The

EUROPA WORLD OF LEARNING

2008

The

EUROPA WORLD OF LEARNING

2008

58th Edition

VOLUME I

INTRODUCTORY ESSAYS
INTERNATIONAL ORGANIZATIONS
AFGHANISTAN–MYANMAR

[redacted]

Routledge
Taylor & Francis Group
LONDON AND NEW YORK

First published 1947
Fifty-eighth Edition 2007

Albert House, 1–4 Singer Street, London, EC2A 4BQ, United Kingdom
(Routledge is an imprint of the Taylor & Francis Group, an Informa business)

ISBN13: 978-1-85743-436-1 (The Set)
ISBN13: 978-1-85743-458-3 (Vol. I)

ISSN 0084-2117

Library of Congress Catalog Card Number 47-30172

Editor: Anthony Gladman

Freelance editorial team: Rebecca Bomford, Karina Holly, Eric Smith,
Nicholas Walmsley, Kristina Wischenkämper, Gareth Wyn Jones

Associate Editor, Directory Research: James Middleton

Editorial Clerical Assistant: Charley McCartney

Editorial Director: Paul Kelly

Typeset in New Century Schoolbook

[redacted]

Typeset by Data Standards Limited, Frome, Somerset
Printed and bound in Great Britain by Polestar Wheatons, Exeter

FOREWORD

THE EUROPA WORLD OF LEARNING first appeared in 1947, and has since become established as an authoritative reference work on academic institutions all over the world. This is the fifty-eighth edition, and appears in two-volume format. Volume I contains introductory essays on academic subjects, information on more than 550 international organizations, and individual chapters on academic institutions in countries from Afghanistan to Myanmar. Volume II contains chapters on countries from Namibia to Zimbabwe, and a comprehensive index of institutions in both volumes.

In this edition, for the first time, introductory surveys feature in every chapter. Information on regulatory and representative bodies in the higher education sector has been included in selected chapters. The section covers ministries, government agencies and departments, funding and accrediting bodies and other organizations of national importance.

We have once again tried to ensure that we provide the latest possible information about institutions included in THE EUROPA WORLD OF LEARNING. Every year, a revision form showing current entry details is sent to each institution; research on the internet and in the world's press, as well as contact with official sources all over the world, supplements this method of revision.

We are always grateful to those individuals and organizations who help us to bring our information up to date with their prompt replies. We particularly emphasize the necessity for revised entries to be returned to us without delay, since important material may otherwise be held over until a later edition. Only by maintaining a strict timetable can the regular production of such a large work as THE EUROPA WORLD OF LEARNING be assured.

We should like to point out that, in the sections on Universities and Colleges, our classification usually follows the practice of the country concerned. This in no way implies any official evaluation on our part. We suggest that readers who are interested in the matter of the equivalence of institutions, degrees or diplomas, should correspond directly with the institutions concerned, or with the national or international bodies set up for this purpose. For selected countries, these organizations now appear in the regulatory and representative bodies section under the heading Accreditation.

An online version of THE EUROPA WORLD OF LEARNING complements the print edition, providing a full range of sophisticated search and browse functions, and regular updates of content. The site offers an unprecedented level of access to institutions of higher education and learning world-wide, and to the people who work within them. For further details of the online version, please see page vi.

August 2007

CONTENTS

• An Index of Institutions is to be found at the end of Volume II

SPECIAL NOTE

Entries within the sections Learned Societies and Research Institutes are grouped under the following headings

GENERAL
AGRICULTURE, FISHERIES AND VETERINARY SCIENCE
ARCHITECTURE AND TOWN PLANNING
BIBLIOGRAPHY, LIBRARY SCIENCE AND MUSEOLOGY
ECONOMICS, LAW AND POLITICS
EDUCATION
FINE AND PERFORMING ARTS
HISTORY, GEOGRAPHY AND ARCHAEOLOGY
LANGUAGE AND LITERATURE
MEDICINE
NATURAL SCIENCES
- *General*
- *Biological Sciences*
- *Mathematical Sciences*
- *Physical Sciences*

PHILOSOPHY AND PSYCHOLOGY
RELIGION, SOCIOLOGY AND ANTHROPOLOGY
TECHNOLOGY

ABBREVIATIONS

AB	Alberta
Abog.	Abogado (lawyer)
Acad.	Academy; Academician
ACT	Australian Capital Territory
Admin.	Administrative, Administration
AFRC	Agricultural and Food Research Council
AIDS	acquired immunodeficiency syndrome
AK	Alaska
AL	Alabama
ALECSO	Arab League Educational, Cultural and Scientific Organization
Apdo	Apartado (Post Box)
approx.	approximately
AR	Arkansas
Arq.	Arquiteto (Portuguese),
Arquitecto	(Spanish)
ASCE	American Society of Civil Engineers
Asscn	Association
Assoc.	Associate
Asst	Assistant
ATC	Art Teacher's Certificate
Atty	Attorney
AUPELF	Association des Universités Partiellement ou Entièrement de Langue Française
Avda	Avenida
Ave	Avenue
Avv.	Avvocato (Advocate)
AZ	Arizona
BA	Bachelor of Arts
BC	British Columbia
Bd, Bld, Blv., Blvd	Boulevard
Bdul	Bulevardul
BILD	Bureau International de Liaison et de Documentation
Bldg	Building
Blvr	Bulevar
BP	Boîte postale
Br.(s)	Branch(es)
Brig.	Brigadier
BRGM	Bureau de Recherches Géologiques et Minières
Bro.	Brother
BSc	Bachelor of Science
B/TEC	Bachelor of Technology
Bul.	Bulvar (boulevard)
bulv.	bulvarȳs (boulevard)
c.	circa (approximately)
CA	California
CAE	College of Advanced Education
CAR	Central African Republic
Ccl	Council
CD-ROM	compact disk read-only memory
CEA	Commissariat à l'Energie Atomique
CEO	Chief Executive Officer
CERN	European Organization for Nuclear Research
CGIAR	Consultative Group on International Agricultural Research
Chair.	Chairman, Chairwoman, Chairperson
CIRAD	Centre de Coopération Internationale en Recherche Agronomique pour le Développement
Cmdr	Commander
CNAA	Council for National Academic Awards
CNR	Consiglio Nazionale delle Ricerche
cnr	corner
CNRS	Centre National de la Recherche Scientifique
Co	Company; County
CO	Colorado
c/o	care of
Col	Colonel
colln	Collection
Comm.	Commission
Commr	Commissioner
Conf.	Conference
Corpn	Corporation
Corresp.	Correspondent, Corresponding
CP	Case postale; Casella postale; Caixa postal (Post Box)
Cr	Contador
CSIRO	Commonwealth Scientific and Industrial Research Organization
CT	Connecticut
CTFT	Centre Technique Forestier Tropical
Cttee	Committee
DC	District of Colombia
DE	Delaware
Del.	Delegate, delegation
Dept	Department
Deptl	Departmental
DES	Department of Education and Science
devt	development
DF	Distrito Federal
Dipl.	Diploma
Dir	Director
Dist.	District
Div.(s)	Division(s)
Doc.	Docent
Dott.	Dottore
Dott.ssa	Dottoressa
Doz.	Dozent (lecturer)
Dr	Doctor
Dr.	Drive
Dra	Doctora
Dr Hab.	Doktor Habilitowany (Assistant Professor)
Drs	Doctorandus (Dutch or Indonesian higher degree)
DSIR	Department of Scientific and Industrial Research
E	East; Eastern
EC	European Community
Econ.	Economics
ECOSOC	Economic and Social Council (UN)
ECSC	European Coal and Steel Community
Edif.	Edificio (Building)
edn	edition
EEC	European Economic Community
e.g.	exempli gratia
Eng.	Engineer; Engineering
EngD	Doctor of Engineering
ESA	European Space Agency
ESCAP	Economic and Social Commission for Asia and the Pacific
esp.	especially
ESRC	Economic and Social Research Council
Est.	Established
etc.	et cetera
ETH	Eidgenössische Technische Hochschule
EU	European Union
Exec.	Executive
f.	founded
FAO	Food and Agriculture Organization
Fed.	Federation, Federal
FL	Florida
fmr(ly)	former(ly)
Fr	Father
F.t.e.	Full-time equivalent (staff)
F.U.T.	Federal University of Technology
GA	Georgia
Gdns	Gardens
Gen.	General
Gov.	Governor
Govt	Government
HQ	Headquarters
HE	His Eminence; His (Her) Excellency
HI	Hawaii
HIV	human immunodeficiency virus
HM	His (Her) Majesty
HND	Higher National Diploma
Hon.	Honourable; Honorary
HRH	His (Her) Royal Highness
IA	Iowa
IAEA	International Atomic Energy Agency
IAU	International Astronomical Union
IBE	International Bureau of Education
ICPHS	International Council for Philosophy and Humanistic Studies
ICSU	International Council of Scientific Unions
ID	Idaho
IEC	International Electrotechnical Commission
IEMVT	Institut d'Elevage et de Médecine Vétérinaire des Pays Tropicaux
IFAN	Institut Fondamental d'Afrique Noire
IFLA	International Federation of Library Associations and Institutions
IGU	International Geographical Union
IICA	Instituto Interamericano de Cooperación para la Agricultura
IL	Illinois
ILO	International Labour Organization
IMU	International Mathematical Union
IN	Indiana
Inc.	Incorporated
incl.	include(s), including
Ind.	Independent

Ing.	Engineer
INRA	Institut National de la Recherche Agronomique
Instn	Institution
Int.	International
Ir	Ingénieur (Engineer)
IRAT	Institut de Recherches Agronomiques Tropicales et des Cultures Vivrières
IRC	Institut de Recherches sur le Caoutchouc
IRCC	Institut de Recherches du Café, du Cacao et autres plantes stimulantes
IRCT	Institut de Recherches du Coton et des Textiles Exotiques
IRFA	Institut de Recherches sur les Fruits et Agrumes
IRHO	Institut de Recherches pour les Huiles et Oléagineux
irreg.	irregular
ISME	International Society for Music Education
ISO	International Organization for Standardization
IUB	International Union of Biochemistry
IUBS	International Union of Biological Sciences
IUCr	International Union of Crystallography
IUGG	International Union of Geodesy and Geophysics
IUGS	International Union of Geological Sciences
IUHPS	International Union of the History and Philosophy of Science
IUIS	International Union of Immunological Societies
IUMS	International Union of Microbiological Societies
IUNS	International Union of Nutritional Sciences
IUPAB	International Union of Pure and Applied Biophysics
IUPAC	International Union of Pure and Applied Chemistry
IUPAP	International Union of Pure and Applied Physics
IUPHAR	International Union of Pharmacology
IUPS	International Union of Physiological Sciences
IUTAM	International Union of Theoretical and Applied Mechanics
Jl	Jalan
Jr	Junior
JSC	Joint Stock Company
jt(ly)	joint(ly)
km	kilometre(s)
KS	Kansas
küç.	küçasi (street)
kv.	kvartal (apartment block), kvartira (apartment)
KY	Kentucky
LA	Louisiana
Lic.	Licenciado
Licda	Licenciada
Lt	Lieutenant
Ltd	Limited
m	metre(s)
m.	million
MA	Master of Arts; Massachusetts
Mag.	Magister (master)
Man.	Manager, Managing
MB	Manitoba
MD	Maryland
ME	Maine
Mem.(s)	Member(s)
Mgr	Monseigneur; Monsignor;
Magister	(Master's degree)
MI	Michigan
Min.	Minister; Ministry
misc.	miscellaneous
MIT	Massachusetts Institute of Technology
mm	millimetre(s)
MN	Minnesota
MO	Missouri
MRC	Medical Research Council
MS	Master of Science; Mississippi
MSc	Master of Science
MSS	Manuscripts
MT	Montana
N	North; Northern
nám	náměstí (square)
NASA	National Aeronautics and Space Administration
Nat.	National
NB	New Brunswick
NC	North Carolina
ND	North Dakota; National Diploma
NE	Nebraska
NERC	Natural Environment Research Council
NGO	Non-Governmental Organization
NH	New Hampshire
NJ	New Jersey
NL	Newfoundland and Labrador
NM	New Mexico
NS	Nova Scotia
NSW	New South Wales
NT	Northwest Territories
NU	Nunavut Territory
NV	Nevada
NY	New York
NZ	New Zealand
OAS	Organization of American States
obl.	oblast
ODA	Overseas Development Administration
OECD	Organisation for Economic Co-operation and Development
Of.	Oficina
OFS	Orange Free State
OH	Ohio
OIC	Organization of the Islamic Conference
OK	Oklahoma
On.	Onorevole (Italian)
ON	Ontario
ONERA	Office National d'Etudes et de Recherches Aérospatiales
opp.	opposite
OR	Oregon
Org.	Organization
OU	Open University
PA	Pennsylvania
PE	Prince Edward Island
PEN	Poets, Playwrights, Essayists, Editors and Novelists (Club)
PhD	Doctor of Philosophy
pl.	place; platz; ploshchad (square)
PMB	Private Mail Bag
POB	Post Office Box
pr.	prospekt (avenue)
Pres.	President
Prin.	Principal
Prof.	Professor
Publ.(s)	Publication(s)
QC	Québec
q.v.	quod vide (to which refer)
rd	road
Rep.	Representative; Represented
retd	retired
Rev.	Reverend
RI	Rhode Island
RP	Révérend Père
Rr.	Rruga
Rt Hon.	Right Honourable
Rt Rev.	Right Reverend
S	South; Southern
SA	South Africa(n); South Australia
SAR	Special Administrative Region
SC	South Carolina
SD	South Dakota
SDI	Selective Dissemination of Information
Sec.	Secretary
SERC	Science and Engineering Research Council
SK	Saskatchewan
s/n	sin número (without number)
Soc.	Society
spec.	special
Sq.	Square
Sr	Senior
St	Saint, Sint; Street
Sta	Santa
Ste	Sainte
str.	strada, stradă, Strasse (street)
tel.	telephone
TN	Tennessee
Treas.	Treasurer
TX	Texas
u.	utca (street)
UK	United Kingdom
ul.	ulica, ulitsa (street)
UN	United Nations
UNDP	United Nations Development Programme
UNESCO	United Nations Educational, Scientific and Cultural Organization
UNICEF	United Nations International Children's Emergency Fund
Univ.	University
UNRWA	United Nations Relief and Works Agency
UNU	United Nations University
URSI	Union Radio-Scientifique Internationale
USA	United States of America
USIS	United States Information Service
UT	Utah
VA	Virginia
Vols	Volumes
VT	Vermont
vul.	vulitsa, vulytsa (sreet)
W	West; Western
WA	Western Australia; Washington (State)
WHO	World Health Organization
WI	Wisconsin
WTO	World Trade Organization
WV	West Virginia
WY	Wyoming
YT	Yukon Territory

INTERNATIONAL TELEPHONE CODES

To make international calls to telephone and fax numbers listed in *The Europa World of Learning*, dial the international code of the country from which you are calling, followed by the appropriate country code for the institution you wish to call (listed below), followed by the area code (if applicable) and telephone or fax number listed in the entry.

	Country code	+ or – GMT*
Afghanistan	93	+4½
Albania	355	+1
Algeria	213	+1
Andorra	376	+1
Angola	244	+1
Antigua and Barbuda	1 268	–4
Argentina	54	–3
Armenia	374	+4
Australia	61	+8 to +10
Australian External Territories:		
Australian Antarctic Territory	672	+3 to +10
Christmas Island	61	+7
Cocos (Keeling) Islands	61	+6½
Norfolk Island	672	+11½
Austria	43	+1
Azerbaijan	994	+5
Bahamas	1 242	–5
Bahrain	973	+3
Bangladesh	880	+6
Barbados	1 246	–4
Belarus	375	+2
Belgium	32	+1
Belize	501	–6
Benin	229	+1
Bhutan	975	+6
Bolivia	591	–4
Bosnia and Herzegovina	387	+1
Botswana	267	+2
Brazil	55	–3 to –4
Brunei	673	+8
Bulgaria	359	+2
Burkina Faso	226	0
Burundi	257	+2
Cambodia	855	+7
Cameroon	237	+1
Canada	1	–3 to –8
Cape Verde	238	–1
Central African Republic	236	+1
Chad	235	+1
Chile	56	–4
China, People's Republic	86	+8
Special Administrative Regions:		
Hong Kong	852	+8
Macao	853	+8
China (Taiwan)	886	+8
Colombia	57	–5
Comoros	269	+3
Congo, Democratic Republic	243	+1
Congo, Republic	242	+1
Costa Rica	506	–6
Côte d'Ivoire	225	0
Croatia	385	+1
Cuba	53	–5
Cyprus	357	+2
'Turkish Republic of Northern Cyprus'	90 3-92	+2
Czech Republic	420	+1
Denmark	45	+1
Danish External Territories:		
Faroe Islands	298	0
Greenland	299	–1 to –4
Djibouti	253	+3
Dominica	1 767	–4
Dominican Republic	1 809	–4
Ecuador	593	–5
Egypt	20	+2
El Salvador	503	–6
Equatorial Guinea	240	+1
Eritrea	291	+3
Estonia	372	+2
Ethiopia	251	+3
Fiji	679	+12
Finland	358	+2
Finnish External Territory:		
Åland Islands	358	+2
France	33	+1
French Overseas Regions and Departments:		
French Guiana	594	–3
Guadeloupe	590	–4
Martinique	596	–4
Réunion	262	+4
French Overseas Collectivities:		
French Polynesia	689	–9 to –10
Mayotte	262	+3
Saint Pierre and Miquelon	508	–3
Wallis and Futuna Islands	681	+12
Other French Overseas Territory:		
New Caledonia	687	+11
Gabon	241	+1
Gambia	220	0
Georgia	995	+4
Germany	49	+1
Ghana	233	0
Greece	30	+2
Grenada	1 473	–4
Guatemala	502	–6
Guinea	224	0
Guinea-Bissau	245	0
Guyana	592	–4
Haiti	509	–5
Honduras	504	–6
Hungary	36	+1
Iceland	354	0

	Country code	+ or – GMT*
India	91	+5½
Indonesia	62	+7 to +9
Iran	98	+3½
Iraq	964	+3
Ireland	353	0
Israel	972	+2
Italy	39	+1
Jamaica	1 876	–5
Japan	81	+9
Jordan	962	+2
Kazakhstan	7	+6
Kenya	254	+3
Kiribati	686	+12 to +13
Korea, Democratic People's Republic (North Korea)	850	+9
Korea, Republic (South Korea)	82	+9
Kuwait	965	+3
Kyrgyzstan	996	+5
Laos	856	+7
Latvia	371	+2
Lebanon	961	+2
Lesotho	266	+2
Liberia	231	0
Libya	218	+1
Liechtenstein	423	+1
Lithuania	370	+2
Luxembourg	352	+1
Macedonia, former Yugoslav republic	389	+1
Madagascar	261	+3
Malawi	265	+2
Malaysia	60	+8
Maldives	960	+5
Mali	223	0
Malta	356	+1
Marshall Islands	692	+12
Mauritania	222	0
Mauritius	230	+4
Mexico	52	–6 to –7
Micronesia, Federated States	691	+10 to +11
Moldova	373	+2
Monaco	377	+1
Mongolia	976	+7 to +9
Montenegro	382	+1
Morocco	212	0
Mozambique	258	+2
Myanmar	95	+6½
Namibia	264	+2
Nauru	674	+12
Nepal	977	+5¾
Netherlands	31	+1
Netherlands Dependencies:		
Aruba	297	–4
Netherlands Antilles	599	–4
New Zealand	64	+12
New Zealand's Dependent and Associated Territories:		
Tokelau	690	–10
Cook Islands	682	–10
Niue	683	–11
Nicaragua	505	–6
Niger	227	+1
Nigeria	234	+1
Norway	47	+1

	Country code	+ or – GMT*
Norwegian External Territory:		
Svalbard	47	+1
Oman	968	+4
Pakistan	92	+5
Palau	680	+9
	970	
Palestinian Autonomous Areas	or 97-	
	2	+2
Panama	507	–5
Papua New Guinea	675	+10
Paraguay	595	–4
Peru	51	–5
Philippines	63	+8
Poland	48	+1
Portugal	351	0
Qatar	974	+3
Romania	40	+2
Russian Federation	7	+2 to +12
Rwanda	250	+2
Saint Christopher and Nevis	1 869	–4
Saint Lucia	1 758	–4
Saint Vincent and the Grenadines	1 784	–4
Samoa	685	–11
San Marino	378	+1
São Tomé and Príncipe	239	0
Saudi Arabia	966	+3
Senegal	221	0
Serbia	381	+1
Seychelles	248	+4
Sierra Leone	232	0
Singapore	65	+8
Slovakia	421	+1
Slovenia	386	+1
Solomon Islands	677	+11
Somalia	252	+3
South Africa	27	+2
Spain	34	+1
Sri Lanka	94	+5½
Sudan	249	+2
Suriname	597	–3
Swaziland	268	+2
Sweden	46	+1
Switzerland	41	+1
Syria	963	+2
Tajikistan	992	+5
Tanzania	255	+3
Thailand	66	+7
Timor-Leste	670	+9
Togo	228	0
Tonga	676	+13
Trinidad and Tobago	1 868	–4
Tunisia	216	+1
Turkey	90	+2
Turkmenistan	993	+5
Tuvalu	688	+12
Uganda	256	+3
Ukraine	380	+2
United Arab Emirates	971	+4
United Kingdom	44	0
United Kingdom Crown Dependencies	44	0
United Kingdom Overseas Territories:		

	Country code	+ or – GMT*
Anguilla	1 264	–4
Ascension Island	247	0
Bermuda	1 441	–4
British Virgin Islands	1 284	–4
Cayman Islands	1 345	–5
Diego Garcia (British Indian Ocean Territory)	246	+5
Falkland Islands	500	–4
Gibraltar	350	+1
Montserrat	1 664	–4
Pitcairn Islands	872	–8
Saint Helena	290	0
Tristan da Cunha	290	0
Turks and Caicos Islands	1 649	–5
United States of America	1	–5 to –10
United States Commonwealth Territories:		
Northern Mariana Islands	1 670	+10
Puerto Rico	1 787	–4
United States External Territories:		
American Samoa	1 684	–11
Guam	1 671	+10
United States Virgin Islands	1 340	–4
Uruguay	598	–3
Uzbekistan	998	+5
Vanuatu	678	+11
Vatican City	39	+1
Venezuela	58	–4
Viet Nam	84	+7
Yemen	967	+3
Zambia	260	+2
Zimbabwe	263	+2

* Time difference in hours + or – Greenwich Mean Time (GMT). The times listed compare the standard (winter) times. Some countries adopt Summer (Daylight Saving) Time — i.e. +1 hour — for part of the year.

MASS TERTIARY EDUCATION IN THE DEVELOPING WORLD: DISTANT PROSPECT OR DISTINCT POSSIBILITY?

Sir JOHN DANIEL

ASHA KANWAR and STAMENKA UVALIĆ-TRUMBIĆ

In the coming decades the global profile of tertiary education will be transformed by the multiplication and growth of institutions in the developing world. Age participation rates in tertiary education are below 10% in many poorer countries. To achieve the rate of 35% considered the threshold for 'developed' status, these countries will greatly expand forms of provision that are marginal in richer countries today: private for-profit institutions; distance learning; and cross-border operations. When today's developing countries account for the majority of college students, tertiary education worldwide will look even more diversified as commercial providers adopt the systems and technologies of production and service industries. With appropriate international safeguards and national regulation, however, the benefits to individuals of this global expansion of access to tertiary education will outweigh any concerns that higher learning is losing its soul in a huge marketplace.

INTRODUCTION

Some economists consider that the world was more 'globalized' at the beginning of the 20th century than today (Hirst and Thompson, 1996—see Bibliographical References below). Similarly, international education is not a new phenomenon. Even the wandering medieval scholar, Erasmus of the Dutch city of Rotterdam, who has given his name to contemporary student exchanges in Europe, was following a much older tradition. Xuanzang (perhaps more familiar as Hsuan Tsang) was one among many Chinese scholars who studied in India in the first millennium of the modern era. Nalanda University (in modern Bihar), where he studied, can claim to be the world's first international university (Tribune, 2003). We do well to recall the 1,500-year history of academic exchange between China and India as contemporary developments there transform the scope and style of tertiary education.

China, India and other large developing countries will dominate tertiary education numerically in the 21st century. Their methods will effectively define the global profile of provision, which will evolve for both economic and technological reasons. Even with annual economic growth of 8% or more, neither public nor private funds will be adequate to create conventional campuses at the rate required. Fortunately, technology is making other alternatives available. The galloping increase in connectivity will link people with institutions more easily, and the burgeoning corpus of open educational resources (OER) could dramatically reduce the cost of creating learning materials.

How will these opportunities be exploited? There will be steady increases in three types of provision (Daniel, Kanwar and Uvalić-Trumbić, 2006). First, private for-profit education will play a relatively larger role in developing countries than it does in the Organisation for Economic Co-operation and Development (OECD) countries today, simply because the public sector will neither be able to afford the necessary investments nor manage the scale of expansion required. Second, distance learning, conducted at scale, which already accounts for a larger proportion of tertiary enrolments in Asia and South Africa than elsewhere in the world, will occupy an even larger place. Third, more tertiary education will be conducted across borders and import–export patterns will change. India, because of its facility in English and low costs, could become the predominant cross-border provider of tertiary education within two decades.

However, even in the developing countries where for-profit providers are prevalent, such providers and distance-teaching institutions still only reach the more privileged sectors of the population. Can the new technological combination of online connectivity and OER allow distance learning to achieve a quantum shift towards lower costs and higher access while providing good quality?

In *The Fortune at the Bottom of the Pyramid*, C. K Prahalad (2004) shows how certain large corporations have radically redesigned their business models. By aiming for low margins and high volume, they have brought new goods and services to the rural poor, to the benefit both of their companies and of their new customers. For developing countries to achieve the threshold 35% age participation rate that goes with developed status, we shall need a similar breakthrough in the provision of tertiary education. Where will it originate and what will be its knock-on effects? How will a much larger, more industrialized and more commoditized system work? How will governments regulate and assure the quality of these large tertiary systems in the interests of protecting their citizens as consumers?

STUDENTS IN THEIR MILLIONS

For two decades world-wide enrolment growth in tertiary education has exceeded the most optimistic forecasts. A milestone of 100m. enrolments was passed some years ago and a forecast of 120m. students by 2020 looks likely to be reached by 2010. Indeed, there are already 130m. tertiary students if we count part-timers. Growth is, if anything, accelerating as more governments see the rapid expansion of tertiary education as a key factor in their transition from developing to developed country status.

Thus, enrolments in the People's Republic of China doubled between 2000 and 2003 and, with 21m. students, China has overtaken the USA as the world's largest tertiary education system, although further expansion has now slowed for fear of having unemployed graduates. India lags behind, but demography and democracy will likely propel its tertiary enrolments past those of both the USA and the People's Republic of China in the coming decades: 60% of India's population are under 25 years of age; and, in the world's largest democracy, the Government will be forced to respond to the desire for access to tertiary education.

Growth has been rapid in other developing countries as well, but usually from a very low base, which creates a massive disparity in the age participation rates (APRs) in tertiary education of 18-to-23 year-olds across the world. APRs of around 50% are now common in OECD countries, whereas in many developing countries they languish below 10%. In these countries, low APRs are accompanied by demographic profiles with median ages in the low 20s or below. The scale of change in tertiary education in the coming decades can be shown simply by applying the threshold target of a 35% APR to the 4,000m. people in the world's poorest countries. This would yield 150m. additional students, which is more than today's global total.

A comparison with the US experience puts potential solutions in perspective. With a population of 300m. and over 1,000 universities, the USA has an APR of over 50%. This averages out at one university per 300,000 people. If we assume that the 18-to-23 year-old age group accounts for 5%–10% of the total population, there will be between 15,000 and 30,000 students of conventional age among those 300,000 souls seeking entrance to one university. However, there are also large numbers of students aged over 25 seeking university study, and these lifelong learners must be factored in too. This implies that the population base for a conventional university is actually fewer than 300,000.

Using this metric, India alone would need nearly 2,400 additional universities in the next 25 years—roughly two new universities per week—which puts into perspective the June 2007 announcement by the Indian Government that it plans to create one central (federal) university in each of the 28 states. For all its symbolic importance, that would only contribute a drop in the bucket of demand. It also raises the question of what types of institutions are needed.

Just as generals plan for the previous war, educational planners and development agencies tend to prefer the creation of new versions of previous generations of elite institutions. Establishing copies of India's prestigious institutes of science and technology in Africa is a good example. Such developments may be necessary, but they are far from sufficient. A wide diversity of tertiary education establishments is needed, as becomes apparent if we examine the expectations of students.

THE FIVE As TEST

Tens of millions of third-world young adults and older lifelong learners, for whom tertiary education was previously an unattainable aspiration, will be seeking it in the coming decades. All these students will look for relevant tertiary education that passes the '5 A' test of being accessible, affordable, appropriate, accredited and accepted. Conventional public institutions that teach face to face will satisfy these criteria for some learners, but will have difficulty operating at the low cost and large scale required.

Affordability is a major challenge. Many developing countries are trying to transform tertiary education from an elite to a mass system aimed at the needs of a democracy. Can public or private (for-profit or not-for-profit) providers devise a business model that can take them beyond the elite to reach out to the masses, in order to realize the cost efficiencies associated with large numbers of students, and to respond to national educational aspirations? In particular, can tertiary education conducted for profit work for the public good?

Tertiary Education and the Public Good

Tertiary education is a private good, with direct benefits to those who participate, but also a public good. A fire service is a more obviously useful public service than having accessible tertiary education, but the proportion of people with tertiary education does correlate well with a society's state of economic and civic development. Accessible tertiary education is in the public interest.

By tradition, governments control public goods like emergency services and defence in order to extend their benefits to all citizens and give full accountability to the electorate. Private militias are a sure indicator of the breakdown of civic order. However, how far should the principle of public control apply to education? Until recently many developing countries have assumed that if tertiary education is a public good, then the state must be the sole or main provider. We contend that practice, principle and pragmatism all argue against treating tertiary education as a public monopoly.

Past practice reveals that private bodies, notably churches and foundations, were providing tertiary education long before governments took an interest. The purpose of state involvement, when it came, was to make tertiary education truly a public good by widening access.

The challenge from principle concerns the right role of government and holds that, apart from services like defence, government is most effective when it monitors and regulates the provision of public services by others, rather than controlling them directly.

Demography and demand present pragmatic challenges. In this era of lifelong learning, there is no way that governments can provide, at no cost, all the education that people will need throughout life. Governments have to focus their contributions.

Some years ago the World Bank briefly promoted the idea of fee-paying private education at the primary level, but it now believes that universal primary education will only be achieved if education at that level is free and compulsory. No government has the resources to pay for basic education for all from the public purse and to fund all of tertiary education as well, so a choice must be made between inadequate provision of tertiary education by a public-sector monopoly or meeting the demand by a combination of public and private institutions. This is a political dilemma for many developing-country governments, which have relied solely on the first option but now realize that it is a serious drag on national development.

In response to these pressures for growth, private tertiary education has become the fastest growing segment of tertiary education worldwide, especially so in Latin America and Asia but also in Africa. In East Asia, 80% of students are enrolled in private tertiary education institutions in Japan, the Philippines, South Korea (Republic of Korea) and Taiwan ('Republic of China'), where governments regulate the private higher education sector tightly. Western Europe, with only 10% of enrolments in private tertiary education, is the least affected (Altbach and Levy, 2005).

Private providers include both not-for-profit and for-profit providers. In the latter category, Phoenix university, Kaplan and Laureate are well known, although Kinser (2006) points out that they are not typical of the generality of the US for-profit sector. Nor is this only a US phenomenon. Universities in the Philippines have been listed on the stock exchanges for decades and, more recently, South Africa has seen a growing number of for-profit providers, often through public-private partnerships. As tertiary education institutions cross borders, however, the notions of public and private, not for profit and for profit are becoming blurred.

Tertiary Education for Profit

In countries that do not have a clear legislative framework for charitable organizations, the distinction between private tertiary institutions that are non-profit foundations and those that operate commercially, for profit, can also be blurred. How many family members can a private foundation support from the revenues of its tertiary college before it is considered to be operating for profit? This question may not have a clear answer in some jurisdictions and we shall not try to answer it here. In looking at the private sector we shall, however, focus our attention on institutions that operate overtly for profit.

That is because we assume that for-profit institutions will be more motivated than others to tackle the challenges of large numbers and will have access to the capital necessary to pursue their plans. How can the governments of developing countries best take advantage of for-profit tertiary education? The challenge is to achieve a balance between accessibility for students and quality of provision, along with returns for the investor. The heart of the issue is fees. In North America almost all tertiary education students pay tuition fees, but in the rest of the world—not only the developing world—they are a hot issue.

Fees are a special problem for those countries that made tertiary education free (i.e. totally subsidized by the state) in the days when only a tiny proportion of the population was expected to go to university. At that time entry to tertiary education was highly competitive, but many citizens believed—and still believe—that the combination of competitive entry and free tuition would produce equitable participation in tertiary education from all socio-economic groups. Research now shows that this is simply not true (for example, Levin, 1990). The socio-economic profile of students in countries that charge fees while providing scholarships and loans for poorer students is more broadly based than in those that do not charge fees. This is a very important finding, and one that governments are gradually finding the courage to act on.

Changes in public fees policy are important, because what the public sector does in relation to fees clearly constrains the for-profit sector. Having a free public sector alongside an expensive for-profit sector does not create an effective tertiary education system. As countries gradually introduce fees in the public sector, either because of a conviction that it is more socially equitable or because there is no financial alternative, the for-profit sector finds itself on a more level playing field.

That, in turn, makes it easier for the for-profit sector to build arrangements for need-based scholarships and loans into their fees regimes. Obviously it takes time to build up enough scholarship funds for admissions policies to be truly blind to student or parental wealth, but if for-profit institutions are to play a major role in the expansion of tertiary education, they must be able to attract a diversity of people. Only then can they truly claim that private investment in tertiary education is making its contribution to widening access and thus contributing to the public good.

By helping to widen access, for-profit institutions also foster good relations with governments and the public tertiary education sector, thereby gradually reducing the scepticism of many governments about expanding the for-profit sector. The net result will be that within a decade or two, private, for-profit provision, already estimated at a worth of US $385,000m. annually worldwide, is likely to account for a larger proportion of tertiary education in the developing countries than it now does in the industrialized world.

How will the for-profit sector provide tertiary education to the developing nations? Much of it will likely follow traditional patterns of classroom teaching on locally owned campuses, but two other forms of provision will have a higher profile: distance learning; and cross-border offerings.

Distance Learning

Distance learning is already providing a significant answer to the challenge of the second 'A', accessibility, in countries such as India, where it is a significant component of tertiary education. Today 24% of all Indian enrolments—well over 2m. students—are in distance education, specifically in 13 national and state open universities and 106 other institutions, mostly public, which teach both on campus and by correspondence. The Government's target, although it seems unlikely to be reached, is to have 40% of all tertiary education participation occurring through distance education by 2010.

The Indira Gandhi National Open University now has 1.5m. students, and India's state open universities are growing fast. For example, the Yashwantrao Chavan Maharashtra Open University expects to grow from 200,000 to 400,000 students in the next three or four years. The West Bengal Netaji Subhas Open University had fewer than 10,000 students in 2000, but reached 100,000 students (and mega-university status) in 2007. The Tamil Nadu Open University, only created in 2003, already has 60,000 students. Some other state open universities, such as those in the states of Bihar, Rajasthan and Uttar Pradesh, have not yet enrolled large numbers but the potential is there.

Despite increasing use of India's educational satellite, those institutions use relatively traditional methods of distance education and may have reached their limits in reducing costs through such older technologies while maintaining an acceptable level of quality. However, a series of developments in the ways that technology is used for distance learning could now stimulate the quantum reduction in operating costs required for a further radical widening of access. The question is whether existing public institutions will be able to harness these disruptive technologies (Christensen, 1997) or whether the for-profit sector will do it better. A look at the past is instructive.

New methods of education have always attracted private providers. In 1837 Isaac Pitman offered the first correspondence course (in shorthand), even before the United Kingdom standardized the penny post in 1840. For-profit providers subsequently dominated the correspondence education industry. The next wave of distance education, led by the large multimedia open universities in the 20th century, was dominated by the public sector. In addition to widening access dramatically in some countries, these institutions also showed that distance learning can be of higher quality, as well as less expensive, than conventional tertiary education, because it has to be developed and delivered in a much more systematic way.

The current wave of distance learning, often called eLearning because of its extensive online components, seems once again to have a special appeal to the for-profit sector. It has a cost structure in which a higher up-front investment is rewarded by lower marginal costs when volume is achieved. The for-profit institutions' access to capital markets allows them to make those investments.

Moreover, providers wishing to use eLearning now have available a rapidly growing body of open educational resources: freely available learning materials that can be adapted to particular local needs. This is a crucial development. The combination of expanding connectivity and the swelling reservoir of OER is potentially revolutionary, not least because it may allow institutions to achieve low per-student costs without having to achieve huge volumes. Course development costs are a major item for quality distance education. OER allow the widespread adaptation and use of good learning material. Such resources could be the key to implementing, in distance education, Prahalad's injunction (Prahalad, 2004) to create 'highly distributed, small-scale operations married to world-scale capabilities'.

Accessibility also means access to the technology and allied infrastructure through which distance education is delivered. Internet connectivity is particularly important, yet the proportion of people online is only 4% in India, 1% in Africa (half of them in South Africa) and 0.1% in Bangladesh, for example. However, in contemplating the limited use of the internet in sub-Saharan Africa and South Asia, we should recall that 20 years ago the online technology now permeating the West hardly existed. Communication links are already beginning to alter the way that poor villages in the developing world function. As bandwidth costs go down, increased internet connectivity will accelerate that trend.

Cross-Border Provision

Distance learning is becoming an increasingly important vehicle for cross-border provision, as connectivity and electronically-held open educational resources become major features of its teaching and student-support systems.

UNESCO and the OECD (2006), in their guidelines for *Quality Provision in Cross-Border Higher Education*, state that cross-border higher education (CBHE) is:

> 'higher education that takes place in situations where the teacher, student, programme, institution/provider or course materials cross national jurisdictional borders. [It] may include higher education by public/private and not-for-profit/for-profit providers. It encompasses a wide range of modalities, in a continuum from face-to-face (taking various forms such as students travelling abroad and campuses abroad) to distance learning (using a range of technologies and including e-learning).'

Those cross-border providers include not just conventional or open universities but also media companies, multinational companies, corporate universities, networks of universities, professional organizations and information technology (IT) companies. Note that nearly all cross-border tertiary education is effectively offered for profit in the receiving country. Even if the originating institution is a public institution in its home country, it must make 'excess revenue'—profit0151on its work in other countries in order to sustain those operations.

The border is a symbol for the special political, social and cultural identity found within the national space. Accepting borders implies recognition of the roles and responsibilities of national governments within their jurisdictions, not simply for deciding whom to let into their country but also for overseeing the national tertiary education system.

National sovereignty over tertiary education has been reinforced by the General Agreement on Trade in Services (GATS) of the World Trade Organization—WTO (COL and UNESCO, 2006). The GATS recognizes four modes of supply. First, *consumption abroad* is where students travel to another country to study. Second, the *presence of natural persons* means, in academic terms, visiting scholars or teachers. Here, however, we are more interested in the other two forms of supply, defined by the GATS as *cross-border supply* and *commercial presence*, but better known as distance education and the establishment of branch campuses. These are the forms of cross-border tertiary education of most interest to for-profit providers.

Such providers often fail the test of our third 'A', appropriateness. Their subject offerings are limited and liberal education often loses out to an exclusive focus on market-driven programmes such as business and information technology, which sometimes prove ephemeral. Students from a variety of cultures and linguistic backgrounds follow the curriculum of the country of origin—baseball or cricket metaphors and all—with no recognition of social, cultural and ethnic differences (Daniel, Kanwar and Uvalić-Trumbić, 2005).

Cross-border provision will become fully relevant only when it responds to country priorities, which is best done through strong partnerships between the overseas provider and local institutions to develop curricula and methods of delivery and student support. Such linkages also help with the fourth 'A' that students seek: accreditation. Some jurisdictions will not accredit foreign providers unless they have local partners.

Students like many characteristics of the newer forms of provision. They respond well to the strong customer focus of good for-profit institutions. They like the convenience and flexibility of distance learning, often finding that, with an effective student support system, human contact in distance learning is both more personal and more effective than in conventional systems. Some students value the overseas qualification that comes with cross-border provision.

However, students prefer their institutions to have more than formal accreditation. They seek a fifth 'A', that of acceptability in their community. They want their academic titles to enjoy a good reputation. The reputation that the public accords to educational institutions changes slowly—rightly in our view. It takes time to build up an institutional reputation and, barring egregious mistakes, it also takes time to lose one. For-profit providers, distance learning and cross-border programmes face greater challenges in the areas of accreditation and reputation than nationally based conventional providers.

For example, even the oldest of India's open universities is barely 20 years old, so they have hardly had time to acquire a reputation for quality, even where they might deserve it. Furthermore, the open universities in India have had to contend with the poor reputation created for distance education by some correspondence courses offered by India's conventional universities. These longstanding operations, which enrol hundreds of thousands of students were, and mostly still are, poor-quality operations with shoddy learning materials and minimal student support. The universities use them as cash cows to subsidize their campus operations.

The irony is that, although the students in these correspondence programmes have a poor experience, they have the advantage of being associated with prestigious institutions such as the University of Delhi and the University of Madras (in Chennai). Students looking for distance learning have a choice between low-quality courses, with no support, that carry the name of a well-known university, and higher-quality programmes from an open university that has yet to acquire its reputation. We can only hope that with time each institution's reputation will become aligned with the inherent quality of its offering. Can this process be speeded up?

QUALITY ASSURANCE

Within two decades the global tertiary education enterprise could have more than doubled in size, be predominantly based in what today we call developing countries and present a greater diversity of both providers and provision.

How will the world ensure the quality of such a vast enterprise? Specifically, how are governments to protect their citizens from fraudulent providers and bogus qualifications, especially when they emanate from another country? So-called eLearning is attractive to unscrupulous operators, because they can close down a website even faster than a post-office box. Cross-border tertiary education makes students particularly vulnerable to scams. Some for-profit providers only seek commercial benefit, ignoring developmental objectives and intellectual advancement. How can we create an international ethic of integrity and quality assurance?

As tertiary education expands, governments' role will increasingly be to monitor and regulate it, rather than to provide it. Many developing countries currently lack quality-assurance mechanisms and, where they do exist, as in India, they are not always properly equipped to cope with diversifying types of provision. However, countries realize that the GATS has created an inexorable trend towards increasing cross-border education supply. Governments will best respond to this trend by building strong frameworks for regulation, quality assurance and accreditation that cover all tertiary education provision within their borders. The task for UNESCO, the Commonwealth of Learning (COL) and other intergovernmental organizations is to support national and regional developments effectively.

The tertiary education market already has plenty of dubious providers and bodies offering accreditation, with some of the latter even claiming a phoney affiliation with UNESCO. Clipping the wings of such operations is in the public interest, but how do we do it? Empowering students, parents and employers to make informed decisions is the best bulwark against deception and fraud. There are no easy solutions, but here are five of the tools that already exist or are emerging.

First, UNESCO has published *Study Abroad*, its international guide to tertiary education institutions and scholarships, for nearly 60 years (UNESCO, 2006). It covers over 150 countries. Recent editions include more on open/distance learning and have a section 'Tools for Students'. This is based in part on the excellent work of South Africa's Council on Higher Education on promoting quality literacy about tertiary education among secondary students (Naidoo, 2005).

Second, UNESCO and the OECD, in an alliance covering both exporting and importing countries, have developed the *Quality Provision in Cross-Border Higher Education* guidelines. This publication addresses all six stakeholder groups: governments; institutions and their staff; quality assurance agencies; student associations; professional groups; and qualification-recognition bodies (UNESCO and OECD, 2006).

Third, since the WTO's GATS is still making waves in international education, COL and UNESCO have published a simple guide to what GATS is and is not (COL and UNESCO, 2006).

Fourth, in 2006 UNESCO launched the pilot of an online portal on recognized tertiary institutions, in order to explore the feasibility of maintaining such a facility at the world level. The project follows naturally from the CBHE quality provision guidelines and shares the objective of protecting students from low-quality offerings and of empowering them to make informed decisions, based on transparent information on the quality of higher education provision. The basic concept is that UNESCO hosts the portal, with the competent national authorities of participating countries providing reliable information on the recognized, registered and/or accredited institutions in their country and keeping this information up to date. This obligation will stimulate some countries to rethink the issue of how they define institutions of quality and how they create the capacity to assess them.

Fifth, the various stakeholders concerned with the quality of international education now meet under the aegis of the Global Forum on International Quality Assurance, Accreditation and the Recognition of Qualifications. It convened for the third time in Tanzania in 2007 under the theme, 'Learners and New Higher Education Spaces'.

PUTTING IT ALL TOGETHER

We have argued that the rapid expansion of tertiary education in developing countries will give for-profit institutions, distance learning and cross-border provision a much greater role. We have assumed that this trend, allied with the use of constantly improving educational technologies, will help to make tertiary education accessible to the masses at an affordable price. Is this merely wishful thinking or is there evidence that it is happening?

For-Profit Providers

Most for-profit providers are content to operate within the same broad parameters as the rest of tertiary education. When they are able to achieve economies of scale and superior efficiency, as in the case of Phoenix University, they tend to grow their profits rather than cutting their fees. However, one exception, which is consciously trying to apply Professor Prahalad's ideas (Prahalad, 2004) to tertiary education, combines the three trends we have identified: a for-profit institution using distance-learning technologies across national borders.

Best Associates, a US merchant bank, is creating educational enterprises that are aimed squarely at combining greater learning effectiveness with dramatically lower costs. At the national level it is slashing the cost and improving the relevance of professional development for teachers through the American College of Education. This for-profit institution, already one of the 10 largest teacher education operations in the USA, teams up with school systems to offer M.Ed. degrees that meet the schools' need for teacher development better than existing programmes and do so at one-fifth of the cost.

At the global level, Best's Whitney International University System is expanding rapidly, both by acquiring universities in other countries and creating joint ventures with existing universities. Having begun its expansion in South America, it is now launching ventures in Morocco, Jordan, Saudi Arabia, India and Indonesia. The mode of delivery is distance learning that blends the remote-classroom and asynchronous approaches. Lectures from senior professors are carried to remote classrooms by satellite or computer and these are underpinned by supporting professors who interact individually with relatively small groups of students online. Unlike conventional remote-classroom teaching, this model is scalable because of the network of supporting professors, which is an essential feature for achieving a low price point. Another cost-saving principle is to use existing facilities, study centres and tele-centres.

Best Associates implements Prahalad's vision (Prahalad, 2004) by setting a low price point as 'step one' of the planning process and then building a teaching-learning system to achieve it. It is too early to predict the success of the model in developing countries, although the US example of the American College of Education is encouraging.

Improving Educational Technologies

Our other key hypothesis is that the combination of expanding connectivity and OER will radically reduce costs. We can be confident about the continuing advance of connectivity, but will institutions really take advantage of OER? The world's smaller states, where populations are too small to amortize course development costs over large numbers of students, may be showing the way. The Virtual University for Small States of the Commonwealth is an attempt by 28 small countries to develop OER jointly on a wiki (collaborative website) and to adapt them into courses at the national level (Commonwealth of Learning, 2007).

The OER movement is too new for us to assert with confidence that these electronic learning materials will always bridge the last mile to the individual student in the form of courses that carry credit. However, the signs are promising. We foresee the day when institutions will turn to repositories of OER to obtain and contribute courses in the same way that individuals now turn to the web to find and publish information in a variety of media.

CONCLUSION

Starting with the objective of a significantly lower price point and of using technology and good management to achieve it with a quality programme is still a revolutionary concept in education. Most for-profit institutions are still content to be 'cream skimmers', operating just a little more cost effectively than their rivals. Most public institutions assume a direct correlation between cost and quality and resist attempts to achieve lower price points.

However, the millions who still thirst for tertiary education must hope that some providers, both public and for-profit, will espouse this revolutionary concept successfully. In so doing they will create a tectonic shift that will make access to higher learning in the developing world a distinct possibility rather than a distant prospect.

BIBLIOGRAPHICAL REFERENCES

Altbach, P. G., and Levy, D. C. (Eds). *Private Higher Education: A Global Revolution*. Rotterdam and Boston, MA, Sense Publishers and Boston College Center for International Higher Education, 2005.

Chandigarh *Tribune*—see the *Tribune* below

Christensen, C. M. *The Innovator's Dilemma: When New Technologies Cause Great Firms to Fail*. Boston, MA, Harvard Business School Press, 1997.

Commonwealth of Learning (COL). 'A Virtual University for Small States of the Commonwealth' (www.col.org/vussc). 2007.

COL and UNESCO. *Higher Education Crossing Borders: A Guide to the Implications of the General Agreement on Trade in Service (GATS) for Cross-border Education*, a report by Knight, J. (www.col.org/colweb/site/pid/4059). Vancouver, BC, and Paris, COL and UNESCO, 2006.

Daniel, J. S., Kanwar, A., and Uvalić-Trumbić, S. 'Who's Afraid of Cross-border Higher Education? A Developing World Perspective', presentation to the final plenary session of the Quality Assurance in Transnational Issues (INQAAHE) 2005 annual conference 2005 at Wellington ((www.col.org/colweb/site/pid/3617). 1 April 2005.

Daniel, J., Kanwar, A., and Uvalić-Trumbić, S. ('A Tectonic Shift in Global Higher Education', in *Change: The Magazine of Higher Learning*, Vol. 38, No. 4 (pp. 16—23). 2006.

Daniel, J., and Uvalić-Trumbić, S. 'Going Global: In What Direction?', presentation to the British Council's GoingGlobal2 Conference at Edinburgh (www.col.org/colweb/site/pid/4254). 2006.

Hirst, P., and Thompson, G. *Globalization in Question*. Cambridge, Oxford and Malden, MA, Polity Press, 1996.

Kanwar, A.—see Daniel et al. above.

Kinser, K. 'What Phoenix Doesn't Teach Us about For-Profit Higher Education', in *Change: The Magazine of Higher Learning*, Vol. 38, No. 4 (pp. 24—29). 2006.

Levin, B. 'Tuition Fees and University Accessibility', in *Canadian Public Policy*, Vol. XVI, No. 1 (pp. 51—59). 1990.

Naidoo, P. 'Student Quality Literacy and Empowerment', report of the Higher Education Quality Committee. Pretoria, Council on Higher Education (CHE), 2005.

Organisation for Economic Co-operation and Development (OECD)—see UNESCO and OECD below.

Prahalad, C. K. *The Fortune at the Bottom of the Pyramid: Eradicating Poverty through Profits*. Old Tappan, NJ, Wharton School Publishing, 2004.

South African Government (CHE)—see Naidoo above.

Tribune, Chandigarh (www.tribuneindia.com/2003/20030822/cth2.htm). 2003.

UNESCO. *Study Abroad* (publishing.unesco.org/details.aspx?-Code_Livre=44). Paris, UNESCO Publishing, 2006.

UNESCO and COL—see COL and UNESCO above.

UNESCO and OECD. *Quality Provision in Cross-Border Higher Education*, guidelines (portal.unesco.org/education/en/ev.php-URL_ID=41508&URL_DO=DO_TOPIC&URL_-SECTION=201.html). 2006

Uvalić-Trumbić, S.—see Daniel et al. above.

GLOBAL STUDENT MOBILITY: MOVING TOWARDS BRAIN EXCHANGE

RAJIKA BHANDARI and PEGGY BLUMENTHAL

Global higher education mobility is a rapidly growing phenomenon, with over 2.5m. students seeking an education outside their home country (UNESCO, 2006—see Bibliographical References below). This number represents a 41% increase since 1999 and the greatest surge in international student enrolments in recent decades. However, although the rapid growth of mobility is relatively recent, the desire to acquire a higher education beyond national borders is itself not new: students and scholars have always sought learning at the best higher education institutions around the world, as a way to broaden their educational and cultural horizons. The renaissance Dutch scholar, Erasmus, after whom the first European Union (EU) mobility schemes were named, embodied the tradition of travel and study, which existed as well in Asia and the Middle East. More recently, not only has the number of internationally mobile students grown, but the overall context of global mobility—both in terms of who is going where and the mix of host and sending countries—has also changed significantly. Most countries now view international academic mobility and educational exchanges as critical components for sharing knowledge, building intellectual capital and remaining competitive in an increasingly flattening and globalizing world.

The rising number of mobile students is perhaps partly an outcome of the worldwide growth in higher education. Globally, domestic higher education enrolment increased to 132m. students, up from 68m. in 1991, with countries in Asia and the Pacific seeing the largest growth (UNESCO, 2006). Some rapidly growing Asian countries, such as Malaysia and the People's Republic of China, have recently almost doubled their higher education enrolments. At the same time, these burgeoning populations have put enormous pressure on the higher education systems of many developing countries, especially at the post-graduate level, leading large numbers of their students to seek higher education outside their home country. India is one such example, where the large college-age population has outpaced the capacity of the country's existing higher education institutions. There remains, therefore, an enormous unmet and growing demand for international education and a huge capacity worldwide to absorb more international students.

In this chapter we examine current trends in international mobility and explore factors that contribute to these trends. In doing so, we draw upon the extensive research in this area by the Institute of International Education (IIE—based in New York, USA), as well as research conducted by other experts who have examined this issue from a variety of angles. The chapter begins by addressing the issue of how to define and measure global student mobility, as this lays the groundwork for discussing trends and variations in global mobility patterns. Next, we examine some key developments that have contributed to the shifting picture of global mobility. Having explored the current status and drivers of mobility trends, we conclude the chapter by examining the implications of these trends at the national- and institutional-level. In doing so, we expand our focus beyond higher education to include skilled employment, because the two are inextricable and critical components of the education-to-employment pipeline in countries that attract international students and skilled migrants.

WHO IS AN INTERNATIONAL STUDENT? THE CHALLENGES OF MEASURING GLOBAL MOBILITY

Which are the largest sending and host countries? Where do the students come from and where do they go? In attempts to answer these critical questions, many countries have established their own systems for collecting information on international students. In the USA, for example, IIE has been collecting this type of data since the 1920s, which have been published as the Open Doors reports on international educational exchange since 1954, with support from the US Department of State since 1972.[1] An annual census of US international educational exchange, Open Doors presents mobility statistics based on data collected from all regionally accredited US higher education institutions. Similar data for Australia is gathered by Australian Education International (AEI), for the United Kingdom by the Higher Education Statistics Agency and for Germany by the German Academic Exchange Service (DAAD). Countries such as the People's Republic of China (through the China Scholarship Council—CSC) and Mexico (Association of Universities and Higher Education Institutions—ANUIES) have only more recently developed mechanisms to collect this type of data.

However, country-specific data by themselves are limited in that they tell us little about the implications of each country's mobility statistics within a global context. Although global mobility involves over 2.5m. students, the worldwide data on this phenomenon are limited and imperfect. Transnational comparisons can be problematic, because different countries use different data definitions and time frames. The variation in national degree and qualifications structures across countries also makes comparative analysis difficult.

While UNESCO and the Organisation for Economic Co-operation and Development (OECD) have instituted large-scale data collection efforts to collect mobility data for all countries, they face a number of well-recognized limitations. For one, there is typically a time lag between the year the data are collected and released. Second, because the data are primarily collected through ministries of education, they do not always capture enrolments at private institutions. The result is an underestimate of international students, since private institutions represent the fastest growing education sector in many countries. Third, according to the definitions used by UNESCO and OECD, only students enrolled for the duration of a year or more are counted in the data. Since internationally mobile students from the USA, Japan and the EU often study abroad for less than a full academic year, it can be safely assumed that the actual number of students who are globally mobile might significantly exceed the 2.5m. counted by UNESCO.

One effort to build upon the work of UNESCO and OECD and that addresses some of its limitations is Project Atlas, a Ford Foundation-supported programme, which is building a community of researchers from around the world to share more current and direct data on student mobility.[2] Project Atlas provides a comprehensive global picture of international student mobility for 27 leading destination countries, and enrolment by students from 75 places of origin. Current project partners include ANUIES, the Association of Indian Universities (AIU), AEI, the British Council, the CSC, DAAD, the International Education Association of South Africa (IEASA) and the Netherlands Organization for International Co-operation in Higher Education (NUFFIC), among others. The project allows researchers, policy-makers and other stakeholders to situate mobility trends within a global context and to understand their implications for higher education and the labour market. Another key feature of the project is that it allows users to examine international education patterns in relation to other national developments, such as home-country investment in human capital, population growth and the expansion of technological capacity.

While Anglophone and Western European countries such as the USA, the United Kingdom, Australia, France and Germany

[1] See opendoors.iienetwork.org and IIE (2006) in Bibliographical References below.

[2] See atlas.iienetwork.org and IIE (2007) below.

have historically attracted the largest number of international students, other countries have boosted their internationalization strategies in recent years to attract more students, build university linkages and develop joint research programmes. In an effort to illuminate the national policies that facilitate global mobility, Atlas partner organizations use the project website to share the strategies and initiatives that their countries and governments have undertaken to increase international educational exchange. To capture more fully the increasingly important role that newer 'host' countries are now playing in global mobility, an ongoing challenge for Project Atlas is to identify and involve more partners from Asia, Latin America, the Middle East and Africa.

CURRENT TRENDS: WHO IS GOING WHERE?

Many factors, real or perceived, can affect a student's choice of a study destination, ranging through: the cost and quality of higher education programmes; the value of the degree or professional credential for future careers; the availability of certain areas of specialization; access to the education system and a country (including, but not limited to, obtaining visas for entry); and important historical, linguistic and geographic links between the home and destination countries. Drawing upon statistical sources such as Open Doors, Project Atlas and the UNESCO and OECD data, this section presents key trends in global education mobility and examines past and current projections of growth in this area.

At the turn of the millennium several studies documented the rise in international student mobility and suggested that the numbers would inevitably increase. In a prominent report published in 2002, IDP Education Australia projected a dramatic expansion in the demand for international education, doubling over the next 10 years and then perhaps doubling again, with as many as 7m. students studying outside their home country by 2025 (Bohm et al., 2002). Five years after those initial projections it appeared that the high estimates did not fully account for the rapid expansion of the higher education sector in countries such as the People's Republic of China, which have since made the transition from their role as primarily sending countries to also becoming attractive host destinations, especially for students from within the region. For example, in just one year, international enrolment in Chinese universities rose from 141,000 students in 2005 to 162,695 students in 2006, a 15% increase (Project Atlas—IIE, 2007).

Despite the inherent limitations of their methodology, the estimates released by UNESCO and OECD have remained fairly stable over time. In 2000 UNESCO estimated that almost 2m. higher education students were being educated in countries other than their homes; current estimates indicate that approximately 2.5m. students (most from the developing world) are currently mobile, a large proportion of whom—42%—are in major Anglophone host countries. Students from the traditional destination countries in Europe and in the USA are also pursuing international education in increasing numbers. Data from Open Doors show that the number of US students studying abroad more than quadrupled from the mid-1980s (IIE, 2006). Countries within the EU have experienced even greater expansion of their internationally mobile student populations, due to EU-funded programmes such as Erasmus, Socrates and Leonardo, as well as the structural reforms initiated through the Bologna process. The EU estimates that 1.4m. European students have already participated in the Erasmus programme.

Based on the data sources mentioned above, we summarize below some key trends that have emerged recently:

Six countries host 67% of the world's mobile students: the USA (23%), the United Kingdom (12%), Germany (11%), France (10%), Australia (7%) and Japan (5%). Anglophone countries such as Australia and the United Kingdom have seen large percentage increases in their international student populations, while the USA has seen a modest decline. However, the USA continues to host the largest number of international students pursuing a higher education outside their home country (576,466 students in 2005/06), followed by the United Kingdom at 344,335 students (IIE, 2007).

Newer 'host' countries such as the People's Republic of China are seeing rapid increases in the numbers of international students. Several other countries in the Asia-Pacific region—Thailand, Malaysia, Singapore and New Zealand, to name some—have stepped up their efforts to internationalize and to attract more international students.

The largest groups of internationally mobile students come from East Asia and the Pacific (31%). Students from China represent the largest share of internationally mobile students (14%), followed by students from India, the Republic of Korea (South Korea), Japan and Germany.

In terms of world regions, sub-Saharan Africa has the highest outbound mobility share of its total higher education population (6%), almost three times greater than the world average. North America has the lowest outbound ratio, with only 0.4% of the region's tertiary students pursuing their education abroad.

THE EXPANDING UNIVERSE OF ACADEMIC MOBILITY: OLD AND NEW PLAYERS

Developed countries in Europe and North America, and Australia and New Zealand in the Pacific region, have dominated the global mobility picture of the late 1900s and into the early 21st century. The USA, United Kingdom, France and Germany, in particular, have long attracted large numbers of international students. For the most part, the movement of students has been from developing to developed countries (Altbach, 2007; Altbach and Knight, 2007; UNESCO, 2006). While this overall trend continues today, the situation is none the less changing for these key countries, with interesting variations emerging and several unexpected players now engaged in what might best be described as a 'global competition' for international students. As a result, international students are not only choosing non-traditional destinations but are also pursuing non-traditional forms of learning.

These changes have been propelled by a combination of factors, such as: the expanding capacity of countries like the People's Republic of China not only to provide more higher education opportunities for their own students but also to host an increasing number of international students; the availability and global spread of alternative modes of educational delivery; and domestic economic, demographic and work-force conditions, which might affect students' decisions regarding an overseas education. For example, it is quite possible that the recent declines in international students pursuing science and engineering degrees in the USA might have more to do with the growing value of degrees in business and management in key sending countries such as India and China, and less to do with the presumed decline in America's appeal as a destination for studying science and engineering. In this section, we examine in detail four interrelated developments in international education that have contributed to a significant shift in the demand and supply equation of global mobility.

Increased Recruiting of International Students

Government-supported efforts by key host countries, including nationally co-ordinated campaigns by the United Kingdom, Australia, Germany, France, New Zealand and others with sophisticated marketing strategies and expedited visa policies, are proving very persuasive, especially to self-funded students from some of the large sending countries in Asia. Several of these host countries, along with newer players in Asia and Europe, have allocated tens of millions of dollars to launch large-scale initiatives over the past few years.

Launched in 1998, the United Kingdom's £5m. Prime Minister's Initiative was one of the earliest; it was updated in 2000 as the Education UK brand, a co-ordinated approach to marketing British institutions abroad that is available for use by any British campus. Other recent British initiatives include the Science and Engineering Graduate Scheme (2004), the United Kingdom-China Higher Education Programme (2005) and the United Kingdom-India Education and Research Initiative (2006).

Countries that were primarily sending countries have now also developed their own internationalization strategies to attract foreign students and encourage international educational exchange. Singapore has been making strides in this area with the establishment of Education Singapore, an agency charged with promoting and marketing Singapore abroad and with attracting 150,000 foreign students by 2015. Malaysia seeks to attract 100,000 international students by 2010 (up from 45,000 in 2005); Jordan announced plans to increase the number of international students to 100,000 by 2020; the People's Republic of China seeks to host 300,000 by 2020; and Japan has reportedly set the ambitious goal of hosting 1m. foreign students by 2025 (up from the current 120,000).[3]

Many countries are also formalizing the link between higher education and the skilled job market by implementing policies that encourage international graduates to enter the work-force of the host country, especially in scientific and technical fields. In the United Kingdom, Scotland has announced a Fresh Talent Initiative, aimed at attracting 8,000 foreign professionals per year from now until 2009, by allowing international students who graduate from a Scottish university to remain for two years of employment. Supplementing efforts by individual host countries in Europe, the EU has also launched initiatives to recruit science and technology researchers from around the world in an attempt to compete with America's well-funded research universities and labs, which reputedly attract the world's best and brightest science and technology talent.

Home Country Higher Education Capacity

In the People's Republic of China, India, South Korea and many other countries, the number of higher education seats at home has grown dramatically (with key Chinese and Indian universities aiming to double their enrolments) as national and provincial/state governments increase their investments in public education. Within some countries, especially in Asia and Latin America, the private higher education sector is also dramatically expanding to meet the growing demand. However, despite the rapid expansion of the public and private education sector in many countries, it is worth noting that the burgeoning college-age population in China and India continues to exceed the domestic higher education capacity of these countries, a demand-supply imbalance that probably partly explains the growing numbers of Chinese and Indian students who continue to seek an overseas education

Growth in Other Forms of International Education

A range of new institutions and alternative approaches to international study have emerged to meet the growing need for a cost-effective education and, as a result, many students are choosing to stay home while also acquiring an 'international' education (Blumenthal, 2002). These new modes of education include, among others, distance learning, joint degrees, branch campuses and 'sandwich' programmes involving short-term study abroad. According to David Gray (presenting to the US National Science Foundation—NSF in 2006), these types of non-traditional academic arrangements have succeeded because they offer alternative modes of organization and operation, such as: new programme offerings (e.g. short courses, night classes); new pedagogical approaches; asynchronous and collaborative learning; and distributed physical infrastructure including, but not limited to, remote campuses and distance education via the internet.

Perhaps the most significant development in alternative forms of international education has been the advent of the branch campus, often referred to as trans-national education (TNE), borderless education or cross-border education. Broadly speaking, this approach involves the 'the movement of education across national jurisdictional or geographic borders' (Knight, 2006)—that is, 'internationalization abroad', as compared with the more traditional form of 'internationalization at home' (IAU—Knight, 2005). As in the case of more traditional forms of global student mobility, the movement and spread of cross-border education has primarily been from the developed North to the developing South. US institutions continue to dominate this type of overseas delivery and account for more than one-half of all overseas higher education, followed by Australia, the United Kingdom and Ireland (Verbik and Merkley, 2006). Key host countries for overseas campuses include Singapore and the People's Republic of China in eastern Asia, and Dubai (Knowledge Village) and Qatar (Education City) in the Middle East.

Cross-border education has significant implications for domestic and international higher education (Knight, 2006). It is conceivable, for example, that as prospective international students choose branch campuses located in their own countries over the institution's home campus, traditional student mobility, as we know it, might decline. The expansion of 'virtual mobility' through internet-based learning might also undercut the need for students to cross physical borders to obtain an international credential. Conversely, it is also possible that these diverse forms of internationalization will continue to grow rapidly, serving different types of students with varying educational needs.[4]

Non-traditional Mobility Patterns

Although there are no hard data to support this assertion, anecdotal evidence suggests that international mobility or skilled migration no longer follow a strictly linear pattern, where people move between just two countries, typically from South to North. In an increasingly connected and flattening world, a student from Asia, for example, might choose to obtain an undergraduate degree in her home country, a master's degree in the USA and a doctoral degree in the United Kingdom, returning home subsequently to work for a European multinational firm. The mobility of international scientists and researchers, too, has become increasingly complex, as the field of science and engineering itself has evolved into a borderless enterprise. Not surprisingly, this type of multi-country mobility is difficult to measure. For instance, even though Michael Finn's groundbreaking research (published in 2005) on the stay rates of international post-doctoral researchers and scholars in the USA sheds light on who remains in the USA and who leaves, it is not able to tell us whether those that leave are heading to another country or back to their home country, or even whether those staying on in the USA are commuting between the USA and their home country regularly to work in joint ventures.

THE BRAIN EXCHANGE: IMPLICATIONS OF GLOBAL MOBILITY TRENDS

Although many researchers use the framework of 'brain-drain' and 'brain-gain' to analyse trends and outcomes of global mobility and skilled migration, this implies a uni-directional, linear approach to mobility that does not fully capture the current reality of international flows. Early assessments of skilled migration emphasized the 'brain drain' aspect of such mobility, arguing that because mobility was primarily from the developing to the developed world, it resulted in a drain of the former's human resources; later interpretations of skilled migration rejected the inequitable aspect of mobility and suggested that the drain should be regarded as a 'brain gain' situation, whereby sending countries actually stand to benefit, primarily financially, from skilled migration.[5]

Like many others in the field, we employ the 'brain' metaphor, while also offering a new and more nuanced interpretation of it that takes into account current mobility trends. We prefer the terms 'brain circulation' or 'brain exchange' to account for the increasingly multi-directional nature of mobility and the growing awareness that such mobility or exchanges are mutually beneficial for sending and receiving countries, albeit in varying ways. It is important to mention, however, that the one major exception to this shift is Africa, as it continues to lose a disproportionate size of its human resources

[3] Projected numbers for these countries are based on reports in national and international media.

[4] In the interest of conserving space, we guide readers to the Observatory on Borderless Higher Education (OBHE—www.obhe.ac.uk).

[5] We do not provide a detailed summary of the brain-drain debate here, as this topic has been covered extensively in other publications; see, for example, Docquier and Marfouk (2004) and Kapur and McHale (2005).

to skilled migration. That, coupled with the widespread destruction of human capital caused by the AIDS epidemic and repeated political upheavals, has taken a heavy toll on the continent's social, economic, and educational sectors.

While there is as yet limited empirical evidence in support of the circulation of global knowledge and talent, related trends and anecdotal reports present an interesting picture. Combining findings for the USA from Finn's stay rates analysis with data from Open Doors, we find that two of the major sending places, South Korea and Taiwan ('Republic of China'), also have the lowest stay rates in the USA (Finn, 2005; Open Doors, 2006). In other words, although large numbers of students from Taiwan and South Korea seek a higher education in the USA, a large proportion, many of whom might be scientists or engineers, are also likely to take their knowledge and skills back to their places of origin. However, this was not always the case. Taiwan's stay rates in the 1950s and 1960s rivalled India's today, but the rapid expansion of Taiwan's economy and the political reforms of the 1980s and 1990s made opportunities at home more attractive to recent graduates of US universities. We are seeing similar trends with Chinese graduates, whose career opportunities in Shanghai (People's Republic of China) or Singapore draw them back to Asia within a few years of graduating from the USA or the United Kingdom.

The strengthening of overseas higher education partnerships, facilitated by advances in telecommunications and the internet, have also contributed to the shift from a drain to a balance in the sharing of knowledge and information. For instance, faculty and researchers at foreign and US universities have significantly increased their collaboration, with research activities now spanning multiple countries while capitalizing on worldwide knowledge and talent (Adams et al., 2004).

To take advantage of the global knowledge and skills required in a knowledge economy, and to meet the demand for skilled labour, many countries have launched extensive efforts and initiatives to recruit back home scientists and engineers. Returning skilled workers are seen as improving a country's productivity and global competitiveness, because of the direct transfer of knowledge and skills and the indirect benefits that accrue through returnees' access to overseas professional and trade networks, which can have a positive impact on domestic growth and development (Thorn and Holm-Nielsen, 2006).

It is not surprising that countries such as Singapore, South Korea and Taiwan, which have well-developed industrial and science and technology sectors that offer attractive opportunities and compensation for highly skilled professionals, are also the ones with the most successful return rates (Meyer and Brown, 1999). For example, Taiwan has focused its efforts on providing challenging opportunities for returning young researchers through the establishment of science-based industrial parks. Keeping in mind the higher standard of living in the developed countries in which its nationals typically reside, Malaysia used the strategy of providing tax exemptions to returning nationals to compensate for the potentially lower income (Lowell, 2001). Between 1991 and 2000, at a total cost of US $56m., the Presidential Fund for Retention in Mexico successfully repatriated 2,000 overseas Mexican-born researchers (NSF, 2000).

Some countries are also experimenting with the Western model of competitive funding for research and innovation as a repatriation strategy (Thorn and Holm-Nielsen, 2006). The Chinese research system provides an interesting example. In an attempt to attract back its researchers and scientists, the Government of the People's Republic is shifting from a Soviet-style centralized research system to one that provides competitive research grants through an impartial, peer-review process (Jonkers, 2004). According to one estimate, the number of returnees almost doubled between 2001 and 2002, reaching close to 18,000 in 2002 (Zweig et al., 2004). A similar approach has been adopted in Chile, Brazil, Mexico, Venezuela and Viet Nam through the Millennium Science Initiative, an international programme designed to build capacity in modern science and engineering and their uses in developing countries.

One of the newest players in the Asian region is Pakistan. The Pakistani Higher Education Commission (HEC), launched in 2002, is an umbrella organization vested with creating academic linkages between Pakistani higher education institutions and foreign universities through an initial investment of US $5.07m. (Atta-ur-Rahman, 2007). Among key strategies to promote bi-directional exchange is the Foreign Faculty Hiring Programme, which recruits highly qualified faculty members from abroad, both on short- and long-term appointments. So far, over 270 faculty have participated in the programme. Efforts to attract back highly skilled Pakistani migrants are complemented by the desire to provide more Pakistani students with the opportunity to obtain an international education and to reinvigorate their country's higher education sector with their newly acquired knowledge: close to 4,200 students are eligible for a variety of scholarships, including those available through the NSF's Fulbright programme, which would enable them to acquire advanced research training overseas. Similar efforts are underway in Saudi Arabia, with the establishment of a multi-million dollar overseas scholarship fund, as well as the creation of a new 'world-class' university to attract international students in 2007.[6]

Key Implications for Developed and Developing Countries

The emergence and growing popularity of alternative higher education destinations, coupled with increasing return rates for a few key 'source' countries, lead to the inevitable question: can the perennial favourite hosts—most of which are large, developed countries—maintain their competitive edge by attracting the best and the brightest from around the world? Here we examine the case of the USA, which remains to date the top choice of international students and scholars, and is therefore affected most by current trends in global student mobility and skilled migration. US reliance on foreign-born talent grew in both absolute numbers and as a share of the science and engineering work-force during the 1990s (National Science Board, 2006). In 2003 foreign-born students earned over 40% of all doctoral degrees in mathematics, computer sciences and engineering. The proportion of foreign-born faculty with US doctoral degrees at US institutions had also more than doubled, from 11% in 1973 to 23% in 2003.

In 2003/04, for the first time in almost three decades, there was a decline in international student enrolment at US campuses. Not surprisingly, these declines were attributed to the events of 9/11 (the terrorist attacks on US cities of 11 September 2001), which led to more restrictive visa procedures and the perception on the part of many international students that the USA no longer offered a safe and welcoming environment. While it is true that two consecutive years of declining enrolments were cause for concern, especially for large research institutions seeing a significant drop in international graduate students, these developments must be viewed within a wider context that takes into account the multiple and complex factors that affect mobility patterns.

First, the overall declines in enrolment—2.4% in 2003/04 and 1.3% in 2004/05—were, statistically speaking, fairly small, despite the disproportionate attention they generated in the press and in countries that compete to recruit international students. Second, even as international enrolments rebound, the rate of growth in US international enrolment will likely be less than those of other countries, which are starting out from a much smaller base. The USA had hosted over 0.5m. students for eight years before 2006, while Australia, for example, hosted only 167,954 students in 2006 and so was likely to experience a steeper rate of increase. Third, and perhaps most important, the overall market for global mobility is expanding, with more countries emerging as important destinations for international students. Even though this has resulted in a somewhat smaller market share for the USA, we believe that this is a positive development, as it has brought more countries into the field of international education and has changed the dynamic between sending and receiving countries from a uni-directional, 'brain-drain' type of mobility to one of true, mutual exchange.

[6] See www.kaust.edu.sa.

The key challenge for countries like the USA that have come to rely on international talent is to strike the right balance between increasing domestic science and technology capacity while also attracting the best and the brightest from around the world. To view these strategies as mutually exclusive is to impose boundaries upon the science and innovation enterprise that, by its very nature, has become global and borderless. Keeping the doors open to international students and scholars, many of whom go on to become immigrants, also has multiplier effects: the children of immigrants seem to show a very high interest in science and technology. According to the National Foundation for American Policy, 60% of top science students and 60% of top mathematics students in US high schools are children of immigrants (Anderson, 2004). A detailed study of engineering and technology companies started in the USA between 1995 and 2005 found that over one-quarter of them were founded by immigrants (primarily Indians, followed people from the United Kingdom, the People's Republic of China, Taiwan and Japan), employing 450,000 workers nationwide and accounting for US $52,000m. in total sales (Wadhwa et al., 2007).

However, underlying the tension between creating opportunities for Americans while also attracting global talent is perhaps the more fundamental issue of the number of college graduates required to meet the USA's future work-force needs. In other words, is it just a matter of science and technology capacity, or is there an overall shortage of highly skilled workers? According to a recent report released under the Making Opportunity Affordable Initiative (Lumina Foundation), there is a significant 'degree gap' in the USA as compared with other leading developed nations—that is, the difference between degrees produced in the USA and those produced by nations that are the main competitors (Reindl, 2007). At the current pace of production, the USA will produce about 41m. degrees by 2025, leaving a gap of 22m. When adjusted for net gains from immigrants with degrees (that is, those entering the USA with post-secondary degrees minus degree-holders leaving the USA), the degree gap will amount to 16m. degrees.

Developing countries have traditionally been the 'suppliers' of international students, but interesting challenges are now faced as they also become hosts to international students. Developing countries that are poised to become popular study destinations are likely to face a dilemma: how to increase the capacity of their higher education systems to provide adequate opportunities for their expanding college-age population, while also accommodating incoming international students and engaging in the type of international educational exchange that is necessary in today's globally competitive world. The IIE has recently launched a study to examine the issue of study abroad capacity. While focused primarily on increasing the numbers of US students going abroad, the study will also assess the capacity of receiving countries—especially those in the developing world—to host a larger number of short-term non-degree study abroad students. Last but not the least, a related challenge for developing countries hoping to attract back their nationals will be to ensure adequate employment opportunities and an appropriate standard of living.

CONCLUSION

The movement of students and scholars across borders is growing rapidly, driven by many factors and involving a wide range of vehicles and modalities. There are a variety of objectives and approaches in 'doing' academic exchange, and countries and institutions that are most effective in internationalizing are characterized by flexibility and a willingness to adapt to new realities in the complex world of higher education. Common to the best of them are certain elements such as commitment to academic excellence, to fair and open access for candidates and to a diverse range of participants. Most also face other similar challenges, such as how to cope with rapidly expanding opportunities and interest in study abroad on limited or shrinking resources.

Indeed, according to some estimates, the desire for international education is expanding so rapidly that in 20 years there will not be enough classroom seats in the whole world to meet the needs of students who want to pursue higher education. Creative and collaborative solutions will be needed to provide higher education and training to those who seek it. Distance learning, joint degree programmes and new approaches that we cannot yet imagine will all be needed to address the educational needs of the hundreds of millions of undergraduates around the world. Governments will of course be the primary responders to this need, but the private and non-profit sectors are also likely to play key roles.

At the institutional level, many universities in a few countries are starting to develop 'joint degree' programmes and branch campuses abroad, so that they can reach the billions of students who cannot afford to study abroad but who desire access to international education. These programmes have their own challenges, and need to be very responsive to the needs and requirements of the host country. They can never fully replace the intense cultural learning experience of plunging into a foreign environment and mastering the linguistic, cultural and academic challenges of studying abroad. Thus, we see an important role for both kinds of 'international education' and hope that they can reinforce each other in the coming decades.

Finally, we cannot ignore the growth of 'virtual mobility', the use of the internet to deliver courses anywhere in the world to anyone who has access to a computer and modem. Among the many challenges of internet-based education are monitoring of quality and equity of access. One creative response to both challenges has been the 'open courseware' offered by the USA's Massachusetts Institute of Technology (MIT), which posted hundreds of its courses on-line and made them available without cost to anyone in the world. Other universities around the globe are also developing creative ways of delivering education remotely and of reaching students and professionals who might never have thought about studying abroad. The internet can also be an invaluable tool for alumni of study abroad programmes staying in touch with their host campuses once they return home and benefiting from the continuing educational opportunities available on-line. The Erasmus student of the 21st century would look quite different from her ancestor, with an iPod loaded with courses from dozens of universities, as well as a well-worn passport including short- and long-term international academic sojourns abroad and frequent mobility throughout her professional career.

BIBLIOGRAPHICAL REFERENCES

Adams, J. D., Black, G. C., Clemmons, J. R. and Stephan, P. E. *Scientific Teams and Institutional Collaborations: Evidence from US Universities*, 1981–1999, NBER Working Paper, No. 10640. Cambridge, MA, National Bureau of Economic Research, 2004.

Altbach, P. G. *Tradition and Transition: The International Imperative in Higher Education*. Boston, MA, Boston College (Center for International Higher Education), 2007.

Altbach, P. G., and Knight, J. 'Higher Education's Landscape of Internationalization: Motivations and Realities', in Altbach, 2007 (see above).

Anderson, S. *The Multiplier Effect* (www.nfap.com/research-activities/studies/TheMultiplierEffectNFAP.pdf). Arlington, VA, National Foundation for American Policy, 2004.

Atlas—see IIE (2007) below.

Atta-ur-Rahman. 'Higher Education in Pakistan: A Silent Revolution' in *IIENetworker* (IIE-B0107/5888). Spring 2007.

Blumenthal, P. 'Virtual and Physical Mobility: A View from the USA', in Wachter, B. (Ed.). *The Virtual Challenge to International Cooperation in Higher Education*, ACA Papers on International Co-operation. Bonn, Lemmens, 2002.

Bohm, A., Davis, D., Meares, D., and Pearce, D. *Global Student Mobility 2025: Forecast of the Demand for International Higher Education*. Sydney, NSW, IDP Education Australia, 2002.

Docquier, F., and Marfouk, A. *Measuring the International Mobility of Skilled Workers (1990-2000)* (Release 1.0), World Bank Policy Research Working Paper, No. 3381. Washington, DC, World Bank, 2004.

Finn, M. G. *Stay Rates of Foreign Doctorate Recipients from US Universities, 2003* (orise.orau.gov/sep/files/stayrate05.pdf), Science and Engineering Education. Oak Ridge, TN, Oak Ridge Institute for Science and Education, 2005.

Gray, D. 'Global Engagement in a Virtual World', paper presented to the Assuring a Globally Engaged Science and Engineering Workforce Workshop of the National Science Foundation at Washington, DC, on 20–22 September 2006.

Institute of International Education (IIE). *Open Doors 2006: Report on International Educational Exchange in the USA*. New York, IIE, 2006.

Atlas of Global Student Mobility 2007. New York, IIE, 2007.

International Association of Universities (IAU)—see Knight (2005) below.

Jonkers, K. *The Role of Return Migrants in the Development of Beijing's Plant Biotechnological Cluster*, paper presented to the Second Globelics Conference: Innovation Systems and Development at Beijing on 16–20 October 2004.

Kapur, D., and McHale, J. *Give Us your Best and Brightest: The Global Hunt for Talent and its Impact on the Developing World*. Washington, DC, Center for Global Development, 2005.

Knight, J. *Internationalization of Higher Education: New Directions, New Challenges*, 2005 IAU Global Survey Report. Paris, International Association of Universities, 2005.

'Crossborder Education: An Analytical Framework for Program and Provider Mobility', in Smart, J. C. (Ed.). *Higher Education: Handbook of Theory and Research*, Vol. XXI (pp. 345–95). Dordrecht, Springer, 2006.

Lowell, L. B. *Policy Responses to the International Mobility of Skilled Labour* (www.ilo.org/public/english/protection/migrant/download/imp/imp45.pdf), International Migration Papers, No. 45 (December). Geneva, International Labour Organization (International Migration Branch), 2001.

Lumina Foundation (Making Opportunity Affordable Initiative)—see Reindl below.

Meyer, J. B., and Brown, M. *Scientific Diasporas: A New Approach to the Brain Drain*, paper presented to the UNESCO and ICSU (International Council for Science) World Conference on Science at Budapest (June–July). Paris, UNESCO, 1999.

National Foundation for American Policy—see Anderson (2004) above.

National Science Board. *Science and Engineering Indicators 2006* (two vols). Arlington, VA, National Science Foundation, 2006.

National Science Foundation (NSF). 'Graduate Education Reform in Europe, Asia and the Americas, and International Mobility of Scientists and Engineers', proceedings of an NSF Science Resources Studies Workshop (Directorate for Social, Behavioral and Economic Sciences). Washington, DC, NSF, 2000.

Open Doors—see IIE (2006) above.

Project Atlas—see IIE (2007) above.

Reindl, R. *Hitting Home: Quality, Cost, and Access Challenges Confronting Higher Education Today* (www.makingopportunityaffordable.org/wp-content/file_uploads/Hitting_Home_030107.pdf), Making Opportunity Affordable Initiative. Indianapolis, IN, Lumina Foundation, 2007.

Thorn, K., and Holm-Nielsen, L. B. *International Mobility of Researchers and Scientists: Policy Options for Turning a Drain into a Gain* (www.wider.unu.edu/publications/rps/rps2006/rp2006-83.pdf), Research Paper, No. 2006/83. Helsinki, United Nations University (World Institute for Development Economics Research), 2006.

UNESCO. *Global Education Digest 2006: Comparing Education Statistics across the World*. Montreal, PQ, UNESCO Institute for Statistics, 2006.

Verbik, L., and Merkley, C. *The International Branch Campus: Models and Trends*. London, Observatory on Borderless Higher Education, 2006.

Wadhwa, V., Saxenian, A., Rissing, B., and Gereffi, G. *America's New Immigrant Entrepreneurs: Part I* (ssrn.com/abstract=990152), Working Papers Series. New York, Social Science Research Network, 2007.

Zweig, D., Changgui, C., and Rosen, S. 'Globalization and Transnational Human Capital: Overseas and Returnee Scholars to China' in *China Quarterly*, No. 179 (pp. 735–57). September 2004.

PUBLIC AND PRIVATE HIGHER EDUCATION: A GROWING GLOBAL ENTERPRISE

RON PERKINSON

INTRODUCTION

All individuals at the different levels of the world's social and economic pyramid should have the right to access systems for education, training and lifelong learning. There is a growing demand for access to both formal and informal education and to training that will provide skills that are of economic relevance, where individuals can update or relearn knowledge and skills that will make them more employable. Lifelong learners should be able to enter or re-enter formal systems of education and training and receive educational recognition or 'credit' for what has been learned, both at their own pace and throughout their working lives.

However, how will world governments create the capacity for increased access in new systems of education, training and lifelong learning, especially when they have struggled or failed to do so in the past? How will governments also cater for the even greater numbers of young people who are still in school and who are yet to compete for places in their local higher education systems,[1] where problems of unmet demand and supply exist today? The global impact of increasing demographics and increased demand for places in formal systems for education and training have posed some daunting challenges for many governments, especially those in the world's most populous countries.

All countries today are reflecting on a global enterprise that is struggling to reach the threshold of one-quarter of 18-to-25 year-olds being enrolled in higher education today. Countries are having difficulty coming to terms with how the converging forces of change in international higher education are forcing providers to find alternative and more innovative ways of resourcing and financing their future development. Given the growing demographics ahead and the decline in public financing in international higher education, the increasing role of the private sector in the areas of financing and of provision of higher education has become the norm. It provides the most practical way for governments to find alternative ways to fill the demand 'gaps' left by their state-owned institutions. The need for universities to become more entrepreneurial in how they will contribute to local development through more innovative models in financing and delivery will only happen in new systems where both public and private higher education can co-exist and work in partnership for the public good. There are growing examples of positive regulatory environments that are helping to foster and mobilize private sector investment in formal systems of higher education. The growing importance of public and private partnerships is becoming the norm in the changing landscape of international higher education.

CONVERGING FORCES OF CHANGE IN HIGHER EDUCATION

The Knowledge Revolution

There are some important drivers behind the knowledge revolution across the world that are forcing the public and private sectors to work more closely together than ever before. Rapid advances in information technologies are reducing the costs of processing and transmitting information. This, in turn, is impacting on how goods are produced and distributed, how learners will interact in society, how we organize our lives and how we will continue to advance knowledge itself. The power of innovation, ideas, skills, productivity and competitiveness is driving the world economy, which gives more weight to intangibles such as research and development, education, training, software development, marketing, logistics and networks. Acceleration in the creation and dissemination of knowledge is leading to shorter time lags between new inventions, the application of knowledge and product life cycles. The reduction of product life cycles is now integral to sectors such as the software and electronics industries, but this is also occurring more generally across a much broader range of products and services than ever before. Knowledge development and its dissemination across borders lead to increasing globalization and competition in services, as well as an increase in international networks and affiliations across the international higher education sector.

Globalization and Increased Competition

As trade increases globally, there is increasing competition across the world. Production is often being outsourced to the lower-cost producer and greater added value is now coming from innovation and from the outsourcing of services. Innovation and higher education are now more entwined and are becoming even more important for economic growth. Economic studies of growth have found that innovation and productivity are predetermined by the strength of education systems, and better ways of producing products and services account for a greater share of economic growth than increases in simple capital and labour inputs in production. This new wave of change poses growing challenges for keeping up with new knowledge and for restructuring economic activities to take advantage of new and better ways of producing goods and services.

Without private sector involvement, governments will not be able to transform the demands of the labour market in economies throughout the world, whereby every citizen can constantly update, absorb and apply new knowledge and skills that are relevant for the work-force.

International Networks and Affiliations

Internationalization has also increased the number of institutional relationships and networking alliances, with many affiliations leading to commercial initiatives involving both public and private sector players. It has also contributed to greater transferability of knowledge through international research networks, as well as joint recognition of both public and private higher education provider qualifications, both within nations and across borders.

The Entrepreneurial University

There is an international trend encouraging universities to become more entrepreneurial and to be agents of positive social, cultural and economic development. Nevertheless, in markets of extreme unmet demand and supply, where there are already insufficient places for academically worthy students to gain admission, there has been little inclination on the part of public universities to change the way that they operate, especially where additional financial or human resources are required. For-profit higher education institutions (HEIs), however, have earned reputations for having a sharper focus on student needs and for offering a more career-orientated education than many of their public sector counterparts.

Increasing Demographics

World population growth is forcing change in the way tertiary education systems have historically provided access to higher education. Between 1988 and 2001 the world population grew from 5,000m. to 6,000m. people, with indicators also predicting that more than one-half of the next billion ('000 million) people will come from Asia. Future demographic analysis of the world's more populous nations emphasizes the daunting task

[1] 'Higher education' is used to denote different levels of post-secondary education, sometimes referred to as 'tertiary university' and 'tertiary non-university' education. Higher education in this context therefore also applies to the parallel world of training, including formal and non-formal technical and vocational education and training, and 'certified' industry, corporate and information technology training.

ahead for governments if they are to cater for future growth in demand for places in their tertiary education systems.

Indonesia has 81 public and 2,236 private higher education institutions. Demand is increasing, with over 2m. students annually graduating from high school. In 2004 around 900,000 or 32% of its students were enrolled in the country's public universities, compared with around 2.1m. students or 68% enrolled in private sector institutions. Indonesia's gross enrolment rate (GER) in higher education is nearly 10% for the age participation group of 18-to-25 years of age, with little or no additional capacity in the public system to create more places for worthy students. As state university enrolments decline, the institutions remain highly oversubscribed.

In Malaysia around 60%of the population is under 30 years of age. Of those enrolled, 10%of 18-to-25 year-olds are enrolled in universities, with another 24% enrolled in tertiary non-university institutions. The private higher education institutions enrol 12% of university students and 51% of tertiary non-university enrolments. Another 30% of that population is still in school and the demand for places in higher education will increase substantially in the years ahead.

Viet Nam has similar challenges, with the population predicted to increase from 81m. to around 120m. by 2030. Around 65% of the population is under 30 years of age in a country where the GER in higher education is currently around 10%. In 2004 there were 1.2m. school leavers, with only 100,000 university places in the public system.

In India around 60% of the population is under 30 years of age. The country has struggled to raise its GER of 18-to-25 year-olds to 10%, of which students, 75% are enrolled in private colleges and universities.

Pakistan has even higher challenges. The country has a population of 160m., with only around 590,000 students enrolled in higher education in 2006. The Government expects this number to increase to 1.3m. students by 2010 (29% compound average growth rate—CAGR). Approaching 60% of the population is under 30 years of age, but this is still less than the average 70% of the population being under 30 years of age across the Middle East and North Africa region.[2]

Looking ahead in the People's Republic of China, the estimated enrolment numbers in higher education by 2010 and 2020 create another conundrum. There were 23m. students enrolled in China's higher education system in 2005. Between 2000 and 2006 the annual growth rate in student numbers was 16%. If China were to grow at a conservative rate of only 5% annually in the coming years, the country's higher education enrolment would total 27m. by 2010 and around 44m. by 2020. How will China finance its real future growth requirements? Alternative forms of financing will be necessary as the People's Republic faces increased demand for places in the world's largest higher education system.

With the increase in demographics across most of the developing world, how will these countries resource the future development of their higher education systems on their own, after experiencing a rapid decline in public financing for higher education since the 1980s?

DECLINE IN PUBLIC FINANCING

In 40 of the world's largest developing countries, enrolments in higher education increased by an estimated 170% between 1991 and 2001.[3] Public spending over the same period struggled to keep pace with the rising demand for places and, from 1997/98 onwards, actual spending remained flat. In the eight most populous Asian countries,[4] student enrolments over the same period increased by 260%. Most of this exponential growth was absorbed by the private sector (see Table 1). Governments across the world no longer have the resources to develop modern systems of post-secondary education, training and lifelong learning on their own. Meaningful engagement with the private sector to mobilize non-state financing and provision will need to take place and on more level playing fields compared with the less favourable treatment experienced by many investors in a number of countries in the past.

ENROLMENT IN PRIVATE HIGHER EDUCATION (% OF TOTAL)

Korea, Republic	80
Japan	77
Brazil	75
India	75
El Salvador	69
Indonesia	68
Philippines	68
Colombia	64
Belgium	63
Chile*	58
Paraguay	47
Portugal	38
Peru	34
Mexico	33
USA	32
Argentina	20

* Incl. seven publicly funded private Catholic universities.

Sources: World Bank, Edstat; IFC staff assessments and statistics; OECD Government Statistics.

The potential of non-state/private sector investment in higher education is far from realized in most countries. This will need to change if international higher education is to stand any chance of meeting its obligations to create true social equity. History shows that it is the private sector that invests more than double what the public sector invests across all sectors of developing economies. In the education sector, however, the trend has been quite the opposite, with around 83% of all education-sector financing still coming from the public sector.[5] The potential gains from private sector investment are far from being realized. With the convergence of tightening fiscal, demographic and market-led pressures, governments can no longer afford to fund the future changes that are necessary on their own. As an industry, the higher education sector has yet fully to optimize the gains of public-private partnerships in both the financing and the provision of higher education.

Trends in Private and Public Investment in Developing Countries, 1970–2000

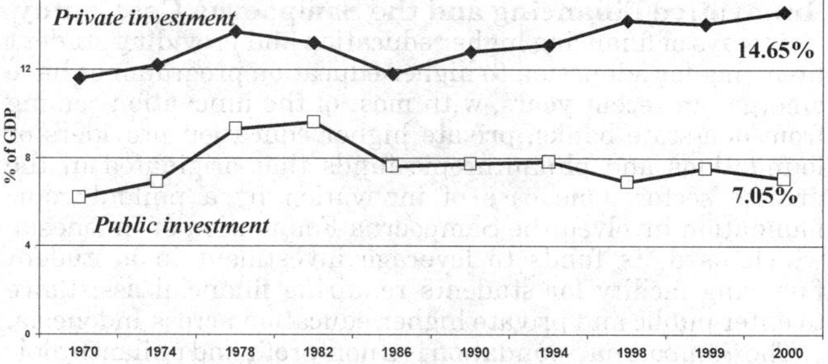

Source: International Finance Corporation, 2000 – Trends in Private Investment

Between 1995 and 2002 the share of public funding in total spending on all levels of education fell by around 50% in nearly

[2] This estimate includes the Arab states of the Persian (Arabian) Gulf and was carried out by the author drawn from available 2005–06 World Bank data and government statistics and from incorporating IFC staff estimates.

[3] Based on IFC staff research and estimates, 2004—the world's 40 largest developing countries are: Angola, Argentina, Bangladesh, Bolivia, Brazil, Bulgaria, Cambodia, Chile, People's Republic of China, Colombia, Dominican Republic, Ecuador, Egypt, Ghana, Guatemala, Hungary, India, Indonesia, Jamaica, Jordan, Kenya, Madagascar, Malaysia, Mauritius, Mexico, Mozambique, Pakistan, Peru, Philippines, Poland, Romania, Russia, Senegal, South Africa, Thailand, Trinidad and Tobago, Turkey, Uganda, Uruguay and Viet Nam.

[4] The eight Asian countries are Bangladesh, People's Republic of China, India, Indonesia, Malaysia, Philippines, Thailand and Viet Nam.

[5] Based on internal IFC staff estimates, carried out in 2004 during the author's tenure as Principal Education Specialist.

half of all Organisation for Economic Co-operation and Development (OECD) countries. The share of tertiary spending from private sources helped to offset this trend, with the share of funds from private sources for tertiary education at 22%, reflecting higher student tuitions in public tertiary institutions, as well as increased numbers and enrolments in private tertiary institutions. By 2003/04 global education expenditures as a percentage of global gross domestic product (GDP) were estimated to be a little above 5%, with OECD countries spending 6.1% of their GDP on education. In the European Union (EU) many countries have tried to hold to the notion of a free higher education for those who are academically worthy, where all member countries invest on average around 1.2% of their GDP on higher education, compared with 2.6% in the USA. Recent EU discussions have also recommended that EU state-supported systems start introducing tuition fees. Higher education systems globally are being forced to balance the needs of their education systems with fiscal realities, forcing higher education institutions to become more reliant on future financing from non-state sources.

Cross-Border Investment

Cross-border investment in higher education, which has mainly involved the private sector, has still done very little to date compared to other economic sectors. Since 2000 Apollo Group (through Western International University, based in Arizona, USA) has invested in India, the Netherlands and the People's Republic of China; CIBT of Canada and the United Kingdom's Nottingham and Napier universities (Edinburgh, Scotland) have also made investments in China; Jinan University is the first such Chinese institution to open a branch campus outside China, in Thailand; Raffles Education (Singapore) has campuses in Australia, Malaysia, Hong Kong and India; by way of return, the University of New South Wales (Australia) is establishing its own campus in Singapore; Manipal University (formerly Manipal Academy of Higher Education—Karnataka, India) has invested in Nepal, Malaysia and Antigua and Barbuda; Estacia University Group in Brazil has invested in a campus in Paraguay; Laureate Education Inc. of the USA had made higher education investments in 15 countries by 2006; the Netherlands Business School (Nyenrode Business Universitiet) has opened a branch campus in Nigeria; the Royal Melbourne Institute of Technology (RMIT—Victoria, Australia), with financing assistance from the International Finance Corporation (IFC—World Bank), has invested in campuses in Viet Nam (Ho Chi Minh City and Hanoi); and Whitney International University System, which is a US-led initiative, made investments in some Latin American universities during 2006. However, considering the global situation of unmet supply and demand in higher education, overall cross-border investment has been modest and does not reflect the reality of the huge unmet demand that exists for places in the tertiary sector worldwide.

A TIME FOR INNOVATION

Innovative Financing and the Sampoerna Case Study

New ways of financing higher education and providing student financing for admission to higher education programmes have emerged in recent years, with most of the innovation coming from non-state banks, private higher education providers or foundations and philanthropic funds that originated in the private sector. One case of innovation by a philanthropic foundation involved the Sampoerna Foundation of Indonesia, which used its funds to leverage investment in a student financing facility for students requiring financial assistance to enter public and private higher education across Indonesia.

The Sampoerna Foundation is a non-profit and philanthropic organization dedicated to improving the education sector in Indonesia and to providing young people who have a proven record of academic achievement with the opportunity to attend higher education. The Sampoerna Foundation provided over 18,000 scholarships to young students between 2000 and 2006. The foundation was established in 2000 by Mr Putera Sampoerna and former shareholders of PT HM Sampoerna Tbk, a major Indonesian cigarette company. The Sampoerna Foundation receives significant annual donations (US $5.8m. during 2005), mostly from institutional and corporate sponsors engaged in Indonesia. It is one of the largest education foundations in the Association of South East Asian Nations (ASEAN) region.

The Sampoerna Foundation led a student financing initiative by establishing a risk-sharing facility with Bank Internasional Indonesia (BII) and the IFC, part of the World Bank Group. The initiative extends loans to parents and students who have difficulty affording tuition and university entrance fees. The parent is the primary borrower, with the student also signing the loan agreement. The student loans: are limited to tuition and entrance costs; mature in 12–36 months; and are offered in some cases as a supplement to Sampoerna scholarships or personal savings. Sampoerna Foundation funds are deposited in a first loss participation account. The remaining losses are shared equally between the IFC and BII, the latter also acting as manager of the facility, by funding and administering the portfolio. The facility covers the costs and risk associated with the portfolio by deriving income both from the borrowers, who pay interest on the loans, and from the participating institutions, which pay fees to the facility in exchange for up-front payments for tuition.

The project was the first private student-loan financing facility in Indonesia and the first facility internationally to use a risk-sharing mechanism to leverage contributions from education foundations into a portfolio of student loans.

Innovative Delivery

Public universities in many countries have been starved of the financing and resources necessary to open up new market-led learning opportunities that foster career pathways for students. However, in many cases it is the private universities that have been more innovative in the way that they have stepped in to help fill the demand gap, by diversifying teaching portfolios, including shorter degrees and by offering alternative learning routes for attaining degrees, which include technical and vocational shorter-cycle courses, as well as continuing education and non-degree options for graduates. As a result, innovative delivery models have tended to become the domain of the private sector.

Innovative financing and new delivery models will play an increasingly important part in improving access and affordability in higher education, both national and cross-border. That financing and delivery will also help to fill the demand and supply gaps that await the growing numbers of young people who are yet to graduate from secondary school across the developing world.

THE GROWING IMPORTANCE OF THE PRIVATE SECTOR

Government policy makers are not usually in the best position to determine industry needs, at least better than industry can itself.

According to the 2000 OECD Programme for International Student Assessment (PISA) study, 6% of 15 year-old students in OECD countries were in government-independent private schools (i.e. privately managed and predominantly privately financed) and 10% of 15 year-old students were in government-dependent (i.e. privately managed and predominantly publicly financed) private schools.

In the USA, evidence shows that private higher education provision has also thrived over many decades, achieving higher results with rigorous regulatory standards, while also serving a disproportionate share of minority and lower income students. Recent trends internationally also indicate that public and private higher education are recognizing the benefits of working more closely together to optimize the gains in internationalizing higher education with the developing world. Evidence of this can be exemplified in the internationalized activities of Australian higher education, where the public universities have engaged in numerous 'Public Private Partnerships' to promote their offshore programmes. The number of Australian offshore programs rose from just 25 in 1991 to almost 1,600 by 2003, with most of them in Asia. Over 70% of the partnerships that Australian universities have developed with foreign HEIs are with private universities and colleges, as well as with a small number of local private training entities (PTEs).

Internationally, there are growing numbers of private firms, corporate universities, private training organizations and international certification bodies that are becoming major players in higher education, in the approval and conferring of certification and qualifications in growth sectors. Government dominance in these sectors cannot hope to keep pace with technological change in the major global information technology (IT) companies, where ongoing training, reskilling and recertification require a more flexible system for technical and vocational certification for lifelong learners. Private sector and industry training groups continue to play an increasingly important role by setting their own standards for learning and qualifications, so that investment in their human capital can make the work-force more productive and competitive.

The private sector can also work alongside education and training providers to ensure that the programmes, courses and qualifications offered are relevant to constantly changing needs. Government policy-makers are not usually in the best position to determine industry needs, at least no better than industry itself can. Industry and business are likely to engage with their governments more readily, and to support further education and training of the work-force, if they can have a greater say in what is taught in the formal and non-formal sectors, along with how training is delivered.[6] Many OECD countries have learned that the private sector can play an important role in advising on updating the accuracy of content and what should be taught.

In the more industrialized countries, academic and vocational education are being forced to navigate towards a new system, which involves both public and private sector representation wherever both sectors are involved–where the standards and processes of quality assurance, including assessment, accreditation, qualifications and certification, have the ownership and commitment of both. For example, even the structured and centralized approach to industry engagement found in many OECD countries today engages industry in education, training, governance and policy development, through to delivery, with representation being well supported by government, industry and the public, in most cases.

Mobilizing the Private Sector

The People's Republic of China is a country example where the education and training market has gone through major change since the 1980s, from there being virtually a sole public player in what was a highly centralized economy, to a fostering multiple players in today's system. To promote private sector development, the Government also enacted a provisional law to allow appropriate returns for private investment in higher education. According to Ministry of Education statistics (see Bibliographical References below), by 2004 China had a total of 78,500 private schools and educational institutions (excluding vocational training institutions), with 17.7m. students enrolled.

Although private education is playing an increasingly important role, in many countries it still faces some policy and regulatory constraints that are impediments to mobilizing private investment. Those constraints can include those listed below.

Lack of strong legal protection and institutional consistency. Although many private education laws and regulations have been enacted, they are sometimes not well implemented, leaving the preferred or intended policies stipulated by law not to be fully realized.

Institutional barriers. To a large extent, in many countries public institutions are still regarded as the official representative of education and receive higher status compared to the private sector providers, which are often perceived as more inferior. Again China provides such an example: by January 2003 only 131 out of 1,280 private higher education institutions were recognized by the Ministry of Education as eligible to participate in the admission process of the national higher education entrance examinations. In practice, many governments exert tight control over the operations of private universities and colleges and have been known to intervene inappropriately. In many countries private education institutions do not receive equal treatment with their public sector counterparts, where qualifications are at times not officially recognized, leaving the institutions undervalued in their societies.

Unfair competition. Due to the lack of a well-defined government role, in some Asian countries favourable treatment of public sector higher education has continued to provide inadequate protection and uneven treatment, resulting in commercial and operating uncertainties for private providers.

Governance and management. Private institutions can fall short of clearly defining the roles and responsibilities of their board of trustees or directors and of their senior management in areas of academic and administrative management and leadership. Family-controlled boards, especially in Latin American and Asian institutions, have in practice been known to micromanage and intervene in the academic operational affairs of their institutions.

Lack of clear tax, student finance and financial incentives. There are now many precedents in place across the globe where not-for-profit education is not taxed and where other tax incentives, which support social development, can be awarded to private institutions, particularly when their public sector counterparts are also not taxed for providing the same services.

THE NEED FOR POSITIVE REGULATORY ENVIRONMENTS

Quality private sector providers welcome even-handed regulations and strict quality standards.

The role and effectiveness of universities in the changing landscape for global higher education, including the notion of fostering partnerships between state and non-state institutions, will be substantially predetermined by the regulatory environments under which the institutions operate.

Opportunities exist for regulatory authorities in higher education to advance their non-state and private sector financing in the higher education industry. The IFC's experience between 2000 and 2006 emphasizes that quality-led private sector providers welcomed even-handed regulations and strict quality standards, which is also validated by how the private higher education sector has thrived in the USA.[7] Generally, achieving higher quality standards and delivery from private providers is predetermined by the positive regulatory environments in which they operate.

Governments can play a critical role in fostering non-state investment in higher education ventures. Investors look for positive regulatory environments as part of their investment strategies, avoiding smothering regulations that create commercial uncertainty. For example, the 'capping' or limiting of tuition fees has the potential to jeopardize commercial objectives and increase the risk of marginal returns, as well as unfairly restricting a provider from reinvesting surpluses in education ventures to improve quality. Capping tuition fees can also result in financial returns that are insufficient to service debt or provide fair returns to shareholders.

Uneven playing fields, where public-sector institutions receive more favourable treatment, along with added inconsistencies and inefficient approval processes, cause investors to

[6] Drawn from the author as Principal Education Specialist of IFC/World Bank; he was the task manager of an international study of best practice in technical and vocational education and training (TVET), covering four continents in 2005 and 2006, on behalf of the Chinese Ministry of Finance, with support from the Minister of Education at the Victoria Department of Education and Training (Australia) plus the Swedish Investment Development Agency (SIDA).

[7] Based on the author's observations and experience as Principal Education Specialist at the IFC (World Bank Group) between 2000 and 2006.

shy away from investing in educational ventures. In many developing countries these barriers have also applied to national investment in e-learning initiatives, leaving cross-border delivery the sole option for interested students.

Another disincentive for the private sector to invest in education markets can be the existence of 'quota systems', which in some countries remain a legacy of the past. Quota systems, despite their original intention, may no longer be practical for supporting a reformed education and training system in a modern knowledge society. The People's Republic of China is a country example where a student quota system still exists. Quota systems arguably fail to identify with provider needs or with business and industry needs in local markets, plus they seldom serve to meet the lifelong learning needs of people in a modern knowledge society. A quota system can also stifle private sector growth and investment, thereby restricting system capacity and perhaps jeopardizing scalability and the underlying commercial objectives of investors. Importantly, a quota system can also act as a barrier to access and participation in formal post-secondary systems for many worthy individuals.

New Regulatory Systems for Public and Private Participation

While the trend worldwide is to have universities transform and become more entrepreneurial entities that are drivers of social, cultural and economic development, this in turn requires new systems with positive regulations and policies for both public and private sector participation. In the future landscape for higher education, new systems will demand more relevant and flexible programmes that are market driven and able to be customized to meet the needs of different student profiles. Governments are being pressured by their economic ministries to facilitate new policies and regulations that will: cater for new student diversity; accommodate programme flexibility in a way that will meet the demand for new skills and for the retraining to acquire more relevant skills; accommodate the needs of lifelong learners and of training for adults, particularly the unemployed; provide incentives for private investment and participation, on a level regulatory playing field; promote academic and vocational education credit transfer, both nationally and across institutions; and facilitate equity, by blending financial subsidies or grants with student financing on market-driven terms.

Most governments across the world have also accepted that the days of formal systems of education for only a limited number of years have become a thing of the past. Constantly changing markets are demanding lifelong learning systems, which are comprehensive in their coverage from early childhood to retirement, producing graduates with new or appropriate skills that are relevant to the needs of the market. Governments have accepted for some time that there is no way that they will be able to resource and fund these changing needs without increasing their reliance on multiple providers from the private and public sector, as well as on foreign and domestic providers that can cater for the constantly changing role that new technologies play in international and local markets, as well as the way that learning will be delivered into those markets. Newer, more innovative and flexible forms of education delivery, financing, quality assurance, certification and recognition of attainment, will only be accommodated in systems where both the public and private sectors can play a meaningful role.

What will a country need to move along the continuum towards a more effective framework and system for lifelong learning, where vocational and academic qualifications can be more evenly valued? It will require qualifications progression or frameworks for career pathways that will help to blur the distinction between vocational and academic education, and the system will have to be more responsive to the changing needs of private enterprise and of the local markets and societies in which it operates.

Career Pathways

This term is used to describe a pathway throughout a working life, which could include a range or groupings of careers that share similar characteristics and where parallel disciplines or employment requirements call for either similar or common skills and competencies. 'Career pathways' should cater for lifelong learners and allow for student or learner choice to align different career opportunities in the workplace. To accommodate career pathways, governments are being forced to reconsider how they will build capacity across systems of higher education, training and lifelong learning and how they will mobilize non-state financing and provision, to invest in and structure the frameworks and programmes necessary to accommodate and foster such career pathways.

Public-Private Partnerships and the SAC Case Study

Shanghai Aerospace Corporation: a public private partnership for both public and private good.

The use of public-private partnerships will continue to grow as governments manage the transition from state-funded higher education towards alternative models of financing and provision. However, public-private partnerships need not be limited to conventional campus-based delivery. In the areas of education technologies, there are growing numbers of cases where the private sector can play an important role in providing and maintaining the technologies required to enable different mass delivery models. One such case is the Shanghai Aerospace Corporation (SAC) partnership with leading medical universities in the People's Republic of China.

SAC is a private medical education service provider that has developed a satellite- and internet-based communications platform for the delivery of distance medical education programmes in partnership with leading public medical universities and nursing colleges. It partners with leading public medical university providers to develop the programmes, which are then delivered to independent distance learning centres (DLCs) located in regional medical and nursing schools and continuing medical education (CME) centres located in leading hospitals across China.

SAC commenced its nursing and medical education operations in 2002. Each public partner university confers its own degrees through a joint venture called Shanghai Eryida Distance Education College (SEDEC), supported under the umbrella of the Government's Medical Distance Education Project (CMDE). Through joint-venture partnerships under SEDEC, SAC delivers health sector and medical post-secondary continuing education courses at both certificated vocational and bachelor (undergraduate) levels. SAC and its partners provide distance education operations to all parts of the People's Republic. As the private partner, SAC's role is to coordinate all investment and the operations of SEDEC, which includes: strategy formulation; the design, development and establishment of all platform technologies; the establishment of the distance learning and CME centres transmission-and-receiving technologies; distance learning and CME administration support centres; and all other technical investments, systems and course-ware development provided by SEDEC.

SAC and each joint-venture university work closely with the National Education Centre of Higher Clinical Medicine (NECHCM), which is the central qualifications standards-setting agency for the Chinese Ministry of Education, as well as with the medical doctors associations in each of the regions across China. By September 2006 SAC had established more than 90 DLCs in medical schools covering 24 provinces, with a total enrolment of over 20,000 students. SAC has been awarded a special Torch award in China for its work on the Government's CMDE initiative and for advancing the innovative use of information and communications technologies in the education sector. The award was issued by the High Technology Industry Development Centre, which is part of the Ministry of Science and Technology.[8]

[8] Information printed with the permission of Shanghai Aerospace Corporation (SAC), March 2007, and drawn from a presentation to the International Investment Forum for Higher Education of the IFC at Washington, DC (USA), in February 2006.

CONCLUSION

Higher education has become a global enterprise that is for the public good, as well as being a potential market for commercial interests.

Higher education has become a global enterprise that is for the public good, as well as being a potential market for commercial interests. However, the full scope of non-state or private sector investment is still far from being optimized internationally. With barely 19% of all 18-to-25 year-olds enrolled in tertiary colleges and universities globally,[9] higher education has yet to meet its obligations to create sufficient access to higher studies and greater social equity in the way that the systems are resourced and regulated. The growth of private education is both inevitable and desirable, especially at the tertiary level. The future horizon for both public and private higher education will become brighter as both realize the gains that can come from public-private partnerships (PPPs) and from working together for both public and private good.

It is generally accepted that public and private good are not easily measured, particularly in a sector where traditional services are not always easily divisible. It is also generally accepted that governments should provide a free and universal primary education for their children. Nevertheless, as students move up the compulsory levels of the education system, higher secondary and technical education have become elements of both public and private participation, which has, in turn, led to different degrees of openness depending on each country. Notwithstanding this trend, governments will in the future still have an all-important role to play in public higher education in areas of high expense, such as research universities, as well as in important disciplines for local economies, for which market demand may not be very high.

The private higher education industry is riding on a wave of opportunity for investment in developing countries, which for some is already paying off. Without increased private sector participation, global higher education will fail to break the 20% gross enrolment rate threshold for 18-to-25 year-olds that is in sight. However, to reach this threshold, further change is required in the ways that the higher education sector will be financed and regulated.

Seizing the Opportunity

Drivers of change impacting on higher education globally will govern future opportunities for growth and investment across the sector. While financing in particular will tighten, the international higher education sector will learn to become more innovative, with a greater proportion of future financing coming from the private sector.

Demographics will also outweigh fiscal realities, forcing governments to seek more innovative ways of pricing and structuring the delivery of education and training, creating more openings for private sector participation. There will be improved systems and more relevant curricula developed to accommodate lifelong learners, in changing economies where education and training will become more market-led and of economic relevance. Private providers will continue to be a dominant force in the financing and delivery of programmes for lifelong learners.

Knowledge societies will continue to be all-important for economic development, fostering innovation and competitiveness through a more educated and skilled work-force. As globalization and internationalization take hold, they will change the future landscape of public and private higher education, both national and cross-border, in ways that will challenge older delivery models, in turn opening up new areas of opportunity for private investment in commercialized initiatives.

The information and communications technologies (ICT) revolution and the internet will also continue to challenge the higher education industry in optimizing the use of new technologies and the ways that higher education has always operated. Better use of new technologies will help create new commercial opportunities in higher education, where most of the new investment will be private. New and more scalable, innovative and quality-based delivery models will allow commercial interests to make a positive difference in mass education delivery, to reach marginalized constituencies and settings that the industry has not yet reached.

[9] Based on IFC staff estimates, February 2006.

BIBLIOGRAPHICAL REFERENCES

Chinese Government—see Dahlman below.

Chinese Government—Ministry of Education. *National Educational Development Statistics Bulletin*, April 2005.

Chinese Government—see Perkinson below.

CIBT School of Business and Technology Corporation at www.cibtcorp.com/aboutus.html (website—last accessed by author 2 April 2007).

Dahlman, C. 'Challenges of the Knowledge Economy for Education and Training in China: Developing the Architecture of an Effective Lifelong Learning System', (unpublished—project commissioned by the Chinese Government. 2005.

Human Development Network, Education (HDNED)—see World Bank below.

International Finance Corporation (IFC)—see Kallierekos and Perkinson below.

Kallierekos, K., presentation to the IFC International Investment Forum for Higher Education, at Washington, DC, in February 2004.

Malaysian Government—Ministry of Education. *Malaysian Educational Statistics and Quick Facts 2003*.

Mann, M., presentation to the Victorian Technical and Further Education (TAFE) Association conference in Melbourne, Vic., in April 2005.

Organisation for Economic Co-operation and Development (OECD). *Education at a Glance*, 2000, 2002 and 2005.

Perkinson, R. 'Technical and Vocational Education and Training: International Cases of Best Practice Characteristics', IFC report for Chinese Ministry of Finance. 2006.

Royal Melbourne Institute of Technology (RMIT International University Vietnam)—see Mann above.

UNESCO. *Global Education Digest*. 2002.

Victorian TAFE Association—see Mann above.

World Bank. *Development Indicators*. 2005.

Edstats. 2005.

Pakistan: An Assessment of the Medium Term Development Framework, report for the Government of Pakistan. June 2006.

World Bank—HDNED. *Lifelong Learning in the Global Knowledge Economy: Challenges for Developing Countries*. October 2002.

Data were also drawn from other IFC and World Bank sources, the Indian Government's Ministry of Education and the Sampoerna Foundation.

ACCESS TO HIGHER EDUCATION: SOCIAL MOBILITY AND STRATIFICATION IN THE KNOWLEDGE SOCIETY

WILLIAM G. TIERNEY

Education has long been seen as a key vehicle for a way out of poverty. During the 20th century elementary school education increased dramatically in much of the world, and in the more developed countries high school or secondary education became a requirement. As Mark Gradstein and Denis Nikitin (2004—see Bibliographical References below) point out:

> 'The last several decades have witnessed a remarkable expansion of schooling around the world. The increase in various measures of schooling in particular, at the primary and secondary level, has been rapid and steady. In particular, the average years of schooling for the adult population (15 years and above), grew from 3.7 years in 1960 to 5.0 in 1980 and 6.3 in 2000.'

A truism has been that the wealthier a country the better developed the educational system; countries that have sought to improve their economic well-being have invested heavily in schooling. The assumption is, if a country's citizens wish to prosper, then the populace needs those skills taught mainly in formal venues such as schools—literacy, mathematics and the like.

Less well established has been the role and scope of tertiary education. Throughout the world prior to the 20th century a university education was reserved primarily for the wealthy or those who desired a religious education. The purpose of a university education had more to do with educating the life of the mind or the soul rather than as a state tool to combat poverty or to enhance the economic well-being of the state. In the late 19th and early 20th centuries, however, the purpose of tertiary education began to shift. In Europe and North America, in particular, a post-secondary education developed a dual purpose: to enhance the life of the mind or soul; and to serve as a way to enter the middle class. Today, as Michael Gibbons (1998) has noted, 'gone is the high-mindedness of a von Humboldt or a Newman, with its pursuit of knowledge for its own sake'. In its place is an economic assumption that a well-educated citizenry benefits not only the individual but the state.

Although universities and post-secondary institutions have existed for centuries throughout the world, the history of higher education is also relatively recent in some countries. The United Kingdom's Oxford University, for example, began in 1096, while Peru's San Marcos University (Universidad Nacional Mayor de San Marcos) was chartered in 1551. Afghanistan, however, did not have its first post-secondary institution until 1932, with a faculty of medicine affiliated to the University of Lyons (Université de Lyon) in France. Both Korea University (based in Seoul) and the University of Tehran (Iran) were founded in the 20th century (1905 and 1934, respectively).

After the Second World War tertiary education became somewhat more important in the developed world, but in the developing world the emphasis remained on mass education geared towards primary, and to a certain extent secondary, education. Most countries in the world, however, had at least one university by 1950. If they did not have such an institution, then the wealthy were likely to send their children abroad to gain a bachelor's (first or undergraduate) degree. Further, by the 1960s many countries in Europe, as well as the USA and Canada, not only had universities, but fully elaborated post-secondary systems had been developed, with multiple functions. Tertiary education educated the young for the life of the mind and soul, but also served as training grounds for particular segments of the populace, as well as a research engine for society in areas such as science, engineering, and medicine.

A significant transformation has occurred over the last generation with regard to the import and role of tertiary education. There is, in general, a common acceptance today that a high school education is no longer sufficient for a society that desires high-wage jobs in a global society. Globalization and technology have not only impacted on how businesses or companies function and interact, but also affected the kinds of skills that a society needs its citizens to acquire in order to be competitive. The result is that there is currently a worldwide push toward the expansion of tertiary education (Clancy and Goastellec, 2007). This increase not only pertains to the number of students who graduate from high school and go on to college, but also concerns an expansion and diversification of the opportunities for post-secondary education for adult students, an expansion of the kinds of educational opportunities and formats that post-secondary students shall receive and an expansion of the kinds of learning experiences and degrees that a student may earn (Pont, 2004). However, while such expansion is occurring on multiple levels throughout the world, one reduction is that tertiary education is increasingly seen less as a place where the life of the mind is nurtured and more as a training engine for multiple kinds of jobs. Countries now believe that a nation's colleges and universities promote social mobility for its citizens, which in turn increases the capacity of the state to develop (Haveman and Smeeding, 2006).

In what follows, I shall track these changes in three manners. First, I shall elaborate on the patterns that have occurred and are currently taking place with regard to access to higher education. I also consider why these patterns are occurring and how they dovetail with the economic needs of the state. Second, I elaborate on the characteristics of who attends and who does not attend post-secondary institutions. In doing so, I consider the characteristics of what blocks and promotes access to higher education. In the third section I turn to state and organizational responses geared toward increasing access and whether these various actions have increased access to academe and 'dumbed down' post-secondary education in the process. I conclude with a summative thought about the consequences of these actions for stratification and equity in the knowledge society. One point I shall make throughout the text is that although the success and impact varies across countries, one common denominator across the world is that post-secondary education is seen as a societal 'good' and as a growth industry, but the manner in which this 'good' is conveyed is increasingly privatized. Nevertheless, even the manner in which countries are trying to increase access to higher education is more similar than different.

PATTERNS AND GOALS OF TERTIARY EDUCATION

The Transformation of Providers

With the exception of the USA and a handful of other countries the typical provider of post-secondary education has been the state, as defined by a federal or national government. Public higher education has been and continues to be where the vast majority of students attend college or university and has been seen as the main vehicle to increase access. Accordingly, until recently the assumption has been that the government of a country sets higher education policy in general and with regard to admissions formulas and cost in particular. The USA has had something of a different model in two respects. First, throughout its history private non-profit institutions have had a robust history, especially with regard to elite education. Second, rather than a federal policy, the USA has a decentralized system where each of the 50 states sets policies.

Although private religious institutions, especially Roman Catholic and particularly Jesuit, have been a staple in many Latin American and European countries, their overall responsibility for educating a country's populace has been relatively meagre. Similarly, the assumption has been that the primary responsibility for an institution's finances has been the state and not the institution or student. That is, the budget of a university, whether that institution was in Malaysia or Guatemala, was determined by the national government. The role of the leader of the institution was not to solicit funds, but to manage funds. The role of the student and his/her family was not to pay for one's education, but to consume that education.

Three trends are occurring that have direct consequences on access to post-secondary education. First, institutions and students now have different expectations placed upon them. The governments of many countries have decentralized budgetary responsibility, such that a university's vice-chancellor, rector or president now has more responsibility, not only to manage a budget but also to be responsible for generating income. Similarly, as I elaborate below, cost sharing and student fees are rising as the assumption shifts toward the belief that a consumer of a university education has a responsibility to pay some part of the cost of post-secondary education. Second, as fees have risen, governments have begun to shift their concerns from the institution to the student. The result is that private tertiary education and forms other than universities are increasing throughout the world. In 1993, for example, even one of the world's poorest countries—Bangladesh—allowed one private university to open, because some saw it as a way to increase access (Quddus, 1999). By the end of 2005 the number of private universities in Bangladesh had increased to over 50 (Kitamura, 2006). The People's Republic of China now has more than 800 private post-secondary institutions, although the ministry only recognizes a few, and over 60% of Brazil's tertiary-level students attend private institutions (World Bank, 2000). Indonesia, South Africa and the Philippines are examples of other countries that have increased access to tertiary education, and one key vehicle is private institutions.

Third, a relatively recent phenomenon is that a new organizational type is emerging—that of for-profit higher education and corporate universities. A private college or university always has been a non-profit organization. The purpose has been to educate a particular clientele (such as Catholics or women) and not to make a profit for investors. For-profit tertiary institutions, however, exist in order to make a profit for their investors. Such a development is of interest for two reasons. First, the business community recognizes that higher education is a growth industry—which suggests that access will increase. Indeed, one merely needs to peruse the report of the World Bank (2000) to recognize that over the last quarter century enrolments in tertiary education have quadrupled and that by 2025 the expectation is that tertiary students will increase from 100m. to 150m. Further, corporate universities have quadrupled in a decade; there are now more than 1,600 such institutions worldwide (World Bank, 2002). The result, then, is that competition for 'consumers' (that is, students) has entered into what was once the rarefied atmosphere of the academy as access to tertiary education explodes.

A Shift in for Whom the Institution Exists

Insofar as most universities have been public institutions funded by the state, the norm has been that academic staff or faculty have been public employees. Nevertheless, for at least a century academic staff has had a privileged position in much of the world's tertiary institutions. The professorate determines whether students pass or fail, whether they receive a degree and the nature of the curricula. When courses are offered and for how long, and who is to offer them, has in general been the purview of academic staff. Although Latin American universities have had a particular tradition of student involvement, in general, the academic staff has been seen as centrally involved in the governance of the institution. If students are unable to pass an examination or unable to take a class during the day because they work, the traditional thinking has been that they will then not qualify for a post-secondary degree. This viewpoint has had the effect of controlling who goes to college. Clearly, if one is poor and needs to earn an income during the day to support one's family and if classes are only offered during the day, then that individual will not gain access to a bachelor's degree. Such a view of students was largely that of passive recipients. Those who were lucky enough to attend a college or university were there to mature and to learn. Their interests and opinions were of little relevance for those who directed the institution—the staff, the administration and the government.

Over the last generation, however, the view has shifted. When higher education becomes a 'market' and students become 'consumers' and when institutions vie for one or another type of 'consumer' in order to help balance their budgets, competition exists in ways that heretofore were largely absent. Whereas the faculty could determine when they wanted to offer a course in the past, such simple determinations are no longer so simple. If a university degree was once for a set period of time—or with regard to the doctorate an indeterminate period of time—in the 21st century such a position is increasingly less tenable. The dramatic increase in students due to the desire of governments and individuals for tertiary degrees, combined with the effects of the market, globalization and technology, has increased the voice of the consumer—the students—and lessened the voice of the provider—the academic staff.

The Redefinition of Academic Cartography

Until recently if someone said he or she was a university student most individuals would assume a specific place—a campus—where the student took classes. To be sure, some campuses were more pleasant than others; in the late 20th century an urban campus for day students might have been only a handful of buildings in the centre of a city but, nevertheless, the place where one took courses was in those buildings. Similarly, study abroad also had a specific connotation. In the late 20th century students in the more elite institutions had programmes made available to them where they might take a term in a foreign country, for often unclear pedagogical reasons other than to gain a cross-cultural experience. Although study-abroad programmes had dramatically increased by the turn of the 21st century, the portrait was still quite fixed: one student from a campus in one country visited another campus in another country for a semester.

Globalization and technology are changing those portraits. As the Organisation for Economic Co-operation and Development (OECD) noted in 2004, 'An increasing number of students are being offered, and taking advantage of, a new option—taking a degree or other post-secondary course offered by a foreign university without leaving their home country' (p. 3). Cross-border education, although still not common, will dramatically increase as technology improves and the hold of the state on student fees lessens (Li and Bray, 2007). An increase in access to tertiary education means that a variety of options now exists for today's students. Twenty percent of foreign students enrolled in Australian universities, for example, study at off-shore campuses (Bennell and Pearce, 1998). Whereas in the past the university and the academic staff had a greater determination on who was to come to campus, today student voice enables them choice—and not simply about one or another campus. Different temporal and curricular modalities exist and students will show less concern or allegiance to a particular institution if another institution is able to demonstrate the worth of its offerings. If education is geared toward employment, who cares about attending institution 'A', on a campus in a traditional format, if institution 'B' offers the same employment opportunities, but in a format that is more conducive for the student?

An increase in access in a market economy has created a relationship with a feedback loop. The entry of more students into the marketplace has created the need for more providers. An increase in the number of providers has enabled incoming students to have more choices about how they conceive of a post-secondary degree. The cartography of what we once meant by a campus is lessening, both by institution and by country.

The Redefinition of Transition Points and Relationships

Throughout the 20th century secondary and post-secondary institutions have had a distant relationship. As countries have moved from elite to mass post-secondary education, high schools in general have not seen their role to be a preparation for a university degree. Similarly, most universities have not considered a relationship with secondary schools to be part of their role or mission. Indeed, until recently in the vast majority of high schools throughout the world the completion of the terminal year was a success; students had achieved what the country had determined was the requisite terminal degree. Of consequence, what universities required or expected of incoming students was largely ignored. True, some countries had entrance examinations, which I will discuss in the next section, but the vast majority of these students were like every other country's students—they did not attend a university. In other countries, such as India, because schools were looked on as weak, an extensive private tutoring system existed (Agarwal, 2006). Thus, if one looks back at the 20th century, a fair assessment would be that primary and secondary education operated in separate spheres from tertiary education.

The consequence of dramatically increasing access to higher education, however, demands new relationships between high schools and tertiary providers. Instead of separate entities with separate missions, more discussion now occurs about inter-organizational relationships that are synthetic and complementary. Some will argue that massification has devalued a post-secondary degree. Ru-Jer Wang (2003), for example, has noted how in Taiwan students once went to the USA for a bachelor's degree, but since the 1990s less qualified students have gone to less prestigious institutions in Taiwan. Although one can certainly make the argument that more students suggest less quality, what needs to be taken into account is that students also attend different kinds of post-secondary institutions. All students are not attending elite institutions, so to hold the same benchmarking standards for all students would be mistaken. Simply stated, whereas a century ago a student may not have needed a post-secondary vocational degree to work in a vocational sphere, that is no longer the case. However, that student attending a polytechnic for vocational training is certainly not getting the same education as his or her peers at elite institutions.

An additional transformation is how countries are constructing transition points between secondary and post-secondary education. For much of the 20th century elite schools in developed countries offered a variety of courses in a student's final year or two in high school that might provide credit in college. Advanced Placement, the International Baccalaureate and the like are examples of college-level courses that might be earned while in secondary school. Such courses were the exception to the norm and reserved for the elite few. Those elite students who graduated from high school also made an automatic transition to university.

The consequence of increasing access has been that more college-level courses are now being taken by students prior to going to university and, rather than make an immediate transition to university, numerous students delay entry for any number of reasons. The result is that, rather than separate spheres that are unrelated to one another, schools and post-secondary institutions of necessity are forging closer relationships, and the boundaries between the two are dissolving, or at least are much less rigid than a generation ago.

From Privilege to Merit to Equity

As noted in the previous section, the earliest history of higher education involved training for the privileged elite. One's academic background was not tested to see if one deserved to gain entrance to the academy; one's background defined who deserved a university degree. Towards the end of the 19th century the idea of a meritocracy took hold and the assumption became that one needed to merit entry into academe. For much of the 20th century, especially in the developed world and its colonies, entrance examinations were concocted that aimed to do away with prejudices and enable everyone the same right to gaining admission to a post-secondary institution. The result was that those individuals who were excluded from higher education because they were not from a particular class, race or gender were able to improve their chances at being admitted.

Although multiple merit-based examinations still exist and most countries still hold to some version of merit-based admissions, the desire to increase access to tertiary education has also caused a movement away from merit and toward equity. On some levels such a plan suggests 'open admissions' to an institution. The reality is that, because most countries have some sort of co-ordinated system, a blend of merit and equity exists, where a student takes an exam and/or high school transcripts are used to determine which students might attend an elite institution and which might attend less prestigious ones. In institutions where there is limited space, the idea of merit still reigns supreme and, of consequence, the upper class remains over-represented. As McCowan noted in 2007 about Brazil, for example (p. 579):

> 'Access to higher education is to a large extent restricted to the higher socio-economic groups. Public universities have limited places and entry is determined by highly competitive exams, thereby excluding those who have not had a high quality secondary education or attended an expensive preparatory course.'

The result has been that those who traditionally attended elite universities are still over-represented, and those who are the first in their families to attend a post-secondary institution are lodged at the less prestigious institutions within a country.

CHARACTERISTICS OF POST-SECONDARY STUDENTS

As with the patterns discussed above, which cut across countries, those individuals who have traditionally attended university share several characteristics. Of consequence, efforts are being made around the world to conceive of ways to boost enrolments of potential students who share membership in groups previously denied entrance to higher education, because of either prejudice or benign neglect. In particular, examples of inclusion and exclusion revolve around three characteristics: gender, race (and to a certain extent, religion) and class.

Gender and Access

Throughout the history of higher education more men than women have participated in academic life. In some countries, such as those in Western Europe and North America, significant advances have been made with regard to an increase of female participants in the post-secondary system. Indeed, in the USA, Australia and New Zealand, currently more women than men participate in higher education. However, discrepancies remain with regard to institutional type and disciplinary preference. Women are over-represented in low-income professions, such as nursing and social work, and under-represented in high-status, high-income professions, such as medicine and engineering.

Those areas where the least progress has been made with regard to gender equity are in developing countries, in particular in sub-Saharan Africa and in South Asia. As the World Bank reported in 2002, for example, in Yemen the female enrolment ratio is only 1% of the eligible age cohort, as against 7% for men; in Bangladesh women account for only 24% of the student population. In those countries that are deeply conservative with regard to gender relations increasing access has frequently meant creating ways that more men and women might enter the system, but not making it any easier for women to participate as equals. Thus, men attend elite institutions and study in more prestigious academic areas and women are confined to the margins. As André Mazawi (2005) notes (p. 152):

> 'Higher education institutions are replete with arrangements which marginalize or confine women whether socially or academically. In Saudi Arabia, in which gender-specific institutions or facilities are the law and the norm women are not able to access technical and vocational education and training.

The result is that even in a country that seeks to increase access to tertiary education women remain far behind their male counterparts. A further problem to overcome with regard to increasing access for women in countries where gender discrimination exists in access to post-secondary education is that a woman's economic prospects and employment possibilities are also circumscribed.

Race, Ethnicity and Access

Just as we know that more men than women have participated in post-secondary education, we also know that throughout the

Country and Region	Combined primary- and secondary-level enrolment ratio (%)*		Tertiary-level students per 1,000 population		Proportion of women in tertiary education (%)
	male	female	male	female	
Africa					
Botswana	93	90	5.5	6.4	47
Madagascar	51	51	1.6	1.9	45
South Africa	40	47	14.6	15.9	48
Asia					
Cambodia	68	86	0.3	1.7	16
China, People's Rep.	95	98	3.3	6.1	n.a.
India	62	81	4.8	7.9	36
Indonesia	79	85	8.1	15.2	35
Kuwait	68	69	25.9	19.3	62
Yemen	34	90	1.1	7.3	13
Latin America					
Brazil	n.a.	n.a.	11.7	10.1	53
Colombia	89	87	18.2	17.1	52
Guyana	87	85	8.9	10.2	48
Industrialized countries					
Austria	102	104	28.2	31.3	48
New Zealand	108	105	49.9	40.1	56
USA	99	100	58.4	48.2	56

* Proportion of the population age 6–17 attending primary or secondary school. Source: United Nations (2000).

world, one's racial and ethnic background impacts one's ability to access a post-secondary education. Institutionalized and societal discrimination has existed for various minority groups throughout the world for as long as tertiary education has existed. African Americans were barred from and remain under-represented in post-secondary institutions in the USA; apartheid in South Africa excluded blacks from participation and its vestiges still have an impact upon the country; in India members of castes and particular tribes were banned from participation in academe and are still marginalized; aboriginals in Australia and the Maoris in New Zealand were similarly shunned and remain under-represented; Kurds and Armenians in Turkey or Berbers in Morocco have faced the same discrimination, which has resulted in their meagre participation in the tertiary system; indigenous people throughout North and South America remain under-represented in tertiary institutions. The unhappy conclusion any student of such data will make is that one's racial and ethnic identity has impacted, and continues to impact, upon whether an individual is likely to graduate from high school and go on to a post-secondary institution.

As with the discussion about women, some progress has been made in some countries. In general, more progress has been made in industrial nations than in the developing world. The USA, for example, still has discrepancies between the participation rates of African-American and white students, but the gap has narrowed over the last century. In post-conflict societies, such as South Africa, significant changes have occurred but problems remain. However, in the developing world the challenge of significantly increasing access to higher education for those racial and ethnic groups that have been historically discriminated against remains a significant challenge. Although the strict exclusion of someone from higher education based on racial or ethnic identity is eschewed in most of the world, the problem remains that without vigorous policies to overcome a legacy of discrimination the change has been insignificant.

Class, Socio-Economic Status and Access

Obviously, an individual has more than one characteristic of his or her identity that influences the ability to access higher education. One's gender and race interact, for example, as do one's religious and familial background. Those from the upper class throughout the world are more likely to make the transition from secondary school than those who are less wealthy.

Indeed, class and socio-economic status (SES) have had as deep and enduring an impact on one's ability to participate in tertiary education as any other characteristic that exists, except when societal mores have forbidden participation because of one's gender, such as when the Taliban ruled Afghanistan in the 1990s, or because of one's race, such as the USA for African-Americans in the 19th century. Thus, class and SES are significant indicators as to whether a child will graduate from high school and go on to a post-secondary institution, whether that poor student is in Canada, Hungary or Singapore. As the World Bank commented in 2002 (p. 52):

> 'In Latin America the share of students from the lowest third of the income distribution enrolled in tertiary education is only 6 percent in Peru, 11 percent in Chile and 18 percent in Uruguay. In francophone Sub-Saharan Africa the children of white-collar employees account for 40 percent of tertiary enrolment even though this group of professionals represents only 6 percent of the total labour force.'

Family income matters for multiple reasons. When one is poor, regardless of country, the likelihood is greater that one's parents and siblings will not have a post-secondary degree. One is less likely to live in a neighbourhood where a significant number of individuals have a post-secondary degree. There is less opportunity to attend quality primary and secondary schools and to have access to private tutoring and after-school activities. The culture of students in low-income schools is focused less on college-going and more on gainful employment upon graduation from high school. Fewer low-income students leave secondary schools with qualifications and fewer pass entrance examinations to university than their well-off counterparts. More low-income students who graduate from high school are in need of remedial assistance than upper-class students, and we know that remediation makes it more difficult to gain a post-secondary degree.

The ability to pay for a tertiary education is harder for low-income families than those from other classes. Insofar as racial and ethnic minorities are disproportionately lodged in the lower class, the impact of one's race and ethnicity gets commingled with poverty to make educational attainment that much more difficult. Further, as Marta Kisilevsky (1999) has noted, even in a country such as Argentina, where open-access is prevalent upon graduation from secondary school, academic outcomes are influenced by SES. Twenty percent of Argentina's poorest students who gain access to higher education eventually graduate, whereas virtually everyone succeeds among the wealthiest. Those who are wealthy also attend more prestigious institutions, and the poor end up over-represented in the weakest academic institutions in a country's system, such as the community college in the USA.

To be sure, other factors also make it difficult to increase access to tertiary education. Physical disability, regional origin, whether one lives in an urban or rural area and the language one speaks at home are examples of factors that may impact upon the likelihood that someone will be able to have access to the post-secondary system. Those who have physical disabilities, especially in developing countries, face specific challenges that make access difficult. Speaking an indigenous language at home, such as Q'eqchi' (Quiché or Kiche) in Guatemala, where the country's language of instruction is Spanish, would suggest that the individual will have a harder time graduating from high school and going on to college. Likewise, urban students are more likely to go to a college or university than those who are rural. Nevertheless, of all these multiple factors, the three greatest challenges to overcome are the discrimination encountered because of one's race or gender, and the challenges faced by those who are poor.

STATE AND ORGANIZATIONAL RESPONSES TO PROMOTE ACCESS

Certain findings about what enables or retards access to college are static and unchangeable. For example, although the research is quite certain that having parents who have a post-secondary degree makes it more likely that a child will go on to college, there is nothing that can be done to change one's birth parents. However, as Ann Matear (2006) astutely summarizes about access in Chile, but pertains to a majority of countries: 'The principal barriers to access are found in institutional funding arrangements, the admissions process and the quality of education at secondary level.'

Paying for Higher Education

State governments are turning to fiscal policies as a way to increase access and to generate resources to pay for the maintenance and expansion of post-secondary institutions. Whereas in the past many countries frequently provided free, or nearly free, tuition and fee policies, such a stance has come under renewed analysis. Although many critics allege that forcing the consumer to pay for a tertiary degree will decrease access, a significant amount of research exists that points out that the greatest beneficiary of tuition-free policies are the upper and middle classes. In effect, such parents are able to pay a considerable amount to send their children to private elementary and high schools that prepare them for admissions examinations and entrance to university, and they then receive a government subsidy for their children's post-secondary education.

The challenge with what has come to be known as 'cost sharing' is that if tuition policies are raised and access remains a central objective, then some form of government subsidy needs to be provided to those who cannot afford the cost of tuition and fees. Means testing is useful in industrialized countries that have verifiable measures of family income and family assets, but such a process is much more difficult in the less developed world (Johnstone and Marcucci, 2003). Similar problems exist with regard to the management of student loan programmes or income-contingent loans such as have existed in Australia. Countries with an infrastructure that enables the tracking of loan repayments and/or income over time have greater latitude in the creation of such policies than those in the developing world. In perhaps the most cogent work on cost-sharing in international perspective, Bruce Johnstone (2006) makes the case for an increase in public resources, as well as, 'the construction of less costly forms of higher education, and the kinds of financial assistance and loan programs that can combine significant cost recovery with protection to those whose participation in higher education is most at risk.'

Institutional Admissions Policies

Corrupt admission practices, where students gain entry to an institution because of one or another vagary such as family privilege or bribes, remain an unfortunate occurrence; however, such practices are now seen for what they are and are largely in decline. Merit-based examinations, which are presumed to be objective, coupled with the grades a student receives in high school remain a norm for entry into elite institutions, but they too, have their own problems. Students from less privileged backgrounds are usually less well prepared and do less well in such exams. A more holistic process, which takes into account multiple criteria of a candidate, is being utilized in some institutions and countries but, at the moment, examinations are more similar than different from a generation ago.

What has changed is the expansion of the tertiary system. Whereas admission to 'university' was the only viable option an aspiring applicant once had, as noted above, three changes are underway throughout the world. First, the public system in most countries today is more diversified than it once was. Students have the ability to attend a vocational or polytechnic institution, a less demanding academic institution or the historic elite university. Second, private institutions have opened that frequently have different admissions standards than a simple examination. Third, for-profit institutions seek to admit students by way of a quite different formula. Whereas merit-based examinations focus on how to keep students out, for-profit institutions strive to develop policies to get students in. By no means is the expansion of the system a cure-all. The result of the entry of new providers and the expansion of the public system is that new forms of stratification exist. Whereas in the past less well-prepared students were denied entry to academe, there are now places for them, but they are in less demanding institutions.

The Quality of Secondary Schooling

As with admissions requirements, some progress is being made. As secondary education becomes more widespread, greater opportunity exists than without. However, the quality of public education is of serious concern in most of the world. The result is that the wealthy are able to send their children to private school and/or hire private tutors. Public schools for the poor are understaffed and poorly staffed. The result is that, while the poor are able to access tertiary education, as noted above, where they go varies from where the wealthy are able to go. As Matear (2006) comments, 'There is a clear hierarchy between institutions, which correlates with the average points score on admission and the type of school attended by applicants' (p. 40).

The problem of public schooling is not soon to be resolved. Issues of teacher preparation and quality, building facilities and technological infrastructure, among others, are topics that will circumscribe how students are able to access tertiary education. Although progress has obviously occurred, stratification within country and across countries is likely to increase, while at the same time massification takes place.

CONCLUSION

As Quddus (1999) has noted, 'An important selling point for supporting public universities in a developing society is that higher education can be a powerful instrument for building a more equitable society' (p. 16). What we have also seen is that how one defines 'public' —who pays—is also under reconsideration. New providers appear to be another way to increase access. The demand for education is driven by the world's technological progress and the forces of globalization, which increase the returns to skills investment on an individual and state level (Gradstein and Nikitin, 2004).

Tertiary education provides skills for all sorts of jobs in the global economy. To the extent that a society underinvests in a network of institutions that support the production of higher-order capacity in its citizens, that country will be less able to prosper. The problem remains an issue of the 'haves' and 'have nots'. Those who are best prepared to increase access to tertiary education are those countries that have an elaborated secondary and post-secondary system; those that are least prepared are in the developing world, especially the world's poorest countries. The future in large part belongs to those who are able to construct a knowledge society. Such a construction is premised on access to tertiary education. Although the trends are similar from country to country in the world, the ability of a society to advance or change a particular trend varies in large part due to its wealth. The result is that stratification is likely to continue, if not increase, unless those who are less wealthy are provided with significant forms of social and economic investment.

Note: The author wishes to acknowledge the helpful comments of Sarjit Kaur, Richard James, Lisa Garcia and Redouane Assad.

BIBLIOGRAPHICAL REFERENCES

Agarwal, P. 'Private Tutoring in India', in *International Higher Education*, No. 45 (pp. 21–23). 2006.

Bennell, P., and Pearce, T. *The Internationalization of Higher Education: Exporting Education to Developing and Transitional Economies*, Institute of Development Studies Working Paper, No. 75. Brighton, University of Sussex (Institute of Development Studies), 1998.

Clancy, P., and Goastellec, G. 'Exploring Access and Equity in Higher Education: Policy and Performance in a Comparative Perspective', in *Higher Education Quarterly*, Vol. 61, No. 2 (pp. 136–54). 2007.

Gibbons, M. *Higher Education Relevance in the 21st Century*, paper presented at the UNESCO World Conference on Higher Education, at Paris, in October 1998.

Gradstein, M., and Nikitin, D. (2004, March). *Educational Expansion: Evidence and Interpretation*, World Bank Policy Research Working Paper, No. 3245. Washington, DC, World Bank, March 2004.

Haveman, R., and Smeeding, T. 'The Role of Higher Education in Social Mobility' in *The Future of the Children*, Vol. 16, No. 2, (pp. 125–50). 2006.

Johnstone, B. 'Cost Sharing in Higher Education: Tuition, Financial Assistance and Accessibility in Comparative Perspective', in Johnstone, B. (Ed.). *Financing Higher Education: Cost-Sharing in International Perspective* (pp. 3–31). Rotterdam, Sense Publishers, 2006.

Johnstone, B., and Marcucci, P. 'Cost Sharing and Higher Education Access in Southern and Eastern Africa', in *International Higher Education*, No. 30 (pp. 9–11). 2003.

Kisilevsky, M. 'Circuitos públicos y privados en la universidad Argentina: Señales desde la encuesta de hogares', in *Pensamiento Universitario*, Vol. 8, No. 6 (pp.61–68). 1999.

Kitamura, Y. 'Expansion and Quality in Bangladesh', in *International Higher Education*, No. 44 (pp. 23–24). 2006.

Li, M., and Bray, M. 'Cross-border Flows of Students in Higher Education: Push-pull Factors and Motivations of Mainland Chinese Students in Hong Kong and Macau', in *Higher Education*, Vol. 53, No. 6 (pp. 791–818). 2007.

Matear, A. 'Barriers to Equitable Access: Higher Education Policy and Practice in Chile since 1990', in *Higher Education Policy*, Vol. 19, No. 1 (pp. 31–49). 2006.

Mazawi, A. E. 'Contrasting Perspectives on Higher Education Governance in the Arab States', in Smart, J. C. (Ed.). *Higher Education: Handbook of Theory and Research*, Vol. XX (pp. 133–90). Dordrecht, Springer, 2005.

McCowan, T. 'Expansion without Equity: An Analysis of Current Policy on Access to Higher Education in Brazil', in *Higher Education*, Vol. 53, No. 5 (pp. 579–98). 2007.

Organisation for Economic Co-operation and Development (OECD). *Internationalization of Higher Education*, Policy Brief. Paris, OECD, August 2004.

Pont, B. 'Improving Access to and Participation in Adult Learning in OECD Countries', in *European Journal of Education*, Vol. 39, No. 1 (pp. 31–45).

Quddus, M. 'Access to Higher Education in Bangladesh: The Case of Dhaka University', in *International Higher Education*, No. 17, (pp. 15–16). 1999.

United Nations (2000). *The World's Women: Trends and statistics*. New York: Author.

Wang, R. 'From Elitism to Mass Higher Education in Taiwan: The Problems Faced', in *Higher Education*, Vol. 46, No. 3 (pp. 261–87). 2003.

World Bank. *Higher Education in Developing Countries: Peril and Promise*. Washington, DC, World Bank, February 2000.

Constructing Knowledge Societies: New Challenges for Tertiary Education. Washington, DC, World Bank, February 2002.

VALUING EDUCATION

ANNA VIGNOLES

INTRODUCTION

'Education, education, education.' (Tony Blair, 1997.)

So said Tony Blair when he was setting out the case for his party's election to power in the United Kingdom in 1997. For many policy-makers across the world, education is like 'motherhood and apple pie', as the Americans would say—something inherently wholesome and good, and certainly something you can never have too much of. To hard-nosed economists, by contrast, education is like any other investment. It offers the potential for an economic return, by yielding better labour market prospects for the individual and higher productivity for the state as a whole. However, education also incurs a cost for both the individual and, in most societies that have some degree of subsidized education, the state. To an economist, therefore, any investment in education by the individual or the state should be done on the basis of careful (albeit often implicit) calculations of the rate of return on that educational investment. In terms of determining the level of state subsidy of education, another important consideration is whether it is largely the individual who reaps the benefit of the educational investment, in terms of higher earnings or better employability, as opposed to society as a whole, in terms of a more productive work-force.

Of course to any serious educator, the notion that one invests in education purely as a means to reap an economic benefit is anathema. Education arguably imparts a range of skills, attitudes and values and has both individual and social benefits that go well beyond the narrow confines of the labour market. An important criticism, therefore, that any economist must answer when making the case for valuing education, is whether the economic approach to valuing education is conceptually narrow and limiting. Most importantly, might the economic approach cause us, as a society, to underinvest in education because the full breadth of the impact of education on individuals, families and society as a whole is ignored?

With these important issues in mind, I present the economist's case for valuing education. I show how economic theory can be used to value education, and how these same economic tools can measure the wider benefits of education, i.e. benefits beyond those accruing in the labour market. I start by outlining the theory that underlies most attempts to value education by economists, namely human capital theory, acknowledging both its strengths as a conceptual tool and its significant limitations. I then present some empirical evidence on the labour-market value of a degree—the earnings and employment effects of higher education (HE)—across a range of countries. I then show how the same methodology has been used to quantify the value of higher education in terms of some non-economic outcomes, such as better health. I end with some concluding remarks.

THE ECONOMIST'S CASE FOR HUMAN CAPITAL THEORY

Economists have a particular way of thinking about education, namely they see it as a form of investment. As far back as Adam Smith (1776—see Bibliographical References below), it has been argued by economists that individuals primarily invest in education in order to improve their skills, and hence their employability and productivity in the labour market. Education and training, it is argued, is largely a means to make individuals more productive. Individuals who are more productive will, according to economic theory, also have higher earnings and be more employable. Thus, the private return to the individual from an investment in education can be measured by the net gain in lifetime earnings accruing as a result of their investment in education. We can also think about a social return on education, arising from the net gain in productive output accruing due to any education investments made by the state. Formally, this theory is known as the human capital theory, as first set out by Gary Becker in his treatise on Human Capital (1964).[1] Human capital theory is still the main theoretical paradigm accepted by most labour economists today.

Human capital theory implies that one can value education by determining the benefits and costs of a particular education investment. The individual or state incurs a cost now, which for the individual is their lost income while studying or the direct costs of tuition, and for the state is the level of subsidy. This cost is compared to the gain in income in the future. Higher income may arise not only from higher earnings but also by improved employability. For this theory to hold, however, a number of assumptions need to be made. First, education must genuinely make the individual more skilled and productive in the labour market. Policy-makers around the world generally take this as given, with most proclaiming the importance of human capital for economic growth and national prosperity. However, this is actually a surprisingly contentious issue among economists. Many have argued that individuals who are more able and productive also tend to invest in more education (Spence, 1973; Arrow, 1973). In other words, education does not make you more productive, it simply acts as an expensive sorting device, to enable employers to identify more able individuals. Alison Wolf (2002) claims that the policy emphasis on education and skills as the main driver of economic growth overstates the importance of human capital investments and that a major function of education is as a sorting device and to some extent a social discriminator, and that this yields more benefit for the individual (as he or she is sorted into a higher paid and higher status job) than it does for the state.

Furthermore, even if one accepts that education genuinely does enhance individuals' productivity in the labour market, it is not clear that wages always accurately reflect individuals' productivity level, as suggested by economic theory. For instance, most people would agree that nurses and teachers are no less productive than bankers and advertising executives, but it is certainly the case that the former earn a lot less. Clearly the assumption that wages reflect workers' productivity levels is particularly problematic in the public sector, where the state has a greater influence on wages than in the private sector. This issue is also significant when determining the value of education for work in the home, such as child rearing. Home working is not waged, so using human capital theory to value education in this context is difficult. In summary, we should apply human capital theory somewhat cautiously when making judgements about the desirability of public investments in education.

Despite these caveats, this essentially simple theory retains its power because it provides a means for us to determine whether we, as individuals or as a state, should invest in a wide variety of forms of human capital, from schooling to on-the-job training. Furthermore, the conceptual framework of human capital theory can be applied in such a way as to produce specific estimates of the labour-market value of education and training. Producing such concrete financial estimates is desirable from a policy-maker's perspective, as it enables judgements to be made about the efficacy of one type of education subsidy as compared to another. Of course we need first to agree that the labour-market value of education is at least one of several potentially desirable criteria on which state investments in education or training might be made.

RATES OF RETURN TO HIGHER EDUCATION

Many thousands of academic articles having been written, estimating the rate of return to education, across a range of countries, across time and in different contexts (including Harmon, Walker and Westergaard-Nielsen, 2001; Psacharopoulos, 1994; Psacharopoulos and Patrinos, 2002; Bennell, 1996). I do not in any way attempt to provide a comprehensive guide to this massive literature, but instead emphasize key

[1] See also Schultz 1961.

findings pertaining to the value of higher education. I also show how the tools provided by human capital theory can help us identify where investments in education are particularly valuable to both individuals and society as a whole.

The value of education as measured by the rate of return will reflect the relative supply of and demand for education in a particular country or setting. Thus, a very high return for a particular qualification, such as a degree, suggests relatively low supply of graduate labour and/or relatively high demand, although determining which is extremely problematic. What this implies is that we would expect to see a different value of higher education across different countries at different stages of development and with a different mix of supply and demand conditions. Conclusions about the economic value of HE therefore need to be context specific. In addition, we need to understand how private rates of return, which reflect only the private costs of education and the benefits accruing to the individual, compare to the social rate of return to education, which reflects the social costs of education and the benefits accruing to the state. Comparing private and social rates of return enables us to determine the optimal mix of state subsidy and private tuition for HE. For example, where private rates of return to a degree are particularly high relative to the social rate of return, this suggests that the rate of subsidy of HE is too high from a purely economic perspective, and that the individual would continue to invest in their own HE if the state subsidy were to be reduced. Reducing the state subsidy might then enable the state to finance other types of education, such as nursery education, where potentially the social rates of return might exceed the private rates of return.

So, can anything useful be said about the average global value of higher education? The pioneer in the field of international comparative work on the value of education was George Psacharopoulos. Early work by Psacharopoulos (1981; 1994), which has since been updated (Psacharopoulos and Patrinos, 2002), suggested that the mean Organisation for Economic Co-operation and Development (OECD) social rate of return to HE is around 10.8% (lower than the rate of return to both primary education (18.9%) and secondary education (13.1%)). Returns to HE are quite similar for men and women. These averages are derived from large numbers of academic studies, which have used data from a range of countries, spanning a period from the early 1970s to the turn of the century. These same studies have also found that, on average, the value of one year of education is somewhat higher in lower income countries (confirmed by Denny et al., 2003). For instance, the social rate of return to HE ranges from 8.5% for OECD countries to 11%–12% for Latin America and the Caribbean, Asia and sub-Saharan Africa. This confirms the so-called 'law of diminishing returns', whereby the return on any investment is likely to fall as the level of investment rises. Thus, one year of higher education in a country where most people do not go on to tertiary education is likely to have higher value in the labour market than one year of HE in a more developed country where a high proportion of each cohort has a degree. Of course these cross-country studies hide large amounts of variation, and studies that set out to determine universal trends in the value of education have been roundly criticized (Bennell, 1996).

Psacharopoulos and Patrinos (2002) also reported the private rate of return to higher education, which in all regions exceeds the social rate of return to HE. On average, the private rate of return to HE is 19%, compared to a 10.8% social rate of return. In low-income regions, such as sub-Saharan Africa, the private rate of return to tertiary education is particularly high (28%). Thus, on average, it appears that the private labour market value of higher education exceeds the value of HE to society as a whole, at least as measured in terms of any wage gain, an important caveat that I return to below. The very high private rates of return to HE reflect the substantial state subsidy of HE in most countries. Economic theory would suggest that where the private rate of return greatly exceeds the social rate of return, policy-makers might consider reducing subsidies. It is important to note, however, that persistently high returns to tertiary education may also indicate that there are significant barriers to entry into universities. If degrees are very highly valued in the labour market, this should encourage more individuals to enrol in HE. This will, in turn, increase the supply of graduates and eventually reduce the return on a degree. Therefore, sustained high private returns may suggest some barrier exists that prevents individuals from enrolling in tertiary education. One obvious barrier is that students cannot afford tuition fees and cannot borrow the funds to do so. This would imply a policy that both increased the contribution made by individuals to the cost of their HE—reduced subsidies—but at the same time introduced a mechanism to enable students to finance fees would be optimal. Many commentators have argued in favour of income-contingent loans that enable students to repay fees after they enter the labour market and are earning high wages.

Certainly the decision about the optimal level of subsidy of higher education is complex and requires information on both the private and social value of a degree. In practice most of the empirical evidence available is for private rates of return. For example, Harmon et al. (2001) have estimated private returns to schooling across a range of countries using the same data source and the same point in time. Such work may generate more comparable estimates of the value of education than collections of estimates such as those presented by Psacharopoulos and Patrinos (2002). However, a major problem for those particularly interested in the value of HE is that such studies tend to estimate only the rate of return to a year of schooling, rather than to a year of higher education specifically. That said, such studies are still informative for developed countries at least, where the return to a year of HE and a year of upper secondary education are not dissimilar. Harmon et al. (2001), for example, find that the average rate of return to one year of schooling across a range of European countries[2] is around 6.5%.[3]

Another issue to consider is the quality of the estimate of the return to education. Many of the studies underlying Psacharopoulos and Patrinos (2002) do not allow for the problem I identified earlier, namely that higher ability individuals may tend to invest in more education and that some of the apparent return to a degree is actually down to the individual's own ability.[4] Comparative studies that take this into account are rare (see Denny et al., 2003, for an exception). So, as a note of caution, policy-makers would be advised, when making decisions about educational investments, to use country-specific studies that tend to be much more sophisticated in isolating the causal effect of HE on earnings.

EFFECTS OF RISING PARTICIPATION IN HIGHER EDUCATION

Education generally, and higher education specifically, has high economic value in that it gives individuals higher wages. However, an important question is whether the value of HE is rising or falling over time. It is well known that in almost all OECD countries there has been a massive expansion of HE, so that younger generations are much more likely to have higher education than older workers. In the OECD as a whole, only 22% of 45–54 year-olds have tertiary education, compared to 29% of 25–34 year-olds (OECD, 2006). Such averages certainly hide differences across the OECD. None the less, in 18 out of 30 OECD countries, the participation rate in HE exceeds 20%, reflecting the substantial expansion of this sector of education. One might have expected this expansion in the supply of graduates to reduce the value of a degree in the labour market. Yet evidence from a number of countries, including the United

[2] The countries considered were the United Kingdom, Germany (West), Portugal, Switzerland, Finland, Greece, Spain, France, Italy, Austria, Netherlands, Norway, Denmark and Sweden.

[3] This estimate is lower than that produced by Psacharopoulos and Patrinos (2002—see Bibliographical References below) partly because the Harmon et al. study (2001) only focuses on developed European countries, which will tend to have lower rates of return to education than the developing countries included in the Psacharopoulos and Patrinos study.

[4] See Card, 1999, for a comprehensive account of the methodological issues arising in calculating the rate of return to education, including the problem of ability bias.

Kingdom, suggests that the return to a degree has remained remarkably stable and sizeable in recent decades. For instance, the wage return to a year of HE remains around 7%–10% in the United Kingdom (Blundell et al., 2005; Dickerson, 2005), even though participation in HE has risen rapidly since the 1960s and now tops 50% by some measures. Globally, Psacharopoulos and Patrinos (2002) found that the private rate of return to HE has actually increased over time, although the average rate of return to all schooling has declined very marginally (by 0.6 percentage points).

Continued expansion of higher education is, however, likely to lead to a fall in the economic value of a degree in the labour market. In the United Kingdom at least, there are some very tentative signs that the value of a degree may be falling for very new graduates. The most recent cohorts of graduates entering the labour market in the early 2000s have earned a lower wage return than previous cohorts (Vignoles and Powdthavee, 2006). This does not necessarily mean that the lifetime value of a degree, in terms of higher earnings, is falling in the United Kingdom. It may mean, however, that young graduates are finding it harder to integrate into the labour market, partly due to increased competition from other graduates. There is indeed evidence for this from the United Kingdom where, although graduate unemployment is low, around one-third of new graduates appear to find it difficult to enter the labour market and end up in non-graduate level jobs, earning less as a result of this (Dolton and Vignoles, 2000; Green et al., 2002).

Despite concerns about an oversupply of graduates leading to so-called overeducation (graduates doing non-graduate jobs), in general graduates face optimistic employment prospects in most OECD countries. Most graduates only search for around six months to find employment and the average unemployment rate is low (around 4%), although this hides a lot of variation in the experiences of graduates across different countries (Paul et al., 2000). In some countries initial search times can be up to three times higher than average.

DIVERSITY

Another key feature of modern higher education is its increasing diversity, in terms of both its student intake and their subsequent labour market outcomes. As participation in HE has increased, so different types of individuals are drawn into it, including those students who historically might not have achieved a degree. This will have consequences for graduate outcomes. It may no longer make sense to talk of a single type of graduate. Instead, graduate outcomes will vary depending on what type of HE institution the person studied at and what particular degree subject he or she took. We already see this in the United Kingdom. Many of the subject areas that have expanded most dramatically now offer lower wage returns than other, more traditional subjects. Thus, although the rate of return to higher education across the piece has remained high (Blundell et al., 2005; McIntosh, 2005), in particular degree subjects there has been a fall in the return for recent graduates (Purcell et al., 2005; Sloane and O'Leary, 2004; Walker and Zhu, 2005). For example, for recent male graduates in the United Kingdom the private return to a degree in arts and humanities has fallen away to zero. This is obviously an issue that merits further monitoring. Of course, as the private costs of higher education increase, via increased student contributions in the form of tuition fees, one would expect that students become increasingly aware of the value of different types of degrees. We may therefore see a slowdown in the expansion of, or even a fall away in, student numbers in degree subjects that offer little in the way of financial return.

GOING BEYOND THE ECONOMIC VALUE OF HIGHER EDUCATION

Measuring the value of higher education purely in terms of its impact on earnings or employability is to miss the potential impact of education on a wide range of other non-economic outcomes (Schuller et al., 2001). In particular, researchers have identified effects from education on individuals' health, their participation in civic life, likelihood of voting in elections, as well as involvement in crime. These potential effects of education are hugely important in their own terms and, recently, social scientists have started to place a financial value on these outcomes, although valuing such things as better health is of course highly contentious.[5]

The literature on the non-economic benefits of education is still developing, and so distilling global estimates of the health benefits from higher education, for example, is not possible. Specific studies have however, found strong relationships between education and a variety of non-economic outcomes. For instance, Lochner and Moretti (2004) found that a 10-percentage-points increase in the high school graduation rate would cut the murder arrest rate by around 13%–27%. British evidence suggests that higher pay has a causal impact on property crime, implicitly suggesting that investing in education will result in higher wages and, indirectly, lower crime rates (Machin and Meghir, 2004). A number of studies have also found strong links between education and health behaviours, such as smoking and exercise (Wadsworth, 1997; Kenkel, 1991; Sander, 1995) as well as actual physical outcomes in old age (Ross and Mirowsky, 1999). Most of these studies have, however, investigated the effects of secondary educational achievement on non-economic outcomes, rather than the effects of higher education per se. It is generally thought that primary and secondary education is likely to have a greater impact on health and crime behaviours, as compared to the impact of tertiary education. Thus, although it is important to recognize the potential non-economic benefits of tertiary education, such benefits may be less important than for earlier phases of education.

MARKET FAILURES: THE PROBLEM OF EXTERNALITIES

Thus far I have focused on the value of education for the individual. However, some of the gain from an individual's higher education may accrue to society as a whole. For example, if a graduate makes others around her more productive, the total benefit from a degree is likely to exceed any gain in an individual's earnings. Instead, the rise in the productivity of other workers needs to be valued and included in our calculations of the true social rate of return to higher education. Where the benefits of education accrue not to the individual but to others, economists term this an externality. There is an extensive economic literature that has focused on establishing the existence and magnitude of productivity externalities (Moretti, June and July–August 2004; Acemoglu and Angrist, 2000). In general, the evidence is supportive of positive productivity externalities arising from education, although the estimates vary in magnitude. Moretti (July–August 2004) in particular estimated the productivity externalities associated with higher education in the USA. He found that in areas with a greater number of college graduates, the wages (and by implication the productivity level) of high school dropouts and high school graduates were higher. This implies that university graduates make other workers in the area more productive and hence earn them higher wages. The effects were sizeable: a one-percentage-point increase in the number of college graduates increased the wages of high school dropouts by nearly 2%, high school graduates by 1.6% and college graduates by 0.4%. This evidence would imply that the true social rate of return to education is likely to be higher than suggested by estimates of the impact of education on an individual's wages.

Positive externalities from education, such as higher productivity among other workers, are a good thing. However, the problem with these externalities is that they cause individuals to underinvest in education. As some of the benefit of education goes to society rather than to the individual, and the individual only takes his or her personal gain from education into account when making investment decisions, the net result is that we as a society underinvest in education. This requires state intervention to bring about higher levels of educational investment. This is the most compelling argument for state subsidy of education, including higher education.

[5] See Feinstein, April and October 2002, for a fuller argument on this issue in relation to valuing crime and health.

CONCLUDING REMARKS

The evidence suggests that higher education is a valuable economic investment. Generally, higher education yields very high benefits, in terms of higher wages, to the individual and substantial returns to society as a whole. The massive expansion in the supply of graduates over the last two decades has done little to reduce the economic value of a degree, suggesting that the demand for highly skilled labour has increased over time, driven by technological developments, globalization and many other features of a modern economy. I would argue, however, that, if anything, we tend to underestimate the value of education. First, this is because too readily policy-makers ignore the non-economic value of education, particularly in terms of its impact on crime, health and civic participation. Secondly, many of the benefits of education accrue not to the individuals themselves but potentially to their co-workers, families and friends. Thus, although economists have much to contribute to the debate about the value of HE, and the level of state subsidy that is optimal, we must be conscious of the broader benefits of education to our society, which are often not easily measured.

BIBLIOGRAPHICAL REFERENCES

Acemoglu, D., and Angrist, J. 'How Large are Human-Capital Externalities? Evidence from Compulsory Schooling Laws', in Bernanke, B., and Rogoff, K. (Eds). *NBER Macroeconomics Annual 2000*, Vol. 15 (pp. 9–59). Cambridge, MA, MIT Press, 2001.

Arrow, K. 'Higher Education as a Filter', in *Journal of Public Economics*, No. 2 (pp. 193–216). 1973.

Becker, G. *Human Capital: A Theoretical Analysis with Special Reference to Education. New York*, Columbia University Press, 1964.

Bennell, P. 'Using and Abusing Rates of Return: A Critique of the World Bank's 1995 Education Review', in *International Journal of Education Development*, Vol. 16 No. 3 (pp. 235–48). 1996.

Blundell, R., Dearden, L., and Sianesi, B. 'Evaluating the Effect of Education on Earnings: Models, Methods and Results from the National Child Development Study', in *Journal of the Royal Statistical Society*, Series A., Vol. 168, No. 3 (pp. 473–512). 2005.

Card, D. 'The Causal Effect of Education on Earnings', in Ashenfelter, O., and Card, D. (Eds). *Handbook of Labor Economics*, Vol. 3. Amsterdam, Elsevier, 1999.

Denny, K., Harmon, C., and Redmond, S. *Functional Literacy, Educational Attainment and Earnings: Evidence From the International Adult Literacy Survey*, Institute for Fiscal Studies (IFS) Working Paper, No. 00/09. London, IFS, 2000.

Denny, K., Harmon, C, and O'Sullivan, V. *Functional Literacy, Educational Attainment and Earnings: A Multi-Country Comparison*, University College Dublin Working Paper, WP03/19. 2003.

Dickerson, A. P. *A Study on Rates of Return to Investment in Level 3 and Higher Qualifications*, University of Warwick mimeo. Warwick, Warwick Institute of Employment Research, 2005.

Dolton, P., and Vignoles, A. 'The Incidence and Effects of Overeducation in the Graduate Labour Market', in *Economics of Education Review*, Vol. 19, No. 2 (pp. 179–98). 2000.

Feinstein, L. *Quantitative Estimates of the Social Benefits of Learning, 1: Crime*, Wider Benefits of Learning research papers, No. 5. London, Institute of Education, April 2002.

Quantitative Estimates of the Social Benefits of Learning, 2: Health (Depression and Obesity), Wider Benefits of Learning research papers, No. 6. London, Institute of Education, October 2002.

Green, F., McIntosh, S., and Vignoles, A. 'Overeducation and Skills: Clarifying the Concepts', in *Manchester School*, Vol. 70, No. 6 (pp. 792–811). 2002.

Harmon, C., Walker, I., and Westergaard-Nielsen, N. 'Returns to Education across Europe', in Harmon, Walker and Westergaard-Nielsen (Eds). *Education and Earnings in Europe: A Cross-Country Analysis of the Returns to Education* (pp. 13–21). Cheltenham, Edward Elgar, 2001.

Kenkel, D. S. 'Health Behavior, Health Knowledge and Schooling', in *Journal of Political Economy*, Vol. 99, No. 2 (pp. 287–305). Chicago, IL, University of Chicago Press, 1991.

Lochner, L., and Moretti, E. 'The Effect of Education on Crime: Evidence from Prison Inmates, Arrests, and Self-Reports', in *American Economic Review* (American Economic Association), Vol. 94, No. 1 (pp. 155–89). March 2004.

Machin, S., and Meghir, C. 'Crime and Economic Incentives', in *Journal of Human Resources*, Vol. 39, No. 4 (pp. 958–79). 2004.

McIntosh, S. *Skills and Labour Market Outcomes*, London School of Economics (LSE) mimeo. London, LSE, 2005.

Moretti, E. 'Workers' Education, Spillovers and Productivity: Evidence from Plant-level Production Functions', in *American Economic Review*, Vol. 94, No. 3 (pp. 656–90). June 2004.

'Estimating the Social Return to Higher Education: Evidence from Longitudinal and Repeated Cross-section Data', in *Journal of Econometrics*, Vol. 121, Issue 1–2 (pp. 175–212). July–August 2004.

Organisation for Economic Co-operation and Development (OECD). *Education Policy Analysis: Focus on Higher Education, 2005-2006*. Paris, OECD Publishing, 2006.

Paul, J, Teichler, U., and van der Velden, R. (Eds). 'Higher Education and Graduate Employment', in *European Journal of Education*, Vol. 35, No. 2 (special issue). June 2000.

Psacharopoulos, G. 'Returns to Education: An Updated International Comparison', in Blaug, M. (Ed.). *The Economic Value of Education: Studies in the Economics of Education*, International Library of Critical Writings in Economics, Vol. 17. Aldershot, Edward Elgar, 1981.

'Returns to Investment in Education: A Global Update', in *World Development*, Vol. 22, No. 9 (pp. 1325–43). 1994.

Psacharopoulos, G., and Patrinos, H. *Returns to Investment in Education: A Further Update*, World Bank Working Paper Series, No. 2881. September 2002.

Purcell, K., Elias, P., Davies, R., and Wilson, N. *The Class of '99: A Study of the Early Labour Market Experiences of Recent Graduates*, Department for Education and Skills (DfES) research paper (www.dfes.gov.uk/research). London, DfES, 2005.

Ross, C. E., and Mirowsky, J. 'Refining the Association between Education and Health: The Effects of Quantity, Credential and Selectivity', in *Demography*, Vol. 36, No. 4 (pp. 445–60). 1999.

Sander, W. 'Schooling and Quitting Smoking', in *Review of Economics and Statistics*, Vol. 77, No. 1 (pp. 191–98). 1995.

Schuller, T., Bynner, J., Green, A., Blackwell, L., Hammond, C., Preston, J., and Gough, M. *Modelling and Measuring the Wider Benefits of Learning: A Synthesis*, Wider Benefits of Learning research papers, No. 1. London, Institute of Education, 2001.

Schultz, T. 'Investment in Human Capital', in *American Economic Review*, 51 (pp. 1–17). 1961.

Sloane, P. J., and O'Leary, N. C. *The Return to a University Education in Great Britain*, IZA Discussion Paper, No. 1199. Bonn, IZA (Institute for the Study of Labour), 2004.

Smith, A. *An Inquiry into the Nature and Causes of the Wealth of Nations*. 1776.

Spence, M. 'Job Market Signalling', in *Quarterly Journal of Economics*, Vol. 87, No. 3 (pp. 355–74). 1973.

Vignoles, A., and Powdthavee, N. *Using Rate of Return Analyses to Understand Sector Skill Needs*, CEE Discussion Paper, No. 70. London, London School of Economics (Centre for the Economics of Education), 2006.

Wadsworth, M. E. J. 'Changing Social Factors and their Long-term Implications for Health', in *British Medical Bulletin*, Vol. 53, No. 1 (pp. 198–209). 1997.

Walker, I., and Zhu, Y. *The College Wage Premium, Overeducation and the Expansion of Higher Education in the UK*, IZA Discussion Paper, No. 1627. Bonn, IZA (Institute for the Study of Labour), 2005.

Wolf, A. *Does Education Matter? Myths about Education and Economic Growth*. London, Penguin, 2002.

INTERNATIONAL ORGANIZATIONS

INTERNATIONAL ORGANIZATIONS

UNITED NATIONS EDUCATIONAL, SCIENTIFIC AND CULTURAL ORGANIZATION (UNESCO)

7 place de Fontenoy, 75352 Paris 07 SP, France
Telephone: 1-45-68-10-00
Fax: 1-45-67-16-90
E-mail: bpi@unesco.org
Internet: www.unesco.org

Founded UNESCO was established in 1946 'for the purpose of advancing, through the educational, scientific and cultural relations of the peoples of the world, the objectives of international peace and the common welfare of mankind'.

Functions

UNESCO's activities are funded through a regular budget provided by member states and also through other sources, particularly the UNDP.

International Intellectual Co-operation

UNESCO assists the interchange of experience, knowledge and ideas through a world network of specialists. Apart from the work of its professional staff, UNESCO co-operates regularly with the national associations and international federations of scientists, artists, writers and educators, some of which it helped to establish.

UNESCO convenes conferences and meetings, and co-ordinates international scientific efforts; it helps to standardize procedures of documentation and provides clearing house services; it offers fellowships; and it publishes a wide range of specialized works, including source books and works of reference.

UNESCO promotes various international agreements, including the Universal Copyright Convention and the World Cultural and Natural Heritage Convention, which member states are invited to accept.

Operational Assistance

UNESCO has established missions which advise governments, particularly in the developing member countries, in the planning of projects; and it appoints experts to assist in carrying them out. The projects are concerned with the teaching of functional literacy to workers in development undertakings; teacher training; establishing of libraries and documentation centres; provision of training for journalists, radio, television and film workers; improvement of scientific and technical education; training of planners in cultural development; and the international exchange of persons and information.

Promotion of Peace

UNESCO organizes various research efforts on racial problems, and is particularly concerned with prevention of discrimination in education, and improving access for women to education. It also promotes studies and research on conflicts and peace, violence and obstacles to disarmament, and the role of international law and organizations in building peace. It is stressed that human rights, peace and disarmament cannot be dealt with separately, as the observance of human rights is a prerequisite to peace and vice versa.

Member States

(July 2007)

Afghanistan
Albania
Algeria
Andorra
Angola
Antigua and Barbuda
Argentina
Armenia
Aruba (Associate Member)
Australia
Austria
Azerbaijan
Bahamas
Bahrain
Bangladesh
Barbados
Belarus
Belgium
Belize
Benin
Bhutan
Bolivia
Bosnia and Herzegovina
Botswana
Brazil
British Virgin Islands (Associate Member)
Brunei
Bulgaria
Burkina Faso
Burundi
Cambodia
Cameroon
Canada
Cape Verde
Cayman Islands (Associate Member)
Central African Republic
Chad
Chile
China, People's Republic
Colombia
Comoros
Congo, Democratic Republic
Congo, Republic
Cook Islands
Costa Rica
Côte d'Ivoire
Croatia
Cuba
Cyprus
Czech Republic
Denmark
Djibouti
Dominica
Dominican Republic
Ecuador
Egypt
El Salvador
Equatorial Guinea
Eritrea
Estonia
Ethiopia
Fiji
Finland
France
Gabon
Gambia
Georgia
Germany
Ghana
Greece
Grenada
Guatemala
Guinea
Guinea-Bissau
Guyana
Haiti
Honduras
Hungary
Iceland
India
Indonesia
Iran
Iraq
Ireland
Israel
Italy
Jamaica
Japan
Jordan
Kazakhstan
Kenya
Kiribati
Korea, Democratic People's Republic
Korea, Republic
Kuwait
Kyrgyzstan
Laos
Latvia
Lebanon
Lesotho
Liberia
Libya
Lithuania
Luxembourg
Macao (Associate Member)
Macedonia, former Yugoslav republic
Madagascar
Malawi
Malaysia
Maldives
Mali
Malta
Marshall Islands
Mauritania
Mauritius
Mexico
Micronesia, Federated States
Moldova
Monaco
Mongolia
Montenegro
Morocco
Mozambique
Myanmar
Namibia
Nauru
Nepal
Netherlands
Netherlands Antilles (Associate Member)

New Zealand
Nicaragua
Niger
Nigeria
Niue
Norway
Oman
Pakistan
Palau
Panama
Papua New Guinea
Paraguay
Peru
Philippines
Poland
Portugal
Qatar
Romania
Russia
Rwanda
St Christopher and Nevis
St Lucia
St Vincent and the Grenadines
Samoa
San Marino
São Tomé and Príncipe
Saudi Arabia
Senegal
Serbia
Seychelles
Sierra Leone
Slovakia
Slovenia
Solomon Islands
Somalia
South Africa
Spain
Sri Lanka
Sudan
Suriname
Swaziland
Sweden
Switzerland
Syria
Tajikistan
Tanzania
Thailand
Timor-Leste
Togo
Tokelau (Associate Member)
Tonga
Trinidad and Tobago
Tunisia
Turkey
Turkmenistan
Tuvalu
Uganda
Ukraine
United Arab Emirates
United Kingdom
United States of America
Uruguay
Uzbekistan
Vanuatu
Venezuela
Viet Nam
Yemen
Zambia
Zimbabwe

Organization

GENERAL CONFERENCE

The supreme governing body of the Organization. Meets in ordinary session once in two years and is composed of representatives of the member states and associate members.

EXECUTIVE BOARD

Consists of 58 members with a four-year term of office. Prepares the programme to be submitted to the Conference and supervises its execution. Meets twice or three times a year.

SECRETARIAT

Director-General KOÏCHIRO MATSUURA.

The Director-General has an international staff of some 2,500 civil servants. Of the professional staff (specialists in various disciplines and administrators), about two-thirds are on technical assistance missions in member states.

CO-OPERATING BODIES

In accordance with UNESCO's constitution, national commissions have been set up in most member states. These help to integrate work within the member states and the work of UNESCO.

UNESCO LIAISON OFFICES

UNESCO Liaison Office New York: Suite 900, 2 United Nations Plaza, New York, NY 10017, USA; tel. (212) 963-5995; fax (212) 963-8014; e-mail newyork@unesco.org; Dir HELENE-MARIE GOSSELIN

UNESCO Liaison Office Geneva: Villa 'Les Feuillantines', Palais des Nations, 1211 Geneva, Switzerland; tel. 229173381; fax 229170064; e-mail geneva@unesco.org; Dir INGEBORG BREINES.

UNESCO FIELD OFFICES

(See also under relevant country)

Africa: Bujumbura (Burundi), Yaoundé (Cameroon), Kinshasa (Democratic Republic of Congo), Brazzaville (Congo), Addis Ababa (Ethiopia), Libreville (Gabon), Accra (Ghana), Nairobi (Kenya), Bamako (Mali), Maputo (Mozambique), Windhoek (Namibia), Abuja (Nigeria), Dakar (Senegal), Dar es Salaam (Tanzania), Harare (Zimbabwe).

Arab States: Cairo (Egypt), Amman (Jordan), Beirut (Lebanon), Rabat (Morocco), Ramallah (Palestinian Authority), Doha (Qatar).

Asia and the Pacific: Kabul (Afghanistan), Dhaka (Bangladesh), Phnom Penh (Cambodia), Beijing (People's Republic of China), New Delhi (India), Jakarta (Indonesia), Tehran (Iran), Almaty (Kazakhstan), Kathmandu (Nepal), Islamabad (Pakistan), Apia (Samoa), Bangkok (Thailand), Tashkent (Uzbekistan), Hanoi (Viet Nam).

Europe and North America: Venice (Italy), Bucharest (Romania), Moscow (Russia)

Latin America and the Caribbean: Santiago de Chile (Chile), San José (Costa Rica), Havana (Cuba), Guatemala, Port-au-Prince (Haiti), Kingston (Jamaica), México (Mexico), Lima (Peru), Montevideo (Uruguay).

Activities

EDUCATION

UNESCO has an overall policy of regarding education as a lifelong process. As an example, one implication is the increasing priority given to basic education for all, including early childhood care and development, primary education and adult education. This approach has been the guideline for many of the projects recently planned.

Each year expert missions are sent to member states on request to advise on all matters concerning education. They also help with programmes for training abroad, and UNESCO provides study fellowships; in these forms of assistance priority is given to the rural regions of developing member countries. The issues and problems involved in human resources development have been at the forefront of UNESCO's education programme since the Organization's foundation. Objectives include the eradication of illiteracy, universal primary education, secondary education reform, technical and vocational education, higher education, adult, non-formal and permanent education, population education, and education of women and girls. 1990 was 'International Literacy Year', in the course of which a world conference on 'Education for All' was held in Thailand. In addition to its regular programme budget, UNESCO's extra-budgetary sources include the UN Development Programme (UNDP), the UN Children's Fund (UNICEF), the UN Population Fund (UNFPA) and the World Bank.

NATURAL SCIENCES

UNESCO's activities under the programme 'The Sciences in the Service of Development' aim to support and foster its member states' endeavours in higher education, advanced training and research in the natural sciences as well as in the application of these sciences to development, while at the same time attaching great importance to integrated and transdisiplinary approaches in its programmes. Activities in the natural sciences focus on the advancement, sharing and transfer of scientific and technological knowledge. At the same time, UNESCO continues to enhance human resources development and capacity building through fellowships, grants, workshops, and seminars, and has produced a number of training tools. At national level, upon request, UNESCO also assists member states in policy-making and planning in the field of science and technology generally, and by organizing training programmes in these fields.

At the international level, UNESCO has over the years set up various forms of intergovernmental co-operation concerned with the environmental sciences and research on natural resources.

The Man and Biosphere Programme (MAB) gives emphasis to the reinforcement of the World Network of Biosphere Reserves, which aims to reconcile the conservation of biodiversity, the quest for social and economic development and the maintenance of associated cultural values. The Man and the Biosphere Programme also promotes an interdisciplinary approach to solving land-use problems through research and training, covering topics such as arid-land crops, sacred sites, coastal regions, the Sahel-Sahara observatories and the biology and fertility of tropical soils.

The International Geological Correlation Programme (IGCP), networking in more than 150 countries, contributes to comparative studies in earth sciences, including the history of the earth and its geological heritage. Geoscientific programmes have resulted in the production of thematic geological maps, postgraduate training, the application of remote sensing and geodata handling, and studies on climate change and industrial pollution. Guidelines and other awareness-building material on disaster prevention, preparedness and mitigation are also prepared.

The International Hydrological Programme (IHP) deals with the scientific aspects of water resources assessment and management; and the Intergovernmental Oceanographic Commission (IOC) (*q.v.*) promotes scientific investigation into the nature and resources of the oceans through the concerted action of its member states.

UNESCO provides the secretariat for the World Solar Programme (instituted in 1996) and has been designated lead agency for the Global Renewable Energy Education and Training Programme.

Major disciplinary programmes are promoted in the fields of physics (including support to the Abdus Salam Centre for Theoretical Physics), the chemical sciences, life sciences, including applied microbiology, mathematics, informatics, engineering sciences and new sources of energy.

SOCIAL AND HUMAN SCIENCES

UNESCO promotes teaching and research in the field of social and human sciences and encourages their application to a number of priority issues relating to education, development, urbanization, migration, youth, human rights, democracy and peace. The social sciences constitute a link between the Organization's two main functions: international intellectual co-operation leading to reflection on major problems, and action to solve these problems.

Among the Organization's subjects of research are the complex relations between demographic changes and socio-cultural transformation on a global scale; the ways in which societies react to global climatic and environmental change; and changes affecting women and families.

UNESCO's programme gives high priority to the problems of young people who are the first victims of unemployment, economic and social inequalities and the widening gap between developing and industrialized countries. Under the mobilizing project 'Youth shaping the Future', an International Youth Clearing House and Information Service was to be established in order to increase awareness among public and private decision-makers of the needs, aspirations and potential of young people.

The struggle against all forms of discrimination is a central part of the Organization's programme. It disseminates scientific information aimed at combating racial prejudice, works to improve the status of women and their access to education, and promotes equality between men and women.

CULTURE

In the field of cultural heritage, the programme concentrates on three major lines of action: activities designed to foster the worldwide application of three international conventions aiming at protecting and preserving cultural property and inserting it into the life of contemporary societies; operational activities such as international safeguarding campaigns designed to help member states to conserve and restore monuments and sites; activities designed to improve the quality of museum management, to train specialists, to disseminate information, such as the most up-to-date conservation methods and techniques, and to promote greater public awareness of the value of cultural heritage.

In addition to a new edition of the *History of the Scientific and Cultural Development of Mankind,* work is continuing on histories of Africa, Latin America, the Caribbean and the civilizations of Central Asia, as well as on a six-volume publication on the various aspects of Islamic culture. A 10-year programme for the collection and safeguarding of the non-physical heritage (oral traditions, traditional music, dance, medicine, etc.) was launched in 1988.

With respect to the cultural dimension of development, the programme includes continuing assistance to member states in the preparation and evaluation of cultural development policies, plans and projects and in the training of cultural development personnel. Proclaimed by the UN General Assembly in December 1986, the World Decade for Cultural Development was launched in January 1988 and ended in 1997. The principal objectives of the Decade were: acknowledging the cultural dimension in development; asserting and enhancing cultural identities; broadening participation in cultural life; and promoting international cultural co-operation.

Following the approval by the General Conference of the Recommendation Concerning the Status of the Artist, efforts are being made to encourage its systematic application in the member states. Particular attention is given to the promotion of music, dance, theatre, architecture, fine arts, design and arts and crafts, as well as the organization of interdisciplinary workshops and other experimental workshops related to the use of new technologies in artistic creation. To contribute to the mutual appreciation of cultures, UNESCO fosters, in the framework of the UNESCO Collection of Representative Works, translation and publication of literary masterpieces, publishes art albums, and produces and disseminates records, cassettes, audio-visual programmes and travelling art exhibitions.

UNESCO's programme for the promotion of books and reading includes activities for the development of book publishing, production and distribution infrastructures as well as for the training of personnel in all the book fields (including editing, layout and design, ad hoc management courses and courses at university level). A major thrust of the programme is aimed at reinforcing the development of reading at all levels of society (and especially that of children) through promotional activities, reading animation programmes, book weeks and book years.

COPYRIGHT

UNESCO's programme in the field of copyright consists of the following types of activities: (i) those aimed at heightening member states' awareness of the role played by copyright as a stimulant to intellectual creativity; (ii) the preparation of international instruments, the implementation of which is assured by the Secretariat (among these instruments should be cited the Universal Copyright Convention which, guaranteeing the minimal protection of authors, facilitates the circulation of intellectual and cultural materials); (iii) activities intended to ensure the adequacy of traditional laws vis-à-vis the means of reproduction and of successive diffusion made possible by the latest technological revolutions in the field of reprography, satellites, computers, cable television, cassettes and magnetic discs; (iv) the organization of individual or group training courses intended mainly for the nationals of developing countries; (v) activities to promote access to protected works; (vi) publications and a database on legislation for copyright specialists; (vii) production of a video to increase public awareness of the importance of copyright.

COMMUNICATION, INFORMATION AND INFORMATICS

UNESCO's Communication, Information and Informatics Programme is designed to encourage the free flow of ideas and to help reinforce communication, information and informatics capacities in developing countries. Its major innovation is the extension of the 'free flow' principle to all forms of information contributing to the progress of societies, coupled with a comprehensive approach to challenges posed by the converging communication, information and informatics technologies.

Priorities in the area of communication include support for press freedom and the independence and pluralism of the media, reflection on their educational and cultural dimensions and efforts to reduce violence on the screen. A series of regional seminars on independence and pluralism of the media has resulted in the declarations and plans of action adopted by those fora being implemented in collaboration with professional media organizations. Furthermore, World Press Freedom Day, initiated by UNESCO in commemoration of the Windhoek Declaration, is celebrated every year on 3 May. UNESCO supports the International Freedom of Expression Exchange network (IFEX), which counts some 260 subscribers committed to protecting press freedom and the safety of journalists. The network of UNESCO Chairs in Communication (ORBICOM), which counts sixteen chairs in all regions of the world, provides an enlarged framework for co-operation among media practitioners, researchers and industries. UNESCO also supports the Global Network of Journalism Training (JOURNET) and the International Network of Women in the Media (WOMMED). The main operational arm of UNESCO's communication strategy, and a major funding channel, is the International Programme for the Development of Communication (IPDC) which focuses on strengthening news agencies, media training, community media and endogenous audiovisual production in developing countries. Since 1992, IPDC has given priority to projects in favour of independent and pluralist media. The Programme is governed by a Council of 39 member states.

The General Information Programme (PGI) pursues its efforts to promote international co-operation in the fields of libraries, archives and documentation, with emphasis on appropriate policies, in particular for the widest possible access to information in the public domain, and for methodologies and tools for information management. Among recent initiatives is the launching of the UNESCO Network of Associated Libraries (UNAL) which already includes some 300 members. The Memory of the World Programme aims at safeguarding the recorded memory of humanity, with a number of pilot projects under way in different countries. Furthermore, UNESCO organizes international aid campaigns in this field, such as the programme for the restoration of the National and University Library of Bosnia and Herzegovina. PGI's enlarged mandate covers trends and societal impacts of information technologies. The International Congress on Ethical, Legal and Societal Aspects of Digital Information (InfoEthics), held for the first time in Monte Carlo in March 1997, provided a forum for reflection and debate in this field.

UNESCO also supports the development of computer networking and the training of informatics specialists, through its Intergovernmental Informatics Programme (IIP). UNESCO-sponsored regional informatics networks—RINAF (Africa), RINAS (Arab States), RINSCA and RINSEAP (Asia/Pacific) and RINEE (Eastern Europe)—serve as test grounds for effective networking options, including links to the Internet.

PUBLICATIONS

(Mostly in English, French and Spanish editions; Arabic, Chinese and Russian versions are also available in many cases.)

Atlas of the World's Languages in Danger of Disappearing (online).

Copyright Bulletin (quarterly).

Encyclopedia of Life Support Systems (online).
International Review of Education (quarterly).
International Social Science Journal (quarterly).
Museum International (quarterly).
Nature and Resources (quarterly).
The New Courier (quarterly).
Prospects (quarterly review on education).
UNESCO Sources (monthly).
UNESCO Statistical Yearbook.
World Communication Report.
World Educational Report (every 2 years).
World Heritage Review (quarterly).
World Information Report.
World Science Report (every 2 years).

INTERNATIONAL BUREAU OF EDUCATION (IBE)

CP 199, 1211 Geneva 20, Switzerland
Telephone: 229177800
Fax: 229177801
E-mail: doc.centre@ibe.unesco.org
Internet: www.ibe.unesco.org

Founded 1925, the IBE became an intergovernmental org. in July 1929 and was incorporated into UNESCO in January 1969 as an int. centre of comparative education.

COUNCIL

The Council of the IBE is composed of representatives of 28 member states designated by the General Conference of UNESCO.

Dir: PIERRE LUISONI (Switzerland).

FUNCTIONS

International Conference on Education (irregular).

International Education Library: 120,000 vols; c. 1,000 journals received regularly; 500,000 research reports on microfiche.

BUDGET

Financed from the budget of UNESCO.

PUBLICATIONS

Educational Innovation and Information (quarterly newsletter).

Prospects, international comparative education review (quarterly).

INTERNATIONAL INSTITUTE FOR EDUCATIONAL PLANNING (IIEP)

7–9 rue Eugène Delacroix, 75116 Paris, France
Telephone: 1-45-03-77-00
Fax: 1-40-72-83-66
E-mail: information@iiep.unesco.org
Internet: www.unesco.org/iiep

(Regional office: IIPE–Buenos Aires, Aguero 2071, 1425 Buenos Aires, Argentina; tel. (114) 806-9366; fax (114) 806-9458; e-mail webmaster@iipe-buenosaires.org.ar)

Founded 1963 to serve as a world centre for advanced training and research in educational planning. Its purpose is to help all member states of UNESCO in their social and economic development efforts, by enlarging the fund of knowledge about educational planning and the supply of competent experts in this field.

Legally and administratively a part of UNESCO, the Institute enjoys intellectual autonomy, and its policies and programme are controlled by its own Governing Board, under special statutes voted by the General Conference of UNESCO.

Chair. of Governing Board: Dato' ASIAH BT ABU SAMAH (Malaysia)

Dir: Dr GUDMUND HERNES (Norway)

Publication: A catalogue of publications, listing 440 titles, is available on request.

UNITED NATIONS UNIVERSITY

53–70, Jingumae 5-chome, Shibuya-ku, Tokyo 150-8925, Japan
Telephone: (3) 3499-2811
Fax: (3) 3499-2828
E-mail: mbox@hq.unu.edu
Internet: www.unu.edu

(Office in Europe: c/o UNESCO, 1 rue Miollis, 75732 Paris Cedex 15, France; tel. 1-45-68-30-08; fax 1-40-65-91-86)

(Office in North America: Room DC2-1462-70, United Nations, New York, NY 10017, USA; tel. (212) 963-6387; fax (212) 371-9454)

The University is an autonomous institution within the UN framework and is sponsored jointly by UN and UNESCO. It is guaranteed academic freedom by a charter approved by the General Assembly in 1973. Its work began in September 1975. The UNU is governed by a 24-mem. Council who are appointed by the Sec.-Gen. of the UN and the Dir-Gen. of UNESCO to serve for six years. They come from various regions of the world and have diverse academic backgrounds.

The UNU is funded by voluntary contributions from the govts of many countries, bilateral and multilateral development assistance agencies, foundations, and other public and private sources. The UNU receives no funds from the regular budget of the UN; contributions are made to the UNU Endowment Fund, which yields investment income, and to its operating funds, as well as to specific programmes and projects.

The UNU undertakes problem-oriented, multidisciplinary research on the problems of human survival, development and welfare that are the concern of the UN and its agencies, and works to strengthen research and training capabilities in developing countries. The programme covers the areas of peace and governance, development, environment, and science and technology. Although the UNU has no students or degree courses, it conducts various training activities in association with its programme and provides fellowships for post-graduate scientists and scholars from developing countries.

The research, training and dissemination activities of the UNU are carried out mainly through networks of collaborating institutions and individual scientists and scholars. These include associated institutions, which are universities and research institutes linked with the University under general agreements of co-operation. The programme is co-ordinated by the University Centre in Tokyo and by research and training centres and programmes (RTC/Ps) that are being established by the UNU to deal with long-term problems and needs. UNU's research and training centres and programmes include: the UNU World Institute for Development Economics Research (UNU/WIDER) in Helsinki, Finland; the UNU Institute for New Technologies (UNU/INTECH) in Maastricht, Netherlands; the UNU International Institute for Software Technology (UNU/IIST) in Macao; the UNU Institute for Natural Resources in Africa (UNU/INRA) in Accra, Ghana, with a mineral resources unit in Lusaka, Zambia; the UNU Institute of Advanced Studies (UNU/IAS) in Tokyo, Japan; the UNU Programme for Biotechnology in Latin America and the Caribbean (UNU/BIOLAC) in Caracas, Venezuela; the UNU International Leadership Academy (UNU/ILA) in Amman, Jordan; and the UNU International Network on Water, Environment and Health (UNU/INWEH) in Ontario, Canada; the UNU Programme on Comparative Regional Integration Studies (UNU/CRIS) in Bruges, Belgium; the UNU Food and Nutrition Programme for Human and Social Development, based at Cornell University, USA; the UNU Geothermal Training Programme (UNU/GTP) and UNU fisheries Training Programme (UNU/FTP), both based in Iceland; and the initiative on Conflict Resolution and Ethnicity (INCORE), jointly managed by UNU and the University of Ulster, UK.

Rector: Prof. HANS J. A. VAN GINKEL

Sr Vice-Rectors: Prof. ITARU YASUI (Environment and Sustainable Development Programme), Prof. RAMESH THAKUR (Peace and Governance Programme)

UNIVERSITY FOR PEACE

Apdo postal 138, Ciudad Colón, Costa Rica
Telephone: 2-49-10-72
Fax: 2-49-19-29
E-mail: info@upeace.org
Internet: www.upeace.org

Founded 1980 by the UN but financially independent; conducts academic research on all aspects of peace, including disarmament, conflict resolution and mediation, the relation between peace and development, and the effects on peace of migration and refugees; various intl and governmental institutions are collaborating with the university; initiated a programme of extensive reforms and expansion in 1999. World Centre for Research and Training in Conflict Resolution established in Bogotá, Colombia, in 2001.

Library of 8,000 vols

First students were admitted in 1985.

Chancellor: Dr GRAÇA MACHEL (Mozambique)
Rector: JULIA MARTON-LEFÈVRE (France)

Number of teachers: 16
Number of students: 130

Publication: *Peace and Conflict Monitor* (monthly, in English).

INTERNATIONAL COUNCIL OF SCIENTIFIC UNIONS

International Council of Scientific Unions (ICSU)/Conseil International des Unions Scientifiques: 51 blvd de Montmorency, 75016 Paris, France; tel. 1-45-25-03-29; fax 1-42-88-94-31; e-mail secretariat@icsu.org; internet www.icsu.org; f. 1931; succeeded the Int. Research Council (f. 1919), to co-ordinate int. efforts in the different brs of science and its applications; to initiate the formation of int. asscns or unions deemed to be useful to the progress of science; to enter into relations with the govts of the countries adhering to the Council in order to promote investigations falling within the competence of the Council; adhering orgs represent 103 countries and 27 int. unions; in December 1946 an agreement was signed between UNESCO and ICSU recognizing the latter as the co-ordinating and representative body of int. scientific unions; Pres. JANE LUBCHENKO; Sec.-Gen. ANA MARIA CETTO (Mexico); Treas. ROGER ELLIOTT (UK); publ. *Newsletter* (quarterly).

UNIONS FEDERATED TO THE ICSU

International Astronomical Union (IAU)/Union Astronomique Internationale: 98 bis blvd Arago, 75014 Paris, France; tel. (1) 43-25-83-58; fax (1) 43-25-26-16; e-mail iau@iap.fr; internet www.iau.org; f. 1919 to facilitate co-operation between astronomers internationally and to advance the study of astronomy in all aspects; 66 affiliated countries, 9,000 individual mems; Pres. RONALD D. EKERS (Australia); Gen. Sec. ODDBJØRN ENGVOLD (Norway); publs *Transactions of the International Astronomical Union and Symposia organized by the International Astronomical Union*, *Highlights of Astronomy* (every 3 years).

International Geographical Union (IGU)/Union Géographique Internationale: c/o Prof. Ronald F. Abler, 2246 North Pollard St, Arlington, VA 22207-3805, USA; tel. (202) 431-6271; fax (703) 527-3227; e-mail igu@aag.org; internet www.igu-net.org; f. 1922 to encourage the study of problems relating to geography, to promote and co-ordinate research requiring int. co-operation, and to organize int. congresses and commissions; 83 mem. countries; Pres. Prof. ADALBERTO VALLEGA; Sec.-Gen. and Treas. Prof. RONALD F. ABLER; publs *Bulletin* (annual), *Newsletter* (quarterly).

International Mathematical Union (IMU): c/o Phillip A. Griffiths, Institute for Advanced Study, Einstein Dr., Princeton, NJ 08540, USA; fax (609) 683-7605; internet www.mathunion.org; f. 1950 to promote int. co-operation in mathematics; to support the Int. Congress of Mathematicians and other int. scientific meetings or conferences; to encourage and support other int. mathematical activities which contribute to the devt of mathematical science—pure, applied, or educational; 52 mem. countries; 2 commissions: Int. Comm. on Mathematical Instruction, Comm. for Devt and Exchange; Jt Int. Comm. on the History of Mathematics, with the Int. Comm. on the History of Mathematics; Pres. JOHN M. BALL (UK); Sec. PHILLIP A. GRIFFITHS (USA).

International Union for Physical and Engineering Sciences in Medicine (IUPESM): c/o Prof. Heikki Terio, Biomedical Eng., MTA C2:44, Karolinska, Univ. Hospital, Huddinge, Stockholm 14186, Sweden; tel. (8) 585-808-52; fax (8) 585-862-90; e-mail heikki.terio@karolinska.se; internet www.iupesm.org; f. 1982; organizes and co-ordinates the triennial World Congress for Medical Physics and Biomedical Eng.; organizes and/or co-ordinates int. meetings or conferences for constituent orgs; represents the interests of members in the Int. Council for Science; disseminates, promotes and/or develops standards of practice in the fields of medical physics and biomedical eng. to enhance the quality of health care worldwide; 40,000 mems; Pres. Prof. JOACHIM NAGEL (Germany); Sec.-Gen. Prof. HEIKKI TERIO (Sweden).

International Union for Pure and Applied Biophysics (IUPAB): c/o Prof. Fritz G. Parak, Physik-Department E-17, Technische Universität München, James-Franck-Str., 85747 Garching, Germany; tel. (89) 28912551; fax (89) 28912548; e-mail fritz.parak@ph.tum.de; internet www.iupab.org; f. 1961 to organize int. co-operation in biophysics and promote communication between biophysics and allied subjects, to encourage nat. co-operation between biophysical socs, and to contribute to the advancement of biophysical knowledge; mems: adhering bodies in 50 countries; Pres. Prof. IAN SMITH (Canada); Sec.-Gen. Prof. Dr FRITZ G. PARAK (Germany); publ. *Quarterly Reviews of Biophysics*.

International Union of Biochemistry and Molecular Biology (IUBMB): c/o Prof. Jacques-Henry Weil, Institut de Botanique, 28 rue Goethe, 67083 Strasbourg Cedex, France; tel. 3-90-24-18-32; fax 3-90-24-19-21; e-mail jacques-henry.weil@ibmp-ulp.u-strasbg.fr; internet www.iubmb.org; f. 1955 to encourage the continuance of a series of Int. Congresses and Conferences of Biochemistry and Molecular Biology; to promote int. co-ordination of research, discussion and publication; to organize permanent co-operation between the socs representing biochemistry and molecular biology in the adherent countries; to contribute to the advancement of biochemistry and molecular biology in all its int. aspects; mems: 49 adhering bodies, 24 assoc. adhering bodies, 7 assoc. orgs; Pres. Prof. MARY OSBORN (Germany); Sec.-Gen. Prof. JACQUES-HENRY WEIL (France); Treas. Prof. JAN JOEP DE PONT (Netherlands); publs *Trends in Biochemical Sciences* (monthly), *Biochemistry and Molecular Biology Education* (monthly), *IUBMB Life* (monthly), *Biofactors* (quarterly), *Biotechnology and Applied Biochemistry* (6 a year), *Molecular Aspects of Medicine* (6 a year).

International Union of Biological Sciences (IUBS)/Union Internationale des Sciences Biologiques: 51 blvd de Montmorency, 75016 Paris, France; tel. 1-45-25-00-09; fax 1-45-25-20-29; e-mail secretariat@iubs.org; internet www.iubs.org; f. 1919 for the promotion of int. co-operation in biology; mems: 41 countries and 83 intl scientific orgs are represented; Exec. Dir Dr TALAL YOUNES; publ. *Biology International* (2 a year).

International Union of Crystallography (IUC)/Union Internationale de Cristallographie: c/o M. H. Dacombe, Executive Secretary, 2 Abbey Square, Chester, CH1 2HU, UK; tel. (1244) 345431; fax (1244) 344843; e-mail execsec@iucr.org; internet www.iucr.org; f. 1947 to promote intl co-operation in crystallography; to contribute to the advancement of crystallography in all its aspects, including related topics concerning the non-crystalline states; to facilitate intl standardization of methods, of units, of nomenclature and of symbols used in crystallography; and to form a focus for the relations of crystallography to other sciences; 17 commissions; 40 mem. countries; Pres. Prof. Y. OHASHI (Japan); Gen. Sec. and Treas. Prof. S. LIDIN (Sweden); Exec. Sec. M. H. DACOMBE; publs *Acta Crystallographica* (Sections A and B, 6 a year; Sections C, D and E and F, monthly), *Journal of Applied Crystallography* (6 a year), *Journal of Synchrotron Radiation* (6 a year).

International Union of Food Science and Technology (IUFoST): POB 61021, No. 19, 511 Maplegrove Rd, Oakville, ON L6J 6X0, Canada; tel. (905) 815-1926; fax (905) 815-1574; e-mail secretariat@iufost.org; internet www.iufost.org; f. 1970; encourages int. co-operation and exchange of scientific and technical information among scientists, food technologists and specialists of member nations; supporting int. progress in both theoretical and applied areas of food science; advances technology in the processing, manufacturing, preservation, storage and distribution of food products; encourages appropriate education and training in food science and technology; fostering professionalism and professional organization among food scientists and technologists; nat. representatives in 65 mem. countries; Pres. ALAN MORTIMER (Australia); Sec.-Gen. and Treas. JUDITH MEECH; publs *The International Review of Food Science and Technology* (annual), *Food Science and Technology* (6 a year), *Trends in Food Science and Technology* (monthly), *The World of Food Science* (online, jtly with Institute of Food Technologists).

International Union of Geodesy and Geophysics (IUGG)/Union Géodésique et Géophysique Internationale: c/o Jo Ann Joselyn, CIRES, University of Colorado, UCB 216, Boulder, CO 80309-0216, USA; tel. (303) 497-5147; fax (303) 497-3645; e-mail secretariat@iugg.org; internet www.iugg.org; f. 1919 to promote the study of problems relating to the form and physics of the earth; to initiate, facilitate and co-ordinate research into those problems of geodesy and geophysics which require international co-operation; federation of 7 associations representing Geodesy, Seismology and Physics of the Earth's Interior, Physical Sciences of the Ocean, Volcanology and Chemistry of the Earth's Interior, Hydrological Sciences, Meteorology and Atmospheric Physics, Geomagnetism and Aeronomy, which meet at the General Assemblies of the Union; jt cttees of the various associations either among themselves or with other unions; organizes scientific meetings and sponsors various permanent services, the object of which is to collect, analyze and publish geophysical data; 66 mem. countries; Pres. URI SHAMIR (Israel); Vice-Pres. TOM BEER (Australia); Sec.-Gen. J. A. JOSELYN (USA); publs *IUGG E-Journal*, *IUGG Year-book*, *Proceedings of Assemblies*.

International Union of Geological Sciences (IUGS)/Union Internationale des Sciences Géologiques: IUGS Secretariat, Geological Survey of Norway, Lade, POB 3006 Lade, 7002 Trondheim, Norway; tel. 73-92-15-00; fax 73-50-22-30; e-mail iugs.secretariat@ngu.no; internet www.iugs.org; f. 1961 from the International Geological Congress; mems from 110 countries; Pres. Prof. ZHANG HONGREN (People's Republic of China); Vice-Presidents Prof. SYLVI HALDORSEN (Norway), Prof. ELDRIDGE M. MOORES (USA); Sec.-Gen. Dr PETER T. BOBROWSKY (Canada); publs *Episodes*, *International Geoscience Newsmagazine* (quarterly),

Reviews or Annotated bibliographies on geological topics of current interest (irregular).

International Union of Immunological Societies (IUIS)/Union Internationale des Sociétés d'Immunologie: c/o Sylvia Trittinger, Vienna Academy of Postgraduate Medical Education and Research, Alser Str. 4, 1090 Vienna, Austria; tel. (1) 405138313; fax (1) 405138323; e-mail iuis-central-office@medacad.org; internet www.iuisonline.org; f. 1971; mems: 54 nat. and regional socs; Pres. ROLF M. ZINKERNAGEL (Switzerland); Sec.-Gen. MOHAMED R. DAHA (Netherlands); publ. *The Immunologist* (6 a year).

International Union of Microbiological Societies (IUMS)/Union Internationale des Sociétés de Microbiologie: c/o Dr Robert Samson, Head of Applied and Industrial Mycology, Centraalbureau voor Schimmelcultures, Utrecht, 3508 AD, The Netherlands; tel. (30) 2122600; fax (30) 2512097; e-mail samson@cbs.knaw.nl; internet www.iums.org; f. 1930; mems: 90 nat. socs; Pres. KARL-HEINZ SCHLEIFER (Germany); Sec.-Gen. Dr ROBERT SAMSON (Australia); publs *Archives of Virology* (monthly), *Biological* (quarterly), *International Journal of Food Microbiology* (fortnightly), *International Journal of Systematic and Evolutionary Microbiology* (monthly).

International Union of Nutritional Sciences (IUNS)/Union Internationale des Sciences de la Nutrition: c/o Dr Osman Galal, UCLA School of Public Health, Community Health Sciences, 36-081 CHS, POB 951772, Los Angeles, CA 90095-1772, USA; tel. (310) 206-9639; fax (310) 794-1805; e-mail info@iuns.org; internet www.iuns.org; f. 1946 to study the science of nutrition and its applications; 80 adhering bodies; Pres. Dr RICARDO UAUY (Chile); Sec.-Gen. Dr OSMAN GALAL (USA).

International Union of Pharmacology (IUPHAR)/Union Internationale de Pharmacologie: c/o Lindsay Hart, Dept of Pharmacology, College of Medicine, University of California, Irvine, CA 92697, USA; tel. (949) 824-1178; fax (949) 824-4855; e-mail l.hart@iuphar.org; internet www.iuphar.org; f. 1959 as section of Int. Union of Physiological Sciences, independent 1966; promotes international co-ordination of research, discussion, symposia, and publication in the field of pharmacology; co-operates with WHO in matters concerning drugs and drug research, and with related intl unions; four-yearly intl congresses; 52 national and 3 regional mem. socs; integral Division of Clinical Pharmacology and sections of Toxicology, Drug Metabolism and Gastro-intestinal Pharmacology, which also arrange intl meetings; Pres. Prof. PAUL M. VANHOUTTE (People's Republic of China); Sec.-Gen. Dr SUE PIPER DUCKLES (USA).

International Union of Physiological Sciences (IUPS)/Union Internationale des Sciences Physiologiques: c/o Susan Orsoni, LGN, Bâtiment CERVI, Hôpital de la Pitié Salpêtrière, 83 blvd de l'Hôpital, 75013 Paris, France; tel. 1-42-17-75-37; fax 1-42-17-75-3; e-mail orsoni@chups.jussieu.fr; internet www.iups.org; f. 1953 for the advancement of physiological sciences, to facilitate the dissemination of knowledge in the field of physiology, to promote the Int. Congresses of Physiology and such other meetings as may be useful for the advancement of physiological sciences; 54 mem. countries; Pres. Prof. AKIMICHI KANEKO (Japan); Sec.-Gen. Prof. OLE PETERSEN (UK); publs *IUPS Newsletter*, *Physiology* (quarterly).

International Union of Psychological Science (IUPsyS)/Union Internationale de Psychologie Scientifique: c/o Pierre Ritchie, Ecole de Psychologie, Université d'Ottawa, 145 Jean-Jacques Lussier, CP 450, Succursale A, Ottawa, ON K1N 6N5, Canada; tel. (613) 562-5800 ext. 4827; fax (613) 562-5169; e-mail pritchie@uottawa.ca; internet www.iupsys.org; f. 1951 at the 13th Int. Congress of Psychology; Int. Congress of Psychology held every 4 years; WHO spec. consultative status; mem. of UN Economic and Social Council, Int. Council for Science, Int. Social Science Council; 70 nat. mems; Pres. BRUCE OVERMIER (USA); Sec.-Gen. PIERRE RITCHIE (Canada); publs *International Journal of Psychology* (6 a year), *Psychology Resource CD-ROM* (annual).

International Union of Pure and Applied Chemistry (IUPAC)/Union internationale de chimie pure et appliquée: POB 13757, Research Triangle Park, NC 27709-3757, USA; tel. (919) 485-8700; fax (919) 485-8706; e-mail secretariat@iupac.org; internet www.iupac.org; f. 1919 to promote co-operation among chemists of the mem. countries; to study topics of int. importance which require regulation, standardization or codification; to co-operate with other int. orgs which deal with topics of a chemical nature; to contribute to the advancement of pure and applied chemistry in all its aspect; 49 mem. countries; Pres. Prof. BRYAN R. HENRY (Canada); Exec. Dir Dr JOHN W. JOST (USA); Sec.-Gen. Prof. DAVID ST C. BLACK (Australia); publs *Chemistry International* (6 a year), *Pure and Applied Chemistry* (monthly).

International Union of Pure and Applied Physics (IUPAP)/Union internationale de physique pure et appliquée: c/o Jackie Beamon-Kiene, American Physical Society, One Physics Ellipse, College Park, MD 20740-3844, USA; tel. (301) 209-3269; fax (301) 209-0865; e-mail beamon@aps.org; internet www.iupap.org; f. 1922 to promote and encourage intl co-operation in physics; 45 countries are affiliated; 19 international commissions; Pres. Y. PETROFF (France); Sec.-Gen. JUDY FRANZ (USA); publ. *IUPAP News Bulletin* (5 or 6 a year).

International Union of the History and Philosophy of Science (IUHPS): c/o Prof. Juan José Saldaña, National University of Mexico, Apdo Postal 21-388, 04000 Mexico, DF, Mexico; tel. (55) 5622-1864; fax (55) 5544-6316; e-mail dhs@servidor.unam.mx; f. 1956; divisions of History of Science and of Logic, Methodology and Philosophy of Science; Sec.-Gen. Prof. JUAN JOSÉ SALDAÑA.

International Union of Theoretical and Applied Mechanics (IUTAM)/Union Internationale de Mécanique Théorique et Appliquée: c/o Prof. Dick H. van Campen, Dept of Mechanical Eng., Technische Universiteit Eindhoven, Den Dolech 2, POB 513, 5600 MB Eindhoven, The Netherlands; fax (40) 2461418; e-mail sg@iutam.net; internet www.iutam.net; f. 1946; provides a forum for persons and orgs engaged in scientific work (theoretical or experimental) in mechanics and related sciences; organizes int. meetings for subjects in this field; and engages in other activities to promote the devt of mechanics as a science; the Union is directed by its Gen. Assembly, which is composed of representatives of the orgs affiliated to the Union and of elected mems; 51 mem. countries; Pres. Prof. BEN FREUND (USA); Sec.-Gen. Prof. DICK H. VAN CAMPEN (Netherlands); publs *Newsletter* (irreg.), *Proceedings of IUTAM Symposia* (irreg.), *Proceedings of IUTAM World Congress* (every 4 years).

International Union of Toxicology (IUTOX): 1821 Michael Faraday Drive, Suite 300, Reston, VA 20190, USA; tel. (703) 438-3103; fax (703) 438-3113; e-mail iutoxhq@iutox.org; internet www.iutox.org; f. 1980; fosters intl scientific co-operation among toxicologists and promotes global acquisition, dissemination, and use of knowledge in the science of toxicology; ensures continued training and development of toxicologists worldwide; International Congress on Toxicology (ICT) every 3 years; sponsors Congresses on Toxicology in Developing Countries (CTDCs) every 3 years; affiliated to WHO; 47 nat. and regional mems representing approx. 20,000 toxicologists; Pres. Prof. Dr ALI ESAT KARAKAYA (Netherlands); Sec.-Gen. Dr A. WALLACE HAYES; publ. *Newsletter* (annually).

Union Radio-Scientifique Internationale (URSI)/International Union of Radio Science: c/o INTEC, Ghent Univ., Sint-Pietersnieuwstraat 41, 9000 Ghent, Belgium; tel. (9) 264-33-20; fax (9) 264-42-88; e-mail info@ursi.org; internet www.ursi.org; f. 1919; encourages and co-ordinates research in the field of radio, telecommunication and electronic sciences, and facilitates the establishment of common radio measurement techniques and standards; 44 nat. cttees; Pres. Prof. FRANÇOIS LEFEUVRE (France); Sec.-Gen. Prof. PAUL LAGASSE (Belgium); Exec. Sec. INGE HELEU (Belgium); Adm. Sec. INGE LIEVENS (Belgium); publs *The Radio Science Bulletin* (quarterly), *Records of General Assemblies* (every 3 years).

COMMITTEES

Tasks which fall within the sphere of activities of two or more Unions have been undertaken by the following Scientific or Special Committees set up by the ICSU:

Committee on Capacity Building in Science (CCBS): c/o Dr Shirley Malcom, AAAS, 1200 New York Ave, Washington, DC 20005, USA; tel. (202) 326-6720; f. 1993; promotes to the public and to policy-makers an understanding and appreciation of the role of science in modern society and provides science education information to primary school teachers worldwide; Chair. Dr SHIRLEY MALCOM.

Committee on Data for Science and Technology (CODATA): c/o Kathleen Cass, 51 blvd de Montmorency, 75016 Paris, France; tel. (1) 45-25-04-96; fax (1) 42-88-14-66; internet www.codata.org; f. 1966 by ICSU to improve the quality, reliability and accessibility of scientific data, including quantitative information on the properties and behaviour of matter, and other experimental and observational data; 19 nat. and 15 scientific union mems; Pres. Prof. SHUICHI IWATA (Japan); Exec. Dir KATHLEEN CASS (France); Sec.-Gen. Dr ROBERT CHEN (USA); publs *CODATA Newsletter* (quarterly), *International Compendium of Numerical Data Projects*, *International Conference Proceedings*.

Committee on Space Research (COSPAR): c/o CNES, 2 pl. Maurice Quentin, 75039 Paris Cedex 01, France; tel. 1-44-76-75-10; fax 1-44-76-74-37; e-mail cospar@cosparhq.cnes.fr; internet cosparhq.cnes.fr; f. 1958 to promote scientific research in space on an int. level, with an emphasis on the exchange of results, information and opinions; promotes the use of space science for the benefit of mankind and for its adoption by developing countries and new space-faring nations; organizes scientific assemblies every 2 years; advises the UN and other int. orgs on space research matters and on the assessment of scientific issues in which space can play a role; prepares scientific and technical standards related to space research; mems: 44 countries and 13 int. scientific unions; Pres. Prof. R.-M. BONNET (France); Exec. Dir Dr I. REVAH; Assoc. Dir A. JANOFSKY; publs *Advances in Space Research (ASR)*, *Space Research Today (SRT)*.

Scientific Committee on Antarctic Research (SCAR): SCAR Secretariat, c/o Scott Polar Research Institute, Lensfield Rd, Cambridge, CB2 1ER, UK; tel. (1223) 336550; fax (1223) 336549; e-mail info@scar.org; internet www.scar.org; f. 1958 by ICSU to continue the promotion of int. co-operation in scientific research in the Antarctic; holds biennial conference; organizes meetings, workshops and symposia; establishes and co-ordinates int. programmes to address major scientific questions in Antarctica; 30 full mems(nat. acads of science), 4 assoc. mems; Pres. Prof. CHRIS G. RAPLEY (UK); Exec. Dir Dr COLIN P. SUMMERHAYES; Exec. Officer (vacant); publs *SCAR Bulletin* (quarterly), *SCAR Report* (irreg.).

Scientific Committee on Oceanic Research (SCOR): c/o Dr Ed Urban, Dept of Earth and Planetary Sciences, Johns Hopkins Univ., Baltimore, MD 21218, USA; tel. (410) 516-4070; fax (410) 516-4019; e-mail scor@jhu.edu; internet www.jhu.edu/~scor; f. 1957 to advance int. scientific activity in all brs of oceanic research; scientific advisory body to UNESCO and to Intergovernmental Oceanographic Commission; c. 20 active working Groups, Cttees and Panels investigate a broad range of oceanographic problems; mems: nominated mems by Cttees for Oceanic Research in 38 countries; rep. mems of affiliated orgs; invited mems by the exec. cttee; Pres. Prof. BJØRN SUNDBY (Canada); Sec. Dr JULIE HALL (New Zealand); Exec. Dir Dr EDWARD R. URBAN, JR (USA); publ. *SCOR Proceedings* (annual).

Scientific Committee on Problems of the Environment (SCOPE): 51 blvd de Montmorency, 75016 Paris, France; tel. 1-45-25-04-98; fax 1-42-88-14-66; e-mail secretariat@icsu-scope.org; internet www.icsu-scope.org; f. 1969; interdisciplinary research in the environmental field; mems: 40 Nat. Cttees and 22 International Unions; Pres. Dr JERRY M. MELILLO (USA); Sec.-Gen. Prof. OSVALDO SALA (Argentina); publ. *SCOPE Reports*.

Scientific Committee on Solar-Terrestrial Physics (SCOSTEP): HAO/NCAR, 3080 Center Green Drive, Boulder, CO 80301, USA; tel. (303) 497-1591; fax (303) 497-1580; e-mail ganglu@ucar.edu; internet www.scostep.ucar.edu; f. 1966 as an Inter-Union Commission by ICSU and became a Scientific Cttee in 1978 to promote and co-ordinate intl interdisciplinary programmes in solar-terrestrial physics and to work with other ICSU bodies in the co-ordination of symposia in the field of solar-terrestrial physics; 400 mems; Pres. M. A. GELLER (USA); Scientific Sec. Dr GANG LU (USA).

SERVICES AND INTER-UNION COMMISSIONS

Federation of Astronomical and Geophysical Data Analysis Services (FAGS): c/o Dr Niels Andersen, Kort and Matrikelstyrelsen, Rentemestervej 8, 2400 Copenhagen NV, Denmark; fax 35-87-50-57; e-mail fags@kms.dk; internet www.kms.dk/fags/index.html; f. 1956; federates the following Permanent Services: International Earth Rotation Service, Bureau Gravimetrique International, International GPS Service for Geodynamics, International Center for Earth Tides, Permanent Service for Mean Sea Level, International Service of Geomagnetic Indices, Quarterly Bulletin of Solar Activity, International Space Environment Service, World Glacier Monitoring Service, Centre des Données Stellaires, Sunspot Index Data Center; Pres. D. PUGH (UK); Sec. N. ANDERSEN (Denmark).

Scientific Committee on Frequency Allocations for Radio Astronomy and Space Science (IUCAF)/Comité scientifique pour l'allocation des fréquences à la radio astronomie et la recherche spatiale: c/o Observatoire de Paris, 5 place Jules Janssen, 92195 Meudon, France; tel. 1-45-07-77-31; fax 1-45-07-77-09; e-mail iucafchair@iucaf.org; internet www.iucaf.org; f. 1960 under auspices of URSI with representatives of URSI, IAU and COSPAR, to study the requirements for frequency bands and radio frequency protection for research in the fields of radio astronomy, earth exploration and space science; and to make their requirements known to the appropriate frequency-allocation authorities; 10 mems; Chair. WIM VAN DRIEL (France).

INTERNATIONAL COUNCIL FOR PHILOSOPHY AND HUMANISTIC STUDIES

International Council for Philosophy and Humanistic Studies (ICPHS)/Conseil International de la Philosophie et des Sciences Humaines: Secretariat Maison de l'UNESCO, 1 rue Miollis, 75732 Paris Cedex 15, France; tel. 1-45-68-48-85; fax 1-40-65-94-80; e-mail cipsh@unesco.org; internet www.unesco.org/cipsh; f. 1949 under the auspices of UNESCO to encourage respect for cultural autonomy by the comparative study of civilization, to contribute towards int. understanding through a better knowledge of man, to develop int. co-operation in philosophy, humanistic and related studies, to encourage the setting up of int. orgs, to promote the dissemination of information in these fields, to sponsor works of learning, etc.; the Council is composed of 13 int. NGOs listed below; these orgs represent 145 countries; in 1951 an agreement was signed between UNESCO and ICPHS recognizing the latter as the co-ordinating and representative body of orgs in the field of philosophy and humanistic studies; Pres. CHA IN-SUK (Korea); Sec.-Gen. MAURICE AYMARD (France); publs *Bulletin of Information* (every 2 years), *Diogenes* (quarterly).

UNIONS FEDERATED TO THE ICPHS

International Union of Academies/Union Académique Internationale: Palais des Académies, 1 rue Ducale, 1000 Brussels, Belgium; tel. 550-22-00; fax 550-22-05; e-mail info@uai-iua.org; internet www.uai-iua.org; f. 1919 to promote intl co-operation through collective research in philology, archaeology, history, social sciences and humanities in general; affiliated countries: Argentina, Australia, Austria, Belgium, Bulgaria, Canada, Chile, China, Costa Rica, Croatia, Czech Republic, Denmark, Egypt, Estonia, Finland, France, Georgia, Germany, Ghana, Greece, Hungary, India, Iran, Ireland, Israel, Italy, Japan, Repub. of Korea, Latvia, Luxembourg, former Yugoslav republic of Macedonia, Madagascar, Mexico, Moldova, Morocco, Netherlands, Norway, Paraguay, Peru, Poland, Portugal, Romania, Russia, Serbia and Montenegro, Slovakia, Slovenia, South Africa, Spain, Sweden, Switzerland, Tunisia, Turkey, Ukraine, UK, USA, Uruguay, Vatican City; associate member: International Academy of History of Science; Pres. AGOSTINO PARAVICINI BAGLIANI (Switzerland); Vice-Pres. CÉSAR A. GARCÍA BELSUNCE (Argentina), PASQUALE SMIRAGLIA (Italy); Admin. Sec JEAN-LUC DE PAEPE (Belgium); publs *Novum Glossarium*, *Archivum Latinitatis Medii Aevi* (every 2 years), *Compte rendu (de la session annuelle) du Comité* (annually).

International Association for the History of Religions/Association Internationale pour l'Histoire des Religions: c/o Prof. Tim Jensen, IFPR, Univ. of Southern Denmark, Campusvej 55, 5230 Odense M, Denmark; tel. 6550-3315; fax 3887-5095; e-mail t.jensen@ifpr.sdu.dk; internet www.iahr.dk; f. 1950 by the 7th Int. Congress for the Study of the History of Religions, to promote the study of the history of religions through the int. collaboration of scholars who research the subject, to organize congresses and to encourage the production of publs; 37 mem. countries, 5 regional assoc. mems; Pres. Prof. ROSALIND HACKETT (USA); Gen. Sec. Prof. TIM JENSEN (Denmark); publs *Numen* (quarterly), *Science of Religion* (2 a year).

International Committee of Historical Sciences/Comité International des Sciences Historiques: c/o Prof. Jean-Claude Robert, Dépt d'Histoire, Université du Québec à Montréal, CP 8888, Succursale Centre ville, Montréal, QC H3C 3P8, Canada; tel. (514) 987-30-00, poste 8433; fax (514) 987-78-13; e-mail cish@uqam.ca; internet www.cish.org; f. 1926; int. congresses since 1900 to work for the advancement of historical sciences by means of int. co-ordination; mems in 53 countries; gen. assembly every 2–3 years; Pres. Prof. JÜRGEN KOCKA (Germany); Sec.-Gen. Prof. JEAN-CLAUDE ROBERT (Canada); publs *Bulletin d'Information*, *Bibliographie Internationale des Sciences Historiques*.

International Committee for the History of Art/Comité international d'histoire de l'art: c/o Philippe Sénéchal, Institut national d'histoire de l'art, 2 rue Vivienne, 75084 Paris, France; tel. 1-47-03-79-25; fax 1-47-03-86-36; e-mail philippe.senechal@inha

.fr; internet www.esteticas.unam.mx/ciha; f. 1930 by the 12th Int. Congress on the History of Art, for collaboration in the scientific study of the history of art; mems in 31 countries; int. congress every 4 years; int. colloquium every year; Pres. Prof. STEPHEN BANN (UK); Scientific Sec. PHILIPPE SÉNÉCHAL (France); Treas. and Admin. Sec. Prof. Dr OSKAR BÄTSCHMANN (Switzerland); publ. *Bibliography of the History of Art* (CD-ROM, quarterly).

International Congress of African Studies/Congrès International des Études Africaines: c/o Prof. Yusuf Fadhl Hassan, Vice-Chancellor, University of Khartoum, POB 321, Khartoum, Sudan; tel. 75100; f. 1900 to develop int. co-operation in the field of African studies through periodic meetings and pbls, to organize and promote research on an int. basis and to serve as a body which shall encourage Africans to have a growing consciousness of their membership of the human race and to express themselves in all fields of human endeavour; Sec.-Gen. Prof. HURREIZ (Sudan); publ. *Proceedings* (in English and French).

International Federation for Modern Languages and Literatures/Fédération Internationale des Langues et Littératures Modernes: c/o Anders Pettersson, Umeå Univ., 901 87 Umeå, Sweden; tel. (90) 786-5797; e-mail anders.pettersson@littvet.umu.se; internet www.fillm.ulg.ac.be; f. 1928 as the Int. Cttee on Modern Literary History; present name and status 1951; to establish permanent contact between historians of literature, to develop or perfect facilities for their work and to promote the study of the history of modern literature; 19 mem. asscns, with mems in 92 countries; Pres. Prof. DAVID A. WELLS (UK); Sec.-Gen. Prof. ANDERS PETTERSSON (Sweden); publ. *Acts of the Triennial Congresses.*

International Federation of Philosophical Societies/Fédération Internationale des Sociétés de Philosophie: c/o Ioanna Kuçuradi, Dept of Philosophy, Hacettepe Univ., Beytepe, 06542 Ankara, Turkey; tel. (312) 2978300; fax (312) 4410297; e-mail ioanna@fisp.org.tr; internet www.fisp.org.tr; f. 1948 under the auspices of UNESCO, to encourage int. co-operation in the field of philosophy, and to promote congresses, symposia and pbls; 108 mem. socs from 50 countries and 26 int. mem. socs; Pres. IOANNA KUÇURADI (Turkey); Sec.-Gen. PETER KEMP (Denmark); publs under the auspices of FISP: *Newsletter, Proceedings of the International Congresses of Philosophy.*

International Federation of the Societies of Classical Studies/Fédération Internationale des Associations d'Etudes Classiques: c/o Prof. Paul Schubert, 7 rue des Beaux-Arts, 2000 Neuchâtel, Switzerland; e-mail paul.schubert@lettres.unige.ch; internet www.fiecnet.org; f. 1948 under the auspices of UNESCO to encourage research on the ancient civilizations of Greece and Rome; to group the main nat. asscns of this field; to ensure collaboration with relevant int. orgs; affiliated bodies incl. the Int. Soc. for Classical Bibliography, Int. Soc. for Classical Archaeology, Int. Soc. for Byzantine Studies, Int. Asscn for Greek and Latin Epigraphy, Int. Asscn of Papyrologists, Unione internazionale degli Istituti di Archaeologia, Storia e Storia dell'Arte in Roma, Société d'histoire des droits de l'antiquité, Comité int. des Etudes mycéniennes, Asscn int. des Etudes patristiques, etc.; 79 mem. socs in 44 countries; Pres. Prof. HEINRICH VON STADEN (USA); Sec. Gen. Prof. PAUL SCHUBERT (Switzerland); publ. *L'Année Philologique* (bibliography, annual).

International Musicological Society/Société Internationale de Musicologie: Nadelstr. 60, 8706 Feldmeilen, Switzerland; tel. (1) 9231022; fax (1) 9231027; e-mail imsba@swissonline.ch; internet www.ims-online.ch; f. 1927 to promote musicological research, to encourage study in the field and to co-ordinate the work of musicologists world-wide; int. congress every 5 years, intercongressional symposia, int. study groups; 48 mem. countries, 1,000 individual mems; Pres. Prof. Dr TILMAN SEEBASS (Austria); Sec.-Gen. Dr DOROTHEA BAUMANN (Switzerland); publs *Acta Musicologica* (2 a year, online), *Documenta Musicologica* (irreg.), *Catalogus Musicus* (irreg.), *International Repertory of Music Literature* (RILM, annual, online), *International Repertory of Musical Iconography* (RIDIM, online databases), *International Inventory of Musical Sources* (RISM, online and print), *Répertoire International de la Presse Musicale* (RIPM, online and print), *Doctoral Dissertations in Musicology* (published jtly with the American Musicological Society, online at www.music.indiana.edu/ddm).

International Union of Anthropological and Ethnological Sciences (IUAES)/Union Internationale des Sciences Anthropologiques et Ethnologiques: see under ISSC.

International Union of Oriental and Asian Studies/Union Internationale des Etudes Orientales et Asiatiques: c/o György Hazai, Közraktár u. 12/A, II/2, 1093 Budapest, Hungary; f. 1951 as the International Union of Orientalists under the auspices of UNESCO, name changed 1973; to promote contacts between orientalists worldwide, and to organize congresses, research and publications; 26 mem. countries; Pres. TATSURO YAMAMOTO; Sec.-Gen. GYÖRGY HAZAI; publs *Philologiae Turcicae Fundamenta, Materialien zum Sumerischen Lexikon, Sanskrit Dictionary, Corpus Inscriptionum Iranicarum, Linguistic Atlas of Iran, Matériels des parlers iraniens, Bibliographie Egyptologique.*

International Union of Prehistoric and Protohistoric Sciences/Union Internationale des Sciences Préhistoriques et Protohistoriques: c/o Prof. Jean Bourgeois, Dept of Archaeology, University of Ghent, 2 Blandijnberg, 9000 Ghent, Belgium; tel. (9) 264-41-11; fax (9) 264-41-73; e-mail uispp@ping.be; internet www.geocities.com/Athens/Ithaca/7152; f. 1931 to promote congresses and scientific work in the fields of pre- and protohistory; 120 mem. countries; Pres. Prof. PIERRE P. BONENFANT (Belgium); Sec.-Gen. Prof. JEAN BOURGEOIS (Belgium); publs *Inventaria archaeologica, Archaeologia urbium.*

Permanent International Committee of Linguists/Comité International Permanent des Linguistes: c/o Prof. P. G. J. van Sterkenburg, Instituut voor Nederlandse Lexicologie, Postbus 9515, 2300 RA Leiden, The Netherlands; tel. (71) 514-16-48; fax (71) 527-21-15; e-mail sterkenburg@inl.nl; internet www.ciplnet.com; f. 1928 to work for the advancement of linguistics worldwide and to encourage intl co-operation in this field; 34 mem. countries and 2 intl orgs; Pres. Prof. F. KIEFER (Hungary); Sec.-Gen. Prof. P. G. J. VAN STERKENBURG; publ. *Linguistic Bibliography* (annually).

INTERNATIONAL SOCIAL SCIENCE COUNCIL

International Social Science Council (ISSC)/Conseil International des Sciences Sociales: Maison de l'UNESCO, 1 rue Miollis, 75732 Paris Cedex 15, France; tel. 1-45-68-48-60; fax 1-45-66-76-03; e-mail issc@unesco.org; internet www.unesco.org/ngo/issc; f. 1952; advancement of the social sciences world-wide and their application to the major problems of the world and cooperation at an int. level between specialists in the social sciences; Standing Cttees on Int. Human Dimensions of Global Environmental Change Program (IHDP, co-sponsored by ICSU), Comparative Research Programme on Poverty (CROP) and Globalization, Gender and Democratization (GGD), Int. Global Social Change Programme, Research on Ethnic Conflicts and Approaches to Peace (RECAP); 13 mem. assocs, 22 mem. orgs, 18 assoc. mems; Pres. Prof. LOURDES ARIZPE (Mexico); Sec.-Gen. Dr ALI KAZANCIGIL (France); publ. *e-bulletin* (online).

ASSOCIATIONS FEDERATED TO THE ISSC

International Association of Legal Sciences/Association Internationale des Sciences Juridiques: c/o ISSC, UNESCO, 1 rue Miollis, 75015 Paris, France; tel. (1) 45-68-25-58; fax (1) 43-06-87-98; e-mail leker.meir@libertysurf.fr; f. 1950 to promote the mutual knowledge and understanding of nations and the increase of learning by encouraging worldwide the study of foreign legal systems and the use of the comparative method in legal science; governed by a President and an executive bureau of ten members known as the International Committee of Comparative Law; national cttees in 46 countries; Pres. Prof. MARY ANN GLENDON (USA); Sec.-Gen. MEIR M. LEKER; Dir of Scientific Research Prof. P. SARCEVIĆ (Croatia).

International Economic Association/Association Internationale des Sciences Economiques: 23 rue Campagne-Première, 75014 Paris, France; tel. 1-43-27-91-44; fax 1-42-79-92-16; e-mail iea@iea-world.org; internet www.iea-world.org; f. 1949 to promote intl collaboration for the advancement of economic knowledge, to develop personal contacts between economists, and to encourage provision of means for the dissemination of economic knowledge; mem. associations in 57 countries; Pres. JANOS

KORNAI (Hungary); Sec.-Gen. JEAN-PAUL FITOUSSI (France).

International Federation of Social Science Organizations/Fédération Internationale des Organisations de Science Sociale: c/o Treasurer's Office, 14 Via dei Laghi, 00198 Rome, Italy; f. 1979 to succeed the Conference of Nat. Social Science Councils and Analogous Bodies (f. 1975) to encourage int. co-operation in the social sciences, to advance the devt of the social sciences, especially in the developing world, to advance the exchange of information, ideas and experiences among its mems, to promote a more effective organization of research and teaching and the building of instns in the social sciences; 22 mems; Pres. Prof. Dr CARMENCITA T. AGUILAR (Philippines); Sec.-Gen. Prof. J. BLAHOZ (Czech Republic); publs *Newsletter*, *International Directory of Social Science Organizations*.

International Geographical Union/Union Géographique Internationale: see under ICSU.

International Institute of Administrative Sciences/Institut International des Sciences Administratives: 1 rue Defacqz, Bte 11, 1000 Brussels, Belgium; tel. (2) 536-08-80; fax (2) 537-97-02; e-mail iias@iiasiisa.be; internet www.iiasiisa.be; f. 1930 for the comparative examination of admin. experience in mem. countries; research and programmes for improving admin. law and practices and for technical assistance; consultative status with ECOSOC, ILO and UNESCO; int. congresses; considers impact of new technologies on admin., management of multicultural societies, admin. in transitional economies, admin. aspects of political transition, women in public admin., new regulations and new modes of control, implications of globalization and internationalization for nat. and local admin., interaction between NGOs and public admin., public admin. and the social sectors, innovations in int. admin.; 45 mem. states, 63 nat. sections, 11 int. governmental orgs, 75 corporate and individual mems; library of 13,000 vols; Pres. Prof. FRANZ STREHL (Austria); Dir-Gen. ROLET LORETAN (Switzerland); publs *International Review of Administrative Sciences/Revue internationale des sciences administratives* (quarterly), *Newsletter* (3 a year).

International Law Association/Association de Droit International: Charles Clore House, 17 Russell Sq., London, WC1B 5DR, UK; tel. (20) 7323-2978; fax (20) 7323-3580; e-mail info@ila-hq.org; internet www.ila-hq.org; f. 1873 for the study and advancement of int. law, public and private, and the promotion of int. understanding and goodwill; 50 regional brs world-wide; 4,200 mems; 25 int. cttees; Pres. Prof. KARL-HEINZ BOCKSTIEGEL; Chair. Exec. Council Lord SLYNN OF HADLEY (UK); Sec.-Gen. DAVID J. C. WYLD.

International Peace Research Association/Association Internationale de Recherche pour la Paix: c/o Luc Reychler, University of Leuven, Van Evenstraat 2B, Leuven, Belgium; tel. (16) 323241; fax (16) 323088; e-mail luc.reychler@soc.kuleuven.ac.be; internet www.human.mie-u.ac.jp/~peace/about-ipra; f. 1964 to encourage the development of interdisciplinary research into the conditions of peace and the causes of war; mems in 93 countries: 1,050 individuals, 400 corporate, 10 nat. and regional asscns; Sec-Gen. LUC REYCHLER (Belgium); publ. *IPRA Newsletter* (4 a year).

International Political Science Association (IPSA)/Association Internationale de Science Politique: 1590 ave Docteur-Penfield, bureau 331, Montreal, QC H3G 1C5, Canada; tel. (514) 848-8717; fax (514) 848-4095; e-mail info@ipsa.ca; internet www.ipsa.ca; f. 1949; promotes internationally planned research and scholarly collaboration, organizes triennial world congresses, and provides documentary and reference services; nat. asscns in 41 countries: 102 assoc. mems, 2,200 individual mems; Pres. Prof. MAX KAASE (Germany); Sec.-Gen. Prof. GUY LACHAPELLE (Canada); publs *Directory* (annual), *International Political Science Abstracts* (6 a year), *International Political Science Review* (quarterly), *Participation* (bulletin, 3 a year).

International Sociological Association/Association Internationale de Sociologie: Facultad CC. Políticas y Sociología, Universidad Complutense, 28223 Madrid, Spain; tel. 91-352-76-50; fax 91-352-49-45; e-mail isa@isa-sociology.org; internet www.isa-sociology.org; f. 1949; promotes sociological research, develops personal contacts among the sociologists of all countries and ensures the exchange of sociological information; 53 research cttees on a wide variety of sociological topics; holds World Congresses every four years; 3,500 individual, 150 collective mems; Pres. Prof. MICHEL WIEVIORKA (France); Exec. Sec. Dr IZABELA BARLINSKA (Poland); publs *Current Sociology/Sociologie Contemporaine* (4 a year), *e-Bulletin* (3 a year), *International Sociology* (4 a year).

International Studies Association: 324 Social Sciences Bldg, University of Arizona, Tucson, AZ 85721, USA; tel. (520) 621-7715; fax (520) 621-5780; e-mail isa@u.arizona.edu; internet www.isanet.org; f. 1959; promotes research and co-operation into international studies; 3,000 mems in 80 countries; Pres. JACEK KUGLER (USA); Exec. Dir THOMAS J. VOLGY (USA); publs *International Studies Quarterly*, *International Studies Newsletter*, *International Studies Notes*.

International Union of Anthropological and Ethnological Sciences (IUAES)/Union Internationale des Sciences Anthropologiques et Ethnologiques: c/o Prof. Peter Nas, University of Leiden, Institute of Cultural and Social Studies, POB 9555, 2300 RB Leiden, Netherlands; tel. (71) 5273992; fax (71) 5273619; e-mail nas@leidenuniv.nl; internet www.leidenuniv.nl/fsw/iuaes/index.htm; f. 1948 under the auspices of UNESCO to promote research and co-operation among anthropological and ethnological institutions; mems: 20 national, 80 institutional and over 200 individuals world-wide; also federated to ICPHS, ISSC and ICSU; Pres. Prof. LUIS ALBERTO VARGAS (Mexico); Sec.-Gen. Prof. Dr PETER NAS (Netherlands); publ. *Newsletter* (3 a year).

International Union of Psychological Science (IUPsyS)/Union International des Sciences Psychologiques: see under ICSU.

International Union for the Scientific Study of Population/Union Internationale pour l'Etude Scientifique de la Population: 3–5 rue Nicolas, 75980, Paris Cedex 20, France; tel. 1-56-06-21-73; fax 1-56-06-22-04; e-mail iussp@iussp.org; internet www.iussp.org; f. 1928, reconstituted 1947, to advance the progress of quantitative and qualitative demography as a science; mems: 1,900 scientists in 124 countries; Pres. JACQUES VALLIN (France); Exec. Dir ERIK KLIJZING (Netherlands); Sec.-Gen. MARY KRITZ (USA); publs *Proceedings* (conferences and seminars), *IUSSP Newsletter*, *IUSSP papers*.

World Association for Public Opinion Research/Association Mondiale pour l'Etude de l'Opinion Publique: c/o UNL Gallup Research Center, Univ. of Nebraska, 200 North 11th St, Lincoln, NE 68588-0242, USA; tel. (402) 458-2030; fax (402) 458-2038; e-mail wapor@unl.edu; internet www.unl.edu/wapor; f. 1947; to establish and promote contacts between persons in the field of survey research on opinions, attitudes and behaviour of people world-wide, and to advance the use of scientific survey research in nat. and int. affairs; 500 individual mems in 55 countries; Pres. Dr KATHLEEN A. FRANKOVIC (USA); Gen. Sec. Prof. Dr ALLAN L. MCCUTCHEON (USA); publs *WAPOR Newsletter* (quarterly), *International Journal for Public Opinion Research* (quarterly).

World Federation for Mental Health/Fédération Mondiale pour la Santé Mentale: POB 16810, Alexandria, VA 22302-0810, USA; tel. (703) 838-7543; fax (703) 519-7648; e-mail info@wfmh.com; internet www.wfmh.org; f. 1948 to promote among all people and nations the highest possible standard of mental health in the broadest biological, medical, educational, and social aspects; to work with ECOSOC, UNESCO, the WHO, and other agencies of the UN, to promote mental health; to help other voluntary associations in the improvement of mental health services; 2,600 individual mems, 150 voting orgs, 139 affiliated orgs; Pres. Dr PATT FRANCIOSI (USA); Sec.-Gen. PRESTON GARRISON (USA); publs *Annual Report*, *WFMH Newsletter* (4 a year).

INTERNATIONAL ASSOCIATION OF UNIVERSITIES (IAU)

1 rue Miollis, 75732 Paris Cedex 15, France; tel. 1-45-68-48-00; fax 1-47-34-76-05; e-mail iau@unesco.org; internet www.unesco.org/iau; f. 1950 to provide a centre of co-operation at int. level among univs and similar instns of higher education of all countries; 650 univs and instns of higher education in 150 countries; 12 assoc. mems (int. and nat. univ. orgs).

Organization

GENERAL CONFERENCE

Composed of the full and assoc. mems. Meets every 5 years. Discusses topics of importance for the future of univ. education, determines gen. policy and elects the Pres. and mems of the Admin. Board. Twelfth Gen. Conference was held in São Paulo, Brazil, in 2004.

ADMINISTRATIVE BOARD

Chaired by the Pres/ of the IAU, and composed of 20 eminent univ. leaders and scholars and a maximum of 20 deputy mems from all continents. Meets annually, ensures that decisions of the Gen. Conference are implemented and guides the work of the Int. Univs Bureau.

Pres.: GOOLAM MOHMAEDBHAI (Rector, Univ. of Mauritius).

INTERNATIONAL UNIVERSITIES BUREAU (IUB)

The IUB, created in 1949, provides the Permanent Secretariat for the IAU. It is the principal instrument for the execution of the activities of the IAU. Its main tasks include facilitating and promoting the exchange of information, experience and ideas, of students, teachers, researchers and administrators, and of publications and material for teaching and research.

Sec.-Gen. EVA EGRON-POLAK.

Principal Activities

Information

Under a formal Agreement with UNESCO, the IAU operates a joint IAU/UNESCO Information Centre on Higher Education at its Int. Univs Bureau. The Centre holds 40,000 vols and a large colln of unpublished materials; it has subscriptions to 300 current specialized periodicals and maintains a colln of 4,000 prospectuses of higher education instns, as well as conference reports, occasional papers, CD-ROMs, etc. The Centre was fully computerized in 1989, and all holdings were subsequently catalogued in the Centre's own database (IAUDOC). All references can be found in the int. bibliographical database (HEDBIB), accessible via the IAU website . The database links to nat. and int. information centres and data networks. IAU acts as the co-ordinating agency for the World Academic Database (WAD).

Studies, Research and Meetings

The IAU co-ordinates and carries out studies and research on issues of higher education and higher education policies which are either common to instns and systems worldwide, or where a comparative analysis between different situations and approaches is of particular benefit to higher education instns. Conferences, symposia, colloquia, seminars, round tables and workshops provide an int. forum for the discussion of topics of common concern to higher education leaders and specialists.

Co-operation

The IAU provides an important clearing-house function to its mems for academic exchange and co-operation. The IAU has adopted the *Kyoto Declaration and Agenda for Sustainable Development 1993*, to promote and support univ. co-operation; the *Durban Declaration on Internationalization 2000* to ensure that higher education instns seize the initiative in the process of internationalization rather than reacting to the forces of globalization and the market; and the *São Paolo Declaration on Information and Communication Technologies (ICTs) 2004*, to act as a platform for information-sharing in regard to the use of ICTs in higher education.

SELECTED PUBLICATIONS

Guide to Higher Education in Africa (irreg.).

Higher Education Policy (English; quarterly).

IAU Newsletter (English and French; 6 a year).

International Handbook of Universities (English; every 2 years).

Issues in Higher Education (English; 3 or 4 a year).

World Academic Database (WAD) (CD-ROM; English and French; annual).

World Higher Education Database (CD-ROM; English; annual).

World List of Universities and Other Institutions of Higher Education (English and French; every 2 years).

OTHER INTERNATIONAL ORGANIZATIONS

General

Academia Europaea: 4th Fl., 76 Portland Pl., London, W1B 1NT, UK; tel. (20) 7323-5834; fax (20) 7323-5844; e-mail admin@acadeuro.org; internet www.acadeuro.org; f. 1988; a free asscn of individual scholars working in Europe in all disciplines; aims to encourage European activities in scholarship and the undertaking of ind. studies on matters of European importance; holds meetings, symposia, study groups, etc.; 2,000 mems; Pres. Prof. JÜRGEN MITTELSTRASS (Germany); Exec. Sec. Dr DAVID COATES; publ. *European Review* (quarterly).

Academia Scientiarum et Artium Europaea (European Academy of Sciences and Arts): Mönchsberg 2, 5020 Salzburg, Austria; tel. (662) 84-13-45; fax (662) 84-13-43; e-mail office@european-academy.at; internet www.european-academy.at; f. 1990; promotes an overall view of the sciences and arts on a European level; 1,200 mems; Pres. FELIX UNGER; Vice-Pres ERICH HÖDL NIKOLAUS LOBKOWICZ FRANCISCO JOSÉ RUBIA; publs *Annales* (annually), *Litterae Academiae Scientiarum et Artium Europaeae* (quarterly).

Islamic World Academy of Sciences (IAS): POB 830036, Amman 11183, Jordan; tel. (6) 5522104; fax (6) 5511803; e-mail secretariat@ias-worldwide.org; internet www.ias-worldwide.org; f. 1986, present name 2005; int., ind., non-political, NGO of scientists and technologists, working to promote science, technology and devt in the Islamic and developing worlds; organizes conferences and seminars; supervises training workshops; commissions research; acts as the scientific advisor to the OIC (Org. of the Islamic Conference) and developing countries; collaborates with other nat., regional and int. academies of science; 100 fellows and 9 hon. fellows from 30 countries; Dir-Gen. MONEEF R. ZOU'BI; publs *Islamic Thought and Scientific Creativity* (quarterly), *Medical Journal* (quarterly), *Newsletter* (quarterly), *Proceedings* (annual).

Agriculture and Veterinary Science

Food and Agriculture Organization of the United Nations/Organisation des Nations Unies pour l'Alimentation et l'Agriculture: Viale delle Terme di Caracalla, 00100 Rome, Italy; tel. 06-57051; fax 06-57053152; e-mail FAO-HQ@fao.org; internet www.fao.org; f. 1945 to raise level of nutrition and living standards, improve production and distribution of food and agricultural products and improve the conditions of rural populations; the policy and budget are determined by the 187 mem. nations and 1 org. mem. (EU) at the biennial Conference; the Conference elects a 49-mem. Council which is served by specialist cttees; there are 4,000 staff, 1,500 of whom are engaged in the Field Programme with 1,850 projects in 135 countries; there are 3 main sources of funding: regular contributions from mem. nations, used for financing the secretariat and Technical Co-operation Programmes; trust funds mainly provided by govts for use in FAO Field Programmes; and UNDP funding; FAO's main activities are concentrated on: improving production in all areas of agriculture, forestry and fisheries; promoting the conservation and management of plant and animal genetic resources; increasing investment in agriculture through irrigation, fertilizer, seed and other rural devt schemes; collecting, analyzing and disseminating information needed by govts and int. bodies; making available technical data through the FAO-co-ordinated AGRIS, CARIS and FAOSTAT computer-based int. information systems; working towards greater world food security by ensuring production of adequate food supplies, maximizing stability in the flow of supplies, and securing access to available supplies by those who need them; and by promoting rural devt schemes; the interpretation and dissemination of information obtained from satellites to predict crop failure and locust migration is an illustration of FAO's GIEWS and ARTEMIS systems to monitor the world food situation; library: FAO David Lubin Memorial Library (fao.org/library) holds 1,000,000 vols and 7,000 periodicals; Dir-Gen. Dr JACQUES DIOUF (Senegal); publs *Animal Health and Fertilizers*, *Commodity Review and Outlook*, *FAO Quarterly Bulletin of Statistics* (quarterly), *Food and Agricultural Legislation* (2 a year), *Forestry and Fisheries*, *Plant Protection Bulletin*, *Rural Development* (annual), *The State of Food and Agriculture* (annual), *State of Food Insecurity in the World*, *Unasylva* (quarterly), *World Animal Review* (quarterly), *Yearbooks of Trade and Production in Agriculture*.

OTHER ORGANIZATIONS

CAB International (CABI): Nosworthy Way, Wallingford, Oxon, OX10 8DE, UK; tel. (1491) 832111; fax (1491) 833508; e-mail corporate@cabi.org; internet www.cabi.org; f. 1929; global non-profit organization specializing in sustainable solutions for agricultural and environmental problems; CAB International offices in Wallingford (UK), New Delhi (India); CABI Bioscience: centres in Ascot and Egham (UK), Rawalpindi (Pakistan), Delémont (Switzerland); CABI regional centres for Africa (Nairobi, Kenya), Caribbean and Latin America (Curepe, Trinidad), South-East Asia (Serdang, Malaysia), China (Beijing); CABI Publishing: offices in Wallingford (UK) and Cambridge, MA (USA); CABI Trust in Wallingford (UK); Dir-Gen. Dr DENIS BLIGHT; publs (a selection), *Pig News and Information* (quarterly), *Horticultural Science Abstracts* (monthly), *Plant Breeding Abstracts* (monthly), *Plant Genetics Resources* (3 a year), *Seed Science Research* (quarterly), *Soils Use and Management* (quarterly), *Forestry Abstracts* (monthly), *Leisure, Recreation and Tourism Abstracts* (quarterly), *Rural Development Abstracts* (quarterly), *British Journal of Nutrition* (monthly), *Animal Health Research Reviews* (2 a year), *Bulletin of Entomological Research* (every 2 months), *Renewable Agriculture and Food Systems* (quarterly), *Journal of Helmintology* (4 a year), *Aquatic Resources, Culture & Development* (quarterly), *Chinese Journal of Agricultural Biotechnology* (3 a year), *Equine and Comparative Exercise Physiology* (quarterly), *World Poultry Science* (quarterly), *International Journal of Tropical Insect Science* (quarterly).

Commonwealth Forestry Association: 2 Webbs Barn Cottage, Witney Rd, Kingston Bagpuize, Abingdon, Oxfordshire, OX13 5AN, UK; tel. (1865) 820935; fax (870) 011-6645; e-mail cfa@cfa-international.org; internet www.cfa-international.org; f. 1921; 1,500 mems; Pres. D. BILL; Chair. J. BURLEY; Sec. K. LEEKS; publ. *Commonwealth Forestry Review* (quarterly).

Consultative Group on International Agricultural Research (CGIAR): 1818 H St, NW, MSN G6-601, Washington, DC 20433, USA; tel. (202) 473-8951; fax (202) 473-8110; e-mail cgiar@cgiar.org; internet www.cgiar.org; f. 1971; co-sponsors: World Bank, FAO, IFAD and UNDP; 58 mems incl. govts, int. orgs and private foundations; Dir FRANCISCO J. B. REIFSCHNEIDER.

Institutions supported by CGIAR:

Africa Rice Center (WARDA)/Centre du Riz pour l'Afrique (ADRAO): 01 BP 2031, Cotonou 01, Benin; tel. 35-01-18; fax 35-05-56; e-mail warda@cgiar.org; internet www.warda.cgiar.org; f. 1970; 17 West and Central African mem states; funds provided through CGIAR and by mem. states, donor nations and orgs, and various foundations; library of 16,442 monographs, 1,523 periodicals; Dir-Gen. Dr KANAYO F. NWANZE; publs *Participatory Rice Improvement and Gender/user Analysis Proceedings* (annual workshop papers), *Program Report* (annual), *Rice Interspecific Hybridization Project Research Highlights* (annual), *WARDA Current Contents* (monthly), *West Africa Rice Research Brief* (in French and English, irreg.).

Bioversity International: Via dei Tre Denari 472A, 00057 Maccarese, Rome, Italy; tel. 06-61181; fax 06-61979661; e-mail bioversity@cgiar.org; internet www.cgiar.org; f. 1974 to advance the collection, conservation and use of crop genetic resources world-wide and to encourage research; Dir-Gen. Dr EMILE A. FRISON; publ. *Geneflow*.

Center for International Forestry Research (CIFOR): POB 6596 JKPWB, Jakarta 10065, Indonesia; located at: Jl. CIFOR, Situ Gede, Sindangbarang, Bogor Barat 16680, Indonesia; tel. (251) 622622; fax (251) 622100; e-mail cifor@cgiar.org; internet www.cifor.cgiar.org; seeks the balanced management of forests and forest lands through collaborative strategic and applied research and related activities; regional offices in Brazil, Cameroon and Zimbabwe; Dir-Gen. DAVID KAIMOWITZ.

International Center for Agricultural Research in the Dry Areas (ICARDA): POB 5466, Aleppo, Syria; tel. (21) 2213433; fax (21) 2213490; e-mail icarda@cgiar.org; internet www.icarda.cgiar.org; f. 1977; serves the entire developing world for the improvement of lentil, barley and faba bean production; all dry-area developing countries for the improvement of on-farm water-use efficiency, rangeland and small-ruminant production; and West and Central Asia and North Africa for the improvement of bread, durum wheat and chickpea production, and farming systems; promotes sustainable natural-resource management practices; library of 16,129 vols, 958 periodicals; Dir-Gen. Prof. Dr ADEL EL-BELTAGY; publ. *ICARDA Caravan* (2 a year).

International Centre for Tropical Agriculture/Centro Internacional de Agricultura Tropical: Apdo aéreo 6713, Cali, Colombia; tel. (2) 4450000; fax (2) 4450073; internet www.ciat.cgiar.org; f. 1967; research on cultivation of beans, cassava, rice, tropical fruit and fodder, combined with applied social sciences; library of 100,000 records and documents; 1,300 mems; Dir-Gen. JOACHIM VOSS; publ. *Pasturas Tropicales* (3 a year).

International Crops Research Institute for the Semi-Arid Tropics (ICRISAT): Patancheru Andhra Pradesh 502 324, India; tel. (40) 23296161; fax (40) 23296180; e-mail icrisat@cgnet.com; internet www.icrisat.org; f. 1972 as world centre for genetic improvement of sorghum, millets, pigeonpea, chickpea and groundnut production, and for research on the management of resources in the world's semi-arid tropics; research covers all physical and socio-economic aspects of improving farming systems on un-irrigated land; Dir-Gen. WILLIAM D. DAR (India); publs *ICRISAT Report* (annual), *International Arachis Newsletter* (annual), *International Chickpea and Pigeonpea Newsletter* (annual), *International Sorghum and Millet Newsletter* (annual), *Research and Information Bulletins*, *Workshop Proceedings*.

International Food Policy Research Institute: 2033 K St NW, Washington, DC 20006, USA; tel. (202) 862-5600; fax (202) 467-4439; e-mail ifpri@cgiar.org; internet www.ifpri.org; f. 1975 to identify and analyse alternative nat. and int. strategies for improving the food situation of the low-income countries; 6 divs: Environment and Production Technology (EPT), Food Consumption and Nutrition (FCN), Markets, Trade and Institutions (MTI), Int. Service for Nat. Agricultural Research (ISNAR), Devt Strategy and Governance (DSG), Communications and 2020 Vision Initiative; library of 4,200 research reports, 3,000 monographs, 175 periodicals; Dir-Gen. JOACHIM VON BRAUN; publs research reports, abstracts, working papers, newsletters, etc.

International Institute of Tropical Agriculture: c/o Lambourn (UK) Ltd, Carolyn House, 26 Dingwall Rd, Croydon, CR9 3EE, UK; field office: Oyo Rd, PMB 5320, Ibadan, Oyo State, Nigeria; tel. (2) 241-2626; fax (2) 241-2221; e-mail iita@cgiar.org; internet www.iita.org; f. 1967; projects incl. preserving and enhancing germplasm and agrobiodiversity; developing biological control options; impact, policy and systems analysis; starchy and grain staples in eastern and southern Africa; diverse agricultural systems in the Humid Zone of West and Central Africa; improving and intensifying cereal-legume systems in the moist and dry savannahs of West and Central Africa; library of 76,500 vols and in-house database of 105,500 records; Dir-Gen. PETER HARTMANN; publ. *WASNET Newsletter*.

International Livestock Research Institute: POB 30709, Nairobi 00100, Kenya; tel. (20) 422-3000; fax (20) 422-3001; internet www.ilri.cgiar.org; POB 5689, Addis Ababa, Ethiopia; tel. (1) 463-215; fax (1) 463-252; f. 1995 as an interdisciplinary research, training and information centre to promote and improve livestock production world-wide; principal research units in Kenya and Ethiopia and field programmes in Ethiopia, Kenya, Niger and Nigeria; library: 37,500 vols, 32,000 microfiches, 1,800 periodicals; Dir-Gen. Dr CARLOS SERÉ; publs *Bulletin*, *Systems Studies Monographs*, progress and research reports, manuals, newsletters, bibliographies.

International Maize and Wheat Improvement Center/Centro Internacional de Mejoramiento de Maíz y Trigo: Apdo 6-641, 06600 México, DF, Mexico; tel. (55) 5804-2004; fax (55) 5804-7558; e-mail cimmyt@cgiar.org; internet www.cimmyt.org; f. 1966; supported by Mexican Min. of Agriculture, various int.

agencies, govts and private foundations; aims to help impoverished people in developing countries by improving maize and wheat productivity and promoting environmentally-sound farming practices; regional offices in Africa, Asia and South and Central America; Dir-Gen. Dr MASA IWANAGA.

International Potato Center/Centro Internacional de la Papa: POB 1558, Lima 12, Peru; tel. (1) 349-6017; fax (1) 317-5326; e-mail cip@cgiar.org; internet www.cipotato.org; f. 1971; non-profit instn dedicated to the increased and more sustainable use of potato, sweet potato and other roots and tubers in developing countries, and to the improved management of agricultural resources in mountain areas; regional offices in Lima, Nairobi, Bogor and New Delhi; library of 13,000 vols, 131 online journals, 16,000 reprints, 65,000 references; Dir-Gen. Dr PAMELA K. ANDERSON; publ. *Program Report* (every 2 years).

International Rice Research Institute: DAPO Box 7777, Metro Manila, Philippines; tel. (2) 580-5600; fax (2) 580-5699; e-mail irri@cgiar.org; internet www.irri.org; f. 1960; research on rice and rice-based cropping systems; library of 120,000 vols; Dir-Gen. Dr WILLIAM G. PADOLINA (acting); publs *Facts about Cooperation* (annual), *IRRI Hotline* (quarterly), *IRRI Notes* (2 a year), *Rice Literature Update* (2 a year), *Rice Today Magazine* (annual).

International Water Management Institute (IWMI): POB 2075, Colombo, Sri Lanka; located at: 127 Sunil Mawatha, Pelawatte, Battaramulla, Sri Lanka; tel. (11) 278-7404; fax (11) 278-6854; e-mail iwmi@cgiar.org; internet www.iwmi.cgiar.org; conducts collaborative research on the sustainable use of water and land resources in agriculture and on the water needs of developing countries; regional offices in India, Pakistan, South Africa, Sri Lanka and Thailand; sub-regional offices in the People's Republic of China, Ghana, Kenya, Nepal, Senegal and Uzbekistan; Dir-Gen. Prof. FRANK RIJSBERMAN.

World Agroforestry Centre: United Nations Ave, Gigiri, POB 30677, 00100 Nairobi, Kenya; tel. (20) 7224000; fax (20) 7224001; e-mail ICRAF@cgiar.org; internet www.worldagroforestry.org; f. 1977; conducts collaborative research on sustainable forestry and its impact on farming, to alleviate poverty and protect the environment; research sites in 23 tropical countries; Dir-Gen. DENNIS PHILIP.

WorldFish Center: POB 500, GPO 10670 Penang, Malaysia; located at: Jl. Batu Maung, Batu Maung, 11960 Bayan Lepas, Penang, Malaysia; tel. (4) 6261606; fax (4) 6265530; e-mail worldfishcenter@cgiar.org; internet www.worldfishcenter.org; f. 1977; non-profit org. involved in collaborative research in developing countries to promote the sustainable use of living aquatic resources based on environmentally sound management; library of 16,000 books, monographs and reprints, 1,376 periodicals; Dir-Gen. Dr STEPHEN HALL; publ. *NAGA – WorldFish Center Quarterly*.

European Confederation of Agriculture/Confédération Européenne de l'Agriculture: 23–25 rue de la Science, Boîte 23, 1040 Brussels, Belgium; tel. (2) 230-43-80; fax (2) 230-46-77; e-mail cea@pophost.eunet.be; f. 1889 as International Confederation of Agriculture, re-formed in 1948 as European Confederation of Agriculture; represents the interests of European agriculture in the international field; 300 mems from 30 countries; Pres. HANS JONSSON (Sweden); publs *CEA Dialog*, publs on current technical, economic, social and cultural problems affecting European Agriculture, Annual Report on the General Assembly.

Inter-American Institute for Co-operation on Agriculture/Instituto Interamericano de Cooperación para la Agricultura: Apdo 55, 2200 Coronado, San José, Costa Rica; tel. (506) 216-02-22; fax (506) 216-02-33; e-mail iicahq@iica.int; internet www.iica.int; f. 1942; a specialized agency of the inter-American system; aims to encourage, promote and support the efforts of the mem. states to achieve agricultural devt and rural well-being; offices in 29 of its 33 countries; Dir-Gen. CHELSTON W. D. BRATHWAITE (Barbados); publ. *Turrialba* (quarterly).

International Association of Agricultural Economists/Conférence Internationale des Economistes Agricoles: 1211 West 22nd St, Suite 216, Oak Brook, IL 60523-2197, USA; tel. (630) 571-9393; fax (630) 571-9580; e-mail iaae@farmfoundation.org; internet www.iaae-agecon.org; f. 1929 to foster the application of the science of agricultural economics to the improvement of the economic and social conditions of rural communities; to advance knowledge of agricultural processes and the economic organization of agriculture; and to facilitate communication and exchange of information among those concerned with rural welfare worldwide; 1,700 mems in 95 countries; Pres. PRABHU PINGALI (Italy); Sec.-Treas. WALTER J. ARMBRUSTER (USA); publ. *Agricultural Economics: the Journal of the International Association of Agricultural Economists* (incl. Proceedings of Conferences).

International Association of Horticultural Producers/Association Internationale des Producteurs de l'Horticulture: Pasteurlaan 6, POB 280, 2700 AG Zoetermeer, Netherlands; tel. (79) 347-07-07; fax (79) 347-04-05; internet www.aiph.org; f. 1948 to represent through its professional mem. orgs the common interests of commercial horticultural producers by means of frequent meetings, regular pbls, press notices, resolutions and addresses to govts and int. authorities; mems: Australia, Austria, Belgium, Canada, China, Colombia, Czechoslovakia, Denmark, Finland, Luxembourg, Netherlands, Norway, Poland, Spain, Sweden, Switzerland, UK, USA; Pres. Dr DOEKE FABER; Sec.-Gen. (vacant).

International Centre for Advanced Mediterranean Agronomic Studies/Centre International de Hautes Etudes Agronomiques Méditerranéennes: Secretariat 11 rue Newton, 75116 Paris, France; tel. 1-53-23-91-00; fax 1-53-23-91-01; internet www.ciheam.org; f. 1962 to provide a supplementary technical, economic and social education for graduates of the higher schools and faculties of agriculture in Mediterranean countries at a postgraduate level; to examine the int. problems posed by rural devt and regional planning; to develop methods of investigation in ecological topics; to contribute to the devt of int. co-operation among agronomists and economists in Mediterranean countries; scholarships may be granted by the governing body; mems: Albania, Algeria, Egypt, France, Greece, Italy, Lebanon, Malta, Morocco, Portugal, Serbia and Montenegro, Spain, Tunisia, Turkey; Chair. MOUÏN HAMZÉ (Lebanon); Sec.-Gen. BERNARD HERVIEU (France); publ. *Options Méditerranéennes*.

Component institutes:

Mediterranean Agronomic Institute of Bari: c/o Cosimo Lacirignola, Via Ceglie 9, 70010 Valenzano, Bari, Italy; tel. 080-4606204; fax 080-4606206; internet netserver.iamb.it; courses on irrigation and drainage, soil conservation, pathology of Mediterranean fruit tree species; Dir COSIMO LACIRIGNOLA.

Mediterranean Agronomic Institute of Chania: c/o Alkinoos Nikolaidis, Alsyllio Agrokepiou, POB 85, Chania 73100, Crete, Greece; tel. 28-21035000; fax 28-21035001; internet www.maich.gr; courses on cultivation of vegetables and flowers under protective covering, Mediterranean forestry and range management, integrated rural devt; Dir ALKINOOS NIKOLAIDIS.

Mediterranean Agronomic Institute of Montpellier: c/o Vincent Dollé, 3191 route de Mende, 34093 Montpellier Cedex 5, France; tel. 4-67-04-60-00; fax 4-67-54-25-27; internet www.iamm.fr; courses on econ. and politics of the agricultural sector and food supplies, econ. and agricultural policies, rural devt and popularization; Dir VINCENT DOLLÉ.

Mediterranean Agronomic Institute of Zaragoza: c/o Miguel Valls Ortiz, Apdo 202, Zaragoza, Spain; tel. (76) 57-60-13; fax (76) 57-63-77; internet www.iamz.ciheam.org; courses on animal husbandry and rural environment, selection, nutrition and animal reproduction, agricultural and food products, marketing, pisciculture, rural environment, plant genetics; Dir MIGUEL VALLS ORTIZ.

International Commission for Food Industries/Commission internationale des industries agricoles et alimentaires: 16 rue Claude Bernard, 75005 Paris, France; tel. 1-43-31-30-36; fax 1-43-31-32-02; e-mail ciia@wanadoo.fr; f. 1934 to develop international co-operation in promoting agricultural and food industries; to organize periodical international congresses and annual study sessions for agricultural and food industries; Sec.-Gen. GUY DARDENNE (France); publs *Food and Agriculture Industries Journal*, Proceedings of Congresses and Symposia.

International Commission of Agricultural Engineering: see under Engineering.

International Committee on Veterinary Gross Anatomical Nomenclature (ICVGAN)/Commission Internationale de la Nomenclature Macroanatomique Vétérinaire: Dept. of Veterinary Anatomy, Bischofsholer Damm 15, 30173 Hanover, Germany; tel. (511) 856-7211; fax (511) 856-7683; f. 1957; language of instruction English; 40 mems; Chair. Prof. HELMUT WAIBL (Germany); Sec. Prof. HAGEN GASSE (Germany); publ. *Nomina Anatomica Veterinaria*.

International Congress on Animal Reproduction/Congrès Internationale de Physiologie et Pathologie de la Reproduction Animale: Dept of Animal Science, University of Sydney, NSW 2006, Australia; tel. (2) 9351-3363; fax (2) 9351-3957; e-mail garethe@vetsci.usyd.edu.au; internet www.vetsci.usyd.edu.au/icar; f. 1948 following the first congress in Milan; Pres. W. THATCHER (USA); Sec.-Gen. Prof. G. EVANS (Australia); publ. *ICAR Proceedings* (every 4 years).

International Dairy Federation/Fédération Internationale de Laiterie: Diamant Bldg, Blvd Auguste Reyers 80, 1030 Brussels, Belgium; tel. (2) 733-98-88; fax (2) 733-0413; e-mail info@fil-idf.org; internet www.fil-idf.org; f. 1903 to link all dairy asscns in order to encourage the solution of scientific, technical and economic problems affecting the dairy industry; mems: nat. cttees in 35 countries; Pres. JIM BEGG; Dir-Gen. EDWARD HOPKIN; publs *Bulletin* (online), *International Standards* (online).

International Federation of Agricultural Producers/Fédération Internationale des Producteurs Agricoles: 60 rue Saint-Lazare, 75009 Paris, France; tel. 1-45-26-05-53; fax 1-48-74-72-12; e-mail ifap@ifap.org; internet www.ifap.org; f. 1946 to represent, in the int. field, the interests of agricultural producers, by laying the co-ordinated views of the nat. member orgs before any appropriate int. body; to act as a forum in which leaders of nat. farmers' orgs can meet to exchange information, experiences and ideas, and bring farmers' concerns to the attention of int. meetings of govts and other bodies; 114 nat. farmers' orgs in 82 countries; Pres. JACK WILKINSON (Canada); Sec.-Gen. DAVID KING; publs *World Farmer* (monthly newsletter), *General Conference Reports* (every 2 years).

International Organization for Biological Control of Noxious Animals and Plants (IOBC)/Organisation Internationale de Lutte Biologique Contre les Animaux et les Plantes Nuisibles: c/o M. Montes de Oca, Agropolis, Ave Agropolis, 34394 Montpellier, Cedex 5, France; tel. 4-67-04-75-30; fax 4-67-04-75-99; e-mail iobc@agropolis.fr; f. 1956 to promote and co-ordinate research on biological and integrated control of pests and weeds; comprises regional sections based on biogeographical zones; mems: public or private from over 50 countries; Pres. Dr J. K. WAAGE (UK); Gen. Sec. Dr E. WAJNBERG (France); publs *Entomophaga* (quarterly), *Bulletin* and Newsletters.

International Seed Testing Association/Association Internationale d'Essais de Semences: Zürichstr. 50, POB 308, 8303 Basserdorf, Switzerland; tel. 448386000; fax 448386001; e-mail ista.office@ista.ch; internet www.seedtest.org; f. 1924; promotes uniformity in the testing and judgement of seeds, through research and by organizing triennial congresses, annual ordinary meetings and periodic training courses; 70 mem. countries, 163 mem. laboratories; Pres. PIETER OOSTERVELD (Netherlands); Sec.-Gen. MICHAEL MUSCHICK (Switzerland); publs *Seed Science and Technology* (3 a year), *ISTA News Bulletin* (2 a year), *ISTA International Rules for Seed Testing* (annually).

International Society for Horticultural Science/Société Internationale de la Science Horticole: POB 500, 3001 Leuven 1, Belgium; located at: Decroylaan 42 (01.21), 3001 Leuven, Belgium; tel. (16) 22-94-27; fax (16) 22-94-50; e-mail info@ishs.org; internet www.ishs.org; f. 1959 to promote and to encourage research in all branches of horticulture and to facilitate co-operation of scientific activities and knowledge transfer on a global scale by means of its publs, events and scientific structure; 6,500 mems in 150 countries; Pres. Dr NORMAN E. LOONEY (Canada); Exec. Dir JOZEF VAN ASSCHE; publs *Chronica Horticulturae* (quarterly), *Acta Horticulturae* (about 35 a year).

International Society for Tropical Crop Research and Development (ISTCRAD): c/o Prof. N. K. Nayar (Associate Director of Research (Planning)), Kerala Agricultural University, Trichur 680654, Kerala, India; tel. (487) 370497; fax (487) 370019; e-mail kauhqr@ren.nic.in; f. 1990; provides a forum for interaction among scientists, progressive farmers and entrepreneurs; Sec.-Gen. Prof. N. K. NAYAR; publs *News Bulletin* (quarterly), *Scientific Journal* (quarterly).

International Society for Tropical Root Crops (ISTRC): c/o I.S.H.S., Englaan 1, 6703 ET Wageningen, Netherlands; tel. (8370) 21747; fax (8370) 21586; f. 1964; 300 mems; Pres. Dr S. K. HAHN; Sec. Ir H.H. VAN DER BORG; publ. *Newsletter* (annually).

International Union of Soil Science (IUSS)/Association Internationale de la Science du Sol/Internationale Bodenkundliche Gesellschaft: c/o Prof. Stephen Nortcliff, Dept of Soil Science, Univ. of Reading, POB 233, Reading, RG6 6DW, UK; tel. (118) 378-6559; fax (118) 378-6666; e-mail iuss@rdg.ac.uk; internet www.iuss.org; f. 1924 to promote soil science and its applications; federated to ICSU; 45,000 mems in 70 countries; Pres. Prof. R. SWIFT; Sec.-Gen. Prof. STEPHEN NORTCLIFF; publ. *Bulletin* (2 a year).

International Union of Forest Research Organizations/Union Internationale des Instituts de Recherches Forestières/Internationaler Verband Forstlicher Forschungsanstalten: Hauptstr. 7, 1140 Vienna–Hadersdorf, Austria; tel. (1) 877-01-51-0; fax (1) 877-01-51-50; e-mail office@iufro.org; internet www.iufro.org; f. 1892 for international co-operation in the various branches of forestry research and related fields; mems: 700 orgs in 115 countries (15,000 scientists), including forestry faculties, experimental stations, research institutions, etc.; Pres. Prof. DON K. LEE (Republic of Korea); Exec. Dir Dr PETER MAYER (Austria); publs *Annual Report, Congress Proceedings, IUFRO News* (online, 10 a year), *IUFRO World Series, Scientific Papers*.

World Association for Animal Production: Via Tomassetti 3 - 1/A, 00161 Rome, Italy; tel. 06-44202639; fax 06-86329263; e-mail waap@waap.it; internet www.waap.it; f. 1965; organizes a conference every 5 years; regional discussions; mems: 17 societies (nat. and regional); Pres. ASSEFAW MEDHIN TEWOLDE (Ethiopia); Sec.-Gen. ANDREA ROSATI (Italy); publ. *News Items* (2 a year).

World Veterinary Association/Association Mondiale Vétérinaire: c/o Dr Lars Holsaae, Emdrupvej 28A, 2100 Copenhagen Ø, Denmark; tel. 38-71-01-56; fax 38-71-03-22; internet www.worldvet.org; f. 1863; mem. organizations in 80 countries, 20 assoc. mems; Pres. Dr HERBERT SCHNEIDER (Namibia); Exec. Sec. Dr LARS HOLSAAE (Denmark); publs *World Veterinary Directory, Bulletin* (2 a year).

Arts

Asociación de Lingüística y Filología de América Latina/Latin American Association of Linguistics and Philology: c/o Adolfo Elizaincín, Universidad de la República, CP 1410, 11000 Montevideo, Uruguay; e-mail aelizain@gmail.com; internet www.mundoalfal.org; f. 1964; 1,009 mems; Pres. ALBA VALENCIA ESPINOSA (Chile); Sec.-Gen. ADOLFO ELIZAINCÍN (Uruguay); publs *Actas de los Congresos, Revista Lingüística*.

Association for Commonwealth Literature and Language Studies: POB 715, Osmania Univ. Post Office, Hyderabad 500 007, India; tel. (40) 27005301; internet www.aclals.org; f. 1965 as an ind. org.; encourages study in Commonwealth literatures and languages, incl. comparative studies between literatures in English and indigenous literatures and languages, new kinds of English and use of mass media; holds triennial conferences and regional meetings; organizes visits and exchanges; collects source material and publishes creative, critical, historical and bibliographical material; 1,600 mems; Chair. MEENAKSHI MUKHERJEE (India); Vice-Chair. HARISH TRIVEDI (India); Vice-Chair. and Sec. C. VIJAYASREE (India); publ. *Bulletin*.

Commonwealth Association of Museums: POB 30192, Chinook Postal Outlet, Calgary, AB T2H 2V9, Canada; tel. (403) 938-3190; fax (403) 938-3190; e-mail irvinel@fclc.com; internet www.maltwood.uvic.ca/cam; f. 1974; aims to maintain and strengthen links between mems of the museum profession; encourages and assists mems to obtain additional training and to attend appropriate conferences, seminars; promotes professional excellence; collaborates with nat. and regional museum asscns; runs conferences and workshops, internships, distance-learning programme in basic museum studies; nat., institutional and individual mems in 38 countries; general assembly every three years with elections; annual meeting; 230 mems; Pres. MARTIN SEGGER (Canada); Sec.-Gen. LOIS IRVINE (Canada); publs *Bulletin* (irreg.), *Conference and Workshop Proceedings*.

Communauté Africaine de Culture: c/o Présence africaine, 25 bis rue des Ecoles, 75005 Paris, France; tel. (1) 43-54-13-74; fax (1) 43-25-96-67; f. 2005 to create unity and friendship among African scholars for the encouragement of their own cultures; mems from 22 countries; Pres. WOLE SOYINKA; Sec.-Gen. Mme CHRISTIANE DIOP; publ. *Présence Africaine* (quarterly).

Europa Nostra (Our Europe): Lange Voorhout 35, 2514 EC The Hague, The Netherlands; tel. (70) 3024050; fax (70) 3617865; e-mail office@europanostra.org; internet www.europanostra.org; f. 1991 by merger of Europa Nostra and the Int. Castles Institute; pan-European org. for the protection of Europe's architectural and natural heritage, and the promotion of high standards in architecture and in town and country planning; undertakes campaigns, conferences, research, exhibitions and an annual award scheme; language of instruction French; 1,500 mem. orgs and individuals; Pres. HRH THE PRINCE CONSORT OF DENMARK; Exec. Pres. ANDREA SCHULER; Sec.-Gen. SNESKA QUAEDVLIEG-MIHAILOVIC; publs *Awards Review* (annual), *Europa Nostra Scientific Bulletin* (annual), *European Cultural Heritage Review* (annual).

European Cultural Foundation/Fondation Européenne de la Culture: Jan van Goyenkade 5, 1075 HN Amsterdam, Netherlands; tel. (20) 573-38-68; fax (20) 675-22-31; e-mail eurocult@eurocult.org; internet www.eurocult.org; f. 1954 as an ind., non-profit organization to promote cultural co-operation in Europe; an operating foundation, which initiates and manages its own projects and programmes and gives grants to other bodies for European-level cultural activities; emphasizes the importance of developing a pluralistic civil society in Europe by encouraging the linkage of cultural activity and social responsibility; supports a network of nat. cttees based in 23 European countries; Pres. HRH Princess MARGRIET OF THE NETHERLANDS; Dir GOTTFRIED WAGNER; publ. *Beyond Borders* (3 a year).

European Society of Culture/Società Europea di Cultura/Société Européenne de Culture: Villa Hériot, Giudecca 54, 30133 Venice, Italy; tel. 041-5230210; fax 041-5231033; internet www.societaeuropeacultura.it; f. 1950 to unite artists, poets, scientists, philosophers and others through mutual interests and friendship to safeguard and improve the conditions required for creative activity; 2,000 mems; library of 5,000 vols; Pres. VINCENZO CAPPELLETTI (Italy); Premier Vice-Pres. ARRIGO LEVI (Italy); International Gen. Sec. MICHELLE CAMPAGNOLO BOUVIER (Italy); publ. *Comprendre* (irregular).

Fédération Internationale des Ecrivains de Langue Française (FIDELF): 3492 ave Laval, Montreal, QC H2X 3C8, Canada; tel. (515) 849-62-39; f. 1982; 18 mem. asscns; Pres. ALIOUNE BADARA BEYE (Senegal); Sec.-Gen. MAMADOU TRAORÉ DIOP (Senegal).

International Amateur Theatre Association—Organization for Understanding and Education through Theatre: Vene 6, 10123 Tallinn, Estonia; tel. 6418-405; fax 6418-406; e-mail secretariat@aitaiata.org; internet www.aitaiata.org; f. 1952; mems in 70 states; composed of nat. centres; organizes int. conferences, colloquia, seminars, workshops, festivals incl. world festival of amateur theatre (every 4 years); Administrator ENE JÜRNA; publ. *Bulletin AITA/IATA*.

International Association for Caribbean Archaeology/Association Internationale d'Archéologie de la Caraïbe/Asociación Internacional de Arqueología del Caribe: BP 4030, Terres Sainvilles Cedex, 97254 Fort-de-France, Martinique; tel. 63-65-51; fax 63-65-51; internet museum-server .archanth.cam.ac.uk/iaca.www/iaca.htm; f. 1962; 59 mems; Pres. Dr JAY HAVISER (Netherlands Antilles); Sec. QUETTA KAYE (UK); publ. *Newsletter* (1 or 2 a year).

International Association of Applied Linguistics/Association Internationale de Linguistique Appliquée: c/o Prof. Karlfried Knapp, Dept of Applied Linguistics, POB 900221, 99105 Erfurt, Germany; tel. (361) 737-4321; fax (361) 737-4329; e-mail aila@uni-erfurt.de; internet www.aila.info; f. 1964 to promote the application of linguistic theories to the solution of language and language-related problems in society; 8,000 mems; Pres. SUSAN M. GASS (USA); Sec.-Gen. Prof. KARLFRIED KNAPP (Germany); publs *AILA Book Series* (3 a year), *AILA News* (2 a year), *AILA Review* (annually).

International Association of Art/Association internationale des arts plastiques: UNESCO House, 1 rue Miollis, 75732 Paris, France; tel. 1-45-68-26-55; fax 1-45-67-16-90; f. 1954; 81 national cttees; Pres. EDUARDO ARENILLAS.

International Association of Art Critics/Association Internationale des Critiques d'Art: 15 rue Martel, 75010 Paris, France; tel. 1-47-70-17-42; fax 1-47-70-17-81; e-mail office.paris@aica-int.org; internet www.aica-int.org; f. 1949 to promote intl co-operation in the world of plastic arts (painting, sculpture, graphic arts, architecture); consultative status with UNESCO; 3,750 individual mems and 72 National Sections; Pres. HENRY MEYRIC HUGHES (UK); Gen. Sec. RAMON TIO BELLIDO (France); publ. *Annuaire AiCA*.

International Association of Literary Critics/Association Internationale des Critiques Littéraires: 38 rue du Faubourg-St-Jacques, 75014 Paris, France; tel. 1-53-10-12-00; fax 1-53-10-12-12; f. 1969; UNESCO consultative status B; organizes congresses, etc.; Pres. ROBERT ANDRÉ; publ. *Revue* (annually).

International Association of Museums of Arms and Military History (IAMAM)/Association Internationale des Musées d'Armes et d'Histoire Militaire: c/o J. P. Puype, Legermuseum, Korte Geer 1, 2611 CA Delft, Netherlands; tel. (15) 2150500; fax (15) 2150544; f. 1957; org. to establish contact between museums and other scientific institutions with colln s of arms and armour, military equipment, uniforms, etc., which may be visited by the public; to promote the study of relevant groups of objects; triennial conferences; 300 instns in 51 countries; Pres. CLAUDE GAIER (Belgium); Sec.-Gen. J. P. PUYPE (Netherlands); publs *Repertory of Museums of Arms and Military History*, *Glossarium Armourum: Arma Defensiva*, *Triennial Reports*.

International Centre for Ancient and Modern Tapestry/Centre International de la Tapisserie Ancienne et Moderne: 4 ave Villamont, 1005 Lausanne, Switzerland; tel. 213230757; fax 213230721; f. 1961; documentation centre; organizes a biennial international exhibition of contemporary art in Lausanne and subsequently shown in other countries; library of 1,400 vols; Pres. Mayor of Lausanne; Exec. Sec. PHILIPPE JEANLOZ; publ. biennial exhibition catalogue.

International Centre for the Study of the Preservation and Restoration of Cultural Property (ICCROM): Via di San Michele 13, 00153 Rome, Italy; tel. 06-585531; fax 06-58553349; e-mail iccrom@iccrom.org; internet www.iccrom.org; f. 1959; inter-governmental org.; UNESCO Class A; assembles documentation and disseminates knowledge by way of publications and meetings; co-ordinates research, organizes training of specialists and short courses; offers technical advice; int. documentation centre; financed by 113 mem. countries; library of 80,000 items; Dir-Gen. NICHOLAS STANLEY-PRICE; publ. *Newsletter* (annually, in Arabic, English, French and Spanish).

International Centre of Films for Children and Young People/Centre International du Film pour l'Enfance et la Jeunesse: Bureau 200, 3774 rue St Denis, Montréal, QC H2W 2M1, Canada; tel. (514) 284-9388; fax (514) 284-0168; e-mail info@cifej.com; internet www.cifej.com; f. 1955; research centre and clearing-house of information about entertainment films (cinema and television) for children all over the world; 153 mems from 55 countries; Pres. ATHINA RIKAKI (Greece); Sec.-Gen. MONIC LESSARD (Canada); publ. *CIFEJ Info* (6 a year).

International Comparative Literature Association/Association internationale de littérature comparée: c/o Prof. Steven P. Sondrup, Brigham Young University, HRCB. Provo, UT 84602-4538, USA; e-mail ailc.icla@gmail.com; internet www.byu.edu/~ida; f. 1954 to promote the development of the comparative study of literature; 4,000 mems (socs and individuals) in 65 countries; Pres. Prof. DOROTHY FIGUEIRA (USA); Secs Prof. SYLVIE ANDRÉ (French Polynesia), Prof. STEVEN P. SONDRUP (USA); publs *ICLA Bulletin AILC* (2 a year), *Recherche Littéraire* (2 a year).

International Council for Film, Television and Audiovisual Communication/Conseil International du Cinéma, de la Télévision et de la Communication audiovisuelle: 1 rue Miollis, Bureau B7.2.23–2.25, 75732 Paris Cedex 15, France; tel. 1-45-68-48-55; e-mail cict@unesco.org; internet www.unesco.org/iftc; f. 1958 under auspices of UNESCO; seeks to provide a link of information and jt action between member orgs, and to assist them in their int. work in film and television; mems: 36 int. asscns and feds and 12 assocs; Sec.-Gen. GIULIO C. GIORDANO.

International Council of Graphic Design Associations (ICOGRADA): POB 5, Forest 2, 1190 Brussels, Belgium; tel. (2) 344-58-43; fax (2) 344-71-38; e-mail secretariat@icograda.org; internet www.icograda.org; f. 1963 to raise the standards of graphic design and professional practice and the professional status of graphic designers; to collect and exchange information relating to graphic design; to organize exhibitions and congresses and to issue reports and surveys; 71 assoc. mems in 44 countries; library: slide and book library at Design Museum, London; poster and records archives at University of Reading, UK; Pres. MERVYN KURLANSKY (Denmark); publ. *Board Message* (4 a year).

International Council of Museums (ICOM): Maison de l'UNESCO, 1 rue Miollis, 75732 Paris Cedex 15, France; tel. 1-47-34-05-00; fax 1-43-06-78-62; e-mail secretariat@icom.museum; internet icom.museum; f. 1946; professional org., open to all mems of the museum profession, established to provide an appropriate org. to advance int. co-operation among museums, and to be the co-ordinating and representative int. body furthering museum interests; in 115 countries an ICOM Nat. Cttee on int. co-operation among museums has been organized, each as widely representative as possible of museum interests; maintains UNESCO-ICOM Museum Information Centre, a library and information service specializing in the field of museology and museum practice world-wide; 30 int. cttees and 15 int. affiliated asscns on specialized subjects; 21,000 individual and institutional members in 140 countries; Pres. ALISSANDRA CUMMINS (Barbados); publs *ICOM News/Nouvelles de l'ICOM/Noticias del ICOM* (quarterly), *Study Series/Cahier d'Etude* (annual).

International Council on Monuments and Sites (ICOMOS)/Conseil International des Monuments et des Sites: 49–51 rue de la Fédération, 75015 Paris, France; tel. 1-45-67-67-70; fax 1-45-66-06-22; e-mail secretariat@icomos.org; internet www.international.icomos.org; f. 1965 to promote the study and preservation of monuments and sites; 7,000 mems, 110 national cttees, 22 int. cttees; library: Documentation Centre on preservation and restoration of monuments and sites: 30,000 vols, 350 periodicals, 25,000 slides; Pres. MICHAEL PETZET (Germany); Sec.-Gen. DINU BUMBARU (Canada); publs *Icomos Newsletter*, *Icomos Scientific Journal*.

International Federation for Theatre Research/Fédération Internationale pour la Recherche Théâtrale: c/o Prof. David Whitton, Dean of Arts and Humanities, Lancaster Univ., Lancaster, LA1 4YN, UK; internet www.firt-iftr.org; f. 1955 by 21 countries at the Int. Conference on Theatre History, London; int. seminars in theatre history; attached research institute Istituto Internazionale per la Ricerca Teatrale: see Italy chapter; Pres. Prof. BRIAN SINGLETON (Ireland); Jt Secs-Gen. Prof. FRÉDÉRIC MAURIN (Canada), Prof. DAVID WHITTON (UK); publ. *Theatre Research International* (quarterly).

International Institute for Conservation of Historic and Artistic Works/Institut International pour la Conservation des Objets d'Art et d'Histoire: 6 Buckingham St, London, WC2N 6BA, UK; tel. (20) 7839-5975; fax (20) 7976-1564; e-mail iic@iiconservation.org; internet www.iiconservation.org; f. 1950; permanent org. for co-ordinating and improving the knowledge, methods and working standards needed to protect and preserve precious materials of all kinds; publishes information on research into all processes connected with conservation, both scientific and technical, and on the devt of those processes; congress held every 2 years; 2,500 individual mems, 500 institutional mems; Pres. ANDREW ODDY; Sec.-Gen. DAVID LEIGH; Exec. Sec. GRAHAM VOCE; publs *Studies in Conservation* (quarterly), *IIC Bulletin* (6 a year), *Reviews in Conservation* (annual).

International Literary and Artistic Association/Association Littéraire et Artistique Internationale: c/o Kimbrough et Associés, 7 bis rue de Monceau, 75008 Paris, France; tel. 1-53-30-24-24; fax 1-53-30-24-25; internet alai.org; f. 1878 at Congress of Paris, presided over by Victor Hugo; seeks to protect the rights and interests of writers and artists of all lands, through the extension of copyright conventions, etc.; mems: nat. groups in Argentina, Austria, Belgium, Canada, Colombia, Croatia, Denmark, Finland, France, Germany, Greece, Hungary, Ireland, Israel, Italy, Japan, Kazakhstan, Mexico, Netherlands, Norway, Portugal, Russia, Spain, Sweden, Switzerland, UK, Uruguay, USA; Pres. VICTOR NABHAN; Sec.-Gen. YVES GAUBIAC.

International Numismatic Commission/Commission internationale de numismatique: Cabinet des Médailles, Bibliothèque Nationale de France, 75084 Paris, France; internet www.inc-cin.org; f. 1927 to facilitate co-operation among individuals and instns in the field of numismatics; mems: nat. orgs in 38 countries; Pres. MICHEL AMANDRY (UK); Sec. Dr CARMEN ARNOLD (USA); publs *Compte rendu* (annual), *International Numismatic Newsletter* (2 a year).

International PEN (A World Association of Writers): 9–10 Charterhouse Bldgs, Goswell Rd, London, EC1M 7AT, UK; tel. (20) 7253-4308; fax (20) 7253-5711; e-mail intpen@dircon.co.uk; internet www.internationalpen.org.uk; f. 1921 by Mrs Dawson Scott under the presidency of John Galsworthy to promote co-operation between writers all over the world in the interests of literature, freedom of expression and int. goodwill; 138 autonomous centres worldwide; 14,000 mems; Int. Pres. JIRI GRUSA; Int. Sec. TERRY CARLBOM; publ. *PEN International* (in English, French and Spanish, in asscn with UNESCO, 2 a year).

International Pragmatics Association (IPrA): POB 33, 2018 Antwerp 11, Belgium; tel. (3) 230-55-74; fax (3) 230-55-74; e-mail ipra@uia.ua.ac.be; internet www.ipra.be; f. 1986; aims to create a framework for the discussion and comparison of results of research in all aspects of language use or functions of language and to disseminate knowledge about pragmatic aspects of language; incorporates a research centre; 1,400 individual mems; Sec.-Gen. JEF VERSCHUEREN; Exec. Sec. ANN VERHAERT; publ. *Pragmatics* (4 a year).

International Robert Musil Society/Internationale Robert-Musil-Gesellschaft: POB 151150, Univ. des Saarlandes, 66041 Saarbrucken, Germany; tel. (681) 302-3334; fax (681) 302-3034; e-mail info@i-r-m-g.de; internet www.i-r-m-g.de; f. 1974 under the patronage of Bruno Kreisky (Austria), to promote int. co-operation in research and publications on Musil and edns of his writings; 267 mems; organizes colloquia; Pres. Prof. Dr PETER HENNINGER (France); Secs.-Gen. Prof. Dr PIERRE BÉHAR (Germany), Prof. Dr ROSMARIE ZELLER (Switzerland); publ. *Musil-Forum* (every 2 years).

International Theatre Institute/Institut International du Théâtre: UNESCO, 1 rue Miollis, 75732 Paris Cedex 15, France; tel. (1) 45-68-48-80; fax (1) 45-66-50-40; e-mail iti@unesco.org; internet www.iti-worldwide.org/amt; f. 1948 to facilitate cultural exchanges and int. understanding in the domain of the performing arts; conferences, workshops, pbls; language of instruction French, English; mems: 102 mem. nations; Pres. MANFRED BEILHARZ (Germany); Sec. Gen. JENNIFER WALPOLE (France); publs *News* (3 a year), *The World of Theatre* (every 2 years), *World Theatre Directory* (online).

International Union of Architects/Union Internationale des Architectes: 51 rue Raynouard, 75016 Paris, France; tel. 1-45-24-36-88; fax 1-45-24-02-78; e-mail uia@uia-architectes.org; internet www.uia-architectes.org; f. 1948; mems in 106 countries; publ. *Newsletter* (monthly).

International Union of Cinema/Union Internationale du Cinéma: c/o Jan P. Essing, Lente 33, 8251 NT Dronten, The Netherlands; tel. (321) 319529; fax (321) 312739; e-mail essing.jan@hetnet.nl; internet www.unica-web.com; f. 1937 to encourage devt of art, techniques and critical judgment among amateurs, to facilitate contacts between nat. asscns and to promote the exchange of films; mems: nat. feds in 35 countries; library of 500 films and videos; Annual Congress; Sec.-Gen. JAN ESSING; publ. *UNICA News*.

Organization for Museums, Monuments and Sites of Africa/Organisation pour les Musées, les Monuments et les Sites d'Afrique: Centre for Museum Studies, PMB 2031, Jos, Plateau State, Nigeria; f. 1975; aims to foster the collection, study and conservation of the natural and cultural heritage of Africa; co-operation between mem. countries through seminars, workshops, conferences, etc., exchange of personnel, developing training facilities, and drawing up legislative and admin. measures; mems from 30 countries; Pres. Dr J. M. ESSOMBA (Cameroon); Sec.-Gen. K. A. MYLES (Ghana).

World Academy of Art and Sciences: see under International—Science.

World Crafts Council: El Comendador 1916, Providencia, 6640064 Santiago, Chile; tel. (2) 3545636; fax (2) 2325811; internet www.wccwis.cl; f. 1964; a non-profit organization to maintain the status of crafts as a vital part of cultural life and to promote fellowship among the world's craftsmen; offers help and advice to craftsmen, consults with govts, nat. and intl institutions; mem. bodies in approx 90 countries; Pres. MARÍA CELINA RODRÍGUEZ OLEA (Chile); Sec.-Gen. (vacant); publ. *World Crafts Council – Asia Pacific* (2 a year).

Bibliography

Association for Health Information and Libraries in Africa: c/o WHO Regional Office for Africa, BP 6, Brazzaville, Republic of Congo; tel. 241-39425; fax 241-39673; internet www.ahila.org; f. 1984, name changed 1989; promotes co-operation among African health information centres and libraries, to enhance health information services and to develop an African *Index Medicus*; Pres. IBRAHIMA BOB; Sec. BACHIR CHAIBOU; publ. *AHILA Newsletter* (quarterly).

Association Internationale de Bibliophilie/International Association of Bibliophiles: c/o Bibliothèque Nationale de France, Réserve des livres rares, Quai François Mauriac, 75706 Paris Cedex 13, France; tel. 1-53-79-54-76; fax 1-53-79-54-60; f. 1963 to form a meeting point for bibliophiles from different countries, to organize conferences; international congresses every 2 years; 500 mems; Pres. CONDE DE ORGAZ (Spain); Sec.-Gen. JEAN-MARC CHATELAIN (France); publ. *Le Bulletin du Bibliophile* (2 a year).

Association of Caribbean University, Research and Institutional Libraries: POB 23317, San Juan, Puerto Rico 00931-3317; tel. (787) 790-8054; internet acuril.rrp.upr.edu; f. 1969 to facilitate the development and use of libraries, archives and information services; identification, collection and preservation of information resources in support of intellectual and educational endeavours in the area; 200 mems; Pres. ANIQUE SYLVESTRE (Martinique); Exec. Sec. ONEIDA RIVERA DE ORTIZ (Puerto Rico); publs *ACURILEANA* (online), *Conference Proceedings*, *Cybernotes* (newsletter, online).

Bibliothèques Européennes de Théologie (BETH)/Europäische Bibliotheken für Theologie/European Theological Libraries: 5 Swanston Crescent, Edinburgh, EH10 7BS, UK; tel. (131) 445-1691; e-mail prjhall@aol.com; internet www.beth.be; f. 1961; holds Annual General Assembly; 35 mems (12 ordinary, 13 extraordinary, 10 individuals); Pres. PIERRE BEFFA (Switzerland); Sec. Prof. PENELOPE HALL.

Commonwealth Library Association: c/o University of the West Indies, Bridgetown Campus, Learning Resources Centre, POB 64, Bridgetown, Barbados; tel. 417-4201; fax 424-8944; e-mail watsone@uwichill.edu.bb; f. 1972 to support and encourage library asscns in the Commonwealth; to create and strengthen professional relationships between librarians; to promote the status and education of librarians and the reciprocal recognition of qualifications; to improve libraries; to initiate research projects designed to promote library provision and to advance technical development of libraries in the Commonwealth; language of instruction English; 52 mems incl. 40 nat. asscns, 130 affiliated mems; Pres. ELIZABETH WATSON (Barbados); publ. *COMLA Bulletin* (3 a year).

European Association for Health Information and Libraries: c/o Leijte & Regoort, POB 1388 , 3600 BJ Maarssen, Netherlands; fax (346) 550876; e-mail eahil@nic.surfnet.nl; internet www.eahil.net; f. 1987, to bring together and represent health librarians and information officers in Europe; 1,150 mems; Pres. SUZANNE BAKKER (Netherlands); Sec. TONY MCSEÀN (UK); publ. *Journal* (quarterly).

International Association for Mass Communication Research/Association internationale des études et recherches sur l'information: C/o Hamid Mowlana, School of International Service, American University, 4400 Massachusetts Ave NW, Washington, DC 20016, USA; tel. (202) 885-1621; fax (202) 855-2494; e-mail mowlana@american.edu; internet www.humfak.auc.dk/iamcr; f. 1957 to disseminate information on teaching and research in mass media; to encourage research; to provide a forum for the exchange of information; to bring about improvements in communication practice, policy and research; and to encourage the improvement of training for journalism; over 1,000 mems in 63 countries; Pres. HAMID MOWLANA.

International Association for the Development of Documentation, Libraries and Archives in Africa: BP 375, Dakar, Senegal; tel. 24-09-54; f. 1957 to promote planning and organization of archives, libraries, documentation centres and museums in all African countries; Permanent Sec. EMMANUEL K. W. DADZIE.

International Association of Agricultural Information Specialists/Association Internationale des Spécialistes de l'Information Agricole: POB 63, Lexington, KY 40588-0063, USA; tel. (859) 254-0752; fax (859) 254-0752; e-mail info@iaald.org; internet www.iaald.org; f. 1955 unites agricultural information specialists worldwide, organizes meetings and annual conferences in various parts of the world, communicates the value of knowledge and information, collaborates with partner orgs;

400 mems, representing 80 countries; Pres. PETER BALLANTYNE; Sec. and Treas. ANTOINETTE P. GREIDER; publ. *Quarterly Bulletin*.

International Association of Law Libraries (IALL)/Association Internationale des Bibliothèques de Droit: POB 5709, Washington, DC 20016-1309, USA; tel. (202) 707-9866; fax (202) 707-1820; e-mail ann.morrison@dal.ca; internet www.iall.org; f. 1959 to offer world-wide co-operation in the devt of law libraries and the collection of legal documentation; holds annual conference; 680 mems in 60 countries; Pres. JULES WINTERTON (UK); Sec. ANN MORRISON (Canada); publ. *International Journal of Legal Information* (3 a year).

International Association of Music Libraries, Archives and Documentation Centres (IAML)/Association Internationale des Bibliothèques, Archives et Centres de Documentation Musicaux/ Internationale Vereinigung der Musikbibliotheken, Musikarchive und Musikdokumentationszentren: c/o Music Room, National Library of New Zealand, POB 1467, Wellington, New Zealand; tel. (4) 474-3039; fax (4) 474-3035; e-mail roger.flury@natlib .govt.nz; internet www.iaml.info/; f. 1951 to facilitate co-operation between music libraries and information centres, compile music bibliographies, and to promote the professional training of music librarians and documentalists; languages of instruction French, German, English; 2,000 mems in 53 countries, incl. 24 nat. brs; Sec.-Gen. ROGER FLURY (New Zealand); publ. *Fontes artis musicae* (4 a year).

International Association of Technological University Libraries (IATUL)/ Association Internationale des Bibliothèques d'Universités Polytechniques: c/o Judith Palmer, Radcliffe Science Library, Univ. of Oxford, Parks Rd, Oxford, OX1 3QP, UK; internet www.iatul.org; f. 1955 to promote co-operation between mem. libraries and conduct research on library problems; mems: 200 univ. libraries in 41 countries; Pres. GAYNOR AUSTEN (Australia); Sec. JUDITH PALMER; publs *IATUL News* (quarterly), *IATUL Proceedings* (annual).

International Board on Books for Young People (IBBY): Nonnenweg 12, Postfach, 4003 Basel, Switzerland; tel. 612722917; fax 612722757; e-mail ibby@ibby.org; internet www.ibby.org; f. 1953 to support and unify those forces in all countries connected with children's book work; to encourage the production and distribution of good children's books especially in the developing countries; to promote scientific investigation into problems of juvenile books; to organize Int. Children's Book Day and a biennial int. congress; to present the Hans Christian Andersen Award every 2 years to a living author and illustrator whose work is an outstanding contribution to children's literature, and the IBBY-Asahi Reading Promotion Award annually to an org. that has made a significant contribution to children's literature; to make a biennial selection of outstanding books to form the IBBY Honour List; Mems: Nat. Sections and individual mems in 68 countries; Pres. PETER SCHNECK (Austria); Admin. Dir LIZ PAGE (Switzerland); publ. *Bookbird* (quarterly).

International Committee for Social Science Information and Documentation/Comité International pour l'Information et la Documentation des Sciences Sociales: c/o Clacso, Callao 875 (3° piso), 1023 Buenos Aires, Argentina; e-mail saugy@clacso.edu.ar; f. 1950 to collect and disseminate information on documentation services in social sciences, help improve documentation, advise socs on problems of documentation and to draw up rules likely to improve the presentation of all documents; mems from int. asscns specializing in social sciences or in documentation, and from other specialized fields; Pres. KRISHANA G. TYAGI (India); Sec.-Gen. CATALINA SAUGY (Argentina); publs *Newsletter*, *International Bibliography of the Social Sciences* (annual, 4 series).

International Council on Archives/Conseil international des archives: 60 rue des Francs-Bourgeois, 75003 Paris, France; tel. 1-40-27-63-06; fax 1-42-72-20-65; e-mail ica@ica.org; internet www.ica.org; f. 1948; 1,690 mems from 190 countries and territories; Pres. LORENZ MIKOLETZKY (Austria); Sec.-Gen. JOAN VAN ALBADA (France); publs *COMMA International Journal on Archives* (3 a year), *FLASH* (3 a year).

International Federation of Film Archives/Fédération Internationale des Archives du Film: 1 rue Defacqz, 1000 Brussels, Belgium; tel. (2) 538-30-65; fax (2) 534-47-74; e-mail info@fiafnet.org; internet www.fiafnet.org; f. 1938 to encourage the creation of archives worldwide for the collection and conservation of the film heritage of each country; to facilitate co-operation and exchanges between these film archives; to promote public interest in the art of the cinema; to aid research in this field and to compile new documentation; conducts research; publishes manuals, etc.; holds annual congresses; 108 affiliates in 62 countries; Pres. EVA ORBANZ (Germany); Sec.-Gen. MEG LABRUM (Australia).

International Federation of Library Associations and Institutions (IFLA)/ Fédération Internationale des Associations de Bibliothécaires et des Bibliothèques: POB 95312, 2509 CH, The Hague, Netherlands; tel. (70) 314-08-84; fax (70) 383-48-27; e-mail ifla@ifla.org; internet www.ifla.org; f. 1927; to promote int. library co-operation in all fields of library activity, and to provide a representative body in matters of int. interest; 1,700 mems in 150 countries; Pres. ALEX BYRNE (Australia); Sec.-Gen. P. J. LOR (South Africa); publs *IFLA Journal* (quarterly), *International Cataloguing Bibliographic Control* (quarterly), *IFLA Directory* (every 2 years), *IFLA Professional Reports*, *IFLA Publication Series* (6 a year).

Associated centre:

International Association of Metropolitan City Libraries (INTAMEL): c/o Swedish Nat. Council for Cultural Affairs, POB 7843, 10398 Stockholm, Sweden; tel. (8) 679-3110; fax (8) 611-1349; f. 1967 to encourage int. co-operation between large city libraries, in particular the exchange of books, exhibitions, staff and information and participation in the work of the Int. Fed. of Library Asscns; Pres. DAN WILSON (USA); Sec.-Treas. JAN BOMAN (Sweden).

International Institute for Children's Literature and Reading Research/Institut für Jugendliteratur/Institut International de Littérature pour Enfants et de Recherches sur la Lecture: 1040 Vienna, Mayerhofgasse 6, Austria; tel. (1) 505-03-59; fax (1) 505-03-59-17; e-mail office@ jugendliteratur.net; internet www .jugendliteratur.net; f. 1965 as an intl documentation and advisory centre of juvenile literature; promotes intl research; arranges conferences and exhibitions; compiles recommendation lists; mems: individual and group members in 26 countries; Dir Mag. KARIN HALLER (Austria); publ. *1000 und 1 Buch* (4 a year).

International Society for Knowledge Organization (ISKO): C/o Peter Ohly, Social Science Information Center, Lennestr. 30, 53113 Bonn, Germany; tel. (228) 2281-142; e-mail isko@iz-soz.de; internet is.gseis .ucla.edu/orgs/isko; f. 1989 to promote research, development, and application of all methods for the organization of knowledge; advises on the construction, perfection and application of classification systems, thesauri, terminologies, etc; organizes int. conference every 2 years; 400 mems; Pres. Prof. MARÍA JOSÉ LÓPEZ-HUERTAS PÉREZ (Spain); Sec. and Treas. PETER OHLY (Germany); publs *Advances in Knowledge Organization* (English and German, irreg.), *ISKO News*, *Knowledge Organization* (quarterly), *Knowledge Organisation in Subject Areas 1994–* (irreg.).

International Youth Library/Internationale Jugendbibliothek: Schloss Blutenburg, 81247 Munich, Germany; tel. (89) 891211-0; fax (89) 8117553; e-mail bib@ijb .de; internet www.ijb.de; f. 1949; an associated project of UNESCO since 1953. Objects: to encourage intl exchange and co-operation in children's book publishing, research, and promotion of reading; to provide information and advice to students, teachers, publishers, etc.; to organize exhibitions; library: largest collection of int. children's literature in the world: 540,000 vols in over 100 languages; Dir Dr BARBARA SCHARIOTH; publs *Report* (2 a year), *White Ravens* (a selection of international children's and youth literature, annually).

Ligue des Bibliothèques Européennes de Recherche (LIBER): LIBER Secretariat, Susan Vejlsgaard, The Royal Library, POB 2149, 1016 Copenhagen K, Denmark; tel. 33-93-62-22; fax 33-91-95-96; e-mail sv@ kb.dk; internet www.kb.dk/liber; f. 1971; 360 mems from more than 40 European countries; represents and promotes the interests of research libraries in Europe, particularly to assist them to create a functional research network across national boundaries; Pres. ERLAND KOLDING NIELSEN (Denmark); Asst Sec. SUSAN VEJLSGAARD (Denmark); publ. *LIBER Quarterly*.

Economics, Political Science and Sociology

International Labour Organisation (ILO): 4 route des Morillons, 1211 Geneva 22, Switzerland; tel. (22) 799-61-11; fax (22) 798-86-85; e-mail ilo@ilo.org; internet www .ilo.org; f. 1919, became Specialized Agency of UN in 1946; aims to build a code of intl labour law and practice, is concerned with the safety, health and social security of workers and provides technical expertise where required by member countries; seeks to improve labour conditions, raise living standards and promote productive employment in all countries; library: see under Switzerland; mems: 179 countries; Dir-Gen. JUAN SOMAVIA; publs *International Labour Review*, *Official Bulletin*, *Bulletin of Labour Statistics*, *Yearbook of Labour Statistics*, *International Labour Documentation*, *World of Work*, studies, manuals and reports.

Associated institutions:

International Institute for Labour Studies: CP 6, 1211 Geneva 22, Switzerland; tel. (22) 799-61-28; fax (22) 799-85-42; e-mail inst@ilo.org; internet www.ilo .org/public/english/bureau/inst; f. 1960 by ILO; aims: to provide a global forum for interaction between business, labour, policy-makers and academics on emerging labour policy issues; to promote research networks on policy implications of changing relationships between labour, business and the State; to develop the research capacities of ministries of labour and employers' and workers' organizations; Dir G. RODGERS.

International Training Centre of the ILO/Centre International de Formation de l'OIT: Viale Maestri del Lavoro 10, 10127 Turin, Italy; tel. 011-693-6111; fax 011-663-8842; e-mail communication@itcilo.org; internet www.itcilo.org; f. 1964 by International Labour Organisation to offer advanced training facilities for managers, trainers and social partners, and technical specialists from ILO mem. states; Exec. Dir FRANÇOIS EYRAUD.

OTHER ORGANIZATIONS

African Training and Research Centre in Administration for Development/Centre Africain de Formation et de Recherche Administratives pour le Développement (CAFRAD): Pavillon International, Blvd Mohammed V, BP 310, 90001 Tangier, Morocco; tel. (61) 30-72-69; fax (39) 32-57-85; e-mail cafrad@cafrad.org; internet www.cafrad.org; f. 1964 by agreement between Morocco and UNESCO; training of African senior civil servants; research into administrative problems in Africa, documentation or results, and the provision of a consultation service for governments and organizations in Africa; holds frequent seminars; mems: Algeria, Angola, Benin, Burkina Faso, Burundi, Cameroon, Cape Verde, Central African Republic, Chad, Côte d'Ivoire, Dem. Rep. of Congo, Djibouti, Equatorial Guinea, Gabon, Gambia, Ghana, Guinea, Guinea-Bissau, Liberia, Libya, Madagascar, Mali, Mauritania, Mauritius, Morocco, Namibia, Niger, Nigeria, São Tomé e Príncipe, Sierra Leone, Somalia, South Africa, Sudan, Swaziland, Togo, Tunisia; UNESCO provided assistance 1964–1970 and UNDP 1971–1983; Pres. MOHAMED BOUSSAID; Dir-Gen. Dr SIMON LELO MAMOSI; publs *African Administrative Studies* (2 a year), *Web Newsletter* (monthly), *Studies and Documents* (irregular), *Directory of African Consultants in Public Administration*, *Directory of African Training and Research Institutions*, *Proceedings of Pan-African Conference of Ministers of the Civil Service* (every 2 years), *African Public Service Charter*.

Association of International Accountants: South Bank Bldg, Kingsway, Team Valley, Newcastle upon Tyne, NE11 0JS, UK; tel. (191) 4824409; fax (191) 4825578; e-mail aia@aia.org.uk; internet www.aia.org.uk; f. 1928; promotes and supports the advancement of the accountancy profession worldwide; offers a professional qualification for accountants and company auditors; 18,000 mems and students; Chair. R.I. IRVING; Chief Exec. P.J.J. TURNBULL; publ. *International Accountant* (4 a year).

Association of Social Anthropologists of the Commonwealth: c/o The Royal Anthropological Institute, 50 Fitzroy St, London, W1T 5BT, UK; tel. (20) 7387-0455; internet www.theasa.org; f. 1946; 570 mems; Chair. Prof. RICHARD FARDON; Hon. Sec. Dr IRIS JEAN-KLEIN; publs *ASA Annals*, *ASA Studies*, *ASA Essays*, *ASA Methods in Social Anthropology*.

Centre for Democracy and Development (Centre pour la Démocratie et le Développement): Unit 2L Leroy House, 436 Essex Rd, London, N1 3QP, UK; tel. (20) 7359-7775; fax (20) 7359-2221; e-mail cdd@cdd.org.uk; internet www.cddwestafrica.org; f. 1997; non-profit NGO dedicated to research, information and exchange of ideas on questions of democratic devt and peace-building in West Africa; offers strategic training in promoting democracy and devt; regional offices in Abuja and Lagos, Nigeria; Dir Dr JIBRIN IBRAHIM; publ. *Democracy & Development: Journal of West African Affairs* (2 a year).

Centre International des Civilisations Bantu/International Centre of Bantu Civilization: BP 770, Libreville, Gabon; tel. 70-40-96; fax 77-50-90; e-mail ciciba@caramail.com; f. 1983; intergovernmental organization founded by 10 countries containing members of the Bantu peoples: Angola, Central African Republic, Comoros, Democratic Republic of the Congo, Republic of the Congo, Gabon, Equatorial Guinea, Rwanda, São Tomé and Príncipe, Zambia; research and documentation centre for the conservation and promotion of the cultural heritage of the Bantu peoples; activities in all fields of culture, science and education; 50 staff; library: library: 4,000 vols, and special collection of university theses (microfiche) on ten member states; Dir-Gen. VATOMENE KUKANDA; publs *Muntu* (2 a year), *CICIBA-Informations* (quarterly).

Econometric Society: Dept of Economics, Northwestern University, 2003 Sheridan Rd, Evanston, IL 60208-2600, USA; tel. (847) 491-3615; fax (847) 491-5427; internet www.econometricsociety.org; f. 1930 to promote studies on the unification of the theoretical-quantitative and the empirical-quantitative approach to economic problems; 6,700 mems; Pres. THOMAS J. SARGENT (USA); Sec. JULIE P. GORDON (USA); publ. *Econometrica* (every 2 months).

European Association for Population Studies/Association Européenne pour l'Étude de la Population: POB 11676, 2502 AR The Hague, Netherlands; tel. (70) 3565200; fax (70) 3647187; e-mail contact@eaps.nl; internet www.eaps.nl; f. 1983 to promote the study of population in Europe through co-operation between persons interested or engaged in European demographics; mems: demographers and other population scientists from all European countries; Pres. JANINA JÓZWIAK (Poland); Sec.-Gen. and Treas. FRANCESCO BILLARI (Italy); Exec. Sec. GYS BEETS; publs *European Journal of Population/Revue Européenne de Démographie*, *European Studies of Population*.

European Centre for Social Welfare Policy and Research: Berggasse 17, 1090 Vienna, Austria; tel. (1) 3194505-0; fax (1) 3194505-19; e-mail ec@euro.centre.org; internet www.euro.centre.org; non-profit autonomous intergovernmental organization affiliated to the UN; conducts research, and provides training and information, in the fields of welfare and social development; library of 8,000 vols; Exec. Dir Prof. Dr BERND MARIN; publ. *Eurosocial Reports Series* (in English, French and German).

European Economic Association: Univ. of Warwick, Dept of Economics, Coventry, CV4 7AL, UK; tel. (24) 7652-3046; fax (24) 7652-3032; e-mail eea@warwick.ac.uk; internet www.eeassoc.org; f. 1986 to contribute to the devt and application of econ. as a science in Europe, to improve communication and exchange between teachers, researchers and students in econ. in the different European countries, to develop and sponsor co-operation between teaching instns of univ. level and research instns in Europe; organizes annual congress; 2,000 mems; Pres. Prof. GUIDO TABELLINI; Sec. Prof. IAN WALKER; publ. *Journal of the European Economic Association (JEEA)* (6 a year).

European Foundation for Management Development (EFMD): 88 rue Gachard, Boîte 3, 1050 Brussels, Belgium; tel. (2) 629-08-10; fax (2) 629-08-11; e-mail info@efmd.org; internet www.efmd.be; f. 1971; provides forum for worldwide co-operation in management development; European Quality Initiative (EQUAL) project seeks intl co-operation in assessing quality in management education; mem. orgs (business schools, management centres, companies, consultancies) in 41 countries; Pres. GERARD VAN SCHAIK; Dir-Gen. ERIC CORNUEL; publ. *Forum* (3 a year).

Futuribles International: 55 rue de Varenne, 75007 Paris, France; tel. (1) 53-63-37-70; fax (1) 42-22-65-54; internet www.futuribles.com/home.html; f. 1960; aims to act as an early-warning system to identify major trends and challenges of the future; to undertake research on current economic and social issues; to serve as a consulting group for futures studies and strategic planning; major fields of expertise: development strategies, and multi-disciplinary studies on economic, technological, social and cultural changes in industrialized countries; library and documentation centre containing 90,000 vols; Scientific Council: 41 mems in 15 countries; Pres. JACQUES LESOURNE; Dir-Gen. HUGUES DE JOUVENEL (France); publs *Futuribles* (monthly), *Vigie Info* (quarterly).

Inter-American Statistical Institute/Instituto Interamericano de Estadística: Balcarce 184 (of. 211), 1327 Buenos Aires, Argentina; tel. (11) 4349-5777; fax (11) 4349-5778; e-mail efabb@indec.mecon.gov.ar; internet www.indec.mecon.ar/iasi; f. 1940; fosters statistical devt in the Western Hemisphere; holds seminars and meetings; 307 mems (262 individual, 34 ex-officio, 11 affiliated institutional); Pres. Dr VÍCTOR M. GUERRERO (Mexico); Technical Sec. Prof. EVELIO O. FABBRONI; publs *Estadística* (2 a year), *Newsletter* (quarterly).

International African Institute (IAI)/Institut Africain International: School of Oriental and African Studies, Thornhaugh St, Russell Square, London, WC1H 0XG, UK; tel. (20) 7898-4420; fax (20) 7898-4419; e-mail iai@soas.ac.uk; internet www.iaionthe.net; f. 1926; encourages the study of African society and disseminates the results of research; language of instruction French; Chair. Prof. V. Y. MUDIMBE; Hon. Dir Prof. PHILIP BURNHAM; publs *Africa* (quarterly), *Africa Bibliography* (annually).

International Association for South-East European Studies/Association Internationale d'Etudes du Sud-Est Européen (AIESEE): Apt. 18, Nicolae Racota 12–14, 713123 Bucharest, Romania; tel. (21) 2242965; fax (21) 2242964; e-mail solist@fx.ro; f. 1963; 23 mem. countries; Pres. Prof. ANDRÉ GUILLOU (France); Sec.-Gen. Prof. RĂZVAN THEODORESCU (Romania); publ. *Bulletin* (annually).

International Association for the Study of Insurance Economics/Geneva Association: 53 route de Malagnou, 1208 Geneva, Switzerland; tel. (22) 707-66-00; fax (22) 736-75-36; e-mail secretariat@genevaassociation.org; internet www.genevaassociation.org; mems: up to 80 CEOs from the world's insurance companies; Pres. HENRI DE CASTRIES; Sec.-Gen. and Man. Dir PATRICK LIEDTKE.

International Association of Schools of Social Work (IASSW): c/o Prof. Lynne Healy, Center for International Social Work Studies, University of Connecticut, School of Social Work, 1798 Asylum Ave, West Hartford, CT 06117, USA; tel. (860) 570-9149; fax (860) 570-9139; e-mail iasswsec@comcast.net; internet www.iassw.soton.ac.uk; f. 1928 to provide intl leadership and encourage high standards in social work education;

mems: 1,700 schools of social work in 90 countries and 35 nat. associations of schools; Pres. Prof. TASSE ABYE (France); Sec. Prof. LYNNE HEALY (USA).

International Center for Monetary and Banking Studies/Centre International d'Etudes Monétaires et Bancaires: 11a ave de la Paix, 1202 Geneva, Switzerland; tel. 227349548; fax 227333853; internet heiwww.unige.ch/icmb; f. 1973; independent, associated with the Graduate Institute of International Studies; scientific study of international monetary, financial and banking issues; organises conferences, public lectures; Pres. TOMMASO PADOA-SCHIOPPA; Dir Prof. CHARLES WYPLOSZ; publ. *Geneva Reports on the World Economy*.

International Centre for Ethnic Studies: 554/6A Peradeniya Rd, Kandy, Sri Lanka; tel. (81) 2232381; fax (81) 2234892; e-mail info@ices.lk; internet www.ices.lk; f. 1982 to provide an institutional focus and identity for the study and management of ethnic conflict; encourages cross-national comparative research in ethnic policy studies; library of 6,200 vols, special collections on ethnicity and women's issues; Exec. Dir Prof. MATHIAS DEWATRIPONT (Sri Lanka); publs *Ethnic Studies Report* (2 a year), *Nethra* (social issues, 4 a year).

International Commission for the History of Representative and Parliamentary Institutions/Commission Internationale pour l'Histoire des Assemblées d'Etats: Dept of History, 43–46 North Bailey, Durham, DH1 3EX, UK; tel. (191) 386-4299; fax (191) 334-1041; e-mail j.m.rogister@dur.ac.uk; f. 1936 to encourage research on the origin and history of representative and parliamentary institutions; mems: individuals in 40 countries; languages of instruction French, English, German; organizes annual conferences, publishes monographs; Presidents Prof. W. BRAUNEDER (Austria), Prof. J. ROGISTER (UK); Sec. ESTEVAO DE REZENDE MARTINS (Brazil); publ. *Parliaments, Estates and Representation* (annually).

International Council on Social Welfare/Conseil International de l'Action Sociale: c/o Netherlands Institute of Care and Welfare, POB 19152, 3501 DD Utrecht, Netherlands; tel. (30) 2306336; fax (30) 2306540; e-mail icsw@icsw.org; internet www.icsw.org; f. 1928 to promote forms of social and economic development which aim to reduce poverty, hardship and vulnerability worldwide, especially in developing countries; 104 mem. orgs worldwide; Pres. SOLVEIG ASKJEM (Norway); Exec. Dir DENYS CORRELL; publ. *Proceedings of International Conferences on Social Welfare* (every 2 years).

International Federation of Business and Professional Women (BPW International)/Federación Internacional de Mujeres de Negocios y Profesionales: POB 568, Horsham, West Sussex, RH13 9ZP, UK; tel. (1403) 739343; fax (1403) 734432; e-mail members@bpw-international.org; internet www.bpwi.org; f. 1930 to promote the interests of business and professional women, and in particular to bring their specialized knowledge and skills to play a more effective part in intl governmental organizations; 250,000 mems; Pres. ANTOINETTE RÜEGG; Exec. Sec. ANN SWAIN; publ. *BPW News International* (monthly newsletter).

International Fiscal Association: World Trade Center, Beursplein 37, POB 30215, 3001 DE Rotterdam, Netherlands; tel. (10) 4052990; fax (10) 4055031; e-mail n.gensecr@ifa.nl; internet www.ifa.nl; f. 1938; to study and advance intl and comparative law with regard to public finance and especially intl and comparative fiscal law and the financial and economic aspects of taxation; 9,500 mems in 90 countries, national brs in 47 countries; Pres. J. B. LIDIN (USA); Sec.-Gen. Prof. M. J. ELLIS; publs *Cahiers de Droit Fiscal International* (Studies on International Fiscal Law), *Yearbook of the International Fiscal Association*.

International Institute for Ligurian Studies/Istituto Internazionale di Studi Liguri: Museo Bicknell, Via Romana 39, 18012 Bordighera, Italy; tel. (184) 263601; fax (184) 266421; f. 1947 to conduct research on ancient monuments and regional traditions in the north-west arc of the Mediterranean; library of 82,000 vols; mems in France, Italy, Spain, Switzerland; Dir Prof. CARLO VARALDO (Italy).

International Institute of Philosophy (IIP)/Institut International de Philosophie: 8 rue Jean-Calvin, 75005 Paris, France; tel. 1-43-36-39-11; e-mail INST.INTERN.PHILO@wanadoo.fr; f. 1937; aims: to clarify fundamental issues of contemporary philosophy in annual meetings, and, by several series of publications, to promote mutual understanding among thinkers of different traditions and cultural backgrounds; a maximum of 115 mems, considered eminent in their field, chosen from all countries and representing different tendencies, are elected; present mems: 106 mems in 43 countries; Pres. HANS LENK (France); Sec.-Gen. P. AUBENQUE (France); publs *Actes des congrès internationaux* (annually), *Bibliography of Philosophy* (4 a year), *Philosophical Problems Today*, *Surveys (Chroniques) of Philosophy*.

International Institute of Sociology/Institut International de Sociologie: c/o Prof. Karen S. Cook, Dept of Sociology, Stanford University, Stanford, CA 94305, USA; e-mail iisoc@post.tau.ac.il; internet www.tau.sc.il/~iisoc; f. 1893 to advance the study of sociology; 300 mems in 45 countries; Pres. ELIEZER BEN-RAFAEL (Israel); Gen. Sec. and Treas. Prof. KAREN S. COOK (USA); publ. *Annales de l'Institut International de Sociologie / The Annals of the International Institute of Sociology*.

International Monetary Fund Institute: Washington, DC 20431, USA; tel. (202) 623-6660; fax (202) 623-6490; f. 1964 to provide specialist training in economic analysis and policy, statistics, public finance, and bank supervision, for officials of mem. countries; courses and seminars in Arabic, English, French and Spanish; library; Dir PATRICK DE FONTENAY; publ. *Courier*.

International Peace Academy: 777 United Nations Plaza, New York, NY 10017-3521, USA; tel. (212) 687-4300; fax (212) 983-8246; e-mail ipa@ipacademy.org; internet www.ipacademy.org; f. 1970; acts as independent, intl institution, working closely with the UN and other governmental and non-governmental organizations, to promote the prevention and settlement of armed conflicts between and within states, through policy research and development; Pres. TERJE ROD-LARSEN; publs *IPA Initiatives* (1 or 2 a year), *International Peacekeeping* (co-edited by IPA, 4 a year).

International Society for Ethnology and Folklore: Meertens Institute, Joan Muyskenweg 25, 1096 CJ Amsterdam, The Netherlands; tel. (20) 4628500; fax (20) 4628555; e-mail sief@meertens.knaw.nl; internet www.siefhome.org; f. 1964 to establish and maintain collaboration between specialists in folklore and ethnology; organizes commissions, symposia, congresses, etc.; affiliated to Int. Union of Anthropological and Ethnological Sciences and ICPHS; close links with Int. Folk Music Council and Int. Council of Museums; mems: 504; Pres. REGINA BENDIX (Romania); Vice-Pres BJARNE ROGAN, PETER JAN MARGRY; publ. *Bulletin d'Informations SIEF* (annual).

International Society for the Study of Medieval Philosophy/Société Internationale pour l'Etude de la Philosophie Médiévale: Academic Secretariat: c/o Prof. Dr Maarten Hoenen, Philosophisches Seminar, Werthmannplatz 3, 79098 Freiburg im Breisgau, Germany; fax (761) 203-9260; e-mail maarten.hoenen@philosophie.uni-freiburg.de; internet www.siepm.uni-freiburg.de; Administrative Secretariat: c/o Chantal Mertens, Hoger Instituut voor Wijsbegeerte, Kardinaal Mercierplein 2, 3000 Leuven, Belgium; tel. (761) 203-2440; f. 1958 to promote the study of medieval thought and the collaboration between individuals and institutions engaged in this field; organizes intl congresses every five years and annual colloquium between congresses; 695 mems in 45 countries; Pres. Prof. Dr JACQUELINE HAMESSE (Germany); Sec.-Gen. Prof. Dr MAARTEN J. F. M. HOENEN (Belgium); publ. *Bulletin de Philosophie Médiévale* (annually).

International Society for Third-Sector Research (ISTR): Wyman Park Building (Room 559), 3400 N. Charles St, Baltimore, MD 21218-2688, USA; tel. (410) 516-4678; fax (410) 516-4870; e-mail istr@jhu.edu; internet www.istr.org; f. 1992; encourages research relevant to civil society, non-profit orgs, voluntarism and philanthropy; regional research networks in Africa, Asia, Europe, Latin America and the Caribbean, and Arab-speaking countries; conference every 2 years; 675 mems; Pres. ALAN F. FOWLER (South Africa); Exec. Dir MARGERY B. DANIELS; publ. *Voluntas* (4 a year).

International Society of Social Defence and Humane Criminal Policy/Société Internationale de Défense Sociale pour une Politique Criminelle Humaniste: c/o Centro nazionale di prevenzione e difesa sociale, Palazzo comunale delle scienze sociali, Piazza Castello 3, 20121 Milan, Italy; tel. (2) 86460714; fax (2) 72008431; e-mail cnpds.ispac@iol.it; internet www.defensesociale.org; f. 1946; non-governmental org. in consultative status with UN Economic and Social Council; the study of crime-related problems in the perspective of a system of reactions which, through prevention and resocialization of deviants, aims to protect the individuals and society at large; 350 mems; Pres. LUIS ARROYO ZAPATERO (Spain); Sec.-Gen. EDMONDO BRUTI LIBERATI (Italy); publ. *Cahiers de défense sociale* (annually, in English, Spanish and French).

Inter-Parliamentary Union/Union Interparlementaire: 5 chemin du Pommier, CP 330, 1218 Le Grand-Saconnex, Geneva, Switzerland; tel. 229194150; fax 229194160; e-mail postbox@mail.ipu.org; internet www.ipu.org; f. 1889 to promote contacts among members of the world's parliaments and unite them in common action for intl peace and co-operation; to promote democracy by strengthening and developing the means of action of representative institutions; studies political, economic, social, juridical, cultural and environmental problems of intl significance, notably through conferences; promotes free and fair elections and provides assistance to representative assemblies; helps to solve cases of violation of parliamentarians' rights; promotes status of women in political life; gathers and disseminates information on parliamentary matters; mems: 146 nat. parliaments; Pres. PIER

FERDINANDO CASINI (Italy); Sec.-Gen. ANDERS B. JOHNSSON (Sweden); publs *Chronicle of Parliamentary Elections* (annually), *IPU Review: The World of Parliaments* (4 a year), *Panorama of Parliamentary Elections* (annually), *World Directory of Parliaments* (annually).

Italian–Latin American Institute/Istituto Italo-Latino Americano: Piazza B. Cairoli 3, 00186 Rome, Italy; tel. 06-684921; fax 06-6872834; e-mail info@iila.org; internet www.iila.org; f. 1966 to develop and co-ordinate research and documentation on the problems, achievements and prospects of mem. countries in cultural, scientific, economic, technical and social fields; organizes meetings and promotes activities representative of the development process of Latin America in its social, economic, cultural and technical-scientific aspects; 21 mem. countries; library: documentation 90,000 vols, 4,500 periodicals; Sec.-Gen. PAOLO FAIOLA; publ. *Quaderni IILA* (series *Economia, Scienza*, Cooperazione).

Nordisk Institut for Asienstudier/Nordic Institute of Asian Studies: Leifsgade 33, 2300 Copenhagen S, Denmark; tel. 35-32-95-00; fax 35-32-95-49; e-mail sec@nias.ku.dk; internet www.nias.ku.dk; f. 1967; non-profit org. funded through Nordic Council of Ministers; research and documentation centre for modern Asian studies within humanities and social sciences to promote research and publish books on Asia; library of 28,000 vols and 750 current journals; Chair. Dekan TAGE BILD; Dir Dr JØRGEN DELMAN; publ. *NIASnytt* (newsletter, 4 a year).

Organisation for Economic Co-operation and Development (OECD): 2 rue André-Pascal, 75775 Paris Cedex 16, France; tel. 1-45-24-82-00; fax 1-45-24-85-00; e-mail webmaster@oecd.org; internet www.oecd.org; f. 1961; concerned with the impact of science, technology, education and the changing pattern of employment structures on the balance of economic and social development of its member countries (in Europe, North America and the Pacific area) and with the implications of technological development for the environment as well as with the broader aspects of policy to meet new social objectives; it seeks to co-ordinate its mems' economic and social policies, and aims at being informative, promotional and catalytic through surveys of the current situation, identification of tentative policies and the establishment of a statistical and methodological base in support of government decision making; serves as an international clearing-house for exchanges of information and provides a forum where experts and policy-makers can discuss common issues and benefit from mutual co-operation; conducts economic analysis of emerging and transition economies; special programmes include the Programme for Educational Building and the Centre for Educational Research and Innovation (*q.v.*); 30 mem. countries; library: online library of books, periodicals and statistics (www.sourceoecd.org); Sec.-Gen. ANGEL GURRÍA; publs note: certain titles are published in more than one language, *Main Economic Indicators* (monthly), *Monthly Statistics of International Trade*, *International Trade by Commodity Statistics* (5 a year), *Quarterly Labour Force Statistics*, *Quarterly National Accounts*, *Indicators of Industry and Services* (quarterly), *Creditor Reporting System on Aid Activities* (every 2 months), *Oil, Gas, Coal and Electricity – Quarterly Statistics*, *Main Science and Technology Indicators* (2 a year), *The OECD Observer* (every 2 months), *OECD Papers* (monthly), *OECD Economic Surveys* (18 a year), *OECD Economic Outlook* (2 a year), *OECD Economic Studies* (2 a year), *OECD Journal of Competition Law and Policy* (quarterly), *Financial Market Trends* (3 a year), *Journal of Business Cycle Measurement and Analysis* (3 a year), *OECD Journal of Budgeting* (quarterly), *The DAC Journal* (quarterly), *Energy Prices and Taxes* (quarterly), *Nuclear Law Bulletin* (2 a year), *NEA News* (2 a year), *PEB Exchange* (3 a year and online), *Higher Education Management and Policy* (3 a year).

Pan-African Institute for Development/Institut Pan-Africain pour le Développement: BP 4056, Douala, Cameroon; tel. 332-28-06; fax 332-28-06; e-mail ipd.sg@camnet.cm; f. 1964 for the training of African development staff; 2 regional institutes in Cameroon and 1 each in Burkina Faso and Zambia supply support services to development agencies; Sec.-Gen. Dr MBUKI V. MWAMUFIYA; publs *Yearly Progress Report*, *PAID Report* (2 a year).

Society for International Development/Société Internationale pour le Développement: Via Panisperna 207, 00184 Rome, Italy; tel. 06-487-2172; fax 06-487-2170; e-mail info@sidint.org; internet www.sidint.org; f. 1957; a global network of individuals and institutions concerned with development that is participative, pluralistic and sustainable; mobilizes and strengthens civil society groups by building partnerships among them and with other sectors; fosters local initiatives and new forms of social experimentation; 3,000 mems in 125 countries, with 65 local chapters and 55 institutional mems; Pres. ENRIQUE IGLESIAS; Sec.-Gen. ROBERTO SAVIO; publ. *Development* (6 a year).

Statistical Institute for Asia and the Pacific: JETRO-IDE Bldg, 3-2-2 Wakaba, Mihama-ku, Chiba-shi, Chiba 261-8787, Japan; tel. (43) 299-9782; fax (43) 299-9780; e-mail staff@unsiap.or.jp; internet www.unsiap.or.jp; f. 1970; subsidiary body of the Economic and Social Commission for Asia and the Pacific (ESCAP) to provide training in official statistics to govt statisticians in the Asia-Pacific region as recommended by resolution 75 (XXIII) of ESCAP; mems: 33 Fellows (Core Official Statistics course), 20 Fellows (ICT Course), 10 Fellows (AIOS Course), 8 Fellows (CA course); library of 20,000 vols; Dir TOMAS P. AFRICA.

Stockholm International Peace Research Institute (SIPRI): Signalistgatan 9, 169 70 Solna, Sweden; tel. (8) 6559700; fax (8) 6559733; e-mail sipri@sipri.org; internet www.sipri.org; f. 1966 for research into problems of peace and conflict with particular attention to the problems of disarmament and arms control; library of 43,000 vols; Chair. ROLF EKÉUS (Sweden); Dir ALYSON J. K. BAILES (UK); publ. *SIPRI Yearbook*.

UNESCO Institute for Statistics: CP 6128, Succ. Centre-Ville, Montréal, QC H3C 3J7, Canada; tel. (514) 343-6880; fax (514) 343-6882; e-mail information@uis.unesco.org; internet www.uis.unesco.org; f. 1999 to meet the needs of UNESCO member states and the intl community for a wide range of policy-relevant and reliable statistics in the fields of education, science and technology, culture and communication; Dir HENDRIK VAN DER POL.

United Nations Institute for Training and Research (UNITAR)/Institut des Nations Unies pour la formation et la recherche: Palais des Nations, 1211 Geneva 10, Switzerland; located at: International Environment House, 11–13 chemin des Anémones, 1219 Chatelaine Geneva, Switzerland; tel. 229178455; fax 229178047; internet www.unitar.org; f. 1965 as an autonomous body within the framework of the UN; aims, by training and research, to enhance the effectiveness of the UN in achieving the major objectives of the Organization, in particular the maintenance of peace and security and the promotion of economic and social development; conducts seminars for diplomats and others who work in the UN system and carries out training, either at UN headquarters or in the field, which has special relevance for developing countries; conducts research into problems of concern to the UN system; Asst Sec.-Gen. and Exec. Dir MARCEL A. BOISARD (Switzerland); publ. more than 50 titles in English and some in French, Spanish and Russian.

Vienna Institute for Development and Co-operation/Wiener Institut für Entwicklungsfragen und Zusammenarbeit: Moellwaldpl. 5/3, 1040 Vienna, Austria; tel. (1) 713-35-94; fax (1) 713-35-94-73; e-mail office@vidc.org; internet www.vidc.org; f. 1987 as successor to Vienna Institute for Development; aims to disseminate information on problems and achievements of developing countries by all possible means in order to convince the public or industrialized nations of the necessity to increase devt aid and to strengthen int. co-operation; research programmes; organizes cultural exchanges between South and North; engages in anti-racism and anti-discrimination activities in sport at nat. and European levels; Pres. Mag. BARBARA PRAMMER (Austria); Dir Mag. WALTER POSCH.

World Bank Institute: 1818 H St, NW, Washington, DC 20433, USA; tel. (202) 473-1000; fax (202) 477-6391; e-mail wbi_infoline@worldbank.org; internet www.worldbank.org/wbi; f. 1955; provides learning programmes and policy advice in the areas of environment and natural resources, economic policy for poverty reduction, governance, regulation, and finance, human development, knowledge networks and outreach; delivers training activities for policymakers in 149 countries through direct and distance learning; has formal partnerships with 130 academic and training institutions in developed nations and client countries; Vice-Pres. FRANNIE A. LÉAUTIER; publs *Development Outreach* (4 a year), *WBI News* (3 a year).

World Institute for Development Economics Research of the United Nations University (UNU-WIDER): Katajanokanlaituri 6B, 00160 Helsinki, Finland; tel. (9) 6159911; fax (9) 61599333; e-mail wider@wider.unu.edu; internet www.wider.unu.edu; f. 1984; conducts policy-oriented research into inequality and poverty, global economic development and related issues; Dir Prof. TONY SHORROCKS.

World Intellectual Property Organization (WIPO): 34 chemin des Colombettes, 1211 Geneva 20, Switzerland; tel. 223389111; fax 227335428; e-mail wipo.mail@wipo.int; internet www.wipo.int; f. 1970; UN specialized agency; promotes the protection of intellectual property rights world-wide; aims to extend benefits of the int. intellectual property system to all mem. states; main activities are: progressive devt of int. intellectual property law, assisting developing countries and providing services to facilitate the process of obtaining intellectual property rights in multiple countries; 184 mem. states; Dir-Gen. Dr KAMIL IDRIS; publs *WIPO Gazette of International Marks* (weekly), *International Designs Bulletin* (monthly), *PCT Newsletter* (monthly), *Appelations of Origin* (irreg.).

World Society for Ekistics: c/o Athens Center of Ekistics, 24 Strat. Syndesmou St,

10673 Athens, Greece; tel. 210-3623216; fax 210-3629337; e-mail ekistics@otenet.gr; internet www.ekistics.org; f. 1965; aims to promote the devt of knowledge and ideas concerning human settlements by research and through publs, conferences, etc.; to encourage the devt and expansion of education in ekistics; to educate public opinion concerning ekistics; to recognize the benefits and necessity of an interdisciplinary approach to the needs of human settlements, and to promote and emphasize such an approach; 191 mems; Pres. Dr SUZANNE KELLER (USA); Sec.-Gen. and Treas. PANAYIS PSOMOPOULOS; publ. conference papers publ. in *Ekistics,* the journal of the Athens Center of Ekistics.

Education

African and Mauritius Council on Higher Education/Conseil africain et mauricien de l'enseignement supérieur: BP 134, Ouagadougou, Burkina Faso; tel. 346-74; f. 1968 to ensure co-ordination between member states in the fields of higher education and research; mems: governments of 15 French-speaking African countries; Pres. DANIEL ABIBI; Sec.-Gen. HENRY VALERE KINIFFO.

Agence Universitaire de la Francophonie: BP 400 Succ. Côte-des-Neiges, Montréal, QC H3S 2S7, Canada; tel. (514) 343-6630; fax (514) 343-2107; internet www.auf.org; f. 1961; aims: documentation, co-ordination, co-operation, exchange; Pres. CHARLES GOMBE MBALAWA (Republic of the Congo); Rector MICHÈLE GENDREAU-MASSALOUX (France).

Arab Bureau of Education for the Gulf States: POB 94693, Diplomatic Quarters, Riyadh 11614, Saudi Arabia; tel. (1) 4800555; fax (1) 4802839; e-mail abegs@abegs.org; internet www.abegs.org; f. 1975 to co-ordinate and integrate the efforts of the mem. states (Bahrain, Kuwait, Oman, Qatar, Saudi Arabia and the United Arab Emirates) in the fields of education, science and culture; aims to unify the educational system for all the mem. states; Gulf Arab States Educational Research Center: see Kuwait chapter; established Arabian Gulf University in Bahrain; Dir-Gen. Dr SAEED ALMULLAIS; publ. *Rissalat al-Khaleej al Araby* (Message of the Arab Gulf, 4 a year).

Asian Association of Open Universities: 160 Fuxingmennei St, Beijing, 100031, People's Republic of China; tel. (10) 66490029; fax (10) 66412407; e-mail aaou@crtvu.edu.cn; internet www.aaou.net; Pres. Prof. YAOXUE ZHANG; Sec.-Gen. Prof. YAWAN LI.

Association for Teacher Education in Europe: 60 Rue de la Concorde, 1050 Brussels, Belgium; fax (2) 629-26-23; e-mail arno.libotton@skynet.be; internet www.atee.org; f. 1976 to establish contacts between institutions for teacher education and those responsible for that education; arranges working groups, annual conference, etc.; undertakes consultancy work for European organizations; Pres. Prof. Dr ARNO LIBOTTON (Belgium); Vice-Pres. MAUREEN KILLEAVY (Ireland); publ. *European Journal of Teacher Education* (3 a year).

Association Internationale de Pédagogie Universitaire: Service Guidance Étude, Bâtiment B33, Université de Liège au Sart Tilman, 4000 Liège, Belgium; tel. (4) 366-20-73; fax (4) 366-29-88; e-mail mdelhaxhe@ulg.ac.be; internet www.ulg.ac.be/aipu; f. 1979; Francophone org. promoting research and development in teaching and higher education; 800 mems; Pres. JACQUES TARDIF (Canada); Sec.-Gen. MICHEL DELHAXHE (Belgium); publ. *Res Academica* (2 a year).

Association Montessori Internationale: Koninginneweg 161, 1075 CN Amsterdam, Netherlands; tel. (20) 679-8932; fax (20) 676-7341; e-mail info@montessori-ami.org; internet www.montessori-ami.org; f. 1929 to propagate the ideals and educational methods of Dr Maria Montessori and to spread knowledge on child devt without racial, religious or political prejudice; activities: supervises affiliated training courses for teachers in several countries; sponsors int. congresses and study conferences on Montessori education; creates new training centres and offers affiliation to Montessori societies; Pres. A. ROBERFROID; Sec. M. HAYES; publs *AMI Newsletter* (3 or 4 a year), *Communications* (2 a year).

Association of African Universities/Association des Universités Africaines: POB 5744, Accra-North, Ghana; tel. (21) 774495; fax (21) 774821; e-mail info@aau.org; internet www.aau.org; f. 1967 to collect, classify and disseminate information on higher education and research in Africa; to promote co-operation among African instns in training, research, community services and higher education policy, in curriculum development and in the determination of equivalence in academic degrees; to encourage increased contacts between mems and the intl academic world; to encourage the development and wide use of African languages and support training of univ. teachers and administrators to deal with problems in African education in general; mems: 151 university institutions in 43 African countries; Pres. Prof. NJABULO NDEBELE (South Africa); Sec.-Gen. Prof. AKILAGPA SAWYERR (Ghana); publs *Newsletter* (3 a year), *Handbook* (every 2 years).

Association of American International Colleges and Universities: c/o Dr John Bailey, American College of Greece, 6 Gravias St, Aghira Paraskevi, 153 42 Athens, Greece; e-mail acg@hol.gr; internet www.aaicu.org; f. 1971 to promote co-operation among independent institutions offering intl education in Europe and the Near East; 12 mem. univs and colleges; Pres. Dr JOHN S. BAILEY (Greece); Sec. and Treas. CRAIG SEXSON (Greece).

Association of Arab Universities: POB 401, Jubeyha, Amman, Jordan; tel. 5345131; fax 5332994; e-mail secgen@aaru.edu.jo; f. 1964 to consolidate co-operation between Arab universities and institutions of higher education; mems: 161 universities; Sec.-Gen. Dr MARWAN R. KAMAL; publs *Bulletin* (annually), *Directory of Arab Universities*, *Directory of Teaching Staff of Arab Universities*, *Proceedings of Seminars*.

Association of Caribbean Universities and Research Institutes (UNICA): C/o Prof. Mervyn C. Alleyne, Department of Liberal Arts, University of the West Indies, St Augustine, Trinidad; f. 1968 to foster contact and collaboration between member universities and institutes; conferences, meetings, seminars, etc.; circulation of information through newsletters, bulletins; facilitates co-operation and the pooling of resources in research; encourages exchanges of staff and students; mems: 50 institutions; Sec.-Gen. Prof. MERVYN C. ALLEYNE; publ. *Caribbean Educational Bulletin* (4 a year).

Association of Commonwealth Universities (ACU): Woburn House, 20–24 Tavistock Sq., London, WC1H 9HF, UK; tel. (20) 7380-6700; fax (20) 7387-2655; e-mail info@acu.ac.uk; internet www.acu.ac.uk; f. 1913; promotes contact and co-operation in higher education throughout the Commonwealth; provides assistance with staff and student mobility and devt programmes; researches and disseminates information about univs and relevant policy issues; organizes major meetings of Commonwealth univs and their representatives; provides the secretariats for, and administers, various scholarship and fellowship schemes (incl. the Commonwealth Scholarship Commission in the UK, the Marshall Aid Commemoration Commission and the Commonwealth Univs Study Abroad Consortium); also administers the Commonwealth Foundation Medical Electives Bursaries, the ACU Devt Fellowships, the DFID Shared Scholarship Scheme, the T. H. B. Symons Fellowship, and the Canada Memorial Foundation Scholarships); operates various subject specialist networks for higher education staff; provides an appointments, advertising and publicity service; operates a policy research unit; addresses the gender imbalance in higher education leadership through its women's programme; organizes various training workshops; hosts the Observatory on Borderless Higher Education; provides the secretariat for the Staff and Educational Devt Asscn; hosts an Africa Unit; mems: 487 univs; library of 18,500 vols; Sec. Gen. Dr JOHN ROWETT; publs *Commonwealth Universities Yearbook*, *Who's Who of Executive Heads, Vice-Chancellors, Presidents, Principals, Rectors* (every 2½ years), *Trends in Academic Recruitment and Retention: a Commonwealth Perspective*.

European University Association/Association Européenne de l'Université: Rue d'Egmont 13, 1000 Brussels Belgium; tel. (2) 230-55-44; fax (2) 230-57-51; e-mail info@eua.be; internet www.eua.be; f. 2001 through merger of Association of European Universities and Confederation of European Union Rectors' Conferences; facilitates partnership in higher education and research within Europe and between Europe and the rest of the world; aims to enhance the contribution of European univs to European integration, principally through the creation of a European Space for Higher Education; 687 individual, collective and affiliate mems in 45 countries; Pres. Prof. GEORG WINCKLER (Austria); Sec.-Gen. LESLEY WILSON (Belgium); publs *EUA News* (online), *Thema* (irregular).

Association of Southeast Asian Institutions of Higher Learning: c/o Dr Ninnat Olanvoravuth, Jamjuree 1 Bldg, Chulalongkorn University, Phayathai Rd, Bangkok 10330, Thailand; tel. 2516966; fax 253-7909; internet www.seameo.org/asaihl; f. 1956 to promote the economic, cultural and social welfare of the people of Southeast Asia by means of educational co-operation and research programmes; to foster the cultivation of a sense of regional identity and interdependence and to co-operate with other regional and international organizations; serves as a clearing-house for information, provides opportunities for discussion and recognizes distinctive academic achievements; 150 mem. instns; Sec.-Gen. Dr NINNAT OLANVORAVUTH; publs *Handbook*, *Newsletter*, *Seminar Proceedings*.

Association of Universities of Asia and the Pacific (AUAP): c/o Centre for International Affairs, Suranaree University of Technology, 111 University Ave, Suranaree Sub-District, Muang, Nakhon Ratchasima 30000, Thailand; tel. (44) 224141; fax (44) 224140; e-mail auap@ccs.sut.ac.th; internet sut2.sut.ac.th/auap; f. 1995; Pres. Drs. ec. WIBISONO HARDJOPRANOTO (Indonesia); Sec. Prof. RUBEN C. UMALY; publ. *Gazette* (4 a year).

Caribbean Network of Educational Innovation for Development (CARNEID): The Towers, 25 Dominica Drive,

3rd Fl., Kingston 5, Jamaica; tel. 427-4771; fax 436-0094; e-mail unesco@caribsurf.com; f. 1981 by UNESCO to advance educational innovation for development through networking among educational institutions and personnel in the Caribbean; publ. *Education Annual*.

Caribbean Regional Council for Adult Education: c/o Azad Hosein, Adult Education Unit, Ministry of Education, 51 Frederick St, Port-of-Spain, Trinidad and Tobago; tel. 625-4091; internet carcae.tripod.com; f. 1978 to promote and facilitate co-operation among national adult education organizations and agencies in non-Spanish-speaking territories of the region; to advocate awareness and recognition of the importance of adult education and to seek funding from governments and other sources; to hold conferences, seminars, training courses, etc.; to advise governments and other bodies on adult education; library of 5,000 vols; Chair. VILMA MCCLENAN (Jamaica); Exec. Sec.-Treas. AZAD HOSEIN; publ. *Newsletter*.

OECD Centre for Educational Research and Innovation (CERI): 2 rue André Pascal, 75775 Paris Cedex 16, France; tel. 1-45-24-82-00; fax 1-44-30-63-94; e-mail ceri.contact@oecd.org; internet www.oecd.org/edu/ceri; f. 1968; projects include: futures thinking in education, university futures, evidence-based policy research in education, national reviews on educational research and development, learning sciences and brain research, formative assessment, systemic innovation; vocational education and training; open educational resources, measuring the social outcomes of learning; globalization and linguistic competencies; Head TOM SCHULLER.

Commonwealth Association of Polytechnics in Africa: c/o Kenya Polytechnic, POB 52428, Nairobi, Kenya; tel. (2) 338232; fax (2) 219689; e-mail polymis@swiftkenya.com; f. 1978 to provide a forum for exchange of professional ideas and practices in technical and business education and training, and to improve the content and methods of polytechnic teaching, to disseminate information through publications and workshops, and to create a data centre and reference library; 135 mem. polytechnics; library of 2,000 vols; Sec.-Gen. WILLIAM RWAMBULLA; publs *CAPA Newsletter* (quarterly), *CAPA Journal of Technical Education and Training* (2 a year).

Commonwealth of Learning: 1055 West Hasting St, Suite 1200, Vancouver, BC V6E 2E9, Canada; tel. (604) 775-8200; fax (604) 775-8210; e-mail info@col.org; internet www.col.org; f. 1988 by Commonwealth Heads of Govt to promote co-operation among Commonwealth countries, utilizing distance education techniques, including communications technologies, to strengthen mem. countries' capacities in human resources development; works with ministries of education, schools, colleges, universities and NGOs to increase access to opportunities for learning; mems are the 53 Commonwealth countries; library of 7,800 vols; Pres. and CEO Sir JOHN DANIEL; publs *Connections/EdTech News* (3 a year), *World Review of Distance Education and Open Learning* (annually).

Commonwealth Secretariat, Education Department, Social Transformation Programmes Division: Marlborough House, Pall Mall, London, SW1Y 5HX, UK; tel. (20) 7747-6460; fax (20) 7747-6287; e-mail education@commonwealth.int; internet www.thecommonwealth.org; encourages and supports educational consultation and co-operation between Commonwealth countries through conferences, seminars, workshops, meetings of experts, and training courses for educational personnel (with assistance from the Commonwealth Fund for Technical Co-operation); contributes to national educational development through studies of particular problems, handbooks, directories and training manuals, and by providing information on educational subjects; undertakes consultancies for govts on request; triennial conference of Ministers of Education; Dir NANCY SPENCE; publs *Annual Report*, *LinkIn* (4 a year).

Community of European Management Schools and International Companies (CEMS): CEMS European Office, 1 rue de la Libération, 78350 Jouy-en-Josas, France; tel. 1-39-67-74-57; fax 1-39-67-74-81; e-mail info@cems.org; internet www.cems.org; f. 1988; mems: 17 European business schools, 8 non-European assoc. members, 53 corporate partners; Chair. Prof. BERNARD RAMANANTSOA (France); Exec. Dir FRANÇOIS COLLIN; publ. *European Business Forum* (quarterly; print and online, in association with PricewaterhouseCoopers).

Confederation of Central American Universities/Confederación Universitaria Centroamericana: Apdo 37-2060, Ciudad Universitaria Rodrigo Facio, San Pedro de Montes de Oca, San José, Costa Rica; tel. 225-27-44; fax 234-00-71; f. 1948; promotes regional co-operative initiatives in public higher education; promotes quality assurance and defends university autonomy and human rights in education; mems: Univ. of S. Carlos, Guatemala, Univ. College of Belize, Univ. of El Salvador, Univ. of Costa Rica, National Univ., Costa Rica, National Autonomous Univ. of Honduras, National Autonomous Univ. of Nicaragua-Managua, National Autonomous Univ. of Nicaragua-León, Univ. of Engineering, Nicaragua, Univ. of Panama; Pres. Dr LUIS GARITA (Costa Rica); Sec-Gen. Dr RICARDO SOL-ARRIAZA.

Conférence des Recteurs des Universités Africaines: BP 69, Brazzaville, Republic of Congo; f. 1976; aims to strengthen and develop inter-university co-operation in Africa; library of 20,000 vols and documentation centre; mems: 41; Pres. Mgr TSHIBANGU TSHISHIKU; Sec.-Gen. Prof. D. ABIBI.

Consorcio-Red de Educación a Distancia (Inter-American Distance Education Consortium): c/o Dr Armando Villarroel, Fischler Graduate School of Education and Human Services, Nova Southeastern University, 1750 NE 167th St, N. Miami Beach, FL 33162-8569, USA; tel. (954) 262-8569; e-mail axv4@omnibus.ce.psu.edu; internet www.cde.psu.edu/DE/CREAD/cread.html; f. 1990; networks of individuals and instns in North, Central and South America; Exec. Dir Dr ARMANDO VILLARROEL.

Council for Cultural Co-operation: Council of Europe, 67075 Strasbourg Cedex, France; tel. 3-88-41-20-00; fax 3-88-41-27-88; f. 1962 to draw up and implement the educational and cultural programme of the Council of Europe; mems: 47 states; publs *Newsletter Education*, *European Heritage*, *EUDISED European Educational Research Yearbook*.

Education International (EI)/Internationale de l'Education (IE): 5 blvd du Roi Albert II, 1210 Brussels, Belgium; tel. (2) 224-0611; fax (2) 224-0606; e-mail headoffice@ei-ie.org; internet www.ei-ie.org; f. 1993 from the merger of the World Confederation of Organizations of the Teaching Profession (WCOTP/CMOPE) and the International Federation of Free Teachers' Unions (IFFTU/SPIE); to advance the cause of organizations of teachers and education employees, promote status, interests and welfare of mems and defend their trade union and professional rights; to promote free, quality, public education for all; to promote peace, democracy, social justice, equality and the application of the Universal Declaration on Human Rights through the development of education and the collective strength of teachers and education employees; World Congress every three years; mems: 305 nat. orgs in 155 countries; Pres. THULAS NXESI (South Africa); Gen. Sec. FRED VAN LEEUWEN (Netherlands); publs *The EI Monthly Monitor* (in English, French and Spanish), *The Education International Quarterly Magazine* (in English, French and Spanish).

Education Network Association: Turan University Bldg, Floor 4, Chaikina 12, 480020 Almaty, Kazakhstan; tel. (3272) 61-92-75; e-mail info@ednetca.org; Toktogula 211, 720010 Bishkek, Kyrgyzstan; tel. (612) 60-08-20; fax (612) 60-08-30; e-mail omoevm@ednetca.org; Dekhoti 1/2, Floor 4, 734055 Dushanbe, Tajikistan; tel. (372) 21-29-05; fax (372) 23-01-49; e-mail lsaidmuradov@ednetca.org; c/o American Councils, Makhtymguli 78, Floor 1, Ashkhabad, Turkmenistan; tel. (12) 39-53-32; fax (12) 39-53-32; e-mail rnebe@online.tm; Uzbekistansky pr. 49, Floors 12–13, 700063 Tashkent, Uzbekistan; tel. (71) 132-61-69; fax (71) 132-61-70; e-mail anartaev@ednetca.org; internet www.ednetca.org; f. 2001; funded by United States Agency for International Development (USAID) and administered by CARANA Corporation with the aim of supporting the development of economics and business education in Central Asia through an international resource network; maintains Country Resource Centers in Kazakhstan, Kyrgyzstan, Tajikistan and Uzbekistan; offers training in economics and business administration to teachers in higher education through EdNet Academy; organizes seminars and conferences and administers grants, fellowships and scholarships; mems include 300 higher education institutions and NGOs in Central Asia; Exec. Dir JOHN KNIGHT.

ERASMUS (European Community Action Scheme for the Mobility of University Students): 70 rue Montoyer, 1040 Brussels, Belgium; tel. (32) (2) 233-01-11; fax (32) (2) 233-01-50; f. 1987 by the Council of Ministers of the European Community; aims to encourage greater student and staff mobility throughout the EU and EFTA (European Free Trade Association) countries by means of the creation of a European University Network, the award of 'mobility' grants to students, arrangements for mutual recognition of qualifications and courses, and other supporting measures; publs *ERASMUS and Lingua Action II Directory* (annually), *Guidelines for Applicants*.

European Association for the Education of Adults: 27 rue Liedts, 1030 Brussels, Belgium; tel. (2) 513-52-05; fax (2) 513-57-34; e-mail eaea-main@eaea.org; internet www.eaea.org; f. 1953 to encourage co-operation between adult education organizations on questions of methods, materials, and exchange of individuals; arranges study sessions and tours; also has offices in Girona (Spain) and Helsinki (Finland); mems in 30 European countries; Gen. Sec. Dr ELLINOR HAASE; publ. *Newsletter*.

European Association of Distance Teaching Universities: Postbus 2960, 6401 DL Heerlen, Netherlands; located at: Valkenburgerweg 177, 6419 AT Heerlen, Netherlands; tel. (45) 5762214; fax (45) 5741473; e-mail secretariat@eadtu.nl; internet www.eadtu.nl; f. 1987; aims to promote higher distance education, to support bilateral and multilateral contacts between academic staff, to support co-operation in research, course development, course transfer and credit transfer, to develop new methods for higher distance education, and to organize common projects in co-operation with European authorities; European Open University Network (f. 1995) acts as executive arm and is responsbile for 60 EuroStudy Centres; mems: 19 mem. univs and 5 observer univs from in European countries; Pres. DAVID VINCENT; Sec.-Gen. PIET HENDERIKX (Belgium).

European Distance and E-Learning Network (EDEN): c/o Budapest Univ. of Technology and Economics, 1111 Budapest, Egry J.u. 1, Hungary; tel. (1) 463-1628; fax (1) 463-1858; e-mail secretariat@eden-online.org; internet www.eden-online.org; f. 1991; to foster devts in flexible, distance and e-learning; 1,078 mems, of which 178 instns, and 900 individuals in the Network of Academics and Professionals; Pres. INGEBORG BØ (Norway); Sec.-Gen. Dr ANDRÁS SZŰCS; publs *Conference Proceedings* (annual), *European Journal of Open and Distance Learning* (online).

European Documentation and Information System for Education (EUDISED): Bibliotheca di Documentazione Palazzo Gerini, Via M. Buonarroti 10, 50122 Florence, Italy; tel. (055) 238011; fax (055) 2380330; e-mail turchi@bdp.it; f. 1968; two main components: a database containing abstracts in English, French or German on educational research in 34 European countries, and a multilingual thesaurus (European Education Thesaurus) available in 11 languages for indexing educational information; publ. *European Yearbook of Educational Research*.

European Institute of Education and Social Policy: Université Paris IX-Dauphine, 1 place du Maréchal de Lattre de Tassigny, 75775 Paris Cedex 16, France; tel. (1) 44-05-40-01; fax (1) 44-05-40-02; internet www.eiesp.org; f. 1975 by the European Cultural Foundation, the European Commission, the International Council for Educational Development; studies specific issues in education, employment and social policy; policy-oriented and research programmes and seminars undertaken for European governments, intl organizations, universities, or regional and local bodies; Chair. HYWEL CERI JONES; Dir JEAN GORDON; publs *European Journal of Education* (quarterly in English), *Newsletter* (annually in English and French).

Fédération Internationale des Professeurs de Français/International Federation of Teachers of French: 1 ave Léon Journault, 92318 Sèvres Cedex, France; tel. 1-46-26-53-16; fax 1-46-26-81-69; internet www.fipf.org; f. 1969 to unite and assist teachers of French as a first or second language worldwide; mems: 173 associations in 108 countries; Pres. DARIO PAGEL (Brazil); Sec.-Gen. MARTINE DEFONTAINE (France); publs *Dialogues and Cultures* (annually), *L'Univers du Français: Lettre FIPF* (quarterly).

Inter-American Council for Education, Science and Culture: General Secretariat of the Organization of American States, 1889 F St, NW, Washington, DC 20006, USA; f. 1970 as an organ of the OAS, replacing the Inter-American Cultural Council; aims: to promote friendly relations and mutual understanding among the people of the Americas through educational, scientific and cultural co-operation and exchange; to help prepare the inhabitants of member states to contribute fully to their progress; to encourage intellectual and artistic expression and help protect, preserve and increase the cultural heritage; to recommend procedures for intensifying the integration of the countries' efforts and periodically to evaluate these efforts; mems: the 25 mems of OAS; Exec. Sec. ENRIQUE MARTÍN DEL CAMPO (Mexico).

Inter-American Organization for Higher Education/Organisation Universitaire Interaméricaine: 333 Grande-Allée est, bureau 230, Québec, QC G1R 2H8, Canada; tel. (418) 650-1515; fax (418) 650-1519; e-mail secretariat@oui-iohe.qc.ca; internet www.oui-iohe.qc.ca; f. 1980; inter-university co-operation and exchange; 360 mems; library of 1,500 vols; Pres. GERSON LUIZ JONER DA SILVEIRA (Brazil); Exec. Dir and Treas. MARCEL HAMELIN (Canada).

International Association for Educational and Vocational Guidance/Association Internationale d'Orientation Scolaire et Professionnelle: c/o Linda Taylor, South London Connexions Ltd, Canius House, 1 Scarbrook Rd, Croydon, CR0 1SQ, UK; tel. (20) 8929-4707; fax (20) 8929-4763; e-mail lindataylor@connexions-southlondon.org.uk; internet www.iaevg.org/IAEVG; f. 1951 to contribute to the devt of vocational guidance and promote contact between associated persons; 40,000 mems in 80 countries; Pres. Dr BERNHARD JENSCHKE (Germany); Sec.-Gen. LINDA TAYLOR; publs *Bulletin—AIOSP* (2 a year), *Newsletter* (3 a year).

International Association for Educational and Vocational Information/Association internationale d'information scolaire universitaire et professionnelle: 20 rue de l'Estrapade, 75005 Paris, France; f. 1956 to facilitate co-operation between national organizations concerned with supplying information to university and college students and secondary pupils and their parents, to compare methods and act as an international documentation centre, and to encourage the establishment of other national organizations; mems: national organizations in 30 countries; Pres. C. VIMONT (France); Vice-Pres. Dr LEVERKUS (Germany), M. KAWKA (Poland), M. AMARA (Tunisia), E. LAMA (Italy); Sec.-Gen. L. TODOROV (France); publ. *Informations universitaires et professionnelles internationales* (quarterly).

International Association for the Exchange of Students for Technical Experience (IAESTE): IAESTE (UK), Central Bureau, 10 Spring Gardens, London, SW1A 2BN, UK; internet www.iaeste.org; f. 1948 to organize exchange of students for work experience; 62 national committees; Gen. Sec. Dr A. SFEIR; publs *Annual Report*, *Activity Report*.

International Association of Dental Students: c/o FDI World Dental Federation, 13 Chemin du Levant, L'Avant Centre, 01210, Ferney-Voltaire, France; tel. 4-50-40-50-50; fax 4-50-40-55-55; e-mail gsecretary@iads-web.org; internet www.iads-web.org; f. 1951 to promote international contact between dental students, to advance and encourage their interest in the science and art of dentistry, to promote exchanges and intl congresses; mems: 88,000 students globally; Pres. ANDREA VEITOVA (Czech Republic); Sec.-Gen. TAYLAN AKCA (Turkey); publ. *Bulletin* (2 a year).

International Baccalaureate Organization (IBO): 15 route des Morillons, 1218 Grand-Saconnex, Geneva, Switzerland; tel. 227917740; fax 227910277; e-mail ibhq@ibo.org; internet www.ibo.org; f. 1968; non-profit foundation encouraging students to be active learners, well-rounded individuals and engaged world citizens; works with 1,834 schools in 124 countries to develop and offer 3 programmes to more than 200,000 students aged 3 to 19 years; Dir-Gen. JEFFREY BEARD; publs *IB World* (3 a year), *Journal of Research in International Education* (3 a year).

International Bureau of Education: see chapter on UNESCO.

International Centre for Agricultural Education (CIEA)/Internationales Studienzentrum für landwirtschaftliches Bildungswesen: Federal Office of Agriculture, 3003 Berne, Switzerland; tel. 313222619; fax 313222634; internet www.ciea.ch; f. 1958; organizes international courses on vocational education and teaching in agriculture every two years; Dir ROLAND STÄHLI.

International Council for Adult Education: 18 de Julio 2095, apt. 301, 11200 Montevideo, Uruguay; tel. and fax (2) 409-79-82; e-mail secretariat@icae.org.uy; internet www.icae.org.uy; f. 1973; global network of NGOs promoting adult and life-long learning; areas of activity: adult literacy, primary healthcare reform, adult education in prison, global citizenship and gender justice, peace education and conflict resolution, globalization, Adult Learners' Week, education and transformative capacity of work spaces; 800 mems in 50 countries; Pres. PAUL BÉLANGER (Canada); publ. *Convergence* (quarterly).

International Council for Open and Distance Education: Lilleakerveien 23, 0283 Oslo, Norway; tel. 22-06-26-30; fax 22-06-26-31; e-mail icde@icde.org; internet www.icde.org; f. 1938 as Intl Council for Correspondence Education, present name 1982; dedicated to furthering the aims and methods of distance education worldwide by promoting and funding research and scholarly publs, encouraging the formation of regional asscns, facilitating communications and information exchange, and organizing conferences and workshops; 7,000 mems in 120 countries; Pres. ARMANDO ROCHA TRINDADE (Portugal); Sec.-Gen. and CEO REIDAR ROLL; publ. *Open Praxis* (every 6 months).

International Federation of Catholic Universities/Fédération Internationale des Universités Catholiques (FIUC): c/o Institut Catholique, 21 rue d'Assas, 75270 Paris Cedex 06, France; tel. 1-44-39-52-26; fax 1-44-39-52-28; e-mail sgfiuc@bureau.fiuc.org; f. 1949 to ensure a strong bond of mutual assistance among all Catholic universities in the search for truth to help to solve problems of growth and development, and to co-operate with other international organizations; 206 mems in 52 countries; Pres. JAN PETERS (Netherlands); Sec.-Gen. GUY-RÉAL THIVIERGE (Canada); publs *Idem Aliter* (monthly), *Proceedings of General Assemblies*.

International Federation of University Women/Fédération Internationale des Femmes Diplômées des Universités: 10 rue du Lac, 1207 Geneva, Switzerland; tel. 227312380; fax 227380440; e-mail info@ifuw.org; internet www.ifuw.org; f. 1919 to promote understanding and friendship between university women irrespective of race, nationality, religion or political opinions, to encourage intl co-operation, to advance the development of education, to represent university women in intl organizations, to encourage the full application of their knowledge and skills to the problems which arise at all levels of public life and to encourage their participation in the resolution of these problems; consultative status with appropriate inter-governmental organizations; offers fellowships and study grants; undertakes studies dealing with the status of women; affiliates in 81 countries with 150,000 mems; Pres. GRISELDA KENYON (UK); Sec.-Gen. LEIGH BRADFORD RATTEREE (USA).

International Federation of Workers' Education Associations: 227 Royal Exchange, Manchester, M2 7DD, United Kingdom; tel. (161) 819-1200; fax (161) 819-1222; e-mail dave.spooner@ifwea.org; internet www.ifwea.org; f. 1947 to promote co-operation between national non-governmental bodies concerned with adult and workers' education, through clearing-house services, exchange of information, publications, conferences, summer schools, etc.; 105 affiliated orgs; Pres. JOÃO PROENCA (Portugal); Gen. Sec. DAVE SPOONER (United Kingdom); publ. *Workers' Education* (quarterly, in English).

International Institute for Educational Planning: see chapter on UNESCO.

International Phonetic Association (IPA): c/o Dr Katerina Nicolaidis, Dept of Theoretical and Applied Linguistics, School of English, Aristotle Univ. of Thessaloniki, Thessaloniki 54124, Greece; tel. (2310) 997429; fax (2310) 997432; e-mail knicol@enl.auth.gr; internet www.arts.gla.ac.uk/IPA/ipa.html; f. 1886 to promote the scientific study of phonetics and its applications; hosts quadrennial Int. Congress of Phonetic Sciences; offers examinations in phonetics; 550 mems; Pres. Prof. Dr JOHN WELLS (UK); Sec. Asst Prof. Dr KATERINA NICOLAIDIS (Greece); publ. *Journal of the International Phonetic Association* (3 a year).

International Reading Association: 800 Barksdale Rd, POB 8139, Newark, DE 19714-8139, USA; tel. (302) 731-1600; fax (302) 731-1057; e-mail pubinfo@reading.org; internet www.reading.org; f. 1956; sets standards for effective reading instruction; improves the quality of reading instruction through the study of the reading process and teaching techniques; promotes lifetime reading habit and public awareness about global literacy; annual convention, regional conferences, and biennial World Congress; 90,000 mems; library of 6,000 vols; Pres. Prof. LINDA GAMBRELL (USA); Exec. Dir ALAN E. FARSTRUP; publs *Lectura y Vida* (quarterly), *Reading Research Quarterly*, *The Reading Teacher* (8 a year), *Journal of Adolescent and Adult Literature*.

International Schools Association (ISA): c/o Drs Bert Timmermans, Alpenroos 11, 2317 EX Leiden, Netherlands; tel. (715) 210280; fax (715) 727803; internet www.isaschools.org; f. 1951 to co-ordinate work in International Schools and promote their development; merged in 1968 with the Conference of Internationally-minded Schools (CIS) and now counts in its membership a number of selected national schools; member schools maintain the highest standards and accept pupils of all nationalities, irrespective of sex, race and creed; ISA carries out curriculum research; convenes annual Conferences on problems of curriculum and educational reform; has consultative status with UNESCO, UNICEF, UNHCR, UNEP and ECOSOC; 85 mem. schools worldwide; Chair. CLIVE CARTHEW (Spain); Exec. Dir Drs BERT TIMMERMANS (Netherlands); publ. *Educational Bulletin* (3 a year).

International Society for Business Education/Société Internationale pour l'Enseignement Commercial: POB 20457, Carson City, NV 89721, USA; tel. (775) 882-1445; fax (775) 882-1449; e-mail kantin@charter.net; internet www.siec-isbe.org; f. 1901 to organize international courses and congresses on business education; 2,000 mems organized in 21 national groups; Pres. Dr HANS WERER (Switzerland); Gen. Sec. G. LEE KANTIN (USA); publ. *International Review for Business Education* (2 a year).

International Society for Education through Art (InSEA)/Société Internationale pour l'Education Artistique: c/o Peter Hermans, POB 1109, 6801 BC Arnhem, Netherlands; fax (26) 3521202; e-mail insea@cito.nl; f. 1951 to unite art teachers worldwide, to exchange information and co-ordinate research into art education; non-governmental global organization for the study of art education, international congresses, exhibitions and other activities; *c.* 1,500 mems; Pres. DIEDERIK W. SCHÖNAU; Sec. PETER HERMANS; publ. *InSEA News* (3 a year).

International Union of Students/Union Internationale des Etudiants: POB 58, 17th November St, 1101 Prague 01, Czech Republic; tel. and fax 271731257; e-mail ius@cfs-fcee.ca; internet www.stud.uni-hannover.de/gruppen/ius; f. 1946 by World Student Congress in Prague; objects: to defend the rights and interests of students, to strive for peace, national independence, academic freedom and democratic education and to unite the student movement in furtherance of these objectives; activities include conferences, meetings, solidarity campaigns, relief projects, award of scholarships, travel and exchange, sports events, cultural projects, publicity and other activities in the furtherance of the Union's aims; mems: 99 full mem. countries, 25 consultative; Pres. MANISH TEWARI (India); Sec.-Gen. FRAGE SHERIF; publs *World Student News*, *Newsletter*, *Democratization of Education*, various regional and other bulletins (quarterly).

International Young Christian Workers/Jeunesse Ouvrière Chrétienne Internationale: 4 Ave Georges Rodenbach, 1030 Brussels, Belgium; tel. (2) 242-18-11; fax (2) 242-48-00; e-mail joci@jociycw.net; internet www.jociycw.net; f. 1925 to train, organize and defend the rights of young workers; develops analysis and action on areas such as informal work, the conditions for young female workers, unemployment, apprenticeships, and temporary and dangerous employment; holds int. councils and training sessions at local, nat. and int. level; mems: nat. orgs in 60 countries; Pres. YOVEL THIRUVALLUVAR; Sec.-Gen. BRIDGET RAUCH.

Inter-University Council for East Africa: 3rd Fl., Plot 4, Nile Ave, East African Development Bank Bldg, POB 7110, Kampala, Uganda; tel. (41) 256251; fax (41) 342007; e-mail exsec@iucea.org; internet www.iucea.org; f. 1984 as Association of Eastern and Southern African Universities; to encourage and develop mutually beneficial collaboration between mem. universities, and between them and nat. govts and other organizations; helps its mems to contribute to meeting nat. and regional development needs, to the resolution of problems in every appropriate sector of activity in the region, and to the development of human resource capacity in the academic arena; Chair. Prof. FREDERICK I. B. KAYANJA (Uganda); Exec. Sec. Prof. CHACHA NYAIGOTTI-CHACHA (Kenya).

Islamic Educational, Scientific and Cultural Organization (ISESCO)/Organisation Islamique pour l'Education, les Sciences et la Culture: Ave des F. A. R., Hay Ryad, BP 2275, 10104 Rabat, Morocco; tel. (3) 7-56-60-52; fax (3) 7-56-60-12; internet www.isesco.org.ma; f. 1982 under the aegis of the Islamic Conference Organization to strengthen co-operation between mem. states in the fields of education, culture and science; 51 mems; Islamic Data Bank service (BIDI); Dir-Gen. Dr ABDULAZIZ OTHMAN AL-TWAIJRI; publs *ISESCO Bulletin* (quarterly), *ISESCO Triennial*, *ISESCO Yearbook*, *Islam Today* (2 a year).

Latin American Institute for Educational Communication/Instituto Latinoamericano de la Comunicación Educativa: Calle del Puente 45, Col. Ejidos de Huipulco, Del. Tlalpan, 14380 México, DF, Mexico; tel. (55) 5728-6500 ext. 2100; e-mail contacto@ilce.edu.mx; internet www.ilce.edu.mx; f. 1956; supported by the Mexican Government to provide leadership in educational communication and technical assistance to mems; regional co-operation in research, experimentation, production and distribution of AV materials; produces and broadcasts educational television programmes; offers online educational services; training at the Center for Training and Advanced Studies on Educational Communication (CETEC); operates Center of AV Documentation for Latin America (CEDAL); 13 mem. countries; library of 34,000 vols; Dir-Gen. Lic. DAVID DE LA GARZA LEAL; publ. *Tecnología y Comunicación Educativas* (quarterly).

Organisation of the Catholic Universities of Latin America/Organización de Universidades Católicas de América Latina (ODUCAL): c/o Juan Alejandro Tobías, Viamonte 1856, CP 1056, Buenos Aires, Argentina; tel. (11) 4814-9630; fax (11) 4812-4625; f. 1953; aims to assist the cultural development of Latin America and to promote the activities of Catholic higher education in the region; mems: 34 Catholic univs in Argentina, Brazil, Colombia, Cuba, Ecuador, Mexico, Peru, Puerto Rico, and Venezuela; Pres. JUAN ALEJANDRO TOBIAS; Sec. Gen. Dr EDUARDO MIRAS.

Organization of Ibero-American States for Education, Science and Culture/Organización de Estados Iberoamericanos para la Educación, la Ciencia y la Cultura (OEI): C/ Bravo Murillo 38, 28015 Madrid, Spain; tel. (91) 594-43-82; fax (91) 594-32-86; e-mail weboei@oei.es; internet www.oei.es; f. 1949 as Ibero-American Bureau of Education, name changed 1985; intergovernmental organization for educational, scientific and cultural co-operation within the Ibero-American countries; provides technical assistance to Ibero-American development systems in the above areas; provides information and documentation on the development of education, science and culture; encourages exchanges in these fields; organizes training courses; the General Assembly (at ministerial level) meets every four years; mems: govts of 20 Ibero-American countries; library of 8,000 vols, 500 periodicals; Sec.-Gen. FRANCISCO JOSÉ PIÑÓN.

Pacific Islands Regional Association for Distance Education: c/o Ruby Va'a, University of the South Pacific, (Dir, USP Centre) POB 3014, Apia, Samoa; tel. 20874; fax 23424; e-mail vaa_r@samoa.usp.ac.fj; internet www.col.org/pirade; Pres. RUBY VA'A; Sec. PEPE LUTERU.

Pan-African Association for Literacy and Adult Education: Rue 10, Bâtiment 306, BP 10358 Dakar, Senegal; fax (1) 824-44-13; e-mail anafa@sentoo.sn; internet www.icae.org.uy/eng/paalae.html; f. 1984; non-political, non-governmental, voluntary partnership; founder regional member of the International Council for Adult Education; composed of national adult education associations, non-governmental organizations, institutions and individuals active in the provision and promotion of literacy and adult education throughout Africa; 19 national asscns, 167 institutional mems; 867 individual mems; 30 assoc. mems; Co-ordinator LAMINE KANE.

Pax Romana: 15 rue du Grand-Bureau, CP 315, 1211 Geneva 24, Switzerland; tel. 228230707; fax 228230708; e-mail miicmica@paxromana.int.ch; internet www.paxromana.org; f. 1921; two brs since 1947; student br—*International Movement of Catholic Students* (80 nat. federations); graduate branch—*International Catholic Movement for Intellectual and Cultural Affairs* (60 nat. federations and 5 intl specialized secretariats); Pres. PATRICIO RODE; Sec.-Gen. PAUL ORTEGA; publ. *Convergence* (in English, French and Spanish, 2 a year).

Southeast Asian Ministers of Education Organization (SEAMEO): 920 Sukhumvit Rd, Bangkok 10110, Thailand; tel. (2) 3910144; fax (2) 3812587; internet www.seameo.org; f. 1965 to promote co-operation among the Southeast Asian nations through jt projects and programmes in education, science and culture; 15 regional centres; mems: Brunei, Cambodia, Indonesia, Laos, Malaysia, Myanmar, Philippines, Singapore, Thailand, Viet Nam; associate mems: Australia, Canada, France, Germany, Netherlands, New Zealand; Pres. HE Pehin Orang Kaya Laila Wijaya Dato Haji ABDUL AZIZ UMAR (Brunei); Dir Dr EDILBERTO C. DE JESUS; publs reports of conferences and seminars, annual reports, periodical (3 a year), technical publications, journals, bulletins.

Steering Committee for Higher Education and Research (CDESR): c/o Council of Europe, Higher Education Section, 67075 Strasbourg Cedex, France; tel. 3-88-41-20-00; fax 3-88-41-27-06; e-mail katia.dolgova-dreyer@coe.int; internet www.coe.int/higher-education; f. 1978 under the Council for Cultural Co-operation (CDCC), set up within the Council of Europe by the signatories of the European Cultural Convention, to promote co-operation among European countries in the field of higher education and research; the CDESR is a steering cttee under the Committee of Ministers of the Council of Europe; work programme: univ. policy, academic mobility (especially jt Council of Europe-UNESCO network of information centres on equivalences and mobility and a new jt convention on recognition); main contributor to the Bologna Process aiming to establish a European Higher Education Area by 2010; projects on higher education as a public responsibility, higher education governance, the heritage of European univs, intercultural dialogue; assistance in higher education reform in countries of South-Eastern Europe and newly independent states; 96 delegates (2 per country), who are representatives higher education instns and senior govt officials from the 48 countries party to the European Cultural Convention; Chair. LUC WEBER (Switzerland); Sec. KATIA DOLGOVA-DREYER.

UNESCO European Centre for Higher Education/Centre Européen pour l'Enseignement Supérieur (CEPES): Str. Stirbei Voda 39, 010102 Bucharest, Romania; tel. (21) 313-08-39; fax (21) 312-35-67; e-mail info@cepes.ro; internet www.cepes.ro; f. 1972; centre for policy development and the promotion of international higher education co-operation in Europe, North America and Israel; Secretariat of Joint UNESCO/Council of Europe European Recognition Convention, and of the ENIC Network of Information Centres on Recognition and Mobility in Europe; library of 6,000 books, 135 periodicals, 3,200 documents; Dir Dr JAN SADLAK; publ. *Higher Education in Europe* (4 a year in English, online in French and Russian).

UNESCO Institute for Lifelong Learning/Institut de l'UNESCO pour l'apprentissage tout au long de la vie/UNESCO-Institut für Lebenslanges Lernen: Feldbrunnenstr. 58, 20148 Hamburg, Germany; tel. (40) 448041-46; fax (40) 4107723; e-mail uil-lib@unesco.org; internet www.unesco.org/uil/documentation; f. 1951; an int. research institute of UNESCO; main concern is the content and quality of education in the framework of lifelong learning, with an emphasis on adult learning, non-formal education and adult literacy; main activities are research, diffusion, promotion, research-based training and documentation; a worldwide network for exchange of information on literacy; a research-oriented training programme; library of 63,000 vols, 170 periodicals; spec. collns: sample learning materials on literacy, post-literacy and continuing education from 120 countries; Dir ADAMA OUANE; publ. *International Review of Education* (6 a year).

UNESCO Institute for Information Technologies in Education: Ul. Kedrova 8, Bldg 3, 117292 Moscow, Russia; tel. (095) 129-29-90; fax (095) 129-12-25; e-mail info@iite.ru; internet www.iite.ru; f. 1997; to develop policy and strategy regarding information and communication technologies (ICTs) in education, to monitor and support use of ICTs in education, to provide training for those working in education, and to assist UNESCO member states in problems relating to ICTs; Chair. Prof. Dr SALEH ABDULRAHMAN AL-ATHEL (Saudi Arabia); Dir VLADIMIR KINELEV; publ. *Newsletter* (4 a year).

UNESCO-UNEVOC International Centre for Technical and Vocational Education and Training: UN Campus, Hermann-Ehlers-Str. 10, 53113 Bonn, Germany; tel. (228) 815-0100; fax (228) 815-0199; e-mail info@unevoc.unesco.org; internet www.unevoc.unesco.org; f. 2000; Dir RUPERT MACLEAN (Australia); publ. *UNESCO-UNEVOC Bulletin* (in Arabic, Chinese, English, French, Russian and Spanish, 2 a year).

UNESCO International Institute for Capacity Building in Africa: POB 2305, Addis Ababa, Ethiopia; tel. (11) 5445284; fax (11) 5514936; e-mail info@unesco-iicba.org; internet www.unesco-iicba.org; f. 1999; the institute's primary responsibility is the development of the capacity of institutions in Africa in the fields of teacher education, curriculum development, educational policy, planning and management, and distance education; Governing Board of 12 mems, sitting for three years each, selected from UNICEF, UNDP, World Bank, OAU, African Development Bank, Association for the Development of Education in Africa, and from representatives of Africa's geographical and linguistic groups; Deputy Dir Dr JOSEPH NGU.

UNESCO International Institute for Higher Education in Latin America and the Caribbean/Instituto Internacional de la UNESCO para la Educación en América Latina y el Caribe: Edificio Asovincar, Avda Los Chorros con Calle Acueducto, Altos de Sebucán, Apdo Postal 68.394, Caracas 1062-A, Venezuela; tel. (212) 2861020; fax (212) 2860527; internet www.iesalc.unesco.org.ve; seeks to promote co-operation between member states in the region, and their institutions and establishments of higher education, the improvement of higher education systems, comparisons with and research into higher education in other parts of the world, regional integration, development of nat. and regional systems of evaluation and accreditation, the utilization of new information and communication technologies in higher education, and co-operation with UNESCO and implementation of its programmes; library: Documentation and Information Centre founded in 1979: online public catalogue, 11,325 bibliographies, 2,500 abstracts, 900 digital monographs and occasional papers; Dir CLAUDIO RAMA VITALE.

Union of the Universities of Latin America/Unión de Universidades de América Latina: Circuito Norponiente s/n, Ciudad Universitaria, Apdo 70-232, Del. Coyocoan, 04510 México, DF, Mexico; tel. (55) 5622-0091; fax (55) 5616-1414; e-mail udual@servidor.unam.mx; internet www.unam.mx/udual; f. 1949 to link the Latin American universities and contribute to the cultural and academic integration of the regional nations; organizes General Assemblies and Conferences; permanent statistical work; mems: 167 universities in 21 countries; library of 7,000 vols, 300 serials, records, microforms; Pres. Dr JUAN VELA VALDÉS (Cuba); Sec.-Gen. RAFAEL CORDERA CAMPOS (Mexico); publs *Revista Universidades* (2 a year), *Gaceta UDUAL* (quarterly), *Window* (4 a year), *Boletín UDUAL* (monthly), *Proceedings of Latin American Universities Conferences*.

University of the Arctic: POB 122, 96101 Rovaniemi, Finland; tel. (16) 3413954; fax (16) 3413950; e-mail uarctic@urova.fi; internet www.uarctic.org; f. 2001; international co-operating network of 31 'high latitude' universities, colleges and higher education and research institutions; the university's secretariat, the Circumpolar Co-ordination Office, is hosted by the University of Lapland, Finland; Dir LARS KULLERUD (Finland); Academic programmes: Bachelor of Circumpolar Studies (BCS), Arctic Learning Environment (ALE), Circumpolar Mobility Program (CMP), Northern Research Forum (NRF), UArctic Field School.

World Association for Educational Research (WAER)/Asociación Mundial de Ciencias de la Educación (AMCE)/Association Mondiale des Sciences de l'Education (AMSE): c/o Yves Lenoir, Faculté d'Éducation, Université de Sherbrooke, 2500 blvd de l'Université, Sherbrooke, QC J1K 2R1, Canada; tel. (819) 821-8000 ext. 1339; fax (819) 829-5343; e-mail amseamcewaer@USherbrooke.ca; internet www.amseamcewaer.usherbrooke.ca; f. 1953, present title adopted 2004; aims: to encourage research in educational sciences by organizing congresses, issuing publications, the exchange of information, etc.; 500 individual mems in 32 countries; Pres. YVES LENOIR; Gen. Sec. ABDELKRIM HASNI (Canada); publ. *Recherche en Education autour du Monde* (2 a year).

World Education Fellowship-International (WEF): 54 Fox Lane, Palmers Green, London, N13 4AL, UK; tel. and fax (20) 8245-4561; e-mail generalsecretary@wef-international.org; internet www.wef-international.org; f. 1921 to promote the exchange and practice of progressive educational ideas worldwide; organizes workshops and one-day conferences; sections and groups in 22 countries; Chair. CHRISTINE WYKES; Gen. Sec. GUADALUPE G. DE TURNER; publ. *The New Era in Education* (3 a year).

World Maritime University: POB 500, 201 24 Malmö, Sweden; tel. (40) 356300; fax (40) 128442; e-mail info@wmu.se; internet www.wmu.se; f. 1983 by the Int. Maritime Organization (IMO); offers postgraduate programmes in maritime affairs for students from around the world; language of instruction English; library of 18,000 vols (special collection: IMO depository); 300 students; Pres. KARL LAUBSTEIN; publ. *Journal of Maritime Affairs* (2 a year).

World Student Christian Federation (WSCF)/Fédération Universelle des Associations Chrétiennes d'Etudiants: WSCF Inter-Regional Office, 5 route des Morillons, Ecumenical Centre, POB 2100, 1211 Geneva 2, Switzerland; tel. 227916358; fax 227916152; e-mail wscf@wscf.ch; internet www.wscfglobal.org; f. 1895; an ecumenical student, univ. and secondary school org. with participants from all major Christian confessions; consultative status with the UN through ECOSOC and UNESCO; affiliated student Christian movements in 105 countries; languages of instruction French, English, Spanish; Chair. Dr KENNETH GUEST (USA); Sec-Gen. Rev. MICHAEL WALLACE (New Zealand); publs *Student World*, *Federation News* (2 a year), *WSCF Journal*, *Newsletter* (2 a year).

World Union of Jewish Students: Rechov King George 58, POB 7114, Jerusalem 91070, Israel; Located at: 4th Fl., Heichal Shlomo, Rechov King George 58, Jerusalem, Israel; tel. (2) 6251682; fax (2) 6251688; e-mail office@wujs.org.il; internet www.wujs.org.il; f. 1924 to act as a global organization for national Jewish student bodies; organizes educational programmes, leadership training seminars, women's seminars and Project Areivim, a service programme for Diaspora communities; divided into 6 regions; organizes Congress every three years; 51 nat. unions; c. 700,000 students; NGO mem. of UNESCO, youth affiliate of World Jewish Congress, mem. org. of World Zionist Organization; Chair. VIKTORIA DOLBURD; Exec. Dir NIR ORTAL; publs *WUJS Leads*, *HERitage and HIStory* (Jewish student activist yearbook).

World University Service: WG-Plein 400, 1054 SH Amsterdam, Netherlands; tel. (20) 4122266; fax (20) 4122267; e-mail wus-i@antenna.nl; internet antenna.nl/wus-i; f. 1920; independent non-governmental organization composed of cttees of academics, students and staff in post-secondary institutions in 50 countries; finances and administers post-secondary scholarships for political refugees and those denied equal educational opportunities; supports community development programmes linking human and technical resources of universities to social and economic development; Pres. CALEB FUNDANGA (Zambia); Gen. Sec. XIMENA ERAZO (acting) (Chile); publs *WUS and Human Rights*, *Academic Freedom Report* (annually).

Engineering and Technology

International Union of Technical Associations and Organizations/Union Internationale des Associations et Organismes Techniques (UATI): 1 rue Miollis, 75732 Paris Cedex 15, France; tel. (1) 45-68-48-28; fax (1) 43-06-29-27; e-mail uati@unesco.org; internet www.unesco.org/uati; f. 1951; activities: working groups and cttees to identify, promote and co-ordinate actions of mem. asscns in areas of common interest, and to facilitate relations with international bodies, in particular UNESCO, UNIDO and ECOSOC; mems: 25 organizations; Pres. JACQUES ROUSSET (France); Sec.-Gen. ROLAND BRESSON (France); publ. *Convergence* (3 a year).

MEMBER ORGANIZATIONS

International Association of Hydraulic Engineering and Research: Paseo Bajo de la Virgen del Puerto 3, 28005 Madrid, Spain; tel. 91-335-79-08; fax 91-335-79-35; e-mail iahr@iahr.org; internet www.iahr.org; f. 1935; 2,300 individual mems, 270 corporate mems; Exec. Dir Dr C. B. GEORGE; publs *Journal of Hydraulic Research* (6 a year, in English or French, and a summary in either language), *Journal of River Basin Management* (published in partnership with IAHS and INBO, quarterly), *Newsflash* (monthly), *Newsletter* (6 a year), *Proceedings of Biennial Congresses* (quarterly), *Journal of HydroEnvironment Research*.

International Commission of Agricultural Engineering/Commission Internationale du Génie Rural (CIGR): c/o Prof. Dr. P. Schulze Lammers, Institut für Landtechnik, Universität Bonn, Nussallee 5, 53115 Bonn, Germany; tel. (228) 73-23-89; fax (228) 73-96-44; e-mail cigr@uni-bonn.de; internet www.ucd.ie/cigr; f. 1930; application of soil and water sciences to agricultural engineering; conservation, irrigation, land improvement and reclamation; rural construction and equipment; agricultural machinery; distribution of electricity in rural areas and its application in the general energy context; scientific organization of agricultural work; food processing; mem. asscns in 30 countries, individual mems in 6 countries; Pres. Prof. LUIS SANTOS (Portugal); Sec.-Gen. Prof. Dr P. SCHULZE LAMMERS (Germany).

International Commission on Glass (ICG): c/o F. Nicoletti, Stazione Sperimentale del Vetro, Via Briati 10, 30140 Murano (VE), Italy; tel. 041-2737011; fax 041-2737048; e-mail fnicoletti@spevetro.it; internet www.shef.ac.uk/~icg; f. 1933 in Venice to promote the dissemination of information on the art, history, science and technology of glass; mems: national societies in 31 countries; Pres. A. YARAMAN (Turkey); Hon. Sec. Dr F. NICOLETTI (Italy).

International Commission on Irrigation and Drainage/Commission Internationale des Irrigations et du Drainage: 48 Nyaya Marg, Chanakyapuri, New Delhi 110021, India; tel. (11) 26116837; fax (11) 26115962; e-mail icid@icid.org; internet www.icid.org; f. 1950; 66 mem. countries; Pres. Ir. Hj. KEIZRUL BIN ABDULLAH (Malaysia); Sec.-Gen. M. GOPALAKRISHNAN (India).

International Commission on Large Dams/Commission Internationale des Grands Barrages: 151 blvd Haussmann, 75008 Paris, France; tel. 1-40-42-68-24; fax 1-40-42-60-71; e-mail secretaire.general@icold-cigb.org; internet www.icold-cigb.org; f. 1928; mems: national cttees in 80 countries; Pres. C. B. VIOTTI (Brazil); Sec.-Gen. A. BERGERET (France); publs *ICOLD Congress Proceedings and Transactions* (every 3 years), *World Register of Dams*.

International Congress on Fracture (ICF): c/o A. T. Yokobori Jr, Tohoku University, 1-31-15 Tajiroku Aoyama, Sendai, Japan; tel. (3) 3534-2310; fax (3) 3534-2207; e-mail m_kitagawa@ihi.co.jp; internet www.icf11.com; f. 1965; aims to foster research in the mechanics and phenomena of fracture, fatigue, and strength of materials; to promote co-operation among scientists in the field; holds Intl Conference every four years; 30 mem. orgs; President Prof. T. YOKOBORI (Japan); President Prof. Y. W. MAI (Australia); Sec.-Gen. A. T. YOKOBORI, Jr (Japan); publ. *Proceedings* (every 4 years).

International Dairy Federation: see under Agriculture.

International Federation of Automatic Control (IFAC)/Fédération Internationale de l'Automatique: Schlosspl. 12, 2361 Laxenburg, Austria; tel. (2236) 71447; fax (2236) 72859; e-mail secr@ifac.co.at; internet www.ifac-control.org; f. 1957 to promote the science and technology of control in the broadest sense in all systems, e.g. engineering, physical, biological, social and economical, in both theory and application; mems: 49 nat. mem. orgs; Pres. WOOK-HYUN KWON (Republic of Korea); Sec. KURT SCHLACHER (Austria); publs *Automatica* (mainly selected papers of IFAC-sponsored symposia, monthly), *Control Engineering Practice* (6 a year), *IFAC Newsletter*.

International Gas Union/Union Internationale de l'Industrie du Gaz: c/o DONG A/S, POB 550, Agern Allé 24–26, 2970 Hoersholm, Denmark; tel. 45-17-12-00; fax 45-17-19-00; e-mail secr.igu@dong.dk; internet www.igu.org; f. 1931; mem. orgs in 65 countries; Pres. GEORGE H. B. VERBERG; Sec.-Gen. PETER K. STORM.

International Institute of Welding/Institut International de la Soudure: BP 50362, 95942 Roissy CDG Cedex, France; tel. 1-49-90-36-08; fax 1-49-90-36-80; e-mail iiwceo@wanadoo.fr; internet www.iiw-iis.org; f. 1948; mem societies in 46 countries; Pres. CHRIS SMALLBONE (Australia); Chief Exec. DANIEL BEAUFILS (France); publ. *Welding in the World* (every 2 months).

International Academy for Production Engineering/Collège International pour la Recherche en Productique: 9 rue Mayran, 75009 Paris, France; tel. 1-45-26-21-80; fax 1-45-26-92-15; e-mail cirp@cirp.net; internet www.cirp.net; f. 1950; aims to promote by scientific research the study of mechanical processing of all solid materials including checks on efficiency and quality of work; 540 mems; Sec.-Gen. Prof. DIDIER DUMUR; publs *Annals–Manufacturing Technology* (2 vols, annually), *Dictionaries of Production Engineering*, *Proceedings of Manufacturing Systems Seminars* (annually).

International Measurement Confederation (IMEKO)/Confédération Internationale de la Mesure: POB 457, 1371 Budapest, Hungary; tel. 3531-562; fax 3531-562; e-mail imeko.ime@mtesz.hu; internet www.imeko.org; f. 1958; promotes the int. exchange of scientific and technical information relating to devts in measuring techniques, instrument design and manufacture and in the application of instrumentation in scientific research and industry; promotes co-operation among scientists and engineers in the field, and with other int. orgs; organizes congresses, symposia, etc.; 36 mem. orgs, 23 technical cttees; Sec. Gen. Prof. MLADEN BORSIC; publs *IMEKO Bulletin* (2 a year), *Measurement* (6 a year).

International Navigation Association/Association Internationale de Navigation: Graaf de Ferraris, 11ème étage, Boîte 3, blvd du Roi Albert II 20, 1000 Brussels, Belgium; tel. (2) 553-71-61; fax (2) 553-71-55; e-mail info@pianc-aipcn.org; internet www.pianc-aipcn.org; f. 1885 to promote inland and ocean navigation by fostering and encouraging progress in the design, construction, improvement, maintenance and operation of inland and maritime waterways, ports, and of coastal areas for the benefit of mankind; 2,002 individual mems, 533 corporate mems; Pres ERIC VAN DEN EEDE; Sec.-Gen. LOUIS VAN SCHEL; publ. *PIANC Bulletin* (4 a year).

International Union of Testing and Research Laboratories on Materials and Structures/Réunion Internationale des Laboratoires d'Essais et de

Recherches sur les Matériaux et les Constructions (RILEM): 157 rue des Blains, 92220 Bagneux Cedex, France; tel. (331) 45-36-10-20; fax (331) 45-36-63-20; e-mail sg@rilem.org; internet www.rilem.org; f. 1947 to advance scientific knowledge related to construction materials, systems and structures and to encourage the transfer and application of this knowledge worldwide; 940 mems; Pres. Prof. ARNON BENTUR (Israel); Sec.-Gen. MICHEL BRUSIN; publ. *Materials and Structures—Matériaux et Constructions* (10 a year).

World Energy Council (WEC)/Conseil Mondial de l'Energie (CME): 5th Fl., Regency House, 1–4 Warwick St, London, W1B 5LT, UK; tel. (20) 7734-5996; fax (20) 7734-5926; e-mail info@worldenergy.org; internet www.worldenergy.org; f. 1924 in London as World Power Conference to consider the potential resources and all means of production, transportation, transformation and utilization of energy in all their aspects, and also to consider energy consumption in its overall relationship to the growth of economic activity; collects and publishes data; holds triennial congress; promotes regional symposia and technical studies; mem. cttees in 96 countries; Chair. ANDRÉ CAILLÉ (Canada); Sec.-Gen. GERALD DOUCET (Canada); publs *World Survey of Energy Resources* (every 3 years), *Performance of Generating Plant* (every 3 years), *Energy Efficiency Policies and Indicators* (every 3 years).

World Foundrymen Organization: National Metalforming Centre, 47 Birmingham Rd, West Bromwich, West Midlands B70 6PY, UK; tel. (121) 601-6976; fax (1544) 340332; e-mail secretary@thewfo.com; internet www.thewfo.com; f. 1927 to promote int. co-operation between member asscns and other orgs; congress every 2 years; mems: 28 nat. technical asscns; Pres. Dr Ing. GOTTHARD WOLF (Germany); Sec.-Gen. Eur. Ing. ANDREW TURNER (UK); publs *E-Newsletter* (monthly), *International Foundry Research* (quarterly).

World Road Association/Association Mondiale de la Route: La Grande Arche, Paroi Nord-Niveau 8, 92055 Paris-La Défense, Cedex, France; tel. (1) 47-96-81-21; fax (1) 49-00-02-02; e-mail piarc@wanadoo.fr; internet www.piarc.org; f. 1909 to share information about roads and transport; 1,640 mems; Pres. COLIN JORDAN (Australia); Sec.-Gen. JEAN-FRANÇOIS CORTÉ (France); publs *Routes/Roads* (4 a year), *Reports to World Road Congress* (every 4 years), *Reports to International Winter Road Congress* (every 4 years), *CD-Route* (technical reports, every 2 years).

OTHER ORGANIZATIONS

Arab Petroleum Training Institute: POB 6037, Al Tajeyat, Baghdad, Iraq; tel. (1) 5234100; fax (1) 5210526; f. 1979; training of high-level personnel in all aspects of the oil industry; 11 OAPEC mem. states; library of 5,000 vols, bibliographic and non-bibliographic data bases; Dir-Gen. Dr TAL'AT NAJEEB HATTAB.

Council of Academies of Engineering and Technological Sciences (CAETS): c/o William C. Salmon, 3601 North Peary St, Arlington, VA 22207, USA; tel. (703) 527-5782; fax (703) 526-0570; e-mail caets@nae.edu; internet www.caets.org; f. 1978 to promote the devt of engineering and technology worldwide and to provide an int. forum for the discussion of technological and engineering issues; encourages int. engineering efforts to promote economic growth and social welfare; 24 nat. mem. acads; Sec. and Treas. WILLIAM C. SALMON (USA).

European Organisation for Civil Aviation Equipment (EUROCAE)/Organisation Européenne pour l'Equipement de l'Aviation Civile: 17 rue Hamelin, 75116 Paris, France; tel. (1) 45-05-71-88; fax (1) 45-05-72-30; e-mail eurocae@eurocae.com; internet www.eurocae.org; f. 1963; studies and advises on problems related to the application of equipment to aviation and prepares minimum performance specifications which administrations in Europe may use for approving equipment; 92 mems; Pres. MICHEL LESAGE; Sec. GILBERT AMATO.

European Society for Engineering Education (SEFI)/Société Européenne pour la Formation des Ingénieurs/Europäische Gesellschaft für Ingenieur-Ausbildung: 119 rue de Stassart, 1050 Brussels, Belgium; tel. (2) 502-36-09; fax (2) 502-96-11; e-mail info@sefi.be; internet www.ntb.ch/sefi; f. 1973 to promote the quality of initial and continuing engineering education and to encourage co-operation throughout Europe; provides services and information about engineering education; encourages exchanges between teachers, researchers and students of engineering; Pres. Dr ALFREDO SOEIRO (Portugal); Sec.-Gen. FRANÇOISE CÔME (Belgium); publs *European Journal for Engineering Education* (4 a year), *SEFI News* (4 a year).

ICHCA International Ltd: Suite 2, 85 Western Rd, Romford, Essex, RM1 3LS, UK; tel. (1708) 735295; fax (1708) 735225; e-mail info@ichcainternational.co.uk; internet www.ichcainternational.co.uk; f. 2003 to promote safety and efficiency in the handling and movement of goods; 900 mems from more than 80 countries; Hon. Pres. JOSÉ ARNAIZ BRÁ (Spain); Chair. JAMES HARTUNG (USA); publs *Cargo World* (annually), *Cargo World – The Newsletter* (online, 6 a year).

International Association for Bridge and Structural Engineering (IABSE)/Association Internationale des Ponts et Charpentes/Internationale Vereinigung für Brückenbau und Hochbau: Secretariat ETH-Hönggerberg, 8093 Zürich, Switzerland; tel. 446332647; fax 446331241; e-mail secretariat@iabse.org; internet www.iabse.org; f. 1929; aims: international co-operation among scientists, engineers, researchers and manufacturers; interchange of knowledge, ideas and the results of research work in the sphere of bridge and structural engineering in general, whether in steel, concrete or another material; 3,900 mems from 100 countries; Pres. Prof. MANFRED A. HIRT (Switzerland); Exec. Dir UELI BRUNNER; publs *Structural Engineering International* (4 a year), *Conference Report* (irregular), *Structural Engineering Document* (annually).

International Association of Public Transport/Union Internationale des Transports Publics (UITP)/Internationaler Verband für Öffentliches Verkehrswesen: 6 rue Ste Marie, 1080 Brussels, Belgium; tel. (2) 673-61-00; fax (2) 660-10-72; e-mail administration@uitp.com; internet www.uitp.com; f. 1885 to study all problems related to the operation of public transportation; 2,500 mems; library of 25,000 vols, 200 journals; online library (MOBI +); Pres. (vacant); Sec.-Gen. HANS RAT (Netherlands); publ. *Public Transport International* (6 a year, published in English, French, German and Spanish).

International Centre for Science and High Technology (ICS): AREA Science Park, Padriciano 99, 34012 Trieste, Italy; tel. 040-9228111; fax 040-9228101; e-mail info@ics.trieste.it; internet www.ics.trieste.it; f. 1988; an international centre of the United Nations Industrial Development Organization (UNIDO); promotes technology transfer for the sustainable industrial development of developing countries; Man. Dir LUISA MESTRONI.

International Commission on Illumination/Commission Internationale de l'Éclairage: Kegelgasse 27, 1030 Vienna, Austria; tel. (1) 714-31-87-0; fax (1) 714-31-87-18; e-mail ciecb@ping.at; internet www.cie.co.at; f. 1900 as Int. Commission on Photometry, reorganized as CIE 1913; objectives: to provide an int. forum for the discussion of all matters relating to science, technology and art in the fields of light and lighting; to develop basic standards and procedures of metrology in the fields of light and lighting; to provide guidance in the application of basic principles and procedures to the devt of int. standards in the fields of light and lighting; to prepare and publish reports and standards; to maintain liaison and technical interaction with relevant int. orgs; mems: 40 affiliated Nat. Illumination Cttees; Gen. Sec. CHRISTINE HERMANN.

International Council for Research and Innovation in Building and Construction: Postbox 1837, 3000 BV Rotterdam, Netherlands; Located at: Kruisplein 25G, 3000 BV Rotterdam, Netherlands; tel. (10) 4110240; fax (10) 4334372; e-mail secretariat@cibworld.nl; internet www.cibworld.nl; f. 1953 to encourage co-operation in building research, studies and documentation in all aspects; mems: 450 institutes and individuals in 70 countries; Pres. RODNEY MILFORD (South Africa); Sec.-Gen. Dr WIM BAKENS (Netherlands); publs *Directory of Building Research and Development Organizations*, *CIB Congress and Symposium Proceedings*, *Newsletter* (6 a year).

International Council for Scientific and Technical Information/Conseil International pour l'Information Scientifique et Technique: 51 blvd de Montmorency, 75016 Paris, France; tel. 1-45-25-65-92; fax 1-42-15-12-62; e-mail icsti@icsti.org; internet www.icsti.org; f. 1952 as ICSU Abstracting Board, present name 1984; aims to increase accessibility to and awareness of scientific and technical information, and to foster communication and interaction among participants in the information transfer chain, to take advantage of the progress made independently by each information activity sector; ICSTI is a Scientific Associate of ICSU; 50 nat. and organizational mems in 12 countries; Pres. GÉRARD GIROUD (Germany); Exec. Dir BARRY MAHON (France).

International Council on Large Electric Systems/Conseil International des Grands Réseaux Électriques(CIGRE): 21 rue d'Artois, 75008 Paris, France; tel. 1-53-89-12-90; fax 1-53-89-12-99; e-mail secretary-general@cigre.org; internet www.cigre.org; f. 1921; electrical aspects of electricity generation, sub-stations and transformer stations, high voltage electrical lines, interconnection of systems and their operation and protection; 4,000 mems; Pres. DAVID CROFT (Australia); Sec.-Gen. M. HEROUARD (France); publs *Electra* (every 2 months), *Session Papers and Proceedings* (every 2 years).

International Electrotechnical Commission/Commission Electrotechnique Internationale: 3 rue de Varembé, POB 131, 1211 Geneva 20, Switzerland; tel. 229190211; fax 229190300; e-mail info@iec.ch; internet www.iec.ch; f. 1906 to promote intl co-operation in the electrotechnical industry; administers int. conformity assessment schemes in the areas of electrical equipment and components testing and certification (IECEE), quality of electronic components, materials and processes (IECQ) and certification of electrical equipment operated in explosive atmospheres (IECEx); prepares and publishes int. standards for all electrical, electronic and related technologies; creator of the 'International System' (SI) of units of measurement; has compiled a multi-language electronic vocabulary with more than 20,000 terms; Pres. JACQUES RÉGIS (Canada); Gen. Sec. AHARON AMIT (Switzerland); publ. *Bulletin* (6 a year).

International Federation for Housing and Planning (IFHP)/Fédération Internationale pour l'Habitation, l'Urbanisme et l'Aménagement des Territoires (FIHUAT)/Internationaler Verband für Wohnungswesen, Städtebau und Raumordnung (IVWSR): Wassenaarseweg 43, 2596 CG The Hague, Netherlands; tel. (70) 324-45-57; fax (70) 328-20-85; e-mail info@ifhp.org; internet www.ifhp.org; f. 1913; global network of professionals from the field of housing and planning; corporate and individual mems; annual congress; Pres. FRANCESC X. VENTURA I TEIXIDOR (Spain); Sec.-Gen. ELSBETH VAN HYLCKAMA VLIEG (Netherlands); publs *Newsletter* (4 a year), *Latest Developments in the Field of Housing and Planning* (annually).

International Federation for Information Processing: Hofstr. 3, 2361 Laxenburg, Austria; tel. (2236) 73616; fax (2236) 736169; e-mail ifip@ifip.org; internet www .ifip.org; f. 1960; aims to promote information science and technology by fostering intl co-operation in this field, stimulating research, development and the application of information processing in science and human activity, furthering the dissemination and exchange of information about the subject, and encouraging education in information processing; 55 mem. organizations in 70 countries; Pres. K. BRUNNSTEIN (Germany); Sec. R. JOHNSON (UK); publs *Computers in Industry*, *Computers and Security*, *Information Bulletin*, newsletters (quarterly).

International Federation of Automotive Engineering Societies/Fédération Internationale des Sociétés d'Ingénieurs des Techniques de l'Automobile (FISITA): 1 Birdcage Walk, London, SW1H 9JJ, UK; tel. (20) 7973-1275; fax (20) 7973-1285; e-mail info@fisita.com; internet www.fisita.com; f. 1947 to promote the exchange of information between member societies, ensure standardization of techniques and terms, to publish research on technical and managerial problems and generally to encourage the technical development of mechanical transport; mem. organizations in 36 countries; Pres. DANIEL M. HANCOCK (USA); Exec. Dir IAN DICKIE (UK); publ. *Global Automotive Network* (6 a year).

International Federation of Operational Research Societies (IFORS): c/o Mary Thomas Magrogan, 901 Elkridge Landing Rd, Suite 400, Linthicum, MD 21090, USA; tel. (410) 691-7858; fax (410) 691-6127; e-mail secretary@ifors.org; internet www .ifors.org; f. 1959; aims: the development of operational research as a unified science and its advancement worldwide; 44 nat. socs, 4 kindred socs; Pres. Prof. THOMAS MAGNANTI (USA); Sec. MARY THOMAS MAGROGAN (USA); publs *International Abstracts* (in Operations Research Bulletin), *International Transactions* (in Operational Research Bulletin).

International Federation of Robotics: IFR Secretariat, c/o Symap, Maison de la Mécanique, 45 rue Louis-Blanc, 92400 Courbevoie, France; tel. 1-47-17-67-07; fax 1-47-17-67-25; e-mail secretariat@ifr.org; internet www.ifr.org; f. 1987; 25 nat. mem. orgs; Chair. PAUL JOHNSTON (Canada); Sec. HERMAN VERBRUGGE (Germany); publs *Newsletter* (quarterly), *World Robotics* (annually); publ. *Industrial Robotics*; publ. *Service Robotics*.

International Federation of Surveyors/Fédération Internationale des Géomètres/Internationale Vereinigung der Vermessungsingenieure: Lindevangs Allé 4, 2000 Frederiksberg, Denmark; tel. 38-86-10-81; fax 38-86-02-52; e-mail fig@fig.net; internet www.fig.net; f. 1878; nine technical commissions; 73 nat. mem. assocs; Pres. Prof. Dr-Ing. HOLGER MAGEL (Germany); Admin. Dir MARKKU VILLIKKA (Denmark).

INFOTERM – International Information Centre for Terminology: Mariahilfer Str. 123/3, 1060 Vienna, Austria; tel. (1) 6643446-181; fax (1) 5240606-99; e-mail infopoint@infoterm.org; internet www.infoterm.info; f. 1971 under UNESCO contract; affiliated to Austrian Standards Institute; operates the secretariat of ISO/TC 37 'Terminology and Other Language and Content Resources'; library of 5,600 vols, 15,000 vocabulary standards; Dir Dr CHRISTIAN GALINSKI; publs *INL – Infoterm Newsletter* (quarterly), *BIT – BiblioTerm* (quarterly), *STT – StandardTerm* (quarterly), *TSH – Terminology, Standardization and Harmonization* (quarterly).

International Institute of Communications: Regent House, 24–25 Nutford Place, London, W1H 5YN, UK; tel. (20) 7323-9622; fax (20) 7323-9623; e-mail enquiries@iicom .org; internet www.iicom.org; f. 1969 as Int. Broadcast Inst.; worldwide research and education on telecommunications, broadcasting and information technology; hosts seminars and annual conference; mems in 70 countries; library: 15,000 items, 200 periodicals; Pres. BERNARD COURTOIS; Dir-Gen. BRIAN QUINN; publ. *InterMedia* (every 2 months).

International Institute of Refrigeration/Institut International du Froid: 177 blvd Malesherbes, 75017 Paris, France; tel. 1-42-27-32-35; fax 1-47-63-17-98; e-mail webmaster@iifiir.org; internet www.iifiir.org; f. 1908; intergovernmental organization; object: the study of all technical, scientific and industrial issues concerning refrigeration systems, cryogenics, air conditioning, heat pumps and their applications; studies are undertaken, under the direction of a Science and Technology Council, by 10 Commissions; organizes congresses and conferences; large library, also computerized abstract database; provides bibliographical searches; mems: 61 countries and private and corporate members; Dir DIDIER COULOMB (France); publs *Bulletin of the IIR* (bibliographical, in French and English), *Proceedings of Conferences*, *International Journal of Refrigeration*.

International Iron and Steel Institute (IISI)/Institut International du Fer et de l'Acier: 120 rue Col. Bourg, 1140 Brussels, Belgium; tel. (2) 702-89-00; fax (2) 702-88-99; e-mail steel@iisi.be; internet www.worldsteel .org; f. 1967 to promote the interests of the world's steel industries; to undertake research in all aspects of steel industries; to serve as a forum for exchange of knowledge and discussion of problems relating to steel industries; to collect, disseminate and maintain statistics and information; to serve as a liaison body between intl and nat. steel organizations; mems in 50 countries; Chair. JOHN SURMA (USA); Sec.-Gen. IAN CHRISTMAS; publs *Crude Steel Production Monthly*, *Iron Production Monthly*.

International Organization for Standardization/Organisation internationale de normalisation: 1 rue de Varembé, CP 56, 1211 Geneva 20, Switzerland; tel. 227490111; fax 227333430; e-mail central@iso.org; internet www.iso.org; f. 1947 to promote the development of standardization and related activities in the world with a view to facilitating the international exchange of goods and services, and to developing mutual co-operation in the spheres of intellectual, scientific, technological and economic activity; 150 mems; reference library holding full collns of ISO and IEC standards; Pres. MÅKAN MURBY (until 31 Dec. 2008 (Sweden); Sec.-Gen. ALAN BRYDE; publs *ISO International Standards*, *ISO Focus* (11 a year), *ISO Management Systems* (6 a year).

International Society for Photogrammetry and Remote Sensing (ISPRS)/Société Internationale de Photogrammétrie et de Télédétection: c/o Orhan Eltan, ITU Insaat Fakultesi, 34669 Maslak-, Istanbul, Turkey; tel. (212) 285-3810; fax (212) 285-6587; e-mail oaltan@itu-edu.tr; internet www.isprs.org; f. 1910; research and information on the application of aerial and space photography and remote sensing to exploration and mapping; federated to ICSU; 90 nat. mem. orgs, 11 assoc. mems and 12 regional mem. assocs.; Pres. IAN DOWMAN (United Kingdom); Sec.-Gen. OHRAN ALTAN (Turkey); publs *International Archives of Photogrammetry and Remote Sensing* (every 2 years), *Journal of Photogrammetry and Remote Sensing* (every 2 months), *ISPRS Highlights* (quarterly), *Annual Report*.

International Society for Soil Mechanics and Geotechnical Engineering/Société Internationale de Mécanique des Sols et de la Géotechnique: City Univ., Northampton Sq., London, EC1V 0HB, UK; tel. (20) 7040-8154; fax (20) 7040-8832; e-mail secretariat@issmge.org; internet www.issmge.org; f. 1936; 77 mem. socs, 17,000 individual mems; Pres. Prof. PEDRO SÊCO E PINTO (Portugal); Sec.-Gen. Prof. R. NEIL TAYLOR (UK).

International Water Association: Alliance House, 12 Caxton St, London, SW1H 0QS, UK; tel. (20) 7654-5500; fax (20) 7654-5555; e-mail water@iwahq.org.uk; internet www.iwahq.org.uk; f. 1999 by the merger of the International Association on Water Quality and the International Water Supply Association; develops effective and sustainable approaches to global water management; members includes academic researchers, research centres, energy utilities, consultants, water industry regulators, industrial water users and water equipment manufacturers; Pres. LASZLO SOMLYODY; Exec. Dir PAUL REITER; publs *Nordic Hydrology* (5 a year), *Journal of Water and Health* (quarterly), *Journal of Hydroinformatics* (quarterly), *Journal of Water Supply: Research & Technology – AQUA* (8 a year), *Water Science & Technology* (24 a year), *Water Science & Technology: Water Supply* (6 a year), *Water Research* (20 a year), *Water21* (6 a year), *Water Policy* (6 a year).

Textile Institute: International Headquarters, 1st Fl., St James's Bldgs, Oxford St, Manchester, M1 6FQ, UK; tel. (161) 237-1188; fax (161) 236-1991; e-mail tiihq@textileinst.org.uk; internet www.texi.org; f. 1910, Royal Charter 1925 and 1955; the international body for those concerned with any aspect of textiles and related industries; promotion of education and training, professional standards and exchange of information within the industry by means of publications, conferences, meetings and information services; 60 national and regional brs; 8,000 mems in 85 countries; library of 1,500 vols, 120 journals; Professional Affairs Dir HELEN YEOWART; Hon. Sec. M. PARKINSON; publs *Journal* (4 a year), *Textile Horizons* (6 a year), *Textiles* (4 a year), *Textile Progress* (4 a year).

Tin Technology Ltd: Unit 3, Curo Park, Frogmore, St Albans, AL2 2DD, UK; tel. (1727) 875544; fax (1727) 871341; e-mail info@tintechnology.com; internet www.tintechnology.biz; f. 1932; aims to maintain and extend the use and effectiveness of tin in modern technology; its work is directed to develop the use of tin and is based on scientific and technical study of the metal, its alloys and compounds, and of industrial processes which use tin or may provide future markets; 200 mems in 35 countries; Man. Dir DAVID BISHOP.

World Wide Web Consortium (W3C): c/o Massachusetts Institute of Technology, Computer Science and Artificial Intelligence Laboratory (CSAIL), 32 Vassar St, Cambridge, MA 02139, USA; tel. (617) 253-2613; fax (617) 258-5999; internet www.w3.org; f. 1994; provides an open forum for discussing the technical evolution of the World Wide Web; develops technical specifications for the Web's infrastructure; 500 mem. orgs worldwide; Chief Operating Officer STEVE BRATT; Dir TIM BERNERS-LEE.

Law

Hague Academy of International Law: Peace Palace, Carnegieplein 2, 2517 KJ The Hague, Netherlands; tel. (70) 3024242; fax (70) 3024153; e-mail hagueacademy@registration.nl; internet www.hagueacademy.nl; f. 1923 as a centre of higher studies in international law (public and private) and cognate sciences, in order to facilitate a thorough and impartial examination of questions bearing on international juridical relations; Sec.-Gen. Prof. G. BURDEAU.

Associated centre:

Centre for Studies and Research in International Law and International Relations: The Hague, Netherlands; tel. (70) 3024242; fax (70) 3024153; e-mail hagueacademy@registration.nl; internet www.hagueacademy.nl; f. 1957; postdoctoral 4-week research courses in August and September after courses held by Academy; open only to participants who are highly qualified by intellectual maturity and experience (12 French-speaking, 12 English-speaking); library: use of Peace Palace Library; Head of Secretariat M. CROESE.

Hague Conference on Private International Law/Conférence de La Haye de droit international privé: Scheveningseweg 6, 2517 KT The Hague, Netherlands; tel. (70) 3633303; fax (70) 3604867; e-mail secretariat@hcch.net; internet www.hcch.net; f. 1893 to work for the unification of the rules of private international law; 65 mems: governments of Albania, Argentina, Australia, Austria, Belarus, Belgium, Bosnia and Herzegovina, Brazil, Bulgaria, Canada, Chile, China, Croatia, Cyprus, Czech Republic, Denmark, Egypt, Estonia, Finland, France, Georgia, Germany, Greece, Hungary, Iceland, Ireland, Israel, Italy, Japan, Jordan, Republic of Korea, Latvia, Lithuania, Luxembourg, former Yugoslav republic of Macedonia, Malaysia, Malta, Mexico, Monaco, Morocco, Netherlands, New Zealand, Norway, Panama, Paraguay, Peru, Poland, Portugal, Romania, Russia, Serbia and Montenegro, Slovakia, Slovenia, South Africa, Spain, Sri Lanka, Suriname, Sweden, Switzerland, Turkey, Ukraine, UK, USA, Uruguay, Venezuela; Sec.-Gen. J. H. A. VAN LOON; publs *The Judges' Newsletter–International Child Protection* (2 a year), *Proceedings of the Conference's Sessions/Actes et documents des Sessions de la Conférence*.

Institute of International Law/Institut de Droit International: 24 rue de Morsaint, 1390 Grez-Doiceau, Belgium; tel. 229085720; fax 229085710; e-mail gerardi@hei.unige.ch; internet www.idi-iil.org; f. 1873 to promote the devt of int. law by endeavouring to formulate general principles in accordance with civilized ethical standards, and by giving assistance to achieve the gradual and progressive codification of int. law; 132 mems and assocs world-wide; Sec.-Gen. Prof. JOE VERHOEVEN; publ. *Tableau général des Résolutions*.

Inter-American Bar Association/Federación Interamericana de Abogados/Federação Interamericana de Advogados/Fédération Inter-Américaine des Avocats: 1211 Connecticut Ave NW, Ste. 202, Washington, DC 20036, USA; tel. (202) 466-5944; fax (202) 466-5946; e-mail iaba@iaba.org; internet www.iaba.org; f. 1940; mems: 51 bar assocs and individual lawyers in 33 countries; Pres. MERCEDES ARAÚZ DE GRIMALDO; Sec.-Gen. HARRY A. INMAN; publs *Newsletter* (4 a year), *Conference Proceedings* (annually), *Inter-American Journal of International and Comparative Law* (annually).

Intergovernmental Committee of the Universal Copyright Convention: UNESCO, 7 Place de Fontenoy, 75700 Paris, France; tel. 1-45-68-47-11; fax 1-45-68-55-89; internet www.unesco.org/culture/copyright; f. 1952; studies the problems concerning the application and operation of the Universal Copyright Convention; makes preparation for periodic revisions of this Convention; mems: Algeria, Argentina, Austria, Cameroon, China, Croatia, Cuba, France, Greece, Guatemala, India, Israel, Japan, Morocco, Portugal, Russia, Ukraine and USA; Chair. ABDULLAH OUADRHIRI (Morocco); publ. *Copyright Bulletin* (4 a year).

International Association for Penal Law/Association Internationale de Droit Pénal: BP 1146, 64013 Pau Université Cedex, France; tel. 5-59-98-08-24; fax 5-59-27-24-56; e-mail aidp-pau@infonie.fr; internet www.penal.org; f. 1924 to promote co-operation between bodies and individuals engaged in the study or practice of criminal law; to study crime, its causes and the means of preventing it, and to advance the theoretical and practical development of intl penal law; 2,000 mems; Pres. JOSÉ LUIS DE LA CUESTA; Gen. Sec. Magistrat H. EPP; publ. *Revue Internationale de Droit Pénal* (2 a year).

International Association for Philosophy of Law and Social Philosophy (IVR)/Internationale Vereinigung für Rechts- und Sozialphilosophie: c/o Aleksander Peczenik, Källerekroken 34, 226 47 Lund, Sweden; tel. (46) 152441; fax (46) 2224444; e-mail ap@ivr2003.net; internet www.cirfid.unibo.it/ivr; f. 1909 for scientific research in philosophy of law and social philosophy; holds intl congresses every 2 years; 44 national sections; 2,300 mems; national sections in 44 countries; Pres. ALEKSANDER PECZENIK (Sweden); Sec.-Gen. CHRISTIAN DAHLMAN (Sweden); publs *IVR Newsletter* (2 a year), *Archiv für Rechts- und Sozialphilosophie* (quarterly).

International Association of Democratic Lawyers (IADL)/Association Internationale des Juristes Démocrates: 21 rue Brialmont, 1210 Brussels, Belgium; tel. (2) 223-33-10; fax (2) 223-33-10; e-mail jsharma@del3.vsnl.net.in; internet www.iadllaw.org; f. 1946; aims to facilitate contacts and exchanges of view between lawyers and lawyers' assocs and to foster understanding and goodwill; to work together to achieve the aims of the Charter of the UN; mems in 102 countries; in consultative status with UN Economic and Social Council and UNESCO; Pres. JITENDRA SHARMA (India); Sec.-Gen. BEINUSZ SZMUKLER (Argentina); publ. *Revue Internationale de Droit Contemporain* (2 a year, also published in English and Spanish).

Union Internationale des Avocats (UIA) (International Association of Lawyers): 25 rue du Jour, 75001 Paris, France; tel. 1-44-88-55-66; fax 1-44-88-55-77; e-mail uiacentre@uianet.org; internet www.uianet.org; f. 1927 to promote the independence and freedom of lawyers, and defend their ethical and material interests on an intl level; to contribute to the development of an intl order based on law; mems: 250 organizations, 3,000 individuals; Pres. PAUL NEMO (France); Sec.-Gen. GUY ARENDT (France); publ. *Juriste International*.

International Bar Association: 1 Stephen St, 10th Fl., London, W1T 1AT, UK; tel. (20) 7691-6868; fax (20) 7691-6544; e-mail editor@int-bar.org; internet www.ibanet.org; f. 1947; mems: 195 nat. bar asscns and law socs and 30,000 individual lawyers from 183 countries; Exec. Dir MARK ELLIS; publs *Business Law International* (3 a year), *International Bar News* (6 a year), *Journal of Energy and Natural Resources Law* (quarterly).

International Bureau of Fiscal Documentation: POB 20237, 1000 HE Amsterdam, Netherlands; located at: H. J. E. Wenckebachweg 210, 1096 AS Amsterdam, Netherlands; tel. (20) 554-01-00; fax (20) 622-86-58; e-mail customerservice@ibfd.org; internet www.ibfd.nl; an ind. non-profit foundationf. 1938 to supply information on fiscal law and its application; tax treaties database, European taxation database, and OECD database, on CD-ROM; library of 30,000 vols, 1,000 periodicals; CEO WILLEM FALTER; publs *Bulletin for International Fiscal Documentation* (monthly), *European Taxation* (monthly), *International VAT Monitor* (6 a year), *International Transfer Pricing Journal* (6 a year), *Asia–Pacific Tax Bulletin* (monthly), *Derivatives and Financial Instruments* (6 a year), *Tax News Service* (weekly).

Attached academy:

IBFD International Tax Academy: Sarphatistraat 500, 1018 AV Amsterdam, Netherlands; tel. (20) 554-01-60; fax (20) 620-93-97; e-mail ita@ibfd.org; internet www.ibfd.nl; f. 1989 to provide education and training on international and comparative tax law through conferences, courses and traineeships; Head ARCOTIA HATSIDIMITRIS.

International Commission of Jurists/Commission Internationale de Juristes: BP 216, 81A ave de Châtelaine, 1219 Châtelaine-Geneva, Switzerland; tel. 229793800; fax 229793801; e-mail info@icj.org; internet www.icj.org; f. 1952 to promote and protect human rights, and to strengthen the Rule of Law in all its practical manifestations—institutions, legislation, procedures, etc.—and defend it through the mobilization of world legal opinion in cases of general and systematic violation of, or serious threat to, such principles of justice; library of 2,000 vols; Pres. ARTHUR CHASKALSON (South Africa); Sec.-Gen. NICHOLAS HOWEN (Switzerland); publ. *Attacks on Justice* (online only).

International Confederation of Societies of Authors and Composers/Conféd-

ération Internationale des Sociétés d'Auteurs et Compositeurs: 20–26 blvd du Parc, 92200 Neuilly sur Seine, France; tel. 1-55-62-08-50; fax 1-55-62-08-60; e-mail cisac@cisac.org; internet www.cisac.org; f. 1926 to ensure more effective protection of the rights of authors and composers, to improve legislation on literary and artistic rights, and to organize research on problems concerning the rights of authors on the internet; participates in preparatory work for inter-governmental conferences on authors' rights; 203 mem. societies in 104 countries; Pres. CHRISTIAN BRÜHN; Dir-Gen. ERIC BAPTISTE; publ. *CISAC News* (4 a year).

International Development Law Organization: Via di San Sebastianello 16, 00187 Rome, Italy; tel. 06-6979261; fax 06-6781946; e-mail idlo@idlo.int; internet www.idli.org; f. 1983 for mid-career training and technical assistance, primarily for developing and transition country lawyers, legal advisers and judges; Rome-based courses and seminars in English and French address legal topics related to economic development and governance, including negotiation, intl contracting and economic law reform; also designs and organizes in-country training workshops on law-related economic development topics; library in process of formation; Dir-Gen. WILLIAM T. LORIS.

International Federation for European Law/Fédération Internationale pour le Droit Européen (FIDE): Via Nicolò Tartaglia 5, 00197 Rome, Italy; fax 80-80-731; f. 1961 to advance studies on European law among members of the European Community by co-ordinating activities of member societies and by organizing regular colloquies on topical problems of European law; mems: 17 national associations; Pres. Hon. Mr Justice NIALL FENNELLY; Sec.-Gen. PATRICK MCCANN.

International Institute for the Unification of Private Law/Institut International pour l'Unification du Droit Privé (Unidroit): Via Panisperna 28, 00184 Rome, Italy; tel. 06-696211; fax 06-69941394; e-mail info@unidroit.org; internet www.unidroit.org; f. 1926, to prepare for the establishment of uniform legislation, to prepare draft uniform laws and intl conventions for adoption by diplomatic conferences, to prepare drafts of intl agreements on private law, to undertake studies in comparative law, and to organise conferences and publish works on such subjects; meetings of organizations concerned with the unification of law; international congresses on private law; mems: governments of 59 countries; library of 235,000 vols; Pres. Prof. BERARDINO LIBONATI (Italy); Sec.-Gen. Prof. HERBERT KRONKE (Germany); publs *Uniform Law Review* (quarterly), *Digest of Legal Activities of International Organizations*.

International Institute of Space Law (IISL)/Institut International de Droit de l'Espace: 8–10 rue Mario-Nikis, 75015 Paris, France; tel. (1) 45-67-42-60; fax (1) 42-73-21-20; e-mail secretary@iafastro-iisl.com; internet www.iafastro-iisl.com; f. 1959 at the XI Congress of the International Astronautical Federation; holds meetings, makes studies on juridical and sociological aspects of astronautics; publishes reports; makes awards; holds an annual Colloquium; mems: 386 individuals elected for life; Pres. Dr N. JASENTULIYANA (USA); Sec. TANJA L. MASSON-ZWAAN (Netherlands); publ. *Proceedings of Colloquia*.

International Juridical Institute/Institut Juridique International: Permanent Office for the Supply of International Legal Information, Spui 186, 2511 BW, The Hague, Netherlands; tel. (70) 346-0974; fax (70) 362-5235; e-mail iji@worldonline.nl; f. 1918 to supply information in connection with any matter of int. interest, not being of a secret nature, respecting int., municipal and foreign law and the application thereof; Chair. Prof. A. V. M. STRUYCKEN; Sec. T. HEUKELS; Dir A. L. G. A. STILLE.

International Maritime Committee/Comité Maritime International (CMI): Mechelsesteenweg 196, 2018 Antwerp, Belgium; tel. (3) 227-35-26; fax (3) 227-35-28; e-mail admini@cmi-imc.org; internet www.comitemaritime.org; f. 1897 to contribute to the unification of maritime and commercial law, maritime customs, usages and practices; promotes the establishment of national associations of maritime law and co-operates with other intl asscns or organizations having the same object; work includes drafting of conventions on collisions at sea, salvage and assistance at sea, limitation of shipowners' liability, maritime mortgages, etc.; mems: associations in 51 countries; Pres. JEAN-SERGE ROHART (France); Sec-Gen. NIGEL FRAWLEY (acting) (Canada); publs *CMI News Letter*, *Year Book*.

World Jurist Association (WJA): Suite 202, 1000 Connecticut Ave NW, Washington, DC 20036, USA; tel. (202) 466-5428; fax (202) 452-8540; e-mail wja@worldjurist.org; internet www.worldjurist.org; f. 1963 to promote the continued development of intl law and world order; biennial world conferences, World Law Day, demonstration trials, research programmes and publications have contributed to the growth of law and legal institutions by focusing on matters of intl concern; mems: lawyers, jurists and legal scholars in over 150 countries; Pres. VALERIJ O. YEVDOKIMOV (Ukraine); Exec. Vice-Pres. MARGARET M. HENNEBERRY (USA); publs *World Jurist* (6 a year), *Law / Technology* (4 a year).

Affiliated bodies:

World Association of Center Associates (WACA): Suite 202, 1000 Connecticut Ave NW, Washington, DC 20036, USA; tel. (202) 466-5428; fax (202) 452-8540; e-mail wja@worldjurist.org; f. 1979 to mobilize interested individuals not in the legal profession to promote the objects of the WJA; Pres. RICK BALTZERSEN (USA).

World Association of Judges (WAJ): Suite 2, 1000 Connecticut Ave NW, Washington, DC 20036, USA; tel. (202) 466-5428; fax (202) 452-8540; e-mail wja@worldjurist.org; f. 1966 to mobilize judicial leaders on important transnational legal issues and to improve the administration of justice; over 23 cttees studying int. law; Pres. Prince BOLA AJIBOLA (Nigeria).

World Association of Law Professors (WALP): Suite 202, 1000 Connecticut Ave NW, Washington, DC 20036, USA; tel. (202) 466-5428; fax (202) 452-8540; e-mail wja@worldjurist.org; f. 1975 to focus the attention of legal scholars and teachers on transnational legal issues, and improve scholarship and education in intl legal matters, including training, practice, administration of justice, human rights, the environment and co-ordination of legal systems; Pres. SALVADOR B. LAO (Philippines).

World Association of Lawyers (WAL): Suite 202, 1000 Connecticut Ave NW, Washington, DC 20036, USA; tel. (202) 466-5428; fax (202) 452-8540; e-mail wja@worldjurist.org; f. 1975 to develop transnational law and improve lawyers' expertise in related areas; over 100 committees studying the development of intl law; Pres. JACK STREETER (USA).

Medicine and Public Health

World Health Organization/Organisation Mondiale de la Santé: Ave Appia 20, 1211 Geneva 27, Switzerland; tel. 227912111; fax 227913111; e-mail info@who.int; internet www.who.int; f. 1948; WHO, a specialized agency of the UN, is governed by its mem. states, which decide the organization's priorities and monitor its work. WHO has been given the mandate to help all people—in particular the poor and the vulnerable—to achieve the highest possible level of health; WHO's work includes reducing the global burden of disease by taking action against the main diseases of the world, reducing the risk factors for ill health, increasing the knowledge base on health issues through co-ordinating and supervising research, setting standards and guidelines, and assisting countries in improving their health systems and making them more equitable; 191 mem. states; library: Library: see entry in Switzerland chapter; Dir-Gen. Dr JONG-WOOK LEE (Republic of Korea); publs *Bulletin* (scientific papers: in English, monthly; in French and English, 2 a year), *International Digest of Health Legislation* (online only, 4 a year), *Weekly Epidemiological Record* (51 a year and online), *WHO Drug Information* (4 a year and online), *World Health Report* (annually and online).

OTHER ORGANIZATIONS

Council for International Organizations of Medical Sciences (CIOMS)/Conseil des Organisations Internationales des Sciences Médicales: Secretariat c/o WHO, 20 ave Appia, 1211 Geneva 27, Switzerland; tel. 227913406; fax 227910746; e-mail cioms@who.int; internet www.cioms.ch; f. 1949 to facilitate and co-ordinate the activities of its members, to act as a co-ordinating centre between them and the national institutions, to maintain collaboration with the UN, to promote international activities in the field of medical sciences, to serve the scientific interests of the intl biomedical community; mems: 66 intl associations, national academic and research councils in 30 countries; Pres. Dr M. B. VALLOTTON; Sec.-Gen. Dr JUHANA E. IDÄNPÄÄN-HEIKKILÄ; publs *International Nomenclature of Diseases*, *International Ethical Guidelines for Biomedical Research Involving Human Subjects*, *International Guidelines for Ethical Review of Epidemiological Studies*.

INTERNATIONAL MEMBERS OF CIOMS

FDI World Dental Federation/Fédération Dentaire Internationale (FDI): 13 Chemin du Levant, L'Avant Centre, 01210 Ferney-Voltaire, France; tel. 4-50-40-50-50; fax 4-50-40-55-55; e-mail info@fdiworldental.org; internet www.fdiworldental.org; f. 1900; 900,000 individual mems, 157 mem. assocs in 136 countries; Pres. Dr HEUNG-RYUL YOON (Repub. of Korea); Pres.-Elect Dr MICHÈLE AERDEN (Belgium); Treas. Dr BRENT STANLEY (New Zealand); Exec. Dir Dr J. T. BARNARD (France); publs *International Dental Journal* (6 a year), *Ferney Communiqué* (online newsletter, 6 a year), *Community Dental Health* (quarterly), *European Journal of Prosthodontics and Restorative Dentistry* (quarterly), *Journal of the International Academy of Periodontology* (quarterly), *Developing Dentistry* (2 a year).

International Association for the Study of the Liver: c/o Dr Wolfgang H. Caselmann, Bavarian State Ministry of the Environment, Public Health and Consumer

Protection, POB 810140, 81901 Munich, Germany; tel. (89) 9214-2141; fax (89) 9214-2384; e-mail secretariat@iaslonline.com; internet www.iaslonline.com; f. 1958 to foster training of experts in hepatology; encourages research on the liver and its diseases and helps to facilitate prevention, recognition and treatment of liver and biliary tract diseases in the intl community; Pres. DING-SHINN CHEN (Taiwan); Sec. and Treas. Dr WOLFGANG H. CASELMANN (Germany).

International College of Surgeons/Collège International de Chirurgiens: 1516 North Lake Shore Dr., Chicago, IL 60610, USA; tel. (312) 642-3555; fax (312) 787 1624; e-mail info@icsglobal.org; internet www.icsglobal.org; f. 1935 Geneva, inc. Washington 1940; organized as a world-wide instn to advance the art and science of surgery by bringing together surgeons of all nations, irrespective of nationality, creed or colour; through its Surgical Congresses, Research and Scholarship Project and Surgical Teams Project of volunteers to developing countries, an exchange of surgical knowledge is facilitated in the highest interest of patients; also operates the Int. Museum of Surgical Science located at HQ; 7,000 mems; World Pres. Dr FIDEL RUIZ-HEALY; Exec. Dir MAX C. DOWNHAM; publ. *International Surgery* (6 a year).

International Council of Nurses (ICN)/Conseil International des Infirmières (CII): 3 place Jean-Marteau, 1201 Geneva, Switzerland; tel. 229080100; fax 229080101; e-mail icn@icn.ch; internet www.icn.ch; f. 1899; works to ensure universal quality nursing care, sound health policies worldwide and advancement of nursing knowledge; Council of National Representatives meets every 2 years; congress every 4 years; mems: 125 national nurses' associations; Pres. CHRISTINE HANCOCK; Exec. Dir JUDITH A. OULTON; publ. *International Nursing Review*.

International Diabetes Federation/Fédération Internationale du Diabète: 19 ave Emile De Mot, 1000 Brussels, Belgium; tel. (2) 538-55-11; fax (2) 538-51-14; e-mail info@idf.org; internet www.idf.org; f. 1949; 172 member associations in 134 countries; holds triennial congresses; Pres. PIERRE LEFÈBVRE (Belgium); Exec. Dir LUC HENDRICKX; publs *Diabetes Voice* (3 a year), *Triennial Report*, *Diabetes Atlas* (annually).

International Federation of Clinical Neurophysiology/Fédération Internationale de Neurophysiologie Clinique: c/o Venue Vest Conference Services Ltd, Suite 100, 873 Beatty St, Vancouver, BC V6B 2M6, Canada; tel. (604) 681-5226; fax (604) 681-2503; e-mail ifcn@ifcn.info; internet www.ifcn.info; f. 1949 to attain the highest level of knowledge in the field of electro-encephalography and clinical neurophysiology worldwide; 58 mem. orgs (nat. socs); Pres. HIROSHI SHIBASAKI (Japan); Sec. Prof. REINHARD DENGLER (Germany); publs *Clinical Neurophysiology* (monthly), *Evoked Potentials* (every 2 months), *EMG and Motor Control* (every 2 months).

International Federation of Oto-Rhino-Laryngological Societies/Fédération Internationale des Sociétés Oto-rhino-laryngologiques: POB 124, 1135 ZK Edam, Netherlands; fax (299) 373723; e-mail ifos@cest-bien.com; internet www.ifosworld.org; f. 1965; aims: to promote scientific and clinical research into oto-rhino-laryngology; to improve aural health in developing countries; to register educational programmes and promote co-operation; mems from 98 countries and 10 intl socs; Pres. NASSER KOTBY (Egypt); Gen. Sec. JAN J. GROTE (Netherlands); publ. *IFOS Newsletter* (quarterly).

International Federation of Surgical Colleges/Fédération Internationale des Collèges de Chirurgie: Secretariat: La Panetière, 1279 Bogis-Bossey, Switzerland; Administration: c/o Royal College of Surgeons in Ireland, 121 St Stephen's Green, Dublin 2, Ireland; tel. (1) 4022707; fax (1) 4022230; e-mail ifsc@rcsi.ie; internet www.ifsc-net.org; f. 1958 in Stockholm; objectives: the improvement and maintenance of the standards of surgery worldwide, by establishment and maintenance of co-operation and interchange of medical and surgical information; encouragement of high standards of education, training and research in surgery and its allied sciences; particularly assisting developing countries in surgical advancement; mems: 70 national colleges or societies and 500 associates; Pres. P. MCLEAN (Ireland); Sec. Prof. S. W. A. GUNN (Switzerland); publs *Electronic Journal*, *IFSC News* (2 a year).

International Leprosy Association/Association Internationale contre la Lèpre: c/o Dr Cornelius S. Walter, The Leprosy Mission Trust – India, CNI Bhavan, 16 Pandit Pant Marg, New Delhi 110 001, India; fax (11) 23710803; e-mail walterc@tlm-india.org; internet www.leprosy-ila.org; f. 1931 to promote intl co-operation into research on and treatment of leprosy; 1,200 mems; Pres. Dr S. K. NOORDEEN (India); Sec. Dr CORNELIUS S. WALTER (India); publ. *International Journal of Leprosy and Other Mycobacterial Diseases* (quarterly).

International Pediatric Association/Association Internationale de Pédiatrie: 17 rue du Cendrier, POB 1726, 1211 Geneva 1, Switzerland; tel. 229069152; fax 227322852; e-mail adminoffice@ipa-world.org; internet www.ipa-world.org; f. 1912; holds regional and int. seminars and symposia; organizes int. paediatric congresses every 3 years; 165 mem. socs; Pres. CHOK WAN CHAN (China (Hong Kong)); Exec. Dir JANE G. SCHALLER (USA); publ. *IPA News* (4 a year).

International Rhinologic Society: c/o Prof. P. A. R. Clement, ENT Dept, AZ-VUB, Laarbeeklaan 101, 1090 Brussels, Belgium; tel. (2) 477-64-22; fax (2) 477-64-23; e-mail knoctp@az-vub.ac.be; f. 1965; aims to create a central organization with which all national and regional societies of rhinology may be affiliated, organize intl congresses and courses of instruction, and encourage study, research and scientific advancement in the field of rhinology and related sciences; national and regional society mems in 31 countries; Pres. Prof. IN YONG PARK (Republic of Korea); Sec.-Treas. Prof. P.A.R. CLEMENT (Belgium); publs *Journal of Rhinology*, *American Journal of Rhinology*.

International Society of Audiology/Société Internationale d'Audiologie: c/o Dr J. Verschuure, Dept ENT/Audiology, Erasmus MC, Dr Molewaterplein 40, 3015 GD Rotterdam, Netherlands; tel. (10) 463-92-22; fax (10) 463-42-40; e-mail info@isa-audiology.org; internet www.isa-audiology.org; f. 1952 to advance the study of audiology and protect human hearing; 300 individual mems; Pres. Dr BILL NOBLE (Australia); Sec.-Gen. Dr J. VERSCHUURE; publs *International Journal of Audiology* (12 a year), *Audinews* (4 a year).

International Society of Internal Medicine/Société Internationale de Médecine Interne: c/o Prof. Rolf A. Streuli, SRO Hospital, 4901 Langenthal, Switzerland; tel. 629163102; fax 629164155; e-mail r.streuli@sro.ch; internet www.acponline.org/isim; f. 1948 to encourage research and education in internal medicine; sponsors the International Congress of Internal Medicine every other year; 52 national mem. societies; Pres. Prof. THOMAS KJELLSTRÖM (Sweden); Sec.-Gen. Prof. ROLF A. STREULI.

International Society of Physical and Rehabilitation Medicine (ISPRM): Medicongress, Waalpoel 28–34, 9960 Assenede, Belgium; tel. (9) 344-39-59; fax (9) 344-40-10; e-mail info@isprm.org; internet www.isprm.org; Pres. Prof. LINAMARA BATTISTELLA (Brazil); Exec. Dir WERNER VAN CLEEMPUTTE.

International Union Against Cancer/Union Internationale contre le Cancer: 62 route de Frontenex, 1207 Geneva, Switzerland; tel. 228091811; fax 228091810; e-mail info@uicc.org; internet www.uicc.org; f. 1933; non-governmental org. devoted to promoting on an intl level the campaign against cancer in its research, therapeutic and preventive aspects; mems: 276 organizations in 85 countries; Pres. Dr JOHN SEFFRIN (USA); Exec. Dir ISABEL MORTARA; publs *International Calendar of Meetings on Cancer* (2 a year), *International Journal of Cancer* (30 a year), *UICC News* (quarterly).

Medical Women's International Association: Wilhelm-Brand-Str. 3, 44141 Dortmund, Germany; tel. (231) 9432771; fax (231) 9432773; e-mail secretariat@mwia.net; internet www.mwia.net; f. 1919 to facilitate contacts between medical women and to encourage their co-operation in matters connected with international health problems; MWIA Congresses and General Assemblies every three years; mems: national associations in 48 countries, with 20,000 mems; Pres. Dr GABRIELLE CASPER (Australia); Sec.-Gen. Dr WALTRAUD DIEKHAUS (Germany); publs *MWIA Update* (3 a year), *Congress Report* (every 3 years).

World Allergy Organization (WAO): 555 East Wells St, 11th Fl., Milwaukee, WI 53202-3823, USA; tel. (414) 276-1791; fax (414) 276-3349; e-mail info@worldallergy.org; internet www.worldallergy.org; f. 1951 to advance work in the educational, research and practical medical aspects of allergy diseases; 38,000 mems from 58 nat. and regional socs; Pres. Prof. CARLOS E. BAENA-CAGNANI (Argentina); Sec.-Gen. Prof. G. WALTER CANONICA (Italy); publ. *Allergy & Clinical Immunology International* (every 2 months).

World Federation for Medical Education: Faculty of Health Sciences, Københavns Universitet, Panum Institute, Blegdamsvej 3, 2200 Copenhagen N, Denmark; tel. 35-32-71-03; fax 35-32-70-70; e-mail wfme@wfme.org; internet www.sund.ku.dk/wfme; f. 1972 to promote and integrate the study and implementation of medical education worldwide; engaged on programme for worldwide reorientation of medical training; non-governmental relations with WHO, UNICEF, UNESCO, UNDP and the World Bank; 6 regional asscns on a global level; Chair. Dr HANS KARLE; Exec. Dir ULRIK MEYER.

World Federation of Associations of Pediatric Surgeons: c/o Prof. J. Boix-Ochoa, Clinica Infantil 'Vall d'Hebron', Dpto de Cirugía Pediatrica, Fac. de Medicina, Univ. Autónoma, PO Valle de Hebron, s/n, 08035 Barcelona, Spain; f. 1974; 60 mem. asscns world-wide; Pres. S. CYWES (South Africa); Sec. and Treas. Prof. J. BOIX-OCHOA.

World Federation of Neurology: c/o Dr Raad Shakir, 12 Chandos St, London, W1G 9DR, UK; tel. (20) 7323-4011; fax (20) 7323-4012; e-mail wfnlondon@aol.com; internet www.wfneurology.org; f. 1957; 96 constituent nat. socs of neurology, representing 24,000 mems; Pres. Dr JOHAN AARLI (Norway); Sec.

and Treas.-Gen. Dr RAAD SHAKIR; publs *Journal of the Neurological Sciences*, *World Neurology* (quarterly).

World Heart Federation: 7 rue des Battoirs, 1211 Geneva, Switzerland; tel. 228070320; fax 228070339; e-mail admin@worldheart.org; internet www.worldheart.org; f. 1978; aims to promote the study, prevention and relief of cardiovascular diseases and strokes through scientific and public education programmes, particularly in low- and middle-income countries; organizes the exchange of materials between its affiliated socs and foundations and with related agencies; world congress every 4 years; 194 mems: 158 nat., 8 continental, 6 individual, 22 int. assocs; Pres. Dr SHAHRYAR A. SHEIKH (Pakistan); CEO JANET VOÛTE (Switzerland); publs *Nature, Prevention & Control* (quarterly), *Heartbeat* (e-newsletter).

World Medical Association/Association Médicale Mondiale: 13 chemin du Levant, CIB – Bâtiment A, 01210 Ferney-Voltaire, France; tel. 4-50-40-75-75; fax 4-50-40-59-37; e-mail wma@wma.net; internet www.wma.net; f. 1947 to serve humanity by endeavouring to achieve the highest intl standards in medical education, medical science, medical art and medical ethics, and health care for all people; the unit of membership is the national medical association; has established relations with UNESCO, WHO and other intl bodies; six regions; mems: 68 nat. assocs; Pres. Dr YANK D. COBLE (USA); Sec.-Gen. Dr OTMAR KLOIBER (Germany); publ. *World Medical Journal*.

World Organization of Gastroenterology/Organisation Mondiale de Gastroentérologie (OMGE): c/o Prof. Meinhard Classen, Dept of Internal Medicine, Technical University, Munich, Germany; fax (89) 41404871; f. 1935 to conduct research and contribute to the progress generally of the study of gastroenterology; mem. societies and groups in 68 countries; Pres. Prof. I. A. D. BOUCHIER; Sec.-Gen. Prof. MEINHARD CLASSEN; publ. *Bulletin* (annually).

World Psychiatric Association/Association Mondiale de Psychiatrie/Asociación Mundial de Psiquiatría: Geneva Univ. Psychiatric Hospital, 2 chemin du Petit-Bel-Air, 1225 Geneva, Switzerland; tel. 223055737; fax 223055735; e-mail wpasecretariat@wpanet.org; internet www.wpanet.org; f. 1950 at the 1st World Congress of Psychiatry in Paris; a not-for-profit charity; aims: to encourage the highest possible standards of clinical practice, to enhance the work of the mem. socs irrespective of their size, to fight stigma and advocate the human right to mental health, to support psychiatrists and other mental health professionals, to disseminate knowledge of the effect of mass violence on mental health, to encourage multi-centre research and enhance standards of training, to organize the World Congress every 3 years and Int. Congresses, and to work with the WHO and other governmental agencies to advance public health; 130 mem. socs; Pres. Prof. JUAN MEZZICH (USA); Sec.-Gen. Prof. JOHN COX (UK); publ. *World Psychiatry* (3 a year).

ASSOCIATE MEMBERS OF CIOMS

American College of Chest Physicians: 3300 Dundee Rd, Northbrook, IL 60062-2348, USA; tel. (847) 498-1400; fax (847) 498-5460; e-mail accp@chestnet.org; internet www.chestnet.org; f. 1935; postgraduate medical education; 15,000 mems; Pres. Dr RICHARD S. IRWIN; Exec. Vice-Pres. and CEO ALVIN LEVER; publ. *Chest* (monthly).

International Committee of Military Medicine/Comité International de Médecine Militaire: Hôpital Militaire Reine Astrid, 1120 Brussels, Belgium; tel. (2) 264-43-48; fax (2) 264-43-67; e-mail info@cimm-icmm.org; internet cimm-icmm.org; f. 1921 to promote world co-operation on questions of military medicine and to foster its international and humanitarian character; holds congress every two years; 100 countries are represented on the Committee; Pres. Dr W. WINKENWERDER, Jr (USA); Sec.-Gen. Dr J. SANABRIA (Belgium); publ. *Revue Internationale des Services de Santé des Forces Armées* (in French and English, 4 a year).

International Congress on Tropical Medicine and Malaria/Congrès International de Médecine Tropicale et de Paludisme: c/o Dr E. C. Garcia, Institute of Public Health, University of the Philippines, POB EA-460, Manila, Philippines; Congresses are held quinquennially; Sec.-Gen. Dr E. C. GARCIA.

International Council on Alcohol and Addictions: CP 189, 1001 Lausanne, Switzerland; tel. 213209865; fax 213209817; e-mail secretariat@icaa.ch; internet www.icaa.ch; f. 1907; aims to reduce and prevent the harmful effects of the use of alcohol and other drugs by the study of addiction problems and the development of programmes in this field, the study of concepts and methods of prevention, treatment and rehabilitation, and the dissemination of knowledge in the interests of public health and personal and social well-being; holds Int. Institute annually and Int. Congress every three or four years, symposia, study courses, training courses on substance abuse in developing countries, etc.; mems: 135 organizations, 500 individuals from 85 countries; library: library: special collection of 6,000 vols on drug dependence, 12,000 pamphlets, reprints, etc., 120 periodicals; Pres. Dr PETER VAMOS; Exec. Dir Dr SHARAFUDDIN MALIK; publs *ICAA News* (quarterly), reports, etc.

International Federation of Clinical Chemistry and Laboratory Medicine: Via Carlo Farini 81, 20159 Milan, Italy; tel. 02-66809912; fax 02-60781846; e-mail ifcc@ifcc.org; internet www.ifcc.org; f. 1952; mems: 63 national socs (30,000 individuals); Pres. Prof. MATHIAS M. MÜLLER (Austria); Sec. Dr RENZE BAIS (Australia); publs *Journal* (every 2 months), *Annual Report*.

International Federation of Medical Students' Associations: c/o WMA, BP 63, 01212 Ferney-Voltaire Cedex, France; fax 4-50-40-59-37; e-mail gs@ifmsa.org; internet www.ifmsa.org; f. 1951 to serve medical students worldwide and to promote intl co-operation; organizes professional exchanges in pre-clinical and clinical fields of medicine; holds Gen. Assembly annually; 63 mem. asscns; Pres. ANDREAS RUDKJØBING; Gen. Sec. STEFANIE BÖTTCHER; publ. *Newsletter* (quarterly).

International Society of Blood Transfusion/Société Internationale de Transfusion Sanguine: c/o Jan van Goyenkade 11, 1075 HP Amsterdam, Netherlands; tel. (20) 679-3411; fax (20) 673-7306; e-mail isbt@eurocongres.com; internet www.isbt-web.org; f. 1937; mems: 2,080 in 108 countries; Pres. Dr FRANCINE DÉCARY; Sec.-Gen. Dr PAUL F. W. STRENGERS; publs *Vox Sanguinis*, *Transfusion Today*, *World Directory of Blood Transfusion*.

Rehabilitation International—International Society for Rehabilitation of the Disabled/Société Internationale pour la Réadaptation des Handicapés: 25 E 21st St, New York, NY 10010, USA; tel. (212) 420-1500; fax (212) 505-0871; e-mail ri@riglobal.org; internet www.rehab-international.org; f. 1922; world congress and regional conferences every 4 years; Pres. MICHAEL FOX; Sec.-Gen. TOMAS LAGERWALL; publs *International Rehabilitation Review*, *One in Ten*, www.disabilityworld.org (online journal, in Spanish and English, 6 a year).

OTHER ORGANIZATIONS

African Medical and Research Foundation: Langata Rd, POB 00506-27691, Nairobi, Kenya; tel. (20) 605220; fax (20) 609518; e-mail fundraising@amrefhq.org; internet www.amref.org; f. 1957; independent, non-profit organization working to improve the health of people in Eastern Africa; funds from governmental and non-governmental aid agencies in Africa, Europe and North America, and private donors; official relations with WHO; activities: primary health care, training, teaching aids, health behaviour and education, airborne medicine, flying doctor service, medical radio communication, ground mobile medicine, emergency intervention in famine and other crises, research, consultancies; library of 6,000 vols, 122 periodicals; Chair. Prof. MIRIAM K. WERE (Kenya); Dir-Gen. Dr MICHAEL SMALLEY (Kenya); publs *AMREF News* (quarterly), *AFYA* (quarterly), *Defender* (quarterly), *COBASHECA* (quarterly), *Helper* (quarterly), *HEN* (quarterly).

Asociación Latinoamericana de Análisis y Modificación del Comportamiento (Latin American Association of Analysis and Behavioural Modification): POB 88754, Bogota, Colombia; f. 1974; professional society for psychology in research and teaching on experimental analysis of behaviour; 1,583 mems; Pres. MIGUEL A. ESCOTET; Vice-Pres. CARLOS M. QUIRCE; publs *Alamoc Newsletter* (4 a year), *Learning and Behavior* (2 a year).

Association for Medical Education in Europe: Tay Park House, 484 Perth Rd, Dundee, DD2 1LR, Scotland; tel. (1382) 631953; fax (1382) 631987; e-mail amee@dundee.ac.uk; internet www.amee.org; f. 1972 to promote and integrate the study of medical education in the countries of Europe; mems: asscns for medical education in most European countries, assoc. corporate mems in countries without nat. asscns, and individual mems worldwide; Pres. Prof. MARGARITA BARÓN-MALDONADO (Spain); Gen. Sec. Prof. RONALD M. HARDEN (UK); publ. *Medical Teacher* (8 a year).

European Academy of Anaesthesiology: Waversebaan 319A, 3001 Heverlee, Belgium; tel. and fax (16) 405151; e-mail secretariat@euro-anaesthesiology.org; internet eaa.euro-anaesthesiology.org; f. 1978 to improve the standard of training, practice and research in anaesthesiology in Europe; 441 mems (251 full, 190 assoc.); Pres. THOMAS PASCH (Switzerland); Hon. Sec. KLAUS OLKKOLA (Finland); publ. *European Journal of Anaesthesiology*.

European Federation of Internal Medicine: c/o Dr C. Davidson, Department of Cardiology, Royal Sussex County Hospital, Eastern Rd, Brighton, BN2 5BE, UK; tel. (1273) 696955; fax (1273) 684554; e-mail chris.davidson@bsuh.nhs.uk; internet www.efim.org; f. 1996; 27 nat. mem. socs; Pres. Prof. J. MERINO (Spain); Sec.-Gen. Dr C. DAVIDSON (UK); publ. *European Journal of Internal Medicine* (4 a year).

European Society of Cardiology: c/o The European Heart House, 2035 Route des Colles, Les Templiers, BP 179, 06903 Sophia Antipolis France; tel. 4-92-94-76-00; fax 4-92-94-76-01; e-mail webmaster@escardio.org; internet www.escardio.org; f. 1950; aims to bring together societies of cardiology in all

European countries, and to provide a forum for working groups on subjects of common interest; 52,000 mems; Pres. Prof. K. FOX (UK); CEO A. J. HOWARD (France); publs *Cardiovascular Research* (14 a year), *The European Heart Journal* (24 a year), *European Journal of Cardiovascular Prevention and Rehabilitation* (6 a year), *European Journal of Heart Failure* (monthly), *Europace* (monthly).

International Association for Humanitarian Medicine (IAHM): 3 chemin du Milieu, 1279 Bogis-Bossey, Switzerland; tel. 227762161; fax 227766417; e-mail swagunn@bluewin.ch; internet www.iahm.org; f. 1984; aims to promote and deliver health care on the principles of humanitarian medicine through the provision of equitable medical, surgical, nursing and rehabilitation care to patients in or from developing countries; brings relief to disaster victims where health aid is lacking; mobilizes hospitals and health specialists in developed countries to receive and treat such patients free of charge; and advocates humanitarian principles in the practice of medicine, on the principle of health as a human right; limited to 100 on invitation; Pres. Prof. S. WILLIAM A. GUNN (Switzerland); Sec. Prof. LEO KLEIN (Czech Republic); publ. *Journal of Humanitarian Medicine* (quarterly).

Inclusion International: c/o The Rix Centre, University of East London, Docklands Campus, 4–6 University Way, London E16 2RD, UK; tel. (20) 8223-7709; fax (20) 8223-7411; e-mail info@inclusion-international.org; internet www.inclusion-international.org; f. 1960 to promote the interests of the mentally handicapped without regard to nationality, race, religion, age, or degree of handicap; furthers co-operation between national bodies, organizes congresses and symposia; consultative status with UNESCO, UNICEF, WHO, ILO, ECOSOC and the Council of Europe; official relations with IIN, the Comm. of the European Communities and various other orgs; mems: 173 socs in 109 countries; Pres. DIANE RICHLER; Sec.-Gen. THÉRÈSE KEMPENEERS-FOULON; publ. *Proceedings*.

International Academy of Cytology/Academie Internationale de Cytologie/Internationale Akademie für Zytologie/Academia Internacional de Citología: c/o Dr Volker Schneider, Burgunderstr. 1, 79104 Freiburg, Germany; fax (761) 2923802; e-mail centraloffice@cytology-iac.org; internet www.cytology-iac.org; organizes congresses, International Board of Cytopathology examinations; Pres. Dr MATÍAS JIMÉNEZ-AYALA (Spain); Sec.-Gen. Dr VOLKER SCHNEIDER (Germany); publs *Cytopaths* (newsletter, 6 a year), *Acta Cytologica – Journal of Clinical Cytology and Cytopathology* (online).

International Agency for Research on Cancer/Centre International de Recherche sur le Cancer: 150 cours Albert-Thomas, 69372 Lyon Cedex 08, France; tel. 4-72-73-84-85; fax 4-72-73-85-75; f. 1965 as an Agency of the World Health Organization; to promote international collaboration in cancer research; 16 mem. countries; library of 8,200 vols, 211 journals; Dir Dr PETER BOYLE; publ. *Report* (every 2 years).

International Agency for the Prevention of Blindness/Organisation mondiale contre la cécité: L. V. Prasad Eye Institute, L. V. Prasad Marg, Banjara Hills, Hyderabad 500034, India; tel. (40) 23545389; fax (40) 23548271; e-mail iapb@lvpei.org; internet www.iapb.org; f. 1975; umbrella org. in official relationship with WHO; promotes the formation of national cttees and programmes on prevention of blindness and the sharing of information; Chair. and Pres. Dr GULLAPALLI N. RAO (India); Sec.-Gen. Dr LOUIS PIZZARELLO (USA); publ. *IAPB News* (every 6 months).

International Association for Child and Adolescent Psychiatry and Allied Professions/Association Internationale de Psychiatrie de l'Enfant et de l'Adolescent et de Professions Associées: Dept of Child and Adolescent Psychiatry, Developmental Psychiatry Section, University of Cambridge, Douglas House, 18B Trumpington Rd, Cambridge, CB2 2AH, UK; tel. (1223) 336098; fax (1223) 746122; e-mail ig104@cus.cam.ac.uk; internet www.iacapap.org; f. 1948 to promote the study, treatment, care and prevention of mental disorders and deficiencies of children, adolescents and their families by promoting research and practice through collaboration with allied professions; mems: nat. asscns and individual mems in 39 countries; Pres. Dr HELMUT REMSCHMIDT (Germany); Sec.-Gen. Dr IAN M. GOODYER (UK); publs *Yearbooks*, *Newsletter* (annually).

International Association for Radiation Research: c/o Dr Fiona Stewart, Netherlands Cancer Institute, Division of Experimental Therapy, Plesmanlaan 121, 1066 CX Amsterdam, The Netherlands; e-mail fas@nki.nl; f. 1962 to advance radiation research in the fields of physics, chemistry, biology and medicine; 3,246 mems; quadrennial congress; Pres. Prof. ERIC J. HALL (USA); Sec.-Gen. and Treasurer Dr FIONA STEWART (Netherlands); publ. *Proceedings of International Congresses*.

International Association of Agricultural Medicine and Rural Health/Association Internationale de Médecine Agricole et de Santé Rurale: OALI (NIPCH), 33–35 Szabolcs utca, Budapest 1135, Hungary; tel. (1) 450-1768; fax (1) 439-0473; e-mail iaamrhsecr@oali.hu; internet www.iaamrh.org; f. 1961 to study the problems of medicine in agriculture globally and to prevent diseases caused by agricultural production; 500 mems; Pres. Dr ASHOK PATIL (India); Sec.-Gen. Dr ISTVAN SZILARD (acting) (Hungary); publ. *Journal of International Agricultural Medicine and Rural Health* (4 a year).

International Association of Applied Psychology/Association Internationale de Psychologie Appliquée: c/o José M. Prieto, Colegio Oficial de Psicólogos, Cuesta de San Vicente 4, 5°, 28008. Madrid, Spain; tel. 91-3943236; fax 91-3510091; e-mail iaap@psi.ucm.es; internet www.iaapsy.org; f. 1920, present title adopted 1955; aims: to establish contacts between those carrying out scientific work on applied psychology, to promote research and the adoption of measures contributing to this work; mems: 2,000 in 80 countries; Pres. MICHAEL FRESE (Germany); Sec.-Gen. JOSÉ M. PRIETO (Spain); publ. *Applied Psychology: An International Review* (quarterly).

International Association of Asthmology/Association Internationale d'Asthmologie (INTERASMA): c/o Prof. F. B. Michel, Hôpital Aiguelongue, Ave du Major Flandre, 34059 Montpellier Cedex, France; tel. 67-54-54-47; fax 67-52-18-48; f. 1954 to advance medical knowledge of bronchial asthma and allied disorders; *c.* 1,000 mems in 52 countries; Pres. Prof. A. G. PALMA-CARLOS (Portugal); Sec. Dr G. SCHULTZE-WERNINGHAUS (Germany); publ. *News Bulletin* (every 4 months).

International Association of Environmental Mutagen Societies: c/o Lynnette R. Ferguson, Discipline of Nutrition and Auckland Cancer Society Research Centre, University of Auckland, Private Bag 92019, Auckland, New Zealand; tel. (9) 373-7599 ext. 6372; fax (9) 373-7502; e-mail l.ferguson@auckland.ac.nz; internet www.iaems.org.nz; f. 1973 for the stimulation of scientific activity and exchange of information by means of World Conference every 4 years; six mem. socs. (3,000 individuals); Pres. JIM GENTILE (USA); Sec.-Gen. LYNNETTE R. FERGUSON (New Zealand).

International Association of Gerontology (IAG): c/o Dr Gloria Gutman, Gerontology Research Centre, Simon Fraser University, 2800-515 W. Hastings St, Vancouver, BC V6B 5K3, Canada; tel. (604) 268-7972; fax (604) 291-5066; e-mail iag@sfu.ca; internet www.sfu.ca/iag; f. 1950 to promote research and training in gerontology; 40,000 mems in 66 nat. mem. socs in 63 countries; Pres. Dr GLORIA GUTMAN (Canada); Sec.-Gen. Dr JOHN GRAY (Canada); publ. *IAG Newsletter* (2 a year).

International Association of Hydatidology/Asociación Internacional de Hidatidología: Florida 460, 3° piso, 1005 Buenos Aires, Argentina; tel. (11) 4322-3431 ext. 166; fax (11) 4325-8231; f. 1941; 650 mems in 40 countries; library: specialized library; Pres. Dr MIGUEL PÉREZ GALLARDO (Spain); Sec.-Gen. Prof. Dr RAÚL MARTÍN MENDY (Argentina); publs *Archivos Internacionales de la Hidatidosis* (every 4 years), *Boletín de Hidatidosis* (quarterly).

International Association of Oral and Maxillofacial Surgeons: 17 West 220 22nd St, Suite 420, Oakbrook Terrace, IL 60181, USA; tel. (630) 833-0945; fax (630) 833-1382; internet www.iaoms.org; f. 1962 to elevate the quality of health care world-wide through the advancement of the art and science of oral and maxillofacial surgery; int. conference every 2 years; promotes collaborative research; educational programmes in developing countries; 3,710 mems; Pres. Dr JOSÉ LUIS FERRERÍA (Argentina); Exec. Dir Dr JOHN F. HELFRICK (USA); publs *International Journal of Oral and Maxillofacial Surgery* (monthly), *Newsletter* (quarterly).

International Brain Research Organization (IBRO): 255 rue Saint Honoré, 75001 Paris, France; tel. 1-46-47-92-92; fax 1-47-46-42-50; e-mail ibro@wanadoo.fr; internet www.ibro.org; f. 1960 to assist all branches of neuroscience; federated to ICSU; 52,000 mems; Pres. Dr A. J. AGUAYO (Canada); Sec.-Gen. JENNIFER LUND (USA); publs *Neuroscience* (28 a year), *IBRO News* (annually), *IBRO Reporter* (online, monthly).

International Cell Research Organisation/Organisation Internationale de Recherche sur la Cellule: c/o UNESCO, SC/BES/LSC, 1 rue Miollis, 75015 Paris, France; fax 1-45-68-58-18; fax 1-45-68-58-16; e-mail icro@unesco.org; internet www.unesco.org/icro; f. 1962 to create, encourage and promote co-operation between scientists of different disciplines worldwide for the advancement of fundamental knowledge of the cell; organizes international training courses and exchange of scientists, etc.; 400 mems; Chair. Prof. Q. S. LIN (China); Exec. Sec. Prof. G. N. COHEN (France).

International Center of Information on Antibiotics: c/o Prof. M. Welsch, Inst. de Pathologie, Université de Liège, Sart-Tilman, 4000 Liège, Belgium; f. 1961 to gather information on antibiotics and strains producing them; to establish contact with discoverers of antibiotics with a view to obtaining samples and filing information; Dir Prof. M. WELSCH; Senior Scientist in Charge Dr L. DELCAMBE.

International Commission on Occupational Health/Commission Internationale de la Santé au Travail: c/o ISPESL, National Institute for Occupational Safety and Prevention, Via Fontana Candida 1, 00040 Monteporzio Catone (Rome), Italy; tel. 06-94181407; fax 06-94181556; e-mail icohsg@iol.it; internet www.icoh.org.sg; f. 1906 to study new findings in the field of occupational health, to publicize the results of study and investigation in occupational health, and to organize meetings on nat. or intl problems in this field; 2,000 mems in 93 countries; recognised by the UN; official languages: English, French; Pres. Prof. JORMA RANTANEN (Finland); Sec.-Gen. Dr SERGIO IAVICOLI (Italy); publ. *ICOH Newsletter* (quarterly).

International Cystic Fibrosis Association: Avda Campanar 106 (6a), 46015 Valencia, Spain; tel. (96) 346-14-14; fax (96) 349-40-47; e-mail fq@vlc.servicom.es; f. 1964; promotes greater understanding of cystic fibrosis among both lay and medical organizations, in regions of the world where understanding of cystic fibrosis is limited; organizes meetings and symposia; mems: 60 nat. orgs; Pres. IAN A. THOMPSON; Sec. AISHA RAMOS.

International Epidemiological Association/Association Internationale d'Epidémiologie: C/o Prof. Ahmed Mandil, IEA Secretary, 38 Ismailiah St, Apt 201, Mostafa Kamel, Alexandria, Egypt; tel. (3) 5467576; fax (3) 5467576; e-mail ieasecretariat@link.net; internet www.ieaweb.org; f. 1954; int. meetings are held every 3 years in different parts of the world and regional meetings are held regularly throughout the world; 1,500 mems in 100 countries; Pres. Dr JORN OLSEN; Sec. Prof. AHMED MANDIL; publ. *International Journal of Epidemiology* (6 a year).

International Federation for Medical and Biological Engineering/Fédération Internationale du Génie Médical et Biologique: c/o Prof. Ratko Magjarevic, Faculty of Electrical Engineering and Computing, University of Zagreb, Unska 3, 10000 Zagreb, Croatia; tel. (1) 6129-938; fax (1) 6129-652; e-mail office@ifmbe.org; internet www.ifmbe.org; f. 1959 to promote international co-operation and communication among societies interested in life and engineering sciences; mem. orgs in 47 countries and two transnational orgs; Pres. Prof. JOACHIM NAGEL (Germany); Sec.-Gen. Prof. RATKO MAGJAREVIC (Croatia); publs *Medical and Biological Engineering and Computing* (every 2 months), *Proceedings of International Conference on Medical and Biological Engineering* (several times a year).

International Federation of Anatomists/Fédération Internationale des Associations d'Anatomistes: Dept of Anatomy, Medical College of Ohio, POB 10008, Toledo, OH 43699-0008, USA; tel. (419) 381-4111; f. 1903; mems: 52 national and multinational associations; Pres. Prof. Dr LIBERATO J. A. DIDIO (USA); publs *Directory*, *Newsletter*, Proceedings of each Federative International Congress of Anatomy (every 4 or 5 years).

International Federation of Gynaecology and Obstetrics/Fédération Internationale de Gynécologie et d'Obstétrique: FIGO House, Suite 3, Waterloo Court, 10 Theed St London, SE15 6DX, UK; tel. (20) 7928-1166; fax (20) 7928-7099; e-mail figo@figo.org; internet www.figo.org; f. 1954; assists and contributes to research in gynaecology and obstetrics; aims to facilitate the exchange of information and perfect methods of teaching; organizes international congresses; 110 nat. socs; Pres. Dr A. ACOSTA (Paraguay); Sec.-Gen. Prof. S. ARULKUMARAN (UK); publ. *International Journal of Gynecology and Obstetrics* (monthly).

Multiple Sclerosis International Federation: Skyline House, 3rd Fl., 200 Union St, London, SE1 0LX, UK; tel. (20) 7620-1911; fax (20) 7620-1922; e-mail info@msif.org; internet www.msif.org; f. 1967 to co-ordinate and advance the work of nat. multiple sclerosis orgs world-wide, to encourage scientific research in this and related neurological diseases, to collect and disseminate information and to advise and help in advancing the devt of voluntary nat. multiple sclerosis orgs; Pres. SARAH PHILLIPS (UK); Sec. WEYMAN T. JOHNSON (USA); publs *MSIF Annual Review*, *MS in Focus*.

International Federation of Ophthalmological Societies/Fédération Internationale des Sociétés d'Ophtalmologie: c/o Dr Bruce E. Spivey, International Council of Ophthalmology, 945 Green St, San Francisco, CA 94133, USA; fax (415) 409-8403; e-mail info@icoph.org; f. 1857; 75 affiliated national societies; Sec.-Gen. Dr BRUCE E. SPIVEY.

International Federation of Physical Education/Fédération Internationale d'Education Physique: CP 837, 85857-970 Foz do Iguacu, Paraná, Brazil; tel. (45) 525-1272; fax (45) 525-1272; e-mail fiep.brasil@foznet.com.br; internet www.fiepbrasil.org; f. 1923; aims to develop national and international physical education and sport-for-all; organizes congresses and courses; mems in 116 countries; Pres. Prof. Dr MANOEL GOMES TUBINO (Brazil); Gen. Sec. Prof. ALMIR ADOLFO GRUHN (Brazil); publ. *FIEP Bulletin* (in English, French and Spanish; Portuguese edition from Brazil).

International Hospital Federation/Fédération Internationale des Hôpitaux: Immeuble JB Say, 13 chemin du Levant, 01210 Ferney Voltaire, France; tel. 4-50-42-60-00; fax 4-50-42-60-01; e-mail info@ihf-fih.org; internet www.ihf-fih.org; f. 1947; an ind. org. supported by subscribing mems in 100 countries; aims to promote improvements in the planning and management of hospitals and health services through int. conferences, field study courses, training courses, information services, publs and research projects; mems: nat. hospital and health service orgs, governmental and non-governmental, individuals from disciplines and occupations concerned with health services, and professional, commercial and industrial firms working in the health service field; Pres. GÉRARD VINCENT (France); Dir-Gen. Prof. PER-GUNNAR SVENSSON (Sweden); publs *International Hospital Federation Reference Book* (annual), *World Hospitals and Health Services* (quarterly).

International Institute on Ageing: 117 St Paul's St, Valletta, VLT 07, Malta; tel. 21243044; fax 21230248; e-mail info@inia.org.mt; internet www.inia.org.mt; f. 1988 by the UN and Government of Malta; training in gerontology and geriatrics, social gerontology, income security, and physiotherapy; research and data collection, technical co-operation (advisory services, project design, planning and implementation of training programmes); library of 800 vols; Dir Prof. FREDERICK F. FENECH; publ. *BOLD* (4 a year).

International League Against Epilepsy/Ligue Internationale contre l'Epilepsie: 204 ave Marcel Thiry, 1200 Brussels, Belgium; tel. (2) 774-9547; fax (2) 774-9690; internet www.ilae.org; f. 1909 to collect and disseminate information concerning epilepsy, to promote treatment of epileptic patients and to foster co-operation with other int. institutions in similar fields; offices in USA; holds scientific congress every 2 years in conjunction with Int. Bureau for Epilepsy; regional congresses every 2 years; nat. congresses annually be each nat. chapter; 15,000 mems, nat. chapters in 98 countries; Pres. PETER WOLF; Admin. Dir PETER J. BERRY; publs *Epilepsia* (every 2 months), *Epigraph* (newsletter, 2 a year).

International Organization Against Trachoma/Organisation Internationale contre le Trachome: c/o Prof. Georges Cornand, La Bergère, Route de Grenoble, 05140 Aspres-sur-Buëch, France; f. 1923 for the research and study of trachomatous conjunctivitis and ophthalmological tropical and sub-tropical diseases; Pres. Prof. GABRIEL COSCAS (France); Sec.-Gen. Prof. GEORGES CORNAND; publ. *Revue Internationale du Trachome* (4 a year).

International Psychoanalytical Association: 'Broomhills', Woodside Lane, London, N12 8UD, UK; tel. (20) 8446-8324; fax (20) 8445-4729; e-mail ipa@ipa.org.uk; internet www.ipa.org.uk; f. 1908 to hold meetings to define and promulgate the theory and teaching of psychoanalysis, to act as a forum for scientific discussions, to control and regulate training and to contribute to the interdisciplinary area which is common to the behavioural sciences; 9,500 mems; Pres. DANIEL WIDLÖCHER; Sec. DONALD CAMPBELL; publ. *IPA Bulletin*.

International Radiation Protection Association: c/o CEPN, Route du Panorama, BP 48, 92263 Fontenay-aux-Roses Cedex, France; tel. 1-46-54-76-43; fax 1-40-85-90-34; e-mail irpa.exof@irpa.net; internet www.irpa.net; f. 1966 to promote intl contacts and co-operation among those engaged in health physics and radiation protection; to provide for discussion of the scientific and practical aspects of the protection of mankind and his environment from the hazards caused by ionizing and non-ionizing radiation, facilitating the exploitation of radiation and nuclear energy for the benefit of mankind; 37 mem. socs, 16,000 individual mems; Scientific Associate of ICSU, official relations with WHO, ILO, IAEA, ICRP; Pres. PHILIP E. METCALF (South Africa); Exec. Officer JACQUES LOCHARD (France); publ. *IRPA Bulletin* (irregular).

International Scientific Council for Trypanosomiasis Research and Control/Conseil Scientifique International pour la Recherche et la Lutte contre les Trypanosomoses: Secretariat OAU/STRC, Ports Authority Bldg, 26/28 Marina, PMB 2359, Lagos, Nigeria; tel. 2633430; fax 2636093; e-mail oaustrc.lagos@rcl.dircon.co.uk; f. 1949 to review the work on tsetse and trypanosomiasis problems carried out by relevant organizations and workers in laboratories and in the field; to encourage further research and discussion and to promote co-ordination between research workers and organizations in African countries; to provide opportunity for the discussion of related problems and their resolution; Exec. Sec. Prof. JOHNSON A. EKPERE.

International Society for Vascular Specialists: 900 Cummings Center, 221-U, Beverly, MA 01915, USA; tel. (978) 927-8330; fax (978) 524-8890; e-mail iscvs@prri.com; internet www.iscvs.vascularweb.org; f. 1950; present name 2003 (comprising members in North and South America, Africa, the Middle East and Australasia); members in Europe and Asia belong to affiliated International Society for Cardiovascular Surgery; promotes the investigation and study of the art, science and therapy of cardiovascular diseases; facilitates the exchange of ideas in the field of vascular diseases through scientific meetings and personal contact between vascular specialists; 2,000 mems; Pres. JAMES MAY; publs *Cardiovascular Surgery* (6 a year), *Annals of Vascular Surgery* (6 a year), *Journal of Vascular Surgery* (monthly).

International Society for Clinical Electrophysiology of Vision: c/o Daphne L. McCulloch, ISCEV Secretary-General, Dept of Vision Sciences, Glasgow Caledonian University, Glasgow, G4 0BA, UK; tel. (141) 331-3379; e-mail dlmc@gcal.ac.uk; internet www.iscev.org; f. 1958; 400 mems; Pres. Prof. MICHAEL BACH (Germany); Sec.-Gen. Prof. DAPHNE MCCULLOCH; publ. *Documenta Ophthalmologica* (6 a year).

International Society of Art and Psychopathology and Art Therapy/Société Internationale de Psychopathologie de l'Expression et d'Art-Thérapie: c/o Dr Roux, 27 rue Maréchal Joffre, 64000 Pau, France; tel. and fax 5-59-27-69-74; e-mail sipearther@aol.com; internet online-art-therapy.com; f. 1959 to bring together the various specialists interested in the problems of expression and artistic activities in connection with psychiatric, sociological and psychological research, as well as in the use of methods applied in fields other than that of mental illness; 825 mems; Pres. Dr GUY ROUX (France); Sec.-Gen. JEAN-LUC SUDRES (France); publ. SIPE-Newsletter (quarterly).

International Society of Criminology/Société Internationale de Criminologie: 12 rue Charles Fourier, 75013 Paris, France; tel. (1) 45-88-00-23; fax (1) 45-88-96-40; e-mail crim.sic@wanadoo.fr; internet perso.wanadoo.fr/societe.internationale.de.criminologie; f. 1938 to promote the development of the sciences in their application to crime; library; 800 mems; Pres. LAWRENCE W. SHERMAN (USA); Sec.-Gen. GEORGES PICCA (France); publ. *Annales Internationales de Criminologie*.

International Society of Haematology/Société Internationale d'Hématologie: c/o Dr Emin Kansu, Institute of Oncology, Faculty of Medicine, Haceteppe University, Hacettepe, 06100 Ankara, Turkey; tel. (312) 305-28-66; fax (312) 324-20-09; e-mail ekansu@ada.net.tr; internet www.ish-world.org; f. 1946 to promote and foster the exchange and diffusion of information and ideas relating to blood and blood-forming tissues worldwide; to provide a forum for discussion of haematologic problems on an international scale and to encourage scientific investigation of these problems; to promote the advancement of haematology and its recognition as a branch of the biological sciences; to attempt to standardize on an international scale haematological methods and nomenclature; to promote a better understanding of the scientific basic principles of haematology among practitioners of haematology and physicians in general and to foster better understanding and a greater interest in clinical haematological problems among scientific investigators in the field of haematology; Vice-Pres. (European and African Division) GAYLE KENOYER (South Africa), FAYZA HAMMOUDA (Egypt); Sec.-Gen. and Treas. (European and African Division), EMIN KANSU (Turkey).

International Society of Hypnosis: c/o Dr Eric Vermetten, Department of Military Psychiatry, Central Military Hospital, University Medical Center Utrecht, Heidelberglaan 100, 3584 CX Utrecht, Netherlands; tel. (30) 2502589; fax (30) 2502586; e-mail admin@ish-web.org; internet ish.driebit.com; f. 1958 as an affiliate of the World Federation of Mental Health; to encourage and improve professional research, co-operative relations among scientific disciplines with regard to the study and application of hypnosis; to bring together persons using hypnosis and set up standards for professional training and adequacy; Pres. Dr KAREN OLNESS (USA); Sec. and Treas. Dr ERIC VERMETTEN (Australia); publ. *Newsletter* (2 a year).

International Society of Lymphology: Dept of Surgery, Rm 4406, 1501 North Campbell Ave, POB 245063, Tucson, AZ 85724-5063, USA; tel. (520) 626-6118; fax (520) 626-0822; e-mail lymph@u.arizona.edu; internet www.u.arizona.edu/~witte/ISL.htm; f. 1966 to advance progress in lymphology and arelated subjects; organizes intl working groups, co-operates with other nat. and intl organizations; intl congresses and postgraduate courses; 400 mems; Pres. M. OHKUMA (Japan); Sec.-Gen. MARLYS WITTE (USA); publs *Lymphology* (4 a year), *Progress in Lymphology* (every 2 years).

International Society of Neuropathology: c/o Dr Seth Love, Dept of Neuropathology, Institute of Clinical Sciences, Frenchay Hospital, Bristol, BS16 1LE, UK; fax (117) 975-3765; e-mail seth.love@bris.ac.uk; internet www.intsocneuropathol.com; f. 1972 to initiate and maintain permanent co-operation between nat. and regional socs of neuropathology, to foster links with other int. orgs in the same field, to initiate int. congresses, symposia, etc.; 2,500 mems; Pres. Dr BERNARDINO GHETTI (USA); Sec.-Gen. Dr SETH LOVE (UK); publ. *Brain Pathology* (quarterly).

International Society of Radiology/Société Internationale de Radiologie: 7910 Woodmont Ave, Suite 400, Bethesda, MD 20814, USA; tel. (301) 657-2652; fax (301) 907-8768; internet www.isradiology.org; f. 1953 to develop and advance medical radiology by giving radiologists in different countries an opportunity of personally submitting their experiences, exchanging and discussing their ideas, and forming personal bonds with their colleagues; 3 permanent Int. Commissions: (*a*) on Radiological Protection (ICRP), (*b*) on Radiation Units and Measurements (ICRU), (*c*) on Radiological Education (ICRE); these Commissions meet during each Congress, held every 2 years or when necessary; Pres. CLAUDE MANELFE (France); Exec. Dir OTHA W. LINTON (USA).

International Society of Surgery (ISS)/Société Internationale de Chirurgie (SIC): Netzibodenstr. 34, POB 1527, 4133 Pratteln, Switzerland; tel. 618159666; fax 618114775; e-mail surgery@iss-sic.ch; internet www.iss-sic.ch; f. 1902; organizes congresses; 3,500 mems; Sec.-Gen. Prof. Dr FELIX HARDER; publ. *World Journal of Surgery* (monthly).

International Union against Sexually Transmitted Infections: c/o Dr Raj Patel, Royal South Hants Hospital, Brintons Terrace, Southampton, SO14 0YG, UK; tel. (23) 8082-5152; fax (23) 8082-5122; internet www.iusti.org; f. 1923; administrative and educational activities, public health, and technical aspects of sexually transmitted diseases, esp. HIV/AIDS; 800 individual, 50 nat. and soc. mems; consultative status with WHO; Pres. Dr FRANK JUDSON (USA); Sec.-Gen. Dr RAJ PATEL (UK).

International Union against Tuberculosis and Lung Disease/Union Internationale contre la Tuberculose et les Maladies Respiratoires: 68 blvd Saint-Michel, 75006 Paris, France; tel. (1) 44-32-03-60; fax (1) 43-29-90-87; e-mail union@iuatld.org; internet www.iuatld.org; f. 1920 to co-ordinate the efforts of anti-tuberculosis associations, to promote programmes and research in tuberculosis control, chest diseases and community health, to co-operate in these respects with the World Health Organization, to promote intl and regional conferences on the above subjects, to collect and disseminate relevant information, to assist in developing national programmes in co-operation with national associations; mems: associations in 165 countries; 3,000 individual mems; Pres. Prof. ASMA EL SONY (Sudan); Exec. Dir Dr NILS E. BILLO (Switzerland); Sec.-Gen. Dr MOHAMMAD REZA MASJEDI (Iran); publs *International Journal of Tuberculosis and Lung Disease* (monthly, in English), *Newsletter* (in English, French and Spanish).

International Union for Health Promotion and Education/Union Internationale de Promotion de la Santé et d'Education pour la Santé: 42 blvd de la Libération, 93203 St Denis Cedex, France; tel. (1) 48-13-71-20; fax (1) 48-09-17-67; e-mail mclamarre@iuhpe.org; internet www.iuhpe.org; f. 1951; mems: organizations in 21 countries; groups and individuals in 90 countries; Pres. MAURICE MITTELMARK (Norway); Exec. Dir MARIE-CLAUDE LAMARRE (France); publ. *Promotion & Education/International Journal of Health Promotion and Education* (4 a year, in a trilingual edition in English, French and Spanish; special supplement issues throughout the year).

International Vaccine Institute: Kwanak, POB 14, Seoul 151-600, Republic of Korea; tel. (2) 872-2801; fax (2) 872-2803; e-mail iviinfo@ivi.int; internet www.ivi.org; f. 1997; established by the UN Development Programme (UNDP) as an international centre of research, training and technical assistance for vaccination in the developing world; Chair. Prof. SAMUEL L. KATZ (USA); Dir Dr JOHN D. CLEMENS (Republic of Korea); publ. *Newsletter*.

Organisation Ouest Africaine de la Santé (OOAS)/West African Health Organisation (WAHO): 01 BP 153, Bobo-Dioulasso 01, Burkina Faso; tel. 97-57-75; fax 97-57-72; e-mail wahooas@fasonet.bf; f. 1960 to combat endemic and transmitted diseases and malnutrition; conducts research and trains medical workers; mem. states: Benin, Burkina Faso, Côte d'Ivoire, Ghana, Liberia, Mali, Niger, Nigeria, Senegal, Sierra Leone, The Gambia, Togo; library of 2,367 vols, 3 current periodicals, 11,010 technical documents; Dir-Gen. Dr T. JOINER KABBA; publ. *Bulletin bibliographique mensuel*.

Pan-American Medical Association (PAMA): 263 West End Ave, New York, NY 10023, USA; f. 1925 to interchange medical knowledge and research among countries of the western hemisphere; to strengthen, through the medical profession, bonds of friendship among peoples of the western hemisphere; to hold Inter-American congresses; to send seminars to various American countries; to grant postgraduate scholarships to doctors of western hemisphere nations; mems: 6,000 in 38 countries; Pres. WILLIAM E. SORREL.

Société Internationale de Chirurgie Orthopédique et de Traumatologie/International Society of Orthopaedic Surgery and Traumatology: 40 rue Washington, bte 9, 1050 Brussels, Belgium; tel. (2) 648-68-23; fax (2) 649-86-01; e-mail hq@sicot.org; internet www.sicot.org; f. 1929 to advance the science and art of orthopaedics and traumatology at an int. level for the enhancement of patient care, to foster and develop teaching, research and education, to facilitate and encourage the interchange of professional experience, and to promote good fellowship among its members; conference held every year except year of congress, which is held every 3 years; 113 mem. countries, 3,000 individual mems; Pres. CHADWICK SMITH (USA); Sec.-Gen. MAURICE HINSENKAMP (Belgium); publ. *International Orthopaedics* (6 a year).

Société de Neurochirurgie de Langue Française (Society of French-Speaking Neurosurgeons): Cliniques Universitaires Saint-Luc, Service de neurochirurgie, Ave Hippocrate, 1200 Brussels, Belgium; tel. (2) 764-10-85; fax (2) 764-89-61; e-mail neurosurgery.adm@clin.ucl.ac.be; internet www.snclf.com; f. 1948; 700 mems; Pres. J. CHAZAL; Sec. C. RAFTOPOULOS; publ. *Neurochirurgie* (every 2 months).

World Association of Societies of Anatomic and Clinical Pathology/Association Mondiale des Sociétés de Pathologie Anatomique et Clinique: c/o Mikio Mori, Dept of Clinical Pathology, Koshigaya Hospital, Dokkyo University School of Medicine, 2-1-50 Minamikoshigaya, Koshigaya, Saitama 343, Japan; f. 1947 (formerly International Society of Clinical Pathology) to improve health worldwide by promoting the teaching and practice of all aspects of pathology and laboratory medicine; mems: 50 national associations; Pres. WILLIAM B. ZEILER (USA); Sec.-Gen. MIKIO MORI; publ. *Newsletter* (2 a year).

World Association of Veterinary Microbiologists, Immunologists and Specialists in Infectious Diseases/Association Mondiale des Vétérinaires Microbiologistes, Immunologistes et Spécialistes des Maladies Infectieuses: Ecole Nationale Vétérinaire d'Alfort, 7 ave du Général de Gaulle, 94704 Maisons-Alfort Cedex, France; tel. 1-43-96-70-21; fax 1-43-96-70-22; f. 1967 to facilitate international contacts in the field of veterinary microbiologists, immunologists and specialists in infectious diseases; Pres. Prof. CH. PILET (France).

World Confederation for Physical Therapy: Kensington Charity Centre, 4th Fl., Charles House, 375 Kensington High St, London, W14 8QH, UK; tel. (20) 7471-6765; fax (20) 7471-6766; e-mail info@wcpt.org; internet www.wcpt.org; f. 1951 to encourage improved standards of physical therapy in education and practice; to promote exchange of information between mem. orgs; to assist the development of informed public opinion regarding physical therapy; to co-operate with appropriate agencies of UN and national and intl organizations; 92 mem. organisations; Pres. SANDRA MERCER MOORE; Sec.-Gen. BRENDA MYERS (UK); publ. *WCPT News* (quarterly).

World Council of Optometry: 8360 Old York Rd, 4th Fl. West, Elkins Park, PA 19027-1598, USA; tel. (215) 780-1320; fax (215) 780-1325; e-mail wco@pco.edu; internet www.worldoptometry.org; f. 1927; aims to co-ordinate efforts to provide a high standard of ophthalmic optical (optometric) care worldwide; provides a forum for the exchange of ideas between different countries; a large part of its work is concerned with optometric education, and advice upon standards of qualification; involved in getting legislation passed in relation to optometry worldwide; 85 mem. orgs in 52 countries; Pres. Prof. D. D. D. SHENI (South Africa); Exec. Dir ANTHONY F. DI STEFANO; publ. *World Optometry*.

World Federation of Neurosurgical Societies/Fédération Mondiale des Sociétés de Neurochirurgie: c/o Janette A. Joseph, 5 rue du Marché, 1260 Nyon, Vaud, Switzerland; tel. 223624303; fax 223624352; e-mail janjoseph@wfns.ch; internet www.wfns.org; f. 1957 to facilitate the exchange of knowledge and to encourage research; 53 mem. societies and affiliated organizations; Pres. Dr EDWARD R. LAWS; Exec. Sec. JANETTE A. JOSEPH (Switzerland).

World Federation of Societies of Anaesthesiologists (WFSA)/Federación Mundial de Sociedades de Anestesiólogos/Weltverband der Anaesthesisten-Gesellschaften: 21 Portland Place, London, W1B 1YP, UK; tel. (20) 7631-8880; fax (20) 7631-8882; e-mail wfsahq@anaesthesiologists.org; internet www.anaesthesiologists.org; f. 1955 to make available the highest standards of anaesthesia, pain treatment, trauma management and resuscitation globally; 120 national mem. societies; Pres. Prof. ANNEKE E. E. MEURSING (Netherlands); Sec. Prof. JOHN MOYERS (USA); publs *Annual Report*, *Update in Anaesthesia* (2 a year in five languages), *World Anaesthesia* (3 a year in three languages).

Music

International Music Council (IMC)/Conseil International de la Musique: UNESCO, 1 rue Miollis, 75732 Paris Cedex 15, France; tel. 1-45-68-48-51; fax 1-43-06-87-98; e-mail imc@unesco.org; internet www.unesco.org/imc; f. 1949 under the auspices of UNESCO to foster the exchange of musicians, music (written and recorded), and information; to support contemporary composers, traditional music, and young professional musicians; to foster appreciation of music by the public; mems: 40 intl and regional non-governmental organizations, 74 national cttees, 5 individual mems; Pres. Dr KIFAH FAKHOURI (Jordan); Exec. Dir Dr DAMIEN M. PWONO (France); publ. *Resonance* (2 a year).

MEMBERS OF IMC

European Festivals Association/Association Européenne des Festivals: Kasteel Borluut, Kleine Gentstraat 46, 9051 Gent, Belgium; tel. (9) 241-80-80; fax (9) 241-80-89; e-mail info@efa-aef.eu; internet www.efa-aef.eu; f. 1952 to maintain high artistic standards in festivals, widen the field of operation, organize information and publicity; 87 mem. festivals in Austria, Belgium, Bosnia and Herzegovina, Bulgaria, Croatia, Czech Republic, Denmark, Estonia, Finland, France, Germany, Greece, Hungary, Iceland, Ireland, Israel, Italy, Japan, Lebanon, Lithuania, Luxembourg, former Yugoslav republic of Macedonia, Mexico, Netherlands, Norway, Poland, Portugal, Romania, Russia, Serbia, Slovakia, Slovenia, Spain, Sweden, Switzerland, Turkey, UK; Sec.-Gen. HUGO DE GREEF.

International Council for Traditional Music/Conseil International de la Musique Traditionelle: UCLA Dept of Ethnomusicology, 2539 Schoenberg Music Bldg, POB 957178, Los Angeles, CA 90095-7178, USA; tel. (310) 794-1858; fax (310) 206-4738; e-mail ictm@arts.ucla.edu; internet www.ethnomusic.ucla.edu/ICTM; f. 1947 (as International Folk Music Council) to advance the preservation, study, practice and dissemination of traditional music (including dance) worldwide; affiliated to UNESCO; 1,500 mems; Pres. Dr KRISTER MALM (Sweden); Sec.-Gen. Prof. ANTHONY SEEGER (USA); publs *Yearbook for Traditional Music*, *Bulletin* (2 a year), *Directory of Traditional Music* (every 2 years).

International Federation of Musicians/Fédération Internationale des Musiciens: 21 bis rue Victor Massé, 75009 Paris, France; tel. 1-45-26-31-23; fax 1-45-26-31-57; e-mail office@fim-musicians.org; internet www.fim-musicians.com; f. 1948 to promote and protect the interests of musicians in affiliated unions and to institute protective measures to safeguard musicians against the abuse of their performances; promotes the international exchange of musicians; makes agreements with other international organizations in the interest of member unions and of the profession; mems: 70 unions in 65 countries; Pres. JOHN F. SMITH (UK); Gen. Sec. BENOÎT MACHUEL.

International Music and Media Centre/Internationales Musikzentrum und Medienzentrum: Stiftgasse 29, 1070 Vienna, Austria; tel. (1) 889-03-15; fax (1) 889-03-15-77; e-mail office@imz.at; internet www.imz.at; f. 1961 as a non-profit org. for the promotion and dissemination of opera, dance, concert and music documentaries through the audiovisual media (film, television, radio, gramophone); organizes congresses, seminars and screenings on music in the audiovisual media; organizes competitions to strengthen relations between composers, interpreters and directors, with particular emphasis on the promotion of the young generation; mems: 180 broadcasting organizations and other artistic organizations in 26 countries; Pres. HENK VAN DER MEULEN (Netherlands); Sec.-Gen. FRANZ PATAY; publ. *IMZ Newsletter*.

International Musicological Society: see under International Council for Philosophy and Humanistic Studies.

International Research Institute for Media, Communication and Cultural Development (MEDIACULT): Anton-von-Webern-Pl. 1, 1030 Vienna, Austria; tel. (1) 71155-8800; fax (1) 71155-8809; e-mail mediacult@mediacult.mdw.ac.at; internet www.mdw.ac.at/mediacult; f. 1969; library of 1,200 vols; Pres. Prof. RAYMOND WEBER (Luxembourg); Dir Dr ANDREW GEBESMAIR; Sec.-Gen. Dr ALFRED SMUDITS; publ. *Newsletter* (in German, English and French).

International Society for Contemporary Music/Société Internationale pour la Musique Contemporaine: c/o Henk Heuvelmans, Gaudeamus, Swammerdamstraat 38, 1091 RV Amsterdam, Netherlands; tel. (20) 694-73-49; fax (20) 694-72-58; e-mail iscm@xs4all.nl; f. 1922 to promote the development of contemporary music and to organize annual World Music Days; mem. organizations in 47 countries; Pres. ARNE MELLNÄS (Sweden); Sec.-Gen. HENK HEUVELMANS; publ. *World New Music Magazine* (annually).

International Society for Music Education: POB 909, Nedlands WA 6909, Australia; tel. (8) 9386-2654; fax (8) 9386-2658; e-mail isme@isme.org; internet www.isme.org; f. 1953 to promote music education as a part of general education and community life; organizes int. conferences and seminars; co-operates with other int. music orgs; acts as an advisory body to UNESCO; co-operates with orgs representing other fields of education; 1,650 mems; Pres. LIANE HENTSCHKE; Sec.-Gen. JUDY THÖNELL; publs *Conference and Seminar Proceedings* (every 2 years), *International Journal of Music Education (ISME)* (3 a year, No. 1 Research, No. 2 Showcase, No. 3 Practice).

Jeunesses Musicales International: Palais des Beaux-Arts, 10 rue Royale, 1000 Brussels, Belgium; tel. (32) 2-5139774; fax (32) 2-5144755; e-mail mail@jmi.net; internet www.jmi.net; f. 1945 to enable young people to develop through music across all boundaries; runs a World Orchestra and a World

Youth Choir; member organizations in 41 countries; Sec.-Gen. Dag Franzén (acting); publ. *JMI News* (every 2 months).

World Federation of International Music Competitions/Fédération Mondiale des Concours Internationaux de Musique: 104 rue de Carouge, 1205 Geneva, Switzerland; tel. 223213620; fax 227811418; e-mail fmcim@iprolink.ch; internet www.wfimc.org; f. 1957; co-ordinates the activities of members and maintains links between them, arranges the calendar of competitions, helps competition-winners to get to know each other; 118 mem. competitions; Pres. Marianne Granvig; Sec.-Gen. Renate Ronnefeld; publ. *Yearbook*.

OTHER ORGANIZATION

Répertoire International de Littérature Musicale (RILM)/International Repertory of Music Literature/Internationales Repertorium der Musikliteratur: RILM International Center, 365 Fifth Avenue, New York, NY 10016-4309, USA; tel. (212) 817-1990; fax (212) 817-1569; e-mail rilm@gc.cuny.edu; internet www.rilm.org; f. 1966; autonomous body sponsored by International Association of Music Libraries, Archives and Documentation Centers, and International Musicological Society; research and gathering of bibliographic references of all significant writings on music, from all nations, for online, printed and CD-ROM database; 63 mem. national committees; library of 1,200 vols, 500 current music journals; Pres. Barbara Dobbs Mackenzie; publ. *RILM Abstracts of Music Literature* (annually).

Science

Abdus Salam International Centre for Theoretical Physics (ICTP): Strada Costiera 11, 34014 Trieste, Italy; tel. 040-2240111; fax 040-224163; e-mail sci_info@ictp.it; internet www.ictp.it; f. 1964; administered under a tripartite agreement between the International Atomic Energy Agency, UNESCO and the Italian govt; primary focus on training and research into: condensed-matter physics, high-energy and astroparticle physics, pure and applied mathematics, physics of weather and climate, earth physics, living-state physics, applied physics, nuclear physics, turbulence; library of 100,000 vols; Dir Katepalli R. Sreenivasan; publ. *Report of Scientific Activities* (annually).

Academy of Sciences for the Developing World: c/o Abdus Salam International Centre for Theoretical Physics, Strada Costiera 11, 34014 Trieste, Italy; located at: ICTP Enrico Fermi Bldg, 1st Fl., Via Beirut 6, 34014 Trieste, Italy; tel. 040 2240327; fax 040 224559; e-mail info@twas.org; internet www.twas.org; f. 1983 to give recognition and support to research carried out by scientists in developing countries, to facilitate their contacts and foster research in developing countries; awards prizes, research grants, fellowships and associateships to scientists working and living in developing countries; 844 fellows and assoc. fellows; Pres. Jacob Palis (Brazil); Sec.-Gen. Dorairajan Balasubramanian (India); Exec. Dir Mohamed H. A. Hassan (Italy); publs *TWAS Newsletter* (quarterly), *TWAS Year Book*.

African Academy of Sciences: POB 24916, Nairobi, Kenya; tel. (2) 884401; fax (2) 884406; e-mail aas@africaonline.co.ke; f. 1985 to promote and foster the growth of the scientific community in Africa; activities: mobilization and strengthening of the African scientific community (includes the Network of African Scientific Institutions, profiles and data-bank of African scientists and instns, African Dissertation Internship Programme, assistance to regional orgs); research development and public policy; capacity building in science and technology; 111 Fellows; library of 1,500 vols; Pres. Prof. Mohamed H. A. Hassan (Sudan); Exec. Dir Gideon B. A. Okelo (Kenya); publs *Discovery and Innovation* (quarterly), *Whydah* (quarterly).

African Association for the Advancement of Science and Technology: c/o Prof. C. Kamala, KNAAS, POB 47288, Nairobi, Kenya; f. 1978; Sec. Prof. C. Kamala.

African Association of Science Editor-sAfrican Association of Science Editors",4>: POB ST 125, Southerton, Harare, Zimbabwe; tel. (4) 621661; fax (4) 621670; f. 1985 to provide a forum for establishing and strengthening the profession and standards of scientific editing in Africa; promotes training programmes, communication and interchange of views; 160 mems; Chair. Cynthia Sithole; Sec. Mazvita Madondo; publ. *Bulletin* (quarterly).

African Oil Chemists' Society: 78 Hospital Rd, POB 678, Akure, Ondo State, Nigeria; tel. (34) 230183; fax (34) 231633; f. 1995; Pres. Dr Mounir Hanna Iskander; Sec.-Gen. Dr Oliver Adesioye; publ. *AFOCS Journal* (4 a year).

African Organization for Cartography and Remote Sensing/Organisation Africaine de Cartographie et Télédétection: BP 102, 16040 Hussein Dey, Algiers, Algeria; tel. (2) 77-79-38; fax (2) 77-79-34; f. 1988 to encourage the development of cartography and of remote sensing by satellite, organize conferences and other meetings, and promote the establishment of training institutions; co-ordinates four regional training centres, in Burkina Faso, Kenya, Nigeria and Tunisia; 24 mem. countries; Sec.-Gen. Muftah Unis.

Association for the Taxonomic Study of Tropical African Flora/Association pour l'Etude Taxonomique de la Flore d'Afrique Tropicale: c/o Prof. Dr Sebsebe Demissew, Faculty of Science, Addis Ababa University, POB 3434, Addis Ababa, Ethiopia; tel. (1) 114323; fax (1) 552350; e-mail nat.heb@telecom.net.et; internet www.br.fgov.be/research/meetings/aetfat/index.html; f. 1950; language of instruction French; 800 mems from 70 countries; Gen. Sec. Prof. Dr Sebsebe Demissew; publ. *Bulletin* (annually).

Association of Information and Dissemination Centers: POB 3212, Maple Glen, PA 19002-8212; tel. (215) 654-9129; fax (215) 654-9129; e-mail info@asidic.org; internet www.asidic.org; f. 1968; independent organization with 100 centres representing industry, government and academia in the USA, Canada, Europe, Israel, Japan, India, South Africa and Australia; to promote applied technology of information storage and retrieval, and research and development for more efficient use of data bases; Pres. Carolyn Finn; Sec. Donald Hawkins.

BirdLife International: 1 Wellbrook Court, Girton Rd, Girton, Cambridge, CB3 0NA, UK; tel. (1223) 277318; fax (1223) 277200; e-mail birdlife@birdlife.org; internet www.birdlife.org; f. 1922; determines status of bird species worldwide and compiles data on all endangered species; identifies conservation problems and priorities and runs a programme of related field projects; partners and reps in 90 countries; Chair. Peter Schei (Norway); Dir and Chief Exec. Dr Michael Rands (UK); publs *Bird Conservation International*, *State of the World's Birds*, *Threatened Birds of the World*, *World Birdwatch*.

Charles Darwin Foundation for the Galapagos Isles/Fundación Charles Darwin para las Islas Galápagos: c/o Fernando Espinoza, Casilla 17-01-3891, Quito, Ecuador; Located at: Avda 6 de Diciembre N 36-109 y Pasaje California, Quito, Ecuador; tel. 244-803; fax 443-935; internet www.darwinfoundation.org; f. 1959 to organize and maintain the Charles Darwin Research Station in the Galapagos Islands and to advise the Government of Ecuador on scientific research and conservation in the archipelago; Pres. Dr Thomas H. Fritts; Exec. Dir Dr Fernando Espinoza F.; publs *Noticias de Galápagos* (2 a year), *Annual Report*.

Circum-Pacific Council for Energy and Mineral Resources: c/o Michele O'Meara, Secretariat, 12201 Sunrise Valley Drive, MS-917A, Reston, VA 20192, USA; tel. (703) 648-5042; fax (703) 648-4227; internet www.circum-pacificcouncil.org; f. 1974; non-profit int. org. of earth scientists and engineers; develops and promotes research and co-operation among industry, govt and academics, for the sustainable use of natural resources in the Pacific region; co-operation of 46 int. geoscience orgs; sponsors conferences, meetings and research; supports conferences, meetings, research; supports and operates regional projects, incl. the Circum-Pacific Map Project, and int. training schools; Pres. David G. Howell (USA); Chair. Nahum Schneidermann (USA); Sec. Edward Saade (USA).

Commonwealth Geographical Bureau: C/o Prof. Mike Meadows, Environmental and Geographical Science, University of Cape Town, Rondebosch 7700, South Africa; tel. (21) 650-2873; fax (21) 650-3791; e-mail meadows@enviro.uct.ac.za; f. 1968; encourages the development of geographical research and study, particularly in developing Commonwealth countries, through assistance to the profession; regional seminars, assistance for study visits; a board of management represents five regions: Asia, Africa, Americas, Australasia and Europe; Pres. Assoc. Prof. Victor R. Savage; publ. *Newsletter* (annually).

Commonwealth Science Council: Commonwealth Secretariat, Marlborough House, Pall Mall, London, SW1Y 5HX, UK; tel. (20) 7747-6500; fax (20) 7930-0827; e-mail science@commonwealth.int; f. 1975; an intergovernmental body, the Science and Technology Division of the Commonwealth Secretariat; seeks to increase the capability of Commonwealth countries to apply science and technology for social, economic and environmental development; conducts no in-house research, but provides support for putting into practice the results of research carried out by others and helps to produce knowledge required to solve developmental problems through research; programmes are: biological and genetic resources, renewable energy, water and mineral resources, advanced technologies; runs a fellowship scheme providing short-term placements at training programmes or research institutes in developing countries; runs a travel-grant scheme to help scientists from member countries attend scientific meetings; 37 mems; Sec. Dr Ken Lum; publs *Commonwealth Scientist* (4 a year), *Report* (every 2 years).

Council for International Congresses of Entomology/Comité Permanent des Congrès Internationaux d'Entomologie: c/o Dr James H. Oliver, Institute of Arthropodology and Parasitology, Georgia Southern University, Landrum Box 8056, Statesboro, GA 30460-8056, USA; tel. (912) 681-5564; fax (912) 681-0559; e-mail joliver@gasou.edu; f. 1910 to act as a link between periodic congresses and to arrange the venue for each congress; the committee is also the entomology section of the International Union of Biological Sciences; Chair. Dr MAX WHITTEN (Philippines); Sec. Dr JAMES H. OLIVER (USA).

European Atomic Energy Community (Euratom): 200 rue de la Loi, 1049 Brussels, Belgium; tel. (2) 235-11-11; internet euratom .org; based on a formal treaty signed in Rome in March 1957, at the same time as the treaty establishing the EEC; aims to integrate the programmes of member states for the peaceful uses of atomic energy; since 1967 combined with the ECSC and EEC.

European Centre for Medium-Range Weather Forecasts: Shinfield Park, Reading, Berks., RG2 9AX, United Kingdom; tel. (118) 949-9000; fax (118) 986-9450; e-mail ecmwf-director@ecmwf.int; internet www .ecmwf.int; f. 1975; aims include the development of numerical methods for medium-range weather forecasting, the collection and storage of data and products, providing operational forecasts to the mem. states and co-operating states, and providing advanced training in numerical weather prediction; 18 mem. states; Dir D. MARBOUTY.

European Geosciences Union: Max-Planck-Str. 13, 37191 Katlenburg-Lindau, Germany; tel. (49) 5556-1440; fax (49) 5556-4709; e-mail egu@copernicus.org; internet www.copernicus.org/EGU; f. 2002 by merger of the European Geophysical Society and the European Union of Geosciences; promotes the sciences of the Earth and its environment and of planetary and space sciences, and encourages co-operation between scientists; organizes annual General Assemblies, topical conferences and short courses; Pres. PETER FABIAN; Exec. Sec. Dr ARNE K. RICHTER; publs *Advances in Geosciences*, *Advances in Radio Science*, *Annales Geophysicae*, *Astrophysics and Space Sciences Transactions*, *Atmospheric Chemistry and Physics*, *Atmospheric Chemistry and Physics Discussions*, *Biogeosciences*, *Geophysical Research Abstracts*, *Hydrology and Earth System Sciences*, *Hydrology and Earth System Sciences Discussions*, *Natural Hazards and Earth System Sciences*, *Nonlinear Processes in Geophysics*, *Ocean Science*, *Ocean Science Discussions*, *Social Geography*, *The Eggs* (newsletter).

European Institute of Environmental Medicine: Odos Kerasundos 2, Athens 162 32, Greece; tel. 210-7628460; fax 210-7628675; e-mail eiem@otonet.gr; f. 1970 to bring together scientists and scholars with cross-sectional background and research interests and to conduct multi-disciplinary educational and research activities studying the interactions between man and his environment (natural and technical); Dir Prof. C. K. KYRILOV.

European Molecular Biology Laboratory: Meyerhofstr. 1, 69117 Heidelberg, Germany; tel. (6221) 3870; fax (6221) 3878306; e-mail info@embl.de; internet www.embl-heidelberg.de; f. 1974; financed by 15 European states and Israel; basic research in molecular biology; outstations in Hinxton, nr Cambridge (European Bioinformatics Institute), Grenoble, Hamburg and Monterotondo (Rome); library of 22,200 vols; Dir-Gen. Prof. FOTIS C. KAFATOS; publs *Annual Report*, *Handbook of Statistics* (annually), *Research Report* (annually).

European Molecular Biology Organization (EMBO)/Organisation Européenne de Biologie Moléculaire: Postfach 1022.40, 69012 Heidelberg, Germany; Located at: Meyerhofstr. 1, 69117 Heidelberg, Germany; tel. (6221) 88910; fax (6221) 8891200; e-mail embo@embo.org; internet www.embo.org; f. 1964 to promote excellence in the molecular life sciences in Europe; awards research fellowships; sponsors scientific meetings; awards installation grants to build scientific capacity in selected countries; provides opportunities for career development to young group leaders in the EMBO Young Investigator Programme; offers fellowships and training for scientists outside Europe; offers scientific advice on European science policy; provides quality reviews of national science programmes, and information and online services for life sciences communities; 1,200 mems; Exec. Dir Prof. FRANK GANNON; publs *EMBO Journal* (24 a year), *EMBO Reports* (monthly), *Molecular Systems Biology* (online, every 2 weeks).

European Organization for Nuclear Research (CERN)/Organisation Européenne pour la Recherche Nucléaire: 1211 Geneva 23, Switzerland; tel. 227676111; fax 227676555; e-mail cern.reception@cern.ch; internet www.cern.ch; f. 1954; mems: Austria, Belgium, Czech Republic, Denmark, Finland, France, Germany, Greece, Hungary, Italy, Netherlands, Norway, Poland, Portugal, Slovakia, Spain, Sweden, Switzerland and UK; carries out and co-ordinates research on fundamental particles; research is undertaken mostly by teams of visiting scientists who remain based at their parent instns; in general the staff is drawn from mem. states, but scientists from any country may be invited to spend a limited period at CERN; research is carried out with the aid of a proton synchrotron of 28 GeV (the PS), the super proton synchrotron (SPS) of 450 GeV and the 27 km LEP electron-positron collider; Pres. of the Council Prof. ENZO IAROCCI; Dir-Gen. Dr ROBERT AYMAR; publs *Annual Report* (in English and French), *CERN Courier* (monthly in English and French).

European Physical Society: 6 rue des Frères Lumière, 68060 Mulhouse Cedex, France; tel. 3-89-32-94-40; fax 3-89-32-94-49; internet www.eps.org; f. 1968; aims to promote the advancement of physics in Europe and neighbouring countries by all suitable means; 39 nat. mem. orgs; 6,500 individual mems; 80 assoc. mems; Sec.-Gen. DAVID LEE; publs *Europhysics News* (every 2 months), *European Journal of Physics* (every 2 months).

European Science Foundation: 1 quai Lezay-Marnésia, 67080 Strasbourg Cedex, France; tel. 3-88-76-71-00; fax 3-88-37-05-32; f. 1974 to promote research in all branches of fundamental science and the humanities; to advance co-operation in European research; to examine and advise on research and science policy issues; to promote the mobility of research workers and the free flow of information and ideas; to facilitate co-operation in the planning and use of research facilities; to plan and manage collaborative research activities; mems: 76 research funding agencies from 29 countries; Pres. Dr REINDER VAN DUINEN (Netherlands); CEO BERTIL ANDERSSON; publs *Annual Report* (in English), *ESF Communications* (2 a year).

European Southern Observatory/Organisation Européenne pour des Recherches Astronomiques dans l'Hémisphère Austral: Karl-Schwarzschild-Str. 2, 85748 Garching bei München, Germany; tel. (89) 320060; fax (89) 3202362; internet www .eso.org; f. 1962; aims: astronomical research in the southern hemisphere, construction and operation of an international observatory in Chile (see under Chile), fostering European co-operation in astronomy; mems: govts of Belgium, Denmark, Germany, France, Italy, The Netherlands, Portugal, Sweden, Switzerland; Dir-Gen. Dr CATHERINE CESARSKY; publs *Annual Report*, *The Messenger*.

European Space Agency: 8–10 rue Mario Nikis, 75738 Paris Cedex 15, France; tel. 53-69-76-54; fax 53-69-75-60; internet www.esa .int; f. 1964, name changed 1975, to provide for, and to promote collaboration among European states in space research and technology and their space applications exclusively for peaceful purposes; provides scientific agencies of the member countries with the necessary technical facilities for the carrying out of space experiments, ranging from the study of the near terrestrial environment to that of stellar astronomy; also responsible for a European programme of application satellite projects, including telecommunications and meteorology, also for Spacelab and Ariane Launcher; supports the following establishments: European Space Research and Technology Centre (ESTEC), Noordwijk, Netherlands; European Space Operations Centre (ESOC), Darmstadt, Germany; European Space Research Institute (ESRIN), Frascati, Italy; European Astronaut Centre (EAC), Cologne, Germany; mems: Austria, Belgium, Denmark, Finland, France, Germany, Ireland, Italy, Netherlands, Norway, Portugal, Spain, Sweden, Switzerland and UK; Canada is linked by a special co-operation agreement; library (ESTEC) of 48,000 vols, 1 million microfiche, 42,000 reports and standards; Dir-Gen. ANTONIO RODOTÀ (Italy); publs *Annual Reports*, *Bulletin*, *Earth Observation Quarterly*, *Reaching for the Skies* (all quarterly), *News and Views* (every 2 months), conference proceedings, scientific and technical reports.

Federation of Arab Scientific Research Councils: POB 13027, Baghdad, Iraq; tel. 8881709f. 1976 to strengthen scientific and technological co-operation and co-ordination between Arab countries; holds conferences, seminars, workshops and training courses; publs Directory of Arab Scientific Research Institutions; 15 mem. countries; Sec.-Gen. Dr TAHA TAYIH AL-NAIMI; publs *Proceedings of Scientific Activities*, *Newsletter*, *Computer Research*.

Federation of Asian Scientific Academies and Societies (FASAS): c/o Malaysian Scientific Association, Bangunan Sultan Salahuddin Abdul Aziz Shah (Room 1, 2nd Floor), 16 Jalan Utara, POB 48, 46700 Petaling Jaya, Malaysia; tel. (3) 7957-8930; fax (3) 7954-1644; e-mail malsci@tm.net.my; f. 1984 to promote regional co-operation and national and regional self-reliance in science and technology by organizing meetings, training and research programs and encouraging exchange of scientists and information; 16 mems (national scientific academies and societies in Afghanistan, Australia, Bangladesh, People's Republic of China, India, Republic of Korea, Malaysia, Nepal, New Zealand, Pakistan, Philippines, Singapore, Sri Lanka, Thailand); Pres. Prof. LEO TAN (Singapore); Sec. Prof. TING-KUEH SOON (Malaysia).

Foundation for International Scientific Co-ordination/Fondation 'Pour la Science', Centre international de Synthèse: Acta – UMS 2267 CNRS, 4 rue Lhomond, 75005 Paris, France; tel. 1-55-42-83-13; fax 1-55-42-83-19; e-mail Fondation .pourlascience.cis@ens.fr; internet www .ehess.fr/acta/synthese; f. 1924; Founder HENRI BERR; Co-Dirs MICHAEL BLAY, ERIC BRIAN; publs *Revue de Synthèse* (4 a year), *Revue d'Histoire des Sciences* (4 a year), *Semaines de Synthèse*, *L'Evolution de l'Humanité*.

Institute of Mathematical Statistics: POB 22718, Beachwood, OH 44122, USA; tel. (216) 295-2340; fax (216) 295-5661; e-mail ims@imstat.org; internet www.imstat.org; f. 1935; 4,000 mems; Pres. THOMAS G. KURTZ; Exec. Sec. ELYSE GUSTAFSON; publs *Annals of Probability*, *Annals of Statistics* (every 2 months), *Statistical Science*, *Annals of Applied Probability* (all quarterly), *IMS Bulletin* (every 2 months), *IMS Lecture Notes—Monograph Series*, *CBMS Regional Conference Series in Probability and Statistics*.

Intergovernmental Oceanographic Commission (IOC)/Commission Océanographique Intergouvernementale: c/o UNESCO, 1 rue Miollis, 75015 Paris, France; tel. 1-45-68-39-84; fax 1-45-68-58-10; internet ioc.unesco.org; f. 1960 to promote scientific investigation with a view to learning more about the nature and resources of the oceans, through the concerted action of its members; mems: 125 governments; Chair. Dr DAVID T. PUGH (UK); Exec. Sec. Dr PATRICIO BERNAL (Chile); publs *IOC Manuals and Guides*, *IOC Technical Series*, *IOC Training Course Reports* (irregular), *IOC Workshop Reports*, *Summary Reports of Sessions*.

International Academy of Astronautics (IAA)/Académie Internationale d'Astronautique: BP 1268-16, 75766 Paris Cedex 16, France; 6 rue Galilée, 75116 Paris, France; tel. 1-47-23-82-15; fax 1-47-23-82-16; internet www.iaanet.org; f. 1960; aims to foster the development of astronautics for peaceful purposes, recognizing individuals who have distinguished themselves in the field, and provides a programme through which mems can contribute to intl co-operation; liaises with nat. academies of science; developing a multilingual (20 languages) Database; maintains the following cttees: Space Sciences, Intl Space Plans and Policies, Life Sciences, Benefits to Society from Space Activities, Economics of Space Operations, Interstellar Space Exploration, Search for Extraterrestrial Intelligence, Safety and Rescue, Space and Environmental Change, History of Astronautics, Scientific Legal Liaison; mems: 975 in 56 countries; Pres. Prof. E. C. STONE (USA); Vice-Pres. Prof. H. CURIEN (France), Prof. K. KASTURIRANGAN (India), Dr Y. N. KOPTEV (Russia), Dr H. MATSUO (Japan); Sec.-Gen. Dr J. M. CONTANT (France); publs *Acta Astronautica* (12 issues a year), *Proceedings of Symposia*.

International Association for Mathematics and Computers in Simulation/Association Internationale pour les Mathématiques et Calculateurs en Simulation: c/o Dept of Computer Science, Hill Center, Busch Campus, Rutgers University, New Brunswick, NJ 08903, USA; internet www.research.rutgers.edu/~imacs; f. 1955 to advance the study of general methods for modelling and computer simulation of dynamic systems; Pres. R. VICHNEVETSKY (USA); Sec.-Gen. R. BEAUWENS (Belgium); publs *Mathematics and Computers in Simulation*, *Applied Numerical Mathematics* (every 2 months).

International Association for Plant Physiology (IAPP): Food Science Australia, CSIRO, POB 52, North Ryde, NSW 1670, Australia; tel. (2) 9490-8333; fax (2) 9490-3107; e-mail douglas.graham@foodscience.afics.csiro.au; f. 1955 to promote the development of plant physiology at the international level, especially collaboration between developed and developing nations, through international congresses and symposia and by the publication of plant physiology matters and the promotion of co-operation between national and international associations and scientific journals; represents plant physiologists on the IUBS; mems: 40 national societies of plant physiology and related international groups; Pres. Prof. S. MIYACHI; Sec.-Gen. Dr D. GRAHAM; publ. *Annual Newsletter*.

International Association for Plant Taxonomy/Association Internationale pour la Taxonomie Végétale: Bureau for Plant Taxonomy and Nomenclature, Institute of Botany, Univ. of Vienna, Rennweg 14, 1030 Vienna, Austria; tel. (1) 427754098; fax (1) 427754099; e-mail office@iapt-taxon.org; internet www.iapt-taxon.org; f. 1950 to promote the development of plant taxonomy and encourage contacts between people and institutes interested in this work; mems: institutes and individuals in 87 countries; Exec. Sec. Dr ALESSANDRA RICCIUTI LAMONEA (Austria); publs *Regnum vegetabile* (irreg.), *Taxon* (quarterly).

International Association for the Physical Sciences of the Ocean (IAPSO)/Association Internationale des Sciences Physiques de l'Océan: POB 820440, Vicksburg, MS 39182-0440, USA; tel. (601) 636-1363; fax (601) 629-9640; internet www.olympus.net/IAPSO; f. 1919 to promote the study of scientific problems relating to the oceans, chiefly by the aid of mathematics, physics and chemistry; to initiate, facilitate and co-ordinate research; to provide for discussion, comparison and publication; 81 mem. states; Pres. Prof. SHIRO IMAWAKI (Japan); Sec.-Gen. Dr FRED E. CAMFIELD (USA); publs *Publications Scientifiques* (irregular), *Procès-Verbaux* (every 2–4 years).

International Association for Vegetation Science/Association Internationale pour l'Etude de la Végétation: c/o Dr J. H. J. Schaminée, Alterra, Green World Research, Postbus 47, 6700 AA Wageningen, Netherlands; tel. (317) 477914; fax (317) 424988; e-mail joop.schaminee@wur.nl; internet www.iavs.org; f. 1937; aims for the development of phytosociology; 1,300 mems; Pres. Prof. E. O. BOX (USA); Sec. Dr J. H. J. SCHAMINÉE; publs *Journal of Vegetation Science*, *Phytocoenologia*, *Applied Vegetation Science*.

International Association of Biological Oceanography: Leigh Marine Laboratory, Univ. of Auckland, POB 349, Warkworth, New Zealand; e-mail m.costello@auckland.ac.nz; internet www.iabo.org; f. 1966 to promote the study of the biology of the sea; attached to Int. Union of Biological Sciences; Pres. Dr ANNALIES PIERROT-BULTS (Netherlands); Sec.-Gen. Dr MARK J. COSTELLO (New Zealand).

International Association of Geodesy/Association Internationale de Géodésie: University of Copenhagen, Dept of Geophysics, Juliane Maries Vej 30, 2100 Copenhagen Ø, Denmark; tel. 35-32-06-00; fax 35-36-53-57; e-mail iag@gfy.ku.dk; internet www.gfy.ku.dk/~iag; f. 1922 to promote the study of all scientific problems of geodesy and encourage geodetic research; to promote and co-ordinate intl co-operation in this field; to publish results; a mem. assn of IUGG; mems: national cttees in 78 countries; Pres. Prof. G. BEUTLER; Sec.-Gen. C. C. TSCHERNING; publs *Journal of Geodesy* (monthly), *Travaux de l'AIG* (every 4 years).

International Association of Geomagnetism and Aeronomy (IAGA)/Association Internationale de Géomagnétisme et d'Aéronomie: c/o Prof. Bengt Hultqvist, Swedish Institute of Space Physics, Box 812, 98128. Kiruna, Sweden; tel. (980) 79060; fax (980) 79091; internet www.iugg.org/IAGA; f. 1919; aims: the study of magnetism and aeronomy of the earth and other bodies of the solar system, and of the interplanetary medium and its interaction with these bodies; mems: countries which adhere to the International Union of Geodesy and Geophysics are eligible; Pres. Dr CHARLES BARTON (Australia); Sec.-Gen. Prof. BENGT HULTQVIST (Sweden); publs *IAGA Bulletins* (irregular), *Geomagnetic Data* (annually), *IAGA News* (annually).

International Association of Hydrological Sciences/Association Internationale des Sciences Hydrologiques: c/o Dr Pierre Hubert, Ecole des Mines de Paris, 35 rue St Honoré, 77305 Fontainebleau, France; tel. 1-64-69-47-40; fax 1-64-69-47-03; e-mail iahs@ensmp.fr; internet www.iahs.info; f. 1922; part of IUGG; aims to promote the study of hydrology, to provide means for discussion, comparison and publication of research findings, and the initiation and co-ordination of research requiring intl co-operation; organizes general assemblies, symposia, etc.; 84 national cttees; Pres. Prof. KUNIYOSHI TAKEUCHI (Japan); Sec.-Gen. Dr PIERRE HUBERT (France); publs *Hydrological Sciences Journal* (6 a year), *Newsletter* (3 a year).

International Association of Meteorology and Atmospheric Sciences (IAMAS)/Association Internationale de Météorologie et de Sciences de l'Atmosphère: c/o Prof. R. List, University of Toronto, Dept of Physics, Toronto, ON M5S 1A7, Canada; f. 1919 to organize research symposia and co-ordinate research in atmospheric science fields; an Association of the International Union of Geodesy and Geophysics; Pres. Prof. R. DUCE (USA); Sec.-Gen. Prof. R. LIST; publ. *IAMAP Assembly Proceedings* (every 2 years).

International Association of Sedimentologists: c/o Dr José-Pedro Calvo, Dpto Petrología y Geoquímica, Fac. Ciencias Geólogicas, Universidad Complutense, 28040 Madrid, Spain; tel. 91-394-49-05; fax 91-544-25-35; e-mail jpcalvo@geo.ucm.es; internet www.iasnet.org; f. 1952; 2,000 mems; Pres. Prof. JUDITH A. MCKENZIE (Switzerland); Sec.-Gen. Dr JOSÉ-PEDRO CALVO; publ. *Sedimentology* (6 a year).

International Association of Theoretical and Applied Limnology/Association internationale de Limnologie Théorique et Appliquée: Dept of Environmental Sciences and Engineering, University of North Carolina, Chapel Hill, NC 27599-7431, USA; tel. (919) 843-4916; fax (919) 843-4072; e-mail rwetzel@unc.edu; internet www.limnology.org; f. 1922; 3,100 mems; Pres. Prof. Dr GENE E. LIKENS (USA); Gen. Sec. and Treas. Prof. ROBERT G. WETZEL (USA); publs *Verhandlungen*, *Mitteilungen*.

International Association of Volcanology and Chemistry of the Earth's Interior (IAVCEI)/Association Internationale de Volcanologie et de Chimie de l'Intérieur de la Terre: c/o S. R. McNutt, Alaska Volcano Observatory, Geophysical Institute UAF, POB 757320, Fairbanks, AK 99775, USA; tel. (907) 474-7131; fax (907) 474-5618; e-mail steve@giseis.alaska.edu; internet www.iavcei.org; f. 1919 to promote scientific investigation and discussion on volcanology and in those aspects of petrology and geochemistry relating to the composition of the interior of the Earth; holds scientific general assemblies; sponsors workshops; participates in IUGG general assemblies; 840 individual mems and nat. correspondents; Pres. Prof. ODED NAVON (Israel); Sec.-Gen. Prof. STEPHEN R. MCNUTT (USA); publs *Bulletin of Volcanology*, *Catalogue of the Active Volcanoes of the World*, *Proceedings in Volcanology*.

International Association of Wood Anatomists/Association Internationale des

Anatomistes du Bois: c/o Nationaal Herbarium Nederland, Universiteit Leiden Branch, POB 9514, 2300 RA Leiden, Netherlands; fax (71) 527-3511; internet www.kuleuven.ac.be/bio/sys/iawa; f. 1931 for the purpose of study, documentation and exchange of information on the anatomy of wood; 600 mems in 60 countries; Exec. Sec. Dr REGIS B. MILLER (USA); publ. *IAWA Journal* (quarterly).

International Astronautical Federation (IAF)/Fédération Internationale d'Astronautique: 8–10 rue Mario-Nikis, 75015 Paris, France; Located at: 94 bis ave de Suffren, 75015 Paris, France; tel. 1-45-67-42-60; fax 1-42-73-21-20; e-mail iaf@iafastro.org; internet www.iafastro.com; f. 1950 to foster the development of astronautics for peaceful purposes at nat. and intl levels; the IAF created the International Academy of Astronautics (IAA), the International Institute of Space Law (IISL) (for information on these bodies, see elsewhere in this chapter), and cttees on Activities and Membership; Allan D. Emil Award; Finances; Publications; Liaison with Intl Organizations and Developing Nations; Education; Student Activities; SYRE, Solar Sail; Astrodynamics; Earth Observations; Satellite Communications; Natural Disaster Reduction; Life Sciences; Microgravity Science and Processes; Space Exploration; Space Power; Space Propulsion; Space Transportation; Space Stations; Space Systems; Materials and Structures; annual student awards; mems: 137 national astronautical societies in 45 countries; Pres. JAMES V. ZIMMERMAN (USA); Vice-Pres MUKUND RAO (India), STUART W. THOMSON (USA), YUAN JIA-JUN (China), ROBERT C. PARKINSON (UK), YASUNORI MATOGAWA (Japan), VICTOR REGLERO (Spain), ANNE-MARIE MAINGUY (France), VIRENDRA K. JHA (Canada), ANATOLY I. GRIGORIEV (Russia), KLAUS BERGE (Germany); Exec. Dir YVES BEGUIN; publ. *Proceedings* (of Annual Congresses).

International Atomic Energy Agency (IAEA): Vienna International Centre, POB 100, 1400 Vienna, Austria; tel. (1) 2600; fax (1) 26007; e-mail official.mail@iaea.org; internet www.iaea.org; f. 1956 by 80 nations; the Board of Governors, consisting of 36 members designated or elected on a regional basis, carries out the functions of the Agency; aims: the contribution of atomic energy to peace, health and prosperity worldwide; to provide materials, services, equipment and facilities; to foster the exchange of scientific and technical information on peaceful uses of atomic energy; to encourage the exchange and training of scientists and experts in the field of atomic energy; to establish health and safety standards and to prepare a comprehensive set of safety codes and guides covering all aspects of building and operating nuclear power plants; establishes safeguards against the military use of civil nuclear materials or equipment provided through the Agency and applies these safeguards in accordance with the Treaty on the Non-Proliferation of Nuclear Weapons, the Treaty for the Prohibition of Nuclear Weapons in Latin America, the Treaty for a Nuclear-Weapon-Free Zone in Africa, the Treaty for a Nuclear-Weapon-Free Zone in South-East Asia and the Treaty of the South Pacific Nuclear-Free Zone; 133 mem. states; library: jt library (with UNIDO and other UN organizations) of 80,000 vols, 708,000 technical reports in microfiche and hard-copy, 3,569 current periodicals, 350 audiovisual items, 1.26m. documents; micro-card clearing-house; the International Nuclear Information System (INIS) provides world-wide coverage of literature on all aspects of peaceful uses of nuclear energy; the IAEA Energy and Economic Data Bank provides information on the world's energy situation and related economic parameters, based on data obtained from member states; Dir-Gen. Dr MOHAMED ELBARADEI; publs *Nuclear Fusion* (monthly), *Atomic Energy Review*, *IAEA Bulletin* (4 a year), *Meetings on Atomic Energy* (quarterly), *INIS Atomindex* (2 a month).

International Biometric Society (IBS)/ Société Internationale de Biométrie: 1444 I St, NW, Suite 700, Washington, DC 20005, USA; tel. (202) 712-9049; fax (202) 216-9646; e-mail ibs@bostrom.com; internet www.tibs.org; f. 1947; dedicated to the development and application of statistical and mathematical theory and methods in the biosciences; 19 regional organizations and 19 national groups; affiliated to the International Statistical Institute and the World Health Organization, and constitutes the section of Biometry of the International Union of Biological Sciences; mems: 5,200 in more than 70 countries; Pres. GEERT MOLENBERGHS (Belgium); Exec. Dir CLAIRE SHANLEY (USA); publs *Biometrics* (quarterly), *Biometric Bulletin* (quarterly), *Journal of Agricultural, Biological and Environmental Statistics* (quarterly).

International Botanical Congress/Congrès International de Botanique: c/o Dr Josef Greimler, Botany, University of Vienna, Rennweg 14, 1030 Vienna, Austria; e-mail office@ibc2005.ac.at; internet www.ibc2005.ac.at; f. 1864 to inform botanists of progress in plant sciences; nomenclature, metabolism and bioenergetics, developmental botany, genetics, breeding and biotechnology, structural botany, systematics and evolution, environmental botany.

International Bureau of Weights and Measures/Bureau International des Poids et Mesures: Pavillon de Breteuil, 92312 Sèvres Cedex, France; tel. 1-45-07-70-70; fax 1-45-34-20-21; e-mail info@bipm.org; internet www.bipm.org; f. 1875 for the preservation of standards of the International System of Units (SI) and world-wide unification of the units of measurement; determination of national standards; precision measurements in physics; establishment of the intl atomic time-scale; 48 mem. states; Pres. Prof. E. O. GÖBEL (Germany); Sec. Dr R. KAARLS (Netherlands); Dir Prof. A. J. WALLARD; publs *Procès-Verbaux* (annually), *Sessions des dix Comités consultatifs auprès du Comité International* (every few years for each committee), *Metrologia*, *Comptes Rendus des Conférences Générales* (every 4 years).

International Centre of Insect Physiology and Ecology: POB 30772-00100, Nairobi, Kenya; tel. (20) 861686; fax (20) 860110; internet www.icipe.org; f. 1970 to develop, through research, plant-borne, human and animal disease management and control strategies, and to promote research and the conservation of arthropods; library of 7,500 vols, 3,500 volumes bound periodicals, 200 periodicals; Chair. Prof. PETER ESBJERG (Denmark); Dir-Gen. and CEO Dr HANS R. HERREN; publs *ICIPE Annual Report*, *Insect Science and Its Application*.

International Commission for Optics (ICO)/Commission Internationale d'Optique: c/o María L. Calvo, Departamento de Optica, Facultad de Ciencias Físicas, Universidad Complutense de Madrid, Ciudad Universitaria s/n, 28040 Madrid, Spain; tel. 91-394-46-84; fax 91-394-46-83; e-mail icosec@fis.ucm.es; internet www.ico-optics.org; f. 1948 to contribute on an int. basis to the progress of theoretical and instrumental optics and its application, through conferences, colloquia, summer schools, etc., and to promote int agreement on nomenclature, specifications, etc.; 50 mem. countries; Pres. Prof. ARI T. FRIBERG (Sweden); Sec.-Gen. Prof. MARÍA L. CALVO (Spain); publs *ICO Newsletter* (quarterly), *International Trends in Optics* (every 3 years).

International Commission for the Scientific Exploration of the Mediterranean Sea/Commission Internationale pour l'Exploration Scientifique de la Mer Méditerranée (CIESM): 16 blvd de Suisse, 98000 Monaco; tel. 93-30-38-79; fax 92-16-11-95; e-mail ciesm@ciesm.org; internet www.ciesm.org; f. 1919 for scientific exploration of the Mediterranean Sea, the study of physical and chemical oceanography, marine geosciences, living resources, marine biodiversity, marine biotechnology, coastal environment; 23 mem. states, 2,500 individual mems; Pres. H.S.H. The Prince ALBERT OF MONACO; Dir-Gen. Prof. FRÉDÉRIC BRIAND; Sec.-Gen. Prof. FRANÇOIS DOUMENGE; publ. *Congress Proceedings* (every 3 years).

International Commission on Zoological Nomenclature/Commission Internationale de Nomenclature Zoologique: c/o The Natural History Museum, Cromwell Rd, London, SW7 5BD, UK; tel. (20) 7942-5653; e-mail iczn@nhm.ac.uk; internet www.iczn.org; f. 1895; the Commission, formerly a standing organ of the Int. Zoological Congresses, now reports to the General Assembly of IUBS; the Commission has judicial powers to determine all matters relating to the interpretation of the *International Code of Zoological Nomenclature* and also plenary powers to suspend the operation of the *Code* where strict application would lead to confusion and instability of nomenclature; the Commission is responsible also for maintaining and developing the *Official Lists of Names in Zoology* and the *Official Indexes of Rejected and Invalid Names in Zoology*; Pres. Prof. D. J. BROTHERS (South Africa); Exec. Sec. Dr A. POLASZEK (UK); publ. *Bulletin of Zoological Nomenclature*.

International Confederation for Thermal Analysis and Calorimetry (ICTAC): c/o Prof. M. E. Brown, Chemistry Dept, Rhodes University, Grahamstown 6140, South Africa; tel. (46) 6038254; fax (46) 6225109; e-mail m.brown@ru.ac.za; internet www.ictac.org; f. 1968; 600 mems in 40 countries, 5,000 affiliate mems in 20 affiliated regional and national societies and groups; co-ordinates these groups and supplies information on their scientific activities; supports national regional seminars and symposia; quadrennial intl conference; Pres. Dr JEAN ROUQUEROL (France); Sec. Prof. MICHAEL E. BROWN (South Africa); publ. *News* (2 a year).

International Council for the Exploration of the Sea (ICES)/Conseil International pour l'Exploration de la Mer: H. C. Andersens Blvd 44-46, 1553 Copenhagen V, Denmark; tel. 33-38-67-00; fax 33-93-42-15; e-mail info@ices.dk; internet www.ices.dk; f. 1902 to promote and encourage research and investigations for the study of the sea, particularly those related to its living resources; area of interest: the Atlantic Ocean (primarily the North Atlantic) and its adjacent seas; mems: 19 national governments; Pres. MICHAEL SISSENWINE (USA); Gen. Sec. DAVID GRIFFITH; publs *ICES Journal of Marine Science*, *ICES Marine Science Symposia*, *ICES Fisheries Statistics*, *ICES Techniques in Marine Environmental Sciences*, *ICES Cooperative Research Reports*.

International Earth Rotation and Reference Systems Service (IERS): Bundesamt für Kartographie und Geodäsie, Richard-Strass-Allee 11, 60598 Frankfurt am Main, Germany; tel. (69) 6333273; fax (69) 6333425; internet www.iers.org; f. 1988 to replace Int. Polar Motion Service and the earth-rotation section of the Int. Time Bureau; organized jtly by the IAU and IUGG; responsible for defining and maintaining a conventional terrestrial reference system based on observing stations that use the high-precision techniques of space geodesy; defining and maintaining a conventional celestial reference system based on extragalactic radio sources, and relating it to other celestial reference systems; determining the earth orientation parameters connecting these systems; organizing operational activities for observation and data analysis, collecting and archiving appropriate data and results, and disseminating the results; Dir of Central Bureau Dr BERND RICHTER.

International Federation for Cell Biology/Fédération Internationale de Biologie Cellulaire: c/o Dr Denys Wheatley, University of Aberdeen, MacRobert Bldg, Room 8.05, 581 King St, Aberdeen, AB24 5UA, UK; tel. (1224) 274173; internet www.ifcbiol.org; f. 1972; sponsors an intl congress every 4 years; Pres. Dr CHENG-WEN WU (China (Taiwan)); Sec.-Gen. Dr DENYS WHEATLEY; publ. *Cell Biology International*.

International Federation of Societies for Microscopy/Fédération Internationale des Sociétés de Microscopie: c/o Prof. C. Barry Carter, Dept of Chemical, Materials and Biomolecular Engineering, 191 Auditorium Rd, Unit 3222, Univ. of Connecticut, Storrs, CT 06269-3222, USA; tel. (860) 486-4020; fax (860) 486-2959; e-mail cbcarter@engr.uconn.edu; internet www.ifsm.umn.edu; f. 1955; mems: representative orgs of 39 countries; Pres. Prof. D. COCKAYNE; Sec. Prof. C. B. CARTER.

International Food Information Service: IFIS Publishing, Lane End House, Shinfield, Reading, RG2 9BB, UK; tel. (118) 988-3895; fax (118) 988-5065; e-mail ifis@ifis.org; internet www.ifis.org; f. 1968; governed by CAB International (UK), Institute of Food Technologists (USA), the Centrum voor Landbouwpublikaties en Landbouwdocumentatie (Netherlands) and the Bundesministerium für Landwirtschaft Ernährung und Forsten (represented by Deutsche Landwirtschafts-Gesellschaft eV) in Germany, for the promotion of education and research in food science and technology; Gen. Man. J. SELMAN; publs *Food Science and Technology Abstracts* (monthly in print, online, CD-ROM), *Food Science Profiles* (monthly in print and on diskette), *Viticulture and Enology Abstracts* (quarterly, in print and online).

International Foundation of the High-Altitude Research Stations, Jungfraujoch and Gornergrat/Fondation internationale des stations scientifiques du Jungfraujoch et du Gornergrat: 5 Sidlerstr, 3012 Bern, Switzerland; tel. 316314052; fax 316314405; e-mail louise.wilson@phim.unibe.ch; internet www.ifjungo.ch; f. 1931; Dir Prof. E. FLUECKIGER.

International Genetics Federation: c/o Elaine Strass, IGF Admin. Office, 9650 Rockville Pike, Bethesda, MD 20814-3998, USA; tel. (301) 634-7300; fax (301) 634-7310; e-mail estrass@genetics-gsa.org; internet www.intergenetics.org; f. 1968 to encourage understanding, co-operation and friendship among geneticists worldwide and to plan and support intl congresses of genetics; 37 mem. countries; Pres. Dr JOHN W. DRAKE (USA); Exec. Administrator ELAINE STRASS.

International Geological Congress/Congrès Géologique International: 77–79 rue Claude Bernard, 75005 Paris, France; f. 1878 to contribute to the advancement of investigations relating to the study of the Earth and other planets, considered from theoretical and practical points of view; the congress is held every four years; Pres. V. Y. KHAIN; Sec.-Gen. (vacant); publs *Extended Abstracts*, *General Proceedings*.

International Glaciological Society: Scott Polar Research Institute, Lensfield Rd, Cambridge, CB2 1ER, UK; tel. (1223) 355974; fax (1223) 354931; e-mail igsoc@igsoc.org; internet www.igsoc.org; f. 1936 to encourage interest in and encourage research into the scientific and technical problems of snow and ice in all countries; publishes int. symposia; 850 mems; Pres. Prof. ATSUMU OHMURA (Switzerland); Sec-Gen. MAGNÚS MÁR MAGNÚSSON; publs *Annals of Glaciology* (2 or 3 a year), *Ice* (news bulletin, 3 a year), *Journal of Glaciology* (quarterly).

International Hydrographic Organization/Organisation Hydrographique Internationale: BP 445, 4 quai Antoine 1er, Monte Carlo, 98011 Monaco Cedex; tel. 93-10-81-00; fax 93-10-81-40; e-mail info@ihb.mc; internet www.iho.shom.fr; f. 1921 to establish a close and permanent association among the hydrographic offices of its mem. states; to co-ordinate the activities of the national hydrographic offices of mem. states in order to render maritime navigation easier and safer; to obtain uniformity in nautical charts and documents; to encourage the adoption of the best methods of conducting hydrographic surveys and improvement in the theory and practice of hydrography; to encourage surveying in those areas where accurate charts are lacking; to encourage co-ordination of hydrographic surveys with relevant oceanographic activities and to provide for co-operation between the IHO and international organizations in the fields of maritime safety and oceanography; to extend and facilitate the application of oceanographic knowledge for the benefit of navigators; 76 mem. states; library of 750 vols, 100 periodicals, 26,000 charts published by member states; Pres. Vice-Adm. ALEXANDROS MARATOS (Greece); Dirs Rear Adm. KENNETH BARBOR (USA), Capt. HUGO GORZIGLIA (Chile); publ. var. online publications (see website).

International Institute for Applied Systems Analysis (IIASA): Schlossplatz 1, 2361 Laxenburg, Austria; tel. (2236) 807; fax (2236) 71313; e-mail inf@iiasa.ac.at; internet www.iiasa.ac.at; f. 1972 on the initiative of the USA and the USSR; non-governmental research organization; concerned with global environmental change, global economic and technological transition, and systems methods for the analysis of global change; mems: organizations from 16 countries; Chair. Prof. SIMON LEVIN; Dir Prof. LEEN HORDIJK; publ. *Options* (4 a year).

International Institute of Seismology and Earthquake Engineering: Building Research Institute, Ministry of Construction, 1 Tatehara, Tsukuba-shi, Ibaraki Prefecture 305-0802, Japan; tel. (298) 79-0680; fax (298) 64-6777; e-mail iisee@kenken.go.jp; internet iisee.kenken.go.jp; f. 1962 to carry out training and research works on seismology and earthquake engineering for the purpose of fostering these research activities in the developing countries, and undertakes survey, research, guidance and analysis of information on earthquakes and their related matters; 12 mems; Dir TOSHIBUMI FUKUTA; publs *Bulletin of IISEE* (annually), *Individual Studies by Participants at the IISEE* (annually), *Year Book*.

International Mineralogical Association (IMA): c/o Maryse Ohnenstetter, CNRS-CRPG, 15 rue Notre Dame des Pauvres, BP 20, 54501 Vandoeuvre-lès-Nancy Cedex, France; tel. 3-83-59-42-46; fax 3-83-51-17-98; e-mail mohnen@crpg.cnrs-nancy.fr; internet www.ima-mineralogy.org; f. 1958 to further intl co-operation in the mineralogical sciences; organizes meetings and field excursion; maintains 7 commissions and 5 working groups which examine and report on certain aspects of mineralogical practice; Commission on New Minerals, Nomenclature and Classification regularly reports on the acceptance of new minerals, and on mineral classification; mems: 38 mineralogical societies or groups in 38 countries; Pres. Prof. TAKAMITSU YAMANAKA (Japan); Sec. MARYSE OHNENSTETTER; publ. *World Directories* (Mineralogists; Mineral Collections).

International Organization of Legal Metrology/Organisation Internationale de Métrologie Légale: 11 rue Turgot, 75009 Paris, France; tel. 1 48-78-12-82; fax 1 42-82-17-27; internet www.oiml.org; f. 1955 documentation and information centre on methods of verifying and checking legal measurements, to study ways of harmonization and to determine the general principles of legal metrology; mems: governments of 59 countries and 54 corresp. mems; Pres. ALAN E. JOHNSTON (acting) (Canada); Dir JEAN-FRANÇOIS MAGAÑA; publs *Bulletin* (quarterly), *International Recommendations and Documents*.

International Ornithological Congress/Congrès International Ornithologique: c/o Prof. Dr Dominique G. Homberger, Dept of Biological Sciences, 202 Life Sciences Bldg, Louisiana State Univ., Baton Rouge, LA 70803-1715, USA; tel. (225) 578-1747; fax (225) 578-2597; internet www.i-o-c.org; f. 1884; int. congress every 4 years; Pres. Prof. Dr JOHN WINGFIELD (USA); Permanent Sec. Prof. Dr DOMINIQUE G. HOMBERGER.

International Palaeontological Association: Palaeontological Institute, Room 121, Lindley Hall, 1475 Jayhawk Blvd, Univ. of Kansas, Lawrence, KA 66045, USA; tel. (785) 864-3338; fax (785) 864-5276; e-mail rmaddocks@uh.edu; internet ipa.geo.ukans.edu; f. 1933 following the meeting of the Int. Geological Congress; affiliated to the Int. Union of Geological Sciences and the Int. Union of Biological Sciences; meets every 4 years at Int. Geological Congress; mems: nat. orgs, research groups; Pres. RICHARD ALDRIDGE (UK); Sec.-Gen. ROSALIE MADDOCKS (USA); publs *Lethaia*, *Directory of Palaeontologists of the World*, *IPA Fossil Collections of the World*.

International Society for Human and Animal Mycology (ISHAM)/Société Internationale de Mycologie Humaine et Animale: c/o Dr Malcolm Richardson, Dept of Bacteriology and Immunology, Haartman Institute, University of Helsinki, Haartmaninkatu 3, POB 21, 00014 Helsinki, Finland; tel. (9) 191-26894; fax (9) 26382; e-mail malcolm.richardson@helsinki.fi; internet www.isham.org; f. 1954 to encourage the practice and study of all aspects of medical and veterinary mycology; 990 mems in 74 countries; Pres. Dr DAVID W. WARNOCK (USA); Gen. Sec. Dr MALCOLM RICHARDSON; publs *Medical Mycology* (annually in 6 parts), *ISHAM Mycoses Newsletter* (2 a year).

International Society for Tropical Ecology: c/o Botany Dept, Banaras Hindu University, Varanasi 5, India; tel. (542) 317099; fax (542) 317074; f. 1956 to promote and develop the science of ecology in the tropics in the service of man; to publish a journal to aid ecologists in the tropics in communication of their findings; and to hold symposia from time to time to summarize the state of knowledge in particular of general fields of tropical ecology; mems: 500; Pres. Prof. HELMUT LIETH; Sec. Prof. J. S. SINGH; publ. *Tropical Ecology* (2 a year).

International Society of Biometeorology: c/o Dr Scott Greene, Department of Geography, University of Oklahoma, Norman, OK 73071, USA; tel. (405) 325-4319; fax (405) 447-8455; e-mail jgreene@ou.edu; internet www.biometeorology.org; f. 1956; aims: to unite biometeorologists working in the fields of agricultural, botanical, cosmic, entomological, forestry, human, veterinary, zoological and other branches of biometeorology; 243 individual mems in 44 countries; Pres. Dr IAN BURTON (Canada); Sec.-Gen. Dr SCOTT GREENE; publs *International Journal of Biometeorology* (4 a year), *Progress in Biometeorology*, *Biometeorology Bulletin* (2 a year).

International Society of Cryptozoology: POB 43070, Tucson, AZ 85733, USA; located at: Dept of Zoological Collections, International Wildlife Museum, 4800 W. Gates Pass Rd, Tucson, AZ 85745, USA; tel. (520) 884-8369; fax (520) 884-8369; e-mail isc-rg@cox.net; internet www.internationalsocietyofcryptozoology.org; f. 1982 to serve as focal point for the investigation, analysis, publication, and discussion of all matters related to animals of unexpected form or size, or unexpected occurrence in time or space, and to encourage scientific examination of all evidence related to these matters; 800 mems; Pres. Prof. CHRISTINE M. JANIS (acting) (USA); Sec. J. RICHARD GREENWELL (USA); publs *Cryptozoology* (annually), *The ISC Newsletter* (quarterly).

International Society of Developmental Biologists: c/o Prof. Ben Scheres, Dept of Molecular Cell Biology, Utrecht University, Padualaan 8, 3584 CH Utrecht, Netherlands; tel. (30) 2533133; tel. (30) 2513655; internet www1.elsevier.com/homepage/sah/isdb; f. 1911 as International Institute of Embryology; to promote study of developmental biology and to promote intl co-operation among researchers in this field; Developmental Biology Section of the International Union of Biological Sciences (*q.v.*); mems: 900 individual, 7 corporate; Pres. Prof. EDWARD M. DE ROBERTIS (USA); Int. Sec. Prof. BEN SCHERES.

International Society of Electrochemistry: c/o Dr Otmar Dossenbach, Executive Secretary, Ave Vinet 19, 1004 Lausanne, Switzerland; tel. 526323044; fax 216483975; e-mail info@ise-online.org; internet www.ise-online.org; f. 1949 to promote the advance of electrochemical science and technology and to organize the free exchange of information in basic and applied electrochemistry; 1,300 mems in 60 countries; Sec.-Gen. D. KOLB (Germany); Pres. Prof. Dr R. HILLMAN (UK); publ. *Electrochimica Acta*.

International Society of Exposure Analysis: c/o JSI Research and Training Institute, 44 Farnsworth St, Boston, MA 02210-1211, USA; tel. (617) 482-9485; fax (617) 482-0617; e-mail iseamail@jsi.com; internet www.iseaweb.org; f. 1989 to foster and advance the science of exposure analysis relating to environmental contaminants, both for human populations and ecosystems; holds annual conferences; 400 mems; Pres. Dr CLIFFORD WEISEL; Sec. Dr NATALIE FREEMAN; publ. *Journal of Exposure Science and Environmental Epidemiology* (6 a year).

International Statistical Institute/Institut International de Statistique: Prinses Beatrixlaan 428, POB 950, 2270 AZ Voorburg, Netherlands; tel. (70) 3375737; fax (70) 3860025; e-mail isi@cbs.nl; internet www.cbs.nl/isi; f. 1885; autonomous soc. devoted to the devt and improvement of statistical methods and their application world-wide; provides a forum for the int. exchange of knowledge between mems, and aims to mobilize mems' expertise to play an effective role in the practical solution of global problems; administers int. statistical education programme, incl. statistical education centre in Kolkata, India, and Indian Statistical Institute; conducts statistical research to undertake operational activities in the field of statistics which help to improve the data used in planning and policy formation, to the benefit of the countries concerned; to advance integration of statistics and promote appropriate use of statistical methods in different socio-cultural settings; 2,020 elected mems, also 11 hon., 145 ex-officio, 65 corporate; Pres. DENISE LIEVESLEY (UK); Dir Permanent Office DANIEL BERZE; publs *Bernoulli Journal* (quarterly), *International Statistical Review / Short Book Reviews* (3 a year).

International Table of Selected Constants/Tables Internationales de Constantes Sélectionnées: Université P. et M. Curie (Paris VI), Faculté des Sciences, Tour 13, 4 place Jussieu, 75252 Paris Cedex 05, France; f. 1909 to publish all the constants and numerical data concerning the pure and applied physico-chemical sciences; Pres. J.-M. FLAUD (France).

International Union for Quaternary Research (INQUA): c/o Prof. Peter Coxon, Dept of Geography, Museum Bldg, Trinity College, Dublin 2, Ireland; tel. (1) 608-1213; internet www.inqua.tcd.ie; f. 1928; geology, geography, prehistory, palaeontology, palynology, pedology; Pres. Exec. Comm. Prof. JOHN J. CLAGUE (Canada); Sec.-Gen. Prof. PETER COXON; publs *Proceedings of Congresses*, *Quaternary International*, *Quaternary Perspective* (newsletter).

International Union for the Study of Social Insects/Union Internationale pour l'Etude des Insectes Sociaux: c/o Dr M. Brown, Dept of Zoology, Trinity College Dublin, Dublin 2, Ireland; e-mail wolfgang.h.kirchner@ruhr-uni-bochum.de; internet www.iussi.org; f. 1951; mems: 500 individuals from 24 countries; comprises seven regional and national sections; Pres. WALTER TSCHINKEL; Sec.-Gen. WOLFGANG H. KIRCHNER; publs *Insectes sociaux*, *Congress Proceedings*, etc.

International Union of Speleology/Union Internationale de Spéléologie: c/o Institute of Karst Research, Titov trg 2, Postojna, Slovenia; internet www.uis-speleo.org; f. 1965; karstology, speleology; 60 mem. countries; Pres. JOSÉ AYRTON LABEGALINI (Brazil); Sec.-Gen. Dr PAVEL BOSÁK (Czech Republic); publs *Bulletin* (1 or 2 a year), *International Journal of Speleology* (annually), *Speleological Abstracts* (annually).

OECD Nuclear Energy Agency (NEA)/Agence de l'OCDE pour l'Energie Nucléaire: Le Seine St-Germain, 12 blvd des Îles, 92130 Issy-les-Moulineaux, France; tel. 1-45-24-10-15; fax 1-45-24-11-10; e-mail nea@nea.fr; internet www.nea.fr; f. 1958, name changed 1972; an intergovernmental organization with the primary objective of assisting its member countries to maintain and further develop, through international co-operation, the scientific, technological and legal bases required for a safe, environmentally friendly and economical use of nuclear energy for peaceful purposes; provides authoritative assessments and forges common understandings on key issues, as input to government decisions on nuclear energy policy and to broader OECD policy analyses in areas such as energy and sustainable development; non-partisan, unbiased source of information, data and analyses, drawing on one of the best international networks of technical experts; mems: 28 countries; Dir-Gen. LUIS ECHÁVARRI; publs *Annual Report*, *NEA News* (2 a year), *Nuclear Law Bulletin* (2 a year).

Pacific Science Association/Association Scientifique du Pacifique: Bishop Museum, 1525 Bernice St, Honolulu, HI 96817, USA; tel. (808) 848-4124; fax (808) 847-8252; e-mail psa@pacificscience.org; internet www.pacificscience.org; f. 1920 to co-operate in the study of scientific problems relating to the Pacific region; sponsors congresses and inter-congresses; mems: scientists and scientific institutions interested in the Pacific; Pres. Dr R. GERARD WARD (Australia); Exec. Sec. JOHN BURKE BURNETT; publ. *Information Bulletin*.

Pan-American Institute of Geography and History/Instituto Panamericano de Geografía e Historia: Ex-Arzobispado 29, Col. Observatorio, 11860 México, DF, Mexico; tel. (55) 5277-5888; fax (55) 5271-6172; e-mail secretariageneral@ipgh.org; internet www.ipgh.org; f. 1928; to encourage, coordinate and promote the study of cartography, geophysics, geography, history, anthropology, archaeology and other related scientific studies; mems: countries of the Org. of American States; library of 60,000 vols and 24,000 maps, periodicals colln of 54,000 vols; Sec.-Gen. MSc SANTIAGO BORRERO (Mexico); publs *Boletín de Antropología Americana* (annual), *Revista de Arqueología Americana*, *Revista Cartográfica* (annual), *Revista Geofísica*, *Revista Geográfica* (2 a year), *Revista de Historia de América* (2 a year).

Wetlands International: POB 471, 6700 AL Wageningen, Netherlands; located at: Droevendaalsesteeg 3A, 6708 PB Wageningen, Netherlands; tel. (317) 478854; fax (317) 478850; e-mail post@wetlands.org; internet www.wetlands.org; f. 1954 to sustain and restore wetlands, their resources and biodiversity through worldwide research, information exchange and conservation activities; 58 mem. countries; CEO J. MADGWICK.

World Academy of Art and Science: c/o Dr Walter Truett Anderson, 760 Market St, Suite 315, San Francisco, CA 94102, USA; tel. (415) 915-2449; fax (415) 781-8227; internet www.worldacademy.org; f. 1960; a forum for discussion of the social consequences and policy implications of knowledge; 471 Fellows in 62 countries; Pres. Dr WALTER TRUETT ANDERSON (USA); publ. *WAAS Newsletter* (2 a year).

World Conservation Union (IUCN)/Union Mondiale pour la Nature (UICN)/Unión Mundial para la Naturaleza: Rue Mauverney 28, 1196 Gland, Switzerland; tel. 229990000; fax 229990002; e-mail mail@iucn.org; internet www.iucn.org; f. 1948 to influence, encourage and assist societies worldwide to conserve the integrity and diversity of nature and to ensure that any use of natural resources is equitable and ecologically sustainable; mems: 1,000 mems (government agencies, NGOs, affiliate orgs and individual scientists) in 150 countries; Pres. MOHAMMED VALLI MOOSA (South Africa); Dir-Gen. ACHIM STEINER (Switzerland); publs *World Conservation* (in English, French and

Spanish), *Red Lists: Environmental Policy and Law Papers*, *Best Policy Guidelines*.

World Meteorological Organization/Organisation Météorologique Mondiale: Secretariat CP 2300, 7 bis ave de la Paix, 1211 Geneva 2, Switzerland; tel. 227308111; fax 227308181; e-mail wmo@wmo.int; internet www.wmo.int; f. 1950; objectives: world-wide co-operation in making and standardizing meteorological, climatological, hydrological and related geophysical observations and their exchange and publication; assists in training, research and technology transfer; furthers the application of meteorology to aviation, shipping, water problems, agriculture, environmental problems (incl. climate and climate change) and to sustainable development; constituent bodies: Congress, Executive Council, six regional associations, eight technical commissions; mems: 181 states and six territories maintaining their own meteorological or hydrometeorological services; Pres. Dr A. I. BEDRITSKY (Russia); Sec.-Gen. M. JARRAUD (France); publs *Annual Report and other publications* (see catalogue of WMO Publications), *WMO Bulletin* (4 a year), *World Climate News* (4 a year).

World Organisation of Systems and Cybernetics/Organisation Mondiale pour la Systémique et la Cybernétique: c/o Dr Alex Andrew, 95 Finch Rd, Earley, Reading, Berks. RG6 7JX, UK; tel. (118) 926-9328; fax (118) 926-9328; e-mail alexandrew@tiscali.co.uk; internet www.cybsoc.org/wosc; f. 1969 to act as focal point for all socs concerned with cybernetics, systems and allied subjects, to aim for the recognition of cybernetics as a bona fide science and to maintain liaison with other int. bodies; holds int. congresses every 3 years; awards Norbert Wiener Memorial Gold Medal; 25 hon. fellows, nat. orgs in more than 20 countries; Pres. Prof. ROBERT VALLÉE; Dir-Gen. Dr ALEX ANDREW; publ. *Kybernetes* (10 a year).

AFGHANISTAN

The Higher Education System

The higher education system in Afghanistan was established with the foundation of Kabul University in 1932. However, during more than 20 years of civil war from 1979 higher education was disrupted by the departure of many teaching staff from Afghanistan. In 1991 there were six institutions of higher education with a total enrolment of 17,000 students. In September 1996 the Islamist Taliban movement gained control of Kabul and issued decrees enforcing their fundamentalist interpretation of Islam, which included banning women from receiving education. In late 2001 a US-led military coalition ousted the Taliban regime following the September 11 terrorist attacks on the USA, which were blamed on the on the al-Qa'ida organization of Osama bin Laden, a Saudi dissident based in Afghanistan. In March 2002 Kabul University was re-opened for men and women. University-level education in Afghanistan is offered by seven universities. Other higher education institutions include agricultural, art, commercial, religious and technical schools. In 2002 some 22,717 students were enrolled at the higher education level.

All higher education is publicly-funded from the government budget. Foreign universities as well as governments and non-governmental organizations have donated books and teaching materials to help revive the higher education sector.

In order to be admitted to higher education students must complete the Baccalauria and pass an entrance examination (Concours). There are three levels of university degrees: Bachelors/Licence, Masters and Doctori. The Bachelors or Licence is usually four years in duration, but engineering and veterinary medicine degrees last five years, while degrees in medicine are seven years in length (including one year pre-medical and a one-year internship). Masters degrees were introduced in 1982 at the University of Kabul and the Institute of Social Sciences, and are two years in length. The Master of Science degree at Kabul Polytechnic is a five-year first degree course. Doctorate courses are three years in length in the following subjects: Architecture, Arts, Engineering, Natural sciences, Social Sciences.

Learned Societies

GENERAL

Academy of Sciences of Afghanistan: Sher Alikhan St, Char Rahe Sher Poor, Kabul; tel. (20) 2102919; fax (20) 2100268; f. 1979; research in science, technology, humanities and culture; 4 main divs: Centre of Natural Sciences (*q.v.*), Institute of Social Sciences (*q.v.*), Institute of Language and Literature (*q.v.*), Int. Centre of Pushtu Studies (*q.v.*); Islamic Studies Centre added 2000; further units incl. Int. Research Centre of Kushan Studies and Archeology, Publication and Literature Dept, Encyclopedia and Dictionaries Dept.; library: Central Library of 5,000 vols, Central Archives; Pres. Dr ABDUL BARI RASHID.

UNESCO Office Kabul: POB 5, UN Compound, Kabul; located at: UN Compound, Kabul; tel. (2) 214522; fax (2) 214379; e-mail martin.hadlow@undpafg.org.pk; Dir MARTIN HADLOW.

LANGUAGE AND LITERATURE

Goethe-Institut: c/o Embassy of the Federal Republic of Germany, POB 83, Kabul; located at: Wazir Akbar Khan, Shahmahmod St, Kabul; e-mail il@kabul.geothe.org; internet www.goethe.de/kabul; promotes cultural exchange with Germany, and contributes to the reconstruction of cultural and educational institutions in Afghanistan since the fall of the Taliban regime in 2001; Dir GERTI HINTERBERGER.

Research Institutes

GENERAL

Afghanistan Research and Evaluation Unit (AREU): Flower St (corner of St 2), Shahr-i-Naw, Kabul; e-mail areu@areu.org.af; internet www.areu.org.af; f. 2002; promotes a culture of research and learning by strengthening analytical capacity in Afghanistan and facilitating reflection and debate; library of 3,000 vols, periodicals, maps, CDs and DVDs; Dir PAUL FISHSTEIN.

Institute of Social Sciences: Kabul; attached to Afghanistan Acad. of Sciences; philosophy, economics, history, archaeology; Pres. Dr HAKIM HELALI; publs *Afghanistan* (quarterly in English, French and German), *Ariana* (quarterly in Pashtu and Dari).

LANGUAGE AND LITERATURE

Institute of Languages and Literature: Kabul; attached to Afghanistan Acad. of Sciences; linguistics, literature and folklore; study of Pashtu and Dari languages, and Afghanistan dialects; publs *Kabul* (monthly, Pashtu), *Zayray* (weekly, Pashtu).

International Centre for Pashtu Studies Kabul: Kabul; attached to Afghanistan Acad. of Sciences; research, compilation and translation; publ. *Pashtu Quarterly*.

MEDICINE

Institute of Public Health: Ansari Wat, Kabul; f. 1962; public health training and research; govt reference laboratory; Dir Dr S. M. SADIQUE; publs *Afghan Journal of Public Health* (every 2 weeks), books and pamphlets.

NATURAL SCIENCES

General

Centre of Natural Sciences: Kabul; attached to Afghanistan Acad. of Sciences; institutes of botany, zoology, geology and chemistry, seismology; computer centre, plants museum and botanical garden.

Physical Sciences

Department of Geology and Mineral Survey: Ministry of Mines and Industries, Kabul; tel. 25848; f. 1955; research, mapping, prospecting and exploration; library of 8,300 vols; Pres. Dip. Eng. Haji MOHAMAD NAWZADI; publs *Journal of Mines and Industries* (quarterly), maps and other reference works.

Libraries and Archives

Kabul

Kabul University Library: c/o Min. of Information and Culture, Mohammad Jan Khan Wat, Kabul; tel. 42594; f. 1931; 250,000 vols; Dir Prof. ABDUL RASOUL RAHIN.

Library of the National Bank: c/o Min. of Information and Culture, Mohammad Jan Khan Wat, Kabul; located at: Bank Millie Afghan, Ibn Sina Wat, Kabul; f. 1941; 5,600 vols; Dir A. AZIZ.

Library of the Press and Information Department: c/o Min. of Information and Culture, Mohammad Jan Khan Wat, Kabul; located at: Sanaii Wat, Kabul; f. 1931; 28,000 vols and 800 MSS; Dir MOHAMMED SARWAR RONA.

Ministry of Education Library: c/o Min. of Information and Culture, Mohammad Jan Khan Wat, Kabul; f. 1920; 30,000 vols; Chief Officer MOHAMAD QASEM HILAMAN; publ. *Erfan* (monthly journal in Pashtu and Dari).

Public Library: c/o Min. of Information and Culture, Mohammad Jan Khan Wat, Kabul; located at: Charaii-i-Malik Asghar, Kabul; f. 1920; attached to Min. of Information and Culture; 60,000 vols, 433 MSS, 30 current periodicals; Dir MOHAMAD OMAR SEDDIQUI.

Nazo Annah Library: c/o Min. of Information and Culture, Mohammad Jan Khan Wat, Kabul; f. 2001 to enable and empower young women through literacy and education; attached to Noor Education Centre; fmrly Women's Welfare Soc. Library; 680 vols; publ. *Baztab Noor* (newsletter, monthly).

Museums and Art Galleries

Ghazni

Ghazni Museum: c/o Min. of Information and Culture, Mohammad Jan Khan Wat, Kabul; located in: Ghazni.

Herat

Herat Museum: c/o Min. of Information and Culture, Mohammad Jan Khan Wat, Kabul; located in: Herat.

Kabul

Kabul Museum: c/o Min. of Information and Culture, Mohammad Jan Khan Wat, Kabul; tel. 42656; f. 1922; archaeology; Dir ORMA KHAN MASSOUDI.

Kandahar

Kandahar Museum: c/o Min. of Information and Culture, Mohammad Jan Khan Wat, Kabul; located in: Kandahar.

Maimana

Maimana Museum: c/o Min. of Information and Culture, Mohammad Jan Khan Wat, Kabul; located in: Maimana.

Mazar-i-Sharif

Mazar-i-Sharif Museum: c/o Min. of Information and Culture, Mohammad Jan Khan Wat, Kabul; located in: Mazar-i-Sharif.

Universities

BALKH UNIVERSITY

Mazar-i-Sharif, Balkh
Telephone: 503487
Fax: 503554

Founded 1988

Pres.: Prof. HABIBULLAH

Number of teachers: 83
Number of students: 4,739

Faculties of Economics, Engineering, Journalism, Law, Literature, Medicine and Science.

UNIVERSITY OF EDUCATION

Kabul

Founded 2002

Number of teachers: 140
Number of students: 1,744.

HERAT UNIVERSITY

Herat

Founded 1986
State control

Vice-Chancellor: Dr ABDUL RAOOF
Deputy Vice-Chancellor: ABDUL RAHMAN MANSURI
Librarian: SAID KHALLIL

Library of 2,000 vols
Number of teachers: 76
Number of students: 2,324

DEANS

Faculty of Agriculture: Prof. GH. RASSOL AMIRI
Faculty of Language and Literature: M. SABBAH

KABUL UNIVERSITY

Jamal Mina, Kabul
Telephone: 40341
Internet: www.ku.edu.af

Founded 1932
State control
Academic year: March to January
Language of instruction: Dari

Rector: Prof. MOHAMMAD AKBAR POPAL
Librarian: REYHANA POPALZAI

Library of 200,000 vols
Number of teachers: 450
Number of students: 7,000

Publication: *Natural Science and Social Science* (quarterly)

Faculties of Agriculture, Economics, Engineering, Fine Arts, History and Philosophy, Islamic Law, Journalism, Law, Linguistics, Pharmacology, Psychology, Veterinary Science, Science, Social Sciences

DEANS

Faculty of Education: Prof. GUL RAHMAN HAKIM
Faculty of Law and Political Science: Prof. IQRAL WASIL
Faculty of Social Sciences: Prof. M. DAUD RAWOSH

ATTACHED RESEARCH CENTRE

National Centre for Policy Research: f. 2003 to promote democracy in Afghanistan; depts of Economics, Law and Political Sciences and Social Science; offers scholarships to Afghani researchers for carrying out post-graduate studies in Germany; financed by Konrad-Adenauer Stiftung (Germany).

KABUL MEDICAL UNIVERSITY

Kabul

Founded 2004; fmrly Faculty of Medicine of Kabul University
State control

Dir: SAYED GAZANFAR.

KANDAHAR UNIVERSITY

Kandahar

Founded 1988
State control

Vice-Pres.: SHAH MAHMUD BARAI

Number of students: 747.

BAYAZID ROSHAN UNIVERSITY OF NANGARHAR

Darunta, Jalalabad, Nangarhar

Founded 1963 from Medical Faculty of Kabul University, reorganized 1978
State control
Language of instruction: Pashtu

Vice-Chancellor: Dr MOHAMMAD TAYAB
Dean: Prof. ABDUL QADIR FAZLI

Number of teachers: 96
Number of students: 3,263

DEANS

Faculty of Medicine: Prof. ASSADULLAH SHINWARI
Faculty of Political Science: MIRWAIS AHMADZAI

There are also faculties of Agriculture, Education and Engineering

Colleges

Institute of Agriculture: Kabul; f. 1924; veterinary medicine, forestry.

Institute of Arabic and Religious Study: Kabul; Other centres incl.: the Najmul-Madares, Nangrahar; the Jamé and Fakhrul Madares, Herat; the Asadia Madrasa, Mazar-i-Sharif; the Takharistan Madrasa, Kunduz; the Zahir Shahi Madrasa, Maimana.

Kabul Art School: Bibi Mahro, nr Kabul; music, painting and sculpture courses.

School of Commerce: Kabul; f. 1943; banking, commercial law, economics, business admin., finance.

School of Mechanics: Kabul; for apprentice trainees.

ALBANIA

The Higher Education System

Higher education is offered through universities and higher schools and is governed by legislation enacted in 1999 and 2003. In 2007 there were eight universities, the oldest of which is the Alexsander Xhuvani University of Elbasan, founded in 1909. The Law on Higher Education of 1999 introduced and guarantees state funding for public higher education. Albania joined the Bologna Process in 2003, and in the same year implemented a new higher education act that introduced a two-tier Bachelors and Masters degree structure. This new system was scheduled to be fully implemented (with the exception of a few subject areas) by the 2006 academic year.

University Rectors and Higher School Directors and Headmasters belong to the Conference of Rectors, the highest decision-making body in Albania's higher education system. All universities consist of faculties, which are governed by faculty councils, and sometimes of higher schools; the highest decision-making body in a higher school is the school council. Both faculties and higher schools consist of departments, in which the department council is the highest decision-making body.

Admission to higher education is conducted according to quotas and is subject to main and secondary fees. Main admission fees are proposed by the Ministry of Education and Science, following recommendations from the universities and higher schools, and are approved by the Council of Ministers. Secondary fees are levied for specialist education and can equate to a maximum of 10% of the main fees. Admission to public universities and higher schools is based on competitive examinations which are organized by the Ministry of Education and Science on the advice the Conference of Rectors. Successful students are then admitted subject to the established fees.

There are three levels of university qualifications: Diplomë (Diploma), Kandidat i Shkencave (Candidate of Sciences) and Doktor mi Shkencave (Doctor of Sciences). The Diplomë is usually a four-year undergraduate degree, however degrees in engineering, technology and dentistry last five years, and courses in medicine last six years. The Kandidat i Shkencave is a first postgraduate degree of two to three years. The Doktor mi Shkencave is based on a significant period of research. There is no grading system for this level of study. Qualifications from the three military institutions (the Higher Military Academies in Tirana and Vlora, and the Higher Unified Military School in Tirana) have the same equivalency as civilian qualifications.

Quality assessment of universities and higher schools and academic accreditation is carried out by the Accrediting Agency and the Accrediting Council, under the authority of the Council of Ministers.

Learned Societies

GENERAL

Academy of Sciences of Albania: Fan. S. Noli Sq., 35542 Tiranë; tel. and fax (4) 227476; e-mail esulstar@akad.edu.al; internet www.academyofsciences.net; f. 1972; attached research institutes: see Research Institutes; 28 mems; Pres. YLLI POPA; Scientific Sec. EDUARD SULSTAROVA; publs *Studia Albanica* (2 a year), *Philological Studies* (2 a year), *Historical Studies* (2 a year), *Ilyria* (2 a year), *Albanian Journal of Natural and Technical Sciences* (2 a year), *Folk Culture* (2 a year), *Our Language* (2 a year), *Issues of Albanian Folklore* (irreg.), *Biological Studies* (2 a year), *Art Studies* (2 a year), *Geographical Studies* (irreg.).

Komiteti Shqiptar për Marrëdhënie Kulturore me botën e jashtme (Albanian Committee for Cultural Relations Abroad): Tiranë; Pres. JORGO MELIKA.

LANGUAGE AND LITERATURE

Alliance Française: French Embassy, Rr. Elbasanit, Shkolla E Mesme E Gjuheve Te Huaja 'Asim Vokshi', Tiranë; tel. (4) 364932; fax (4) 347589; e-mail alliancefr_tirane@yahoo.fr; offers courses and examinations in French language and culture and promotes cultural exchange with France; attached teaching centres in Elbasan and Korçë.

British Council: Rr. 'Ded Gjo Luli' 3/1, Tiranë; tel. (4) 240856; fax (4) 240858; e-mail info@britishcouncil.org.al; internet www2.britishcouncil.org/albania; offers courses and examinations in English language and British culture and promotes cultural exchange with the UK; library of 3,000 vols; Dir JOAN CURRY.

Lidhja e Shkrimtarëve dhe e Artistëve të Shqipërisë (Union of Writers and Artists of Albania): Tiranë; f. 1957; 1,750 mems; Pres. DRITËRO AGOLLI; Secs FEIM IBRAHIMI, PETRO KOKUSHTA, NASI LERA; publs *Drita* (journal, weekly), *Les Lettres Albanaises* (quarterly), *Nëntori* (Review, monthly).

PEN Centre of Albania: Rr. 'Ded Gjo Luli', Pallati 5, shk. 3/4, Tiranë; e-mail albania@aol2.albaniaonline.net; Pres. BESNIK MUSTAFAJ.

NATURAL SCIENCES

Physical Sciences

Shoqata e Gjeologëve te Shqipërisë (Geologists' Association of Albania): Blloku 'Vasil Shanto', Tiranë; tel. (4) 226597; f. 1989; 450 mems; Chair. ALEKSANDËR ÇINA; Sec.-Gen. ILIR ALLIU; publ. *Buletini i Shkencave Gjeologjike*.

Research Institutes

AGRICULTURE, FISHERIES AND VETERINARY SCIENCE

Instituti i Duhanit (Tobacco Institute): Cërrik; tel. (581) 2800; f. 1956; library of 1,000 vols; Dir BELUL GIXHARI; publ. *Bulletin des sciences de l'agriculture* (quarterly).

Instituti i Kërkimeve Bujqësore Lushnje (Lushnje Institute of Agricultural Research): Lushnje; f. 1952; focuses on cultivating new varieties of bread and durum wheat, cotton, sunflower and dry bean; library of 8,000 vols; Dir VLADIMIR MALO.

Instituti i Kërkimeve Pyjore dhe Kullotave (Forest and Pasture Research Institute): Tiranë; f. 1992; Dir SPIRO KARADUMI.

Instituti i Kërkimeve të Foragjere (Forage Research Institute): Fushë-Krujë; tel. (4) 233354; f. 1973; Dir VASILLAQ DHIMA.

Instituti i Kërkimeve të Pemëve Frutore dhe Vreshtave (Institute of Fruit Growing and Vineyard Research): Tiranë; tel. (4) 229704; f. 1984; library of 70 vols; Dir STEFAN GJOKA; publs *Pemëtaria*, *Bulletini i Shkencave Bujqësore*.

Instituti i Kërkimeve të Zooteknisë (Institute of Animal Husbandry Research): Laprake, Tiranë; tel. (4) 223135; f. 1955; library of 1,900 vols; Dir MINA SPIRU.

Instituti i Kërkimeve Veterinare (Institute of Veterinary Research): Tiranë; tel. and fax (4) 372912; e-mail instvet@icc.al.eu.org; f. 1928; Dir Prof. Dr KRISTAQ BERXHOLI; publ. *Veterinaria* (3 a year).

Instituti i Kerkimit te Bimeve te Arave, Stacioni Eksperimental (Experimental Station of the Research Institute for Arable Farming): Rr. Voskopojës, Korçë; fax (824) 3086; e-mail stacionieksperimental@yahoo.com; f. 1953; attached to Min. of Agriculture and Food; library of 600 vols; Dir Dr EQREM MEÇOLLARI; publ. *Bulletin* (annual).

Instituti i Mbrojtjes Bimeve (Institute of Plant Protection Research): Durrës; tel. and fax (52) 64527; e-mail imb@anep.al.eu.org; f. 1971; library of 2,410 vols; Dir Dr SKENDER VARRAKU.

Instituti i Misrit dhe Orizit (Institute of Maize and Rice): Shkodër; tel. (225) 1200; fax (224) 2507; e-mail imoshkoder@yahoo.com; f. 1971; library of 4,860 vols; Dir Prof. KOSTANDIN HAJKOLA; publ. *Agriculture Science Bulletin* (quarterly).

Instituti i Perimeve dhe i Patates (Institute of Vegetables and Potatoes): Rr. Skënder Kosturi, Tiranë; tel. (4) 228422; e-mail instpp@albmail.com; f. 1980; library of 6,000 vols; Dir XHEVAT SHIMA; publs *Bulletin of Agricultural Sciences*, *Bulletin of Vegetables and Potatoes*, *Bulletin of Vegetables*.

Instituti i Studimeve dhe i Projektimeve të Veprave të Kullimit dhe Ujitjes (Institute of Irrigation and Drainage Studies and Designs): Tiranë; f. 1970; Dir DHIMITËR VOGLI.

Instituti i Studimit të Tokave (Institute of Soil Studies): Tiranë; tel. (4) 223278; fax (4) 228367; f. 1971; library of 5,000 vols; Dir ALBERT DUBALI.

Instituti i Ullirit dhe i Agrumeve (Institute of Olives and Citrus Plants): 'Uji i Jtohtë', Vlorë; tel. and fax (33) 23225; f. 1971; library of 500 vols; Dir Dr HAIRI ISMAILI; publ. *Bulletin*.

Stacioni i Studimeve dhe i Kërkimeve të Peshkimit (Fisheries Research): Durrës; f. 1960; Dir EQREM KAPIDANI.

ARCHITECTURE AND TOWN PLANNING

Instituti i Monumenteve të Kulturës (Institute of Cultural Monuments): Rr. Murat Toptani 9, Tiranë; tel. and fax (4) 227511; e-mail imk@albmail.com; f. 1965; research and restoration of ancient and medieval architecture, cultural bldgs and artistic monuments; library of 9,000 vols; Dir ARTAN SHKRELI; publ. *Monumentet* (Monuments, 2 a year).

Instituti i Studimeve e Projektimeve Urbanistikë (Institute of Urban Planning and Design): Rr. M. Gjollesha Istn, Tiranë; tel. and fax (4) 223361; f. 1991; library of 400 vols; Dir GJERGJ KOTMILO.

ECONOMICS, LAW AND POLITICS

Instituti i Studimeve të Marrëdhënieve Ndërkombëtare (Institute of International Relations): Tiranë; tel. (4) 229521; fax (4) 232970; f. 1981; Dir SOKRAT PLAKA; publ. *Politika ndërkombëtare* (International Politics, quarterly).

EDUCATION

Instituti i Studimeve Pedagogjike (Institute of Pedagogical Studies): Rr. Naim Frashëri 37, Tiranë; tel. (4) 222573; fax (4) 225858; f. 1970; Dir LUAN HAJDARAGA; publs *Revista Pedagogjike* (quarterly), *Yllkat* (monthly), *Chemistry and Biology in School* (2 a year), *Mathematics and Physics in School* (2 a year), *Vocational Schools* (2 a year), *Social Materials in School* (2 a year), *Albanian Language and Literature in School* (2 a year), *Elementary School* (annual), *Nursery School 3–6* (annual), *Foreign Languages in School* (annual).

FINE AND PERFORMING ARTS

Qendra e Studimeve të Artit (Centre for Art Studies): Rr. Don Bosko 60, Tiranë; tel. (4) 259667; fax (4) 228274; e-mail betim@sizmo.albnet.net; f. 1984; research in fine arts, music, choreography, theatre, cinema, art and culture instns; attached to Acad. of Sciences of Albania; Dir. Prof. JOSIF PAPAGJONI; publ. *Studime për Artin* (Studies for Art, 2 a year).

HISTORY, GEOGRAPHY AND ARCHAEOLOGY

Instituti i Arkeologjisë (Institute of Archaeology): Bulevardi Deshmoret e Kombit, Sheshi Nënë Tereza, Tiranë; tel. (4) 226541; fax (4) 240712; e-mail instark@albmail.com; f. 1976; attached to Acad. of Sciences of Albania; Dir. Prof. Dr MUZAFER KORKUTI; publ. *Iliria* (in Albanian , English and French, annual).

Instituti i Historisë (Institute of History): Rr. Naim Frashëri 7, Tiranë; tel. (4) 225869; fax (4) 225869; e-mail analalaj@worldmailer.com; f. 1972; attached to Acad. of Sciences of Albania; study of ancient and modern Albanian history and people; library of 52,000 vols, 10,000 periodicals; Dir Prof. Dr ANA LALAJ; publ. *Studime Historike* (Historical Studies, quarterly).

Qendra e Kërkimeve Gjeografike (Centre for Geographical Research): Qendri e Studimeve Hidraulike, Sheshi Fan S. Noli, Tiranë; tel. (4) 227985; fax (4) 227985; f. 1986; attached to Acad. of Sciences of Albania; library of 3,200 vols; Dir Prof. Dr ARQILE BERXHOLI; publ. *Studime Gjeografike* (Geographical Studies, annual).

LANGUAGE AND LITERATURE

Instituti i Gjuhësisë dhe i Letërsisë (Institute of Linguistics and Literature): Rr. Naim Frashëri 7, Tiranë; tel. (4) 351134; fax (4) 222509; e-mail bulo@igji.tirana.al; f. 1972; study of Albanian language and literature; attached to Acad. of Sciences of Albania; Dir Prof. Dr JORGO BULO; publs *Studime Filologjike* (Philological Studies, quarterly), *Gjuha Jonë* (Our Language, quarterly).

Qendra e Enciklopedisë Shqiptare (Centre for the Albanian Encyclopedical Dictionary): Sheshi Fan S. Noli 7, Tiranë; tel. (4) 250369; fax (4) 227476; e-mail enciklոped@yahoo.com; f. 1988 to prepare revised edn of the *Albanian Encyclopedical Dictionary*; sections of social sciences, natural and technical sciences; attached to the Acad. of Sciences of Albania; Dir Prof. Dr EMIL LAFE.

MEDICINE

Instituti i Mjekësisë Popullore (Institute of Folk Medicine): Tiranë; tel. (4) 223493; f. 1977; Dir Dr GËZIM BOCARI; publ. *Përmbledhje Studimesh* (Collections of Studies, irreg.).

Instituti i Shëndetit Publik (Institute of Public Health): Aleksander Moisiu 80, Tiranë; tel. (4) 374756; fax (4) 370058; f. 1969 as Research Institute of Hygiene, Epidemiology and Immunobiological Products; present name 1995; Dir Prof. EDUARD KAKARRIQI; publ. *Revista Mjekesore* (Medical Magazine, 6 a year).

NATURAL SCIENCES

Biological Sciences

Instituti i Kërkimeve Biologjike (Institute of Biological Research): Rr. Sami Frasheri 5, Tiranë; tel. (4) 222638; fax (4) 222638; e-mail ikbiol@albmail.com; f. 1978; attached to Acad. of Sciences of Albania; Dir Prof. EFIGJENI KONGJIKA.

Mathematical Sciences

Instituti i Informatikës dhe i Matematikës së Aplikuar (Institute of Informatics and Applied Mathematics): Rr. Lek Dukagjini 3, Tiranë; tel. (4) 362968; fax (4) 362122; e-mail inima@inima.al; f. 1971; attached to Acad. of Sciences of Albania; Dir Prof. Dr GUDAR BEQIRAJ.

Physical Sciences

Instituti i Energjetikës (Institute of Energetics): Tiranë; f. 1982; Dir LLAZAR PAPAJORGJI.

Instituti i Fizikës Bërthamore (Institute of Nuclear Physics): POB 85, Tiranë; tel. (4) 376341; fax (4) 362596; e-mail inp@albaniaonline.net; f. 1970; attached to Acad. of Sciences of Albania; Dir Prof. Dr FATOS YLLI.

Instituti i Hidrometeorologjisë (Institute of Hydrometeorology): Rr. e Durrësit 219, Tiranë; tel. (4) 223518; fax (4) 223518; e-mail mitats@yahoo.com; f. 1962; attached to Acad. of Sciences of Albania; Dir Prof. Dr MITAT SANXHAKU.

Instituti i Sizmologjise (Institute of Seismology): Tiranë; tel. and fax (4) 228274; e-mail aliaj@sizmo.albnet.net; f. 1993; attached to Acad. of Sciences of Albania; Dir Prof. Dr SHYQYRI ALIAJ.

Instituti i Studimeve dhe Projektimeve të Gjeologjisë (Geological Research Institute): Blloku 'Vasil Shanto', Tiranë; tel. (4) 226597; f. 1962; library of 20,000 vols; Dir ALAUDIN KODRA; publ. *Buletini i Shkencave Gjeologjike* (quarterly).

RELIGION, SOCIOLOGY AND ANTHROPOLOGY

Instituti i Kulturës Popullore (Institute of Folk Culture): Rr. Kont Urani 3, Tiranë; tel. (4) 222323; fax (4) 224555; e-mail ikp.alb@icc.al.org; f. 1961, present status 1979; depts of ethnology, ethnomusic and ethnochoreography, prose and poetry; library of 10,000 vols, 1.5m. verses of poetry; attached to Acad. of Sciences of Albania; Dir Asst Prof. AFËRDITA ONUZI; publ. *Folk Culture* (2 a year).

TECHNOLOGY

Infraproject Consulting SH.p.K.: Rr. Sami Frasheri; Tiranë; tel. (4) 225206; fax (4) 228321; e-mail vguri@icc.al.eu.org; road, railway and waterway engineering; library of 900 vols; Dir-Gen. VEHIP GURI.

Instituti i Kerkimeve të Ushqimit (Food Research Institute): Rr. M. Gjollesha 56, Tiranë; tel. (4) 226770; fax (4) 226770; e-mail iku@anep.al.eu.org; f. 1961; Dir Prof. Dr RUSTEM ZENELAJ; publ. *Përmbledhje Studimesh* (Collections of Studies, irreg.).

Instituti i Studimeve dhe i Projektimeve Gjeologjike të Naftës e të Gazit (Institute for Studies and Design of Oil and Gas Geology): Fier; f. 1965; Dir DRINI MEZINI; publ. *Buletini Nafta dhe Gazi* (2 a year, summaries in English).

Instituti i Studimeve dhe i Projektimeve të Hidrocentraleve (Institute of Hydraulic Studies and Design): Tiranë; f. 1966; Dir EGON GJADRI.

Instituti i Studimeve dhe i Projektimeve të Metalurgjise (Institute for Metallurgical Studies and Designs): Elbasan; tel. and fax (54) 55565; f. 1978; metallurgy of iron, chrome, copper, nickel; library of 6,100 vols; Dir ALFRED MALKJA.

Instituti i Studimeve dhe i Projektimeve të Minierave (Mining Research Institute): Blloku 'Vasil Shanto', Tiranë; tel. (4) 229445; f. 1983; library of 10,000 vols; Dir ENGJELL HOXHAJ; publ. *Buletini i Shkencave Minerare* (2 a year, summaries in English).

Instituti i Studimeve dhe i Projektimeve të Teknologjisë Kimike (Institute of Chemical Studies and Technological Design): Tiranë; f. 1981; Dir GASTOR AGALLIU.

Instituti i Studimeve dhe i Projektimeve të Teknologjisë Mekanike (Institute of Mechanical Technology Studies and Design): Tiranë; f. 1969; Dir ROBERT LAPERI.

Instituti i Studimeve dhe i Projektimeve Teknologjike të Mineraleve (Institute for Studies and Technology of Minerals): Tiranë; tel. (4) 225582; f. 1979; mineral processing research; library of 1,480 vols; Dir JLIR LAKRORI.

Instituti i Studimeve dhe i Projektimeve Teknologjike të Naftës e të Gazit (Institute for Studies and Design of Oil and Gas Technology): Tiranë; f. 1981; Dir PERPARIM HOXHA; publ. *Nafta dhe Gazi* (Oil and Gas, 6 a year).

Instituti i Studimeve dhe i Teknologjisë Ndërtimit (Institute of Building Technology Studies): Tiranë; tel. and fax (4) 223811; f. 1979; library of 1,500 vols; Dir Ing. MUHANEM DELIU.

Instituti i Studimeve dhe Projektimeve Mekanike (Mechanics Research Institute):

Rr. 'Ferit Xajko', Tiranë; tel. (4) 228543; f. 1970; library of 3,000 vols; Dir NEDIM KAMBO.

Qendra e Kerkimeve Hidraulike (Centre of Hydraulic Research): Rr. Sami Frasheri 5, Tiranë; tel. (4) 227322; fax (4) 227322; f. 1957; attached to Acad. of Sciences of Albania; Dir Prof. Dr STAVRI LAMI.

Libraries and Archives

Durrës

Durrës Public Library: Durrës; tel. (52) 22281; f. 1945; 180,462 vols; Dir FLORA DERVISHI.

Elbasan

Elbasan Public Library: Elbasan; f. 1934; 284,000 vols.

Gjirokastër

Gjirokastër Public Library: Gjirokastër; 90,000 vols.

Korçë

Korçë Public Library: Korçë; f. 1938; 139,000 vols.

Shkodër

Shkodër Public Library: Shkodër; f. 1935; 250,000 vols.

Tiranë

Centre for Scientific and Technical Information and Documentation: Rr. Lek Dukagjini 5, Tiranë; tel. and fax (4) 222491; f. 1981; attached to Min. of Education and Science; Dir HYDAI MYFTIU; publ. *Buletin Analitik Fushor* (Disciplinary Analytical Bulletin, monthly).

National Library: Sheshi Skenderbej, Tiranë; tel. and fax (4) 223843; e-mail plasari@natlib.tirana.al; f. 1922; 1,000,000 vols; Dir Dr AUREL PLASARI; publs *National Bibliography of Albanian Books* (quarterly), *National Bibliography of Albanian Periodicals* (monthly).

Scientific Library: Tiranë; f. 1972; attached to Acad. of Sciences of Albania; Dir NATASHA PANO.

State Archives: Tiranë; document conservation and research; Dir SHABAN SINANI.

Museums and Art Galleries

Berat

District Historical Museum: Berat; tel. (32) 32595; f. 1948; Dir ARBEM JANPAJ.

'Onufri' Iconographic Museum: Berat; f. 1986; sited in the town's castle; exhibits incl. icons by the medieval painter, Onufri.

Durrës

Archaeological Museum: Durrës; f. 1951; exhibits representing life in ancient Durrës.

Elbasan

Kristoforidhi, K., House-Museum: Elbasan; birth-place of the patriot and linguist; Dir LIMAN VAROSHI.

Stafa, Q., House-Museum: Elbasan; birth-place of the nat. hero; Dir LIMAN VAROSHI.

Fier

Archaeological Museum: Fier; f. 1958; exhibits incl. archaeological items from the fmr town of Apollonia.

District Historical Museum: Fier; tel. (34) 2583; f. 1948; Dir PETRIT MALUSHI.

Korçe

Mio, V., House-Museum: Korcë; house where the painter worked; contains works of art by Mio.

Museum of Education: Korçë; devt of education in Albania.

Museum of the Struggle for National Liberation: Bulevard Repuplika, Korçë; tel. (824) 2888; f. 1977; library of 400 vols.

National Museum of Medieval Art: Korçë; tel. (824) 3022; fax (824) 2022; f. 1980; Dir LORENC GLOZHENI.

Kruja

Scanderbeg Museum: Kruja; memorabilia of the nat. hero.

Përmet

Frashëri Brothers Museum: Përmet; birth-place of the brothers Frashëri.

Shkodër

Gurakuqi, Luigi, House-Museum: Shkodër; house where the patriot lived.

Migjeni House-Museum: Shkodër; where the writer Migjeni lived.

Pascha, Vaso, House-Museum: Shkodër; house where the patriot lived.

Tiranë

Albanian National Culture Museum: Tiranë; attached to Institute of Nat. Culture; exhibits incl. agricultural tools of all periods, stock-breeding equipment, interiors and exteriors, household objects, textiles and customs, local crafts and ceramics up to the present day.

Fine Arts Gallery: Bulevardi Dëshmorët Ekombit, Tiranë; tel. and fax (4) 233975; e-mail natgal@albaniaonline.net; f. 1952; Dir GËZIM QËNDRO.

National Historical Museum: Skenderbe Sq., Tiranë; tel. and fax (4) 228389; f. 1981; Illyrian and Greco-Roman artefacts, history of modern Albania; Dir VILSON KURI.

National Museum of Archaeology: Tiranë; tel. (4) 226541; f. 1948; attached to the Institute of Archaeology of the Acad. of Sciences of Albania; exhibits from prehistoric and historic times up to Middle Ages; responsible for archaeological museums at Durrës, Apollonia and Butrinti; library of 7,200 vols, film and photograph libraries; Curator ILIR GJIPALI; publ. *Illyria* (2 a year).

Natural Science Museum: Tiranë; attached to Univ. of Tiranë; zoology, botany, geology.

Vlorë

District Historical Museum: Vlorë; tel. (63) 2646; f. 1953; archaeology, history of art, history.

Independence Museum: Vlorë; tel. (63) 2481; f. 1962; Chief Officer BASLUKIM FIFO.

Nushi Brothers Museum: Vuno, Vlorë.

Universities

ALEKSANDER XHUVANI UNIVERSITY OF ELBASAN

Rinia, Elbasan

Telephone: (54) 52593
Fax: (54) 52593
E-mail: jdode@uniel.edu.al
Internet: www.uniel.edu.al

Founded 1909
Academic year: October to July

Rector: Prof. Dr JANI DODE

Library of 100,000 vols
Number of teachers: 245
Number of students: 11,000

Publications: *Scientific Bulletin* (quarterly), *Studenti* (magazine)

DEANS

Economics: Dr ALBERT DELIMETA
Elementary School Teaching: Prof. Dr FATBARDHA GJINI
Foreign Languages: Assoc. Prof. Dr VILMA TAFANI
Human Sciences: Prof. Dr MEHMET ÇELIKU, Prof. Dr ZISO THOMOLLARI
Natural Sciences: Prof. Dr JANI DODE, Prof. Dr AGRON TATO, Prof. Dr ZISO THOMOLLARI
Nursery High School: Dr SKENDER TOPI
Social Sciences: Prof. Dr VILSON KURI

EQREM ÇABEJ UNIVERSITY OF GJIROKASTRA

Gjirokastra
Telephone: (726) 3776
Founded 1971
State control.

FAN S. NOLI UNIVERSITY

Rr. Gjergj Kastrioti, Korçë
Telephone: (82) 42230
Fax: (82) 42230
Internet: www.unkorce.edu.al

Founded 1971 as Higher Agricultural Institute; present name and title 1992
State control
Languages of instruction: Albanian, English
Academic year: October to July

Rector: Asst Prof. Dr GJERGJI PENDAVINJI
Vice-Rector: Assoc. Prof. Dr EVRI PEPO
Chief Admin. Officer: PETRIKA PETRO
Int. Relations Officer: ILO SHANO
Librarian: ANA VELO

Library of 24,000 vols
Number of teachers: 82
Number of students: 3,080 (incl. part-time and corresp. students)

Publication: *Bulletin*

DEANS

Faculty of Agriculture: Assoc. Prof. Dr NIKO ROSHANJI
Faculty of Economics: Prof. Dr FRIDA ZEFI
Faculty of Education: Asst Prof. Dr BASHKIM JAHOLLARI
Department of Nursing: JETONA MYTEVELIU

PROFESSORS

JASHARI, A., Education
MANOKU, Y., Economics
PENDAVINJI, G., Education
TENEQEXHIU, K., Agriculture
ZEFI, E., Economics

LUIGJ GURAKUQI UNIVERSITY OF SHKODËR

2 Prilli Sq., Shkodër
Telephone: (224) 2235
Fax: (224) 3747
E-mail: rektori@unishk.tirana.al

Founded 1991; based on fmr Instituti i Lartë Pedagogjik (Higher Pedagogical Institute), Shkodër (f. 1957)
State control
Language of instruction: French
Academic year: September to July

Rector: Prof. Dr MAHIR HOTI
Vice-Rector: Asst Prof. Dr ARTAN HAXHI
Librarian: GJOVALIN ÇUNI

Number of teachers: 134
Number of students: 6,050 (2,050 full-time, 4,000 part-time)

Publication: *Scientific Bulletin* (separate series on Natural Sciences, Social Sciences, Didactics, each 2 a year)

DEANS

Faculty of Economics: Assoc. Prof. Dr SADIJE BUSHATI
Faculty of Education: Assoc. Prof. Dr VEHBI HOTI
Faculty of Languages: Prof. Dr REFIK KADIJA
Faculty of Law: ARENCA TRASHANI
Faculty of Natural Sciences: Assoc. Prof. Dr FADIL GALIQI
Faculty of Social Sciences: Prof. Dr TRIFON ZIU

UNIVERSITETI BUJQËSOR I TIRANËS
(Agricultural University of Tiranë)

Kamëz, Tiranë
Telephone: (4) 353873
Fax: (4) 353874
Internet: www.ubt.edu.al

Founded 1951
State control
Academic year: October to July

Rector: Prof. Dr VELESIN PEÇULI
Vice-Rector: Assoc. Prof. BIZENA BIJO
Library Dir: ENGJELLUSHE SULA

Library of 10,000 vols
Number of teachers: 212
Number of students: 5,122

Publication: *Albanian Review of Agricultural Sciences*

DEANS

Faculty of Agriculture: Prof. Dr FATOS HARIZAJ
Faculty of Forestry Science: Prof. Dr MIHALLAQ KOTRO
Faculty of Veterinary Science: Prof. Dr NEFAIL BIBA

UNIVERSITETI POLITEKNIK I TIRANËS
(Polytechnic University of Tirana)

Sheshi 'Nene Tereza', Nr 4, Tiranë
Telephone: (4) 227914
Fax: (4) 227914
Internet: www.upt.edu.al

Founded 1957; present status 1991
State control

Rector: TAMARA EFTIMI
Vice-Rector: AGIM ANXHAKU

Library of 250,000 vols
Number of teachers: 470
Number of students: 2,565

DEANS

Faculty of Civil Engineering: HASAN JAHO
Faculty of Electrical Engineering: PIRO CIPO
Faculty of Geology and Mining: SELAM MEÇO
Faculty of Mechanical Engineering: ANDONAQ LONDO

UNIVERSITETI TEKNOLOGJIK 'ISMAIL QEMAL VLORA'
('Ismail Qemal Vlora' Technological University)

Lagija 'Pavaresia', Skele Vlore, Vlorë
Telephone: (63) 24952
Fax: (63) 24952

Founded 1994
State control

Rector: BILAL SHKURTAJ
Chancellor: KASTRIOT BRESHANI

Library of 10,100 vols
Number of teachers: 195
Number of students: 1,250

DEANS

Faculty of Naval Engineering and Navigation: KRENAR IBRAHIMI
Faculty of Nursing: VITORI HASANAJ
Faculty of Trade: NATASHA AHMETAJ

UNIVERSITETI I TIRANËS
(University of Tiranë)

Deshmoret e Kombit, Tiranë
Telephone: (4) 228258
Fax: (4) 228258
Internet: albaniaonline.net/ut

Founded 1957
Academic year: September to June

Rector: Dr HALIL SYKJA
Vice-Rector: SULEJMAN KODRA
Library Dir: ARJANA KITA

Library of 700,000 vols
Number of teachers: 750
Number of students: 8,755

Publications: *Buletini i Shkencave Mjekësore* (Medicine, quarterly), *Buletini i Shkencave të Natyrës* (Natural Sciences, quarterly), *Përmbledhje studimesh* (Collection of Studies, quarterly, with Institutes of Geological Research)

DEANS

Faculty of Economics: Dr KADRI XHULALI
Faculty of Foreign Languages: Doc. AVNI XHELILI
Faculty of History and Linguistics: Dr PASKAL MILO
Faculty of Law: ZEF BROZI
Faculty of Mechanics and Electronics: Dr GËZIM KARAPICI
Faculty of Medicine: , Doc. KRISTO PANO
Faculty of Natural Science: Prof. Dr LLUKAN PUKA
Faculty of Philosophy and Sociology: Doc. LUAN PIRDENI

Higher Institute

Akademia e Arteve, Tiranë (Academy of Arts, Tiranë): Dëshmorët e Kombit St, Tiranë; tel. and fax (4) 225488; e-mail majlinda_h@yahoo.com; f. 1966; faculties of fine arts, music and drama; 105 teachers; 776 students; library: 60,000 vols; Rector Prof. KASTRIOT CAUSHI.

ALGERIA

The Higher Education System

The Higher education system in Algeria falls under the authority of the Ministry of Higher Education and Scientific Research. In 2002/03 the number of students receiving higher education was 624,364. In addition, several thousand students go abroad to study.

Students are admitted to higher education on the basis of the Baccalauréat de l'Enseignement Secondaire. The three levels of higher education qualifications are the Diplôme d'études universitaires appliqué (DEUA) or Diplôme d'études supérieures (Licence), Maitrise and Doctorat d'état. The DEUA is awarded after three years of study, whilst the Licence is usually awarded in scientific fields. Engineering, medicine, dentistry and pharmacy degrees and other professional courses last for five years, while the Doctor of Medicine is awarded after seven years. The second degree-level (and first postgraduate) is the Maitrise. This is a two-year taught course including a thesis. Finally, following a Maitrise awarded with a grade of at least *assez bien*, a Doctorat d'état is awarded after three to five years of study.

Students may also undertake technical or vocational training at university level. On completion of basic education, vocational training is offered by Centres de formation professionnelle, and on completion of the three-year course a student is awarded the Certificat d'aptitude professionnelle (also called the Certificat de technicien), whilst completion of a four-year course leads to the Brevet de maîtrise.

Instituts de technologie (technological institutes) are educational establishments operated by other ministries or national corporations. Degrees offered include the Diplôme d'études universitaires appliquées (DEUA) (two-and-a-half or three years) and the Diplôme d'ingénieur (five years). These institutes are regulated by the ministry or national corporation responsible, and programmes are not standardized.

Learned Societies

GENERAL

El-Djazairia el-Mossilia: 1 rue Hamitouche, Algiers; f. 1930; cultural soc., particularly concerned with Arab classical music; 452 mems; Pres. ALI BENMERABET; Sec.-Gen. ABDELHADI MERAOUBI.

HISTORY, GEOGRAPHY AND ARCHAEOLOGY

Société Archéologique du Département de Constantine (Constantine Archaeological Society): Musée Gustave Mercier, Constantine; f. 1852; 250 mems; library of 10,000 vols; Pres. Dr BAGHLI (acting); publ. *Recueil des Notices et Mémoires*.

Société Historique Algérienne (Algerian Historical Society): c/o Faculté des Lettres, Univ. d'Alger, Algiers; f. 1963; 600 mems; publ. *Revue d'Histoire et Civilisation du Maghreb*.

LANGUAGE AND LITERATURE

British Council: c/o Hotel Hilton International Alger, 7th Fl., Pins Maritimes, Palais des Expositions, El Mohammadia, Algiers; tel. (21) 23-00-68; fax (21) 23-07-51; e-mail rachida.banyahia@fco.gov.uk; offers courses and examinations in English language and British culture and promotes cultural exchange with the UK; Office Man. RACHIDA BENYAHIA.

Instituto Cervantes: 9 rue Khelifa Boukhalfa, 16000 Algiers; tel. (21) 63-38-02; fax (21) 63-41-36; e-mail cenarg@cervantes.es; internet argel.cervantes.es; offers courses and examinations in Spanish language and culture and promotes cultural exchange with Spain and Spanish-speaking Latin and Central America; Dir EDUARDO CALVO GARCÍA.

MEDICINE

Union Médicale Algérienne (Algerian Medical Association): POB 8, Aadun St, Algiers; tel. (21) 73-36-00; fax (21) 63-27-77; publ. *Algérie Médicale*.

Research Institutes

GENERAL

Organisme National de la Recherche Scientifique (National Bureau of Scientific Research): Route de Dély Ibrahim, Ben Aknoun, Algiers; main executive body for govt policy; Dir (vacant).

Research centres:

Centre de Co-ordination des Etudes et des Recherches sur les Infrastructures, les Equipements du Ministère de l'Enseignement et de la Recherche Scientifique (Centre for the Co-ordination of Studies and Research on the Infrastructure and Facilities of the Ministry of Education and on Scientific Research): 1 rue Bachir Attar, Algiers; Dir A. GUEDIRI.

Centre de Développement des Energies Renouvelables (CDER) (Centre for the Development of Renewable Energy): BP 62, Route de l'Observatoire, Bouzaréah Algiers; tel. (21) 90-15-03; fax (21) 90-15-60; e-mail mail@cder.dz; internet www.cder.dz; f. as Centre National d'Etudes et de Recherche en Energie Renouvelable (CRENO); Dir M. BELHAMEL.

Centre d'Etudes et de Recherches en Biologie Humaine et Animale (CERBHA) (Study and Research Centre for Human and Animal Biology): BP 9, Université des Sciences et de la Technologie Houari Boumédienne, Algiers; Dir K. BENLATRACHE.

Centre d'Etudes et de Recherche sur le Développement Régional, Annaba (CERDA) (Annaba Study and Research Centre for Regional Development): Université d'Annaba, Annaba; Dir M. AMIRI.

Centre d'Etudes et de Recherche sur le Développement Régional, Oran (CERDO) (Oran Study and Research Centre for Regional Development): Université d'Oran, Es-Senia, Oran; Dir M. TALEB.

Centre d'Information Scientifique et Technique et de Transferts Technologiques (CISTTT) (Centre for Scientific and Technical Information and for Technological Transfer): BP 315, blvd Frantz Fanon, Algiers (Gare); Dir M. TIAR (acting).

Centre National d'Astronomie, d'Astrophysique et de Géophysique (CNAAG) (National Centre of Astronomy, Astrophysics and Geophysics): Observatoire de Bouzaréah, Algiers; Dir H. BENHALLOU.

Centre National de Documentation et de Recherche en Pédagogie (CNDRP) (National Documentation and Research Centre for Education): Université d'Alger, 2 rue Didouche Mourad, Algiers; Dir M. D. CHABOU.

Centre National d'Etudes et de Recherches pour l'Aménagement du Territoire (CNERAT) (National Centre for Studies and Research in National and Regional Development): 3 rue Professor Vincent, Telemly, Algiers; Dir MESSAOUD TAIEB.

Centre National de Recherches et d'Application des Géosciences (CRAG) (National Centre for Geoscientific Research and Application): 2 rue Didouche Mourad, Algiers; Dir R. ABDELHALIM.

Centre National de Recherche sur les Zones Arides (CNRZA) (National Centre for Research on Arid Zones): Université d'Alger, 2 rue Didouche Mourad, Algiers; Dir N. BOUNAGA (acting).

Centre National de Traduction et de Terminologie Arabe (CNTTA) (National Centre for Arab Translation and Terminology): 3 blvd Franklin Roosevelt, Algiers; Dir A. MEZIANE.

Centre de Recherches Anthropologiques, Préhistoriques et Ethnographiques (CRAPE) (Centre for Anthropological, Prehistoric and Ethnographical Research): 3 blvd Franklin Roosevelt, Algiers; f. 1957; Dir M. BELKAID.

Centre de Recherches en Architecture et Urbanisme (CRAU) (Centre for Research in Architecture and Town Planning): BP 2, El-Harrach, Algiers; Dir AMEZIANE IKENE.

Centre de Recherches en Economie Appliquées pour le Développement (CREAD) (Centre for Research in Applied Economics for Development): rue Djamal

Eddine El-Afghani, El Hamadia-Bouzareah, Algiers; tel. (21) 94-23-67; fax (21) 94-17-16; e-mail cread@wissal.dz; internet www.cread.edu.dz; f. 1985; Dir MOHAMED YACINE FERFERA; publ. *Les Cahiers du CREAD*.

Centre de Recherches Océanographiques et des Pêches (CROP) (Centre for Oceanographic and Fisheries Research): Jetée Nord, Amirauté, Algiers; Dir RACHID SEMROUD.

Centre de Recherches sur les Ressources Biologiques Terrestres (CRBT) (Centre for Research on Biological Resources of the Land): 2 rue Didouche Mourad, Algiers; Dir (vacant).

Centre Universitaire de Recherches, d'Etudes et de Réalisations (CURER) (University Centre for Research, Study and Application): Université de Constantine, 54 rue Larbi Ben M'Hidi, Constantine; agriculture, forestry, energy resources; Dir FELLAH LAZHAR.

AGRICULTURE, FISHERIES AND VETERINARY SCIENCE

Institut National de la Recherche Agronomique (INRAA) (National Institute of Agronomic Research): 2 ave des Frères Ouadak, Belfort, El Harrach, Algiers; tel. (21) 75-63-15; f. 1966; library of 6,500 vols; Dir M. BEKKOUCHE; publ. *Bulletin d'Agronomie Saharienne*.

Institut National de Recherche Forestière (National Institute of Forestry Research): Arboretum de Bainem, Algiers; tel. (21) 79-72-96; fax (21) 78-32-11; f. 1981; library of 4,000 vols; Dir FATEH DAHIEDINE; publ. *Annale de la recherche forestière*.

BIBLIOGRAPHY, LIBRARY SCIENCE AND MUSEOLOGY

Institut de Bibliothéconomie et des Sciences Documentaires (Institute of Library Economics and Documentation): Univ. d'Alger, 2 rue Didouche Mourad, Algiers; tel. and fax (21) 93-15-10; e-mail allahoum@yahoo.fr; f. 1975; Dir RABAH ALLAHOUM.

HISTORY, GEOGRAPHY AND ARCHAEOLOGY

Centre National de Recherches Préhistoriques Anthropologiques et Historiques (National Centre for Prehistorical, Anthropological and Historical Research): 3 rue F. D. Roosevelt, Algiers; tel. and fax (21) 74-79-29; f. 1993; library of 35,000 vols; Dir N. E. SAOUDI; publs *Libyca*, *Madjallat et Tarikh*.

Institut National de Cartographie (National Institute of Cartography): 123 rue de Tripoli, BP 69, Hussein-Dey, Algiers; f. 1967; under trusteeship of Min. of Defence; Dir NADIR SAADI; publ. maps (100 to 150 a year).

MEDICINE

Institut National d'Hygiène et de Sécurité (National Institute of Hygiene and Safety): Lotissement Meridja, BP 07, 42395 Saoula; f. 1972; research in the fields of hygiene and safety at work; library of 8,000 vols, 110 periodicals, 45,000 microfiches; Dir Gen. CHÉRIF SOUAMI; publ. *Revue Algérienne de Prévention* (quarterly).

Institut Pasteur d'Algérie (Pasteur Institute in Algeria): rue du Dr Laveran, Algiers; tel. (21) 65-88-60; fax (21) 67-25-03; f. 1910; research and higher studies in microbiology, parasitology and immunology; preparation of vaccines and sera in conjunction with the health services of Algeria; library of 47,000 vols, 500 periodicals; Dir Prof. F. BOULAHBAL; publ. *Archives* (annual).

TECHNOLOGY

Commissariat aux Energies Nouvelles (Commission for New Sources of Energy): BP 1017, Algiers Gare; tel. (21) 61-14-18; f. 1983; research and devt in the field of renewable sources of energy, incl. atomic, solar, wind and geothermal energy; incl. centres for energy conversion and for nuclear and solar studies.

Office National de la Recherche Géologique et Minière/Service Géologique de l'Algérie (National Office of Geological and Mining Research): Cité Ib Khaldoun, BP 102, Boumerdès 35000; tel. (24) 81-75-99; fax (24) 81-83-79; e-mail orgm-dg@ogrm.com.dz; internet www.orgm.com.dz; f. 1883; 5 regional divs: East (located in Tebessa), Central (Tizi Ouzou), West (Sidi Bel Abbes), South West (Bechar) and South (Tamanrasset); library of 50,000 vols, periodicals, maps and aerial photographs; Gen.-Man. ABDELKADER SEMIANI; publs *Bulletins du Service Géologique d'Algérie* (2 a year), *Mémoires du Service Géoloqique de l'Algérie* (annual).

Libraries and Archives

Algiers

Archives Nationales d'Algérie (National Archives of Algeria): BP 61, Algiers-Gare; tel. (21) 54-21-60; fax (21) 54-16-16; e-mail dgan@ist.cezist.dz; f. 1971; Dir ABDELKRIM BADJADJA.

Bibliothèque de l'Université d'Alger (Library of the University of Algiers): 2 rue Didouche Mourad, Algiers; tel. (21) 64-02-15; fax (21) 61-31-44; f. 1880; 800,000 vols.

Bibliothèque Nationale (National Library): 1 ave Frantz Fanon, Algiers; tel. (21) 63-06-32; f. 1835; 950,000 vols; spec. collns incl. Africa and the Maghreb; Dir MUHAMMAD AÏSSA-MOUSSA; publs *Bibliographie de l'Algérie* (2 a year), *Publications*, several collns in Arabic and French.

Section de Diffusion Scientifique et Technique du Centre Culturel Français d'Alger (Department for the Distribution of Scientific and Technical Information at the French Cultural Centre in Algiers): 7 rue du Médecin Capitaine Hassani Issad, 16000 Algiers; tel. (21) 63-61-83; 25,000 vols, 350 periodicals; Dir MARC SAGAERT.

Constantine

Bibliothèque Municipale (Municipal Library): Hôtel de Ville, Constantine; f. 1895; 25,000 vols.

Museums and Art Galleries

Algiers

Direction du Patrimoine Culturel (Office of Cultural Heritage): Ministère de la Culture et du Tourisme, Kouba, Algiers; f. 1901; gen. admin. of museums, restoration, conservation and archaeological excavations; library of 8,000 vols, 300 periodicals; Dir S. A. BAGHLI; publ. *Bulletin d'Archéologie Algérienne* (annual).

Musée National des Antiquités (National Museum of Antiquities): Parc de la Liberté, Algiers; tel. (21) 74-66-86; fax (21) 74-74-71; f. 1897; library of 3,100 vols, 102 periodicals; Dir DRIAS LAKHDAR; publ. *Annales du Musée National des Antiquités*.

Musée National des Beaux Arts d'Alger (National Fine Arts Museum of Algiers): pl. Dar-el-Salem, El-Hamma, Algiers; tel. and fax (21) 66-49-16; f. 1930; library of 17,000 vols, 300 periodicals; Dir DALILA ORFALI; publ. *Revue* (annual).

Musée National du Bardo: 3 rue F. D. Roosevelt, Algiers; tel. (21) 74-76-41; fax (21) 74-24-53; f. 1930; prehistory, ethnography; library of 3,000 vols; Dir FATIMA AZZOUG.

Musée National du Djihad: El Madania, Algiers; tel. (21) 65-34-88; f. 1983; contemporary history; publ. *Actes du Musée*.

Constantine

Musée de Cirta: Blvd de la République, Constantine; f. 1853; archaeology, art; library of 20,000 vols; Dir AHMED GUEDDOUDA; publ. *Recueil et Mémoires de la Société Archéologique de Constantine*.

Oran

Musée National Zabana: Blvd Zabana, Oran; tel. (41) 34-37-81; f. 1935; prehistory, Roman and Punic archaeology, ethnography, zoology, geology, botany, sculpture and painting; Dir Dr MALKI NORDINE.

Sétif

Musée National de Sétif: Rue de l'A.L.N., 19000 Sétif; tel. (36) 84-35-36; fax (36) 84-58-13; e-mail mns@elhidhab.cerist.dz; f. 1991; prehistoric, Roman, Byzantine and medieval Islamic antiquities; Curator CHERIF RIACHE.

Skikda

Musée de Skikda: Skikda; Punic and Roman antiquities, modern art.

Tlemcen

Musée de Tlemcen: pl. Khemisti, 13000 Tlemcen; tel. (43) 26-55-06; Islamic art, minerals, botany, Numidian and Roman archaeology.

Universities

UNIVERSITE D'ADRAR

rue 11 Décembre, Adrar 01960
Telephone: (49) 96-85-32
Fax: (49) 96-75-71

Founded 2001
State control

Number of teachers: 35
Number of students: 1,030

Faculties of Arts and Humanities, Science and Engineering, Social Sciences and Islamic Studies.

UNIVERSITÉ D'ALGER

2 rue Didouche Mourad, Algiers
Telephone: (21) 64-69-70
Internet: www.univ-alger.dz

Founded 1879 (reorganized 1909)
Languages of instruction: Arabic, French
State control
Academic year: September to June

Rector: AMAR SAKHRI
Vice-Rectors: S. BABA-AMEUR (Pedagogy), RABAH KHIMA (Planning), A. E. R. AZZI (Postgraduates and Scientific Research)
Librarian: ABDELLAH ABDI

Number of teachers: 1,400
Number of students: 32,000.

UNIVERSITY INSTITUTES

Centre Intensif des Langues: 2 rue Didouche Mourad, Algiers; Dir Mr BOUCHAIB.

Institut d'Archéologie: 2 rue Didouche Mourad, Algiers; Dir Mr BENGUERBA.

Institut de Bibliothéconomie: f. 1975; EXEMEPS, Dely-Ibrahim, Algiers; Dir Mr TIAR.

Institut d'Histoire: c/o Ecole supérieure des transmissions, Bouzaréah, Algiers; Dir Mr BEN-AMIRA.

Institut de l'Information et de la Communication: 11 chemin Mokhtar Doudou ITFC, Ben-Aknoun; Dir Mr BEN-ZAOUI.

Institut d'Interprétariat et traduction: 2 rue Didouche Mourad, Algiers; Dir AHMED ABBACHI.

Institut des Langues Etrangères: c/o Ecole supérieure des transmissions, Bouzaréah, Algiers; Dir Mr HASSAINE.

Institut de Langue et Littérature Arabes: 2 rue Didouche Mourad, Algiers; Dir Mr HADJAR.

Institut de Philosophie: c/o Ecole supérieure des transmissions, Bouzaréah, Algiers; Dir Mr ZEKKI.

Institut de Psychologie et Sciences de l'Education: c/o Ecole supérieure des transmissions, Bouzaréah, Algiers; Dir Mr LABOUDI.

Institut des Sciences Economiques: 2 rue Colonel Azzoug, Côte Rouge, Hussein Dey, Algiers; Dir DJILLALI DJELLATOU.

Institut de Sciences Juridiques et Administratives: 11 chemin Mokhtar Doudou ITFC, Ben-Aknoun; f. 1885; library of 60,000 vols, 500 periodicals; Dir Mr ZOUINA; publ. *Revue algérienne des sciences juridiques*.

Institut des Sciences Politiques et Relations Internationales: 11 Cchemin Mokhtar Doudou ITFC, Ben-Aknoun; Dir Mr DEBÈCHE.

Institut de Sociologie: c/o Ecole supérieure des transmissions, Bouzaréah, Algiers; Dir Mr GHALAMALLAH.

UNIVERSITÉ BADJI MOKHTAR ANNABA

BP 12, 23000 Annaba

Telephone: (38) 87-26-78
Fax: (38) 87-24-36
E-mail: mtlaskri@wissal.dz
Internet: www.univ-annaba.org

Founded 1975
State control
Languages of instruction: Arabic, French
Academic year: September to June

Rector: MOHAMED TAYEB LASKRI
Vice-Rectors: Z. DJEGHABA (Postgraduate Studies and Research), M. OUCHEFFOUN (Planning), M. S. BOULAKOUD (Graduate Studies)
Chief Admin. Officer: S. ARABI
Librarian: N. MANCEUR

Number of teachers: 1,221
Number of students: 37,978

Publications: *Synthese* (science and technology, 2 a year), *Et-Tawassol* (humanities and social sciences, 2 a year)

DEANS

Faculty of Earth Sciences: TAYEB SERRADJ
Faculty of Economics and Management: CHERIF HAMZAOUI
Faculty of Engineering: NASR-EDDINE DEBBACHE
Faculty of Law: DJAMEL ABDELNASSER MANAA
Faculty of Letters, Humanities and Social Sciences: MOHAMED AÏLANE
Faculty of Medicine: ABDESSLEM KAÏDI
Faculty of Science: FAOUZIA REBBANI

UNIVERSITÉ DE BATNA

ave Chahid Boukhlouf, 05000 Batna
Telephone: (33) 81-40-39
Fax: (33) 81-53-75
E-mail: recteur@univ-batna.dz
Internet: www.univ-batna.dz

Founded 1977 as Centre Universitaire de Batna

Rector: MOHAMED KHEZZAR
Vice-Rectors: MOUSSA ZEREG, TAYEB BOUZID
Sec.-Gen.: ALI LABOUEL

Library of 60,000 vols

Publications: *Revue Sciences Sociales et Humaines* (annual), *Revue des Sciences Agronomiques et Forestières* (annual), *Revue II IIA* (annual)

Faculties of Science and Technology, Humanities and Social Sciences, Economics, Agronomic and Veterinary Sciences, Medicine, Hydraulic and Civil Engineering.

UNIVERSITE ABDERRAHMANE MIRA DE BEJAÏA

Route de Targua Ouzemour, Bejaïa 6000

Telephone: (34) 21-43-33
Fax: (34) 21-43-32
E-mail: infobej@univbej.dz
Internet: www.univbej.dz

Founded 1983
State control

Rector: DJOUDI MERABET
Number of students: 3,900

DEANS

Faculty of Arts and Humanities: SALAH DERRADJI
Faculty of Economics and Law: FARID YAICI
Faculty of Natural and Life Sciences: (vacant)
Faculty of Science and Engineering Science: BOUALEM SAIDANI

UNIVERSITE MOHAMED KHIDER DE BISKRA

BP 145, Biskra 07000

Telephone: (33) 73-20-53
Fax: (33) 74-61-62

Founded 1998
State control

Number of teachers: 300
Number of students: 11,285

Faculties of Arts, Humanities and Social Sciences, Law and Economics and Science and Engineering.

UNIVERSITÉ DE BLIDA

Route de Soumaa Blida, BP 270, Blida

Telephone: (25) 41-10-00
Fax: (25) 41-78-13
Internet: www.univ-blida.edu.dz

Founded 1981 as Centre Universitaire de Blida

Rector: ZETILI NOUREDDINE
Vice-Rectors: GUEND ABDELHANI (Admin.), NADER SALAH (Teaching), KHELIL AMARA (Postgraduate Affairs)

Number of teachers: 644
Number of students: 7,990

Publication: *Revue de l'Université*

Depts of Mechanics, Aeronautics, Electronics, Industrial Chemistry, Architecture, Civil Engineering, Agronomy, Agricultural Engineering, Medicine, Veterinary Science, Economics, Mathematics, Physics, Law, Social Sciences, Language and Literature.

UNIVERSITÉ DE BOUMERDES

Boumerdes

Founded 1981.

CONSTITUENT INSTITUTES

Institut Algérien de Pétroléum.

Institut National d'Electricité et d'Electronique.

Institut National de Génie Mécanique.

Institut National des Hydrocarbures.

Institut National des Industries Légères.

Institut National de Productivité et Développement

UNIVERSITE HASSIBA BEN BOUALI, CHLEF

Hay Salam, BP 151, Chlef 02000

Telephone: (27) 72-17-30
Fax: (27) 72-17-88
E-mail: info@univ-chlef.dz
Internet: www.univ-chlef.dz

Founded 1983; present status 2001
State control

Rector: A. OUAGUED

Library of 10,220 vols, 127 periodicals
Number of teachers: 275
Number of students: 12,522

Faculties of Science and Engineering, Earth Science and Agronomy, Humanities and Social Sciences.

UNIVERSITE DES SCIENCES ISLAMIQUES EMIR ABDELKADER, CONSTANTINE

BP 137, Constantine 25000

Telephone: (31) 93-92-92
Fax: (31) 93-80-73
Internet: www.univ-emir.dz

Founded 1984
State control
Academic year: September to June

Rector: ABDULLAH BOUKHELKAL

Library of 16,000 vols
Number of teachers: 112
Number of students: 2,476

Faculties of Literature and Humanities and Oussoul Eddine, Sharia and the Islamic Civilization.

UNIVERSITE DE GUELMA (8 MAI 1945)

BP 401, Guelma 24000

Telephone: (37) 20-71-52

Founded 2001
State control

Number of teachers: 137
Number of students: 6,716

Faculties of Economics and Management, Law, Humanities and Social Sciences, Science and Engineering.

UNIVERSITE ABDELHAK BENHAMOUDA DE JIJEL

BP 98, Ouled Aissa, Jijel

Telephone: (34) 49-80-16
Fax: (34) 49-55-78
Internet: www.univ-jijel.dz

Founded 1998
State control

Number of teachers: 137
Number of students: 3,757

Faculties of Engineering, Law, Management, Science.

UNIVERSITE AMAR TLEDJI DE LAGHOUAT

Route de Ghardaia, BP 37G, Laghouat 03000
Telephone: (29) 93-17-91
Fax: (29) 93-26-98
E-mail: rectorat@mail.lagh-univ.dz
Internet: www.lagh-univ.dz
Founded 1986 as Ecole Normale Supérieure de l'Enseignement Technique; univ. status 2001
State control
Languages of instruction: Arabic, French
Academic year: October to July
Rector: AÏSSA BENHORMA
Librarian: NOUIOUA HADJIRA
Library of 65,427 vols, 10 periodicals
Number of teachers: 312
Number of students: 9,417, 41 foreign students
Faculties of Engineering Science, Economics and Management, Law and Humanities.

UNIVERSITÉ MENTOURI

Route d'Aïn El Bey, BP 325, Constantine
Telephone: (31) 92-51-13
Fax: (31) 92-51-20
Internet: www.univ-constantine.dz
Founded 1969
Languages of instruction: Arabic, French
Rector: ABDELHAMID DJEKOUNE
Vice-Rectors: EMBAREK FERGAG (Orientation, Planning and Information), SALAH EDDINE BOUAOUD (Postgraduate and Scientific Research), BELKACEM SLATINA (Teaching)
Sec.-Gen.: FOUDIL BELAOUIRA
Librarian: TEBOURA BENKAID-KESBA
Library of 240,000 vols
Number of teachers: 1,503
Number of students: 27,995
Institutes of Law and Administration, Arabic, Social Sciences, Psychology, Biology, Architecture and Town Planning, Physics, Chemistry, Mathematics, Earth Sciences, Economics, Foreign Languages, Computer Science, Civil and Mechanical Engineering, Agriculture and Nutrition, Veterinary Science, Technology, Industrial Chemistry, Electronics, Sociology, Physical Education; also a pre-univ. centre and audio-visual dept.

UNIVERSITE ABDELHAMID IBN BADIS DE MOSTAGANEM

Ex-ITA, Mostaganem
Telephone: (45) 26-54-55
Fax: (45) 26-54-52
Internet: www.univ-mosta.dz
Founded 1978
State control
Rector: SID EL MAHI LAMINE KADI
Publication: *Annales du Patrimoine* (Arabic and French, 2 a year)
Faculties of Arts and Letters, Law and Commerce, Science and Engineering, Social Sciences, Physical Training and Sports.

UNIVERSITE DE M'SILA

BP 166, Draa El Hadjar, M'sila
Telephone: (35) 55-09-06
Fax: (35) 55-04-11
E-mail: cubmsila@ist.cerist.dz
Founded as Centre Universitaire de M'sila; present status 2001
State control
Number of teachers: 246
Number of students: 10,355
Faculties of Arts and Social Sciences, Economics, Management and Commercial Sciences, Law,Science and Engineering.

UNIVERSITÉ D'ORAN ES-SENIA

BP 1524, Es-Senia, Oran El-M'Naouer, Oran
Telephone: (41) 41-69-54
Fax: (41) 41-01-57
Internet: www.univ-oran.dz
Founded 1967
State control
Languages of instruction: Arabic, French
Academic year: September to July (2 semesters)
Rector: ABDELKADER DERBAL
Vice-Rector for Pedagogy and Registration: AHMED BENAYED
Vice-Rector for Planning and Equipment: MOHAMMED DELLIL
Vice-Rector for Postgraduate Studies, Research and External Relations: AHMED AMRANI
Sec.-Gen.: MABROUK IKHLEF
Librarian: S. CHAÏB DRAA
Library of 800,000 vols
Number of teachers: 1,200
Number of students: 45,000
Publications: *Al Bahith Ilqtissady* (2 a year), *Cahiers du Centre de Documentation des Sciences Humaines*, *Cahiers de Géographie de l'Ouest Algérien*, *El Moutarjeem* (annual), *Proceedings of the Research Unit in Social and Cultural Anthropology*, *Revue des Langues*, *Social Sciences Review* (annual), *University Letters* (quarterly)

DIRECTORS

Faculty of Arabic Language, Foreign Languages and Fine Arts: Prof. CHEIKH BOUGUERBA
Faculty of Economics: Prof. BOULANDUAR BACHIR
Faculty of Geography and Land Management: Prof. MEKAHLI LARBI
Faculty of Humanities and Religious Studies: Prof. BEKRI A. KRIM
Faculty of Law and Admin.: Prof. YELLES CHAOUCH BACHIR
Faculty of Medical Studies: Prof. ZOUBIR FOUATIH
Faculty of Sciences: Prof. ABDELGHANI KRALEFAT
Faculty of Social Sciences: Prof. AHMED LALAOUI
IGLAEIL Institute: Prof. MOHAMED MELIANI
Institute of Natural Sciences: ZITOUNI BOUTIBA

UNIVERSITE DE OUARGLA

Route de Ghardaia, Ourgla
Telephone: (29) 71-24-68
Fax: (29) 71-51-61
Internet: www.ouargla-univ.dz
Founded 1987 as Ecole Nationale Supérieure; present status 2001
State control
Academic year: September to June
Dir: MOHAMED EL-KHAMES TIDJANI
Number of teachers: 465
Number of students: 10,118

DEANS

Faculty of Law and Economics: NASREDDINE SEMAR
Faculty of Letters and Languages: SALAH KENNOUR
Faculty of Science and Engineering: BELKHEIR DADA MOUSSA

UNIVERSITÉ DES SCIENCES ET DE LA TECHNOLOGIE HOUARI BOUMEDIENNE

BP 32, El Alia, Bab Ezzouar, Algiers
Telephone: (21) 24-72-83
Fax: (21) 24-79-92
E-mail: benrect@hotmail.com
Internet: www.usthb.dz
Founded 1974
Languages of instruction: Arabic, French
Academic year: September to June
Rector: Prof. BENALI BENZAGHOU
Vice-Rectors: MALEK BOUHADEF, MAHREZ DRIR, ABDELKRIM TOUABET
Sec.-Gen.: REDA DJELLID
Librarian: SAIDA BOUAOUNE
Number of teachers: 1,371
Number of students: 19,177
Publication: *Annales des Sciences et de la Technologie*

DIRECTORS

Institute of Chemistry: OUIZA CHERIFI
Institute of Civil Engineering: MOHAMED CHABAAT
Institute of Computer Science: HABIBA DRIESS
Institute of Earth Sciences: MOULOUD IDRESS
Institute of Electronics: MOKHTAR ATTARI
Institute of Higher Technical Studies: MOHAMED AREZKI BOUZEGHOUB
Institute of Industrial Engineering: RACHIDA MAACHI
Institute of Mathematics: MOHAMED BENTARZI
Institute of Mechanical Engineering: ABDELAZIZ ATTI
Institute of Natural Sciences: RABEA SERIDJI
Institute of Physics: EL KHIDER SI AHMED

UNIVERSITÉ DES SCIENCES ET DE LA TECHNOLOGIE D'ORAN – MOHAMED BOUDIAF

BP 1505, El M'naouer, Oran
Telephone: (41) 42-25-61
Fax: (41) 42-15-81
E-mail: vrase@mail.univ-usto.dz
Internet: www.univ-usto.dz
Founded 1975
Languages of instruction: Arabic, French
Academic year: September to July
Rector: DJAMEL EDDINE KERDAL
Vice-Rectors: MOHAMED TEBBAL (Planning and Orientation), BENYOUNES MAZART (Postgraduate Studies, Research and External Relations), MAAMAR BOUDIA (Teaching and Re-training)
Sec.-Gen.: ELOUADI DORGHAM
Librarian: BACHIR YAKOUBI
Number of teachers: 582
Number of students: 11,491

DEANS

Architecture and Civil Engineering: HAMID P. KHELAFI
Electrical Engineering: ABDELHAMID MIDOUN
Mechanical Engineering: OMAR IMINE
Sciences: MOHAMED BENYETTOU

FACULTIES

Faculty of Architecture and Civil Engineering: BP 1505, El M'naouer, Oran; tel. and fax (41) 42-06-82; Depts of Architecture, Civil Engineering, Hydraulics.

Faculty of Electrical Engineering: BP 1505, El M'naouer, Oran; tel. and fax (41) 42-06-81; Depts of Electronics, Electrotechnics.

Faculty of Mechanical Engineering: BP 1505, El M'naouer, Oran; tel. and fax (41) 41-92-69; Depts of Marine Engineering, Mechanical Engineering, Metallurgy.

Faculty of Sciences: BP 1505, El M'naouer, Oran; tel. and fax (41) 42-06-80; Depts of Biology, Computer Sciences, Industrial Chemistry, Languages, Mathematics, Physical Education, Physics.

UNIVERSITÉ FERHAT ABBAS – SÉTIF

Route de Scipion, 19000 Sétif
Fax: (36) 90-38-79
Founded 1978
State control
Languages of instruction: Arabic, French
Academic year: September to June

Pres.: DJAFAR BENACHOUR
Vice-Pres: Dr TACHRAFT (Planning and Information), Dr N. HADDAOUI (Research and Graduate Studies), M. BENKHEDIMALIAH (Undergraduate Studies)
Sec.-Gen.: N. BOUGHESSA
Librarian: CHÉRIF CHIDEKH

Number of teachers: 594
Number of students: 12,700

Publication: *Annales* (quarterly)

DIRECTORS

Institut d'Architecture: TAHAR BELLAL
Institut de Biologie: RACHID GHARZOULI
Institut de Chimie Industrielle: B. DJELLOULI
Institut de Droit: M. KARMED
Institut d'Electronique: S. BERRETILI
Institut d'Electrotechnique: SAAD BELKHIAT
Institut de Génie Civil: M. MIMOUN
Institut d'Informatique: SAMIR AKROUF
Institut des Langues Etrangères: ABDELKRIM ZEGHAD
Institut des Lettres Arabes: BELKACEM NOUICER
Institut de Mathématiques: BOUBEKEUR MEROUANI
Institut de Mécanique: AHMED MANALLAH
Institut de Physique: ABDELAZIZ MANSOURI
Institut des Sciences Economiques: H. SAHRAOUI
Institut des Sciences Médicales: R. TALBI
Institut de Tronc-Commun et Technologie: MABROUK BENKHEDIMALLAH

UNIVERSITE DJILLALI LIABES, SIDI BEL ABBÈS

BP 89, Sidi Bel Abbès 22000

Telephone: (48) 54-30-18
Fax: (48) 54-11-52
E-mail: rectorat@univ-sba.dz
Internet: www.uviv-sba.dz

Founded 1978; present status 1989
State control

Rector: A. TADJER

Library of 70,000 vols
Number of students: 15,000

DEANS

Faculty of Economics: M. DANI ELKBIR
Faculty of Engineering: A. KHALFI
Faculty of Humanities: N. SEBBAR
Faculty of Law: B. MEKELKEL
Faculty of Medicine: A. DJADEL
Faculty of Science: M. BENYAHYA
Research Centre: F. TEBBOUNE (Dir)

UNIVERSITE DE SKIKDA

BP 26, Route El-Hadaiek, Skikda 21000

Telephone: (38) 70-10-32
Fax: (38) 70-10-04
E-mail: univskikda@wissal.dz
Internet: www.univ-skikda.dz

Founded 2001
State control

Rector: MOHAMED TAIBI

Faculties of Law and Social Sciences, Management and Economics, Science and Engineering.

UNIVERSITÉ IBN KHALDOUN DE TIARET

BP 78, 14000 Tiaret
Telephone: (46) 42-42-13
Fax: (46) 42-41-47
E-mail: univ-tiaret@mail.univ-tiaret.dz
Internet: www.univ-tiaret.dz

Founded 1980 as Institut National d'Enseignement Supérieur de Tiaret; became Centre Universitaire de Tiaret 1992; present name and status 2001
Languages of instruction: Arabic, French
Academic year: October to July

Dir: NASSREDINE HADJ-ZOUBIR
Vice-Dir of Planning, Orientation and Information: SAHNOUNE MOHAMED
Vice-Dir of Postgraduate Studies and Scientific Research: SAHUAOUI HADJ-ZIANE
Vice-Dir of Studies: MADANI HASSANE
Librarian: ABED MAKHLOUFI

Number of teachers: 229
Number of students: 10,493

depts of Arabic Literature, Biology, Economics, Law, Physics, Technology; institutes of Agronomy, Civil Engineering, Electronic Engineering, Environment, Mechanical Engineering, Veterinary Medicine.

UNIVERSITE MOULOUD MAMMERI TIZI-OUZOU

Oued-Aissi, Tizi-Ouzou

Telephone: (26) 40-56-51
Fax: (26) 21-29-68

Founded 1977; present status 2001
State control

Rector: RABAH KAHLOUCHE

Faculties of Arts and Humanities, Biology and Agronomy, Construction Engineering, Economics and Management, Electrical and Computer Engineering, Law, Medicine and Science.

UNIVERSITÉ ABOU BEKR BELKAID TLEMCEN

22 rue Abi Ayed Abdelkrim, Faubourg Pasteur, BP 119, 13000 Tlemcen

Telephone: (43) 20-09-22
Fax: (43) 20-41-89
Internet: www.univ-tlemcen.dz/

Founded 1974 as Centre Universitaire de Tlemcen

State control (by Min. of Higher Education and Scientific Research)
Languages of instruction: Arabic, French
Academic year: September to July

Rector: ZOUBIR CHAOUCHE-RAMDANE
Vice-Rectors: SIDI MOHAMMED BOUCHENAK-KHELLADI (External Relations), FOUAD GHOMARI (Planning), GHAOUTI MEKANCHA (Teaching)
Sec.-Gen.: ABDELDJALIL SARI ALI
Librarian: NOUREDDINE HADJI

Library of 66,000 vols
Number of teachers: 514
Number of students: 9,989

PROFESSORS

Medicine:

ALLAL, M. R., Radiology
BENKALFAT, F. Z., Cardiology
BENKALFAT, M., General Surgery
HADJ ALLAL, F., Otorhinolaryngology

Science:

BABA AHMED, A., Physical Chemistry
BENMOUANA, M., Nuclear Engineering
BENYOUCEF, B., Energy Physics
BOUAMOUD, M., Atomic Physics
BOUCHERIF, A., Applied Mathematics
HADJIAT, M., Mathematics
TALEB BENDIAB, S. A., Chemistry

Social Sciences and Humanities:

BELMOKADEM, M., Quantitative Technology
BENDIABDALLAH, A., Management
BOUCHENAK KHELLADI, S. M., Management
DENDOUNI, H., Civil Law
DERRAGUI, Z., Literature
KAHLOULA, M., Private Law
KALFAT, C., Criminology
SOUTI, M., Finance

DIRECTORS

Institute of Arabic Language and Literature: MOHAMMED ABBAS
Institute of Biology: KEBIR BOUCHERIT
Institute of Civil Engineering: MUSTAPHA DJAFFOUR
Institute of Earth Sciences: MOHAMED EL KHAMIS BAGHLI
Institute of Economics: MOHAMMED ZINE BARKA
Institute of Electronics: FETHI TARIK BENDIMERAD
Institute of Exact Sciences: ABDERRAHIM CHOUKCHOU BRAHAM
Institute of Foreign Languages: ZOUBIR DENDEN
Institute of Forestry: RACHID BOUHRAOUA
Institute of Hydraulics: ZINE EL ABIDINE CHERIF
Institute of Law and Administration: MOHAMMED BENAMAR
Institute of Mechanical Engineering: FETHI METALSI-TANI
Institute of Medical Sciences: FOUZI TALEB
Institute of Popular Culture: OKACHA CHAIF
Institute for the Promotion of the Arabic Language and for Intensive Language Training: BOUMÉDIÈNE BENMOUSSAT

Colleges

Conservatoire de Musique et de Déclamation: 2 blvd Ché Guévara, Algiers; f. 1920; library: 6,800 vols; 82 teachers; 2,300 students; Dir-Gen. BACHETARZI MOHIEDDINE; Sec.-Gen. KADDOUR GUECHOUD.

Ecole Nationale d'Administration: 13 chemin Gadouche Hydra, Algiers; tel. (21) 60-14-16; fax (21) 60-49-41; e-mail ena@wissel.dz; internet www.cerist.dz/ena; f. 1964; provides training for entrance into the civil service; library: 30,000 vols, 600 periodicals.

Ecole Nationale Polytechnique: BP 182, ave Pasteur, El-Harrach, 16200 Algiers; tel. (21) 52-14-94; fax (21) 52-29-73; e-mail berrah@wissal.dz; internet www.enp.edu.dz; f. 1962; undergraduate and postgraduate courses in civil engineering, electronics control, electrical engineering, telecommunications, chemical engineering, mechanical engineering, environmental engineering, hydraulic engineering, mining engineering, metallurgy, industrial engineering; library: 45,000 vols; 200 teachers; 2,000 students (1,500 undergraduate, 500 postgraduate); Dir Prof. M. K. BERRAH; Deans Dr D. HARIK (Graduate School), Dr A. BELOUCHRANI (Undergraduate School); publ. *Algerian Journal of Technology* (French and English).

Ecole Nationale Vétérinaire: BP 161, ave Pasteur, El-Harrach, Algiers; tel. (21) 52-47-81; fax (21) 52-59-04; f. 1974; 60 teachers; 900 students; library: 8,000 vols, 40 periodicals; Dir A. OTHMANI.

Ecole Polytechnique d'Architecture et d'Urbanisme: BP 2, El Harrach, Algiers; tel.

(21) 52-47-27; fax (21) 52-58-89; e-mail contact@epau.edu.dz; internet www.epau.edu.dz; f. 1970; library: 8,000 vols, 100 periodicals; 127 teachers; 1,523 students; Dir Prof. M. CHEMROUK.

Ecole Supérieure des Beaux-Arts: blvd Krim Belkacem, Parc Zyriab, Algiers; tel. (21) 74-90-09; fax (21) 74-91-14; f. 1881; painting, sculpture, ceramics, design; library: 9,000 vols; 65 teachers; 350 students; Dir MOHAMMED DJEHICHE.

Ecole Supérieure de Commerce d'Alger: BP 313, Rampe F. Chasseriau, Algiers; f. 1900; attached to Univ. of Algiers 1966; 4-year first degree courses; 34 teachers; 485 students.

Institut Hydrométéorologique de Formation et de Recherches (IHFR): BP 7019, Seddikia, Oran; tel. (41) 42-28-01; fax (41) 42-13-12; e-mail ihfr@djazair-connect.com; f. 1970; library: 15,000 vols; 200 students; Dir A. LAGHA.

Institut National Agronomique: 1 ave Pasteur, Hacen-Badi, El-Harrach, Algiers; tel. (21) 52-19-87; fax (21) 82-27-29; e-mail ina@wissal.dz; f. 1905; library: 70,000 vols, 200 periodicals; 141 teachers; 1,100 students; Dir M. M. BELLAL; publ. *Annales* (2 a year).

Institut National de la Planification et des Statistiques: 11 chemin Doudou Mokhtar, Ben Aknoun, Algiers; tel. and fax (21) 91-21-39; f. 1983; planning and statistics.

Institut des Sciences Politiques et de l'Information: 11 chemin Doudou Mokhtar, Ibn-Aknoun, Algiers; tel. (21) 78-15-18; fax (21) 79-66-41; f. 1948 as result of merger between Ecole Supérieure de Journalisme and Institut d'Etudes Politiques; attached to Univ. of Algiers; 100 teachers; 2,000 students; Dir Dr ISMAIL DEBECHE.

ANDORRA

The Higher Education System

University-level education is generally undertaken abroad, although there is one university, the Universitat d'Andorra. The University maintains two centres for vocational training, the School of Nursing and the School of Information Technology and Management, and a School of Virtual Learning for distance education. The Ministry of Culture and Higher Education oversees higher education. In 2002/03 1,288 students were in higher education; 307 students were studying in Andorra, 218 in France and 746 in Spain.

Learned Societies

GENERAL

Amics de la Cultura (Friends of Culture): Plaça Co-Prínceps 4 bis, Despatx no. 1, Escaldes-Engordany.

Associació Cultural i Artística Els Esquirols (Els Esquirols Cultural and Arts Association): Sala Parroquial, Plaça de l'Església, La Massana.

Centre de Trobada de les Cultures Pirenenques (Centre for the Understanding of Pyrenean Culture): Edif. Prada Casadet, Prat de la Creu, Andorra la Vella; tel. 860768; fax 861998; f. 1983; attached to Comunitat de Treball dels Pirineus; database on the Pyrenees; Dir ELISENDA VIVES BALMAÑA.

Cercle de les Arts i de les Lletres (Arts and Letters Circle): Avda Carlemany 24, Escaldes-Engordany; tel. 821233; f. 1968; Pres. JOAN BURGUÉS MARTISELLA.

BIBLIOGRAPHY, LIBRARY SCIENCE AND MUSEOLOGY

International Council of Museums, Andorran National Committee: Patrimoni Cultural d'Andorra, Carretera de Bixessarri s/n, Aixovall; tel. 844141; fax 844343; e-mail pca.gov@andorra.ad; f. 1988; 28 mems; Pres. MARTA PLANAS DE LA MAZA; Sec. LOURDES LÓPEZ MONTANYA.

LANGUAGE AND LITERATURE

Alliance Française: Avda Princep Benlloch 30, Andorra la Vella; tel. 342852; fax 866955; offers courses and examinations in French language and culture and promotes cultural exchange with France.

NATURAL SCIENCES

General

Societat Andorrana de Ciències (Andorra Scientific Society): Centre Cultural La Llacuna, C/M. C. Verdaguer 4, 500 Andorra la Vella; tel. 829729; fax 852383; e-mail sac@andorra.ad; internet www.sac.ad; f. 1983; carries out research; organizes talks, conferences and symposiums; 292 mems; Pres. ANGELS MACH; Sec. PERE CAVERO; publs *Diada Andorrana a la UCE* (annual), *El Sac* (monthly), *Jornades* (annual), *Recull de Conferències* (annual), *Papers de Recerca Històrica* (annual), *Trobades Culturals Pirinenques* (annual).

Biological Sciences

Associació per a la Defensa de la Natura (Association for Nature Conservation): Apartat de Correus Espanyols 96, Andorra la Vella; tel. 866086; fax 866586; e-mail adn@andorra.ad; internet www.andorra.ad; f. 1986; 300 mems; Pres. ÀNGELS CODINA FARRÁS; Sec. JORDI PALAUI PUIGVERT; publ. *Aigüerola*.

Research Institutes

GENERAL

Institut d'Estudis Andorrans (Institute of Andorran Studies): Edifici Molí, 3r pis, Avda Rocafort 21–23, 600 Sant Julià de Lòria; tel. 742630; fax 843585; e-mail iea@iea.ad; f. 1976; centres in Barcelona and Toulouse; Dir JORDI GUILLAMET.

Attached institutes:

Centre de Biodiversitat (Centre for Biodiversity): Edifici El Molí, 3r pis, Avda Rocafort 21–23, 600 Sant Julià de Lòria; tel. 742630; fax 843585; e-mail cbdiea@andorra.ad; internet www.iea.ad/cbd/index2.html; f. 1998; study and monitoring of Andorra's biological diversity; library of 450 vols; Dir MARTA DOMÈNECH FERRÉS; publ. *Hàbitats* (2 a year).

Centre d'Estudis de la Neu i de la Muntanya d'Andorra: Edifici Molí, 3r pis, Avda Rocafort 21–23, 600 Sant Julià de Lòria; tel. 742630; fax 843585; e-mail cenma@iea.ad.

Centre de Recerca en Ciències de la Terra (CRECIT) (Centre for Earth Sciences Research): Edifici El Molí, 3r pis, Avda Rocafort 21–23, 600 Sant Julià de Lòria; tel. 742630; fax 843585; e-mail crecit@andorra.ad; internet www.iea.ad/crecit/index2.html; f. 2001.

Centre de Recerca Sociològica (CRES) (Centre for Sociological Research): Edifici El Molí, 3r pis, Avda Rocafort 21–23, 600 Sant Julià de Lòria; tel. 742630; fax 843585; e-mail cres@andorra.ad; internet www.iea.ad/cres/noticies/; f. 2000.

Libraries and Archives

Andorra la Vella

Arxiu Nacional d'Andorra (National Archive of Andorra): Prat de la Creu 8–12, Edif. Prada Casadet, Andorra la Vella; tel. 802289; fax 868645; e-mail ana.gov@andorra.ad; internet www.arxius.ad; f. 1975; 280,000 documents; Head of Service SUSANNA VELA PALOMARES.

Biblioteca Nacional d'Andorra (Andorra National Library): Placeta de Saint Esteve, Casa Bauró, Andorra la Vella; tel. 826445; fax 829445; e-mail bncultura.gov@andorra.ad; internet www.bibliotecanacional.ad; f. 1974; legal deposit, Andorran standard book number agency (ISBN); 13,000 vols, 120 periodicals; Chief Librarian PILAR BURGUES MONSERRAT.

Canillo

Biblioteca Comunal de Canillo (Canillo Community Library): Comú de Canillo, Canillo; tel. 851888; f. 1988; 3,000 vols; Librarian DOLORS CALVÓ.

Encamp

Biblioteca Comunal d'Encamp (Encamp Community Library): Complex Socio-Cultural i Esportiu, Prat del Bau, Encamp; tel. 831080; fax 832034; f. 1980; 17,000 vols.

Escaldes-Engordany

Biblioteca del Centre Cultural d'Escaldes-Engordany (Library of the Escaldes-Engordany Cultural Centre): Passeig del Valira 9, Escaldes-Engordany; tel. 860729; fax 828959; f. 1972; 26,000 vols; Librarian ALEXIA CARRERAS SIRES.

La Massana

Biblioteca Comunal de la Massana (Massana Community Library): Cap del Carrer, La Massana; tel. 836920; fax 835834; f. 1990; 6,500 vols; Librarian NURIA PORQUERES.

Museums and Art Galleries

Andorra la Vella

Museu Filatèlic i Postal (Philatelic and Postal Museum): Casa de la Vall, Andorra la Vella; tel. 829129; f. 1986.

Encamp

Museu Nacional de l'Automòbil (National Motor Car Museum): Avda Co-Princep Episcopal 64, Encamp; tel. 832266; f. 1988; cars, motorbikes and bicycles from 1898 to 1950, components, miniature cars in porcelain and iron.

Escaldes-Engordany

Museu Viladomat: Avda Josep Viladomat s/n, Escaldes-Engordany; tel. 829340; fax 829340; e-mail museuviladomat@andorra.ad; f. 1987; Curator GLORIA PUJOL.

Ordino

Museu Casa Areny de Plandolit: Ordino; tel. 836908; f. 1987; typical 17th-century house, with later alterations; furniture, porcelain, costumes.

University

UNIVERSITAT D'ANDORRA

Plaça de la Germandat 7, 600 Sant Julià de Lòria

Telephone: 743000
Fax: 743043
E-mail: uda@uda.ad
Internet: www.uda.ad

Founded 1997

Language of instruction: Catalan

Rector: DANIEL BASTIDA OBIOLS
Dir: JOAN OBIOLS

DIRECTORS

School of Information Technology and Management: FLORENCI PLA ALTISENT
School of Nursing: ROSA MARIA MANDICÓ
School of Virtual Learning: RAMONET CASALPRIM

ANGOLA

The Higher Education System

Higher education was established when Angola was still a Portuguese colony, initially with the foundation in 1958 of institutes for training Catholic priests. In 1962 the Estudos Gerais Universitários de Angola was established in Luanda and became the Universidade de Luanda in 1968; a branch was also set up in Huíla. Following independence in 1975, all non-state institutions were closed and in 1979 the Universidade de Luanda was renamed Universidade de Angola, which in turn became the Universidade Agostinho Neto in 1985; it remains Angola's only public university. Independent Angola's first private university, the Universidade Católica de Angola, was founded in 1992. In 1997/8 there were 8,337 students in higher education.

Under legislation passed in 1995 full autonomy was conferred on Universidade Agostinho Neto, and staff were empowered to elect organs and officials. Financing for higher education depends on the status of the university: Universidade Agostinho Neto is heavily reliant on state funding, while the private universities rely on students' fees and donations from individuals and non-governmental organizations.

To attend university students must hold the Habilitação Literárias (secondary school leaving certificate), pass the entrance examinations and complete either a period of state employment or pre-university education.

The first undergraduate qualification is the Bacharel, study for which lasts for four years. Students may continue for a further two years, after which the Licenciado is awarded. The Licenciado may also be awarded on completion of a five-year university course, or a six-year course for medical students. A doctorate requires a further two or three years' research following the award of the Licenciado.

Learned Societies

LANGUAGE AND LITERATURE

Alliance Française: Largo da Sagrada Familia, Traversa Barbosa do Bocage 12, CP 1578, Luanda; tel. and fax (2) 321993; e-mail afluanda@ebonet.net; offers courses and examinations in French language and culture and promotes cultural exchange with France; attached teaching centres in Benguela, Cabinda and Lubango.

União dos Escritores Angolanos (Association of Angolan Writers): CP 2767-C, Luanda; tel. and fax (2) 323205; e-mail uea@uea-angola.org; internet www.uea-angola.org; f. 1975; 75 mems; library of 2,000 vols; Sec.-Gen. LUANDINO VIEIRA; publs *Lavra & Oficina* (monthly), *Criar* (quarterly).

Research Institutes

AGRICULTURE, FISHERIES AND VETERINARY SCIENCE

Centro de Investigação Científica Algodoeira (Cotton Scientific Research Centre): Instituto do Algodão de Angola, Estação Experimental de Onga-Zanga, Catete; fibre technology laboratory, agricultural machinery station, crop irrigation station (Bombagem); library; Dir Eng. Agr. JOAQUIM RODRIGUES PEREIRA.

Instituto de Investigação Agronómica (Agronomic Research Institute): CP 406, Estação Experimental Agrícola da Chianga, Huambo; f. 1962; incorporates agrarian documentation centre; publs *Comunicações*, *Relatório Anual*, *Série Divulgação*.

Instituto de Investigação Veterinária (Institute for Veterinary Research): CP 405, Lubango; tel. (2) 322094; f. 1965; Dir Dr A. M. POMBAL; publs *Acta Veterinaria-separatas* (annual), *Relatório Anual*.

NATURAL SCIENCES

Physical Sciences

Direcção Provincial dos Serviços de Geologia e Minas de Angola (Angolan Directorate of Geological and Mining Services): CP 1260-C, Luanda; f. 1914; geology, geological mapping and exploration of mineral deposits; library of 40,000 vols; Dir J. TRIGO MIRA; publs *Boletim*, *Carta Geológica de Angola*, *Memória*.

Libraries and Archives

Luanda

Arquivo Histórico Nacional (National Historical Archive): Rua Pedro Félix Machado 49, Luanda; tel. (2) 333512; fax (2) 334410; e-mail ahadg@nexus.ao; f. 1977; 20,000 vols, 3,000 periodicals; Dir ROSA CRUZ E SILVA; publ. *Guias de Informação Documental para o Estudo da História de Angola*.

Biblioteca Municipal (Municipal Library): CP 1227, Luanda; tel. (2) 392297; fax (2) 333902; f. 1873; 31,470 vols; Dir CUSTA GANHAR FILIPE.

Biblioteca Nacional de Angola (National Library of Angola): Largo António Jacinto, CP 2915, Luanda; tel. (2) 326331; e-mail bibliotecanacional@netangola.com; f. 1969; 84,000 vols; IFLA colln legal deposit, nat. deposit for UNESCO and FAO publs; Dir MARIA JOSÉ F. RAMOS.

Museums and Art Galleries

Luanda

Instituto Nacional do Patrimonio Cultural (National Institute for Cultural Heritage): CP 1267, Luanda; tel. (2) 332575; e-mail ipc@snet.co.ao; nat. antiquities dept; Dir FRANCISCO XAVIER YAMBO.

Affiliated museums:

Museu Central das Forças Armadas (Central Museum of the Armed Forces): CP 1267, Luanda; Dir SILVESTRE A. FRANCISCO.

Museu do Dundo (Dundo Museum): CP 14, Chitato, Lunda Norte; ethnography; Dir SONY CAMBOL CIPRIANO.

Museu da Escravatura (Museum of Slavery): CP 1267, Luanda; Dir ANICETE DO AMARAL GOURGEL.

Museu Nacional de Antropologia (National Anthropology Museum): CP 2159, Luanda; tel. (2) 337024; Dir AMERICO A. CUONONOCA.

Museu Nacional de Arqueologia (National Archaeology Museum): CP 79, Benguela; Dir JOAQUIM PAIS PINTO.

Museu Nacional de História Natural (National Museum of Natural History): CP 1267, Luanda; Dir ANA PAULA DOS SANTOS C. VICTOR.

Museu Regional de Cabinda (Cabinda Regional Museum): CP 283, Cabinda; ethnography; Dir TADEU DOMINGOS.

Museu Regional da Huila (Huila Regional Museum): CP 445, Lubango; ethnography; Dir JOSÉ FERREIRA.

Universities

UNIVERSIDADE AGOSTINHO NETO

CP 815, Avda 4 de Fevereiro 7, 2o andar, Luanda

Telephone: (2) 330517
Fax: (2) 330520
E-mail: depinf@diee.fe.uan.ao
Internet: www.uan.ao

Founded 1963

Language of instruction: Portuguese
Academic year: October to June

Rector: JOÃO SEBASTIÃO TETA

Number of teachers: 700
Number of students: 6,800

DEANS

Faculty of Agriculture: Dr AMILCAR MATEUS DE OLIVEIRA SALUMBO
Faculty of Economics: Dr LAURINDA DE JESUS FERNANDES HOYGAARD
Faculty of Engineering: CARLOS ALBERTO ABREU SERENO
Faculty of Law: Dr ADERITO CORREIA
Faculty of Medicine: Dr PAULO ADÃO CAMPOS
Faculty of Sciences: Dr ABILO ALVES FERNANDES

AFFILIATED INSTITUTES

Centro Nacional de Investigação Científica: Avda Revolução de Outubro, Luanda; tel. (2) 350762; Co-ordinator Dr NANIZEYI KINDUDI ANDRÉ.

Instituto Superior de Ciências da Educação: CP 230, Lubango; tel. (6) 120243; Dir Dr NARCISO DAMASIO DOS SANTOS BENEDITO.

UNIVERSIDADE CATÓLICA DE ANGOLA

Rua N. Sra da Muxima 29, CP 2064, Luanda

Telephone: (2) 331973
Fax: (2) 398759
E-mail: info@ucan.edu
Internet: www.ucan.edu

Founded 1997

Controlled by Episcopal Conference of Angola and São Tomé

Academic year: May to December

Chancellor and Rector: Archbishop DAMIÃO FRANKLIN

Vice-Rector: Fr Dr FILOMENO VIEIRA DIAS

Head of Admin.: Fr Dr MANUEL S. GONÇALVES

Head of Library and Documentation: Fr Dr JOSÉ CACHADINHA

Number of teachers: 99
Number of students: 1,800

Faculties of Economics, Informatics, Law, Management.

Publications: *UCAN Boletim Informativo*, *Revista Academica*.

UNIVERSIDADE JEAN PIAGET DE ANGOLA

Campus Universitário de Viana, Bairro Capalanka, Viana 10365, Brito Godins

Telephone: (2) 301148
Fax: (2) 290872
E-mail: info@angola.ipiaget.org
Internet: www.ipiaget.org/campus.asp?id=89

Founded 1998 as a result of collaboration between the Min. for Education and Culture of the Republic of Angola and the Instituto Piaget in Portugal

Courses offered in social sciences and education, science and technology and health.

College

Instituto Médio Industrial de Luanda: Largo de Soweto, CP 2513, Luanda; tel. 343200; e-mail imil@netangola.com; internet www.netangola.com/imil; f. 1956 as Escola Industrial de Luanda; courses in civil engineering, mechanics, chemistry.

ANTIGUA AND BARBUDA

The Higher Education System

Higher education is provided by an extra-mural department of the University of the West Indies, which offers several foundation courses leading to higher study at branches elsewhere, and at several other institutes and colleges. Teacher-training and technical training are available at the Antigua State College in St John's, which absorbed the Antigua and Barbuda School of Nursing in 2000. There is also an Institute of Technology, a Hotel Training Centre and a private University of Health Sciences.

Admission to tertiary education is usually dependent upon award of the Caribbean Advanced Proficiency Examination (CAPE). Grading in higher education is based on the system used by the University of the West Indies.

Learned Societies

BIBLIOGRAPHY, LIBRARY SCIENCE AND MUSEOLOGY

Library Association of Antigua and Barbuda: c/o Org. of Eastern Caribbean States, Economic Affairs Secretariat, Documentation Centre, POB 822, St John's; tel. 462-3500; fax 462-1537; f. 1983; 40 mems; Pres. MOLIVAR SPENCER; Sec. TRACY SAMUEL.

LANGUAGE AND LITERATURE

Alliance Française: POB 2086, St John's; tel. 462-3625; offers courses and exams in French language and culture and promotes cultural exchange with France.

Archives

St John's

Antigua and Barbuda National Archives: Victoria Park, Factory Rd, St John's; tel. 462-4959; fax 462-4970; e-mail archives@antigua.gov.ag; f. 1982; Dir Dr MARION BLAIR.

Universities

UNIVERSITY OF HEALTH SCIENCES ANTIGUA

POB 510, St John's
Telephone: 753-0253
Fax: 753-0265
E-mail: fmcp@uhsa.edu.ag
Internet: www.uhsa.ag

Founded 1982

Pres.: Dr AKIN OMITOWOJU
Registrar: IVORY TAYLOR
Librarian (vacant)
Dean, School of Medicine: Dr N. OLOWOPOPO

Library: Library in process of formation
Number of teachers: 32
Number of students: 203.

Colleges

Antigua and Barbuda International Institute of Technology (ABIIT): POB 736, St John's; tel. 480-2400; fax 480-2411; e-mail info@abiit.edu.ag; internet www.abiit.edu.ag; f. 2001; Pres. GLADWIN HENRY; Dean of Academics EUSTACE HILL.

Antigua State College: POB 193, Golden Grove, St John's; tel. 462-1434; fax 460-9476; f. 1977 by merger of Leeward Islands Teachers' Training College and Golden Grove Technical College, absorbed Antigua and Barbuda School of Nursing in 2000; hospitality and tourism management, teacher-training, technical training.

University of the West Indies School of Continuing Studies (Antigua and Barbuda): POB 142, St John's; tel. 462-1355; fax 462-2968; e-mail university@candw.ag; f. 1949; adult education courses; BSc in Management Studies, first year of BSc in Social Sciences, Cert. in Business Admin., in Education, in Public Admin., in Pre-School Education, in Professional (Admin.) Secretarial skills; BSc General Degree with double major in Agribusiness and Management, B.Ed. in Educational Admin., Certificate in Adult Education, Advanced Diploma in Construction Management; also spec. programmes for women, summer courses for children, occasional seminars and workshops; library: 10,000 vols; 23 part-time tutors; 350 students; Resident Tutor Dr ERMINA OSOBA.

ARGENTINA

The Higher Education System

The Federal Law of Education of 1993 decentralized the education system, with administration devolving to each of the 23 individual provinces and to the Municipality of Buenos Aires. The federal Ministry of Education, Science and Technology is responsible for the provision of university education, while each provincial ministry of education is responsible for education provision at post-secondary, non-university level. Technical education is supervised by the Consejo Nacional de Educación Técnica.

Admission to higher education is dependent upon successful completion of the secondary qualification. There are two levels of higher qualification: first, a Professional Title (Licenciado), study for which lasts for between four and six years depending on the subject; and secondly the Doctorado, which requires a further two years of study. Vocational and professional post-secondary education and training is available at higher technical schools or institutes of technology, also known as polytechnic institutes, and at higher commercial schools. Courses at these institutions are usually two years in length, and successful students are awarded a title such as Técnico Superior or Técnico Universitario in the area of specialization.

Argentina is a member state of the Mercado Común del Sur (MERCOSUR—Southern Common Market) and as such is a participant in its accreditation programme: El Mecanismo Experimental de Acreditación de Carreras del MERCOSUR. This programme has so far accredited Argentine degrees in agronomy, medicine and engineering.

In 2004 there were 1,805,491 students in higher education, of whom 1,273,156 were enrolled at universities, 512,002 at general non-university institutions and a further 20,333 at specialized institutions.

Regulatory and Representative Bodies

GOVERNMENT

Ministry of Education, Science and Technology: Pizzurno 935, C1020ACA Buenos Aires; tel. (11) 4129-1000; e-mail info@me.gov.ar; internet www.me.gov.ar; Minister DANIEL FERNANDO FILMUS.

ACCREDITATION

Comisión Nacional de Evaluación y Acreditación Universitaria (CONEAU) (National Commission for University Evaluation and Accreditation): Avda Santa Fe 1385, 4o, C1059ABH, Buenos Aires; tel. (11) 4815-1767; fax (11) 4815-0744; e-mail consulta@coneau.gov.ar; internet www.coneau.gov.ar; f. 1996 to foster improvements of univ. education in Argentina; govt agency under Min. of Education, Science and Technology; functions according to the Higher Education Act No 24.521; composed of 12 mems appointed by the Govt for 4 years, the National University Council (CIN), the Federal Senate and the Federal Chamber of Deputies nominate 3 mems each, the Council of Heads of Private Universities (CRUP), the National Academy of Education and the Min. of Education, Science and Technology nominate 1 mem. each; evaluates projects submitted by new public and private univs; performs external evaluation of univs; grants accreditation to govt regulated undergraduate programs; grants accreditation to graduate programs; conducts evaluation processes for accreditation of private evaluation and accreditation orgs; serves as Secretariat of Red Iberoamericana para la Acreditación de la Calidad de la Educación Superior (RIACES) and plays an active role in the initiatives carried out by the International Network for Quality Assurance Agencies in Higher Education (INQAAHE); contributes to devt of MERCOSUR experimental accreditation mechanism (MEXA); Pres. FRANCISCO JOSE MIGUEL TALENTO CUTRIN; Sec. Gen. NÉSTOR RAUL PAN.

NATIONAL BODIES

Academia Nacional de Educación (National Academy of Education): Pacheco de Melo 2084, C1126AAF, Buenos Aires; tel. (11) 4806-2818; fax (11) 4806-8817; e-mail info@acaedu.edu.ar; internet www.acaedu.edu.ar; f. 1984 as Argentine Academy of Education; incl. within the national academies rule (Decree number 4362/55) by Min. of Education and Justice (ruling no. 107, dated 27 June 1989; ratified by Decree number 1124, dated 26 October 1989); promotes educational creativity and innovation; Pres. AVELINO JOSÉ PORTO; Vice-Pres. LUIS RICARDO SILVA, MARÍA CELIA AGUDO DE CÓRSICO; Sec. ALFREDO VAN GELDEREN.

Consejo Interuniversitario Nacional (CIN) (National University Council): Pacheco de Melo 2084, C1126AAF, Buenos Aires; tel. (11) 4806-2269; e-mail info@cin.edu.ar; internet www.cin.edu.ar; f. 1985; proposes and co-ordinates policy for mem. univs; defines and co-ordinates academic, research and management programmes of mem. instns; creates regional orgs for inter-univ. co-operation; consults on creation or closure of nat. univs; generates and supports self-evaluation and external evaluation policies for mems; promotes compatibility and quality assurance of study programmes; Pres. Ing. OSCAR FEDERICO SPADA.

Consejo de Rectores de las Universidades Privadas (CRUP) (Council of Rectors of Private Universities): Montevideo 1910 PB, C1021AAH, Buenos Aires; tel. (11) 4811-6435; fax (11) 4811-0947; internet www.crup.org.ar; representative and consultative org.; co-ordinates teaching in private univs in conjunction with Min. of Education, Science and Technology and the Provincial Councils of Rectors; fosters collaboration between mem. univs; Pres. Dr HORACIO O'DONNELL; Vice-Pres. Lic. LUIS VELASCO, Mgr Dr ALFREDO ZECCA; Sec. Dr HECTOR SAURET.

Learned Societies

AGRICULTURE, FISHERIES AND VETERINARY SCIENCE

Academia Nacional de Agronomía y Veterinaria (Academy of Agronomy and Veterinary Science): Avda Alvear 1711 (2o), 1014 Buenos Aires; tel. (11) 4815-4616; fax (11) 4812-4168; e-mail academia@inta.gov.ar; f. 1909; 98 mems; library of 3,000 vols; Pres. Dr NORBERTO RAS; Sec.-Gen. Dr ALBERTO CANO; publ. *Anales* (annual).

Asociación Argentina de la Ciencia del Suelo (Argentine Association of Soil Science): Pabellón INGEIS, Ciudad Universitaria, 1428 Buenos Aires; tel. (11) 4783-3021; fax (11) 4783-3024; internet www.suelos.org.ar; f. 1958; 800 mems; Pres. G. MOSCATELLI; Sec. R. ALVAREZ; publs *Ciencia del Suelo* (2 a year), *Boletín* (3 a year).

Sociedad Rural Argentina (Argentine Agricultural Society): Florida 460, 1005 Buenos Aires; tel. (11) 4322-0468; fax (11) 4325-8231; internet www.sra.org.ar; f. 1866; 10,000 mems; library: see Libraries and Archives; Pres. Dr LUCIANO MIGUENS.

ARCHITECTURE AND TOWN PLANNING

Sociedad Central de Arquitectos (Architects' Association): Montevideo 938, C1019ABT Buenos Aires; tel. (11) 4812-3644; fax (11) 4813-6629; e-mail info@socearq.org; internet www.socearq.org; f. 1886; 8,500 mems; library of 9,200 vols, 90 periodicals; Pres. Arq. DANIEL SILBERFADEN; Sec. Arq. LUIS MARÍA ALBORNOZ; publ. *Revista SCA* (6 a year).

BIBLIOGRAPHY, LIBRARY SCIENCE AND MUSEOLOGY

Asociación Argentina de Bibliotecas y Centros de Información Científicos y Técnicos (Argentine Association of Scientific and Technical Libraries and Information Centres): Santa Fé 1145, 1059 Buenos Aires; tel. (11) 4393-8406; f. 1937; 84 mems; Pres. ABILIO BASSETS; Tech. Sec. ERNESTO G. GIETZ; publ. *Union Catalogue of Scientific and Technical Publications*.

Asociación de Bibliotecarios Graduados de la República Argentina (ABGRA) (Association of Argentine Librarians): Tucumán 1424 (8o piso D), C1050AAB Buenos Aires; tel. (11) 4373-0571; fax (11) 4371-5269; e-mail abgra@ciudad.com.ar; internet abgra.sisbi.uba.ar; f. 1953; 1,650 mems; Pres. ANA MARÍA PERUCHENA ZIMMERMANN; Sec.-Gen. ROBERTO JORGE SERVIDIO; publ. *Revista REFERENCIAS* (3 a year).

Comisión Nacional de Museos y de Monumentos y Lugares Históricos (National Commission for Museums and

Historic Monuments and Sites): Avda de Mayo 556, Buenos Aires; tel. (11) 4331-6151; f. 1938; supervises museums and protects the nat. historical heritage; library; Pres. JORGE E. HARDOY; Gen. Sec. MATILDE I. ORUETA; publ. *Boletín*.

Comisión Nacional Protectora de Bibliotecas Populares (Commission for the Protection of Public Libraries): Ayacucho 1578, 1112 Buenos Aires; tel. (11) 4803-6545; f. 1870; Pres. DANIEL RÍOS; Sec. Prof. ANA T. DOBRA; publ. *Boletín*.

ECONOMICS, LAW AND POLITICS

Academia Nacional de Ciencias Económicas (National Academy of Economic Sciences): Avda Alvear 1790, 1014 Buenos Aires; tel. (11) 4813-2344; fax (11) 4813-2078; f. 1914; 35 mems; library of 13,500 vols; Pres. Dr LUIS GARCÍA MARTÍNEZ; Sec. Dra LUISA MONTUSCHI; publ. *Anales*.

Academia Nacional de Ciencias Morales y Políticas (National Academy of Moral and Political Sciences): Avda Alvear 1711, PB, 1014 Buenos Aires; tel. (11) 4811-2049; f. 1938; 35 mems; library of 13,536 vols; Pres. Dr JORGE A. AJA ESPIL; Sec. CARLOS A. SÁNCHEZ; publ. *Anales*.

Academia Nacional de Derecho y Ciencias Sociales (National Academy of Law and Social Sciences): Avda Alvear 1711 (1o), 1014 Buenos Aires; tel. (11) 4821-3522; f. 1874; 25 mems; Pres. Dr SEGUNDO LINARES QUINTANA; Secs Dr A. G. PADILLA, L. MORENO; publ. *Anales*.

Academia Nacional de Derecho y Ciencias Sociales (Córdoba) (National Academy of Law and Social Sciences, Córdoba): Artigas 74, 5000 Córdoba; tel. (351) 421-4929; fax (351) 421-4929; e-mail acader@interactive.com.ar; f. 1941; 110 mems (26 ordinary, 31 corresp., 53 foreign); Pres. Dr LUIS MOISSET DE ESPANÉS; Sec. Dr RICARDO HARO; publs *Anales*, *Cuaderno de Federalismo*, *Cuaderno de Historia*.

Colegio de Abogados de la Ciudad de Buenos Aires (Buenos Aires City Bar Association): Montevideo 640, 1019 Buenos Aires; tel. (11) 4371-1110; fax (11) 4375-5442; e-mail abogados@colabogados.org.ar; internet www.colabogados.org.ar; f. 1913; 1,600 mems; library of 45,000 vols; Pres. Dr RAFAEL LA PORTA DRAGO; Exec. Dir Dr IGNACIO ALPERIN BRUVERA; publs *Revista* (2 a year), *Actualidad* (6 a year).

FINE AND PERFORMING ARTS

Academia Nacional de Bellas Artes (National Academy of Fine Arts): Sánchez de Bustamante 2663, 1425 Buenos Aires; tel. (1) 802-2469; e-mail anba@via-net-works.net.ar; f. 1936; 30 mems, 30 foreign corresp. mems; library of 6,000 vols; Pres. Prof. NELLY KIRGER DE PERAZZO; Sec.-Gen. Prof. ALEJANDRO PUENTE; publs *Monografías de Artistas Argentinos*, *Serie Estudios de Arte en la Argentina*, *Cuaderno Especial: 'Escenas del Campo Argentino' 1885–1900*, *Documentos de Arte Argentino*, *Documentos de Arte Colonial Sudamericano*, *Anuario*.

Fondo Nacional de las Artes (National Arts Foundation): Alsina 673, C1087AAI Buenos Aires; tel. (11) 4343-1590; e-mail fnartes@fnartes.gov.ar; internet www.fnartes.gov.ar; f. 1958; promotes and supports the arts; 15 mems; library of 7,000 vols; Pres. Lic. HÉCTOR W. VALLE; publs *Informativo*, *Anuario del Teatro Argentino*, *Bibliografía Argentina de Artes y Letras*.

HISTORY, GEOGRAPHY AND ARCHAEOLOGY

Academia Nacional de Geografía (National Academy of Geography): Avda Cabildo 381 (7o piso), C1426AAD Buenos Aires; tel. (11) 4771-3043; fax (11) 4771-3043; e-mail ang_secretaria@velocom.com.ar; internet www.an-geografia.org.ar; f. 1956; 32 mems; Pres. Prof. EFI EMILIA OSSOINAK DE SARRAILH; Sec. SUSANA ISABEL CURTO; publ. *Anales*.

Academia Nacional de la Historia (National Academy of History): Balcarce 139, 1064 Buenos Aires; tel. (11) 4331-5147; fax (11) 4331-4633; e-mail admite@an-historia.org.ar; internet www.an-historia.org.ar; f. 1893; study of Argentine and American history; 257 mems (34 ordinary, 223 foreign corresp.); Pres. Dr MIGUEL ANGEL DE MARCO; publs *Boletín*, *Investigaciones y Ensayos*.

Instituto Bonaerense de Numismática y Antigüedades (Buenos Aires Institute of Numismatics and Antiquities): San Martín 336, 1004 Buenos Aires; tel. (11) 449-2659; f. 1872; 107 mems; Pres. HUMBERTO F. BURZIO; publ. *Boletín*.

Junta de Historia Eclesiástica Argentina (Council of Argentine Ecclesiastical History): Reconquista 269, 1003 Buenos Aires; tel. (11) 4331-6239; f. 1942; 100 mems; Pres. Dr CARLOS MARIA GELLY Y OBES; Sec. ALBERTO S. J. DE PAULA; publs *Revista Archivum* (annual), *Boletín*.

Sociedad Argentina de Estudios Geográficos (Argentine Society of Geographical Studies): Rodríguez Peña 158 (4o piso Dpto 7), 1020 Buenos Aires; tel. (11) 440-2076; fax (11) 4382-3305; f. 1922; 4,000 mems; library of 12,000 vols; Pres. Dra SUSANA I. CURTO DE CASAS; Sec. Lic. ANALÍA S. CONTE; publs *Anales*, *GAEA Boletín*, *Geografía de la República Argentina*, *Contribuciones Científicas*.

LANGUAGE AND LITERATURE

Academia Argentina de Letras (Argentine Academy of Letters): Sánchez de Bustamante 2663, 1425 Buenos Aires; tel. (11) 4802-3814; fax (11) 4802-8340; internet www.aal.universia.com.ar; f. 1931; 77 mems (24 ordinary, 53 corresp.); Pres. PEDRO LUIS BARCIA; Sec.-Gen. RODOLFO MODERN; publ. *Boletín* (quarterly).

Alliance Française: Avda Cordoba 946, 1054 Buenos Aires; tel. (11) 4322-0068; fax (11) 4326-6655; e-mail info@alianzafrancesa.org.ar; internet www.alianzafrancesa.org.ar; offers courses and examinations in French language and culture and promotes cultural exchange with France; attached teaching offices in Alta Gracia, Azul, Bahia Blanca, Banfield, Baradero, Bell Ville, Bella Vista, Bernal, Bragado, Brandsen, Buenos Aires (Belgrano, Flores and Fortabat), Campana, Campana-Escobar, Chacabuco, Chajari, Chivilcoy, Cinco Saltos, Colon, Comodoro Rivadavia, Concepcion del Uruguay, Córdoba, Coronel-Pringles, Coronel-Suarez, El Trebol, Esperanza, Formosa, Gualeguay, Gualeguaychu, Jesus Maria, Junin, La Plata, Las Varillas, Lincoln, Mar del Plata, Marcos-Juarez, Marcos-Paz, Martinez, Martinez-Olivos, Martinez-San Isidro, Mendoza, Mercedes, Mercedes-Lujan, Neuquén, Neuquén-General Roca, Nogoya, Olavarria, Paraná, Pehuajo, Pergamino, Pigue, Posadas, Quilmes, Rafaela, Reconquista, Resistencia, Rio Cuarto, Rio Gallegos, Rivadavia, Roque Saenz Peña, Rosario, Salta, San Carlos de Bariloche, San Francisco, San Jorge, San Jose, San Juan, San Luis, San Nicolas, San Rafael, San Salvador de Jujuy, Santa Fé, Santa Rosa, Santiago del Estero, Tandil, Trelew, Tres Arroyos, Tucumán, Tuerto, Ushuala, Venado, Vicente Lopez, Vicente Lopez-San Martín, Villa Elisa, Villa Maria, Villa Mercedes and Villaguay; Dir of Operations, Argentina FRANÇOISE COCHAUD.

British Council: Marcelo T. de Alvear 590, C1058AAF Buenos Aires; tel. (11) 4311-9814; fax (11) 4311-7747; e-mail info@britishcouncil.org.ar; internet www2.britishcouncil.org/argentina; offers courses and examinations in English language and British culture and promotes cultural exchange with the UK; Dir Dr PAUL DICK.

Goethe-Institut: Avda Corrientes 319/343, C1043AAD Buenos Aires; tel. (11) 4311-8964; fax (11) 4315-3327; e-mail goethe@buenosaires.goethe.org; internet www.goethe.de/hs/bue/deindex.htm; offers courses and examinations in German language and culture and promotes cultural exchange with Germany; library of 15,000 vols, 37 periodicals; Dir RUDOLF BARTH.

PEN Club Argentino—Centro Internacional de la Asociación PEN (International PEN Centre): Rivadavia 4060, 1205 Buenos Aires; f. 1930; 100 mems; Pres. MIGUEL A. OLIVERA; publ. *Boletín*.

Sociedad Argentina de Autores y Compositores de Música (SADAIC) (Argentine Society of Authors and Composers): Lavalle 1547, 1048 Buenos Aires; tel. (11) 4374-2730; f. 1936; library of 4,000 vols, 13,000 music scores; Pres. ARIEL RAMIREZ; Cultural Dir EUGENIO INCHAUSTI.

Sociedad General de Autores de la Argentina (Argentores) (Argentine Society of Authors): J. A. Pacheco de Melo 1820, 1126 Buenos Aires; tel. (11) 4811-2582; f. 1910; 2,000 mems; library of 60,000 vols; Pres. ISAAC AISEMBERG; Sec. AUGUSTO GIUSTOZZI; publ. *Boletín* (quarterly).

MEDICINE

Academia Argentina de Cirugía (Argentine Academy of Surgery): Marcelo T. de Alvear 2415, 1122 Buenos Aires; tel. (11) 4925-3649; f. 1911; Pres. Dr E. ROBERTO VIDAL; Sec.-Gen. JORGE SIVORI.

Academia de Ciencias Médicas: CC 130, 5000 Córdoba; f. 1975; 350 mems; Pres. Dr REMO BERGOGLIO; Sec. Dr JESÚS R. GIRAUDO.

Academia Nacional de Medicina (National Academy of Medicine): Las Heras 3092, 1425 Buenos Aires; tel. (11) 4805-6890; fax (11) 4806-6638; e-mail acamedbai@acamedbai.org.ar; internet www.acamedbai.org.ar; f. 1822; 35 mems; library of 50,000 vols; Pres. Acad. RÓMULO L. CABRINI; Sec.-Gen. Acad. JUAN M. GHIRLANDA; publ. *Boletín* (2 a year).

Asociación Argentina de Biología y Medicina Nuclear (Argentine Association for Biology and Nuclear Medicine): Avda Santa Fé 1145, 1059 Buenos Aires; tel. (11) 4393-5682; f. 1963; 190 mems; Pres. Dr JUAN J. O'FARRELL; Sec. Dr CARLOS CAÑELLAS.

Asociación Argentina de Cirugía (Argentine Association of Surgery): Marcelo T. de Alvear 2415, 1122 Buenos Aires; tel. (11) 4822-2905; fax (11) 4822-6458; f. 1930; 4,000 mems; Pres. LUIS V. GUTIÉRREZ; Dir MARTIN MIHURA; publs *Revista Argentina de Cirugía* (8 a year), *Boletín Informativo* (every 2 weeks), *Anuario*.

Asociación Argentina de Farmacia y Bioquímica Industrial (Argentine Industrial Biochemistry and Pharmacy Association): Uruguay 469 (2o B), 1015 Buenos Aires; tel. (11) 4373-8900; fax (11) 4372-7389; f. 1952; 1,100 mems; library of 500 vols; Pres. Dr HUMBERTO TORRIANI; Sec. Dr RAÚL ALBERTO REVILLA; publs *Revista SAFYBI*, *Boletín Informativo* (3 a year).

Asociación Argentina de Ortopedia y Traumatología (Argentine Orthopaedic and Traumatology Association): Vicente López 1878, C1128ABC Buenos Aires; tel. (11) 4801-2320; fax (11) 4801-7703; e-mail gerencia@aaot.org.ar; internet www.aaot.org.ar; f. 1936; 2,944 mems; library of 1,460 vols, 67 periodicals; Pres. Dr. GREGORIO M. ARENDAR; Sec. Dr CARLOS F. SANCINETO; publ. *Revista* (quarterly).

Asociación Médica Argentina (Argentine Medical Association): Santa Fé 1171, 1059 Buenos Aires; tel. (11) 4814-2182; fax (11) 4811-3850; e-mail info@ama-med.com; internet www.ama-med.org.ar; f. 1891; 3,520 mems; library of 32,000 vols, 290,000 periodicals; Pres. Dr ELÍAS HURTADO HOYO; Sec. MIGUEL A. GALMÉS; publs *Revista AMA* (quarterly), *Boletín Informativo* (monthly).

Asociación Odontológica Argentina (Argentine Dental Association): Junín 959, 1113 Buenos Aires; tel. (11) 4961-6141; fax (11) 4961-1110; f. 1896; incl. postgraduate school for dentists; 8,000 mems; library of 7,200 vols, 11,300 periodicals; Pres. CARLOS A. SPIELBERG; Sec. GUILLERMO ROSSI; publ. *Revista*.

Asociación para la Lucha contra la Parálisis Infantil (Association for Combating Infantile Paralysis): Salguero 1639, 1425 Buenos Aires; tel. (11) 484-1034; f. 1943; 30 mems; library of 3,000 vols; Pres. VERÓNICA S. M. DE BUSTO; publ. *Memoria y Balance Anual*.

Federación Argentina de Asociaciones de Anestesiología (Argentine Federation of Anaesthesiology Associations): J. F. Aranguren 1323, 1405 Buenos Aires; tel. (11) 4431-2463; fax (11) 4431-2463; f. 1970; 1,113 mems; Pres. Dr ALFREDO PAIRETTI; Admin. Sec. Dr ALFREDO CATTANEO; publs *Revista Argentina de Anestesiología*, *Boletín Informativo*.

Liga Argentina contra la Tuberculosis (Argentine Anti-Tuberculosis League): Santa Fé 4292, Buenos Aires; f. 1901; library of 140 series of periodicals; Pres. Dr RODOLFO CUCCHIANI ACEVEDO; Sec.-Gen. Dr GERMÁN QUINTELA NOVOA; publs *Revista Argentina del Tórax*, *La Doble Cruz*.

Sociedad Argentina de Ciencias Fisiológicas (Argentine Physiological Society): Solís 453, 1078 Buenos Aires; tel. (11) 4378-1151; fax (11) 4381-0323; e-mail safis@safisiol.org.ar; internet www.safisiol.org.ar; f. 1950; 300 mems; library of 600 vols; mem. of IUPS; Pres. Dr VALERIA RETTORI; Sec. Dr B. FERNANDEZ; publ. *Physiological Mini-Reviews* (monthly).

Sociedad Argentina de Ciencias Neurológicas, Psiquiátricas y Neuroquirúrgicas (Argentine Neurological, Neurosurgical and Psychiatric Society): Santa Fé 1171, 1059 Buenos Aires; tel. (11) 441-1633; f. 1920; 400 mems; library of 35,000 vols; Pres. Prof. Dr DIEGO BRAGE; Sec. Prof. Dr CARLOS MÁRQUEZ; publ. *Revista* (monthly).

Sociedad Argentina de Dermatología (Argentine Society of Dermatology): Avda Callao 852 (2o piso), 1023 Buenos Aires; tel. (11) 4815-4649; fax (11) 4814-4919; e-mail sad@sad.org.ar; internet www.sad.org.ar; f. 1934; 2,100 mems; Pres. Prof. Dr HORACIO CABO; Sec.-Gen. Dra PATRICIA TROIELLI; publ. *Dermatología, Argentina* (5 a year).

Sociedad Argentina de Endocrinología y Metabolismo (Argentine Society of Endocrinology and Metabolism): Avda Díaz Vélez 3889, C1200AAF Buenos Aires; tel. (11) 4963-7166; fax (11) 4961-5106; f. 1941; 550 mems; Pres. Dr LÉON SCHURMAN; Sec. Dr ANA ORLANDI; publ. *Revista* (quarterly).

Sociedad Argentina de Farmacología y Terapéutica (Argentine Society of Pharmacology and Therapeutics): Santa Fé 1171, 1059 Buenos Aires; tel. (11) 441-1633; f. 1929; 100 mems; Pres. Prof. Dr MANUEL LITTER; Sec. Dr JOSÉ A. L. CHIESA.

Sociedad Argentina de Gastroenterología (Argentine Society of Gastroenterology): Santa Fé 1171, 1059 Buenos Aires; tel. (11) 441-1633; f. 1927; 900 mems; Pres. Dr ERMAN E. CROSETTI; Sec.-Gen. Dr LEONARDO PINCHUK; publ. *Acta Gastroenterológica Latinoamericana*.

Sociedad Argentina de Gerontología y Geriatría (Argentine Gerontological and Geriatrics Society): San Luis 2538, C1056AAD Buenos Aires; fax (11) 4961-0070; e-mail sagg@connmed.com.ar; internet www.sagg.org.ar; f. 1950; 1,500 mems; Pres. Dr ISIDORO FAINSTEIN; Sec. Dr HUGO ALBERTO SCHIFIS; publs *Revista Argentina de Gerontología y Geriatría* (6 a year), *Vivir en Plenitud* (6 a year).

Sociedad Argentina de Hematología (Argentine Society of Haematology): Avda Angel Gallardo 899, 1405 Buenos Aires; f. 1948; 350 mems; Pres. Dr GUILLERMO CARLOS VILASECA; Sec. Dr EDUARDO DIBAR.

Sociedad Argentina de Investigación Clínica (Argentine Society of Clinical Research): Instituto de Investigaciones Médicas, U.B.A., Donato Alvares 3150, 1427 Buenos Aires; tel. (11) 4573-2619; fax (11) 4573-2619; f. 1960; 500 mems; Pres. BASILIO A. KOTSIAS; Sec. ADRIANA FRAGA; publ. *Medicina*.

Sociedad Argentina de Oftalmología (Argentine Ophthalmological Society): Santa Fé 1171, 1059 Buenos Aires; tel. (11) 4241-0392; f. 1920; 2,000 mems; Pres. Dr ROBERTO SAMPOALESI; Sec. Dr JOSÉ A. BADIA; publ. *Archivos de Oftalmología de Buenos Aires* (monthly).

Sociedad Argentina de Patología (Argentine Society of Pathology): Santa Fé 1171, 1059 Buenos Aires; tel. (11) 441-1633; f. 1933; 220 mems; Pres. Dr ALBERTO SUNDBLAD; Sec. Dra MABEL POMAR DE GIL; publ. *Archivos*.

Sociedad Argentina de Pediatría (Argentine Paediatric Society): Coronel Díaz 1971, 1425 Buenos Aires; tel. (11) 4824-2063; f. 1911; 7,500 mems; library of 5,000 vols; Pres. Dr CARLOS A. GIANANTONIO; Sec. Dra MARÍA LUISA AGEITOS; publ. *Archivos Argentinos de Pediatría* (6 a year).

Sociedad de Cirugía de Buenos Aires (Buenos Aires Surgical Society): Santa Fé 1171, 1059 Buenos Aires; tel. (11) 444-0664; Pres. IVAN GOÑI MORENO; Sec.-Gen. GUILLERMO I. BELLEVILLE.

Sociedad de Psicología Médica, Psicoanálisis y Medicina Psicosomática (Society of Medical Psychology, Psychoanalysis and Psychosomatic Medicine): Avda Santa Fé 1171, 1059 Buenos Aires; tel. (11) 4814-2182; f. 1939; 80 mems; Pres. Dr JOSÉ CUKIER; Sec. Dr A. STISMAN.

NATURAL SCIENCES

General

Academia Nacional de Ciencias de Buenos Aires (National Academy of Sciences of Buenos Aires): Avda Alvear 1711 (3o piso), 1014 Buenos Aires; tel. (11) 441-3066; f. 1935; 35 mems; Pres. Dr JULIO H. G. OLIVERA; Sec. Dr HUGO F. BAUZÁ; publs *Anales*, *Escritos de Filosofía* (quarterly).

Academia Nacional de Ciencias en Córdoba (National Academy of Sciences in Córdoba): CC 36, Avda Vélez Sarsfield 229, 5000 Córdoba; tel. (351) 433-2089; fax (351) 421-6350; e-mail gamezg@acad.uncor.edu; f. 1869; 79 mems; library of 12,000 vols, 3,800 periodicals; Pres. Dr ALBERTO PASCUAL MAIZTEGUI; Sec. Dr ALFREDO ELIO COCUCCI; publs *Actas*, *Boletín*, *Miscelánea*.

Academia Nacional de Ciencias Exactas, Físicas y Naturales (National Academy of Exact, Physical and Natural Sciences): Avda Alvear 1711 (4o), 1014 Buenos Aires; tel. (11) 4811-2998; fax (11) 4811-6951; e-mail acad@ancefn.org.ar; internet www.ancefn.org.ar; f. 1874; 130 (36 full voting, 27 nat. corresp., 61 foreign corresp., 6 hon.); library of 400 collns of periodicals; Pres. Dr ALEJANDRO J. ARVIA; Sec.-Gen. Dr JORGE V. CRISCI; publ. *Anales* (annual).

Asociación Argentina de Ciencias Naturales (Argentine Association of Natural Sciences): Avda Angel Gallardo 470, C1405DJR Buenos Aires; tel. (11) 4982-8370; fax (11) 4982-4494; e-mail physis@muambe.gov.ar; f. 1912; 450 mems; Pres. JUAN CARLOS GIACCHI; Sec. Dra CRISTINA MARINONE; publ. *Physis* (2 a year).

Asociación Argentina para el Progreso de las Ciencias (Association for the Advancement of Science): Avda Alvear 1711 (4o piso), 1014 Buenos Aires; tel. (11) 4811-2998; fax (11) 4811-6951; f. 1933; 215 mems (200 ordinary, 15 assoc.); Pres. Dr EDUARDO HERNÁN CHARREAU; Sec. Dr AUGUSTO F. GARCÍA; publ. *Ciencia e Investigación*.

Sociedad Científica Argentina (Argentine Scientific Society): Avda Santa Fé 1145, 1059 Buenos Aires; tel. (11) 4816-4745; fax (11) 4816-5406; e-mail postmaster@sociar.org.ar; f. 1872; affiliations in Santa Fé, La Plata, San Juan; 698 mems; library of 80,337 vols; Pres. ARTURO OTAÑO SAHORES; publ. *Anales* (annual).

Biological Sciences

Asociación Argentina de Micología (Argentine Mycological Society): Universidad de Buenos Aires, Facultad de Medicina, Departamento de Microbiología, Paraguay 2155 (Piso 11), 1121 Buenos Aires; tel. (11) 4962-7274; fax (11) 4962-5404; e-mail micomuniz@connmed.com.ar; f. 1960; studies in medical and veterinary mycology, and mycotoxins; 150 mems; library; Pres. Dra CRISTINA IOVANNITTI; Sec. Dra ALICIA ARECHAVALA; publ. *Revista Argentina de Micología* (3 a year).

Asociación Paleontológica Argentina (Argentine Association of Palaeontology): Maipú 645 (1o piso), C1006ACG Buenos Aires; tel. (11) 4326-7463; fax (11) 4326-7463; e-mail secretaria@apaleontologica.org.ar; internet www.apaleontologica.org.ar; f. 1955; 500 mems; Pres. Dr SERGIO F. VIZCAÍNO; Sec. Dra MARÍA DE LAS MERCEDES DI PASQUO; publ. *Ameghiniana* (quarterly).

Sociedad Argentina de Biología (Argentine Biological Society): Vuelta de Obligado 2490, 1428 Buenos Aires; tel. (11) 4783-2869; e-mail biologia@dna.uba.ar; internet proteus.dna.uba.ar/biologia; f. 1920; 140 mems; Pres. Dra ISABEL LÜTHY; Sec. Dr HÉCTOR COIRINI; publ. *Revista* (annual).

Sociedad Argentina de Fisiología Vegetal (Argentine Society of Plant Physiology): Departamento de Agronomía, UNS, 8000 Bahía Blanca; tel. (291) 43-4775; fax (291) 42-1942; f. 1958; 260 mems; Pres. Dr GUSTAVO A. ORIOLI; Sec. Dr LUIS F. HERNANDEZ.

Sociedad Entomológica Argentina (SEA) (Argentine Entomological Society): Miguel Lillo 205, 4107 San Miguel de Tucumán; tel. and fax (381) 423-2965; e-mail seatuc@csnat.unt.edu.ar; internet www.sea.secyt.gov.ar; f. 1925; 400 mems; library of 815 vols, 590 periodicals; located in the Museo de la Plata, Buenos Aires, e-mail bibsea@museo.fcnym.unlp.edu.ar; Pres. MER-

CEDES LIZARRALDE DE GROSSO; Sec. CARMEN REGUILÓN; publs *Revista de la Sociedad Entomológica Argentina* (2 a year), *Publicación Especial de la Sociedad Entomológica Argentina* (irreg.).

Mathematical Sciences

Unión Matemática Argentina (Argentine Mathematical Union): Facultad Ciencias Físico Matemáticas y Naturales, Universidad Nacional de San Luis, Ejército de los Andes 950, 5700 San Luis; tel. (2652) 422803; fax (2652) 430224; f. 1936; 600 mems; Pres. Dr FELIPE ZÓ; Sec. Dr HUGO ALVAREZ; publ. *Revista*.

Physical Sciences

Asociación Argentina Amigos de la Astronomía (Argentine Association for the Friends of Astronomy): Avda Patricias Argentinas 550, C1405BWS Buenos Aires; tel. and fax (11) 4863-3366; e-mail info@amigosdelaastonomia.org; internet www.amigosdelaastronomia.org; f. 1929; maintains an observatory and museum; 1,000 mems; library of 6,000 vols; Pres. CARLOS E. ANGUEIRA VÁZQUEZ; Sec. LUIS MANTEROLA; publ. *Revista Astronómica* (quarterly).

Asociación Argentina de Astronomía (Argentine Astronomy Association): Observatorio Astronómico, B1900FWA La Plata; tel. (221) 423-6593; fax (221) 423-6591; e-mail aaacd@fcaglp.fcaglp.unlp.edu.ar; internet www.astronomiaargentina.org.ar; f. 1958; 312 mems; Pres. MARTA GRACIELA ROVIRA; Sec. ROSA BEATRIZ ORELLANA; publ. *Boletín* (annual).

Asociación Argentina de Geofísicos y Geodestas (Argentine Association of Geophysicists and Geodesists): c/o Observatorio Astronómico de La Plata, Paseo del Bosque s/n, 1900 La Plata; e-mail jero@aagg.org.ar; internet www.aagg.org.ar; f. 1959; Pres. Dra MARÍA L ALTINGER; Sec. Dra MARÍA C. POMPOSIELLO; publs *Geoacta* (annual), *Boletín* (3 a year).

Asociación Bioquímica Argentina (Argentine Biochemical Association): Venezuela 1823, 1096 Buenos Aires; tel. (11) 438-2907; f. 1934.

Asociación Geológica Argentina (Argentine Geological Association): Maipú 645 (1o piso), 1006 Buenos Aires; tel. (11) 4325-3104; fax (11) 4325-3104; e-mail postmaster@aga.edu.ar; f. 1945; 1,750 mems; Pres. Dr A. C. RICCARDI; Sec. Dr S. DAMBORENEA; publ. *Revista* (quarterly).

Asociación Química Argentina (Argentine Chemical Association): Sánchez de Bustamante 1749, 1425 Buenos Aires; tel. (11) 4822-4886; fax (11) 4822-4886; e-mail info@aqa.org.ar; internet www.aqa.org.ar; f. 1912; 1,000 mems; library of 10,000 vols, 500 periodicals; Pres. Dr EDUARDO A. CASTRO; Sec. Dr EDUARDO J. BOTTANI; publs *Anales de la Asociación Química Argentina* (Scientific), *Industria y Química* (Technical).

Centro Argentino de Espeleología (Argentine Centre of Speleological Studies): Avda de Mayo 651 (1o piso), 1428 Buenos Aires; tel. (11) 4331-6798; f. 1970; 60 mems; library of 250 vols; Pres. JULIO GOYÉN AGUADO; Sec. ROBERTO OSCAR BERMEJO; publ. *Las Brujas* (annual).

Grupo Argentino del Color (Argentine Colour Group): c/o Secretary of Research, School of Architecture, Buenos Aires Univ., Ciudad Universitaria, Pav. 3 (4o), C1428BFA Buenos Aires; tel. (11) 4789-6289; fax (11) 4702-6009; e-mail gac@fadu.uba.ar; internet www.fadu.uba.ar/sicyt/color/gac.htm; f. 1979; study of colour science; 159 mems; Pres. Dr MARÍA L. DE MATTIELLO; publ. *GAC Revista* (3 a year).

PHILOSOPHY AND PSYCHOLOGY

Sociedad Argentina de Psicología (Buenos Aires Psychological Society): Callao 435 (1o), 1022 Buenos Aires; tel. (11) 4432-3760; f. 1930; Pres. JUAN CUATRECASAS.

RELIGION, SOCIOLOGY AND ANTHROPOLOGY

Asociación Argentina de Estudios Americanos (Argentine Association of American Studies): Maipú 672, 1424 Buenos Aires; tel. (11) 4392-4971.

Sociedad Argentina de Antropología (Argentina Anthropological Society): Moreno 350, 1091 Buenos Aires; f. 1936; 255 mems; Pres. M. M. PODESTÁ; Sec. I. GONZÁLEZ; publ. *Relaciones* (annual).

Sociedad Argentina de Sociología: Trejo 241, 5000 Córdoba; tel. (351) 44-5901; f. 1950; Pres. Prof. ALFREDO POVIÑA; Sec.-Gen. Prof. ODORICO PIRES PINTO.

TECHNOLOGY

Asociación Argentina del Frío (Argentine Refrigeration Association): Avda Mayo 1123 (5o), 1085 Buenos Aires; tel. (11) 4381-7544; f. 1932; 178 mems; small library; Pres. Ing. ROBERTO RICARDO AGUILO; Sec. Ing. FLORENTINO ROSON RODRIGUEZ; publ. *Clima* (monthly).

Asociación Electrotécnica Argentina (Argentine Electrotechnical Association): Posadas 1659, 1112 Buenos Aires; tel. (11) 4804-3454; f. 1913; 2,000 mems; library of 2,500 vols; Pres. ERNESTO H. RODIL; publ. *Revista Electrotécnica*.

Centro Argentino de Ingenieros (Argentine Centre of Engineering): Cerrito 1250, 1010 Buenos Aires; tel. (11) 4811-4961; fax (11) 4812-0475; f. 1895; 10,231 mems; library of 11,000 vols; Pres. Ing. ROBERTO P. ECHARTE; publ. *Políticas de la Ingeniería*.

Federación Lanera Argentina (Argentine Wool Federation): Avda Paseo Colón 823, C1063ACI Buenos Aires; tel. (11) 4300-7661; fax (11) 4361-6517; e-mail federacionlanera@speedy.com.ar; f. 1929; concerned with all aspects of wool trade, from breeding to sales; 50 mems; Pres. RICARDO VON GERSTENBERG; Sec. CLAUDIO ULRICH; publ. *Argentine Wool Statistics* (monthly).

Research Institutes

GENERAL

Instituto Torcuato Di Tella: Miñones 2159/77, 1428 Buenos Aires; tel. (11) 4783-8630; fax (11) 4783-3061; f. 1958; promotes scientific research and artistic creativity on a nat. and int. scale; administers research centres and higher education instns; postgraduate courses in economics, sociology and admin.; library of 85,000 vols; Pres. GREGORIO KLIMOVSKY; Dir Dr ADOLFO CANITROT.

AGRICULTURE, FISHERIES AND VETERINARY SCIENCE

Estación Experimental Agro-Industrial 'Obispo Colombres' ('Obispo Colombres' Agro-Industrial Experimental Research Station): CC 9, Las Talitas, 4101 Tucumán; tel. (381) 427-6561 ext. 221; fax (381) 427-6404 ext. 231; e-mail biblioteca@eeaoc.org.ar; internet www.eeaoc.org.ar; f. 1909; library of 8,000 vols, 75,000 periodicals; Technical Dir Ing. Agr. LEONARDO D. PLOPER; publs *Avance Agro-Industrial* (quarterly), *Gacetilla Agro-Industrial* (irreg.), *Revista Industrial y Agrícola de Tucumán* (annual).

Instituto Agrario Argentino de Cultura Rural (Argentine Agricultural Institute for Rural Education): Florida 460, 1005 Buenos Aires; tel. (11) 4392-2030; f. 1937; library of 2,000 vols; Dir Dr CORNELIO J. VIERA; Sec. MARÍA LUIS RIVAS; Technical Sec. EURIFUE ALFREDO VIVANA; publs *Reseñas Argentinas*, *Reseñas*, *Comunicados*.

Instituto de Edafología Agrícola (Institute of Agricultural Soil Science): Cerviño 3101, 1425 Buenos Aires; tel. (11) 484-9623; f. 1944; library of 3,200 vols; Dir Ing. Agr. JORGE I. BELLATI; publs *Técnicas Apartados de Artículos Tiradas Internas*, *Suelos*.

Instituto Nacional de Investigación y Desarrollo Pesquero (National Institute for Fisheries Research and Development): Casilla 175, 7600 Mar del Plata; tel. (223) 486-0963; fax (223) 486-1830; e-mail biblio@inidep.edu.ar; internet www.inidep.edu.ar; f. 1977; library of 4,260 vols, 750 periodicals; Dir Ing. LUIS M. BARLETTA; publs *INIDEP Informe Técnico* (irreg.), *Revista de Investigación y Desarrollo Pesquero* (irreg.).

Instituto Nacional de Tecnología Agropecuaria (INTA) (National Institute for Agricultural Technology): Rivadavia 1439, 1033 Buenos Aires; tel. (11) 4383-5095; fax (11) 4383-5090; e-mail ctorres@correo.inta.gov.ar; internet www.inta.gov.ar; f. 1956; 42 experimental stations, 13 research institutes; Pres. Ing. Agr. CARLOS CHEPI; Nat. Dir Ing. Agr. ROBERTO BOCHETTO; publs *Revista de Investigaciones Agropecuarias* (3 a year), *Idia XXI* (3 a year).

Main research centre:

Centro Nacional de Investigación Agropecuaria (National Centre for Agricultural Research): CC 25, 1712 Castelar, Buenos Aires; tel. (11) 4621-1819; research in all aspects of farming; Dir Dr Vet. HUMBERTO CISALE.

Instituto Nacional de Vitivinicultura (National Vine Growing and Wine Producing Institute): San Martín 430, 5500 Mendoza; tel. (261) 449-6300; fax (261) 449-6306; f. 1959; library of 20,000 vols, 690 journals; Nat. Dir Lic. FELIX ROBERTO AGUINAED; publs *Estadística Vitivinícola* (annual), *Exportaciones Argentinas de Productos Vitivinícolas* (annual), *Revista Vinifera*, *Superficie de Vinos por Variedades Implatada en la República Argentina*.

ARCHITECTURE AND TOWN PLANNING

Instituto de Planeamiento Regional y Urbano (IPRU) (Regional and Urban Planning Institute): Calle Posadas 1265 (7o), 1011 Buenos Aires; fax (11) 4815-8673; f. 1952; Dir FERNANDO PASTOR; publs *Plan*, *Cuadernos de IPRU*.

BIBLIOGRAPHY, LIBRARY SCIENCE AND MUSEOLOGY

Centro de Documentación Bibliotecológica (Centre for Library Science Documentation): Universidad Nacional del Sur, Avda Alem 1253, 8000 Bahía Blanca; tel. (291) 42-8035; fax (291) 455-1447; f. 1962; teaching and research in library science; library of 2,980 vols, 332 periodicals; Chief Librarian MARTA IBARLUCEA DE RUIZ; publs *Bibliografía Bibliotecológica Argentina 1978–81*, *Documentación Bibliotecológica*, *Revista de Revistas*.

Instituto de Bibliografía del Ministerio de Educación de la Provincia de Buenos Aires (Bibliographical Institute of Ministry of Education of the Province of Buenos Aires): Calle 47 No. 510 (6o), 1900 La Plata; tel. (221) 43-5915; Dir MARÍA DEL CARMEN CRESPI DE BUSTOS; publs *Bibliografía Argen-*

tina de Historia, *Boletín de Información Bibliográfica*.

ECONOMICS, LAW AND POLITICS

Centro de Investigaciones Económicas (Economic Research Centre): Instituto Torcuato Di Tella, Miñones 2159/77, 1428 Buenos Aires; tel. (11) 4781-5014; fax (11) 4786-2636; f. 1960; library of 85,000 vols; Dir ADOLFO CANITROT; publ. *Documentos de Trabajo*.

Instituto de Desarrollo Económico y Social (Institute of Economic and Social Development): Aráoz 2838, 1425 Buenos Aires; tel. (11) 4804-4949; fax (11) 4804-5856; e-mail ides@ides.org.ar; internet www.ides.org.ar; f. 1960; library of 15,000 vols; Pres. ADRIANA MARSHALL; Dir JUAN CARLOS TORRE; publ. *Desarrollo Económico – Revista de Ciencias Sociales* (quarterly).

Instituto Nacional de Estadística y Censos (National Institute of Statistics and Censuses): Avda Pte. Julio A. Roca 609, 1067 Buenos Aires; tel. (11) 4349-9609; fax (11) 4349-9601; e-mail ces@indec.mecon.gov.ar; internet www.indec.mecon.gov.ar; f. 1894; library of 30,000 vols; Dir LELIO MARMORA; publs *INDEC Informa* (monthly), *Comercio Exterior Argentino* (annual), *Anuario Estadístico de la República Argentina* (annual).

Instituto para el Desarrollo de Empresarial en la Argentina (Institute for Management Development): Moreno 1850, 1094 Buenos Aires; tel. (11) 4372-7667; fax (11) 449-6944; f. 1960; library of 10,000 vols, 50 periodicals; Dir RUBEN D. PUENTEDURA; publ. *IDEA*.

Instituto para la Integración de América Latina y el Caribe (Institute for the Integration of Latin America and the Caribbean): Esmeralda 130 (pisos 16 y 17), C1035ABD Buenos Aires; tel. (11) 4320-1850; fax (11) 4320-1865; e-mail int/inl@iadb.org; internet www.iadb.org/intal; f. 1965 following an agreement between the Inter-American Devt Bank and the govt of Argentina; undertakes research and provides support in all aspects of regional integration and co-operation, incl. infrastructural links among countries, regional devt of border areas, trade liberalization, legal aspects of integration and accession to new agreements; provides technical support for hemispheric integration processes agreed during Summit of the Americas 1994, and to fulfil WTO disciplines; organizes policy-orientated fora for govt officials and other interested parties; library: Documentation Centre of 100,000 documents, 12,000 vols, 400 periodicals; Dir RICARDO CARCIOFI; publs *Caricom Report* (in English, annual), *Informe Andino* (Andean Report, in Spanish and English, annual), *Informe Centroamericano* (Central American Report, in Spanish and English, annual), *Informe Mercosur* (Mercosur Report, annual), *Integración & Comercio* (Integration & Trade, 2 a year).

FINE AND PERFORMING ARTS

Instituto Nacional de Estudios de Teatro (National Institute for the Study of Theatre): Avda Córdoba 1199, 1055 Buenos Aires; tel. and fax (11) 4816-7212; f. 1936; library of 16,000 vols, archives; also nat. theatre museum; Dir Prof. CRISTINA LASTRA BELGRANO.

HISTORY, GEOGRAPHY AND ARCHAEOLOGY

Departamento de Estudios Históricos Navales (Department of Naval History Studies): Jefatura del Estado Mayor General de la Armada, Avda Almirante Brown 401, 1155 Buenos Aires; tel. (11) 4362-1248; fax (11) 4362-1130; e-mail estudioshistoricosnavales@yahoo.com.ar; internet www.ara.mil.ar; f. 1957; large number of publs, also paintings and medals; Dir Capt. GUILLERMO ANDRÉS OYARZABAL.

Dirección Nacional del Antártico (National Antarctic Office): Cerrito 1248, C1010AAZ Buenos Aires; tel. (11) 4813-0072; fax (11) 4813-7807; e-mail dna@dna.gov.ar; internet www.dna.gov.ar; f. 1970; scientific colln; maintains Yubany station at King George Island, Antarctica; library of 15,000 vols; Dir Dr MARIANO A. MEMOLLI; publs *Contribuciones Científicas* (irreg.), *Revista Antártica*, *Boletín del SCAR* (3 a year, Spanish edn of SCAR Bulletin).

Attached institute:

Instituto Antártico Argentino (Argentine Antarctic Institute): Cerrito 1248, C1010AAZ Buenos Aires; tel. and fax (11) 4813-7807; e-mail diriia@dna.gov.ar; internet www.antartida.gov.ar; f. 1951; Dir Dr SERPIO MAREUSSI.

Instituto Geográfico Militar (Military Geographical Institute): Avda Cabildo 381, 1426 Buenos Aires; tel. (11) 4576-5545; fax (11) 4576-5595; e-mail public@mapas.igm.gov.ar; internet www.igm.gov.ar; f. 1879; topographic survey of Argentina; Dir Coronel FERNANDO MIGUEL GALBÁN; publ. *Revista* (annual).

MEDICINE

Administracion Nacional de Laboratorios e Institutos de Salud 'Carlos G. Malbran' ('Carlos G. Malbran' National Administration for Laboratories and Institutes of Health): Avda Vélez Sarsfield 563, 1281 Buenos Aires; tel. (11) 4303-1804; fax (11) 4303-1433; f. 1916; library of 6,500 vols; Dir Dr ELSA L. SEGURA.

Centro de Investigaciones Neurobiológicas 'Prof. Dr Christfried Jakob' (Christfried Jakob Centre for Neurobiological Research): Avda Amancio Alcorta 1602, 1283 Buenos Aires; tel. and fax (11) 4306-7314; f. 1899; attached to Min. of Public Health and Welfare; Dir Prof. Dr MARIO-FERNANDO CROCCO; publ. *Folia Neurobiológica Argentina*.

Instituto de Biología y Medicina Experimental (Institute of Biology and Experimental Medicine): Vuelta de Obligado 2490, 1428 Buenos Aires; tel. (11) 4783-2869; fax (11) 4786-2564; e-mail ibyme@dna.uba.ar; internet proteus.dna.uba.ar/ibyme; f. 1944; library of 15,000 vols; Dir Dr EDUARDO H. CHARREAU; publ. *Memoria* (annual).

Instituto de Investigaciones Médicas 'Alfredo Lanari' (Alfredo Lanari Institute of Medical Research): Avda Donato Alvarez 3150, 1427 Buenos Aires; tel. (11) 4522-1438; f. 1957; clinical and basic medical research, teaching; library of 4,185 vols, 6,738 periodicals; Research Dir AQUILES J. RONCORONI.

NATURAL SCIENCES

General

Consejo Nacional de Investigaciones Científicas y Técnicas (CONICET) (National Council of Scientific and Technical Research): Avda Rivadavia 1917, 1033 Buenos Aires; tel. (11) 4953-3609; fax (11) 4953-4345; e-mail postmaster@conica.gov.ar; f. 1958; supports 6 regional research centres and 114 research institutes; maintains several scientific services; Pres. ANDRÉS CARRASCO.

Main research institutes:

Centro Argentino de Datos Oceanográficos (CEADO) (Argentine Centre of Oceanographic Data): Avda Montes de Oca 2124, 1271 Buenos Aires; tel. (11) 4303-2240; fax (11) 4303-2299; e-mail postmaster@ceado.edu.ar; Dir Capt. ADOLFO GIL VILLANUEVA.

Centro Argentino de Etnología Americana (CAEA) (Argentine Centre for American Ethnology): Avda de Mayo 1437 (1o piso Dpto. A), 1085 Buenos Aires; tel. (11) 4381-1821; e-mail caea@caea.gov.ar; Dir Dr MARIO CALIFANO.

Centro Argentino de Primates (CAPRIM) (Argentine Primates Centre): San Cayetano CC 145, 3400 Corrientes; tel. (3783) 42-7790; fax (3783) 42-7790; e-mail ruiz@caprim.edu.ar; Dir Dr JULIO CÉSAR RUIZ.

Centro Austral de Investigaciones Científicas (CADIC) (Southern Centre for Scientific Research): Avda Malvinas Argentinas s/n, CC 92, Ruta Nacional No. 3, Barrio La Misión, Camino Lapataia, 9410 Ushuaia; tel. (2901) 42-2310; fax (2901) 43-0644; e-mail postmaster@cadica.edu.ar; f. 1975; biology, geology, archaeology, anthropology, hydrography, climatology; library of 1,000 vols; Dir Dr EDUARDO B. OLIVERO; publs *Boletín*, *Publicaciones especiales del CADIC*, *Contribuciones Científicas del CADIC*.

Centro de Diagnóstico e Investigaciones Veterinarias Formosa (CEDIVEF) (Formosa Centre of Veterinary Diagnosis and Research): Ruta Nacional No. 11, km 1164, CC 292, 3600 Formosa; fax (3717) 45-1334; Dir Dr CARLOS M. MONZON.

Centro de Ecofisiología Vegetal (CEVEG) (Centre for Plant Ecophysiology): Serrano 669 (pisos 5 y 6), 1414 Buenos Aires; tel. (11) 4856-7110; fax (11) 4856-7110; e-mail postmaster@ceveg.gov.ar; Dir Dr OSVALDO H. CASO.

Centro de Ecología Aplicada del Litoral (CECOAL) (Centre of Coastal Applied Ecology): Ruta Prov. No. 5, Km 2·5, CC 291, 3400 Corrientes; tel. (3783) 45-4418; fax (3783) 45-4421; internet www.cecoal.com.ar; Dir Prof. JUAN JOSÉ NEIFF.

Centro de Estudios e Investigaciones Laborales (CEIL) (Centre of Labour Study and Research): Corrientes 2470 (6o piso, of. 24 y 25), 1046 Buenos Aires; tel. (11) 4952-5273; fax (11) 4952-5273; e-mail postmaster@ceil.edu.ar; f. 1971; Dir Dr JULIO CÉSAR NEFFA; publ. *Boletín – Serie Documentos*.

Centro de Estudios Farmacológicos y Botanicos (CEFYBO) (Centre for Pharmacological Studies and Botany): Serrano 669, 1414 Buenos Aires; tel. (11) 4856-2751; fax (11) 4856-2751; e-mail postmaster@cefybo.edu.ar; f. 1975; Dirs Dra LEONOR STERIN DE BORDA, Dra MARÍA ANTONIETA DEL PERO.

Centro de Estudios Fotosintéticos y Bioquímicos (CEFOBI) (Centre for Studies in Photosynthesis and Biochemistry): Suipacha 531, 2000 Rosario; tel. (341) 437-1955; fax (341) 437-0044; e-mail rncefobi@arcride.edu.ar; f. 1976; Dir Dr RUBÉN H. VALLEJOS.

Centro de Investigación y Desarrollo en Criotecnología de Alimentos (CIDCA) (Research and Development Centre for Food Cryotechnology): Calles 47 y 116, CC 553, 1900 La Plata; tel. (221) 424-9287; fax (221) 425-4853; Dir Dra MARÍA C. AÑON.

Centro de Investigación y Desarrollo en Fermentaciones Industriales (CINDEFI) (Research and Development Centre for Industrial Fermentation): Calles 47 y 115, 1900 La Plata; tel. (221) 483-3794; fax (221) 425-4533; e-mail voget@biol.unlp.edu.ar; Dir Dr RODOLFO J. ERTOLA.

Centro de Investigación y Desarrollo en Procesos Catalíticos (CINDECA) (Research and Development Centre for Catalytic Processes): Calle 47 No. 257, CC 59, 1900 La Plata; tel. (221) 421-1353; fax (221) 425-4277; e-mail cindeca@nahuel.biol.unlp.edu.ar; Dir Dr HORACIO J. THOMAS.

Centro de Investigación y Desarrollo en Tecnología de Pinturas (CIDEPINT) (Research and Development Centre for Paint Technology): Calle 52 a 121 y 122, 1900 La Plata, Buenos Aires; tel. (221) 421-6214; fax (221) 427-1537; e-mail cielsner@isis.unlp.edu.ar; Dir Dr VICENTE J. D RASCIO.

Centro de Investigación y Estudios Ortopédicos y Traumatológicos (CINEOT) (Research and Study Centre for Orthopaedics and Traumatology): Potosí 4215, 1199 Buenos Aires; tel. (11) 4958-4011; fax (11) 4981-0991; e-mail cineot@impsat1.com.ar; Dir Dr DOMINGO L. MUSCOLO.

Centro de Investigaciones en Antropología Filosófica y Cultural (CIAFIC) (Centre for Research in Philosophical and Cultural Anthropology): Juramento 142, 1609 Boulogne, Buenos Aires; Federico Lacroze 2100, 1426 Buenos Aires; tel. and fax (11) 4776-0913; e-mail postmaster@ciafic.edu.ar; internet www.ciafic.edu.ar; f. 1976; research into education, philosophy, linguistics, epistemology, anthropology; library of 12,000 vols and periodicals; Sec. Mag. CLOTILDE DE LA BARRA; publs *Archivos* (anthropology, annual), *Servicio de Información Bibliográfica Especializada* (2 a year).

Centro de Investigaciones en Recursos Geológicos (CIRGEO) (Centre for Research into Geological Resources): Ramírez de Velasco 847, 1414 Buenos Aires; tel. (11) 4772-9729; fax (11) 4771-3742; e-mail pompo@cirgeo.edu.ar; f. 1976; library of 6,000 vols, 90 periodicals; Dir Dr BERNABÉ J QUARTINO.

Centro de Investigaciones Endocrinológicas (CEDIE) (Centre of Endocrinological Research): Gallo 1330, 1425 Buenos Aires; tel. (11) 4963-5931; fax (11) 4963-5930; e-mail master@fend.sld.arg; Dir Dr CÉSAR BERGADÁ.

Centro de Investigaciones Opticas (CIOP) (Centre for Optical Research): Camino Parque Centenario e/505 y 506, Gonnet, CC 124, 1900 La Plata, Buenos Aires; tel. (221) 484-0280; fax (221) 453-0189; e-mail postmaster@ciop.edu.ar; Dir Dr MARIO GALLARDO.

Centro de Investigaciónes sobre Regulación de Poblacion de Organismos Nocivos (CIRPON) (Centre for Research into Controlling Harmful Organisms): Pasaje Caseros 1050, CC 90, 4000 San Miguel de Tucumán; fax (381) 434-6940; e-mail postmaster@cirpon.untmre.edu.ar; Dir Dr ALBERTO A. P. FIDALGO.

Centro de Referencia para Lactobacilos (CERELA) (Reference Centre for Lactobacillus): Chacabuco 145, 4000 San Miguel de Tucumán; tel. (381) 431-1720; fax (381) 431-1720; e-mail crl@cerela.edu.ar; Dir Dra AÍDA A. P. DE RUIZ HOLGADO.

Centro de Tecnología en Recursos Minerales y Cerámica (CETMIC) (Technology Centre for Mineral and Ceramic Resources): CC 49, 1897 Gonnet, Buenos Aires; Camino Centenario y 506, 1897 Gonnet, Buenos Aires; tel. (221) 484-0247; fax (221) 471-0075; e-mail postmaster@cetmic.edu.ar; Dir Dr ENRIQUE PEREIRA.

Centro Experimental de la Vivienda Económica (CEVE) (Experimental Centre for Low-Cost Housing): Igualdad 3585, Villa Siburu, 5003 Córdoba; tel. (351) 489-4442; fax (351) 489-4442; e-mail postmaster@ceve.org.ar; Dir Arq. HORACIO BERRETTA.

Centro Nacional Patagónico (CNP) (National Patagónia Centre): Blvd Alte. Brown s/n, 9120 Puerto Madryn, Chubut; tel. (2965) 45-1375; fax (2965) 47-2885; e-mail postmaster@cenpat.edu.ar; Dir Dr ADAN E. PUCCI.

Instituto Argentino de Investigaciónes de las Zonas Aridas (IADIZA) (Argentine Institute for Arid Zones Research): Dr Adrián Ruiz Leal s/n, Parque Gral San Martín, 5500 Mendoza; fax (261) 428-7995; e-mail cricyt@planet.losandes.com.ar; f. 1974; Dir Ing. Agr. JUAN CARLOS GUEVARA (acting); publ. *Boletín Informativo*.

Instituto Argentino de Nivologia, Glaciologia y Ciencias Ambientales (IANIGLA) (Argentine Institute for Snow, Ice and Environmental Sciences): Dr Adrián Ruiz Leal s/n, Parque Gral San Martín, CC 131, 5500 Mendoza; tel. (261) 428-7029; fax (261) 428-7029; e-mail cricyt@planet.losandes.com.ar; Dir Dr WOLFGANG VOLKHEIMER.

Instituto Argentino de Oceanografía (IADO) (Argentine Oceanographic Institute): Edificio E3, Complejo de la Carrindanga, Florida 4000, 8000 Bahía Blanca, Buenos Aires; tel. (291) 42-3555; fax (291) 486-1112; e-mail postmaster@criba.edu.ar; f. 1969; Subdirector-in-Charge Dr JOSÉ KOSTADINOFF; publ. *Contribuciones Científicas IADO*.

Instituto Argentino de Radioastronomía (IAR) (Argentine Institute of Radioastronomy): Casilla de Correo 5, 1894 Villa Elisa, Buenos Aires; tel. (221) 482-4903; fax (221) 425-4909; e-mail webmaster@irma.iar.unlp.edu.ar; internet www.iar.unlp.edu.ar; f. 1963; library of 6,000 vols, 100 periodicals; Dir Dr RICARDO MORRAS.

Instituto de Botánica del Nordeste (IBONE) (Northeastern Institute of Botany): Sargento Cabral 2131, CC 209, 3400 Corrientes; tel. (3783) 42-7309; fax (3783) 42-7131; e-mail postmaster@unneib.edu.ar; Dir Ing. ANTONIO KRAPOVICKAS.

Instituto de Desarrollo Tecnológico para la Industria Química (INTEC) (Technological Development Institute of the Chemical Industry): Güemes 3450, 3000 Santa Fé; tel. (342) 455-9174; fax (342) 455-0944; e-mail director@intec.unl.edu.ar; Dir Dr ALBERTO E. CASSANO (acting).

Instituto de Geocronología y Geología Isotópica (INGEIS) (Institute of Isotope Geochronology and Geology): Pabellón INGEIS, Ciudad Universitaria, 1428 Buenos Aires; tel. (11) 4784-7798; fax (11) 4783-3024; e-mail postmaster@ingeis.uba.ar; Dir Dr ENRIQUE LINARES.

Instituto de Investigación de Productos Naturales, de Análisis y de Síntesis Orgánica (IPNAYS) (Institute for Research, Analysis and Organic Synthesis of Natural Products): Santiago del Estero 2829, 3000 Santa Fé; tel. (342) 455-3958; fax (342) 456-1146; e-mail rmalizia@fiqus.unl.edu.ar; Dir Ing. J. A. RETAMAR.

Instituto de Investigación Médica 'Mercedes y Martín Ferreyra' (INIMEC) (Mercedes and Martín Ferreyra Medical Research Institute): CC 389, 5000 Córdoba; Friuli 2434, Colinas de V. Sarfield, 5016 Córdoba; tel. (351) 468-1465; fax (351) 469-5163; e-mail lbeauge@immf.uncor.edu; Dir Dr LUISA BEAUGE.

Instituto de Investigaciones Bioquímicas (INIBIBB) (Institute for Biochemical Research): Edificio E1, Complejo de la Carrindanga, Florida 4000, 8000 Bahía Blanca, Buenos Aires; tel. (291) 486-1201; fax (291) 486-1200; e-mail rtfjb1@criba.edu.ar; f. 1975; Dir Prof. Dr FRANCISCO JOSÉ BARRANTES.

Instituto de Investigaciónes en Catálisis y Petroquímica (INCAPE) (Catalysis and Petrochemistry Research Institute): Santiago del Estero 2654, 3000 Santa Fé; tel. (342) 453-3858; fax (342) 453-1068; e-mail parera@fiqus.unl.edu.ar; Dir Ing. JOSÉ M. PARERA.

Instituto de Investigaciones Estadísticas (INIE) (Statistical Research Institute): Avda Independencia 1900, CC 209, 4000 San Miguel de Tucumán; tel. (381) 436-4093; fax (381) 436-4105; e-mail postmaster@untiie.edu.ar; Dir Dr RAÚL P. MENTZ.

Instituto de Investigaciones Farmacológicas (ININFA) (Pharmacological Research Institute): Junín 956 (5o), 1113 Buenos Aires; tel. (11) 4961-6784; fax (11) 4963-8593; e-mail ininfa@huemul.ffyb.uba.ar; Dir Dra EDDA ADLER DE GRASCHINSKY.

Instituto de Investigaciones Geohistóricas (IIGHI) (Institute of Geohistorical Research): Avda Castelli 930, CC 438, 3500 Resistencia, Chaco; tel. (3722) 42-7798; fax (3722) 43-9983; e-mail postmaster@iighi.gov.ar; Dir Dr ERNESTO J. A. MAEDER.

Instituto de Limnología Dr Raul A. Ringuelet (ILPLA) (Limnology Institute): CC 712, 1900 La Plata, Buenos Aires; e-mail postmaster@ilpla.edu.ar; Dir Dr HUGO LOPEZ (acting).

Instituto de Matemática (INMABB) (Mathematics Institute): Avda Alem 1253, 8000 Bahía Blanca; tel. (291) 43-3382; fax (291) 455-1447; e-mail inmabb@arcriba.edu.ar; f. 1956; Dir Dra AURORA GERMANI.

Instituto de Mecánica Aplicada (IMA) (Institute of Applied Mechanics): Gorriti 43, 8000 Bahía Blanca; tel. (291) 44-5154; fax (291) 455-1447; e-mail ima@criba.edu.ar; Dir Dr PATRICIO A. A. LAURA.

Instituto de Neurobiología (IDNEU) (Neurobiology Institute): Serrano 669, 1414 Buenos Aires; tel. (11) 4855-7674; fax (11) 4856-7108; e-mail postmaster@fuacta.sld.ar; Dir Dr JUAN H. TRAMEZZANI.

Instituto Latinoamericano de Investigaciones Comparadas Oriente y Occidente (ILICOO) (Latin-American Institute for Comparative East-West Studies): Callao 853, 1023 Buenos Aires; tel. (11) 4811-2270; e-mail postmaster@uscsoc.edu.ar; f. 1973; library of 2,000 vols, 1,500 periodicals; Dir Prof. MARÍA M. TERREN; publ. *Oriente – Occidente*.

Instituto Multidisciplinario de Biología Celular (IMBICE) (Multidisciplinary Institute of Cellular Biology): Calle 525, e/ 10 y 11, CC 403, 1900 La Plata, Buenos Aires; tel. (221) 421-0112; fax (221) 425-3320; e-mail imbice@imbice.edu.ar; Dir Dr NÉSTOR O. BIANCHI.

Instituto Rosario de Investigaciónes en Ciencias de la Educación (IRICE) (Rosario Education Research Institute): Blvd 27 de Febrero 210 'bis', 2000 Rosario; tel. (341) 482-1769; fax (341) 482-1772;

e-mail irice@ifir.ifir.edu.ar; Dir Dr NÉSTOR DIRECTORIO ROSELLI.

Fundación Miguel Lillo: Miguel Lillo 251, 4000 JFE San Miguel de Tucumán; tel. and fax (381) 433-0868; internet www.lillo.org.ar; f. 1931; scientific research in natural history; incl. institutes of Botany (Dir Lic. ANA MARÍA FRÍAS DE FERNANDEZ), Geology (Dir Dr CARLOS GONZALEZ) and Zoology (Dir Dr SONIA TURK), Geobiological Information Centre (135,000 documents, Dir Prof. ROSALINA CORROTO), a botanic garden (Dir MARÍA E. CRISTOBAL DE HINOJO), a museum (Dir Lic. LILIA LÓPEZ DE LEGUIZAMÓN) and a cultural centre (Dir Prof. FLORENCIA ARAOZ); Pres. Dr JORGE L. ROUGES; Dir Dr JOSÉ ANTONIO HAEDO ROSSI; publs *Genera et Species Plantarum Argentinarum, Genera et Species Animalium Argentinorum, Lilloa* (botanical), *Acta Zoologica Lilloana, Acta Geologica Lilloana, Opera Lilloana, Miscelánea, Serie Conservación de la Naturaleza, Extensión Científica y Cultural.*

Biological Sciences

Estación Hidrobiológica (Hydrobiology Station): 7631 Quequén, Buenos Aires; f. 1928; attached to 'B. Rivadavia' Argentine Museum of Natural Sciences; concerned especially with marine hydrobiology; Dir Prof. ENRIQUE BALECH; publ. *Trabajos de la Estación Hidrobiológica* (irreg.).

Instituto de Botánica 'C. Spegazzini' (Botanical Institute): Calle 53 No. 477, 1900 La Plata, Buenos Aires; tel. and fax (221) 421-9845; e-mail speg-lps@museo.fcnym.unlp.edu.ar; internet www.fcnym.unlp.edu.ar/institutos/spegazzini/indexibs.html; f. 1930; affiliated to Museo de La Plata; mycological research, biodiversity of saprotrophic and biotrophic fungi; mycological collns from Argentina and all South America; germplasm bank of arbuscular mycorrhizal fungi; Dir Prof. Dr MARTA NOEMI CABELLO.

Instituto de Botánica 'Darwinion' (Darwinian Botanical Institute): Labardén 200, CC 22, B1642HYD San Isidro; tel. 4743-4800; fax 4747-4748; e-mail secretaria@darwin.edu.ar; internet www.darwin.edu.ar; f. 1911; attached to the Academia Nacional de Ciencias Exactas, Físicas y Naturales and the Consejo Nacional de Investigaciones Científicas y Técnicas; fields of research: systematic botany, phytogeography, plant anatomy and cytogenetics, palynology, ethnobotany, archaeobotany; 45 mems; library of 160,000 vols, 2,600 periodicals; Dir Dr FERNANDO O. ZULOAGA; publs *Hickenia* (irreg.), *Revista Darwiniana* (2 a year).

Instituto Municipal de Botánica, Jardín Botánico 'Carlos Thays' (Municipal Botanical Institute, Carlos Thays Botanical Gardens): Sante Fé 3951, 1407 Buenos Aires; tel. (11) 469-3954; f. 1898; library of 1,000 vols, 7,000 periodicals; Dir ANTONIO AMADO GARCÍA; publs *Index Seminum, Revista del Instituto de Botánica.*

Instituto Nacional de Limnología (National Institute of Limnology): José Maciá 1933, 3016 Santo Tomé, Santa Fé; tel. (342) 474-0723; fax (342) 475-0394; e-mail inali@arcride.edu.ar; f. 1962; library of 3,000 vols, 385 periodicals; Dir Prof. ELLY CORDIVIOLA DE YUAN.

Physical Sciences

Comisión Nacional de Actividades Espaciales (CONAE) (National Commission on Space Activities): Avda Paseo Colón, 1063 Buenos Aires; internet www.conae.gov.ar; f. 1991; develops Argentina's Nat. Space Programme.

Comisión Nacional de Energía Atómica (National Atomic Energy Commission): Avda del Libertador 8250, 1429 Buenos Aires; tel. (11) 4704-1209; fax (11) 4704-1154; f. 1950; govt agency; promotes and undertakes scientific and industrial research and applications of nuclear transmutations and reactions; research centres in Buenos Aires, Constituyentes, Ezeiza and Bariloche; library: information centre: see Libraries; Pres. Ing. EDUARDO SANTOS.

Observatorio Astronómico (Astronomical Observatory): Laprida 854, 5000 Córdoba; tel. (351) 433-1064; fax (351) 433-1063; e-mail library@mail.oac.uncor.edu; internet www.oac.uncor.edu; f. 1871; attached to the Univ. of Córdoba; research and undergraduate and postgraduate teaching; library of 5,000 vols; Dir Prof. Dr LUIS A. MILONE; publs *Resultados, Reprints* (40 a year).

Observatorio Astronómico (Astronomical Observatory): Paseo del Bosque s/n, 1900 La Plata; tel. (221) 423-6593; fax (221) 423-6591; e-mail academic@fcaglp.fcaglp.unlp.edu.ar; internet www.fcaglp.unlp.edu.ar; f. 1883; library of 25,000 vols, 500 periodicals; Dean Dr JUAN CARLOS MUZZIO.

Servicio Geológico Minero Argentino (Argentine Geological and Mining Service): Avda Julio A. Roca 651 (10o), 1322 Buenos Aires; tel. (11) 4349-3162; fax (11) 4349-3160; e-mail dnsg@secind.mecon.ar; internet www.segemar.gov.ar; f. 1904; attached to the State Secretariat of Mining of Min. of Economy and Public Works; Dir Dr ROBERTO PAGE; publ. *Estadística Minera de la República Argentina* (annual).

Servicio Meteorológico Nacional (National Meteorological Service): 25 de Mayo 658, 1002 Buenos Aires; tel. (11) 4312-4481; fax (11) 4311-3968; f. 1872; library of 45,000 vols; Dir RAMON AGUSTIN SONZINI; publs *Boletín informativo, Boletín climatológico.*

RELIGION, SOCIOLOGY AND ANTHROPOLOGY

Departamento de Estudios Etnográficos y Coloniales (Department of Ethnographical and Colonial Studies): Calle 25 de Mayo 1470, 3000 Santa Fé; tel. (342) 457-3550; fax (342) 457-3550; e-mail etnosfe@ceride.gov.ar; internet www.santafe.gov.ar/cultura/cultura/htm; f. 1940; Dir Arq. LUIS MARIA CALVO; publ. *America* (annual).

Instituto Nacional de Antropología y Pensamiento Latinoamericano (National Institute of Anthropology and Latin American Thought): Calle 3 de Febrero 1378, 1426 Buenos Aires; tel. (11) 4784-3371; fax (11) 4784-3371; e-mail postmaster@bibapl.edu.ar; f. 1943; attached to the Secretariat for Culture at the President's Office; library of 15,000 vols, 1,600 periodicals; Dir Dra DIANA BOLANDI DE PERROT; publ. *Cuaderno.*

TECHNOLOGY

Instituto Argentino de Normalización (IRAM) (Argentine Standards Institute): Perú 552/556, C1068AAB Buenos Aires; tel. (11) 4346-0600; fax (11) 4346-0601; e-mail iram4@vianetworks.net.ar; internet www.iram.com.ar; f. 1935; library of 174,300 standards; Dir-Gen. Ing. JOSÉ F. LÓPEZ; publ. *Boletín IRAM* (monthly).

Instituto de Mecánica Aplicada y Estructuras (Institute of Applied Mechanics and Structures): Riobamba y Berutti, 2000 Rosario, Santa Fé; tel. (341) 480-8538; fax (341) 480-8540; e-mail imaesecr@eie.fceia.unr.edu.ar; f. 1963; library of 1,000 vols, 3,000 periodicals; Dir Ing. FERNANDO OSCAR MARTÍNEZ.

Instituto Nacional de Tecnología Industrial (INTI) (National Institute of Industrial Technology): Avda Leandro N. Alem 1067 (7o), 1001 Buenos Aires; tel. (11) 4313-3013; fax (11) 4313-2130; internet www.inti.gov.ar; f. 1957; library of 32,000 vols, 2,216 periodicals, 105,000 standards; Pres. Ing. LEÓNIDAS J. F. MONTAÑA; publs *Boletín técnico* (irreg.), *Dendroenergía* (2 a year), *Noticiteca* (quarterly).

Research institutes:

Centro de Investigación y Desarrollo en Construcciones (Centre for Construction Research and Development): Avda Gral Paz e/ Avda Albarellos 33/10, CC 157, 1650 San Martin, Buenos Aires; Dir Ing. R. LEONARDO CHECMAREW.

Centro de Investigación y Desarrollo en Física (Centre for Physics Research and Development): Avda Gral Paz e/ Avda de los Constituyentes y Avda Albarellos 3/44, CC 157, 1650 San Martin, Buenos Aires; fax (11) 4713-4140; Dir Lic. GUSTAVO RANGUGNI.

Centro de Investigación en Tecnologías de Industrialización de Alimentos (Centre for Research on Technologies for the Industrialization of Food Production): Avda Gral Paz e/ Avda de los Constituyentes y Avda Albarellos 40, CC 157, 1650 San Martin, Buenos Aires; Dir Ing. GUILLERMO CAMBIAZZO.

Centro de Investigación de Tecnologías de Granos (Centre for Research on Technologies for the Industrialization of Grain Production): Avda Alte. Brown e/ Reconquista y Juan Jose Paso, 6500 Nueve de Julio, Buenos Aires; Dir Ing. NICOLÁS APRO.

Centro de Investigación y Desarrollo de Ingeniería Ambiental (Centre for Environmental Engineering Research and Development): Paseo Colón 850 (4o), 1063 Buenos Aires; tel. (11) 4345-7541; fax (11) 4331-5362; Dir Ing. LUIS A. DE TULIO.

Centro de Investigación y Desarrollo para el Uso Racional de la Energía (Centre for Research and Development for the Rational Use of Energy): Avda Gral Paz e/ Avda de los Constituyentes y Avda Albarellos 5, CC 157, 1650 San Martin, Buenos Aires; Dir Ing. MARIO OGARA.

Centro de Investigación y Desarrollo de Métodos y Técnicas para Pequeñas y Medianas Empresas (Centre for Methods and Techniques Research and Development for Small and Medium-Size Industries): Avda Gral Paz e/ Avda de los Constituyentes y Avda Albarellos 12, CC 157, 1650 San Martin, Buenos Aires; Dir Ing. ROBERTO LÓPEZ.

Centro de Investigación de los Reglamentos Nacionales de Seguridad para Obras Civiles (Centre for Research for National Regulations on Civil Work Safety): Avda de los Immigrantes 1950 (Of. 22 y 24), 1104 Buenos Aires; Dir Ing. MARTA PARMIGIANI.

Centro de Investigación y Desarrollo sobre Contaminantes Especiales (Centre for Special Pollutants Research and Development): Avda Gral Paz e/ Avda de los Constituyentes y Avda Albarellos 38, CC 157, 1650 San Martin, Buenos Aires; tel. (220) 4754-4074; fax (220) 4753-5749; Dir Ing. ISABEL FRAGA.

Centro de Investigación y Desarrollo Textil (Centre for Textile Research and Development): Avda Gral Paz e/ Avda de los Constituyentes y Avda Albarellos 15, CC 157, 1650 San Martin, Buenos Aires; Dir Ing. PATRICIA MARINO.

Centro de Investigación y Desarrollo del Cuero (Centre for Leather Research and Development): Camino Centenario e/ 505 y 508, CC 6, 1897 Manuel Gonnet,

Buenos Aires; tel. 484-1876; fax 484-0244; Dir Ing. ALBERTO SOFÍA.

Centro de Investigación y Desarrollo de Carnes (Centre for Meat Research and Development): Avda Gral Paz e/ Avda de los Constituyentes y Avda Albarellos 47, CC 157, 1650 San Martin, Buenos Aires; Dir Ing. NÉLIDA PROLA.

Centro de Investigación y Desarrollo de Electrónica e Informática (Centre for Electronics and Computer Science Research and Development): Avda Gral Paz e/ Avda de los Constituyentes y Avda Albarellos 42, CC 157, 1650 San Martin, Buenos Aires; tel. (220) 4754-4064; fax (220) 4754-5194; Dir Ing. DANIEL LUPI.

Centro de Investigación y Desarrollo en Mecánica (Centre for Mechanics Research and Development): Avda Gral Paz e/ Avda de los Constituyentes y Avda Albarellos 9/46, CC 157, 1650 San Martin, Buenos Aires; tel. (220) 4752-0818; fax (220) 4754-5301; Dir Ing. MARIO QUINTEIRO.

Centro de Investigación y Desarrollo en Química y Petroquímica (Centre for Chemistry and Petrochemistry Research and Development): Avda Gral Paz e/ Avda de los Constituyentes y Avda Albarellos 38, CC 157, 1650 San Martin, Buenos Aires; Dir Lic. GRACIELA ENRIQUEZ.

Centro de Investigación y Asistencia Técnica a la Industria (Centre for Research and Technical Assistance to Industry): Avda Mitre y 20 de Junio, CC 548, 8336 Villa Regina, Rio Negro; tel. (2941) 46-2810; Dir Ing. RODOLFO ARDENGHI.

Centro de Investigación de Celulosa y Papel (Centre for Cellulose and Paper Research): Avda Gral Paz e/ Avda de los Constituyentes y Avda Albarellos 15, CC 157, 1650 San Martin, Buenos Aires; Dir Ing. HUGO VELEZ.

Centro de Investigación y Desarrollo sobre Electrodeposición y Procesos Superficiales (Centre for Electroplating and Superficial Processes Research and Development): Avda Gral Paz e/ Avda de los Constituyentes y Avda Albarellos 46, CC 157, 1650 San Martin, Buenos Aires; Dir Ing. ALICIA NIÑO GÓMEZ.

Centro de Investigación y Desarrollo de la Industria de la Madera y Afines (Centre for the Wood Industry and Related Research and Development): Juana Gorriti 3520, 1708 Hurlingham, Buenos Aires; Dir Ing. GRACIELA RAMIREZ.

Centro de Investigación y Desarrollo de Envases y Embalajes (Centre for Packaging Research and Development): Avda Gral Paz e/ Avda de los Constituyentes y Avda Albarellos 48, CC 157, 1650 San Martin, Buenos Aires; Dir Ing. CARLOS LOMO.

Centro de Investigación y Desarrollo de Tecnológico de la Industria del Caucho (Centre for Research and Technological Development of the Rubber Industry): Avda Gral Paz 5445, CPB1650KNA San Martin, Buenos Aires; fax (11) 4753-5781; Dir Lic. LILIANA REHAK.

INTI-Plásticos (INTI-Plastics): Avda Gral Paz e/ Avda de los Constituyentes y Avda Albarellos 16, CC 157, B1650WAB San Martin, Buenos Aires; tel. (11) 4724-6373; fax (11) 4753-5773; e-mail plasticos@inti.gov.ar; internet www.inti.gov.ar/citip; f. 1978; research and devt; technology transfer; 45 mems; library of 500 vols; Dir Ing. ALEJANDRO ARIOSTI.

Libraries and Archives

Bahía Blanca

Asociación Bernardino Rivadavia—Biblioteca Popular (People's Library of the Bernardino Rivadavia Association): Avda Colón 31, 8000 Bahía Blanca; tel. (291) 455-4055; fax (291) 455-9677; e-mail abr@abr.org.ar; internet www.abr.org.ar; f. 1882; funded by its members; 4,500 mems; 158,319 vols, 1,000 periodicals, 1,000 video cassettes and a large archive of newspapers; Pres. Dr NÉSTOR J. CAZZANIGA; Sec. MIGUEL A. LALANNE.

Biblioteca Central de la Universidad Nacional del Sur (Central Library of the National University of the South): Avda Alem 1253, 8000 Bahía Blanca; tel. (291) 42-8035; fax (291) 459-5110; e-mail unsbc@criba.edu.ar; internet bc.uns.edu.ar; f. 1948; 164,000 vols, 7,293 periodicals; Chief Librarian LUIS A. HERRERA; publs *Memoria Anual*, *Ultimas Adquisiciones*.

Buenos Aires

Archivo General de la Nación (National Archives): Avda Leandro N. Alem 246, 1003 Buenos Aires; tel. (11) 4331-5531; fax (11) 4334-0065; e-mail archivo@mininterior.gov.ar; internet www.archivo.gov.ar; f. 1821; Supervisor ENRIQUE TANDETER.

Biblioteca Argentina para Ciegos (Argentine Library for the Blind): Lezica 3909, C1202AAA Buenos Aires; tel. (11) 4981-0137; fax (11) 4981-0137 ext. 15; e-mail bac@bac.org.ar; internet www.bac.org.ar; f. 1924; 14,000 vols in Braille, talking books; Dir FERNANDO GALARRAGA; publs *Burbujas* (in Braille, for children), *Hacia La Luz* (in Braille, for adults), *Con Fundamento* (in Braille, for young people).

Biblioteca Central de la Armada (Central Library of the Navy): Estado Mayor General de la Armada, Calle Comodoro Py 2055 (3o), 1104 Buenos Aires; tel. (11) 4317-2039; f. 1914; 160,000 vols; 50 brs; Dir Capt. LUIS ALBERTO PONS; publ. *Revista de Publicaciones Navales*.

Biblioteca Central de la Universidad del Salvador 'Padre Guillermo Furlong' (Fr Guillermo Furlong Central Library of the University of the Saviour): Presidente Perón 1818, 1040 Buenos Aires; tel. (11) 4371-0422; e-mail uds-bibl@salvador.edu.ar; f. 1956; 55,000 vols; Dir LAURA MARTINO; publ. *Boletín Bibliográfico*.

Biblioteca de Arte (Art Library): Avda Libertador General San Martín 1473, 1425 Buenos Aires; tel. (11) 4803-0714; f. 1910; part of the Museo Nacional de Bellas Artes; visual arts; 40,000 vols; Dir RAQUEL EDELMAN.

Biblioteca de la Sociedad Rural Argentina (Library of Argentine Agricultural Society): Florida 460, 1005 Buenos Aires; tel. (11) 4322-3431; fax (11) 4325-8231; f. 1866; 47,500 vols; Dir Dr VÍCTOR LUIS FUNES; publs *Anales de la Sociedad Rural Argentina* (quarterly), *Boletín*, *Memoria* (annual).

Biblioteca de Leprología 'Dr Enrique P. Fidanza' (Dr Enrique P. Fidanza Leprosy Library): Federación del Patronato del Enfermo de Lepra de la República Argentina, Beruti 2373/77, 1106 Buenos Aires; tel. (11) 483-1815; f. 1930; 4,000 vols, 35,000 cards in its catalogues; museum of histopathology of skin; publ. *Temas de Leprología*.

Biblioteca del Banco Central de la República Argentina (Library of the Central Bank of the Republic of Argentina): San Martín 216, C1004AAF Buenos Aires; tel. (11) 4348-3772; fax (11) 4348-3771; e-mail biblio@bcra.gov.ar; internet www.bcra.gov.ar; f. 1935; 100,000 vols; Dir MARTA S. GUTIÉRREZ; publs *Boletín Estadístico* (monthly), *Boletín Monetario y Financiero* (quarterly), *Informe Anual del Presidente al Congreso* (annual), *Notas Técnicas* (irreg.), *Documentos de Trabajo* (irreg.), *Información de Entidades Financieras* (monthly).

Biblioteca del Bibliotecario 'Dr Augusto Raúl Cortazar' (Library of the Librarian Dr Augusto Raúl Cortazar): México 564, 1097 Buenos Aires; f. 1944; is a section of the Escuela Nacional de Bibliotecarios (Instituto Superior de Enseñanza); 2,500 vols; Dir RUBY A. ESCANDE.

Biblioteca del Colegio de Escribanos 'José A. Negri' (José A. Negri Library of the College of Notaries): Callao 1540, 1024 Buenos Aires; tel. and fax (11) 4807-1637; e-mail bibnegri@colegio-escribanos.org.ar; internet www.colegio-escribanos.org.ar; f. 1886; law and social science; 32,500 vols; Librarian ANA MARÍA DANZA; publs *Revista del Notariado*, *Boletín de Legislación*.

Biblioteca del Congreso de la Nación (Library of the National Congress): Rivadavia 1850, 1033 Buenos Aires; tel. (11) 4476-1641; fax (11) 4954-1067; f. 1859; 2,000,000 vols; Dir DOMINGO A. BRAVI; publ. *Boletín*.

Biblioteca del Ministerio de Relaciones Exteriores y Culto (Ministry of Foreign Affairs and Religion Library): Arenales 761, 1061 Buenos Aires; tel. (11) 441-1498; 50,000 vols; Dir HORACIO R. PIÑEYRO.

Biblioteca del Servicio Geológico Minero Argentino (Library of the Argentine Mining Geology Service): Avda Julio A. Roca 651 (9o), 1322 Buenos Aires; tel. (1) 349-3200; fax (1) 349-3198; e-mail mjanit@secind.mecon.gov.ar; internet www.segemar.gov.ar; f. 1904; 150,000 vols, 45,000 pamphlets, 15,000 maps; Dir Lic. MARA JANITENS; publs *Boletines*, *Anales*.

Biblioteca Nacional (National Library): Agüero 2502, 1425 Buenos Aires; tel. (11) 4806-6155; fax (11) 4806-6157; e-mail postmaster@siscor.bibnal.edu.ar; internet www.bibnal.edu.ar; f. 1810; 2,000,000 vols, 46,177 MSS; Dir Dr FRANCISCO DELICH.

Biblioteca Nacional de Aeronáutica (National Aeronautics Library): CC 3389, 1000 Buenos Aires; located at: Paraguay 748, 1057 Buenos Aires; tel. (11) 4312-9038; e-mail binae@ciudad.com.ar; internet www.binae.org.ar; f. 1927; aeronautics, astronautics, aeronautical law; 50,000 vols; Dir Brig. MIGUEL ANGEL AGUILAR; Chief Librarian ANGÉLICA A. LLORCA; publs *Aeroespacio*, *Boletín Bibliográfico* (2 a year).

Biblioteca Nacional de Maestros (National Library for Teachers): Pizzurno 953, 1020 Buenos Aires; tel. (11) 4129-1272; fax (11) 4129-1299; e-mail bnminfo@me.gov.ar; internet www.bnm.me.gov.ar; f. 1870; 150,000 vols; general reference and education; Dir Lic. GRACIELA PERRONE.

Biblioteca Nacional Militar (National Military Library): Santa Fé 750, 1059 Buenos Aires; tel. (11) 4311-4560; f. 1938; 150,000 vols; Librarian MARTÍN SUÁREZ.

Biblioteca Tornquist (Tornquist Library): Ernesto Tornquist & Cía Ltda, Bartolomé Mitre 559, 1036 Buenos Aires; tel. (11) 433-4006; f. 1916; economics and social sciences; 55,000 vols; Dir JUAN JOSÉ GALLI.

Centro Argentino de Información Científica y Tecnológica (CAICYT) (Argentine Centre of Scientific and Technological Information): Saavedra 15 (1o), C1083ACA Buenos Aires; tel. (11) 4951-6975; fax (11) 4951-8334; e-mail postmaster@caicyt.edu.ar; internet www.caicyt-conicet.gov.ar; f. 1958; attached to Consejo Nacional de Investigaciones Científicas y Técnicas; Dir TITO SUTER.

Centro de Documentación e Información Internacional (International Centre of Documentation and Information): Dirección Nacional General de Cooperación Internacional, Ministerio de Cultura y Educación, Agüero 2502 (3o), 1425 Buenos Aires; f. 1959; publs by UN, Organization of American States, etc.; 5,000 vols; Dir FRANCISCO PIÑÓN.

Centro de Información de la Comisión Nacional de Energía Atómica (Information Centre of the National Atomic Energy Commission): Avda del Libertador 8250, 1429 Buenos Aires; tel. (11) 4701-9380; f. 1950; 36,700 vols, 450 current periodicals, 450,000 microcards and reports; Librarian ALEJANDRA NARDI; publs *Informes CNEA*, *Memoría CNEA*.

Centro de Información y Estadística Industrial (Centre for Industrial Information and Statistics): c/o INTI, Avda Leandro N. Alem 1067 (7o), 1101 Buenos Aires; attached to Instituto Nacional de Tecnología Industrial; Dir Ing. ALFREDO P. GALLIANO.

Dirección General de Bibliotecas Municipales (Public Libraries Administration): Calle Talcahuano 1261, 1014 Buenos Aires; tel. (11) 4811-9027; fax (11) 4811-0867; f. 1928; comprises 25 public municipal libraries in Buenos Aires with an aggregate of 350,000 vols; Dir-Gen. Prof. JOSEFINA DELGADO; publs *Cuadernos de Buenos Aires*, *Guía Cultural de Buenos Aires*.

Sistema de Bibliotecas y de Información, Universidad de Buenos Aires (Library and Information System of the University of Buenos Aires): Azcuénaga 280 (2o), 1029 Buenos Aires; tel. (11) 4951-1366 ext. 500; fax (11) 4952-6557; e-mail postmaster@sisbi.uba.ar; internet www.sisbi.uba.ar; f. 1941; 17 constituent faculty libraries; Gen. Co-ordinator ELSA ELENA ELIZALDE (acting).

Córdoba

Biblioteca de la Universidad Católica de Córdoba (Library of Córdoba Catholic University): Obispo Trejo 323, 5000 Córdoba; tel. (351) 493-8090; fax (351) 493-8091; e-mail bibdir@uccor.edu.ar; internet www.uccor.edu.ar; f. 1956; 51,000 vols, 700 periodicals; Dir Mag. SANDRA GISELA MARTÍN; publs *Diálogos Pedagógicos* (2 a year), *Studia Politicae* (2 a year).

Biblioteca Mayor de la Universidad Nacional de Córdoba (Main Library of Córdoba National University): Calle Obispo Trejo 242 (1° piso), CC 63, 5000 Córdoba; tel. (351) 433-1072; fax (351) 433-1079; e-mail rbestani@sri.trejo.unc.edu.ar; f. 1613; 150,000 vols, 3,890 periodicals and pre-1860 newspapers; partial depository for UN publs; Dir Lic. ROSA M. BESTANI.

La Plata

Biblioteca de la Universidad Nacional de La Plata (Library of La Plata National University): Plaza Rocha 137, 1900 La Plata; tel. (221) 425-5004; fax (221) 425-5004; f. 1884; 450,000 vols, 5,000 periodicals; spec. collns incl. South American newspapers relating to the Independence movement, South American history and geography and first travels in South America; 60 br. libraries within the univ.; Dir CARLOS JOSÉ TEJO; publ. *Informaciones*.

Biblioteca del Ministerio de Gobierno de la Provincia de Buenos Aires (Library of the Buenos Aires Province Ministry of the Interior): Casa de Gobierno, 1900 La Plata; law, politics and economics; 20,000 vols.

Biblioteca y Centro de Documentación del Ministerio de Economía de la Provincia de Buenos Aires (Library and Documentation Centre of the Ministry of the Economy of the Province of Buenos Aires): Calle 8 entre 45 y 46 (piso 1 Of. 25), 1900 La Plata; tel. (221) 429-4400 ext. 4702; 13,800 vols; Dir (vacant); publs *Noticias de Economía* (6 a year), *Cuadernos de Economía* (6 a year).

Mendoza

Biblioteca Central de la Universidad Nacional de Cuyo (Central Library of the National University of Cuyo): CC Mendoza, Parque Gral San Martín, 5500 Mendoza; tel. (261) 425-7463; e-mail biblio@raiz.uncu.ed.ar; f. 1939; 120,000 vols; Dir Lic. JUAN GUILLERMO MILIA; publs *Boletín Bibliográfico* (irregular), *Cuadernos de la Biblioteca* (irregular).

Biblioteca Pública General San Martín (General San Martín Public Library): Remedios Escalada de San Martín 1843, 5500 Mendoza; tel. (261) 423-1674; f. 1822; 120,000 vols; special collections: local authors, children's books; Dir ANA MARIA GARCIA BUTTINI; publs *BAL* (Biblioteca de Autor Local, annually), *BIL* (Biblioteca Infanto/Juvenil), *Versión II epocá* (annually).

Pergamino (Buenos Aires)

Biblioteca Pública Municipal 'Dr Joaquín Menéndez' (Dr Joaquín Menéndez Municipal Public Library): San Martín 838, 2700 Pergamino, Buenos Aires; f. 1901; 58,000 vols; Librarian ALICIA D. PARODI.

Resistencia

Centro de Información Bioagropecuaria y Forestal (CIBAGRO) (Bio-Farming and Forestry Information Centre): Dirección de Bibliotecas, Universidad Nacional del Nordeste, Avda Las Heras 727, 3500 Resistencia, Chaco; tel. (3722) 44-3742; fax (3722) 44-3742; e-mail jencinas@bib.unne.edu.ar; f. 1976; 2,500 books, 2,800 pamphlets, 1,000 periodicals; special collections: FAO and other int. agricultural orgs; Dir JULIO E. ENCINAS; publs *Ciencias Forestales – Bibliografía, Agronea, Bibliografía sobre El Quebracho, Bibliografía sobre El Picudo del Algodonero, Bibliografía Forestal Nacional*.

Forest Information Network for Latin America and the Caribbean (RIFALC): CIBAGRO, Dirección de Bibliotecas, Universidad Nacional del Nordeste, Avda Las Heras 727, 3500 Resistencia, Chaco; tel. and fax (3722) 44-3742; e-mail jencinas@bib.unne.edu.ar; f. 1985; co-ordinates and integrates at regional level the efforts made by individual networks, and makes accessible in each country all the information available; mems: 19 orgs in 12 countries; Exec. Sec JULIO E. ENCINAS; publ. *Boletín Informativo*.

Rosario

Biblioteca Argentina 'Dr Juan Alvarez' de la Municipalidad de Rosario (Dr Juan Alvarez Argentine Library of the Municipality of Rosario): Pte Roca 731, 2000 Rosario; tel. (341) 480-2538; fax (341) 480-2561; e-mail biblarg@rosario.gov.ar; f. 1912; 180,000 vols; Dir MARÍA DEL CARMEN D'ANGELO.

Biblioteca Pública 'Estanislao S. Zeballos' (Estanislao S. Zeballos Public Library): Bv. Oroño 1261, 2000 Rosario; tel. (341) 480-2793 ext. 128; fax (341) 480-2797 ext. 110; f. 1915; economics, accountancy, business studies, statistics; 111,000 vols; Dir BEATRIZ LODEZANO; publs *Revista de la Facultad de Ciencias Económicas y Estadística* (irregular), *Ciudad y Región* (3 a year).

San Miguel (Buenos Aires)

Biblioteca de las Facultades de Filosofía y Teología S.I. (Library of the Faculties of Philosophy and Theology): Avda Mitre 3226, 1663 San Miguel, Buenos Aires; tel. (11) 4455-7992; fax (11) 4455-6442; e-mail gerardo@bibusv.edu.ar; f. 1931; central deposit library; 153,000 vols, 700 current periodicals; Librarian Prof. GERARDO LOSADA; publ. *Stromata* (4 a year).

Tucumán

Biblioteca Central de la Universidad Nacional de Tucumán (Central Library of the National University of Tucuman): Lamadrid 817, CC 167, 4000 San Miguel de Tucumán; tel. (381) 424-7752; fax (381) 424-8025; e-mail bibcen@unt.edu.ar; f. 1917; 48,000 vols; Dir JUAN RICARDO ACOSTA; publ. *Boletín Bibliográfico*.

Museums and Art Galleries

Buenos Aires

Museo Argentino de Ciencias Naturales 'Bernardino Rivadavia'—Instituto Nacional de Investigación de las Ciencias Naturales (Bernardino Rivadavia Argentine Museum of Natural Sciences—National Research Institute of Natural Sciences): Avda Angel Gallardo 470, Suc. 5, 1405 Buenos Aires; tel. (11) 4982-0306; fax (11) 4982-5243; e-mail secretaria@macn.gov.ar; internet www.macn.gov.ar; f. 1823; zoology, botany, palaeontology, geology and ecology; library of 500,000 vols; Dir Dr EDGARDO ROMERO; publ. *Revista* (2 a year).

Museo de Armas de la Nación (National Arms Museum): Santa Fé 750, 1059 Buenos Aires; tel. (11) 4312-9774; f. 1904; library of 1,000 vols; Dir JULIO E. SOLDAINI.

Museo de Arte Español 'Enrique Larreta' (Enrique Larreta Museum of Spanish Art): Juramento 2291 y Obligado 2139, 1428 Buenos Aires; tel. (11) 4784-4040; fax (11) 4783-2640; e-mail museolarreta@infovia.com.ar; f. 1962; 13th- to 18th-century wood carvings, gilt objects and painted panels, paintings of Spanish School from 16th to 20th centuries, tapestries, furniture; library of 9,700 vols; Dir MERCEDES DI PAOLA DE PICOT.

Museo de Arte Hispanoamericano 'Isaac Fernández Blanco' (Isaac Fernández Blanco Museum of Spanish-American Art): Suipacha 1422, 1011 Buenos Aires; tel. (11) 4327-0183; f. 1947; 16th- to 19th-century Spanish- and Portuguese-American art, silver, furniture; library of 5,000 vols; Dir Arq. ALBERTO PETRINA.

Museo de Arte Moderno (Museum of Modern Art): Avda San Juan 350, 1147 Buenos Aires; tel. (11) 4361-1121; f. 1956; Latin American paintings, especially Argentine, and contemporary schools; Co-ordinator LAURA BUCCELLATO.

Museo de Bellas Artes de la Boca (Boca Fine Arts Museum): Pedro Mendoza 1835, 1169 Buenos Aires; tel. (11) 421-1080; painting, sculpture, engravings, and maritime museum; Dir Dr GUILLERMO C. DE LA CANAL.

Museo de la Dirección Nacional del Antártico (Museum of the National Antarctic Administration): Angel Gallardo 470, 1405 Buenos Aires; tel. (11) 4812-7327; natural and physical sciences of the Antarctic; Dir Dr RICARDO CAPDEVILA.

Museo de la Policía Federal Argentina (Argentine Federal Police Museum): San Martín 353 (pisos 7 y 8), 1004 Buenos Aires; tel. (11) 4394-2017; f. 1899; Dir JOSÉ A. GUTIÉRREZ.

Museo Etnográfico 'Juan B. Ambrosetti' (Juan B. Ambrosetti Ethnographical

Museum): Moreno 350, 1091 Buenos Aires; tel. (11) 4331-7788; fax (11) 4331-7788; e-mail etnogra@mail.retina.ar; f. 1904; attached to the Faculty of Philosophy and Letters of the Univ. of Buenos Aires; ethnography and archaeology of Argentina, the Americas, Africa, Asia and Oceania; library of 80,000 vols; Dir Dr JOSÉ ANTONIO PÉREZ GOLLÁN; publ. *Runa* (annual).

Museo Histórico de la Ciudad de Buenos Aires 'Brigadier-General Cornelio de Saavedra' (Brig.-Gen. Cornelio de Saavedra Historical Museum of the City of Buenos Aires): Calle Larralde 6309, 1431 Buenos Aires; tel. (11) 4572-0746; fax (11) 4574-1328; e-mail museosaavedra@uolsinectis.com.ar; internet www.museos.buenosaires.gov.ar; f. 1921; library of 3,600 vols; Dir ALBERTO GABRIEL PIÑEIRO.

Museo Histórico Nacional (National History Museum): Defensa 1600, 1143 Buenos Aires; tel. (11) 4307-1182; fax (11) 4307-3157; e-mail mnh_biblioteca@yahoo.com.ar; f. 1889; library of 15,000 vols, 20,000 artefacts; Dir Dr JUAN JOSÉ CRESTO; publ. *El Museo Histórico Nacional* (annual).

Museo Histórico Sarmiento (Sarmiento History Museum): Cuba 2079, 1428 Buenos Aires; tel. (11) 4783-7555; fax (11) 4788-5157; f. 1938; library of 13,000 vols; Dir BEATRIZ ARTAZA DE GLEZER.

Museo Mitre (Mitre Museum): San Martín 336, 1004 Buenos Aires; tel. (11) 4394-7659; f. 1907; preserves the household of Gen. Bartolomé Mitre; antique maps, coins and medals; library of 66,621 vols on American history, geography and ethnology, archive of 80,000 historical documents; Dir Dr JORGE CARLOS MITRE.

Museo Nacional de Aeronáutica (National Museum of Aeronautics): Obligado 4550, 1425 Buenos Aires; tel. (11) 4773-0665; f. 1960; Dir Cmdr SANTOS A. DOMINGUEZ KOCH (RETD).

Museo Nacional de Arte Decorativo (National Museum of Decorative Art): Avda del Libertador 1902, 1425 Buenos Aires; tel. (11) 4801-8248; fax (11) 4802-6606; e-mail museo@mnad.org; internet www.mnad.org; f. 1937; furniture, sculpture, tapestries, European and South American works; library of 2,000 vols; Dir ALBERTO GUILLERMO BELLUCCI.

Museo Nacional de Arte Oriental (National Museum of Oriental Art): Avda del Libertador 1902 (1o), 1425 Buenos Aires; tel. (11) 4801-5988; fax (11) 4801-5988; e-mail mnao@cultura.gov.ar; f. 1966; Asian and African art; library of 1,500 vols, 2,500 periodicals; Dir Lic. MARÍA DEL VALLE GUERRA.

Museo Nacional de Bellas Artes (National Museum of Fine Arts): Avda del Libertador 1473, 1425 Buenos Aires; tel. (11) 4803-0714; fax (11) 4803-4062; f. 1895; Argentine, American and European painting since 19th century, classical painting and sculpture, pre-Colombian art; library of 50,000 vols, 200,000 booklets; Dir Arq. ALBERTO G. BELLUCCI.

Museo Naval de la Nación (National Museum of Naval History): Paseo Victorica 602, Tigre, 1648 Buenos Aires; tel. (11) 4749-0608; e-mail museonaval@hotmail.com; f. 1892; library of 3,000 vols; Dir Capt. HORACIO MOLINA PICO (RETD).

Museo Numismático 'Dr José Evaristo Uriburu' (Dr José Evaristo Uriburu Numismatics Museum): Banco Central de la República Argentina, Calle San Martín 216, 1o, 1004 Buenos Aires; tel. (11) 4348-3882; fax (11) 4348-3699; e-mail museo@bcra.gob.ar; internet www.bcra.gov.ar; f. 1935; attached to Central Bank of Argentina; Dir DANIEL ANTONIO REY.

Museo Social Argentino (Argentine Museum of Sociology): Avda Corrientes 1723, 1042 Buenos Aires; tel. (11) 4375-4601; fax (11) 4375-4600; f. 1911; library of 80,000 vols; Pres. Dr GUILLERMO GARBARINI ISLAS; publs *Foro Economico* (2 a year), *Foro Político* (3 a year).

Córdoba

Museo Botánico (Botanical Museum): Universidad Nacional de Córdoba, CC 495, 5000 Córdoba; tel. (351) 4332104; fax (351) 4332104; e-mail museo@imbiv.unc.edu.ar; f. 1870; conducts research as a unit of Instituto Multidisciplinario de Biología Vegetal (run by CONICET and Universidad Nacional de Córdoba); library of 8,000 vols; Dir Dr. ANA M. ANTON; publs *Kurtziana* (annual), *Lorentzia* (irreg.).

Museo Provincial de Bellas Artes 'Emilio A. Caraffa' (Emilio A. Caraffa Provincial Museum of Fine Arts): Avda Hipólito Irigoyen 651, 5000 Córdoba; tel. (351) 469-0786; f. 1916; Argentine and foreign paintings, sculptures, drawings and engravings; library and archive; Dir Lic. GRACIELA ELIZABETH PALELLA.

Museo Provincial de Ciencias Naturales 'Bartolomé Mitre' (Bartolomé Mitre Provincial Museum of Natural Sciences): Avda Hipólito Irigoyen 115, 5000 Córdoba; tel. (351) 422-1428; f. 1919; geology, zoology, botany; library of 3,400 vols and periodicals; Dir MARTA CANO DE MARTIN.

Corrientes

Museo Histórico de Corrientes (Corrientes Historical Museum): Calle 9 de Julio 1044, 3400 Corrientes; internet www.museosargentinos.org.ar; f. 1929; history of Corrientes Province; library of 1,900 vols; Dir MIGUEL FERNANDO GONZÁLEZ AZCOAGA; publ. *Boletín de Extensión Cultural* (quarterly).

La Plata

Museo de La Plata (La Plata Museum): Paseo del Bosque s/n, 1900 La Plata; tel. (221) 43-9125; fax (221) 425-7527; f. 1884; anthropology, archaeology, geology, natural history (incl. palaeontological colln of Patagonian mammalia); library of 60,000 vols, 240,000 periodicals; Dir Dr EDGARDO O. ROLLERI; publs *Anales, Revista, Notas, Novedades, Obra del Centenario, Obra del Cincuentenario, Serie Técnica y Didáctica*.

Luján

Complejo Museografico 'Enrique Udaondo' (Enrique Udaondo Museographic Complex): Lezica y Torrezuri 917, 6700 Luján; tel. (2323) 42-0245; f. 1923; comprises 4 museums: Museo Colonial e Histórico (history, archaeology, silver, paintings, furniture), Museo de Transportes (transport), Museo del Automóvil and Pabellón 'Belgrano' y Depósitos (vintage cars); Dir CARLOS A. SCANNAPIECO.

Mendoza

Museo de Ciencias Naturales y Antropológicas 'Juan Cornelio Moyano' (Juan Cornelio Moyano Museum of Anthropology and Natural Sciences): Extremo Sur del Lago, Parque General San Martín, 5500 Mendoza; tel. and fax (261) 428-7666; f. 1911; library of 18,900 vols on American and Argentine history; Asst Dir Prof. CLARA ABAL DE RUSSO; publ. *Boletín* (2 a year).

Paraná

Museo de Ciencias Naturales y Antropológicas 'Prof. Antonio Serrano' (Prof. Antonio Serrano Museum of Anthropology and Natural Sciences): Carlos Gardel 62, E3100FWB Paraná; tel. (343) 420-8894; e-mail museoserrano@msn.com; f. 1917; library of 35,000 vols; Dir Prof. GISELA BAHLER; publs *Memorias, Catalogos*.

Museo Histórico 'Martiniano Leguizamón' (Martiniano Leguizamón Historical Museum): Laprida y Buenos Aires, 3100 Paraná; tel. (343) 41-2735; f. 1948; library of 27,000 vols; library and archive; Dir TERESA ROCHA.

Rosario

Museo Histórico Provincial de Rosario 'Dr Julio Marc' (Rosario Dr Julio Marc Provincial History Museum): Parque Independencia, 2000 Rosario; tel. (341) 472-1457; fax (341) 472-1457; e-mail museomarc@citynet.net.ar; internet www.santafe.gov.ar/cultura/museos/historo.htm; f. 1939; library of 33,000 vols; Dir Prof. IRMA B. MONTALVAN.

Museo Municipal de Arte Decorativo 'Firma y Odilo Estevez' (Firma y Odilo Estevez Municipal Decorative Arts Museum): Santa Fé 748, 2000 Rosario; tel. (341) 480-2547; fax (341) 480-2547; e-mail museo@museoestevez.gov.ar; internet www.museoestevez.gov.ar; f. 1968; Curator P. A. SINOPOLI.

Museo Municipal de Bellas Artes 'Juan B. Castagnino' (Juan B. Castagnino Municipal Fine Arts Museum): Avda Pellegrini 2202, 2000 Rosario; tel. (341) 421-7310; fax (341) 421-7310; f. 1937; library of 2,500 vols; Dir Prof. BERNARDO MIGUEL BALLESTEROS.

San Carlos de Bariloche

Museo de la Patagonia 'Dr Francisco P. Moreno' (Dr Francisco P. Moreno Museum of Patagonia): Centro Cívico, 8400 San Carlos de Bariloche, Río Negro; tel. (2944) 42-2309; fax (2944) 42-2309; e-mail museo@bariloche.com.ar; f. 1940; political history of Patagonia, ethnology, natural sciences, archaeology; library of 2,500 vols; Dir Lic. CECILIA GIRGENTI; publs *Antropología, Diversidad Cultural de la Argentina*.

Santa Fé

Museo de Bellas Artes 'Rosa Galisteo de Rodriguez' (Rosa Galisteo de Rodriguez Museum of Fine Arts): 4 de Enero 1510, 3000 Santa Fé; tel. (342) 459-6142; fax (342) 459-6142; f. 1922; contemporary Argentine and modern art; library of 4,200 vols; Dir Prof. NYDIA DE IMPINI.

Museo Histórico Provincial de Santa Fé (Santa Fé Provincial Museum of History): San Martín 1490, 3000 Santa Fé; tel. (342) 459-3760; f. 1943; Dir Prof. ALICIA TALSKY DE RONCHI.

Museo Provincial de Ciencias Naturales 'Florentino Ameghino' (Florentino Ameghino Provincial Museum of Natural History): 1o Junta 2859, 3000 Santa Fé; tel. (342) 457-3770; fax (342) 457-3730; e-mail ameghino@ceride.gov.ar; internet www.unl.edu.ar/santafe/museocn.htm; f. 1914; zoology, botany, geology, palaeobiology; library: public library of 50,000 vols; Dir Lic. CARLOS A. VIRASORO.

Santiago del Estero

Museo Provincial de Arqueología 'Wagner' (Wagner Provincial Archaeological Museum): Calle Avellaneda, 4200 Santiago del Estero; tel. (385) 41064; archaeology of Chaco-Santiagueno and later cultures; Dir OLIMPIA L. RIGHETTI.

Tandil

Museo Municipal de Bellas Artes de Tandil (Tandil Municipal Museum of Fine Arts): Chacabuco 357, 7000 Tandil; tel.

(2293) 43-2067; fax (2293) 43-0667; e-mail museotandil@hotmail.com; f. 1920; paintings of Classical, Impressionist, Cubist and Modern schools, Argentinian contemporary art (20th-century), small statues, furniture, engravings; small library; Dir CRISTIAN SEGURA.

Ushuaia

Museo del Fin del Mundo (The End of the World Museum): Maipú 175/179, 9410 Ushuaia, Tierra del Fuego; tel. (2901) 42-1863; fax (2901) 42-1201; e-mail museo@tierradelfuego.ml.org; f. 1979; history and natural sciences; library of 5,000 vols; Dir OSCAR PABLO ZANOLA; publs *Museo Territorial*, *Arqueología de la Isla Grande de Tierra del Fuego*, *Raíces del Fin del Mundo* (3 a year).

Universities

There are three main categories of Universities in Argentina: National (or Federal), which are supported by the Federal Budget; Provincial (or State), supported by the Provincial Budgets; and Private Universities, created and supported entirely by private initiative, but authorized to function by the Ministry of Education.

National Universities

UNIVERSIDAD DE BUENOS AIRES

Calle Viamonte 430/444, 1053 Buenos Aires
Telephone: (11) 4511-8120
Internet: www.uba.ar
Founded 1821
Academic year: March to November
Rector: GUILLERMO JAIM ETCHEVERRY
Vice-Rector: Dra SUSANA LAURA MIRANDE
Library Dir: Dra SUSANA SOTO
Number of teachers: 21,688
Number of students: 325,000
Library: see under Libraries
Publications: *Encrucijadas* (quarterly), *Oikos* (quarterly)

DEANS

Faculty of Agriculture (Avda San Martín 4453): Ing. Agr. FERNANDO VILELLA
Faculty of Architecture, Design and Town Planning (Ciudad Universitaria, Pabellón 3, Núñez): Arq. BERARDO DUJOVNE
Faculty of Dentistry (M. T. de Alvear 2142): Dr MÁXIMO GIGLIO
Faculty of Economic Sciences (Avda Córdoba 2122): Dr JUAN CARLOS CHERVATIN
Faculty of Engineering (Paseo Colón 850): Ing. CARLOS ALBERTO RAFFO
Faculty of Exact and Natural Sciences (Ciudad Universitaria, Pabellón 2, Núñez): Dr PABLO MIGUEL JACOVKIS
Faculty of Law and Social Sciences (Avda Pte Figueroa Alcorta 2263): Dr ANDRÉS JOSÉ D'ALESSIO
Faculty of Medicine (Paraguay 2155): Dr SALOMÓN SCHÄCHTER
Faculty of Pharmacy and Biochemistry (Junín 954): Dra REGINA WIGDOROVITZ DE WIKINSKI
Faculty of Philosophy and Letters (Puan 470): Dr FRANCISCO RAÚL CARNESE
Faculty of Psychology (Hipólito Irigoyen 3238/46): Lic. RAÚL COUREL
Faculty of Social Sciences (Marcelo T. de Alvear 2230): Dr FORTUNATO MACIMACCI
Faculty of Veterinary Sciences (Chorroarín 280): Med. Vet. ANÍBAL FRANCO

SELECTED AFFILIATED INSTITUTES

Colegio Nacional de Buenos Aires: Bolívar 263, 1066 Buenos Aires; tel. 331-6777; Rector Dr HORACIO SANGUINETTI.

Escuela Superior de Comercio 'Carlos Pellegrini': Marcelo T. de Alvear 1851, 1122 Buenos Aires; tel. (11) 4811-7547; f. 1890; incorporated in the Univ. of Buenos Aires 1912; 6-year course in commercial education; Rector Dr ABRAHAM LEONARDO GAK.

Hospital de Clínicas 'José de San Martín': Avda Córdoba 2351, Buenos Aires; tel. (11) 4508-3888; Dir Dr JORGE ITALA.

Instituto de Investigaciones Médicas: see under Research Institutes.

Instituto Modelo de Clínica Médica 'Luis Agote': Avda Córdoba 2351, 11o, Buenos Aires; tel. (1) 961-6001; Exec. Dir Dr FLORENTINO SANGUINETTI.

Instituto de Oncología 'Angel H. Roffo': Avda San Martín 5481, 1417 Buenos Aires; tel. (11) 4580-2800; f. 1966; library of 3,000 vols, 180 periodicals; Dir Dr ALEJO A. L. CARUGATTI.

Instituto de Perfeccionamiento Médico-Quirúrgico 'Prof. Dr José María Jorge': Avda Córdoba 2351, 7o, Buenos Aires; tel. (11) 4961-6001; Exec. Dir Dr FLORENTINO SANGUINETTI.

UNIVERSIDAD NACIONAL DE CATAMARCA

Esquiu 612, 4700 Catamarca
Telephone: (3833) 42-4099
Fax: (3833) 43-1200
E-mail: siuc@catam.unca.edu.ar
Internet: www.unca.edu.ar
Founded 1972
Academic year: February to December
Rector: Agrim. JULIO LUIS SALERNO
Vice-Rector: Lic. ROLANDO E. CORONEL
Sec.-Gen.: Ing. CARLOS RUBEN MICHAUD
Librarian: MARÍA EMILIA MARTÍNEZ
Number of teachers: 304
Number of students: 1,666
Publication: *Aportes*

DEANS

Faculty of Agricultural Sciences: Ing. Agr. EDMUNDO JOSÉ A. AGUERO
Faculty of Economics and Administration: CPN DANIEL EDUARDO TOLOZA
Faculty of Exact and Natural Sciences: Ing. Qco. BLANCA STELLA SOSA
Faculty of Health Sciences: Dr JORGE DANIEL BRIZUELA DEL MORAL
Faculty of Humanities: Lic. ROLANDO EDGARDO CORONEL
Faculty of Technology and Applied Sciences: Agrim. FÉLIX RAMÓN DOERING
School of Archaeology: Lic. MÓNICA CATOGGIO DE ACOSTA (Dir)
School of Law: Dra IRMA DEL TRÁNSITO ROMERO NIEVA (Dir)
Fray Mamerto Esquiu Higher School: Prof. HORTENCIA DURANTI DE ALVAREZ (Dir)

UNIVERSIDAD NACIONAL DEL CENTRO DE LA PROVINCIA DE BUENOS AIRES

General Pinto 399, 7000 Tandil
Telephone: (2293) 42-2062
Fax: (2293) 42-1608
E-mail: rector@rec.unicen.edu.ar
Internet: www.unicen.edu.ar
Founded 1974
State control
Academic year: February to December
Rector: Agrimensor CARLOS ALBERTO NICOLINI
Vice-Rector: Dr EDUARDO MIGUEZ
Gen. Sec.: Ing. GILLERMO AMILCAR CORRES
Academic Sec.y: Lic. SILVIA MARZORATTI
Admin. Sec.: Cr VICTOR MILANI
Library Dir: Prof. ZULEMA GRANDINETTI DE CAGLIOLO
Number of teachers: 1,585
Number of students: 7,000
Publications: *Alternativas*, *Anuario IEHS*

DEANS

Faculty of Agricultural Sciences: Med. Vet. ARNALDO PISSANI
Faculty of Economics: Cr ROBERTO TASSARA
Faculty of Engineering: Ing. EDUARDO F. IRASSAR
Faculty of Humanities: Lic. ALEJANDRO DILLON
Faculty of Sciences: Dr GERY BIOUL
Faculty of Social Sciences: Lic. CRISTINA BACCIN
Faculty of Theatre: Dr CARLOS CATALANO
Faculty of Veterinary Science: Dr PEDRO STEFFAN

ATTACHED INSTITUTES

Instituto de Física Arroyo Seco: Dir Dr HÉCTOR DI ROCCO.

Instituto de Física de Materiales: Dir Dr RICARDO ROMERO.

Instituto de Sistemas Tandil: Dir Ing. JEAN PIERRE DESCHAMPS.

UNIVERSIDAD NACIONAL DEL COMAHUE

Buenos Aires 1400, Q8300BCX Neuquén
Telephone: (299) 449-0300
Fax: (299) 449-0351
E-mail: sprector@uncoma.edu.ar
Internet: www.uncoma.edu.ar
Founded 1972
State control
Academic year: March to March
Rector: Dra ANA MARIA PECHEN DE D'ANGELO
Vice-Rector: Dr CARLOS CALDERON
Academic Sec.: Prof. MARINA BARBABELLA
Admin. Sec.: Lic. OSCAR LUSETTI
Librarian: EUGENIA LUQUE
Number of teachers: 1,700
Number of students: 30,000

DEANS

Faculty of Agricultural Sciences: Ing. Ftal. JORGE LUIS GIRARDIN
Faculty of Economics and Administration: Lic. SUSANA GRACIELA LANDRISCINI
Faculty of Education: Lic. GUILLERMO VILLANUEVA
Faculty of Engineering: Ing. DANIEL BOCCANERA
Faculty of Humanities: Lic. PEDRO BARREIRO
Higher School of Languages: Prof. MARÍA ELENA AGUILAR
Faculty of Law and Social Sciences: Dr JUAN MANUEL SALGADO
Faculty of Tourism: Dra ADRIANA OTERO
Bariloche Regional University Centre: Lic. FEDERICO HORACIO PLANAS
Zona Atlantica Regional University Centre: Ing. Agr. MIGUEL ANGEL SILVA

UNIVERSIDAD NACIONAL DE CÓRDOBA

Calle Raúl Haya de la Torre s/n (2o piso), Pabellón Argentina, Ciudad Universitaria, 5000 Córdoba
Telephone: (351) 433-4081
Fax: (351) 433-4081
Internet: www.uncor.edu

Founded 1613; charter received from Philip III of Spain 1622; fully established by Pope Urban VIII 1634; nationalized 1856
Academic year: February to December

Rector: Ing. JORGE GONZÁLEZ
Vice-Rector: Ing. DANIEL DI GIUSTO
Sec.-Gen.: Ing. GABRIEL TAVELLA
Librarian: Lic. ROSA M. BESTANI

Library: see Libraries and Archives
Number of teachers: 7,753
Number of students: 114,918

Publication: *Revista*

DEANS

Faculty of Agrarian Sciences: Ing. Agr. HECTOR FONTÁN
Faculty of Architecture and Town Planning: Arq. MIGUEL ANGEL ROCA
Faculty of Chemical Sciences: Dr GERARDO FIDELIO
Faculty of Dentistry: Dr NAZARIO KUYUMLLIAM
Faculty of Economics: Dr HEBE G. DE ROITTER
Faculty of Exact, Physical and Natural Sciences: Ing. ERNESTO ALVAREZ
Faculty of Languages: Dra CRISTINA ELQUE DE MARTINI
Faculty of Law and Social Sciences: Dra RAMÓN PEDRO YANZI FERREYRA
Faculty of Mathematics, Astronomy and Physics: Dr CRISTIAN URBANO SÁNCHEZ
Faculty of Medicine: Dr PEDRO LEÓN SARACHO CORNET
Faculty of Philosophy and Humanities: Dra SILVIA CAROLINA SCOTTO
Faculty of Psychology: Lic. ANA ALDERETE

DIRECTORS

'Manuel Belgrano' Higher School of Commerce: JOSÉ MARIA ALDAY
Monserrat National College: FRANCISCO BOBONE

UNIVERSIDAD NACIONAL DE CUYO

Centro Universitario, Parque General San Martín, 5500 Mendoza
Telephone: (261) 420-5115
Fax: (261) 423-3296
Internet: www.uncu.edu.ar

Founded 1939
State control
Academic year: April to October

Rector: Ing. ARMANDO BERTRANOU
Vice-Rector: Lic. JOSÉ FRANCISCO MARTIN
Admin. Dir: Cont. GERARDO ONTIVERO
Librarian: Lic. JUAN GUILLERMO MILIA

Library: see Libraries and Archives
Number of teachers: 4,794
Number of students: 22,000

Publication: *Boletín Oficial*

DEANS

Faculty of Agricultural Sciences: Ing. JORGE TACCHINI
Faculty of Applied Science: Ing. ERNESTO MUÑOZ
Faculty of Arts: Prof. ELIO ORTIZ
Faculty of Dentistry: Dr ONOFRE CIPOLLA
Faculty of Economics: Cont. RODOLFO SÍCOLI
Faculty of Engineering: Ing. JUAN MANUEL GOMEZ
Faculty of Law: Dr LUIS ABBIATI
Faculty of Medical Sciences: Dr ISAAC RIVERO
Faculty of Philosophy and Letters: Prof. MIGUEL VERSTRAETE
Faculty of Political and Social Sciences: Lic. CARLOS FINOCHIO
Teacher Training College: MARÍA VICTORIA GOMEZ DE ERICE
Zona Sur: Dis. Ind. ADRIANA RUIZ

ATTACHED INSTITUTE

Centro Regional de Investigaciones Científicas y Tecnológicas (CRICYT): Calle Bajada del Cerro s/n, Parque General San Martín, Casilla de Correo 131, 5500 Mendoza; tel. (261) 428-8314; fax (261) 428-7370; Dir Dr RICARDO PAULINO DEI.

UNIVERSIDAD NACIONAL DE ENTRE RÍOS

Eva Perón 24/32, 3260 Concepción del Uruguay, Entre Ríos
Telephone: (3442) 42-2108
Fax: (3442) 42-5573
Internet: www.uner.edu.ar

Founded 1973
State control
Academic year: April to March

Rector: Cont. CÉSAR GOTTFRIED
Vice-Rector: Psic. JUAN CARLOS ROQUEL
Dir-Gen. of Admin.: Cont. PEDRO SANDOVAL
Academic Sec.: Prof. MARÍA ANGÉLICA G. F. DE MARCO
Library Dir: Prof. JORGE TITO MARTÍNEZ

Number of teachers: 1,219
Number of students: 8,000

Publications: *Ciencia*, *Docencia y Tecnología* (3 a year), *Guía de Carreras*.

CONSTITUENT INSTITUTIONS

Facultad de Bromatología (Bromatology): 25 de Mayo 709, POB 243, 2820 Gualeguaychú; Dean Lic. SUSANA NOVELLO DE METTLER.

Facultad de Ciencias de la Administración (Administration): Alvear 1424, 3200 Concordia; Dean Cont. EDUARDO ASUETA.

Facultad de Ciencias Agropecuarias (Agrarian Sciences): Ruta Provincial 11, Km 13, 3114 Oro Verde; Dean Ing. FRANCISCO RAMÓN ETCHEVERS.

Facultad de Ciencias de la Alimentación (Nutritional Sciences): Monseñor Tavella 1450, 3200 Concordia; Dean Ing. JORGE AMADO GERARD.

Facultad de Ciencias Económicas (Economics): Urquiza 52, 3100 Paraná; Dean Cont. JULIO CÉSAR YODICE.

Facultad de Ciencias de Educación (Education): Rivadavia 106, 3100 Paraná; Dean Prof. MARTHA BENEDETTO DE ALBORNOZ.

Facultad de Ciencas de la Salud (Health Sciences): 8 de Junio 600, 3260 Concepción del Uruguay; Dean Dr JULIO SIMOVICH.

Facultad de Ingeniería (Engineering): Ruta Provincial 11, Km 13, 3114 Oro Verde; Dean Ing. AGUSTÍN CARPIO.

Facultad de Servicio Social (Social Services): La Rioja 6, Subsuelo, 3100 Paraná; Dean A. S. ALICIA MERCEDES GONZÁLEZ ALARCÓN.

UNIVERSIDAD NACIONAL DE FORMOSA

Don Bosco 1082, 3600 Formosa
Telephone: (3717) 423-926
Fax: (3717) 423-928
E-mail: adminweb@unf.edu.ar
Internet: www.unf.edu.ar

Founded 1988
State control

Rector (vacant)
Vice-Rector: Ing. MARTÍN RENÉ ROMANO
Secretary-General (Academic): Ing. JULIO RENÉ ARÁOZ
Secretary-General (Management and Development): Cont. JOSÉ ASSAF GAIT
Secretary-General (Science and Technology): Dr CARLOS ENRIQUE PELOZO
Secretary-General (Student Affairs and University Extension): Dr RAFAEL PORTOCARRERO CURAY

Library of 12,000 vols

DEANS

Faculty of Economics and Business Administration: Lic. HECTOR CARMELO QUIJANO
Faculty of Health: Dr JOSÉ TRINIDAD ESCOBAR
Faculty of Humanities: Prof. MARÍA DE LA CRUZ COLOMBERA DE CASTAÑEDA
Faculty of Natural Resources: (vacant)

HEADS OF DEPARTMENTS

Faculty of Economics and Business Administration (Campus Universitario, Avda Gobernador Gutnisky 3200, 3600 Formosa; tel. (3717) 451-792; e-mail faen@unf.edu.ar):
- Accounting: Cdor JUAN RAMÓN BOGADO
- Foreign Trade: Lic. EDUARDO FERNÁNDEZ REY

Faculty of Health (Campus Universitario, Avda Gobernador Gutnisky 3200, 3600 Formosa; tel. (3717) 451-836; e-mail adminsalud@unf.edu.ar):
- Bromatology: Ing. LUIS ROMPATTO
- Clinical Analysis: Dra SUSANA SOMOZA
- Nursing: Lic. NOEMÍ JUÁREZ
- Nutrition: Lic. YOLANDA GIGLI

Faculty of Humanities (Campus Universitario, Avda Gobernador Gutnisky 3200, 3600 Formosa; tel. (3717) 452-473; e-mail fhumanidades@unf.edu.ar):
- Biology: Prof. ABEL VERA
- Geography: Prof. EDUARDO VARELA
- History: Prof. ALVIS GÓMEZ
- Letters: Prof. MIRTHA RUBIANO
- Mathematics: Prof. MARIA ELENA GONZÁLEZ DE CERUTTI
- Psychology: Lic. RAMONA FERNÁNDEZ DE POSSE
- Special Education: MARIA OLGA MAYOR DE BRUNELLI

Faculty of Natural Resources (Campus Universitario, Avda Gobernador Gutnisky 3200, 3600 Formosa; tel. (3717) 452-241; e-mail frecursosnat@unf.edu.ar):
- Agribusiness: Ing. GRISELDA RODAS
- Civil Engineering: Ing. OSCAR LEMOS
- Forestry Engineering: Ing. ILDA C. VILLALBA
- Zootechnical Engineering: Ing. JUAN MARCELO DOMINGUEZ

UNIVERSIDAD NACIONAL DE GENERAL SAN MARTÍN

Avda 25 de Mayo e Irigoyen, San Martín, Buenos Aires
Telephone: (11) 4512-5151
Internet: www.unsam.edu.ar

Founded 1992
State control

Rector: DANIEL MALCOLM
Vice-Rector: AGUSTÍN PIERONI
Secretary-General: HUGO NIELSON
Secretary (Academic): NORBERTO FERRÉ
Secretary (Administration): HUGO NIELSON (acting)
Secretary (Science and Technology): CARLOS GIANELLA
Secretary (Student Affairs and University Extension): AMANDA BALLESTER DE RULAND

Library of 4,700 vols, 350 periodicals

Publications: *Educación en Ciencias*, *Educación en Ciencias Sociales, Política y Gestión*, *Revista de la Escuela de Economía y Negocios*

DIRECTORS

School of Economics and Business: HORACIO VAL

School of Government and Politics: MARCELO CAVAROZZI
School of Humanities: CARLOS RAFAEL RUTA
School of Science and Technology: DANIEL DI GREGORIO
School of Postgraduate Studies: ALBERTO POCHETTINO
Institute of Biotechnical Research: ALBERTO FRASCH
Institute of Higher Social Studies: JOSÉ NUN
Institute of Industrial Quality: JOAQUÍN VALDÉS
Institute of Rehabilitation Sciences and Movement: HUGO RODRÍGUEZ ISARN
Prof. Jorge A. Sabato Institute of Technology: JOSÉ RODOLFO GALVELE

HEADS OF DEPARTMENTS

School of Humanities (e-mail humanidades@unsam.edu.ar):
Arts: JOSÉ VILLELLA, BEATRIZ MASTRÁNGELO
Education: NORBERTO FERRÉ, ALICIA RAPACIOLI
Primary Education: JORGE STEIMAN
Teaching of Science: HUGO TRICÁRICO, ALFREDO GARCÍA ECHAM
Teaching of Social Sciences: PATRICIA MOGLIA, GABRIEL ÁLVAREZ
Philosophy: EDGARDO ALBIZU, CRISTINA LÓPEZ
Humanities: DANIELA VERÓN, CRISTINA MANTEGARI
Language and Literature: GUSTAVO BOMBINI
Psychology: HAYDÉE ECHEVERRÍA, PATRICIA VILA
Latin American Poetry: JUAN GELMAN, JORGE BOCCANERA

School of Science and Technology (Calle 78 3901, 1653 Villa Ballester, Buenos Aires; fax (11) 4512-5151; e-mail escuelacyt@unsam.edu.ar):
Biology: Dra DEBORAH TASAT
Chemistry: Dr HUGO BIANCHI
Electronics: Ing. JOREG SINDERMAN
Informatics: Lic. ROBERTO BEVILACQUA
Mathematics: Dra ROSA PIOTRKOWSKI
Physics: Dr ANDRÉS KREINER

ATTACHED RESEARCH INSTITUTES

Centro de Apoyo y Desarrollo a Empresas: Co-ordinator MARIELA BALBO.

Centro de Aprendizaje.

Centro de Capacitación Pymes: Dir DANIEL PÉREZ ENRRI.

Centro de Economia de la Educacion y Capital Humano: Co-ordinator HORACIO VAL.

Centro de Economía de la Innovación y del Desarrollo: Co-ordinator DANIEL RUBY HERNÁNDEZ.

Centro de Estudios Desarrollo y Territorio: tel. (11) 4374-7300; e-mail cedet@unsam.edu.ar; internet www.cedet.edu.ar; Dir OSCAR MADOERY.

Centro de Estudios en Didácticas Específicas.

Centro de Estudios de Historia de la Ciencia y la Técnica 'José Babini'.

Centro de Estudios Latinoamericanos.

Centro de Estudios para la Sustentabilidad: e-mail ceps@unsam.edu.ar.

Centro de Investigaciones Jorge Furt.

Centro de Investigación y Medición Económica: Dir VÍCTOR PÉREZ BARCIA.

Centro de Investigación y Producción de Juguetes.

Centro de Investigación y Producción en Teatro de Objetos.

Centro de Producción Audiovisual.

Observatorio Permanente de las Pyme del Conurbano Bonaerense–Observatorio Regional Norte: Co-ordinator MARIO BRUZZESI.

UNIVERSIDAD NACIONAL DE GENERAL SARMIENTO

Campus Universitario, José M. Gutiérrez entre José L. Suárez y Verdi, 1613 Los Polvorines, Buenos AiresTelephone: (11) 4469-7500
Fax: (11) 4451-4575
E-mail: info@ungs.edu.ar
Internet: www.ungs.edu.ar

Founded 1993
State control
Academic year: October to April

Rector: Lic. SILVIO ISRAEL FELDMAN
Vice-Rector: Ing. MARCELO OSCAR FERNÁNDEZ
Secretary-General: Lic. ALEJANDRO LUIS LOPEZ ACCOTTO
Secretary (Academic): Prof. ELSA BEATRIZ PEREYRA
Secretary (Administration): DANIELA LETICIA GUARDADO
Secretary (Legal and Technical): Lic. HAYDÉE NÉLIDA UGRIN
Secretary (Research): Lic. CARLOS EDUARDO REBORATTI

Library of 18,000 vols, 121 periodicals
Number of students: 5,547

DIRECTORS

Institute of Human Development: Dr EDUARDO RINESI
Institute of Industry: Ing. NÉSTOR BRUNO BRAIDOT
Institute of Science: Lic. ROSA ELENA BELVEDRESI
Institute of Urban Studies: Lic. MAGDALENA GRACIELA CHIARA

UNIVERSIDAD NACIONAL DE JUJUY

Avda Bolivia 1239, 4600 San Salvador de Jujuy
Telephone: (388) 422-1515
Fax: (388) 422-1507
E-mail: info@unju.edu.ar
Internet: www.unju.edu.ar

Founded 1972
State control
Academic year: March to December

Rector: Ing. Qco OSCAR GUILLERMO INSAUSTI
Vice-Rector: CPN OSCAR ALBERTO FERNANDEZ
Secretary for Academic Affairs: Lic. JOSÉ ANDRÉS ALCALDE
Secretary for Administrative Affairs: CPN PATRICIA CUELLAR DE COMAS
Secretary for Science and Technology: Dr FERMÍN DE VEGA
Secretary for Student Welfare: JULIO TENTOR
Secretary for University Extension: Ing. EDUARDO BERRAFATO
Librarian: MARÍA E. C. DE MARTÍNEZ

Library of 18,000 vols
Number of teachers: 700
Number of students: 6,000

DEANS

Faculty of Agriculture: Dra SUSANA MURUAGA DE L'AGENTIER
Faculty of Economics: CPN LUIS SALVADOR FORTUNI
Faculty of Engineering: Ing. ENRIQUE MATEO ARNAU
Faculty of Humanities and Social Sciences: Lic. MARIO RABEY
School of Mining: Ing. Qco ALBERTO CONSTANTINO ALBESA

ATTACHED RESEARCH INSTITUTES

Institute of Geology and Mining: Avda Bolivia 2355, 4600 San Salvador de Jujuy; tel. (388) 422-1593; fax (388) 422-1594; Dir Dra BEATRIZ COIRA.

Institute of Marine Biology: Avda Bolivia No. 2345/55, 4600 San Salvador de Jujuy; tel. (388) 422-1596; fax (388) 422-1597; Dir Lic. MARTHA G. ARCE DE HAMITY.

UNIVERSIDAD NACIONAL DE LA MATANZA

Florencio Varela, 1903 San Justo, Buenos Aires
Telephone: (11) 4480-8900
Fax: (11) 4480-8919
E-mail: info@unlm.edu.ar
Internet: www.unlm.edu.ar

Founded 1990
State control
Academic year: March to December (two semesters)

Rector: Prof. Lic. DANIEL EDUARDO MARTÍNEZ
Vice-Rector: Dr JUAN CARLOS BUSNELLI
Secretary-General: Dr GUSTAVO ALBERTO CASTRO
Secretary (Academic): Dr FERNANDO LUJÁN ACOSTA
Secretary (Administration):
Secretary (Legal and Technical): Dr CRISTIAN JAVIER CABRAL
Secretary (Information Technology and Communications): Ing. JORGE E. ETEROVIC
Secretary (Management and Planning): Dr GUSTAVO ALBERTO CASTRO
Secretary (Postgraduate Affairs): Dr MARIO ENRIQUE BURKÚN
Secretary (Science and Technology): Lic. RICARDO O. CASTRO
Secretary (University Public Relations): Lic. ROBERTO LUIS AYUB

DEANS

Economics: Prof. Dr JUAN CARLOS BUSNELLI
Engineering and Technological Research: Prof. Ing. MARCELO ESTAYNO
Humanities and Social Sciences: Prof. Dr ENRIQUE VALIENTE
Law and Political Science: Dr ALEJANDRO FINOCCHIARO

HEADS OF DEPARTMENTS

Economics (tel. (11) 4480-8900):
Accounting: Dr ALBERTO LONGO
Administration: Lic. DANIEL ROMERO
International Trade: Lic. MARCELO FRANCO

Engineering and Technological Research (tel. (11) 4480-8900):
Computer Engineering: Ing. OSVALDO SPOSITTO
Electronic Engineering: Ing. ISABEL WEINBERG
Industrial Engineering: Ing. ALDO SACERDOTI

Humanities and Social Sciences (tel. (11) 4651-3749):
Labour Relations: Lic. ENRIQUE DEIBE
Physical Education: Prof. WALTER NESTOR TOSCANO
Social Communication: Lic. OSCAR MARGAROLA
Social Work: Lic. GRACIELA TONON

Law and Political Science (tel. (11) 4480-8900; e-mail derecho@unlm.edu.ar):
Law: (vacant)

UNIVERSIDAD NACIONAL DE LA PAMPA

9 de Julio 149, 6300 Santa Rosa, La Pampa
Telephone: (2954) 43109
Internet: www.unlpam.edu.ar

Founded 1958
Academic year: April to November
Rector: Dr Marcelo Iván Aguilar
General Secretary: Juan José Costa
Academic Secretary: Lic. Luis María Morete
Librarian: Lic. Atilio Denouard
Number of teachers: 632
Number of students: 2,000

DEANS
Faculty of Agronomy: Ing. Agr. Guillermo Covas
Faculty of Economics: CPN Roberto Oscar Vassia
Faculty of Exact and Natural Sciences: Profa. Nora D. Andrada de Guesalaga
Faculty of Human Sciences: Prof. José Rufino Villarreal
Faculty of Veterinary Science: Dr Raúl Antonio Alvarez

UNIVERSIDAD NACIONAL DE LA PATAGONIA AUSTRAL

Lisandro de la Torre 860, 8400 Río Gallegos, Santa Cruz
Telephone: (2966) 442-376
Fax: (2966) 442-376
E-mail: rector@unpa.edu.ar
Internet: www.unpa.edu.ar
Founded 1994
State control
Rector: Ing. Héctor Aníbal Billoni
Vice-Rector: Eugenia María Márquez
Secretary-General (Academic): Ing. Hugo Santos Rojas
Secretary (Administration and Finance): Lic. Marcelo Miljak
Secretary (Planning): Lic. Roberto Palma
Secretary (Science and Technology): Ing. Rafael Oliva
Secretary (University Public Relations): Lic. María Victoria Hernández

CAMPUS DEANS
Caleta Olivia: Ing. Daniel Lorenzetti
Río Gallegos: Dr Alejandro Súnico
Río Turbio: Prof. Virginia Barbieri
San Julian: Arq. Juan Carlos Díaz

UNIVERSIDAD NACIONAL DE LA PATAGONIA SAN JUAN BOSCO

CC 786, Correo Central, 9000 Comodoro Rivadavia, Chubut
Telephone: (297) 43-3446
Fax: (297) 43-4442
Internet: www.unp.edu.ar
Founded 1980 by merger of Universidad de la Patagonia San Juan Bosco and Universidad Nacional de la Patagonia
Academic year: February to December
Rector: Lic. Arturo Canero
Vice-Rector: Ing. Aldo Lopez Guidi
Academic Secretary: Lic. Eduardo Bibiloni
Librarian: Mario D'Orta
Number of teachers: 850
Number of students: 7,000
Library of 40,000 vols
Publication: *Naturalia Patagónica* (4 a year)

DEANS
Faculty of Economics: Cr Jorge Stacco
Faculty of Engineering: Ing. Roberto Aguirre
Faculty of Humanities and Social Sciences: Lic. Dolores del Castaño
Faculty of Natural Sciences: Lic. Omar Cesaris

HEADS OF DEPARTMENTS
Faculty of Engineering:
Civil Engineering: Ing. Jorge Huberman
Civil and Hydraulic Engineering: Ing. Juan José Ramón Serra
Forestry Engineering: Ing. Pedro Esteban Guerra
Industry: Ing. Enrique Rost
Mathematics: Profa María Gabina Romero
Physics: Ing. Manuel Schaigorodsky
Stability and Materials: Ing. Júlio César Mora
Surveying: Agr. Carlos Mistó
Systems: C. C. Patricia Uviña
Faculty of Humanities and Social Sciences:
Education: Profa Elizabeth Guglielmino
Geography: Profa Ana Burcheri
History: Profa Cristina Barile
Literature: Prof. José M. Gutiérrez
Social Communication: Lic. Luis Sandoval
Social Work: Prof. Celia Vicari
Faculty of Natural Sciences:
Biochemistry: Bioq. Laerte Massari
Chemistry: Dra Vilma Balzaretti
Geology: Geo. Raúl Gia
Human Biology: Ing. Mónica Stronati
Nursing: Enf. Lidia Blanco
Pharmacy: Phar. Rita Curdelas
Faculty of Economics:
Accounting: Cra Rudel de Walter
Administration: Cra Patricia Kent
Economics: Lic. Ester Badenas
Human Sciences: Lic. Virgilio Zampini
Law: Dra R. Rosalía de Alcaro
Mathematics: Prof. Estela Tolosa

REGIONAL FACULTIES
Esquel: Alvear 1021, 3 piso, 9200 Esquel; tel. (2945) 43729; Dir Lic. Roberto Viera; forestry and economics.

Puerto Madryn: Bv. Almirante Brown 3700, CC 164, 9120 Puerto Madryn; tel. (2965) 45-1024; Dir Dr Miguel A. Haller; marine biology, computer science.

Trelew: Faculty of Economics and Faculty of Humanities and Social Sciences, Fontana 488, 9100 Trelew; tel. (2965) 43-1532; fax (2965) 43-1276Faculty of Engineering and Faculty of Natural Sciences, Belgrano 507, 9100 Trelew; tel. (2965) 43-3305; Dir Juan Pérez Amat.

Ushuaia: CADIC, 9410 Ushuaia; tel. (2901) 43-0892; Dir Dr Oscar Lobo; tourism, computer science.

UNIVERSIDAD NACIONAL DE LA PLATA

Avda 7 No. 776, 1900 La Plata
Telephone: (221) 421-5501
Fax: (221) 43-0563
Internet: www.unlp.edu.ar
Founded 1905
Academic year: March to December
President: Dr Angel L. Plastino
Vice-President: Prof. Lic. Angel Tello
Secretary-General: Ing. Marcelo Rastelli
Librarian: Dr Carlos Tejo
Library: see Libraries and Archives
Number of teachers: 6,300
Number of students: 50,000
Publication: *Revista de la Universidad*

DEANS
Faculty of Agriculture: Ing. Guillermo Miguel Hang
Faculty of Architecture and Town Planning: Arq. Jorge Alberto Lombardi
Faculty of Astronomy and Geophysics: Prof. César Augusto Mondinalli
Faculty of Dentistry: Alfredo V. Ricciardi
Faculty of Economic Sciences: (vacant)
Faculty of Engineering: Ing. Luis Julián Lima
Faculty of Exact Sciences: Dr Enrique Pereyra
Faculty of Fine Arts: Prof. Roberto Oscar Rollié
Faculty of Humanities and Education: Dr José Panettieri
Faculty of Juridical and Social Sciences: Ricardo Pablo Reca
Faculty of Medical Sciences: Dr Jaime Trajtenberg
Faculty of Natural Sciences: Dr Isidoro A. Schalamuck
Faculty of Veterinary Sciences: Dr Alberto Dibbern

SELECTED AFFILIATED SCHOOLS AND INSTITUTES
Colegio Nacional 'Rafael Hernández' (National College): Avda 1 y 49, La Plata; Dir Prof. Graciela Teresa Ibarra.

Escuela Graduada 'Joaquín V. González' (Graduate School 'Joaquín V. González'): Calle 50 y 119, La Plata; Dir Prof. Martha S. Betti de Milichio.

Escuela Práctica de Agricultura y Ganadería 'María Cruz y Manuel L. Inchausti' (School of Agriculture and Stockbreeding): Estación Valdés, 6660 Veinticinco de Mayo, Pca de Buenos Aires; Dir Dr Ricardo Luis Cabassi.

Escuela Superior de Periodismo y Comunicación Social (School of Journalism): Avda 44 No 676, La Plata; Dir Lic. Jorge Luis Bernetti.

Instituto de Física de Líquidos y Sistemas Biológicos: Calle 59 No 789, 1900 La Plata; tel. (221) 44-7545f. 1981; theoretical and applied research; 9 researchers; library of 582 vols, in process of formation; Dir Dr Antonio E. Rodríguez.

UNIVERSIDAD NACIONAL DE LA RIOJA

Avda Laprida y V. Bustos, 5300 La Rioja
Telephone: (3822) 45-7000
Fax: (3822) 45-7061
E-mail: postmast@unlar.edu.ar
Internet: www.unlar.edu.ar
Founded 1972
State control
Academic year: February to December
Rector: Dr Enrique Tello Roldán
Vice-Rector: Ing. Manuel Jesús Mamaní
Administrative Secretary: Santiago Romero
Librarian (vacant)
Library of 23,000 vols
Number of teachers: 1,154
Number of students: 15,630
Publication: *Research Projects* (6 a year)
Faculties of economics, humanities and arts, social sciences, engineering.

UNIVERSIDAD NACIONAL DE LANÚS

29 de Septiembre 3901, 1826 Lanús, Buenos Aires
Telephone: (11) 6322-9200
Fax: (11) 6322-9200
E-mail: info@unla.edu.ar
Internet: www.unla.edu.ar
Founded 1995
State control
Academic year: March to December (two semesters)
Rector: Ana María Jaramillo
Vice-Rector and Secretary (Academic): Dr Juan Carlos Geneyro
Secretary-General: Cdor. Jorge Cartocio
Secretary (Administration): Cdor. Guillermo Grosskopf
Secretary (Public Service and Co-operation): Lic. Georgina Hernández

Secretary (Research, Science and Technology): Ing. NORBERTO CAMINOA
Librarian: Lic. ELVIRA LOFIEGO

DIRECTORS

Arts and Humanities: Prof. HECTOR MUZZOPAPPA
Community Health: Dr DANIEL RODRÍGUEZ
Planning and Public Policy: Dr ALEJANDRO KAWABATA
Production and Labour Development: Dr JORGE MOLINA

ATTACHED RESEARCH INSTITUTES

Centre for Ethical Research: Dir Dr RICARDO MALIANDI.
Centre for Historical Research: Dir Dr HUGO BIAGINI.
Centre for Human Rights: Dir Dr LEONARDO FRANCO.
Centre for Scientific Theory and Practice: Dir Dra ESTHER DÍAZ.
Centre for the Study of Politics, Employment and Society: Dir Dr ALFREDO ERIC CALCAGNO.
Centre for Urban Planning and Management: Dir Arq. JORGE MOSCATO.
International Information and Study Centre of Resilience: Dir Dr NÉSTOR SUÁREZ OJEDA.

UNIVERSIDAD NACIONAL DEL LITORAL

Blvd Pellegrini 2750, S3000ADQ Santa Fé
Telephone: (342) 457-1110
Fax: (342) 457-1248
E-mail: dcopint@unl.edu.ar
Internet: www.unl.edu.ar
Founded 1919
State control
Academic year: March to December
Rector: Ing. MARIO D. BARLETTA
Vice-Rector: Dr MARIO T. CADIOTI
General Secretary: Ing. EDUARDO MATOZO
Administrative Secretary: Esc. RODOLFO M. R. ACANFORA GRECO
Secretary for International Co-operation: Ing. JULIO C. THEILER
Librarian: MARISA PULIOTTI DE FERRARI
Number of teachers: 2,171
Number of students: 23,740
Publications: *Science and Technology*, *Society and Culture*

DEANS

Faculty of Agrarian Sciences: Ing. Agr. HUGO ARMANDO ERBETTA
Faculty of Architecture, Design and Town Planning: Arq. JULIO ALEJANDRO TALÍN
Faculty of Biochemistry and Biological Sciences: Bioq. EDUARDO RAMÓN VILLARREAL
Faculty of Chemical Engineering: Ing. PEDRO MÁXIMO MANCINI
Faculty of Economics: Cont. FRANCISCA SÁNCHEZ DE DUSSO
Faculty of Education: Prof. LEONOR JUANA CHENA
Faculty of Law and Social Sciences: Dr MARIANO T. CANDIOTI
Faculty of Teacher Training: Prof. LEONOR J. CHENA
Faculty of Veterinary Sciences: Med. Vet. EDUARDO BARONI
Faculty of Water Resources Engineering and Sciences: Ing. CRISTÓBAL VICENTE LOZECO

DIRECTORS

Higher Institute of Music: Prof. MARIANO CABRAL MIGNO
Higher School of Health Services: Dr CARLOS PRONO
Higher School of Industry: Ing. JORGE OSVALDO BASILICO
Institute of Food Technology: Ing. HUGO SÁNCHEZ
Institute of Technological Development for the Chemical Industry (INTEC): Dr ALBERTO ENRIQUE CASSANO
School of Agriculture, Stockbreeding and Farming: Ing. Agr. OSVALDO MARIO HERMANN
University School of Food Analysis: Ing. ALEJANDRO BERNABEU
University School of Food Science: Bioq. LUIS MARÍA NICKISH

UNIVERSIDAD NACIONAL DE LOMAS DE ZAMORA

Ruta Provincial No. 4 Km. 2, Llavaloll, Buenos Aires
Telephone: (11) 4282-8046
Fax: (11) 4282-8046
E-mail: secpriv@unlz.edu.ar
Internet: www.unlz.edu.ar
Founded 1972
State control
Chancellor: GUIDO DI TELLA
Rector: HORACIO GEGUNDE
Vice-Rector: PABLO MARTÍNEZ SAMECK
Secretary-General: NÉSTOR PAN
Librarian: MARIA LUISA ISHIKAWA
Number of teachers: 3,800
Number of students: 35,000

DEANS

Faculty of Agrarian Science: Ing. FERNANDO RUMIANO
Faculty of Economics: Cdr ALEJANDRO KURUC
Faculty of Engineering: Ing. OSCAR PASCAL
Faculty of Law: Dr ALEJANDRO TULLIO
Faculty of Social Sciences: Lic. GABRIEL MARIOTTO

UNIVERSIDAD NACIONAL DE LUJÁN

CC 221, 6700 Luján, Buenos Aires
Telephone: (2323) 42-3171
Fax: (2323) 42-5795
Internet: www.unlu.edu.ar
Founded 1973
Academic year: February to December
Rector: Lic. ANTONIO F. LAPOLLA
Vice-Rector: Dr NORBERTO KRYMKIEWICZ
Registrar: Lic. MARCELO BUSALACCHI
Librarian: Lic. EDUARDO ZEISS
Number of teachers: 1,000
Number of students: 1,200
Publications: *Cuadernos de Economía Política*, *Cuadernos de Historia Regional*

DEANS

Department of Basic Sciences: Dr JOSÉ AGUIRRE
Department of Education: Prof. HÉCTOR CUCUZZA
Department of Social Sciences: Lic. AMALIA TESTA
Department of Technology: Vef. JUAN TREGONING

UNIVERSIDAD NACIONAL DE MAR DEL PLATA

Juan Bautista Alberdi 2695, 7600 Mar del Plata, Pca de Buenos Aires
Telephone: (223) 492-1705
Fax: (223) 492-1705
Internet: www.mdp.edu.ar
Founded 1961
State control
Academic year: March to November
Rector: Ing. JORGE DOMINGO PETRILLO
Vice-Rector: Dr ARMANDO DANIEL ABRUZA
Secretary-General (Planning and Institutional Development): Arq. ARIEL MAGNONI
Academic Secretary: Lic. MONICA VAN GOOL
Secretary for Economics and Finance: C. P. JORGE HERRADA
Secretary for Extension: Prof. ADRIANA CORTES
Secretary for Technological Development: Lic. OLGA DELLA VEDOVA
Secretary for the University Community: Lic. PAULA PAZ
Librarian: Lic. OSCAR FERNÁNDEZ
Number of teachers: 1,600
Number of students: 17,000
Publication: *Revista de Letras* (3 a year)

DEANS

Faculty of Agriculture: Ing. Agr. JOSÉ LUIS BODEGA
Faculty of Architecture and Town Planning: Arq. MANUEL TORRES CANO
Faculty of Economics and Social Sciences: Cont. OTTORINO OSCAR MUCCI
Faculty of Engineering: Ing. MANUEL LORENZO GONZÁLEZ
Faculty of Exact and Natural Sciences: Dr JULIO LUIS DEL RIO
Faculty of Health Sciences and Social Services: Lic. GRISELDA SUSANA VICENS
Faculty of Humanities: Prof. CRISTINA ROSENTHAL
Faculty of Law: Dr LUIS PABLO SLAVIN
Faculty of Psychology: Lic. MARÍA CRISTINA DI DOMÉNICO

DIRECTORS

Centre for Coastal and Quaternary Geology: Lic. DANIEL MARTINEZ
Institute of Biological Research: Dr JORGE JULIAN SANCHEZ
Institute of Science and Materials Technology Research: Dr SUSANA ROSSO

UNIVERSIDAD NACIONAL DE MISIONES

Ruta 12 km. 7½, 3304 Estafeta Miguel Lanus, Posadas
Telephone: (3752) 48-0916
Fax: (3752) 48-0500
Internet: www.unam.edu.ar
Founded 1973
State control
Academic year: February to December
Rector: Ing. LUIS ESTEBAN DELFREDERICO
Vice-Rector: Ing. JORGE CARLOS BETTAGLIO
Number of teachers: 900
Number of students: 8,800
Publications: *Boletín*, *Revista*

DEANS

Faculty of Arts: Prof. ADA SARTORI DE VENCHARUTTI
Faculty of Economics: JOSE LUIS LIBUTTI
Faculty of Engineering: Ing. OSCAR EDUARDO PERRONE
Faculty of Forestry: Ing. JUAN CARLOS MULARCZUK KOSARIK
Faculty of Humanities and Social Sciences: Prof. ANA MARÍA CAMBLONG
Faculty of Sciences: Ing. RAUL MARUCCI

UNIVERSIDAD NACIONAL DEL NORDESTE

25 de Mayo 868, 3400 Corrientes
Telephone: (3783) 42-5060
Fax: (3783) 42-5064
Internet: www.unne.edu.ar
Founded 1957
Academic year: March to December
Rector: Dr ADOLFO DOMINGO TORRES
Vice-Rector: Prof. ANTONIO BADICAN MAHAVE

Secretaries-General: Arq. OSCAR V. VALDES (Academic Affairs), Dr HUGO A. PEIRETTI (Administration), CPN GABRIEL E. OJEDA (Planning), Ing. Dr JORGE R. AVANZA (Science and Technology), Dr SERGIO M. FLINTA (Social Affairs), Dr LUCIANO R. FABRIS (University Extension), CPN GABRIEL E. OJEDA (Planning)

Librarian: Prof. ITALO JUAN L. METTINI

Number of teachers: 4,327

Number of students: 28,459

Publications: *Cuadernos Serie Agro*, *Revista de la Facultad de Ciencias Veterinarias*, *Revista de la Facultad de Derecho*, *Revista Nordeste*, *Serie Medicina*, *Serie Planeamiento*

DEANS

Faculty of Agricultural Industries: Ing. MARÍA ALICIA JUDIS

Faculty of Agricultural Sciences: Ing. Agr. LUIS AMADO MROGINSKY

Faculty of Architecture and Town Planning: Arq. HECTOR LUIS CABALLERO

Faculty of Dentistry: Dr VÍCTOR MENDEZ

Faculty of Economics: CPN EDGARDO MARTÍN AYALA

Faculty of Engineering: Ing. MARIO BRUNO NATALINI

Faculty of Humanities: Prof. ANA MARÍA FOSCHIATTI DE DELL'ORTO

Faculty of Law and Social and Political Sciences: Dr JORGE MARIÑO FAGES

Faculty of Medicine: Dr SAMUEL BLUVSTEIN

Faculty of Natural Sciences and Surveying: Lic. MARÍA SILVIA AGUIRRE

Faculty of Veterinary Sciences: Dr ROBERTO A. JACOBO

DIRECTORS

Institute of Administration of Agriculture and Fishing Business: Ing. Agr. ALBERTO DEZA

Institute of Agrotechnology: Ing. CARLOS ENRIQUE TOMEI

Institute of Criminal Sciences: Lic. FRANCISCO CAMACHO

Institute of Economics of Agriculture and Fishing: Ing. Agr. JULIO JORGE ESPERANZA

Institute of Regional Pathology: Dr JORGE O. GORODNER

Industrial Relations, Social Communication and Tourism: Prof. IRMA QUIJANO

Patterns of Foreign Trade: CPN JUAN CARLOS BARBAGALLO

UNIVERSIDAD NACIONAL DE QUILMES

Roque Sáenz Peña 180, 1876 Bernal, Buenos Aires

Telephone: (11) 4365-7100

Fax: (11) 4365-7101

Internet: www.unq.edu.ar

Founded 1989

State control

Rector: Dr MARIO ERMÁCORA

Vice-Rector: Prof. ROQUE DABAT

Secretary (Academic): Dr MARTÍN BECERRA

Secretary (Administration): Cdora CARMEN CHIARADONNA

Secretary (Communication and Information Technology): Lic. SERGIO NAPOLITANO

Secretary (Legal and Technical): Abog. LORENA LAMPOLIO

Secretary (Postgraduate Affairs): Dr DIEGO GOLOMBEK

Secretary (Research): Dra ANAHÍ BALLENT

Secretary (University Public Relations): Lic. MARCELO GÓMEZ

Librarian: LAURA MANZO

Library of 16,000 vols

Number of students: 11,000

Publications: *Prismas. Revista de historía intelectual* (intellectual history), *Redes* (science and technology), *Revista de Ciencias Sociales* (social sciences)

DIRECTORS

Department of Science and Technology: Dr DANIEL GHIRINGHELLI

Department of Social Sciences: Prof. RODOLFO PASTORE

Centre for Research and Study: Lic. ALBERTO DÍAZ

UNIVERSIDAD NACIONAL DE RÍO CUARTO

Ruta Nacional 36 Km 601, X5804BYA Río Cuarto, Córdoba

Telephone: (358) 467-6300

Fax: (358) 468-0280

E-mail: postmaster@unrc.edu.ar

Internet: www.unrc.edu.ar

Founded 1971

State control

Academic year: February to December

Rector: Ing. Agr. LEONIDAS CHOLAKY SOBARI

Vice-Rector: Ing. OSCAR SPADA

General Secretary: Méd Vet. JUAN JOSÉ BUSSO

Academic Secretary: Lic. MARISA MOYANO

Science and Technology Secretary: Dr JORGE DANIEL ANUNZIATA

Extension and Development Secretary: Ing. Agr. VÍCTOR HUGO BECERRA

Economic Secretary: Lic. LEONILDA BROLL

Welfare Secretary: Lic. GUILLERMO HUCK

Co-ordinator of Institutional Communication: Lic. MIGUEL A. TRÉSPIDI

Head of Postgraduate School: Dr Lic. ENRIQUE GROTE

Librarian: CRISTINA CH. DE FAUDA

Number of teachers: 1,280

Number of students: 17,000

Publications: *Contextos de Educación* (2 a year), *Crónia* (2 a year), *Fundamentos* (2 a year), *Interciencia* (2 a year), *Revista* (2 a year), *Voces de la Universidad* (2 a year)

DEANS

Faculty of Agriculture and Veterinary Science: Med. Vet. HÉCTOR PAGLIARICCI

Faculty of Economics: Lic. FERNANDO LAGRAVE

Faculty of Engineering: Ing. DIEGO MOITRE

Faculty of Exact, Physical, Chemical and Natural Sciences: Lic. HÉCTOR AGNELLI

Faculty of Humanities: Dr MARÍA ZULMA LARREA

UNIVERSIDAD NACIONAL DE ROSARIO

Córdoba 1814, 2000 Rosario

Telephone: (341) 480-2620

E-mail: webmaster@unr.edu.ar

Internet: www.unr.edu.ar

Founded 1968

State control

Academic year: April to November

Rector: Cont. RICARDO SUÁREZ

Vice-Rector: Ing. ALDO OMAR GIMBATTI

Head of Administration: Dr CARLOS A. DULONG

Number of teachers: 5,741

Number of students: 54,319

DEANS

Faculty of Agricultural Sciences: Ing. LILIANA MARGARITA

Faculty of Architecture, Planning and Design: Dr HÉCTOR DANTE FLORIANI

Faculty of Biochemistry and Pharmacy: Dra CLAUDIA ELIZABETH BALAGUE

Faculty of Dentistry: Dr HÉCTOR DARÍO MASIA

Faculty of Economic Sciences and Statistics: Cont. ALICIA INÉS CASTAGNA

Faculty of Exact Sciences, Engineering and Surveying: Ing. DAVID ESTEBAN ASTEGGIANO

Faculty of Humanities and Arts: Prof. DARIO MAIORANA

Faculty of Law: Dr RICARDO ISIDORO

Faculty of Medical Sciences: Dra RAQUEL MADIS CHIARA

Faculty of Political Science and International Relations: Lic. FABIÁN ARIEL BACCIRE

Faculty of Psychology: Dr OVIDE JUAN MENIN

Faculty of Veterinary Sciences: Dr CLAUDIO JUAN GIUDICI

UNIVERSIDAD NACIONAL DE SALTA

Buenos Aires 177, 4400 Salta

Telephone: (387) 432-0563

Fax: (387) 431-1611

E-mail: rector@unsa.edu.ar

Internet: www.unsa.edu.ar

Founded 1972

Academic year: March to December

Rector: Ing. Agr. STELLA MARIS PÉREZ DE BIANCHI

Vice-Rector (vacant): Dr CARLOS CADENA

General Secretary (vacant)

Academic Secretary: Prof. MARÍA TERESA ALVAREZ DE FIGUEROA

Administrative Secretary: Cr HÉCTOR FLORES

Library of 57,633 vols, 42,300 periodicals

Number of teachers: 1,390

Number of students: 12,399

DEANS

Faculty of Economics, Juridical and Social Sciences: CPN LUIS ALBERTO MARTINO

Faculty of Engineering: Ing. JORGE FÉLIX ALMAZÁN

Faculty of Exact Sciences: Ing. JUAN FRANCISCO RAMOS

Faculty of Health Sciences: Med. JOSÉ OSCAR ADAMO

Faculty of Humanities: Lic. EMILIANA CATALINA BULIUBASICH

Faculty of Natural Sciences: Ing. STELLA MARIS PÉREZ DE BIANCHI

ATTACHED INSTITUTE

Consejo de Investigación (Research Council): Pres. Ing. EDGARDO LING SHAM.

UNIVERSIDAD NACIONAL DE SAN JUAN

Avda José Ignacio de la Roza 391 (Este), 6° piso, 5400 San Juan

Telephone: (264) 421-4510

Fax: (264) 421-4586

Internet: www.unsj.edu.ar

Founded 1973

State control

Academic year: April to March

Rector: Ing. TULIO DEL BONO

Vice-Rector: Lic. PEDRO O. MALLEA

Admin. and Financial Secretary: Lic. ALEJANDRO LARREA

Librarian: RAÚL I. LOZADA

Number of teachers: 2,001

Number of students: 11,596

DEANS

Faculty of Architecture, Town Planning and Design: Arq. ROMEO BERNABÉ PLATERO

Faculty of Engineering: Ing. ROBERTO ROMUALDO GOMEZ GUIRADO

Faculty of Exact, Physical and Natural Sciences: Ing. JESÚS ABELARDO ROBLES

Faculty of Humanities, Philosophy and Arts: Prof. ZULMA LUCÍA CORZO

Faculty of Social Sciences: Lic. LUIS FRANCISCO MERITELLO

UNIVERSIDAD NACIONAL DE SAN LUIS

Lavalle 1189, 5700 San Luis
Telephone: 42-4689
Internet: www.unsl.edu.ar
Founded 1974
Academic year: March to December
Rector: Lic. ALBERTO F. PUCHMULLER
Vice-Rector: Lic. EDGARDO E. MONTINI
Librarian: MIGUEL A. LUCERO
Number of teachers: 255
Number of students: 8,500

DEANS

Faculty of Chemistry, Biochemistry and Pharmacy: Dr ROBERTO OLSINA
Faculty of Education: Lic. NILDA E. PICCO DE BARBEITO
Faculty of Engineering and Business Administration (25 de Mayo 374, 5736 Villa Mercedes, San Luis): Ing. RAÚL A. MERINO
Faculty of Physical, Mathematical and Natural Sciences: Dr JULIO C. BENEGAS

UNIVERSIDAD NACIONAL DE SANTIAGO DEL ESTERO

Avda Belgrano (S) 1912, 4200 Santiago del Estero
Telephone: (385) 450-9500
Fax: (385) 422-2595
E-mail: info@unse.edu.ar
Internet: www.unse.edu.ar
Founded 1973
Academic year: February to December
Rector: Dr HUMBERTO HERRERA
Vice-Rector: Geologo ARNALDO TENCHINI
Secretary-General: Ing. GUILLERMO SAN MARCO
Librarian: JORGE LUJAN GEREZ
Library of 20,000 vols
Number of teachers: 848
Number of students: 9,067 (excluding postgraduates)
Publications: *Cuadernos de la UNSE*, *Revista de Ciencia y Técnica* (annually), *Revista 'Quebracho'* (forestry, annually), *Revista 'Unase'* (6 a year)

DEANS

Faculty of Agriculture and Agricultural Industry: Ing. JOSÉ M. SALGADO
Faculty of Forestry: Ing. VICTORIO MARIOT
Faculty of Humanities: CPN SANTIAGO ÁNGEL DRUETTA
Faculty of Science and Technology: Ing. CARLOS ALBERTO BONETTI

ATTACHED INSTITUTES

Centro Educativo Rural: Dir Ing. LUIS E. LUQUE.
Centro de Investigaciones Apícolas: Dir Dr EDUARDO MARIO BIANCHI.
Instituto de Control Biológico: Dir Dr DANTE C. FIORENTINO.
Instituto de Estudios para la Administración Pública: Dir CPN MARÍA ANGÉLICA LEDESUIA.
Instituto de Estudios para el Desarrollo Social: Dir Lic. HORTENCIA CIAUCIA DE SOLOMÓN.
Instituto de Silvicultura y Manejo de Bosques: Dir Ing. ANA MARÍA GIMÉNEZ DE BOLSÓN.
Instituto de Tecnología de la Madera: Dir Ing. VÍCTOR RAÚL TABOADA.
Jardín Botánico: Dir Ing. LUCAS DOMINGO ROIC.

UNIVERSIDAD NACIONAL DEL SUR

Avda Colón 80, B8000FTN Bahía Blanca
Telephone: (291) 459-5015
Fax: (291) 459-5016
E-mail: rectorado@uns.edu.ar
Internet: www.uns.edu.ar
Founded 1956
Academic year: February to December
Rector: Dr LUIS MARÍA FERNÁNDEZ
Vice-Rector: Dr EDGARDO NORBERTO GÜICHAL
General Secretaries: Dra MARÍA FERNANDA CRAVERO (Academic), Lic. MARÍA DEL CARMEN VAQUERO (Communication and Culture), Dr GUILLERMO CRAPISTE (Institutional Relations and University Extension), Dr GUSTAVO ADOLFO ORIOLI (Scientific and Technological), Lic. CLAUDIA LEGNINI (Student Affairs), Lic. GUILLERMO LUCANERA (Technical-Administrative), Lic. SANDRA BAIONI (University Superior Council)
Library: see Libraries
Number of teachers: 2,069
Number of students: 22,571
Publications: *Capacitando en Calidad* (3 a year), *Escritos Contables* (2 a year), *Latin American Applied Research* (4 a year), *Reflexiones* (economics), *Revista Diálogos* (4 a year), *Revista Estudios Económicos* (annually), *Revista Universitaria de Geografía* (annually)

DIRECTORS

Department of Agriculture: Dr JUAN CARLOS LOBARTINI
Department of Biology, Biochemistry and Pharmacy: Mag. MARCELO SAGARDOY
Department of Business Administration: Cra ALICIA DIETERT
Department of Chemical Engineering: Dr JORGE LOZANO
Department of Chemistry: Dr JULIO CÉSAR PODESTÁ
Department of Computing Engineering Sciences: Dr GUILLERMO SIMARI
Department of Economics: Mag. ANDREA S. CASTELLANO
Department of Electrical Engineering: Dr JAVIER D. OROZCO
Department of Engineering: Ing. RICARDO CASAL
Department of Geography: Dr ROBERTO NICOLÁS BUSTOS CARA
Department of Geology: Dr PEDRO MAIZA
Department of Humanities: Dra SUSANA C. SCABUZZO
Department of Law: Abog. TOMÁS LOBATO
Department of Mathematics: Dr MANUEL ABAD
Department of Physics: Dr ALFREDO JUAN

ATTACHED RESEARCH INSTITUTES

Centro de Recursos Naturales Renovables de la Zona Semiárida (CERZOS): Altos del Barrio Palihue, 8000 Bahía Blanca; tel. (291) 486-1127; Dir Dr NÉSTOR CURVETTO.
Centro Regional de Investigaciones Básicas y Aplicadas Bahía Blanca (CRIBABB): Camino La Carrindanga Km 7, 8000 Bahía Blanca; tel. (291) 486-1666; Dir Ing. MARTÍN URBICAIN.
Instituto Argentino de Oceanografía (IADO): Camino La Carrindanga Km 7, 8000 Bahía Blanca; tel. (291) 486-1112; run in conjunction with CONICET; Dir Dra MARÍA CIMTIA PÍCCOLO.
Instituto de Investigaciones Bioquímicas (INIBIBB): Camino La Carrindanga Km 7, 8000 Bahía Blanca; tel. (291) 486-1201; Dir Dr FRANCISCO JOSÉ BARRANTES.
Instituto de Matemática Bahía Blanca (INMABB): Avda Alem 1253, 8000 Bahía Blanca; tel. (291) 459-5116; Vice-Dir Mg. AURORA GERMANI.
Planta Piloto de Ingeniería Química (PLAPIQUI): Camino La Carrindanga Km 7, 8000 Bahía Blanca; tel. (291) 486-1700; Dir Dr ENRIQUE MARCELO VALLÉS.

UNIVERSIDAD NACIONAL DE TRES DE FEBRERO

Avda San Martín 2921, 1678 Caseros, Buenos Aires
Telephone: (11) 4759-9810
Fax: (11) 4759-9810
E-mail: info@untref.edu.ar
Internet: www.untref.edu.ar
Founded 1995
State control
Academic year: March to December
Rector: Lic. ANÍBAL Y. JOZAMI
Vice-Rector: Lic. MARTÍN KAUFMANN
Secretary (Academic): Ing. CARLOS MUNDT
Secretary (Research and Co-operation): Dr FÉLIX PEÑA

DIRECTORS

Administration and Economics: Dr MARTÍN GRAS
Art and Culture: Lic. FERMÍN FÈVRE
Health Sciences and Social Security: Dr CARLOS TORRES
Mathematics, Statistics and Methodology: Lic. ERNESTO ROSA
Social Sciences: Dr CÉSAR LORENZANO

ATTACHED RESEARCH INSTITUTES

CEiArte: Dir RICARDO DAL FARRA.
Centro de Investigación y Docencia en Economía para el Desarrollo: Dir Dr LUIS BLAUM.
Centro de Investigaciones en Estadística Aplicada: Dir Lic. ERNESTO ROSA.
Instituto de Artes y Ciencias de la Diversidad Cultural: Dir DANIEL FEIERSTEIN, HAMURABI NOUFOURI.
Instituto de Cooperación para el Desarrollo de la Educación: Dir NORBERTO FERNÁNDEZ LAMARRA.
Instituto de Estudios Históricos.
Instituto de Estudios Metropolitanos: Dir Dr MARTÍN GRAS.
Instituto de Etnomusicología y Creación en Artes Tradicionales y de Vanguardia: Dirs Dra ISABEL ARETZ, Lic. ALEJANDRO IGLESIAS ROSSI.
Instituto de Investigaciones de la Adolescencia y la Juventud: Dir Lic. FABIÁN RUOCCO.
Instituto de Políticas Culturales: Dir Prof. PATRICIO LÓIZAGA.
Núcleo Interdisciplinario de Arte, Cultura y Comunicación: Dirs Dr NORBERTO GRIFFA, Lic. FERMÍN FÈVRE.
Núcleo Interdisciplinario de Estudios Internacionales.

UNIVERSIDAD NACIONAL DE TUCUMÁN

Ayacucho 491, 4000 San Miguel de Tucumán
Telephone: (381) 424-7762
Fax: (381) 424-8654
E-mail: postmaster@unt.edu.ar
Internet: www.unt.edu.ar
Founded 1914
Language of instruction: Spanish
Academic year: April to December
Rector: Pr. Cr. MARIO ALBERTO MARIGLIANO
Vice-Rector: Dr CARLOS ROBERTO FERNÁNDEZ
Secretary (Administration): Ing. JUAN CARLOS REIMUNDIN

Secretary (Academic Affairs): Dr RITA WASERMAN DE CUNIO
Secretary (Postgraduate Affairs): Dr SUSANA MAIDANA
Secretary (Science and Technology): Dr FAUSTINO SIÑERIZ
Secretary (University Extension and Environment): Arq. DIEGO LECUONA
Director of International Relations: Dr RAMIRO ALBARRACÍN
General Sec.: Dr FLORENCIO ACEÑOLAZA

Library: see Libraries and Archives
Number of teachers: 3,967
Number of students: 42,946

DEANS

Faculty of Agriculture and Animal Husbandry: Dr CARLOS HUGO BELLONE
Faculty of Architecture and Town Planning: Dr PABLO HOLGADO
Faculty of Biochemistry, Chemistry and Pharmacy: Dr ALICIA BARDÓN
Faculty of Dentistry: Dr GUILLERMO RAIDEN LAZCANO
Faculty of Economics: JUAN ALBERTO CERISOLA
Faculty of Exact Sciences and Technology: Ing. MARIO DONZELLI
Faculty of Fine Arts: Arq. MARCOS FIGUEROA
Faculty of Law and Social Sciences: Prof. PEDRO MARCOS ROUGES
Faculty of Medicine: Dr HORACIO DEZA
Faculty of Natural Sciences and Miguel Lillo Institute: Dr FERNANDO PRADO
Faculty of Philosophy and Letters: Dr ELENA ROJAS
Faculty of Psychology: Prof. MARIA LUISA ROSSI DE HERNANDEZ

UNIVERSIDAD NACIONAL DE VILLA MARÍA

San Juan 1270, 5900 Villa María, Córdoba
Telephone: (353) 453-9100
Fax: (353) 453-9117
E-mail: comunica@unvm.edu.ar
Internet: www.unvm.edu.ar

Founded 1995
State control
Academic year: March to November (two semesters)

Rector: Cr CARLOS OMAR DOMÍGUEZ
Secretary-General: Abog. GERMÁN CARIGNANO
Secretary (Academic): Mgr EDUARDO A. MARZOLLA
Secretary (Finance): Cr EDUARDO REMIGIO ROMANO
Secretary (Welfare): Lic. MARÍA DEL ROSARIO GALARZA
Number of students: 3,000

DIRECTORS

Institute of Basic and Applied Sciences: Cr CARLOS OMAR DOMÍNGUEZ
Institute of Human Sciences: Dr CARLOS DANIEL LASA
Institute of Social Sciences: Lic. DANTE LA ROCCA MARTÍN
Dr Antonino Sobral University Centre: Lic. SILVIA MARÍA PAREDES
University Centre of Mediterranean Studies: Ing. JORGE LUIS FERRERO

SUBJECT CO-ORDINATORS

Institute of Basic and Applied Sciences:
- Agricultural Engineering: Ing. JOSÉ ROMANO
- Food Technology Engineering: Ing. JUAN PABLO BERTELLO
- Information Technology: Ing. EDUARDO GONZÁLEZ

Institute of Human Sciences:
- Castilian Language: Lic. BEATRIZ VOTTERO
- Educational Psychology: SILVIA CARTECHINI
- Educational Science: SILVIA PAREDES
- English Language: Lic. MARTA ANCARANI
- Image Design and Production: Prof. HÉCTOR GENTILE
- Mathematics: Lic. RICARDO DANIEL JUAN
- Musical Composition and Popular Music: Prof. JUAN CARLOS CIALLELA
- Nursing: MARTHA TORRE
- Occupational Therapy: SANDRA WESTMAN
- Physical Education: MARIO BACHIOCHI

Institute of Social Sciences:
- Accounting: Mgr GUSTAVO SADER
- Administration: Lic. NICOLÁS SALVADOR BELTRAMINO
- Communication: Lic. ANA EMAIDES
- Economics: Lic. SILVIA BUCCIARELLI
- Local and Regional Development: Lic. CARLOS ALBERTO SEGGIARO
- Political Science: Lic. OMAR BARBERIS
- Social Services: Lic. ADRIANO ROCHETTI
- Sociology: Lic. ADA BEATRIZ CARACCIOLLO

UNIVERSIDAD TECNOLÓGICA NACIONAL

Sarmiento 440, 6° piso, 1347 Buenos Aires
Telephone: (11) 4394-8075
Fax: (11) 4322-0674
Internet: www.utn.edu.ar

Founded 1959
Academic year: April to November

Rector: Ing. HECTOR C. BROTTO
Vice-Rector: Ing. BENITO POSSETTO
General Secretary: Ing. CARLOS FANTINI
Academic Secretary: Ing. CIRIO MURAD
Secretary for Finance: Ing. CARLOS RAPP
Secretary for Institutional Relations: Prof. CARLOS RÍOS
Secretary for Student Affairs: Ing. RUBÉN SORO MARTÍNEZ
Secretary for Technological Research: Ing. JORGE FERRANTES
Secretary for University Extension: Ing. DANIEL FERRADAS

Number of teachers: 16,185
Number of students: 70,087

Publication: *Boletín Informativo*.

REGIONAL FACULTIES

Avellaneda: Ing. Marconi 775, 1870 Avellaneda, Buenos Aires; mechanical, electrical and electronic engineering; Dean Ing. HÉCTOR R. GONZÁLEZ.

Bahía Blanca: 11 de Abril 461, 8000 Bahía Blanca, Buenos Aires; construction, electrical and mechanical engineering; Dean Ing. VICENTE EGIDI.

Buenos Aires: Medrano 951, 1179 Buenos Aires; textile, chemical, metallurgical, electronic, construction, electrical and mechanical systems analysis engineering; Dean Arq. LUIS A. DE MARCO.

Concepción del Uruguay: Ing. Pereyra 676, 3260 Concepción del Uruguay, Entre Ríos; electromechanical and construction engineering; Dean Ing. JUAN CARLOS PITER.

Córdoba: Uladíslao Frías s/n, 5000 Córdoba; chemical, metallurgical, mechanical, electronic and electrical engineering; Dean Ing. RUBÉN SORO MARTÍNEZ.

Delta: San Martín 1171, 2804 Campana, Buenos Aires; electrical, mechanical and chemical engineering; Dean Ing. GUSTAVO BAUER.

General Pacheco: Avda Irigoyen 2878, 1617 General Pacheco, Buenos Aires; mechanical engineering; Dean Ing. EUGENIO B. RICCIOLINI.

Haedo: París 532, 1707 Haedo, Buenos Aires; aeronautical engineering, electronics, mechanical engineering; Dean Ing. ELIO BIAGINI.

La Plata: Calle 60 esq. 124, 1900 La Plata, Buenos Aires; chemical, mechanical, electrical and construction engineering; Dean Ing. CARLOS FANTINI.

Mendoza: Rodríguez 273, 5500 Mendoza; construction, electromechanical, chemical, electronic engineering, systems analysis; Dean Ing. JULIO CÉSAR CLETO COBOS.

Paraná: Almafuerte 1033, 3100 Paraná, Entre Ríos; electromechanical and construction engineering; Dean Ing. RAÚL E. ARROYO.

Rafaela: Blvd Roca y Artigas, 2300 Rafaela, Santa Fé; electromechanical and construction engineering; Dean Ing. OSCAR DAVID.

Resistencia: French 414, 3500 Resistencia, Chaco; electromechanical engineering, systems analysis; Dean Ing. SEBASTIÁN VICENTE MARTÍN.

Río Grande: Belgrano 777, 9420 Río Grande, Tierra del Fuego; electronic and industrial engineering; Dean Ing. MARIO FERREIRA.

Rosario: Estanislao Zeballos 1341, 2000 Rosario, Santa Fé; electrical, mechanical, construction, chemical engineering and systems analysis; Dean Ing. DANIEL OSCAR BADÍA.

San Francisco: Avda Gral. Savio 501, 2400 San Francisco, Córdoba; electromechanical engineering, electronics, information technology; Dean Ing. RAÚL C. ALBERTO.

San Nicolás: Colón 332, 2900 San Nicolás, Buenos Aires; electromechanical and metallurgical engineering; Dean Ing. NEORÉN P. FRANCO.

San Rafaél: Comandante Salas 370, 5600 San Rafaél, Mendoza; construction, electromechanical, chemical and civil engineering; Dean Ing. HORACIO P. PESSANO.

Santa Fé: Lavaise 610, 3000 Santa Fé; construction, electrical and mechanical engineering and systems analysis; Dean Ing. RICARDO O. SCHOLTUS.

Tucumán: Rivadavia 1050, 4000 San Miguel de Tucumán; construction, mechanical and civil engineering, information technology; Dean Ing. HUGO E. CELLERINO.

Villa María: Avda Universidad 450, Barrio Bello Horizonte, 5900 Villa María, Córdoba; mechanical and chemical engineering; Dean Ing. CARLOS R. RAPP..

ACADEMIC UNITS

Concordia: Salta 277, 3200 Concordia, Entre Ríos; construction and electromechanical engineering; Dir Ing. JOSÉ BOURREN.

Confluencia: Juan Manuel de Rosas y Juan Soufal, 8318 Plaza Huincul, Neuquén; electronic and chemical engineering; Dir Ing. SUSANA L. TARGHETTA DUR.

La Rioja: Facundo Quiroga y Beccar Varela, 5330 La Rioja; electromechanical engineering; Dir Dr MAURICIO KEJNER.

Rawson: Mitre 764, 9100 Rawson, Chubut; electromechanical and industrial engineering; Dir Ing. ERNESTO A. PASCUALICH.

Reconquista: Freyre 980, 3560 Reconquista, Santa Fé; electromechanical engineering; Dir Ing. OSVALDO DEL VALLE FATALA.

Río Gallegos: Maipú 53, 9400 Río Gallegos, Santa Cruz; electromechanical and industrial engineering; Dir Lic. SERGIO RAÚL RAGGI.

Trenque Lauquen: Villegas y Pereyra Rosas, 6400 Trenque Lauquen, Buenos Aires; electromechanical and construction engineering; Dir Ing. GUILLERMO A. GIL.

Venado Tuerto: Castelli 501, 2600 Venado Tuerto, Santa Fé; electromechanical and construction engineering; Dir Ing. ALFREDO ANÍBAL GUILLAUMET.

INSTITUTO UNIVERSITARIO AERONÁUTICO

Avda Fuerza Aérea, Km. 6½, 5022 Guarnicíon Aérea Córdoba
Telephone: (351) 433-3916
Fax: (351) 433-3916
E-mail: rector@iua.edu.ar
Internet: www.iua.edu.ar

Founded 1947
State control
Language of instruction: Spanish
Academic year: February to December

Rector: Brig. (R) RAÚL JUAN CARLOS CAMUSSI
Vice-Rector (Academic): Lic. HÉCTOR OSCAR BENZA
Vice-Rector (Distance Learning): Ing. JAVIER ETCHEGOYEN
General Secretary: Ing. PEDRO EMILIO MURILLO
Librarian: MARCELA A. DUCASSE

Library of 8,000 vols
Number of teachers: 185
Number of students: 4,800

Publication: *Acortando Distancia* (4 a year)

DIRECTORS

Department of Aeronautical Engineering: Ing. ALBERTO FIDEL BAZAN
Department of Business Management: Cont. CATALINA ROSA TINARI
Department of Electrical Engineering: Ing. SERGIO ALFREDO MEDINA
Department of Languages: Prof. NICOLÁS ERICO GERMAN ANDERSEN
Department of Systems Engineering: Lic. SUSANA B. BARRIONUEVO DE BUSTOS ACUÑA
Centre for Applied Research: Vicecomodoro LADISLAO MATHE

Five-year courses for military personnel and civilians.

Private Universities

UNIVERSIDAD DEL ACONCAGUA

Catamarca 147, 5500 Mendoza
Telephone: (261) 423-2281
Fax: (261) 423-2281
Internet: www.uda.edu.ar

Founded 1965
Academic year: April to October

Rector: Dr OSVALDO S. CABALLERO
Secretary-General: OSCAR DAVID CERUTTI
Librarian: HAYDEE TORRES BOUSOÑO

Number of teachers: 451
Number of students: 2,150

DEANS

Faculty of Economics and Commerce: Dr ROLANDO GALLI REY
Faculty of Phono-audiology: Dr GUSTAVO MAURICIO
Faculty of Psychology: Lic. HUGO LUPIAÑEZ
Faculty of Social Sciences and Administration: Dr JUAN FARRES CAVAGNARO

UNIVERSIDAD ARGENTINA DE LA EMPRESA
(Argentine University of Administration Sciences)

Lima 717, C1073AAO Buenos Aires
Telephone: (11) 4372-5454 or (800) 122-8233
E-mail: contactcenter@uade.edu.ar
Internet: www.uade.edu.ar

Founded 1962
Academic year: March to December

Rector: Dr GERMÁN GUIDO LAVALLE
Provost: Lic. ANA MARÍA MASS
Secretary for Student Affairs: ROBERTO PEDRAZA
Librarian: RODOLFO LÖHE

Library of 50,000 vols, 865 periodicals
Number of teachers: 750
Number of students: 14,400

Publication: *@ UADE* (monthly)

DEANS AND DIRECTORS

School of Economics: Dr JORGE DEL ÁGUILA
School of Engineering and Exact Sciences: Dr RICARDO OROSCO
School of Legal, Social and Communication Sciences: Dr MARIO SERRAFERO

DEPARTMENTAL DIRECTORS

Accounting and Taxation: Dr ALEJANDRO TELIAS
Administration and Human Resources: Lic. ALEJANDRO CARDOZO
Communication and Design: Arq. RICARDO MENDEZ
Economics and Finance: Lic. SILVIA CAVIOLA
Food Technology: Eng. ALBERTO ETIENNOT
Industrial and Service Technology: Dr AXEL LARRETEGUY
Languages: Lic. MARISA LÓPEZ
Law: Dra SILVIA TOSCANO
Marketing: JUAN HUDSON
Mathematics and Quantitative Methods: Lic. SUSANA MASTRANGELO
Social Sciences and Humanities: Lic. MARTÍN CUESTA
Technology and Computers: Lic. ALEJO RUBÍN AYMÁ

ATTACHED INSTITUTES

Advanced Research Center: Dir Dr DIEGO PETRECOLLA.

Institute of Economics: Dir Dr GUSTAVO FERRO.

Institute of Economic Regulation Studies: Dir Dr DIEGO PETRECOLLA.

Institute of Labour Studies: Dir Dr DANIEL FUNES DE RIOJA.

UADE Research: Dir Dr DIEGO PETRECOLLA.

UNIVERSIDAD ARGENTINA 'JOHN F. KENNEDY'

Calle Bartolomé Mitre 1411, 1037 Buenos Aires
Telephone: (11) 4476-4338
Fax: (11) 4476-2271
Internet: www.kennedy.edu.ar

Founded 1961

Rector: Dr MIGUEL HERRERA FIGUEROA
Vice-Rector: Dr PEDRO R. DAVID
Secretary-General: Ing. MIGUEL HERRERA FILAS

Library of 50,000 vols
Number of teachers: 1,800
Number of students: 10,000

HEADS OF DEPARTMENTS

Anthropology: Dr LUIS FERNANDO RIVERA
Architecture: Arq. ALDO DE LORENZI
Biology: Dr ALDO IMBRIANO
Building and Construction: Ing. M. HERRERA FILAS
Business Studies: Dr FRANCISCO RISSO PATRÓN
Chemistry: Dr EDMUNDO SAVASTANO
Clinical Psychology: Dr MARIO COSCIO
Communications: Prof. HUMBERTO PACHECO MILESI
Computer Studies: CARLOS VIDAL
Criminology: Dr HORACIO MALDONADO
Demography and Tourism: Dr RAÚL GÓMEZ FUENTEALBA
Design: JULIO CÉSAR ABRAMOF
Development and Planning: Dr MIGUEL HERRERA FIGUEROA
Economics: Cont. OLVER BENVENUTO
Education: Lic. ELISA HERREN DE DAVID
Educational Psychology: Dr MARIO COSCIO
History: Dr ENRIQUE DE GANDIA
Labour Studies: Dr EMILIO PETRARCA
Law: Dr JOSÉ ALBERTO VIDAL DÍAZ
Literature: Prof. MARÍA DEL VALLE ROMANELLI
Mathematics: Ing. MIGUEL HERRERA FILAS
Philosophy: FRANCISCO GARCÍA BAZÁN
Political Science: Prof. LUIS M. PREMOLI
Psychology: Dr ELEONORA ZENEQUELLI
Public Relations: Dr JUAN CARLOS IGLESIAS
Social Work: JULIO ENRIQUE APARICIO
Sociology: Dr FERNANDO CUEVILLAS
Systems Analysis: RODOLFO NAVEIRO
University Extension: Dra CRISTINA HERRERA FILAS

UNIVERSIDAD DE BELGRANO

Zabala 1837, 1426 Buenos Aires
Telephone: (11) 4788-5400
Fax: (11) 4576-3912
E-mail: beker@ub.edu.ar
Internet: www.ub.edu.ar

Founded 1964
Language of instruction: Spanish
Private control
Academic year: March to November

Rector: Dr AVELINO JOSÉ PORTO
Vice-Rector for Academic Affairs: Prof. BRIGANTE NILDA
Vice-Rector for Institutional Affairs: Prof. ALDO PÉREZ
Vice-Rector for Legal and Technical Admin.: Dr EUSTAQUIO CASTRO
Librarian: MERCEDES PATALANO

Library of 49,303 vols, 2,500 periodicals
Number of teachers: 1,097
Number of students: 10,441

Publications: *Académicos* (monthly), *Postcátedra* (quarterly), *UB News* (weekly)

DEANS

Faculty of Agriculture: Eng. CARLOS MENDEZ ACOSTA
Faculty of Architecture and Urban Planning: Arq. MÓNICA FERNÁNDEZ
Faculty of Distance Learning: Dr CLARA BONFILL
Faculty of Economics: Dr GUILLERMO VINITZKY
Faculty of Engineering and Information Technology: Eng. LUIS R. VACA ARENAZA
Faculty of Health Sciences: Dr MARCELO VERNENGO
Faculty of Humanities: Dr SUSANA SEIDMANN
Faculty of Law and Social Sciences: Dr ASTRID GOMEZ
Faculty of Languages and Foreign Studies: Prof. RAQUEL ALBORNOZ
Faculty of Natural and Exact Sciences: Dr MARCELO VERNENGO
Faculty of Graduate Studies: Dr ANDRÉS FONTANA
Graduate School of Economics and International Business: Dr CARLOS STEIGER
Department of Graduate Studies and Continuing Education: Dr CARLOS STEIGER

UNIVERSIDAD CAECE

Avda de Mayo 1400, 1085 Buenos Aires
Telephone: (11) 4381-3229
Fax: (11) 4381-6520
Internet: www.caece.edu.ar

Founded 1967
Private control

Rector: JORGE E. BOSCH
General Vice-Rector: NICOLÁS PATETTA
Academic Vice-Rector: ROBERTO P. J. HERNÁNDEZ
Chief Administrative Officer: OLGA VILLAVERDE
University Librarian: SUSANA BUONO

Library of 9,000 vols

Number of teachers: 300
Number of students: 2,000
Publication: *Elementos de Matemática*

HEADS OF DEPARTMENTS

Biology: CLAUDIA AGUILAR
Education: MARTA L. LOCATELLI
Mathematics: ROBERTO P. J. HERNÁNDEZ
Systems Analysis: ELENA I. GARCÍA

PONTIFICIA UNIVERSIDAD CATÓLICA ARGENTINA 'SANTA MARÍA DE LOS BUENOS AIRES'

Alicia Moreau de Justo 1300, C1107AAZ Buenos Aires
Telephone: (11) 4349-0200
Fax: (11) 4349-0246
E-mail: rrii@uca.edu.ar
Internet: www.uca.edu.ar
Founded 1958
Academic year: March to November
Rector: Monseñor Dr ALFREDO HORACIO ZECCA
Vice-Rector: Lic. ERNESTO JOSÉ PARSELIS
Academic Secretary: Dr JORGE NICOLÁS LAFFERRIÈRE
Director of International Relations: Dr CARLOS EZCURRA
Number of teachers: 3,200
Number of students: 12,000
Publications: *Boletín de Ciencias Económicas* (6 a year), *Colección* (political science, 2 a year), *Letras* (Argentinian and comparative literature, 2 a year), *Prudentia Juris* (2 a year), *Sapientia* (2 a year), *Teología* (2 a year), *Valores* (economics and social ethics, 3 a year)

DEANS

Faculty of Agriculture: Dr CARLOS PACÍFICO
Faculty of Arts and Music: GUILLERMO SCARABINO
Faculty of Canon Law: Lic. VICTOR PINTO
Faculty of Chemistry and Engineering (Mendoza): Lic. LUIS SCOZZINA
Faculty of Economics (Mendoza): Ing. ALFREDO DOMINGO VIOTTI
Faculty of Economic Sciences (Rosario): Cr. RICARDO PARÍS
Faculty of Economic and Social Sciences: Dr LUDOVICO VIDELA
Faculty of Health Sciences: Dr CARLOS ALVAREZ
Faculty of Humanities and Education (Mendoza): Prof. ADRIANA MENÉNDEZ DE ZUMER
Faculty of Humanities 'Teresa de Avila' (Paraná): Dr MIGUEL ANGEL NESA
Faculty of Law and Political Sciences: Dr EDUARDO VENTURA
Faculty of Law and Social Sciences (Rosario): Dr GUSTAVO GUILLERMO LO CELSO
Faculty of Philosophy and Letters: Dr HÉCTOR DELBOSCO
Faculty of Physical Sciences, Mathematics and Engineering: Ing. HORACIO CARLOS REGGINI
Faculty of Theology: Dr CARLOS M. GALLI

DIRECTORS

Institute of Bioethics: Dr ALBERTO BOCHATEY
Institute of Social Communication, Journalism and Publicity: Lic. ALICIA PERESON
Institute of Spirituality and Pastoral Action: GUSTAVO LUIS BOQUIN
Institute of University Extension: Dr ALFREDO ZECCA

UNIVERSIDAD CATÓLICA DE CÓRDOBA

Obispo Trejo 323, 5000 Córdoba
Telephone: (351) 493-8000
Fax: (351) 493-8002
E-mail: secrec@uccor.edu.ar
Internet: www.uccor.edu.ar
Founded 1956
Academic year: February to December
Chancellor: Mgr CARLOS JOSÉ ÑAÑEZ (Archbishop of Córdoba)
Vice-Chancellor: R. P. ALVARO RESTREPO
Rector: Dr MIGUEL AMBROSIO PETTY
Vice-Rector (Academic) (vacant)
Vice-Rector (Development): Dr CARLOS VIDO KESMAN
Vice-Rector (Economy): Cont. NORBERTO ANTONIO BERTAINA
Vice-Rector (University Community) (vacant): Lic. CARLOS VIGIL AVALOS
Academic Secretary: Lic. JUAN SARDO
Librarian (vacant)
Library: see Libraries and Archives
Number of teachers: 1,305
Number of students: 7,156

DEANS

Faculty of Agriculture: Dr JUAN CARLOS BOGGIO
Faculty of Architecture: Arq. ESTEBAN TRISTÁN REMIRO BONDONE
Faculty of Chemical Sciences: Bioq. PAULA MARÍA COOKE
Faculty of Economics and Administration: Mag. CARLOS ORLANDO PÉREZ
Faculty of Education: Dr ENRIQUE NÉSTOR BAMBOZZI
Faculty of Engineering: Ing. RAÚL JUAN VACA NARVAJA
Faculty of Law and Social Sciences: Abog. JOSÉ NARCISO REY NORES
Faculty of Medicine: Mag. CARLOS EMILIO GATTI
Faculty of Philosophy and Humanities: Dr CARLOS FEDERICO SCHICKENDANTZ
Faculty of Political Sciences and International Relations: Lic. MARIO GERMÁN RIORDA
Institute of Administrative Sciences: ADOLFO MARTÍN GUSTAVO BERTOA

UNIVERSIDAD CATÓLICA DE CUYO

Avda Ignacio de la Roza 1516, Rivadavia, 5400 San Juan
Telephone: (264) 429-2300
Fax: (264) 429-2310
E-mail: extension@uccuyo.edu.ar
Internet: www.uccuyo.edu.ar
Founded 1953
Rector: Dr JUAN CARLOS GUILLERMO KREBS
Vice-Rector: Dr CARLOS QUIROGA CONTE GRAND
Secretary-General: Arq. CARLOS PUJADAS
Director of Library: EUGENIA CARRASCOSA DE YUNES
Library of 25,000 vols
Number of teachers: 408
Number of students: 3,072
Publications: *Revista Cuadernos*, *La Verdad*

DEANS

Faculty of Economics: C. P. JOSÉ ANTONIO OLIVER
Faculty of Food Sciences: Lic. GRACIELA BEATRIZ MARTÍN DE ROCA
Faculty of Health Sciences: Dr HUGO CAMPAYO
Faculty of Law and Social Sciences: Dr GILBERTO RIVEROS
Faculty of Philosophy and Humanities: Dra MARÍA ISABEL LARRAURI

UNIVERSIDAD CATÓLICA DE LA PLATA

Calle 13 No. 1227, 1900 La Plata
Telephone: (221) 43-4779
Internet: www.ucalp.edu.ar
Founded 1968
Academic year: March to November
Grand Chancellor: Mons. Dr CARLOS GALAN
Rector: Cr CAYETANO A. LICCIARDO
General Secretary: Dr JORGE I. BENZRIHEN
General Secretary in charge of Colleges and Institutes: Prof. NANCY DI PIERO DE WARR
Librarian: GLADYS R. MARDUEL
Number of teachers: 635
Number of students: 3,000
Publication: *Revista*

DEANS

Faculty of Applied Mathematics: Ing. EDUARDO FULCO
Faculty of Architecture: Arq. CARLOS ALBERTO RUOTOLO
Faculty of Economics: Cr MARIO LUIS SZYCHOWSKI
Faculty of Education: Prof. NANCY DI PIERO DE WARR
Faculty of Law: Dr JORGE O. PERRINO
Faculty of Social Sciences: Dr JORGE O. PERRINO
Department of Theology: Pbro Ing. RUBEN A. GARINO (Dir)

AFFILIATED COLLEGES AND INSTITUTE

Colegio José Manuel Estrada: Dir MONICA INES ROLANDELLI.
Colegio Ministro Luis R. MacKay: Dir Prof. SILVIA LAPORTE.
Colegio San Miguel de Garicoits: Dir Prof. JOSE MARIA DELGADO ZURETTI.
Instituto José Manuel Estrada: Rector Prof. NOEMI HILDA CARIONE.

UNIVERSIDAD CATÓLICA DE SALTA

Ciudad Universitaria, Campo Castañares, Casilla 18, 4400 Salta
Telephone: (387) 423-3270
Internet: www.ucasal.net
Founded 1963
Academic year: March to December
Chancellor: Mons. MARIO ANTONIO CARGNELLO
Rector: Dr PATRICIO GUSTAVO E. COLOMBO MURÚA
Academic Vice-Rector: Prof. ALFREDO TAGLIABUE
Administrative Vice-Rector: Ing. MANUEL CORNEJO TORINO
Secretary-General: Dr LUIS MARTÍNEZ
Librarian: WARTHA ANSALDI DE VINANTE
Library of 42,000 vols
Number of teachers: 750
Number of students: 13,000

DEANS

Faculty of Architecture and Urban Planning: Arq. ROQUE GÓMEZ
Faculty of Economics and Administration: Lic. ROBERTO CADAR
Faculty of Engineering and Informatics: Ing. FERNANDO ROMAIN
Faculty of Law: Dr LUIS MARTÍNEZ
School of Physical Education: Lic. DOLORES MEDINA BOUQUET
School of Social Service: Lic. SONIA ZAMORA
School of Tourism: Lic. CARLOS FRANCISCO SÁNCHEZ

UNIVERSIDAD CATÓLICA DE SANTA FÉ

Echagüe 7151, 3000 Santa Fé
Telephone: (342) 460-3030
Fax: (342) 460-3030
E-mail: postmaster@ucsfre.edu.ar
Internet: www.ucsf.edu.ar
Founded 1957
Academic year: February to December

Grand Chancellor: Mons. EDGARDO GABRIEL STORNI
Rector: Arq. JOSÉ MARÍA PASSEGGI
Vice-Rector for Academic Affairs: Lic. TOMÁS GUTIERREZ
Vice-Rector for Training: Lic. MARCELO MATEO
Secretary-General: Dra MARTA D. V. OLMOS
Library Director: Dr JUAN CARLOS P. BALLESTEROS
Number of teachers: 480
Number of students: 3,864

DEANS

Faculty of Architecture: Arq. RICARDO MARÍA ROCHETTI
Faculty of Economic Sciences: Cont. LUIS ELIO BONINO
Faculty of Education: Dr JUAN CARLOS PABLO BALLESTEROS
Faculty of Engineering, Geoecology and the Environment: Lic. TOMÁS GUTIERREZ
Faculty of Law: Dr RICARDO ANDRÉS VILLA
Faculty of Philosophy: Prof. DANIEL VASCHETTO (acting)
Faculty of Social Communication: Lic. CARLOS TEALDI

UNIVERSIDAD CATÓLICA DE SANTIAGO DEL ESTERO

Avda Alsina y Núñez de Prado, 4200 Santiago del Estero
Telephone: (385) 421-3820
Fax: (385) 421-9754
Internet: www.ucse.edu.ar
Founded 1960
Language of instruction: Spanish
Academic year: April to November
Grand Chancellor: Mons. GERARDO EUSEBIO SUELDO
Rector: Ing. JORGE LUIS FEIJÓO
Administrative Director: Lic. MARÍA ÉLIDA CERRO DE ÁBALOS
Librarian: Prof. Dr MATIAS ZUZEC
Library of 19,000 vols
Number of teachers: 450
Number of students: 4,000
Publication: *Nuevas Propuestas*

DEANS

Faculty of Applied Mathematics: Ing. OCTAVIO JOSÉ MÉDICI
Faculty of Economics: Lic. VÍCTOR MANUEL FEIJÓO
Faculty of Education: Hna Lic. LILIANA BADALONI
Faculty of Politics, Social Sciences and Law: Abogada MARIA TERESA TENTI DE VOLTA

PROFESSORS

Faculty of Applied Mathematics:
- CORONEL, J. C., Introduction to Mathematical Analysis
- KORSTANJE, A. P., Operational Research
- MARTÍNEZ, E., Systems Evaluation
- PASTORINO, M. I., Numerical Methods
- TRAJTENBERG, J. O., Introduction to Data Processing

Faculty of Economics:
- ALEGRE, J. C., Bankruptcy Law
- BRAVO, W., Auditing
- CHAYA, H. N., Administration and Personnel
- CORONEL, J. C., Budgeting
- FERRERO DE AZAR, A. M., Company Law
- MARIGLIANO, M., Business Organization
- MARTELEUR, R., Introduction to Economics
- MORELLINI, P. A., Accounting, Budget Sheet Analysis
- OSTENGO, H., Accounting
- PASTORINO, M. I., Statistics
- TERUEL, R., General Administration

Faculty of Education:
- CASTIGLIONE, J. C., Theology
- GELID, T., General Sociology and Sociology of Education
- MUHN, G., Vocational Orientation
- RIERA DE LUCENA, E., Philosophical Anthropology, Basic Epistemology
- SGOIFO, M. DEL V., Psychology

Faculty of Politics, Social Sciences and Law:
- ALEGRE, J. C., Agricultural and Mining Law
- ARGAÑARAZ ORGAZ, C., Administrative Law
- ARGUELLO, L. R., Roman Law
- ARNEDO, E., Private International Law
- AUAD, A., Social Philosophy
- BENEVOLE DE GAUNA, T., Legal Consultation
- BONACINA, R. A., Introduction to Economics
- BRIZUELA, N., General and Social Psychology
- BRUNELLO DE ZURITA, A., Civil Law
- CASTIGLIONE, J. C., Philosophy of Law
- CERRO, F. E., Theory of the State
- CHRISTENSEN, E., Finance and Financial Law
- HARO DE SURIAN, E., Economic Geography
- LEDESMA, A. E., Civil and Penal Procedural Law
- NAVARRO, J. V., Penal Law
- PAZ, G. M., Civil Law
- PAZ, M. J., Commercial Law
- RETAMOSA, J. R., History of Ideas and Political Institutions, History of the World, History of Argentina
- RIGOURD, C., Public Law
- RIMINI, J. C., Commercial Law
- SALERA, J. B., Sociology
- VICTORIA, M. A., Agricultural and Mining Law
- ZURITA DE GONZÁLEZ, M., Civil Law

UNIVERSIDAD DE CONCEPCIÓN DEL URUGUAY

8 de Junio 522, 3260 Concepción del Uruguay, Entre Ríos
Telephone: (3442) 42-5606
Fax: (3442) 42-7721
Internet: www.ucu.edu.ar
Founded 1971
Private control
Academic year: February to December
Rector: Dr ROBERTO PERINOTTO
Vice-Rector: JULIO CESAR VEGA
Chief Administrative Officer: BEATRIZ MERELLO
Chief Librarian: Prof. ROSA MURILLO DE ROUSSEAUX
Library of 4,300 vols
Number of teachers: 222
Number of students: 850
Publication: *Ucurrencias*

DEANS

Faculty of Agronomy: Ing. CARMEN BLÁZQUEZ
Faculty of Architecture: Arq. CRISTINA BONUS
Faculty of Economics: Cr. MARCELO GRANILLO

UNIVERSIDAD DE LA MARINA MERCANTE (University of the Merchant Navy)

Avda Rivadavia 2258, C1034ACO Capital Federal
Telephone: (11) 4953-9000
Fax: (11) 4953-9000
E-mail: informes@udemm.edu.ar
Internet: www.udemm.edu.ar
Founded 1974
Private control
Academic year: March to December
President: Ing. GUSTAVO ZOPATTI
Rector: Dr NORBERTO E. FRAGA
General Secretary: Ing. LUIS E. FRANCHI
Administrative Secretary: Dr DANTE STERRANTINO
Number of teachers: 283
Number of students: 2,035

DEANS

Faculty of Administration and Economics: Lic. MIRKO EDGARDO MAYER
Faculty of Engineering: Ing. NELSON NOZIGLIA
Faculty of Human and Social Sciences: Lic. SYLVIA FABIÁN DE ETKIN

UNIVERSIDAD DE MENDOZA

Avda Boulogne-sur-Mer 683, 5500 Mendoza
Telephone: (261) 420-2017
Fax: (261) 420-1100
E-mail: unimen@um.edu.ar
Internet: www.um.edu.ar
Founded 1960
Language of instruction: Spanish
Academic year: March to November
Rector: Dr JUAN C. MENGHINI
Vice-Rectors: Dr Ing. SATURNINO LEGUIZAMÓN, Arq. RICARDO PEROTTI
Administrative Officer: Cont. ROSA CELESTE
Number of teachers: 785
Number of students: 4,600
Publications: *Idearium*, *Ideas*, *Revista*

DEANS

Faculty of Architecture and Town Planning: Arq. RICARDO BEKERMAN
Faculty of Engineering: Dr Ing. SALVADOR NAVARRÍA
Faculty of Health Sciences: Dr JUAN CARLOS BEHLER
Faculty of Law and Social Sciences: Dr EMILIO VÁZQUEZ VIERA

DIRECTORS

Centre of Higher Research: Dr JUAN C. MENGHINI
Department of Evaluation: Arq. CRISTINA INZIRILLO
Department of Scientific Research: Dr Ing. SATURNINO LEGUIZAMÓN
Department of Technology: Ing. DIEGO NAVARRO
Institute of Architectural Technology: Arq. RICARDO BEKERMAN
Institute of Architectural and Urban Culture: Arq. ELIANA BORMIDA
Institute of Design: Dr AURELIO ALVAREZ CAMPI
Institute of Energy: Ing. RUTH GRAVINA
Institute of Environmental, Urban and Regional Research: Arq. RAÚL AMPRIMO
Institute of Informatics: Arq. OSCAR GARCÍA VILA
Institute of Natural Sciences: Prof. RUTH LEITON
Institute of Practical Philosophy: Dr NOLBERTO ESPINOSA
Institute of Private Law: Dra CATALINA A. DERONCHIETTO
Institute of Public Law: (vacant)
Institute of Social Housing: Arq. ALFREDO MÉNDEZ
Institute of Telecommunications: Ing. JORGE MARTÍNEZ
Institute of Virtual Technology: Lic. DANIEL LILLO

UNIVERSIDAD DE MORÓN

Cabildo 134, B1708JPD Morón, Buenos Aires
Telephone: (11) 5627-2000
Fax: (11) 5627-4598
E-mail: postmaster@unimoron.edu.ar
Internet: www.unimoron.edu.ar
Founded 1960

Private control
Academic year: March to December
Rector: Dr Mario Armando Mena
Vice-Rector in charge of Presidency: Ing. Agr. Jorge Raúl Ottone
Secretaries: Dr Eduardo Néstor Cozza (Academic and Research), Dr Jorge Eduardo Marcos (Administrative), Dr José Maria Baños (General)
Library Director: Dr Graciela Susana Puente
Library of 40,000 vols
Number of teachers: 2,000
Number of students: 14,000
Publication: *UM Saber* (2 a month)

DEANS AND DIRECTORS
Faculty of Agronomy and Food Sciences: Ing. Agr. Antonio Angrisani
Faculty of Architecture, Design, Art and Urban Planning: Arq. Oscar Anibal Borrachia
Faculty of Computer Sciences, Communication Sciences and Special Technology: Ing. Hugo René Padovani
Faculty of Economic and Business Sciences: Dr Jorge Raúl Lemos
Faculty of Engineering: Dr Ing. Ezequiel Pallejá
Faculty of Exact, Chemical and Natural Sciences: Dr Aquiles Carlos Ferranti
Faculty of Law, Political and Social Sciences: Dr Héctor Norberto Porto Lemma
Faculty of Medicine: Dr Domingo Santos Liotta
Faculty of Philosophy, Education and Humanities: Dr Roberto Mario Paterno
Faculty of Sciences applied to Tourism and Population: Lic. Alejandro Gavric
High School of Social Services: Lic. María Cristina Devita

UNIVERSIDAD DEL MUSEO SOCIAL ARGENTINO
(University of the Argentine Museum of Sociology)

Avda Corrientes 1723, 1042 Buenos Aires
Telephone: (11) 4375-4601
Fax: (11) 4375-4600
Internet: www.umsa.edu.ar
Founded 1912
Rector: Dr Guillermo E. Garbarini Islas
Librarian: Lic. Gabriel Medina Ernst

DEANS
Faculty of Human Recovery Sciences: Lic. Estela Salazar
Faculty of Information and Opinion Science: Lic. Adriana Adamo
Faculty of Political, Juridical and Economic Sciences: Dr Luis J. Zaballa
Faculty of Social Services: Dr Gustavo Pinard
School of Economics: Cont. Elba Font de Malugani
University School of Translation: Lic. Alicia Bermolen
Institute of Political Sciences: Dra Marta Biagi
Institute of Professional Training: Lic. Maria E. Pellanda

UNIVERSIDAD DEL NORTE SANTO TOMÁS DE AQUINO

9 de Julio 165, T4000IHC San Miguel de Tucumán
Telephone: (381) 430-0698
Fax: (381) 422-4494
E-mail: info@unsta.edu.ar
Internet: www.unsta.edu.ar
Founded 1965
Academic year: March to November
Grand Chancellor: Fr Javier Pose
Rector: Dr Pedro Wenceslao Lobo
Vice-Rector: Ing. Juan Carlos Muzzo
General Secretary: Ing. Juan A. Balzaretti
Academic Secretary: Lic. Jorge Abatte
Director of the Library: Lilian Gartner
Number of teachers: 700
Number of students: 5,000

DEANS
Faculty of Economics and Administration: Cont. Efraín David
Faculty of Engineering: Ing. Raul Alcaide
Faculty of Humanities: Lic. Francisco Torres Nieto
Faculty of Law and Political Sciences: Dra Gilda Pedicone de Valls
Faculty of Philosophy: Fr Jorge Scampini
Faculty of Psychology and Health Sciences: Dr Gustavo Marangoni
School of Education: Profa Ana M. Barbado de Fiorito (Dir)
Department of Humanistic-Christian Training: Fr Carlos María Izaguirre (Dir)

ATTACHED INSTITUTES
Historical Research Institute 'Prof. Manuel García Soriano': Dir Fr Rubén González.
Institutional Studies Centre: Defensa 422, 1065 Buenos Aires; Dean Fr Jorge Scampini.
University Centre in Concepción: Pres. Julio A. Roca 32, 4146 Concepción, Tucumán; General Co-ordinator Arq. Eduardo E. Kern.

UNIVERSIDAD NOTARIAL ARGENTINA
(Argentine University for Lawyers)

Avda 51 No. 435, 1900 La Plata
Telephone: (221) 421-9283
Fax: (221) 421-0552
E-mail: uninotlp@universidadnotarial.edu.ar
Founded 1964
Academic year: March to November
Chancellor: Not. Jorge F. Dumon
Rector: Néstor O. Pérez Lozano
Vice-Rector: Dr Oscar E. Sarubo
General Director: Prof. Alicia Palaia
Librarian: Dra Dora C. Tálice de Seco Villalba
Number of teachers: 150
Number of students: 2,300
Publication: *Cuadernos Notariales*.

UNIVERSIDAD DEL SALVADOR
(University of the Saviour)

Viamonte 1856, 1056 Buenos Aires
Telephone: (11) 4813-9630
Internet: www.salvador.edu.ar
Founded 1956
Academic year: January to December
Rector: Lic. Juan Alejandro Tobias
Academic Vice-Rector: Lic. Javier Alonso Hidalgo
Vice-Rector (Economics): Dr Enrique A. Betta
Vice-Rector (Religious Training): Lic. Juan Alejandro Tobias (acting)
Vice-Rector (Research and Development): Dr Fernando Lucero Schmidt
Secretary-General: Prof. Pablo Gabriel Varela
Librarian: Lic. Laura Martino
Library: see under Libraries and Archives
Number of teachers: 2,800
Number of students: 16,500
Publications: *Anales*, *Bulletin of Number Theory and Related Topics*, *Signos*

DEANS
Faculty of Administration: Ing. Aquilino López Diez
Faculty of Economics: Dr Sergio García
Faculty of Educational Sciences and Social Communication: Dr Gustavo Martínez Pandianj
Faculty of Law: Dr Práxedes Sagasta
Faculty of Medicine: Dr Adolfo Lizarraga
Faculty of Philosophy, History and Arts: Dr Juan Carlos Lucero Schmidt
Faculty of Psychology and Psychopedagogy: Lic. Bernardo Béguet
Faculty of Science and Technology: Ing. Miguel Guerrero
Faculty of Social Sciences: Lic. Eduardo Suárez

DIRECTORS
School of Oriental Studies: Prof. Luisa Rosell
School of Theatre Arts: Prof. Alice D. de Beitía

National University-Level Institutions

INSTITUTO DE ENSEÑANZA SUPERIOR DEL EJÉRCITO
(Institute of Higher Military Education)

Avda Cabildo 65, 1426 Buenos Aires
Telephone: (11) 4576-5648
E-mail: dieseext@iese.edu.ar
Internet: www.iese.edu.ar
Founded 1990
State control
Director: Gen. de Bgda Dr Luis Eduardo Pierri
Vice-Rector: Col Miguel Angel Podestá
Secretary-General: Lt-Col Dr Victorio Cándido Fontana
Secretary (Academic): Col Dr Julio Horacio Bergallo
Secretary (Evaluation): Col Dr Hector Eduardo Gallardo
Secretary (University Extension): Col Dr Alejandro Alberto Diaz Bessone
Departments of Modern Languages, Information Technology and Distance Learning.

CONSTITUENT SCHOOLS
Colegio Militar de la Nación: Avda Matienzo y Ruta 201, 1684 El Palomar, Buenos Aires; tel. (11) 4751-8001; fax (11) 4751-0767; e-mail ingresocmn@ejercito.mil.ar; internet www.colegiomilitar.mil.arf. 1869.
Escuela Superior de Guerra: Avda Luis María Campos 480, 1426 Buenos Aires; tel. (11) 4576-5689; fax (11) 4576-5692; e-mail esg@iese.edu.ar; internet www.escuelasuperiordeguerra.iese.edu.arf. 1900; library: library of 30,000 vols, 44 periodicals; Dir Col Raúl Alberto Aparicio; publ. *La Revista* (quarterly).
Escuela Superior Técnica: Avda Cabildo 15, 1426 Buenos Aires, Capital Federal; tel. (11) 4576-5555; fax (11) 4576-5681; e-mail estextuniv@iese.edu.ar; internet www.ingenieriaest.iese.edu.arf. 1930; library: library of 30,000 vols, 100 periodicals; Dir Col Jorge Gómez; publ. *Ingeniería Militar*.

INSTITUTO UNIVERSITARIO AERONÁUTICO

Avda Fuerza Aérea 6500, 5022 Córdoba
Telephone: (351) 568-8800
Fax: (351) 466-1562

E-mail: informes@iua.edu.ar
Internet: www.iua.edu.ar
Founded 1947; integrated into National University System 1971
State control
Language of instruction: Spanish
Academic year: February to December
Rector: Brig. Ing. HÉCTOR EDUARDO RÉ
Vice-Rector (Academic): Cmdr Ing. MIGUEL ANGEL LLABRES
Vice-Rector (Planning): Brig. Ing. ROBERTO ANÍBAL GÓMEZ
Secretary-General: Ing. PEDRO EMILIO MURILLO
Library of 10,000 vols
Associated academic units: Escuela de Aviación Militar; Escuela Superior de Guerra Aérea; Instituto Nacional de Derecho Aeronáutico y Espacial; Escuela de Defensa Electrónica; Liceo Aeronáutico Militar; Escuela de Suboficiales de la Fuerza Aérea; Centro de Instrucción, Perfeccionamiento y Experimentación; Instituto de Formación Ezeiza; Instituto Nacional de Aviación Civil; Unidad de Educación a Distancia en el Exterior; Escuela de Ciencias de la Salud.

DEANS
Faculty of Administration: Brig. Ing. ROBERTO ANÍBAL GÓMEZ
Faculty of Engineering: Brig. Ing. FERNANDO ANÍBAL ÁLVAREZ

ATTACHED RESEARCH INSTITUTES
Centro de Investigaciones Aplicadas: Dir Vice-Cmdr Ing. JORGE MUÑOZ.

INSTITUTO UNIVERSITARIO DE LA POLICÍA FEDERAL ARGENTINA

Rosario 532, 1424 Buenos Aires, Capital Federal
Telephone: (11) 4901-9783
Fax: (11) 4901-9783
E-mail: academica@universidad-policial.edu.ar
Internet: www.universidad-policial.edu.ar
Founded 1974 as Academia Federal de Estudios Policiales; current name and status since 1995
State control
Academic year: March to December (two semesters)
Rector: Dr LUIS MARÍA DESIMONI
Vice-Rector: Lic. CARLOS DANIEL MUSSO
Secretary (Academic): Dr HUGO ALBERTO MÉNDEZ
Secretary (Administration): Com. Gen. ANGEL JUAN ANTONIO RAMÍREZ
Library of 20,500 vols
Number of students: 3,200
Publication: *Editorial Policial*

DEANS
Faculty of Biomedical Sciences: Dr ENRIQUE LAFRENZ
Faculty of Criminal Sciences: Lic. NORBERTO ANTONIO SANCHEZ
Faculty of Law and Social Sciences: Dr HORACIO TOMAS ARACAMA
Faculty of Security Sciences: Gen. ROBERTO CÉSAR ROSSET

INSTITUTO UNIVERSITARIO DE SEGURIDAD MARÍTIMA

Avda Eduardo Madero 235, 1106 Buenos Aires, Capital Federal
Telephone: (11) 4314-2434
E-mail: arl@arnet.com.ar
Internet: www.prefecturanaval.edu.ar/iupna
Founded 2002
Rector: Prefecto Gen. OSVALDO DANIEL TOURN
Secretary (Academic): Lic. AMALIA INÉS VILLALUSTRE.

INSTITUTO UNIVERSITARIO NACIONAL DEL ARTE

Paraguay 786, 1057 Buenos Aires, Capital Federal
Telephone: (11) 4516-0992
Fax: (11) 4516-0992
Internet: www.iuna.edu.ar
Founded 1996
State control
Rector: Lic. RAÚL OSVALDO MONETA
Secretary-General: Prof. ROBERTO DE ROSE
Publication: *Boletín*

HEADS OF DEPARTMENTS
Audiovisual Arts: ALFREDO BENAVÍDEZ BEDOYA
Criticism of Art: Dr OSCAR TRAVERSA
Dramatic Arts: Prof. LILIANA SILVIA DEMAIO
Folklore: Prof. AZUCENA COLATARCI
Moving Arts: Prof. SILVIA CÉSAR
Multimedia: Prof. MARCELO SAITTA
Music: Prof. JULIO GARCIA CÁNEPA
Teacher Training: Prof. SUSANA SILVIA VEGA
Visual Arts: Prof. RODOLFO AGÜERO

INSTITUTO UNIVERSITARIO NAVAL

Avda del Libertador 8209, 1429 Buenos Aires, Capital Federal
Telephone: (11) 4704-8200
Fax: (11) 4704-8261
E-mail: administra@inun.edu.ar
Internet: www.inun.edu.ar
Founded 1978 as Instituto Universitario de Estudios Navales y Martimes; current name and status 1991
Controlled by the Armada Argentina (Argentine Navy)
Rector: Ing. JULIO MARCELO PÉREZ
Secretary (Academic): Lic. JULIO E. GROSSO

DIRECTORS
School of Marine Sciences: DANIEL HINDRYCKX
School of Military Naval Studies: CARLOS LUIS MAZZONI
School of Nautical Science: ARMANDO GROSO
School of Navy Officer Studies: EDUARDO OSCAR GUELFO
School of Navy Warfare: PEDRO LUIS DE LA FUENTE

Provincial University

UNIVERSIDAD AUTÓNOMA DE ENTRE RÍOS

Avda Ramírez 1143, 3100 Paraná, Entre Ríos
Telephone: (343) 420-7908
E-mail: rectorado@uader.edu.ar
Internet: www.uader.edu.ar
Independent control
Rector: Cr MARIO MATHIEU
Secretary (Academic): Prof. ROBERTO FARIÑA.

Colleges

Escuela Nacional de Bibliotecarios: Agüero 2502, 1425 Buenos Aires; tel. (11) 4808-6095; fax (11) 4863-8805; e-mail escuelabib@red.bibnal.edu.ar; internet www.bibnal.edu.ar/paginas/escuelabib.htm; f. 1956; 15 teachers; Rector Prof. JOSÉ EDMUNDO CLEMENTE.

Escuela Nacional de Educación Técnica 'Gral Ing. Enrique Mosconi': Calle Schreiber 892 Cutralco, 8318 Plaza Huincul, Neuquén; tel. (299) 46-3288; f. 1953; specializes in mechanical and petroleum engineering; 600 students; Dir Ing. ARMANDO PARIS.

Instituto Tecnológico de Buenos Aires: Avda Eduardo Madero 399, 1106 Buenos Aires; tel. (11) 4314-7778; fax (11) 4314-0270; e-mail postmaster@itba.edu.ar; internet www.itba.edu.ar; f. 1959; private; library: 16,010 books; 350 teachers; 2,010 students; Rector Almirante Dr ENRIQUE E. MOLINA PICO; publs *Revista del Instituto Tecnológico de Buenos Aires*, *Boletín General*, *Acontecer*.

Schools of Art and Music

Conservatorio Municipal de Música 'Manuel de Falla': Sarmiento 1551, 1042 C.P., Buenos Aires; tel. (11) 4371-5898; f. 1919; 3,000 mems; library: library of 8,000 scores and vols; Dir AUGUSTO B. RATTENBACH.

Escuela Nacional de Arte Dramático (National School of Drama): French 3614, 1425 Buenos Aires; tel. (11) 4804-7970; f. 1924; 300 students; library: 4,200 vols; Rector CARLOS ALBARENGA.

Escuela Nacional de Bellas Artes 'Prilidiano Pueyrredón': Las Heras 1749, 1018 Buenos Aires; tel. (11) 442-0657; f. 1878; depts of painting, engraving and sculpture; library: 5,923 vols; 373 students; Dir DOMINGO MAZZONE.

Escuela Nacional de Danzas: Esmeralda 285, 1035 Buenos Aires; tel. (11) 445-5478; Rector Prof. GLADYS S. DE MUTTER.

Escuela Superior de Bellas Artes 'Ernesto de la Cárcova': Tristán Achaval Rodríguez 1701, 1107 Buenos Aires; tel. (11) 4361-5144; f. 1923; painting, sculpture, engraving and décors; museum of tracings; library: 4,500 vols; Rector Prof. EDUARDO A. AUDIVERT.

ARMENIA

The Higher Education System

The oldest university in Armenia is the Yerevan State University, which was founded in 1919. Most institutions of higher education were founded while Armenia was a full Union Republic of the Union of Soviet Socialist Republics (USSR). Armenia declared independence from the USSR in 1991. Higher education is overseen by the Ministry of Education and Science, and is governed by the constitution (1995), which states that all citizens have the right to receive an education, and by the Law on Education (1999) which outlines the system's structure. In 2000 the National Assembly approved the State Programme for Education Sector Development 2001–2005, which outlined a five-year programme of reforms aimed at rationalizing and modernizing the entire education system. In 2002 the Law on Higher and Postgraduate Professional Education (2002) was passed, outlining the reforms to prepare Armenia for the Bologna process.

To enter higher education students must hold the Mijnakarg Yndhanur Krtoutian Attestat (Certificate of Completed Secondary Education) and pass at least one university entrance examination one month after their high school examinations, depending upon their intended area of study. However, as part of higher education reforms, an independent body is to be established to administer university entrance examinations in place of the ministry.

There are three levels of higher education degrees in Armenia, one undergraduate and two postgraduate. The main undergraduate degree is the Bakalavr (Bachelors), which is usually a four-year programme. The Specialist Diploma, meanwhile, is a Soviet-style degree, which lasts for five years and is offered at professional institutions. The first postgraduate degree is the Magistros (Masters), a one- or two-year course, admission to which is by examination. The second and final level of postgraduate education is the Aspirantura (Doctorate), which is split into two stages: the Candidate of Science and the Doctor of Science. The first stage lasts for two years and consists of taught and research components, while the second stage is purely research and necessary only for those who wish to pursue a career in higher education.

The first level of non-university technical and vocational education is Preliminary Professional (Vocational) Education and is open to holders of the Himnakan Yndhanur Krtutyan Attestat (Certificate of Basic Education) or the Certificate of Completed Secondary Education. Courses run for between one and three years. The second level of technical and vocational education is known as Middle Level Professional (Vocational) Education and is open to holders of the Certificate of Completed Secondary Education. The principal aim is to train specialists in fields such as the arts, finance, health, the humanities, pedagogy and technology. Training may last between two and five years. Upon qualification students gain the title Junior Specialist. There are also two levels of teacher-training: Junior Specialist for primary and basic school teaching; and Bachelors or Specialist Diploma for secondary school teaching.

The Licensing and Accreditation Service, founded in 2000 as a separate unit under the aegis of the Ministry of Education and Science, is responsible for the licensing and accreditation of all public and private institutions under the terms of the Law on Education (1999). The final decision on the licensing and accreditation of an institution, however, lies with Minister of Education and Science for approval. In 2004/05 total enrolment in higher schools (including universities) was 62,500 students; 41,500 students were enrolled at universities.

Learned Societies

GENERAL

National Academy of Sciences of Armenia: 0019 Yerevan, Marshal Baghramyan Ave 24; tel. (10) 52-70-31; fax (10) 56-92-81; e-mail academy@sci.am; internet www.sci.am; f. 1943; depts of Physical, Mathematical and Technological Sciences, Natural Sciences, Humanities; research institutes attached to depts: see Research Institutes; 119 mems; Pres. F. T. Sargasian; Acad.-Sec. and Vice-Pres. V. B. Barkhudarian; publs *Doklady* (Reports), *Izvestiya* (Bulletins: Mathematics, Mechanics, Physics, Engineering Sciences, Earth Sciences), *Astrofizika* (Astrophysics), *Neirokhimiya* (Neurochemistry), *Khimicheskii Zhurnal Armenii* (Chemical Journal of Armenia), *Biologicheskii Zhurnal Armenii* (Biological Journal of Armenia), *Vestnik Obshchestvennykh Nauk* (Herald of Social Sciences), *Meditsinskaya Nauka Armenii* (Medical Science of Armenia), *Vestnik Khirurgii Armenii* (Herald of Armenian Surgery), *Istoriko-Filologicheskii Zhurnal* (Historical and Philological Journal), *Soobshcheniya Byurakanskoi Observatorii* (Reports of the Byurakan Astrophysical Observatory).

LANGUAGE AND LITERATURE

Alliance Française: 0010 Yerevan, ul. Aigestan 74; tel. and fax (10) 52-04-01; e-mail alliancefr_arm@hotmail.com; offers courses and examinations in French language and culture and promotes cultural exchange with France.

British Council: 0019 Yerevan, Baghramian Ave 24; tel. (10) 56-99-23; fax (10) 56-99-29; e-mail info@britishcouncil.am; internet www2.britishcouncil.org/armenia.htm; offers courses and examinations in English language and British culture and promotes cultural exchange with the UK; Dir Roger Budd.

Research Institutes

GENERAL

Institute of the Arts: 0019 Yerevan, Pr. Marshala Bagramyana 24G; tel. (10) 58-37-02; fax (10) 52-83-18; e-mail instart@sci.am; f. 1958; attached to Armenian Nat. Acad. of Sciences; depts of Architecture, Fine Arts, Music, Folk Arts, Theatre and Cinema; Dir A. Aghasyan.

AGRICULTURE, FISHERIES AND VETERINARY SCIENCE

Institute of Hydroponics Problems: 0082 Yerevan, Noragyugh 108; tel. (10) 56-51-62; fax (10) 56-55-90; e-mail hydrop@netsys.am; internet www.sci.am; f. 1947; attached to Armenian Nat. Acad. of Sciences; devt of basic science and technology for hydroponic cultivation of valuable, rare and endangered medicinal, aromatic and dye-bearing plants, trees and shrubs; 47 mems; library of 9,200 vols; Dir Khachatur Mairapetyan; publ. *Communications of IHP* (every 3 years).

Scientific Center of Agriculture and Plant Protection: 1110 Echmiadzin, Armavir Marz, St Isy le Moulino St 1; tel. (23) 15-34-54; attached to Min. of Agriculture; 143 staff, 6 depts, 11 laboratories; Dir H. Hovsepian.

ECONOMICS, LAW AND POLITICS

Armenian Center for National and International Studies: 0033 Yerevan, Yerznkian St 75; tel. (10) 52-87-80; fax (10) 52-48-46; e-mail root@acnis.am; internet www.acnis.am; f. 1994 to research issues of public policy, civic education, foreign relations, conflict resolution and the global environment; Pres. R. K. Hovannisian; publ. *Hayatsk Yerevanits* (monthly).

Institute of Economics: 0001 Yerevan, ul. Abovyana 15; tel. (10) 58-19-71; fax (10) 56-92-81; e-mail nas_ie@sci.am; f. 1955; attached to Armenian Nat. Acad. of Sciences; Dir V. E. Khojabekyan.

HISTORY, GEOGRAPHY AND ARCHAEOLOGY

Institute–Museum of Genocide: 0028 Yerevan, Tsitsernakaberd; tel. (10) 39-09-81; e-mail lbars@sci.am; f. 1995; attached to Armenian Nat. Acad. of Sciences; Dir L. A. Barseghyan.

Institute of Archaeology and Ethnography: 0025 Yerevan, Charents 15; tel. and fax (10) 55-68-96; e-mail setako@arminco.com; f.

1959; attached to Armenian Nat. Acad. of Sciences; library of 15,000 vols; Dir A. A. Kalantaryan.

Institute of History: 0019 Yerevan, Pr. Marshala Bagramyana 24G; tel. (10) 52-92-63; fax (10) 56-92-81; e-mail history@sci.am; f. 1943; attached to Armenian Nat. Acad. of Sciences; Dir A. Melkonyan.

Institute of Oriental Studies: 0019 Yerevan, Pr. Marshala Bagramyana 24G; tel. (10) 58-33-82; fax (10) 50-50-75; e-mail armarev@sci.am; f. 1971; attached to Armenian Nat. Acad. of Sciences; Dir N. O. Hovhanesyan.

Shirak Armenological Study Center: 3100 Gyumri, Ankakhutyan Sq. 1; tel. (31) 13-31-73; fax (31) 56-92-81; e-mail academy@sci.am; f. 1997; attached to Armenian Nat. Acad. of Sciences; Dir S. Hayrapetyan.

LANGUAGE AND LITERATURE

Abegyan Institute of Literature: 0015 Yerevan, ul. Grikora Lusavoricha 15; tel. and fax (10) 56-32-54; e-mail lit.inst@best.am; f. 1943; attached to Armenian Nat. Acad. of Sciences; Dir A. K. Eghiazaryan.

Atcharian Institute of Linguistics: 0001 Yerevan, ul. Abovyana 15; tel. (10) 56-53-37; fax (10) 56-92-81; e-mail inslang@sci.am; f. 1943; attached to Armenian Nat. Acad. of Sciences; Dir G. B. Djaukyan.

MEDICINE

Armenian Institute of Spa Treatment and Physiotherapy: 0028 Yerevan, ul. Bratev Orbeli 41,; e-mail libspa@medlib.am; internet www.medlib.am/spa; f. 1930; library of 30,000 vols; Dir Prof. G. Agadjanian.

Armenian Research Centre of Maternal and Child Health Care: 0002 Yerevan, Mesrop Mashtots Ave 22; tel. (10) 53-01-72; fax (10) 53-01-92; e-mail info@armobgyn.com; internet www.armobgyn.com; f. 1931; library of 25,000 vols; Dir Prof. G. Okoyev.

Center of Medical Genetics: 0010 Yerevan, Zakyan St 5/1; tel. (10) 54-43-67; fax (10) 56-92-81; e-mail tamsar@sci.am; f. 1999; attached to Armenian Nat. Acad. of Sciences; Dir Dr T. F. Sargsian.

Center of Traumatology, Orthopaedics, Burns and Radiology: 0047 Yerevan, Marash 9th St; tel. (10) 65-00-40; fax (10) 65-30-40; e-mail aav@arm.r.am; internet www.ctooir.narod.ru; f. 1945; fmrly Yerevan Scientific Research Institute of Orthopaedics and Traumatology; functioning depts: acute trauma, polytrauma, post-traumatic complications, infection complication, bone pathology, adult orthopaedics, paediatric orthopaedics, morphology, experimental biology; research departments: bone defect reconstruction, joint replacement, vertebral surgery, bone matrix preparation, bone tumour surgery, complex burns treatment; 28 mems; Dir Aivazyan Vachagan; publ. *Abstracts of Annual Congress of Traumatologists & Orthopaedic Surgeons of Armenia* (annual).

Mikaelian Research Institute of Surgery: Yerevan, Hasratyan 9; tel. (10) 28-19-90; fax (10) 28-22-22; e-mail surgery@netsys.am; f. 1974; library of 5,000 vols; Dir H. S. Tamazian.

Research Centre for Epidemiology, Virology and Medical Parasitology: 0009 Yerevan, ul. Gevorga Kochara 21A; tel. (10) 56-21-02; Dir Yu. T. Aleksanyan.

NATURAL SCIENCES

Biological Sciences

Buniatian, H., Institute of Biochemistry: 0014 Yerevan, ul. Paruyra Sevaga 5/1; tel. (10) 28-18-40; fax (10) 28-19-51; e-mail galoyan@sci.am; f. 1961; attached to Armenian Nat. Acad. of Sciences; Dir A. A. Galoyan; publ. *Neurokhimija* (quarterly).

Centre for Ecological-Noosphere Studies: 0025 Yerevan, Abovian 68; tel. (10) 56-93-31; fax (10) 58-02-54; e-mail ecocentr@sci.am; internet www.ecocentre.am; f. 1989; attached to Armenian Nat. Acad. of Sciences; Dir A. K. Saghatelyan.

Institute of Botany: 0063 Yerevan, Avan; tel. (10) 62-17-81; fax (10) 56-92-81; e-mail academy@sci.am; f. 1939; attached to Armenian Nat. Acad. of Sciences; Dir A. A. Charchoglyan.

Institute of Microbiology: 2210 Abovian; tel. (222) 2-16-22; fax (222) 2-16-23; e-mail microbio@sci.am; f. 1961; attached to Armenian Nat. Acad. of Sciences; library of 5,000 vols; Dir J. I. Akopian.

Institute of Molecular Biology: 0014 Yerevan, Hasratyan 7; tel. (10) 28-16-26; fax (10) 28-26-22; e-mail konstant@mb.sci.am; f. 1966; attached to Armenian Nat. Acad. of Sciences; Dir K. G. Karageuzyan.

Institute of Zoology: 0044 Yerevan, ul. Paruyra Sevaka 7; tel. (10) 28-14-70; fax (10) 28-13-60; e-mail zool@sci.am; f. 1943; attached to Armenian Nat. Acad. of Sciences; Dir S. H. Movsesian.

Orbeli Institute of Physiology: 0028 Yerevan, ul. Bratev Orbeli 22; tel. and fax (10) 27-22-47; e-mail vvfanardjian@neuroscience.am; f. 1943; attached to Armenian Nat. Acad. of Sciences; library of 4,000 vols, 25,000 periodicals; Dir V. V. Fanardjian.

Sevan Institute of Hydroecology and Ichthyology: 1510 Sevan, ul. Kirova 186; tel. (10) 56-85-54; fax (10) 56-94-11; e-mail rhovan@sci.am; f. 1923; attached to Armenian Nat. Acad. of Sciences; Dir R. Hovhannisyan.

State Microbial Depository Centre: 2210 Abovian; tel. and fax (222) 2-32-40; e-mail microbio@sci.am; f. 1993; attached to Armenian Nat. Acad. of Sciences; Dir E. G. Afrikian.

Mathematical Sciences

Institute of Mathematics: 0019 Yerevan, Pr. Marshala Bagramyana 24B; tel. (10) 52-47-91; fax (10) 52-48-01; e-mail arakelian@instmath.sci.am; internet math.sci.am; f. 1971; 30 mems; attached to Armenian Nat. Acad. of Sciences; Dir Norair U. Arakelian; Scientific Sec. Bagrat T. Batikyan; publ. *Journal of Contemporary Mathematical Analysis* (6 a year).

Physical Sciences

Byurakan Astrophysical Observatory: 0213 Byurakan, Ashtarak raion; tel. (10) 24-85-75; fax (10) 56-92-81; e-mail ekhach@bao.sci.am; internet www.sci.am/ac/bao.html; f. 1946; attached to Armenian Nat. Acad. of Sciences; Dir E. Khachikian.

Garni Geophysical Observatory: 0019 Yerevan, Pr. Marshal Baghramyana 24A; tel. (10) 27-95-39; fax (10) 56-92-81; e-mail hakhleon@sci.am; f. 1982; attached to Armenian Nat. Acad. of Sciences; Dir L. A. Hakhverdyan.

Garni Space Astronomy Institute: 2215 Garni, Kotayk; tel. (10) 64-90-01; fax (10) 56-92-81; e-mail gurzad@arminco.com; f. 1982; attached to Armenian Nat. Acad. of Sciences; Dir G. A. Gurzadyan.

Institute of Chemical Physics: 0004 Yerevan, ul. Paruyra Sevaka 5/2; tel. (10) 28-16-41; fax (10) 28-17-42; e-mail adolph@ichph.sci.am; internet chph.sci.am; f. 1975; attached to Armenian Nat. Acad. of Sciences; Dir Prof. A. A. Mantashyan.

Institute of Fine Organic Chemistry: 0014 Yerevan, Pr. Azatutyana 26; tel. (10) 28-83-34; fax (10) 28-83-32; e-mail ifoc@msrc.am; f. 1955; attached to Armenian Nat. Acad. of Sciences; Dir B. T. Gharibjanian.

Institute of General and Inorganic Chemistry: 0051 Yerevan, ul. Fioletova 11110; tel. (10) 23-07-38; fax (10) 23-12-75; f. 1957; attached to Armenian Nat. Acad. of Sciences; Dir S. S. Karakhanian.

Institute of Geology: 0019 Yerevan, Pr. Marshala Bagramyana 24A; tel. (10) 52-44-26; fax (10) 56-80-72; e-mail hrshah@sci.am; f. 1935; attached to Armenian Nat. Acad. of Sciences; Dir R. T. Jrbashian.

Institute of Geophysics and Engineering Seismology: 3115 Gjumry, Pr. Leningradyana 5; tel. and fax (312) 3-12-61; e-mail as_iges@shirak.am; f. 1961; attached to Armenian Nat. Acad. of Sciences; Dir S. M. Hovhannisyan.

Institute of Organic Chemistry: 0091 Yerevan, ul. Zakaria Kanakertsy 167A; tel. and fax (10) 28-35-21; e-mail mvm@ioc.armenia.su; f. 1935; attached to Armenian Nat. Acad. of Sciences; Dir Sh H. Badanyan.

Research Institute of Radiophysical Measurements: 0014 Yerevan, ul. Komitasa 49/4; tel. (10) 23-49-90; Dir P. M. Geruni.

Yerevan Physics Institute: 0036 Yerevan, ul. Bratev Alikhanyan 2; tel. (10) 34-15-00; fax (10) 35-00-30; e-mail hrachia@jerewqan1.yerphi.am; internet www.yerphi.am; f. 1942; particle and nuclear physics; library of 10,000 vols; Dir H. Asatrian.

PHILOSOPHY AND PSYCHOLOGY

Institute of Philosophy and Law: 0010 Yerevan, ul. Arami 44; tel. (10) 53-05-71; fax (10) 50-59-47; e-mail gevork@sci.am; f. 1969; attached to Armenian Nat. Acad. of Sciences; Dir G. A. Poghoysan.

TECHNOLOGY

Institute for Physical Research: 0210 Ashtarak; tel. (10) 28-81-50; fax (10) 56-92-81; e-mail ifi@ipr.aci.am; f. 1968; attached to Armenian Nat. Acad. of Sciences; Dir Prof. E. S. Vardanyan.

Institute of Applied Problems in Physics: 0014 Yerevan, ul. H. Nersesiana 25; tel. (10) 24-58-96; fax (10) 24-85-75; e-mail malpic@iapp.sci.am; internet www.sci.am/ac/iapp.html; f. 1980; attached to Armenian Nat. Acad. of Sciences; Dir. A. R. Mkrtchyan.

Institute of Mechanics: 0019 Yerevan, Pr. Marshala Bagramyana 24B; tel. (10) 52-48-90; fax (10) 56-81-89; e-mail mechins@sci.am; f. 1955; attached to Armenian Nat. Acad. of Sciences; Dir L. A. Aghalovian.

Institute of Problems in Informatics and Automation: 0014 Yerevan, ul. Paruyra Sevaka 1; tel. and fax (10) 28-58-12; e-mail shouk@sci.am; internet ipia.sci.am; f. 1957; attached to Armenian Nat. Acad. of Sciences; Dir Yu. H. Shoukourian.

Institute of Radiophysics and Electronics: 0210 Ashtarak, ul. Bratev Alikhanyan; tel. (10) 28-78-50; e-mail office@irphe.am; internet www.irphe.am; f. 1960; library of 12,000 vols; attached to Armenian Nat. Acad. of Sciences; Dir R. M. Martirosyam.

Special Experimental Design Technological Institute: 3101 Gjumry, Sarkisyana 5A; tel. (312) 4-56-63; fax (10) 56-92-81; e-mail academy@sci.am; f. 1976; attached to Armenian Nat. Acad. of Sciences; Dir R. Y. Sarkissyan.

Yerevan Automated Control Systems Scientific Research Institute: 0003 Yerevan, ul. A. Akopyana 3; tel. (10) 27-77-79;

internet www.yercsi.am; f. 1992; Dir R. ATOIAN.

Yerevan Computer Research and Development Institute: 0033 Yerevan, Hagop Hagopyan 3; tel. (10) 27-77-79; fax (10) 27-68-52; e-mail ghovhan@ycrdi.am; internet www.ycrdi.am; f. 1956; Dir G. T. HOVHANNISIAN.

Yerevan Telecommunications Research Institute: 0015 Yerevan, Dzorapy 26; tel. (10) 56-60-61; fax (10) 56-17-37; e-mail mark@yetri.am; internet www.yetri.am; f. 1978.

Libraries and Archives

Yerevan

Armenian Centre for Scientific and Technical Information (ACSTI): 0051 Yerevan, Komitas 49/3; tel. (10) 23-67-74; fax (10) 23-80-29; e-mail info@acsti.am; internet www.acsti.am; f. 1961; 22,000,000 vols; Dir S. A. AGHAJANYAN.

Armenian Scientific-Medical Library: Yerevan; tel. (10) 24-96-77; e-mail staff@medlib.am; internet www.medlib.am; attached to Nat. Acad. of Sciences; 500,000 vols, theses, serials, micro-fiche and audio-visual items; Dir A. E. SHIRINIAN.

Fundamental Scientific Library of the National Academy of Sciences of Armenia: 0019 Yerevan, Pr. Marshala Baghramyana 24D; tel. and fax (10) 52-47-50; e-mail nerses@flib.sci.am; internet www.flib.sci.am; f. 1935; 3,000,000 vols; Dir Acad. A. B. NERSESSIAN.

Matenadaran Institute of Ancient Armenian Manuscripts: Yerevan, Mashtots Ave 53; tel. (10) 56-25-78; internet www.matenadaran.am; f. 1959; incorporates research institute of Armenian textology and codicology; 17,000 Armenian MSS dating from 5th–18th centuries, miniature paintings, 100,000 archival documents and works by Greek, Syrian, Persian, Arabic, Latin, Georgian and Ethiopian authors; Dir S. AREVSHATIAN; publ. *Banber Matenadarani*.

National Library of Armenia: 0009 Yerevan, Teryan 72; tel. (10) 58-42-59; fax (10) 52-97-11; e-mail nla@arm.r.am; internet www.nla.am; f. 1919; 6,248,043 vols; Dir DAVIT SARGSYAN.

Yerevan State University Library: 0049 Yerevan, ul. Mravyana 1,; internet www.ysu.am/~library; 1,500,000 vols; Dir V. S. ARSLANIAN.

Museums and Art Galleries

Yerevan

Armenian State Historical Museum: 0010 Yerevan, Republic Sq.; tel. (10) 58-27-61; fax (10) 56-53-22; f. 1919; Archaeological, documentary and other evidence charting the history and culture of Armenia from prehistoric times; Dir ANELKA GRIGORIAN.

Geological Museum of the Institute of Geology: Yerevan, ul. Aboviana 10; tel. (10) 58-06-63; f. 1937; colln mainly from Armenia; Dir G. B. MEZHLUMYAN.

National Gallery of Armenia: 0010 Yerevan, ul. Arami 1; tel. and fax (10) 58-08-12; e-mail gallery@nga.sci.am; internet www.gallery.am; f. 1921; West European, Armenian, Russian and Oriental art; library of 10,330 vols; Dir S. KHATCHATURIAN.

Yegishe Charents State Museum of Literature and Art: Yerevan, Mashtots St 17; tel. (10) 53-55-94; fax (10) 56-36-61; f. 1921; Armenian literature (since 18th century), theatre, cinema and music; library of 84,526 vols, 862,252 MSS; Dir H. BAKHCHINYAN.

Yerevan Children's Picture Gallery: Yerevan, ul. Aboviana 13; tel. (10) 52-78-93; f. 1970; works of art by children of Armenian and other nationalities; Dir H. IKITIAN.

Universities

ABOVIAN ARMENIAN STATE PEDAGOGICAL UNIVERSITY

0070 Yerevan, Khandyjan 5

Telephone: (10) 52-26-04
Fax: (10) 56-00-82
E-mail: armped@netsys.am

Founded 1922; present status 2000
State control
Academic year: September to July

Rector: MISAK DAVTYAN

Number of teachers: 620
Number of students: 4,200

Publication: *Mankavarzh* (monthly)

DEANS

Armenian Language and Literature: MARTIN GILAVIAN
Art and Aesthetic Education: ARKADIY SHEKUNTS
Biology and Chemistry: MEZHLUM YERITSIAN
Culture: RUBEN MIRZAKHANIAN
History and Geography: POGHOS SIMONIAN
Industrial Pedagogy: KLEMENT ANANIAN
Mathematics and Physics: ALEXANDER GHUSHCHIAN
Primary Education and Defectology: DIMITRIY NAZARIAN
Psychology and Pedagogics: ROBERT DASHIAN
Public Professions: KAMO MKRYTCHIAN

ARMENIAN–RUSSIAN (SLAVIC) STATE UNIVERSITY

0051 Yerevan, Valutin St 123

Telephone: (10) 55-33-62
E-mail: rectorat@rau.am
Internet: www.rau.am

Founded 1998 by govts of Russia and Armenia
State control

Rector: LEVON MKRTČYAN

Library of 47,000 vols, 2,000 journals
Number of teachers: 156
Number of students: 1,600

DEANS

Faculty of Applied Mathematics and Informatics: Doc. VLADIMIR S. YEGIAZARYAN
Faculty of Economics: ALBERT YE. VARDANYAN
Faculty of Journalism: RAFAEL GR. AIRAPETYAN
Faculty of Law: Prof. Dr ARMEN A. ARUTYUNYAN
Faculty of Politology: Doc. ASHOT P. YENGOYAN
Faculty of Social and Cultural Services and Tourism: NINA I. KEVORKOVA

FRENCH UNIVERSITY OF ARMENIA

0067 Yerevan, Aigestan 8

Telephone: (10) 57-16-04
Fax: (10) 57-84-57
E-mail: ufa@arminco.com
Internet: www.ufa.am

Founded 2000
State control

Rector: PAUL ROUSSET
Secretary-General and Director of Studies: LUCIE HUCHOT

DEANS

Faculty of Business: NORAYR SAFARIAN
Faculty of Commerce: ARTAK MELKONIAN
Faculty of Law: GRIGOR BADIRIAN

GAVAR STATE UNIVERSITY

1230 Gavar, Azatutian 1
Telephone: (264) 2-38-03

Founded 1993
State control
Language of instruction: Armenian
Academic year: September to June

Rector: HRANT HAKOBIAN
Vice-Rector: VARDAN HAYRAPETIAN

Number of teachers: 146
Number of students: 1,180

DEANS

Faculty of Economics: SAMVEL AMIRKHANIAN
Faculty of Humanities: VICTOR KATVALIAN
Faculty of Natural Sciences: MARTIN AVAGIAN

STATE ENGINEERING UNIVERSITY OF ARMENIA

0009 Yerevan, ul. Teryana 105

Telephone: (10) 52-05-20
Fax: (10) 15-10-68
E-mail: president@seua.am
Internet: www.seua.am

Founded 1933
State control

Rector: Y. L. SARKISSIAN

Library of 667,000 vols
Number of teachers: 1,000
Number of students: 8,000

Faculties of Chemical Technology and Environmental Engineering, Electrical Engineering, Power Engineering, Mechanics and Machine Science, Machine Building, Automation and Instrumentation, Informatics and Computer Systems, Cybernetics, Radio Technology and Communications Systems, Mining and Metallurgy and Transport Systems.

YEREVAN STATE UNIVERSITY

0049 Yerevan, Alex Manoogian 1

Telephone: (10) 55-46-29
Fax: (10) 55-46-41
E-mail: rector@ysu.am
Internet: www.ysu.am

Founded 1919
State control
Language of instruction: Armenian
Academic year: September to June

Rector: RADIK M. MARTIROSIAN
Vice-Rectors: EDWARD CHUBARIAN (Academic Affairs: Natural Sciences), SEMION HAKHUMIAN (Academic Affairs: Humanities), RAFAEL MATEVOSIAN (International Relations), ROMEN SHARKHATUNIAN (Economic Development), EDWARD KAZARIAN (Education Development)
Director of Library: VARDGES ASLANIAN

Number of teachers: 1,200
Number of students: 9,000

Publications: *Bulletin* (annual), *Transactions* (quarterly), *Yerevan University* (annual)

DEANS

Faculty of Applied Arts: SPARTAK SARGSYAN
Faculty of Armenian Philology: ARTSRUN AVAGYAN
Faculty of Biology: EMIL GEVORGIAN
Faculty of Chemistry: AIDA AVETISIAN

Faculty of Computer Science and Applied Mathematics: VAHRAM DUMANYAN
Faculty of Economics: HAIK SARKISSIAN
Faculty of Geography: AŠOT KHOYETSYAN
Faculty of Geology: MARAT GRIGORIAN
Faculty of History: BABKEN HARUTIUNIAN
Faculty of International Relations: EDIK ZOHRABYAN
Faculty of Law: GAGIK GHAZINIAN
Faculty of Mathematics: ROMEN SHAHBAGIAN
Faculty of Mechanics: VLADIMIR SARKISIAN
Faculty of Oriental Studies: GURGEN MELIKIAN
Faculty of Philosophy, Psychology and Sociology: HRACHIK MIRZOYAN
Faculty of Physics: SAMVEL HAROUTINIAN
Faculty of Radiophysics: YURI VARDANIAN
Faculty of Romanic-Germanic Philology: KARO KARAPETIAN
Faculty of Russian Philology: KAREN MKRTČIAN
Faculty of Theology: Archbishop SHAHE AJEMIAN

YEREVAN STATE UNIVERSITY OF LINGUISTICS, 'V. BRUSOV'

0002 Yerevan, Toumanian 42
Telephone: (10) 53-05-52
Fax: (10) 50-64-29
E-mail: ysifl@edu.am
Internet: www.brusov.am

Founded 1935
State control

Rector: SUREN ZOLYAN

Number of teachers: 440
Number of students: 2,200

Faculties of Foreign Languages, Social Sciences, Russian Language and Literature and Foreign Languages, Romance and Germanic languages.

YEREVAN STATE MEDICAL UNIVERSITY, M. HERATSI

0025 Yerevan, ul. Koryan 2
Telephone: (10) 58-18-02
Fax: (10) 52-96-05
E-mail: meduni@ysmu.am
Internet: www.ysmu.am

Founded 1920
State control

Rector: VILEN P. HAKOPIAN
Vice-Rector for Int. Relations: YERVAND S. SAHAKYAN
Vice-Rector for Post-Graduate Studies: MIKHAIL Z. NARIMANYAN
Vice-Rector for Post-Graduate Studies: VLADIMIR A. SHEKOYAN

Library of 613,000 vols
Number of teachers: 715
Number of students: 4,568

Publications: *Future Physician* (monthly), *Medicus* (monthly), *Doctor and Officer* (6 a year), *Medical Science of Armenia* (quarterly), *Actual and Fundamental Problems of Medicine* (2 a year)

Faculties of General Medicine, Stomatology, Pharmacy, Military Medicine.

Other Higher Educational Institutes

Armenian Agricultural Academy: 0009 Yerevan, ul. Teryana 74; tel. (10) 52-45-41; fax (10) 52-23-61; e-mail agacad@arminco.com; internet www.arminco.com/homepages/usdaes/acad/acad.htm; f. 1994 from merger of Armenian Agricultural Institute (f. 1930) and Yerevan Zootechnical and Veterinary Institute (f. 1928); Faculties of Agrarian Studies, Economics, Technology, Zootechnical and Veterinary Studies, Engineering, Advanced Studies; 152 full professors; 419 teachers; 4,322 students; library: 563,389 vols; Rector A. KHACHATRIAN; publs *Agronews* (weekly), *Agroscience* (monthly), *News* (weekly).

Armenian State Institute of Physical Education: 0070 Yerevan, Alex Manoogian 11; tel. (10) 55-24-31; f. 1945; State control; Rector VAHRAM ARAKELIAN; Faculties of Education, Sports.

Gyumri M. Nalbandian State Pedagogical Institute: 3126 Gyumri, Paruir Sevak 4; tel. (312) 3-77-32; fax (312) 3-21-99; e-mail postmaster@shirak.am; f. 1935; state control; Rector HOURIK HARUTUNIAN; Faculties of Foreign Languages, History and Philology, Natural Sciences and Geography, Pedagogy, Physical Education, Physics and Mathematics.

Vanadzor State Pedagogical Institute: 2000 Vanadzor, Tigran Mets 36; tel. (322) 4-63-87; fax (322) 2-04-68; e-mail mankocol@hragir.aua.am; f. 1969; state control; Rector RAFIK YEDOVAN; Vice-Rector SHVAITS SAHAKIAN; 310 teachers; 1,900 students; Faculties of Biology, History and Geography, Mathematics and Physics, Philology and Pre-school Education, Psychology.

Yerevan Institute of Architecture and Construction: 0009 Yerevan, ul. Teryana 105; tel. (10) 58-01-77; fax (10) 56-59-84; internet yeriac.iatp.irex.am; f. 1989; Faculties of Architecture, Industrial and Civil Construction, Construction Technology, Hydrotechnical Studies, Construction and Urban Economy, Transport Construction; 262 teachers; 1,624 students; library: 1,373,203 vols; Rector A. G. BEGLARIAN.

Yerevan Komitas State Conservatoire: 0001 Yerevan, Sayat-Nova 1A; tel. (10) 58-11-64; fax (10) 56-35-40; e-mail ysc@edu.am; f. 1920; orchestral, chamber, choral, folk music; library: 130,000 vols; 386 teachers; 1,045 students; Rector Prof. ARMEN SMHATYAN.

Yerevan State Academy of Fine Arts: 0009 Yerevan, Isahakian 36; tel. (10) 56-07-26; fax (10) 54-27-06; e-mail ysifa@edu.am; internet www.iatp.am/yafa; f. 1945; Faculties of Art, Design, Decorative Arts; brs in Gjumri and Dilijan; library: 25,000 vols; 98 teachers; 428 students; Rector Prof. ARAM ISABEKIAN.

Yerevan State Institute of Economics: 0025 Yerevan, Nalbandian St 164; tel. (10) 52-17-21; fax (10) 52-88-64; e-mail ysine@ysine.am; internet www.ysine.am; f. 1975; Faculties of Economic Planning, Finance and Accounting, Economics of Labour and Sociology, Economics and Organization of Labour, Economics of Trade and Commodities; 326 teachers; 5,600 students; Rector G. KIRAKOSIAN; publ. *Economics*.

Yerevan Zootechnical and Veterinary Institute: Ul. Nalbandyana 128, 375025 Yerevan; tel. (10) 56-13-42; f. 1929; library: 210,000 vols; faculties of livestock management, veterinary science, technology of milk and dairy products, improvement of qualifications; 200 teachers; 2,900 students; Rector M. S. MELKONIAN; publ. *Trudy*.

AUSTRALIA

The Higher Education System

In 2004 there were 48 public universities and two private universities, as well as several public institutions of higher education. A total of 830,058 students were enrolled in universities in that year. Under the federal system of government in Australia, the six states and two territories are responsible for providing education services for their own residents. The Australian Constitution, however, empowers the Federal Government to make special-purpose financial grants to the states for education in both government and non-government schools. Responsibility for educational policy rests with the Minister for Education, Science and Training. An education department headed by a Director-General deals with all aspects of education within each state.

The Federal Government is the most important source of funding for universities; in 2003 the Government contributed 41% accounted of funding. Most Australian students contribute to the cost of their courses under the Higher Education Contribution Scheme (HECS), with the amount of the student's contribution depending on the cost of the course and likely future earnings. Financial assistance is available to certain students subject to a means test. In addition, there are a limited number of equity and merit scholarships which exempt students from the HECS charge.

Universities are administered by a Governing Body such as a Council, Senate or Board of Governors, chaired by a Chancellor. A Chief Executive, usually a Vice-Chancellor or President, oversees the day-to-day running of the university and reports to the Governing Body.

In 1990 a Unified National System was established, replacing the previously existing binary system of universities and non-university institutions. The Australian Qualifications Framework (AQF) was introduced in 1995 and implemented by 1999, leading to the development of a comprehensive national framework for post-secondary education and training. The AQF identifies six post-secondary levels of qualification: Diploma, Advanced Diploma, Bachelors degree, Graduate Certificate and Graduate Diploma, Masters degree and Doctoral degree.

Universities administer their own admissions processes. Admission is usually based on a combination of completion of Year 12, leading to the award of the Senior Secondary Certificate of Education (the name may vary in each state or territory), and entrance test scores. The Diploma and Advanced Diploma, requiring two and three years of study respectively, are sub-degree qualifications that may in certain circumstances allow entry to the second year of a Bachelors degree. The Bachelors degree may be rated either Ordinary/Pass after three years of study or Honours after four years of study. The Graduate Certificate and Graduate Diploma require one or two semesters of full-time study respectively following a Bachelor degree. The Masters degree is awarded after two years of study following an Ordinary/Pass Bachelors or after one year of study following an Honours Bachelors. Finally, the Doctoral degree requires three years of full-time study and research plus submission of a thesis. Other, more recent, Doctoral-level awards include the Professional Doctorate and the Higher Doctorate.

Vocational education and training (VET) is supervised by the Australian National Training Authority, established in 1994. The Australian Recognition Framework approves VET qualifications. VET programmes are offered at upper-secondary schools, Technical and Further Education colleges and State- or Territory-accredited private providers. VET programmes require between one and three years study depending upon the requirements of the course and the level of qualification sought. The range of VET qualifications are as follows: Certificates I, II, III, IV; Diploma; Advanced Diploma. Teacher training usually requires either a three-year Bachelors degree in the subject to be taught, followed by a one- to two-year (Graduate) Diploma in Education, or the four-year Bachelor of Education.

Regulatory and Representative Bodies

GOVERNMENT

Department of Education, Science and Training: GPOB 9880, Canberra, ACT 2601; located at: 16 Mort St, Canberra, ACT 2601; tel. (2) 6240-8111; fax (2) 6240-8571; internet www.dest.gov.au; Minister JULIE BISHOP.

Ministerial Council on Education, Employment, Training and Youth Affairs (MCEETYA): POB 202, Carlton, Vic. 3053; tel. (03) 9639-0588; fax (03) 9639-1790; e-mail enquiries@mceetya.edu.au; internet www.mceetya.edu.au; f. 1993 by merger of the Australian Education Council (AEC), the Council of Ministers of Vocational Education, Employment and Training (MOVEET) and the Youth Ministers Council (YMC); responsible fo pre-primary education, primary and secondary education, vocational education and training, higher education, employment and links between employment/labour market programs and education and training, adult and community education, youth policy programs and cross-sectoral matters; works in close interaction with the Ministerial Council for Vocational and Technical Education (MCVTE); functions incl. co-ordination of strategic policy at nat. level, negotiation and devt of nat. agreements on shared objectives and interests (incl. principles for Australian Govt/State relations) in the Council's areas of responsibility, negotiations on scope and format of nat. reporting on areas of responsibility, sharing of information and collaborative use of resources towards agreed objectives and priorities, and co-ordination of communication with, and collaboration between, related nat. structures; Chair. PAUL HENDERSON.

ACCREDITATION

Australian Qualifications Framework Advisory Board (AQFAB): POB 609, Carlton, Vic. 3053; located at: Level 3, 15–31 Pelham St, Carlton, Vic. 3053; tel. (3) 9639-1606; fax (3) 9639-1315; e-mail aqfab@aqf.edu.au; internet www.aqf.edu.au; f. 1995 to protect the Australian Qualifications Framework (AQF) qualifications guidelines and to promote and monitor nat. implementation of the AQF; operates as a high-level, cross-sectoral forum; Chair. WARREN GRIMSHAW; Secretariat Exec. Officer Dr JUDY FORSYTH.

ENIC/NARIC Australia: AEI-NOOSR, Australian Education Int./Nat. Office of Overseas Skills Recognition, GPO Box 1407, Canberra ACT 2601; tel. (3) 8341-3611; fax (2) 6240-8448; e-mail noosr@dest.gov.au; internet aei.dest.gov.au/aei/qualificationsrecognition; Dir MARGARET PROCTOR.

NATIONAL BODIES

Adult Learning Australia Quest: GPO Box 260, Canberra City, ACT 2601; tel. (2) 6274-9500; fax (2) 9274-9513; e-mail info@ala.asn.au; internet www.ala.asn.au; f. 1961; mem. of ICAE, ASPBAE, ICEA; co-ordinates and encourages adult and community education at nat. level; publishes educational books; lobbies govts and appropriate depts; holds national conferences, etc.; 500 mems, also corporate mems; Pres. GREG PEART; Exec. Dir. RON ANDERSON; publs *Australian Journal of Adult Learning* (3 a year), *Adult Learning Australia* (4 a year).

Australian Research Council: GPO Box 2702, Canberra, ACT 2601; tel. (2) 6284-6605; fax (2) 6284-6601; internet www.arc.gov.au; f. 1965, present name 1988; responsible for the allocation of grants for research in the physical sciences, biological sciences, chemical sciences, earth sciences, applied sciences, social sciences and the humanities by individuals or research teams; and provides advice to relevant Minister on national research priorities and the co-ordination of research policy; 14 mems; Chief Exec. Prof. PETER HØJ; publ. annual reports.

Australian Vice-Chancellors' Committee: GPO Box 1142, Canberra, ACT 2601; tel. (2) 6285-8200; fax (2) 6285-8211; e-mail avcc@avcc.edu.au; internet www.avcc.edu.au; f. 1920; represents Australian univs; 38 mems; Pres. Prof. GERARD SUTTON; Vice-Pres. Prof. RICHARD LARKINS; Chief Exec. DAVID ROME.

Centre for Adult Education (CAE): 253 Flinders Lane, Melbourne, Vic. 3000; tel. (3) 9652-0611; fax (3) 9654-6759; e-mail international@cae.edu.au; internet www.cae.edu.au; f. 1947; statutory body engaged in providing adult education and business training in Vic.; funded in part through the Govt of Vic.; library of 50,000 vols; Dir JOHN WILLS; publs *Program Guide* (5 a year), *Dialogue* (every 3 years, catalogue of book, film and music titles available for self-directed learning groups).

Learned Societies

GENERAL

Academy of the Social Sciences in Australia: GPO Box 1956, Canberra, ACT 2601; tel. (2) 6249-1788; fax (2) 6247-4335; e-mail ASSA.Secretariat@anu.edu.au; internet www.assa.edu.au; f. 1971; 447 fellows; Pres. Prof. STUART MACINTYRE; Exec. Dir Dr JOHN BEATON; publs *Dialogue* (3 a year), *Occasional Paper* (irregular).

Australian Academy of the Humanities: GPO Box 93, Canberra, ACT 2601; tel. (2) 6125-9860; fax (2) 6248-6287; e-mail aah@anu.edu.au; internet www.humanities.org.au; f. 1969; language, literature, history, philosophy, fine arts; 400 mems; Pres. Prof. IAIN MCCALMAN; Exec. Dir, Secretariat JOHN BYRON; Hon. Sec. Prof. GRAEME CLARKE; Librarian and Archivist Dr JANET H. WILLIAMS; publ. *Proceedings*.

AGRICULTURE, FISHERIES AND VETERINARY SCIENCE

Australian Institute of Agricultural Science and Technology: Level 2, 21 Burwood Rd, Hawthorn, Vic. 3122; tel. (3) 9815-3600; fax (3) 9815-3633; e-mail members@aiast.com.au; internet www.aiast.com.au; f. 1935; 2,500 mems; Pres. CHARLES DREW; Exec. Dir ALLAN JONES; publ. *Agricultural Science* (4 a year).

Australian Veterinary Association: Unit 40, 2A Herbert St, St Leonards, NSW 2065; tel. (2) 9431-5000; fax (2) 9437-9068; e-mail members@ava.com.au; internet www.ava.com.au; f. 1921; professional asscn; 5,000 mems; Pres. KERSTI SEKSEL; Chief Exec. MARGARET CONLEY; publ. *Australian Veterinary Journal* (monthly).

Dairy Industry Association of Australia Inc.: 84 William St, Melbourne, Vic. 3000; tel. (3) 9760-0422; fax (3) 9642-8144; e-mail kmanser@ozemail.com.au; internet www.diaa.asn.au; f. 1946; divisions in each State; 1,600 mems; Pres. JO DAVEY; Sec. KRISTINE MANSER; publs *The Australian Journal of Dairy Technology* (3 a year), *Australian Dairy Foods* (6 a year).

Primary Industries Ministerial Council: Dept of Agriculture, Fisheries and Forestry, Barton, Canberra, ACT 2600; tel. (2) 6272-5216; fax (2) 6272-4772; internet www.affa.gov.au/docs/operating_environment/armcanz/armcanz.html; f. 2001; mems: Commonwealth, State, Territory and New Zealand ministers responsible for agriculture and rural adjustment; advised by a Standing Committee comprising heads of Commonwealth, State, Territory and New Zealand agencies responsible for agriculture, and representatives from CSIRO and the Bureau of Meteorology; Exec. Dir Dr MAXINE COOPER.

ARCHITECTURE AND TOWN PLANNING

Australian Council of National Trusts: POB 1002, Civic Sq., ACT 2612; tel. (2) 6247-6766; fax (2) 6249-1395; e-mail acnt@nationaltrust.org.au; internet www.nationaltrust.org.au; f. 1965; Federal Council of the State and Territory National Trusts established for the conservation of lands and buildings of beauty or of national, historic, scientific, architectural or cultural interest and Aboriginal relics and wildlife; 80,000 mems of the National Trust movement; Chair. SIMON R. MOLESWORTH; Exec. Officer ALAN GRAHAM.

Australian Institute of Quantity Surveyors: National Office, POB 301, Deakin West, ACT 2600; tel. (2) 6282-2222; fax (2) 6285-2427; e-mail contact@aiqs.com.au; internet www.aiqs.com.au; f. 1971; 3,700 mems; Pres. PETER COX; Gen. Man. TERRY SANDERS; publs *Australian Journal of Construction Economics and Building* (2 a year), *The Building Economist* (4 a year).

Planning Institute of Australia: GPO Box 1491, Canberra, ACT; tel. (2) 6248-7299; fax (2) 6262-9970; e-mail act@planning.org.au; internet www.planning.org.au; f. 1951; professional asscn for town and regional planners; 3,444 mems; Nat. Pres. MARCUS SPILLER; Pres. CLAIRE MIDDLETON; publs *Australian Planner* (quarterly), *National Office News* (6 a year).

Royal Australian Institute of Architects: 2A Mugga Way, Red Hill, Canberra, ACT 2603; tel. (2) 6208-2100; fax (2) 6208-2106; e-mail act@raia.com.au; internet www.raia.com.au; inc. 1930; 8,500 mems; Nat. Pres. ALEX TZANNES; CEO DAVID PARKEN; ACT Man. SOPHIE CLEMENT; publs *Architecture Australia* (every 2 months), occasional newsletters, research papers, seminar and workshop papers, management and law notes.

BIBLIOGRAPHY, LIBRARY SCIENCE AND MUSEOLOGY

Australian Library and Information Association: POB 6335, Kingston, ACT 2604; tel. (2) 6215-8222; fax (2) 6282-2249; e-mail enquiry@alia.org.au; internet alia.org.au; f. 1937; 6,000 mems; Pres. ROXANNE MISSINGHAM; Exec. Dir SUE HUTLEY; publs *Australian Academic and Research Libraries* (quarterly), *Australian Library Journal* (quarterly), *inCite* (monthly, except a jt issue for Jan.–Feb.).

Bibliographical Society of Australia and New Zealand: c/o The Secretary/Treasurer, POB 1463, Wagga Wagga, NSW 2650; tel. and fax (3) 9654-4347; e-mail rsalmond@pobox.com; internet www.csu.edu.au/community/BSANZ; f. 1969 to promote research in bibliography; 248 mems; Pres. P. EGGERT; publs *Broadsheet* (3 or 4 a year), *Bulletin* (quarterly).

Museums Australia: POB 266, Civic Sq., ACT 2608; tel. (2) 6273-2437; fax (2) 6273-2451; e-mail national.director@museumsaustralia.org.au; internet www.museumsaustralia.org.au; f. 1993 to promote museums and galleries to all levels of govt and the community, and to foster high standards in all aspects of museum operations through nat. advocacy, professional development, training, research, policy formulation, publications, collaborative facilitation and partnerships; 2,000 mems; Nat. Pres. PATRICIA SABINE; Nat. Dir BERNICE L. MURPHY; publ. *Museums Australia Magazine* (quarterly).

ECONOMICS, LAW AND POLITICS

Australasian Political Studies Association: Political Science Program, RSSS, ANU, Canberra, ACT 0200; tel. (2) 6125-2117; fax (2) 6125-3051; e-mail roderick.rhodes@anu.edu.au; internet www.auspsa.anu.edu.au; f. 1952; organises an annual conference; workshops; 269 mems; Pres. Assoc. Prof. DEBORAH BRENNAN; Sec. and Treasurer Prof. ROD RHODES; publ. *Australian Journal of Political Science* (quarterly).

Australian Bar Association: Bar Association of Queensland, Level 5, Inns of Court, 107 North Quay, Brisbane, Qld 4000; tel. (7) 3236-2477; fax (7) 3236-1180; e-mail president@qldbar.asn.au; internet qldbar.asn.au; f. 1962 to advance the interests of barristers; to maintain and strengthen the position of the Bar, maintaining its independence and the rule of law; to maintain and improve standards of instruction and training of barristers; 3,440 mems; Pres. GLENN MARTIN; Vice-Pres. PETER LYONS; Treas. MARTIN DAUBNEY; Sec. DOUGLAS MURPHY.

Australian Institute of Credit Management: Suite 202, 619 Pacific Highway, St Leonards, NSW 2065; tel. (2) 9906-4563; fax (2) 9906-5686; e-mail terry@aicm.com.au; internet www.aicm.com.au; f. 1937 to provide a national and professional organization for credit managers and those engaged in the control of credit; holds conferences, discussions; maintains educational programmes at CAEs; divisions in all States; Pres. B. J. FULMER; CEO T. J. COLLINS.

Australian Institute of International Affairs: 32 Thesiger Court, Deakin, ACT 2600; tel. (2) 6282-2133; fax (2) 6285-2334; e-mail ceo@aiia.asn.au; internet www.aiia.asn.au; f. 1933; 1,500 mems; Pres. CLIVE HILDEBRAND; Exec. Dir MELISSA H. CONLEY TYLER; publs *Australian Journal of International Affairs* (quarterly), *Australia in World Affairs* (every 5 years).

Australian Institute of Management: 181 Fitzroy St, St. Kilda, Vic. 3182; tel. (3) 9534-8181; fax (3) 9534-5050; e-mail enquiry@aimvic.com.au; internet www.aim.com.au; f. 1941; professional management association; information and training services; divisions in all states; 30,000 professional mems, 7,500 corporate mems; library of 20,000 vols; publ. *National Management Today Magazine* (monthly).

Australian Property Institute: 6 Campion St, Deakin, ACT 2600; tel. (2) 6282-2411; fax (2) 6285-2194; e-mail national@api.org.au; internet www.api.org.au; f. 1927; 7,500 mems; Pres. BARRY BRAKEY; Dir MARK HOWLAND; publs *Australian Property Journal* (4 a year), *Professional Practice* (annually), *Valuation Principles and Practices*.

Committee for Economic Development of Australia: Level 5, 136 Exhibition St, Melbourne, Vic. 3000; tel. (3) 9662-3544; fax (3) 9663-7271; e-mail info@ceda.com.au; internet www.ceda.com.au; f. 1960 to facilitate discussion, research and interdisciplinary communication in the interests of the devt of the nat. economy and the future of Australia; holds more than 250 events, seminars and exec. roundtables each year; 1,000 orgs; Chair. IVAN DEVESON; Chief Exec. DAVID BYERS; publs *Australian Chief Executive* (mem. magazine, quarterly), *Growth Reports* (multi-author long reports on selected research themes), *Information Papers* (single author short reports on selected research themes).

Economic Society of Australia: POB 937, St Ives, NSW 2075; tel. (2) 9402-7635; internet www.ecosoc.org.au; f. 1925; 1,400 mems; brs in each State; Pres. NEVILLE

NORMAN; Sec. JEFFREY SHEEN; Treas. ANDREW HUGHES; publs *The Economic Record*, *Economic Papers*.

Institute of Public Affairs: Level 2, 410 Collins St, Melbourne, Vic. 3000; tel. (3) 9600-4744; e-mail ipa@ipa.org.au; internet www.ipa.org.au; f. 1943; non-profit educational org. to study economic and industrial problems and to advance the cause of free enterprise in Australia; supported by 550 companies and 3,500 individuals; Chair. ALAN STOCKDALE; Exec. Dir MIKE NAHAN; publs *IPA Review* (quarterly), *Backgrounder* (10 a year), *Current Issues* (5 a year).

Law Council of Australia: GPO Box 1989, Canberra, ACT 2601; premises at: 19 Torrens St, Braddon, ACT 2612; tel. (2) 6246-3788; fax (2) 6248-0639; e-mail mail@lawcouncil.asn.au; internet www.lawcouncil.asn.au; f. 1933; 15 constituent bodies representing 50,000 mems; Sec.-Gen. PETER WEBB; publs *Australian Family Lawyer* (4 a year), *Australian Law Management Journal* (4 a year).

Law Society of New South Wales: 170 Phillip St, Sydney, NSW; tel. (2) 9926-0333; fax (2) 9231-5809; internet www.lawsocnsw.asn.au; f. 1884; 20,000 mems; library of 32,000 vols; Sec. C. CAWLEY; publs *Law Society Journal* (11 a year), *Caveat* (irregular).

Local Government Managers Australia: POB 615, Unit D3.1, 63–85 Turner St, Port Melbourne, Vic. 3207; tel. (3) 9676-2755; fax (3) 9676-2311; e-mail national@lgma.org.au; internet www.lgma.org.au; f. 1936; professional local govt assoc. for general managers, chief executives and officers; 2,500 mems; CEO JIM ELVEY; publ. *Local Government Manager* (6 a year).

EDUCATION

Australian College of Educators: 42 Geils Court, Deakin, ACT 2600; tel. (2) 6281-1677; fax (2) 6285-1262; e-mail ace@austcolled.com.au; internet www.auscolled.com.au; f. 1959; an independent professional association of educators from every field of education throughout Australia; encourages professional advancement of its members and the nat. development of education; brs and regional groups in each state and territory; conducts nat. and state conferences, surveys and studies, etc.; 6,000 mems; CEO CHERYL O'CONNOR; publs *Education Review* (incl. *ACE Perspectives*, monthly), chapter newsletters, *Professional Educator* (quarterly).

IDP Education Australia Ltd: GPO Box 2006, Canberra, ACT 2601; tel. (2) 6285-8222; fax (2) 6285-3036; e-mail info@idp.com; internet www.idp.com; f. 1969 as the Int. Development Program of Australian Universities and Colleges Ltd, renamed 1994; 37 mem. Australian univs; an independent company owned by the Australian Universities; seeks to promote Australian education and training services overseas; 53 overseas network offices; Chief Exec. L. HYAM; publs *Annual Report*, newsletters in Asia-Pacific languages.

Open and Distance Learning Association of Australia Inc.: Teaching and Learning Centre, University of New England, Armidale NSW 2351; tel. (2) 6773-3628; fax (2) 6773-3510; e-mail secretary@lists.odlaa.org; internet www.odlaa.org; f. 1974 to advance the practice and study of distance education in Australia; Pres. Prof. RON OLIVER; Vice-Pres. JOHN HEDBERG; Sec. Dr CHRIS BROOK; publ. *Distance Education* (3 a year).

FINE AND PERFORMING ARTS

Australia Council for the Arts: 372 Elizabeth St, Surry Hills, NSW 2010; tel. (2) 9215-9000; e-mail mail@ozco.gov.au; internet www.ozco.gov.au; f. 1968; aims to foster the development of the arts through the programmes of seven funds: Music, Dance, Theatre, New Media, Literature, Visual Arts/Craft, Community Cultural Development, and one board: Aboriginal and Torres Straits Islander Arts; library of 6,500 vols; Chair. DAVID GONSKI; Deputy Chair. TERREY ARCUS; CEO JENNIFER BOTT; publ. *Artforce* (quarterly).

Australian and New Zealand Association for Medieval and Early Modern Studies: c/o Pippa Maddern, School of Humanities, M208, The University of Western Australia, Crawley, WA 6009; e-mail pipma@cyllene.uwa.edu.au; internet www.anzamems.arts.uwa.edu.au; f. 1996 by merger of ANZAMRS (Australian and New Zealand Association of Medieval and Renaissance Studies) and AHMEME (Australian Historians of Medieval and Early Modern Europe); organizes conferences every 2 years; 300 mems; Pres. KIM PHILLIPS (University of Auckland); Sec. ANNE SCOTT (University of Western Australia); publ. *Parergon* (2 a year).

Musicological Society of Australia: GPO Box 2402, Canberra, ACT 2601; e-mail secretary@msa.org.au; internet www.msa.org.au; f. 1963; the advancement of musicology; 290 mems; Pres. VICTORIA ROGERS; National Sec. DOROTTYA FABIAN; publs *Musicology Australia* (annually), *Newsletter* (2 a year).

Royal Art Society of New South Wales: 25–27 Walker St, North Sydney, NSW 2060; tel. (2) 9955-5752; fax (2) 9925-0064; e-mail lavender@cia.com.au; f. 1880; for the promotion of high standards in Australian art; school for painting (beginners to Diploma RAS of NSW); 400 mems; Pres. RON STANNARD; Sec. CHRISTINE FEHER; publ. *Newsletter* (monthly).

Royal Queensland Art Society Inc.: Box 1602, GPO, Brisbane, Qld 4001; tel. (7) 3831-3455; fax (7) 3831-3452; e-mail rqasi@oznetcom.com.au; internet www.rqas.ozevents.com; f. 1887; 500 mems; Sec. KAREN KANE; publ. *Newsletter* (6 a year).

Royal South Australian Society of Arts: Edmund Wright House, 59 King William St, Adelaide, SA 5000; tel. (8) 8226-8579; fax (8) 8226-8505; f. 1856; 702 mems; Pres. BEVERLY M. BILLS; Hon. Sec. JAMES E. G. RAGGATT; publ. *Kalori* (irregular).

Victorian Artists' Society: 430 Albert St, East Melbourne, Vic. 3002; tel. (3) 9662-1484; fax (3) 9662-2343; e-mail vicartists@vicnet.net.au; internet www.vicnet.net.au/~vicartists; f. 1870; 1,000 mems; four galleries and a studio; Pres. JOHN HUNT; Sec. TED DANSEY; publs *Newsletter*, *Annual Report*, *Gallery on Eastern Hill*.

HISTORY, GEOGRAPHY AND ARCHAEOLOGY

Australian Numismatic Society: POB 366, Brookvale, NSW 2096; tel. (2) 9223-4578; fax (2) 9401-3788; e-mail rodsell@rodsell.com; f. 1913; promotes the study of coins, banknotes and medals with particular reference to Australasia and the Pacific region; monthly meetings in Sydney and Brisbane; 204 mems (incl. overseas); Pres. C. PITCHFORK; Sec. R. CLIMPSON; publs *Report* (2 a year), *Journal* (annual).

Geographical Society of New South Wales Inc.: POB 162, Ryde, NSW 1680; tel. (2) 9807-3586; fax (2) 9807-3589; e-mail office@gsnsw.org.au; internet www.gsnsw.org.au; f. 1927; 300 mems; Hon. Sec. E. TARANTO; publ. *Australian Geographer* (3 a year).

Mapping Sciences Institute, Australia: GPO Box 1817, Brisbane, Qld 4000; tel. (7) 3343-7706; fax (7) 3219-2281; e-mail msiau@gil.com.au; internet www.mappingsciences.org.au; f. 1952; holds biennial conferences; 1,250 mems; Nat. Pres. JOHN MCCORMACK; Hon. Sec. K. H. SMITH; publ. *Cartography* (2 a year).

Royal Australian Historical Society: History House, 133 Macquarie St, Sydney, NSW 2000; tel. (2) 9247-8001; fax (2) 9247-7854; e-mail history@rahs.org.au; internet www.rahs.org.au; f. 1901; 2,000 mems; library: 20,000 items; Exec. Officer DAVID LEWIS; publs *Journal* (2 a year), *History Magazine* (4 a year).

Royal Geographical Society of Queensland Inc.: 237 Milton Rd, Milton, Qld 4064; tel. (7) 3368-2066; fax (7) 3367-1011; e-mail admin@rgsq.org.au; internet www.rgsq.org.au; f. 1885; 450 mems; library of 2,500 monographs, 320 periodicals, maps; Pres. PAUL FEENEY; Sec. KEITH SMITH.

Royal Historical Society of Queensland: POB 12057, George St, Brisbane, Qld 4003; tel. (7) 3221-4198; fax (7) 3221-4698; e-mail info@queenslandhistory.org.au; internet queenslandhistory.org.au; f. 1913; Welsby library; research; historical documents preserved and filed; photographic collection; social history; museum; 600 mems; Pres. Dr IAN HADWEN; Man. ALLAN R. BELL; publs *Bulletin* (monthly), *Journal* (quarterly).

Royal Historical Society of Victoria: 239 A'Beckett St, Melbourne, Vic. 3000; tel. (3) 9326-9288; fax (3) 9326-9477; e-mail office@historyvictoria.org.au; internet www.historyvictoria.org.au; f. 1909; research; collection of historical material; exhibitions; 1,600 mems; library of 8,000 vols, MSS, photographs, paintings and prints; Pres. Prof. WESTON BATE; Exec. Officer Dr ELIZABETH RUSHDEN; publs *Journal* (every 6 months), *History News* (monthly).

Royal Western Australian Historical Society: Stirling House, 49 Broadway, Nedlands, WA 6009; tel. (8) 9386-3841; fax (8) 9386-3309; e-mail histwest@git.com.au; internet www.histwest.org.au; f. 1926; runs museum and research library; 1,000 mems; Pres. REG APPLEYARD; publs *Early Days* (annually), *History West* (monthly).

Society of Australian Genealogists: Richmond Villa, 120 Kent St, Sydney, NSW 2000; tel. (2) 9247-3953; fax (2) 9241-4872; e-mail info@sag.org.au; internet www.sag.org.au; f. 1932; 7,500 mems; library of 20,000 vols, 1,000 microfilm reels, 1 m. names on microfiche, 40,000 photographs, 30,000 MSS; Exec. Officer H. E. GARNSEY; Librarian ANGELA PHIPPEN; publ. *Descent* (quarterly).

LANGUAGE AND LITERATURE

Alliance Française: 66 McCaughey St, Turner, Canberra, ACT 2601; tel. (2) 6247-5027; fax (2) 6257-6696; e-mail general@alliancefrancaise.com.au; internet www.alliancefrancaise.com.au; offers courses and exams in French language and culture and promotes cultural exchange with France; attached teaching centres in Albury, Alice Springs, Armidale, Atherton, Ballarat, Blue Mountains, Brisbane, Cairns, Callaghan, Darwin, Don, Esperance, Eurobodolla, Figtree, Geelong, Hobart, Illawarra, Katoomba, Kooringal, Launceston, Melbourne, Milton, Nedlands, Perth, Port Macquerie, St Kilda South, Sunshine Coast, Sydney, Thuringowa Central, Toowoomba, Townsville, Tuross

Head, Wagga Wagga and Wayville; Dir BERTRAND CALMY.

Australasian and Pacific Society for Eighteenth-Century Studies: c/o Humanities Research Centre, Australian National University, ACT 0200; f. 1970; one of the sponsoring bodies of the David Nichol Smith Seminars; 80 mems; Pres. Prof. IAIN MCCALMAN.

Australian Society of Authors Ltd: POB 1566, Strawberry Hills, NSW 2012; tel. (2) 9318-0877; fax (2) 9318-0530; e-mail asa@asauthors.org; internet www.asauthors.org; f. 1963; 3,000 mems; Chair. SUSAN HAYES; publ. *The Australian Author* (3 a year).

British Council: POB 88, Edgecliff, NSW 2027; tel. (2) 9326-2022; fax (2) 9327-4868; e-mail enquiries@britishcouncil.org.au; internet www2.britishcouncil.org/au.htm; offers courses and exams in English language and British culture and promotes cultural exchange with the UK; Dir (vacant).

English Association Sydney Inc.: Box 91, Wentworth Bldg, University of Sydney, Sydney, NSW 2006; e-mail r.madelaine@unsw.edu.au; f. 1923; organizes conferences for teachers and study days for students; 170 mems; Pres. Assoc. Prof. RICHARD MADELAINE; Treasurer CERIDWEN LEE; publ. *Southerly* (quarterly).

Fellowship of Australian Writers NSW Inc.: POB 488, Rozelle, NSW 2039; tel. (2) 9810-1307; e-mail fawnsw@bigpond.com; internet www.fawnsw.org.au; f. 1928; 3,500 nat. mems; brs in all states and territories; Pres. TREVAR LANGLANDS; Sec. ELAINE BURTON; publ. *Writers' Voice* (every 2 months).

Goethe-Institut: 90 Ocean St, Woollahra, Sydney, NSW 2025; tel. (2) 8356-8333; fax (2) 8356-8314; e-mail info@sydney.goethe.org; internet www.goethe.de/an/syd/deindex.htm; offers courses and exams in German language and culture and promotes cultural exchange with Germany; Dir DR ROLAND GOLL.

PEN International (Sydney Centre): Faculty of Humanities and Social Sciences, University of Technology, Sydney, NSW 2007; tel. (2) 9514-2738; fax (2) 9514-2778; e-mail sydney@pen.org.au; internet www.pen.org.au; f. 1926; promotes friendship and intellectual co-operation among writers; 160 mems; Pres. NICHOLAS JOSE; publ. *Newsletter* (quarterly).

MEDICINE

Australasian Association of Clinical Biochemists: POB 278, Mt Lawley, WA 6929; tel. (8) 9370-5224; fax (8) 9370-4409; e-mail office@aacb.asn.au; internet www.aacb.asn.au; f. 1961; 1,400 mems; Chair. MARY CONROY; Sec. CONCHITA KUEK; publs *Clinical Biochemist Newsletter* (4 a year), *Clinical Biochemist Reviews* (4 a year).

Australasian Chapter of Sexual Health Medicine: 145 Macquarie St, Sydney, NSW 2000; tel. (2) 9256-9643; fax (2) 9256-9693; e-mail sexualhealthmed@racp.edu.au; internet www.racp.edu.au; f. 1988; aims to further the professional devt of medical practitioners in the discipline of sexual health medicine; 184 mems; Chair. Prof. KATHERINE BROWN; Exec. Officer SUZANNE MARKS.

Australasian College of Dermatologists: POB 2065, Boronia Park, NSW 2111; tel. (2) 9879-6177; fax (2) 9816-1174; e-mail admin@dermcoll.asn.au; internet www.dermcoll.asn.au; f. 1966; 360 mems; undertakes training of dermatologists and scientific research; provides public education in skin protection; Pres. Dr ANNE HOWARD; Hon. Sec. Dr STEPHEN LEE; publ. *The Australasian Journal of Dermatology* (3 a year).

Australian Association of Neurologists: Royal Australasian College of Physicians, 145 Macquarie St, Sydney, NSW 2000; tel. (2) 9256-5443; fax (2) 9241-4083; e-mail aansyd@hotkey.net.au; internet www.medeserv.com.au/aan/index.cfm; f. 1950 to bring together clinical neurologists and scientific workers in the field of the nervous system and its diseases by such means as meetings, provision of special facilities and assistance in any publications on these matters; 450 mems; Pres. Prof. GEOFFREY DONNAN; Hon. Sec. Assoc. Prof. RICHARD MACDONNELL; publ. *Clinical and Experimental Neurology* (annually).

Australian Dental Association: 75 Lithgow St, St Leonards, POB 520, NSW 2065; tel. (2) 9906-4412; fax (2) 9906-4676; e-mail adainc@ada.org.au; internet www.ada.org.au; f. 1928 to promote the art and science of dentistry and to promote dental health to the public; 9,500 mems; Chief Exec. ROBERT N. BOYD-BOLAND; publs *News Bulletin* (monthly), *Australian Dental Journal* (quarterly).

Australian Institute of Holistic Medicine: POB 3079, Jandakot, WA 6164; tel. (8) 9417-3553; fax (8) 9417-1881; f. 1946; education and research in the field of natural medicine; Dean of Studies Dr S. JAYAWARDANA.

Australian Medical Association: 42 Macquarie Street, Barton, ACT 2600; tel. (2) 6270-5400; fax (2) 6270-5499; e-mail ama@ama.com.au; internet www.ama.com.au; Sec.-Gen. Dr ROBYN MASON; publs *Medical Journal of Australia*, *Australian Medicine*.

Australian Physiological Society: c/o Dr David Saint, School of Molecular and Biomedical Science, University of Adelaide, Adelaide, SA 5005; tel. (8) 8303-3931; fax (8) 8303-3356; e-mail david.saint@adelaide.edu.au; internet www.aups.org.au; f. 1960 for the advancement of sciences of physiology; 350 mems; Pres. Prof. DAVID ADAMS; National Sec. Dr DAVID SAINT; publ. *Proceedings* (2 a year).

Australian Physiotherapy Association: Level 3, 201 Fitzroy St, St Kilda, Melbourne, Vic. 3182; tel. (2) 9534-9400; fax (2) 9534-9199; e-mail national.office@physiotherapy.asn.au; internet www.physiotherapy.asn.au; f. 1905; provides postgraduate courses and professional services; 3,000 mems; Nat. Pres. CATHERINE MICKEL; CEO DAVID MALONE; publ. *NSW Physiotherapy Bulletin* (monthly).

Australian Society of Clinical Hypnotherapists: POB 471, Eastwood, NSW 2122; tel. and fax (2) 9874-2776; e-mail secretary@asch.com.au; internet www.asch.com.au; f. 1974; to advance knowledge and practice of hypnosis and to maintain the highest ethical standards in its use; 350 mems; Pres. LYNDALL BRIGGS; Sec. EDWARD ZWICKI; publ. *The Australian Journal of Clinical Hypnotherapy and Hypnosis* (2 a year).

Medical Foundation: Edward Ford Bldg A27, University of Sydney, Sydney, NSW 2006; tel. (2) 9351-7315; fax (2) 9351-3299; e-mail medfdn@med.usyd.edu.au; internet www.medicalfoundation.usyd.edu.au; f. 1958 to raise funds for medical research; awards Program Grants for medical research, and postgraduate scholarships for study, at the University of Sydney; Pres. RICHARD CALDWELL; Man. WENDY MARCEAU.

Optometrists Association Australia: POB 185, Carlton South, Vic. 3053; tel. (3) 9663-6833; fax (3) 9663-7478; e-mail oaanat@optometrists.asn.au; internet www.optometrists.asn.au; f. 1918; promotes optometry and public education on vision care; 3,600 mems; Pres. IAN BLUNTISH; Exec. Dir JOSEPH CHAKMAN; publs *Clinical and Experimental Optometry* (every 2 months), *Australian Optometry* (monthly).

Royal Australasian College of Dental Surgeons: 64 Castlereagh St, Sydney, NSW 2000; tel. (2) 9232-3800; fax (2) 9221-8108; e-mail registrar@racds.org; internet www.racds.org; f. 1965; holds scientific meetings and administers examinations; 1,233 fellows; Pres. NEIL J. PEPPITT; Hon. Sec. STEPHEN C. DAYMOND; publs *Annals* (2 a year), *Lecture Notes in Anatomy* (annually), *Lecture Notes in Biochemistry* (annually), *Lecture Notes in Histology* (annually), *Lecture Notes in Microbiology* (annually), *Lecture Notes in Pathology* (annually), *Lecture Notes in Physiology* (annually), *Sedation Guidelines* (irregular).

Royal Australasian College of Physicians: 145 Macquarie St, Sydney, NSW 2000; tel. (2) 9256-5444; fax (2) 9252-3310; e-mail racp@racp.edu.au; internet www.racp.edu.au; f. 1938; charitable, educational and scientific activities; 7,000 fellows; library of 40,000 vols; History of Medicine library containing Ford Collection of rare Australiana; Pres. Dr JILL SEWELL (Vic.); CEO CRAIG PATTERSON; publs *Internal Medicine Journal* (monthly), *Journal of Paediatrics and Child Health* (6 a year).

Royal Australasian College of Surgeons: Spring St, Melbourne, Vic. 3000; tel. (3) 9249-1200; fax (3) 9249-1219; e-mail surgeons.sec@hen.net.au; internet www.racs.edu.au; CEO ANNE KOLBE; Vice-Pres. PETER W. H. WOODRUFF; Hon. Treasurer ANDREW D. SUTHERLAND; publ. *Australian and New Zealand Journal of Surgery* (monthly).

Royal Australian and New Zealand College of Ophthalmologists: 94–98 Chalmers St, Surry Hills, Sydney, NSW 2010; tel. (2) 9690-1001; fax (2) 9690-1321; e-mail ranzco@ranzco.edu; internet www.ranzco.edu; f. 1969 (formerly Ophthalmological Society of Australia); 1,322 mems; CEO ROBERT GUEST; Pres. Dr PETER HENDERSON; Vice-Pres. MICHAEL TREPLIN; Hon. Sec. CRAIG DONALDSON; publ. *Clinical and Experimental Ophthalmology* (6 a year).

Royal Australian and New Zealand College of Psychiatrists: 309 La Trobe St, Melbourne, Melbourne, Vic. 3000; tel. (3) 9640-0646; fax (3) 9642-5652; e-mail ranzcp@ranzcp.org; internet www.ranzcp.org; f. 1963, present name 1976; 2,429 fellows, 650 trainees; Pres. Prof. PHILIP BOYCE; publs *Australasian and New Zealand Journal of Psychiatry*, *Australasian Psychiatry*.

Royal Australian and New Zealand College of Radiologists: Level 9, 51 Druitt St, Sydney, NSW 2000; tel. (2) 9268-9777; fax (2) 9268-9799; e-mail ranzcr@ranzcr.edu.au; internet www.ranzcr.edu.au; f. 1935; 2,301 mems; CEO DON SWINBOURNE; publ. *Australasian Radiology*.

Royal College of Nursing, Australia: 1 Napier Close, Deakin West, ACT 2600; tel. (2) 6282-5633; fax (2) 6282-3565; e-mail canberra@rcna.org.au; internet www.rcna.org.au; f. 1949; aims to promote improvement in nursing practice through education and research; grants membership to graduates of approved courses; administers nat. scholarships and research grants; conducts policy and development programme, distance education programme; 10,000 mems; Pres. DI TWIGG; Exec. Dir ROSEMARY BRYANT; publs *Collegian* (4 a year), *Nursing Review* (monthly), *RCNA News* (monthly).

Royal College of Pathologists of Australasia: Durham Hall, 207 Albion St, Surry

Hills, NSW 2010; tel. and fax (2) 8356-5858; e-mail rcpa@rcpa.edu.au; internet www.rcpa.edu.au; f. 1956; 1,817 Fellows; Pres. Dr VINCE CARUSO; CEO Dr DEBRA GRAVES; publ. *Pathology*.

NATURAL SCIENCES

General

Australian Academy of Science: GPO Box 783, Canberra, ACT 2601; tel. (2) 6201-9400; fax (2) 6201-9494; e-mail eb@science.org.au; internet www.science.org.au; f. 1954; independent non-profit organization for Australia's leading research scientists, elected for their personal contributions to science; recognizes research excellence, advises government, organizes scientific conferences, publishes scientific books and journals; administers intl exchange programmes and promotes science education and public awareness of science and technology; 396 fellows; Pres. Prof. KURT LAMBECK; Exec. Sec. SUE SERJEANTSON; Sec. (Biological Sciences) Prof. JOHN SHINE; Sec. (Education and Public Awareness) Prof. JULIE CAMPBELL; Sec. (Physical Sciences) Dr ROBERT FRATER; Sec. (Science Policy) Dr PHILIP KUCHEL; Foreign Sec. Prof. JENNY GRAVES; Treasurer Prof. PHIL MCFADDEN; publs *Records*, *Science and Industry Forum reports*, *Year Book*.

Australian and New Zealand Association for the Advancement of Science (ANZAAS): University of Adelaide, Adelaide, SA 5005; tel. (8) 8303-4965; fax (8) 8177-1732; e-mail mail@anzaas.org.au; internet anzaas.org.au; f. 1886; 1,000 mems; Divisions in NSW, Vic., SA, WA, Tas., ACT and NT, also overseas mems; Sec. ROBERT PERRIN; publ. *ANZAAS Mercury* (4 a year).

Australian Conservation Foundation: Floor 1, 60 Leicester St, Carlton, Vic. 3053; tel. (3) 9345-1112; fax (3) 9345-1166; e-mail acf@acfonline.org.au; internet www.acfonline.org.au; f. 1965; non-profit org. working for an ecologically sustainable society; 60,000 mems and supporters; library of 15,000 vols; Pres. Prof. IAN LOWE; Dir DON HENRY; publs *Bilby Bulletin*, *Habitat* (6 a year).

Federation of Australian Scientific and Technological Societies: POB 218, Deakin West, Canberra, ACT 2600; tel. (2) 6257-2891; fax (2) 6257-2897; e-mail fasts@anu.edu.au; internet www.fasts.org; f. 1985 to foster close relations between the scientific and technological socs in Australia and to take concerted action for promoting science and technology in Australia; 60 mem. socs; Pres. Prof. CHRIS FELL; Pres.-Elect Prof. SNOW BARLOW; Exec. Dir BRADLEY SMITH; publ. *FASTS Circular* (monthly).

Royal Society of New South Wales: 6/142 Herring Rd, North Ryde, POB 1525 Macquarie Centre, NSW 2113; tel. (2) 9887-4448; fax (2) 9887-4448; internet www.science.uts.edu.au/rsnsw; f. 1821; collection of monographs and periodicals relating to the history of Australian science, manuscripts of original research results; 305 mems; Pres. K. F. KELLY; Hon. Sec. Prof. Dr P. A. WILLIAMS; publs *Journal and Proceedings* (2 a year), *Bulletin* (monthly).

Royal Society of Queensland: POB 21, St Lucia, Qld 4067; f. 1884; natural and applied sciences; 250 mems; library of 75,000 vols; Pres. Dr JULIA PLAYFORD; Hon. Sec. C. WALTON; publs *Proceedings* (annually), *Symposia*, *Science Queensland* (4 a year).

Royal Society of South Australia Inc.: South Australian Museum, North Terrace, Adelaide, SA 5000; tel. (8) 8223-5360; e-mail roysocsa@gmail.com; internet www.ees.adelaide.edu.au/industry/rssa/index.html; f. 1853; natural sciences; 270 mems; Pres. Dr ALAN PRING; Hon. Sec. Dr ROBERT LAVIGNE; publs *Transactions* (annual), *Regional Natural Histories* (irreg.).

Royal Society of Tasmania: GPO Box 1166, Hobart, Tas 7001; tel. (3) 6211-4147; fax (3) 6211-4112; e-mail royal.society@tmag.tas.gov.au; f. 1843; 360 mems; library of 40,000 vols; Pres. Dr MICHAEL READETT; Hon. Sec. CAROL BACON; publ. *Papers and Proceedings* (annually).

Royal Society of Victoria: 9 Victoria St, Melbourne, Vic. 3000; tel. (3) 9663-5259; fax (3) 9663-2301; e-mail admin@sciencevictoria.org.au; internet www.sciencevictoria.org.au; f. 1854; 750 mems; library: large colln of scientific periodicals; Pres. Prof. GRAHAM D. BURROWS; Hon. Sec. Prof. T. FRED SMITH; publ. *Proceedings* (2 a year).

Royal Society of Western Australia: c/o Western Australian Museum, Locked Bag 49, Welshpool DC, WA 6986; tel. (8) 9212-3771; fax (8) 9212-3882; e-mail rswa@museum.wa.gov.au; internet www.ecu.edu.au/pa/rswa; f. 1913; to promote and foster natural and physical science and facilitate interdisciplinary interaction; study of botany, zoology, geology, anthropology, geography, physics and chemistry; 395 mems; Pres. Dr COLIN WALKER; Joint Secs Dr LYNNE MILNE, MARGARET BROCX; publ. *Journal* (4 a year).

Biological Sciences

Australian Society for Fish Biology: WA Marine Research Laboratories, POB 20, North Beach, WA 6020; tel. (8) 9246-8418; e-mail dgaughan@fish.wa.gov.au; internet www.asfb.org.au; f. 1971 to promote the study of fish and fisheries in Australia and provide a communications medium for Australian fish workers; 530 mems; Pres. Dr DAN GAUGHAN; Sec. and Vice-Pres. KIM SMITH; publ. *Newsletter* (2 a year).

Australian Society for Limnology: Museum of Victoria, GPO Box 666, Melbourne, Vic. 3001; tel. (3) 8341-7433; fax (3) 8341-7750; e-mail rmarch@museum.vic.gov.au; internet www.asl.org.au; f. 1961; study and management of inland waters; 600 mems, incl. researchers, managers, engineers, teachers and tertiary-level students; Sec. Dr RICHARD MARCHANT; publ. *ASL Newsletter* (quarterly).

Australian Society for Microbiology Inc.: Unit 23, 20 Commercial Rd, Melbourne, Vic. 3004; tel. (3) 9867-8699; fax (3) 9867-8722; e-mail theasm@asm.auz.com; f. 1959; 3,200 mems; Pres. Assoc. Prof. JOHN FINLAY-JONES; Sec. Dr J. LANSER; publs *Microbiology Australia* (5 a year), *Recent Advances in Microbiology* (annually).

Australian Society for Parasitology: c/o Dr M. K. Jones, Queensland Institute of Medical Research, Herston, Qld 4006; tel. (7) 3362-0405; fax (7) 3362-0104; e-mail malcolmj@qimr.edu.au; internet www.parasite.org.au; f. 1964; all aspects of parasitology, including immunology and vaccinology; 380 mems; 27 fellows; Pres. Dr MALCOLM JONES; Sec. Dr DANIELLE SMYTH; publ. *International Journal for Parasitology* (12 a year).

Ecological Society of Australia Inc.: POB 1564, Canberra, ACT 2601; tel. (8) 8952-4480; fax (8) 8952-4480; e-mail executiveofficer@ecolsoc.org.au; internet www.ecolsoc.org.au; f. 1960 to promote the scientific study of plants and animals in relation to their environment, and publication of the results of research; to facilitate the exchange of ideas amongst ecologists; to promote the application of ecological principles to the development, utilization and conservation of Australian natural resources; to advise government and other agencies; to foster the reservation of natural areas for scientific and recreational purposes; 1,564 mems; Pres. Dr C. D. JAMES; Sec. Dr G. EDWARDS; Exec. Officer T. HOWARD; publs *Bulletin* (4 a year), *Austral Ecology* (6 a year), *Environmental Management and Restoration* (3 a year).

Entomological Society of New South Wales Inc.: Entomology Dept, The Australian Museum, 6–8 College St, Sydney, NSW 2000; e-mail tanya.james@agric.nsw.gov.au; internet entsocnsw.netfirms.com; f. 1953; 180 mems; Pres. MARTIN HORWOOD; Hon. Sec. TANYA JAMES; publ. *General and Applied Entomology* (annually).

Entomological Society of Queensland: POB 537, Indooroopilly, Brisbane, Qld 4072; e-mail esq@uqconnect.net; internet www.esq.org.au/entomologist.html; independent; f. 1923; 300 mems; Pres. Dr P. ALLSOPP; Sec. G. MAYWALD; publs *News Bulletin* (10 a year), *The Australian Entomologist* (3–4 a year).

Field Naturalists Club of Victoria: Locked Bag 3, Post Office, Blackburn, Vic. 3130; tel. (3) 9877-9860; fax (3) 9877-9860; e-mail fncv@vicnet.net.au; internet www.vicnet.net.au/~fncv; f. 1880; study of natural history and conservation of environment; 1,000 mems; Pres. KAREN MUSCAT; publs *The Victorian Naturalist* (6 a year), *Field Nats News* (11 a year).

Malacological Society of Australasia: c/o Dept of Malacology, Australian Museum, 6 College St, Sydney, NSW 2010; tel. (2) 9320-6275; fax (2) 9320-6050; e-mail des@phm.gov.au; f. 1955; 400 mems; Pres. D. L. BEECHEY; Sec. MICHAEL KEATS; publs *Australasian Shell News* (4 a year), *Molluscan Research* (2 a year).

Royal Australasian Ornithologists Union & Birds Australia: 415 Riversdale Rd, Hawthorn East, Vic. 3123; tel. (3) 9882-2622; fax (3) 9882-2677; e-mail mail@birdsaustralia.com.au; internet www.birdsaustralia.com.au; f. 1901; for conservation and scientific study of Australasian birds; extensive library and database; 7,000 mems; CEO JIM DOWNEY; publs *Wingspan*, *Emu*, *Stilt* (bulletin of Australasian Wader Studies Group, 2 a year), *Eclectus* (bulletin of Parrot Group, 2 a year), *ASE News* (Seabird Group newsletter), *ARA News* (Raptor Group newsletter, 2 a year).

Royal Zoological Society of New South Wales: POB 20, Mosman, NSW 2088; tel. (2) 9969-7336; fax (2) 9969-7336; f. 1879; 1,000 mems; Pres. Dr PAT HUTCHINGS; Exec. Officer GILLIAN SIMPSON; publ. *Australian Zoologist* (2 a year).

Royal Zoological Society of South Australia Inc.: Frome Rd, Adelaide, SA 5000; tel. (8) 8267-3255; fax (8) 8239-0637; internet www.adelaidezoo.com.au; f. 1878; maintains public zoo and open-range park; plays an active role in the conservation of endangered species, conservation education and in conservation research; 19,000 mems; library of 2,800 vols; books, audiovisual and digital media; Chief Exec. Prof. C. WEST.

Wildlife Preservation Society of Australia Inc.: POB 42, Brighton Le Sands, NSW 2216; e-mail wildlifepreservation@optusnet.com.au; f. 1909; independent, voluntary, non-profit organisation, committed to the preservation of Australia's flora and fauna; provides advice to government agencies and institutions regarding environmental and conservation issues; national environmental education programmes, political lobbying, advocacy and practical conservation work; 1,000 mems; Pres. PATRICK W. MEDWAY; Hon. Sec. SUZANNE MEDWAY; publ. *Australian Wildlife Magazine* (quarterly).

Zoological Parks and Gardens Board: POB 74, Parkville, Vic. 3052; tel. (3) 9285-9300; fax (3) 9285-9330; e-mail zpgb@zoo.org.au; internet www.zoo.org.au; f. 1937 as successor to Royal Zoological and Acclimatisation Society of Victoria (f. 1857); responsible for the management of the Royal Melbourne Zoological Gardens, Healesville Sanctuary and Victoria's Open Range Zoo at Werribee; 9 mems; Chair. TINA MCMECKAN.

Mathematical Sciences

Australian Mathematical Society: Dept of Mathematics, Univ. of Queensland, Brisbane, Qld 4072; tel. (7) 3365-2313; fax (7) 3365-1477; e-mail secretary@austms.org.au; internet www.austms.org.au; f. 1956; 900 mems; Pres. Prof. P. G. HALL; Sec. Dr E. J. BILLINGTON; publs *Journal* (6 a year), *Bulletin* (6 a year), *Gazette* (5 a year), *ANZIAM Journal* (quarterly).

Statistical Society of Australia, Inc.: POB 5111, Braddon, ACT 2612; tel. (2) 6249-8266; fax (2) 6249-6558; e-mail admin@statsoc.org.au; internet www.statsoc.org.au; f. 1959; 800 mems; Pres. Prof. KAYE BASFORD; Sec. Dr DOUGLAS SHAW; publs *Australian & New Zealand Journal of Statistics* (4 a year), *SSAI Newsletter* (quarterly).

Physical Sciences

Astronomical Society of Australia: c/o School of Physics, Univ. of Sydney, NSW 2006; tel. (2) 9351-3184; fax (2) 9351-7726; e-mail j.obyrne@physics.usyd.edu.au; internet asa.astronomy.org.au; f. 1966 as the organization of professional astronomers in Australia; 400 mems; Pres. Prof. GARY DA COSTA; Sec. Dr JOHN O'BYRNE; publ. *Publications of the Astronomical Society of Australia* (online, quarterly).

Astronomical Society of South Australia (Inc.): GPO Box 199, Adelaide, SA 5001; tel. (8) 8821-1751; internet www.assa.org.au; f. 1892; 500 mems; library of 400 vols; Pres. P. A. ELLIN; Sec. B. M. NEYLON; publ. *The Bulletin* (monthly).

Astronomical Society of Tasmania Inc.: c/o The Secretary, POB 1654, Hobart, Tas. 7001; tel. (3) 6323-3777; fax (3) 6323-3776; internet www.ast.net.au; f. 1934; 100 mems; Pres. S. W. MATHERS; Sec. LAURIE. PRIEST; publs *Bulletin* (every 2 months), *Annual Ephemeris for Tasmania*.

Astronomical Society of Victoria Inc.: GPO Box 1059, Melbourne, Vic. 3001; tel. (3) 9888-7130; internet www.asv.org.au; f. 1922; 1,000 mems; library of 3,000 vols; Pres. B. ADCOCK; Sec. G. WILLIAMS; publs *Newsletter 'Crux'* (every 2 months), *Astronomical Yearbook*.

Australasian College of Physical Scientists and Engineers in Medicine: c/o Dept of Physical Sciences, Peter MacCallum Cancer Institute, Locked Bag 1, A'Beckett St, Melbourne, Vic. 8006; tel. (3) 9656-1253; fax (3) 9650-4870; e-mail secretary@acpsem.org.au; internet www.acpsem.org.au; f. 1977 to promote the development of the physical sciences as applied to medicine, to facilitate the exchange of information and ideas among mems and others, to disseminate knowledge relating to physical sciences and their application to medicine; 450 mems (179 corporate, 232 assoc.); Pres. Dr H. ROUND; Hon. Sec. Dr JOHN R. COLES; publ. *Australasian Physical and Engineering Sciences in Medicine* (quarterly).

Australian Acoustical Society: POB 903, Castlemaine, Vic. 3450; tel. (3) 5470-6381; fax (3) 5470-6381; e-mail watkinsd@castlemaine.net; internet www.acoustics.asn.au; f. 1971; 420 mems; Pres. KEN MIKL; Gen. Sec. D. WATKINS; publ. *Acoustics Australia* (3 a year).

Australian Institute of Physics: 1/21 Vale Street, North Melbourne, Vic. 3051; tel. (3) 9326-6669; fax (3) 9328-2670; e-mail physics@raci.org.au; internet www.physics.usyd.edu.au/aipaust; f. 1963; 2,500 mems; Pres. Prof. ROBERT ELLMAN; Hon. Sec. Dr IAN BAILEY; publ. *The Physicist* (6 a year).

Geological Society of Australia: Suite 706, 301 George St, Sydney, NSW 2000; tel. (2) 9290-2194; fax (2) 9290-2198; e-mail info@gsa.org.au; internet www.gsa.org.au; f. 1953; 2,300 mems; publs *Australian Journal of Earth Sciences* (8 a year), *Alcheringa* (quarterly).

Royal Australian Chemical Institute: 21 Vale St, North Melbourne, Vic. 3051; tel. (3) 9328-2033; fax (3) 9328-2670; e-mail member@raci.org.au; internet www.raci.org.au; f. 1917, inc. by Royal Charter 1932; it is both the qualifying body for professional chemists and a learned society which aims to promote the science and practice of chemistry in all its branches; 9,500 mems; Pres. DAVID EDMONDS; Hon. Gen. Sec. Dr JANE WEDER; publ. *Chemistry in Australia* (monthly).

PHILOSOPHY AND PSYCHOLOGY

Australasian Association of Philosophy: Dept of Philosophy, La Trobe Univ., Melbourne, Vic. 3086; tel. (3) 9479-3605; fax (3) 9479-3639; e-mail t.oakley@latrobe.edu.au; internet www.uq.edu.au/hprc/aap; f. 1923; brs throughout Australia and New Zealand; 400 mems; Pres. GRAHAM PRIEST; Sec. TIM OAKLEY; publ. *Australasian Journal of Philosophy* (quarterly).

Australian Psychological Society: POB 38, Flinders Lane, Vic 8009; located at: 11th Fl., 257 Collins St, Melbourne, Vic. 3000; tel. (3) 8662-3300; fax (3) 9663-6177; e-mail assessments@psychology.org.au; internet www.psychology.org.au; f. 1966; 15,500 mems; Pres. AMANDA GORDON; Exec. Dir Dr LYNDEL LITTLEFIELD; publs *Australian Journal of Psychology* (3 a year), *Australian Psychologist* (3 a year), *In-Psych* (6 a year).

RELIGION, SOCIOLOGY AND ANTHROPOLOGY

Australian Sociological Association: School of Social Science, Univ. of Queensland, St. Lucia, Qld 4072; tel. (7) 3365-7516; fax (7) 3365-1544; e-mail admin@tasa.org.au; internet www.tasa.org.au; f. 1963; aims to promote devt of sociology in Australia; 650 mems; Pres. Prof. MICHAEL GILDING; Vice-Pres. Dr TIM MARJORIBANKS; Sec. EILEEN CLARK; Treasurer Dr WENDY HILLMAN; publs *Journal of Sociology* (quarterly), *Nexus Newsletter*, *Health Sociology Review*.

TECHNOLOGY

Australasian Ceramic Society: c/o Dept of Applied Physics, Curtin University of Technology, GPOB U1987, Perth, WA 6845; tel. (8) 9266-7544; fax (8) 9266-2377; e-mail j.low@curtin.edu.au; internet www.austceram.com; f. 1961; to promote ceramic science and technology and its applications for Australian ceramic industry and art; 250 mems; Fed. Pres. Dr DAN PERERA; Fed. Sec. Assoc. Prof. JIM LOW; publs *Journal* (2 a year), *Newsbulletin* (4 a year).

Australasian Institute of Mining and Metallurgy: Level 3, 15–31 Pelham St, Carlton, Vic. 3053; tel. (3) 9662-3166; fax (3) 9662-3662; e-mail publications@ausimm.com.au; internet www.ausimm.com.au; f. 1893; incorporated by Royal Charter 1955; 8,500 mems; Pres. IAN GOULD; publ. *The AusIMM Bulletin* (every 2 months).

Australian Academy of Technological Sciences and Engineering: Ian McLennan House, 197 Royal Parade, Parkville, Vic. 3052; tel. (3) 9347-0622; fax (3) 9347-8237; e-mail paulaw@atse.org.au; internet www.atse.org.au; f. 1976; promotion of scientific and engineering knowledge for practical purposes; 670 fellows (incl. 8 hon., 9 foreign, 1 Royal); Pres. Dr J. W. ZILLMAN; CEO Dr JOHN DODGSON; publs *Annual Report*, *Annual Symposia Proceedings*, *ATSE Focus (Quarterly)*.

Australian Institute of Energy: POB 268, Toukley, NSW 2263; tel. and fax (2) 4393-1114; e-mail aie@aie.org.au; internet www.aie.org.au; f. 1978; 1,500 mems; Pres. Dr MALCOLM MESSENGER; Sec. COLIN PAULSON; Treasurer Dr DAVID ALLARDICE; publ. *Energy News* (quarterly).

Australian Institute of Food Science and Technology, Inc.: Suite 2, Level 2, 191 Botany Rd, Waterloo, NSW 2017; tel. (612) 8399-3996; fax (612) 8399-3997; e-mail aifst@aifst.asn.au; internet www.aifst.asn.au; f. 1967; national association for professionals involved in the science and technology of food; Pres. Prof. PAUL BAUMGARTNER; Treasurer Dr JEFF FAIRBROTHER; publ. *Food Australia* (monthly).

Australian Institute of Nuclear Science and Engineering: PMB No. 1, Menai, NSW 2234; tel. (2) 9717-3376; fax (2) 9717-9268; e-mail ainse@ansto.gov.au; internet www.ainse.edu.au; f. 1958; consortium of Australian universities and the University of Auckland, New Zealand, in partnership with the Australian Nuclear Science and Technology Organization; aims to assist research and training in nuclear science and engineering and to make the facilities of the Lucas Heights Research Laboratories available to research staff and students from mem. institutions; projects in advanced materials, biomedicine, environmental science, applications of nuclear physics, nuclear technology and engineering; organizes Australian Numerical Simulation and Modelling Services and Australian Radioisotope Services; organizes conferences, awards postgraduate studentships and research grants; 49 mems; Pres. Prof. JOHN WHITE; Vice-Pres. Prof. BRIAN O'CONNOR; Scientific Sec. Dr DENNIS MATHER; publs *AINSE Annual Report*, *AINSE Conference Books*.

Australian Robotics and Automation Association Inc.: GPO Box 1527, Sydney, NSW 2001; tel. (2) 9959-3239; fax (2) 9959-4632; internet www.araa.asn.au; f. 1981; professional society concerned with robots, their applications and implications, and related automation technologies; Pres. GORDON WYETH; Vice-Pres. JONATHAN ROBERTS; Sec. MATTHEW DUNBABIN; publ. *Newsletter* (quarterly).

Chartered Institute of Logistics and Transport: POB A2333, Sydney South, NSW 1235; tel. (2) 9267-7538; fax (2) 9864-4738; e-mail cilta@bigpond.net.au; internet www.ciltia.com.au; f. 1935; professional society concerned with logistics and transport; 30,000 members worldwide; Admin Man. DIANNE DAVIS; publ. *Australian Transport Review* (2 a year).

Institution of Engineers, Australia: 11 National Circuit, Barton, ACT 2600; tel. (2) 6270-6555; fax (2) 6273-1488; e-mail memberservices@engineersaustralia.org.au; internet www.engineersaustralia.org.au; f. 1919; incorporates colleges of Biomedical Engineers, Chemical Engineers, Civil Engineers, Electrical Engineers, Environmental Engineers, Information Telecommunications and Electronics Engineers, Mechanical Engineers, and Structural Engineers; 75,000 mems; Chief Exec. PETER TAYLOR; publs *Engineers Australia* (monthly), *Engineers Australia Civil* (monthly), *Engineering World* (6 a year), *Australian Journal of Civil Engineering*, *Australian Journal of Electrical and Electronics Engineering*, *Australian Journal of Mechanical Engineering*, *Chemical Engineering in Australia*, *Australian Journal of Multidisciplinary Engineering*, *Transport Engineering in Australia*, *Australian Journal of Water Resources*.

Institution of Surveyors, Australia: 27–29 Napier Close, Deakin, Canberra, ACT 2600; tel. (2) 6282-2282; fax (2) 6282-2576; e-mail info@isaust.org.au; internet www.isaust.org.au; f. 1952; 3,800 mems; CEO JOHN D. CRICKMORE; publs *The Australian Surveyor* (annually), *Trans Tasman Surveyor* (annually), *Geomatics Research Australasia* (2 a year).

Royal Aeronautical Society, Australian Division: POB 573, Mascot, NSW 2020; tel. (2) 9523-4332; fax (2) 9523-7158; e-mail austdivision@raes.org.au; internet www.raes.org.au; f. 1927; Pres. P. G. NICHOLSON; Hon. Sec. R. D. BARKLA; Treasurer R. H. STEVENS; publ. *Australian Aeronautics* (every 2 years).

Research Institutes

GENERAL

Australian Research Council: GPO 2702, Canberra, ACT 2601; tel. (2) 6287-6600; fax (2) 6287-6601; e-mail info@arc.gov.au; internet www.arc.gov.au; f. 2001; advises the nat. govt on how best to allocate funding for research in science, social science and the humanities; accountable to the Federal Minister for Education, Science and Training; Chief Exec. Prof. PETER HØJ; Exec. Dirs Prof. MARGARET CLAYTON (Biological Sciences and Biotechnology), Dr IAN MACKINNON (Engineering and Environmental Science), Prof. ELIM PAPADAKIS (Social, Behavioural and Economic Sciences), Dr MANDY THOMAS (Humanities and the Creative Arts), Dr DAVID FALVEY, Prof. JONATHAN MANTON; publs *Discovery* (newsletter, quarterly), *Strategic Plan* (every 2 years).

AGRICULTURE, FISHERIES AND VETERINARY SCIENCE

Department of Infrastructure, Planning and Natural Resources: GPO Box 39, Sydney, NSW 2001; tel. (2) 9228-6111; fax (2) 9228-6455; e-mail infocentre@dipnr.nsw.gov.au; internet www.dipnr.nsw.gov.au; conservation and management of crown land, rivers and water resources and containment of salinity and acid sulphate soils; Dir-Gen. JENNIFER WESTACOTT.

EDUCATION

Australian Council for Educational Research Ltd: 19 Prospect Hill Rd (Private Bag 55), Camberwell, Vic. 3124; tel. (3) 9277-5555; fax (3) 9277-5500; e-mail info@acer.edu.au; internet www.acer.edu.au; f. 1930; independent; educational research and publishing; books for teachers at all levels, students, parents, psychologists, counsellors, administrators, curriculum writers; educational, psychological and personnel tests; CEO Prof. GEOFFEREY MASTERS; publs *Australian Education Index* (quarterly), *Australian Journal of Career Development* (3 a year), *Australian Journal of Education* (3 a year), *Australian Thesaurus of Education Descriptors* (annually), *Bibliography of Education Theses in Australia* (annually), *Newsletter* (3 a year), *Professional Education* (4 a year), *Teacher Education Magazine* (11 a year).

National Centre for Vocational Education Research (NCVER) Ltd: Level 11, 33 King William St, Adelaide, SA 5000; tel. (8) 8230-8400; fax (8) 8212-3436; e-mail ncver@ncver.edu.au; internet www.ncver.edu.au; f. 1981; independent org. established by the Federal, State and Territory ministers responsible for vocational and technical education; Australia's principal provider of vocational education and training (VET) research and statistics; responsible for collecting and managing national VET and New Apprenticeship statistics; provides VET research findings from Australian and international sources through its VOCED research database; library of 20,000 vols; Chair. PETER GRANT; Man. Dir Dr TOM KARMEL; publs *Insight* (news and information, quarterly), *Vocational Education and Training Research Database (VOCED)* (4 a year).

HISTORY, GEOGRAPHY AND ARCHAEOLOGY

Tasmanian Historical Research Association: POB 441, Sandy Bay, Tas. 7006; tel. (3) 6260-2515; fax (3) 6260-2438; e-mail dsnowdon@iinet.net.au; internet www.thra.tascom.net; f. 1951; 400 mems; Pres. and Chair. Dr STEFAN PETROW; Sec. DIANNE SNOWDEN; publ. *Papers and Proceedings* (4 a year).

MEDICINE

Australian Radiation Protection and Nuclear Safety Agency (Australian Department of Health and Ageing): 619 Lower Plenty Rd, Yallambie, Vic. 3085; tel. (3) 9433-2211; fax (3) 9432-1835; e-mail arpansa@arpansa.gov.au; internet www.arpansa.gov.au; f. 1929; works to protect the environment and the health and safety of the public from the harmful effects of radiation; library of 10,000 vols; CEO Dr JOHN LOY; publ. *ARPANSA technical reports* (irregular).

Australian Society for Medical Research: 145 Macquarie St, Sydney, NSW 2000; tel. (2) 9256-5450; fax (2) 9252-0294; e-mail asmr@world.net; internet www.asmr.org.au; f. 1961 to provide a forum for discussion of medical research across disciplinary boundaries, and to encourage recent graduates to consider research as a career; holds Nat. Scientific Conference; 1,400 mems; Hon. Sec. Dr BRONWYN KINGWELL; Hon. Treasurer Dr ROHAN BAKER; publ. *Proceedings*.

Baker Medical Research Institute: POB 6492, St Kilda Rd Central, Melbourne, Vic. 3004; tel. (3) 8532-1111; fax (3) 8532-1100; e-mail baker@baker.edu.au; internet www.baker.edu.au; f. 1926; basic, clinical and applied research on cardiovascular disease, physiology, pharmacology, endocrinology, molecular and cell biology; affiliated to WHO, Monash University, Alfred Hospital including the Alfred-Baker Medical Unit (f. 1949); library of 15,000 vols; Dir Prof. GARRY JENNINGS; Pres., Board of Management NORMAN O'BRYAN; CEO ERICA HUGHES; publs *Annual Report*, *Research*.

CSL Ltd: 45 Poplar Rd, Parkville, Vic. 3052; tel. (3) 9389-1911; fax (3) 9389-1434; f. 1916 for research, production and marketing of biologicals; library: Knowledge Library of 8,500 vols; CEO Dr BRIAN MCNAMEE; publ. *Annual Report of Activities*.

Institute of Dental Research: Westmead Millenium Institute, POB 412, Westmead NSW 2145; f. 1946; for research into biological problems relating to dental health; Head Prof. NEIL HUNTER (acting).

Institute of Medical and Veterinary Science: Frome Rd, Adelaide, SA 5000; tel. (8) 8222-3000; fax (8) 8222-3538; f. 1938 for purposes of research into diseases of human beings and animals, and to provide a diagnostic pathology service for the Royal Adelaide Hospital and for the State through 12 regional laboratories; teaching is provided for the Univ. of Adelaide Medical School; Dir BARRIE VERON-ROBERTS; publ. *Annual Report*.

Kolling Institute of Medical Research: Royal North Shore Hospital, Pacific Highway, St Leonards, NSW 2065; tel. (2) 9926-8486; fax (2) 9926-8484; e-mail kolling@med.usyd.edu.au; internet www.kolling.usyd.edu.au; f. 1930; Exec. Officer CAMILLA SCANLAN; Technical Officer HELEN YU; research in allergic diseases, molecular genetics and growth factors; publ. *Biennial Report*.

Mental Health Research Institute: 155 Oak St, Parkville, Vic. 3052; tel. (3) 9388-1633; fax (3) 9387-5061; e-mail rj@mhri.edu.auj; internet www.mhri.edu.au; f. 1956; studies aspects of the nature and treatment of psychiatric illnesses with a particular emphasis on a neuroscience approach to Alzheimer's Disease and to the major psychoses, especially schizophrenia; Chair. Prof. BRUCE R. KEAN; Dir Prof. DAVID COPOLOV.

National Health and Medical Research Council: GPO Box 9848, Canberra, ACT 2601; tel. (2) 6289-9184; fax (2) 6289-9197; e-mail exec.sec@nhmrc.gov.au; internet www.nhmrc.gov.au; f. 1936 to advise on the achievement and maintenance of the highest practicable standards of individual and public health, and to foster research in the interests of improving those standards; CEO Prof. ALAN PETTIGREW; publs *Annual Report*, *Triennial Strategic Plan*.

National Vision Research Institute of Australia: 386 Cardigan St, Carlton, Melbourne, Vic. 3053; tel. (3) 9349-7480; fax (3) 9349-7473; e-mail nvri@optometry.unimelb.edu.au; internet www.optometry.unimelb.edu.au/nvri/nvri.htm; f. 1972; basic, applied and clinical research into vision and visual dysfunction; Chair. S. F. KALFF; Dir of Research Prof. P. R. MARTIN; publ. *Annual Report and Newsletter* (for members).

Queensland Institute of Medical Research: PO Royal Brisbane Hospital, Brisbane, Qld 4029; tel. (7) 3362-0222; fax (7) 3362-0111; e-mail info@qimr.edu.au; internet www.qimr.edu.au; f. 1945; research into medical problems important in the Australian and Asian Pacific region; current areas are tropical medicine, virology, oncology, cell biology, molecular biology, epidemiology, liver disease; library of 19,100 vols; Chair. of Council BRUCE WATSON; Dir Prof. MICHAEL F. GOOD; publ. *Annual Report*.

Walter and Eliza Hall Institute of Medical Research: 1G, Royal Parade, Parkville, Vic. 3050; tel. (3) 9345-2555; fax (3) 9347-0852; e-mail information@wehi.edu.au; internet www.wehi.edu.au; f. 1916; research into cellular and molecular immunology, cancer, immunopathology and immunoparasitology, genome science and bioinformatics; 500 staff; library of 20,000 vols; Dir Prof. SUZANNE CORY.

NATURAL SCIENCES

General

Commonwealth Scientific and Industrial Research Organisation (CSIRO): Bag 10, Clayton South, Vic. 3169; tel. (3) 9545-2176; fax (3) 9545-2175; e-mail enquiries@csiro.au; internet www.csiro.au; f. 1926; researches all fields of the physical and biological sciences except defence science, nuclear energy and clinical medicine; Sectors: Field Crops; Food Processing; Forestry, Wood and Paper Industries; Horticulture; Meat, Dairy and Aquaculture; Wool and Textiles; Biodiversity; Climate and Atmosphere; Land and Water; Marine; Information Technology and Telecommunications; Built Environment; Measurement Standards; Radio Astronomy; Services; Chemicals and Plastics; Integrated Manufactured Products; Pharmaceuticals and Human Health; Energy; Mineral Exploration and Mining; Mineral Processing and Metal Production; Petroleum; library: library: see Libraries and Archives; Chair. CATHERINE LIVINGSTONE; Chief Exec. Dr GEOFF GARRETT; publs *Australian Journal of: Agricultural Research* (8 a year), *Australian Systematic Botany* (4 a year), *Botany* (6 a year), *Chemistry* (monthly), *ECOS* (4 a year), *Experimental Agriculture* (6 a year), *The Helix* (6 a year), *Invertebrate Taxonomy* (6 a year), *Marine and Freshwater Research* (6 a year), *Physics* (6 a years), *Plant Physiology* (6 a year), *Reproduction, Fertility and Development* (6 a year), *Soil Research* (6 a year), *Wildlife Research* (6 a year), *Zoology* (6 a year).

National Facility within CSIRO:

CSIRO–Australia Telescope National Facility: POB 76, Epping, NSW 1710; tel. (2) 9372-4100; fax (2) 9372-4310; e-mail atnf-enquiries@csiro.au; internet www.atnf.csiro.au; f. 1988; a radio telescope array consisting of six 22-m antennas at the Paul Wild Observatory, Narrabri, NSW, a 22-m antenna at Mopra, west of Coonabarabran, NSW, and a 64-m antenna near Parkes, NSW; Dir Prof. BRIAN BOYLE.

Biological Sciences

Australian Institute of Marine Science: PMB 3, Townsville MC, Qld 4810; tel. (7) 4753-4444; fax (7) 4772-5852; e-mail reception@aims.gov.au; internet www.aims.gov.au; f. 1972; to advance knowledge, sustainable use and protection of the marine environment, through scientific and technological research; 165 mems; library of 10,000 vols, 1,875 periodicals, 1,544 electronic journals, 450 maps, 55 video cassettes; Chair. Dr IAN GOULD; CEO Prof. IAN R. POINER; publ. *Annual Report*.

Australian National Botanic Gardens: POB 1777, Canberra, ACT 2601; located at: Clunies Ross St, Black Mountain, Canberra; tel. (2) 6250-9450; fax (2) 6250-9599; e-mail anbg-info@anbg.gov.au; internet www.anbg.gov.au; f. 1970; grows a colln of Australian native plants (6,500 species); jtly manages with CSIRO the Centre for Plant Biodiversity Research and Australian National Herbarium with about 1.2m. specimens; manages the Australian Plant Image Index, the largest colln of photographs of Australian native plants; 1,500 mems; library of 13,356 vols, 650 serial titles, 5000 maps; Dir ANNE DUNCAN.

Royal Botanic Gardens Melbourne: Private Bag 2000, S. Yarra, Vic. 3141; tel. (3) 9252-2300; fax (3) 9252-2350; e-mail rbg@rbg.vic.gov.au; internet www.rbg.vic.gov.au; f. 1846; 36-ha (94-acre) garden with more than 10,000 different species and cultivars of Australian and exotic plants; herbarium of 1,000,000 specimens; library of 50,000 vols; also Royal Botanic Gardens, Cranbourne, for growing display and study of native Australian plants; also Australian Research Centre for Urban Ecology; Dir Dr PHILIP MOORS; publ. *Muelleria*.

Royal Botanic Gardens Sydney: Mrs Macquaries Rd, Sydney, NSW 2000; tel. (2) 9231-8111; fax (2) 9251-4403; e-mail inquiries@rbgsyd.nsw.gov.au; internet www.rbgsyd.nsw.gov.au; f. 1816; 470-hectare living plant collection in three botanic gardens and herbarium of 1,000,000 specimens; library of 50,000 vols; Mount Tomah Botanic Garden for cool-climate plants; Mount Annan Botanic Garden for native plants; specialization in research on Australian native plants; Exec. Dir TIM ENTWISLE; publs *Telopea*, *Cunninghamia*.

Therapeutic Goods Administration Laboratories: POB 100, Woden, ACT 2606; tel. (2) 6232-8400; fax (2) 6232-8442; e-mail tga-information-officer@health.gov.au; internet www.tga.gov.au; f. 1958 as National Biological Standards Laboratories to ensure the quality, safety, efficacy and timely availability of therapeutic goods used in or exported from Australia; part of the Therapeutic Goods Administration, Dept of Health and Aged Care; library of 30,000 vols and 5,000 microfiche; Dir Dr R. J. SMITH; publ. *TGA Laboratory Information Bulletin* (annually).

Mathematical Sciences

Australian Bureau of Statistics: Locked Bag 10, Belconnen, ACT 2616; tel. (2) 6252-5000; fax (2) 6251-6009; e-mail client.services@abs.gov.su; internet www.abs.gov.au; f. 1905; library of 38,000 vols, 9,600 periodicals; Australian Statistician DENNIS TREWIN; publs *Yearbook Australia* (annual), and some 400 other titles listed in *Catalogue of ABS Publications*.

Physical Sciences

Australian Nuclear Science and Technology Organisation (ANSTO): Attention: Access ANSTO, PMB 1, Menai, NSW 2234; tel. (2) 9717-3111; fax (2) 9717-9274; internet www.ansto.gov.au; f. 1987; Australia's nat. atomic org.; aims to bring the benefits of atomic science and technology to industry, medicine and the community; research and devt programmes focusing on industrial and other applications of atomic science, environmental science, advanced materials, biomedicine and health; operates nat. facilities, provides technical advice and training; library of 40,000 vols, 900,000 fiches; Exec. Dir Dr IAN SMITH; publ. scientific papers and reports.

Commonwealth Bureau of Meteorology: GPO Box 1289K, Melbourne, Vic. 3001; tel. (3) 9669-4000; fax (3) 9669-4699; internet www.bom.gov.au; f. 1908; regional offices in Perth, Adelaide, Brisbane, Sydney, Hobart, Darwin and Melbourne; library of 80,000 vols; Chair. Prof. VICKI SARA; Dir Dr GEOFF LOVE; publs daily weather bulletins and charts, monthly, seasonal and annual rainfall maps and statistical summaries, publications on special subjects, climatological reviews, *Australian Meteorological Magazine* (4 a year).

Geological Survey of New South Wales: Dept of Mineral Resources, POB 536, St Leonards, NSW 1590; tel. (2) 9901-8888; fax (2) 9901-8777; e-mail webcoord@minerals.nsw.gov.au; internet www.minerals.nsw.gov.au; f. 1874; advice on geology and mineral resources of NSW, incl. preparation of standard series geological, geophysical and metallogenic maps; research studies in tectonics, palaeontology, petrology and selected mineral commodities; Dir. Gen. ALAN COUTTS; publs *Quarterly Notes*, *Geological Memoirs*, *Palaeontological Memoirs*, *Bulletins*, *Records*, *Mineral Resources*, *Mineral Industry*, *Geological and Metallogenic Maps* (with notes).

Geological Survey of Victoria: Dept of Primary Industries, POB 500, East Melbourne, Vic. 3002; tel. (3) 9412-5042; fax (3) 9412-5155; e-mail customer.service@dpi.vic.gov.au; internet www.dpi.vic.gov.au; f. 1852; Man. TOM DICKSON; publs Reports, Bulletins, Geological Maps, etc.

Geological Survey of Western Australia: Mineral House, 100 Plain St, East Perth, WA 6004; tel. (8) 9222-3333; fax (8) 9222-3633; e-mail geological.survey@doir.wa.gov.au; internet www.doir.wa.gov.au/GSWA/index.asp; library: library; Exec. Dir Dr TIM GRIFFIN; publs *Bulletin*, *Mineral Resources Bulletin*.

Geoscience Australia (GA): GPO Box 378, Canberra, ACT 2601; tel. (2) 6249-9111; fax (2) 6249-9999; e-mail ref.library@ga.gov.au; internet www.ga.gov.au; f. 1946 as Bureau of Mineral Resources, Geology and Geophysics (BMR) to develop a comprehensive, scientific understanding of the geology of Australia, its offshore area, and the Australian Antarctic Territory; library of 21,000 vols, 4,000 serials; CEO Dr NEIL WILLIAMS; publ. *Bulletin*.

Mineral Resources Tasmania: POB 56, Rosny Park, Tas. 7018; tel. (3) 6233-8333; fax (3) 6233-8338; e-mail info@mrt.tas.gov.au; internet www.mrt.tas.gov.au; f. 1885; library of 10,000 books, 300 periodicals; Chief Geologist A. V. BROWN; publs *Explanatory Reports*, *Geological Survey Maps*, *Tasmanian Geological Survey Bulletins*, *Tasmanian Geological Survey Records*.

Mount Stromlo and Siding Spring Observatories: Cotter Rd, Weston Creek, ACT 2611; tel. (2) 6125-0230; fax (2) 6125-0233; e-mail director@mso.anu.edu.au; internet www.mso.anu.edu.au; f. 1924 as Commonwealth Solar Observatory; research in astrophysics, incl. all phases of stellar, galactic and extra-galactic astronomy; transferred to Australian National University 1957; library of 17,000 vols; Dir Prof. PENNY D. SACKETT; Sec. TERRY GALLAGHER.

Perth Observatory: 337 Walnut Rd, Bickley, WA 6076; tel. (8) 9293-8255; fax (8) 9293-8138; e-mail perthobs@calm.wa.gov.au; internet www.wa.gov.au/perthobs; f. 1896; astronomy research, education and outreach and information provision; research areas incl. optical astronomy, variable and transient monitoring, photometry, planetary observations, microlens monitoring and minor-body tracking; public star-viewing, guided tours and museum; library of 20,000 vols; Govt Astronomer JAMES BIGGS.

Primary Industries and Resources South Australia: 101 Grenfell St, GPO Box 1671, Adelaide, SA 5001; tel. (8) 8463-3000; fax (8) 8204-1880; internet www.pir.sa.gov.au; f. 1892; Geological Survey of South Australia, mining, energy and energy conservation, oil and gas; library of 25,000 vols (special coll. on early South Australian mining); Chief Exec. JIM HALLION; publs *Geological Survey Bulletin*, *MESA Journal* (quarterly), *Annual Report*.

Queensland Department of Natural Resourcesand Water: GPO Box 2454, Brisbane, Qld 4001; located at: 41 George St, Brisbane, Qld 4000; tel. (7) 3224-8790; fax (7) 3224-7571; e-mail library@nrw.qld.gov.au; internet www.nrw.qld.gov.au; f. 1874; climate change, natural resource management, geological mapping, sedimentary basin studies, metallogenic studies, biostratigraphy, geophysics, mineral, petroleum, coal and oil shale resources assessment, extractive industries and environmental management, land use planning, mining safety and technology, energy management, resource economics, computer and information services; library of 8,800 monographs, 27,000 reports, 1,000 serials, records, maps, map commentaries, guidebooks; Dir-Gen. (vacant); publs *Minerals and Energy Review*, *Queensland Geology*, *DME Reviews*, *Records*,

Queensland Government Mining Journal (monthly).

Riverview College Observatory: Lane Cove, NSW 2066; tel. (2) 9882-8295; fax (2) 9882-8455; e-mail bwmarsh@riverview.nsw.edu.au; f. 1908; meteorological observations, world-wide standard seismograph network station (1962); Dir R. W. MARSH.

RELIGION, SOCIOLOGY AND ANTHROPOLOGY

Australian Institute of Aboriginal and Torres Strait Islander Studies: GPO Box 553, Canberra, ACT 2601; tel. (2) 6246-1111; fax (2) 6261-4285; e-mail corporate@aiatsis.gov.au; internet www.aiatsis.gov.au; f. 1961; statutory body since 1964; provides funds, promotes research and publishes books on all aspects of Aboriginal and Torres Strait Islander studies, traditional and contemporary; library: 11,000 books, 1,220 serial titles, 32,000 book and journal analytics, 2,500 language books, 1,400 rare books, 14,000 pamphlets, 30,000 hours of audio tapes, 9,500 MSS, 650,000 prints and colour slides, 2.5 million feet of film and 5,000 video tapes; Chair. Prof. MICHAEL DODSON; publ. *Australian Aboriginal Studies* (2 a year).

Australian Institute of Archaeology: LaTrobe University, Vic. 3086; tel. (4) 2159-5966; e-mail director@aiarch.org.au; f. 1946 to investigate discoveries and results which the Institute or any other organization publishes, which relate to the authenticity, historicity, accuracy and inspiration of the Bible; teaching programmes and exhibitions on the ancient Near East and Biblical archaeology; library of 10,000 vols (special coll. on Palestinian, Egyptian and Mesopotamian archaeology); Dir CHRISTOPHER DAVEY; publ. *Buried History* (annually).

Australian Institute of Criminology: GPO Box 2994, Canberra, ACT 2601; tel. (2) 6260-9200; fax (2) 6260-9201; e-mail frontdesk@aic.gov.au; internet www.aic.gov.au; f. 1973; conducts criminology research, training courses, conferences and seminars, provides library and information services, publs results of research and other materials, and services the Criminology Research Council; library: see Libraries and Archives; Dir TONI MAKKAI (acting); publ. *Trends and Issues in Crime and Criminal Justice* (20 a year).

Elda Vaccari Collection of Multicultural Studies: Library, Victoria Univ. of Technology, POB 14428, Melbourne City Mail Centre, Melbourne, Vic. 8001; tel. (3) 9919-4809; fax (3) 9919-4920; e-mail mark.armstrong-roper@vu.edu.au; f. 1982; research on immigrant and minority groups in Australia; supported by Vaccari Italian Historical Trust; library of 4,000 vols; Librarian MARK ARMSTRONG-ROPER.

TECHNOLOGY

AMDEL: 1868 Dandenong Rd, Clayton, Vic. 3168; tel. (3) 9538-6777; fax (3) 9538-6704; f. 1960; analysis, testing, services in mineral engineering, chemical metallurgy, materials technology, mineralogy and petrology, process control instrument development, petroleum, geoanalysis, chemical analysis; offices and laboratories around Australia and New Zealand and representatives worldwide; 400 staff; Group Gen. Man. RAY DOYLE; publ. *Annual Report*.

ARRB Group Ltd: 500 Burwood Highway, Vermont South, Vic. 3133; tel. (3) 9881-1555; fax (3) 9887-8104; e-mail info@arrb.com.au; internet www.arrb.com.au; f. 1960; research related to the design, planning, construction, maintenance and use of roads, and transport; library of 42,000 vols and journals; Man. Dir GERARD WALDRON; Company Sec. TOM WOOD; publs *ARRB Briefing*, *ARRB Research Reports* (irreg.), *Australian Transport Index database*, *Proceedings of Biennial Conference*, *Road and Transport Research* (quarterly), *Special Reports* (irreg.), *Transport and Road Update* (monthly).

Defence Science and Technology Organisation: Building R1, Level 6, Russell Offices, Canberra, ACT 2600; tel. (2) 6265-9111; fax (2) 6265-2741; internet www.dsto.defence.gov.au; attached to Dept of Defence; Chief Defence Scientist Dr ROGER LOUGH.

Associated research laboratory:

Defence Science and Technology Organization, Fishermens Bend: 506 Lorimer St, Fishermens Bend, Vic. 3207; e-mail information@dsto.defence.gov.au; internet www.dsto.defence.gov.au; f. 1939; incl. divisions of Air Operations, Guided Weapons, and Airframes and Engines.

Water Research Foundation of Australia: c/o Centre for Resource and Environmental Studies, Australian National University, Canberra, ACT 0200; tel. (2) 6125-0651; fax (2) 6125-0757; e-mail office@cres.anu.edu.au; f. 1956; a non-profit research organization; research into the development, control, use and re-use of Australia's water resources; publs *Water and the Environment* (6 a year), *Annual Report*.

Libraries and Archives

Australian Capital Territory

Australian Institute of Criminology, J. V. Barry Library: GPO Box 2944, Canberra, ACT 2601; tel. (2) 6260-9264; fax (2) 6260-9299; e-mail jvbarry@aic.gov.au; internet www.aic.gov.au; f. 1974; material is collected in English in the field of criminology; 30,000 monographs, 800 periodicals; articles and monographs of Australian criminological interest are indexed for CINCH–The Australian Criminology Database, publicly available on the INFORMIT ONLINE network; Dir, Information Services JANET SMITH.

Australian National University Library: J. B. Chifley Bldg (15), Canberra, ACT 0200; tel. (2) 6125-2003; fax (2) 6125-6662; e-mail librarian@anu.edu.au; internet anulib.anu.edu.au; f. 1948; 2,200,000 vols; Librarian VIC ELLIOTT.

DEST Library Services, Department of Education, Science and Training: Loc. 702, GPO Box 9880, Canberra, ACT 2601; tel. (2) 6240-8848; fax (2) 6240-8861; e-mail library@dest.gov.au; internet www.dest.gov.au/library; f. 1945; 40,000 vols; Library Man. ROBYN SPRY.

High Court of Australia Library: POB 6309, Kingston, ACT 2604; tel. (2) 6270-6922; fax (2) 6273-2110; internet www.hcourt.gov.au/library; f. 1903; private library of the Justices of the Court and barristers appearing before it; 149,000 vols in Canberra; Librarian PETAL KINDER.

IP Australia Library: Discovery House, POB 200, Woden, ACT 2606; tel. (2) 6283-2999; fax (2) 6283-7999; e-mail library@ipaustralia.gov.au; internet www.ipaustralia.gov.au; f. 1904; 14,000 vols, 300 periodicals; Australian and foreign patent specifications from all patent countries, science and technology and industrial property.

National Archives of Australia: POB 7425, Canberra Mail Centre, ACT 2610; tel. (2) 6212-3600; fax (2) 6212-3699; e-mail archives@naa.gov.au; internet www.naa.gov.au; f. 1945; archival authority of the Commonwealth since 1952; responsible for the management of Commonwealth records: survey, storage, preservation, retention or destruction, retrieval and access; provides information to the public on nature and location of Commonwealth records and on agencies and persons responsible for them; collections of documents, maps, plans, films, photographs, records, paintings, models, microforms and electronic records (487,522 shelf metres); holdings date from the early 19th c., but most date from Federation (1901), derived from a variety of sources; offices in Canberra, Darwin and all state capitals; Dir-Gen. ROSS GIBBS; publs *Annual Report*, *Memento* (4 a year).

National Library of Australia: Parkes Place, Canberra, ACT 2600; tel. (2) 6262-1111; fax (2) 6257-1703; e-mail www@nla.gov.au; internet www.nla.gov.au; f. 1901; maintains a national colln of Australian library materials and provides a gateway to national and international sources of information; 2,852,901 vols, 41,031 current serial titles, 643,792 maps, 12,895 m of manuscript material, 16,297 oral history recordings, 189,031 music scores, 64,373 pictures and prints, 750,299 photographs, 860,187 aerial photographs, 3,812 electronic media; Dir-Gen. JAN FULLERTON; publs *Annual Report* (electronic and print), *APAIS* (online only), *Gateways* (electronic only, 6 a year), *NLA News* (electronic and print, monthly).

University of Canberra Library: The Library, University of Canberra, ACT 2601; tel. (2) 6201-2282; fax (2) 6201-5068; e-mail info@cts.canberra.edu.au; internet www.canberra.edu.au/library/index.html; f. 1968; 480,000 vols; collection includes audiovisual material, access to electronic information services; Librarian ANITA CROTTY.

New South Wales

Charles Sturt University–Division of Library Services: Locked Bag 7003, Bathurst, NSW 2795; tel. (2) 6338-4732; fax (2) 6338-4986; e-mail soakley@csu.edu.au; internet www.csu.edu.au/division/library; f. 1947; 637,904 vols, 2,005 CAUL Statistics non-serial items; libraries at Albury, Bathurst, Wagga Wagga, Burlington (Ontario, Canada), Orange and Dubbo; Exec. Dir, Library Services SHIRLEY OAKLEY.

City of Sydney Library: Town Hall House, Level 3, 456 Kent St, Sydney, NSW 2000; tel. (2) 9242-8555; fax (2) 9242-8561; e-mail library@cityofsydney.nsw.gov.au; internet www.cityofsydney.nsw.gov.au; f. 1877; 9 brs, 2 library links; 473,805 items, including books, CDs, DVDs, audio-books, magazines; 100 newspaper titles; special collns: Australiana, local govt, Olympic Games, koori (Aboriginal) material; Man. Library Services PATRICK CONDON.

Macquarie University Library: Bldg C7A, Macquarie University, NSW 2109; tel. (2) 9850-7546; fax (2) 9850-9236; e-mail maxine.brodie@library.mq.edu.au; internet www.library.mq.edu.au; f. 1964; 962,061 vols; University Librarian MAXINE BRODIE.

Newcastle Region Public Library: War Memorial Cultural Centre, Laman St, Newcastle, NSW 2300; tel. (2) 4974-5300; fax (2) 4974-5396; e-mail library@ncc.nsw.gov.au; internet www.ncc.nsw.gov.au/library; f. 1948; 406,242 vols; 2,663 periodicals; 121 newspaper titles; special facilities: Information Works, Local Studies, Hunter Photo Bank, Earthquake Database; publs *Newcastle Morning Herald Index* (1861–84, annually), *Monographs* (irregular).

Parliamentary Library of New South Wales: Parliament House, Sydney, NSW

2000; tel. (2) 9230-2383; fax (2) 9231-1932; e-mail libreq@parliament.nsw.gov.au; internet www.parliament.nsw.gov.au; f. 1840; 200,000 vols; Parliamentary Librarian GREIG TILLOTSON.

State Library of New South Wales: Macquarie St, Sydney, NSW 2000; tel. (2) 9273-1414; fax (2) 9273-1255; e-mail library@sl.nsw.gov.au; internet www.sl.nsw.gov.au; f. 1826; 5,000,000 items; State legal deposit privileges; special collections: Australiana, historical pictures, maps, MSS, of Australasia and the Pacific; State Librarian and Chief Exec. REGINA A. SUTTON.

State Records New South Wales: POB 516, Kingswood, NSW 2747; tel. (2) 6773-2165; fax (2) 6773-3943; e-mail srecords@records.nsw.gov.au; internet www.records.nsw.gov.au; f. 1961; incl. Univ. Archives and Heritage Centre; Exec. Dir. DAVID ROBERTS.

University of New England Library: Dixson Library, University of New England, Armidale, NSW 2351; tel. (2) 6773-2165; fax (2) 6773-3943; e-mail eve.woodberry@une.edu.au; internet www.une.edu.au/library; f. 1954; 905,000 vols; agriculatural sciences, Australian law, humanities and social sciences, health, education; special collns: Campbell Howard (Australian plays in manuscript), Gordon Athol Anderson (music), New England, Royal Society of New South Wales, Australian League of Rights, Saunders Colln in War and Peace; University Librarian EVELYN WOODBERRY.

University of New South Wales Library: Sydney, NSW 2052; tel. (2) 9385-2615; fax (2) 9385-8002; e-mail information@unsw.edu.au; internet info.library.unsw.edu.au; f. 1949; 2,850,000 items at Kensington and other centres; University Librarian ANDREW WELLS.

University of Newcastle Library: Callaghan, NSW 2308; tel. (2) 4921-5851; fax (2) 4921-5833; internet www.newcastle.edu.au/services/library; f. 1965; 1,300,000 vols; Librarian GREG ANDERSON.

University of Sydney Library: University of Sydney, NSW 2006; tel. (2) 9351-2993; fax (2) 9351-2890; e-mail loanenq@library.usyd.edu.au; internet www.library.usyd.edu.au; f. 1852; network of 18 libraries containing 5,186,229 vols, 68,130 electronic journals and 281,600 electronic books; University Librarian JOHN SHIPP.

Northern Territory

Northern Territory Library: Parliament House, POB 42, Darwin, NT 0801; tel. (8) 8999-7177; fax (8) 8999-6927; e-mail ntlinfo.dcdsca@nt.gov.au; internet www.ntl.nt.gov.au; f. 1950 as Darwin Public Library; 130,000 books, 4,132 periodicals, 80,000 photographs, 3,000 maps, 2,500 films and videos, 7,000 microforms; includes the Northern Territory Colln (one copy of all types of library material dealing with North and Central Australia, and NT in particular); Dir JO MCGILL.

Queensland

Queensland Parliamentary Library: Parliamentary Annex, Alice St, Brisbane, Qld 4000; tel. (7) 3406-7219; fax (7) 3210-0172; e-mail library.inquiries@parliament.qld.gov.au; f. 1860; information service to members of State Legislature; statistics, economics, politics, law and education; 120,000 vols; special collection: O'Donovan Collection of 19th century literature; Librarian MARY SEEFRIED; publ. *Queensland Parliamentary Record* (every 3 years).

Queensland University of Technology Library: GPO Box 2434, Brisbane, Qld 4001; tel. (7) 3864-1821; fax (7) 3864-2485; e-mail c2.davies@qut.edu.au; internet www.library.qut.edu.au; f. 1989; 73,000 vols, 5,000 print and microform periodicals, 36,000 electronic periodicals; Dir GAYNOR AUSTEN.

State Library of Queensland: POB 3488, Brisbane, Qld 4101; tel. (7) 3840-7666; fax (7) 3846-2421; internet www.slq.qld.gov.au; f. 1896; State Reference Library, non-lending except for music scores and to libraries, groups and organizations; includes John Oxley Library of Queensland History and James Hardie Library of Australian Fine Arts; has library deposit privileges; State Librarian LEA GILES-PETERS.

Supreme Court Library: POB 15019, City East, Brisbane, Qld 4002; tel. (7) 3247-4373; fax (7) 3247-9233; e-mail librarian@sclqld.org.au; internet www.scqld.org.au; f. 1862; 160,000 vols; Librarian ALADIN RAHEMTULA; publ. *Qld Legal Indexes*.

University of Queensland Library: Qld 4072; tel. (7) 3365-6551; fax (7) 3365-7317; e-mail universitylibrarian@library.uq.edu.au; internet library.uq.edu.au; f. 1911; 2,500,000 vols; 10,853 print journals, 47,744 electronic journals, 1,014 networked databases, 370,974 electronic books, 32,645 videos ; manuscript, microform and pictorial collns mainly in Australian literature; Librarian KEITH WEBSTER.

South Australia

Flinders University Library: Bedford Park, SA 5042; tel. (8) 8201-2131; fax (8) 8201-2508; e-mail libinfo@flinders.edu.au; internet www.lib.flinders.edu.au; f. 1963; 1,500,000 vols; Univ. Librarian W. T. CATIONS.

State Library of South Australia: North Terrace, GPO Box 419, Adelaide, SA 5001; tel. (8) 8207-7200; fax (8) 8207-7247; e-mail info@slsa.sa.gov.au; internet www.slsa.sa.gov.au; f. 1884; State general reference library and legal depository; online services incl. networked CD-ROMs; Bray Reference Colln (400,000 vols, 21,000 serial titles, 6,000 current, 109,000 maps); South Australiana Colln (62,000 vols, 12,000 serial titles, 8,000 current, Archival Collns of 4,500 m); spec. collns incl. Children's Literature Research Colln (55,000 vols), Edwardes Coln of Shipping Photographs (8,000), Arbon-Le Maistre Colln of Shipping Photographs (70,000), Mountford-Sheard Colln of Aboriginal Ethnology, Thomas Hardy Wine Library (1,000 vols), Paul McGuire Maritime Library (3,000 vols), Rare Books Colln (92,000 vols), Royal Geographical Soc. of South Australia Inc. Library, J. D. Somerville Oral History Colln (1,500 cassette tapes), Pictorial Colln (350,000 images); Bradman Coln of Cricketing Memorabilia; supports 138 public libraries (1.5m. vols); Dir ALAN SMITH; publ. *Extra Extra* (2 a year).

University of Adelaide Library: University of Adelaide, Adelaide, SA 5005; tel. (8) 8303-5370; fax (8) 8303-4369; e-mail library@library.adelaide.edu.au; internet library.adelaide.edu.au; f. 1876; 2,100,000 items; Librarian RAY CHOATE.

University of South Australia Library: Mawson Lakes Blvd, Mawson Lakes, SA 5095; tel. (8) 8302-6231; fax (8) 8302-3746; e-mail dels@unisa.edu.au; internet www.library.unisa.edu.au; libraries located at City East Campus, North Terrace, Adelaide, SA 5000; Mawson Lakes Campus, Mawson Lakes, SA 5095; Magill Campus, Lorne Avenue, Magill, SA 5072; City West Campus, North Terrace, Adelaide, SA 5000; Whyalla Campus, Nicolson Avenue, Whyalla Norrie, SA 5608; f. 1991 (as School of Art 1856); 1,000,000 vols; special collections include Oregon Collection of Theses in Physical Education and Sport, Doris Taylor Collection on Ageing, Gavin Walkley collection on Architectural History; Clearinghouse in Australia for Adult Basic Education and Literacy, Aboriginal and Torres Strait Islander Special Collection, Australian Bureau of Statistics Collection, HOPE Collection; Dir, Library Services HELEN LIVINGSTON.

Tasmania

State Library of Tasmania: 91 Murray St, Hobart, Tas. 7000; tel. (3) 6233-7511; fax (3) 6231-0927; e-mail state.library@education.tas.gov.au; internet www.statelibrary.tas.gov.au; f. 1850; 964,707 items; state legal deposit privileges; 46 brs, 5 reference and spec. collns; Dir SIOBHAN GASKELL.

University of Tasmania Library: Private Bag 25, GPO Hobart, Tas. 7001; tel. (3) 6226-2223; fax (3) 6226-2878; internet www.utas.edu.au/library/index.html; f. 1892; 996,832 vols; Sandy Bay Campus libraries: Law, Morris Miller (social sciences and humanities) and Science; Centre for the Arts Library, Hunter St, Hobart; Clinical Library, 43 Collins St, Hobart; Launceston Campus Library, Newnham, Launceston; special collections on Quakerism; houses the Royal Soc. of Tasmania Library; Librarian LINDA LUTHER.

Victoria

Commonwealth Scientific and Industrial Research Organisation, Information Services: Bag 10, Clayton South, Vic. 3169; fax (3) 9545-2715; e-mail aswr@csiro.au; internet www.csiro.au; publs and communicates science information in print, video and multimedia, and electronic databases; disseminates science and research information through CSIRO Library Network, search and inquiry services SEARCH PARTY; archival services for CSIRO research and records; Gen. Man. JINETTE DE GOOIJER.

La Trobe University Library: Bundoora, Vic. 3086; tel. (3) 9479-2922; fax (3) 9471-0993; internet www.lib.latrobe.edu.au; f. 1964; 1,469,906 vols; special emphasis on humanities and social sciences, allied health sciences; area studies: Latin America, India, Canada; University Librarian G. E. GOW.

Monash University Library: Monash University, Vic. 3800; tel. (3) 9905-5054; fax (3) 9905-2610; e-mail library@lib.monash.edu.au; internet www.lib.monash.edu.au; f. 1961; 2,900,000 vols, 17,800 periodicals; also libraries at Caulfield Campus, Caulfield East, Vic. 3145; Peninsula Campus, Frankston, Vic. 3199; Gippsland Campus, Churchill, Vic. 3842; and Berwick Campus, Berwick, Vic. 3806; Pharmacy College, Royal Parade, Parkville, Vic. 3052; Roodepoort 1725, South Africa; Petaling Jaya, 46150 Selangor, Malaysia; Librarian C. HARBOE-REE.

Parliamentary Library: Parliament of Victoria, Spring St, Melbourne, Vic. 3002; tel. (3) 9651-8640; fax (3) 9650-9775; e-mail bruce.davidson@parliament.vic.gov.au; internet www.parliament.vic.gov.au; f. 1851; reference and research service for MPs and associated staff; statistics, economics, politics, law, government publs; Parliamentary Librarian B. J. DAVIDSON; publ. *Victorian Parliamentary Handbook* (every 4 years).

Public Record Office of Victoria: POB 2100, North Melbourne, Vic. 3051; tel. (3) 9348-5600; fax (3) 9348-5656; e-mail ask.prov@dpc.vic.gov.au; internet www.prov.vic.gov.au; f. 1973; 67,074 linear metres of public records; Dir and Keeper of Public Records JUSTINE HAZLEWOOD; publs *Profile* (quarterly), *Journal* (annually, online).

State Library of Victoria: 328 Swanston St, Melbourne, Vic. 3000; tel. (3) 8664-7000; fax (3) 9639-4737; e-mail info@slv.vic.gov.au; internet www.slv.vic.gov.au; f. 1854; theoldest publicly-funded library in Australia and Victoria's primary general reference and research library; legal deposit library responsible for collecting, preserving and making available all published materials and associated material relating to the heritage of the state of Victoria; offers community outreach and learning programmes; works with other library sectors, cultural institutions and the education sector to provide access to information and promote Victorian cultural heritage; 2,000,000 vols and periodicals; special collections include La Trobe Colln (Australiana), art, newspapers, music and performing arts, Anderson Chess Colln, maps, manuscripts and pictures; digitization of 200,000 items from the Pictures Colln and a broader range of formats including text, audio and music are available online; CEO and State Librarian ANNE-MARIE SCHWIRTLICH; publs *La Trobe Journal* (2 a year), *State Library of Victoria News* (3 a year).

University of Melbourne Library: Vic. 3010; tel. (3) 8344-9590; fax (3) 8344-9588; internet www.lib.unimelb.edu.au; f. 1855; 3,000,000 vols; spec. collns incl. Australiana, East Asia; responsible for University Archives and Grainger Museum; Librarian HELEN HAYES; publs *Ex Libris* (4 a year), *Annual report*.

Western Australia

Curtin University of Technology Library and Information Service: POB U1987, Perth, WA 6845; tel. (8) 9266-7205; fax (8) 9266-3213; e-mail i.garner@curtin.edu.au; f. 1967; 390,526 vols, 11,917 current serial titles; Librarian IMOGEN GARNER.

State Library of Western Australia: Alexander Library Bldg, Perth Cultural Centre, Perth, WA 6000; tel. (8) 9427-3111; fax (8) 9427-3256; e-mail info@liswa.wa.gov.au; internet www.liswa.wa.gov.au; Reference and Information Services: 490,000 vols, 21,000 serial and newspaper titles, 60,000 music scores, 15,000 music recordings, 28,000 microfilm reels, 19,000 video cassettes and 16mm films, 3,500 oral history transcripts, 467,000 pictorial images, 82,000 ephemera, 52,000 cartographic items; Public Library and Lending Services: provides stock and support services for 229 public libraries; J. S. Battye Library of West Australian History (f. 1887): legal deposit library of West Australian publs; special collns of music, business, genealogy and Australian children's literature; CEO and State Librarian MARGARET ALLEN (acting); Dir of Public Library Services SUSAN FEENEY; Dir, State Reference Library BARBARA PATISON; Dir, J. S. Battye Library JENNY CARTER; publs *Annual Report*, *Directory of Public Library Services* (annually), *Legal Deposit Publications in Western Australia* (4 a year), *LISWA Newsletter* (6 a year), *Statistical Bulletin for Public Libraries in Western Australia* (annually).

University of Western Australia Library: 35 Stirling Highway, Crawley, WA 6009; tel. (8) 6488-1777; fax (8) 6488-1012; e-mail uwalibrary@library.uwa.edu.au; internet www.library.uwa.edu.au; f. 1913; 1m. vols; Librarian JOHN ARFIELD.

Museums and Art Galleries

Australian Capital Territory

Australian War Memorial: GPO Box 345, Canberra, ACT 2601; tel. (2) 6243-4211; fax (2) 6243-4325; internet www.awm.gov.au; f. 1917; national war memorial, museum, research centre and art gallery illustrating and recording aspects of all wars in which the Armed Forces of Australia have been engaged; dioramas of historical battles, and a total collection of over 3.5m. items; works of art, relics, documentary and audio-visual records; library: books, serials, pamphlets, photographs, maps, film and sound recordings on military history; repository of operational records of Australian fighting units; Dir Maj.-Gen. STEVE GOWER; publ. *Wartime* (4 a year).

National Gallery of Australia: POB 1150, Canberra, ACT 2601; tel. (2) 6240-6411; fax (2) 6240-6529; e-mail information@nga.gov.au; internet www.nga.gov.au; f. 1975; the National Collection has 100,000 works of Australian and international art; Australian collection includes fine and decorative arts, folk art, commercial art, architecture and design; other collections include arts of Asia and Southeast Asia, Oceania, Africa and Pre-Columbian America, European art, also prints, drawings, illustrated books since 1800, photography; library of 120,000 monographs, 35,000 auction sales catalogues, 1,200 current serials, 47,000 microfiches, 1,000,000 ephemeral materials; Dir BRIAN P. KENNEDY; publs *Annual Report*, *Artonview* (4 a year).

National Museum of Australia: POB 1901, Canberra, ACT 2601; tel. (2) 6208-5000; fax (2) 6208-5099; e-mail information@nma.gov.au; internet www.nma.gov.au; f. 1980; Australian history, Aboriginal and Torres Strait Island cultures, social history and environment; library of 35,000 vols; Dir CRADDOCK MORTON (acting); publ. *National Museum of Australia Annual Report*.

New South Wales

Art Gallery of New South Wales:; tel. (2) 9225-1700; fax (2) 9221-1701; e-mail artmail@ag.nsw.gov.au; internet www.artgallery.nsw.gov.au; f. 1874; representative collection of Australian art, Aboriginal and Melanesian art; collections of British art since 18th century; European painting and sculpture (since 15th century); Asian art, particularly Chinese and Japanese ceramics and Japanese painting; Australian, British and European prints and drawings, contemporary Australian and foreign art; photography; Pres., Board of Trustees STEVEN LOWY; Dir EDMUND CAPON.

Australian Museum: 6 College St, Sydney, NSW 2010; tel. (2) 9320-6000; fax (2) 9320-6050; e-mail library@austmus.gov.au; internet www.amonline.net.au; f. 1827; natural history, museology, anthropology, palaeontology, mineralogy, biodiversity; library of 90,000 vols; Dir FRANK HOWARTH; publs *Records of the Australian Museum* (quarterly), *Technical Reports of the Australian Museum* (irregular).

Australian National Maritime Museum: POB 5131, Sydney, NSW 2001; tel. (2) 9298-3777; fax (2) 9298-3780; internet www.anmm.gov.au; f. 1985, open 1991; illustrates maritime history as exemplified by the Colonial Navies, the Royal Australian Navy, merchant shipping and trade, whaling and the fishing industry, explorers and cartographers, immigration, the design and use of leisure and sporting craft and int. competition, surfing, surf life saving and the culture of the beach, and the maritime activities of the Aborigines; models, prints and drawings, glass plate negatives, uniforms, relics, full-size vessels; library of 12,000 vols, 750 periodicals; Chair. MARK BETHWAITE; Dir MARY-LOUISE WILLIAMS; publ. *Signals* (quarterly).

Macleay Museum: Gosper Lane, off Science Rd, Univ. of Sydney, Sydney, NSW 2006; tel. (2) 9351-2274; fax (2) 9351-5646; e-mail macleay@macleay.usyd.edu.au; internet www.usyd.edu.au/su/macleay/welcome.htm; f. 1888 based on colln begun in 1790; entomology, zoology, ethnology, 19th c. scientific instruments; Australian photographs since 1850s; Dir DAVID ELLIS.

Museum of Applied Arts and Sciences: POB K346, Haymarket, NSW 1238; tel. (2) 9217-0111; fax (2) 9217-0333; e-mail info@phm.gov.au; internet www.powerhousemuseum.com; f. 1880; comprises Powerhouse Museum (decorative arts, history, science and technology), Sydney Observatory astronomical museum; Dir Dr KEVIN FEWSTER; publ. *Annual Report*.

Museum of Contemporary Art: POB R1286, Royal Exchange, NSW 1223; located at: Level 5, 140 George St, Sydney, NSW 2000; tel. (2) 9252-4033; fax (2) 9252-4361; e-mail mail@mca.com.au; internet www.mca.com.au; f. 1991; Dir ELIZABETH ANN MACGREGOR.

Nicholson Museum: Univ. of Sydney, Sydney, NSW 2006; tel. (2) 9351-2812; fax (2) 9351-7305; e-mail m.turner@usyd.edu.au; internet www.usyd.edu.au/museums/about/nicholson.shtml; f. 1860; collection of Egyptian, Near Eastern, Cypriot, European, Greek and Roman antiquities; Dir DAVID ELLIS; Senior Curator MICHAEL TURNER.

Wilson, J. T., Museum of Human Anatomy: Anderson Stuart Bldg, Dept of Anatomy, Univ. of Sydney, NSW 2006; e-mail hod@anatomy.usyd.edu.au; f. 1886; Curator PETER MILLS; includes 1,000 dissected parts and cross-sections of the human body.

Northern Territory

Museum and Art Gallery of the Northern Territory: GPO Box 4646, Darwin, NT 0801; Conacher St, Bullocky Point, Darwin, NT; tel. (8) 8999-8264; fax (8) 8999-8289; e-mail museum@nt.gov.au; f. 1969; art, history, culture, and natural history of the Northern Territory, particularly Aboriginal visual arts and material culture; South-east Asian and Oceanic art and material culture; maritime archaeology; five major permanent galleries; touring gallery; educational facilities for students; library of 10,000 vols, 1,000 serials; Dir ANNA MALGORZEWICZ; publ. *Research Reports* (irregular).

Queensland

Queensland Art Gallery: POB 3686, South Brisbane, Qld 4101; Melbourne St, South Brisbane, Qld 4101; tel. (7) 3840-7333; fax (7) 3844-8865; e-mail gallery@qag.qld.gov.au; internet www.qag.qld.gov.au; f. 1895; State collection of Australian and foreign paintings, prints, drawings and photographs, sculpture and decorative arts; education and advisory services; library of 25,000 books, 500 periodicals, photographs, catalogues; Dir DOUG HALL.

Queensland Herbarium: Brisbane Botanic Gardens Mt Coot-tha, Mt Coot-tha Rd, Toowong, Qld 4066; tel. (7) 3896-9326; fax (7) 3896-9624; e-mail queensland.herbarium@env.qld.gov.au; internet www.env.qld.gov.au; f. 1874; as Botanic Museum and Herbarium; studies of flora and mapping of vegetation of Queensland, rare and threatened plant species, plant ecology, weeds, poisonous plants and economic botany; 650,000 plant specimens; library of 10,000 vols; Dir G. P. GUYMER; publ. *Austrobaileya* (annually).

Queensland Museum: Cultural Centre, South Bank, South Brisbane, Qld 4101; tel. (7) 3840-7555; fax (7) 3846-1918; e-mail inquirycentre@qm.qld.gov.au; internet www.qm.qld.gov.au; f. 1871; zoology, geology, palaeontology, history, anthropology, technology; library of 95,000 vols; publ. *Memoirs of the Queensland Museum*; Dir Dr IAN GALLOWAY.

South Australia

Art Gallery of South Australia: North Terrace, Adelaide, SA 5000; tel. (8) 8207-7000; fax (8) 8207-7070; e-mail agsa.info@saugov.sa.gov.au; internet www.artgallery.sa.gov.au; f. 1881; comprehensive collection of Australian works of art, British and European painting, prints, drawings and sculpture 16th c. to present; British, European and Asian decorative arts; early South Australian pictures; library; education services; Dir CHRISTOPHER MENZ; publs *Annual Report*, *Newsletter* (6 a year).

South Australian Museum: North Terrace, Adelaide, SA 5000; tel. (8) 8207-7500; fax (8) 8207-7430; internet www.samuseum.sa.gov.au; f. 1856; anthropological, geological and zoological material mainly related to South Australia; Australian ethnological colln; education and advisory services; library of 45,000 vols; Dir Dr S. MILLER; publ. *Transactions of the Royal Society of South Australia (incorporating Records of the South Australian Museum)*.

Tasmania

Queen Victoria Museum and Art Gallery: 2 Wellington St, Launceston, Tas. 7250; tel. (3) 6323-3777; fax (3) 6323-3776; e-mail enquiries@qvmag.tas.gov.au; internet www.qvmag.tas.gov.au; f. 1891; collections comprise pure and applied art, Tasmanian history, Tasmanian and general anthropology, Tasmanian botany, geology, palaeontology and zoology; library of 8,500 vols; Dir C. B. TASSELL; publs *Records*, *Annual Report*.

Tasmanian Museum and Art Gallery: 40 Macquarie St, GPO Box 1164M, Hobart, Tas. 7001; tel. (3) 6211-4177; fax (3) 6211-4112; e-mail tmagmail@tmag.tas.gov.au; internet www.tmag.tas.gov.au; f. 1852; applied science, art and natural and human history, with emphasis on Tasmania and Australia generally; includes Tasmanian Herbarium, coin collections, early photography, collections relating to the Aboriginal people of Tasmania; colln also at the West Coast Pioneers' Museum at Zeehan (mining, local history and minerals); and the Australasian Golf Museum at Bothwell (golfing memorabilia); Dir BILL BLEATHMAN; publ. *Research Journal—Kanunnah* (annually).

Victoria

Museum Victoria: GPO Box 666E, Melbourne, Vic. 3001; tel. (3) 8341-7777; fax (3) 8341-7778; e-mail webmaster@museum.vic.gov.au; internet www.museum.vic.gov.au; f. 1854; CEO Dr J. PATRICK GREENE.

Constituent museums:

Immigration Museum: Old Customs House, 400 Flinders St, Melbourne, Vic. 3000; tel. (3) 9927-2700; fax (3) 9927-2701; e-mail webmaster@museum.vic.gov.au; internet immigration.museum.vic.gov.au; f. 1998.

Melbourne Museum: Carlton Gardens, Carlton, Vic. 3053; tel. (3) 8341-7777; fax (3) 8341-7778; e-mail webmaster@museum.vic.gov.au; internet melbourne.museum.vic.gov.au; f. 2000; science, technology, Australian society, environment, indigenous cultures and human mind and body; incl. Aboriginal Centre, Children's Museum, living forest gallery, IMAX theatre and Royal Exhibition Building.

Scienceworks Museum: 2 Booker St, Spotswood, Vic. 3015; tel. (3) 9392-4800; fax (3) 9391-0100; e-mail webmaster@museum.vic.gov.au; internet scienceworks.museum.vic.gov.au; f. 1992; science and technology, Melbourne Planetarium, Spotswood Pumping Station.

National Gallery of Victoria: POB 7259, Melbourne, Vic. 8004; tel. (3) 9208-0222; fax (3) 9208-0245; e-mail enquiries@ngv.vic.gov.au; internet www.ngv.vic.gov.au; f. 1861; Old Masters and depts of Prints and Drawings, Modern European Art, Australian Art, Aboriginal and Oceanic Art, Decorative Art and Design, Asian Art, Antiquities, Photography, Pre-Columbian Art, Costume and Textiles; library of 45,000 vols, and slides; Dir Dr GERARD VAUGHAN; publs *Art Bulletin of Victoria* (annually), *Gallery* (6 a year).

Western Australia

Art Gallery of Western Australia: Perth Cultural Centre, Perth, WA 6000; tel. (8) 9492-6600; fax (8) 9492-6655; e-mail admin@artgallery.wa.gov.au; internet www.artgallery.wa.gov.au; f. 1895; Aboriginal art, Australian and foreign paintings, sculpture, decorative arts and crafts; library of 16,000 vols; Dir ALAN R. DODGE; publ. *Annual Report*.

Western Australian Museum: 49 Kew St, Welshpool, Perth, WA 6106; tel. (8) 9427-2700; fax (8) 9427-2882; e-mail reception@museum.wa.gov.au; internet www.museum.wa.gov.au; f. 1891; natural history, archaeology, history, earth sciences, anthropology; library of 20,000 vols, 1,500 journal titles; Dir Dr DAWN CASEY; Exec. Officer and Foundation Dir CATHRIN CASSARCHIS; publs *Annual Report*, *Records*, *Records Supplements*.

Universities

UNIVERSITY OF ADELAIDE

Adelaide, SA 5005

Telephone: (8) 8303-4455
Fax: (8) 8303-4401
E-mail: council.secretary@adelaide.edu.au
Internet: www.adelaide.edu.au

Founded 1874

Autonomous institution established by Act of Parliament

Academic year: March to December

Chancellor: ROBERT CHAMPION DE CRESPIGNY
Deputy Chancellor: B. CROSER
Vice-Chancellor: Prof. JAMES MCWHA
Deputy Vice-Chancellor: Prof. P. BOUMELHA
Deputy Vice-Chancellor (Research) (vacant)
Pro-Vice-Chancellor (International): Prof. J. TAPLIN
Librarian: R. C. CHOATE

Number of teachers: 929 (full-time)
Number of students: 12,950

Publications: *Adelaide Law Review* (2 a year), *Australian Economic Papers* (2 a year), *Australian Feminist Studies* (2 a year), *Australian Journal of Legal History* (2 a year), *Australian Journal of Social Research* (4 a year), *Australian Women's Studies* (annually), *Corporate and Business Law Journal* (2 a year), *Economic Briefings* (3 a year), *The Joseph Fisher Lecture in Commerce* (irregular), *Research Report* (annually), *Social Analysis* (2 a year)

EXECUTIVE DEANS

Faculty of Engineering, Computer and Mathematical Sciences: Prof. A. PARKER (acting)
Faculty of Health Sciences: Prof. D. B. FREWIN
Faculty of Humanities and Social Sciences: M. INNES
Faculty of the Professions: F. M. MCDOUGALL
Faculty of Sciences: P. D. RATHJEN

PROFESSORS

Faculty of Engineering, Computer and Mathematical Sciences (tel. (8) 8303-4700; fax (8) 8303-4361; e-mail eng.cs.maths@adelaide.edu.au; internet www.adelaide.edu.au/ecms):

- BARTER, C. J., Computer Science
- BEGG, S. H., Petroleum Engineering and Management
- BEHRBRUCH, P., Petroleum Engineering and Management
- BRATVOLD, R. B., Petroleum Engineering and Management
- BROOKS, M. J., Computer Science
- COLE, P. H., Electrical and Electronic Engineering
- COUTTS, R. P., Telecommunications
- DANDY, G. D., Civil Engineering
- GRAY, D. A., Sensor Signal Processing
- HANSEN, C. H., Mechanical Engineering
- IRELAND, V., Education Centre for Innovation and Commercialisation
- KHURANA, A. K., Petroleum Engineering and Management
- KING, K. D., Chemical Engineering
- LINTON, V. M., Welded Structures (Cooperative Research Centre)
- MCLEAN, A. J., Road Accident Research
- SARMA, H. K., Petroleum Engineering and Management
- WHITE, L. B., Electrical and Electronic Engineering

Faculty of Health Sciences (Medical School North, Frome Rd, Adelaide; tel. (8) 8303-5336; fax (8) 8303-3788; e-mail health.sciences@adelaide.edu.au; internet www.health.adelaide.edu.au):

- BARRETT, R. J., Psychiatry
- BARTOLD, P. M., Dentistry
- BEILBY, J. J., General Practice
- BOCHNER, F., Clinical and Experimental Pharmacology
- DEKKER, G., Obstetrics and Gynaecology
- FREWIN, D. B., Clinical and Experimental Pharmacology
- GOLDNEY, R. D., Psychiatry
- GOSS, A. N., Dentistry
- HENNENBERG, M., Anatomical Sciences
- HILLER, J. E., Public Health
- HOROWITZ, J. D., Medicine
- HOROWITZ, M., Medicine
- HOWIE, D. W., Orthopaedics, Trauma
- JAMIESON, G. G., Surgery
- JONES, N., Surgery
- KOTLARSKI, I., Health Sciences Faculty Office
- LUDBROOK, G. L., Anaesthesia and Intensive Care
- MCFARLANE, A. C., Psychiatry
- MACLENNAN, A. H., Obstetrics and Gynaecology
- MADDERN, G. J., Surgery
- MOYES, D. G., Anaesthesia and Intensive Care
- NETTELBECK, T. J., Psychology
- NORMAN, R. J., Obstetrics and Gynaecology
- ROBERTON, D. M., Paediatrics
- ROBINSON, J. S., Obstetrics and Gynaecology
- RUFFIN, R. E., Medicine
- RUNCIMAN, W. B., Anaesthesia and Intensive Care

SAMPSON, W. J., Dentistry
SAWYER, M. G., Paediatrics
SLADE, G. D., Dentistry
SOMOGYI, A. A., Clinical and Experimental Pharmacology
SPENCER, A. J., Dentistry
TAN, H. L., Paediatrics
TAPLIN, J. E., Psychology
THOMPSON, P. D., Medicine
TIERNEY, A. J., Clinical Nursing
TILLEY, W. D., Medicine
TOWNSEND, G. C., Dentistry
VERNON-ROBERTS, B., Pathology
WHITE, J. M., Clinical and Experimental Pharmacology
WORMALD, P. J., Surgery

Faculty of Humanities and Social Sciences (tel. (8) 8303-5345; fax (8) 8303-4382; e-mail humss.office@adelaide.edu.au; internet www.arts.adelaide.edu.au/arts-web):

BODMAN RAE, C., Music
BOUMELHA, P. A., English
BULBECK, C., Social Inquiry
HARVEY, N., Geographical and Environmental Studies
HUGO, G. J., Social Applications of Geographical Information Systems
JAIN, P. C., Asian Studies
MORTENSEN, C. E., Philosophy
MUHLHAUSLER, P., European Studies, General Linguistics
PREST, W. R., History
SHAPCOTT, T. W., English
WILLIAMS, M. A., Geographical and Environmental Studies

Faculty of the Professions (tel. (8) 8303-3986; fax (8) 8303-4416):

ANDERSON, K., Economics
BRADBROOK, A. J., Law
DETMOLD, M. J., Law
FAIRALL, P. A., Law
MCDOUGALL, F. M., Graduate School of Business
MARJORIBANKS, K. M., Graduate School of Education
NAFFINE, N. M., Law
PARKER, L. D., Commerce
POMFRET, R. W., Economics
QUESTER, P. G., Commerce
RADFORD, A. D., Architecture, Landscape and Urban Design
SHERIDAN, K., Graduate School of Business
SMOLICZ, J. J., Graduate School of Education
TAYLOR, D. W., Commerce

Faculty of Sciences (tel. (8) 8303-5673; fax (8) 8303-4386; internet www.sciences.adelaide.edu.au):

AUSTIN, A. D., School of Earth and Environmental Sciences
BOWIE, J. H., School of Chemistry and Physics
BRUCE, M. I., School of Chemistry and Physics
BURRELL, C. J., School of Molecular and Biomedical Sciences
COVENTRY, D. R., School of Earth and Environmental Sciences
FINCHER, G. B., School of Agriculture and Wine
GREENHALGH, S. A., School of Earth and Environmental Sciences
HILLIS, R. R., Petroleum Geology and Geophysics (National Centre)
HYND, P. I., School of Agriculture and Wine
KALDI, J. G., Petroleum Geology and Geophysics (National Centre)
LANGRIDGE, P., School of Agriculture and Wine
LINCOLN, S. F., School of Chemistry and Physics
MCMILLEN, I. C., School of Molecular and Biomedical Sciences
MILES, T. S., School of Molecular and Biomedical Sciences
MUNCH, J., School of Chemistry and Physics
OWENS, J. A., School of Molecular and Biomedical Sciences
PATON, J. C., School of Molecular and Biomedical Sciences
RANDLES, J. W., School of Agriculture and Wine
RATHJEN, P. D., School of Molecular and Biomedical Sciences
SCHMIDT, O., School of Agriculture and Wine
SEDGLEY, M., School of Agriculture and Wine
SEYMOUR, R. S., School of Earth and Environmental Sciences
SMITH, S. E., School of Earth and Environmental Sciences
TYERMAN, S. D., School of Agriculture and Wine
VINCENT, R. A., School of Chemistry and Physics
WALLACE, J. C., School of Molecular and Biomedical Sciences
WHAN, B., Molecular Plant Breeding (Co-operative Research Centre)

ATTACHED RESEARCH INSTITUTES

Australian Centre for Plant Functional Genomics: Dir Prof. P. LANGRIDGE.

Australian Petroleum Co-operative Research Centre: Dir Dr J. KALDI.

Co-operative Research Centre for Signal and Information Processing: Dir Prof. M. BROOKS.

Co-operative Research Centre for Tissue Growth and Repair: Dir Dr J. BALLARD.

Co-operative Research Centre for Viticulture: Dir Dr J. HARDIE.

Co-operative Research Centre for Weed Management Systems: Dir Assoc. Prof. R. ROUSH.

Co-operative Research Centre for Welded Structure: Dir Prof. V. LINTON.

Key Centre for Social Applications of Geographical Information Systems: Dir Prof. G. HUGO.

Research Data Network Co-operative Research Centre: Dir Dr A. WENDELBORN.

SA Partnership for Advanced Computing: Dir Dr A. G. WILLIAMS.

Special Research Centre for the Subatomic Structure of Matter: Dir Dr A. WILLIAMS.

AFFILIATED RESIDENTIAL COLLEGES

Aquinas College Inc.: North Adelaide; f. 1947; 150 students; Rector Fr M. HEAD.

Kathleen Lumley College Inc.: North Adelaide; f. 1967; 63 students (postgraduate); Master Dr D. L. CLEMENTS.

Lincoln College Inc.: North Adelaide; f. 1951; 240 students; Principal Dr P. GUNN.

Roseworthy College, Inc.: Roseworthy; f. 1991; 250 students; Principal Dr D. TAPLIN.

St Ann's College Inc.: North Adelaide; f. 1939; 154 students; Principal Dr R. BROOKS.

St Mark's College Inc.: North Adelaide; f. 1924; 204 students; Master C. R. ASHWIN.

AUSTRALIAN CATHOLIC UNIVERSITY

POB 968, North Sydney, NSW 2059
Telephone: (2) 9739-2929
Fax: (2) 9739-2905
Internet: www.acu.edu.au

Founded 1991 by amalgamation of Catholic College of Education, Sydney, Institute of Catholic Education, Victoria, McAuley College, Brisbane, and Signadou College, Canberra

Academic year: February to December

Chancellor: Br JULIAN MCDONALD
Pro-Chancellor: EDWARD EXELL
Vice-Chancellor: Prof. PETER W. SHEEHAN
Pro-Vice-Chancellor (Academic): Prof. GABRIELLE MCMULLEN
Pro-Vice-Chancellor (Quality and Outreach): Prof. JOHN O'GORMAN
Pro-Vice-Chancellor (Research and International): Prof. JOHN COLL
Executive Director, University Services: JOHN CAMERON

Library of 460,903 vols, 2,296 periodicals, 5,415 online journals
Number of teachers: 514
Number of students: 12,156

Publications: *Interlogue* (2 a year), *Journal of Religious Education* (4 a year)

DEANS

Arts and Sciences: Dr GAIL CROSSLEY (acting)
Education: Prof. MARIE EMMITT
Health Sciences: Prof. ELIZABETH CAMERON-TRAUB

AUSTRALIAN NATIONAL UNIVERSITY

Canberra, ACT 0200
Telephone: (2) 6125-5111
Fax: (2) 6125-9062
Internet: www.anu.edu.au

Founded 1946 for postgraduate research. Now consists of Institute of Advanced Studies (postgraduate), The Faculties (all levels)

Academic year: March to December

Chancellor: Prof. P. E. BAUME
Vice-Chancellor: Prof. IAN CHUBB
Deputy Vice-Chancellor (Education): Prof. MALCOLM GILLIES
Deputy Vice-Chancellor (Research): Prof. LAWRENCE CRAM
Pro Vice-Chancellor: Prof. ROBIN STANTON
Director, Student and Academic Services: GILLIAN LUCK
Librarian: VIC ELLIOT

Library: See under Libraries and Archives

Publications: *Annual Report*, *ANU Reporter*.

INSTITUTE OF ADVANCED STUDIES

Institute of Advanced Studies: Chair of the Institute of Advances Studies Forum Prof. G. FARQUHAR (acting); number of academic staff: 727; number of postgraduate students: 949..

Constituent schools:

Research School of Biological Sciences: Director Prof. JONATHAN STONE

PROFESSORS

ANDREWS, T. J., Molecular Genetics
BADGER, M., Photosythetic Functional Genomics
CLARK-WALKER, D., Molecular Genetics
FARQUHAR, G., Environmental Biology
GIBSON, J., Molecular and Poulation Genetics
GRAVES, J., Comparative Genomics
HARDHAM, A., Phytophthora Laboratory
NOBLE, I., Theoretical Ecology
SRINIVASAN, M., Insect Vision
WILLIAMSON, R., Cell Wall Laboratory

Research School of Chemistry: Dean Prof. DENIS EVANS

PROFESSORS

BANWELL, M., Organic Chemistry

COLLINS, M., Physical and Theoretical Chemistry
EASTON, C., Organic Chemistry
EVANS, D., Physical and Theoretical Chemistry
HILL, A., Inorganic Chemistry
KRAUSZ, E., Physical and Theoretical Chemistry
MANDER, L., Organic Chemistry
OTTING, G., Organic Chemistry
RADOM, L., Physical and Theoretical Chemistry
WELBERRY, T., Physical and Theoretical Chemistry
WHITE, J., Physical and Theoretical Chemistry
WILD, S., Iorganic Chemistry
WITHERS, R., Inorganic Chemistry

Research School of Earth Sciences: Director Prof. MARK HARRISON

PROFESSORS

CHAPPELL, J., Earth Environment
COX, S., Earth Materials
GRIFFITHS, R., Earth Physics
GRUN, R., Earth Environment
JACKSON, I., Earth Materials
KENNETT, B. L. N., Earth Physics
LAMBECK, K., Earth Physics
LISTER, G., Earth Materials
MCCULLOCH, M., Earth Environment
O'NEILL, H. ST C., Earth Materials

John Curtin School of Medical Research: Director Prof. J. WHITWORTH

PROFESSORS

BOARD, P., Molecular Genetics
DULHUNTY, A., Muscle Research
GAGE, P., Membrane Physiology
YOUNG, I., Cytokine Molecular Biology

Research School of Pacific and Asian Studies: Director Prof. J. FOX

PROFESSORS

ANDERSON, A. J., Archaeology and Natural History
BABBAGE, R.
BALL, D. J., Strategic and Defence Studies
BARMÉ, G. R.
BELLWOOD, P.
CROUCH, H.
DENOON, D. J. N., Pacific and Asian History
FANE, G.
FOX, J. J., Anthropology
HILL, H.
HOPE, G.
HORNER, D. M.
JHA, R.
JOLLY, M. A.
KERKVLIET, B. J. T., Political and Social Change
LAL, B.
MARR, D.
MCCORMACK, G. P., Pacific and Asian History
MCKIBBEN, W., Economics
MOSKO, M.
NELSON, H. N., Pacific and Asian History
PAWLEY, A. K., Linguistics
RAVENHILL, J.
SPRIGGS, M.
TRYON, D.
WARR, P. G., Agricultural Economics

Research School of Information Sciences and Engineering: Director Prof. JOHN RICHARDS

PROFESSORS

ANDERSON, B. D. O., Information Engineering
BRENT, R. P., Computer Science
HARTLEY, R., Information Engineering
LLOYD, J., Computer Sciences Laboratory
MOORE, J., Information Engineering

Research School of Physical Sciences and Engineering: Director Prof. J. WILLIAMS

PROFESSORS

BATCHELOR, M., Theoretical Physics
BAZHANOV, V., Theoretical Physics
DEWAR, R. L., Plasma Physics and Theoretical Physics
DRACOULIS, G. D., Nuclear Physics
ELLIMAN, R. G., Electronic Materials Engineering
HAMBERGER, S. M., Plasma Research
HYDE, S., Applied Mathematics
JAGADISH, C., Electronic Materials Engineering
LUTHER-DAVIES, B., Laser Physics
MARCELJA, S., Applied Mathematics
MITCHELL, D. J., Optical Sciences Centre
MOORE, J. B., Systems Engineering
SPEAR, R. H., Nuclear Physics
WEIGOLD, E., Atomic and Molecular Physics
WILLIAMS, J., Electronic Materials Engineering

Research School of Social Sciences: Director Prof. F. C. JACKSON

PROFESSORS

BOOTH, A., Economics
BRAITHWAITE, J., Regulatory Institutions Network
BRENNAN, H. G., Economics and Social and Political Theory
CANE, P., Law
CHALMERS, D., Philosophy
CHAPMAN, B., Economics
CHARLESWORTH, H., Regulatory Institutions Network
DAVIES, M., Philosophy
DEACON, D., History
DRAHOS, P., Regulatory Institutions Network
DRYZEK, J. S., Political Science
GODFREY-SMITH, P., Philosophy
GOODIN, B., Philosophy
GRABOSKY, P., Regulatory Institutions Network
GREGORY, R. G., Economics
GUNNINGHAM, N., Regulatory Institutions Network
HAJEK, A., Philosophy
HIGMAN, B., History
HINDESS, B., Political Science
HULL, T., Demography
JACKSON, F. C., Philosophy
JALLAND, P., History
MCALLISTER, A., Political Science
MCDONALD, P., Demography
MCGRATH, A., History
MCMILLEN, J., Regulatory Institutions Network
PAGAN, A. R., Economics
RHODES, R., Political Science
RITCHIE, J. D., Australian Dictionary of Biography
SAWER, M., Political Science
SHEARING, C., Regulatory Institutions Network
SNOOKS, G. D., Economic History
STAPLETON, J., Law
STERELNY, K., Philosophy
WAJCMAN, J., Demography and Sociology
WANNA, J., Political Science

Research School of Astronomy and Astrophysics: Director Prof. PENNY D. SACKETT

PROFESSORS

BESSELL, M., Astronomy
BRIGGS, F. H., Astronomy
DA COSTA, G., Astronomy
DOPITA, M. A., Astronomy
FREEMAN, K. C., Astronomy
NORRIS, J. E., Astronomy
SACKETT, P. D., Astronomy
SCHMIDT, B. P., Astronomy

School of Mathematical Sciences: Dean Prof. A. L. CAREY

PROFESSORS

BATCHELOR, M., Mathematics
BAXTER, R. J., Mathematics
BAZHANOV, V., Mathematics
DALEY, D., Mathematics
GANI, J., Mathematics
HALL, P. J., Statistics
HEATHCOTE, C., Mathematics
HEYDE, C., Mathematics
HUTCHINSON, J., Mathematics
MCINTOSH, A., Mathematics
NEEMAN, A., Mathematics
NEWMAN, M., Mathematics
OSBORNE, M. R., Advanced Computation
ROBINSON, D., Mathematics
TRUDINGER, N., Mathematics
URBAS, J., Mathematics
WELSH, A., Statistics
WICKRAMASINGHE, D., Mathematics
WILSON, S. R., Statistics

THE FACULTIES

The Faculties: Chair of the Faculties Forum Prof. A. KUMAR (acting); number of academic staff: 586; number of students: 1,836 postgraduate, 8,279 undergraduate

DEANS

Faculty of Arts: Prof. A. SHOEMAKER
Faculty of Asian Studies: Prof. A. C. MILNER
Faculty of Economics and Commerce: Prof. K. HOUGHTON
Faculty of Engineering and Information Technology: Prof. R. B. STANTON
Faculty of Law: Prof. M. D. COPER
Faculty of Medicine: Prof. P. A. GATENBY
Faculty of Science: Prof. T. C. BROWN

PROFESSORS

Faculty of Arts:

BELLWOOD, P., Archaeology
CAMPBELL, R. J., Philosophy
CURTHOYS, A., History
GREENHALGH, C. M. B., Art History
GRISHIN, S., Art History
GROVES, C., Archaeology
MERLAN, F. C., Anthropology
MILLER, S., Philosophy
PAPADAKIS, E., Social Sciences
SAIKAI, A., Political Sciences
SITSKY, A., Composition
SPRIGGS, M., Archaeology
WARHURST, J. L., Political Science
WIERZBICKA, A. C., Linguistics
WILLIAMS, D., Visual Arts
WRIGHT, I. R., English

Faculty of Asian Studies:

CORBETT, J., Asian Studies
HOOKER, V., Oriental Studies
LOUIE, K., Chinese Studies
MILNER, A. C., Southeast Asian History
WELLS, K., Korean Studies

Faculty of Economics and Commerce:

CRAIG, R., Commerce
DOWRICK, S., Economics
GREGOR, S., Business Information Management
HATTON, T., Economics
HEATHCOTE, C. R., Mathematical Statistics
MALLER, R., Finance and Applied Statistics
MONROE, G., Business Information Management
NICHOLLS, D. F., Statistics
O'NEILL, T., Applied Statistics
RICHARDSON, M., Economics
SMITH, T., Applied Statistics
TYERS, R., Economics

Faculty of Engineering and Information Technology:

BLAKERS, A., Engineering
CARDEW-HALL, M., Engineering
CUEVAS, A., Engineering
GEDEON, T., Engineering
JAMES, M., Engineering
MCKAY, B., Engineering
QIN, Q., Engineering

Faculty of Law:

CAMPBELL, T. D., Law
COPER, M. D., Law
DAVIS, J. L. R., Law
DISNEY, J. P., Law
GREIG, D. W., Law
GUNNINGHAM, N. A., Law
HAMBLEY, A. D., Law
PEARCE, D. C., Law
SWEENEY, M. D., Law
ZINES, L. R., Law

Faculty of Science:

CLARK, I., Biochemistry
COCKBURN, A., Botany and Zoology
COX, S., Structural Geology
DE DECKKER, P., Geology
ELLIS, D., Igneous Petrology
GUNNINGHAM, N., Resources, Environment and Society
KANOWSKI, P. J., Resources, Environment and Society
KIRK, K., Biochemistry
LEVICK, B., Psychology
MCCLELLAND, D., Physics
PASHLEY, R., Colloid Chemistry
RIDE, D., Geology
STANTON, R., Palaeontology
TURNER, J., Psychology

UNIVERSITY CENTRES

Asia-Pacific College of Diplomacy: Dir Prof. W. MALEY.

Asia-Pacific School of Economics and Government (APSEG): Dir Prof. CHONG JU CHOI

APSEG CENTRES

Australia–Japan Research Centre: Exec. Dir Prof. P. DRYSDALE
Australia–South Asia Research Centre: Exec. Dir Prof. R. JHA
National Centre for Development Studies: Exec. Dir Prof. R. C. DUNCAN
Graduate Program in Public Policy: Exec. Dir Prof. G. WITHERS

Centre for Aboriginal Economic Policy Research: Dir Prof. J. C. ALTMAN.

Centre for Advanced Legal Studies in International and Public Law: Dir Prof. H. CHARLESWORTH.

Centre for Arab and Islamic Studies: Dir Prof. AMIN SAIKAL.

Centre for Commercial Law: Dir Prof. STEPHEN BOTTOMLEY.

Centre for Cross-Cultural Research: Dir Prof. H. MORPHY.

Centre for Educational Development and Academic Methods: Dir Dr L. HORT.

Centre for Environmental Law: Dir DON ANTON.

Centre for Mental Health Research: Dir Prof. A. JORM.

Centre for the Public Awareness of Science: Dir SUE STOCKLMAYER.

Centre for Resource and Environmental Studies: Dir Prof. M. HUTCHINSON.

Centre for Sustainable Energy Systems: Dir Prof. ANDREW BLAKERS.

Humanities Research Centre: Dir Prof. I. DONALDSON (acting).

National Centre for Epidemiology and Population Health: Dir Prof. T. MCMICHAEL.

UNIVERSITY OF BALLARAT

POB 663, Ballarat, Vic. 3353
Telephone: (3) 5327-9000
Fax: (3) 5327-9544
Internet: www.ballarat.edu.au

Founded 1976 as Ballarat College of Advanced Education; University status acquired 1994

Vice-Chancellor: Prof. KERRY O. COX
Number of students: 22,000 (higher education and Technical and Further Education—TAFE)

DEANS

Arts Academy: Prof. PETER MATTHEWS
School of Behavioural and Social Sciences and Humanities: Assoc. Prof. ROSEMARY GREEN
School of Business: Prof. JULIAN LOWE
School of Business Services—TAFE: RUSSELL BRAY
School of Education: Prof. LAWRIE ANGUS
School of Human Movement and Sport Sciences: Assoc. Prof. LEONIE OTAGO
School of Human Sciences—TAFE: GREG HAINES
School of Information Technology and Mathematical Sciences: Prof. SID MORRIS
School of Manufacturing Services—TAFE: CARLA READING
School of Nursing: Assoc. Prof. HANNELORE BEST
School of Science and Engineering: Prof. MARTIN WESTBROOKE

BOND UNIVERSITY

Qld 4229
Telephone: (7) 5595-1111
Fax: (7) 5595-1140
E-mail: information@bond.edu.au
Internet: www.bond.edu.au

Founded 1987
Private control
Academic year: January to December

Chancellor: TREVOR ROWE
Vice-Chancellor: Prof. R. STABLE
Registrar: ALAN FINCH
Director, Commercial and Financial Services: JOHN LELIEVRE
Director, Library Services: GULCIN CRIBB
Director, Marketing and Student Recruitment: ANDREA HARCOURT
Number of teachers: 337
Number of students: 2,743

Publications: *Bond Law Review*, *Bond Management Review*, *Revenue Law Journal*

DEANS

Business: Prof. G. MARCHANT
Health Sciences: Prof. C. DEL MAR
Humanities and Social Sciences: Prof. R. MORTLEY
Information Technology: Prof. R. DAVISON
Law: Prof. D. BENTLEY

PROFESSORS

Faculty of Business:

BERTIN, W., Finance
CROUCH, A., Organizations and Management
FISHER, C., Management
GASTON, N., Economics
ISELIN, E., Accounting
JOHNSON, P., Entrepreneurship
MOORES, K., Accounting
SHAW, J. B., Management

Faculty of Health Sciences:

HENLY, D., Biomedical Sciences
MAGUIRE, E., Surgery
YOUNGMAN, J., Population Health

Faculty of Humanities:

BOYLE, G., Psychology
EDWARDS, M., Psychology
HARRISON, P., Philosophy
HICKS, R., Psychology
MOLLOY, B., Film and Television
PEARSON, M., Communication and Media
WILSON, P., Criminology

Faculty of Information Technology:

FINNIE, G., Information Systems
KRISHNAN, P., Computer Science

Faculty of Law:

ALLAN, D., Contract and Commercial Law
BOULLE, L., Alternative Dispute Resolution
CARNEY, G., Constitutional and Administrative Law
COLVIN, E., Criminal Law
CORKERY, J., Corporate and Taxation Law
HISCOCK, M., Contract, Comparative and Commercial Law
LUPTON, M., Law and Medicine
WADE, J., Mediation

UNIVERSITY OF CANBERRA

University of Canberra, ACT 2601
Telephone: (2) 6201-5111
Fax: (2) 6201-5999
Internet: www.canberra.edu.au

Founded 1990 from former Canberra CAE
Government control
Academic year: February to November (two semesters)

Chancellor: WENDY MCCARTHY
Vice-Chancellor: Prof. ROGER DEAN
Deputy Vice-Chancellor: Prof. ELIZABETH MORE
Pro Vice-Chancellors: Prof. JOHN DEARN (Academic Affairs), Prof. PETER DOWLING (Division of Business, Law and Information Sciences), Prof. PETER PUTNIS (Division of Communication and Education), Dr SUE THOMAS (Division of Health, Design and Science), Prof. ANDREW CHEETHAM (Research and Information Management)
University Librarian: ANITA R. M. CROTTY

Library: see Libraries and Archives
Number of teachers: 388 (full-time)
Number of students: 10,625

Publications: *Annual Report*, *Handbook* (annually)

PROFESSORS

ALDERMAN, B. Y., Children's Literature
ARBON, P., Acute Care Nursing
BARTINIK, R., Mathematics
BLOOD, R. W., Professional Communication
BREMNER, C., Design
CREAGH, D. C., Physics
DEARN, J., Higher Education
DOWLING, P. J., International Management and Strategy
DUNK, A., Accounting
EDWARDS, P. J., Electronics Engineering and Applied Physics
FRITH, S. H., Architecture
GEORGES, A., Applied Ecology
HALLIGAN, J., Public Administration
HANDING, A., Applied Economics and Social Policy
HORRIGAN, B., Law
JONES, G., Freshwater Science
KYN, J., Forensics Studies
LEWIS, P. E. T., Economics
MAHER, W., Environmental Chemistry
MORRISON, P. A., Nursing
NANDAN, S. P., English and Commonwealth Studies
NORRIS, R. H., Freshwater Ecology

PUTNIS, P., Communication
SHADDOCK, A. J., Special Education and Counselling
TAYLOR, P. J., Mathematics Education
TURNER, M., Public Administration
WAGNER, M., Computing

CENTRAL QUEENSLAND UNIVERSITY

Bruce Highway, Rockhampton, CQ Mail Centre, Qld 4702
Telephone: (7) 4930-9368
Fax: (7) 4930-9438
E-mail: publicrelations@cqu.edu.au
Internet: www.cqu.edu.au

Founded 1967 as Queensland Institute of Technology (Capricornia); became Capricornia Institute of Advanced Education in 1971; became University College of Central Queensland in 1990 and University of Central Queensland in 1992; present name 1994

Chancellor: RENNIE FRITSCHY
Vice-Chancellor: Prof. JOHN RICKARD
Deputy Vice-Chancellors: Prof. JIM MIENCZAKOWSKI, Prof. JOHN NELSON, JACK WOOD
Registrar: KEN WINDOW
Librarian: GRAHAM BLACK

Number of teachers: 321
Number of students: 18,000

Publications: *Annual Report*, *Handbook*

DEANS

Arts, Health and Sciences: Prof. ERROL PAYNE
Business and Law: Prof. CATHERINE SMITH
Education and Creative Arts: Prof. RICHARD SMITH (acting)
Engineering and Physical Systems: Prof. ELIZABETH TAYLOR
Informatics and Communication: Assoc. Prof. KEVIN TICKLE (acting)

Campuses at Brisbane, Bundaberg, Emerald, Gladstone, Mackay, Melbourne, Rockhampton, Sydney and Fiji

CHARLES DARWIN UNIVERSITY

Darwin, NT 0909
Telephone: (8) 8946-6666
Fax: (8) 8927-0612
Internet: www.cdu.edu.au

Founded 2003 by the merger of Northern Territory University and Centralian College
Federal control
Academic year: February to November

Chancellor: R. RYAN
Vice-Chancellor: Prof. HELEN GARNETT
Pro Vice-Chancellor (Community and Access): DAN ZOELLNER
Pro Vice-Chancellor (Teaching and Learning): Prof. C. WEBB
Deputy Vice-Chancellor: Prof. ROBERT WASSON
Executive Director, Corporate Services: Dr SCOTT SNYDER

Number of academic staff: 400
Number of students: 18,000

DEANS

Education, Health and Science: Prof. G. HILL
Law, Business and Arts: ADRIAN WALTER
Technology: Dr S. SHANHAN

CHARLES STURT UNIVERSITY

Chancellery, The Grange, Panorama Ave, Bathurst, NSW 2795
Telephone: (2) 6338-4000
Fax: (2) 6338-6001
E-mail: inquiry@csu.edu.au
Internet: www.csu.edu.au

Founded 1989 by amalgamation of Mitchell College of Advanced Education (f. 1951) and Riverina-Murray Inst. of Higher Education (f. 1947); campuses at Albury, Bathurst, Dubbo and Wagga Wagga
State control
Academic year: January to December

Chancellor: LAWRENCE WILLETT
Vice-Chancellor: Prof. IAN GOULTER
ProViceChancellor (Research and Graduate Training): Prof. P. BURNETT
Sec.: MARK BURDACK
Univ. Librarian: SHIRLEY OAKLEY

Number of teachers: 620
Number of students: 34,246

DEANS

Faculty of Arts: Assoc. Prof. TRACEY GREEN
Faculty of Commerce: Prof. JOHN HICKS
Faculty of Education: Prof. TONI DOWNES
Faculty of Science: Prof. MARK BURTON

PROFESSORS

Faculty of Arts (POB 588, Wagga Wagga, NSW 2678; tel. (2) 6933-2861; fax (2) 6933-2868; internet www.csu.edu.au/faculty/arts):
ALSTON, M. M., Centre for Rural Social Research
BRADLEY, B. S., Social Sciences and Liberal Studies
CAMPBELL, T., Centre for Applied Philosophy and Public Ethics
GORMAN, L.
GREEN, D. L., Visual and Performing Arts
LUPTON, D. A., Social Sciences and Liberal Studies
MARCUS, J., Social Sciences and Liberal Studies
MILLER, S. R. M., Centre for Applied Philosophy and Public Ethics
OALMER, J., Graduate School of Policing
THOMSON, D. M., Social Sciences and Liberal Studies

Faculty of Commerce (Panorama Ave, Bathurst, NSW 2795; tel. (2) 6338-4285; fax (2) 6338-4250; internet www.csu.edu.au/faculty/commerce):
FARRELL, M.
FISH, B. S., International School of Business
HEAZLEWOOD, C. T.
HICKS, J.
JARRATT, D. G.
MATHEWS, M. R., Accounting
OCZKOWSKI, E.
TRAVAGLIONE, A., Marketing and Management

Faculty of Education (Panorama Ave, Bathurst, NSW 2795; tel. (2) 6338-4444; fax (2) 6338-4182; internet www.csu.edu.au/faculty/educat):
GREEN, W. C., Teacher Education
KEMMIS, S., Education
MEYENN, R., Teacher Education
ZEVENBERGEN, R., Murray Education Unit

Faculty of Health Studies (POB 789, Aubury, NSW 2640; tel. (2) 6051-9806; fax (2) 6051-9900; internet www.csu.edu.au/faculty/health):
BALL, P., Biomedical Sciences
BURTON, M. A., School of Biomedical Sciences

Faculty of Science and Agriculture (POB 588, Wagga Wagga, NSW 2678; tel. (2) 6933-2864; fax (2) 6933-2868; internet www.csu.edu.au/faculty/sciagr):
ABBOTT, K., School of Agriculture and Veterinary Sciences
BATTEN, G. D., School of Agriculture
BOWMER, K., Science and Agriculture
BOSSOMAIER, T. R. J., School of Information Technology
CURTIS, A., School of Environmental and Information Sciences
HARVEY, R., School of Information Studies
KHAN, S., School of Information Studies
KLOMP, N., School of Environmental and Information Sciences
POON, S. P., School of Information Studies
ROBARDS, K., School of Information Studies
SCOLLARY, G. R., School of Wine and Food Sciences
SILLENCE, M. N., Agriculture
WECKERT, J., School of Information Studies

CONSTITUENT CAMPUSES

Albury–Wodonga Campus

POB 789, Albury, NSW 2640
Telephone: (2) 6051-6000
Fax: (2) 6051-6629
E-mail: inquiry@csu.edu.au
Internet: www.csu.edu.au

Founded 1989

Head of Campus: Prof. GAIL WHITEFORD

Bathurst Campus

Panorama Ave, Bathurst, NSW 2795
Telephone: (2) 6338-4000
Fax: (2) 6331-9634
E-mail: inquiry@csu.edu.au
Internet: www.csu.edu.au

Founded 1989

Principal: Assoc. Prof. GREG WALKER.

Dubbo Campus

Locked Bag 49, Dubbo East, NSW 2830
Telephone: (2) 6884-7209
Fax: (2) 6884-7218
E-mail: inquiry@csu.edu.au
Internet: www.csu.edu.au

Founded 1995

Head of School: HEATHER BELL (acting).

Orange Campus

Orange, NSW
Telephone: (2) 6365-7555
Fax: (2) 6360-5590
E-mail: inquiry@csu.edu.au
Internet: www.csu.edu.au

Principal: Prof. KEVIN PARTON.

Wagga Wagga Campus

Locked Bag 588, Wagga Wagga, NSW 2678
Telephone: (2) 6933-2000
Fax: (2) 6933-2639
E-mail: inquiry@csu.edu.au
Internet: www.csu.edu.au

Founded 1989

Head of Campus: Prof. DAVID GREEN.

CURTIN UNIVERSITY OF TECHNOLOGY

GPO Box U1987, Perth, WA 6845
Telephone: (8) 9266-9266
Fax: (8) 9266-2255
Internet: www.curtin.edu.au

Founded 1967 as Western Australian Inst. of Technology; present name and status 1987
Academic year: February to November (two semesters)

Chancellor: RICHARD TASTULA (acting)
Vice-Chancellor: Prof. LANCE TWOMEY
Senior Deputy Vice-Chancellor: Prof. LESLEY PARKER
Deputy Vice-Chancellor (Research and Development): Prof. PAUL ROSSITER
Pro Vice-Chancellor (Academic Services): Prof. JANE DEN HOLLANDER
Pro Vice-Chancellor (International and Enterprise): Prof. JEANETTE HACKETT

Executive Dean (Curtin Business School): Prof. MICHAEL WOOD
Executive Dean (Engineering, Science and Computing): PETER LEE
Executive Dean (Health Sciences): Prof. CHARLES WATSON
Executive Dean (Humanities): Prof. TOM STANNAGE
Executive General Manager (University Resources): PETER WALTON
University Librarian: VICKI WILLIAMSON

Number of teachers: 1,200
Number of students: 27,000

DEANS

Faculty of Built Environment, Art and Design: L. HEVGOLD
Faculty of Education, Language Studies and Social Work: Dr G. DELLAR
Research and Development (Graduate Studies): Prof. L. RENNIE

HEADS OF DEPARTMENTS

Department of Applied Geology: L. COLLINS
Department of Applied Physics: Dr A. RIESSEN
Department of Architecture: Dr J. STEPHENS
Department of Art: H. HUMMERSTON
Department of Chemical Engineering: M. O'TADÉ
Department of Civil Engineering: D. SCOTT
Department of Communication and Cultural Studies: JON STRATTON
Department of Construction Management: D. J. BACCARINI
Department of Dental Hygiene and Therapy: R. KENDELL
Department of Design: G. BORZYSKOWSKI
Department of Education: H. JENKINS
Department of Electrical and Computer Engineering: SYED ISLAM
Department of Environmental Biology: Prof. J. MAJER
Department of Environmental Health: R. PICKETT
Department of Exploration Geophysics: Assoc. Prof. N. UREN
Department of Health Information Management: B. POSTLE
Department of Health Policy and Management: Prof. D. BOLDY
Department of Health Promotion: Assoc. Prof. P. HOWAT
Department of Human Biology: Dr M. GARDINER
Department of Languages and Intercultural Education: K. DUNWORTH
Department of Mathematics and Statistics: Prof. L. CACCETTA
Department of Mechanical Engineering: Dr A. LUCEY
Department of Medical Imaging Science: T. KNIGHTS
Department of Petroleum Engineering: Prof. R. RAJESWARAN
Department of Podiatry: Prof. T. WRIGHT
Department of Social Science: A. PILGRIM
Department of Social Work and Policy: S. LEITMANN
Department of Spatial Sciences: GRAEME WRIGHT
Department of Urban and Regional Planning: D. A. HEDGCOCK
Graduate School of Business: Assoc. Prof. M. NOWAK
School of Accounting: J. NEILSON
School of Applied Chemistry: R. DE MARCO
School of Applied Science: Prof. B. O'CONNOR
School of Architecture, Construction and Planning: Prof. L. HEGVOLD
School of Biomedical Sciences: J. WETHERALL
School of Business Law: D. GUTHRIE
School of Communication and Cultural Studies: Prof. B. DIBBLE
School of Computing: Prof. G. WEST
School of Design: A. PRICE
School of Economics and Finance: I. A. KERR
School of Information Systems: J. VENABLE
School of Management: R. GRAINGER
School of Marketing: Assoc. Prof. R. RAMASESHAN
School of Media and Information: K. SMITH
School of Nursing: Prof. J. DOWNIE
School of Occupational Therapy: Dr R. MARQUIS
School of Pharmacy: M. J. GARLEPP
School of Physiotherapy: Prof. T. WRIGHT
School of Psychology: L. SMITH
School of Public Health: M. CLINTON
Centre for Aboriginal Studies: P. DUDGEON
Centre for International Health: P. FERRONI
Centre for Marine Science and Technology: Prof. J. PENROSE
Science and Mathematics Education Centre: Prof. B. FRASER

ATTACHED INSTITUTES

Australian Telecommunications Research Institute: Dir Prof. S. NORDHAM.

Curtin Sarawak: campus in Malaysia; Dir Prof. K. MCKENNA.

Institute for Research into International Competitiveness: Dir Prof. P. KENYON.

Muresk Institute of Agriculture: Northam, WA 6401; Dir G. HEPWORTH.

National Drug Research Institute: Dir Prof. T. STOCKWELL.

Research Institute for Cultural Heritage: Dir Prof. D. DOLAN.

Western Australian School of Mines: PMB 22, Kalgoorlie, WA 6430; f. 1902, coll. of univ. since 1969; Dir G. LODWICK.

DEAKIN UNIVERSITY

Geelong, Vic. 3217
Campuses: Melbourne (Burwood), Geelong, Rusden, Toorak, Warrnambool and Geelong Waterfront

Telephone: (3) 5227-1100
Fax: (3) 5227-2001
Internet: www.deakin.edu.au

Founded 1974
Academic year: February to November

Chancellor: R. H. SEARBY
Vice-Chancellor and President: Prof. SALLY WALKER
Deputy Vice-Chancellor (Academic): Prof. JOHN ROSENBERG
Pro Vice-Chancellor (International Relations): ERIC MEADOWS
Pro Vice-Chancellor (Online Services): Prof. BRIAN CORBITT
Pro Vice-Chancellor (Research): Prof. PHILIP HAMILTON
Pro Vice-Chancellor (Rural and Regional): Prof. ROB WALLIS
Librarian: S. MCKNIGHT

Library of 1,434,864 vols, 15,959 current periodical titles
Number of teachers: 790
Number of students: 20,460

DEANS

Faculty of Arts: Prof. JOAN BEAUMONT
Faculty of Business and Law: Prof. PHILIP CLARKE
Faculty of Education: Prof. SHIRLEY GRUNDY
Faculty of Health and Behavioural Sciences: Prof. JOHN CATFORD
Faculty of Science and Technology: Prof. RICHARD RUSSELL

HEADS OF SCHOOLS

Faculty of Arts (Pigdons Rd, Geelong, Vic. 3217; tel. (3) 5227-1335; fax (3) 5227-2018; e-mail arts@deakin.edu.au; internet www.arts.deakin.edu.au):

School of Australian and International Studies: Assoc. Prof. GARY SMITH
School of Contemporary Arts: Assoc. Prof. LOUISE JOHNSTON
School of Literary and Communication Studies: Dr LYN MCCREDDEN (acting)
School of Social Inquiry: Prof. ALLAN JOHNSTON

Faculty of Business and Law (Pigdons Rd, Geelong, Vic. 3217; tel. (3) 5227-1100; fax (3) 5227-2001; internet www.deakin.edu.au/fac_buslaw):

Bowater School of Management and Marketing: Prof. DAVID SHILBURY
School of Accounting and Finance: Dr BEVERLEY JACKLING
School of Economics: Prof. BHARAT HAZARI
School of Law: Prof. JEAN DU PLESSIS (acting)
School of Management Information Systems: Prof. PAUL SWATMAN

Faculty of Education (221 Burwood Highway, Burwood, Vic. 3125; tel. (3) 9244-6281; fax (3) 9244-6687; e-mail teached-enquiries@deakin.edu.au; internet education.deakin.edu.au):

School of Social and Cultural Studies in Education: Prof. MARIE EMMITT
School of Scientific and Developmental Studies in Education: Assoc. Prof. SUSIE GROVES (acting)

Faculty of Health and Behavioural Sciences (221 Burwood Highway, Burwood, Vic. 3217; tel. (3) 9244-6135; fax (3) 9244-6019; e-mail hbs.info@deakin.edu.au; internet www.hbs.deakin.edu.au):

Institute of Disability Studies: Prof. BARRIE O'CONNOR
School of Health Sciences: Prof. MARK HARGREAVES
School of Nursing: Assoc. Prof. PAULINE NUGENT
School of Psychology: Assoc. Prof. HILDE LOVEGROVE

Faculty of Science and Technology (662 Blackburn Rd, Clayton, Vic. 3168; tel. (3) 9244-7100; fax (3) 9244-7134; internet www.deakin.edu.au/fac_st):

School of Architecture and Building: Assoc. Prof. NICK BEATTIE
School of Biological and Chemical Sciences: Prof. RICHARD RUSSELL
School of Computing and Mathematics: Prof. ANDRZEJ GOSCINSKI
School of Ecology and Environment: Prof. ROB WALLIS
School of Engineering and Technology: Prof. PETER HODGSON

ATTACHED RESEARCH INSTITUTES

Cell and Organism Bio-engineering: Dir Prof. JULIAN MERCER.

Cellular Metabolism in Health and Disease: Dirs Prof. GREG COLLIER, Prof. MARK HARGREAVES.

Citizenship and Globalization: Dir Dr MICHAEL MUETZELFELDT.

Information Technology for the Information Economy: Dir Prof. GEOFFREY WEBB.

Metals Manufacturing and Performance: Dir Prof. PETER HODGSON.

Palaeoenvironments and Global Change: Dir Prof. NEIL ARCHBOLD.

Quality of Life: Dirs Prof. ROBERT CUMMINS, Dr LIZ ECKERMANN.

Sustainable Environment Management: Dir Prof. GORDON DUFF.

EDITH COWAN UNIVERSITY

Pearson St, Churchlands, WA 6018
Telephone: (8) 9273-8333
Fax: (8) 9387-7095
Internet: www.ecu.edu.au

Founded 1991
State control
Academic year: February to November (2 semesters)

Chancellor: Hon. Justice R. NICHOLSON
Vice-Chancellor: Prof. MILLICENT POOLE
Deputy Vice-Chancellor (Academic): Prof. PATRICK GARNETT
Deputy Vice-Chancellor (Students, Advancement and International Affairs): Prof. JOHN WOOD
Pro Vice-Chancellor (Equity and Indigenous Affairs): Prof. ROBERT HARVEY
Pro Vice-Chancellor (Research): Prof. BILL LOUDEN
Pro Vice-Chancellor (Teaching and Learning): Prof. ROBYN QUIN
Pro Vice-Chancellor (Technology and Information Systems): Prof. TONY WATSON
Vice President (Resources) and Chief Financial Officer: WARREN SNELL

Number of teachers: 772
Number of students: 23,000

Publications: *Digest* (quarterly), *Handbook* (annually), *Quest* (quarterly), *Research & Postgraduate Studies* (annually)

DEANS

Faculty of Business and Public Management: Prof. ROBERT HARVEY
Faculty of Communications and Creative Industries: Prof. ROBYN QUIN
Faculty of Community Services, Education and Social Sciences: Prof. WILLIAM LOUDEN
Faculty of Computing, Health and Science: ANTHONY WATSON
Faculty of Regional Professional Studies: ELIZABETH HATTON

HEADS OF SCHOOL

Faculty of Business and Public Management (Pearson St, Churchlands, WA 6018; tel. (8) 9273-8696; fax (8) 9273-8754; e-mail business@ecu.edu.au; internet www.business.ecu.edu.au):

Accounting, Finance and Economics: Assoc. Prof. ATIQUE ISLAM
Justice and Business Law: Prof. PAUL MOYLE
Management: Assoc. Prof. PETER STANDEN
Management Information Systems: Prof. JANICE BURN
Marketing, Tourism and Leisure: Assoc. Prof. ROSS DOWLING

Faculty of Communications and Creative Industries (100 Joondulup Drive, Joondulup, WA 6027; tel. (8) 9400-5514; fax (8) 9400-5613; e-mail fchs@ecu.edu.au; internet www.chs.ecu.edu.au):

Communications and Multimedia: Prof. ARSHAD OMARI (acting)
School of Contemporary Arts: Assoc. Prof. DOMENICO DE CLARIO
Western Australian Academy of Performing Arts: Assoc. Prof. PATRICK CRICHTON (acting)

Faculty of Community Services, Education and Social Sciences (2 Bradford St, Mount Lawley, WA 6050; tel. (8) 9370-6187; fax (8) 9370-6664; e-mail csess@ecu.edu.au; internet www.ecu.edu.au/ses):

Education: Prof. MAXWELL ANGUS
International, Cultural and Community Studies: Assoc. Prof. GRAHAM MCKAY
Kurongkurl Katitjin School of Indigenous Australian Studies: GRAEME GOWER
Psychology: Dr CRAIG SPEELMAN

Faculty of Computing, Health and Science (tel. (8) 6304-5505; e-mail a.elam@ecu.edu.au):

Biomedical and Sports Science: Assoc. Prof. BARRY GIBSON
Computer and Information Science: Assoc. Prof. WOJCIECH KUCZBORSKI
Engineering and Mathematics: Prof. KAMRAN ESHRAGHIAN
Natural Sciences: Assoc. Prof. PAUL LAVERY
Nursing and Public Health: Assoc. Prof. KATHRYN WHITE

Faculty of Regional Professional Studies (tel. (8) 9780-7711; e-mail r.bailey@ecu.edu.au):

Enterprise and Technology: TERENCE HAINES
Professional Community Services: KEN ROBINSON

ATTACHED INSTITUTES

Australian Institute for Research in Primary Mathematics Education: Head P. SWAN.

Cancer, Palliative Care and Family Health Collaborative Research Team: Head Prof. LINDA KRISTJANSON.

Centre for Applied Language and Literary Research: Heads Prof. IAN MALCOLM, Dr MARY ROHL.

Centre for Asian Communication, Media and Cultural Studies: Head Dr B. SHOESMITH.

Centre for Disability, Research and Development: Head Dr R. JACKSON.

Centre for Ecosystem Management: Head Dr PIERRE HORWITZ.

Centre for Health and Ageing: Head Prof. ALAN BITTLES.

Centre for Human Genetics: Heads Prof. A. BITTLES, Assoc. Prof. L. KELAYDJIEVA.

Centre for Regional Development and Research: Head Dr KEN ROBINSON.

Centre for Research for Women: Head Dr E. REID-BOYD.

Centre for Social Research: Head Prof. ALAN BLACK.

Centre for Very High Speed Microelectronic Systems: Head Prof. K. ESHRAGHIAN.

Data Modelling and Analysis Research Group: Head Assoc. Prof. LYNETTE BLOOM.

Exercise and Sports Science Research Group: Head Dr P. SACCO.

Finance and Capital Markets Research Group: Head Prof. DAVID ALLEN.

Health Promotion Research Group: Head GLENDA JACKSON.

Institute for the Service Professions: Dir Dr HELEN WILDY.

Interactive Information Technology Group: Head Prof. RON OLIVER.

Internet and Computer Security Laboratory Group: Head Prof. ANTHONY WATSON.

Mathematics, Science and Technology Education Centre: Head Dr J. BANA.

Mental Health Research Forum: Head Prof. EAMONN SHANLEY.

Mining Health and Safety Research Forum: Heads Assoc. Prof. MILOS NEDVED, JANIS MUSSETT.

Public Health Research Network: Head Prof. NEIL THOMSON.

Security and Applied Technology Research Group: Head Assoc. Prof. CLIFTON SMITH.

Sellenger Centre in Collaboration with the Western Australia Police Force: Head Assoc. Prof. IRENE FROYLAND.

Small and Medium Enterprise Research Centre: Head Assoc. Prof. DIETER FINK.

Software Engineering Group: Head Dr JAMES MILLAR.

Sport and Physical Activity Research Centre: Head Assoc. Prof. ANDREW TAGGART.

Visual Information Processing Research Group: Head Assoc. Prof. ABDESSELAM BOUZERDOUM.

Working for e-Business (We-B) Centre: Head Prof. JANICE BURN.

FLINDERS UNIVERSITY

GPO Box 2100, Adelaide, SA 5001
Telephone: (8) 8201-3911
Fax: (8) 8201-3000
E-mail: central.records@flinders.edu.au
Internet: www.flinders.edu.au

Founded 1966; merged in 1991 with Sturt Campus of South Australian College of Advanced Education
Academic year: March to November (2 semesters)

Chancellor: Sir ERIC NEAL
Vice-Chancellor: Prof. A. R. EDWARDS
Pro-Vice-Chancellor (Academic): Prof. J. A. COOPER
Pro-Vice-Chancellor (International): Prof. D. FORBES
Pro-Vice-Chancellor (Research): Prof. C. D. MARLIN
Director of Administration: B. FERGUSSON
Registrar: B. SIMONDSON
Librarian: W. T. CATIONS

Library: see Libraries and Archives
Number of teachers: 625
Number of students: 14,700

Publications: *Australian Bulletin of Labour* (quarterly), *Australian Economic Papers* (with University of Adelaide), *Australian Journal of Political Science*, *Health Sociology Review*

EXECUTIVE DEANS

Education, Humanities, Law and Theology: Prof. F. H. E. TRENT
Health Sciences: Prof. R. GOLDIE
Science and Engineering: Prof. J. F. WHELDRAKE
Social Sciences: Assoc. Prof. J. G. BROWETT

PROFESSORS

AYLWARD, P., Medicine
BARRITT, G. T., Medical Biochemistry
BAUM, F., Public Health
BEAL, R. W., Medicine
BERSTEN, A. A., Medicine
BLESSING, W. W., Medicine
BREWSTER, P., Northern Territory Clinical School
BULL, M., Biological Sciences
BURGOYNE, L., Biological Sciences
BUTCHER, A. R., Communication Disorders
CATCHESIDE, D. E. A., Biological Sciences
CLARE, J. M. R., Nursing
CLARK, D. J., Law
CONDON, J., Psychiatry
COOPER, L. L., Social Administration and Social Work
COSTA, M., Human Physiology
COSTER, D. J., Ophthalmology
CROCKER, A. D., Clinical Pharmacology
CROTTY, M., Rehabilitation, Aged and Extended Care
CURROW, D. C., Palliative Care
DEBATS, D. A., American Studies
DE CRESPIGNY, C. F. C., Nursing and Midwifery
DODDS, P. G., Mathematics and Statistics
DOWNING, A. R., Engineering (Biomedical)
DUNBAR, J., Rural Health
DUNN, S. V., Nursing

FAIRWEATHER, P. G., Biological Sciences
FORBES, D. K., Geography
FORSYTH, K. D., Paediatrics and Child Health
GIBBINS, I. L., Anatomy and Histology
GOLDSMITH, A. J., Law
GOODMAN, A. E., Biology
GORDON, T. P., Immunology, Allergy and Arthritis
HASSAN, R. U., Sociology
HAY, I. M., Geography
HEARN, T. C., Orthopaedic Research
HENDERSON, D. W., Medicine
HOLLEDGE, J., Drama
KALUCY, R. S., Psychiatry
KEIRSE, M., Obstetrics and Gynaecology
KNOWLES, G. P., Computer Systems Engineering
KRISHNAN, J., Surgery
LAWRANCE, W., Chemistry
LAWSON, M. J., Education
LEONARD, D., Economics
LUSZCZ, M. A., Psychology
MACKENZIE, P. I., Clinical Pharmacology
MACKINNON, A., Medicine
MALTBY, R. G., Screen Studies
MARLIN, C. D., Computer Science
MATISONS, J. G., Chemistry, Physics and Earth Sciences
MCDONALD, J. M., Economics
MCMAHON, R., Commerce
MINERS, J. O., Environmental Health Unit
MORLEY, A. A., Haematology
MORLEY, M. W., Drama
OWEN, H., Anaesthesia and Intensive Care
PARKIN, A., Political and International Studies
PHILLIPS, P., Medicine
PILLER, N. B., Public Health
PILOTTO, L. S. J., General Practice
PRIDEAUX, D. J., Teaching Research
RICHARDS, E. S., History
RICHARDSON, S., National Institute of Labour Studies
ROACH ANLEU, S. L., Sociology
ROCHE, A. M., School of Medicine
RODDICK, J. F., Computer Science
RUSH, R. A., Human Physiology
RYALL, R. L., Surgery
SAGE, M. R., Diagnostic Radiology
SHERIDAN, S. M., Women's Studies
SKINNER, J., Pathology
SMITH, M. D., Medicine
STEWART, A. J., Law
STORER, R., Physics
STUHLMILLER, C., School of Nursing
TEUBNER, P. J. O., Physics
TIGGEMANN, M., Psychology
TOMCZAK, M., Earth Sciences
TONKIN, A. M., Medicine
TOOULI, J., Surgery
TRENT, F. H., Education
TULLOCH, G. J., English
WATSON, D., Surgery
WHELDRAKE, J., Biological Sciences
WILLOUGHBY, J. O., Medicine
WING, L. M. H., Medicine
WITHERS, R. T., Education
WORLEY, P. S., Rural and Remote Health
YOUNG, G. P., Gastroenterology
ZOLA, H., Paediatrics and Child Health

ATTACHED RESEARCH INSTITUTES

(The mailing address is that of the University)

Airborne Research Australia: Dir Assoc. Prof. J. M. HACKER.

Australian Centre for Community Services Research: Dir Prof. L. L. COOPER.

Centre for Ageing Studies: Dir Prof. G. ANDREWS.

Centre for Applied Philosophy: Dir Dr I. A. HUNT.

Centre for Development Studies: Dir Dr S. SCHECH.

Centre for Groundwater Studies: Contact Dr C. T. SIMMONS.

Centre for Neuroscience: Convenor Assoc. Prof. J. MORRIS.

Centre for Research in the New Literatures in English: Dir Dr S. C. HARREX.

Centre for Scandinavian Studies: Dir Dr A. R. G. GRIFFITHS.

Centre for Theology, Science and Culture: Dir Revd Dr A. DUTNEY.

Flinders Centre for Epidemiology and Biostatistics: Dir Prof. L. S. J. PILOTTO.

Flinders Institute of Public Policy and Management: Dir Dr L. ORCHARD.

Flinders Institute for the Study of Teaching: Dir Prof. J. SMYTH.

Flinders Institute for Health and Medical Research: Dir Prof. G. BARRITT.

Flinders University Institute of International Education: Dir Assoc. Prof. G. R. TEASDALE.

International Institute of Palliative and Supportive Services: Dir Prof. D. C. CURROW.

Lincoln Marine Science Centre: Dir Dr T. BOLTON (acting).

National Centre for Education and Training on Addiction: Dir Prof. A. ROCHE.

National Institute of Labour Studies Inc.: Dir Prof. S. RICHARDSON.

Pan Pacific Institute: Dir Prof. D. A. DEBATS.

Primary Health Care Research and Information Services: Dirs Prof. L. S. J. PILOTTO, Assoc. Prof. L. KALUCY.

Research Centre for Injury Studies: Dir Assoc. Prof. J. E. HARRISON.

South Australian Centre for Economic Studies: run jointly with the University of Adelaide; Contact G. SCOTT.

South Australian Centre for Lifelong Learning and Development: Dir Prof. D. RALPH.

GRIFFITH UNIVERSITY

Qld 4111
Telephone: (7) 3735-7111
Fax: (7) 3735-7965
Internet: www.griffith.edu.au
(Griffith Univ. Gold Coast Campus, Parklands Dr., Southport, Qld 4215; tel. (7) 5552-8800; fax (7) 5552-8777)
(Griffith Univ. Mount Gravatt Campus, Messines Ridge Rd, Mt Gravatt, Qld 4122; tel. (7) 3735-7111; fax (7) 3735-7965)
(Griffith Univ. Nathan Campus, Kessels Rd, Nathan, Qld 4111; tel. (7) 3735-7111; fax (7) 3735-7965)
(Griffith Univ. Logan Campus, University Dr., Meadowbrook, Qld 4131; tel. (7) 3382-7111; fax (7) 3735-7965)
(Queensland College of Art, Griffith Univ., 226 Grey St, South Bank, Qld 4101; tel. (7) 3735-3111; fax (7) 3735-3199; f. 1881, became a college of Griffith Univ. 1992)
(Queensland Conservatorium, Griffith Univ., 16 Russell St, South Bank, Qld 4101; tel. (7) 3735-6111; fax (7) 3735-6282; f. 1957, became a college of Griffith Univ. 1991)

Founded 1971
State control
Academic year: February to November

Chancellor: LENEEN FORDE
Vice-Chancellor and Pres.: Prof. I. O'CONNOR
Deputy Vice-Chancellor (Research) and Deputy Pres.: Prof. L. JOHNSON
Deputy Vice-Chancellor (Academic) and Deputy Pres.: Prof. J. DEWAR
Pro-Vice-Chancellor (Admin.): COLIN MCANDREW
Pro-Vice-Chancellor (Arts, Education and Law): Prof. M. MCMENIMAN
Pro-Vice-Chancellor (Business): Prof. M. POWELL
Pro-Vice-Chancellor (Community Partnerships): Prof. M. STANDAGE
Pro-Vice-Chancellor (Health): Prof. A. CRIPPS
Pro-Vice-Chancellor (Information Services): JANICE RICKARDS
Pro-Vice-Chancellor (Int.): C. MADDEN
Pro-Vice-Chancellor (Science, Environment, Engineering and Technology): Prof. N. PANKHURST
Academic Registrar: Dr RICHARD AMOUR
Dir, Queensland College of Art: Prof. P. CLEVELAND
Dir, Queensland Conservatorium: Prof. P. ROENNFELDT

Library of 800,000
Number of teachers: 1,254
Number of students: 35,335
Publication: *Griffith Review* (quarterly)

DEANS

Faculty of Arts: Prof. K. FERRES
Faculty of Education: Prof. C. WYATT-SMITH
Griffith Business School: Prof. W. SHEPHERD (Academic: Prof. L. FULOP (Research: Prof. L. FRAZER (Learning and Teaching)
Griffith Health: Prof. D. CREEDY (Academic: Prof. K. HALFORD (Research: Assoc. Prof. N. BUYS (Learning and Teaching)
Griffith Law School: Prof. P. BARON
Science, Environment, Engineering and Technology: Assoc. Prof. C. WILD (Academic: G. BUSHELL (Research: D. EDWARDS (Learning and Teaching)
Griffith Graduate Research School: Prof. J. CUMMING

PROFESSORS

AITKEN, L., Nursing
ARTHINGTON, A. H., Environmental Science
AULD, C., Tourism, Leisure, Hotel and Sports Management
BAGNALL, R., Education
BALASUBRAMANIAM, A. B., Engineering
BALFOUR, M., Education
BAMBER, G., Business
BARKER, M., Management
BEACHAM, I., Medical Science
BERNS, S., Law
BORBASI, S., Nursing
BRADDOCK, R., Environmental Sciences
BRAMLEY-MOORE, M., Queensland College of Art
BROWN, L., Environmental Sciences
BROWN, P., Leisure Studies
BUCKLEY, R., Engineering
BUNN, S., Environmental Studies
BURCH, D., Science
BURTON, B., Education
BUSHELL, G., Science
CHABOYER, W., Nursing
CHENOWETH, L., Human Services
CHU, C., Public Health
CLARKE, F., Biomolecular and Physical Sciences
COUCHMAN, P., Management
CREED, P., Psychology
CREEDY, D., Health
CRIPPS, A., Health
CUMMING, J., Education
DALY, K., Criminology and Criminal Justice
DAVIDSON, M. C., Tourism, Leisure, Hotel and Sports Management
DEHNE, F., Information and Communication Technology
DE LEO, D., Suicide Research and Prevention
DEMPSTER, N., Education
DEWAR, J. K., Law
DIMITRIJEV, S., Microelectronic Engineering
DOBSON, J., Science

DRAPER, P., Music
DREW, R., Environmental Studies
DREW, R., Biomolecular and Physical Sciences
DROMEY, R. G., Computing and Information Technology
DYCK, M. J., Business
ELKINS, J., Education
ESTIVILL-CASTRO, V., Information and Communication Technology
FARQHAR, M., International Business and Asian Studies
FERRES, K., Arts
FINNANE, M. J., Arts, Postgraduate Studies
FRAZER, L., Marketing
FULOP, E., Marketing and Management
GAMMACK, J., Management
GIDDINGS, J., Law
GLEESON, B., Environmental Planning
GRIFFITHS, L., Medical Science
GUEST, R., Graduate School of Management
GUILDING, C., Tourism, Leisure, Hotel and Sports Management
HALFORD, G., Psychology
HALFORD, W. K., Health and Applied Psychology
HARRISON, H. B., Microelectronic Engineering
HEAD, B., Law
HEADRICK, J., Medical Science
HEALY, P., Science
HOMEL, R. J., Criminology and Criminal Justice
HOPE, G., Science
HUDSON, C. W., Humanities
HUGHES, J., Environmental Sciences
HUNTER, R., Law
HYDE, M. B., Education
ISLAM, Y., International Business and Asian Studies
IVANOVSKI, S., Dentistry and Oral Health
JENKINS, I., Science
JOHNSON, L., Research
JOHNSON, N. W., Dentistry and Oral Health
JOHNSTONE, R., Law
KANE, J., Politics and Public Policy
KEITH, R., International Business and Asian Studies
KITCHING, R. L., Environmental Science
KNIGHT, A. E., Science
KNIGHT, K., International Business and Asian Studies
KWON, O. Y., International Business and Asian Studies
LAM, A. K., Medicine
LEE, S., Environmental Studies
LISNER, P., Microelectronic Engineering
LOO, Y.-C., Engineering
MACKAY-SIM, A., Biomolecular and Biomedical Sciences
MACKERRAS, C. P., International Business and Asian Studies
MCDONALD, J., Law
MCLURE, R. J., Medicine
MCMENIMAN, M., Education
MCQUEEN, R. I., Law
MCROBBIE, C., Education
MCTAINSH, G., Environmental Studies
MAKIN, A., Accounting, Finance and Economics
MERRILEES, W., Marketing and Management
MIA, L., Accounting and Finance
MORAN, A., Arts
MOYLE, W., Nursing
MUIRHEAD, B. D., Education
NESDALE, A. R., Commerce, Management and Applied Psychology
NG, A. C., Accounting
NGUYEN, D. T.
O'CONNOR, I., Economics
O'FAIRCHEALLAIGH, C. S., Politics and Public Policy
O'TOOLE, J., Education
PALIWAL, K., Microelectronic Engineering
PARRY, K., Management
PATEL, B., Biomolecular and Physical Sciences
PEETZ, D., Industrial Relations
PEGG, D. T., Science
POWELL, M. J., Business
QUINN, R. J., Science
RICKARD, C., Nursing
RICKSON, R., Environmental Studies
ROEMFELDT, P. J., Music
SADLER, D. R., Education
SAMPFORD, C. J., Criminology and Criminal Justice
SATTAR, A., Information Technology
SCHULTZ, J., Public Culture
SCHUMAN, A. D., Business
SCUFFHAM, P., Medicine
SEARLE, J., Medicine
SELVANATHAN, A., International Business and Asian Studies
SELVANATHAN, S., Accounting, Finance and Economics
SHEPHERD, W., International Business and Asian Studies
SHORT, S. D., Public Health
SMITH, C., Accounting, Finance and Economics
SPARKS, B., Tourism and Hotel Management
STANDAGE, M., Science and Health
STEVENSON, J. C., Education
STRACHAN, G., Commerce and Business
SUN, C., Computing and Information Technology
TACON, P., Arts
THIEL, D. V., Microelectronic Engineering
TOH, S. H., Multi-faith Centre
TOMLINSON, R., Environmental Engineering
TOPOR, R. W., Computing and Information Technology
TURNBULL, P. G., Arts
VON ITZTEIN, M., Biomolecular Science
VLACIC, L., Microelectronic Engineering
WALLIS, M., Nursing
WANNA, J., Politics and Public Policy
WELLER, P. M., Politics and Public Policy
WISEMAN, H. M., Science
XU, Z., Environmental Studies
YEO, R., Humanities
ZEVENBERGEN, R., Education

ACADEMIC CENTRES AND INSTITUTES

Centre for Applied Linguistics and Languages: tel. (7) 3735-7089; fax (7) 3875-7090; e-mail call@griffith.edu.au; internet www.griffith.edu.au/centre/call; Dir MARGARET CASEY.

Centre for Applied Studies in Deafness: tel. (7) 5552-8619; e-mail m.hyde@griffith.edu.au; internet www.griffith.edu.au/centre/casd; Dir Prof. MERVYN HYDE.

Centre for Credit and Consumer Law: tel. (7) 3735-4211; fax (7) 3735-5599; e-mail n.howell@griffith.edu.au; internet www.griffith.edu.au/centre/cccl; Dir NICOLA HOWELL.

Centre for Environmental and Population Health: tel. (7) 3735-7458; fax (7) 3735-5318; e-mail c.chu@griffith.edu.au; internet www.griffith.edu.au/centre/ceph; Dir Prof. CORDIA CHU.

Centre for Leadership and Management in Education: tel. (7) 3735-5626; fax (7) 3735-6877; e-mail clme@griffith.edu.au; internet www.griffith.edu.au/centre/clme; Dir (vacant).

Centre for Professional Development: tel. (7) 5552-8452; fax (7) 5552-9076; e-mail b.mclellan@griffith.edu.au; internet www.griffith.edu.au/centre/cpd; Dir Dr M. COOPER.

Griffith Graduate Research School: tel. (7) 3735-5958; e-mail j.cumming@griffith.edu.au; internet www.griffith.edu.au/ggrs; Dir Prof. JOY CUMMING.

Griffith Institute for Higher Education: tel. (7) 3735-5982; fax (7) 3735-5998; e-mail c.birch@griffith.edu.au; internet www.griffith.edu.au/centre/gihe; Dir Prof. KERRI-LEE KRAUSE.

GUMURRII Student Support Centre: tel. (7) 3735-7676; fax (7) 3735-7033; e-mail kerryn.brown@griffith.edu.au; internet www.griffith.edu.au/centre/gumurrii; Dir Prof. B. ROBERTSON.

Institute for Educational Research, Policy and Evaluation: Dir (vacant).

Queensland Centre for Public Health (Griffith Node): tel. (7) 3735-3241; fax (7) 3735-3272; e-mail donald.stewart@griffith.edu.au; internet www.griffith.edu.au/centre/qcph; Dir Prof. DONALD STEWART.

Unit for Italian Studies: Dir C. KENNEDY.

ATTACHED RESEARCH CENTRES

Applied Cognitive Neuroscience Research Centre: tel. (7) 3735-3456; fax (7) 3735-3388; e-mail acnrc@griffith.edu.au; internet www.griffith.edu.au/school/psy/acnrc; Dir Assoc. Prof. DAVID SHUM.

Australian Centre for Intellectual Property in Agriculture: tel. (7) 3346-7506; fax (7) 3346-7480; e-mail acipa@law.uq.edu.au; internet www.acipa.edu.au; Dir Prof. B. SHERMAN.

Australian Institute for Suicide Research and Prevention: tel. (7) 3735-3382; internet www.griffith.edu.au/school/psy/aisrap; Dir Prof. DIEGO DE LEO.

Centre for Applied Language, Literacy and Communication Studies: tel. (7) 3735-5497; fax (7) 3735-5921; Dir Prof. C. WYATT-SMITH.

Centre for Aquatic Processes and Evolution: tel. (7) 5552-9185; fax (7) 5552-8067; e-mail cpp-capp@griffith.edu.au; internet www.griffith.edu.au/centre/capp; Dir Prof. JOE LEE.

Centre for Forestry and Horticultural Research: tel. (7) 3735-6709; fax (7) 3735-7656; e-mail cfhr@griffith.edu.au; internet www.griffith.edu.au/centre/cfhr; Dir Prof. Z. XU.

Centre for Governance and Public Policy: tel. (7) 3735-7723; fax (7) 3735-7737; e-mail p.weller@griffith.edu.au; internet www.griffith.edu.au/centre/cgpp; Dir Prof. PATRICK WELLER.

Centre for Infrastructure Engineering and Management: tel. (7) 5552 8575; fax (7) 5552 8065; e-mail ; internet www.griffith.edu.au/centre/iem; Dir Prof. SHERIF MOHAMED.

Centre for Innovative Conservation Strategies: tel. (7) 5552 9234; internet www.griffith.edu.au/centre/cics/home.html; Dir Assoc. Prof. JEAN MARC HERO (acting).

Centre for Learning Research: tel. (7) 3735-5724; fax (7) 3735-6868; e-mail h.middleton@griffith.edu.au; internet www.griffith.edu.au/centre/clr; Dir Assoc. Prof. HOWARD MIDDLETON.

Centre for Organisational Governance and Performance Management: tel. (7) 3735-6621; fax (7) 3735-7760; e-mail g.warry@griffith.edu.au; internet www.griffith.edu.au/centre/cogap; Dir Assoc. Prof. NAVA SUBRAMANIAN.

Centre for Public Culture and Ideas: tel. (7) 3735-4131; fax (7) 3735-4132; e-mail j.dragisic@griffith.edu.au; internet www.griffith.edu.au/centre/cpci; Co-Dirs Assoc. Prof. A. HAEBICH, Dr F. PAISLEY.

Centre for Quantum Dynamics: tel. (7) 3735-7279; fax (7) 3735-7773; e-mail h.wiseman@griffith.edu.au; internet www.griffith.edu.au/centre/quantumdynamics; Dir Prof. HOWARD WISEMAN.

Centre for Riverine Landscapes: tel. and fax (7) 3735-7403; e-mail a.arthington@griffith.edu.au; internet www.griffith.edu.au/centre/riverlandscapes; Dir Prof. ANGELA ARTHINGTON.

Centre for Wireless Monitoring and Applications: tel. (7) 3735-7192; fax (7) 3735-5198; e-mail d.thiel@griffith.edu.au; internet www.griffith.edu.au/centre/cwma; Dir Prof. DAVID THIEL.

Centre for Work, Leisure and Community Research: tel. (7) 3735-3714; fax (7) 3735-4298; e-mail h.gray@griffith.edu.au; internet www.griffith.edu.au/centre/wlcr; Dir Prof. ADRIAN WILKINSON (acting).

Eskitis, The Institute for Cell and Molecular Therapies: tel. (7) 3735-6006; fax (7) 3735-7656; e-mail eskitis@griffith.edu.au; internet www.griffith.edu.au/centre/eskitis; Dir Prof. RON QUINN.

Forensic Science Research and Innovation Centre: tel. (7) 3735 5069; fax (7) 3735 7773; e-mail dennis.burns@griffith.edu.au; Dir Assoc. Prof. DENNIS BURNS.

Genomics Research Centre: Dir Prof. L. GRIFFITHS.

Griffith Asia Institute: tel. (7) 3735-7370; fax (7) 3735-3731; e-mail gai@griffith.edu.au; internet www.griffith.edu.au/business/griffith-asia-institute; Dir Prof. MICHAEL WESLEY.

Griffith Centre for Coastal Management: tel. (7) 5552-8506; fax (7) 5552-8067; e-mail r.tomlinson@griffith.edu.au; internet www.griffith.edu.au/centre/gccm; Dir Prof. RODGER TOMLINSON.

Griffith Psychological Health Research Centre: tel. (7) 3732-8052; fax (7) 3732-8291; e-mail r.tomlinson@griffith.edu.au; internet www.griffith.edu.au/centre/gphrc; Dir Prof. SHARON DAWE.

Heart Foundation Research Centre: tel. (7) 5552-8314; fax (7) 5552-8802; e-mail m.john@griffith.edu.au; internet www.griffith.edu.au/centre/hfrc; Dir Prof. JOHN HEADRICK.

Institute for Ethics, Governance and Law: tel. (7) 3735-6987; fax (7) 3735-6985; e-mail iegl-enquiry@griffith.edu.au; internet www.griffith.edu.au/centre/iegl; Dir Prof. CHARLES SAMPFORD.

Institute for Glycomics: tel. (7) 5552-7025; fax (7) 5552-8098; e-mail m.vonitzstein@griffith.edu.au; internet www.griffith.edu.au/centre/glycomics; Dir Prof. MARK VON ITZSTEIN.

Institute for Integrated and Intelligent Systems: tel. (7) 3735-3757; fax (7) 3735-4066; e-mail n.dunstan@griffith.edu.au; internet iiis.griffith.edu.au; Dir Prof. ABDUL SATTAR.

International Centre for Ecotourism Research: tel. (7) 5552-8677; fax (7) 5552-8895; e-mail r.buckley@griffith.edu.au; internet www.griffith.edu.au/centre/icer; Dir Prof. RALF BUCKLEY.

International Fruit Fly Research Centre: tel. (7) 3735-3696; fax (7) 3735-3697; e-mail d.drew@griffith.edu.au; internet www.griffith.edu.au/centre/icmpff; Dir Prof. RICHARD DREW.

Key Centre for Ethics, Law, Justice and Governance: tel. (7) 3735-6988; fax (7) 3735-6985; e-mail s.stewart@griffith.edu.au; internet www.griffith.edu.au/centre/kceljag; Dir Prof. ROSS HOMEL.

Nanoscale Science and Technology Centre: tel. (7) 3735-7240; fax (7) 3735-7656; e-mail e.gray@griffith.edu.au; internet www.griffith.edu.au/centre/nstc; Dir Assoc. Prof. EVAN GRAY.

Queensland Conservatorium Research Centre: tel. (7) 3735-6335; fax (7) 3735-6262; e-mail qcrc@griffith.edu.au; internet www.griffith.edu.au/centre/qcrc; Dir Assoc. Prof. HUIB SCHIPPERS.

Queensland Microtechnology Facility: tel. (7) 3735-5053; fax (7) 3735-8021; e-mail barry.harrison@griffith.edu.au; internet www.griffith.edu.au/centre/qmf; Dir Prof. H. BARRY HARRISON.

Research Centre for Clinical Practice Innovation: tel. (7) 5552-8931; e-mail cpi-research@griffith.edu.au; internet www.griffith.edu.au/centre/rccpi; Dir Prof. WENDY CHABOYER.

Service Industry Research Centre: tel. (7) 5552-8790; e-mail c.guilding@griffith.edu.au; internet www.griffith.edu.au/centre/sirc; Dir Prof. CHRIS GUILDING.

Socio-Legal Research Centre: tel. (7) 3735-3747; fax (7) 3735-5169; e-mail slrc@griffith.edu.au; internet www.griffith.edu.au/centre/slrc; Dir Prof. R. JOHNSTONE.

Software Quality Institute: tel. (7) 3735-5209; fax (7) 3735-5207; e-mail sqi@cit.gu.edu.au; internet www.sqi.gu.edu.au; Dir Prof. GEOFF DROMEY.

Urban Research Program: tel. (7) 3735-3742; fax (7) 3735-4026; e-mail j.pascoe@griffith.edu.au; internet www.griffith.edu.au/centre/urp; Dir Prof. BRENDAN GLEESON.

JAMES COOK UNIVERSITY

Townsville, Qld 4811Telephone: Townsville: (7) 4781-4111, Cairns: (7) 4042-1111
Fax: Townsville: (7) 4779-6371, Cairns: (7) 4042-1300
E-mail: ViceChancellor@jcu.edu.au
Internet: www.jcu.edu.au

Founded 1970
Academic year: February to November

Chancellor: Lt-Gen. J. GREY
Deputy Chancellor: G. N. WHITMORE
Rector: Prof. SCOT BOWMAN
Vice-Chancellor: Prof. B. P. MOULDEN
Deputy Vice-Chancellor: Prof. H. HYLAND
Pro Vice-Chancellors: B. LILLIS, Prof. R. MCTAGGART, Prof. T. N. PALMER, Prof. A. VANN
Registrar: M. KERN
Librarian: J. W. MCKINLAY

Number of teachers: 444 full-time
Number of students: 13,587

Publications: *Academic Calendar*, *Annual Report*, *JCU Outlook* (monthly)

EXECUTIVE DEANS

Faculty of Arts, Education and Social Sciences: Prof. J. D. GREELEY
Faculty of Law, Business and the Creative Arts: Prof. S. SPEEDY
Faculty of Medicine, Health and Molecular Sciences: Prof. I. WRONSKI
Faculty of Science and Engineering: Prof. NED PANKHURST

PROFESSORS

BAXTER, A. G., Biochemistry
BELL, T. H., Earth Sciences
BURNELL, J. N., Biochemistry
CARTER, R. M., Earth Sciences
CLARK, G., Law
COLLINS, B., Tropical Environment
CROZIER, R., Zoology
DAVIS, D. F., Creative Arts
GADEK, P., Tropical Biology
GILBERT, R., Education
GILLIESON, D., Tropical Environment
GLASS, B., Pharmacy
GRAW, S. B., Law
HASSALL, A. J., English
HAVEMANN, P., Law
HAYES, B. A., Nursing
HELMES, E., Psychology
HENDERSON, R. A., Earth Sciences
HERBERT, H. J., Indigenous Australian Studies
HERON, M. L., Physics
HO, Y. H., Medicine
HUGHES, T. P., Marine Biology
KEENE, F. R., Chemistry
KENNEDY, L., Medicine
KINGSFORD, M., Marine Biology
LANKSHEAR, C., Education
LAVERY, B., Information Technology
LAWN, R. J., Tropical Crop Science and CRC for Sustainable Sugar Production
LEAKEY, R., Tropical Biology
LOUGHRAN, J., Engineering
MARSH, H. D., Environmental Science
MILLER, D., Biochemistry and Molecular Biology
NOTT, J., Tropical Environment
OLIVER, N. H. S., Economic Geology
PATTERSON, J. C., Environmental Engineering
PEARCE, P. L., Tourism
PEARSON, R. G., Biological Science
PIERCE, P. F., Australian Literature
PORTER, R., Medicine
PRIDEAUX, B., Business
RANE, A., Medicine
REICHELT, R., CRC Reef Research
SPEARE, R., Public Health and Tropical Medicine
STORK, N. E., CRC Rainforest
SUMMERS, P. M., Tropical Veterinary Science
THORPE, R. M., Social Work
WHITTINGHAM, I., Mathematics and Physics
YELLOWLEES, D., Pharmacy

LA TROBE UNIVERSITY

Bundoora, Vic. 3086
Telephone: (3) 9479-1111
Fax: (3) 9478-5814
E-mail: international@latrobe.edu.au
Internet: www.latrobe.edu.au

Founded 1964
Academic year: March to November

Chancellor: Emeritus Prof. N. MILLIS
Vice-Chancellor: Prof. M. J. OSBORNE
Deputy Vice-Chancellor: Prof. G. H. MCDOWELL
Deputy Vice-Chancellor (Research): Prof. T. F. SMITH
Pro-Vice-Chancellor (Equity and Access): Prof. K. FERGUSON
Pro-Vice-Chancellor (Information Technology): Prof. E. R. SMITH
Pro-Vice-Chancellor (International): Prof. D. STOCKLEY
Pro-Vice-Chancellor (La Trobe Albury-Wodonga): J. HILL
Pro-Vice-Chancellor (La Trobe Bendigo): Prof. L. A. KILMARTIN
University Secretary: D. F. BISHOP
Chief Librarian: G. E. GOW

Number of teachers: 1,253
Number of students: 22,317

DEANS

Health Sciences: Prof. S. DUCKETT
Humanities and Social Sciences: Prof. R. J. WALES
Law and Management: Prof. G. C. O'BRIEN
Science, Technology and Engineering: Prof. D. FINLAY
Bendigo Campus: Prof. L. A. KILMARTIN

PROFESSORS

AIKHENVALD, A., Research Centre for Linguistics Typology
ALTMAN, D., Politics
ARNASON, J. P., Sociology and Anthropology
BEILHARZ, D. M., Sociology and Anthropology
BERNARD, C., Psychology

BLAKE, B. J., Linguistics
BOLAND, R. C., European Studies
BRANSON, J. E., Education
BROWN, D. F., Accounting and Management
CAHILL, L. W., Electronics Engineering
CAMILLERI, J., Politics
CHANOCK, M., Law and Legal Studies
CROUCH, G., Tourism and Hospitality
DILLON, T. S., Computer Science and Computer Engineering
DIXON, R. M. W., Research Centre for Linguistics Typology
DYSON, P., Physics
ENDACOTT, R., Mental Health
FITZGERALD, J. J., Asian Languages
FOOK, J., Health Sciences
FREADMAN, R. B., English
FROST, A. J., History
GATT-RUTTER, J. A., Italian Studies
GAUNTLETT, E., Hellenic Studies
HANDLEY, C., Human Biosciences
HARBRIDGE, R. J., Management
HOFFMAN, A., Genetics and Human Variation
HOOGENRAAD, N. J., Biochemistry
JEFFREY, R., Politics
KAHN, J., Sociology and Anthropology
KELLEHEAR, S., Public Health
KING, J. E., Economics and Finance
LAKE, M., History
LECKEY, R. C. G., Physics
LEDER, G., Education
LIN, V., Health
LINDQUIST, B. I., Occupational Therapy
LUMLEY, J. M., Mothers' and Children's Health
MCDONALD, S. J., Midwifery
MCDOWELL, G. H., Agriculture
MILLS, T. M., Mathematics
MOOSA, I. A., Economics and Finance
MORRIS, M. E., Physiotherapy
MURPHY, P., Tourism and Hospitality
MURRAY, T. A., Archaeology
NAY, R. M., Nursing
O'MALLEY, P., Law and Legal Studies
PARISH, R. W., Botany
PEARSON, A., Nursing
PERRY, A. R., Human Communication Science
PITTS, M. K., Health and Sexuality
PORTER, R. S., Business
PRATT, C., Psychological Sciences
RAYMOND, K., Pharmacy
REILLY, S., Human Communication Sciences
ROSENTHAL, D. A., Health Sciences
SALMOND, J. A., History
STEPHENSON, D., Zoology
STREET, A. F., Nursing
SUGIMOTO, Y., Sociology and Anthropology
SULLIVAN, P. A., Education
TAMIS, A., Hellenic Studies
THORNTON, M. R., Law and Legal Studies
TORRANCE, C., Nursing
WALKER, G. R., Law and Legal Studies
WHITE, C. M., Graduate School of Management
WILLIS, E. M., Humanities

MACQUARIE UNIVERSITY

Balaclava Rd, North Ryde, , NSW 2109
Telephone: (2) 9850-7111
Fax: (2) 9850-7433
E-mail: mqinfo@mq.edu.au
Internet: www.mq.edu.au

Founded 1964 (opened 1967)
Chancellor: MORRISH ALEXANDER BESLEY
Deputy Chancellor: His Hon. Dr J. F. LINCOLN
Vice-Chancellor: Prof. STEVEN SCHWARTZ
Deputy Vice-Chancellor (Academic): Prof. J. LOXTON
Deputy Vice-Chancellor (Administration): Prof. C. MARTIN
Deputy Vice-Chancellor (Research): Prof. PETER BERGQUIST
Registrar and Vice-Principal: B. J. SPENCER
Librarian: MAXINE BRODIE

Number of teachers: 775
Number of students: 17,954

Publications: *Annual Report*, *Calendar*, *Research Report*, *Study at Macquarie* (all annually), *University News* (monthly)

DEANS

College of Commerce: JOHN LOXTON
College of Humanities and Social Sciences: JACK BASSETT
College of Science and Technology: JAMES PIPER

DIRECTORS OF INTERDISCIPLINARY CENTRES

Graduate School of the Environment: Prof. PETER NELSON
Graduate School of Management: JOHN HEWSON

PROFESSORS

College of Commerce:
ABELSON, P. W., Economics
CROUCHER, J., Statistics
DAVIS, E., Management
EDDEY, P. H., Accounting, Graduate Accounting and Commerce Center
HARRISON, G. L., Accounting and Finance
HORNE, J., Economics
HUDSON, M., Statistics
JONG, P. DE, Actuarial Studies
O'DONNELL, R., Economics
QUINN, B., Statistics
THROSBY, C., Economics
WOOD, G., Statistics
YUSUF, F., Business

College of Humanities and Social Sciences:
GIBBS, A. M., English and Cultural Studies
GOOT, M., Politics
HAYWARD, P., Contemporary Music Studies
JEFFERY, M., Law
KANAWATI, N., Ancient History
KANE, D., Chinese
LIEU, S. N., History

College of Science and Technology:
BASSETT, J., Biology
BEATTIE, A.,
BERGQUIST, P., Biology
BURNS, A., Linguistics
CANDLIN, C., Linguistics
COLTHEART, M., Psychology
COOPER, D, Biological Sciences
CURSON, P., Health and Chiropractic
DEANE, E., Biology
FAGAN, R., Human Geography
JOSS, J., Biology
MATTHIESSEN, C., Linguistics
MURRAY, D., Linguistics
NEWALL, P., Linguistics
O'REILLY, S., Earth and Planetary Sciences
ORR, B., Chemistry
PITMAN, A., Physical Geography
RAPEE, R., Psychology
VEAL, D., Biology
WESTOBY, M., Biology
WALTER, M., Earth and Planetary Sciences
WENDEROTH, P., Psychology
WILLIAMS, K., Psychology
SMITH, P., Mathematics
STREET, R., Mathematics

ATTACHED RESEARCH INSTITUTES

Centre for Biodiversity and Bioresources: Dir ANDREW J. BEATTIE.

Centre of Language Technology: Dir ROBERT DALE.

Centre for Lasers and Applications: Dir Prof. BRIAN ORR.

Joint Research Centre for Advanced Systems Engineering (JRCASE): Dir Prof. RAY OFFEN.

UNIVERSITY OF MELBOURNE

Melbourne, Vic. 3010
Telephone: (3) 8344-4000
Fax: (3) 8344-5104
E-mail: vc@unimelb.edu.au
Internet: www.unimelb.edu.au

Founded 1853 (opened 1855)
Autonomous institution established by Act of Parliament (State of Victoria) and financed mainly by Commonwealth Government
Academic year: February to December
Chancellor: FAY MARLES
Deputy Chancellor: IAN RENARD
Vice-Chancellor and Principal: Prof. GLYN DAVIS
Senior Deputy Vice-Chancellor (vacant)
Deputy Vice-Chancellor (Research): Prof. FRANCIS LARKINS
Deputy Vice-Chancellor (Students and Staff): Prof. KWONG LEE DOW
Pro Vice-Chancellor: Prof. FIELD RICKARDS
Pro Vice-Chancellor: Prof. LOANE SKENE
Deputy Vice-Chancellor: Prof. PETER MCPHEE
Assistant Vice-Chancellor: Prof. ROBERT RICHARDSON
Senior Vice-Principal: IAN MARSHMAN
Vice-Principal (Information): LINDA O'BRIEN
Vice-Principal (University Development): ROGER PEACOCK
Vice-Principal and Academic Registrar: LIN MARTIN
Vice-Principal and Chief Financial Officer: DAVID PERCIVAL
Vice-Principal and General Counsel: CHRIS PENMAN
Vice-Principal (Human Resources): LIZ BARÉ
Vice-Principal (Property and Buildings): Dr DOUGLAS DAINES
University Secretary: LENNARD CURRIE

Number of teachers: 2,733
Number of students: 39,873

DEANS

Faculty of Architecture, Building and Planning: Prof. R. FINCHER
Faculty of Arts: Prof. S. MACINTYRE
Faculty of Economics and Commerce: Prof. M. ABERNETHY
Faculty of Education: Prof. B. CALDWELL
Faculty of Engineering: Prof. J. VAN DEVENTER
Institute of Land and Food Resources: Prof. R. RICHARDSON
Faculty of Law: Prof. B. M. L. CROMMELIN
Faculty of Medicine, Dentistry and Health Sciences: Prof. J. ANGUS
Melbourne Business School: Prof. JOHN SEYBOLT
Faculty of Music: Prof. W. A. BEBBINGTON
Faculty of Science: Prof. J. MCKENZIE
Faculty of Veterinary Science: Prof. I. W. CAPLE
School of Graduate Studies: Prof. B. EVANS

PROFESSORS

H=Head of Department

Faculty of Architecture, Building and Planning (tel. (3) 8344-6429; fax (3) 8344-5532; e-mail apb-info@unimelb.edu.au; internet www.arbld.unimelb.edu.au):
BRAWN, G. W., Architecture
BULL, C., Landscape Architecture
DOVEY, K. G., Architecture and Urban Design
FINCHER, R., Urban Planning
GOAD, P., Architecture, Building and Planning
GREEN, R., Landscape Architecture (H)
HUTSON, A., Architecture (H)
KING, R. J., Environmental Planning
LEWIS, M. B.
ROBINSON, J. R. W., Property and Construction

RODGER, A., Architecture, Building and Planning
YENCKEN, D., Architecture, Building and Planning

Faculty of Arts (tel. (3) 8344-6395; fax (3) 9347-0424; e-mail arts-enquiries@unimelb.edu.au; internet www.arts.unimelb.edu.au):

ANDERSON, J., Fine Arts, Classical Studies and Archaeology
AUSTIN, P. K., Linguistics and Applied Linguistics
BUDIMAN, A., Indonesian
CLARKE, A. F., Equine Studies
COALDRAKE, W. H., Japanese
DURING, S., English
ENRIGHT, N. J., Anthropology, Geography and Environmental Studies
FINLAYSON, B., Anthropology, Geography and Environmental Studies
FREIBERG, A., Criminology
GALLIGAN, B. J., Political Science
GELDER, K., English
GRIMSHAW, P. A., History
HAJEK, J., French and Italian Studies (H)
HOLM, D., Chinese
HOLMES, L. T., Political Science
HOME, R. W., History and Philosophy of Science
HURST, A., School of French (H)
JACKSON, A. C., Social Work
LANGTON, M. L., Australian Indigenous Studies
MCINNES, C. V., Higher Education
MACINTYRE, S. F., History
MCPHEE, P. B., History
MALCOLM, E. L., Irish Studies
NETTELBECK, C., School of Languages
O'BRIEN, A., Creative Arts (H)
PIKE, K., Criminology
PRIEST, P. G., Philosophy
RICKLEFS, M., Melbourne Institute of Asian Languages and Societies
RIDLEY, R., History
SEAR, F. B., Classics and Archaeology
STEELE, P. D., English
WALLACE-CRABBE, C. K., English
WEBBER, M. J., Geography

Faculty of Economics and Commerce (tel. (3) 8344-5328; fax (3) 9347-3986; e-mail commerce-enquiries@unimelb.edu.au; internet www.ecom.unimelb.edu.au):

ABERNETHY, M. A., Accounting and Business Information Systems
BARDSLEY, P., Economics
BORLAND, J., Economics
BROWN, R., Finance
CREEDY, J., Economics
DAVIS, K. T., Finance
DAWKINS, P. J., Melbourne Institute of Applied Economic and Social Research
DICKSON, D., Economics
FREEBAIRN, J. W., Economics
GRIFFITHS, B., Economics
HARDY, C., Management
HOUGHTON, K. A., Accounting
KING, S. P., Economics
KOFMAN, P., Finance
KULIK, C., Management
LEECH, S., Accounting and Business Information Systems
LLOYD, P. J., Economics
MCDONALD, I. M., Economics
MARCHANT, G., Accounting and Business Information Systems
MARTIN, V., Economics
NASSER, S., Accounting and Business Information Systems
NICHOLAS, S., Management
PERKINS, E. J., Economics
SAMSON, D., Management
SHAPIRO, P., Economics
TOURKY, R., Economics
WHEATLEY, S., Finance
WIDING, R. E., Management
WILLIAMS, R. A., Econometrics
WOODEN, M., Melbourne Institute of Applied Economics and Social Research

Faculty of Education (tel. (3) 8344-8628; fax (3) 8344-8529; e-mail enquiries@edfac.unimelb.edu.au; internet www.edfac.unimelb.edu.au):

CALDWELL, B. J., Education (Leadership and Management)
CHRISTIE, F., Language, Literacy and Arts Education
EVANS, G., Learning and Educational Development
GRIFFIN, P. E., Assessment
HILL, P., Education (Leadership and Management)
LAKOMSKI, G., Education
LEE DOW, K., Education
MAGLEN, L. R., Asian Pacific Economics of Education and Training
RABAN-BISBY, B., Early Childhood Studies
RICKARDS, F. W., Education (Learning, Assessment and Special Education)
STACEY, K. C., Science and Mathematics Education
START, B., Learning and Educational Development

Faculty of Engineering (tel. (3) 8344-6703; fax (3) 9349-2182; e-mail eng-info@unimelb.edu.au; internet www.eng.mu.oz.au):

BISHOP, I. D., Geomatics
BOGER, D. V., Chemical Engineering
CHING, M. S., Mechanical and Manufacturing Engineering
EVANS, R. J., Electrical Engineering
FENTON, J. D., Civil and Environmental Engineering
FRASER, C. S., Geomatics
GOOD, M. C., Mechanical and Manufacturing Engineering
HUTCHINSON, G. L., Civil and Environmental Engineering
KOTAGIRI, R., Computer Science and Software Engineering
KRISHNAMURTHY, V., Electrical and Electronic Engineering
MCMAHON, T. A., Environmental Hydrology
MAREELS, I. M. V., Electrical Engineering
MOFFAT, A. M., Computer Science and Software Engineering
MORAN, W., Electronic and Electrical Engineering
STERLING, L. S., Computer Science and Software Engineering
STEVENS, G. W., Chemical Engineering
STUCKLEY, P. J., Computer Science and Software Engineering
TUCKER, R. S., Electrical Engineering
VAN DEVENTER, J., Mineral and Process Engineering
WATSON, H. C., Mechanical and Manufacturing Engineering
WILLIAMSON, I. P., Surveying and Land Information
WOOD, D. G., Engineering
YOUNG, D. M., Engineering Construction Management
ZUCKERMAN, M., Electronic and Electrical Engineering

Institute of Land and Food Resources (tel. (3) 8344-0276; fax (3) 9348-2156; e-mail enquiries@landfood.unimelb.edu.au; internet www.landfood.unimelb.edu.au):

BRITZ, M., Food Science
CHAPMAN, D. F., Pasture Science
COUSENS, R. D., Crop Science
EGAN, A. R., Agriculture (Animal Science)
FALVEY, J. L., Agriculture
FERGUSON, I. S., Forest Science
GODDARD, M., Agriculture
HEMSWORTH, P., Agriculture
HILLIER, A. J., Agriculture
KOLLMORGEN, J. F., Agriculture
MACMILLAN, K. L., Agriculture
RICHARDSON, R. A., Land and Food Resources
ROSS, E. W., Agriculture
VINDEN, P., Forest Industries

Faculty of Law (tel. (3) 8344-6164; fax (3) 9347-2392; e-mail post@law.unimelb.edu.au; internet www.law.unimelb.edu.au):

BRYAN, M., Law
CHRISTIE, A. F., Intellectual Property
COLMAN, P. M., Medical Biology
COWMAN, A. F., Medical Biology
CROMMELIN, B. M. L., Law
MCCORMACK, T. L. H., International Humanitarian Law
MITCHELL, R. J., Law
MORGAN, J. J., Law
RAMSAY, I. M., Commercial Law
RICKETSON, S., Law
SAUNDERS, C. A., Law
SKENE, L., Law
SMITH, M. D. H., Asian Law
TRIGGS, G., Law

Faculty of Medicine, Dentistry and Health Sciences (tel. (3) 8344-5894; fax (3) 9347-7854; e-mail medicine-info@unimelb.edu.au; internet www.medfac.unimelb.edu.au/med):

ADAMS, J. M., Medical Biology
ALCORN, D., Anatomy
ANDERSON, I. P., Public Health
ANDERSON, J. N., Public Health
ANDERSON, V., Psychology
BERK, M., Psychiatry
BERKOVIC, S. F., Medicine
BEST, J. D., Medicine
BHATHAL, P. S., Pathology
BLOCH, S., Psychiatry
BOWES, G., Paediatrics
BREARLEY-MESER, L., Paediatrics
BRENNECKE, S. P., Obstetrics and Gynaecology
BROWN, G. V., Medicine
BYRNE, E., Experimental Neurology
CARLIN, J. B., Public Health
CHAN, S. T. F., Surgery
CHIU, E., Psychiatry
CLEMENT, J. G., Forensic Odontology
CORY, S., Medical Biology
CREAMER, M., Psychiatry
DENNERSTEIN, L., Psychiatry
DOHERTY, P., Microbiology and Immunology
DONNAN, G., Medicine
DOWELL, R. C., Otolaryngology
DUNNING, T., Nursing
FAIRLEY, C. K., Sexual Health
FUNDER, J., Medicine
FURNESS, J. B., Anatomy
GALEA, M. P., Physiotherapy
GAYLER, K. R., Biochemistry and Molecular Biology
GETHING, M. J., Biochemistry and Molecular Biology
GIBSON, R. M., Radiology
GOODWIN, A. W., Anatomy
GRAHAM, H. K., Orthopaedic Surgery
GRAVES, S. E., Orthopaedic Surgery
HARRAP, S. B., Physiology
HARRIS, P. J., Physiology
HARRISON, L. C., Medical Biology
HOPPER, J. L., Public Health
JACKSON, H. J., Psychology
KAYE, A. H., Surgery
LOUIS, W. J., Clinical Pharmacology and Therapeutics
MCCALMAN, J. S., Public Health
MCCLUSKEY, J., Microbiology and Immunology
MCMEEKEN, J., Physiotherapy
MANDERSON, L. H., Women's Health
MASTERS, C. L., Pathology
MESSER, H. H., Restorative Dentistry
MESSER, L. J. B., Child Dental Health
MILLGROM, J., Psychology
MORGAN, T. O., Physiology
MORRISON, W. A., Surgery

MULHOLLAND, E. K., Paediatrics
NELSON, S., Nursing
NICHOLSON, G. C., Medicine
NICOLA, N., Medical Biology
NOLAN, T. M., Public Health
O'BOYLE, M. W., Psychology
OLEKALNS, M., Psychology
PARKER, J. M., Postgraduate Nursing
PATTISON, P. E., Psychology
PERMEZEL, J. M. H., Obstetrics and Gynaecology
PIERCE, R., Medicine
PRIOR, M., Psychology
PROIETTO, J., Medicine
REYNOLDS, E. C., Dental Science
ROBINS-BROWN, R. M., Microbiology and Immunology
SCHWEITZER, I., Psychiatry
SHORTMAN, K. D., Medical Biology and Developmental Immunology
SINGH, B. S., Psychiatry
SMALLWOOD, R. A., Medicine
SPEED, T. P., Medical Biology
STRUGNELL, R. A., Microbiology and Immunology
TAYLOR, H. R., Ophthalmology
TILLER, J. W. G., Psychiatry
TRESS, B. M., Radiology
TRINDER, J. A., Psychology
TYAS, M. J., Dental Science
VADJA, F., Medicine
WARD, T., Psychology
WARK, J. D., Medicine
WATTERS, D. A. K., Surgery
WEARING, A. J., Psychology
WETTENHALL, R. E. H., Biochemistry
WICKS, I. P., Medical Biology
WILLIAMS, D. A., Physiology
YEOMANS, N. D., Medicine
YOUNG, D., General Practice
ZAJAC, J. D., Medicine

Melbourne Business School (Leicester St, Carlton, Vic. 3053; tel. (3) 9349-8403; fax (3) 9349-8404; e-mail mbs@unimelb.edu.au; internet www.mbs.unimelb.edu.au):

ALFORD, J. L., Public Sector Management
DAINTY, P., Human Resources Management and Employee Relations
GANS, J. S., Management
GRUNDY, B., Finance
HARPER, I. R., Commerce and Business Administration
KING, S., Economics
LEWIS, G., Strategy
MANN, L., Organizational Behaviour and Decision Making
MISHRA, D., Marketing
OLEKALNS, M., Leadership and Decision Making
RIZZO, P., Finance and Management
SAMSON, D. A., Manufacturing Management
SINCLAIR, A. M. A., Management (Diversity and Change)
SPEED, R., Marketing Management and Advanced Marketing Strategy
WILLIAMS, P. L., Management (Law and Economics)

Faculty of Music (tel. (3) 8344-5256; fax (3) 8344-5346; e-mail enquiries@music.unimelb.edu.au; internet www.music.unimelb.edu.au):

BEBBINGTON, W. A., Music
BROADSTOCK, B., Music
GRIFFITHS, J. A., Music

Faculty of Science (tel. (3) 8344-6404; fax (3) 8344-5803; e-mail science-queries@unimelb.edu.au; internet www.science.unimelb.edu.au):

BACIC, A., Botany
BAKER, A. J. M., Botany
CAMPBELL, G. D., Zoology
CHAN, D. Y. C., Mathematics
CLARKE, A. E., Botany
COLE, B. L., Optometry
FERGUSON, I. S., Forest Science
GHIGGINO, K. P., Chemistry
GRIESER, F., Chemistry
GUTTMANN, A. J., Mathematics
HYNES, M. J., Genetics
KOTAGIRI, R., Computer Science
KLEIN, A. G., Physics
LADIGES, P. Y., Botany
MCBRIEN, N. A., Optometry
MCKELLAR, B. H. J., Theoretical Physics
MCKENZIE, J. A., Genetics
MILLER, C. F., Mathematics
MORRISON, I., Information Systems
NUGENT, K. A., Physics
PICKETT-HEAPS, J. D., Botany
PLIMER, I. R., Geology
RENFREE, M. B., Zoology
RUBINSTEIN, J. H., Mathematics
SCHIESSER, C., Chemistry
SONENBERG, E. A., Information Systems
STERLING, L. S., Computer Science
TAYLOR, G. N., Physics
THOMPSON, C. J., Mathematics
WEDD, A. G., Chemistry

Faculty of Veterinary Science (tel. (3) 8344-7356; fax (3) 8344-7374; e-mail vet-info@unimelb.edu.au; internet www.vet.unimelb.edu.au):

CAHILL, R. N. P., Veterinary Biology
CAPLE, I. W., Veterinary Medicine
CLARKE, A. F., Equine Studies
SLOCOMBE, R. F., Veterinary Pathology

Victorian College of the Arts (234 St Kilda Rd, Southbank, Vic. 3010; tel. (3) 9685-9300; fax (3) 9682-1841; internet www.vca.unimelb.edu.au):

HULL, A. (Dir)

ASSOCIATED INSTITUTES

Austin Research Institute.
Australian Antarctic Division.
Australian Artificial Intelligence Institute Ltd.
Australian Institute of Family Studies.
Australian Institute of Judicial Administration Inc.
Bionic Ear Institute.
Bureau of Meteorology.
Centre for the Study of Sexually Transmitted Diseases.
CSIRO.
Hawthorn International Institute of Education Ltd.
Howard Florey Institute of Experimental Physiology and Medicine.
Leo Cussen Institute for Continuing Legal Education.
Macfarlane Burnet Centre for Medical Research Ltd.
Melbourne College of Divinity.
Mental Health Research Institute of Victoria Inc.
Murdoch Institute for Research into Birth Defects Ltd.
National Ageing Research Institute Inc.
Royal Botanic Gardens Board.
St Vincent's Institute of Medical Research.
Skin and Cancer Foundation Inc.
Tasman Institute Ltd and Tasman Area Pacific Pty Limited.
Turning Point Alcohol and Drug Centre Inc.
Victorian College of Optometry.
Victorian Institute of Forensic Pathology.
Victorian Institute of Marine Sciences.
Zoological Board of Victoria

MONASH UNIVERSITY

Wellington Rd, Clayton, Vic. 3800
Telephone: (3) 9905-4000
Fax: (3) 9905-4007
E-mail: inquiries@adm.monash.edu.au
Internet: www.monash.edu.au

Founded 1958 (opened 1961); merged with Chisholm Institute of Technology and Gippsland Institute of Advanced Education 1990, and with Victorian College of Pharmacy 1992

Academic year: March to November

Chancellor: JEREMY K. ELLIS
Vice-Chancellor: Prof. R. LARKINS
Senior Deputy Vice-Chancellor: Prof. S. PARKER
Deputy Vice-Chancellor (Research): Prof. E. CORNISH
Pro-Vice-Chancellor, Gippsland: Prof. B. MACKENZIE
Pro-Vice-Chancellor, Monash Malaysia: Prof. M. LIDDELL
Pro-Vice-Chancellor, Monash South Africa: Prof. T. B. PRETORIUS
Vice-President (Administration): P. MARSHALL
Vice-President (International): T. POLLOCK
Director, Monash Centre, Prato: Dr A. PAGLIARO
Director, Monash University Centre, London: Prof. M. EVANS
Librarian: C. HARBOE-REE

Number of teachers: 2,797
Number of students: 51,296

Publications: *Annual Report*, *Asia-Pacific Journal of Clinical Nutrition* (online), *Eras: School of Historical Studies Online Journal*, *Journal of Australian Taxation* (6 a year), *Journal of Intercultural Studies* (3 a year), *Monash Bioethics Review* (4 a year), *Monash Law Review* (2 a year)

DEANS

Faculty of Art and Design: Prof. J. K. REDMOND
Faculty of Arts: Prof. H. LE GRAND
Faculty of Business and Economics: Prof. G. PALMER
Faculty of Education: Prof. S. WILLIS
Faculty of Engineering: Prof. T. SRIDHAR
Faculty of Information Technology: Prof. R. WEBER
Faculty of Law: Prof. A. FREIBERG
Faculty of Medicine, Nursing and Health Sciences: Prof. E. BYRNE
Faculty of Science: Prof. R. NORRIS
Victorian College of Pharmacy: Prof. C. B. CHAPMAN

PROFESSORS

Faculty of Art and Design (900 Dandenong Rd, Caulfield East, Vic. 3145; tel. (3) 9903-2707; fax (3) 9903-2845; e-mail enquiries@artdes.monash.edu.au; internet www.artdes.monash.edu.au):

HOFFERT, B. J., Fine Arts
REDMOND, J., Industrial Design
TERSTAPPEN, C., Contemporary Installation and Photography

Faculty of Arts (tel. (3) 9905-2100; fax (3) 9905-2148; e-mail deansec@arts.monash.edu.au; internet www.arts.monash.edu.au):

BENJAMIN, A., Comparative Literature and Cultural Studies
BIGELOW, J. C., Philosophy and Bioethics
BOUMA, G. D., Political and Social Enquiry
BURRIDGE, K., Languages, Cultures and Linguistics
CAINE, B., Historical Studies
COCKLIN, C., Philosophy and Bioethics
DAVISON, G. J., Historical Studies

EDWARDS, I., International Studies
FELIX, U., Languages, Cultures and Linguistics
FITZPATRICK, P., Drama and Theatre Studies
HART, K. J., Comparative Literature and Cultural Studies
JACOBS, J. B., Languages, Cultures and Linguistics
KARTOMI, M. J., Music – Conservatorium
KENT, F. W., Historical Studies
KERSHAW, P. A., Geography and Environmental Science
LIPSIG-MUMME, C., Political and Social Enquiry
LOVE, H. H. R., Literary, Visual and Performance Studies
LYNCH, A., Geography and Environmental Science
MARKUS, A., Jewish Studies
MILNER, A., Comparative Literature and Cultural Studies
MOUER, R., Languages, Cultures and Linguistics
NELSON, B., Languages, Cultures and Linguistics
OPPY, G., Philosophy and Bioethics
PROBYN, C. T., Literary, Visual and Performance Studies
QUARTLY, M., Historical Studies
RUSSELL, L., Australian Indigenous Studies
TAPPER, N., Geography and Environmental Science
VICZIANY, M., Asian Studies
WALTER, J., Political and Social Enquiry

Faculty of Business and Economics (POB 197, Caulfield East, Vic. 3145; tel. (3) 9903-2327; fax (3) 9903-2148; e-mail enquiries.caulfield@buseco.monash.edu.au; internet www.buseco.monash.edu.au):
ARIFF, M., Accounting and Finance
BROOKS, B., Business and Economics
BROOKS, D., Econometrics and Business Statistics
CHENHALL, R. H., Accounting and Finance
CULLEN, R., Business Law and Taxation
DHALIWAL, D., Accounting and Finance
DINGLE, A. E., Economics
DIXON, P. B., Policy Studies
EWING, M., Marketing
FAFF, R., Accounting and Finance
FORSYTH, P. J., Economics
GABBOTT, T. M., Marketing
GODFREY, J. M., Accounting and Finance
HUGHES, O. E., Management
HYNDMAN, R. J., Econometrics and Business Statistics
IN, F., Accounting and Finance
KING, M. L., Business and Economics
LANGFIELD-SMITH, K., Accounting and Finance
MCLAREN, K. R., Econometrics and Business Statistics
MITCHELL, R., Business Law and Taxation
NG, Y., Economics
NYLAND, C., Management
OPPEWAL, H., Marketing
PEARSON, K., Policy Studies
POSKITT, D. S., Econometrics
RAINNIE, A. F., Management
RATNATUNGA, J. T., Accounting and Finance
RICHARDSON, J., Health Programme Evaluation
SARROS, J. C., Management
SILVAPULLE, M., Econometrics and Business Statistics
SKULLY, M. T., Accounting and Finance
SMYTH, R., Economics
SOHAL, A., Management
SMYTH, R. L., Economics
TAM, O. K., MBA Programme
TEICHER, J., Management
VON NESSEN, P., Business Law and Taxation
WEILER, B. V., Management
WILLIS, R. J., MBA Programme
WORTHINGTON, J. S., Marketing
YANG, X., Economics

Faculty of Education (POB 6, Monash University, Clayton, Vic. 3800; tel. (3) 9905-2888; fax (3) 9905-5400; e-mail enquiry@education.monash.edu.au; internet www.education.monash.edu.au):
BURKE, G.
FLEER, M.
GRONN, P.
GUNSTONE, R. F.
KENWAY, J.
LOUGHRAN, J.
MARGINSON, S.
SEDDON, T.
WILLIS, S. G.

Faculty of Engineering (POB 72, Clayton, Vic. 3800; tel. (3) 9905-3404; fax (3) 9905-3409; e-mail enginfo@eng.monash.edu.au; internet www.eng.monash.edu.au):
CURRIE, G., Civil Engineering
DEMIDENKO, S., Electrical and Computer Systems Engineering
EGAN, G. K., Electrical and Computer Systems Engineering
FORSYTH, M., Materials Engineering
HOURIGAN, K., Mechanical Engineering
JARVIS, R. A., Electrical and Computer Systems Engineering
JESSON, D., Materials Engineering
JONES, R., Mechanical Engineering
LEWIS, R. A., Physics
MORGAN, D. L., Electrical and Computer Systems Engineering
MUDDLE, B. C., Materials Engineering
PRINCE, I., Chemical Engineering
PUDLOWSKI, Z. J., UNESCO International Centre for Engineering Education
RHODES, M. J., Chemical Engineering
SHERIDAN, J., Mechanical Engineering
SIMON, G., Materials Engineering
SORIA, J., Mechanical Engineering
SRIDHAR, T., Chemical Engineering
YOUNG, W., Civil Engineering
ZHAO, X.-L., Civil Engineering

Faculty of Information Technology (900 Dandenong Rd, Caulfield East, Vic. 3145; tel. (3) 9903-2433; fax (3) 9903-2745; e-mail admissions@infotech.monash.edu.au; internet www.infotech.monash.edu.au):
ABRAMSON, D., School of Computer Science and Software Engineering
ARNOTT, D. R., School of Information Management and Systems
CROSSLEY, J., School of Computer Science and Software Engineering
DOOLEY, L. S., Gippsland School of Computing and Information Technology
GEORGEFF, M., Dean's Office
GREEN, D., School of Computer Science and Software Engineering
GUPTA, G., Business Systems
KENDALL, E. A., School of Network Computing
MCKEMMISH, S. M., School of Information Management Systems
MARRIOTT, K., School of Computer Science and Software Engineering
SCHAUDER, D., School of Information Management and Systems
SCHMIDT, H. W., School of Computer Science and Software Engineering
SHANKS, G., School of Business Systems
SRINIVASAN, B., School of Computer Science and Software Engineering
WALLACE, M., School of Business Systems
WEBB, G., School of Computer Science and Software Engineering
WEBER, R., Dean

Faculty of Law (POB 12, Monash University, Clayton, Vic. 3800; tel. (3) 9905-9335; fax (3) 9905-5868; e-mail law-general@law.monash.edu.au; internet www.law.monash.edu.au):
BOROS, E., Company Law
CAMPBELL, S.
FOX, R. G., Criminal Law
FREIBERG, A., Dean
GOLDSWORTHY, J., Legal Philosophy and Constitutional Law
HAMPEL, G., Advocacy Training
HODGE, G., Privatization and Public Accountability
JOSEPH, S., International Human Rights and Constitutional Law
KINLEY, D., Human Rights Law
LEE, H. P., Constitutional and Administrative Law
MCSHERRY, B., Criminal Law, Mental Health Law and Bioethics
PITTARD, M., Industrial Relations and Employment Law
SCHEEPERS, T., International Development Law
WAINCYMER, J., Taxation and International Trade Law
WILLIAMS, C. R., Criminal Law and Evidence

Faculty of Medicine, Nursing and Health Sciences (Bldg 64, Monash University, Clayton, Vic. 3800; tel. (3) 9905-4327; fax (3) 9905-4302; e-mail enquiries@lmed.monash.edu.au; internet www.med.monash.edu.au):
ABRAMSON, M. J., Epidemiology and Preventative Medicine
ADLER, B., Microbiology
ANDERSON, W. P., Physiology/School of Biomedical Sciences
BERTRAM, J., Anatomy and Cell Biology
BROWN, T., Social Work and Human Services
BROWNE, C., Medical and Health Sciences Education
BURROWS, R. F., Obstetrics and Gynaecology
BYRNE, E., Dean
CAMPBELL, D., Health Sciences Research
COLEMAN, G., Psychology
COPPEL, R. L., Microbiology
CORDNER, S. M., Forensic Medicine
CROWE, S., Medicine
DAVIES, J., Microbiology
DAVIS, S. R., Medicine
DE KRETSER, D. M., Reproduction and Development
DOHERTY, R. R., Paediatrics
FRANCIS, K., Nursing
GIBSON, P., Medicine
GODDARD, C. R., Social Work
GODING, J. W., Pathology and Immunology
GOODCHILD, C. S., Anaesthesia
GRIGG, M. J., Surgery
HARDING, R., Physiology
HEALY, D. L., Obstetrics and Gynaecology
HOLDSWORTH, S. R., Medicine
HUMPHREYS, J. S., Rural Health
IRVINE, D., Psychology
JANS, D. A., Biochemistry and Molecular Biology
JENKIN, G., Physiology
JOLLY, B. C., Medical and Health Sciences Education
JUDD, F. K., Psychological Medicine
KOSSMAN, T., Medicine
KRUM, H., Epidemiology and Preventive Medicine
KULKARNI, J., Psychological Medicine
LEWIN, S., Medicine
MACKINNON, A., Psychological Medicine
MCGRATH, B., Medicine
MCNEIL, J. J., Epidemiology and Preventive Medicine
MEADOWS, G., Psychological Medicine
MITCHELL, C., Biochemistry and Molecular Biology

MULLEN, P. E., Psychological Medicine
NAGLEY, P., Biochemistry and Molecular Biology
OAKLEY-BROWN, M., Psychological Medicine
O'CONNOR, D. W., Psychological Medicine
O'CONNOR, M. M., Nursing
OGLOFF, J., Psychological Medicine
O'HEHIR, R. E., Medicine
PITERMAN, L., General Practice
POLGLASE, A., Surgery
PONSFORD, J. L., Psychology
PRIESTLEY, B. G., Epidemiology and Preventative Medicine
PROSKE, U., Physiology
REUTENS, D., Neurosciences
RICHARDS, J., General Practice
ROOD, J., Microbiology
ROSENFELD, J. V., Neurosurgery
SALEM, H. H., Medicine
SCHMIDT, H., Pharmacology
SMITH, J., Surgery
SOLARSH, G., Rural Health
STOELWINDER, J., Epidemiology and Preventive Medicine
STOREY, E., Neurosciences
SUMMERS, R. J., Pharmacology
THOMSON, N. M., Medicine
TOH, B. H., Pathology and Immunology
TONGE, B. J., Psychological Medicine
TROUNSON, A. O., Early Human Development
WHYTE, G., Bendigo Regional Clinical School
WORKMAN, G., Geriatric Medicine
ZIMMET, P., Biochemistry and Molecular Biology

Faculty of Science (POB 19, Clayton, Vic. 3800; tel. (3) 9905-4610; fax (3) 9905-5692; e-mail enquiries@sci.monash.edu.au; internet www.sci.monash.edu.au):

ADELOJU, S. B., Applied Sciences
BARBNIK, R. A., Mathematical Science
BOND, A., Chemistry
CALLY, P., Mathematical Sciences
CAS, R. A. F., Geosciences
CLAYTON, M., Biological Sciences
CULL, J. P., Geosciences
DEACON, G. B., Chemistry
HAMILL, J. D., Biological Sciences
HEARN, M., Chemistry
JACKSON, R., Chemistry
JACKSON, W. R., Chemistry
JESSON, D., Physics and Material Engineering
KEAYS, R., Geosciences
KLEBANER, F., Mathematical Sciences
LAKE, P. S., Biological Sciences
LEWIS, R., Physics and Material Engineering
MACFARLANE, D. R., Chemistry
MONAGHAN, J. J., Mathematical Sciences
MURRAY, K. S., Chemistry
NORRIS, R., Dean
REEDER, M., Mathematical Sciences
SIMON, G., Physics and Material Engineering
SMYTH, D. R., Biological Sciences
VICKERS-RICH, P., Geosciences

Victorian College of Pharmacy (381 Royal Parade, Parkville, Vic. 3052; tel. (3) 9903-6000; fax (3) 9903-9581; e-mail info@vcp.monash.edu.au; internet www.vcp.monash.edu.au):

CHAPMAN, C. B., Immunology
CHARMAN, W. N., Pharmaceutics
DOOLEY, M., Pharmacology
NATION, R. L., Pharmaceutics
POUTON, C. W., Pharmaceutics
REED, B. L., Biopharmaceutics
SCAMMELLS, P. J., Biopharmaceutics
STEWART, P. J., Pharmaceutics

DIRECTORS

Accident Research Centre: Dr I. JOHNSTON
Facility for Anti-infective Drug Development and Innovation: Prof. R. NATION
Australian APEC Study Centre: A. OXLEY
Australian Centre for Biodiversity: Assoc. Prof. R. MCNALLY
Australian Centre for Human Health Risk Assessment: Prof. B. G. PRIESTLEY
Australian Centre for the Study of Jewish Civilisation: Prof. A. MARKUS
Australian Centre for Research in Employment and Work: Assoc. Prof. H. DE CIERCI
Australian Centre for Retail Studies: A. WYOUNG
Australian Crustal Research Centre: Prof. R. CAS
Australian Geodynamics Co-operative Research Centre: Dr G. PRICE
Australian Pulp and Paper Institute: Prof. I. PARKER
Australian Sustainable Industry Research Centre: R. EDWARDS
Australian Telecommunications Co-operative Research Centre: Prof. G. EGAN
Bendigo Regional Clinical School: Prof. G. WHYTE
Castan Centre for Human Rights: Prof. S. JOSEPH
Central and Eastern Clinical School: Prof. N. THOMSON
Centre for Advanced Materials Technology: Prof. B. MUDDLE
Centre for Ambulance and Paramedic Studies: Assoc. Prof. F. ARCHER
Centre of Archaeology and Ancient History: Dr C. HOPE
Centre for Australian Indigenous Studies: Prof. L. RUSSELL
Centre for Biography and Life Writing: Prof. B. CAINE
Centre for Biomedical Engineering: Assoc. Prof. T. I. H. BROWN
Centre for Childhood Studies: Prof. M. FLEER
Centre for Community Networking Research: Prof. G. JOHANSON
Centre for Comparative Literature and Cultural Studies: Prof. K. RIGBY
Centre for Developmental Disability Health Victoria: Prof. H. SCHMIDT
Centre for Developmental Psychiatry and Psychology: Prof. B. TONGE
Centre for Distributed Systems and Software Engineering: Prof. H. SCHMIDT
Centre for Drama and Theatre Studies: Prof. P. SNOW
Centre for Drug Candidate Optimisation: Prof. B. CHARMAN, Assoc. Prof. S. CHARMAN
Centre for Dynamical Meteorology and Oceanography: Dr S. SIEMS
Centre for Economics of Education and Training: Prof. G. BURKE
Centre for Educational Multimedia: B. HOLKNER
Centre for Electronic Media Art: (vacant)
Centre for Environmental Stress and Adaptation Research: Assoc. Prof. S. MCKECHNIE
Centre for European Studies: Assoc. Prof. M. PAVLYSHYN
Centre for Functional Genomics and Human Diseases: Prof. B. HERTZOG
Centre for Gippsland Studies: Dr M. FLETCHER
Centre for Green Chemistry: Prof. M. HEARN
Centre for Heart and Chest Research: Prof. R. HARPER
Centre for Health Economics: Prof. J. RICHARDSON
Centre for Higher Education Quality: Prof. G. WEBB
Centre for Human Bioethics: Dr J. OAKLEY
Centre for Increasing Returns and Economic Organization: (vacant)
Centre for Law and Reconstruction in Southern Africa: Prof. R. SCHEEPERS
Centre for Learning and Teaching Support: Prof. D. KIRKPATRICK
Centre for Mathematics and Science Education: Prof. R. GUNSTONE
Centre for Medical and Health Sciences Education: Prof. C. BROWNE
Centre for Modelling of Stochastic Systems: Prof. F. KLEBANER
Centre for Monash Cluster Computing: Dr L. MORESI
Centre for Multidiscipline Studies: Dr D. PEDLER
Centre for Multimedia and Hypermedia Research: Prof. J. HARRIS
Centre of Policy Studies: Prof. P. ADAMS
Centre for Population and Urban Research: Dr R. J. BIRRELL
Centre for Postcolonial Writing: Dr C. LOKUGE
Centre for Rural Mental Health: Prof. F. JUDD
Centre for Science, Mathematics and Technology Education: Prof. D. GUNSTONE
Centre for Stellar and Planetary Astrophysics: Dr J. LATTANGZIO
Centre of Studies in Religion and Theology: Dr C. MEWS
Centre for the Study of Ethics in Medicine and Society: Assoc. Prof. P. KOMESAROFF
Centre for Telecommunications and Information Engineering: Prof. G. K. EGAN
Centre for Urological Research: Prof. G. RISBRIDGER
Centre for Women's Mental Health Studies: Prof. J. KULKARNI
Centre for Women's Studies and Gender Research: Dr M. DEVER
Centre for X-Ray Physics and Imaging: Prof. R. LEWIS
Clinical Psychology Centre: Prof. J. OGLOFF
Commonwealth Key Centre of Institute of Transport Studies: Assoc. Prof. G. ROSE
Co-operative Research Centre for Asthma: Dr E. SEVERIN
Co-operative Research Centre for Australian Telecommunications: Prof. G. EGAN
Co-operative Research Centre for Cast Metal Manufacturing: Prof. B. MUDDLE
Co-operative Research Centre for Catchment Hydrology: Prof. R. VERTESSY
Co-operative Research Centre for Clean Power from Lignite: Prof. T. SRIDHAR
Co-operative Research Centre for Fresh Water Ecology: Prof. G. JONES
Co-operative Research Centre for Integrated Engineering Asset Management: Prof. J. PRICE
Co-operative Research Centre for Polymers: Dr G. SIMON
Co-operative Research Centre for Water Quality and Treatment: Prof. D. BURSILL
Elwyn Morey Child Study Centre: Assoc. Prof. D. HARVEY
Facilitated Learning for Information Technology Education (FLITE) Centre: A. ELLIS
Food and Agricultural Centre of Excellence in Food Quality, Safety and Nutrition: M. WAHLQVIST
Gippsland Centre for Art and Design: J. ADAMS
Gippsland Regional Clinical School: Dr D. PEDLER
Institute of Railway Technology: G. TEW
Institute of Reproduction and Development: Prof. D. DE KRETSER
Institute of Transport Studies: The Australian Key Centre in Transport Management: Prof. G. ROSE
Intelligent Robotics Research Centre: Prof. R. A. JARVIS
International Institute for Forensic Studies: Prof. Hon. G. HAMPEL
Krongold Centre: Dr D. MOORE
Language and Society Centre: Dr H. BOWE
Melbourne Centre for Japanese Language Education: A. DE KRETSER
Mildura Regional Clinical School: Dr J. RUSSELL

Monash Ageing Research Centre: Prof. B. WORKMAN
Monash Asia Institute: Prof. A. M. VICZIANY
Monash Centre for Research in International Education: Prof. S. MARGINSON
Monash Centre of Clinical Research Excellence in Therapeutics: Assoc. Prof. C. REID
Monash Data Mining Centre: T. DIX, K. SMITH
Monash Environment Institute: Prof. C. COCKLIN
Monash Institute of Health Services Research: Prof. D. CAMPBELL
Monash Institute for the Study of Global Movements: (vacant)
Monash Maintenance Technology Institute: J. RUCINSKI
Monash Regional Centre for Information and Communications Technology: Prof. L. DOOLEY
Monash Science Centre: Prof. P. VICKERS-RICH
Monash Timber Engineering Centre: Prof. H. R. MILNER
Nanotechnology Victoria: Prof. B. MUDDLE
National Centre for Australian Studies: J. ARNOLD
National Centre for Coronial Information: D. RANSON
National History Centre: Dr A. TAYLOR
National Key Centre for Advanced Materials Technology: Prof. B. C. MUDDLE
National Stem Cell Centre: Prof. A. TROUNSON
Research Centre for Mobile Commerce (mCommerce Centre): Prof. C. MINGINS
Research Centre for New Media in Language Learning: (vacant)
Research Evaluation and Practice Unit: Dr A. VANCE
Ritchie Centre for Baby Health: Prof. A. WALKER
UNESCO International Centre for Engineering Education: Prof. Z. J. PUDLOWSKI
Van Cleef / Roet Centre for Nervous Diseases / Dept of Neurosciences: Prof. E. STOREY
Water Studies Centre: Dr B. T. HART

AFFILIATED INSTITUTIONS

Baker Medical Research Institute: Commercial Rd, Melbourne, Vic. 3004; tel. (3) 8532-1111; Dir Prof. G. JENNINGS.

Bureau of Meteorology: 150 Lonsdale St, Melbourne, Vic. 3000; tel. (3) 9669-4915; Dir J. W. ZILLMAN.

MacFarlane Burnet Institute for Medical Research and Public Health Ltd (Burnet Institute): Commercial Rd, Melbourne, Vic 3004; tel. (3) 9282-2111; Dir Prof. S. WESSELINGH.

Mannix College: Wellington Rd, Monash University, Clayton, Vic. 3800; tel. (3) 9544-8895; Master Rev. K. SAUNDERS.

Mental Health Research Institute of Victoria: Locked Bag No. 11, Parkville, Vic. 3052; tel. (3) 9388-1633; Dir Prof. D. COPOLOV.

Prince Henry's Institute of Medical Research: Monash Medical Centre, Level 4, Block E, 246 Clayton Rd, Clayton, Vic. 3168; tel. (3) 9594-4372; Dir Prof. E. SIMPSON.

MURDOCH UNIVERSITY

South St, Murdoch, WA 6150
Telephone: (8) 9360-6000
Fax: (8) 9360-6847
Internet: www.murdoch.edu.au

Founded 1973; postgraduate courses began 1974; undergraduate courses began 1975
State control
Academic year: February to November

Chancellor: The Hon. GEOFFREY BOLTON
Pro-Chancellor: Judge KATE O'BRIEN
Vice-Chancellor: Prof. JOHN YOVICH
Pro Vice-Chancellor (Academic): Prof. JANETTE THOMAS
Pro Vice-Chancellor (Research): Prof. ANDRIS STELBOVICS
Pro Vice-Chancellor (Regional Development): KATERYNA LONGLEY
Pro Vice-Chancellor (Resource Management): Prof. CRAIG SPENCE (acting)
Pro Vice-Chancellor (Strategy): GARY MARTIN
President, Academic Council: MICHAEL BOROWITZKA
Director of Library Services: MARGARET JONES

Number of teachers: 455
Number of students: 12,343

Publications: *Annual Report*, *In Touch* (2 a year), *On Campus* (8 a year), *Research Report* (annually), *Synergy* (4 a year)

DEANS

Division of Arts (Information Technology): Assoc. Prof. ARNOLDATHERINE DEPICKERE
Division of Science and Engineering: Exec. Dean Prof. YIANNI ATTIKOUZEL
Division of Social Sciences, Humanities and Education: Exec. Dean Prof. K. LONGLEY
Division of Veterinary and Biomedical Sciences: Exec. Dean Prof. J. YOVICH
School of Education: Prof. DAVID ANDRICH
School of Engineering: Prof. MAURICE ALLEN
School of Health Sciences: Prof. JIM REYNOLDSON (acting)
School of Law: Prof. CHRISTOPHER KENDALL

PROFESSORS

Division of Business, Information Technology and Law (tel. (8) 9360-2414; fax (8) 9360-2994; internet www.murdoch.edu.au/bitl):

FORBES, R., Law
MCLEOD, N. D. B., Law
PENDLETON, M. D., Law
ROBISON, R., Asian and International Politics
SIMMONDS, R., Law
THOMPSON, H. M., Economics

Division of Science (tel. (8) 9360-2161; fax (8) 9360-6304; internet www.science.murdoch.edu.au):

BLOOM, W. R., Mathematics and Statistics
CARNEGIE, P., Biotechnology
DILWORTH, M. J., Biology
GILES, R. G. F., Organic Chemistry
HOBBS, R., Environmental Science
JAMES, I., Mathematics
JENNINGS, P., Physics, Energy Studies
JONES, M. G. K., Plant Sciences
LYONS, T. J., Environmental Science
NICOL, M. J., Mineral Science
POTTER, I. C., Animal Biology
RITCHIE, I. M., Chemistry
WEBB, J. M., Chemistry

Division of Science and Engineering (Rockingham Campus, Dixon Rd, Rockingham, WA; tel. (8) 9360-7100; fax (8) 9360-7104; internet wwweng.murdoch.edu.au):

LEE, P. L., Instrumentation and Control Engineering
ROY, G., Software Engineering

Division of Social Sciences, Humanities and Education (tel. (8) 9360-6045; fax (8) 9360-6367; internet www.sshe.murdoch.edu.au):

ANDRICH, D., Education
BALDOCK, C., Sociology
DE GARIS, B., History
DUREY, M., History
FRODSHAM, J. D., English and Comparative Literature
HILL, B. V., Education
HILL, D., Asian Studies (Head)
INNES, M., Psychology
LOADER, B., Social Enquiry (Head)
MISHRA, V., English and Comparative Literature
NEWMAN, P., Science and Technology Policy
O'TOOLE, L. M., Communication Studies
RUTHROF, H. G., Philosophy

Division of Veterinary and Biomedical Sciences (tel. (8) 9360-2566; fax (8) 9310-7390; internet wwwvet.murdoch.edu.au/home.html):

HAMPSON, D., Microbiology and Immunobiology
SWAN, R. A., Veterinary Clinical Studies
THOMPSON, A., Parasitology
WILCOX, G. E., Virology

DIRECTORS

A. J. Parker Co-operative Research Centre for Hydrometallurgy: MARK WOFFENDEN
Asia-Pacific Centre for Human Rights and the Prevention of Ethnic Conflicts: Dr F. DE VARENNES
Asia-Pacific Intellectual Property Law Institute: (vacant)
Asia Research Centre on Social, Political and Economic Change: (vacant)
Australian Co-operative Research Centre for Renewable Energy: Dr F. REID
Centre for Atomic, Molecular and Surface Physics (jointly with Univ. of Western Australia): Assoc. Prof. A. T. STELBOVICS, Prof. J. F. WILLIAMS
Centre for Curriculum and Professional Development: Assoc. Prof. S. WILLIS
Centre for Enterprise Development and Entrepreneurship: G. HERPS
Centre for Federal and Regional Studies: Dr F. HARMAN
Centre for Irish Studies: Assoc. Prof. R. REECE
Centre for Labour Market Research: (vacant)
Centre for Necrotrophic Fungal Pathogens: Prof. RICHARD OLIVER
Centre for Organic Waste Management: Prof. ARTHUR MCCOMB
Centre for Production Animal Research: Assoc. Prof. D. H. HAMPSON
Centre for Research in Culture and Communication: Dr T. O'REGAN
Centre for Research on Women: A. GOLDFLAM
Centre for Rhizobium Studies: Assoc. Prof. J. HOWIESON
Co-operative Research Centre for Legumes in Mediterranean Agriculture: Prof. J. HAMBLIN (University of Western Australia)
Energy Research Institute: Dr T. PRYOR
Institute for Environmental Science: Prof. G. HO
Institute for Molecular Genetics and Animal Disease: Prof. A. THOMPSON
Institute for Research in Safety and Transport: Assoc. Prof. L. R. HARTLEY
Institute for Science and Technology Policy: Prof. P. NEWMAN
Institute for Social Programme Evaluation: Prof. D. ANDRICH
Office of Continuing Veterinary Education: Dr M. G. BREDHAUER
Rumen Biotech: Prof. RUDOLPH APPELS
State Agricultural Biotechnology Centre: Prof. M. G. K. JONES
Western Australia Biotechnology Research Institute: Prof. SIMON CARROLL (Curtin)

UNIVERSITY OF NEW ENGLAND

Armidale, NSW 2351
Telephone: (2) 6773-3333
Fax: (2) 6773-3122
E-mail: admissions@une.edu.au
Internet: www.une.edu.au

Founded 1954; previously New England University College (f. 1938); Armidale College of Advanced Education merged with the University in 1989

Commonwealth govt control
Academic year: February to November (2 semesters)

Chancellor: J. CASSIDY
Deputy Chancellor: J. HARRIS
Vice-Chancellor: Prof. I. MOSES
Pro Vice-Chancellor (International and Entrepreneurial Affairs): Prof. R. POLLARD
Pro Vice-Chancellor (Research and Development): Prof. P. FLOOD
Pro Vice-Chancellor (Teaching and Learning): Prof. D. RICH
Executive Director: G. DENNEHY (Business and Administration)
Secretary to Council: H. ARTHURSON
Librarian: E. WOODBERRY

Library: see under Libraries and Archives
Number of teachers: 484
Number of students: 18,863

Publications: *Australian Folklore: A Yearly Journal of Folklore Studies*, *Australasian Victorian Studies Journal* (annually), *Journal of Australian Colonial History* (2 a year), *South Asia* (annually), *TalentEd* (3 a year), *The University of New England Law Journal* (2 a year), *Wool Technology and Sheep Breeding* (4 a year)

DEANS

Faculty of Arts: Dr M. MACKLIN
Faculty of Economics, Business and Law: Prof. R. PIGGOTT
Faculty of Education, Health and Professional Studies: Prof. V. MINICHIELLO
Faculty of the Sciences: Prof. M. SEDGLEY

PROFESSORS

BINDON, B., CRC for Cattle and Beef Quality
BOULTON, A. J., Environmental Sciences and Natural Resources Management
BRASTED, H. V., Classics, History and Religion
BRUNCKHORST, D., Institute for Rural Futures/UNESCO Centre for Bioregional Resource Management
BYRNE, B. J., Psychology
CARRINGTON, K. L., Social Science
CHOCT, M., Rural Science and Agriculture
COLBRAN, S., Law
COOKSEY, R. W., New England Business School
COTTLE, D., Rural Science and Agriculture
DAVIDSON, I., Human and Environmental Studies
DOLLERY, B. E., Economics
ECKERMAN, A.-K., Professional Development and Leadership
FLOOD, P., Pro Vice-Chancellor (Research and Development)
FORD, H. A., Environmental Sciences and Natural Resources Management
FORREST, P. R. H., Social Science
FRANZMANN, M., Classics, History and Religion
GEISER, F., Environmental Sciences and Natural Resources Management
GIBSON, J., Rural Science and Agriculture
GODDARD, C. W., Languages, Cultures and Linguistics
GOSSIP, C. J., Languages, Cultures and Linguistics
GUNTER, M. J., Biological and Molecular Sciences
HORSLEY, G. H. R., Classics, History and Religion
HUTCHINSON, P. J., New England Business School
KAUR, A., Economics
KENT, D. A., Classics, History and Religion
KIERNANDER, A. R. D., English, Communication and Theatre
KINGHORN, B. P., Rural Science and Agriculture
LLOYD, C., Economics
MAGNER, E. S., Law
MEEK, V. L., Professional Development and Leadership
MOSES, I., Vice-Chancellor
NOBLE, W., Psychology
NOLAN, J. V., Rural Science and Agriculture
PEGG, J. E., Education
POLLARD, R., Pro Vice-Chancellor (International Affairs)
RICH, D. C., Pro-Vice Chancellor (Teaching and Learning)
ROGERS, L. J., Biological, Biomedical and Molecular Sciences
ROWE, J. B., Rural Science and Agriculture
RUVINSKY, A., Rural Science and Agriculture
SAJEEV, A. S. M., Mathematics, Statistics and Computing Science
SCOTT, J. M., Rural Science and Agriculture
SIMPSON, R. D., Environmental Sciences and Natural Resources Management
TAJI, A., Rural Science and Agriculture
THOMPSON, J. M., Rural Science and Agriculture
TREADGOLD, M. L., Economics
UNSWORTH, L., Education
WALMSLEY, D. J., Human and Environmental Studies
WARE, H. R., Professional Development and Leadership
WATSON, K., Biological, Biomedical and Molecular Sciences

ATTACHED RESEARCH INSTITUTES

(The mailing address is that of the University, Armidale)

Agricultural Business Research Institute: Man. Dir P. A. RICKARDS.

Animal Genetics and Breeding Unit: Dir Dr H. GRASER.

Australian Centre for Agriculture and Law: Dir P. MARTIN.

Australian Poultry Co-operative Research Centre: CEO Prof. M. CHOCT.

Australian Sheep Industry Co-operative Research Centre: CEO Prof. J. ROWE.

Centre for Agricultural and Applied Economics: Dir Prof. C. LLOYD (acting).

Centre for Animal Health and Welfare: Co-ordinator S. W. WALKDEN-BROWN.

Centre for Behavioural and Physiological Ecology: Co-ordinator F. GEISER.

Centre for Bioactive Discovery in Health and Ageing: Dir Prof. K. WATSON.

Centre for Ecological Economics and Water Policy Research: Dir Dr R. GILL.

Centre for Ecology, Evolution and Systematics: Co-ordinator Dr J. BRUHL.

Centre for Environmental Dispute Resolution: Co-ordinator J. C. PRIOR.

Centre for Higher Education Management and Policy: Dir Prof. V. L. MEEK.

Centre for Language and Cognition: Dir Prof. C. W. GODDARD.

Centre for Local Government: Dir Prof. B. E. DOLLERY.

Centre for Molecular Biology: Co-ordinator B. F. CHEETHAM.

Centre for Neuroscience and Animal Behaviour: Co-ordinator Prof. L. ROGERS.

Centre for North Coast Aquatic Linkages: Co-ordinator A. J. BOULTON.

Centre for Peace Studies: Co-ordinator R. D. SPENCE.

Centre for Research in Aboriginal and Multicultural Studies: Dir Prof. A. D. ECKERMANN.

Centre for Research in Context: Co-ordinator P. M. NINNES.

Centre for Rural Crime, Safety and Security: Programme Leader E. BARCLAY.

Centre for Small and Medium Research Enterprise Research: Dir Prof. P. J. HUTCHINSON (acting).

Centre for Spatial Sciences: Co-ordinator L. KUMAR.

Centre for Sustainable Farming Systems: Co-ordinator Prof. J. M. SCOTT.

Co-operative Research Centre for Cattle and Beef Quality: Dir Prof. B. BINDON.

Co-operative Research Centre for Viticulture: Supervisor D. W. LAMB.

Heritage Future Research Centre: Dir Prof. I. DAVIDSON.

Institute for Genetics and Bioinformatics: Dir J. P. GIBSON.

Institute for Rural Futures: Dir Prof. D. J. BRUNCKHORST.

International Livestock Resource Information Centre: CEO G. STASSEN.

Language Training Centre: Dir D. WILLIAM.

National Centre of Science, Information and Communication Technology, and Mathematics, Education for Rural and Regional Australia: Dir Prof. J. E. PEGG.

National Marine Science Centre: Dir Prof. R. SIMPSON.

UNE Asia Centre: Dir Prof. H. V. BRASTED.

UNESCO Centre for Bioregional Resource Management: Dir D. J. BRUNCKHORST.

UNIVERSITY OF NEW SOUTH WALES

Sydney, NSW 2052
Telephone: (2) 9385-1000
Fax: (2) 9385-2000
Internet: www.unsw.edu.au

Founded 1948

incorporated by Act of Parliament 1949
Academic year: February to November (2 sessions)

Chancellor: DAVID GONSKI
Vice-Chancellor and Principal: Professor FRED HILMER
Deputy Vice-Chancellor (Academic): Prof. ROBERT KING
Deputy Vice-Chancellor (Int.): Prof. JOHN INGLESON
Deputy Vice-Chancellor (Research): Prof. LES FIELD
Pro-Vice-Chancellor (Education): Prof. RICHARD HENRY
Chief Financial Officer: GARRY MCLENNAN
Chief Information Officer: TIM COPE
Principal Librarian: ANDREW WELLS

Number of teachers: 2,300
Number of students: 38,000

Publications: *Calendar* (annual), *Faculty Handbooks*, *news@unsw* (fortnightly online staff newsletter.), *Research@UNSW* (annual), *Uniken* (official univ. magazine, 10 a year.)

DEANS

Faculty of Arts and Social Sciences: Prof. ANNETTE HAMILTON
Faculty of the Built Environment: Prof. PETER MURPHY
Faculty of Engineering: Prof. BRENDON PARKER
Faculty of Commerce and Economics: Prof. JOHN PIGGOTT (acting)
Faculty of Law: Prof. DAVID DIXON (acting)
Faculty of Medicine: Prof. PETER SMITH
Faculty of Science: MIKE ARCHER
Australian Graduate School of Management: Prof. ROBERT MCLEAN
Univ. College, Australian Defence Force Academy: Assoc. Prof. JOHN BAIRD (Rector)
College of Fine Arts: Prof. IAN HOWARD

PROFESSORS

Faculty of Arts and Social Sciences:

ALEXANDER, C., English
ALEXANDER, P., English
ASHCROFT, W., English
BELL, P., History and Philosophy of Science
BELL, R., History
BENNETT, B., Humanities
CAHILL, D, History
CASS, B, Social Policy
CHAN, J., Social Science and Policy
CHANDLER, P., Education
CONDREN, C., Politics and International Politics
COOPER, M., Education
COTTON, J., Humanities
DANIEL, A., Sociology
DENNIS, P., Humanities
DONALD, J., Media, Film and Theatre
EGGERT, P., Humanities
GASCOIGNE, J., History
GREY, J., Humanities
GROSS, M, Education
HALL, R., Social Science and Policy
HUGMAN, R., Social Work
HUMPHREY, M., Sociology
JOHNSON, R., History
KATZ, I, Social Policy
KITCHING, G., Politics and International Relations
LYONS, M., History
OLDROYD, D., History and Philosophy of Science
PATTON, P., Philosophy
PEARSON, M., History
SAUNDERS, P, Social Policy
SCHUSTER, J., Media and Communications
SWELLER, J., Education
THAYER, C., Humanities
TYRRELL, I., History
WILLIAMS, M., Politics and International Relations
WOODMAN, S., Humanities

Faculty of the Built Environment:

CUTHBERT, A., Architecture
LANG, J., Architecture
LOOSEMORE, M., Built Environment
RUAN, X., Architecture
WEIRICK, J., Landscape Architecture

Faculty of Engineering:

ACWORTH, R, Civil Engineering
ADESINA, A, Chemical Engineering
ASHBOLT, N., Civil and Environmental Engineering
BRADFORD, M., Civil and Environmental Engineering
CARMICHAEL, D., Civil and Environmental Engineering
CELLER, B., Electrical Engineering
CHATTOPADHYAY, G., Civil and Environmental Engineering
COMPTON, P. J., Computer Science
CROSKY, A, Materials Science and Engineering
DAVIS, T., Chemical Engineering
DOCTORS, L., Mechanical Engineering
DZURAK, A., Electronic Engineering and Telecommunications
FANE, A., Chemical Engineering
FELL, R., Civil and Environmental Engineering
FLEET, G, Chemical Engineering
FOO, N., Computer Science
FORSTER, B., Surveying and Spatial Information Systems
FOSTER, N., Chemical Engineering
GALVIN, J., Mining Engineering
GILBERT, R., Civil and Environmental Engineering
HEISER, G., Computer Science
HEBBLEWHITE, B., Mining Engineering
HOUGH, R, Engineering
JEFFERY, R., Computer Science
KAEBERNICK, H., Mechanical Engineering
KELLY, D., Mechanical Engineering
LEONARDI, E., Mechanical Engineering
MAROSSZEKY, M., Civil and Environmental Engineering
MORRISON, G., Mechanical Engineering
NOWOTNY, J., Materials Science and Engineering
OSTROVSKI, O., Materials Science and Engineering
PINCZEWSKI, W., Petroleum Engineering
RANDALL, R., Mechanical Engineering
RIZOS, C., Surveying and Spatial Information Systems
SAHAJWALLA, V., Materials Science and Engineering
SAMMUT, C., Computer Science
SAVKIN, A., Electrical Engineering
SCHINDHELM, K., Biomedical Engineering
SENEVIRATNE, A., Electrical Engineering
SHARMA, A., Civil and Environmental Engineering
SHAW, J., Computer Science
SKYLLAS-KAZACOS, M., Chemical Engineering
SOLO, V., Electrical Engineering
SORRELL, C., Materials Science and Engineering
TIN LOI, F., Civil and Environmental Engineering
TRIMM, D., Chemical Engineering
TRINDER, J., Surverying and Spatial Information Systems
VALLIAPPAN, S., Civil and Environmental Engineering
WAITE, D., Civil and Environmental Engineering
WENHAM, S., Photovoltaic Engineering
YU, A., Materials Science and Engineering

Faculty of Law:

ARONSON, M.
BROWN, D.
BYRNES, A
CUNNEEN, C
DISNEY, J.
DIXON, D.
GREENLEAF, G.
KINGSFORD-SMITH, D.
KRYGIER, M.
REDMOND, P.
WILLIAMS, G.

Faculty of Medicine:

ANDERSON, D., Medicine
ANDREWS, J., Psychiatry
BARRY, P., Physiology
BENNETT, M., Obstetrics and Gynaecology
BRODATY, H., Psychiatry
CALVERT, G., Medicine
CAMPBELL, T., Medicine
CHESTERMAN, C., Medicine, Pathology
CHISHOLM, D., Medicine, Metabolic Research
CHONG, B., Medicine
COIERA, E, Medical Sciences
COOPER, D., Medicine
CORONEO, M., Ophthalmology
DAY, R., Medicine, Clinical Pharmacology
DEANE, S., Surgery
DICKSON, H., Rehabilitation, Aged and Extended Care
EISENBUCH, I., Medicine
EISMAN, J., Medicine, Bone and Mineral Research
GANDEVIA, S., Medicine
GECZY, C., Pathology
GRAHAM, R., Medicine
HALL, B., Medicine
HARRIS, M., Medicine
HARRISON, G., Anaesthetics
HARVEY, R., Medicine
HENRY, R., Paediatrics
HILLMAN, K., Anaesthetics and Intensive Care
HOGG, P., Pathology
HOLDEN, B. A., Optometry
HOWES, L., Medicine, Physiology
KALDOR, J., Epidemiology
KEARSLEY, J., Surgery
KHACHIGIAN, L., Pathology
KIPPAX, S, HIV Social Research Centre
KRILIS, S., Medicine
KUMAR, R., Pathology
LAWSON, J., Health Services Management
LEE, A., Medical Microbiology
LLOYD, A., Pathology
LORD, R., Surgery
LUMBERS, E., Physiology
MACDONALD, G., Medicine
MCLACHLAN, E., Physiology, Medical Research
MORRIS, D., Surgery
O'ROURKE, M., Medicine
O'SULLIVAN, W., Medical Biochemistry
PARKER, G., Psychiatry
POOLE, M., Surgery
RICHMOND, R., Medicine
ROTEM, A., Medical Education
ROWE, M., Physiology
RUSSELL, P., Medicine
SCHINDHELM, K., Biomedical Engineering
SILOVE, D., Psychiatry
TARANTOLA, D, Medicine
TORDA, T. A., Anaesthetics and Intensive Care
WAKEFIELD, D., Pathology
WHITE, L., Paediatrics
ZWAR, N., Paediatrics
ZWI, A., Paediatrics

Faculty of Science:

ADAMS, M, Biological Earth and Environmental Science
BALLARD, J, Biotechnology and Biomolecular Science
BISHOP, R., Chemical Sciences
BLACK, D. ST. C., Chemical Sciences
BRYANT, R., Psychology
CADOGAN, M, Physics
CAMPBELL, S., Physical, Environmental and Mathematical Sciences
CLARK, R, Physics
COOPER, D., Biological, Earth and Environmental Science
COUCH, W., Physics
COWLING, M., Mathematics
DAIN, S, Optometry
DADDS, M., Psychology
DAWES, W., Biotechnology and Biomolecular Science
DORAN, P., Biotechnology and Biomolecular Science
DUNSMUIR, W., Mathematics
ENGLAND, M, Mathematics
FLAMBAUM, V, Physics
FORGAS, J., Psychology
GAL, M, Physics
GILLAM, B., Psychology
GRAY, P., Biotechnology and Biomolecular Science
HIBBERT, D., Chemical Sciences
HUON, G., Psychology
JACKSON, W., Physical, Environmental and Mathematical Sciences
KEHOE, J., Psychology
KINGSFORD, R., Biological, Earth and Environmental Science
KJELLEBERG, S., Biotechnology and Biomolecular Science
LAMB, R., Chemical Sciences
LESLIE, L., Mathematics
LITTLE, F., Biotechnology and Biomolecular Science
LOVIBOND, P., Psychology
MCLEAN, R., Physical, Environmental and Mathematical Sciences
MCCONKEY, K., Psychology
MCMURTRIE, R., Biological, Earth and Environmental Science
MIDDLETON, J., Mathematics
NEILAN, B, Biotechnology and Biomolecular Science
NEILSON, D., Physics

PASK, C., Physical, Environmental and Mathematical Sciences
ROGERS, C., Mathematics
SAMMUT, R., Physical, Environmental and Mathematical Sciences
SIMMONS, M., Physics
SLOAN, I., Mathematics
STEINBERG, P., Biological, Earth and Environmental Science
STOREY, J., Physics
SUSHKOV, O., Physics
SUTHERLAND, C., Mathematics
SUTHERLAND, P, Mathematics
TAFT, M., Psychology
WAND, M., Mathematics
WARD, C., Biological, Earth and Environmental Science
WEBB, J., Physics
WILKINS, M., Biotechnology and Biomolecular Science
WOLFE, J., Physics

Faculty of Commerce and Economics:
ANDERSON, E, AGSM
BALZER, L, Banking and Finance
BROWN, R, Accounting
DWYER, L, Accounting
FELDMAN, D, Banking and Finance
FIEBIG, D, Economics
FOSTER, F, Banking and Finance
FOX, K, Economics
HILL, R, Economics
KOHN, R, Economics
LAYTON, R, Marketing
MORRISON, P, Marketing
MOSHIRIAN, FARIBOZ, Banking and Finance
UNCLES, M, Marketing

ASSOCIATE COLLEGES

Faculty of the College of Fine Arts: Selwyn St, Paddington, NSW 2021; tel. (2) 9385-0888; f. 1990 following merger of the City Art Institute and the Univ.; Dean and Dir IAN HOWARD.

University College, Australian Defence Force Academy: Northcott Drive, Campbell, ACT 2601; tel. (2) 6268-8111; f. 1981 by agreement between the Commonwealth of Australia and the Univ. of NSW; degree courses started 1986; Rector Prof. ROBERT KING; Exec. Officer T. HODSON

PROFESSORS

BENNETT, B., Language, Literature and Communication
DENNIS, P., History
DUGGINS, R. K., Mechanical Engineering
EGGERT, P., Language, Literature and Communication
HALL, P., Business
JACKSON, G., Chemistry
LOVELL, D., Politics
THAYER, C., Politics
YOUNG, J., Civil Engineering
YOUNG, P., Civil Engineering

ASSOCIATED INSTITUTES

Australian Graduate School of Management: Sydney, NSW 2052; tel. (2) 9931-9200; f. 1975; postgraduate MBA and PhD courses, residential courses for execs; 42 faculty mems; library of 25,000 vols; Dir Prof. ROBERT MCLEAN; publ. *Australian Journal of Management*, *AGSM Working Paper Series*

PROFESSORS

ANDERSON, E.
COLLINS, R.
DAVIS, J.
DEVINNEY, T.
DONALDSON, D.
DOWLING, G.
EAGLESON, G.
HIRST, M.
MARKS, R.
PARKER, S.
POWELL, T.
ROBERTS, J.
SHEATHER, S.
TURNER, D.
VITALE, M.
YETTON, P.

UNIVERSITY OF NEWCASTLE

University Drive, Callaghan, NSW 2308
Telephone: (2) 4921-5000
Fax: (2) 4985-4200
Internet: www.newcastle.edu.au

Founded 1965
State control
Academic year: March to November (2 semesters)

Chancellor: Prof. TREVOR WARING
Vice-Chancellor and President: Prof. ROGER HOLMES
Pro-Vice-Chancellor and President: Prof. TERRY LOVAT
Deputy Vice-Chancellor: Prof. BRIAN ENGLISH
Deputy Vice-Chancellor (Research): Prof. RON MACDONALD
Deputy Vice-Chancellor (University Services): Dr SUE GOULD
Director, Central Coast Campus: Dr BARRY MCKNIGHT

Library: see under Libraries and Archives
Number of teachers: 800
Number of students: 25,000

Publications: *Annual Report*, *Cetus* (annually), *UniNews*

PRO VICE-CHANCELLORS

Faculty of Business and Law: Prof. B. CAREY
Faculty of Education and Arts: Prof. T. LOVAT
Faculty of Engineering and Built Environment: Prof. A. W. PAGE
Faculty of Health: Prof. J. MARLEY
Faculty of Science: Prof. B. HOGARTH

PROFESSORS

Faculty of Business and Law (internet www.newcastle.edu.au/faculty/bus-law):
BATES, F. A., Law
BRAY, M., Employment Studies
CATLEY, B., Management
CLARKE, F.
EASTON, S., Finance
GILLARD, P., e-Business
HOLMES, S., Accounting
MITCHELL, W. F., Economics
O'CASS, A., Marketing
PURCELL, B., International Business
REES, N. R., Law
SCHAPER, M., Entrepreneurship and Small Business
WINSEN, J. K., Commerce
WRIGHT, T., Law

Faculty of Education and Arts (internet www.newcastle.edu.au/faculty/educ-artsl):
BOURKE, S., Education
CONNOR, L., Social Sciences
CONSTABLE, R., Music
CRAIG, H.
EMELJANOW, V., Drama
FOREMAN, P., Education
GORE, J., Curriculum Teaching and Learning
GRAHAM, A., Fine Art
GRAY, M., Social Work
HOOKER, C., Philosophy
LAURA, R., Education
LAVAT, T.
LESTER, J., Aboriginal Studies
RYAN, L., Australian Studies
SAMUEL, G., Social Sciences
TARRANT, H., Classics

Faculty of Engineering and Built Environment (internet www.eng.newcastle.edu.au):
ANTONIA, R. A., Mechanical Engineering
BELOVA, I., Materials Engineering
CHEN, S., Building and Construction Management
EVANS, G., Chemical Engineering
FELLOWES, M., Computer Science
FRYER, J. G., Photogrammetry
FU, M., Electrical Engineering
GOODWIN, G. C., Electrical Engineering
JAMESON, G. J., Chemical Engineering
JONES, M., Bulk Solids
KALMA, J. D., Environmental Engineering
KUCZERA, G., Water Engineering
LAKSHMI, N., Sofware Engineering
MELCHERS, R., Civil Engineering
MIDDLETON, R., Electrical Engineering
MURCH, G. E., Materials Engineering
OSTWALD, M., Architecture
PAGE, A. W., Civil Engineering
PAGE, N., Mechanical Engineering
SLOAN, S., Civil Engineering
WALL, T. G., Fuels and Combustion Engineering
WEIHE, K., Software Engineering

Faculty of Health (internet www.newcastle.edu.au/faculty/health):
ASHMAN, L., Medical Biochemistry
BOULTON, J., Medical Practice and Population Health
BURNS, G., Medical Biochemistry
CALFORD, M., Human Physiology
CAPRA, M., Health Sciences
CAPRA, S.
CARR, V., Medical Practice and Population Health
COCKBURN, J.
DAY, T.
DUNKLEY, P., Medical Biochemistry
FAHY, K., Nursing and Midwifery
FITZGERALD, M., Clinical Nursing Research
FLETCHER, P.
FORBES, J.
HAZELTON, M.
HENRY, D.
HENSLEY, M., Medicine
KEATINGE, D., Paediatrics
KELLY, B.
MADJAR, I., Nursing
MARLEY, J.
MCMILLAN, M., Nursing
POND, D., Medical Practice and Population Health
POW, D.
ROBERTSON, V.
ROSTAS, J., Medical Biochemistry
SANSON-FISHER, W.
SCOTT, S.
SMITH, R.
SMITH, W.

Faculty of Science (internet www.newcastle.edu.au/faculty/science-it/):
AITKEN, J. R., Biological Sciences
AISBETT, J., Design, Communication and Information Technology
EDDISON, A., Design, Communication and Information Technology
FRASER, B. J., Physics
HOGARTH, W.
LAWRANCE, G. A., Chemistry
MENGERSON, K., Statistics
MICHIE, P., Psychology
PATRICK, J., Environmental and Life Sciences
RAEBURN, I.
RODGER, J.
STARTUP, M.
WILLS, R. B. H., Food Technology

ATTACHED RESEARCH INSTITUTES

Centre for Asia-Pacific Social Transformation Studies: Dir Dr SANTI ROZARIO.

Centre for Biotechnology and Development: Dir Prof. JOHN AITKEN.

Centre for Bulk Materials Handling: Dir Emer. Prof. A. ROBERTS.

Centre for Clinical Epidemiology and Biostatistics: Dir Prof. WAYNE SMITH.

Centre of Excellence for Integrative Legume Research: Dir Assoc. Prof. RAY ROSE.

Centre of Full Employment and Equity: Dir Prof. BILL MITCHELL.

Centre for Health Services Research: Dir Assoc. Prof. ROBERT GIBBERD.

Centre for the Interdisciplinary Study of Property Rights: Dir Dr NANCY E. WRIGHT.

Centre for Literary and Linguistic Computing: Dir Prof. HUGH CRAIG.

Centre for Mental Health Studies: Dir Prof. VAUGHAN CARR.

Centre for Research and Education in Aging: Dir Prof. JULIE BYLES.

Centre for Special Education and Disability Studies: Dir Assoc. Prof. ROBERT CONWAY.

Centre for the Study of Research Training and Impact (SORTI): Dir Assoc. Prof. ALLYSON HOLBROOK.

Centre for Sustainable Use of Coasts and Catchments: Dir Dr BILL GLADSTONE.

Centre for Urban and Regional Studies: Dir Dr PHILLIP O'NEILL.

Children and Education Research Centre: Dir Assoc. Prof. LAURIE MAKIN.

Co-operative Research Centre for Coal in Sustainable Development: Chief Exec Officer FRANK VAN SCHAGEN.

CRC for Satellite Systems: Program Coordinator Prof. B. FRASER.

Cultural Industries and Practices Research Centre: Dir Assoc. Prof. DAVID ROWE.

Employment Studies Centre: Dir Assoc. Prof. JOHN BURGESS.

Family Action Centre: Dir JUDI GEGGIE.

Hunter Medical Research Institute: Dir Prof. JOHN ROSTAS.

Indigenous Higher Education Centre: Dir Prof. JOHN LESTER.

Justice Policy Research Centre: Dir Prof. TED WRIGHT.

Mothers and Babies Research Centre: Dir Prof. ROGER SMITH.

Problem-Based Learning Assessment and Research Centre: Contact KATHY BYRNE.

Research Centre for Gender and Health: Deputy Dir Dr PENNY WARNER-SMITH.

Special Education Centre: Dir Assoc. Prof. ROBERT CONWAY.

Special Research Centre for Industrial Control Science: Dir Prof. G. GOODWIN.

University of Newcastle Legal Centre: Dir (vacant).

NOTRE DAME UNIVERSITY

19 Mouat St, POB 1225, Fremantle 6959, WA
Telephone: (8) 9239-5650
Fax: (8) 9239-5653
E-mail: enquiries@nd.edu.au
Internet: www.nd.edu.au

Founded 1990 by Act of Parliament

Campuses at Broome, Fremantle and Sydney (Broadway and Darlinghurst)
Private control (Archdiocese of Perth)
Language of instruction: English
Academic year: February to December

Vice-Chancellor: Dr PETER TANNOCK
Deputy Vice-Chancellor: Prof. PETER DALLIMORE
Provost: Prof. JENNIFER NICOL
Executive Director, Division of the Vice Chancellery: ALEC O'CONNELL
Executive Director, Finance: GOREY GOREY
Executive Director, Sydney: PETER GLASSON

Library:
Number of teachers: 170
Number of students: 3,000

DEANS

(Broome and Fremantle Campuses):

- College of Arts: Assoc. Prof. SIMON ADAMS
- College of Business: Prof. DEREK PARKIN
- College of Education: Assoc. Prof. MICHAEL O'NEILL
- College of Medicine: Prof. ADRIAN BOWER
- College of Nursing: Assoc. Prof. SELMA ALLIEX
- College of Science and Technology: Prof. BRIAN COLLINS
- College of Theology: Prof. DENNIS ROCHFORD
- School of Law: Prof. MICHAEL GILLOOLY

Sydney Campus:

- College of Arts: Assoc. Prof. SIMON ADAMS
- College of Business: Prof. GEORGE KAILIS
- College of Education: Prof. ALLAN COMAN
- College of Medicine: Prof. MARK MCKENNA
- College of Nursing: Prof. MARGOT KEARNS
- College of Medicine: Prof. MARK MCKENNA
- School of Law: Assoc. Prof. MARY MCCOMISH

UNIVERSITY OF QUEENSLAND

Qld 4072
located at: St Lucia, Brisbane, Qld 4072
Telephone: (7) 3365-1111
Fax: (7) 3365-1199
E-mail: marketing.communications@uq.edu.au
Internet: www.uq.edu.au

Founded 1910

Academic year: January to December (two semesters, and summer semester)

Chancellor: Hon. Sir LLEWELLYN EDWARDS
Deputy Chancellor: Hon. Justice M. J. WHITE
Vice-Chancellor: Prof. J. A. HAY
Senior Deputy Vice-Chancellor: Prof. P. F. GREENFIELD
Deputy Vice-Chancellor for Academic Affairs: Prof. M. D. KENIGER
Deputy Vice-Chancellor for Int. and Devt Affairs: Prof. T. J. GRIGG
Deputy Vice-Chancellor for Research: Prof. D. SIDDLE
Pro-Vice-Chancellor for Teaching and Learning: Prof. DEBBIE J. TERRY
Pro-Vice-Chancellor for Ipswich Campus: Prof. A. G. RIX
Pres. of Academic Board: Prof. M. D. GOULD
Univ. Sec. and Registrar: Prof. D. PORTER
Librarian: K. G. WEBSTER

Library: see Libraries and Archives
Number of teachers: 1,261
Number of students: 38,139

Publication: *University News*

EXECUTIVE DEANS

Faculty of Arts: Assoc. Prof. R. A. FOTHERINGHAM (acting)
Faculty of Biological and Chemical Sciences: Prof. M. MCMANUS
Faculty of Business, Economics and Law: Prof. I. R. ZIMMER
Faculty of Engineering, Physical Sciences and Architecture: Prof. S. J. WALKER
Faculty of Health Sciences: Prof. P. M. BROOKS
Faculty of Natural Resources, Agriculture and Veterinary Science: Prof. R. SWIFT
Faculty of Social and Behavioural Sciences: Prof. D. J. TERRY

HEADS OF SCHOOL

School of Agronomy and Horticulture: Assoc. Prof. A. WEARING
School of Animal Studies: Prof. W. BRYDEN
School of Biomedical Sciences: Prof. D. ADAMS
Business School: Prof. T. BRAILSFORD
School of Dentistry: Prof. L. J. WALSH
School of Economics: Prof. J. FOSTER
School of Education: Prof. P. D. RENSHAN (acting)
School of Engineering: Prof. J. D. LITSTER
School of English, Media Studies and Art History: Prof. T. A. O'REGAN (acting)
School of Geography, Planning and Architecture: Dr M. BELL (acting)
School of Health and Rehabilitation Sciences: Prof. L. HICKSON
School of History, Philosophy, Religion and Classics: Assoc. Prof. R. A. HUTCH
School of Human Movement Studies: Prof. D. MACDONALD
School of Information Technology and Electrical Engineering: Prof. P. BAILES (acting)
School of Integrative Biology: Prof. S. O'NEILL
School of Journalism and Communication: Prof. J. SERVAES
School of Land, Crop and Food Sciences: Assoc. Prof. K. BASFORD
School of Languages and Comparative Cultural Studies: Assoc. Prof. A. MARTINEZ EXPOSITO
School of Law: Prof. C. RICKETT
School of Medicine: Prof. D. WILKINSON
School of Molecular and Microbial Sciences: Prof. A. MCEWAN
School of Music: Prof. P. K. BRACANIN
School of Natural and Rural Systems Management: Assoc. Prof. O. BOSCH
School of Nursing and Midwifery: Prof. E. DAVIES
School of Pharmacy: Prof. P. N. SHAW
School of Physical Sciences: Prof. H. RUBINSZTEIN-DUNLOP
School of Political Science and International Studies: Assoc. Prof. S. R. BELL
School of Population Health: Prof. A. LOPEZ
School of Psychology: Prof. C. E. LEE
School of Social Science: Prof. G. LAWRENCE
School of Social Work and Applied Human Sciences: Assoc. Prof. J. E. R. WILSON
School of Tourism: (vacant)
School of Veterinary Science: Prof. N. MCMENIMAN

PROFESSORS

Arts (Room E206, Level 2, Forgan Smith Bldg, St Lucia Campus, Qld 4072; tel. (7) 3365-1333; fax (7) 3365-2866; e-mail arts@uq.edu.au; internet www.arts.uq.edu.au):

- ALMOND, P. C., History of European Discourses
- BRACANIN, P., Music
- CRYLE, P. M., History of European Discourses
- ELSON, R., History, Philosophy, Religion and Classics
- GRIFFITHS, P., History, Philosophy, Religion and Classics
- HUNTER, I. R., History of European Discourses
- KELLY, V. E., English, Media Studies and Art History
- LATTKE, M. S., History, Philosophy, Religion and Classics
- MOORHEAD, J. A., History, Philosophy, Religion and Classics
- O'REGAN, T., English, Medial Studies and Art History
- SUSSEX, R. D., Languages and Comparative Cultural Studies
- TIFFIN, H. M., English, Media Studies and Art History
- TURNER, G., Critical and Cultural Studies

WHITLOCK, G., English, Media Studies and Art History

Biological and Chemical Sciences (Room 313, Level 3, Computer Science Bldg, St Lucia Campus, Qld 4072; tel. (7) 3365-1888; fax (7) 3365-1613; e-mail bacs.enquiries@uq.edu.au; internet bacs.uq.edu.au):

ADAMS, D. J., Biomedical Sciences
BIRCH, R., Integrative Biology
BOWLING, F., Molecular and Microbial Sciences
BROAD, T., Biological and Chemical Sciences
CAMPBELL, G. R., Biomedical Sciences
CAMPBELL, J. H., Bioengineering and Nanotechnology
CRITCHLEY, C., Integrative Biology
DEGNAN, B. M., Integrative Biology
DRENNAN, J., Microscopy and Microanalysis
GRESSHOFF, P. M., Integrative Legume Research
GRIGG, G. C., Integrative Biology
HOEGH-GULDBERG, O., Marine Studies
IRWIN, J. A. G., Integrative Biology, Tropical Plant Protection
JENNINGS, M. P., Molecular and Microbial Sciences
KEY, B., Biomedical Sciences
KITCHING, W., Molecular and Microbial Sciences
MCEWAN, A., Molecular and Microbial Sciences
MCMANUS, M. E., Biological and Chemical Sciences
MINCHIN, R., Biomedical Sciences
NORTON, G. A., Biological Information Technology
O'NEILL, S., Integrative Biology
PETTIGREW, J. D., Vision, Touch and Hearing Research
POSSINGHAM, H., Integrative Biology; Ecology Centre
SMITH, R. W., Molecular and Microbial Sciences
SMITH, S., Molecular and Microbial Sciences
TAYLOR, S. M., Biomedical Sciences
TINDLE, R. W., Clinical Medical Virology Centre
TOTH, I., Molecular and Microbial Sciences
TRAU, M., Bioengineering and Nanotechnology
WENTRUP, C., Molecular and Microbial Sciences
ZALUCKI, M. P., Integrative Biology

Business, Economics and Law (Room 233, Level 2, Colin Clark Bldg, St Lucia Campus, Qld 4072; tel. (7) 3365-7111; fax (7) 3365-4788; e-mail facbel@bel.uq.edu.au; internet www.bel.uq.edu.au):

ALLAN, J. F. P., Law
ASHKANASY, N. M., Business
BALLANTYNE, R. R., Tourism
BRAILSFORD, T., Business
CALLAN, V. J., Business
CAMPBELL, H. F., Economics
CLARKSON, P., Business
COELLI, T., Economics
COOPER, C., Tourism
CORNWELL, T. B., Business
DE LACY, T., Tourism and Leisure Management
DEVEREUX, J., Law
DODGSON, M., Technology and Innovation Management
FINN, F. J., Business, Economics and Law
FOSTER, J., Economics
GRANTHAM, R. B., Law
GRAY, S., Business
KIEL, G. C., Business
LIESCH, P. W., Business
MCCOLL-KENNEDY, J., Business
MANGAN, J. E., Economics
O'KEEFE, T., Business
PURI, K., Law
QUIGGIN, J., Economics
RAO, P., Economics
RATNAPALA, A. S., Law
RICKETT, C., Law
SHERMAN, B. G., Law
WILTSHIRE, K. W., Business
ZIMMER, I., Business, Economics and Law

Engineering, Physical Sciences and Architecture (Room S204, Level 2, Hawken Engineering Bldg, St Lucia Campus, Qld 4072; tel. (7) 3365-4777; fax (7) 3365-4444; e-mail admin@epsa.uq.edu.au; internet www.epsa.uq.edu.au):

ANDRESEN, B., Architecture
BAILES, P. A., Information Technology and Electrical Engineering
BELL, M. J., Geography, Planning and Architecture
BERGMANN, N., Information Technology and Electrical Engineering
BHATIA, S. K., Chemical Engineering
BIALKOWSKI, M. E., Information Technology and Electrical Engineering
BLACKALL, L. L., Advanced Wastewater Management Centre
BRACKEN, A. J., Mathematics
BREMHORST, K., Mechanical Engineering
BRERETON, D., Social Responsibility in Mining
BURRAGE, K., Advanced Computational Modelling Centre
CAMERON, I. T., Chemical Engineering
CHARLES, P. M., Civil Engineering
COLLERSON, K. D., Earth Sciences
CROZIER, S., Information Technology and Electrical Engineering
DARVENIZA, M., Information Technology and Electrical Engineering
DO, D. D., Chemical Engineering
DOBSON, A. J., Population Health
DRUMMOND, P. D., Physics
ECCLESTON, J. A., Physical Sciences
FRANZIDIS, J., Mineral Research Centre
GALLOWAY, G. J., Magnetic Resonance
GURGENCI, H., Mechanical Engineering
HANSON, G. R., Magnetic Resonance
HAYES, I. J., Information Technology and Electrical Engineering
HAYES, P. C., Mining and Minerals Process Engineering
HUNDLOE, T. J., Geography, Planning and Architecture
JAMES, D. C., Chemical Engineering
JOY, J., Minerals Industry Safety and Health Centre
KELLER, J., Advanced Wastewater Management Centre
KUBIK, K. K. T., Information Technology and Electrical Engineering
LEVER, P. J., Mining and Minerals Process Engineering
LINDSAY, P., Information Technology and Electrical Engineering
LITSTER, J. D., Engineering
LU, G., Engineering
MCKEE, D. J., Sustainable Minerals Institute
MCLACHLAN, G. J., Mathematics
MILBURN, G. J., Quantum Computer Technology
MORA, P., Earth Systems Science Computational Centre
MORGAN, R., Mechanical Engineering
MÜHLHAUS, H. B., Earth System Science Computational Centre
NIELSEN, L. K., Chemical Engineering
NIELSEN, M. A., Physical Sciences
ORLOWSKA, M. E., Information Technology and Electrical Engineering
PAILTHORPE, B., Physical Sciences
POLLETT, P. K., Mathematics
RADCLIFFE, D. F., Mechanical Engineering
RUBINSZTEIN-DUNLOP, H., Physics
RUDOLPH, V., Chemical Engineering
SAHA, T. K., Information Technology and Electrical Engineering
SANDERSON, P., Information Technology and Electrical Engineering
SCHAFFER, G. B., Materials Engineering
SIMMONS, J. M., Mechanical Engineering
ST JOHN, D. H., Materials Engineering
STALKER, R. J., Mechanical Engineering
STIMSON, R. J., Geography, Planning and Architecture
WHITEN, W. J., Mineral Research Centre
WHITTAKER, A. K., Magnetic Resonance
ZHOU, X., Information Technology and Electrical Engineering

Health Sciences (Level 1, Edith Cavell Bldg, Royal Brisbane Hospital, Herston, Qld; tel. (7) 3365-5342; fax (7) 3365-5533; e-mail healthsciences@uq.edu.au; internet www.uq.edu.au/health):

ABERNETHY, A. B., Human Movement Studies
BELLAMY, N., Population Health; Medicine
BETT, J., Medicine
BICKEL, M., Dentistry
BLACK, B., Surgery
BOWLING, F. G., Medicine
BOYD, A. W., Experimental Haematology
BROOKS, P., Health Sciences
BROWN, W. J., Human Movement Studies
BURGESS, P., Health Systems Division
BUSH, R., Population Health
CARSON, R. G., Human Movement Studies
CATTS, S., Psychiatry
CHAN, F. Y., Medicine
CLEGHORN, G. J., Medicine
COLDITZ, P. B., Obstetrics and Gynaecology
COMAN, W. B., Surgery
COOKSLEY, W. G. E., Medicine
DAVIES, E. A., Nursing and Midwifery
DICKINSON, R. G., Medicine
DOBSON, A. J., Population Health
DODD, B. J., Obstetrics and Gynaecology
DONALD, K. J., Medicine
ELLIS, N. M., Centre for Military and Veterans' Health
EVANS, L. E. J., Psychiatry
FAWCETT, J., Surgery
FRAZER, I. H., Immunology and Cancer Research
GEFFEN, L. B., Psychiatry
GONDA, T. J., Immunology and Cancer Research
GOTLEY, D., Surgery
GOUGH, I. R., Surgery
GRAY, L., Medicine
HALL, W. D., Population Health
HODGES, P., Health and Rehabilitation Sciences
HOY, W. E., Medicine
JAMROZIK, K. D., Health Systems Division
JOHNSON, D. W., Medicine
JONES, I. S. C., Obstetrics and Gynaecology
JULL, G. A., Health and Rehabilitation Sciences
KAVANAGH, D. J., Psychiatry
KHOO, S. K., Obstetrics and Gynaecology
LAKHANI, S., Molecular and Cellular Pathology
LAVIN, M. F., Surgery
LOPEZ, A., Population Health
MACDONALD, D., Human Movement Studies
MARTIN, G., Psychiatry
MARWICK, T., Medicine
MEYERS, I. A., Dentistry
MOORE, M. R., Environmental Toxicology
MORTIMER, R., Medicine
MURDOCH, B. E., Health and Rehabilitation Sciences
MYERS, P. T., Human Movement Studies
NAJMAN, J. M., Public Health
O'ROURKE, M. G. E., Medicine
OWEN, N., Population Health
PEARN, J. H., Medicine
PENDER, M. P., Medicine

RILEY, I. D., Population Health
ROBERTS, M. S., Medicine
SAUNDERS, J. B., Psychiatry
SEYMOUR, G. J., Dentistry
SHAW, P. N., Pharmacy
SMITH, M. T., Pharmacy
STRONG, J., Health and Rehabilitation Sciences
TAYLOR, R. J., Population Health
TETT, S., Pharmacy
THOMAS, R., Immunology, Metabolic Medicine and Cancer Research
TINNING, R. I., Human Movement Studies
TOTH, I., Pharmacy
TUDEHOPE, D. I., Paediatrics and Child Health
WALSH, L. J., Dentistry
WHITEFORD, H. A., Health Systems
WILKINSON, D., Medicine
WILLIAMS, G. M., International Health
WILSON, A., Public Health
WOOTTON, R., Online Health
YELLOWLEES, P. M., Military and Veterans' Health

Natural Resources, Agriculture and Veterinary Science (N. W. Britton Admin. Bldg (No. 8101), Gatton Campus, Qld; tel. (7) 5460-1276; fax (7) 5460-1204; e-mail nravs.enquiries@uqg.uq.edu.au; internet www.uq.edu.au/nravs):

ATWELL, R. B., Veterinary Science
BASFORD, K. E., Land, Crop and Food Sciences
BOSCH, O. J. H., Natural and Rural Systems Management
BRYDEN, W. L., Animal Studies
BURNS, R. G., Land, Crop and Food Sciences
D'OCCHIO, M., Beef Genetic Technologies
FUKAI, S., Land, Crop and Food Sciences
GIDLEY, M., Nutrition and Food Sciences
HUNDLOE, T., Geography, Planning and Architecture
JOYCE, D. C., Native Floriculture
PHILLIPS, C. J., Animal Welfare and Ethics
POLLITT, C. C., Veterinary Science
RAND, J. S., Veterinary Science
ROSS, H., Natural and Rural Systems Management
TAYLOR, J. A., Natural and Rural Systems Management
WILLIAMS, R. R., Land, Crop and Food Sciences
WOODS, E. J., Natural and Rural Systems Management

Social and Behavioural Sciences (Room S423, Level 4, Social Sciences Bldg, St Lucia Campus, Qld 4072; tel. (7) 3365-7487; fax (7) 3346-9136; e-mail sbs@uq.edu.au; internet www.uq.edu.au/sbs):

ASHMAN, A. F., Education
BARTLETT, H., Ageing
BAXTER, J. H., Social Science
BOREHAM, P., Political Science and International Studies; Social Research
CLEMENTS, K., Australian Centre for Peace and Conflict
GALLOIS, C., Psychology; Social Research in Communication
GEFFEN, G. M., Psychology
HOGG, M. A., Psychology
HUMPHREYS, M.., Psychology; Human Factors and Applied Cognitive Psychology
LAWRENCE, G., Social Science
LEE, C., Psychology
LUKE, C., Education
NAJMAN, J. M., Social Science
OEI, T. P. S., Psychology
PETERSON, C. L., Psychology
PITMAN, J., Education
POWER, C., Education
QUIGGIN, J., Economics
ROSENMAN, L. S., Social Work and Applied Human Sciences
SANDERS, M. R., Psychology
SERVAES, J., Journalism and Communication
TERRY, D., Social and Behavioural Sciences

AFFILIATED RESIDENTIAL COLLEGES

Cromwell College: Principal Rev. Dr H. M. BEGBIE.

Duchesne College: Principal N. KAY.

Emmanuel College: Principal Dr S. GILL.

Gatton Halls of Residence: Principal S. SCOTT.

Grace College: Principal Dr S. FAIREY.

International House: Dir Dr C. TROMANS.

King's College: Master G. EDDY.

St. John's College: Warden Rev. Prof. J. MORGAN.

St Leo's College: Rector V. SKELLY.

Union College: Warden P. E. FRASER.

The Women's College: Principal Dr M. G. W. AITKEN.

ATTACHED RESEARCH INSTITUTES; (ALL AT UNIVERSITY OF QUEENSLAND, BRISBANE, UNLESS NOTED OTHERWISE)

Aboriginal Environments Research Centre: Dir Assoc. Prof. P. C. MEMMOTT.

Advanced Computational Modelling Centre: Dir Prof. K. BURRAGE.

Advanced Wastewater Management Centre: Dir Dr J. KELLER.

Australasian Centre on Ageing: Dir Prof. H. BARTLETT.

Australian Biosecurity Co-operative Research Centre: Emerging Infectious Disease: Dir Dr S. PROWSE.

ARC Centre for Complex Systems: Dir Prof. P. LINDSAY.

ARC Centre of Excellence for Quantum Computer Technology (University of Queensland node): Man. Assoc. Prof. T. C. RALPH.

ARC Centre for Functional Nanomaterials: Dir Prof. G. Q. LU.

Australian Centre for Complementary Medicine, Education and Research: Dir Prof. S. P. MYERS.

Australian Centre for Intellectual Property in Agriculture: Dir Prof. B. SHERMAN.

Australian Centre for International and Tropical Health and Nutrition (ACITHN): Dir Prof. H. B. KAY.

Australian Centre for Minerals Extension and Research: Man. R. MCLEAN.

Australian Centre for Peace and Conflict Studies: Dir Prof. K. P. CLEMENTS.

Australian Equine Genetics Research Centre (AEGRC): Dir Prof. A. E. O. TRESIZE.

Australian Institute for Bioengineering and Nanotechnology: Dir PETER GRAY.

Australian Research Council Centre of Excellence for Integrative Legume Research: Dir Prof. P. M. GRESSHOFF.

Australian Research Council Centre of Excellence for Quantum-Atom Optics (Queensland node): Dir Prof. P. D. DRUMMOND.

Australian Research Council Centre of Excellence in Biotechnology and Development (Queensland node): Dir Prof. P. KOOPMAN.

Australian Research Council Key Centre for Human Factors and Applied Cognitive Psychology: Dir Prof. P. SANDERSON.

Australian Studies Centre: Dir Dr D. CARTER.

Behaviour Research and Therapy Centre: Dir Dr P. H. HARNETT.

Brisbane Surface Analysis Facility: Dir Assoc. Prof. I. R. GENTLE.

Burns, Trauma and Critical Care Research Centre: Dir Prof. J. LIPMAN.

Cancer Prevention Research Centre: Dir Prof. N. OWEN.

Catalyst Research Centre for Society and Technology: Dir Prof. D. RADCLIFFE.

Centre for Animal Welfare and Ethics: Dir Prof. C. J. C. PHILLIPS.

Centre for Applied History and Heritage Studies: Dir Dr G. A. C. GINN.

Centre for Bacterial Diversity and Identification: Dir Assoc. Prof. L. I. SLY.

Centre for Biological Information Technology: Dir Prof. G. NORTON.

Centre for Biomolecular Engineering: Dir Prof. A. P. J. MIDDLEBERG.

Centre for Biophotonics and Laser Science: Dir Prof. H. RUBINSZTEIN-DUNLOP.

Centre for Buddhist Studies: Co-Dirs Prof. T. DITRICH, Dr P. PECENKO.

Centre for Burden of Disease and Cost-Effectiveness: Dir Assoc. Prof. T. VOS.

Centre for Business Forensics: Dir Dr L. CHAPPLE.

Centre for Companion Animal Health: Dir Prof. J. RAND.

Centre for Computational Molecular Science: Dir Prof. S. C. SMITH.

Centre for Corporate Valuation: Co-Dirs Prof. A. GRAY, Prof. T. O'KEEFE.

Centre for Critical and Cultural Studies: Dir Prof. G. TURNER.

Centre for Discrete Mathematics and Computing: Dir Assoc. Prof. E. J. BILLINGTON.

Centre for Efficiency and Productivity Analysis: Dir Prof. D. S. P. RAO.

Centre for High Performance Polymers: Dir Assoc. Prof. P. HALLEY.

Centre for History of European Discourses: Dir Prof. P. CRYLE.

Centre for Hypersonics: Dir Prof. R. G. MORGAN.

Centre for Immunology and Cancer Research (CICR): Dir Prof. I. H. FRAZER.

Centre for Integrated Resource Management (CIRM): Exec. Dir Assoc. Prof. J. J. MOTT.

Centre for International Journalism: Dir Dr E. LOUW.

Centre for Magnetic Resonance (CMR): Dir Prof. I. M. BRERETON.

Centre for Marine Studies (CMS): Dir Prof. O. HOEGH-GULDBERG.

Centre for Mathematical Physics: Dir Dr J. R. LINKS.

Centre for Mathematics and Statistics of Complex Systems: an Australian Research Council Centre of Excellence (Queensland node): Dir Prof. P. K. POLLETT.

Centre for Medical Education: Dir Assoc. Prof. R. PETERSON.

Centre for Metals in Biology: Dir Prof. P. V. BERNARDT.

Centre for Microscopy and Microanalysis (CMM): Dir Prof. J. DRENNAN.

Centre for Military and Veterans' Health: Dir Prof. N. ELLIS.

Centre for Mined Land Rehabilitation (CMLR): Dir Dr D. MULLIGAN.

Centre for Nanotechnology and Biomaterials: Dir Prof. M. TRAU.

Centre for Native Floriculture: Dir Prof. D. C. JOYCE.

Centre for Nutrition and Food Sciences: Dir Prof. M. GIDLEY.

Centre for Online Health: Dir Prof. R. WOOTTON.

Centre for Organisational Psychology: Dir Dr R. MARTIN.

Centre for Pesticide Application and Safety: Dir A. J. HEWITT.

Centre for Physical Activity and Sport Education: Man. M. SIMJANOVIC.

Centre for Public, International and Comparative Law: Dir Prof. S. RATNAPALA.

Centre for Remote Sensing and Spatial Information Science: Dir Assoc. Prof. S. R. PHINN.

Centre for Research in Language Processing and Linguistics: Co-Dirs Assoc. Prof. J. WILES, Assoc. Prof. H. CHENERY, Dr J. INGRAM.

Centre for Research in Vascular Biology: Dir Prof. J. H. CAMPBELL.

Centre for Research into Sustainable Urban and Regional Futures (CRSURF): Dir Prof. R. J. STIMSON.

Centre for Research on Group Processes: Dir Dr M. HORNSEY.

Centre for Research on Women, Gender, Culture and Social Change: Dir Assoc. Prof. C. FERRIER.

Centre for Rural and Regional Innovation–Queensland: Dir Assoc. Prof. J. ALLISON.

Centre for Social Research in Communication: Dir Prof. C. GALLOIS.

Centre for Social Responsibility in Mining: Dir Prof. D. BRERETON.

Centre for Statistics: Dir Prof. G. J. MCLACHLAN.

Centre for Sustainable Design: Dir Assoc. Prof. R. HYDE.

Centre for Transport Strategy: Dir Prof. P. M. CHARLES.

Centre for Water Futures: Dir Dr D. A. LOCKINGTON.

Centre for Water in the Minerals Industry: Dir Prof. C. MORAN.

Centre of National Research on Disability and Rehabilitation Medicine (CONROD): Dir Prof. N. BELLAMY.

Children's Nutrition Research Centre: Dir Prof. G. CLEGHORN.

Clinical Medical Virology Centre: Dir Prof. R. TINDLE.

Cognitive Psychophysiology Laboratory: Co-Dirs Prof. G. M. GEFFEN, Prof. L. B. GEFFEN.

Communication Disability in Ageing Research Centre: Co-Dirs Assoc. Prof. L. HICKSON, Prof. L. E. WORRALL.

Co-operative Research Centre for Aboriginal Health: Dir Prof. A. LOPEZ.

Co-operative Research Centre for Australasian Invasive Animals: Dir Prof. W. BRYDEN.

Co-operative Research Centre for Beef Genetic Technologies: Dir Prof. M. D'OCCHIO.

Co-operative Research Centre for Cast Metals Manufacturing (CAST): CEO Prof. D. ST JOHN.

Co-operative Research Centre for Chronic Inflammatory Diseases: CEO Prof. J. HAMILTON.

Co-operative Research Centre for Coal in Sustainable Development: Dir F. VAN SCHAGEN.

Co-operative Research Centre for Coastal Zone, Estuary and Waterway Management: CEO Dr R. FEARON.

Co-operative Research Centre for Contamination Assessment and Remediation of the Environment: Dir Prof. R. SWIFT.

Co-operative Research Centre for Enterprise Distributed Systems Technology: CEO M. GIBSON.

Co-operative Research Centre for Environmental Biotechnology: Exec. Dir Dr D. GARMAN.

Co-operative Research Centre for Interaction Design: Co-Dirs Dr M. BRERETON, Dr M. DOCHERTY.

Co-operative Research Centre for Mining: CEO Prof. M. HOOD.

Co-operative Research Centre for Polymers: Dir Assoc. Prof. P. HALLEY.

Co-operative Research Centre for Rail: CEO Prof. D. ROACH.

Co-operative Research Centre for Sugar Industry Innovation through Biotechnology: Dir Dr P. TWINE.

Co-operative Research Centre for Sustainable Aquaculture of Finfish: Dir Dr P. MONTAGUE.

Co-operative Research Centre for Sustainable Resource Processing: Dir Prof. D. MCKEE.

Co-operative Research Centre for Sustainable Tourism: Dir Prof. T. DE LACY.

Co-operative Research Centre for Tropical Plant Protection: CEO Prof. J. IRWIN.

Co-operative Research Centre for Tropical Rainforest Ecology and Management: Dir Prof. N. STORK.

Co-operative Research Centre for Tropical Savannas Management: Dir Prof. G. DUFF.

Co-operative Research Centre for Water Quality and Treatment: Dir Prof. D. BURSILL.

Earth Systems Science Computational Centre (ESSC): Dir Prof. P. MORA.

The Ecology Centre: Dir Prof. H. PAOSSINGHAM.

Endocrine Hypertension Research Centre: Dir Assoc. Prof. M. STOWASSER.

Environmental Management Unit: Dir Dr D. MCPHEE.

Fred and Eleanor Schonell Special Education Research Centre: Dir Dr C. E. VAN KRAAYENOORD.

ISMC Solutions Pty Ltd: Dir (vacant).

Institute for Molecular Bioscience: Dir Prof. B. J. WAINWRIGHT.

International Relations and Asian Politics Research Unit: Dir (vacant).

Julius Kruttschnitt Mineral Research Centre (JKMRC): Dir Prof. B. J. I. ADAIR.

Marine and Shipping Law Unit: Dir Assoc. Prof. S. DERRINGTON.

Minerals Industry Safety and Health Centre: Dir Prof. J. JOY.

Motor Speech Research Centre: Dir Prof. B. E. MURDOCH.

National Heart Foundation and Prince Charles Hospital Foundation Cardiovascular Research Centre: Dir Prof. M. J. WEST.

Nanomaterials Centre (NanoMac): Dir Prof. G. Q. LU.

National Research Centre for Environmental Toxicology (NRCET): Dir Prof. M. R. MOORE.

Neuroimmunology Research Centre: Dir Prof. M. P. PENDER.

Parker CRC for Integrated Hydrometallurgy Solutions: Dir M. WOFFENDEN.

Particle and Systems Design Centre: Co-Dirs Assoc. Prof. I. T. CAMERON, Prof. J. D. LISTER.

Perinatal Research Centre: Dir Prof. P. B. COLDITZ.

Protein Research Centre: Dir Assoc. Prof. P. A. KROON.

Pyrometallurgy Research Centre: Dir Prof. P. HAYES.

Queensland Alcohol and Drug Research Education Centre: Dir Prof. J. NAJMAN.

Queensland Brain Institute: Dir Prof. P. BARTLETT.

Queensland Centre for Intellectual and Developmental Disability: Dir Assoc. Prof. N. LENNOX.

Queensland Centre for Population Research: Dir Prof. M. BELL.

Queensland Centre for Public Health: UQ Coordinator Dr A. CLAVARINO.

Queensland Liver Transplant Unit: Dir Prof. J. FAWCETT.

Rangelands Australia: Dir Prof. J. TAYLOR.

Renal Research Centre: Dir Prof. D. JOHNSON.

Rotary Centre for International Studies in Peace and Conflict Resolution: Dir Dr M. HANSON.

Social Research Centre: Co-Dirs Prof. P. BOREHAM, Assoc. Prof. M. WESTERN.

Special Research Centre for Functional and Applied Genomics: Deputy Dir Prof. D. HUME.

Sustainable Minerals Institute: Dir Prof. D. MCKEE.

Technology and Innovation Management Centre: Dir Prof. M. DODGSON.

Tropical and Subtropical Weeds Research Unit: Dir Assoc. Prof. S. ADKINS.

University of Queensland Archeological Services Unit: Dir Dr J. M. PRANGNELL.

University of Queensland Blue Care Research and Practice Development Centre: Dir Prof. D. HEGNEY.

Vision, Touch and Hearing Research Centre: Dir Prof. J. D. PETTIGREW.

W. H. Bryan Mining Geology Research Centre: Dir C. G. ALFORD.

QUEENSLAND UNIVERSITY OF TECHNOLOGY

GPO Box 2434, Brisbane, Qld 4001
Telephone: (7) 3864-2111
Fax: (7) 3864-1510
E-mail: qutinformation@qut.edu.au
Internet: www.qut.edu.au

Founded 1965; Brisbane CAE merged with the Univ. 1990
State control
Chancellor: Dr C. HIRST
Vice-Chancellor: Prof. O. P. COALDRAKE
Deputy Vice-Chancellor: Prof. D. GARDINER (acting)
Pro Vice-Chancellor (Information and Academic Services): T. COCHRANE
Pro Vice-Chancellor (Research and Advancement): Prof. J. GOUGH (acting)
Executive Director, Finance and Resource Planning: P. SULLIVAN (acting)
Registrar: Dr C. DICKENSON
Librarian: G. AUSTEN
Library of 672,000 vols
Number of students: 34,000
Publications: *Inside QUT*, *Annual Report*

DEANS

Built Environment and Engineering: Prof. W. P. CHANG
Business: Prof. S. HARDING
Creative Industries: Prof. JOHN HARTLEY
Education: Prof. V. MCLEAN
Health: Prof. K. J. BOWMAN
Information Technology: Prof. K. J. GOUGH
Law: Prof. M. COPE
QUT Carseldine: Prof. RUTH MATCHETT
Science: Prof. G. GEORGE

PROFESSORS

ABBEY, J., Nursing
ARMSTRONG, H., Design and Built Environment
ARNOLD, N., Advertising, Marketing and Public Relations
ARTHURS, A., Music
BETTS, M., Faculty Office (Built Environment and Engineering)
BOASHASH, B., Electrical and Electronic Systems
BOULTON-LEWIS, G., Learning and Professional Studies
BOWMAN, K., Faculty Office (Health)
BOYCE, G., International Business
BOYD, T., Construction Management and Property
BROMLEY, M., Journalism
CAELLI, W., Data Communications
CARNEY, L., Optometry
CHANG, A., Nursing
CLEMENTS, J., Life Science
COALDRAKE, P., Chancellery
COLLIER, B., Law
COOPER, T., Mathematics, Science and Technology Education
COPE, M., Faculty Office (Law)
CORONES, S., Law Research
COURTNEY, M., Nursing
CRAWFORD, R., Mechanical, Manufacturing and Medical Engineering
CUNNINGHAM, S., Creative Industries Research and Applications Centre
DALE, J., Faculty Office (Science)
DAWSON, E., Data Communications
DOUGLAS, E., Brisbane Graduate School of Business
DUNCAN, W., Law
EDWARDS, H., Nursing
ENGLISH, L., Mathematics, Science and Technology Education
FERREIRA, L., Civil Engineering
FISHER, D., Law
FITZGERALD, B., Law School
GABLE, G., Information Systems
GARDINER, D., Chancellery
GARDNER, I., Life Science
GEORGE, G., Faculty Office (Science)
GIBSON, D., Chancellery
GOUGH, J., Research and Advancement
GRIFFIN, M., Faculty Office (Business)
HAMPSON, K., Co-operative Research Centre for Construction
HARDING, S., Faculty Office (Business)
HARTLEY, J., Faculty Office (Creative Industries)
HERINGTON, A., Life Science
HOCKINGS, J., Design and Built Environment
HUDSON, P., Life Science
HURN, A., Economics and Finance
JONES, J., Creative Industries Research and Applications Centre
KABANOFF, B., Management
LANE, W., Law School
LAVERY, P., Creative Industries Faculty Advancement
LAYTON, A., Economics and Finance
LEDWICH, G., Electrical and Electronic Systems
LEHMANN, S., Design and Built Environment
LITTLE, P., Accountancy
MAEDER, A., Electrical and Electronic Systems
MAHENDRAN, M., Civil Engineering
MATCHETT, R., QUT Carseldine
MATHEW, J., Mechanical, Manufacturing and Medical Engineering
MCELWAIN, D., Mathematics
MCGREGOR-LOWNDES, M., Centre of Philanthropy and Non-profit Studies
MCLEAN, V., Faculty Office (Education)
MCROBBIE, C., Mathematics, Science and Technology Education
MCWILLIAM, E., Cultural and Language Studies in Education
MOODY, M., Electrical and Electronic Systems Engineering
NEWMAN, B., Public Health
OLDENBURG, B., Public Health
PARKER, A., Human Movement Studies
PATTI, C., Advertising, Marketing and Public Relations
PATTON, W., Learning and Professional Studies
PEARCY, M., Mechanical, Manufacturing and Medical Engineering
PETTITT, A., Mathematics
PHAM, B., Information Technology
POPE, J., Physical Sciences
RENFORTH, W., Business
RYAN, N., Management
SARA, V., Life Science
SHEEHAN, M., Psychology and Counselling
SIDWELL, A., Construction Management and Property
SKITMORE, R., Construction Management and Property
SRIDHARAN, S., Electrical and Electronic Systems
TAYLER, C., Early Childhood
THAMBIRATNAM, D., Civil Engineering
TOWERS, S., Creative Industries Faculty Academic Programs
TROCKI, C., Humanities and Human Services
TROUTBECK, R., Civil Engineering
WALDERSEE, R., Business
WILLETT, R., Accountancy
WISSLER, R., Research and Advancement
YOUNG, R., Psychology and Counselling

ROYAL MELBOURNE INSTITUTE OF TECHNOLOGY

GPO Box 2476V, Melbourne, Vic. 3001
Telephone: (3) 9925-2000
Fax: (3) 9663-2764
Internet: www.rmit.edu.au

Founded 1887; university status 1992
Academic year: February to November

Chancellor: Prof. DENNIS GIBSON
Vice-Chancellor Higher Education and TAFE: Prof. RUTH DUNKIN
Pro Vice-Chancellors: Prof. MARGARET JACKSON (Business), Prof. BELINDA PROBERT (acting) (Design and the Social Context), CAMERON MORONEY (Finance and Business Services), Dr MADELEINE REEVE (International Enterprise and Community Development), COLIN SHARP (Organisational Capability and Development), Prof. NEIL FURLONG (Research and Innovation), Prof. DAINE ALCORN (Science, Engineering and Technology), Prof. HELEN PRAETZ (Students), Prof. GAIL HART (Teaching and Learning)
Academic Registrar: SUE JELLETT
Library Director: KAREN JOHNSON (acting)

Library of 1,221,500 vols
Number of students: 55,515

Publications: *Annual Report*, *Research Highlights* (annually), *RMIT Openline* (university news, 5 a year)

DEANS

Faculty of Applied Science: Prof. MALCOLM MCCORMICK
Faculty of Art, Design and Communication: Prof. ROBIN WILLIAMS
Faculty of Business: Prof. MARGARET JACKSON
Faculty of Constructed Environment: Prof. BELINDA PROBERT
Faculty of Education, Language and Community Services: Prof. MARY KALANTZIS
Faculty of Engineering: Prof. ROBERT SNOW
Faculty of Life Sciences: Prof. ALEX RADLOFF

ATTACHED CENTRES

Centre for Advanced Technology in Telecommunications (CATT): Dir Prof. RICHARD HARRIS.

Centre for Applied Social Research: Dir Assoc. Prof. JOHN MURPHY.

Centre for Design at RMIT: Dir HELEN LEWIS (acting).

Centre for Management Quality Research: Dir Prof. JOHN DALRYMPLE.

Centre for Youth Affairs Research and Development: Dir DAVID MACKENZIE.

Co-operative Research Centre for Advanced Composite Structures: RMIT Contact Prof. ROBERT SNOW.

Co-operative Research Centre for Australian Photonics: RMIT Contact Prof. IAN BATES.

Co-operative Research Centre for Australian Telecommunications: RMIT Contact Prof. NEIL FURLONG.

Co-operative Research Centre for Construction Innovation: RMIT Contact Prof. ARUN KUMAR.

Co-operative Research Centre for Intelligent Manufacturing Systems and Technologies: RMIT Contact Prof. IAN BATES.

Co-operative Research Centre for Microtechnology: RMIT Contact Prof. DAVID MAINWARING.

Co-operative Research Centre for Polymers: RMIT Contact Prof. DAVID MAINWARING.

Co-operative Research Centre for SMART Internet Technology: RMIT Contact Prof. NEIL FURLONG.

Co-operative Research Centre for Water Quality and Treatment: RMIT Contact Prof. IAN BATES.

Microelectronics and Materials Technology Centre: Dir Prof. MICHAEL AUSTIN.

Rheology and Materials Processing Centre: Dir Prof. SATI N. BHATTACHARYA.

RMIT Multimedia Database Systems: Dir Prof. RON SACKS-DAVIS.

Sir Lawrence Wackett Centre for Aerospace Design Technology: Dir Prof. MURRAY SCOTT.

Transport Research Centre: Dir Assoc. Prof. JENNY MORRIS.

UNIVERSITY OF SOUTH AUSTRALIA

GPO Box 2471, Adelaide, SA 5001
Telephone: (8) 8302-6611
Fax: (8) 8302-2466
Internet: www.unisa.edu.au

Founded 1991 by the merger of the South Australian Institute of Technology and three campuses of the South Australian College of Advanced Education; campuses at City East, City West, Magill, Mawson Lakes, Underdale and Whyalla
Autonomous (established by Act of Parliament)
Academic year: January to December

Chancellor: DAVID KLINGBERG
Vice-Chancellor and President: Prof. DENISE BRADLEY

Executive Director and Vice-President (Finance and Resources): PAUL BEARD
Executive Director and Vice-President (International and Development): Dr ANNA CICCARELLI
Pro-Vice-Chancellor (Access and Learning Support): Prof. PETER LEE
Pro-Vice-Chancellor (Division of Business and Enterprise): Prof. GERRY GRIFFIN
Pro-Vice-Chancellor (Division of Health Sciences): Prof. ROBYN MCDERMOTT
Pro-Vice-Chancellor (Division of Information Technology, Engineering and the Environment): Prof. ROBIN KING
Pro-Vice-Chancellor (Education, Arts and Social Sciences): Prof. MICHAEL ROWAN
Pro-Vice-Chancellor (Organisational Strategy and Change): Prof. HILARY WINCHESTER
Pro-Vice-Chancellor (Research and Innovation): Prof. CAROLINE MCMILLEN
Director of Student and Academic Services: LUCY SCHULZ
Director of Library Services: HELEN LIVINGSTON

Library of 1,000,000 vols
Number of teachers: 983
Number of students: 32,187

Publications: *Bi-Annual Report*, *UniSA Researcher* (electronic, 6 a year)

HEADS OF SCHOOLS

Division of Education, Arts and Social Sciences:
- School of Education (Underdale Campus): Prof. MARIE BRENNAN
- School of Education (Magill Campus): Assoc. Prof. J. HARPER
- School of Communication,Information and New Media: Assoc. Prof. MICHAEL GALVIN
- School of International Studies: Dr GIANCARLO CHIRO
- School of Psychology: Dr JACQUES METZER
- School of Social Work and Social Policy: Assoc. Prof. ADRIAN VICARY
- Louis Laybourne-Smith School of Architecture and Design: Prof. MADS GAARDBOE
- South Australian School of Art: Prof. KAY LAWRENCE
- Unaipon School: Assoc. Prof. DAVID ROBERTS
- DeLissa Institute of Early Childhood and Family Studies: Prof. WENDY SCHILLER

Division of Business and Enterprise:
- School of Accounting and Information Systems: Assoc. Prof. DAVID RIVETT
- School of International Business: Assoc. Prof. GEOFF PAGE
- School of Marketing: Prof. GUS GEURSEN (acting)
- International Graduate School of Management: Prof. HELEN THORNE

Division of Health Sciences:
- School of Health Sciences: Dr SARA JONES
- School of Nursing and Midwifery: Prof. ANNETTE SUMMERS
- School of Pharmacy and Medical Sciences: Prof. KENNETH ATKINS (acting)

Division of Information Technology, Engineering and the Environment:
- School of Advanced Manufacturing and Mechanical Engineering: Prof. LEE LUONG
- School of Computer and Information Science: Prof. ANDY KORONIOS
- School of Electrical and Information Engineering: Prof. ANDREW NAFALSKI
- School of Mathematics: BRENTON R. DANSIE
- School of Mathematics and Statistics: Assoc. Prof. DAVID PANTON
- School of Natural and Built Environments: Prof. PATRICK JAMES

ATTACHED RESEARCH INSTITUTES

Aboriginal Research Institute: Dir Assoc. Prof. MARTIN NAKATA.

Advanced Computing Research Centre: Dir Assoc. Prof. JIM WARREN.

Agricultural Machinery Research and Design Centre: Dir Assoc. Prof. JOHN FIELKE.

Centre for Advanced Sensor Technology and Microelectronics: Leader Assoc. Prof. DENNIS MULCAHY.

Centre for Advanced Manufacturing Research: Dir Prof. GRIER LIN.

Centre for Allied Health Research: Dir Assoc. Prof. KAREN GRIMMER.

Centre for Applied Behavioural Science: Dir Prof. DREW DAWSON.

Centre for Biomolecular Studies: Dir Prof. ALLAN BRETAG.

Centre for Building and Planning Studies: Co-Leader Prof. STEPHEN HAMNETT; Co-Leader GEORGE ZILLANTE.

Centre of Business Analysis and Research: Dir Prof. MALCOLM SMITH.

Centre for Environmental and Recreation Management: Leader Dr IAN CLARK.

Centre for Industrial and Applicable Mathematics: Dir Prof. PHIL HOWLETT.

Centre for International and Cross-Cultural Studies: Leader Dr DAVID LUNDBERG.

Centre for Pharmaceutical Research: Dir Assoc. Prof. ALLAN EVANS.

Centre for Research in Education, Equity and Work: Dir Assoc. Prof. ROGER HARRIS.

Centre for Research in Education and Sports Science: Leader Assoc. Prof. KEVIN NORTON.

Centre for Research into Nursing and Health Care: Dir Prof. JULIANNE CHEEK.

Centre for Rural And Remote Area Studies: Leader PETER MUNN.

Centre for Settlement Studies: Leader SCOTT DRAKE.

Centre for Studies in Literacy, Policy and Learning Cultures: Dir Assoc. Prof. BARBARA COMBER.

Co-operative Research Centre for Intelligent Manufacturing Systems and Technologies Ltd: Dir Prof. G. LIN.

Commonwealth Special Research Centre for Particle and Material Interfaces: Dir Prof. JOHN RALSTON.

Co-operative Research Centre for Railway Engineering and Technology: Dir Prof. P. HOWLETT.

Co-operative Research Centre for Satellite Systems: Dir Prof. B. COWLEY.

Co-operative Research Centre for Sensor Signal and Information Processing: Dir Prof. D. SINNOTT.

Co-operative Research Centre for Sustainable Tourism: Dir J. DAVIES.

Co-operative Research Centre for Water Quality and Treatment: Dir Assoc. Prof. D. BURSILL.

de Lissa Research Centre: early childhood and family studies; Leader Prof. MARJORY EBBECK.

Food Science and Technology Centre: Leader FRANK PEDDIE.

Ian Wark Research Institute: technological research; Dir Prof. JOHN RALSTON.

Institute for Telecommunications Research: Dir Prof. BILL COWLEY.

International Centre for Management and Organisational Effectiveness: Leader Prof. TRICIA VILKINAS.

Marketing Science Centre: Dir Assoc. Prof. BYRON SHARP.

Quality Use of Medicines and Pharmacy Research Centre: Dir Assoc. Prof. ANDREW GILBERT.

Research Centre for Gender Studies: Dir Assoc. Prof. JUDITH GILL.

Research Centre for Languages and Cultures: Leader ANGELA SCARINO.

Sustainable Energy Centre: Dir Assoc. Prof. WASIM SAMAN.

Systems Engineering and Evaluation Centre: Dir Prof. STEPHEN COOK.

Transport Systems Centre: Dir Prof. MICHAEL TAYLOR.

Urban Water Resources Centre: Leader Assoc. Prof. TONY MINNS.

SOUTHERN CROSS UNIVERSITY

POB 157, Lismore, NSW 2480
Campuses at Lismore, Coffs Harbour and Tweed Heads
Telephone: (2) 6620-3000
Fax: (2) 6622-1300
E-mail: marketing@scu.edu.au
Internet: www.scu.edu.au

Founded 1993 from Northern Rivers and Coffs Harbour components of the University of New England
Academic year: February to November (2 semesters)

Vice-Chancellor: Prof. JOHN RICKARD
Pro Vice-Chancellors: Prof. B. BAVERSTOCK, Prof. A. C. B. DELVES, Prof. L. Z. KLICH
Executive Director and Vice-President (Corporate Services): M. H. MARSHALL

Number of teachers: 350
Number of students: 12,000

Publications: *Annual Report*, *Research Report* (annually)

HEADS OF SCHOOL

School of Arts: Assoc. Prof. MICHAEL HANNAN
School of Commerce and Management: Assoc. Prof. KEITH SLOAN
School of Education: Prof. MARTIN HAYDEN
School of Environmental Science and Management: Prof. DON GARTSIDE
School of Exercise Science and Sport Management: Assoc. Prof. R. BRONKS
School of Indigenous Studies: MARCELLE TOWNSEND-CROSS
School of Law and Justice: RICHARD HARRIS
School of Multimedia and Information Technology: Prof. SAM MURUGESAN
School of Natural and Complementary Medicine: PAUL ORROCK
School of Nursing and Health Care Practices: CHRIS GAME
School of Psychology: Prof. PETER WILSON
School of Social Sciences: M. A. WALLACE
School of Tourism and Hospitality Management: PERRY HOBSON
Graduate College of Management: Assoc. Prof. MICHAEL EVANS
Graduate Research College: Prof. PETER R. BAVERSTOCK

PROFESSORS

ATKINSON, J., Indigenous Australian Peoples
BAVERSTOCK, P., Graduate Research College (and PVC Research)
BRAITHWAITE, R., Tourism and Hospitality Management
DELVES, A., University Enterprise and International Activities (PVC)
GARTSIDE, D. F., Resource Science and Management
GRAHAM, J., Health and Applied Sciences Division (Executive Dean)
HAYDEN, M., Teaching and Learning Unit
HENRY, R. J., Plant Conservation Genetics

JACKSON, J. G., Law and Justice
KLICH, Z., University Academic and Quality Matters (PVC)
KOUZMIN, A., Graduate College of Management
LEIPER, N., Tourism and Hospitality Management
MCCONCHIE, D., Environmental Science and Management
MEREDITH, G., Business Administration
MURUGESAN, S., Multimedia and Information Technology
NECK, P., Business Administration
RICKARD, J., Vice-Chancellor
ROTHWELL, B., Manager, Tweed Gold Coast Campus
SAENGER, P., Environmental Science and Management
SAVERY, L., Business Division (Executive Dean)
SCOTT, D., Commerce and Management
SIMPSON, R., National Marine Science Centre
SPECHT, R., Environmental Science and Management
SPEEDY, G., Teaching and Learning Centre
TAYLOR, B., Nursing and Health Care Practices
THOM, P., Arts Division (Executive Dean)
VANCLAY, J., Environmental Science and Management
WILSON, P., Psychology
YEO, S. M. H., Law and Justice
ZANN, L. P., Environmental Science and Management

UNIVERSITY OF SOUTHERN QUEENSLAND

Toowoomba, Qld 4350
Telephone: (7) 4631-2100
Fax: (7) 4631-2892
Internet: www.usq.edu.au

Founded 1992 (fmrly the University College of Southern Queensland, founded 1991 from the Darling Downs Institute of Advanced Education)
State control
Academic year: January to December

Chancellor: DONALD STEVENS
Vice-Chancellor: Prof. WILLIAM LOVEGROVE
Deputy Vice-Chancellor (Academic and Global Learning): Prof. JAMES TAYLOR
Pro-Vice-Chancellor (International Quality) (vacant)
Pro-Vice-Chancellor (Learning and Teaching): Prof. MAURICE FRENCH
Pro-Vice-Chancellor (Planning and Quality): Prof. WILLIAM MACGILLIVRAY
Pro-Vice-Chancellor (Regional Engagement and Social Justice): Prof. FRANK CROWTHER
Pro-Vice-Chancellor (Research): Prof. GRAHAM BAKER
Provost (Wide Bay Campus): Dr KENNETH STOTT
General Manager, University Services: STEVE TANZER
Librarian: M. MCPHERSON

Library of 309,000 vols
Number of teachers: 480
Number of students: 26,500

DEANS

Faculty of Arts: Prof. M. FRENCH
Faculty of Business: Assoc. Prof. R. ST HILL
Faculty of Education: Prof. F. CROWTHER
Faculty of Engineering and Surveying: Prof. G. BAKER
Faculty of Sciences: Prof. W. MACGILLIVRAY
School of Transdisciplinary Graduate Studies and Continuing Education: Prof. A. BARNETT

PROFESSORS

BILLINGSLEY, J., Engineering and Surveying
ERWEE, R., Business
FOGARTY, G., Sciences
HEGNEY, D., Sciences
HORSFIELD, B., Arts
MCMILLEN, D., Arts
ROBERTS, A., Sciences
ROSS, D., Engineering and Surveying
SMITH, R., Engineering and Surveying
TERRY, P., Sciences
TRAN-CONG, T., Engineering and Surveying
VAN ERP, G., Engineering and Surveying

ATTACHED CENTRES

European Center of Study and Research: Bretten, Baden-Württemberg, Germany.

Land Use Research Centre: Dir Prof. C. ZAMMIT.

Performance Centre: Dir Dr K. FOY.

UNIVERSITY OF THE SUNSHINE COAST

Maroochydore D.C., Qld 4558
located at: Sippy Downs Dr., Sippy Downs, Qld 4556
Telephone: (7) 5430-1234
Fax: (7) 5430-1111
E-mail: information@usc.edu.au
Internet: www.usc.edu.au

Founded 1996
Academic year: February to December

Vice-Chancellor: Prof. PAUL THOMAS
Deputy Vice-Chancellor: Prof. GREG HILL
Pro-Vice-Chancellor: Prof. ROBERT ELLIOT

Number of teachers: 123 full-time
Number of students: 4,760

DEANS

Faculty of Arts and Social Sciences: Assoc. Prof. PAM DYER
Faculty of Business: Prof. EDMOND FITZGERALD
Faculty of Science, Health and Education: Prof. ROD SIMPSON

PROFESSORS

Faculty of Arts and Social Sciences:
ELLIOT, R.
QUINN, S.
Faculty of Business:
FITZGERALD, E.
HEDE, A.
RALSTON, D.
Faculty of Science:
SIMPSON, R.

ATTACHED RESEARCH INSTITUTES

Centre for Healthy Activities, Sport and Exercise (CHASE): Sippy Downs, Qld; tel. (7) 5459-4656; fax (7) 5459-4682; e-mail chase@usc.edu.au; internet www.usc.edu.au/chase; Dir Assoc. Prof. BRENDAN BURKETT.

Centre for Multicultural and Community Development: tel. (7) 5430-1259; fax (7) 5430-2859; e-mail ngopalkr@usc.edu.au; Dir NARAYAN GOPALKRISHNAN.

National Seniors Productive Ageing Centre: POB 1450, Brisbane, Qld 4001; tel. (7) 3321-7074; fax (7) 3321-9339; e-mail info@productiveageing.com.au; internet www.productiveageing.com.au; Dir (vacant).

SWINBURNE UNIVERSITY OF TECHNOLOGY

POB 218, Hawthorn, Vic. 3122
Hawthorn, Wantirna, Croydon, Healesville, Prahran, Lilydale, Laem Chambeng (Thailand), Sarawak (Malaysia)Telephone: (3) 9214-8000
Fax: (3) 9819-5454
E-mail: info@swin.edu.au
Internet: www.swin.edu.au

Founded 1908 as Eastern Suburbs Technical College; present name and status 1992
Academic year: March to November

Chancellor: Dr DOUGLAS MITCHELL
Vice-Chancellor: Prof. IAN YOUNG
Deputy Vice-Chancellor: F. G. BANNON
Deputy Vice-Chancellor (Division of Higher Education, Hawthorn and Prahran): Prof. DALE MURPHY
Divisional Deputy Vice-Chancellor (Lilydale): Prof. BARBARA VAN ERNST
Divisional Deputy Vice-Chancellor, Technical and Further Education (TAFE Division): ALISTAIR CROZIER
Vice President, Resources: STEPHEN MURBY
Vice President, Student Affairs: SARAH DAVIES
Registrar: T. KILSBY (Deputy Registrar)
Librarian: D. WHITEHEAD

Library of 250,000 vols
Number of teachers: 657 (362 Higher Education, 295 TAFE)
Number of students: 38,000 (incl. 14,118 Higher Education, 23,882 TAFE)

Publications: *Annual Report*, *Research Report*

HEADS OF SCHOOLS

School of Biophysical Sciences and Electrical Engineering: Assoc. Prof. RUSSELL CRAWFORD
School of Business: BARBARA J. CARGILL
School of Engineering and Science: Dr IAN K. JONES
School of Information Technology: Prof. DOUG GRANT
School of Mathematical Sciences: PETER JONES
School of Social and Behavioural Sciences: Dr JULIE MULVANY

UNIVERSITY OF SYDNEY

Sydney, NSW 2006
Telephone: (2) 9351-2222
Internet: www.usyd.edu.au

Founded 1850
Private control
Academic year: February to December

Chancellor: The Hon. Justice KIM SANTOW
Deputy Chancellor: Emeritus Prof. ANN SEFTON
Vice-Chancellor and Principal: Prof. GAVIN BROWN
Deputy Vice-Chancellor (Academic and International): Prof. JOHN HEARN
Deputy Vice-Chancellor (Infrastructure): Prof. ANN BREWER
Deputy Vice-Chancellor (Research): Prof. TIM HIRST
Pro-Vice-Chancellor (Employee Relations): Prof. BERYL HESKETH (acting)
Pro-Vice-Chancellor (Health Sciences): Prof. DON NUTBEAM
Pro-Vice-Chancellor (Humanities and Social Sciences): Prof. JUNE SINCLAIR
Pro-Vice-Chancellor (Sciences and Technology): Prof. BERYL HESKETH (acting)
Pro-Vice-Chancellor (Teaching and Learning): Prof. JUDYTH SACHS (acting)
Chief Financial Officer: BOB KOTIC
Registrar: Dr WILLIAM ADAMS
Librarian: JOHN SHIPP

Library: see under Libraries and Archives
Number of teachers: 5,812
Number of students: 47,296

DEANS

Faculty of Agriculture, Food and Natural Resources: Prof. L. COPELAND
Faculty of Architecture: Prof. G. T. MOORE
Faculty of Arts: Prof. S. GARTON
Faculty of Dentistry: Prof. ELI SCHWARTZ

Faculty of Economics and Business: Prof. P. WOLNIZER
Faculty of Education and Social Work: Assoc. Prof. D. ARMSTRONG (acting)
Faculty of Engineering: Prof. GREGORY HANCOCK (acting)
Faculty of Health Sciences: Prof. GWYNETH LLEWELYN (acting)
Faculty of Law: Prof. RON MCCALLUM
Faculty of Medicine: Prof. ANDREW J. S. COATS
Faculty of Nursing and Midwifery: Prof. JOCALYN LAWLER
Faculty of Pharmacy: Prof. SHALOM CHARLIE BENRIMOJ
Faculty of Science: Prof. D. DAY (acting)
Faculty of Veterinary Science: Assoc. Prof. L. JEFFCOTT (acting)
Sydney College of the Arts: Prof. RON NEWMAN
Sydney Conservatorium of Music: Assoc. Prof. K. WALKER (acting)
Graduate School of Government: Prof. D. RICHMOND
Graduate School of Management: Prof. R. MCLEAN

PROFESSORS

ADAM, C. M., MBA Programs
ALLARS, M., Law
ALLEN, D. G., Physiology
APPS, P. F., Law
ARMITAGE, S., Nursing Practice
ASTOR, H., Law
AUSTIN-BROOS, D. J., Anthropology
BAKER, A. B., Anaesthesia
BANDLER, R. J., Anatomy and Histology
BARNETSON, R. ST. C., Dermatology
BASTEN, A., Immunology
BAXTER, R. C., Medicine
BENNETT, M. R., Physiology
BENRIMOJ, S. I., Pharmacy Practice
BEREND, N., Respiratory Medicine
BERRY, G., Public Health and Community Medicine
BEUMONT, P. J. V., Psychiatry
BILGER, R. W., Mechanical Engineering
BILLSON, F. A., Clinical Ophthalmology
BOAKES, R. A., Psychology
BOER, B. W., Environmental Law
BOKEY, E. L., Colorectal Surgery
BOYCE, P., Psychiatry
BOYD, A. E., Music
BRYANT, R. W., Conservative Dentistry
BURGESS, L., Agriculture
CARNEY, T. R., Law
CARSANIGA, G., Italian Studies
CARTER, J. P., Civil Engineering
CARTER, J. W., Law
CASS, B., Faculty of Arts
CATERSON, I. D., Endocrinology
CHAMBERLAIN, M., Family and Community Health in Nursing
CHRISTOPHERSON, R. I., Biochemistry
CLARKE, H. D. B., Asian Studies
CLUNIES ROSS, M. B., English
CODE, C., Speech Pathology
COLE, T. W., Electrical Engineering
COLLINS, R. E., Applied Physics
CONNELL, R. W., Social and Policy Studies in Education
COOK, D., Physiology
COSSART, Y. E., Infectious Diseases
COUSINS, M. J., Anaesthesia and Pain Management
CRAM, L. E., Astrophysics
CRITTENDEN, P. J., Philosophy
CURTHOYS, I., Psychology
DAMPNEY, R., Physiology
DANCER, E. N., Mathematics and Statistics
DAVIES, P. J., Geology and Geophysics
DAVIS, J., Astronomy
DELBRIDGE, L. W., Surgery
DREHER, B., Anatomy and Histology
DUNN, R. A., Sydney College of the Arts
DUNSTAN, H., Asian Studies
DURRANT-WHYTE, H., Mechanical and Mechatronic Engineering
EASTMAN, C. J., Clinical Professor (Medicine)
EBIED, R. Y., Semitic Studies
EGERTON, J. R., Animal Health
FARRELL, G. C., Hepatic Medicine
FARROW, B. R. H., Veterinary Clinical Sciences
FIELD, L. D., Chemistry (Organic Chemistry)
FISHER, M. MCD., Clinical Professor (Medicine)
FLETCHER, J. P., Surgery
FOLEY, W. A., Linguistics
FRASER, D. R., Animal Science
FRASER, I. S., Reproductive Medicine
FREEDMAN, B., Cardiology
GALLERY, E. D. M., Clinical Professor (Medicine)
GATENBY, P., Canberra Clinical School
GAUKROGER, S., Traditional and Modern Philosophy
GERO, J. S., Architectural and Design Science
GETHING, L., Nursing Research Centre
GIBSON, W. P. R., Otolaryngology
GILBERT, G. L., Clinical Professor (Medicine)
GILBERT, R. G., Theoretical Chemistry
GILL, G. J., Government and Public Administration
GRAYCAR, R., Law
GREEN, J. R., Classical Archaeology
GROENEWEGEN, P. D., Economics
GYÖRY, A. Z., Medicine
HANCOCK, G. J., Steel Structures
HANDELSMAN, D. J., Medicine
HARLAND, D. J., Law
HARPER, C. G., Neuropathology
HARRIS, J. P., Vascular Surgery
HARRIS, M. A., English Literature
HAYMET, A. D. J., Theoretical Chemistry
HAYNES, B., Chemical Engineering
HENDERSON-SMART, D. J., Perinatal Medicine
HENSHER, D. A., Institute of Transport Studies
HESKETH, B., Science
HIGGS, J., Physiotherapy
HILL, D., Electrical Engineering
HORVATH, J. S., Clinical Professor (Medicine)
HOUGHTON, C. R. S., Gynaecological Oncology
HUME, I. D., Biology
HUNT, N. H., Pathology
HUSBAND, A. J., Veterinary Pathology
IRWIG, L., Public Health and Community Medicine
JACKSON, M. W., Government and Public Administration
JANSEN, R. P. S., Clinical Professor (Medicine)
JEFFREYS, M. J., Modern Greek
JOHNSON, G. F. S., Psychiatry
JOHNSTON, G. A. R., Pharmacology
KEFFORD, R. F., Medical Oncology
KELLY, D. T., Cardiology
KENDIG, H., Health Sciences
KENNEDY, I., Agricultural Chemistry and Soil Science
KIDD, M., General Practice
KLINEBERG, I. J., Prosthetic Dentistry
KUCHEL, P. W., Biochemistry
KWOK, K. C. S., Civil Engineering
LANSBURY, R. D., Industrial Relations
LARKUM, A. W. D., Biological Sciences
LAWLER, J., Nursing
LAWRENCE, J. R., Medicine
LAY, P., Chemistry
LEE, K. H., Classics
LEEDER, S. R., Public Health and Community Medicine
LEHRER, G. I., Mathematics and Statistics
LESTER, K., Dentistry
LINDOY, L. F., Chemistry
LUSBY, R. J., Surgery
LYLE, D., Rural Health
MACAULAY, T. G., Agricultural Economics
MCBRATNEY, A. B., Agricultural Chemistry and Soil Science
MCCALLUM, R. C., Industrial Law
MCCARTHY, W. H., Melanoma and Skin Oncology
MCINTOSH, R. A., Cereal Genetics and Cytogenetics
MCKENZIE, D., Physics
MCLEOD, J. G., Medicine and Neurology
MACLEOD, R. M., History
MCPHEDRAN, R. C., Physics (Electromagnetic Physics)
MAHER, M., Architectural and Design Science
MAI, Y.-W., Mechanical Engineering
MARKUS, G., Philosophy
MARSHALL, D. R., Plant Breeding
MARTIN, A. A., French
MARTIN, C. J., Surgery
MARTIN, P. M., Urban Horticulture
MASON, I. M., Geosciences
MATHER, L. E., Anaesthesia and Analgesia
MAY, J., Surgery
MEARES, R. A., Psychiatry
MELROSE, D. B., Theoretical Physics
MILLS, G., Economics
MINDEL, A., Sexual Health
MOORE, G., Architecture
MORGAN, M., Neurosurgery
MORRIS, B., Physiology
NADE, S. M. L., Clinical Professor (Medicine)
NARAQI, S., Medicine and Infectious Diseases
PATRICK, J., Computer Science
PATTERSON, D. J., Biology
PESMAN, R., History
PETRIE, J. G., Chemical Engineering
PHAN-THIEN, N., Mechanical Engineering
PHEGAN, C. S., Law
PHOON, W.-O., Occupational Health
POLLARD, J., Medicine
POTTS, D. T., Middle Eastern Archaeology
POULOS, H. G., Civil Engineering
PRETTY, S., Sydney Conservatorium of Music
PRICE, H., Philosophy
RAPER, J., Engineering
RASMUSSEN, H. H., Medicine
REED, V., Communication Disorders
REES, S. J., Social Work
REEVES, P. R., Microbiology
REID, B., Health Information Management
ROBINSON, B. G., Medicine (Endocrinology)
ROBINSON, J., Mathematical Statistics
ROMAGNOLI, J. A., Process Systems Engineering
ROSE, R. J., Veterinary Clinical Sciences
ROSS, D. L., Medicine
ROUFOGALIS, B. D., Pharmaceutical Chemistry
ROWE, P. B., Dir, Children's Medical Research Foundation
RUBIN, G., Public Health and Community Medicine
SACHS, J. M., Teaching and Curriculum Studies
SADURSKI, W., Legal Philosophy
SAUNDERS, D. M., Obstetrics and Gynaecology
SEALE, J. P., Clinical Pharmacology
SENETA, E., Mathematical Statistics
SHEARER, I. A., International Law
SHEIL, A. G. R., Surgery (Transplantation)
SHEPHERD, R. B., Physiotherapy
SHEPPARD, C. J. R., Physical Optics
SHERINGTON, G. E., Education
SHINE, R., Evolutionary Biology
SILLENCE, D. O., Medical Genetics
SKURRAY, R. A., Biology (Genetics)
SMITH, D. S., Rehabilitation Medicine
SMITH, T., Art History and Theory
SORRELL, T. C., Clinical Infectious Diseases
SPATE, V. M., Contemporary Art
SPRINGBORG, P., Government and Public Administration
STAINTON, M. C., Family and Community Health in Nursing
STEVEN, G. P., Aeronautical Engineering
STONE, J., Anatomy
SULLIVAN, C. E., Medicine
SWAIN, M., Biomaterials Science
TALLEY, N., Medicine

TANNER, R. I., Mechanical Engineering
TATTERSALL, M. H. N., Cancer Medicine
TAY, A. E.-S., Jurisprudence
TAYLOR, T. K. F., Orthopaedics and Traumatic Surgery
TAYLOR, W. C., Organic Chemistry
TEIWES, F. C., Chinese Politics
TENNANT, C. C., Psychiatry
TILLER, D. J., Clinical Professor (Medicine)
TOUYZ, S., Psychology
TRENT, R. J. A., Medical Molecular Genetics
TROMPF, G., Studies in Religion
TRUDINGER, B. J., Obstetrics and Gynaecology
TRUSWELL, A. S., Human Nutrition
TURTLE, J. R., Endocrinology
UNDERWOOD, A. J., Experimental Ecology
USHERWOOD, T., General Practice
UTHER, J. F. B., Clinical Professor (Medicine)
VANN, R. J., Law
VUCETIC, B., Electrical Engineering
WAKE, R. G., Biochemistry
WALKER, D. M., Oral Pathology
WALTER, T. S., Accounting
WATTS, G., Academic Director of Kolej Antarabangsa
WEBBER, G. P., Architecture
WEBBER, J., Law
WEBBY, E. A., Australian Literature
WEISBROT, D., Law
WILDING, R. M., English and Australian Literature
WILSON, P. R., Applied Mathematics
WOLNIZER, P., Economics
WOODLAND, A. D., Econometrics
YAN, H., Electrical Engineering
YOUNG, J. A., Physiology
YUE, D. K., Medicine

ATTACHED COLLEGES

Sydney College of the Arts: Dir Prof. RON NEWMAN.

Sydney Conservatorium of Music: Principal Prof. S. E. PRETTY.

ATTACHED INSTITUTES

A.W. Morrow Gastroenterology and Liver Centre.

Accounting Research Centre.

Ageing and Alzheimer's Disease Research and Education Institute.

ANZAC Health and Medical Research Institute.

Asian Agribusiness Research Centre.

Australian Archaeological Institute at Athens.

Australian Centre for Advanced Risk and Reliability Engineering.

Australian Centre for Applied Research in Music Performance.

Australian Centre for Effective Healthcare.

Australian Centre for Environmental Law.

Australian Centre for Field Robotics.

Australian Centre for Health Promotion.

Australian Centre for Industrial Relations Research and Training.

Australian Centre for Innovation and International Competitiveness.

Australian Centre for Precision Agriculture.

Australian Graduate School of Engineering Innovation.

Australian Health Policy Institute.

Australian Key Centre for Microscopy and Microanalysis.

Australian Key Centre in Transport Management.

Australian Marine Mammal Research Centre.

Australian Marketing Science Institute.

Australian Mekong Resource Centre.

Australian Membrane and Biotechnology Research Institute.

Australian National Genomic Information Service.

Australian Pharmacy Research Centre.

Australian Photonics Cooperative Research Centre.

Australian Research Council Special Research Centre for Offshore Foundation Systems.

Australian Stuttering Research Centre.

Centenary Institute of Cancer Medicine and Cell Biology.

Central Sydney Area Health Service Drug and Alcohol Unit.

Centre for Advanced Materials Technology.

Centre for Advanced Structural Engineering.

Centre for Animal Immunology Research.

Centre for Applied Marketing: jtly with the University of New South Wales.

Centre for Asian and Pacific Law.

Centre for Celtic Studies.

Centre for Classical Civilisation.

Centre for Conservation Biology.

Centre for Continuing Education.

Centre for Corporate Change: jointly with the University of New South Wales.

Centre for Cypriot Archaeology.

Centre for English Teaching.

Centre for European Studies.

Centre for Geotechnical Research.

Centre for Health Economics Research and Evaluation.

Centre for Heavy Metals Research.

Centre for Human Aspects of Science and Technology.

Centre for Immunisation Research.

Centre for International and Public Affairs.

Centre for Lesbian and Gay Research.

Centre for Medieval Studies.

Centre for Microeconomic Policy Analysis.

Centre for the Mind.

Centre for Nursing Research.

Centre for Oral Health Research.

Centre for Pain Management and Research.

Centre for Peace and Conflict Studies.

Centre for Performance Studies.

Centre for Practitioner Research.

Centre for Research and Teaching in Civics.

Centre for Research in Finance: jointly with the University of New South Wales.

Centre for Risk, Environment and Systems Technology Analysis.

Centre for Salinity Assessment and Management.

Centre for South Asian Studies.

Centre for the Study and Treatment of Dieting Disorders.

Centre for the Study of the History of Economic Thought.

Centre for Values, Ethics and the Law in Medicine.

Centre for Wave Physics.

Children's Cochlear Implant Centre.

Children's Hospital Education Research Institute (CHERI).

Children's Medical Research Institute.

China Education Centre.

Classical Languages Acquisition Research Centre.

Clinical Immunology Research Centre.

Coastal Studies Unit.

Competitive Tendering and Contracting Research Unit.

Co-operative Research Centre for Advanced Composite Structures.

Co-operative Research Centre for Asthma.

Co-operative Research Centre for Biological Control of Pest Animals.

Co-operative Research Centre for Cochlear Implant, Speech and Hearing Research.

Co-operative Research Centre for Construction Innovation.

Co-operative Research Centre for Mining Technology and Equipment.

Co-operative Research Centre for Polymers.

Co-operative Research Centre for Smart Internet Technology.

Co-operative Research Centre for Sustainable Cotton Production.

Co-operative Research Centre for Sustainable Rice Production.

Co-operative Research Centre for Welded Structures.

Coral Reef Research Institute.

Cumberland Health and Research Centre.

Dairy Research Unit.

Dental Health Education and Research Foundation.

Department of Anatomical Pathology, Royal Prince Alfred Hospital.

Department of Endocrinology, Royal Prince Alfred Hospital.

Ecological Impacts of Coastal Cities—An Australian Research Council Special Research Centre.

Educational Technology Centre.

Effective Healthcare Australia.

Electron Microscope Unit.

European Studies Centre.

Evelyn McCloughan Children's Centre.

Family Medicine Research Centre.

Finite Element Analysis Research Centre.

Fruit Fly Research Centre.

Fujitsu Centre: jointly with the University of New South Wales.

Health Education Unit.

Heart Research Institute.

Herbal Medicines Research and Education Centre.

IA Watson Grains Research Centre.

Ian Buchan Fell Housing Research Centre.

Innovative Dairy Products Cooperative Research Centre.

Institute for Biomedical Research.

Institute for Immunology and Allergy Research.

Institute for Information Technology and the Knowledge Economy.

Institute for International Health Research and Development.

Institute for Marine and Ocean Sciences.
Institute for Teaching and Learning.
Institute of Astronomy.
Institute of Bone and Joint Research.
Institute of Clinical Neurosciences.
Institute of Criminology.
Institute of Magnetic Resonance Research.
Institute of Marine Ecology.
Institute of Paediatric Endocrinology, Diabetes and Metabolism.
Institute of Respiratory Medicine.
Institute of Transport Studies.
Institute of Wildlife Research.
International Institute for Educational Development.
Julius Stone Institute of Jurisprudence.
Kanematsu Laboratories.
Key Centre for Design Computing and Cognition.
Key Centre for Polymer Colloids.
Kolling Institute of Medical Research.
Koori Centre.
Language Centre.
Medical Psychology Unit.
Menzies School of Health Research.
Micro-Economic Modelling Laboratory.
Molonglo Observatory.
Multicultural Research Centre.
NHMRC Clinical Trials Centre.
N.W.G. Macintosh Centre for Quaternary Dating.
National Centre for Classification in Health.
National Centre for Health Promotion.
National Children's and Youth Law Centre.
National Health and Medical Research Council Clinical Trials Centre.
National Innovation Centre.
National Micro-Economic Modelling Laboratory.
National Voice Centre (with Sydney Conservatorium of Music).
NOVAE Research Group.
NSW Breast Cancer Institute.
NSW Centre for Perinatal Health Services Research.
Nursing History Research Unit.
Nursing Professional Development Unit.
Nursing Research Centre for Adaptation in Health and Illness.
Ocean Sciences Institute.
One Tree Island Research Station.
Optical Fibre Technology Centre.
Pacioli Society.
Pain Management and Research Centre.
Planning Research Centre.
Plant Breeding Institute.
Polymer Research Centre.
Poultry Research Centre.
Power Institute of Fine Arts.
Public Affairs Research Centre.
Quality Wheat Cooperative Research Centre.
Rehabilitation Research Centre.
Rehabilitation Studies Unit.
Reprogen Advanced Technologies in Animal Genetics and Reproduction.
Research Centre for Adaptation in Health and Illness.
Research Centre for Theoretical Astrophysics.
Research Institute for Asia and the Pacific.
Research Institute for Humanities and Social Sciences.
Save Sight Institute.
Securities Industry Research Centre of Asia-Pacific.
Shakespeare Globe Centre Australia.
Sydney Category Theory Seminar.
Sydney Melanoma Unit.
Sydney Nursing Research Centre.
Sydney Regional Visualisation Laboratory (VISLAB).
Sydney University and Royal Prince Alfred Hospital Macromolecular Analysis Centre (SUPAMAC).
Sydney University Biological Information and Technology Centre: jtly between the Faculties of Science and Medicine, with the Australian National Genomic Information Service and the Faculty of Veterinary Science.
Sydney University Nitrogen Fixation Centre.
Sydney University Stellar Interferometer.
Teaching Resources and Textbooks Research Unit.
Technology Enabled Capital Markets Cooperative Research Centre.
University of Sydney AHURI Housing and Urban Research Centre.
Value Added Wheat Cooperative Research Centre.
Warren Centre for Advanced Engineering.
Westmead Millennium Institute and Research Centres.
WHO Collaborating Centre for Nursing Development in Primary Health Care.
WHO Collaborating Centre for Rehabilitation.
WHO Collaborating Centre in Health Promotion.
Women's Studies Centre

UNIVERSITY OF TECHNOLOGY, SYDNEY

POB 123, Broadway, Sydney, NSW 2007
Telephone: (2) 9514-2000
Fax: (2) 9514-1551
E-mail: info.office@uts.edu.au
Internet: www.uts.edu.au

Founded 1965 as NSW Institute of Technology; university status 1988
Academic year: March to December

Chancellor: Prof. VICKI SARA
Deputy Chancellor: KENNETH RENNIE
Vice-Chancellor and President: Prof. ROSS MILBOURNE
Deputy Vice-Chancellor and Vice-President (Academic): Prof. PETER BOOTH
Pro-Vice-Chancellor and Vice-President (Teaching and Learning): Prof. RICHARD. A. JOHNSTONE
Pro-Vice-Chancellor and Vice-President (Research): Prof. SUSAN ROWLEY
Pro-Vice-Chancellor and Vice-President (International): Prof. DAVID GOODMAN
Registrar: Dr JEFF M. FITZGERALD
Librarian: ALEX BYRNE

Library of 626,983 vols, 37,929 e-journals, 3,775 print journals
Number of teachers: 809 (full-time)
Number of students: 30,587
Publications: *CREArTA* (research and education in the arts, 2 a year), *Form/Work* (irregular), *Literacy and Numeracy Studies* (education and training of adults, 2 a year), *Locality* (3 a year), *Pacific Rim Property Research Journal* (4 a year), *Public History Review* (annually), *UTS Law Review* (annually), *Cultural Studies Review* (published jtly with University of Melbourne; 2 a year), *UTS Writer's Anthology* (annually)

DEANS

Faculty of Business: Prof. ROB LYNCH
Faculty of Design, Architecture and Building: Prof. DESLEY LUSCOMBE
Faculty of Education: Prof. SHIRLEY ALEXANDER
Faculty of Engineering: Prof. ARCHIE JOHNSTON
Faculty of Humanities and Social Sciences: Prof. THEO VAN LEEUWEN
Faculty of Information Technology: Prof. THARAM DILLON
Faculty of Law: Prof. DAVID BARKER
Faculty of Nursing, Midwifery and Health: Prof. JILL F. WHITE
Faculty of Science: Prof. J. RICE

ATTACHED RESEARCH INSTITUTES

ARC Centre of Excellence for Autonomous Systems (jtly with University of Sydney and University of New South Wales): Dir Prof. GAMINI DISSANAYAKE.
ARC Centre of Excellence for Ultra-High Bandwidth Devices for Optical Systems: Dir Prof. LINDSEY BOTTEN.
Australian Centre for Cooperative Research and Development: Co-Dirs Prof. MARK LYONS JUDY JOHNSTON.
Australian Centre for Event Management: Dir ROB HARRIS.
Australian Centre for Independent Journalism: Exec. Dir Assoc. Prof. CHRIS NASH.
Australian Centre for Olympic Studies: Exec. Officer STEPHEN FRAWLEY.
Australian Centre for Public Communication: Co-Dirs REBECCA HARRIS, MAI HANSFORD, JANNET PENDLETON.
Australian Centre for Public History: Co-Dirs Dr PAULA HAMILTON, Dr PAUL ASHTON.
Australasian Legal Information Institute: with University of New South Wales; Exec. Dir PHILIP CHUNG.
Australian Technology Park Innovations Pty Ltd: CEO Dr MARK BRADLEY.
Centre for Australian Community Organisations and Management: Dir Assoc. Prof. JENNY ONYX.
Centre for Complex Systems Research: Co-Dirs Dr JOHN GALLOWAY, SURESH SOOD.
Centre for e-Business and Knowledge Management: Man. ROBERT LAI.
Centre for Ecotoxicology: Dir Assoc. Prof. ROD BUCKNEY.
Centre for Electrical Machines and Power Electronics: Dir Dr JIANGUO ZHU.
Centre for Forensic Science: Dir Assoc. Prof. CLAUDE ROUX.
Centre for Health Economics Research and Evaluation: Dir Prof. JANE HALL.
Centre for Health Services Management: Dir Prof. CHRISTINE DUFFIELD.
Centre for Language and Literacy: Co-Dirs Prof. LIAM MORGAN, CHRIS NESBITT.
Centre for Local Government: Dir Assoc. Prof. GRAHAM SANSOM.

Centre for Midwifery and Family Health: Dir Prof. CAROLINE HOMER (acting).

Centre for New Writing: Dir JOHN DALE (acting).

Centre for Object Technology Applications and Research: Dir Prof. BRIAN HENDERSON-SELLERS.

Centre for Popular Education: Dir RICK FLOWERS.

Centre for Research and Education in the Arts: Dir Dr ROSEMARY JOHNSTON.

Centre for Research on Provincial China: Dir Prof. DAVID GOODMAN.

Cooperative Research Centre for Enterprise Distributed Systems Technology: Dir Dr TIM MANSFIELD.

Cooperative Research Centre for Satellite Systems: Dir Assoc. Prof. SAM REISENFELD.

Cooperative Research Centre for the Sustainable Aquaculture of Finfish: Dir Prof. ROBERT RAISON.

Cooperative Research Centre for Sustainable Tourism: Dir TONY GRIFFIN.

Cooperative Research Centre for Technology-Enabled Capital Markets: Dir Prof. DONALD J. STOKES.

Institute for the Biotechnology of Infectious Diseases: Dir Prof. MICHAEL WALLACH.

Institute for Information and Communication Technologies: Dir Prof. JOHN HUGHES.

Institute for Interactive Media and Learning: Dir Prof. SHIRLEY ALEXANDER.

Institute for International Studies: Dir Prof. LYN SHOEMARK.

Institute for Nanoscale Technology: Dir Prof. MICHAEL CORTIE.

Institute for Sustainable Futures: Dir Prof. STUART WHITE.

Institute for Water and Environmental Resource Management: Dir Prof. DEREK EAMUS.

Jumbunna Indigenous House of Learning: Dir Prof. LARISSA BEHRENDT.

Key University Research Centre for Built Infrastructure Research: Dir Prof. BIJAN SAMALI.

Key University Research Centre for Corporate Governance: Dir Prof. THOMAS CLARKE.

Key University Research Centre for Cultural Studies–Transforming Cultures: Dir Prof. STEPHANIE HEMELRYK DONALD.

Key University Research Centre for Health Technologies: Co-Dirs Prof. HUNG NGUYEN, Prof. ASHLEY CRAIG.

Key University Research Centre for Innovative Collaborations, Alliances and Networks: Dir Prof. STEWART CLEGG.

Key University Research Centre for Organisational, Vocational and Adult Learning: Co-Dirs Dr CLIVE CHAPPELL, Dr NICKY SOLOMON.

Key University Research Centre for Quantitative Finance Research: Dir Prof. TONY HALL.

National Centre for Groundwater Management: Dir Dr NOEL MERRICK (acting).

UTS Community Law Centre: Dir JENNIFER BURN.

UTS Shopfront: Dir Dr PAUL ASHTON.

UTS Training and Development Services: Dir ANNE HALLARD.

UNIVERSITY OF TASMANIA

Burnie campus: POB 447, Burnie, Tas. 7320
Hobart campus: POB 252C-52, Hobart, Tas. 7001
Launceston campus: Locked Bag 1, Launceston, Tas. 7250
Telephone: Hobart campus, (3) 6226-2999; Burnie campus, (3) 6430-4999; Launceston campus, (3) 6324-3999
Fax: Hobart campus, (3) 6226-7871; Burnie campus, (3) 6430-4950; Launceston campus, (3) 6324-3799
E-mail: course.info@utas.edu.au
Internet: www.utas.edu.au
Founded 1991 through merger of the University of Tasmania (f. 1890) and the Tasmanian State Institute of Technology
Academic year: February to October (two terms)
Chancellor: Dr M. VERTIGAN
Vice-Chancellor and Principal: Prof. D. LE GREW
Deputy Vice-Chancellor: Prof. R. LIDL
Pro-Vice-Chancellor (Research): Prof. A. R. GLENN
Pro-Vice-Chancellor (Teaching and Learning): Prof. S. JOHNSTON
Executive Director of Finance and Administration: A. FERRALL
Academic Registrar: C. P. CARSTENS
Librarian: L. L. LUTHER
Library: see under Libraries and Archives
Number of teachers: 800
Number of students: 15,207
Publication: *Law Review*

DEANS

Faculty of Arts: Prof. J. PAKULSKI
Faculty of Commerce: Prof. P. G. H. CARROLL
Faculty of Education: Prof. R. M. ARNOLD
Faculty of Health Science: Prof. A. CARMICHAEL
Faculty of Law: Prof. D. R. C. CHALMERS
Faculty of Science, Engineering and Technology: Prof. J. B. REID
Board of Graduate Studies by Research: Assoc. Prof. C.J. DENHOLM

PROFESSORS

at Hobart campus:

Faculty of Arts (Private Bag.44, Hobart, Tas. 7001; tel. (3) 6226-1874; fax (3) 6226-7842; e-mail N.Foster@utas.edu.au; internet www.arts.utas.edu.au):

BENNETT, M. J., History and Classics
BLAND, R., Sociology
FRANKHAM, N. H., Fine Art
KELLOW, A. J., Government
KNEHANS, D., Music
MALPAS, J. E., Philosophy
PAKULSKI, J., Sociology
REYNOLDS, H., History and Classics
WHITE, R., Sociology and Social Work

Faculty of Commerce (Private Bag 84, Hobart, Tas. 7001; tel. (3) 6226-2160; fax (3) 6226-2170; e-mail course.info@utas.edu.au; internet www.utas.edu.au/commerce):

CARROLL, P. G. H., Accounting and Finance
GODFREY, J., Accounting and Finance
KEEN, C. D., Information Systems
RAY, R., Economics

Faculty of Education (Locked Bag 1308, Launceston, Tas. 7250; tel. (3) 6324-3446; fax (3) 6324-3303; e-mail secretary@utas.edu.au; internet www.educ.utas.edu.au):

ARNOLD, R. M., Empathic Intelligence and Pedagogy
HOGAN, D. J., Sociology of Education
MULFORD, W. R., Educational Leadership
WILLIAMSON, J. C., Teaching Studies and Teacher Education

Faculty of Health Science (POB 252C-99, Hobart, Tas. 7001; tel. (3) 6226-4757; fax (3) 6226-4747; e-mail shssec@utas.edu.au; internet www.healthsci.utas.edu.au):

CARMICHAEL, A., Paediatrics and Child Health
CLARK, M. G., Biochemistry
CLEMENT, C., Obstetrics and Gynaecology
DWYER, T., Population Health
KIRKBY, K. C., Psychiatry
MUDGE, P., General Practice
PETERSON, G., Pharmacy
STANTON, P. D., Surgery
VICKERS, J. C., Pathology
WALTERS, H., Medicine

Faculty of Law (Private Bag 89, Hobart, Tas. 7001; tel. (3) 6226-2066; fax (3) 6226-7623; e-mail secretary@law.utas.edu.au; internet www.law.utas.edu.au):

CHALMERS, D. R. C., Law
WARNER, C. A., Law

Faculty of Science, Engineering and Technology (Private Bag 50, Hobart, Tas. 7001; tel. (3) 6226-2125; fax (3) 6226-7809; e-mail alex.hamiltonsmith@utas.edu.au; internet www.utas.edu.au/scieng):

BUDD, W. F., Antarctic and Southern Ocean Environment
BULLEN, F., Engineering
BUXTON, C. D., Aquaculture and Fisheries
CANTY, A. J., Chemistry
CLARK, R. J., Agricultural Science
CRAWFORD, A., Earth Sciences
DAVIS, M. R., Civil and Mechanical Engineering
FORBES, L., Mathematics
GRIFFIN, R., Co-operative Research Centre for Sustainable Production Forestry
HADDAD, P. R., Chemistry
JOHNSON, C., Zoology
KIRKPATRICK, J. B., Geography and Environmental Studies
LARGE, R. R., Earth Sciences
MCMEEKIN, T. A., Agricultural Science
NGUYEN, D. T., Electrical Engineering and Computer Science
REID, J. B., Plant Science
SALE, A., Computing
SUMMERS, J. J., Psychology
VANCLAY, F., Agricultural Science

at Launceston campus:

Faculty of Arts (Private Bag 44, Hobart, Tas. 7001; tel. (3) 6226-1874; fax (3) 6226-7842; e-mail N.Foster@utas.edu.au; internet www.arts.utas.edu.au):

BLAND, R., Sociology and Social Work
HATLEY, B., Asian Languages and Studies
MCGRATH, V. F., Visual and Performing Arts

Faculty of Education (Locked Bag 1308, Launceston, Tas. 7250; tel. (3) 6324-3446; fax (3) 6324-3303; e-mail secretary@utas.edu.au; internet www.educ.utas.edu.au):

MULFORD, W. R., Educational Leadership
WILLIAMSON, J. C., Secondary and Post-compulsory Education

Faculty of Health Science (Private Bag 99, Hobart, Tas. 7001; tel. (3) 6226-4757; fax (3) 6226-4747; e-mail shssec@utas.edu.au; internet www.healthsci.utas.edu.au):

BALL, M., Biomedical Science
FARRELL, G., Nursing
WALKER, J. H., Rural Health

Faculty of Science, Engineering and Technology (Private Bag 50, Hobart, Tas. 7001; tel. (3) 6226-2125; fax (3) 6226-7809; e-mail alex.hamiltonsmith@utas.edu.au; internet www.utas.edu.au/scieng):

CHOI, Y. J., Computing
FAY, R., Architecture and Urban Design
PANKHURST, N. W., Aquaculture

ATTACHED INSTITUTES

The mailing address is that of the Hobart campus unless indicated otherwise

Central Science Laboratory: Dir J. A. HUTTON.

Centre for Biodiversity and Evolutionary Biology: Dir Assoc. Prof. A. RICHARDSON.

Centre for Furniture Design: Co-ordinator K. PERKINS.

Centre for Regional Economic Analysis: Dir Dr J. R. MADDEN.

Centre for Tasmanian Historical Studies: Dir Prof. M. BENNETT.

Co-operative Research Centre for the Antarctic and Southern Ocean Environment: Dir Prof. G. W. PALTRIDGE.

Co-operative Research Centre for Sustainable Production Forestry: Dir Prof. J. B. REID.

English Language Centre: Dir R. R. STODDART.

Institute of Antarctic and Southern Ocean Studies: Dir Prof. G. W. PALTRIDGE.

Menzies Centre for Population Health Research: Dir Prof. T. DWYER.

Special Research Centre for Ore Deposit Research: Dir Prof. R. R. LARGE.

Tasmanian Aquaculture and Fisheries Institute: Dir Dr C. BUXTON.

Tasmanian Electronic Commerce Centre: Dir J. MCCANN.

Tasmanian Institute of Agricultural Research: Dir Prof. R. CLARK.

University Department of Rural Health: Dir Assoc. Prof. J. H. WALKER.

VICTORIA UNIVERSITY

POB 14428, Melbourne, Vic. 8001
Telephone: (3) 9688-4000
Fax: (3) 9689-4069
Internet: www.vu.edu.au

Founded 1990 by merger of Footscray Institute of Technology and the Western Institute; merged with Western Melbourne Institute of Technical and Further Education 1998

Academic year: March to November

Chancellor: His Honour Mr Justice FRANK VINCENT

President and Vice-Chancellor: Prof. ELIZABETH HARMAN

Deputy Vice-Chancellors: RICHARD CARTER, Prof. MICHAEL HAMERSTON, Prof. JOHN MCCALLUM

Pro Vice-Chancellor (International): BRIAN STODDART

Pro Vice-Chancellor (Research): Prof. VAUGHAN BECK

Pro Vice-Chancellor (Staffing and Students): CHRISTINE KOTUR

University Secretary and General Counsel: Dr STEVEN STERN

University Librarian: DOREEN PARKER

Number of teachers: 1,118

Number of students: 52,207

Publications: *Beanland Lectures* (annually), *Jipam* (journal of inequalities in pure and applied mathematics, irregular)

DEANS

Faculty of Arts: Prof. ROBERT PASCOE
Faculty of Business and Law: Prof. ROMAN TOMASIC
Faculty of Human Development: Prof. CAROL MORSE
Faculty of Science, Engineering and Technology: Prof. ALBERT MCGILL

PROFESSORS

ADAMS, R., Europe–Australia Institute
ANDERSON, R., Accounting
ANDREWS, N., Law
ARMSTRONG, A., School of Management
ARUP, C., Law
BAKER, H., Nursing
BROCK, D., Faculty of Arts
CARLSON, J., Centre for Rehabilitation
CARY, J., Key Research Area of Integrated Food Value Chain
CLARK, C., Accounting
DAVIDSON, J., History
DEERY, P., Dept of Asian and International Studies
DRAGOMIR, S., Engineering
EADE, R., Arts
FAIRCLOUGH, R., Science
FAULKNER, M., Telecommunications
GABB, R., Centre for Educational Development and Support
GEORGE, G., Accounting
GLASBEEK, H., Faculty of Business and Law
GREWAL, B., Centre for Strategic Economic Studies
HOUGHTON, J., Centre for Strategic Economic Studies
JAGO, L., Tourism and Hospitality Studies
KALAM, A., Engineering
KING, B., School of Hospitality, Tourism and Marketing
LEUNG, C., Computer Science
MCGRATH, M., Information Systems
MCQUEEN, R., Law
MARTIN, E., Postgraduate Studies
MATTHEWS, B., Europe–Australia Institute
MORRIS, A., Faculty of Human Development
MUTZELFELDT, M., Management
PATIENCE, A., Arts
POLONSKY, M., Marketing
PRIESTLY, I., Accounting
PRILLELTENSKY, I., Psychology
ROBERTS, T., School of Human Movement, Recreation and Performance
ROBINSON, R., Intermodal Transport Systems
RYAN, M., Education
SEEDSMAN, T., Faculty of Human Development
SHEEHAN, P., Centre for Strategic Economic Studies
SINCLAIR, J., Faculty of Arts
THOMAS, I., Centre for Environmental Safety and Risk Engineering
THORPE, G., School of the Built Environment
TURNER, L., School of Applied Economics
WILSON, K., Economics
XIE, M., Engineering

UNIVERSITY OF WESTERN AUSTRALIA

35 Stirling Highway, Crawley, WA 6009
Telephone: (8) 6488-6000
Fax: (8) 6488-1380
E-mail: general.enquiries@uwa.edu.au
Internet: www.uwa.edu.au

Founded 1911

Academic year: February to October

Chancellor: Dr K. C. MICHAEL
Pro-Chancellor: Hon. Justice C. A. WHEELER
Vice-Chancellor: Prof. A. D. ROBSON
Deputy Vice-Chancellor: Prof. M. SEARES
Pro Vice-Chancellor (Academic): Prof. B. PROBERT
Executive Director (Academic Services) and Registrar: P. W. CURTIS
Executive Director (Finance and Resources): G. MCMATH
Pro Vice-Chancellor (Research and Innovation): Prof. D. MCEACHERN
Librarian: J. ARFIELD
Number of teachers: 1,162
Number of students: 16,659

Publications: *Annual Report*, *Research Expertise* (annually), *Uniview* (3 a year)

DEANS

Faculty of Architecture, Landscape and Visual Arts: D. C. BALL
Faculty of Arts, Humanities and Social Sciences: Prof. A. PAUWELS
Faculty of Economics and Commerce: Dr T. HORTON
Faculty of Education: Assoc. Prof. M. H. O'NEILL
Faculty of Engineering, Computing and Mathematics: Prof. M. BUSH
Faculty of Law: Prof. W. J. FORD
Faculty of Life and Physical Sciences: Prof. G. STEWART
Faculty of Medicine and Dentistry: Prof. I. PUDDEY
Faculty of Natural and Agricultural Sciences: Prof. A. ROBERTSON

PROFESSORS

ABBOTT, L. K., Soil Science and Plant Nutrition
ABBOTT, P. V., Clinical Dentistry
ALMEIDA, O. P., Geriatric Psychiatry
ARNOLDA, L. F., Cardiology
ATKINS, C. A., Plant Biology
ATLAS, M. D., Otolaryngology
BADCOCK, D. R., Psychology
BADDELEY, A. J., Mathematics and Statistics
BAILEY, W. J., Animal Biology
BARLEY, M. E., Earth and Geographical Sciences
BARTLETT, R. H., Law
BASSOM, A., Mathematics and Statistics
BEAZLEY, L. D., Animal Biology
BEILIN, L. J., Medicine
BERNERS-PRICE, S. J., Biological Chemistry
BLAIR, D. G., Physics
BLANKSBY, B. A., Human Movement and Exercise Science
BOSWORTH, A. B., Classics and Ancient History
BOSWORTH, R. J. B., History
BOWDLER, S., Archaeology
BRADSHAW, S. D., Animal Biology
BRENNAN, A. A., Philosophy
BUSH, M., Mechanical Engineering
CANTONI, A., Electrical and Electronic Engineering
CAWOOD, P., Tectonic Special Research Centre
CHISHOLM, J. S., Anatomy and Human Biology
CHRISTIANSEN, F. T., Pathology
CLEMENTS, K. W., Economics
COCKS, P. S., Plant Biology
CONSIDINE, J. A., Plant Biology
CONSTABLE, I. J., Ophthalmology and Visual Science
CORAM, A. T., Political Science and International Relations
CORDERY, J. L., Management
CRAWFORD, P. M., History
DAINTITH, T. C., Law
DAVIES, P., Animal Biology
DAVIS, T. M. E., Medicine
DAWKINS, R. L., Pathology
DAY, D. A., Biochemistry
DEEKS, A. J., Civil Engineering
DHARMARAJAN, A. M., Anatomy and Human Biology
DODSON, J. R., Geography
DYSKIN, A. V., Civil and Resource Engineering
EGGLETON, I. R. C., Accounting and Finance
ELLIOTT, B. C., Human Movement and Exercise Science
EMERY, J., General Practice
ETHERINGTON, N. A., History
EVERETT, J. E., Information Management
FAHEY, M., Civil Engineering
FARAONE, L., Electrical and Electronic Engineering

FLETCHER, D. R., Surgery
FLICKER, L., Geriatric Medicine
FRASER, H. D., English
GARRY, R., Paediatrics and Clinical Gynaecology
GILKES, R. J., Agriculture
GRIFFITHS, G., English
GROUNDS, M. D., Anatomy and Human Biology
GROVE, J. R., Human Movement and Exercise Science
GROVES, D. I., Geology and Geophysics
HALL, J. C., Surgery
HALL, S. R., Crystallography
HAO, H., Civil Engineering
HARTMANN, P. E., Biochemistry
HARVEY, A. R., Anatomy and Human Biology
HASKELL, D. J., English
HOLMAN, D., Population Health
HOPPER, S., Soil Science and Plant Nutrition
HOUGHTON, S. J., Education
HURLE, B., Oil and Gas Engineering
HULSE, G. K., Alcohol and Drug Studies
IMBERGER, J., Environmental Engineering
IVEY, G. N., Water Research
IZAN, H. Y., Management
JABLENSKY, A. V., Psychiatry
JANCA, A., Psychiatry
JELINEK, G. A., Emergency Medicine
JOHNSON, M. S., Animal Biology
KAKULAS, B. A., Neuropathology
KENNEDY, D. L., Classics and Ancient History
KIRSNER, P. K., Psychology
KLINKEN, S. P., Clinical Biochemistry
KUSTER, M. S., Orthopaedics
LAING, N. G., Neurology
LAMBERS, J. T., Plant Biology
LANDAU, L. I., Medicine and Dentistry
LEEDMAN, P. J., Cancer Medicine
LESOUËF, P. N., Paediatrics
LEVINE, M. P., Philosophy
LEWANDOWSKY, S., Psychology
LINDNER, R. K., Agriculture
LONDON, G. L., Architecture
MCALEER, M., Economics
MCCORMICK, P. G., Materials Engineering
MCEACHERN, D., Research and Innovation
MCGEACHIE, J. K., Anatomy and Human Biology
MACLEOD, C., Psychology
MCMENAMIN, P. G., Anatomy and Human Biology
MCSHANE, S. L., Management
MALLER, R., Accounting and Finance
MARTIN, G. B., Animal Biology
MASTAGLIA, F. L., Neurology
MILLER, P. W., Economics
MILLWARD, M. J., Medicine and Pharmacology
MILNE, G. J., Computer Science
MITCHELL, H. W., Physiology
MIZERSKI, R. W., Marketing
MURDOCH, C., Rural and Remote Medicine
NEWNHAM, J. P., Maternal–Fetal Medicine
NIVBRANT, B., Surgery
NOAKES, J. L., Mathematics
O'DONOGHUE, T. A., Education
O'DONOVAN, J., Law
OH, T. E., Anaesthesia
OLYNYK, J. K., Gastroenterology
OWENS, R. A., Computer Science
PALMER, L., Population Health
PAN, J., Mechanical Engineering
PANNELL, D. J., Agriculture
PATTIARATCHI, C., Water Research
PAUWELS, A., Arts, Humanities and Social Sciences
PAYNE, R., Psychology
PLOWMAN, D. H., Management
PORTER, P. H., International Relations
POWLES, S. B., Plant Biology
PRAEGER, C. E., Pure Mathematics
PROBERT, B., Vice-Chancellery
PUDDEY, I., Medicine
PUNCH, K. F., Education
RAKOCZY, P. E., Ophthalmology and Visual Science
RANDOLPH, M. F., Civil Engineering
RASTON, C. L., Chemistry
RAVINE, D., Medical Genetics
REDGRAVE, T. G., Physiology
RENGEL, Z., Agriculture
RHODES, G., Psychology
RILEY, T. V., Microbiology
ROBERTSON, A., Natural and Agricultural Sciences
ROBERTSON, D., Physiology
ROBINSON, B. W. S., Medicine
ROBSON, A. D., Soil Science and Plant Nutrition
SAMPSON, D. D., Electrical and Electronic Engineering
SAUNDERS, C. M., Surgery
SEARES, M., Vice-Chancellery
SHELLAM, G. R., Microbiology
SIDDIQUE, K., Agriculture
SIMMER, K., Paediatrics
SIVAPALAN, M., Water Research
SIVASITHAMPARAM, K., Agriculture
SLY, P. D., Paediatrics
SOUTAR, G. N., Management
STACEY, M. C., Surgery
STACHOWIAK, G. W., Mechanical Engineering
STANLEY, F. J., Paediatrics
STARKSTEIN, S. E., Psychiatry
STEWART, G., Life and Physical Sciences
STEWART, G. A., Microbiology
STOCKPORT, G. J., Management
STONE, B. J., Mechanical Engineering
TAPLIN, J. H. E., Information Management
TRIGGER, D. S., Anthropology
TURKINGTON, D. A., Economics
WADDELL, B. J., Anatomy and Human Biology
WADE, L., Plant Biology
WALKER, D. I., Plant Biology
WATTS, G. F., Medicine
WEINSTEIN, P., Population Health
WHITE, A. H., Chemistry and Crystallography
WHITE, R. S., English
WILLIAMS, J. F., Physics
WITHERS, P. C., Animal Biology
WOOD, D. J., Orthopaedics
YU, D. Y., Ophthalmology
ZHENG, M. H., Surgery

UNIVERSITY OF WESTERN SYDNEY

Locked Bag 1797, Penrith, South DC, NSW 1797
Telephone: (2) 9852-5555
Fax: (2) 9852-5556
E-mail: international@uws.edu.au
Internet: www.uws.edu.au

Founded 1989
State control
Academic year: March to December

Chancellor: M. JOHN PHILLIPS
Vice-Chancellor: Prof. JANICE REID
Deputy Vice-Chancellor (Academic and Services): Prof. ROBERT COOMBES
Deputy Vice-Chancellor (Development and International): Prof. CHUNG-TONG WU
Academic Registrar: COLIN HAWKINS
Librarian: LIZ CURACH

Library of 1,000,606 vols
Number of teachers: 1,001
Number of students: 32,000

DEANS

College of Arts, Education and Social Sciences: Prof. WAYNE MCKENNA
College of Law and Business: Prof. ROBIN WOELLNER
College of Science, Technology and Environment: Prof. MICK WILSON
College of Social and Health Sciences: Prof. JOHN MCCALLUM

HEADS OF SCHOOL

College of Arts, Education and Social Sciences:
- Communication, Media and Design: KAYE SHUMACK
- Contemporary Arts: JULIAN KNOWLES
- Education and Early Childhood: Assoc. Prof. TONI DOWNES
- Humanities: Dr CAROL LISTON
- Languages and Linguistics: Prof. STUART CAMPBELL
- Psychology: Prof. JIM MCKNIGHT
- Sociology and Lifelong Learning: Dr STEVE WILSON

College of Law and Business:
- Accounting: Prof. GARRY TIBBITS
- Construction, Property and Planning: Assoc. Prof. GRAHAM MILLER
- Economics and Finance: Dr BRIAN PINKSTONE
- Law: Prof. CAROLYN SAPPIDEEN
- Marketing and International Business: Prof. HARRY IRWIN
- Quantitative Methods and Mathematical Science: Assoc. Prof. ROBERT MELLOR
- School of Management: DENNIS MORTIMER

College of Science, Technology and Environment:
- Computing and Information Technology: Assoc. Prof. GEORGE BRYAN
- Engineering and Industrial Design: Prof. STEVEN RILEY
- Environment and Agriculture: Assoc. Prof. ROBERT MULLEY
- Science, Food and Horticulture: Dr JIM BERGAN

College of Social and Health Sciences:
- Applied Social and Human Services: Assoc. Prof. KEITH BENNETT
- Exercise and Health Sciences: Dr GODFREY ISOUARD
- Nursing, Family and Community Health: Prof. JOHN DALY

UNIVERSITY OF WOLLONGONG

Northfields Ave, Wollongong, NSW 2522
Telephone: (2) 4221-3555
Fax: (2) 4221-3477
Internet: www.uow.edu.au

Founded 1961 as a College of the University of New South Wales; merged with Wollongong Inst. of Education 1982
Academic year: March to November (two sessions), and a summer session from December to February

Chancellor: MICHAEL CODD
Vice-Chancellor and Principal: Prof. GERARD SUTTON
Vice-Principal (Administration): CHRIS GRANGE
Vice-Principal (International): JAMES LANGRIDGE
Pro-Vice-Chancellor (Academic): Prof. ROB CASTLE
Pro-Vice-Chancellor (Operations): Prof. JOHN PATTERSON
Pro-Vice-Chancellor (Research): Prof. MARGARET SHEIL
Director of the Dubai Campus: Dr NICE VAN DER WELT
Registrar: Dr DAVID CHRISTIE (acting)
Librarian: FELICITY MCGREGOR

Number of teachers: 656
Number of students: 21,148

Publications: *Annual Report*, *Australian Journal of Information Systems*, *Australian Journal of Natural Resources Law and Policy*, *Boxkite* (creative arts), *Campus News* (weekly), *Illawarra Unity* (labour history), *International Journal of Forensic Psychology*, *Journal of University Teach-*

ing and Learning Practice, *Rhizome* (2 a year)

FACULTY DEANS

Faculty of Arts: Prof. ANDREW WELLS
Faculty of Commerce: Prof. JOHN GLYNN
Faculty of Creative Arts: Prof. ANDREW SCHULTZ
Faculty of Education: Prof. BARRY HARPER
Faculty of Engineering: Prof. CHRIS COOK (acting)
Faculty of Health and Behavioural Sciences: Prof. DON IVERSON
Faculty of Informatics: Prof. JOE CHICHARO
Faculty of Law: Prof. STUART KAYE
Faculty of Science: Prof. ROB WHELAN

PROFESSORS

Faculty of Arts:

BERN, J., Social Sciences, Media and Communication
BEDER, S., Social Sciences, Media and Communication
KITLEY, P., Social Sciences, Media and Communication
VICKERS, A., History and Politics

Faculty of Commerce:

BARRETT, M., GSBPD
EAGAR, K., Centre for Health Services Development
EKLUND, P., Economics and Information Systems
FUNNELL, W., Accounting and Finance
GAFFIKIN, M., Accounting and Finance
LEWIS, D., Economics and Information Systems
ROSSITER, J., Management, Marketing and Employment Relations
SPEDDING, T., Management and Marketing
TURPIN, T., Management, Marketing and Employment Relations
VILLE, S., Economics and Information Systems
WORTHINGTON, A., Accounting and Finance

Faculty of Creative Arts:

KNOWLES, J., Music
LAWSON, J., Visual Arts and Graphic Design

Faculty of Education:

DINHAM, S., Australian Centre for Educational Leadership
WRIGHT, J., Associate Dean Research

Faculty of Engineering:

ARNOLD, P., Mechanical Engineering
BRINSON, G., Mechanical Materials and Mechatronics
BROWN, H., Steel Institute
CHOWDURY, R., Civil Mining and Environmental Engineering
DIPPENAAR, R., Steel Institute
DOU, S., Mechanical Materials and Mechatronics
FISHER, P., Engineering Physics
INDRARATNA, B.
LIU, H., ISEM
MCCARTHY, G., Civil Mining and Environmental Engineering
NORRISH, J.
ROZENFELD, A., Engineering Physics
SINGH, R., Civil Mining and Environmental Engineering
SPINKS, G., Mechanical Materials and Mechatronics
TIEU, A.
UY, B., Civil Mining and Environmental Engineering
VARIN, R. A., Mechanical Materials and Mechatronics
WEST, M., Mechanical Materials and Mechatronics
ZHANG, C., Engineering Physics

Faculty of Health and Behavioural Science:

BARRY, R., Psychology
CALVERT, G. D., Graduate School of Public Health
DEANE, F., Psychology
HOGG, J., Medicine
IVERSON, D.
STEELE, J., Biomedical Sciences
TAPSELL, L., Biomedical Sciences

Faculty of Informatics:

BUNDER, M., Mathematics and Applied Statistics
EKLUND, P.
FULCHER, J., Information Technology and Computer Science
GHOSE, A., Information Technology and Computer Science
GOSBELL, V., Electrical, Computer and Telecommunications Engineering
GRIFFITHS, D. A., Mathematics and Applied Statistics
HILL, J., Mathematics and Applied Statistics
OGUNBONA, P., Information Technology and Computer Science
SAFAEI, F., Electrical, Computer and Telecommunications Engineering
SEBERRY, J., Information Technology and Computer Science
STEEL, D., Mathematics and Applied Statistics

Faculty of Law:

FARRIER, M., Natural Resources Law and Policy
TSAMENYI, M., Centre for Maritime Policy

Faculty of Science:

AYRE, D., Biological Sciences
BREMNER, J., Chemistry
CHIVAS, A., Geosciences
GRIFFITH, D., Chemistry
KANE-MAGUIRE, L., Chemistry
MORRISION, J., Environmental Science
NANSON, G., Geosciences
OLSSEN, M., Biological Sciences
PYNE, S., Chemistry
WALKER, M., Biological Sciences
WALLACE, G., Intelligent Polymer Research Institute

Colleges

Ansto Training: Private Mail Bag 1, Menai, NSW 2234; tel. (2) 9717-9430; fax (2) 9717-9449; internet www.ansto.gov.au; f. 1964; the training arm of the University of NSW and the Australian Nuclear Science and Technology Organisation; short courses in use of radioisotopes, radionuclides in medicine, radiation protection and occupational health and safety; Exec. Dir and Chief Exec. Dr IAN SMITH; publ. *Annual Report*.

Australian Film, Television and Radio School: POB 126, North Ryde, NSW 2113; tel. (2) 9805-6611; fax (2) 9887-1030; f. 1973; library: 20,000 vols; 100 full-time, 3,000 part-time/short course students; courses: 1- and 2-year courses (postgraduate level), 7-month commercial radio course, short industry courses; Dir MALCOLM LONG; Library Man. MICHELE BURTON.

Australian Maritime College: POB 986, Launceston, Tas. 7250; tel. (3) 6335-4711; fax (3) 6326-6493; e-mail amcinfo@amc.edu.au; internet www.amc.edu.au; f. 1978; library: 36,800 vols; 75 teachers; 1,300 students; Principal Dr NEIL OTWAY; Asst Registrar ELIZABETH VAGG; Library Officer MICHELLE STEVENS; publs *Annual Report*, *Handbook*, *AMC News*, *Course Brochures*

FACULTY DIRECTORS

Fisheries and Marine Environment: Dr PAUL MCSHANE
Maritime Transport and Engineering: Dr BARRIE LEWARN

National Art School: Forbes St, Darlinghurst, NSW 2010; tel. (2) 9339-8744; fax (2) 9339-8740; e-mail nas@det.nsw.edu.au; internet www.nas.edu.au; f. 1843; honours and masters courses offered in ceramics, painting, photography, printmaking, sculpture with painting and art history and art theory; organises a visual arts public programme; 100 teachers; 400 students; Dir BERNARD OLLIS; Deputy Dir GEOFF IRELAND.

National Institute of Dramatic Art: UNSW, Sydney, NSW 2052; tel. (2) 9697-7600; fax (2) 9662-7415; e-mail nida@unsw.edu.au; internet www.nida.unsw.edu.au; f. 1958; degree, graduate diploma and advanced diploma courses; library: 28,000 vols, 55 periodicals; 150 full-time students, 5,000 part-time students in Open Program; Dir JOHN R. CLARK.

AUSTRIA

The Higher Education System

Austria's oldest institution is the University of Vienna, established in 1365. Institutes of adult education (Volkshochschulen) are found in all provinces, as are other centres operated by public authorities, church organizations and the Austrian Trade Union Federation. The central controlling and funding body is the Federal Ministry of Education and Research. University-level education is free, and the guiding framework is based on the General Law for University Education (1966) and the University Organization Law (1975). Since 2003 extensive reforms of the higher education system have been enacted. Universities have become quasi-autonomous institutions, independent of state control. A more 'top-down' form of management has been introduced, with university councils responsible for appointing senior managers (Rektorat). Other reforms include the separation of the three medical universities from their parent institutions, the accreditation of private universities and the introduction of competitive hiring practices for recruitment of academic staff. However, reforms have been hampered by the lack of additional funding beyond inflation-level increases.

Admission to higher education is based on award of the Reifeprüfung (the certificate received upon successful completion of secondary education). In addition, all Austrian citizens over the age of 24 years, and with professional experience, may attend certain university courses in connection with their professional career or trade. However, for certain courses of study offered at Fachhochschulen students may be required to take extra examinations. Students without the Reifeprüfung can gain admission to university study by completing a preparatory course and the Studienberechtigungsprüfung examination. Successful completion of this course gives access to study in the fields in which the examinations were taken.

As one of the original signatories to the Bologna Process, Austria has implemented the two-tier system of undergraduate and graduate Bachelor and Masters level degrees alongside the traditional degrees, with a view to phasing the latter out entirely. However, medical degree programmes and upper-secondary teaching qualifications are exempt from the new system. The following degrees are available: Bakkalaureat, Diplomstudium/Magister, Fachhochschuldiplom and Kurzstudium (all undergraduate); Magisterstudium (Bologna), Aufbaustudium and Doktoratstudium (both postgraduate). The traditional undergraduate degree is the Diplomstudium, leading to the title Magister or Diplom and lasting four to six years. The Bologna equivalent is the Bakkalaureat, lasting three to four years. Students with the Diplom or Magister traditionally proceeded directly to Doctoral studies, which usually lasted between one and three years and required the writing of a thesis and the passing of final examinations, known as Rigorosum. Under the Bologna Process students are now expected to study for up to two years after the Bakkalaureat and earn the Magisterstudium before undertaking doctoral studies.

Non-university higher education is offered in Hochschulen for students, graduates and those who do not have the Reifeprüfung. Fachhochschulen were launched in 1993, entry into which requires the Reifeprüfung. These offer professional training in technology, finance and social affairs which lasts for three to four years and allows admission to doctoral studies. Akademien and Kollegs also offer vocational training.

Learned Societies

GENERAL

Österreichische Akademie der Wissenschaften (ÖAW) (Austrian Academy of Sciences (AAS)): Dr Ignaz Seipel-Pl. 2, 1010 Vienna; tel. (1) 51581-0; fax (1) 5139541; e-mail webmaster@oeaw.ac.at; internet www.oeaw.ac.at; f. 1847; sections of Mathematics and Natural Sciences (Prof. Dr GEORG STINGL), Humanities and Social Sciences (Prof. Dr HERWIG FRIESINGER (acting)); attached institutes: see Research Institutes; 160 mems, 456 corresp. mems, 16 hon. mems; library: see Libraries and Archives; Gen. Sec. Prof. Dr HERBERT MANG; Pres. Prof. Dr HERWIG FRIESINGER; Sec. Prof. Dr GEORG STINGL; publs *Almanach*, *Anzeiger math.-nat. Klasse*, *Anzeiger phil.-hist. Klasse*, *Sitzungsberichte math.-nat. Klasse Abt. I, II*, *Sitzungsberichte phil.-hist. Klasse*, *Denkschriften der Gesamtakademie*, *Denkschriften math.-nat. Klasse*, *Denkschriften phil.-hist. Klasse*, *Monatshefte für Chemie*.

AGRICULTURE, FISHERIES AND VETERINARY SCIENCE

Österreichische Gesellschaft der Tierärzte (Austrian Society of Veterinary Medicine): Veterinärpl. 1, 1210 Vienna; tel. (1) 25077-1800; fax (1) 71606-900; e-mail sekretariat@oegt.at; internet www.oegt.at; f. 1919; 1,200 mems; Pres. Prof. Dr. PETRA WINTER; Sec. Dr MICHAEL WILLMANN; publ. *Wiener Tierärztliche Monatsschrift* (monthly).

ARCHITECTURE AND TOWN PLANNING

Österreichische Gesellschaft für Raumplanung (Austrian Society for Regional Planning): Wiedner Hauptstr. 8-10, 1040 Vienna; tel. (1) 58801-26633; fax (1) 58801-26699; e-mail oegr@oegr.at; internet www.oegr.at; Pres. Prof. Dr RUDOLF GIFFINGER; publs *FORUM Raumplanung* (2 a year), *Schriftenreihe* (irregular).

Österreichischer Ingenieur- und Architekten-Verein (Austrian Society of Engineers and Architects): Eschenbachgasse 9, 1010 Vienna; tel. (1) 5873536; fax (1) 5873536-5; e-mail office@oiav.at; internet www.oiav.at; f. 1848; 4,000 mems; Pres. HEINZ BRANDL; Gen. Sec. GEORG WIDTMANN; publ. *Österreichische Ingenieur- und Architekten-Zeitschrift* (6 a year).

Zentralvereinigung der Architekten Österreichs-ZV (Central Association of Austrian Architects): Salvatorgasse 10, 1010 Vienna; tel. (1) 5334429; e-mail zv@aaf.or.at; internet www.zv-architekten.at; f. 1907; 700 mems; Pres. HANS HOLLEIN.

BIBLIOGRAPHY, LIBRARY SCIENCE AND MUSEOLOGY

Gesellschaft für Landeskunde von Oberösterreich (Upper Austrian Cultural Heritage Society): Landstr. 31/II/ zi 225, LKZ Ursulinenhof, 4020 Linz; tel. (732) 770218; fax (732) 770218; e-mail ooelandeskunde@aon.at; internet www.ooelandeskunde.at; f. 1833; 860 mems; Chair. HR Mag. Dr GERHARD WINKLER; publs *Beiträge zur Landeskunde von Oberösterreich*, *Jahrbuch*, *Mitteilungen* (4 a year), *Schriftenreihe*.

Österreichische Gesellschaft für Dokumentation und Information (Austrian Society for Documentation and Information): Klosterwiesgasse 32/I, 8010 Graz; tel. (316) 818228; fax (316) 818228-30; e-mail office@oegdi.at; internet www.oegdi.at; f. 1951; organizes vocational training courses for information professionals, workshops, conference; 90 mems; Chair. Prof. Dr WALTER KOCH; Exec. Sec. Dr HERMANN HUEMER.

Vereinigung Österreichischer Bibliothekarinnen und Bibliothekare (Austrian Librarians Association): Fluherstr. 4, 6901 Bregenz; tel. (5574) 51144010; fax (5574) 51144095; e-mail harald.weigel@vorarlberg.at; internet voeb.uibk.ac.at; f. 1946; 1,100 mems; Pres. Dr HARALD WEIGEL; publ. *Mitteilungen* (4 a year).

ECONOMICS, LAW AND POLITICS

Nationalökonomische Gesellschaft (Austrian Economics Association): Klagenfurt Unive., c/o Economics Dept, Universitätsstr. 65–67, 9020 Klagenfurt; tel. (463) 2700-4102; fax (463) 2700-4191; internet www.noeg.ac.at; f. 1918; 240 mems; Pres. Prof. REINHARD NECK; Vice-Pres. Prof. GOTTFRIED HABER; publ. *Empirica* (applied economics and economic policy, 5 a year).

Österreichische Gesellschaft für Aussenpolitik und Internationale Beziehungen (Austrian Association for Foreign Policy and International Relations): Hofburg/Schweizerhof/Brunnenstiege, 1010 Vienna;

tel. (1) 5354627; fax (1) 5322605; e-mail oega@afa.at; internet afa.at/oega; f. 1958; 500 mems; Pres. Dr WOLFGANG SCHALLENBERG; Sec.-Gen. MICHAEL F. PFEIFER.

Österreichische Gesellschaft für Kirchenrecht (Austrian Society for Ecclesiastical Law): Freyung 6/2/2/4, 1010 Vienna; tel. (1) 427735811; fax (1) 427735899; internet www.univie.ac.at/recht-religion/ogk; f. 1949; 200 mems; Pres. Prof. Dr LUDGER MÜLLER; Vice-Pres. Dr WERNER JISA; publ. *Österreichisches Archiv für Recht und Religion*.

Österreichische Statistische Gesellschaft (Austrian Statistical Society): c/o Statistik Austria, Guglgasse 13, 1110 Vienna; tel. (1) 71128-7851; fax (1) 7158667; e-mail osg@statistik.gv.at; internet www.osg.or.at; f. 1951; 600 mems; Pres. Prof. Dr WILFRIED GROSSMANN; publ. *Österreichische Zeitschrift für Statistik* (irregular).

Wiener Juristische Gesellschaft (Vienna Legal Association): Heinestr. 38, 1020 Vienna; tel. (1) 21300-611; fax (1) 21300-609; e-mail office@wjg.at; internet www.wjg.at; f. 1867; 600 mems; Pres. Prof. Dr WALTER BARFUSS.

EDUCATION

Österreichische Rektorenkonferenz (Austrian Rectors' Conference): Liechtensteinstr. 22, 1090 Vienna; tel. (1) 313360; fax (1) 31336777; e-mail publicu@reko.ac.at; internet www.reko.ac.at; f. 1911; 21 mems; Pres. Prof. Dr CHRISTOPH BADELT; Sec.-Gen. HERIBERT WULZ.

Verband der Akademikerinnen Österreichs (Austrian Association of University Women): Reitschulgasse 2, 1010 Vienna; tel. (1) 5339080; internet www.vaoe.at; f. 1922; promotes scientific and professional advancement of university women graduates; 650 mems; Pres. MARIANNE BARGIL; Vice-Pres. Dr HELGA SZABO; publ. *VAÖ-Mitteilungen* (quarterly).

FINE AND PERFORMING ARTS

Bundesdenkmalamt (Federal Office for the Care and Protection of Monuments): Hofburg, Säulenstiege, 1010 Vienna; tel. (1) 53415-0; fax (1) 53415-252; e-mail service@bda.at; internet www.bda.at; f. 1850; protection and restoration of historical, artistic and cultural monuments; has control of excavations and art export; 200 mems; library of 40,000 vols; Pres. Dr WILHELM GEORG RIZZI; publs *Corpus der mittelalterlichen Wandmalereien Österreichs*, *Corpus Vitrearum Medii Aevi Österreich*, *Dehio Handbuch*, *Die Kunstdenkmäler Österreichs*, *Fundberichte aus Österreich*, *Österreichische-Kunsttopographie*, *Österreichische Zeitschrift für Kunst und Denkmalpflege*, *Studien zu Denkmalschutz und Denkmalpflege*, *Studien zur österreichischen Kunstgeschichte*, *Wiener Jahrbuch für Kunstgeschichte*.

Gesellschaft der Musikfreunde in Wien (Society of Friends of Music in Vienna): Bösendorferstr. 12, 1010 Vienna; tel. (1) 5058190; fax (1) 5058190-94; e-mail office@musikverein.at; internet www.musikverein.at; f. 1812; organizes concerts; 11,000 mems; choir of 300 mems; library: see Libraries; collection of music, MSS, instruments etc.; Pres. Dr DIETRICH KARNER; Exec. and Artistic Dir Dr THOMAS ANGYAN; publ. *Musikfreunde* (8 a year).

Internationale Franz Lehár-Gesellschaft (International Franz Lehár Society): Lothringerstr. 20, 1030 Vienna; tel. (1) 7132761; fax (1) 8873967; e-mail alleslehar@aon.at; internet www.franz-lehar-gesellschaft.com; f. 1949; Gen. Sec. Prof. HARALD SERAFIN.

Johann Strauss-Gesellschaft Wien (Johann Strauss Society of Vienna): Hetzgasse 19/9, 1030 Vienna; tel. and fax (1) 5339194; e-mail johann-strauss-gesellschaft@utanet.at; internet www.johann-strauss-gesellschaft.at; f. 1936; 300 mems; Pres. Prof. FRANZ MAILER; Sec.-Gen. Prof. Mag. FRIEDRICH FALTUS; publ. *Wiener Bonbons* (quarterly).

Kunsthistorische Gesellschaft (Art History Society): 1090 Vienna, Universitätscampus AAKH, Spitalgasse 2 (Eingang Garnisongasse 13); tel. (1) 427741410; fax (1) 42779414; e-mail eva-maria.grohs@univie.ac.at; f. 1956; 200 mems; Dir Prof. Dr HANS AURENHAMMER.

Künstlerhaus (Gesellschaft Bildender Künstler Österreichs) (Austrian Artists Association): Karlsplatz 5, 1010 Vienna; tel. (1) 5879663; fax (1) 5878736; e-mail office@k-haus.at; internet www.kuenstlerhaus.at; f. 1861; 460 mems; Pres. Arch. DI MANFRED NEHRER.

Österreichische Gesellschaft für Kommunikationswissenschaft (Austrian Society of Communications): Institut für Kommunikationswissenschaft, Universität Salzburg, Rudolfskai 42, 5020 Salzburg; tel. (662) 80444150; fax (662) 80444190; e-mail oegk@sbg.ac.at; internet www.ogk.at; f. 1976; encourages co-operation between communication researchers and communication practitioners (journalists, mediaworkers); 480 mems; Sec. Gen. Dr THOMAS STEINMAURER; Dir Dr MICHAEL MANFÉ; publ. *Medien Journal* (quarterly).

Österreichische Gesellschaft für Musik (Austrian Music Society): Hanuschgasse 3, 1010 Vienna; tel. (1) 5123143; fax (1) 5124299; e-mail oegm@music.at; internet www.music.at/oegm; f. 1964; 1,000 mems; library of 1,000 vols mainly on contemporary music, and records; Pres. Dr WALBURGA LITSCHAUER; Vice-Pres. Prof. Dr HARALD GOERTZ; Dir Dr CARMEN OTTNER; publ. *Beiträge* (every 2 years).

Österreichischer Komponistenbund (Association of Austrian Composers): Baumannstr. 8–10, 1031 Vienna; tel. (1) 7147233; fax (1) 7147233; e-mail info@komponistenbund.at; internet www.komponistenbund.at; f. 1913; 360 mems; Pres. Univ. Prof. KLAUS AGER; Vice-Pres KURT BRUNTHALER, MANFRED SPIES.

Wiener Beethoven Gesellschaft (Vienna Beethoven Society): Heiligenstadt, Probusgasse 6, 1190 Vienna; tel. (1) 3188215; f. 1954; 300 mems; Pres. Prof. ALEXANDER JENNER; publ. *Mitteilungsblatt* (quarterly).

Wiener Konzerthausgesellschaft (Vienna Concert Hall Society): Lothringerstr. 20, 1030 Vienna; tel. (1) 24200-333; fax (1) 24200-111; e-mail mail@konzerthaus.at; internet www.konzerthaus.at; f. 1913; 6,700 mems; Pres. Dr THERESA JORDIS; publ. *Konzerthaus Nachrichten* (8 a year).

Wiener Secession (Vienna Secession Association of Visual Artists): Friedrichstr. 12, 1010 Vienna; tel. (1) 5875307; fax (1) 5875307-34; e-mail office@secession.at; internet www.secession.at; f. 1897; promotes exhibitions of contemporary art in its own gallery; 260 mems; Pres. BARBARA HOLUB.

HISTORY, GEOGRAPHY AND ARCHAEOLOGY

Geschichtsverein für Kärnten (Historical Association of Carinthia): Museumgasse 2, 9020 Klagenfurt; tel. (463) 53630573; fax (463) 53630550; e-mail geschichtsverein@landesmuseum-ktn.at; internet www.geschichtsverein-ktn.at; f. 1844; 2,440 mems; Dir Dr CLAUDIA FRÄSS-EHRFELD; Sec. Prof. Dr GERNOT PICCOTTINI; publs *Carinthia I* (annual), *Archiv für Vaterländische Geschichte und Topographie* (irreg.), *Aus Forschung und Kunst* (irreg.).

Heraldisch-Genealogische Gesellschaft 'Adler' ('Eagle' Heraldry and Genealogy Society): Universitätstr. 6/9 B, 1096 Vienna; fax (1) 8775493; e-mail office@adler-wien.at; internet www.adler-wien.at; f. 1870; 700 mems; library of 40,000 vols; Pres. Dr GEORG KUGLER; Sec.-Gen. Dr ANDREAS CORNARO; publs *Jahrbuch*, *Zeitschrift* (quarterly).

Historische Landeskommission für Steiermark (Styrian Historical Land Commission): Karmeliterpl. 3/II, 8010 Graz; tel. (316) 8773013; fax (316) 8775504; f. 1892; 30 mems; Pres. Mag. FRANZ VOVES; Sec. Prof. Dr ALFRED ABLEITINGER; publs *Forschungen zur geschichtlichen Landeskunde der Steiermark*, *Arbeiten zur Quellenkunde*, *Quellen zur geschichtlichen Landeskunde der Steiermark*, *Forschungen und Darstellungen zur Geschichte des Steiermärkischen Landtages*, *Geschichte der Steiermark*, *Mitteilungsblatt der Korrespondenten*.

Historischer Verein für Steiermark (Styrian Historical Association): Karmeliterplatz 3, 8010 Graz; tel. and fax (316) 8772366; e-mail histor.verein.stmk@aon.at; internet members.aon.at/histor.verein.stmk; f. 1850; 1,360 mems; Chair. Prof. Dr GERHARD PFERSCHY; Sec. Dr GERNOT OBERSTEINER; publs *Beiträge zur Erforschung Steirischer Geschichtsquellen*, *Blätter für Heimatkunde*, *Zeitschrift*.

Kommission für Neuere Geschichte Österreichs (Commission for Modern Austrian History): Fachbereich Geschichte Universität Salzburg, Rudolfskai 42, 5020 Salzburg; tel. (662) 80444776; fax (662) 8044413; e-mail franz.adlgasser@sbg.ac.at; f. 1900; research into and pbls about modern Austrian history since the 16th century; 27 mems; Chair. Prof. Dr FRITZ FELLNER; Sec. Dr FRANZ ADLGASSER; publ. *Veröffentlichungen*.

Orientalische Gesellschaft (Oriental Society): IX, Spitalgasse 2/4, 1090 Vienna; tel. (1) 427743401; f. 1952; Pres. Prof. Dr HERMANN HUNGER.

Österreichische Byzantinische Gesellschaft (Austrian Byzantine Society): Postgasse 7–9, 1010 Vienna; tel. (1) 427742001; fax (1) 42779420; e-mail byzneo@univie.ac.at; internet www.univie.ac.at/byzneo; f. 1946; 145 mems; Pres. Prof. Dr JOHANNES KODER; publ. *Mitteilungen aus der österreichischen Byzantinistik und Neogräzistik* (annually).

Österreichische Geographische Gesellschaft (Austrian Geographical Society): Karl Schweighofer-Gasse 3, 1071 Vienna; tel. and fax (1) 5237974; internet www.oegg.info; f. 1856; 1,400 mems; Pres. Dr CHRISTIAN STAUDACHER; Hon. Pres. Dr INGRID KRETSCHMER; library: see Libraries; publ. *Mitteilungen* (annual).

Österreichische Gesellschaft für Archäologie (Austrian Archaeological Society): c/o Institut für Alte Geschichte, Altertumskunde und Epigraphik, Universität Wien, Dr Karl Lueger-Ring I, 1010 Vienna; e-mail oega@univie.ac.at; internet www.univie.ac.at/oega; f. 1972; publishes on topics relevant to Austria in archaeology, ancient history and numismatics; public lectures, excursions; 190 mems; Pres. Doz. Dr PETER SCHERRER; publs *Römisches Österreich* (annual), *Althistorisch-epigraphische Studien* (irreg.), *Austria Antiqua* (irreg.).

Österreichische Gesellschaft für Ur- und Frühgeschichte (Austrian Society for Pre- and Early History): Franz-Klein-Gasse 1, 1190 Vienna; tel. (1) 4277-40473; fax (1)

4277-9404; internet www.oeguf.ac.at; f. 1950; 1,050 mems; Gen. Sec. Mag. ALEXANDRA KRENN-LEEB; publ. *Archäologie Österreichs* (2 a year).

Österreichische Numismatische Gesellschaft (Austrian Numismatic Society): Burgring 5, 1010 Vienna; tel. (1) 52524-381; fax (1) 52524-353; e-mail office@oeng.at; internet oeng.at; f. 1870; 400 mems; library of 5,000 vols; Pres. Ing. HELMUT HIRSCHBERG; Vice-Pres. Prof. GÜNTHER DEMBSKI; Sec. Dr MICHAEL ALRAM; publs *Mitteilungen* (every 3 months), *Numismatische Zeitschrift* (irregular).

Verband Österreichischer Historiker und Geschichtsvereine (Union of Austrian Historians and Historical Associations): Postfach 263, 1015 Vienna; tel. (1) 79540-100; fax (1) 79540-199; f. 1949; 130 mem. socs; Man. Vice-Pres. Prof. Dr LORENZ MIKOLETZKY; Gen. Sec. Dr ERWIN A. SCHMIDL; publ. *Veröffentlichungen des Verbands Österreichischer Historiker und Geschichtsvereine* (every 2 or 3 years).

Verein für Geschichte der Stadt Wien (Association for the History of the City of Vienna): Wiener Stadt- und Landesarchiv, Rathaus, 1082 Vienna; tel. (1) 400084808; fax (1) 400084809; e-mail post@m08.magwien.gv.at; internet www.wien.gv.at/ma08/vgw; f. 1853; 1,592 mems; Pres. Dr KLARALINDA MA-KIRCHER; Vice-Pres. Dr HELMUT KRETSCHMER; Sec. Dr KARL FISCHER; publs *Studien zur Wiener Geschichte* (annually), *Wiener Geschichtsblätter* (4 a year).

LANGUAGE AND LITERATURE

Austria Esperantista Federacio (Austrian Esperanto Society): Postfach 39, 1014 Vienna; tel. (1) 8934196; e-mail aef@esperanto.at; internet aef.esperanto.at; f. 1935; 500 mems; library of 1,500 vols, 1,000 pamphlets; Pres. Mag. HERBERT MAYER; Vice-Pres. Prof. Dr HANS-MICHAEL MAITZEN; Gen. Sec. RICHARD HABLE; publs *Austria-Esperanto-Revuo*, *Esperanto-Servo* (quarterly).

British Council: Siebensterngasse 21, 1070 Vienna; tel. (1) 533-2616; fax (1) 533-261685; e-mail bc.vienna@britishcouncil.at; internet www.britishcouncil.at; f. 1946; offers courses and exams in English language and British culture and promotes cultural exchange with the UK; library contains large collection of modern British fiction, titles on British studies and English language-learning materials; access to British websites, databases and learning software; Dir WILL TODD.

Eranos Vindobonensis: Institut für Klassische Philologie, Mittel- und Neulatein, Universität Wien, Dr Karl Lueger-Ring 1, 1010 Vienna; tel. (1) 4277-41916; fax (1) 4277-9419; internet www.univie.ac.at/klassphil/eranos.html; f. 1885; philological soc.; 90 mems; Pres. Prof. Dr B. PALME; Sec. Dr P. LORENZ.

Gesellschaft für Klassische Philologie in Innsbruck (Classical Philological Society of Innsbruck): Institut für Klassische Philologie, Universität Innsbruck, Innrain 52, Innsbruck; tel. (512) 5074082; fax (512) 5072982; e-mail klassphil@uibk.ac.at; internet www.uibk.ac.at/sci-org/klassphil; f. 1958; 200 mems; Dir Mag. FLORIAN SCHAFFERNATH; Sec. Mag. STEFAN TILG; publ. *Acta philologica Aenipontiana*.

Gesellschaft zur Förderung Slawistischer Studien (Society for Slavic Studies): Teschnergasse 4/17, 1180 Vienna; f. 1983; Dir AAGE HANSEN-LÖVE; publs *Journal* (2 a year), *Wiener Slawistischer Almanach*, monograph series (quarterly).

Instituto Cervantes: Schwarzenbergplatz 2, 1010 Vienna; tel. (1) 5052535; fax (1) 505253518; e-mail cenvie@cervantes.es; internet viena.cervantes.es; offers courses and exams in Spanish language and culture and promotes cultural exchange with Spain and Spanish-speaking Latin and Central America; library: library of 19,000 vols, 70 periodicals; Dir FRANCISCO FERRERO CAMPOS.

Österreichische Gesellschaft für Literatur (Austrian Literary Society): Herrengasse 5, 1010 Vienna; tel. (1) 5338159; fax (1) 5334067; e-mail office@ogl.at; internet www.ogl.at; f. 1961; Pres. MARIANNE GRUBER.

Wiener Goethe-Verein (Vienna Goethe Association): Stallburggasse 2, 1010 Vienna; internet www.univie.ac.at/Goethe-Verein; f. 1878; 300 mems; library of 2,000 books; Pres. Prof. Dr HERBERT ZEMAN; publ. *Jahrbuch*.

Wiener Humanistische Gesellschaft: Institut für Klassische Philologie, Mittel- und Neulatein, Universität Wien, Dr-Karl-Lueger-Ring 1, 1010 Vienna; tel. (1) 4277-41917; fax (1) 4277-9419; e-mail kurt.smolak@univie.ac.at; f. 1947; philological society; 550 mems; Joint Pres. Prof. HEINRICH STREMITZER; Joint Pres. Prof. KURT SMOLAK; Sec. Dr MARGIT KAMPTNER; publ. *Wiener Humanistische Blätter*.

Wiener Sprachgesellschaft (Vienna Language Society): Institut für Sprachwissenschaft, Universität, 1010 Vienna; internet www.univie.ac.at/indogermanistik/wsg; f. 1947; 150 mems; Pres. Prof. GERHARD BUDIN; Sec. Dr H. CH. LUSCHÜTZKY; publ. *Die Sprache* (annual).

MEDICINE

Gesellschaft der Ärzte in Wien (Vienna Society of Physicians): Postfach 147, Frankgasse 8, 1096 Vienna; tel. (1) 4054777; fax (1) 4023090; e-mail info@billrothhaus.at; internet www4.billrothhaus.at; f. 1837; 1,278 mems; library of 200,000 vols, 25,900 monographs; Pres. Prof. Dr SEPP LEODOLTER; Secs Prof. Dr PAUL AIGINGER, Prof. Dr FRANZ KAINBERGER; publ. *Wiener Klinische Wochenschrift*.

Gesellschaft der Chirurgen in Wien (Vienna Society of Surgeons): Postfach 80, 1096 Vienna; tel. (1) 4087920; fax (1) 4081328; e-mail chirurgie@billrothhaus.at; internet www.chirurgie-ges.at; f. 1935; 137 mems; Dir Prof. Dr RAIMUND JAKESZ; Sec. Prof. Dr RUDOLF ROKA.

Internationale Paracelsus-Gesellschaft: Duerlingerstr. 23, 5020 Salzburg; tel. (662) 826773; e-mail info@paracelsus-ipg.com; internet www.teamforweb.at/kunden/paracelsus-ipg; f. 1951; 315 mems; 27 mem. asscns; Pres. Prof. Dr HEINZ DOPSCH; Gen. Sec. GERTRAUD WEISS; publs *Parcelsus-Briefe*, *Salzburger Beiträge zur Paracelsusforschung*.

Österreichische Gesellschaft für Anästhesiologie, Reanimation und Intensivmedizin (Austrian Society of Anaesthesiology, Resuscitation and Intensive Care Medicine): Höfergasse 13, 1090 Vienna; tel. (1) 4064810; fax (1) 4064811; e-mail office@oegari.at; internet www.oegari.at; f. 1951; 1,300 mems; Pres. Prof. Dr HANS GOMBOTZ; Sec. Prof. Dr C.-G. KRENN; publ. *A + IC News* (4 a year).

Österreichische Gesellschaft für Arbeitsmedizin (Austrian Society for Occupational Health): Kaplanhofstr. 1, 4020 Linz; tel. (732) 781560-0; fax (732) 784594; internet www.gamed.at; f. 1954; 350 mems; Pres. Dr REINHARD JÄGER; publ. *Jahresbericht*.

Österreichische Gesellschaft für Chirurgie (Austrian Society for Surgery): Frankgasse 8, POB 80, 1096 Vienna; tel. (1) 4087920; fax (1) 4081328; e-mail chirurgie@billrothhaus.at; internet www.chirurgie-ges.at; f. 1958; includes the associated Austrian societies for Traumatology, Orthopaedic, Thoracic and Cardiac Surgery, Vascular Surgery, Neurosurgery, Obesity Surgery, Paediatric Surgery, Plastic, Aesthetic and Reconstructive Surgery, Surgical Oncology, Osteosynthesis, Coloproctology, Hand Surgery, Surgical Research, Maxillo-Facial Surgery, Surgical Endocrinology, Keyhole Surgery, Medical Videography, Surgical Endoscopy, Hernia Surgery, Implantology and Tissue-Integrated Prosthesis; 4,440 mems; Sec. Gen. Prof. Dr RUDOLF ROKA; publ. *European Surgery/Acta Chirurgica Austriaca* (6 a year).

Österreichische Gesellschaft für Dermatologie und Venereologie (Austrian Dermatological and Venereological Society): c/o Wiener Medizinische Akademie für ärztliche Fortbildung und Forschung, Alserstr. 4, 1090 Vienna; tel. (1) 405138320; fax (1) 405138323; internet www.oegdv.at; 876 mems; Pres. Dr H. J. RAUCH; Vice-Pres. Prof. Dr H. PEHAMBERGER.

Österreichische Gesellschaft für Geriatrie und Gerontologie (Austrian Society for Geriatrics and Gerontology): Sozialmedizinisches Zentrum, Apollogasse 19, 1020 Vienna; tel. (1) 521031307; fax (1) 521031309; internet www.geriatrie-online.at; f. 1955; 200 mems; library of 2,000 vols; Pres. Dr FRANZ BÖHMER; Vice-Pres. Dr HANNES PLANK; publs *Aktuelle Gerontologie* (monthly), *European Journal of Geriatrics*, *Scriptum Geriatricum* (annually).

Österreichische Gesellschaft für Hals-, Nasen-, Ohrenheilkunde Kopf- und Halsschirurgie (Austrian Society of Ear, Nose and Throat Science, Head and Neck Surgery): Ebene 8, Währinger Gürtel 18–20, 1090 Vienna; tel. (1) 40400-3321; fax (1) 40400-3350; e-mail hno-lehre@meduniwien.ac.at; internet www.hno.at; f. 1892; 640 mems; Pres. Prof. Dr P. ZOROWKA; Gen. Sec. Prof. Dr KLAUS ALBEGGER; publ. *Zeitschrift*.

Österreichische Gesellschaft für Innere Medizin (Austrian Society for Internal Medicine): St.-Peter-Gasse 21, 1170 Vienna; tel. (1) 4850003; fax (1) 4850005; e-mail oegim@oegim.at; internet www.oegim.at; f. 1886; 400 mems; Pres. Prof. Dr ERNST PILGER; Sec. Dr J. PIDLICH; publ. *Wiener Zeitschrift für Innere Medizin*.

Österreichische Gesellschaft für Kinder- und Jugendheilkunde (Austrian Society for Paediatrics): c/o Frau Liesbeth Kautschitsch, LKH Klagenfurt, Abteilung für Kinder- und Jugendheilkunde, St Veiter Str. 47, 9026 Klagenfurt; tel. (463) 538-39403; fax (463) 538-39408; e-mail praesident.oegkj@kabeg.at; internet www.docs4you.at; f. 1962; 805 mems; Pres. Prof. Dr WILHELM KAULFERSCH; Sec. Prim. MARTIN EDLINGER; publs *Monatsschrift Kinderheilkunde* (online), *Pädiatrie und Pädologie* (6 a year).

Österreichische Gesellschaft für Klinische Neurophysiologie (Austrian Clinical Neurophysiological Society): Institut für Neurophysiologie der Universität Wien, Währingerstr. 18-20, 1090 Vienna; internet www.oegkn.at; f. 1954; 250 mems; Pres Prof Dr CHRISTOPH BAUMGARTNER, Dr MARTIN GRAF; Secs Prof. Dr WOLFGANG SERLES, Dr EUGEN TRINKA; publs *EEG/EMG*, *Thieme* (quarterly).

Österreichische Gesellschaft für Urologie und Andrologie (Austrian Society for Urology and Andrology): SMZOst-Donauspital, Abteilung f. Urologie und Andrologie, Langobardenstr. 122, 1220 Vienna; tel. (1) 28802-3702; fax (1) 28802-3780; internet www.uro.at; 511 mems; Pres. Prof. Dr WALTER STACKL; Sec. Dr MICHAEL RAUCHENWALD.

Österreichische Gesellschaft zum Studium der Sterilität und Fertilität (Austrian Society for the Study of Sterility and Fertility): Währinger Gürtel 18–20, 1090 Vienna; tel. (1) 404002813; internet www.univie.ac.at/Frauenheilkunde/endokrinologie; Pres. Prof. Dr G. TSCHERNE; Sec. Prof. Dr J. C. HUBER.

Österreichische Ophthalmologische Gesellschaft (Austrian Ophthalmological Society): Schlüsselgasse 9, 1080 Vienna; tel. (1) 4028540; fax (1) 4027935; e-mail oeog@augen.at; internet www.augen.at; f. 1955; 730 mems; library of 2,100 vols; Pres. Prof. Dr SUSANNE BINDER; Sec. Prof. Dr GÜNTHER GRABNER; publ. *Spectrum der Augenheilkunde* (every 2 months).

Österreichische Röntgengesellschaft—Gesellschaft für Medizinische Radiologie und Nuklearmedizin (Austrian Radiography Society): Alser Str. 4, 1090 Vienna; tel. (1) 404005803; fax (1) 404003777; e-mail osteo-mr@meduniwien.ac.at; internet www.oerg.at; f. 1946; 800 mems; Pres. Prof. Dr HERWIG IMHOF; publ. *ÖRG- Mitteilungen* (quarterly).

Verein für Psychiatrie und Neurologie (Society for Psychiatry and Neurology): Neurologische Universitätsklinik, Währinger Gürtel 18–20, 1090 Vienna; tel. (1) 404003514; internet www.meduniwien.ac.at/akh/verpsychneur; f. 1867; Pres. Prof. Dr KENNETH THAU; Secs Prof. Dr GABRIELE SACHS, Dr BERNHARD VOLLER.

Wiener Medizinische Akademie für Ärztliche Fortbildung und Forschung (Vienna Academy of Postgraduate Medical Education and Research): Alser Str. 4, 1090 Vienna; tel. (1) 4051383-0; fax (1) 4051383-23; e-mail rk@medacad.org; internet www.medacad.org; f. 1896; Pres. Prof. Dr H. GRÜBER; Exec. Dirs JEROME DEL PICCHIA, ROMANA KÖNIG; Secs Prof. Dr C. ZIELINSKI, Prof. Dr A. TUCHMANN.

NATURAL SCIENCES

General

Naturwissenschaftlicher Verein für Kärnten (Carinthian Association of Natural Sciences): Museumgasse 2, 9021 Klagenfurt; tel. (463) 53630574; fax (463) 53630597; e-mail nwv@landesmuseum-ktn.at; internet www.naturwissenschaft-ktn.at; f. 1848; 1,300 mems; Pres. Dr HELMUT ZWANDER; publ. *Carinthia II* (annually with special issues).

Biological Sciences

Österreichische Mykologische (Pilzkundliche) Gesellschaft (Austrian Mycological Society): Rennweg 14, 1030 Vienna; tel. (1) 4277-54050; fax (1) 4277-9541; e-mail irmgard.greilhuber@univie.ac.at; internet www.botanik.univie.ac.at/mycology/omg; f. 1919; 300 mems; library of 1,000 vols; mycological herbarium collection, fungal records database, excursions, lectures, newsletter; Pres. Dkfm. A. HAUSKNECHT; publ. *Österreichische Zeitschrift für Pilzkunde* (annually).

Zoologisch-Botanische Gesellschaft in Österreich (Zoological-Botanical Society of Austria): Althanstr. 14, Postfach 207, 1091 Vienna; fax (1) 4277-9542; e-mail wolfgang.punz@univie.ac.at; internet www.univie.ac.at/zoobot; f. 1851; 610 mems; Pres. Dr ERICH HÜBL; Gen. Sec. Dr W. PUNZ; publs *Koleopterologische Rundschau* (annually), *Verhandlungen* (annually), *Abhandlungen* (irregular).

Mathematical Sciences

Mathematisch-Physikalische Gesellschaft in Innsbruck (Mathematics and Physics Society of Innsbruck): c/o Manfred P. Leubner, Institut für Astrophysik, Universität Innsbruck, Technikerstr. 25, 6020 Innsbruck; tel. (512) 512-6060; fax (512) 512-2923; e-mail math-phys-ges@uibk.ac.at; internet www.uibk.ac.at/sci-org/math-phys-ges; f. 1936; 126 mems; Chair. MANFRED P. LEUBNER.

Österreichische Mathematische Gesellschaft (Austrian Mathematical Society): Technische Universität, E118, Wiedner Hauptstr. 8–10, 1040 Vienna; tel. (1) 5880111823; e-mail oemg@oemg.ac.at; internet www.oemg.ac.at; f. 1903; 537 mems; Chair. R. F. TICHY; publs *International Mathematical News* (3 a year), *Monatshefte für Mathematik* (12 a year).

Physical Sciences

Chemisch-Physikalische Gesellschaft in Wien (Vienna Chemical-Physical Society): Strudlhofgasse 4, 1090 Vienna; tel. (1) 427751153; f. 1869; 260 mems; Sec. Prof. Dr GEORG REISCHL; publ. *Bulletin* (2 a year).

Gesellschaft Österreichischer Chemiker (Austrian Chemical Society): Nibelungengasse 11/6, 1010 Vienna; tel. (1) 5874249; fax (1) 5878966; e-mail office@goech.at; internet www.goech.at; f. 1897; educational programme for professional advancement in chemistry; 1,900 mems in attached socs; Pres. D Dr HAIO HARMS; Vice-Pres. Prof. Dr WOLFGANG BUCHBERGER; Exec. Dir Dr ERICH LEITNER; publs *Chemiereport.at* (online at: www.chemiereport.at), *Chemistry–A European Journal* (co-author), *Monatshefte für Chemie*.

Österreichische Geologische Gesellschaft (Austrian Geological Society): Geologische Bundesanstalt, Neulinggasse 38, 1030 Vienna; tel. (1) 7125674-0; fax (1) 7125674-56; e-mail oegg@geologie.ac.at; internet www.geol-ges.at; f. 1907; 714 mems; Pres. WOLFGANG NACHTMANN; Vice-Pres. CHRISTIAN SPÖTL; publ. *Austrian Journal of Earth Sciences*.

Österreichische Gesellschaft für Analytische Chemie (Austrian Society for Analytical Chemistry):; tel. (1) 427752300; internet www.asac.at; f. 1948; 400 mems; Pres. Prof. Dr WOLFGANG LINDNER; Sec. Prof. Dr W. BUCHBERGER.

Österreichische Gesellschaft für Biochemie und Molekularbiologie (Austrian Society for Biochemistry and Molecular Biology): c/o Max. F. Perutz Laboratories, Medizinische Universität Wien, Dr. Bohrgasse 9/3, 1030 Vienna; internet www.ogbm.org; promotion of research and education in biochemistry, molecular biology and cell biology; 825 mems; Pres. ANDREA BARTA; Vice-Pres. MICHAEL BREITENBACH; publ. *ÖGBM Nachrichten* (quarterly).

Österreichische Gesellschaft für Erdölwissenschaften (Austrian Society for Petroleum Sciences): c/o Wirtschaftskammer Österreich, Wiedner Hauptstr. 63, Zimmer 4208, 1045 Vienna; tel. (5) 909004891; e-mail oegew@oil-gas.at; internet www.oegew.org; f. 1960; 502 mems; Pres. JOSEF HIEBLINGER; publs *Erdöl Erdgas Kohle*, scientific papers.

Österreichische Gesellschaft für Laboratoriumsmedizin und Klinische Chemie (Austrian Society of Laboratory Medicine and Clinical Chemistry): Tullnertalgasse 72, 1230 Vienna; tel. and fax (1) 8896238; e-mail office@oeglmkc.at; internet www.oeglmkc.at; f. 2004; Pres. Prof. Dr ILSE SCHWARZINGER; Sec. Doz. Dr WOLFGANG HÜBL.

Österreichische Gesellschaft für Meteorologie (Austrian Meteorological Society): Hohe Warte 38, 1190 Vienna; tel. (1) 36026-2002; fax (1) 3691233; e-mail dion@zamg.ac.at; internet www.boku.ac.at/oegm; f. 1865; 230 mems; Pres. Prof. Dr REINHOLD STEINACKER; Sec. Doz. Dr FRITZ NEUWIRTH.

Österreichische Physikalische Gesellschaft (Austrian Physical Society): c/o Dr Max E. Lippitsch, Institut für Experimentalphysik, Karl-Franzens-Universität Graz, Universitätsplatz 5, 8010 Graz; tel. (316) 380-5192; fax (316) 380-9816; e-mail office@oepg.at; internet www.oepg.at; f. 1950; 870 mems; Chair. Prof. Dr HELMUT RAUCH; Exec. Dir Prof. Dr MAX E. LIPPITSCH; publ. *Newsletter* (4 a year).

Österreichischer Astronomischer Verein (Austrian Astronomical Association): Hasenwartgasse 32, 1238 Vienna; tel. (1) 8893541-0; fax (1) 8893541-11; e-mail astbuero@astronomisches-buero-wien.or.at; internet members.ping.at/astbuero; f. 1924; astronomical phonomenology; 1,500 mems; Pres. JOHANN ALBRECHT; Sec. Prof. HERMANN MUCKE; publs *Der Sternenbote* (monthly), *Österreichischer Himmelskalender* (annual), *Seminarpapiere* (annual).

PHILOSOPHY AND PSYCHOLOGY

Österreichische Gesellschaft für Parapsychologie und Grenzbereiche der Wissenschaften (Austrian Society for Parapsychology and Frontier Areas of Science): c/o Manfred Kremser, Institute for Social and Cultural Anthropology, Vienna University, Universitätsstr. 7, 1010 Vienna; tel. (1) 427748507; fax (1) 4173119; e-mail office@parapsychologie.ac.at; internet parapsychologie.ac.at; f. 1927; 200 mems; library of 1,200 vols; Pres. Prof. Dr MANFRED KREMSER; Vice-Pres. and Sec.-Gen. Prof. W. PETER MULACZ.

Philosophische Gesellschaft Wien (Philosophical Society of Vienna): Universitätsstr. 7/2/2, 1010 Vienna; tel. (1) 4277-47402; fax (1) 4277-47492; f. 1954; 100 mems; Dir Prof. Dr HANS-DIETER KLEIN.

Sigmund Freud-Gesellschaft (Sigmund Freud Society): Berggasse 19, 1090 Vienna; tel. (1) 3191596; fax (1) 3170279; e-mail office@freud-museum.at; internet www.freud-museum.at; f. 1968; history and application of psychoanalysis; 1,000 mems; library of 8,000 vols, 15,000 off-prints, 45 journals; archives; Sigmund Freud museum; Pres. Doz. Dr H. LEUPOLD-LÖWENTHAL; Vice-Pres. Prof. Dr E. WEINZIERL; publ. *Newsletter* (4 a year).

Wiener Psychoanalytische Vereinigung (Vienna Psychoanalytical Association): Gonzagagasse 11, 1010 Vienna; tel. and fax (1) 5330767; e-mail office@wpv.at; internet www.wpv.at; f. 1908; 71 mems; Pres. Dr CHRISTINE DIERCKS; Sec. Mag. GUDRUN WOLFGRUBER.

RELIGION, SOCIOLOGY AND ANTHROPOLOGY

Anthropologische Gesellschaft in Wien (Vienna Anthropological Society): Burgring 7, 1010 Vienna; tel. (1) 52177-569; fax (1) 52177-309; e-mail ag@nhm-wien.ac.at; internet www.nhm-wien.ac.at/ag; f. 1870; 300 mems; Pres. HR Dr HERBERT KRITSCHER; Sec. HR Dr ANTON KERN; publs *Mitteilungen* (annually), *Prähistorische Forschungen* (irregular), *Anthropologische Forschungen* (irregular), *Völkerkundliche Veröffentlichungen* (irregular).

Evangelische Akademie Wien (Evangelical Academy in Vienna): Schwarzspanierstr. 13, 1090 Vienna; tel. (1) 4080695; fax (1) 408069533; e-mail akademie@evang.at; internet www.evang.at/akademie; f. 1955; Protestant adult education; documentation on church and society; Dir ROLAND RITTER-WERNECK.

Gesellschaft für die Geschichte des Protestantismus in Österreich (Society for History of Protestantism in Austria): Rooseveltplatz 10, 1090 Vienna; f. 1879; 300 mems; Chair. Prof. Dr GUSTAV REINGRABNER; publ. *Jahrbuch*.

Österreichische Gesellschaft für Soziologie (Austrian Sociological Society): Institut für Soziologie der Universität Graz, Universitätsstr. 15/G4, 1160 Graz; tel. (316) 3803544; fax (316) 3809515; e-mail kontakt@oegs.ac.at; internet www.oegs.ac.at; f. 1950; 430 mems; Pres. Prof. Dr CHRISTIAN FLECK; publ. *Österreichische Zeitschrift für Soziologie* (quarterly).

Verein für Landeskunde von Niederösterreich (Association for Regional Studies of Lower Austria): Landhausplatz 1, 3109 St Pölten; tel. (2742) 9005-16255; fax (2742) 9005-16550; e-mail postk2institut@noel.gv.at; internet www.noel.gv.at/service/k/k2/verein-landeskunde.htm; f. 1864; 1,300 mems; Pres. Hofrat Dr ANTON EGGENDORFER; Gen. Sec. Mag. WILLIBALD ROSNER; publs *Unsere Heimat* (4 a year), *Jahrbuch für Landeskunde von Niederösterreich*, *Forschungen zur Landeskunde von Niederösterreich*.

Verein für Volkskunde (Society of Ethnography and Popular Culture): Laudongasse 15–19, 1080 Vienna; tel. (1) 4068905; fax (1) 4085342; e-mail verein@volkskundemuseum.at; internet www.volkskundemuseum.at; f. 1894; 900 mems; Pres. Dr KONRAD KÖSTLIN; Sec. Dr MARGOT SCHINDLER; publs *Österreichische Zeitschrift für Volkskunde* (quarterly), *Volkskunde in Österreich* (monthly), *Österreichische Volkskundliche Bibliographie* (every 2–3 years), *Buchreihe der Österreichischen Zeitschrift für Volkskunde* (irregular), *Documenta Ethnographica* (irregular), *Sonderschriften*.

Wiener Katholische Akademie (Vienna Catholic Academy): Ebendorferstr. 8/10, 1010 Vienna; tel. (1) 4023917; fax (1) 4022355; internet stephanscom.at/edw/akademie.html; f. 1945; seminars and lectures, symposia, publications; 110 mems; library of 7,000 vols; Protector Erzbischof Cardinal Dr C. SCHÖNBORN; Dir Dr E. MAIER; publ. *Schriften der Wiener Katholischen Akademie*.

TECHNOLOGY

Österreichische Gesellschaft für Artificial Intelligence (Austrian Association for Artificial Intelligence): POB 177, 1014 Vienna; tel. (1) 427763117; e-mail anfrage@oegai.at; internet www.oegai.at; f. 1981; 150 mems; Pres. ERNST BUCHBERGER; publ. *ÖGAI-Journal* (quarterly).

Österreichische Gesellschaft für Vermessung und Geoinformation (Austrian Society for Surveying and Geological Information): Schiffamtsgasse 1–3, 1025 Vienna; tel. and fax (1) 2167551; e-mail office@ovg.at; internet www.ovg.at; f. 1973; 600 mems; library of 3,000 vols; Pres. Dipl.-Ing. GERT STEINKELLNER; Sec. Dipl.-Ing. KARL HAUSSTEINER; publ. *Österreichische Zeitschrift für Vermessung und Geoinformation* (quarterly).

Österreichische Studiengesellschaft für Kybernetik (Austrian Society for Cybernetic Studies): Freyung 6/6, 1010 Vienna; tel. (1) 5336112-60; fax (1) 5336112-77; e-mail sec@ofai.at; internet www.ofai.at; f. 1969; 1,238 mems (38 ordinary, 1,200 corresp.); Pres. Prof. Dr ROBERT TRAPPL; publs *Cybernetics and Systems: An International Journal* (8 a year), *Reports* (irregular).

Research Institutes

AGRICULTURE, FISHERIES AND VETERINARY SCIENCE

Bundesamt und Forschungszentrum für Landwirtschaft, Wien (Federal Office and Research Centre for Agriculture, Vienna): Spargelfeldstr. 191, Postfach 400, 1226 Vienna; tel. (1) 73216-0; fax (1) 73216-2100; e-mail office@bfl.at; internet www.bfl.ac.at; f. 1995; library of 100,000 vols; Dir-Gen. Hofrat Dipl.-Ing. A. KÖCHL; publs *Die Bodenkultur* (quarterly), *Pflanzenschutz* (quarterly), *Pflanzenschutzberichte* (2 a year).

Bundesamt und Forschungszentrum für Wald (Federal Office and Research Centre for Forests): Seckendorff-Gudent-Weg 8, 1131 Vienna; tel. (1) 878380; fax (1) 878381250; e-mail direktion@bfw.gv.at; internet bfw.ac.at; f. 1874; library of 48,000 vols; Dir HARALD MAUSER; publs *BFW-Berichte* (irregular), *Tätigkeitsbericht* (annually).

Bundesanstalt für Agrarwirtschaft (Federal Institute of Agricultural Economics): Marxergasse 2, 1030 Vienna; tel. (1) 8773651; fax (1) 8773651-7490; e-mail office@awi.bmlfuw.gv.at; internet www.awi.bmlfuw.gv.at; f. 1960; applied research; library of 65,000 vols, 420 periodicals; Dir HUBERT PFINGSTER; Librarian HUBERT SCHLIEBER; publs *Agrarpolitische Arbeitsbehelfe* (irregular), *Schriftenreihe der Bundesanstalt* (irregular).

Bundesanstalt für Alpenländische Landwirtschaft, Gumpenstein (Federal Research Institute for Agriculture in Alpine Regions, Gumpenstein): Steiermark, 8952 Irdning; tel. (3682) 22451-0; fax (3682) 22451-21; e-mail office@raumberg-gumpenstein.at; internet www.gumpenstein.at; f. 1947; library of 21,000 vols; Dir Dr ALBERT SONNLEITNER; publs *BAL-Berichte*, *BAL-Sortenversuchsergebnisse*, *BAL-Veröffentlichungen*.

ARCHITECTURE AND TOWN PLANNING

Österreichisches Institut für Raumplanung (Austrian Institute for Regional Studies and Spatial Planning): Franz Josefs Kai 27, 1010 Vienna; tel. (1) 5338747-0; fax (1) 5338747-66; e-mail oir@oir.or.at; internet www.oir.at; f. 1957; library of 38,000 vols; Dir Mag. PETER SCHNEIDEWIND; publ. *RAUM* (quarterly).

ECONOMICS, LAW AND POLITICS

Dr Karl Kummer Institut für Sozialreform, Sozial- und Wirtschaftspolitik (Institute for Social Reform and Social Politics): Ebendorferstr. 6/4, 1010 Vienna; tel. (1) 4052674; fax (1) 4052674-99; e-mail office@kummer-institut.at; internet www.kummer-institut.at; f. 1953; Exec. Dirs DORIS PALZ, ALEXANDER RAUNER; publ. *Gesellschaft und Politik*.

Institut für Europäische Integrationsforschung (EIF) (Institute for European Integration Research): Prinz Eugen-Str. 8, 1040 Vienna; tel. (1) 51581-7565; fax (1) 51581-7566; e-mail eif@oeaw.ac.at; internet www.eif.oeaw.ac.at; f. 1998; attached to Austrian Acad. of Sciences; Dir Prof. SONJA PUNTSCHER RIEKMANN.

Institut für Höhere Studien (Institute for Advanced Studies): 1060 Vienna, Stumpergasse 56; tel. (1) 59991-0; fax (1) 59991-162; e-mail ihs@ihs.ac.at; internet www.ihs.ac.at; f. 1963; postgraduate training and research in economics and finance, sociology and political science; library of 20,300 vols, 500 current periodicals; Dir Prof. Dr BERNHARD FELDERER; publs *Empirical Economics* (4 a year), *European Societies* (4 a year), *German Economic Revue* (4 a year).

Österreichische Forschungsstiftung für Entwicklungshilfe (Austrian Foundation for Development Research): Berggasse 7, 1090 Vienna; tel. (1) 3174010; fax (1) 3174015; e-mail office@oefse.at; internet www.oefse.at; f. 1967; documentation and information on development aid, developing countries and int. development, particularly relating to Austria; library of 50,000 vols, 140 periodicals; publs *BZA Newsletter* (3 a year), *ÖFSE-Edition* (irregular), *ÖFSE-Forum* (irregular), *Österreichische Entwicklungspolitik*. *Berichte-Analysen-Informationen* (annually).

Österreichisches Institut für Wirtschaftsforschung (Austrian Institute of Economic Research): Postfach 91, 1103 Vienna; tel. (1) 7982601; fax (1) 7989386; e-mail office@wifo.ac.at; internet www.wifo.ac.at; f. 1927; Dir Prof. Dr KARL AIGINGER; publs *Austrian Economic Quarterly*, *Empirica* (3 a year, with Austrian Economic Assen), *Monatsberichte* (monthly).

Österreichisches Meinungs- und Marktforschungsinstitut (Austrian Public Opinion and Market Research Institute): c/o Karmasin Marktforschung, Österreichisches Gallup Institut, Anastasius-Grün-Gasse 32, 1180 Vienna; tel. (1) 4704724; fax (1) 470472419; e-mail office@gallup.at; internet www.gallup.at; f. 1964; Dirs ROSWITHA HASSLINGER, Prof. FRITZ KARMASIN.

Österreichisches Ost- und Südosteuropa-Institut (Austrian Institute of East and South-East European Studies): Josefsplatz 6, 1010 Vienna; tel. (1) 5121895; fax (1) 512189553; e-mail office@osi.ac.at; internet www.osi.ac.at; f. 1958; library of 43,150 vols, 1,639 (339 current) periodicals and documents; Chair. of Exec. Board Prof. Dr A. SUPPAN; Dir Doz. Dr PETER JORDAN; publs *Österreichische Osthefte* (quarterly), *OSI-aktuell* (newsletter, irregular).

Statistik Austria: Guglgasse 13, 1033 Vienna; tel. (1) 71128-0; fax (1) 71128-7728; e-mail info@statistik.gv.at; internet www.statistik.gv.at; f. 1829; library of 210,000 vols; Pres. Prof. Dr PETER HACKL; publs *Statistisches Handbuch für die Republik Österreich* (annually), *Statistische Nachrichten* (monthly).

Wirtschaftsförderungsinstitut der Wirtschaftskammer Österreich (Institute of Business Promotion of the Austrian Federal Economic Chamber): Wiedner Hauptstr. 63, 1045 Vienna; tel. (1) 476-77; e-mail InfoCenter@wifiwien.at; internet www.wifi.at; f. 1946; adult education, management and vocational training, public relations for Austrian economy, consulting service, international business skills exchange; Man. Dir Dr MICHAEL LANDERTSHAMMER.

FINE AND PERFORMING ARTS

Abteilung für Inventarisation und Denkmalforschung (Department of Art Research and Inventory): Hofburg, Schweizerhof, Säulenstiege, 1010 Vienna; tel. (1) 53415-121; fax (1) 53415-5120; e-mail denkmalforschung@bda.at; internet www.bda.at; f. 1911; research and documentation on works of art in Austria; library of 22,000 vols; Chief Officer Dr ANDREAS LEHNE.

Gesellschaft für vergleichende Kunstforschung (Society of Comparative Art Research): Universitätscampus AAKH, Spitalgasse 2 (Eingang Garnisongasse 13), 1090 Vienna; tel. (1) 427741425; fax (1) 42779414; e-mail walter.krause@univie.ac.at; f. 1932; 300 mems; Sec.-Gen. Prof. Dr WALTER KRAUSE; publ. *Mitteilungen* (3 a year).

Wiener Gesellschaft für Theaterforschung (Viennese Society for Theatre Research): Hofburg, Batthyanystiege, 1010 Vienna; tel. (1) 427748401; fax (1) 42779484; e-mail otto.schindler@univie.ac.at; f. 1944; Pres. Prof. Dr WOLFGANG GREISENEGGER; Gen. Sec. Dr OTTO G. SCHINDLER; publs *Jahrbuch*, *Theater in Österreich* (annually).

HISTORY, GEOGRAPHY AND ARCHAEOLOGY

Forschungsgesellschaft Wiener Stadtarchäologie (Research Unit for Archaeology in Vienna): Apollogasse 7, 1070 Vienna; tel. (676) 7215105; internet www.archaeologie-wien.at; Chair. Dr ORTOLF HARL; publ. *Onomasticon Provinciarum Europae Latinarum*.

Institut für Demographie (Institute of Demography): Prinz-Eugen-Str. 8, 1040 Vienna; tel. (1) 515817702; fax (1) 515817730; e-mail vid@oeaw.ac.at; internet www.oeaw.ac.at/vid; attached to Austrian Acad. of Sciences; Dir Dr WOLFGANG LUTZ.

Institut für Realienkunde des Mittelalters und der Frühen Neuzeit (Institute for Research into Daily Life and Material Culture in Medieval and Early Modern Times): Körnermarkt 13, 3500 Krems an der Donau; tel. (2732) 84793; fax (2732) 84793-1; e-mail imareal@oeaw.ac.at; internet www.imareal.oeaw.ac.at; f. 1969; attached to Austrian Acad. of Sciences; Dir Dr ELISABETH VAVRA; publs *Veröffentlichungen* (every 2 years), *Medium Aevum Quotidianum* (3 or 4 a year), *Forschungen* (every 2 years).

LANGUAGE AND LITERATURE

Institut für Österreichische Dialekt- und Namenlexika (Institute for Lexicography of Austrian Dialects and Names): Postgasse 7, 1010 Vienna; tel. (1) 51581-3493; fax (1) 51581-3495; e-mail dinamlex@oeaw.ac.at; internet www.oeaw.ac.at/dinamlex; attached to Austrian Acad. of Sciences; Dir INGEBORG GEYER.

MEDICINE

Institut für Biomedizinische Alternsforschung (Institute of Biomedical Research on Ageing): Rennweg 10, 6020 Innsbruck; tel. (512) 583919-0; fax (512) 583919-8; e-mail iba@oeaw.ac.at; internet www.iba.oeaw.ac.at; f. 1992; attached to Austrian Acad. of Sciences; Dir BEATRIX GRUBECK-LOEBENSTEIN.

NATURAL SCIENCES

General

Fonds zur Förderung der wissenschaftlichen Forschung (Austrian Science Fund): Weyringergasse 35, 1040 Vienna; tel. (1) 5056740; fax (1) 5056739; e-mail office@fwf.ac.at; internet www.fwf.ac.at; f. 1967; all Austrian universities with their faculties, the art schools and the Austrian Academy of Sciences are represented, also delegates of non-univ. research instns and professional asscns; Pres and Exec. Dir CHRISTOPH KRATKY.

Institut für Wissenschaft und Kunst (Institute for Science and Art): Berggasse 17, 1090 Vienna; tel. (1) 3174342; fax (1) 3174342; e-mail iwk.institut@utanet.at; internet www.univie.ac.at/iwk; f. 1946; Gen. Sec. Dr HELGA KASCHL; publ. *Mitteilungen*.

Institut für Wissenschaftstheorie (Institute for the Philosophy of Science): Internationales Forschungszentrum, 5020 Salzburg, Mönchsberg 2; tel. (662) 842521; fax (662) 842521118; f. 1961; philosophy of science, foundations of logic, mathematics and ethics, philosophy of religion; library of 12,000 vols; Dir Prof. Dr PAUL WEINGARTNER; publs *Forschungsgespräche* (irregular), *Wissenschaft und Religion* (annually).

Biological Sciences

Biologische Station Neusiedler See (Biological Station Neusiedler See): Amt d. Burgenl. Landesregierung, Abt. 5, 7142 Illmitz; tel. (2175) 2328; fax (2175) 232810; e-mail biol.stat@aon.at; f. 1971; nature conservation, limnology, ornithology, botany; Dir Prof. Dr A. HERZIG; publ. *BFB (Biologisches Forschungsinstitut Burgenland)–Berichte* (irregular).

Institut für Biophysik und Röntgenstrukturforschung (Institute of Biophysics and X-Ray Structure Research): Schmiedlstr. 6, 8042 Graz; tel. (316) 4120-300; fax (316) 4120-390; e-mail ibr.office@oeaw.ac.at; internet www.ibr.oeaw.ac.at; f. 1847; attached to Austrian Acad. of Sciences; Dir Prof. Dr PETER LAGGNER.

Institut für Botanik der Universtät Wien (Institute of Botany of the University of Vienna): Rennweg 14, 1030 Vienna; tel. (1) 4277-54100; fax (1) 4277-9541; e-mail botanik@univie.ac.at; internet www.botanik.univie.ac.at; f. 1754 (Garden) and 1844 (Institute); library of 40,000 vols; Dir Prof. Dr T. F. STUESSY; publs *Taxon* (2 a year), *Österreichische Zeitschrift für Pilzkunde* (Austrian Journal of Mycology, annually), *Neilreichia* (annually).

Institut für Limnologie (Institute of Limnology): Mondseestr. 9, 5310 Mondsee; tel. (6232) 3125; fax (6232) 3578; internet www.oeaw.ac.at/limno; f. 1972; attached to Austrian Acad. of Sciences; Dir Dr THOMAS WEISSE.

Institute of Molecular Biotechnology (IMBA): Dr Bohr-Gasse 3, 1030 Vienna; tel. (1) 79044; fax (1) 79044110; internet www.imba.oeaw.ac.at; attached to Austrian Acad. of Sciences; Scientific Dir Prof. Dr JOSEF PENNINGER; Admin Dir MICHAEL KREBS.

Physical Sciences

Atominstitut der Österreichischen Universitäten (Atomic Institute of the Austrian Universities): Stadion allee 2, 1020 Vienna; tel. (1) 58801-14111; fax (1) 58801-14199; f. 1958; training of advanced students and basic research; Dir Prof. Dr HELMUT RAUCH.

BMLFUW Abteilung VII/3–Wasserhaushalt (Federal Ministry of Agriculture, Forestry, Environment and Water Management Sub-Department VII/3–Water Balance): Marxergasse 2, 1030 Vienna; tel. (1) 71100-6942; fax (1) 71100-6851; e-mail wasserhaushalt@bmlfuw.gv.at; internet www.lebensministerium.at; f. 1893; library of 8,000 vols; Head of Division VII/3 Dr Ing. REINHOLD GODINA; publs *Hydrographisches Jahrbuch von Österreich* (annually), *Mitteilungsblatt des Hydrographischen Dienstes von Österreich* (irregular), *Hydrological Atlas of Austria*.

Geologische Bundesanstalt (Geological Survey of Austria): Neulinggasse 38, Postfach 127, 1031 Vienna; tel. (1) 7125674-0; fax (1) 7125674-56; e-mail office@geologie.ac.at; internet www.geologie.ac.at; f. 1849; library of 259,000 vols, 45,000 geological maps, 9,500 aerial photographs, 15,000 archive items, 14,000 microforms; Dir Prof. Dr H. P. SCHÖNLAUB; publs *Abhandlungen*, *Archiv für Lagerstättenforschung*, *Berichte*, *Jahrbuch*, *Jahresberichte* (annually), geological maps.

Institut für Astron- und Teilchenphysik, Universität Innsbruck (Institute of Astro– and Particle Physics, University of Innsbruck): Technikerstr. 25, 6020 Innsbruck; tel. (512) 5076031; fax (512) 5072923; e-mail astro@uibk.ac.at; internet astro.uibk.ac.at; f. 1904; library of 4,598 vols; Dir Prof. Dr SABINE SCHINDLER; publ. *Mitteilungen* (irregular).

Institut für Astronomie der Universität Wien (Vienna University Observatory): 1180 Vienna, Türkenschanzstr. 17; tel. (1) 427751801; fax (1) 42779518; e-mail admin@astro.unvie.ac.at; internet www.astro.univie.ac.at; f. 1755; joined with L. Figl Observatory for Astrophysics; library of 117,300 vols; Pres. Prof. GERHARD HENSLER; publ. *Communications in Asteroseismology*.

Associated body:

Figl Observatorium für Astrophysik (Figl Observatory for Astrophysics): Türkenschanzstr. 17, 1180 Vienna; St Corona at Schöpfl (Vienna Forest); tel. (1) 427751801; fax (1) 42779518; e-mail admin@astro.univie.ac.at; internet 131.130.36.120/~foa; f. 1969; Head of Dept Dr H. M. MAITZEN.

Institut für Hochenergiephysik (Institute of High Energy Physics): Nikolsdorfergasse 18, 1050 Vienna; tel. (1) 5447328; fax (1) 544732854; internet wwwhephy.oeaw.ac.at; attached to Austrian Acad. of Sciences; Dir Prof. Dr WALTER MAJEROTTO.

Institut für Mittelenergiephysik (Institute of Medium Energy Physics): Boltzmanngasse 3, 1090 Vienna; tel. (1) 3108616; fax (1) 3108801; e-mail imep@oeaw.ac.at; internet www.oeaw.ac.at/imep; f. 1910; attached to Austrian Acad. of Sciences; Dir Prof. Dr mg. PAUL KIENLE.

Institut für Schallforschung (Acoustics Research Institute): Reichsratsstr. 17, 1010 Vienna; tel. (1) 4277-29501; fax (1) 4277-9295; e-mail christiane.herzog@oeaw.ac.at; internet www.kfs.oeaw.ac.at; attached to Austrian Acad. of Sciences; Dir Prof. Dr WERNER DEUTSCH.

Institut für Weltraumforschung (Space Research Institute): Schmiedlstr. 6, 8042 Graz; tel. (316) 4120-400; fax (316) 4120-490; e-mail office.iwf@oeaw.ac.at; internet www.iwf.oeaw.ac.at; attached to Austrian Acad. of Sciences; Dir Prof. Dr WOLFGANG BAUMJOHANN.

Kuffner-Sternwarte (Kuffner Observatory): Johann-Staud-Str. 10, 1160 Vienna; tel. (1) 9148130; fax (1) 914813031; e-mail admin@kuffner.ac.at; internet www.kuffner.ac.at; f. 1884; library of 500 vols; Dir PETER HABISON.

Ludwig Boltzmann Institut für Festkörperphysik (Ludwig Boltzmann Institute for Solid State Physics): VI, Kopernikusgasse 15, 1060 Vienna; tel. (1) 5863408-22; fax (1) 5863409-22; internet www.ludwigboltzmann.at; f. 1965; research into semiconductors, conducting polymers and high-temperature superconductors; Dir Prof. Dr ALFRED PHILIPP.

Österreichische Geodätische Kommission (Austrian Geodetic Commission): 1030 Vienna, Landstrasser Hauptstr. 55–57; tel. (1) 71100-8213; fax (1) 71100-93-8213; e-mail christoph.twaroch@bmwa.gv.at; internet www.cis.TUGraz.at/ivm/oegk; f. 1863; Pres. Prof. Dr FRITZ K. BRUNNER; Sec. Univ. Doz. Dipl.-Ing. Dr CHRISTOPH TWAROCH; publ. *Geodätische Arbeiten Österreichs für die Internationale Erdmessung*.

Sonnenobservatorium Kanzelhöhe der Universität Graz (Kanzelhöhe Solar Observatory of the University of Graz): 9521 Treffen; tel. (4248) 2717; fax (4248) 271715; internet www.solobskh.ac.at; f. 1943; small library; Dir Prof. Dr HEINZ KRENN.

Sternwarte Kremsmünster (Kremsmünster Observatory): 4550 Kremsmünster; tel. and fax (7583) 5275450; e-mail sternwarte

.kremsmuenster@telecom.at; internet members.nextra.at/stewar; f. 1748; library of 25,000 vols; Dir Mag. Dr P. AMAND KRAML; publ. *Naturwissenschaftliche Sammlungen Kremsmünster* (irregular).

Umweltbundesamt (Federal Environment Agency): Spittelauer Lände 5, 1090 Vienna; tel. (1) 31304; fax (1) 31304-5400; e-mail office@umweltbundesamt.at; internet www.umweltbundesamt.at; f. 1985; elaboration of scientific studies and basic data for fed. environmental protection policy in Austria; library of 20,000 vols, 300 periodicals; Dir GEORG REBERNIG.

Zentralanstalt für Meteorologie und Geodynamik (Central Institute for Meteorology and Geodynamics): Hohe Warte 38, 1191 Vienna; tel. (1) 36026; fax (1) 3691233; e-mail dion@zamg.ac.at; internet www.zamg.ac.at; f. 1851; provides national weather service; acts in all fields of meteorology except aeronautical field; nat. body responsible for geophysics; library of 80,000 vols; Dir Prof. FRITZ NEUWIRTH; publ. *Oesterreichische Beitraege zu Meteorologie und Geophysik* (irregular).

PHILOSOPHY AND PSYCHOLOGY

Institut für Kultur- und Geistesgeschichte Asiens (Institute for the Cultural and Intellectual History of Asia): Prinz-Eugen-Str. 8–10, 1040 Vienna; tel. (1) 51581-6400; fax (1) 51581-6410; e-mail office.ias@oeaw.ac.at; internet ikga.oeaw.ac.at; attached to Austrian Acad. of Sciences; Dir Doz. Dr HELMUT KRASSER.

Konrad-Lorenz-Institut für Vergleichende Verhaltensforschung (Konrad Lorenz Institute of Comparative Behavioural Research): Savoyenstr. 1A, 1160 Vienna; tel. (1) 4515812700; fax (1) 515812800; e-mail initial.name@klivv.oeaw.ac.at; internet www.oeaw.ac.at/klivv; f. 1945; attached to Austrian Acad. of Sciences; Dir Dr DUSTIN PENN.

Psychotechnisches Institut (Psychotechnical Institute): Augasse 9, 2103 Langenzersdorf; tel. (2244) 30996-0; fax (2244) 30996-22; e-mail psychotech@utanet.at; internet www.psychotech.at; f. 1926; training of supervisors of all levels; library of 8,500 vols; Dirs DDr HANS-RICHARD GRÜMM, Dr SUSANNE HACKL-GRÜMM.

RELIGION, SOCIOLOGY AND ANTHROPOLOGY

Institut für den Christlichen Osten (Institute of the Christian East): Mönchsberg 2A, Salzburg; tel. (662) 80442919; fax (662) 842521-143; e-mail dietmar.winkler@sbg.ac.at; internet www.kirchen.net/ifz/institute/christlicherosten.htm; f. 1961; library of 3,000 vols; Dir Prof. Dr DIETMAR WINKLER.

Institut für Kirchliche Zeitgeschichte (Institute for Contemporary Ecclesiastical History): Mönchsberg 2A, 5020 Salzburg; tel. (662) 842521161; fax (622) 84252118; e-mail kirchliche-zeitgeschichte@ifz.kirchen.net; internet www.kirchen.net/ifz/institute/kirchlzeitgeschichte.htm; f. 1961; library of 8,500 vols; Dir Doz. Dr ALFRED RINNERTHALER; publs *Hirtenbriefe aus Deutschland, Österreich und der Schweiz* (annually), *Publikationen des Instituts für Kirchliche Zeitgeschichte*.

Institut für Stadt und Regionalforschung (Institute of Urban and Regional Research): Postgasse 7/4/2, 1010 Vienna; tel. (1) 51581-3520; fax (1) 51581-3533; e-mail isr@oeaw.ac.at; internet www.oeaw.ac.at/isr; attached to Austrian Acad. of Sciences; Dir Prof. Dr HEINZ FASSMANN.

TECHNOLOGY

Erich-Schmid-Institut für Materialwissenschaft (Erich Schmid Institute of Solid Material Sciences): Jahnstr. 12, 8700 Leoben; tel. (3842) 804112; fax (3842) 804116; internet www.oeaw.ac.at/esi; f. 1971; attached to Austrian Acad. of Sciences; Dir Prof. Dr G. DEHM.

Holzforschung Austria (Wood Research Austria): Arsenal, Franz Grillstr. 7, 1030 Vienna; tel. (1) 7982623-0; fax (1) 7982623-50; e-mail hfa@holzforschung.at; internet www.holzforschung.at; f. 1948; research institute of the Austrian Wood Research Society; library of 35,000 vols; Dir Dipl.-Ing. Dr MANFRED BRANDSTÄTTER; publs *Holzforschung und Holzverwertung* (every 2 months), *Literature Database of the Austrian Wood Research Society* (2 a month).

Institut für Diskrete Mathematik (Institute of Discrete Mathematics): Fleischmarkt 22, 1010 Vienna; tel. (1) 5129184-91; fax (1) 5129184-92; e-mail herbert.fleischner@oeaw.ac.at; internet www.ricam.oeaw.ac.at/dismat; f. 1999; attached to Austrian Acad. of Sciences; Dir Prof. Dr HERBERT FLEISCHNER.

Institut für Technikfolgen-Abschätzung (Institute of Technology Assessment): Strohgasse 45/5, 1030 Vienna; tel. (1) 51581-6582; fax (1) 7109883; internet www.oeaw.ac.at/ita; attached to Austrian Acad. of Sciences; Dir Univ. Doz. Dr MICHAEL NENTWICH.

Institut für Wasserbau und Hydrometrische Prüfung (Institute for Hydraulic Engineering and the Calibration of Hydrometrical Current-Meters): Severingasse 7, 1090 Vienna; tel. (1) 4026802-0; fax (1) 4026802-30; e-mail office.iwb@baw.bmlfuw.gv.at; internet www.iwbhp.at; f. 1913; attached to Federal Office of Water Resources Management; calculation and implementation of measures concerning the protection and maintenance of waters, as well as flood protection; physical model tests and mathematical models for studies in the field of hydraulic engineering; consulting in hydraulic engineering; 13 mems; library of 5,600 vols, database containing 26,200 articles; Dir Dipl.-Ing. Dr techn. MICHAEL HENGL.

KMU Forschung Austria (Austrian Institute for SME Research): Gusshausstr. 8, 1040 Vienna; tel. (1) 5059761; fax (1) 5034660; e-mail office@kmuforschung.ac.at; internet www.kmuforschung.ac.at; f. 1952 as Österreichisches Institut für Gewerbeforschung; conducts social and economic research with focus on small and medium-sized enterprises; prepares and supplies information and data to facilitate decision-making for businesses and their advisors, for institutions responsible for economic policy and business promotion as well as for universities, colleges of higher education and other research institutions; member of the Austrian Co-operative Research (ACR) and the European Network for Small- and Medium-sized Enterprise Research (ENSR); 800 mems; library of 3,200 vols; Pres. Prof. Dr J. HANNS PICHLER; Dir Dr WALTER BORNETT.

Österreichisches Forschungsinstitut für Artificial Intelligence (Austrian Research Institute for Artificial Intelligence): Freyung 6/6, 1010 Vienna; tel. (1) 5336112-60; fax (1) 5336112-77; e-mail sec@ofai.at; internet www.ofai.at; f. 1984; a research institute of the Austrian Soc. for Cybernetic Studies; library of 3,000 vols; Dir Prof. Dr ROBERT TRAPPL; publs *Applied Artificial Intelligence: An International Journal* (10 a year), *Technical Reports* (irregular).

Österreichisches Forschungsinstitut für Technikgeschichte (ÖFiT) am Technischen Museum in Wien (Austrian Research Institute for the History of Technology at the Museum of Technology in Vienna): Mariahilfer Str. 212, 1140 Vienna; tel. (1) 89998-2500; fax (1) 89998-1111; e-mail helmut.lackner@tmw.at; internet www.tmw.at; f. 1931; Pres. Prof. Dr REINHOLD REITH; publ. *Blätter für Technikgeschichte* (annually).

Österreichisches Forschungszentrum Seibersdorf GmbH (Austrian Research Centre, Seibersdorf): 2444 Seibersdorf; tel. (50550) 2110; fax (50550) 2131; e-mail seibersdorf@arcs.ac.at; internet www.seibersdorf-research.at; f. 1956; contract research and development in instrumentation and information technology, process and environmental technologies, engineering, life sciences and systems research; library of 15,500 vols; Dir KONRAD FREYBORN; publ. OEFSZ Reports.

Österreichisches Giesserei-Institut (Austrian Foundry Research Institute): Parkstr. 21, 8700 Leoben; tel. (3842) 431010; fax (3842) 431011; e-mail office.ogi@unileoben.ac.at; internet www.ogi.at; f. 1952; library of 2,140 vols; Man. and Tech. Dir Prof. Dr PETER SCHUMACHER; publ. *Giesserei Rundschau* (6 a year).

Österreichisches Normungsinstitut (ON) (Austrian Standards Institute): Postfach 130, Heinestr. 38, 1021 Vienna; tel. (1) 21300; fax (1) 21300-818; e-mail office@on-norm.at; internet www.on-norm.at; f. 1920; govt-supervised private institute for standardization in all fields; library of 1,000 vols, 30 periodicals, 600,000 foreign standards; Pres. Prof. Dr Dr WALTER BARFUß; Man. Dir Ing. Dr GERHARD HARTMANN; publ. *ON top news* (monthly).

Österreichisches Textil-Forschungsinstitut (Austrian Textile Research Institute): Spengergasse 20, 1050 Vienna; tel. (1) 5442543-0; fax (1) 5442543-10; e-mail office@oeti.at; internet www.oeti.at; f. 1967; Dir Dipl.-Ing. Dr ERICH ZIPPEL.

Physikalisch-Technische Versuchsanstalt für Wärme- und Schalltechnik am Technologischen Gewerbemuseum (Physical-technical Institute for Research on Heat and Noise Technology at the Technological Industrial Museum): Wexstr. 19–23, 1200 Vienna; tel. (1) 33126411; fax (1) 3305925; Dir Ing. Mag. MATHIAS STANI.

Zentrum für Elektronenmikroskopie Graz (Graz Centre for Electron Microscopy): Steyrergasse 17, 8010 Graz; tel. (316) 8738320; fax (316) 811596; e-mail office@felmi-zfe.at; internet www.felmi-zfe.tugraz.at; f. 1959; library of 2,000 vols; Pres. Prof. Dipl.-Ing. Dr h.c. HELMUT LIST; Dir Komm. Rat Dipl.-Ing. ULRICH SANTNER.

Libraries and Archives

Admont

Bibliothek der Benediktinerabtei (Library of the Benedictine Abbey): 8911 Admont; tel. (3613) 2312602; fax (3613) 2312359; e-mail tomaschek@stiftadmont.at; internet www.stiftadmont.at; f. 1074; 200,000 vols, 1,400 MSS, 530 incunabula; Librarian Mag. Dr JOHANN TOMASCHEK.

Bregenz

Vorarlberger Landesarchiv (Vorarlberg State Archives): Kirchstr. 28, 6901 Bregenz; tel. (5574) 51145005; fax (5574) 51145095; e-mail landesarchiv@vorarlberg.at; internet www.landesarchiv.at; f. 1898; Dir Prof. Dr ALOIS NIEDERSTÄTTER; publ. *Zeitschrift Montfort* (quarterly).

Vorarlberger Landesbibliothek (Vorarlberg State Library): Fluherstr. 4, 6901 Bregenz; tel. (5574) 511-44100; fax (5574) 511-44095; e-mail info.vlb@vorarlberg.at; internet www.vorarlberg.at/vlb; f. 1904; 450,000 vols; Dir Dr HARALD WEIGEL.

Eisenstadt

Burgenländische Landesbibliothek (Burgenland Provincial Library): Europaplatz 1, Landhaus, 7000 Eisenstadt; tel. (2682) 6002356; fax (2682) 6002058; e-mail post.kultur@bgld.gv.at; internet www.burgenland.at; f. 1922; 110,000 vols; Chief Librarian Mag. NORBERT FRANK; publs *Burgenländische Forschungen* (2 or 3 a year), *Burgenländische Heimatblätter* (4 a year), *Burgenländische Landesbibliographie* (annually).

Burgenländisches Landesarchiv (Burgenland Provincial Archives): Europapl. 1, 7000 Eisenstadt; tel. (2682) 6002358; fax (2682) 6002058; e-mail post.kultur@bgld.gv.at; f. 1922; Dir Dr JOHANN SEEDOCH; publ. *Burgenländische Heimatblätter* (quarterly).

Graz

Steiermärkische Landesbibliothek (Styrian Federal State Library): Kalchberggasse 2, Graz; tel. (316) 80164600; fax (316) 80164633; e-mail stlbib@stmk.gv.at; f. 1811; 700,000 vols, 2,800 periodicals, 2,300 MSS; Dir OBR Dr CHRISTOPH BINDER; publs *Arbeiten aus der Steiermärkischen Landesbibliothek* (irregular), *Steierische Bibliographie* (irregular).

Steiermärkisches Landesarchiv (Styrian Provincial Archives): Karmeliterplatz 3, 8010 Graz; tel. (316) 8772361; fax (316) 8772954; e-mail fa1d@stmk.gv.at; internet www.landesarchiv.steiermark.at; f. 1811; Dir Hofrat Hon.-Prof. Dr JOZEF RIEGLER; publs *Mitteilungen* (annually), *Veröffentlichungen* (irregular), *Styriaca* (irregular), *Quellen aus steirischen Archiven* (irregular), *Ausstellungsbegleiter* (irregular).

Universitätsbibliothek der Technischen Universität Graz (Technical University Library): Technikerstr. 4, 8010 Graz; tel. (316) 873-6151; fax (316) 873-6671; e-mail service.bibliothek@tugraz.at; internet www.ub.tugraz.at; f. 1875; 600,000 vols, 1,250 periodicals; Dir EVA BERTHA.

Universitätsbibliothek Graz (University Library, Graz): Universitätspl. 3, 8010 Graz; tel. (316) 3803102; fax (316) 384987; e-mail ubgraz@uni-graz.at; internet ub.uni-graz.at; f. 1573; 3,000,000 vols, 10,500 periodicals, 2,203 MSS, 1,150 incunabula; Dir Dr WERNER SCHLACHER; publs *Jahresbericht* (annually), *News* (4 a year).

Heiligenkreuz bei Baden

Stiftsarchiv des Zisterzienserstiftes (Cistercian Abbey Archives): 2532 Heiligenkreuz; tel. (2258) 8703; fax (2258) 8703-114; e-mail information@stift-heiligenkreuz.at; internet www.stift-heiligenkreuz.at; archives since foundation of the monastery in 1133; Archivist DDr WILHELM KUNDRATITZ.

Innsbruck

Tiroler Landesarchiv (Tyrolese Provincial Archives): Michael-Gaismair-Str. 1, 6020 Innsbruck; tel. (512) 508-3534; fax (512) 508-3505; e-mail landesarchiv@tirol.gv.at; internet www.tirol.gv.at/landesarchiv; f. 13th century; records from 11th century; Dir Dr RICHARD SCHOBER; publs *Tiroler Erbhöfe* (irregular), *Tiroler Geschichtsquellen* (irregular), *Veröffentlichungen des Tiroler Landesarchivs* (irregular).

Universitätsbibliothek Innsbruck (University Library, Innsbruck): Innrain 50, 6010 Innsbruck; tel. (512) 5072401; fax (512) 5072893; e-mail ub-hb@uibk.ac.at; internet www.uibk.ac.at/ub; f. 1746; 3,200,000 vols, 7,470 current periodicals, 1,100 MSS, 2,000 incunabula; Dir Dr MARTIN WIESER.

Klagenfurt

Kärntner Landesarchiv (Carinthian Provincial Archives): St Ruprechter Str. 7, 9020 Klagenfurt; tel. (463) 56234; fax (463) 56234-20; e-mail post.landesarchiv@ktn.gv.at; internet www.landesarchiv.ktn.gv.at; f. 1904; Dir Dr WILHELM WADL; publ. *Das Kärntner Landesarchiv* (annually).

Universitätsbibliothek Klagenfurt: Universitätsstr. 65–67, 9020 Klagenfurt; tel. (463) 2700-9565; fax (463) 2700-9599; e-mail info.bibliothek@uni-klu.ac.at; internet www.uni-klu.ac.at/ub; f. 1775; open to the public; 750,000 vols; Dir Dr MANFRED LUBE.

Klosterneuburg

Bibliothek des Augustiner-Chorherrenstiftes (Library of the Augustine Abbey): Stiftsplatz 1, 3400 Klosterneuburg; tel. (2243) 411-151; fax (2243) 411-156; e-mail bibliothek@stift-klosterneuburg.at; internet www.stift-klosterneuburg.at; f. 1114; 240,000 vols, 1,250 MSS, 836 incunabula; Dir Dr HEINZ RISTORY.

Leoben

Universitätsbibliothek Leoben (University Library Leoben): Franz-Josef-Str. 18, 8700 Leoben; tel. (3842) 4027800; fax (3842) 46380; e-mail univbibl@unileoben.ac.at; internet www.unileoben.ac.at/bibliothek; f. 1840; 250,000 vols, 173 current periodicals; Librarians Dr JOHANN DELANOY, Dr LIESELOTTE JONTES.

Linz

Bibliothek der Oberösterreichischen Landesmuseen (Library of the Upper Austrian Provincial Museums): Postfach 91, Museumstr. 14, 4010 Linz; tel. (732) 774482-41; fax (732) 774482-66; e-mail bibliothek@landesmuseum-linz.ac.at; internet www.landesmuseum.at; f. 1836; 140,000 vols; Chief Librarian WALTRAUD FAISSNER.

Oberösterreichische Landesbibliothek (Federal State Library of Upper Austria): Schillerpl. 2, 4021 Linz; tel. (732) 664071-00; fax (732) 664071-44; e-mail landesbibliothek@ooe.gv.at; internet www.landesbibliothek.at; f. 1774; 400,000 vols; Dir Dr CHRISTIAN ENICHLMAYR.

Oberösterreichisches Landesarchiv (Provincial Archives of Upper Austria): Anzengruberstr. 19, 4020 Linz; tel. (732) 772014601; fax (732) 772014619; e-mail landesarchiv@ooe.gv.at; internet www.landesarchiv-ooe.at; f. 1896; Dir Dr GERHART MARCKHGOTT; publs *Forschungen zur Geschichte Oberösterreichs* (irreg.), *Beiträge zur Zeitgeschichte Oberösterreichs* (irreg.), *Quellen zur Geschichte Oberösterreichs* (irreg.), *Mitteilungen* (irreg.).

Universitätsbibliothek der Johannes Kepler Universität Linz: Altenbergerstr. 69, 4040 Linz; tel. (732) 2468 9380; fax (732) 2468 1233; e-mail bibliothek@jku.at; internet www.ubl.jku.at; f. 1965; 900,000 vols, 2,500 periodicals; Dir Dr MONIKA SCHENK.

Melk

Bibliothek des Benediktinerklosters Melk in Niederösterreich (Library of the Melk Benedictine Monastery in Lower Austria): 3390 Stift Melk; tel. (2752) 555; fax (2752) 55552; e-mail bibliothek@stiftmelk.at; internet www.stiftmelk.at; 80,000 vols (mostly pre-19th-century), 1,800 codices, 750 incunabula; Librarian GOTTFRIED GLASSNER.

Salzburg

Bibliothek der Benediktiner Erzabtei St Peter (Library of the Benedictine Abbey of St Peter): Postfach 113, 5010 Salzburg; tel. (662) 844576-58; fax (662) 844576-80; e-mail scriptorium@stift-stpeter.at; internet www.stift-stpeter.at; f. 700; 120,000 vols, 1,300 MSS, 923 incunabula; Dir P. PETRUS EDER.

Salzburger Landesarchiv (Salzburg Provincial Archives): Postfach 527, 5010 Salzburg; tel. (662) 80424527; fax (662) 80424661; e-mail landesarchiv@salzburg.gv.at; internet www.salzburg.gv.at/archive.htm; f. 1875; Dir Dr FRITZ KOLLER.

Universitätsbibliothek Salzburg (Salzburg University Library): Hofstallgasse 2–4, 5020 Salzburg; tel. (662) 8044-77550; fax (662) 8044-103; e-mail info.hb@sbg.ac.at; internet www.uni-salzburg.at/bibliothek; f. 1623; 2,000,000 vols, 1,100 MSS, 2,400 incunabula; Dir Mag. Dr URSULA SCHACHL-RABER.

Sankt Florian

Bibliothek des Augustiner-Chorherrenstiftes (Library of the Augustine Canonical Foundation): Stiftstrasse 1, 4490 St Florian; tel. (7224) 8902-54; fax (7224) 8902-60; e-mail bibliothek@stift-st-florian.at; internet www.stift-st-florian.at; f. 1071; 150,000 vols, 920 MSS, 800 incunabula; Dir Prof. Dr KARL REHBERGER.

Sankt Pölten

Niederösterreichisches Landesarchiv (Lower Austrian Provincial Archives): Landhauspl. 1, 3100 St Pölten; tel. (2742) 9005-12044; fax (2742) 9005-12052; e-mail post.k2archiv@noel.gv.at; internet www.noel.gv.at/service/k/k2/landesarchiv.htm; f. 16th century; 31,000 vols; Dir Dr ANTON EGGENDORFER; publs *Mitteilungen*, *NÖLA*.

Niederösterreichische Landesbibliothek (Lower Austrian Provincial Library): Landhausplatz 1, 3109 St Pölten; tel. (2742) 9005-12847; fax (2742) 9005-13860; e-mail post.k3@noel.gv.at; internet www.noe.gv.at/service/k/k3/k3.htm; f. 1813; 196,000 vols; Dir Dr GEBHARD KOENIG.

Seckau

Bibliothek der Benediktinerabtei (Library of the Benedictine Abbey): 8732 Seckau; f. 1883; 160,000 vols; Dir Dr P. BENNO ROTH.

Vienna

Archiv, Bibliothek und Sammlungen der Gesellschaft der Musikfreunde in Wien (Archives, Library and Collections of the Society of Friends of Music in Vienna): Bösendorferstr 12, 1010 Vienna; tel. (1) 505868144; fax (1) 505868166; f. 1812; 23,000 vols; 73,000 scores, historical material; Dir Prof. Dr OTTO BIBA.

Archiv der Universität Wien (Archives of the University of Vienna): Postgasse 9, 1010 Vienna; tel. (1) 427717201; fax (1) 42779172; e-mail archiv@univie.ac.at; internet www.univie.ac.at/archiv; f. 1365; records since 13th century; Archivist Dr KURT MÜHLBERGER.

Archiv des Stiftes Schotten (Schotten Abbey Archives): Freyung 6, 1010 Vienna; tel. (1) 53498-0; fax (1) 53498-105; e-mail archiv.bibliothek@schottenstift.at; internet www.schottenstift.at; f. 1155; archives of the Benedictine monastery; Archivist Abt Dr P. HEINRICH FERENCZY.

Bibliothek der Akademie der Bildenden Künste (Library of the Academy of Fine Arts): Schillerpl. 3, 1010 Vienna; tel. (1) 58816166; fax (1) 58816227; internet www.akbild.ac.at/bib; f. 1773; exhibitions, presentation of new books; 136,000 vols; Dir Doz. Dr BEATRIX BASTL.

Bibliothek der Mechitharistenkongregation: Mechitaristengasse 4, 1070 Vienna; tel. (1) 5236417; fax (1) 5236417101; e-mail pvahan@mechitaristen.at; f. 1773; literature related to Armenia; 150,000 vols, 3,000 Armenian MSS, all current Armenian newspapers and periodicals; Dir P. VAHAN HOVAGIMIAN; publ. *Handes Amsorya* (annually).

Bibliothek der Österreichischen Akademie der Wissenschaften (Library of the Austrian Academy of Sciences): Dr-Ignaz-Seipel-Platz 2, 1010 Vienna; tel. (1) 515811262; fax (1) 515811256; e-mail bibliothek@oeaw.ac.at; internet www.oeaw.ac.at/biblio; f. 1847; 320,900 vols; Dir Prof. Dr CHRISTINE HARRAUER.

Bibliothek der Österreichischen Geographischen Gesellschaft (Library of the Austrian Geographical Society): Nottendorfer Gasse 2, 1030 Vienna; tel. (1) 5237974; internet arcims.isr.oeaw.ac.at/website/oegg/oegg.htm; f. 1856; 21,000 vols; Librarian Dr PETER FRITZ.

Bibliothek der Veterinärmedizinischen Universität Wien (Library of Vienna University of Veterinary Medicine): Veterinärpl. 1, 1210 Vienna; tel. (1) 25077-1414; fax (1) 25077-1490; e-mail bibliothekinfo@vu-wien.ac.at; internet www.vu-wien.ac.at/bibl; f. 1767; 201,000 vols; Dir Dr GÜNTER OLENSKY.

Bibliothek der Wirtschaftskammer Wien (Vienna Chamber of Commerce Library): Stubenring 8–10, 1010 Vienna; tel. (1) 51450-1370; fax (1) 51450-1469; e-mail bibliothek@wkw.at; internet bibliothek.wkw.at; f. 1849; 200,000 vols; Dir Dr HERBERT PRIBYL.

Bibliothek des Bundesministeriums für Finanzen (Library of the Ministry of Finance): Himmelpfortgasse 4, 1015 Vienna; tel. (1) 514331247; fax (1) 514331246; internet www.bmf.gv.at; f. 1810; 290,000 vols; Librarian HEINZ RENNER.

Bibliothek des Bundesministeriums für Land- und Forstwirtschaft, Umwelt und Wasserwirtschaft (Library of the Federal Ministry of Agriculture, Forestry, the Environment and Water Management): Stubenring 1, 1012 Vienna; tel. (1) 71100; fax (1) 7103254; e-mail ingrid.saberi@lebensministerium.at; f. 1868; 127,500 vols; Librarian Mag. INGRID SABERI.

Bibliothek des Bundesministeriums für Soziale Sicherheit, Generationen und Konsumentenschutz (Library of the Federal Ministry for Social Security and Consumer Protection): Stubenring 1, 1010 Vienna; tel. (1) 711006143; fax (1) 718947011-80; e-mail ilga.kubela@bmsg.gv.at; f. 1917; 150,000 vols; Dir ILGA ANNA KUBELA.

Bibliothek des Instituts für Österreichische Geschichtsforschung (Library of the Institute of Austrian Historical Research): Dr Karl Lueger Ring 1, 1010 Vienna; tel. (1) 427727201; fax (1) 42779272; internet www.univie.ac.at/geschichtsforschung; f. 1854; 75,000 vols; Librarian Dr PAUL HEROLD.

Bibliothek des Österreichischen Patentamtes (Library of the Austrian Patents Office): Dresdner Str. 87, 1200 Vienna; tel. (1) 53424153; fax (1) 53424110; e-mail info@patentamt.at; internet www.patent.bmvit.gv.at; f. 1899; 45,000,000 vols; Dir Dr INGRID WEIDINGER; publs *Jahresbericht*, *Österreichisches Gebrauchsmusterblatt*, *Österreichischer Markenanzeiger*, *Österreichischer Musteranzeiger*, *Österreichisches Patentblatt*, *Patentschriften*.

Bibliothek des Österreichischen Staatsarchivs (Library of the Austrian State Archives): Nottendorferg. 2, 1030 Vienna; tel. (1) 79540-113; fax (1) 79540-109; e-mail bibpost@oesta.gv.at; internet www.oesta.gv.at; history, military history; 400,000 vols; Dir Dr ADOLF GAISBAUER.

Bibliothek des Österreichischen Statistischen Zentralamtes (Library of the Austrian Central Statistical Office): Postfach 9000, 1033 Vienna; tel. (1) 71128-7800; fax (1) 7146251; e-mail alois.gerhart@oestat.gv.at; f. 1829; 210,000 vols; Dir Dr ALOIS GEHART.

Büchereien Wien (Municipal Libraries of Vienna): Urban-Loritz-Platz 2A, 1070 Vienna; tel. (1) 4000-84500; fax (1) 4000-9984510; e-mail post-stb@m13.magwien.gv.at; internet www.buechereien.wien.at; f. 1945; 1,600,000 vols, 120,000 audio media items; central library and 41 brs; Dir Dr ALFRED PFOSER.

Bundesstaatliche Paedagogische Bibliothek beim Landesschulrat für Niederösterreich (Library of the Lower Austrian Education Authority): Rennbahnstr. 29, 3109 St Poelten; tel. (2742) 2801482; fax (2742) 2801111; e-mail pbn@lsr-noe.gv.at; internet pbn.lsr-noe.gv.at; f. 1923; 160,000 vols, 460 periodicals; Dir Mag. ERNST CHORHERR.

Diözesanarchiv Wien (Vienna Diocesan Archives): Erzbischöfliches Palais, Wollzeile 2, 1010 Vienna; tel. (1) 51552-3239; fax (1) 51552-3240; e-mail daw@edw.or.at; internet stephanscom.at/edw/kulissen/archiv_v.html; f. 1936; history of archdiocese of Vienna and of parishes and convents in Vienna and the eastern part of Lower Austria; 45,000 vols, 800 periodicals, 6,000 documents and files; Dir Dr ANNEMARIE FENZL.

Fakultätsbibliothek für Rechtswissenschaften (Faculty Library of Legal Studies): Schottenbastei 10–16, 1010 Vienna; tel. (1) 4277-16311; fax (1) 4277-9163; e-mail thomas.luzer@univie.ac.at; internet www.univie.ac.at/fbrecht; f. 1922; 238,000 vols, 1,100 periodicals; Dir Dr THOMAS LUZER.

Oesterreichische Zentralbibliothek für Physik (Austrian Central Library for Physics): Boltzmanngasse 5, 1090 Vienna; tel. (1) 3190011; fax (1) 42779276; e-mail zb@zbp.univie.ac.at; internet www.zbp.univie.ac.at; f. 1946; 357,000 vols, 2,890 periodicals, 1,175,000 microfiches; Dir Dr WOLFGANG KERBER.

Österreichische Nationalbibliothek (Austrian National Library): Josefsplatz 1, 1015 Vienna; tel. (1) 53410; fax (1) 53410-1280; e-mail onb@onb.ac.at; internet www.onb.ac.at; f. in 14th c.; consists of 10 special collections and main library; 3,342,944 books, 11,577 periodicals, 8,017 incunabula, 388,422 MSS, 126,673 vols of printed music, 50,648 music MSS, 265,164 maps, 231,984 papyri; Austrian literature archive, portrait colln and picture archive; International Esperanto Museum; Dir-Gen. Dr JOHANNA RACHINGER; publs *Biblios. Beiträge zu Buch, Bibliothek und Schriftt* (2 a year), *NB-Newsletter* (4 a year), *Nilus* (1 or 2 a year), *Profile. Magazin des Österreichischen Literaturarchivs* (2 or 3 a year), *Sichtungen* (annually), *Ausstellungskataloge* (irregular), *Jahresberichte* (annually), *Corpus Papyrorum Raineri*, *Mitteilungen aus der Papyrussammlung* (annually).

Österreichisches Staatsarchiv (Austrian State Archives): Nottendorfer Gasse 2, 1030 Vienna; tel. (1) 79540-0; fax (1) 79540-199; e-mail gdpost@oesta.gv.at; internet www.oesta.gv.at; f. 1945; Domestic, Court and State Archives, General Administrative Archives, Finance and Treasury Archives, War Archives, Archives of the Austrian Republic; Gen. Dir Prof. Dr LORENZ MIKOLETZKY; publ. *Mitteilungen des österreichischen Staatsarchivs*.

Parlamentsbibliothek (Library of Parliament): Dr Karl Renner-Ring 3, 1017 Vienna; tel. (1) 40110-2285; fax (1) 40110-2825; e-mail bibliothek@parlinkom.gv.at; internet www.parlament.gv.at/bibliothek; f. 1869; 323,300 vols; Dir Dr ELISABETH DIETRICH-SCHULZ.

Sozialwissenschaftliche Bibliothek der Kammer für Arbeiter und Angestellte für Wien (Social Sciences Library of the Vienna Chamber of Labour): Prinz Eugenstr. 20–22, 1040 Vienna; tel. (1) 501652466; fax (1) 501652229; e-mail bibliothek@akwien.at; internet wien.arbeiterkammer.at/bibliothek; f. 1922; 440,000 vols, 900 periodicals; Dir Dr HERWIG JOBST.

Universitätsbibliothek Bodenkultur Wien (Library of the University of Natural Resources and Applied Life Sciences, Vienna): Peter-Jordanstr. 82, 1190 Vienna; tel. (1) 47654-2060; fax (1) 47654-2092; e-mail ub.information@boku.ac.at; internet www.boku.ac.at/bib.html; f. 1872; 500,000 vols, 1,300 periodicals, 12,500 dissertations, 3,600 e-journals; Dir Dr WERNER HAINZ-SATOR.

Universitätsbibliothek der Technischen Universität Wien (Vienna University of Technology Library): Resselgasse 4, 1040 Vienna; tel. (1) 58801-44051; fax (1) 58801-44099; e-mail info@mail.ub.tuwien.ac.at; internet www.ub.tuwien.ac.at; f. 1815; 1,300,081 vols; Dir Mag. Dr PETER KUBALEK.

Universitätsbibliothek der Universität für Musik und darstellende Kunst Wien (Library of the Vienna University for Music and Dramatic Art): Lothringerstr. 18, 1030 Vienna; tel. (1) 71155-8101; fax (1) 71155-8199; e-mail infobib@mdw.ac.at; internet www.mdw.ac.at/bib; f. 1909; 170,000 vols, 52,000 audiovisual media items; Bruno Walter Archive; Dir Dr SUSANNE ESCHWÉ.

Universitätsbibliothek der Wirtschaftsuniversität Wien (Library of the Vienna University of Economics and Business Administration): Augasse 2–6, 1090 Vienna; tel. (1) 313364990; fax (1) 31336745; e-mail ubww@wu-wien.ac.at; internet www.wu-wien.ac.at/bib; f. 1898; 800,000 vols; Dir Dr BETTINA SCHMEIKAL.

Universitätsbibliothek Wien (Vienna University Library): Dr Karl Lueger Ring 1, 1010 Vienna; tel. (1) 427715001; fax (1) 42779150; e-mail ilse.dosoudil@univie.ac.at; internet ub.univie.ac.at; f. 1365; 5,800,000 vols; Dir Hofrätin Mag. MARIA SEISSL.

Wiener Stadt- und Landesarchiv (Municipal and Provincial Archives of Vienna): Rathaus, 1082 Vienna; located at Vienna 11, Guglgasse 14, Gasometer D; tel. (1) 4000-84808; fax (1) 4000-84809; e-mail post@m08.magwien.gv.at; internet www.magwien.gv.at/ma08; f. 1889; records since 13th c.; Dir Prof. Dr FERDINAND OPLL; publ. *Veröffentlichungen*.

Wiener Stadt- und Landesbibliothek (Vienna City and Provincial Library): Rathaus, 1082 Vienna; tel. (1) 400084920; fax (1) 40007219; e-mail post@wienbibliothek.at; internet www.stadtbibliothek.wien.at; f. 1856; 426,000 vols, 220,000 MSS, 65,000 musical items, 16,000 MSS musical items, 150,000 posters; Dir SYLVIA MATTL-WURM.

Zentralarchiv des Deutschen Ordens: Singerstr. 7, 1010 Vienna; tel. (1) 5137014; f. 1852; 11,668 vols; Archivist Dr BERNHARD DEMEL.

Zentralbibliothek im Justizpalast (Central Library of the Palace of Justice): Museumstr. 12, Vienna; tel. (1) 52152-3351;

fax (1) 52152-3677; e-mail ogh.bibliothek@justiz.gv.at; internet www.ogh.gv.at/zentralbibliothek; f. 1829; 114,000 vols, 160 current periodicals; Dir WINFRIED KMENTA.

Zentrale Verwaltungsbibliothek und Dokumentation für Wirtschaft und Technik (Central Library for Economics and Technology): Bundesministerium für Wirtschaftliche Angelegenheiten,I, Stubenring 1, 1011 Vienna; tel. (1) 711005483; fax (1) 711002384; internet www.bmwa.gv.at/BMWA/Service/Bibliothek/default.htm; f. 1850; 514,000 vols; Dir Dr BRIGITTA KOHLERT-WINDISCH.

Museums and Art Galleries

Bad Deutsch-Altenburg

Archäologisches Museum Carnuntinum (Carnuntinum Archaeological Museum): Badgasse 40–46, 2405 Bad Deutsch-Altenburg; tel. (2165) 62480; fax (2165) 62480-20; f. 1904; Roman archaeology; library of 12,000 vols; Curator Mag. FRANZ HUMER.

Bregenz

Vorarlberger Landesmuseum (Vorarlberg Provincial Museum): Kornmarkt 1, 6900 Bregenz; tel. (5574) 46050; fax (5574) 4605020; e-mail info@vlm.at; internet www.vlm.at; f. 1857; archaeology, art and folklore of the region; Dir TOBIAS G. NATTER; publ. *Jahrbuch*.

Eggenburg

Krahuletz Museum: Krahuletzpl., 3730 Eggenburg; tel. (2984) 3400; fax (2984) 34005; e-mail gesellschaft@krahuletzmuseum.at; internet www.krahuletzmuseum.at; colln f. 1866; geology, prehistory, ethnology; Dir Dr JOHANNES M. TUZAR; publ. *Katalogreihe*.

Eisenstadt

Burgenländisches Landesmuseum (Burgenland Provincial Museum): Museumgasse 1–5, 7000 Eisenstadt; tel. (2682) 600-1209; fax (2682) 600-1277; e-mail landesmuseum@bgld.gv.at; internet www.burgenland.at/landesmuseum; f. 1926; archaeology, geology, history of art, natural history, ethnology, numismatics, history of music; library of 31,000 vols; Dir Dr JOSEF TIEFENBACH; publ. *Wissenschaftliche Arbeiten aus dem Burgenland*.

Furth bei Göttweig

Graphische Sammlung und Kunstsammlungen Stift Göttweig (Stift Göttweig Graphic Art Collection): Stift Göttweig 1, 3511 Furth bei Göttweig; tel. (2732) 85581226; fax (2732) 71848; e-mail graph.kab.gtwt@eunet.at; internet www.stiftgoettweig.at; f. 1960; graphic art from the 16th century to the present, music, coins and medals; library of 280,000 vols (history, law, theology, history of art, sciences), 1,110 MSS, 1,120 incunabula, 2,750 archives (1054–1900); Curator Prof. Dr GREGOR MARTIN LECHNER.

Graz

Steiermärkisches Landesmuseum Joanneum (Provincial Museum of Styria): Raubergasse 10, 8010 Graz; tel. (316) 8017-9660; fax (316) 8017-9669; e-mail post@museum-joanneum.at; internet www.museum-joanneum.at; f. 1811; history, natural history, art (exhibits housed on several sites); picture and sound archives; Dir Dr WOLFGANG MUCHITSCH.

Innsbruck

Kaiserliche Hofburg (Imperial Palace): Rennweg 1, 6020 Innsbruck; tel. (512) 587186; fax (512) 587186-13; e-mail hofburg.ibk@burghauptmannschaft.at; internet www.hofburg-innsbruck.at; f. 15th century; spec. exhibitions throughout the year; Dir WALTRAUD SCHREILECHNER.

Kunsthistorische Sammlungen (Collections of Historical Art): Schloss-str. 20, Schloss Ambras, 6020 Innsbruck; tel. (1) 52524-4802; fax (1) 52524-4899; e-mail info.ambras@khm.at; internet www.khm.at/ambras; f. 1580; armour, furniture, pictures, sculpture; Curator Dr ALFRED AUER.

Museum im Zeughaus (Zeughaus Museum): Zeughausgasse, 6020 Innsbruck; tel. (512) 59489-311; fax (512) 59489-318; e-mail zeughaus@tiroler-landesmuseum.at; internet www.tiroler-landesmuseum.at; f. 1973; geology, history, technology of the Tyrol; Pres. ANDREAS TRENTINI; Curator Dr MEINRAD PIZZININI.

Tiroler Landesmuseum Ferdinandeum (Tyrol Provincial Museum): Museumstr. 15, 6020 Innsbruck; tel. (512) 59489-102; fax (512) 59489-109; e-mail sekretariat@tiroler-landesmuseum.at; internet www.tiroler-landesmuseum.at; f. 1823; ancient and early history, art; library of 150,000 vols; Dir ANJA LUTTINGER; publs *Ferdinandea* (4 a year), *Veröffentlichungen des Tiroler Landesmuseums Ferdinandeum* (annually).

Tiroler Volkskunstmuseum (Tyrol Popular Art Museum): Universitätsstr. 2, 6020 Innsbruck; tel. (512) 584302; fax (512) 584302-70; e-mail volkskunstmuseum@tirol.gv.at; internet www.tiroler-volkskunstmuseum.at; f. 1880; local folk arts and crafts; library of 2,940 vols; Dir Dr HERLINDE MENARDI; Librarian HANSJÖRG BADER.

Klagenfurt

Landesmuseum Kärnten, Kärntner Botanikzentrum (Carinthian Botanic Centre): Prof.-Dr-Kahler-Pl. 1, 9020 Klagenfurt; tel. (463) 502715-12; e-mail kbz@landesmuseum-ktn.at; internet www.landesmuseum-ktn.at; f. 1862; cultivation of central and southern Alpine flora; school and adult education in botany and nature conservation; collns of orchids, succulents and carnivorous plants, poisonous and medicinal herbs, spices and useful plants, fossils (2,000 specimens); ethnobotanical and carpological colllns; herbarium of 150,000 phanerogams and 50,000 cryptogams; garden for the blind; library of 12,000 vols; offprint, slide, biographical and bibliographical colllns; Head Mag. Dr ROLAND K. EBERWEIN; publs *Wulfenia* (annual), *Index Seminum* (annual).

Landesmuseum für Kärnten (Provincial Museum of Carinthia): Museumgasse 2, 9021 Klagenfurt; tel. (50) 53630599; fax (50) 53630540; e-mail info@landesmuseum-ktn.at; internet www.landesmuseum-ktn.at; f. 1844; history, natural history, archaeology, art, folk arts and crafts; library of 120,000 vols; Dir CHRISTIAN WALTL; publs *Archiv für Vaterländische Geschichte und Topographie*, *Carinthia I* (archaeology, history, history of art, and folklore), *Carinthia II* (science), *Kärntner Heimatleben*.

Krems

WEINSTADTMuseum (Museum of the Wine City): Körnermarkt 14, 3500 Krems; tel. (2732) 801-567; fax (2732) 801-576; e-mail museum@krems.gv.at; internet www.weinstadtmuseum.at; f. 1996; located in fmr Dominican monastery; primitive art; Romanesque and Gothic sculptures; Kremser Schmidt's paintings; Dir Dr FRANZ SCHÖNFELLNER.

Linz

Lentos Kunstmuseum Linz: Ernst-Koref-Promenade 1, 4020 Linz; tel. (732) 70703600; fax (732) 70703604; e-mail info@lentos.at; internet www.lentos.at; f. 1947 as Neue Galerie der Stadt Linz; current name 2003; gallery of Contemporary Art with paintings (ranging from Klimt, Schiele and Kokoschka to Arnulf Rainter, Karel Appel and Hermann Nitsch), drawings, prints, posters and sculptures since 19th c.; library: library incl. 30,000 catalogues; Dir of Art STELLA ROLLIG; Exec. Dir GERNOT BAROUNIG.

Oberösterreichische Landesmuseen (Regional Museums for Upper Austria): Museumstr. 14, 4010 Linz; tel. (732) 774482-0; fax (732) 774482-66; internet www.landesmuseum.at; f. 1833; library of 130,000 vols; Dir Mag. Dr PETER ASSMANN; publs *Stapfia*, *Studien zur Kulturgeschichte von Oberösterreich* (annual), *Denisia*, *Linzer biologische Beiträge*, *Beiträge zur Naturkunde Oberösterreichs*, *Vogelkundliche Nachrichten aus Oberösterreich*, *Neues Museum*.

Salzburg

Haus der Natur (Natural History Museum): Museumplatz 5, 5020 Salzburg; tel. (662) 842653-0; fax (662) 847905; e-mail office@hausdernatur.at; internet www.hausdernatur.at; f. 1924; zoology, botany, anthropology, geology; reptile zoo, aquarium, space hall; Dir Prof. Dr EBERHARD STÜBER.

Mozarteum: Schwarzstr. 26, 5020 Salzburg; tel. (662) 88940-0; fax (662) 88940-36; e-mail office@mozarteum.at; internet www.mozarteum.at; f. 1914 by 'Internationale Stiftung Mozarteum'; concert rooms, a library of MSS, books and other Mozart memorabilia; Pres. Dr FRIEDRICH GEHMACHER.

Mozarts Wohnhaus: Makartpl. 8, 5020 Salzburg,; tel. (662) 87422740; fax (662) 872924; e-mail archiv@mozarteum.at; internet www.mozarteum.at; multivision 'Mozart and Salzburg'; the world of Mozart 1773–80; instruments from Mozart's time.

Residenzgalerie Salzburg: Residenzplatz 1, 5010 Salzburg; tel. (662) 840451-0; fax (662) 84045116; e-mail residenzgalerie@salzburg.gv.at; internet www.residenzgalerie.at; f. 1923; 16th- to 19th-c. European paintings; Dir Dr ROSWITHA JUFFINGER.

Salzburger Museum Carolino Augusteum: Museumsplatz 6, 5020 Salzburg; tel. (662) 620808-0; fax (662) 620808-720; e-mail office@smca.at; internet www.smca.at; f. 1834; prehistoric and Roman remains, art, coins, musical instruments, costumes, toys; library of 100,000 vols, archives; Dir Dr ERICH MARX.

Schloss Hellbrunn (Hellbrunn Palace): 5020 Salzburg; tel. (662) 820372-0; fax (662) 820372-4931; e-mail info@hellbrunn.at; internet www.hellbrunn.at; f. 1612; furnished 17th-century palace, with water gardens, deer park and open-air theatre; Dir INGRID SONVILLA.

St Pölten

Niederösterreichisches Landesmuseum (Provincial Museum of Lower Austria): Kulturbezirk 5, 3109 St Pölten; tel. (2742) 908090; fax (2742) 908099; e-mail info@landesmuseum.net; internet www.landesmuseum.net; f. 1907; natural history, history of art (since the medieval period; many attached deptl museums are located in Lower Austria, incl. Haydn's birthplace at Rohrau; information centre; Dirs CHRISTIAN

BAUER, CORNELIA LAMPRECHTER; publ. *Newsletter*.

Stillfried/March

Museum für Ur- und Frühgeschichte (Museum for Pre- and Early History): Hauptstr. 23, 2262 Stillfried/March (Niederösterreich); tel. (676) 6113979; e-mail stillfried@aon.at; internet www.museumstillfried.at; f. 1914; local archaeology and palaeontology; Dir Dr WALPURGA ANTL; publ. *Museumsnachrichten* (3 or 4 a year).

Vienna

Erzbischöfliches Dom- und Diözesanmuseum (Archiepiscopal Cathedral and Diocesan Museum): Stephansplatz 6, 1010 Vienna; tel. (1) 51552-3689; fax (1) 51552-3599; e-mail dommuseum@edw.or.at; internet www.dommuseum.at; f. 1933; ecclesiastical art; Dir GERHARD EDERNDORFER.

Gemäldegalerie der Akademie der Bildenden Künste Wien (Vienna Academy of Fine Arts Gallery): Schillerplatz 3, 1010 Vienna; tel. (1) 58816228; fax (1) 5863346; e-mail gemgal@akbild.ac.at; internet www.akademiegalerie.at; f. 1822; paintings since 14th c.; Dir Dr RENATE TRNEK.

Graphische Sammlung Albertina (Albertina Graphic Art Collection): Albertinaplatz 1, 1010 Vienna; tel. (1) 53483-0; fax (1) 53483-430; e-mail info@albertina.at; internet www.albertina.at; f. 1776; prints, drawings, posters; library of 40,000 vols; Dir THERES KOLARZ-LAKENBACHER.

Heeresgeschichtliches Museum (Military History Museum): III, Arsenal, Vienna; tel. (1) 79561-0; fax (1) 79561-17707; e-mail bmlv.hgm@magnet.at; internet www.hgm.or.at; f. 1891; exhibits dating from Thirty Years War to Second World War; library of 70,000 vols; Dir Dr MANFRIED RAUCHENSTEINER.

Kunsthistorisches Museum (Museum of Fine Arts): Burgring 5, 1010 Vienna; tel. (1) 52524-401; fax (1) 52524503; e-mail info@khm.at; internet www.khm.at; f. 1891 from Hapsburg Imperial collections; paintings, Egyptian and other antiquities, numismatics, armour, historical costume, plastics and handicrafts, musical instruments, secular and ecclesiastical relics of the Holy Roman Empire and the Hapsburg dynasty, state carriages (at Schönbrunn palace); library of 85,000 vols; Gen. Dir Dr WILFRIED SEIPEL.

Kupferstichkabinett der Akademie der Bildenden Künste (Graphic Art Collection of the Academy of Fine Arts): Makartgasse 3, 1010 Vienna; tel. (1) 5813040; fax (1) 5813040-31; e-mail m.knofler@akbild.ac.at; internet www.akbild.ac.at/kuka; f. 1689; drawings, prints, photographs, architecture; library: see Libraries and Archives; Dir Dr MONIKA KNOFLER.

Leopold Museum: Museumspl. 1, 1070 Vienna; tel. (1) 52570-0; fax (1) 52570-1500; e-mail office@leopoldmuseum.org; internet www.leopoldmuseum.org; f. 2001; fmrly private art colln of Rudolf and Elisabeth Leopold; works by Schiele, Klimt, Kokoschka and others; Dir Prof. Dr RUDOLF LEOPOLD.

Medizinhistorische Sammlungen am Josephinum: Währingerstr. 25, 1090 Vienna; tel. (1) 427763404; internet www.meduniwien.ac.at/medizingeschichte/medhistmus_uebersicht.htm; f. 1785 as acad. for military surgeons; 18th-century wax anatomical colln, museum of the 2 Vienna Medical Schools and museum of medical endoscopy; library of 80,000 historical medical books; Head of Medicohistorical Collections Assoc. Prof. Dr MANFRED SKOPEC.

Museum für Völkerkunde (Museum of Ethnology): Neue Hofburg, Ringstrassentrakt, 1010 Vienna; tel. (1) 53430-0; fax (1) 53430-230; e-mail v*@ethno-museum.ac.at; internet www.ethno-museum.ac.at; f. 1928; ethnology of non-European peoples; closed for renovation until early 2007; library of 130,000 vols; Dir Prof. Dr CHRISTIAN FEEST; publs *Archiv für Völkerkunde* (annually), *Veröffentlichungen zum Archiv für Völkerkunde*.

Museum Moderner Kunst Stiftung Ludwig Wien (Museum of Modern Art Ludwig Foundation Vienna): Museumspl. 1, 1070 Vienna; tel. (1) 52500-0; fax (1) 52500-1300; e-mail info@mumok.at; internet www.mumok.at; f. 1991; modern and contemporary art, incl. American Pop Art and concurrent European movements; library of 25,000 vols; Dir EDELBERT KÖB.

Naturhistorisches Museum (Natural History Museum): I, Burgring 7, 1014 Vienna; tel. (1) 52177; fax (1) 935254; internet www.nhm-wien.ac.at; f. 1748; geology, palaeontology, zoology, botany, anthropology, prehistory, speleology; library of 400,000 books; Dir Prof. Dr BERNHARD LÖTSCH; Librarian ANDREA KOURGLI; publ. *Annalen*.

Österreichische Galerie Belvedere (Austrian Gallery): Oberes Belvedere, Prinz Eugenstr. 27, 1030 Vienna; tel. (1) 79557-112; fax (1) 7984337; e-mail public@belvedere.at; internet www.belvedere.at; Austrian painting and sculpture from Middle Ages to present, foreign painting and sculpture since 19th c., spec. colln of sculpture by G. Ambrosi; library of 17,000 vols; Dir Dr GERBERT FRODL (acting); publ. *Belvedere*.

Österreichisches Gesellschafts- und Wirtschafts-Museum (Austrian Museum for Economics and Social Affairs): Vogelsanggasse 36, 1050 Vienna; tel. (1) 5452551; fax (1) 5452551-55; e-mail wirtschaftsmuseum@oegwm.ac.at; internet www.oegwm.ac.at; f. 1925; archives, maps, photographs; public library on 'Austria Yesterday and Today'; Dir HANS HARTWEGER; publ. *Österreichs Wirtschaft im Überblick* (annually; also in English).

Österreichisches Museum für angewandte Kunst (Austrian Museum of Applied Arts): Stubenring 5, 1010 Vienna; tel. (1) 711360; fax (1) 7131026; e-mail office@mak.at; internet www.mak.at; f. 1864; applied arts from Roman to modern times, incl. furniture and woodwork, textiles and carpets, glass and ceramics, Islamic and East Asian art, metalwork, Vienna workshop colln and contemporary art; library of 200,000 vols, 300 periodicals, 500,000 prints; Dir PETER NOEVER.

Österreichisches Museum für Volkskunde (Austrian Museum of Folk Life and Folk Art): Laudongasse 15–19, 1080 Vienna; tel. (1) 4068905; fax (1) 4085342; e-mail office@volkskundemuseum.at; internet www.volkskundemuseum.at; f. 1895; incl. nat. furniture colln and other spec. collns (housed on separate sites); Dir Dr FRANZ GRIESHOFER; publs *Kataloge* (1–3 issues a year), *Veröffentlichungen* (irregular).

Österreichisches Theatermuseum: Lobkowitzpl. 2, 1010 Vienna; tel. (1) 52524-3460; fax (1) 52524-5399; e-mail info@theatermuseum.at; internet www.theatermuseum.at; f. 1991; library of 80,000 vols; Dir Dr THOMAS TRABITSCH.

Schloss Schönbrunn Kultur- und Betriebsges. m.b.H. (Schönbrunn Palace): Schönbrunn, 1130 Vienna, Schloss; tel. (1) 81113–239; fax (1) 8121106; internet www.schoenbrunn.at; mid 18th c. fmr Imperial summer residence of the Habsburg dynasty; baroque and botanical gardens; zoological garden opened 1752; Dirs Dipl.-Ing. WOLFGANG KIPPES, Dr FRANZ SATTLECKER.

Technisches Museum Wien (Museum of Technology in Vienna): Mariahilferstr. 212, 1140 Vienna; tel. (1) 89998-6000; fax (1) 89998-3333; e-mail museumsbox@tmw.at; internet www.tmw.at; f. 1907; library of 40,000 vols; Dir Mag. PETER DONHAUSER; publ. *Blätter für Technikgeschichte* (annually).

Wien Museum: Karlsplatz, 1040 Vienna; tel. (1) 5058747-0; fax (1) 5058747-7201; e-mail office@wienmuseum.at; internet www.wienmuseum.at; f. 1887; local history from prehistoric times to the present; among many associated museums are premises once occupied by Beethoven, Haydn, Mozart, Schubert and Johann Strauss; Dir Dr WOLFGANG KOS.

Universities

(All institutions of higher education have university status)

AKADEMIE DER BILDENDEN KÜNSTE WIEN (Academy of Fine Arts Vienna)

Schillerplatz 3, 1010 Vienna
Telephone: (1) 588-160
Fax: (1) 588-16137
E-mail: rektor@akbild.ac.at
Internet: www.akbild.ac.at

Founded 1692
State control
Academic year: October to June

Rector: Prof. Dr STEPHAN SCHMIDT-WULFFEN
Pro-Rectors: Mag. ANDREAS SPIEGL, Mag. ANNA STEIGER
Librarian: BEATRIX BASTL

Library: see Libraries and Archives
Number of teachers: 190
Number of students: 929

PROFESSORS

ALLIEZ, E., Aesthetics and Sociology of Art
BAATZ, W., Conservation and Restoration
BAUER, U. M., Theory, Practice and Transfer of Contemporary Art
BISCHOF, E., Textile Art
DAMISCH, G., Drawing and Graphic Techniques
GIRONCOLI, B., Sculpture
GRAF, F., Expanded Artistic Environment
GRAF, O., Art History
GREEN, R., Conceptual Art
HASPEL, F., Textile Art
KOGLER, P., Computer and Video Art
LAINER, R., Architectural Design
OBHOLZER, W., Abstract Art
PRUSCHA, C., Architectural Design and Habitat, Environment and Conservation
ROSENBLUM, A., Representational Painting and Drawing
SAMSONOW, E., Philosophical and Historical Anthropology of the Arts
SCHLEGEL, E., Photography and Art
SCHMALIX, H., Art in Public Space
SCHREINER, M., Natural Science and Technology in Art
SCHULZ, J., Textile Arts and Crafts, Tapestry
SLOTERDIJK, P., Cultural Philosophy and Media Theory
WAGNER, K., Construction and Technology
WONDER, E., Stage Design
ZENS, H., Education and Science of Art
ZOBERNIG, H., Sculpture

UNIVERSITÄT FÜR ANGEWANDTE KUNST IN WIEN
(University of Applied Arts in Vienna)

Oskar Kokoschkaplatz 2, 1010 Vienna

Telephone: (1) 71133-0
Fax: (1) 71133-222
E-mail: pr@uni-ak.ac.at
Internet: www.dieangewandte.at

Founded 1868

Rector: Dr GERALD BAST
Vice-Rectors: Prof. Dipl.-Ing. SILKE PETSCH, Prof. Dipl.-Ing. WOLF D. PRIX
Chair. of the Academic Senate: Prof. Mag. art. SIGBERT SCHENK
Dean of Studies: Prof. Mag. art. JOSEF KAISER
University Director: Mag. iur. Dr HEINZ ADAMEK
Registrar: SENTA SCHWANDA
Head Librarian: Dr phil. GABRIELE KOLLER

Library of 85,000 vols, 300 periodicals
Number of teachers: 380
Number of students: 1,350

Publications: exhibition catalogues (6–8 a year), *Prospect* (2 a year), *Studienführer*

HEADS OF INSTITUTES

Institute of Aesthetics and Cultural Studies/Art Pedagogy: Prof. Mag. art. BARBARA PUTZ-PLECKO
Institute of Architecture: Prof. Dipl.Ing. WOLF D. PRIX
Institute of Conservation Sciences and Restoration Technology: Prof. Dipl.-Ing. Dr techn. ALFRED VENDL
Institute of Design: Prof. Mag. arch. PAOLO PIVA
Institute of Fine Arts: (vacant)
Institute of Media Art: Prof. Dipl.-Ing. BERNHARD LEITNER

HEADS OF DEPARTMENTS

Institute of Aesthetics and Cultural Studies/Art Pedagogy:
- Art History: Prof. Dr phil. GABRIELE WERNER
- Art Teacher Education (Crafts): Prof. JAMES SKONE
- Art Teacher Education (Fine Arts): Prof. Mag. art. ERWIN WURM
- Art Teacher Education (Textiles): Prof. Mag. art. BARBARA PUTZ-PLECKO
- History of Culture and Civilization: Prof. Dr phil. MANFRED WAGNER
- Sociology of Art and Cultural Sociology: Prof. Dr phil. ROMAN HORAK

Institute of Architecture:
- Architectural History and Theory: Prof. Dr phil. LIANE LEFAIVRE
- Architecture: Prof. ZAHA HADID
- Architecture: Prof. Mag. arch. GREG LYNN
- Architecture: Prof. Dipl.-Ing. WOLF D. PRIX
- Building Construction: Prof. Dipl.-Ing. ERNST MACZEK-MATEOVICS
- Building Technology: Prof. Dipl.-Ing. ROLAND BURGARD
- Model Construction: Prof. Prof. Ing. FRANZ HNIZDO
- Statics: Prof. Dipl.-Ing. Dr techn. KLAUS BOLLINGER

Institute of Conservation Studies and Restoration Technology:
- Archeometry: Prof. Dipl.-Ing. Dr techn. BERNHARD PICHLER
- Conservation and Restoration: Prof. Mag. art. Dr phil. GABRIELA KRIST
- Metal Technology: AUGUST KORISCHUM
- Technical Chemistry: Prof. Dipl.-Ing. Dr techn. ALFRED VENDL
- Textile Technology: Prof. Mag. art. BEATRIX KASER
- Timber Techology: REINHOLD KROBATH

Institute of Design:
- Computer Studio: HELGA RÖSSLER
- Fashion Design: Prof. RAF JAN SIMONS
- Graphic Design: Prof. Dipl. des. MATTHIAS HICKMANN
- Graphic Design and Advertising: Prof. WALTER LÜRZER
- History and Theory of Design: Prof. Dr phil. ALISON CLARKE
- Industrial Design: Prof. Mag. arch. PAOLO PIVA
- Industrial Design: Prof. Dr BOREK SIPEK
- Landscape Design: Prof. Mag. art. MARIO TERZIC
- Repro Technology: Akad. Maler ROBERT LETTNER
- Video: Mag. art. WOLFGANG NEIPL

Institute of Fine Arts:
- Artistic Book Design: Prof. Mag. art. ANDREA FRANKL
- Ceramics: Prof. Mag. art. OTTO LORENZ
- Graphics: Prof. Mag. art. SIGBERT SCHENK
- Nude Drawing: Prof. Mag. art. JOSEF KAISER
- Painting: Prof. ADOLF FROHNER
- Painting: Prof. Mag. art. WOLFGANG HERZIG
- Painting, Movie Cartoon and Tapestry: Prof. Mag. art. CHRISTIAN LUDWIG ATTERSEE
- Philosophy: Prof. Dr RUDOLF BURGER
- Sculpture: Prof. Mag. art. GERDA FASSEL

Institute of Media Art (internet www.vis-med.ac.at):
- Artistic and Scientific Transfer: Prof. Dr rer. pol. CHRISTIAN REDER
- Communication Theory: Prof. Dr rer. pol. MANFRED FASSLER
- Digital Art: Prof. PETER WEIBEL, Prof. THOMAS FÜRSTNER
- Visual Media and Space (Intermedia Art): Prof. Mag. art. BRIGITTE KOWANZ
- Visual Media, Space and Sound (Intermedia Art): Prof. Dipl.-Ing. BERNHARD LEITNER

UNIVERSITÄT FÜR BODENKULTUR WIEN
(University of Natural Resources and Applied Life Sciences, Vienna)

Gregor Mendelstr. 33, 1180 Vienna

Telephone: (1) 47654-0
Fax: (1) 47654-2606
E-mail: bdr@boku.ac.at
Internet: www.boku.ac.at

Founded 1872
State control
Academic year: October to June

Rector: Prof. Dipl.-Fw. Dr Dr HUBERT DÜRRSTEIN
Vice-Rector (Research): Prof. Dipl.-Ing. Dr MARTIN H. GERZABEK
Vice-Rector (Studies and International Affairs): Prof. Dipl. Ing. Dr ERIKA STAUDACHER
Librarian: Dr phil. WERNER HAINZ-SATOR

Library: see under Libraries and Archives
Number of teachers: 330
Number of students: 4,364

Publications: *Blick ins Land* (monthly), *Die Bodenkultur*, *Ökoenergie* (every 2 months), *Zentralblatt für das gesamte Forstwesen* (quarterly)

HEADS OF DEPARTMENTS

Department for Agrobiotechnology: MATHIAS MÜLLER
Department of Applied Plant Sciences and Plant Biotechnology: FLORIAN M.W. GRUNDLER
Department of Biotechnology: DAVID PHILIP KREIL
Department of Chemistry: PAUL KOSMA
Department of Civil Engineering and Natural Hazards: KONRAD BERGMEISTER
Department of Economics and Social Sciences: HANS KARL WYTRZENS
Department of Forest- and Soil Sciences: HUBERT STERBA
Department of Integrative Biology and Biodiversity Research: EMMERICH BERGHOFER
Department of Landscape, Spatial and Infrastructure Sciences: GERD SAMMER
Department of Material Sciences and Process Engineering: STEFANIE TSCHEGG
Department of Sustainable Agricultural Systems: WERNER ZOLLITSCH
Department of Water, Atmosphere and Environment: HERWIG WAIDBACHER

PROFESSORS

KOSMA, P., Organic Chemistry
LICKA, L., Landscape Architecture
LISCHKA, H., Soil Science
MINSCH, J., Sustainable Economic Development
ROSENAU, T., Organic Chemistry
SCHNEIDER, W., Surveying, Remote Sensing and Land Information
SCHOPF, A., Forest Entomology, Forest Pathology and Forest Protection
SÖLKNER, J., Livestock Sciences
STINGEDER, G. J., Analytical Chemistry
TREBERSPURG, M., Structural Engineering
TSCHEGG, S., Material Sciences and Process Engineering
WIMMER, R., Wood Science and Technology
WINCKLER, C., Livestock Sciences
WINDISCH, W. M., Animal Food and Nutrition
WU, W., Geotechnical Engineering

ATTACHED RESEARCH CENTRES

Centre for Applied Genetics: internet www.boku.ac.at/zag; Dir Prof. J. GLÖSSL.

Centre for Environmental Studies and Nature Conservation: internet www.boku.ac.at/zun; Dir Prof. W. HOLZNER.

DONAU-UNIVERSITÄT KREMS/UNIVERSITÄT FÜR WEITERBILDUNG
(Danube University Krems/University of Continuing Education)

Dr-Karl-Dorrek-Str. 30, 3500 Krems

Telephone: (2732) 893-0
Fax: (2732) 893-4000
E-mail: info@donau-uni.ac.at
Internet: www.donau.uni.ac.at

Founded 1995
State control
Languages of instruction: German, English
Academic year: October to June

Rector: Prof. Dr HELMUT KRAMER
Vice-Rectors: Prof. Mag. Dr ADA PELLERT, Dilp.-Ing. Dr PETER STRIZIK
University Director: Dr HELMUT DORN
Director of Communications: GISELA GRUBER

Number of teachers: 939
Number of students: 3,100

Publications: *Annual Report*, *campus_aktuell* (4 a year), *Study Program* (annually), *timnews* (4 a year), *Uni-Bilanz* (4 a year), *upgrade* (4 a year)

PROFESSORS

BAUMGARTNER, P., Interactive Media and Educational Technology
BRAININ, M., Clinical Medicine and Preventive Medicine
BRANDTWEINER, R., Management and Economics
DOCKNER, E., Banking and Finance
FALKENHAGEN, D., Environmental and Medical Sciences
FILZMAIER, P., Political Communication
FINA, S., European Integration
GRAU, O., Applied Cultural Studies

LENK, K., New Public Management and E-Governance
MIKSCH, S., Information and Knowledge Engineering
PELLERT, A., Continuing Education Research and Educational Management
RISKU, H., Knowledge and Communication Management
STRAUBE, M., European Integration
WILLER, J., Interdisciplinary Dentistry and Technology
ZECHNER, J., Banking and Finance

INTERNATIONAL UNIVERSITY

Mondscheingasse 16, 1070 Vienna
Telephone: (1) 7185068-12
Fax: (1) 7185068-9
E-mail: info@iuvienna.edu
Internet: www.iuvienna.edu

Founded 1980 as European Christian College, became International Christian University 1991, current name 1998
Private control, liberal arts institution of higher learning
Language of instruction: English
Academic year: September to July
President: Dr WILL C. GOODHEER
Administrative Vice-President: LINDA BOYER
Director of Marketing: SABRINA NILL
Assistant to Academic Dean: OLA NYKOLYSHYN
Library of 9,000 vols
Number of teachers: 54
Number of students: 270
Schools: business administration, diplomatic studies; Masters courses: MBA, MIB, MA Diplomatic and Strategic Studies.

JOHANNES KEPLER UNIVERSITÄT LINZ
(Johannes Kepler University Linz)

4040 Linz
Telephone: ()732) 2468-0
Fax: (732) 2468-8822
E-mail: rektor@jku.at
Internet: www.jku.at

Founded as College 1966 present name 1975
State control
Languages of instruction: German, English
Academic year: October to June
Rector: Prof. Dr RUDOLF ARDELT
Vice-Rectors: Dr FRANZ WURM (Finance and Resource Management), Prof. Dr FRIEDRICH SCHNEIDER (Foreign Affairs), Prof. Dr GÜNTER PILZ (Research), Prof. Dr HERBERT KALB (Teaching)
Administrative Director: Dr JOSEF SCHMIED
Librarian: Dr MONIKA SCHENK

Library: see Libraries and Archives
Number of teachers: 554
Number of students: 12,307

Publications: *Mitteilungsblatt der Universität* (weekly), *News vom Campus* (6 a year), *UNIVATIONEN - Forschungsmedienservice der Johannes Kepler Universität Linz* (4 a year)

DEANS

Faculty of Engineering and Natural Sciences: Prof. Dipl.-Ing. Dr RICHARD HAGELAUER
Faculty of Law: Prof. Dr HERIBERT FRANZ KÖCK
Faculty of Social Sciences, Economics and Business: Prof. Dipl.-Ing. Dr Dr JOHANN BRUNNER

PROFESSORS

Faculty of Engineering and Natural Sciences (Altenberger Str. 69, 4040 Linz; tel. (732) 2468-3220; fax (732) 2468-3225; e-mail tnf-dekanat@jku.at; internet www.tn.jku.at):

AMRHEIN, W., Electrical Drives and Power Electronics
BAUER, G., Semiconductor Physics
BAUER, S., Soft Matter Physics
BÄUERLE, D., Applied Physics
BIERE, A., Formal Models and Verification
BREMER, H., Robotics
BUCHBERGER, W., Analytical Chemistry
CHROUST, G., Systems Engineering and Automation
COOPER, J. B., Functional Analysis
DEL RE, L., Design and Control of Mechatronical Systems
ENGL, H., Industrial Mathematics
FALK, H., Organic Chemistry
FERSCHA, A., Pervasive Computing
GITTLER, P., Fluid Mechanics and Heat Transfer
GRITZNER, G., Chemical Technology of Inorganic Materials
HAGELAUER, R., Integrated Circuits
HOCHREITER, S., Bioinformatics
IRSCHIK, H., Technical Mechanics
JAKOBY, B., Microelectronics
JANTSCH, W., Solid State Physics
JÜTTLER, B., Applied Geometry
KLEMENT, E. P., Fuzzy Logic
KNÖR, G., Inorganic Chemistry
KOTSIS, G., Telecooperation
KROTSCHECK, E., Many Particle Systems
LANGER, U., Computational Mathematics
LARCHER, G., Financial Mathematics
MÖSSENBÖCK, H., System Software
MÜHLBACHER, J., Information Processing and Microprocessor Technology
PAULE, P., Symbolic Computation
PILZ, G., Algebra
POHL, P., Biophysics
SAMHABER, W., Process Engineering
SARICIFTCI, N. S., Physical Chemistry
SCHÄFFLER, F., Semiconductor Physics
SCHEIDL, R., Machine Design and Hydraulic Drives
SCHLACHER, K., Automatic Control and Control Systems Technology
SCHLÖGLMANN, W., Mathematics Education
SCHMIDT, H., Chemical Technology of Organic Materials
SOBCZAK, R., Polymer Science
SPRINGER, A., Communications and Information Engineering
TITULAER, U. M., Condensed Matter Theory
VOLKERT, J., Graphics and Parallel Processing
WAGNER, R., Applied Knowledge Processing
WEIß, P., Stochastics
WIDMER, G., Computational Perception
WINKLER, F., Symbolic Computation
ZAGAR, B., Electrical Measurement Technology
ZEMAN, K., Computer-aided Methods in Mechanical Engineering
ZEPPENFELD, P., Atomic Physics and Surface Science

Faculty of Law (tel. (732) 2468-3201; fax (732) 2468-3205; e-mail re-dekanat@jku.at; internet www.re.jku.at):

ACHATZ, M., Administrative Law and Management
ACHATZ, M., Research Department for Tax Law and Tax Management
APATHY, P., Roman Law
BINDER, B., Administrative Law and Administrative Sciences
BURGSTALLER, A., European and Austrian Civil Procedure Law
DOLINAR, H., Civil Procedure
FLOSZMANN, U., History of Austrian and German Law
FUNK, B.-C., University Law
HAUER, A., Public Law with Special Reference to Austrian Administrative Law
HENGSTSCHLÄGER, J., Constitutional Law and Political Science
JABORNEGG, P., Labour Law and Social Security
KALB, H., Canon Law
KAROLLUS, M., Commercial and Securities Law
KEINERT, H., Commercial and Securities Law
KERSCHNER, F., Civil Law and Environmental Law
KLINGENBERG, G., Roman Law
KÖCK, H., Public International Law and European Law
LEITL, B., Correspondence Course
OBERNDORFER, P., Administrative Law and Administrative Sciences
REISCHAUER, R., Civil Law
RIEDLER, A., Correspondence Course
RUMMEL, P., Civil Law
SPIELBUECHLER, K., Civil Law
WEGSCHEIDER, H., Criminal Law and Procedure
WIDDER, H., Constitutional Law and Political Science
VELTEN, P., Criminal Law and Procedure

Faculty of Social Sciences, Economics and Business (tel. (732) 2468-3211; fax (732) 2468-3215; e-mail sowi-dekanat@jku.at; internet www.sowi.jku.at):

ALTRICHTER, H., Education and Educational Psychology
BACHER, J., Sociology
BATINIC, B., E-learning
BECKER, P., Modern and Contemporary History
BÖHNISCH, W., Business Administration (Management), Human Resources Management
BRUNNER, J., Economics
COCCA, T., Asset Management
DULLECK, U., Economics
DYK, I., Socio-politics
EULER, H. P., Sociology
FELDBAUER-DURSTMÜLLER, B., Business Administration (Accountancy, Auditing, Business Taxation and Controllership)
FRÜHWIRTH-SCHNATTER, S., Applied Statistics and Econometrics
GADENNE, V., Philosophy and Theory of Science
HAUCH, G., Modern and Contemporary History, Gender Studies
KAILER, N., Entrepreneurship and Business Development
LANDESMANN, M., National Economy
MALINSKY, A. H., Environmental Management in Business and Regional Policy
MATZLER, K., Business Administration
MÜLLER, W. G., Applied Statistics
PERNSTEINER, H., Corporate Finance
PILS, M., Data Processing
PÖLL, G., Economics
POMBERGER, G., Software Engineering
ROHATSCHEK, R., Business Administration (Accountancy, Auditing, Business Taxation and Controllership
ROITHMAYR, F., Information Engineering
SANDGRUBER, R., Social and Economic History
SCHAUER, R., Business Administration (Public Administration and Non-Profit Organizations)
SCHNEIDER, F., Economics, Public Economics, Public Choice
SCHREFL, M., Data and Knowledge Engineering
SCHURER, B., Economic and Business Education
SCHUSTER, H., Economics
STARY, C., Communications Engineering
STREHL, F., Business Administration

TUMPEL, M., Business Administration, Accountancy, Auditing, Business Taxation and Controllership
WEIDENHOLZER, J., Social Policy
WINTER-EBMER, R., Economics
WÜHRER, G., Business Administration (Marketing)

HEADS OF DEPARTMENTS

General and Inorganic Chemistry: Prof. Dr GÜNTHER KNÖR
Analytical Chemistry: Prof. Dr WOLFGANG BUCHBERGER
Chemical Technology of Inorganic Materials: Prof. Dr GERHARD GRITZNER
Chemical Technology of Organic Materials: Prof. Dr HARALD SCHMIDT
Organic Chemistry: Prof. Dr HEINZ FALK
Physical Chemistry: Prof. Dr NIYAZI SERDAR SARICIFTCI
Polymer Science: Prof. Dr RUDOLF SOBCZAK
Process Engineering: Prof. Dr WOLFGANG SAMHABER
Organic Solar Cells: Prof. Dr NIYAZI SERDAR SARICIFTCI
Applied Knowledge Processing: Prof. Dr ROLAND WAGNER
Bioinformatics: Prof. Dr SEPP HOCHREITER
Computational Perception: Prof. Dr GERHARD WIDMER
Formal Models and Verification: Prof. Dr ARMIN BIERE
Graphics and Parallel Processing: Prof. Dr JENS VOLKERT
Informatics in Business and Government: Prof. Dr ROLAND WAGNER
Information Processing and Microprocessor Technology: Prof. Dr JÖRG MÜHLBACHER
Integrated Circuits: Prof. Dr RICHARD HAGELAUER
Pervasive Computing: Prof. Dr ALOIS FERSCHA
Systems Engineering and Automation: Prof. Dr GERHARD CHROUST
System Software: Prof. Dr HANSPETER MÖSSENBÖCK
Telecooperation: Prof. Dr GABRIELE KOTSIS
Algebra: Prof. Dr GÜNTER PILZ
Analysis: Prof. Dr JAMES BELL COOPER
Applied Geometry: Prof. Dr BERT JÜTTLER
Mathematics Education: Prof. Dr WOLFGANG SCHLÖGLMANN
Financial Mathematics: Prof. Dr GERHARD LARCHER
Industrial Mathematics: Prof. Dr HEINZ ENGL
Computational Mathematics: Prof. Dr ULRICH LANGER
Stochastics: Prof. Dr PETER WEIß
Symbolic Computation: Prof. Dr FRANZ WINKLER
Knowledge-Based Mathematical Systems: Prof. Dr ERICH PETER KLEMENT
Special Research Program "Numerical and Symbolic Scientific Computing": Prof. Dr PETER PAULE
Design and Control of Mechatronical Systems: Prof. Dr LUIGI DEL RE
Electrical Drives and Power Electronics: Prof. Dr WOLFGANG AMRHEIN
Electrical Measurement Technology: Prof. Dr BERNHARD ZAGAR
Machine Design and Hydraulic Drives: Prof. Dr RUDOLF SCHEIDL
Microelectronics: Prof. Dr BERNHARD JAKOBY
Communications and Information Engineering: Prof. Dr ANDREAS SPRINGER
Computer-Aided Methods in Mechanical Engineering: Prof. Dr KLAUS ZEMAN
Automatic Control and Control Systems Technology: Prof. Dr KURT SCHLACHER
Robotics: Prof. Dr-Ing. HARTMUT BREMER
Fluid Mechanics and Heat Transfer: Prof. Dr PHILIPP GITTLER
Technical Mechanics: Prof. Dr HANS IRSCHIK
Applied Physics: Prof. Dr DIETER BÄUERLE
Biophysics: Prof. Dr PETER POHL
Experimental Physics: Prof. Dr PETER ZEPPENFELD
Semiconductor and Solid State Physics: Prof. Dr GÜNTHER BAUER
Theoretical Physics: Prof. Dr ECKHARD KROTSCHECK
Finance: Prof. Dr HELMUT PERNSTEINER
Business Taxation: Prof. Dr MICHAEL TUMPEL
Environmental Management in Business and Regional Policy: Prof. Dr ADOLF HEINZ MALINSKY
Public and Nonprofit Management: Prof. Dr REINBERT SCHAUER
Controlling and Consulting: Prof. Dr BIRGIT FELDBAUER-DURSTMÜLLER
Marketing: Prof. Dr GERHARD WÜHRER
Production and Logistics Management: Prof. Dr GÜNTHER ZÄPFEL
Strategic Management: Prof. Dr FRANZ STREHL
Human Resources Management: Prof. Dr WOLF BÖHNISCH
International Management: Prof. Dr KURT MATZLER
Entrepreneurship and Business Development: Prof. Dr NORBERT KAILER
Accounting and Auditing: Prof. Dr ROMAN ROHATSCHEK
Education and Psychology: Prof. Dr HERBERT ALTRICHTER
Philosophy and Theory of Science: Prof. Dr VOLKER GADENNE
Modern and Contemporary History: Prof. Dr PETER BECKER
Social and Economic History: Prof. Dr ROMAN SANDGRUBER
Social and Societal Policy: Prof. Dr JOSEF WEIDENHOLZER
Sociology: Prof. Dr JOHANN BACHER
Applied Statistics: Prof. Dr SYLVIA FRÜHWIRTH-SCHNATTER
Economics: Prof. Dr REINER BUCHEGGER
Data Processing: Prof. Dr MANFRED PILS
Communication Engineering: Prof. Dr CHRISTIAN STARY
Data and Knowledge Engineering: Prof. Dr MICHAEL SCHREFL
Information Engineering: Prof. Dr FRIEDRICH ROITHMAYR
Software Engineering: Prof. Dr GUSTAV POMBERGER
Research Institute for Banking and Finance: Prof. Dr FRIEDRICH SCHNEIDER
Cultural Economy and Cultural Research: Prof. Dr INGO MÖRTH
Health Systems Research: Prof. Dr REINER BUCHEGGER
Interdisciplinary Research Institute for Development Cooperation: Prof. Dr ROMAN SANDGRUBER
Center for Knowledge Management: Prof. Dr CHRISTIAN STARY
Administrative Law and Management: Prof. Dr MARKUS ACHATZ
Research Department for Tax Law and Tax Management: Prof. Dr MARKUS ACHATZ
Roman Law: Prof. Dr PETER APATHY
European and Austrian Civil Procedure Law: Prof. Dr ALFRED BURGSTALLER
Civil Procedure: Prof. Dr HANS DOLINAR
History of Austrian and German Law: Prof. Dr URSULA FLOSSMANN
University Law: Prof. Dr BERND CHRISTIAN FUNK
Constitutional Law and Political Science: Prof. Dr JOHANNES HENGSTSCHLAEGER
Labour Law and Social Security: Prof. Dr PETER JABORNEGG
Canon Law: Prof. Dr HERBERT KALB
Commercial and Securities Law: Prof. Dr MARTIN KAROLLUS
Environmental Law: Prof. Dr FERDINAND KERSCHNER
Roman Law: Prof. Dr GEORG KLINGENBERG
Public International Law and European Law: Prof. Dr HERIBERT FRANZ KOECK
Correspondence Course: Prof. Dr ANDREAS RIEDLER
Civil Law: Prof. Dr PETER RUMMEL
Criminal Law: Prof. Dr HERBERT WEGSCHEIDER

KARL-FRANZENS-UNIVERSITÄT GRAZ
(Graz University)

Universitätsplatz 3, 8010 Graz
Telephone: (316) 380-0
Fax: (316) 380-9140
E-mail: udion@email.kfunigraz.ac.at
Internet: www.uni-graz.at

Founded 1585
State control
Academic year: October to June (two terms)

Rector: Prof. Dr ALFRED GUTSCHELHOFER
Chief Administrative Officer: Dr MARIA EDLINGER
Librarian: HRat Dr WERNER SCHLACHER

Library: see Libraries and Archives
Number of teachers: 2,532
Number of students: 24,059

DEANS

Faculty of Business Administration and Economics: Dr LUTZ BEINSEN
Faculty of Catholic Theology: Dr GERHARD LARCHER
Faculty of Law: Dr h.c. Dr GERNOT KOCHER
Faculty of Liberal Arts: Dr WALTER HÖFLECHNER
Faculty of Medicine: Dr HELMUT WURM
Faculty of Science: Dr GEORG HOINKES

PROFESSORS

Faculty of Business Administration and Economics (Universitätsstr. 15, 8010 Graz; fax (316) 380-9400):

ACHAM, K., Sociology
BAIGENT, N., Public Economy
BEINSEN, L., Political Economy
HALLER, M., Sociology
HÜLSMANN, J., Statistics, Econometry and Operations Research
KRAUS, H., Organization and Industrial Data Processing
KURZ, H. D., Political Economy
LIEBMANN, H. P., Marketing
MANDL, D., Business, Methodology of Economics
MANDL, G., Industrial Economics
RAUCH, W., Computer Science
SCHLEICHER, ST., Political Economy
SCHNEIDER, U., Industrial Economics
SCHÖPFER, G., Economic and Social History
STEINER, P., Industrial Economics
STREBEL, H., Business Administration
WAGENHOFER, A., Business Administration

Faculty of Catholic Theology (fax (316) 380-9300):

ANGEL, H. F., Catechetics
BUCHER, R. M., Pastoral Theology
ESTERBAUER, R., Philosophy
HIRNSPERGER, J., Canon Law
JENSEN, A., History of Doctrine and Ecumenical Theology
KÖRNER, B., Dogmatics
LARCHER, G., Fundamental Theology
MARBÖCK, J., Old Testament
WOSCHITZ, K., Bible Knowledge

Faculty of Law (Universitätsstr. 15, 8010 Graz; fax (316) 380-9400):

BRÜNNER, CH., Public Law
BYDLINSKI, P., Civil Law
HINTEREGGER, M., Civil Law
JELINEK, W., Civil Procedure, Private International Law, Agricultural Law
JUD, W., Commercial Law
KOCHER, G., History of Austrian Law

KOLLER, P., Philosophy of Law, Legal Theory, Sociology of Law
MANTL, W., Political Science and Constitutional Law
MARHOLD, F., Labour Law
NOVAK, R., Austrian Administrative Law
PICHLER, J., European Legal Development
POSCH, W., Civil Law
RUPPE, H. G., Financial Law
SCHICK, P., Criminal Law and Criminology
SCHILCHER, B., Private Law
SIMOTTA, D., Civil Procedure
THÜR, G., Roman Law

Faculty of Liberal Arts (fax (316) 380-9700):

CSÁKY, M., Austrian History
EISMANN, W., Slavonic Philology
FILL, A., English Philology
GOLTSCHNIGG, D., German Philology
HÄRTEL, R., Medieval History
HELMICH, W., Roman Philology
HIEBEL, H., Austrian Literature and Theory of Literature
HÖRANDNER, E., Folklore
HOSSENFELDER, M., Philosophy
HUMMEL, M., Roman Philology
HURCH, B., General and Applied Linguistics
KAMITZ, R., Philosophy
KASER, K., South-East European History
KONRAD, H., Contemporary History
KRUMMEM, E., Classical Philology
LENZ, W., Pedagogics
MITTELBERGER, H., Comparative Linguistics
PIEPER, R., Economic and Social History
POCHAT, G., Art History
PORTMANN, P., German Philology
PRUNČ, E., Translation and Interpreting
RIEHLE, W., English Philology
SCHWOB, A., German Philology
SUST, M., Sports Science
TOŠOVIĆ, B., Slavonic Philology
WALTER, M., Musicology
WOLF, W., English Philology

Faculty of Medicine (fax (316) 380-9600):

ANDERHUBER, F., Anatomy
DENK, H., Pathological Anatomy
DOHR, G., Histology and Embryology
FAULBORN, J., Ophthalmology
GELL, G., Medical Statistics
HÖLLWARTH, M., Paediatric Surgery
HUBMER, G., Urology
KERL, H., Venereal and Skin Diseases
KOSTNER, G., Medical Biochemistry
KREJS, G., Internal Medicine
KURZ, R., Paediatrics
LEINZINGER, E., Forensic Medicine
MARTH, E., Hygiene
MISCHINGER, H. J., Surgery
MOSER, M., Oto-rhino-laryngology
NOACK, R., Social Medicine
PESKAR, B., Pharmacology
PIERINGER, W., Medical Psychology and Psychotherapy
REIBNEGGER, G., Medical Chemistry
RIENMÜLLER, R., Radiology
SCHAUENSTEIN, K., Functional Pathology
SZYSZKOWITZ, R., Orthopaedic Surgery
TRITTHART, H., Medical Physics
WINDHAGER, E., Orthopaedics and Orthopaedic Surgery
WINTER, R., Midwifery and Gynaecology

Faculty of Science (fax (316) 380-9800):

ALBERT, D., Psychology
BAUER, R., Pharmacognosy
BLANZ, P., Botany
FABER, K., Organic Chemistry
FLOR, P., Mathematics
FRANCESCONI, K., Analytical Chemistry
HALTER-KOCH, F., Mathematics
HASLINGER, E., Pharmaceutical Chemistry
HEINRICH, G., Plant Anatomy and Physiology
HÖGENAUER, G., Microbiology
HOINKES, G., Mineralogy
HUBER, H., Psychology
JANOSCHEK, R., Theoretical Chemistry
KAPPEL, F., Mathematics
KOHLWEIN, S., Biochemistry
KRATKY, CH., Physical Chemistry
KRENN, H., Experimental Physics
KUNISCH, K., Mathematics
MAYER, B. M., Pharmacology and Toxicology
NETZER, F., Experimental Physics
PILLER, W., Geology and Palaeontology
PÖTZ, W., Theoretical Physics
REICH, L., Mathematics
ROEMER, H., Zoology
SCHNEIDER, J., Inorganic Chemistry
STURMBAUER, CH., Zoology
WAKONIGG, H., Geography
WALLBRECHER, E., Geology and Palaeontology
ZIMMERMANN, F., Geography

UNIVERSITÄT KLAGENFURT
(University of Klagenfurt)

Universitätsstr. 65-67, 9020 Klagenfurt
Telephone: (463) 2700-9200
Fax: (463) 2700-9299
E-mail: uni@uni-klu.ac.at
Internet: www.uni-klu.ac.at

Founded 1970
State control
Academic year: October to February, March to June

Rector: Prof. Dr HEINRICH C. MAYR
Vice-Rectors: Prof. Dr PETRA HESSE, O. Univ. Prof. MMag. Dr JUTTA MENSCHIK-BENDELE, Univ. Prof. Dr HUBERT LENGAUER
Librarian: Dr MANFRED LUBE

Number of teachers: 520
Number of students: 7,000

DEANS

Faculty of Economics, Business Administration and Informatics: (vacant)
Faculty of Humanities: Prof. Dr KARL STUHLPFARRER
Faculty of Interdisciplinary Research and Education: Prof. Dr ROLAND FISCHER

PROFESSORS

Faculty of Economics, Business Administration and Informatics (tel. (463) 2700-6229):

BODENHÖFER, H.-J., Economics of Education
BÖSZÖRMÉNYI, L., Computer Science
DÖRFLER, W., Mathematics
EDER, J., Computer Science
FISCHER, R., Mathematics
FRIEDRICH, G., Computer Science
HELLWAGNER, H., Computer Science
HITZ, M., Computer Science
HORSTER, P., Computer Science
KALSS, S., Law
KALUZA, B., Business Administration
KELLERMANN, P., Sociology of Education
KOFLER, H., Business Administration
KROPFBERGER, D., Business Administration
MAYR, H., Computer Science
MITTERMEIR, R., Computer Science
MÜLLER, W., Mathematics
NADVORNIK, W., Business Administration
NECK, R., Business Administration
PILZ, J., Applied Statistics
POTACS, M., Law
RENDL, F., Mathematics
RIECKMANN, H.-J., Business Administration
RONDO-BROYETTO, P., Business Administration
SAUBERER, M., Geography
SCHNEIDER, D., Business Administration
SCHWARZ, E., Business Administration
SEGER, M., Geography
STETTNER, H., Mathematics

Faculty of Humanities (tel. (463) 2700-6227):

ARNOLD, U., Philosophy
ASPETSBERGER, F., German Philology
BAMMÉ, A., Educational Science
BERGER, A., German Philology
BRANDSTETTER, A., German Philology
GSTETTNER, P., Educational Science
HEINTEL, P., Philosophy and Group Dynamics
HÖDL, G., Medieval History and Studies Related to History
HOVORKA, H., Special Educational Theory Relating to Disabilities
JAMES, A., English and American Studies
KARMASIN, M., Communications
KLINGLER, J., Educational Theory
KUNA, F. M., English and American Studies
LARCHER, D., Educational Science
LÖSCHENKOHL, E., Psychology and Developmental Psychology
MAYERTHALER, W., General and Applied Philology
MELEZINEK, A., Teaching Methods
MENSCHIK, J., Educational Science
METER, H., Romance Studies
MORITSCH, A., History of Southern and Eastern Europe
NEUHÄUSER, R., Slavic Studies
NEWEKLOWSKY, G., Slavic Studies
OTTOMEYER, K., Social Psychology
POHL, H.-D., General Philology
POSCH, P., Curriculum Studies
RUMPLER, H., Modern and Austrian History
SCHAUSBERGER, N., Modern Austrian History
STROBEL, K., Ancient History and Archaeology
STUHLPFARRER, K., History
VÖLKL, F., Educational Psychology
WANDRUSZKA, U., Romance Studies
ZIMA, P. V., General Comparative Literature

ATTACHED INSTITUTE

Interuniversitäres Institut für Interdisziplinäre Forschung und Fortbildung: Sterneckstr. 15, 9020 Klagenfurt,; tel. (463) 2700-754; fax (463) 2700-759; f. 1980; development of innovative research projects in such fields as man-machine relationship, preventive health policy, in-service teacher training; Dir Prof. Dr ROLAND FISCHER; publ. *Perspektiven für Fernstudien*.

UNIVERSITÄT FÜR KÜNSTLERISCHE UND INDUSTRIELLE GESTALTUNG LINZ
(University of Art and Industrial Design Linz)

Hauptpl. 8, 4010 Linz
Telephone: (732) 7898-0
Fax: (732) 783508
E-mail: kunstunilinz@ufg.ac.at
Internet: www.ufg.ac.at

Founded 1947, present status 1998

Rector: Prof. Dr REINHARD KANNONIER
Vice-Rectors: Dr MANFRED LECHNER, Dr iur. CHRISTINE WINDSTEIGER, Mag. art. RAINER ZENDRON
Librarian: URSULA GANGLBAUER

Library of 50,000 vols
Number of teachers: 140
Number of students: 800

HEADS OF DEPARTMENTS

Aesthetic Education: Prof. Mag. art. WOLFGANG STIFTER
Architecture: Prof. Mag. arch. Ir. ROLAND GNAIGER

Industrial Design: Prof. Dipl.-Ing. AXEL THALLEMER
Space and Design Strategies: Prof. Mag. arch. ELSA PROCHAZKA

MEDIZINISCHE UNIVERSITÄT GRAZ

Universitätsplatz 3, 8010 Graz
Telephone: (316) 380-0
Fax: (316) 380-9140
E-mail: rektor@meduni-graz.at
Internet: www.meduni-graz.at
Founded 1863 as Medical Faculty of Graz University; university status 2002
State control
Language of instruction: German
Rector: Prof. Dr GERHARD FRANZ WALTER
Vice-Rector for Clinical Affairs: Prof. Dr KARLHEINZ TSCHELIESSNIGG
Vice-Rector for Research Management and International Co-operation: Dr SABINE HERLITSCHKA
Vice-Rector for Strategy and Innovation: Prof. Dr HELLMUT SAMONIGG
Vice-Rector for Teaching and Studies: Prof. Dr GILBERT REIBNEGGER
Director of the Organizational Unit for Central Infrastructure: Mag. Dr GERALD WALLAND
Librarian: Dr ULRIKE KORTSCHAK
Number of teachers: 741
Number of students: 4,900

HEADS OF DEPARTMENTS

Department of Dentistry: Prof. Dr PETER STAEDTLER
Department of Medicine (University Clinic): Prof. Dr ERNST PILGER

MEDIZINISCHE UNIVERSITÄT INNSBRUCK

Christoph-Probst-Platz, Innrain 52, 6020 Innsbruck
Telephone: (512) 507- 0
E-mail: i-master@uibk.ac.at
Internet: www.i-med.ac.at
Founded 2004 from the medical faculty of the University of Innsbruck
State control
Rector: Prof. Dr CLEMENS SORG
Vice-Rector for Clinical Studies: Prof. Dr ROLAND STAUDINGER
Vice-Rector for Human Resources, Human Resources Development and Gender Equality: Prof. Dr MARGARETHE HOCHLEITNER
Vice-Rector for Teaching and Studies: Prof. Dr MANFRED DIERICH
Departments of Anatomy, Histology, and Embryology, of Medical Statistics, Computer Sciences and Health Management, of Hygiene, Microbiology and Social Medicine, of Medical Genetics, Molecular and Clinical Pharmacology and of Physiology and Medical Physics; Innsbruck Biocentre (Divisions of Biological Chemistry, Cell Biology, Clinical Biochemistry, Experimental Pathophysiology and Immunology, Genomics and RNomics, Medical Biochemistry, Molecular Biology, Molecular Pathophysiology, Neurobiochemistry); University Medical Centre (Departments of Anesthesiology and Critical Care Medicine, Dentistry and Oral Surgery, Dermatology and Venereology, Diagnostic Radiology, Gynaecology, Internal Medicine, Neurology, Neurosurgery, Nuclear Medicine, Medical Psychology and Psychotherapy, Ophthalmology, Orthopedic Surgery, Otorhinolaryngology, Paediatrics, Plastic and Reconstructive Surgery, Psychiatry, Radiotherapy, Surgery, Traumatology and Sport Traumatology and Urology; Institute for Addiction Research); Central Laboratory Animal Facilities, Ethics Commission, Gene Discovery Core Facility; Institutes of Legal Medicine, Neuroscience, Pathology and of Pharmacology; School of Public Health.

MEDIZINISCHE UNIVERSITÄT WIEN

Spitalgasse 23, 1090 Vienna
Telephone: (1) 40160-0
Fax: (1) 40160-910000
E-mail: rektor@meduniwien.ac.at
Internet: www.meduniwien.ac.at
Founded 2004
Library of 520,000 vols, 2,400 periodicals
Rector: Prof. Dr WOLFGANG SCHÜTZ
Vice-Rector (Academic): Prof. Dr RUDOLF MALLINGER
Vice-Rector (Clinical Affairs): Mag. PETER SOSWINSKI
Vice-Rector (Finance): Mag. ELISABETH CHALUPA-GARTNER
Vice-Rector (Research and International Relations): Prof. HANS-GEORG EICHLER.

MONTANUNIVERSITÄT LEOBEN (University of Leoben)

Franz-Josef Str. 18, 8700 Leoben
Telephone: (3842) 402-0
Fax: (3842) 402-7012
Internet: www.unileoben.ac.at
Founded 1840
Languages of instruction: German, English
Academic year: October to September
Rector: Prof. Dr WOLFHARD WEGSCHEIDER
Administrator (vacant)
Librarian: Dr LIESELOTTE JONTES
Library: see Libraries and Archives
Number of students: 2,200
Publications: *BHM- Berg- und Hüttenmannische Monatshefte* (12 a year), *Triple M* (4 a year)

PROFESSORS

BIEDERMANN, H., Economics, Industrial Management and Industrial Engineering
BÜHRIG-POLACZEK, A., Foundry Technology
DANZER, R., Ceramics
EBNER, F., Geology and Mineral Resources
ENGELHARDT, C., Industrial Logistics
EICHLSEDER, W., Mechanical Engineering
FISCHER, D., Mechanics
GOLSER, J., Sublevel Construction
HARMUTH, H., Refractory Materials, Ceramics, Glass and Cement
HEINEMANN, Z., Reservoir Engineering
IMRICH, W., Applied Mathematics
JEGLITSCH, F., Physical Metallurgy and Material Testing
KEPPLINGER, W., Industrial Environmental Protection
KESSLER, F., Conveying Technology
KIRSCHENHOFER, P., Mathematics
KNEISSL, A., Metallography
KRIEGER, W., Ferrous Metallurgy
KUCHAR, F., Physics
LANG, R., Plastics
LANGECKER, G., Plastics Technology
LEDERER, K., Chemistry of Plastics
LORBER, K., Decontamination
MAURITSCH, H., Geophysics
MEISEL, T., General and Analytical Chemistry
MILLAHN, K., Applied Geophysics
O'LEARY, P., Automation
PASCHEN, P., Nonferrous Metallurgy
RUTHAMMER, G., Petroleum Engineering
SACHS, H., Applied Geometry
SCHWENZFEIER, W., Deformation Processing and Steel Mill Machineries
SITTE, W., Physical Chemistry
STEINER, H., Mineral Processing
VORTISCH, W., Applied Sedimentology
WAGNER, H., Mining Engineering
WEISS, G., Electrical Engineering
WOERNDLE, R., Plastics
WOLFBAUER, J., Business Economics

UNIVERSITÄT MOZARTEUM SALZBURG (University Mozarteum Salzburg)

Schrannengasse 10a, 5020 Salzburg
Telephone: (662) 6198-0
Fax: (662) 6198-3033
E-mail: moz@moz.ac.at
Internet: www.moz.ac.at
Founded 1841
State control
Academic year: October to June
Rector: Dr ROLAND HAAS
Deputy Rectors: Prof. Mag. GOTTFRIED HOLZER-GRAF, Dr BERND LANGE
Librarian: Dr MANFRED KAMMERER
Number of teachers: 458
Number of students: 1,600
Publications: *International Summer Academy Mozarteum Brochure* (annually), *Jahresbericht* (annually), *UniArt* (monthly)

DIRECTORS

Department of Brass, Wind and Percussion Studies: Prof. HANSJÖRG ANGERER
Department of Conducting, Composition and Music Theory: Prof. ERNST LUDWIG LEITNER
Department of Drama: Prof. Mag. MARKUS TRABUSCH
Department of Fine Arts, Art and Crafts Education: Prof. Mag. DIETER KLEINPETER
Department of Keyboard Studies: Prof. KLAUS KAUFMANN
Department of Music and Dance Education (Orff Institute): Mag. MANUELA WIDMER
Department of Music Education: Prof. Dr MONIKA OEBELSBERGER
Department of Musicology and Interdisciplinary Studies: Prof. Dr PETER MARIA KRAKAUER
Department of Sacred Music: Prof. ALBERT ANGLBERGER
Department of Stage Design: Prof. HERBERT KAPPLMÜLLER
Department of String Studies: Prof. HARALD HERZL
Department of Vocal Studies: Prof. Mag. MICHAEL HORNIG
Innsbruck Department of Music Education: Prof. Dr ARMIN LANGER

UNIVERSITÄT FÜR MUSIK UND DARSTELLENDE KUNST GRAZ (University of Music and Dramatic Arts, Graz)

Leonhardstr. 15, POB 208, Palais Meran, 8010 Graz
Telephone: (316) 389-0
Fax: (316) 389-1101
E-mail: info@kug.ac.at
Internet: www.kug.ac.at
Founded 1963
State control
Language of instruction: German
Academic year: October to June
Rector: Prof. Em. Dr OTTO KOLLERITSCH
Vice-Rector (Management of Resources and Infrastructure) and Administrative Director: Dr HERMANN BECKE
Vice-Rector (Personnel Policies and Gender Mainstreaming): Ao. Univ. Prof. Dr RENATE BOZIĆ
Vice-Rector (Teaching): Ao. Univ. Prof. Mag. Mag. Dr GEORG SCHULZ
Librarian: Mag. ROBERT SCHILLER
Number of teachers: 422
Number of students: 1,862

HEADS OF INSTITUTES

Institute of Church Music and Organ: Prof. Dr JOHANN TRUMMER
Institute of Composition, Music Theory, Music History and Conducting: Prof. WOLFGANG BOZIC
Institute of Drama: Prof. Doz. Dr EVELYN DEUTSCH-SCHREINER
Institute of Early Music and Performance Practice: Prof. Mag. Dr KLAUS HUBMANN
Institute of Electronic Music and Acoustics: Prof. Dipl.-Ing. Mag. Dr ROBERT HÖLDRICH
Institute of Ethnomusicology: Prof. Dr GERD GRUPE
Institute of Jazz: Prof. Dr HARALD NEUWIRTH
Institute of Jazz Research: Prof. Dr FRANZ KERSCHBAUMER
Institute of Music Criticism and Aesthetical Research: Prof. Dr ANDREAS DORSCHEL
Institute of Music Drama: Prof. CHRISTIAN PÖPPELREITER
Institute of Music Education: Prof. Mag. GERHARD WANKER
Institute of the Oberschützen Campus: Prof. HERBERT WEIßBERG
Institute of Piano: Prof. EUGEN JAKAB
Institute of Stage Design: Prof. HANS SCHAVERNOCH
Institute of String Instruments: Prof. CHRISTIAN EULER
Institute of Voice, Song and Oratorio: Prof. MARTIN KLIETMANN
Institute of Wind and Percussion Instruments: Prof. Mag. JOSEF MAIERHOFER

UNIVERSITÄT FÜR MUSIK UND DARSTELLENDE KUNST WIEN
(University of Music and Performing Arts, Vienna)

Anton-von-Webern-Pl. 1, 1030 Vienna
Telephone: (1) 71155
Fax: (1) 71155-199
E-mail: rektor@mdw.ac.at
Internet: www.mdw.ac.at

Founded 1812 as 'Conservatorium der Gesellschaft der Musikfreunde', nationalized 1909

Rector: Prof. Mag. Dr WERNER HASITSCHKA
Vice-Rectors: Prof. Dr IRMGARD BONTINCK, Prof. Mag. RUDOLF HOFSTÖTTER, Prof. WOLFGANG KLOS
Library Director: Dr SUSANNE ESCHWÉ

Number of teachers: 807
Number of students: 2,327

HEADS OF INSTITUTES

Bruckner Institute (Theory, Aural Training and Conducting): ALOIS GLASSNER
Film Academy: PETER MAYER
Hellmesberger Institute (Stringed Instruments): WOLFGANG AICHINGER
Institute of the Analysis, Theory and History of Music: CORNELIA SZABO-KNOTIK
Institute of Chamber Music and Special Ensembles: AVO KOUYOUMDJIAN
Institute of Composition and Sound Technology: DIETMAR SCHERMANN
Institute of Conducting: THOMAS KREUZBERGER
Institute of Cultural Management: FRANZ-OTTO HOFECKER
Institute of Folk Music Research and Ethnomusicology: GERLINDE HAID
Institute of Keyboard Instruments: HEINZ MEDJIMOREC
Institute of Music and Movement Education and Music Therapy: ANGELIKA HAUSER
Institute of Music Teaching: FRANZ NIERMANN
Institute of Organ, Organ Research and Church Music: ERWIN ORTNER
Institute of Research into Musical Style: HARTMUT KRONES
Institute of the Sociology of Music: IRMGARD BONTINCK
Institute of Song and Musicals: LEOPOLD SPITZER
Institute of Stringed Instruments: STEFAN KROPFITSCH
Institute of Wind and Percussion Instruments: BARBARA GISLER
Ludwig van Beethoven Institute (Keyboard Instruments): URSULA KNEIHS
Max Reinhardt Seminar: HUBERTUS PETROLL
Popular Music: WOLFGANG PUSCHNIG
Salieri Institute (Song): MARIA BAYER
Schubert Institute (Wind and Percussion Instruments): WALTER WRETSCHITSCH
Vienna Institute of Sound: GREGOR WIDHOLM

UNIVERSITÄT SALZBURG
(Salzburg University)

Kapitelgasse 4–6, 5020 Salzburg
Telephone: (662) 8044-0
Fax: (662) 8044214
E-mail: uni.service@sbg.ac.at
Internet: www.uni-salzburg.at

Founded 1622; closed 1810; College 1810–50, independent faculty of Catholic Theology 1850–1962; reconstituted 1962
State control
Academic year: October to end of June

Rector: Prof. Dr HEINRICH SCHMIDINGER
Pro-Rectors: Prof. Dr ALBERT DUSCHL, Prof. Dr RUDOLF MOSLER, Prof. Dr SONJA PUNTSCHER-RIEKMANN
Librarian: Dr URSULA SCHACHL-RABER

Library: see under Libraries and Archives
Number of teachers: 750
Number of students: 11,000

Publications: *University Prospectuses*, *Yearbook*

DEANS

Faculty of Arts: Prof. Dr GERHARD PETERSMANN
Faculty of Catholic Theology: Prof. Dr Dr HANS-JOACHIM SANDER
Faculty of Law: Prof. Dr KURT SCHMOLLER
Faculty of Natural Science: Prof. Dr URS BAUMANN

PROFESSORS

Faculty of Arts:
BETTEN, A., German
BOTZ, G., History
BRUCHER, G., History of Austrian Art
DALFEN, J., Classical Philology
DOPSCH, H., History
EHMER, J., Modern History
FABRIS, H., Journalism and Communications
FELTEN, F., Classical Archaeology
GOEBL, H., Romance Languages
GRASSL, H., Ancient History
GRÖSSING, S., Sport
HAAS, H., Austrian History
HAIDER, H., Linguistics
HASLINGER, A., German
JALKOTZY, S., Ancient History
KLEIN, H. M., English
KNOCHE, M., Journalism and Communications
KOLMER, L., Medieval History and Historic Auxiliary Sciences
KRONSTEINER, O., Slavic Languages
KRUMM, V., Education
KUON, P., Romance Philology
MAYER, G., Slavic Languages
MESSNER, D., Romance Languages
MORSCHER, E., Philosophy
MÜLLER, E., Physical Education
MÜLLER, U., German
PANAGL, O., Linguistics
PATRY, J. L., Education
PETERSMANN, G., Classical Philology
PIEL, F., Medieval and Modern History of Art
ROSSBACHER, K., German
SCHMOLKE, M., Journalism and Communications
STAGL, J., Sociology
STENZL, J., Music Science
TRUCHLAR, L., English
WEINGARTNER, P., Philosophy
ZAIC, F., English

Faculty of Catholic Theology:
BACHL, G., Dogmatics
BEILNER, W., New Testament Studies
BUCHER, A., Catechism and Religious Education
KÖHLER, W., Christian Philosophy and Psychology
MÖDLHAMMER, J., Ecumenical Theology
NIKOLASCH, F., Liturgy
PAARHAMMER, J., Church Law
PAUS, A., Epistemology and Religious Studies
SCHLEINZER, F., Pastoral Theology
SCHMIDINGER, H., Christian Philosophy
WINKLER, G. B., Church History
WOLBERT, W., Moral Theology

Faculty of Law:
BERKA, W., General Theory of the State, Theory of Administration, Constitutional and Administrative Law
BUSCHMANN, A., German Legal History, German Private and Civil Law
GRILLBERGER, K., Industrial Law
HACKL, K., Roman and Civil Law
HAGEN, J., Sociology of Law
HAMMER, R., Management
HARRER, F., Civil and Commercial Law
KARL, W., International Law
KOJA, F., General Constitutional Law
KOPPENSTEINER, H.-G., Austrian and International Commercial Law
KYRER, A., Economics
MAYER-MALY, TH., German and Austrian Private Law
MIGSCH, E., Civil Law
RAINER, J., Roman and Modern Private Law
SCHÄFFER, H., Public Law
SCHMOLLER, K., Austrian Criminal Law
SCHUMACHER, W., International Commercial Law and Civil Law
SCHWIMANN, M., International Civil Law
STOLZLECHNER, H., Public Law
TRIFFTERER, O., Austrian and International Criminal Law

Faculty of Natural Sciences:
AMTHAUER, G., Geology
BAUMANN, U., Psychology
BENTRUP, F. W., Plant Physiology and Anatomy
BREITENBACH, M., Molecular Genetics
CLAUSEN, H., Systems Analysis
CZIHAK, G., Genetics
FÜRNKRANZ, D., Botany
GERL, P., Mathematics
HERMANN, A., Zoology
NEUBAUER, F., Geology
PERNER, J., Psychology
PFALZGRAF, J., Computer Science
RIEDL, H., Geography
SCHWEIGER, F., Mathematics
STADEL, CH., Geography
STEINHÄUSLER, F., Biophysics
STRACK, H.-B., Biochemistry
WALLBOTT, H., Psychology
WERNER, H., Sciences Education
ZINTERHOF, P., Mathematics

Inter-faculty Institutes:
CROLL, G., Music History of Salzburg
FAUPEL, K., Political Science
GACHOWETZ, H., Organizational Psychology
HAUPTMANN, W., Criminal Psychology
KOPPENSTEINER, H. G., European Law
LAUBER, V., Political Science

MAYER-MALY, TH., Energy Law, Law of Liechtenstein
MIGSCH, E., Private Insurance Law
MORSCHER, E., Philosophy, Technology, Economics
ZINTERHOF, P., Software Technology

TECHNISCHE UNIVERSITÄT GRAZ (Graz University of Technology)

Rechbauerstr. 12, 8010 Graz
Telephone: (316) 873-0
Fax: (316) 873-6009
E-mail: info@tugraz.at
Internet: www.tugraz.at
Founded 1811
Academic year: October to July
Rector: O. Univ.-Prof. Dipl.-Ing. Dr techn. HANS SÜNKEL
Vice-Rector (Academics): O. Univ.-Prof. Dipl.-Ing. Dr mont. HORST-HANNES CERJAK
Vice-Rector (Finances and Personnel): O. Univ.-Prof. Dipl.-Ing. Dr techn. ULRICH BAUER
Vice-Rector (Infrastructure): Dipl.-Ing. Dr techn. JOHANN THEURL
Vice-Rector (Research and Technology): O. Univ.-Prof. Dipl.-Ing. Dr rer. nat. WOLFGANG VON DER LINDEN
Librarian: Dipl.-Ing. EVA BERTHA
Library: see Libraries and Archives
Number of teachers: 569
Number of students: 8,279

DEANS

Faculty of Architecture: Prof. Dipl. Architekt LEONARD HIRSCHBERG
Faculty of Chemistry, Chemical and Process Engineering: Prof. Dipl.-Ing. Dr techn. FRANZ STELZER
Faculty of Civil Engineering: Prof. Dipl.-Ing. Dr techn. HAROLD KAINZ
Faculty of Computer Science: Prof. Dipl.-Ing. Dr phil. HERMANN MAURER
Faculty of Constructional Engineering: Prof. Dipl.-Ing. Dr techn. KLAUS RIESSBERGER
Faculty of Mechanical Engineering and Economics: Prof. Dipl.-Ing. Dr sc. techn. REINHARD HABERFELLNER
Faculty of Electrical and Information Engineering: Prof. Dipl.-Ing. Dr techn. GEORG BRASSEUR
Faculty of Mathematical and Physical Engineering: Prof. Dipl.-Ing. Dr phil. ROBERT TICHY
Faculty of Natural Sciences: Prof. Mag. Dr HANS VOGLER

PROFESSORS

ARRIGONI, E., Theoretical Physics
AURENHAMMER, F., Basics of Information Processing
BAUER, U., Industrial Management
BEER, G., Building Statics
BERKES, I., Probablility Theory and Statistics
BESENHARD, O. J., Inorganic Chemical Technology
BRASSEUR, G., Electrical Measurement and Measurement Signals Processing
BRENN, G., Fluid Mechanics
BRUNNER, F. K., Geodesy
BURKARD, R., Mathematics
CELIGOJ, CH., Strength of Materials
CERJAK, H., Materials Science and Welding
DOURDOUMAS, N., Automatic Control
EICHLSEDER, H., Combustion Engines
ERNST, W., Experimental Physics
FICKERT, L., Electrical Installations
FRANK, A., Manufacturing Technology
FRANK, I., Interior Design
GAMERITH, H., Building and Design
GESCHEIDT-DEMNER, G., Material Testing
GRAMPP, G., Physical Chemistry
GREINER, R., Timberwork and Elevation
GRIENGL, H., Organic Chemistry
HABERFELLNER, R., Management
HEIGERTH, G., Hydraulic Design and Water Resources Management
HEITMEIR, F., Thermo Turbo-Machinery
HIRSCHBERG, W., Automotive Engineering
HOFMANN-WELLENHOF, B., Theoretical Geodesy
JABERG, H., Hydraulic Turbo-machinery
JÜRGENS, G., Machine Principles
KAHLERT, H., Solid State Physics
KAINZ, H., Hydraulics, Agricultural and Industrial Hydraulic Engineering
KERN, G., Analysis and Applications
KNAPP, G., Analytical Chemistry
KOUDELKA, O., Telecommunications
KUBIN, G., Non-linear Signals Processing
KUPELWIESER, H., Artistic Forms
LEBERL, F., Computer-aided Geometry and Graphics
LECHNER, H., Project Envelopment and Project Management
LEITGEB, N., Hospital Technology
MAASS, W., Information Processing
MACHEROUX, P., Biochemistry
MARR, R. J., Process Engineering
MAURER, H., Information Processing
MEUWISSEN, J. M. C., Building and Town Planning
MORITZ, H., Geodesy
MUHR, H. M., Electrical Power Systems and High Voltage Engineering
NIDETSKY, B., Biotechnology
OSER, J., Materials Handling and Mechanical Engineering Design
PFANNHAUSER, W., Food Chemistry
POSCH, R., Applied Information Processing and Communications Technology
RENTMEISTER, M., Electrical Engineering
RIESSBERGER, K., Railways
RÖSCHEL, O., Geometry
SCHUBERT, W., Rock Mechanics and Tunnelling
SCHWAB, H., Biotechnology
SEMPRICH, S., Soil Mechanics and Foundation Engineering
SPAROWITZ, L., Concrete Construction
STADLER, G., Building
STADLOBER, E., Probability Theory and Statistics
STAUDINGER, G., Instrument Construction and Mechanical Techniques
STELZER, F., Chemical Technology of Organic Materials
STIGLER, H., Electricity Economy and Energy Innovation
SÜNKEL, H., Theoretical Geodesy
TICHY, R., Mathematics
TSCHOM, H., Domestic Architecture
VON DER LINDEN, W., Theoretical Physics
VÖSSNER, S., Mechanical Engineering and Industrial Informatics
WACH, P., Theoretical Methods in Mechanical Engineering and Industrial Informatics
WEISS, R., Computer Engineering
WOESS, W., Mathematics
WOHINZ, J., Industrial Management
WOLFBAUER, O., Chemical and Process Engineering
WÜRSCHUM, R., Materials Science and Physical Methods

ATTACHED INSTITUTES

Institute of Applied Geosciences: Rechbauerstr. 12, 8010 Graz; Dir Univ.-Prof. Dipl.-Min. Dr rer. nat. MARTIN DIETZEL.

Institute of Architecture and Landscape: Rechbauerstr. 12, 8010 Graz; Dir Univ.-Prof. Dipl. Architekt DANIELE MARQUES.

Institute of Architecture and Media: Inffeldgasse 10/II, 8010 Graz; Dir Vertragsprof. Dipl. Architekt ETH URS LEONHAND HIRSCHBERG.

Institute of Architectural Science and Architectural Design: Rechbauerstr. 12/II, 8010 Graz; Dir Univ.-Prof. Dr. phil. ULLRICH SCHWARZ.

Institute of Architectural Technology: Rechbauerstr. 12/I, 8010 Graz; Dir Dipl.-Ing. Architekt ROGER RIEWE.

Institute of Architectural Typologies: Lessingstr. 25/IV, 8010 Graz; Dir Univ.-Prof. Dipl.-Ing. Architekt HRVOJE NJIRIC.

Institute of Building Construction and Industrial Architecture: Lessingstr. 25/III, 8010 Graz; Dir O. Univ.-Prof. Dipl.-Ing. Dr techn. Architekt HORST GAMERITH.

Institute of Building and Energy: Rechbauerstr. 12, 8010 Graz; Dir Vertragsprof. BSc. CEng MCIBSE BRIAN CODY.

Institute of Contemporary Art: Inffeldgasse 10/II, 8010 Graz; Dir O. Univ.-Prof. HAND KUPELWIESER.

Institute of Construction Management and Economics: Lessingstr. 25/II, 8010 Graz; Dir Univ.-Prof. Dipl.-Ing. HANS LECHNER.

Institute of Domestic Architecture: Rechbauerstr. 12, 8010 Graz; Dir Univ.-Prof. Dipl.-Ing. Dr. techn. Architekt HANS-JÖRG TSCHOM.

Institute of Engineering Geodesy and Measurement Systems: Steyrergasse 30/II, 8010 Graz; Dir O. Univ.-Prof. Dipl.-Ing. Dr techn. KARL BRUNNER.

Institute of General Mechanics: Technikerstr. 4/II, 8010 Graz; Dir Univ.-Prof. Dr.-Ing. Priv.-Doz. MARTIN SCHANZ.

Institute of Highway Engineering and Transport Planning: Rechbauerstr. 12/II, 8010 Graz; Dir Ao. Univ.-Prof. Dipl.-Ing. Dr techn. tit. Univ.-Prof. WERNER GOBIET.

Institute of History of Art and Cultural Studies: Technikerstr. 4/III, 8010 Graz; Dir Vertragsprof. Dr. phil. SUSANNE HAUSER.

Institute of Hydraulic Engineering and Water Resources Management: Stremayrgasse 10/II, 8010 Graz; Dir O. Univ.-Prof. Dipl.-Ing. Dr techn. GÜNTHER HEIGERTH.

Institute of Project Development and Management: Lessingstr. 25/I, 8010 Graz; Dir Vertragsprof. Dr techn. Dipl.-Bauing. ULRICH WALDER.

Institute of Railway Engineering and Transport Economy: Rechbauerstr. 12/II, 8010 Graz; Dir O. Univ.-Prof. Dipl.-Ing. Dr techn. KLAUS RIEßBERGER.

Institute of Rock Mechanics and Tunnelling: Rechbauerstr. 12, 8010 Graz; Dir O. Univ.-Prof. Dipl.-Ing. Dr mont. WULF SCHUBERT.

Institute of Soil Mechanics and Foundation Engineering: Rechbauerstr. 12, 8010 Graz; Dir O. Univ.-Prof. Dipl.-Ing. Dr techn. STEPHAN SEMPRICH.

Institute of Spatial Design: Rechbauerstr. 12/II, 8010 Graz; Dir Univ.-Prof. Mag.arch. Mag.art. Architektin IRMGARD FRANK.

Institute of Structural Design: Technikerstr. 4/IV, 8010 Graz; Dir O. Univ.-Prof. Dipl.-Ing. Dr. techn. LUTZ SPAROWITZ.

Institute of Steel Structures and Shell Structures: Lessingstr. 25/III, 8010 Graz; Dir O. Univ.-Prof. Dipl.-Ing. Dr techn. RICHARD GREINER.

Institute of Structural Analysis: Lessingstr. 25/II, 8010 Graz; Dir O. Univ.-Prof. Dipl.-Ing. Dr techn. GERNOT BEER.

Institute of Structural Concrete: Lessingstr. 25, 8010 Graz; Dir O.Univ.-Prof. Dipl.-Ing. Dr techn. LUTZ SPAROWITZ.

Institute of Structural Engineering: Inffeldgasse 24, 8010 Graz; Dir Dipl.-Ing. Dr techn. BERNHARD FREYTAG.

Institute of Technology and Testing of Building Materials: Stremayrgasse 11, 8010 Graz; Dir Univ.-Prof. Dipl.-Ing. Dr techn. tit. Ao. Univ.-Prof. PETER MAYDL.

Institute of Timber Engineering and Wood Technology: Inffeldgasse 24, 8010 Graz; Dir Univ.-Prof. Dipl.-Ing. Dr techn. GERHARD SCHICKHOFER.

Institute of Urbanism: Rechbauerstr. 12, 8010 Graz; Dir Prof. Dipl. Architekt ERNST HUBELI.

Institute of Urban Water Management and Landscape Water Engineering: Stremayrgasse 10/I, 8010 Graz; Dir Univ.-Prof. Dipl.-Ing. Dr techn. HARALD KAINZ.

TECHNISCHE UNIVERSITÄT WIEN (Vienna University of Technology)

Karlsplatz 13, 1040 Vienna

Telephone: (1) 58801-0
Fax: (1) 58801-40199
E-mail: pr@zv.tuwien.ac.at
Internet: www.tuwien.ac.at

Founded 1815
State control
Academic year: October to June (two terms)

Rector: Prof. Dipl. Ing. Dr techn. PETER SKALICKY
Vice-Rector: Prof. Dipl. Ing. Dr techn. GERHARD SCHIMAK
Vice-Rector for Academic Affairs: Prof. Dr phil. HANS KAISER
Vice-Rector for Research: Prof. Dipl. Ing. Dr techn. G. RAMMERSTORFER
Director: Mag. iur EVELINE URBAN
Librarian: Dr PETER KUBALEK

Library: see under Libraries and Archives
Number of teachers: 2,715
Number of students: 15,851

Publications: *Mitteilungsblatt*, *Schriftenreihe*, *ZID-Line*

DEANS

Faculty of Architecture and Planning: Prof. Dr KLAUS SEMSROTH
Faculty of Civil Engineering: Prof. Dr JOHANN LITZKA
Faculty of Electrical Engineering and Information Technology: Prof. Dr MARKUS RUPP
Faculty of Informatics: Prof. Dr GERALD STEINHARDT
Faculty of Mathematics and Geoinformation: Prof. Dr DIETMAR DORNINGER
Faculty of Mechanical Engineering: Prof. Dr BRUNO GRÖSEL
Faculty of Physics: Prof. Dr GERALD BADUREK
Faculty of Technical Chemistry: Prof. Dr JOHANNES FRÖHLICH

PROFESSORS

Faculty of Architecture and Planning (Karlsplatz 13, 1040 Vienna; tel. (1) 58801-25001; fax (1) 58801-25099; e-mail E250@tuwien.ac.at; internet www.rpl-arch.tuwien.ac.at):

ALSOP, W., Building Construction and Building Systems for Architects
BÖKEMANN, D., Town and Country Planning
BRÜLLMANN, K., Residential Building
CERWENKA, P., Transport Systems Planning
DANGSCHAT, J., Urban and Regional Research
FRANCK-OBERASPACH, G., Computer-aided Design and Planning Methods
HIERZEGGER, H., Local Area Planning
JORMAKKA, K. J., Architectural History and Historic Building Survey
JOURDA, F. H., Spatial Design
LESAK, F., Model Construction
MAHDAVI, A., Building Physics and Human Ecology
RICHTER, H., Structural Engineering for Architects
SCHÖNBÄCK, W., Public Finance and Infrastructure Policy
SEMSROTH, K., Urban Design and Planning
STILES, R., Landscape Planning and Garden Architecture
STRAUBE, M., Banking and Securities Law
WEBER, G., History of Art and Cultural Conservation
WEHDORN, M., History of Art, Architectural Conservation, and Industrial Archaeology
WINTER, W., Studies of Structural Design and Timber Construction
WOLFF-PLOTTEGG, M., Building Design and Theory
ZEHETNER, F., Public Law

Faculty of Civil Engineering (Karlsplatz 13, 1040 Vienna; tel. (1) 58801-20001; fax (1) 58801-20099; e-mail info@bauwesen.tuwien.ac.at; internet www.bauwesen.tuwien.ac.at):

BRANDL, H., Foundations
BRUNNER, P. H., Waste Management
DREYER, J., Building Material Sciences, Building Physics and Fire Protection
DROBIR, H., Water Plant Construction, Navigable Waterways and Environmental Hydraulics
GUTKNECHT, D., Hydraulics, Hydrology and Water Supply
JODL, H. G., Construction Practice and Methods
KNOFLACHER, H., Traffic Planning and Engineering
KOLBITSCH, A., Building Construction and Industrial Buildings
KOLLEGGER, J., Reinforced Concrete Construction and Massive Construction
KROISS, H., Water Supply, Sewage Purification and Prevention of Water Pollution
LITZKA, J., Road Engineering and Maintenance
MANG, H., Elasticity and Strength
MATSCHE, N., Water Quality and Waste Management
OBERNDORFER, W. J., Construction and Planning
OGRIS, H., Experimental Hydraulics
RAMBERGER, G., Steel Girder Construction
RUBIN, H., Structural Analysis
SCHIMMERL, J., Rational Mechanics
SCHNEIDER, U., Building Materials
TENTSCHERT, E. H., Geology
ZIEGLER, F., Applied Mechanics

Faculty of Electrical Engineering and Information Technology (Gusshausstr. 25-29, 1040 Vienna; tel. (1) 58801-35001; fax (1) 58801-35099; e-mail goppenhe@pop.tuwien.ac.at; internet www.info.tuwien.ac.at/et):

BERTAGNOLLI, E., Solid-State Electronics
BONEK, E., High Frequency and Communications Technology
BRAUNER, G., Power Systems
CHABICOVSKY, R., Industrial Electronics and Materials Science
DETTER, H., Precision Engineering
DIETRICH, D., Computer Technology
EIER, R., Data Processing
FALLMANN, W., Industrial Electronics and Materials Science
GORNIK, E., Solid State Electronics
HAAS, H., Fundamentals and Theory of Electrical Engineering
KRAUSZ, F., Photonics
LEEB, W., Communications and Radio-Frequency Engineering
MAGERL, G., Electrical Measurement Technology
MECKLENBRÄUKER, W., Low Frequency Technology
PFUNDNER, P., Industrial Electronics and Materials Science
PRECHTL, A., Theory of Electrical Engineering
RUMMICH, E., Electrical Drives and Machines
RUPP, M., Communications and Radio-Frequency Engineering
SCHMIDT, A., Quantum Electronics and Lasers
SCHRÖDL, M., Electrical Machines and Drives
SELBERHERR, S., Software Technology for Microelectronic Systems
VAN AS, H. R., Communication Networks
VELLEKOOP, M., Industrial Electronics and Materials Science
WEINMANN, A., Electrical Control, Navigation and Power Engineering
WEINRICHTER, J., Communications and Radio-Frequency Engineering
ZACH, F., Electrical Drives and Machines
ZEICHEN, G., Flexible Automation
ZIMMERMANN, H., Electrical Measurements and Circuit Design

Faculty of Informatics (Getreidemarkt 9, 1060 Vienna; tel. (1) 58801-10000; fax (1) 58801-10099; e-mail dek100@mail.zserv.tuwien.ac.at; internet www.cs.tuwien.ac.at):

BREITENEDER, C., Software
BROCKHAUS, M., Information Technology
EITER, T., Information Systems
FLEISSNER, P., Design and Assessment/Social Cybernetics
GOTTLOB, G., Applied Informatics
GRÜNBACHER, H., Computer Engineering (VLSI-Design)
JAZAYERI, M., Information Systems
KAPPEL, G., Software Technology and Interactive Systems
KOPETZ, H., Software Technology
KROPATSCH, W., Design and Manufacturing
KUICH, W., Mathematical Logic and Computer Languages
LEITSCH, A., Computer Languages
MUTZEL, P., Computer Graphics and Algorithms
PURGATHOFER, W., Computer Graphics and Algorithms
SCHILDT, G.-H., Automation Systems
TJOA, A. M., Software Engineering
VIERTL, R., Applied Statistics and Information Science
WAGNER, I., Design and Assessment of Technology

Faculty of Mathematics and Geoinformation (Getreidemarkt 9, 1060 Vienna; tel. (1) 58801-10000; fax (1) 58801-10099; e-mail dekmug@mail.zserv.tuwien.ac.at; internet www.math.tuwien.ac.at):

BARON, G., Geometry
CARSTENSEN, C., Applied and Numerical Mathematics
DIRSCHMID, H., Analysis and Technical Mathematics
DORNINGER, D., Algebra and Computational Mathematics
DUTTER, R., Technical Statistics
EBEL, H., Technical Physics
FRANK, A., Surveying and Geoinformation
GRUBER, P., Mathematical Analysis
HERTLING, J., Applied and Numerical Mathematics
KAHMEN, H., General Geodesy
KAISER, H., Algebra and Computational Mathematics
KELNHOFER, F., Cartography and Reproduction Technology
KUICH, W., Mathematical Logic and Computer Languages
MLITZ, R., Applied and Numerical Mathematics
LANGER, H., Applied Analysis
POTTMANN, A., Geometry
SCHACHERMAYER, W., Statistics and Probability Theory

SCHNABL, R., Analysis and Technical Mathematics
SCHUH, H., Geodesy and Geophysics
STACHEL, H., Geometry
TROCH, I., Analysis and Technical Mathematics
VANA, N., Dosimetry
VIERTL, R., Applied Statistics and Information Science
WERTZ, W., Financial and Actuarial Mathematics

Faculty of Mechanical Engineering (Karlsplatz 13, 1040 Vienna; tel. (1) 58801-30001; fax (1) 58801-30099; e-mail mrosen@pop.tuwien.ac.at; internet www.tuwien.ac.at/maschinenbau):

BIBERSCHICK, D., Industrial Engineering, Ergonomics and Business Economics
DEGISCHER, H. P., Materials Science and Testing
GAMER, U., Mechanics
GRÖSEL, B., Handling and Transport Technology and General Design Engineering
HASELBACHER, H., Thermal Turbo-Machinery and Power Plants
JÖRGL, H. P., Machine- and Process-Engineering
KLUWICK, A., Hydrodynamics
KOPACEK, P., Handling Devices and Robotics
LENZ, H. P., Internal Combustion Vehicles
LINZER, W., Theory of Heat
LUGNER, P., Mechanics
MATTHIAS, H. B., Water-powered Machines and Pumps
PATZAK, G., Industrial Engineering, Ergonomics and Business Economics
RAMMERSTORFER, F., Light Engineering, Aeroplane Engineering
RINDER, L., Machine Parts
SCHNEIDER, W., Gas and Thermodynamics
SCHUÖCKER, D., Non-conventional Processing, Forming and Laser Technology
SCHWAIGER, W., Accounting and Controlling
SEIDLER, S., Materials Science and Testing
SPRINGER, H., Machine Dynamics and Measurement
STEPAN, A., Industrial Business Management
TROGER, H., Mechanics
UHLIR, H., Industrial Engineering, Ergonomics and Business Economics
VARGA, T., Welding
WESESLINDTNER, H., Computer Integrated Manufacturing
WOJDA, F., Business Management
ZEMAN, J., Pressure Vessel and Plant Technology

Faculty of Physics (Wiedner Hauptstr. 8-10, 1040 Vienna; tel. (1) 58801-10000; fax (1) 58801-10099; internet www.physik.tuwien.ac.at):

AIGINGER, J., Ionizing Radiation
BADUREK, G., Nuclear Solid State Physics
BALCAR, E., Neutron and Solid-State Physics
BENES, E., General Physics
BRÜCKL, E., Geophysics
BURGDÖRFER, J., Theoretical Physics
EBEL, H., Technical Physics
FLECK, M. C., Neutron Physics
KIRCHMAYR, H., Experimental Physics
KRAUS, K., Photogrammetry
KUMMER, W., Theoretical Physics
RAUCH, H., Experimental Nuclear Physics
SCHUH, H., Geodesy and Geophysics
SCHWEDA, M., Theoretical Physics
SKALICKY, P., Applied Physics
WEBER, H. W., Low Temperature Physics
WINTER, H., General Physics

Faculty of Technical Chemistry (Getreidemarkt 9, 1060 Vienna; tel. (1) 58801-10000; fax (1) 58801-10099; e-mail Johannes.Froehlich@tuwien.ac.at; internet www.chemie.tuwien.ac.at):

FABJAN, C., Technical Electrochemistry and Solid-State Chemistry
GRASSERBAUER, M., Analytical Chemistry
GRUBER, H., Chemical Technology of Organic Materials
HAMPEL, W., Biochemical Technology
HOFBAUER, H., Chemical Engineering, Fuel Technology and Environmental Technology
KNÖZINGER, E., Physical Chemistry
KUBEL, F., Mineralogy, Crystallography and Structural Chemistry
MARINI, I., Chemical Engineering, Fuel Technology and Environmental Technology
SCHMID, R., Inorganic Chemistry
SCHUBERT, U., Inorganic Chemistry
SCHWARZ, K., Physical and Theoretical Chemistry
STACHELBERGER, H., Botany, Technical Microscopy and Organic Raw Materials
WEINBERGER, P., Technical Electrochemistry and Solid State Chemistry
WRUSS, W., Chemical Technology of Inorganic Materials
WURST, F., Applied Botany, Technical Microscopy, and Organic Raw Materials Science

UNIVERSITÄT WIEN
(Vienna University)

Dr Karl Lueger-Ring 1, 1010 Vienna
Telephone: (1) 4277-0
Fax: (1) 4277-9120
E-mail: public@univie.ac.at
Internet: www.univie.ac.at
Founded 1365
Academic year: October to June

Rector: Prof. Dr GEORG WINCKLER
Vice-Rectors: JOHANN JURENITSCH, ARTHUR METTINGER, MARTHA SEBÖK, GÜNTHER VINEK
Librarian: MARIA SEISSL

Library: see under Libraries and Archives
Number of teachers: 4,040
Number of students: 63,000

DEANS

Faculty of Business, Economics and Statistics: UDO WAGNER
Faculty of Catholic Theology: P. M. ZULEHNER
Faculty of Chemistry: FRANZ DICKERT
Faculty of Computer Science: GÜNTER HARING
Faculty of Earth Sciences, Geography and Astronomy: WOLFRAM RICHTER
Faculty of Historical–Cultural Sciences: ALFRED KOHLER
Faculty of Law: Prof. Dr W. RECHBERGER
Faculty of Life Sciences: CHRISTIAN NOE
Faculty of Mathematics: HARALD RINDLER
Faculty of Philological–Cultural Sciences: FRANZ RÖMER
Faculty of Philosophy and Educational Sciences: PETER KAMPITS
Faculty of Physics: WALTER KUTSCHERA
Faculty of Protestant Theology: Prof. Dr G. ADAM
Faculty of Psychology: CHRISTIANE SPIEL
Faculty of Social Sciences: RUDOLF RICHTER
Centre for Sports Sciences and University Sports: NORBERT BACHL
Centre for Translation Studies: DIETER KASTOVSKY

PROFESSORS

Faculty of Business, Economics and Statistics (tel. (1) 4277-37030; fax (1) 4277-37045; e-mail dekanat-win@univie.ac.at; internet www.univie.ac.at/Wirtschaftswissenschaften):

ALTENBERGER, O., Business Studies
BONZE, I., Economics
CLEMENZ, G., Economics
DIAMANTOPOULOS, A., Business Studies
DOCKNER, E., Business Studies
FINSINGER, J., Business Studies
FITZSIMONS, C. O., Business Languages
HARTL, R., Business Studies
HEIDENBERGER, K., Business Studies
KUNST, R., Computer Science and Business Informatics
LECHNER, E., Commercial Law
MUELLER, D., Economics
NERMUTH, M., Economics
OROSEL, G., Economics
PFEIFFER, T., Business Studies
PFLUG, G., Statistics and Decision Support Systems
PÖTSCHER, B., Statistics and Decision Support Systems
SORGER, G., Economics
TRAXLER, F., Government
VAN DER BELLEN, A., Economics
WAGENER, A., Economics
WAGNER, U., Business Studies
WEILINGER, A., Commercial Law
WINCKLER, G., Economics
WIRL, F., Business Studies
ZECHNER, J., Business Studies

Faculty of Catholic Theology (tel. (1) 4277-3001; fax (1) 4277-9300; internet www.univie.ac.at/ktf):

FEULNER, H.-J., Liturgical Studies
FIGL, J., Study of Religion
JÄGGLE, M., Religious Education
GABRIEL, I., Social Ethics
KÜHSCHELM, R., Ethics and Social Sciences
LANGTHALER, R., Christian Philosophy
MÜLLER, L., Canon Law
PROKSCHI, R., Theology and History of Eastern Churches
REIKERSTORFER, J., Fundamental Theology and Apologetics
SCHLOSSER, M., Theology of Spirituality
STUBENRAUCH, B., Dogmatics
VIRT, G., Moral Theology

Faculty of Chemistry (tel. (1) 4277-51001; fax (1) 4277-9510; e-mail chemie.dekanat@univie.ac.at; internet chemie.univie.ac.at):

BRINKER, U., Organic Chemistry
DICKERT, F., Analytical Chemistry and Food Chemistry
DJINOVIC-CARUGO, K., Biomolecular Structural Chemistry
FRINGELI, U. P., Biophysical Chemistry
IPSER, H., Inorganic Chemistry
KEPPLER, B., Inorganic Chemistry
KONRAT, R., Biomolecular Structural Chemistry
LINDNER, W., Analytical Chemistry and Food Chemistry
LISCHKA, H., Theoretical Chemistry
MULZER, J., Organic Chemistry
SCHMID, W., Organic Chemistry
SCHUSTER, P., Theoretical Chemistry
SONTAG, G., Analytical Chemistry and Food Chemistry
STEINHAUSER, O., Biomolecular Structural Chemistry

Faculty of Computer Science (tel. (1) 4277-39001; fax (1) 4277-9390; internet www.cs.univie.ac.at):

EDER, JOHANN, Knowledge and Business Engineering
GROSSMANN, WILFRIED, Computer Science
HARING, GÜNTER, Faculty of Computer Science

KARAGIANNIS, DIMITRIS, Knowledge and Business Engineering
KLAS, WOLFGANG, Computer Science
QUIRCHMAYR, GERALD, Distributed and Multimedia Systems
ZIMA, HANS, Department of Scientific Computing

Faculty of Earth Sciences, Geography and Astronomy (tel. (1) 4277-53001; fax (1) 4277-9530; internet www.univie.ac.at/geowissenschaften):

BREGER, M., Astronomy
FAßMANN, H., Geography and Regional Research
FERGUSON, D. K., Palaeontology
HENSLER, G., Astronomy
HOFMANN, T., Environmental Geosciences
KAINZ, W., Geography and Regional Research
HANTEL, M., Meteorology and Geophysics
RABEDER, G., Palaeontology
RICHTER, W., Lithospheric Sciences
STEINACKER, R., Meteorology and Geophysics
STEINHAUSER, P., Meteorology and Geophysics
TILLMANNS, E., Mineralogy and Crystallography
WEICHHART, P., Geography and Regional Research
WOHLSCHLÄGL, H., Geography and Regional Research

Faculty of Historical-Cultural Sciences (tel. (1) 4277-40001; fax (1) 4277-9400; e-mail guntram.schneider@univie.ac.at; internet www.univie.ac.at/dekanat-hist-kult):

ASH, M., History
BACH, F. T., Art History
BIETAK, M., Egyptology
BOTZ, G., Contemporary History
BRUCKMÜLLER, E., Social and Economic History
BRUNNER, K., History
DIENST, H., History
DOBESCH, G., Ancient History, Papyrology and Epigraphy
DONNERMAIR, C., Social and Economic History
DREKONJA, G., History
EHMER, J., Social and Economic History
FRIESINGER, H., Prehistoric and Mediaeval Archaeology
HAHN, W., Numismatics and Monetary History
HASELSTEINER, H., East and Southern European History
KAPPELER, A., East and Southern European History
KLIMBURG-SALTER, D., Art History
KODER, J., Byzantine and Modern Greek Studies
KOHLER, A., History
KÖSTLIN, K., European Ethnology
KRESTEN, O., Byzantine and Modern Greek Studies
KRINZINGER, F., Classical Archaeology
LANGE, A., Jewish Studies
LIPPERT, A., Prehistoric and Mediaeval Archaeology
LORENZ, H., Art History
MALECZEK, W., History
MEYER, M., Classical Archaeology
PALME, B., Ancient History, Papyrology and Epigraphy
PILLINGER, R., Classical Archaeology
ROSENAUER, A., Art History
SACHSE, C., Contemporary History
SAURER, E., History
SCHMALE, W., History
SCHMIDT-COLINET, A., Classical Archaeology
SCHMITT, O., Eastern and Southern European History
SCHWARZ, M., Art History
SIEWERT, P., Institute of Ancient History, Papyrology and Epigraphy
STELZER, W., History
STEMBERGER, G., Jewish Studies
STERN, F., Contemporary History
STIEFEL, D., Social and Economic History
SUPPAN, A., Eastern and Southern European History
THEIS, L., Art History
WEBER, E., Institute of
WERNER, F., Jewish Studies

Faculty of Law (Schottenbastei 10–16, 1010 Vienna; tel. (1) 4277-34001; fax (1) 4277-9340; e-mail dekanat-jur@univie.ac.at; internet www.juridicum.at):

AICHER, J., Commercial Law
BAJONS, E. M., Procedural Law
BENKE, N., Roman Law and Ancient Legal History
BÖHM, P., Civil Procedural Law
BRANDSTETTER, W., Criminal Law and Criminology
BRAUNEDER, W., Austrian and European Legal History
BURGSTALLER, M., Criminal Law and Criminology
DORALT, W., Financial Law
FENYVES, A., Civil Law
FISCHER-CZERMAK, C., Civil Law
FUCHS, H., Criminal Law and Criminology
FUNK, B. CHR., State and Administrative Law
HAFNER, G., International Law and International Relations
HÖPFEL, F., Criminal Law and Criminology
IRO, G., Civil Law
KONECNY, A., Procedural Law
KOPETZKI, C., Commercial and Business Law
KREJCI, H., Commercial Law
LUF, G., Legal Philosophy and Legal Theory
MAYER, H., State and Administrative Law
MAZAL, W., Labour Law and Social Law
MEISSEL, F. S., Roman Law and Antique Legal History
NEUHOLD, H. P., International Law and International Relations
OFNER, H., European, International and Comparative Law
ÖHLINGER, T., State and Administrative Law
PIELER, P. E., Roman Law and History of Ancient Law
POTZ, R., Cultural and Religious Law
RASCHAUER, B., State and Administrative Law
REBHAHN, R., Labour Law and Law of Social Security
RECHBERGER, W., Civil Procedural Law
RIEDL, K., Civil Law
SCHAUER, M., Civil Law
SCHRAMMEL, W., Labour Law and Social Law
SCHREUER, CHR., International Law and International Relations
SIMON, T., Legal and Constitutional History
STELZER, M., State and Administrative Law
TANZER, M., Financial Law
THIENEL, R., State and Administrative Law
VERSCHRÄGEN, B., Comparative Law
WELSER, R., Civil Law
WILHELM, G., Civil Law
WILLVONSEDER, R., Roman Law and Ancient Legal History

Faculty of Mathematics (tel. (1) 4277-56001; fax (1) 4277-9560; e-mail dekanat.mathematik@univie.ac.at; internet www.mat.univie.ac.at):

FRIEDMAN, S.-D., Mathematics
GRÖCHENIG, K.-H., Mathematics
KOTH, M., Mathematics
LOSERT, V., Mathematics
MARKOWICH, P., Mathematics
MITSCH, H., Mathematics
MUTHSAM, H., Mathematics
NEUMAIER, A., Mathematics
RINDLER, H., Mathematics
SCHMIDT, K., Mathematics
SCHWERMER, J., Mathematics
SIGMUND, K., Mathematics

Faculty of Philological–Cultural Sciences (tel. (1) 4277-45001; fax (1) 4277-9450; internet www.univie.ac.at/dekanat-phil-kult):

ALLGAYER-KAUFMANN, R., Musicology
BESTERS-DILGER, J., Slavonic Studies
BIRKHAN, H., German Studies
CAVIC-PODGORNIK, N. A., Slavonic Studies
CYFFER, N., African Studies
DÖNT, E., Classical Philology, Medieval and Neo-Latin Studies
DORMELS, R., East Asian Studies
DRESSLER, W., Linguistics
EBENBAUER, A., German Studies
EICHNER, H., Linguistics
FAISTAUER, R., German Studies
FROSCH, F., Romance Studies
GREISENEGGER, W., Theatre Arts
GRUBER, G., Musicology
HAIDER, H., Theatre Arts
HARRAUER, C., Classical Philology, Medieval and Neo-Latin Studies
HASSAUER, F., Romance Studies
HOLUBOWSKY, E., East Asian Studies
HUBER, W., English and American Studies
HUNGER, H., Near Eastern Studies
HÜTTNER, J., Theatre Arts
KASPER, C., European and Comparative Literature and Language Studies
KASTOVSKY, D., English and American Studies
KÖHBACH, M., Near Eastern Studies
KREMNITZ, G., Romance Studies
KRUMM, H.-J., German Studies
LAAKSO, J., European and Comparative Literature and Language Studies
LINHART, S., East Asian Studies
LIPOLD-STEVENS, I., English and American Studies
LOHLKER, R., Musicology
MARTINO, A., European and Comparative Literature and Language Studies
MEHLMAUER-LARCHER, B., English and American Studies
MENGEL, E., English and American Studies
METZELTIN, M., Romance Studies
MIKLAS, H., Slavonic Studies
NEWEKLOWSKY, G., Slavonic Studies
NEWERKLA, S. M., Slavonic Studies
POLJAKOV, F., Slavonic Studies
PREISENDANZ, K., South Asian, Tibetan and Buddhist Studies
ROHRWASSER, M., German Studies
RÖMER, F., Classical Philology, Medieval and Neo-Latin Studies
ROSSEL, S. H., European and Comparative Literature and Language Studies
RUBIK, M., English and American Studies
SCHENDL, H., English and American Studies
SCHJERVE-RINDLER, R., Romance Studies
SCHMIDT-DENGLER, W., German Studies
SEIDLHOFER, B., English and American Studies
SCHICHO, W., African Studies
SELZ, G., Near Eastern Studies
SMOLAK, K., Classical Philology, Medieval and Neo-Latin Studies
SODEYFI, H., Slavonic Studies
SOOMAN, I., European and Comparative Literature and Language Studies
STEINKELLNER, E., South Asian, Tibetan and Buddhist Studies
VAN UFFELEN, H., European and Comparative Literature and Language Studies
WAGNER, B., Romance Studies

WEIGELIN-SCHWIEDRZIK, S., East Asian Studies
WIESINGER, P., German Studies
WOLDAN, A., Slavonic Studies
WOYTEK, E., Classical Philology, Medieval and Neo-Latin Studies
WIESINGER, P., German Studies
ZEMAN, H., German Studies

Faculty of Philosophy and Educational Sciences (tel. (1) 4277-46001; fax (1) 4277-9460; internet homehobel.phl.univie.ac.at):
BIEWER, G., Educational Sciences
BREINBAUER, I. M., Educational Sciences
HÄMMERLE, M., Educational Sciences
GIAMPIERI-DEUTSCH, P., Philosophy
HOPMANN, S., Educational Sciences
KAMPITS, P., Philosophy
KLEIN, H.-D., Philosophy
NAGL, H., Philosophy
OESER, E., Philosophy of Science
PIAS, C., Philosophy
PÖLTNER, G., Philosophy
POLLMEISTER, K., Educational Sciences
SWERTZ, C., Educational Sciences
WALLNER, F., Philosophy

Faculty of Physics (tel. (1) 4277-51001; fax (1) 4277-9510; e-mail dekanat.physik@univie.ac.at; internet physics.univie.ac.at):
AICHELBURG, P. C., Theoretical Physics
BARTL, A., Theoretical Physics
DELLAGO, C., Experimental Physics
HAFNER, J., Materials Physics
HORVATH, H., Experimental Physics
KARNTHALER, H.-P., Materials Physics
KUTSCHERA, W., Isotope Research and Nuclear Physics
RUPP, R., Experimental Physics
VOGL, G., Materials Physics
YNGVASON, J., Theoretical Physics
ZEILINGER, A., Experimental Physics

Faculty of Protestant Theology (Rooseveltplatz 10, 1090 Vienna; tel. (1) 4277-32001; fax (1) 4277-9320; internet www.univie.ac.at/etf):
ADAM, G., Religious Education
DANZ, C., Systematic Theology
DEEG, M., Systematic Theology
HEINE, S., Pastoral Theology and Psychology of Religion
KÖRTNER, U., Systematic Theology
LEEB, R., Christian History, Art and Archaeology
LOADER, J., Old Testament and Biblical Archaeology
PRATSCHER, W., New Testament Studies
WISCHMEYER, W., Christian History, Art and Archaeology

Faculty of Psychology (tel. (1) 4277-47001; fax (1) 4277-9470; internet www.univie.ac.at/psychologie):
BAUER, H., Clinical, Biological and Differential Psychology
FORMANN, A., Psychological Basic Research
HERKNER, W., Psychological Basic Research
KIRCHLER, E., Economic Psychology, Educational Psychology and Evaluation
KUBINGER, K., Developmental Psychology and Psychological Assessment
KRYSPIN-EXNER, I., Clinical, Biological and Differential Psychology
LEDER, H., Psychological Basic Research
SPIEL, C., Economic Psychology, Educational Psychology and Evaluation
VORACEK, M., Psychological Basic Research

Faculty of Social Sciences (tel. (1) 4277-49001; fax (1) 4277-9490; internet www.univie.ac.at/sowi):
AMANN, A., Sociology
BAUER, T. A., Communication
DUCHKOWITSCH, W., Communication
FELT, U., Vienna Interdisciplinary Research Unit for the Study of (Techno) Science and Society
GOTTSCHLICH, M., Communication
GERLICH, P., Government
GINGRICH, A., Social and Cultural Anthropology
GOTTWEIS, H., Political Science
GRIMM, J., Communication
KRAMER, H., Political Science
KREISKY, H. E., Political Science
LANGENBUCHER, W., Communication
RICHTER, R., Sociology
ROSENBERGER, S., Political Science
SAUER, B., Political Science
SCHULZ, W., Sociology
SEGERT, D., Political Science
SEIDL, E., Nursing Science
TÁLOS, E., Government
UCAKAR, K., Government
VITOUCH, P., Communication

Centre for Sports Sciences and University Sports (tel. (1) 4277-59001; fax (1) 4277-9590; e-mail sportwissenschaft@univie.ac.at; internet www.univie.ac.at/sportwissenschaft):
ANKNER, P.
BACHL, N.
BENDA, F.
HACKL-JAGENBREIN, S.
KELLNER, A.
KOLB, M.
MUNZAR, S.
WEIß, O.

Centre for Translation Studies (tel. (1) 4277-58001; fax (1) 4277-9580; e-mail translation@univie.ac.at; internet www.univie.ac.at/transvienna):
BUDIN, G.
FRANK, G.
KASTOVSKY, D.
KLAMBAUER, E.
LEIMEIER, C.
MOLDAU, S.
RESCH, R.
SCHÄTTLE, M.
SNELL-HORNBY, M.
WILDMANN, D.

VETERINÄRMEDIZINISCHE UNIVERSITÄT WIEN (University of Veterinary Medicine, Vienna)

Veterinärplatz 1, 1210 Vienna
Telephone: (1) 25077-0
Fax: (1) 25077-1090
E-mail: rektor@vu-wien.ac.at
Internet: www.vu-wien.ac.at
Founded 1765
State control
Academic year: October to June
Rector: Dr WOLF-DIETRICH FREIHERR VON FIRCKS
Vice-Rector (Academic Affairs): A. Univ. Prof. Dr WOLFGANG KÜNZEL
Vice-Rector (Animal Hospital): Univ. Prof. Dr LASZLO SOLYI
Vice-Rector (Research): Prof. Dr PETER SWETLY
Vice-Rector (Resources): A. Univ. Prof. Dr ERICH MÖSTL
Administrative Director: Dr MANFRED KISLING
Library: see Libraries and Archives
Number of teachers: 206
Number of students: 2,538
Publications: *Uni Vet Wien Report* (4 a year), *Wiener Tierärztliche Monatsschrift* (monthly)

PROFESSORS
ARNOLD, W., Wildlife Biology
AURICH, J. E., Obstetrics, Gynaecology and Andrology
BAMBERG, E., Biochemistry
BAUMGARTNER, W., Internal Medicine and Contagious Diseases of Ruminants and Swine
BÖCK, P., Histology and Embryology
FRANZ, C., Applied Botany
GEMEINER, M., Medical Chemistry
GÜNZBURG, W., Virology
HOFECKER, G., Physiology
KÖNIG, H., Anatomy
MAYRHOFER, E., Radiology
MÜLLER, M., Stock Breeding, Genetics
NIEBAUER, G., Surgery and Ophthalmology
NOHL, H., Pharmacology and Toxicology
ROSENGARTEN, R., Bacteriology, Mycology, Hygiene
SCHMIDT, P., Pathology, Forensic Medicine
SMULDERS, F., Meat Hygiene, Meat Technology, Food Science
STANEK, CH., Orthopaedics in Ungulates
THALHAMMER, J. G., Small Animals and Horses
TROXLER, J., Animal Husbandry, Animal Welfare
WINDISCHBAUER, G., Medical Physics, Biostatistics
ZENTEK, J., Nutrition

WIRTSCHAFTSUNIVERSITÄT WIEN (Vienna University of Economics and Business Administration)

Augasse 2–6, 1090 Vienna
Telephone: (1) 313 36-0
Fax: (1) 313 36-740
E-mail: presse@wu-wien.ac.at
Internet: www.wu-wien.ac.at
Founded 1898
State control
Languages of instruction: German, English
Academic year: October to June
Rector: Prof. Dr CHRISTOPH BADELT
Vice-Rectors: Dr HORST BREITENSTEIN, Prof. Dr EVA EBERHARTINGER, a.o. Prof. Dr KARL SANDNER, a.o. Prof. Dr BARBARA SPORN
Librarian: Dr BETTINA SCHMEIKAL
Library: see Libraries and Archives
Number of teachers: 400
Number of students: 20,000
Publication: *Journal für Betriebswirtschaft* (Journal for Business Administration, 6 a year)

PROFESSORS
ABELE, H., Economic Theory and Policy
AFF, J., Economics
ALEXANDER, R. J., English Business Communication
AMBOS, B., International Marketing and Management
BAUER, L., Economic Theory and Policy
BERGMAN, E. M., Urban and Regional Studies
BERTL, R., Auditing, Accounting and International Accounting
BOGNER, ST., Department of Corporate Finance
BREUSS, F., Research Institute for European Affairs
DORALT, P., Corporate Law
DORFLEITNER, G., Corporate Law
EBERHARTINGER, E., Tax-oriented Business Management
FINK, G., Research Institute for European Affairs
FISCHER, M., Economic and Social Geography
FRANKE, N., Entrepreneurship and Foundation Research
GAREIS, R., Project Management
GRILLER, S., Research Institute for European Affairs
GRÜN, O., Business Organization and Materials Management

HANAPPI-EGGER, E., Gender and Diversity in Organizations
HANSEN, H., Management and Computer Science
HOLOUBEK, M., Constitutional and Administrative Law
HORNIK, K., Mathematical and Statistical Methods
JAMMERNEGG, W., Industrial Information Processing
JANKO, W., Information Processing and Information Economics
KALSS, S., Business Law
KASPER, H., General Management
KLAUSINGER, H.-J., Political Economy
KUBIN, I., International Economics and Development Planning
KUMMER, S., Transportation
LANG, M., International Tax Law
LAURER, H. R., Constitutional and Administrative Law
LIENBACHER, G., Austrian and European Public Law
LOISTL, O., Finance and Financial Markets
LUPTÁČIK, M., Economic Theory and Policy
MATIS, H., Economic and Social History
MAUTNER, G., English Business Communication
MAYRHOFER, W., Business and Government Management
MAZANEC, J., Tourism
MEYR, H., Transport and Logistics
MEYER, M., Non-profit Management
MIKL-HORKE, G., General Sociology and Economic Sociology
MOSER, R., International Business
MUGLER, J., Small Business
NEUMANN, G., Business Informatics and New Media
NOWOTNY, C., Commercial Law
NOWOTNY, E., Financial Politics
OBENAUS, W., English Business Communication
OBERMANN, G., Public Finance
PANNY, W., Applied Computer Science
PFEIFFLE, H, Theory of Education
PICHLER, J. H., Economic Theory and Policy
PICHLER, S., Economic Theory and Policy
RAINER, F., Romance Languages
RATHMAYR, R., Slavonic Languages
RIEGLER, C., Integrated Business Accounting
RUNGGALDIER, U., Labour Law, Social Law
SANDNER, K., General Management
SCHEUCH, F., Marketing
SCHLEGELMILCH, B., International Marketing and Management
SCHNEDLITZ, P., Retail Management
SCHNEIDER, U., Social Policy
SCHNEIDER, W., Business Education
SCHUCH, J., International Tax Law
SCHÜLEIN, J. A., General and Economic Sociology
SCHWEIGER, G., Advertising and Market Research
SEICHT, G., Industrial Management
SPECKBACHER, G., Business Management
SPRINGER, R., Export
STARINGER, C., Tax Law
STEGU, M., Romance Languages
STRASSER, H., Experimental Methods of Mathematics and Statistics
STREMITZER, H., Insurance Management
TAUDES, A., Industrial Information Processing
TITSCHER, C., Sociology and Empirical Sociological Research
TOPRITZHOFER, E., Operations Research
VOGEL, G., Technology and Commodity Economics
VON ECKARDSTEIN, D., Human Resources Management
WALTHER, H., Employment Theory and Policy
WEISS, C., Economic Theory
WENTGES, P., Business Management
WIEBE, A., Information Technology Law and Intellectual Property Law

Schools of Applied Science

Fachhochschule IMC Krems: Piaristengasse 1, 3500 Krems; tel. (2732) 802; fax (2732) 802-4; e-mail information@fh-krems.ac.at; internet www.imc-krems.ac.at; f. 1994; courses in corporate governance and e-business management, export-oriented management, health management, medical and pharmaceutical biotechnology and tourism management; library: 4,500 vols, 50 periodicals; 216 teachers; 1,300 students; Dir Prof. Mag. HANS LICHTENWAGNER.

Fachhochschul-Studiengang Bauingenieurwesen-Baumanagement (School of Applied Construction Engineering and Management): Daumegasse 1, 2nd Fl., 1100 Vienna; tel. (1) 6066877-2120; fax (1) 6066877-2129; e-mail bau@fh-campuswien.ac.at; internet www.fachhochschulen.at/FH/Studium/Bauingenieurwesen-_Baumanagement_147.htm; f. 1996; State control; languages of instruction: German, English; bachelor and master's courses in construction engineering and management; Dir Dr DORIS LINK.

Fachhochschul-Studiengänge bfi Wien (School of Applied Science bfi Vienna): Wohlmutstr. 22, 1020 Vienna; tel. (1) 7201286-0; fax (1) 7201286-19; e-mail info@fh-vie.at; internet www.fh-vie.at; f. 1996, present status 2002; languages of instruction: German, English; courses in banking and finance, European economics and business, logistics and transport management and project management and information technology; MBAs in Central, South and East Europe Studies and Risk Management; 27 teachers; 1,100 students; Dir HELMUT HOLZINGER.

Fachhochschul-Studiengang Burgenland (School of Applied Sciences Burgenland): Haydngasse 1, 7000 Burgenland; tel. (5) 9010609-0; fax (5) 9010609-15; e-mail officefh@burgenland.at; internet www.fh-eisenstadt.ac.at; f. 1994; language of instruction: German; bachelor and master's courses in economics, environmental and energy management, health studies, information technology and management; 68 teachers; 866 students; Dir Mag. INGRID SCHWAB-MATKOVITS.

Fachhochschul-Studiengänge Campus Wien (School of Applied Sciences Vienna Campus): Daumegasse 3, 1100 Vienna; tel. (1) 6066877-100; fax (1) 6066877-109; e-mail office@fh-campuswien.ac.at; internet www.fh-campuswien.ac.at; f. 1999; language of instruction: German; diploma courses in bioengineering, biotechnology, information technology and telecommunications, social work, and technical project and process management; bachelor courses in construction engineering and management; master's courses in local management and economics, and social management; Dir Ing. WILHELM BEHENSKY; publ. *Aktuell* (monthly).

Fachhochschul-Studiengänge Kufstein (School of Applied Sciences Kufstein): Andreas Hofer Str. 7, 6330 Kufstein; tel. (5372) 71819; fax (5372) 71819-104; e-mail info@fh-kufstein.ac.at; internet www.fh-kufstein.ac.at; f. 1997; diploma course in property economics and facility management; bachelor's courses in business information technology, sport, culture and event management, European energy economics, facility management and property economics and international economics and management ; master's courses in crisis and decontamination management; library: 8,500 vols, 90 periodicals; 120 teachers; 2,000 students (1,000 full-time, 1,000 exchange); Dir Mag. NORBERT WITTING.

Fachhochschul-Studiengang Oberösterreich (School of Applied Sciences of Upper Austria): Franz-Fritsch-Str. 11/3, 4600 Wels; tel. (7242) 44808-0; fax (7242) 44808-77; e-mail info@fh-ooe.at; internet www.fh-ooe.at; f. 1994; language of instruction: German; bachelor and master's courses; campuses in Hagenberg (software, information technology and media), Linz (health and social welfare), Steyr (business and management studies) and Wels (engineering and environment and energy studies); Dir KARIN AUSSERSDORFER.

Fachhochschul-Studiengang Salzburg (School of Applied Sciences Salzburg): Schillerstr. 30, 5020 Salzburg; tel. (43) 50-2211-0; e-mail office@fh-sbg.ac.at; internet www.fh-sbg.ac.at; f. 1995; incorporated Holztechnikum Kuchl in 2003; campuses in Kuchl and Urstein; bachelor and master's courses in business and technology, media and design and health and welfare; 81 teachers; 1,375 students; Dir ERHARD BOJANOVSKY.

Fachhochschul-Studiengänge St Pölten (School of Applied Sciences St Pölten): Herzogenburger Str. 68, 3100 St. Pölten; tel. (2742) 313228; fax (2742) 313229; e-mail office@fh-stpoelten.ac.at; internet www.fh-stpoelten.ac.at; f. 1996; language of instruction: German; courses in economics, social sciences and technology; 95 teachers; 1,000 students; Dirs Prof. Ing. Dr JOHANN GÜNTHER, Dipl.-Ing. GERNOT KOHL; publ. *FACTS* (2 a year).

Fachhochschul-Studiengänge Technikum Joanneum (School of Applied Sciences Technikum Joanneum): Alte Poststr. 149, 8020 Graz; tel. (316) 5453-8800; e-mail info@fh-joanneum.at; internet www.fh-joanneum.at; f. 1995; degrees in business and technology, architecture and civil engineering, business, information engineering, mobility, media and design, social services and public health; language of instruction: German; library: 27,000 vols, 600 periodicals; 270 teachers; 1,424 students; Dir Prof. Mag. Dr PETER REININGHAUS.

Fachhochschul-Studiengänge der Wiener Neustadt (School of Applied Sciences Wiener Neustadt): Johannes Gutenberg Str. 3, 2700 Vienna-Neustadt; tel. (2622) 89084-0; fax (2622) 89084-99; e-mail office@fhwn.ac.at; internet www.fhwn.ac.at; f. 1994; languages of instruction: German, English; diploma and master's courses in business consultancy, business and engineering, information technologies, mechatronics and microsystems engineering, logistics, geographic information technologies, product marketing and project management, management for rural areas and biotechnological processes; 200 teachers; 1,800 students; Dirs Prof. Dr HELMUT DETTER, Prof. Mag. WERNER JUNGWIRTH.

Fachhochschul-Studiengänge WIFI Steiermark (School of Applied Sciences WIFI Styria): Körblergasse 111–113, 8021 Graz; tel. (316) 602-1234; e-mail info@stmk.wifi.at; internet www.stmk.wifi.at; campuses in Graz, Niklasdorf and Unterpremstätten; courses in business management, business studies, modern languages, information technology, engineering, health and welfare, tourism and gastronomy; Pres. Ing. Mag. PETER HOCHEGGER.

Fachhochschule Technikum Kärnten (School of Applied Science Carinthia): Villacher Str. 1, 9800 Spittal; tel. (4762) 90500-0; fax (4762) 90500-1110; e-mail international@fh-kaernten.at; internet www.fh-kaernten.ac.at; f. 1995; courses in civil engineering, electronic engineering, geoinformation, healthcare management, medical information technology, public management, social work, telematics/network engineering; international master's degree programmes in communication engineering for information technology, geographic information science and operations research, healthcare information technology, integrated systems and circuit design and remote engineering, and spatial decision support systems; Dir Doz. Dipl.-Ing. Dr HERBERT STÖGNER.

Fachhochschule Technikum Wien (School of Applied Science Vienna): Mariahilfer Str. 37–39, 1060 Vienna; tel. (1) 58839-46; fax (1) 58839-49; e-mail info@technikum-wien.at; internet www.technikum-wien.at; f. 1994; bachelor's programmes in biomedical engineering, business informatics, computer science, electronics and information and communication systems; master's programmes in biomedical engineering sciences, business informatics, embedded systems, industrial economics, information management and computer security, software development and media informatics, technology and management and telecommunications and internet technologies; diploma engineer courses in intelligent transport systems, international business engineering, mechatronics/robotics and sports equipment technology; library: 3,000 vols; 400 teachers; 1,500 students; Dir Ing Dr MICHAEL WÜRDINGER; publ. *Technikum News* (4 a year).

Fachhochschule Vorarlberg (School of Applied Sciences Vorarlberg): Hochschulstr. 1, 6850 Dornbirn; tel. (5572) 792-0; fax (5572) 792-9500; e-mail info@fhv.at; internet www.tvlbg.ac.at; f. 1994; bachelor's, master's and diploma programmes in business administration, computer science, mechatronics, media design; diploma programme in social work; other programmes in engineering and business administration; office for continuing education; library: 35,000 vols, 300 periodicals, 1,500 CDs 800 DVDs; 86 teachers; 850 students; Dir Prof. Dipl.-Ing. RUDI FEURSTEIN.

Other Colleges

Berg- und Hüttenschule Leoben (Leoben School of Mining and Foundry Engineering): Max-Tendler-Str. 3, 8700 Leoben; tel. (3842) 44888; fax (3842) 44888-3; e-mail schule@htl-leoben.at; internet www.htl-leoben.at; f. 1865; mechanical engineering and metallurgy, industrial engineering, industrial logistics; 27 teachers; 161 students; Dir Prof. DI HERIBERT RESCH.

Diplomatische Akademie Wien (Diplomatic Academy of Vienna): Favoritenstr. 15A, 1040 Vienna; tel. (1) 5057272; fax (1) 5042265; e-mail info@da-vienna.ac.at; internet www.da-vienna.ac.at; f. 1964; Diploma and Master of Advanced International Studies programmes prepare Austrian and foreign graduates for careers in diplomacy, international business and finance, international organizations and public administration; library: 35,000 vols, 330 newspapers in German, English, French, Spanish, Italian and Russian; 80 students; Dir Dr JIŘÍ GRUSA; publ. *Jahrbuch* (annually).

Schools of Art and Music

Kärntner Landeskonservatorium (Carinthian Conservatory of Music): Miesstalerstr. 8, 9020 Klagenfurt; tel. (463) 511421; fax (463) 511421-40508; e-mail klk@aon.at; internet www.lonse.at; f. 1827; 74 teachers; 920 students; library: 40,000 vols; Dir Mag. ROLAND STREINER; publ. *Jahresbericht* (annual report).

Konservatorium Wien (Vienna Municipal Conservatory): Johannesgasse 4A, 1010 Vienna; tel. (1) 512-7747; fax (1) 512-7747-7913; e-mail office@konswien.at; internet www.konservatorium-wien.ac.at; f. 1938; consists of Konservatorium (247 teaching staff; 1,240 students), affiliated to it are 17 Musikschulen (301 teaching staff; 4,215 students) and the Kindersingschule (36 teaching staff; 2,836 students); Dirs GOTTFRIED EISL, RANKO MARKOVIC; Librarian EVA SMEKAL; publ. *Fidelio* (5 a year).

Musikschule der Stadt Innsbruck: Innrain 5, 6010 Innsbruck; tel. (512) 585425-0; fax (512) 585425-5; e-mail musikschule@magibk.at; f. 1818; 70 teachers; 1,800 students; Dir WOLFRAM ROSENBERGER.

Tiroler Landeskonservatorium (Tirol Conservatory of Music): Paul-Hofhaimer-Gasse 6, 6020 Innsbruck; tel. (512) 508-6850; fax (512) 508-6855; internet www.tirol.gv.at/konservatorium; f. 1818; 75 teachers; 500 students; library: 100,000 vols and musical notes; Dir Dr THOMAS JUEN; Librarian FRANZ BAUER.

AZERBAIJAN

The Higher Education System

The higher education system was established when Azerbaijan was a full Union Republic of the Union of Soviet Socialist Republics (USSR). The main language of instruction is Azerbaijani, but there are also Russian-language schools and some teaching in Georgian and Armenian. From 1992 a Turkic version of the Latin alphabet was used in Azerbaijani-language schools (replacing the Cyrillic script). In June 1999 legislation entitled The Program of Education Reforms of the Republic of Azerbaijan was passed by presidential decree, effecting reforms at all levels of education. In 2005 Azerbaijan signed up to the Bologna Process, under which all European countries will endeavour to adopt a universal two-tier Bachelors and Masters degree structure. Azerbaijan intends to adopt this system by 2010. In 2005/06 there were 129,948 students in higher education.

The state oversees educational policy, dispenses funding and lays down guidelines for quality assurance. Individual institutions are responsible for employing teaching staff and establishing curricula. In 2006 the Ministry of Education established the Standing Commission on Accreditation to act as the main quality assurance body for higher education institutions and secondary specialized institutions. Institutions are subject to inspection every four years. Since 2004/05 entrance examinations for state institutions have been organized by a central body, the Talaba Qabulu üzre Dövlat Komissiyasi (TQDK—State Students Admission Commission). An estimated 20% of school-leavers enter higher education through this process.

The three levels of higher education qualifications are Bachelors, Masters and Doctorates. Study for the Bachelors degree lasts for four years, while the Soviet-style Specialist Diploma, which is still offered in some disciplines, lasts for five years. The Masters degree was introduced in 1997/98 and lasts for up to two years. Finally, the Soviet-style Aspirantura and Doctorantura remain the main doctoral degrees, though Bologna Process reforms are being implemented.

Learned Societies

GENERAL

Azerbaijan National Academy of Sciences: 1141 Baku, F. Ağayev küç. 9; tel. (12) 441-72-81; fax (12) 441-72-81; e-mail secretary@iit.ab.az; internet www.science.az; f. 1945; depts of Physical, Mathematical and Technical Sciences (Academician-Sec. A. J. HAJIYEV), Chemical Sciences (Academician-Sec. A. A. EFENDIYEV), Earth Sciences (Academician-Sec. A. M. ALIZADEH), Biological Sciences (Academician-Sec. M. A. MUSAYEV), Humanities and Social Sciences (Academician-Sec. A. A. AKHUNDOV; attached research institutes: see Research Institutes; Pres. M. K. KERIMOV; Academician-Sec. T. N. SHAKHTAKHTINSKIY; publs *Proceedings* (in Russian and Azeri, quarterly), *Elm* (Newsletter, in Azeri and Russian, fortnightly), *Transactions* (series: Physical, Mathematical and Technical Sciences, Biological Sciences, Historical, Philosophical and Juridical, Economics, Literature, Philology and Art, Geological), *Journal of Physics* (in Azeri, Russian and English, quarterly), *Azerbaijan Journal of Physics* (in Azeri, Russian and English, quarterly), *Azerbaijan Journal of Chemistry* (in Azeri and Russian, quarterly), *Processes of Petrochemistry and Oil Refining Journal* (in Russian and English, 6 a year), *Journal of Turkology* (in Azeri and Russian, annual), *Journal of Problems of Eastern Philosophy* (In Azeri, Arabic, Farsi, Turkish, English, German and French, 2 a year), *Azerbaijan and Azerbaijanists* (in English and Russian, monthly), *Applied and Computational Mathematics* (2 a year).

LANGUAGE AND LITERATURE

British Council: 1000 Baku, Vali Mammadov küç. 1, Icheri Sheher; tel. (12) 497-20-13; fax (12) 498-92-36; e-mail enquiries@britishcouncil.az; internet www2.britishcouncil.org/azerbaijan.htm; office opened 1993; offers courses and examinations in English language and British culture and promotes cultural exchange with the UK; Dir MARGARET JACK.

Research Institutes

AGRICULTURE, FISHERIES AND VETERINARY SCIENCE

Agricultural Research Institute: 1016 Baku, U. Hadjibeyov küç. 40; tel. (12) 497-49-31; fax (12) 497-50-45; e-mail musayev@artel.net.az; f. 1950; attached to Min. of Agriculture; Dir A. MUSAYEV.

Institute of Genetic Resources: 1106 Baku, Azadlyg Ave; tel. (12) 462-94-62; fax (12) 449-92-20; e-mail akparov@yahoo.com; f. 2003; attached to Azerbaijan Acad. of Sciences; Dir Z. I. AKPAROV; publ. *Transactions* (in Azeri and Russian, irreg.).

Institute of Soil Science and Agrochemistry: 1073 Baku, M. Arif küç. 5; e-mail soiman@dcacs.ab.az; f. 1945; attached to Azerbaijan Acad. of Sciences; Dir M. P. BABAYEV; publ. *Transactions* (in Azeri and Russian, annual).

Karaev, A. I., Institute of Physiology: 1100 Baku, Sharif-Zade küç. 2; tel. (12) 432-15-20; e-mail inphys@dcacs.ab.az; f. 1968; attached to Azerbaijan Acad. of Sciences; Dir T. M. AQAYEV; publ. *Transactions* (in Azeri and Russian, annual).

Rajably Scientific Research Institute of Horticulture and Sub-Tropical Plants: 4035 Quba, Zardabi; tel. (169) 45-37-17; fax (12) 493-08-84; f. 1926; Dir D. BAYRAMOVA.

ARCHITECTURE AND TOWN PLANNING

Institute of Architecture and Art: 1143 Baku, Pr. Narimanova 31; tel. (12) 439-35-39; e-mail senet@lan.ab.az; f. 1945; attached to Azerbaijan Acad. of Sciences; Dir. R. S. EFENDIYEV.

BIBLIOGRAPHY, LIBRARY SCIENCE AND MUSEOLOGY

Institute of Manuscripts: 1001 Baku, Istiglaliyyat küç. 8; tel. and fax (12) 492-31-97; e-mail dr.adilov@mail.ru; f. 1950; attached to Azerbaijan Acad. of Sciences; library of 40,000 MSS, documents and vols; Dep.-Dir M. M. ADILOV; publs *Älyazmalar khäzinäsinda* (irreg.), *Kechmishimizdän gälän säslär* (irreg.), *Orta äsr älyazmalari vä Azärbaycan mädäniyyäti problemläri* (every 2 years).

ECONOMICS, LAW AND POLITICS

Institute of Economics: 1143 Baku, Pr. H. Javid 31; tel. (12) 439-43-98; fax (12) 435-31-12; e-mail economy@eco.ab.az; f. 1958; attached to Azerbaijan Acad. of Sciences; Dir S. M. MURADOV.

Institute of Philosophy and Law: 1143 Baku, Pr. H. Javid 31; tel. (12) 439-37-28; f. 1945; attached to Azerbaijan Acad. of Sciences; Dir A. ABASOV; publ. *Qendershunaslig* (in Azeri and English, 11 a year).

HISTORY, GEOGRAPHY AND ARCHAEOLOGY

Institute of Archaeology and Ethnography: 1143 Baku, Pr. H. Javid 31; tel. (12) 439-36-49; fax (12) 439-39-91; e-mail abbasov@arch.ab.az; attached to Azerbaijan Acad. of Sciences; Dir A. A. ABBASOV.

Institute of Geography: 1143 Baku, Pr. H. Javid 31; tel. (12) 438-29-00; fax (12) 439-35-41; e-mail azgeog@geo.ab.az; f. 1945; attached to Azerbaijan Acad. of Sciences; research into natural resources, industrial and infrastructural problems, desertification, hydrometeorology of the Caspian sea and its coastal dynamics; 250 mems; library of 53,000 vols; Dir Acad. B. A. BUDAGOV; publ. *Khabarlar* (2 a year).

Institute of History: 1143 Baku, Pr. H. Javid 31; tel. (12) 439-36-15; f. 1940; attached to Azerbaijan Acad. of Sciences; Dep. Dir J. A. BAHRAMOV.

Institute of Oriental Studies: 1143 Baku, Pr. H. Javid 31; tel. and fax (12) 439-23-51; e-mail sharq@lan.ab.az; f. 1958; attached to Azerbaijan Acad. of Sciences; Dir G. B. BAKHSHALIYEVA.

LANGUAGE AND LITERATURE

Nasimi Institute of Linguistics: 1143 Baku, Pr. H. Javid 31; tel. (12) 439-35-71; f. 1932; attached to Azerbaijan Acad. of Sciences; library of 6,000 vols, 50 periodicals; Dir Prof. A. A. AKHUNDOV; publ. *Turkology* (quarterly).

Nizami Institute of Literature: 1143 Baku, 5th Fl., H. Javid 31; tel. (12) 439-56-51; fax (12) 439-56-68; e-mail adib@aas.ab.az; f. 1932; attached to Azerbaijan Acad. of Sciences; Dir B. A. NABIYEV.

MEDICINE

Azerbaijan Institute of Orthopaedics and Traumatology: 1007 Baku, 32 Abbas Sakhat küç.; tel. (12) 496-62-62.

Azerbaijan Institute of Tuberculosis and Pulmonology: 1001 Baku, 2514 kv., 8 km settlement; tel. (12) 421-22-62.

Azerbaijan Medical Association: 1000 Baku, S. Akhundov küç. 2/1; tel. (12) 31-88-66; fax (12) 31-51-36; e-mail azer.ma@medmail.com; internet azma.aznet.org; f. 1998; 600 ; Dir NARIMAN SAFARLI.

Azerbaijan Research Institute of Haematology and Blood Transfusion: 1007 Baku, M. Kaskkay 87; tel. (12) 440-53-18; fax (12) 440-63-34; e-mail hajiev_azad@yahoo.com; f. 1943; Dir AZAD HAJIYEV; publ. *Azerbaijan Medical Journal* (quarterly).

Azerbaijan Research Institute of Ophthalmology: 1065 Baku, 6-ya Kommunisticheskaya küç. 5; tel. (12) 421-22-62.

Research Institute of Gastroenterology: 1110 Baku, Leningradsky pr. 111; tel. (12) 464-45-09; f. 1988; Dir B. A. AGAYEV; publ. *Actual Questions of Gastroenterology* (annual).

Research Institute of Medical Rehabilitation and Natural Therapeutic Factors: 1008 Baku, Khatai Ave 3; tel. (12) 466-31-93; fax (12) 466-58-35; f. 1936; Dir Prof. Dr A. V. MUSAYEV.

NATURAL SCIENCES

Biological Sciences

Botanical Garden: 1073 Baku, Patamdartskoe shosse 40; e-mail cbg@lan.ab.az; f. 1934; attached to Azerbaijan Acad. of Sciences; Dir O. V. IBADLI.

Institute of Botany: 1073 Baku, Patamdartskoe shosse 40; tel. (12) 439-32-30; fax (12) 439-33-80; e-mail botanica@baku.ab.az; f. 1936; attached to Azerbaijan Acad. of Sciences; Dir V. H. HAJIYEV.

Institute of Microbiology: 1073 Baku, Patamdart Ave 40; f. 1972; attached to Azerbaijan Acad. of Sciences; Dir M. A. SALMANOV; publ. *Transactions* (in Azeri and Russian, annual).

Institute of Zoology: 1073 Baku, Proezd 1128, kv. 504, A. Abbasov; tel. (12) 439-73-71; fax (12) 439-73-53; e-mail zoology@dcacs.ab.az; f. 1936; attached to Azerbaijan Acad. of Sciences; Dir M. A. MUSAYEV; publ. *Transactions* (in Azeri and Russian, irreg.).

Mardakan Arboretum: 1044 Baku; tel. (12) 454-30-12; fax (12) 454-03-74; e-mail office@dendrary.in-baku.com; f. 1926; attached to Azerbaijan Acad. of Sciences; Dir T. S. MAMEDOV.

Mathematical Sciences

Institute of Mathematics and Mechanics: 1141 Baku, Agaeva küç. 9; tel. (12) 439-39-24; fax (12) 439-01-02; e-mail frteb@aas.ab.az; attached to Azerbaijan Acad. of Sciences; Dir A. J. HAJIYEV; publ. *Proceedings* (in Azeri, Russian and English, quarterly).

Physical Sciences

Azerbaijan National Aerospace Agency: 1106 Baku, Pr. Azadlyg 159; tel. (12) 462-93-87; fax (12) 462-17-38; e-mail aflatun_hasanov@anasa.baku.az; f. 1975; Dir-Gen. Dr AFLATUN HASANOV.

Institute of Chemical Problems: 1143 Baku, Pr. H. Javid 29; tel. (12) 439-29-08; fax (12) 438-77-56; e-mail itpcht@lan.ab.az; f. 1935; attached to Azerbaijan Acad. of Sciences; Dir T. N. SHASKHTAKHTINSKI.

Institute of Geology: 1143 Baku, Pr. H. Javid 29A; tel. (12) 438-62-30; fax (12) 497-52-85; e-mail gia@azdata.net; internet www.gia.az; f. 1938; attached to Azerbaijan Acad. of Sciences; 250 mems; library of 24,000 vols, 70,000 periodicals; Dir A. A. ALI-ZADEH; publs *Proceedings* (annual), *Sciences of the Earth* (quarterly).

Institute of Physics: 1143 Baku, Pr. H. Javid 33; tel. (12) 439-41-51; fax (12) 439-59-61; e-mail azhep@physics.ab.az; f. 1945; attached to Azerbaijan Acad. of Sciences; Dir Dr A. M. GASHIMOV.

Institute of Radiation Problems: 1143 Baku, Pr. H. Javid 31A; tel. (12) 439-33-91; fax (12) 439-83-18; e-mail azerecolab@azerin.com; f. 1969; attached to Azerbaijan Acad. of Sciences; Dir A. A. GARIBOV.

Şamaxı Astro-Physical Observatory: 5600 Şamaxı, Pos. Mamedalieva; tel. (12) 497-52-68; fax (12) 497-52-68; e-mail shao@lan.ab.az; f. 1960; attached to Azerbaijan Acad. of Sciences; Dir A. S. GULUYEV; publ. *The Azerbaijan Astronomical Journal* (in Azeri, Russian and English, quarterly).

TECHNOLOGY

Azerbaijan Energy Research Institute: 1602 Baku, Pr. H. Zardabi 94; tel. (12) 432-80-76; fax (12) 498-13-68; f. 1941; library of 6,000 vols; Dir RAMAZANOV KERIM NAZIR OGLU; publ. *Transactions of the Azerbaijan Energy Research Institute* (annual).

Azerbaijan Petroleum Machinery Research and Design Institute (Azinmash): 1029 Baku, 4 Araz küç.; tel. (12) 467-08-88; fax (12) 467-28-88; e-mail office@azinmash.azeri.com; internet www.azinmash.com; f. 1930; Dir R. DJABBAROV.

Azerbaijan Scientific Gas Research and Projects Institute: 1000 Baku, Yusif Safarov küç. 23; tel. (12) 490-43-59.

Guliyev, A.M., Institute of Additive Chemistry: 1603 Baku, Beyukshorskoe shosse, kv. 2062; tel. (12) 467-65-33; fax (12) 493-33-64; e-mail aki@lan.ab.az; f. 1965; attached to Azerbaijan Acad. of Sciences; lubricant and fuel additives, cutting fluids and erosion inhibitors; library of 9,000 vols; Dir Dr V. M. FARZALIYEV.

Institute of Cybernetics: 1141 Baku, Agaeva küç. 9, kv. 553; tel. (12) 439-01-51; fax (12) 439-26-33; e-mail cyber@cyber.ab.az; internet www.science.az/en/cyber/index.htm; f. 1965; attached to Azerbaijan Acad. of Sciences; Dir T. A. ALIYEV; publ. *Transactions* (2 a year).

Institute of Deep Oil and Gas Deposits: 1143 Baku, Pr. H. Javid 33; tel. (12) 439-21-40; fax (12) 497-58-52; e-mail arif.guliyev@lan.ab.az; attached to Azerbaijan Acad. of Sciences; Dir A. M. GULIYEV.

Institute of Information Technology: 1141 Baku, F. Agayev; tel. (12) 439-01-67; fax (12) 439-61-21; e-mail secretary@iit.ab.az; f. 2003; attached to Azerbaijan Acad. of Sciences; Dir R. M. ALGULIYEV.

Institute of Polymer Materials: 5004 Sumqayıt, Samed Vargun küç. 124; tel. (12) 497-60-38; fax (164) 42-04-00; e-mail ipoma@dcacs.ab.az; f. 1966; attached to Azerbaijan Acad. of Sciences; Dir A. A. EFENDIYEV.

Mamedaliev, Yu. G., Institute of Petrochemical Processes: 1025 Baku, N. Rafiyev 30; tel. (12) 490-24-76; fax (12) 490-35-20; e-mail anipcp@dcacs.ab.az; f. 1929; attached to Azerbaijan Acad. of Sciences; Dir M. I. RUSTAMOV; publ. *Process of Petrochemistry and Oil Refining* (in Russian and English, 6 a year).

Oil Research and Design Institute (AzNIPIneft): 1033 Baku, Aga Neimatully küç. 39; tel. (12) 493-64-29.

Research and Design Institute for Oil Engineering: 1000 Baku, Aga Neymatully küç. 39; tel. (12) 466-21-69; fax (12) 467-79-39.

Research Institute of Photoelectronics: 1000 Baku, Block 555, Agaeva küç.,; tel. (12) 439-13-08; f. 1972; library of 1,095 vols; Dir Prof. S. E. YUNISOGLU.

Libraries and Archives

Baku

Akhundov, M. F., State Library of Azerbaijan: 1601 Baku, Hagani küç. 29; tel. (12) 493-64-03; fax (12) 493-56-05; internet www.anl.aznet.org; f. 1923; 4,406,636 vols (incl. 1,300,294 periodicals), 26,723 sound recordings, 52,204 microforms; Dir L. YU GAFUROVA; publs *Azerbaijan in Foreign Press, New Literature on Culture and Art, Information and Bibliographic Indexes.*

Azerbaijan Scientific and Technical Library: 1001 Baku, G. Gadzhieva küç. 3; tel. (12) 492-08-07; 9,000,000 vols; Dir G. D. MAMEDOV.

Baku State University Central Library: 1145 Baku, Z. Khalilova küç. 23; tel. (12) 439-08-58; fax (12) 438-05-82; e-mail sara_ibragimova@yahoo.com; f. 1919; 2,003,515 vols; Librarian S. IBRAGIMOVA.

Central Library of the Azerbaijan Academy of Sciences: 1143 Baku, Pr. Narimanova 31; tel. (12) 438-60-17; f. 1925; 2.5m. vols, periodicals and serials; Dir M. M. CASANOVA.

Museums and Art Galleries

Baku

Azerbaijan State Museum of Art: 1001 Baku, Niyazi 9–11; tel. (12) 492-57-89; fax (12) 492-67-69; f. 1920; library of 11,000 vols; Dir A. R. ASRAFILOV.

Baku Museum of Education: 1001 Baku, Niazi küç. 11; tel. (12) 492-04-53; f. 1940; library of 52,000 vols; Dir T. Z. AHMEDZADE.

Huseyn Javid Memorial Flat–Museum: 1000 Baku, Istiglaliyat 8; tel. (12) 492-06-57; f. 1995; attached to Azerbaijan Acad. of Sciences; Dir T. H. JAVID.

Museum of the History of Azerbaijan: 1005 Baku, H. Z. Tagiyev 4; tel. (12) 493-36-48; fax (12) 498-52-11; f. 1920; attached to Azerbaijan Acad. of Sciences; history of the Azerbaijani people since ancient times; Dir N. M. VALIKHANLI.

Nizami Gandjavi State Museum of Azerbaijan Literature: 1001 Baku, Isteglal küç. 53; tel. (12) 492-18-64; f. 1939; history of Azerbaijani literature since ancient times; Dir R. B. HUSEYNOV.

State Museum Palace of Shirvan-Shakh: 1004 Baku, Zamkovski pereulok 76; tel. (12) 492-95-73; fax (12) 492-83-04; e-mail shirvanshah@bakililar.az; internet www.culture.az:8101/museums/shirv/titlerus.htm; f. 1964; historical and architectural museum; Dir SEVDA DADASHEVA.

Stepano-Kert

Stepanakert Museum of the History of Nagornyi-Karabakh: 2600 Xankandi (Stepanakert), Gorkogo küç. 4,; history of the Armenian people of Arthakh (Nagornyi Karabakh).

Universities

AZERBAIJAN ARCHITECTURE AND CONSTRUCTION UNIVERSITY/ AZERBAIJAN CIVIL ENGINEERING UNIVERSITY

1073 Baku, A. Sultanova küç. 5
Telephone: (12) 439-05-97
Fax: (12) 498-78-36

Founded 1920
State control

Pres.: G. MAMMADOVA

Faculties of Architecture, Civil Engineering, Construction, Construction Automation, Construction Technology, Economics, Hydrotechnical Machines, Road Building.

AZERBAIJAN MEDICAL UNIVERSITY

1022 Baku, Bakizkhanova küç. 23
Telephone: (12) 495-35-66
Fax: (12) 495-38-14
E-mail: amu_rector@baku-az.net

Founded 1930
State control

Rector: A. AMIRASLANOV

Library of 600,000 vols
Number of teachers: 2,000
Number of students: 7,186

Faculties of Dentistry, General Medicine, Paediatrics, Pharmacy, Prophylactic Medicine, Biology.

AZERBAIJAN STATE ECONOMIC UNIVERSITY

1001 Baku, Istiqlaliyyat 6
Telephone: (12) 492-60-43
Fax: (12) 492-59-40
E-mail: aseu@aseu.ab.az
Internet: www.aseu.ab.az

Founded 1929, current name and status 2000
State control

President: ALI ABBASOV

Faculties of Accountancy, Commerce, Economics, Finance, Management.

AZERBAIJAN STATE PEDAGOGICAL UNIVERSITY 'NASREDDIN TUSI'

1000 Baku, Uzeir Hajibejov 34
Telephone: (12) 493-00-32
Fax: (12) 493-00-32

Founded 1921
State control
Languages of instruction: Azeri, Russian

President: BAHLUL AGAJEV

Faculties of Azeri Language and Literature, Chemistry and Biology, Drawing and Imitation Arts, Elementary Military Education and Physical Training, Geography, History, Mathematics, Pedagogy and Psychology, Physics.

AZERBAIJAN STATE UNIVERSITY OF CULTURE AND FINE ARTS

1065 Baku, Pr. Insaatchilar 9
Telephone: (12) 439-07-78
Fax: (12) 438-93-48
E-mail: inchmed@azeri.com

Founded 1945
State control
Academic year: September to July

Rector: TEYMURCHIN AFANDIYEV
Vice-Rector: RAFIQ SADIQOV

Library of 115,000 vols
Number of teachers: 190
Number of students: 1,562

DEANS

Faculty of Cultural Studies: ALEKPER MAMMADOV
Faculty of Fine Arts: VEFA ALIYEV
Faculty of Management: BAYRAM HADJIYEV
Faculty of Music: VAMIG MAMMEDALIYEV
Faculty of Painting: DJABBAR HASSANOV
Faculty of Theatre and Cinema: MAMMEDSHAH ATAYEV

AZERBAIJAN STATE UNIVERSITY OF LANGUAGES

1055 Baku, Rashid Bahbudov 60
Telephone: (12) 440-35-05
Fax: (12) 440-85-46
E-mail: ibiyev@yahoo.com

Founded 1937
State control

Rector: SAMAD SEYIDOV

Faculties of Russian, English, French, Romance and Germanic languages.

AZERBAIJAN TECHNICAL UNIVERSITY

1073 Baku, H. Javid Ave 25
Telephone: (12) 438-33-43
Fax: (12) 438-32-80
E-mail: aztu@aztukm.baku.az
Internet: www.aztu.az

Founded 1950
State control
Languages of instruction: Azeri, Russian
Academic year: September to July

Rector: Dr H. A. MAMEDOV
Vice-Rector for Inte. Relations: S. M. SULTANZADE
Vice-Rector for Learning and Education: Dr F. G. MAMEDOV
Vice-Rector for Research and Devt: Dr A. N. ALIZADE
Vice-Rector for Student Affairs: SHIKAR M. GASIMOV
Registrar and Chief Admin. Officer: AZIZA B. GASIMLI
Librarian: NARINGUL KHALAFOVA

Library of 600,000 vols
Number of teachers: 695
Number of students: 4,828

Publications: *Research Works* (quarterly), *Ziya* (monthly)

DEANS

Faculty of Automation and Computing Equipment: Dr R. A. HASANOV
Faculty of Business and Management for the Engineering Industry: Dr I. A. ASLANDAZE
Faculty of Electrical Engineering and Energy: Dr H. S. ALIYEV
Faculty of Machine-Building: Dr N. M. RASULOV
Faculty of Machine Sciences: Dr M. H. GARIBOV
Faculty of Metallurgy: Dr A. I. BABAYEV
Faculty of Radio Engineering and Communications: Dr A. N. HASANOV
Faculty of Transportation: Dr F. A. HASANOV

PROFESSORS

Faculty of Automation and Computing Technology (tel. (12) 438-94-06):

ABILOV, C. I., Automation
ALIYEV, A. B., Higher Mathematics
ALIZADE, A. N., Applied Mathematics
ASLANOV, G. I., Higher Mathematics
BAYRAMOV, K. T., Computers and Systems
DUNYAMALIEV, M. A., Applied Mathematics
HACHIYEV, M.A., Design and Manufacture of Computers
ISKENDERZADE, Z. A., Applied Physics and Microelectronics
MAMEDOV, H. A., Automation and Control
MELIKOV, A. Z., Automation
NOVRUZBEKHOV, I. G., Applied Mathematics
RZAYEV, T. G., Automation

Faculty of Business and Management for the Engineering Industry (tel. (12) 439-13-96):

ABBASOV, M. A., History
ALIYEV, A. A., Theory of Economics
ALIYEV, A. H., Philosophy and Political Science
ALIYEV, R. Z., Physical Education and Sport
GULIYEV, R. I., Theory of Economics
HUSEYNOV, S. Y., Philosophy and Political Science
ISMAYILOV, R. A., French
JUMSHUDOV, S. Q., Economy and Management of Transportation
NACAFOV, B. I., History
RAMAZANOV, F. F., Philosophy and Political Science
SAMEDZADE, SH. A., Management, Economics and Organization

Faculty of Electrical Engineering and Energy (tel. (12) 439-12-47):

ABDALOV, S. I., Theoretical Electrical Engineering
GURBANOV, M. A., Physics
GURBANOV, T. B., Automation
LAZIMOV, T. M., Automation
NAZIYEV, Y. M., Thermal Engineering and Heating Mechanisms
SHAKHVERDIYEV, A. H., Thermal Engineering and Heating Mechanisms

Faculty of Machine-Building (tel. (12) 439-13-56):

ABBASOV, T. F., Physics
ABBASOV, V. A., Metal-cutting Machines and Tools
EFENDIYEV, SH. M., Physics
GODJAYEV, E. M., Physics
HUSEYNOV, S. O., Hydraulics
MIRZAJANOV, J. B., Machine-building Technology
MOVLAZADE, V. Z., Machine-building Technology
RASULOV, N. M., Machine-building Technology
RUSTAMOV, M. I., Metal-cutting Machines and Tools
SADYKHOV, A. H., Repair Technology of Machines

Faculty of Machine Sciences (tel. (12) 438-94-70):

ABDULLAYEV, A. H., Lift Transport Machines
BAGIROV, SH. M., Mechanical Theory
HUSEYNOV, H. A., Automated Design Systems in Machine-building
KENGERLI, A. M., Mechanical Theory
KHALILOV, A. M., Mechanical Theory
MAMMEDOV, V. A., Mechanical Theory
MUSTAFAYEV, M. R., Mechanical Theory
QAFAROV, A. M., Metrology and Standardization

Faculty of Metallurgy (tel. (12) 438-34-69):

AMIROV, S. T., Construction Materials Technology, Powder Metallurgy and Corrosion
ASKEROV, K. A., Industrial Ecology and Safety
BABAYEV, F. R., Chemistry
EYVAZOV, B. Y., Construction Materials Technology, Powder Metallurgy and Corrosion

HUSEYNOV, R. G., Construction Materials Technology, Powder Metallurgy and Corrosion
MAMEDOV, Z. G., Metallurgy and Science of Metals
MAMMEDOV, A. A., Industrial Ecology and Safety
MAMMEDOV, A. T., Metallurgy and Science of Metals
NOVRUZOV, H. D., Powder Metallurgy and Corrosion
RUSTAMOV, M. A., Chemistry
SHARIFOV, Z. Z., Powder Metallurgy and Science of Metals
SHUKUROV, R. I., Metallurgy and Science of Metals
ZAMANOVA, E. N., Physics

Faculty of Radio-Engineering and Communications (tel. (12) 438-50-13):

EFENDIYEV, C. A., Television and Radio Systems
HASANOV, A. N., Telecommunications
IMAMVERDIYEV, G. M., Electronic Communications
ISMIBEYLI, E. G., Electrodynamics and High Frequency Instruments
KENGERLI, U. S., General Theoretical Radio-Engineering
MAGARRAMOV, V. A., General Theoretical Radio-Engineering
MAMEDOV, F. H., Telecommunications
MAMEDOV, I. R., General Theoretical Radio-Engineering

Faculty of Transportation (tel. (12) 439-12-51):

AHMEDOV, H. M., Road Transport and Road Safety
BAGIROV, S. M., Automation
EFENDIYEV, V. S., Internal Combustion Engine and Refrigeration Machinery
MAKHMUDOV, R. N., Theoretical Mechanics
MIRSALIMOV, V. M., Automechanics of Materials Resistance
NASIBOV, N. E., Theoretical Mechanics
TAGIZADE, A. G., Road Transport and Road Safety

AZERBAIJAN TECHNOLOGICAL UNIVERSITY

2000 Ganca, 28 May küç. 103
Telephone: (22) 23-56-29
Founded 1970
State control
Faculties of Food Production, Industrial Textile Technology, Light Industry Technology.

BAKU ISLAMIC UNIVERSITY

1000 Baku, Mirza Fatali 7
Telephone: (12) 492-82-23
State control
President: Haj SABIR HASANLI.

BAKU STATE UNIVERSITY

1045 Baku, ul. Z. Khalilova 23,
Telephone: (12) 438-64-58
Fax: (12) 498-33-76
E-mail: ir_bsu@box.az
Internet: www.bsu.az
Founded 1919
Academic year: September to July
Rector: ABEL MAMMADALI MAHARRAMOV
Pro-Rectors: BAKHRAM MEKHRALI ASKEROV, VUSAT AMIR EFENDIYEV, SHAHVALAD BINNAT KHALILOV, IZZAT ASHRAF RUSTAMOV
Librarian: SARA IBRAGIMOVA
Library: see Libraries and Archives
Number of teachers: 1,380
Number of students: 13,000
Publications: *Baki Universiteti* (newspaper, weekly), *Estestvennikh nauk* (quarterly), *Gumanitarnikh nauk* (quarterly), *Sotsialno-politicheskikh nauk* (quarterly), *Vestnik Bakinskogo Universiteta: Fiziko - Matematicheskikh nauk* (quarterly)
depats of Applied Mathematics, Biology, Chemistry, Commerce, Geology and Geography, Hebrew Studies, Int. Law and Int. Relations, Journalism, Law, Library Sciences, Mathematics, Oriental Studies, Philology, Philosophy and Psychology, Physics, Religion, Preparatory Studies.

GANCA STATE UNIVERSITY

2000 Ganca, Pr. Khatai 187
Telephone: (22) 56-33-58
Fax: (22) 56-19-63
E-mail: nabiyev@azeranline.com
Founded 1938
State control
Rector: MUBAZIZ YUSIFOV
Faculties of Chemistry and Biology, Educational Psychology, Engineering Education, Foreign Languages, History, Mathematics and Computer Science, Philology.

KHAZAR UNIVERSITY

1096 Baku, Mehseti 11
Telephone: (12) 421-79-27
Fax: (12) 498-93-79
E-mail: contact@khazar.org
Internet: www.khazar.org
Founded 1991
Private control
Languages of instruction: English, Azeri, Russian
Academic year: September to August
Pres.: Prof. HAMLET ISAXANLI
Vice-Pres.: Prof. MOHAMMAD NOURIYEV
Dir of the Academic Library (vacant)
Library of 60,000 vols, 87 periodicals
Number of teachers: 70
Number of students: 970 (850 undergraduate, 120 postgraduate)
Publications: *Azerbaijani Archaeology* (quarterly), *Journal of Azerbaijani Studies* (quarterly), *Khazar View* (literary and scientific, fortnightly)

DEANS

Faculty of Economics and Management: Prof. MOHAMMAD NOURIYEV
Faculty of Engineering and Applied Sciences: Assoc. Prof. RAFIG AHMADOV
Faculty of Humanities: Prof. AFGAN ABDULLAYEV
Faculty of Law and Social Sciences: Prof. CABIR KHALILOV
Faculty of Medical Sciences: Assoc. Prof. NIGAR BAGHIROVA

LANKARAN STATE UNIVERSITY

4230 Lankaran, Gen. H. Aslanov 50
Telephone: (171) 5-30-88
Fax: (171) 5-27-86
E-mail: lsu@aznet.org
Founded 1991
State control
Rector: MIRZA A. BAGIROV
Faculties of Economics, Humanities, Natural Sciences, Pedagogy.

NAXÇIVAN STATE UNIVERSITY

7001 Naxçıvan, Mardanov Gardashlari 99
Telephone: (12) 94-99-97
Fax: (12) 95-93-29
Internet: www.ndu.edu.az
Founded 1967
State control
Rector: ISSA HABIBBEYLI
Vice-Rector: ZORAB VALIYEV.

Other Higher Educational Institutes

Azerbaijan Agricultural Institute: 2000 Ganca, Azizbekova küç. 262; tel. (22) 2-10-64; depts of Agrochemistry and Soil Science, Agronomy, Fruit and Vegetable Growing, Viticulture; Animal Husbandry, Veterinary Science, Silkworm Breeding, Mechanization, Electrification, Economics and management, Accounting; library: 200,000 vols; Rector N. A. SAFAROV.

Azerbaijan State Academy for Physical Training and Sports: 1072 Baku, Fatali Khan Khoyski; tel. (12) 464-09-05; fax (12) 493-86-17; f. 1930; State control; languages of instruction: Azeri, Russian; Rector AGADJAN ABIYEV; Faculties of Physical Education, Sports.

Azerbaijan State Marine Academy: 1000 Baku, Pr. Azerbaijan 18; tel. (12) 493-09-19; fax (12) 493-86-17; e-mail agma@azerin.com; f. 1881; State control; languages of instruction: Azeri, Russian; Pres. SAMBUR HAMDULLAH; library: 90,000 vols; 55 doctoral staff; 350 students.

Azerbaijan State Oil Academy: 1010 Baku, Pr. Azadlyg 20; tel. (12) 493-45-57; fax (12) 498-29-41; e-mail ihm@adna.baku.az; internet www.adna.baku.az; f. 1920; faculties of Oil and Gas Exploitation, Power Engineering, Oil Mechanical Engineering, Chemical Technology, Automation of Production, Engineering Economics; brs in Sumqayit and Mingaçevir; library: 860,000 vols; 870 teachers; 5,483 students; Rector S. QARAYEV.

Uzeir Hajibeyov Baku Academy of Music: 1014 Baku, Shamsi Badalbeyli 98; tel. (12) 493-22-48; fax (12) 498-13-30; f. 1920; courses: piano, orchestral instruments, folk instruments, singing, choral conducting, composition, musicology; library: 220,000 vols and 25,000 scores; 290 lecturers; 630 students; Rector F. SH. BADALBEYLI.

BAHAMAS

The Higher Education System

The Bahamas is a contributing country to the University of the West Indies (UWI). The UWI Centre for Hotel and Tourism Management is located in Nassau. Other institutions of higher education include the College of the Bahamas (a community college), the Bahamas Hotel Training College and Bahamas Law School (part of the UWI). The Ministry of Education, Science and Technology is responsible for education. To gain admission to degree programmes students must have at least two GCE A-level subjects or equivalent. Available degrees available include Associates, Bachelors and Masters. Associate degrees are taken after GCE O-levels and last for two years. Bachelors degrees last for three years, and Masters degrees last for two years after the Bachelors. Associate degrees are mostly available at the College of the Bahamas.

Learned Societies

GENERAL

Bahamas National Trust: POB N-4105, Nassau; tel. 393-1317; fax 393-4978; e-mail bnt@batelnet.bs; internet www.bahamasnationaltrust.com; f. 1959; preservation of bldgs, wildlife and areas of beauty or historic interest; manages 21 nat. parks and protected areas; 2,500 mems; Exec. Dir CHRISTOPHER HAMILTON (acting); publ. *Trust Notes* (6 a year).

HISTORY, GEOGRAPHY AND ARCHAEOLOGY

Bahamas Historical Society: POB SS-6833, Nassau-New Providence; tel. 322-4231; e-mail info@bahamashistoricalsociety.com; internet www.bahamashistoricalsociety.com; f. 1959; 400 mems; collection and preservation of material relating to the history of the Bahamas; Pres. STEPHEN B. ARANHA; Corresp. Sec. JOAN CLARKE; publ. *Journal* (annual).

LANGUAGE AND LITERATURE

Alliance Française: Suite 60, Grosvenor Close, Shirley St, POB CB-13002, Nassau-New Providence; tel. 356-0961; fax 326-5662; e-mail afbahamas@hotmail.com; offers courses and examinations in French language and culture and promotes cultural exchange with France.

Libraries and Archives

Freeport

Sir Charles Hayward Public Lending Library: POB F-40040, Freeport, Grand Bahama; f. 1966; 40,000 vols; Librarian ELAINE B. TALMA.

Nassau

College of the Bahamas–Libraries and Instructional Media Services: POB N-4912, Nassau; tel. 302-4552; fax 326-7803; e-mail library@cob.edu.bs; f. 1974; 75,000 vols; spec. collns incl. Bahamiana, Caribbean dissertations; document delivery and inter-library loans; deposit collns of the UN, WHO and Pan-American Health Organization; Dir WILLAMAE M. JOHNSON; publ. *Library Informer*.

Nassau Public Library: POB N-3210, Nassau; f. 1837; 80,000 vols; Dir (vacant).

Public Records Office: Dept of Archives, POB SS-6341, Nassau; tel. 393-2175; fax 393-2855; e-mail archives@bahamas.net.bs; internet www.bahamas.net.bs/archives; f. 1971; nat. archival depository; 2,689 linear ft of records; Dir Dr GAIL SAUNDERS; publ. *Preservum* (annual).

Museum

Nassau

Bahamia Museum: POB N-1510, Nassau.

Colleges

University of the West Indies (Bahamas Office): POB N-1184, Nassau; tel. 323-6593; fax 328-0622; e-mail matwilliam@hotmail.com; f. 1965; Representative MATTHEW WILLIAM.

College of the Bahamas: Thompson Blvd, POB N-4912, Nassau; tel. 323-8550; fax 326-7834; internet www.cob.edu.bs; f. 1974; 4-year college; assoc. degrees in arts, natural and social sciences, business, technology, nursing, teaching; Bachelors degrees in banking and finance, management, accounting, nursing, education; continuing education; 160 teachers; 3,463 students; library: 68,000 vols; Pres. Dr LEON HIGGS; publs *College Forum* (2 a year), *COBLA Journal* (2 a year), *At Random* (annual).

BAHRAIN

The Higher Education System

The University of Bahrain was founded in 1986 by Amiri decree as a merger of two pre-existing institutions of higher education. The other main institutions of higher education are the College of Health Sciences, founded in 1976, the Arabian Gulf University, founded in 1980 as a joint venture between six (now seven) Arab Governments and the Gulf College of Hospitality and Tourism.

Admission to higher education is based on a test score of 70% or higher in the Tawjihiya examinations. The main undergraduate qualifications are the Associate and Bachelors degrees, whilst the main postgraduate qualifications are the Masters degree, Doctorate, and Postgraduate Diploma. The undergraduate degrees are based on the US credits system: Associate degrees last for two years and require 60–70 credits, and Bachelors degrees are four years in length and require 130–140 credits. The Masters degree and Postgraduate Diploma are based on the British Masters degree, and last for two to four years, with an equal division between taught classes and research. Finally, the Doctorate, usually PhD, requires three to five years of full-time study and research. All Bahraini students studying abroad are required to have their degrees submitted for recognition by the Commission for the Evaluation of Academic Degrees.

Non-university level education is offered at the University of Bahrain in the form of two-year diploma courses in a number subjects. The admissions criteria are the same as those for a full degree course. The College of Health Sciences offers Certificates, Associate degrees, Post-basic diplomas and Bachelors degrees in mostly medical-related subjects. Vocational and technical training is also offered at the Bahrain Training Institute, the Hotel and Catering Training Centre and the Vocational and Training Centre (the latter being run by the Ministry for Labour and Social Affairs).

Learned Societies

ECONOMICS, LAW AND POLITICS

Bahrain Bar Society: POB 5025, Manama; tel. 17720566; fax 17721219; f. 1977; 65 mems; Pres. Hassan Ali Radhi; publ. *Al Muhami*.

FINE AND PERFORMING ARTS

Bahrain Arts Society: POB 26264, Manama; tel. 17590551; fax 17594211; e-mail tbartss@batelco.com.bh; internet www.bahartsociety.org.bh/; f. 1983; promotes fine arts of Bahrain nationally and internationally; includes a school of fine arts and art gallery, and the official photography club; 184 mems; library: small library; Pres. Ali Al-Mahmeed.

Bahrain Contemporary Art Association: POB 26232, Manama; tel. 17728046; fax 17723341; e-mail bcaa7@hotmail.com; f. 1970; 60 mems; library of 250 vols; Pres. Rashid al-Orafi; Dir Yousef al-Mahmoud; publs magazine, *Newsletter* (quarterly).

HISTORY, GEOGRAPHY AND ARCHAEOLOGY

Bahrain Historical and Archaeological Society: POB 5087, Manama; tel. 17727895; f. 1953; 143 mems; library: reference library; Pres. Dr Essa Amin; Hon. Sec. Dr Khalid Khalifa al-Khalifa; publ. *Dilmun* (2 a year).

LANGUAGE AND LITERATURE

Alliance Française: POB 840, Manama; tel. 17683295; fax 17781137; e-mail allfranc@batelco.com.bh; internet www.allliancefrancaise-bahrein.com; offers courses and exams in French language and culture and promotes cultural exchange with France.

Bahrain Writers and Literature Association: POB 1010, Manama; tel. and fax 17274866; f. 1969; 40 mems; library of 700 vols; Pres. Ali al-Shargawi; Sec. Fareed Ramadan.

British Council: AMA Centre, 146, Shaikh Salman Highway, Manama 356, POB 452; tel. 17261555; fax 17241272; e-mail bc.enquiries@britishcouncil.org.bh; internet www2.britishcouncil.org/bahrain.htm; office opened 1959; attached teaching centre; offers courses and exams in English language and British culture and promotes cultural exchange with the UK; library of 9,000 vols; Dir Amanda Burrell.

MEDICINE

Bahrain Medical Society: POB 26136, Adliya; tel. 17827818; fax 17827814; f. 1972; 350 mems; library of 300 vols; Pres. Dr Ali Mohd Matar; Gen. Sec. Dr Faisal A. Alnasir; publ. *Journal* (quarterly).

RELIGION, SOCIOLOGY AND ANTHROPOLOGY

Bahrain Society of Sociologists: POB 26488, Manama; tel. 17727483; f. 1979; 65 mems; library of 423 vols; Pres. Dr Ahmed al-Sharyan; Sec.-Gen. Ebrahim Alalawi.

Islamic Association: POB 22484, Manama; tel. 17671788; fax 17676718; f. 1979; teaches the Qur'an, Fiqh, Hadith, Sunnah; distributes zakat and donations; 200 mems; Pres. Abdulrahman Ebrahim Abdulsalam.

TECHNOLOGY

Bahrain Information Technology Society: POB 26089, Manama; tel. 17741770; fax 17741772; e-mail bits@batelco.com.bh; internet www.bits.org.bh/; f. 1981; promotes information technology in the kingdom; 260 mems; Pres. Mohammed Ahmed al-Amer; publ. *BITS Update* (monthly).

Bahrain Society of Engineers: POB 835, Manama; tel. 17727100; fax 17729819; e-mail mohandis@batelco.com.bh; internet www.mohandis.org; f. 1972; 900 mems; Pres. Mohamed K. Alsayed; Admin Man. Jawad Jaffar al-Jabal; publ. *Al-Mohandis* (quarterly).

Research Institute

NATURAL SCIENCES

General

Bahrain Centre for Studies and Research: POB 496, Manama; tel. 17754757; fax 17754678; e-mail bcsr@batelco.com.bh; internet www.bcsr.gov.bh; f. 1981; scientific study and research ineconomics, politics and strategy, marketing and consumer behaviour, social, educational and tourism studies, international and intercivilization studies; library of 6,000 vols, 40 periodicals; Sec.-Gen. Dr Hasan Mahmood al-Bastaki; publs *Arab Magazine for Food and Nutrition* (2 a year), *Journal of Strategic Research* (irregular).

Libraries and Archives

Isa Town

University of Bahrain Libraries and Information Services: POB 32038, Isa Town; tel. 17838808; fax 17449838; e-mail library@admin.uob.bh; internet http://libwebserver.uob.edu.bh/assets/; f. 1986; 150,000 vols, 700 periodicals; Dir Hedi Talbi.

Manama

Ahmed Al-Farsi Library (College of Health Sciences): POB 12, Manama; tel. 17255555 ext. 5202; fax 17242485; e-mail a.khatem@health.gov.bh; internet www.chs.edu.bh/library; f. 1976; serves Min. of Health staff, also public and reference service; 29,000 vols, 545 periodicals, 375 audiovisual items; Librarian Abbas Al-Khatem.

Educational Documentation Library: POB 43, Manama; tel. 17710599; fax 17710376; e-mail edudoc@batelco.com.bh; internet www.education.gov.bh/english/edu-library/index.asp; f. 1976; part of Min. of Education; 22,000 vols, 197 periodicals, 300 files of documents; Chief Officer Faiqa Saeed al-Saleh; publs *Acquisitions List* (monthly), *Bibliographical Lists* (annually), *Educational Index of Arabic Periodicals*, *Educational Index of Foreign Periodicals*, *Educational Indicative Abstracts* (3 a year), *Educational Information Abstracts* (3 a year), *Educational Legislation Index*, *Educational Selective Articles* (every 2 months).

Historical Documents Centre: POB 28882, Manama; tel. 17664454; fax 17651050; f. 1978; attached to the Crown Prince's Court; maintains historical documents and MSS on the history of Bahrain and the Gulf; 4,000 vols; Pres. Shaikh Abdullah bin Khalid al-Khalifa; Dir Dr

ALI ABA-HUSSAIN; publ. *Al-Watheeka* (2 a year).

Manama Central Library: c/o Ministry of Education, POB 43, Manama; tel. 17231105; fax 17274036; e-mail libman@batelco.com.bh; f. 1946; 171,622 vols, 734 periodicals, 1,475 cassettes; Dir of Public Libraries MANSOOR MOHAMED SARHAN; publ. *Bahrain National Bibliography* (every 4 years).

Museum

Manama

Bahrain National Museum: POB 2199, Manama; tel. 17292977; fax 17297871; e-mail musbah@batelco.com.bh; internet www.bnmuseum.com; f. 1970; archaeology, ethnography, natural history, art; Dir ABDUL RAHMAN MUSAMAH.

Universities

ARABIAN GULF UNIVERSITY

POB 26671, Manama
Telephone: 17239999
Fax: 17272555
Internet: www.agu.edu.bh

Founded 1980 by the seven Gulf States
Languages of instruction: Arabic, English
Academic year: September to June

President: Dr RAFIA O. GHUBASH
Director of Administration and Financial Affairs (vacant)
Director of Student Affairs: Dr AMENA AL-JAAR
Registrar: Dr WAHIB AL-KHAJAH
Librarian: SUAD AL-KHALIFA

Number of teachers: 86
Number of students: 368

Publications: *AGU Annual Catalogue*, *Journal of Scientific Research* (3 a year)

DEANS

College of Applied Sciences: (vacant)
College of Education: Prof. FATHI ABD-EL RAHIM (acting)
College of Medicine: Prof. HASAM HAMDY
College of Postgraduate Studies: Prof. MAHMED JABER AL-ANSARI

PROFESSORS

AL-AAQIB, AR-R., Water Engineering, Energy
AL-ABADIN, M. Z., Physiology
AL-ANSARI, M. J.
BANDARANAYAKE, R. C.
BOTTA, G.
AD-DIN, M. N., Microbiology
AKBAR, M. M.
AL-DIN, N. A.
AL-KHOLY, U.
AL-QAISI, K. A., Botany, Algae
ASH-SHAZALI, H., Paediatrics
FULEIHAN, F., Internal Medicine
GRANGULY, P. K.
GRANT, N. I.
GREALLY, J.
HAMDY, H.
ISSA, A. A.
KHADER, M. H. A., Organic Chemistry
MATHUR, V., Pharmacology
MATHUR, V. S.
NASSER, A. I., Mechanical Engineering
NAYAR, U.
PRASAD, K.
RAKHA, I., General Surgery, Orthopaedics
RAHIM, F. AS-A. A., Education and Psychology
SACHDEVA, U.
SATIR, A. A.
SKERMAN, J. H.

UNIVERSITY OF BAHRAIN

POB 32038, Isa Town
Telephone: 17682748
Fax: 17681465
Internet: www.uob.bh

Founded 1986 by merger of University College of Arts, Science and Education, and Gulf Polytechnic
Autonomous control
Language of instruction: Arabic
Academic year: October to August

Chairman of Board of Trustees: THE MINISTER OF EDUCATION
President: Dr IBRAHIM AL-HASHEMI
Vice-President for Academic Programmes and Research: Dr NIZAR AL-BAHARNA
Vice-President for Administration and Finance: Dr SAMIR FAKHRO
Vice-President for Planning and Community Service: Dr GEORGE NAJJAR
Registrar: Dr ISA AL-KHAYAT
Director of Library and Information Services: WARWICK PRICE

Library: see Libraries and Archives
Number of teachers: 320
Number of students: 6,760

DEANS

College of Arts: Dr HILAL AL-SHAIJI
College of Business: Dr GEORGE NAJJAR (acting)
College of Education: Dr ABBAS ADEBI
College of Engineering: Dr HANNA MAKHLOUF
College of Information Technology: Dr YOSIF AL-BASTAKI
College of Science: Dr WAHEEB AL-NASER

HEADS OF DEPARTMENTS

College of Arts:
- Arabic and Islamic Studies: Dr IBRAHIM GHOLOOM
- Foreign Languages and Literature: Dr A. NEWBURY
- Information, Tourism and Arts: Dr FAWWAZ TUQAN
- Social Studies: Dr RAJAB ABDUL-HALEEM

College of Business:
- Accounting: Dr JAWAHER AL-MADHAKI
- Continuing Management Education: Dr PARIS ANDREOU
- Economics and Finance: Dr NADHEM AL-SALEH
- Management and Marketing: Dr FAROUK A. SALEH

College of Education:
- Continuing Education: Dr KHALIL SHOBAR
- Curricula and Teaching Methods: Dr HUSSEIN AL-SADEH
- Education Technology: Dr MOHSIN AL-JAMLAN
- Physical Education: Dr MOHAMMED AL-MOTAWA
- Psychology: Dr MUSTAFA HEJAZI

College of Engineering:
- Chemical Engineering: Dr ABDERRAHIM ABBAS
- Civil and Architectural Engineering: Dr SAMI ALI HASSAN QAMBER
- Electrical Engineering and Computer Science: Dr ABDUL IMAM AL-SAMMAK
- Mechanical Engineering: Dr ABDUL JALIL ABDULLA YOUSIF SINGACE
- Continuing Engineering Education: Dr BASHAR HABIB AHMADI

College of Information Technology:
- Computer Engineering: Dr SALAH AL-MAJDOUB
- Computer Engineering: Dr NEDZAD MEHIC

College of Science:
- Biology: Dr E. GHANEM
- Chemistry: Dr MOHAMMAD AL-ARAB
- Mathematics: Dr ABDUL SAMIE' MOHAMMAD ABU SAFIYA
- Physics: Dr MOHAMMED KAYSAROUN MERZAA

Colleges

College of Health Sciences: POB 12, Ministry of Health, Bahrain; tel. 17279664; fax 17251360; e-mail chs@health.gov.bh; internet www.chs.edu.bh; f. 1976; library: see entry for Ahmed Al-Farsi Library; 111 teachers; Dean BATOOL AL-MUHANDIS; Head of Registration and Student Affairs AMAL Z. AKLEH; Librarian ABBAS KHATEM (Ahmed Al-Farsi Library))

CHAIRPERSONS OF DIVISIONS

Allied Health: HASSAN AL-JAROODI
Educational Development Centre: ELIZABETH POPOVICH
English: MOHAMMAD YOUSIF ABDUMAJEED
Integrated Science: Dr MUNA BUHAZZA
Nursing: Dr MOUZA SUWAILEH

Gulf College of Hospitality and Tourism: POB 22088, Muharraq; tel. 17320191; fax 17332547; e-mail mancat5@batelco.com.bh; internet www.gulf-college.com; f. 1976; higher nat. diploma and degree courses in hospitality management and travel and tourism; library: 10,000 vols; Dean TONY SPICER; Dir DAVID PATTERSON.

BANGLADESH

The Higher Education System

In 2005 there were 26 public and 53 private higher education institutions recognized by the University Grants Commission (UGC). Both public and private universities are governed by the UGC, founded by an Act of Parliament in 1973; private universities are also subject to the Private Universities Act (1992). The Government accounts for 95% of university funding, with the rest coming from students' tuition fees and other compulsory fees. There are four categories of university: General, Special, Open, and Affiliating. The President and/or Prime Minister of Bangladesh acts as the Chancellor of a university and appoints the Vice-Chancellors and the academic and executive heads of the universities. The Syndicate is the university's executive body. Its decisions are ratified by the Senate, a board that also approves the accounts. The Academic Council of a university consists of professors and other teaching representatives. Deans of Faculty are either elected by the faculty or appointed by the Academic Council, depending on the institution in question. Most public universities are modelled on the University of London (United Kingdom), consisting of a central department with affiliated colleges and institutions.

Admission is based on completion of 12 years' general education, receipt of the Higher Secondary Certificate, or equivalent, and success in entrance examinations. The main university degrees are the Bachelors, Masters and Doctor of Philosophy. A Bachelors from affiliated colleges of public universities are known as 'Pass' degrees and are three years in length; Bachelors degrees from public universities are known as 'Honours' degrees and last four years. Most private universities have adopted the US-style 'major' and 'minor' subject system with a Grade Point Average grading system. A Masters degree requires two years of further study after a 'Pass' degree, and one year after an 'Honours' degree. The Doctorate requires three years of study and research.

There is a formal system of Islamic education, consisting of a two-year Fazil, roughly equivalent to the Bachelors, and the two-year Kamil, equivalent to the Masters. Students are examined in fields such as Arabic, Hadith, and Tafsir (Koranic interpretation). Technical and vocational education is overseen by the Bangladesh Technical Education Board (BTEB). There are three levels of technician award: SSC, HSC and Diploma. The BTEB also administers a four-year diploma.

There is no formal system of accreditation and quality assurance, and institutions are not legally obliged to seek quality assurance. However, there are legislative plans to establish an Accreditation Council.

Learned Societies

GENERAL

Society of Arts, Literature and Welfare: Society Park, K. C. Dey Rd, Chittagong; f. 1942; 500 mems; Gen. Sec. NESAR AHMED CHOWDHURY.

UNESCO Office Dhaka: GPO Box 57, Dhaka 1207; located at: IDB Bhaban, 16th Floor, E/8-A Rokeya Sharani, Sher-e-Bangla Nagar, Dhaka 1207; tel. (2) 9123469; fax (2) 9123468; e-mail dhaka@unesco.org; Dir (vacant).

BIBLIOGRAPHY, LIBRARY SCIENCE AND MUSEOLOGY

Bangladesh Association of Librarians, Information Scientists and Documentalists: CDL, House 39, Rd 14/A, Dhanmandi R/A, Dhaka 1209; e-mail mmr@northsouth.edu; internet www.balid.org; f. 1986; runs courses in library and information sciences; Chair. Dr M. MOSTAFIZUR RAHMAN; Sec.-Gen. Dr M. HANIF UDDIN.

ECONOMICS, LAW AND POLITICS

Bangladesh Bureau of Statistics: E-27/A, Agargaon, Sher-e-banglanagar, Dhaka 1207; tel. (2) 9118045; fax (2) 9111064; e-mail ndbp@bangla.net; internet www.bbsgov.org; f. 1971; collection, analysis and publication of statistics covering all sectors of society and the economy; Dir-Gen. WALIUL ISLAM; publs *Child Nutrition Survey* (annually), *Foreign Trade Statistics* (annually), *Labour Force Survey* (annually), *Statistical Bulletin* (monthly), *Statistical Pocket Book* (annually), *Statistical Yearbook* (annually), *Yearbook of Agricultural Statistics* (annually).

Bangladesh Economic Association: c/o Department of Economics, 4/C Eskaton Garden Rd, Dhaka; tel. and fax (2) 9345996; e-mail becoa@bdlink.com; f. 1958; Pres. Dr QAZI KHOLIQUZZAMAN AHMAD; Sec.-Gen. Dr ABUL BARKAT.

EDUCATION

Association of Universities of Bangladesh: House 47, Rd 10/A Dhanmondli R/A, Dhaka 1209; tel. and fax (2) 8126101; e-mail vc-iu@kushtia.com; co-ordinates activities of all 17 public universities in Bangladesh, and liaises with the government and the University Grants Commission (UGC) in administrative and financial matters; Chair. MUHAMMAD MUSTAFIZUR RAHMAN; Exec. Sec. S. M. SAIFUDDIN.

LANGUAGE AND LITERATURE

Alliance Française: Rd 108, House 18, Gulshan, Dacca 1212; tel. (2) 8813811; fax (2) 8823612; e-mail french@gononet.net; offers courses and exams in French language and culture and promotes cultural exchange with France; attached teaching centre in Chittagong.

Bangla Academy: Burdwan House, Dhaka 2; f. 1972; promotes culture and development of the Bengali language and literature; produces dictionaries, translates scientific and reference works into Bangla; library of 102,000 vols; Dir-Gen. Dr ASHRAF H. SIDDIQI; Sec. ABDUS SATTAR KHAN; publs *Dhan Shaliker Desh* (juvenile, monthly), *Journal* (2 a year, in English), *Research Journal*, *Science Journal* (quarterly, in Bangla), *Uttaradhikar* (literary, monthly).

British Council: 5 Fuller Rd, POB 161 Dhaka 1000; tel. (2) 8618905; fax (2) 8613375; e-mail dhaka.enquiries@bd.britishcouncil.org; internet www.britishcouncil.org/bangladesh; teaching centre; offers courses and exams in English language and British culture and promotes cultural exchange with the UK; attached teaching centre in Chittagong; Dir Dr JUNE ROLLINSON.

Attached Centre:

Teaching Centre: 754b Satmasjid Rd, Dhanmondi, Dhaka 1205; tel. (2) 9116171; fax (2) 8116554; e-mail dhaka.teachingcentre@bd.britishcouncil.org; Man MARK BARTHOLOMEW.

Goethe-Institut: House 10, Rd 9 (new), Dhanmondi R/A, Dhaka 1205; tel. (2) 9126525; fax (2) 8110712; e-mail verw@dhaka.goethe.org; internet www.goethe.de/su/dha/enindex.htm; offers courses and exams in German language and culture and promotes cultural exchange with Germany; library of 4,000 vols, 20 periodicals; Dir Dr MARCUS LITZ.

MEDICINE

Bangladesh Medical Association: BMA House, 15/2 Topkhana Rd, Dhaka 2; f. 1971; 10,000 mems; library of 8,000 vols; Pres. Dr M. A. MAJED; Sec.-Gen. Dr GAZI ABDUL HOQUE; publ. *Bangladesh Medical Journal* (quarterly).

NATURAL SCIENCES

General

Bangladesh Academy of Sciences: 3/8 Asad Ave, Mohammadpur, Dhaka 1207; tel. (2) 9110425; e-mail bas@bdmail.net; f. 1973; 49 mems (43 fellows, 6 foreign fellows); Pres. Prof. A. K. M. SIDDIQ; Sec. Prof. MAHMUD-UL AMEEN; publs *Journal* (2 a year), *Year Book*.

Biological Sciences

Zoological Society of Bangladesh: c/o Dept of Zoology, University of Dhaka, Dhaka 1000; tel. (2) 7168321; fax (2) 8615583; e-mail mnnaser@udhaka.net; f. 1972; 1,500 mems; Pres. Prof. MOHAMED ABUL BASHAR; Gen. Sec. Prof. MOHAMED MOKSED ALI HOWLADER; publs *Bangladesh Journal of Zoology* (2 a year), *Bulletin* (irregular), *Proceedings of National Conference* (every 2 years).

RELIGION, SOCIOLOGY AND ANTHROPOLOGY

Asiatic Society of Bangladesh: 5 Old Secretariat Rd (Nimtali), Ramna, Dhaka 1000; tel. (2) 9667586; e-mail asb@bangla.net; f. 1952; study of Man and Nature of Asia; 1,788 mems; library of 10,000 vols, 500 Urdu and Persian MSS; Pres. Prof. ABDUL MOWIAN CHOWDHURY; Gen. Sec. Prof. SYED RASHIDUL HASAM; publs *Journal of the Asiatic Society of Bangladesh – Humanities* (2 a year), *Journal of the Asiatic Society of Bangladesh – Science* (2 a year).

TECHNOLOGY

Institution of Engineers, Bangladesh: Ramna, Dhaka; f. 1948; 6,000 mems; library of 4,050 vols; Pres. Eng. S. M. AL-HUSAINY; Hon. Gen. Sec. Eng. MD ABUL QUASSEM; publs *Engineering News* (monthly), *Journal* (quarterly).

Research Institutes

GENERAL

Bangladesh Council of Scientific and Industrial Research: Dr Qudrat-I-Khuda Rd, Dhanmondi, Dhaka 1205; tel. (2) 8620106; fax (2) 8613022; e-mail bcsir@bangla.net; internet www.bcsir.org; f. 1973; library of 15,000 vols, 100 periodicals; Chair. Prof. Dr MD. AMJAD HOSSAIN; publs *Bangladesh Journal of Scientific and Industrial Research*, *Bigganer Joyjattra*, *News Letter*, *Purogami Bijnan*, *Science, Technology & Development*, *Scientific & Technological Contributions of BCSIR*.

Attached research institutes:

BCSIR Laboratory, Chittagong: Chittagong; four divisions: chemistry, botany, pharmacology, microbiology; Dir Dr M. MANZUR-I-KHUDA.

BCSIR Laboratory, Dhaka: Dhaka; seven divisions: natural products; glass and ceramics; fibres and polymers; leather technology; physical instrumentation; analytical; industrial physics; Dir Dr MIR AMJAD ALI.

BCSIR Laboratory, Rajshahi: Rajshahi; four divisions: lac research; fats and oils; fibres; fruit processing and preservation; Dir Dr M. A. KHALEQUE.

Institute of Food Science and Technology, Dhaka: Dhaka; seven divisions: technology of foodgrains; animal food products; plant food products; microbiology; food science and quality control; biochemistry and applied nutrition; industrial development; Dir Dr S. F. RUBBI.

Institute of Fuel Research and Development, Dhaka: Dhaka; seven divisions: solar energy; biomass and hydrocarbon research; combustion, application and pilot plant; Dir Dr M. EUSUF.

AGRICULTURE, FISHERIES AND VETERINARY SCIENCE

Animal Husbandry Research Institute: Comilla; f. 1947; Prin. Scientific Officer SALIL KUMAR DHAR.

Bangladesh Jute Research Institute: Manik Miah Ave, Dhaka 1207; f. 1951; Dir-Gen. Dr MD A. ISLAM.

BIBLIOGRAPHY, LIBRARY SCIENCE AND MUSEOLOGY

Varendra Research Museum: Rajshahi; f. 1910; under control of University of Rajshahi; museum-based research instn; history, archaeology, anthropology, literature, art; library of 14,000 vols; museum colln; Dir Dr M. SAIFUDDIN CHOWDHURY; publ. *Journal* (annually).

ECONOMICS, LAW AND POLITICS

Bangladesh Institute of Development Studies: E-17 Agargaon, Sher-e-Bangla Nagar, Dhaka 1207; tel. (2) 9125004; fax (2) 8113023; internet www.bids-bd.org; f. 1957; divisions: agriculture and rural development, general economic, human resources, industries and physical infrastructures, population studies; 81 mems; library: see Libraries and Archives; Dir-Gen. Dr QUAZI SHAHABUDDIN; publs *Bangladesh Development Studies* (quarterly), *Bangladesh Unnayan Samikhha* (annually), *Research Monograph Series*, *Research Report Series*.

MEDICINE

Centre for Medical Education (CME): 2nd Fl., IPH Building, Mohakhali, Dhaka 1212; e-mail cmed-dk@bangla.net; f. 1983; conducts research related to health care services, health manpower development and the education of health professionals; library of 2,000 vols, 15,000 journals; Dir Prof. Dr FATIMA PARVEEN CHOWDHURY.

ICDDR,B: Centre for Health and Population Research: GPO Box 128, Dhaka 1000; located at: Mohakhali, Dhaka 1212; tel. (2) 8871751; fax (2) 8823116; e-mail info@icddrb.org; internet www.icddrb.org; f. 1960; funded by 50 countries and NGOs; library of 40,611 vols, 14,600 documents; Exec. Dir Prof. DAVID A. SACK; publs *Annual Report*, *Glimpse* (newsletter, 4 a year), *Health and Science Bulletin* (4 a year), *Journal of Health, Population and Nutrition* (4 a year), *Shasthya Sanglap* (newsletter in Bangla, 3 a year), *SUZY Newsletter* (2 a year).

Institute of Epidemiology, Disease Control and Research (IEDCR): Mohakhali, Dhaka 1212; tel. and fax (2) 8821237; e-mail iedcrdir@hotmail.com; internet www.iedcr.org; f. 1976; epidemiology, medical social science, biostatistics, virology, parasitology, microbiology, zoonosis, medical entomology and vector bionomics; library of 4,000 vols; Dir Prof. MAHMUDUR RAHMAN.

NATURAL SCIENCES

Physical Sciences

Geological Survey of Bangladesh: 153 Pioneer Rd, Segun bagicha, Dhaka 1000; tel. (2) 9349502; fax (2) 9339309; e-mail gsb@dhaka.agni.com; f. 1972; govt org. under Ministry of Energy and Mineral Resources; library of 7,000 vols, 97 journals; Dir-Gen. M. NAZRUL ISLAM; publ. *Records* (irregular).

TECHNOLOGY

Bangladesh Atomic Energy Commission: 4 Kazi Nazrul Islam Ave, POB 158, Dhaka 1000; fax (2) 8613051; e-mail baec@agni.com; f. 1973; library of 25,375 vols, 192 periodicals; Chair. Dr M. A. MANNAN; publ. *Nuclear Science & Applications* (Series A: Biological Sciences, Series B: Physical Sciences).

Attached institutes include:

Atomic Energy Centre: POB 164, Ramna, Dhaka 2; basic and applied research in physics, electronics and chemistry; library of 10,728 vols, 100 periodicals..

Atomic Energy Research Establishment: Ganak Bari, Savar, POB 3787, Dhaka; consists of Institute of Nuclear Science and Technology, Institute of Computer Sciences, Institute of Electronics and Materials Science, Institute of Food and Radiation Biology, Institute of Nuclear Medicine.

Libraries and Archives

Chittagong

Divisional Government Public Library: POB 771, K. C. Dey Rd, Chittagong; tel. (31) 611578; f. 1963; 62,910 vols, 121 periodicals; Senior Librarian A. D. M. ALI AHAMMED.

Dhaka

Bangladesh Central Public Library: 3 Liaquat Ave, Dhaka 1000; tel. (2) 8500819; f. 1958; 1,014,870 vols, 2,300 periodicals; spec. colln: depository for UNESCO publs; Dir A. F. M. BADIUR RAHMAN.

Bangladesh Institute of Development Studies Library: E-17, Agargaon, Sher-e-Bangla Nagar, Dhaka 1207; tel. (2) 9125004; fax (2) 8113023; e-mail sparveen@sdnbd.org; internet www.bids-bd.org; f. 1957; 130,000 vols, 600 peridocals; Chief Librarian SHAHANA PARVEEN (acting).

Bangladesh National Scientific and Technical Documentation Centre (BANSDOC): Mirpur Rd, Dhanmondi, Dhaka 1205; tel. (2) 8610224; fax (2) 8613900; e-mail bansdoc@bansdoc.gov.bd; f. 1963; 19,000 vols, 114 national periodical, 350 foreign periodicals; Dir SUNIL KANTI BOSE; publs *Bangladesh Science and Technology Abstracts* (annually), *Current Scientific and Technological Research Projects of Bangladesh* (every 2 years), *National Catalogue of Scientific and Technological Periodicals of Bangladesh* (every 2 years), *Report of the Survey of Research and Development Activities in Bangladesh* (every 2 years).

Directorate of Archives and Libraries: National Library Building, Sher-e-Bangla Nagar (Agargaon), Dhaka 1207; tel. (2) 9129992; fax (2) 9118704; e-mail nab@accesstel.net; f. 1971; co-ordinating centre for archives and libraries at nat. level; 500,000 vols, 5,00,000 105 Bengali periodicals, 10 foreign periodicals, 20 maps, 3,000 microfilms, 60 rolls of microfiche, 235 issues of National Bibliography (1972–1991); Dir Dr SHARIF UDDIN AHMED.

Institutions under the control of the Directorate:

National Archives of Bangladesh: National Library Building, Sher-e-Bangla Nagar, Agargaon, Dhaka 1207; f. 1973; 225,000 vols of records and documents, 3,500 books, 58 rolls of microfilm, 10,000 press clippings; Dir Dr SHARIF UDDIN AHMED; publs *Annual Reports 1973–84*, *Bulletin of Dissertations and Theses by Bangladeshi Scholars 1947–73*, *SWARBICA Journal Vol III*, etc.

National Library of Bangladesh: Sher-e-Bangla Nagar Agargaon, Dhaka 1207; f. 1968; 1,000,000 books, 2,000 journals; Dir Dr SHARIF UDDIN AHMED; publs *Articles Index*, *Bangladesh National Bibliography*.

University of Dhaka Library: Ramna, Dhaka 1000; tel. (2) 9661900; fax (2) 8615583; e-mail duregstr@bangla.net; f. 1921; 5,500,000 vols, 30,000 rare manuscripts and a large number of tracts (booklets, leaflets, pamphlets, and puthis) in microfilm format; rare books and reports, puthis, Bengali Tracts and private collection of Buchanan on Bengal have been acquired from the British Museum, UK; Librarian Dr MD. SERAJUL ISLAM.

Rajshahi

Rajshahi University Library: Rajshahi; tel. (721) 750666; fax (721) 750064; e-mail rajucc@citechno.net; f. 1953; 250,000 vols, 2,000 journals; Administrator Prof. OBAIDUR RAHMAN PRAMANIK.

Museums and Art Galleries

Dhaka

Ahsan Manzil Museum: Nawab Ahsanulla Rd, Shadarghat, Dhaka; tel. (2) 282790; fmr home of the Nawab of Dhaka; 23 galleries displaying portraits, furniture and other objects used by the Nawab.

Balda Museum: Dhaka; f. 1927; art, archaeology; Superintendent MUHAMMAD HANNAN.

Bangabandhu Memorial Museum: House 10 Rd 32, Dhanmondi Residential Area, Dhaka; tel. (2) 8110046; residence of the father of the nation, Bangabandhu Sheikh Mujibur Rahman (1920–75); colln of personal effects and photographs of his lifetime.

Bangladesh National Museum: POB 355, Shahbag, Dhaka 1000; tel. (2) 8619396; fax (2) 8615585; e-mail dgmuseum@bdonline.com; internet www.bangladeshmuseum.org; f. 1913; history and classical art, ethnography and decorative art, natural history, contemporary art and world civilization; library of 34,388 vols; Dir-Gen. Dr IFTIKHAR-UL-AWWAL; publ. *Bangladesh Jadughar Samachar* (4 a year).

Dhaka Zoo: Mirpur-1, Dhaka; tel. (2) 9002954; f. 1964; attached to Min. of Fisheries and Livestock; colln of more than 2,000 native and non-native animals and wildlife; Curator KAZI FAZLUL HAQUE.

Mukti Juddha Museum: 5 Segun Bagicha, Dhaka; tel. (2) 9559091; fax (2) 9559092; f. 1996; concerns Bangladesh's Liberation War (1971); ancient Bengali artefacts, and items from the British Raj period and the Pakistani period, photographs of the war and items used by the freedom fighters during the period; Man. Dir AKKU CHOWDHURY.

National Art Gallery: Shilpakala Academy, Segun Bagicha, Dhaka 1000; tel. (2) 9562801; f. 1965; colln of folk art and paintings by Bangladeshi artists.

National Botanical Garden: Mirpur-1, Dhaka; tel. (2) 8018092; f. 1961; attached to Min. of Environment and Forests; colln of 50,000 plants, herbs, shrubs and trees on a 200-acre site.

National Science and Technology Museum: Agargaon, Sher-e-Bangla Nagar, Dhaka 1207; tel. (2) 9112084; fax (2) 9114831; f. 1965 to popularize science and technology; Dir NURUL HAQ.

Universities

AHSANULLAH UNIVERSITY OF SCIENCE AND TECHNOLOGY

20 West Testuri Bazar Rd, Dhaka 1215
Telephone: (2) 9130613
Fax: (2) 8113010
E-mail: regr@aust.agni.com
Internet: www.aust.edu
Private control, sponsored by Dhaka Ahsania Mission
Faculties of Engineering and Architecture.

AMERICAN INTERNATIONAL UNIVERSITY BANGLADESH

House 83 Rd 4, Kamal Ataturk Ave, Banani, Dhaka 1213
Telephone: (2) 9885907
Fax: (2) 881233
E-mail: info@aiub.edu
Internet: www.aiub.edu

Founded 1994
Private control
Academic year: January to December
Number of teachers: 100
Number of students: 2,500
Vice-Chancellor: CARMEN Z. LAMAGNA
Pro Vice-Chancellor: Prof. Dr TAFAZZAL HOSSAIN
Schools of Science, Engineering, Business.
Publications: *AIUB Journal of Business and Economics* (2 a year), *AIUB Journal of Science and Engineering* (annually).

BANGABANDHU SHEIKH MUJIB MEDICAL UNIVERSITY

POB 3048, Dhaka 1000
Telephone: (2) 8612550
Fax: (2) 9661063
E-mail: bsmmu@bangla.net
Internet: www.bsmmu.edu
Founded 1965 as Institute of Postgraduate Medicine and Research; present name and status 1998
Academic year: July to June
Vice-Chancellor: Prof. M. A. HADI
Pro Vice-Chancellors: Prof. MD. TAHIR, Prof. M. A. MANNAN
Registrar: M. A. GAFUR
Chief Librarian: MD. SHAHADAT HUSSAIN
Library of 23,000 vols, 100 periodicals
Number of teachers: 200
Number of students: 600
Publications: *Journal of the Institute of Postgraduate Medicine and Research* (2 a year), *Bangladesh Journal of Neurology* (2 a year), *Bangladesh Journal of Psychiatry* (2 a year).

BANGABANDHU SHEIKH MUJIBUR RAHMAN AGRICULTURAL UNIVERSITY

Salna, Gazipur 1703
Telephone: (2) 9252850
Fax: (2) 9252873
E-mail: bsmrau@bttb.net.bd
Founded 1983 as Bangladesh College of Agricultural Sciences; became Institute of Postgraduate Studies in Agriculture 1994; present name 1998
State control
Academic year: November to October
Vice-Chancellor: Prof. Dr M. A. HALIM KHAN
Deans: Prof. Dr ABDUL MANNAN AKANDA (Graduate Studies), Prof. Dr M. A. HALIM KHAN (Faculty of Agriculture)
Registrar: MOHAMMAD ABUL KALAM AZAD
Asst Librarian: MOHAMMAD ABDUR ROUF MIAN
Number of teachers: 47
Number of students: 244
Publication: *Annals of Bangladeshi Agriculture* (every 2 years).

BANGLADESH AGRICULTURAL UNIVERSITY

PO Agricultural University, Mymensingh
Telephone: (91) 55695
Fax: (91) 55810
E-mail: bau@drik.bgd.toolnet.org
Internet: www.bau.mymensingh.org
Founded 1961
Autonomous control
Languages of instruction: English, Bengali
Academic year: July to June (two semesters)
Chancellor: Prof. Dr IAJUDDIN AHMED
Vice-Chancellor: Prof. Dr M. AMIRUL ISLAM
Registrar: MD. NAZIBUR RAHMAN
Public Relations and Publications Director: DIWAN RASHIDUL HASSAN
Committee for Advanced Studies and Research Co-ordinator: Prof. AHMED ALI
Librarian: ABDUL GAFUR DEWAN
Library of 179,213 vols
Number of teachers: 484
Number of students: 4,586
Publications: *Bangladesh Journal of Agricultural Economics*, *Bangladesh Journal of Aquaculture*, *Bangladesh Journal of Agricultural Science*, *Bangladesh Journal of Animal Science*, *Bangladesh Journal of Crop Science*, *Bangladesh Journal of Environmental Science* (annually), *Bangladesh Journal of Extension Education*, *Bangladesh Journal of Fisheries* (4 a year), *Bangladesh Journal of Horticulture* (2 a year), *Bangladesh Journal of Plant Pathology*, *Bangladesh Journal of Seed Science and Technology* (2 a year), *Bangladesh Journal of Training and Development*, *Bangladesh Journal of Agricultural Engineering*, *Bangladesh Veterinary Journal*, *Journal of Veterinary Medicine*, *Progressive Agriculture*, *The Bangladeshi Veterinarian*

DEANS

Faculty of Agricultural Economics and Rural Sociology: Prof. Dr M. ABUL BASHAR
Faculty of Agricultural Engineering and Technology: Prof. K. S. RAHMAN
Faculty of Agriculture: Prof. Dr M. R. H. BHUIYA
Faculty of Animal Husbandry: Prof. Dr M. R. ALAM
Faculty of Fisheries: Prof. M. JAHIR UDDIN MIAH
Faculty of Veterinary Science: Prof. Dr M. M. SEN

PROFESSORS

Faculty of Agricultural Economics and Rural Sociology:

AHMED, A. R., Agricultural Statistics
AKBAR, M. A., Co-operation and Marketing
ALAM, M. F., Agricultural Finance
ALAM, S., Co-operation and Marketing
ALI, M. H., Co-operation and Marketing
ALI, R., Rural Sociology
BASAR, M. A., Agricultural Finance
DEBNATH, S. C., Agricultural Statistics
HOSSAIN, M. I., Agricultural Statistics
ISLAM, M. S., Agricultural Economics
KHAN, M. Z. A., Agricultural Statistics
MANDAL, A. S., Agricultural Economics
MIA, M. I. A., Co-operation and Marketing
MIAN, M. T. H., Agricultural Economics
MODAK, P. C., Agricultural Statistics
MOLLA, M. A. R., Agricultural Economics
MURSHED, S. M. M., Agricultural Economics
QUDDUS, M. A., Agricultural Statistics
RAHA, S. K., Co-operation and Marketing
RAHMAN, M. H., Agricultural Economics
RAHMAN, M. M., Agricultural Economics
RAHMAN, M. M., Agricultural Finance
SABUR, S. A., Co-operation and Marketing
TALUKDER, M. R. K., Agricultural Economics
ZAIM, W. M. H., Agricultural Economics

Faculty of Agricultural Engineering and Technology:

ABEDIN, M. Z., Farm Structure
AHMED, M., Irrigation and Water Management
AKHTARUZZAMAN, M., Farm Power and Machinery
ALAM, M. M., Farm Power and Machinery
ALAM, M. MURSHED, Farm Power and Machinery

ALI, M. M., Computer Science and Mathematics
AWAL, A. S. M. A., Farm Structure
BALA, B. K., Farm Power and Machinery
BASAK, N. K., Computer Science and Mathematics
BISWAS, M. R., Irrigation and Water Management
HAQUE, M. M., Computer Science and Mathematics
HAQUE, M. N., Farm Structure
HAQUE, M. R., Irrigation and Water Management
HASSANUZZAMAN, K. M., Irrigation and Water Management
HUSSAIN, A. A. MAINUL, Farm Power and Machinery
HUSSAIN, M. D., Farm Power and Machinery
HUSSAIN, M. M., Farm Power and Machinery
ISLAM, M. N., Irrigation and Water Management
ISLAM, M. NURUL, Food Technology and Rural Industries
ISLAM, MD. N., Food Technology and Rural Industries
KHAIR, A., Irrigation and Water Management
KHAN, L. R., Irrigation and Water Management
KHAN, M. M. R., Irrigation and Water Management
MONAYEMDAD, M., Farm Structures
RAHMAN, K. S., Farm Structures
RASHID, M. A., Farm Structure
SARKER, M. R. I., Farm Power and Machinery
SATTER, M. A., Farm Power and Machinery
SHAMSUDDIN, M., Food Technology and Rural Industries
TALUKDER, M. S., Irrigation and Water Management
UDDIN, B. M., Food Technology and Rural Industries
ZIAUDDIN, A. T. M., Farm Power and Machinery

Faculty of Agriculture:

AHMAD, K. N. U., Genetics and Plant Breeding
AHMAD, M. U., Plant Pathology
AHMED, M., Agronomy
AHMED, M., Entomology
ALAM, M. S. E., Genetics and Plant Breeding
ALI, M. S., Agricultural Chemistry
ANWAR, A. B. M., Agricultural Extension Education
ASHRAFUZZAMAN, M., Plant Pathology
BHUIYAN, M. R. H., Biochemistry
BHUIYAN, M. S. U., Agronomy
CHOUDHURY, A. K. M. S., Agronomy
CHOUDHURY, M. A. KH., Agricultural Chemistry
CHOUDHURY, M. S. H., Horticulture
CHOWDHURY, B. L. D., Biochemistry
CHOWDHURY, M. A. H., Agricultural Chemistry
FAKIR, M. G. A., Plant Pathology
FAKIR, M. S. A., Crop Botany
FAROOQUE, A. M., Horticulture
HALIM, A., Agricultural Extension Education
HAQUE, M. A., Horticulture
HAQUE, M. A., Entomology
HAQUE, M. M., Agricultural Extension Education
HAQUE, S. A., Soil Science
HASHEM, M. A., Soil Science
HASSAN, L., Genetics and Plant Breeding
HOSSAIN, I., Plant Pathology
HOSSAIN, M. A., Biochemistry
HOSSAIN, M., Entomology
HOSSAIN, M. A., Agroforestry
HOSSAIN, M. A., Soil Science
HOSSAIN, M. M., Plant Pathology
ISLAM, K. S., Entomology
ISLAM, M. A., Agronomy
ISLAM, M. A., Genetics and Plant Breeding
ISLAM, M. M., Agricultural Extension Education
ISLAM, M. R., Soil Science
ISLAM, M. T., Plant Pathology
ISLAM, N., Agronomy
KAMAL, A. M. A., Agronomy
KARIM, A. S. M. Z., Agricultural Extension Education
KARIM, M. A., Crop Botany
KARIM, M. M., Agronomy
KARIM, M. R., Entomology
KARIM, M. S., Chemistry
KARIM, S. M. R., Agronomy
KASEM, M. A., Agricultural Extension Education
KHAN, A. B., Entomology
KHAN, M. A. H., Crop Botany
MAMUN, A. A., Environmental Science
MIAH, M. A. M., Agricultural Extension Education
MIAH, M. B., Plant Pathology
MIAN, M. J. A., Soil Science
MIAN, M. M. H., Soil Science
MOMEN, A., Plant Pathology
MONDAL, M. F., Horticulture
MOTIN, M. A., Soil Science
NEWAZ, M. A., Genetics and Plant Breeding
NEWAZ, N., Biochemistry
PATWARI, M. A. K., Genetics and Plant Breeding
PRODHAN, A. K. M. A., Crop Botany
QUDDUS, M. A., Genetics and Plant Breeding
RABBANI, M. G., Horticulture
RAHIM, M. A., Horticulture
RAHMAN, A. K. M. M., Entomology
RAHMAN, G. M. M., Agroforestry
RAHMAN, L., Genetics and Plant Breeding
RAHMAN, M. A., Chemistry
RAHMAN, M. M., Crop Botany
RAHMAN, M. M., Soil Science
RAHMAN, M. M., Agricultural Extension Education
RASHID, A. Q. M. B., Plant Pathology
RASHID, M. H., Agricultural Extension Education
RASHID, M. R., Biochemistry
RAZZAQUE, M. A., Languages
ROY, P. K., Biochemistry
SAHA, K. C., Chemistry
SALIM, M., Agronomy
SAMAD, M. A., Agronomy
SARDER, M. M. A., Entomology
SARJER, A. K., Chemistry
SARKER, A. R., Chemistry
SARKER, A. U., Agronomy
SARKER, M. A. R., Agronomy
SATTER, M. A., Environmental Science
SEAL, H. P., Chemistry
SHAHJAHAN, M., Entomology
SHAMSUDDIN, A. K. M., Genetics and Plant Breeding
SHARFUDDIN, A. F. M., Horticulture
SIDDIKA, A., Biochemistry
SIDDIQUE, M. A., Horticulture
TALUKDER, M. N., Agricultural Chemistry
UDDIN, M. J., Soil Science
UDDIN, N., Biotechnology
UDDIN, S. G., Biochemistry
WAHID-UZZAMAN, Agricultural Chemistry
WAZIUDDIN, M., Genetics and Plant Breeding

Faculty of Animal Husbandry:

AHMED, S. U., Poultry Science
AKBAR, M. A., Animal Nutrition
AKHTAR, S., Animal Science
ALAM, M. R., Animal Science
ALI, A., Animal Breeding and Genetics
ALI, M. A., Poultry Science
ALI, S. Z., Animal Breeding and Genetics
AMIN, M. R., Animal Breeding and Genetics
AMIN, M. R., Animal Science
BHUIYA, A. K. F. H., Animal Breeding and Genetics
BULBUL, S. M., Poultry Science
CHOWDHURY, S. D., Poultry Science
FARUQUE, M. O., Animal Breeding and Genetics
HAMID, M. A., Poultry Science
HAQUE, M. A., Animal Science
HASSAN, M. N., Dairy Science
HOSSAIN, S. M. I., Dairy Science
HOSSAIN, S. S., Animal Breeding and Genetics
HOWLIDER, M. A. R., Poultry Science
HUSSAIN, M. M., Animal Science
ISLAM, M. M., Animal Nutrition
ISLAM, M. N., Dairy Science
KHAN, M. A. S., Dairy Science
KHAN, M. J. UDDIN, Animal Nutrition
KHANDAKER, Z. H., Animal Nutrition
MANNAN, A. K. M. A., Dairy Science
MOKTARUZZAMAN, M., Dairy Science
REZA, A., Animal Nutrition
SADULLAH, M., Animal Science
SAMAD, M. A., Animal Science
SARKER, D. R. D., Animal Science
SHAHJALAL, M., Animal Nutrition
TAREQ, A. M. M., Animal Nutrition
WADUD, A., Dairy Science

Faculty of Fisheries:

AHMED, G. U., Aquaculture
ALAM, A. K. M. N., Fisheries Technology
ALAM, M. S., Fisheries Biology and Genetics
ALI, M. M., Aquaculture
AMIN, M. R., Aquaculture
CHANDRA, K. Z., Aquaculture
CHAKRABORTY, S. C., Fisheries Technology
CHOWDHURY, M. B. R., Aquaculture
DAS, M., Aquaculture
DEWAN, S., Fisheries Management
HABIB, M. A. B., Aquaculture
HAQUE, M. M., Fisheries Management
HAQUE, M. S., Fisheries Management
HASAN, M. R., Aquaculture
HOSSEIN, M. A., Aquaculture
HUSSIN, L., Fisheries Biology and Genetics
ISLAM, M. A., Aquaculture
ISLAM, M. AMINUL, Fisheries Biology and Genetics
ISLAM, M. NAZRUL, Fisheries Technology
KAMAL, M., Fisheries Technology
KHATOON, F., Fisheries Biology and Genetics
MANSUR, M. A., Fisheries Technology
MIAH, M. I., Fisheries Management
MIAN, M. Z. U., Aquaculture
MOLLAH, M. F. A., Fisheries Biology and Genetics
RAHMAN, M. S., Fisheries Management
RAHMATULLAH, S. M., Aquaculture
RASHID, M. M., Aquaculture
UDDIN, M. N., Fisheries Technology
WAHAB, M. A., Fisheries Management

Faculty of Veterinary Science:

AHMAD, M. U., Medicine
AHMED, J. U., Surgery and Obstetrics
AHMED, M., Anatomy and Histology
AHMED, N., Physiology
ALAM, M. G. S., Surgery and Obstetrics
AMIN, M. M., Microbiology and Hygiene
ANAM, M. K., Anatomy and Histology
ASADUZZAMAN, M., Anatomy and Histology
AWAL, M., Pharmacology
AWAL, M. A., Anatomy and Histology
BAKI, M. A., Pathology
BARI, A. S. M., Pathology
BEGUM, N., Parasitology
CHOWDHURY, K. A., Microbiology and Hygiene
DAS, P. M., Pathology
HAQUE, S., Parasitology
HASAN, Q., Pharmacology

HASHIM, M. A., Surgery and Obstetrics
HOSSAIN, M. A., Surgery and Obstetrics
HOSSAIN, M. I., Anatomy and Histology
HOSSAIN, M. M., Pathology
HOSSAIN, W. I. M. A., Microbiology and Hygiene
HUQUE, A. K. M. F., Medicine
ISLAM, A. W. M. S., Parasitology
ISLAM, K. S., Medicine
ISLAM, M. R., Pathology
KARIM, M. J., Parasitology
KASEM, M. A., Anatomy and Histology
KHAN, J. I., Anatomy and Histology
KHAN, M. A. B., Anatomy and Histology
KHAN, M. A. I., Pharmacology
MIAH, A. K. M., Anatomy and Histology
MONDAL, M. M. H., Parasitology
MUSTAFA, M., Pharmacology
MYRNUDDIN, M., Physiology
NOORUDDIN, M., Medicine
RAHMAN, M., Physiology
RAHMAN, M. A., Microbiology and Hygiene
RAHMAN, M. A., Microbiology and Hygiene
RAHMAN, M. H., Parasitology
RAHMAN, M. H., Pathology
RAHMAN, M. M., Microbiology and Hygiene
RAHMAN, M. M., Microbiology and Hygiene
SAMAD, M. A., Medicine
SEN, M. M., Medicine
SHAHJAHAN, M., Anatomy and Histology
SHAMSUDDIN, M., Surgery Obstetrics
UDDIN, M., Pathology

DIRECTORS

Agricultural University Extension Centre: Prof. M. MUTTAQUIMUR RAHMAN
Agricultural University Research System: Prof. M. R. I. SARKOR
Central Laboratory: Prof. Dr LUTFUR RAHMAN
Graduate Training Institute: Prof. M. TAZUL ISLAM
Seed Pathology Centre: Prof. MUYEEN UDDIN AHMED
Veterinary Clinic: Prof. Dr M. GOLAM SHAHI ALAM

CHAIRS

Bureau of Research, Testing and Consultation: Prof. K. S. RAHMAN
Bureau of Socio-economic Research and Training: Prof. Dr MD ABUL BASHAR

BANGLADESH OPEN UNIVERSITY

Board Bazar, Gazipur 1704
Telephone: (2) 9800801
Fax: (2) 9800822
E-mail: boupvc@citechco.net
Internet: www.citechco.net/bou

Founded 1992
State control

Chancellor: PRIME MINISTER OF THE PEOPLE'S REPUBLIC OF BANGLADESH
Vice-Chancellor: Prof. M. AMINUL ISLAM
Pro-Vice-Chancellor: Prof. R. I. SHARIF
Registrar: MD. MONZUR-E-KHODA TARAFDAR
Librarian: MUHAMMAD SAADAT ALI

Library of 11,000 vols
Number of teachers: 62
Number of students: 103,000

DEANS

School of Agriculture and Rural Development: Dr A. H. M. FARUQUE
School of Business: Prof. ABDUL AWAL KHAN
School of Education: Prof. M. SHAMSUL KABIR
School of Science and Technology: Prof. Dr MOFIZ UDDIN AHMED
School of Social Science, Humanities and Languages: Prof. Dr SHIREEN HUQ
Open School: MUSTAFIZUR RAHMAN

BANGLADESH UNIVERSITY OF ENGINEERING AND TECHNOLOGY

Palassy, Ramna, Dhaka 1000
Telephone: (2) 9665650
Fax: (2) 8613026
E-mail: shah@regtr.buet.ac.bd
Internet: www.buet.ac.bd

Founded 1962
State control
Language of instruction: English
Academic year: January to December

Chancellor: PRIME MINISTER OF THE PEOPLE'S REPUBLIC OF BANGLADESH
Vice-Chancellor: Prof. Dr MD. ALEE MURTUZA
Registrar: MOHAMMAD SHAHJAHAN
Librarian: MOHAMMAD ZAHIRUL ISLAM

Library of 132,586 vols
Number of teachers: 501
Number of students: 7,501

Publications: *Annual Report, Bangladesh Journal of Water Resource Research, Chemical Engineering Research Bulletin, Electrical and Electronic Engineering Research Bulletin, Industrial and Production Engineering Research Bulletin, Journal of Energy and Environment, Journal of Mechanical Engineering Research and Development, Protibesh Journal of the Dept of Architecture*

DEANS

Faculty of Architecture and Planning: Prof. A. S. M. MAHBUB-UN-NABI
Faculty of Civil Engineering: Prof. Dr MD. KHORSHED ALAM
Faculty of Electrical and Electronic Engineering: Prof. Dr SHAHIDUL ISLAM KHAN
Faculty of Engineering: Prof. Dr M. MOHAR ALI BEPARI
Faculty of Mechanical Engineering: Prof. Dr MD. QUAMRUL ISLAM

HEADS OF DEPARTMENTS

Architecture: Prof. Dr MD. SHAHIDUL AMEEN
Chemical Engineering: Prof. Dr IJAZ HOSSEIN
Chemistry: Prof. Dr MD. RAFIQUE ULLAH
Civil Engineering: Prof. Dr MD. ABDUR ROUF
Computer Science and Engineering: Dr MD. ABUL KASHEM MIA
Electrical and Electronic Engineering: Prof. Dr M. M. SHAIDUL HASAN
Humanities: MD. MURSHIKUL ALAM
Industrial and Production Engineering: Prof. Dr MOHIUDDIN AHMED
Materials and Metallurgical Engineering: Prof. Dr A. K. M. BAZLUR RASHID
Mathematics: Prof. Dr MUSTAFA KAMAL CHOWDHURY
Mechanical Engineering: Prof. Dr MAGLUB-AL-NOOR
Naval Architecture and Marine Engineering: Prof. Dr REAZ HASAN KHONDOKER
Petroleum and Mineral Resources Engineering: Prof. Dr MOHAMMAD TAMIM
Physics: Prof. Dr NAZMA ZAMAN
Urban and Regional Planning: Prof. Dr SARWAR JAHAN
Water Resources Engineering: Prof. Dr MOHAMMAD ALI BHUIYAN

ATTACHED INSTITUTES

Accident Research Centre: Dir Prof. Dr MD. MAZHARUL HOQUE.

Bio-Medical Engineering Centre: Dir Prof. Dr M. ABU TAHER ALI.

Centre for Energy Studies: Dir Prof. Dr EDMOND GOMES.

Centre for Environmental and Resource Management: Dir Prof. Dr MD. MUJIBUR RAHMAN.

Directorate of Continuing Education: Dir Prof. Dr MD. GOLAM MOIUDDIN.

Institute of Appropriate Technology: Dir Dr MD. KAMAL UDDIN.

Institute of Information and Communication Technology: Dir Prof. Dr S. M. LUTFUL KABIR.

Institute of Water and Flood Management: Dir Prof. Dr A. K. M. JAIRUDDIN CHOWDHURY.

BRAC UNIVERSITY

66 Mohakhali C/A Dhaka 1212
Telephone: (2) 9881265
Fax: (2) 8823542
E-mail: info@bracuniversity.net
Internet: www.bracuniversity.net

Founded 2001
Private control, under BRAC non-governmental development organization

Vice-Chancellor: Prof. JAMILUR REZA CHOUDHURY
Registrar: MUHAMMAD SAHOOL AFZAL

Faculties of Natural Sciences, and Arts and Social Sciences.

UNIVERSITY OF CHITTAGONG

University Post Office, Chittagong 4331
Telephone: (31) 682042
Fax: (31) 726310
E-mail: vc-cu@spnetctg.com
Internet: www.cu.ac.bd

Founded 1966
Languages of instruction: Bengali, English
Academic year: July to June

Vice-Chancellor: Prof. A. J. M. NURUDDIN CHOWDHURY
Pro Vice-Chancellor: Prof. Dr MOHAMMED SHAMSUDDIN
Registrar: Prof. IDRIS MIYAN
Librarian: SYED MOHAMED ABU TAHER

Library of 201,514 vols
Number of teachers: 643
Number of students: 14,844

DEANS

Faculty of Arts: Prof. Dr MOHAMMED SIRAJUL ISLAM
Faculty of Commerce: Prof. Dr MONJUR MORSHED MAHMUD
Faculty of Law: Dr MORSHED MAHMUD KHAN
Faculty of Medicine: Prof. CHOWDURY B. MAHMUD
Faculty of Science: Prof. Dr ABU SALEH
Faculty of Social Science: Prof. Dr MUINUL ISLAM
Faculty of Veterinary Medicine: Prof. Dr NITISH CHANDRA DEBNATH

PROFESSORS

Faculty of Arts

Arabic and Islamic Studies:

AHMED, R.
DOZA, H. M. B
HAQUE, A. F. M. A.
KHATIBI, M. A. H.
QUADER, A. K. M. A.
RASHID, M.

Bengali:

ALAM, M. S.
AMIN, M. N.
AZIM, A.
AZIZ, M. M.
BISWAS, S. N.
CHOWDHURY, A. U. M. Z. H.
DASTIDAR, S. R.
IQBAL, B. M.
ISLAM, A. K. M. N.
MANIRUZZAMAN, M.
QUASEM, M. A.
SHAHJAHAN
ZAMAN, A. L.

English:

ALAM, M. U.
BARUA, T. J.
BILLA, Q. M.
CHOWDHURY, G. S.
DUTTA, S. K.
ISLAM, M. S.
MOHMOOD, A. B. M. M.

Fine Arts:

ALI, S. M. A.
AZIM, F.
BANU, N.
ISLAM, M. S.
KARIM, M. M.
KHALED, S. A.
MANSUR, A.
RAHIM, M.
ROY, A.

History:

CHOWDHURY, M. A.
HOQUE, M.
HOSSAIN, E.
HOSSAIN, H.
KABIR, E.
KHALED, A. M. M. S.
SAYED, A.
SHAH, M.

Islamic History and Culture:

AHMED, A.
AHMED, S.
ALAM, A. Q. M. S.
BHUIYAN, G. K.
CHOWDHURY, M. T. H.
HUQ, M. I.
SHAFIQ ULLAH, S. M.
YUSUF, A.

Oriental Languages:

BARUA, D. S.
BARUA, R. K.
HALDER, S. R.

Philosophy:

AHMED, R.
ALI, M. A.
ALAM, M. S.
ANWAR, A. J.
CHOWDHURY, M. A.
KHALEQUE, A. S. M. A.
RAHMAN, A. K. M. S.
RAHMAN, A. M. M. W.
RAHMAN, M. B.
RAHMAN, M. L.

Faculty of Commerce

Accounting and Information Systems:

AHMED, S.
BHATTACHARJEE, M. K.
CHOWDHURY, R. K.
DAS, S. R.
DATTA, D. K.
MAHMUD, M. M.
MOHIUDDIN, K. M. G.
NAG, A. B.
PURAHIT, K. K.
RASHID, H.
SALAUDDIN, A.
SHARMA, B. K.

Finance and Banking:

HOQUE, M. J.
LOQMAN, M.
MOQTADIR, A. N. M. A.
NABI, K. A.
RASHID, M. H.

Management:

ALAM, M. F.
ALI, A. F. M. A.
ARIF, M. A. A.
ATHER, S. M.
MAMUN, M. A.
MANNAN, M. A.
SIKDER, Z. H.
TAHER, M. A.

Marketing:

B-HUIYAN, S. M. S. U.
CHOWDHURY, A. J. M.
KARIM, A. N. M. N.
MEHER, M. S.
SHAHIN, S.
SOLAIMAN, M.

Faculty of Law

Law:

ALAM, M. S.

Faculty of Science

Applied Physics and Electronics:

BHUIYAN, M. A. S.
HOSSAIN, A.
KHAN, M. R. H.
SAHA, S. L.

Biochemistry and Molecular Biology:

ALAUDDIN, M.

Botany:

AHMED, M.
ALAMGIR, A. N. M.
BASET, Q. A.
BHADRA, S. K.
CHOWDHURY, A. M.
GAFUR, M. A.
MRIDHA, M. A.
PASHA, M. K.
RAHMAN, M. A.
RAHMAN, M. A.

Chemistry:

AHMED, M. J.
AHMED, M. S. U.
AKHTAR, S.
BEGUM, S. A.
CHOWDHURY, D. A.
CHOWDHURY, M. Z. A.
DEY, B. K.
HABIB ULLAH, M.
HAZARI, S. K. S.
ISLAM, M.
KABIR, A. K. M. S.
NAZIMUDDIN, M.
PALIT, D.
RAHMAN, K. M. M.
ROY, T. G.
SALAM, M. A.
SALEH, M. A.
UDDIN, M. H.

Computer Science:

MOSTAFA, M. N.

Mathematics:

AHMED, M.
AZAD, A. K.
BHATTACHARJEE, N. R.
ISLAM, M. A.
ISLAM, M. N.
MOHIUDDIN, M.
RAHMAN, M. M.

Microbiology:

ANWAR, M. N.
HAKIM, M. A.

Physics:

AHMED, F. K.
AHMED, M.
BANU, H.
BARUA, B. P.
BEGUM, D. A.
DEB, A. K.
ISLAM, M. N.
ISLAM, M. N.
MIYA, M. M. H.
NABI, S. R.
PAUL, D. P.
ROY, M. K.
SAFIULLAH, M. A.
SAHA, S. K.
SIDDIQA, N.

Soil Science:

OSMAN, K. T.

Statistics:

ISLAM, S. M. S.
PAUL, J. C.
RAHMAN, M. M.
RASUL, M. A.
ROY, M. K.
SHAMSUDDIN, M.
SHIL, R. N.
YAHYA, N. S. M.

Zoology:

AHMED, B.
AHSAN, M. F.
ALAM, M. S.
ASMAT, G. S. M.
AZADI, M. A.
BANU, Q.
BHUIYAN, A. M.
BHUIYAN, M. A.
HAFIZUDDIN, A. K. M.
ISLAM, M. A.
KHAN, M. A. G.
MEAH, M. I.
NASIRUDDIN, M.
ULLAH, G. M. R.

Faculty of Social Sciences

Anthropology:

CHOWDHURY, A. F. H.

Economics:

ASHRAF, M. A.
AZAD, A. K.
CHOWDHURY, M. A. M.
DEY, H. K.
DUTTA, J. P.
HOQ, M.
HOQUE, M. S.
HOSSAIN, B.
ISLAM, M.
KHAN, I. K.
KHAN, M. S.
MAHBUB, U.
NAG, N. C.
SALEHUDDIN, M.
TAHERA, B. S.

Political Science:

AHMED, A. N. M. M.
AHMED, S. Z.
AKHTER, M. Y.
ALAM, M. B.
CHOWDHURY, M. H.
CHOWDHURY, S. A.
HAKIM, M. A.
HASSAN, M.
HOQUE, M. E.
KABIR, B. M. M.
KHAN, Z. N.
KHANAM, J.
KHANAM, R.
MUSHRAFI, M. E. M.
SHAMSUDDIN, M.

Public Administration:

AHMED, N. U.
AHMED, T.
AMIN, M. R.
BEGUM, A.
ISLAM, M. N.
MASHREQUE, M. S.
NOOR, A.
WAHHAB, M. A.

Sociology:

ALI, A. F. I.
B-HUIYAN, M. A.
CHOWDHURY, A. Q.
CHOWDHURY, H. Z.
CHOWDHURY, I. U.
HUSSAIN, M.
KARIM, M. O.
MAHABUBULLAH, M.
QUDDUS, A. H. G.
SALEHUDDIN, G.
SEN, A.

There are 130 affiliated colleges

ATTACHED INSTITUTES

Institute of Community Ophthalmology: f. 1990; Dir Dr MOHAMMED FAZLUL HAQUE.

Institute of Forestry and Environmental Sciences: f. 1977; Dir Dr M. SHAFIUL ALAM.

Institute of Marine Sciences: f. 1982; Dir MOHAMMAD ZAFAR.

Research Centre for Mathematical and Physical Science: Chittagong; f. 1988; Dir Prof. MOHAMMED ABUL MUNSUR CHOWDHURY.

Social Science Research Institute: f. 2004; Dir Dr ABUL KALAM AZAD.

CHITTAGONG UNIVERSITY OF ENGINEERING AND TECHNOLOGY

Chittagong 4349
Telephone: (31) 714946
Fax: (31) 714910
E-mail: registrar@cuet.ac.bd
Internet: www.cuet.ac.bd

Founded 1968 as Engineering College, Chittagong; Bangladesh Institute of Technology, Chittagong 1986; present name and status 2003
State control
Language of instruction: English
Vice-Chancellor: Prof. Dr MIR SHAHIDUL ISLAM
Registrar: Dr MAHMUD OMAR IMAM

HEADS OF DEPARTMENTS

Chemistry: ROWSHON ARA BEGUM
Civil Engineering: Dr MD HAZRAT ALI
Computer Science and Engineering: Dr MD TAZUL ISLAM
Electrical and Electronic Engineering: ANIL KANTI DHAR
Mathematics and Humanities: ASHUTOSE SAHA
Mechanical Engineering: Dr P. K. MD OMAR FARUQUE
Physics: Dr FARUQUE-UZ-ZAMAN CHOWDHURY

UNIVERSITY OF DHAKA

Ramna, Dhaka
Telephone: (2) 9661900
Fax: (2) 9661920
E-mail: duregstr@bangla.net
Internet: www.univdhaka.edu

Founded 1921
Independent
Languages of instruction: Bengali, English
Academic year: July to June (three terms)
Chancellor: PRESIDENT OF THE PEOPLE'S REPUBLIC OF BANGLADESH
Vice-Chancellor: Prof. S. M. A. FAIZ
Pro Vice-Chancellor: Prof. A. F. M. Y. HAIDER
Treasurer: S. R. HASAN (acting)
Registrar: M. A. HUSSAIN (acting)
Librarian: Dr M. S. ISLAM (acting)
Library: see Libraries and Archives
Number of teachers: 1,492
Number of students: 24,060
Publications: *Annual Report*, *Calendar*, *Dhaka University Studies* (2 a year), *Dhaka Viswa Vidyalaya Bartra* (quarterly), *Dhaka Viswa Vidyalaya Patrika* (3 a year), *Sahitya Patrika* (3 a year)

DEANS

Faculty of Arts: Prof S. AMIN
Faculty of Business Studies: Prof M. S. ISLAM
Faculty of Biological Sciences: Prof. S. S. QADRI
Faculty of Education: M. SHAH JAHAN
Faculty of Law: Dr N. HUQ
Faculty of Medicine: Dr A. Z. M. Z. HOSSAIN
Faculty of Pharmacy: Prof. M. A. RASHID
Faculty of Social Sciences: H. RASHID (acting)
Faculty of Science: Dr R. I. M. A. RASHID
Faculty of Postgraduate Medical Sciences and Research: Prof. T. AHMED

PROFESSORS

ABEDIN, K. M., Physics
ABRAR, C. R., International Relations
ABULULAYEE, S. K. M., Philosophy
ADBDULLAH, A. S. A., Accounting and Information Systems
ADEEB, K., Nutrition and Food Science
ADITYA, S. K., Applied Physics and Electronics
AFROEZ, D., Psychology
AFTABUDDIN, M., Biochemistry and Molecular Biology
AHAD, S. A., Soil, Water and the Environment
AHMAD, N., Arabic
AHMED, A., Economics
AHMED, A., Political Science
AHMED, A. F., Public Administration
AHMED, A. I. M. U., Sociology
AHMED, A. K. M. U., Economics
AHMED, A. T. A., Zoology
AHMED, A. U., Nutrition and Food Science
AHMED, E., Chemistry
AHMED, E., International Relations
AHMED, F., Applied Physics and Electronics
AHMED, F., Economics
AHMED, I., Business Administration
AHMED, J. U., Finance
AHMED, K. U., Political Science
AHMED, M., Accounting and Information Systems
AHMED, M., Clinical Pharmacy and Pharmacology
AHMED, M., Economics
AHMED, M., Physics
AHMED, M., Public Administration
AHMED, M. F., Finance
AHMED, M. G., Chemistry
AHMED, N., Geography and the Environment
AHMED, S., Anthropology
AHMED, S., Economics
AHMED, S., Economics
AHMED, S., Management Studies
AHMED, S. A., Chemistry
AHMED, S. J., Theatre and Music
AHMED, S. U., History
AHMED, S. U., Management Studies
AHMED, S.G., Public Administration
AHMED, W., Bengali
AHMED, Z., History
AHMED MAJIB, U., Accounting and Information Systems
AHMED MAMATAJ, U., Accounting and Information Systems
AHSAN, A., Management Studies
AHSAN, C. R., Microbiology
AHSAN, M., Pharmaceutical Chemistry
AHSAN, M. A., Education and Research
AHSAN, M. Q., Chemistry
AHSAN, R. M., Geography and the Environment
AKHTER, N., Botany
AKHTER, R., Philosophy
AKHTER, S. H., Geology
AKHTERUZZAMAN, M., Islamic History and Culture
AKKAS, M. A., Management Studies
AKTER, S., Education and Research
ALAM, A. F., Marketing
ALAM, A. M. S., Chemistry
ALAM, B., Physics
ALAM, F., English
ALAM, H. A., Philosophy
ALAM, K. M. U., Geology
ALAM, K. S., Marketing
ALAM, M., Geology
ALAM, M. D., Soil, Water and the Environment
ALAM, M. K., Soil, Water and the Environment
ALAM, M. M., Economics
ALAM, M. M., Geology
ALAM, M. R., Fine Arts
ALAM, S. S., Botany
ALI, A. H. M. M., Fine Arts
ALI, A. K. M. I., Islamic History and Culture
ALI, A. M., Mass Communication and Journalism
ALI, M. A., Education and Research
ALI, M. S., Physics
ALI, M. S., Zoology
ALI, R., Psychology
ALI, S. M. K., Nutrition and Food Science
ALVI, S. A. B., Fine Arts
AMIN, M. R., Islamic Studies
AMIN, S., English
AMIN, S. N., History
AMINUZZAMAN, S. M., Development Studies
ANISUZZAMAN, Philosophy
ANOWAR, A. J., Philosophy
ANOWAR, S. F., Business Administration
ANSARUDDIN, M., Islamic Studies
ARA, R., Philosophy
AREFEEN, H. K. S., Anthropology
ASADUZZAMAN, M., Public Administration
AWAL, A. Z. M. I., History
AZAD, S. A. K., Marketing
AZIM, F., English
AZIZ, A., Botany
BANOO, R., Pharmaceutical Chemistry
BANU, K., Statistics
BANU, N., Zoology
BANU, R., Modern Languages
BANU, S., Mathematics
BANU, S., Psychology
BANU, U. A. B. R. A., Political Science
BAPARY, M. N. A., Political Science
BAQI, A., Islamic Studies
BAQUEE, A. H. M. A., Geography and the Environment
BARI, M. E., Law
BARKAT, M. A., Economics
BARMAN, D. C., Peace and Conflict Studies
BARUA, S., Nutrition and Food Science
BASHAR, M. H., Chemistry
BASHER, A., Zoology
BEGUM, A., Islamic History and Culture
BEGUM, A., Physics
BEGUM, F., Sanskrit and Pali
BEGUM, H. A., Education and Research
BEGUM, H. A., Psychology
BEGUM, H. J., Physics
BEGUM, K., Education and Research
BEGUM, L., Philosophy
BEGUM, M., Botany
BEGUM, N., Economics
BEGUM, N., Islamic History and Culture
BEGUM, R., Botany
BEGUM, R., Clinical Psychology
BEGUM, R., Education and Research
BEGUM, R., Marketing
BEGUM, S., Zoology
BEGUM, S. F., Social Welfare and Research
BEGUM, Z. N. T., Botany
BHATTACHARJEE, D. D., Management Studies
BHATTACHARJEE, H., Marketing
BHOWMIK, D. K., Sanskrit and Pali
BHOWMIK, N. C., Applied Physics and Electronics
BHUIYAN, G. M., Physics
BHUIYAN, M. A. H., Nutrition and Food Science
BHUIYAN, M. M. R., Statistics
BHUIYAN, M. S., Management Studies
BHUIYAN, M. S., Political Science
BHUIYAN, M. Z. H., Marketing
BHUIYAN, S., History
BILLAH, M. M., Statistics
BISWAS, N. C., Sanskrit and Pali
BORHANUDDIN, Geography and the Environment
BSAHAR, M. A., Botany
CHAKMA, N. K., Philosophy
CHOWDHURY, A., Zoology
CHOWDHURY, A. A. M. U., Finance
CHOWDHURY, A. B. M. H., Islamic Studies

CHOWDHURY, A. K. A., Clinical Psychology
CHOWDHURY, A. M., History
CHOWDHURY, A. M. S. U., Applied Chemistry and Chemical Technology
CHOWDHURY, A. R., Law
CHOWDHURY, A. U., Anthropology
CHOWDHURY, B., Bengali
CHOWDHURY, D. K., Accounting and Information Systems
CHOWDHURY, F., Mathematics
CHOWDHURY, G. M., Business Administration
CHOWDHURY, H. U., Political Science
CHOWDHURY, I. G., Business Administration
CHOWDHURY, L. H., Public Administration
CHOWDHURY, M. A., Economics
CHOWDHURY, M. A. I., Marketing
CHOWDHURY, M. A. M., Management Studies
CHOWDHURY, M. H., Social Welfare and Research
CHOWDHURY, M. M., Political Science
CHOWDHURY, M. M. R., Sociology
CHOWDHURY, M. R., Biochemistry and Molecular Biology
CHOWDHURY, M. R., Mathematics
CHOWDHURY, M. S., Physics
CHOWDHURY, M. S., Soil, Water and the Environment
CHOWDHURY, N., Statistics
CHOWDHURY, N., Women's Studies
CHOWDHURY, P. B., Management Studies
CHOWDHURY, Q. A., Sociology
CHOWDHURY, R. R., Accounting and Information Systems
CHOWDHURY, S., Physics
CHOWDHURY, S. Q., Geology
CHOWDHURY, T. A., Chemistry
DAS, A. K., Chemistry
DATTA, B. K., Pharmaceutical Chemistry
ELAHI, S. F., Soil, Water and the Environment
EUSUF, A. Z., Geography and the Environment
FAIZ, B., Soil, Water and the Environment
FAIZ, S. M. A., Soil, Water and the Environment
FAROUK, A. B. M., Pharmaceutical Technology
FERDAUSI, N., Physics
FERDAUSI, R. R., Mathematics
GHOSH, B., Bengali
GHOSH, S. N., Accounting and Information Systems
GOMES, D. J., Microbiology
HADIUZZAM, S., Botany
HAIDER, A. F. M. Y., Physics
HAIDER, A. R. M. A., Islamic Studies
HAKIM, M. A., Accounting and Information Systems
HALDER, A. K., Mathematics
HALIM, M. A., International Relations
HANNAN, F., Sociology
HAQ, M., Fine Arts
HAQ, M., Psychology
HAQ, M. M., Microbiology
HAQ, M. R., International Relations
HAQ, P., Psychology
HAQUE, A. N. M. S., Marketing
HAQUE, I., Sociology
HAQUE, K. B., Management Studies
HAQUE, M., Geology
HAQUE, M. A., Geology
HAQUE, M. E., Biochemistry and Molecular Biology
HAQUE, M. M. N., Education and Research
HAQUE, S. A., Bengali
HAROON, S. M. I., Mass Communication and Journalism
HASAN, C. M., Pharmaceutical Chemistry
HASAN, M. A., Botany
HASAN, M. N., Nutrition and Food Science
HASAN, M. S., Population Sciences
HASAN, P., Islamic History and Culture
HASAN, S. R., Marketing
HASHEM, A., Accounting and Information Systems
HASSAN, S. A., Political Science
HAYE, A. H. M. A., Modern Languages
HOSSAIN, A., Chemistry
HOSSAIN, A., International Relations
HOSSAIN, A., Public Administration
HOSSAIN, A. H. M. M., Islamic Studies
HOSSAIN, A. M. M. M., Nutrition and Food Science
HOSSAIN, B., Marketing
HOSSAIN, K. M., Sociology
HOSSAIN, K. M. A., English
HOSSAIN, M., Bengali
HOSSAIN, M. A., Biochemistry and Molecular Biology
HOSSAIN, M. A., Marketing
HOSSAIN, M. A., Mathematics
HOSSAIN, M. A., Pharmaceutical Chemistry
HOSSAIN, M. F., Political Science
HOSSAIN, M. H., Education and Research
HOSSAIN, M. I., Zoology
HOSSAIN, M. K., Finance
HOSSAIN, M. M., Botany
HOSSAIN, M. M., Mathematics
HOSSAIN, M. N., Arabic
HOSSAIN, M. Q., Geology
HOSSAIN, M. S., Geology
HOSSAIN, M. S., Geology
HOSSAIN, M. S., Physics
HOSSAIN, M. S., Soil, Water and the Environment
HOSSAIN, M. T., Physics
HOSSAIN, M. Z., Business Administration
HOSSAIN, N. M., Microbiology
HOSSAIN, S., English
HOSSAIN, S. A., Bengali
HOSSAIN, S. A., Soil, Water and the Environment
HOSSAIN, S. H., Geography and the Environment
HOSSAIN, S. M., Accounting and Information Systems
HOSSAIN, S. S., Statistical Research and Training
HOWLADER, M. M. A., Zoology
HOWLADER, S. R., Health Economics
HUDA, S. N., Nutrition and Food Science
HUQ, A. K. M. M. S., Political Science
HUQ, A. Q. M. F., Bengali
HUQ, D., Applied Chemistry and Chemical Technology
HUQ, K. M. H., English
HUQ, M. I., Botany
HUQ, R., English
HUQ, S., Soil, Water and the Environment
HUQ, S. A., English
HUQ, S. A., History
HUQ, S. M. F., English
HUQ, S. M. I., Soil, Water and the Environment
HUQ, Z. S. M. M., Geography and the Environment
IBRAHIM, M., Islamic History and Culture
IBRAHIM, M., Physics
ILYAS, K. S. M., Psychology
IMAM, M. B., Geology
IMAM, M. O., Finance
ISLAM, A., Philosophy
ISLAM, A. F. M. M., Business Administration
ISLAM, A. K. M. N., Botany
ISLAM, A. N., Philosophy
ISLAM, K., Nutrition and Food Science
ISLAM, K. M. S., Information Science and Library Management
ISLAM, L. N., Biochemistry and Molecular Biology
ISLAM, M. A., Chemistry
ISLAM, M. A., Marketing
ISLAM, M. A., Mathematics
ISLAM, M. A., Statistics
ISLAM, M. A., Zoology
ISLAM, M. M., History
ISLAM, M. M., Statistics
ISLAM, M. N., Mathematics
ISLAM, M. N., Political Science
ISLAM, M. N., Social Welfare and Research
ISLAM, M. N., Statistics
ISLAM, M. NAZRUL, Sociology
ISLAM, M. NURAL, Sociology
ISLAM, M. S., Applied Physics and Electronics
ISLAM, M. S., Biochemistry and Molecular Biology
ISLAM, M. S., Clinical Pharmacy and Pharmacology
ISLAM, M. S., English
ISLAM, M. S., Management Studies
ISLAM, N., Geography and the Environment
ISLAM, N., Psychology
ISLAM, R., Applied Chemistry and Chemical Technology
ISLAM, S. N., Nutrition and Food Science
ISLAM, T. S. A., Chemistry
ISLAM, Z., Anthropology
JAHAN, K., Nutrition and Food Science
JAHAN, N., Botany
JAHANGIR, M., Modern Languages
JALIL, R., Pharmaceutical Technology
JINNAH, M. A., Public Administration
KABIR, A., Bengali
KABIR, K. A., Physics
KABIR, M. H., Statistical Research and Training
KABIR, Y., Biochemistry and Molecular Biology
KADER, D. A., Modern Languages
KALAM, A., Microbiology
KALIMULLAH, N. A., Public Administration
KAMAL, A. H. A., History
KAMAL, B. A., Bengali
KAMAL, M. M. U., Marketing
KARIM, M. N., Management Studies
KARIM, N., Sociology
KARIM, R., Nutrition and Food Science
KARIM, S. F., Psychology
KARMAKER, J. L., Botany
KARMAKER, S. S., Management Studies
KHAIR, A., Chemistry
KHALEQUE, M. A., Physics
KHALILY, M. A. B., Finance
KHAN, A. A., Geology
KHAN, A. A., Management Studies
KHAN, A. K. M. S. I., Microbiology
KHAN, A. M. M. A. U., Geography and the Environment
KHAN, A. N. M. A. M., Arabic
KHAN, A. T. M. N. R., Bengali
KHAN, A. Z. M. N. A., Botany
KHAN, G. A., Philosophy
KHAN, H., Genetic Engineering and Biotechnology
KHAN, H. R., Zoology
KHAN, M. A. A., Education and Research
KHAN, M. A. H., Fine Arts
KHAN, M. A. H., Soil, Water and the Environment
KHAN, M. A. R., Banking
KHAN, M. A. R., Microbiology
KHAN, M. H., Fine Arts
KHAN, M. H. R., Economics
KHAN, M. H. R., Soil, Water and the Environment
KHAN, M. M., Accounting and Information Systems
KHAN, M. M., Public Administration
KHAN, M. M. I., Sociology
KHAN, M. N. I., Nutrition and Food Science
KHAN, M. S. H., Statistical Research and Training
KHAN, R. U., Bengali
KHAN, S., Public Administration
KHAN, S. A., Mass Communication and Journalism
KHAN, T. H., Soil, Water and the Environment
KHAN, Z. R., Public Administration
KHANAM, B. K., Fine Arts
KHANAM, H., Zoology
KHANAM, M., Psychology
KHANDAKER, M., Botany
KHANDAKER, M., Marketing
KHANDAKER, N., Economics
KHATUN, H., Geography and the Environment
KHATUN, H., Islamic History and Culture

KHATUN, K., Statistical Research and Training
KHATUN, M., Botany
KHATUN, R., Sociology
KHATUN, S., Arabic
KHUDA, B. A., Economics
KIBRIA, R., International Relations
KOWSER, F., Bengali
LATIFA, G. A., Zoology
MABUD, M. A., Arabic
MAHBUB, A. Q. M., Geography and the Environment
MAHMUD, A. H. W. U., Economics
MAHMUD, A. J., Chemistry
MAHMUD, S., Biochemistry and Molecular Biology
MAHMUD, S. H., Psychology
MAHMUDA, S., Bengali
MAHTAB, N., Women's Studies
MAJID, A. K. M. S., Business Administration
MAJUMDER, A. R., Physics
MALEK, M. A., Islamic Studies
MALEK, M. A., Microbiology
MALEK, M. A., Nutrition and Food Science
MALLICK, S. A., Statistics
MAMUM, M. K., History
MAMUN, M. A. A., Chemistry
MAMUN, M. Z., Business Administration
MANNAN, K. A., Mass Communication and Journalism
MANNAN, K. A. I. F. M., Physics
MANNAN, M. A., Management Studies
MANNAN, S. M., Information Science and Library Management
MATIN, A., Botany
MATIN, K. A., Statistical Research and Training
MATIN, M. A., Mathematics
MAWLA, A., Nutrition and Food Science
MAWLA, G., Nutrition and Food Science
MAZUMDAR, M. A. R., Soil, Water and the Environment
MAZUMDER, K. A. B., Persian and Urdu
MAZUMDER, R. K., Applied Physics and Electronics
MAZUMDER, T. I. M. A., Botany
MIAH, M. S., Bengali
MIAH, M. S., Education and Research
MIAH, M. S., Philosophy
MINA, M. S., Finance
MOHIUDDIN, M., Management Studies
MOHSIN, A., International Relations
MOKADDEM, M., Economics
MOLLAH, M. G., Political Science
MOLLAH, M. Y. A., Chemistry
MONDAL, A. C., Mathematics
MONDAL, R., Soil, Water and the Environment
MONSUR, M. H., Geology
MORSHED, A. J. M. H., Finance
MORSHED, M. S., Botany
MOSHIHUZZAMAN, M., Chemistry
MOWLA, S. G., Management Studies
MOYEEN, M. A., Management Studies
MUNSHI, M. S. H., Political Science
MUSA, A. M. M. A., Modern Languages
MUSTAFA, A. I., Applied Chemistry and Chemical Technology
MUTTAQUI, M. I. A., Education and Research
NABI, A. K. M. N., Population Sciences
NABI, M. R., Fine Arts
NAHAR, B., Nutrition and Food Science
NAHAR, L., Nutrition and Food Science
NAHAR, N., Chemistry
NASIRUDDIN, M., Finance
NASREEN, G. A., Mass Communication and Journalism
NAZNEEN, D. R. Z. A., Peace and Conflict Studies
NIZAMI, A. B. M. S. R., Arabic
OSMAN, B., Fine Arts
OSMANY, S. H., History
PAHA, N. A., Chemistry
PARVEEN, K. N., Political Science
PARVEEN, Z., Soil, Water and the Environment
PERVIN, S., Mathematics
QADRI, S. S., Biochemistry and Molecular Biology
QAIS, N., Clinical Pharmacy and Pharmacology
QUADER, M. A., Chemistry
QUASEM, M. A., Philosophy
QUDDUS, M. A., Marketing
QUDDUS, M. A., Mathematics
QUDDUS, M. M. A., Zoology
QUYYUM, M. A., Applied Chemistry and Chemical Technology
RAB, M. A., Geography and the Environment
RABBANI, K. S. E., Physics
RAFIQ, S., Applied Physics and Electronics
RAHIM, K. A., Biochemistry and Molecular Biology
RAHIM, T., Botany
RAHMA, P. K. M. M., Statistical Research and Training
RAHMAN, A., Health Economics
RAHMAN, A., Information Science and Library Management
RAHMAN, A., Modern Languages
RAHMAN, A. H. M. A., Political Science
RAHMAN, A. H. M. H., Finance
RAHMAN, A. H. M. M., Applied Chemistry and Chemical Technology
RAHMAN, A. H. M. M., Soil, Water and the Environment
RAHMAN, A. K. M. M., Information Technology
RAHMAN, A. M. M. H., Modern Languages
RAHMAN, A. S. M. A., Social Welfare and Research
RAHMAN, A. Z. M. A., Accounting and Information Systems
RAHMAN, B. W., Education and Research
RAHMAN, J., Applied Physics and Electronics
RAHMAN, K. M., Nutrition and Food Science
RAHMAN, K. M. M., Statistical Research and Training
RAHMAN, K. R., English
RAHMAN, M., Accounting and Information Systems
RAHMAN, M., Biochemistry and Molecular Biology
RAHMAN, M., Marketing
RAHMAN, M., Public Administration
RAHMAN, M. A., Chemistry
RAHMAN, M. A., Clinical Psychology
RAHMAN, M. A., Law
RAHMAN, M. A., Marketing
RAHMAN, M. A., Mathematics
RAHMAN, M. A., Physics
RAHMAN, M. A., Political Science
RAHMAN, M. F., Arabic
RAHMAN, M. F., Zoology
RAHMAN, M. G., Mass Communication and Journalism
RAHMAN, M. H., Pharmaceutical Technology
RAHMAN, M. H., Sociology
RAHMAN, M. K., Biochemistry and Molecular Biology
RAHMAN, M. K., Soil, Water and the Environment
RAHMAN, M. K., Zoology
RAHMAN, M. L., Computer Science and Engineering
RAHMAN, M. M., Arabic
RAHMAN, M. M., Chemistry
RAHMAN, M. M., Clinical Psychology
RAHMAN, M. M., Marketing
RAHMAN, M. M., Mathematics
RAHMAN, M. M., Microbiology
RAHMAN, M. M., Nutrition and Food Science
RAHMAN, M. M., Philosophy
RAHMAN, M. M., Physics
RAHMAN, M. M., Soil, Water and the Environment
RAHMAN, M. M., Statistics
RAHMAN, M. S., Bengali
RAHMAN, M. S., Education and Research
RAHMAN, M. S., Soil, Water and the Environment
RAHMAN, M. S., Statistics
RAHMAN, M. T., Mathematics
RAHMAN, N., Business Administration
RAHMAN, N., Sociology
RAHMAN, N. N., Pharmaceutical Chemistry
RAHMAN, R., Biochemistry and Molecular Biology
RAHMAN, S. M. L., Bengali
RAHMAN, S. M. M., Banking
RAISUDDIN, A. N. M., Islamic Studies
RASHED, K. B. S., Geography and the Environment
RASHID, A. H. M. H., Philosophy
RASHID, G. H., Soil, Water and the Environment
RASHID, H., Management Studies
RASHID, M. A., Pharmaceutical Chemistry
RASHID, M. H., Accounting and Information Systems
RASHID, M. H., Political Science
RASHID, M. H., Soil, Water and the Environment
RASHID, P., Botany
RASHID, R. I. M. A., Physics
ROY, K. N., English
ROY, P. K., Philosophy
SAHA, M., Applied Chemistry and Chemical Technology
SAHA, M. L., Botany
SAHA, P. K., Education and Research
SAHA, S. K., Accounting and Information Systems
SALAM, S. A., Mass Communication and Journalism
SALAMATULLAH, K., Nutrition and Food Science
SALEH, M. A., Management Studies
SALMA, U., Persian and Urdu
SAMAD, A., Biochemistry and Molecular Biology
SAMAD, M., Social Welfare and Research
SARKER, A. H., Social Welfare and Research
SARKER, A. M., Fine Arts
SARKER, N., Fisheries
SARKER, N. R., Psychology
SARKER, R. H., Botany
SATTER, M. A., Fine Arts
SATTER, M. A., Physics
SEN, K., Statistics
SERAJ, Z. I., Biochemistry and Molecular Biology
SHAFEE, A., Physics
SHAFEE, S., Physics
SHAFI, M., Geology
SHAH, A. K. F. H., Marketing
SHAH, A. S., Fine Arts
SHAHED, S. M., Bengali
SHAHED, S. N., Bengali
SHAHEEN, N., Nutrition and Food Science
SHAHIDULLAH, A. K. M., Political Science
SHAHIDULLAH, K., History
SHAHIDULLAH, S. M., Psychology
SHAHIDUZZAMAN, M., International Relations
SHAMIM, I., Sociology
SHAMSI, S., Botany
SHARIF, M. R. I., Applied Physics and Electronics
SHEIKH, M. D. H., Education and Research
SIDDIQ, A. F. M. A. B., Arabic
SIDDIQ, M. A. B., Arabic
SIDDIQUE, A. A. M. S. A., Mass Communication and Journalism
SIDDIQUE, A. H., Management Studies
SIDDIQUE, S. A., Accounting and Information Systems
SIDDIQUE, T. A., Political Science
SIKDER, S. A., Fine Arts
SUFI, G. B., Zoology
SUKLADAS, J. C., Accounting and Information Systems
SULTANA, A., Mass Communication and Journalism
SULTANA, A., Philosophy
SYED, S., Nutrition and Food Science
TAHER, M. A., Social Welfare and Research
TALUKDER, A. S., Marketing
TASLIM, M. A., Economics

THAKURATA, M. G., International Relations
UDDIN, M. J., Education and Research
ULLAH, A. S. M. O., Geology
ULLAH, S. M., Soil, Water and Environment
WADUD, N., Psychology
WAHID, A. Q. F., Philosophy
YUSUF, H. K. M., Biochemistry and Molecular Biology
ZAFAR, M. A., Bengali
ZAMAN, F., Fine Arts
ZAMAN, N., English
ZAMAN, S. U., Economics

CONSTITUENT AND AFFILIATED COLLEGES

There are 58 constituent colleges and 3 affiliated colleges

DHAKA UNIVERSITY OF ENGINEERING AND TECHNOLOGY

Gazipur 1700
Telephone: (2) 9264021
Fax: (2) 9261234
E-mail: aazim@duet.ac.bd
Internet: www.duet.ac.bd
Founded 1980; present name and status 2003
State control
Language of instruction: English
Vice-Chancellor: Prof. Dr Ing. M. ANWARUL AZIM
Registrar: ALIM DAD.

HAJEE MOHAMMAD DANESH UNIVERSITY OF SCIENCE AND TECHNOLOGY

Dinajpur 5200
Telephone: (531) 65429
Fax: (531) 61344
E-mail: vcmdstu@dhaka.net
Founded 1976; present name and status 2002
State control
Vice-Chancellor: Prof. Dr MOSARARAF HOSSAIN MIAH
Registrar: Prof. MOHAMED KHALILUR RAHMAN
Librarian: MOHAMED ALAUDDIN KHAN.

INDEPENDENT UNIVERSITY, BANGLADESH

House 3, Rd 14, Baridhara, Dhaka 1212
Telephone: (2) 9881681
Fax: (2) 8823959
E-mail: info@iub-bd.edu
Internet: www.iub.bd.edu
Founded 1992
Private control
Language of instruction: English
Academic year: August to May
Chancellor: PRESIDENT OF THE PEOPLE'S REPUBLIC OF BANGLADESH
Vice-Chancellor: Prof. BAZLUL MOBIN CHOWDHURY
Director, Finance and Accounts: MUHAMMAD NURUL HASSAN
Associate Dean, Undergraduate Admissions: YAZMIN Z. MAHMUD
Registrar: Dr TANVIR AHMED KHAN
Librarian: MUHAMMAD HOSSAM HAIDER CHOWDHURY (Associate Librarian)
Library of 21,733 vols; 176 journal subscriptions
Number of teachers: 152, (127 full-time, 25 part-time)
Number of students: 3,042

DIRECTORS OF SCHOOLS

School of Business: Prof. BORHAN UDDIN
School of Engineering and Computer Science: Prof. MOHAMMED ANWER
School of Environmental Science and Management: Prof. HAROUN-ER-RASHID
School of Liberal Arts and Science: Prof. M. MOUFAKHARUL ISLAM

PROFESSORS

School of Business:
KUMAR SEN, D. ROWSHAN KAMAL, R.
School of Engineering and Computer Science:
ANWER, M. KHODADAT KHAN, A. F. M. NURUZZAMAN, M. SUFDERUL HUQ, S.

ATTACHED RESEARCH INSTITUTES

Centre for Social Science and Public Policy Research: House 58, Park Rd, Baridhara, Dhaka 1212; Executive Director ABUL AHSAN.

Extension and Continuing Education Centre: House 58, Park Rd, Baridhara, Dhaka 1212; Director MAHMOOD-UL HAQ.

INTERNATIONAL UNIVERSITY OF BUSINESS, AGRICULTURE AND TECHNOLOGY

4 Embankment Drive Rd, Sector 10, Uttara Model Town, Dhaka 1230
Telephone: (2) 8963523
Fax: (2) 8922625
E-mail: info@iubat.edu
Internet: www.iubat.edu
Founded 1991
Private control
Academic year: January to December
Chancellor: President of the People's Republic of Bangladesh
Vice-Chancellor: Prof. M. ALIMULLAH MIYAN
Pro-Chancellor: Prof. MAHMUDA KHANUM
Registrar: Dr M. A. HANNAN
Librarian: MONOWARA SARWAR
Number of teachers: 150
Number of students: 700
Publication: *Newsletter* (2 a year)
Colleges of Agricultural Sciences, Arts and Sciences, Business Administration, Engineering and Technology, Nursing and Tourism and Hospitality Management.

ISLAMIC UNIVERSITY

Shantidanga-Dulalpur, Kushtia
Telephone: (71) 53029
Fax: (71) 54400
Founded 1980
Vice-Chancellor: Prof. MOHAMMAD M. RAHMAN
Registrar: K. M. ASHRAF HOSSAIN
Librarian (vacant)
Library of 22,000 vols
Number of teachers: 65
Number of students: 1,500

DEANS

Faculty of Social Sciences: Dr M. MAMUN
Faculty of Theology and Islamic Studies: Prof. M. A. HAMID (acting)

ISLAMIC UNIVERSITY OF TECHNOLOGY

Board Bazar, Gazipur 1704
Telephone: (2) 9291250
Fax: (2) 9291260
E-mail: vc@iut-dhaka.edu
Internet: www.iutoic-dhaka.edu
Founded 1981 as Islamic Centre for Technical and Vocational Training and Research; became Islamic Institute of Technology 1994; present name 2001
Subsidiary of the Organization of the Islamic Conference
Academic year: December to September
Vice-Chancellor: Prof. Dr MOHAMMAD FAZLI ILAHI
Registrar: MOHAMMAD AHSAN HABIB
Librarian: Dr MIRZA MOHAMMAD REZAUL ISLAM
Library of 26,500 vols, 17 periodicals
Number of teachers: 103
Number of students: 696
Publications: *Calendar* (annually), *Journal of Engineering and Technology* (2 a year), *News Bulletin* (annually), *Newsletter* (4 a year)

HEADS OF DEPARTMENTS

Computer Science and Information Technology: Prof. Dr MOHAMMAD ABDUL MOTTALIB
Electrical and Electronic Engineering: Prof. Dr FAZLI QAYYUM YOUSAF-ZAI
Instructor Training and General Studies: Prof. Dr MOHAMMAD SHAHJAHAN MIAN (TAPAN)
Mechanical and Chemical Engineering: Prof. Dr MOHAMMAD ABDUR RAZZAQ AKHANDA

ATTACHED CENTRES

Department of Research, Extension, Advisory Services and Publication: Dir Prof. Dr MOHAMMAD SHAHJAHAN MIAN (TAPAN).

Energy and Environment Centre: Head Prof. Dr A. K. M. IQBAL HUSSAIN.

JAHANGIRNAGAR UNIVERSITY

Savar, Dhaka 1342
Telephone: (2) 7708469
Fax: (2) 7708069
E-mail: vc@juniv.edu
Internet: www.juniv.edu
Founded 1970
Languages of instruction: Bengali, English
Academic year: July to June (three terms)
Chancellor: PRESIDENT OF THE REPUBLIC
Vice-Chancellor: Prof. KHANDAKER MUSTAHADIR RAHMAN
Pro-Vice-Chancellor (Academic): Prof. MD ENMUL HUQ KHAN
Pro-Vice-Chancellor (Administration): Prof. M. IMAMUDDIN
Registrar: KAZI MAHIUDDIN
Librarian: Prof. SUBASH CHANDRA DAS
Library of 103,000 vols, 193 periodicals
Number of teachers: 423
Number of students: 7,376
Publications: *Asian Studies*, *Bangladesh Geoscience Journal*, *Bangladesh Journal of Life Sciences* (biological and life sciences), *Clio* (History), *Copula* (Philosophy), *Harvest* (English Studies), *Jahangirnagar Economic Review*, *Jahangirnagar Physics Studies*, *Jahangirnagar Planning Review*, *Jahangirnagar Review* (arts and humanities), *Jahangirnagar Review* (social sciences), *Jahangirnagar University Chemical Review*, *Jahangirnagar University Journal of Sciences* (mathematical and physical sciences), *Journal of Business Research*, *Journal of Electronic and Computer Science*, *Journal of Mathematics and Mathematical Sciences*, *Journal of Statistical Studies*, *Nre Baggan Patrica* (Anthropology), *Pratnatattva* (Archaeology), *Theatre Studies*, *Vhasa Shahitta Patra* (Bengali Studies), *Vogal Patrica* (Geography)

DEANS

Faculty of Arts and Humanities: Prof. MD NASIRUDDIN
Faculty of Biological Sciences: Prof. SHAHABUDDIN KABIR CHOWDHURY (Dir)
Faculty of Mathematical and Physical Sciences: Prof. MAHMOODA GHANI AHMED

Faculty of Social Sciences: Prof. AMIN MUHAMMAD ALI

HEADS OF DEPARTMENTS

Anthropology: Dr MD JAHIR UDDIN AHMED
Archaeology: Prof. MD MOZAMMEL HOQUE
Bengali: Prof. SAUDA AKHTER
Biochemistry and Molecular Biology: Dr MD SAHADAT HOSSAIN
Botany: NAZMUL ALAM
Business Administration: CHOWDHURY GOLAM KIBRIA
Chemistry: Prof. MD RABIUL ISLAM
Drama and Dramatics: MD HAROONAR RASHID KHAN
Economics: Prof. ZINATUNESSA R. M. M. KHUDA KHANDAKAR
Computer Sciences and Engineering: Prof. AKRAM HOSSAIN
English: Dr MONIRUZZAMAN
Environmental Sciences: Dr MAHFUZA SHARIFA SULTANA
Geography and Environment: Prof. AL AMIN MOHAMMAD
Geological Sciences: Prof. A. T. M. SHAKHAWAT HOSSAIN
Government and Politics: Dr NAIM SULTAN
History: Prof. MD NASIR UDDIN
International Relations: Prof. TAREQUE SHAMSUR RAHMAN
Mathematics: Prof. SATRAJIT KUMAR SAHA
Pharmacy: Dr MD SOHEL RANA
Philosophy: MAHAMMAD KAMRUL AHSAN
Physics: Prof. MIR MD AKRAMUZZAMAN
Statistics: Prof. SWAMAN KUMAR DHAR
Urban and Regional Planning: Prof. MD SAJED ASHRAF KARIM
Zoology: Prof. MOHAMMAD MOSTAFA FEEROZ

ATTACHED INSTITUTE

Computer Science and Information Technology Institute: Dir Prof. MD NURUL ALAM KHAN.

Institute of Remote Sensing: Dir Prof. MD SAJED ASHRAF KARIM.

Language Centre: Dir Prof. U. H. M. SHAMSUN NAHAR.

KHULNA UNIVERSITY

Khulna 9208
Telephone: (41) 721393
Fax: (41) 731244
E-mail: ku@bdonline.com
Founded 1987
State control
Language of instruction: English
Academic year: July to June
Vice-Chancellor: Prof. Dr S. M. NAZRUL ISLAM
Registrar: GAZI ABDULLA-HEL BAQUI (acting)
Librarian: MOKLESUR RAHMAN (acting)
Library of 30,000 vols
Number of teachers: 154
Number of students: 3,038
Publications: *Business Review* (2 a year), *Khulna University Studies* (2 a year)

DEANS

School of Arts, Humanities and Social Science: Prof. Dr MOHAMED MAHBUBUR RAHMAN
School of Business Administration: Prof. Dr MOHAMED MAHBUBUR RAHMAN
School of Life Science: Prof. MOHAMED ABDUL MALIN
School of Science, Engineering and Technology: Prof. Dr MOHAMED RAZAUL KARIM

HEADS OF DISCIPLINE

Agrotechnology: Dr KHAN GOLAM QUDDUS
Architecture: MOZAMMEL H. MRIDHA
Biology: SELINA AHMED
Biotechnology: Prof. Dr MOHAMED RAIHAN ALI
Business Administration: FEROZ AHMED
Computer Science and Engineering: Dr MOHAMED MAHBUBUR RAHMAN
Economics: SHAHNEWAZ NAZIMUDDIN AHMED
Electronics and Communication Engineering: MOHAMMAD ISMAT KADIR
English: Dr MOHAMMAD EMDADUL HUQ
Environmental Science: Dr RAKIB UDDIN
Fisheries and Marine Resource Technology: Prof. Dr MD. SAIFUDDIN SHAH
Forestry and Wood Technology: Prof. MOHAMED OBAIDULLAH HANNAN
Mathematics: Dr MOHAMMAD MAHMUD ALAM
Pharmacy: Dr MOHAMMAD MEHEDI MASUD
Soil Science: Dr MIZANUR RAHMAN BHUIYAN
Urban and Rural Planning: MOHAMED REZAUL KARIM

KHULNA UNIVERSITY OF ENGINEERING AND TECHNOLOGY

Fulbarigate, Khulna 9203
Telephone: (41) 774584
Fax: (41) 774403
E-mail: registrar@kuet.ac.bd
Internet: www.kuet.ac.bd
Founded 1974 as Khulna Engineering College; Bangladesh Institute of Technology, Khulna 1986; present name and status 2003
State control
Vice-Chancellor: Prof. Dr EHSANUL HAQUE
Registrar (vacant)
Library of 35,000 vols
Number of teachers: 132
Number of students: 1,887

DEANS

Faculty of Civil Engineering: Prof. Dr MOHAMED MONJUR HOSSAIN
Faculty of Electrical and Electronic Engineering: Prof. Dr ABDUR RAHIM MOLLAH
Faculty of Mechanical Engineering: Prof. Dr MOHAMED KUTUB UDDIN

HEADS OF DEPARTMENTS

Faculty of Civil Engineering:
- Chemistry: MOHAMED SHOFIUR RAHMAN
- Civil Engineering: Prof. Dr MUHAMMED ALAMGIR
- Humanities: MUNSHI TOUHIDUZZAMAN
- Mathematics: Prof. Dr MOHAMED BAZLAR RAHMAN
- Physics: Prof. Dr SHIBENDRA SHEKER SIKDER

Faculty of Electrical and Electronic Engineering:
- Biomedical Engineering: (vacant)
- Computer Science and Engineering: Prof. Dr M. M. A. HASHEM
- Electrical and Electronic Engineering: Prof. Dr MOHAMED ABUL KALAM AZAD
- Electronic and Communication Engineering: Prof. Dr BASHUDEB CHANDRA GHOSH

Faculty of Mechanical Engineering:
- Energy Technology: (vacant)
- Industrial Engineering and Management: Prof. Dr MOHAMED SAYED ALI MOLLAH
- Mechanical Engineering: Prof. Dr A. N. M. MIZANUR RAHMAN

MAWLANA BHASANI UNIVERSITY OF SCIENCE AND TECHNOLOGY

Santosh, Tangail 1902
Telephone: (2) 9136969
Fax: (2) 9130374
Founded 1999
State control
Vice-Chancellor: Prof. Dr YUSUF SHARIF AHMED KHAN
Registrar: Shah MOHAMED SARWAHUL ISLAM.

NATIONAL UNIVERSITY

Gazipur 1704
Telephone: (2) 9800667
Fax: (2) 8110261
E-mail: nulib@bdonline.com
Founded 1992
State control
Chancellor: Prime Minister of the People's Republic of Bangladesh
Vice-Chancellor: Prof. AMINUL ISLAM
Dean of the School of Undergraduate Studies: Prof. QUAZI BILLAH
Publications: *Journal* (4 a year), *Jatiya Bishawvidalaya Patrika* (4 a year), *Jatiya Bishawvidalaya Newsletter*.

NORTH SOUTH UNIVERSITY

12 Banani Commercial Area, Kemal Ataturk Ave, Dhaka 1213
Telephone: (2) 9885611
Fax: (2) 8823030
E-mail: registrar@northsouth.edu
Internet: www.northsouth.edu
Founded 1992
Private control
Academic year: January to December (three semesters)
Number of teachers: 155 (84 full-time, 71 visiting)
Number of students: 4,281.

PATUAKHALI UNIVERSITY OF SCIENCE AND TECHNOLOGY

Dumki, Patuakhali 8602
Telephone: (441) 62678
Founded 2002
State control
Vice-Chancellor: Prof. Dr A. K. M. ABDUL HANNAN BHUIYAN
Librarian: MOHAMED ANWAR HOSSEIN.

UNIVERSITY OF RAJSHAHI

Rajshahi 6205
Telephone: (721) 750041
Fax: (721) 750064
E-mail: rajucc@cilechco.net
Founded 1953
Languages of instruction: English, Bengali
Academic year: July to June (three terms)
Chancellor: PRESIDENT OF THE PEOPLE'S REPUBLIC OF BANGLADESH
Vice-Chancellor: Prof. SAYEEDUR RAHMAN KHAN
Registrar: M. ABDUS SALAM
Librarian (vacant)
Library: see Libraries and Archives
Number of teachers: 804
Number of students: 24,032 (university)
Publications: *Calendar* (every 2 years), *Rajshahi University Studies* (annually)

DEANS

Faculty of Agriculture: Prof. M. ABDUL KHALEQUE
Faculty of Arts: Prof. KHANAM MUMTAZ AHMED
Faculty of Business Studies: Prof. A. K. M. ABDUL MAJID
Faculty of Law: Prof. MOHAMMAD HABIBUR RAHMAN
Faculty of Life and Earth: MOHAMMAD ABDUS SALAM
Faculty of Medicine: Prof. ABU BAKER SIDDIQUE
Faculty of Science: Prof. FAISUL ISLAM FARUQUI
Faculty of Social Science: Prof. MUHAMMAD ABDUR RAHMAN

PROFESSORS

Faculty of Agriculture:

JOARDER, M. O. I., Genetics and Breeding
KABIR, G., Agronomy and Agricultural Extension
KHALEQUE, M. A., Genetics and Breeding

Faculty of Arts:

ADHIKARY, M. N., Philosophy
AHMED, K. M., Philosophy
AHMED, S., Islamic History and Culture
AHMED, W., History
ALI, A. K. M. Y., Islamic History and Culture
ALI, M. A., English
ALI, M. W., History
ASADULLAH-AL-GHALIB, M., Arabic
BARI, M. A., Islamic History and Culture
CHOWDHURY, N. H., History
FARUK-UZ-ZAMAN, M., History
FAZUL, M. A., Bengali
GHOSE, R. N., Philosophy
HAMID, M. A., Philosophy
HAQUE, A., Philosophy
HAQUE, K. S., Bengali
HAQUE, M. E., English
HARUN-OR-RASHID, M., Bengali
HASSAN, M. A. D., English
HOSSAIN, K. F., Bengali
HOSSAIN, S., History
IBRAHIMI, M. S. A., Arabic
JALIL, M. A., Bengali
JALIL, M. A., Folklore
KHALEQUE, A., Bengali
KHAN, M. A. A., Arabic
MATIN, C. Z., Bengali
MISRA, C. R., History
MOHIUDDIN, A. K. M., English
MONDAL, A. A., Philosophy
NAHAR, S., Islamic History and Culture
QAIYUM, M. N., History
QUASEM, M. A., History
RAHIM, M. A., History
RAHMAN, A. F. M. S., History
RAHMAN, A. K. M. A., Bengali
RAHMAN, M. M., History
RAHMAN, M. M., Islamic History and Culture
RAHMAN, Q., Islamic History and Culture
REHMAN, A. A., English
ROY, K. L., Languages
SALAM, M. A., Arabic
SAMADI, S. S., Bengali
SARKAR, J. N., Philosophy
SARKAR, M. S. A., Philosophy
SHAFI, M., History
SHAFIQULLAH, M., Islamic Studies
SHAHIDULLAH, M., English
SHAHJAHAN, M., Philosophy
SHAMSUDDIN, Philosophy
SHIBLY, A. H., History
TALUKDAR, M. A. H., Philosophy
TAQI, F. M. A. H., Islamic Studies

Faculty of Business Studies:

ADBULLAH-AL-HAROON, M., Accounting
AKAM, M. H. R., Accounting
ALAM, M. S., Accounting
ALI, A. S. M. N., Management
ALI, M. O., Management
ALI, M. S. N., Management
ANJUM, M. N., Management
ANSARI, M. R., Finance and Banking
DEY, M. M., Accounting
HOSSAIN, M. M., Accounting
HOSSAIN, S. Z., Accounting
ISLAM, M. A., Management
ISLAM, M. N., Accounting
MOJID, A. K. M. A., Finance and Banking
PAUL, P., Accounting
PRAMANIK, M. A. R., Accounting
RAHMAN, M. M., Management
SAHA, A. C., Accounting
SAHA, S. K., Marketing

Faculty of Law:

HOSSAIN, M. M.
RAHMAN, M. H.
SIDDIQUE, M. A. B.

Faculty of Life and Earth:

AFSARUDDIN, M., Psychology
AHMED, A., Botany
AHMED, M., Geology and Mining
AHMED, M., Psychology
AHMED, R., Geography and Environmental Studies
AHMED, S. S., Geology and Mining
AHMED, S. T., Geology and Mining
ALAM, M. S., Geography and Environmental Studies
ALAM, M. S., Botany
ALI, M. M., Zoology
ALI, M. S., Zoology
AMIN, M. N., Botany
ARA, S., Psychology
BHUIYAN, M. A. S., Zoology
FARUK, T., Psychology
HAQUE, A. B. M. J., Psychology
HAQUE, M. E., Geography and Environmental Studies
HAQUE, M. M., Psychology
HOSSAIN, M. A., Psychology
HOSSAIN, M. A., Zoology
HOSSAIN, M. M., Information and Communication Technology
HOSSAIN, M. MONZUR, Botany
HOSSAIN, M. MOZAHED, Botany
HOSSAIN, N., Botany
HUSSAIN, M. Z., Geography and Environmental Studies
ISLAM, A. K. M. R., Botany
ISLAM, M. A., Geology and Mining
ISLAM, M. B., Geology and Mining
ISLAM, M. S., Zoology
JAHAN, M. S., Zoology
KHALEQUE, M. A., Botany
KHALEQUZZAMAN, M., Zoology
KHAN, J. R., Geography and Environmental Studies
KUNDU, P., Botany
LATIF, M. A., Psychology
MAJUMDER, Q. H., Geology and Mining
MANNAN, M. A., Zoology
NADERUZZAMAN, A. T. M., Botany
NAHAR, S., Botany
PARVEEN, S., Zoology
PAUL, N. K., Botany
RAHMAN, A. S. M. S., Zoology
RAHMAN, M. A., Botany
RAHMAN, M. A., Geography and Environmental Studies
RAHMAN, M. A., Zoology
RAHMAN, M. HABIBUR, Geology and Mining
RAHMAN, M. HAMIDUR, Geology and Mining
RAHMAN, M. S., Botany
RAHMAN, M. S., Zoology
RAHMAN, M. S., Zoology
RAHMAN, S. M., Zoology
RAQUIBUDDIN, M., Geology and Mining
RUMI, S. R. A., Geography and Environmental Studies
SALAM, M. A., Zoology
SHAIKH, M. A. H., Geography and Environmental Studies
TAHA, M. A., Geography and Environmental Studies
WAHAB, M. A., Geography and Environmental Studies
ZAMAN, M., Botany
ZUBERI, M. I., Botany

Faculty of Science:

ABEDIN, S., Statistics
ABSAR, N., Biochemistry
AHMED, M., Mathematics
AHMED, N., Chemistry
AHMED, S. U., Chemistry
ALI, D. M., Mathematics
ALI, M. A., Chemistry
ALI, M. K., Population Science and Human Resource Development
ALI, M. U., Chemistry
ALI, M. Y., Chemistry
ALI, S. M. M., Applied Chemistry and Chemical Technology
ANSARI, M. A., Mathematics
AZAD, M. A. K., Applied Chemistry and Chemical Technology
BAKER, M. A., Applied Chemistry and Chemical Technology
BANU, K., Physics
BASAK, A. K., Physics
BHATTACHARJEE, S., Physics
BHATTACHARJEE, S. K., Mathematics
BHATTACHARJEE, S. K., Statistics
BISWAS, R. K., Applied Chemistry and Chemical Technology
CHAKRAVARTY, P. K., Chemistry
CHOWDHURY, G. M., Physics
DAS, B. K., Chemistry
DEBNATH, R. C., Applied Physics and Electronics
FARUQUI, F. I., Applied Chemistry and Chemical Technology
HAKIM, M. O., Physics
HAQUE, M. E., Chemistry
HAQUE, M. E., Pharmacy
HAQUE, M. E., Physics
HASHEM, M. A., Applied Physics and Electronics
HOSSAIN, M. D., Applied Physics and Electronics
HOSSAIN, M. L., Chemistry
HOWLADER, M. B. H., Chemistry
ISLAM, A. K. M. A., Physics
ISLAM, G. S., Physics
ISLAM, M. A., Chemistry
ISLAM, M. A., Physics
ISLAM, M. F., Applied Chemistry and Chemical Technology
ISLAM, M. N., Chemistry
ISLAM, M. N., Physics
ISLAM, M. S., Applied Chemistry and Chemical Technology
ISLAM, M. S., Physics
ISLAM, M. S., Chemistry
ISLAM, M. W., Mathematics
ISLAM, S. N., Physics
KARMAKER, A. K., Applied Physics and Electronics
KERAMAT, M., Applied Physics and Electronics
KHAN, M. A R., Chemistry
KHAN, M. K. A., Applied Physics and Electronics
KHAN, M. S. R., Applied Physics and Electronics
LATIF, M. A., Mathematics
MAHATABOALLY, S. Q. G., Physics
MAJUMDER, S., Mathematics
MALLICK, A. K., Mathematics
MIA, M. A. A., Applied Physics and Electronics
MIAH, M. A. B., Statistics
MIAH, M. A. J., Chemistry
MOLLA, M. A. H., Applied Chemistry and Chemical Technology
MONDAL, M. A. S., Physics
MORTUZA, M. G., Physics
MOSTAFA, M. G., Statistics
MOSTOFA, C. H., Applied Chemistry and Chemical Technology
NOOR, A. S. A., Mathematics
NOOR, A. S. A., Population Science and Human Resource Development
PAUL, A. C., Mathematics
PAUL, S. C., Chemistry
RAHMAN, M. A., Applied Chemistry and Chemical Technology
RAHMAN, M. B., Chemistry
RAHMAN, M. L., Chemistry
RAHMAN, M. M., Physics
RAHMAN, M. S., Applied Chemistry and Chemical Technology
RAHMAN, M. Z., Mathematics
RAQIB-UZ-ZAMAN, M., Applied Chemistry and Chemical Technology
RAZZAQUE, M. A., Statistics
SAHA, R. K., Biochemistry

SARKER, M. A. R., Applied Physics and Electronics
SARKER, M. J. A., Physics
SARKER, M. S. A., Mathematics
SATTAR, M. A., Mathematics
SATTAR, M. A., Chemistry
SAYEED, M. A., Applied Chemistry and Chemical Technology
SHAHJAHAN, M., Biochemistry
SOBHAN, M. A., Applied Physics and Electronics
SOBHAN, M. A., Applied Physics and Electronics
TORAFDER, M. T. H., Chemistry

Faculty of Social Science:
AKBAR, M. A., Social Work
ALI, M. M., Economics
BEGUM, H. A., Social Work
BHUIYAN, M. A. Q., Sociology
EUNUS, M., Economics
HABIB, A. H. M. A., Economics
HALIM, M. A., Social Work
HOSSAIN, A. M. M., Economics
HOSSAIN, K. T., Sociology
IMAM, M. H., Sociology
ISLAM, A. S. M. N., Social Work
ISLAM, M. S., Political Science
ISLAM, T. S., Economics
KARIM, A. H. M. Z., Anthropology
KHAN, F. R., Sociology
KHANUM, S. M., Sociology
MIZANUDDIN, M., Sociology
MOAZZEM, M., Economics
MORSHED, G., Political Science
MOSTUFA, S. K., Political Science
NATH, D. K., Economics
NATH, J., Sociology
OBAIDULLAH, A. T. M., Public Administration
QUASEM, M. A., Political Science
QUAYUM, M. A., Economics
RAHMAN, A. H. M. M.., Sociology
RAHMAN, M. A., Economics
RAHMAN, M. F., Sociology
RAHMAN, M. M., Political Science
RAHMAN, M. S., Public Administration
RAHMAN, S. M. H., Economics
RAHMAN, S. M. Z., Sociology
SADEQUE, M., Social Work
SAHA, M. S. K., Economics
SARKAR, P. C., Social Work
SIDDIQUI, A. R., Sociology

There are 241 affiliated colleges

ATTACHED INSTITUTES

Institute of Bangladesh Studies: Dir Prof. PRITI KUMAR MITRA.

Institute of Biological Science: Dir Prof. M. SOHRAB ALI.

Institute of Business Administration: Dir Prof. M. NASIM ANZUM.

Institute of Education and Research: Dir Prof. M. SHAHIDUL ISLAM.

Institute of Environmental Science: Dir Prof. MUSHFIQ AHMED.

RAJSHAHI UNIVERSITY OF ENGINEERING AND TECHNOLOGY

Kajla, Rajshahi 6204

Telephone: (721) 6254
Fax: (721) 6254
Internet: www.geocities.com/uddinfarid/bitraj/bit_rajshahi.html

Founded 1986 as Engineering College, Rajshahi; present name and status 2003
State control

Vice-Chancellor: Prof. Dr KERAMAT ALI MOLLAH.

SHAHJALAL UNIVERSITY OF SCIENCE AND TECHNOLOGY

PO University 3114, Sylhet

Telephone: (821) 713491
Fax: (821) 715257
E-mail: reg@sust.edu

Founded 1987
State control
Languages of instruction: English, Bengali
Academic year: July to June

Chancellor: PRESIDENT OF THE PEOPLE'S REPUBLIC OF BANGLADESH
Vice-Chancellor: Prof. MUSLEH UDDIN AHMED
Registrar: JAMIL AHMED CHOWDHURY
Librarian: MOHAMED ABDUL HAYEE SAMENI (Deputy Librarian)

Library of 41,000 vols

Number of teachers: 307
Number of students: 4,638

Publication: *SUST Studies* (annually)

DEANS

School of Agriculture and Mineral Science: Prof. M. ZAFAR IQBAL (acting)
School of Applied Sciences and Technology: Prof. M. ZAFAR IQBAL
School of Business Administration: Prof. M. HABIBUR RAHMAN (acting)
School of Life Sciences: Prof. MOSLEH UDDIN
School of Medical Science: Prof. N. K. PAUL
School of Physical Sciences: Prof. G. D. ROY
School of Social Sciences: Prof. HABIBUR RAHMAN

SHER-E-BANGLA AGRICULTURAL UNIVERSITY

Sher-e-Banglanagar, Dhaka 1207

Telephone: (2) 9110351
Fax: (2) 9112649

Founded 2001
State control

Vice-Chancellor: Prof. Dr A. M. FARUQUE
Registrar: Prof. ABU AKBAR MIA (acting)
Librarian: MOHAMED MAHBUBUR RAHMAN.

Colleges

Bangladesh Agricultural Research Institute: Joydebpur, Gazipur 1701; tel. (2) 9261501; fax (2) 9252713; e-mail biis@bttb.net.bd; f. 1976; library: 28,092 vols, 150 periodicals; Dir-Gen. Dr MOHAMMED SAHIDUL ISLAM; Sr Librarian A. B. M. FAZLUR RAHMAN; publ. *Bangladesh Journal of Agricultural Research* (quarterly).

Bangladesh College of Textile Technology: Tejgaon I/A, Dhaka 1208; f. 1950; a constituent college of Dhaka University; degree courses; 27 teachers; library: 8,535 vols; Principal Dr M. RAHMAN.

Institute of Leather Technology: Dhaka.

BARBADOS

The Higher Education System

The main institution of higher education on the island is a branch campus of the University of the West Indies. Non-university post-secondary education is offered by the Samuel Jackson Prescod Polytechnic and Barbados Community College.

Admission to the University is based on satisfactory performance in the Caribbean Advanced Proficiency Examinations. The University offers Associate, Bachelors, Masters and Doctoral degrees programmes. The Associate degree lasts for two years, the Bachelors three years, the Masters two years after the Bachelors and the Doctorate two more years after the Masters.

The Samuel Jackson Prescod Polytechnic trade and craft programmes leading to City and Guilds qualifications and Royal Society of Arts qualifications. Two-year Associate degrees are available from the Barbados Community College.

Learned Societies

GENERAL

Caribbean Conservation Association: The Garrison, St Michael; tel. 426-5373; fax 429-8483; e-mail admin@cca.net; internet www.cca.net; f. 1967; independent, non-profit-making; preservation and development of the environment, and conservation of the cultural heritage in the Caribbean as a whole; c. 200 mems; small library; Pres. ATHERTON MARTIN; Exec. Dir Dr JOTH SINGH.

BIBLIOGRAPHY, LIBRARY SCIENCE AND MUSEOLOGY

Library Association of Barbados: POB 827E, Bridgetown; f. 1968 to unite qualified librarians, archivists and information specialists, and all other persons engaged or interested in information management and dissemination in Barbados, and to provide opportunities for their meeting together; to promote the active development and maintenance of libraries in Barbados and to foster co-operation between them; to interest the general public in the library services available; 60 mems; Pres. SHIRLEY YEARWOOD; Sec. HAZELYN DEVONISH; publ. *Update* (irregular).

HISTORY, GEOGRAPHY AND ARCHAEOLOGY

Barbados Museum and Historical Society: see Museum.

LANGUAGE AND LITERATURE

Alliance Française: 17 Pine Rd, Belleville, St Michael; tel. 436-4675; e-mail afbb@cariaccess.com; academic year offers courses and exams in French language and culture and promotes cultural exchange with France.

MEDICINE

Barbados Association of Medical Practitioners: BAMP Complex, Spring Garden, St Michael; tel. 429-7569; fax 435-2328; e-mail bamp@sunbeach.net; internet www.bamp.org.bb; f. 1973; 348 mems; Pres. Dr JEROME WALCOTT; Gen. Sec. RANDOLPH CARRINGTON; publ. *BAMP Bulletin* (5 a year).

Barbados Pharmaceutical Society: POB 820 E., St Michael; f. 1948, inc. 1961; 155 mems; Pres. DELORES MORRIS; Sec. GEORGE ALLEYNE; publ. *Pharmacy in Progress*.

Research Institute

GENERAL

Bellairs Research Institute: Holetown, St James; tel. 422-2087; fax 422-0692; e-mail bellairs@caribsurf.com; internet www.mcgill.ca/bellairs; f. 1954; affiliated with McGill University, Canada; field courses, workshops and research and teaching in all aspects of tropical environments; library of 200 vols; Dir Dr BRUCE R. DOWNEY.

Libraries and Archives

Bridgetown

Public Library: Coleridge St, Bridgetown; tel. 436-6081; fax 436-1501; f. 1847; an island-wide service is provided from the central library in Bridgetown by means of 7 brs, 6 centres, and a mobile service to 66 primary schools; acts as a national repository for legal deposit printed materials; 165,000 vols; special Barbadian and West Indian research collection; Dir JUDY BLACKMAN; publ. *National Bibliography of Barbados* (2 a year with, annual cumulations).

University of the West Indies Main Library: POB 1334, Bridgetown; tel. 417-4444; fax 417-4460; e-mail mlrefdesk@uwichill.edu.bb; internet mainlibrary.uwichill.edu.bb/; f. 1963; 155,000 vols, special West Indies collection, OAS, UN, UNESCO and World Bank depository library; Librarian NEL BRETNEY.

St James

Department of Archives: Black Rock, St James; tel. 425-5150; fax 425-5911; e-mail archives@sunbeach.net; f. 1963; part of the Prime Minister's Office; 990 linear m of archives, 2,366 vols and pamphlets, 922 serials, 391 microfilm reels, 2,747 fiches, 220 sound recordings; Chief Archivist DAVID WILLIAMS.

Museum

St Ann's Garrison

Barbados Museum and Historical Society: St Ann's Garrison, St Michael; tel. 427-0201; fax 429-5946; e-mail museum@caribsurf.com; internet www.barbmuse.org.bb; f. 1933; collections illustrating the island's geology, prehistory, history, natural history and marine life; European decorative arts, militaria, furniture; library of 5,000 vols; 1,000 mems; Pres. Dr TREVOR CARMICHAEL; Dir ALISSANDRA CUMMINS; publs *Journal* (annually), *Newsletter* (4 a year).

University

THE UNIVERSITY OF THE WEST INDIES, CAVE HILL CAMPUS

POB 64, Bridgetown

Telephone: 417-4000
Fax: 425-1327
E-mail: jwade@uwichill.edu.bb
Internet: www.cavehill.uwi.edu

Founded 1963
Language of instruction: English
Academic year: August to July (2 semesters)
Private control

Chancellor: Sir GEORGE ALLEYNE
Vice-Chancellor: Prof. E. NIGEL HARRIS
Pro-Vice-Chancellor and Principal: Prof. HILARY M. BECKLES
Registrar: JACQUELINE E. WADE
Campus Librarian: KAREN LEQUAY

Library of 180,815 vols, 2,346 serial titles
Number of teachers: 528 (incl. 363 part-time)
Number of students: 7,547

Publications: *Caribbean Journal of Mathematics* (annually), *Caribbean Law Bulletin* (2 a year), *Caribbean Law Review* (2 a year), *Journal of Eastern Caribbean Studies* (4 a year)

one of the three campuses of the University of the West Indies, intended to serve Barbados, the Leeward and Windward Islands; see also Jamaica and Trinidad and Tobago; teaching programmes cover humanities, education, law, pure and applied sciences, social sciences and clinical studies in medicine

DEANS

Faculty of Humanities and Education: Prof. HAZEL SIMMONS-MCDONALD
Faculty of Law: Prof. SIMEON MCINTOSH
Faculty of Pure and Applied Sciences: Prof. C. M. SEAN CARRINGTON
Faculty of Social Sciences: Dr GEORGE A. V. BELLE
School of Clinical Medicine and Research: Prof. HENRY FRASER

PROFESSORS

ANDERSON, W., International & Environmental Law
BARRITEAU, E., Gender and Public Policy
BARROW, C., Sociology
BECKLES, H., Economic and Social History
BURGESS, A., Corporate and Commercial Law
CARNEGIE, A., Law
CARRINGTON, S., Plant Biology
CHAUDHURI, P., Computer Science
COBLEY, A., South African and Comparative History
DOWNES, A., Economics
FAIDJOE, A., Public Law

FRASER, H., Medicine and Clinical Pharmacology
HOWARD, M., Economics
HUNTE, W., Ecology and Environmental Sciences
KHAN, J., Development Administration
KING, W., Science Education & Curriculum Studies
KODILYNE, G., Property Law
LAVOIE, M., Microbiology
MARSHALL, S., Distance Education
MAHON, R., Resource Management & Environmental Studies
MCDOWELL, S., Theoretical & Computational Chemistry
MCINTOSH, S., Jurisprudence
MCWATT, M., West Indian Literature
MOSELEY, L., Physics
NEWTON, V., Law Librarianship
O'GARRO, L., Plant Pathology
PUNNETT, B. J., Management Studies
RICHARDSON, A., Educational Psychology
ROBERTS, P., Creole Linguistics
THOMPSON, A., Caribbean History
TINTO, W., Organic Chemistry
ZBAR, A., Surgery

ATTACHED RESEARCH INSTITUTES

Caribbean Law Institute Centre: POB 64, Bridgetown 11000; tel. 417-4560; fax 424-1318; Exec. Dir Prof. RALPH CARNEGIE.

Centre for Gender and Development Studies: POB 64, Bridgetown 11000; tel. 417-4490; fax 424-3822; e-mail gender@uwichill.edu.bb; internet gender.uwichill.edu.bb; Head Prof. V. EUDINE BARRITEAU.

Centre for International Services: Dir (vacant).

Centre for Management Development: Dir Dr JEANNINE COMMA.

Sir Arthur Lewis Institute of Social and Economic Studies (SALISES): Dir Prof. ANDREW DOWNES.

Tertiary Level Institutions Unit: Dir Dr BEVIS F. PETERS.

College

Barbados Community College: 'The Eyrie', Howell's Cross Rd, St Michael; tel. 426-2858; fax 429-5935; e-mail eyrie@bcc.edu.bb; internet www.bcc.edu.bb; f. 1968; commerce, liberal arts, health sciences, fine arts, science, technology, Barbados Language Centre, Hospitality Institute, general and continuing education, computer studies, physical education; library: 35,000 vols; 449 teachers (149 full-time, 300 part-time); 3,697 students; Principal NORMA J. I. HOLDER; Registrar SYDNEY O. ARTHUR.

Samuel Jackman Prescod Polytechnic: Wildey, St Michael; tel. 426-1920; fax 426-0843; e-mail info@sjpp.edu.bb; internet www.sjpp.edu.bb; f. 1969 in Bridgetown; merged with Barbados Technical Institute in 1972; div of Agriculture established at Eckstein Village and main br. relocated in 1975; relocation to present site 1982; attached to Min. of Education, Youth Affairs and Culture; divs of Building, Electrical Engineering, Mechanical Engineering and Printing, Human Ecology, Business Studies, General Studies, Agriculture, Motor Vehicle and Welding, Distance and Continuing Education, Open and Flexible Learning Centre.

BELARUS

The Higher Education System

Until its independence in 1991 Belarus was part of the Union of Soviet Socialist Republics (USSR), and its education system was based on the Soviet model. Following independence the Government began to introduce greater provision for education in the Belarusian language and more emphasis on Belarusian, rather than Soviet or Russian, history and literature. Higher education is the responsibility of the Ministry of Education. while research is co-ordinated by the National Academy of Sciences of Belarus. Reform of the higher education system began in 1993, including the introduction of a standardized syllabus and increased institutional autonomy. All Belarusians have the right to free higher education. In 2005/06 383,000 students were enrolled in higher education.

The Ministry of Education administers admission to higher education on the joint basis of the Certificate of General Secondary Education (or equivalent) and competitive university entrance examinations. The main undergraduate degree is the Bachelors, taken in conjunction with the Diploma of Higher Education, lasting four to five years. The first level of postgraduate study is the Magister (Masters), requiring one to two years' study, culminating in research and presentation of a thesis. The final level of postgraduate education includes the Aspirantura, leading to the Kandidat Nauk (Candidate of Sciences), and Doctorantura (Doctorate), leading to the title Doctor of Sciences.

Non-university post-secondary education is provided by technical and vocational schools, sometimes known as technicums. Courses vary in length from one to four years, depending on the level of specialization. There are currently 174 technicums, 26 colleges, 49 intermediate professional education institutions, four higher colleges and eight private secondary specialized establishments.

Learned Societies

GENERAL

National Academy of Sciences of Belarus: 220072 Minsk, pr. Nezavisimosti 66; tel. (17) 284-18-01; fax (17) 239-31-63; e-mail academy@presidium.bas-net.by; internet www.ac.by; f. 1929; depts of Biological Sciences (Academician-Sec. I. D. VOLOTOVSKIY, Scientific Sec. V. A. VOINILO), Chemical and Earth Sciences (Academician-Sec. N. P. KRUTKO, Scientific Sec. N. M. LITVINKO), Humanities and Arts (Academician-Sec. P. G. NIKITENKO, Scientific Sec. V. I. LEVKOVICH), Medical Sciences (Academician-Sec. E. D. BELOENKO, Scientific Sec. L. P. MALAEVA), Physical and Technical Sciences (Academician-Sec. S. A. ZHDANOK, Scientific Sec. V. A. GAIKO), and Physics, Mathematics and Information Science (Academician-Sec. S. V. ABLAMEIKO, Scientific Sec. G. A. BUTKIN); 210 mems; (94 academicians; 129 corresp.; 17 foreign; 3 hon.); attached research institutes: see Research Institutes; library and archive: see Libraries and Archives; Chairperson MIKHAIL V. MYASNIKOVICH (acting); Chief Scientific Sec. NIKOLAI S. KAZAK; publs *Computational Methods in Applied Mathematics* (4 a year), *Doklady* (Reports, 6 a year), *Inzhenerno-Fizicheskii Zhurnal* (Journal of Engineering Physics and Thermophysics, 6 a year), *Litasfera* (Lithosphere, 12 a year), *Materialy, Technologii, Instrumenty* (Materials, Technologies, Tools, 4 a year), *Nonlinear Phenomena in Complex Systems* (4 a year), *Prirodnye Resurcy* (Natural Resources, 4 a year), *Trenie i Iznos* (Friction and Wear, 6 a year), *Vestsi* (Bulletins: Physical-Technical Sciences, Biological Sciences, Biomedical Sciences, Physical-Mathematical Sciences, Humanities, Chemistry, 4 a year), *Zhurnal Prikladnoi Spektroskopii* (Journal of Applied Spectroscopy, 6 a year).

AGRICULTURE, FISHERIES AND VETERINARY SCIENCE

Department of Agricultural Sciences of the National Academy of Sciences of the Republic of Belarus: 220049 Minsk, vul. Nezavisimosti 1; tel. (17) 284-18-12; fax (17) 284-09-95; e-mail agro@presidium.bas-net.by; comprises 16 research institutes and 8 experimental stations; attached to Nat. Acad. of Sciences; 13 academicians; 19 corresp. mems; attached research institutes: see Research Institutes; library: see Libraries and Archives; Pres. VLADIMIR G. GUSAKOV; Scientific Sec. SVETLANA A. KASYANCHIK; publ. newsletter (quarterly).

HISTORY, GEOGRAPHY AND ARCHAEOLOGY

Department of Humanitarian Sciences and Arts of the National Academy of Sciences of Belarus: 220072 Minsk, pr. Nezavisimosti 66; tel. (17) 284-07-74; fax (17) 239-31-63; e-mail humanity@presidium.bas-net.by; internet www.ac.by/organizations/departments/ogum.html; fields of study include: history; historical geography and cartography; comparative historical and structural-typological studies of Belarusian and other languages; Belarusian literature, poetry and folklore; history of philosophy and politics in Belarus; sociolinguistic and psycholinguistic investigation; Acad.-Sec. Acad. PYOTR G. NIKITENKO.

LANGUAGE AND LITERATURE

Goethe-Institut: 220034 Minsk, vul. Frunze 5; tel. (17) 236-34-33; fax (17) 236-73-14; e-mail info@minsk.goethe.org; internet www.goethe.de/minsk; offers courses and exams in German language and culture and promotes cultural exchange with Germany; library of 8,840 vols; Dir BARBARA FRAENKEL-THONET.

MEDICINE

Department of Medical Sciences of the National Academy of Sciences of Belarus: 220072 Minsk, pr. Nezavisimosti 66; tel. and fax (17) 284-07-78; e-mail medicine@presidium.bas-net.by; internet www.ac.by/organizations/departments/omed.html; develops and co-ordinates research in the fields of: physiology of self-regulation; development of a theoretical basis for management of compensatory-recombinatory processes; modern ecosystems and their effects on the physiological state and health of humans; and the development of medical-biological problems connected with the consequences of the Chornobyl (Chernobyl) nuclear accident in 1986; Acad.-Sec. Acad. EVGENIY D. BELOYENKO.

NATURAL SCIENCES

Department of Biological Sciences of the National Academy of Sciences of Belarus: 220072 Minsk, pr. Nezavisimosti 66; tel. (17) 284-03-79; fax (17) 284-28-21; e-mail biology@presidium.bas-net.by; internet www.ac.by/organizations/departments/obio.html; fields of study include: biodiversity of plants and animals in Belarus; development of methods of protection of flora and fauna; and reproduction and rational use of biological resources in conditions of anthropogenic pressure; Acad.-Sec. Acad. IGOR D. VOLOTOVSKIY.

Department of Chemistry and Earth Sciences of the National Academy of Sciences of Belarus: 220072 Minsk, pr. Nezavisimosti 66; tel. and fax (17) 284-03-71; e-mail chemistry@presidium.bas-net.by; internet www.ac.by/organizations/departments/ochi.html; develops and co-ordinates research in the fields of: chemistry of polymers and their application; organic synthesis of substances with valuable properties; chemistry of inorganic materials; physical chemistry; chemistry of proteins, nucleic acids and low-molecular bioregulators; Acad.-Sec. Acad. NIKOLAI P. KRUTKO.

Department of Physical and Engineering Sciences of the National Academy of Sciences of Belarus: 220072 Minsk, pr. Nezavisimosti 66; tel. (17) 284-03-77; fax (17) 284-03-75; e-mail engine@presidium.bas-net.by; internet www.ac.by/organizations/departments/ochi.html; develops and co-ordinates research and applied scientific investigations in the fields of: power engineering; conservation of energy and resources; materials and high-energy technologies; and machine building, modelling and diagnostics; Acad.-Sec. Acad. SERGEI A. ZHDANOK.

Department of Physics, Mathematics and Informatics of the National Academy of Sciences of Belarus: 220072 Minsk, pr. Nezavisimosti 66; tel. and fax (17) 284-03-76; e-mail physics@presidium.bas-net.by; internet www.ac.by/organizations/departments/ochi.html; develops and co-ordinates research in the fields of: optics, spectroscopy, laser and plasma physics; atomic and molecular analysis and diagnostics; study and control of the natural environment (incl. laser-sensing and air-space spectrometry); development of materials with electrical, magnetic, optical, and physical-mechanical properties; advanced information technologies (incl. fibre optics, design of automated technical systems); image processing (digital cartography, processing of space images), modelling of intelligent processes (incl. voice-recognition and neurocomputing); Acad.-Sec. Prof. SERGEI V. ABLAMEYKO.

Research Institutes

AGRICULTURE, FISHERIES AND VETERINARY SCIENCE

Belarus Research Institute for Potato Cultivation: 223013 Minsk obl., pos. Samokhvalovichi, vul. Kovaleva 2A; tel. (17) 506-61-45; fax (17) 506-70-01; e-mail bripotat@mshp.minsk.by; internet http://mshp.minsk.by/science/kartof/index.htm; f. 1957; attached to Nat. Acad. of Sciences of Belarus; Dir SERGEI A. BANADYSEV; publ. *Potato Growing* (annually).

Belarus Research Institute of Power Engineering for Agro-industrial complex: 220024 Minsk, vul. Stebeneva 20; tel. (17) 275-19-07; fax (17) 275-10-20; e-mail energetika@forenet.by; f. 1994; attached to Acad. of Agricultural Sciences of the Republic of Belarus; Dir Prof. VIKENTIY I. RUSAN; publs *Problems in the Development of Power Engineering and Electrification for Agro-industrial complex*, *Use of Renewable Energy*.

Belarus Research Institute for Soil Science and Agrochemistry: 220108 Minsk, vul. Kazintsa 62; tel. (17) 277-08-21; fax (17) 277-44-80; e-mail brissa@mail.belpak.by; internet mshp.minsk.by/science/niiagrhru.htm; f. 1931; attached to Acad. of Agricultural Sciences of the Republic of Belarus; Dir Prof. IOSIF M. BOGDEVICH; publs *Soil Investigation and Fertilizer Application* (every 2 years), *Soil Science and Agrochemistry* (annually).

Belarus Research and Technological Institute of the Meat and Dairy Industry: 220075 Minsk, Partizansky pr. 72; tel. (17) 244-38-52; fax (17) 244-38-91; attached to Acad. of Agricultural Sciences of the Republic of Belarus; Dir NIKOLAY A. PROKOPEV.

Grodno Zonal Planting Institute: 231510 Grodno raion, Shchuchin, Akademicheskaya 21; tel. (1514) 2-36-90; fax (1514) 2-36-87; e-mail gznii@tut.by; f. 1910; attached to National Acad. of Sciences of Belarus; 87 mems; library of 22,000 vols; Dir VLADIMIR KURILOVICH.

Institute of Agricultural Economics: 220108 Minsk, vul. Kazintsa 103; tel. (17) 277-04-11; fax (17) 278-69-21; e-mail agrecinst@mail.belpak.by; f. 1958; attached to Acad. of Agricultural Sciences of the Republic of Belarus; library of 20,000 vols; Dir Dr VLADIMIR G. GUSAKOV; publ. *Agricultural Economics* (monthly).

Institute of Agricultural Radiology: 246050 Gomel, vul. Feduninskogo 16; tel. (23) 251-68-21; fax (23) 253-75-60; e-mail firs@biar.gomel.by; attached to Acad. of Agricultural Sciences of the Republic of Belarus; Dir SLAVA K. FIRSAKOVA.

Institute of Animal Production: 222160 Minsk obl., Zhodino, vul. Frunze 11; tel. (1775) 3-34-26; fax (1775) 3-52-83; e-mail belniig@tut.by; f. 1949; attached to Nat. Acad. of Sciences of Belarus; library of 68,000 vols; Dir Prof. IVAN P. SHEYKO; publ. *Zootechnic Science of Belarus* (annually).

Institute of Arable Farming: 222160 Minsk raion, Zhodino, vul. Timiryazeva 1; tel. (1775) 3-25-68; fax (1775) 3-70-66; e-mail izis@tut.by; internet www.izis.basnet.by; f. 1928 as Institute of Socialist Agriculture; present name 1956; attached to Nat. Acad. of Sciences of the Republic of Belarus; conducts applied and basic research in arable farming, plant growing, selection, genetics and crop protection; creation of highly productive varieties of agricultural crops, working with resource-saving technologies; library of 61,000 vols; Gen. Dir Dr FEDOR IVANOVICH; publ. *Transactions on Arable Farming and Plant Growing* (annual).

Institute of Experimental Veterinary Medicine 'S. N. Wyshelesski': 223020 Minsk raion, pos. Kuntsevshchina, Vyshelessky 2; tel. and fax (17) 508-81-31; f. 1930; attached to Acad. of Agricultural Sciences of the Republic of Belarus; Dir ALIAKSANDR P. LYSENKA; publ. *Veterinarnaya Nauka-Proisvodstvu* (annually).

Institute of Fisheries: 220024 Minsk, vul. Stebeneva 22; tel. (17) 275-36-46; fax (17) 275-36-60; e-mail belniirh@infonet.by; f. 1958; attached to National Acad. of Sciences of Belarus; Dir VICTOR V. KONCHITS; publ. *Belarus Fish Industry Problems* (Russian—summary in English—annually).

Institute of Forestry: 246001 Gomel, Praletarskaya vul. 71; tel. (232) 53-73-73; fax (232) 53-53-89; e-mail forinst@server.by; f. 1930; attached to Nat. Acad. of Sciences of Belarus; Dir Prof. Dr VIKTOR A. IPATEV; publ. *Questions in Forest Sciences* (annually).

Institute of Fruit Cultivation: 223013 Minsk raion, pos. Samokhvalovichi, vul. Kovalevea 2; tel. and fax (17) 506-61-40; e-mail belhort@it.org.by; internet mshp.minsk.by/science/niipl.htm; attached to Acad. of Agricultural Sciences of the Republic of Belarus; Dir VYACHESLAV A. SAMUS.

Institute of Land Reclamation and Grass Management: 220040 Minsk, Vul. M. Bogdanovicha 153; tel. (17) 232-49-41; fax (17) 232-64-96; e-mail niimel@mail.ru; internet www.niimelio.niks.by; f. 1930; attached to Nat. Acad. of Sciences of Belarus; Dir ANATOLI LIKHATSEVICH; publ. *Reclamation of Overmoistened Land* (2 a year).

Institute for the Mechanization of Agriculture: 220049 Minsk, vul. Knorina 1; tel. and fax (17) 266-02-91; e-mail belniimsh@tut.by; f. 1947; attached to Acad. of Agricultural Sciences of the Republic of Belarus; Dir VLADIMIR N. DASHKOV.

Institute of Plant Protection: 223011 Minsk raion, Pos. Priluki, vul. Mira 2; tel. and fax (17) 509-23-39; e-mail entom@izr.belpak.minsk.by; attached to Acad. of Agricultural Sciences of the Republic of Belarus; Dir SERGEY V. SOROKA.

Institute of Vegetable Crops: 220028 Minsk, vul. Mayakovskogo 127a; tel. (17) 221-37-11; e-mail inst@belniio.belpak.minsk.by; internet mshp.minsk.by/science/niiov.htm; attached to Acad. of Agricultural Sciences of the Republic of Belarus; Dir GENNADY I. GANUSH.

ARCHITECTURE AND TOWN PLANNING

Research and Design Institute of Construction Materials 'BelNIIS': 220114 Minsk, Staroborisovskiy tr.; tel. (17) 264-10-01; fax (17) 264-87-92; e-mail lmdp@nsys.by; Dir NADEZHDA N. TSYBULKO.

ECONOMICS, LAW AND POLITICS

Economic Research Institute of the Ministry of the Economy: 220086 Minsk, vul. Slavinskogo 1, korp. 1; tel. (17) 264-02-78; fax (17) 264-64-40; e-mail niei@main.gov.by; f. 1962; library of 51,425 vols; Dir STEPAN S. POLONIK.

Institute of Economics of the National Academy of Sciences of Belarus: 220072 Minsk, vul. Surganava 1–2, Korpus 2; tel. (17) 284-24-43; fax (17) 284-07-16; e-mail directorship@economics.basnet.by; internet economics.bas-net.by; f. 1931; attached to Nat. Acad. of Sciences of Belarus; Dir Prof. PETR G. NIKITENKO; publ. *Organizatsiya i upravleniye* (Organization and Management, in Russian, 4 a year).

Institute for State and Law: 220072 Minsk, vul. Surganava 1, Korpus 2; tel. (17) 284-18-64; fax (17) 284-18-24; e-mail philos@bas-net.by; f. 1999; attached to Nat. Acad. of Sciences of Belarus; Dir Dr VLADIMIR P. IZOTKO.

Research Institute of Criminalistics and Forensic Expertise: 220073 Minsk, Kalvariiskaya vul. 43; tel. and fax (17) 226-72-79; e-mail sudexpertiza@adsl.by; internet www.sudexpertiza.by; f. 1929; attached to Ministry of Justice; library of 10,000 vols; Dir Dr ALEXANDER RUBIS; publ. *Issues of Criminalistics, Criminology and Forensic Expertise* (annual).

EDUCATION

National Institute of Education: 220004 Minsk, vul. Korolja 16; tel. (17) 220-59-09; fax (17) 220-56-35; e-mail nieby@minsk.sovam.com; f. 1990; library of 20,000 vols; Dir Dr BORIS KRAIKO; publ. *Adulcatsia i Wychawanne*.

HISTORY, GEOGRAPHY AND ARCHAEOLOGY

Institute of History: 220072 Minsk, vul. Akademicheskaya 1; tel. and fax (17) 284-02-19; f. 1929; attached to Nat. Acad. of Sciences of Belarus; Dir Prof. ALEKSANDR A. KOVALENYA (acting).

LANGUAGE AND LITERATURE

Institute of Linguistics 'Ya. Kolas': 220072 Minsk, vul. Surganava 1, Korpus 2; tel. (17) 268-48-84; fax (17) 284-18-85; e-mail inlinasbel@tut.by; f. 1929; attached to Nat. Acad. of Sciences of Belarus; Dir ALEKSANDR A. LUKASHANETS.

Institute of Literature: 220072 Minsk, pr. Nezavisimosti 66; tel. (17) 268-58-86; e-mail inlit@bas-net.by; f. 1931; attached to Nat. Acad. of Sciences of Belarus; Dir VLADIMIR V. GNILOMEDOV.

MEDICINE

Alexandrov, N. N., Research Institute of Oncology and Medical Radiology: 223052 Minsk, pos. Lesnoy-2; tel. (17) 269-95-05; fax (17) 202-47-04; e-mail ooncobel@omr.med.by; internet www.omr.med.by; f. 1960; library of 15,000 vols, 55 periodicals; Dir IOSIF V. ZALUTSKY; publ. *Topical Problems in Oncology and Medical Radiology* (annually).

Institute of Pulmonology and Phthisiology: 223059 Minsk raion, pos. Novinki; tel. (17) 289-87-95; fax (17) 289-89-50; e-mail niipulm@users.med.by; f. 1923; library of 7,000 vols; Dir VALENTIN V. BORSHCHEVSKIY; publ. *Research Report* (annually).

Republican Scientific Practical Centre of Hygiene: 220012 Minsk, Akademicheskaya 8; tel. (17) 284-13-70; fax (17) 284-03-45; e-mail rspch@rspch.by; internet www.rspch

.by; f. 1927; library of 11,982 vols; Dir SERGEY SOKOLOV.

Research Institute of Cardiology: 220036 Minsk, ul. R. Lyuksemburga 110; tel. (17) 256-07-69; fax (17) 256-29-05; e-mail cardio@bcsmi.minsk.by; f. 1977; Dir GEORGIY I. SIDORENKO.

Research Institute of Epidemiology and Microbiology: 220114 Minsk, vul. Filimonova 23; tel. (17) 267-30-50; fax (17) 267-30-93; e-mail info@riem.bn.by; internet www.belriem.org; f. 1924 as Belarusian Pasteur Institute; research to improve surveillance of infectious diseases, study of molecular mechanisms of pathogenicity of main infectious and immune diseases, development of immuno- and molecular biologic diagnostic preparations against the agents of main infections, elaboration and implementation into medical practice of up-to-date diagnostic, medical, and vaccine preparations, quality controls of immunobiological products, medical information support in the control of infectious and immune diseases; library of 9,000 vols; Dir Prof. LEONID P. TITOV.

Research Institute for Evaluation of the Working Capacity of Disabled People: 220114 Minsk, Staroborisovsky trakt 24; tel. and fax (17) 264-25-08; f. 1974; library of 35,000 vols; Dir Prof. V. B. SMYCHEK.

Research Institute of Neurology, Neurosurgery and Physiotherapy: 220061 Minsk, vul. Filatova 9; tel. (17) 246-40-88.

Research Institute of Traumatology and Orthopaedics: Minsk, vul. Gorkogo 2..

Skin and Venereological Research Institute: Minsk, Prilukskaya vul. 46A..

NATURAL SCIENCES

Biological Sciences

Central Botanical Garden: 220012 Minsk, vul. Surganava 2A; tel. (17) 284-14-84; fax (17) 284-14-83; e-mail cbg@it.org.by; internet hbc.bas-net.by/cbg; f. 1932; attached to Nat. Acad. of Sciences of Belarus; Dir Acad. VLADIMIR N. RESHETNIKOV.

Institute of Biochemistry: 230017 Grodno, bul. Leninskogo Komsomola 50; tel. (15) 233-41-61; fax (15) 233-41-21; e-mail val@biochem.unibel.by; f. 1985; attached to Nat. Acad. of Sciences of Belarus; library of 40,000 vols; Dir Prof. PAVEL S. PRONKO.

Institute of Bio-organic Chemistry: 220141 Minsk, vul. Akad. V. F. Kuprevicha 5; tel. (17) 264-87-61; fax (17) 263-71-32; e-mail iboch@ns.igs.ac.by; internet iboch.bas-net.by; f. 1974; attached to Nat. Acad. of Sciences of Belarus; Dir Acad. FYODOR A. LAKHVICH.

Institute of Biophysics and Cell Engineering: 220072 Minsk, vul. Akademicheskaya 27; tel. (17) 284-17-49; fax (17) 284-23-57; e-mail ipb@biobel.bas-net.by; internet biobel.bas-net.by/biophys; f. 1973; attached to Nat. Acad. of Sciences of Belarus; Dir IGOR D. VOLOTOVSKIY; publ. *Godnev's Lectures: Plant Photobiology and Photosynthesis* (annual).

Institute of Experimental Botany 'V. Kuprevich': 220072 Minsk, vul. Akademicheskaya 27; tel. (17) 284-15-64; fax (17) 284-18-53; e-mail expbot@biobel.bas-net.by; f. 1931; attached to Nat. Acad. of Sciences of Belarus; Dir Prof. Dr NIKOLAI A. LAMAN.

Institute of Genetics and Cytology: 220072 Minsk, vul. Akademicheskaya 27; tel. (17) 284-18-48; fax (17) 284-19-17; e-mail dromash@biobel.bas-net.by; internet biobel.bas-net.by/igc; f. 1965; attached to Nat. Acad. of Sciences of Belarus; Dir ALEKSANDR V. KILCHEVSKIY.

Institute of Microbiology: 220141 Minsk, vul. Akad. V. F. Kuprevicha 2; tel. (17) 202-99-46; fax (17) 264-47-66; e-mail microbio@mbio.bas-net.by; internet www.mbio.bas-net.by; f. 1975; attached to Nat. Acad. of Sciences of Belarus; Dir EMILIYA I. KOLOMETS.

Institute of Physiology: 220072 Minsk, vul. Akademichnaya 28; tel. (17) 284-24-61; fax (17) 284-16-30; e-mail biblio@fizio.bas-net.by; f. 1953; attached to Nat. Acad. of Sciences of Belarus; basic and applied research in biomedicine; Dir VLADIMIR S. ULASHCHYK.

Institute for Problems of Natural Resources Use and Ecology: 220114 Minsk, Starobonsovsky trakt 10; tel. (17) 264-26-32; fax (17) 264-24-13; e-mail ipnrue@ns.ecology.ac.by; internet www.ecology.ac.by; f. 1932; attached to Nat. Acad. of Sciences of Belarus; Dir Prof. VLADIMIR F. LOGIMOV.

Institute of Radiobiology: 246007 Gomel, vul. Fedyuninskogo 4; tel. and fax (232) 57-07-06; e-mail irb@mail.gomel.by; f. 1987; attached to Nat. Acad. of Sciences of Belarus; Dir Acad. EVGENIY KONOPLYA.

Institute of Zoology: 220072 Minsk, vul. Akademichnaya 27; tel. (17) 284-22-75; fax (17) 284-10-36; e-mail zoo@biobel.bas-net.by; internet biobel.bas-net.by/zoo; f. 1958; attached to Nat. Acad. of Sciences of Belarus; Dir MIKHAIL E. NIKIFOROV.

Mathematical Sciences

Institute of Mathematics: 220072 Minsk, vul. Surganava 11; tel. (17) 284-17-01; fax (17) 284-22-59; e-mail senko@im.bas-net.by; internet im.bas-net.by; f. 1959; attached to Nat. Acad. of Sciences of Belarus; Dir Acad. IVAN V. GAISHUN.

Physical Sciences

Institute of Applied Optics: 212793 Mogilev, vul. Bialynitskaga-Biruli 11; tel. and fax (22) 226-46-49; f. 1970; attached to Nat. Acad. of Sciences of Belarus; Dir V. P. REDKO.

Institute of General and Inorganic Chemistry: 220072 Minsk, vul. Surganava 9; tel. (17) 284-27-23; fax (17) 284-27-03; e-mail secretar@igic.bas-net.by; f. 1959; attached to Nat. Acad. of Sciences of Belarus; Dir NIKOLAI P. KRUTKO.

Institute of Geochemistry and Geophysics: 220141 Minsk, vul. Kuprevicha 7; tel. (17) 264-53-15; fax (17) 263-63-98; e-mail geology@igig.org.by; internet www.igig.org.by; f. 1971; attached to Nat. Acad. of Sciences of Belarus; Dir Prof. ANATOLIY A. MAKHNACH; publ. *Lithosphere* (2 a year).

Institute of Molecular and Atomic Physics: 220072 Minsk, pr. Nezavisimosti 70; tel. (17) 284-16-35; fax (17) 284-00-30; e-mail imafbel@imaph.bas-net.by; internet imaph.bas-net.by; f. 1992; attached to Nat. Acad. of Sciences of Belarus; Dir Dr SERGEY V. GAPONENKO; publ. *Journal of Applied Spectroscopy*.

Institute of Physical Organic Chemistry: 220072 Minsk, vul. Surganava 13; tel. (17) 284-23-38; fax (17) 284-16-79; tel. ifoch@ifoch.bas-net.by; fax ifoch.bas-net.by; f. 1929; attached to Nat. Acad. of Sciences of Belarus; Dir Prof. ALEKSANDR V. BILDYUKEVICH (acting).

Institute of Physics 'B. I. Stepanov': 220072 Minsk, pr. Nezavisimosti 68; tel. (17) 284-17-55; fax (17) 284-08-79; e-mail ifanbel@ifanbel.bas-net.by; internet ifanbel.bas-net.by; f. 1955; attached to Nat. Acad. of Sciences of Belarus; Dir Prof. VLADIMIR V. KABANOV (acting).

Institute of Solid State and Semiconductor Physics: 220072 Minsk, vul. P. Brovki 17; tel. (17) 284-28-14; fax (17) 284-13-13; e-mail ifttpanb@iftt.basnet.minsk.by; f. 1963; attached to Nat. Acad. of Sciences of Belarus; library of 72,000 items; Dir Prof. VALERY M. FEDOSYUK.

PHILOSOPHY AND PSYCHOLOGY

Institute of Philosophy: 220072 Minsk, vul. Surganava 1, korp. 2; tel. (17) 284-18-63; fax (17) 284-29-25; e-mail philos@anitex.by; internet ip.basnet.by; f. 1931; attached to Nat. Acad. of Sciences of Belarus; research in the field of theory and methodology of natural scientific and socio-humanitarian cognition, philosophical anthropology, social ecology, ethics and aesthetics; elaboration of innovative strategies of social, spiritual, cultural and scientific progress; study of the actual problems of contemporary socio-political and cultural devt; study and summary of the achievements of the world and national philosophical thought; Dir Dr VASILY N. NOVIKOV.

RELIGION, SOCIOLOGY AND ANTHROPOLOGY

Institute of Arts, Ethnography and Folklore: 220072 Minsk, vul. Surganava 1, korp. 2; tel. (17) 239-59-21; f. 1957; attached to Nat. Acad. of Sciences of Belarus; Dir M. P. PILIPENKO.

Institute of Sociology: 220072 Minsk, vul. Surganava 1, korp. 2; tel. (17) 239-48-65; fax (17) 239-59-28; f. 1990; attached to Nat. Acad. of Sciences of Belarus; Dir E. M. BABOSOV.

TECHNOLOGY

Belarus Institute for the Science, Research and Design of Food Products: 220037 Minsk, Kozlova 29; tel. (17) 285-39-70; fax (17) 285-39-71; e-mail info@harteh.com; f. 2000; library of 20,000 vols; Dir ZENON LOVKIS.

Belarusian Institute of System Analysis and Information Support for Scientific and Technical Sphere (BELISA): 220004 Minsk, pr. Pobeditelei 7; tel. (17) 203-14-87; fax (17) 203-35-40; e-mail isa@belisa.org.by; internet www.belisa.org.by; operated by the State Committee on Science and Technologies of Belarus; Dir VALERJY E. KRATENOK.

Engineering Centre 'Plazmoteg': 220141 Minsk, vul. Akad. V. F. Kuprevicha 1, korp. 3; tel. (17) 263-93-41; fax (17) 263-59-20; e-mail pec@bas-net.by; f. 1990; attached to Nat. Acad. of Sciences of Belarus; Dir EDUARD I. TOCHITSKY.

Institute of Applied Physics: 220072 Minsk, vul. Akademicheskaya 16; tel. (17) 284-17-94; fax (17) 284-10-81; e-mail admcom@iaph.bas-net.by; internet iaph.bas-net.by; f. 1963; attached to Nat. Acad. of Sciences of Belarus; physics of non-destructive testing; Dir Prof. Dr NIKOLAI P. MIGUN.

Institute of Chemistry of New Materials: 220141 Minsk, vul. Akad. V. F. Kuprevicha 16; tel. and fax (17) 263-19-23; e-mail dvas@ichnm.ac.by; internet www.ichnm.ac.by; f. 1993; attached to Nat. Acad. of Sciences of Belarus; Dir Acad. VLADIMIR E. AGABEKOV.

Institute of Electronics: 220090 Minsk, Logoiskiy trakt 22; tel. (17) 265-34-13; fax (17) 283-91-51; e-mail inel@inel.bas-net.by; f. 1973; attached to Nat. Acad. of Sciences of Belarus; Dir YURIY V. TROFIMOV.

Institute of Energetics Problems: 220109 Minsk, vul. Akad. Krasina; tel. and fax (17) 246-70-55; e-mail ipep@sosny.bas-net.by; f. 1991; attached to Nat. Acad. of Sciences of Belarus; Dir Dr YURIY V. KLIMENKOV.

Institute of Engineering Cybernetics: 220012 Minsk, vul. Surganava 6; tel. (17)

268-51-71; fax (17) 231-84-03; e-mail cic@newman.basnet.minsk.by; f. 1965; attached to Nat. Acad. of Sciences of Belarus; Dir Prof. VYACHESLAV S. TANAYEV.

Institute for Heat and Mass Transfer 'A. V. Lykov': 220072 Minsk, vul. P. Brovki 15; tel. (17) 284-21-36; fax (17) 232-25-13; f. 1952; attached to Nat. Acad. of Sciences of Belarus; Dir Acad. SERGEY A. ZHDANOK.

Institute of Machine Mechanics and Reliability: 220072 Minsk, vul. Akademicheskaya 12; tel. (17) 210-07-48; fax (17) 284-02-41; e-mail admin@inmash.bas-net.by; f. 1971; attached to Nat. Acad. of Sciences of Belarus; Dir Dr YURIY V. KLIMENKOV.

Institute of Radiation Physical-Chemical Problems: 220109 Minsk, Akad. Krasina 99; tel. (17) 246-77-50; fax (17) 246-73-17; e-mail fokov@sosny.bas-net.by; f. 1991; attached to Nat. Acad. of Sciences of Belarus; Dir SERGEY E. CHIGRINOV.

Institute of Radioecological Problems: 220109 Minsk, Sosny; tel. (17) 246-72-53; fax (17) 246-70-17; e-mail irep@sosny.basnet.minsk.by; f. 1991; attached to Nat. Acad. of Sciences of Belarus; Dir G. A. SHAROVAROV.

Institute of Technical Acoustics: 210717 Vitebsk, pr. Lyudnikova 13; tel. (212) 25-41-89; fax (212) 24-39-53; e-mail ita@vitebsk.by; internet www.belpak.vitebsk.by/ita; f. 1995; attached to Nat. Acad. of Sciences of Belarus; library of 43,000 vols; Dir Prof. VASILIY V. RUBANIK.

Institute of Technology of Metals: 212030 Mogilev, vul. Bialynitskaga-Biruli 11; tel. (222) 26-46-43; fax (222) 32-65-93; e-mail inmet@mogilev.unibel.by; internet www.ussr.to/belarus/itm; f. 1992; attached to Nat. Acad. of Sciences of Belarus; Dir Dr EVGENIY MARUKOVICH.

Medical Biotechnological Institute: 220029 Minsk, vul. Varvasheny 17; tel. and fax (17) 234-32-06; e-mail mbirb@mail.bn.by; internet www.medbiotech.bn.by; f. 1972; 120 mems; Dir VICTOR N. TERECHOV; Dir of Scientific Research K. M. BELIAVSKY.

Metal–Polymer Research Institute 'V. A. Belyi': 246050 Gomel, vul. Kirova 32a; tel. (232) 77-52-12; fax (232) 77-52-11; e-mail mpri@mail.ru; internet mpri.org.by; f. 1969; attached to Nat. Acad. of Sciences of Belarus; library of 19,519 vols; Dir Prof. NIKOLAI K. MYSHKIN; publs *Friction and Wear* (6 a year), *Materials, Technologies and Tools* (4 a year).

Non-Traditional Energetics and Energy-Saving Scientific and Engineering Centre: 220109 Minsk, Sosny; tel. (17) 246-76-61; f. 1992; attached to Nat. Acad. of Sciences of Belarus; Dir V. N. YERMASHKEVICH.

Physical-Technical Institute: 220141 Minsk, vul. Akad. V. F. Kuprevicha 10; tel. (17) 264-60-10; fax (17) 263-76-93; e-mail phti@tut.by; internet phti.at.tut.by; f. 1931; attached to Nat. Acad. of Sciences of Belarus; Dir .ANATOLIY I. GORDIENKO.

Republican Scientific and Engineering Centre for Environmental Remote Sensing 'Ecomir': 220012 Minsk, vul. Surganava 2; tel. (17) 284-00-49; fax (17) 284-00-47; e-mail ecomir@open.by; internet www.ecomir-eeica.com; f. 1990; attached to Nat. Acad. of Sciences of Belarus; Dir Prof. A. A. KOVALEV.

Scientific-Engineering Republican Unitary Enterprise 'Belavtotraktorostroenie': 220072 Minsk, vul. Akademicheskaya 12; tel. (17) 210-07-49; fax (17) 284-02-41; e-mail bats@ncpmm.bas-net.by; internet www.bats.basnet.by; f. 1993; attached to Nat. Acad. of Sciences of Belarus; Dir Acad. M. S. VYSOTSKY.

Libraries and Archives

Brest

Brest Oblast Library 'M. Gorky': 210601 Brest, bul. Kosmanavtov 48; tel. and fax (162) 22-22-01; e-mail brl@tut.by; internet grl.brest.by; f. 1940; regional centre for 19 central libraries and 818 brs; 740,000 vols; Dir TAMARA P. DANILYUK; publ. *Bibliopanorama* (irregular).

Gomel

Gomel Oblast Universal Library 'V. I. Lenin': 246000 Gomel, pl. Pobedy 2a; tel. (232) 77-36-51; e-mail goub@it.org.by; Dir VALENTINA P. DUBROVA.

Minsk

Belarus Agricultural Library: 220108 Minsk, vul. Kazintsa 86/2; tel. (17) 212-15-61; fax (17) 212-00-66; e-mail belal@belal.minsk.by; internet belal.by; f. 1960; attached to Nat. Acad. of Sciences of Belarus; 500,000 vols; Dir VALENTINA YURCHENKO.

Belarus State University Library: 220050 Minsk, pr. Skoriny 4; tel. (17) 220-78-23; fax (17) 226-59-40; e-mail lapo@bsu.by; internet www.library.bsu.by; f. 1921; 2,040,000 vols; Dir PETR M. LAPO.

Central Scientific Archive of the National Academy of Sciences of Belarus: 220072 Minsk, pr. Nezavisimosti 66; tel. (17) 284-22-87; fax (17) 239-31-63; f. 1931; Head MIKHAIL M. SMOLYANINOV.

Central Scientific Library of the National Academy of Sciences of Belarus 'Ya. Kolas': 220072 Minsk, vul. Surganava 15; tel. and fax (17) 284-14-28; e-mail csl@kolas.bas-net.by; internet www.csl.bas-net.by; f. 1925; 3,108,000 vols; Dir NATALIYA YU. BEREZKINA.

National Library of Belarus: 220636 Minsk, vul. Chyrvonaarmeyskaya 9; tel. (17) 227-54-63; fax (17) 229-24-94; e-mail sol@nacbibl.org.by; internet natlib.org.by; f. 1922; 8,000,000 vols; Dir RAMAN S. MATULSKI; publs *Chernobyl: Bibliographical Index* (2 a year), *New Literature on the Culture and Art of Belarus* (monthly), *Novyja Knigi* (monthly), *Social Sciences* (monthly).

Republican Library for Science and Technology of Belarus: 220004 Minsk, pr. Pobediteley 7; tel. and fax (17) 203-31-38; e-mail rlst@rlst.org.by; internet www.rlst.org.by; f. 1977; 32,440,600 vols (excl. patents); Dir RAISA SUKHORUKOVA.

Republican Scientific Medical Library: 220007 Minsk, vul. Fabritsiusa 28; tel. (17) 226-21-52; fax (17) 216-20-43; e-mail rsml@rsml.med.by; internet www.rsml.med.by; f. 1941; 860,000 vols; Dir VLADIMIR N. SOROKO.

Mogilev

Mogilev Oblast Library 'V. I. Lenin': 212030 Mogilev, vul. Krylenko 8; tel. and fax (222) 25-07-58; e-mail adm@mlib.basnet.by; internet www.mlib.basnet.by; f. 1935; Dir ALLA M. VASILENKO; publs *Bibliographic Indices* (irregular), *Bulletin* (irregular).

Vitebsk

Vitebsk Oblast Library 'V. I. Lenin': 210601 Vitebsk, vul. Lenina 8a; tel. (212) 37-45-21; fax (212) 37-30-58; e-mail vrlib@lib.vitebsk.net; f. 1921; Dir ALEKSANDR SEMKIN.

Museums and Art Galleries

Belovezhskaya Pushcha

'Belovezhskaya Pushcha' National Park Museum: 225063 Brestskaya oblast, Kamenetzky raion; tel. (1631) 5-63-96; fax (1631) 2-50-56; e-mail box@npbprom.belpak.brest.by; internet www.npbp.cis.by; f. 1960; displays flora and fauna of the Belovezhskaya Pushcha Primeval Forest, and shows work being done to preserve the biological diversity in the primeval forest, particularly with respect to the European Bison; Dir NIKOLAI N. BAMBIZA.

Grodno

Grodno State Historical and Archaeological Museum: 230023 Grodno, Zamkovaya vul. 22; tel. and fax (152) 74-08-33; e-mail grodno_museum@tut.by; f. 1920; museum collection contains 186,000 items; library of 35,000 vols; Dir Dr YURY KITURKA; publ. *Krayaznauchya zapiski* (Journal of Regional Studies, every two years).

Minsk

Great Patriotic War Museum: 220030 Minsk, pr. Nezavisimosti 25A; tel. and fax (17) 227-11-66; e-mail museumww2@tut.by; internet nacbibl.org.by/war_museum; f. 1943; Soviet Army and partisans' war history 1941–1945; library of 14,000 vols; Dir GENNADIY I. BARKUN.

National Art Museum of the Republic of Belarus: 220030 Minsk, vul. Lenina 20; tel. and fax (17) 227-56-72; internet www.artmuseum.by; f. 1939; Belarusian art from 11th c. to early 20th c.; European art from 16th c. to early 20th c.; Russian art 18th c. to early 20th c.; temporary exhibitions; Dir VLADIMIR I. PROKOPTSOV.

National Museum of the History and Culture of Belarus: 220050 Minsk, vul. K. Marksa 12; tel. (17) 286-63-75; fax (17) 227-36-65; e-mail nmiikb@mail.ru; f. 1957; history and local natural history; archaeological, ethnographical and coin collections; library of 20,000 vols; Dir PETR S. KHOTKO.

Universities

BARANOVICHI STATE UNIVERSITY

225404 Baranovichi, vul. Voikova 21
Telephone: (163) 45-78-60
Fax: (163) 45-78-31
E-mail: barsu@brest.by
Internet: www.barsu.by
Founded 2004
Rector: Prof. VASILIY I. KOCHURKO
Library of 221,890 vols
Number of teachers: 360
Number of students: 5,500
Faculties of Engineering, Foreign Languages, Pedagogy, Finance and Jurisprudence, Pre-University Training, Qualifications Improvement and Personnel Retraining; External Faculties of Engineering, Pedagogy and Finance and Jurisprudence.

BELARUS STATE ECONOMIC UNIVERSITY

220070 Minsk, Partizanskiy pr. 26
Telephone: (17) 249-40-32
Fax: (17) 249-51-06
E-mail: mo@bseu.by
Internet: www.bseu.by
Founded 1933

Rector: Prof. Dr V. N. SHIMOV
Library of 1,500,000 vols
Number of teachers: 1,400
Number of students: 28,000

DEANS

Faculty of Accounting and Economics: G. P. MATETSKY
Faculty of Commerce, Economics and Management: V. N. PLATONOV
Faculty of Finance and Banking: V. S. BASS
Faculty of International Economic Relations: M. V. MISHKEVICH
Faculty of Language Studies: N. V. POPOK
Faculty of Law: L. M. RYABTSEV
Faculty of Management: V. A. SIMKHOVICH
Faculty of Marketing: O. I. KARPEKO
Faculty of Pre-University Training: V. N. LIPOVTSEV
Higher School of Business and Management: S. YU. KRYCHEVSKIY
Higher School of Tourism: N. I. KABUSHKIN
Special Faculty of Psychology and Pedagogy for Teachers of Economics: G. V. BOROZDINA

ATTACHED INSTITUTES

Institute of Qualifications Improvement and Retraining of Economists: Dir A. A. LAPKO.

Institute of Social Sciences and Humanities Education: Dir YADVIGA S. YASKEVICH.

BELARUS STATE TECHNOLOGICAL UNIVERSITY

220050 Minsk, vul. Sverdlova 13
Telephone: (17) 226-14-32
Fax: (17) 227-62-17
E-mail: root@bstu.unibel.by
Internet: www.bstu.unibel.by
Founded 1930
Rector: IVAN M. ZHARSKIY
Pro-Rector for Academic Affairs: ALEKSANDR S. FEDORENCHIK
Pro-Rector for Administrative Affairs: BORIS V. ALDANOV
Pro-Rector for Economic Affairs: ALEKSANDR I. KUPTSOV
Pro-Rector for Education: GENNADY M. KVESKO
Pro-Rector for Research: PETR A. LYSHCHIK
Library of 1,200,000 vols
Number of teachers: 607
Number of students: 9,103

DEANS

Faculty of Chemical Technology and Engineering: SVETLANA E. OREKHOVA
Faculty of Engineering Economics: MIKHAIL I. BARANOV
Faculty of External Studies: ANDREY R. GORONOVSKIY
Faculty of Forestry: VALERIY K. GVOZDEV
Faculty of Forestry Technology: NIKOLAY P. VYRKO
Faculty of Organic Substance Technology: VALERIY N. FARAFONTOV
Faculty of Publishing and Printing: LEONID M. DAVIDOVICH
Faculty of Qualifications Improvement and Retraining of Specialists: ANDREY I. ROVKACH

BELARUSIAN-RUSSIAN UNIVERSITY

212005 Mogilev, pr. Mira 43
Telephone: (222) 23-61-00
Fax: (222) 22-58-21
E-mail: bru@bru.mogilev.by
Internet: www.bru.mogilev.by
Founded 1961
Rector: IGOR S. SAZONOV
First Pro-Rector: FEDOR G. LOVSHENKO
Pro-Rectors for Academic Affairs: ALEKSANDR A. KATKALO, ALEKSANDR A. ZHOLOBOV
Pro-Rector for Academic, Economic and International Affairs: GRIGORIY P. KOSYACHENKO
Library of 1,500,000 vols
Number of teachers: 1,100
Number of students: 6,300

DEANS

Faculty of Automotive and Mechanical Engineering: STANISLAV B. PARTNOV
Faculty of Construction: SERGEY D. GALYUZHIN
Faculty of Economics: NIKOLAY S. ZHELTOK
Faculty Electrotechnology: ALEKSANDR S. KOVAL
Faculty of Machine Building: VIKTOR A. POPKOVSKY

BELARUSIAN NATIONAL TECHNICAL UNIVERSITY

220027 Minsk, pr. Nezavisimosti 65
Telephone: (17) 232-74-26
Fax: (17) 232-74-26
E-mail: bntu@bntu.by
Internet: www.bntu.by
Founded 1920
Rector: Prof. BORIS M. KHRUSTALEV
Library of 2,035,737 vols
Number of teachers: 2,643
Number of students: 15,000
Publications: *Energetica* (4 a year), *Mir Technologij* (4 a year), *Vestnik BNTU* (4 a year)
Faculties of Architecture, Construction, Economics and Management, Instrument-Making, Mechanics and Technology, Motor Vehicles and Tractors, Power Engineering, Road Construction and Robots and Robot Systems.

BELARUSIAN STATE AGRARIAN TECHNICAL UNIVERSITY

220023 Minsk, pr. Nezavisimosti 99
Telephone: (17) 264-47-71
Fax: (17) 264-41-16
E-mail: rektorat@batu.edu.by
Internet: www.batu.edu.by
Founded 1954
Rector: Prof. NIKOLAY V. KAZAROVETS
Library of 381,968 vols
Number of teachers: 519
Number of students: 8,783
Faculties of Agroenergy, Agromechanics, Business and Management, Humanities and Ecology in Social Work, Pre-University Training and Technical Service, Qualifications Improvement and Personnel Retraining and Vocational Guidance.

BELARUSIAN STATE PEDAGOGICAL UNIVERSITY 'M. TANK'

220050 Minsk, ul. Sovetskaya 18
Telephone: (17) 226-40-20
Fax: (17) 226-40-24
E-mail: rector@bspu.unibel.by
Internet: www.bspu.unibel.by
Founded 1922
Rector: PETR D. KUKHARCHUK
First Pro-Rector: ALEKSANDR I. ANDARALO
Pro-Rector for Academic Affairs: SERGEY M. BYKADOROV
Pro-Rector for Administrative Affairs: VLADIMIR V. YADLOVSKIY
Pro-Rector for Education and Social Affairs: SVETLANA I. KOPTEVA
Pro-Rector for Information and Analytical Affairs: VALERIY B. TARANCHUK
Pro-Rector for Research: VASILIY V. BUSHCHIK
Librarian: N. P. KOPTEVA
Library of 1,300,000 vols
Number of teachers: 1,180
Number of students: 9,000

DEANS

Faculty of Mathematics: PAVEL V. KIKEL
Faculty of National Culture: MIKHAIL M. KRUTALEVICH
Faculty of Natural History: MARAT G. YASOVEEV
Faculty of Physics: IGOR S. TASHLYKOV
Faculty of Pre-University Training: VIKTOR L. TSYBOVSKIY
Faculty of Primary Education: NIKOLAY I. MITSKEVICH
Faculty of Russian Philology: VASILIY D. STARICHENOK
Faculty of Social Pedagogy and Technology: TATYANA P. MIKHNEVICH

BELARUSIAN STATE UNIVERSITY

220050 Minsk, pr. Nezavisimosti 4
Telephone: (17) 209-52-03
Fax: (17) 226-59-40
E-mail: bsu@bsu.by
Internet: www.bsu.by
Founded 1921
State control
Languages of instruction: Belarusan, Russian
Academic year: September to June
Rector: VASILIY I. STRAZHEV
First Pro-Rector: SERGEY K. RAKHMANOV
Pro-Rectors for Academic Affairs: VLADIMIR L. KLYUNYA, VIKTOR V. SAMOKHVAL
Pro-Rector for Administration and Finance: VLADIMIR V. ROGOVITSKIY
Pro-Rector for Economic and Commercial Affairs: IGOR V. VOYTOV
Pro-Rector for Education and Social Affairs: VLADIMIR V. SUVOROV
Pro-Rector for International Affairs: VLADIMIR A. ASTAPENKO
Library of 2,000,000 vols
Number of teachers: 2,400
Number of students: 16,500
Publications: *Belarusskiy Universitet* (24 a year), *Higher School* (6 a year), *Sociology* (4 a year), *Vestnik BGU* (monthly)

DEANS

Faculty of Applied Mathematics: P. A. MANDRIK
Faculty of Biology: V. V. LYSAK
Faculty of Chemistry: G. A. BRANITSKY
Faculty of Economics: M. M. KOVALEV
Faculty of Geography: I. I. PIROZHNIK
Faculty of History: S. N. KHODZIN
Faculty of International Relations: A. V. SHARAPO
Faculty of Journalism: V. P. VOROBIOV
Faculty of Law: S. A. BALASHENKO
Faculty of Management and Social Technologies: V. G. BULAVKO
Faculty of Mechanics and Mathematics: N. I. YURCHUK
Faculty of Philology: I. S. ROVDO
Faculty of Philosophy and Social Studies: A. I. ZELENKOV
Faculty of Physics: V. M. ANISCHIK
Faculty of Radiophysics and Electronics: S. G. MULIARCHIK
International Graduate School of Business and Management of Technology: V. V. APANASOVICH

ATTACHED INSTITUTES

International Humanities Institute.

Institute for the Retraining of Judges, Staff of the Office of the Public Prosecutor, Courts and Legal Establishment.

Republican Institute of Higher Schooling.

Research Institute of Applied Mathematics and Informatics.

Research Institute of Applied Physics 'A. N. Sevchenko': Dir A. F. CHERNIAVSKY.

Research Institute for Nuclear Problems: Dir V. G. BARYSHEVSKY.

Research Institute for Physical and Chemical Problems: Dir O. A. IVASHKEVICH.

State Institute of Management and Social Technology

BELARUSIAN STATE UNIVERSITY OF INFORMATICS AND RADIOELECTRONICS

220013 Minsk, ul. Brovska
Telephone: (17) 232-04-51
Fax: (17) 231-09-14
E-mail: oms.bsuir@unibel.by
Internet: www.bsuir.unibel.by

Founded 1964

Rector: Prof. MIKHAIL P. BATURA
First Pro-Rector: Dr STEPAN V. LUKYANETS
Pro-Rector for Administration: VLADIMIR I. TARASEVITCH
Pro-Rectors for Education: Prof. VIKTOR E. BORISENKO, Prof. ALEXANDER A. KHMYL, Doc. VLADIMIR I. KRASOVSKIY
Pro-Rector for Research and Development: Prof. ALEXANDER P. KUZNETSOV

Library of 1,398,300 vols
Number of teachers: 692
Number of students: 10,000

DEANS

Faculty of Computer-Aided Design: Dr ANATOLY N. OSIPOV
Faculty of Computer Systems and Networks: Dr BORIS V. NIKULSHIN
Faculty of Engineering Economics: Dr EDUARD A. AFITOV
Faculty of Extramural, Evening and Distance Education: Dr ALEXANDER V. LOMAKO
Faculty of Information Technologies and Control Systems: Dr VITALY L. BUSKO
Faculty of Pre-University Preparation and Occupational Guidance: Dr GALINA F. SMIRNOVA
Faculty of Radioengineering and Electronics: Dr VITALY I. PACHININ
Faculty of Telecommunications: Dr OLEG D. TCHERNUKHO

BELARUSIAN STATE UNIVERSITY OF PHYSICAL CULTURE

220020 Minsk, pr. Pobeditelei 105
Telephone: (17) 250-80-08
Fax: (17) 250-80-08
E-mail: rector@bgafk.unibel.by
Internet: www.bgafk.unibel.by

Founded 1937

Rector: MIKHAIL E. KOBRINSKIY
First Pro-Rector: OLGA A. GUSAROVA
Pro-Rector for Economic Affairs: GRIGORIY P. KOSYACHENKO
Pro-Rector for Research: TATYANA D. POLYAKOVA
Pro-Rector for Sport: VLADIMIR M. VASILEVSKIY

DEANS

Faculty of Pre-University Education: VLADIMIR M. LITVINOVICH
Faculty of Rehabilitative Physical Culture and Tourism: NATALYA M. MASHARSKAYA
Faculty of Sports Education for Individual and Team Sports: ALEXANDR M. SHAKHLAY
Faculty of Sports Education for Popular Sports: MIKHAIL I. KORBIT

ATTACHED INSTITUTE

Institute of Qualifications Improvement and Retraining of Leaders and Specialists in Physical Culture, Sport and Tourism: Dir GENNADIY D. DYLYAN.

BELARUSIAN STATE UNIVERSITY OF TRANSPORT

246653 Gomel, ul. Kirova 34
Telephone: (232) 95-20-96

Founded 1953

Rector: Prof. VENIAMIN I. SENKO
First Pro-Rector and Pro-Rector for Academic Affairs: Prof. VIKTOR YA. NEGREY
Pro-Rector for Academic Affairs: SERGEY I. SUKHOPAROV
Pro-Rector for Administrative Affairs: VALERIY V. BABIY
Pro-Rector for Economics: GALINA M. BYCHKOVA
Pro-Rector for Education: GALINA M. CHAYANKOVA
Pro-Rector for Research: Prof. KONSTANTIN A. BOCHKOV

Library of 650,000 vols
Number of teachers: 358
Number of students: 3,390

Publication: *Vestnik BelGUTa: Nauka i Transport* (quarterly)

DEANS

Faculty of Continuing Education: VLADIMIR V. PIGUNOV
Faculty of Electrical Engineering: ALEKSANDR V. GRAPOV
Faculty of Engineering: VIKTOR A. BERBILO
Faculty of Foreign Students: IRINA G. PASHKO
Faculty of Humanities and Economics: YURI P. LYCH
Faculty of Industrial and Civil Construction: ANATOLIY G. TASHNIKOV
Faculty of Mechanical Engineering: YURI G. SAMODUM
Faculty of Military Transportation: Col VLADIMIR V. LEVTRINSKIY
Faculty of Transport Management: NIKOLAY P. BERLIN
Faculty of Vocational Guidance and Pre-University Training: OLEG P. GORAEV

BELARUSIAN TRADE AND ECONOMIC UNIVERSITY OF CONSUMER CO-OPERATIVES

246029 Gomel, pr. Oktyabrya 50
Telephone: (232) 78-17-07
Fax: (232) 47-80-68
E-mail: priem@bteu.by
Internet: www.bteu.by

Founded 1964

Rector: Doc. ANNA A. NAUMCHIK
First Pro-Rector: Doc. PAVEL G. PONOMARENKO
Pro-Rectors for Academic Affairs: Doc. VASILIY V. BOGUSH, Doc. LYUBOMIR M. SKORIK
Pro-Rector for Academic Research: Doc. LYUDMILA V. MISINKOVA
Pro-Rector for Administration: Dr VASILIY D. POTAPOV
Pro-Rector for Education and Information Technology: Dr ALEKSANDR I. KAPSHTYK
Pro-Rector for Scientific Research: Dr GEORGIY S. MITYURICH

Library of 500,000 vols
Number of teachers: 330
Number of students: 8,450

DEANS

Faculty of Accounting and Finance: VALENTINA A. ASTAFEVA
Faculty of Commerce: KLAVDIYA I. LOKTEVA
Faculty of Economics and Management: TATYANA V. EMELYANOVA
External Faculty of Commerce and Management: GALINA S. TURILKINA
External Faculty of Economics and Management: ANDREY A. KOLESNIKOV

BREST STATE TECHNICAL UNIVERSITY

224017 Brest, vul. Moskovskaya 267,
Telephone: (162) 42-33-93
Fax: (162) 42-21-27
E-mail: canc@bstu.by
Internet: www.bstu.by

Founded 1966

Rector: Prof. Dr P. S. POJTA

Library of 395,000 vols
Number of teachers: 499
Number of students: 6,438

Faculties of Civil Engineering (civil engineering, production of building elements and structures, construction of roads and transport facilities, architecture), Economics (accounting, analysis, audit; world economy and international economic relations; marketing), Electronic and Mechanical Engineering (technology, equipment and automation of machine-building; automatic data processing systems; computers, systems and networks), Extramural Studies and Preparatory Training and Water Supply Systems and Soil Conservation (water supply and sewage disposal systems, soil conservation and water resources management).

BREST STATE UNIVERSITY 'A. S. PUSHKIN'

224016 Brest, bul. Kosmonavtov 21
Telephone: (162) 23-33-40
Fax: (162) 23-09-96
E-mail: box@brsu.brest.by
Internet: www.brsu.brest.by

Founded 1945

Rector: Prof. MECHISLAV E. CHESNOVSKIY
First Pro-Rector: Prof. ANDREY A. GORBATSKIY
Pro-Rector for Academic Affairs: Prof. STANISLAV G. RACHEVSKIY
Pro-Rector for Academic and Socio-Economic Affairs: Prof. ANNA N. SENDER
Pro-Rector for Educational and Social Affairs: Dr LYUDMILA A. GODUYKO

DEANS

Faculty of Biology: ALEXANDR N. TARASYUK
Faculty of Foreign Languages: ALEKSANDR N. GARBALEV
Faculty of Geography: ELENA N. GRIGOROVICH
Faculty of History: NATALYA P. GALIMOVA
Faculty of Law: BORIS M. LEPESHKO
Faculty of Mathematics: ALEXANDR E. BUDKO
Faculty of Philology: ZOYA P. MELNIKOVA
Faculty of Physical Education: NIKOLAY I. PRISTUPA
Faculty of Physics: VLADIMIR A. PETYUKHOV
Faculty of Pre-School Education: LARISA D. GUSAROVA
Faculty of Pre-University Education: ELENA I. MIRSKAYA
Faculty of Psychology and Pedagogy: ALEKSANDR I. OSTAPUK

ATTACHED INSTITUTE

Institute of Qualifications Improvement and Retraining of Leaders and Specialists in Physical Culture, Sport and Tourism: Dir GENNADIY D. DYLYAN.

GOMEL STATE MEDICAL UNIVERSITY

224016 Gomel, vul. Lante 5
Telephone: (232) 74-41-21
Fax: (232) 74-98-31
E-mail: medinst@mail.gomel.by
Internet: www.medinstitut.gomel.by

Founded 1990

Rector: Prof. SERGEY V. ZHAVORONOK
First Pro-Rector: Prof. ANATOLIY N. LYZIKOV
Pro-Rector for Medicine, Postgraduate Education and International Relations: Prof. VLADIMIR V. ANICHKIN
Pro-Rector for Research: Prof. ANDREY L. LYZIKOV

Library of 154,163 vols

DEANS

Faculty of Medical Diagnostics: IRINA A. NOVIKOVA
Faculty of Medicine: ALEKSANDR A. KOZLOVSKIY
Faculty of Preparation of Specialists for Foreign Countries: (vacant)
Faculty of Pre-University Education: IVAN M. OTROSHCHENKO
Faculty of Preventative Medicine: LYUDMILA P. MAMCHITS

GOMEL STATE TECHNICAL UNIVERSITY 'P. SUKHOI'

246746 Gomel, pr. Oktyabrya 48
Telephone: (23) 248-16-00
Fax: (23) 247-91-65
E-mail: rector@gstu.gomel.by
Internet: www.gstu.gomel.by

Founded 1981
Academic year: September to August

Rector: STANISLAV B. SARELO
First Pro-Rector: SERGEY I. TIMOSHIN
Pro-Rector for Construction: VIKTOR A. SOLOMADZE
Pro-Rector for Economics and Administration: STANISLAV I. PROKOPENKO
Pro-Rector for Research: VIKTOR M. KENKO
Pro-Rector for Studies and Education: VIKTOR V. KIRIENKO

Founded 1981

Library of 460,000 vols
Number of teachers: 700
Number of students: 7,985

DEANS

Faculty of Automation and Information Systems: GEORGIY I. SELIVESTROV
Faculty of External Studies: PETR V. LYCHEV
Faculty of Humanities and Economics: RAISA I. GROMYKO
Faculty of Machine Building: ALEKSEY T. BELSKY
Faculty of Mechanical Engineering and Technology: VLADIMIR P. RUSOV
Faculty of Power Engineering: LEONID I. EVMINOV
Faculty of Pre-University Training: SERGEY A. YURIS
Faculty of Qualifications Improvement: OLEG G. SHIROKOV

GOMEL STATE UNIVERSITY 'F. SKORINA'

246699 Gomel, Sovetskaya vul. 104
Telephone: (232) 56-31-13
Fax: (232) 57-81-11
E-mail: selkin@gsu.unibel.by
Internet: www.gsu.unibel.by

Founded 1969
State control
Languages of instruction: Russian, Belarusan
Academic year: September to July

Rector: Prof. Dr MIKHAIL V. SELKIN
First Pro-Rector: ALEKSANDR P. KARMAZIN

Library of 1,026,587 vols
Number of teachers: 570
Number of students: 5,843

Publications: *Belarusan Language*, *Problems in Algebra*, *University News* (in Russian, Belarusan and English, 6 a year)

Faculties of Biology, Economics, Foreign Languages, Geology and Geography, History, Law, Mathematics, Philology, Physical Training, Physics, , Psychology and Preparatory Training; France–Belarus Institute of Management, Institute of Qualification Improvement.

GRODNO STATE AGRARIAN UNIVERSITY

230008 Grodno, vul. Tereshkovoy 28
Telephone: (152) 77-01-68
Fax: (152) 72-13-65
E-mail: ggay@uni-agro.grodno.by
Internet: www.uni.agro-grodno.com

Founded 1951
State control

Rector: VITOLD K. PESTIS
First Pro-Rector: ALEKSANDR A. DUDUK
Pro-Rector for Administrative Affairs: VALERIY N. TRIKUTS
Pro-Rector for Education: FEDOR N. LEONOV
Pro-Rector for Research: ALEKSANDR V. GLAZ
Librarian: NADEZHDA P. KHODOTCHUK

Library of 300,000 vols
Number of teachers: 209
Number of students: 3,842

DEANS

Faculty of Agronomy: FEDOR F. SEDLYAR
Faculty of Economics: IOSIF I. DEGTYAREVICH
Faculty of Plant Protection: GALINA A. ZEZYULINA
Faculty of Pre-University Training: REGINA K. YANKELEVICH
Faculty of Qualifications Improvement and Retraining of Agricultural Personnel: OLEG E. MOLYAVKO (Pro-Rector)
Faculty of Veterinary Medicine: MIKHAIL A. KAVRUS
Faculty of Zooengineering: EVGENIY A. DOBRUK

GRODNO STATE MEDICAL UNIVERSITY

230015 Grodno, vul. Gorkogo 80
Telephone: (152) 233-03-65
Fax: (152) 233-53-41
E-mail: mailbox@grsmu.by
Internet: www.grsmu.by

Founded 1958
State control

Rector: PETR V. GARELIK
First Pro-Rector: IGOR G. ZHUK
Pro-Rector for Administrative and Economic Affairs: VLADIMIR P. KUZMICH
Pro-Rector for Commercial Activities and International Relations: VIKTOR V. ZINCHUK
Pro-Rector for Information and Pedagogical Affairs: VITALY V. VOROBYOV
Pro-Rector for Medical Affairs: SERGEY M. SMOTRIN
Pro-Rector for Research: SERGEY M. ZIMATKIN

DEANS

Faculty of Foreign Students: IGOR P. BOGDANOVICH
Faculty of General Medicine: GENNADIY G. MARMYSH
Faculty of Medical Nurses with Higher Education: EVGENY M. TISCHENKO
Faculty of Medical Psychology: TATYANA M. SHAMOVA
Faculty of Paediatrics: NELLA S. PARAMONOVA

GRODNO STATE UNIVERSITY 'YANKA KUPALA'

230023 Grodno, vul. Ozheshko 22
Telephone: (152) 44-85-78
Fax: (152) 44-06-19
E-mail: mail@grsu.by
Internet: www.grsu.by

Founded 1940
State control
Academic year: September to June

Rector: Prof. SIARHEI MASKEVICH
First Vice-Rector: Prof. EVGENY ROVBA
Vice-Rector (Academic Affairs and Information Technology): Dr YURY BEITIUK
Vice-Rector (Academic Affairs and International Relations): Dr LIUDMILA RYCHKOVA
Vice-Rector (Academic Research): Prof. VLADIMIR BARUSKOV
Vice-Rector (Education and Social Issues): Prof. TATSIANA BADZIUKOVA

Library of 620,000 vols
Number of teachers: 1,154
Number of students: 20,776

Publications: *Vestnik GrGU – Humanities Series* (4 a year), *Vestnik GrGU – Natural Sciences Series* (2 a year)

DEANS

Faculty of Biology and Ecology: Dr GALINA E. MINYUK
Faculty of Economics and Management: Dr YURY E. BELYKH
Faculty of History: Prof. ALEXANDR N. NECHUKHRYN
Faculty of Humanities: Dr IOSIF I. VELENTO
Faculty of Law: Dr MARIA ZHUK
Faculty of Mathematics: Dr VALERY K. BOIKO
Faculty of Pedagogy: Dr VICTOR P. TARANTEI
Faculty of Philology: (vacant): Dr VITALY TSARLYUKEVICH
Faculty of Physical Training: Dr ANDREI I. NAVOICHIK
Faculty of Physics and Mathematics: Dr GENNADY A. GACHKO
Faculty of Psychology: Dr PAVEL R. GALUZO
Institute for Post-Diploma Education: Dr YURY GNEZDOVSKY (Director)
Grodno Pedagogical College: DANUTA NASHKEVICH (Director)
Lida Pedagogical College: NATALIA KUDERKO (Director)
Volkovysk Pedagogical College: LEONID DASHKOVSKY (Director)
Grodno School of Management: Dr YURY VAITUKEVICH (Director)
Technological College of Grodno: Dr VASILY SENKO (Director)
Lida Technical College: YULIAN GRINEVICH (Director)

INTERNATIONAL SAKHAROV ENVIRONMENTAL UNIVERSITY

220009 Minsk, vul. Dolgobrodskaya 23
Telephone: (17) 230-69-98
Fax: (17) 230-68-88
E-mail: rector@iseu.by
Internet: www.iseu.by

Founded 1992
State control

Rector: Prof. SEMYON P. KUNDAS

Library of 150,000 vols
Number of teachers: 105
Number of students: 600

DEANS

Faculty of Advanced Training and Retraining: IVAN I. MATVEENKO

Faculty of Environmental Medicine: Asst Prof. MIKHAIL S. MAROZIK
Faculty of Environmental Monitoring: Prof. NIKOLAY S. LESHENYUK
Faculty of Pre-University Training: Asst Prof. LYUDMILA M. SHEIKO

ATTACHED INSTITUTE

Research Institute of Environmental Problems: Dir Dr SERGEY S. PAZNIAK.

MINSK STATE LINGUISTIC UNIVERSITY

220034 Minsk, vul. Zakharova 21
Telephone: (17) 284-80-67
Fax: (17) 236-75-04
E-mail: mslu@mslu.by
Internet: www.mslu.by

Founded 1948

Rector: NATALYA P. BARANOVA

Library of 1,000,000 vols and periodicals
Number of teachers: 560
Number of students: 6,030

Publications: *Foreign Languages in the Republic of Belarus* (4 a year), *Methodology of Teaching Foreign Languages* (annually), *Studies in Romanic and Germanic Languages* (annually), *Vestnik of MSLU: History, Philosophy and Economics* (annually), *Vestnik of MSLU: Phylology and Linguistics* (2 a year), *Vestnik of MSLU: Psychology, Didactics and Methods of Foreign Language Teaching* (annually)

Schools of English, French, German, Intercultural Communication, Retraining and Teacher Development, Russian as a Foreign Language, Spanish and Translation and Interpreting.

MOGILEV STATE FOODSTUFFS UNIVERSITY

212027 Mogilev, pr. Shmidta 3
Telephone: (22) 244-03-63
Fax: (22) 244-00-11
E-mail: info@mgup.net
Internet: www.mgup.net

Founded 1973
State control

Rector: Prof. VYACHESLAV SHARSHUNOV

Library of 500,000 vols
Number of teachers: 250
Number of students: 5,530

DEANS

Faculty of Chemical Technology: T. I. PISKUN
Faculty of Economics: NADEZHDA V. ABRAMOVICH
Faculty of External Studies: A. V. OBOTUROV
Faculty of Mechanical Engineering: VALERIY P. CHIRKIN
Faculty of Pre-University Training: ELENA N. ANDREYCHIKOVA
Faculty of Technology: LIDIYA A. KASYANOVA

MOGILEV STATE UNIVERSITY 'A. A. KULESHOV'

220009 Minsk, vul. Dolgobrodskaya 23
Telephone: (17) 230-69-98
Fax: (17) 230-68-88
E-mail: rector@iseu.by
Internet: msu.mogilev.by

Founded 1913; present name and status 1997

Rector: KONSTANTIN M. BONDARENKO
First Pro-Rector: MIKHAIL I. VISHNEVSKIY
Pro-Rector for Academic Affairs: VLADIMIR I. POPOV
Pro-Rector for Research: NIKOLAY P. BUZUK

Library of 500,000 vols
Number of teachers: 450
Number of students: 7,600.

ATTACHED INSTITUTE

Institute of Qualifications Improvement and Retraining: Rector ZHANNA A. BARSUKOVA.

POLOTSK STATE UNIVERSITY

211440 Novopolotsk, vul. Blokhina 29
Telephone: (214) 53-20-12
Fax: (214) 53-42-63
E-mail: post@psu.by
Internet: www.psu.by

Founded 1968
State control

Rector: DMITRIY N. LAZOVSKIY
First Pro-Rector: NATALYA N. BELORUSOVA
Pro-Rector for Academic Affairs: VASILIY V. BULAKH
Pro-Rector for Administrative Affairs: VLADIMIR P. STRIZHAK
Pro-Rector for Education and Social Affairs: VIKENTIY G. TSYGANOK
Pro-Rector for the Environment: VLADIMIR K. LIPSKIY
Pro-Rector for Information Systems: DMITRIY O. GLUKHOV
Pro-Rector for Innovation: NIKOLAY N. POPOK
Pro-Rector for International Affairs: SERGEY V. PESHKUN
Pro-Rector for Maintenance and Construction: VILEN S. LEVIN
Pro-Rector for Research: FEDOR I. PANTALEENKO

Library of 427,000 vols
Number of teachers: 500
Number of students: 6,000.

VITEBSK STATE MEDICAL UNIVERSITY

210023 Vitebsk, pr. Frunze 27
Telephone: (212) 24-04-33
Fax: (212) 37-21-07
E-mail: admin@vgmu.vitebsk.by
Internet: www.vgmu.vitebsk.by

Founded 1934
State control

Rector: ALEKSANDR N. KOSINETS
Pro-Rector for Academic Affairs: VASILIY V. BULAKH
Pro-Rector for Administrative Affairs: ALEKSANDR P. SOLODKOV
Pro-Rector for Clinical and Pharmaceutical Affairs: ALEKSANDR P. SOLODKOV
Pro-Rector for Educational work and International Affairs: VALERY P. DEIKALO
Pro-Rector for Ideological Affairs: OLGA A. SYRODOYEVA
Pro-Rector for Scientific and Research Affairs: ALEKSANDR P. SOLODKOV

Library of 408,000 vols
Number of teachers: 390
Number of students: 4,500

Publications: *Herald* (4 a year), *Immunopathology, Allergology, Infectology* (4 a year), *Maternity and Child Protection* (4 a year), *Pharmacy News* (4 a year), *Surgery News* (4 a year).

VITEBSK STATE TECHNOLOGICAL UNIVERSITY

210035 Vitebsk, Moskovskiy pr. 72
Telephone: (212) 27-50-26
Fax: (212) 27-74-01
E-mail: vstu@vstu.vitebsk.by
Internet: www.vstu.vitebsk.by

Founded 1959
State control

Rector: Prof. VALERIY S. BASHMETOV
First Pro-Rector: IVAN A. MOSKALEV
Pro-Rector for Administrative Affairs: ALEKSEY N. SHUT
Pro-Rector for Education: ANATOLIY A. BELOV
Pro-Rector for Research: SERGEY M. BASHMETOV
Pro-Rector for Social and Economic Affairs and Construction: BORIS E. RYKLIN

Library of 300,000 vols
Number of teachers: 293
Number of students: 5,500 (incl. 2,500 external)

DEANS

Faculty of Arts and Technology: GALINA V. KAZARNOVSKAYA
Faculty of Civil Engineering and Technology: VITALIY K. SMELKOV
Faculty of External Studies: ANATOLIY M. TIMOFEEV
Faculty of Mechanical Engineering and Technology: VALERIY I. OLSHANSKIY
Faculty of Economics: VLADIMIR P. SHARSTNEV
Faculty of Pre-University Training and Vocational Guidance: ALEKSANDR P. SUVOROV
Faculty of Qualifications Improvement: IGOR M. KONTOROVICH

VITEBSK STATE UNIVERSITY 'P. M. MASHEROV'

210038 Vitebsk, Moskovskiy pr. 33
Telephone: (212) 21-58-66
E-mail: vsu@vsu.by
Internet: www.vsu.by

Founded 1910 as Teacher Training Institute; present name and status 1955
State control

Rector: Prof. ARKADIY V. RUSETSKIY
First Pro-Rector: IOSIF E. ANDRUSHKEVICH
Pro-Rector for Research: GENNADY I. MIKHASYOV
Pro-Rector for Studies: TATYANA G. ALEYNIKOVA

Publications: *departmental publications*, *My i Chas*, *Vestnik VGU*

DEANS

Faculty of Belarusian Philology and Culture: VIKTOR I. NESTOROVICH
Faculty of Biology: VITALIY YA. KUZMENKO
Faculty of Graphic Arts: VALENTIN P. KLIMOVICH
Faculty of History: VENIAMIN A. KOSMACH
Faculty of Law: VYACHESLAV I. PUSHKIN
Faculty of Mathematics: NIKOLAY E. BOLSHAKOV
Faculty of Pedagogy: ANATOLIY I. MURASHKIN
Faculty of Philology: LEONID M VARDOMATSKIY
Faculty of Physics: ILLARION V. GALUZO
Faculty of Social Pedagogy and Psychology: SERGEY A. MOTOROV

ATTACHED INSTITUTE

Institute of Qualifications Improvement and Retraining

Other Institutes of Higher Education

Academy of the Ministry of Internal Affairs: 220771 Minsk, pr. Pobeditelei 6; tel. (17) 284-31-15; fax (17) 288-27-58; e-mail info@amia.unibel.by; internet amia.nsys.by; f. 1958; faculties of distance education, forensic medicine, investigation, military studies, officer training and professional training; Rector VITALIY I. APARASEVICH.

Academy of Public Administration of the President of the Republic of Belarus: 220007 Minsk, vul. Moskovskaya

17; tel. and fax (17) 222-82-05; e-mail rector@pacademy.edu.by; internet www.pacademy.edu.by; f. 1991 as an instn of higher and advanced education for the training of public administration personnel; library: 200,000 vols; Rector PETR KUKHARCHYK; publ. *Issues of Management*..

Constituent institutes:

Centre for Education and Youth Initiatives.

Centre for Educational Technology.

Centre for Information Technology.

Centre for Innovation.

Centre for International Co-operation and Educational Programmes.

Editorial and Publishing Centre.

Institute of Public Administration.

Institute of Public Service.

Institute of Senior Management Personnel.

Research Institute for the Theory and Implementation of Public Administration: Dir YAUHEN MATUSEVICH.

Belarusian Medical Academy of Post-graduate Education: 220013 Minsk, vul. P. Brovki 3; tel. and fax (17) 232-25-83; e-mail rector@belmapo.edu.by; internet www.belmapo.edu.by; f. 1931; faculties of dentistry, public health and protection, paediatrics, surgery and therapy; attached Laboratory of Scientific Research; 16,000 students; Rector Prof. GENNADIY Y. KHULUP; Librarian ANNA A. KOLBASKO.

Belarus State Academy of Arts: 220012 Minsk, pr. Nezavisimosti 81; tel. (17) 232-15-42; fax (17) 232-20-41; e-mail belam@user.unibel.by; internet belam.by.com; f. 1945; faculties of decorative-applied arts, fine arts and design and theatre; postgraduate courses in theatre art, television, cinema and visual arts, fine and decorative-applied arts and architecture, theory of arts, technical aesthetics and design; library: 83,538 vols; Rector Prof. RICHARD B. SMOLSKIY.

Belarusian State Academy of Music: 220030 Minsk, Internatsionalnaya vul. 30; tel. (17) 227-49-42; fax (17) 206-55-01; e-mail bgam@tut.by; internet www.bgam.edu.by; f. 1932; courses: piano, orchestral and folk instruments, singing, composition, pedagogics, musicology, ethnomusicology, choir and symphony conducting; library: 211,702 vols; 307 teachers; 979 students; Rector M. A. KOZINETS.

Belarus State Agricultural Academy: 213410 Mogilev raion, Gorki, vul. Michurina 5; tel. and fax (2233) 5-14-20; internet www.belagro.org.by; f. 1840; faculties of accounting, agribusiness and law, agronomy, agroecology, animal husbandry, economics, mechanization, land management and hydromelioration; library: 1,000,000 vols; 800 teachers; 11,000 students; Rector Prof. ALEKSANDR R. TSYGANOV; publ. collection of research works (annually).

Minsk Institute of Management: 220102 Minsk, vul. Lazo 12; tel. (17) 242-97-97; fax (17) 243-67-61; e-mail mik@mikby.com; internet www.miu.by; f. 1991; faculties of accounting and finance, economics and law; Rector Dr NIKOLAY V. SUSHA.

Minsk State Higher Education College of Civil Aviation: 220096 Minsk, vul. Uborevitcha 17; tel. (17) 201-02-81; fax (17) 241-66-32; e-mail aviakollege@ivcavia.com; internet www.avia.by/mgvak_en.shtml; f. 1974; trains specialists in aircraft and engine technical exploitation, lifting and transportation, operation of building and road machinery, technical exploitation of aviation technology (electrical devices and light technical equipment), information technology systems and networks and air traffic control and operation; Head ALEXANDER I. NAUMENKO.

Vitebsk State Academy of Veterinary Medicine: 210026 Vitebsk, vul. 1-ya Dovatora 7/11; tel. (212) 37-20-44; fax (212) 37-02-84; e-mail vet@lib.belpak.vitebsk.by; f. 1924; faculties of correspondence studies, specialist upgrading, veterinary medicine and zooengineering; library: 340,000 vols; 348 teachers; 3,109 students; Rector A. I. YATUSEVICH.

BELGIUM

The Higher Education System

The higher education system in Belgium reflects divisions of language, with separate ministries of education for the Dutch (or Flemish), French (Walloon) and German-speaking communities. This division was enshrined in legislation passed in 1963, under which French was established as the medium of instruction in Wallonia, Flemish in Flanders and German in the East-Cantons (Ostkantone). Brussels, the capital, is officially bilingual (French and Flemish). Both public and private universities are funded through their respective communities, but Roman Catholic institutions are regarded as 'free' and account for about 60% of Belgium's students. In 2002/03 a total of 119,484 students were enrolled in university-level establishments. Non-university institutions of higher education provide arts education, technical training and teacher training; in 2002/03 a total of 178,903 students were enrolled in such institutions. In that year enrolment at tertiary level was equivalent to 61.1% of those in the relevant age-group (males 55.9%; females 66.5%). A national study fund provides grants where necessary and almost 20% of students receive scholarships.

The requirement for university entrance is the Certificat d'Enseignement Secondaire or Diploma Secundair Onderwijs. Hogescholen (see below) are open to all applicants holding the required certificates or wishing to attend courses as a 'free' student. The latter category of students are only eligible for certificates, not diplomas, after completing part of these studies. Generally, there are no entrance examinations or selective admission systems in use. However, in specific areas like nautical sciences and some art courses (audio-visual arts, music and dance), entrance examinations are compulsory.

The French community controls four universities, while the Flemish community controls three; in addition, there are 11 university centres or faculties (six French, five Flemish). Courses are divided into a period of general preparation followed by a period of specialization, each lasting two to three years. Belgium began implementing the Bologna Process in the 2004/05 academic year; reforms are being carried out by all three communities. The Bachelors is intended to replace a number of different degrees, notably one-cycle programmes of up to three years, resulting in either Gegradueerde (Flemish) or Graduat (Walloon), and two-cycle programmes of four or more years consisting of Candidat and Licencié (Walloon) or Kandidaat and Licentiaat (Flemish). The first part of the two-cycle degree (Candidat/Kandidaat) provides a general education, and lasts two years, whilst the second part (Licencié/Licentiaat) provides more specialized training over two or more years. The Masters is broadly equivalent to the old degrees of complementary education, the Gediplomeerde in de Aanvullende Studiën (Flemish) and Diplômé d'Etudes Complémentaires (Walloon), and degrees of advanced studies, Diplômé d'Etudes Approfondies (Walloon) and Diploma van Grondige Studies (Flemish). The final, and highest, level of academic degree is the Doctorate, which has no time limit but cannot be awarded until at least two years after completion of the second-cycle degree (now Bachelors).

Non-university post-secondary education is provided by Hautes Ecoles (in Wallonia) Hogescholen (in Flanders) and a number of specialist colleges of technology, agriculture, paramedical studies, economics, social studies and teacher training. In Walloon-controlled institutions courses are divided into eight subject categories, leading either to a Graduat after a 'short' course of three years or a Licencié after a 'long' course of four years. Programmes in the Hogescholen are also divided in 'long/short' courses of one or two cycles. Technical and vocational training is available either through an employer or an institution and is divided into three categories: apprenticeship contract; industrial apprenticeship contract and part-time work and/or training.

Regulatory and Representative Bodies

GOVERNMENT

Ministry of Flanders and the Dutch-speaking Community, Department of Education and Training: Hendrik Consciencegebouw, Koning Albert II-laan 15, 1210 Brussels; tel. (2) 553-86-11; fax (2) 553-95-25; internet www.ond.vlaanderen.be; Minister FRANK VANDENBROUCKE.

Ministry of the French-speaking Community, Office for Higher Education, Scientific Research and International Relations: Rue Belliard 9–13, 1040 Brussels; tel. (2) 213-35-11; fax (2) 231-35-23; Minister MARIE-DOMINIQUE SIMONET.

Ministry of the German-speaking Community, Department of Education and Training: Gosperstr. 1, 4700 Eupen; tel. (8) 759-64-81; fax (8) 755-64-75; e-mail unterricht@dgov.be; Minister OLIVER PAASCH.

REGIONAL AND COMMUNITY BODIES

Conseil Interuniversitaire de la Communauté française de Belgique (CIUF) (Interuniversity Council of the French-speaking Community in Belgium): rue d'Egmont 5, 1000 Brussels; tel. (2) 504-92-91; fax (2) 502-27-68; e-mail info@ciuf.be; internet www.ciuf.be; f. 2003; represents 9 univs. and univ.-level instns in the French-speaking community; advises on education policy; promotes co-operation between univs and univ.-level instns; Pres. BERNARD RENTIER.

Conseil des Recteurs des Universités Francophones de Belgique(CREF) (Rectors' Conference for Francophone Universities in Belgium): 5 rue d'Egmont, 1000 Brussels; tel. (2) 504-92-11; fax (2) 514-00-06; e-mail kokkelkoren@cref.be; internet www.cref.be; f. 1990 by rectors of French-speaking Belgian univs, to address issues of higher education and scientific research; 9 mems; Pres. BERNARD COULIE.

Vlaamse hogescholenraad (VLHORA) (Flemish Council for Non-university Higher Education): Wolvengracht 38/2, 1000 Brussels; tel. (2) 211-41-90; fax (2) 211-41-99; internet www.vlhora.be; f. 1996, awarded statute of public utility institution by decree in 1998; gives advice to the Flemish authorities on all policy aspects regarding college education, scientific project research, social services and the practice of the arts; organizes and stimulates consultation between the institutions on all issues related to the univ. colleges (hogescholen); Sec.-Gen. LUC VAN DE VELDE.

Vlaamse Interuniversitaire Raad (VLIR) (Flemish Interuniversity Council): VLIR algemeen secretariaat, Egmontstraat 5, 1000 Brussels; tel. (2) 550-15-72; fax (2) 512-29-96; e-mail administratie@vlir.be; internet www.vlir.be; f. 1976; autonomous body financed by univs; advises on and presents proposals to minister with regard to univ. education; research activities; Dir ANNE-MARIE DE JONGHE.

Learned Societies

GENERAL

Académie Royale des Sciences, des Lettres et des Beaux-Arts de Belgique (Royal Academy of Science, Letters and Fine Arts of Belgium): Palais des Académies, 1 rue Ducale, 1000 Brussels; tel. (2) 550-22-11; fax (2) 550-22-05; e-mail arb@cfwb.be; internet www.arb.cfwb.be; f. 1772; divisions of Science (Dir JEAN MAWHIN), Letters and Moral and Political Sciences (Dir JACQUES POUCET), Fine Arts (Dir PHILIPPE ROBERTS-JONES); 300 mems (90 ordinary, 60 corresp., 150 assoc.); library of 420,000 vols; Pres. JEAN MAWHIN; Permanent Sec. LÉO HOUZIAUX; Librarian FRANÇOISE THOMAS; publs *Bulletin de la Classe des Sciences* (2 a year), *Year Book*, *Nouvelle Biographie Nationale* (every 2 years), *Bulletin de la Classe des Sciences morales et politiques* (2 a year), *Bulletin de la Classe des Beaux-Arts* (2 a year), *Mémoires de l'Académie Royale de Belgique* (5–10 a year).

Académie Royale des Sciences d'Outre-Mer/Koninklijke Academie voor Overzeese Wetenschappen (Royal Academy of Overseas Sciences): 1 rue Defacqz, boîte 3, 1000 Brussels; tel. (2) 538-02-11; fax (2) 539-23-53; e-mail kaowarsom@skynet.be; internet www.kaowarsom.be; f. 1928; the promotion of scientific knowledge of overseas areas, especially those with particular development problems; Permanent Sec. DANIELLE SWINNE; 298 mems (68 hon., 48 ordinary, 32 hon. assoc., 53 assoc., 44 hon. corresp., 53 corresp.); publs *Actes Symposiums/Acta Symposia*, *Biographie belge d'Outre-Mer/ Belgische Overzeese Biografie*, *Bulletin des Séances/Mededelingen der Zittingen*, *Mémoires/Verhandelingen*, *Recueils d'études historiques/Historische bijdragen*

HEADS OF DEPARTMENTS

NAHAVANDI, F., Moral and Political Science
OZER, A., Natural and Medical Science
MARCHAL, J., Technical Science

Koninklijke Vlaamse Academie van België voor Wetenschappen en Kunsten (Royal Flemish Academy of Belgium for Science and the Arts): Paleis der Academiën, Hertogsstraat 1, 1000 Brussels; tel. (2) 550-23-23; fax (2) 550-23-25; e-mail info@kvab.be; internet www.kvab.be; f. 1938; divs of Natural Science (Dir J. VANDEKERCKHOVE), Humanities and Social Sciences (Dir C. STEEL), Arts (Dir V. NEES); 289 mems (90 ordinary, 30 corresp., 19 hon., 150 foreign assoc.); library of 50,000 vols; Pres. M. EYSKENS; Permanent Sec. N. SCHAMP; publs *Academiae Analecta*, *Memoirs*, *Year Book*, *Iuris Scripta Historica*, *Collectanea Maritima*, *Fontes Historiae Artis Neerlandicae*, *Iusti Lipsi Epistolae*, *Collectanea Biblica et Religiosa Antiqua*, *Collectanea Hellenistica*.

Attached institute:

Commission Royale d'Histoire/ Koninklijke Commissie voor Geschiedenis (Royal Historical Commission): Palais des Académies, 1 rue Ducale, 1000 Brussels; e-mail academie .royaledebelgique@cfwb.be; internet www .kbr.be/crh-kcg; f. 1834; research, analysis and publication of written sources concerning the history of Belgium; Pres. L. MILIS; Vice-Pres. J.-H. DUVOSQUEL; Sec. C. BRUNEEL; Admin. Sec. J.-L. DE PAEPE; publs *Bulletin* (quarterly), *Actes des Princes Belges* (irreg.), *Instruments de Travail* (irreg.).

AGRICULTURE, FISHERIES AND VETERINARY SCIENCE

Fédération Wallonne de l'Agriculture: Chaussée de Namur 47, 5030 Gembloux; tel. and fax (81) 60-00-60; e-mail fwa@fwa.be; internet www.fwa.be; f. 1930; protects professional interests.

Attached Institute:

Committee of Agricultural Organizations in the EU (COPA-COGECA): Rue de Trèves 61 1040 Brussels; tel. (2) 287-27-11; fax (2) 287-27-00; e-mail mail@ copa-cogeca.be; internet www.copa-cogeca .be; Pres. N. DEWISCH.

ARCHITECTURE AND TOWN PLANNING

Association Royale des Demeures Historiques de Belgique (Royal Association for Historic Buildings): 24 rue Vergote, 1200 Brussels; tel. (2) 735-09-65; fax (2) 735-99-12; f. 1934; Pres Prince ALEXANDRE DE MERODE; publ. *La Maison d'Hier et d'Aujourd'hui* (quarterly).

Fédération Royale des Sociétés d'Architectes de Belgique: 27 rue Ernest Allard, 1000 Brussels; tel. (2) 512-34-52; fax (2) 502-82-04; Sec.-Gen. E. DRAPS.

Société Belge des Urbanistes et Architectes Modernistes: 366 ave Brugmann, Brussels 18; f. 1919; Sec. L. OBIZINSKI.

Société Centrale d'Architecture de Belgique: Hôtel Ravenstein, 3 rue Ravenstein, 1000 Brussels; tel. (2) 511-34-92; f. 1872; promotion of architecture and town planning; 180 mems; library: *c.* 1,500 vols; Pres. WENLI KAO; Sec. MAURICE HEISTERCAMP; publ. *Bulletin mensuel* (monthly).

BIBLIOGRAPHY, LIBRARY SCIENCE AND MUSEOLOGY

Archives et Bibliothèques de Belgique: 4 blvd de l'Empereur, 1000 Brussels; tel. (2) 519-53-93; fax (2) 519-56-10; e-mail frankd@ kbr.be; f. 1907; a sub-committee of UNESCO, studies methods of standardization of bibliography; 350 mems; Pres. Dr FRANK DAELEMANS; publs *Archives et Bibliothèques de Belgique*, *Coll* (annual).

Association Professionnelle des Bibliothécaires et Documentalistes: Ave Rêve d'or 30, 7100 La Louvière; tel. (71) 61-43-35; fax (71) 61-16-34; e-mail library.ipg@ mail.interpac.be; f. 1975; 300 mems; Pres. LAURENCE BOULANGER; Vice-Pres ALEXANDRE LEMAIRE, ANDRÉ MORUE; publ. *Bloc-Notes* (4 a year).

Service Belge des Echanges Internationaux/Belgische Dienst Internationale Ruil (Belgian International Exchange Service): 4 blvd de l'Empereur, 1000 Brussels; tel. (2) 519-54-01; fax (2) 519-54-04; e-mail paul.de.ridder@kbr.be; f. 1889; information, documentation, exchange and transmission; Dir Dr PAUL DE RIDDER.

Vereniging van Antwerpse Bibliofielen (Antwerp Association of Bibliophiles): Museum Plantin-Moretus, Vrijdagmarkt 22, 2000 Antwerp; tel. (3) 221-14-50; fax (3) 221-14-71; f. 1877 to advance the study of the history of the printed book, particularly in Belgium and the Netherlands; frmrly Vereeniging der Antwerpsche Bibliophielen; 155 mems; Pres. Dr F. DE NAVE; Sec. Lic. M. DE SCHEPPER; publ. *De Gulden Passer* (annual).

Vereniging van Religieus-Wetenschappelijke Bibliothecarissen (Association of Theological Librarians): Minderbroederstraat 5, 3800 St Truiden; f. 1965; Pres. E. D'HONDT; Sec. K. VAN DE CASTEELE; publ. *V. R. B.-Informatie* (quarterly).

Vlaamse Museumvereniging (Flemish Museums Association): Plaatsnydersstraat 2, 2000 Antwerp; tel. (3) 216-03-60; fax (3) 257-08-61; e-mail info@museumvereniging .be; internet www.museumvereniging.be; f. 1962 to defend the interests of museums and museum personnel; 650 mems; Pres. S. THOMAS; publs *Museumkatern* (4 a year), *VMV Nieuwsbrief*.

ECONOMICS, LAW AND POLITICS

Institut Belge de Droit Comparé: 14 rue Bosquet, 1060 Brussels; f. 1907; Pres. M. VAUTHIER, Hon. Pres. of the Conseil d'Etat; Sec. PAUL LANDRIEN; 400 mems; publ. *La Revue de Droit International et de Droit Comparé* (quarterly).

Institut Belge des Sciences Administratives/Belgisch Instituut voor Bestuurswetenschappen (Belgian Institute of Administrative Sciences): Voorlopig Bewindstraat 15, 1000 Brussels; f. 1936; Pres. W. LAMBRECHTS; studies and research in public administration, also studies questions submitted by the International Institute of Administrative Sciences; 150 mems; publ. *Administration publique* (quarterly and monthly).

Politologisch Instituut (Institute of Political Science): Van Evenstraat 2 B, 3000 Leuven; tel. (16) 32-32-54; fax (16) 32-30-88; e-mail res.publica@soc.kuleuven.ac.be; internet www.respublica.be; f. 1958; annual conference; PhD seminars; 600 mems; Pres. Prof. MARC HOOGHE; publs *Res Publica* (French, English, Dutch, quarterly), *Belgian Political Yearbook* (Dutch, French, English), *Res Publica Library*.

Société Royale d'Economie Politique de Belgique (Royal Belgian Society of Political Economy): c/o CIFOP, 1 B ave Gén. Michel, 6000 Charleroi; tel. (71) 32-73-94; fax (71) 32-86-76; f. 1855; for popularization and progress in political economy; 400 mems; Pres. RENÉ LAMY; Sec.-Gen. ALBERT SCHLEIPER; publ. *Comptes rendus des travaux* (5 or 6 a year).

Union Royale Belge pour les Pays d'Outre-Mer (UROME): 22 rue de Stassart, 1050 Brussels; internet www.urome.be; f. 1912; 28 mems; Chair. PIERRE ANDRÉ.

FINE AND PERFORMING ARTS

Association Belge de Photographie et de Cinématographie: 57 rue Claessens, 1020 Brussels; f. 1874; 130 mems; Pres. J. PEETERS; publ. *Informations* (monthly).

Société Belge de Musicologie (Belgian Society of Musicology): 30 rue de la Régence, 1000 Brussels; e-mail vanhulst@ulb.ac.be; f. 1946; encourages the study and progress of the science and history of music; 300 mems; Pres. R. WANGERMEE; Sec. H. VANHULST; publ. *Revue belge de Musicologie* (French, English, German and Flemish) (annually).

Société Royale des Beaux-Arts: 25 ave Jef. Lambeaux, Brussels; f. 1893; organizes exhibitions of paintings, sculpture and engravings in Brussels; Pres. Baron ALBERT HOUTART; Sec. (vacant); publ. exhibition catalogues.

HISTORY, GEOGRAPHY AND ARCHAEOLOGY

Académie Royale d'Archéologie de Belgique/Koninklijke Academie voor Oudheidkunde van België (Royal Academy of Archaeology of Belgium): Musées Royaux d'Art et d'Histoire, 10 Parc du Cinquantenaire, 1000 Brussels; e-mail info@acad.be; internet www.acad.be; f. 1842; to promote study of the art history of the Southern Low Countries, Liège and Belgium; 100 mems (60 ordinary, 40 corresp.); Pres. NORBERT BASTIN; Sec. ALAIN JACOBS; publs *Bibliography of the History of the National Art* (online), *Revue Belge d'Archéologie et d'Histoire de l'Art/ Belgisch Tijdschrift voor Oudheidkunde en Kunstgeschiednis* (annually).

Association Egyptologique Reine Elisabeth/Egyptologisch Genootschap Kongingin Elisabeth: Parc du Cinquantenaire 10, 1000 Brussels; tel. (2) 741-73-64; fax (2) 733-77-35; e-mail aere.egke@kmkg-mrah.be; f. 1923 to encourage Egyptological and papyrological studies; 650 mems; library of 30,000 vols; Pres. Comte D'ARSCHOT; Dirs H. DE MEULENAERE, A. MARTIN; publs *Bibliographie Papyrologique* (quarterly), *Chronique d'Egypte* (2 a year).

Belgische Vereniging voor Aardrijkskundige Studies/Société Belge d'Etudes Géographiques (Belgian Society for Geographical Studies): W. de Croylaan 42, 3001 Heverlee (Leuven); tel. (16) 32-24-27; fax (16) 32-29-80; f. 1931; Pres. J. CHARLIER; Sec. F. WITLOX; centralizes and co-ordinates geographical research in Belgium; 150 mems; publ. *BELGEO* (2 a year).

Institut Archéologique du Luxembourg: 13 rue des Martyrs, 6700 Arlon; tel. (63) 21-28-49; fax (63) 22-47-65; e-mail info@ial.be; internet www.ial.be; f. 1847; Luxembourgeois Museum covers prehistoric period, Belgian-Roman period, Frankish period; Musée Gaspar displays works by Jean-Marie Gaspar and local art since the 16th century; 500 mems; library of 25,000 vols; Pres. LOUIS LEJEUNE; publs *Annales*, *Bulletin* (quarterly).

Institut Archéologique Liégeois: Musée Curtius, 13 quai de Maastricht, 4000 Liège; tel. (4) 221-94-04; fax (4) 221-94-32; f. 1850; studies of history and archaeology and related sciences in the District of Liège; language of instruction: French; 490 mems (450 ordinary, 40 corresp.); Pres. PHILIPPE GEORGE; Sec. JULIEN MAQUET; publ. *Bulletin* (annually).

Institut Géographique National/Nationaal Geografisch Instituut: Abbaye de la Cambre 13, 1000 Brussels; tel. (2) 629-82-11; fax (2) 629-82-12; e-mail sales@ngi.be; internet www.ign.be; f. 1831; land surveying and cartography; 267 mems; library: 15,000 maps; Dir.-Gen. INGRID VANDEN BERGHE; publs *Catalog* (annually), *Rapport Annuel—Jaarverslag* (annually).

Société Archéologique de Namur: Hôtel de Croix, 3 rue Saintraint, 5000 Namur; tel. (81) 22-43-62; fax (81) 22-43-62; f. 1845; museum and library; 450 mems; Pres. M. PACCO; Sec. J. JEANNEART; publ. *Annales*.

Société Belge d'Études Byzantines/Belgisch Genootschap voor Byzantijnse Studies: 1 rue Ducale, 1000 Brussels; tel. (9) 264-40-39; fax (9) 264-41-64; e-mail floris.bernard@ugent.be; f. 1956; 57 mems; Pres. Prof. ANNE TIHON; Sec. FLORIS BERNARD; publ. *Byzantion*.

Société Royale Belge de Géographie: Laboratoire de géographie humaine, Campus de la Plaine ULB, accès 5, Blvd du Triomphe, CP 246, 1050 Brussels; tel. (2) 650-50-72; fax (2) 650-50-92; e-mail srbg@ulb.ac.be; internet www.srbg.be; f. 1876; 130 mems; library of 9,500 vols; Pres. Prof. Dr C. VANDERMOTTEN; Sec.-Gen. Dr B. WAYENS; publ. *Belgeo* (4 a year).

Société Royale d'Archéologie de Bruxelles: 185 ave Winston Churchill, 1180 Brussels; tel. (2) 344-46-20; f. 1887; sections for archaeology proper, and the history of art; other collections in Musées Royaux d'Art et d'Histoire; library of 20,000 vols; 450 mems; Pres. P. P. BONENFANTI; Sec.-Gen. A. VANRIE; Librarian R. LAURENT; publs *Bulletins*, *Annales*.

Société Royale de Numismatique de Belgique: Bibliothèque Royale de Belgique, Cabinet des Médailles, 4 blvd de l'Empereur, 1000 Brussels; tel. (2) 639-00-00; fax (2) 466-86-02; e-mail jm@bvdmc.com; f. 1841; promotion of numismatics through publications and conferences; 277 mems (50 full, 15 hon., 112 nat. corresp., 100 foreign corresp.); Pres. RAF VAN LAERE; Sec. JAN MOENS; publ. *Revue Belge de Numismatique et de Sigillographie* (annually).

LANGUAGE AND LITERATURE

Académie Royale de Langue et de Littérature Françaises (Royal Academy of French Language and Literature): Palais des Académies, 1 rue Ducale, 1000 Brussels; tel. (2) 550-22-72; fax (2) 550-22-75; e-mail alf@cfwb.be; internet www.academiedelitterature.be; f. 1920; sections of Literature, Philology; 30 Belgian mems; 10 foreign mems; Dir RAYMOND TROUSSON; Permanent Sec. ANDRÉ GOOSSE; publs *Bulletin*, *Annuaire*, *Mémoires*.

Alliance Française: 59 Ave de l'Emeraude, 1030 Brussels; tel. (2) 732-11-03; fax (2) 502-33-77; e-mail info@alliancefr.be; internet www.alliancefr.be; offers courses and exams in French language and culture and promotes cultural exchange with France; attached offices in Antwerp, Condroz-Meuse-Hesbaye, Hainaut, Kortrijk, Limburg and Verviers; library of 5,000 vols; Chair, Belgium FRANK ARTS; Chair, Brussels Comte JEAN-PIERRE DE LAUNOIT.

Association des Ecrivains Belges de Langue Française (Association of Belgian Writers in the French Language): Maison Camille Lemonnier-Maison des Ecrivains, 150 chaussée de Wavre, 1050 Brussels; tel. (2) 512-29-68; fax (2) 502-43-73; internet www.ecrivainsbelges.be; f. 1902; 500 mems; library of 11,000 vols; awards prizes for essays, poetry and prose; Camille Lemonnier museum; Pres. FRANCE BASTIA; Vice-Pres MARIE NICOLAÏ, EMILE KESTEMAN; publ. *Nos Lettres* (10 a year).

British Council: Leopold Plaza, Rue du Trône 108, 1050 Brussels; tel. (2) 227-08-40; fax (2) 227-08-49; e-mail enquiries@britishcouncil.be; internet www.britishcouncil.be; offers courses and exams in English language and British culture and promotes cultural exchange with the UK; also responsible for Luxembourg; Dir Dr ROMAN STEPHAN.

Goethe-Institut: 58 Rue Belliard, 1040 Brussels; tel. (2) 230-39-70; fax (2) 230-77-25; e-mail info@bruessel.goethe.org; internet www.goethe.de/bruessel; offers courses and examinations in German language and culture and promotes cultural exchange with Germany; library of 20,000 vols, 90 periodicals; Dir MARGARETA HAUSCHILD.

Instituto Cervantes: 64 ave de Tervurenlaan, 1040 Brussels; tel. (2) 737-01-90; fax (2) 735-44-04; e-mail cenbru@cervantes.es; internet bruselas.cervantes.es; offers courses and exams in Spanish language and culture and promotes cultural exchange with Spain and Spanish-speaking Latin and Central America; library: library of 13,500 vols; Dir JOSÉ EDUARDO MIRA GONZÁLEZ.

International PEN Club, French-speaking Branch: c/o Huguette de Broqueville, 10 ave des Cerfs, 1950 Kraainem; tel. (2) 731-48-47; fax (2) 731-48-47; e-mail huguette.db@skynet.be; f. 1922; 540 mems; Pres. HUGUETTE DE BROQUEVILLE; Gen. Sec. VINCENT MALACOR.

International PEN Club, PEN-Centre Belgium: c/o Paul Koeck, Wiesbeek 41, 9255 Buggenhout; tel. (52) 35-11-18; fax (52) 35-11-19; Dutch-speaking branch; f. 1935; 140 mems; Pres. Gov. MONIKA VAN PAEMEL; Gen. Sec. PAUL KOECK; publ. *PEN-Tijdingen* (quarterly).

Koninklijke Academie voor Nederlandse Taal- en Letterkunde (Royal Academy of Dutch Language and Literature): Koningstraat 18, 9000 Ghent; tel. (9) 265-93-40; fax (9) 265-93-49; e-mail secretariaat@kantl.be; internet www.kantl.be; f. 1886; 69 mems (30 ordinary, 4 extraordinary., 10 hon., 25 foreign hon.); library of 40,000 vols; Permanent Sec. G. DE SCHUTTER; publs *Jaarboek*, *Verslagen en Mededelingen* (3 a year).

Société Belge des Auteurs, Compositeurs et Editeurs (SABAM): 75–77 rue d'Arlon, Brussels 1040; tel. (2) 286-82-11; fax (2) 230-05-89; e-mail info@sabam.be; internet www.sabam.be; f. 1922; collection and distribution of copyrights; 25,000 mems; Gen. Dir JACQUES LION; Man. Dirs CHRISTOPHE DEPRETER, LUC VAN OYCKE WILLY HEYNS, SERGE VLOEBERGHS, DIRK VAN SOOM, INGRID CLAES, THIERRY DACHELET; publs *Sabam Magazine* (4 a year), *Tempo* (4 a year), *Synopsis* (4 a year).

Société de Langue et de Littérature Wallonnes (Society for Walloon Language and Literature): Université de Liège, 7 place du XX Août, 4000 Liège; tel. (86) 34-44-32; e-mail sllw.be@skynet.be; internet users.skynet.be/sllw; f. 1856; 400 mems; library of 20,000 vols (Bibliothèque des Dialectes de Wallonie, 8 Place des Carmes, 4000 Liège; tel. (41) 23-19-60 ext. 139); Pres. GUY BELLEFLAMME; Sec. V. GEORGE; publs *Wallonnes* (4 a year), *Dialectes de Wallonie* (annually), *Littérature dialectale d'aujourd'hui* (annually), *Mémoire Wallonne* (annually).

Société d'Etudes Latines de Bruxelles (Brussels Society for Latin Studies): 6 rue du Palais St Jacques, 7500 Tournai; tel. (69) 21-47-13; fax (69) 21-47-13; e-mail latomus@belgacom.net; internet users.belgacom.net/latomus; f. 1937; languages of instruction: French, English; languages of instruction: German, Spanish; languages of instruction: Italian, Latin; 750 mems; Pres. C. DEROUX; publs *Review Latomus* (quarterly), *Collection Latomus*.

MEDICINE

Académie Royale de Médecine de Belgique (Royal Academy of Medicine of Belgium): Palais des Académies, 1 rue Ducale, 1000 Brussels; tel. (2) 550-22-55; fax (2) 550-22-65; e-mail academie.de.medecine@beon.be; internet www.armb.be; f. 1841; divisions of Biological Sciences, Human Medicine, Surgery and Obstetrics, Microbiology, Parasitology, Immunology, Public Health and Forensic Medicine, Pharmacy, Veterinary Medicine; 332 mems (80 ordinary, 37 corresp., 12 hon., 127 hon. foreign, 76 foreign corresp.); Pres. Prof. G. FRANCK; Permanent Sec. Prof. A. DE SCOVILLE; publ. *Bulletin et Mémoires* (monthly).

Association Belge de Santé Publique (Belgian Public Health Association): c/o Scientific Institute of Public Health, 14 rue Juliette Weytsman, 1050 Brussels; tel. (2) 642-54-07; fax (2) 642-54-10; f. 1938; promotes public health research in Belgium; 200 mems; Pres. Prof. Dr G. VAN HAL; publ. *Archives de Santé Publique*.

Association Royale des Sociétés Scientifiques Médicales Belges: 138A ave Circulaire, 1180 Brussels; tel. (2) 374-51-58; fax (2) 374-96-28; e-mail amb@skynet.be; internet www.ulb.ac.be/medecine/loce/amb.htm; f. 1945; 4,000 mems; Pres. Dr G. STALPAERT; Sec.-Gen. Dr P. DOR; publs *Acta Anaesthesiologica Belgica*, *Acta Chirurgica Belgica*, *Acta Gastro-Enterologica Belgica*, *Acta Neurologica Belgica*, *Acta Orthopedica Belgica*, *JBR-BTR* (Belgian Journal of Radiology).

Koninklijke Academie voor Geneeskunde van België (Royal Academy of Medicine of Belgium): Paleis der Academiën, Hertogsstraat 1, 1000 Brussels; tel. (2) 550-23-00; fax (2) 550-23-05; e-mail academiegeneeskunde@vlaanderen.be; internet www.academiegeneeskunde.be; f. 1938; divisions of Human Medicine, Pharmacy, Veterinary Medicine; 168 mems (76 ordinary, 63 foreign corresp., 29 hon.); Pres. (vacant); Sec.-Gen. Prof. Dr BERNARD HIMPENS; publs *Dissertationes–Series Historica*, *Proceedings*, *Year Book*.

Société Belge de Médecine Tropicale/Belgische Vereniging voor Tropische Geneeskunde: Nationalestraat 155, Antwerp; tel. (3) 247-62-01; fax (3) 237-67-31; e-mail dir@itg.be; f. 1920; 569 mems (24 Belgian and foreign hon., 66 assoc., 85 titular, 394 corresp.); Sec. Prof. Dr B. GRYSEELS; publ. *Tropical Medicine and International Health* (monthly).

Société Belge d'Ophtalmologie, section francophone (Belgian Society of Ophthalmology, French-speaking section): 126 ave P. Hymans, 1200 Brussels; f. 1896; Sec. Prof. J. M. LEMAGNE; publ. *Bulletin* (quarterly).

NATURAL SCIENCES

General

Association pour la Promotion des Publications Scientifiques (APPS): 26 ave de l'Amarante, 1020 Brussels; tel. (2) 268-29-33; fax (2) 268-25-14; f. 1981; 80 mems and 20 assoc. mems; Pres. Dr J. C. BAUDET; publ. *Ingénieur et Industrie* (monthly).

Société Royale des Sciences de Liège (Royal Society of Sciences of Liège): Institut de Mathématique B37, Université de Liège, 4000 Liège I; tel. (4) 366-38-41; fax (4) 366-95-47; e-mail srsl@guest.ulg.ac.be; internet www.srsl-ulg.net; f. 1835; promotion of biological, chemical, mathematical mineral and physical sciences; 200 mems; Pres. PASCAL PONCIN; Sec.-Gen. Prof. JACQUES AGHION; publ. *Bulletin* (online, 6 a year).

Société Scientifique de Bruxelles: 61 rue de Bruxelles, 5000 Namur; tel. (81) 72-46-71; fax (81) 72-44-65; e-mail charles.courtoy@fundp.ac.be; f. 1875; 140 mems; Pres. TH. DE BARSY; Sec. C. COURTOY; publ. *Revue des Questions Scientifiques* (4 a year).

Biological Sciences

Koninklijke Maatschappij voor Dierkunde van Antwerpen (Royal Zoological Society of Antwerp): 26 Koningin Astridplein, 2018 Antwerp; tel. (3) 202-45-40; fax (3) 231-00-18; internet www.zooantwerpen.be; f. 1843; Zoological and Botanical Gardens, Aquarium, Nature Reserve, Laboratories; educational and cultural services and scientific research; 32,000 mems; library of 34,000 vols; Dir R. VAN EYSENDEYK; publ. *Zoo* (quarterly, Dutch).

Naturalistes Belges, Les: 29 rue Vautier, 1000 Brussels; f. 1918; 1,000 mems; library of 5,000 vols; zoology, botany, geology, nature conservancy, etc.; Pres. ALAIN QUINTART; publ. *Les Naturalistes Belges* (quarterly).

Société Belge de Biochimie et de Biologie Moléculaire/Belgische Vereniging voor Biochemie en Moleculaire Biologie (SBBBM/BVBMB): 75 ave Hippocrate, UCL-ICP 74.39, 1200 Brussels; tel. (2) 764-74-39; fax (2) 762-68-53; e-mail secretary@biochemistry.be; internet www.biochemistry.be; f. 1951; 950 mems; Pres. Prof. Y. ENGELBORGHS; Sec. Prof. FRED R. OPPERDOES.

Société Belge de Biologie: Europawijk, 2440 Geel; 110 mems; Sec. A. LEONARD.

Société Royale Belge d'Entomologie (Royal Belgian Entomological Society): 29 rue Vautier, 1000 Brussels; tel. (2) 627-43-21; fax (2) 627-41-32; e-mail srbe@naturalsciences.be; internet www.sciencesnaturelles.be/srbe/page1.htm; f. 1855; 250 mems; library of 23,000 vols; Pres. G. WAUTHY; Sec. P. GROOTAERT; publs *Belgian Journal of Entomology* (2 a year), *Mémoires* (irregular), *Catalogue des Coléoptères de Belgique* (irregular), *Bulletin* (2 a year).

Société Royale de Botanique de Belgique: c/o Anne-Laure Jacquemart, Unité d'Ecologie et de Biogéographie, 5 Place Croix-du-Sud, 1348 Louvain-la-Neuve; tel. (10) 47-34-56; fax (10) 47-34-90; e-mail jacquemart@ecol.ucl.ac.be; internet www.biol.ucl.ac.be/socbota/socbotaun.htm; f. 1862; 250 mems; Pres. P. MEERTS; Sec. A.-L. JACQUEMART; publ. *Belgian Journal of Botany* (2 a year).

Société Royale Zoologique de Belgique/Koninklijke Belgische Vereniging voor Dierkunde: 50 ave F. D. Roosevelt, 1050 Brussels; tel. (2) 650-22-63; fax (2) 650-22-31; e-mail kbvd@uia.ua.ac.be; internet kbvd-www.uia.ac.be/kbvd; f. 1863; 400 mems; library of 1,500 periodicals; Pres. G. JOSENS; Sec. H. LEIRS; publ. *Belgian Journal of Zoology* (2 a year).

Mathematical Sciences

Belgian Mathematical Society: Dept of Mathematics and Computer Science, Univ. of Antwerp, Middelheimlaan 1, 2020 Antwerp; tel. (3) 265-38-89; fax (3) 265-37-77; e-mail bms@ulb.ac.be; internet bms.ulb.ac.be; f. 1921; promotion of mathematical activities; 240 mems (incl. 60 libraries, with which there is an exchange agreement); library of 200 vols; Sec. Prof. JAN VAN CASTEREN; publ. *Bulletin* (4 or 5 a year).

Conseil Supérieur de Statistique: 44 rue de Louvain, 1000 Brussels; tel. (2) 548-62-11; fax (2) 548-62-62; f. 1841; 36 mems; Pres. M. DESPONTIN; Sec. G. DUPONT.

Physical Sciences

Geologica Belgica: 13 rue Jenner, 1000 Brussels; tel. (2) 788-76-30; fax (2) 647-73-59; e-mail wdevos@naturalsciences.be; internet www.ulg.ac.be/geolsed/GB; f. 1887; 360 mems; Pres. D. LADURON; Sec. E. GROESSENS; Librarian and Treasurer W. DE VOS; publ. *Geologica Belgica* (2 a year).

Koninklijk Sterrenkundig Genootschap van Antwerpen/Société Royale d'Astronomie d'Anvers (Royal Astronomical Society of Antwerp): c/o Willy de Kort, Kapelsesteenweg 340, 2930 Brasschaat; tel. (3) 664-28-93; e-mail ksga@pandora.be; f. 1905; dissemination, teaching and aid for the promotion of astronomy; 180 mems; Pres. WILLY DE KORT; Sec. F. DELATIN; publ. *Astronomische Gazet* (6 a year).

Société Astronomique de Liège (Liège Society of Astronomy): Avenue de Cointe 5, B-4000 Liège; tel. (4) 253-35-90; fax (4) 252-74-74; e-mail sal@astro.ulg.ac.be; internet www.astro.ulg.ac.be/~sal/; f. 1938; brings together amateurs of astronomy, and promotes public understanding; 800 mems; library of 500 vols; Pres. A. LAUSBERG; Sec. L. PAUQUAY; publ. *Le Ciel* (monthly).

Société Géologique de Belgique (Belgian Geological Society): Unité de documentation, B6 Allée de la Chimie, 4000 Liège; tel. (4) 366-53-56; fax (4) 366-56-36; e-mail a.anceau@ulg.ac.be; f. 1874; 458 mems; Pres. F. BOULEVAIN; Sec.-Gen. A. ANCEAU; publ. *Geologica Belgica* (2 a year).

Société Royale Belge d'Astronomie, de Météorologie et de Physique du Globe: 3 ave Circulaire, 1180 Brussels; tel. (2) 373-02-53; fax (2) 374-98-22; internet www.srba.be; f. 1894; 800 mems; Pres. M. VANDIEPENDEECK; Sec. Gen. R. DEJAIFFE; publ. *Ciel et Terre* (every 2 months).

Société Royale de Chimie: ULB, CP 160/07, 50 ave F. Roosevelt, 1050 Brussels; tel. (2) 650-52-08; fax (2) 650-51-84; e-mail src@ulb.ac.be; internet www.ulb.ac.be/assoc/src/; f. 1887; 1,000 mems; library at 48 ave Depage, Brussels; Pres. Prof. J. M. FRÈRE; Gen. Sec. Prof. J. C. BRAEKMAN; publ. *Chimie Nouvelle* (quarterly).

PHILOSOPHY AND PSYCHOLOGY

Société Philosophique de Louvain: c/o Institut Supérieur de Philosophie, Place du Cardinal Mercier 14, 1348 Louvain-la-Neuve; tel. (10) 47-48-15; fax (10) 47-82-93; e-mail destree@sofi.ucl.ac.be; internet www.isp.ucl.ac.be/associations/socphil.html; f. 1888; 71 mems; Pres. B. FELTZ; Sec. P. DESTRÉE.

RELIGION, SOCIOLOGY AND ANTHROPOLOGY

Centre pour l'Etude des Problèmes du Monde Musulman Contemporain (Study Centre for Problems of the Contemporary Muslim World): 44 ave Jeanne, 1050 Brussels; tel. (2) 642-33-59; f. 1958; Dir Mme A. DESTREE; publ. *Le Monde Musulman Contemporain—Initiations*.

Institut Belge des Hautes Etudes Chinoises: c/o Musées Royaux d'Art et d'Histoire, 10 parc du Cinquantenaire, 1000 Brussels; tel. and fax (2) 741-73-55; e-mail inst.chin@kmkg-mrah.be; f. 1929; Sinology and Buddhism; lectures, courses on Chinese art, history, painting and calligraphy; library: *c.* 60,000 vols; *c.* 300 mems; Dir J.-M. SIMONET; publ. *Mélanges Chinois et Bouddhiques* (every 2 years).

Ruusbroecgenootschap: Prinsstraat 13, 2000 Antwerp; tel. (3) 220-43-69; fax (3) 220-44-20; f. 1925, inc. as Centrum voor Spiritualiteit of Universiteit Antwerpen in 1973; soc. of mainly Flemish Jesuits engaged in spiritual studies of the Low Countries; library of 115,000 vols (incl. 30,000 old and rare books), 500 MSS, 35,000 devotional prints; Dir Prof. Dr TH. MERTENS; publ. *Ons Geestelijk Erf* (quarterly).

Société des Bollandistes: 24 blvd St Michel, 1040 Brussels; tel. (2) 740-24-21; fax (2) 740-24-24; e-mail info@bollandistes.be; internet www.bollandistes.be; f. 1630; research and publication in critical hagiography; library of 500,000 vols; Dir Dr ROBERT GODDING; publs *Analecta Bollandiana* (critical hagiography, 2 a year), *Subsidia Hagiographica* (irregular), *Tabularium Hagiographicum* (irregular).

Société Royale Belge d'Anthropologie et de Préhistoire: 29 rue Vautier, 1000 Brussels; tel. (2) 627-43-85; fax (2) 627-41-13; e-mail annehauzeur@kbinirsub.be; f. 1882; Pres. MARTINE VERCAUTEREN; Sec.-Gen. A. HAUZEUR; 130 mems; publs *Anthropologie et Préhistoire* (annually), *Hominid Remains* (series).

TECHNOLOGY

Institut Belge de Normalisation (IBN) (Belgian Standards Institute): 29 ave de la Brabançonne, 1000 Brussels; tel. (2) 738-01-11; fax (2) 733-42-64; f. 1946; Belgian member of the International Organization for Standardization; 962 mems; Pres. F. SONCK; Dir-Gen. P. CROON; publs *Normes Belges*, *Revue IBN* (monthly), *Rapport annuel*.

Koninklijke Vlaamse Ingenieursvereniging (Royal Flemish Association of Engineers): KVIV Ingenieurshuis, Desguinlei 214, 2018 Antwerp; tel. (3) 216-09-96; fax (3) 216-06-89; internet www.kviv.be; f. 1928; 11,000 mems; Pres. Ir G. KESTENS; Sec.-Gen. Ir J. MARYNEN; publs *Het Ingenieursblad* (monthly), *KVIV-Direkt* (every 2 weeks), *Journal A* (quarterly).

Société Belge de Photogrammétrie, de Télédétection et de Cartographie (Belgian Society for Photogrammetry, Remote Sensing and Cartography): C.A.E.-Tour Finances (Bte 38), 50 blvd du Jardin Botanique, 1010 Brussels; f. 1931; 163 mems; Pres. R. THONNARD; Sec. J. VAN HEMELRIJCK; publ. *Bulletin* (quarterly).

Société Royale Belge des Electriciens: c/o VUB-TW-ETEC, 2 Blvd de la Plaine, 1050 Brussels; tel. (2) 629-28-19; fax (2) 629-36-20; e-mail srbe-kbve@vub.ac.be; f. 1884; 1,600 mems; Sec.-Gen. BRIGITTE SNEYERS; publ. *Revue E Tijdschrift* (quarterly).

Société Royale Belge des Ingénieurs et des Industriels: 3 rue Ravenstein, 1000

Brussels; tel. (2) 511-58-56; fax (2) 514-57-95; f. 1885; 2,000 mems; Pres. PIERRE KLEES; publ. *Bulletin Mensuel*.

Research Institutes

AGRICULTURE, FISHERIES AND VETERINARY SCIENCE

Centre de Recherches Agronomiques de Gembloux: 9 rue de Liroux, 5030 Gembloux; tel. (81) 62-65-55; fax (81) 62-65-59; e-mail cra@cra.wallonia.be; internet www.cragx.fgov.be; f. 1872; agricultural research at 8 research depts; Dir R. BISTON; publ. *Rapport d'activité*.

Centre d'Economie Agricole: WTC-3, 30 ave Simon Bolivar, 1000 Brussels; f. 1960; study and research in agricultural economics and rural sociology; Dir A. MOTTOULLE.

Centrum voor Onderzoek in Diergeneeskunde en Agrochemie/Centre d'Etude et de Recherches Vétérinaires et Agrochimiques (Veterinary and Agrochemical Research Centre): Groeselenberg 99, 1180 Brussels; tel. (2) 379-04-00; fax (2) 379-04-01; e-mail info@var.fgov.be; internet www.var.fgov.be; f. 1997; research sites in Brussels, Tervuren and Machelen; Pres. and Dir Dr J. E. PEETERS; publ. *Activiteitsverlag/Rapport d'activité* (annually).

ECONOMICS, LAW AND POLITICS

Centre for European Policy Studies (CEPS): 1 place du Congrès, Brussels 1000; tel. (2) 229-39-11; fax (2) 219-41-51; e-mail info@ceps.eu; internet www.ceps.eu; f. 1983; ind. instn dedicated to producing sound policy research leading to constructive solutions to the challenges facing Europe today; CEO KAREL LANNOO.

Institut Royal des Relations Internationales: 69 rue de Namur, 1000 Brussels; tel. (2) 223-41-14; fax (2) 223-41-16; e-mail info@egmontinstitute.be; internet www.egmontinstitute.be; f. 1947; 1,000 mems; research in int. relations, int. economics, int. politics, int. law, European affairs; documentation centre covering EU integration, central Africa, European security and defence policy; archives; library of 3,000 vols; Dir-Gen. CLAUDE MISSON; publs *Studia Diplomatica* (quarterly), *Egmont Papers* (irreg.).

FINE AND PERFORMING ARTS

Centre d'Etude de la Peinture du XVe Siècle dans les Pays-Bas Méridionaux et la Principauté de Liège/Studiecentrum voor de 15de-Eeuwse Schilderkunst in de Zuidelijke Nederlanden en het Prinsbisdom Luik (Centre for the Study of 15th Century Painting in the Southern Netherlands and the Principality of Liège): 1 Parc du Cinquantenaire, 1000 Brussels; tel. (2) 739-68-66; fax (2) 732-01-05; e-mail helene.mund@kikirpa.be; internet xv.kikirpa.be; f. 1950; research into 15th-century Flemish painting; language of instruction: French; 15 mems; library of 6,400 vols; Pres. P. COLMAN; Dir M. SERCK-DEWAIDE; Scientific Secs H. MUND, B. FRANSEN; publs *Corpus de la Peinture des Pays-Bas Méridionaux et de la Principauté de Liège au 15e Siècle*, *Répertoire*, *Contributions*.

MEDICINE

Born-Bunge Research Foundation: Universiteitsplein 1, 2610 Antwerp (Wilrijk); tel. (3) 820-26-02; fax (3) 820-22-48; e-mail jjmneuro@uia.ac.be; internet www.bbf.uia.ac.be/BBF; f. 1963; research in neurological sciences and cardiology; Dir Dr J. J. MARTIN.

Fondation Médicale Reine Elisabeth: 3 ave J. J. Crocq, 1020 Brussels; tel. (2) 478-35-56; fax (2) 478-24-13; e-mail fmre.gske@skymet.be; f. 1926; supports medical research in the field of neurobiology through several Belgian university laboratories; Dir Prof. TH. DE BARSY.

Institut Neurologique Belge: 152 rue de Linthout, Brussels 4; f. 1924; Pres. Comte EDOUARD D'OULTREMONT; publs *Acta Neurologica, Psychiatrica Belgica*.

Institut Pasteur de Bruxelles: 642 rue Engeland, 1180 Brussels; tel. (2) 373-31-11; fax (2) 373-32-82; e-mail lschoofs@pasteur.be; internet www.pasteur.be; f. 1900; scientific biomedical research, analyses; Dir JEAN CONTENT.

NATURAL SCIENCES

General

Institut Royal des Sciences Naturelles de Belgique/Koninklijk Belgisch Instituut voor Natuurwetenschappen: 29 rue Vautier, 1000 Brussels; tel. (2) 627-42-11; fax (2) 627-41-13; e-mail info@naturalsciences.be; internet www.naturalsciences.be; f. 1846; library: see Libraries; biology, zoology, palaeontology, geology, anthropology; Dir C. PISANI; publs *Bulletin: Biology*, *Bulletin: Entomology*, *Bulletin: Palaeontology*, *Study Documents* (irregular).

Biological Sciences

Jardin Botanique National de Belgique/Nationale Plantentuin van België: Domein van Bouchout, 1860 Meise; tel. (2) 260-09-20; fax (2) 260-09-45; e-mail office@br.fgov.be; internet www.br.fgov.be; f. 1870; botanical taxonomy and geography, especially of African and European plants, including Cryptogams; gene bank of Phaseolinae; herbarium with over 2,000,000 specimens; library: *c.* 200,000 vols; Dir J. RAMMELOO; publs *Systematics and Geography of Plants* (2 a year), *Flore illustrée des champignons d'Afrique Centrale* (annually), *Dumortiera* (3 a year), *Flore d'Afrique Centrale* (irregular), *Distributiones plantarum africanarum* (irregular), *Icones mycologicae* (irregular), *Opera Botanica Belgica* (irregular), *Scripta Botanica Belgica* (irregular).

Mathematical Sciences

Institut National de Statistique: 44 rue de Louvain, 1000 Brussels; tel. (2) 548-62-11; fax (2) 548-63-67; internet statbel.fgov.be; f. 1831; Dir-Gen. CLAUDE CHERUY; publs *Bulletin de Statistique* (monthly), *Annuaire statistique de la Belgique*, etc.

Physical Sciences

Centre d'Etude de l'Energie Nucléaire (Studiecentrum voor Kernenergie): Boeretang 200, 2400 Mol; tel. (14) 33-21-11; fax (14) 31-50-21; internet www.sckcen.be; f. 1952; nuclear research and development, reactor safety, fuel and materials irradiation, characterization and geological disposal of waste, decontamination and dismantling of facilities, radioprotection, nuclear services incl. irradiation in BR2 and post-irradiation examination; Chair. FRANK DECONINCK; Man. Dir CLAUDE TRUFFIN; publ. *Scientific Report* (annually).

Institut d'Aéronomie Spatiale de Belgique: Ave Circulaire 3, 1180 Brussels; tel. (2) 373-04-13; fax (2) 375-93-36; e-mail bira-iasb_webmaster@aeronomie.be; internet www.aeronomie.be; f. 1964 to undertake research in aeronomy (physics and chemistry of the atmosphere) from information gained from space vehicles; library of 3,000 vols and 150 periodicals; Dir Prof. PAUL C. SIMON; Sec. MARC DELANCKER.

Institut Royal Météorologique de Belgique: Ave Circulaire 3, 1180 Brussels; tel. (2) 373-05-08; fax (2) 375-05-28; e-mail irni_info@oma.be; internet www.meteo.be; f. 1913; departments for Climatology, Aerometry, Aerology, Applied Meteorology, Geophysics and Numerical Calculus; Dir Dr H. MALCORPS; publs *Bulletin Quotidien du temps* (daily), *Observations climatologiques*, *Observations synoptiques*, *Observations géophysiques*, *Observations ionosphériques* (monthly), *Observations d'ozone* (quarterly), *Climatologie*, *Rayonnement solaire*, *Magnétisme terrestre*, *Marées terrestres à Dourbes*, *Hydrologie* (annually).

Observatoire Royal de Belgique/Koninklijke Sterrenwacht van Belgie: Ave Circulaire 3, 1180 Brussels; tel. (2) 373-02-11; fax (2) 374-98-22; internet www.astro.oma.be/KSB-ORB; f. 1826; fundamental astronomy, satellite positioning, time service, seismology, gravimetry, earth tides, celestial mechanics, astrometry, astrophysics, solar physics, radioastronomy; Dir Prof. P. PÂQUET; publs *Annuaire*, *Bulletin Astronomique*, *Communications*.

PHILOSOPHY AND PSYCHOLOGY

Centre National de Recherches de Logique: Fondation Universitaire, 11 rue d'Egmont, 1000 Brussels; internet www.lofs.ucl.ac.be/cnrl; f. 1951; 32 mems; Pres. J. P. VAN BENDEGEM; Sec. SONIA SMETS; publ. *Logique et Analyse* (4 a year).

RELIGION, SOCIOLOGY AND ANTHROPOLOGY

Centre d'Etudes et de Recherches Arabes: Université de l'Etat à Mons, 24 ave Champ de Mars, 7000 Mons; tel. (65) 37-36-15; fax (65) 84-06-31; e-mail prof.h.safar@worldonline.be; f. 1978; includes the dept of Arabic of the Ecole d'Interprètes Internationaux; teaching and research in translation and interpretation, Arabic language, culture, curriculum development in underdeveloped countries, immigration, international relations, transfer of technology, Euro-Arab dialogue, subtitling, dubbing and multimedia; library of 2,000 vols; Dir Prof. H. SAFAR.

Centrum voor Interdisciplinair Antropologisch Onderzoek (Centre for Interdisciplinary Anthropological Research): Maria-Christinastraat 8, 3070 Kortenberg; f. 1967; Dir KAMEL DE VOS.

Institut d'Etudes du Judaïsme (Institute for the study of Judaism): 17 ave Roosevelt, 1050 Brussels; tel. (2) 650-33-48; fax (2) 650-33-47; e-mail iej@ulb.ac.be; internet www.ulb.ac.be/philo/judaism/; f. 1959; studies, publications and documentation on contemporary Judaism; library of 8,000 vols; Dir THOMAS GERGELY; publs *Nouvelles* (quarterly), *Mosaïque* (annually).

TECHNOLOGY

Institut Meurice (IIF–IMC–ISI): 1 ave Emile Gryzon, Anderlecht, 1070 Brussels; tel. (2) 526-73-00; fax (2) 524-30-82; e-mail cv@meurice.heldb.be; internet www.heldb-meurice.be; f. 1892; research and training centre for industrial engineers in chemistry and biochemistry; Dir Dr Ir PATRICK DYSSELER.

Institut Scientifique de Service Public (ISSeP): 200 rue du Chéra, 4000 Liège; tel. (4) 229-83-11; fax (4) 252-46-65; e-mail direction@issep.be; internet www.issep.be; f. 1990; applied research, development and demonstration relating to natural resources, the environment, technical and industrial security, solid fuels, radiocommunications; library of 11,000 vols; Gen. Man. J. JADIN.

Von Karman Institute for Fluid Dynamics: Chaussée de Waterloo 72, 1640 Rhode-St-Genese; tel. (2) 359-96-11; fax (2) 359-96-00; e-mail secretariat@vki.ac.be; internet www.vki.ac.be; f. 1956; multinational postgraduate teaching and research in aerodynamics, supported by the countries of NATO; depts of aeronautics/aerospace, turbomachinery and propulsion, environmental fluid dynamics; library of 2,000 vols, 55,000 reports; Dir Prof. MARIO CARBONARO; publ. *Lecture Series Monographs* (10 to 12 a year).

Libraries and Archives

Antwerp

AMVC—Letterenhuis (AMVC—Literary Centre): Minderbroedersstraat 22, 2000 Antwerp; tel. (3) 222-93-20; fax (3) 222-93-21; e-mail amvc.letterenhuis@stad.antwerpen.be; internet museum.antwerpen.be/amvc_letterenhuis; f. 1933; archives of Flemish literature, theatre, music, arts and culture; files and MSS can be seen on application; 55,000 files, 2m. letters and MSS, 35,000 posters, 130,000 photographs; Dir LEEN VAN DIJCK.

Bibliotheek Middelheimcampus–Universiteit Antwerpen: Middelheimlaan 1, 2020 Antwerp; tel. (3) 265-37-94; fax (3) 265-06-52; e-mail helpdesk@lib.ua.ac.be; internet lib.ua.ac.be; f. 1965; 75,000 vols; (Third World Development: Middelheimlaan 1, 2020 Antwerp; Science and Medicine: Groenenborgerlaan 171, 2020 Antwerp); Chief Librarian Dr B. VAN STYVENDAELE.

Bibliotheek Universitaire Instelling Antwerpen: Universiteitsplein 1, 2610 Antwerp; tel. (3) 820-21-41; fax (3) 820-21-59; e-mail uia@lib.ua.ac.be; internet lib.ua.ac.be; f. 1972; 400,000 vols; Dir J. VAN BORM.

Rijksarchief te Antwerpen (Antwerp State Archives): Door Verstraetepl. 5, 2018 Antwerp; tel. and fax (3) 236-73-00; e-mail rijksarchief.antwerpen@arch.be; internet arch.arch.be/frame_nl_d2.htm; f. 1896; history of the province of Antwerp; documents since 12th c.; Dir ERIK HOUTMAN.

FelixArchief/Stadsarchief (City Archives): Oudeleeuwenrui 29, 2000 Antwerp; tel. (3) 292-94-11; fax (3) 292-94-10; e-mail stadsarchief@stad.antwerpen.be; internet www.felixarchief.be; f. 1796; 16 km of documents concerning the admin. of Antwerp since the 13th century; history, genealogy, heraldry, cartography, sigillography; 11,000 specialized vols, 245 periodicals; Archivist INGE SCHOUPS.

Rubenianum: Kolveniersstraat 20, 2000 Antwerp; tel. (3) 201-15-77; fax (3) 231-93-87; e-mail info@rubenianum.be; internet www.rubenianum.be; documentation centre for the study of 16th and 17th c. Flemish art, especially the works of Jordaens, Rubens and Van Dyck; 45,000 vols; Curator NORA DE POORTER; publ. *Corpus Rubenianum Ludwig Burchard*.

Stadsbibliotheek: Hendrik Conscienceplein 4, 2000 Antwerp; tel. (3) 206-87-10; fax (3) 206-87-75; e-mail sba@antwerpen.be; internet stadsbibliotheek.antwerpen.be; f. 1481, reorganized 1834; Flemish and Dutch literature, history, humanities, local press; open to the public; 1,000,000 vols; Dir R. RENNENBERG.

Universiteit Antwerpen–Bibliotheek der Universitaire Faculteiten Sint-Ignatius: Prinsstraat 9, 2000 Antwerp; tel. (3) 220-49-96; fax (3) 220-44-37; e-mail ufsia@lib.ua.ac.be; internet lib.ua.ac.be; f. 1852; 870,000 vols; Dir TH. BOECKX; Chief Librarian L. SIMONS.

Arlon

Archives de l'Etat à Arlon: Parc des Expositions, 6700 Arlon; tel. and fax (63) 22-06-13; e-mail archives.arlon@arch.be; internet arch.arch.be/arlon.htm; f. 1849; documents concerning the Province of Luxembourg since 12th c.; 18 km of shelving; 100,000 vols; Archivist P. HANNICK; publs guides, inventories, exhibition catalogues, minutes of symposia.

Bruges

Rijksarchief te Brugge: Academiestraat 14, 8000 Bruges; tel. (50) 33-72-88; fax (50) 61-09-18; e-mail rijksarchief.brugge@arch.be; internet arch.arch.be; f. 1796; documents on Western Flanders since 12th c.; Archivist M. NUYTTENS.

Brussels

Archives de la Ville de Bruxelles: 65 rue des Tanneurs, 1000 Brussels; tel. (2) 279-53-20; fax (2) 279-53-29; e-mail archives@brucity.be; internet bold.belnet.be/BOLD/HTML/FR/AVB.html; historical archives of the city of Brussels; 20,000 reference vols, 100 periodicals; Archivist ANNE VANDENBULCKE.

Archives et Musée du Centre Public d'Action Sociale de Bruxelles: 298A rue Haute, Brussels; tel. (2) 543-60-55; fax (2) 543-61-06; e-mail dguilardian@cpasbru.irisnet.be; f. 1796; archives concerning hospitals and welfare since 12th century; approx. 20,000 archives; 15,000 vols; Archivist D. GUILARDIAN.

Archives Générales du Royaume: 2–4 rue de Ruysbroeck, 1000 Brussels; tel. (2) 513-76-80; fax (2) 513-76-81; e-mail archives.generales@arch.be; internet arch.arch.be; f. 1815; 50 km documents concerning the Low Countries, Belgium and Brabant since 11th c.; execution of legislation on Public Records; 254,000 vols; Gen. Archivist D. VAN OVERSTRATEN (acting).

Attached centre:

Centre de recherches et d'études historiques de la seconde guerre mondiale: Résidence Palace, 155/B2 rue de la Loi, 1040 Brussels; tel. (2) 287-48-11; fax (2) 287-47-10; Dir J. GOTOVITCH.

Bibliothèque artistique, Académie Royale des Beaux-Arts: 144 rue du Midi, 1000 Brussels; tel. (2) 506-10-35; fax (2) 506-10-38; e-mail bib.aca@brunette.brucity.be; internet www.e-monsite.com/biblioartistique; f. 1886; 18,155 vols, 400 rare books from the 17th and 18th centuries; more than 2,000 books on the applied arts from the 19th century, collections of photographs from the 19th and early 20th centuries (architecture, applied arts, travel); Librarian CHRISTINE FERON.

Bibliothèque Centrale du Ministère de l'Education, de la Recherche et de la Formation (Communauté Française): 43 rue de Stassart, 1050 Brussels; f. 1879; contains vols on administration and law, all branches of science and pedagogy, educational books; 400,000 vols, 900 periodicals; open only to teachers and mems of French Dept; Dir J.-M. ANDRIN.

Bibliothèque d'Art, Ecole Nationale Supérieure des Arts Visuels de la Cambre: 21 abbaye de la Cambre, 1000 Brussels; tel. (2) 626-17-86; fax (2) 640-96-93; e-mail bibliotheque@lacambre.be; internet www.lacambre.be; f. 1926; 60,000 vols; Librarian RÉGINE CARPENTIER.

Bibliothèque de l'Institut Royal des Sciences Naturelles de Belgique/Bibliotheek en Documentatiedienst van het Koninklijk Belgisch Instituut voor Natuurwetenschappen (Library and Documentation Service of the Royal Belgian Institute of Natural Sciences): 29 rue Vautier, 1000 Brussels; tel. (2) 627-41-89; fax (2) 627-41-13; e-mail bib@naturalsciences.be; internet www.naturalsciences.be; f. 1846; 750,000 vols, 2,900 periodicals; Dir CAMILLE PISANI; Librarian LAURENT MEESE; publs *Bulletin de l'Institut Royal des Sciences Naturelles de Belgique, Série Biologie*, *Bulletin de l'Institut Royal des Sciences Naturelles de Belgique, Série Sciences de la Terre*, *Bulletin de l'Institut Royal des Sciences Naturelles de Belgique, Série Entomologie*.

Bibliothèque des Facultés Universitaires Saint-Louis: 43 blvd du Jardin Botanique, 1000 Brussels; tel. (2) 211-79-09; fax (2) 211-79-97; e-mail lib@fusl.ac.be; internet www4.fusl.ac.be; f. 1858; 260,000 vols; Librarians M.-C. MINGUET, N. PETIT.

Bibliothèque, Documentation, Publications du Ministère de l'Emploi et du Travail: 51 rue Belliard, 1040 Brussels; tel. (2) 233-44-44; fax (2) 233-44-55; f. 1896 (since the foundation of the Board of Labour); 80,000 specialized vols, 500 periodicals on social sciences and labour relations; Dir J.-C. CASSIMONS.

Bibliothèque du Parlement: rue de la Loi 13, 1000 Brussels; tel. (2) 549-92-12; e-mail bibliotheque@lachambre.be; f. 1831; 500,000 vols, 1,200 periodicals, collections on microfilms; Librarians ROLAND VAN NIEUWENBORGH, BERNARD VANSTEELANDT.

Bibliothèque Fonds Quetelet (Fonds Quetelet Library): 50 Vooruitgangstraat, 1210 Brussels; tel. (2) 277-55-55; fax (2) 277-55-53; e-mail quetelet@mineco.fgov.be; internet www.mineco.fgov.be/informations/quetelet/home_en.htm; f. 1841; library of the Federal Public Service Economy, SMEs, Self-Employed and Energy; open to the public; reference and computer-assisted bibliographic services; 1,200,000 vols on statistics, economic and social sciences, 8,000 periodicals (of which 3,000 current); Chief Librarian STEFAAN JACOBS; publ. *Aanwinsten=Accroissements* (online at www.economie.fgov.be/informations/quetelet/acquisitions_nl.htm).

Bibliothèque Royale de Belgique/Koninklijke Bibliotheek van België (Belgian National Library): 4 blvd de l'Empereur, 1000 Brussels; tel. (2) 519-53-11; fax (2) 519-55-33; e-mail contacts@kbr.be; internet www.kbr.be; f. 1837; national depository library; 5,000,000 vols, 18,000 periodicals, 35,000 MSS, 35,000 rare printed books, 700,000 prints, 140,000 maps, 200,000 coins and medals, 10,000 records; Dir and Head Librarian RAPHAËL DE SMEDT (acting).

Bibliothèques de l'Université Libre de Bruxelles: 50 ave Franklin D. Roosevelt, CP 180, 1050 Brussels; tel. (2) 650-23-70; fax (2) 650-41-86; e-mail bibdir@ulb.ac.be; internet www.bib.ulb.ac.be; f. 1846; 2,000,000 vols including periodicals and theses; Librarian Prof. JEAN-PIERRE DEVROEY.

Central Library of the European Commission: VM18 1/18, 1049 Brussels; tel. (2) 295-04-28; fax (2) 296-11-49; e-mail biblio-library@ec.europa.eu; internet ec.europa.eu/libraries/doc/index_en.htm; f. 1958; a central library linking a system of specialized library/documentation units; forms part of the EC's Directorate-General for Education and Culture; 450,000 vols and periodicals on European integration and European Union policies; also br. library in the Bech bldg in Luxembourg (tel. 4301-33341); Head of Unit ROBERTA PERSICHELLI-SCOLA.

NATO Library, Public Diplomacy Division: Room Nb 123, 1110 Brussels; tel. (2) 707-44-14; fax (2) 707-42-49; e-mail library@hq.nato.int; internet www.nato.int/structur/library/library-e.htm; f. 1950; serves the Int. Staff, Int. Military Staff, delegations and PfP countries; subject areas: politics, military science, strategy, int. orgs, biography, current affairs, international law; 22,000 vols, 200 periodicals; Librarian JEAN-ARTHUR CREFF; publs *Acquisitions List* (monthly), *Current Affairs Awareness Service* (monthly), *Thematic Bibliographies* (monthly).

Service Fédéral d'Information/Federale Voorlichtingsdienst (Federal Information Service): Résidence Palace, 11e étage, 155 rue de la Loi, 1040 Brussels tel. (2) 287-41-11 fax (2) 287-41-00 Information Centre: 54 blvd du Régent, 1000 Brussels; tel. (2) 514-08-00; fax (2) 512-51-25; e-mail fvdsfi@belgium.fgov.be; f. 1962; aims to make Belgium better known abroad with the help of information technology, collects documentation about Belgium's heritage and activities, provides information about Belgium, information and public relations programmes, audiovisual information, organizes exhibitions, etc.; Pres. JEAN-PIERRE HUBENS; Gen. Man. MIEKE VAN DEN BERGHE; publs *Faits / Feiten*, *Répertoire de l'Information / Repertorium van de Voorlichting*, etc.

SIST-DWTI (Scientific and Technical Information Service): 4 blvd de l'Empereur, 1000 Brussels; tel. (2) 519-56-40; fax (2) 519-56-45; e-mail stis@kbr.be; f. 1964; provides information in the fields of medicine, science and technology; focal point for library, documentation and information networks (national and international); Head of Unit Dr JEAN MOULIN.

Vrije Universiteit Brussel, Universiteitsbibliotheek: Pleinlaan 2, 1050 Brussels; tel. (2) 629-26-09; fax (2) 629-26-93; e-mail mjvcauwe@vub.ac.be; internet www.vub.ac.be/BIBLIO/index_en.html; f. 1972; 500,000 vols; Librarian P. VANOUPLINES.

Gembloux

Bibliothèque de la Faculté Universitaire des Sciences Agronomiques: 2 passage des Déportés, 5030 Gembloux; tel. (81) 62-21-02; fax (81) 61-45-44; e-mail bibliotheque@fsagx.ac.be; internet www.bib.fsagx.ac.be; f. 1860; 100,000 vols, 1,000 journals; Chief Librarian BERNARD POCHET; publ. *Biotechnologies, Agronomie, Société et Environnement* (4 a year).

Ghent

Leeszaal Faculteit Landbouwkundige en Toegepaste Biologische Wetenschappen (Reading room, Faculty of Agricultural and Applied Biological Sciences): Universiteit, Coupure links 653, 9000 Ghent; 65,000 vols.

Rijksarchief te Gent: Geraard de Duivelstraat 1, 9000 Ghent; tel. (9) 225-13-58; fax (9) 225-52-01; e-mail rijksarchief.gent@arch.be; internet arch.arch.be; f. 1830; 7 km of documents (since 9th century): mainly County of Flanders (until 1795), Diocese of Ghent (until 1801), Province of Oost-Vlaanderen (until 1870), District of Ghent; Archivists WILLY BUNTINX, Dr CHANTAL VANCOPPENOLLE.

Universiteitsbibliotheek Gent: Rozier 9, 9000 Ghent; tel. (9) 264-38-51; fax (9) 264-38-52; e-mail libservice@ugent.be; internet www.lib.ugent.be; f. 1797/1817; 3,000,000 vols, 5,060 MSS; open to the public; Chief Librarian Dr S. VAN PETEGHEM.

Liège

Archives de l'Etat à Liège: 79 rue du Chéra, 4000 Liège; tel. (41) 252-03-93; fax (41) 229-33-50; e-mail archives.liege@arch.be; internet arch.arch.be/frame_fr_d3.htm; state archives, Belgian federal scientific and cultural institute; 18 km of public and private records relating to the history of the Liège district since the 9th c.; Archivist Dr BRUNO DUMONT.

Bibliothèque 'Chiroux-Croisiers': 8 place des Carmes, 4000 Liège; tel. (41) 23-19-60; fax (41) 23-20-62; e-mail chiroux@liege.be; internet www.bib.chiroux-croisiers.liege.be; f. 1907; general library, MSS, ancient works, maps; 1,300,000 vols, local history, architecture, Walloon dialectology, *c.* 1,000 periodicals; Dir J. P. ROUGE.

Bibliothèque de l'Institut Archéologique Liégeois:e-mail monique.merland@crmsf.be Musée Curtius, 13 quai de Maastricht, 4000 Liège; tel. and fax (4) 232-98-60; f. 1850; archaeology, decorative arts; 27,000 vols (mostly periodicals); Librarian MONIQUE MERLAND; publs *Bulletin de l'Institut Archéologique Liégeois* (annually), *Chroniques d'Archéologie et d'Histoire du Pays de Liège* (quarterly).

Bibliothèques de l'Université: 1 place Cockerill, 4000 Liège; tel. (4) 366-52-06; fax (4) 366-57-02; e-mail joseph.denooz@ulg.ac.be; internet www.ulg.ac.be/libnet; f. 1817; spec. collns incl. Fonds Chauvin (orientalism), Fonds Québecois (French Canadian literature and society), Fonds Creame (research on Latin American history); language of instruction: French; 2,600,000 vols and pamphlets (incl. 12,000 current serials, 6,000 MSS and 500 early printed books); Chief Librarian Dr J. DENOOZ; publ. *Bibliotheca Universitatis Leodiensis*.

Louvain

Universiteitsbibliotheek-K.U. Leuven: Mgr Ladeuzeplein 21, 3000 Louvain; tel. (16) 32-46-60; fax (16) 32-46-16; e-mail centrale.bibliotheek@bib.kuleuven.be; internet www.bib.kuleuven.be; f. 1636; 4,300,000 vols (of which 3m. in faculty and dept libraries), c. 1,000 MSS; Chief Librarian Prof. MEL COLLIER.

Louvain-la-Neuve

Bibliothèques de l'Université Catholique de Louvain: c/o Service central des bibliothèques, 1 place de l'Université, 1348 Louvain-la-Neuve; tel. (10) 47-82-99; fax (10) 47-82-98; e-mail sceb@sceb.ucl.ac.be; internet www.bib.ucl.ac.be; 2,000,000 vols, 8,000 current periodicals; Chief Librarian CH.-H. NYNS.

Maredsous

Bibliothèque de l'Abbaye de Saint-Benoît: Maredsous, 5537 Denée; tel. (82) 69-82-11; fax (82) 69-83-21; f. 1872; books of learning, especially history and theology; 400,000 vols, 50,000 brochures; Chief Librarian Dom DANIEL MISONNE; publ. *Revue Bénédictine*.

Mechelen

Archdiocesan Archives, Mechelen: Varkensstraat 6, 2800 Mechelen; tel. (15) 29-84-22; fax (15) 21-90-94; e-mail archiv@diomb.be; archives of the archdiocese of Mechelen and its predecessors since 12th c.; MSS and books; photographs, iconographs, souvenirs; Archivist Drs GERRIT VANDEN BOSCH.

Archief en Stadsbibliotheek: Goswin de Stassartstraat 145, 2800 Mechelen; tel. (15) 20-43-46; e-mail stadsarchief@mechelen.be; f. 1802; archives of the city of Malines (Mechelen) since the 13th century and the library of the Great Council of the Netherlands; Archivist H. INSTALLÉ; publs *Inventaire des Archives de la ville de Malines* (8 vols), *Catalogue méthodique de la Bibliothèque de Malines* (1 vol).

Mons

Archives de l'Etat: 23 place du Parc, 7000 Mons;; tel. (65) 35-45-06; e-mail archives.mons@arch.be; internet arch.arch.be/mons.htm; 25,000 vols; archives since 10th c.; the buildings were badly damaged during the war and many records lost; ongoing renovation and additions to archives; archives from the Abbeys and noble families of Hainaut; Dir P.-J. NIEBES.

Bibliothèque Centrale de la Faculté Polytechnique de Mons: 9 rue de Houdain, 7000 Mons; tel. (65) 37-40-10; fax (65) 37-45-00; e-mail biblio@fpms.ac.be; internet bib.fpms.ac.be; f. 1837; 48,500 vols; Chief Librarian CATHERINE MASSELUS.

Bibliothèque de l'Université de Mons-Hainaut: 2 rue Marguerite Bervoets, 7000 Mons; tel. (65) 37-30-55; fax (65) 37-30-68; e-mail bibliotheque.centrale@umh.ac.be; internet www.umh.ac.be/Bibli/index.html; f. 1797; 785,305 vols, 3,622 MSS and incunabula, maps, prints; Dir Dr RENÉ PLISNIER.

Namur

Archives de l'Etat à Namur: 45 rue d'Arquet, 5000 Namur; tel. (81) 22-34-98; fax (81) 65-41-99; e-mail archives.namur@arch.be; internet arch.arch.be/namur.htm; f. 1848; documents concerning the County and Province of Namur since the 8th c.; Dir A. VANRIE.

Bibliothèque Universitaire Moretus Plantin: 19 rue Grandgagnage, 5000 Namur; tel. (81) 72-46-46; fax (81) 72-46-45; e-mail bump@fundp.ac.be; internet www.bump.fundp.ac.be; f. 1921; history of Western Europe, Classical, Roman and German philology, philosophy, law, economics, art, biomedical sciences, life sciences, earth sciences; 800,000 vols; special collection: rare books on natural sciences; Chief Librarian Prof. JEAN-MARIE ANDRÉ; Sec. Y. WILQUET-DEHERVE.

Sint Niklaas Waas

Bibliotheek voor Hedendaagse Dokumentatie (Library on Contemporary Documentation): Parklaan 2, 9100 Sint Niklaas Waas; tel. (3) 776-50-63; e-mail bhd@skynet.be; f. 1964; private political, social and economic library; *c.* 120,000 vols, 4,000 periodicals, 15,000 maps; special collections on governmental research, public administration; US govt documents depository collection; Librarian YVAN VAN GARSSE; publs *Bibliographical Series* (irreg), *Bulletin* (monthly), *Governmental Publications Survey* (annually).

Ypres

Stedelijke Openbare Bibliotheek: St-Jansstraat 7, 8900 Ypres; tel. (57) 23-94-20; fax (57) 23-94-29; e-mail bibliotheek@ieper.be; internet www.ieper.be; f. 1839; general interest; 120,000 vols, 400 periodicals; Librarian EDDY BARBRY.

Museums and Art Galleries

Antwerp

Etnografisch Museum: Suikerrui 19, 2000 Antwerp; tel. (3) 220-86-00; fax (3) 227-08-71; e-mail etnografisch.museum@stad.antwerpen.be; internet museum.antwerpen

.be/etnografisch_museum; f. 1988; arts and crafts of pre-literate and non-European people; library of 12,000 vols; Dir JAN VAN ALPHEN; publ. *Bulletin van de Vrienden van het Etnografisch Museum Antwerpen*.

Koninklijk Museum voor Schone Kunsten (Royal Museum of Fine Arts): Leopold De Waelplaats, 2000 Antwerp; tel. (3) 238-78-09; fax (3) 248-08-10; e-mail info@kmska.be; internet www.kmska.be; f. 1890; collns of Flemish Primitifs, early foreign schools, Rubens, 16th–17th-century Antwerp School, 17th-century Dutch School, works of Belgian artists since 19th century; important works of Leys, De Braekeleer, Ensor, Wouters, Smits, Magritte, Permeke; library of 50,000 vols; Dir Dr PAUL HUVENNE; publs *Dossiertentoonstelling* (2 a year), *Jaarboek* (annual), *Museumkrant* (quarterly), *Restauratie Schone Kunst* (2 a year).

Middelheimmuseum (Openluchtmuseum voor beeldhouwkunst) (Open-air Museum of Sculpture): Middelheimlaan 61, 2020 Antwerp; tel. (3) 827-15-34; fax (3) 825-28-35; e-mail middelheimopenluchtmuseum@stad.antwerpen.be; internet www.middelheimmuseum.be; f. 1950; important colln of contemporary sculpture, including Cragg, Gargallo, Graham, Kirkeby, Maillol, Manzu, Marini, Moore, Muñoz, Rodin and Zadkine, exhibited in a large park; exhibitions devoted to modern sculpture; library of 50,000 vols; Dir MENNO MEEWIS.

Museum Brouwershuis: Adriaan Brouwerstraat 20, 2000 Antwerp; tel. (3) 232-65-11; fax (3) 232-65-11; internet museum.antwerpen.be/brouwershuis; f. 1933; 16th c. installations for water-supply to breweries, council chamber; Curator F. DE NAVE.

Museum Mayer van den Bergh: Lange Gasthuisstraat 19, 2000 Antwerp; tel. (3) 232-42-37; fax (3) 231-73-35; e-mail museum.mayervandenbergh@stad.antwerpen.be; internet museum.antwerpen.be/mayervandenbergh; f. 1904; paintings, including Breughel, Metsys, Aertsen, Mostaert, Bronzino, Heda, de Vos, and medieval sculpture, ivories, etc.; Chief Curator HANS NIEUWDORP.

Museum Plantin-Moretus/Prentenkabinet Unesco World Heritage: Vrijdagmarkt 22, 2000 Antwerp; tel. (3) 221-14-50; fax (3) 221-14-71; e-mail museum.plantin.moretus@stad.antwerpen.be; internet www.museumplantinmoretus.be; f. 1876; print room f. 1938; UNESCO World Heritage site; 16th to 18th-century patrician house with ancient printing office and foundry, engravings on copper and wood; typographical collns, drawings, prints and paintings by Rubens; illuminated MSS; ancient rare maps and atlases; library of 30,000 vols (15th to 18th century), family and business archives; special collns: Max Horn Legacy, Ensemble Emile Verhaeren; Dir Dr FRANCINE DE NAVE.

Museum Smidt van Gelder: Lange Nieuwstraat 24, 2000 Antwerp; tel. (3) 239-06-52; fax (3) 230-22-81; e-mail museum.smidtvangelder@stad.antwerpen.be; internet museum.antwerpen.be/smidtvangelder; f. 1950; Chinese and European porcelains, Dutch 17th c. paintings, 18th c. French furniture; Curator CLARA VANDERHENST.

Museum Vleeshuis: Vleeshouwersstraat 38, 2000 Antwerp; tel. (3) 233-64-04; fax (3) 231-47-05; e-mail vleeshuis@stad.antwerpen.be; internet museum.antwerpen.be/vleeshuis; f. 1913; archaeology, local history, Egyptian, Greek and Roman antiquities, numismatics, sculpture, applied art, ceramics, furniture, arms, posters, musical instruments; library of 15,000 vols; Asst Curator KAREL MOENS.

Nationaal Scheepvaartmuseum (Steen) (National Maritime Museum): Steenplein 1, 2000 Antwerp; tel. (3) 201-93-40; fax (3) 201-93-41; e-mail scheepmus@stad.antwerpen.be; internet museum.antwerpen.be/scheepvaartmuseum; f. 1952; maritime history, especially concerning Belgium; library of 43,000 vols; Asst Dir R. JALON.

Rubenshuis (Rubens' House): Wapper 9–11, 2000 Antwerp; tel. (3) 201-15-55; fax (3) 227-36-92; e-mail info.rubenshuis@stad.antwerpen.be; internet www.antwerpen.be/cultuur/rubenshuis; f. 1946; reconstruction of Rubens' house and studio; original 17th-century portico and pavilion; paintings by P. P. Rubens, his collaborators and pupils; 17th-century furnishings; Curator CARL DEPAUW.

Stedelijk Prentenkabinet: Vrijdagmarkt 22, 2000 Antwerp; tel. (3) 221-14-50; fax (3) 221-14-60; e-mail prentenkabinet@stad.antwerpen.be; internet www.antwerpen.be/cultuur/stedelijk_prentenkabinet; f. 1938; prints and drawings from the 16th century to the present; library of 15,000 ; Keeper Dr F. DE NAVE.

Volkskundemuseum: Gildekamersstraat 2–6, 2000 Antwerp; tel. (3) 220-86-66; fax (3) 220-83-68; internet museum.antwerpen.be/volkskunde; f. 1907; folklore of the Flemish provinces, especially folk art and craft; library of 18,000 vols; Curator WERNER VAN HOOF.

Bouillon

Musée Ducal 'Les Amis de Vieux Bouillon': Rue du Petit 1–3, 6830 Bouillon; tel. (61) 46-41-89; fax (61) 46-41-99; e-mail courrier@museeducal.be; internet www.museeducal.be; f. 1947; archives, historical manuscripts and documents; archaeology, folklore; exhibition of the history of Godefroy de Bouillon; small library; Curator Mme MICHEL GOURDIN.

Bruges

Arentshuis: Dijver 16, 8000 Bruges; tel. (50) 44-87-11; fax (50) 44-87-78; e-mail musea@brugge.be; internet www.brugge.be/musea/nl/mbran.htm; 18th c. manor house, contains a collection of lace and a permanent exhibition of works by Frank Brangwyn; additional exhibitions from the Groeningemuseum; Chief Curator Dr MANFRED SELLINK.

Bruggemuseum–Archeologie (Bruges Museum–Archaeology): Mariastr. 36 A, 8000 Bruges; tel. (50) 44-87-11; fax (50) 44-87-37; e-mail musea@brugge.be; internet www.brugge.be/musea/fr/marf.htm; f. 1997; Dir HUBERT DE WITTE.

Bruggemuseum–Gruuthuse: Dijver 17, 8000 Bruges; tel. (50) 44-87-11; fax (50) 44-87-37; e-mail bruggemuseum@brugge.be; internet www.brugge.be; f. 1895; one of seven locations of the Bruggemuseum; a municipal collection in the 15th c. Palace of the Lords of Gruuthuse; furniture, sculpture, ceramics, tapestries, metalwork, instruments; Chief Curator HUBERT DE WITTE.

Groeningemuseum (Municipal Art Gallery): Dijver 12, 8000 Bruges; tel. (50) 44-87-11; fax (50) 44-87-78; e-mail musea@brugge.be; internet www.brugge.be/musea/fr/groeningefrans.htm; Belgian and Dutch paintings and etchings from late medieval times to present; Art Dir MANFRED SELLINK.

Hospitaalmuseum Sint-Janshospital: St John's Hospital, Mariastraat 38, 8000 Bruges; tel. (50) 44-87-11; fax (50) 44-87-35; e-mail musea@brugge.be; internet www.brugge.be/musea; f. *c.*1150; paintings by Hans Memling and Jan Provost, furniture and sculpture from 15th–19th c.; mediaeval instruments and books; 17th c. pharmacy; Chief Curator EVA TAHON.

Museum Onze-Lieve-Vrouw ter Potterie: Potterierei 79, 8000 Bruges; tel. (50) 44-87-11; fax (50) 44-87-78; e-mail musea@brugge.be; internet www.brugge.be/musea/nl/mpotn.htm; f. 1276 old hospital, museum and church; church ornaments, furniture, paintings, sculptures, 17th c. tapestries, etc.; Chief Curator Dr MANFRED SELLINK.

Stedelijk Museum voor Volkskunde (Municipal Museum of Folklore): Rolweg 40, 8000 Bruges; tel. (50) 33-00-44; fax (50) 33-54-89; e-mail volkskundemuseum@skynet.be; internet www.brugge.be; f. 1973; popular art, 19th c. trades and crafts (shoemaker, grocer, cooper, confectioner, chemist, hatter, tailor), domestic interiors, classroom, devotional objects, pipes and tobacco, typical Flemish living room, period tavern *The Black Cat*; Curator W. LE LOUP.

Brussels

Koninklijk Museum voor Midden-Afrika/Musée Royal de l'Afrique Centrale: Leuvensesteenweg 13, 3080 Tervuren; tel. (2) 769-52-11; fax (2) 767-02-42; e-mail biblita@africamuseum.be; internet www.africamuseum.be; f. 1897; large collections in the fields of prehistory, ethnography, native arts and crafts; geology, mineralogy, palaeontology; zoology (entomology, ornithology, mammals, reptiles, etc.); history, economics; library of 110,000 vols; 37 scientific staff; Dir G. GRYSEELS; publ. *Annales* (5 publs dealing with botany, geology, zoology, the humanities and economics).

Musée d'Ixelles: 71 rue Jean Van Volsem, Ixelles, 1050 Brussels; tel. (322) 515-64-21; fax (322) 515-64-24; e-mail musee-ixelles@skynet.be; internet www.musee-ixelles.be; f. 1892; ancient and modern masters, watercolours, drawings, engravings, sculptures, posters, etc.; works of Belgian and foreign schools; library of 3,000 vols (bibliography); Curator NICOLE D'HUART.

Musée Royal de l'Armée et d'Histoire Militaire: Parc du Cinquantenaire 3, 1000 Brussels; tel. (2) 737-78-11; fax (2) 737-78-02; e-mail infocom@klm-mra.be; internet www.klm-mra.be; f. 1910; colln incl. military history of Belgium from 10th century onwards; arms, uniforms, decorations, paintings, sculpture, maps; library of 450,000 vols and archives; Dir-Gen. PHILIPPE THILLY; publs *Revue Belge d'Histoire Militaire/Belgisch Tijdschrift voor Militaire Geschiedenis* (quarterly), *AELR (Air et Espace, Lucht en Ruimtevaart) Militaria Belgica* (quarterly).

Musées Royaux d'Art et d'Histoire: Parc du Cinquantenaire 10, 1000 Brussels; tel. (2) 741-72-11; fax (2) 733-77-35; e-mail info@kmkg-mrah.be; internet www.kmkg-mrah.be; f. 1835; Dir ANNE CAHEN-DELHAYE.

Component museums:

Musée du Cinquantenaire: 10 parc du Cinquantenaire, 1000 Brussels; tel. (2) 741-72-11; fax (2) 733-77-35; e-mail info@kmkg-mrah.be; internet www.kmkg-mrah.be; f. 1835; archaeology of Belgium, the Americas, Asia, the Pacific and North Africa, and of ancient Iran and the Near East, Egypt, Greece and Rome; European decorative arts; library of 100,000 vols; Dir ANNE CAHEN-DELHAYE; publ. *Musze* (3 a year).

Musée des Instruments de Musique: 2 Montagne de la Cour, 1000 Brussels; tel. (2) 545-01-30; fax (2) 545-01-78; e-mail info@kmkg-mrah.be; internet www.mim.fgov.be; f. 1877; musical instruments; Dir MALOU HAINE.

Pavillon Chinois et Tour Japonaise: 44 ave Van Praet, 1020 Brussels; tel. (2) 268-16-08; fax (2) 268-16-08; e-mail info@kmkg-mrah.be; internet www.kmkg-mrah.be; f. 1904; Chinese art, porcelain and furniture; Japanese architecture and decorative arts; Dir CHANTAL KOZYREFF.

Pavillon Horta-Lambeaux: Parc du Cinquantenaire, 1000 Brussels; tel. (2) 741-72-11; fax (2) 733-77-35; e-mail info@kmkg-mrah.be; internet www.kmkg-mrah.be; f. 1899; marble relief of the Human Passions; Dir ANNE CAHEN-DELHAYE.

Porte de Hal/Hallepoort: Blvd du Midi, 1000 Brussels; tel. (2) 534-15-18; e-mail info@kmkg-mrah.be; internet www.kmkg-mrah.be; f. 1835; temporary exhibitions; Dir ELS VAN DER ELST.

Musées Royaux des Beaux-Arts de Belgique: 9 rue du Musée, 1000 Brussels; tel. (2) 508-32-11; fax (2) 508-32-32; e-mail info@fine-arts-museum.be; internet www.fine-arts-museum.be; f. 1801; Brussels, medieval, Renaissance and modern pictures, drawings and sculpture; library of 164,000 vols; Chief Curator MICHEL DRAGUET; publ. *Bulletin*.

Attached museums:

Musée d'Art Ancien: 3 rue de la Régence, 1000 Brussels; tel. (2) 508-32-11; fax (2) 508-32-32; e-mail info@fine-arts-museum.be; internet www.fine-arts-museum.be; f. 1801; 15th–18th-century paintings, drawings and sculpture; Chief Curator MICHEL DRAGUET.

Musée d'Art Moderne: 1–2 Place Royale, 1000 Brussels; tel. (2) 508-32-11; fax (2) 508-32-32; e-mail info@fine-arts-museum.be; internet www.fine-arts-museum.be; f. 1984; paintings since 19th century, drawings and sculpture; Chief Curator MICHEL DRAGUET.

Musée Constantin Meunier: 59 rue de l'Abbaye, 1000 Brussels; tel. (2) 508-32-11; fax (2) 508-32-32; e-mail info@fine-arts-museum.be; internet www.fine-arts-museum.be; f. 1978; paintings, drawings and sculptures by Constantin Meunier, the artist's house and studio; Dir MICHEL DRAGUET.

Musée Wiertz: 62 rue Vautier, 1000 Brussels; tel. (2) 508-32-11; fax (2) 508-32-32; e-mail info@fine-arts-museum.be; internet www.fine-arts-museum.be; f. 1868; paintings by Antoine Wiertz; the artist's house and studio; Chief Curator MICHEL DRAGUET.

Museum Erasmus: 31 rue du Chapitre, 1070 Brussels; tel. (2) 521-13-83; fax (2) 527-12-69; e-mail erasmushuis.maisonerasme@skynet.be; f. 1932; documents, paintings, early editions and manuscripts relating to Erasmus and other Humanists of the 16th century; library of 5,000 vols; Curator A. VANAUTGAERDEN.

Ghent

Museum voor Schone Kunsten (Museum for Fine Arts): Ch. de Kerchovelaan 187A, 9000 Ghent; tel. (9) 240-07-00; fax (9) 240-07-90; e-mail museum.msk@gent.be; internet www.mskgent.be; f. 1902; contains ancient and modern paintings, sculpture, tapestries, prints and drawings, icons from the Middle Ages to the first half of the 20th century; library; Dir ROBERT HOOZEE.

Oudheidkundig Museum van de Stad Gent: Godshuizenlaan 2, 9000 Ghent; tel. (9) 225-11-06; fax (9) 233-34-59; e-mail museum.bijloke@gent.be; internet www.gent.be; f. 1833; prehistory, local history, applied arts, furniture, arms, numismatics, collection of Chinese art, tapestries, costumes; Dir JEANNINE BALDEWIJNS.

Stedelijk Museum voor Actuele Kunst (Museum of Contemporary Art): Citadelpark, 9000 Ghent; tel. (9) 221-17-03; fax (9) 221-71-09; e-mail museum.smak@gent.be; internet www.smak.be; f. 1975; paintings, sculpture, drawings, etchings; featured movements incl. Cobra, Pop Art, Minimalism, Conceptualism, Arte Povera; library of 40,000 vols, 195 periodicals; Dir JAN HOET.

Liège

Collections artistiques de l'Université de Liège: 7 place du 20 août, 4000 Liège; tel. (4) 366-56-07; fax (4) 366-58-54; e-mail wittert@ulg.ac.be; internet www.ulg.ac.be/wittert; f. 1903; 30,000 prints and drawings, paintings of 15th and 16th c.; modern Belgian paintings; 5,483 coins; collection of Zairian art and craft; Curator Dr JEAN-PATRICK DUCHESNE.

Musées d'Archéologie et d'Arts Décoratifs de Liège: Institut Archéologique Liégeois, 13 quai de Maastricht, 4000 Liège; tel. (4) 221-94-04; fax (4) 221-94-32; Curator ANN CHEVALIER.

Attached museums include:

Musée d'Ansembourg: 114 Féronstrée, 4000 Liège; tel. (4) 221-94-02; f. 1905; collections of 18th c. decorative arts of Liège; reconstituted interiors.

Musée Curtius: 13 quai de Maastricht, 4000 Liège; tel. (4) 221-83-83; fax (4) 221-94-80; f. 1909; chief sections: pre-history, Romano-Belgian and Frankish, Liège coins, decorative arts (from the Middle Ages to the 19th c.); Annexe: lapidary collection in Palais de Justice; the museum is the headquarters of the Archaeological Institute of Liège (*q.v.*).

Musée du Verre: 13 quai de Maastricht, 4000 Liège; tel. (4) 221-94-04; fax (4) 221-94-32; f. 1959; all the main centres of production, from the earliest times to present, are represented.

Musée d'Art Moderne et d'Art Contemporain: 3 parc de la Boverie, 4020 Liège; tel. (4) 343-04-03; fax (4) 344-19-07; e-mail mamac@skynet.be; internet www.mamac.org; f. 1981; modern paintings, sculptures and abstracts of the Belgian School, French and foreign masters; Curators FRANCINE DAWANS, FRANÇOISE DUMONT FRANÇOISE SAFIN.

Musée de la Vie Wallonne: Cour des Mineurs, 4000 Liège; tel. (4) 237-90-40; fax (4) 237-90-89; internet www.viewallonne.be; f. 1912; varied collection covering south Belgium in the fields of ethnography, folklore, arts and crafts and history; 450,000 documents; library of 35,000 vols; Man. Dir MARIE-CLAUDE THURION; publ. *Enquêtes* (annually).

Mariemont

Musée Royal et Domaine de Mariemont: 100 Chaussée de Mariemont, 7140 Morlanwelz, Mariemont; tel. (64) 21-21-93; fax (64) 26-29-24; e-mail info@musee-mariemont.be; internet www.musee-mariemont.be; f. 1920; contains antiquities from Egypt, Greece, Rome, China, Japan; national archaeology; Tournai porcelain; bookbindings; library of 100,000 vols; Directors FRANÇOIS MAIRESSE, MARIE-CÉCILE BRUWIER; publs *Les Cahiers de Mariemont* (annually), *Bulletin d'Information* (4 a year).

Mechelen

Stadsmuseum: Hof van Busleyden-Fred. de Merodestraat 65–67, 2800 Mechelen; tel. (15) 29-40-30; fax (15) 29-40-31; e-mail stedelijkemusea@mechelen.be; internet www.mechelen.be/stedelijkemusea; f. 1844; municipal museum; history, art, applied art; Curator HEIDI DE NIJN.

Verviers

Musée d'Archéologie et de Folklore: 42 rue des Raines, 4800 Verviers; tel. (87) 33-16-95; e-mail musees.verviers@skynet.be; internet www.lesmuseesenwallonie.be; f. 1959; history of art, archaeology, folklore, local history; Curator MARIE-PAULE DEBLANC.

Musée des Beaux-Arts et de la Céramique: 17 rue Renier, 4800 Verviers; tel. (87) 33-16-95; e-mail musees.verviers@skynet.be; internet www.lesmuseesenwallonie.be; f. 1884; sculpture, paintings; ceramics of Europe and Asia; MARIE-PAULE LEBLANC; publ. *Guide du Visiteur*.

Musée de la Laine: 8 rue de Séroule, Verviers; f. 1985; history of wool-making before the industrial revolution of 1800.

Universities

UNIVERSITEIT ANTWERPEN
(University of Antwerp)

Prinsstraat 13 2000 Antwerp
Telephone: (3) 220-41-11
Fax: (3) 220-44-20
E-mail: info@ua.ac.be
Internet: www.ua.ac.be

Founded 2003 by merger of Universitair Centrum Antwerpen, Universitaire Faculteiten Sint-Ignatius Antwerpen and Universitaire Insteling Antwerpen

State control
Language of instruction: Dutch
Academic year: September to July

Library of 1,351,000 vols

Rector: Prof. Dr FRANCIS VAN LOON
Pres.: Prof. Dr ALAIN VERSCHOREN
Vice-Rector for Education: Prof. Dr JOKE DENEKENS
Vice-Rector for Research: Prof. Dr DIRK VAN DYCK
Vice-Rector for Services to Science and the Community: Prof. Dr BEA CANTILLON
Man.: Prof. Dr BART HEIJNEN
Librarian: TRUDI NOORDERMEER

Number of teachers: 2,200
Number of students: 10,330

Publications: *Antwerpse Studies over Nederlandse Literatuurgeschiedenis*, *Bijdragen tot de Geschiedenis*, *Computer Assisted Language Learning*, *CSB-Berichten*, *Discussion Papers of the Centre for the Economic Study of Innovation and Technology*, *Discussion Papers of the Centre for Asian Studies*, *Economische Didaktiek*, *Economisch en Sociaal Tijdschrift*, *Exchange to Change (and Annual Report and Discussion Papers) of the Institute of Development Policy and Management*, *Genetic Joyce Studies* (e-journal on the works of James Joyce), *Gezelliana, Kroniek van de Gezellestudie*, *Het Teken van de Ram*, *In de Steigers*, *Jaarboek*, *Miscellanea Neerlandica*, *OASeS Cahiers and Documenten*, *Ons Geestelijk Erf*, *Pragmatics*, *Research Topics University of Antwerp*, *Working Papers of the Faculty of Applied Economics*

DEANS

Faculty of Applied Econ.: Prof. Dr KAREL SOUDAN
Faculty of Arts: Prof. Dr JEF VERSCHUEREN
Faculty of Law: Prof. Dr JOHAN MEEUSEN
Faculty of Medicine: Prof. Dr PAUL VAN DE HEYNING

Faculty of Pharmaceutical, Biomedical and Veterinary Sciences: Prof. Dr FRANS VAN MEIR
Faculty of Political and Social Sciences: Prof. Dr RIA JANVIER
Faculty of Science: Prof. Dr JAN PAREDAENS

ATTACHED RESEARCH INSTITUTES

Aisthesis: tel. (3) 220-43-04; fax (3) 220-45-46; e-mail luc.vandendries@ua.ac.be; internet www.ua.ac.be/main.aspx?c=*faclw=18390; Dir Prof. Dr LUC VAN DEN DRIES.

Antwerps Innovatie Centrum: Drie Eikenstraat 661, 2650 Edegem; tel. (3) 826-93-04; fax (3) 826-93-78; e-mail luc.lammens@antwerpinnovation.com; internet www.antwerpinnovation.com; Gen. Manager LUC LAMMENS.

Antwerp University Hospital: Wilrijkstraat 10, 2650 Edegem; tel. (3) 821-00-00; fax (3) 821-42-96; e-mail info@uza.be; internet www.uza.be/uza; Dir JOHNNY VAN DER STRAETEN.

Austrian Centre Antwerp: tel. (3) 220-42-48; fax (3) 220-42-59; e-mail octant@ua.ac.be; internet www.ua.ac.be/octant; Dir Prof. Dr CLEMENS RUTHNER.

Centre for ASEAN Studies: Kipdorp 61, 2000 Antwerpen; tel. (3) 275-50-34; fax (3) 275-50-26; e-mail ludo.cuyvers@ua.ac.be; internet webh01.ua.ac.be/cas; Dir Prof. Dr LUDO CUYVERS.

Centre for European and International Business Education and Research: tel. (3) 275-50-28; fax (3) 275-50-26; e-mail liliane.vanhoof@ua.ac.be; Dir Prof. Dr LILIANE VAN HOOF.

Centre for Grammar, Cognition and Typology: tel. (3) 220-45-50; fax (3) 220-45-46; e-mail johan.vanderauwera@ua.ac.be; internet webhost.ua.ac.be/cgct/id11.htm; Dir Prof. Dr JOHAN VAN DER AUWERA.

Centre for Psycholinguistics: tel. (3) 220-42-47; fax (3) 220-42-59; e-mail dominiek.sandra@ua.ac.be; internet www.cpl.ua.ac.be; Dir Prof. Dr DOMINIEK SANDRA.

Centre for International Management and Development: Lange Sint Annastraat 7 , 2000 Antwerpen; tel. (3) 220-45-25; fax (3) 220-48-53; e-mail filip.debeule@ua.ac.be; internet www.ua.ac.be/cimda; Dir Prof. Dr DANNY VAN DEN BULCKE.

Centre for Mexican Studies: Prinsstraat 9, 2000 Antwerpen; tel. (3) 220-44-42; fax (3) 220-44-20; e-mail ingeborg.jongbloet@ua.ac.be; internet www.ua.ac.be/cms; Dir Prof. Dr JEAN VAN HOUTTE.

Centre for Migration and Intercultural Studies (CeMIS): Lange Nieuwstraat 55, 2000 Antwerpen; tel. (3) 275-59-65; fax (3) 275-59-26; e-mail ina.lodewyckx@ua.ac.be; internet www.ua.ac.be/cemis; Dir Prof. Dr CHRISTIANE TIMMERMAN.

Centre for Philosophical Psychology: tel. (3) 220-43-08; fax (3) 220-44-20; e-mail joachim.leilich@ua.ac.be; internet www.ua.ac.be/main.aspx?c=.philosophyofmind; Dir Prof. Dr JOACHIM LEILICH.

Centre for Proteomics and Mass Spectrometry: Groenenborgerlaan 171, 2020 Antwerpen; tel. (3) 265-34-96; fax (3) 265-34-88; e-mail eddy.esmans@ua.ac.be; internet www.ceproma.ua.ac.be/ceproma.html; Dir Prof. Dr EDDY ESMANS.

Centre for Social Policy Herman Deleeck: Sint-Jacobsstraat 2, 2000 Antwerpen; tel. (3) 275-53-74; fax (3) 275-57-90; e-mail ingrid.vanzele@ua.ac.be; internet webhost.ua.ac.be/csb/eng/index.php; Dir Prof. Dr BEA CANTILLON.

Centre for the Economic Study of Innovation and Technology: tel. (3) 220-40-54; fax (3) 220-40-26; e-mail sigrid.suetens@ua.ac.be; internet webh01.ua.ac.be/cesit/; Dirs Prof. Dr WIM MEEUSEN, Prof. Dr JEF PLASMANS.

Centre for the Evaluation of Vaccination: Universiteitsplein 1, 2610 Antwerpen-Wilrijk; tel. (3) 820-26-52; fax (3) 820-26-40; e-mail cev@ua.ac.be; internet www.ua.ac.be/cev; Dir Prof. Dr PIERRE VAN DAMME.

Centre for the Study of the Great Lakes Region of Africa: Lange Sint Annastraat 7 , 2000 Antwerpen; tel. (3) 275-56-99; fax (3) 275-57-71; e-mail stefaan.marysse@ua.ac.be; internet www.ua.ac.be/main.aspx?c=.gralac; Dir Prof. Dr STEFAAN MARYSSE.

Centrum Nascholing Onderwijs: Universiteitsplein 1, 2610 Antwerpen-Wilrijk; tel. (3) 820-29-60; fax (3) 820-29-57; e-mail paul.reynders@ua.ac.be; internet www.ua.ac.be/cno; Dir Prof. Dr PAUL MAHIEU.

Centrum voor Bedrijfsgeschiedenis: tel. (3) 220-42-52; fax (3) 220-45-46; e-mail greta.devos@ua.ac.be; internet www.ua.ac.be/main.aspx?c=*faclw=3314; Dir Prof. Dr GRETA DEVOS.

Centrum voor Begaafdheidsonderzoek: Grote Steenweg 40, 2600 Antwerpen-Berchem; tel. (3) 297-30-88; fax (3) 297-31-86; e-mail marianne.remon@cbo-antwerpen.be; internet www.ua.ac.be/main.aspx?c=cbo; Dir Dr TESSA KIEBOOM.

Centrum voor Bekkenbodemkunde: Universiteitsplein 1, 2610 Antwerpen-Wilrijk; tel. (3) 820-25-35; fax (3) 820-25-01; e-mail jeanjacques.wyndaele@ua.ac.be; Dir Prof. Dr JEAN-JACQUES WYNDAELE.

Centrum Technologie voor Gehandicapte Personen: Universiteitsplein 1, 2610 Antwerpen-Wilrijk; tel. (3) 820-23-12; fax (3) 820-23-12; e-mail ctg@ua.ac.be; internet webh01.ua.ac.be/ctg; Dir VICTOR CLAES.

Centrum voor Beroepsvervolmaking Rechten: Venusstraat 35, 2000 Antwerpen; tel. (3) 275-54-48; fax (3) 275-59-79; e-mail cbr@ua.ac.be; internet www.ua.ac.be/cbr; Dir PASCALE BUYCK.

Centrum voor Biomedische Beeldvorming: Groenenborgerlaan 171 , 2020 Antwerpen; tel. (3) 265-32-30; fax (3) 265-32-33; e-mail annemie.vanderlinden@ua.ac.be; internet www.ua.c.be/biomedischebeeldvorming; Dir Prof. Dr ANNEMIE VAN DER LINDEN.

Centrum voor de Filosofie van de Religie: Koningstraat 8, 2000 Antwerpen; tel. (3) 220-46-60; fax (3) 220-44-20; e-mail luc.braeckmans@ua.ac.be; Dir Prof. Dr LUC BRAECKMANS.

Centrum voor Ethiek: tel. (3) 220-43-07; fax (3) 220-44-20; e-mail johan.taels@ua.ac.be; Dir Prof. Dr JOHAN TAELS.

Centrum voor Filosofie van de Kunst en Literatuur: tel. (3) 220-43-08; fax (3) 220-44-20; e-mail erik.oger@ua.ac.be; Dir Prof. Dr ERIK OGER.

Centrum voor Kankerpreventie: Universiteitsplein 1, 2610 Antwerpen-Wilrijk; tel. (3) 820-26-53; fax (3) 820-26-40; e-mail rsc@ua.ac.be; internet www.ua.ac.be/main.aspx?c=esoc; Dir Prof. Dr JOOST WEYLER.

Centrum voor Longitudinaal en Levenslooponderzoek: Sint-Jacobsstraat 2, 2000 Antwerpen; tel. (3) 275-55-35; fax (3) 275-57-93; e-mail dimitri.mortelmans@ua.ac.be; internet webh01.ua.ac.be/cello; Dir Prof. Dr DIMITRI MORTELMANS.

Centrum voor Metafysica en Cultuur: tel. (3) 220-43-41; fax (3) 220-44-20; e-mail guy.vanheeswijck@ua.ac.be; Dir Prof. Dr GUIDO VANHEESWIJCK.

Centrum voor Nederlandse Taal en Spraak: Universiteitsplein 1, 2610 Antwerpen-Wilrijk; tel. (3) 820-27-66; fax (3) 820-27-62; e-mail walter.daelemans@ua.ac.be; internet www.cnts.ua.ac.be/cnts; Dir Prof. Dr WALTER DAELEMANS.

Centrum voor Rechtssociologie: tel. (3) 220-41-11; fax (3) 220-44-20; e-mail francis.vanloon@ua.ac.be; Dir Prof. Dr FRANCIS VAN LOON.

Centrum voor Roemenië Studies: tel. (3) 220-45-50; fax (3) 220-45-46; e-mail liliane.tasmowski@ua.ac.be; Dir Prof. Dr LILIANE TASMOWSKI.

Centrum voor Stadsgeschiedenis: tel. (3) 220-42-78; fax (3) 220-44-20; e-mail bruno.blonde@ua.ac.be; Dir Prof. Dr BRUNO BLONDÉ.

Centrum voor Tekstgenetica: tel. (3) 220-42-57; fax (3) 220-45-46; e-mail geert.lernout@ua.ac.be; Dir Prof. Dr GEERT LERNOUT.

Centrum voor Thoracale Oncologie Groep Antwerpen: Universiteitsplein 1, 2610 Antwerpen-Wilrijk; tel. (3) 820-26-39; fax (3) 820-25-01; e-mail paul.germonpre@ua.ac.be; Dir Prof. Dr PAUL GERMONPRÉ.

Collaborative Antwerp Psychiatric Research Institute: Universiteitsplein 1, 2610 Antwerpen-Wilrijk; tel. (3) 820-24-01; fax (3) 820-24-14; e-mail astrid.janssens@ua.ac.be or sofie.houthoofd@ua.ac.be; internet www.ua.ac.be/main.aspx?c=.capri; Dirs ASTRID JANSSENS, SOFIE HOUTHOOFD.

Department of General Practice: Universiteitsplein 1, 2610 Antwerpen-Wilrijk; tel. (3) 820-25-29; fax (3) 820-25-26; e-mail chris.monteyne@ua.ac.be; internet webh01.ua.ac.be/cha; Dirs Prof. Dr JOKE DENEKENS, Prof. Dr PAUL VAN ROYEN.

Expertise Centrum Hoger Onderwijs: Lange Nieuwstraat 55, 2000 Antwerpen; tel. (3) 212-16-83; fax (3) 212-16-81; e-mail echo@ua.ac.be; internet www.ua.ac.be/echo; Dir Prof. Dr PETER VAN PETEGEM.

Europacentrum Jean Monnet: tel. (3) 220-40-88; fax (3) 220-44-20; e-mail evrard.claessens@ua.ac.be; Dir Prof. Dr EVRARD CLAESSENS.

European Institute of Maritime and Transport Law: tel. (3) 220-42-13; fax (3) 238-67-14; e-mail eric.vanhooydonk@ua.ac.be; internet www.ua.ac.be; Dir Prof. Dr ERIC VAN HOOYDONK.

India Study Centre: Universiteitsplein 1, 2610 Antwerpen-Wilrijk; tel. (3) 820-27-87; fax (3) 820-27-86; e-mail india@ua.ac.be; internet www.ua.ac.be/indiastudiecentrum; Dir GINNY DE VOS.

Institute of Development Policy and Management: Lange St. Annastraat 7, 2000 Antwerpen; tel. (3) 275-57-70; fax (3) 275-57-71; e-mail dev@ua.ac.be; internet www.ua.ac.be/iob; Dir Prof. Dr FILIP REYNTJENS.

Institute of Education and Information Sciences: Universiteitsplein 1, 2610 Antwerpen-Wilrijk; tel. (3) 820-29-51; fax (3) 820-29-62; e-mail ailo@ua.ac.be; internet www.ua.ac.be/ioiw; Dir Prof. Dr PETER VAN PETEGEM.

Institute of Environmental Studies: Universiteitsplein 1, 2610 Antwerpen-Wilrijk; tel. (3) 820-21-14; fax (3) 820-21-28; e-mail milieu@ua.ac.be; internet www.ua.ac.be/main.aspx?c=*milknd; Dir Prof. Dr AVIEL VERBRUGGEN.

Institute of Jewish Studies: tel. (3) 275-52-43; fax (3) 275-52-41; e-mail ijs@ua.ac.be; internet www.ua.ac.be/ijs; Dir Prof. Dr VIVIAN LISKA.

Institute of Molecular Neurosciences: Universiteitsplein 1, 2610 Antwerpen-Wilrijk; tel. (3) 265-10-02; fax (3) 265-10-12; e-mail gisele.smeyers@ua.ac.be; internet www.molgen.ua.ac.be; Dir Prof. Dr CHRISTINE VAN BROECKHOVEN.

Institute of Transport and Maritime Management, Antwerp: Keizerstraat 64, 2000 Antwerpen; tel. (3) 275-51-51; fax (3) 275-51-52; e-mail itmma@ua.ac.be; internet www.ua.ac.be/itmma; Dir Prof. Dr THEO NOTTEBOOM.

Instituut Sociale Economie: Sint-Jacobsstraat 2, 2000 Antwerpen; tel. (3) 275-52-65; fax (3) 275-57-98; e-mail marleen.denef@ua.ac.be; internet www.ua.ac.be/psw; Dir Prof. Dr MARLEEN DENEF.

Instituut voor de Geschiedenis van de Spiritualiteit in de Nederlanden tot ca. 1750: tel. (3) 275-57-80; fax (3) 220-44-20; e-mail thom.mertens@ua.ac.be; Dir Prof. Dr THOM MERTENS.

Instituut voor de Geschiedenis van de Geneeskunde en de Natuurwetenschappen: Universiteitsplein 1, 2610 Antwerpen-Wilrijk; tel. (3) 820-25-37; fax (3) 820-21-28; e-mail robrecht.vanhee@ua.ac.be; Dir Prof. Dr ROBRECHT VAN HEE.

Instituut voor Onderwijs- en Informatiewetenschappen: Venusstraat 35, 2000 Antwerpen; tel. (3) 820-29-51; fax (3) 820-29-62; e-mail lieve.billion@ua.ac.be; internet www.ua.ac.be/ioiw-ua; Dir Prof. Dr PETER VAN PETEGEM.

Instituut voor Samenwerking tussen Universiteit en Arbeidersbeweging: Venusstraat 23, 2000 Antwerpen; tel. (3) 275-58-86; fax (3) 275-59-77; e-mail els.peeters@ua.ac.be; internet www.ua.ac.be/isua; Dir Prof. Dr MARC RIGAUX.

Instituut voor de Studie van de Letterkunde in de Nederlanden: tel. (3) 220-42-91; fax (3) 220-44-20; e-mail els.crauwels@ua.ac.be; internet www.ua.ac.be/isln; Dir Prof. Dr PIET COUTTENIER.

International Pragmatics Association: tel. (3) 220-45-63; fax (3) 220-55-74; e-mail ann.verhaert@ua.ac.be; internet ipra.ua.ac.be; Dir Prof. Dr JEF VERSCHUEREN.

Linguapolis: Institute for Language and Communication: Prinsstraat 8, 2000 Antwerpen; tel. (3) 220-48-03; fax (3) 220-46-37; e-mail info@linguapolis.be; internet www.linguapolis.be; Dir Prof. Dr POL CUVELIER.

Louis Paul Boon Documentatiecentrum: tel. (3) 275-52-50; fax (3) 275-52-24; e-mail kris.humbeeck@ua.ac.be; internet www.lpbooncentrum.be; Dir Prof. Dr KRIS HUMBEECK.

Micro and Trace Analysis Center: Universiteitsplein 1, 2610 Antwerpen-Wilrijk; tel. (3) 820-23-40; fax (3) 820-23-76; e-mail rene.vangrieken@ua.ac.be; Dir Prof. Dr RENÉ VAN GRIEKEN.

Referentiecentrum voor Biologische Merkers van Geheugenstoornissen: Universiteitsplein 1, 2610 Antwerpen-Wilrijk; tel. (3) 820-26-20; fax (3) 820-26-69; e-mail peter.dedeyn@ua.ac.be; Dir Prof. Dr PETER DE DEYN.

Reflectiecentrum Pieter Gillis: tel. (3) 220-44-77; fax (3) 220-49-38; e-mail nina.vleugels@ua.ac.be; internet www.ua.ac.be/main.aspx?c=pietergil; Dir Prof. Dr GUY VANHEESWIJCK.

Research Centre on Technology, Energy and Environment: Kleine Kauwenberg 12, 2000 Antwerpen; tel. (3) 220-49-00; fax (3) 220-49-01; e-mail aviel.verbruggen@ua.ac.be; internet www.ua.ac.be/stem; Dir Prof. Dr AVIEL VERBRUGGEN.

Research Park Waterfront: Drie Eikenstraat 661, 2650 Edegem; tel. (3) 826-93-00; fax (3) 826-93-09; e-mail chris.deceulaerde@ubca.be; internet www.waterfront.be; Dir CHRIS DE CEULARDE.

Steunpunt Buitenlands Beleid: Lange Sint-Annastraat 7, 2000 Antwerpen; tel. (3) 275-56-37; fax (3) 275-57-98; e-mail vsbb@ua.ac.be; internet www.ua.ac.be/vsbbe; Dir ANNICK SCHRAMME.

Steunpunt Gelijkekansenbeleid: Lange Nieuwstraat 55, 2000 Antwerpen; tel. (3) 275-59-43; e-mail steunpuntgeka@ua.ac.be; internet www.ua.ac.be/sgk; Dir NICO STEEGMANS.

Studie Centrum voor Onderneming en Beurs: Middelheimlaan 1, 2020 Antwerpen; tel. (3) 265-35-38; e-mail frans.buelens@ua.ac.be; internet www.scob.be; Dir Prof. Dr LUDO CUYVERS.

Studie- en Documentatiecentrum Hugo Claus: tel. (3) 220-52-49; fax (3) 220-44-20; e-mail georges.wildemeersch@ua.ac.be; internet www.clauscentrum.be/main.aspx?c=claus; Dir Prof. Dr GEORGES WILDEMEERSCH.

Universitair Wetenschappelijk Instituut voor Drugproblemen: tel. (3) 220-40-65; fax (3) 220-44-20; e-mail a.uwid@antwerpen.be; internet www.uwid.be; Dir Prof. Dr BOB VERMERGHT.

University of Antwerp Legal School: Venusstraat 23, 2000 Antwerpen; tel. (3) 275-54-45; fax (3) 275-51-20; e-mail mieke.briels@ua.ac.be; internet www.ua.ac.be/uals; Dir Prof. Dr MAURICE ADAMS.

University of Antwerp Management School: Sint-Jacobsmarkt 9-13, 2000 Antwerpen; tel. (3) 220-47-58; fax (3) 220-47-59; e-mail info@uams.be; internet www.uams.be/en; Dir Prof. Dr FRANK BOSTYN.

KATHOLIEKE UNIVERSITEIT BRUSSEL
(Catholic University of Brussels)

Vrijheidslaan 17, 1081 Brussels

Telephone: (2) 412-42-11
Fax: (2) 412-42-00
E-mail: info@kubrussel.ac.be
Internet: www.kubrussel.ac.be

Founded 1968; present name 1991; previously Universitaire Faculteiten Sint-Aloysius
Language of instruction: Dutch
Private control
Academic year: October to July

Rector: Prof. Dr M. VAN HOECKE
Librarian: Prof. Dr E. DEFOORT

Library of 70,000 vols
Number of teachers: 51
Number of students: 800

DEANS

Department of Economic Sciences: I. VAN DE W. DE STYNE
Department of Germanic Philology: M. DE CLERCK
Department of History: E. DEFOORT
Department of Law: F. FLEERACKERS
Department of Philosophy: J. F. LINDEMANS
Department of Social and Political Sciences: J. DELWAIDE

PROFESSORS

ACX, R., Bank and Credit Sciences
BOUSSET, H., Dutch Literature
BRAEKMAN, W. L., English Literature
CARPENTIER, N.
DE BOECK, A.
DE CLERCQ, M., European Literature and Introduction to Modern Literature
DEFOORT, E., Modern French Texts
DEGADT, J., Economic Science and Social Statistics
DE LATHOUWER, L.
DELWAIDE, J.
DE MARTELAERE, P., Philosophic Anthropology
DEPREEUW, E.
DE SCHRYVER, J.
DESMET, J.
DE VIN, D., Dutch Literature
DEWINTER, L.
ELST, M.
FLEERACKERS, F.
FOBLETS, M.-C.
GEERAERTS, R.
GOOSSENS, W., Historic Introduction to Philosophy
GOTZEN, F., Introduction to Law
HEMMERECHTS, L.
HEYSSE, T.
JAKOBS, D.
JANSSENS, J., History of Medieval Dutch Literature
JANSSENS, P., Modern Times
LINDEMANS, J.-F., Traditional Logics
LOOSVELDT, G., Methods and Techniques of Social Sciences
MOONS, T., History of Antiquity
MUYLLE, J., Art and Cultural History
NELDE, P. H., Germanic Linguistics
OOSTERBOSCH, A., Physics
SCHOENMAECKERS, R.
SWYNGEDOUW, M.
TACQ, J., Sociology
VANDEN BROECKE, S.
VANDEN WYNGAERD, G.
VAN DEN WIJNGAERT, M., History of Modern Times
VAN DE WOESTYNE, I.
VANHEMELRYCK, F., History of Modern Times
VAN HOECKE, M., Introduction to Law
VERRETH, H.
VERSTRAELEN, L., Mathematics
VERTONGHEN, R., Accountancy
WINTGENS, L.

UNIVERSITÉ LIBRE DE BRUXELLES
(Free University of Brussels)

50 ave Franklin Roosevelt, 1050 Brussels

Telephone: (2) 650-23-17
Fax: (2) 650-36-30
E-mail: elennertz@admin.ulb.ac.be
Internet: www.ulb.ac.be

Founded 1834; became independent from the Vrije Universiteit Brussel in 1970
Language of instruction: French
Private control
Academic year: September to July

President: JEAN-LOUIS VANHERWEGHEM
Vice-President: FABRIZIO BUCELLA
Rector: PIERRE DE MARET
Secretary: SERGE BODSON
Librarian: Prof. JEAN-PIERRE DEVROEY

Library: see Libraries and Archives
Number of teachers: 1,300
Number of students: 20,000

Publication: *Esprit Libre* (magazine, monthly)

DEANS

Faculty of Applied Sciences: Prof. PHILIPPE VINCKE
Faculty of Law: Prof. PAUL-ALAIN FORIERS
Faculty of Medicine: Prof. ELIE COGAN
Faculty of Philosophy and Letters: Prof. JEAN-PIERRE DEVROEY
Faculty of Psychology and Education: Prof. ASSAAD ELIA AZZI
Faculty of Science: Prof. GUY LATOUCHE
Faculty of Social, Political and Economic Sciences: Prof. ANDRÉ FARBER

INSTITUTES

Institute of Environmental Management and Development Planning: Dir Prof. EDWIN ZACCAÏ.

Institute of European Studies: Pres. Prof. FRANÇOISE THYS-CLEMENT.

Institute of Labour: Pres. Prof. MICHEL SYLIN.

Institute of Modern Languages and Phonetics: Pres. Prof. EMILE KNOPS.

Institute of Pharmacy: Pres. Prof. JEAN NÈVE.

Institute of Physical Education and Kinesitherapy: Pres. Prof. GUY CHÉRON.

Institute of Statistics and Operational Research: Pres. Prof. MARC HALLIN.

School of Criminology: ave Paul Héger, 1050 Brussels; f. 1935; Pres. HUGUETTE JONES.

School of Public Health: Pres. Prof. CHRISTOPHE DE BROUWER.

Solvay Business School: Dir Prof. PHILIPPE BILTIAU.

ASSOCIATED INSTITUTES AND SCHOOLS

Centre Emile Bernheim: Pres. ANDRÉ FARBER.

Centre d'Etudes Canadiennes (Centre for Canadian Studies): Pres. GINETTE KURGAN-VAN HENTENRYK.

Centre Interdisciplinaire D'Etude des Religions et de la Laïcité (CIERL): Dir JEAN-PHILIPPE SCHREIBER.

Centre de Recherches Industrielles et Agronomiques (CRIA): Pres. JEAN-CLAUDE LEGROS.

Département d'Economie Appliquée (Applied Economics Department): 2 ave Paul Héger, 1050 Brussels; Dirs HENRI CAPRON, ROBERT PLASMAN.

Ecole de Commerce Ernest Solvay (Ernest Solvay Business School): Pres. PHILIPPE BILTIAU.

Ecole d'Infirmières annexée à l'Université (Nursing School attached to the University): Campus Erasme, 808 Route de Lennik, 1070 Brussels; Dir GABRIELLE BUSCARLET.

European Centre for Advanced Research in Economics and Statistics (ECARES): Dirs VICTOR GINSBURGH, MARC HALLIN.

Groupe d'Etudes sur l'Ethnicité, le Racisme, les Migrations et l'Exclusion (GERME): Dir ANDREA REA.

Institut Jules Bordet (Jules Bordet Institute): 1 rue Héger-Bordet, 1000 Brussels; tel. (2) 538-28-20; diagnosis and treatment of tumours; Dir JEAN KLASTERSKY.

Institut de Recherche Interdisciplinaire en Biologie Humaine et Moléculaire (IRIBHM): Dir GILBERT VASSART.

Institut de Sociologie (Institute of Sociology): 44 ave Jeanne, 1050 Brussels; f. 1901; Dir FIROUZEH NAHAVANDI.

VRIJE UNIVERSITEIT BRUSSEL (Free University of Brussels)

Pleinlaan 2, 1050 Brussels
Telephone: (2) 629-21-11
Fax: (2) 629-22-82
E-mail: infovub@vub.ac.be
Internet: www.vub.ac.be

Founded 1834; became independent from the Université Libre de Bruxelles in 1970
Languages of instruction: Dutch, English
Private control
Academic year: October to July

President: R. VAN AERSCHOT
Rector: B. VAN CAMP
Vice-Rectors: J. CORNELIS, R. S'JEGERS
Director-General: J. VAN LEEMPUT
Librarian: P. VANOUPLINES

Number of teachers: 700
Number of students: 10,000

Publications: *Akademos*, *Newsletter* (electronic), *Nieuw Tijdschrift van de VUB*, *VUB-Press*

DEANS

Faculty of Applied Science: J. WASTIELS
Faculty of Law: M. MAGITS
Faculty of Medicine: A. VAN STEIRTEGHEM
Faculty of Physical Education and Kinesiology: J. P. CLARIJS
Faculty of Philosophy and Letters: W. GOEGEBUER
Faculty of Psychology and Education: I. PONJAERT-KRISTOFFERSEN
Faculty of Science: L. WYNS
Faculty of Social, Political and Economic Sciences: E. VANDIJK

CONSTITUENT COLLEGE

Vesalius College: Pleinlaan 2, 1050 Brussels; tel. (2) 629-28-22; fax (2) 629-36-37; f. 1987 in assn with Boston Univ.; degree courses in arts, sciences and engineering; language of instruction: English; Dean JEAN-PIERRE DE GRÈVE.

UNIVERSITEIT GENT (Ghent University)

St-Pietersnieuwstraat 25, 9000 Ghent
Telephone: (9) 264-31-11
Fax: (9) 264-82-93
E-mail: communicatie@ugent.be
Internet: www.ugent.be

Founded 1817
Language of instruction: Dutch
State control
Academic year: October to July

Rector: PAUL VAN CAUWENBERGE
Vice-Rector: LUC MOENS
Government Commissioner: YANNICK DE CLERCQ
Academic Administrator: KOEN GOETHALS
Logistic Administrator: DIRK MANGELEER
Sec. of the Board: LIEVE BRACKE

Library: see Libraries and Archives
Number of teachers: 800
Number of students: 28,000

Publication: *Universiteit Gent* (8 a year)

DEANS

Faculty of Bioscience Engineering: H. VAN LANGENHOVE
Faculty of Arts and Philosophy: F. MORTIER
Faculty of Economics and Business Admin.: R. PAEMELEIRE
Faculty of Eng.: D. DE ZUTTER
Faculty of Law: E. SOMERS
Faculty of Medicine and Health Sciences: J. L. PANNIER
Faculty of Pharmaceutical Sciences: J.-P. REMON
Faculty of Political and Social Sciences: J. VINCKE
Faculty of Psychology and Educational Sciences: G. DE SOETE
Faculty of Sciences: H. DEJONGHE
Faculty of Veterinary Medicine: H. DE BRABANDER

PROFESSORS

Faculty of Bioscience Engineering (Coupure Links 653, 9000 Ghent; tel. (9) 264-59-01; fax (9) 264-62-45):

DEBEVERE, J., Food Safety and Food Quality
GABRIËLS, D., Soil Management and Soil Care
LEMEUR, R., Applied Ecology and Environmental Biology
OTTOY, J. P., Applied Mathematics, Biometrics and Process Control
REHEUL, D., Plant Production
SORGELOOS, P., Animal Production
STEURBAUT, W., Crop Protection
STEVENS, M., Forest and Water Management
VAN OOSTVELDT, P., Molecular Biotechnology
VERHÉ, R., Organic Chemistry
VERLOO, M., Applied Analytical and Physical Chemistry
VERSCHOORE, R., Agricultural Engineering
VERSTRAETE, W., Biochemical and Microbial Technology
VIAENE, J., Agricultural Economics

Faculty of Arts and Philosophy (Blandijnberg 2, 9000 Ghent; tel. (9) 264-39-32; fax (9) 264-41-95):

ART, J., Modern History
COMMERS, M., Philosophy and Moral Sciences
DECREUS, F., Latin and Greek
DEVOS, M., Dutch Linguistics
DEVREKER, J., Archaeology and Ancient History of Europe
KABUTO, N., African Languages and Cultures
LAUREYS, G., Nordic Studies
LEMAN, M., Art, Music and Theatre Sciences
MOERLOOSE, E., Languages and Cultures of South and East Asia
PINXTEN, H., Comparative Sciences of Culture
REYNAERT, J., Dutch Literature
ROEGIEST, E., Language and Communication
SLEMBROUCK, S., English
SYMOENS, H., Early Modern History
TANRET, M., Languages and Cultures of the Near East and North Africa
THOEN, E., Medieval History
VAN UYTFANGHE, M., Romance Languages other than French
VEREECKEN, J., Slavonic and East-European Studies
WILLEMS, D., French
WILLEMS, K., German

Faculty of Economics and Business Administration (Hoveniersberg 24, 9000 Ghent; tel. (9) 264-36-61; fax (9) 264-35-92):

DE BEELDE, I., Accountancy and Corporate Finance
DE CLERCQ, M., General Economics
HEENE, A., Management and Entrepreneurship
OMEY, E., Social Economics
PAEMELEIRE, R., Management Information, Operations Management and Technology Policy
VANDER VENNET, R., Financial Economics
VAN KENHOVE, P., Marketing

Faculty of Engineering (Jozef Plateaustraat 22, 9000 Ghent; tel. (9) 264-37-13; fax (9) 264-41-90):

BRUNEEL, H., Telecommunications and Information Processing
DEGRIECK, J., Mechanical Construction and Production
HOUBAERT, Y., Metallurgy and Materials Science
KIEKENS, P., Textiles
LAGASSE, P., Information Technology
LEYS, C., Applied Physics
MARIN, G., Chemical Engineering and Technical Chemistry
MELKEBEEK, J., Electrical Energy, Systems and Automation
SIERENS, R., Flow, Heat and Combustion Mechanics
TAERWE, L., Structural Engineering

Van Campenhout, J., Electronics and Information Systems
Van Keer, R., Mathematical Analysis
Van Landeghem, H., Industrial Management
Verdonck, P., Civil Engineering
Verschaffel, B., Architecture and Urban Planning

Faculty of Law (Universiteitstraat 4, 9000 Ghent; tel. (9) 264-67-62; fax (9) 264-69-99):

Bocken, H., Civil Law
Bouckaert, B., Legal Theory and Legal History
Erauw, J., Procedural Law, Arbitration and Private International Law
Humblet, P., Labour Law and Social Security
Maresceau, M., European Institute
Somers, E., International Public Law
Van Acker, C., Economic Law
Van Crombrugge, S., Public and Tax Law
Veny, L., Public Law
Vermeulen, G., Penal Law and Criminology

Faculty of Medicine and Health Sciences (Campus Heymans, De Pintelaan 185, 9000 Ghent; tel. (9) 240-41-93; fax (9) 240-49-90):

De Backer, G., Public Health
De Clercq, D., Movement and Sports Sciences
De Hemptinne, B., Surgery
De Maeseneer, J., General Practice and Primary Health Care
De Vos, M., Internal Medicine
De Wagter, C., Radiotherapy and Nuclear Medicine
Dhont, M., Uro-gynaecology
Kestelyn, P., Ophthalmology
Lefebvre, R., Pharmacology
Matthys, D. M., Paediatrics and Medical Genetics
Mortier, E., Anaesthesiology
Naeyaert, J. M., Dermatology
Pannier, J., General, Human and Pathophysiology, Pathology and Forensic Medicine
Piette, M., Forensic Medicine
Plum, J., Clinical Chemistry, Microbiology and Immunology
Van Cauwenberge, P., Otorhinolaryngology
Vandekerckhove, J., Biochemistry
Van Heeringen, C., Psychiatry and Medical Psychology
Verdonk, R., Physical Medicine and Orthopaedic Surgery
Verstraete, K., Radiology

Faculty of Pharmaceutical Sciences (Campus Heymans, Harelbekestraat 72, 9000 Ghent; tel. (9) 264-80-40; fax (9) 264-81-94):

Nelis, H., Pharmaceutical Analysis
Remon, J. P., Pharmaceutics
Van Peteghem, C., Bio-analysis

Faculty of Political and Social Sciences (Universiteitstraat 4, 9000 Ghent; tel. (9) 264-67-80; fax (9) 264-69-86):

Coolsaet, H., Political Sciences
Verstraeten, H., Communication Studies
Vincke, J., Sociology
Walraet, A., Third World Studies

Faculty of Psychology and Educational Sciences (Henri Dunantlaan 2, 9000 Ghent; tel. (9) 264-63-41; fax (9) 264-64-98):

Broekaert, E., Special Education
Claes, R., Personnel Management, Work and Organizational Psychology
De Bie, M., Social Welfare Studies
Hartsuiker, R., Experimental Psychology
Mervielde, I., Developmental, Personality and Social Psychology
Schuyten, G., Data Analysis
Spoelders, M., Pedagogy
Valcke, M., Educational Studies
Van Oost, P., Experimental Clinical and Health Psychology
Verhaeghe, P., Psychoanalysis and Clinical Consulting

Faculty of Sciences (K. L. Ledeganckstraat 35, 9000 Ghent; tel. (9) 264-50-42; fax (9) 264-53-40):

Antrop, M., Geography
Clauws, P., Solid State Sciences
De Clerck, F., Pure Mathematics and Computer Algebra
De Clercq, P., Organic Chemistry
Depicker, A., Molecular Genetics
De Vos, P., Biochemistry, Physiology and Microbiology
Hoste, S., Inorganic and Physical Chemistry
Huysseune, A., Biology
Jacobs, P., Geology and Soil Science
Ryckbosch, D., Subatomic and Radiation Physics
Sarlet, W., Mathematical Physics and Astronomy
Strijckmans, K., Analytical Chemistry
Vanden Berghe, G., Applied Mathematics and Computer Science
Van Roy, F., Molecular Biology

Faculty of Veterinary Sciences (Salisburylaan 133, 9820 Merelbeke; tel. (9) 264-75-03; fax (9) 264-77-99):

De Backer, P., Pharmacology, Pharmacy and Toxicology
De Brabanter, H., Veterinary Public Health and Food Safety
de Kruif, A., Obstetrics, Reproduction and Herd Health
Deprez, P., Internal Medicine and Clinical Biology of Large Animals
Duchateau, L., Physiology and Biometry
Gasthuys, F., Surgery and Anaesthesiology of Domestic Animals
Haesebrouck, F., Pathology, Bacteriology and Poultry Diseases
Simoens, P., Morphology
Van Bree, H., Medical Imaging of Domestic Animals
Van Ham, L., Medicine and Clinical Biology of Small Animals
Van Zeveren, A., Animal Nutrition, Genetics, Breeding and Ethology
Vercruysse, J., Virology, Parasitology and Immunology

HASSELT UNIVERSITEIT

Campus Diepenbeek Agoralaan, Gebouw D, 3590 Diepenbeek
Telephone: (11) 26-81-11
Fax: (11) 26-81-99
E-mail: info@uhasselt.be
Internet: www.uhasselt.be

Founded 1971; incorporated Economische Hogeschool Limburg in 1991; the University of Limburg (www.tul.edu) was established in 2001, in partnership with Universiteit Maastricht (see chapter on the Netherlands)
State control
Languages of instruction: Dutch, English

Rector: Marie-Paule Jacobs
Librarian: Prof. Dr Leo Egghe

Number of teachers: 380
Number of students: 2,219

Faculties of Applied Economics, Medicine, Sciences.

ATTACHED RESEARCH INSTITUTES

Biomedical Research Institute: Dir Prof. Dr P. Stinissen.

Centre for Environmental Sciences: Dir Prof. Dr Jaco Vangronsveld,.

Center for Statistics (CenStat): Dir Prof. Dr Geert Molenberghs.

Expertise Centre for Digital Media: Dir Prof. Dr Eddy Flerackers.

Institute for Entrepreneurship and Innovation: Dir Prof. Dr Wim Vanhaverbeke.

Institute for Materials Research: Dir Prof. Dr Harry Martens.

Socio-economic Institute: Dir Prof. Dr Mieke Van Haegendoren.

Transportation Research Institute: Dir Prof. Dr Geert Wets.

UNIVERSITÉ DE LIÈGE (University of Liège)

Place du 20-Août 7, 4000 Liège
Telephone: (4) 366-21-11
Fax: (4) 366-57-00
E-mail: International@ulg.ac.be
Internet: www.ulg.ac.be

Founded 1817
Language of instruction: French
Academic year: October to September

Rector: W. Legros
Vice-Rector: B. Rentier
Administrator: L. Bragard

Library: see under Libraries
Number of teachers: 470
Number of students: 13,069

DEANS

Faculty of Applied Sciences: A. Germain
Faculty of Economics, Business Administration and Social Sciences: A. Corhay
Faculty of Law: G. de Leval
Faculty of Medicine: R. Limet
Faculty of Philosophy and Letters: P. Somville
Faculty of Psychology and Educational Sciences: S. Bredart
Faculty of Sciences: J.-M. Bouquegneau
Faculty of Veterinary Medicine: P. Lekeux

PROFESSORS WITH CHAIRS

Faculty of Applied Sciences (Chemin des Chevreuils, 1, B52/3 Sart Tilman, 4000 Liege):

Beckers, P.
Bozet, J., Mechanical Engineering
Cantraine, G., Electronics
Cescotto, S., Mechanics of Materials
Coheur, J. P., Iron and Steel Metallurgy
Dendal, J., Applied Acoustics
Destine, J., Microelectronics
Dimanche, F., Applied Geology
Dupagne, A., Methodology of Architectonic Composition
Essers, J. A., Aerodynamics
Etienne, J., Mathematics
Fawe, A., Telecommunications
Fleury, Cl., Aerospatial Structures
Fonder, G., Structural Mechanics
Geradin, M., Aeronautical Engineering
Germain, A., Industrial Chemistry
Hogge, M., Thermomechanics
Lebrun, J., Thermodynamics, Nuclear Engineering
Legros, W., Electrical Engineering
Lejeune, A., Hydraulics
L'Homme, G., Chemical Engineering
Litt, F. X., Applied Mathematics
Maquoi, R., Mechanics of Materials, Stability of Structures
Marchal, J., Transport Systems and Shipbuilding
Monjoie, A., Engineering and Hydrogeology
Nguyen-Dang, H., Mechanics of the Rupture of Solid Bodies
Mme Pavella, M., Electrical Circuits
Peters, F., Architecture
Pirard, J. P., Applied Physical Chemistry

PIROTTE, P., Transport and Distribution of Electrical Energy
RIBBENS, D., Computer Science
RONDAL, J., Mechanics of Materials
VANDERSCHUEREN, H., Electrical Measurements
VAN MELLAERT, L., Automatics
WOLPER, P., Computer Science

Faculty of Economics, Business Administration and Social Sciences (7 Boulevard du Rectorat, B 31 Sart Tilman, 4000 Liege):
BAIR, J., Mathematics in Economic and Management Sciences
BAWIN-LEGROS, B., Sociology of the Family and General Sociology
CHOFFRAY, J.-M., Computing applied to Economics and Business
CRAMA, Y., Operational Research and Production Management
DE BRUYN, C., Quantitative Management Methods
DE COSTER, M., Sociology
DISTER, G., Management Sociology
FELD, S., Development Economics
GAZON, J., Economics
JURION, B., Political Economy
LANGASKENS, Y., Economics
MICHEL, P. A., Financial Analysis
MINGUET, A., Economics
PESTIEAU, P., Economic Science
QUADEN, G., Political Economy and Economic Systems
THIRY, B., Political Economy and Applied Microeconomics

Faculty of Law (7 Boulevard du Rectorat, B 31 Sart Tilman, 4000 Liege):
BEAUFAYS, J., General and Regional Political Studies
BENOIT-MOURY, A., Commercial Law
DE LEVAL, G., Civil Law
DELNOY, P., Civil Law and Juridical Methodology
DEMARET, P., European Economic Law
FRANÇOIS, L., General Theory of Law
GOTHOT, P., Comparative and International Law
HANSENNE, J., Civil Law
HERBIET, M., Public and Administrative Law
Mme JAMOULLE, M., Social Law
KELLENS, G., Criminology
LEWALLE, P., Public and Administrative Law
MELCHIOR, M., Private International Law
Mme MOREAU-MARGRÈVE, I., Civil Law
PAPPALARDO, A., European Competition Law
SCHOLSEM, J. CL., Public Law and Public Finance
Mme VANWIJCK-ALEXANDRE, M., Civil Law
VIGNERON, R., Roman Law

Faculty of Medicine (CHU level 0, B 35 Sart Tilman, 4000 Liege):
ANGENOT, L., Pharmacy
BONIVER, J., Anatomy and Pathological Cytology
DANDRIFOSSE, G., General Biochemistry and Physiology
DELARGE, J., Pharmaceutical Chemistry
DE LEVAL, J., Urology
DRESSE, A., Pharmacology
FILLET, G., Haematology
FISETTE, J., Topographical and Intestinal Human Anatomy
FOIDART, J. M., General and Cellular Biology
FRANCK, G., Neurology
FRANÇOIS, M., Stomatology
GIELEN, J., Medical Chemistry
HENNEN, G., Human and Pathological Biochemistry
JACQUET, N., Abdominal Surgery
KULBERTUS, H., Medical Clinic
LAMY, M., Anaesthesiology
LEFEBVRE, P., Clinical Medicine
LEMAIRE, R., Surgery of Locomotor System
LIMET, R., Cardiovascular Surgery
MOONEN, G., Normal and Pathological Physiology
PIERON, M., Physical Education
RORIVE, G., Nephrology
SENTERRE, J., Paediatrics
STEVENAERT, A., Neurosurgery

Faculty of Philosophy and Letters (Place du 20-Août, A1 (Centre Ville), 4000 Liege):
BAJOMEE, D., Contemporary French Literature
BARRERA VIDAL, A., Special Methodology of Romance Languages, French and Spanish
DELBOUILLE, P., French Stylistics and Analysis of Modern Authors
DESAMA, CL., Economic and Social History
DOR, J., Medieval English Language and Literature
DUBOIS, J., Modern French Authors and Contemporary Literature
JODOGNE, P., Italian Language and Literature
JOSET, J., Spanish Language and Literature
KLINKENBERG, J.-M., Rhetoric and Semiology
KUPPER, J. L., History of the Middle Ages and Historical Geography
LEROY, R., Modern German Literature
LOICQ, J., Roman History and Archaeology
MALAISE, M., Oriental History and Philology
MASSAUT, J. P., Modern History
MICHEL, P., Modern English and American Literature
MOTTE, A., Moral Philosophy and History of Ancient Philosophy
PASTOR, E., German Literature and Historical Philology
SOMVILLE, P., Aesthetics and Philosophy of Art
THEISSEN, S., Modern Dutch Philology
WATHELET, P., Greek Language, Literature and Civilization

Faculty of Psychology and Educational Sciences (5 Boulevard du Rectorat, B 32 Sart Tilman, 4000 Liege):
BORN, M., Psychology of Criminality and Psycho-Social Development
CRAHAY, M., Experimental Education
Mme DE KEYSER, V., Business and Administrative Psychology
FONTAINE, O., Psychology of Health, Behavioural Therapy Unit
LECLERCQ, D., Educational Technology
RONDAL, J. A., Language Psychology
VAN DER LINDEN, M., Neuropsychology

Faculty of Sciences (Institut de Chimie, B6 Sart Tilman, 4000 Liege):
AGHION, P., Vegetal Biochemistry
BECKERS, J., Theoretical and Experimental Physics
BERNIER, G., Vegetal Physiology
CUGNON, J., Theoretical Physics
DESREUX, J. F., Inorganic Chemistry and Co-ordination Chemistry
DE WILDE, M., Differential Geometry
DUCHESNE, J.-C., Petrology and Geochemistry
EVRARD, R., Experimental Physics
FRANSOLET, A. M., Mineralogy
FRÈRE, J. M., Enzymology Laboratory
GERDAY, C., Biochemistry Laboratory
GILLES, R., Physiology
GOESSENS, G., Cell and Tissue Biology
HOUSSIER, C. I., Macromolecular and Physical Chemistry
JEROME, R., Macromolecular Chemistry and Organic Materials
LAMBINON, J., Vegetal Systematics and Geography
LAZLO, P., Organic Physical Chemistry
LEBON, G., Thermomechanics of Irreversible Phenomena
LORQUET, J., Physical Chemistry
MARTIAL, J., Molecular Biology and Genetic Engineering
MATAGNE, R. F., Genetics of Micro-organisms
MERENNE-SCHOUMAKER, B., Economic Geography
NIHOUL, J., Analytical Mechanics
RENTIER, B., Basic Virology
ROUBENS, M., Statistics and Quantitative Management Methods
RUWET, J.-C., Animal Ethology and Psychology
SCHMETS, J., Mathematics
THONART, PH., Microbiology
THOREZ, J., Geology of Clays
VAN DE VORST, A., Experimental Physics

Faculty of Veterinary Medicine (Boulevard du Colonster, B 43 Sart Tilman):
ANSAY, M., Pharmacology and Treatment of Domestic Animals
COIGNOUL, F., Pathological Anatomy and Autopsies
DESSY-DOIZE, C., Histology, Embryology, Cytology
ECTORS, F., Obstetrics and Pathology
GODEAU, J. M., Biochemistry
HENROTEAUX, M., Semiology and Medical Treatment of Small Animals
LEROY, P., Information Science Applied to Animal Husbandry
LOMBA, F., Medical and Clinical Pathology
MAGHUIN-ROGISTER, G., Analysis of Foodstuffs derived from Animals
PASTORET, P. P., Virology and Immunology
VINDEVOGEL, H., Treatment of Birds, Food Hygiene

ATTACHED INSTITUTES

Ecole Liégeoise de Criminologie Jean Constant: President MICHEL BORN.

KATHOLIEKE UNIVERSITEIT LEUVEN
(Catholic University of Leuven)

Naamsestraat 22, 3000 Louvain (Leuven)
Telephone: (16) 32-40-67
Fax: (16) 32-41-96
E-mail: info@kuleuven.be
Internet: www.kuleuven.ac.be

Founded 1425 by Papal Bull; in 1970 the Katholieke Universiteit Leuven was officially split into two autonomous universities: the Katholieke Universiteit Leuven and the Université Catholique de Louvain
Languages of instruction: Dutch, English
Private control
Academic year: October to July

Rector: ANDRE OOSTERLINCK
Vice-Rector for Biomedical Sciences: GUY MANNAERTS
Vice-Rector for Exact Sciences: GUIDO LANGOUCHE
Vice-Rector for Humanities: MARC VERVENNE
Vice-Rector for Kortrijk Campus: PIET VANDEN ABEELE
Librarian: R. DEKEYSER
Library: see Libraries and Archives
Number of students: 28,057

Publication: *Campuskrant* (monthly)

DEANS

Faculty of Agricultural and Applied Biological Sciences: R. SCHOONHEYDT
Faculty of Arts: W. EVENEPOEL
Faculty of Canon Law: R. TORFS
Faculty of Economics and Applied Economics: F. ABRAHAM
Faculty of Engineering: Y. WILLEMS
Faculty of Law: F. VANISTENDAEL

Faculty of Medicine: J. JANSSENS
Faculty of Pharmaceutical Sciences: P. DE CLERCK
Faculty of Philosophy: A. VAN DE PUTTE
Faculty of Physical Education and Physiotherapy: M. BUEKERS
Faculty of Psychology and Educational Sciences: J. CORVELEYN
Faculty of Science: A. VERBEURE
Faculty of Social Sciences: E. GERARD
Faculty of Theology: M. LAMBERIGTS

INTERFACULTY INSTITUTES

Catholic Documentation and Research Centre: Pres. E. LAMBERTS.

Centre for Risk and Insurance Studies: Dirs H. COUSY.

Energy Institute: Dirs R. BELMANS, W. D'HAESELEER, S. PROOST.

European Centre for Ethics: Pres. H. DE DIJN; publ. *Ethical Perspectives* (Journal of the European Ethics Network).

Institute of Labour Studies: Pres. J. RENDERS.

Institute of Modern Languages: Pres. A. VAN AVERMAET.

Vlerick–Leuven–Gent Management School: Dir L. SLEUWAEGEN.

UNIVERSITÉ CATHOLIQUE DE LOUVAIN
(Catholic University of Louvain)

Place de l'Université 1, 1348 Louvain-la-Neuve
Telephone: (10) 47-21-11
Fax: (10) 47-38-03
E-mail: info-portail@uclouvain.be
Internet: www.ucl.ac.be

Founded 1425 by Papal Bull; became independent when the Katholieke Universiteit Leuven split into two autonomous universities in 1970
Private control
Language of instruction: French
Academic year: September to May

Rector: M. CROCHET
Vice-Rectors: M. MOLITOR, X. RENDERS
General Administrator: A.-M. KUMPS
Librarian: CH. H. NIJNS

Library: see Libraries and Archives
Number of teachers: 1,260
Number of students: 20,517

Publication: *Bulletin des Amis de Louvain*

DEANS

Faculty of Applied Sciences: J.-D. LEGAT
Faculty of Biological, Agricultural and Environmental Engineering: J. DUFEY
Faculty of Economic, Political and Social Sciences: A. SPINEUX
Faculty of Economic and Social Policy: P. REMAN
Faculty of Law: H. SIMONART
Faculty of Medicine: J.-J. ROMBOUTS
Faculty of Philosophy and Letters: B. COULIE
Faculty of Psychology and Education: G. LORIES
Faculty of Sciences: J. FASTREZ
Faculty of Theology and Canon Law: C. FOCANT
Higher Institute of Philosophy: M. DUPUIS

HEADS OF DEPARTMENTS

Faculty of Agriculture (tel. (10) 47-37-19; fax (10) 47-47-45):
- Applied Chemistry and Bio-Industries: M. BOUTRY
- Biology and Agricultural Production Department: Y. LARONDELLE
- Environmental Sciences and Rural Management Department: B. DELVAUX

Faculty of Applied Sciences (tel. (10) 47-24-60; fax (10) 47-24-66):
- Architecture: J. FR THIMUS
- Computer Engineering: M. LOBELLE
- Electricity: J. D. LEGAT
- Materials Science: P. BERTRAND
- Mathematical Engineering: M. GEVERS
- Mechanics: J. CL. SAMIN

Faculty of Economic, Political and Social Sciences (tel. (10) 47-85-91; fax (10) 47-29-97):
- Administration and Business: P. SEMAL
- Communication: PH. VERHAEGEN
- Economics: L. BAUWENS
- Political and Social Sciences: CH. DE VISSCHER
- Population and Development Science: J.-M. WAUTELAT

Faculty of Law (tel. (10) 47-86-00; fax (10) 47-46-01):
- Criminology and Penal Law: FR. DIGNEFFE
- Economic and Social Law: M. BOURLARD
- International Law: M. FALLON
- Private Law: J.-L. DENCHON
- Public Law: H. SIMONART

Faculty of Medicine (Ave E. Mounier 50, 1200 Brussels; tel. (2) 764-50-30; fax (2) 764-50-35):
- Biochemistry and Cellular Biology: Y. EECKHOUT
- Dentistry and Stomatology: J. VREVEN
- Gynaecology, Obstetrics and Paediatrics: J.-P. BUTS
- Internal Medicine: M. BUYSSCHAERT
- Microbiology, Immunology and Genetics: P. COULIE
- Morphology: J. RAHIER
- Neurology and Psychiatry: CH. SINDIC
- Pharmaceutics: R. K. VERBEECK
- Physical Education and Rehabilitation: P. WILLEMS
- Physiology and Pharmacology: J. CL. HENQUIN
- Public Health: A. DECCACHE
- Radiology: B. MALDAGUE
- Surgery: P. GIANELLO

Faculty of Philosophy and Letters (tel. (10) 47-26-40; fax (10) 47-20-53):
- Archaeology and History of Art: R. BRULET
- Germanic Studies: S. VANDERLINDEN
- Greek, Latin and Oriental Studies: P. A. DEPROOST
- History: P. SERVAIS
- Romance Studies: L. COLLES

Faculty of Sciences (tel. (10) 47-33-24; fax (10) 47-28-37):
- Biology: PH. VAN DEN BOSCH DE AGUILAR
- Chemistry: J. PH. SOUMILLON
- Geology and Geography: E. LAMBIN
- Mathematics: J. P. TIGNOL
- Physics: J. P. ANTOINE

PRESIDENTS OF INSTITUTES

Higher Institute of Religious Studies: A. HAQUIN
Institute for Developing Countries: J.-PH. PEEMANS
Institute of Family Studies and Sexology: J. SOSSON
Institute of Labour Studies: C. DEMEZ
'Open' Faculty of Economic and Social Politics: G. LIENARD
Oriental Institute: B. COULIE

UNIVERSITÉ DE MONS-HAINAUT
(University of Mons-Hainaut)

20 place du Parc, 7000 Mons
Telephone: (65) 37-31-11
Fax: (65) 37-30-54
E-mail: martine.vanelslande@umh.ac.be
Internet: www.umh.ac.be

Founded 1965
Language of instruction: French
State control
Academic year: October to September

Rector: BERNARD LUX
Vice-Rector: MICHEL HECQ
Administrator: D. VINCE
Librarian: RENÉ PLISNIER

Number of teachers: 250
Number of students: 3,000

Publication: *UMH Dedicace* (4 a year)

DEANS

Faculty of Applied Economics: KARIN COMBLÉ
Faculty of Medicine and Pharmacy: HENRI ALEXANDRE
Faculty of Psychology and Educational Sciences: BERNARD HARMEGNIES
Faculty of Sciences: CATHERINE FINET

PROFESSORS

ALEXANDRE, H., Biology and Embryology
BELAYEW, A., Molecular Biology
BIEMONT, E., Astrophysics and Spectroscopy
BREDAS, J.-L., Chemistry of New Materials
BRIHAYE, Y., Theoretical Physics and Mathematics
BRUYÈRE, V., Theoretical Computer Science
BRUYNINCKX, H., Linguistics and Data Processing
CHERON, G., Electrophysiology
COMBLÉ-DARJA, K., Accountancy and Finance
COUVREUR, P., Applied Statistics
DANG, N. N., Probability and Statistics
DE CONINCK, J., Molecular Modelling
DEFRAITEUR, R., Fiscal System
DEPOVER, C., Moulding Technology
DESMET, H., Social and Community Psychology
DONNAY-RICHELLE, J., Clinical Psychology
DOSIERE, M., Physics and Chemistry of Polymers
DUBOIS, P., Polymeric and Composite Materials
DUFOUR, P., Computer Sciences
DUPONT, P., Methodology and Formation
ESCARMELLE, J.-F., Public Economy
FALMAGNE, P., Biological Chemistry
FINET, C., Mathematical Analysis
FORGES, G., Language Teaching
GILLIS, P., Experimental and Biological Physics
GOCZOL, J., Microeconomics and Marketing
GODAUX, E., Neurosciences
HARMEGNIES, B., Metrology in Psychology and Education
HECQ, M., Analytical and Inorganic Chemistry
HERQUET, P., Physics
ISAAC-VANDEPUTTE, M.-T., Historical Bibliography
JANGOUX, M., Marine Biology
LAUDE, L., Solid State Physics
LEBRUN-CARTON, C., Mathematics
LOWENTHAL, F., Cognitive Sciences
LUX, B., Company Management and Economics
MAGEROTTE, G., Education of the Handicapped
MAHY, B., Economic Analysis
MICHAUX, CH., Logic Mathematics
PAGANO, G., Public Finance and Management
PLATTEN, J., General Chemistry
POURTOIS, J.-P., Psychosociology of Family and School Education
RADOUX, C., Mathematics and Number Theory
RASMONT, P., Zoology
SAUSSEZ, S., Anatomy
SPILLEBOUDT-DETERCK, M., Finance
SPINDEL, P., Mechanics and Gravitation
STANDAERT, S., International Economic Analysis
TEGHEM-LORIS, J., Mathematics and Actuarial Science

THIRY, P., Management Information Science
TOUBEAU, G., Histology
TROESTLER, C., Numerical Analysis
VAN DAELE, A., Psychology of Labour
VAN HAVERBEKE, Y., Organic Chemistry
VANSNICK, J.-C., Quantitative Methods
VERHEVE, D., Chemical Technology
WAUTELET, H., Experimental Photonics
WIJSEN, J., Information Systems Science

ATTACHED INSTITUTES

Centre de Didactique des Sciences: 8 ave Maistriau, 7000 Mons; Dir PHILIPPE HERQUET.

Centre d'Informatique, de l'Audiovisuel et du Multimédia: 6 ave du Champ de Mars, 7000 Mons; Dir CHANTAL POIRET.

Ecole d'Interprètes Internationaux: Ave du Champ de Mars, 7000 Mons; tel. (65) 37-36-09; fax (65) 37-36-22; Dir ALAIN PIETTE.

Institut de Linguistique: 19 place du Parc, 7000 Mons; Dir BERNARD HARMEGNIES.

Institutions with University Status

FAÇULTÉ UNIVERSITAIRE DE THÉOLOGIE PROTESTANTE DE BRUXELLES/UNIVERSITAIRE FACULTEIT VOOR PROTESTANTSE GODGELEERDHEID TE BRUSSEL

40 rue des Bollandistes, 1040 Brussels
Telephone: (2) 735-67-46
Fax: (2) 735-47-31
E-mail: info@protestafac.ac.be
Internet: www.protestafac.ac.be

Founded 1942
Languages of instruction: French, Dutch
Private control (United Protestant Church)

Rector: W. WILLEMS
Chairman of Administrative Board: C. PEETERS
Dean of Dutch-speaking Section: J. WIERSMA
Dean of French-speaking Section: B. HORT
Secretary: A. JOUÉ
Librarian: E. EVRARD

Library of 41,134 vols
Number of teachers: 20
Number of students: 110

Publications: *Analecta Bruxellensia* (annually), *Belgische Protestantse Biografieën/Biographies Protestantes Belges* (quarterly), *FACtualité/FACtualiteit* (quarterly), *Programme et Horaire des Cours/Studiegids* (annually)

PROFESSORS

Dutch-speaking Section:
DE LANGE, J., Practical Theology
REIJNEN, A. M., Ethics
SMELIK, K., Old Testament Studies, Hebrew
TOMSON, P., New Testament Studies, Greek
WIERSMA, J., Dogmatics, Philosophy
WILLEMS, W., Church History, History of Dogma and 16th-century History

French-speaking Section:
HORT, B., Dogmatics, History of Philosophy and Religious Philosophy
MUTOMBO, F., Old Testament Studies and Hebrew
REIJNEN, A. M., Church History, Ethics
ROUVIÈRE, C., Practical Theology
VAN MOERE, R., New Testament Studies
WILLEMS, W., Church History and Methodology

FACULTÉ UNIVERSITAIRE DES SCIENCES AGRONOMIQUES DE GEMBLOUX

2 passage des Déportés, 5030 Gembloux
Telephone: (81) 62-21-11
Fax: (81) 62-25-20
E-mail: fsagx@fsagx.ac.be
Internet: www.fsagx.ac.be

Founded 1860, university status 1947
Language of instruction: French
State control
Academic year: September to June

Rector: A. THEWIS
Vice-Rector: J.-J. CLAUSTRIAUX
Dean: C. DEBOUCHE
Secretary: J. P. WATHELET

Library: see under Libraries
Number of teachers: 52
Number of students: 1,100

Publication: *BASE* (4 a year)

PROFESSORS

AUBINET, M., Physics
BAUDOIN, J.-P., Phytotechnology of Tropical Zones
BOCK, L., Soil Sciences
BODSON, M., General Horticulture
CHARLES, C., Applied Mathematics
CLAUSTRIAUX, J.-J., Statistics and Data Processing
CULOT, H., Microbial Ecology and Wastewater Treatment
DAUTREBANDE, S., Agricultural Hydraulics
DEBOUCHE, C., Fluid Mechanics and Environment
DOUCET, J. L., Tropical Forestry
DEROANNE, C., Food Technology, Organic and Biological Chemistry
DESTAIN, M.- F., Machinery and Construction
DU JARDIN, P., Plant Biology
FALISSE, A., Phytotechnology of Temperate Zones
FELTZ, C., Land Planning
HAUBRUGE, E., General and Applied Zoology
LEBAILLY, J.-P., Economics and Rural Development
LEPOIVRE, P., Phytopathology
LOGNAY, G., Analytical Chemistry
MAHY, G., Ecology
MARLIER, M., General and Organic Chemistry
PAQUOT, M., Industrial Biological Chemistry
PAUL, R., Environmental Toxicology
PORTETELLE, D., Animal and Microbial Biology
RONDEUX, J., Forest Management and Economics
THEWIS, A., Stockbreeding
THONART, P., Bio-industries
VERBRUGGE, J.-C., Strength of Materials, Agricultural Engineering Constructions

FACULTÉ POLYTECHNIQUE DE MONS

9 rue de Houdain, 7000 Mons
Telephone: (65) 37-41-11
Fax: (65) 37-42-00
E-mail: recteur@fpms.ac.be
Internet: www.fpms.ac.be

Founded 1837
Academic year: September to June

President of the Board: R. URBAIN
Rector: Prof. S. BOUCHER
Dean: Prof. J. HANTON

Library: see under Libraries
Number of teachers: 70
Number of students: 1,000

Publications: *Bulletin de l'AIMS* (monthly), *Mons Mines* (4 a year), *PolyTech News* (4 a year)

PROFESSORS

ANCIA, PH., Mining Engineering
BLONDEL, M., Electromagnetism and Telecommunications
BOUCHER, S., Theoretical Mechanics
BOUQUEGNEAU, C., General Physics
BROCHE, C., Electrotechnics
CONTI, C., Theoretical Mechanics
COUSSEMENT, G., Fluid Mechanics, Applied Mechanics
CRAPPE, R., Microelectronics
DE HAAN, A., General Chemistry, Electrochemistry
DE MEYER, M., Applied Chemistry and Biochemistry
DEHOMBREUX, P., Mechanical Engineering
DELHAYE, M., Electrotechnology
DELVOSALLE, C., Chemical and Biochemical Engineering
DUMORTIER, C., Metallurgy
DUPUIS, C., Geology
DURAND, Y., Mechanical Engineering
DUTOIT, T., Signals Processing
FILIPPI, E., Mechanical Engineering
FORTEMPS, P., Mathematics, Operational Research
FRÈRE, M., Thermodynamics
GUERLEMENT, G., Strength of Materials, Stability of Buildings
HANCQ, J., Signal Processing
HANTON, J., Fluid Mechanics, Applied Mechanics
LAMBLIN, D., Strength of Materials, Stability of Buildings
LAMQUIN, M., Electromagnetism and Telecommunications
LIBERT, G., Computer Science
LIÉNARD, PH., Metallurgy
LOBRY, J., Transport and Distribution of High-Voltage Electricity
LYBAERT, P., Heat Transfer
MACQ, D., Electronics
MANNEBACK, P., Computer Science
MEGRET, P., Electromagnetism and Telecommunications
MOINY, F., General Physics
PILATTE, A., Thermodynamics
PIRLOT, M., Mathematics, Operational Research
QUINIF, Y., Geology
REMY, M., Automation
RENGLET, M., Electronics
RENOTTE, CH., Automation
RIQUIER, Y., Metallurgy
SAUCEZ, PH., Mathematics, Operational Research
TEGHEM, J., Mathematics, Operational Research
TRÉCAT, J., Transport and Distribution of High-Voltage Electricity
TSHIBANGU, J. P., Mining Engineering
TUYTTENS, D., Mathematics, Operational Research
VANDER WOUWER, A., Automation
VANKERKEM, M., Business Administration
VERLINDEN, O., Theoretical Mechanics
WILQUIN, H., Architecture

FACULTÉS UNIVERSITAIRES CATHOLIQUES DE MONS

Chaussée de Binche 151, 7000 Mons
Telephone: (65) 32-32-11
Fax: (65) 31-56-91
E-mail: international@fucam.ac.be
Internet: www.fucam.ac.be

Founded 1896 as Institut Supérieur Commercial et Consulaire; university status 1965
Private control
Language of instruction: French
Academic year: October to September

Rector: Prof. CHRISTIAN DELPORTE
Vice-Rector: Prof. MICHEL DELATTRE

Number of teachers: 120
Number of students: 1,400
Courses in economics, management science and political science.

FACULTÉS UNIVERSITAIRES NOTRE-DAME DE LA PAIX

61 rue de Bruxelles, 5000 Namur
Telephone: (81) 72-41-11
Fax: (81) 23-03-91
E-mail: relations_exterieures@fundp.ac.be
Internet: www.fundp.ac.be

Founded 1831
Language of instruction: French
Academic year: September to June

Rector: M. SCHEUER
Secretary: R. LESUISSE
Chief Librarian: J. M. ANDRÉ

Library: see Libraries and Archives
Number of teachers: 210
Number of students: 4,100

DEANS

Faculty of Economics, Social Sciences and Management: P. WYNANTS
Faculty of Law: Y. POULLET
Faculty of Medicine: B. FLAMION
Faculty of Philosophy and Letters: M. PETERS
Faculty of Sciences: J. DELHALLE
Institute of Computer Science: J.-L. HAINAUT

PROFESSORS

Faculty of Economics, Social Sciences and Management (8 Rempart de la Vierge, 5000 Namur; tel. (81) 72-48-53; fax (81) 72-48-40; internet www.fundp.ac.be/eco/eco.html):

BALAND, J.-M., Development Economics
BERTELS, K., Information Management
BODART, F., Management Information Systems
COIPEL, M., Commercial Law
DE COMBBRUGGHE DE PICQUENDAELE, A., International Trade Project Evaluation
DESCHAMPS, R., Macro-economics
DUPLAT, J.-L., Fiscal Law
GLEJSER, H., Econometrics, International and Interregional Economics
GREGOIRE, P., Corporate Finance and Portfolio Management
HOTTE, L., Industrial Economics, Development Economics
JACQUEMIN, J.-C., International Trade, Methods of Economic Investigation
JACQUES, J.-M., Business Policy, International Strategy
JAUMOTTE, CH., Political Economy, Regional and Sectoral Economic Analysis
LEGRAND, M., Epistemology, Philosophical Anthropology
LESUISSE, R., Computer Science
LOUVEAUX, F., Mathematical Statistics, Mathematical Programming, Operations Research
MANIQUET, F., Micro-economics
MIGNOLET, M., Fiscal Policy and Business Strategies, Macro-economics
NIZET, J., Sociology
PLATTEAU, J.-PH., Economic Development, Institutional Economics
PLATTEN, I., Finance and Financial Modelling
REDING, P., Money and Banking, Monetary Theory and Policy, International Monetary Economics
RIGAUX, N., Sociology
SCHEPENS, G., Operations Management, Management Information Systems
VALOGNES, F., Advanced Mathematics
VAN WYMEERSCH, C., Managerial Finance, Business Forecasting, Accounting
VAN YPERSELE, T., Public Economics, Regional Economics
WALLEMACQ, A., Human Resources Management
WERY, P., European Law, Common Law, Private Economic Law
WUIDAR, J., Mathematics
WYNANTS, P., History

Faculty of Law:

BRACKELAIRE, J. L., Psychology
CHEFFERT, J. M., Micro-economics
COIPEL, N., Methodology and Legal Sources
COLSON, B., Political Sociology and Comparative History of Institutions
DIJON, X., Natural Law
FIERENS, J., Legal Methodology and Human Rights
HOTTE, L., Macro-economics
KIGANAHÉ, Criminal Law
POULLET, Y., Roman Law
ROBAYE, R., History of Private Law
THIRY, PH., General Theory of Knowledge and Philosophy
THUNIS, X., Comparative Law and Law of Obligation
VUYE, H., Constitutional Law, Dutch Legal Terminology
WÉRY, P., General Principles of Private Law
WYNANTS, B., Introduction to Sociology
WYNANTS, P., History of Belgian Institutions: Modern and Contemporary History

Faculty of Medicine (place du Palais de Justice, 5000 Namur; tel. (81) 72-43-47; internet www.fundp.ac.be/medecine):

BOSLY, A., Immunology
DONCKIER, J., Endocrinology
DULIEU, J., Human Anatomy
FLAMION, B., Physiology, Pharmacology
GOFFINET, A., Special Physiology
HÉRIN, M., Histology, Embryology
JADOT, M., Human Biochemistry, General Biochemistry
LALOUX, P., Physiopathology
MARCHANOL, E., Human Physiology
MERCIER, M., Psychology and Medical Psychology
PIRONT, A., General Physiology
POUMAY, Y., General Histology
TRIGAUX, J. P., Radiological Anatomy
VANDERPAS, J., Epidemiology
ZECH, F., Microbiology

Faculty of Philosophy and Letters (1 rue J. Grafé, 5000 Namur; tel. (81) 72-42-04; fax (81) 72-42-03; internet www.fundp.ac.be/philo_lettres):

ALLARD, A., Classical Philology
BOSSE, A., German and Comparative Literature
BRACKELAIRE, J.-L., Psychology
BURNEZ, L., Prehistoric Art, Archaeology
DELABASTITA, D., English, General and Comparative Literature
DE RUYT, C., History of Ancient Art, Archaeology
DOYEN, A.-M., Greek Language and Literature
GANTY, E., Modern Philosophy
GIOT, J., French Linguistics
HANTSON, A., English Language, Linguistics
LEGROS, G., Romance Philology, Theory of Literature
LEIJNSE, E., Dutch, General and Comparative Literature
LENOIR, Y., History of Music
MARCHETTI, P., Classical Philology, Antiquity and Latin Authors
MORENO, P., Italian Language
NOËL, R., Medieval History
PETERS, M., German Language, Linguistics
PHILIPPART, G., Medieval History
RIZZERIO, L., Ancient Philosophy
SAUVAGE, P., History of the 19th and 20th Centuries
SELDESLACHTS, H., Latin Language, Greek and Latin Linguistics
VANDEN BEMDEN, Y., History of Post-Classical Art, Archaeology
VAN DEN BERGHE, K., Spanish Language
WEISSHAUPT, J., Dutch Language, Linguistics
WYNANTS, P., History of Belgian Institutions

Faculty of Sciences (61 rue de Bruxelles, 5000 Namur; tel. (81) 72-73-74; fax (81) 72-53-06; internet www.fundp.ac.be/sciences):

ANDRE, J.-M., Quantum Chemistry, Physical Chemistry
B'NAGY, J., General Chemistry, Spectroscopy
BLANQUET, GH., Molecular Infrared Spectroscopy and General Physics
BODART, F., Experimental Physics, Atomic and Nuclear Physics
CALLIER, F., Differential and Integral Calculus, Graph Theory
DE BOLLE, X., Statistics, Biostatistics, Bioinformatics
DELHALLE, J., General Chemistry
DEMORTIER, G., X-ray Physics, General Physics and Nuclear Physics
DEPIEREUX, E., Statistics, Biostatistics, Bioinformatics
DESCY, J.-P., Ecology
DEVOS, P., Endocrinology and Zoology
DUCHENE, J., Philosophy of Science
DURANT, F., Radiocrystallography and General Chemistry
EVRARD, G., Radiocrystallography
GIFFROY, J.-M., Anatomy, Embryology and Ethology of Animals
HALLET, V., Mineralogy, Geology
HARDY, A., Mathematics and Statistics
HENRARD, J., Mathematics, Celestial Mechanics, Astronomy
HEVESI, L., Organic Chemistry
HOUSSIAU, L., Experimental Physics, Thermodynamics
KESTEMONT, P., Ecology
KRIEF, A., Organic Chemistry
LAMBERT, D., Philosophy of Science
LAMBERTS, L., Analytical Chemistry
LAMBIN, P., Analytical Mechanics, Theoretical Physics
LETESSON, J. J., Microbiology, Immunology
LUCAS, A., Theoretical Solid State Physics and Quantum Physics
MAES, A., Mathematics, Differential and Integral Calculus
MASEREEL, B., Pharmaceutical Sciences, Biochemistry and Cytology
MEKHALIF, Z., General Chemistry, Physical Chemistry, Polymers
MESSIAEN, J., General Biology, Vegetal Physiology
MICHA, J.-CL., Ecology
NGUYEN, V. H., Differential and Integral Calculus, Optimization and Applied Mathematics
ORBAN-FERAUGE, F., Geography, Cartography
PAQUAY, R., Animal Physiology
PIREAUX, J.-J., Experimental Physics, Atomic and Molecular Physics
PIRSON, P., Methodology of Chemistry
RAES, M., Biochemistry
RASSON, J.-P., Probabilities
REMACLE, J., Biochemistry
REMON, M., Programming Statistics
ROUSSELET, D., Methodology of Biology
SCHNEIDER, M., Methodology of Mathematics
STOIKEN, R., Physics, Electronics
STRODIOT, J.-J., Optimization
SU, B. L., General Chemistry
THILL, G., Philosophy of Science
THIRAN, J.-P., Numerical Analysis
THIRY, P., Solid State Physics, General Physics

TOINT, PH., Algebra, Numerical Analysis
VAN CUTSEM, P., Biotechnology
VANDENHAUTE, J., Genetics
VERCAUTEREN, D., General Chemistry, Kinetics, Physical Chemistry
VIGNERON, J.-P., Solid State Physics

Institute of Computer Science (21 rue Grandgagnage, 5000 Namur; tel. (81) 72-49-66; fax (81) 72-49-67; internet www.info.fundp.ac.be):

BERLEUR, J., Informatics and Sciences, Informatics and Rationality (Epistemological questions), Informatics and Society
BODART, F., Information Systems Design, Decision Support System, User/Machine Interface Engineering
BONAVENTURE, O., Computer Architecture, Computer Networks
FICHEFET, J., Graph Theory, Linear Programming, Numerical Analysis, Operations Research, Multicriteria Decision Aid, Management
HABRA, N., Software Engineering, Software Development
HAINAUT, J. L., Database Technology, Database Design, Database Engineering
JACQUET, J.-M., Programming Methodology, Programming Projects, Artificial Intelligence Techniques, Theory of Programming Languages
LE CHARLIER, B., Programming Methodology, Theory of Programming Languages, Abstract Interpretation
LECLERCQ, J.-P., Scientific Methods and Applications, Graph Theory
LESUISSE, R., Organization Design, Strategic Management and Information Systems, Organization Theory
LOBET-MARIS, C., Organization Theories, Psychological Aspects of Information Systems, Communication
NOIRHOMME-FRAITURE, M., Stochastic Processes, Simulation of Systems, Data Mining and Database Analysis, Performance Models and Evaluation
RAMAEKERS, J., Operating Systems, Performance and Measurement of Computer Systems, Computer System Reliability and Security, Operating Systems
SCHOBBENS, P.-Y., Artificial Intelligence Techniques, Automatic Testing and Program Testing, Artificial Intelligence in DSSs, Language Theory

FACULTÉS UNIVERSITAIRES SAINT-LOUIS

43 blvd du Jardin Botanique, 1000 Brussels
Telephone: (2) 211-78-11
Fax: (2) 211-79-97
E-mail: webmaster@fusl.ac.be
Internet: www.fusl.ac.be

Founded 1858
Language of instruction: French
Academic year: October to May

Rector: J. P. LAMBERT
Vice-Rector: F. OST

Library: see Libraries and Archives
Number of teachers: 82
Number of students: 1,200

Publications: *Revue interdisciplinaire d'Etudes Juridiques* (2 a year), *Revue internationale des droits de l'Antiquité*

DEANS

Faculty of Economic, Social and Political Sciences: M. HUBERT
Faculty of Law: H. DUMONT
Faculty of Philosophy and Letters: J. P. NANDRIN

PROFESSORS

Faculty of Economic, Social and Political Sciences:

BERTRAND, P., Physics
CALLUT, J. P., English Language
CITTA-VANTHEMSCHE, M., Mathematics
D'ASPREMONT LYNDEN, C., Philosophy and Social Sciences
DE KERCHOVE DE DENTERGHEM, A. M., Economics
DEPRINS, D., Statistics
DE RONGE, Y., Accountancy
DE SAINT-GEORGES, P., Social Communication
DE STEXHE, G., Philosophy and Ethics
EVERAERT-DESMEDT, N., Semiology
FRANCK, C., Political Science
GILLARDIN, J., Introduction to Law
GUERRA, F., Accountancy
HARDY, A., Mathematics
HUBERT, M., Sociology
LAMBERT, J. P., Economics
LECLERCQ, N. C., Civil Law
LEPERS, A., Accountancy
LOUTE, E., Mathematics and Computer Science
MARQUET, J., Sociology
MITCHELL, J., Economics
RIGAUX, M.-F., Introduction to Law, Public Law
SERVAIS, P., Economic and Social History
SIMAR, L., Statistics
SOETE, J. L., Contemporary History
SONVEAUX, E., Chemistry
STREYDIO, J. M., Physics
STRODIOT, J. J., Mathematics
TULKENS, H., Political Economy
VAN CAMPENHOUDT, L., Sociology
VAN RILLAER, J., Social and Industrial Psychology
VERHOEVEN, J., International Law
WIBAUT, S., Political Economy
WITTERWULGHE, R., Political Economy

Faculty of Law:

CARTUYVELS, Y., Introduction to Law
DE BROUWER, J. L., Political Science
DE JEMEPPE, B., Dutch Language
DE THEUX, A., Introduction to Law
DEVILLE, A., Sociology
DILLENS, A. M., Philosophy
DUMONT, H., Public Law
GERARD, P., Introduction to Law
HANARD, G., Roman Law
JACOB, R., Private Law
LORIAUX, C., English
MAHIEU, M., Introduction to Law
NANDRIN, J. P., History
OST, F., Introduction to Law
SEGERS, M. J., Psychology
STROWEL, A., Introduction to Law
VAN DE KERCHOVE, M., Introduction to Law
VAN GEHUCHTEN, P. P., Law
WANTHY, X., Political Economy

Faculty of Philosophy and Letters:

BOUSSET, H., Dutch Authors and Literature
BRAIVE, J., History
BRISART, R., Philosophy
CAUCHIES, J. M., History
CHEYNS, A., Greek Philology and Authors
CUPERS, J.-L., English Authors and Literature
DAUCHY, S., History
DE RUYT, C., Ancient History and History of Art
DUCHESNE, J.-P., History of Art
HEIDERSCHEIDT, J., English Phonetics and Grammar
JONGEN, R., German Phonetics and Grammar, Linguistics
LENOBLE-PINSON, M., Modern French Grammar, Philology
LEONARDY, E., German Literature
LOGE, T., French Literature
LONGREE, D., Latin Philology and Authors
MAESCHALCK, M., Philosophy
MARRANT, A., Latin Authors
MATTENS, W., Dutch Grammar and Philology
RENARD, M. C., French Authors, Modern Literatures, Italian and Spanish
TOCK, B. M., History
WILLEMS, M., Medieval French Literature
XHARDEY, D., History of Greek and Latin Literature and Greek Philology

ATTACHED INSTITUTE

Ecole des Sciences Philosophiques et Religieuses: Brussels; f. 1925; Pres. A.-M. DIBLEUR; 10 teachers; 230 students.

LIMBURGS UNIVERSITAIR CENTRUM

Universitaire Campus, Gebouw D, 3590 Diepenbeek
Telephone: (11) 26-81-11
Fax: (11) 26-81-99
E-mail: luc-rect@luc.ac.be
Internet: www.luc.ac.be

Founded 1971
Private control; state-aided
Academic year: October to July

Chairman: T. KELCHTERMANS
Vice-Chairman: L. GELDERS
Rector: L. DE SCHEPPER
Vice-Rector: M. VAN HAEGENDOREN
Permanent Secretary: W. GOETSTOUWERS
Librarian: L. EGGHE

Number of teachers: 110 (full-time)
Number of students: 2,116

DEANS

Faculty of Applied Economics: G. HEEREN
Faculty of Medicine: E. VAN KERKHOVE
Faculty of Sciences: E. NAUWELAERTS

HEADS OF DEPARTMENTS

Basic Medical Sciences: M. VANDERSTEEN
Chemistry, Biology and Geology: D. VANDERZANDE
Economics and Law: T. THEWYS
Human Sciences and Languages: W. CLIJSTERS
Management: K. VANHOOF
Mathematics, Physics and Informatics: G. MOLENBERGHS

INSTITUTES OF THE UNIVERSITY

Biomedical Research Institute: Dir P. STINISSEN.

Centre for Environmental Sciences: Dir J. VANGRONSVELD.

Centre for Statistics: Dir G. MOLENBERGHS.

Expertise Centre for Digital Media: Dir E. FLERACKERS.

Institute for Materials Research: Dir L. DE SCHEPPER.

Institute of Social and Economic Sciences: Dir M. VAN HAEGENDOREN.

KIZOK–Institute for Entrepreneurship and SMEs: Dir W. VANHAVERBEKE.

Transportation Research Institute: Dir G. WETS.

ATTACHED INSTITUTES

IMOMEC: Dir H. MARTENS.

Science Park Limburg: Dir I. BREESCH.

WTCM: Scientific Consultant H. MARTENS.

University Level Institutions

COLLEGE OF EUROPE

Dijver 11, 8000 Bruges
Telephone: (50) 47-71-11
Fax: (50) 47-71-10
E-mail: info@coleurop.be
Internet: www.coleurop.be
Founded 1949; institute of postgraduate European studies
Languages of instruction: English, French
Academic year: September to June
President of Board of Trustees: JEAN-LUC DEHAENE
Rector: Prof. PAUL DEMARET
Librarian: JOHN MILLER
Library of 100,000 vols
Number of teachers: 140
Number of students: 360
Publication: *Collegium*

DIRECTORS

Department of Administration: D. MAHNCKE
Department of Development of Human Resources: R. PICHT
Department of Economics: J. TINBERGEN
Department of Law: I. GOVAERE
Programme of European General and Interdisciplinary Studies: R. PICHT

CAMPUS IN POLAND

College of Europe: ul. Nowoursynowska 84, Box 120, 02-797 Warsaw 78; tel. (22) 545-94-01; fax (22) 649-13-52; e-mail info@natolin.edu.pl; Dir PIOTR NOWINA-KONOPKA.

ÉCOLE DES HAUTES ÉTUDES COMMERCIALES

14 rue Louvrex, 4000 Liège
Telephone: (4) 232-72-11
Fax: (4) 232-72-40
E-mail: info@hec.be
Internet: www.hec.be
Founded 1898
Language of instruction: French
Academic year: September to June
President: YVES NOEL
Director-General: M. DUBRU
Academic Director: LOUIS ESCH
Secretary-General: JACQUES DEFER
Librarian: M.A. THOMAS
Library of 12,000 vols
Number of teachers: 217
Number of students: 1,620

HEADS OF DEPARTMENTS

Economics: M. HERMANS
Finance and Law: M. RENOUPREZ
Management: J. ROBERT
Languages: L. NACHTERGAELE
Operations: D. DUBOIS

ECONOMISCHE HOGESCHOOL SINT-ALOYSIUS

Stormstraat 2 , 1000 Brussels
Telephone: (2) 210-12-11
Fax: (2) 217-64-64
E-mail: info@ehsal.be
Internet: www.ehsal.be
Founded 1925
Languages of instruction: Dutch, English
Academic year: September to June
A university-level school of economics
Director: Prof. Dr D. DE CEULAER
Number of teachers: 150
Number of students: 5,000
Publications: *Arcade* (in Dutch), *In4you* (information for students, in Dutch and English), *International programme brochures* (in English)

DEAN

Department of Economics and Management: WALTER PLATTEAU

DIRECTOR

Centre for External Co-operation: INGEBORG VANDENBULCKE

ERASMUSHOGESCHOOL-BRUSSEL

Nijverheidskaai 170, 1070 Brussels
Telephone: (2) 523-37-37
E-mail: info@ehb.be
Internet: www.ehb.be
Founded 1991 by the amalgamation of the Administratieve en Economische Hogeschool (f. 1938) and the School for Translators and Interpreters (f. 1958)
Language of instruction: Dutch, but multilingual for postgraduate studies
Private control
Director-General and Delegate Administrator: H.-J. VERMEYLEN
Assistant Director: J. TERWECOREN
Publications: *Tijdschrift voor Bestuurswetenschappen en Publike Recht* (monthly), *Medium—Tijdschrift voor Toegepaste Taalwetenschap* (3 a year).

FACULTEIT VOOR VERGELIJKENDE GODSDIENSTWETENSCHAPPEN (Faculty for Comparative Study of Religions)

Bist 164, 2610 Antwerp (Wilrijk)
Telephone: (3) 830-51-58
Fax: (3) 825-26-73
E-mail: info@antwerpfvg.org
Internet: www.antwerpfvg.org
Founded by Royal Decree in 1980
Languages of instruction: Dutch, English
Languages of instruction: German, French
Academic year: October to June
Chairman of Board: JEREMY ROSEN
Rector: CHRISTIAAN J. G VONCK
Deans: LYDIA BONTE, JAMNADAS GOHIL, Frank STAPPAERTS
Joint Librarians: WU JEN, EDDY VAN LAERHOVEN, HUGO PEERLINCK, CHRISTIAN VANDEKERKHOVE
Library of 30,000 vols
Number of teachers: 44
Number of students: 84
Publication: *Acta Comparanda* (annual)
An int. univ.-level org for the comparative study of religions.

PROFESSORS

BOCKEN, I., Gnosticism
BRIOT, P., Philosophy
DETHIER, H., Humanism
GERDING, H., Parapsycholological Approach in Religion
KAPOOR, S., Sikhism
KERSTEN, H., Bahá'í
KUMAR, V., Indology
MERTENS, H., Christianity
PEEL, K. A., Buddhism
ROSEN, J., Judaism
SHAH, N., Jainism
TAYLOR, FR., American Natives
VAN DEN BROECK, L., Islam
VONCK, CH., Protestantism

HAUTE ÉCOLE DE BRUXELLES

34 rue Joseph Hazard, 1180 Brussels
Telephone: (2) 340-12-95
Fax: (2) 347-52-64
E-mail: heb@heb.be
Internet: www.heb.be
Academic year: September to June
President and Director: JEAN-MARIE VAN DER MEERSCHEN
Librarians: J. P. GAHIDE, O. GALMA
Library of 45,000 vols
Number of teachers: 189
Number of students: 2,200
Publication: *Équivalences* (2 a year)

DIRECTORS

Institute of Economics and Technology: MARIANNE COESSENS
Institute of Teacher-Training: LUC BARBAY
Institute of Translating and Interpreting: FRANS DE LAET

HOGER INSTITUUT VOOR ARCHITECTUURWETENSCHAPPEN HENRY VAN DE VELDE (Henry van de Velde Higher Institute for Architectural Sciences)

Mutsaardstraat 31, 2000 Antwerp
Telephone: (3) 205-71-70
Fax: (3) 226-04-11
E-mail: designsciences@ha.be
Internet: www.ontwerpwetenschappen.be
Founded 1663 by Teniers; independent 1952
Publication: *Antwerp Design Sciences Cahiers (ADSC)* (every 6 months).

INSTITUT CATHOLIQUE DES HAUTES ÉTUDES COMMERCIALES

2 blvd Brand Whitlock, 1200 Brussels
Telephone: (2) 739-37-11
Fax: (2) 739-38-03
E-mail: communication@ichec.be
Internet: www.ichec.be
Founded 1934
Languages of instruction: French, Dutch, English
Rector: CHRISTIAN OST
President: E. DAVIGNON
General Secretary: P. FLAHAUT
Librarian (vacant)
Library of 16,000 vols
Number of teachers: 170
Number of students: 2,000
Publication: *Reflets et Perspectives de la Vie Economique*

HEADS OF DEPARTMENTS

Auditing: P. LURKIN
Commercial Engineering: G. JANNES
Finance: P. VAN NAMEN
Human Resources Management: C. DE BRIER
Information Science: J.-M. PONCELET
International Economics: E. CRACCO
Marketing: R. SAINTROND

ATTACHED SCHOOLS

Ecole Supérieure des Sciences Fiscales: 2 blvd Brand Whitlock, 1150 Brussels; f. 1958; library of 2,000 vols; 28 teachers; 200 students; Pres. Prof. P. DUPRIEZ; Librarian M.-C. SIBILLE-VAN GRIEKEN.

INSTITUT COOREMANS

11 place Anneessens, 1000 Brussels
Telephone: (2) 551-02-10
Fax: (2) 551-02-16
Internet: www.brunette.brucity.be/ferrer/eco
Founded 1911
Academic year: September to June
Language of instruction: French (English in some postgraduate programmes)
President: P. LAMBERT

Dean: L. COOREMANS
Number of teachers: 80
Number of students: 400
Courses at bachelors and masters degree level in commerce and administration
Publication: *ECOO* (4 a year).

INSTITUT GRAMME LIÈGE INSTITUT SUPÉRIEUR INDUSTRIEL

28 quai du Condroz, 4030 Angleur (Liège)
Telephone: (4) 340-34-30
Fax: (4) 343-30-28
E-mail: secr.direction@gramme.hemes.be
Internet: www.gramme.be
Founded 1906
Language of instruction: French
Director: JEAN-PIERRE POSTULA
Librarian: NICOLE GRAVIER
Library of 11,528 vols
Number of teachers: 64
Number of students: 480
Courses in industrial engineering
Publications: *Nouvelles de l'Union Gramme* (quarterly), *Annuaire*.

INSTITUT SUPÉRIEUR D'ARCHITECTURE DE LA COMMUNAUTÉ FRANÇAISE — LA CAMBRE

19 place Eugène Flagey, 1050 Brussels
Telephone: (2) 640-96-96
Fax: (2) 647-46-55
E-mail: isacf@lacambre-archi.org
Internet: www.lacambre-archi.be
Founded 1926
State control
Language of instruction: French
Director: Prof. J.-L. GENARD
Deputy Director: Dr GUY PILATE
Head of Academic Affairs (vacant)
Librarian: MARIE-MICHÈLE BOSMANS
Library of 8,000 vols.

INSTITUT SUPÉRIEUR D'ARCHITECTURE INTERCOMMUNAL (ISAI)

Site Victor Horta, CP 248, Blvd du Triomphe, 1050 Brussels
Telephone: (2) 650-50-52
Fax: (2) 650-50-93
E-mail: isahorta@ulb.ac.be
Internet: horta.ulb.ac.be
Founded 1711; associated with Free University of Brussels and schools of architecture at Liège and Mons (ISAI)
Language of instruction: French
Director: GERARD VAN GOOLEN
Library of 30,000 vols
Number of teachers: 60
Number of students: 650
Publication: *I.S.A.Br* (monthly)
Courses in architecture, urban design, restoration and heritage conservation.

LESSIUS HOGESCHOOL

Jozef de Bomstraat 11, 2018 Antwerp
Telephone: (3) 206-04-80
Fax: (3) 206-04-99
E-mail: paul.pauwels@lessius-ho.be
Internet: www.lessius-ho.be
Founded 2000 following the merger of Handelshogeschool (f. 1923) and Katholieke Vlaamse Hogeschool (f. 1919)
Language of instruction: Dutch
Academic year: October to July
Vice-Chancellor: Prof. Dr FLORA CARRIJN
Dean of Academic Affairs: Prof. Dr PAUL PAUWELS
Number of teachers: 300
Number of students: 2,800

HEADS OF DEPARTMENTS

Applied Language Studies: Prof. Dr FRIEDA STEURS
Applied Psychology: Prof. Dr HUGO SCHOUPPE
Business Studies: Prof. Dr PAUL VERHEYEN
Speech Therapy and Audiology: KRIS LAMBERS

PRINS LEOPOLD INSTITUUT VOOR TROPISCHE GENEESKUNDE/ INSTITUT DE MÉDECINE TROPICALE PRINCE LÉOPOLD (Prince Leopold Institute for Tropical Medicine)

Nationalestraat 155, 2000 Antwerp
Telephone: (3) 247-66-66
Fax: (3) 216-14-31
E-mail: dvmelle@itg.be
Internet: www.itg.be
Founded 1906, Royal Decree 1931
Languages of instruction: Dutch, French, English
Academic year: September to July
President: C. PAULUS
Director: Prof. Dr B. GRYSEELS
Administrative Director: L. SCHUEREMANS
Librarian: D. SCHOONBAERT
The library contains 30,000 books and 15,000 pamphlets
Number of teachers: 30
Number of students: 300 postgraduates
Publication: *Journal of Tropical Medicine and International Health* (monthly)

PROFESSORS

BERKVENS, D., Animal Health
BRANDT, J., Helminthology
BUSCHER, PH., Serology
COLEBUNDERS, B., Clinical Services
COOSEMANS, M., Entomology
CRIEL, B., Public Health
D'ALESSANDRO, U., Parasitology
DE BROUWERE, V., Public Health
DE MUYNCK, A., Epidemiology
GEERTS, S., Veterinary Pathology
GRYSEELS, B., Medical Helminthology
KEGELS, G., Public Health
KESTENS, L., Immunology
KOLSTEREN, P., Nutrition and Child Health
LAGA, M., Epidemiology, Sexually-transmitted Diseases
LE RAY, D., Protozoology
PORTAELS, F., Microbiology
SWINNE, D., Mycology
UNGER, J. P., Public Health
VAN DEN ENDE, J., Tropical Pathology
VAN DER GROEN, G., Virology
VAN DER STUYFT, P., Epidemiology, Public Health
VAN GOMPEL, A., Tropical Pathology
VAN LERBERGHE, W., Public Health
VERVOORT, T., Clinical Sciences

ATTACHED INSTITUTE

Leopold II Kliniek: Kronenburgstraat 43, 2000 Antwerp; tropical and travel medicine; treats sexually-transmitted diseases; Dir Dr F. VAN GOMPEL.

VLERICK LEUVEN GENT MANAGEMENT SCHOOL

Ghent campus: Bellevue 6, 9050 Ghent
Leuven campus: Vlamingenstraat 83, 3000 Leuven/ Louvain
Telephone: (9) 210-97-11
Fax: (9) 210-97-00
E-mail: info@vlerick.be
Internet: www.vlerick.be
Founded 1953
Academic year: September to July
Associated with the Autonomous Management School of Ghent University and Katholieke Universiteit Leuven
Dean: Prof. ROLAND VAN DIERDONCK
Librarian: ALEC VUIJLSTEKE
Library of 11,000 books and 135 serials
Number of teachers: 60
Number of students: 370 undergraduate students
Number of students: 4,000 executives

PROFESSORS

(The list indicates whether the professor holds a position at either Katholieke Universiteit Leuven or Ghent University)

Accounting and Finance:
- BRUGGEMAN, W. (Ghent University)
- KEULENEER, L. (Katholieke Universiteit Leuven and Ghent University)
- MANIGART, S. (Ghent University)
- OOGHE, H. (Ghent University)
- ROODHOOFT, F. (Katholieke Universiteit Leuven)
- VAN HULLE, C. (Katholieke Universiteit Leuven)
- VANTHIENEN, L.
- WILLEKENS, M. (Katholieke Universiteit Leuven)

Entrepreneurship, Governance and Strategy:
- BEGHIN, P. (Ghent University)
- BOUCKAERT, L. (Katholieke Universiteit Leuven)
- CRIJNS, H. (Ghent University)
- DE BONDT, R. (Katholieke Universiteit Leuven)
- HASPESLAGH, P. (Ghent University)
- LINT, O.
- SLEUWAEGAN, L. (Katholieke Universiteit Leuven)
- VAN DEN BERGHE, L. (Ghent University)
- VEUGELERS, R. (Katholieke Universiteit Leuven)

Marketing:
- DE WULF, K. (Ghent University)
- GEUENS, M. (Ghent University)
- MUYLLE, S.
- VAN OSSEL, G.
- VANDEN ABEELE, P. (Katholieke Universiteit Leuven)

Operations and Technology Management:
- CLARYSSE, B. (Ghent University)
- DE MEYER, A.
- DEBACKERE, K. (Katholieke Universiteit Leuven)
- DESCHOOLMEESTER, D. (Ghent University)
- DIRICKX, Y. (Katholieke Universiteit Leuven)
- GEMMEL, P. (Ghent University)
- VANTHIENEN, J. (Katholieke Universiteit Leuven)
- VEREECKE, A. (Ghent University)

People and Organization:
- BOUWEN, R.
- BUELENS, M. (Ghent University)
- BUYENS, D. (Ghent University)
- DEVOS, G.
- TAILLIEU, T. (Katholieke Universiteit Leuven)
- VAN DEN BROECK, H. (Ghent University)
- VAN POUCKE, D. (Ghent University)
- VANDERHEYDEN, K.

Colleges

Ecole Royale Militaire/Koninklijke Militaire School: 30 ave de la Renaissance, 1000

Brussels; tel. (2) 737-60-01; fax (2) 737-60-32; internet www.rma.ac.be; f. 1834; academic education of officers for Army, Navy, Air Force, Medical Service and Gendarmerie; languages of instruction: French, Dutch; 117 teachers; 900 students; library: 100,000 vols; Dir, Academic Studies Col.-Adm JEAN MARSIA; Dir of Support Maj. EDDY DELPORTE; Library Dir RITA LAMOTE

PROFESSORS

ACHEROY, M. P. J., Electrical Engineering
BAUDOIN, Y., Applied Mecanics
BISSCHOP, H., General Chemistry
BOSSCHAERTS, W., Applied Mechanics
BOURGOIS, R. A., Construction Engineering
DE BISSCHOP, H., Chemistry
DECUYPERE, R. H., Applied Mechanics
DE VOS, L., History
LEFEBVRE, M., Applied Chemistry
LEYSEN, J., Economics and Management
MANIGART, R., Sociology
PASTYN, H. J., Mathematics and Operations Research
SCHWEICHER, E. J. P., Opto-electronics
STRUYS, W. R., Economics
THOMAS, FR., Law
VAN HAMME, J., Mathematics
VANTOMME, J., Construction Engineering
VLOEBERGHS, C., Telecommunications
WEYNANTS, R., Physics

Horeca en Sportinstituut Wemmel: Zijp 14–16, 1780 Wemmel; tel. (2) 456-01-01; fax (2) 456-51-91; e-mail kta.hsiw.wemmel@rago.be; internet schoolweb.rago.be/kta/wemmel; Dir NORA DE CALUWÉ (acting).

Institut des Hautes Études de Belgique: 44 ave Jeanne, 1050 Brussels; f. 1894; language of instruction: French; courses in natural sciences, mechanics, history, philosophy, arts and letters, economics, social and political sciences; Pres. S. HUYBERECHTS; Gen. Sec. G. SAMUEL..

Attached school:

Ecole d'Ergologie: 50 ave F. D. Roosevelt, 1050 Brussels; f. 1925; Dir J. HOFMANS.

Institut Libre Marie Haps: 11 rue d'Arlon, 1050 Brussels; tel. (2) 511-92-92; fax (2) 511-98-37; e-mail information@ilmh.be; internet www.ilmh.be; f. 1919; two- and three-year courses for translators and interpreters; three-year courses in psychology and speech therapy, audiology; languages of instruction: Dutch, English; languages of instruction: German, French; languages of instruction: Italian, Russian; languages of instruction: Spanish, Chinese; languages of instruction: Turkish, Arabic; library: 17,700 vols; 161 teachers; 1,500 students; Dir C. CAMPOLINI; Sec.-Gen. B. QUOILIN-CLAUDE; Librarian M. VAN LIL; publ. *Le langage et l'homme* (3 a year).

Koninklijke Belgische Marine Academie/Académie Royale de Marine de Belgique: Steenplein 1, 2000 Antwerp; tel. (3) 232-08-50; f. 1935; Pres CHRISTIAN KONINCKX; Sec.-Gen. LIONEL TRICOT; publs *Mededelingen, Communications* (annually).

Schools of Music, Art and Architecture

Académie Royale des Beaux-Arts de Bruxelles (Brussels Royal Academy of Fine Arts): 144 rue du Midi, 1000 Brussels; tel. (2) 511-04-91; fax (2) 513-27-54; e-mail info@aca-bxl.be; internet www.aca-bxl.be; f. 1711; drawing, painting, sculpture, interior design, illustration, publicity and visual communication, engraving, tapestry-textile creation, environmental art; 80 teachers; 450 students; library: see Libraries and Archives; Dir M. BAUDSON.

Conservatoire Royal de Bruxelles: 30 rue de la Régence, 1000 Brussels; tel. (2) 511-04-27; fax (2) 512-69-79; e-mail administration@conservatoire.be; internet www.conservatoire.be; f. 1832; library: 1,000,000 vols; 250 teachers; 500 students; Dir FRÉDÉRIC DE ROOS; Librarian PAUL PROSPÉ.

Conservatoire Royal de Musique de Liège: 14 rue Forgeur, Liège; tel. (4) 222-03-06; fax (4) 222-03-84; f. 1826; 80 professors; students taken from 15 years of age; all branches of music and theatre; Dir B. DEKAISE; Admin. Sec. CLAUDETTE VAN HOLSAET; Librarian PHILIPPE GILSON.

Conservatoire Royal de Musique de Mons: 7 rue de Nimy, 7000 Mons; tel. (65) 34-73-77; fax (65) 34-99-06; f. 1926; 420 students; library: 30,000 vols; Dir HENRI BARBIER.

Ecole Nationale Supérieure des Arts Visuels de la Cambre: Abbaye de La Cambre 21, 1000 Brussels; tel. (2) 648-96-19; fax (2) 640-96-93; e-mail lacambre@lacambre.be; internet www.lacambre.be; f. 1926; library: see Libraries and Archives; 500 students; Dir CAROLINE MIEROP.

Hogeschool Antwerpen, Herman Teirlinck Instituut: Maarschalk Gérardstraat 4, 2000 Antwerp; tel. (3) 231-54-65; fax (3) 232-22-34; e-mail hti@ha.be; internet www.teirlinckinstituut.be; f. 1946; 4-year full-time academic education and professional training in theatre and related performing arts; Dir JOHAN VAN ASSCHE.

Insas (Institut National Supérieur des Arts du Spectacle et Techniques de Diffusion): Rue Thérésienne 8, 1000 Brussels; tel. (2) 511-92-86; fax (2) 511-02-79; e-mail sec@insas.be; internet www.insas.be; f. 1962 for advanced studies in dramatic art, cinema and broadcasting technique, including television; 3- and 4-year courses; Dir J. P. CASIMIR.

Koninklijk Vlaams Conservatorium Antwerpen (Royal Flemish Conservatoire Antwerp): Desguinlei 25, 2018 Antwerp; tel. (3) 244-18-00; fax (3) 238-90-17; e-mail secr@ha.be; internet www.conservatorium.be; f. 1898; languages of instruction: Dutch, English; languages of instruction: German, French; library: 600,000 vols; 180 teachers; 350 students; Principal PASCALE DE GROOTE; Admin. Sec. ROGER QUADFLIEG; Librarian JAN DEWILDE.

Nationaal Hoger Instituut en Koninklijke Academie voor Schone Kunsten-Antwerpen (National Higher Institute and Royal Academy of Fine Arts, Antwerp): Mutsaertstraat 31, 2000 Antwerp; tel. (3) 232-41-61; f. 1663; awards first and Master's degrees; 100 staff; library: 20,000 vols and prints, 250 periodicals; Dir G. GAUDAEN; Scientific Librarian Dr G. PERSOONS..

BELIZE

The Higher Education System

The main institution of higher education is the University of Belize, which was established in 2000 as an amalgam of six previously existing institutions. There is also an extra-mural branch of the University of the West Indies in Belize.

Admission to university is on the basis of GCE A-level or Caribbean Advanced Proficiency Examination. Holders of the Caribbean Examinations Council Secondary Education Certificate or GCE O-level take a preliminary year before entry to a degree. There are two degree levels, Associate and Bachelors, with the latter available from either University of Belize or University of the West Indies. The Associate degree lasts for two years and the Bachelors for three.

Other post-secondary non-university education and training is available either through the workplace or at colleges. Courses can be taken leading to qualifications from City and Guilds, London Chamber of Commerce and the Royal Society of Arts. The Belize School of Nursing offers three-year professional course leading to a Diploma in Professional Nursing.

Learned Society

NATURAL SCIENCES

Belize Audubon Society: POB 1001, Belize City; fax 223-4985; internet www.belizeaudubon.org; f. 1969; sustainable management of natural resources; manages 8 protected areas; 1,200 mems; Pres. DAVID CRAIG; Hon. Sec. LYDIA WAIGHT; publ. *Newsletter* (quarterly).

Research Institute

NATURAL SCIENCES

Biological Sciences

Carrie Bow Marine Field Station – Caribbean Coral Reef Ecosystems (CCRE): c/o Invertebrate Zoology Section, National Museum of Natural History – Smithsonian Institution, 10th and Constitution Ave, NW, Washington, DC 20560, USA; located at: Carrie Bow Cay, Belize; internet www.mnh.si.edu/biodiversity/ccre.htm; f. 1972; field laboratory; part of the Smithsonian Marine Science Network; attached to the Smithsonian Institution's National Museum of Natural History (USA); Dir KLAUS RUETZLER.

Libraries and Archives

Belize City

Leo Bradley Library: POB 287, Belize City; located at: Princess Margaret Drive, Belize City; tel. 223-4248; fax 223-4246; f. 1935; nat. library service for Belize; incl. National Collection; 100,000 vols; 40 brs throughout Belize; Chief Librarian JOY YSAGUIRRE.

Belmopan

Belize Archives Department: 26/28 Unity Blvd, Belmopan; tel. 822-2247; fax 822-3140; e-mail archives@btl.net; internet www.belizearchives.org; f. 1965; 150,000 documents; Chief Archivist CHARLES A. GIBSON.

University

UNIVERSITY OF BELIZE

University Dr., POB 340, Belmopan City
Telephone: 223-0256
Fax: 233-0255
Internet: www.ub.edu.bz
Founded 2000
President: Dr CORINTH MORTER-LEWIS
Provost: HENRY ANDERSON

DEANS

Faculty of Agriculture and Natural Science: (vacant)
Faculty of Education and the Arts: Dr VILMA JOSEPH
Faculty of Management and Social Science: Dr KEVIN GEBAN
Faculty of Nursing, Health Science and Social Work: Dr ISMAEL HOARE
Faculty of Science and Technology: Dr AARON LEWIS

ATTACHED INSTITUTES

Adult and Continuing Education Centre: Freetown Rd, POB 990, Belize City.

Institute of Marine Studies: Freetown Rd, POB 990, Belize City

Colleges

Corozal Community College: POB 63, Corozal Town; tel. 422-2541; fax 422-3597; internet www.corozal.com/ccc/; f. 1978 by merger of Fletcher College and St Francis Xavier College to form an ecumenical (Roman Catholic, Methodist, Anglican) college; four- and two-year courses in academic and business studies; 41 teachers; 650 students; Principal ENDEVORA JORGENSON.

University of the West Indies School of Continuing Studies: POB 229, University Centre, Belize City; tel. and fax 223-2038; e-mail uwibze@btl.net; internet www.uwi.edu/scs; f. 1949; continuing education, particularly adult learning; 20 teachers; 200 students; library: 10,000 vols; Resident Tutor LUZ. M. LONGWORTH.

Wesley College: POB 543, 34 Yarborough Rd, Belize City; tel. 227-6302; fax 227-0278; f. 1882; 4-year arts, science and commercial courses; 20 teachers; 336 students; library: 3,000 vols; Principal BRENDA J. ARMSTRONG.

BENIN

The Higher Education System

The structure of the higher education system in Benin (known as Dahomey until 1975) is a legacy of its period as a French colony (1890–1960). It is dominated by the Université d'Abomey-Calavi, which was founded in 1970 as Université de Dahomey. The university changed its name to Université Nationale du Bénin in 1975 and adopted its current name in 2001. In 1999/2000 it had approximately 9,000 students. A second university, in Parakou, with a student capacity of approximately 3,000, opened in 2001.

The Ministry of Higher Education and Professional Training is responsible for the higher education sector. The university rectors are government appointees, but deans of faculty are elected by their peers. State funding for higher education has been affected by economic problems and poor management, with the effect that more specialized private institutions have begun to emerge.

The Baccalauréat is required for admission to university. Qualifications are arranged in three cycles. The first cycle lasts for two years and leads to one of four Diplomas. The second cycle lasts for either one year after the Diplomas for the Licence, or two years for the Maîtrise. Finally, the third cycle is a programme of doctoral research for two or more years leading to the award of Doctorat de Troisième Cycle.

Research Institutes

GENERAL

Centre Régional de Recherche Sud-Bénin: Attogon; f. 1904; library of 2,000 vols and periodicals; Dir Dr J. DETONGNON.

Institut de Recherches Appliquées: BP 6, Porto Novo; f. 1942; library of 8,000 vols; Dir S. S. ADOTEVI; publ. *Etudes*.

AGRICULTURE, FISHERIES AND VETERINARY SCIENCE

Institut National des Recherches Agricoles du Bénin (INRAB): 01 BP 884 Cotonou; tel. 21-30-37-70; fax 21-30-07-36; e-mail inrabdg4@bow.intnet.bj; internet www.bj.refer.org/benin_ct/rec/inrab/inrab.htm; f. 1992 to replace the Direction de la Recherche Agronomique (DRA); Dir-Gen. DAVID YAO ARODOKOUN.

Station de Recherches sur le Cocotier de Semé-Podji: Semé-Podji; tel. 20-24-07-01; coconut research; f. 1949; attached to Institut des Recherches sur les Huiles et Oléagineux, France; Dir HONORÉ TCHIBOZO.

Station de Recherches sur le Palmier à Huile de Pobe: BP 1, Pobe; tel. and fax 20-25-00-66; f. 1922; palm oil station; attached to Direction de la Recherche Agronomique/Ministère des Affaires Rurales, France; library of 70 vols, 54 reviews; Dir Dr MOÏSE HOUSSOU.

NATURAL SCIENCES

General

Institut de Recherche pour le Développement (IRD):; see main entry in France chapter.

TECHNOLOGY

Office Béninois de Recherches Géologiques et Minières: BP 249, Cotonou; tel. 21-31-03-09; fax 21-31-41-20; e-mail obrgm@intnet.bj; f. 1977; branch of Ministry of Mining, Energy and Hydraulics; library of 8,000 vols, 10 current periodicals; Dir-Gen. NESTOR VEDOGBETON; publ. *OBRGM Actu* (4 a year).

Libraries and Archives

Porto Novo

Archives Nationales de la République du Bénin: BP 629, Porto Novo; tel. and fax 20-21-30-79; e-mail a.plathe@unesco.org; internet www.unesco.org/webworld/archives/benin/anb.htm; f. 1914; Dir ELISE PARAISO; publs *Bulletin* (annually), *Mémoire du Bénin* (irregular), *Répertoire d'archives* (irregular).

Bibliothèque Nationale: BP 401, Porto Novo; tel. 20-21-25-85; f. 1976; 35,000 vols; Dir H. N. AMOUSSOU.

Museums and Art Galleries

Abomey

Musée Historique d'Abomey: BP 25, Abomey; tel. and fax 22-50-03-14; e-mail musabome@intnet.bj; internet epa-prema.net/abomey/; f. 1943; collection includes craftwork, drawings, jewellery and royal paraphenalia; Curator ZÉPHIRIN DAAVO.

Porto Novo

Musée National: c/o IRA, BP 6, Porto Novo; premises at Cotonou; Curator MARTIN AKABIAMU.

Universities

UNIVERSITÉ D'ABOMEY-CALAVI

Abomey-Calavi, BP 526, Cotonou
Telephone: 21-36-00-74
Fax: 21-30-16-38
Internet: www.bj.refer.org/benin_ct/edu/univ-be/univ-be.htm
Founded 1970 as Université du Dahomey; became Université Nationale du Bénin 1975; present name 2001
State control
Language of instruction: French
Academic year: October to July
Rector: Prof. ISSIFOU TAKPARA
Vice-Rector, and Director of Academic Affairs: TAOFIKI AMINOU
Director of Administrative and Financial Affairs: EFIOTODJI ACHI NOUMAGNON
Secretary-General: Dr SOUMANOU SEIBOU TOLEBA
Librarian: PASCAL A. I. GANDAHO
Library of 50,000 vols
Number of teachers: 650
Number of students: 18,533

DEANS

Faculty of Agriculture: MATHURIN NAGO
Faculty of Arts, Letters and Humanities: ASCENSION BOGNIAHO
Faculty of Economics and Management: FULBERT GÉRO AMOUSSOUGA
Faculty of Health Sciences: Prof. CÉSAR AKPO
Faculty of Science and Technology: CYPRIEN GNANVO

DIRECTORS

Benin Centre for Foreign Languages: BIENVENU AKOHA
Institute of Mathematics and Physics: JEAN-PIERRE EZIN
National Institute of Youth, Physical Education and Sport: PIERRE H. DANSOU
National School of Administration and the Magistrature: NOEL GBAGUIDI
National School of Applied Economics and Management: SIMÉON FAGNISSE
University Institute of Technology: EZÉCHIEL ALLOBA
University Polytechnic College: MARC KPODEKON

UNIVERSITÉ DE PARAKOU

BP 123, Parakou
Telephone: and fax 23-61-07-12
E-mail: universite_parakou2001@yahoo.fr
Founded 2001
State control
Academic year: October to July
Rector: Prof. ALEXIS HOUNTONDJI
Vice-Rector: Dr AGNÈS THOMAS-ODJO
Registrar: Dr MOUHAMED PARAPE
Librarian: BIO TIKANDE
Library of 3,657 vols
Number of teachers: 28
Number of students: 3,020

DEANS

Faculty of Agricultural Sciences: Dr NESTOR SOKPON
Faculty of Economics: Prof. BARTHÉLÉMY BIAO
Faculty of Law and Policy: Dr OMAR FORTUNÉ ALAPINI
Institute of Technology and Management: Dr SIMÉON FAGNISSE
School of Medicine: Prof. SIMON A. AKPONA

BHUTAN

The Higher Education System

Traditionally, education in Bhutan was purely monastic; the establishment of the contemporary state education system was the result of the reforming zeal of the third King, Jigme Dorji Wangchuck (r. 1952–72). There are five main linguistic groups in Bhutan; Dzongkha, spoken in western Bhutan, is the official language but English is the medium of school instruction. Tertiary education includes various first degree courses offered by institutes under the supervision of the Royal University of Bhutan (RUB), which was established in 2003. Adult literacy and non-formal education (NFE) programmes began in Bhutan in 1992, with the establishment of 10 pilot NFE centres targeting those who had left school before completing the curriculum and those without a formal education. The programme offered a one-year basic literacy programme together with a nine-month post-literacy course in Dzongkha covering practical issues such as agriculture, health and sanitation. By 2006 about 24,000 persons had completed the courses, and there were 646 NFEs with some 18,550 adults enrolled (of whom some 70% were women).

Admission to higher education is made on the basis of completion of grade 12 and passing of examinations leading to award of either the Indian School Certifcate or Bhutan Higher Secondary Education Certificate. Bachelors degrees last for three to four years are offered at the RUB as well as other colleges and non-university institutions. The Masters degree is currently offered on a very limited basis. There are no doctoral programmes in Bhutan.

The Department of Human Resources of the Ministry of Labour and Human Resources was founded in 1999 to supervise technical and vocational education and training. Within the Department, the Department of Occupational Standards (formerly Bhutan Vocational Qualifications Authority) has developed a three-tier Bhutan Vocational Qualifications Framework. The grades of occupational training are Apprenticeship Training Programmes, Special Skills Development Programmes and Village Skills Development Programmes. Constituent colleges of the RUB also offer technical and vocational programmes of education.

Libraries and Archives

Thimphu

National Library of Bhutan: POB 185, Thimphu; tel. (2) 324314; fax (2) 322693; e-mail nlibrary@druknet.net.bt; internet www.library.gov.bt/nlb.htm; f. 1967; 1,600 vols of Tibetan MS and block-print books, 90,000 Tibetan books in other forms; 15,000 foreign (mainly English) books; Eastern branch: Kuenga Rabten, nr Tongsa; Dir MYNAK TULKU (acting); publ. *Rigter* (2 a year).

Thimphu Public Library: POB 295 Thimphu; f. 1980; inc. the Jigme Dorji Wangchuk Library (f. 1978); UN depository library; 6,000 vols; Librarian Mrs TSHEWANG ZAM.

Museum and Art Gallery

Paro

National Museum of Bhutan: Ta Dzong, Paro; tel. (8) 271257; fax (8) 271510; e-mail nmb@druknet.net.bt; f. 1968; housed in seven-storey 17th-c. fortress; gallery of paintings (Thankas), images, decorative art, arms, jewellery; copper, bronze, wood and bamboo objects, philately, photographs; natural history of Bhutan; reference library with books on Bhutan, Northern Buddhism, Tibetology, museology and conservation; Dir Dr C. T. DORJI.

University

ROYAL UNIVERSITY OF BHUTAN (RUB)

POB 708, Semtokha, Thimphu
Telephone: (2) 351626
Fax: (2) 351710
E-mail: tshetenwangyel@yahoo.com
Internet: www.rub.edu.bt

Founded 2003
State control

Chancellor: HM JIGME KHESAR NAMGYEL WANGCHUCK
Vice-Chancellor: DASHO ZANGLEY DUKPA

Number of teachers: 354
Number of students: 3,820

10 mem. instns: College of Natural Resources (located in Lobesa, Thimphu), College of Science and Technology (Rinchhending, Phuntsholing), Institute of Language and Culture Studies (Stemokha, Thimphu), Jigme Namgyel Polytechnic (Dewathang), National Institute of Traditional Medicine (Thimphu), Paro College of Education (Paro), Royal Institute of Health Science (Thimphu), Royal Institute of Management (Semtokha, Thimphu), Samtse College of Education (Samtse), Sherubtse College (Kanglung, Trashigang).

Colleges

National Institute of Education: Samtse; tel. (5) 365273; fax (5) 365363; e-mail dorjee@druknet.net.bt; f. 1968; three-year B.Ed. course, two-year certificate course, one-year postgraduate certificate course in Education, five-year distance-learning course; academic year August to July; 35 teachers; 273 students; library: 15,000 vols, 20 periodicals; Dir DORJEE TSHERING; Principal TSHEWANG CHHODEN WANGDI.

Royal Bhutan Polytechnic: Deothang; tel. 51146; f. 1974; three-year diploma courses in civil, mechanical and electrical engineering; two-year certificate courses in surveying and draughtsmanship; library: 2,000 vols; Principal KEZANG CHADOR.

Royal Institute of Management: POB 416, Simtokha, Thimphu; tel. (2) 351013; fax (2) 351029; internet www.rim.edu.bt; f. 1986; training courses for civil service and private sector at certificate, diploma and postgraduate diploma levels; Dir NAMGAY OM; library: 13,000 vols, 60 periodicals; 32 teachers; 292 students; publ. *dZinchong Rigphel* (2 a year).

Royal Technical Institute: Kharbandi; tel. (5) 252317; fax (5) 252171; e-mail rti@druknet.net.bt; f. 1965; three- and five-year certificate courses for electricians, draughtsmen, mechanics, motor mechanics; 42 teachers; 313 students; Principal SANGAY DORJEE.

Sherubtse Degree College: Kanglung, Trashigang; tel. (4) 535208; fax (4) 535129; e-mail shercol@druknet.bt; internet www.sherubtse.edu.bt; f. 1983; affiliated college of Delhi University; three-year honours degree courses in economics, English, geography, Dzongkha and commerce, and general degree courses in sciences; two-year pre-university course in science; language of instruction: English; 46 teachers; 484 students; library: 22,000 vols; Principal Dr JAGAR DORJI; Assistant Principal LOPON JAMPEL CHOGYEL, LHATO JAMBA, NIDUP DORJI; publ. *Sherub Doenme* (journal, in English, 2 a year).

Ugyen Wangchuck University: in process of formation.

BOLIVIA

The Higher Education System

Higher education is the responsibility of the Ministry of Education and Culture. University admission is based on award of the Bachiller Humanístico after four years of secondary education and success in the Pre-Grado entrance examination. The university degree systems comprises of Licenciado (undergraduate), Maestría and Doctorado (both postgraduate). The Licenciado lasts four to five years, after which the Maestría requires a further two to three years' study. The Doctorado consists of a period of research culminating in the submission of a thesis.

Post-secondary vocational and technical education is available at universities, institutos normales and state technical colleges. Entrance is based on examination and completion of secondary education. Courses lasts three to fours years and lead to the title of Técnico, whilst the title Técnico Superio is awarded after seven years of study for disciplines such as engineering.

Learned Societies

GENERAL

Academia Boliviana (Bolivian Academy): Casilla 4145, La Paz; f. 1927; Corresponding Academy of the Real Academia Española in Madrid; 26 mems; Dir Mons. JUAN QUIRÓS; Permanent Sec. CARLOS CASTAÑÓN BARRIENTOS; Pro-Sec. MARIO FRÍAS INFANTE; publ. *Revista*.

UNESCO Office La Paz: Casilla 5112, La Paz; located at: Edificio del B.B.A. Piso 10, Ave Camacho 1413, La Paz; tel. (2) 204009; fax (2) 204029; e-mail unesco.la-paz@unesco.org; Dir YVES DE LA GOUBLAYE DE MENORVAL.

AGRICULTURE, FISHERIES AND VETERINARY SCIENCE

Sociedad Rural Boliviana (Agricultural Society): Casilla 786, Edif. El Condor piso 10, Of. 1005, La Paz; f. 1934; 30 assoc. mems; Pres. Ing. JOSÉ LUIS ARAMAYO V.; publs *IFAP News*, *El Surco*, *Cotar*, *Universitas*.

ARCHITECTURE AND TOWN PLANNING

Colegio de Arquitectos de Bolivia: Casilla 8779, La Paz; tel. 39-15-68; fax 39-15-68; f. 1940; architecture and town planning; 3,000 mems; library of 5,000 vols; Pres. FROILÁN CAVERO M.; Sec. JUAN C. BARRIENTOS M.; publs *Punku*, *Arquitectura y Ciudad*, *CDALP Informa*.

FINE AND PERFORMING ARTS

Círculo de Bellas Artes (Fine Arts Circle): Plaza Teatro, La Paz; f. 1912; Pres. ERNESTO PEÑARANDA.

HISTORY, GEOGRAPHY AND ARCHAEOLOGY

Academia Nacional de la Historia (National Academy of History): Avda Abel Iturralde 205, La Paz; f. 1929; 18 mems; Pres. Dr DAVID ALVESTEGUI; Sec.-Gen. Dr HUMBERTO VÁZQUEZ-MACHICADO.

Sociedad de Estudios Geográficos e Históricos (Geographical and Historical Society): Plaza 24 de Setiembre, Santa Cruz de la Sierra; f. 1903; Pres. Dr HERNANDO SANABRIA FERNÁNDEZ; Vice-Pres. Lic. PLÁCIDO MOLINA B.; Sec. AVELINO PEREDO; publ. *Boletín*.

Sociedad Geográfica de La Paz (La Paz Geographical Soc.): Casilla 1487, Edif. Santa Mónica, 13 Plaza Abaroa, La Paz; f. 1889; depts of pre-history, history, folklore, geography; 580 mems; Pres. Dr GREGORIO LOZA BALSA; publ. *Boletín* (2 a year).

Sociedad Geográfica y de Historia 'Potosí' (Geographical and Historical Society): Casilla 39, Potosí; tel. (62) 2-27-77; fax (62) 2-27-77; f. 1905; 20 mems; library of 4,000 vols; Pres. Prof. ALFREDO TAPIA VARGS; Sec. WALTER ZAVAL; publ. *Boletín*.

Sociedad Geográfica y de Historia 'Sucre': Plaza 25 de Mayo, Sucre; f. 1887; 8 mems; library of 3,000 vols; Dir Dr JOAQUÍN GANTIER V.; publ. *Boletín*.

LANGUAGE AND LITERATURE

Alliance Française: Calle Guachalla 399 Esq., Avda 20 de Octubre, Casilla 10220, La Paz; tel. (2) 442075; fax (2) 391950; e-mail alflapaz@ceibo.entelnet.bo; internet www.afbolivia.org; offers courses and exams in French language and culture and promotes cultural exchange with France; attached teaching offices in Cochabamba, Santa Cruz and Sucre; Dir JEAN-FRANÇOIS GUEGANNO.

Goethe-Institut: Avda 6 de Agosto 2118, Casilla 2195, La Paz; tel. (2) 2442453; fax (2) 2441469; e-mail ita@lapaz.goethe.org; internet www.goethe.de/hn/lap/deindex.htm; offers courses and exams in German language and culture and promotes cultural exchange with Germany; library of 10,000 vols; Dir DR MANUEL NEGWER.

PEN Club de Bolivia–Centro Internacional de Escritores (International PEN Centre): Calle Goitia 17, Casilla 149, La Paz; f. 1931; 40 Bolivian mems; 7 from other South American countries; Pres. (vacant); Sec. YOLANDA BEDREGAL DE CÓNITZER.

MEDICINE

Ateneo de Medicina de Sucre (Athenaeum of Medicine): Sucre; Pres. Dr AGUSTÍN BENÁVIDES; Vice-Pres. Dr ABERTO MARTÍNEZ; Sec.-Gen. Dr ROMELIO A. SUBIETA.

Sociedad de Pediatría de Cochabamba (Paediatrics Soc.): Casilla 1429, Cochabamba; f. 1945; 14 mems; Pres. Dr JULIO CORRALES BADANI; Sec. Dr MOISÉS SEJAS.

NATURAL SCIENCES

General

Academia Nacional de Ciencias de Bolivia (Bolivian National Academy of Sciences): POB 5829, Avda 16 de Julio 1732, La Paz; tel. (2) 363990; fax (2) 379681; f. 1960; 42 mems; library of 8,000 vols; Pres. Dr CARLOS AGUIRRE BASTOS; Sec.-Gen. Ing. ISMAEL MONTES DE OCA; Librarian Ing. ANTONIO SAAVEDRA; publs *Publicaciones* (irregular), *Boletín Informativo* (monthly), *Revista* (2 a year).

Physical Sciences

Colegio de Géologos de Bolivia: Edif. Sergeomin, calle Federico Zuazo, Esq. Reyes Ortiz 1673, Casilla 8941, La Paz; f. 1961 as Sociedad Geológica Boliviana; present name 1996; Pres. Ing. DIONISIO GARZÓN MARTINEZ.

TECHNOLOGY

Asociación de Ingenieros y Geólogos de Yacimientos Petrolíferos Fiscales Bolivianos (AIG—YPFB): Casilla 401, La Paz; f. 1959; 210 mems in 4 brs: La Paz, Camiri, Cochabamba, Santa Cruz; Pres. Ing. JUAN CARRASCO; publ. *Revista Técnica de Yacimientos Petrolíferos Fiscales Bolivianos* (quarterly).

Research Institutes

GENERAL

Institut de Recherche pour le Développement (IRD): CP 9214, La Paz; tel. (2) 784925; fax (2) 782944; e-mail cecilia.ird@mail.megalink.com; geology, hydrobiology, medical entomology, agronomy, nutrition, hydrology, climatology, social sciences; Dir Dr JEAN-PIERRE CAMOUZE; (see main entry under France).

AGRICULTURE, FISHERIES AND VETERINARY SCIENCE

Sistema Boliviano de Tecnología Agropecuaria (SIBTA): Avda Camacho 1471, Ministerio de Agricultura, Ganadería y Desarrollo Rural, Dirección General de Desarrollo Tecnológico, Casilla 5783, La Paz; tel. (2) 376050; fax (2) 375572; e-mail dgdt@kolla.net; f. 1975; 380 mems; library of 47,000 vols, 260 periodicals; Dir Dr GONZALO ROMERO G.; publ. *SIBTA* (annual report).

ECONOMICS, LAW AND POLITICS

Instituto Nacional de Estadística (National Institute of Statistics): Calle J. Carrasco 1391, Miraflores, La Paz; tel. (2) 2222333; fax (2) 222693; e-mail ceninf@ine.gov.bo; internet www.ine.gov.bo; f. 1937; national, economic and social statistics and censuses; library of 10,500 vols, 370 periodicals; Exec. Dir JOSÉ LUIS CARJAVAL B.; publs *Actualidad Estadística* (weekly), *Actualidad Estadística Departamental* (monthly), *Anuaro Estadística*, *Encuenta Integrada de Hogares* (annual).

HISTORY, GEOGRAPHY AND ARCHAEOLOGY

Instituto Geográfico Militar (Military Institute of Geography): Avda Saavedra 2303, Cuartel General, Miraflores, La Paz; tel. (2) 220513; fax (2) 228329; e-mail igm@chilepac.net; f. 1936; geodesy, nat. topographical survey; Commandant Brig.-Gen. CARLOS BELMONTE CORDANO; publ. *Boletín Informativo*.

Instituto Nacional de Arqueología de Bolivia: Calle Tiwanaku 93, Casilla 20319, La Paz; tel. 329624; f. 1975; *c.* 26 mems; library of 6,000 vols; Dir CARLOS URQUIZO SOSSA; publ. *Arqueología Boliviana*.

LANGUAGE AND LITERATURE

Instituto Nacional de Estudios Lingüísticos (INEL): Junín 608, Casilla 7846, La Paz; f. 1965; part of *Instituto Nacional de Historia, Literatura y Antropología*; linguistic, social and educational research and teaching; specializations: Quechua and Aymara; library of 1,200 vols; Dir VITALIANO HUANCA TORREZ; publs specialized papers, *Yatiñataki*, *Notas y Noticias Lingüísticas* (monthly).

MEDICINE

Instituto de Cancerología 'Cupertino Arteaga': Hospital de Clínicas, Plaza de Libertad, Sucre; f. 1947; Dir Dr H. NUNEZ R..

Instituto Médico Sucre (Medical Inst.): San Alberto 8 y 10, Casilla 82, Sucre; f. 1895; 27 mems, 3 hon., and 130 corresp.; library of 8,000 vols, including *Flora Peruviensis* and 16th-century edition of *Aforismos de Hipocrates*, 6,000 pamphlets; research and production of vaccines and sera; Pres. Dr EZEQUIEL L. OSORIO; Sec. Dr JOSÉ AGUIRRE; Librarian Dr GUSTAVO VACA GUZMÁN; publ. *Revista* (quarterly).

Instituto Nacional de Medicina Nuclear (National Institute of Nuclear Medicine): Casilla 5795, Calle M. Zubieta 1555, Miraflores, La Paz; tel. (2) 226116; fax (2) 811-27-84; e-mail inamen@wara.bolnet.bo; f. 1962; Dir Prof. LUIS F. BARRAGÁN M..

NATURAL SCIENCES

Physical Sciences

Observatorio San Calixto: Casilla 12656, La Paz; tel. (2) 2406222; fax (2) 2116723; e-mail oscdrake@ceibo.entelnet.bo; internet www.observatoriosancalixto.org.bo; f. 1913; meteorology and seismology; library of 11,000 vols; Dir Dr LAWRENCE A. DRAKE.

Servicio Nacional de Geología y Técnico de Minas (SERGEOTECMIN): Federico Zuazo 1673, Casilla 2729, La Paz; tel. (2) 2330766; fax (2) 2391725; e-mail sergeotecmin@sergeomin.gov.bo; internet www.sergeomin.gov.bo; f. 1956 as a national department, reorganized 1965 and 1996; 136 mems; 10 laboratories; library of 3,692 vols; Exec. Dir Ing. CARLOS FREDDY VARGAS; publs *Boletín Informativo*, geological maps.

RELIGION, SOCIOLOGY AND ANTHROPOLOGY

Instituto de Sociología Boliviana (ISBO) (Inst. of Sociology): Apdo 215, Sucre; f. 1941; investigates economic, juridical and sociological problems; library of 15,000 vols; Dir TOMÁS LENZ B.; publ. *Revista del Instituto de Sociología Boliviana*.

TECHNOLOGY

Instituto Boliviano de Ciencia y Tecnología Nuclear: Avda 6 de Agosto 2905, Casilla 4821, La Paz; tel. (02) 356877; f. 1983; Exec. Dir Ing. JUAN CARLOS MÉNDEZ FERRY (acting).

Instituto Boliviano del Petróleo (IBP): Casilla 4722, La Paz; f. 1959 to support and co-ordinate scientific, technical and economic studies on the oil industry in Bolivia; 50 mems; library of 1,000 technical vols; Pres. Ing. JOSÉ PATIÑO; Gen. Sec. Ing. REYNALDO SALGUEIRO PABÓN; publs *Boletín*, *Manual de Signos Convencionales*.

Libraries and Archives

Cochabamba

Biblioteca Central Universitaria 'José Antonio Arze' (Universidad Mayor de San Simón): Avda Oquendo esq. Sucre, Casilla 992, Cochabamba; tel. (42) 31733; fax (42) 31691; f. 1930; 30,000 vols; Dir LUIS ALBERTO PONCE; publ. *Boletín Bibliográfico*.

La Paz

Biblioteca Central de la Universidad Mayor de San Andrés: CC 6548, La Paz; f. 1930; 121,000 vols; Dir Lic. ALBERTO CRESPO RODAS.

Biblioteca del Honorable Congreso Nacional (Congress Library): Calle Ayacucho esquina Mercado No. 308, La Paz; tel. (2) 314731; f. 1912; 22,000 vols; Dir VÍCTOR BERNAL SOLARES; Chief Librarian NELLY ARRAYA VASQUEZ; publ. *Reports of Congress*.

Biblioteca del Instituto Boliviano de Estudio y Acción Social: Avda Arce 2147, La Paz; special collections on social science, Boliviana, education and government documents; 12,000 vols; Dir ELENA PEDDLE.

Biblioteca del Ministerio de Relaciones Exteriores (Library of the Ministry of Foreign Affairs): Plaza Murillo, La Paz; f. 1930; 10,039 vols; private library; Dir Prof. PACÍFICO LUNA QUIJARRO.

Biblioteca Municipal 'Mariscal Andrés de Santa Cruz' (Municipal Library): Plaza del Estudiante, La Paz; tel. (2) 378477; f. 1838; 35,000 vols; Dir MARIA FEDAK KURPEL.

Centro Nacional de Documentación Científica y Tecnológica (Bolivian National Scientific and Technological Documentation Centre): CP 9357, Calle Ayacucho, La Paz; tel. (2) 359586; fax (2) 359491; f. 1967 to provide extensive information service for research and development; depository library for FAO, WHO and ILO; 9,800 vols; Dir RUBÉN VALLE VERA; publ. *Actualidades* (quarterly).

Potosí

Biblioteca Central Universitaria: Universidad Autónoma 'Tomás Frías', Casilla 54, Avda del Maestro, Potosí; tel. 27313; f. 1942; 43,796 vols, 1,471 periodicals; one central library, eight specialized libraries; Dir JULIA B. DE LÓPEZ; publs *Revista Orientación Pedagógica*, *Revista Científica*, *Revista de Ciencias*.

Biblioteca Municipal 'Ricardo Jaime Freires': Potosí; f. 1920; 30,000 vols; Dir LUIS E. HEREDIA.

Sucre

Biblioteca Central de la Universidad Mayor de San Francisco Xavier: Plaza 25 de Mayo, Apdo 212, Sucre; Dir AGAR PEÑARANDA.

Biblioteca y Archivo Nacional de Bolivia (Nat. Library and Archives): Calle Bolívar, Sucre; f. 1836; 150,000 vols; Dir GUNNAR MENDOZA.

Museums and Art Galleries

La Paz

Museo 'Casa de Murillo': Calle Jaén 790, La Paz; f. 1950; folk and colonial art; paintings, furniture, national costume, herb medicine and magic; Dir (vacant).

Museo Costumbrista: Parque Riosinhio, La Paz; f. 1979; history of La Paz.

Museo del Oro: Calle Jaén 777, Casilla 609, La Paz; f. 1983; pre-Columbian archaeology (especially gold and silver); Dir JOSÉ DE MESA.

Museo Nacional de Arqueología (National Museum): Calle Tihuanaco 93, Casilla oficial, La Paz; f. 1846, reinaugurated 1961; archaeological and ethnographical collections; Lake Titicaca district exhibits; Dir Lic. MAX PORTUGAL ORTIZ; publ. *Anales*.

Museo Nacional de Arte: Calle Socabaya esq. Calle Comercio, CP 11390, La Paz; tel. (2) 408542; fax (2) 408600; f. 1964; housed in 18th-century Baroque palace; colonial art, sculpture and furniture; Bolivian and Latin-American modern art; Dir TERESA VILLEGAS DE ANEIVA.

Potosí

Museo Nacional de la Casa de Moneda de Potosí (Nat. Museum of the Potosí Mint): Casilla 39, Potosí; f. 1938; housed in 'Casa Real de la Moneda', the Royal Mint, founded 1542, now restored, said to be the most outstanding civic monument of the Colonial period in South America; colonial art, 18th-century wooden machinery, coins, historical archives, mineralogy, weapons, Indian ethnography, archaeology, modern art; Dir LUIS ALFONSO FERNÁNDEZ; publ. see under Sociedad Geográfica y de Historia de Potosí.

Sucre

Casa de la Libertad: Plaza Casilla Postal 101, 25 de Mayo (Mayor), Sucre; tel. 064-24200; fmrly Casa de la Independencia; historical collection concerned with Independence, including Bolivian Declaration of Independence; library of 4,000 vols, 1,000 maps; publ. *Memorias*.

Museo Charcas: Universidad Boliviana Mayor, Real y Pontificia de San Francisco Xavier, Bolívar 401, Apdo 212, Sucre; f. 1944; anthropological collection with pre-Inca archaeology: Dir JAIME URIOSTE ARANA; ethnographical and folklore collection: Dir ELIZABETH ROJAS TORO; colonial and modern art section, including Princesa de la Glorieta collection: Dir MANUEL GIMÉNEZ CARRAZANA; publ. *Boletín Antropológico*.

Universities

UNIVERSIDAD AMAZÓNICA DE PANDO

Calle Enrique Cornejo 77, Pando, Cobija
Telephone: (3) 842-2411
Fax: (3) 842-9710
E-mail: recuap@hotmail.com

Founded 1993
State control

Rector: ADOLFO MEJIDO.

UNIVERSIDAD AUTÓNOMA 'GABRIEL RENÉ MORENO'

CP 702, Santa Cruz de la Sierra
Telephone: (3) 372898
Fax: (3) 342160
E-mail: uagrmrec@bibosi.scz.entelnet.bo

Internet: www.uagrm.edu.bo
Founded 1879
State control
Language of instruction: Spanish
Academic year: February to December

Rector: Lic. SAUL BENJAMIN ROSAS FERRUFINO
Vice-rector: Dr JULIO ARGENTINO SALEK MERY
Secretary-General: Dr JOSÉ MIRTENBAUM KNIEVEL
University Director of Academic Affairs: Ing. JOSÉ FREDDY SÁNCHEZ SÁNCHEZ
Director of Administration and Finance: Lic. WALDO LOPEZ APARICIO
University Director of Extension: Arq. ROBERT RIVERA CAMACHO
University Director of Research: Dr ALFREDO MENACHO VACA
University Director of Social Welfare: Ing. PILAR DÁVALOS SÁNCHEZ
Librarian: Lic. JOSÉ MELCHOR MANSILLA

Library of 40,000 vols
Number of teachers: 1,019
Number of students: 27,600

Publication: *Universidad*

DEANS

Faculty of Agriculture: Ing. ALFREDO PÉREZ ANGULO
Faculty of Economics and Finance: Lic. ALFREDO JALDÍN FARELL
Faculty of Exact Sciences and Technology: Ing. WALTER YABETA SÁNCHEZ
Faculty of Habitat, Integral Design and Art: Arq. CARLOS BARRERO SUAREZ
Faculty of Health Sciences: Lic. NELSON VILLEGAS ROJAS
Faculty of Humanities: Dr EMILIO DURÁN RIVERA
Faculty of Juridical, Political and Social Sciences: Dr OSVALDO ULLOA PEÑA
Faculty of Veterinary Medicine and Zootechnology: Dr SERGIO SANTA CRUZ GIL
Polytechnic Faculty: Ing. LUIZ ALBERTO VACA PINTO
Polytechnic Faculty of Camiri: Ing. ROBERTO SAAVEDRA ARÉVALO

ATTACHED INSTITUTES

Centre for the Improvement of Bovine Livestock: Dir Dr MANUEL JESÚS ANGULO.

'El Prado' Centre for Research and Production: Dir Dr NAVIL CORCUY.

'El Remanso' Centre for Research and Production: Dir Dr NAVIL CORCUY.

'El Vallecito' Institute of Agricultural Research: Dir Ing. WALBERTO PRADA.

'ICAP' Institute for Post-Secondary Education: Dir Ing. FERNANDO JIMENEZ CUELLAR.

'ISTACH' Higher Technical Institute of Agriculture: Dir Ing. JORGE DANTE EGÜEZ PREXELL.

UNIVERSIDAD AUTÓNOMA 'JUAN MISAEL SARACHO'

Avda Victor Paz 149, CP 51, Tarija
Telephone: (66) 43110
Fax: (66) 43403
E-mail: rector@uajms.edu.bo
Internet: www.uajms.edu.bo

Founded 1946
State control
Academic year: March to December

Rector: Lic. EDUARDO CORTEZ BALDIVIEZO

Number of teachers: 611
Number of students: 12,634

Publications: *Astro Información* (monthly), *Visión Universitaria* (monthly)

DEANS

Faculty of Agriculture and Forestry: Ing. WILFREDO BENÍTEZ
Faculty of Dentistry: Dr ALBERTO VARGAS LIRA
Faculty of Economics and Finance: Lic. FRANZ RODRIGUEZ O.
Faculty of Health Sciences: Dra SARA PACHECO
Faculty of Humanities: Lic. EDWIN JIJENA
Faculty of Law and Political Sciences: Dr CARLOS PÉREZ RIVERO
Faculty of Sciences and Technology: Ing. VICTOR MASTAJO R.

ATTACHED RESEARCH INSTITUTES

Facultad Gran Chaco Yacuiba.

Facultad Integrada de Bermejo.

Instituto Agronomia El Palmar.

Instituto Agropecuario de Bermejo.

UNIVERSIDAD AUTÓNOMA 'TOMÁS FRÍAS'

Casilla 36, Avda del Maestro, Potosí
Telephone: (62) 27300
Fax: (62) 26663
E-mail: rector@rect.nrp.edu.bo
Founded 1892
State control
Academic year: April to November

Rector: Lic. ABDÓN SOZA YÁÑEZ
Vice-Rector: Ing. GERMÁN LIZARAZU PANTOJA
Chief Librarian: Dr CARLOS LOAYZA MENDIZABAL

Number of teachers: 380
Number of students: 7,551

Publication: *Vida Universitaria*

DEANS

Faculty of Agriculture and Stockbreeding: Ing. AMILCAR MARISCAL CORTEZ
Faculty of Arts: Lic. LUIS TORRICO GAMARRA
Faculty of Economics, Finance and Administration: Lic. VALETÍN VIÑOLA QUINTANILLA
Faculty of Engineering: Ing. ALBERTO SCHMIDT QUEZADA
Faculty of Geological Engineering: Ing. DANIEL HOWARD BARRÓN
Faculty of Humanities and Social Sciences: Dr NESTOR GOITIA IRAHOLA
Faculty of Law: Dr JORGE QUILLAGUAMÁN SÁNCHEZ
Faculty of Mining: Ing. EDDY ROMAY MORALES
Faculty of Sciences: Lic. GONZALO POOL GARCÍA
Polytechnic: Téc. Sup. ENRIQUE ARROYO MAMANI

HEADS OF DEPARTMENTS

Accountancy: Cr. JUÁN MEDINACELI LLANO
Accountancy (Tupiza Site): Lic. JOSÉ ANTONIO SURRIABLE BAREA
Agricultural Engineering: Ing. RODOLFO PUCH CABRERA
Auditing: Lic. VICTOR ANGEL SUBIETA
Automobile Engineering: Ing. MARIO SAAVEDRA MONTERO
Business Management: Lic. AVELINO AIZA AVILA
Chemistry: Ing. WILLY VARGAS ENRIQUEZ
Civil Construction: Ing. EDGAR SANGÜEZA FIGUEROA
Civil Engineering: Ing. ALFREDO ARANCIBIA CHAVEZ
Computing: Lic. ROSARIO VÁSQUEZ ARAUJO
Economics: Lic. OCTAVIO MARTÍNEZ CHURA
Electricity: Téc. Sup. ZENOBIO SILES SOLIZ
Electronics: Egr HERNÁN ACEBEY OÑA
Geology: Ing. HERNÁN CHUMACERO ENRIQUEZ
Law: Dr FÉLIX COLLAZOS MORALES
Linguistics and Language: Prof. LOURDES WAYLLACE GASPAR
Mathematics: Lic. OSCAR BARRIENTOS ENRIQUEZ
Mechanics: Téc. Sup. DULFREDO ZULETA SÁNCHEZ
Mining: Ing. EPIFANIO MAMANI ALIZARES
Musical Arts: Lic. MAGDALENA CAVERO GARNICA
Nursing: Lic. ALCIRA MENESES CAMACHO
Physics: Lic. SANTIAGO MAMANI HUANACO
Plastic Arts: Téc. Sup. JUÁN VILLARROEL SOLA
Process Engineering: Ing. JORGE SOTELO
Social Work: Lic. YOLANDA MUÑOZ BURGOS
Statistics: Lic. MARIO SOTO
Topography: Top. OMAR RIVERA ALVAREZ
Tourism: Lic. EDGAR VALDA MARTÍNEZ
Veterinary Science and Zootechnics: Lic. WILBERT PEREIRA MAMANI

UNIVERSIDAD CATÓLICA BOLIVIANA 'SAN PABLO'

Avda 14 de Septiembre 4807 esq. calle 2 (Obrajes), CP 4805, La Paz
Telephone: (2) 2782222
Fax: (2) 2786707
E-mail: rrppint@ucb.edu.bo
Internet: www.ucb.edu.bo

Founded 1966
Church Control
Language of instruction: Spanish
Academic year: February to December

Grand Chancellor: Mons. EDMUNDO ABASTOFLOR MONTERO
Rector: Dr CARLOS GERKE MENDIETA
Pro-Rector: Ing. HÉCTOR CORDOVA EGUIVAR
Vice-Rector (Administration and Finance): Lic. FERNANDO MOSCOSCO SALMÓN
Regional Vice-Rector (Cochabamba): Dr RENÉ SANTA CRUZ R.
Regional Vice-Rector (La Paz): Lic. CARLOS MACHICADO
Regional Vice-Rector (Santa Cruz): Dr NABOR DURÁN SAUCEDO
Director for Academic Planning: Lic. GABRIEL PONCE
General Manager: Lic. JAIME RIVERO
SecretaryGeneral: Dr MARIO HOYES
Academic Secretary: Lic. ELIZABETH ALVAREZ R.

Number of teachers: 778
Number of students: 11,000

Publication: *Ciencia y Cultura* (2 a year)

HEADS OF DEPARTMENTS

Cochabamba Campus:

Business Administration: Mgr RAFAEL A. TERRAZAS PASTOR
Communication Sciences: Mgr FERNANDO ANDRADE RUIZ
Education: Mgr JACQUELINE ROBLIN DE PAREJA
Environmental Engineering: Mgr CHRISTIAN BOMBLAT
Exact Sciences: Dr OSCAR PINO ORTIZ
Industrial Engineering: Dr MARCOS LUIS LUJÁN PÉREZ
Law: Dra AMANDA ARRIARÁN DE ZAPATA
Nursing: MARÍA ANGELES GONZALES
Philosophy and Letters: Lic. LUIS ALBERTO VACA CUÉLLAR
Religious Science: Lic. VICTOR ROMERO MORALES
Systems Engineering: Dr REYNALDO VARGAS ALTAMIRANO
Theology: Lic. ALVARO RESTREPO, Dr HANS VAN DEN BERG

La Paz Campus:

Accountancy: Lic. GABRIEL FUENTES
Architecture: Arq. GUSTAVO MEDEIROS
Business Administration: J. ALEJANDRO BLACUTT O.

Communication Sciences: Dr RAÚL RIVADENEIRA PRADA
Culture and Art: Mtro CARLOS ROSSO
Economics: Lic. MARCELA APARICIO DE GUZMÁN
Education: Lic. ROCIO PEREDO VIDEA
Exact Sciences: Ing. JOSÉ GIL I.
Industrial Engineering: Ing. MARIANO SAUCEDO
Law: Dr CARLOS ANTONIO MIRANDA GUMUCIO
Postgraduate Studies: Dr MANUEL EDUARDO CONTRERAS CABEZAS
Psychology: Lic. FELIX VÍA ORELLANA
Religious Science: Lic. P. FERNANDO FORGUES
Rural Studies Unit: Lic. HUGO OSSIO S.
Systems Engineering: Lic. IRMA PRADO
Tourism: Lic. VICTOR HUGO AMURRIO

Santa Cruz Campus:

Accountancy: Lic. RUBIN DORADO LEIGUE
Agriculture: Dr DANTE INVERNIZZI
Architecture: Arq. JORGE ROMERO PITTARI
Business Administration: Lic. CARLOS CALDERÓN GUTIÉRREZ
Education: Lic. MARTHA AGUIRRE
Educational Psychology: WILMA FOREST
Industrial Engineering: Ing. JUAN ALBERTO MOLLO MAMANI
Medicine: Dr JUAN CARLOS GIANELLA PEREDO
Religious Science: BERNARDITTA TAVAROZI
Systems Engineering: Ing. CARLOS BARROSO

ATTACHED INSTITUTES

Instituto de Investigaciones Socio-Económicas: Avda Hernando Siles 4737, CP 4805, La Paz; tel. (2) 784159; Dir Lic. JUSTO ESPEJO.

Servicio de Capacitación en Radiodifusión para el Desarrollo: Avda Hernando Siles 4737, CP 4805, La Paz; Dir Lic. MARIOLA MATERNA.

UNIVERSIDAD EMPRESARIAL MATEO KULJIS

Calle 24 de Septiembre 444, CP 2321 Santa Cruz
Telephone: (3) 332-2211
Fax: (3) 336-5173
E-mail: universidad@unikuljis.edu.bo
Internet: www.unikuljis.edu.bo

Founded 2000

Rector: Lic. IVO KULJIS FUTCHNER.

UNIVERSIDAD MAYOR DE 'SAN ANDRÉS'

Casilla 4787, La Paz
Telephone: 359490
Fax: (591-2) 359491
Internet: www.umsanet.edu.bo

Founded 1930
State control
Academic year: January to December
Rector: Ing. ANTONIO SAAVEDRA MUÑOZ
Vice-Rector: Dr GONZALO TABOADA LOPEZ
Administrative Director: Lic. EMILIO PÉREZ LARREA
Librarian: Lic. ELIANA MARTINEZ DE ASBUN
Library: see Libraries
Number of teachers: 2,266
Number of students: 37,109
Publications: *Boletín Tesis*, *Gaceta Universitaria*, *Memorias Universitarias*

DEANS

Faculty of Agronomy: Ing. PERCY BAPTISTA
Faculty of Architecture: Arq. DAVID BARRIENTOS ZAPATA
Faculty of Dentistry: Dra NELLY SANDOVAL DE MOLLINEDO
Faculty of Economics and Finance: Lic. CARLOS CLAVIJO VARGAS
Faculty of Engineering: Ing. ADHEMAR DAROCA MORALES
Faculty of Geology: Ing. JOSÉ PONCE VILLAGOMEZ
Faculty of Humanities and Education: Dr RENE CALDERÓN SORIA
Faculty of Law and Political Science: Dr RAMIRO OTERO LUGONES
Faculty of Medicine: Dr BUDDY LAZO DE LA VEGA
Faculty of Pharmacy and Biochemistry: Dr OSWALDO TRIGO FREDERICKSEN
Faculty of Pure and Natural Sciences: Lic. JUAN ANTONIO ALVARADO KIRIGIN
Faculty of Social Sciences: Lic. TERESA MORENO
Faculty of Technology: Lic. LAURENTINO SALCEDO AGUIRRE

ATTACHED RESEARCH INSTITUTES

Centro de Investigaciones Geológicas: Ciudad Universitaria Calle 27 Cota Cota, La Paz; tel. 793392; Dir (vacant).

Instituto de Biología de la Altura: Avda Saavedra 2246, Facultad de Medicina, Piso 11, La Paz; tel. 376675; Dir Dr ENRIQUE VARGAS PACHECO.

Instituto de Ecología: Ciudad Universitaria Calle 27 Cota Cota, Casilla 20127, La Paz; tel. 7924416; Dir CECIL DE MORALES.

Instituto de Ensayo de Materiales: Avda Villazón 1995, Edificio Central, La Paz; tel. 359577; Dir Ing. MARIO TERAN.

Instituto de Genética Humana: Avda Saavedra 2246, Facultad de Medicina Piso 11, La Paz; tel. 359613; Dir Dr JORGE OLIVARES PLAZA.

Instituto de Hidráulica e Hidrología: Ciudad Universitaria Calle 27 Cota Cota, La Paz; tel. 795724; Dir Ing. FREDDY CAMACHO V..

Instituto de Ingenieria Sanitaria: Avda Villazón 1995, Pabellón 103, La Paz; tel. 359519; Dir Ing. JOSÉ DÍAZ BENAVENTE.

Instituto de Investigaciones Arquitectónicas: Calle Lisímaco Gutiérrez, Facultad de Arquitectura, La Paz; tel. 359568; Dir Arq. CRISTINA DAMM PEREIRA.

Instituto de Investigaciones Económicas: Avda 6 de Agosto 2170, Edificio HOY, 5° Piso, La Paz; tel. 359618; Dir Lic. PABLO RAMOS SANCHEZ.

Instituto de Investigaciones Físicas: Ciudad Universitaria Calle 27 Cota Cota, Casilla 8635, La Paz; tel. 792622; Dir Lic. ALFONSO VELARDE.

Instituto de Investigaciones Históricas y Estudios Bolivianos: Avda 6 de Agosto 2080, La Paz; tel. 359602; Dir Lic. RAUL CALDERÓN GENIO.

Instituto de Investigaciones Químicas: Ciudad Universitaria Calle 27 Cota Cota, Casilla 303, La Paz; tel. 792238; Dir Lic. LUIS MORALES ESCOBAR.

UNIVERSIDAD MAYOR DE SAN SIMON

Avda Ballivián esq. Reza 591, Casilla 992, Cochabamba
Telephone: (4) 4524768
Fax: (4) 4524779
E-mail: rector@umss.edu.bo
Internet: www.umss.edu.bo

Founded 1832
Language of instruction: Spanish
State control
Academic year: July to December
Rector: Lic. AUGUSTO ARGANDOÑA YÁÑEZ
Vice-Rector: Ing. RAÚL RICO GAMBOA
Secretary-General: Arq. CARLOS VALDIVIESO SULFO
Librarian: RUTH VALENCIA
Library: see Libraries and Archives
Number of teachers: 1,149
Number of students: 40,641
Publication: *Guía de Proyectos* (current research projects, annually)

DEANS

Faculty of Agriculture and Stockbreeding: Ing. FERNANDO RODRIGUEZ MÉNDEZ
Faculty of Architecture: Arq. RAFAEL ANEIVA SOLIZ
Faculty of Biochemistry and Pharmacy: Dr FÉLIX QUIROGA FLORES
Faculty of Dentistry: Dr JUVENAL LÓPEZ MIRANDA
Faculty of Economics: Lic. ELMER PÉREZ AMADOR
Faculty of Humanities and Education: Dr ROLANDO LÓPEZ HERBAS
Faculty of Law and Political Sciences: Dr OSCAR ALBA SALAZAR
Faculty of Medicine: Dr ENRIQUE SANTIAGO MONTENEGRO
Faculty of Science and Technology: Ing. OSCAR ANTEZANA MENDOZA
Higher Technical School of Agriculture: Ing. ARTURO MOREIRA RÍOS (Dir)
University Polytechnic Institute: Ing. ROLANDO DÍAZ COIMBRA (Dir)

HEADS OF DEPARTMENTS

Faculty of Agriculture and Stockbreeding (Avda Petrolera Km. 4, Cochabamba; tel. (4) 4234123; fax (4) 4234123; e-mail facyp@supernet.com.bo):

- Crop Cultivation: Ing. RUTH LÓPEZ DE RODRIGUEZ
- Veterinary Medicine and Zootechnics: Dra ELFY VACA ALFARO

Faculty of Architecture (Final Calama Este, Casilla 992, Cochabamba; tel. (4) 4231172; fax (4) 4231172; internet www.arq.umss.edu.bo):

- Design: Arq. AUGUSTO CARBALLO ANGULO
- Social Sciences: Arq. FREDDY SURRIABRE GARCÍA
- Technology: Arq. NELSON OLIVARES ARANA

Faculty of Biochemistry and Pharmacy (Avda Aniceto Arce frente Parque la Torre, Casilla 992, Cochabamba; tel. (4) 4250651; fax (4) 4231511; e-mail bioquimica@bio.umss.edu.bo):

- Biochemistry: Dra ZULEMA BUSTAMANTE GARCÍA
- Pharmacy: Dra SILVIA ZABALAGA VIA

Faculty of Dentistry (Avda Aniceto Arce frente Parque la Torre, Casilla 992, Cochabamba; tel. (4) 4225511; fax (4) 4251526; e-mail mfernandez@odo.umss.edu.bo):

- Dentistry: Dra DELIA AYALA ARAMBURO (Acad. Dir)

Faculty of Economics (Final Calama Este, Casilla 4973, Cochabamba; tel. (4) 4231733; fax (4) 4231691; e-mail decano@faces.umss.edu.bo):

- Auditing: Lic. WALTER LÓPEZ VALENZUELA
- Business Administration: Lic. GONZALO RAMIREZ MOLINA
- Economics: Lic. HERNÁN DELGADILLO DORADO
- Social Communication: Lic. MARCO VELEZ OCAMPO VILLAROEL

Faculty of Humanities and Education (Avda Oquendo esq. Sucre, Casilla 992, Cochabamba; tel. (4) 4233891; fax (4) 4233891; e-mail decano@hum.umss.edu.bo; internet www.hum.umss.edu.bo):

- Languages: Lic. MARÍA ESTHER CORTEZ LÓPEZ
- Pedagogy: Lic. JORGE PAREDES GUZMÁN
- Psychology: Lic. MARIO BARRAZA BARADAN

Faculty of Law and Political Sciences (Avda Oquendo esq. Sucre, Casilla 928, Cochabamba; tel. (4) 4253225; fax (4) 4259278; e-mail waparicio@sderecho.der.umss.edu.bo):

Political Sciences: Dr JUAN M. TERRAZAS ROJAS
Postgraduate: Dr LUIS A. ARELLANO RODRIGUEZ

Faculty of Medicine (Avda Aniceto Arce 371, Casilla 3119, Cochabamba; tel. (4) 4259833; fax (4) 4232206; e-mail decano@med.umss.edu.bo):

Medicine: Dr CARLOS VARGAS (Acad. Dir)
Nursing: Lic. INGRID VEGA SUAZNABAR

Faculty of Science and Technology (Calle Sucre y Parque la Torre, Casilla 5474, Cochabamba; tel. (4) 4231765; fax (4) 4231765; e-mail decanato@fcyt.umss.edu.bo; internet www.fcyt.umss.edu.bo):

Biology: Lic. FREDDY NAVARRO ANTEZANA
Chemistry: Lic. OMAR ARCE GARCÍA
Civil Engineering: Ing. RAMIRO SAAVEDRA ANTEZANA
Computing: Lic. BORIS CALANCHA NAVIA
Electrical Engineering: Ing. JAIME ORELLANA JIMÉNEZ
Industrial Engineering: Ing. ROBERTO MANCHEGO CASTELLÓN
Mathematics: Lic. ROBERTO ZEGARRA DORADO
Mechanical Engineering: Ing. JULIO MEDINA GAMBOA
Physics: Lic. NESTOR AVILÉS RÍOS

RESEARCH INSTITUTES

Centro de Aguas y Saneamiento Ambiental: Dir Lic. GASTON JOFFRE LARA.

Centro de Alimentos y Productos Naturales: Dir Dr GONZALO ALFARO DENUS.

Centro de Biotecnología: Dir Ing. ROBERTO SOTO SOLIZ.

Centro de Bioversidad y Genética: Dir Lic. AMPARO BRUCKNER BAZOBERRY.

Centro de Estudios de Población: Dir Lic. ROSSEMARY SALAZAR.

Centro de Estudios Superiores Universitarios: Dir Lic. RENATO CRESPO C.

Centro de Geotecnica: Dir Ing. MAURICIO SALINAS PEREIRA.

Centro de Hidraúlica: Dir Ing. MARCO ESCOBAR SELEME.

Centro de Investigación Carrera de Sociologia: Dir Lic. ALBERTO RIVERA PIZARRO.

Centro de Levantamientos Aerospaciales SIG par el Desarrollo Sostenible de los Recursos Naturales: Dir Dr CARLOS VALENZUELA.

Centro de Limnología y Recursos Acuáticos: Dir Lic. MABEL MALDONANDO MALDONADO.

Centro de Medioambiente y Recursos Renovables: Dir Ing. MABEL MAGARIÑOS VILLARROEL.

Centro de Planificación y Gestión: Dir Lic. MANUEL DE LA FUENTE.

Centro de Semillas Forestales: (vacant).

Centro de Tecnologías Agroindustriales: Dir Ing. EDUARDO ZAMBRANA MONTÁN.

Centro Universitario de Medicina Tropical: Dir Dr HERNÁN BERMUDEZ PAREDES.

Dentro de Desarrollo de Tecnologías de Fabricación: Dir Ing. ANDRES GARRIDO VARGAS.

Instituto de Estudios Sociales y Económicos: Dir Lic. CRECENCIO ALBA PINTO.

Instituto de Investigaciones de Arquitectura: Dir Arq. ANTONIO SALINAS MORENO.

Instituto de Investigaciones de la Facultad de Bioquímica y Farmacia: Dir Ing. VICTOR MEÍJA URQUIETA.

Instituto de Investigacíon de la Facultad de Ciencias Agrícolas y Pecuarias: Dir Ing. CARLOS ROJAS RALDE.

Instituto de Investigaciones de la Facultad de Ciencias y Tecnología: Dir Ing. JOSÉ LUIS VALDERRAMA IDINA.

Instituto de Investigaciones de la Facultad de Humanidades y Ciencias de la Educación: Dir Lic. GUIDO DE LA ZERDA.

Instituto de Investigación de la Facultad de Medicina: Dir Dr WALTER SALINAS ARGANDOÑA.

Instituto de Investigaciones de la Facultad de Odontología: Dir Dr LUIS MORALES ARLANDO.

Instituto de Investigaciones Jurídicas y Políticas: Dir Dra JAROSLAVAB Z. DE BALLÓN.

Instituto de Medicina Nuclear: Dir Dr DANIEL VILLAGRA GONZÁLES.

Semillas Forrajeras: Dir Ing. GASTÓN SAUMA.

UNIVERSIDAD MAYOR, REAL Y PONTIFICIA DE SAN FRANCISCO XAVIER DE CHUQUISACA

Apdo 212, Sucre
Internet: www.usfx.edu.bo

Founded 1624 by Papal Bull of Gregory XV dated 1621 and Royal Charter of Philip III, 1622
Autonomous control
Academic year: two semesters beginning March and August

Rector: Dr JORGE ZAMORA HERNÁNDEZ
Vice-Rector: Lic. FRANCISCO CAMACHO PUENTES
Administrative Officer: Lic. WÁLTER YAÑEZ FLORES
Librarian: Dr RONALD GANTIER LEMOINE

Number of teachers: 438
Number of students: 10,156

Publications: *Archivos bolivianos de Medicina*, *Revista del Instituto de Sociología Boliviana*

DEANS

Faculty of Agriculture: Prof. ARMANDO GANTIER ALFARO
Faculty of Economics, Finance and Administration: Lic. MARCEL CIVERA GIL
Faculty of Health Sciences: Dr ENRIQUE AZURDUY VACAFLOR
Faculty of Humanities: Prof. GERMÁN PALACIOS CORS
Faculty of Law, Political and Social Sciences: Dr RUFFO OROPEZA DELGADO
Faculty of Technology: Ing. DANIEL ALVAREZ GANTIER
Polytechnic Institute: Ing. GERSON ANDRADE TABOADA

ATTACHED INSTITUTES

Centro de Medicina Nuclear: Destacamento 111, No 1, Sucre.

Instituto de Anatomía Patológica: Destacamento 111, No 1, Sucre.

Instituto de Cancerología 'Cupertino Arteaga': Destacamento 111, No 1, Sucre.

Instituto Experimental de Biología: Dalence 207, Sucre.

Instituto de Investigaciones Biológicas: Dalence 207, Sucre.

Instituto de Investigaciones Económicas: Grau 107, Sucre.

Instituto de Investigación Mal de Chagas: Colón final, Sucre.

Instituto de Investigaciones Tecnológicas: Regimiento Campos No 181, Sucre.

Instituto de Sociología Boliviana: Estudiantes esq. Junín, Sucre.

UNIVERSIDAD NACIONAL 'SIGLO XX'

CP 27, Llallagua
(Office in La Paz: CP 8721, La Paz)
Telephone: (052) 54385
Founded 1985

Rector: CIRILO JIMÉNEZ ALVAREZ
Vice-Rector: EDGAR F. VÁSQUEZ PALENQUE
Chief Administrative Officer: MARIO TÓRREZ MIRANDA
Librarian: FLAVIO FERNÁNDEZ MARISCAL
Academic Co-ordinator: VICENTE CÁCERES B.
Director-General for Extension: EDGAR F. VÁSQUEZ P.
Director-General for Research: DIÓGENES ROQUE T.

Number of teachers: 65
Number of students: 1,526

HEADS OF DEPARTMENTS

Communication: MARUJA SERRUDO
Complementary Education: JOSÉ MORATÓ
Health: RUTH FUENTES VENEROS
Languages: CRISTOBAL SOTO
Mining and Metallurgy: WILLY FLORES O.
Political Training: EDGAR LIMA TÓRREZ
Stockbreeding: JORGE PLAZA

UNIVERSIDAD TÉCNICA DE ORURO

CP 49, Avda 6 de Octubre 1209, Oruro
Telephone: (52) 50100
Fax: (52) 42215
E-mail: recuto@uto.edu.bo
Internet: www.uto.edu.bo

Founded 1892
Autonomous control
Language of instruction: Spanish
Academic year: January to November

Rector: Ing. RUBÉN MEDINACELI ORTIZ
Vice-Rector: Lic. RAÚL ARIAS MURILLO
Administrative Director: Lic. VICTORIANO HUGO CANAVIRI CHÁNEZ
Librarian: SOFÍA A. ZUBIETA

Number of teachers: 487
Number of students: 10,403

Publications: *Revista de Cultura Boliviana*, *Revista de Derecho*, *Revista de Economía*, *Revista de Mecánica*, *Revista Metalúrgica*, *Revista Universitaria*

DEANS

Faculty of Agricultural Sciences: Ing. HARRY CARREÑO PEREYRA
Faculty of Architecture and Town Planning: Arq. RUBÉN URQUIOLA MURILLO
Faculty of Economics and Finance: Lic. ROLANDO MALDONADO ALFARO
Faculty of Engineering: Ing. EDDY NISTTAHUZ GISBERT
Faculty of Legal, Political and Social Sciences: Dr VIDAL VILLARROEL VEGA
University Polytechnic: HUMBERTO QUISPE GONZALES

ATTACHED RESEARCH INSTITUTES

Institute of Economic Research.

Institute of Social Research.

UNIVERSIDAD TÉCNICA DEL BENI 'MARISCAL JOSÉ BALLIVIÁN'

Casilla de Correo 38, Trinidad, Beni
Telephone: 21590
Fax: 20236

Founded 1967
State control

Rector: Dr HERNAN MELGAR JUSTINIANO
Vice-Rector: Dr CARMELO APONTE VÉLEZ
Registrar: Ing. VIDAL CHÁVEZ PERALES
Librarian: LORGIA S. DE TANAKA

Library of 9,600 vols
Number of teachers: 155
Number of students: 1,039

Publications: *Boletines de los Institutos de Investigaciones, Ictícola del Beni, Investigaciones Forestales y de Defensa de la Amazonía, Socio-económicas*

DEANS

Faculty of Agriculture: Lic. CASTO PLAZA CUENCA
Faculty of Economics: RODOLFO ARTEAGA CÉSPEDES
Faculty of Stockbreeding: Dr PABLO MEMM DORADO

AFFILIATED INSTITUTES

Instituto de Investigaciones Forestales y Defensa del Medio Ambiente de la Amazonia: Casilla 12, Riberalta, Beni; tel. 82484; Dir OSCAR LLANQUE.

Instituto de Investigaciones Icticolas del Beni: Casilla 38, Trinidad, Beni; tel. 21705; Dir Dr RENÉ VASQUEZ PÉREZ.

Instituto de Investigaciones Socio-económicas: Casilla 38, Trinidad, Beni; tel. 21566; Dir Lic. CARLOS NAVIA RIBERA.

Schools of Art and Music

Conservatorio Nacional de Música: CP 11226, Avda 6 de Agosto 2092, La Paz; tel. (2) 373297; fax (2) 361798; f. 1907; state control; library: 420 books, 3,900 scores; Dir ANTONIO ROBERTO BORDA.

Escuela Superior de Bellas Artes 'Hernando Siles': Calle Rosendo Gutiérrez 323, La Paz; tel. 371141; f. 1926; 18 teachers; 206 students; Dir ALBERTO MEDINA MENDIETA; Registrar WALLY DE MONTALBAN.

BOSNIA AND HERZEGOVINA

The Higher Education System

Bosnia and Herzegovina emerged in its present form from the conflict that, from 1991, engulfed the republics hitherto constituting Yugoslavia. In accordance with the General Framework Agreement for Peace in Bosnia and Herzegovina, signed in 1995, Bosnia and Herzegovina is a single state, which consists of two political entities: the Federation of Bosnia and Herzegovina, principally comprising the Bosniak (Muslim)- and Croat-majority areas, and Republika Srpska, principally comprising the Serb-majority area. Although there is a central (state) Government of Bosnia and Herzegovina, based in Sarajevo, both constituent entities have their own governments. In the Federation of Bosnia and Herzegovina, higher education is the responsibility of the Ministry of Education and Science, based in Sarajevo, and in the Republika Srpska higher education is overseen by the Ministry of Education and Culture, based in Banja Luka.

In 2002/03 in the Federation of Bosnia and Herzegovina, 53,985 students attended higher education institutions. In 2007 there were eight universities, as well as other university faculties, specialist institutes and Visoke skole (high schools). In August 2003 officials of the Federation, Republika Srpska, the cantonal Governments and the Interim District Government of Brčko signed an agreement to replace the country's three ethnically-based education systems with a single unified system. (However, some local authorities remained resistant to the unification of the education system.) In the same year Bosnia and Herzegovina became a signatory to the Bologna Process. However, Bosnia and Herzagovina has yet to implement this.

Higher education admission is made on the basis of a Secondary School Leaving Certificate. There are four university degrees: two at undergraduate level (Diploma Višeg Obrazovanje and Diploma Visokog Obrazovanja) and two at postgraduate level (Magistar and Doktor Nauka). The Diploma Višeg Obrazovanje (Diploma of Higher Education) is a two- to three-year course, resulting in a professional title, but is not a full degree. The Diploma Visokog Obrazovanja (Advanced Diploma of Higher Education) is a full degree course of four to six years leading to a professional title. At postgraduate level the Magistar (Masters) requires two years of research and defence of a thesis, and the Doktor Nauka (Doctor of Science) requires further research and defence of a thesis, but in a non-specified timeframe.

Learned Societies

GENERAL

Akademija Nauka i Umjetnosti BiH (Academy of Arts and Sciences of Bosnia and Herzegovina): Bistrik 7, 71000 Sarajevo; tel. (33) 206-034; fax (33) 206-033; e-mail akademija@anubih.ba; f. 1952; attached research institute: see Research Institutes; 57 mems; library of 50,000 vols; Pres. Dr Božidar Matić; Sec.-Gen. Dr Slobodan Loga; publs *Radovi* (Works, irregular), *Godišnjak* (Annals, annually), *Ljetopis* (Yearbook, annually).

Hrvatsko Kulturno Društvo Napredak ('Napredak' Croatian Cultural Society): Maršala Tita 56, Sarajevo; tel. (33) 213-767; fax (33) 663-380; e-mail trebevic@bih.net.ba; internet www.napredak.com.ba; f. 1902; 20,000 mems; publ. *Stecak* (cultural and social issues, monthly).

Srpsko Prosvjetno Kulturno Drustvo 'Prosvjeta' Sarajevo ('Prosvjeta' Serbian Cultural Society, Sarajevo): Sime Milutinovića-Sarajlije 1, 71000 Sarajevo; tel. (33) 444-230; fax (33) 444-230; e-mail prosveta@bih.net.ba; f. 1902; science, art and literature; 140 mems; library of 3,000 vols; Pres. Teodor Romanić; Sec. Dragan Seleda; publ. *Bosanska Vila*.

Udruženje Gradjana Bošnjačka Zajednica Kulture Preporod u BiH ('Preporod' Cultural Association of the Bosniak Community of Bosnia and Herzegovina): Branilaca Sarajeva 30, Sarajevo; tel. (33) 205-553; fax (33) 205-553.

UNESCO Office Sarajevo: Aleja Bosna Srebrene, UN House, 71000 Sarajevo; tel. (33) 497-314; fax (33) 497-312; e-mail colin.kaiser@unmibh.org; Dir Colin Kaiser.

AGRICULTURE, FISHERIES AND VETERINARY SCIENCE

Bosnia and Herzegovina Small Animal Veterinary Association: Alipašina 37, Sarajevo; tel. (33) 442-303; fax (33) 442-303; e-mail veterins@bih.net.ba; Pres. Dr Josip Krasni.

ARCHITECTURE AND TOWN PLANNING

Drustvo Urbanista Bosne i Hercegovine (Society of Town Planning of Bosnia and Herzegovina): Zavod za urbanizam, Aleja bosanskih vladara 6, 75000 Tuzla; tel. (35) 252-038; fax (35) 251-575; e-mail jpurbanizam@max.ba; f. 1993; 500 ; Pres. Zehra Morankić; publ. *URBO* (annually).

BIBLIOGRAPHY, LIBRARY SCIENCE AND MUSEOLOGY

Društvo Arhivskih Radnika Bosne i Hercegovine (Association of Archive Workers of Bosnia and Herzegovina): Franje Ledera 1, 75000 Tuzla; tel. (35) 252-620; fax (35) 252-620; Pres. Dr Azem Kožar; publ. *Glasnik Arhiva i Društva Arhivski Radnika Bosne i Hercegovine* (annually).

Društvo Bibliotekara BiH (Librarians' Society of Bosnia and Herzegovina): Zmaja od Bosne 8B, 71000 Sarajevo; tel. (33) 275-325; fax (33) 212-435; f. 1949; 450 mems; Pres. Nevenka Hajdarović; publs *Bibliotekarstvo* (annually), *Bilten*.

ECONOMICS, LAW AND POLITICS

Avokatska Komora Bosne i Hercegovine (Law Society of Bosnia and Herzegovina): Čemaluša 2, Sarajevo; tel. (33) 471-156; fax (33) 471-156.

Udruženje Sudija i Sudaca u Federacije Bosne i Hercegovine (Association of Judges of the Federation of Bosnia and Herzegovina): Valtera Perića 15, Sarajevo; tel. (33) 668-035; fax (33) 668-035; f. 1996; 320 mems; Pres. Hajrudin Hajdarević; Sec. Izet Baždarević; publ. *Mjesečni Časopis*.

Udruženje Sudija i Tužilaca Republike Srpske (Judges' and Prosecutors' Association of Republika Srpska): Kralja Petra 1 Karadjordjevica 12, 58000 Banja Luka; tel. (51) 212-725; fax (51) 212-725; e-mail maja@inneco.net; f. 1998; 400 mems; Pres. Mirko Dabić; Sec. Živana Bajić; publs *Glasnik Pravde* (3 a year), *Bulletin* (6 a year).

EDUCATION

Pedagoško Društvo BiH (Pedagogical Society of Bosnia and Herzegovina): Djure Djakovića 4, 71000 Sarajevo.

FINE AND PERFORMING ARTS

Muzička Omladina Sarajeva BiH (Bosnia and Herzegovina Musical Youth, Sarajevo): C/o Open Society Fund – Bosnia-Herzegovina, Maršala Tita 19/III, 71000 Sarajevo; tel. (33) 665-713; fax (33) 665-713; e-mail muzomlsa@soros.org.ba; f. 1958; organizes concerts and theatre events; 12,000 mems; library of 1,000 vols, record library of 1,000 items; Pres. Rešad Arnautović; Sec. Slavica Špoljarić.

Udruženje Muzičkih Umjetnika BiH (Association of Musicians of Bosnia and Herzegovina): Sv. Markovicá 1, 71000 Sarajevo.

HISTORY, GEOGRAPHY AND ARCHAEOLOGY

Društvo Istoričara BiH (Historical Society of Bosnia and Herzegovina): Račkog 1, Filozofski fakultet, 71000 Sarajevo.

Geografsko Društvo BiH (Geographical Society of Bosnia and Herzegovina): Prirodnomatematički fakultet, Vojvode Putnika 43A, 71000 Sarajevo; f. 1947; 1,541 mems; Pres. Dr Miloš Bjelovitić; Vice-Pres. Dr Krešimir Papić; publs *Geografski list* (5 a year), *Geografski pregled*, *Nastava geografije* (annually).

Geografsko Društvo Republike Srpske (Society of Geographers of Republika Srpska): Bana Lazarevića 1, 78000 Banja Luka; tel. (51) 235-625.

LANGUAGE AND LITERATURE

British Council: Ljubljianska 9, 71 000 Sarajevo; tel. (33) 250-220; fax (33) 250-240;

e-mail British.Council@britishcouncil.ba; internet www.britishcouncil.ba; offers courses and exams in English language and British culture and promotes cultural exchange with the UK; library of 6,500 vols; Dir CHRIS RAWLINGS.

Društvo Pisaca BiH (Association of Writers of Bosnia and Herzegovina): Kranjčevićeva 24, Sarajevo; tel. (33) 443-514; fax (33) 443-514; e-mail d_pisaca@soros.org.ba; f. 1993; 95 mems; library of 1,500 vols; Pres. NEDŽAD IBRIŠIMOVIĆ; Sec. ZLATKO TOPČIĆ; publs *Slovo* (monthly), *Lica i Život* (4 a year).

Goethe-Institut: Bentbaša 1a, 71000 Sarajevo; tel. (33) 570-000; fax (33) 570-030; e-mail goethe@sarajevo.goethe.org; internet www.goethe.de; offers courses and exams in German language and culture and promotes cultural exchange with Germany; Dir MICHAEL SCHROEN.

PEN Centar BiH (PEN Centre of Bosnia and Herzegovina): Vrazova 1, 71000 Sarajevo; tel. (33) 200-155; fax (33) 217-854; e-mail krugpen@bih.net.ba; internet www.penbih.ba; f. 1992; 58 mems; Pres. ZDENKO LEŠIĆ; Sec. FERIDA DURAKOVIĆ; publ. *Novi Izraz* (4 a year).

MEDICINE

Društvo Ljekara BiH (Physicians' Society of Bosnia and Herzegovina): Zavod za zdravst-venu zaštitu BiH, Maršala Tita 7, 71000 Sarajevo.

Paediatric Association of Bosnia and Herzegovina: Bolnička 25, Sarajevo; tel. (33) 472-406; fax (33) 472-406; Pres. Dr ESMA ĆEMERLIĆ-ZEČEVIĆ; Sec.-Gen. Dr ZLATAN DŽUMHUR.

Udruženje Farmakologa FBiH Federacije Bosne i Hercegovine (Association of Pharmacologists of the Federation of Bosnia and Herzegovina): Čekaluša 90/II, 71000 Sarajevo; tel. (33) 441-813; fax (33) 441-895; e-mail farma@bih.net.ba; f. 1980; 48 mems; library of 5,000 vols; Pres. Prof. Dr NEDŽAD MULABEGOVIĆ; Sec. Asst Prof. SVJETLANA LOGA; publs *Bosnian Journal of Basic Medical Sciences* (6 a year), *Drug Plus* (monthly).

Udruženje Stomatologa BiH (Dental Association of Bosnia and Herzegovina): School of Dentistry, Bolnička 4A, 71000 Sarajevo; tel. (33) 652-831; fax (33) 214-259; e-mail usbih@bih.net.ba; f. 1997; 400 mems; Pres. Dr HALID SULEJMANAGIĆ; publs *Bilten Stomatologa BiH* (in the nat. languages of Bosnia and Herzegovina and in English, 3 a year), *Stomatološki vjesnik* (in the nat. languages of Bosnia and Herzegovina and in English, 2 a year).

NATURAL SCIENCES

General

Društvo Matematičara, Fizičara i Astronoma BiH (Society of Mathematicians, Physicists and Astronomers of Bosnia and Herzegovina): Prirodnomatematički fakultet, Zmaja od Bosne 35, 71000 Sarajevo; tel. (33) 659-377.

Mathematical Sciences

Drustvo Matematicara Republike Srpske (Society of Mathematicians of Republika Srpska): Bana Lazarevića 1, 78000 Banja Luka; tel. (51) 268-686.

PHILOSOPHY AND PSYCHOLOGY

Društvo Psihologa BiH (Association of Psychologists of Bosnia and Herzegovina): Aleja lipa 81, Sarajevo; tel. (33) 659-184.

Research Institutes

GENERAL

Bošnjački Institut—Fondacija Adila Zulfikarpašića (Bosniak Institute—Adil Zulfikarpašić Foundation): M. Mustafe Bašeskie 21, 71000 Sarajevo; tel. (33) 279-800; fax (33) 279-777; e-mail bosinst@bosnjackiinstitut.org; internet www.bosnjackiinstitut.org; f. 1988 in Zurich; 2001 in Sarajevo; research into the history, literature, art, language and religion of the Bosniaks and other peoples of Bosnia and Herzegovina and the promotion of their cultural heritage; library: reference library of 80,000 vols, open to the public; Dir AMINA RIZVANBEGOVIC DZUVIC.

Centre for Philosophical Research: Bistrik 7, 71000 Sarajevo; tel. (33) 210-902; fax (33) 206-033; e-mail akademija@anubih.ba; internet www.anubih.ba; attached to Acad. of Arts and Sciences of Bosnia and Herzegovina; Dir ARIF TANOVIC; publ. *Dialogue* (4 a year).

Kantonalni Zavod a Zaštitut Kulturni-Historisjkog i Prirodnog Naslijedja Sarajevo (Institute for the Protection of the Cultural, Historical and Natural Heritage of the Canton of Sarajevo): Kaptol 16, Sarajevo; tel. (33) 260-980; fax (33) 663-298; e-mail heritsa@bih.net.ba; f. 1965; library of 15,000 vols; Dir VALIDA ČELIĆ ĆEMERLIĆ; publ. *Annual Report*.

Orijentalni Institut u Sarajevu (Oriental Institute, Sarajevo): Zmaja od Bosne 8, 71000 Sarajevo; tel. (33) 670-353; fax (33) 670-353; e-mail ois@bih.net.ba; f. 1950; history, philology and culture of the Ottoman Balkans and the Middle East; library of 10,000 vols, 470 periodicals; Dir Dr BEHIJA ZLATAR; publ. *Prilozi za orientalnu filologiju/Revue de philologie orientale* (annually).

Zavod za Zaštitu Kulturnog, Historijskog i Prirodnog Naslijedja BiH (Institute for the Protection of the Cultural, Historical and Natural Heritage of Bosnia and Herzegovina): Alekse Šantića 8/III, 71000 Sarajevo; tel. (33) 663-299; fax (33) 663-299; e-mail h_c_bih@bih.net.ba; f. 1947; Dir DŽIHAD PAŠIĆ.

ECONOMICS, LAW AND POLITICS

Ekonomski Institut Sarajevo (Institute of Economics, Sarajevo): Branilaca Sarajevo 47, 71000 Sarajevo; tel. (33) 442-576; fax (33) 664-047; f. 1950; library of 12,400 vols; Dir Dr KEMAL HRELJA.

Ekonomski Institut Tuzla (Tuzla Institute of Economics): Zvonka Cerića 1, 75000 Tuzla; tel. (35) 214-120; fax (35) 214-120; Dir SEAD BABOVIĆ.

HISTORY, GEOGRAPHY AND ARCHAEOLOGY

Institut za Istoriju (Institute of History): Sarajevo, Alipašina 9; tel. and fax (33) 217-263; f. 1959; library of 10,000 vols; Dir Dr HUSMJE KOMBEROVIĆ; publ. *Prilozi* (Contributions, annual).

LANGUAGE AND LITERATURE

Institut za Jezik i Književnost (Institute of Language and Literature): Hasana Kikića 12, Sarajevo; tel. (33) 200-117.

Language Institute: Hasana Kikića 12, 71000 Sarajevo; tel. (33) 200-117; f. 1973; library of 3,200 vols; Dir Dr IBRAHIM ČEDIĆ; publs *Dijalektološki Zbornik* (Dialect Collection, irreg.), *Književni jezik* (Literary Language, quarterly), *Radovi* (Works, annual).

Media Plan Institute: Patriotske Lige 30/3, 71000 Sarajevo; tel. (33) 206-542; fax (33) 213-078; e-mail mediaplan@mediaplan.ba; internet www.mediaplan.ba; f. 1994; research into and analysis of the media; 14 mems; President ZORAN UDOVIĆIĆ.

NATURAL SCIENCES

Mathematical Sciences

Agencija za Statistiku Bosne i Hercegovine (Agency for Statistics of Bosnia and Herzegovina): Zelenih beretki 26, Sarajevo; tel. (33) 220-626; fax (33) 220-622; e-mail bhas@bhas.ba; internet www.bhas.ba; f. 1998; directors consist of one Serb, one Croat, one Muslim, and two deputies; Dirs MAIDA HASANBEGOVIĆ, ZDENKO MILINOVIĆ, SLAVKA POPOVIĆ; publs *First Release* (monthly), *Statistical Bulletins* (6–8 annually).

Federalni Zavod za Statistiku (Institute of Statistics of the Federation of Bosnia and Herzegovina): Zeleni beretki 26, 71000 Sarajevo; tel. (33) 206-452; fax (33) 664-553; f. 1997; library of 6,940 vols; Dir MUNIRA ZAHIRAGIĆ; publs *Statistički Godisnjak* (annually), *Federacija BiH u Brojkama* (annually), *Kanton u Brojkama* (annually), *Statistički Podaci o Privrednim i Drugim Kretanjima u Federacije BiH* (monthly), *Statistički Podaci o Privrednim i Drugim Kretanjim o Kantonima* (monthly), *Socjalna Zaštita* (Statistical Bulletin, annually), *Obrazovanje* (annually), *Pravosudje* (annually), *GDP* (annually), *Zaposlenost i Plaće* (annually), *Poljoprivedra* (annually).

Republički Zavod za Statistiku Republike Srpske (Institute of Statistics of Republika Srpska): Veljka Mlađenovića BB, 78000 Banja Luka; tel. (51) 301-492; fax (51) 303-583; e-mail stat_rs@inecco.net; internet www.rzs.rs.ba; f. 1992; Dir SLAVKO ŠOBOT; publs *Bulletin of Monthly Statistical Reviews* (12 a year), *Annual Demographic Review*, *Data on Industrial Production* (in Serbian, annually), *Quarterly Statistical Review*, *Education Statistics Bulletin (Basic and Secondary Education)* (annually), *Social Welfare Bulletin* (annually), *Forestry Statistics Bulletin* (annually), *Agricultural Statistics Bulletin* (annually), *Gender Statistics Bulletin* (annually).

Physical Sciences

Federalni Meteorološki Zavod (Institute of Meteorology of the Federation of Bosnia and Herzegovina): Bardakčije 12, Sarajevo; tel. (33) 663-508; fax (33) 524-040; e-mail fmzbih@bih.net.ba; Dir ENES SARAČ.

Geodetski Zavod Bosne i Hercegovine (Geodetic Institute of Bosnia and Herzegovina): Bulevar Meše Selimovića 95, 71000 Sarajevo; tel. (33) 469-357; fax (33) 468-989.

Institute of Meteorology: Hadži Loje 4, Sarajevo; f. 1891; Dir M. V. VEMIĆ.

Metalurški Institut 'Kemal Kapetanović' (Kemal Kapetanović Metallurgical Institute): Travnička 7, 72000 Zenica; tel. (32) 417-336; fax (32) 287-666; e-mail miz@miz.ba; internet www.miz.ba; f. 1961; Dir Dr MIRSADA ORUČ.

Zavod za Geologiju (Institute of Geology): Ustanička 3, Sarajevo; tel. (33) 621-567.

TECHNOLOGY

Institut za standarde, mjeriteljstvo i intelektualno vlasništvo (Institute for Standards, Metrology and Intellectual Property of Bosnia and Herzegovina): Hamdije Čemerlića br. 2/VII, 71000 Sarajevo; tel. (33) 652-765; fax (33) 652-757; e-mail info@basmp.gov.ba; internet www.basmp.gov.ba; f. 1992; library of 950 vols; Dir ŽARKO SAVIĆ (acting); publs *Glasnik Standardi i Mjeriteljstvo* (4 a year), *Glasnik Intelektualo Vlasništvo* (4 a year).

Rudarski Institut: Rudarska 72, 75000 Tuzla; tel. (35) 282-406; fax (35) 282-700; mining technology; Dir RASIM PIRIĆ.

Libraries and Archives

Banja Luka

Arhiv Republike Srpske (Archives of Republika Srpska): Ul. Svetog Save 1, 58000 Banja Luka; tel. (51) 231-528; fax (51) 231-528; f. 1953; 2,500 metres of records from all periods; 12,000 vols, 15,000 photographs; Dir Prof. DUŠAN VRŽINA.

Narodna i Univerzitetska Biblioteka Republike Srpske (National and University Library of Republika Srpska): Jevrejska 30, 78000 Banja Luka; tel. (51) 215-894; fax (51) 217-040; e-mail nubrs@urc.bl.ac.yu; internet www.nubrs.rs.ba; f. 1936; organizes continuous educational programmes for librarians; 500,000 vols; Dir RANKO RISOJEVIĆ; publs *Information Bulletin ISBN/ISMN*, *National Bibliography of Republika Srpska*.

Bihać

Arhiv Unsko-sanskog Kantona Bihać (Una-Sana Canton Archives, Bihać): Ul. Bosanskih banova 7, 77000 Bihać; tel. (37) 327-384; fax (37) 327-384; f. 1988; Dir Prof. OSMAN ALTIĆ.

Javna Biblioteka Unsko-sanskog Kantona (Una-Sana Canton Public Library): Trg slobode 8, 77000 Bihać; tel. (37) 333-372; fax (37) 333-372; f. 1954; Dir REUF MUSTAFIĆ.

Fojnica

Franjevački Samostan Fojnica, Biblioteka (Library of the Franciscan Monastery, Fojnica): Fojnica; tel. (33) 837-410; fax (33) 837-412; f. 1668; 12,500 vols, 13 incunabula; archives incl. documents in Turkish and Bosnian; Guardian Fra STJEPAN DUVNJAK.

Kraljevska Sutjeska

Franjevački Samostan Kraljeva Sutjeska, Biblioteka (Library of the Franciscan Monastery, Kraljeva Sutjeska): 72244 Kraljeva Sutjeska; tel. (32) 779-015; fax (32) 779-291; e-mail samostan@kraljeva-sutjeska.com; internet www.kraljeva-sutjeska.com; f. 1664; archives incl. parish registers and MSS in Bosnian Cyrillic and Turkish; 11,000 vols, 31 incunabula; Guardian Fra VJEKO TOMIĆ.

Kreševo

Franjevački Samostan Kreševo, Biblioteka (Library of the Franciscan Monastery, Kreševo): Kreševo; tel. (30) 806-075; f. 1767; 25,000 vols; archive; Guardian Fra MATO CVIJETKOVIĆ.

Mostar

Arhiv Hercegovine Mostar (Archives of Herzegovina, Mostar): Trg 1 Maj 17, 88000 Mostar; tel. (36) 551-047; fax (36) 551-047; e-mail arhiv@cob.net.ba; f. 1954; records from the 13th century onwards; spec. Oriental colln of 800 MSS and 2,000 documents; 9,000 vols; Dir EDIN ČELEBIĆ; publ. *Hercegovina* (annually).

Narodna Biblioteka Mostar (Mostar Public Library): Marsala Tita b.b., 88000 Mostar; tel. (36) 551-487; fax (36) 551-487; Dir RASIM PRGUDA.

Sarajevo

Arhiv Bosne i Hercegovine (Archive of Bosnia and Herzegovina): Ul. Reisa Čauševića 6, 71000 Sarajevo; tel. (33) 663-863 ext. 224; fax (33) 665-365; f. 1947; national archive; 11,000 metres of documents from the 14th century to the present; 20,000 vols; Dir Prof. MATKO KOVAČEVIĆ; publ. *Glasnik*.

Arhiv Federacije Bosne i Hercegovine (Archive of the Federation of Bosnia and Herzegovina): Ul. Reisa Čauševića 6, 71000 Sarajevo; tel. (33) 214-481; fax (33) 214-481; f. 1994; entity archive; Dir AMIRA ŠEHOVIĆ.

Biblioteka Grada Sarajeva (Sarajevo City Library): Mis Irbina 4, Sarajevo; tel. (33) 444-580; fax (33) 442-314; f. 1948; 300,000 vols; Dir HATIDŽA DEMIROVIĆ.

Gazi Husrevbegova biblioteka (Gazi Husrevbeg Library): Hamdije Kreševljakovića 58, Sarajevo; tel. (33) 658-143; fax (33) 205-525; e-mail ghbibl@bih.net.ba; f. 1537; oriental library; 80,000 vols, 11,000 Islamic MSS; Dir MUSTAFA JAHIĆ; publs *Anali Gazi Husrevbegove biblioteke*, *Katalog arapskih, turskih i perzijskih rukopisa*.

Istorijski Arhiv Sarajevo (Sarajevo Historical Archives): Ul. Alipašina 19, 71000 Sarajevo; tel. (33) 209-685; fax (33) 209-675; f. 1948; archive of the canton and city of Sarajevo; 3,000 metres of documents; spec. colln of Ottoman MSS; Dir Prof. TONČI GRBELJA.

Nacionalna i univerzitetska biblioteka Bosne i Hercegovine (National and University Library of Bosnia and Herzegovina): Zmaja od Bosne 8B, 71000 Sarajevo; tel. (33) 275-312; fax (33) 533-204; e-mail nubbih@nub.ba; f. 1945; copyright and deposit library; 2,000,000 vols; Head Dr ENES KUJUNDŽIĆ.

Zemaljski Muzej Bosne i Hercegovine, Biblioteka (National Museum of Bosnia and Herzegovina, Library): Zmaja od Bosne 3, 71000 Sarajevo; tel. (33) 668-027; fax (33) 262-710; e-mail z.muzej@zemaljskimuzej.ba; internet www.zemaljskimuzej.ba; f. 1888; archaeology, ethnology and natural sciences; 230,000 vols; Chief Librarian OLGA LALEVIC; publ. *Glasnik Zemaljskog muzeja BiH* (scientific reports of the museum of Bosnia and Herzegovina; 3 series: Archaeology, Ethnology, Natural History, in Bosnian and German).

Travnik

Kantonalni-Županijski Arhiv Travnik (Cantonal and County Archive, Travnik): Ul. Školska b.b., 72000 Travnik; tel. (30) 511-580; fax (30) 518-979; f. 1954; 8,900 metres of documents; Dir Prof. JASMINA HOPIĆ.

Tuzla

Narodna i Univerzitetska Biblioteka 'Derviš Sušić' Tuzla (Derviš Sušić Public and University Library, Tuzla): Mihajla i Živka Crnogorčevića 7, 75000 Tuzla; tel. (35) 272-626; fax (35) 266-343; e-mail nubt@nubt.ba; internet www.nubt.ba; f. 1946; 200,000 vols, 10,000 periodicals; Dir ENISA ŽUNIĆ.

Regionalni Historijski Arhiv Tuzla (Regional Historical Archives, Tuzla): Ul. Franje Ledera 1, 75000 Tuzla; tel. (35) 252-620; fax (35) 252-620; f. 1954; 1,380 metres of documents from all periods; Dir Dr AZEM KOZAR.

Zenica

Javna Biblioteka Zenica (Zenica Public Library): Školska 6, 72000 Zenica; tel. (32) 401-971; fax (32) 401-971; e-mail biblioteka_zenica@yahoo.com; f. 1954; 78,000 vols; Dir SLAVICA HRNKAŠ.

Museums and Art Galleries

Banja Luka

Galerija Likovnah Umjetnosti Republike Srpske (Art Gallery of Republika Srpska): Srpskih Junaka 2, 78000 Banja Luka; tel. (51) 215-364; fax (51) 304-994; e-mail galrs@inecco.net; f. 1971; contemporary works in different media; Dir NIKOLA GALIĆ.

Muzej savremene umjetnosti Republike Srpske (Museum of Contemporary Art of Republika Srpska): Trg srpskih junaka 2, 78000 Banja Luka; tel. (51) 215-364; fax (51) 215-366; e-mail galrs@inecco.net; internet www.msurs.org; f. 1971; history, archaeology, ethnography, history of art, contemporary art, natural history of Republika Srpska; library of 5,500 vols, 500 periodicals; Man. LJILJANA LABOVIČ MARINKOVIČ; publ. *Zbornik* (irregular).

Bihać

Muzej Unsko-sanskog Kantona (Una-Sana Canton Museum): Ul. 5 Korpusa 2, 77000 Bihać; tel. (37) 229-743; f. 1953; archaeology, history, natural history, ethnography; Dir DŽAFER MAHMUTOVIĆ.

Bijeljina

Muzej Semberija (Semberija Museum): Karadjordjeva 1, 76300 Bijeljina; tel. (65) 401-293; fax (65) 471-625; f. 1970; archaeology, history, ethnography; Dir MIRKO BABIĆ.

Doboj

Regionalni Muzej Doboj (Doboj Regional Museum): Ul. Vidovdanska br. 4, Doboj; tel. (32) 231-220; f. 1956; archaeology, history, ethnography; Dir DOBRILA BIJELIĆ.

Mostar

Muzej Hercegovine (Museum of Herzegovina): Maršala Tita b.b., Mostar; f. 1950; archaeology, history, ethnography, art, numismatics; Dir SABIT HODŽIĆ.

Prijedor

Muzej Kozara (Kozara Museum): Nikole Pašića, 79101 Prijedor; tel. (62) 221-334; f. 1953; regional museum; archaeology, history, ethnography, art; Dir MILENKO RADIVOJEC.

Sarajevo

Istorijski Muzej Bosne i Hercegovine (History Museum of Bosnia and Herzegovina): Zmaja od Bosne 9, 71000 Sarajevo; tel. (33) 210-416; fax (33) 656-629; f. 1945; history since medieval times; archives of documents and photographs; library of 20,000 vols; Dir Dr AHMED HADŽIROVIĆ.

Muzej Književnosti BiH (Literary Museum of Bosnia and Herzegovina): Sime Milutinovića Sarajlije 7, Sarajevo; tel. (33) 471-828; fax (33) 471-828; e-mail ljiljak@bih.net.ba; literature and theatre arts; Dir ALEKSANDAR LJILJAK; publ. *Baština*.

Muzej Sarajeva (Museum of Sarajevo): Josipa Štedlera 32, 71000 Sarajevo; tel. (33) 475-741; fax (33) 475-749; e-mail muzejsarajeva@bih.net.ba; internet muzejsarajeva.ba; f. 1949; history, archaeology, fine and applied art; Dir MEVLIDA SERDAREVIĆ.

Branch museums:

Despića Kuća (Despić House): Despićeva 2, 71000 Sarajevo; tel. (33) 215-531; fax (33) 215-532; Serbian merchant's house; Dir MEVLIDA SERDAREVIĆ.

Muzej Jevreja BiH (Jewish Museum of Bosnia and Herzegovina): Velika Avlija b.b., Sarajevo; tel. (33) 535-688; Dir ŽANKA DODIĆ-KARAMAN.

Muzej Sarajevska 1878–1918 (Museum of Sarajevo 1878–1918): Zelenih beretki b.b., Sarajevo; tel. (33) 533-288; Curator MIRSAD AVDIĆ.

Svrzina Kuća (Svrzo House): Glodjina 8, Sarajevo; tel. (33) 535-264; house of the Ottoman period; Curator AMRA MADIŽAREVIĆ.

Umjetnička galerija Bosne i Hercegovine (Art Gallery of Bosnia and Herzegovina): Zelenih beretki br. 8, 71000 Sarajevo; tel. (33) 667-532; fax (33) 664-162; e-mail ugbih@bih.net.ba; f. 1946; collections of modern art from Serbia and Montenegro and Bosnia and Herzegovina; also ancient icons and art; library of 3,000 vols; Dir Prof. SEID HASANEFENDIĆ; publ. publs catalogues.

Zemaljski Muzej Bosne i Hercegovine (National Museum of Bosnia and Herzegovina): Zmaja od Bosne 3, 71000 Sarajevo; tel. and fax (33) 262-710; e-mail z.muzej@zemaljskimuzej.ba; internet www.zemaljskimuzej.ba; f. 1888; prehistoric, Roman, Greek and Medieval periods, ethnological, botanical, zoological, geological sections; botanical garden; museum closed October 2004 due to lack of funds; reported to have reopened early 2005; library: see Libraries and Archives; Dir Dr AIŠA SOFTIĆ; publs *Glasnik Zemaljskog muzeja–Arheologija* (annually), *GZM–Etnologija* (annually), *GZM–Prirodne nauke* (annually), *Wissenschaftliche Mitteilungen A (Archäologie)* (irreg.), *Wissenschaftliche Mitteilungen B (Volkskunde)* (irreg.), *Wissenschaftliche Mitteilungen C (Naturwissenschaft)* (irreg.).

Travnik

Zavićajni Muzej Travnik (Regional Museum, Travnik): Memed-paše Kukavice 1, 72270 Travnik; tel. (30) 518-140; fax (30) 518-140; e-mail zmt99@bih.net.ba; Dir FATIMA MASLIĆ.

Trebinje

Muzej Herzegovine – Trebinje (Museum of Herzegovina, Trebinje): Stari Grad b.b., Trebinje; tel. (59) 220-220; f. 1956; archaeology, history, ethnography, art; Dir DJORDJO ODAVIĆ.

Tuzla

Medjunarodna Galerija Portreta Tuzla (Tuzla International Portrait Gallery): Tuzla; tel. (35) 234-897; fax (35) 235-211; internet www.tuzla.net/mpg; f. 1964; works by artists from Bosnia and Herzegovina and abroad; spec. colln of works by Izmet Mujezinović, whose studio forms a br. museum; Dir ČAZIM SARAJLIĆ.

Muzej Istočne Bosne Tuzla (Museum of East Bosnia, Tuzla): Džindić mahala 21, 75000 Tuzla; tel. (35) 318-321; fax (35) 318-320; e-mail muzej.ib@bih.net.ba; f. 1947; archaeology, history, ethnography, natural history, art, numismatics; library of 15,000 vols, 30,000 exhibits; Dir VESNA ISABEGOVIĆ; Curator MIRSAD BAKALOVIĆ; publ. *Clanci i gradja za kulturnu historiju sjeveroistočne Bosne* (Articles and study materials for the cultural history of East Bosnia—annually).

Muzej Solane Tuzla (Tuzla Saltworks Museum): Solanska 1, 75000 Tuzla; tel. (35) 214-167; fax (35) 214-167; devoted to the Tuzla saltworks industry.

Zenica

Muzej Grada Zenica (Zenica Town Museum): Jevrejska 1, Zenica; tel. (32) 421-732; fax (32) 436-724; f. 1979; archaeology, history, ethnography, geology, art; Dir ZDRAVKO BALTAN.

Universities

UNIVERZITET U BANJOJ LUCI (University of Banja Luka)

Trg srpskih vladara 2, 78000 Banja Luka
Telephone: (51) 218-997
Fax: (51) 315-694
E-mail: uni-bl@blic.net
Internet: unibl.org

Founded 1975
State control
Academic year: October to September

Rector: Prof. Dr DRAGOLJUB MIRJANIĆ
Vice-Rectors: Prof. RAJKO GNJATO, Prof. Dr RADOSLAV GRUJIĆ
Head of Administration: DJORDJE MARKEZ
International Relations Officer: DJORDJE MARJANOVIĆ
Librarian: RANKO RISOJEVIĆ

Number of teachers: 802
Number of students: 12,664

DEANS

Faculty of Agriculture: Prof. Dr NICOLA MIČIČ
Faculty of Civil Engineering: Prof. Dr JELA BOŽIČ
Faculty of Economics: Prof. Dr STANKO STANIĆ
Faculty of Electrical Engineering: Prof. Dr MILORAD BOŽIČ
Faculty of Forestry: Prof. Dr ZORAN MAUNAGA
Faculty of Law: Prof. Dr MILORAD ŽIVANOVIĆ
Faculty of Mathematics and Natural Sciences: Prof. Dr RAJKO GNJATO
Faculty of Mechanical Engineering: Prof. Dr MILAN SLJIVIČ
Faculty of Medicine: Prof. Dr SLOBODAN BILBIJA
Faculty of Philosophy: Prof. Dr DRAGO BRANKOVIĆ
Faculty of Technology: Prof. Dr RADOSLAV GRUJIČ

ATTACHED INSTITUTES

Institute of Agriculture: Dir Prof. Dr JOVE STOJČIČ.

Institute of International Law and International Relations: Dir Prof. Dr VITOMIR POPOVIĆ.

UNIVERZITET U BIHAĆU (University of Bihać)

Ul. Kulina Bana 2/II, 37000 Bihać
Telephone: (37) 322-022
Fax: (37) 322-022
Internet: www.unbi.ba

Founded 1997

Rector: Prof. ISAK KARABEGOVIĆ
Librarian: HALILAGIĆ DŽENITA

Number of teachers: 333
Number of students: 3,400

Faculties of Biotechnology, Economics, Law, Pedagogy and Technology.

UNIVERZITET 'DŽEMAL BIJEDIĆ' MOSTAR (Džemal Bijedić University of Mostar)

USRC Midhat-Hujdur-Hujka, 88104 Mostar
Telephone: (36) 570-727
Fax: (36) 570-032
E-mail: uni_mo@cob.net.ba
Internet: www.cob.net.ba/univerzitet_mostar

Founded 1977
State control
Academic year: October to September

Rector: Prof. Dr ELBISA USTAMUJIĆ
Vice-Rector (Finance): Prof. Dr ADIL TRGO
Vice-Rector (Scientific Research): Prof. Dr SEAD PAŠIĆ
Vice-Rector (Teaching): Prof. Dr HAMID DRLJEVIĆ
Secretary-General: ZIJADA BEČIĆ
Chief Librarian: EMINA ĐAPO

Publication: *Revija za pravo i ekonomiju* (Law and Economics Review, 2 a year)

Library of 11,850 vols
Number of teachers: 232
Number of students: 4,050 (4,000 undergraduate, 50 postgraduate)

DEANS

Agromediterranean Faculty: Doc. Dr AHMED DŽUBUR
Faculty of Civil Engineering: Prof. Dr FUAD ČATOVIĆ
Faculty of Economics: Prof. Dr DAMIR ZAKLAN
Faculty of Humanities: Prof. Dr ELBISA USTAMUJIĆ
Faculty of Information Technology: Prof. Dr SAFET KRKIĆ
Faculty of Law: Prof. Dr SUZANA BUBIĆ
Faculty of Mechanical Engineering: Doc. Dr JUSUF KEVELJ
Academy of Education: Prof. ĐULSA BAJRAMOVIĆ

SVEUČILIŠTE U MOSTARU (University of Mostar)

Trg hrvatskih velikana bb, 88000 Mostar
Telephone: (36) 310-778
Fax: (36) 320-885
E-mail: mail@sve-mo.ba
Internet: www.sve-mo.ba

Founded 1977; present name and status 1992
State control
Language of instruction: Croatian
Academic year: September to August

Rector: Prof. Dr FRANO LJUBIĆ
Pro-Rectors: Prof. Dr VOJO VIŠEKRUNA (Academic Affairs and Students), Prof. Dr ŽELJKO ŠUMAN (International Relations), Prof. Dr ŠIMUN MUSA, Prof. Dr LJUBOMIR ZOVKO
General Secretary: MARINKO JURILJ
Librarian: SLAVICA JUKA

Library of 15,200 vols
Number of teachers: 500
Number of students: 7,500

Publications: *Mostariensia* (2 a year), *Znanstveni glasnik* (2 a year)

DEANS

Faculty of Agriculture: Dr MARKO MATIC
Faculty of Civil Engineering: Prof. Dr PERO MARIJANOVIĆ
Faculty of Economics: Prof. Dr IVAN PAVLOVIĆ
Faculty of Education: Prof. Dr ŠIMUN MUSA
Faculty of Law: Prof. Dr DRAGO RADIĆ
Faculty of Mechanical Engineering: Prof. Dr VLADO MAJSTOROVIĆ
Faculty of Medicine: Prof. Dr FILIP ČUSO
College of Nursing: LJUBO ŠIMIĆ

ATTACHED INSTITUTES

Institute of Agriculture: research and development in agriculture and agroeconomics; Dir Dr JAKOV PEHAR.

Institute for Biology and Chemistry.

Institute of Civil Engineering: Dir Prof. Dr HRVOJE SOČE.

Institute of Croatian Language, Literature and History: Dir Prof. Dr STOJAN VRLJIĆ.

Institute for Economic Development: Dir Prof. Dr DANE KORDIĆ.

Institute of Mechanical Engineering: Dir Prof. Dr VOJISLAV VIŠEKRUNA.

Institute for Planning and Testing of Materials and Construction.

International Centre for Philosophy

UNIVERZITET U SARAJEVU
(University of Sarajevo)

Obala Kulina bana 7/II, 71000 Sarajevo
Telephone: (33) 663-392
Fax: (33) 663-393
E-mail: rektorat@unsa.ba
Internet: www.unsa.ba

Founded 1949
Academic year: October to September

Rector: Prof. Dr HASAN MURATOVIĆ
Vice-Rectors: Prof. Dr LJERKA BABIĆ, Prof. Dr MENSUR HAJRO, Prof. Dr NIKOLA KOVAČ
Secretary-General: ZORAN SELESKOVIĆ
Director, National and University Library: Dr ENES KUJUNDŽIĆ

Number of teachers: 1,680
Number of students: 50,000

Publications: *Bulletin* (every 2 years), *Doctoral Dissertations–Bibliography* (annually), *Preglad* (quarterly), *Preglad Predavanja* (annually)

DEANS

Faculty of Agriculture: Prof. Dr VJEKOSLAV SELAK
Faculty of Architecture: Prof. Dr MUHAMED HAMIDOVIĆ
Faculty of Civil Engineering: Prof. Dr MUHAMED ZLATAR
Faculty of Criminology: Prof. Dr HIDAJET REPOVAC
Faculty of Dentistry: Prof. Dr HAJRIJA KONJHODŽIĆ
Faculty of Economics: Prof. Dr MURIS ČIČIĆ
Faculty of Electrical Engineering: Prof. Dr KEMO SOKOLIJA
Faculty of Forestry: Prof. Dr FARUK MEKIĆ
Faculty of Law: Prof. Dr FUAD SALTAGA
Faculty of Mechanical Engineering: Prof. Dr STJEPAN MARIĆ
Faculty of Medicine: Prof. Dr OSMAN DURIĆ
Faculty of Natural Sciences: Prof. Dr SULEJMAN REDŽIĆ
Faculty of Pharmacy: Prof. Dr ADLIJA JEVRIĆ-ČAUŠEVIĆ
Faculty of Philosophy: Prof. Dr SALIH FOČO
Faculty of Physical Education: Prof. Dr SALIH FOČO
Faculty of Political Sciences: Prof. Dr ISMET GRBO
Faculty of Transportation: Prof. Dr ŠEFKIJA ČEKIĆ
Faculty of Veterinary Sciences: Prof. Dr FARUK ČAKLOVICA
Academy of Dramatic Art: Prof. ADMIR GLAMOČAK
Academy of Fine Arts: METKA KRAIGHER-HOZO
Academy of Music: Prof. Dr SELMA FEROVIĆ
Teacher-Training Academy: Prof. Dr SAFET SMAJKIĆ

DIRECTORS

Institute of Architecture and Urbanization: (vacant)
Institute of Biology: (vacant)
Institute of Economics: (vacant)
Institute of Genetic Engineering and Biotechnology: Prof. Dr KASIM HADŽISELIMOVIĆ
Institute of History: Prof. Dr HUSNIJA BAJROVIĆ
Institute of Oriental Research: Dr BEHIJA ZLATAR
Institute for Research into Crimes against Humanity and International Law: Dr SMAIL ČEKIĆ
Institute of Thermo-technics and Nuclear Technics: (vacant)

UNIVERZITET U ISTOČNOM SARAJEVU
(University of East Sarajevo)

Lukavica, Vuka Karadžića br.30, 71123 Istočno Sarajevo
Telephone: (57) 340-464
Fax: (57) 340-263
E-mail: univerzitet@paleol.net
Internet: www.unssa.rs.ba

Founded 1992 as University of Serb Sarajevo; present name 2005
State control
Language of instruction: Serbian

Rector: Prof. Dr MITAR NOVAKOVIĆ
Pro-Rector for Education: Prof. Dr ZORAN LJUBOJE
Pro-Rector for Finance: Prof. Dr ALEKSA MILOJEVIĆ
Pro-Rector for Research: Prof. Dr DANIMIR MANDIĆ
Pro-Rector for Students: IVANA ŠARABA

Number of teachers: 919
Number of students: 11,054

DEANS

Faculty of Economics: Prof. Dr MIROSLAV BOGDANOVIĆ
Faculty of Economics (Brčko): Prof. Dr MARIN GUŽALIĆ
Faculty of Economics (Pale): Prof. Dr NOVO PLAKALOVIĆ
Faculty of Electrotechnology: Prof. Dr BOŽIDAR KRSTAJIĆ
Faculty of Law: Prof. Dr RADOMIR LUKIĆ
Faculty of Mechanical Engineering: Prof. Dr MOMIR ŠARENAC
Faculty of Medicine: Prof. Dr VELJKO MARIĆ
Faculty of Pedagogy: Prof. Dr MOMČILO PELEMIŠ
Faculty of Philosophy: Prof. Dr MILENKO PIKULA
Faculty of Physical Sciences: Prof. Dr DANKO PRŽULJ
Faculty of Production and Management: Prof. Dr LJUBOMIR ŠIBALIJA
Faculty of Stomatology: Prof. Dr PETAR GRGIĆ
Faculty of Technology: Prof. Dr MILOVAN JOTANOVIĆ
Faculty of Theology: Prof. Dr PREDRAG PUZOVIĆ
Academy of Music: Prof. Dr OGNJEN BOMOŠTAR
Academy of Fine Arts: MIRKO TOLJIĆ

UNIVERZITET U TUZLI
(University of Tuzla)

M. Fizovića-Fiska 6, POB 528, 75000 Tuzla
Telephone: (35) 252-061
Fax: (35) 251-405
E-mail: unitz@untz.ba
Internet: www.untz.ba

Founded 1976

Rector: Prof. Dr IZUDIN KAPETANOVIĆ
Vice-Rector for Finance and Development: Prof. Dr MIRJANA RADIĆ
Vice-Rector for International Relations: Prof. Dr MIRSAD ĐONLAGIĆ
Vice-Rector for Science and Research: Prof. Dr BOŽO BANJANIN
Vice-Rector for Teaching and Students: Prof. Dr DŽEMO TUFEKČIĆ
Secretary-General: JASMINA BERBIĆ
General Secretary: AIDA HODŽIĆ

Number of teachers: 425
Number of students: 5,000

DEANS

Faculty of Economics: MEHMED DEDIĆ
Faculty of Electrical and Mechanical Engineering: MIRZA KUŠLJUGIĆ
Faculty of Medicine: AHMED HALILBAŠIĆ
Faculty of Mining and Geology: SADUDIN HODŽIĆ
Faculty of Philosophy: ENVER HALILOVIĆ
Faculty of Special Education: DŽEVDET SARAJLIĆ
Faculty of Technology: MAHMUT AHMETBAŠIĆ
Academy of Drama: MIRALEM ZUPČEVIĆ

UNIVERZITET U ZENICI
(University of Zenica)

Fakultetska 3, 72000 Zenica
Telephone: (32) 444-420
Fax: (32) 444-431
E-mail: rektorat@unze.ba
Internet: www.unze.ba

Founded 2000
Languages of instruction: Bosnian, Serbianand
Language of instruction: Croatian

Rector: Prof. Dr SABAHUDIN EKINOVIĆ
Vice-Rector for Education: Dr ŽELJKO ŠKULJEVIĆ
Vice-Rector for Scientific Research, Development and International Co-operation: Dr DARKO PETKOVIĆ
Secretary-General: ARIFA ĆURUKOVIĆ

Number of teachers: 210
Number of students: 3,200

Publications: *Didaktički putokazi* (education), *Mašinstvo* (mechanical engineering)

DEANS

Faculty of Economics: (vacant)
Faculty of Education: REFIK CATIĆ
Faculty of Health: (vacant)
Faculty of Law: (vacant)
Faculty of Mechanical Engineering: SAFET BRDAREVIĆ
Faculty of Metallurgy and Materials Science: FUAD BEGOVAĆ

BOTSWANA

The Higher Education System

Tertiary education is provided by the University of Botswana and the affiliated College of Technical and Vocational Education. There are also technical and vocational training centres, including the Botswana College of Agriculture, the Botswana Institute of Administration and Commerce, the Botswana Polytechnic and the Institute of Development Management. The University of Botswana was founded in 1963 as the University of Basutoland (now Lesotho), Bechuanaland (now Botswana) and Swaziland at Roma, in Lesotho. It became the University of Botswana, Lesotho and Swaziland (UBLS) following the independence of Botswana and Lesotho in 1966, and has been known under its current name since 1982. The University of Botswana is funded mainly by the Government and receives some income from students' fees. The Ministry of Education is responsible for higher education.

Admission to the University of Botswana requires the Botswana General Certificate of Secondary Education, the local variant of the Cambridge Overseas School Certificate, either first or second division, with a credit in English language. The standard undergraduate degree is the Bachelors, which comprises two two-year cycles; the main postgraduate degree is the Masters, taken after the Bachelors. Non-university technical and vocational education and training is mainly provided by institutions affiliated to the University of Botswana, with the most common awards being Diplomas and Certificates.

Learned Societies

GENERAL

Botswana Society: POB 71, Gaborone; tel. 3919673; fax 3919745; e-mail botsoc@botsnet.bw; internet www.botsnet.bw/botswanasociety.htm; f. 1968, in association with the National Museum and Art Gallery, to encourage knowledge and research on Botswana in all fields; 450 mems; Chair. Dr I. NDZINGE; Exec. Sec. TREVOR BURNETT; publ. *Botswana Notes and Records* (annually).

BIBLIOGRAPHY, LIBRARY SCIENCE AND MUSEOLOGY

Botswana Library Association: POB 1310, Gaborone; tel. 3552295; fax 3957291; e-mail mbangiwa@noka.ub.bw; f. 1978; 60 mems; Chair. F. M. LAMUSSE; Sec. A. M. MBANGIWA; publs *Journal*, *Botswana Journal of Library and Information Science* (2 a year).

LANGUAGE AND LITERATURE

Alliance Française: POB 1817, Gaborone; tel. 3951650; fax 3584433; e-mail af.gaborone@info.bw; internet www.ibis.bw/~all.francaise/; offers courses and exams in French language and culture and promotes cultural exchange with France.

British Council: British High Commission Bldg, Queen's Rd, The Mall, POB 439, Gaborone; tel. 3953602; fax 3956643; e-mail general.enquiries@britishcouncil.org.bw; internet www.britishcouncil.org/botswana; offers courses and exams in English language and British culture and promotes cultural exchange with the UK; Dir DAVID KNOX.

Research Institute

NATURAL SCIENCES

Physical Sciences

Geological Survey of Botswana: Private Bag 14, Lobatse; tel. 5330327; fax 5332013; e-mail geosurv@global.bw; internet www.gov.bw/government/geology.htm; f. 1948; library of 2,000 vols, 151 periodicals; Dir T. P. MACHACHA; publs *Annual Report*, *Bulletin*, *Bibliography of the Geology of Botswana* (every 5 years), *District Memoir*.

Libraries and Archives

Gaborone

Botswana National Archives and Records Services: Khama Crescent, Government Enclave, POB 239, Gaborone; tel. 3911820; fax 3908545; e-mail kkgabi@gov.bw; f. 1967; central govt, district, tribal, business and private archives since c. 1885; audio-visual and machine-readable archives; records management for central govt, districts and Parastatal orgs; oral tradition programmes; educational programmes and exhibitions; 14,000 vols; Dir K. P. KGABI; Senior Archivist C. T. NENGOMASHA; Librarian A. R. ADEKANMBI; publ. *Archives Library Accessions List*.

Botswana National Library Service: Private Bag 0036, Gaborone; tel. 3952288; fax 3901149; e-mail natlib@global.bw; f. 1968; nationwide public library service; also acts as a national library (legal deposit); 282,383 vols; 23 branch libraries, 3 mobile libraries; 286 book box service points; 64 village reading rooms; Dir CONSTANCE B. MODISE; publs *Annual Report*, *National Bibliography of Botswana* (3 a year), *Quarterly Accessions List*, *Statistical Bulletin*, *Newsletter*.

Museums and Art Galleries

Gaborone

National Museum, Monuments and Art Gallery: Independence Ave, Private Bag 00114, Gaborone; tel. 3974616; fax 3902797; e-mail national.museum@gov.bw; internet www.gov.bw/tourism/attractions/thenational.html; f. 1968; provides, through dioramas and graphic displays, a visual education in the development of man in Botswana; preserves and promotes Botswana's cultural and natural heritage; operates mobile education service for rural primary schools; repository for scientific collections relating to Botswana; National Herbarium contains 20,000 plant specimens; art gallery holds a collection of art of all races of Africa south of the Sahara, and exhibits works from the rest of the world; library of 7,000 vols and numerous journals; Dir SUSO R. MWEENDO; publs *The Zebra's Voice* (newsletter), *Zebra's Tales* (4 a year).

Mochudi

Phuthadikobo Museum: POB 367, Mochudi; tel. 5777238; f. 1976; ethnography, photographic collections, conservation, community education; Dir PAT KOLLARS; publ. *Annual Report*.

University

UNIVERSITY OF BOTSWANA

Private Bag 0022, Gaborone

Telephone: 3550000

Fax: 3956571

Internet: www.ub.bw

Founded 1963 as Univ. of Basutoland (now Lesotho), Bechuanaland (now Botswana) and Swaziland at Roma (Lesotho); became Univ. of Botswana, Lesotho and Swaziland (UBLS) following the independence of Botswana and Lesotho in 1966; adopted present name 1982

State control

Language of instruction: English

Academic year: August to May

Vice-Chancellor: Prof. BOJOSI K. OTLHOGILE

Deputy Vice-Chancellor (Academic Affairs): Prof. FRANK YOUNGMAN

Deputy Vice-Chancellor (Finance and Administration): DAVID BENJAMIN KATZKE

Deputy Vice-Chancellor (Student Affairs): Dr BURTON MGUNI

Library of 370,001 vols

Number of teachers: 796

Number of students: 15,720

Publications: *Annual Report* (annually), *Pula* (2 a year)

DEANS

Faculty of Business: S. V. CHINYOKA

Faculty of Education: Prof. L. NYATI-RAMAHOBO

Faculty of Engineering and Technology: Dr. M. T. OLADIRAN

Faculty of Humanities: Dr N. L. RASEBOTSA

Faculty of Science: Prof. O. TOTOLO

Faculty of Social Sciences: Prof. B. TSIE

School of Graduate Studies: Prof. C. O. HAAVIK

HEADS OF DEPARTMENTS

Faculty of Business (Private Bag UB 00701, Gaborone; tel. 3552234; fax 3185102; e-mail business@mopipi.ub.bw):

Accounting and Finance: Dr E. G. KITINDI
Management: J. P. W. SHUNDA
Marketing: Prof. O. IYANDA

Faculty of Education (Private Bag UB 00702, Gaborone; tel. 3552171; fax 3185096; e-mail educiao@mopipi.ub.bw):

Adult Education: Prof. A. B. ODUARAN
Educational Foundations: Dr B. CHILISA
Educational Technology: Dr P. T. NLEYA
Home Economics: Dr L. R. MBEREBGWA
Languages and Social Science Education: Dr T. MOOKO
Mathematics and Science Education: Prof. R. B. PROPHET
Nursing Education: Dr E. S. SELOILWE
Physical Education: Dr M. M. MOKGWATHI
Primary Education: Dr G. TSAYANG

Faculty of Engineering and Technology (Private Bag UB 0061, Gaborone; tel. 3554222; fax 3952309; e-mail fet@mopipi.ub.bw):

Architecture and Planning: Prof. A. C. MOSHA
Civil Engineering: Prof. A. B. NGOWI
Electrical Engineering: Prof. G. O. ANDERSON
Industrial Design and Technology: Prof. K. L. KUMAR
Mechanical Engineering: Prof. J. UZIAK

Faculty of Humanities (Private Bag UB 00703, Gaborone; tel. 3552196; fax 3185098; e-mail human@mopipi.ub.bw):

African Languages and Literature: Dr P. S. SELOMA
English: Prof. J. T. MATHANGWANE
French: Dr T. KITENGE-NGOY
History: Dr G. A. SEKGOMA
Library Studies and Information: Dr K. H. MOAHI
Media Studies: Prof. D. KERR
Theology and Religious Studies: Dr F. NKOMAZANA

Faculty of Science (Private Bag UB 00704, Gaborone; tel. 3552470; fax 3185097; e-mail science@mopipi.ub.bw):

Biology: Dr M. DITLHOGO
Chemistry: Prof. R. R. T. MAJINDA
Computer Science: Dr S. O. OJO
Environmental Sciences: Prof. R. CHANDA
Geology: Dr R. T. CHAOKA
Mathematics: Dr J. B. GATSINZI
Physics: Dr J. S. NKOMA

Faculty of Social Sciences (Private Bag UB 00705, Gaborone; tel. 3552743; fax 3185099; e-mail socialsc@mopipi.ub.bw):

Economics: Dr H. K. SIPHAMBE
Law: Prof. E. K. QUANSAH
Political and Administrative Studies: Prof. G. S. MAIPOSE
Population Studies: R. G. MAJELANTLE
Psychology: Prof. I. E. PLATTNER
Social Work: Assoc. Prof. L.-K. J. MWANSA
Sociology: Dr M. MULINGE
Statistics: Dr N. FORCHEH

ATTACHED INSTITUTE

Centre for Academic Development: Dir Prof. A. P. N. THAPISA.

Centre for Continuing Education: Dir Dr T. NHUNDU.

Directorate for Research and Development: Dir Prof. I. N. MAZONDE (acting).

Harry Oppenheimer Okavango Research Centre: Dir Prof L. RAMBERG.

Colleges

Botswana College of Agriculture: Content Farm, Sebele, Gaborone; Private Bag 0027, Gaborone; tel. 3650100; fax 3928753; internet www.bca.bw; f. 1967; associated instn of University of Botswana; library: 29,810 vols, 118 periodicals; 79 teachers; 425 students; Principal E. J. KEMSLEY.

Botswana Institute of Administration and Commerce: POB 10026, Gaborone; tel. 3956324; fax 3959768; f. 1970; library: 7,000 vols; 73 teachers; Principal L. L. SEBINA; publ. *Newsletter* (4 a year).

Botswana Polytechnic: Private Bag 0061, Gaborone; tel. 3952305; fax 3952309; library: 13,000 vols; 120 teachers; 800 students; Principal A. KERTON; Registrar T. MOGKWATI

HEADS OF DEPARTMENTS

Civil Engineering: H. PARAMESWAR
Electrical Engineering: D. DAWOOD
Mechanical Engineering: D. JACKSON
Technology and Education: M. KEWAGAMANG

Institute of Development Management: POB 1357, Gaborone; tel. 3952371; fax 3973144; e-mail idm@info.bw; f. 1974; management training in business management, education management, information management, administration of legal services; library: 8,000 vols (including special World Bank and SADCC collections); 25 teachers; 965 students; certificate courses; Regional Dir Dr M. KHAKHETLA.

BRAZIL

The Higher Education System

In 2003 there were 1,859 institutions of higher education in Brazil, with total student enrolment of 4,619,409. Universities fall into five categories: federal, state, municipal, private and Catholic. Federal universities are the most popular and competition to enter them is very fierce; they are administered by the federal Government. State universities are funded by the individual states, while municipal universities usually focus on one subject or provide professional training. Private universities are funded by private organizations and students' fees, and Catholic universities, while supported principally by the Catholic Church, are in fact open to students of all denominations. The Ministry of Education has ultimate control of higher education, and the establishment of new institutions is authorized by the Conselho Nacional de Educação (CNE—National Education Council).

Both public (federal, state, municipal) and private (including Catholic) universities base admissions on a combination of the secondary school diploma and entrance examinations (Vestibular). There are three qualifications each at undergraduate and postgraduate level. Undergraduate degrees are between four and five years long, and consist of the Bacharel (excludes teacher-training), Licenciado (includes teacher-training) and Título Profissional (professional title). Parallel to these degrees are cursos seqüenciais, which are non-degree courses in subjects such as business and management, and the Provão, an obligatory test designed to monitor teaching standards.

Postgraduate qualifications are divided into sensu stricto ('strict sense') and sensu lato ('wide sense'). Sensu stricto encompasses the classical postgraduate schema, consisting of the Mestrado (Masters), which requires two years of study, and the Doutorado (Doctorate), which is awarded after four years of study and research following the Mestrado. Sensu lato covers professional qualifications which do not hold graduate 'credit' but are of value in the private sector; Especialista (Specialist) is the title often bestowed by Sensu lato.

The CNE accredits and assesses all federal and private universities at the undergraduate graduate level, while state and municipal universities are accredited and assessed by the respective state council. The Brazilian Higher Education Funding Agency is the body within the Ministry of Education responsible for evaluating graduate programmes, with courses generally requiring a score of 3 on a scale of 7 to meet the minimum requirements.

Vocational and technical training is separate from academic education, and is governed according to the Educational Guidelines Law of 1996, which established three levels of non-university, post-secondary education and training. The three levels are: nivel básico, a first stage open to students of any educational attainment, and leading to a certificate of basic competency in a specific job or skill; nivel técnico, which lasts one to two years, requires at least 11 years of basic education and is regulated by the Ministry of Education or State authorities; and nivel tecnológica, the third and final level, providing vocational education of a higher education standard and lasting two to three years.

Regulatory and Representative Bodies

GOVERNMENT

Ministry of Culture: Esplanada dos Ministérios, Bloco B, 4o andar, 70068-900 Brasília, DF; tel. (61) 3316-2171; fax (61) 3225-9162; e-mail gm@minc.gov.br; internet www.cultura.gov.br; Minister GILBERTO PASSOS GIL MOREIRA.

Ministry of Education: Esplanada dos Ministérios, Bloco L, 70047-900 Brasília, DF; tel. (61) 2104-8731; fax (61) 2104-9172; e-mail henriquepaim@mec.gov.br; internet www.mec.gov.br; Minister FERNANDO HADDAD.

Institute Nacional de Estudos e Pesquisas Educacionais Anício Teixeira (INEP): Inep/MEC, Esplanada dos Ministérios, Bloco L, Anexos I e II, 4o andar, 70047-900 Brasília, DF; tel. (61) 2104-8406; fax (61) 2104-9850; internet www.inep.gov.br; f. 1937; govt agency; promotes study and research of Brazilian education system; supports formation and implementation of education policy; Pres. REYNALDO FERNANDES.

Secretaria de Educação Superior (SESU): Ministério da Educação, Esplanada dos Ministérios, Bloco L, 70047-900 Brasília, DF; tel. (61) 2104-8710; internet portal.mec.gov.br/sesu; attached to Min. of Education; Sec. RONALDO MOTA.

ACCREDITATION

Conselho Nacional de Educação (CNE): SGAS, Av. L/2, Quadra 607, Lote 50, 70200-670 Brasília, DF; tel. (61) 2104-6339; fax (61) 2104-6224; e-mail edsonnunes@mec.gov.br; internet portal.mec.gov.br/cne; f. 1995; Pres. EDSON DE OLIVEIRA NUNES.

FUNDING

Co-ordenação de Aperfeiçoamento de Pessoal de Nível Superior (CAPES) (Federal Agency for Postgraduate Education): Ministério da Educação, Anexos I e II, 2° andar, 70359-970 Brasília, DF; tel. (61) 321-3200; internet www.capes.gov.br; f. 1951; govt agency; funds *sensu stricto* postgraduate study of the sciences in Brazil and abroad; main objects are to deploy the human resources of graduate schools to help govt and public enterprises, to give student grants, to evaluate and co-ordinate Masters and Doctors courses; funds over half of all eligible postgraduate students in Brazil; Pres. JORGE ALMEIDA GUIMARÃES.

NATIONAL BODIES

Associação de Educação Católica do Brasil (Association for Catholic Education in Brazil): SBN Q01, Bloco H, Loja 40, 70040-000 Brasília, DF; tel. (61) 223-2947; fax (61) 226-3081; f. 1945; supervises 27 sections, with a total of 1,750 schools and seminaries; Pres. P. AGUSTÍN CASTEJÓN; publs *Cadernos de Educação, Revista de Educação AEC*.

Conselho de Reitores das Universidades Brasileiras (Council of Brazilian University Rectors): SEUP/Norte, Quadra 516, Conj. D, 70770-535 Brasília, DF; tel. (61) 349-9010; fax (61) 274-4621; e-mail crub@nutecnet.com.br; internet www.crub.org.br; f. 1966; study of problems affecting higher education; 128 mems; library of 15,000 vols; Pres. JOSÉ CARLOS ALMEIDA DA SILVA; Gen. Sec. MARIA HELENA ALVES GARCIA; publs *Educação Brasileira, Estudos e Debates, Anais, Sistema de Informação das Universidades Brasileiras, Cadernos CRUB, CRUB Informa*.

Instituto Brasileiro de Educação, Ciência e Cultura (IBECC) (Brazilian Institute of Education, Science and Culture): UNESCO National Commission, Av. Marechal Floriano 196, 3° andar, Palácio Itamaraty, 20080 Rio de Janeiro, RJ; tel. (21) 516-2458; fax (21) 516-2458; e-mail ibecc@unisys.com.br; f. 1946; library of 1,500 vols; Pres. (vacant); Exec. Sec. JOAQUIM CAETANO GENTIL NETO; publ. *Boletim: Correio do IBECC*.

Learned Societies

GENERAL

Fundação Santista (Santista Foundation): Av. M.C. Aguiar 215, Bl. D, 5° andar, 05804-905 São Paulo, SP; tel. (11) 3741-6832; fax (11) 3741-1288; e-mail fsantista@vol.com.br; f. 1955; to promote the advancement of science, letters and arts in Brazil by granting every year the Santista prizes and the Santista prizes for young people, consisting of the following: gold and silver medals, diploma of recognition for outstanding service in any of the scientific, literary or artistic fields, plus a sum of money; Chair. Prof. MIGUEL REALE; Exec. Sec. RENATO WENTER.

UNESCO Brasilia Office: CP 08563, 70070-000 Brasilia, DF; located at: SAS Quadra 5 Bloco H Lote 6, Edificio CNPQ/IBICT/UNESCO, 9° andar, 70070-914 Brasilia, DF; tel. (61) 2106-3500; fax (61) 321-8577; e-mail uhbrz@unesco.org; internet www

.unesco.org.br; f. 1972; Dir JORGE WERTHEIN; publ. *Unesco News* (4 a year).

AGRICULTURE, FISHERIES AND VETERINARY SCIENCE

Associação Brasileira de Mecânica dos Solos (Brazilian Society for Soil Mechanics): CP 7141, 01064-970 São Paulo, SP; tel. (11) 268-7325; fax (11) 268-7325; f. 1950; 865 mems; Pres. Eng. SUSSUMU NIYAMA; Sec. MARCUS PACHECO; publ. *Solos e Rochas – Revista Brasileira de Geotecnia*.

Sociedade Nacional de Agricultura (National Agricultural Society): Av. General Justo 171, 20021-130 Rio de Janeiro, RJ; tel. (21) 2533-0088; fax (21) 2240-4189; e-mail sna@sna.agr.br; internet www.sna.agr.br; f. 1897; 10,000 mems; library of 45,000 vols; Pres. OCTÁVIO MELLO ALVARENGA; Dir and First Sec. ELVO SANTORO; publ. *A Lavoura* (6 a year).

BIBLIOGRAPHY, LIBRARY SCIENCE AND MUSEOLOGY

Associação dos Arquivistas Brasileiros: Rua da Candelária 9-sala 1.004, 20091-020 Rio de Janeiro, RJ; tel. (21) 233-7142; fax (21) 233-7142; e-mail aab@imagelink.com.br; f. 1971; co-operates with the Government, national and international organizations on all matters relating to archives and documentation; organizes national congresses, study courses, conferences, etc.; has achieved national legislation on archives; 300 mems; Pres. MARIZA BOTTINO; Sec. TANIA SOUZA PIMENTA; publs *Boletim* (quarterly), *Revista Arquivo & Administraçao*.

Federação Brasileira de Associações de Bibliotecários (FEBAB) (Brazilian Federation of Library Associations): Rua Avanhandava 40, conj. 110, 01306 São Paulo, SP; tel. (11) 257-99-79; f. 1959 to act for the regional library associations at a national level; to serve as a centre of documentation and bibliography for Brazil; biennial national congress; 27 mem. associations; Pres. JOÃO CARLOS GOMES RIBEIRO; Sec. Gen. WILMA ROSA; publs *Revista Brasileira de Biblioteconomia e Documentação*, *Boletim*.

ECONOMICS, LAW AND POLITICS

Instituto Brasileiro de Economia (Brazilian Institute of Economics): Getúlio Vargas Foundation, CP 62-591, Rio de Janeiro, RJ; f. 1951; Chair. ANTÔNIO SALAZAR P. BRANDÃO; publs *Conjuntura Econômica* (monthly), *Revista Agroanalysis* (monthly).

Instituto dos Advogados Brasileiros (Institute of Brazilian Lawyers): Av. Marechal Câmara 210, 5° andar, Castelo, 20020-080 Rio de Janeiro, RJ; f. 1843; 1,141 mems; Pres. RICARDO CÉSAR PEREIRA LIRA; library: see Libraries; publ. *Revista*.

Instituto Municipal de Administração e Ciências Contábeis (Municipal Institute of Administration and Business Science): Parque Municipal, CP 1914, Belo Horizonte, MG; f. 1954; library of 33,000 vols; Pres. RAUL LOPES MURADAS.

EDUCATION

Fundação Carlos Chagas: CP 11478, Av. Prof. Francisco Morato 1565, 05513-900 São Paulo, SP; tel. (11) 3723-3000; fax (11) 3721-1059; e-mail fcc@fcc.org.br; internet www.fcc.org.br; f. 1964; activities in the fields of human resources, educational research and educational evaluation; 184 mems; library of 41,000 vols; Pres. Prof. Dr RUBENS MURILLO MARQUES; Sec.-Gen. Prof. Dr NELSON FONTANA MARGARIDO; publs *Cadernos de Pesquisa* (3 a year), *Estudos em Avaliação Educacional* (2 a year).

Fundação de Desenvolvimento de Pessoal (FUNDESP): Av. João Pessoa 5609, Damas, 60435 Fortaleza, CE; tel. (85) 292-1877; f. 1974; language courses; library of 6,128 vols; Pres. MARIA DO CARNO MAGALHÃES.

Fundação Getúlio Vargas: Praia de Botafogo 190, 22253-900 Rio de Janeiro, RJ; tel. (21) 2559-6000; fax (21) 2553-6372; e-mail fgv@fgv.br; f. 1944; technical, scientific, educational and philanthropic activities; includes 3 educational institutes; 385 mems in General Assembly; library: over 120,000 vols; Pres. Dr CARLOS IVAN SIMONSEN LEAL; publs *Conjuntura Econômica* (monthly), *Correio da UNESCO* (monthly), *Revista de Administração de Empresas* (every 2 months), *Revista de Administração Pública* (quarterly), *Revista Brasileira de Economia* (quarterly), *Agroanalysis* (monthly), *Estudos Históricos* (2 a year).

HISTORY, GEOGRAPHY AND ARCHAEOLOGY

Instituto Arqueológico, Histórico e Geográfico Pernambucano (Archaeological, Historical and Geographical Institute): Rua do Hospício 130, Recife, PE; f. 1862; library of 20,000 vols; 50 mems; 130 corresp. mems; 5 hon. mems; Pres. Dr JOSÉ ANTÔNIO GONSALVES DE MELO; First Sec. Prof. J. L. MOTA MENEZES; Librarian Prof. FERNANDA IVO NEVES; publ. *Revista*.

Instituto do Ceará (Ceará Institute): Rua Barão do Rio Branco 1594, 60025-061 Fortaleza, CE; tel. (85) 32316152; fax (85) 32544116; e-mail institutodoceara@secrel.com.br; internet www.institutodoceara.org.br; f. 1887; includes the following commissions; History, Manuscripts and Periodicals, Geography, Anthropology; 40 mems; library of 52,000 vols; Pres. MANUEL EDUARDO PINHEIRO CAMPOS; Gen. Sec. VALDELICE CARNEIRO GIRÃO; publ. *Revista* (annually).

Instituto Genealógico Brasileiro (Genealogical Institute): Rua Dr Zuquim 1525, São Paulo, SP; library of 972 vols; Pres. Colonel SALVADOR DE MOYA; Sec. Dr JORGE BUENO DE MIRANDA; publs *Anuário Genealógico Brasileiro*, *Anuário Genealógico Latino*, *Revista Genealógica Brasileira*, *Biblioteca Genealógica Brasileira*, *Biblioteca*, *Genealógica Latina*, *Indices Genealógicos Brasileiros*, *Subsídios Genealógicos*.

Instituto Geográfico e Histórico da Bahia (Bahia Geographical and Historical Institute): Av. 7 de Setembro 94A, Piedade, 40060-001 Salvador, BA; tel. (71) 322-2453; fax (71) 321-4787; f. 1894; 300 mems; library of 35,000 vols; Pres. Profa CONSUELO PONDÉ DE SENA; Sec. Dr LAMARTINE DE ANDRADE LIMA; publ. *Revista* (annually).

Instituto Geográfico e Histórico do Amazonas (IGHA): Rua Bernardo Ramos 117, Manaus, AM; tel. 232-7077; f. 1917; 120 mems; library of 45,158 vols; Pres. Dr ROBERIO DOS SANTOS PEREIRA BRAGA; Gen. Sec. Dr JOSÉ ROBERTO TADROS; Admin. Sec. JOSÉ GERALDO XAVIER DOS ANJOS; publs *Revista*, *Boletim*.

Instituto Geológico (Geological Institute): Av. Miguel Stefano 3900, Agua Funda, 04301-903 São Paulo, SP; tel. (11) 5077-1155; fax (11) 5077-2219; e-mail igeologico@igeologico.sp.gov.br; internet www.igeologico.sp.gov.br; f. 1886; 100 mems; library of 8,500 vols, 1,850 periodicals, 10,000 maps; map collection, geological museum; Dir Dr CLÁUDIO JOSÉ FERREIRA; publs *Boletim*, *Revista*.

Instituto Histórico de Alagoas (Alagoas Historical Institute): Rua João Pessoa 382, 57000 Maceió, AL; f. 1869; 40 mems; library of 15,000 vols; Pres. Dr JOSÉ LAGES FILHO; Sec. Dr ABELARDO DUARTE; publ. *Revista*.

Instituto Histórico e Geográfico Brasileiro (Brazilian Historical and Geographical Institute): Av. Augusto Severo 8, 20021-040 Rio de Janeiro, RJ; tel. (21) 509-5107; fax (21) 252-4430; e-mail ihgbpresidencia@unikey.com.br; f. 1838; library of 560,000 vols; archive of 110,000 documents; museum of 1,100 items; Pres. ARNO WEHLING; Sec. CYBELLE MOREIRA DE IPANEMA; publ. *Revista* (quarterly).

Instituto Histórico e Geográfico de Goiás (Historical and Geographical Institute): Rua 82, No 455, S. Sul, Goiânia; tel. 224-4622; f. 1933; 60 mems; library of 20,000 vols; rare collections of letters and newspapers; Dir Dr COLEMAR NATAL E SILVA; publs *Boletim* (quarterly), *Review* (annually).

Instituto Histórico e Geográfico de Santa Catarina (Santa Catarina Historical and Geographical Institute): Praça XV de Novembro/Palácio Cruz e Sousa, CP 1582, Florianópolis, SC; tel. (48) 212-2363 ext. 216; fax (48) 222-5111; e-mail ihgsc@ihgsc.org.br; internet www.ihgsc.org.br; f. 1896; 235 mems; library of 8,000 vols; Pres. Prof. Dr CARLOS HUMBERTO PEDERNEIRAS CORRÊA; Sec. Prof. JALI MEIRINHO; publs *Revista* (annually), *Anais*, *Boletim* (monthly), *Coleção Catariniana*, *Coleção Ensaios*.

Instituto Histórico e Geográfico de São Paulo (São Paulo Historical and Geographical Institute): Rua Benjamim Constant 158, 01005-000 São Paulo, SP; f. 1894; library of 40,000 vols; Pres. HERNÂNI DONATO; Sec. MARIO SAVELLI; publ. *Revista*.

Instituto Histórico e Geográfico de Sergipe (Sergipe Historical and Geographical Institute): Rua de Itabaianinha 41, 49000 Aracajú; f. 1912; Pres. Prof. MARIA THETIS NUENS; publ. *Revista*.

Instituto Histórico e Geográfico do Espírito Santo (Historical and Geographical Institute): Av. República 374, CP 29020-620, Vitória; tel. (27) 3223-5934; e-mail ihges.vix@zaz.com.br; f. 1916; 400 mems; Pres. Profa LEA BRÍGIDA DE ALVARENGA ROSA; Gen. Sec. VITOR BIASUTTI; publ. *Revista* (annually).

Instituto Histórico e Geográfico do Maranhão (Maranhão Historical and Geographical Institute): Rua Santa Rita 230, 65000 São Luíz, MA; f. 1925; Pres. Dr JOSÉ RIBAMAR SEGUINS; Sec.-Gen. Dr FRANCISCO MARIALVA MONT'ALVERNE FROTA; publ. *Revista*.

Instituto Histórico e Geográfico do Pará (Pará Historical and Geographical Institute): Rua d'Aveiro-Cidade Irmã 62 (Antiga Thomazia Perdigão), CP 547, 66000 Belém; f. 1900; Pres. Dr JOSÉ RODRIGUES DA SILVEIRA NETTO; First Sec. Dr ALAÚDIO DE OLIVEIRA MELLO.

Instituto Histórico e Geográfico do Rio Grande do Norte (Rio Grande do Norte Historical and Geographical Institute): Rua da Conceição 622, 59000 Natal; f. 1902; library: library of 50,000 vols; Pres. Dr ENÉLIO LIMA PETROVICH; Librarian OLAVO DE MEDEIROS FILHO; publ. *Revista*.

Instituto Histórico e Geográfico do Rio Grande do Sul (Rio Grande do Sul Historical and Geographical Institute): Rua Riachuelo 1317, 90010-271 Porto Alegre, RS; tel. and fax (51) 3224-3760; e-mail ihgrgs@terra.com.br; internet www.ihgrgs.org.br; f. 1920; 30 mems; Pres. Prof. GERVÁSIO RODRIGO NEVES; publs *Revista* (annually), *O Pensamento Político* (annually).

Instituto Histórico e Geográfico Paraíbano (Paraíba Historical and Geographical Institute): Rua Barão do Abiaí 64, CP 37, 58013-080 João Pessoa; f. 1905; library of 30,000 vols; 50 mems; 30 corresp.; Pres. LUIZ

HUGO GUIMARÃES; Sec. DOMINGOS A. RIBEIRO; publ. *Revista*.

Instituto Histórico, Geográfico e Etnográfico Paranaense (Historical, Geographical, Ethnographic Institute of Paraná): Rua José Loureiro 43, 80000 Curitiba; f. 1900; Pres. Gen. LUÍZ CARLOS PEREIRA TOURINHO; Sec. NEY FERNANDO PERRACINI DE AZEVEDO; publ. *Boletim*.

Sociedade Brasileira de Cartografia (SBC): Av. Presidente Wilson 210, 7° andar, Centro, 20030-021 Rio de Janeiro, RJ; tel. (21) 2240-6901; fax (21) 2262-2823; e-mail sbc.rlk@terra.com.br; internet www.rio.com.br/sbcgfsr; f. 1958; cartography, geodesy, surveying, photogrammetry and remote sensing; 2,000 mems; Pres. Dr Eng. PAULO CESAR TEIXEIRA TRINO; Sec. Eng. JOSÉ HENRIQUE DA SILVA; publs *Proceedings of the Brazilian Congress of Cartography* (every 2 years), *Revista Brasileira de Cartografia* (papers and contributions, 1 or 2 a year), *Boletim* (news and updates, 6 a year).

Sociedade Brasileira de Geografia (Brazilian Geographical Society): Praça da República 54, 1° andar, Rio de Janeiro, RJ; f. 1883; library of 13,712 vols; 284 mems; Pres. Prof. JURADYR DE CASTRO PIRES FERREIRA; Sec.-Gen. General HENRIQUE GUILHERME MULLER; publs *Boletim*, *Estante Paranista*.

LANGUAGE AND LITERATURE

Academia Amazonense de Letras (Amazonas Academy of Letters): Rua Ramos Ferreira 1009, Manaus, AM; f. 1918; Pres. DJALMA BATISTA; Sec. GENESINO BRAGA; Librarian MÁRIO YPIRANGA MONTEIRO; 40 mems; library of 3,500 vols; publ. *Revista*.

Academia Brasileira de Letras (Brazilian Academy of Letters): Av. Presidente Wilson 203, 20030 Rio de Janeiro, RJ; tel. (21) 524-8230; fax (21) 220-6695; e-mail abl2@openlink.com.br; internet www.academia.org.br; f. 1897; preparing exhaustive *Dictionary of the Portuguese Language*; annual prizes awarded for best Brazilian works in prose, verse and drama; 40 mems; library of 50,000 vols; Pres. (vacant); Sec.-Gen. ABGAR RENAULT; Librarian BARBOSA LIMA SOBRINHO; publ. *Revista Brasileira* (annals, 3 a year).

Academia Cearense de Letras (Ceará Academy of Letters): Biblioteca, Rua do Rosario 1, Palacio da Luz, 60055-090 Fortaleza, CE; tel. (85) 253-4275; fax (85) 253-4275; e-mail aceletras@accvia.com.br; f. 1894; 40 mems; 21 hon. mems; library of 18,000 vols; Pres. ARTUR EDUARDO BENEVIDES; Sec.-Gen. PEDRO PAULO MONTENEGRO; publ. *Revista*.

Academia de Letras da Bahia (Bahia Academy of Letters): Av. Joana Angélica 198, Nazaré, 40050 Salvador, BA; tel. (71) 243-7614; f. 1917; 40 mems; 19 corresponding in Brazil, 6 abroad; library of 10,000 vols; Pres. CLÁUDIO VEIGA; Vice-Pres. WILSON LINS; Sec. EDIVALDO M. BOAVENTURA; publ. *Revista* (annually).

Academia de Letras e Artes do Planalto (Planalto Academy of Arts and Letters): Rua do Santissimo Sacramento 32, 72800-000 Luziânia, GO; tel. (61) 3621-1184; e-mail alan@viggiano.com.br; f. 1976; 40 mems; library of 8,000 vols; Pres. MARCO ANTONIO MARTINS DE ARAUJO.

Academia Mineira de Letras (Minas Gerais Academy of Letters): Rua da Bahia 1466, 30160 Belo Horizonte, MG; Pres. VIVALDI MOREIRA.

Academia Paraibana de Letras (Paraíba Academy of Letters): Rua Duque de Caxias 25, CP 334, 58000 João Pessoa, PB; f. 1941; 40 mems; Pres. AFONSO PEREIRA DA SILVA; Gen. Sec. AURÉLIO MORENO DE ALBUQUERQUE; publs *Revista*, *Boletim Informativo*, *Discursos e Ensaios*.

Academia Paulista de Letras (São Paulo Academy of Letters): Largo do Arouche 312, 01219 São Paulo, SP; f. 1909; 40 mems; library of 50,000 vols; Pres. ANTONIO A. S. AMORA; publ. *Revista*.

Academia Pernambucana de Letras (Pernambuco Academy of Letters): Av. Rui Barbosa 1596, Graças, 52050-000 Recife, PE; fax (81) 268-2211; f. 1901; library of 12,000 vols; 40 mems, unlimited number of hon. and corresp. mems in Brazil and abroad; Pres. LUIZ DE MAGALHAES MELO; Sec. Dr LUCILO VAREJÃO FILHO; publ. *Revista*.

Academia Piauiense de Letras (Piauí Academy of Letters): 64001-490 Teresina, PI; Pres. MANOEL PAULO NUNES; publ. *Revista*.

Academia Riograndense de Letras (Rio Grande Academy of Letters): Rua Cândido Silveira 43, Porto Alegre, RS; publ. *Revista*.

Alliance Française: Rua Duvivier, 43/103 Copacabana, 20020-020 Rio de Janeiro; tel. (21) 2244-6950; fax (21) 2543-7656; e-mail dgafpbr@rioaliancafrancesa.com.br; internet www.aliancafrancesa.com; offers courses and exams in French language and culture and promotes cultural exchange with France; attached teaching offices in Aracaju, Batatais, Bauru, Belém, Belo Horizonte, Blumenau, Brasília, Campina Grande, Campinas, Campo Grande, Caxias do Sul, Curitiba, Florianopolis, Fortaleza, Franca, Goiânia, Guarulhos, João Pessoa, Joinville, Juazeiro do Norte, Juíz de Fora, Jundiai, Londrina, Maceió, Manaus, Natal, Niterói, Nova Friburgo, Petropolis, Porto Alegre, Recife, Resende, Ribeirão Preto, Salvador, Santana do Livramento, Santo André, Santos, São Caetano do Sul, São Carlos, São Gonçalo, São João del Rei, São Jose dos Campos, São Luis, São Paulo, Sete Lagoas, Sorocaba, Tatuape, Teresopolis, Vicosa and Vitoria; Dir of Operations, Brazil LUCE RUDENT.

British Council: Ed. Centro Empresarial Varig, SCN Quadra 04 Bloco B, Torre Oeste Conjunto 202, 70710-926 Brasilia, DF; tel. (61) 2106-7500; fax (61) 2106-7599; e-mail brasilia@britishcouncil.org.br; internet www.britishcouncil.org.br; offers courses and exams in English language and British culture and promotes cultural exchange with the UK; attached offices in Curitiba, Recife, Rio de Janeiro (teaching centre) and São Paolo; Dir Dr DAVID COOKE.

Goethe-Institut: Rua Lisboa 974, 05413-001 São Paulo, SP; tel. (11) 3088-4288; fax (11) 3060-8413; e-mail institut@saopaulo.goethe.org; internet www.goethe.de/br/sap/deindex.htm; offers courses and exams in German language and culture and promotes cultural exchange with Germany; attached centres in Curitiba, Porto Alegre, Rio de Janeiro and Salvador/Bahia; library of 15,000 vols, 60 periodicals; Dir and Regional Dir, South America Dr BRUNO FISCHLI.

Instituto Cervantes: Rua do Carmo 27, Segundo Andar, 20011-020 Rio de Janeiro; tel. (21) 3231-6555; fax (21) 2531-9647; e-mail cenrio@cervantes.es; internet riodejaneiro.cervantes.es; offers courses and exams in Spanish language and culture and promotes cultural exchange with Spain and Spanish-speaking Latin and Central America; attached centre in São Paulo; Dir FRANCISCO CORRAL SÁNCHEZ-CABEZUDO.

PEN Clube do Brasil—Associação Universal de Escritores (International PEN Centre): Praia do Flamengo 172, 10° andar, Rio de Janeiro, RJ; f. 1936; 106 mems; monthly free lectures; theatrical performances; Pres. Prof. MARCOS ALMIR MADEIRA; publ. *Boletim*.

Sociedade Brasileira de Autores (SBAT) (Society of Playwrights): Av. Almirante Barroso 97, 3° andar, 20031-005 Rio de Janeiro, RJ; tel. (21) 2240-7231; fax (21) 2240-7431; e-mail sbat@sbat.com.br; internet www.sbat.com.br; f. 1917; non-profit-making organization; 6,000 mems; library of 6,000 vols, 30,716 plays; Pres. CARLOS EDUARDO NOVÃES; Communications Dir EWA PROCTER; publ. *Revista de Teatro* (6 a year).

MEDICINE

Academia de Medicina de São Paulo (Medical Academy of São Paulo): Rua Teodoro Sampaio 115, 2° andar, 05405 São Paulo, SP; tel. 853-9677; f. 1895 as Sociedade de Medicina e Cirurgia; Pres. Prof. RAUL MARINO JUNIOR; Gen. Sec. Prof. CLAUDIO COHEN.

Academia Nacional de Medicina (National Academy of Medicine): Av. General Justo 365, 7° andar, 20021-130 Rio de Janeiro, RJ; tel. (21) 2524-2164; fax (21) 2240-8673; e-mail anm@anm.org.br; internet www.anm.org.br; f. 1829; 100 mems; library of 22,000 vols, 1,200 periodicals; Pres. Dr AUGUSTO PAULINO-NETTO; Sec.-Gen. Dr MARCOS F. MORÃES; publ. *Anais* (2 a year).

Associação Bahiana de Medicina (Medical Society): Av. Sete de Setembro 48, 1°, Salvador, BA; f. 1894; Pres. Dr JOSÉ SILVEIRA; Sec.-Gen. Dr MENANDRO NOVÃES; publ. *Anais*.

Associação Brasileira de Farmacêuticos (Brazilian Pharmaceutical Association): Rua dos Andradas 96 (10° Andar), Centro 2005-1000, Rio de Janeiro, RJ; tel. (21) 2263-0791; fax (21) 2233-3672; e-mail abf@abf.org.br; internet www.abf.org.br; f. 1916; comprises the following Comms: *Econômica e Etica Farmacêutica* (Pharmaceutical Economics and Ethics); *Desenvolvimento Cultural* (Cultural Development); *Propaganda e Intercambio Associativo* (Propaganda and Exchange); *Legislação Comercial* (Commercial Legislation); *Legislação Sanitaria* (Sanitary Legislation); *Legislação Tributaria* (Tax Legislation); *Legislação de Marcas e Patentes* (Trade Marks and Patents); library; 950 mems (hon. and corresp.); Pres. Dr JORGE CAVALCANTI DE OLIVEIRA; Vice-Pres. Dr JOSÉ LIPORAGE TEIXEIRA; publ. *Revista Brasileira de Farmácia* (3 a year).

Associação Médica Brasileira (Brazilian Medical Association): Rua São Carlos do Pinhal 324, CP 8094, São Paulo; f. 1951; professional association; 35,000 mems; Pres. Dr PEDRO KASSAB; Sec.-Gen. Dr RADION SCHUELER BARBOZA; publs *Journal AMB* (weekly), *Boletim AMB and Revista AMB(-monthly)*, *Revista Brasileira de Ortopedia*, *Arquivos Brasileiros de Endocrinologia e Metabologia*, *Jornal Brasileira de Nefrologia*, *Anais Brasileiros de Geriatria e Gerontologia* (quarterly), *Revista Brasileira de Reumatologia* (every 2 months).

Associação Paulista de Medicina (São Paulo Medical Association): Av. Brigadeiro Luís Antônio 278, CP 2103, 01318-901 São Paulo; tel. (11) 232-3141; e-mail apm@apm.org.br; f. 1930; 22,000 active mems; 432 corresp. mems; Pres. Dr ELEUSES VIEIRA DE PAIVA; Scientific Dir Dr ÁLVARO NAGIB ATALLAH; publs *Revista Paulista de Medicina* (6 a year), *Jornal da APM* (monthly), *Revista Diagnóstico & Tratamento* (4 a year).

Sociedade Brasileira de Dermatologia (Brazilian Dermatological Society): CP 389, 20001-970 Rio de Janeiro, RJ; tel. (21) 253-6747; f. 1912; 16 hon. mems; 56 corresponding mems; 3,800 mems; library of 4,000 vols,

200 periodicals; Sec.-Gen. Dr MARIA DE LOURDES VIEGAS; publ. *Anais Brasileiros de Dermatologia*.

Sociedade de Medicina de Alagoas (Alagoas Medical Society): Rua Barão de Anadia 5 (centro), CP 57025 Maceió, AL; tel. 223-3463; fax (82) 223-3463; f. 1917; 1,200 mems; library of 2,500 vols; Pres. Dr SERGIO TOLEDO BARBOSA; publs *Consulta*, *Boletim da SMA*.

Sociedade de Pediatria de Bahia (Paediatrics Society): Hospital Martagão Gesteira, Rua José Duarte 114, Salvador, BA; f. 1930; 200 mems; Pres. ELIEZER AUDÍFACE; publ. *Pediatria e Puericultura*.

NATURAL SCIENCES

General

Academia Brasileira de Ciências (Brazilian Academy of Sciences): Rua Anfilófio de Carvalho 29, 3° andar, 20030-060 Rio de Janeiro, RJ; tel. (21) 3907-8100; fax (21) 3907-8101; e-mail abc@abc.org.br; internet www.scielo.br/aabc; f. 1916; 602 mems (393 full, 146 foreign, 85 assoc., 2 collaborating); Pres. EDUARDO MOACYR KRIEGER; Vice-Pres. JACOB PALIS JUNIOR; Secs LUIZ DAVIDOVICH, HERNAN CHAIMOVICH GURALNIK, IVÁN IZQUIERDO, CARLOS EDUARDO ROCHA MIRANDA; publ. *Anais da Academia Brasileira de Ciências* (4 a year, also online).

Sociedade Brasileira para o Progresso da Ciência (Brazilian Society for the Advancement of Science): Rua Maria Antonia 294, 4° andar, 01222-010 São Paulo, SP; tel. (11) 259-2766; fax (11) 3106-1002; e-mail diret@www.sbpcnet.org.br; internet www.sbpcnet.org.br; f. 1948; 3,000 mems; Pres. Profa Dra GLACI ZANCAN; Sec.-Gen. Prof. Dr ALDO MALAVASI; publs *Ciência e Cultura* (every 2 months), *Ciência Hoje* (every 2 months), *Jornal da Ciência* (every 2 weeks), *Revista Ciência Hoje das Crianças* (monthly).

Biological Sciences

Sociedade Brasileira de Entomologia (Brazilian Entomological Society): CP 42672, 04299-970 São Paulo, SP; tel. (11) 6161-3504; fax (11) 6161-3504; e-mail sbe@ib.usp.br; internet zoo.bio.ufpr.br/sbe; f. 1937; 400 mems; Pres. PEDRO GNASPINI NETTO; Sec. SÉRVIO TÚLIO PIRES AMARANTE; publ. *Revista Brasileira de Entomologia* (quarterly).

Physical Sciences

Associação Brasileira de Química (Brazilian Chemical Association): Av. Presidente Vargas 633 sala 2208, CEP 20071-004, Rio de Janeiro, RJ; tel. (21) 2224-4480; fax (21) 2224-6881; e-mail abqrj@alternex.com.br; f. 1922; affiliated to IUPAC; 3,000 mems; library of 3,000 vols; regional brs in Amazonas, Pará, Maranhão, Ceará, Rio Grande do Norte, Pernambuco, Paraíba, Bahia, Rio de Janeiro, São Paulo, Rio Grande do Sul and Brasília; Pres. HARRY SERRUYA; publs *Anais da Associação Brasileira de Química*, *Revista de Química Industrial*.

PHILOSOPHY AND PSYCHOLOGY

Sociedade Brasileira de Filosofia (Brazilian Philosophical Soc.): Praça da República 54, Rio de Janeiro, RJ; f. 1927; 80 mems; 8 hon., 5 Brazilian corresp., 12 foreign; Pres. Dr HERBERT CANABARRO REICHARDT; Sec.-Gen. Prof. ARNALDO CLARO DE SÃO THIAGO; publ. *Anais*.

RELIGION, SOCIOLOGY AND ANTHROPOLOGY

Comissão Nacional de Folclore (National Folklore Commission): Palácio Itamaraty, Av. Marechal Floriano 196, CEP 20080-002 Rio de Janeiro, RJ; fax (21) 516-2458; Dept of the Brazilian Institute of Education, Science and Culture (IBECC); Pres. ÁTICO VILAS BOAS DA MOTA; publ. *Boletim*.

Sociedade Hebraico Brasileira Renascença: Rua Prates 790, Bom Retiro, 01121-000 São Paulo; tel. (11) 3311 0778; fax (11) 3311-0778; internet www.renascenca.br; f. 1922 as Gymnasio Hebraico-Brasileiro Renascença; Exec. Dir MAX WAINTRAUB.

Attached faculties:

Faculdades Integradas Hebraico Brasileira Renascença: see separate entry under Colleges.

TECHNOLOGY

Associação Brasileira de Metalurgia e Materiais (ABM) (Brazilian Metallurgy and Materials Society): Rua Antônio Comparato 218, 04605-030 São Paulo, SP; f. 1944; 5,500 mems; library of 5,000 vols, periodicals; Pres. SYLVIO N. COUTINHO; Vice-Pres. MARCUS J. A. TAMBASO; publ. *Metalurgia & Materiais* (monthly).

Associação de Engenharia Química (Society of Chemical Engineers): Conjunto das Químicas, Bloco 19, Cidade Universitária, São Paulo, SP; f. 1944; 500 mems; Pres. ALDO TONSO; Sec. UDO HUPFELD.

Research Institutes

AGRICULTURE, FISHERIES AND VETERINARY SCIENCE

Centro de Energia Nuclear na Agricultura (CENA) (Centre of Nuclear Energy in Agriculture): Univ. de São Paulo, Campus de Piracicaba, CP 96, 13400-970 Piracicaba, SP; tel. (19) 429-4600; fax (19) 429-4610; f. 1966; 52 researchers; plant biochemistry, entomology, plant nutrition, radiogenetics, phytopathology, electron microscopy, soil fertility, soil physics, soil microbiology, animal nutrition, hydrology, radiochemistry, radiation protection, ecology, water pollution, genetic engineering; library of 9,000 vols and 366 periodicals; special collection: IAEA publs on life sciences; Dir Dr AUGUSTO TULMANN NETO; publs *Annual Report*, *Scientia Agrícola*.

Centro de Pesquisas Veterinárias 'Desidério Finamor' (Institute of Veterinary Research): CP 2076, 90001-970 Porto Alegre, RS; tel. (51) 4813711; fax (51) 4813337; f. 1949; research and training in all aspects of animal health; library of 1,400 vols; Dir Dr AUGUSTO CÉSAR DA CUNHA; publ. *Pesquisa Agropecuária Gaúcha*.

Empresa Brasileira de Pesquisa Agropecuária (EMBRAPA) (Brazilian Agricultural Research Enterprise): Parque Estacão Biológica s/n, Ed. Sede Plano Piloto, CP 04-0315, 70770-901 Brasília, DF; tel. (61) 3448-4433; fax (61) 3347-1041; e-mail presid@sede.embrapa.br; internet www.embrapa.br; f. 1972; attached to Ministry of Agriculture; controls agricultural research throughout the country; library of 120,000 vols; Pres. SILVIO CRESTANA; publs *Cadernos de Ciência e Tecnologia* (4 per year), *Pesquisa Agropecuaria Brasileira* (monthly), *Textos para Discussão* (irregular).

Research centres:

Centro de Pesquisa Agroflorestal da Amazônia Oriental: Travessa Dr Enéas Pinheiro s/n, Bairro do Marco, 66095-100 Belém, PA; tel. (91) 276-6333; fax (91) 276-0323; internet www.cpatu.embrapa.br; f. 1975.

Centro Nacional de Pesquisa de Florestas: Estrada da Ribeira km 111, CP 319, 83411-000 Colombo, PR; tel. (41) 666-1313; fax (41) 666-1276; internet www.cnpf.embrapa.br; f. 1978; forest research.

Centro de Pesquisa de Pecuária dos Campos sul Brasileiros: Rodovia 153, km 595, Vila Industrial, Zona Rural, 96400-970 Bagé, RS; tel. (32) 42-8499; fax (32) 42-4395; internet www.cppsul.embrapa.br; f. 1975.

Centro de Pesquisa de Pecuária do Sudeste: Rodovia Washington Luiz km 234, 13560-970 São Carlos, SP; tel. (16) 261-5611; fax (16) 261-5754; internet www.cppse.embrapa.br; f. 1975.

Centro Nacional de Pesquisa de Caprinos: Fazenda Três Lagoas/Estrada Sobral/Groaíras km 4, 62011-970 Sobral, CE; tel. (88) 677-7000; fax (88) 677-7055; internet www.cnpc.embrapa.br; e-mail Postmaster@cnpc.embrapa.br; f. 1975; research on goats.

Centro de Pesquisa Agropecuária dos Cerrados: BR 020 km 18, Rodovia Brasília/Fortaleza, 73301-970 Planaltina, DF; tel. (61) 388-9898; fax (61) 389-9879; internet www.cpac.embrapa.br; f. 1975.

Centro Nacional de Recursos Genéticos e Biotecnologia: Parque Estacão Biológico s/n, Plano Piloto (final W-3 Norte), 70770-900 Brasília, DF; tel. (61) 448-4700; fax (61) 448-3624; internet www.cenargem.embrapa.br; f. 1976.

Centro Nacional de Pesquisa de Hortaliças: Rodovia BR 060 Brasília-Anápolis km 09, Fazendo Tamandué, 70359-970 Brasília; tel. (61) 385-9000; fax (61) 556-5744; internet www.cnph.embrapa.br; f. 1975; vegetable research.

Centro Nacional de Pesquisa de Arroz e Feijão: Rodovia Goiânia o Nova Veneza km 12, 75375-000, Santo Antônio de Góias, GO; tel. (62) 533-2110; fax (62) 533-2100; internet www.cnpaf.embrapa.br; f. 1975; research on beans, cowpeas and rice.

Centro Nacional de Pesquisa de Gado de Leite: Rua Eugênio do Nascimento 610, Bairro Dom Bosco, 36038-330 Juiz de Fora, MG; tel. (32) 3249-4700; fax (32) 3249-4701; internet www.cnpgl.embrapa.br; f. 1976; dairy research.

Centro de Pesquisa Agropecuária de Clima Temperado: Rodovia BR 392 km 78, 9° Distrito de Pelotas, 96001-970 Pelotas, RS; tel. (532) 275-8100; fax (532) 275-8221; internet www.cpact.embrapa.br; f. 1975; research on temperate fruit and vegetable crops and food technology.

Centro de Pesquisa Agroflorestal do Acre: Rodovia BR 364, km 14, 69908-970 Rio Branco, AC; tel. (68) 212-3200; fax (68) 212-3284; internet www.cpafac.embrapa.br; f. 1976.

Centro Nacional de Pesquisa de Suínos e Aves: Rodovia BR 153, km 110, Vila Tamanduá, 89700-000 Concórdia, SC; tel. (49) 442-8555; fax (49) 442-8559; internet www.cnpsa.embrapa.br; f. 1975; research on pigs and poultry; library of 4,000 vols, 800 periodicals..

Centro Nacional de Pesquisa de Mandioca e Fruticultura Tropical: Rua EMBRAPA s/n, 44380-000 Cruz das Almas, BA; tel. (75) 621-8000; fax (75) 621-1118; internet www.cnpmf.embrapa.br; f. 1975; research on pineapple, banana, citrus, mango, cassava; Head Dr JOSÉ CARLOS NASCIMENTO.

Centro Nacional de Pesquisa de Milho e Sorgo: Rodovia MG 424, km 65; 35701-970, Sete Lagoas, MG; tel. (31) 3779-1000; fax (31) 3779-1088; internet www.cnpms.embrapa.br; f. 1975; research on maize and sorghum; library of 5,500 books, 65 periodicals; Head Dr ANTÔNIO FERNANDINO C. BAHIA F.

Centro de Pesquisa Agropecuária dos Tabuleiros Costeiros: Av. Beira Mar 3250, 49025-040 Aracaju, SE; tel. (79) 226-1300; fax (79) 226-6145; internet www.cpatc.embrapa.br; f. 1974.

Centro Nacional de Pesquisa de Uva e Vinho: Rua Livramento 515, 95700-000 Bento Gonçalves, RS; tel. (54) 451-2144; fax (54) 451-2792; internet www.cnpuv.embrapa.br; f. 1975; research and development in viticulture and the wine industry.

Centro de Pesquisa Agroflorestal de Rondônia: Rodovia BR 364, km 5.5, 78970-900 Porto Velho, RO; tel. (69) 216-6500; fax (69) 216-6543; f. 1975.

Centro de Pesquisa Agropecuária do Oeste: Rodovia BR 163, km 253.6, 79804-970 Dourados, MS; tel. (67) 425-5122; fax (67) 425-0811; internet www.cpao.embrapa.br; f. 1976.

Centro de Pesquisa Agroflorestal de Roraima: BR 174, km 08, Distrito Industrial, 69301-970 Boa Vista, RR; tel. (95) 626-7125; fax (95) 626-7104; internet www.cpafrr.embrapa.br; f. 1981.

Centro de Pesquisa Agroflorestal da Amazônia Ocidental: Rodovia AM-010 km 29, Estrada Manaus/Itacoatiara, 69011-970 Manaus, AM; tel. (92) 621-0300; fax (92) 621-0322; internet www.cpaa.embrapa.br; f. 1975; rubber and oil palm research.

Centro Nacional de Pesquisa de Gado de Corte: Rodovia BR 262 km 04, 79002-970 Campo Grande, MS; tel. (67) 368-2000; fax (67) 368-2150; internet www.cnpgc.embrapa.br; f. 1976; research on beef cattle.

Centro de Pesquisa Agropecuária do Pantanal: Rua 21 de Setembro 1880, 79320-900 Corumbá, MS; tel. (67) 233-2430; fax (67) 233-1011; internet www.cpap.embrapa.br; research on beef cattle and pasture land.

Centro Nacional de Pesquisa de Soja: Rodovia Carlos João Strass (Londrina/Warta), Acesso Orlando Amaral, Distrito de Warta, 86001-970 Londrina, PR; tel. (43) 3371-6000; fax (43) 3371-6100; internet www.cnpso.embrapa.br; f. 1975; research on soya beans and sunflowers.

Centro de Pesquisa Agropecuária do Trópico Semi-Árido: Rodovia BR 428 km 152, Zona Rural, 56300-000 Petrolina, PE; tel. (87) 3862-1711; fax (87) 3862-1744; internet www.cpatsa.embrapa.br; f. 1975.

Centro Nacional de Pesquisa de Algodão: Rua Osvaldo Cruz 1143, Bairro Centenário, 58107-720 Campina Grande, PB; tel. (83) 341-3608; fax (83) 322-7751; internet www.cnpa.embrapa.br; f. 1975; research on cotton.

Centro Nacional de Pesquisa de Embrapa Solos: Rua Jardim Botânico 1024, 22460-000 Rio de Janeiro, RJ; tel. (21) 2179-4500; fax (21) 2274-5291; internet www.cnps.embrapa.br; f. 1974; soil survey and conservation.

Centro Nacional de Pesquisa de Tecnologia Agroindustrial de Alimentos: Av. das Americas 29501-B, Guaratiba, 23020-470 Rio de Janeiro, RJ; tel. (21) 2410-9500; fax (21) 2410-1090; internet www.ctaa.embrapa.br; f. 1971; food science and technology centre.

Centro Nacional de Pesquisa de Trigo: Rodovia BR 285 km 174, 99001-970 Passo Fundo, RS; tel. (54) 311-3444; fax (54) 311-3617; internet www.cnpt.embrapa.br; f. 1974; wheat research centre.

Centro Nacional de Pesquisa de Agrobiologia: Rodovia Rio/São Paulo km 47, BR 465, 23851-970 Seropédica, RJ; tel. (21) 2682-1500; fax (21) 2682-1230; internet www.cnpala.embrapa.br.

Centro de Pesquisa Agropecuária do Meio Norte: Av. Duque de Caxias 5.650, Bairro Buenos Aires, 64006-220 Teresina, PI; tel. (86) 225-1141; fax (86) 225-1142; internet www.cnpmn.embrapa.br.

Centro Nacional de Pesquisa de Monitoramento e Avaliaçao de Impacto Ambiéntal – CNPMA: Rodovia SP 340, km 127.5, Bairro Tanquinho Velho, 13820-000 Jaguariúna, SP; tel. (19) 3867-8700; fax (19) 3867-8740; internet www.cnpma.embrapa.br.

Centro de Pesquisa Agroflorestal do Amapá: Rodovia Juscelino Kubitschek, km 05, (Macapá/Fazendinha), 68903-000 Macapá, AP; tel. (96) 241-1551; fax (96) 241-1480; internet www.cpafap.embrapa.br.

Núcleo de Monitoramento Ambiental de Recursos Naturais por Satélite: Av. Dr Júlio Soares de Arruda 803, Parque São Quirino, 13088-300 Campinas, SP; tel. (19) 3256-6030; fax (19) 3254-1100; internet www.cnpm.embrapa.br.

Centro Nacional de Pesquisa Tecnológica em Informática para a Agricultura: Cidade Universitária Zeferino Vaz, Campus da Universidade Estadual de Campinas – UNICAMP, Bairro de Barão Geraldo, 13083-970 Campinas, SP; tel. (19) 3789-5700; fax (19) 3789-5711; internet www.cnptia.embrapa.br.

Centro Nacional de Pesquisa e Desenvolvimento de Instrumentação Agropecuária: Rua XV de Novembro 1452, Centro, 13561-160 São Carlos, SP; tel. (16) 274-2477; fax (16) 272-5958; internet www.cnpdia.embrapa.br.

Centro Nacional de Pesquisa de Agroindústria Tropical (CNPAT): Rua Dra Sara Mesquita 2270, Bairro Pici, 60511-110 Fortaleza, CE; tel. (85) 299-1800; fax (85) 299-1803; internet www.cnpat.embrapa.br.

Instituto Agronômico (Institute of Agronomy): CP 28, 13020-902 Campinas, SP; tel. (19) 2315422; fax (19) 2314943; f. 1887; basic and applied research on plants, soils, environment, farming methods and agricultural machinery; Divisions: Biology, Experimental Stations, Agricultural Engineering, Food Plants, Industrial Plants, Soil; Technical Scientific Information Service; library of 200,000 vols; 20 experimental stations in the State of São Paulo; Gen. Dir Dr EDUARDO BULISONI; publs *Bragantia* (2 a year), *O Agronômico* (irregular).

Instituto Brasileiro do Meio Ambiente e dos Recursos Naturais Renováveis (IBAMA) (Brazilian Institute for the Environment and Renewable Natural Resources): SCEN trecho 2, Edifício Sede Ibama, 70818-900 Brasília, DF; tel. (61) 316-1205; fax (61) 226-5094; e-mail cnia.sede@ibama.gov.br; internet www.ibama.gov.br; f. 1989; library of 65,000 vols; Pres. Dr MARCUS LUIZ BARROSO BARROS.

Instituto de Economia Agrícola (Agricultural Economics Institute): Av. Miguel Stefano 3900, Água Funda, CP 68029, 04301-903 São Paulo, SP; tel. (11) 5073-0244; fax (11) 5073-4062; e-mail iea@iea.sp.gov.br; internet www.iea.sp.gov.br; f. 1968; affiliated to SP Secretariat of Agriculture and Provision; provides information for state and federal governments and other interested bodies; library of 70,000 vols, 2,700 periodicals; Dir Dr JOSÉ SIDNEY GONÇALVES; publs *Agricultura em São Paulo* (irregular), *Informações Econômicas* (monthly), *Informações Estatística da Agricultura* (annually).

Instituto de Zootecnia (Institute of Animal Science and Pastures): Rua Heitor Penteado 56, CP 60, 13460-000 Nova Odessa, SP; tel. (19) 3466-9400; fax (19) 3466-6415; e-mail diretoria@iz.sp.gov.br; internet www.iz.sp.gov.br; f. 1905; 92 researchers; pastures, beef cattle, dairy cattle, pigs, sheep, goats, water buffaloes, information science, reproduction and genetics; library of 10,710 vols, 1,610 periodicals; Dir-Gen. ANTONIO ALVARO DUARTE DE OLIVEIRA; publs *Boletim de Indústria Animal* (2 a year), *Boletim Tecnicos*.

Instituto Florestal (Estado de São Paulo) (São Paulo State Forestry Institute): Rua do Horto 931, CP 1322, 02377-000 São Paulo, SP; tel. (11) 6231-8555 ext. 2100; fax (11) 6132-5767; e-mail nuinfo@iflorest.sp.gov.br; internet www.iflorestsp.br; f. 1896; 1,107 staff; library of 7,500 vols, 2,000 periodicals; Dir MARIA CECÍLIA WEY DE BRITO; publs *Revista do Instituto Florestal* (2 a year), *Revista IF-Serie Registros* (irregular).

Serviço de Defesa Sanitária Vegetal (Plant Health Protection Service): Secretaria de Defesa Sanitária Vegetal, Ministério da Agricultura, Esplanada dos Ministérios, Bloco 8, Anexo 3° andar, Brasília, DF; tel. (61) 224-6543; f. 1920; library of 5,000 vols, pamphlets and periodicals; Sec. HÉLIO PALMA DE ARRUDA; publs *Boletim Fitossanitário*, *Monografias*.

ECONOMICS, LAW AND POLITICS

Centro de Estatística e Informações (Statistics and Information Centre): Centro Administrativo da Bahia, Av. 435 4a, 41750-300 Salvador, BA; tel. (71) 371-9665; fax (71) 371-9664; f. 1983; statistics, natural resources, economic indicators; library of 15,448 vols; Dir RENATA PROSERPIO; publ. *Bahia Análise e Dados* (every 4 months).

EDUCATION

Instituto Nacional de Estudos e Pesquisas Educacionais (National Institute for Educational Studies and Research): INEP/MEC, Esp. dos Ministérios, Bloco L, Anexos I e II (4° andar), 70047-900 Brasília, DF; internet www.inep.gov.br; f. 1938; 130 mems; library of 50,000 vols, 985 periodicals; Pres. Dr MARIA HELENA GUIMARÃES DE CASTRO; publs *Revista Brasileira de Estudos Pedagógicos*, *Bibliografia Brasileira de Educação*, *Em Aberto*.

HISTORY, GEOGRAPHY AND ARCHAEOLOGY

Fundação Instituto Brasileiro de Geografia e Estatística (Brazilian Institute of Geography and Statistics): Av. Franklin Roosevelt 166, 20021-120 Rio de Janeiro, RJ; internet www.ibge.gov.br; f. 1936; produces and analyses statistical, geographical, cartographic, geodetic, demographic, socio-economic, natural resources and environmental information; Pres. EDUARDO PEREIRA NUNES; publs *Revista Brasileira de Estatística*, *Anuário Estatístico do Brasil*, *Revista Brasileira de Geografia*.

MEDICINE

Fundacão Oswaldo Cruz (Oswaldo Cruz Foundation): Av. Brasil 4365, Manguinhos, CP 926, 21045-900 Rio de Janeiro, RJ; tel. (21) 2598-4242; fax (21) 2270-7444; e-mail ferreirj@fiocruz.br; internet www.fiocruz.br; f. 1900; tropical medicine, infectious and parasitic diseases, public health; immunology, virology, entomology, epidemiology, history of science; library of 800,000 vols, 2,000 current periodicals; Pres. Dr PAULO MARCHIORI BUSS; publs *Memórias* (6 a year), *Cadernos de Saúde Pública* (4 a year), *História, Ciências, Saúde – Manguinhos* (3 a year).

Instituto 'Adolfo Lutz': Av. Dr Arnaldo 355, Pacaembú, 01246-902 São Paulo, SP; fax (11) 3085-3505; f. 1892; Central Laboratory of Public Health for the State of São Paulo; library of 50,000 vols, incl. periodicals; Dir.-Gen. CRISTIANO CORRÊA DE AZEVEDO MARQUES; publ. *Revista*.

Instituto 'Benjamin Constant': Av. Pasteur 350/368, Urca, 22290-240 Rio de Janeiro, RJ; tel. (21) 2295-4498; fax (21) 2543-1137; e-mail ibc@ibcnet.org.br; internet www.ibcnet.org.br; f. 1854; educational institute for the blind; library: braille and general library of 5,000 vols; Dir ERICA DESLANDES MAGNO OLIVEIRA; publs *Revista Brasileira para Cegos* (4 a year), *Pontinhos* (4 a year), *Revista Benjamin Constant*.

Instituto Brasileiro de Estudos e Pesquisas de Gastroenterologia (IBEPEGE): Rua Dr Seng 320, Bairro da Bela Vista, 01331-020 São Paulo; tel. (11) 288-2119; fax (11) 289-2768; f. 1963; study and research in gastroenterology, nutrition and psychosomatic medicine; postgraduate courses; library of 10,000 vols; Pres. Prof. JOSÉ FERNANDES PONTES; Vice-Pres. Dr JOSÉ VICENTE MARTINS CAMPOS; publ. *Arquivos de Gastroenterologia* (quarterly).

Instituto Butantan (Butantan Institute): Av. Vital Brazil 1500, CP 65, 05504 São Paulo, SP; tel. (11) 813-7222; fax (11) 815-1505; f. 1901; library of 72,826 vols, on ophiology and bio-medical sciences; famous snake farm; Public Health Institute for research and the production of vaccines, sera, etc.; also research in genetics, virology, pathology, etc.; Hospital Vital Brasil (snake, spider and scorpion accidents); Tech. Dir Prof. HISAKO GOWDO HIGASHI; publ. *Memórias* (annually).

Instituto de Saúde (Institute of Health): Av. Dr Eneas Carvalho de Aguiar 188, CP 8027, 01051 São Paulo; f. 1969; organization and supervision of study, research and activities in the fields of mother and child care, phthisiology, hansenology, dermatology, ophthalmology, nutrition and degenerative diseases; library: see Libraries; Dir-Gen. Dr EDMUR F. PASTORELO; publ. *Hansenologia Internationalis* (2 a year).

Instituto Evandro Chagas (MS-Fundação Nacional de Saúde): Av. Almirante Barroso 492, CP 1128, 66090-000 Belém, PA; tel. (91) 246-1022; fax (91) 226-1284; f. 1936; research in bacteriology, parasitology, pathology, virology, mycology, medical entomology, human ecology and environment; library of 50,000 vols, 134 current periodicals, 4,000 reprints; Dir Dr JORGE FERNANDO SOARES TRAVASSOS DA ROSA.

Instituto Nacional de Cancer, Co-ordenação de Pesquisa: Rua André Cavalcanti 37/2 andar-Centro, 20231-050 Rio de Janeiro, RJ; tel. (21) 3233-1414; fax (21) 3233-1355; internet www.inca.org.br; f. 1958; genetics, experimental oncology, pharmacology, molecular biology, cell biology; Head of Research Dra MARISA BREITENBACH.

Instituto 'Oscar Freire' (Oscar Freire Institute): Rua Teodoro Sampaio 115, CP 05405-000 São Paulo, SP; f. 1918; for instruction and research in forensic medicine; assoc. with Univ. of São Paulo; library of 4,200 vols; Chair. Prof. Dr CLÁUDIO COHEN.

Instituto Pasteur: Av. Paulista 393, 01311 São Paulo, SP; tel. (11) 288-00-88; f. 1903; practical measures and theoretical studies aimed at preventing rabies in humans; 15 staff; library of 904 vols and 1,083 periodicals; Technical Dir SOSTHENES VITAL DE KERBRIE.

Instituto 'Penido Burnier': Rua Dr Mascarenhas 249, POB 284, 13020-050 Campinas, SP; tel. (19) 3232-5866; fax (19) 3233-4492; e-mail penido@penidoburnier.com.br; f. 1920; ophthalmology, otolaryngology, anaesthesiology; library of 11,585 vols; Chief Librarians Dr HILTON DE MELLO E OLIVEIRA; VANDA REGINA SILVA JUCÁ; publ. *Arquivos IPB* (2 a year).

NATURAL SCIENCES

General

Centro de Ciências, Letras e Artes (Science, Letters and Arts Centre): Rua Bernardino de Campos 989, CP 76, Campinas, SP; f. 1901; library: *c.* 30,000 vols; Pres. Dr JOÃO DE SOUSA COELHO; Gen. Sec. ARISTIDES DA COSTA VERDADE; Librarian G. ZINCK; publ. *Revista*; museum and art gallery attached.

Conselho Nacional de Desenvolvimento Científico e Tecnológico (National Council of Scientific and Technological Development): Av. W-3 Norte Quadra 507, Bl. B, 70740-905 Brasília, DF; tel. (61) 348-9400; f. 1951; Pres. JOSÉ GALIZIA TUNDISI.

Institut de Recherche pour le Développement (IRD): CP 7091, 71619-970 Brasília, DF; tel. (61) 248-5323; fax (61) 248-5378; e-mail orstom@apis.com.br; f. 1979; headquarters of the Brazilian delegation to Latin America; missions at various universities and research institutes; Delegate to Brazil MAURICE LOURD. (See main entry under France.).

Instituto Nacional de Pesquisas da Amazônia (National Research Institute for Amazonia): Alameda Cosme Ferreira Aleixo, 1756, CP 478, 69083 Manaus, AM; tel. (92) 643-3097; fax (92) 643-3095; e-mail ozorio@cr-am.rap.br; f. 1954; agronomics, biology, medicine, ecology, technology, forestry, and special projects; 1,003 staff; library of 48,000 items; herbarium; wood collection; Dir OZÓRIO JOSE DE MENEZES FONSECA; publ. *Acta Amazônica* (quarterly).

Biological Sciences

Campo de Santana: Praça da República, Rio de Janeiro, RJ; laid out 1870 by Auguste F. M. Glaziou, who collected 23,000 plants, including 700 trees; Herbário Glaziou forms the most noteworthy exhibit in the Botanical Division of the National Museum.

Centro de Pesquisa e Gestão de Recursos Pesqueiros Continentais (CEPTA) (Research and Management Centre for Continental Fish Resources): Rod. Pref. Euberto N. P. de Godoy s/n, CP 64, Km 6.5, 13630-970 Pirassununga, SP; tel. (19) 3565-1299; fax (19) 3565-1318; e-mail cepta@cepta.ibama.gov.br; f. 1938; library of 26,024 vols; Dir LAERTE BATISTA DE OLIVEIRA ALVES; publ. *Boletim Técnico* (annually).

Departamento de Planejamento Ambiental (FEEMA) (Department of Environmental Planning): Rua Fonseca Teles 121, 16°, 20940-200 Rio de Janeiro, RJ; f. 1975; library of 13,100 vols; Dir EDUARDO RODRIGUES.

Fundação Ezequiel Dias: Centro de Pesquisa e Desenvolvimento, CP 26, Rua Conde Pereira Carneiro 80, Gameleira, 30510-10 Belo Horizonte, MG; tel. (31) 371-9433; fax (31) 371-9432; f. 1907; attached to the Secretariat of Health and Public Welfare; health and welfare, biotechnology, immunology research; library; Superintendent Dr ROBERTO PORTO FONSECA; Dir Prof. CARLOS RIBEIRO DINIZ.

Herbário 'Barbosa Rodrigues': Av. Marcos Konder 800, 88301-122 Itajaí, SC; tel. (47) 348-8725; e-mail hbr@cttmar.univali.br; internet www.cttmar.univali.br/~hbr; f. 1942; botany of Southern Brazil, taxonomy, ecology; 123 mems; library of 13,562 vols; Dir VICTUS SCHLICKMANN ROETGER; publs *Sellowia* (annually), *Flora Ilustrada Catarinense* (annually).

Instituto Biológico (Biological Institute): Av. Cons. Rodrigues Alves 1252, 04014-002 São Paulo; tel. (11) 5579-4234; fax (11) 5087-1796; e-mail divulgacao@biologico.sp.gov.br; internet www.biologico.sp.gov.br; f. 1927; animal and plant protection; library of 13,000 vols, 105,000 periodicals; Dir-Gen. ANTONIO BATISTA FILHO; publs *Arquivos do Instituto Biológico* (quarterly), *O Biológico* (2 a year), *Boletim Técnico* (irregular).

Instituto de Botânica (Botanical Institute): CP 4005, 01061-970 São Paulo; tel. (11) 5073-6300; fax (11) 5073-3678; e-mail biblioteca@ibot.sp.gov.br; internet www.ibot.sp.gov.br; f. 1938; herbarium of 370,000 plants; postgraduate course in plant diversity and the environment; library of 90,000 vols; Dir Dr LUIZ MAURO BARBOSA; publs *Hoehnea* (3 a year), *Boletim* (irregular).

Instituto de Pesquisas do Jardim Botânico do Rio de Janeiro: Rua Jardim Botânico 1008, Jardim Botânico, Rio de Janeiro, RJ; tel. (21) 511-0511; fax (21) 259-5041; e-mail jbrj@gov.br; internet www.jbrj.gov.br; f. 1808; attached to Min. of the Environment, Water Resources and Amazonia; botanical research in systematics, wood anatomy (7,148 samples and 17,000 microscope plates), cytomorphology and ecology; botanical garden with 7,800 species and 11,000 specimens; herbarium with 350,000 samples; library of 15,000 vols, 50,000 periodicals, antiquarian collection of 3,000 vols; Dir SERGIO DE ALMEIDA BRUNI; publs *Arquivos*, *Rodriguésia*.

Physical Sciences

Associação Internacional de Lunologia (International Association of Lunology): CP 322, Franca, São Paulo; f. 1969; to publish a review on lunar research carried out by all countries.

Centro Brasileiro de Pesquisas Físicas (Brazilian Centre for Physics Research): Rua Xavier Sigaud 150, 4° andar, Urca, 22290-180 Rio de Janeiro, RJ; tel. (21) 541-0337; fax (21) 541-2047; f. 1949; library of 18,951 vols, 811 periodicals; Dir AMÓS TROPER; publs *Notas de Físicas*, *Notas Técnicas*, *Ciência e Sociedade*.

Departamento Nacional da Produção Mineral (National Department of Mineral Production): Setor de Autarquias Norte, Quadra 1, Projeção E, Bloco B, Esplanada dos Ministérios, Brasília, DF; f. 1907; Dept of Ministry of Mines and Energy; Dir YVAN BARRETTO DE CARVALHO; publs *Boletim*, *Anuário Mineral Brasileiro*, *Avulso*, *Boletim de Preços*, *Balanço Mineral Brasileiro*.

Instituto Nacional de Meteorologia (National Institute of Meteorology): Eixo Monumental Via S1, 70680-900 Brasília, DF; tel. (61) 344-3333; internet www.inmet.gov.br; publ. *Boletim Agroclimatológico*.

Laboratório de Análises (Analytical Laboratory): Av. Rodrigues Alves 81, 20081-250 Rio de Janeiro, RJ; tel. (21) 223-7743; f. 1889; covers organic, inorganic and pharmaceutical chemistry, biochemistry and materials; library of 4,000 vols; Dir Prof. MARCELO DE M. MOURA.

Observatório Nacional do Brasil (National Observatory): Rua General Bruce 586, 20921 Rio de Janeiro, RJ; tel. (21) 580-6087; f. 1827; library; astronomical and geophysical research programmes using 7 refractors, a Time Service at Rio de Janeiro and a Time Station at Brasília; operates 2 magnetic observatories; Dir SAYD JOSE CODINA LANDABERRY; Sec. SANDRA C. P. SILVA; publs *Efemérides Astronômicas* (annually), *Contribuições Científicas*.

PHILOSOPHY AND PSYCHOLOGY

Instituto Neo-Pitagórico (Neo-Pythagorean Institute): CP 1047, 80011-970 Curitiba, PR; located at: Templo das Musas, Rua Prof. Dario Vellozo 460, Vila Izabel, 80320-050 Curitiba, PR; tel. (41) 242-1840; internet www.pitagorico.org.br; f. 1909; courses in philosophy, history of religion, psychical research, theosophy, occultism, hierology, Pythagorean studies; 486 mems; library of 21,000 vols; Pres. Dr ROSALA GARZUZE; publs *A Lâmpada* (4 a year), *Circulares* (annually), *Biblioteca Neo-Pitagórica* (annually), *Boletim Informativo* (4 a year), *Templo da Paz* (3 a year).

RELIGION, SOCIOLOGY AND ANTHROPOLOGY

Fundação Joaquim Nabuco: Av. 17 de Agosto 2187, Casa Forte, 52061-540 Recife, PE; tel. (81) 441-5500; fax (81) 441-5600; f. 1949; sociological, anthropological, economic, historical, political, educational, geographical, statistical and population studies about Brazil's north and north-east; 600 mems; library: specialized library of 60,238 vols and museum; Dir FERNANDO DE MELLO FREYRE; publs *Ciência & Trópico* (2 a year), *Cadernos de Estudos Sociais* (2 a year).

TECHNOLOGY

Centro de Pesquisas e Desenvolvimento (CEPED) (Research and Development Centre): Rodovia BA 512, Km 0, CP 09, 42800-000 Camaçari, BA; tel. (71) 834-7300; fax (71) 832-2095; e-mail ceped@bahianet.com.br; f. 1969; research in agroindustrial and food technology, energy, chemistry and petrochemistry, metallurgy, ores treatment, mineralogy, environmental engineering, building materials, quality control, materials testing, analysis; library of 26,702 vols; Dir Dr SYLVIO DE QUEIROS MATTOSO; publ. *Tecbahia* (3 a year).

Centro de Pesquisas e Desenvolvimento Leopoldo A. Miguez de Mello (PETROBRÁS) (PETROBRÁS Research and Development Centre): Ilha do Fundão, Quadra 7, CP 21949-900 Rio de Janeiro, RJ; tel. (21) 280-1101; fax (21) 598-6363; f. 1966; research into exploration, exploitation and refining of petroleum resources; 757 mems; library: specialized library of 35,000 vols, 520 current titles of periodicals; Gen. Man. ANTONIO SERGIO FRAGOMENI; publs *Boletim Técnico da PETROBRÁS* (quarterly), *Ciência-Tecnica-Petróleo*, *Boletim de Geociências da PETROBRÁS* (quarterly).

Comissão Nacional de Energia Nuclear (CNEN) (Commission for Nuclear Energy): Rua General Severiano 90, Botafogo, 22294-900 Rio de Janeiro, RJ; tel. (21) 2546-2320; fax (21) 2546-2282; internet www.cnen.gov.br; f. 1956; supervisory nuclear agency, coordinates planning and financing of nuclear activities, promotes and executes research programmes, trains scientists and technicians; Pres. JOSÉ MANUO ESTEVES DOS SANTOS.

Attached institutes:

Instituto de Engenharia Nuclear (IEN) (Nuclear Engineering Institute): CP 2186, Rio de Janeiro, RJ; tel. (21) 2560-4113; fax (21) 2590-2692; e-mail ien@ien.gov.br; internet www.ien.gov.br; f. 1962; pure and applied research and development of uses of atomic energy, especially fast breeder reactors, instrumentation and control, cyclotron physics; Dir LUIZ ALBERTO ILHA ARRIETA.; Dir SERGIO CHAVES CABRAL.

Instituto de Radioproteção e Dosimetria (IRD) (Radiation Protection and Dosimetry Institute): Av. Salvador Allende s/n, Jacarepaguá, CP 37750, 22780-160 Rio de Janeiro, RJ; tel. (21) 442-2530; fax (21) 442-2530; e-mail ird@ird.gov.br; internet www.ird.gov.br; f. 1972; research and development of radiation protection and dosimetry methods and standards; Dir ELIANA AMARAL.

Instituto de Pesquisas Energéticas e Nucleares (IPEN) (Energetics and Nuclear Research Institute): CP 11049, São Paulo, SP; tel. (11) 3816-9095; fax (11) 212-3546; e-mail webmaster@net.ipen.br; internet www.ipen.br; f. 1956; conducts pure and applied research in energy, mainly in nuclear sector; offers training courses; energy information centre; Dir CLAUDIO RODRIGUES.

Centro de Desenvolvimento da Tecnologia Nuclear (CDTN) (Nuclear Technology Development Centre): Belo Horizonte, MG; tel. (31) 3499-3261; fax (31) 3499-3444; e-mail webmaster@urano.cdtn.br; internet www.cdtn.br; f. 1952; Co-ordinator SILVESTRE PAIANO SOBRINHO; environmental and atomic energy research.

Centro de Energia Nuclear na Agricultura (CENA): see under Agriculture.

Instituto Brasileiro de Petróleo (Brazilian Institute of Petroleum): Av. Almirante Barroso 52, 26° Andar, 20043, Centro, Rio de Janeiro, RJ; tel. (21) 532-1610; fax (21) 220-1596; internet www.ibp.org.br; f. 1957; holds Brazilian standards for petroleum products and equipment; research in petroleum and petrochemical industries; mems: 146 companies; Pres. GUILHERME DE OLIVEIRA ESTRELLA.

Instituto de Pesquisas Tecnológicas do Estado de São Paulo S.A. (IPT) (Institute for Technological Research of the State of São Paulo): Cidade Universitária Armando de Salles Oliveira, n. 532, 05508-901 São Paulo, SP; tel. (11) 3767-4000; fax (11) 3767-4002; internet www.ipt.br; f. 1899; non-profit making public corporation, owned by the State of São Paulo; has eight technical divisions: civil engineering, economy and systems engineering, geology, metallurgy, transport technology, mechanical and electrical engineering, forest products, chemistry; has four technical centres: technological information, leather and footwear technology, information technology and telecommunications, technological improvement; library of 98,200 books, 4,315 periodicals, 1,100,000 national and international active and historical standards; Dir Dr GUILHERME ARY PLONSKI; publ. *Tecnologia em dia* (6 a year).

Instituto de Tecnologia do Paraná (Paraná Institute of Technology): Rua Algacyr Munhoz Mader 2400, 81310-020 Curitiba, PR; tel. (41) 346-3141; fax (41) 247-6788; f. 1940; research in all aspects of technology for the development of the state; produces vaccines; national and int. exchange with orgs in the same field; library of 8,000 vols, 1,054 periodicals; Dir/Pres. ALEXANDRE FONTANA BELTRÃO; publs *Arquivo de Biologia e Tecnologia* (quarterly), *Boletim Técnico* (every 2 months).

Instituto Nacional de Pesquisas Espaciais (INPE) (National Institute for Space Research): Av. Dos Astronautas 1758, CP 515, 12227-010 São José dos Campos, SP; tel. (12) 3945-6000; fax (12) 3945-6919; internet www.inpe.br; f. 1961, renamed in 1971; astrophysics, solar physics, geomagnetism, ionosphere, upper atmosphere, medium and low atmosphere, plasma physics, basic meteorology, meteorological instrumentation, meteorological satellite services, meteorological applications, remote sensing for mineral resources, remote sensing for forestry and agronomic resources, remote sensing for sea resources, environmental analysis, image production, ground stations, control and tracking stations, structure and thermic control of space platforms, space telecommunications, energy supply, analogic and digital systems, orbital dynamics and control, payloads for space platforms, assembly, integration and tests of space platforms, qualification of components, units and systems for space applications, centre for satellite operation and missions, balloon launching centre, systems engineering, informatics, materials, combustion processes, sensors, space geodesy, human resources, technology transfer; library of 47,000 vols, microforms, CD-ROMs, microfilms and tapes, 1,600 periodicals, 21,000 specialized papers, 10,000 INPE reports, 5,800 maps; Dir LUIZ CARLOS MOURA MIRANDA; publ. *Climanálise*.

Instituto Nacional de Tecnología (National Technological Institute): Av. Venezuela 82, 20081-310 Rio de Janeiro, RJ; tel. (21) 2206-1135; fax (21) 2253-4361; internet www.int.gov.br/principal.html; f. 1922; research in chemical industry, chemistry of natural products, metallurgy, rubber and plastics, corrosion, pollution control, industrial design, energy conservation, computer-aided projects; library of 17,000 vols, 1,000 periodicals, 100,000 microfiches; Dir JOAO LUIZ HANRIOTT SELASCO; publ. *Informativo do INT*.

Instituto Tecnológico do Estado de Pernambuco (ITEP) (Technological Institute of the State of Pernambuco): Av. Prof. Luis Freire 700, Cidade Universitária, Recife, PE; tel. (81) 3272-4399; fax (81) 3272-4272; e-mail itep@itep.br; internet www.itep.br; f. 1942; industrial research; library of 10,000 vols; Pres. FÁTIMA MARIA MIRANDA BRAYER; publ. *Revista Pernambucana de Tecnologia* (2 a year).

Libraries and Archives

Aracajú

Biblioteca Pública do Estado de Sergipe (Sergipe State Public Library): Aracajú, SE; f. 1851; Dir ALFREDO MONTES DE ARAÚJO PINTO; 153,750 vols, including periodicals.

Belém

Arquivo Público do Estado do Pará (Pará Public Archives): Rua Campos Sales, 273, 66019-050 Belém, PA; tel. (91) 241-9700; fax (91) 241-9097; f. 1901; 500 vols; special collection of 742 vols; Dir GERALDO MÁRTIRES COELHO; publ. *Anais do Arquivo Público do Pará* (every 2 years).

Biblioteca Central da Universidade Federal do Pará: Rua Augusto Corrêa 1, Campus Universitário, Guamá, 66075-110 Belém, PA; tel. (91) 211-1140; fax (91) 211-1351; e-mail bc@ufpa.br; internet www.ufpa.br/bc; f. 1962; 157,000 vols, 4,440 periodicals; Dir SILVIA MARIA BITAR DE LIMA MOREIRA.

Biblioteca do Grêmio Literário e Comercial Português (Library of the Portuguese Literary and Commercial Union): Rua Senador Manuel Barata 237, Belém, PA; f. 1867;

Sec. ANÍSIO DE SOARES TEIXEIRA; 29,568 vols; exchange service.

Belo Horizonte

Biblioteca Pública Estadual Luiz de Bessa (Public Library): Praça da Liberdade 21, 30140-010 Belo Horizonte, MG; tel. (31) 337-1265; fax (31) 269-1108; f. 1954; 280,000 vols, 5,124 vols of Braille, 300 talking books; 600 brs.

Universidade Federal de Minas Gerais, Biblioteca Universitária/Sistema de Bibliotecas da UFMG: Av. Presidente Antônio Carlos 6627, 31270-901 Belo Horizonte, MG; tel. (31) 499-4611; fax (31) 499-4611; e-mail dir@bu.ufmg.br; internet www.bu.ufmg.br; f. 1927; collection of special documents; 650,000 vols, 6,000 maps, 14,763 rare works, 22,000 periodicals, 15,000 music scores; Dir SIMONE APARECIDA DOS SANTOS.

Brasília

Biblioteca Central, Universidade de Brasília: Campus Universitário, Asa Norte, 70910 Brasília, DF; tel. (61) 348-2402; f. 1962; 530,292 vols, 7,864 periodicals; Dir Prof. ODILON PEREIRA DA SILVA.

Biblioteca Demonstrativa de Brasília FBN/minc (Public Library): Av. W/3 Sul, Entrequadras 506/507, 70350-580 Brasília, DF; tel. (61) 243-5682; fax (61) 243-3163; f. 1970; 92,000 vols, 2,400 periodicals on general subjects; also maps, microfilms, slides, pictures; Dir MARIA DA CONCEIÇÃO MOREIRA SALLES.

Biblioteca do Ministério da Justiça (Library of Ministry of Justice): Esplanada dos Ministérios, Ed. Sede Térreo, 70064-900 Brasília, DF; tel. (61) 3429-3323; fax (61) 3429-9161; e-mail biblioteca@mj.br; f. 1941; 130,000 vols, of which many are on law, economics, sociology, labour, and political science; very rare collection of laws of Portuguese colonial period; 6,000-vol. Goethe collection; Dir DOROTI TEREZITA HOF; publ. *Revista Arquivos do Ministério da Justiça*.

Biblioteca do Ministério das Relações Exteriores (Library of the Ministry of Foreign Affairs): Esplanada dos Ministérios, Anexo II, Térreo, 70170-900 Brasília, DF; tel. (61) 211-6359; fax (61) 223-7362; f. 1906; 80,000 vols, including periodicals (history collection in Rio de Janeiro, *q.v.*); law, history, politics and economics; collection of UN documents; Chief Librarian MARIA SALETE CARVALHO REIS.

Biblioteca do Ministério do Trabalho e Emprego (Library of Ministry of Labour and Employment): Esplanada dos Ministérios, Bloco F, Anexo, Ala B, Térreo, 70059-900 Brasília, DF; tel. (61) 317-6186; fax (61) 226-7536; e-mail biblioteca@mte.gov.br; f. 1871; 18,000 vols; 120 collections of newspapers; Librarian MARIA PAULA GARCIA CAMPOS DE ARAYO; publ. *Relação Anual de Informações Sociais*.

Biblioteca do Senado Federal (Library of the Federal Senate): Praça dos Três Poderes, Palácio do Congresso (Anexo II – Térreo), 70165-900 Brasília, DF; tel. (61) 224-9784; fax (61) 311-1765; e-mail SSBIB@admass.senado.gov.br; f. 1826; specializes in social sciences, law, politics, public administration, legislation; also works on literature, history, geography, etc.; 150,000 vols; Dir SIMONE BASTOS VIEIRA; publs *Bibliografia Brasileira de Direito* (annually), *Dados Biográficos dos Senadores*.

Centro de Documentação e Informação da Câmara dos Deputados do Brasil (Documentation and Information Centre of the Brazilian House of Representatives): Palácio do Congresso Nacional, Camara dos Deputados (Anexo II), 70160-900 Brasília, DF; tel. (61) 216-5501; fax (61) 216-5515; e-mail cedi@camara.gov.br; internet www.camara.gov.br; f. 1971; (1) Archives (Dir LAMBERTO RICARTE SERRA JÚNIOR), (2) Central Inquiry Unit (Dir EDILSON SARAIVA ALENCAR), (3) Legislative Studies (Dir SIMONE MARIA FREITAS E SILVA), (4) Library (Dir CHRISTIANE COELHO DE PAIVA), (5) Preservation of Cultural Goods (Dir MÁRCIO COUTINHO VARGAS), (6) Publications (Dir PEDRO AQUINO NOLETO); 400,000 vols, 3,500 periodicals; Dir JORGE HENRIQUE CARTAXO.

Centro de Informação e Biblioteca em Educação: Ministério da Educação, Esplanada dos Ministérios, Bloco L, Térreo, CP 08866, 70047-900 Brasília, DF; tel. (61) 410-9052; fax (61) 223-5137; e-mail cibec@inep.gov.br; internet www.inep.gov.br/cibec; f. 1981; 21,000 vols, 844 periodicals; specialized library on education; Dir ÉRICA MÁSSIMO MACHADO.

Co-ordenação Geral de Informação Documental Agrícola (CENAGRI) (National Centre of Agricultural Documentary Information): CP 02432, Ministério da Agricultura, Anexo I, Bl.B, Térreo e 1° andar, 70043-970 Brasília, DF; tel. (61) 218-2613; fax (61) 226-8190; f. 1974; central unit of National System of Agricultural Information and Documentation (SNIDA); responsible for establishing State libraries of agriculture in order to decentralize information sources; 50,000 vols, 7,032 serial titles, 216,000 microfiche documents; Co-ordinator CLAITON PIMENTEL; publs *Série Aptidão Agrícola das Terras*, *Série Estudos sobre o Desenvolvimento Agrícola*, *Série Levantamentos Bibliográficos*, *Bibliografia Brasileira de Agricultura*, *Banco de Bibliografias da América Latina e do Caribe*, *Bibliografias Agrícolas* (national series), *Bibliografias Agrícolas* (international series), *Thesaurus para Indexação/Recuperação da Literatura Agrícola Brasileira*.

Instituto Brasileiro de Informação em Ciência e Tecnologia (IBICT): SAS Quadra 05, Lote 06, Bloco H, 70070-000 Brasília, DF; fax (61) 226-2677; f. 1954 as IBBD, renamed 1976; co-ordinates scientific and technical information services throughout the country; provides technical assistance, and training; maintains the following databases available for public access, through the National Telecommunications Network: *ACERVO*(Library and Information Science, holds records from 1982 to present, updated daily), *EVENTOS*(current meetings, updated daily), *BEN*(directory of Brazilian institutions in science and technology, updated daily), *BPS*(Union Catalog of Serials Publications, updated daily), *TESES*(theses and dissertations from 1984 to present, updated daily), *FILMES*(Films and videos in science and technology from 1988 to present), *BASES*(directory of Brazilian databases from 1989), *EMPRESAS*(directory of software institutions), *CIENTE*(scientific and technological policy, updated daily); runs a postgraduate course in Information Science and a special course on scientific documentation; 205,000 vols; Dir JOSÉ RINCON FERREIRA; publs *Ciência da Informação* (3 a year), *Calendário de Eventos em Ciência e Tecnologia* (quarterly), *Qualidade & Produtividade: Eventos e Cursos* (quarterly), *Informativo IBICT* (every 2 months).

Curitiba

Biblioteca Central da Universidade Federal do Paraná (University of Paraná Library): CP 441, Rua Gen. Carneiro 370/80, 80001-970 Curitiba, PR; tel. (41) 264-5545; fax (41) 262-7784; e-mail bc@bc.ufpr.br; internet www.bc.ufpr.br; f. 1956; 350,000 vols; 13 specialized libraries; Dir LIGIA ELIANA SETENARESKI.

Biblioteca Pública do Paraná (Paraná Public Library): Rua Cândido Lopes 133, 80020-901 Curitiba, PR; tel. (41) 322-9800; fax (41) 225-6883; f. 1954; 416,000 vols, 6,000 periodicals; Dir MARILENE ZICARELLI MILARCH.

Florianópolis

Biblioteca Pública do Estado de Santa Catarina (Santa Catarina State Public Library): Rua Tenete Silveira 343, 88010 Florianópolis, SC; tel. (482) 22-1378; f. 1854; 60,000 vols; collections of rare books, Braille and talking books; Dir ISABELA SALUM FETT.

Fortaleza

Biblioteca Pública Governador Menezes Pimentel (Ceará Public Library): Av. Presidente Castelo Branco 255, Centro, CEP 60010-000, Fortaleza, CE; tel. (85) 3101-2546; fax (85) 3101-2544; e-mail bpublica@secult.ce.gov.br; internet www.secult.ce.gov/br; f. 1867 as a Provicial Library; 100,000 vols, incl. books, periodicals, rare books, videos, spoken books, Braille books and CDs; Man. MARIA HELENA LYRA.

Biblioteca Universitária da Universidade Federal do Ceará: Campus do Pici, CP 6025, Fortaleza, CE; tel. (85) 243-9506; fax (85) 243-9513; f. 1958, renamed 1982; 164,429 vols; Dir GABRIELITA CARRHÁ MACHADO.

João Pessôa

Biblioteca Pública do Estado da Paraíba (Paraíba Public Library): Av. General Osório 253, João Pessôa, PB; f. 1859; 10,000 vols; Dir GERALDO EMILIO PÔRTO.

Manaus

Biblioteca e Arquivo Público de Manaus (Manaus Public Library and Archives): Praça Pedro II 265, 69005 Manaus, AM; tel. (92) 232-3878; f. 1852; *c.* 3,000 vols; Dir Com. JUNOT C. FREDERICO; publ. *Arquivo do Amazonas*.

Niterói

Biblioteca Pública do Estado do Rio de Janeiro (Public Library of the State of Rio): Praça da República, Niterói, RJ; f. 1927; possesses rare early works, newspapers and valuable first editions; 80,000 vols, notably dictionaries, encyclopædias, reference books; Dir ALBERTINA FORTUNA BARROS.

Ouro Prêto

Biblioteca da Escola de Minas da Universidade Federal de Ouro Prêto (Library of the Ouro Prêto School of Mines): Praça Tiradentes 20, 35400-000 Ouro Prêto, MG; tel. (31) 551-1666; f. 1876; 50,000 vols, 1,900 periodicals; Dir MARIA DA GLÓRIA RIBEIRO SOARES ARAÚJO; publ. *Revista*.

Pelotas

Biblioteca Pública Pelotense (Public Library): Praça Coronel Pedro Osório 103, Pelotas, RS; tel. (532) 223856; f. 1875; 150,000 vols; museum, cultural exhibition; Pres. JOAQUIM SALVADOR COELHO PINHO.

Petrópolis

Biblioteca Municipal (Municipal Library): Petrópolis, RJ; f. 1871; Librarian MARIA HELENA DE AVELLAR PALMA; 100,000 vols; 2 branches.

Porto Alegre

Biblioteca Central da Universidade Federal do Rio Grande do Sul: Av. Paulo Gama 110, Térreo da Reitoria, 90046-900 Porto Alegre, RS; tel. (51) 3316-3065; fax (51)

3316-3984; e-mail bcentral@bc.ufrgs.br; internet www.biblioteca.ufrgs.br; f. 1971; 32 br. libraries; 1,044,830 vols; Dir VIVIANE CARRION CASTANHO.

Biblioteca Pública do Estado do Rio Grande do Sul (Rio Grande do Sul State Public Library): Rue Riachuelo s/n, Porto Alegre, RS; f. 1871; 775,863 vols; Dir JULIANA VIANNA ROSA.

Recife

Biblioteca Central da Universidade Federal de Pernambuco: Av. dos Reitores s/n, Cidade Universitária, 50670-901 Recife, PE; fax (81) 271-8090; f. 1968; 405,291 vols (including all departmental libraries), 8,603 periodicals; a regional centre for the national bibliographic network organized by the Instituto Brasileiro de Informação em Ciência e Tecnologia (*q.v.*); Dir Profa ANA MARIA FERRACIN; publs *Sumários de Periódicos* (monthly), *BC-informa* (monthly).

Biblioteca Pública Estadual de Pernambuco (Pernambuco State Public Library): Recife, PE; f. 1852; 150,000 vols; Dir CLEA DUBEUX PINTO PIMENTEL.

Rio de Janeiro

Arquivo Nacional (National Archives): Rua Azeredo Coutinho 77, 20230-170 Rio de Janeiro, RJ; tel. (21) 2252-2617; fax (21) 2232-8430; e-mail diretorgeral@arquivonacional.gov.br; internet www.arquivonacional.gov.br; f. 1838; specializes in history of Brazil, technique of archives and legislation; 28,000 vols; 45 shelf-km. of documents; Dir-Gen. JAIME ANTUNES DA SILVA; publs *BIBA*, *Revista Acervo*.

Biblioteca Bastos Tigre da Associação Brasileira de Imprensa (Library of Brazilian Press Association): Rua Araújo Porto Alegre 71, 12° andar, 20030-010 Rio de Janeiro, RJ; tel. 2262-9822; fax 2262-3893; e-mail abi@abi.org.br; f. 1908; 40,473 vols, 6,788 periodical titles; Dir MAURÍCIO AZÊDO.

Biblioteca da Sociedade Brasileira de Cultura Inglesa: CP 5215, Rua Raul Pompéia 231, 3° andar, Rio de Janeiro, RJ; tel. 287-0990 ext. 300; fax 267-6474; f. 1934; 3 brs; 34,000 vols; Head Librarian MARIA DE FÁTIMA BORGES GONÇALVES; publ. *Library News*.

Biblioteca do Centro Cultural Banco do Brasil (Library of the Banco do Brasil Cultural Centre): Rua Primeiro de Março 66, 5° andar, Centro, 20010-000 Rio de Janeiro, RJ; tel. (21) 216-0212; fax (21) 216-0216; f. 1931; social sciences, literature and arts; 100,000 vols; special collections: rare books, Brazilian music and folklore; Dir KLEUBER DE PAIVA PEREIRA.

Biblioteca do Exército (Army Library): Praça Duque de Caxias 25, Ala Marcillo Dias (3 and.), 20221-260 Rio de Janeiro; fax (21) 519-5569; e-mail bibliex@ism.com.br; internet www.bibliex.eb.br; f. 1881; 60,000 vols; general collections to supply cultural needs of the army; Dir Cel LUIZ EUGÊNIO DUARTE PEIXOTO; publs *Revista A Defesa Nacional* (3 a year), *Revista do Exército Brasileiro* (3 a year), *Revista Militar de Ciência e Tecnologia* (3 a year).

Biblioteca do Instituto dos Advogados Brasileiros (Library of Lawyers' Institute): Av. Marechal Câmara 210, 5° andar, 20020-080 Rio de Janeiro, RJ; tel. (21) 240-3921; fax (21) 240-3173; f. 1843; 32,000 vols; Dir ROBERTO DE BASTOS LELIS.

Biblioteca do Ministério da Fazenda no Estado do Rio de Janeiro (Library of the Ministry of Finance of Rio de Janeiro State): Av. Pres. Antonio Carlos 375, sala 1238, 12° andar, 20020 Rio de Janeiro, RJ; tel. (21) 240-1120; f. 1943 by incorporation of various departmental libraries; 145,000 vols, 100 current periodicals; Librarian KATIA APARECIDA TEIXEIRA DE OLIVEIRA; publs *A Legislação Tributária no Brasil*, *Informe*.

Biblioteca do Ministério das Relações Exteriores no Rio de Janeiro (Library of the Ministry of Foreign Affairs in Rio de Janeiro): Av. Marechal Floriano 196, Centro 20080-002 Rio de Janeiro, RJ; tel. 253-5730; f. 1906; history; 270,000 vols including periodicals; rare books; Dir SONIA DOYLE; (See also under Brasília.).

Biblioteca do Mosteiro de S. Bento (Library of the St Benedict Monastery): CP 2666, 20001-970 Rio de Janeiro, RJ; tel. (21) 291-7122; f. 1600; 125,000 vols; Librarian D. MIGUEL VEESER; also in the towns of São Paulo, Salvador (Bahia) and Olinda; publs *Pergunte e Responderemos*, *Liturgia e Vida*.

Biblioteca Nacional (National Library): Av. Rio Branco 219-39, 20040-008 Rio de Janeiro, RJ; tel. (21) 262-8255; fax (21) 220-4173; e-mail gabinete@bn.br; internet www.bn.br; f. 1810 with 60,000 vols from the Real Biblioteca brought to Brazil by the Royal Family of Portugal in 1808; 9,000,000 documents; special collections: Col. De Angelis (Brazilian and Paraguayan History), Col. Tereza Cristina Maria (donated by Emperor D. Pedro II, 1891), Col. Alexandre Rodrigues Ferreira (description with illustrations of travels in Amazônia by A. R. Ferreira, 1783–1792); Pres. PEDRO CORREA DO LAGO; publ. *Anais da Biblioteca Nacional*.

Biblioteca Popular do Leblon-Vinicius de Moraes: Av. Bartolomeu Mitre 1297, 22431-050, Rio de Janeiro, RJ; f. 1954; 8,000 vols; Dir MARIA ALICE AMARAL PATERNOT.

Biblioteca Pública do Estado do Rio de Janeiro: Av. Presidente Vargas 1261, 20071-004 Rio de Janeiro, RJ; tel. 224-6184; fax 252-6810; e-mail bperj@callnet.com.br; f. 1873; attached to the State Office of Culture; 175,000 vols; Dir ANA LIGIA SILVA MEDEIROS.

Biblioteca Regional de Copacabana: Av. N.S. de Copacabana 702B, 3° andar, Rio de Janeiro, RJ; tel. (21) 237-8607; f. 1954; 29,706 vols; Dir ANA MARIA COSTA DESLANDES.

Fundação Casa de Rui Barbosa (Rui Barbosa Foundation): Rua S. Clemente 134, 22260-000 Rio de Janeiro, RJ; tel. (21) 2537-0036; fax (21) 2537-1114; e-mail mario@rb.gov.br; internet www.casaruibarbosa.gov.br; f. 1930, became Foundation 1966; includes a centre for research in law, philology and history, a centre of Brazilian literature (over 50,000 documents), a documentation centre, with a library, Rui Barbosa archive, a microfilm laboratory and a paper restoration laboratory; museum and auditorium; 100,000 vols; Pres. MARIO BROCKMANN MACHADO; Exec. Dir LUIZ EDUARDO CONDE.

Fundação Instituto Brasileiro de Geografia e Estatística – Centro de Documentação e Disseminação de Informações, Divisão de Biblioteca e Acervos Especiais: Rua General Canabarro 706, Térreo Maracanà, 20271-201 Rio de Janeiro, RJ; fax (21) 2142-4933; e-mail ibge@ibge.gov.br; internet www.ibge.gov.br; f. 1977; documentation and dissemination of research and studies in geoscience, environment, demography, social and economic indicators, national accounts, statistics; 48,000 vols, 2,105 periodicals, 20,000 maps, 115,000 photographs; Dir MARIA TERESA PASSOS BASTOS.

Serviço de Documentação da Marinha (Documentation Service of the Navy): Praça Barão de Ladário (Ilha das Cobras), Centro, 20091-000 Rio de Janeiro, RJ; tel. (21) 3870-6721; fax (21) 3870-6716; e-mail admin@sdm.mar.mil.br; internet www.sdm.mar.mil.br; f. 1943; maritime history of Brazil; includes a naval museum and archives; naval library of 110,000 vols; Dir CMG LUIS HENRIQUE DE AZEVEDO BRAGA; publ. *Revista Marítima Brasileira* (3 a year).

Sistema de Bibliotecas e Informação da Universidade Federal do Rio de Janeiro (Library and Information System of the University of Rio de Janeiro): Av. Pasteur 250, Urca, 22295-900 Rio de Janeiro, RJ; tel. (21) 295-1595 ext. 119; fax (21) 295-1397; f. 1989; maintains Nat. Catalogue of Periodicals; 3,500,000 vols, 1,900,000 periodicals; Dir MARIZA RUSSO.

Rio Grande

Biblioteca Rio-Grandense (Rio Grande Library): Rua General Osório 430, 96200-400 Rio Grande, RS; f. 1846; 400,000 vols, 7,600 maps; Pres. Dr JOÃO MARINONIO CARNEIRO LAGES; Dir Dr GILBERTO M. CENTENO CARDOSO.

Rio Negro

Biblioteca do Convento dos Franciscanos (Library of Franciscan Monastery): Rio Negro, PR; f. 1922; 20,000 vols; Sec. FREI ALFREDO SETÁRO.

Salvador

Biblioteca do Gabinete Português de Leitura (Portuguese Reading Room and Library): Praça da Piedade s/n, 40070-010, Salvador, BA; tel. 322-1580; fax 322-1299; 15,000 vols; Librarian AGNÚBIA OLIVEIRA.

Biblioteca Pública do Estado da Bahia (Bahia State Central Library): Rua Gen. Labatut 27, Barris – Salvador, BA; f. 1811, name changed 1984; 114,698 vols; Dir LÍDIA MARIA BASTISTA BRANDÃO.

São José dos Campos

Biblioteca Pública 'Cassiano Ricardo' ('Cassiano Ricardo' Public Library): Rua Sebastião Humel 110, São José dos Campos, SP; tel. (123) 29-2000, ext. 3071; f. 1968; 49,300 vols and 8,500 periodicals; Dir ANA ELISABETE MARTINELLI GODINHO.

São Luis

Biblioteca Pública do Estado (Public State Library): Praça de Panteon, São Luis, MA; f. 1829; 38 mems; 45,000 vols; collections of more than 15,000 engravings, and newspapers since 1821; Dir MARIA JOSÉ VAZ DOS SANTOS; Librarian ROBERTO TAMARA.

São Paulo

Arquivo do Estado de São Paulo (São Paulo State Archives): Rua Voluntários da Pátria 596, Santana, 02010-000 São Paulo, SP; tel. (11) 6221-2850; fax (11) 6221-4785; e-mail supervisao@arquivoestado.sp.gov.br; internet www.arquivoestado.sp.gov.br; f. 1721; 45,000 vols; 10,000 files of loose documents; 1m. images (negatives, photographs, postcards, caricatures and illustrations); State records, collections of rare books, MSS, periodicals, maps and plans; Dir Dr FAUSTO COUTO SOBRINHO; publ. *Revista Histórica* (print and online, monthly).

Biblioteca do Conservatório Dramático e Musical de São Paulo (Library of Academy of Music and Drama): Av. São João 269, São Paulo, SP; f. 1906; 30,000 vols; Dir Dr LUÍS CORRÊA FRAGOSO; Sec. JOSÉ RAYMUNDO LOBO.

Biblioteca do Instituto de Saúde (Health Institute Library): Av. Enéas Carvalho Aguiar 188, CP 8027, 01051 São Paulo, SP; f. 1969; 41,000 vols, valuable collection of works, reviews, maps on dermatology and

Hansen's disease, and rare works since 1600; Librarian ASTRID B. WIESEL.

Biblioteca 'George Alexander' (George Alexander Library): Rua da Consolação 896, Prédio 02, Higienópolis, 01302-907 São Paulo, SP; tel. (11) 3236-8302; fax (11) 3236-8302; e-mail biblio.per@mackenzie.com.br; internet www.mackenzie.com.br; f. 1870 as Mackenzie Library, present name 1926; 246,342 vols; Dir KAO SHIN.

Biblioteca Municipal Mário de Andrade (Municipal Library): Rua da Consolação 94, 01302-000 São Paulo, SP; tel. (11) 3241-5630; fax (11) 3259-5728; f. 1925; municipal library; 344,000 vols and 11,000 journal titles; incorporates former Biblioteca Pública do Estado de São Paulo; specialized collections of 40,000 rare editions and MSS, 25,000 drawings and art books, 5,500 maps; microfilms, legislation and multi-media sections; Dir of Municipal Library LUÍS FRANCISCO CARVALHO FILHO; publ. *Revista da Biblioteca Mário de Andrade*.

BIREME – Centro Latino-Americano e do Caribe de Informação em Ciências da Saúde (Latin American and Caribbean Centre on Health Sciences Information): Rua Botucatu 862, CP 20381, 04023-901 São Paulo, SP; tel. (11) 5576-9801; fax (11) 5575-8868; e-mail bireme@bireme.br; internet www.bireme.org; f. 1967 under the auspices of the Pan American Health Organization to promote a regional network of health libraries and information centres; aims to index all health literature produced in the region; provides bibliographic searches, document delivery, training, etc.; co-ordinates and promotes the Virtual Health Library (VHL); 400,000 issues of scientific journals, 3,500 current periodicals, 3,000 discontinued periodicals; Dir ABEL LAERTE PACKER; publ. *LILACS/CD-ROM* (3 a year).

British Council Library and Information Centre: Rua Ferreira Araújo, 741 terreo Pinheiros, 05428-000 São Paolo SP; tel. (11) 2126-7560; fax (11) 2126-7564; e-mail centro.info@britishcouncil.org.br; 7,000 vols; Library and Customer Services Officer ANA LUIZA MATTOS.

Discoteca Oneyda Alvarenga: Centro Cultural São Paulo, Rua Vergueiro 1000, 01504-000 São Paulo, SP; tel. (11) 277-3611 ext. 244; fax (11) 277-3611 ext. 231; e-mail ccsp@eu.ansp.br; f. 1935; study and diffusion of Brazilian and international classical, folk and popular music; 42,000 vols of music scores and 8,300 books; collection of 74,000 records, 400 periodical titles; museum of folklore; Dir MARIA CRISTINA MAGALHÃES MARINHO.

Sistema Integrado de Bibliotecas da Universidade de São Paulo (São Paulo University Integrated Library System): Av. Prof. Luciano Gualberto, Trav. J, 374-1°andar, 05508-010 São Paulo, SP; tel. (11) 3031-7448; fax (11) 3815-2142; e-mail dtsibi@org.usp.br; internet www.usp.br/sibi; f. 1981; 39 libraries, with 6,007,946 vols; Technical Dir ADRIANA CYBELE FERRARI.

Vitória

Biblioteca Estadual: Av. Pedro Palácios 76, Vitória, ES; f. 1855; 31,981 vols.

Biblioteca Municipal Vitória: Rua Barão Itapemirim 204, 1° andar, Vitória, ES; f. 1941; 12,859 vols.

Museums and Art Galleries

Belém

Museu Paraense Emílio Goeldi (Pará Museum): Av. Magalhães Barata 376, CP 399, 66017-970 Belém, PA; tel. (91) 249-1233; fax (91) 249-0466; e-mail postmaster@museu-goeldi.br; f. 1866; part of MCT/CNPq; natural history, archaeology, anthropology and ethnography of the Amazon region; zoological and botanical garden; library of 200,000 vols; collection of rare books; Dir PETER MANN TOLEDO; publs *Boletim* (four separate series on anthropology, botany, geology and zoology), *Guia*.

Belo Horizonte

Museu Histórico Abílio Barreto (Historical Museum): Av. Prudente de Morais 202, Barrio Cidade Jardim, 30380-000 Belo Horizonte, MG; tel. (31) 3277-8573; fax (31) 3277-8572; e-mail mhab@pbh.gov.br; internet www.pbh.gov.br/cultura; f. 1943; local collection; special collections: original documentation of the Belo Horizonte Construction Commission, Minas Gerais provincial laws (1849–89); library; Dir THAÏS VELLOSO COUGO PIMENTEL.

Campinas

Museu de História Natural (Natural History Museum): Rua Coronel Quirino 2, Bosque dos Jequitibás, Campinas, SP; tel. (192) 310555 ext. 372; f. 1938; history, folklore and anthropology; Dir TEREZA CRISTINA SILVA MELLO BORGES.

Campo Grande

Museu Regional D. Bosco (D. Bosco Regional Museum): Rua Barão do Rio Branco 1885, CP 415, 79100 Campo Grande, MTS; f. 1951; ethnographic, shell and insect collections; Dir JOÃO FALCO.

Curitiba

Museu Paranaense (Paraná Museum): Praça Generoso Marques s/n, 80020-230 Curitiba, PR; tel. (41) 323-1411; fax (41) 222-5824; e-mail museupr@pr.gov.br; internet www.pr.gov.br/museupr; f. 1876; historical, ethnographical and archaeological collections; library of 6,000 vols, 2,200 periodicals; Dir JAYME ANTONIO CARDOSO; publ. *Arquivos do Museu Paranaense*.

Fortaleza

Museu do Ceará: Rua São Paulo 51, CEP 60030-100 Fortaleza, CE; historical collection.

Goiânia

Museu Goiano Zoroastro Artiaga (Zoroastro Artiaga State Museum): Praça Cívica 13, Goiânia, GO; tel. (62) 223-1763; e-mail muza.go@zipmail.com; f. 1946; history, geology, anthropology, local art, folklore; Dir Dr HENRIQUE DE FREITAS.

Itu

Museu Republicano 'Convenção de Itu' (Itu Convention Republican Museum): Rua Barão de Itaim 67, 13300-160 Centro, SP; tel. (11) 4023-0240; fax (11) 4023-2525; e-mail jonasouz@usp.br; internet www.mp.usp.br/mr; f. 1923; attached to Museu Paulista da Universidade de São Paulo (*q.v.*); historical; library of 35,000 vols, 113 periodicals, photographs; spec. collns incl. Prudente de Morais colln, database 1870–1930; Suprervisor Prof. Dr CARLOS DE ALMEIDA PRADO BACELLAR; Curator Prof. JONAS SOARES DE SOUZA; publ. *Boletim Informativo—SAMUR*.

Macapá

Museu Territorial do Amapá (Amapá Territorial Museum): Fortaleza de S. José de Macapá, Macapá (Território do Amapá); f. 1948; zoology, archaeology, ethnography and numismatics; expeditions.

Olinda

Museu Regional de Olinda (Regional Museum of Olinda): Rua do Amparo 128, Olinda, PE; f. 1934; historic and regional art.

Ouro Prêto

Museu da Inconfidência (History of Democratic Ideals and Culture): Praça Tiradentes 139, Ouro Prêto, MG; tel. (31) 551-1121; fax (31) 551-1121; f. 1944; 18th- and 19th-century music MSS and works of art, documents related to Inconfidência Mineira, documents from the Notary Public's Office during the Colonial Period; library of 19,000 vols; Dir RUI MOURÃO; publ. *Anuário do Museu da Inconfidência*.

Museu de Ciência e Técnica da Escola de Minas (Science and Technology Museum of the School of Mines): Praça Tiradentes 20, 35400-000 Ouro Prêto, MG; tel. (31) 551-5257; fax (31) 551-5261; e-mail museuct@ouropreto.feop.com.br; f. 1995; affiliated to the Universidade Federal de Ouro Prêto; Dir Prof. Dr LEONARDO BARBOSA GODEFROID.

Petrópolis

Museu Imperial (Imperial Museum): Rua da Imperatriz 220, 25610-320 Petrópolis, RJ; tel. (24) 2237-8000; fax (24) 2237-8000 ext. 252; e-mail museu@museuimperial.gov.br; internet www.museuimperial.gov.br; f. 1940; 11,024 period exhibits of Brazilian Empire (1808–89) and Petrópolis history, notably imperial regalia, jewels and apparel; library: special library on the history of Brazil, 35,770 vols; historic archives of 100,000 MSS on Brazilian history in the 19th century; 4,000 photos, 500 maps and 700 iconographic items; Dir MARIA DE LOURDES PARREIRAS HORTA; publ. *Anuário*.

Porto Alegre

Museu de Arte do Rio Grande do Sul: Praça da Alfândega s/n, 90010-150 Porto Alegre, RS; tel. (51) 3227-2311; fax (51) 3227-2519; e-mail museu.margs@terra.com.br; internet www.margs.org.br; f. 1954; paintings, statues, prints; library: art library of 2,500 vols; Dir PAULO CESAR BRASIL DO AMARAL; publ. *Jornal do MARGS* (11 a year).

Museu 'Julio de Castilhos' (State Historical Museum): Rua Duque de Caxias 1205 e 1231, 90010-283 Porto Alegre, RS; tel. and fax (51) 3221-3959; e-mail museujulio.castilhos@terra.com.br; f. 1903; 10,100 exhibits of national history, including the 1835 Revolutionary period, the Paraguayan War, and collection of Indian pieces; armoury, antique furniture and slave pieces; library of 5,000 vols; Dir NARA MARIA MACHADO NUNES.

Recife

Museu do Estado de Pernambuco (State Museum): Av. Rui Barbosa 960, Graças, CEP 52011-040 Recife, PE; tel. (81) 427-9322; fax (81) 427-0766; f. 1929; local history, paintings; library of 4,000 vols, 110 periodicals; Dir SYLVIA PONTUAL.

Rio de Janeiro

Museu Carpológico do Jardim Botânico do Rio de Janeiro (Museum of Carpology of the Botanical Garden): Rua Pacheco Leão 915, 22460-030 Rio de Janeiro, RJ; tel. (21) 511-2749; fax (21) 511-2749; f. 1915; specializes in botany; collection of 6,200 fruits; Dir Dra NILDA MARQUETE.

Museu da Fauna (Wildlife Museum): Quinta da Boa Vista, São Cristónão, Rio de Janeiro, RJ; tel. 2280556; f. 1939; collections include vertebrates, mammals, birds, butterflies and reptiles from the principal regions of Brazil; part of Tijuca National Park; scientific expeditions; publ. *Monograph*.

Museu da República (Museum of the Republic): Rua do Catete 153, 22220-000 Rio de Janeiro, RJ; tel. (21) 265-9747; fax (21) 285-6320; e-mail musrepublica@ax.ibase.org.br; f. 1960; sited in Catete Palace, built 1858–67, fmr seat of Government; exhibits of items belonging to former Presidents; special collections: history of Brazil, historical archive with 85,000 photographs and documents; library of 10,000 vols; Dir ANELISE PACHECO.

Museu de Arte Moderna do Rio de Janeiro (Museum of Modern Art): Av. Infante Dom Henrique 85, 20021-140 Rio de Janeiro, RJ; tel. (21) 2240-4944; fax (21) 2240-4899; e-mail mamrio@mamrio.org.br; internet www.mamrio.org.br; f. 1948; collections representing different countries; film archive; library of 25,000 vols; Pres. GILBERTO CHATEAUBRIAND.

Museu de Ciências da Terra, Departamento Nacional da Produção Mineral (Earth Sciences Museum, National Department of Mineral Production at the Ministry of Mines and Energy): Av. Pasteur 404, 2° andar, Praia Vermelha, 22290-240 Rio de Janeiro, RJ; tel. (21) 2295-6673; fax (21) 2295-4896; e-mail wmuseu@yahoo.com.br; internet www.dnpm.gov.br; f. 1907; collection of fossils, minerals, rocks, gems, ore minerals and meteorites from Brazil and other countries; Dir DIOGENES DE ALMEIDA CAMPOS.

Museu do Índio (Museum of the Indian): Rua das Palmeiras 55, Botafogo, 22270-070 Rio de Janeiro, RJ; tel. (21) 286-2097; fax (21) 286-8899; e-mail atividades@museudoindio.org.br; internet www.museudoindio.org.br; f. 1953; ethnology, ethnohistory, museology, linguistics, documentation; conducts research into Indian societies and cultures; library of 28,000 vols; scientific archives (documents, photographs, films and music); Chair. JOSÉ CARLOS LEVINHO; publs *Boletim*, *Museo ao Vivo*.

Museu do Instituto Histórico e Geográfico Brasileiro (Museum of the Brazilian Historical and Geographical Institute): Av. Augusto Severo 8, 20021-040 Rio de Janeiro, RJ; f. 1838; history, geography and ethnography collection.

Museu e Arquivo Histórico do Centro Cultural Banco do Brasil (Museum and Historical Archives of the Banco do Brasil Cultural Centre): Rua Primeiro de Março 66, Centro, 20010-000 Rio de Janeiro, RJ; tel. (21) 216-0620; fax (21) 263-6314; f. 1955; collection of banknotes and coins from Brazil and other countries, documents relating to the economic history of Brazil and to the Banco do Brasil; library: see Libraries; Dir KLEUBER DE PAIVA PEREIRA.

Museu Histórico da Cidade do Rio de Janeiro (Historical Museum of the City): Estrada Santa Marinha, s/n, Parque da Cidade, Gávea, 22451 Rio de Janeiro, RJ; f. 1934; art and history of the City; library of 4,000 vols; Dir BEATRIZ DE VICQ CARVALHO.

Museu Histórico Nacional (National Historical Museum): Praça Marechal Âncora s/n, 20021-200 Rio de Janeiro, RJ; tel. (21) 2550-9221; fax (21) 2550-9220; e-mail mhn02@visualnet.com.br; internet www.museuhistoriconacional.com.br; f. 1922; collections of coins, medals, ceramics, ivory, vehicles, weapons, furniture, prints, paintings, besides historical exhibits; organizes courses in museology, national history, arts; library of 50,000 vols, historical archive; Dir VERA LÚCIA BOTTREL TOSTES.

Museu Nacional (National Museum): Quinta da Boa Vista, 20940-040 Rio de Janeiro, RJ; tel. (21) 254-4320; fax (21) 568-8262 ext. 232; e-mail museu@acd.ufrj.br; internet acd.ufrj.br/museu/; f. 1818; sections: anthropology, botany, entomology, geology and palaeontology, invertebrates and vertebrates, archaeology, ethnolinguistics; 4,000,000 specimens; library of 473,000 vols; Dir Prof. LUIZ FERNANDO DIAS DUARTE; publs *Arquivos* (irregular), *Boletim: Antropologia* (irregular), *Boletim: Botânica* (irregular), *Boletim: Geologia* (irregular), *Boletim: Zoologia* (irregular), *Estudos de Antropologia Social* (2 a year).

Museu Nacional de Belas Artes (National Museum of Fine Arts): Av. Rio Branco 199, Rio de Janeiro, RJ; tel. 240-9869; f. 1937; collections of Brazilian and European paintings and sculpture; graphic arts and furniture; primitive art, numismatics, posters, photographs; exhibitions and educational services; library of 12,000 vols; Dir Prof. HELOISA A. LUSTOSA; publ. *Boletim*.

Museus Raymundo Ottoni de Castro Maya: R. Murtinho Nobre 93, 20241-050 Santa Teresa, Rio de Janeiro, RJ; tel. (21) 224-8524; fax (21) 507-1932; e-mail c.maya01@visualnet.com.br; f. 1962 by Raymundo Ottoni de Castro Maya, now run by the Ministry of Culture; two museums: Museu da Chácara do Céu (modern Brazilian and European art, Chinese pottery and sculpture, Luso-Brazilian furniture etc.) and Museu do Açude (17th- to 19th-century Portuguese tiles and sculpture, Luso-Brazilian furniture etc. in 19th-century manor house); library: *c.* 2,000 vols; Dir VERA DE ALENCAR.

Rio Grande

Museu Oceanográfico 'Prof. Eliézer de C. Rios' (Oceanographic Museum): CP 379, 96200-970, Rio Grande, RS; tel. (532) 32-34-96; fax (532) 32-96-33; f. 1953; attached to Univ. of Rio Grande; oceanography, ichthyology, malacology, mammalogy; large shell collection, cetaceans collection; library; Dir Oc. Ms. LAURO BARCELLOS.

Sabará

Museu do Ouro (Gold Museum): Rua da Intendência, 34500 Sabará, MG; tel. (31) 671-1848; fax (31) 671-1848; f. 1945; museum housed in a building dated 1730; sections: technical, historical, artistic; antique methods of gold mining and smelting; gold ingots, 18th-century silverware, 18th-century furniture and typical handicrafts of the mining districts; library of 3,000 vols, 35,000 documents; Dir SELMA MELO MIRANDA.

Salvador

Museu de Arte da Bahia (Bahia Art Museum): Av. 7 de Setembro 2340, Vitória, Salvador, BA; f. 1918; library of 8,000 vols; 9,209 exhibits; general collection, with emphasis given to art, particularly Bahian Colonial art; Dir LUIZ JASMIN; publ. *Publicações do Museu*.

Museu Henriqueta Catharino, Instituto Feminino da Bahia (Henriqueta Catharino Museum, Bahia Women's College): Rua Monsenhor Flaviano 2, 40080-150 Salvador, BA; tel. (71) 329-5522; fax (71) 329-5681; e-mail ifbmuseu@terra.com.br; f. 1933; collections of religious art, Brazilian art and feminine apparel; also the Museu de Arte Popular; gold, silver, jewellery, clothing, weapons, furniture, porcelain, textiles; Dir TEREZA MARIA PEREIRA TOURINHO.

São Paulo

Museu de Arqueologia e Etnologia da Universidade de São Paulo e Serviço de Biblioteca e Documentação: Av. Prof. Almeida Prado 1466, CEP 05508-900 São Paulo, SP; tel. (11) 3091-4978; fax (11) 3091-5042; f. 1964; 88 staff; library of 60,000 vols, incl. 19,000 books and 32,000 vols of print periodicals; Museum Dir Dr MURILLO MARA; Library Dir ELIANA ROTOLO; publs *Revista do Museu de Arqueologia e Etnologia* (annually), *Sumários de Periódicos* (6 a year).

Museu de Arte Contemporânea da Universidade de São Paulo (Contemporary Art Museum of São Paulo University): Rua da Reitoria 160, CEP 05508-900 São Paulo, SP; tel. (11) 3818-3538; fax (11) 212-0218; e-mail informac@edu.usp.br; internet http://www.mac.usp.br/; f. 1963; a permanent exhibition of international and Brazilian plastic arts; library of 6,000 vols, 30,000 catalogues, 20,500 slides, 4,000 posters; Dir Prof. Dr JOSÉ TEIXEIRA COELHO.

Museu de Arte de São Paulo: Av. Paulista 1578, 01310-200 São Paulo, SP; tel. 251-5644; fax 284-0574; e-mail atemasp@masp.art.br; internet www.masp.art.br; f. 1947; classical and modern paintings, Italian, Spanish, Dutch, Flemish, and French schools; also representative works by Portinari and Lasar Segall; departments of theatre, music, cinema, art history, exhibitions, printing, photography and education; Dir JULIO NEVES.

Museu de Arte Sacra: Av. Tiradentes 676, CEP 01102-Luz, São Paulo, SP; tel. 227-7694; fax 227-7687; e-mail museu@artesacra.com.br; internet www.cultura.sp.gov.br/arte_sacra.htm; f. 1970, formerly Museu da Curia Metropolitana; sacred art, furniture, numismatics, paintings, silverware, jewellery, textiles, etc.; library of 3,400 vols; Dirs Eng. Dr JOÃO MARINO, MARI MARINO.

Museu de Zoologia, Universidade de São Paulo (Museum of Zoology, University of São Paulo): Av. Nazaré 481, CP 42694, 04299-970 São Paulo, SP; tel. (11) 6165-8100; fax (11) 6165-8113; e-mail mz@edu.usp.br; internet www.mz.usp.br; f. 1939; 7,000,000 specimens of neotropical and world fauna; library of 104,000 vols; Dir Dr CARLOS ROBERTO FERREIRA BRANDÃO; publs *Arquivos de Zoologia*, *Papeis Avulsos de Zoologia*.

Museu Florestal 'Octávio Vecchi' (Forestry Museum): Rua do Horto 931, Bairro Horto Florestal, CEP 02377-000, São Paulo, SP; tel. 952-8555; fax (11) 204-8067; f. 1931; a dependency of the Forestry Institute of the Sec. of State for Environment; forestry and forest technology, collections of local timber; Dir DALMO DIPPOLD VILAR.

Museu Paulista da Universidade de São Paulo (São Paulo University Museum): Parque da Independência s/n, Ipiranga, CP 42503, 04218-970 São Paulo, SP; tel. (11) 6165-8012; fax (11) 6165-8051; e-mail mp@edu.usp.br; internet www.mp.usp.br; f. 1895; history, material culture, historical and numismatic specimens; also collections of furniture and stamps; library of 26,000 vols, 2,300 periodical titles; Dir ENI DE MESQUITA SAMARA; publs *Anais do Museu Paulista*, *Cadernos de São Paulo*.

Pinacoteca do Estado de São Paulo (State Art Museum): Praça da Luz 02–Luz, 01120-010 São Paulo, SP; tel. (11) 3229-9844; fax (11) 3226-7876; f. 1905; Brazilian art from 19th century to the present; temporary and permanent exhibitions, workshops, lectures, int. meetings; library: specialized library of 10,000 vols, 3,440 exhibition catalogues; Exec. Dir MARCELO MATTOS ARAUJO.

Terezina

Museu do Piauí: Praça Marechal Deodoro, 64000 Terezina, PI; tel. 2226027; f. 1980; historical, cultural and artistic exhibitions; Dir SELMA DUARTE FERREIRA; publ. *Boletim*.

Vitória

Museu Solar Monjardim: Av. P. Müller, Jucutuquara, Vitória, ES; f. 1939 as State Museum; inc. Jan. 1967 to Federal Univ.; history, sacred art, furniture, porcelain, paintings, arms, books, silverware and photographs; publ. *Boletim* (weekly).

Universities

UNIVERSIDADE FEDERAL DO ACRE

CP 500, Campus Universitario, BR 364, Km 04, 69915-900 Rio Branco, AC
Telephone: (68) 229-2244
Fax: (68) 229-1246
Internet: www.ufac.br

Founded 1971

Rector: FRANCISCO CARLOS DA SILVEIRA CAVALCANTI
Librarian: VALCI AUGUSTINHO

Library of 46,000 vols
Number of teachers: 274
Number of students: 2,013

DIRECTORS

Law: ANA ROSA BAYMA AZEVEDO
Economics: VICENTE ABREU NETO
Education: JOAQUIM LOPES DA CRUZ FILHO
Language and Literature: LINDA BARBARY MESQUITA
Geography: MARIA DAS DORES SILVA LUSTOSA
History: PEDRO MARTINELLO
Mathematics and Statistics: AROLDO CARDOSO CAMPOS
Social Sciences and Philosophy: PEDRO VICENTE COSTA SOBRINHO
Health Sciences: PASCOAL TORRES MUNIZ
Natural Sciences: MAURO LUIZ ALDRIGUE
Physical Education: WALTER FÉLIX DE SOUZA
Technology of Civil Construction: JAIR VICENTE MANOEL
Agrarian Science: JOSÉ DE RIBAMAR TORRES DA SILVA

UNIVERSIDADE FEDERAL DE ALAGOAS

Campus A. C. Simões, BR/104, Km 97, Tabuleiro do Martins, 57072-970 Maceió, AL
Telephone: (82) 214-1100
Fax: (82) 322-2345
Internet: www.ufal.br

Founded 1961
State (Federal) control
Language of instruction: Portuguese
Academic year: March to December (two semesters)

Rector: ROGÉRIO MOURA PINHEIRO
Vice-Rector: Prof. JOSÉ M. MALTA LESSA
Chief, Rector's Office: Prof. ELIAS PASSOS TENÓRIO
Pro-Rector (Academic Affairs): Prof. EDUARDO ALMEIDA SILVA
Pro-Rector (Community Affairs): Prof. WILD SILVA
Pro-Rector (Planning Affairs): Prof. JOÃO FERREIRA AZEVEDO
Pro-Rector (Postgraduate and Research Affairs): Prof. MANOEL M. RAMALHO AZEVEDO

Number of teachers: 907
Number of students: 6,128

Publication: *Boletim da UFAL*

DEANS

Centre of Exact and Natural Sciences: Prof. EDMILSON DE VASCONCELOS PONTES
Centre of Human Sciences, Letters and Arts: Profa GEORGETTE CASTRO DE ALMEIDA
Centre of Biological Sciences: Profa DELZA LEITE GITAI
Centre of Technology: Prof. REINALDO MARINHO
Centre of Health Sciences: Prof. ÚLPIO PAULO DE MIRANDA
Centre of Agrarian Sciences: Prof. PAULO GALINDO MARTINS
Centre of Applied Social Sciences: Prof. JAIR GALVÃO FREIRE

UNIVERSIDADE REGIONAL INTEGRADA DO ALTO URUGUAI E DAS MISSÕES

Av. Sete de Setembro 1558 (1° andar), Centro, CP 290, 99700-000 Erechim, RS
Telephone: (54) 522-2348
Fax: (54) 522-1255
E-mail: urireitoria@st.com.br
Internet: www.uri.com.br

Founded 1992

Rector: CLÉO JOAQUIM ORTIGARA

Library: Libraries with 204,000 vols, 5,130 periodicals
Number of teachers: 425
Number of students: 8,337.

UNIVERSIDADE DA AMAZONIA

Av. Alcindo Cacela 287, 66060-000 Belém, PA
Telephone: (91) 210-3000
Fax: (91) 225-3909
Internet: www.unama.br

Founded 1974
Private control

Rector: ÉDSON RAYMUNDO PINHEIRO DE SOUZA FRANCO

Library: Libraries with 121,000 vols, 3,219 periodicals
Number of teachers: 383
Number of students: 10,328.

UNIVERSIDADE DO AMAZONAS

Av. Gen. Rodrigo Otávio Jordão Ramos 3000, Campus Universitário, Aleixo, 69077-000 Manaus
Telephone: (92) 644-2244
Fax: (92) 644-1620
Internet: www.fua.br

Founded 1962
Federal control
Academic year: March to December

Rector: Prof. WALMIR DE ALBUQUERQUE BARBOSA
Vice-Rector: Dr SILAS GUEDES
Sub-Rectors: Profa IERECÊ BARBOSA MONTEIRO (Academic Affairs), Profa SEVERINA OLIVEIRA DOS REIS (Planning), Prof. RAIMUNDO NONATO QUEIROZ DE ARAÚJO (Administrative Affairs), Prof. RUTÊNIO CASTRO (Research and Graduate Affairs), Prof. ALMIR LIBERATO (Community Affairs), Prof. GEDEÃO TIMÓTEO AMORIM (Extension Services)
Librarian: ELIZABETH HEITOR PINTO

Number of teachers: 777
Number of students: 15,605

Publications: *Relatório de Atividades, Boletim Estatístico, Orçamento Programa, Catálogo de Teses, Boletim Bibliográfico, Plano Diretor, Caderno de Humanidades e Ciências Sociais*

DIRECTORS

Institute of Exact Sciences: Prof. ADEMAR MAURO TEIXEIRA
Institute of Human Sciences and Literature: Prof. MARCO FREDERICO KRÜGER ALEIXO
Institute of Technology: Prof. JORGE ANDRADE FILHO
Faculty of Social Studies: Prof. ROSALVO MACHADO BENTES
Faculty of Health Sciences: Prof. MENA BARRETO SEGADILHA FRANÇA
Faculty of Law: Prof. JOSÉ RUSSO
Centre for Environmental Sciences: Prof. JOSÉ AMÉRICO LEITE
Computer Centre: EDUARDO JAMES PEREIRA SOUTO
Centre for Arts: Prof. FRANCISCO CARNEIRO DA SILVA FILHO

UNIVERSIDADE FEDERAL DA BAHIA

Palácio da Reitoria, Rua Augusto Viana s/n, Canela, 40110-060 Salvador, BA
Telephone: (71) 245-9002
Fax: (71) 245-2460
Internet: www.ufba.br

Founded 1946
State control

Rector: LUIZ FELIPE PERRET SERPA
Vice-Rector: MARIA GLEIDE SANTOS BARRETO
Administrative Officer: NICE MARIA AMERICANO DA COSTA PINTO
Secretary-General: JUSSARA BARBARA MARTINS PINHEIRO
Librarian: VERA DELIA ABRAMO PEREIRA

Library: Central library and 35 departmental libraries, with 531,000 vols
Number of teachers: 1,812
Number of students: 16,836

Publication: *Universitas*

DIRECTORS

Faculty of Architecture: MANOEL JOSÉ FERREIRA DE CARVALHO
Faculty of Communication: MARCOS SILVA PALACIOS
Faculty of Economics: SERGIO GABRIELLI DE AZEVEDO
Faculty of Law: JOSÉ TEIXEIRA CAVALCANTE FILHO
Faculty of Medicine: JOSÉ ANTÔNIO DE ALMEIDA SOUZA
Faculty of Dentistry: EDMAR JOSÉ BORGES DE SANTANA
Faculty of Education: IRACY SILVA PICANÇO
Faculty of Pharmacy: NADIA ANDRADE DE MOURA RIBEIRO
Faculty of Philosophy and Humanities: SYLVIA MARIA DOS REIS MAIA
Polytechnic School: MAERBAL BITTENCOURT MARINHO
School of Fine Arts: MARIA DAS GRAÇAS MOREIRA RAMOS
School of Librarianship: OTHON FERNANDO JAMBEIRO BARBOSA
School of Nursing: GEORGINA ALMEIDA LOMANTO
School of Administration: OSVALDO BARRETO FILHO
School of Agriculture: WASHINGTON LUIZ COTRIM DUETE
School of Veterinary Medicine: RICARDO CASTELO BRANCO ALBINATI
School of Dietetics: CARMEM CELIA CARNEIRO CARVALHO SMITH
School of Music: OSCAR NASCIMENTO DOURADO
School of Dance: SUZANA MARIA COELHO MARTINS
School of Theatre: DEOLINDO CHECCUCCI NETO
Institute of Mathematics: ILKA REBOUÇAS FREIRE
Institute of Physics: MANUEL BLANCO MARTINEZ
Institute of Chemistry: WILSON ARAÚJO LOPEZ

Institute of Biology: VIRGINIA GUIMARÃES ALMEIDA
Institute of Geology: FRANCISCO JOSÉ GOMES MESQUITA
Institute of Letters: EVELINA DE CARVALHO SÁ HOISEI
Institute of Health Sciences: ROBERTO PAULO CORREIA DE ARAÚJO
Institute of Community Health: NAOMAR MONTEIRO DE ALMEIDA FILHO
Human Resources Centre: ALBA REGINA NEVES RAMOS
Data Processing Centre: MARCIA TEREZA RANGEL DE OLIVEIRA
Centre of Afro-Oriental Studies: JEFERSON AFONSO BACELAR
Centre of Bahian Studies: FERNANDO DA ROCHA PEREZ
Centre of Inter-disciplinary Studies for Public Services: DORA LEAL ROSA
University Hospital: ANTONIO CARLOS MOREIRA LEMOS
Maternity Hospital: BENEDITO SOARES METZKER

CENTRO UNIVERSITÁRIO DE BARRA MANSA – UBM

Rua Vereador Pinho de Carvalho, 267 Centro, Barra Mansa, RJ 27330-550
Telephone: (24) 3325-0262
Fax: (24) 3323-9565
E-mail: pro.com@ubm.br
Internet: www.ubm.br
Founded 1961 as an institution of higher education; university status and present name 1997
Private control
Rector: GUILHERME DE CARVALHO CRUZ
Pro-Rector (Administration): FÉRES OSRRAIA NADER
Pro-Rector (Communications): LEANDRO ÁLVARO CHAVES
Librarian: ANA MARIA DINARDI BARBOSA BARROS
Library of 43,151 books, 500 periodicals
Publications: *Revista Cientifica* (2 a year), *UBM Noticias* (quarterly), *Caderno de Cultura Referencia* (quarterly)

ACADEMIC CO-ORDINATORS
Accountancy: ROSÂNGELA DOS SANTOS
Biological Sciences: ZILANI DE OLIVEIRA MACHADO
Business Administration: JOSE GONCALVES BARBOSA
Communication Disorders and Sciences: DEBORA LUDERS
Computer Engineering: RICARDO DE OLIVEIRA ALVES
Computer Science: JOSE NILTON CANTARINO GIL
Geography: MARIA ILDA FIDÉLIS E SILVA
History: MARIA ILDA FIDÉLIS E SILVA
Letters: MARIA DO CARMO M. BASTOS
Mass Communication: ANA LUCIA CORREA DE SOUZA
Mathematics: JACQUELINE BERNARDO PEREIRA OLIVEIRA
Nursing: SUELI SOLDATI ABRANCHES
Nutrition: MARILENE DE OLIVEIRA LEITE
Pedagogy: MARIA APARECIDA M. GLEIZER
Pharmacy: (vacant)
Physiotherapy: ANDRÉ LUIS VIEIRA CAVALLEIRO
Secondary Teacher Training: ROSA MARIA GOUVEA ESTEVES
Systems Analysis: JOSE CLAUDIO DE A. FILHO
Tourism: MARIA ILDA FIDÉLIS E SILVA
Veterinary Medicine: FRANCISCO RICARDO C. NOGUEIRA
Visual Arts: RONALDO AUAD MOREIRA

INSTITUTO METODISTA BENNETT

Rua Marquês de Abrantes 55, Flamengo, 22230-060 Rio de Janeiro, RJ
Telephone: (21) 557-1001
Fax: (21) 205-9159
E-mail: imb@bennett.br
Internet: www.bennett.br
Founded 1887
Academic year: February to December
Director-General: CARLOS HENRIQUE GARCIA DE OLIVEIRA
Library: Libraries with 46,000 vols, 978 periodicals
Number of teachers: 258
Number of students: 3,548.

UNIVERSIDADE REGIONAL DE BLUMENAU

Rua Antônio da Veiga 140, Sala C 106, 89012-900 Blumenau, SC
Telephone: (47) 3321-0200
Fax: (47) 3322-8818
E-mail: reitoria@furb.br
Internet: www.furb.br
Founded 1968
Under control of the Fundação Universidade Regional de Blumenau
Language of instruction: Portuguese
Academic year: January to December
Rector: Prof. EGON JOSÉ SCHRAMM
Vice-Rector: Prof. RUI RIZZO
Pro-Rectors: Prof. ANTONIO ANDRÉ CHIVANGA BARROS, Prof. EMARDI FEIJÓ VIEIRA, Profa LUCIA SEVEGNANI, Prof. EDÉSIO LUIZ SIMIONATTO
Head, Informatics Laboratory: ALDÍRIO VICENTE
Head, Language Laboratory: IARA JANE WOLLSTEIN
Librarian: MAURO TESSARI
Informatic Centre: MAURO SCHRAMM
Library of 461,103 vols
Number of teachers: 834
Number of students: 12,314
Publications: *Dynamis–Revista Tecno-Científica*, *Revista de Divulgação Cultural*, *Revista de Estudos Ambientais*, *Revista Jurídica*, *Revista de Negócios*

DIRECTORS
Communication and Human Sciences Centre: CLÓVIS REIS
Education Sciences Centre: MARILENE DE LIMA K. SCHRAMM
Health Sciences Centre: Prof. ÉLIDE KURBAN
Juridical Sciences Centre: PATRÍCIA LUÍZA KEGEL
Natural Exact Sciences Centre: SÉRGIO STRINGARI
Technology Centre: CLARISSE ODEBRECHT

HEADS OF DEPARTMENTS
Accountancy Department: Prof. JOSANI MILENE FINK
Administration Department: Prof. ARLINDO SCHULZ
Architecture and City Planning Department: Prof. MÁRCIA CRISTINA SARDÁ
Arts Department: Prof. EUSÉBIO NICOLAU KOHLER
Chemical Engineering Department: Prof. ATILANO ANTÔNIO VEGINI
Chemistry Department: Prof. MAURO SCHARF
Civil Engineering Department: Prof. PAULO OSCAR BAIER
Communication Department: Prof. VENILTON REINERT
Economy Department: Prof. RALF MARCOS EHMKE
Education Department: Prof. MARIA ADÉLIA BENTO SCHMITT
Electrical and Telecommunication Engineering: Prof. RICARDO JOSÉ DE OLIVEIRA CARVALHO
Forest Engineering Department: Prof. ALEXANDER CHRISTIAN VIBRANS
History and Geography Department: Prof. CRISTINA FERREIRA
Law Department: Prof. FELICIANO ALCIDES DIAS
Letter Department: Prof. VICTOR CÉSAR DA SILVA NUNES
Mathematics Department: Prof. VIVIANE CLOTILDE DA SILVA
Medicine Department: Prof. KARLA FERREIRA RODRIGUES
Natural Sciences Department: Prof. ANDRÉ PAULO NASCIMENTO
Odontology Department: Prof. IVENS FRISHKNECHT
Pharmaceutical Sciences Department: Prof. CAIO MAURÍCIO MENDES DE CÓRDOVA
Physical Education and Sports Department: Prof. ARTUR JOSÉ NOVAES
Physics Department: Prof. ÉLCIO SCHUHMACHER
Physiotherapy Department: Prof. EDISON SANFELICE ANDRÉ
Production Engineering and Design Department: Prof. ANDRÉ LUIS ALMEIDA BASTOS
Psychology Department: Prof. GESELDA BARATTO
Social Sciences and Philosophy Department: Prof. VERA ITEN TEIXEIRA
Social Service Department: Prof. RÚBIA DOS SANTOS
Systems and Computer Department: Prof. MAURO MARCELO MATTOS

PROFESSORS
International Relations Office: Prof. JORGE GUSTAVO BARBOSA DE OLIVEIRA

ATTACHED RESEARCH INSTITUTES
Environmental Research Institute: tel. (47) 3321-0540; fax (47) 3321-0556; e-mail ipa@furb.br; internet www.furb.br/2005/ipa.php?secao=1502; Dir Dra NOEMIA BOHN.
Social Research Institute: Rua São Paulo 1525, Ed. Cristiana, Blumenau; tel. (47) 3321-0350; fax (47) 3321-0338; e-mail ips@furb.br; internet www.furb.br/2005/ips.php?secao=1837; Dir Prof. MARCOS ANTONIO MATTEDI.
Technological Research Institute of Blumenau: Rua São Paulo 3250, Bloco B, Blumenau; tel. (47) 3321-6082; fax (47) 3321-6081; e-mail iptb@furb.br; internet www.furb.br/2005/iptb.php?secao=1828; Dir Dr CLODOALDO MACHADO.

UNIVERSIDADE DO BRASIL

Av. Brig. Trompowski s/n, Cidade Universitária, Ilha do Fundão, CP 68536, 21949-900 Rio de Janeiro, RJTelephone: (21) 290-2112
Fax: (21) 260-7750
E-mail: reitoria@reitoria.ufrj.br
Internet: www.ufrj.br
Founded 1920 as Universidade do Rio de Janeiro; became Universidade do Brasil 1937 and Universidade Federal do Rio de Janeiro 1965; reverted to present name 2000
State control
Rector: Prof. PAULO ALCÂNTARA GOMES
Vice-Rector: Prof. JOSÉ HENRIQUE VILHENA DE PAIVA
Secretary-General: Dr IVAN RODRIGUES DA SILVA
Director of Central Library: MARIZA RUSSO
Library: 42 faculty libraries
Number of teachers: 3,580
Number of students: 40,000

Publications: *Anais*, *Boletim*

DIRECTORS OF CENTRES

Mathematics and Natural Sciences Centre: Prof. MARCO ANTONIO FRANÇA FARIA
Literature and Arts Centre: Prof. CARLOS ANTONIO KALIL TANNUS
Philosophy and Humanities Centre: Prof. CARLOS ALBERTO MESSEDER PEREIRA
Technology Centre: Prof. OSCAR ACSELRAD
Law and Economic Sciences Centre: Prof. CARLOS LESSA
Health Sciences Centre: Profa VERA LUCIA RABELO DE CASTRO HALFOUN
Forum for Science and Culture: Profa MYRIAN DAVELSBERG

DEANS AND DIRECTORS OF FACULTIES, SCHOOLS AND INSTITUTES

Mathematics and Natural Sciences Centre:
- Institute of Physics: Prof. CARLOS ALBERTO ARAGÃO DE CARVALHO FILHO
- Institute of Geosciences: Prof. JORGE SOARES MARQUES
- Institute of Mathematics: Prof. LUIS PAULO VIEIRA BRAGA
- Institute of Chemistry: Prof. ROBERTO MARCHIORI
- Computer Science Centre: Prof. EDUARDO PAES
- Valongo Observatory: Profa HELOÍSA MARIA BOECHAT ROBERTY

Literature and Arts Centre:
- Faculty of Architecture and Town Planning: Profa MARIA ANGELA DIAS ELIAS
- Faculty of Literature: Prof. EDIONE TRINDADE DE AZEVEDO
- School of Fine Arts: Prof. VICTORINO DE OLIVEIRA NETO
- School of Music: Prof. JOSÉ ALVES DA SILVA (Dir)

Philosophy and Humanities Centre:
- Faculty of Education: Profa MARLENE DE CARVALHO
- School of Communications: Prof. ANDRE DE SOUZA PARENTE
- School of Social Services: Profa MARIA DURVALINA FERNANDES BASTOS
- Institute of Philosophy and Social Sciences: Profa NEYDE THEML
- Institute of Psychology: Profa MARIA INÁCIA D'AVILLA NETTO
- School of Teacher Training: Prof. MOACYR BARRETO DA SILVA JUNIOR

Technology Centre:
- School of Engineering: Prof. HELOI JOSÉ FERNANDES MOURA
- School of Chemistry: Prof. CARLOS AUGUSTO GUIMARÃES PERLINGEIRO
- Institute of Macromolecules: Prof. AÍLTON DE SOUZA GOMES
- Coordination of Graduate Programmes in Engineering: Prof. SEGEN FARID ESTEFEN

Law and Economic Sciences Centre:
- Faculty of Law: Prof. AYRTON DA COSTA PAIVA
- Faculty of Business Administration and Accounting: Prof. CARLOS ALBERTO BESSA
- Institute of Economics: Prof. JOÃO CARLOS FERRAZ
- Institute of Research, Regional and Town Planning: Prof. HERMES MAGALHÃES TAVARES
- Graduate School of Business Administration: Prof. AGRÍCOLA DE SOUZA BETHLEM

Health Sciences Centre:
- Institute of Biomedical Sciences: Prof. ANÍBAL GIL LOPES
- School of Nursing: Profa IVONE EVANGELISTA CABRAL
- Faculty of Pharmacy: Prof. JOSÉ CARLOS DA SILVA LIMA
- Faculty of Medicine: Profa SYLVIA DA SILVEIRA DE MELLO VARGAS
- Institute of Microbiology: Prof. SÉRGIO EDUARDO LONGO FRANCALANZZA
- Institute of Nutrition: Profa REJANE ANDRÉA RAMALHO NUNES DA SILVA
- Faculty of Dentistry: Prof. NÉLIO VICTOR DE OLIVEIRA
- School of Physical Education and Sport: Prof. JOSÉ MAURICIO CAPINASSO
- Institute of Biology: Prof. SERGIO LUIS COSTA BONECKER
- Institute of Biological and Health Sciences: Prof. ANIBAL GIL LOPES
- Institute of Biophysics: Prof. ANTONIO CARLOS CAMPOS DE CARVALHO
- Institute of Gynaecology: Prof. PASCHOAL MARTINI SIMÕES
- Institute of Neurology: Prof. GIANNI MAURELIO TEMPONI
- Institute of Psychiatry: Prof. JOÃO FERREIRA DA SILVA FILHO
- Institute of Child Care and Education: Prof. LUÍS AFONSO HENRIQUE MARIZ
- Institute of Thoracic Diseases: Prof. ALFREDO RISSON PEYNEAU
- Maternity School Hospital: Prof. JOFFRE AMIM JUNIOR
- Clementino Fraga Filho University Hospital: Prof. AMANCIO PAULINO
- São Francisco de Assis School Hospital: Profa SONIA REGINA CARVALHAL GOMES
- Technology Education Institute for Health: Profa ELIANA CLÁUDIA DE OTERO RIBEIRO
- Institute of Natural Product Research: Prof. ANTONIO JORGE RIBEIRO DA SILVA
- Community Health Study Centre: Profa DIANA MAUL DE CARVALHO

UNIVERSIDADE DE BRASÍLIA

Campus Universitário Darcy Ribeiro, Asa Norte, CP 4399, 70910-900 Brasília, DF
Telephone: (61) 307-2022
Fax: (61) 272-0003
E-mail: unb@unb.br
Internet: www.unb.br

Founded 1961; inaugurated 1962
Under the control of the Fundação Universidade de Brasília
Language of instruction: Portuguese
Academic year: March to December

Rector: LAURO MORHY
Vice-Rector: TIMOTHY MARTIN MULHOLLAND
Dean of Graduate Studies and Research: NORAÍ ROMEU ROCCO
Dean of Administration and Finance: ERICO PAULO SIEGMAR WEIDLE
Dean of Extension: DORIS SANTOS DE FARIA
Dean of Undergraduate Studies: MICHELÂNGELO GIOTTO S. TRIGUEIRO
Dean of Community Affairs: THÉRÈSE HOFMANN GATTI
Central Library Director: CLARIMAR ALMEIDA VALLE

Library: see Libraries
Number of teachers: 1,342
Number of students: 25,000

Publications: *Revista Humanidades* (4 a year), *UnB Revista* (4 a year)

DIRECTORS

Institute of Exact Sciences: HAYDÉE WERNECK POUBEL
Institute of Biological Sciences: IVONE DOZONDE DIMIZ
Institute of Humanities: DENISE BOMTEMPO BIRCHE DE CARVALHO
Institute of Literature: HENRYK SIEVIERSKI
Institute of Arts: SUZETE VENTURELLI
Institute of Geosciences: NILSON FRANCISQUINI BOTELHO
Institute of Psychology: MARIA ANGELA GUIMARÃES FEITOSA
Institute of Physics: ANTONIO LUCIANO DE A. FONSECA
Institute of Chemistry: MARCAL DE OLIVEIRA NETO
Institute of Political Science and International Relations: VAMIHED CHACON (acting)
Faculty of Law: JOSÉ GERALDO DE SOUSA JÚNIOR
Faculty of Architecture and Town Planning: GERALDO SÁ NOGUEIRA BATISTA
Faculty of Technology: HUMBERTO ABEDALLA JUNIOR
Faculty of Health Sciences: REYNALDO FELIPE TARELHO
Faculty of Applied Social Studies: GILENO FERNANDES MAREELINO (acting)
Faculty of Education: ERASTO FORKS MENDOZA
Faculty of Communications: MURILO CEZAR DE OLIVEIRA RAMOS
Faculty of Medicine: TANIO TORRES ROSA
Faculty of Physical Education: IRAN JUNQUEIRA DE CASTRO
Faculty of Agricultural Engineering and Veterinary Medicine: EVERALDO A. PEREIRA
Institute of Social Science: ELLEN FENSTERSEIFER WOORTMANN

HEADS OF DEPARTMENTS

Institute of Exact Sciences (Universidade de Brasília, Campus Universitário Darcy Ribeiro, 70910-900 Brasília, DF; tel. (61) 307-2291; fax (61) 273-1155; e-mail ie@exatas.unb.br; internet www.unb.br/ie/index.htm):
- Mathematics: ARTHUR VICENTE FERREIRA DE AZEVEDO
- Statistics: ANA MARIA NOGALES VASCONCELOS
- Computer Science: GERSON HENRIQUE PFITSCHER

Institute of Biological Sciences (Universidade de Brasília, Campus Universitário Darcy Ribeiro, Asa Norte, 70910-900 Brasília, DF; tel. (61) 307-2260; fax (61) 272-1497; e-mail ibd@unb.br; internet www.unb.br/ib-n/index.htm):
- Cell Biology: JAIME MARTINS DE SANTANA
- Genetics and Morphology: UMBERTO EUZÉBIO
- Physiological Sciences: ELISABETH NOGUEIRA FERROUI SCHWARTZ
- Ecology: MUNDAYTAN HARIDASAN
- Phytopathology: JOSÉ CARMINE DIANESE
- Botany: MARIA ELISA RIBEIRO CALBO
- Zoology: PAULO CESAR MOTTA

Institute of Humanities (Universidade de Brasília, Campus Universitário Darcy Ribeiro, ICC-Ala Norte, 70910-900 Brasília, DF; tel. (61) 340-2290; fax (61) 274-5362; e-mail mbc1957@unb.br; internet www.unb.br/ih/index.htm):
- Economics: FLÁVIO VERSIANI
- Social Services: CAROLINA CÁSSIA BATISTA SANTOS
- Philosophy: SAMUEL JOSÉ SIMON RODRIGUES
- Geography: MÁRIO DINIZ DE ARAÚJO NETO
- History: ELEONORA ZICARI COSTA DE BRITO

Institute of Literature (Universidade de Brasília, Campus Universitário Darcy Ribeiro, CP 4467, 70910-900 Brasília, DF; tel. (61) 307-2359; fax (61) 273-0255; e-mail il@unb.br; internet www.unb.br/il-n/index.htm):
- Linguistics, Classical and Vernacular Languages: DJALMA CAVALCANTE MELO
- Literary Theory and Literature: MARIA ISABEL EDOM PIRES
- Foreign Languages and Translation: GLÓRIA PACITA FRÁGUAS VÁSQUEZ

Institute of Arts (Universidade de Brasília, Campus Universitário Darcy Ribeiro, SG1-Asa Norte, 70910-900 Brasília, DF; tel. (61)

307-2879; fax (61) 307-2027; e-mail ida@unb.br; internet www.unb.br/ida-n/index.htm):

Scenic Arts: José Mauro Barbosa Ribeiro
Visual Arts: Shirley Gomes de Queiroz
Music: Marírs Lima Brasil

Institute of Geosciences (Universidade de Brasília, Campus Universitário Darcy Ribeiro, Asa Norte, 70910-900 Brasília, DF; tel. (61) 307-2433; fax (61) 272-4286; e-mail igd@unb.br; internet www.unb.br/ig-n/index.htm):

Mineralogy and Petrology: Elí Mendes Guimaraes
General and Applied Geology: Demerval Aparecido do Carmo
Geochemistry and Mineral Resources: Roberto Ventura Santos
Seismological Observatory: Lucas Vieira Barros

Institute of Psychology (Universidade de Brasília, Campus Universitário Darcy Ribeiro, ICC (Minhorão) Ala Sul, CP 4500, 70910-900 Brasília, DF; tel. (61) 307-2633; fax (61) 273-6378; e-mail ipd@unb.br; internet www.unb.br/ip-n/index.htm):

Clinical Psychology: Maria de Fátima Olivier Sudbrack
Basic Psychological Processes: Rachel Nunes da Cunha
Education and Developmental Psychology: Silviane Bonaccorsi Barbato
Social and Occupational Psychology: Gardémia Abbad de Oliveira Castro (acting)
Centre for Psychological Studies and Services: Ileno Izidio da Costa

Institute of Social Sciences (Universidade de Brasília, Campus Universitário Darcy Ribeiro Prédio Multiuso II (1° Andar), 70910-900 Brasília, DF; tel. (61) 307-2892; fax (61) 274-7570; e-mail ics@unb.br; internet www.unb.br/ics):

Sociology: Sadi Dal Rosso
Anthropology: Aleida Rita Ramos

Institute of Political Science and International Relations (Universidade de Brasília, Campus Universitário Darcy Ribeiro, CP 04359, 70910-900 Brasília, DF; tel. (61) 307–2865; fax (61) 273–3930; e-mail pol@unb.br; internet www.unb.br/ipr/index.htm):

Political Science: Lucia Merces Merces de Avelar
International Relations: Antônio Jorge Ramalho Jorge

Faculty of Law (Universidade de Brasília, Campus Universitário Darcy Ribeiro, Asa Norte, 70910-900 Brasília, DF; tel. (61) 307-2349; fax (61) 273-3532; e-mail fdir@unb.br; internet www.unb.br/fd-n/index.htm):

Law: José Geraldo de Sousa Júnior

Faculty of Architecture and Town Planning (Universidade de Brasília, ICC Norte – Bloco A, Campus Universitário Darcy Ribeiro, Asa Norte, CP 04431, 70910-900 Brasília, DF; tel. (61) 307-2453; fax (61) 273-2070; e-mail fau-unb@unb.br; internet www.unb.br/fau-n/index.htm):

Project, Expression and Representation in Architecture and Town Planning: Cláudia da Conceicão Gareia
Architectural and Town Planning Engineering: Cláudia Estrela Porto
Theory and History of Architecture and Town Planning: Gabriel Dorfman

Faculty of Technology (Universidade de Brasília, Campus Universitário Darcy Ribeiro, Asa Norte, 70910-900 Brasília, DF; tel. (61) 307-2305; fax (61) 273-8893; e-mail ftd@unb.br; internet www.unb.br/ft/index.htm):

Civil Engineering: Ennio Marquez Palmeira
Electrical Engineering: Francisco Damasceno Freitas
Mechanical Engineering: Sadek Crisóstomo Absi Altaro
Forestry Engineering: Alexandre Florian da Costa

Faculty of Health Sciences (Universidade de Brasília, Campus Universitário da Asa Norte, CP 4370, 70910-900 Brasília, DF; tel. (61) 273-3862; fax (61) 273-0105; e-mail jeesar@unb.br; internet www.unb.br/fe-n/index.htm):

Collective Medicine: Ximena Pamela
Nursing: Moema da Silva Borges
Nutrition: Yolanda Mercedes Silva de Oliveira
Odontology: Lilian Marly de Paula

Faculty of Applied Social Studies (Universidade de Brasília, Campus Universitário Darcy Ribeiro, Asa Norte, 70910-900 Brasília, DF; tel. (61) 307-2348; fax (61) 273-1105; e-mail lourim@unb.br; internet www.unb.br/fa/index.htm):

Administration: Geraldo Sardinha Almeida
Information and Documentation Science: Antônio Lisboa Carvalho de Miranda
Accounting: Elivânio Geraldo de Andrade

Faculty of Education (Universidade Brasília, Campus Universitário Darcy Ribeiro, Asa Norte, 70910-900 Brasília, DF; tel. (61) 307-2124; fax (61) 307-3826; e-mail postweb@fe.unb.br; internet www.unb.br/fe-n/index.htm):

Theory and Basic Education: Cláudia Valéria de Assis Dansa (acting)
Methods and Techniques: Sandra M. Von Tiesenhausen de S. Carmo
Planning and Administration: Hélène Leblanc

Faculty of Communications (Universidade de Brasília, Campus Universitário Darcy Ribeiro, ICC Norte, 70910-900 Brasília, DF; tel. (61) 307-2463; fax (61) 307-2461; e-mail fac@unb.br; internet www.unb.br/fac-n/index.htm):

Audio-Visual Communication and Publicity: Érika Bauer
Journalism: Susana Guedes Cardoso

Faculty of Medicine (Universidade de Brasília, Campus Universitário Darcy Ribeiro, Asa Norte, 70910-090 Brasília, DF; tel. (61) 307-2535; fax (61) 273-3907; e-mail fmd@unb.br; internet www.unb.br/fm/index.htm):

Surgery: João Batista de Sousa
Paediatrics: Maria Lígia Robalinho Lima
Pathology: Albino Verçosa de Magalhães
Gynaecology and Obstetrics: Carlos Resende de Miranda
Morphology: Yolanda Galindo Pacheco
Clinical Medicine: Cleudson Nery de Castro
Tropical Medicine: Flávio Alberto de Andrade Goulart

Faculty of Physical Education (Universidade de Brasília, Campus Universitário Darcy Ribeiro, Asana Norte, 70910-090 Brasília, DF; tel. (61) 307-2252; fax (61) 307-1779; e-mail fef@unb.br; internet www.unb.br/fef-n/index.htm):

Olympic Centre: Ana Maria Renne Lapa

UNIVERSIDADE CATÓLICA DE BRASÍLIA

QS 07, Lote 01, EPCT, Águas Claras, 71966-700 Taguatinga Sul, DF

Telephone: (61) 356-9000
Fax: (61) 356-3010
E-mail: ucb@ucb.br
Internet: www.ucb.br

Founded 1994

Rector: Dr Debora Pinto Niquini

Library: Libraries with 193,000 vols, 19,280 periodicals
Number of teachers: 879
Number of students: 16,926 (15,130 undergraduate, 1,796 postgraduate)

Publications: *Direito em Ação* (2 a year), *Revista Brasileira de Ciência e Movimento* (4 a year), *Revista Brasileira de Economia de Empresa* (3 a year), *Revista Technologia da Informação* (2 a year).

UNIVERSIDADE 'BRAZ CUBAS'

Av. Francisco Rodrigues Filho 1233, CP 511, 08773-380 Mogi das Cruzes, SP

Telephone: (11) 469-6444
Fax: (11) 4790-3844
Internet: www.brasilnet.com/brascubas

Founded 1940, university status 1986
Private control
Language of instruction: Portuguese
Academic year: February to December

Rector: Prof. Maurício Chermann
Pro-Rectors: Dr Jacks Grinberg (Teaching, Research and Extension), Dr Benedicto Laporte Vieira da Motta (Finance), Dr Israel Alves dos Santos (Administration), Isaac Grinberg (Community), Dr Saul Grinberg (Planning)
Secretary-General: Pércio Chamma Junior
Librarian: Jandira Maria Coutinho

Library of 97,000 vols
Number of teachers: 512
Number of students: 10,494

DIRECTORS

Centre for Applied Social Studies: Dr Marco Antonio Rodrigues Nahum
Centre for Exact and Technological Sciences: Dr Benedito Luiz Franco
Centre for Human Sciences, Literature and Education: Prof. Dilson Del Bem

COURSE CO-ORDINATORS

Law: Profa Marcia D. Nigro Conceição
Executive Bilingual Secretarial and Communication: Francisco J. Arouche Ornellas
Economics, Administration and Accountancy: Prof. Jair Gonçalves da Cunha
Basic and Natural Sciences: Prof. Pio Torre Flores
Architecture and Town Planning: Prof. Ciro Felice Pirondi
Human Sciences: Prof. Cesar Bilitardo
Postgraduate Courses: Jarbas Vargas Nascimento
Engineering and Technology: Prof. Pio Torre Flores
Odontology: Prof. Tadaaki Ando

UNIVERSIDADE DA REGIÃO DE CAMPANHA

Av. Tupy Silveira 2099, Centro, CP 141, 96400-110 Bagé, RS

Telephone: (532) 42-2244
Fax: (532) 42-2898
E-mail: urcamp@attila.urcamp.tche.br
Internet: attila.urcamp.tche.br

Founded 1989

Rector: Morvan Meirelles Ferrugem

Library: Libraries with 160,000 vols, 2,350 periodicals
Number of teachers: 578
Number of students: 6,985.

UNIVERSIDADE FEDERAL DE CAMPINA GRANDE

Rua Aprígio Veloso 882, Bodocongó CP 10049, 58109-000 Campina Grande, PB

Telephone: (83) 310-1089
Fax: (83) 310-1089
E-mail: bcufcg@zipmail.com.br

Founded 2002 from four existing campuses of the Universidade Federal da Paraíba

Publications: *Ariús–Revista do Centro de Humanidades* (annually), *Raizes–Revista do Centro de Humanidades* (2 a year), *Sheculum* (Revista de História, annually), *Revista Brasileira de Engenharia Agrícola e Ambiental (AGRIAMBI)* (quarterly)

DIRECTORS

Campina Grande Campus (58109-000 Campina Grande, PB; tel. (83) 310-1463):
- Centre for Science and Technology: BENEDITO GUIMARÃES AGUIAR NETO
- Centre for Humanities: JOSÉ EDILSON AMORIM
- Centre for Biological Sciences and Health: VILMA LÚCIA FONSECA MENDOZA

Cajazeiras Campus (58900-000 Cajazeiras, PB; tel. (83) 531-3046):
- Teacher Training Centre: JOSÉ MARIA GURGEL

Sousa Campus (58800-970 Sousa, PB; tel. (83) 521-1363):
- Centre for Law and Social Sciences: JOAQUIM CAVALCANTE DE ALENCAR

Patos Campus (58700-970 Patos, PB; tel. (83) 421-3397):
- Centre for Veterinary and Rural Technology: CARLOS PEÑA ALFARO

PONTIFÍCIA UNIVERSIDADE CATÓLICA DE CAMPINAS

Rodovia Dom Pedro I, Km 136 -Parque das Universidades, 13086-900 Campinas, SP

Telephone: (19) 3756-7000
Fax: (19) 3256-8477
E-mail: reitoria@puc-campinas.edu.br
Internet: www.puc-campinas.edu.br

Founded 1941
Private control
Academic year: February to December

Chancellor: Dom BRUNO GAMBERINI
Rector: Prof. Pe. JOSÉ BENEDITO DE ALMEIDA DAVID
Vice-Rector: Prof. Pe. WILSON DENADAI
Pro-Rector (Administration): Prof. ANTÔNIO SERGIO CELLA
Pro-Rector (Extension and Communitarian Subjects): Profa CARMEN CECÍLIA DE CAMPOS LAVRAS
Pro-Rector (Research and Graduate and Postgraduate Courses): Profa VERA SILVIA MARÃO BERAQUET
Pro-Rector (Undergraduate Courses): Prof. MARCO ANTONIO CARNIO
Secretary-General: Prof. MARCEL DANTAS DE CAMPOS
Librarian: ROSA MARIA VIVONA B. OLIVEIRA

Number of teachers: 1,091
Number of students: 21,315

Publications: *Cadernos do CCH*, *Cadernos de Extensão*, *Cadernos da FACECA*, *Cadernos de Serviço Social*, *Revista Bióikos*, *Revista de Ciências Médicas*, *Revista Comunicarte*, *Revista de Educação*, *Revista Estudos de Psicologia*, *Revista Humanitas*, *Revista Jornalismo*, *Revista Jurídica*, *Revista Letras*, *Revista Notícia Bibliográfica e Histórica*, *Revista de Nutrição*, *Revista Oculum Ensaios*, *Revista Phrónesis*, *Revista Reflexão*, *Revista TransInformação*, *Série Acadêmica*

DIRECTORS OF CENTRES

Centre for Applied Social Sciences: Prof. MARINA DE MACEDO ARRUDA
Centre for Communication Sciences: Prof. LAURA UMBELINA SANTI
Centre for Economics and Administration: Prof. MAURÍCIO DE OLIVEIRA
Centre for Humanities: Prof. PAULO SÉRGIO LOPES GONÇALVES
Centre for Life Sciences: Prof. LUIZ MARIA PINTO
Centre for Mathematical, Environmental and Technological Sciences: Prof. ORANDI MINA FALSARELLA

DIRECTORS OF FACULTIES

Centre for Applied Social Sciences (Rodovia Dom Pedro I, Km 136 Parque das Universidades, 13086-900 Campinas, SP; tel. (19) 3735-5869; fax (19) 3735-5820; e-mail ccsa@puc-campinas.edu.br; internet www.puc-campinas.edu.br/ccsa):
- Faculty of Education: Prof. EDWIGES PEREIRA ROSA CAMARGO
- Faculty of Library Science: Profa MARISA MARQUES ZANATTA
- Faculty of Physical Education and Sports: Profa MÁRCIA CÂNDIDA TEIXEIRA GOZZI
- Faculty of Social Services: Profa VÂNIA MARIA CAIO

Centre for Communication Sciences (Rodovia Dom Pedro I, Km 136 Parque das Universidades, 13086-900 Campinas, SP; tel. (19) 3756-7192; fax (19) 3756-7191; e-mail clc@puc-campinas.edu.br; internet www.puc-campinas.edu.br/clc):
- Faculty of Advertising and Publicity: Prof. MÁRCIO ANTÔNIO BRAS ROQUE
- Faculty of Journalism: Profa CECÍLIA HELENA TOLEDO VIEIRA
- Faculty of Letters: Prof. CARLOS DE AQUINO PEREIRA
- Faculty of Public Relations: Profa MARIA ROSANA FERRARI NASSAR
- Faculty of Tourism: Profa CECÍLIA HELENA M. A. PIOVESAN
- Faculty of Visual Arts: Profa ROBERTA PUCCETTI

Centre for Economics and Administration (Rodovia Dom Pedro I, Km 136 Parque das Universidades, 13086-900 Campinas, SP; tel. (19) 3756-7099; fax (19) 3756-7129; e-mail cea@puc-campinas.edu.br; internet www.puc-campinas.edu.br/cea):
- Faculty of Accounting: Prof. GIDEON CARVALHO DE BENEDICTO
- Faculty of Administration: Prof. PAULO ANTÔNIO G. L. ZUCCOLOTTO
- Faculty of Economics: Prof. CÂNDIDO FERREIRA DA SILVA FILHO

Centre of Humanities Sciences (Rodovia Dom Pedro I, Km 136 Parque das Universidades, 13086-900 Campinas, SP; tel. (19) 3756-7299; fax (19) 3756-7298; e-mail cch@puc-campinas.edu.br; internet www.puc-campinas.edu.br):
- Faculty of History: Prof. LILIA INÊS ZANOTTI DE MEDRANO
- Faculty of Law: Prof. JAMIL MIGUEL
- Faculty of Philosophy: Prof. TARCÍSIO MOURA
- Faculty of Social Sciences: Profa SÔNIA REGINA DA CAL S. G. BARBOSA
- Faculty of Theology and Religious Studies: Prof. ELISIÁRIO CÉSAR CABRAL

Centre for Life Sciences (Av. John Boyd Dunlop s/n - Jardim Ipaussurama, 13059-900 Campinas, SP; tel. (19) 3729-6801; fax (19) 3729-6806; e-mail ccv@puc-campinas.edu.br; internet www.puc-campinas.edu.br/ccv):
- Faculty of Biological Sciences: Profa MARIÂNGELA CAGNONI RIBEIRO
- Faculty of Dentistry: Prof. EMERSON COCCO LANARO
- Faculty of Medicine: Prof. JOSÉ FRANCISCO KERR SARAIVA
- Faculty of Nursing: Profa MARIA TERESA C. T. L. MARTINS
- Faculty of Nutrition: Prof. KÁTIA REGINA L. S. L. Q. GUIMARÃES
- Faculty of Occupational Therapy: Profa ROSIBETH DEL CARMEN M. PALM
- Faculty of Pharmacy: (vacant)
- Faculty of Physical Therapy: Prof. AIRTON JOSÉ MARTINS
- Faculty of Psychology: Prof. NILTON JÚLIO DE FARIA
- Faculty of Speech Therapy and Audiology: Profa MARIENE TERUMI UMEOKA HIDAKA

Centre for Mathematical, Environmental and Technological Sciences (Rodovia Dom Pedro I, Km 136 Parque das Universidades, 13086-900 Campinas, SP; tel. (19) 3756-7314; fax (19) 3756-7177; e-mail ceatec@puc-campinas.edu.br; internet www.puc-campinas.edu.br/ceatec):
- Faculty of Architecture and Urban Planning: Prof. WILSON RIBEIRO SANTOS JÚNIOR
- Faculty of Chemistry: Prof. RONALDO LUIZ MINCATO
- Faculty of Civil Engineering: Prof. LOIR AFONSO MOREIRA
- Faculty of Computer Engineering: Prof. RICARDO PANNAIN
- Faculty of Electrical Engineering: Prof. DAVID BIANCHINI
- Faculty of Environmental Engineering: Prof. SUELI DO CARMO BETTINE
- Faculty of Geography: Prof. DAMARIS PUGA DE MORÃES
- Faculty of Mathematics: Prof. ELIANA DAS NEVES AREAS
- Faculty of Systems Analysis: Prof. JOSÉ ESTEVÃO PICARELLI

UNIVERSIDADE ESTADUAL DE CAMPINAS

Cidade Universitária 'Zeferino Vaz', 13083-970 Campinas, SP

Telephone: (19) 3788-4720
Fax: (19) 3788-4789
E-mail: gabinete@rei.unicamp.br
Internet: www.unicamp.br

Founded 1966
State control
Academic year: March to December

Rector: Prof. Dr CARLOS HENRIQUE DE BRITO CRUZ
Vice-Rector: Prof. Dr JOSÉ TADEU JORGE
Dean for Research: Prof. Dr FERNANDO FERREIRA COSTA
Dean for University Development: Prof. Dr PAULO EDUARDO M. RODRIGUES DA SILVA
Dean for Undergraduate Studies: Prof. Dr JOSÉ LUIZ BOLDRINI
Dean for Graduate Studies: Prof. Dr DANIEL HOGAN
Dean for Extension and Community Matters: Prof. Dr RUBENS MACIEL FILHO
Secretary-General: RENATO ATÍLIO JORGE
Librarian (vacant)

Number of teachers: 1,800
Number of students: 28,000

Publication: *Jornal da Unicamp* (monthly)

DIRECTORS

Institute of Fine Arts: Prof. Dr JOSÉ ROBERTO ZAN
Institute of Biology: Prof. Dr MOHAMED HABIB
Institute of Philosophy and Humanities: Prof. Dr RUBEM MURILO LEÃO RÊGO
'Gleb Wataghin' Institute of Physics: Prof. Dr DANIEL PEREIRA

Institute of Language Studies: Profa Dra Charlotte Marie Chamberland Galves
Institute of Mathematics, Statistics and Computer Science: Prof. Dr João Frederico da Costa Azevedo Meyer
Institute of Chemistry: Prof. Dr Francisco de Assis Machado Reis
Institute of Geosciences: Prof. Dr Archimedes Peres Filho
Institute of Economics: Prof. Dr Marcio Percival Alves Pinto
Institute of Computer Science: Prof. Dr Ricardo de Oliveira Anido
School of Medical Sciences: Profa Dra Lilian Tereza Lavras Costallat
School of Education: Prof. Dr Jorge Megid Neto
School of Agricultural Engineering: Prof. Dr Roberto Testezlaf
School of Food Engineering: Prof. Dr Carlos Anjos
School of Mechanical Engineering: Prof. Dr Kamal Abdel Radi Ismail
School of Civil Engineering: Prof. Dr João Alberto Venegas Requena
School of Electrical Engineering: Prof. Dr Léo Pini Magalhães
School of Chemical Engineering: Prof. Dr Milton Mori
School of Dentistry: Prof. Dr Thales Rocha de Mattos Filho
School of Physical Education: Prof. Dr Roberto Rodrigues Paes
Technology Centre: Prof. Dr Cláudio Bianor Sverzut
Computer Centre: Prof. Dr Luiz Eduardo Buzato

UNIVERSIDADE CASTELO BRANCO

Av. Santa Cruz 1631, Realengo, 21710-250 Rio de Janeiro, RJ
Telephone: (21) 331-1207
Fax: (21) 331-6090
E-mail: info@castelobranco.br
Internet: www.castelobranco.br
Founded 1994
Private control
Rector: Vera Costa Gissoni
Library of 33,000 vols
Number of teachers: 167
Number of students: 5,914.

UNIVERSIDADE DE CAXIAS DO SUL

CP 1352, Rua Francisco Getúlio Vargas 1130, Bairro Petrópolis, 95070-560 Caxias do Sul, RS
Telephone: (54) 212-1133
Fax: (54) 212-1049
E-mail: informa@ucs.tche.br
Internet: www.ucs.tche.br
Founded 1967
Private control
Language of instruction: Portuguese
Academic year: March to December
Rector: Prof. Ruy Paulettti
Vice-Rector: Prof. Luiz Antonio Rizzon
Pro-Rector (Undergraduate): Prof. Luiz Antonio Rizzon
Pro-Rector (Postgraduates): Profa Olga Maria Perazzolo
Pro-Rector (Extension and University Relations): Prof. Armando Antonio Sachet
Pro-Rector (Finance): Prof. Enestor José Dallegrave
Pro-Rector (Planning): Prof. José Carlos Köche
Pro-Rector (Administration): Prof. Emir José Alves da Silva
Pro-Rector (Head of Office): Profa Gelça Regina Lusa Prestes
Chief Librarian: Lígia Goncalves Hesseln
Number of teachers: 1,098
Number of students: 27,599
Publications: *Revista Chronos*, *Caderno da Editora da Universidade de Caxias do Sul*, *Boletim Atos e Fatos*, *Guia Acadêmico*, *Jornal Multicampi e Cadernos de Pesquisa*, *Revista Jovens Pesquisadores* (annually), *Revista do CCET* (2 a year), *Revista Faculdade de Direito* (2 a year), *Conjectura* (2 a year), *Cadernos de Pequisa* (irregular), *Sensu* (2 a year), *Coletânea, Cultura e Saber* (2 a year), *Comunicado* (irregular), *Revista de Ciências Médicas* (2 a year)

DIRECTORS

Centre of Science and Technology: Prof. Roberto Itacyr Mandelli
Centre of Humanities and Arts: Prof. Olivar Maximino Mattia
Centre of Applied Social Studies: Prof. Nelson Goulart Ramos
Centre of Biological Sciences and Health: Prof. Celso Piccoli Coelho
Centre of Philosophy and Education: Prof. Aldo Francisco Migot
Centre of Arts and Architecture: Profa Ana Mery Sehbe de Carli
University Campus of the Winery Region: Prof. Pedro Ernesto Gasperin
University Campus of Vacaria: Prof. Nelson Francisco Benvenutti
University Branch of Canela: Profa Liane Beatriz Moretto Ribeiro
University Branch of Farroupilha: Prof. Raul Bampi
University Branch of Guaporé: Profa Myrian Rotta
University Branch of Nova Prata: Prof. José Reovaldo Oltramari
Unit in the Valley of Caí: Prof. Clóvis José Assmann

HEADS OF DEPARTMENTS

Centre of Science and Technology:
- Department of Mechanical Engineering: Prof. Carlos Roberto Altafini
- Department of Chemical Engineering: Profa Lisete Cristina Scienza
- Department of Physics and Chemistry: Profa Ivete Ama Schmitz Booth
- Department of Mathematics, Statistics and Computation: Profa Isolda Giani de Lima
- Department of Computer Science: Prof. Alexandre Moreto Ribeiro

Centre of Humanities and Communication:
- Department of Languages: Profa Isabel Maria Paese Pressanto
- Department of Sociology: Prof. Paulo Luiz Zungo
- Department of History and Geography: Profa Luiza Horn Iotti
- Department of Communication: Profa Silvana Padilha Flores
- Department of Psychology: Profa Siloe Pereira

Centre of Applied Social Studies:
- Department of Juridical Science: Prof. Ambrósio Luiz Bonalume
- Department of Economics: Profa Lodonha M. Portela Coimbra Soares
- Department of Accountancy: Prof. Jaime Luiz Prux Jr
- Department of Business Administration: Profa Marta Sílvia Buffon Martins

Centre of Biological Sciences and Health:
- Department of Biological Science: Prof. Ronaldo Adelfo Wasum
- Department of Nursing: Profa Roseane Maria Medeiros
- Department of Clinical Surgery: Prof. Wilson Paloschi Spiandorello
- Department of Clinical Medicine: Prof. Petrônio Fagundes de Oliveira Filho
- Department of Physical Education: Prof. Paulo Eugênio Gedoz de Carvalho
- Department of Biomedical Sciences: Profa Bárbara Catarina de Antoni Zoppas

Centre of Philosophy and Education:
- Department of Education: Profa Corina Michelon Dotti
- Department of Philosophy: Profa Fátima Jeanette Marinato

University Campus of the Winery Region:
- Department of Humanities, Social Sciences and Languages: Profa Bernardete S. Caprara
- Department of Exact and Natural Sciences: Prof. Igino Santo Damo
- Department of Economic and Administrative Sciences: Prof. Roberto José Possamai

University Campus of Vacaria:
- Department of Social Studies and Communication: Prof. Homero Francisco Peixoto Camargo
- Department of Education: Profa Clenia Maria Zanela

UNIVERSIDADE ESTADUAL DO CEARÁ

Campus do Itaperi, Av. Paranjana 1700, CP 1531, 60740-000 Fortaleza, CE
Telephone: (85) 292-4499
Fax: (85) 292-4299
E-mail: coopint@uece.br
Internet: www.uece.br
Founded 1975
State control
Academic year: March to December
Rector: Prof. Dr Manassés Claudino Fonteles
Vice-Rector: Prof. Francisco de Assis Moura Araripe
Registrar: Prof. Dr Fábio Perdigão Vasconcelos
Librarian: Ângela Maria Pinho de Barros
Library of 60,338 vols, 586 periodicals
Number of teachers: 1,071
Number of students: 11,970
Publication: *Revista Lumen Ad Viam*

DEANS

Health Science Centre: Prof. Antônio de Pádua Valença da Silva
Science and Technology Centre: Prof. Raimundo Santiago dos Santos
Applied Social Studies Centre: Prof. Gedyr Lírio Almeida
Humanities Centre: Prof. João Nogueira Mota Morais
Veterinary College: Prof. José Mário Girão Abreu
Faculty of Education, Sciences and Arts at Iguatu: Profa Maria Auxiliadora Benedine O. Bezerra
Faculty of Education, Sciences and Arts of the Central Interior: Profa Fátima Maria Leitão Araújo
Faculty of Philosophy 'Dom Aureliano Matos': Prof. Arnobio Santiago de Freitas
Faculty of Education at Crateús: Profa Elda Maria de Freire Maciel
Faculty of Education at Itapipoca: Prof. João Batista Carvalho Nunes
Centre for Education, Science and Technology at Sertão dos Inhamuns: Prof. João Alcimo Viana Lima
Advanced Campus at Baturite: Prof. Rômulo Mascarenhas dos Santos Júnior
Advanced Campus at Senador Pompeu: Profa Cleide Maria dos Santos Amorin
Advanced Campus at Pentecoste: Prof. Manoel Lopes Martins

Centre for Continuing and Distance Education: Profa LÚCIA HELENA FONSECA GRANGEIRO

HEADS OF DEPARTMENTS

Health Sciences Centre:
- Department of Nutrition: Profa ANA MARIA MACDOWELL COSTA
- Department of Biology: Prof. LUIZ MENEZES DE ARRUDA
- Department of Nursing: Profa MARIA EURIDES DE CASTRO
- Department of Physiology: Profa LIA MAGALHÃES ALMEIDA SILVA
- Department of Physical Education: Prof. EDUARDO HUMBERTO GARCIA ELLERY
- Department of Public Health: Profa CLAYRE ANNE HOLANDA VERAS

Applied Social Studies Centre:
- Department of Accountancy: Prof. ARTUR LINHARES MENDES
- Department of Economics: Prof. FRANCISCO DAS CHAGAS GOUVEIA
- Department of Law: Prof. MÁRCIO MALVEIRA DE QUEIROZ
- Department of Administration: Profa ANAHID BOYADJIAN DE MIRANDA SOARES
- Department of Foundations of Education: Profa BERNARDETE CÂNDIDO FURTADO
- Department of Education, Methods and Techniques: Profa SELMA MAIA DE OLIVEIRA
- Department of Methods and Techniques of Social Work: Prof. PAULO ROBERTO DE AGUIAR LOPES

Humanities Centre:
- Department of Portuguese Language: Prof. ROSILMAR ALVES DOS SANTOS
- Department of Foreign Languages: Prof. FRANCISCO LÚCIO CABRAL PINHEIRO
- Department of Social Sciences: Prof. BELISA MARIA VELOSO HOLANDA
- Department of Arts: Profa MARIA JOSÉ BENEVIDES DI CALVACANTI
- Department of Philosophy: Prof. ADAUTO LOPES DA SILVA FILHO
- Department of History: Prof. FRANCISCO AGILEU DE LIMA GADELHA
- Department of Psychology: Profa SANDRA MARIA MUNIZ REBOUÇAS

Sciences and Technology Centre:
- Department of Statistics and Computation: Profa ROBERTA SOUSA PONTES
- Department of Mathematics: Prof. LUCIANO MOURA CAVALCANTE
- Department of Physics and Chemistry: Prof. PAULO AUBER ROUQUAYROL
- Department of Geo-Science: Prof. ANTÔNIO DE OLIVEIRA GOMES NETO

Veterinary College:
- Department of Animal Production and Rural Extension: Prof. JOSÉ EDUARDO CABRAL MAIA
- Department of Veterinary Medicine: Prof. OLACÍLIO LOPES DE SOUZA

Faculty of Education, Sciences and Arts at Iguatu:
- Department of Education: Profa LIDUINA MARIA DUARTE DOS REIS

Faculty of Education at Itapipoca:
- Department of Education and Arts: Profa MARIA ROMELIA DOS SANTOS

Faculty of Education, Sciences and Arts of the Central Interior:
- Department of Humanities: Profa FÁTIMA MARIA LEITÃO ARAÚJO
- Department of Natural Sciences: JOSE MAILDO NUNES

Faculty of Philosophy 'Dom Aureliano Matos':
- Department of Geosciences: Profa FRANCISCA MARIA DO OLIVEIRA
- Department of Education: Profa MARIA DO SOCORRO HOLANDA
- Department of Arts: Prof. JOSE MENDES DE ANDRADE
- Department of Social Sciences: FRANCISCO EDBERTO JORGE

UNIVERSIDADE FEDERAL DO CEARÁ

Av. da Universidade 2853, Benfica, CP 2600, 60020-181 Fortaleza, CE
Telephone: (85) 281-4333
Fax: (85) 281-5383
Internet: www.ufc.br

Founded 1955

Rector: Prof. ROBERTO CLÁUDIO FROTA BEZERRA
Administrative Officer: VERA MARIA BEZERRA RAE
Librarian: NORMA HELENA PINHEIRO DE ALMEIDA

Number of teachers: 1,452
Number of students: 11,924

HEADS OF DEPARTMENTS

Sciences Centre:
- Mathematics: JOSÉ OTHON DANTAS LOPES
- Statistics: Profa ELIANA MIRANDA SAMPAIO
- Physics: Prof. FRANCISCO ERIVAN DE ABREU MELO
- Chemistry: Prof. NILO DE MORAES BRITTO FILHO
- Geography: Prof. ANTÔNIO JEOVAH DE ANDRADE MEIRELES
- Geology: Prof. FRANCISCO MARQUES JÚNIOR
- Biology: Profa MARIA APARECIDA OLIVEIRA ALVES
- Computer Sciences: Profa LUCY VIDAL SILVA

Humanities Centre:
- Social Sciences: Prof. CÉSAR BARREIRA
- Social Communications: Profa OLGA MARIA RIBEIRO GUEDES
- History: Prof. PEDRO AIRTON QUEIROZ LIMA
- Letters: Profa COEMA ESCÓRCIO DE ATHAYDE DAMASCENO

Technology Centre:
- Civil Engineering: Prof. JOSÉ ADEMAR GONDIM VASCONCELOS
- Mechanical Engineering: Prof. CARLOS ANDRÉ DIAS BEZERRA
- Electrical Engineering: Prof. FERNANDO LUIZ MARCELO ANTUNES
- Architecture and Town Planning: Profa MARGARIDA JÚLIA FARIAS DE SALLES ANDRADE

Agricultural and Food Sciences Centre:
- Agronomy: Prof. PAULO TEODORO DE CASTRO
- Fisheries: Prof. LUÍS PESSOA DE ARAÚJO
- Domestic Science: Profa ELISA MARIA MAIA GOMES
- Food Technology: Prof. ANTÔNIO CLÁUDIO LIMA GUIMARÃES

Health Sciences:
- Medicine: Prof. ELIAS GEOVANI BOUTALA SALOMÃO
- Dentistry: Prof. FRANCISCO BESSA NOGUEIRA
- Pharmacy: Profa VERBENA LIMA VALE

DIRECTORS OF FACULTIES

Faculty of Economics, Management and Accounting: Profa MARIA DA GLÓRIA ARRAIS PETER
Faculty of Education: Prof. OZIR TESSER
Faculty of Law: Prof. ÁLVARO MELO FILHO

UNIVERSIDADE DO CONTESTADO

Rua Itororó 800, 89500-000 Caçador, SC
Telephone: (49) 663-2033
Fax: (49) 663-0941
E-mail: reitoria@unc-cdr.rct-sc.br
Internet: www.unc-cni.rct-sc.br

Founded 1990
State control

Rector: MÁRIO BANDIERA

Library of 51,400 vols
Number of teachers: 305
Number of students: 5,549.

UNIVERSIDADE DE CRUZ ALTA

Rua Andrade Neves 308, Centro, CP 858, 98025-810 Cruz Alta, RS
Telephone: (55) 322-8400
Fax: (55) 322-8400
E-mail: webmaster@main.unicruz.tche.br
Internet: www.unicruz.tche.br

Founded 1988

Rector: LUCIA MARIA BAIOCCHI AMARAL

Library of 14,000 vols, 864 periodicals
Number of teachers: 236
Number of students: 3,492.

UNIVERSIDADE CRUZEIRO DO SUL

Campus I, Av. Dr Ussiel Cirilo 225, São Miguel Paulista, 08060-070 São Paulo, SP
Telephone: (11) 956-9177
Fax: (11) 956-9177 ext. 105
Internet: www.unicsul.br

Founded 1993
Private control

Rector: WILSON JOÃO ZAMPIERI

Library of 43,000 vols, 194 periodicals
Number of teachers: 239
Number of students: 9,771.

UNIVERSIDADE DE CUIABÁ

Av. Beira Rio 3100, Jardim Europa, 78015-480 Cuiabá, MT
Telephone: (65) 615-1000
Fax: (65) 615-1100
E-mail: unic@nutecnet.com.br

Founded 1988
Private control

Rector: ALTAMIRO BELO GALINDO

Library: Libraries with 58,000 vols, 261 periodicals
Number of teachers: 408
Number of students: 9,053.

UNIVERSIDADE CATÓLICA DOM BOSCO

Jardim Seminário, Av. Tamandaré 6000, CP 801, 79002-905 Campo Grande, MS
Telephone: (67) 765-2040
Fax: (67) 765-2041
E-mail: reitoria@unibosco.br
Internet: www.unibosco.br

Founded 1993 from Faculdades Unidas Católicas de Mato Grosso

Rector: Pe JOSÉ MARINONI

Library of 175,000 vols
Number of teachers: 217

Publications: *Jornal UCDB* (monthly), *Revista Koembá Pytã* (2 a year), *Revista do Direito* (every 2 months)

Faculties of Philosophy, Science and Literature, Law, Economics, Accounting and Administration, Social Work.

UNIVERSIDADE FEDERAL DO ESPÍRITO SANTO

Campus Universitário, Av. Fernando Ferrari, Goiabeiras, 29060-900 Vitória, ES
Telephone: (27) 335-2244
Fax: (27) 335-2210
E-mail: reitoria@server.npd.ufes.br
Internet: www.ufes.br

Founded as State University in 1954, as Federal University in 1961
Federal control
Language of instruction: Portuguese
Academic year: March to December

Rector: José Weber Freire Macedo
Vice-Rector: Rubens Sergio Rasseli
Registrar: Eliana Mara Bortoloni Frizera
Librarian: Angela Maria Becalli

Number of teachers: 1,036
Number of students: 10,187

Publications: *Dados Estatísticos, Revista de Cultura da UFES, Caderno de Pesquisa da UFES, RCP — Revista Universo Pedagógico, Jornal Laboratório, Revista de História, Primeira Mão, Revista Você da Secretaria de Cultura da UFES, Revista Sofia do Departamento de Filosofia, Journal UFES*

DIRECTORS

Agricultural and Animal Husbandry Centre: José Augusto Teixeira do Amaral
Arts Centre: Kleber Perini Frizzera
Biomedical Centre: Wilson Mário Zanotti
Education Centre: Maria José Campos Rodrigues
General Studies Centre: Luiz Mário Có, Santinho Ferreira de Souza
Law and Economic Sciences Centre: Ana Maria Petroneto Serpa
Physical Education and Sports Centre: José Christofari Frade
Technology Centre: Edson Baptista
Exact Sciences Centre: Maria José Schwartz Ferreira

HEADS OF DEPARTMENTS

Agricultural Engineering: Rosembergue Bragança
Phytotechnics: José Carlos Lopes
Animal Husbandry and Agricultural Economics: Ary Caetano Gonçalves Macedo
Architecture and Urban Planning: Marco Antonio C. Romanelli
Industrial and Decorative Arts: Marcia Braga Capovilla Alves
Artistic Formation: Rosana Lucia Paste
Technical-Artistic Foundations: Marcia Jardim Calgaro
Physiological Sciences: Adércio João Marquezini
Clinical Surgery: Johnson Joaquim Gouvea
Clinical Medicine: Ayrton Gomes da Fonseca Filho
Clinical Odontology: Armelindo Roldi
Nursing: Angela Maria de Castro Simões
Gynaecology and Obstetrics: Luiz Cláudio Franca
Specialized Medicine: Adelson João da Cunha
Social Medicine: Décio Neves da Cunha Filho
Morphology: Gilton Coutinho Barros
Pathology: José Benedito Malta Varejão
Dental Prosthesis: João Helvécio Xavier Pinto
Administration: Regina Maria Monteiro
Library Management: Maria de Fátima Barreto
Accountancy Sciences: Geraldo Antonio M. de Oliveira
Social Communication: Ruth de Cássia dos Reis
Law: Geraldo Vieira Simões Filho
Economics: Pedro José Mansur
Social Service: Maria Madalena do Nascimento Sartim
Sports: Og Garcia Negrão
Gymnastics: Valter Bracht
Biology: Celso Oliveira Azevedo
Social Sciences: Luis Muramatsu
Statistics: Maria Angelica F. de Oliveira
Philosophy: Anacleto Rodrigues da Silva
Physics and Chemistry: Reinaldo Centoducatte
Geosciences: Jara de Almeida
History: Gilvan Ventura da Silva
Languages and Literature: Walkyria Puppim
Mathematics: Standard Silva
Psychology: Elizabeth Maria Andrade Aragão
Administration and Student Supervision: Ana Lucia Baptista Rocha
Didactics and Practice of Teaching: Maria José Campos Rodrigues
Foundations of Education and Educational Orientation: Izabel Cristina Novães
Electrical Engineering: Edson Pereira Cardoso
Industrial Engineering and Computer Science: Maria Christina Pedrosa Valli
Mechanical Engineering: Oswaldo Paiva Almeida Filho
Structures and Buildings: José Maria Rodrigues Nicolau
Hydraulics and Sanitation: Alexandre José Serafim
Transport: Marco Antonio Barboza da Silva

ATTACHED INSTITUTES

Institute of Technology: Superintendent Annibal Ewald Martins.

Institute of Dental Medicine: Superintendent Ranulfo Gianordoli Neto.

UNIVERSIDADE ESTADUAL DE FEIRA DE SANTANA

BR 116, Km 3, Campus Universitário, CP 294, 44031-460 Feira de Santana, BA
Telephone: (75) 224-8200
Fax: (75) 224-2284
Internet: www.uefs.br

Founded 1976
State control
Language of instruction: Portuguese
Academic year: March to December

Rector: Anaci Bispo Paim
Vice-Rector: Joaquim Pondé Filho
Academic Pro-Rector: Anaci Bispo Paim
Administrative Pro-Rector: Eutímio de Oliveira Almeida
Academic Director: Antônio Raimundo Bastos Melo
Administrative Director: Roberto Gomes da Silva Neto
Financial Director: Gildince Lima Ferreira
Director of Student Affairs: Antonio Roberto Seixas da Cruz
Librarian: Vera Vilene Ferreira Nunes

Library of 72,700 vols
Number of teachers: 508
Number of students: 4,253

Publications: *Sitientibus* (2 a year), *Intercampus*

HEADS OF DEPARTMENTS

Letters and Arts: Rubens Edson Alves Pereira
Applied Social Sciences: Jorge Jesus Almeida
Biological Sciences: Cleide Mércia Soares Pereira
Exact Sciences: Inácio de Souza Fadigas
Technology: Genival Correia de Souza
Human Sciences and Philosophy: Maria Lúcia Cintra Barreto
Health: Denice Vitória de Brito
Education: Eunice Freitas Ferreira

UNIVERSIDADE FEDERAL FLUMINENSE

Rua Miguel de Frias 9, Icaraí, 24220-000 Niterói, RJ
Telephone: (21) 620-8080
Fax: (21) 719-6084
E-mail: garaai@vm.uff.br
Internet: www.uff.br

Founded 1960 as Federal University of the State of Rio de Janeiro; present title 1965
Academic year: March to December

Rector: Luiz Pedro Antunes
Vice-Rector: Fabiano da Costa Carvalho
Pro-Rector (Academic Affairs): Prof. Maria Helena da Silva Paes Faria
Pro-Rector (Extension): Profa Aydil de Carvalho Preis
Pro-Rector (Research and Postgraduate): Prof. Marcos Moreira Braga
Pro-Rector (Planning): Prof. Walter Pinho da Silva Filho
Chief Administrative Officer: Alderico Mendonça Filho
Librarian: João Carlos Gomes Ribeiro

Library: Libraries with 420,000 vols
Number of teachers: 2,637
Number of students: 26,050 (23,982 undergraduate, 2,068 postgraduate)

Publications: *Revista da Faculdade de Educação, Revista de Ciências Médicas*

DIRECTORS OF CENTRES

General Studies Centre: Esther Hermes Luck
Applied Social Studies Centre: Raul de Albuquerque Filho
Nilo Peçanha Agricultural School: Fernando Gonçalves da Cruz, Jr
Ildefonso Bastos Technical Agricultural School: José Bastos Cavichini
Medical Sciences Centre: José Celestino Bicalho de Figeiredo
Technology Centre: Heitor Luiz Salles Soares de Moura

DIRECTORS OF INSTITUTES

General Studies Centre:
- Institute of Arts and Social Communications: Ana Maria Lopes Pereira
- Institute of Biology: Luiz Antônio Botelho Andrade
- Institute of Human Sciences and Philosophy: Humberto Fernandes Machado
- Institute of Physics: Paulo Roberto Silveira Gomes
- Institute of Language and Literature: Laura Cavalcanti Padilha
- Institute of Mathematics: Luiz Antonio dos Santos Cruz
- Institute of Chemistry: Leonor Reise de Almeida
- Institute of Earth Sciences: Walter Ronaldo Nunes
- Institute of Biomedical Science: Alexandre Sampaio de Martino

Applied Social Studies Centre:
- Institute of Law: Maria Arair Pinto Paiva
- Institute of Economics and Administration: Alberto Santos Lima Filho
- Institute of Education: Maria Felisberta Baptista Trindade
- School of Social Service: Maria Auxiliadora da Costa Simão
- Department of Social Service (Campos): Geralda Freire Bello de Campos

Medical Sciences Centre:
- School of Nursing: Carlos Alberto Mendes
- School of Pharmacy: Antonio Carlos Carrera Freitas
- School of Medicine: José Carlos Carraro Eduardo

School of Veterinary Science: MARIO AUGUSTO RONCONI
School of Dentistry: RAUL FERES MONTE ALTO FILHO
Rodolfo Albino University Laboratory: CARLOS DE CASTRO PEREIRA JORGE
School of Nutrition: STELA MARIA PEREIRA DE GREGÓRIO
Veterinary Experimental Centre (Iguaba): ADEMIL DE SOUZA PINTO
Technology Centre:
School of Engineering: JOSÉ JAIRO ARAÚJO DE SOUZA
School of Architecture and Town Planning: PEDRO ALFREDO MORAES LENTINO
School of Industrial Metallurgy: ANTONIO FONTANA

UNIVERSIDADE DE FORTALEZA

CP 1258, Av. Washington Soares 1321, Edson Queiroz Block, 60811-341 Fortaleza, CE
Telephone: (85) 273-2833
Fax: (85) 273-1667
E-mail: webmaster@cr.unifor.br
Internet: www.unifor.br
Founded 1973
Private control (Fundação Edson Queiroz)
Chancellor: AIRTON JOSÉ VIDAL QUEIROZ
Rector: Prof. ANTÔNIO COLAÇO MARTINS
Librarian: LEONILHA BRASILEIRO DE OLIVEIRA
Library of 87,453 vols
Number of teachers: 601
Number of students: 11,076.

ATTACHED CENTRES

Administrative Sciences Centre: 81 Rua da Paz, Apto 100, Meireles, 60165-180 Fortazela, CE; Dir Prof. JOSÉ MARTÔNIO ALVES COELHO.

CCS: Rua Paschoal de Castro Alves 350/401, 60155-420 Fortaleza, CE; Dir Profa FÁTIMA MARIA FERNANDES VERAS.

Human Sciences Centre: 626 Léa Pompeu St, 60821-490 Fortaleza, CE; Dir Prof. JOSÉ BATISTA DE LIMA.

Technological Sciences Centre: 758 Prof. Heráclito St, 60155-440 Fortaleza, CE; Dir Profa NISE SANFORD FRAGA.

UNIVERSIDADE DE FRANCA

Av. Dr Armando Salles Oliveira 201, Parque Universitário, 14404-600 Franca, SP
Telephone: (16) 724-2211
Fax: (16) 722-086
Internet: www.unifran.br
Founded 1970
Private control
Rector: ABIB SALIM CURY
Library of 58,000 vols, 1,300 periodicals
Number of teachers: 221
Number of students: 6,258.

UNIVERSIDADE GAMA FILHO

Rua Manoel Vitorino 625, Piedade, 20748-900 Rio de Janeiro, RJ
Telephone: (21) 599-7100
Fax: (21) 289-8394
Internet: www.ugf.br
Founded 1972
Private control
Language of instruction: Portuguese
Academic year: February to December
Chancellor: Prof. Dr PAULO GAMA FILHO
Vice-Chancellors: Prof. Ms PAULO CESAR GAMA FILHO, Prof. LUIZ ALFREDO GAMA FILHO
Rector: Prof. SÉRGIO DE MORAES DIAS
Vice-Rectors: Dr MANOEL JOSÉ GOMES TUBINO (Academic), Prof. SÉRGIO DE MORAES DIAS (Planning and Co-ordination), Prof. PERALVA DE MIRANDA DELGADO (Community), Prof. AYRTON LUIZ GONÇALVES (Development), Prof. PREDUÊNCIO FERREIRA (Administrative)
Secretary General: Dra MARIA CECÍLIA NUNES AMARANTE
Librarian: Profa LÚCIA BEATRIZ R. T. PARANHOS DE OLIVEIRA
Library of 146,000 vols, 130,000 periodicals
Number of teachers: 1,080
Number of students: 15,500
Publications: *Artus* (every 6 months), *Ciência* (every 6 months), *Ciência Humana* (every 6 months), *Ciência Social* (every 6 months)

DEANS

Sciences and Technology Centre: Prof. SÉRGIO FLORES DA SILVA
Biological and Health Sciences Centre: Prof. JOAQUIM JOSÉ DO AMARAL CASTELLÕES
Social Sciences Centre: Prof. HENRIQUE LUÍS ARIENTE
Human Sciences Centre: Profa PAULINA CELI GAMA DE CARVALHO

ATTACHED INSTITUTES

Instituto de Pesquisas Gonzaga da Gama Filho: Rio de Janeiro; Admin. Dir Prof. UBIRAJARA PEÇANHA ALVES; Scientific Dir Prof. JOÃO CARLOS DE OLIVEIRA TÓRTORA.

Instituto de Estudos de Linguas Estrangeiras: Rio de Janeiro; Co-ordinator REGINA LUCIA MORAES MARIN.

UNIVERSIDADE CATÓLICA DE GOIÁS

Av. Universitária 1069, Setor Universitário, CP 86, 74605-010 Goiânia, GO
Telephone: (62) 227-1239
Fax: (62) 227-1010
E-mail: Gil@ucg.br
Internet: www.ucg.br
Founded 1959
Private control
Academic year: March to December
Chancellor: Father JOSÉ PEREIRA DE MARIA
Rector: Prof. MARISVALDO CORTEZ AMADO
Vice-Rector for Academic Affairs: Prof. LUIZ DE GONZAGA VIEIRA
Vice-Rector for Research and Graduate Studies: Prof. NELSON JORGE DA SILVA J.
Vice-Rector for Administrative Affairs: JOÃO DE CARMELO XAVIER
Vice-Rector for Community and Student Affairs: Prof. PABLO SANTIAGO VALLADARES DIEZ
Registrar: DAGMAR MARTINS DAS GRAÇAS
Librarian: IRENE TOSCANO PASCOAL
Number of teachers: 1,317
Number of students: 22,179
Publications: *Estudos* (6 a year), *Flash* (weekly), *Momento* (weekly), *Fragmentos de Cultura* (6 a year)

DIRECTORS

Languages: CELINA MARIA DE JESUS
History, Geography and Social Sciences: LAÍS APARECIDA MACHADO
Law: HELENISA M. GOMES
Philosophy and Theology: LUÍZ GIRARDI, UENE JOSÉ GOMES
Education: OLGA IZILDA RONCHI
Nursing: MARIA SALETE S. P. NASCIMENTO
Biomedical Sciences: PAULO ROBERTO DE MELO REIS
Engineering: MANOEL DA SILVA ALVARES
Architecture: DEUSA MARIA RODRIGUÊS BOAVENTURA
Mathematics and Physics: MILTON OLIMPIO ALVES
Psychology: ANTÔNIO CARLOS G. SANTOS
Speech and Language Therapy: MAIONE MARIA MILÉO
Economics: JOSÉ AUGUSTO COSTA
Accounting: NAZARENO ROCHA JÚNIOR
Business Administration: JOÃO BOSCO DE BARROS
Computer Science: JOSÉ ROLDÃO GONÇALVES BARBOSA
Zootechnics: ROBERTO CAMARGO WASCHECK
Biology: JOSÉ WELLINGTON G. LEMOS
Food Science: CLELIA ALVES S. DE SOUZA
Manufacturing Engineering: PAULO JOSÉ MASCARENHAS RORIZ
Electrical Engineering: RUI BARBOSA COELHO
Environmental Engineering: HARLEM INÁCIO DOS SANTOS
Computer Engineering: JOSÉ ROLDÃO GONÇALVES BARBOSA
Physiotherapy: ROSÂNGELA ALVES MOTEFUSCO
Occupational Therapy: IVONE PORTILHO DO NASCIMENTO
Aeronautical Science: RAUL FRANCÉ MONTEIRO
Design: TAI HSUAN NA
Bilingual Executive Secretariat: ROQUE TOSCANO
Tourism Management: CARLA BAYLÃO DE CARVALHO

ATTACHED INSTITUTES

Institute of Prehistory and Anthropology: Dir MANOEL FERREIRA LIMA FILHO.

Centre for Biological Studies and Research: Dir MARTA REGINA MAGALHÃES.

Sub-humid Tropics Institute: Dir ALTAIR SALES BARBOSA.

Education Research Institute: Dir MARIA DE ARAÚJO NEPOMUCENO.

Social Sciences Research Unit: Dir MARIA DO ESPIRITO S. R. CAVALCANTE.

Social Policies and Movements Research Unit: Dir WALDEREZ LOUREIRO MIGUEL.

Urban Studies Research Unit: Dir EVERALDO ANTÔNIO PASTORE.

Literature and Language Research Unit: Dir ALBERTINA VICENTII ASSUMPÇÃO.

Semiconductors Research Unit: Dir ANTÔNIO NEWTON BORGES.

Food Science Research Unit: Dir ADOLFO FRANCO JR.

Animal Science Research Unit: Dir MARIA SILVIA RODRIGUES MONTEIRO.

Brazil–African Study Centre: Dir SARA TALEB RASSI.

Youth Village Study, Research and Extension Centre: Dir MARIA LUÍSA.

UNIVERSIDADE FEDERAL DE GOIÁS

CP 131, Campus Samambaia, Km 7, 74000-970 Goiânia, GO
Telephone: (62) 205-1777
Fax: (62) 205-1327
E-mail: cai@cai.ufg.br
Internet: www.ufg.br
Founded 1960
Rector: Prof. Dra MILCA SEVERINO PEREIRA
Pro-Rectors: Profa ILKA MARIA DE ALMEIDA MOREIRA (Administration and Finance), Enfa IVETE SANTOS BARRETO (Community Affairs), Prof. EMILSON ROCHA DE OLIVEIRA (Development and Human Resources), Prof. Dr ANA LUIZA LIMA SOUZA (Extension), Prof. Dra ELIANA MARTINS LIMA (Research and Postgraduate), Prof. Dr CELENE CUNHA MONTEIRO ANTUNES BARREIRA (Undergraduates)
Librarian: VALÉIRA MARIA SOLEDADE DE ALMEIDA
Number of teachers: 1,114
Number of students: 12,384

Publications: *Boletim do Pessoal* (monthly), *Anais da Escola de Agronomia e Veterinária* (annually), *Anais da Universidade* (2 a year), *Inter-Ação, Revista Goiana de Artes* (2 a year), *Revista da Faculdade de Direito* (2 a year), *Boletim Estatístico* (2 a year), *Revista Goiana de Medicina* (4 a year), *Revista de Patologia Tropical* (4 a year), *Letras em Revista* (2 a year), *Ciências Humanas em Revista* (2 a year), *Cerrado* (2 a year)

DIRECTORS

Faculty of Law: Prof. PAULO DE TARSO FLEURY
Faculty of Education: Profa WALDERÊS NUNES LOUREIRO
Faculty of Medicine: Profa ELEUSE MACHADO DE BRITO GUIMARÃES
Faculty of Pharmacy: Prof. JAIR SEBASTIÃO GOMES DE OLIVEIRA
Faculty of Dentistry: Profa TEREZINHA VASCONCELOS CAMPOS
Faculty of Visual Arts: Prof. JOSÉ CÉSAR TEATINE DE SOUZA CLÍMACO
Faculty of Nursing: Profa MARIA ALVES BARBOSA
Faculty of Communication and Library Science: Profa MARIA AUXILIADORA ANDRADE DE ECHEGARAY
Faculty of Physical Education: Prof. ANTONIO CELSO FERREIRA FONSECA
Faculty of Arts: Profa VERA MARIA TIETZMANN SILVA
Faculty of Nutrition: Profa NILCE MARIA DA SILVA CAMPOS COSTA
Faculty of Human Sciences and Philosophy: Profa MARIA CRISTINA TEIXEIRA MACHADO
School of Agronomy: Prof. LÁZARO EURÍPEDES XAVIER
School of Veterinary Science: Prof. HÉLIO LOUREDO DA SILVA
School of Civil Engineering: Prof. OSVALDO LUIZ VALINOTE
School of Electrical Engineering: Prof. ADENONE DINIZ COSTA
School of Music: Profa DILMA BARBOSA YAMADA
Institute of Mathematics and Statistics: Prof. RONALDO ALVES GARCIA
Institute of Tropical Pathology and Public Health: Prof. JOAQUIM CAETANO DE ALMEIDA NETTO
Institute of Biological Sciences: Profa MARIA DE LOURDES BRESEGHELO
Institute of Chemistry: Prof. CELSO MACHADO
Institute of Social and Environmental Studies: Profa CELENE CUNHA MONTEIRO ANTUNES BARREIRA
Institute of Physics: Prof. ORLANDO AFONSO VALLE DO AMARAL
Institute of Information Science: Prof. JOÃO CARLOS DA SILVA
Centre for Teaching and Applied Research in Education: Prof. ARMANDO ALVES DE CARVALHO

HEADS OF DEPARTMENTS

School of Engineering:
- Construction: OSWALDO CASCUDO MATOS
- Hydraulics and Sanitation: Prof. EDWARD BONFIM DE SOUZA
- Structural Engineering: Prof. NEWTON DE CASTRO
- Electronics: Profa GISELE GUIMARÃES
- Electrical Engineering: EMILSON ROCHA DE OLIVEIRA

Faculty of Human Sciences and Philosophy:
- History: Prof. JOÃO ALBERTO DA COSTA PINTO
- Social Sciences: Profa MARIA CRISTINA TEIXEIRA MACHADO
- Philosophy: Prof. RALPH ROMAN KONRAD GNISS
- Social Communication: FRANCISCO EDUARDO P. PIERRE
- Letters: Prof. AGOSTINHO POTENCIANO DE SOUZA

Faculty of Pharmacy:
- Pharmaceutical Technology: Prof. JAIRO DE SOUSA SANTOS
- Clinical Analysis, Toxicology and Bromatology: JAIR SEBASTIÃO G. OLIVEIRA

Institute of Biological Sciences:
- Anatomy: Prof. PAULO ROBERTO DE SOUZA
- General Biology: Prof. JESUÍNO ANDRIOLO
- Biochemistry and Biophysics: MARIA DE LOURDES BRESEGHELO
- Botany: Prof. JOSÉ ÂNGELO RIZZO
- Physiology: Prof. JEFONE DE MELO ROCHA
- Histology and Embryology: Prof. ALVARO JOSÉ DO AMARAL MATEUS
- Morphology: Prof. NOZELMAR BORGES DE SOUZA

Faculty of Medicine:
- Surgery: Prof. HÉLIO MOREIRA
- Clinical Medicine: Prof. CELSO DA CUNHA BASTOS
- Gynaecology and Obstetrics: Profa MARILUZA TERRA SILVEIRA
- Ophthalmology: Prof. ELIEZER FERREIRA DA COSTA
- Otorhinolaryngology: Prof. JOÃO SEBBA NETO
- Orthopaedics, Traumatology and Plastic Surgery: Prof. MÁRIO DA PAZ ALVES
- Paediatrics and Puericulture: Profa FÁTIMA MARIA LINDOSO DA SILVA
- Pathology: Prof. MAURÍCIO SÉRGIO BRASIL LEITE
- Psychiatry and Forensic Medicine: Prof. JOSÉ REINALDO DO AMARAL
- Radiology: Prof. WALSIR FAGANELO FIORI
- Experimental Surgery: Prof. DJALMA RODRIGUES DE SOUSA

Faculty of Nursing and Nutrition:
- Nursing: Profa MARIA DAS GRAÇAS N. DE OLIVEIRA
- Nutrition: Profa MARIA MARGARETH VELOSO N. CABRAL

Faculty of Dentistry:
- Dental Medicine: Prof. WANDERLY CARVALHO LOPES
- Oral Rehabilitation: Prof. MAURO DE MELO
- Social Dentistry: Prof. DISNEI ALVES DA CUNHA
- Polyclinic: Profa ENILZA MARIA MENDONÇA

Institute of Arts:
- Theory and Applied Arts: Profa MARIA IGNES DE GRANDI MÜLLER
- Plastic Arts: Prof. ORLANDO FERREIRA CASTRO
- Vocal: Profa MARIA LÚCIA MASCARENHAS RORIZ
- Figurative Arts: ÂNGELOS ANDRÉ KTENAS
- Complementary Subjects: Profa EVANY DIAS FONSECA
- Keyboard and Percussion Instruments: Profa VITÓRIA HELENA MAIA A. MARTINS

Institute of Tropical Pathology and Public Health:
- Immunology, Pathology: Profa REGINA BEATRIZ BEVILACQUA
- Public Health: Profa IONIZETE GARCIA DA SILVA
- Tropical Medicine and Public Health: Profa LEDICE INÁCIA DE ARAÚJO PEREIRA
- Microbiology: Profa MARCIA ALVES VASCONCELOS RODRIGUES
- Parasitology, Microbiology and Immunology: Profa JULIETA MACHADO PAÇO

Institute of Chemistry and Geoscience:
- Geography: Profa ZELINDA FANUCH DE MENDONÇA
- Topography and Geodesy: (vacant)
- Geology: (vacant)
- Analytical Chemistry: Profa MARIA GISELDA DE OLIVEIRA TAVARES
- Organic Chemistry: Prof. ALBERTO E. FINOTTI
- General and Inorganic Chemistry: Profa CAROLINA MARIA GOETZ

Institute of Mathematics and Statistics:
- Mathematics: (vacant)
- Statistics: (vacant)
- Physics: Prof. ANTONIO CARLOS DE FARIA

Faculty of Education:
- Teaching Practice and School Organization: Profa SANDRAMARA MATIAS CHAVES
- Principles of Education: Prof. ANTONIO CÉSAR DE OLIVEIRA
- Applied Studies: Profa MONIQUE ANDRIES NOGUEIRA

Faculty of Arts:
- Foreign Languages and Literature: Profa HELOÍSA AUGUSTA BRITO DE MELLO
- Linguistics and Literary Studies: Profa MARGARETH CAVALCANTE DE CASTRO LOBATO

Faculty of Law:
- Basic Law: Prof. CARLOS ALBERTO GUIMARÃES
- Private Law: Prof. JOSÉ BEZERRA COSTAS
- Criminal Law: Prof. BYRON SEABRA GUIMARÃES
- Basic and Complementary Studies: Prof. JOVENY SEBASTÃO CÂNDIDO DE OLIVEIRA
- Civil and Labour Law: Prof. ALBERTO ABINAGEM
- Professionalization: Prof. GETÚLIO VARGAS DE CASTRO

School of Agronomy:
- Agriculture: Prof. DOMINGOS TIVERON FILHO
- Horticulture: Profa IRAIDES FERNANDES CARNEIRO
- Rural Economy: Prof. DORIVAL GOMES GERALDINE
- Agricultural Engineering: Prof. ILDEU MATIAS DO NASCIMENTO
- Food Technology: Profa HENRIQUETA MERCON VIEIRA ROLIM
- Plant Hygiene: Profa VALQUÍRIA DA ROCHA SANTOS VELOSO

School of Veterinary Medicine:
- Clinics: Prof. ARY DA SILVA RODRIGUES
- Preventive Medicine: Prof. CARLOS STUART CORONEL PALMA
- Pathology: Prof. JOÃO MAURÍCIO LUCAS GORDO
- Animal Husbandry: Prof. PEDRINHO PAES TEIXEIRA
- Veterinary Medicine: Prof. FRANCISCO DE CARVALHO DIAS FILHO

UNIVERSIDADE DO GRANDE RIO

Rua Prof. José de Souza Herdy 1160, Bairro 25 de Agosto, 25071-200 Duque de Caxias, RJ
Telephone: (21) 671-4251
Fax: (21) 671-4248
E-mail: editora@unigranrio.br
Internet: www.unigranrio.br

Founded 1994
Private control
Academic year: January to December

Rector: ARODY CORDEIRO HERDY
Vice-Rectors: CARLOS DE OLIVEIRA VARELLA (Undergraduate Studies), BENJAMIN, CORDEIRO HERDY (Research and Graduate Studies), MARIA VITÓRIA S. GUIMARÃES (Extension and Community Relations)

Library of 110,535 vols
Number of teachers: 550
Number of students: 10,457

Publications: *Caderno Técnico – Científico da Escola de Medicina Veterinária* (2 a year), *Cadernos de Direito* (2 a year), *Cadernos de*

Gestão (2 a year), *Cadernos de Contabilidade e Economia* (2 a year), *Cadernos de Odontologia* (2 a year), *Cadernos de Educação* (2 a year), *Paidéia: Revista do Instituto de Humanidades* (2 a year), *Cadernos de Meio Ambiente* (2 a year).

UNIVERSIDADE GUARULHOS

Praça Tereza Cristina 01, Centro, 07023-070 Guarulhos, SP
Telephone: (11) 209-9222
Fax: (11) 6440-2030
E-mail: ung@ung.br
Internet: www.ung.br
Founded 1986
Private control
Academic year: February to December
Rector: ALEXANDRE ESTOLANO
Library of 88,000 vols, 840 periodicals
Number of teachers: 875
Number of students: 14,640
Publication: *Geosciences Magazine* (in Portuguese with abstracts in English, 2 a year).

UNIVERSIDADE IBIRAPUERA

Av. Iraí 297, Moema, 04082-000 São Paulo, SP
Telephone: (11) 533-2022
Fax: (11) 241-4529
E-mail: unib@unib.br
Internet: www.unib.br
Founded 1971
Private control
Rector: JORGE BASTOS
Library of 69,000 vols, 1,936 periodicals
Number of teachers: 317
Number of students: 10,829.

UNIVERSIDADE FEDERAL DE ITAJUBÁ

Campus Prof. José Rodrigues Seabra, Av. BPS 103, 37500-903 Itajubá, MG
Telephone: (35) 3629-1124
Fax: (35) 3620-1124
E-mail: maua@unifei.edu.br
Internet: www.unifei.edu.br
Founded 1913 as Instituto Eletrotécnico e Mecânico de Itajubá; became Instituto Eletrotécnico de Itajubá 1936 and Escola Federal de Engenharia de Itajubá 1968; present name and status 2002
Rector: Prof. JOSÉ CARLOS GOULART DE SIQUEIRA
Vice-Rector: Prof. FELÍCIO BARBOSA MONTEIRO
Librarian: MARÍA DE FÁTIMA BASTOS
Library of 26,699 vols
Number of teachers: 183
Number of students: 2,581
Publication: *Pesquisa e Desenvolvimento Tecnológico* (4 a year)

DIRECTORS
Institute of Sciences: Prof. Dr FARNEZIO MOREIRA DE CARVALHO FILHO
Institute of Electrical Engineering: (vacant)
Institute of Mechanical Engineering: Prof. JOSÉ ARNALDO BARRA MONTEVECHI

UNIVERSIDADE DE ITAÚNA

Av. Dona Cota 397, Centro, CP 99, 35680-033 Itaúna, MG
Telephone: (37) 241-2375
Fax: (37) 241-2375
E-mail: fui@prover.com.br
Founded 1965
Private control
Academic year: March to December
President: FAIÇAL DAVID FREIRE CHEQUER
Executive Director: JOSÉ W. TEIXEIRA DE MELO
Librarian: MARIA DA CONCEIÇÃO APARECIDA CARVALHO CARRILHO
Number of teachers: 200
Number of students: 2,154
Publications: *Odonto-Itaúna*, *Cadernos de Extensão*

DIRECTORS
Faculty of Dentistry: JAIR RASO
Faculty of Engineering: FRANCISCO JOSÉ DE CASTRO BIANCHI
Faculty of Law: GERALDO DOS SANTOS
Faculty of Philosophy, Sciences, Languages and Social Sciences: ANNA ALVES VIERA DOS REIS
Faculty of Economics: RAIMUNDO DA SILVA RABELLO

UNIVERSIDADE DA REGIÃO DE JOINVILLE

Campus Universitário s/n, Bairro Bom Retiro, CP 246, 89201-972 Joinville, SC
Telephone: (47) 461-9000
Fax: (47) 473-0131
E-mail: reitoria@univille.com.br
Internet: www.univille.br
Founded 1992
State control
Rector: PAULO IVO KOEHNTOPP
Library: Libraries with 71,000 vols, 1,200 periodicals
Number of teachers: 633
Number of students: 8,532
Publications: *Revista UNIVILLE* (2 a year), *Universo UNIVILLE* (3 a year), *Revista Saúde e Meio Ambiente* (Health and Environmental Journal, 2 a year).

UNIVERSIDADE JOSÉ DO ROSARIO VELLANO

Rodovia MG 179, Km 0, Campus Universitário, CP23, 37130-000 Alfenas, MG
Telephone: (35) 3299-3000
Fax: (35) 3299-3800
E-mail: unifenas@unifenas.br
Internet: www.unifenas.br
Founded 1988 as Universidade de Alfenas; present name 2002
Private control
Academic year: February to December
Rector: EDSON ANTÔNIO VELANO
Library: Libraries with 48,000 vols, 2,514 periodicals
Number of teachers: 668
Number of students: 8,846
Publication: *Jornal da UNIFENAS* (monthly).

UNIVERSIDADE FEDERAL DE JUIZ DE FORA

Rua Benjamim Constant 790, Centro, CP 656, 36015-400 Juiz de Fora, MG
Telephone: (32) 215-5966
Fax: (32) 231-1998
E-mail: ufjf@pet.ufjf.br
Internet: www.ufjf.br
Founded 1960
Federal control
Language of instruction: Portuguese
Academic year: March to December
Rector: Prof. RENÊ GONÇALVES DE MATOS
Vice-Rector: Prof. CARLOS ALBERTO TARCHI CRIVELLARI
Pro-Rectors: MURILO CESAR MENDES GARCIA (Administration), Profa SONIA MARIA ROCHA HECKERT (Community Affairs), Prof. LUIZ ANTONIO VALLE ARANTES (Planning and Development), Profa MARLENE CALIL NETTO (Teaching), Profa MARIA MARGARIDA MARTINS SALOMÃO (Research)
Registrar: Profa MARIA HELENA BRAGA
Librarian: LEOPOLDINA LEONOR FAGUNDES MUNIZ
Number of teachers: 1,020
Number of students: 9,977
Publications: *Revista do Hospital Universitário* (quarterly), *Boletim do Centro de Biologia da Reprodução* (annually), *Boletim do Instituto de Ciências Biológicas* (annually), *Locus* (annually), *Educaçāo em Foco* (2 a year), *Ética e Filosofia Política* (2 a year), *Revista do Instituto de Ciências Exatas* (annually), *Revista Eletrônica de História do Brasil* (2 a year)

DIRECTORS
Faculty of Medicine: Prof. JOSÉ OLINDO D. FERREIRA
Faculty of Dentistry: Prof. HENRIQUE DUQUE M. C. FILHO
Faculty of Economics and Administration: Profa MARIA ISABEL DA SILVA AZEVEDO
Faculty of Pharmacy and Biochemistry: Profa MIRIAM APARECIDA PINTO VILELA
Faculty of Engineering: Prof. JÚLIO CÉSAR DA SILVA PORTELA
Faculty of Law: Prof. JOSÉ ANTÔNIO CÚGULA GUEDES
Faculty of Education: Prof. MANOEL PALÁCIOS DA P. E. MELO
Faculty of Social Services: Profa SANDRA A. HALLACK
Faculty of Physical Education: Prof. PAULO ROBERTO BASSOLI
Faculty of Social Communication: Prof. JOSÉ LUIZ RODRIGUES
Faculty of Nursing: Prof. MARLI SALVADOR
Institute of Biological Sciences: Prof. JOÃO B. PICININI TEIXEIRA
Institute of Human Sciences and Letters: Profa TEREZINHA MARIA SCHER PEREIRA
Institute of Exact Sciences: Prof. EMANOEL DE CASTRO ANTUNES FELÍCIO

UNIVERSIDADE ESTADUAL DE LONDRINA

CP 6001, Campus Universitário, 86051-990 Londrina, PR
Telephone: (43) 371-4000
Fax: (43) 328-4440
E-mail: www.npd@uel.br
Internet: www.uel.br
Founded 1971
Language of instruction: Portuguese
Academic year: February to December
Rector: Profa LYGIA LUMINA PUPATTO
Vice-Rector: EDUARDO DI MAURO
Secretary-General: Profa ANGELA MARIA VERGUE
Librarian: Profa VILMA APARECIDA GIMENEZ DA CRUZ
Library of 143,756 vols, 5,360 periodicals, 6,442 vols of pamphlets
Number of teachers: 1,643
Number of students: 16,582
Publications: *Boletim Informativo da Biblioteca Central* (monthly), *Temática: estudos de administração* (2 a year), *Boletim do CCH* (2 a year), *Revista do Depto de Geociências* (2 a year), *Semina* (4 a year), *Crítica – Revista de Filosofia* (4 a year), *Paradigmas – Revista de Filosofia Brasileira* (2 a year), *Torre de Babel – Reflexões e Pesquisas em Psicologia* (2 a year), *PSI – Revista de Psicologia Social e Institucional* (2 a year), *Informação e Informação* (2 a year), *Olho Mágico* (3 a year), *Revista Medicações* (2 a year), *Biosaúde* (2 a year), *Cadernos Difusão* (2 a year), *Diálogo* (annually), *Entretextos* (annually), *Scientia*

Iuris (annually), *Serviço Social em Revista* (2 a year), *Signum: Estudos da Linguagem* (2 a year), *Signum: estudos literarios* (2 a year), *Todavia* (annually)

DEANS

Centre of Letters and Human Sciences: Profa ESTHER GOMES DE OLIVEIRA
Centre of Biological Sciences: Prof. LUIZ CARLOS BRUSCHI
Centre of Exact Sciences: Prof. MARCOS DE CASTRO FALLEIROS
Centre of Applied Social Studies: Prof. MAURO ONIVALDO TICIANELLI
Centre of Health Sciences: Prof. PEDRO ALEJANDRO GORDAN
Centre of Education, Communication and Arts: Profa NÁDINA APARECIDA MORENO
Centre of Agrarian Sciences: Prof. ERNST ECKEHARDT MÜLLER
Centre of Physical Education: Profa MARIVAL ANTÔNIO MAZZIO
Centre of Technology and Urbanism: Prof. ANTONIO CARLOS ZANI

HEADS OF DEPARTMENTS

Centre of Biological Sciences (tel. (43) 371-4435; fax (43) 371-4079; e-mail bruschi@uel.br):
- General Biology: Prof. MÁRIO SÉRGIO MANTOVANI
- Animal and Plant Biology: (vacant)
- General Pathology: Prof. FRANCISCO JOSÉ DE ABREU OLIVEIRA
- Anatomy: Prof. JUAREZ CEZAR BORGES DE AQUINO
- Histology: NILCE MARZOLLA IDEHIHA
- General Psychology and Behaviour Analysis: ARI BASSI DO NASCIMENTO
- Basic Psychology and Psychoanalysis: Profa LOURDES SÍPOLI COUTINHO
- Social and Institutional Psychology: JOÃO BATISTA MARTINS
- Physiological Sciences: CLAUDETE FARAD NAME
- Microbiology: GALDINO ANDRADE FILHO

Centre of Letters and Human Sciences (tel. (43) 371-4418; fax (43) 371-4408; e-mail cchadm@uel.br):
- History: CLAUDIOMAR DOS REIS GONÇALVES
- Philosophy: Prof. LOURENÇO ZANCANARO
- Social Sciences: NELSON DACIO TOMAZI
- Modern and Foreign Languages: JEAN MARIE BRETON
- Classical and Vernacular Languages: Profa NEUZA CECILIATO DE CARVALHO

Centre of Health Sciences (tel. (43) 337-6574; fax (43) 337-5100; e-mail dirsec@ccs.br):
- General Medicine: RACHID TUMA NETTO
- Surgery: Prof. ANTONIO CARLOS VALEZI
- Nursing: BENEDITA RIBEIRO CORDEIRO
- Applied Pathology and Legal Medicine: Profa LEDA MEZZAROBA
- Restorative Dentistry: AMADEU MOREIRA PULLIN
- Oral Medicine and Odontopaediatrics: SILVIO DE OLIVEIRA RODRIGUES
- Physiotherapy: ANDRÉ LUIZ RODRIGUES DA SILVA
- Community Health: JOÃO JOSÉ BATISTA DE CAMPOS
- Paediatrics and Paediatric Surgery: FERNANDO COSTA
- Gynaecology and Obstetrics: OSMAR HENRIQUES

Centre of Education, Communication and Arts (tel. (43) 371-4308; fax (43) 371-4639; e-mail ceca@uel.br):
- Education: Profa JAQUELINE DELGADO PASCHOAL
- Communication: ZILDA AP. FREITAS DE ANDRADE
- Arts: Profa RENAN DOS SANTOS SILVA
- Library Science: Profa MARIA ELISABETE CATARINO

Centre of Applied Social Sciences (tel. (43) 371-4225; fax (43) 371-4215; e-mail cesasec@uel.br):
- Private Law: Profa ADILOAR FRANCO ZEMUNER
- Public Law: NELSON MILANEZ
- Economy: ANTONIO EDUARDO NOGUEIRA
- Accounting Sciences: JOSÉ AYLTON NOGUEIRA
- Business Administration: LUIZ FERNANDO PINTO DIAS
- Social Services: SANDRA DA CRUZ PERDIGÃO DOMICIANO

Centre of Exact Sciences (tel. (43) 371-4611; fax (43) 371-4216; e-mail ccexatas@uel.br):
- Mathematics: NELSON FERNANDO INFORZATO
- Applied Mathematics: JOÃO BATISTA MARTINS
- Physics: WELLINGTON DA CRUZ
- Chemistry: DIONISIO BORSATO
- Geosciences: JAIME DE OLIVEIRA
- Biochemistry: MARIA ANTONIA PEDRINE COLABONE CELLIGOI
- Computer Science: Prof. DIRCEU MOREIRA GUAZZI

Centre of Agrarian Sciences (tel. (43) 371-4435; fax (43) 371-4079; e-mail muller@uel.br):
- Agronomy: OTÁVIO JORGE GRIGOLI ABI SAAB
- Veterinary Science: Prof. NILVA MARIA FRERES MASCARENHAS
- Preventive Veterinary Medicine: DAISY PONTES NETTO
- Stockbreeding: LEANDRO DAS DORES FERREIRA DA SILVA
- Food and Drug Technology: Prof. FABIO YAMASHITA

Centre of Technology and Town Planning (tel. (43) 371-4505; fax (43) 371-4082; e-mail zani@uel.br):
- Structures: LUIZ ANTONIO DE SOUZA
- Civil Engineering: ARON LOPES PETRUCCI
- Architecture and Town Planning: FAUSTO CARMELO DE LIMA
- Electrical Engineering: REINALDO GONÇALVES NOGUEIRA

Centre of Physical Education (tel. (43) 371-4218; fax (43) 371-4144; e-mail cef@uel.br):
- Gymnastics, Recreation and Dance: DÉBORA BEATRIZ
- Individual and Collective Sports: JOÃO OSVALDO BORGES MONTEIRO
- Fundamentals of Physical Education: Profa JOANA ELIZABETE RIBEIRO PINTO GUEDES

UNIVERSIDADE LUTERANA DO BRASIL

Rua Miguel Tostes 101, São Luiz, 92420-280 Canoas, RS
Telephone: (51) 477-4000
Fax: (51) 477-1313
E-mail: postmaster@luther.ulbra.tche.br
Internet: www.ulbra.br

Founded 1988

Rector: RUBEN EUGEN BECKER

Library: Libraries with 346,000 vols, 1,285 periodicals
Number of teachers: 1,762
Number of students: 17,557.

UNIVERSIDADE MACKENZIE

Rua Itambé 45, Higienópolis, 01239-902 São Paulo, SP
Telephone: (11) 236-8766
Fax: (11) 255-2588
Internet: www.mackenzie.br
Founded 1952
Private control
Academic year: March to December

President: Dr ATHOS VIEIRA DE ANDRADE
Rector: Prof. Dr CLAUDIO SALVADOR LEMBO
Secretary-General: Prof. NELSON CALLEGARI

Number of teachers: 121
Number of students: 14,022

Publications: *O Picareta*, *Revista Mackenzie*, *Jornal Análise*, *Horacinho*, *Oráculo*, *Perfil Mackenzie*

DIRECTORS

School of Engineering: Prof. MARCEL MENDES
School of Architecture and Town Planning: Prof. WALTER SARAIVA KNEESE
School of Letters and Education: Profa MARIA LUCIA MARCONDES CARVALHO VASCONCELOS
School of Economics, Administration and Accounting: Prof. HAMILTON MENEZES FISCINA
School of Law: Prof. FRANCISCO LÉO MUNARI
School of Technology: Prof. OSNY RODRIGUES
School of Sciences: Profa ANA MARIA PORTO CASTANHEIRA
School of Arts and Communication: Profa MARCIA CRISTINA GONÇALVES DE OLIVEIRA

UNIVERSIDADE FEDERAL DO MARANHÃO

Palácio Cristo Rei, Praça Gonçalves Dias 351, Centro, 65020-240 São Luís, MA
Telephone: (98) 221-1055
Fax: (98) 221-5285
E-mail: ufmagr@bacanga.ufma.br
Internet: www.ufma.br
Founded 1966
Federal control
Academic year: March to December

Rector: OTHON DE CARVALHO BASTOS
Vice-Rector: REGINA CELI MIRANDA REIS LUNA
Pro-Rectors: RAIMUNDO NONATO PALHANO SILVA (Administration), SEBASTIÃO MOREIRA DUARTE (Post-graduates and Research), MARIA DA PAZ PORTO MACEDO COSTA (Extension and Student Affairs), CERES COSTAS FERNANDES VAZ DOS SANTOS (Undergraduates)
Librarian: MARIA DA GRAÇA MONTEIRO FONTOURA

Number of teachers: 867
Number of students: 8,895

DIRECTORS

Centre of Health Sciences: JAMILE ALVES DE OLIVEIRA
Centre of Basic Studies: SEBASTIÃO BARBOSA CAVALCANTI FILHO
Centre of Social Sciences: RUBEM RODRIGUES FERRO
Centre of Technology: PEDRO JAFAR BERNIZ

COURSE CO-ORDINATORS

Centre of Health Sciences:
- Medicine: ROSE MARIE DE JESUS J. C. GOMES
- Pharmacy: SANDRA MARIA JANSEN CUTRIM CORRÊA
- Dentistry: MARIA CELESTE DE MESQUITA AGUIAR
- Nursing: NAIR PORTELA SILVA COUTINHO
- Physical Education and Sports Technology: WALDECY DAS DORES VIEIRA VALE
- Biological Sciences: SILMA REGINA PEREIRA MARTINS

Centre of Basic Studies:
- Philosophy: MARIA DE FÁTIMA GARCÊS TEIXEIRA
- Psychology: LOIDE CÉLIA DE BRITO
- Geography: JOSÉ RIBAMAR TROVÃO
- Literature: MARCUS VINÍCIUS MAGALHÃES CATNUDA

Arts: ALDO DE JESUS MUNIZ LEITE
Tourism: MARIA DO SOCORRO ARAÚJO

Centre of Social Sciences:

Librarianship: JOANA RITA VILAS BOAS MUALEM
Accountancy: RAIMUNDO NONATO SERRA CAMPOS FILHO
Economics: ELIZEU SERRA DE ARAÚJO
Social Communication: ADEILCE GOMES DE AZEVEDO
Law: VALÉRIA MARIA PINHEIRO MONTENEGRO
Social Service: ANA MARIA SANTANA NEIVA COSTA
Practical Art: IVALBERTO CASTRO CAMPOS
Social Sciences: LÚCIA HELENA FERNANDES DE SABOIA
Teaching: LUCINETE MARQUES LIMA
Hotel Management: JOSÉ MARIA GOMES DE AGUIAR

Centre of Technology:

Industrial Chemistry: PEDRO EURICO NOLETO CRUZ
Electrical Engineering: MANUEL LEONEL DA COSTA NETO
Computer Science: JORGE HENRIQUE MARQUES CARACAS
Industrial Design: PAULO SERGIO LAGO DE CARVALHO
Mathematics: ABINAEL ASCENÇÃO RIBEIRO
Chemistry: MARIA DA GRAÇA SILVA NUNES
Physics: RAIMUNDO ANTONIO DA SILVA SANTOS

UNIVERSIDADE DE MARÍLIA

Campus I, Campus Universitário, 17525-902 Marília, SP

Telephone: (14) 3402-4111
Fax: (14) 3433-8691
E-mail: proaco@unimar.br
Internet: www.unimar.br

Founded 1956
Private control
Academic year: February to December (two semesters)

Rector: MÁRCIO MESQUITA SERVA
Vice-Rector: REGINA LÚCIA OTTAIANO LOSASSO SERVA
Pro-Rectors: MARIA BEATRIZ DE BARROS MORAES TRAZZI, JOSÉ ROBERTO MARQUES DE CASTRO, SOSÍGENES VICTOR BENFATTI
Sec.-Gen.: GENI DE ALMEIDA COLLA
Head of Library: LUCIANA GARCIA DA SILVA SANTAREM

Library of 110,000 vols, 15,000 periodicals
Number of teachers: 500
Number of students: 9,000

Publications: *Unimar Ciências* (2 a year), *Argumentum* (annually), *Ciências Humanas* (annually), *Ciências Odontológicas* (annually), *Comunicação Veredas* (annually), *Asuntamentos Humanos* (annually), *Unimídia* (6 a year), *Uninformativo* (annually).

UNIVERSIDADE ESTADUAL DE MARINGÁ

Av. Colombo 5790, Zona 7, CP 331, 87020-900 Maringá, PR

Telephone: (44) 261-4040
Fax: (44) 263-4487
E-mail: fadec@wnet.com.br
Internet: www.uem.br

Founded 1970
Academic year: March to December

Rector: LUIZ ANTÔNIO DE SOUZA
Vice-Rector: NEUSA ALTOÉ
Pro-Rectors: JOÃO DIRCEU NOGUEIRA CARVALHO (Administration), SILVIA INES CONEGLIAN CARRILHO DE VASCONCELOS (Teaching), CELSO SOUZA (Extension and Culture), MILTON MIRANDA DE ARAÚJO (Human Resources and Community Affairs), ERIVELTO GOULART (Research and Postgraduates)
Librarian: ANA MARIA MARQUEZINI ALVARENGA

Number of teachers: 1,287
Number of students: 9,804

Publications: *Unimar, Unimar Jurídica, Universidade e Sociedade, Boletim de Geografia, Revista de Educação Física, Revista Apontamentos, Cadernos de Administração, Revista Enfoque-Reflexão Contábil, A Economia em Revista, Revista Tecnológica, Jornal Alfabetizando, Caderno da Semana de Geografia, Revista Diálogos, Caderno de METEP, Revista de Psicologia*

DIRECTORS

Socio-Economic Studies Centre: JOSÉ ROBERTO PINHEIRO DE MELO
Humanities and Arts Centre: ROMILDA MARINS CORREA
Biological Sciences Centre: SANDRA REGINA STÁBILLE
Health Sciences Centre: MARIA JOSÉ SCOCHI
Exact Sciences Centre: LUIZ ROBERTO EVANGELISTA
Technology Centre: MAURO ANTONIO DA SILVA SÁ RAVAGNANI
Agricultural Sciences Centre: GERALDO TADEU DOS SANTOS

HEADS OF DEPARTMENTS

Humanities and Arts Centre:

Geography: JOSÉ CANDIDO STEVAUX
Arts and Letters: JULIANO TAMANINI
Social Sciences: CELENE TONELLA
Education: JORGE CANTOS
Psychology: MARIA TERESA CLARO GONZAGA
Principle of Education: LIZETE SHIZUE BOMURA MACIEL
History: ALBERTO GAWRYSZEWSKI

Socio-Economic Studies Centre:

Private and Procedural Law: FABÍOLA VILELLA MACHADO
Public Law: FAUSTINO FRANCISCO DE SOUZA
Economics: REINALDO CONSONI
Business Administration: LUIZ TATTO
Accountancy: MÁRIO LONARDONI

Biological Sciences Centre:

Biology: ISMAR SEBASTIÃO MOSCHETA
Cellular Biology: VERONICA ELIZA P. VICENTINI
Biochemistry: SÉRGIO PAULO SEVERO DE S. DINIZ
Morphophysiological Sciences: DÍOGENES SANCHES

Health Sciences Centre:

Clinical Analysis: RICARDO ALBERTO MOLITERNO
Medicine: JOSÉ CARLOS DA SILVA
Odontology: ANDRES JOSÉ TUMANG
Physical Education: LUIZ ANTONIO PEREIRA DA SILVA
Nursing: VALMIR RYCHETA CORREIA
Pharmacy and Pharmacology: ROBERTO BARBOSA BAZOTTE

Agricultural Sciences Centre:

Animal Husbandry: ANTONIO CLAUDIO FURLAN
Agronomy: SUELI SATO MARTINS

Exact Sciences:

Chemistry: JONES SOARES
Mathematics: JULIO SANTIAGO PRATES FILHO
Physics: ANTONIO JOSÉ PALANGANA
Statistics: MARGARETH CIZUKA TOYAMA UDO

Technology Centre:

Civil Engineering: LUIZ DOMINGOS MORENO DE CARVALHO
Computer Science: WESLEY ROMÃO
Chemical Engineering: MARCELINO LUIZ GIMENES

DIRECTORS

Centre for the Integration of Children and Adolescents: CLEUZA LUCENA
Languages Institute: CRISTINA MORAES
Applied Psychology Centre: MARIA JOSÉ SARAIVA RIBEIRO
Data Processing Centre: DILVO PAUPITZ

UNIVERSIDADE FEDERAL DE MATO GROSSO

Av. Fernando Corrêa da Costa s/n, Caxipó, 78060-900 Cuiabá, MT

Telephone: (65) 615-8000
Fax: (65) 361-1119
E-mail: janemar@cpd.ufmt.br
Internet: www.ufmt.br

Founded 1970

Rector: FERNANDO NOGUEIRA DE LIMA
Administrative Officer: Profa NEUSA SOUZA DOURADO

Number of teachers: 1,167
Number of students: 9,195

Faculties of agrarian sciences, biological and health sciences, literature and human sciences, social sciences, exact sciences and technology.

FUNDAÇÃO UNIVERSIDADE FEDERAL DE MATO GROSSO DO SUL

CP 649, Cidade Universitária, 79100 Campo Grande, MS

Telephone: (67) 787-7425
Fax: (67) 787-3607
E-mail: ro@nin.ufms.br
Internet: www.ufms.br

Founded 1970
Academic year: March to December

Centres of biology, general studies, physical education, computer studies, education. Campuses in Corumbá, Aquidaúana, Dourados, Três Lagoas.

PONTIFÍCIA UNIVERSIDADE CATÓLICA DE MINAS GERAIS

Av. Dom José Gaspar 500, Bairro Coração Eucarístico, 30535-610 Belo Horizonte, MG

Telephone: (31) 3319-4444
Fax: (31) 3319-4225
E-mail: central@pucminas.br
Internet: www.pucminas.br

Founded 1958
Academic year: February to December

Chancellor: Dom WALMOR OLIVEIRA DE AZEVEDO
Rector: Prof. EUSTÁQUIO AFONSO ARAÚJO
Vice-Rector: Prof. Pe JOAQUIM GIOVANI MOL GUIMARÃES
General Secretary: FLÁVIO AUGUSTO BARROS
Chief Librarian: CÁSSIO JOSÉ DE PAULA

Library of 200,000 vols
Number of teachers: 2,032
Number of students: 44,043

Publications: *Journal PUC Minas* (monthly), *PUC Informa* (weekly), *No Pique da PUC* (weekly)

DIRECTORS

Institute of Psychology: ANA LÚCIA ANDRADE MARÇOLLA
Institute of Biological and Health Sciences: UBIRATAN BARROS DE MELO
Institute of Continuing Education: Dr MARIA REGINA NABUCO BRANDÃO
Institute of Informatics: CARLOS BARRETO RIBAS

Institute for the Study of Fauna and Flora: MIGUEL ALONSO DE GOUVÊA VALLE
Polytechnic Institute: NILSON DE FIGUEIREDO FILHO
Institute of Economic and Managerial Sciences: ÂNGELA MARIA MARQUES CUPERTINO
PUC Minas Virtual (Distance Learning): MARIA BATRIZ OLIVEIRA GONÇALVES
Institute of Labour Relations: Dr ANTONIO MOREIRA DE CARVALHO NETO
Institute of Humanities: AUDEMARO TARANTO GOULART

AFFILIATED FOUNDATION

Fundação Dom Cabral: Rua Bernardo Guimarães 3071, 30140-083, Belo Horizonte, MG; tel. (31) 275-3466; fax (31) 275-1558; f. 1976; Dean Prof. EMERSON DE ALMEIDA.

UNIVERSIDADE FEDERAL DE MINAS GERAIS

Av. Antônio Carlos 6627, Campus Universitário, Pampulha, CP 1621, 31270-901 Belo Horizonte, MG
Telephone: (31) 3499-4025
Fax: (31) 3499-4530
E-mail: info@cointer.ufmg.br
Internet: www.ufmg.br
Founded 1927
State control
Language of instruction: Portuguese
Academic year: February to December
Rector: Profa ANA LÚCIA ALMEIDA GAZZOLA
Vice-Rector: Prof. MARCOS BORATO VIANA
Vice-Chancellor (Administration): LUIZ FELIPE VIEIRA CALVO
Vice-Chancellor (Planning): Prof. RONALDO TADEU PENA
Vice-Chancellor (Undergraduates): Prof. CRISTINA RIBEIRO ROCHA AUGUSTIN
Vice-Chancellor (Research): Profa JOSÉ AURÉLIO GARCIA BERGMANN
Vice-Chancellor (Extension): Prof. EDISON JOSÉ CORRÊA
Vice-Chancellor (Postgraduates): Profa MARIA SUELI DE OLIVEIRA PIRES
Director of Libraries: SIMONE APARECIDA DOS SANTOS
Library of 522,100 vols, 19,400 periodicals
Number of teachers: 2,527
Number of students: 31,000
Publications: *Revista Brasileira de Estudos Políticos*, *Arquivos da Escola de Veterinária da UFMG*, *Estudos Germânicos*, *Barroco*, *Kriterion*, *Diversa* (annually), *Manuelzão* (monthly)

DIRECTORS

Fine Arts: Prof. EVANDRO JOSÉ LEMOS DA CUNHA
Literature: Profa ELIANA AMARANTE DE MENDONÇA MENDES
Music: Prof. LUCAS JOSÉ BRETAS DOS SANTOS
Philosophy and Human Sciences: Prof. JOÃO PINTO FURTADO
Biological Sciences: Prof. CARLOS ALBERTO PEREIRA TAVARES
Exact Sciences: Prof. BISMARCK VAZ DA COSTA
Geo-Sciences: Prof. ANTÔNIO GILBERTO COSTA
Architecture: Prof. LEONARDO BARCI CASTRIOTA
Economic Sciences: Prof. CLÉLIO CAMPOLINA DINIZ
Law: Prof. ALOÍSIO GONZAGA ANDRADE ARAÚJO
Education: Profa ÂNGELA LOUREIRO DE FREITAS DALBEN
Physical Education: Prof. PABLO RUAN GRECO
Nursing: Prof. FRANCISCO CARLOS FELIX LANA
Engineering: Prof. RICARDO NICOLAU NASSAR KOURY
Medicine: Prof. GERALDO BRASILEIRO FILHO
Dentistry: Prof. WELLINGTON CORREA JANSEN
Veterinary Sciences: Prof. ROBERTO BACARAT DE ARAÚJO
Pharmacy: Prof. GERSON ANTÔNIO PIANETTI

AFFILIATED INSTITUTES

Centre for Development and Regional Planning: Rua Curitiba 832, Belo Horizonte, MG; Dir Prof. JOSÉ ALBERTO MAGNO DE CARVALHO.

Astronomical Observatory: Dir Prof. RENATO LAS CASAS.

Institute of Technology and Agriculture: Dir Prof. REGINALDO LAMBERTI NAPOLEÃO.

Centre for the Conservation and Restoration of Movable Cultural Property: Dir ANAMARIA RUEGGER ALMEIDA NEVES.

Centre for Crime and Public Safety Studies: Dir CLÁUDIO BEATO.

UNIVERSIDADE DE MOGI DAS CRUZES

Av. Dr Cândido Xavier de Almeida Souza 200, 08780-911 Mogi das Cruzes, SP
Telephone: (11) 4798-7051
Fax: (11) 4799-1569
E-mail: reitoria@umc.br
Internet: www.umc.br
Founded 1973
Private control
Academic year: February to December
Chancellor: Prof. MANOEL BEZERRA DE MELO
Vice-Chancellor: Profa MARIA COELI BEZERRA DE MELO
Rector: Profa REGINA COELI BEZERRA DE MELO NASSRI
Vice-Rector: Prof. LUIZ FERNANDO GIAZZI NASSRI
Pro-Rector (Administrative): JESUS GONZÁLEZ
Pro-Rector (Research, Graduate Studies and Extension): Prof. JAIR RIBEIRO CHAGAS
Pro-Rector (Undergraduate Studies): Prof. RUBENS GUILHEMAT
General Secretary: CLAUDIO DA SILVA NICOLICHE
Librarian: DECLEIA MARIA FAGANELLO
Library of 107,208 vols
Number of teachers: 678
Number of students: 14,193
Publication: *Entre Nós* (monthly)

CO-ORDINATORS

Accountancy: Prof. JOSÉ CARLOS MARION
Accountancy, Business Administration, Marketing, Administration Services: Prof. ALEXANDRE LUZZI LAS CASAS
Accountancy, Quality and Productivity, Business Management, Personnel Management, Tourism and Hotel Management (São Paulo Campus): Prof. RÔMULO FRANCISCO DE SOUZA MAIA
Administration (São Paulo Campus): Prof. EDMO ALVES MENINI
Architecture and Town Planning, Civil Engineering: Prof. MARCO ANTÔNIO PLÁCIDO DE ALMEIDA
Biological Sciences: Prof. ERICSON ANTONIO AMBROSANO
Biology: Prof. LUIZ ROBERTO NUNES
Chemistry and Chemical Engineering: Prof. ANDRÉ FERNANDO DE OLIVEIRA
Dentistry: Prof. CAMILLO ANAUATE NETTO
Development of Computer Systems, Internet and Computer Networks Management (São Paulo Campus): Prof. ROBERTO AFFONSO DA COSTA, JR
Electrical Engineering: Prof. CARLOS MARCELO GURJÃO DE GODOY
Environmental Sciences Technology: Profa JOSÉ ROBERTO KOCHEL DOS SANTOS
Information Systems, Systems Development Technology, Internet and Computer Networks Management: Prof. HENRIQUE JESUS QUINTINO DE OLIVEIRA
Law: Prof. JOSÉ MOREIRA DE ASSIS
Law (São Paulo Campus): Prof. JOSÉ GERALDO BRITO FILOMENO
Letters (Portuguese, English and Literatures): Profa VERA LÚCIA MEIRA MAGALHÃES
Letters (Portuguese, English and Literatures), Pedagogy (São Paulo Campus): Prof. YÊDA MARIA DA COSTA LIMA VARIOTTA
Mechanical Engineering, Industrial Production Technology and Industrial Automation Technology: Prof. MARCO ANTÔNIO FUMAGALLI
Medicine: Prof. CARLOS MATEUS ROTTA
Nursing: Profa OSVALDO CÉLIO LAGE
Nutrition: Profa SUSANA FONSECA DA SILVEIRA
Pedagogy: Profa MIRIAN APARECIDA ROMANO
Pharmacy: Profa REGINA LÚCIA BATISTA DA COSTA OLIVEIRA
Physical Education: Prof. ZENON SILVA ARANHA FILHO
Physiotherapy: Prof. CESAR AUGUSTO CALONEGO
Psychology: Profa GERALDINA PORTO WITTER
Quality and Productivity, Business Management, Personnel Management, Tourism and Hotel Management (São Paulo Campus): Prof. JOSÉ GALBA DE AQUINO
Social Communications, Design (Visual Programme): Prof. ARMANDO SÉRGIO DA SILVA
Touristic Business Management, Marketing and Sales, Quality and Productivity Management, Enterprising and Business Management: Prof. ROBERTO KANAANE

UNIVERSIDADE ESTADUAL DE MONTES CLAROS

Campus Universitário Prof. Darcy Ribeiro, Vila Mauricéia, 39401-089 Montes Claros, MG
Telephone: (38) 229-8000
Fax: (38) 229-8103
E-mail: reitoria@unimontes.br
Internet: www.unimontes.br
Founded 1962
State control
Rector: JOSÉ GERALDO DE FREITAS DRUMOND
Library of 46,000 vols, 2,609 periodicals
Number of teachers: 368
Number of students: 4,667.

UNIVERSIDADE REGIONAL DO NOROESTE DO ESTADO DO RIO GRANDE DO SUL

Rua do Comércio, Bairro Universitário, 98700-000 Ijuí, Rio Grande do Sul
Telephone: (55) 333-20200
Fax: (55) 333-29100
E-mail: reitoria@unijui.tche.br
Internet: www.unijui.tche.br
Founded 1985
Private control (Fundação de Integração, Desenvolvimento e Educação do Noroeste do Estado)
Language of instruction: Portuguese
Academic year: March to December
Rector: GILMAR ANTÔNIO BEDIN
Vice-Rectors: MARTINHO LUÍS KELM (Administration), DILSON TRENNEPOHL (Graduate Courses), ANTONIA CARVALHO BUSSMAN (Undergraduate Courses)
Academic Secretary: MARISA FRIZZO
Librarian: KENIA M. BERNINI
Library of 180,700 vols
Number of teachers: 569
Number of students: 12,000
Publications: *Contexto & Educação* (4 a year), *Espaços da Escola* (4 a year), *Contabilidade e Informacão* (4 a year), *Contexto e Saúde* (2 a year), *Revista de Estudos de Administracão* (2 a year), *Direito em*

Debate (2 a year), *Formas & Linguagens* (2 a year), *Leitura e Revista* (2 a year), *Educação nas Ciências* (2 a year), *Revista AD Homimen Tomo I* (2 a year), *Desenvolvimento em Questão* (2 a year), *Coleção Situação de Estudos* (2 a year)

HEADS OF DEPARTMENTS

Administration: GUSTAVO ARNO DREWS
Law: CEZAR BUSNELLO
Economics and Accountancy: Dr ARGEMIRO LUIS BRUM
Teaching: Dr JOSÉ PEDRO BOUFFLER
Philosophy and Psychology: VÂNIA DUTRA DE AZEVEDO
Languages, Arts and Communication: MARIA JULIA PADILHA MACAGNAN
Social Sciences: SUIMAR JÃO BRESSAN
Health: ELOISA KOPF
Biology and Chemistry: MARLI DALLGNOL FRISON
Agronomy: Dr BENEDITO SILVA NETO
Technology: Dr FABIANO SALVADORI
Physics, Statistics and Mathematics: SONIA B. TELLES DREWS

UNIVERSIDADE DE NOVA IGUAÇU

Av. Augusto Távora 2134, Jardim Redenção, 26275-580 Nova Iguaçu, RJ
Telephone: (21) 2765-4012
Fax: (21) 2765-1687
E-mail: proeg@unig.br
Internet: www.unig.br
Founded 1993
Private control
Rector: JULIO CÉSAR DA SILVA
Pro-Rector (Administration): JOÃO BATISTA BARRETO LUBANCO
Pro-Rector (Undergraduate Studies): CARLOS HENRIQUE MELO REIS
Pro-Rector (Postgraduate Studies, Research and External Relations): ANTONIO CARLOS CARREIRA FREITAS
Library: Libraries with 59,000 vols, 1,355 periodicals
Number of teachers: 922
Number of students: 12,301
Publications: *InterFace* (Journal of Faculty of Education and Humanities), *In Solidum* (Journal of Faculty of Law and Applied Social Sciences), *Arquivos de Direito*, *Revista de Ciências Biológicas e da Saúde*, *Revista de Ciência & Tecnologia*

DIRECTORS

Faculty of Biological and Health Sciences: UÉLITON VIANNA
Faculty of Education and Humanities: MARIONICE ALEXANDRE BOECHAT
Faculty of Exact Sciences and Technology: JOSÉ CARLOS DA SILVA
Faculty of Law and Applied Social Sciences: JOÃO BATISTA BARRETO LUBANCO

UNIVERSIDADE FEDERAL DE OURO PRÊTO

Rua Diogo de Vasconcelos 122, 35400-000 Ouro Prêto, MG
Telephone: (31) 3559-1218
Fax: (31) 3551-1689
E-mail: reitoria@ufop.br
Internet: www.ufop.br
Founded 1969
Federal state control
Academic year: February to December
Rector: DIRCEU DO NASCIMENTO
Vice-Rector: MARCO ANTONIO TOURINHO FURTADO
Chief Administrative Officer: MÁRCIO GALVÃO
Librarian: JUSSARA SANTOS SILVA
Number of teachers: 390
Number of students: 5,200 (4,800 undergraduate, 400 postgraduate)
Publications: *Revista da Escola de Minas* (4 a year), *Revista de Historia* (3 a year), *Jornal da UFOP* (monthly), *Jornal Revirarte*, *Revista de Pesquisa da UFOP* (4 a year), *Revista Juridica* (annually).

CONSTITUENT INSTITUTES

School of Mines: Praça Tiradentes 20, 35400-000 Ouro Prêto, MG; f. 1876; Dean ANTONIO GOMES.

School of Pharmacy: Rua Costa Sena 171, 35400-000 Ouro Prêto, MG; f. 1839; Dean LISIANE DA SILVEIRA EU.

Institute of Human and Social Sciences: Rua do Seminário, 35420-000 Mariana, MG; f. 1979; Dean IVAN A. ALMEIDA.

Institute of Exact and Biological Sciences: Campus Universitario, Morro do Cruzeiro, 35400-000 Ouro Prêto, MG; f. 1982; Dean JOÃO MARTINS.

Institute of Arts and Culture: Rua Coronel Alves 55, 35400-000 Ouro Prêto, MG; f. 1981; Dean GUIOMAR GRAMONT.

UNIVERSIDADE FEDERAL DO PARÁ

Av. Augusto Corrêa 1, Campus Universitário, Bairro do Guamá, CP 479, 66075-900 Belém, PA
Telephone: (91) 211-2121
Fax: (91) 211-1734
E-mail: postmaster@ufpa.br
Internet: www.ufpa.br
Founded 1957
Federal control
Language of instruction: Portuguese
Academic year: March to December
Rector: Prof. Dr CRISTOVAM WANDERLEY PICANÇO DINIZ
Vice-Rector: Profa TELMA DE CARVALHO LOBO
Central Library Administrator: MARIA DAS GRAÇAS DA SILVA PENA
Number of teachers: 2,179
Number of students: 28,492
Publications: *Cadernos do Centro de Filosofia e Ciências Humanas*, *MOARA*, *Ver a Educação*, *Cadernos de Pós-Graduação em Direito da UFPA*, *Revista do Tecnológico*, *Revista do Centro do Ciências Jurídicas*, *Humanitas*, *Revista do Centro Sócio-Econômico*

DIRECTORS

Exact and Natural Sciences Centre: Prof. RENATO BORGES GUERRA
Biology Centre: Profa SETSUKO NORO DOS SANTOS
Philosophy and Human Sciences Centre: Prof. JOSÉ ALVES DE SOUZA JÚNIOR
Arts and Literature Centre: (vacant)
Health Science Centre: Prof. Dr CLÁUDIO JOSÉ DIAS KLAUTAU
Technology Centre: Profa VERA MARIA NOBRE BRÁZ
Socio-Economic Centre: Prof. MARIO NAZARENO NORONHA FARIA E SOUZA
Education Centre: Profa ANA MARIA ORLANDINA TANCREDI CARVALHO
Geosciences Centre: Prof. MARCONDES LIMA DA COSTA
Law Sciences Centre: Prof. JOÃO BATISTA KLAUTAU LEÃO

UNIVERSIDADE ESTADUAL DA PARAÍBA

CP 791, Av. Mar. Floriano Peixoto 718, CP 781, 58100-001 Campina Grande, PB
Telephone: (83) 341-3300
Fax: (83) 341-4509
E-mail: uepb@uepb.rpp.br
Internet: www.uepb.rpp.br
Founded 1966
Municipal control
Language of instruction: Portuguese
Academic year: March to December
Rector: SEBASTIÃO GUIMARÃES VIEIRA
Vice-Rector: JOSÉ BENJAMIN PEREIRA FILHO
General Secretary: CLEÓMENES LOIOLA CAMINHA
Librarian: IVONETE ALMEIDA GALDINO
Library of 65,000 vols
Number of teachers: 650
Number of students: 10,000
Publications: *Catálogo Geral* (annually), *Roteiro*, *Informativo UEPB*

DIRECTORS

Agricultural College 'Assis Chateaubriand': JOSÉ PAULO DE AMORIM FARIAZ
Faculty of Sciences and Technology: GIVANILDO GONÇALVES DE FARIAS
Faculty of Physical Education: SIDELENE GONSAGA DE MELO
Faculty of Physiotherapy: LÍDIA MARIA ALBUQUERQUE MARQUES
Faculty of Nursing: JOSEFA JOSETE DA SILVA SANTOS
Faculty of Pharmacy and Biology: LUIZA MARIA BARRETO DA SILVEIRA
Faculty of Odontology: CARLTON FERREIRA NÓBREGA
Faculty of Psychology: GUTEMBERG GERMANO BARBOSA
Faculty of Administration and Accounting: FRANCISCO LUIZ DE OLIVEIRA
Faculty of Social Communication: SIMÃO ARRUDA
Faculty of Law: HARRISON ALEXANDRE TARGINO
Faculty of Education, Letters and Social Sciences: ZÉLIA MARIA PEREIRA FERNANDES
Faculty of Social Work: MARIA JOSÉ DA COSTA SILVA
Faculty of Philosophy, Sciences and Letters: TANIA PORPINO MARINHO DO NASCIMENTO
School of Agricultural Engineering, Catolé do Rocha: PEDRO FERREIRA NETO

UNIVERSIDADE FEDERAL DA PARAÍBA

Campus Universitário, 58059-900 João Pessoa, PB
Telephone: (83) 216-7200
Fax: (83) 225-1901
E-mail: gabinete@reitoria.ufpb.br
Internet: www.ufpb.br
Founded 1955
Language of instruction: Portuguese
Academic year: March to December
Rector: JADER NUNES DE OLIVEIRA
Vice-Rector: MÚCIO ANTÔNIO SOBREIRA SOUTO
Registrar: IGUATEMY MARIA DE LUCENA MARTINS
Librarian: BABYNE NEIVA DE G. RIBEIRO
Number of teachers: 1,423
Number of students: 19,203
Publications: *Revista Brasileira de Ciência da Saúde* (4 a year), *Temas em Educação* (annually), *Revista Brasileira de Engenharia Agrícola e Ambiental* (4 a year), *Informação e Sociedade : Estudos* (2 a year), *Nordestina de Biologia* (annually)

DIRECTORS

Campus I—João Pessoa (58059-900 João Pessoa, PB; tel. (83) 216-7200):
Health Sciences: ZORAIDE MARGARET BEZERRA LINS
Applied Social Sciences: JOSÉ DÉCIO DE ALMEIDA LEITE
Human Sciences, Letters and Arts: MARIA YARA CAMPOS MATOS

Education: ANEDITE ALMEIDA DE FREITAS
Exact and Natural Sciences: UMBELINO DE FREITAS NETO
Technology: ORLANDO DE CAVALCANTI VILLAR FILHO
Law: MANOEL ALEXANDRE CAVALCANTE BELO

Campus II—Areia: (58397-000 Areia, PB; tel. (83) 362-2218):

Agricultural Sciences: ALBERÍCIO PEREIRA DE ANDRADE

Campus III—Bananeiras: (58220-000 Bananeiras, PB; tel. (83) 363-2621):

Technologist Training Centre: CHATEAUBRIAND BANDEIRA JÚNIOR

PONTIFICIA UNIVERSIDADE CATÓLICA DO PARANÁ

Rua Imaculada Conceição 1155, Prado Velho, CP 16210, 80215-901 Curitiba, PR
Telephone: (41) 330-1515
Fax: (41) 332-5588
E-mail: postmaster@pucpr.br
Internet: www.pucpr.br

Founded 1959
Private control
Academic year: March to December (two semesters)

Grand Chancellor: PEDRO FEDALTO (Archbishop of Curitiba)
Rector: CLEMENTE IVO JULIATTO
Administrative Pro-Rector: Prof. ARAMIS DEMETERCO
Academic Pro-Rector: Profa NEUZA APARECIDA RAMOS
Community Pro-Rector: ADILSON MORAES SEIXAS
Pro-Rector for Planning and Development: ROBERTO BORGES FRANÇA
Pro-Rector for Graduate Studies, Research and Extension Services: FLÁVIO BORTO
Registrar: OSVALDO ULYSSES MAZAY
Library Director: SILVIANE MÜLLER

Number of teachers: 1,241
Number of students: 20,413 (17,721 undergraduate, 2,692 postgraduate)

Publications: *Estudos de Biologia* (2 a year), *Psicologia Argumento* (annually), *Vida Universitária* (monthly), *Revista de Filosofia* (annually), *Revista Acadêmica* (2 a year), *Revista de Fisioterapia* (2 a year), *Círculo de Estudos Bandeirantes* (annually), *Verba Iuris* (annually), *PUC-PR em Dados* (annually), *Estudos de Medicina* (4 a year), *Locus* (annually), *Diálogo Educacional* (2 a year)

DEANS

Centre for Humanities and Theological Sciences: ANTÔNIO QUIRINO DE OLIVEIRA
Centre for Juridical and Social Sciences: ROBERTO LINHARES DA COSTA
Centre for Exact and Technological Sciences: ROBERT CARLISLE BURNETT
Centre for Biological and Health Sciences: ALBERTO ACCIOLY VEIGA
Centre for Agronomy and Environmental Sciences: SYLVIO PÉLLICO NETO
Centre for Applied and Social Sciences: SÉRGIO PEREIRA LOBO

HEADS OF DEPARTMENTS

Centre for Humanities and Theological Sciences:

Education: SÉRGIO ROGÉRIO JUNQUEIRA
Philosophy: ANTÔNIO EDMILSON PASCHOAL
Theology: MÁRIO ANTÔNIO BETIATO
Physical Education: VILMA SULEI JENTSCH
Languages: MARTA MORAIS DA COSTA

Centre for Juridical and Social Sciences:

Law: MÁRCIA CARLA PEREIRA RIBEIRO
Social Work: MARGARETE APOLÔNIA BUNN ZANON
Social Communication: MÔNICA CRISTINA FORT
Tourism: MARIA IGNEZ MARINS

Centre for Exact and Technological Sciences:

Mathematics: TAMIA MARTA YAMAMOTO
Industrial Design: JAIME RAMOS
Civil Engineering: RICARDO BERTIN
Architecture and Town Planning: LEONARDO TOSSIAK OBA
Computer Science: EDSON EMÍLIO SCALABRIN
Computer Engineering: HENRI FREDERICO EBERSPÄCHER
Mechanical Engineering: JOÃO ELIAS ABDALA FILHO
Electrical Engineering: MARIA GERTRUDES TE VAARWERK
Food Engineering: ADENISE LORENCI WOICIECHOWSKI
Chemical Engineering: NEI HANSEN DE ALMEIDA
Control and Automation Engineering: MARCO ANTÔNIO BUSETTI DE PAULA
Environmental Engineering: CARLOS MELLO GARCIAS
Mechanical Production Engineering: ALFREDO IAROZINSKI NETO
Systems Analysis: MARCOS AUGUSTO HOCHULI SHMEIL
Industrial Chemistry: NERY NISHIMURA DE LIMA

Centre for Biological and Health Sciences:

Psychology: REGINA CELINA CRUZ
Nursing: MARIA LEDA VIEIRA
Medicine: ALBERTO ACCIOLY VEIGA
Dentistry: MONIR TACLA
Nutrition: HELENA MARIA SIMONARD LOUREIRO
Physiotherapy: ANDREA PIRES MÜLLER
Speech Therapy and Audiology: CLEYBE HIOLE VIEIRA
Biology: WALDEMAR ENS
Pharmacy and Biochemistry: ANTONIO CARLOS MIRA

Centre for Agronomy and Environmental Sciences:

Agronomy: MARCELO CABRAL JAHNEL
Veterinary Medicine: ANTÔNIO FELIPE PAULINO DE FIGUEIREDO WOUK
Animal Sciences: HUMBERTO MACIEL FRANÇA MADEIRA

Centre for Applied and Social Sciences:

Administration: NÉLIO MAURO AGUIRRE DE CASTRO
Accounting: ORIVALDO JOSÉ BUSARELLO
Economics: LOURIVAL SCHEIDWEILLER
Law: SIMARA CARVALHO DUARTE BETIER FORTES

Graduate Programmes:

Education: LILIAN ANNA WACHOWICZ
Social and Economic Law: ROBERTO CATALANO BOTELHO FERRAZ
Architecture and Town Planning: LUÍS SALVADOR PETRUCCI GNOATO
Applied Computation: CARLOS ALBERTO MAZIEIRO
Mechanical Engineering: JOÃO ELIAS ABDALLA FILHO
Orthodontics and Odontology: SÉRGIO ROBERTO VIEIRA
Medicine: PAULO ROBERTO SLUD BROFMANN
Business Administration: NÉLIO MAURO AGUIRRE DE CASTRO

ATTACHED INSTITUTES

Higher Institute of Human and Education Sciences: Dir ANTÔNIO QUIRINO DE OLIVEIRA.

Institute of Juridical and Social Sciences: Dir ROBERTO LINHARES DA COSTA.

Institute of Exact and Technological Sciences: Dir ROBERT CARLISLE BURNETT.

Institute of Biological and Health Sciences: Dir ALBERTO ACCIOLY VEIGA.

Institute of Agronomy and Environmental Sciences: Dir SILVIO PÉLLICO NETO.

Higher Institute of Business Administration: Dir SÉRGIO PEREIRA LOBO.

São José dos Pinhais Campus

Seminário dos Sagrados Corações, BR 376, Km 14, 83010-500 São José dos Pinhais, Paraná; tel. (41) 283-4434; fax (41) 382-1223; Director: Prof. SERGIO PEREIRA LOBO

HEADS OF DEPARTMENTS

Accounting: ORIVALDO JOÃO BUSARELO
Law: NOEL SANWAYS
Business Administration: SÉRGIO LOBO
Economics: CARLOS ALBERTO REINCHEN DE SOUZA MIRANDA
Religious Studies: ZÉLIA KOPACHESKI
Management Information Systems: CLÁUDIO DE OLIVEIRA
Sports and Recreation: VILMA SUELI JENTSCH
Agronomy: SYLVIO PELLICO NETO
Veterinary Medicine: DOREI BRANDÃO
Zootechnics: SÍLVIO DEGASPERI
Brazilian Studies and Citizenship: VALÉRIO HOERNER

UNIVERSIDADE FEDERAL DO PARANÁ

Rua 15 de Novembro 1299, CP 441, 80060-000 Curitiba, PR
Telephone: (41) 360-5343
Fax: (41) 264-2243
E-mail: externas@ufpr.br
Internet: www.ufpr.br

Founded 1912
Academic year: March to December

Rector: CARLOS MOREIRA JÚNIOR
Vice-Rector: MARIA TARCISA SILVA BEGA
Chief Administrative Officer: ANTONIO CARLOS GONDIM
Librarian: LÍGIA ELIANA SETENARESKI

Library: Library: see Libraries and Archives
Number of teachers: 1,800
Number of students: 30,000

Publications: *Desenvolvimento e Meio Ambiente* (2 a year), *Dens* (2 a year), *História: Questões & Debates* (2 a year), *Nerítica* (annually), *RAEGA* (annually), *Scientia Agraria* (2 a year), *Boletim Paranaense de Geociências* (2 a year), *Revista de Economia* (2 a year), *Revista Letras* (2 a year), *Revista de Faculdade de Direito* (2 a year)

DIRECTORS

Agriculture: AMADEU BONA FILHO
Applied Social Sciences: LUIZ VAMBERTO DE SANTANA
Biological Sciences: MARCIA HELENA MENDONÇA
Exact Sciences: SILVIA HELENA SOARES SCWAB
Law: LUIZ ALBERTO MACHADO
Earth Sciences: SILVIO ROGÉRIO CORREA DE FREITAS
Education: SERLEI MARIA FISCHER RANZI
Health Sciences: ROGÉRIO ANDRADE MULINARI
Humanities, Letters and Arts: JOSÉ BORGES NETO
Technical School: ALÍPIO SANTOS LEAL NETO
Technology: MAURO LACERDA SANTOS FILHO

UNIVERSIDADE ESTADUAL DO OESTE DO PARANÁ

Rua Universitária 1619, CP 801, 85814-110 Cascavel, PR
Telephone: (45) 224-5353

Fax: (45) 225-4590
Internet: www.unioeste.br
Founded 1987
State control
Rector: ERNELDO SCHALLENBERGER
Library: Libraries with 50,000 vols, 741 periodicals
Number of teachers: 393
Number of students: 5,996.

UNIVERSIDADE DE PASSO FUNDO

Bairro São José, CP 566, 99001-970 Passo Fundo, RS
Telephone: (54) 316-8100
Fax: (54) 311-1307
E-mail: cominfor@upf.tche.br
Internet: www.upf.tche.br
Founded 1968
Private control
Academic year: March to November (two semesters)
Rector: Pe. ELYDO ALCIDES GUARESCHI
Vice-Rector (Academic): LORIVAN FISCH DE FIGUEIREDO
Vice-Rector (Administrative): Prof. ILMO SANTOS
Vice-Rector (Research and Extension): TANIA M. K. RÖSING
Registrar: Prof. LUIS DE CESARO
Librarian: WLADEMIR PINTO
Number of teachers: 839
Number of students: 11,409

DIRECTORS

School of Education: Prof. SELINA MARIA DAL MORO
School of Physical Education: Prof. CARLOS RICARDO SCHLEMMER
School of Economics and Administration: Prof. ACIOLY RÖSING
School of Law: Prof. LUIZ J. NOGUEIRA DE AZEVEDO
School of Engineering: Prof. LUIZ FERNANDO PRESTES
School of Agronomy: Prof. WALTER BOLLER
School of Dentistry: Prof. RUI GETÚLIO SOARES
School of Medicine: Prof. LUIZ SÉRGIO DE MOURA FRAGOMENI
Institute of Philosophy and Humanities: Prof. TELISA GRAEFF
Institute of Biological Sciences: Prof. LORENA GEIB
Institute of Exact and Geosciences: Prof. GERALDO HALLWASS
Institute of Arts: Profa MARIA C. DE BRITTO RAMOS

UNIVERSIDADE PAULISTA

Rua Dr Bacelar 1212, Mirandópolis, 04026-002 São Paulo, SP
Telephone: (11) 5071-8000
Fax: (11) 275-1541
Internet: www.unip-objetivo.br
Founded 1988
Private control
Rector: JOÃO CARLOS DI GENIO
Library of 248,000 vols, 3,300 periodicals
Number of teachers: 2,519
Number of students: 57,064.

UNIVERSIDADE DO OESTE PAULISTA

Rua José Bongiovani 700, Cidade Universitária, CP 1161, 19050-900 Presidente Prudente, SP
Telephone: (18) 221-0666
Fax: (18) 221-0200
Internet: www.unoeste.br
Founded 1972
Private control
Rector: AGRIPINO DE OLIVEIRA LIMA FILHO
Library of 74,000 vols, 43,000 periodicals
Number of teachers: 614
Number of students: 13,744.

UNIVERSIDADE PARA O DESENVOLVIMENTO DO ESTADO E DA REGIÃO DO PANTANAL

Rua Ceará 333, 79003-010 Campo Grande, MS
Telephone: (67) 741-9080
Fax: (67) 741-9210
Internet: www.uniderp.br
Founded 1996
State control
Rector: PEDRO CHAVES DOS SANTOS FILHO
Library: Libraries with 100,000 vols, 1,656 periodicals
Number of teachers: 236
Number of students: 5,111.

UNIVERSIDADE CATÓLICA DE PELOTAS

Rua Félix da Cunha 412, CP 402, 96010-000 Pelotas, RS
Telephone: (53) 284-8000
Fax: (53) 225-3105
E-mail: ucpel@phoenix.ucpel.tche.br
Internet: www.ucpel.tche.br
Founded 1960
Private control
Language of instruction: Portuguese
Academic year: February to December
Chancellor: Dom JAYME HENRIQUE CHEMELLO
Rector: Prof. ALENCAR MELLO PROENÇA
Pro-Rector (Undergraduate): Profa Dra MYRIAM SIQUIERA DA CUNHA
Pro-Rector (Administrative): Cont. CARLOS RICARDO GASS SINNOTT
Pro-Rector (Postgraduate, Research and Extension): Prof. Dr WILLIAM PERES
Library of 91,563 vols
Number of teachers: 443
Number of students: 6,189

DIRECTORS

School of Economics and Business: Prof. RENATO LUIS TAVARES DE OLIVEIRA
School of Education: Profa PAULO DOMINGUES MIERES CARUSO
School of Engineering and Architecture: Prof. DELMAR BROGLIO CARVALHO
School of Environmental Sciences: Profa CLARISSE SIQUEIRA COELHO
School of Informatics: Profa RENATA HAX SANDER REISER
School of Law: Prof. RUBENS BELLORA
School of Medicine: Prof. RENATO AZEVEDO DA SILVA
School of Pharmacy and Biochemistry: Profa IRACI DE LOURDES PACHOLSKI
School of Psychology: Prof. RICARDO AZEVEDO DA SILVA
School of Social Communication: Prof. ANTÔNIO LUIZ OLIVEIRA HEBERLÊ
School of Social Services: Prof. VINI RABASSA SA SILVA

ATTACHED INSTITUTES

Higher Institute of Philosophy: Dir Frei AGEMIR BAVARESCO.

Higher Institute of Theology: Dir Pe ANTONIO REGES BRASIL.

Institute of Religious Culture: Dir Pe ANTONIO REGES BRASIL.

UNIVERSIDADE FEDERAL DE PELOTAS

Campus Universitário s/n, CP 354, 96010-900 Pelotas, RS
Telephone: (53) 3275-7104
Fax: (53) 3275-9023
E-mail: reitor@ufpel.edu.br
Internet: www.ufpel.edu.br
Founded 1883 as Imperial Escola de Medicina Veterinária e de Agricultura Prática; present name 1969
State control
Academic year: March to December
Rector: Dr ANTONIO CESAR GONÇALVES BORGES
Vice-Rector: Dr TELMO PAGANA XAVIER
Pro-Rector (Administrative Affairs): Eng. FRANCISCO CARLOS GOMES LUZZARDI
Pro-Rector (Extension Services and Culture): Dr VITOR HUGO BORBA MANZKE
Pro-Rector (Planning and Developmental Affairs): Prof. ELIO PAULO ZONTA
Pro-Rector (Research and Graduate Studies): Dr ALCI ENIMAR LOECK
Pro-Rector (Undergraduate Studies): Dr LUIZ FERNANDO MINELLO
Number of teachers: 948
Number of students: 9,989
Publications: *Cadernos de Educação* (annually), *Dissertatio* (annually), *Expresso Extensão* (annually), *Histöria da Educação* (annually), *Jornal da UFPel* (monthly), *Revista Acadêmica de Medicina* (annually), *Revista Brasileira de Agrociência* (2 a year)

DIRECTORS

Faculty of Dentistry: Profa ANGELA MARIA ANTUNES NUNES
Faculty of Law: Prof. RENATO OSWALDO FLEISCHMANN
College of Agricultural Engineering: Prof. WOLMER BROD PERES
College of Agronomy: Prof. JOSÉ FRANCISCO GOMES SCHILD
College of Architecture and Urban Planning: Profa NIRCE SAFFER MEDVEDOVSKI
College of Education: Prof. AVELINO DA ROSA OLIVEIRA
College of Home Economics: Profa TÂNIA ELISA MORALES GARCIA
College of Medicine: Prof. FARID IUNAN NADER
College of Meteorology: Prof. JOSÉ HONORATO DE OLIVEIRA FILHO
College of Nursing: Profa EMILIA NALVA FERREIRA DA SILVA
College of Nutrition: Prof. JOSÉ BEIRO CARVALHAL
College of Veterinary Medicine: Prof. MARIO CARLOS ARAÚJO MEIRELES
School of Music: Profa ISABEL PORTO NOGUEIRA
School of Physical Education: Profa TÂNIA BEATRIZ GAMBOA ARAÚJO MORSELLI
Institute of Biology: Prof. GLADIS AVER RIBEIRO
Institute of Chemistry and Geosciences: Prof. SÉRGIO LUIZ DOS SANTOS DO NASCIMENTO
Institute of Human Sciences: Prof. FABIO VERGARA CERQUEIRA
Institute of Arts and Design: Profa ANAIZI CRUZ ESPÍRITO SANTO
Institute of Physics and Mathematics: Prof. ALVARO LEONARDI AYALA FILHO
Institute of Social and Political Sciences: Prof. ALVARO AUGUSTO DE BORBA BARRETO
College of Letters: Prof. PAULO RICARDO SILVEIRA BORGES

UNIVERSIDADE CATÓLICA DE PERNAMBUCO

Rua do Príncipe 526, Boa Vista, 50050-900 Recife, PE
Telephone: (81) 216-4000
Fax: (81) 423-0541
E-mail: postmaster@unicap.br
Internet: www.unicap.br

Founded 1951
Private control
Academic year: February to December (two semesters)

Chancellor: Ferdinand Azevedo
Rector: Fr Theodoro Paulo Severino Peters
Pro-Rectors: Erhard Cholewa (Academic), Altamir Soares de Paula (Administrative), Profa Maria de Fatima da Rocha Breckenfeld (Community Relations)
Registrar: Maria Teresa Barreto de Melo Peretti
Librarian: Rosilda Miranda da Silva

Number of teachers: 575
Number of students: 13,353

Publication: *Symposium* (2 a year)

DEANS

Centre for Social Sciences: Profa Miriam de Sá Pereira
Centre for Sciences and Technology: Prof. Reginaldo Lourenço da Silva
Centre for Theology and Human Sciences: Prof. Junot Cornélio Matos

HEADS OF DEPARTMENTS

Centre for Theology and Human Sciences:
- Department of Theology: Fr Jacques Trudel
- Department of Philosophy: Prof. Karl-Heinz Efken
- Department of Education: Profa Maria Lúcia Cavalcanti Galindo
- Department of Psychology: Profa Maria Lúcia Cavalcanti Galindo
- Department of Language and Literature: Profa Rachel de Hollanda Costa
- Department of History: Profa Maria José Pinheiro

Centre for Sciences and Technology:
- Department of Mathematics: Prof. Nivaldo Pinheiro da Silva
- Department of Physics: Prof. Augusto Otávio Galvão de Lima
- Department of Chemistry: Prof. Antônio Helder Parente
- Department of Statistics and Information Science: Prof. Jessé Gomes de Oliveira
- Department of Engineering: Prof. José Orlando Vieira Filho
- Department of Biology: Prof. Bento Ferreira de Carvalho

Centre for Social Sciences:
- Department of Law: Profa Miriam de Sá Pereira
- Department of Sociology: Profa Davina Maria Guimarães Barros
- Department of Economics and Administration: Prof. Luís Eduardo Carvalheira de Mendonça
- Department of Social Communication: Prof. Paulo César Nunes Fradique
- Department of Geography: Prof. Luiz Ernani de Saboia Campos

UNIVERSIDADE FEDERAL DE PERNAMBUCO

Av. Prof. Moraes Rego 1235, Cidade Universitária, 50670-901 Recife, PE
Telephone: (81) 2126-8000
Fax: (81) 2126-8029
E-mail: gabinete@ufpe.br
Internet: www.ufpe.br

Founded 1946
Academic year: March to December

Rector: Prof. Amaro Henrique Pessoa Lins
Pro-Rector (Academic Affairs): Profa Lícia de Souza Leão Maia
Pro-Rector (Extension): Prof Anísio Brasiliero de Freitas Dourado
Pro-Rector (Personnel Administration and Quality of Life): Profa Ana Cristina Brito Arcoverde
Pro-Rector (Planning and General Co-ordination): Prof. Hermino Ramos de Souza
Pro-Rector (Research and Postgraduate Affairs): Prof. Celso Pinto de Melo

Library: see Libraries
Number of teachers: 1,739
Number of students: 23,200

Publications: *Boletim Oficial*, *Revista de Estudos Universitários*, *Incampus* (information bulletin, monthly)

DIRECTORS

Centre of Applied Social Sciences: Prof. Sérgio Alves de Sousa
Centre of Arts and Communication: Profa Vilma Maria Villarouco Santos
Centre of Biological Sciences: Profa Miriam Camargo Guarnieri
Centre of Exact and Natural Sciences: Prof. Alfredo Mayall Simas
Centre of Health Sciences: Prof. José Thadeu Pinheiro
Centre of Informatics: Profa Ana Carolina Brandão Salgado
Centre of Juridical Sciences: Profa Luciana Grassano de Gouvea Melo
Centre of Philosophy and Humanities: Profa Edvânia Torres Aguias Gomes
Education Centre: Prof. Sergio Paulino Abranches
Technology Centre: Prof. Edmilson Santos de Lima

HEADS OF DEPARTMENTS

Centre of Applied Social Sciences:
- Accountancy: Prof. Mário Hermínio Girard
- Administrative Sciences: Prof. Jairo Simião Dornelas
- Economics: Prof. André Matos Magalhães
- Social Service: Profa Maria Alexandra Monteiro Mustafá

Centre of Arts and Communication:
- Architecture and City Planning: Prof. Nehilde Tragano da Silva
- Art Theory and Artistic Expression: Prof. Dinauro Esteves Filho
- Art Theory–Painting: Prof. João Germano de Almeida Ponte
- Design: Prof. Hans da Nóbrega Waechter
- Literature: Prof. João Alfredo Modesto Sedycias
- Information Science: Profa Cecilia Maria Freire Physthon
- Music: Prof. Paulo Cristóvão de Lima
- Social Communication: Prof. Ari Luiz da Cruz

Centre of Biological Sciences:
- Anatomy: Profa Elizabeth da Silveira Neves
- Antibiotics: Profa Silene Carneiro do Nascimento
- Biochemistry: Profa Maria Tereza dos Santos Correia
- Biophysics and Radiobiology: Profa Claudia Sampaio de Andrade Lima
- Botany: (vacant)
- Genetics: Prof. José Ferreira dos Santos
- Histology and Embryology: Profa Eliete Cavalcanti da Silva
- Mycology: Profa Elza Aurea de Luna Alves Lima
- Physiology and Pharmacology: Profa Maria Bernadete de Souza Maia
- Zoology: Profa Luciana Iannuzzi

Centre of Exact and Natural Sciences:
- Chemistry: Prof. Flamarion Borges Diniz
- Mathematics: Prof. Marcus Vinicius de Medeiros Wanderley
- Physics: Prof. Mário Engelsberg
- Statistics: Profa Maria Cristina Falcão Raposo

Centre of Health Sciences:
- Clinical Medicine: Profa Jocelene Tenório Albuquerque Madruga Godoi
- Clinical and Preventive Odontology: Prof. Caetano Gomes da Silva
- Mother and Child Health: Prof. Sálvio Freire
- Neuro-Psychiatry: Prof. Osmar José Tavares Gouveia de Melo
- Nursing: Profa Maria das Graças Carvalho Barros
- Nutrition: Profa Emília Aureliano de Alencar Monteiro
- Occupational Therapy: Profa Valéria Moura Moreira Leite
- Pathology: Profa Ana Virgínia de Azevedo Guendler
- Pharmacy: Profa Jane Sheila Higino
- Physical Education: Prof. Rómulo de Araújo de Araújo Carneiro Cavalcanti de Lacerda Júnior
- Physiotherapy: Prof. Joaquim Sérgio de Lima Neto
- Prosthesis and Orofacial Surgery: Profa Lúcia Carneiro de Souza Beatrice
- Social Medicine: Prof. Oscar Bandeira Coutinho Neto
- Surgery: Prof. Silvio Romero de Barros Marques
- Tropical Medicine: Prof. Carlos Antônio de Carvalho Arcoverde

Centre of Informatics:
- Computer Science: Prof. Sergio Vanderlei Cavalcante
- Computer Systems: Prof. André Luis de Madeiros
- Information and Systems: Profa Hermana Perrelli de Moura

Centre of Juridical Sciences:
- General and Procedural Law: Profa Dalva Rodrigues Bezerra de almeida
- General Theory of Law and Private Law: Profa Fabíola Santos Albuquerque
- Public Law: Prof. Edson José da Silva

Centre of Philosophy and Humanities:
- Geography: Prof. Aldemir Dantas Barboza
- History: Prof. Severino Vicente da Silva
- Philosophy: Prof. Washington Luiz Martins da Silva
- Psychology: Profa Jorge Tarcísio Da Rocha Falcão
- Social Sciences: Profa Russell Parry Scott

Education Centre:
- Psychology and Educational Orientation: Profa Ana Coelho Vieira Selva
- School Administration and Educational Planning: Prof. Darci Barbosa Lira de Melo
- Socio-Philosophic Bases of Education: Prof. Geraldo Barroso Filho
- Teaching Methods and Techniques: Profa Gilda Lisboa Guimarães

Technology Centre:
- Cartographical Engineering: Prof. Adeildo Antão dos Santos
- Chemical Engineering: Profa Yeda Medeiros Bastos de Oliveira
- Civil Engineering: Profa Suzana Maria Gico Lima Montenegro
- Geology: Prof. Valdir do Amaral Vaz Manso

Electrical Engineering and Potential Systems: Prof. RONALDO RIBEIRO BARBOSA DE AQUINO
Electronics and Systems: Prof. ANTÓNIO JERÓNIMO BELFORT DE OLIVEIRA
Mechanical Engineering: Profa IVAN VIEIRA DE MELO
Mining Engineering: Prof. DORIVAL DE CARVALHO PINTO
Nuclear Energy: Prof. ANTÔNIO CELSO DANTAS ANTONINO
Oceanography: Prof. MOACYR CUNHA DE ARAÚJO FILHO
Production Engineering: Prof. ENRIQUE ANDRÉS LOPEZ DROGUETT

UNIVERSIDADE FEDERAL RURAL DE PERNAMBUCO

CP 2071, Rua D. Manoel de Medeiros s/n, Dois Irmãos, 52171-900 Recife, PE
Telephone: (81) 3302-1001
Fax: (81) 3302-1004
E-mail: reitoria@ufrpe.br
Internet: www.ufrpe.br
Founded 1912
Federal control
Language of instruction: Portuguese
Rector: EMÍDIO CANTÍDIO DE OLIVEIRA FILHO
Vice-Rector: VALMER CORRÊA DE ANDRADE
Administrative Officer: LUCIANO DE AZEVEDO SUARCO NETO
Librarian: NANCI DE OLIVEIRA TOLEDO
Library of 55,947 vols
Number of teachers: 497
Number of students: 6,921
Publications: *Caderno Ômega* (irregular), *Anais* (annually)

HEADS OF DEPARTMENTS

Agronomy: CLODOALDO JOSÉ DA ANUNCIAÇÃO FILHO
Veterinary Medicine: TOMOE NODA SAUKAS
Animal Husbandry: LUIZ GONZAGA DA PAZ
Fishery: ISABEL CRISTINA DE SÁ MARINHO
Education: FRANCISCO FERREIRA DA ROCHA
Domestic Science: CARLA SUELY VITA BEZERRA SANTIAGO
Physics and Mathematics: ALEXANDRE JOSÉ DE MEDEIROS
Chemistry: MARTHA MARIA ANDRADE PESSOA
Biology: MARCELO DE ATAÍDE SILVA
Morphology: ARMANDO JOSÉ RIBEIRO SAMICO
Letters and Humanities: EXPEDITO BANDEIRA DE ARAÚJO
Rural Technology: CLARIVALDO GERMANO DA COSTA
'Dom Agostinho Ikas' Grade 2 College: RICARDO WAGNER DE GUIMARÃES ROCHA

FUNDAÇÃO UNIVERSIDADE DE PERNAMBUCO

Av. Agamenon Magalhães s/n, Santo Amaro, CP 3447, 50100-010 Recife, PE
Telephone: (81) 421-3111
Fax: (81) 423-2248
E-mail: upe@recife.upe.br
Internet: www.upe.br
Founded 1965
President: Prof. HINDENBURG T. LEMOS
Vice-President: Prof. GUSTAVO A. M. TRINDADE HENRIQUES
Rector: Prof. JÚLIO FERNANDO PESSOA CORREIA
Vice-Rector: Prof. EMANUEL DIAS DE OLIVEIRA E SILVA
Administrative Pro-Rector: Prof. ANDRÉ JORGE DE BARROS E SILVA
Pro-Rector (Postgraduate, Research and Extension): Prof. ANTONIO GILDO PAES GALINDO
Pro-Rector (Planning): Prof. CARLOS MAGNO PADILHA CURSINO
Pro-Rector (Undergraduates): Prof. VALDEMAR VIEIRA DE MELO
Librarian: LÍDIA PONTUAL
Library of 8,000 vols, 8,302 periodicals (390 titles)
Number of teachers: 879
Number of students: 11,928 (10,968 undergraduate, 350 postgraduate, 610 extension)

DIRECTORS

Faculty of Medicine: Prof. JOSÉ GUIDO CORREIA DE ARAÚJO
Faculty of Administrative Sciences: Prof. ARANDI MACIEL CAMPELO
Faculty of Dentistry: Prof. JOSÉ RICARDO DIAS PEREIRA
School of Nursing: Profa KÁTIA REJANE VERGUEIRO CÉSAR
School of Physical Education: Prof. RENATO MEDEIROS DE MORAES
Polytechnic: Prof. ARMANDO CARNEIRO P. REGO FILHO
Institute of Biological Sciences: Prof. CARLOS ROBERTO DA SILVA
Oswaldo Cruz University Hospital: Dr ÊNIO LUSTOSA CANTARELLI
Amaury de Medeiros Integrated Health Centre: Dr ARINALDO VASCONCELOS DE ALENCAR
Faculty of Teacher Training (in Garanhuns): Prof. LUIZ TENÓRIO DE CARVALHO
Faculty of Teacher Training (in Petrolina): Prof. JOAQUIM SILVA E SANTANA
Faculty of Teacher Training (in Nazaré da Mata): Prof. LUIZ INTERAMINENSE

UNIVERSIDADE CATÓLICA DE PETRÓPOLIS

Rua Benjamin Constant 213, Centro, CP 90944, 25621-970 Petrópolis, RJ
Telephone: (24) 237-5062
Fax: (24) 242-7747
E-mail: reitoria@risc.ucp.br
Internet: www.ucp.br
Founded 1961
Private control
Academic year: February to December
Rector: Profa MARIA DA GLÓRIA RANGEL SAMPAIO FERNANDES
Vice-Rector: Prof. Dr GETÚLIO CHEHAB
Chief Administrative Officer: Prof. PEDRO RUBENS PANTOLA DE CARVALHO
Registrar: LUIZ HERIQUE SCHAEFFER
Librarian: MARIA DAS NEVES FRANCA LEITE KRÜGER
Number of teachers: 266
Number of students: 3,390
Publications: *Informativo UCP* (6 a year), *Revista UCP* (3 a year), *O Communitário* (monthly)

DIRECTORS

Faculty of Law: Prof. LINDOLPHO DE MORAES MARINHO
Faculty of Economics, Accounting and Administration: Prof. CELSO PERMÍNIO SCHIMID
Faculty of Education: Profa SANDRA TEREZA LA CAVA DE ALMEIDA AMADO
School of Engineering: Prof. RICARDO GRECHI PACHECO
School of Rehabilitation: Prof. GERSON DE AGUIAR LOUREIRO
Institute of Theology, Philosophy and Human Science: Prof. ALFREDO AUGUSTO GARCIA QUESADA
Institute of Exact and Natural Sciences: Prof. GUILHERME CRISTÓVÃO NICODEMUS
Institute of Arts and Communication: Profa RUTH M. RANGEL SAMPAIO FERNANDES
Rehabilitation School: Prof. GERSON DE AGUIAR LOUREIRO

UNIVERSIDADE ESTADUAL DO PIAUÍ

Rua João Cabral s/n, Pirajá, 64002-550 Teresina, PI
Telephone: (86) 213-5195
Fax: (86) 213-2733
Internet: www.uespi.br
Founded 1985
State control
Rector: JONATHAS DE BARROS NUNES
Library: Libraries with 59,000 vols, 5,050 periodicals
Number of teachers: 359
Number of students: 7,001.

UNIVERSIDADE FEDERAL DO PIAUÍ

Campus Universitário, Bairro Ininga, 64049-550 Teresina, PI
Telephone: (86) 232-1212
Fax: (86) 232-2816
E-mail: ufpinet@ufpi.br
Internet: www.ufpi.br
Founded 1968
Controlled by the Fundação Universidade Federal do Piauí
Academic year: March to November
Rector: PEDRO LEOPOLDINO FERREIRA FILHO
Vice-Rector (vacant)
Administrative Director: FRANCISCO JOACY SAMPAIO
Librarian: MARGARETH DE LUCENA MARTINS LIMA
Library of 88,617 vols
Number of teachers: 1,104
Number of students: 11,612
Publication: *Notícias da FUFPI* (monthly)

DIRECTORS

Health Sciences: NATHAN PORTELLA NUNES
Natural Sciences: ANTONIO MACEDO SANTANA
Human Sciences and Letters: JOSÉ DE RIBAMAR FREITAS
Educational Sciences: MARIANO DA SILVA NETO
Technology: RAFAEL V. DO REGO MONTEIRO
Agrarian Sciences: ANTONIO M. G. E. ALMENDRA CASTELO BRANCO FILHO

HEADS OF DEPARTMENTS

Health Sciences:
- Specialized Medicine: WILTON MENDES DA SILVA
- Community Medicine: ANTONIO J. CASTRO AGUIAR
- General Clinic: ANTÔNIO DE DEUS FILHO
- Pathological and Clinical Dentistry: JOSÉ RESENDE LEITE
- Restorative Dentistry: CANDIDA FORTES DA COSTA MENESES
- Nursing: MARIA HELENA BARROS DE ARAÚJO LUZ
- Physical Education: CONRADO NOGUEIRA BARROS
- Mother and Child Care: TERESINHA DAS GRAÇAS DE OLIVEIRA FORTES

Natural Sciences:
- Mathematics: MARIO LUCIO DA COSTA FERREIRA
- Physics: MÔNICA M. MACHADA R. N. CASTRO
- Chemistry: JOSÉ A. DANTAS LAGES
- Biology: ROSA MARIA DA SILVA ARAÚJO
- Biomedical Sciences: ANA ZÉLIA CORREIA L. C. BRANCO

Human Sciences and Letters:
- Law: PEDRO DE ALCÂNTARA FERREIRA TEIXEIRA
- Social Sciences: MAURINO MEDEIROS DE SANTANA
- Letters: CATARINA DE SENA S. MENDES DA COSTA
- Geography and History: MARIA DO SOCORRO ALMEIDA WAQUIM

Philosophy: FRANCISCA MENDES DE SOUSA
Administration and Economics: PRETEXTATO S. Q. GOMES DE OLIVEIRA MELLO

Educational Sciences:
Educational Foundations: CONCEIÇÃO DE MARIA BOAVISTA DE OLIVEIRA
Methods and Techniques of Teaching: LEONTINA P. LOPES DE MENDONÇA
Practical Arts: MARIA DE JESUS SILVA
Artistic Education: MÁRCIA ALVES SEMENTE

Technology:
Civil Construction: AMAURI RIBEIRO BARBOSA
Structures: MARIA DE LOURDES TEIXEIRA MOREIRA
Transportation: ANTÔNIO DE ABREU LOPES
Hydrology and Applied Geology: JOSE GERALDO DE OLIVEIRA FERRO

Agrarian Sciences:
Agricultural Engineering and Soil Science: ADEODATO ARI CAVALCANTE SALVIANO
Phytotechnology: FRANCISCO RODRIGUES LEAL
Zootechnology: MARIA DE NAZARÉ BONA DE ALENCAR ARARIPE
Agricultural Planning and Policy: VICENTE PAULO GOMES
Veterinary Morphology: MARIA ACELINA MARTINS DE CARVALHO
Veterinary and Surgery Clinic: ANTONIO FRANCISCO DE SOUSA

UNIVERSIDADE METODISTA DE PIRACICABA

Rua Rangel Pestana 762, CP 68, 13400-901 Piracicaba, SP
Telephone: (19) 3124-1528
Fax: (19) 3124-1500
E-mail: unimep@unimep.br
Internet: www.unimep.br

Founded 1975
Private control
Languages of instruction: Portuguese, Spanish
Academic year: March to December

President: GUSTAVO JACQUES DIAS ALVIM
Vice-President (Administrative): ARSENIO FIRMINO NOVÃES NETO
Vice-President (Academic): SERGIO MARCUS PINTO LOPES
Registrar: ENIO TRIERVAILER
Librarian: REGINA FRACETO

Library of 360,000 vols
Number of teachers: 680
Number of students: 15,000

Publications: *Revista de Ciência e Tecnologia* (science and technology), *Impulso* (humanities and social sciences), *Revista Brasileira de Educação Especial* (special education), *Saúde em Revista* (health sciences), *Revista de Odontologia* (dental medicine), *Cadernos de Direito* (law)

DIRECTORS

School of Health Sciences: Prof. OLNEY L. FONTES
School of Law: Prof. JOÃO MIGUEL RIVERO
School of Business and Mangement: Prof. DORGIVAL HENRIQUE
School of Human Sciences: Profa THEREZA B. F. SANTOS
School of Engineering, Architecture and Urban Studies: Prof. GILBERTO MARTINS
School of Natural and Computer Sciences: Profa ANGELA MARIA CORREA
School of Dental Medicine: Prof. CARLOS W. WERNER
School of Communication: Prof. BELARMINO CESAR COSTA
School of Religious Studies: (vacant)

UNIVERSIDADE ESTADUAL DE PONTA GROSSA

Av Carlos Cavalcanti 4748, Campus de Uvaranas, 84030-900 Ponta Grossa, PR
Telephone: (42) 220-3232
Fax: (42) 220-3233
E-mail: uepg@uepg.br
Internet: www.uepg.br

Founded 1970
Academic year: March to November

Rector: PAULO ROBERTO GODOY
Vice-Rector: ÍTALO SÉRGIO GRANDE
Pro-Rector (Administrative Affairs): CARLOS LUCIANO SANT'ANA VARGAS
Pro-Rector (Undergraduate): CÂNDIDA LEONOR MIRANDA
Pro-Rector (Research and Graduate): ALTAIR JUSTINO
Pro-Rector (Extension and Cultural Affairs): CARLOS ROBERTO BERGER
Librarian: MARIA LUIZA FERNANDES BERTHOLINO

Number of teachers: 721
Number of students: 11,408

Publications: *Uniletras Review* (annually), *General Catalogue* (annually), *Biological Sciences and Health Review* (4 a year), *Exact and Earth Sciences, Agriculture and Engineering Sciences Review* (3 a year), *Human Sciences, Applied Social Sciences, Linguistics, Letters and Art Review* (2 a year), *UPEG em Números* (2 a year), *Social Emancipation Review* (annually), *Teacher Eyes Review* (annually), *Regional History Review* (2 a year)

DIRECTORS

Sector of Applied Social Sciences: Prof. SILAS GUIMARÃES MORO
Sector of Exact and Natural Sciences: Prof. JOÃO ALFREDO MADALOZO
Sector of Letters and Human Sciences: Prof. GRACIETE TOZETTO GÓES
Sector of Biological Sciences and Health: Prof. ELIAS ZAHI FADEL
Sector of Agricultural Science and Technology: Prof. VICTOR GEORGE CELINSKI

HEADS OF DEPARTMENTS

Mathematics and Statistics: Prof. JOSÉ TADEU TELES LUNARDI
Physics: Prof. FRANCISCO CARLOS SERBENA
Chemistry: JESUAN HENRIQUE RUPEL
Geosciences: GILSON BURIGO GUIMARÃES
Civil Engineering: NADIM BACHOUR SALLOUM
Materials Engineering: OSVALDO MITSUYUKI CINTHO
Agricultural Engineering and Soil Sciences: ANDRÉ BELMONT PEREIRA
Phytotechnology: DAVID DE SOUZA JACCOUD FILHO
Zootechnics: SÉRGIO ROBERTO POSTIGLIONI
Food Technology: IVO MOTTIN DEMIATE
Computer Science: FREDERICO GUILHERME DE PAULA FERREIRA IELO
Biology: ROSEMERI SEGECIN MORO
Structural and Molecular Biology, Genetics: MARIA CRISTINA DE ALMEIDA MATIELLO
Dentistry: EDISON DO ROCIO MEISTER
Pharmacy Sciences: FABIANI POSTIGLIONI MANSANI PEREIRA
Clinical and Toxicological Analysis: ANDRÉA TIMÓTEO DOS SANTOS
Education: ELIZABETH SILVEIRA SCHMIDT
Economics: HERMES YUKIO HIGACHI
Administration: SÉRGIO ESCORSIN
Accounting: JOANI ALVES FERREIRA
History: NILTONCI BATISTA CHAVES
Modern Foreign Languages: MARIA RUTH FERREIRA SCALISE TAQUES FONSECA
Vernacular Languages (Languages and Corresponding Literatures): FRUTOSO DREHER SIMÕES
Teaching Methods: PAULO ROGÉRIO MORO
Social Service: JOSIANE DE FÁTIMA WAMBIER
Physical Education: CONSTANTINO RIBEIRO DE OLIVEIRA
Communication: MARCELO ENGEL BRONOSKI
State Law: ANA MARIA BUSATO DE LIMA
Processual Law: DIRCÉIA MOREIRA
Social Relations Law: ALCÍDIO SOARES JUNIOR
Tourism: MARIA AUGUSTA PEREIRA JORGE

ATTACHED INSTITUTE

Augusto Ribas Agricultural High School: Av. Carlos Cavalcanti 4748, Campus de Uvaranas; Principal VERA MÁRCIA MESSIAS.

Centro de Atenção Integral à Criança e ao Adolescente: Av. Carlos Cavalcanti 4748, Campus de Uvaranas; Principal MARY ANGELA TEIXEIRA BRANDALISE.

UNIVERSIDADE POTIGUAR

Av. Sen. Salgado Filho 1610, Lagoa Nova, 59056-000 Natal, RN
Telephone: (84) 215-1209
Fax: (84) 215-1204
E-mail: proacad@unp.com.br
Internet: www.unp.br

Founded 1981
Private control

Rector: MIZAEL ARAÚJO BARRETO

Library of 32,000 vols, 241 periodicals
Number of teachers: 249
Number of students: 5,813.

UNIVERSIDADE DE RIBEIRÃO PRETO

Av. Costabile Romano 2201, Ribeirania, CP 0098, 14096-380 Ribeirão Preto, SP
Telephone: (16) 627-3300
Fax: (16) 627-5035
Internet: www.unaerp.br

Founded 1985
Private control

Rector: ELMARA LUCIA DE OLIVEIRA BONINI CORAUCI

Library of 96,000 vols, 796 periodicals
Number of teachers: 399
Number of students: 7,479.

UNIVERSIDADE DO RIO GRANDE

Rua Eng. Alfredo Huch 475, CP 474, 96201-900 Rio Grande, RS
Telephone: (532) 31-1990
Fax: (532) 32-3346
E-mail: reitor03@super.furg.br
Internet: www.furg.br

Founded 1969
State control
Language of instruction: Portuguese
Academic year: March to November

Rector: CARLOS ALBERTO EIRAS GARCIA
Vice-Rector: Prof. VICENTE MARIANO PIAS
Chief Administrative Officer: Eng. CARLOS KALIKOWSKI WESKA
Librarian: MARIA DA CONCEIÇÃO DE LIMA HOHMANN

Library of 75,000 vols
Number of teachers: 647
Number of students: 4,722

HEADS OF DEPARTMENTS

Mathematics: Prof. NÉLSON LOPES DUARTE FILHO
Physics: Prof. CARLOS ALBERTO EIRAS GARCIA
Chemistry: Prof. SÉRGIO MENDONÇA GIESTA
Geosciences: Prof. HELEM MARIA VIEIRA
Literature and Arts: Prof. CLÁUDIO GABIATTI
Economics: Prof. JOSÉ VANDERLEI SILVA BORBA
Juridical Sciences: Prof. JOÃO MORENO POMAR

Materials and Construction: Prof. HUMBERTO CAMARGO PICCOLI
Librarianship and History: Prof. HENRIQUETA GRACIELA DORFMANN DE CUARTAS
Education and Behavioural Sciences: Profa DORILDA GROLLI
Oceanography: Prof. LUIZ CARLOS KRUG
Surgery: Prof. NILO CARDOSO DORA
Mother and Child Health: Prof. ANTONIO SAMIR BERTACO
Internal Medicine: Prof. LUIS SUAREZ HALTY
Morphology and Biological Sciences: Prof. JOÃO RENAN SILVA DE FREITAS
Physiology: Prof. FERNANDO AMARANTE SILVA
Pathology: Prof. IVO GOMES DE MATTOS

UNIVERSIDADE FEDERAL DO RIO GRANDE DO NORTE

Campus Universitário, BR 101, Lagoa Nova, CP 59072-970 Natal, RN
Telephone: (84) 215-3125
Fax: (84) 215-3131
E-mail: gabinete@reitoria.ufrn.br
Internet: www.ufrn.br
Founded 1958
Federal control
Language of instruction: Portuguese
Academic year: March to December
Rector: JOSÉ IVONILDO DO RÊGO
Vice-Rector: NILSEN CARVALHO FERNANDES DE OLIVEIRA FILHO
Librarian: RILDECI MEDEIROS
Number of teachers: 1,679
Number of students: 27,605

DEANS
Undergraduate Studies: ANTÔNIO CABRAL NETO
Research: ANANIAS MONTEIRO MARIZ
Graduate Studies: EDNA MARIA DA SILVA
Extension Programmes: ILZA ARAÚJO LEÃO DE ANDRADE
Human Resources: JOÃO CARLOS TENÓRIO ARGOLO
Administration: LUIZ PEDRO DE ARAÚJO
Planning and General Co-ordination: OSWALDO HAJIME YAMAMOTO

DIRECTORS
Centre for Earth and Exact Sciences: Prof. JAZIEL MARTINS SÁ
Centre of Humanities, Letters and Arts: Prof. MÁRCIO MORAES VALENÇA
Centre of Technology: Prof. MANOEL LUCAS FILHO
Centre of Applied Social Sciences: Profa MARIA ARLETE DUARTE DE ARAÚJO
Centre of Biosciences: Prof. RANKE DOS SANTOS SILVA
Centre of Health Sciences: Prof. JUAREZ DA COSTA FERREIRA

UNIVERSIDADE ESTADUAL DO RIO GRANDE DO NORTE

Rua Almino Afonso 478, Centro, CP 70, 59610-210 Mossoró, RN
Telephone: (84) 316-2997
Fax: (84) 316-2770
Internet: www.uern.br
Founded 1968
State control
Rector: Prof. JOSÉ WALTER DA FONSÊCA
Chief Administrative Officer: Profa IÊDA MARIA ARAÚJO CHAVES FREITAS
Librarian: ELVIRA FERNANDES DE ARAÚJO
Number of teachers: 400
Number of students: 5,300
Publications: *Expressão* (2 a year), *Contexto* (2 a year), *Terra e Sal* (2 a year)

DEANS
Faculty of Economic Science: Profa ELIZABETH SILVA VEIGA
Faculty of Social Service: Profa ZÉLIA MARIA RODRIGUES M. VASCONCELAS
Faculty of Arts: Prof. GILBERTO DE OLIVEIRA SILVA
Faculty of Education: Profa MARIA DAS DORES LOPES DE PAIVA
Faculty of Philosophy and Social Science: Prof. WILSON BEZERRA DE MOURA
Faculty of Nursing: Profa MARIA DAS GRAÇAS ALVES DE LIMA
Faculty of Natural and Physical Science: Prof. FRANCISCO VALDOMIRO DE MORAIS
Faculty of Law: Profa MARIA HÉLDERI QUEIRÓZ DIÓGENES NEGREIROS
Faculty of Physical Education: Prof. ANTÔNIO DE PÁDUA LOPEZ ALVES

PONTIFÍCIA UNIVERSIDADE CATÓLICA DO RIO GRANDE DO SUL

Av. Ipiranga 6681, Partenon, CP 1429, 90619-900 Porto Alegre, RS
Telephone: (51) 3320-3500
Fax: (51) 3339-1564
E-mail: gabreit@pucrs.br
Internet: www.pucrs.br
Founded 1948
Private control
Academic year: March to December
Chancellor: Dom DADEUS GRINGS
Rector: Prof. Ir. NORBERTO FRANCISCO RAUCH
Pro-Rectors: Prof. ANTONIO MARIO PASCUAL BIANCHI (Administration), Profa HELENA WILLHELM DE OLIVEIRA (Community Affairs), Prof. Dr Mons. URBANO ZILLES (Research and Graduate Studies), Profa Dra SOLANGE MEDINA KETZER (Undergraduate Studies), Prof. Dr PAULO ROBERTO GIRARDELLO FRANCO (University Extension)
Head of Administration: Prof. MARIO HAMILTON VILELA
Director of Uruguaiana campus: Profa MARIA DE LOURDES SOUZA VILLELA
Librarian: Prof. CÉSAR AUGUSTO MAZZILLO
Number of teachers: 1,896
Number of students: 33,000
Publications: *Agenda PUCRS* (monthly), *Analise* (2 a year), *Anuário* (annually), *Biociências* (2 a year), *Brasil* (2 a year), *Direito e Justiça* (2 a year), *Educação* (2 a year), *Estudos Ibero-Americanos* (2 a year), *Hífen* (2 a year), *Letras de Hoje* (4 a year), *Mundo Jovem* (monthly), *Odontociência* (2 a year), *Psico* (2 a year), *Revista da FAMECOS* (2 a year), *Revista de Medicina da PUCRS* (4 a year), *Teocomunicação* (4 a year), *Veritas* (4 a year)

DIRECTORS
Faculty of Administration, Accountancy and Computer Science (Uruguaiana campus): Prof. Me. CLEITON TAMBELLINI BORGES
Faculty of Administration, Accountancy and Economics: Prof. JORGE ALBERTO FRANZONI
Faculty of Aeronautical Sciences: Profa Me. MARIA REGINA DE MORAES XAUSA
Faculty of Architecture and Urbanization: Prof. IVAN GILBERTO BORGES MIZOGUCHI
Faculty of Biosciences: Profa Me. CLARICE PRADE CARVALHO
Faculty of Chemistry: Prof. Me. ASSIS PEDRO PERIN PICCINI
Faculty of Computer Science: Profa Dra VERA LÚCIA STRUBE DE LIMA
Faculty of Dentistry: Prof. JOÃO MIGUEL MESSINA DA CRUZ
Faculty of Education: Profa Me. MARIA WALESKA CRUZ
Faculty of Engineering: Prof. Me. EDUARDO GIUGLIANI
Faculty of Law: Prof. ATTILA SÁ D'OLIVEIRA
Faculty of Law (Uruguaiana campus): Prof. ROBERTO DURO GICK
Faculty of Letters and Arts: Profa Dra REGINA ZILBERMANN
Faculty of Mathematics: Profa ALAYDES SANT'ANNA BIANCHI
Faculty of Medicine: Prof. Dr LUIZ CARLOS BODANESE
Faculty of Nursing, Nutrition and Physiotherapy: Profa Me. BEATRIZ SEBBEN OJEDA
Faculty of Pharmacy: Prof. Dr SÉRGIO DE MEDA LAMB
Faculty of Philosophy and Sciences: Prof. Dr THADEU WEBER
Faculty of Philosophy, Sciences and Letters (Uruguaiana campus): Profa MARIA DE LOURDES SOUZA VILLELA
Faculty of Physical Education and Sport Sciences: Prof. Dr FRANCISCO CAMARGO NETTO
Faculty of Physics: Profa Me. MARIA EMILIA BALTAR BERNASIUK
Faculty of Psychology: Profa Me. JACQUELINE POERSCH MOREIRA
Faculty of Social Communications: Prof. JERÔNIMO CARLOS SANTOS BRAGA
Faculty of Social Service: Profa Dra JUSSARA MARIA ROSA MENDES
Faculty of Theology: Prof. Dr Pe. GERALDO LUIZ BORGES HACKMANN
Faculty of Zootechnics, Veterinary Science and Agronomy (Uruguaiana campus): Prof. DOUGLAS DE MENDONÇA THOMPSON

UNIVERSIDADE FEDERAL DO RIO GRANDE DO SUL

Av. Paulo Gama 110, 90046-900 Porto Alegre, RS
Telephone: (51) 3316-3601
Fax: (51) 3316-3973
E-mail: relinter@ufrgs.br
Internet: www.ufrgs.br
Founded 1934
Federal control
Language of instruction: Portuguese
Academic year: March to November
Rector: Profa WRANA MARIA PANIZZI
Vice-Rector: Prof. JOSÉ CARLOS FERRAZ HENNEMANN
Pro-Rector (Undergraduate Studies): NORBERTO HOPEN
Pro-Rector (Research): Prof. CARLOS ALEXANDRE NETTO
Pro-Rector (Graduate Studies): Profa JOCELIA GRAZIA
Pro-Rector (Planning and Administration) and Secretary for Technological Development: Profa MARIA ALICE LAHORGUE
Pro-Rector (Human Resources): Prof. DIMITRIOS SAMIOS
Pro-Rector (Extension): Prof. FERNANDO MEIRELLES
Pro-Rector (Infrastructure): Prof. HELIO HENKIN
Pro-Rector, and Secretary for Institutional and International Affairs: Profa SILVIA ROCHA (acting)
Pro-Rector and Secretary for Student Affairs: Prof. ANGELO RONALDO PEREIRA DA SILVA (acting)
Registrar: ANDREA BENITES
Librarian: REJANE RAFFO KLAES
Number of teachers: 2,258
Number of students: 29,117 (22,138 undergraduate, 6,979 postgraduate)
Publications: *Caderno de Farmácia* (pharmacy, 2 a year), *Revista da Faculdade de Odontologia* (dentistry, 2 a year), *Revista Movimento* (sports, 2 a year), *Revista Gaúcha de Enfermagem* (nursing, 2 a year), *Revista Perfil* (sports, 2 a year),

Revista HCPA (University Hospital, 2 a year), *Anos 90* (philosophy and humanities, 2 a year), *Cadernos de Sociologia* (sociology, 2 a year), *Educação e Realidade* (education, 2 a year), *Educação, Subjetividade e Poder* (social and institutional psychology, 2 a year), *Epistéme* (philosophy and history of science, 2 a year), *Humanas* (philosophy and humanities, 2 a year), *Psicologia: Reflexão e Crítica* (psychology, 2 a year), *Horizontes Antropológicos* (social anthropology, 2 a year), *Pesquisas* (earth sciences, 2 a year), *Revista de Informática Teórica e Aplicada* (informatics, 2 a year), *Notas Técnicas* (earth sciences, 2 a year), *Art e Educação em Revista* (arts, 2 a year), *Em Pauta* (music, 2 a year), *Organon* (literature, 2 a year), *Porto Artes* (visual arts, 2 a year), *Boletim do Instituto de Biociências* (biosciences, 2 a year), *Napaea* (botany, 2 a year), *Egatea* (engineering, 2 a year), *Forjamento* (engineering, 2 a year), *Arquivos da Faculdade Veterinária* (veterinary science, 2 a year), *Análise Econômica* (economics, 2 a year), *Intexto* (communication and information, 2 a year), *Jornal do SAJU* (law, 2 a year), *Revista da Faculdade de Direito* (law, 2 a year), *Revista de Biblioteconomia e Comunicação* (librarianship and communication, 2 a year)

DIRECTORS

Faculty of Economic Sciences: Prof. PEDRO CEZAR DUTRA FONSECA
Faculty of Medicine: Prof. WALDOMIRO CARLOS MANFROY
Faculty of Architecture: Prof. EDSON WALDIR MEDEIROS KREBS
Faculty of Dentistry: Prof. JOÃO JORGE DINIZ BARBACHAN
Faculty of Agriculture: GILMAR ARDUINO BETTIO MARODIN
Faculty of Pharmacy: Profa VALQUIRIA LINCK BASSANI
Faculty of Veterinary Medicine: Prof. ANTÔNIO DE PÁDUA FERREIRA DA SILVA FILHO
Faculty of Education: Profa MERION CAMPOS BORDAS
Faculty of Librarianship and Communication: Profa MARCIA BENETTI MACHADO
Faculty of Law: Prof. PLÍNIO DE OLIVEIRA CORRÊA
School of Engineering: Prof. RENATO MACHADA DE BRITO
School of Physical Education: Prof. RICARDO DEMÉTRIO DE SOUZA PETERSEN
School of Nursing: Profa IDA HAUNSS DE FREITAS XAVIER
School of Management: Prof. JOÃO LUIZ BECKER
Institute of Arts: Prof. CIRIO SIMON
Institute of Biological Sciences: Prof. JORGE MARIATH
Institute of Chemistry: Prof. DIMITRIOS SAMIOS
Institute of Food Technology: Prof. MARCO ANTONIO ZACHIA AYUB
Institute of Geological Sciences: Prof. RICARDO NOBERTO AYUP ZOUAIN
Institute of Hydraulic Research: Prof. LUIZ FERNANDO DE ABREU CYBIS
Institute of Letters and Literature: Profa. SARA VIOLA RODRIGUES
Institute of Mathematics: Profa ELSA CRISTINA DE MUNDSTOCK
Institute of Philosophy and Humanities: Prof. JOSÉ VICENTE TAVARES DOS SANTOS
Institute of Physics: Prof. CLAUDIO SCHERER
Institute of Computer Science: PHILIPPE OLIVIER ALEXANDER NAVAUX
Institute of Basic Health Sciences: JOÃO ROBERTO BRAGA MELLO
Institute of Psychology: Prof. CLAUDIO S. HUTZ

ATTACHED RESEARCH CENTRES

Ecology Centre: Dir MARIA TERESA RAYA RODRIGUES.
Technology Centre: Dir IVA GUERRA MACHADO.
Biotechnology Centre: Dir JORGE ALMEIDA GUIMARÃES.
Olympic Centre: Dir ALBERTO RAMOS BISCHOFF.
Veterinary Hospital: Dir HELOISA AZEVEDO SCHERER.
Remote Sensing Centre: Dir JORGE RICARDO DUCATTI.
Astronomical Laboratory: Dir KEPLER DE SOUZA OLIVEIRA FILHO.
Experimental Agronomic Station: Dir CARLOS RICARDO TREIN.
Management Research Centre: Dir LUIZ ANTÔNIO SLONGO.
Economics Research Centre: Dir FERNANDO FERRARI FILHO.
Coastal and Oceanic Geological Research Centre: Dir ELIRIO E. TOLDO JR.
Coastal, Limnological and Oceanic Research Centre: Dir LUIZ PAULO RODRIGUES S. CUNHA.
Computer Centre: Dir JUSSARA ISSA MUSSE.
National Supercomputer Centre: Dir DENISE GRUENE EWALD.

PONTIFÍCIA UNIVERSIDADE CATÓLICA DO RIO DE JANEIRO

Rua Marquês de São Vicente 225, Edif. Pe. Leonel Franca, 8 andar, Gávea, 22453-900 Rio de Janeiro, RJ
Telephone: (21) 3114-1577
Fax: (21) 3115-1094
E-mail: director@ccci.puc-rio.br
Internet: www.puc-rio.br

Founded 1941
Private control
Academic year: March to December
Chancellor: Arcebispo Metropolitano do Rio de Janeiro EUSÉBIO OSCAR SCHEID
Rector: Pe. JESUS HORTAL SÁNCHEZ
Vice-President: Pe. JOSAFÁ CARLOS DE SIQUEIRA
Vice-President for Academic Affairs: Prof. DANILO MARCONDEZ SOUZA FILHO
Vice-President for Administrative Affairs: Prof. LUIZ CARLOS SCAVARDA DO CARMO
Vice-President for Community Affairs: Prof. AUGUSTO LUIZ DUARTE LOPES SAMPAIO
Vice-President for Development Affairs: Eng. NELSON JANOT MARINHO
Registrar: Prof. WASHINGTON BRAGA
Librarian: Dra DOLORES RODRIGUEZ PERES

Library of 600,000 vols
Number of teachers: 1,162
Number of students: 18,254

Publication: *Anuário*

DEANS

Medical Centre: Prof. Dr FRANCISCO DE PAULA AMARANTE NETO
Social Sciences Centre: Profa GISELE GUIMARÃES CITTADINO
Technical and Scientific Centre: Prof. JOSÉ ALBERTO DOS REIS PARISE
Theology and Human Sciences Centre: Profa MARIA CLARA BINGEMER

HEADS OF DEPARTMENTS

Theology and Human Sciences Centre (tel. (21) 3114-1001; fax (21) 3114-1119):
- Theology: Prof. Pe. NILO AGOSTINI
- Philosophy: Profa VERA CRISTINA DE ANDRADE BUENO
- Education: Profa MENGA LUDKE
- Psychology: Profa ANA MARIA RUDGE
- Literature: Profa LUCIA PACHEKO
- Arts: Profa REJANE SPITZ

Social Sciences Centre (tel. (21) 3114-1001; fax (21) 3114-1001):
- History and Geography: Profa FLÁVIA MARIA SCHLEE EYLER
- Sociology and Political Science: Profa SONIA MARIA GIACOMINI
- Economics: Prof. ROGÉRIO FRUQUIM WERNECK
- Law: Prof. Dr JOÃO RICARDO DORNELLES
- Communications: Prof. MIGUEL SERPA PEREIRA
- Social Work: Profa MARIA APARECIDA BARBOSA MARQUES
- Business Administration: Profa HÉLÈNE BERTRAND

Technical and Scientific Centre (tel. (21) 3114-1001; fax (21) 3114-1001):
- Mathematics: Prof. GEOVAN TAVARES DOS SANTOS
- Physics: Prof. FERNANDO LÁZARO FREIRE
- Chemistry: Prof. PÉRCIO FARIAS
- Computer Science: Prof. ARNDT VON STAA
- Civil Engineering: Prof. CELSO ROMANEL
- Electrical Engineering: Prof. RICARDO TANSCHEIT
- Mechanical Engineering: Prof. PAULO ROBERTO DE SOUZA MENDES
- Metallurgical Engineering: Prof. MAURICIO LEONARDO TOREM
- Industrial Engineering: Profa MARIA ANGELA CAMPELO DE MELO

DIRECTORS OF ATTACHED INSTITUTES

Institute of International Relations: Profa SONIA DE CAMARGO
Centre for Telecommunications Research: Prof. FLAVIO JOSÉ VIEIRA
Rio Data Centre (Computer Centre): Prof. JOSÉ RAIMUNDO LOPES DE OLIVEIRA
Dentistry Institute (Post-graduate): Dr RICARDO GUIMARÃES FISCHER
Post-graduate Medical School: Prof. Dr MAURO MEIRELES PENA
Technological Institute: Prof. SÉRGIO LEAL BRAGA

UNIVERSIDADE DO RIO DE JANEIRO

Av. Pasteur 296, Urca, 22290-240 Rio de Janeiro, RJ
Telephone: (21) 295-5737
Fax: (21) 541-8394
Internet: www.unirio.br

Founded 1979
Federal control

Rector: Prof. Dr PIETRO NOVELLINO
Vice-Rector: Prof. Dr JOSÉ DIAS
Pro-Rectors: BRÍGIDA RIBEIRO PONCIANO (Graduate Instruction), Prof. Dra ANA MARIA DE BULHÕES CARVALHO (Postgraduate Research and Extension), MAURÍCIO DE PINHO GAMA (Plannning and Development), BENEDITO CUNHA MACHADO (Administration)
Director of Central Library: EROTILDES DE LIMA MATTOS

Library: Libraries with 87,000 vols, 204 periodicals
Number of teachers: 575
Number of students: 5,620

DEANS

Centre for Biological Sciences and Health: MARIO BARRETO CORRÊA LIMA
Centre for Humanities: MARIA JOSÉ MESQUITA CAVALLEIRO DE MACEDO WEHLING
Centre for Physical Sciences and Technology: LUIZ PEDRO SAN GIL JUTUCA

DIRECTORS

Centre for Biological Sciences and Health (Rua Silva Ramos 32, Tijuca, 20270-330 Rio de Janeiro, RJ; tel. (21) 2569-6643; fax (21) 2509-0422; e-mail ccbs@unirio.br):

School of Biological Sciences: EDUARDO GOMES DOS SANTOS
School of Medicine and Surgery: ANTONIO CARLOS RIBEIRO GARRIDO IGLESIAS
Alfredo Pinto School of Nursing: TERESINHA DE JESUS ESPÍRITO SANTO DA SILVA
School of Nutrition: MARIA APARECIDA CAMPOS
Institute of Biomedicine: ANTONIO BRISOLLA DIUANA

Centre for Humanities (Av. Pasteur 458 (prédio Pe. José de Anchieta), Urca, 22290-240 Rio de Janeiro, RJ; tel. (21) 2541-1839 ext. 2008; fax (21) 2542-2242; e-mail cch@unirio.br):

School of Archaeology: MARIZA BOTINO
School of Education: DAYSE MARTINS HORA
School of Jurisprudence: ÁLVARO REINALDO DE SOUZA
School of Library Studies: MARCOS LUIZ CAVALCANTI DE MIRANDA
School of Museology: JOSÉ MAURO MATHEUS LOUREIRO
Historical Research: MARIA JOSÉ MESQUITA CAVALLEIRO DE MACEDO WEHLING

Centre for Physical Sciences and Technology (Rua Voluntários de Pátria 107, Botafogo, 22270-000 Rio de Janeiro, RJ; tel. (21) 2266-5694; fax (21) 2266-5694; e-mail ccet@uniriotec.br):

School of Applied Informatics: ASTERIO KYIOSHI TANAKA

UNIVERSIDADE DO ESTADO DO RIO DE JANEIRO

Rua São Francisco Xavier 524, Maracanã, 20559-900 Rio de Janeiro, RJ
Telephone: (21) 587-7100
Fax: (21) 591-4803
E-mail: comuns@uerj.br
Internet: www.uerj.br

Founded 1950
State control
Language of instruction: Portuguese
Academic year: March to December (two semesters)

Chancellor: MARCELLO ALENCAR
Rector: Prof. ANTONIO CELSO ALVES PEREIRA
Vice-Rector: Prof. NILCÉA FREIRE
Pro-Vice-Chancellors: Prof. RICARDO VIEIRALVES DE CASTRO (Graduate), Prof. REINALDO GUIMARÃES (Postgraduate and Research), Profa MARIA THEREZINHA NÓBREGA DA SILVA (Culture and Extension)
General Administrative Director: RUBENS SILVA E SILVA
Librarian: SILVIA MARIA GAGO DA COSTA

Number of teachers: 2,005
Number of students: 17,615

Publications: *Cadernos de Antropologia da Imagem*, *Geo UERJ*, *Espaço e Cultura*, *Qfwfq*, *Logos*, *Em Pauta*, *Revista de Enfermagem da UERJ*, *Matraga*, *Revista do Centro de Estudos da Faculdade de Odontologia da UERJ* (all 2 a year)

SENIOR DIRECTORS

Bio-medical Centre: Prof. ELLEN MARCIA PERES
Education and Humanities Centre: Prof. JOSÉ RICARDO DA SILVA ROSA
Faculty of Social Communication: Prof. RICARDO FERREIRA FREITAS
Fernando Rodrigues da Silveira Training College: Profa MARICÉLIA BISPO
Technology and Science Centre: Prof. MAURÍCIO JOSÉ FERRARI REY
Higher School of Industrial Design: Prof. FRANK ANTHONY BARRAL DODD
Social Science Centre: Prof. JOSÉ FLAVIO PESSOA DE BARROS

DEANS

Bio-medical Centre:

Faculty of Medicine: Prof. JOSÉ AUGUSTO FERNANDES QUADRA
Faculty of Dentistry: Prof. MILTON SANTOS JABUR
Faculty of Nursing: Profa VERA RODRIGUES OLIVEIRA ANDRADE
Institute of Biology: Prof. ELIZEU FAGUNDES DE CARVALHO
Institute of Social Medicine: Prof. RICARDO TAVARES
Institute of Nutrition: Profa MARCIA VERONICA DE S. V. BELLA

Education and Humanities Centre:

Faculty of Education: Prof. ISAC JOÃO DE VASCONCELLOS
Institute of Letters: Prof. CLAUDIO CEZAR HENRIQUES
Institute of Physical Education and Sport: JOÃO GONZAGA DE OLIVEIRA
Institute of Psychology: Prof. SOLANGE DE OLIVEIRA SOUTO

Technology and Science Centre:

Faculty of Engineering: Prof. NIVAL NUNES DE ALMEIDA
Institute of Mathematics and Statistics: Profa MARINILZA BRUNO DE CARVALHO
Institute of Geosciences: Profa ANA LÚCIA TRAVASSOS ROMANO
Faculty of Physics: Prof. JADER BERNUZZI MARTINS
Institute of Chemistry: Prof. ILTON JORNADA
Faculty of Geology: Prof. RUI ALBERTO AZEVEDO DOS SANTOS

Social Science Centre:

Faculty of Law: Prof. ANTONIO CELSO ALVES PEREIRA
Faculty of Economics: Prof. RALPH MIGUEL ZERKOUVISKY
Faculty of Administration and Finance: Prof. DOMÊNICO MANDARINO
Faculty of Social Service: Profa ROSANGELA NAIR DE C. BARBOSA
Institute of Philosophy and Human Sciences: Prof. LUIZ EDMUNDO TAVARES

UNIVERSIDADE FEDERAL RURAL DO RIO DE JANEIRO

BR 465 Km 7, Antiga Rodovia Rio–São Paulo, 74504, 23825-000 Seropédica, RJ
Telephone: (21) 682-1210
Fax: (21) 682-1120
E-mail: gabinete@ufrrj.br
Internet: www.ufrrj.br

Founded 1910 as Escola Superior de Agronomia e Medicina Veterinária
Federal control
Language of instruction: Portuguese
Academic year: March to December (two semesters)

Rector: JOSÉ ANTÔNIO DE SOUZA VEIGA
Vice-Rector: MARIA DA CONCEIÇÃO ESTELLITA VIANNI
Chief Administrative Officer: MARCELO SOBREIRO
Librarian: CRISTINA VICTORIA DAL LIN ESTEVES

Library of 44,233 vols
Number of teachers: 612
Number of students: 6,303

Publications: *Ciências da Vida* (2 a year), *Ciências Humanas* (2 a year), *Ciências Exatas e da Terra* (2 a year)

DIRECTORS

Institute of Agronomy: ELSON DE CARVALHO VIEGAS
Institute of Biology: MARCOS ANTONIO JOSÉ DOS SANTOS
Institute of Pure Sciences: ELIZA HELENA DE SOUZA FARIA
Institute of Humanities: SILVESTRE PRADO DE SOUZA NIETO
Institute of Education: ALDA MARIA MAGALHÃES D'ALMEIDA SILVA
Institute of Forestry: RICARDO DA SILVA PEREIRA
Institute of Technology: LUIZ OTÁVIO NUNES DA SILVA
Institute of Animal Husbandry: NELSON JORGE MORAES MATOS
Institute of Veterinary Science: LAERTE GRISI

FUNDAÇÃO UNIVERSIDADE FEDERAL DE RONDÔNIA

BR 364 Km 9.5, Campus Universitário José Ribeiro Filho, 78900-000 Porto Velho, RO
Telephone: (69) 216-8500
Fax: (69) 216-8506
E-mail: reitoria@unir.br
Internet: www.unir.br

Founded 1982
Federal govt control
Academic year: March to December

Rector: Prof. Dr ENE GLORIA DE SILVEIRA
Vice-Rector: Prof. Dr MIGUEL NENEVÉ
Administrative Pro-Rector: EDUARDO MARTINS
Academic Pro-Rector: FABÍOLA LINS CALDAS
Librarian: LUZIMAR BARBOSA CHAVES

Number of teachers: 260
Number of students: 4,800

Publication: *Presença: Cadernos de Criação* (4 a year)

Faculties of Education (depts of Letters, Geography, Mathematics, Physical Education, Teaching), Social Sciences (depts of Business Administration, Accounting, Economics, Law), Health Sciences (depts of Nursing, Psychology, Biology), Exact Sciences (depts of Chemistry, Computing, Engineering).

UNIVERSIDADE FEDERAL DE RORAIMA

BR 174 s/n, Jardim Floresta 1, 69310-270 Boa Vista, RR
Telephone: (95) 623-9067
Fax: (95) 623-9063
Internet: www.ufrr.br/

Founded 1989
Federal control

Rector: FERNANDO ANTÔNIO MENEZES DA SILVA

Library of 18,000 vols, 980 periodicals
Number of teachers: 278
Number of students: 4,200.

UNIVERSIDADE ESTÁCIO DE SÁ

Rua do Bispo 83, Rio Comprido, 20261-060 Rio de Janeiro, RJ
Telephone: (21) 503-7000
Fax: (21) 293-4539
Internet: www.estacio.br

Founded 1988
Private control

Rector: GILBERTO MENDES DE OLIVEIRA CASTRO

Library of 46,000 vols, 710 periodicals
Number of teachers: 634
Number of students: 17,416.

UNIVERSIDADE DO SAGRADO CORAÇÃO

Rua Irmã Arminda 10–50, 17011-160 Bauru, SP
Telephone: (14) 3235-7000
Fax: (14) 3235-7325
E-mail: reitoria@usc.br
Internet: www.usc.br

Founded 1953
Academic year: February to November
Private control

Rector: Dra Sister JACINTA TUROLO GARCIA
Vice-Rector: Sister ILDA BASSO
Pro-Rector (Academic): REGINA CÉLIA BELLUZZO
University Secretary: GESIANE MONTEIRO FOLKIS
Librarian: MÔNICA VALÉRIA P. LOSNAK

Library of 110,000 vols
Number of teachers: 353
Number of students: 6,000

Publications: *Revista Mimesis* (liberal studies, 2 a year), *Revista Salusvita* (science and health, in Portuguese and English), *Boletim Cultural* (cultural studies, annually), *Cadernos de Divulgação Cultural* (Master's theses and doctoral dissertations, annually), *Revista Camoniana* (Portuguese literature studies)

DEANS

College of Business Administration: Ir GENI DA SILVA
College of Sciences: Ir MARISABEL LEITE
College of Liberal Arts: Ir EVANIRA DE SOUZA
College of Social Sciences: VALDEIR R. VIDRIK
Graduate Programmes: Dr JOSÉ JOBSON DE ANDRADE ARRUDA (Dir)
Master's Programme in Dentistry: CARLOS E. FRANCISCHONE (DirImplantology: HUGO NARY FILHO (DirTraumatology, Oral and Maxillofacial Surgery: MARIA CECILIA V. DAHER (DirDentistry: EYMAR S. LOPES (Dir)
Master's Programme in Oral Biology: SÉRGIO A. C. GUIMARÃES (Dir)
Lato Sensu Courses: Dr SONIA SEVILHA MARTINS
Branemark Centre: Dr CARLOS E. FRANCISCHONE (Dir)
Research: Dr SÉRGIO AUGUSTO CATANZARO GUIMARÃES
Committee on Ethics: Dr NILTON AQUILES VON ZUBEN
Scientific Initiation Projects: Dr SÉRGIO AUGUSTO CATANZARO GUIMARÃES

UNIVERSIDADE SALGADO DE OLIVEIRA

Rua Lambari 10, Trindade, São Gonçalo, 24456-420 Niterói, RJ
Telephone: (21) 701-0505
Fax: (21) 701-7444
E-mail: universo@ax.ibase.org.br
Internet: www.universo.br

Founded 1976
Private control

Rector: MARLENE SALGADO DE OLIVEIRA

Library: Libraries with 59,000 vols, 32,859 periodicals
Number of teachers: 426
Number of students: 20,995.

UNIVERSIDADE SALVADOR

Rua Ponciano de Oliveira 126, Garibaldi, 40225-300 Salvador, BA
Telephone: (71) 331-3138
Fax: (71) 235-2911
E-mail: areitoria@unifacs.br
Internet: www.unifacs.br

Founded 1972
Private control

Rector: MANOEL JOAQUIM F. DE BARROS SOBRINHO

Library of 61,000 vols, 485 periodicals
Number of teachers: 151
Number of students: 3,693.

UNIVERSIDADE CATÓLICA DO SALVADOR

Praça Ana Nery s/n, Convento da Palma Mouraria Nazaré, 40040-020 Salvador, BA
Telephone: (71) 321-7199
Fax: (71) 322-4331
E-mail: reitoria@ucsal.br
Internet: www.ucsal.br

Founded 1961
Private control
Languages of instruction: Portuguese, French, English

Chancellor: Cardinal Dom LUCAS MOREIRA NEVES
Rector: Dr JOSÉ CARLOS ALMEIDA DA SILVA
Vice-Rector: LILIANA MERCURI ALMEIDA
Librarian: SONIA RODRIGUES

Number of teachers: 690
Number of students: 12,000

DIRECTORS

Faculty of Education: Profa ITALVA SIMÕES
School of Social Services: Profa EMILIA NORONHA LYRA
School of Business Administration: Prof. HUGO BELEUS
Faculty of Law: Prof. THOMAS BACELLAR
Faculty of Philosophy and Human Sciences: Prof. JURANDYR OLIVEIRA
Faculty of Nursing: Profa MARGARIDA MACHADO
Institute of Sciences: Profa LYGIA PARAGUASSU
Institute of Theology: Pe ADEMAR DANTOS DE SOUZA
School of Engineering: Prof. LUIZ GONZAGA MARQUES
Institute of Letters: Profa TEREZA CHIANCA
Institute of Music: Profa LEDA MARGARIDA DE SOUZA
Institute of Mathematics: NILTON CRUZ
Faculty of Economics: (vacant)
Faculty of Accountancy: (vacant)
School of Physical Education: (vacant)

UNIVERSIDADE DO ESTADO DE SANTA CATARINA

Campus Universitário, Av. Madre Benvenuta 2007, CP D-34, Itacorubi, 88035-001 Florianópolis, SC
Telephone: (48) 231-1550
Fax: (48) 334-6000
E-mail: r4sl@pobox.udesc.br
Internet: www.udesc.br

Founded 1965
State control
Language of instruction: Portuguese
Academic year: March to December

Rector: ANSELMO FÁBIO DE MORAES
Chief Administrative Officer: PIO CAMPOS FILHO
Chief Academic Officer: ANTONIO WALDIMIR LEOPOLDINO DA SILVA
Librarian: NOÊMA SCHOFFEN PRADO

Library of 75,838 vols
Number of teachers: 402
Number of students: 10,000

Publications: *Boletim do Centro de Artes*, *CCII News*, *Jornal da UDESC*

DIRECTORS

Faculty of Education: JARBAS JOSÉ CARDOSO
Faculty of Engineering (Joinville): GERSON VOLNEY LAGEMANN
Faculty of Nursing, Nutritional Studies and Zootechnician: ANTÔNIO WALDIMIR LEOPOLDINO DA SILVA
School of Agronomics and Veterinary Medicine: PAULO CÉSAR CASSOL
Business School: AMILTON GIÁCOMO TOMASI
School of Fine Arts: ALBERTINA PEIREIRA MEDEIROS
School of Physical Education: PAULO HENRIQUE XAVIER DE SOUZA
Distance Learning Centre: RAIMUNDO NONATO GONÇALVES ROBERT

UNIVERSIDADE FEDERAL DE SANTA CATARINA

Campus Universitário, CP 476, 88040-900 Trindade (Florianópolis), SC
Telephone: (48) 331-9000
Fax: (48) 234-4069
Internet: www.ufsc.br

Founded 1960
State control
Language of instruction: Portuguese
Academic year: March to December

Rector: Prof. RODOLFO JOAQUIM PINTO DA LUZ
Vice-Rector: Prof. LÚCIO JOSÉ BOTELHO
Pro-Rector (Graduate Education and Research): Prof. ÁLVARO TOUBES PRATA
Pro-Rector (Undergraduate Education): Profa SÔNIA MARIA HICKEL PROBST
Pro-Rector (Academic Affairs): Prof. PEDRO DA COSTA ARAÚJO
Pro-Rector (Extension and Culture): Profa ROSSANA PACHECO DA COSTA PROENÇA
Pro-Rector (Administration): JOÃO MARIA DE LIMA

Number of teachers: 1,658
Number of students: 27,244

Publications: *Seqüência* (politics and law, 2 a year), *Travessia* (Brazilian literature, 2 a year), *Ciências Humanas* (philosophy and human sciences, 2 a year), *Ilha do Desterro* (language studies and literature, 2 a year), *Perspectiva* (education, 2 a year), *Geosul* (geosciences, 2 a year), *Biotemas* (biological sciences, 2 a year), *Ciências da Saúde* (health sciences, 2 a year), *Motrivivência – Políticas Públicas* (physical education, sport and leisure, 2 a year), *Fragmentos* (foreign language and literature, 2 a year), *Principia* (epistemology, 2 a year), *Graf & Tec* (graphics, 2 a year), *Katalysis* (social services, 2 a year)

DEANS

Agrarian Sciences Centre: Prof. ÊNIO LUIZ PEDROTTI
Engineering and Technology Centre: Prof. ARIOVALDO BOLZAN
Bio-Medical Sciences Centre: Prof. CARLOS ALBERTO JUSTO DA SILVA
Social and Economic Sciences Centre: Prof. ERMES TADEU ZAPELINI
Education Centre: Profa VERA LÚCIA BAZZO
Physical Education Centre: Prof. JÚLIO CÉSAR SCHMITT ROCHA
Communication Centre: Prof. DILVO ILVO RISTOFF
Physics and Mathematics Centre: Prof. IVAN GONÇALVES DE SOUZA
Biological Sciences Centre: Prof. JOÃO DE DEUS MEDEIROS
Philosophy and Social Sciences Centre: Prof. JOÃO EDUARDO PINTO BASTO LUPI
Law Sciences Centre: Prof. JOSÉ LUIZ SOBIERAJSKI

UNIVERSIDADE DO OESTE DE SANTA CATARINA

Rua Jaime Martins Alves 196, Bairro Flor de Serra, 89600-000, Joaçaba, SC
Telephone: (49) 551-2098

Fax: (49) 551-2100
E-mail: reitor@unoesc.edu.br
Internet: www.unoesc.edu.br

Founded 1968
State control
Rector: ARISTIDES CIMADON
Library of 180,099 vols, 21,633 periodicals
Number of teachers: 766
Number of students: 13,645.

UNIVERSIDADE DO SUL DE SANTA CATARINA

Av. José Acácio Moreira 787, Bairro Dehon, 88704-900 Tubarão, SC
Telephone: (48) 621-3000
Fax: (48) 621-3036
E-mail: unisul@unisul.br
Internet: www.unisul.br

Founded 1967
Municipal control
Academic year: March to November
Rector: GERSON LUIZ JONER DA SILVA
Vice-Rector: SEBASTIÃO SALÉSIO HERDT
Library of 161,346 vols
Number of teachers: 1,641
Number of students: 23,113
Publication: *Jornal* (10 a year).

UNIVERSIDADE SANTA CECÍLIA

Rua Oswaldo Cruz 266, CP 1213, 11045-907 Santos, SP
Telephone: (13) 221-3242
Fax: (13) 232-4010
E-mail: scecilia@cat.cce.usp.br
Internet: www.stcecilia.br

Founded 1961
Private control
Academic year: February to December
Chancellor: Dr MILTON TEIXEIRA
President: Dra LÚCIA M. TEIXEIRA FURLANI
Vice-President: Profa MARIA CECÍLIA P. TEIXEIRA
Rector: Dra SÍLVIA ÂNGELA TEIXEIRA PENTEADO
Academic Pro-Rector: Profa ZULEIKA DE A. SENGER GONÇALVES
Administrative Pro-Rector: Dr MARCELO PIRILO TEIXEIRA
Community Pro-Rector: Prof. AQUELINO J. VASQUES
Pro-Rector for University Development: Profa EMÍLIA MARIA PIRILLO
General Secretary: WALDIR GRAÇA
Chief Librarian: ANA MARIA RACCIOPI SILVEIRA
Library of 84,000 vols
Number of teachers: 640
Number of students: 13,000
Publications: *Ceciliana*, *Revista de Estudo*

COORDINATORS

Santa Cecília Campus: Profa LÚCIA MARIA TEIXEIRA FURLANI, Dr MARCELO TEIXEIRA, Profa MARIA CECÍLIA TEIXEIRA
Bandeirante I Campus: Profa ROSINHA GARCIA DE SIQUEIRA VIEGAS
Bandeirante II Campus: Profa CARMEN LÚCIA TABOADA DE CARVALHO

DEANS

Faculty of Arts and Communication: Prof. A. J. VASQUES
Faculty of Sciences and Technology: Prof. R. PATELLA
Faculty of Industrial Engineering: Eng. A. E. P. FIGUEIREDO
Faculty of Civil Engineering: Eng. A DE SALLES PENTEADO
Faculty of Dentistry: Dr R. G. DE SIQUEIRA VIEGAS
Faculty of Education and Human Sciences: Prof. C. M. BAFFA
Faculty of Commercial and Administrative Sciences: Prof. A. PORTO PIRES
Faculty of Chemical Engineering: Eng. A. DE SALLES PENTEADO
Faculty of Physical Education: Prof. V. A. TABOADA DE CARVALHO RAPHAELLI
Faculty of Dance: Prof. L. RACCINI
Faculty of Law: Dr R. MEHANNA KHAMIS

UNIVERSIDADE FEDERAL DE SANTA MARIA

Campus Universitário – Camobi, 97105-900 Santa Maria, RS
Telephone: (55) 220-8000
Fax: (55) 220-8001
E-mail: sai@adm.ufsm.br
Internet: www.ufsm.br

Founded 1960
Federal government control
Academic year: March to December (two semesters)
Rector: Prof. PAULO JORGE SARKIS
Vice-Rector: Prof. CLÓVIS SILVA LIMA
Pro-Rectors: Prof. PAULO TABAJARA CLÓVIS COSTA (Postgraduate and Research), Prof. BALTAZAR SCHIRMER (Undergraduate), Prof. JOÃO LUIS DE OLIVEIRA ROTH (Student Affairs), Prof. AILO VALMIR SACCOL (Extension), Prof. ROBERTO DA LUZ JÚNIOR (Planning), Prof. VALDEMAR SPERONI (Administration)
Librarian: KUZIA SANT'ANNA
Library of 116,000 vols
Number of teachers: 1,301
Number of students: 13,477 (11,727 undergraduate, 1,750 postgraduate, 2,474 at Technical High School)
Publications: *Ciência e Natura*, *Extensão Rural*, *Ciência e Ambiente*, *Ciência Rural*, *Revista Brasilerira de Agroameteorologia*, *Animus Revista Interamericana de Comunicação Mediática*

DIRECTORS OF CENTRES

Technology: Profa NILZA ZAMPIERI
Arts and Letters: Prof. EDEMUR CASANOVA
Rural Science: Prof. FLÁVIO MIGUEL SCHNEIDER
Education: Prof. JORGE LUIS DA CUNHA
Health Sciences: Prof. ALBERTO BINATO
Social and Human Sciences: Prof. JOÃO MANUAL SPINA ROSSETTI
Natural and Exact Sciences: Prof. EDUARDO RAMOS MEDEIROS
Sports Research Centre: Prof. LUIS CELSO GIACOMINI

ATTACHED INSTITUTES

Faculty of Nursing: Av. Presidente Vargas 2777, 97100 Santa Maria, RS; Dir Ir. NOEMI LUNARDI.

Faculty of Philosophy, Sciences and Letters: Rua Andradas 1614, 97100 Santa Maria, RS; Dir Profa MARIA A. MARQUES.

UNIVERSIDADE SANTA ÚRSULA

Rua Fernando Ferrari 75, Botafago, CP 16086, 22231-040 Rio de Janeiro, RJ
Telephone: (21) 551-5542
Fax: (21) 552-0796
E-mail: ascon@ax.apc.org.br
Internet: www.usu.br

Founded 1938
Rector: MARIA DO CARMO BITTENCOURT
Library: Libraries with 123,000 vols, 2,128 periodicals
Number of teachers: 425
Number of students: 7,639.

UNIVERSIDADE SANTO AMARO

Rua Prof. Enéas de Siqueira Neto 340, Jardim dos Imbuias, 04829-300 São Paulo, SP
Telephone: (11) 520-9611
Fax: (11) 520-9160
Internet: www.osec.br

Founded 1994
Private control
Rector: SIDNEY STORCH DUTRA
Library of 57,000 vols, 700 periodicals
Number of teachers: 505
Number of students: 7,789.

UNIVERSIDADE CATÓLICA DE SANTOS

Rua Euclides da Cunha 241, José Menino, 11065-902 Santos, SP
Telephone: (13) 250-5555
Fax: (13) 250-5559
E-mail: unisantos@unisantos.com.br
Internet: www.unisantos.com.br

Founded 1986
Rector: FRANCISCO PRADO DE OLIVEIRA RIBEIRO
Library of 58,000 vols, 945 periodicals
Number of teachers: 537
Number of students: 7,015.

UNIVERSIDADE METROPOLITANA DE SANTOS

Rua da Constituição 374, Vila Mathias, 11015-470 Santos, SP
Telephone: (13) 233-3400
Fax: (13) 235-2990
E-mail: infounimes@unimes.com.br
Internet: www.unimes.com.br

Founded 1996
Private control
Rector: ROSINHA GARCIA DE SIQUEIRA VIEGAS
Library of 59,000 vols, 233 periodicals
Number of teachers: 405
Number of students: 5,034.

UNIVERSIDADE FEDERAL DE SÃO CARLOS

Rodovia Washington Luiz, Km 235, Monjolinho, CP 676, 13565-905 São Carlos, SP
Telephone: (16) 260-8111
Fax: (16) 261-4846
E-mail: ufscar@power.ufscar.br
Internet: www.ufscar.br

Founded 1970
Federal control
Language of instruction: Portuguese
Academic year: March to December
Chancellor: PAULO RENATO DE SOUZA
Rector: Prof. Dr OSWALDO BAPTISTA DUARTE FILHO
Vice-Rector: Prof. Dr ROMEU CARDOSO ROCHA FILHO
Chief Administrative Officer: Profa Dra NANCY V. F. DE ALMEIDA
Librarian: LOURDES DE SOUZA MORAES
Number of teachers: 545
Number of students: 6,959

DIRECTORS

Institute of Sciences and Technology: Prof. Dr NÉLIO BALDIN
Institute of Education and Human Sciences: Prof. Dr VALTER ROBERTO SILVERIO
Institute of Biological and Health Sciences: Profa Dra ROSANA MATTIOLI
Institute of Agricultural Sciences: Prof. Dr SEBASTIÃO ALVES DE LIMA FILHO

HEADS OF DEPARTMENTS

Sciences and Technology (tel. (16) 260-8202; fax (16) 260-8286; e-mail ccetdir@power.ufscar.br):

Computer Science: Prof. Dr ORIDES MORANDIM JUNIOR
Statistics: Profa Dra MARIA CECILIA MENDES BARRETO
Materials Engineering: Prof. Dr PEDRO IRIS PAULIN FILHO
Chemical Engineering: Prof. Dr ERNESTO ANTONIO URQUIETA GONZALEZ
Production Engineering: Prof. Dr FRANCISCO JOSÉ DA COSTA ALVES
Civil Engineering: Prof. Dr ARCHIMEDES AZEVEDO RAIA JUNIOR
Physics: Prof. Dr FERNANDO MANUEL ARAUJO
Mathematics: Prof. Dr IVO MACHADO DA COSTA
Chemistry: Prof. Dr JULIO ZUKERMAN SCHPECTOR

Education and Human Sciences (tel. (16) 260-8351; fax (16) 260-8353; e-mail cech@power.ufscar.br):

Psychology: Profa Dra AZAIR LIANE MATOS DO CANTO SOUZA
Social Sciences: Prof. PIERO DE CAMARGO LEIRNER
Education: Prof. Dr ANTONIO ALVARO SOARES ZUIN
Philosophy and Methodology of Science: Prof. Dr RICHARD THEISEN SIMANKE
Teaching Methodology: Profa Dra DENISE DE FREITAS
Spanish and English: Profa Dra GLADYS M. B. ALMEIDA
Arts: Profa Dra JOSETTE ALVES MONZANI
Information Science: Profa NADEA REGINA GASPAR

Biological and Health Sciences (tel. (16) 260-8301; fax (16) 260-8302; e-mail ccbsdir@power.ufscar.br; internet www.ccbs.ufscar.br):

Ecology and Evolutionary Biology: Profa Dra ANGELICA M. P. M. DIAS
Nursing: Profa Dra MARIZA B. B. DE SOUZA
Physiotherapy: Prof. DARLEI LAZARO BALDI
Occupational Therapy: Profa UMAIA EL-KHATIB
Genetics and Evolution: Profa Dra NORMA MORTARI
Physiological Sciences: Profa Dra HELOISA S. F. ARAUJO
Botany: Prof. Dr MARCOS ARDUIN
Hydrobiology: Prof. Dr IRINEU BIANCHINI
Physical Education: Profa SELVA MARIA G. BARRETO
Morphology: Prof. Dr CLOVIS WESLEY OLIVEIRA DE SOUZA

Agricultural Sciences (tel. (19) 542-4007; fax (19) 542-3773; e-mail diretor@cca.ufscar.br):

Agroindustrial Technology and Rural Development: Prof. Dr CLAUDIO HARTKOPF LOPES
Natural Resources and Environmental Safety: Prof. Dr JOSÉ GEANINI PERES
Vegetal Biotechnology: Prof. Dr ANTONIO CARLOS ARABICANO GHELLER

UNIVERSIDADE DE SÃO FRANCISCO

Av. São Francisco de Assis 218, CP 163, 12900-000 Bragança Paulista, SP

Telephone: (11) 7844-8240
Fax: (11) 7844-0087
E-mail: nogara@usf.com.br
Internet: www.usf.com.br

Founded 1976, university status 1985
Private control
Language of instruction: Portuguese
Academic year: February to December

Chancellor: Fr. CAETANO FERRARI
Rector: Fr. CONSTÂNCIO NOGARA
Vice-Rector: Fr. FÁBIO PANINI
Pro-Rectors: Profa ACÁCIA AP. ANGELI DOS SANTOS (Undergraduate), Profa MARIA APARECIDA BARBOSA MARQUES (Research, Postgraduate and Extension), ANTÔNIO CARLOS DE ALMEIDA (Community), Prof. GILBERTO LUIS MORAES SELBER (Administrative)
General Secretary: Prof. JOSÉ ENIO TRIERVAILER
Librarian: IVANI BENASSI

Library of 132,000 vols, 1,200 periodicals
Number of teachers: 821
Number of students: 17,561

Publications: *Informativo USF* (monthly), *Semeando* (monthly), *Cadernos do IFAN* (4 a year), *InformIPPEX* (monthly), *Anais do Encontro de Iniciação Científica e Pesquisadores* (annually)

DIRECTORS

Câmpus de Bragança Paulista (Av. São Francisco de Assis 218, CP 163, 12900-000 Bragança Paulista, SP):

Faculty of Pharmacy: Prof. EDSON RODRIGUES
Faculty of Medicine: Prof. SÉRGIO LUIZ MARTIN NARDY
Faculty of Law: Prof. JOSÉ NICOLA JANNUZZI
Faculty of Economics and Administration: Profa HILDA MARIA C. BARROSO BRAGA
Faculty of Philosophy, Sciences and Literature: Prof. MIGUEL HENRIQUE RUSSO
Faculty of Dentistry: Prof. ROSSINE AMORIM MACIEL

Câmpus de Itatiba (Rua Alexandre Rodrigues Barbosa 45, 13251-900 Itatiba, SP):

Faculty of Engineering: Prof. WERNER MERTZIG
Faculty of Human Sciences: Profa CARMEM BEATRIZ RODRIGUES FABRIANI
Faculty of Administrative and Exact Sciences: Prof. FÁBIO ALEXANDRE GAION CASOTTI

Câmpus de São Paulo (Rua Hannemann 352, Pari, 03031-040 São Paulo, SP):

Faculty of Education and Social Sciences: Prof. MARINO ANTONIO SEHNEN
Faculty of Business and Administration: Prof. LUIZ MAURÍCIO DE ANDRADE DA SILVA
Faculty of Law: Prof. MARLON WANDER MACHADO

ATTACHED INSTITUTES

Franciscan Institute of Anthropology: Dir Fr ORLANDO BERNARDI.

Institute for Graduate Research and Extension: Dir Profa JOSIANE MARIA DE FREITAS TONELOTTO.

UNIVERSIDADE SÃO JUDAS TADEU

Rua Taquari 546, Mooca, 03166-000 São Paulo, SP

Telephone: (11) 608-1677
Fax: (11) 291-6932
E-mail: webmaster@saojudas.br
Internet: www.saojudas.br

Founded 1985
Private control

Rector: JOSÉ CRISTIANO A. SILVA MESQUITA

Library of 70,000 vols, 2,066 periodicals
Number of teachers: 733
Number of students: 18,410.

UNIVERSIDADE SÃO MARCOS

Rua Clovis Bueno de Azevedo 176, Ipiranga, 04266-040 São Paulo, SP

Telephone: (11) 6163-6877
Fax: (11) 6163-0978
E-mail: reitoria@server.smarcos.br
Internet: www.smarcos.br

Founded 1970
Private control

Rector: PAULO NATHANAEL PEREIRA DE SOUZA

Library of 73,000 vols, 347 periodicals
Number of teachers: 309
Number of students: 8,164.

UNIVERSIDADE DE SÃO PAULO

Cidade Universitária, Rua da Reitoria 109, 05508-900 São Paulo, SP

Telephone: (11) 3091-1000
Fax: (11) 3815-5665
E-mail: gr@usp.br
Internet: www.usp.br

Founded 1934
State control
Academic year: March to November

Rector: Prof. Dr ADOLPHO JOSÉ MELFI
Vice-Rector: Prof. Dr HÉLIO NOGUEIRA DA CRUZ
Pro-Rector (Culture and University Extension): Prof. Dr ADILSON AVANSI DE ABREU
Pro-Rector (Postgraduate Studies): Prof. Dra SUELY VILELA
Pro-Rector (Research): Prof. Dr LUIZ NUNES DE OLIVEIRA
Pro-Rector (Undergraduate Studies): Profa Dra SONIA T. DE SOUSA PENIN
Secretary: Profa Dra NINA BEATRIZ STOCCO RANIERI

Library: see Libraries and Archives
Number of teachers: 4,953
Number of students: 75,962

Publications: *Revista USP* (4 a year), *Revista Paulista de Educação Física* (2 a year), *Revista da Escola de Enfermagem* (4 a year), *Scientia Agrícola — ESALQ* (4 a year), *Sinopses — FAU* (irregular), *Revista Brasileira de Ciências Farmacêuticas — IQ/FCF* (3 a year), *Revista da Faculdade de Direito* (annually), *Educação e Pesquisa — FE* (2 a year), *Revista de Administração* (4 a year), *Revista do Instituto de Medicina Tropical de SP* (6 a year), *Revista de Psicologia USP* (2 a year), *Revista de Terapia Ocupacional* (4 a year), *Revista de Fisioterapia* (2 a year), *Brazilian Journal of Veterinary Research and Animal Science* (6 a year), *Pesquisa Odontológica Brasileira* (4 a year), *Revista de Saúde Pública* (6 a year), *Boletim de Botânica* (annually), *Boletim IG/USP – Série Científica* (annually), *Revista Brasileira de Oceanografia* (2 a year), *Estilos da Clínica* (2 a year), *Revista do Museu de Arqueologia e Etnologia* (annually)

DEANS

Faculty of Animal Husbandry and Food Engineering (Pirassununga): Prof. Dr JOSÉ BENTO STERMAN FERRAZ
Faculty of Architecture and Town Planning: Prof. Dr RICARDO TOLEDO SILVA
School of Communication and Arts: Prof. Dr LUIS AUGUSTO MILANESI
Faculty of Dentistry: Prof. Dr NEY SOARES DE ARÚJO
Faculty of Dentistry (Bauru): Profa Dra MARIA FIDELA DE LIMA NAVARRO
Faculty of Dentistry (Ribeirão Prêto): Profa Dra MARISA SEMPRINI
Faculty of Economics, Administration and Accounting: Profa Dra MARIA TEREZA LEME FLEURY
Faculty of Economics, Administration and Accounting (Ribeirão Preto): Prof. Dr MARCOS CORTEZ CAMPOMAR
Faculty of Education: Profa Dra SELMA GARRIDO PIMENTA
Faculty of Law: Prof. Dr EDUARDO CESAR SILVEIRA VITA MARCHI

Faculty of Medicine: Prof. Dr GIOVANNI GUIDO CERRI
Faculty of Medicine (Ribeirão Prêto): Prof. Dr MARCOS FELIPE SILVA DE SÁ
Faculty of Pharmaceutical Sciences: Profa Dra TEREZINHA DE JESUS ANDREOLI PINTO
Faculty of Pharmaceutical Sciences (Ribeirão Prêto): Profa Dra MARIA DE LOURDES PIRES BIANCHI
Faculty of Philosophy, Literature and Human Sciences: Prof. Dr SEDI HIRANO
Faculty of Philosophy, Sciences and Literature (Ribeirão Prêto): Prof. Dr FRANCISCO DE ASSIS LEONE
Faculty of Public Health: Prof. Dr ARISTIDES ALMEIDA ROCHA
Faculty of Veterinary Medicine and Zootechnics: Prof. Dr CASSIO XAVIER DE MENDONÇA
'Luiz de Queiroz' Higher School of Agriculture: Prof. Dr JOSÉ ROBERTO POSTALI PARRA
School of Engineering (São Carlos): Prof. Dr FRANCISCO ANTONIO ROCCO LAHR
School of Nursing: Profa Dra ANA MARIA KAZUE MIYADAHIRA
School of Nursing (Ribeirão Prêto): Profa Dra ISABEL AMÉLIA COSTA MENDES
School of Physical Education and Sport: Prof. Dr ALBERTO CARLOS AMADIO
Polytechnic School: Prof. Dr VAHAN AGOPYAN
Institute of Biomedical Sciences: Prof. Dr HENRIQUE KRIEGER
Institute of Biosciences: Profa Dra JOÃO STENGHEL MORGANTE
Institute of Chemistry: Prof. Dr HERNAN CHAIMOVICH
Institute of Chemistry (São Carlos): Prof. Dr DOUGLAS WAGNER FRANCO
Institute of Geophysics, Astronomy and Atmospheric Sciences: Profa Dra MÁRCIA ERNESTO
Institute of Geosciences: Prof. Dr JORGE KAZUO YAMAMOTO
Institute of Mathematical Sciences and Computing Systems (São Carlos): Prof. Dr PLACIDO ZOEGA TABOAS
Institute of Mathematics and Statistics: Prof. Dr FRANCISCO CESAR POLCINO MILIES
Institute of Physics: Prof. Dr GIL DA COSTA MARQUES
Institute of Physics (São Carlos): Prof. Dr ROBERTO MENDONÇA FARIA
Institute of Oceanography: Prof. Dr BELMIRO MENDES DE CASTRO FILHO
Institute of Psychology: Profa Dra MARIA HELENA SOUZA PATTO

ATTACHED RESEARCH INSTITUTES

Institute for Advanced Studies: Dir Prof. Dr JOÃO EVANGELISTA STEINER.

Institute of Electrical Engineering and Energy: Dir Prof. Dr GERALDO FRANCISCO BURANI.

Centre of Marine Biology: Dir Profa Dra ELEONORA TRAJANO.

Centre of Nuclear Energy Applied in Agriculture: Dir Prof. Dr REYNALDO LUIZ VICTORIA.

Institute of Brazilian Studies: Dir Prof. Dr ISTVAN JANCSÓ.

Institute of Tropical Medicine: Dir Prof. Dr ANTONIO WALTER FERREIRA.

UNIVERSIDADE BANDEIRANTE DE SÃO PAULO

Rua Maria Candida 1813, V. Guilherme, 02071-013 São Paulo, SP
Telephone: (11) 6967-9000
Fax: (11) 6967-9006
E-mail: uniban@ns.uniban.br
Internet: www.uniban.br

Founded 1994
Private control
Academic year: February to December

Rector: HEITOR PINTO FILHO
Library of 400,000 vols, 900 periodicals
Number of teachers: 1,200
Number of students: 30,000.

UNIVERSIDADE CIDADE DE SÃO PAULO

Rua Cesário Galeno 432/448, 03071-000 São Paulo, SP
Telephone: (11) 6190-1200
Fax: (11) 6190-1415
E-mail: gabreit@unicid.br
Internet: www.unicid.br

Founded 1992
Private control

Rector: RUBENS LOPES DA CRUZ
Chancellor: PAULO EDUARDO SOARES DE OLIVEIRA NADDEO

Library of 103,000 vols, 1,200 periodicals
Number of teachers: 535
Number of students: 12,000.

UNIVERSIDADE ESTADUAL PAULISTA 'JULIO DE MESQUITA FILHO'

Alameda Santos 647, Cerqueira César, 01419-901 São Paulo, SP
Telephone: (11) 3252-0521
Fax: (11) 3252-0316
E-mail: arex@reitoria.unesp.br
Internet: www.unesp.br

Founded 1976, incorporating previous existing Faculties in São Paulo State
State control
Academic year: February to December

Rector: MARCOS MACARI
Vice-Rector: HERMAN JACOBUS CORNELIS VOORLWALD
Head of Administration: KLEBER TOMAS RESENDE
Secretary-General: MARIA DALVA SILVA PAGOTTO
Librarian: MARGARET ALVES ANTUNES

Library: 30 libraries university-wide
Number of teachers: 3,329
Number of students: 43,967, of which 34,346 undergraduate and 9,621 postgraduate

Publications: *Alfa* (linguistics, annually), *Alimentos e Nutrição* (food and nutrition, annually), *ARBS* (biomedical sciences, annually), *ARTunesp* (arts, annually), *Científica* (agronomy, annually), *Didática* (education, annually), *Eclética Química* (chemistry, annually), *Geociências* (geosciences, 2 a year), *História* (history, annually), *Naturália* (biological sciences, annually), *Perspectivas* (social sciences, annually), *Revista de Ciêcias Farmacêuticas* (pharmaceutical sciences, 2 a year), *Revista de Engenharia e Ciências Aplicadas* (engineering and applied sciences, annually), *Revista de Geografia* (geography, annually), *Revista de Matemática e Nutrição* (mathematics and nutrition, annually), *Revista de Odontologia da UNESP* (dentistry, 2 a year), *Transformação* (philosophy, annually), *Veterinária e Zootecnia* (veterinary and husbandry, annually)

DIRECTORS

Araçatuba Campus:

Faculty of Dentistry (Rua José Bonifácio 1193, 16015-050 Araçatuba, SP; tel. (18) 3236-3203; fax (18) 3636-2638; e-mail diretor@foa.unesp.br; internet www.foa.unesp.br):
Prof. Dr PAULO ROBERTO BOTACIN

Araraquara Campus:

Faculty of Dentistry (R. Humaitá 1680, 14801-903 Araraquara, SP; tel. (16) 3301-6431; fax (16) 3301-6433; e-mail diretor@foar.unesp.br; internet www.foar.unesp.br):
Prof. Dr ROSEMARY ADRIANA CHIÉRICI MARCANTONIO

Faculty of Pharmaceutical Sciences (Rodovia Araraquara–Jaú km 1, 14801-902 Araraquara, SP; tel. (16) 3301-6880; fax (16) 3222-0073; e-mail diretor@fcfar.unesp.br; internet www.fcfar.unesp.br):
Prof. Dr IGUATEMI LOURENÇO BRUNETTI

Faculty of Sciences and Humanities (Rodovia Araraquara–Jaú km 1, 14801-901 Araraquara, SP; tel. (16) 3301-4066; fax (16) 3301-6257; e-mail diretor@fclar.unesp.br; internet www.fclar.unesp.br):
Prof. Dr CLÁUDIO BENEDITO GOMIDE DE SOUZA

Institute of Chemistry (R. Prof. Francisco Degni s/n - Bairro Quitandinha, 14800-900 Araraquara, SP; tel. (16) 3301-6679; fax (16) 3322-2308; e-mail diretor@foar.unesp.br; internet www.iq.unesp.br):
Profa Dra MAYSA FURLAN

Assis Campus:

Faculty of Sciences and Humanities (Av. Dom Antonio 2100, 19800-900 Assis, SP; tel. (18) 3302-5802; fax (18) 3302-5804; e-mail diretor@assis.unesp.br; internet www.assis.unesp.br):
Prof. Dr ANTONIO CELSO FERREIRA

Bauru Campus:

Faculty of Architecture, Arts and Communication (Eng. Luiz Edmundo Carrijo Coube s/n, 17033-360 Bauru, SP; tel. (14) 3103-6050; fax (14) 3101-6051; e-mail diretor@faac.unesp.brr; internet www.faac.unesp.br):
Prof. Dr ANTONIO CARLOS DE JESUS

Faculty of Engineering and Technology (Eng. Luiz Edmundo Carrijo Coube s/n, 17033-360 Bauru, SP; tel. (14) 3221-6100; fax (14) 3221-6101; e-mail diretor@feb.unesp.br; internet www.feb.unesp.br):
Prof. Dr LAURO HENRIQUE MELLO CHUEIRI

Faculty of Sciences (Eng. Luiz Edmundo Carrijo Coube s/n, 17033-360 Bauru, SP; tel. (14) 3103-6070; fax (14) 3103-6071; e-mail diretor@fc.unesp.br; internet www.fc.unesp.br):
Prof. Dr JOSÉ BRÁS BARRETO DE OLIVEIRA

Botucatu Campus:

Faculty of Agronomical Sciences (Fazenda Experimental Lageado, 18610-307 Botacatu, SP; tel. (14) 3811-7150; fax (14) 3811-7139; e-mail diretor@fca.unesp.br; internet www.fca.unesp.br):
Prof. Dr LEONARDO THEODORO BÜLL

Faculty of Medicine (Distrito de Rubião Júnior s/n, 18618-970 Botucatu, SP; tel. and fax (14) 3811-6000; e-mail diretor@fmb.unesp.br; internet www.fmb.unesp.br):
Prof. Dr PASCOAL

Faculty of Veterinary Medicine and Animal Husbandry (Distrito de Rubião Júnior s/n, 18618-970 Botucatu, SP; tel. (14) 3811-6002; fax (14) 3815-4398; e-mail diretor@fmvz.unesp.br; internet www.fmvz.unesp.br):
Prof. Dr LUIZ CARLOS VULCANO

Institute of Biosciences (Distrito de Rubião Júnior s/n, 18618-970 Botucatu, SP; tel. and fax (14) 3811-6160; fax (14) 3811-6160; e-mail diretor@ibb.unesp.br; internet www.ibb.unesp.br):
Prof. Dr JOSÉ ROBERTO CÔRREA SAGGLIETTI

Dracena Campus:

Dracena Campus (R. Bahia 332, 17900-000 Métropole, SP; tel. (18) 3821-8101; fax (18) 3821-8100; internet www.dracena.unesp.br): Prof. Dr JOSÉ ANTONIO MARQUES

Franca Campus:

Faculty of History, Law and Social Services (R. Major Claudiano 1.488, 14400-690 Franca, SP; tel. (16) 3711-1804; fax (16) 3711-1807; e-mail diretor@franca.unesp.br; internet www.franca.unesp.br): Prof. Dr HELIO BORGHI

Guaratinguetá Campus:

Faculty of Engineering (Av. Dr Ariberto Pereira da Cunha 333, 12500-000 Guaratinguetá, SP; tel. (12) 3123-2800; fax (12) 3125-2466; e-mail direcao@feg.unesp.br; internet www.feg.unesp.br): Prof. Dr TÂNIA C. A. M. DE AZEVEDO

Ilha Solteira Campus:

Faculty of Engineering (Av. Brasil Centro 56, 15385-000 Ilha Solteira, SP; tel. (18) 3743-1000; fax (18) 3742-2735; e-mail gd@feis.unesp.br; internet www.feis.unesp.br): Prof. Dr VICENTE LOPES JUNIOR

Itapeva Campus:

Itapeva Campus (R. Geraldo Alckmin 519, 18049-010 Itapeva, SP; tel. (15) 3524-9100; fax (15) 3524-9107; internet www.itapeva.unesp.br): Prof. Dr MARCUS TADEU TIBÚRCO GONÇALVES

Jaboticabal Campus:

Faculty of Agricultural and Veterinary Sciences (Prof. Paulo Donato Castellane s/n, 14884-900 Jaboticabal, SP; tel. (16) 322-4250; fax (16) 322-4275; e-mail diretor@fcav.unesp.br; internet www.fcav.unesp.br): Prof. Dr ROBERVAL VIEIRA

Marília Campus:

Faculty of Philosophy and Sciences (Av. Hygino Muzzi Filho 737, 17525-900 Marília, SP; tel. and fax (14) 3402-1300; e-mail diretor@marilia.unesp.br; internet www.marilia.unesp.br): Prof. Dr MARIA CANDIDA SOARES DEL MASSO

Ourinhos Campus:

Ourinhos Campus (R. Dom José Marello 749, 19911-760 Vila Perino, SP; tel. (14) 3302-5800; fax (14) 3302-5802; e-mail joaolima@ourinhos.unesp.br; internet www.ourinhos.unesp.br): Prof. Dr JOÃO LIMA SANT'ANNA NETTO

Presidente Prudente Campus:

Faculty of Science and Technology, Presidente Prudente (R. Roberto Simonsen 305, 19060-900 Presidente Pridente, SP; tel. and fax (18) 229-5300; e-mail dirfct@prudente.unesp.br; internet www.prudente.unesp.br): Prof. Dr NERI ALVES

Registro Campus:

Registro Campus (R. Tamekeshi Takano 05, 11900-000 Centro, SP; tel. (13) 3828-2901; fax (18) 3828-2908; e-mail benez@registro.unesp.br; internet www.registro.unesp.br): Prof. SÉRGIO HUGO BENEZ

Rio Claro Campus:

Institute of Biosciences (Av. 24-A 1515, Bela Vista, 13500-900 Rio Claro, SP; tel. and fax (19) 3526-1400; e-mail dirib@rc.unesp.br; internet www.rc.unesp.br): Prof. Dr AMILTON FERREIRA

Institute of Geosciences and Exact Sciences (Rua Dez 2527, 13500-230 Rio Claro, SP; tel. (19) 534-0326; fax (19) 534-8250; e-mail diretor@caviar.igce.unesp.br): Profa Dra MARIA RITA CAETANO CHANG

Rosana Campus:

Rosana Campus (Av. dos Barrageiros s/n, 19274-000 Primavera, SP; tel. (18) 3284-9201; fax (18) 3284-9209; e-mail coordenadoria@rosana.unesp.br; internet www.rosana.unesp.br): Prof. Dr MESSIAS MENGHETTI JÚNIOR

São José dos Campos Campus:

Faculty of Dentistry (Av. Engenheiro Francisco José Longo 777, 12245-000 São José dos Campos, SP; tel. (12) 3947-9000; fax (12) 3947-9010; e-mail diretor@fosjc.unesp.br; internet www.fosjc.unesp.br): Profa Dra MARIA AMÉLIA MÁXIMO DE ARAÚJO

São José do Rio Preto Campus:

Institute of Biosciences, Humanities and Exact Sciences (Ruo Cristóvão Colombo 2265, 15054-000 São José do Rio Preto, SP; tel. (17) 221-2200; fax (17) 221-8692; e-mail diretor@ibilce.unesp.br; internet www.ibilce.unesp.br): Profa Dr JOHNNY RIZZIERI OLIVEIRA

São Paulo Campus:

Institute of Arts (Rua Dom Luiz Lasagna 400, Ipiranga, 04266-030 São Paulo, SP; tel. (11) 274-4733; fax (11) 274-2190; e-mail diretor@ia.unesp.br; internet www.ia.unesp.br): Profa Dra MARISA TRENCH O. FONTERRADA

Institute of Theoretical Physics (Rua Pamplona 145, 01405-900 São Paulo, SP; tel. (11) 3177-9090; fax (11) 215-1371; e-mail gkrein@iff.unesp.br; internet www.iff.unesp.br): Profa Dr GASTÃO I. KREIN

São Vicente Campus:

São Vicente Campus (Praça Infante Don Henrique s/n, 011330-205 São Vicente, SP; tel. (13) 3569-9403; fax (13) 3469-7374; e-mail coordenadoria@csv.unesp.br; internet www.csv.unesp.br): Prof. Dr MARCELO ANTONIO AMARO PINHEIRO

Sorocaba Campus:

Sorocaba Campus (Av. Três de Marco 511, 18087-180 Alto da Boa Vista, SP; tel. (15) 3238-3401; fax (15) 3228-2842; e-mail direcao@sorocaba.unesp.br; internet www.sorocaba.unesp.br): Prof. Dr GALDENORO BOTURA JÚNIOR

Tupã Campus:

Tupã Campus (Av. Domingas da Costa Lopes 780, 17602-660 Tupã, SP; tel. (14) 3404-4200; fax (14) 3404-4201; e-mail ejsimon@tupa.unesp.br; internet www.tupa.unesp.br): Prof. Dr ELIAS JOSÉ MARELLO

COMPLEMENTARY UNITS

Aquaculture Centre: Rodovia Carlos Tonanni km 5, 14870-000 Jaboticabal, SP; tel. (16) 3203-2500; fax (16) 3203-2268; e-mail fatima@caunesp.unesp.br; Dir Profa Dra ELISABETH CRISCUOLO URBINATI.

Centre for Education and Cultural Radio and Television: Av. Eng. Luiz Edmundo Carrijo Coube s/n°, 17033-360 Bauru, SP; tel. and fax (14) 230-5486; e-mail dir-rad@faac.unesp.br; Dir Prof. Dr MURILO CÉSAR SOARES.

Centre for Environmental Studies (CEA): Av. 24-A 1.515, 13506-900 Rio Claro, SP; tel. (19) 534-7298; fax (19) 534-2358; e-mail cea@life.ibrc.unesp.br; Dir Prof. Dr NIVAR GOBBI.

Centre of Excellence in Dental Care (CAOE): Rod. Marechal Rondon km 527, 16015-050 Araçatuba, SP; tel. (18) 622-4125 ext. 403; fax (18) 622-2638; e-mail saguiar@foa.unesp.br; Dir Profa Dra SANDRA MARIA H. C. AVILA DE AGUIAR.

Centre for the Study of Venom and Venomous Animals (CEVAP): Distrito de Rubião Junior s/n°, 18610-000 Botucatu, SP; tel. (14) 6821-2121 ext. 2054; fax (14) 6821-3963; e-mail cevap@botunet.com.br; Dir Prof. Dr CARLOS ALBERTO DE MAGALHÃES LOPES.

Centre for Tropical Root Crops (CERAT): Fazenda Experimental Lageado, CP 237, 18603-970 Botucatu, SP; tel. (14) 6802-7158; e-mail seccerat@fca.unesp.br; internet www.cerat.unesp.br; Dir Profa Dra ELISABETH CRISCUOLO URBINATI.

Institute of Meteorological Research (IPMet): Av. Eng Luiz Edmundo Carrijo Coube s/n, 17033-360 Bauru, SP; tel. (14) 221-6028; fax (14) 230-3649; e-mail ipmet_geral@ipmet.ipmet.unesp.br; Dir Prof. Dr MAURÍCIO DE AGOSTINHO ANTONIO.

Isotopes Centre: Distrito de Rubião Júnior s/n, 18618-000 Botucatu, SP; tel. (14) 6821-1171; fax (14) 6802-6359; e-mail ducatti@ibb.unesp.br; Dir Prof. Dr CARLOS DUCATTI.

AFFILIATED FACULTIES

Faculty of Technology, Americana: Av. Nossa Senhora de Fátima 567, 13465-000 Americana, SP; tel. (149) 468-1049; e-mail douglas@fatecam.com.br; internet www.fatecam.com.br.

Faculty of Technology, Baixada Santista: Av. Bartolomeu de Gusmão 110, 11045-401 Santos, SP; tel. (13) 227-6003; e-mail cpd_fatecbr@ig.com.br.

Faculty of Technology, Guaratinguetá: Praça Conselheiro Rodrigues Alves 48, 12500-000 Guaratinguetá, SP; tel. (12) 532-5110; e-mail fatec@provale.com.br.

Faculty of Technology, Indaiatuba: Rua D. Pedro I 65, 13330-000 Indaiatuba, SP; tel. (19) 834-9168.

Faculty of Technology, Jahu: Rua Frei Galvão s/n°, Jd. Pedro Ometto, 17212-650 Jaú, SP; tel. (14) 622-8533; e-mail fatec.jau@netsite.com.br; internet www.netsite.com.br/ccf/fatec.

Faculty of Technology, Ourinhos: Av. Vitalina Marcusso 1400, 19900-000 Ourinhos, SP; tel. (14) 323-3031; e-mail fatec@fatecou.com.br; internet www.fatecou.com.br.

Faculty of Technology, São Paulo: Praça Coronel Fernando Prestes 110, 01124-060 São Paulo, SP; tel. (11) 227-0105; e-mail secdir@fatecsp.br; internet www.fatecsp.br.

Faculty of Technology, Sorocaba: Av. Eng. Carlos Reinaldo Mendes 2015, 18013-280 Sorocaba, SP; tel. (15) 228-2381; e-mail fatecso@cruzeironet.com.br.

Faculty of Technology, Taquaritinga: Rua Dr Flávio Henrique Lemos 585, Portal Itamaracá, 15900-000 Taquaritinga, SP; tel. (16) 352-5250; e-mail fatec@tq.com.br; internet www.fatectq.com.br.

Faculty of Technology, Zona Leste: Av. Águia de Haia 2633, 03694-6271 São Paulo, SP; tel. (11) 61436271; e-mail fatec-zl@centropaulasouza.com.br; internet www.fatecsp.br.

PONTIFÍCIA UNIVERSIDADE CATÓLICA DE SÃO PAULO

Rua Monte Alegre 984, Perdizes, 05014-901 São Paulo, SP

Telephone: (11) 3670-8000

Fax: (11) 3670-8504

E-mail: reitoria@pucsp.br

Internet: www.pucsp.br

Founded 1946

Private control

Academic year: March to December (two semesters)

Grand Chancellor: Dom CLÁUDIO HUMMES (Archbishop of São Paulo)
Rector: Prof. Dr ANTONIO CARLOS CARUSO RONCA
Vice-Rector for Academic Affairs: Profa RAQUEL RAICHELIS DEGENSZAJN
Vice-Rector for Administration: Prof. EDUARDO FERNANDES P. MOREIRA
Vice-Rector for Community Affairs: Profa BRANCA JUREMA PONCE
General Secretary: Profa ADRIANA ANCONA DE FARIA
Librarian: ANA MARIA RAPASSI

Library of 250,000 vols
Number of teachers: 1,591
Number of students: 27,268

Publications: *Administração em Diálogo* (annually), *Caderno de Administração* (annually), *Cadernos Metrópole* (2 a year), *Cadernos PUC Economia* (2 a year), *Claritas* (annually), *Cognitio* (annually), *Delta* (2 a year), *Distúrbios da Comunicação* (2 a year), *Educação Matemática Pesquisa* (2 a year), *Galáxia* (2 a year), *Hypnos* (annually), *Intercâmbio* (annually), *Kairós* (2 a year), *Margem* (2 a year), *Natureza Humana* (2 a year), *Projeto História* (2 a year), *Psicologia da Educação* (2 a year), *Psicologia Revista* (2 a year), *Ciências Biológicas e do Ambiente* (4 a year), *Revista da FEA* (annually), *The ESPecialist* (2 a year), *Último Andar* (2 a year)

DIRECTORS

Centre of Law, Economics and Administration: Prof. ADHEMAR DE CAROLI
Centre of Humanities: Prof. EDISON NUNES
Centre of Mathematical, Physical and Technological Sciences: Profa TANIA MARIA MENDONÇA CAMPOS
Centre of Education: Profa NÁDIA DUMARA RUIZ DA SILVEIRA
Centre of Biological and Medical Sciences: Profa CIBELE ISAAC

DEANS

Centre of Law, Economics and Administration (tel. (11) 3670-8304; fax (11) 3670-8533; e-mail ccjea@pucsp.br):
- Faculty of Law: Prof. DIRCEU DE MELO
- Faculty of Economics: Prof. GILBERTO CAETANO

Centre of Humanities (tel. (11) 3670-8306; fax (11) 3670-8289; e-mail centrohumanas@pucsp.br):
- Faculty of Psychology: Profa MARIA DA GRAÇA MARCHINA GONÇALVES
- Faculty of Communications and Philosophy: Profa DIELI VESARO PALMA
- Faculty of Social Work: Profa MARIA ROSÂNGELA BATISTONI
- Faculty of Social Sciences: Profa MARGARIDA LIMENA

Centre of Mathematical, Physical and Technological Sciences (Rua Marquês de Paranaguá 111, 01303-050 São Paulo, SP; tel. (11) 3256-1622; fax (11) 3256-1622; e-mail pgedmat@pucsp.br):
- Faculty of Mathematical and Physical Sciences: Prof. FERNANDO ANTONIO DE CASTRO GIORNO

Centre of Education (tel. (11) 3670-8258; fax (11) 3670-8161; e-mail faceeducacao@pucsp.br):
- Faculty of Education: Profa MARINA FELDMANN

Centre of Biological and Medical Sciences (Praça Dr José Ermírio de Morães 290, 18030-230 Sorocaba, SP; tel. (15) 3212-9900; fax (15) 3212-9879; e-mail ccmb@pucsp.br):
- Faculty of Biological Sciences: Prof. WALTER BARRELLA
- Faculty of Medical Sciences: Profa MARIA HELENA SENGER

UNIVERSIDADE METODISTA DE SÃO PAULO

Rua do Sacramento, Rudge Ramos 230, CP 5002, 09640-000 São Bernardo do Campo, SP

Telephone: (11) 4366-5600
Fax: (11) 4366-5768
E-mail: reitoria@metodista.br
Internet: www.metodista.br

Founded 1997

Rector: Prof. Dr DAVI FERREIRA BARROS

Library of 97,000 vols, 4,900 periodicals
Number of teachers: 548
Number of students: 11,907.

UNIVERSIDADE FEDERAL DE SERGIPE

Av. Marechal Rondon s/n, Jardim Rosa Elze, CP 353, 49100-000 São Cristóvão, SE

Telephone: (79) 241-2848
Fax: (79) 241-3995
E-mail: ufs@ufs.br
Internet: www.ufs.br

Founded 1967
Federal control
Language of instruction: Portuguese
Academic year: March to December

Rector: JOSÉ FERNANDES DE LIMA
Vice-Rector: Prof. JOSÉ PAULINO DA SILVA
President of Council: Dr LUIZ GARCIA
Librarian: JUSTINO ALVES LIMA

Number of teachers: 448
Number of students: 5,908

Publications: *Revista* (irregular), *Jornal* (every 2 weeks), *Relatório Anual de Atividades*

DIRECTORS

Centre of Biological Sciences and Health (Rua Claudio Batista, Bairro Sanatário, Aracaju, Sergipe): Prof. Dr ANTONIO CESAR CABRAL DE OLIVEIRA
Centre of Applied Social Sciences: Prof. NAPOLEÃO DOS SANTOS QUEIROZ
Centre of Education and Humanities: Prof. LUIZ ALBERTO DOS SANTOS
Centre of Exact Sciences and Technology: Prof. JOSÉ AIRTON DOS SANTOS

HEADS OF DEPARTMENTS

Centre of Biological Sciences and Health:
- Biology: Profa MARIA HELENA ZUCON
- Surgery: Profa SÔNIA OLIVEIRA LIMA
- Physical Education: Prof. FERNANDO SANTOS OLIVEIRA
- Nursing and Nutrition: Profa LINDETE AMORIM SANTOS
- Physiology: Prof. ANTONIO EDILSON DO NASCIMENTO
- Internal Medicine: Prof. JOSÉ MARIA RODRIGUES SANTOS
- Morphology: Prof. GILENO DE SÁ CARDOSO
- Odontology: Prof. FERNANDO SANTOS VASCONCELOS
- Community Health: Prof. ANTÔNIO SAMARONE DE SANTANA

Centre of Applied Social Sciences:
- Administration: Prof. NAPOLEÃO DOS SANTOS QUEIROZ
- Law: Profa ARLENE PEREIRA CHAGAS
- Economics: Prof. JOSÉ MANUEL PINTO ALVIDOS
- Social Services: Profa TEREZINHA LEMOS S. DE ARAÚJO
- Accountancy: Prof. CARLOS AUGUSTO DOS SANTOS

Centre of Education and Humanities:
- Education: Profa ANTONIA GONÇALVES MAYNARD DIAS
- Geography: Prof. AGAMENON GUIMARÃES DE OLIVEIRA
- Philosophy and History: Profa LENALDA ANDRADE SANTOS
- Letters: Prof. JOSÉ COSTA ALMEIDA
- Psychology: Prof. JOSÉ CARLOS TOURINHO E SILVA
- Social Sciences: Prof. NADIA FRAGA VILLAS BOAS

Centre of Exact Sciences and Technology:
- Civil Engineering: Prof. JOÃO GALO DOS SANTOS AMARAL
- Chemical Engineering: Prof. EMERALDINO CASALI
- Statistics and Information: Profa YVONETE LOPES DE OLIVEIRA
- Mathematics: Prof. JOSÉ AIRTON BATISTA
- Physics: Prof. JOSÉ FERNANDES DE LIMA
- Chemistry: Prof. MARCIONILO DE MELO LOPES NETO

UNIVERSIDADE SEVERINO SOMBRA

Praça Martinho Nóbrega 40, Centro, 27700-000 Vassouras, RJ

Telephone: (24)2471-8200
Fax: (24) 2471-8225
E-mail: reitoria@uss.br
Internet: www.uss.br

Founded 1969
Private control

Rector: Dr AMÉRICO DA SILVA CARVALHO
Vice-Rector: ANTÓNIO ORLANDO IZOLANI
Pro-Rector: MARCO ANTÓNIO SOARES DE SOUZA
Pro-Rector: PAULO CÉSAR RODRIGUES CASSINO

Library: Libraries with 46,000 vols, 708 periodicals
Number of teachers: 207
Number of students: 2,034.

UNIVERSIDADE DE SOROCABA

Km 92.5, Rod. Raposo Tavares, 18023-000 Sorocaba, SP

Telephone: (15) 229-9200
Fax: (15) 229-9211
E-mail: uniso@uniso.br
Internet: www.uniso.br

Founded 1994
Academic year: February to December

Rector: ALDO VANNUCCHI

Library of 106,616 vols, 1,112 periodicals
Number of teachers: 316
Number of students: 9,992

Publications: *Revista de Estudos Universitários* (2 a year), *Quaestio – Revista de Estudos de Educação* (2 a year).

UNIVERSIDADE DE TAUBATÉ

Rua 4 de Março 432, 12020-270 Taubaté, SP

Telephone: (12) 232-7555
Fax: (12) 232-7660
E-mail: reitoria@lobato.unitau.br
Internet: www.unitau.br

Founded 1976
Municipal control
Academic year: March to November

Rector: Prof. Dr NIVALDO ZÖLLNER
Vice-Rector: Prof. CELSO FERRO
Pro-Rectors: Prof. PAULO GUAYCURÚ SAN-MARTIN (Economics and Finance), Profa MARIA JOSÉ MILHAREZI ABUD (Undergraduates), Profa VANDA APARECIDA VÁRZEA CURSINO (Extension), Profa MARIA JÚLIA FERREIRA XAVIER RIBEIRO (Research and Postgraduate Studies), Prof. WANDERLEY ANTONIO ANGARANO (Administration)

Secretary General: José Luiz Ribeiro do Valle
Chief Librarian: Henny Petersen França

Library of 195,000 vols
Number of teachers: 820
Number of students: 12,538

Publication: *Taubaté*

HEADS OF DEPARTMENTS

Biological Sciences and Health:
- Medicine: Prof. José Carlos de Carvalho
- Biology: Prof. Sérgio de Moura Araújo
- Nursing and Obstetrics: Profa Carmen Lúcia S. Pupio
- Psychology: Profa Cristiana M. Esper Berthoud
- Clinical Psychology: Profa Maria de Fátima C. D. Ferreira
- Dentistry: Prof. Gilson Serra Nogueira
- Physical Education: Prof. Sérgio Luiz Querido
- Agronomy: Prof. Vicente de Jesus Carvalho

Human Sciences and Literature:
- Social Communication: Prof. José Felício Goussain Murade
- Law: Prof. William Beny Block Telles Alves
- Social Work: Profa Maria Célia C. Minamisako
- Social Science and Literature: Prof. Gilio Giacomozzi
- Economics, Accounting and Administration: Prof. Orlandino Roberto Pereira Filho
- Education: Profa Mércia Aparecida da Cunha Oliveira

Sciences and Technology:
- Architecture and Town Planning: Prof. José Roberto Naves Silva
- Civil Engineering: Prof. José Carlos Simões Florençano
- Electrical Engineering: Prof. João Bosco Guaycurú Biscardi
- Mechanical Engineering: Prof. Sebastião Cardoso
- Mathematics and Physics: Prof. Reinaldo Gomes Alvarenga
- Data Processing: Prof. José Alberto Fernandes Ferreira

UNIVERSIDADE TIRADENTES

Av. Murilo Dantes 300, Farolândia, 49032-490 Aracaju, SE

Telephone: (79) 218-2100
Fax: (79) 218-2200
E-mail: asscom@unit.br
Internet: www.unit.br

Founded 1972
Private control

Rector: Jouberto Uchôa de Mendonça

Library of 111,904 vols, 957 periodicals
Number of teachers: 442
Number of students: 11,741

Publication: *Revista Fragmenta* (3 a year).

UNIVERSIDADE FEDERAL DE UBERLÂNDIA

Av. Engenheiro Diniz 1178, Martins, CP 00593, 38401-136 Uberlândia, MG

Telephone: (34) 239-4811
Fax: (34) 235-0099
E-mail: reitoria@ufu.br
Internet: www.ufu.br

Founded 1969
Academic year: February to December

Rector: Prof. Gladstone Rodrigues da Cunha Filho
Vice-Rector: Prof. Gilberto Arantes Carrijo
Pro-Rectors: Prof. Renato Alves Pereira (Planning and Administration), Prof. Osvaldo Freitas de Jesus (Education), Prof. Humberto Eustáquio Coelho (Research and Postgraduates), Prof. Waldenor Barros Moraes Filho (Extension, Culture and Student Affairs), Edna Pereira Alvim de Sousa (Human Resources)
Secretary-General: Elaine da Silveira Magali
Librarian: Elza Maria Pena F. Cosenza

Library of 132,000 vols, 5,200 periodicals
Number of teachers: 1,209
Number of students: 12,432

Publications: *Economia e Ensaios, Letras & Letras, Educação e Filosofia, Sociedade e Natureza, Veterinária e Notícias, Revista do CEBIM, Revista do CETEC, Revista do Direito, Ciência e Engenharia, Ensino em Revista*

DIRECTORS

Centre of Biomedical Sciences: Prof. Sebastião Rodrigues Ferreira Filho
Centre of Exact Sciences and Technology: Prof. Arquimedes Diogenes Ciloni
Centre of Humanities and Arts: Prof. Luiz Gonzaga Barbosa Pires

HEADS OF COURSES

Centre of Biomedical Sciences:
- Physical Education: Prof. Roberto José Tenório Lira
- Biology: Profa Ana Maria Coelho Cavalho
- Medicine: Prof. Eduardo Antônio Andrade
- Veterinary Medicine: Prof. Marcos Silva
- Odontology: Prof. Carlos José Soares
- Agronomy: Prof. Elias Nascentes Borges
- Immunology and Applied Parasitology: Prof. Ernesto Akio Taketomi
- Post-graduate Genetics and Biochemistry: Prof. Warwick Estevam Kerr
- Post-graduate Clinical Medicine: Prof. Renato Enrique Sologuren Achá

Centre of Exact Sciences and Technology:
- Mathematics: Prof. Márcio José Horta Dantas
- Civil Engineering: Profa Ilce Oliveira Campos
- Electrical Engineering: Prof. Keide Matumoto
- Electrical Engineering (Postgraduate): Prof. Darizon Alves de Andrade
- Chemical Engineering: Prof. Alvimar Ferreira Nascimento
- Mechanical Engineering: Prof. Orosimbo Andrade A. Rego
- Mechanical Engineering (Postgraduate): Prof. Álisson Rocha Machado
- Chemistry: Profa Efigênia Amorim
- Computer Science: Profa Márcia Aparecida Fernandes
- Chemical Engineering (Master's): Prof. Eloízio Júlio Ribeiro
- Physics: Prof. Antonio Tadeu Lino

Centre of Humanities and Arts:
- Arts: Profa Heliana Ometto Nardim
- Music: Profa Cíntia Thaís Morato Lopes
- Decorative Arts: Profa Maria Lourdes Pereira Fonesca
- Administration: Prof. Francisco José Wanderlei Osterne
- Economics: Prof. Paulo Antônio de Oliveira Gomes
- Law: Profa Aparecida Monteiro de França
- Geography: Prof. Júlio César Lima Ramirez
- History: Profa Christina Silva Roquete Lopreato
- Letters: Profa Maria Cristina Martins
- Education: Profa Helenice Camargos Viana Diniz
- Education (Master's): Prof. Jefferson Ildefonso da Silva
- Psychology: Profa Marcionila Rodrigues da Silva Brito
- Accountancy: Prof. João Batista Mendes
- Law Internships: Prof. Antônio Caixeta Ribeiro
- Philosophy: Prof. Alexandre Guimarães Tadeu Soares
- Social Sciences: Prof. Antônio Ricardo Micheloto
- Languages: Prof. Evandro Silva Martins
- Development Economics: Prof. Antônio César Ortega

UNIVERSIDADE ESTADUAL DO VALE DO ACARAÚ

Av. da Universidade 850, Betânia, 62040-370 Sobral, CE

Telephone: (85) 613-1213
Fax: (85) 613-1895
E-mail: reitoria@uvanet.br
Internet: www.uvanet.br

Founded 1968
State control

Rector: José Teodoro Soares

Library: Libraries with 26,000 vols
Number of teachers: 257
Number of students: 9,717.

UNIVERSIDADE DO VALE DO ITAJAÍ

Rua Uruguai 458, Centro, 88302-202 Itajaí, SC

Telephone: (47) 341-7500
Fax: (47) 341-7577
E-mail: reitoria@univali.rsc-sc.br
Internet: www.univali.br

Founded 1970
Municipal control

Rector: Edison Villela
International Affairs Office Co-ordinator: Prof. Dr J. M. Luna

Library: Libraries with 103,000 vols, 18,000 periodicals
Number of teachers: 1,180
Number of students: 26,100

Publications: *Alcance* (4 a year), *Turismo e Ação* (2 a year), *Novos Estudos Jurídicos* (2 a year).

UNIVERSIDADE DO VALE DO PARAÍBA

Praça Cândido Dias Castejon 116, 12245-720 São José dos Campos, SP

Telephone: (123) 22-2355
Fax: (123) 22-2668
Internet: www.univap.br

Founded 1992
Private control

Rector: Baptista Gargione Filho

Library of 59,000 vols, 539 periodicals
Number of teachers: 269
Number of students: 6,255.

UNIVERSIDADE DO VALE DO RIO DOS SINOS

Av. Unisinos 950, CP 275, 93022-000 São Leopoldo, RS

Telephone: (51) 590-8237
Fax: (51) 590-8443
E-mail: unisinos@unisinos.br
Internet: www.unisinos.br

Founded 1969
Private control (Society of Jesus)
Language of instruction: Portuguese
Academic year: February to December

President: Prof. Dr Aloysio Bohnen

Vice-President: Prof. Dr MARCELO FERNANDES DE AQUINO
Dean (Academic Affairs): PEDRO GILBERTO GOMES
Dean (Research and Development): Prof. LUDGER TEODORO HERZOG
Registrar: EUSÉBIO SCHNEIDER
Library Director: P. Dr LODOMILO AUGUSTO MALLMANN

Library of 721,098 vols
Number of teachers: 915
Number of students: 28,051

Publications: *Acta Biologica Leopoldensia* (every 4 months), *Acta Geologica Leopoldensia* (every 6 months), *Estudos Tecnológicos* (every 6 months), *Perspectiva Econômica* (online, every 6 months), *Estudos Jurídicos* (every 4 months), *Scientia* (every 6 months), *Verso & Reverso* (every 4 months), *Jornal UNISINOS* (quarterly), *Filosofia UNISINOS* (every 4 months), *Entrelinhas* (every 4 months), *IHU OnLine* (weekly), *Educação Unisinos* (every 4 months), *História Unisinos* (every 4 months), *Ciências Sociais Unisinos* (every 4 months), *Base: revista de Administração e Contabilidade da Unisinos* (every 4 months), *Calidoscópio* (every 4 months), *Fronteiras* (media studies, every 4 months), *Cooperativismo* (every 6months), *AV: Audio Visual* (every 6 months), *Arquitetura revista* (every 6months), *Controvérsia* (every 6months)

DEANS

Communication Sciences: Profa IONE MARIA GHISLENE BENTZ
Economics: Prof. TIAGO WICKSTROM ALVES
Exact and Technological Sciences: Profa SILVIA COSTA DUTRA
Health Sciences: Prof. CORNÉLIA HULDA VOLKART
Human Sciences: Prof. JOSÉ IVO FOLLMANN
Law: Prof. IELBO MARCUS LÔBO DE SOUZA

ATTACHED RESEARCH INSTITUTES

Anchietano Research Institute: Dir Dr PEDRO IGNÁCIO SCHMITZ.

Humanitas: Research and Community Services Institute: Dir P. IGNÁCIO NEUTZLING.

Information Technology Institute: Dir CRISTIANO ANDRÉ DA COSTA.

Instituto de Formação de Professores de Língua Alemão (IFPLA): Dir Prof. DARLI RENEU BREUNING.

Planarian Research Institute: Dir Dra ANA MARIA LEAL ZANCHET.

Unilínguas Languages Institute: Dir Profa SILVIA MATURRO PANZARDI FOSCHIERA.

UNIVERSIDADE VEIGA DE ALMEIDA

Rua Ibituruna 108, Bloco B (5° andar), Maracanã, 20271-020 Rio de Janeiro, RJ
Telephone: (21) 284-2362
Fax: (21) 248-2165
Internet: www.uva.br

Founded 1992
Private control

Rector: MÁRIO VEIGA DE ALMEIDA JUNIOR
Library: Libraries with 66,000 vols, 1,007 periodicals
Number of teachers: 333
Number of students: 6,864.

UNIVERSIDADE FEDERAL DE VIÇOSA

Av. P.H. Rolfs s/n, Campus Universitário, CP 384, 36571-000 Viçosa, MG
Telephone: (31) 3899-2796
Fax: (31) 3899-2203
E-mail: reitoria@mail.ufv.br
Internet: www.ufv.br

Founded 1926; formerly Universidade Rural do Estado de Minas Gerais
State control
Language of instruction: Portuguese
Academic year: March to November

Rector: Prof. EVALDO FERREIRA VILELA
Vice-Rector: Prof. FERNANDO COSTA BAÊTA
Pro-Rectors: Prof. OG FRANCISCO FONSECA DE SOUZA (Research and Postgraduate), Prof. JOSÉ BENÍCIO PAES CHAVES (Undergraduate), Prof. PAULO CÉSAR STRINGHETA (Extension and Culture), Prof. LUIZ CLÁUDIO COSTA (Community Affairs), Prof. LUIZ EDUARDO FERREIRA FONTES (Administration), Prof. JOSÉ MARIA ALVES DA SILVA (Planning and Budget)
Chief Administrative Officer: Prof. VICENTE DE PAULA LELIS
Director of Library: DORIS MAGNA DE AVELAR OLIVEIRA

Number of teachers: 786
Number of students: 9,584 (incl. 815 at high school level)

Publications: *Revista Ceres* (6 a year), *Boletim Técnico de Extensão*, *Revista Brasileira de Armazenamento*, *Revista Brasileira de Zootecnia* (6 a year), *Revista Oikos* (2 a year), *Revista de Educação Física* (2 a year), *Revista de Engenharia na Agricultura* (monthly), *Economia Rural* (6 a year), *Revista Gláuks* (2 a year), *Jornal da UFV* (monthly), *Revista de Ciências Humanas* (2 a year)

DIRECTORS

Agricultural Sciences Centre: Prof. MAURINHO LUIZ DOS SANTOS
Human Sciences and Liberal Arts Centre: Prof. ADRIEL RODRIGUES DE OLIVEIRA
Engineering and Technological Sciences Centre: Prof. LUIZ AURELIO RAGGI
Biological and Health Sciences Centre: Prof. RICARDO JUNQUEIRA DEL CARLO

HEADS OF DEPARTMENTS

Agricultural Sciences Centre (tel. (31) 3899-2161; fax (31) 3899-2266; e-mail cca@mail.ufv.br):

- Agricultural Economics: Prof. FÁTIMA MARÍLIA ANDRADE DE CARVALHO
- Agricultural Engineering: Prof. HAROLDO CARLOS FERNANDES
- Agronomy: Prof. JOSÉ GERALDO BARBOSA
- Forestry Engineering: Prof. AMAURY PAULO DE SOUZA
- Phytopathology: Prof. SÉRGIO HERMÍNIO BROMMONSCHENKEL
- Soil Science: Prof. REINALDO BERTOLA CANTARUTTI
- Animal Science: Prof. SEBASTIÃO DE CAMPOS VALADARES FILHO

Biological and Health Sciences Centre (tel. (31) 3899-2164; fax (31) 3899-2053; e-mail ccb@mail.ufv.br):

- Animal Biology: Prof. JORGE ABDALA DERGAM DOS SANTOS
- Biochemistry and Molecular Biology: Prof. GEORGE HENRIQUE KLING DE MORAES
- General Biology: Prof. MARCOS RIBEIRO FURTADO
- Plant Biology: Prof. ELDO ANTÔNIO MONTEIRO DA SILVA
- Physical Education: Prof. EMMI MYOTIN
- Nutrition and Health: Prof. NEUZA MARIA BRUNORO COSTA
- Microbiology: Prof. ARNALDO CHAER BORGES
- Veterinary Medicine: Prof. JOSÉ ANTÔNIO VIANA

Engineering and Technological Sciences Centre (tel. (31) 3899-2171; fax (31) 3899-2172; e-mail cce@mail.ufv.br):

- Civil Engineering: Prof. KLÉOS MAGALHÃES LENZ CÉSAR JÚNIOR
- Physics: Prof. MARCELO LOBATO MARTINS
- Computer Science: Prof. CARLOS DE CASTRO GOULART
- Architecture: Prof. ÍTALO ITAMAR CAIXEIRO STEPHAN
- Mathematics: Prof. MARGARETH DA SILVA ALVES
- Chemistry: Prof. BENJAMIN GONÇALVES MILAGRES
- Food Technology: Prof. JOSÉ ANTÔNIO MARQUES PEREIRA

Human Sciences and Liberal Arts Centre (tel. (31) 3899-2167; fax (31) 3899-2416; e-mail cch@mail.ufv.br):

- Business Administration: Prof. WALMER FARONI
- Economics: Prof. ADRIANO PROVEZANO GOMES
- Home Economics: Prof. SIMONE CALDAS TAVARES MAFRA
- Education: Prof. LOURDES HELENA DA SILVA
- Languages and Fine Arts: Prof. LÍVIA HELENA REBOUÇAS SANTANA LOURES
- Law: Prof. JOSÉ GERALDO CAMPOS GOUVÊIA

Colleges

GENERAL

Associação de Ensino Unificado do Distrito Federal: SEP/SUL, Eq. 704/904, Conjunto A, 70390-045 Brasília, DF; tel. (61) 321-3838; fax (61) 223-7195; f. 1967; controls Instituto de Ciências Sociais; courses in accountancy, administration, economics, education and law; 290 teachers; library: 42,000 vols; Pres. REZENDE RIBEIRO DE REZENDE.

Centro de Ensino Unificado de Brasília: SEPN 707/907, Campus do UniCEUB, Brasília, DF; tel. 340-1878; fax 340-1578; e-mail biblioteca@uniceub.br; internet www.uniceub.br; f. 1968; controls Faculdade de Direito do Distrito Federal, Faculdade de Filosofia, Ciências e Letras do Distrito Federal, Faculdade de Ciências Econômicas, Contábeis e Administrativas do Distrito Federal, Faculdade de Ciências da Educacão, Faculdade de Ciências da Saudé, Faculdade de Ciências Exatas e Tecnologia, Faculdade de Ciências Sociais e Aplicadas; library: 22,000 vols; 710 teachers; 14,000 students; Rector Dr JOÃO HERCULINO DE SOUZA LOPES; publs *Universitas–Biociencias* (2 a year), *Universitas–Psicologia* (2 a year), *Universitas–Jus* (2 a year).

Faculdades Integradas Hebraico Brasileira Renascença: Rua Prates 790, Bom Retiro, 01121-000 São Paolo; tel. (11) 33110778; fax (11) 2279587; e-mail faculdade.br@renascenca.br; internet www.renascenca.br/faculdade; f. 1975; attached to the Sociedade Hebraico Brasileira Renascença; languages of instruction: Portuguese, English; languages of instruction: Spanish, Hebrew; academic year January to December (two terms); library: 41,157 vols, 868 periodicals, 164 videos, 839 theses; 72 teachers; 1,107 students; Dir-Gen. Prof. BERNARDO ZWEIMAN ABRÃO.

Faculdades Oswaldo Cruz: Rua Brigadeiro Galvão 540, Barra Funda, São Paulo, SP; tel. 3825-4266; fax 3825-4266 ext. 236; e-mail faculdades@oswaldocruz.br; internet www.oswaldocruz.br; f. 1966; library: 36,565 vols; 328 teachers; 4,895 students; Dir CARLOS EDUARDO QUIRINO SIMÕES DE AMORIM;

Librarian VALDENISE MACHADO RIBEIRO FIDELIS..

Constituent institutions:

Faculdade de Ciências Farmacêuticas e Bioquímicas: Rua Brigadeiro Galvão 540, Prédio I 7° andar, Barra Funda, São Paulo, SP; tel. 3825-4266 ext. 259; fax 3825-4266 ext. 236; e-mail farmacia@oswaldocruz.br; internet www.oswaldocruz.brf. 1981; courses in pharmacy and biochemistry; 70 teachers; 504 students; Dir Prof. PAULO ROBERTO MIELE.

Escola Superior de Química: Rua Brigadeiro Galvão 540, Prédio I 7° andar, Barra Funda, São Paulo, SP; tel. 3825-4266 ext. 258; fax 3825-4266 ext. 236; e-mail esq@oswaldocruz.br; internet www.oswaldocruz.brf. 1966; 76 teachers; 1,313 students; courses in industrial chemistry, engineering; Dir Prof. VICTOR ABOU NEHMI.

Faculdade de Ciências Administrativas, Econômicas e Contábeis: Rua Brigadeiro Galvão 540, Prédio I 7° andar, Barra Funda, São Paulo, SP; tel. 3825-4266 ext. 245; fax 3825-4266 ext. 236; e-mail ocfaec@oswaldocruz.br; internet www.oswaldocruz.brf. 1974; 98 teachers; 2,257 students; courses in economics, accountancy and management; Dir Prof. Dr ODUVALDO CARDOSO.

Faculdade de Filosofia, Ciências e Letras: Rua Brigadeiro Galvão 540, Prédio I 7° andar, Barra Funda, São Paulo, SP; tel. 3825-4266 ext. 243; fax 3825-4266 ext. 236; e-mail ffcl@oswaldocruz.br; internet www.oswaldocruz.brf. 1969; 84 teachers; 821 students; courses in chemistry, physics, mathematics, Portuguese, pedagogy; Dir Prof. VICTOR ABOU NEHMI.

Federação de Escolas Superiores: Rua Cobre 200, 30000 Belo Horizonte, MG; f. 1967; controlled by the Fundação Mineira de Educação e Cultura; courses in psychology, education, civil engineering, business administration; 203 professors; 2,691 students; library: 25,000 vols; Pres. HÉLIO LOPES.

Fundação Valeparaibana de Ensino: Praça Cândido Dias Castejón 116, 12245 São José dos Campos, SP; tel. (123) 22-2355; f. 1963; Pres. Dr BAPTISTA GARGIONE FILHO..

Controls the following:

Faculdades Integradas de São José dos Campos: São José dos Campos; SP; 206 teachers; library of 53,000 vols; Dir Gen. JOÃO LUIZ TEIXEIRA PINTO...

Courses are offered by the following faculties:

Faculdade de Ciências Humanas: f. 1967; 48 teachers; 1,130 students; Dir IVONNE TESSIN WEIS.

Faculdade de Ciências Exatas e Tecnologia: f. 1968; 90 teachers; 800 students; Dir LUIZ ANTONIO PEDROSO DE MORAIS.

Faculdade de Ciências Sociais Aplicadas: f. 1952; 68 teachers; 1,560 students; Dir FRANCISCO JOSÉ DE CASTRO PIMENTEL.

Instituição 'Moura Lacerda': Rua Padre Euclides 995, Ribeirão Prêto, SP; tel. 636-1010; f. 1923; consists of the Faculdade de Ciências Econômicas de Ribeirão Prêto, the Instituto Politécnico de Ribeirão Prêto, the Faculdade de Filosofia, Ciências e Letras de Ribeirão Prêto, the Faculdade de Arquitetura e Urbanismo de Ribeirão Prêto, the Faculdade de Educação Física de Jaboticabal, also two teacher training colleges and a music conservatoire; library: 50,000 vols; Pres. Dr OSCAR LUIS DE MOURA LACERDA.

ECONOMICS, POLITICAL SCIENCE, SOCIOLOGY

Escola de Administração de Emprêsas de São Paulo da Fundação Getúlio Vargas: Av. 9 de Julho 2029, 01313-902 São Paulo, SP; tel. 281-7700; fax (11) 284-17-89; e-mail mazzvca@fgvsp.br; internet www.fgvsp.br; f. 1954; library: 70,000 books, 1,200 periodicals; business and public administration; 250 teachers; 4,616 students; Dir ALAIN F. STEMPFER; publs *Revista de Administração de Emprêsas*, *Relatórios de Pesquisa*.

Universidade de Santa Cruz do Sul: Av. Independência 2293, CP 236, Santa Cruz do Sul, RS; tel. (51) 717-7365; fax (51) 715-1855; f. 1964; courses in accountancy; library: 26,000 vols; Course Co-ordinator Prof. RENÊ LUIZ SEIBERT.

Faculdade de Ciências Econômicas do Sul de Minas: Av. Pres. Tancredo de A. Neves 55, CP 37500, Itajubá, MG; f. 1965; Dir HÉCTOR GUSTAVO ARANGO.

Faculdade de Ciências Econômicas e Administrativas de Santo André: Av. Príncipe de Gales 821, CP 247, Santo André, SP; tel. (11) 449-3093; fax (11) 440-2048; f. 1954; supported by the Fundação Santo André; library: 19,340 vols; Dir Prof. CARLOS VIEIRA.

Faculdade de Ciências Econômicas e Administrativas de Taubaté: Rua Visconde do Rio Branco 210, Taubaté, SP; f. 1961; courses in accounting, economics and business administration; Dir Dr ULISSES VIEIRA.

Faculdade de Ciências Políticas e Econômicas de Cruz Alta: Rua Andrade Neves 308, Cruz Alta, RS; f. 1955; independent; library: 4,605 vols; Dir DARIO SILVEIRA NETTO.

Faculdade Estadual de Ciências Econômicas de Apucarana: Rodovia do Café, BR 376-Km 3, CP 98, 86800 Apucarana, PR; f. 1959; state school; Dir Prof. ADRIANO CORRÊA.

Instituto Rio Branco: Anexo II do Palácio Itamaraty, Ministério das Relações Exteriores, 70170-900 Brasília, DF; tel. 211-6194; fax 322-8355; f. 1945; official Brazilian Diplomatic Academy; 2-year graduate courses; also courses for foreign students; Dir Min. ANDRE MATTOSO MAIA AMADO; publ. *Yearbook*.

Instituto Universitário de Pesquisas do Rio de Janeiro: Rua da Matriz 82, Botafogo, 22260-100, Rio de Janeiro, RJ; tel. (21) 537-8020; fax (21) 286-7146; f. 1963; research and graduate training in sociology and political science; 18 teachers; library: 20,000 vols; Dir RENATO LESSA; publs *Dados* (3 a year), *Indice de Ciências Sociais* (2 a year), *Série Estudos* (monthly), *Cadernos de Conjuntura* (irregular).

LAW

Faculdade de Direito Cândido Mendes: Praça 15 de Novembro 101, Rio de Janeiro, RJ; f. 1953; courses in law, sociology and economics; library: 10,000 vols; Dir Prof. CÂNDIDO MENDES DE ALMEIDA; publ. *Dados*.

Faculdade de Direito de Caruarú: Av. Portugal s/n, 55100 Caruarú, PE; f. 1959; library: 6,027 vols; Dir Prof. LUÍZ PINTO FERREIRA; publ. *Revista*.

Faculdade de Direito de São Bernardo do Campo: Rua Java 425, Jardim do Mar, CP 180, 09750-650 São Bernardo do Campo, SP; tel. and fax 4123-0222; e-mail diretoria@direitosbc.br; internet www.direitosbc.br; f. 1964; library: 27,000 vols; 57 teachers; 2,486 students; Dir LUIZ ANTONIO MATTOS PIMENTA ARAÚJO.

Faculdade de Direito de Sorocaba: Rua Dra. Ursulina Lopes Torres 123, 18100 Sorocaba, SP; f. 1957; library: 10,000 vols; Dir Dr HELIO ROSA BALDY; publ. *Revista*.

MEDICINE

Escola de Farmácia e Odontologia de Alfenas: Rua Gabriel Monteiro da Silva 714, 37130-000 Alfenas, MG; tel. (35) 3299-1062; fax (35) 3299-1063; e-mail grad@efoa.int.br; f. 1914; graduate courses in dentistry, biochemical and applied pharmacy, general nursing and obstetrics, biological sciences and nutrition; 127 teachers; library: 16,059 vols; Dean Prof. MACIRO MANOEL PEREIRA; publ. *Revista*.

Universidade Federal de São Paulo: Rua Botucatú 740, 04023-062 São Paulo, SP; tel. (11) 5549-7699; fax (11) 5576-4313; e-mail unifesp@epm.br; f. 1933 (formerly Escola Paulista de Medicina); medicine, biomedical sciences, nursing, phonoaudiology and ophthalmic technology; library: 9,002 vols, 8,079 journals, 10,600 theses; 635 teachers; 3,853 students; Dean Dr HELIO EGYDIO NOGUEIRA; publ. *A Folha Médica* (4 a year).

Faculdade de Ciências Médicas de Pernambuco: Hospital Escola Oswaldo Cruz, Rua Arnóbio Marques 310, Santo Amaro, Recife, PE; tel. (81) 421-1761; f. 1950; supported by the Fundação do Ensino Superior de Pernambuco; 165 teachers; library: 22,763 vols; Dir Prof. JOSÉ GUIDO CORRÊA DE ARAÚJO.

Faculdade de Medicina do Triângulo Mineiro: Rua Frei Paulino 30, 38025-180 Uberaba, MG; tel. (34) 3318-5004; fax (34) 3312-1487; e-mail diretoria@diretoria.fmtm.br; internet www.fmtm.br; f. 1953; 185 teachers; 1,383 students; Dir Prof. EDSON LUIZ FERNANDES.

Faculdade de Odontologia de Lins: Rua Tenente Florêncio Pupo Neto 300, CP 118, 16400 Lins, SP; f. 1954; independent; Dir NICÁCIO GARCIA HERNANDES; publ. *Revista da Faculdade de Odontologia de Lins*.

Faculdade de Odontologia, Universidade de Passo Fundo: Rua Teixeira Soares 817, 99010-080 Passo Fundo, RS; tel. (54) 311-1177; fax (54) 311-1307; f. 1961; dentistry; 44 teachers; 310 students; Dean Dr RUI GETÚLIO SOARES.

Faculdade de Odontologia de Pernambuco: CP 1536, Av. Gral. Newton Cavalcanti 1650, Caramajibe, São Lourenço da Mata, PE; f. 1957; supported by the Fundação da Ensino Superior de Pernambuco; undergraduate and postgraduate courses; 32 teachers; 243 students; Dir Prof. EDRIZIO BARBOSA PINTO.

Faculdade de Odontologia do Triângulo Mineiro: Av. Guilherme Ferreira 217, CP 93, 38100 Uberaba, MG; f. 1947; four-year graduate course in Dentistry; library: 3,500 vols; Dir Prof. JAYME SOARES BILHARINHO NETTO; Sec. Dr ANDRÉ LUÍZ MARTINS COIMBRA.

Fundação Faculdade Federal de Ciências Médicas de Porto Alegre: Rua Sarmento Leite 245, 90050-170 Porto Alegre, RS; tel. 26-79-13; f. 1953; library: 9,000 vols; 211 teachers; Dir Prof. OSCAR BELMIRO MANOEL MAY PEREIRA; publ. *Pesquisa Médica*.

PHILOSOPHY, ARTS AND LITERATURE

Faculdade de Filosofia, Ciências e Letras de Ouro Fino: Rodovia MG 290, Km 59, Ouro Fino, CP 38, MG; f. 1972; run by Associação Sul Mineira de Educação e Cultura; 23 teachers; 1,437 students; library: 8,306 vols, 3,522 periodicals; Pres. Prof. GUILHERME BERNARDES; publ. *Signum*.

Faculdades Salesianas – Unidade de Ensino de Lorens: Rua Dom Bosco 284, CP 41, 12600-000 Lorena, SP; f. 1985; courses in psychology, history, geography, education, law, philosophy and sciences; library: 60,000 vols; Dir Pe. DILSON PASSOS JUNIOR; Sec. GETULINO DO ESPÍRITO SANTO MACIEL; publ. *Revista*.

TECHNICAL

Centro Universitário do Instituto Mauá de Tecnologia: Praça Mauá, CEP 09580-900, São Caetano do Sul, SP; tel. (11) 4239-3000; fax (11) 4239-3041; e-mail ceum@maua.br; internet www.maua.br; f. 1961; civil, electrical, mechanical, industrial, chemical, environmental and food engineering, mechatronics and packaging technology; library: 60,000 vols; 250 teachers; 4,000 students; Dir OTAVIO DE MATTOS SILVARES.

Escola de Engenharia de Lins: Av. Nicolau Zarvos 1925, CP 103, 16400-000 Lins, SP; tel. (145) 22-2300; fax (145) 22-2300; f. 1961; departments of civil and electrical engineering, attached faculties of informatics and of Social Services; 50 teachers; 650 students; Pres. Prof. EDGAR PAULO PASTORELLO; Dir of Engineering Prof. BERNARDO LUIZ COSTAS FUMIÓ..

Attached institute:

Faculdade de Informática de Lins: f. 1986; department of data processing technology; 25 teachers; 280 students; Dir of Data Processing Profa MARIA EMILCE FERREIRA VILLELA PASTORELLO.

Escola de Engenharia de Taubaté: Av. Marechal Deodoro 605, Taubaté, SP; f. 1962; courses in civil, mechanical and electrical engineering; library: 6,000 vols; Dir Eng. ADOLFO FERNANDES ARAÚJO.

Escola Superior de Desenho Industrial: Rua Evaristo da Veiga 95, Rio de Janeiro 20031-040; tel. (21) 2240-1790; fax (21) 2240-1890; e-mail diretoria@esdi.uerj.br; internet www.esdi.uerj.br; f. 1962; state school, affiliated to Univ. do Estado do Rio de Janeiro; courses in product and graphic design; 34 teachers; 160 students; Dean GABRIEL PATROCÍNIO.

Universidad Federal Rural da Amazôn: CP 917, 66077-530 Belém, PA; tel. (91) 274-4518; fax (91) 274-4518; e-mail biblioteca@ufra.edu.br; internet www.ufra.edu.br; f. 1951; agronomic, forestry and veterinary studies, zootechnics, fisheries engineering; library: 18,000 vols, 1,343 periodicals; 118 teachers; 1,900 students; Dir Dr MANOEL MALHEIROS TOURINHO; publs *Revista de Ciências Agrárias* (2 a year), *O Trimestre*, *Informe Técnico* (irregular), *Informe Didático* (irregular), *Cartilhas Didáticas* (irregular), *Livros Técnicos* (irregular).

Faculdade de Ciências de Barretos: Av. Prof. Roberto Frade Monte 389, CP 16, 14783-266 Barretos, SP; tel. (173) 22-6411; fax (173) 22-6205; f. 1969; physics, mathematics, chemistry and food engineering and processing; library: 13,300 vols; Principal LUIZA MARIA PIERINI MACHADO.

Faculdade de Engenharia de Barretos: C/o Fundacão Educacional de Barretos, Av. Prof. Roberto Frade Monte 389, CP 16, 14783-226 Barretos, SP; tel. (17) 3322-6411; fax (17) 3322-6205; e-mail dirgeral@feb.br; internet www.feb.br; f. 1965; part of the Fundação Educacional de Barretos; civil, food and electrical engineering; library: 14,000 vols; 202 teachers; 2,000 students; Academic Dir PATRICIA HELENA RODRIGUES DE SOUZA; Vice-Dir Dr OLIVIO CARLOS NASCIMENTO SOUTO.

Instituto Militar de Engenharia: Praça Gen. Tibúrcio 80, Praia Vermelha, 22290-270 Rio de Janeiro, RJ; tel. (21) 295-8146; fax (21) 275-9047; f. 1792, present name 1959; undergraduate, master's and doctoral courses in sciences and engineering; 200 teachers; 500 students; library: 20,000 vols; Dir JOSÉ CARLOS ALBANO DO AMARANTE.

Instituto Nacional de Telecomunicações de Santa Rita do Sapucaí (INATEL): Av. João de Camargo 510, CP 05, Santa Rita do Sapucaí, MG; tel. (35) 471-9200; fax (35) 471-9314; e-mail informa@inatel.br; f. 1965; electrical engineering (electronics and telecommunications); library: 13,000 vols; Dir Prof. PEDRO SERGIO MONTI.

Instituto Tecnológico de Aeronáutica: Praça Mal. do Ar Eduardo Gomes 50, Vila das Acácias, 12228-900 São José dos Campos, SP; tel. (12) 3947-5731; fax (12) 3941-3500; e-mail reitor@ita.br; internet www.ita.br; f. 1950; divisions of Electronic Engineering, Aeronautical Engineering, Mechanical Engineering, Civil and Basic Engineering, Computer Engineering; 130 teachers; 800 students; library: 98,841 vols and reports, 135,000 microforms, 2,182 periodicals, 5,000 electronic publications; Rector Prof. MICHAL GARTENKRAUT; Dean Prof. FERNANDO TOSHINORI SAKANE; Admin. Officer Cel. DINO ISHIKURA; publ. *Produção Técnico Científica*.

Instituto Tecnológico e Científico 'Roberto Rios' (INTEC): Av. Prof. Roberto Frade Monte 389, 14780 Barretos, SP; f. 1981; soil physics, solar energy, apiculture, civil and electrical engineering; Dir WANDERLEY MAURO DIB.

Schools of Art and Music

Centro de Letras e Artes da UNI-RIO: Av. Pasteur 436, Urca, 22290-240 Rio de Janeiro, RJ; tel. (21) 295-2548; fax (21) 295-1043; f. 1969; four-year course in theatre and music, Masters course in theatre and Brazilian music; 96 teachers; 850 students; library: 25,000 vols, 7,000 scores, 3,000 records; Dean EDIR EVANGELISTA GANDRA; Dirs AUSONIA BERNARDES MONTEIRO, NEREIDA DE ASSIS NOGUEIA DE MOURA RANGEL.

Conservatório Brasileiro de Música: Av. Graça Aranha 57, 12°, Rio de Janeiro; tel. (21) 240-5431; fax (21) 240-6131; f. 1936; undergraduate and postgraduate courses; library: 6,000 vols; Dir-Gen. MARINA H. LORENZO FERNANDEZ SILVA; publ. *Revista Pesquisa e Música*.

Conservatório Dramático e Musical de São Paulo: Av. São João 269, São Paulo; f. 1906; library: 30,000 vols; Dir Dr ALONSO A. DA FONSECA (acting).

Escola de Artes Visuais (School of Visual Arts): Rua Jardim Botânico 414, Parque Lage, 22461-000 Rio de Janeiro, RJ; tel. (21) 2538-1879; fax (21) 2538-1879; e-mail eav@eavparquelage.org.br; internet www.eavparquelage.org.br; f. 1975; linked administratively to the State Department of Culture; courses in painting, drawing, sculpture, photography, video, computer art, art theory and history; library: 5,500 vols; 40 teachers; 1,200 students; Dir REYNALDO ROELS Jr.

Escola de Comunicações e Artes: Av. Prof. Lúcio M. Rodrigues 443, Cidade Universitária, 05508-900 São Paulo; tel. (11) 3818-4066; fax (11) 3818-4304; e-mail rebeca@edu.usp.br; f. 1967; undergraduate and postgraduate training given; mass communication, library and information science, journalism, public relations, film, radio, television, the arts, theatre courses, music, advertising, tourism, publishing; library: 28,000 vols, 1,600 periodical titles, 6,000 records, 10,000 slides, 900 video tapes, 6,000 art exhibition catalogues, 250 films, 3,200 theses, 2,300 photographs, etc; 180 teachers; 1,736 students; Librarian BÁRBARA JÚLIA M. LEITÃO.

Escola de Música e Belas Artes do Paraná: Rua Emiliano Perneta 179, 80000 Curitiba, PR; f. 1948; library: 2,350 vols, also tapes, records; musical instruments, singing, plastic arts; Dir LILIAN M. SCHEEL.

Escola de Música da Universidade Federal do Rio de Janeiro: Rua do Passeio 98, Lapa, 20021-290 Rio de Janeiro, RJ; tel. (21) 240-1391; fax (21) 240-1591; f. 1848; 77 teachers; 478 students; library: 100,000 vols of music; museum of 90 antique instruments; Dir Prof. JOSÉ ALVES; Librarian DOLORES BRANDÃO DE OLIVEIRA; publ. *Revista Brasileira de Música* (irregular)..

Attached to the school:

Centro de Pesquisas Folclóricas: Rio de Janeiro; f. 1943; Dir Prof. SAMUEL MELLO ARAÚJO Jr.; collections of traditional music on records.

Faculdade de Belas Artes de São Paulo: Rua Edmundo Juventino Fuentes 160 (apt 12), Edif. Torino, 03280-000 São Paulo, SP; tel. (11) 6946-1255; fax (11) 6946-1255; e-mail vania.traducoes@originet.com.br; f. 1925; architecture, town planning, industrial arts and design, painting, sculpture, etc.; 130 teachers; library: 10,000 vols; Dir PAULO ANTONIO GOMES CARDIM.

Faculdade de Música Mãe de Deus: Av. São Paulo 651, CP 106, 86100 Londrina, PR; f. 1965; library: 2,650 vols; Dir Profa. THEODOLINDA GERTRUDES MORO; publ. *Fôlha de Londrina*.

Faculdade Santa Marcelina – (FASM): Rua Dr Emílio Ribas 89, 05006-020 Perdizes, SP; tel. (11) 3824-5800; fax (11) 3824-5818; e-mail fasm@fasm.edu.br; internet www.fasm.edu.br; f. 1929; music, musical instruments, singing, composition, art education, visual arts, fashion design, electric-acoustic music, marketing administration, international relations, nursing; 169 teachers; 1,700 students; library: 50,000 vols; Pres. FILOMENA MARIA PEDONE; Dir ÂNGELA RIVERO.

Fundação Armando Alvares Penteado: Rua Alagoas 903, 10242 São Paulo; tel. 826-4233; f. 1947; 1,120 teachers; 12,000 students; Pres. LUCIA C. PINTO DE SOUZA.

Instituto de Letras e Artes: Rua Marechal Floriano 179, 96015-440 Pelotas, RS; tel. (53) 225-9544; fax (53) 222-4318; internet www.ufpel.tche.br; f. 1971; institute of the Universidade Federal de Pelotas; degree courses in plastic arts, music, literature and culture, English, French, Spanish; 60 teachers; 800 students; Dir ANAIZI CRUZ ESPÍRITO SANTO.

BRUNEI

The Higher Education System

The University of Brunei Darussalam (founded in 1985) is the principal institution of higher education. Malay is the official language of instruction, but courses are also taught in English and Arabic (especially Islamic education). The Ministry of Education is responsible for higher education.

Students with adequate 'A' Level passes are eligible for entry to the University of Brunei Darussalam or other tertiary institutions or to be awarded scholarships to study abroad. The Institut Teknologi Brunei provides courses leading to a Higher National certificate (part-time) or a National Diploma (full-time). Bachelors degrees at the University of Brunei Darussalam last for four to six years and programmes operate on a US-style 'credit' system, with a minimum number required for graduation.

Learned Societies

LANGUAGE AND LITERATURE

Alliance Française: No. 1, A24-7 Spg 465, Ting Sing Garden, Kg. Sg. Tilong Jalan Muara, Bandar Seri Begawan BS 8675; tel. (2) 343245; fax (2) 339214; e-mail secretariataf@brunet.bn; offers courses and exams in French language and culture and promotes cultural exchange with France.

British Council: 2nd Fl., Block D, Yayasan Complex Sultan Haji Hassanal Bolkiah Jalan Pretty Bandar Seri Begawan, Brunei Darussalam BS8711; tel. (2) 237742; fax (2) 237392; e-mail all.enquiries@bn.britishcouncil.org; internet www.britishcouncil.org/brunei; offers courses and exams in English language and British culture and promotes cultural exchange with the UK; Dir AMANDA GRIFFITHS.

Research Institutes

AGRICULTURE, FISHERIES AND VETERINARY SCIENCE

Brunei Agricultural Research Centre, Department of Agriculture: Dept of Agriculture, Ministry of Industry and Primary Resources, Kilanas, Jalan Tutong BF2520; tel. (2) 661894; fax (2) 661354; e-mail barc001@brunet.bn; internet www.brunet.bn/gov/doa/barc.htm; f. 1984; present name since 1995; 100 mems; Head of Division Pg Hajah ROSIDAH BINTI PG HG METUSSIN.

HISTORY, GEOGRAPHY AND ARCHAEOLOGY

Brunei History Centre: Ministry of Culture, Youth and Sports, Bandar Seri Begawan; tel. (2) 240167; fax (2) 241958; e-mail sejarah@brunet.bn; internet www.history-centre.gov.bn; f. 1982; government dept under the Ministry of Culture, Youth and Sports; research on Brunei's history and genealogies, and history of Brunei's Sultan, royal families, and state dignitaries; Dir Haj AWANG MOHAMED JAMIL AL-SUFRI; publs *Pusaka* (Heritage, 2 a year), *Darussalam* (The Abode of the Peace, annually).

Library

Bandar Seri Begawan

Language and Literature Bureau Library: Jalan Elizabeth II, Bandar Seri Begawan; tel. (2) 235501; f. 1961; reference and lending facilities open to the public; 300,000 vols in Malay and English; one central and 4 full-time brs; 5 mobile units; Chief Librarian Haji ABU BAKAR BIN Haji ZAINAL; publs *Accessions List*, indexes.

Museums and Art Galleries

Bandar Seri Begawan

Brunei Museum: Jalan Kota Batu, Bandar Seri Begawan BD 1510; tel. (2) 244545; fax (2) 242727; e-mail bmlibry@brunet.bn; internet www.museums.gov.bn; f. 1965; ethnographical, historical, archaeological displays; natural history, oriental arts and cultural heritage colln; library of 77,813 vols, Borneo collection of 2,492 vols, 63,927 local publications; legal depository for Brunei; Dir AWANG HAJI MATASSIM BIN HAJI JIBAH; publs *Berita Muzium* (quarterly), *Brunei Darussalam National Bibliography* (annually), *Brunei Museum Journal* (annually).

Constitutional History Gallery: Jalan Sultan, Bandar Seri Begawan BD 1510; tel. (2) 238360; fax (2) 242727; f. 1984; Dir PENGIRAN Haji HASHIM BIN PENGIRAN Haji MOHAMED JADID.

Malay Technology Museum: Jalan Kota Batu, Bandar Seri Begawan BD 1510; tel. (2) 242861; fax (2) 242727; e-mail bmethno@brunet.bn; internet www.museums.gov.bn/bangunan1.htm; f. 1988; exhibitions of local industries and handicrafts; Dir PENGIRAN Haji HASHIM BIN PENGIRAN Haji MOHD JADID.

Royal Regalia Building: Jalan Sultan, Bandar Seri Begawan BS 8610; tel. (2) 238360; fax (2) 242727; internet www.museums.gov.bn/bangunan2.htm; f. 1992; Dir Haji MATASSIM BIN HAJI JIBAH.

University

UNIVERSITY OF BRUNEI DARUSSALAM

Jalan Tungku Link, Gadong BE 1410

Telephone: (2) 463001

Fax: (2) 461003

Internet: www.ubd.edu.bn

Founded 1985; the Sultan Hassanal Bolkiah Teachers' College was integrated into the University in 1988

State control

Languages of instruction: Malay, English

Academic year: August to May (two semesters)

Chancellor: HM Sultan Haji HASSANAL BOLKIAH MU'IZZADDIN WADDAULAH

Pro-Chancellor: HRH Crown Prince Pengiran MUDA HAJI AL-MUHTADEE BILLAH

Vice-Chancellor: Dr Haji ISMAIL BIN HAJI DURAMAN

Assistant Vice-Chancellor: Pengiran Dr Haji MOHD YUSOP BIN AWG HAJI DAMIT (Administration and Student Affairs)

Registrar and Secretary: Dr Haj MATAMIT BIN RATU

Chief Librarian: NELLIE HAJI SUNNY

Library of 340,000 vols

Number of teachers: 300

Number of students: 2,800

Publications: *Jare* (annually), *Tinjauan* (annually), *Ungkayah* (4 a year)

DEANS

Faculty of Arts and Social Science: Dr MATAIM BIN BAKAR

Faculty of Business, Economics and Policy Studies: Dr AZMAN BIN AHMAD,

Faculty of Science: Dr ZOHRAH BINTI HAJI SULAIMAN

Academy of Brunei Studies: Pengiran Dr Haji ABU BAKAR BIN PENGIRAN HAJI SARIFUDDIN

Communication and Technology Centre: Dr YONG CHEE TUAN

Educational Technology Centre: Haji ANDY AZHAR BIN HAJI SURA

Sultan Hassanal Bolkiah Institute of Education: Dr Haji JUNAIDI BIN HJ ABD RAHMAN

Sultan Haji Omar Ali Saifuddien Institute of Islamic Studies: Pengiran Dr Haji SERBINI BIN HAJI MATAHIR AL-AZHAR

Institute of Medicine: Dr ZULKAMAIN HAJI HANAFI

Language Centre: Haji ROSNAH HAJI RAMLI

Postgraduate Studies and Research: Dr Hajah HAIRUNI BINTI HAJI MOHD ALI MARICAR

Student Affairs: AMPUAN HAJI BRAHIM BIN AMPUAN HAJI TENGAH

Colleges

There are Adult Education Centres attached to colleges and schools

Institut Teknologi Brunei: Tungku Link, Gadong, Bandar Seri Begawan 1410; tel. (2) 461020; fax (2) 461035; internet www.itb.edu.bn; f. 1986; B/TEC HND and BEng courses; library: 35,000 vols; 83 teachers; 483 students; Dir Haji MOHAMED YUSRA BIN HAJI ABDUL HALIM; Registrar Haji MOHAMMAD BIN HAJI HIDUP; Librarian HAJAH PUSPARAINI BINTI HAJI THANI

HEADS OF DEPARTMENTS

Business and Management: HAJAH ROSE BINTI HAJI KARIM

Civil Engineering: Haji KHAIRUL BASHAR MOHAMMAD SHAIFIUDDIN

Computing and Information Systems: SOPHIANA CHUA BINTI ABDULLAH

Electrical and Electronic Engineering: M. MATHEW POULOSE

Mechanical Engineering: Dr HAKIM A. ABBASS

Jefri Bolkiah College of Engineering: POB 63, Kuala Belait 6000; internet www.brunet.bn/php/chongrms/jbcehome.htm; f. 1970; craft, technical, mathematics and English courses; 78 staff; 350 students; Principal MICHAEL LIM (acting).

Seri Begawan Religious Teachers' College: Bandar Seri Begawan.

Sultan Saiful Rijal Technical College: POB 914, Simpang 125, Jalan Muara; tel. (2) 331077; fax (2) 343207; e-mail mtssr@brunet.bn; internet www.mtssr.edu.bn; f. 1985; engineering and business courses; 195 teachers; 1,000 students; Dir PENGIRAN SUHAIMI BIN PENGIRAN HAJI BAKAR (acting).

BULGARIA

The Higher Education System

Higher education is supported by the State through the aegis of the Ministry of Education. During the mid-1990s the higher education system was extensively reorganized, with a degree system introduced and many foundations renamed. Higher education is governed by the Higher Education Act (amended 1999, 2001 and 2004) and the Academic Degrees and Titles Act (amended 1999). In 2004/05 there were 219,477 students enrolled in higher education. Higher education is provided by universities, specialized higher education institutions and colleges. In mid-1999 tuition fees for university students were introduced.

Admission to higher education is on the basis of the Diploma of Completed Secondary Education and successful entrance examinations. Institutions are allowed to set their own criteria for admission. Under the 2001 and 2004 amendments to the Higher Education Act, Bulgaria has implemented the Bologna Process. The principal undergraduate degree is the Bachelors, which requires four years of study culminating in defence of a thesis. There is also a range of Diploma and Diploma Specialist programmes. The Masters degree requires five years of study (or one more year after the Bachelors) ending with either state examinations or defence of a thesis. Finally, there are three types of Doctorate, each requiring at least three years of study following the Masters: Doctors, Doctor of Sciences, and Doctor Honoris Causa.

Vocational and technical training is mostly implemented at the secondary-school level. The National Evaluation and Accreditation Agency is responsible for evaluating and accrediting institutions of higher education.

Learned Societies

GENERAL

Bulgarian Academy of Sciences: 1040 Sofia, 15 Noemvri 1; tel. (2) 989-84-46; fax (2) 981-72-62; e-mail president@eagle.cu.bas.bg; internet www.bas.bg; f. 1869; attached research institutes: see Research Institutes; 204 mems (53 academicians, 88 corresp., 63 foreign); library: see Libraries and Archives; Pres. Prof. Dr IVAN YUCHNOVSKI; Gen. Scientific Sec. Prof. NAUM YAKEMOFF; publs *Balgaristika/Bulgarica* (2 a year), *Comptes rendus de l'Académie Bulgare des Sciences* (monthly), *Spisanie na Balgarskata Akademija na Naukite* (Journal of the Bulgarian Academy of Sciences), (and various specialist publications on science and the arts).

Union of Scientists in Bulgaria: 1505 Sofia, Madrid 39; tel. (2) 944-11-57; fax (2) 944-15-90; e-mail science@usb-bg.org; internet www.usb-bg.org; f. 1944; 4,000 mems; Pres. Prof. D. DAMYANOV; publ. *Nauka* (every 2 months).

AGRICULTURE, FISHERIES AND VETERINARY SCIENCE

Scientific and Technical Union of Specialists in Agriculture: 1000 Sofia, G. Rakovski 108; tel. 87-65-13; fax 987-93-60; f. 1965; Pres. Prof. V. VALOV; Sec. DIMITAR RADULOV; publ. *Buletin Vnedreni Novosti*.

Soil Resources Agency: 1331 Sofia, Shose Bankia 7; tel. (2) 24-87-98; fax (2) 24-02-39; e-mail soilsurv@mailnetplus.bg; internet www.soils-bg.org; f. 1959; analytical research of soil; verifies the quality of agricultural land, and applies finding in legal cases; assesses deterioration risks posed by erosion, contamination, salinity, acidity/akalinity and bogginess; cartographic information and reports; creation and maintenance of the State Digital Map of Soil and Agricultural Land Grades and Soil Resource Geographical Information System, both overseen by the Ministry of Agricultural and Forestry; Exec. Dir D. MIHALEV; Gen.-Sec. T. CHERNOGOROVA.

ARCHITECTURE AND TOWN PLANNING

Union of Architects in Bulgaria: 1504 Sofia, Krakra 11; tel. (2) 943-83-21; fax (2) 943-83-49; e-mail sab@bgnet.bg; internet bularch.org; f. 1965; 4,500 mems; library of 6,000 vols; Pres. Arch. IVAN STANISHEV; publs *Architecture* (every 2 months), *Bulgarian Architect* (information bulletin, every 2 weeks).

ECONOMICS, LAW AND POLITICS

Bulgarian Association of Criminology: 1000 Sofia, Vitosha 2; tel. 87-47-51; fax 986-22-70; f. 1986; Pres. Assoc. Prof. Y. BOYADZHIEVA.

Bulgarian Association of International Law: 1680 Sofia, Belite brezi bl. 6 ap. 31; tel. and fax (2) 859-80-92; e-mail margaritganev@yahoo.com; f. 1962; 55 mems; Pres. Prof. TODOR TODOROV; Sec. Dr MARGARIT GANEV; publ. *Trudove po Mezhdunarodno Pravo* (annually).

Union of Economists: 1000 Sofia, G. Rakovski 108; tel. 87-18-47; fax 984-43-215; f. 1968; Pres. Assoc. Prof. S. ALEXANDROV; Sec. I. POPOV; publ. *Bjuletin*.

FINE AND PERFORMING ARTS

Union of Bulgarian Actors: 1000 Sofia, Narodno Sabranie 12; tel. 87-07-25; fax 88-33-01; e-mail sab@einet.bg; f. 1919; 600 mems; Pres. STEFAN ILIEV; publ. *Teatar*.

Union of Bulgarian Artists: 1504 Sofia, Shipka 6; tel. (2) 943-44-21; fax (2) 946-02-12; e-mail info@sbhart.com; internet www.sbhart.com; f. 1893; Pres. IVAYLO MIRCHEV; publs *Promishlena Estetika*, *Dekorativno Izkustvo*.

Union of Bulgarian Composers: 1000 Sofia, Iv. Vazov 2; tel. (2) 988-15-60; fax (2) 987-43-78; e-mail mail@ubc-bg.com; internet www.ubc-bg.com; f. 1933; 230 mems; library of 25,280 books, scores and recordings; Pres. VELISLAV ZAIMOV; Sec.-Gen. STEFAN ILIEV.

Union of Bulgarian Film Makers: 1504 Sofia, Dondukov 67; tel. and fax (2) 946-10-68; e-mail sbfd@sbfd-bg.com; internet www.filmmakersbg.org; f. 1934; 907 mems; Pres. IVAN PAVLOV; publ. *KINO* (6 a year).

HISTORY, GEOGRAPHY AND ARCHAEOLOGY

Bulgarian Geographical Society: 1000 Sofia, Tsar Osvoboditel 15; tel. (2) 85-82-61; fax (2) 44-64-87; f. 1918; Pres. Prof. P.V. PETROV; Sec. L. TSANKOVA; publs *Geografija*, *Geoecologija*, *Geografijata Dnes*.

LANGUAGE AND LITERATURE

Alliance Française: 4000 Plovdiv, Avxenti Velechki bl. 20, POB 1015; tel. (3) 263-13-42; fax (3) 263-48-07; e-mail afbg@afbg.org; internet www.afbg.org; f. 1904; offers courses and exams in French language and culture and promotes cultural exchange with France; attached offices in Blagoevgrad, Burgas, Kazanlak, Pleven, Stara Zagora, Varna and Veliko Tarnovo; library of 17,000 vols, 40 periodicals; Dir BERNARD ROUHAUD; publ. *Alliances* (2 a year).

Balkanmedia Association: 1407 Sofia, Luibotran 96; tel. (2) 980-70-85; fax (2) 87-16-98; f. 1990; ind. non-profit org. for mass media and communication culture in the Balkan countries; 36 assoc. mems (from all Balkan countries); Pres. ROSEN MILEV; publ. *Balkanmedia*.

British Council: 1504 Sofia, Krakra 7; tel. (2) 942-43-44; fax (2) 942-42-22; e-mail bc.sofia@britishcouncil.bg; internet www.britishcouncil.org/bulgaria; offers courses and exams in English language and British culture and promotes cultural exchange with the UK; teaching centre; library of 20,000 vols, 80 periodicals; Dir IAN STEWART.

Bulgarian Philologists' Society: 1000 Sofia, Moskovska 13; tel. (2) 986-25-61; e-mail vessie@biscom.net; f. 1977; Pres. Prof. S. HADZHIKOSEV; publ. *Ezik i literatura* (4 a year).

Bulgarian Translators' Union: 1000 Sofia, Graf Ignatiev 16, POB 161; tel. (2) 986-45-00; fax (2) 981-09-60; f. 1974; Pres. V. BOYADZHIEVA; publ. *Panorama*.

Goethe-Institut: 1000 Sofia, Budapesta 1; tel. (92) 939-01-00; fax (92) 939-01-99; e-mail vl@sofia.goethe.org; internet www.goethe.de/ms/sof/deindex.htm; offers courses and exams in German language and culture and promotes cultural exchange with Germany; library of 10,000 vols; Dir PETER ANDERS.

Society of Aesthetes and Art and Literary Critics: 1000 Sofia, Krakra 21; f. 1970; Pres. (vacant); Sec. (vacant).

Union of Bulgarian Journalists: 1000 Sofia, Graf Ignatiev 4; tel. (2) 987-27-73; fax (2) 988-30-47; e-mail sbj-bg@mail.bg; f. 1944; 5,500 mems; Pres. MILEN VALKOV.

Union of Bulgarian Writers: 1000 Sofia, Pl. Slavejkova 2A; tel. 88-00-31; fax 88-06-85;

f. 1913; 495 mems; Pres. N. HAITOV; publs *Bulgarian Writer*, *Plamak*, *Slavejche*.

MEDICINE

Bulgarian Society of Neurosciences: 1431 Sofia, Zdrave 2; tel. 51-86-23; fax 51-87-83; f. 1987; Pres. Prof. V. OVCHAROV.

Bulgarian Society of Parasitology: 1113 Sofia, Acad. G. Bonchev bl. 25; tel. (2) 979-23-13; fax (2) 71-01-07; e-mail ieppcom@bas.bg; f. 1965; Pres. Dr YANA MIZINSKA.

Bulgarian Society of Sports Medicine and Kinesitherapy: Dept of Sports Medicine, National Sports Academy, 1000 Sofia, Gurgulyat 1; tel. (2) 88-30-64; f. 1953; 200 mems; Pres. Prof. Dr MARIA TOTEVA; Sec. Dr TODOR TODOROV; publ. *Sport i Nauka* (monthly).

Union of Scientific Medical Societies in Bulgaria: 1431 Sofia, D. Nestorov 15, Hygiene Centre, 12th Floor, Room 19; tel. (2) 954-11-56; fax (2) 954-11-56; f. 1968; 12,000 mems, 64 mem. socs; Pres. Prof. Dr IVAN VALKOV; publ. *Modern Medicine* (4 a year).

NATURAL SCIENCES

Biological Sciences

Bulgarian Botanical Society: c/o Institute of Botany, 1113 Sofia, Acad. G. Bonchev bl. 23; tel. (2) 72-09-51; fax (2) 71-90-32; e-mail dpeev@bio.bas.bg; internet www.bio.bas.bg; f. 1923; Pres. (vacant); Sec. M. ANCHEV.

Bulgarian Society of Natural History: 1164 Sofia, D. Zankov 8; tel. 66-65-94; f. 1896; 1,000 mems; Pres. Prof. D. VODENICHAROV; Sec. S. DIMITROVA; publ. *Priroda i Znanie* (10 a year).

Mathematical Sciences

Union of Bulgarian Mathematicians: 1113 Sofia, Acad. G. Bonchev bl. 8; tel. (2) 72-11-89; fax (2) 971-36-49; e-mail smb@math.bas.bg; f. 1977; 5,000 mems; Pres. Prof. Dr ST. DODUNEKOV; Sec. Dr S. GROZDEV; publ. *Mathematics and Mathematical Education* (annually).

Physical Sciences

Bulgarian Geological Society: 1000 Sofia, Akad. G. Bonchev 24, POB 228; tel. 87-24-50; e-mail cndab@router.geology.bas.bg; f. 1925; 430 mems; library of 21,000 vols; Pres. Prof. CHR. DABOVSKI; Sec. GABRIEL NIKOLOV; publ. *Review* (3 a year).

Union of Physicists in Bulgaria: 1126 Sofia, J. Bourchier 5; tel. 62-76-60; f. 1971; Pres. Prof. L. LALOV; Sec. Prof. M. VELEVA; publ. *Bulgarian Journal of Physics*.

PHILOSOPHY AND PSYCHOLOGY

Bulgarian Pedagogical Society: 1547 Sofia, Shipchenski prohod 69A; tel. (2) 72-08-93; f. 1975; Pres. Prof. G. BIZHKOV.

Bulgarian Philosophical Association: 1303 Sofia, Ing. Ivan Ivanov 88; tel. (2) 931-57-80; fax (2) 931-57-80; e-mail ivan_kaltchev@yahoo.com; f. 1968; 320 mems; Pres. Prof. IVAN KALCHEV; Sec. R. KRIKORIAN; publs *Filosofski Forum* (Philosophical Forum, 4 a year), *Filosofski Vestnik* (Philosophical News, 4 a year), *Filosofski Alternativi* (Philosophical Alternatives, monthly), *Filosofia* (Philosophy, monthly).

Society of Bulgarian Psychologists: 1606 Sofia, Liulin Planina 14, POB 1333; tel. 54-12-95; f. 1969; Pres. Prof. D. GRADEV; Sec. ZH. BALEV; publ. *Balgarsko Spisanie po Psikhologija*.

RELIGION, SOCIOLOGY AND ANTHROPOLOGY

Bulgarian Sociological Association: 1000 Sofia, Lege 5; tel. (2) 88-40-35; fax (2) 52-24-07; f. 1959; Pres. Prof. Dr PETAR-EMIL MITEV; Sec. M. MIRCHEV.

TECHNOLOGY

Bulgarian Astronautical Society: 1113 Sofia, Akad. G. Bonchev bl. 3, Tsentralna laboratoria po slanchevo-zemni vazdeistvia; tel. (2) 979-33-50; f. 1957; 600 mems; library of 500 vols; Pres. Prof. D. MISHEV; Scientific Sec. Prof. A. SIMEONOV.

Federation of Scientific and Technical Unions in Bulgaria: 1000 Sofia, G. Rakovski 108; tel. (2) 989-83-79; fax (2) 987-93-60; e-mail info@fnts-bg.org; internet www.fnts-bg.org; f. 1893; organizes congresses, conferences, symposia, seminars and workshops; participates in the drafting of laws and other normative documents related to science and technology; carries out qualification activity through its Centre for Professional Education and Qualification; 20,000 ; Pres. Acad. V. SGUREV; publ. *Nauka i Obshestvo* (Science and Society).

Scientific and Technical Union of Civil Engineering: 1000 Sofia, G. Rakovski 108; tel. (2) 988-53-03; fax (2) 987-93-60; f. 1965; Pres. Dr E. MILCHEV; Sec. M. RUSEVA; publs *Stroitelstvo*, *Stroitel 2000*.

Scientific and Technical Union of Energetics: 1000 Sofia, G. Rakovski 108; tel. 88-41-58; fax 87-93-60; f. 1965; Pres. Prof. S. BATOV; Sec. Eng. D. TOMOV; publ. *Energetika*.

Scientific and Technical Union of Forestry: 1000 Sofia, G. Rakovski 108; tel. 88-36-83; fax 987-93-60; f. 1965; Pres. V. BREZIN; Sec. S. SAVOV; publs *Darvoobrabotvashta i mebelna Promislenost*, *Celuloza i Hartija*.

Scientific and Technical Union of Mechanical Engineering: 1000 Sofia, G. Rakovski 108; tel. (2) 987-72-90; fax (2) 986-22-40; e-mail nts-bg@tea.bg; internet www.nts-bg.tea.bg; f. 1966; 2,300 mems; Pres. Prof. ALEXANDER SKORDEV; Gen. Sec. DAMIAN DAMIANOV; publ. *Mashinostroene* (monthly).

Scientific and Technical Union of Mining, Geology and Metallurgy: 1000 Sofia, G. Rakovski 108; tel. 87-57-27; fax 986-13-79; f. 1965; Pres. Prof. V. STOYANOV; Sec. V. GENEVSKI; publs *Rudodobiv*, *Metalurgija*.

Scientific and Technical Union of Textiles, Clothing and Leather: 1000 Sofia, G. Rakovski 108; tel. 88-16-41; fax 987-93-60; f. 1965; Pres. Prof. E. KANTCHEV; Sec. I. MECHEV; publs *Tektil i obleklo*, *Kozhi i Obuvki*.

Scientific and Technical Union of the Food Industry: 1000 Sofia, G. Rakovski 108; tel. 87-47-44; fax 987-93-60; f. 1965; Pres. A. PETROV; Sec. TODOROV; publ. *Hranitelna promishlenost*.

Scientific and Technical Union of Transport: 1000 Sofia, G. Rakovski 108; tel. 958-10-36; fax 87-93-60; f. 1965; Pres. K. ERMENKOV; Sec. ST. GAIDAROV; publs *Zelezopaten Transport*, *Patishta*.

Scientific and Technical Union of Water Affairs in Bulgaria: 1000 Sofia, G. Rakovski 108; tel. 988-53-03; fax 987-93-60; f. 1965; Pres. Prof. A. MALINOV; Sec. M. SJAROVA; publ. *Vodno delo*.

Union of Chemists in Bulgaria: 1000 Sofia, G. Rakovski 108; tel. 87-58-12; fax 987-93-60; f. 1901; Pres. Prof. I. SHOPOV; Sec. N. NAIDENOV; publ. *Bulgarian Chemistry and Industry* (4 a year).

Union of Electronics, Electrical Engineering and Telecommunications: Rakovski 108, 1000 Sofia; tel. (2) 287-97-67; fax (2) 987-93-60; e-mail ceec@mail.bg; internet ceec.fnts-bg.org; f. 1965; 1,300 ; Pres. IVAN YATCHEV; Vice-Pres. STEFAN MIRTCHEV; Executive Dir IVAN VASILEV; publ. *Elektrotechnica i Elektronica* (monthly).

Union of Surveyors and Land Managers: 1000 Sofia, G. Rakovski 108; tel. (2) 987-58-52; fax (2) 986-16-19; e-mail milev@bgcict.acad.bg; f. 1922; 200 mems; Pres. Prof. Dr Ing. G. MILEV; Sec. ST. BOGDANOV; publ. *Geodesija, Kartografija, Zemeustrojstvo* (6 a year).

Research Institutes

AGRICULTURE, FISHERIES AND VETERINARY SCIENCE

Agricultural Institute: 9700 Shumen; tel. 6-02-41; fax 6-28-32; e-mail agr_inst@abv.bg; f. 1955; library of 10,900 vols; Dir ST. SLANEV; publs *Bulgarian Journal of Agricultural Science*, *Zhivotnovadni Nauki* (8 a year), *Genetica i selectija* (4 a year).

Barley Research Institute: 8400 Karnobat; tel. 27-31; fax (559) 58-47; f. 1925; library of 17,000 vols; Dir Assoc. Prof. I. MIHOV.

Canning Research Institute: 4000 Plovdiv, V. Aprilov 154; tel. (32) 5-58-04; fax (32) 55-22-86; e-mail canri@main.infotel.bg; f. 1962; library of 19,000 vols; Dir PAVLINA PARASKOVA.

Central Medical Veterinary Research Institute: 1606 Sofia, P. Slaveykov 15; tel. (2) 952-12-77; fax (2) 952-53-06; e-mail director@iterra.net; f. 1901; Dir Prof. Dr S. P. MARTINOV.

Cotton and Durum Wheat Research Institute: 6200 Chirpan; tel. (416) 31-33; fax (416) 31-33; e-mail iptp@abv.bg; f. 1925; library of 16,000 vols; Dir NELI K. VALKOVA.

Dairy Research Institute: 3700 Vidin; tel. 2-32-04; fax 3-46-32; f. 1959; library of 8,000 vols; Dir A. KOZHEV; publs *Dairy Abstracts Bulletin* (monthly), *Advanced Experience* (2 a year).

Fisheries Industry Institute: 8000 Burgas, Industrialna 3; tel. (56) 84-05-22; fax (56) 4-03-31; f. 1965; Dir Dr ZH. NECHEV.

Forage Institute: 5800 Pleven, I. Vazov 89; tel. (64) 2-34-74; fax (64) 3-85-28; f. 1955; Dir Prof. T. ZHELIAZKOV.

Forest Research Institute: 1756 Sofia, Blvd Sv. Kliment Ohridski 132; tel. (2) 962-04-42; fax (2) 962-04-47; e-mail forestin@bulnet.bg; internet www.bulnet.com/forestin; f. 1928; attached to Bulgarian Acad. of Sciences; library of 39,000 vols; Dir Prof. Dr Sci. ALEXANDER H. ALEXANDROV; publs *Nauka za gorata* (Forest Science, 4 a year), *Silva Balcanica* (2 a year).

Freshwater Fisheries Research Institute: 4003 Plovdiv, V. Levski 248; tel. (32) 55-60-33; fax (32) 55-39-24; f. 1978; Dir G. GROZEV.

Fruit-Growing Research Institute: 4004 Plovdiv, Ostromila 12; tel. (32) 77-13-49; fax (32) 67-08-08; f. 1950; Dir Prof. D. DIMITROV.

Institute for the Control of Foot and Mouth Disease and Dangerous Infections: 8800 Sliven, Trakia 75; tel. (44) 2-20-39; fax (44) 2-26-42; f. 1974; Dir R. KASABOV.

Institute of Agricultural Economics: 1618 Sofia, Tsar Boris III 136; tel. 56-28-08; fax 56-28-05; f. 1935; library of 29,463 vols; Dir Prof. R. TRENDAFILOV.

Institute of Animal Science: 2232 Kostinbrod (Sofia District); tel. (721) 32-91-64; f. 1947; library of 25,200 vols; Dir Prof. H. STANCHEV.

Institute of Cattle and Sheep Breeding: 6000 Stara Zagora; tel. (42) 4-10-76; fax (42) 4-71-48; f. 1942; Dir Prof. GEKO GEKOV.

Institute of Fisheries: 9000 Varna, Primorski 4; tel. (52) 23-18-52; fax (52) 25-78-76; e-mail ifr@abcis.bg; f. 1932; library of 24,000 vols; Dir Dr P. KOLAROV; publ. *Proceedings* (annually).

Institute of Fruit Growing: 2500 Kyustendil; tel. (78) 2-75-32; fax (78) 2-40-36; f. 1929; library of 9,000 vols; Dir Assoc. Prof. Dr DIMITAR DOMOZETOV.

Institute of Grains and Feed Industry: 2232 Kostinbrod 2; tel. (721) 20-84; fax (721) 20-84; f. 1965; library of 9,050 vols, 16 periodicals; Dir M. MACHEV.

Institute of Introduction and Plant Genetic Resources: 4122 Sadovo (Plovdiv District); tel. (32) 22-51; fax (32) 493-00-26; f. 1977; library of 30,000 vols; Dir Dr R. KOEVA.

Institute of Soya Bean Growing: 5200 Pavlikeni, POB 8; tel. (610) 22-75; fax (610) 25-41; f. 1925; Dir Dr G. GEORGIEV.

Institute of the Sugar Industry and Bioproducts: 5100 Gorna Orjahovica; tel. (618) 4-18-80; fax (618) 4-05-65; f. 1963; library of 10,600 vols; Dir K. TODOROVA.

Institute of Upland Stockbreeding and Agriculture: 5600 Trojan, V. Devski 281; tel. (670) 2-28-60; fax (670) 2-30-32; e-mail insba@insba.bia-bg.com; f. 1978; Dir P. DONCHEV.

Institute of Viticulture and Oenology: 5800 Pleven, Kala tepe 1; tel. (64) 2-21-61; fax (64) 2-64-70; f. 1902; Dir Prof. P. ABRASHEVA.

Institute of Water Problems: 1113 Sofia, Acad. G. Bonchev bl. 1; tel. (2) 72-25-72; fax (2) 72-25-77; e-mail santur@iwp.bas.bg; internet www.iwp.bas.bg; f. 1961; attached to Bulgarian Acad. of Sciences; water resource systems management, hydraulic structures, water quality, fluvial and structural hydraulics; 73 mems; Dir Prof. OHANES SANTOURDJIAN; publ. *Vodni Problemi* (Water Problems, annually).

Institute of Wheat and Sunflower 'Dobroudja': 9520 General Toshevo (Dobrich District); tel. (58) 2-74-54; fax (58) 2-63-64; f. 1940; library of 32,000 vols; Dir Prof. Dr PETER IVANOV.

Maize Research Institute: 3230 Knezha; tel. (9132) 22-11; fax (9132) 27-11; e-mail mri@main.infotel.bg; f. 1924; Dir Assoc. Prof. K. ANGELOV.

Maritsa Vegetable Crops Research Institute: 4003 Plovdiv, Brezovsko shose 32 (kl. 3), PK 20; tel. (32) 95-12-27; fax (32) 96-01-77; e-mail izk@plov.omega.bg; f. 1930; library of 20,500 vols; Dir Dr STOYKA MASHERA.

'N. Pushkarov' Institute for Soil Science: 1080 Sofia, Shose Bankya 7; tel. 24-61-41; fax 24-89-37; e-mail soil@mail.bg; internet www.iss-poushkarov.org; f. 1947; Dir Assoc. Prof. MARTIN BANOV; publs *Soil Science, Agrochemistry and Ecology* (in Bulgarian with English abstract, 6 a year), *Journal of Balkan Ecology* (in English, 4 a year).

National Wine and Spirituous Beverages Research Institute: 1618 Sofia, Tsar Boris III 134; tel. (2) 855-40-09; fax (2) 955-52-24; e-mail office@wineinbg.org; internet www.wineinbg.org; f. 1951; Exec. Dir CHRISTO BOEVSKY.

'Obraztsov Chiflik' Institute of Agriculture and Seed Science: 7007 Ruse; tel. 22-58-98; fax 22-58-98; e-mail izsruse@elits.rousse.bg; f. 1905; Dir Dr. GENKA PATENOVA.

Plant Protection Institute: 2230 Kostinbrod, POB 238; tel. (721) 20-70; fax (721) 20-71; e-mail protection@infotel.bg; f. 1935; Dir Prof. Dr NIKOLA ATANASOV.

Regional Veterinary Institute: 4000 Plovdiv, Nezavisimost III; tel. (32) 26-08-68; fax (32) 22-33-67; f. 1936; library of 10,000 vols; Dir D. ARNAUDOV.

Regional Veterinary Institute: 5000 Veliko Tarnovo, Slavjanska 5; tel. 2-16-69; fax 2-16-69; e-mail rvmi@vt.bitex.com; f. 1932; library of 11,840 vols; Dir Assoc. Prof. V. RADOSLAVOV.

Regional Veterinary Research Institute and Centre: 6000 Stara Zagora, Slavyanska 58; tel. (42) 2-67-32; fax (42) 2-31-15; f. 1931; Dir Assoc. Prof. N. NIKOLOV.

Research Institute for Irrigation, Drainage and Hydraulic Engineering: 1618 Sofia, Tsar Boris III 136; tel. (2) 56-30-01; fax (2) 55-41-58; e-mail riidhe@bgcict.acad.bg; f. 1953; library of 18,000 vols; Dir Asst Prof. Dr PLAMEN PETKOV; publ. *Proceedings* (every 3 years).

Research Institute for Irrigation, Drainage and Hydraulic Engineering: 1618 Sofia, Tsar Boris III 136; tel. (2) 56-30-01; fax (2) 55-41-58; e-mail riidhe@bgcict.acad.bg; f. 1953; library of 18,000 vols; Dir Asst Prof. Dr PLAMEN PETKOV; publ. *Proceedings* (every 3 years).

Research Institute for Roses, Aromatic and Medicinal Plants: 6100 Kazanlak, Bul. Osvobojdenie 49; tel. (431) 2-20-39; fax (431) 4-10-83; f. 1907; library of 3,600 vols; Dir Dr GEORGE CHAUSHEV.

Scientific and Production Enterprise with Sugar Beet Research Institute 'Prof. Ivan Ivanov': 9747 Carev Brod (Shumen District); tel. (54) 5-51-02; fax (54) 5-69-06; f. 1926; Dir Assoc. Prof. S. KRASTEV.

Scientific and Production Institute for Veterinary Preparations 'Vetbiopharm': 3000 Vraca; tel. 4-94-81; fax 4-75-30; f. 1942; library of 5,000 vols; Dir Dr T. NIKOLOV.

Tobacco and Tobacco Products Institute: 4108 Plovdiv; tel. (32) 67-23-64; fax 77-51-56; f. 1944; library of 40,000 vols; Dir Dr ELENA APOSTOLOVA; publ. *Bulgarian Tobacco* (every 2 months).

Veterinary Institute of Immunology Ltd: 1360 Sofia, Bakareno shose 1; tel. (2) 26-31-70; fax (2) 26-24-85; f. 1942; Pres. Prof. Dr STEFANOV.

ARCHITECTURE AND TOWN PLANNING

Centre for Architectural Studies: 1113 Sofia, Acad. G. Bonchev bl. 1; tel. 72-46-20; f. 1949; attached to Bulgarian Acad. of Sciences; Dir Assoc. Prof. K. BOYADZHIEV.

National Centre for Regional Development and Housing Policy: 1000 Sofia, Alabin 14–16; tel. (2) 980-03-08; fax (2) 980-03-12; f. 1960; library of 9,000 vols; Dir-Gen. Dr V. GARNIZOV; publ. *Series for the Municipalities* (every 2 months).

ECONOMICS, LAW AND POLITICS

Institute of Economics: 1040 Sofia, Aksakov 3; tel. (2) 987-58-79; fax (2) 988-21-08; e-mail ineco@iki.bas.bg; internet www.iki.bas.bg; f. 1949; attached to Bulgarian Acad. of Sciences; Dir Dr MITKO DIMITROV; publs *Ikonomicheska Misal* (6 a year), *Ikonomicheski Izsledvania* (3 a year), *Economic Thought* (annually).

Institute of Legal Studies: 1000 Sofia, Serdika 4; tel. (2) 987-49-02; fax (2) 988-23-69; internet ipn.bas.bg; f. 1947; attached to Bulgarian Acad. of Sciences; library of 33,000 vols; Pres. Prof. Dr KINO LAZAROV; Dir Prof Dr TSVETANA KARNENOVA; publ. *Pravna Misal* (4 a year).

Research Institute of Forensic Sciences and Criminology: 1000 Sofia, POB 934; tel. (2) 987-82-10; fax (2) 987-82-10; e-mail int.27@mvr.bg; f. 1968; forensic science and criminology studies; Dir Prof. K. BOBEV; publs *News Bulletin* (3 a year), *Scientific Proceedings* (annually).

EDUCATION

National Institute for Education: 1113 Sofia, Tsarigradsko shose 125 bl. 5; tel. 71-72-24; fax 70-20-62; e-mail elka_nikolova@hotmail.com; internet www.nie.bg; f. 1996; library of 100,000 vols; publ. *Strategies for Policy in Science and Education*.

FINE AND PERFORMING ARTS

Institute of Art Studies: Krakra bl. 21, 1000 Sofia; tel. (2) 944-24-14; fax (2) 943-30-92; e-mail art@musicart.imbm.bas.bg; internet musicart.imbm.bas.bg; f. 1949; attached to Bulgarian Acad. of Sciences; Dir Assoc. Prof. Dr ALEXANDER YANAKIEV; publs *Art Studies Quarterly* (4 a year), *Bulgarian Musicology* (4 a year).

HISTORY, GEOGRAPHY AND ARCHAEOLOGY

Archaeological Institute: 1000 Sofia, Saborna 2; tel. (2) 988-44-06; fax (2) 988-24-05; e-mail aim-bas@aclubcable.com; f. 1921; research into pre-history, classical antiquity and the middle ages; attached to Bulgarian Acad. of Sciences; Dir Prof. VASIL NIKOLOV; publs *Archaeology* (4 a year), *Reports* (irregular).

Institute of Balkan Studies: 1000 Sofia, Moskovska 45; tel. (2) 980-62-97; fax (2) 980-62-97; e-mail balkani@cl.bas.bg; internet www.cl.bas.bg/Balkan-Studies; f. 1963; attached to Bulgarian Acad. of Sciences; library of 27,000 vols; Dir Assoc. Prof. A. GARABEDYAN; publ. *Études Balkaniques* (4 a year).

Institute of Demography: 1114 Sofia, Akad. G. Bonchev bl. 6 (Et. 6); tel. (2) 70-53-03; fax (2) 70-04-08; f. 1982; attached to Bulgarian Acad. of Sciences; Dir Assoc. Prof. E. KHRISTOV; publ. *Naselenie*.

Institute of Geography: 1113 Sofia, Acad. G. Bonchev bl. 3; tel. (2) 70-02-04; fax (2) 70-02-04; e-mail geograph@bgcict.acad.bg; f. 1950; attached to Bulgarian Acad. of Sciences; library of 17,000 vols; Dir Assoc. Prof. Dr G. GESHEV; publ. *Problems of Geography* (4 a year).

Institute of History: 1113 Sofia, Shipchenski prohod 52 bl. 17; tel. 70-85-13; fax 70-21-91; f. 1947; attached to Bulgarian Acad. of Sciences; Dir Prof. GEORGI MARKOV; publs *Bulgarian Historical Review* (2 a year), *Istoricheski Preglad* (3 a year).

Institute of Thracian Studies 'Prof. Alexnder Fol': 1000 Sofia, Moskovska 13; tel. (2) 981-58-53; fax (2) 988-15-59; e-mail thracologia@abv.bg; f. 1972; attached to Bulgarian Acad. of Sciences; library of 6,000 vols; Dir Prof. KIRIL JORDANOV; publ. *Orpheus* (annually).

LANGUAGE AND LITERATURE

Cyril and Methodius Research Centre: 1000 Sofia, POB 432, Moskovska 13; tel. (2) 987-02-61; fax (2) 986-69-62; e-mail kmnc@bas.bg; internet www.kmnc.bas.bg; f. 1980; attached to Bulgarian Acad. of Sciences; Dir Assoc. Prof. SVETLINA NIKOLOVA; publs *Kirilo-Metodievski studii* (annually), *Palaeobulgarica* (4 a year).

Institute for Literature: 1113 Sofia, Shipchenski prohod 52 bl. 17; tel. 70-18-30; f. 1948; attached to Bulgarian Acad. of Sciences; Dir Assoc. Prof. R. KUNCHEVA.

Institute for the Bulgarian Language: 1113 Sofia, Shipchenski prohod 52 bl. 17; tel.

72-23-02; fax (2) 72-23-02; e-mail ibe@ibl.bas.bg; internet www.ibl.bas.bg; f. 1942; attached to Bulgarian Acad. of Sciences; Dir Assoc. Prof. Y. BALTOVA.

MEDICINE

Centre of Physiotherapy and Rehabilitation: 1618 Sofia, Ovcha kupel 2B; tel. 56-28-24; fax 55-30-23; f. 1949; Dir Assoc. Prof. P. NIKOLOVA; publ. *Journal*.

Clinical Centre for Haemodialysis: 1431 Sofia, G. Sofijski 1; tel. 54-07-40; fax 51-73-43; f. 1967; Dir Prof. ZDRAVKO KIRIAKOV.

Clinical Centre of Gastroenterology: 1527 Sofia, Bialo More 8; tel. (2) 434-45-13; fax (2) 43-26-64; f. 1959; Dir Prof. A. MENDEOVA.

Institute of Obstetrics and Gynaecology: 1431 Sofia, Zdrave 2; tel. (2) 51-72-42; fax (2) 51-70-92; f. 1976; library of 2,000 vols; Dir Assoc. Prof. N. DOGANOV; publ. *Problems of Obstetrics and Gynaecology* (annually).

National Centre of Cardiovascular Diseases: 1309 Sofia, Miko Papo 65; tel. 22-31-34; fax 22-31-28; f. 1972; Dir Dr. L. BOYADZHIEV.

National Centre of Haematology and Transfusiology: 1756 Sofia-Darvenica, Plovdivsko pole 6; tel. 72-25-92; fax 72-25-92; e-mail ncht_bg@hotmail.com; f. 1948; Dir Prof. Dr T. LISICHKOV; publ. *Clinical and Transfusional Haematology*.

National Centre of Public Health Protection: 1431 Sofia, Ivan Ev. Geshov Bul. 15; tel. and fax (2) 954-93-90; e-mail livanov@nchi.government.bg; internet www.ncphp.government.bg; f. 2005 by merger of National Centre of Hygiene, Medical Ecology and Nutrition and National Centre of Public Health; 308 mems; research and development, expert consultancy, methodological and training activities in the field of public health protection; assessment of health risks from occupational and environmental factors, personal behaviour and lifestyle, health promotion and integral diseases prevention, analytical and control services; base organization and co-ordinator for nat. and intl programmes and projects on public health protection; base for post-graduate and continuation training; library of 32,000 vols; Dir Prof. Dr LYUBOMIR IVANOV; publ. *Problems of Hygiene* (3 a year).

National Centre of Radiobiology and Radiation Protection: 1756 Sofia, 132 Kl. Ohridski Blvd; tel. (2) 62-60-36; fax (2) 62-10-59; e-mail ncrrp@ncrrp.org; internet www.ncrrp.org; f. 1963; research, education and training, monitoring and control on occupationally exposed persons and radiological equipment, methodology, diagnostics and prophylaxis of radiation injury, emergency at nuclear accident sites; Dir Prof. Dr RADOSTINA GEORGIEVA (acting).

National Drug Institute: 1504 Sofia, Bul. Yanko Sakazov 26; tel. (2) 943-40-46; fax (2) 943-44-87; e-mail ndi@bg400.bg; f. 1949; registration, analysis and control of drugs; Dir Dr BORISLAV BORISOV.

National Oncological Centre: 1756 Sofia, Plovdivsko Pole 6; tel. (2) 72-06-54; fax (2) 72-06-51; f. 1952; library of 22,000 vols; Dir Prof. I. CHERNOZEMSKI; publ. *Oncology* (4 a year).

'Pirogov' Emergency Medical Institute: 1606 Sofia, Makedonija 21; tel. (2) 52-10-77; fax (2) 951-62-68; f. 1965; Dir Prof. ZLATARSKI.

Research Institute of Infectious and Parasitic Diseases: 1504 Sofia, Yanko Sakazov 26; tel. (2) 4-34-71; fax (2) 943-30-75; e-mail ncipd@ncpd.ndt.bg400.bg; f. 1972; Dir Prof. B. PETRUNOV; publs *Problems of Infectious and Parasitic Diseases*, *Infectology*.

State Institute of Endocrinology and Gerontology: 1303 Sofia, Dame Gruev 6; tel. (2) 987-72-01; fax (2) 87-41-45; f. 1972; Dir Prof. B. LOZANOV.

NATURAL SCIENCES

Biological Sciences

Central Laboratory of General Ecology: 1113 Sofia, Gagarin 2; tel. (2) 73-61-37; fax (2) 70-54-98; e-mail ecolab@ecolab.bas.bg; f. 1956; attached to Bulgarian Acad. of Sciences; library of 8,000 vols; Dir Assoc. Prof. Dr N. CHIPEV.

Centre for Biomedical Engineering: 1113 Sofia, Acad. G. Bonchev bl. 105; tel. 70-03-26; fax 72-37-87; e-mail clbm@bgcict.acad.bg; f. 1979; attached to Bulgarian Acad. of Sciences; Dir Prof. Dr I. K. DASKALOV.

Institute of Biophysics: 1113 Sofia, Acad. G. Bonchev bl. 21; tel. (2) 971-22-64; fax (2) 971-24-93; e-mail biophys@obzor.bio21.bas.bg; f. 1967; attached to Bulgarian Acad. of Sciences; Dir Prof. B. TENCHOV.

Institute of Botany: 1113 Sofia, Acad. G. Bonchev bl. 23; tel. (2) 72-09-51; fax (2) 71-90-32; e-mail botinst@bio.bas.bg; internet www.bio.bas.bg/botany; f. 1919; attached to Bulgarian Acad. of Sciences; Dir Prof. DIMITAR PEEV; Vice-Dir Assoc. Prof. Dr VELISLAV NIKOLOV; Scientific Sec. Assoc. Prof. Dr DIMITER IVANOV; publ. *Phytologia Balcanica* (3 a year).

Institute of Experimental Morphology and Anthropology: 1113 Sofia, Acad. G. Bonchev bl. 25; tel. (2) 979-23-40; fax (2) 71-90-07; e-mail iemabas@bas.bg; internet www.iema.bas.bg; f. 1953; attached to Bulgarian Acad. of Sciences; 89 mems; Dir Prof. Y. AL. JORDANOV; Scientific Sec. Assoc. Prof. D. D. DELEVA; publs *Journal of Anthropology* (annually), *Acta Morphologica et Anthropologica* (annually).

Institute of Experimental Pathology and Parasitology: 1113 Sofia, Acad. G. Bonchev bl. 25; tel. (2) 72-24-26; fax (2) 71-01-07; e-mail ieppcom@bas.bg; f. 1948; attached to Bulgarian Acad. of Sciences; Dir Prof. ILARION YANCHEV; publ. *Experimental Pathology and Parasitology* (4 a year).

Institute of Genetics: 1113 Sofia, Okolovrastno shose 1, POB 96; tel. 75-90-41; fax 75-70-87; e-mail genetika@bas.bg; f. 1940; attached to Bulgarian Acad. of Sciences; Dir Assoc. Prof. B. DIMITROV.

Institute of Microbiology: 1113 Sofia, Acad. G. Bonchev bl. 26; tel. 70-10-81; fax 70-01-09; e-mail microbas@bas.bg; f. 1947; attached to Bulgarian Acad. of Sciences; Dir Prof. A. GALABOV.

Institute of Molecular Biology: 1113 Sofia, Acad. G. Bonchev bl. 21; tel. and fax (2) 72-35-07; internet www.bio21.bas.bg/imb; f. 1960; attached to Bulgarian Acad. of Sciences; 97 mems; library of 5,000 vols; Dir Prof. ILYA GEORGIEV PASHEV.

Institute of Physiology: 1113 Sofia, Acad. G. Bonchev bl. 23; tel. 71-91-08; fax 71-91-09; e-mail books@iph.bio.acad.bg; f. 1947; attached to Bulgarian Acad. of Sciences; Dir Prof. R. RADOMIROV.

Institute of the Biology and Immunology of the Reproduction and Development of Organisms: 1784 Sofia, Carigradsko shose 73; tel. 72-00-18; fax 72-00-22; e-mail kenayov@bgcict.acad.bg; f. 1939; attached to Bulgarian Acad. of Sciences; Dir Prof. I. KEKHAIOV.

Institute of Zoology: 1000 Sofia, Tsar Osvoboditel 1; tel. (2) 988-51-15; fax (2) 988-28-97; e-mail zoology@zoology.bas.bg; internet www.zoology.bas.bg; f. 1889; attached to Bulgarian Acad. of Sciences; Dir Prof. MLADEN ZIVKOV; publs *Acta Zoologica Bulgarica* (3 a year), *Fauna of Bulgaria* (annual), *Catalogus Faunae Bulgaricae* (annual).

'Methodi Popov' Institute of Plant Physiology: 1113 Sofia, Acad. G. Bonchev bl. 21; tel. 72-84-80; fax 73-99-52; e-mail karanov@obzor.bio21.bas.bg; f. 1948; attached to Bulgarian Acad. of Sciences; Dir Prof. E. KARANOV.

Mathematical Sciences

Institute of Mathematics and Informatics: 1113 Sofia, Acad. G. Bonchev bl. 8; tel. (2) 70-10-72; fax (2) 971-36-49; e-mail director@math.bas.bg; f. 1947; attached to Bulgarian Acad. of Sciences; Dir Prof. S. DODUNEKOV; publ. *Serdica* (4 a year).

Physical Sciences

Central Laboratory of Electrochemical Power Sources: 1113 Sofia, Acad. G. Bonchev bl. 10; tel. (2) 72-25-43; fax (2) 72-25-44; e-mail banchem@bgearn.acad.bg; f. 1967; attached to Bulgarian Acad. of Sciences; Dir Prof. Z. STOINOV.

Central Laboratory of Geodesy: 1113 Sofia, Acad. G. Bonchev bl. 1; tel. (2) 72-08-41; fax (2) 72-08-41; e-mail kotzev@bas.bg; f. 1948; attached to Bulgarian Acad. of Sciences; Dir Assoc. Prof. V. KOTZEV; publ. *Geodesy* (2 a year).

Central Laboratory of Optical Storage and the Processing of Information: 1113 Sofia, Acad. G. Bonchev bl. 101; tel. 71-00-18; fax 71-91-65; e-mail vsainov@optics.bas.bg; f. 1975; attached to Bulgarian Acad. of Sciences; Dir Assoc. Prof. V. SAYNOV.

Central Laboratory of Photoprocesses: 1113 Sofia, Acad. G. Bonchev bl. 109; tel. (2) 872-00-73; fax (2) 872-24-65; e-mail clf@clf.bas.bg; internet www.clf.bas.bg; f. 1967; attached to Bulgarian Acad. of Sciences; Dir Assoc. Prof. Dr ATANAS TZVETANOV BUROV.

Central Laboratory of Solar Energy and New Energy Sources: 1784 Sofia, Tzarigradsko shose 72; tel. and fax 75-40-16; e-mail solar@phys.bas.bg; internet www.senes.bas.bg; f. 1977; attached to Bulgarian Acad. of Sciences; 44 mems; Dir Assoc. Prof. PETKO VITANOV.

Geological Institute 'Acad. Str. Dimitrov': 1113 Sofia, Acad. G. Bonchev bl. 24; tel. (2) 72-35-63; fax (2) 72-46-38; e-mail geolinst@geology.bas.bg; internet www.geology.bas.bg; f. 1947; attached to Bulgarian Acad. of Sciences; library of 73,000 vols; Dir Prof. Dr H. HRISCHEV; publs *Geologica Balcanica* (quarterly), *Review of the Bulgarian Geological Society* (3 a year), *Geochemistry, Mineralogy and Petrology* (annually).

Institute of Catalysis: 1113 Sofia, Acad. G. Bonchev St. bl. 11; tel. (2) 971-21-24; fax (2) 971-29-67; e-mail icatalys@ic.bas.bg; internet www.ic.bas.bg; f. 1983; 78 mems; attached to Bulgarian Acad. of Sciences; Dir Prof. Dr L. A. PETROV; publs *Proceedings of the International Symposium on Heterogeneous Catalysis*, *Proceedings of the International Symposium on Electron Paramagnetic Resonance*.

Institute of General and Inorganic Chemistry: 1113 Sofia, Acad. G. Bonchev bl. 11; tel. (2) 72-48-01; fax (2) 70-50-24; e-mail banchem@bas.bg; internet www.bas.bg; f. 1960; attached to Bulgarian Acad. of Sciences; Dir Prof. Dr P. PESHEV.

Institute of Geophysics: Acad. G. Bonchev bl. 3, 1113 Sofia; tel. (2) 971-26-77; fax (2) 971-30-05; e-mail office@geophys.bas.bg; internet www.geophys.bas.bg; f. 1960;

attached to Bulgarian Acad. of Sciences; 133 mems; Dir Assoc. Prof. NIKOLAY MILOSHEV; publ. *Bulgarian Geophysical Journal* (4 a year).

Institute of Mechanics: 1113 Sofia, Acad. G. Bonchev bl. 4; tel. (2) 973-31-40; fax (2) 70-74-98; e-mail e.manoach@info.imbm.bas.bg; internet www.imbm.bas.bg; f. 1977; attached to Bulgarian Acad. of Sciences; research, consultation and experts' reports, metrology measurements, construction of scientific devices and education of highly-qualified specialists in theoretical and applied mechanics, biomechanics and mechatronics; main fields of research incl. mechanics of multibody systems, solid mechanics, fluid mechanics and biomechanics; library of 6,000 vols; Dir Assoc. Prof. Dr EMIL MANOACH; publ. *Journal of Theoretical and Applied Mechanics* (online).

Institute of Nuclear Research and Nuclear Energy: 1784 Sofia, Carigradsko shose 72; tel. (2) 714-44-98; fax (2) 975-36-19; e-mail inrne@inrne.bas.bg; f. 1972; attached to Bulgarian Acad. of Sciences; Dir Prof. I. STAMENOV; publ. *Proceedings of the International School on Nuclear Physics*.

Institute of Oceanology: 9000 Varna, POB 152; located at: 9000 Varna, Kv. Asparuhovo, Parvi May 40; tel. (52) 37-04-84; fax (52) 37-04-83; e-mail office@io-bas.bg; internet www.io-bas.bg; f. 1973; 104 mems; attached to Bulgarian Acad. of Sciences; research in the field of marine physics, chemistry, geology, biology, ecology, coastal dynamics and underwater investigations; consulting and expert services; training; library of 8,266 vols; Dir Dr HRISTO SLABAKOV; publ. *Proceedings* (irregular).

Institute of Organic Chemistry with Centre of Phytochemistry: 1113 Sofia, Acad. G. Bonchev bl. 9; tel. 72-48-17; fax 70-02-25; e-mail iochem@orgchm.bas.bg; f. 1960; attached to Bulgarian Acad. of Sciences; Dir Prof. YU. STEFANOVSKI.

Institute of Physical Chemistry: 1113 Sofia, Acad. G. Bonchev bl. 11; tel. 72-75-50; fax 971-26-88; e-mail physchem@ipchp.ipc.acad.bg; f. 1958; attached to Bulgarian Acad. of Sciences; Dir Prof. H. NANEV.

Institute of Polymers: 1113 Sofia, Acad. G. Bonchev bl. 103-A; tel. (2) 971-28-17; fax (2) 870-75-23; e-mail instpoly@polymer.bas.bg; internet www.polymer.bas.bg; f. 1973; attached to Bulgarian Acad. of Sciences; Dir Prof. KOLIO TROEV.

Institute of Space Research: 1000 Sofia, Moskovska 6, POB 799; tel. (2) 988-35-03; fax (2) 981-33-47; e-mail office@space.bas.bg; internet www.space.bas.bg; f. 1973; attached to Bulgarian Acad. of Sciences; Dir Dr PETAR GETZOV; publ. *Aerospace Research in Bulgaria* (annually).

National Astronomical Observatory – Rozhen: POB 136, 4700 Smoljan; tel. and fax (30) 218-356; e-mail rozhen@mbox.digsys.bg; internet www.astro.bas.bg; f. 1975; attached to Bulgarian Acad. of Sciences.

National Institute of Meteorology and Hydrology: 1184 Sofia, Carigradsko shose 66; tel. (2) 975-39-96; fax (2) 88-44-94; f. 1954; attached to Bulgarian Acad. of Sciences; Dir Assoc. Prof. K. TSANKOV; publ. *Problemi na meteorologia i hidrologia*.

Solar Terrestrial Influences Laboratory: 1113 Sofia, Acad. G. Bonchev bl. 3; tel. 70-02-29; fax 70-01-78; f. 1990; attached to Bulgarian Acad. of Sciences; Dir Prof. D. MISHEV.

'Acad. G. Nadjakov' Institute of Solid State Physics: 1784 Sofia, Tsarigradsko shose 72; tel. (2) 875-80-61; fax (2) 975-36-32; e-mail director@issp.bas.bg; internet www.issp.bas.bg; f. 1972; attached to Bulgarian Acad. of Sciences; Dir Prof. A. G. PETROV.

PHILOSOPHY AND PSYCHOLOGY

Institute for Philosophical Research: 1000 Sofia, Patriarh Evtimij 6; tel. (2) 987-37-02; fax (2) 981-07-91; e-mail office@philosophybulgaria.org; internet www.philosophybulgaria.org; f. 1945, as Institute of Philosophy and Education; 1952–1988 Institute of Philosophy; 1988–95 Institute of Philosophical Sciences; present name 1995; attached to Bulgarian Acad. of Sciences; 65 mems; Dir Prof. VASSIL PRODANOV; Scientific Sec. Assoc. Prof. SONYA KANEVA; publ. *Philosophical Alternatives* (monthly).

Institute of Psychology: 1113 Sofia, Akad. G. Bonchev bl. 6 (Et. 5); tel. (2) 70-32-17; f. 1972; attached to Bulgarian Acad. of Sciences; Dir Assoc. Prof. V. RUSINOVA.

RELIGION, SOCIOLOGY AND ANTHROPOLOGY

Ethnographic Institute: 1000 Sofia, Moskovska 6A; tel. (2) 987-41-91; fax (2) 980-11-62; f. 1947; attached to Bulgarian Acad. of Sciences; Dir Assoc. Prof. R. POPOV.

Institute of Folklore: 1113 Sofia, Acad. G. Bonchev bl. 6; tel. (2) 70-42-09; e-mail folklor@ifolk.bas.bg; internet mail.ifolk.bas.bg/ifolk; f. 1972; attached to Bulgarian Acad. of Sciences; library of 4,200 vols, 73 periodicals; Dir Assoc. Prof. MILA SANTOVA; publ. *Bulgarian Folklore* (4 a year).

Institute of Sociology: 1000 Sofia, Moskovska 13A; tel. (2) 980-90-86; fax (2) 980-58-85; e-mail banis@bgcict.acad.bg; f. 1968; attached to Bulgarian Acad. of Sciences; Dir Prof. G. FOTEV; publs *Sociological Problems* (4 a year), *Sociological Review* (6 a year).

TECHNOLOGY

Central Laboratory of Applied Physics: 4000 Plovdiv, Sankt Peterburg 59; tel. (32) 63-50-19; fax (32) 63-28-10; e-mail ipfban@mbox.digsys.bg; f. 1979; attached to Bulgarian Acad. of Sciences; Dir Prof. R. KAKANAKOV.

Central Laboratory of Mechatronics and Instrumentation: 1113 Sofia, Acad. G. Bonchev bl. 1; tel. 72-35-71; fax 72-35-71; e-mail bogdan@bgearn.acad.bg; f. 1990; attached to Bulgarian Acad. of Sciences; Dir Assoc. Prof. R. ZAKHARIEV.

Central Laboratory of Mineralogy and Crystallography: 1113 Sofia, Acad. G. Bonchev bl. 107; tel. (2) 979-70-55; fax (2) 979-70-56; e-mail mincryst@interbgc.bg; internet www.clmc.bas.bg; f. 1977; attached to Bulgarian Acad. of Sciences; Dir Assoc. Prof. NIKOLA ZIDAROV.

Central Laboratory of Physico-Chemical Mechanics: 1113 Sofia, Acad. G. Bonchev bl. 1; tel. (2) 71-81-82; fax (2) 870-34-33; e-mail clphchm@clphchm.bas.bg; internet www.clphchm.bas.bg; f. 1972; attached to Bulgarian Acad. of Sciences; Dir Prof. Dr G. ZACHARIEV; publ. *Physico-Chemical Mechanics* (2 a year).

Central Laboratory of Seismic Mechanics and Earthquake Engineering: 1113 Sofia, Acad. G. Bonchev bl. 3; tel. (2) 971-24-07; fax (2) 971-24-07; e-mail simeonov@geophys.bas.bg; internet www.clsmee.geophys.bas.bg; f. 1982; attached to Bulgarian Acad. of Sciences; Dir Assoc. Prof. SVETOSLAV SIMEONOV.

Institute of Chemical Engineering: 1113 Sofia, Acad. G. Bonchev bl. 103; tel. 70-42-49; fax 70-75-23; e-mail ichemeng@bgean.acad.bg; f. 1972; attached to Bulgarian Acad. of Sciences; Dir Prof. V. BESHKOV.

Institute of Computer and Communication Systems: 1113 Sofia, Acad. G. Bonchev bl. 2; tel. (2) 72-01-32; fax (2) 72-39-05; e-mail fenerdjiev@iccs.acad.bg; f. 1990; attached to Bulgarian Acad. of Sciences; Dir Assoc. Prof. B. ZHECHEV.

Institute of Control and Systems Research: 1113 Sofia, Acad. G. Bonchev bl. 2, POB 79; tel. (2) 73-26-14; fax (2) 70-33-61; f. 1982; attached to Bulgarian Acad. of Sciences; Dir Prof. CH. RUMENIN.

Institute of Electronics 'Acad. Emil Djakov': 1784 Sofia, Tzarigradsko shose 72; tel. (2) 875-00-77; fax (2) 975-32-01; e-mail die@ie.bas.bg; f. 1963; attached to Bulgarian Acad. of Sciences; Dir Prof. RADOMIR ENIKOV.

Institute of Information Technology: 1113 Sofia, Acad. G. Bonchev bl. 29A, POB 161; tel. 72-04-97; fax 72-04-97; f. 1990; attached to Bulgarian Acad. of Sciences; Dir Assoc. Prof. V. VASILEV.

Institute of Laser Technology: 1326 Sofia, Galichitsa 33A; tel. 68-89-13; fax 68-89-13; f. 1980; Dir Assoc. Prof. I. KHRISTOV.

Institute of Metal Science: 1574 Sofia, Shipchenski prohod 67; tel. (2) 971-32-19; fax (2) 70-32-07; e-mail imst@bgcict.acad.bg; f. 1967; attached to Bulgarian Acad. of Sciences; Dir Prof. Y. ARSOV.

ISOMATIC Labs Ltd: 1797 Sofia, Bul. Universiada 4; tel. (2) 77-45-96; fax (2) 975-30-32; e-mail isomatic@isomatic.com; f. 1992; robotics, electronics; Dir Assoc. Prof. G. NACHEV.

Technological Institute of Agricultural Engineering: 7005 Ruse, Bul. Lipnitsa 106; tel. (82) 44-19-21; fax (82) 45-93-82; f. 1962; Dir T. KAYRIAKOV.

Libraries and Archives

Burgas

Regional Library: 8000 Burgas, A. Bogoridi 21; tel. (56) 84-27-53; e-mail rl_bourgas@burglib.org; internet www.burglib.org; f. 1888; 560,000 vols; Dir K. HRUSANOVA.

Plovdiv

Ivan Vazov National Library: 4000 Plovdiv, Avksentii Veleshki 17; tel. (32) 62-29-15; e-mail nbiv@plovdiv.techno-link.com; f. 1879; 1,313,000 vols, 1,100 periodical titles, 336 MSS, 4,134 incunabula; Dir RADKA KOLEVA; publ. *Plovdivski Kraj* (annually).

Ruse

'Lyuben Karavelov' Regional Library: 7000 Ruse, D. Korsakov 1; tel. (82) 82-01-26; fax (82) 82-01-34; e-mail director@librousse.bg; internet www.librousse.bg; f. 1888; 700,000 vols; Dir Z. KALINOVA.

Shumen

Public Library: 9700 Shumen, Slaviansky 19; tel. 5-70-93; f. 1922; 684,000 vols; Dir Z. KUKUSHKOVA.

Sofia

British Council Library and Information Centre: 9000 Varna, Drin 1; e-mail library.varna@britishcouncil.bg; 7,000 vols; Head of Customer Services MARIANA NIKOLOVA.

Central Agricultural Library: 1113 Sofia, Tsarigradsko shose 125 bl. 1; tel. 870-41-61; e-mail csb@abv.bg; f. 1961; 520,000 vols; Dir MARGARET STAMATOVA.

Central Library of Sofia: 1000 Sofia, Slaveikov 4; tel. 80-22-34; fax 88-22-36; f. 1886; 938,000 vols; Dir NADEZHDA ALEKSANDROVA.

Central Library of the Bulgarian Academy of Sciences: 1040 Sofia, 15 Noemvri 1; tel. (2) 987-89-66; fax (2) 986-25-00; e-mail library@cl.bas.bg; internet www.cl.bas.bg; f. 1869; 1,919,626 vols; 48 affiliated institute libraries; Dir Assoc. Prof. Dr D. KRASTEV; publs *Problemi na spetsialnite biblioteki-tematichen sbornik*, *Bulgaristika / Bulgarica*, *Informatsionen biuletin*.

Central Medical Library: 1431 Sofia, G. Sofijski 1; tel. (2) 952-31-71; fax (2) 952-31-71; e-mail mlib@medun.acad.bg; internet www.medun.acad.bg/Library/1.htm; f. 1918; 524,777 vols; 25 affiliated libraries; Dir P. DABCHEV; publ. *Abstracts of Bulgarian Scientific Medical Literature*.

National Centre for Information and Documentation (NACID) Central Research and Technical Library: 1125 Sofia, Dr G. M. Dimitrov 50; tel. (2) 873-54-00; fax (2) 971-31-20; e-mail ctb@nacid.bg; internet www.nacid.bg; f. 1962; 4,798,620 vols and materials; Dir VALENTINA SLAVCHEVA; publ. *Advances in Bulgarian Science*.

Central State Archive: 1000 Sofia, Moskovska 5; tel. 940-01-04; fax 980-14-43; e-mail gua@archives.government.bg; internet www.archives.government.bg; f. 1952; 110,000 files, documenting the activities of state instns, political parties, state and private companies and enterprises, from the mid 19th century to recent times; personal papers of eminent Bulgarians; Dir G. CHERNEV.

Centre for European Studies: 1125 Sofia, G. M. Dimitrov 52A; tel. (2) 971-24-11; fax (2) 971-24-11; e-mail ces@mail.cesbg.org; f. 1990; European Documentation Centre receiving all official publs of EC; Dir I. SHIKOVA; publ. *Evropa* (monthly).

Centre for Scientific and Technical Information (at the National Centre for Agricultural Science): 1113 Sofia, Tsarigradsko shose 125 bl 1; tel. (2) 870-55-58; fax (2) 870-80-78; e-mail cstiia@yahoo.com; f. 1961; Dir Dr MLADEN MLADENOV.

General Department of Archives at the Council of Ministers: 1000 Sofia, Moskovska 5; tel. (2) 940-01-05; fax (2) 980-14-43; e-mail gua@archives.government.bg; internet www.archives.government.bg; f. 1951; administers two central and 27 regional archives; 34,600 vols, 140 periodicals; Dir A. ATANASOV; publs *Izvestiya na daržavnite arhivi* (2 a year), *Arhiven pregled* (4 a year).

Library of the University of Architecture, Civil Engineering and Geodesy: 1421 Sofia, Bul. Dragan Tzankov 2; tel. (2) 66-52-74; fax (2) 65-68-63; e-mail lib@uacg.acad.bg; internet www.uacg.acad.bg; f. 1942; science and technology; 610,312 vols; Dir PERSIDA RAFAILOVA.

National Centre for Information and Documentation (at the Ministry of Industry): 1125 Sofia, Dr G. M. Dimitrov 52A; tel. 71-92-03; fax 71-01-57; e-mail infdoc@nacid.nat.bg; f. 1993; 4,650,000 vols; Gen. Dir J. KHLEBAROV; publ. *Scientific and Technical Publications in Bulgaria* (in English, 4 a year).

National Centre of Health Information: 1431 Sofia, D. Nestorov 15; tel. 958-19-32; fax 59-01-47; f. 1976; Dir KH. I. GRIVA; publ. *Zdraveopazvane*.

St Cyril and St Methodius National Library: 1037 Sofia, V. Levski 88; tel. (2) 988-28-11; fax (2) 843-54-95; e-mail nl@nationallibrary.bg; internet www.nationallibrary.bg; f. 1878; 2,863,754 books and periodicals, 5,536 MSS, 34,187 old and rare publs, 290,093 maps, prints and portraits, 85,418 scores and gramophone records, 292,437 patents and standards, 3,114,876 archival documents; archive of Bulgarian printed material; nat. ISBN and ISSN agency; spec. archive of documents from the period of Ottoman rule, feudalism and the Bulgarian nat. revival; research institute in library science; Dir Prof. Dr BORYANA HRISTOVA; publs *Biblioteca* (monthly), *Proceedings* (annual).

St Kliment Ohridsky University of Sofia Library: 1504 Sofia, Tsar Osvoboditel 15; tel. (2) 846-75-84; fax (2) 846-71-70; e-mail lsu@libsu.uni-sofia.bg; internet www.libsu.uni-sofia.bg; f. 1888; print and electronic library and information services, database access, inter-library and international inter-library loans; copying and microfiche services and electronic document delivery services; 2,001,000 vols; Dir Dr IVANKA YANKOVA.

Scientific Archives of the Bulgarian Academy of Sciences: 1040 Sofia, 15 Noemvri 1; tel. (2) 88-40-46; fax (2) 981-66-29; e-mail banlib@bgcict.acad.bg; f. 1947; MSS and 110,000 scientific dossiers; Head Assoc. Prof. S. PINTEV.

Stara Zagora

Regional Library: 6000 Stara Zagora, Tsar Kalojan 50; tel. (42) 64-81-31; e-mail lib-sz@prolink.bg; f. 1954; 419,000 vols; Dir SNEZANA MARINOVA.

Varna

'Pencho Slaveykov' Public Library: 9010 Varna, Slivnitsa 34; tel. 22-33-51; fax 22-33-51; 773,000 vols; Dir L. STOYANOVA.

Veliko Tărnovo

'P. R. Slaveykov' Regional Public Library: 5000 Veliko Tărnovo, I. Boteva 2; tel. (62) 62-02-08; e-mail nbvt@mbox.digsys.bg; internet www.library.vtbg.com; f. 1889; 586,873 vols; Dir IVAN ALEXANDROV.

Museums and Art Galleries

Blagoevgrad

Blagoevgrad Regional History Museum: 2700 Blagoevgrad, Rila 1; tel. (73) 88-53-70; fax (73) 88-53-73; e-mail im_bld@yahoo.com; f. 1951; archaeology, history, ethnography, natural history, fine arts; library of 16,500 vols; Dir K. GRANCHAROVA.

Burgas

Regional Burgas Museum: Slavyanska 69, 8000 Burgas; tel. (56) 84-22-93; fax (56) 84-25-88; e-mail main@burgasmuseum.bg; internet www.burgasmuseum.bg; f. 1912; Dir TSONYA GEORGIEVA DRAGEVA; publs *Bulletin of Museums of Southeast Bulgaria* (annually), *Bulletin* (annually).

Dobrich

Literary Museum of Jordan Jovkov: 9300 Dobrich, Gen. Gurko 4; tel. (58) 2-82-13; fax (58) 2-82-13; e-mail dobrichmuseum@abv.bg; f. 1968; literature and theatre art (life and creative work of Jovkov, Dora Gabe, the actress Adriana Budevska, the ballet-master Anastas Petrov and the artist Petar Dachev); Dir DIANA BORISOVA.

Regional Museum of History: 9300 Dobrich, Konstantin Stoilov 18; tel. (58) 2-82-13; fax (58) 2-82-56; e-mail dobrichmuseum@abv.bg; f. 1953; library of 20,000 vols; Dir DIANA BORISOVA; publ. *Dobrudja* (annually).

Haskovo

Regional Museum of History: 6300 Haskovo, Pl. Svoboda; tel. 62-42-37; fax 62-42-37; f. 1952; Dir G. GRAMATIKOV.

Kalofer

Hristo Botev National Museum: 4370 Kalofer, Khr. Botev 5; tel. and fax (3133) 22-71; e-mail musei_botev@abv.bg; f. 1944; birthplace of Hristo Botev, poet, revolutionary and rebel against Ottoman rule; objects and clothes showing Bulgarian life in the past; exhibit of rose oil and lace production; Dir A. NIKOLOVA.

Karlovo

Vasil Levski Museum: 4300 Karlovo, Gen. Kartsov 57; tel. 934-89; e-mail v_levski_museum@mail.orbitel.bg; internet www.vlevskimuseum-bg.org; f. 1937; named after Vasil Levski (1837–1873), founder of the Revolutionary Committee, which liberated Bulgaria from Ottoman rule; consists of Levski's birth house, an exhibition hall with items, photographs, documents and works of art; and a memorial chapel in which the hair of Vasil Levski is preserved; Dir DORA CHAUSHEVA.

Kazanlak

Shipka-Buzludza National Park Museum: 6100 Kazanlak, P. R. Slavejkov 8; tel. (431) 6-29-18; fax (431) 6-47-87; e-mail shipkamuseum@mail.bg; f. 1956; monuments connected with the liberation of Bulgaria from Ottoman rule; Dir D. DANCHEV.

Lovech

Regional Museum of History: 5500 Lovech, Pl. T. Kirkova; tel. (68) 60-13-82; e-mail imlovech@yahoo.com; f. 1895; Dir I. LALEV.

Montana

Regional Museum of History: 3400 Montana, Tsar Boris III 2; tel. 2-84-81; fax 2-25-36; f. 1953; Dir U. DERAKCHIISKA.

Pazardzhik

Regional Museum of History: 4400 Pazardzhik, Pl. K. Velichkov 15; tel. (34) 44-31-13; fax (34) 44-31-44; e-mail museumpz@yahoo.com; internet pa-media.net; f. 1911; library of 11,000 vols; Dir D. MITREV; publ. *Homeland* (every 2 years).

Stanislav Dospevsky Art Gallery: 4400 Pazardzhik, Pl. K. Velichkov 15; tel. 44-41-52; f. 1963; Dir DOYCHEV.

Pernik

Regional Museum of History: 2300 Pernik, Fizkulturna 2; tel. (76) 2-31-18; f. 1954; Dir O. ASPROV.

Pleven

Regional Museum of History: 5800 Pleven, Stoyan Zaimov 3; tel. (64) 82-26-23; fax (64) 82-26-91; e-mail plevenmuseum@dir.bg; internet www.plevenmuseum.dir.bg; f. 1903; library of 13,824 vols; Dir Prof. Dr MIKHAIL GRANCHAROV; publ. *Museum Studies in North-Western Bulgaria* (annual).

Plovdiv

City Gallery of Fine Arts: 4000 Plovdiv, Kniaz Alexander I 15; tel. (32) 63-53-22; e-mail ghgpl@abv.bg; f. 1952; Dir KRASIMIR LINKOV.

Ethnographical Museum: 4000 Plovdiv, Dr Chomakov 2; tel. (32) 62-52-57; fax (32) 62-71-32; e-mail ethnograph@abv.bg; internet ethnograph.org; f. 1917; Dir Dr A. YANKOV.

Natural Science Museum: 4000 Plovdiv, Chr. G. Danov 34; tel. (32) 63-30-96; f. 1955; library of 7,820 vols; Dir I. BASAMAKOV.

Regional Museum of Archaeology: 4000 Plovdiv, Pl. Šaedinenie 1; tel. 23-17-60; f. 1882; library of 12,000 vols; Dir A. PEYKOV; publ. *Pulpudeva*.

Regional Museum of History: 4000 Plovdiv, Pl. Šaedinenie 1; tel. 26-99-55; f. 1948; Dir S. SHIVACHEV.

Rila

Rila Monastery National Museum: Rilski Monastir, 2643 Rila (Sofia District); tel. (771) 2-22-08; f. 1961; Bulgarian art and architecture during the Ottoman period, Bulgarian history and history of the monastery; Dir P. MITEV.

Ruse

Regional Museum of History: 7000 Ruse, Pl. Kniaz Al. Batemberg 3; tel. (82) 23-61-15; e-mail museumrusse@mlnk.net; f. 1904; library of 15,340 vols; Dir Dr NIKOLAY NENOV; publ. *Izvestija*.

Shumen

Regional Museum of History: 9700 Shumen, Slavjanski 17; tel. (54) 5-74-10; f. 1904; Dir D. LECHEV.

Sofia

Boyana Church National Museum: 1616 Sofia, Boyansko ezero 3; tel. (2) 68-53-04; fax (2) 68-72-66; e-mail nmbc@mail.orbitel.bg; internet www.boyanachurch.org; f. 1947; medieval orthodox painting; Dir M. TRIFONOVA.

Dimitr Blagoev Museum: 1606 Sofia, L. Koshut 34; tel. 52-31-45; f. 1948; house of the founder of the Bulgarian Social-Democratic Party, containing documents and personal effects; Dir R. RUSSEV.

Georgi Dimitrov National Museum: 1303 Sofia, Opalchenska 66; tel. 32-01-49; f. 1951; Dir VERA DICHEVA.

Ivan Vazov Museum: 1000 Sofia, I. Vazov 10; tel. 88-12-70; f. 1926; house in which the Bulgarian poet lived; Curator I. BACHEVA.

National Archaeological Museum: 1000 Sofia, Saborna 2; tel. (2) 988-24-06; fax (2) 988-24-05; e-mail aim-bas@aclubcable.com; f. 1879; permanent exhibitions on pre-history, classical antiquity and the middle ages; temporary exhibitions; Dir Prof. VASIL NIKOLOV; publs *Archaeology* (4 a year), *Annual*.

National Art Gallery: 1000 Sofia, Pl. Knyaza Batemberga 1; tel. (2) 980-33-20; fax (2) 980-00-71; e-mail nag@office1.bg; f. 1948; modern Bulgarian art; br. in St Alexander Nevsky Cathedral (icons and ecclesiastical art); Dir Dr R. MARINSKA.

National Ethnographical Museum: 1000 Sofia, Moskovska 6A; tel. (2) 988-19-74; fax (2) 980-11-62; f. 1906; library of 22,221 vols; Dir N. TENEVA; publs *Bulgarian Ethnology*, *Ethnologia Balcanica* (annually).

National Gallery of Decorative Arts: 1000 Sofia, Vasil Levsky 56; tel. (2) 65-41-72; fax (2) 65-41-72; f. 1976; works from the 1950s to the present; library of 2,000 vols; Dir ZDRAVKO MAVRODIEV.

National Museum of Ecclesiastical History and Archaeology: 1000 Sofia, Pl. Sv. Nedelya 19; tel. 89-01-15; Dir N. KHADZHIEV.

National Museum of History: 1000 Sofia, Vitosha 2; tel. (2) 980-22-58; fax (2) 980-42-60; f. 1973; Dir I. PROKOPOV.

National Museum of Literature: 1000 Sofia, G. Rakovski 138; tel. 988-24-93; Dir DZH. KAMENOV.

National Museum of Military History: 1463 Sofia, Gen. Skobelev bl. 23; tel. 952-15-96; fax 952-59-91; e-mail m.museum@bol.bg; internet www.md.government.bg/nvim/_en/index.htm; f. 1916; attached to Min. of Defence; library of 6,100 vols; collects and registers Bulgarian and European military artefacts (arms, uniforms, flags, photographs, etc.); maintains two military mausolea in Sofia; 2 brs in Varna; Dir Dr PETKO YOTOV; publ. *Bulletin* (annually).

National Natural History Museum: 1000 Sofia, Tsar Osvoboditel 1; tel. 988-51-15; fax 88-28-97; f. 1889; library of 7,200 vols; Dir Assoc. Prof. P. BERON; publ. *Historia naturalis bulgarica* (annually).

National Polytechnical Museum: 1303 Sofia, Opalchenska 66; tel. 31-80-18; fax 31-40-36; f. 1968; science and technology; library of 10,000 vols; Dir A. VALCHEV; publs *Annual of the National Polytechnical Museum*, *Technitartché*.

Sofia Museum of History: 1000 Sofia, Exarh Yossif 27; tel. (2) 983-37-55; fax (2) 983-53-51; e-mail p_mitanov@yahoo.com; internet www.oldsofia.bg; f. 1952; library of 16,000 vols.

Sopot

Ivan Vazov Museum: 4330 Sopot, Vasil Levski 1; tel. (3134) 20-70; fax (3134) 21-66; e-mail vazov-muzeum@sopot-municipality.com; internet www.sopot-municipality.com; f. 1935; birthplace of the writer (1850–1921); Dir C. NEDELCHEVA.

Stara Zagora

Regional Museum of History: 6000 Stara Zagora, Graf Ignatiev 11; tel. (42) 60-02-99; fax (42) 60-02-99; e-mail histmuseumsz@mbox.digsys.bg; f. 1907; Dir P. KALCHEV.

Trjavna

Museum of Wood Carving and Icon Paintings: 5350 Trjavna, Pl. Kapitan Nikola 7; tel. (677) 22-78; f. 1963; Dir TSVETAN KOLEV.

Trojan

Museum of Folk Craft and Applied Arts: 5600 Trojan, Pl. Vazrashdane, P.B. 46; tel. 2-20-62; f. 1962; library of 2,700 vols; Dir T. TOTEVSKI; publ. *Cultural and Historical Inheritance of Trojan Region* (annually).

Varna

Regional Museum of History: 9000 Varna, Bul. Maria Luisa 41; tel. (52) 68-10-12; fax (52) 68-10-25; internet www.varna-bg.com; f. 1906; br. open-air museums: Roman Baths, Aladzha Monastery, 'Stone Forest' National Park; library of 25,000 vols; Dir Dr VALENTIN PLETNYOV; publ. *Izvestija na narodniya muzei Varna* (annually).

Veliko Tărnovo

National Museum of Architecture: 5000 Veliko Tarnovo, Ivan Vazov 35, POB 281; tel. 3-05-87; f. 1979; library of 4,600 vols; Man. Dir T. TEOPHILOV.

Regional Museum of History: 5000 Veliko Tărnovo, Nikola Pikolo 6; tel. (62) 62-02-56; fax (62) 63-69-54; e-mail rimvt@yahoo.com; f. 1871; library of 12,000 vols; Dir HRISTO HARITONOV; publ. *Bulletin* (annually).

Vidin

Regional Museum of History: 3700 Vidin, S. Veliki 13; tel. (94) 2-44-21; f. 1910; library of 8,500 vols; Dir A. BANOVA.

Vratsa

Regional Museum of History: 3000 Vratsa, Pl. Hr. Boteva 2; tel. (92) 2-03-73; f. 1952; Dir I. RAJKINSKY.

Universities

AGRAREN UNIVERSITET PLOVDIV
(Agricultural University Plovdiv)

4000 Plovdiv, D. Mendeleev 12
Telephone: (32) 65-42-00
Fax: (32) 63-31-57
E-mail: info@au-plovdiv.bg
Internet: www.au-plovdiv.bg
Founded 1945
State control
Academic year: September to June
Rector: Prof. YORDANKA KUZMANOVA
Pro-Rectors: Assoc. Prof. Dr ANNA ALADJADJIYAN, Prof. GEORGI NESHEV, Assoc. Prof. Dr ZHIVKO TERZIEV
Chief Administrative Officer: HELSIMIRA KIRKOVA
Chief Librarian: E. ANASTASOVA
Number of teachers: 221
Number of students: 2,726
Publication: *Scientific Works* (4 a year)

DEANS

Faculty of Agricultural Economics: Assoc. Prof. Dr GEORGI BOGOEV
Faculty of Agronomy: Assoc. Prof. Dr DIMITAR GREKOV
Faculty of Horticulture: Assoc. Prof. Dr ANGEL IVANOV
Faculty of Plant and Soil Protection: Prof. IVANKA LECHEVA
Faculty of Tropical and Sub-tropical Farming: Assoc. Prof. Dr NANKO POPOV
Centre for Continuous Education: Assoc. Prof. Dr G. RACHOVSKI

PROFESSORS

BABRIKOVA, T., Entomology
BRAIKOV, D., Viticulture
CHOLAKOV, D., Horticulture
DOCHEV, H., Agricultural Economics
GORASTEV, KH., Plant Genetics and Breeding
IVANOV, K., General Chemistry
KAMBUROVA, M., General Chemistry
KUZMANOVA, I., Microbiology
LECHEVA, I., Entomology
MATEEVA, A., Entomology
NESHEV, G., Phytopathology
PANDELIEV, S., Viticulture
PEEV, P., Tourism
POPOV, D., Agricultural Engineering
SPASOV, V., Crop Farming

AMERIKANSKI UNIVERSITET V BULGARIA
(American University in Bulgaria)

2700 Blagoevgrad, 1 G. Izmirliev Sq.
Telephone: (73) 88-55-45
Fax: (73) 88-83-44
Internet: www.aubg.bg
Founded 1991
Private control
Language of instruction: English
Academic year: August to May
President: REYNOLD BLOOM
Chief Administrative Officer: DAVID DURST
Associate Dean (Academic Affairs): STEVEN SULLIVAN
Associate Dean (College of Business): DUDLEY BLOSSOM
Registrar: EVELINA TERZIEVA
Number of teachers: 65 (42 full-time, 23 part-time)
Number of students: 827
Publication: *AUBG Newsletter* (3 a year)
academic departments: arts, languages and literature; European studies, history, and political science/international relations; economics; journalism/mass communica-

tion; business management; computer science; mathematics and science

PROFESSORS

BHARATH, R.
CHRISTOZOV, D.
FAIRCHILD, J.
GALLETLY, J.
MIREE, L.
MUTAFCHIEV, L.
NEDEV, S.
POPOV, A.
STEFANOVICH, M.

BURGAS PROF. ASSEN ZLATAROV UNIVERSITY
(Burgas 'Prof. Assen Zlatarov' University)

8010 Burgas, Prof. Jakimov 1
Telephone: (56) 86-00-41
Fax: (56) 88-02-49
E-mail: office@btu.bg
Internet: www.btu.bg

Founded 1963 (until 1992, Higher Institute of Chemical Technology; until 1995, Burgas University of Technology)
State control
Language of instruction: English
Academic year: September to July

Rector: Prof. DIMITAR KAMENSKI
Vice-Rector (Education): Prof. NIKOLAY RALEV
Vice-Rector (Quality Control): Prof. YONKA BALTADJIEVA
Vice-Rector (Research): Prof. VALENTIN NENOV
Dean (International Relations): Prof. RADOSTIN KUTSAROV
Registrar: IVAN MARKOV
Librarian: IRENA MARKOVSKA

Library of 160,000 vols
Number of teachers: 310
Number of students: 3,918

Publication: *Godishnik*

DEANS

Faculty of Natural Sciences: Prof. D. KETENEV
Faculty of Social Sciences: Prof. IVAN DIMITROV
Faculty of Technical Sciences: Prof. G. KORALSKI

HEADS OF DEPARTMENTS

Faculty of Natural Sciences (tel. (56) 85-82-78; e-mail office_edu@btu.bg):
Analytical Chemistry: Prof. A. DAKASHEV
Ecology and Environmental Protection: Prof. M. DIMOVA-TODOROVA
Inorganic Chemistry: Prof. K. DAVARSKI
Mathematics: Prof. G. STAMOV
Organic Chemistry: Prof. D. ALEXSIEV
Physical Chemistry: Prof. D. DAMJANOV
Physics: Prof. N. SULTANOVA

Faculty of Social Sciences (8010 Burgas, K/s Slaveikov; tel. (56) 86-00-25; fax (56) 86-00-19; e-mail economics@btu.bg):
Bulgarian Language: Prof. M. TERZIEVA
Computer and Information Technology: Prof. S. DIMITROV
Economics and Management: Prof. I. HRISTOV
Industrial Technology: Prof. P. PETKOV
Marketing and Accountancy: Dr K. PETROV
Pedagogy: Prof. E. GEORGIEVA
Social and Natural Sciences: Prof. A. SPIRTOV

Faculty of Technical Sciences (tel. (56) 68-71-83; e-mail office_edu@btu.bg):
Technology of Inorganic Substances and Silicates: Prof. T. DIMOVA
Chemical Engineering: Prof. G. STEFANOV
Organic Chemical Technologies: Prof. E. BALBOLOV
Technology of Materials and Materials Sciences: Prof. D. GEORGIEV
Biotechnology: Prof. T. GODJEVARGOVA
Water Technology: Prof. T. PANAJOTOVA
Fundamentals of Chemical Technologies: Prof. ST. PETROV

Departments not within a faculty:
Creative Arts and Sport: Asst Prof. R. DJENDOVA
Foreign-Language Teaching: Asst Prof. D. TOTEVA

ATTACHED COLLEGES

College of Tourism: 8000 Burgas, Park Ezero; tel. (56) 81-37-61; fax (56) 81-37-69; e-mail cot@cot.bse.bg; Dir Prof. A. KOKINOV.

Medical College: 8000 Burgas, St Stambolov St; tel. (56) 81-32-95; fax (56) 81-32-95; e-mail medical_college@btu.bg; Dir Asst Prof. M. STOICHEVA.

Technical College: 8010 Burgas, Prof. Jakimov 1; tel. (56) 88-12-31; e-mail barzov@crosswinds.net; Dir Prof. P. BARZOV.

BURGASKI SVOBODEN UNIVERSITET
(Burgas Free University)

8001 Burgas, 62 San Stefano
Telephone: (56) 900-520
Fax: (56) 813-912
Internet: www.bfu.bg

Founded 1991
Private control

Rector: Prof. Dr PETKO CHOBANOV
Registrar: DARINA DIMITROVA

Library of 62,000 vols
Number of teachers: 615
Number of students: 5,881

Publications: *Juridical Collection* (2 a year), *University Annual*

DEANS

Faculty for Business Studies: Prof Dr PETKO CHOBANOV
Faculty for Computer Science, Engineering and Natural Studies: Prof. DIMITAR YUDOV
Faculty for Humanities: Assoc. Prof. Dr EVELINA DINEVA
Faculty for Legal Studies: Assoc. Prof. Dr MOMYANA GUNEVA

PROFESSORS

(some professors teach in more than one faculty)

Faculty for Business Studies:
DOGANOV, D.
VELEV, I.

Faculty for Computer Science, Engineering and Natural Sciences:
LANDJEV, I. N.
LAZAROV, A. D.
MAKEDONSKI, D. V.
YARMOV, I. M.
YUDOV, D.

Faculty for Humaities:
STAMOV, V. H.
VALCHEV, R. I.

Faculty for Legal Studies:
CHINOVA, M.
CHOBANOV, P.
GROZDANOV, B.
KANDEVA, E.
KOTZEVA, E.
VASSILEV, A.
VLADIMIROV, I.
ZLATAREV, E.

HIMIKO TEHNOLOGIČEN I METALURGIČEN UNIVERSITET
(University of Chemical Technology and Metallurgy)

1756 Sofia, Bul. Kliment Ohridski 8
Telephone: (2) 868-15-13
Fax: (2) 868-54-88
E-mail: rectorat@uctm.edu
Internet: www.uctm.edu

Founded as a state university 1953
State control
Language of instruction: Bulgarian, some subjects in German, French and English
Academic year: September to July

Rector: Prof. Dr KIRIL STANULOV
Vice-Rector for Education: Prof. Dr KALINA MUTAFCHIEVA
Vice-Rector for Research and International Co-operation: Prof. Dr BORIS STEFANOV
Chief Administrative Officer: Prof. Dr ASSEN PETKOV
Librarian: MAIA PENCHEVA

Library of 66,000 vols
Number of teachers: 371
Number of students: 3,667

Publication: *Godishnik, now Journal of the University of Chemical Technology and Metallurgy* (quarterly published in english)

DEANS

Faculty of Chemical and Systems Engineering: Assoc. Prof. Dr BOGDANA KUMANOVA MINCHEV
Faculty of Chemical Technology: Assoc. Prof. Dr DIMITAR PISHEV
Faculty of Metallurgy and Materials Science: Assoc. Prof. Dr IVAN GRUEV AHMAKOV
Department of Chemical Sciences: Assoc. Prof. Dr ASSEN GIRGINOV
Department of Humanities: Assoc. Prof. Dr MARIANA ILIEVA
Department of Physico-Mathematical and Technical Sciences: Assoc. Prof. Dr TODOR DIMOV
College of Technology: Prof. Dr NIKOLA SHOILEV

HEADS OF DEPARTMENTS

Analytical Chemistry: Assoc. Prof. Dr C. NEDELCHEVA
Applied Mechanics: Assoc. Prof. Dr A. ALEKSANDROV
Automation of Production: Assoc. Prof. Dr V. TZOCHEV
Biotechnologies: Assoc. Prof. Dr I. DOBREV
Chemical Engineering: Assoc. Prof. Dr I. PENCHEV
Chemical Technology of Wood and Poligraphy: Assoc. Prof. Dr D. POZALINOV
Economics and Management: Assoc. Prof. Dr P. GECHEV
Electrical Engineering and Electronics: Assoc. Prof. Dr A. MIREV
Ferrous Metallurgy and Metal Foundry: Assoc. Prof. Dr M. MIHOVSKI
Foreign Languages: Assoc. Prof. Dr M. KUZMENKO
Fundamentals of Chemical Technologies: Assoc. Prof. Dr Z. ZDRAVCHEV
Humanities and Education Quality: Assoc. Prof. Dr S. TERSIEVA
Inorganic Chemistry: Assoc. Prof. Dr M. GEORGIEV
Inorganic and Electrochemical Production: Assoc. Prof. Dr L. FACHIKOV
Mathematics: Assoc. Prof. Dr D. KOLEV
Nonferrous Metallurgy And Semiconductor Technologies: Assoc. Prof. Dr I. MARKOVA
Organic Chemistry: Assoc. Prof. Dr E. NAIDENOVA
Organic Synthesis and Fuels: Assoc. Prof. Dr G. CHOLAKOV

Physical Chemistry: Assoc. Prof. Dr M. Hristov
Physical Metallurgy and Heat Aggregates: Prof. Dr. D. Angelova
Physics: Assoc. Prof. Dr E. Kashchieva
Polymer engineering: Prof. Dr N. Dishovski
Programming and Computer System Application: Assoc. Prof.Dr A. Georgieva
Sports: Assoc. Prof. Dr L. Mateeva
Technology of Silicates and Binding Substances: Assoc. Prof. Dr L. Pavlova
Textile and Leather: Assoc. Prof. Dr V. Vasileva

PROFESSORS

Faculty of Chemical and Systems Engineering:

Velev, K., Automation of Industry
Vuchkov, I., Automation of Industry
Yonchev, H., Automation of Industry

Faculty of Chemical Technology:

Dishovski, N., Polymer engineering
Dombalov, I., Technology of Inorganic Compounds
Grancharov, I., Technology of Inorganic Compounds
Raichev, R., electrochemistry and Corrosion
Simeonov, N., Textile Chemistry
Vladkova, T., Polymer engineering

Faculty of Metallurgy and Materials Science:

Angelova, D., Plastic Deformation and Heat Treatment of Metals
Kojuharov, V., Silicate Technology

Department of Chemical Sciences:

Dukov, I., Inorganic Chemistry
Girginov, A., Physical Chemistry
Veleva, S., Physical Chemistry

Department of Humanities (tel. (2) 816-34-90; e-mail marianao@uctm.edu):

Ilieva, M., education Quality

Department of Physico-Mathematical and Technical Sciences:

Hadjov, K., Applied Mechanics
Panev, S., Applied Mechanics
Shoilev, N., Electrotechnology and Electronics

LESOTEHNIČESKI UNIVERSITY (University of Forestry)

1756 Sofia, Kl. Ohridski 10
Telephone: (2) 9-19-07
Fax: (2) 862-28-30
Internet: www.ltu.acad.bg

Founded as an independent institute 1953
State control
Academic year: September to June (two terms)

Rector: Prof. Dr Dimitar Kolarov
Pro-Rectors: Assoc. Prof. D. Georgiev, Assoc. Prof. I. Iliev, Assoc. Prof. N. Pipkov
Registrar (vacant)
Librarian: Juliana Josifova

Number of teachers: 350
Number of students: 3,500

Publications: *Forest Ideas*, *Management and Sustainable Development*, *Propagation of Ornamental Plants*, *Woodworking and Furniture Production*

DEANS

Faculty of Ecology and Landscape Architecture and Agronomy: Asst Prof. G. Trenchev
Faculty of Forestry: Asst Prof. K. Liubenov
Faculty of Forestry Industry: Prof. B. Dinkov
Faculty of Industrial Management: Asst Prof. Iv. Yovkov
Faculty of Veterinary Medicine: Asst Prof. J. Kostadinov
Postgraduate Centre: Prof. Ek. Pavlova

PROFESSORS

Asparuchov, K., Harvesting Machinery and Technology
Dimitrov, E., Basis of Forestry
Dinkov, B., Wood Technology
Gencheva, S., Ecology and Conservation, Soil Science
Gerasimov, Sv., Zoology
Grigorov, P., Sawing of Timber
Kavalov, A., Furniture Technology
Kolarov, D., Plant Physiology
Kovachev, G., Veterinary Medicine
Kuleliev, J., Planting Trees and Flowers
Kyuchukov, G., Furniture Construction
Michov, I., Forest Mensuration
Pavlov, D., Phytocenology
Pavlova, Ek., Ecology
Puchalev, G., Organization and Planting in Landscape Architecture
Raichev, A., Thermodynamics, Heat and Mass Transfer
Shechtov, Ch., Automation of Technological Processes
Shktilyanova, El., Floriculture
Tasev, G., Machinery and Technology in Agronomy
Vakazelov, I., Dendrology
Videlov, H., Hydrothermal Treatment of Wood
Yorova, K., Soil Science
Yosifov, N., Particle-Board Technology

ATTACHED INSTITUTE

Balkan Centre of Study and Research in Ecology and Environmental Protection: Dir Assoc. Prof. I. Dombalov.

MEDICINSKI UNIVERSITET PLEVEN (Medical University Pleven)

5800 Pleven, 1 Kliment Ochridski
Telephone: (64) 88-41-00
Fax: (64) 80-16-03
E-mail: rector@vmi-pl.bg
Internet: www.vmi-pl.bg

Founded 1974
State control
Academic year: September to June

Rector: Grigor Gorchev
Vice-Rector for Education: Assoc. Prof. Dr Petyo Bochev
Vice-Rector for Research: Assoc. Prof. Dr Maria Sredkova
Vice-Rector for Therapeutic Activities: Assoc. Prof. Dr Ivan Lalev

Library of 82,287 vols, 90 periodicals
Number of teachers: 341
Number of students: 756

Publication: *Science Book* (annually)

DEANS

Faculty of Medicine: Grigor Gorchev
Faculty of Public Health: Gena Grancharova

MEDICINSKI UNIVERSITET SOFIA (Medical University Sofia)

1431 Sofia, D. Nestorov 15
Telephone: 59-00-52
Fax: 59-40-94
E-mail: rtb@bulinfo.net
Internet: www.medun.acad.bg

Founded 1972, as the Academy of Medicine, by the integration of the former Higher Medical Institute and the medical research institutes; present name and status 1995
State control
Academic year: September to June

Rector: Prof. Vladimir Ovcharov
Pro-Rectors: Prof. Todor Peev (Education), Prof. Ivan Asenov (International Relations and Research), Prof. Ilko Karagyozov (Medical Affairs)
Chief Administrative Officer: Khristo Anachkov
Librarian: Dr Dabchev

Number of teachers: 1,819
Number of students: 6,141

Publication: *Acta Medica Bulgarica* (2 a year)

DEANS

Faculty of Medicine: Prof. N. Tsankov
Faculty of Nursing: Assoc. Prof. K. Yurukova
Faculty of Pharmacy: Prof. S. Nikolov
Faculty of Stomatology: Prof. B. Indzhov
Free Faculty: Assoc. Prof. N. Vrabchev

MEDICINSKI UNIVERSITET VARNA (Medical University of Varna)

9002 Varna, Marin Drinov 55
Telephone: (52) 22-56-22
Fax: (52) 22-25-84
E-mail: uni@asclep.muvar.acad.bg
Internet: www.muvar.acad.bg

Founded 1961
Academic year: October to June

Rector: Prof. T. D. Temelkov
Vice-Rector (Education): Assoc. Prof. Dr M. N. Nenova
Vice-Rector (Quality): Assoc. Prof. Dr L. P. Havezova
Vice-Rector (Research): Assoc. Prof. Dr A. D. Klisarova
Vice-Rector (Therapy): Prof. Dr H. B. Tsekov
Chief Librarian: P. A. Mileva

Library of 185,000 vols
Number of teachers: 355
Number of students: 2,360

Publications: *Biomedical Reviews* (annually), *Bulgarska koloproktologia* (2 a year), *Scripta Scientifica Medica* (annually), *Syrtse i Byal Drob* (Heart and Lung, in Bulgarian and English, 4 a year)

DEANS

Faculty of Medicine: Assoc. Prof. Dr D. S. Karastatev
Faculty of Public Health: Assoc. Prof. Dr S. T. Popova
Medical College of Dobrich: Assoc. Prof. Dr N. Spasova (Head)
Medical College of Shumen: Assoc. Prof. Dr N. Stoynov (Head)
Medical College of Varna: Assoc. Prof. Dr D. Radev (Head)

MINNO-GEOLOŽKI UNIVERSITET 'SV. IVAN RILSKI' (UNIVERSITY OF MINING AND GEOLOGY 'ST IVAN RILSKI')

1700 Sofia, Darvenica
Telephone: (2) 962-72-20
Fax: (2) 962-49-40
E-mail: maillist-mgu@mgu.mg
Internet: www.mgu.bg

Founded 1953
Academic year: October to June (two terms)

Rector: Assoc. Prof. Ivan Milev
Pro-Rectors: Assoc. Prof. Nikolay Djerahov, Assoc. Prof. Ventislav Ivanov
Registrar: S. Ivanov
Librarian: K. Draganova

Number of teachers: 230
Number of students: 2,500

Publication: *Godishnik* (annually)

DEANS

Faculty of Geological Prospecting: Assoc. Prof. Radi Radichev
Faculty of Mining Electromechanics: Assoc. Prof. Kancho Ivanov
Faculty of Mining Technology: Assoc. Prof. Luben Totev

Department of Humanities: Sr Prof. STEPHAN FILIPOV

PROFESSORS

Faculty of Geological Prospecting (tel. (2) 962-72-70 ext. 207; e-mail radirad@mgu.bg):

GROUDEV, S., Environmental Science
STAVREV, P., Applied Geophysics

Faculty of Mining Electromechanics (tel. 262-72-28):

DONCHEV, S., Theory of Mechanics
FETVADJIEV, G., Mechanization of Mines

Faculty of Mining Technology (tel. (2) 962-72-20 ext. 206; e-mail ltotev@abv.bg):

KOLEV, K., Rock Mechanics
KUZEV, L., Mineral Processing
METODIEV, M., Mineral Processing
MICHAYLOV, M., Mine Ventilation
VISOKOV, G., Chemistry

Department of Humanities (tel. (2) 962-72-20 ext. 324):

STAMATOV, A., Philosophy

NOV BULGARKI UNIVERSITET (New Bulgarian University)

1618 Sofia, 21 Montevideo
Telephone: (2) 955-52-91
Fax: (2) 955-52-91
E-mail: info@nbu.bg
Internet: www.nbu.bg

Founded 1990
Private control
Languages of instruction: Bulgarian, French, English
Rector: Assoc. Prof. Dr SERGEI IGNATOV
Vice-Rector for Educational Activities: Prof. MIROSLAV DACHEV
Vice-Rector for International and Research Activities: Assoc. Prof. Dr LIUDMIL GEORGIEV
Vice-Rector on Quality Management Research: BOICHO KOKINOV
Library of 90,000 vols, 1,800 reference works, 190 periodicals
Number of teachers: 250

DEANS

School of Basic Education: Assoc. Prof. Dr PLAMEN BOCHKOV
Graduate School: Assoc. Prof. Dr ANTONII TODOROV
Undergraduate School: Prof. Dr RADOSLAV TSONCHEV

HEADS OF DEPARTMENTS

Anthropology: Assoc. Prof. MAGDALENA ELCHINOVA
Applied Arts: Assoc. Prof. EKATERINA ROUSINOVA
Applied Linguistics: Assoc. Prof. PAVLINA STEFANOVA
Archaeology: Prof. IVAN GATSOV
Cinema, Advertising and Show Business: Assoc. Prof. IVAN GEORGIEV
Cognitive Science and Psychology: Assoc. Prof. ELENA PASPALANOVA
Earth and Environmental Sciences: Prof. RANGEL GJUROV
Economics and Business Administration: Prof. RADOSLAV TZONTCHEV
History: Assoc. Prof. VESELIN METODIEV
History of Culture: Prof. IVAN MAZAROV
Informatics: Assoc. Prof. Dr PETIA ASSENOVA
Law: Prof. Dr ROUMEN VLADIMIROV
Mass Communications: Assoc. Prof. Dr RUSI MARINOV
Medicine and Biology: Assoc. Prof. JIVKA VINAROVA
Mediterranean and Eastern Studies: Asst Prof. Dr THEODORE LEKOV
Musical Arts: Prof. MILENA MOLLOVA
New Bulgarian Studies: Assoc. Prof. MIHAIL NEDELTCHEV
Political Sciences: Assoc. Prof. ANNA KRASTEVA
Telecommunications: Prof. ANTONI SLAVINSKI
Theatre: Prof. RUMEN TSONEV
Anthropological and Field Research Centre: Prof. Dr JULIAN KONSTANTINOV
Bulgarian Centre for Human Relations: Assoc. Prof. TOMA TOMOV
Central and East European Center for Cognitive Science: Prof. ELIZABETH BATES, BOICHO KOKINOV
Centre for Public Administration: Assoc. Prof. LIUBOMIR SLAVKOV
Centre for Social Practices: Prof. EVGENI DAINOV
South-East European Center for Semiotic Studies: Prof. MARIA POPOVA

PLOVDIVSKI UNIVERSITET 'PAISII HILENDARSKI' ('Paisii Hilendarski' University of Plovdiv)

4000 Plovdiv, Tsar Asen 24
Telephone: (32) 62-90-94
Fax: (32) 63-50-49
E-mail: pduniv@pu.acad.bg
Internet: www.pu.acad.bg

Founded 1961 from 'Paisij Hilendarski' Higher Pedagogical Institute, Plovdiv; university status 1972
Academic year: October to June
Rector: Prof. O. SAPAREV
Vice-Rectors: Prof. Z. KOZLUDZHOV, Prof. D. LEVTEROVA, Prof. N. SILOV, Prof. G. TOTKOV
Registrar: D. BOIKOV
Librarian: R. PANOVA
Number of teachers: 800
Number of students: 15,000
Publication: *Nauchni Trudove*

DEANS

Faculty of Biology: Prof. AT. DONEV
Faculty of Chemistry: Prof. AT. VENKOV
Faculty of Economics: Assoc. Prof. M. MIHAILOVA
Faculty of Law: Prof. G. PETROVA
Faculty of Mathematics and Computer Science: Prof. D. MEKEROV
Faculty of Pedagogics: Assoc. Prof. P. RADEV
Faculty of Philology: Prof. IV. KUTSAROV
Faculty of Physics: Prof. G. MEKISHEV

PROFESSORS

ALEKSANDROV, A.
ANDREEV, G.
ANGELOV, A.
ANGELOV, P., Zoology
ATANASOV, A., Theoretical Physics
BACHVAROV, G.
BALABANOV, N., Nuclear Physics
DIMITROV, R., Technology of Inorganic Chemistry
DRUMEVA, E.
FUTEKOV, L., Analytical Chemistry
GOLEMINOV, C.
GOLEVA, P.
GRUEV, B.
IVANOV, A., Microbiology
IVANOV, S., Technology of Organic Chemistry
JENKINS, D.
KARTALOV, A.
KATSARKOVA, V.
KIRYAKOV, I.
KOLAROV, N.
KUTSAROV, I., Morphology of Modern Bulgarian Language
KUZMANOVA, A.
LAZAROV, K.
MIHAYLOVA, M.
MIHOVSKI, S.
MINKOV, I., Plant Physiology
MITEV, D., Zoology
MOLLOV, T., Algebra
MRACHKOV, V.
NIKOLOVA, M.
PAPANOV, G.
PETROV, P.
POPCHEV, I.
POPOV, P.
SAPAREV, O.
SAPKOVA, I.
SAVOV, E.
TSEKOV, G.
VELCHEV, N., Physics of Dielectrics
VENKOV, A.
YORDANOV, Y

RUSENSKI UNIVERSITET 'ANGEL KANCHEV' ('Angel Kanchev' University of Ruse)

Studentska 8, 7017 Ruse
Telephone and fax (82) 84-53-62
E-mail: ird@ru.acad.bg
Internet: www.ru.acad.bg

Founded 1954 as Institute of Mechanization and Electrification of Agriculture; became Angel Kanchev Higher Technical School 1982 and Angel Kanchev Technical University of Ruse 1990; present name 1995
State control
Academic year: September to July
Rector: Assoc. Prof. Dr MARKO TODOROV
Vice-Rectors: Assoc. Prof. Dr BORISLAV ANGELOV, Assoc. Prof. Dr IASSEN DOCHEV, Prof. VELIKO IVANOV
Sec.-Gen.: Assoc. Prof. Dr IORDAN NIKOLOV
Director of the International Relations Dept: Assoc. Prof. Dr KIRIL BARZEV
Librarian: E. LEKHOVA
Library of 306,641 vols
Number of teachers: 600
Number of students: 7,700
Publication: *Nauchni Trudove*

DEANS

Faculty of Agricultural Mechanization: Assoc. Prof. Dr HRISTO BELOEV
Faculty of Automative and Transport Engineering: Assoc. Prof. Dr EMIL MARINOV
Faculty of Business and Management: Assoc. Prof. Dr VASIL PENCHEV
Faculty of Electrical Engineering, Electronics and Automation: Assoc. Prof. Dr NIKOLAY MIHAILOV
Faculty of Law: Assoc. Prof. Dr SIMEON BOJANOV
Faculty of Mechanical and Manufacturing Engineering: Assoc. Prof. Dr VALENTIN GAGOV
Faculty of Pedagogy: Assoc. Prof. Dr ROUSSI ROUSSEV
Faculty of Pedagogy (Silistra): Assoc. Prof. Dr ILIANA GORANOVA
Faculty of Postgraduate Studies and Further Education: Assoc. Prof. Dr IULIAN MLADENOV
College of Technical Studies (Razgrad): Assoc. Prof. Dr NEIKO STOYANOV
College of Technical Studies (Silistra): Assoc. Prof. Dr DIMO DIMOV

PROFESSORS

Faculty of Agricultural Mechanization:

ENCHEV, K.
GUZHGULOV, G.
MITKOV, A.
ORLOEV, N.
PARASHKEVOV, I.

Faculty of Automotive and Transport Engineering:

ANDREEV, D.
ILIEV, L.
LIUBENOV, SL.
NENOV, P.

SIMEONOV, D.

Faculty of Business and Management:

PAPAZOV, KR.

Faculty of Electrical Engineering, Electronics and Automatics:

ANDONOV, K.

Faculty of Law:

MICHEV, N.

Faculty of Mechanical and Manufacturing Engineering:

IVANOV, V.
KANEV, M.
POPOV, G.
TOMOV, B.
VELCHEV, S.
VITLIEMOV, VL.

Faculty of Pedagogy:

KOZHUKHAROV, K.

Faculty of Pedagogy (Silistra) (Albena 1, POB 103, 7500 Silistra):

NEDEV, L.

ATTACHED CENTRE

Bulgaria–Romania Interuniversity Europe Centre: 7000 Ruse, Aleksandrovska St 55; tel. (82) 82-56-67; fax (82) 82-56-62; e-mail brie-bg@ru.acad.bg; internet www.brie.ru.acad.bgf. 2001; operates through collaboration between the Rusenski Universitet 'Angel Kanchev' and the Academia de Studii Economice (see Romania chapter); languages of instruction: English, German.

SHUMENSKI UNIVERSITET 'EPISKOP KONSTANTIN PRESLAVSKI' (Bishop Konstantin Preslavski University of Shumen)

9712 Shumen, Universitetska 115
Telephone: (54) 83-04-95
Fax: (54) 83-03-71
E-mail: rector@shu-bg.net
Internet: www.shu-bg.net
Founded 1971
Academic year: September to June
Rector: Prof. Dr DOBRIN DOBREV
Vice-Rector (Academic Affairs): Assoc. Prof. MALCHO MALCHEV
Vice-Rector (Finance, Administration and Economic Affairs): Assoc. Prof. DOBROMIR ENCHEV
Vice-Rector (Scientific and International Affairs): Assoc. Prof. ANA DIMOVA
Number of teachers: 616
Number of students: 10,000
Publications: *Godishnik* (annually), *Liuboslovie* (journal of the Faculty of Humanities)

DEANS

Faculty of Education: Assoc. Prof. GEORGI KOLEV
Faculty of Humanities: Assoc. Prof. STOYAN VITLYANOV
Faculty of Mathematics and Computer Science: Assoc. Prof. DIMCHO K. STANKOV
Faculty of Natural Sciences: Assoc. Prof. VELIKO VELIKOV

ATTACHED RESEARCH INSTITUTES

College Dobritch: Dir Assoc. Prof. SLAVKA SLAVOVA.

Teacher Information and Qualification Centre: Dir Assoc. Prof. MARGARITA GEORGIEVA.

SOFIISKI UNIVERSITET 'SVETI KLIMENT OHRIDSKY' (St Kliment Ohridsky University of Sofia)

1504 Sofia, Tsar Osvoboditel 15
Telephone: (2) 93-08
Fax: (2) 946-02-55
Internet: www.uni-sofia.bg
Founded 1888 as High School; granted charter 1909
State control
Academic year: September to June (two terms)
Rector: Prof. Dr B. BIOLCHEV
Pro-Rectors: Assoc. Prof. D. GIUROV, Assoc. Prof. M. PENCHEVA, Prof. Dr A. POPOV, Assoc. Prof. D. TOPLIISKI
Director of International Relations: R. GRIGOROV
Secretary: R. STANIMIROVA
Director of Library: Prof. ZH. STOYANOV
Library: see under Libraries
Number of teachers: 1,608
Number of students: 25,454
Publication: *Godishnik*

DEANS

Faculty of Biology: Assoc. Prof. R. DIMKOV
Faculty of Chemistry: Prof. Dr I. PANAIOTOV
Faculty of Classical and Modern Philology: Assoc. Prof. M. PENCHEVA
Faculty of Economics: Assoc. Prof. G. CHOBANOV
Faculty of Geology and Geography: Assoc. Prof. M. VODENSKA
Faculty of History: Prof. Dr P. DELEV
Faculty of Journalism: Prof. Dr V. DIMITROV
Faculty of Law: Assoc. Prof. D. KRUSANOV
Faculty of Mathematics and Information Science: Assoc. Prof. I. MITEV
Faculty of Pedagogy: Assoc. Prof. E. VASILEVA
Faculty of Philosophy: Assoc. Prof. V. STEFANOV
Faculty of Physics: Prof. Dr B. SLAVOV
Faculty of Primary and Pre-School Education: Prof. G. BIZHKOV
Faculty of Slavonic Philology: Assoc. Prof. V. STEFANOV
Faculty of Theology: Prof. Dr D. KIROV

PROFESSORS

Faculty of Biology:

BOZHILOVA, E., Botany
IVANOVA, I., Plant Physiology
KIMENOV, G., Plant Physiology
KOLEV, D., Biochemistry
MARGARITOV, N., Hydrobiology and Ichthyology
MINKOV, I., Human and Animal Physiology
TEMNISKOVA, D., Botany
VLAHOV, S., General and Industrial Microbiology

Faculty of Chemistry:

ALEKSANDROV, S., Analytical Chemistry
BONCHEV, P., Analytical Chemistry
DOBREV, A., Organic Chemical Technology
FAKIROV, S., Organic Chemical Technology
GALABOV, B., Organic Chemical Technology
IVANOV, I., Physical Chemistry
KALCHEVA, B., Organic Chemical Technology
KOSTADINOV, K., Inorganic Chemical Technology
LAZAROV, D., Inorganic Chemical Technology
MARKOV, P., Organic Chemistry
PANAYOTOV, I., Physical Chemistry
PETROV, B., Organic Chemical Technology
PETSEV, N., Organic Chemistry
PLATIKANOV, D., Physical Chemistry
RADOEV, B., Physical Chemistry
TOSHEV, B., Physical Chemistry

Faculty of Classical and Modern Philology:

ALEKSIEVA, B., English Philology
BOEV, E., Eastern Languages
BOGDANOV, B., Classical Philology
BOYADZHIEV, D., Classical Philology
DAKOVA, N., German Philology
DELIIVANOVA, B., German Philology
GALABOV, P., Romance Philology
KANCHEV, I., Ibero-Romance Philology
PARASHKEVOV, B., German Philology
PETKOV, P., German Philology
SHURBANOV, A., English Philology

Faculty of Economics:

BEHAR, H., History of Economics
SERGIENKO, R., General Economic Theory

Faculty of Geology and Geography:

BACHVAROV, M., Geography of Tourism
ESKENAZI, G., Mineralogy, Petrology and Economic Geology
KANCHEV, D., Economic Geography
MANDOV, G., Geology and Palaeontology
PETROV, P., Geography

Faculty of History:

BAKALOV, G., Byzantine History
DIMITROV, I., Bulgarian History
DRAGANOV, D., Modern History
GEORGIEV, V., Bulgarian History
GEORGIEVA, I., Ethnography
GETOV, L., Archaeology
GYUZELEV, V., Bulgarian History
ILIEV, I., Modern History
LALKOV, M., Modern History
NAUMOV, G., Bulgarian History
NIKOLOV, J., Medieval History
OGNYANOV, L., Bulgarian History
PANTEV, A., Modern History
POPOV, D., Ancient History and Thracian Studies
SEMKOV, M., Modern History
TACHEVA, M., Ancient History and Thracian Studies
TRIFONOV, S., Modern History

Faculty of Journalism:

DIMITROV, V., Radio Journalism
KARAIVANOVA, P., Journalism
PANAYOTOV, F., History of Journalism
SEMOV, M., Theory of Journalism

Faculty of Law:

BOYCHEV, G., Theory of State Law
GERDZHIKOV, O., Civil Law
MIHAYLOV, D., Criminal Law
PAVLOVA, M., Civil Law
PETKANOV, G., Finance Law
POPOV, P., Civil Law
SREDKOVA, K., Civil Law
STOYCHEV, S., Constitutional and Administrative Law
TSANKOVA, TS., Civil Law
ZAHAROV, V., Theory of State Law
ZIDAROVA, I., International Law

Faculty of Mathematics and Information Science:

BOYANOV, B., Numerical Analysis and Algorithms
DENCHEV, R., Complex Analysis and Topology
GENCHEV, T., Differential Equations
HADZHIIVANOV, N., Education in Mathematics and Computer Sciences
HOROSOV, E., Differential Equations
HRISTOV, E., Complex Analysis and Topology
LILOV, L., Analytical Mechanics
MARKOV, K., Continuous Media Mechanics
POPIVANOV, N., Differential Equations
SKORDEV, D., Mathematical Logic and Applications
STANILOV, G., Education in Mathematics and Computer Sciences
TROYANSKI, S., Mathematical Analysis
ZAPRYANOV, Z., Continuous Media Mechanics

Faculty of Pedagogy:
- ANDREEV, M., Didactics
- BOYCHEVA, V., History of Pedagogy
- DIMITROV, L., Theory of Education
- PAVLOV, D., Didactics
- STOYANOV, P., History of Pedagogy
- VASILEV, D., Didactics

Faculty of Philosophy:
- ALEKSANDROV, P., History of Psychology
- ANDONOV, A., Philosophy
- BOYADZHIEV, T., History of Philosophy
- DESEV, L., Social Psychology
- DINEV, V., Philosophical Anthropology
- FOL, A., History of Culture
- GENCHEV, N., History of Culture
- GERGOVA, A., Book Science
- GINEV, V., Theory of Culture
- GRADEV, D., Social Psychology
- KARASIMEONOV, G., Political Science
- KRUMOV, K., Social Psychology
- MIHAILOVSKA, E., Sociology
- MITEV, P. E., Political Science
- NESHEV, K., Ethics
- PETKOV, K., Sociology
- RADEV, R., History of Philosophy
- SIVILOV, L., Epistemology
- STEFANOV, I. I., Sociology
- VASILEV, N., Philosophy
- VENEDIKOV, Y., Sociology
- ZNEPOLOSKY, I., Theory of Culture

Faculty of Physics:
- APOSTOLOV, A., Solid State Physics
- DENCHOV, G., Geophysics
- DINEV, S., Quantum Electronics
- GEORGIEV, G., Quantum Electronics
- ILIEV, M., Condensed Matter Physics
- IVANOV, G., Astronomy
- KAMENOV, P., Nuclear Physics and Energetics
- KUTSAROV, S., Electronics
- LALOV, I., Condensed Matter Physics
- LUKYANOV, A., Nuclear Physics and Energetics
- MARTINOV, N., Condensed Matter Physics
- MATEEV, M., Theoretical Physics
- NIKOLOV, N., Plasma Physics
- PANCHEV, S., Meteorology and Geophysics
- POPOV, A., Semiconductor Physics
- SALTIEV, S., Quantum Electronics
- SLAVOV, B., Quantum and Nuclear Physics
- ZAHARIEV, Z., Theoretical Physics
- ZHELYASKOV, I., Plasma Physics

Faculty of Primary and Pre-School Education:
- BALTADZHIEVA, A., Special Education
- BIZHKOV, G., Primary Education
- DOBREV, Z., Special Education
- KOLEV, J., Primary Education
- PETROV, P., Primary Education
- RADEVA, B., Anatomy
- TSVETKOV, D., Primary Education
- ZDRAVKOVA, S., Primary Education

Faculty of Slavonic Philology:
- BIOLCHEV, B., Slavonic Literature
- BOEVA, L., Russian Literature
- BOYADZHIEV, T., Bulgarian Language
- BOYADZHIEV, Z., Linguistics
- BRESINSKI, S., Bulgarian Language
- BUNDZHALOVA, B., Russian Language
- BUYUKLIEV, I., Slavonic Linguistics
- CHERVENKOVA, I., Russian Language
- CHOLAKOV, Z., Bulgarian Literature
- DIMCHEV, K., Teaching Methods of Bulgarian Language and Literature
- DOBREV, I., Studies on Cyril and Methodius
- GEORGIEV, N., Theory of Literature
- HADZHIKOSEV, S., Theory of Literature
- MINCHEVA, A., Studies on Cyril and Methodius
- NITSOLOVA, R., Bulgarian Language
- PASHOV, P., Bulgarian Language
- PAVLOV, I., Slavonic Literature
- PAVLOVA, R., Russian Language
- POPIVANOV, L., Theory of Literature
- POPOVA, V., Bulgarian Language
- RADEVA, V., Bulgarian Language
- TROEV, P., Russian Literature
- VASILEV, M., Bulgarian Literature
- VIDENOV, M., Bulgarian Language
- YANEV, S., Bulgarian Literature
- YOTOV, T., Russian Language

Faculty of Theology:
- DENEV, I., Practical Theology
- HUBANCHEV, A., Christian Philosophy
- KIROV, T., Moral Theology
- KOEV, T., Dogmatics
- MADZHUROV, N., Christian Philosophy
- POPTODOROV, R., Canon Law
- SHIVAROV, N., Old Testament Studies
- SLAVOV, S., Old Testament Studies
- STOYANOV, H., Church History

ATTACHED RESEARCH CENTRES

Centre for Ancient Languages and Civilizations: Dir (vacant).

Ivan Duichev Centre for Slavic and Byzantine Studies: Dir Prof. A. DZHUROVA.

TEHNIČESKI UNIVERSITET GABROVO
(Technical University of Gabrovo)

4 Hadzhi Dimităr, 5300 Gabrovo
Telephone: (66) 80-11-44
Fax: (66) 80-11-55
E-mail: rector@tugab.bg
Internet: www.tugab.bg

Founded 1964 as Higher Mechanical and Electrical Engineering Institute of Gabrovo; adopted present name 1990
Academic year: September to June

Rector: Assoc. Prof. Dr ILIYA NEMIGENCHEV
Vice-Rectors: Assoc. Prof. Dr KIRIL KIROV, Assoc. Prof. Dr DESHKA MARKOVA, Assoc. Prof. Dr DIMITAR PETROV
Registrar: NIKOLAY MIRAZCHIEV

Number of teachers: 493
Number of students: 7,219

Publication: *Journal* (2 a year)

DEANS

Faculty of Economics: Assoc. Prof. Dr ANYUTA NIKOLOVA
Faculty of Electrical Engineering and Electronics: Assoc. Prof. Dr TOSHKO NENOV
Faculty of Mechanical and Precision Engineering: Assoc. Prof. Dr HRISTO HRISTOV

AFFILIATED COLLEGE

Technical College of Lovech: 31 Sofiyska, Lovech; Dir Assoc. Prof. Dr VASIL KOCHEVSKI.

TEHNIČESKI UNIVERSITET SOFIA
(Technical University of Sofia)

1000 Sofia, Kliment Ohridski Boulevard 8
Telephone: (2) 965-321-11
Fax: (2) 68-32-15
E-mail: office-tu@tu-sofia.acad.bg
Internet: www.tu-sofia.acad.bg

Founded 1945
Academic year: September to July

Rector: Prof. VENELIN ZHIVKOV
Pro-Rectors: Assoc. Prof. M. HRISTOV, Assoc. Prof. R. IVANOV, Prof. M. LEPAROV, Prof. D. STOYANOV
Sec.-Gen.: V. DIMITROV
Librarian: SL. SKOPTSOVA

Library of 163,384 vols
Number of teachers: 1,309
Number of students: 14,190

Publication: *Nov Tehničeski Avangard* (monthly)

DEANS

Faculty of Applied Mathematics and Information Science: Assoc. Prof. M. MARINOV
Faculty of Automatics: Assoc. Prof. G. SAPUNDZHIEV
Faculty of Communications and Communication Technologies: Assoc. Prof. ARNAUDOV
Faculty of Computer Systems and Control: Assoc. Prof. H. OSKAR
Faculty of Electronics and Electronic Technologies: Assoc. Prof. S. TABAKOV
Faculty of Electrical Engineering: Assoc. Prof. K. ZAKHARINOV
Faculty of Engineering Education and Industrial Management (German Language): Prof. I. BOYADZHIEV
Faculty of Machine Technology: Assoc. Prof. A. DIKOV
Faculty of Management: Prof. G. TSVETKOV
Faculty of Mechanical Engineering: Assoc. Prof. T. NESHKOV
Faculty of Power Engineering and Power Machines: Assoc. Prof. A. KIRII
Faculty of Transport: Assoc. Prof. B. TRAIKOV
Open Faculty: Assoc. Prof. T. ATANASOV
English-Language Department of Engineering: Assoc. Prof. N. KOLEV
French-Language Department of Electrical Engineering: (vacant)

ATTACHED CENTRES

Centre for Continuing Education: Dir Assoc. Prof. E. SOKOLOV.

Department of Applied Physics: Dir Assoc. Prof. N. ANDREEV.

Department of Foreign Languages and Applied Linguistics: Dir ANTONIA VELKOVA.

Department of Physical Education and Sport: Dir Assoc. Prof. I. BOZOV.

TEHNIČESKI UNIVERSITET VARNA
(Technical University Varna)

9010 Varna, Studenska 1, POB 10
Telephone: (52) 30-24-44
Fax: (52) 30-27-71
E-mail: rectorat@ms3.tu-varna.acad.bg
Internet: www.tu-varna.acad.bg

Founded 1962 as Higher Institute of Electrical and Mechanical Engineering; adopted present name in 1990
Academic year: September to July

Rector: Assoc. Prof. Dr STEFAN BARUDOV
Pro-Rectors: Assoc. Prof. Dr HRISTO DRAGANCHEV, Assoc. Prof. Dr HRISTO HRISTOV, Assoc. Prof. Dr VASIL SMARKOV
Registrar: DIMITAR DIMITRAKIEV
Librarian: D. DIMITROVA

Library of 231,786 vols
Number of teachers: 450
Number of students: 6,500

Publications: *Acta Universitatis Pontica Euxinus* (2 a year), *Annual Proceedings*

DEANS

Faculty of Computer Science and Automation: Assoc. Prof. OVID FARHI
Faculty of Electrical Engineering: Assoc. Prof. KOLYO TASEV
Faculty of Electronics: Assoc. Prof. JORDAN KOLEV
Faculty of Law: Assoc. Prof. R. KURTEVA
Faculty of Marine Sciences and Ecology: Assoc. Prof. P. HAJIATANASOV
Faculty of Mechanical Engineering and Technology: Assoc. Prof. R. RADEV
Faculty of Shipbuilding: Assoc. Prof. I. IVANOV

PROFESSORS

- ALEXANDROV, Z., Theory of Machinery
- DIMITROV, D., Electrical Apparatus

GEORGIEV, V., Theoretical Electrical Engineering
GRADINAROV, P., Theoretical Mechanics
IVANOV, I., Law
JOSIFOV, R., Marine Engineering
KANDEVA, E., Law
KOLEV, P., Shipbuilding
KOTSEVA, E., Law
MILANOV, ZH., Law
MILKOV, V., Engineering Mechanics
MINCHEV, N., Engineering Mechanics
MUTAFCHIEV, S., Government
NEDEV, A., Heat Technology
PILEV, D., Transport Machinery and Technology
RUSEV, I., Biology
RUSEV, R, Materials Science
SERAFIMOV, M., Internal Combustion Engine
SHISHKOV, A., Law
SOTIROV, L., Computer Engineering
STAVREV, D., Physical Metallurgy and Metals Engineering
STOYANOV, V., Internal Combustion Engines
VLADIMIROV, R., Law
ZAHAROV, V., Law

TRAKIJSKI UNIVERSITET STARA ZAGORA
(Thracian University Stara Zagora)

6000 Stara Zagora, Students' Campus
Telephone: (42) 69-92-02
Fax: (42) 67-20-09
E-mail: info@uni-sz.bg
Internet: www.uni-sz.bg

Founded 1995, following merger of Higher Institute of Animal Sciences and Veterinary Medicine and Higher Institute of Medicine
State control
Languages of instruction: Bulgarian, English
Academic year: September to July

Rector: Assoc. Prof. Dr SVETLIN TANCHEV
Pro-Rectors: Assoc. Prof. Dr D. DINEV (Administration and Finance), Assoc. Prof. Dr V. GADJEVA (Research), Prof. Dr D. DINEV (Teaching)
General Secretary: Assoc. Prof. Dr A. PAVLOV
Librarian: J. DAKOVSKA

Library of 360,000 vols
Number of teachers: 646
Number of students: 4,000

Publications: *Bulgarian Journal of Veterinary Medicine* (4 a year), *Pro Otology* (4 a year), *Trakia Journal of Sciences* (Biomedical Sciences and Social Sciences series, 4 a year)

DEANS

Faculty of Agriculture: (vacant)Faculty of Medicine: Assoc. Prof. Dr JIVKO KARAKOLEV, Prof. IVAN STANKOV
Faculty of Pedagogy: Assoc. Prof. Dr HRISTO MAKAKOV
Faculty of Veterinary Medicine: Prof. Dr YORDAN NIKOLOV
Medical College, Haskovo: Dr D. KOSTOV (Dir)
Medical College, Sliven: K. HALACHEVA (Dir)
Medical College, Stara Zagora: Dr D. KOSTOV (Dir)
Technical College, Yambol: Assoc. Prof. G. GAYDADJIEV (Dir)
Bulgarian-German Farmers' College: Assoc. Prof. Dr M. PANAYOTOV (Dir)
Department of Information and In-service Teacher Training: Assoc. Prof. Dr G. KOZHUHAORVA

HEADS OF DEPARTMENTS

Faculty of Agriculture:

Agricultural Economics: Assoc. Prof. I. GEORGIEV
Agricultural Management: Prof. V. STANKOV
Agricultural Engineering and Farm Buildings: Assoc. Prof. N. DELCHEV
Animal Genetics and Breeding: Prof. G. NIKOLOV
Animal Hygiene: Assoc. Prof. D. DIMANOV
Animal Nutrition: Prof. N. TODOROV
Animal Physiology: Prof. A. PETKOV
Biochemistry: Prof. O. PETKOVA
Biology and Special Animals: Assoc. Prof. M. STOEVA
Cattle Husbandry: Prof. P. PETKOV
Foreign Languages: N. TANEVA
Horse Breeding: Assoc. Prof. A. BARZEV
Mathematics and Physics: Assoc. Prof. G. BOYCHEV
Morphology of Farm Animals: Assoc. Prof. ST. TENEV
Pig Production: Assoc. Prof. V. KATSAROV
Plant Science: Prof. D. PAVLOV
Poultry Production: Prof. G. KAYTAZOV
Reproduction: Assoc. Prof. IV. MANOLOV
Sheep Production: Prof. S. TYANKOV
Social Science: Assoc. Prof. ST. PASHOV
Special Branches: Assoc. Prof. P. NENCHEV

Faculty of Medicine:

Anaesthesiology and Reanimation: Assoc. Prof. Dr ZH. KARAKOLEV
Anatomy: Prof. Dr CHR. CHUCHKOV
Catastrophe Medicine: Assoc. Prof. Dr V. POPZAKHARIEVA
Chemistry and Biochemistry: Assoc. Prof. B. CHEMISHEV
Clinical Laboratory: Assoc. Prof. Dr V. LAZAROVA
Dermatology and Venereology: Assoc. Prof. P. GARDEV
General Medicine: Assoc. Prof. Dr V. POPZAHARIEVA
Forensic Medicine: Assoc. Prof. Dr M. GROZEVA
General and Operational Surgery: Prof. Dr A. ATANASOV
Hygiene and Professional Diseases: Assoc. Prof. Dr R. DELIRADEVA
Internal Diseases: Prof. Dr ST. MANTOV
Microbiology and Epidemiology: Assoc. Prof. Dr P. SOTIROVA
Molecular Biology and Immunology: Assoc. Prof. ZH. ZHELEV
Neurology: Assoc. Prof. I. MANCHEV
Centre for Neurosurgery: Assoc. Prof. P. VALKANOV
Obstetrics and Gynaecology: Assoc. Prof. Dr L. LAZAROV
Ophthalmology: Assoc. Prof. Dr E. FILIPOV
Orthopaedics and Traumatology: Assoc. Prof. Dr G. PROICHEV
Oto-rhino-laryngology: Assoc. Prof. Dr P. DIMOV
Paediatrics: Assoc. Prof. Dr P. CHAKUROVA
Pathological Anatomy: Prof. Dr GR. VELEV
Pathophysiology: Assoc. Prof. DEMIREVA
Pharmacology: Assoc. Prof. Dr V. SPASSOV
Physics: Assoc. Prof. I. TANEV
Physiology: (vacant)
Physiotherapy, Rehabilitation and Remedial Gym: Assoc. Prof. M. BELCHEV
Propadeutics of Internal Diseases: Prof. Y. VULKOV
Roentgenology and Radiology: Assoc. Prof. Dr VLAHOV
Social Medicine: (vacant)
Special Surgery: Assoc. Prof. Dr A. ANDREEV
Surgery Diseases: Prof. Dr G. DIMITROV
University Hospital: Dr ZH. KARAKOLEV (Dir)
Urology: Assoc. Prof. AT. UZUNOV

Faculty of Veterinary Medicine:

Anatomy of Domestic Animals: Assoc. Prof. S. GADZHEV
Biochemistry: Prof. CH. POPOV
Cytology, Histology and Embryology: Assoc. Prof. S. VITANOV
Epizootology and Infectious Diseases: Assoc. Prof. P. IVANOV
Foreign Languages: N. TANEVA
General and Organic Chemistry: Assoc. Prof. S. CHERVENKOV
Genetics and Private Breeding: Prof. Iv. YOTOVA
Hygiene and Control of Foodstuffs: Prof. L. GEORGIEV
Internal Medicine: Prof. CHR. GEORGIEV
Obstetrics and Gynaecology: Prof. S. TSOLOV
Organization of the Veterinary Service: Prof. I. BOZHKOV
Parasitology: Prof. D. GEORGIEVA
Pathological Anatomy: Prof. A. ANGELOV
Pathological Physiology: (vacant)
Physical Education and Sports: T. GURGURIEV
Pharmacology and Toxicology: Prof. D. PASHOV
Radiobiology and Radioecology: Assoc. Prof. P. GEORGIEV
Surgery: Prof. ZH. FILIPOV
Veterinary Microbiology, Virology and Immunology: Assoc. Prof. K. KOLEV
Veterinary Physiology with Endocrinology: Assoc. Prof. Y. ILIEV
Zoohygiene and Animal Nutrition: Prof. N. NETSOV

UNIVERSITET PO ARHITEKTURA, STROITELSTVO I GEODEZIA
(University of Architecture, Civil Engineering and Geodesy)

1046 Sofia, H. Smirnenski 1
Telephone: (2) 963-52-45
Fax: (2) 963-17-96
E-mail: aceint@uacg.bg
Internet: www.uacg.bg

Founded 1942 (until 1990, Higher Institute of Architecture and Civil Engineering)
State control
Academic year: September to June

Rector: Assoc. Prof. Dr P. D. PENEV
Vice-Rector (Academic Affairs): Prof. Dr P. KALINKOV
Vice-Rector (International Relations and Postgraduate Qualification): Assoc. Prof. Dr I. TOTEV (acting)
Vice-Rector (Management and Development of Material and Technical Equipment): Assoc. Prof. Dr M. RILSKI
Vice-Rector (Research and Design Affairs): Assoc. Prof. Dr K. TOPUROV
Registrar: S. VASILEVA
Librarian: P. RAFAILOVA

Library of 450,000 vols
Number of teachers: 531 (372 full-time, 159 part-time)
Number of students: 3,300

Publication: *Annals* (annual)

DEANS

Faculty of Architecture: Assoc. Prof. Dr N. BONCHEV
Faculty of Geodesy: Assoc. Prof. Dr S. GOSPODINOV
Faculty of Hydrotechnology: Prof. R. ARSOV
Faculty of Structural Engineering: Assoc. Prof. Dr T. DAKOVSKI
Faculty of Transport Engineering: Assoc. Prof. Dr D. DENEV

PROFESSORS

Faculty of Architecture (tel. (2) 865-31-48; fax (2) 865-68-63; e-mail far@uacg.bg):

DIMITROV, S., Urban Planning
HARALAMPIEV, H., Drawing and Modelling
KRASTEV, T., History of Architecture
TROEVA, D., Urban Planning

Faculty of Geodesy (tel. (2) 866-22-01; fax (2) 866-22-01; e-mail fgs@uacg.bg):

VALEV, G., Geodesy

Faculty of Hydrotechnology (tel. (2) 865-66-48; fax (2) 865-68-63; e-mail fhe@uacg.bg):

ARSOV, R., Water Supply and Sewerage
DIMITROV, G., Water Supply and Sewerage
KALINKOV, P., Water Supply and Sewerage
MARADJIEVA, M., Hydraulics and Hydrology
MLADENOV, K., Theoretical Mechanics

Faculty of Structural Engineering (tel. (2) 865-66-74; fax (2) 865-66-74; e-mail dean_fce@uacg.bg):

BARAKOV, T., Reinforced Concrete Structures
BAYCHEV, I., Building Mechanics
DAKOV, D., Steel, Timber and Plastic Structures
DRAGANOV, N., Steel, Timber and Plastic Structures
GOSPODINOV, G., Building Mechanics
JANCHULEV, A., Organization and Economics of Construction
KIROV, N., Building Technology and Mechanization
NAZARSKI, D., Building Materials and Insulation
STAJKOV, P., Steel, Timber and Plastic Structures

Faculty of Transport Engineering (tel. (2) 865-50-79; fax (2) 865-68-63; e-mail fte@uacg.bg):

DOULEVSKI, E., Bridges, Tunnels, Harbours
GICHEV, T., Mathematics
KONSTANTINOV, M., Mathematics
TRIFONOV, I., Road Engineering

UNIVERSITET PO HRANITELNI TECHNOLOGII
(University of Food Technologies)

26 Maritza Blvd, 4000 Plovdiv
Telephone: (32) 64-30-05
Fax: (32) 64-41-02
E-mail: rector@hiffi-plovdiv.acad.bg
Internet: www.vihvp.bg

Founded 1953
State control
Academic year: September to July

BSc and MSc courses in Food Technology, Food Engineering, Biotechnologies, Tourism, Industrial Management, Ecology and Environmental Safety

Rector: Assoc. Prof. GEORGI VALTCHEV
Vice-Rectors: Assoc. Prof. VESELIN DZHAMBAZOV, Prof. ATANAS GEORGIEV, Assoc. Prof. GEORGI SOMOV
Registrar: VOLODYA KAMENOV
Head of Accounts: PENKA PETROVA
Librarian: IVANKA KUNEVA

Number of teachers: 197
Number of students: 3,117 (2,073 full-time, 1,044 part-time)

Publications: *Scientific Journals in Food Technology* (irregular), *Scientific Works of UFT* (annually)

DEANS

Economic Faculty: Assoc. Prof. JORDANKA ALEKSIEVA
Technical Faculty: Assoc. Prof. MILCHO ANGELOV
Technological Faculty: Assoc. Prof. KOSTADIN VASILEV

PROFESSORS

Economic Faculty:

KONAREV, A., Organization and Management
STAMOV, S., Catering and Tourism
ZLATEV, T., Ecology and Environmental Safety

Technical Faculty:

DICHEV, S., Refrigeration
GEORGIEV, A., Automatics, Information and Control Equipment
LAMBREV, A., Technical Equipment in the Food Industry

Technological Faculty:

KABSEV, J., Technology of Fish and Fish Products
MARINOV, M., Beverage Technology
MURGOV, I., Microbiology
OBRETENOV, T., Organic Chemistry
VASILEV, K., Technology of Meat and Fish

UNIVERSITET ZA NACIONALNO I SVETOVNO STOPANSTVO
(University of National and World Economics)

Studentski grad 'Hristo Botev', 1700 Sofia
Telephone: (2) 962-53-05
Fax: (2) 962-13-76
E-mail: bborisov@unwe.acad.bg
Internet: www.unwe.acad.bg

Founded 1920
Academic year: October to July

Rector: Prof. B. BORISOV
Pro-Rectors: Assoc. Prof. I. BLIZNAKOV, Assoc. Prof. P. ORESHARSKY, Assoc. Prof. S. STATTEV, Assoc. Prof. I. VLADIMIROVA
Librarian: S. TSENOVA

Library of 500,000 vols
Number of teachers: 531
Number of students: 19,556

Publications: *Alternativi* (monthly), *Trudove* (2 a year)

DEANS

Faculty of Economics: Assoc. Prof. M. MARKOV
Faculty of Economic Industries: Asst Prof. V. ZLATEV
Faculty of Economics and Infrastructure: Assoc. Prof. H. HRISTOV
Faculty of Finance and Accounting: G. VAZOV
Faculty of International Economics and Politics: Assoc. Prof. G. GENOV
Faculty of Law: Prof. G. BOIANOV
Faculty of Management and Informatics: Assoc. Prof. A. ANGELOV
Economics College: Prof. H. KARAKASHEV (Dir)
Institute for Postgraduate Studies: Assoc. Prof. B. NEDELCHEVA (Dir)

PROFESSORS

Faculty of Economic Industries:

GEORGIEV, I., Industrial Business
ILIEV, I., Industrial Business
KANCHEV, I., Agrarian Business
TODOROV, K., Industrial Business

Faculty of Economics:

BORISOV, B., Economics of Intellectual Property
KOLEV, B., Sociology
MIRKOVICH, K., Economics
NIKOV, A., Economic Psychology and Economic Pedagogy
YANKOV, G., Politology

Faculty of Economics of the Infrastructure:

IVANOV, T., Economics of National Defence and Security
KARAKASHEV, H., Public Administration
LULANSKY, P., Economics of the Social and Cultural Sphere
VASILEV, E., Economics of Transport

Faculty of Finance and Accounting:

MLADENOV, M., Finance
STEFANOVA, P., Finance

Faculty of International Economics and Politics:

BOEVA, B., International Economics
MARINOV, V., International Economics
MIHOV, N., French Language

Faculty of Law:

BALABANOVA, H., Law
BOIANOV, G., Law
KARANIKOLOV, L., Law
KORENZOV, L., Law
SUKAREVA, Z., Law
VASILEV, A., Law

Faculty of Management and Informatics:

BOGINOV, N., Mathematics
GEROV, A., Forecasting and Planning
MANOV, V., Forecasting and Planning
VLADIMIROVA, K., Marketing

VARNENSKI SVOBODEN UNIVERSITET
(Varna University of Economics)

9002 Varna, Bul. Kniaz Boris I 77
Telephone: 66-02-12
Fax: 23-56-80
E-mail: rector@mail.ue-varna.bg
Internet: www.ue-varna.bg

Founded 1920
State control
Academic year: September to June

Rector: Prof. B. ATANASOV
Pro-Rectors: Assoc. Prof. A. APOSTOLOV, Assoc. Prof. N. BAKOLOV, Assoc. Prof. S. RAKADZHIJSKA, Assoc. Prof. V. STANEV
Registrar: Dr S. IVANOV
Librarian: Mag. T. TSANEVA

Library of 268,000 vols
Number of teachers: 262
Number of students: 8,202

Publications: *Economic Research* (3 a year), *Godishnik*, *Izvestya*

DEANS

Faculty of Business Administration: Assoc. Prof. D. ANGELOV
Faculty of Computer Science: Assoc. Prof. A. KANCHEVA
Faculty of Finance and Accounting: Assoc. Prof. V. VLADIMIROV
Faculty of Management: Assoc. Prof. I. ILIEV

PROFESSORS

ATANASOV, B., Econometrics
DIMITROV, G., Economics of Building
DOCHEV, D., Mathematics
DONEV, K., Auditing
GENOV, G., Accountancy
ILIEV, P., Computer Sciences
KARAMFILOV, Z., Informatics
KOTSEV, T., Finance and Credit
KOVACHEV, Z., Economics
MIKHAILOV, P., Economics
MINCHEV, S., Organic Chemistry
SALOVA, N., Economics and Organization of Trade

VELIKO TĂRNOVSKI UNIVERSITET 'SV. KIRIL I METODII'
(Sts Cyril and Methodius University of Veliko Tărnovo)

5003 Veliko Tărnovo, 2 T. Tarnovski
Telephone: (62) 62-01-89
Fax: (62) 62-80-23
E-mail: mbox@uni-vt.bg
Internet: www.uni-vt.bg

Founded 1971 from 'Kiril i Metodii' Higher Pedagogical Institute
Academic year: October to June

Rector: Prof. Dr habil. IVAN HARALAMPIEV
Vice-Rectors: Assoc. Prof. Dr STOYAN BUROV, Assoc. Prof. Dr ATANAS DERMENDZHIEV,

Assoc. Prof. Dr HRISTO GLUSHKOV, Assoc. Prof. Dr MILKO PALANGURSKI
Administrative Officer: OLEG BOZANOV
Librarian: Assoc. Prof. SAVA VASILEV

Number of teachers: 853
Number of students: 9,971

Publications: *Archives of Historical and Geographical Research* (4 a year), *Epochi* (4 a year), *Pir* (annually), *Proglas* (4 a year), *Works of the University* (annually)

DEANS

Faculty of Arts: Prof. IVAN BOCHEV
Faculty of Economics: Assoc. Prof. BAYKO BAYKOV
Faculty of History and Law: Assoc. Prof. MINCHO MINCHEV
Faculty of Letters: Assoc. Prof. BAGRELIA BORISOVA
Pedagogical Faculty: Assoc. Prof. PLAMEN LEGKOSTUP
Faculty of Philosophy: Assoc. Prof. VIHREN BUZOV
Faculty of Theology: Prof. KAZIMIR POPKONSTANTINOV

AFFILIATED COLLEGES

Pedagogical College in Pleven: Dir Assoc. Prof. YORDAN MITEV.
Pedagogical College in Vratsa: Dir Assoc. Prof. YORDAN YOTOV.

YUGOZAPADEN UNIVERSITET 'NEOFIT RILSKI'
('Neofit Rilski' Southwest University)

2700 Blagoevgrad, 66 Ivan Mihailov Blvd
Telephone: (73) 88-55-01
Fax: (73) 88-55-16
E-mail: info@aix.swu.bg
Internet: www.swu.bg

Founded 1976
State control
Academic year: September to July

Rector: Assoc. Prof. Dr ILIYA GYUDZHENOV
Vice-Rector for Credential Activity, Publications and Information Infrastructure: Prof. Dr IVAN MIRCHEV
Vice-Rector for Research and Development, Practical Training and Professional Qualifications: Assoc. Prof. Dr DIMITAR DIMITROV
Vice-Rector for Teaching: Assoc. Prof. Dr ZDRAVKO GARGAROV
Vice-Rector for International Relations: Asst Prof. Dr DOBRINKA GEORGIEVA

Number of teachers: 1,000
Number of students: 10,000

DEANS

Faculty of Arts: Prof. Dr RUMEN POTEROV
Faculty of Economics: Assoc. Prof. Dr CHAVDAR NIKOLOV
Faculty of Law and History: Prof. Dr ALEXANDER VODENICHAROV
Faculty of Mathematics and Natural Sciences: Assoc. Prof. Dr BORISLAV YURUKOV
Faculty of Pedagogy: Assoc. Prof. Dr RUSSI RUSSEV
Faculty of Philology: Assoc. Prof. Dr ALEXANDER RANGELOV
Faculty of Philosophy: Assoc. Prof. Dr ALEXANDER RANGELOV
Technical College: Assoc. Prof. Eng. HRISTO PATEV (Dir)

Academies and Institutes

AKADEMIJA ZA MUZIKALNO I TANZOVO IZKUSTVO
(Academy of Music and Dance)

4025 Plovdiv, T. Samodumov 2
Telephone: (32) 22-83-11
Fax: (32) 63-16-68

Founded 1972
Academic year: September to July

Rector: Prof. A. SLAVCHEV
Pro-Rectors: Prof. Z. DELIRADEVA, Assoc. Prof. I. KOZHUHAROV
Secretary-General (Manager): A. ANTONOV
Librarian: V. PAVLOVA

Number of teachers: 105
Number of students: 972

Publication: *Collection of Articles* (annually).

DARJAVNA MUZIKALNA AKADEMIJA 'PROF. PANČO VLADIGEROV'
('Pančo Vladigerov' State Academy of Music)

1505 Sofia, E. Georgiev 94
Telephone: (2) 943-34-00
Fax: (2) 944-14-54
Internet: www.art.acad.bg/music/index-e.html

Founded 1904; became Conservatoire 1954 and Academy 1995
Academic year: September to June

Rector: Prof. G. KOSTOV
Pro-Rectors: Prof. P. GERDZHIKOV, Prof. YO. KRUSHEV, Assoc. Prof. D. OSHANOV, Prof. A. STANKOV
Registrar: A. ANASTASOV
Librarian: E. PETKOVA

Number of teachers: 220
Number of students: 995

Publication: *Godishnik*

DEANS

Faculty of Instrumentation: Prof. D. MOMCHILOV
Faculty of Musical Theory, Composition and Conducting: Prof. M. PEKOV
Faculty of Vocal Studies: Prof. P. GERDZHIKOV
Dean for Foreign Students: Prof. A. STANKOV

NACIONALNA AKADEMIJA ZA TEATRALNO I FILMOVO IZKUSTVO 'KRUSTYO SARAFOV'
(National Academy of Theatre and Film Arts 'K. Sarafov')

1000 Sofia, G. Rakovski 108A
Telephone: (2) 986-40-19
Fax: (2) 989-73-89
E-mail: natfiz@bitex.com
Internet: natfiz.bg

Founded 1948
Academic year: October to July

Rector: Prof. Dr STANISLAV SEMERDJIEV
Registrar: STOYAN EVTIMOV
Librarian: EMILIA BALDZHIYSKA

Number of teachers: 204
Number of students: 560

DEANS

Faculty of Screen Arts: Prof. LUBOMIR HALATCHEV
Faculty of Stage Arts: Prof. SNEZHINA TANKOVSKA

NACIONALNA HUDOJESTVENA AKADEMIJA
(National Academy of Art)

1000 Sofia, Shipka 1
Telephone: (2) 987-33-28
Fax: (2) 987-33-28
E-mail: art_academy@yahoo.com
Internet: www.nha-bg.org

Founded 1896; reorganized as an academy 1995
Academic year: October to May

Chancellor: Prof. BOJIDAR IONOV
Vice-Chancellor for Economic Matters: Prof. CHRISTO STAYKOV
Vice-Chancellor for Education: Prof. SVETOSLAV KOKALOV
Vice-Chancellor for International Relations: Prof. MITKO DINEV
Librarian: DARINKA DIUKMEDJIEVA

Number of teachers: 131
Number of students: 800

Publication: *The Art of Drawing* (annual)

DEANS

Faculty of Applied and Industrial Arts: Prof. LUCHEZAR LOZANOV
Faculty of Fine Arts: Prof. TOMA VARBANOV

PROFESSORS

Faculty of Applied and Industrial Arts:

ASSA, G.
BALEV, D.
BONCHEV, B.
BOYADZHIEVA, A.
DIMOV, I.
DINEV, M.
DJIDROV, K.
DONCHEV, A.
GRIGOROV, G.
HARALAMPIEVA, V.
KOLKALOV, S.
KOTSEV, M.
KOZAREV, B.
KOZOUHAROVA, Y.
LOZANOV, L.
NIKOLOV, B.
OVCHAROV, V.
PANOVA, S.
POPNEDELEV, V.
PRASHKOV, L.
RAYCHEV, R.
RAYCHINOVA, M.
RAYKOV, R.
SHOSHEV, O.
TSANEV, K.

Faculty of Fine Arts:

ANGELOVA, L.
BAKALOVA, E.
BOYADZHIEV, B.
CHELEBIEV, R.
CHUKLEV, P.
DAMIANOV, K.
DANIEL, A.
DIMOV, I.
DOMUSCHIEV, S.
GAZDOV, I.
GOCHEV, O.
GONDOV, B.
KOEVA, M.
KOLEV, V.
KOSTOVA, K.
MIRCHEV, I.
MINCHEVA, D.
OVCHAROV, D.
PAMUKCHIEV, S.
POPOV, C.
POPOV, E.
SOKEROV, .
STAYKOV, C.
STOYANOV, S.
STOYANOV, Z.
TASSEV, D.
TRENDAFILOV, D.
VARDZHIEV, T.
VURBANOV, T

NACIONALNA SPORTNA AKADEMIJA 'VASSIL LEVSKI'
('Vassil Levski' National Sports Academy)

1700 Sofia, Studentski grad
Telephone: (2) 962-11-82
Fax: (2) 962-90-07
E-mail: rector@nsa.bg
Internet: www.nsa.bg
Founded 1942
State control
Languages of instruction: Bulgarian, English
Languages of instruction: Russian, French
Academic year: September to June
Rector: Prof. Dr LACHEZAR DIMITROV
Vice-Rector for Education: Assoc. Prof. Dr LAZAR KAMENOV
Vice-Rector for Sciences: Prof. PETAR BONOV
Vice-Rector for Social and Economic Affairs, International and Public Relations: Assoc. Prof. Dr KIRIL ANDONOV
Library of 128,000 vols
Number of teachers: 450
Number of students: 2,000

DEANS
Faculty of Coach Training: Assoc. Prof. Dr VALENTINA GIGOVA
Faculty of Kinesitherapy: Assoc. Prof. Dr PENCHO GESHEV
Faculty of Teaching: Assoc. Prof. Dr DIMITAR MIHAJLOV

PROFESSORS
Faculty of Coach Training:
BROGLI, Y., Theory of Sports Training
DIMITROV, L., Football and Tennis
JELJAZKOV, T., Theory of Sports Training
KALAIKOV, Y., History and Management of Sport
SHIJKOV, A., Football and Tennis

Faculty of Kinesitherapy:
JANCHEVA, S., Kinesitherapy and Rehabilitation
JELEV, V., Kinesitherapy
PETKOV, I., Kinesitherapy
TOTEVA, M., Sports Medicine

Faculty of Teaching:
ANTONOV, N., Track and Field Athletics
BONOV, P., Track and Field Athletics
KAJKOV, D., Psychology, Pedagogics and Sociology

STOPANSKA AKADEMIJA 'D. A. TSENOV'
(Tsenov Academy of Economics)

5250 Svishtov, Em. Chakarov 2
Telephone: (631) 2-27-22
Fax: (631) 2-34-72
E-mail: uircomm@comm.uni-svishtov.bg
Internet: www.uni-svishtov.bg
Founded 1936 as D. A. Tsenov Higher School of Commerce; became Higher School of Economics and Social Studies in 1948; reorganized in 1952/53; became D. Tsenov Economic University in 1990; present name 1995
State control
Academic year: September to July
Rector: Assoc. Prof. N. PAVLOV
Vice-Rectors: Assoc. Prof. Dr G. GERGANOV, Assoc. Prof. Dr P. KANEV, Assoc. Prof. Dr L. KIREV, Assoc. Prof. Dr N. PAVLOV
Chief Administrative Officer: V. TANEV
Librarian: S. LALEV
Library of 211,000 vols
Number of teachers: 196
Number of students: 11,618
Publications: *Biznes—Upravlenie* (quarterly), *Economic World Library* (6 a year), *Narodnostopanski Arhiv* (quarterly)

DEANS
Faculty of Accounting: Assoc. Prof. Dr G. BATASHKI
Faculty of Finance: Assoc. Prof. Dr R. LILOVA
Faculty of Industry and Trade: Assoc. Prof. Dr V. PETROV
Faculty of Management and Marketing: Assoc. Prof. Dr S. TONKOVA
Open Faculty: Assoc. Prof. Dr N. GEORGIEV

PROFESSORS
CHONOV, N., Economics
DAMIANOV, D., Accounting
DIMITROV, M., Accounting
DRAGANOV, H., Insurance
KANEV, M., Economics
MOINOV, M., Informatics
PANAIOTOV, D., Strategic Planning
RADKOV, R., Finance
SLAVEV, S., Regional Economics

VISŠ MEDICINSKI INSTITUT PLOVDIV
(Higher Medical Institute Plovdiv)

4000 Plovdiv, V. Aprilov 15A
Telephone: (32) 44-38-39
Fax: (32) 60-25-34
E-mail: unimed@plov.omega.bg
Internet: www.hms-plovdiv.acad.bg
Founded 1945
Academic year: September to May (two terms)
Number of teachers: 636
Number of students: 2,870 (incl. 855 in Medical College)
Rector: Prof. AT. DZHURDZHEV
Publication: *Folia Medica* (4 a year)

DEANS
Faculty of Dentistry: Assoc. Prof. ST. VLADIMIROV
Faculty of Medicine: Assoc. Prof. G. PASCALEV

BURKINA FASO

The Higher Education System

Higher education in Burkina Faso dates from the establishment of a teacher-training institute in 1965 which, after several name changes, became known as the University of Ougadougou (UO) in 1972. In addition to the UO there is a polytechnic university at Bobo-Dioulasso; there are also several private institutions. The number of students enrolled at tertiary-level institutions in 2001/02 was 15,535. The two state-run universities are Government-funded, with additional financial resources provided by bilateral or multilateral agreements and the universities' own revenue streams. Higher education is the responsibility of the Ministry of Secondary and Higher Education and Scientific Research.

The UO and Université Polytechnoque de Bobo-Dioulasso have similar, five-tier administrative structures consisting of a Board of Directors, a University Assembly, a University Council, institutions and departments. The Board of Directors consists of representatives from the Government ministries, the institution's administrative staff, trades' unions representatives, academic staff and students. The University Assembly decides university policy and is summoned by the Rector at least twice year. Its members are drawn from the Directors, teaching, administrative and technical staff, students and representatives from Government ministries. The Rector (or Chancellor) runs the university with the aid of the Vice-Chancellors and a Secretary-General. Finally, institutions are administered by Directors, who report directly to the Rector.

Admission to higher education is based on the award of the Baccalauréat or Bachelier du second degré. Higher education awards are arranged in three cycles. The first cycle lasts two years and leads to award of the Diplôme d'Études Universitaires Générales (DEUG), Premier Cycle d'Études Médicales (PCEM), Diplôme Universitaire d'Études Littéraires (DUEL), Diplôme Universitaire d'Études Scientifiques (DUES) or Diplôme Universitaire de Technologie. The second cycle lasts one year after first cycle for the Licence degree, two years for the Maîtrise or three years for Diplôme d'Ingénieur. Finally, the third cycle comprises doctoral-level studies. The Diplôme d'Études Supérieures Spécialisées (DESS) or the Diplôme d'Études Approfondies (DEA) are awarded after one-year courses in subjects such as mathematics, biology, chemistry, law, economics and linguistics, and the Doctorat de Troisième Cycle or Doctorat de Spécialité are awarded following two further years of study after the DEA. In addition to higher education awards, the main vocational award is the Diplôme, which requires two years of study.

Research Institutes

GENERAL

Centre National de la Recherche Scientifique et Technologique: 03 BP 7047, Ouagadougou 03; tel. 50-32-46-48; fax 50-31-50-03; e-mail dg.cnrst@fasonet.bf; internet www.cnrst.bf; f. 1950, 1968 incorporated into Ministère de l'Education Nationale, 1978 into Ministère de l'Enseignement Supérieur et de la Recherche Scientifique; basic and applied research in humanities, social sciences, natural sciences, agriculture, energy, medicine; library of 20,000 vols; 102 researchers; Dir-Gen. BASILE L. GUISSOU; publs *Sciences et Technique* (2 a year), *CNRST-Information* (every 2 months), *Eurêka* (quarterly).

Institut de Recherche pour le Développement (IRD): BP 182, Ouagadougou 01; tel. 50-30-67-37; fax 50-31-03-85; e-mail direction@ouaga.ird.bf; internet www.ird.bf; f. 1968; hydrology, geography, agronomy, botany, medical entomology, economics, demography, anthropology, pedology, ethnology, geology, sociology; Dir JEAN-PIERRE GUENGANT; (see main entry under France).

AGRICULTURE, FISHERIES AND VETERINARY SCIENCE

Centre de Co-opération Internationale en Recherche Agronomique pour le Développement (CIRAD): Ave du Président Kennedy, BP 596, Ouagadougou 01; tel. 50-30-70-70; fax 50-30-76-17; e-mail jacques .pages@cirad.fr; f. 1963; natural resource management and environmental protection; improved crop and livestock production; agroeconomics; remote sensing and geographical information systems; agrifoods; 15 research staff; Regional Dir for continental West Africa JACQUES PAGÈS; publ. *Rapport scientifique* (annually).

Institut de l'Environnement et de Recherches Agricoles: BP 8645, Ouagadougou 04; tel. 50-34-71-12; fax 50-34-02-71; e-mail inera.direction@fasonet.bf; f. 1978; research in arable and livestock farming, forestry, agricultural machinery, natural resources, management and farming systems; library of 2,500 vols, 2,500 documents; Dir Prof. HAMIDOU BOLY; publ. *Science et Technique* (2 a year).

EDUCATION

Institut Pédagogique du Burkina: BP 7043, Ouagadougou; tel. 50-33-63-63; f. 1976 by the Ministry of National Education, for the development of methods and courses in primary education; library of 16,000 vols (Min. of Education Library); 150 staff; Dir Gen. JUSTINE TAPSOBA; publ. *Action, Réflexion et Culture* (8 a year).

TECHNOLOGY

Bureau de Recherches Géologiques et Minières (BRGM): BP 86, Ouagadougou; tel. 50-33-50-42; (see main entry under France.).

Libraries and Archives

Ouagadougou

Bibliothèque Nationale du Burkina: 03 LP 7007, Ouagadougou 03; tel. 50-32-63-63; internet www.culture.gov.bf/Site_Ministere/M.C.A.T/ministere/ministere_sr_bn.htm; f. 1988; under Min. of Culture, Arts and Tourism; Dir-Gen. ABEL NADIE.

Centre National des Archives: Présidence du Faso, BP 7030, Ouagadougou; tel. 50-33-61-96; fax 50-31-49-26; e-mail didier .ouedrago@presidence.gov.bf; f. 1970; Dir DIDIER E. OUEDRAOGO.

Museum

Ouagadougou

Musée National: 08 BP 11186, Ouagadougou; located at: Ave Oubritenga, Ouagadougou; tel. 50-30-73-89; fax 50-31-25-09; internet www.culture.gov.bf/Site_Ministere/textes/etablissements/etablissements_museenational.htm; f. 2003; 4,000 artefacts; Dir Prof. ALIMATA SAWADOGO.

Universities

UNIVERSITÉ POLYTECHNIQUE DE BOBO-DIOULASSO

01 BP 1091, Bobo-Dioulasso 01
Telephone: 20-98-06-35
Fax: 20-98-25-77
E-mail: akry@univ-ouaga.bf

Founded 1997
State control
Academic year: October to July

Rector: Prof. AKRY COULIBALY
Vice-Rector: Prof. GEORGES A. OUEDRAOGO
Director of External Relations: Dr PATRICE TOE

Number of teachers: 63
Number of students: 886

DIRECTORS

Ecole Supérieure d'Informatique: Pr. THÉODORE TABSOBA
Institut du Développement Rural: Dr JEAN-BAPTISTE OUÉDRAOGO
Institut des Sciences Exactes et Appliquées: Dr SADO TRAORE
Institut des Sciences de la Nature et de la Vie: Pr. CHANTAL Y. ZOUNGRANA
Institut Universitaire de Technologie: Dr BETABOALÉ NAHON

UNIVERSITÉ DE OUAGADOUGOU

03 BP 7021, Ouagadougou 03

Telephone: 50-30-70-64
Fax: 50-30-72-42
E-mail: info@univ-ouaga.bf
Internet: www.univ-ouaga.bf

Founded 1969, university status 1974
Academic year: October to June
State control
Language of instruction: French

President: JOSEPH PARE
Vice-Presidents: JEAN COULIDIATY, GUSTAVE KABRÉ, FRANÇOIS RENÉ TALL
Secretary-General: MAMIDOU KONE
Librarian: MAÏMOUNA SANOKO

Library of 70,000 vols
Number of teachers: 395
Number of students: 21,309

Publications: *Cahiers du Centre d'Etudes, de Documentation et de Recherches Economiques et Sociales* (quarterly), *Revue burkinabé de Droit* (2 a year), *Annales* (2 a year)

DEANS

Faculty of Economics and Management Sciences: DEMBO GADIAGA
Faculty of Health Sciences: MAMADOU SAWADOGO
Faculty of Law and Politics: G. AUGUSTIN LOADA
Faculty of Letters, Arts, Humanities and Social Sciences: ROSAIRE BAMA, JUSTIN KOUTABA
Faculty of Science and Technology: MARTIN LOMPO

Colleges

Centre d'Etudes Economiques et Sociales d'Afrique Occidentale (CESAO): BP 305, Bobo-Dioulasso; tel. 20-97-10-17; fax 20-97-08-02; e-mail cesao.bobo@fasonet.bf; f. 1960; areas of study include the enhancement of rural orgs on an institutional level, the promotion of women, faith and humanity, community health, administration of the development of rural communities, environment and land administration, savings and investments in rural areas, development projects; 16 staff; library: 14,000 vols and 77 periodicals; Dir ROSALIE OUOBA; publ. *Construire Ensemble* (every 2 months).

Ecole Inter-Etats d'Ingénieurs de l'Equipement Rural (EIER): BP 7023, Ouagadougou 03; tel. 50-30-20-53; fax 50-31-27-24; f. 1968 by governments of 14 francophone African states; 3-year postgraduate diploma course; hydraulics, civil engineering, refrigeration technology, sanitary engineering; Dir MICHEL GUINAUDEAU.

BURUNDI

The Higher Education System

The main institution of higher education is the Université de Burundi, founded in 1973 following a merger of several institutions, including the Université Officielle de Bujumbura. In 2002/03 11,915 students were enrolled at the Université de Burundi. The main language of instruction is French. The Minister of National Education and Culture is responsible for higher education, although the Université de Burundi enjoys a relative degree of autonomy. There is also a growing private higher education sector.

The Diplôme des Humanités Complètes is the standard secondary education qualification required for admission to higher education. Undergraduate education consists of three stages: the Candidature is a programme of general studies lasting two years; the Diplôme de Licence requires a further two years of study; and in medicine the professional title Docteur en Médecin is awarded after four years of study following the Candidature. The main postgraduate qualification is the Diplôme d'Études Approfondies.

Several institutes of the Université de Burundi also offer higher vocational education, usually courses of three to four years leading to the award of the Diplôme d'Ingénieur Technicien.

Research Institutes

AGRICULTURE, FISHERIES AND VETERINARY SCIENCE

Institut des Sciences Agronomiques du Burundi: BP 795, Bujumbura; tel. 22223390; fax 22225798; e-mail isabu@usan-bu.net; internet www.asareca.org/naris/isabu; f. 1962; agronomical research and farm management; library of 11,500 vols, 120 periodicals; Dir-Gen. Dr JEAN NDIKURANA.

MEDICINE

Laboratoire Médical: Bujumbura; devoted to clinical analyses, physio-pathological research and nutritional studies.

NATURAL SCIENCES

Physical Sciences

Centre National d'Hydrométéorologie: Bujumbura; Dir E. KAYENGAYENGE.

TECHNOLOGY

Direction Générale de la Géologie et des Mines: Ministère de l'Energie et des Mines, BP 745, Bujumbura; tel. 22222278; fax 22223538; Dir-Gen. Dr AUDACE NTUNGICIMPAYE.

Libraries and Archives

Bujumbura

Archives nationales du Burundi: Ministère de la Jeunesse, de la Culture et des Sports, BP 1095 Rohero II, Bujumbura; located at: ave Kunkiko, Bujumbura; tel. 22225051; fax 22226231; 26,000 vols; Dir NICODÈME NYANDWI.

Bibliothèque de l'Université: BP 1320, Bujumbura; tel. 22222857; f. 1961; 192,000 vols, 554 periodicals; Chief Librarian THARLISSE NSABIMANA.

Museums and Art Galleries

Bujumbura

Musée Vivant de Bujumbura: Ministère de la Jeunesse, de la Culture et des Sports, BP 1095 Rohero II, Bujumbura; located at: ave Kunkiko, Bujumbura; tel. 22226852; f. 1977; part of Centre de Civilisation Burundaise attached to Ministry of Youth, Sport and Culture; reflects the life of the Burundi people in all its aspects; incl. a reptile house, aquarium, aviary, traditional Rugo dwelling, open-air theatre, fishing museum, botanical garden, herpetology centre, musical pavilion, and crafts village; Dir EMMANUEL NIRAGIRA.

Gitega

Musée National de Gitega: 223 Magarama (Pl. de la Révolution), BP 110, Gitega; tel. 22242359; fax 22242357; f. 1955; history, archaeology, ethnography, arts, folk traditions, arms; library: library in process of formation (200 vols); Curator JACQUES MAPFARAKORA.

University

UNIVERSITÉ DU BURUNDI

BP 1550, Bujumbura
Telephone: 22223288
E-mail: rectorat@ub.edu.bi
Internet: www.ubi.edu.bi

Founded 1960, present name 1980
Academic year: October to September

Pres. of Administrative Council: P. NZINAHORA
Rector: Prof. DIDACE NIMPAGARITSE
Vice-Rector: Prof. GÉRARD RUSUKU
Academic Dir: Prof. DOMITIEN NIZIGIYIMANA
Administrative and Finance Dir: VÉNÉRAND NIZIGIYIMANA
Research Dir: Prof. EMILE EMERUSENGE
Librarian: VENANT BUSHUBIJE

Number of teachers: 239
Number of students: 2,749

Publications: *Actes de la Conférence des Universités des Etats Membres de la CEPGL* (annual), *Actes de la Semaine de l'Université* (annual), *Le Flambeau* (annual), *Le Héraut* (every 2 months), *Revue de l'Université* (quarterly)

DEANS

Faculty of Agriculture: PONTIEN NDABANEZE
Faculty of Applied Sciences: THÉOPHILE NDIKUMANA
Faculty of Economic and Administrative Sciences: DÉO NGENDAKUMANA
Faculty of Law: GERVAIS GATUNANGE
Faculty of Letters and Humanities: HENRI BOYI
Faculty of Medicine: EVARISTE NDABANEZE
Faculty of Psychology and Education: GABRIEL NTUNAGUZA
Faculty of Sciences: THÉODORE MUBAMBA

DIRECTORS

Higher Technical Institute: THÉOPHILE NDIKUMANA
Institute of Education: DOMITIEN NIZIGIYIMANA
Institute of Physical Education and Sports: THARCISSE NIYONZIMA

Colleges

Centre Social et Éducatif: Bujumbura; f. 1957; courses in crafts, photography, mechanics; 75 students.

Ecole Supérieure de Commerce du Burundi: BP 1440, Bujumbura; tel. 22224520; f. 1982; 304 students; library: 1,200 vols; Dir PIERRE NZEYIMANA.

Institut Supérieur d'Agriculture: BP 35, Gitega; tel. 22242335; f. 1983; under Min. of Nat. Education; courses in tropical agriculture, stockbreeding, agricultural engineering, food technology; 213 students; Dir (vacant); publ. *Revue des Techniques Agricoles Tropicales* (2 a year).

Institut Supérieur de Techniciens de l'Aménagement et de l'Urbanisme: BP 2720, Bujumbura; tel. 22223694; f. 1983; under the Min. of Public Works and Urban Development; 103 students; library: 863 vols; Dir SALVATOR NAHIMANA.

Lycée Technique: Bujumbura; f. 1949; training apprentices, craftsmen and professional workers; 4 workshops: mechanics, masonry, carpentry, electrical assembling; 450 students.

CAMBODIA

The Higher Education System

The oldest institution of higher education is the Royal University of Phnom-Penh, founded in 1960. The higher education system was greatly affected by the coup of 1975 and the Khmer Rouge regime (1975–79), but has enjoyed a renaissance in recent years with the restoration of pre-Khmer Rouge institutions and foundation of private establishments. Other public institutions of higher education now include universities of agriculture, fine arts and health sciences.

To gain admission to higher education students must possess the Diploma of Upper Secondary Education and pass the competitive national entrance examination. Higher education lasts for up to eight years, including undergraduate and postgraduate study. Until 1993 the most common undergraduate qualification was the Diploma of Higher Education, but since then several other equivalent degree titles have emerged.

Technical and vocational educational and training courses are one to three years in length, and the Department of Technical Vocational Education and Training (DTVET) has established criteria for certificate and Diploma-level studies.

Learned Societies

GENERAL

UNESCO Office Phnom-Penh: POB 29, Phnom-Penh; located at: House 38, Samdech Sothearos Blvd, Phnom-Penh; tel. (23) 426726; fax (23) 426163; e-mail phnompenh@unesco.org; internet www.un.org.kh/unesco; Dir ETIENNE CLEMENT.

AGRICULTURE, FISHERIES AND VETERINARY SCIENCE

Cambodian Society of Agriculture: C/o CIAP, POB 01, Phnom-Penh; located at: CIAP, 29 Km Highway 3, Phnom-Penh; internet www.bigpond.com.kh/users/CIAP/csa.htm; f. 1998; attached to Cambodia-IRRI-Australia Project; 144 mems; Pres. MAK SOLIENG; Sec. TOUCH SAVY; publs *Bulletin* (3 a year), *Cambodian Journal of Agriculture* (irregular).

HISTORY, GEOGRAPHY AND ARCHAEOLOGY

Authority for the Protection and Management of Angkor and the Region of Siem Reap (APSARA): 187 Pasteur St, Chaktomuk, Daun Penh, Phnom-Penh; tel. (23) 720315; fax (23) 990185 Angkor Preservation Compound, Siem Reap; tel. (63) 760080; fax (63) 760080; e-mail apsara-admin@camnet.com.kh; internet www.autoriteapsara.org; f. 1995; departments: Monuments and Archaeology, Research and Culture, Economic and Social Development, Urbanism and Urban Planning, Angkor Tourist Development; publ. *Udaya—Journal of Khmer Studies* (irregular).

Royal Angkor Foundation: POB 255, 1241 Budapest, Hungary; tel. (1) 322-4270; fax (1) 322-4270; e-mail angkor@hu.inter.net; internet www.angkor.iif.hu; f. 1992; safeguards the monuments and relics of the ancient Khmer civilization, establishing projects and gathering data; Hon. Co-Pres. HM NORODOM SIHANOUK (King of Cambodia), ÁRPÁD GÖNCZ (former Pres. of Hungary); Chair. of Supervisory Board GÁBOR BARTA.

NATURAL SCIENCES

Biological Sciences

Parks Society of Cambodia: POB 2680, Phnom-Penh; located at: 280B, Street 146, Group 32, Sangkat Toek Laaok II, Khan Toul Kork, Phnom-Penh; tel. (16) 813700; e-mail vibolparkssociety@hotmail.com; internet parkssociety-cambodia.netfirms.com; NGO responsible for community development, environmental education and the preservation of 10 wildlife reserves, 7 national parks, 3 protected landscapes and 3 multiple-use areas.

RELIGION, SOCIOLOGY AND ANTHROPOLOGY

Buddhist Association: c/o Buddhist Institute Library, POB 1047, Phnom-Penh.

Research Institutes

ECONOMICS, LAW AND POLITICS

Cambodia Development Resource Institute (CDRI): POB 622, Phnom-Penh; located at: 56 St 315, Tuol Kork, Phnom-Penh; tel. (23) 881701; fax (23) 880734; e-mail cdri@camnet.org.kh; internet www.cdri.org.kh; f. 1990; research in macroeconomic policy, rural livelihoods, governance and decentralization, natural resources and the environment, poverty analysis and monitoring; Centre for Peace and Development programme; library of 9,690 vols, 100 periodicals; Dir LARRY STRANGE; Co-ordinator of the Centre for Peace and Development ROMDUOL HUY; publs *Cambodia Annual Economic Review* (annually), *Cambodia Development Review* (4 a year), *Flash Report on the Cambodian Economy* (monthly).

Cambodian Institute for Co-operation and Peace: POB 1007, Phnom-Penh; located at: Room 1G, Government Palace, Sisowath Quay, Wat Phnom, Phnom-Penh; tel. (23) 722759; fax (23) 362520; e-mail cicp@camnet.com.kh; internet www.cicp.org.kh; f. 1994; affiliated with ASEAN Institutes of Strategic and International Studies; library of 4,000 vols in Khmer, English and French; Exec. Dir KAO KIM HOURN.

Cambodian Institute of Human Rights: POB 550, 30, St 57, Sangk at Boeung Keng Kong 1, Khan Chamcar Morn, Phnom-Penh; tel. (23) 210596; fax (23) 362739; e-mail cihr@camnet.com.kh; internet www.ned.org/grantees/cihr; f. 1993 by UN Transitional Authority in Cambodia; Dir KASSIE NEOU.

Center for Social Development: POB 1346, Phnom-Penh; located at: House 19, St 57, Sangkat Boeung Trabek, Keng Kang I Khan Chamkar Mon, Phnom-Penh; tel. and fax (23) 364735; e-mail csd@bigpond.com.kh; internet www.bigpond.com.kh/users/csd; f. 1995; aims to promote democratic values through research, training, advocacy and debate; Pres. CHEA VANNATH; publ. *Bulletin* (monthly).

MEDICINE

National Institute of Public Health: POB 1300, Phnom-Penh; tel. (23) 880345; fax (23) 880346; e-mail nphri@camnet.com.kh; internet www.camnet.com.kh/nphri; attached to Min. of Health; advises on govt policy and trains senior staff.

RELIGION, SOCIOLOGY AND ANTHROPOLOGY

World Buddhism Association for Development, Cambodia Regional Center: 11C, Rd 1986, Sangkat Phnom-Penh, Termei, Khan Kussey Keo, Phnom-Penh; tel. (23) 368506.

Libraries and Archives

Phnom-Penh

Documentation Center of Cambodia: POB 110, Phnom-Penh; located at: 70E, King Norodom Sihanouk Blvd, Phnom-Penh; tel. (23) 211875; fax (23) 210358; e-mail dccam@online.com.kh; internet www.dccam.org/; f. 1995, as field office of the Cambodian Genocide Program at Yale University, USA; became fully autonomous instn in 1997; information resource centre on the Khmer Rouge regime; Dir YOUK CHHANG.

National Archives of Cambodia: POB 1109, Phnom-Penh; tel. (23) 430582; e-mail archives.cambodia@camnet.com.kh; internet www.camnet.com.kh/archives.cambodia; records of Résidence Supérieure du Cambodge (French colonial administration), 1863–1954; post-colonial govt collns; records of Khmer Rouge regime and 1979 genocide tribunal; periodicals and newspapers in French, Khmer, Vietnamese and Chinese.

National Library of Cambodia: Street 92, Daun Penh District, Phnom-Penh; tel. and fax (23) 430609; e-mail contact@bnc-nlc.info; f. 1924; 103,635 vols; special collection of original palm-leaf manuscripts, 700 manuscript titles on microfilm; French Indo-China collection; Dir KHLOT VIBOLLA; publ. *Books-in-Print Cambodia*.

Museums and Art Galleries

Phnom-Penh

Museum of Genocide: Tuol Svay Prey Gymnasium, 103rd St, Phnom-Penh; f. 1979; fmr school converted into prison in

1975 after capture of Phnom-Penh by Khmer Rouge, and used as interrogation, torture and execution facility; following fall of the Khmer Rouge in 1979, converted into a museum depicting crimes of the regime.

National Museum of Arts: POB 2341, Phnom-Penh; located at: 13 Street, Phnom-Penh; tel. (23) 24369; f. 1920; main galleries dedicated to bronzes, sculpture, ethnography and ceramics; Dir KHUN SAMEN.

Universities

UNIVERSITY OF HEALTH SCIENCES

Monivong Blvd, Phnom-Penh
Telephone: (23) 430732
Fax: (23) 430129

Rector: KIM PO VOU.

ROYAL ACADEMY OF CAMBODIA

Campus 2, Federation of Russia Boulevard, Sangkat Tuk Laak 1, Khan Tuol Kok, Phnom Penh 12156
POB 2070, Phnom Penh
Telephone: (23) 890180
Fax: (23) 221408
E-mail: hacademy@camnet.com.kh
Internet: www.rac.edu.kh

Founded 1965; disbanded 1975 due to civil war; re-established 1997
Languages of instruction: Khmer, English
State control; attached to Office of the Council of Ministers
Academic year: October to June
Library of 10,000 vols

President: Dr SORN SAMNANG
Under-General Secretary (Administration and Finance): CHHUN SUM BUN
Under-General Secretary (Training and Research): CHEA NENG

Offers a range of master's and doctoral programmes; promotes research in all major academic areas and organises scientific forums..

SUB-INSTITUTES

Institute of Biology, Medicine and Agriculture: tel. (12) 835306; Dir Dr SAM SOPHEAN.

Institute of Culture and Fine Arts: tel. (12) 733336; Dir Dr CHHAY YIHEANG.

Institute of Humanities and Social Sciences: tel. (11) 919044; Dir Dr ROS CHANTRABOT.

Institute of National Language: tel. (12) 836040; Dir Dr LONG SEAM.

Institute of Science and Technology: tel. (11) 951849; Dir Dr CHAN PORN.

ROYAL UNIVERSITY OF AGRICULTURE

POB 2696, Chamkar Daung, Phnom-Penh
Telephone: (23) 219829
Fax: (23) 219690
E-mail: rua@forum.org.kh

Founded 1964, university status since 1999

Number of teachers: 217
Number of students: 1,097

Rector: NARETH CHAN
Vice-Rector: MUNY PHAT

DEANS

Agricultural Economics and Rural Development: BORA KATHY
Agricultural Technology and Management: BUNTHAN NGO
Agro-Industry: SOK KUNTHY
Agronomy: SOPHAL CHOUNG
Animal Science and Production: PITH LOAN CHUM
Fisheries: CHHOUK BORIN
Forestry: MONIN VON
Information Technology and Telecommunications: MAO NARA
Land Management and Administration: MAK VISAL

ROYAL UNIVERSITY OF FINE ARTS

Street No. 70, Phnom-Penh
Telephone: (23) 910703

Founded 1965, closed 1975, re-opened as School of Fine Arts 1980, original name and status restored 1993

Rector: KEOUN TUK
Vice-Rector and Dean of Choreographic Arts: CHHIENG PROEUNG

Faculties: archaeology, architecture and urban studies, plastic arts, music, choreographic arts.

ROYAL UNIVERSITY OF LAW AND ECONOMICS

Preah Monivong, Phnom-Penh 12305
Telephone: (23) 211565
Fax: (23) 214953
E-mail: fle@khmerson.com

Founded 1948 as National Institute of Law, Politics and Economics; incorporated into the University of Phnom Penh as Faculty of Law and Economics 1957; independent university status 2003
Language of instruction: Khmer
State control
Academic year: October to July
Number of teachers: 266 (84 full-time, 112 visiting Cambodian lecturers and 70 foreign visiting lecturers)
Number of students: 4,802

Rector: YUOK NGOY (acting)

Faculties of Economics and Management; Law; Public Administration; Graduate Schools of Law and Economics and Management.

ROYAL UNIVERSITY OF PHNOM-PENH

Confederation of Russia Blvd, Khan Tuol Kork, Phnom-Penh
Telephone: (12) 812017
Fax: (23) 880116
E-mail: pitch@camnet.com.kh
Internet: www.rupp.edu.kh

Founded 1960 as Khmer Royal University, re-named Phnom-Penh University 1970, closed 1975–1979, re-opened 1980, current name 1996
State control
Languages of instruction: Khmer, English, French
Academic year: September to June

Rector: Prof. PIT CHAMNAM
Vice-Rectors: Dr NETH BAROM, LAV CHHIV EAV
Librarian: SEN SENG

Library of 39,000 vols
Number of teachers: 225
Number of students: 6,500

DEANS

Faculty of Science: HANG CHANTHON
Faculty of Social Science and Humanities: MONH SARY
Institute of Foreign Languages: Dr MAO SOKAN

DIRECTORS

Faculty of Science (tel. (23) 884-320; fax (23) 880-116; e-mail caradvchthon@online.com.kh; internet www.rupp.edu.kh):
- Biology: CHENG MARKPHON
- Chemistry: LONG LAY
- Computer Science: OUK CHHIENG
- Mathematics: SUON SOVAN
- Physics: CHHUM NAVY

Faculty of Social Science and Humanities (tel. (12) 825-284; fax (23) 880-116; internet www.rupp.edu.kh):
- Geography: MENG MOEUN
- History: NGIN VUTH
- Khmer Literature: THEA SOKMENG
- Philosophy: CHHAY YI HEANG
- Psychology: SEK SISOKHOM
- Sociology: PHON SENG

Institute of Foreign Languages (tel. and fax (23) 884-154; e-mail ifl@everyday.com.kh; internet www.rupp.edu.kh):
- English: OM SORYONG
- French: MEAS VANNA

CAMEROON

The Higher Education System

As a result of Cameroon's mixed colonial heritage, there are separate education systems in the former British and French-administered regions. East Cameroon was a French colony from 1916 to 1960, when it became independent and was known as Republic of Cameroon. A merger with the smaller, British-run provinces of Southern Cameroon in the same year led to the creation of United Republic of Cameroon. The official name of the country, Republic of Cameroon, was adopted in 1984. British and French-inspired educational systems now operate in the respective former provinces, and English and French are now the respective official languages of instruction. The Université de Yaoundé I (formerly Federal University of Cameroon) was established in 1962 and operates on a decentralized principle, with five regional campuses, each devoted to a different field of study. Five new state universities were created by Presidential decree in 1993: Buea, Douala, Dschang, Ngaoundéré and Yaoundé II. The Ministry of Education is responsible for maintaining standards in both the public and private higher education sectors. In 2003 seven private institutions signed 'creation agreements' with the Ministry of Education, which initiate the process by which universities seek authorization for establishment.

Chancellors are government appointees and are the executive heads of universities. The Chancellor oversees the appointments of Deans of faculty, Heads of department and Directors of professional schools in consultation with the Vice-Chancellor. The Governing Council is presided over by the Vice-Chancellor, and includes the Deans, Directors, members of the academic staff and representatives from government and labour organizations.

Admission to university requires the Baccalauréat or two GCE Advanced level examinations and four GCE Ordinary level examinations. University education is broken up into three cycles, the first two at undergraduate level and the third at postgraduate level. The first cycle comprises two- or three-year diploma programmes (Diplômes), notably the Diplôme d'Etudes Universitaires Générales (DEUG, two years) and Diplôme d'Etudes Professionnelles Approfondies (three years). The second cycle programmes last for a further one or two years. Awards at this level include the Licence, Bachelors, Maîtrise and Diplôme. The Licence usually requires one year of study after the first cycle, and the Maîtrise two years. The third cycle consists of doctoral studies: two to four years of study after the Maîtrise for the Doctorat du Troisième Cycle; and five years for the award of Doctorat d'Etat.

Specialist institutions offer vocational education and technical training in several fields; the most common awards are diplomas.

Learned Societies

GENERAL

UNESCO Office Yaoundé: POB 12909, Yaoundé; located at: Immeuble Stamatiades, 2e étage, Yaoundé; tel. 222-57-63; fax 222-63-89; e-mail yaounde@unesco.org; f. 1991; designated Cluster Office for Cameroon, Chad and Central African Republic; 19 mems; Dir BERNARD HADJADJ.

LANGUAGE AND LITERATURE

Alliance Française: BP 441, Ngaoundéré; tel. and fax 225-18-26; e-mail alliance.ngaoundere@free.fr; internet alliance.ngaoundere.free.fr; offers courses and exams in French language and culture and promotes cultural exchange with France; attached teaching offices in Bamenda, Buea, Dschang, Garoua and L'Adamaoua; Dir JACQUES LE JOLLEC.

British Council: Immeuble Christo, Ave Charles de Gaulle, BP 818 Yaoundé; tel. 221-16-96; fax 221-56-91; e-mail bc-yaounde@britishcouncil.cm; internet www.britishcouncil.org/cameroon; teaching centre; offers courses and exams in English language and British culture and promotes cultural exchange with the UK; attached teaching centre in Douala; Dir JENNY SCOTT; Teaching Centre Man. TOM HINTON.

Goethe-Institut: Quartier Bastos, BP 1067, Yaoundé; tel. 221-44-09; fax 221-44-19; e-mail goethe.il@camnet.cm; internet www.goethe.de/af/yao/deindex.htm; offers courses and exams in German language and culture and promotes cultural exchange with Germany; library of 6,000 vols; Dir ANDREA JACOB.

Research Institutes

GENERAL

Instituts du Ministère de l'Enseignement Supérieur: BP 1457, Yaoundé; tel. 227-29-83; 5 university institutes and 5 research institutes; soil science, hydrology, nutrition, psycho-sociology, demography, economics, geography, archaeology, botany and vegetal biology, and medical entomology; Sec.-Gen. PIERRE OWONO ATEBA; publs *Annales* (quarterly, in 4 series: languages and literature, human sciences, law, economics), *Revue Science et Technique* (quarterly, in 3 series: agriculture, health sciences, human sciences).

Institut de Recherche pour le Développement (IRD): Représentation ORSTOM, BP 1857, Yaoundé; tel. 220-15-08; fax 220-18-54; e-mail orstyde@ird.uninet.cm; internet www.ird.fr; f. 1944; pedology, sedimentology, hydrology, ecology, medical entomology, cell biology, demography, linguistics, geography, anthropology, ornithology, sociology; Representative FRANÇOIS RIVIÈRE; (see main entry under France).

Institut des Sciences Humaines: Yaoundé; f. 1979; part of Min. of Higher Education; Dir W. NDONGKO.

AGRICULTURE, FISHERIES AND VETERINARY SCIENCE

Humid Forest Ecoregional Center: BP 2008, Nkolbisson, Yaoundé; tel. 223-26-44; f. 1980; forestry research; 170 staff (14 researchers); Dir A. M. MAINO; publ. *Rapport Annuel*.

Institut de la Recherche Agronomique: BP 2123, Yaoundé; tel. 223-26-44; f. 1979; part of Ministry of Higher Education; agriculture, agronomy, phytopathology, entomology, pedology, botany; 6 research centres, 16 stations; 314 staff; library of 2,600 vols, 2,500 brochures, 450 periodicals; Dir Dr J.-A. AYUK-TAKEM; publs *Mémoires et Travaux de l'IRA*, *Rapport Annuel*, *Science et Technique (Series Sciences agronomiques et zootechniques* (quarterly).

Institut de Recherches pour les Huiles et Oléagineux (IRHO): BP 243, Douala; f. 1949; Dir J. N. REGAUD; (See main entry under France).

Institut des Recherches Zootechniques et Vétérinaires (IRZV): BP 1457, Yaoundé; tel. 223-24-86; fax 223-24-86; f. 1974; part of Min. of Higher Education; research on livestock, fisheries and wildlife, and environment; library of 1,800 vols, 358 periodicals; Dir Dr JOHN TANLAKA BANSER; publ. *Science and Technology Review*.

ECONOMICS, LAW AND POLITICS

Institut de Formation et de Recherche Démographiques: BP 1556, Yaoundé; tel. 22-24-71; fax 22-67-93; f. 1972 with the co-operation of the UN; ECA Executing Agency; training and research on demographic phenomena and their links with economic and social factors; library of 17,000 vols; Dir AKOTO ELIWO; publ. *Annales* (3 a year).

Institut des Relations Internationales du Cameroun (IRIC): BP 1637, Yaoundé; tel. and fax 231-03-05; e-mail iric@uycdc.uninet.cm; f. 1971 by the Federal Government, the Carnegie Endowment for International Peace, the Swiss Division for Technical Co-operation and others; a bi-lingual, post-graduate institute for education, training and research in diplomacy and international studies, attached to the university of Yaoundé II; library of 65,000 vols; Dir Dr JEAN-EMMANUEL PONDI; Sec.-Gen. SAMUEL ENOH BESONG; publ. *Cameroon Review of International Studies* (annually).

EDUCATION

Centre National d'Education: Yaoundé; f. 1979; part of Min. of Higher Education; Dir E. BEBEY.

HISTORY, GEOGRAPHY AND ARCHAEOLOGY

Institut Géographique National: BP 157, Ave Mgr.-Vogt, Yaoundé; tel. 222-29-21; fax 223-39-54; f. 1945; survey office; Dirs J. L. LE FLOCH PATRICE NGUELA.

LANGUAGE AND LITERATURE

Centre Régional de Recherche et de Documentation sur les Traditions Orales et pour le Développement des Langues Africaines (CERDOTOLA): BP 479, Yaoundé; tel. 230-31-44; fax 230-31-89; e-mail cerdo@cenadi.cm; f. 1978; research on African languages, oral literature, traditional music; 20 mem. countries; library in process of formation; Exec. Sec. SOUNDJOCK-SOUNDJOCK.

MEDICINE

Institut de Recherches Médicales et d'Etudes des Plantes Médicinales: Yaoundé; tel. 223-13-61; f. 1979; 250 staff; library of 1,000 vols, 50 periodicals; Dir A. ABONDO; publs *Cahiers*, *Science et Technique* (series *Sciences Médicales*).

NATURAL SCIENCES

Physical Sciences

Direction de la Météorologie Nationale: 33 rue Ivy, BP 186, Douala; tel. and fax 342-16-35; f. 1934; Dir EMMANUEL EKOKO ETOUMANN; publs *Annales climatologiques* (irregular), *Bulletin agrométéorologique décadaire*, *RCM: Résumé climatologique mensuel*, *Résumé mensuel du Temps* (both monthly).

TECHNOLOGY

Compagnie Française pour le Développement des Fibres Textiles (CFDT): BP 1699, Douala; brs at Garoua, Maroua, Mora, Touboro and Kaele; textile research.

Institut de Recherches Géologiques et Minières: POB 4110, Yaoundé; tel. and fax 221-03-16; f. 1979; Dir GEORGES E. EKODECK.

Libraries and Archives

Bamenda

British Council Library and Information Centre: Bamenda Urban Council Library, Commercial Ave, POB 622; tel. 336-20-11; fax 336-20-22; e-mail britishcouncil@bamenda.org; jtly run with Bamenda Urban Council; 10,000 vols; Information Officer CATHERINE TAKU.

Yaoundé

Archives Nationales: BP 1053, Yaoundé; tel. 223-00-78; fax 223-20-10; f. 1952; conserves and classifies all documents relating to the Republic; 15,000 vols; Dir AMADOU POKEKO.

Bibliothèque Nationale du Cameroun: Ministère de la Culture, Yaoundé; tel. and fax 223-70-02; 64,000 vols; Dir NGOTOBO NGOTOBO.

Museums and Art Galleries

Bamenda

International Museum and Library—Akum: POB 389, Bamenda, Northwest Province; f. 1948; local and foreign artefacts of interest to researchers and students of sociology, anthropology and archaeology; brasswork, paintings, beaded work, clay figures, animal skins, masks, postage stamps, iron work, sculpture, stools, traditional costumes, films and books; Curator PETER S. ATANGA.

Kumbo-Nso

Musa Heritage Gallery (Mus'Art): POB 21, Kumbo, Northwest Prov.; located at: Bamfem Quarter, street above STS, Kumbo, Northwest Prov.; tel. 506-99-84; e-mail musartgallery@yahoo.com; internet www.musartgallery.info.ms; f. 1996; named after Cameroonian artists Daniel and John Musa; arts and crafts of the Western Grassfields region of Cameroon; 400 artefacts; Dir MANGONG PETER MUSA.

Universities

UNIVERSITÉ DE BUÉA

POB 63, Buea
Telephone: 332-21-34
Fax: 343-25-08

Founded 1977 (opened 1986) as Buea University Centre; present name and status 1992
State control
Languages of instruction: English, French, Spanish
Academic year: September to June

Chancellor: Dr PETER AGBOR TABI
Pro-Chancellor: Prof. VICTOR ANOMAH NGU
Vice-Chancellor: Dr DOROTHY L. NJEUMA
Deputy Vice-Chancellor (Control): Prof. SAMMY BEBAN CHUMBOW
Deputy Vice-Chancellor (Research and Co-operation): Prof. SAMSON ABANGMA
Deputy Vice-Chancellor (Teaching): Prof. VINCENT P. K. TITANJI
Registrar: Dr HERBERT NGANJO ENDELEY
Librarian: ROSEMARY SHAFACK

Library of 35,000 vols
Number of teachers: 93 full-time
Number of teachers: 115 part-time
Number of students: 3,300

Publications: *Epasa Moto* (annually), *Newsletter* (quarterly)

DEANS

Faculty of Arts: Prof. EMMANUEL GWAN ACHU
Faculty of Education: Dr GRACE EWENE
Faculty of Health Sciences: Dr THEODOSA MCMOLI
Faculty of Science: Dr NZUMBE MESAPE NTOKO
Faculty of Social and Management Sciences: Prof. CORNELIUS LAMBI

HEADS OF DEPARTMENTS

Chemistry: Assoc. Prof. SAMUEL FANSO-FREE
Cultural and Sporting Activities: GRACE EWENE
Economics and Management Sciences: Dr ALEXANDER A. ASONG
Education: Prof. LYDIA E. LUMA
English Language and Literature: ADOLF LIMA
French: Prof. ALBERT AZEYEH
Geography: Assoc. Prof. CORNELIUS LAMBI
Geology and Environmental Science: Dr SAMUEL N. AYONGHE
History: Assoc. Prof. VICTOR J. NGOH
Journalism and Mass Communication: Dr ENO TANJONG
Law: JONIE B. FONYAM
Life Sciences: Dr THERESA N. AKENJI
Linguistics: Dr VINCENT TANDA
Mathematics and Computer Science: Assoc. Prof. FRANCIS MBUNTUM
Performing Arts: Dr ASHERI KILO
Physics: Assoc. Prof. NZUMBE-MESAPE NTOKO
Political Science and Administration: Dr BEN N. JUA
Sociology and Anthropology: Dr FRANCIS NYAMNJOH
Women and Gender Studies: Dr JOYCE ENDELEY

CONSTITUENT INSTITUTE

Advanced School of Translators and Interpreters (ASTI): Dir Dr ETIENNE ZÉ AMVELA.

UNIVERSITÉ CATHOLIQUE DE L'AFRIQUE CENTRALE

BP 11628, Yaoundé
Telephone: 223-74-00
Fax: 223-74-02
E-mail: ucac.icy-nk@camnet.cm
Internet: www.cm.refer.org/edu/ram3/univers/ucac/ucac.htm

Founded 1989
Private Control (Catholic Church)
Languages of instruction: French, English
Academic year: October to July

Rector: Abbé OSCAR EONE EONE
Vice-Rector: Abbé OLIVIER MASSAMBA LOUBELO
Secretary-General: JOSEPH KONO OWONA
Director of Development and Co-operation: GILLES NOUDJAG
Head Librarian: Dr PATRICK ADESO (acting)

Library of 39,341 vols
Number of teachers: 90 and 240 assoc. lecturers
Number of students: 1,692

Publication: *Cahiers de l'U.C.A.C.* (annually)

DEANS

Faculty of Philosophy: Prof. Dr GABRIEL NDINGA
Faculty of Social Sciences and Management: Prof. Dr JACQUES FDRY
Faculty of Theology: Père Dr ANTOINE BABÉ

DIRECTORS

Dept of Canon Law: Prof. Dr SILVIA RECCHI
Higher Institute of Technology: ANNAUD DESJONQUÈRES
School of Nursing: Soeur RENÉE GEOFFRAY
2nd Cycle in Douala: Ing. HUGUES WINDAL

UNIVERSITÉ DE DOUALA

BP 2701, Douala
Telephone: 340-64-15
Fax: 340-11-34
E-mail: ud@camnet.com

Founded 1977
State control
Languages of instruction: French, English
Academic year: October to July

Rector: Prof. MAURICE TCHUENTE
Deputy Rector: Prof. ROGER GABRIEL NLEP
Secretary-General: THÉRÈSE WANGUE
Librarian: JEREMIE NSANGOU

Number of teachers: 140
Number of students: 6,500

Publications: *Arts Review* (annually), *Revue de Sciences Economiques et de Management* (quarterly), *Technologie et Développement* (every 2 years).

CONSTITUENT INSTITUTES

Ecole Normale Supérieure de l'Enseignement Technique: BP 1872, Douala; Dir Dr NDEH NTOMAMBANG NINGO.

Ecole Supérieure des Sciences Economiques et Commerciales: BP 1931, Douala; Dir Dr ROBERT BILONGO.

Faculté des Lettres et des Sciences Humaines: BP 3132, Douala; Dean Prof. SYLVESTRE BOUELET IVAHA.

Faculté des Sciences: BP 24157, Douala; Dean Prof. THÉOPHILE NGANDO MPONDO.

Faculté des Sciences Economiques et de Gestion Appliquée: BP 4032, Douala; Dean Prof. BLAISE MUKOKO.

Faculté des Sciences Juridiques et Politiques: BP 4982, Douala; Dean Dr LEKENE DONFACK.

Institut Universitaire de Technologie: BP 8698, Douala; Dir Dr AWONO ONANA.

UNIVERSITÉ DE DSCHANG

POB 96, Dschang

Telephone: 345-10-92
Fax: 340-11-34

Founded 1993
State control
Languages of instruction: French, English
Academic year: October to July

Rector: Prof. RÉMY S. BOUELET
Vice-Rectors: Prof. MBIAPO FÉLICITÉ TCHOUANGUEP (Inspection), Prof. JOHNSON FOYERE AYAFOR (Research and Co-operation), Prof. FRANÇOIS KAMAJOU (Teaching)
Secretary-General: Prof. ANDRÉ MVESSO
Librarian: MICHELINE TCHOUAMO

Number of teachers: 235
Number of students: 8,288

Publications: *Les Echos* (law and politics, 4 a year), *NKA* (arts and humanities, 2 a year), *Sciences et Développement* (agriculture, 2 a year)

DEANS

Faculty of Agronomy and Agricultural Sciences: Dr MBIDA MPOAME
Faculty of Economics and Management Sciences: Prof. SAMUEL NGOGANG
Faculty of Law and Political Science: Prof. FRANÇOIS ANOUKAHA
Faculty of Letters and Social Sciences: Prof. GABRIEL KUITCHE FONKOU
Faculty of Sciences: Prof. MPAOME MBIDA
Fotso Victor Institute of Technology: MÉDARD FOGUE

HEADS OF DEPARTMENTS

African Studies: Dr ENGELBERT DOMCHE TOKO
Agricultural Economics: Dr M. P. AYISSI
Animal Production: Prof. JOSEPH DJOUKAM
Biochemistry: Dr BIKAY V. BIKAY
Botany and Plant Biology: Dr JONAS Y. PINTA
Chemistry: PIERRE TANE
Economic Analysis: MBOG T. NGWEM
Forestry: Dr HERÉ DUCHAFOUR
Geography and History: Prof. MARTIN KUETE
Geology: Dr D. NONO
Law, Common: Dr A. S. EWANG
Law, Private: Dr I. L. MIENDJIEM
Law, Public and Political Sciences: Dr C. KEUTCHA TCHAPNGA
Management Sciences: Dr ARMAND G. NOULA
Mathematics and Computer Sciences: Dr NDOMBOL BITJONG
Philosophy and Social Sciences: Assoc. Prof. ROBERT C. DIMI
Physics: Dr PIERRE K. TALA
Plant Production: Dr PAUL MBOUEMBOUE
Plant Protection: Dr RICHARD GHOGOMU
Rural Education and Sociology: ANDRÉ KAMGA
Soil Sciences: Dr M. OMOKO
Zoology: Dr PAUL TAN

ATTACHED INSTITUTE

Centre Specialisé pour l'Agriculture (CRESA): Co-ordinator JACQUES ROUY.

UNIVERSITÉ DE NGAOUNDÉRÉ

BP 454, Ngaoundéré

Telephone: 222-57-41
Fax: 333-06-43
E-mail: rectorat_ngaoundere@yahoo.fr

Founded 1977, opened 1982; present name since 1993
State control
Languages of instruction: French, English
Academic year: October to July

Rector: Prof. PAUL-HENRI AVZAM ZOLLO
Vice-Rector (Control and Internal Evaluation): Prof. MEGNAMISI BELOMBE
Vice-Rector (Research and Co-operation) and Director of Academic Affairs: Prof. JOSEPH G. KAYEM
Vice-Rector (Teaching): Prof. BOUBA OUMAROU
Secretary-General: Dr ADAMA HAMADOU

Library of 60,000 vols
Number of teachers: 300
Number of students: 9,000

Publications: *Annales de la Faculté des Arts, Lettres et Sciences Humaines* (annually), *Ngaounderé-Apropos* (social science review, annually)

DEANS

School of Agro-Industrial Sciences: Prof. CARL M. F. MBOFUNG (Dir)
Faculty of Arts and Humanities: Dr IYA MOUSSA
Faculty of Economics and Management Science: Prof. VICTOR TSAPI
Faculty of Law and Political Science: Prof. VICTOR BOKALLI
Faculty of Science: Prof. ISMAIL NGOUNOUNO
Institute of Technology: Dr ALI AHMED

PROFESSORS

Faculty of Economics and Management Science:

TSAPI, V.

Faculty of Law and Political Science:

BOKALLI, V. E.

Faculty of Science:

AMVAM ZOLLO, P.-H.
BELOMBE MEGNAMISSI, M.
NGOUNOUNO, I.
OUMAROU, B.

School of Agro-Industrial Science:

DZUDIE, T.
KAMGA, R.
KAPSEU, C.
KAYEM, J.
MBOFUNG, C. M. F.
NGASSOUM, M. B.
TCHIEGANG, C.

UNIVERSITÉ DE YAOUNDÉ I

BP 337, Centre Province, Yaoundé

Telephone: 222-07-44
Fax: 223-53-88
E-mail: cdc@uycdc.uninet.cm

Founded 1962
State control
Languages of instruction: English, French
Academic year: October to July

Rector: JEAN TABI-MANGA
Vice-Rector (Inspection): MAURICE AURÉLIEN SOSSO
Vice-Rector (Research and Co-operation) (vacant)
Vice-Rector (Teaching): MAURICE AURÉLIEN SOSSO
Secretary-General: ELIE-CLAUDE NDJITOYAP NDAM
Librarian: ALEXIS EYANGO MOUEN

Library of 90,000 vols
Number of teachers: 929
Number of students: 20,343

Publications: *Annales de la Faculté des Lettres*, *Annales de la Faculté des Sciences*, *Sosongo* (Cameroon review of the arts, annually), *Syllabus* (review of the Ecole Normale Supérieure)

DEANS

Faculty of Arts: Prof. EMMANUEL GWAN ACHU
Faculty of Medicine and Biomedical Science: Prof. AMOUGOU AKOA
Faculty of Sciences: Prof. MAURICE A. SOSSO

DIRECTORS

Ecole Normale Supérieure: MATHIEU FRANÇOIS MINYONO NKODO
Ecole Nationale Supérieure Polytechnique: AYINA OHANDJA

HEADS OF DEPARTMENTS

Faculty of Arts (POB 755, Yaoundé):

- African Languages and Linguistics: JEAN MARIE ESSONO
- Art and Archaeology: JOSEPH MARIE ESSOMBA
- English: EDWARD O. AKO
- Foreign Languages, Literature and Civilization: SIMO
- French: ANDRÉ MARIE NTSOBE NDJOH
- Geography: EMMANUEL NGWA NEBASINA
- German: SIMO
- History: DANIEL ABWA
- Negro-African Literature: NOL ALEMBONG
- Philosophy: GUILLAUME BWELE
- Psychology: RAYMOND MDEBE
- Sociology: JEAN MFOULOU
- Spanish: ONOMO ABENA SOSTHÈNE

Faculty of Medicine (POB 8290, Yaoundé; tel. 223-12-26; fax 223-18-41):

- Anatomy and Pathology: Prof. AGRÉGÉ ESSAME OYONO SAMUEL
- Biomedical Sciences: MICHEL ASONGANYI TAZOACHA
- Clinical Sciences: PAUL KOUEKE
- Gynaecology and Obstetrics: ROBERT LEKE
- Internal Medicine: MUNA WALLY
- Medical Imagery and Radiotherapy: JOSEPH GONSU FOTSING
- Ophthalmology: ORL
- Paediatrics: JOSEPH MBEDE
- Public Health: JEAN MELI
- Physiology: JEANNE NGOGANG
- Stomatology: GENEVIÈVE BENGONO
- Surgery: EIMO MALONGA

Faculty of Science (POB 812, Yaoundé; tel. 223-56-60):

- Animal Biology and Physiology: NJIFUTIE NJIKAM
- Biochemistry: FRANÇOIS XAVIER ETOA
- Computer Science: EMMANUEL KAMGNIA
- Earth Sciences: PAUL BILONG
- Inorganic Chemistry: DANIEL NJOPWOUO
- Mathematics: DAVID BEKOLLE
- Organic Chemistry: LUC SONDENGAM
- Physics: PIERRE OWONO ATEBA
- Plant Biology and Physiology: AMOUGOU AKOA

Ecole Normale Supérieure (POB 47, Yaoundé; tel. 222-49-34; fax 222-09-13):

- Biology: DENIS OMOKOLO NDOUMOU
- Chemistry: HÉLÈNE TAMBOUE
- Education: THÉRÈSE TCHOMBE
- English: BABILA MUTIA
- French: MATHIEU FRANÇOIS MINYONO NKODO

History and Geography: SAMSON ANGO MENGUE
Languages: MODE DONATIEN
Mathematics: NICHOLAS GABRIEL ANDJIGA
Philosophy: NKOLO FOÉ
Physics: JEAN MARIE MBOUNGA

Ecole National Supérieure Polytechnique (POB 8290, Yaoundé; tel. 223-12-26; fax 223-18-41):
Civil Engineering and Town Planning: TAMO TATIETSE THOMAS
Computer Engineering: ERIC BADOUEL
Electrical Engineering: EMMANUEL TONYE
Mathematics: JEAN NGAHNOU
Physics and Chemistry: NGOHE EKAM

UNIVERSITÉ DE YAOUNDÉ II

POB 18, Soa
Telephone: 221-34-03
Fax: 799-14-23
E-mail: jmanga@uycdc.uninet.cm

Founded 1993
State Control
Academic year: October to July

Rector: Prof. JEAN TABI MANGA
Vice-Rector (Academic Affairs): Prof. PAUL GÉRARD POUGOUÉ
Vice-Rector (Control): Prof. ADOLPHE MINKOA SHE
Vice-Rector (Research and Cooperation): Prof. JEAN ONGLA
Secretary-General: Prof. ADOLPHE MINKOA SHE (acting)

Number of teachers: 271
Number of students: 13,768

Publications: *African Review of Political Strategy* (annually), *Cameroon Review of International Relations* (2 a year), *Fréquence Sud* (2 a year), *Les Cahiers de l'IFORD* (monthly), *Revue Africaine des Sciences Economiques et de Gestion* (2 a year), *Revue Africaine des Sciences Juridiques* (2 a year)

DEANS

Faculty of Economics and Management: Prof. SÉRAPHIN MAGLOIRE FOUDA
Faculty of Law and Political Science: Prof. MAURICE KAMTO

DIRECTORS

Advanced School of Mass Communication: Prof. MARC JOSEPH OMGBA
Institute for Demographic Training and Research: Dr AKOTO ELIWO MANDJALE
International Relations Institute of Cameroon: Prof. JEAN EMMANUEL PONDI

HEADS OF DEPARTMENTS

African Communication: Prof. JACQUES FAME-NDONGO
Banking and Monetary Economics: Prof. BRUNO BEKOLO-EBE
Business Law: Prof. JOSETTE NGUEBOU
Common Law: Prof. EPHRAIM NGWAFOR
Comparative Law, Legal Theory and Science: Assoc. Prof. S. ADOLPHE MINKOA
Diplomacy and Professional Education: Assoc. Prof. LAURENT ZANG
Documentation: Dr MOUEN A. EYANGO
Economic Policy Analysis: Prof. MAMA TOUNA
Fundamental Private Law: Assoc. Prof. ALEXANDRE D. TJOUEN
General Studies and Communication Science: Assoc. Prof. ASSALE L. BOYOMO
Human Resource Economics: Assoc. Prof. EDOKAT E. O. TAFAH
International Economics and Development: Prof. GERMAIN NDJIEUNDE
International Politics: Assoc. Prof. JEAN-EMMANUEL PONDI
International Public Law: Assoc. Prof. MAURICE KAMTO
Management: Dr JEAN M. BEGNE
Political Science: Prof. MICHAEL T. ALETUM
Print Journalism: Dr BAKOUME NDEMBIYEMBE
Public Economics: Assoc. Prof. BATHÉLEMY BIAO
Public Law: Assoc. Prof. WOUM BIPOUM
Public Relations and Advertising: Dr BOLIVINE F. WAKATA
Publishing and Graphic Arts: Dr MARC JOSEPH OMGBA
Quantitative Techniques: Dr BERNADETTE KAMGNIA-DIA
Radio Broadcasting: Assoc. Prof. MENTAN E. TATAH
Television: Dr ALBERT MBIDA

PROFESSORS

Faculty of Economics and Management:
BEKOLO, E. B.
GANKOU, J. M.
NDJIEUNDE, G.
TOUNA, M.

Faculty of Law and Political Science:
ALETUM, M. T.
ANOUKAHA, F.
KONTCHOU, K. A.
MINKOA, S. A.
NGWAFOR, E. N.
NTAMARK, P. Y.
OWONA, J.
POUGOUE, P. G.

Advanced School of Mass Communication:
BOYOMO, A. L. C.
CHINJI, K. F.
FAME, N.

International Relations Institute of Cameroon:
OYONO, D.

ATTACHED INSTITUTES

Centre for Study and Research in Economics and Management: tel. 223-73-89; fax 223-79-12; Co-ordinator Assoc. Prof. SÉRAPHIN FOUDA.

Centre for Study and Research in International Community Law: tel. 221-42-34; fax 231-35-09; Co-ordinator Assoc. Prof. MAURICE KAMTO.

Colleges

Ecole Nationale d'Administration et de Magistrature: BP 7171, Yaoundé; tel. 223-13-08; f. 1959; training for public administration; library: 11,000 vols; 85 teachers (10 full-time, 75 part-time); 1,063 students; Dir. V. MOUTTAPA.

Institut d'Administration des Entreprises: BP 337, Yaoundé; 150 students; Dir G. NDJIEUNDE.

CANADA

The Higher Education System

Under legislation passed in 1982 the 10 provinces and three territories enjoy autonomy over higher education; however the Council of Ministers of Education Canada was created by the provincial and territorial ministers of education to take collective decisions in the national interest. The Association of Universities and Colleges of Canada (AUCC) is the national organization of university executive heads. In 2003/04 an estimated 990,385 students were enrolled in post-secondary education. The official languages of Canada are French and English, but English is the language of instruction in most universities except in the province of Quebec, where French is used.

The standard administrative structure for a university consists of two governing bodies, a Board of Governors or Regents and a Senate or Academic Council. In addition, a Vice-Chancellor, President, Principal or Rector is responsible for administrative and academic management. Higher education funding varies according to the province or territory in question. The only consistent admissions criteria for university include possession of the secondary school equivalent or, in Quebec, the Collège d'enseignement général et professionnel (CEGEP); otherwise, universities are free to set their own criteria.

Though there may be provincial or territorial peculiarities, the university degree system conforms to the Bachelors/Masters/Doctorate schema. The Bachelors (Baccalaureat in Quebecois) is a three- to four-year programme the format of which varies from institution to institution, with some following the US-style credits system. Some Bachelors programmes include an element of research and are known as Honours. Following Bachelors are Masters (Maîtrise) programmes of two years, which fall into two classifications: Taught and Research. Finally, the qualification Doctor of Philosophy (PhD, or Philosophiae Doctor) requires three- to five-years' study following the Masters.

Post-secondary technical and vocational education is provided by community and professional colleges; the most common qualifications are the Certificate and Diploma, the latter requiring two- to three-years' study.

There is no central system of accreditation for post-secondary institutions in Canada, only for certain programs within these institutions. However, procedures and regulations are in place in each province and territory that provide ongoing assessment of the overall quality equivalent to 'accreditation' as it is commonly understood. The Canadian Education and Training Accreditation Commission (CETAC) provides a voluntary system of non-governmental self-regulation of Canada's private post-secondary institutions.

Regulatory and Representative Bodies

GOVERNMENT

Council of Ministers of Education, Canada/Conseil des Ministres de l'Éducation (Canada) (CMEC): Suite 1106, 95 St Clair Ave W, Toronto, ON M4V 1N6; tel. (416) 962-8100; fax (416) 962-2800; e-mail info@cmec.ca; internet www.cmec.ca; f. 1967; intergovernmental body of which all 13 provinces and territories are mems; forum to discuss policy issues; mechanism through which to undertake activities, projects and initiatives in areas of mutual interest; means by which to consult and co-operate with nat. education orgs and the federal govt; instrument to represent the education interests of the provinces and territories internationally; provides leadership in education at the pan-Canadian and int. levels and contributes to the fulfilment of the constitutional responsibility for education conferred on provinces and territories; governed by an Agreed Memorandum approved by all mems; current funding c. C $7.5m. per year of which provinces and territories provide c. C $5.7m. through base amount, calculated according to the population of each province and territory, and additional amounts for specific projects and initiatives; Chair. JOAN BURKE.

National Research Council Canada: Bldg M58, 1200 Montréal Rd, Ottawa, ON K1A 0R6; tel. (613) 993-9101; fax (613) 952-9907; e-mail info@nrc-cnrc.gc.ca; internet www.nrc.ca; f. 1916; carries out research and devt in life sciences, physical sciences, engineering, information technology, technology and industry support; Pres. Dr PIERRE COLOUMBE; Sec.-Gen. MARIELLE PICHÉ.

ACCREDITATION

Canadian Education and Training Accreditation Commission (CETAC): Suite 101, 267 Adelaide St W, Toronto, ON M5H 1Y3; tel. (416) 875-8629; fax (416) 977-5612; e-mail info@accreditations.ca; internet www.accreditations.ca; f. 1984; responsible for institutional accreditation of private post-secondary institutions in Canada; provides nat. accrediting service with established nat. standards; Nat. Commissioners ROSEMARY BOYD, F. RICK KLEIMAN, CAROL LOWTHERS, MONIKA OEPKES, MICHAEL BARRETT, BILL RICHES, CHRISTOPHER HOPE, FRANK T. MIOSI, NELLIE BURKE.

NATIONAL BODIES

Association of Canadian Community Colleges/Association des collèges communautaires du Canada (ACCC): Suite 200, 1223 Michael St N, Ottawa, ON K1J 7T2; tel. (613) 746-2222; fax (613) 746-6721; e-mail info@accc.ca; internet www.accc.ca; f. 1972; nat. voluntary membership org. to represent colleges and institutes to govt, business and industry, both in Canada and world-wide; interacts with fed. depts and agencies on the mems' behalf; links college capabilities to nat. industries; organizes conferences and workshops for college staff, students and Board members to facilitate networking and participation in nat. and int. activities such as sector studies, awards programmes and linkages; Pres. GERALD (GERRY) BROWN.

Association of Universities and Colleges of Canada: 350 Albert St (Suite 600), Ottawa, ON K1R 1B1; tel. (613) 563-1236; fax (613) 563-9745; e-mail info@aucc.ca; internet www.aucc.ca; f. 1911; represents Canadian public and private, not-for-profit univs and univ.-degree level colleges; 90 univ. mems; Pres. CLAIRE MORRIS; Chair. BONNIE PATTERSON.

Canadian Association for Distance Education/Association canadienne de l'éducation à distance: Suite 204, 260 Dalhousie St, Ottawa, ON K1N 7E4; tel. (613) 241-0018; fax (613) 241-0019; e-mail cade-aced@csse.ca; internet www.cade-aced.ca; f. 1983; holds annual conference; 600 .mems; Dir of Admin. TIM G. HOWARD; publ. *Journal of Distance Education* (2 a year).

Canadian Bureau for International Education/Bureau Canadien de l'Education Internationale: 220 Laurier Ave W, Suite 1550, Ottawa, ON K1P 5Z9; tel. (613) 237-4820; fax (613) 237-1073; e-mail info@cbie.ca; internet www.cbie.ca; f. 1966 to promote international development and inter-cultural understanding through a broad range of educational activities in Canada and abroad; 3 divisions: Research, Development and Membership, Scholarships and Awards, Centre for Central and Eastern Europe; library of 300 vols and journals; 120 institutional mems; Chair. Dr BERNARD SHAPIRO; Chair.-designate Dr ROB TURNER; Treasurer M. DENIS COSSETTE; publs *Canadian Internationalist* (4 a year), *Annual Report*, *International Students' Handbook*, *National Report on International Students in Canada* (every 2 years).

Learned Societies

GENERAL

Académie des lettres du Québec: CP 8888, Succursale Centre-ville, Montréal, QC H3C 3P8; tel. (514) 987-3000; fax (514) 987-8484; e-mail secretariat@academiedeslettresduquebec.ca; internet academiedeslettresduquebec.ca; f. 1944 (fmrly Académie canadienne-française) for the promotion of the French language and culture in Canada; 42 chairs; 38 mems; Pres. JACQUES ALLARD; publ. *Les Ecrits* (3 a year).

Canadian Council for International Co-operation/Conseil Canadien pour la Coopération Internationale: 1 Nicholas St, Suite 300, Ottawa, ON K1N 7B7; tel. (613) 247-7007; fax (613) 241-5302; internet www.ccic.ca; f. 1968 (fmrly Overseas Institute of Canada, f. 1961); co-ordination centre for voluntary agencies working in international development; 115 mems; Chair. JEAN-PIERRE MASSÉ; publs *Directory of Canadian NGOs*, *Newsletter* (6 a year).

Royal Canadian Academy of Arts: 401 Richmond St West (Suite 375), Toronto, ON M5V 3A8; tel. (416) 408-2718; fax (416) 408-2286; e-mail rcaarts@interlog.com; internet www.rca-arc.ca; f. 1880; visual arts; Pres. ALISON HYMAS.

Royal Canadian Institute: 700 University Ave., H7-D, Toronto, ON M5G 1X6; tel. (416) 977-2983; fax (416) 962-7314; internet www.royalcanadianinstitute.org; f. 1849, aims to increase public understanding of science; 800 mems; Pres. M. JANE PHILLIPS; Sec. PIPPA WYSONG; Treasurer HAROLD H. HARVEY.

Royal Society of Canada: 283 Sparks St, Ottawa, ON K1R 7X9; tel. (613) 991-6990; fax (613) 991-6996; e-mail adminrsc@rsc.ca; internet www.rsc.ca; f. 1882; 1,600 mems; academies: Academy I (Lettres et Sciences Humaines), Academy II (Humanities and Social Sciences), Academy III (Science); Pres. GILLES PAQUET; Hon. Sec. BERNARD BONIN; publs *Transactions* (annually), *Proceedings* (annually), *Présentations* (annually).

AGRICULTURE, FISHERIES AND VETERINARY SCIENCE

Agricultural Institute of Canada: Suite 900, 280 Albert St, Ottawa, ON K1P 5G8; tel. (613) 232-9459; fax (613) 594-5190; internet www.aic.ca; f. 1920 to organize and unite all workers in scientific and technical agriculture and to serve as a medium where progressive ideas for improvements in agricultural education, investigation, publicity and extension work can be discussed and recommended for adoption; represents 6,500 scientists and agrologists; publs *Canadian Journal of Plant Science*, *Canadian Journal of Soil Science*, *Canadian Journal of Animal Science* (all quarterly).

Canadian Forestry Association: 185 Somerset St West, Suite 203, Ottawa, ON K2P 0J2; tel. (613) 232-1815; fax (613) 232-4210; e-mail cfa@canadianforestry.com; internet www.canadianforestry.com; f. 1900; conservation org. providing educational materials and programmes to raise awareness of the wise use of forest, wildlife and water resources; 354 mems; Pres. BARRY WAITO; General Manager DAVE LEMKAY.

Canadian Society of Animal Science: Suite 900, 280 Albert St, Ottawa, ON K1P 5G8; tel. (613) 232-9459; fax (613) 594-5190; internet www.csas.net; part of the Agricultural Institute of Canada (*q.v.*); f. 1925 to provide opportunities for discussion of problems, improvement and co-ordination of research, extension and teaching and to encourage publication of scientific and educational material relating to animal and poultry industries; holds annual meetings, produces occasional papers and presents awards to members; 550 mems; Pres. DUANE MCCARTNEY; Sec.-Treas. CHRISTIANE GIRARD; publs *Canadian Journal of Animal Science* (quarterly), *CSAS Newsletter* (quarterly, mems only).

Canadian Veterinary Medical Association/Association Canadienne des Médecins Vétérinaires: 339 Booth St, Ottawa, ON K1R 7K1; tel. (613) 236-1162; fax (613) 236-9681; e-mail kallen@cvma-acmv.org; internet www.cvma-acmv.org; f. 1948; 4,000 mems; publs *Canadian Journal of Veterinary Research* (quarterly), *Canadian Veterinary Journal* (monthly).

ARCHITECTURE AND TOWN PLANNING

Canadian Society of Landscape Architects/Association des Architectes Paysagistes du Canada: POB 13594, Ottawa, ON K2K 1X6; tel. (613) 622-5520; fax (613) 622-5870; e-mail info@csla.ca; internet www.csla.ca; f. 1934; 1,100 mems, a federation of seven component asscns; Exec. Dir FRAN PAUZÉ; publs *Landscapes/Paysages* (4 a year), *Bulletin* (6 a year).

Royal Architectural Institute of Canada: 55 Murray St, Suite 330, Ottawa, ON K1N 5M3; tel. (613) 241-3600; fax (613) 241-5750; e-mail info@raic.org; internet www.raic.org; f. 1908; 3,500 mems; Pres. CHRIS FILLINGHAM; Exec. Dir JON F. HOBBS; publs *Update/En Bref* (quarterly), *Bulletin* (online, monthly).

BIBLIOGRAPHY, LIBRARY SCIENCE AND MUSEOLOGY

ASTED (Association pour l'avancement des sciences et des techniques de la documentation) Inc. (Association for the advancement of documentation sciences and techniques): 3414 ave du Parc, Bureau 202, Montréal, QC H2X 2H5; tel. (514) 281-5012; fax (514) 281-8219; e-mail info@asted.org; internet www.asted.org; f. 1973; a professional organization of libraries, librarians and library technicians; 500 mems; Pres. PIERRE TESSIER; Exec. Dir LOUIS CABRAL; publs *Documentation et bibliothèques* (quarterly), *Nouvelles de l'ASTED*.

Bibliographical Society of Canada: POB 575, Postal Station P, Toronto, ON M5S 2T1; e-mail mcgaughe@yorku.ca; internet www.library.utoronto.ca/bsc; f. 1946; 300 mems; Pres. DAVID MCKNIGHT; Sec. ANNE MCGAUGHEY; publs *Bulletin* (2 a year), *Papers/Cahiers* (2 a year).

Canadian Association of Law Libraries: POB 1570, Kingston, ON K7L 5C8; tel. (613) 531-9338; fax (613) 531-0626; e-mail office@callacbd.ca; internet www.callacbd.ca; f. 1961 to promote law librarianship, to develop and increase the usefulness of Canadian law libraries, and to foster a spirit of co-operation among them, to provide a forum for meetings and to co-operate with other similar orgs; 500 mems; Pres. JANINE MILLER; Administrative Officer ELIZABETH HOOPER; publs *CALL Newsletter* (5 a year), *Canadian Law Library* (5 a year).

Canadian Library Association: 328 Frank St, Ottawa, ON K2P 0X8; tel. (613) 232-9625; fax (613) 563-9895; e-mail info@cla.ca; internet www.cla.ca; f. 1946; 3,000 mems; Pres. STEPHEN ABRAM; Exec. Dir DON BUTCHER.

Canadian Museums Association/Association des Musées Canadiens: 280 Metcalfe, Suite 400, Ottawa, ON K2P 1R7; tel. (613) 567-0099; fax (613) 233-5438; e-mail info@museums.ca; internet www.museums.ca; f. 1947; advancement of public museums and art galleries services in Canada; 2,000 mems; Exec. Dir JOHN G. MCAVITY; publ. *Muse* (every 2 months).

ECONOMICS, LAW AND POLITICS

Canadian Bar Association: 500–865 Carling Ave, Ottawa, ON K1S 5S8; tel. (613) 237-1988; fax (613) 237-0185; e-mail info@cba.org; internet www.cba.org; f. 1914 to promote the administration of justice and uniformity of legislation throughout Canada, and to promote a high standard of legal education, training and ethics; 38,000 mems; Pres. SUSAN T. MCGRATH; Exec. Dir. JOHN HOYLES; Treasurer JACK INNES; publs *The National*, *The Canadian Bar Review*.

Canadian Economics Association: c/o Frances Woolley, Dept of Economics, Carleton Univ., 1125 Colonel By Dr., Ottawa, ON K1S 5B6; e-mail frances_woolley@carleton.ca; internet www.economics.ca; f. 1967; non-partisan asscn promoting the advancement of economic knowledge through the encouragement of study and research, the issuing of publs and the furtherance of free and informed discussion of economic questions; 1,400 mems; Pres. GERARD GAUDET; Sec.-Treas. FRANCES WOOLLEY; publs *Canadian Journal of Economics/Revue Canadienne d'Economique*, *Canadian Public Policy/Analyse de Politique*.

Canadian Institute of Chartered Accountants: 277 Wellington St W, Toronto, ON M5V 3H2; tel. (416) 977-3222; fax (416) 977-8585; internet www.cica.ca; f. 1902; professional and examining body; 70,000 mems; Chair. ALAIN BENEDETT; Pres. and CEO KEVIN J. DANCEY; publ. *CA Magazine* (monthly).

Canadian Institute of International Affairs: Suite 302, 205 Richmond St W, Toronto, ON M5V 1V3; tel. (416) 977-9000; fax (416) 977-7521; e-mail mailbox@ciia.org; internet www.ciia.org; f. 1928; 1,400 mems in 15 brs; library of 8,000 vols; Chair. The Hon. ROY MACLAREN; Pres. and CEO DOUGLAS GOOLD; publs *Behind the Headlines*, *International Journal* (4 a year), *Annual Report*, *Canadian Foreign Relations Index* (CD-ROM, annually; online, monthly).

Canadian Political Science Association/Association Canadienne de Science Politique: 260 Dalhousie St, Suite 204, Ottawa, ON K1N 7E4; tel. (613) 562-1202; fax (613) 241-0019; e-mail cpsa@csse.ca; internet www.cpsa-acsp.ca; f. 1913; organizes an annual conference; awards prizes; runs the Parliamentary Internship Programme and Ontario Legislative Internship Programme; 1,250 mems; Administrator MICHELLE HOPKINS; publ. *Canadian Journal of Political Science* (quarterly).

EDUCATION

Canadian Education Association/Association Canadienne d'Education: 317 Adelaide St W, Suite 300, Toronto, ON M5V 1P9; tel. (416) 591-6300; fax (416) 591-5345; e-mail info@cea-ace.ca; internet www.cea-ace.ca; f. 1891; 300 mems; Pres. GILLIAN MCCREARY; Vice-Pres. CAROLE OLSEN; CEO PENNY MILTON; publs *Bulletin* (billingual, monthly), *CEA Handbook/Ki-es-Ki* (annual), *Education Canada* (quarterly).

Canadian Society for the Study of Education: Suite 204, 260 Dalhousie St, Ottawa, ON K1N 7E4; tel. (613) 241-0018; fax (613) 241-0019; e-mail csse-scee@csse.ca; internet www.csse.ca; f. 1972; to enhance educational research in Canada; holds annual conference; 1,000 mems; Dir of Admin. TIM G. HOWARD; publ. *Canadian Journal of Education* (quarterly).

FINE AND PERFORMING ARTS

Canada Council for the Arts/Conseil des Arts du Canada: POB 1047, 350 Albert St, Ottawa, ON K1P 5V8; tel. (613) 566-4365; fax (613) 566-4390; internet www.canadacouncil.ca; f. 1957; the Council provides grants and services to professional Canadian artists and arts organizations; maintains secretariat for Canadian Commission for UNESCO; administers Public Lending Right Comm. and Canada Council Art Bank; administers Killam Program of prizes and fellowships to

Canadian research scholars, and recognizes achievement through a number of prizes, including Governor General's Literary Awards, Molson Prizes and Glenn Gould Prize; 90% state-funded; 11 mems; Chair. NALINI STEWART (acting); Vice-Chair. SIMON BRAULT; Dir JOHN HOBDAY; publ. *Annual Report*.

Canadian Film Institute: 2 Daly Ave, Suite 120, Ottawa, ON K1N 6E2; tel. (613) 232-6727; fax (613) 232-6315; f. 1935 to encourage and promote the study, appreciation and use of motion pictures and television in Canada; division of Cinémathèque Canada; operates CFI Film Library, renting 6,500 educational films and videos; cinema; Canadian Centre for Films on Art; hosts Ottawa International Animation Festival; Dir TOM MCSORLEY.

Canadian Music Centre (Centre de Musique Canadienne): 20 St Joseph St, Toronto, ON M4Y 1J9; tel. (416) 961-6601; fax (416) 961-7198; e-mail info@musiccentre.ca; internet www.musiccentre.ca; f. 1959; for the collection and promotion, in Canada and abroad, of music by contemporary Canadian composers; collection of 16,000 scores; produces Canadian concert recordings (Centrediscs); Exec. Dir ELISABETH BIHL; publ. list of acquisitions (annually).

Sculptors' Society of Canada: 64 Merton St, Toronto, ON M4S 1A1; tel. (416) 214-0389; e-mail gallery@cansculpt.org; internet www.cansculpt.org; f. 1928; Pres. JUDI MICHELLE YOUNG; Vice-Pres. SAULIUS JASKUS; Treasurer JOHN WILES.

Society of Composers, Authors and Music Publishers of Canada (SOCAN): 41 Valleybrook Drive, Toronto, ON M3B 2S6; tel. (416) 445-8700; fax (416) 445-7108; e-mail socan@socan.ca; internet www.socan.ca; f. 1990; copyright collective for the communication and performance of musical works; licenses music in Canada; distributes royalties to its members for the use of their music overseas; offices in Toronto, Montreal, Vancouver, Edmonton and Dartmouth; 80,000 mems; Pres. PIERRE-DANIEL RHEAULT; publs *Music Means Business/Le Rhytme de vos Affaires* (2 a year), *Words & Music/Paroles & Musique* (4 a year).

Visual Arts Ontario: 1153A Queen St West, Toronto, ON M6J 1J4; tel. (416) 591-8883; fax (416) 591-2432; e-mail info@vao.org; internet www.vao.org; f. 1973; federation of professional artists; 3,600 mems; Exec. Dir HENNIE L. WOLFF; publs *Agenda* (4 a year), *Hidden Agenda* (10 a year).

HISTORY, GEOGRAPHY AND ARCHAEOLOGY

Antiquarian and Numismatic Society of Montreal (Château Ramezay Museum)/Société d'Archéologie et de Numismatique de Montréal (Musée du Château Ramezay): 280 Notre Dame St E, Montréal, QC H2Y 1C5; tel. (514) 861-3708; fax (514) 861-8317; e-mail info@chateauramezay.qc.ca; internet www.chateauramezay.qc.ca; f. 1862; 210 mems; library: library of 8,000 books; Dir ANDRÉ J. DELISLE; Sec. SUZANNE LALUMIÈRE; publ. *La Lettre de Ramezay* (Ramezay Letter, 3 a year).

Canadian Association of Geographers: Dept of Geography, McGill Univ, 425-805 Sherbrooke St W, Montréal, QC H3A 2K6; tel. (514) 398-4946; fax (514) 398-7437; e-mail cag@geog.mcgill.ca; internet www.cag-acg.ca; f. 1951; 800 mems; Pres. CHRIS SHARPE; Sec.-Treas. ALAN NASH; publs *The Canadian Geographer* (quarterly), *The CAG Newsletter* (6 a year), *The Directory* (annually).

Canadian Historical Association/Société historique du Canada: 395 Wellington St, Ottawa, ON K1A 0N3; tel. (613) 233-7885; fax (613) 567-3110; e-mail cha-shc@archives.ca; internet www.cha-shc.ca; f. 1922, to encourage historical research and public interest in history; 1,300 mems; Sec. (English) JOHN WILLIS; Sec. (French) PETER BISCHOFF; publs *Journal of the CHA/Revue de la SHC* (annually), *Bulletin* (3 a year), *Register of Dissertations/Répertoire des thèses* (online), *Canada's Ethnic Groups* (2 a year), *Historical Booklets* (2 a year).

Genealogical Association of Nova Scotia: 3045 Robie St, Suite 222, Halifax, NS B3K 4P6; tel. (902) 454-0322; e-mail gans@chebucto.ns.ca; internet www.chebucto.ns.ca/recreation/gans; f. 1982; 1,000 mems; Pres. SCOTT TAYLOR; publ. *The Nova Scotia Genealogist* (3 a year).

Genealogical Institute of the Maritimes (Institut généalogique des provinces Maritimes): POB 36022, Canada Post Postal Office, 5675 Spring Garden Rd, Halifax, NS B3J 1G0; internet nsgna.ednet.ns.ca/gim; f. 1983; education and research in genealogy; offers certification and registration of individuals undertaking genealogical research for the public; 44 mems; publ. *East Coast Roots* (newsletter).

Institut d'Histoire de l'Amérique Française: 261 Bloomfield Ave, Montréal, QC H2V 3R6; tel. (514) 278-2232; fax (514) 271-6369; e-mail ihaf@ihaf.qc.ca; internet www.cam.org/~ihaf; f. 1946; 1,000 mems; Pres. CHRISTIAN DESSUREAULT; Sec. JEAN LAMARRE; publ. *Revue d'histoire de l'Amérique française* (quarterly).

Ontario Historical Society: 34 Parkview Ave, Willowdale, ON M2N 3Y2; tel. (416) 226-9011; fax (416) 226-2740; e-mail ohs@ontariohistoricalsociety.ca; internet www.ontariohistoricalsociety.ca; f. 1888; 300 affiliated societies; 3,000 mems; Exec. Dir PATRICIA K. NEAL; publs *Ontario History* (2 a year), *OHS Bulletin* (5 a year).

Royal Canadian Geographical Society: 39 McArthur Ave, Ottawa ON K1L 8L7; tel. (613) 745-4629; fax (613) 744-0947; e-mail rcgs@rcgs.org; internet www.rcgs.org; f. 1929; 260,000 mems; Pres. GISELE JACOB; publ. *Canadian Geographic* (6 a year).

Royal Nova Scotia Historical Society: POB 2622, Halifax, NS B3J 3P7; internet nsgna.ednet.ns.ca/rnshs/; f. 1878; history, biography, social studies of provincial past; 350 mems; Pres. JUDITH FINGARD; Sec. R. BARBOUR; publs *Collections* (irregular), *Journal* (annually).

Société Généalogique Canadienne Française: 3440 rue Davidson, Montréal, QC H1W 2Z5; tel. (514) 527-1010; fax (514) 527-0265; e-mail info@sgcf.com; internet www.sgcf.com; f. 1943; studies and publications on the origins and history of French Canadian families since 1615; 4,000 mems; library of 17,000 books, 3,000,000 cards on marriages, 4,500 microfilms; Pres. MARCEL FOURNIER; publ. *Mémoires* (4 a year).

Waterloo Historical Society: c/o Kitchener Public Library, 85 Queen St N, Kitchener, ON N2H 2H1; tel. (519) 743-0271 ext. 252; fax (519) 570-1360; internet www.whs.ca; f. 1912; 300 mems; local history; collection at Kitchener Public Library, ON; Sec. IRIS MITTEN; publ. annual volume containing articles on regional history.

LANGUAGE AND LITERATURE

Alliance Française: 352 MacLaren St, Ottawa, ON K2P 0M6; tel. (613) 234-9470; fax (613) 233-1559; e-mail info@af.ca; internet www.af.ca; offers courses and exams in French language and culture and promotes cultural exchange with France; attached offices in Calgary, Edmonton, Halifax, Mississauga, Moncton, North York, Regina, Saskatoon, Toronto, Vancouver, Victoria and Winnipeg; Dir ALAIN LANDRY.

British Council: British High Commission, 80 Elgin St, Ottawa, ON K1P 5K7; tel. (613) 237-1530; fax (613) 569-1478; e-mail education.enquiries@ca.britishcouncil.org; internet www.britishcouncil.org/canada; offers courses and exams in English language and British culture and promotes cultural exchange with the UK; attached office in Montréal; Dir PETER CHENERY.

Canadian Authors Association: Box 419, Campbellford, ON K0L 1L0; tel. (705) 653-0323; fax (705) 653-0593; e-mail admin@canauthors.org; internet www.canauthors.org; f. 1921; 600 mems; administers awards; annual conference; workshops and seminars; Pres. JOAN EYOLFSON CADHAM; publ. *The Canadian Writer's Guide* (irregular).

Canadian Linguistic Association/Association Canadienne de Linguistique: Département d'Études Françaises, University of Toronto, Toronto, ON M5S 1J4; fax (416) 926-1300; internet www.chass.utoronto.ca/~cla-acl; f. 1954 to advance the study of linguistics, languages in Canada; 220 mems; Pres. JOHN ARCHIBALD; Sec. MARTHA MCGINNIS; Treas. MARGUERITE MACKENZIE; publ. *The Canadian Journal of Linguistics/La Revue Canadienne de Linguistique* (quarterly).

Goethe-Institut: 418 Sherbrooke Est, Montréal, QC H2L 1J6; tel. (514) 499-0159; fax (514) 499-0905; e-mail goethe.montreal.il@netaxis.qc.ca; internet www.goethe.de/uk/mon/deindex.htm; offers courses and exams in German language and culture and promotes cultural exchange with Germany; attached centres in Ottawa and Toronto; library of 8,000 vols, 40 periodicals; Dir MECHTILD MANUS.

PEN Canada: 24 Ryerson Ave, Suite 214, Toronto, ON M5T 2P3; tel. (416) 703-8448; fax (416) 703-3870; e-mail pen@pencanada.ca; f. 1982; international literary association; 125 mems; Pres. HAROON SIDDIQUI; Vice-Pres. and Treasurer DAVID SILCOX.

MEDICINE

Academy of Medicine: c/o Fudger Library, University Health Network, Toronto General Hospital, 200 Elizabeth St, EN1-418, Toronto, ON M5G 2C4; tel. (416) 340-3259; fax (416) 340-4384; f. 1907; history of medicine; library of 100,000 vols, 2,270 periodicals; Librarian MARGARET ALIHARAN.

Canadian Association for Anatomy, Neurobiology and Cell Biology/Association Canadienne d'Anatomie, de Neurobiologie et de Biologie Cellulaire: c/o Dr MICHAEL KAWAJA, Dept. of Anatomy and Cell Biology, Queen's University, Kingston, ON K7L 3N6; tel. (613) 533-2864; fax (613) 533-2566; e-mail kawajam@post.queensu.ca; f. 1956; 147 mems; Pres. Dr RIC DEVON; Sec. Dr MICHAEL KAWAJA; publ. *The Bulletin* (annually).

Canadian Association of Optometrists: 234 Argyle Ave, Ottawa, ON K2P 1B9; tel. (613) 235-7924; fax (613) 235-2025; e-mail info@opto.ca; internet www.opto.ca; f. 1948; Pres. Dr SCOTT MUNDLE; Dir-Gen. GLENN CAMPBELL; Sec.-Treasurer Dr DORRIE MORROW; publ. *The Canadian Journal of Optometry/La Revue Canadienne d'Optométrie* (quarterly).

Canadian Dental Association: 1815 Alta Vista Drive, Ottawa, ON K1G 3Y6; tel. (613) 523-1770; fax (613) 523-7736; e-mail reception@cda-adc.ca; internet www.cda-adc.ca; f. 1902; Pres. Dr LOUIS DUBÉ; publs *Journal* (11 a year), *Communiqué* (6 a year).

Canadian Lung Association: 3 Raymond St, Suite 300, Ottawa, ON K1R 1A3; tel. (613) 569-6411; fax (613) 569-8860; e-mail info@lung.ca; internet www.lung.ca; f. 1900; 10 provincial member associations (Alberta, British Columbia, Québec, Nova Scotia, Saskatchewan, Manitoba, New Brunswick, Newfoundland and Labrador, Ontario, Prince Edward Island), 1 territorial association (North West Territories); associated professional societies: Canadian Thoracic Society, Canadian Physiotherapy Cardio-Respiratory Society, Canadian Nurses' Respiratory Society, Respiratory Therapy Society; publ. *Canadian Respiratory Journal* (8 a year).

Canadian Medical Association: 1867 Alta Vista Drive, Ottawa, ON K1G 3Y6; fax (613) 236-8864; e-mail pubs@cma.ca; internet www.cma.ca; f. 1867; 60,000 mems; Pres. Dr COLIN MACMILLAN; Sec.-Gen. WILLIAM THOLL; Hon. Treasurer Dr JOHN RAPIN; publs *Canadian Association of Radiologists Journal* (6 a year), *Canadian Journal of Emergency Medicine* (4 a year), *Canadian Journal of Rural Medicine* (4 a year), *Canadian Journal of Surgery* (6 a year), *Canadian Medical Association Bulletin* (every 2 weeks), *Canadian Medical Association Journal–CMAJ* (25 a year), *Health Care News* (monthly), *Journal of Psychiatry and Neuroscience* (5 a year), *Strategy Magazine*.

Canadian Paediatric Society (Société Canadienne de Pédiatrie): 100–2204 Walkley Rd, Ottawa, ON K1G 4G8; tel. (613) 526-9397; fax (613) 526-3332; e-mail info@cps.ca; internet ww.cps.ca; f. 1923; 2,000 mems; Pres. C. ROBIN WALKER; publ. *Paediatrics and Child Health* (6 a year).

Canadian Pharmacists Association: 1785 Alta Vista Drive, Ottawa, ON K1G 3Y6; tel. (613) 523-7877; fax (613) 523-0445; e-mail cpha@pharmacists.ca; internet www.pharmacists.ca; f. 1907; 9,000 mems; Pres. GARTH MCCUTCHEON; publs *Compendium of Pharmaceuticals and Specialties* (English and French edns, annually), *Patient Self-Care* (English only), *Compendium of Non Prescription Products* (English only), *Therapeutic Choices* (English only).

Canadian Physiological Society: c/o Canadian Federation of Biological Societies, 305-1750 Courtwood Crescent, Ottawa, ON K2C 2B5; tel. (613) 225-8889; fax (613) 225-9621; internet www.cps.cfbs.org; f. 1936; 300 mems; Pres. Dr CHRIS CHEESEMAN; Sec. Dr C. ELAINE CHAPMAN; Treasurer Dr DOUG JONES; publ. *The Canadian Journal of Physiology and Pharmacology* (monthly).

Canadian Psychiatric Association/Association des Psychiatres du Canada: 141 Laurien Ave West, Suite 701, Ottawa, ON K1P 5J3; tel. (613) 234-2815; fax (613) 234-9857; e-mail cpa@cpa-apc.org; internet www.cpa-apc.org; f. 1951 to promote research into psychiatric disorders and foster high standards of professional practice; 2,800 mems; Chair. Dr D. BLAKE WOODSIDE; Chief Exec. Officer ALEX SAUNDERS; publ. *The Canadian Journal of Psychiatry* (14 a year).

Canadian Public Health Association: 1565 Carling Ave, Suite 400, Ottawa, ON K1Z 8R1; tel. (613) 725-3769; fax (613) 725-9826; e-mail info@cpha.ca; internet www.cpha.ca; f. 1910; 2,000 mems; Pres. CHRISTINA MILLS; CEO ELINOR E. WILSON; publ. *Canadian Journal of Public Health* (every 2 months).

Canadian Society for Nutritional Sciences: c/o Dr SUSAN WHITING, Div. Nutrition & Dietetics, College of Pharmacy & Nutrition, 110 Science Place, Univ. of Saskatchewan, Saskatoon, SK S7N 5C9; internet www.nutritionalsciences.ca; f. 1957 to extend knowledge of nutrition by research, discussion of research reports, and exchange of information; 340 mems; Pres. SUSAN WHITING; Sec. GUYLAINE FERLAND; publ. *Nutrition / Forum de Nutrition* (2 a year).

Pharmacological Society of Canada: C/o Dept of Physiology and Pharmacology, M216 Medical Sciences Bldg, Univ. of Western Ontario, London, ON N6A 5C1; e-mail robert.mcneill@usask.ca; internet www.physpharm.med.uwo.ca; f. 1956; 320 mems; Pres. Dr J. ROBERT MCNEILL; Sec. Dr FIONA PARKINSON; publ. *Canadian Journal of Physiology and Pharmacology*.

Royal College of Physicians and Surgeons of Canada: 774 Echo Drive, Ottawa, ON K1S 5N8; tel. (613) 730-8177; fax (613) 730-8830; e-mail info@rcpsc.edu; internet rcpsc.medical.org; f. 1929; sets standards for postgraduate medical education of specialists in Canada; accredits postgraduate specialist education programmes; acts as national examining body to certify medical, surgical and laboratory specialists; offers a professional development programme; 39,270 mems; CEO Dr ANDREW PADMOS; publs *Annual Report*, *Royal College Outlook* (quarterly).

NATURAL SCIENCES

General

Association Francophone pour le Savoir (Acfas): 425 rue De La Gauchetière Est, Montréal, QC H2L 2M7; tel. (514) 849-0045; fax (514) 849-5558; e-mail acfas@acfas.ca; internet www.acfas.ca; f. 1923; aims to popularize science by means of lectures, meetings, awards, publications; 6,000 mems; Pres. CLAIRE V. DE LA DURANTAYE; publs *Découvrir* (6 a year), *Les Cahiers de l'Acfas* (2–3 a year).

Nova Scotian Institute of Science: Ocean Nutrition Canada, 1721 Lower Water St, Halifax, NS B3J 1S5; internet www.chebucto.ns.ca; f. 1862; monthly lecture series; 300 mems; Pres. Dr ARCHIE MCCULLOCH; Vice-Pres. CAROLYN BIRD; Sec. TRUMAN LAYTON; publ. *Proceedings* (irregular).

Biological Sciences

Canadian Phytopathological Society: c/o Joanne McWilliams, KW Neatby Bldg, Agriculture & Agri-Food Canada, 960 Carling Ave, Ottawa, ON K1A 0C6; internet www.cps-scp.ca; f. 1929; 500 mems; Pres. RICHARD MARTIN; Sec. DEENA ERRAMPALLI; publs *News* (quarterly), *Canadian Journal of Plant Pathology* (quarterly).

Canadian Society for Cellular and Molecular Biology: Centre de recherche, Hôtel-Dieu de Québec, 11 Côte du Palais, Quebec, QC G1R 2J6; internet www.csbmcb.ca; f. 1966; 400 mems; Pres. Dr DAVID ANDREWS; Sec. C. CASS; publ. *Bulletin* (3 a year).

Canadian Society for Immunology: c/o Immunology Research Group, University of Calgary, 2500 University Drive NW, Calgary, AB T2N 1N4; tel. (403) 492-0712; fax (403) 439-3439; f. 1966; 400 mems; Pres. Dr JOHN SCHRADER; Sec. and Treas. Dr DONNA CHOW; publ. *Bulletin* (irregular).

Canadian Society of Microbiologists/Société Canadienne des Microbiologistes: 375 W. 5th Ave, Suite 201, Vancouver, BC V5Y 1J6; tel. (604) 484-5698; fax (604) 874-4378; e-mail info@csm-scm.org; internet www.csm-scm.org; f. 1951; 500 mems; Sec. Dr MARTHA DAVIS; Co-ordinator Dr ALEXIS MARTIS; publs *CSM Newsletter* (3 a year), *Programme & Abstracts* (annually).

Cercles des Jeunes Naturalistes: 4101 Sherbrooke est, Suite 262, Montréal, QC H1X 2B2; tel. (514) 252-3023; fax (514) 254-8744; e-mail cjn@cam.org; internet www.cjn.cam.org; f. 1931; 1,500 mems; Pres.-Gen. YVES BREAULT; Dir LAURE BOUCHARD; publs *Nouvelles CJN* (monthly), *Les Naturalistes* (4 a year).

Entomological Society of Canada: 393 Winston Ave, Ottawa, ON K2A 1Y8; tel. (613) 725-2619; fax (613) 725-9349; e-mail entsoc.can@bellnet.ca; internet esc-sec.org; f. 1863; 500 mems, 7 affiliated regional socs; Pres. Dr DAN QUIRING; Sec. Dr RICK WEST; publ. *The Canadian Entomologist* (6 a year).

Genetics Society of Canada/Société de Génétique du Canada: c/o E. K. Consulting, 53 Slalom Gate Rd, Collingwood, ON L9Y 5B1; tel. (613) 232-9459; fax (613) 594-5190; internet www.life.biology.mcmaster.ca/gsc/; f. 1956; 425 mems; Pres. VIRGINIA WALKER; Treasurer JOHN BELL; Sec. CAROLYN J. BROWN; publs *Bulletin* (quarterly), *Genome* (6 a year).

Manitoba Naturalists Society: 401–63 Albert St, Winnipeg, MB R3B 1G4; tel. (204) 943-9029; fax (204) 943-9029; e-mail mns@escape.ca; internet www.manitobanature.ca; f. 1920; 1,500 mems; Pres. LARRY DE MARCH; Exec. Dir GORDON FARDOE; publ. *Bulletin* (10 a year).

Société de Protection des Plantes du Québec: c/o Secretary, 1643 Chemin des Lacs, Vincent Phillion, Station de recherches agricoles, CP 480, Saint-Faustin-Lac carré, QC J0T 1J2; e-mail ltartier@sympatico.ca; internet www.sppq.qc.ca; f. 1908; 225 mems; Pres. DANNY RIOUX; Sec. LÉON TARTIER; Treasurer GAÉTAN BOURGEOIS; publs *Echos phytosanitaires* (quarterly), *Phytoprotection* (3 a year).

Société Linnéenne du Québec: 1040 Belvédère, Sillery, QC G1S 3G3; tel. (418) 683-2432; fax (418) 683-2893; e-mail soclinneque@qc.aira.com; internet ecoroute.uqcn.qc.ca/group/slq; f. 1929; 800 mems; natural history; Pres. JEAN-PAUL L'ALLIER; Dir AGATHE SAVARD; publ. *Le Linnéen* (quarterly).

Vancouver Natural History Society: POB 3021, Vancouver, BC V6B 3X5; tel. (604) 737-3074; fax (604) 876-3313; e-mail mgrcoope@interchange.ubc.ca; internet www.naturalhistory.bc.ca/vhns; f. 1918; aims to promote interest in nature, conservation of natural resources, protection of endangered species and ecosystems; 900 mems; Pres. KELLY SEKHON; publ. *Discovery* (2 a year).

Mathematical Sciences

Canadian Mathematical Society/Société mathématique du Canada: 577 King Edward, Suite 109, Ottawa, ON K1N 6N5; tel. (613) 562-5702; fax (613) 565-1539; e-mail office@cms.math.ca; internet www.cms.math.ca; f. 1945, inc. 1979; promotes the discovery, learning and application of mathematics; 1,400 mems; Pres. H. E. A. EDDY CAMPBELL; Exec. Dir and Sec. Dr GRAHAM P. WRIGHT; Treasurer F. ARTHUR SHERK; publs *Canadian Mathematical Bulletin* (quarterly), *Canadian Journal of Mathematics* (every 2 months), *CMS Notes* (8 a year), *CRUX with Mayhem* (8 a year).

Physical Sciences

Canadian Association of Physicists/Association canadienne des physiciens et physiciennes: MacDonald Bldg (Suite 112), 150 Louis Pasteur, Ottawa, ON K1N 6N5; tel. (613) 562-5614; fax (613) 562-5615; e-mail cap@physics.uottawa.ca; internet www.cap.ca; f. 1945; 2,000 mems; Pres. Dr MICHAEL R. MORROW; Exec. Dir. FRANCINE M.

FORD; Sec. and Treasurer Dr RICHARD HODGSON; publ. *Physics in Canada* (every 2 months).

Canadian Meteorological and Oceanographic Society/Société Canadienne de Météorologie et d'Océanographie: Station 'D', POB 3211, Ottawa, ON K1P 6H7; tel. (613) 990-0300; fax (613) 993-4658; e-mail cmos@meds-sdmm.dfo-mpo.gc.ca; internet www.cmos.ca; f. 1977; 800 mems; Pres. Dr ALLYN CLARKE; Exec. Dir Dr NEIL CAMPBELL; publs *Atmosphere-Ocean* (quarterly), *CMOS Bulletin SCMO* (every 2 months), *Congress Program and Abstracts* (annually).

Canadian Society of Biochemistry, Molecular and Cellular Biology/Société Canadienne de Biochimie et de Biologie Moléculaire et Cellulaire: c/o Dr E. R. Tustanoff, Dept of Biochemistry, University of Western Ontario, London, ON N6A 5C1; tel. (519) 471-1961; fax (519) 661-3175; e-mail etustan@uwo.ca; f. 1958; 1,000 mems; Pres. Dr J. ORLOWSKI; Sec. Dr E. R. TUSTANOFF; publ. *Bulletin* (annually).

Canadian Society of Petroleum Geologists: 540 Fifth Ave SW (Suite 160), Calgary, AB T2P 0M2; tel. (403) 264-5610; fax (403) 264-5898; e-mail cspg@cspg.org; internet www.cspg.org; f. 1927; 3,400 mems; Pres. CRAIG LAMB; Business Man. TIM HOWARD; publs *Bulletin of Canadian Petroleum Geology* (quarterly), *Reservoir* (11 a year).

Chemical Institute of Canada: 130 Slater St, Suite 550, Ottawa, ON K1P 6E2; tel. (613) 232-6252; fax (613) 232-5862; e-mail info@cheminst.ca; internet www.cheminst.ca; f. 1945; 27 local sections, 16 subject divisions, 116 student chapters and 3 constituent societies—Canadian Society for Chemical Engineering, the Canadian Society for Chemical Technology and the Canadian Society for Chemistry; Exec. Dir ROLAND ANDERSSON; publs *Canadian Chemical News* (10 a year), *Canadian Journal of Chemical Engineering* (6 a year).

Geological Association of Canada: Dept of Earth Sciences, Rm ER4063, Memorial University of Newfoundland, St John's, NL A1B 3X5; tel. (709) 737-7660; fax (709) 737-2532; e-mail gac@esd.mun.ca; internet www.gac.ca; f. 1947 to advance the science of geology and related fields of study and to promote a better understanding thereof throughout Canada; 3,000 mems; Pres. Prof. SANDRA BARR; Sec.-Treas. Dr RICHARD WARDLE; publs *Geoscience Canada* (quarterly), *Geolog* (4 a year).

Royal Astronomical Society of Canada: 136 Dupont St, Toronto, ON M5R 1V2; tel. (416) 924-7973; fax (416) 924-2911; e-mail nationaloffice@rasc.ca; internet www.rasc.ca; f. 1890; 28 centres; 4,400 mems; Exec. Sec. BONNIE BIRD; publs *Journal* (every 2 months), *Observers' Handbook* (annually).

Society of Chemical Industry (Canadian Section): 247 Ridgewood Rd, Toronto, ON M1C 2XC; tel. (416) 708-8924; fax (416) 281-8691; e-mail SCICanada@soci.info; internet www.soci.org; f. 1902; fosters contact between chemical industry, universities and govt; rewards achievement in industry and universities; promotes international contact; 150 mems; Administrator BETH GALLOWAY.

Spectroscopy Society of Canada/Société de Spectroscopie du Canada: POB 332, Stn A, Ottawa, ON K1N 8V3; internet www.globalserve.net/~ssccan; f. 1957; 350 mems; provides the annual Herzberg Award, the Barringer Research Award and an award to the Youth Science Foundation; Pres. DIANE BEAUCHEMIN; Sec. TERESA SWITZER; publ. *Canadian Journal of Analytical Sciences and Spectroscopy*.

PHILOSOPHY AND PSYCHOLOGY

Canadian Philosophical Association/Association canadienne de philosophie: POB 450, Stn A, Ottawa, ON K1N 6N5; tel. (613) 562-5367; fax (613) 562-5370; e-mail acpa@uottawa.ca; internet www.acpcpa.ca; f. 1958 to promote philosophical scholarship in Canada and to represent Canadian philosophers; 800 mems; Administrator LOUISE MOREL; publ. *Dialogue* (French and English, quarterly).

Canadian Psychological Association/Société Canadienne de Psychologie: 151 Slater St, Suite 205, Ottawa, ON K1P 5H3; tel. (613) 237-2144; fax (613) 237-1674; e-mail cpa@cpa.ca; internet www.cpa.ca; f. 1939; 4,500 mems; Exec. Dir Dr JOHN C. SERVICE; publs *Canadian Journal of Experimental Psychology* (4 a year), *Canadian Psychology* (4 a year), *Canadian Journal of Behavioral Science* (4 a year), *Psynopsis* (4 a year).

RELIGION, SOCIOLOGY AND ANTHROPOLOGY

Association for the Advancement of Scandinavian Studies in Canada (AASSC): 643 University College, Winnipeg, MB R3T 2M8; tel. (204) 474-6628; fax (204) 261-5764; e-mail neijmann@cc.manitoba.ca; f. 1982; 120 mems; Pres. JOHN TUCKER; Sec. KATHY HANSON; publs *Newsbulletin* (every 6 months), *Scandinavian-Canadian Studies* (annually).

Canadian Association of African Studies/Association Canadienne des Etudes Africaines: CCASLS SB 115, c/o Concordia University, 1455 de Maisonneuve Ouest, Montréal, QC H3G 1M8; tel. (514) 848-2280; fax (514) 848-4514; e-mail caas@bellnet.ca; internet caas.concordia.ca; f. 1970; 310 mems; promotion of the study of Africa in Canada; aims to improve the Canadian public's knowledge and awareness of Africa; provides a link between Canadian and African scholarly and scientific communities; Exec. Dir ANNAMARIA PICCIONI; publs *Canadian Journal of African Studies / Revue Canadienne des Etudes Africaines* (3 a year), *Newsletter / Bulletin* (3 a year).

Canadian Association of Latin American and Caribbean Studies/Association Canadienne des Etudes Latino-Américaines et des Caraïbes: CCASLS SB-115, Concordia University, 1455 de Maisonneuve Ouest, Montréal, QC H3G 1M8; tel. (514) 848-2280; fax (514) 848-4514; e-mail calacs_acelac@bellnet.ca; internet www.can-latam.org; f. 1969; 200 mems; Pres. STUART MCCOOK; Sec. and Treas. KRIS E. INWOOD; publs *Canadian Journal of Latin American and Caribbean Studies* (2 a year), *Newsletter* (quarterly), *Directory of Canadian Scholars and Universities interested in Latin American Studies*.

Canadian Society of Biblical Studies: c/o Michele Murray, Dept of Religion, Bishop's University, Lennoxville, QC J1M 1Z7; tel. (819) 822-9600; e-mail mmurray@ubishops.ca; internet www.ccsr.ca/csbs; f. 1933; the promotion of scholarship in Biblical studies; 287 mems; Pres. DAVID HAWKIN; Exec. Sec. M. MURRAY; publ. *Bulletin* (annually).

TECHNOLOGY

Canadian Academy of Engineering/Académie canadienne du génie: 180 Elgin St, Suite 1100, Ottawa, ON K2P 2K3; tel. (613) 235-9056; fax (613) 235-6861; e-mail acadeng@ccpe.ca; internet www.acad-eng-gen.ca; f. 1987; assesses the changing needs of Canada and the technical resources that can be applied to them; sponsors programmes to meet these needs; provides independent and expert advice on matters of national importance concerning engineering; highlights exceptional engineering achievements; works by co-operation with national and international academies; 260 mems; Pres. RON NOLAN; Sec. and Treasurer Dr JOHN MCLAUGHLIN; Exec. Dir PHILIP COCKSHUTT; publ. *Newsletter* (quarterly).

Canadian Aeronautics and Space Institute: 1685 Russell Rd, Unit 1R, Ottawa, ON K1G 0N1; tel. (613) 234-0191; fax (613) 234-9039; e-mail casi@casi.ca; internet www.casi.ca; f. 1954; 2,000 mems; Pres. P. WHYTE; Exec. Dir I. ROSS; publs *Canadian Aeronautics and Space Journal* (4 a year), *Canadian Journal of Remote Sensing* (4 a year).

Canadian Council of Professional Engineers: 180 Elgin St (Suite 1100), Ottawa, ON K2P 2K3; tel. (613) 232-2474; fax (613) 230-5759; e-mail info@ccpe.ca; internet www.ccpe.ca; f. 1936; co-ordinating body for 12 Provincial and Territorial Licensing Bodies; total membership of constituent associations 152,000; CEO MARIE LEMAY.

Canadian Electricity Association: 1155 rue Metcalfe, bureau 1120, Montréal, QC H3B 2V6; tel. (514) 866-6121; fax (514) 866-1880; e-mail info@canelect.ca; internet www.canelect.ca; f. 1891; represents Canada's electric utility industry; 35 corporate utilities, 38 corporate manufacturers, 109 assoc. cos, 2,500 individual mems; Pres. H. R. KONOW; publs *Reports* (various), *Electricity* (annually), *Connections* (10 a year).

Canadian Institute of Mining, Metallurgy and Petroleum: Xerox Tower, Suite 1210, 3400 de Maisonneuve Blvd West, Montréal, QC H3Z 3B8; tel. (514) 939-2710; fax (514) 939-2714; e-mail cim@cim.org; internet www.cim.org; f. 1898; 10,500 mems; Pres. WARREN HOLMES; Exec. Dir JEAN VAVREK; publs *CIM Bulletin* (10 a year), *CIM Directory* (annually), *Journal of Canadian Petroleum Technology* (10 a year), *CIM Reporter* (2 a year).

Engineering Institute of Canada: 1295 Hwy 2E, Kingston, ON K7L 4V1; tel. (613) 547-5989; fax (613) 547-0195; e-mail info@eic-ici.ca; internet www.eic-ici.ca; f. 1887; 16,000 mems and 5 mem. socs; Pres. GUY GOSSELIN; Exec. Dir B. JOHN PLANT.

Research Institutes

GENERAL

Alberta Research Council Inc.: 250 Karl Clark Rd, Edmonton, AB T6N 1E4; tel. (780) 450-5111; fax (780) 450-5333; internet www.arc.ab.ca; f. 1921; develops and commercializes technologies to give clients a competitive advantage; provides solutions globally to the agriculture, life sciences, energy, environment, forestry and manufacturing sectors; library of 40,000 vols, 3,500 reports, 450 current periodicals; Man. Dir and CEO JOHN R. MCDOUGALL; publs *R & D Newsletter* (3 a year), *Annual Report*.

InNOVAcorp: 101 Research Drive, Woodside Industrial Park, Dartmouth, NS B2Y 4T6; tel. (902) 424-8670; fax (902) 424-4679; e-mail corpcomm@innovacorp.ns.ca; f. 1995; library of 20,000 vols; assists firms based in Nova Scotia to develop and market products, particularly in the fields of life sciences, advanced engineering, information technology and oceans technology; CEO Dr ROSS MCCURDY; publs *Annual Report*, *Progress Report* (4 a year).

National Research Council of Canada/Conseil national de recherches Canada:

1200 Montreal Rd, Bldg M-58, Ottawa, ON K1A 0R6; tel. (613) 993-9101; fax (613) 952-9907; e-mail info@nrc-cnrc.gc.ca; internet www.nrc-cnrc.gc.ca; f. 1916; integrated science and technology agency of the federal govt; provides scientific and technological information through Canada Institute for Scientific and Technical Information and industrial support through Industrial Research Assistance Program; research carried out by 16 research institutes linked to 3 technology groups: biotechnology, information and telecommunications technologies, and manufacturing technologies; Pres. MICHAEL RAYMONT (acting); Sec.-Gen. PAT MORTIMER; publs *Biochemistry and Cell Biology* (6 a year), *Environmental Reviews* (4 a year), *Genome* (6 a year), *Canadian Geotechnical Journal* (6 a year), *Canadian Journal of Botany* (monthly), *Canadian Journal of Chemistry* (monthly), *Canadian Journal of Physics* (monthly), *Canadian Journal of Microbiology* (monthly), *Canadian Journal of Fisheries and Aquatic Sciences* (monthly), *Canadian Journal of Physiology and Pharmacology* (monthly), *Canadian Journal of Zoology* (monthly), *Canadian Journal of Forest Research* (monthly), *Canadian Journal of Civil Engineering* (6 a year), *Canadian Journal of Earth Sciences* (monthly).

North-South Institute: 55 Murray St, Suite 200, Ottawa, ON K1N 5M3; tel. (613) 241-3535; fax (613) 241-7435; e-mail nsi@nsi-ins.ca; internet www.nsi-ins.ca; f. 1976; policy-relevant research on issues of relations between industrialized and developing countries; library of 10,000 vols, 300 periodical titles; Pres. Dr ROY CULPEPER; publs *Review* (newsletter, 2 a year), *Canadian Development Report* (annually).

Nunavut Research Institute: POB 1720, Iqaluit, NU X0A 0H0; tel. (867) 979-7279; fax (867) 979-7109; e-mail slcnri@nunanet.com; internet pooka.nunanet.com/~research; f. 1978; present name 1995; br. in Igloolik; publ. *Research Compendium* (annually).

Process Research ORTECH Corporation: 2395 Speakman Drive, Mississauga, ON L5K 1B3; tel. (905) 822-4111; fax (905) 822-9537; e-mail info@processortech.com; internet www.processortech.com; f. 1928; formed to take over the Process Technologies division of ORTECH Corporation in 1999 (formerly Ontario Research Foundation) under the privatization scheme of the Ontario Govt. Contract research in areas of mining, metallurgical, recycling and chemical industries; Pres. Dr R. SRIDHAR; library of 10,000 vols; publ. *Annual Report*.

RPC (Research and Productivity Council): 921 College Hill Rd, Fredericton, NB E3B 6Z9; tel. (506) 452-1212; fax (506) 452-1395; e-mail info@rpc.ca; internet www.rpc.ca; f. 1962; professional and technical services to help industry develop new products and innovative solutions to operating problems; departments include Engineering Materials and Diagnostics, Inorganic Analytical Services, Food, Fisheries and Aquaculture, Chemical and Biotechnical Services, Product Innovation, and Process and Environmental Technology; library: information centre with 21,000 vols, 250 periodicals, inter-library loan services, access to on-line databases; Exec. Dir Dr P. LEWELL; publ. *Annual Report*.

Saskatchewan Research Council: 125-15 Innovation Blvd, Saskatoon, SK S7N 2X8; tel. (306) 933-5400; fax (306) 933-7446; e-mail info@src.sk.ca; internet www.src.sk.ca; f. 1947; assists the population of Saskatchewan in strengthening the economy and securing the environment by means of research, development and the transfer of innovative scientific and technological solutions, applications and services; library: library (Information Services) of 25,000 vols, 5,500 in-house publs and 300 periodicals; Pres. and CEO LAURIER SCHRAMM.

Vizon SciTech Inc: BC Research Complex, 3650 Wesbrook Mall, Vancouver, BC V6S 2L2; tel. (604) 224-4331; fax (604) 224-0540; e-mail info@vizonscitech.com; internet www.vizonscitech.com; f. 1944 as British Columbia Research Inc. (BCRI), present name 2004; conducts technological research in fields of applied biology, applied chemistry, engineering-physics.

AGRICULTURE, FISHERIES AND VETERINARY SCIENCE

Canadian Forest Service: Ottawa, ON K1A 0E4; f. 1899; forest production, tree improvement, forest statistics and the environmental aspects of forestry, pests, fire, carbon monitoring, industrial competitiveness; supports FPInnovations (see Research Institutes, Technology) and research at Canadian forestry schools; Asst Deputy Minister JIM FARRELL; publs *Annual State of Canada's Forests*, *CFS Research Notes*, *Forestry Technical Reports*, *Information Reports Digest*.

Research establishments:

Great Lakes Forestry Centre: Box 490, 1219 Queen St East, Sault Ste Marie, ON P6A 5M7; Dir-Gen. E. KONDO.

Laurentian Forestry Centre: 1055 rue du P.E.P.S., BP 10380, Ste-Foy, QC G1V 4C7; tel. (418) 648-5847; fax (418) 648-7317; Dir-Gen. N. LAFRENIÈRE.

Maritimes Forestry Service: Box 4000, Fredericton, NB E3B 5P7; Dir-Gen. H. OLDHAM.

Northern Forestry Centre: 5320 122nd St, Edmonton, AB T6H 3S5; Dir-Gen. G. MILLER.

Pacific Forestry Centre: 506 West Burnside Rd, Victoria, BC V8Z 1M5; Dir-Gen. C. WINGET.

Dominion Arboretum: Bldg 72, Central Experimental Farm, Ottawa, ON K1A 0C6; tel. (613) 995-3700; fax (613) 992-7909; f. 1886; part of Agriculture Canada; evaluation of woody plants for cold hardiness and adaptability; display area of 35 ha; special living collections; Dir Dr H. DAVIDSON.

MEDICINE

Canadian Institutes of Health Research: Room 97, 160 Elgin St, Ottawa, ON K1A 0W9; tel. (613) 941-2672; fax (613) 954-1800; e-mail info@cihr.ca; internet www.cihr.ca; f. 2000; aims to make Canadian health services and products more effective and to strengthen the health-care system; Pres. Dr ALAN BERNSTEIN; publs *Communiqué* (in English and French, 4 a year), *Report of the President* (annually).

Cancer Care Ontario: 620 University Ave, Suite 1500, Toronto, ON M5G 2L7; tel. (416) 971-9800; fax (416) 971-6888; e-mail publicaffairs@cancercare.on.ca; internet www.cancercare.on.ca; f. 1943; prevention, diagnosis, treatment, supportive care, education and research in cancer; Pres. and CEO Dr ALAN HUDSON; publ. *Cancer Care*.

Dentistry Canada Fund: 427 Gilmour Street, Ottawa, ON K2P 0R5; tel. (613) 236-4763; fax (613) 236-3935; e-mail information@dcf-fdc.ca; internet www.dcf-fdc.ca; f. 1902; charity promoting oral health; Pres. and Chair. Dr BERNARD DOLANSKY; Exec. Dir RICHARD MUNRO.

National Cancer Institute of Canada: Suite 200, 10 Alcorn Ave, Toronto, ON M4V 3B1; tel. (416) 961-7223; fax (416) 961-4189; e-mail ncic@cancer.ca; internet www.ncic.cancer.ca; f. 1947; grant-awarding agency; Pres. Dr BARBARA WHYLIE; Exec. Dir Dr MICHAEL WOSNICK; publs *Annual Report*, *Annual Scientific Report*, *NCIC Update*, *NCIC CBCRI Breast Cancer Bulletin*.

NATURAL SCIENCES

General

Arctic Institute of North America: Library Tower, University of Calgary, 2500 University Drive NW, Calgary, AB T2N 1N4; tel. (403) 220-7515; fax (403) 282-4609; e-mail anforsch@ucalgary.ca; internet www.ucalgary.ca/aina; f. 1945, became inst. of Univ. of Calgary 1979; multidisciplinary research on physical, biological and social sciences; library of 40,000 vols; Exec. Dir ROSS GOODWIN (acting); publ. *Arctic* (quarterly).

International Development Research Centre: POB 8500, Ottawa, ON K1G 3H9; tel. (613) 236-6163; fax (613) 238-7230; e-mail info@idrc.ca; internet web.idrc.ca; f. 1970 by Act of the Canadian Parliament; to support research in the developing regions of the world in the fields of environment and natural resources; information sciences and systems; health science; social science; training and research utilization; library of 60,000 vols, 5,000 serials, 1,000 pamphlets and annual reports; Pres. MAUREEN O'NEIL; Dir, Finance and Administration JORGE DA SILVA; publs annual report, *IDRC Reports* (quarterly).

Natural Sciences and Engineering Research Council of Canada (NSERC): 350 Albert St, Ottawa, ON K1A 1H5; tel. (613) 995-5992; fax (613) 992-5337; e-mail comm@nserc.ca; internet www.nserc.ca; f. 1978; a crown corporation of the federal Government reporting to Parliament through the Minister of Industry; supports both basic university research through research grants and project research through partnerships of universities with industry, as well as the advanced training of highly qualified people in both areas; Pres. TOM BRZUSTOWSKI; publ. *NSERC Contact* (newsletter).

Biological Sciences

Huntsman Marine Science Centre: 1 Lower Campus Rd, St Andrews, NB E5B 2L7; tel. (506) 529-1200; fax (506) 529-1212; e-mail huntsman@huntsmanmarine.ca; internet www.huntsmanmarine.ca; f. 1969 with the co-operation of universities and the federal government; mems include 9 Canadian universities, Fisheries and Oceans Canada, National Research Council of Canada, the New Brunswick Depts of Education and of Fisheries and Aquaculture, corporations, organizations and individuals; research and teaching in marine sciences and coastal biology; marine education courses for elementary, high school and university groups; Centre includes a public aquarium with local flora and fauna, and the Atlantic Reference Centre which houses a zoological and botanical museum reference collection; Dir Dr MARK J. COSTELLO; publ. *Newsletter* (2 a year).

Jardin botanique de Montréal: 4101 Sherbrooke St East, Montréal, QC H1X 2B2; tel. (514) 872-1400; fax (514) 872-3765; e-mail jardin_botanique@ville.montreal.qc.ca; internet www.ville.montreal.qc.ca/jardin; f. 1931; 22,000 plant species and cultivars, 30 thematic gardens; educational and conservation activities; affiliated botanical and horticultural societies; library of 25,000 vols and 50,000 vols of periodicals

(500 titles); Botanist-Librarian CELINE ARSENAULT; publs *Quatre-temps* (Amis du Jardin botanique, quarterly), *Index Seminum* (every 2 years).

Physical Sciences

Algonquin Radio Observatory: c/o Natural Resources Canada, Geodetic Survey Div., 615 Booth St, Room 440, Ottawa, ON K1A 0E9; tel. (613) 996-4410; fax (613) 995-3215; e-mail information@geod.nrcan.gc.ca; f. 1959; operated by the National Research Council; includes 150 ft-diameter radiotelescope completed in 1966.

David Dunlap Observatory of the University of Toronto: POB 360, Station A, Richmond Hill, ON L4C 4Y6; tel. (905) 884-2112; fax (905) 884-2672; f. 1935; 50 mems; library of 30,000 vols; Assoc. Dir SLAVEK RUCINSKI.

Dominion Astrophysical Observatory: 5071 West Saanich Rd, Victoria, BC V9E 2E7; tel. (250) 363-0001; fax (250) 363-0045; f. 1918; part of Nat. Research Ccl Herzberg Inst. of Astrophysics; 70 mems; library of 20,000 vols; Dir Dr JAMES E. HESSER.

Geological Survey of Canada: 601 Booth St, Ottawa, ON K1A 0E8; tel. (613) 996-3919; fax (613) 943-8742; e-mail esstweb@nrcan-rncan.gc.ca; internet gsc.nrcan.gc.ca; f. 1842; part of Natural Resources Canada; regional centres in Dartmouth, NS, Ste-Foy, QC, Calgary, AB, Vancouver and Sidney, BC, and associated with Nunavut Geoscience Centre, Iqaluit, NU; nat. geoscience agency providing geological information on Canada's landmass and near-offshore regions to support the sustainable devt of the nation's natural resources, to help mitigate against loss from natural disasters and to inform environmental stewardship and health issues; carries out studies and provides information relating to bedrock geology at the surface or at depth, and the derived surficial deposits, that characterize the geological regions of Canada; carries out research assisted by airborne and ground-based mapping of physical properties of these geological materials; has information on mineral deposits of Canada, including exploration guidelines and techniques, and on mineral potential for land-use planning and policy formulation; provides information and advice on natural hazards and terrain stability influenced by permafrost, glaciation and geomorphology, with special emphasis on public safety and the environment; has information on coastal and offshore marine geoscience, hazards and environmental quality of these extensive regions; has geological, geochemical and geophysical information on the coastal zone, seabed, onshore and offshore sedimentary basins and crustal processes; has information on Canada's marine continental margins for United Nations Convention on Law of the Sea; has geoscience knowledge about oil, gas, coal, coalbed methane and gas hydrates resources throughout Canada, both onshore and offshore; has information on climate change evidence, glaciers, ice caps, glacial history, glacial deposits and drift prospecting; has information on groundwater resources and the sustainability of aquifers for potable water; library services; major cartographic service; has extensive publication programme for geological, geophysical and geochemical maps and reports; Asst Deputy Minister MARK COREY; publ. *GSC Information Circular*.

Toronto Biomedical NMR Centre: Dept of Medical Genetics and Microbiology, University of Toronto Medical Sciences Building, Rm 1233, Toronto, ON M5S 1A8; fax (416) 978-6885; f. 1970; a national centre for high field NMR spectroscopy servicing industry, universities and the Government; Dir Dr A. A. GREY.

RELIGION, SOCIOLOGY AND ANTHROPOLOGY

Canadian Federation for the Humanities and Social Sciences: Suite 415, 151 Slater St, Ottawa, ON K1P 5H3; tel. (613) 238-6112; fax (613) 238-6114; e-mail fedcan@fedcan.ca; internet www.fedcan.ca; f. 1941; Exec. Dir PAUL LEDWELL.

International Center for Research on Language Planning/Centre International de Recherche en Aménagement Linguistique: Pavillon De Koninck, Cité Universitaire, Sainte-Foy, QC G1K 7P4; tel. (418) 656-3232; f. 1967; basic research on language planning, description of oral and written Quebec French, new information technologies, learning of a second language; 19 researchers, 80 graduate students, 4 staff; library of 6,000 vols, 50 periodicals; Exec. Dir D. DESHAIES.

Social Sciences and Humanities Research Council of Canada/Conseil de recherches en sciences humaines du Canada: 350 Albert St, Box 1610, Ottawa, ON K1P 6G4; tel. (613) 992-0691; fax (613) 992-1787; e-mail info@sshrc.ca; internet www.sshrc.ca; f. 1977 to promote research and advanced training in the social sciences and humanities; offers grants for basic and applied research; doctoral and postdoctoral fellowships; scholarly publishing journals and conferences; Pres. Dr MARC RENAUD.

TECHNOLOGY

Atomic Energy of Canada, Ltd (AECL): 2251 Speakman Drive, Mississauga, ON L5K 1B2; tel. (905) 823-9040; fax (905) 823-6120; internet www.aecl.ca; f. 1952; development of economic nuclear power, scientific research and development in the nuclear energy field, and marketing of nuclear reactors; Chair. J. RAYMOND FRENETTE; Pres. and CEO ROBERT VAN ADEL.

Attached laboratories:

AECL Research, Chalk River Laboratories: Chalk River, ON K0J 1J0; f. 1944; nuclear reactors (NRU, NRX, Pool Test Reactor and ZED-2), Tandem Accelerating Super Conducting Cyclotron, equipment for nuclear research and engineering development.

AECL Research, Whiteshell Laboratories: Pinawa, MB R0E 1L0; f. 1960; I-10/1 Accelerator, Underground Research Laboratory, equipment for nuclear research and engineering development.

BC Advanced Systems Institute: 1048, 4720 Kingsway, Burnaby, BC V5H 4N2; tel. (604) 438-2752; fax (604) 438-6564; e-mail asi@asi.bc.ca; internet www.asi.bc.ca; f. 1986; promotes research and development in high technology areas such as microelectronics and artificial intelligence; Pres. and CEO VICTOR JONES.

Canada Centre for Inland Waters/Centre Canadien des Eaux Intérieures: 867 Lakeshore Rd, POB 5050, Burlington, ON L7R 4A6; tel. (905) 336-4981; fax (905) 336-6444; f. 1967; a joint freshwater research complex of the Depts of Environment and Fisheries and Oceans; freshwater environmental and fisheries research and monitoring; 600 mems; co-operative management by committee of institutional directors.

Attached research institutes:

Bayfield Institute: 867 Lakeshore Rd, POB 5050, Burlington, ON L7R 4A6; under Dept of Fisheries and Oceans; comprises: Great Lakes Laboratory for Fisheries and Aquatic Sciences; Fisheries and Habitat Management; Canadian Hydrographic Service; Small Craft Harbours br.; and support for shipping. Together with the Freshwater Research Institute in Winnipeg, it provides the federal Fisheries and Oceans programme for the Central and Arctic Region.

National Water Research Institute: 867 Lakeshore Rd, POB 5050, Burlington, ON L7P 3M1; tel. (905) 336-4675; fax (905) 336-6444; e-mail nwriscience.liaison@ec.gc.ca; internet www.nwri.ca; a Directorate of Canada's Environmental Conservation Service; more than 300 mems of staff incl. aquatic ecologists, hydrologists, toxicologists, physical geographers, modelers, limnologists environmental chemists, research technicians and experts in linking water science to environmental policy; centres at the Canada Centre for Inland Waters (Burlington, ON) and at the National Hydrology Research Centre (Saskatoon, SK); staff also located at Gatineau, QC.; Frederiction, NB; and Victoria, BC; works in conjunction with government departments, universities and research orgs to address a variety of water-related issues, focusing on the aquatic ecosystems, protection and management research, science liaison, monitoring and research support; also comprises the National Laboratory for Environmental Testing (NLET) and the program office for the United Nations' Global Environment Monitoring System (GEMS/Water); 300 mems; library of 58,000 vols, 105 print journals, 105 online journals; Dir-Gen. Dr JOHN H. CAREY; publ. *NWRI Contributions*.

FPInnovations - Forintek Division: Head Office and Western Laboratory, 2665 East Mall, Vancouver, BC V6T 1W5; tel. (604) 224-3221; fax (604) 222-5690; Eastern Laboratory, 319 rue Franquet, Sainte-Foy, QC G1P 4R4; f. 1979 (fmrly Forintek Canada Corp.); solid wood products research; Pres. I. A. DE LA ROCHE; Corp. Sec. P. K. P. CHAU.

Institute for Aerospace Studies: 4925 Dufferin St, Toronto, ON M3H 5T6; tel. (416) 667-7700; fax (416) 667-7799; e-mail info@utias.utoronto.ca; internet www.utias.utoronto.ca; f. 1949; part of the Univ. of Toronto; undergraduate and graduate studies; research in aerospace science and engineering, and associated fields; serves industrial research and development needs in government and industry; facilities for experimental and computational research; library of 80,000 vols; Dir Prof. A. A. HAASZ; publ. *Progress Report* (annually).

Pulp and Paper Research Institute of Canada (Paprican): 570 Blvd St-Jean, Pointe-Claire, QC H9R 3J9; tel. (514) 630-4100; fax (514) 630-4134; e-mail info@paprican.ca; internet www.paprican.ca; f. 1925; pulp and paper research, contract research and technical services; postgraduate training programme in co-operation with McGill University and University of British Columbia; library of 20,000 vols; Pres. and CEO J. D. WRIGHT; Sec. and Treasurer. LUCIE LAPOINTE; publ. *Annual Report*.

Libraries and Archives

Alberta

Calgary Public Library: 616 Macleod Trail SE, Calgary, AB T2G 2M2; tel. (403) 260-2600; fax (403) 237-5393; e-mail dearlibrary@calgarypubliclibrary.com; internet www.calgarypubliclibrary.com; f. 1912; 2.4 million items; 16 brs; special sections on petroleum; Dir GERRY MEEK.

City of Edmonton Archives: 10440 108th Ave, Edmonton, AB T5H 3Z9; tel. (780) 496-8711; fax (780) 496-8732; e-mail cms.archives@gov.edmonton.ca; internet www.edmonton.ca/archives; f. 1971; reference library of 10,000 vols, also MSS, newspapers, slides, city records, photographs and maps of the city; Man. (vacant).

Edmonton Public Library: 7 Sir Winston Churchill Square, Edmonton, AB T5J 2V4; tel. (780) 496-7000; fax (780) 496-7097; internet www.epl.ca; f. 1913; 16 brs; 1,766,809 print items, 242,934 audio-visual items; Dir of Libraries LINDA C. COOK.

Glenbow Library and Archives: 130 9th Ave SE, Calgary, AB T2G 0P3; tel. (403) 268-4204; fax (403) 232-6569; internet www.glenbow.org; f. 1955; 80,000 vols, 700,000 photographs and a large collection of manuscript materials, chiefly on Western and Northern Canada.

Legislature Library: 216 Legislature Bldg, 10800 97th Ave, Edmonton, AB T5K 2B6; tel. (780) 427-2473; fax (780) 427-6016; e-mail library@assembly.ab.ca; internet www.assembly.ab.ca/lao/library; f. 1906; parliamentary library of 413,940 vols and documents; extensive colln of most Alberta weekly newspapers; Librarian SANDRA E. PERRY; publs *New Books in the Library* (10 a year), *Selected Periodical Articles List* (10 a year).

Parkland Regional Library: 5404-56 Ave, Lacombe, AB T4L 1G1; tel. (403) 782-3850; fax (403) 782-4650; e-mail psilver@prl.ab.ca; internet www.prl.ab.ca; f. 1959; serves 145 school and public library service points; Dir PATRICIA SILVER.

Provincial Archives of Alberta: 8555 Roper Rd, Edmonton, AB T6E 5W1; tel. (780) 427-1750; fax (780) 427-4646; e-mail paa@gov.ab.ca; internet www.cd.gov.ab.ca/paa; f. 1963; collns of non-current Alberta govt records, private papers, church records, municipal records, photographs, taped oral history interviews, films, videotapes and maps pertaining to the history of Alberta; special colln of Western Canadiana, local histories and archival literature (10,000 vols); thematic exhibitions; Dir and Provincial Archivist LESLIE LATTA-GUTHRIE.

University of Alberta Library: 5-07 Cameron Library, Edmonton, AB T6G 2J8; tel. (403) 492-3790; fax (403) 492-8302; f. 1909; 4,809,303 vols, 3,690,989 microforms; Chief Librarian ERNIE INGLES; Dir KAREN ADAMS; publ. *Library Editions* (2 a year).

University of Calgary Library: 2500 University Drive NW, Calgary, AB T2N 1N4; tel. (403) 220-5953; fax (403) 282-1218; e-mail libinfo@ucalgary.ca; internet library.ucalgary.ca; f. 1966; 7,678,394 items (2,540,294 print items, 3,528,108 microforms, 1,430,467 maps and aerial photographs, 179,525 audiovisual items), 2,917 m of archives; University Librarian H. THOMAS HICKERSON.

British Columbia

British Columbia Archives: 655 Belleville St, Victoria, BC V8W 9W2; tel. (250) 387-1952; fax (250) 387-2072; e-mail access@bcarchives.gov.bc.ca; internet www.bcarchives.gov.bc.ca; f. 1893; 71,000 items of printed material, 7,000 linear metres of MSS and government records, 5,000,000 photographs, 9,000 paintings, 35,000 maps, charts and architectural plans, 25,000 hours of sound recordings, 4,000 cans of moving images; Provincial Archivist GARY A. MITCHELL.

Fraser Valley Regional Library: Headquarters: 34589 Delair Rd, Abbotsford, BC V2S 5Y1; tel. (604) 859-7141; fax (604) 852-5701; e-mail jean.dirksen@fvrl.bc.ca; internet www.fvrl.bc.ca; f. 1930; 23 brs; 733,000 vols, 10,000 talking books; Chief Admin. Officer JEAN DIRKSEN.

Greater Victoria Public Library: 735 Broughton St, Victoria, BC V8W 3H2; tel. (250) 382-7241; fax (250) 382-7125; internet www.gvpl.ca; f. 1864; 940,749 vols; CEO SANDRA ANDERSON.

Legislative Library: Parliament Buildings, Victoria, BC V8V 1X4; tel. (250) 387-6510; fax (250) 356-1373; internet www.llbc.leg.bc.ca; f. 1863; 200,000 vols; Dir JANE TAYLOR.

Public Library InterLINK: c/o Burnaby Public Library, 7252 Kingsway, Burnaby, BC V5E 1G3; tel. (604) 517-8441; fax (604) 517-8410; e-mail plilink@moon.bcpl.gov.bc.ca; internet www.bcpl.gov.bc.ca/interlink; f. 1994; a federation of 17 autonomous public libraries sharing resources and services and providing open access to all member libraries to all area residents; special services: audio books for the visually impaired (37,000 vols), multilingual books, staff training videotapes, children's educational videotapes; Man. of Operations RITA AVIGDOR.

Simon Fraser University, W. A. C. Bennett Library: 8888 University Blvd, Burnaby, BC V5A 1S6; tel. (604) 291-3265; fax (604) 291-3023; e-mail libhelp@sfu.ca; internet www.lib.sfu.ca; f. 1965; 1,214,111 vols, 937,181 microforms; University Librarian LYNN COPELAND.

University of British Columbia Library: Vancouver, BC V6T 1Z1; tel. (604) 822-3871; fax (604) 822-3893; internet www.library.ubc.ca; f. 1915; 14 brs; 4,600,000 vols, 5,000,000 microforms, 44,722 journal, e-journal and series subscriptions; Librarian CATHERINE QUINLAN.

Vancouver Island Regional Library: Headquarters: 6250 Hammond Bay Rd, Box 3333, Nanaimo, BC V9R 5N3; tel. (250) 758-4697; fax (250) 758-2482; e-mail virl@virl.bc.ca; internet virl.bc.ca; f. 1936; 37 brs; 1,172,571 vols; Exec. Dir PENNY GRANT.

Vancouver Public Library: 350 West Georgia St, Vancouver, BC V6B 6B1; tel. (604) 331-3600; fax (604) 331-4080; e-mail info@vpl.ca; internet www.vpl.ca; f. 1887; 2,000,000 vols; 21 brs; City Librarian PAUL WHITNEY.

Vancouver School of Theology Library: 6050 Chancellor Blvd, Vancouver, BC V6T 1X3; tel. (604) 822-9430; fax (604) 822-9372; e-mail geraldt@vst.edu; internet www.vst.edu; f. 1971; 85,000 vols; Librarian GERALD TURNBULL.

Manitoba

Archives of Manitoba: 200 Vaughan St, Winnipeg, MB R3C 1T5; tel. (204) 945-3971; fax (204) 948-2008; e-mail archives@gov.mb.ca; internet www.gov.mb.ca/archives/index.html; f. 1884; 5,500 linear ft private MSS, 65,000 linear ft Manitoba government and court records, 8,000 linear ft Hudson's Bay Co Archives records, 130,000 architectural drawings, 1,200,000 photographs, 32,000 maps, 300 paintings, 5,500 prints and drawings, 7,000 sound records; special collections: Red River Settlement and Red River Disturbance, Lt-Governors' papers, Winnipeg General Strike, Canadian Airways Ltd, Archives of the Ecclesiastical Province of Rupert's Land, records of local govts and school divisions, Archives of Manitoba legal and judicial history; Archivist of Manitoba GORDON DODDS.

Legislative Library of Manitoba: Rm 100, 200 Vaughan St, Winnipeg, MB R3C 1T5; tel. (204) 945-4330; fax (204) 948-1312; e-mail legislative_library@gov.mb.ca; internet www.manitoba.ca/leglib; f. 1870; 1.4m. items; special collns: Canadian, Western Canadian and Manitoba history, economics, political and social sciences, urban, rural and ethnic language newspapers of Manitoba, govt publs; Legislative Librarian SUSAN BISHOP; publs *Monthly Checklist of Manitoba Government Publications* (also available online), *Selected New Titles* (10 a year, also available online).

Manitoba Culture, Heritage and Tourism: Public Library Services: Unit 200, 1525 1st St, Brandon, MB R7A 7A1; tel. (204) 726-6590; fax (204) 726-6868; e-mail pls@gov.mb.ca; f. 1972; 172,688 vols, 4,000 government publs, 5,286 talking books, 7,139 video tapes; Dir (vacant); publ. *Manitoba Public Library Statistics* (annually).

Manitoba Justice Great Library: 331-408 York Ave, Winnipeg, MB R3C 0P9; tel. (204) 945-1958; fax (204) 948-2138; internet www.cbsc.org; f. 1877; 50,000 vols; Librarian R. GARTH NIVEN.

University of Manitoba Libraries: Winnipeg, MB R3T 2N2; tel. (204) 474-9881; fax (204) 474-7583; e-mail marina_webster@umanitoba.ca; internet www.umanitoba.ca/libraries; f. 1877; collections supporting 18 faculties and 4 schools; special collections: Slavic, Icelandic; 2,000,000 vols, 520,000 government publications, 157,500 other print items (maps, performance music, text book collection, etc.), 2,700,000 microforms, 31,000 audio-visual items, 9,000 serial titles; Dir CAROLYNNE PRESSER.

New Brunswick

Mount Allison University Libraries and Archives: Mount Allison University, 49 York St, Sackville, NB E4L 1C6; tel. (506) 364-2562; fax (506) 364-2617; e-mail bgnassi@mta.ca; internet www.mta.ca/library; f. 1840; 454,000 vols, 515,000 microforms, 282,000 documents; University Librarian BRUNO GNASSI.

Bibliothèque Champlain (Université de Moncton): Moncton, NB E1A 3E9; tel. (506) 858-4012; fax (506) 858-4086; internet www.umoncton.ca/champ; f. 1965; general academic collections; 518,000 vols, 1,555 current periodicals; Head Librarian SONIA POULIN.

Harriet Irving Library: University of New Brunswick, POB 7500, Fredericton, NB E3B 5H5; tel. (506) 453-4740; fax (506) 453-4595; e-mail library@unb.ca; internet www.lib.unb.ca; f. 1790; 1,141,807 vols and 3,103,813 (equivalent vols) microforms; Dir of Libraries JOHN D. TESKEY.

Legislative Library: Box 6000, Fredericton, NB E3B 5H1; tel. (506) 453-2338; fax (506) 444-5889; e-mail library.biblio-info@gnb.ca; f. 1841; 35,000 vols; Librarian MARGARET PACEY.

Provincial Archives of New Brunswick: POB 6000, Fredericton, NB E3B 5H1; tel. (506) 453-2122; fax (506) 453-3288; e-mail provincial.archives@gnb.ca; internet archives.gnb.ca; f. 1968; 25,000 ft of govt and private textual documents, 250,000 photographs, 300,000 cartographic and architectural documents, 4,600 hours audio recordings, 1,800 video tapes and films, 60,000 microfiches, 14,000 reels microfilm; Provincial Archivist MARION BEYEA.

Newfoundland and Labrador

Newfoundland and Labrador Public Libraries Service: 48 St George's Ave, Stephenville, NL A2N 1K9; tel. (709) 643-0900; fax (709) 643-0925; internet www.nlpubliclibraries.ca; f. 1934; 1,300,000 vols at 96 libraries; provides public library services incl. books, magazines, newspapers, large-print and spoken-word books, computers with free internet access, digital cameras; Provincial Dir SHAWN TETFORD.

The Rooms Corporation Provincial Archives: POB 1800, Station C, St John's, NL A1C 5P9; located at: 9 Bonaventure Ave, St John's, NL A1C 5P9; tel. (709) 757-8030; fax (709) 757-8031; e-mail information@therooms.ca; internet www.therooms.ca; f. 1960, refounded 2005; provincial govt archives, genealogical collection, cartographic and architectural archives, sports archives, film and still images; Dir GREG WALSH.

Provincial Resource Library: Arts and Culture Centre, St John's, NL A1B 3A3; tel. (709) 737-3946; fax (709) 737-2660; f. 1934; Newfoundland Collection open to the public; back-up resource library for the provincial system; 181,604 vols (incl. Newfoundland Collection); Man. MICHELLE WALTERS.

Queen Elizabeth II Library: Memorial University of Newfoundland, St John's, NL A1B 3Y1; tel. (709) 737-7428; fax (709) 737-2153; e-mail rhellis@mun.ca; internet www.library.mun.ca/; f. 1925; 1,724,807 vols, 1,977,982 microform units; Librarian RICHARD H. ELLIS.

Nova Scotia

Angus L. Macdonald Library: St Francis Xavier University, Box 5000, Antigonish, NS B2G 2W5; tel. (902) 867-2267; fax (902) 867-5153; internet libmain.stfx.ca/newlib; f. 1853; 762,000 vols; special collection: Celtic history, literature and language; Librarian LYNNE MURPHY; publ. *The Antigonish Review* (quarterly).

Dalhousie University Libraries: Halifax, NS B3H 4H8; tel. (902) 494-3601; internet www.library.dal.ca; 1,844,000 vols; University Librarian WILLIAM R. MAES.

Halifax Regional Library: 60 Alderney Drive, Dartmouth, NS B2Y 4P8; tel. (902) 490-5744; fax (902) 490-5762; internet www.halifax.library.ns.ca; f. 1996; 1,027,418 books, 1,588 current periodicals, 33 microfilms, 197 films/filmstrips, 210 CD-ROMs, 56,215 sound recordings, 7,622 talking books, 63,171 videos, 272 alternate format videos; CEO JUDITH HARE.

Nova Scotia Archives and Records Management: 6016 University Ave, Halifax, NS B3H 1W4; tel. (902) 424-6060; fax (902) 424-0628; e-mail nsarm@gov.ns.ca; internet www.gov.ns.ca/nsarm; f. 1929; provincial govt records; family, political, personal and business papers; maps, plans, charts; photographs, paintings; microfilmed files of leading newspapers; film, television and sound archives; research library of about 50,000 titles; Provincial Archivist BRIAN SPEIRS.

Nova Scotia Legislative Library: Province House, 1726 Hollis St, Halifax, NS B3J 2P8; tel. (902) 424-5932; fax (902) 424-0220; e-mail murphymf@gov.ns.ca; internet www.gov.ns.ca/legislature/LIBRARY; f. 1862; Nova Scotiana Collection; 170,000 vols; Librarian MARGARET MURPHY; publ. *Publications of the Province of Nova Scotia* (monthly and annually).

Vaughan Memorial Library, Acadia University: POB 4, 50 Acadia St, Wolfville, NS B4P 2P6; tel. (902) 585-1249; fax (902) 585-1748; internet library.acadiau.ca; f. 1843; 800,000 vols and govt documents; University Librarian SARA LOCHHEAD.

Nunavut Territory

Nunavut Public Library Services: POB 189A, Iqaluit, NU X0A 0H0; tel. (867) 979-5400; fax (867) 979-1373; e-mail nuic@gov.nu.ca; br. libraries in Arctic Bay, Arviat, Baker Lake, Cambridge Bay, Clyde River, Igloolik, Kugluktuk, Pangnirtung, Pond Inlet and Rankin Inlet.

Branch library:

Iqaluit Centennial Library: POB 189A, Iqaluit, NU X0A 0H0; tel. (867) 979-5400; fax (867) 979-1373; e-mail nuic@gov.nu.ca; T. H. Manning archival collection of polar materials; Librarian TORI-LYNNE EVANS.

Ontario

Canada Institute for Scientific and Technical Information (CISTI): Montreal Rd, M-55, Ottawa, ON K1A 0R6; tel. (613) 993-9251; fax (613) 993-7619; e-mail info.cisti@nrc.ca; internet cisti-icist.nrc-cnrc.gc.ca; operated by National Research Council Canada; f. 1974, fmrly National Science Library; focal point of a national scientific and technical information network; resources of over 50,000 serial titles are made available through loan, copies and consultation; information services include operation of a national computerized current awareness service and an online table of contents service (CISTI SOURCE), Customized Literature Search Service providing custom bibliographies on requested topics, MEDLARS co-ordinator for Canada; Dir. Gen. BERNARD DUMOUCHEL.

Canadian Agriculture Library: Sir John Carling Bldg, Agriculture and Agri-Food Canada, Ottawa, ON K1A 0C5; tel. (613) 759-7068; fax (613) 759-6643; internet www.agr.gc.ca/cal; f. 1910; 1,000,000 vols, 22,200 serials; specializes in agriculture, biology, biochemistry, plant science, entomology, veterinary medicine, food sciences, economics; serves 24 field libraries; Dir DANIELLE JACQUES.

Canadian Postal Archives: 344 Wellington St, Ottawa, ON K1A 0N3; tel. (613) 992-3744; internet www.collectionscanada.ca; f. 1971; Chief CIMON MORIN.

Carleton University Library: 1125 Colonel By Drive, Ottawa, ON K1S 5B6; tel. (613) 520-2735; fax (613) 520-2750; e-mail university.librarian@carleton.ca; internet www.library.carleton.ca; f. 1942; 1,782,483 vols, 10,486 serial subscriptions, 1,513,714 items (microforms, maps, audio-visual items), 12,025 electronic journals; Librarian MARTIN FOSS.

Departmental Library, Indian and Northern Affairs Canada: Ottawa, ON K1A 0H4; tel. (819) 997-0811; fax (819) 953-5491; e-mail reference@ainc-inac.gc.ca; internet www.ainc-inac.gc.ca; f. 1966; 100,600 vols, 20,000 bound periodicals, 2,000 rare books, 3,500 government documents, 3,000 microfilm reels, incl. records relating to Indian Affairs; service to Native people, researchers, libraries; Chief Librarian JULIA FINN.

Earth Sciences Information Centre: 601 Booth St, Ottawa, ON K1A 0E8; tel. (613) 996-3919; fax (613) 943-8742; e-mail esic@nrcan.ac.ca; internet www.nrcan.gc.ca/ess/esic; f. 1842; component of Natural Resources Canada; interlibrary loans, on-line retrospective searching; 400,000 vols, 260,000 geological maps; Head of ESIC Services PAULINE MCDONALD (acting).

Hamilton Public Library: 55 York Blvd, POB 2700, Station A, Hamilton, ON L8N 4E4; tel. (905) 546-3200; fax (905) 546-3202; e-mail kroberts@hpl.ca; internet www.hpl.hamilton.on.ca; f. 1889; special collections of local history, Canadiana to 1950, govt documents; 1,492,467 vols and 1,876 periodicals; 24 br. libraries; 2 bookmobiles; Chief Librarian KEN ROBERTS.

John W. Graham Library, University of Trinity College: 6 Hoskin Ave, Toronto, ON M5S 1H8; tel. (416) 978-2653; fax (416) 978-2797; internet www.trinity.utoronto.ca; f. 1851; 185,000 vols; special collections: Strachan Collection, SPCK Collection, Churchill Collection, G8 Collection, Anglican Church of Canada; Librarian LINDA WILSON CORMAN.

Library and Archives Canada: 395 Wellington St, Ottawa, ON K1A 0N3; tel. (613) 996-5115; fax (613) 995-6274; e-mail reference@lac-bac.gc.ca; internet www.collectionscanada.ca; f. 2004, following merger of National Library of Canada (f. 1953) and National Archives of Canada (f. 1872); includes Canadian Postal Archives; depository of all Canadian publications, public records and historical material; 71,000 films and documentaries, 2.5m. architectural drawings, plans and maps, 21.3m. photographic images, 270,000 hours of audio and visual recordings, 343,000 works of art, Canadian sheet music and 200,000 recordings related to music in Canada, Canadian postal archive, medals, seals, posters and coats of arms, national, provincial and territorial newspapers, periodicals, MSS, microforms and theses, more than 1m. portraits of Canadians; Librarian and Archivist Dr IAN E. WILSON; publs *Annual Review*, *The Archivist/L'Archiviste* (annually).

Library of Parliament: Ottawa, ON K1A 0A9; tel. (613) 995-1166; fax (613) 992-1269; e-mail info@parl.gc.ca; internet www.parl.gc.ca; f. 1867; 407,500 vols in integrated systems, 510,000 microforms; Parliamentary Librarian RICHARD PARÉ; publs *Quorum* (daily, during session), *Articles* (weekly during session), *Current Issue Reviews* (monthly).

Library of the Pontifical Institute of Medieval Studies: 4th Fl., 113 St Joseph St, Toronto, ON M5S 1J4; tel. (416) 926-7146; e-mail james.farge@utoronto.ca; internet www.pims.ca; f. 1929; principal resource for the Institute's Mellon Fellows, post-doctoral candidates for the Licence in Medieval Studies, and for doctoral students of the University of Toronto Centre for Medieval Studies; 120,000 vols, 210 periodicals, 10,000 folios of MSS on photostats, 250,000 folios of MSS on microfilm; Pres. JAMES K. MCCONICA; Librarian JAMES K. FARGE.

London Public Library: 251 Dundas St, London, ON N6A 6H9; tel. (519) 661-4600; fax (519) 663-5396; internet www.lpl.london.on.ca; f. 1894; 982,581 vols, 110,813 non-book materials; CEO DARREL SKIDMORE (acting).

McMaster University Libraries: 1280 Main St West, Hamilton, ON L8S 4L6; tel. (905) 525-9140; fax (905) 546-0625; e-mail libinfo@mcmaster.ca; internet www.mcmaster.ca/library; f. 1887; 1,717,799 vols, 1,488,305 microform items, 175,000 non-print items, 10,976 linear metres archival material, 6,292 serial subscriptions; contains among others Vera Brittain archives, Bertrand Russell archives and 18th c. collection; Librarian GRAHAM R. HILL.

National Defence Headquarters Library: 101 Colonel By Drive, Ottawa, ON K1A 0K2; tel. (613) 995-2213; fax (613) 995-8176; e-mail Grier.jb@forces.ca; internet www.collectionscanada.ca; f. 1903; library services, inter-library loans, information retrieval; 30,000 vols incl. military Canadiana; Librarian J. BRIAN GRIER.

Natural Resources Canada, Headquarters Library: 580 Booth St, Ottawa, ON K1A 0E4; tel. (613) 996-8282; fax (613) 992-7211; internet www.nrcan-rncan.gc.ca; f. 1958; 65,000 vols and bound periodicals, 3,000 reports; mineral and energy economics, policy, taxation, legislation and statistics, energy conservation; Dir S. E. HENRY.

Ontario Legislative Library: Legislative Bldg, Queen's Park, Toronto, ON M7A 1A9; tel. (416) 325-3900; fax (416) 325-3925; f. 1867; 58,440 monograph titles; Exec. Dir (vacant).

Ottawa City Archives: 1st Floor, Bytown Pavilion, 111 Sussex Drive, Ottawa, ON K1N 1J1; tel. (613) 580-2424; e-mail archives@ottawa.ca; f. 1976; repository of public records of civic administration and other historical material; special collections: genealogy, heraldry, local railroad history; City Archivist DAVE BULLOCK.

Ottawa Public Library (Bibliothèque publique d'Ottawa): 120 Metcalfe St, Ottawa, ON; tel. (613) 580-2940; fax (613) 567-4013; e-mail feedback@biblioottawalibrary.ca; internet www.biblioottawalibrary.ca; f. 1906; 2,500,000 vols; Chief Librarian BARBARA CLUBB.

Queen's University Library: Kingston, ON K7L 5C4; tel. (613) 533-2519; fax (613) 533-6362; internet library.queensu.ca; f. 1842; 2,380,675 vols, 3,792,624 other items; University Librarian PAUL WIENS.

Supreme Court of Canada Library: 301 Wellington St, Ottawa, ON K1A 0J1; tel. (613) 996-8120; fax (613) 952-2832; e-mail library@scc-csc.gc.ca; internet www.scc-csc.gc.ca/aboutlibrary/index_e.html; 200,000 vols; Dir ROSALIE FOX.

Toronto Public Library: 789 Yonge St, Toronto, ON M4W 2G8; tel. (416) 393-7131; internet www.tpl.toronto.ca; 99 brs; 1,200,000 vols; City Librarian JOSEPHINE BRYANT; publ. *What's On* (4 a year).

University of Ottawa Library Network: 65 University Private, Ottawa, ON K1N 6N5; tel. (613) 562-5883; fax (613) 562-5195; e-mail wwwbib@uottawa.ca; internet www.biblio.uottawa.ca; f. 1848; library contains more than 4.5m. items incl. more than 1,250,000 monographs, 19,000 current periodicals, 1,900,000 microforms; tens of thousands of music scores, sound recordings and audiovisual items; hundreds of thousands of slides, aerial photographs, maps and govt publications; electronic resources; University Chief Librarian LESLIE WEIR.

University of Toronto Libraries: Toronto, ON M5S 1A5; tel. (416) 978-8580; fax (416) 978-7653; e-mail utweb@library.utoronto.ca; internet www.library.utoronto.ca; f. 1891; 10,342,574 vols, 32,485 serials, 5,372,000 microforms, 1,695,060 other non-book items (maps, sound recordings, audio-visual, manuscript titles, aerial photographs, etc.), 32,912 online journals; Chief Librarian CAROLE MOORE.

University of Waterloo Library: 200 University Ave, Waterloo, ON N2L 3G1; tel. (519) 888-4567; fax (519) 888-4320; f. 1957; 2,006,887 vols, 1,707,697 microfiches, 7,017 periodicals, 13,011 online periodicals; University Librarian K. MARK HASLETT; publ. *Bibliography* (irregular).

University of Western Ontario Libraries: London, ON N6A 3K7; tel. (519) 661-2111; fax (519) 661-3911; internet www.lib.uwo.ca; f. 1878; 3,077,381 vols, 34,745 serials, 3,883,392 microforms; 2,183,098 other items; University Librarian JOYCE C. GARNETT.

Victoria University Library: 71 Queen's Park Crescent East, Toronto, ON M5S 1K7; tel. (416) 585-4471; fax (416) 585-4591; e-mail vic.library@utoronto.ca; internet library.vicu.utoronto.ca; f. 1836; 275,000 vols; special colls: humanities (general), religions and theology; William Blake and his contemporaries, S. T. Coleridge, V. Woolf, Bloomsbury Group, Hogarth Press, Tennyson, Wesleyana, Northrop Frye, Norman Jewison Archive, E. J. Pratt; George Baxter (books and prints); 19th-century Canadian Poetry, French and French-Canadian Literature (Rièse colln); folklore; Senator Keith Davey; posters (Paris riots of 1968); contemporary poets; Chief Librarian ROBERT C. BRANDEIS.

Prince Edward Island

Confederation Centre Public Library: Box 7000, Charlottetown, PE C1A 8G8; tel. (902) 368-4642; fax (902) 368-4652; e-mail ccpl@gov.pe.ca; f. 1773; 72,000 vols; Librarian BARB KISSICK.

Prince Edward Island Provincial Library: POB 7500, Morell, PE C0A 1S0; tel. (902) 961-7320; fax (902) 961-7322; e-mail plshq@gov.pe.ca; internet www.library.pe.ca; f. 1933; 310,000 vols in regional system of 23 rural and town public libraries; Provincial Librarian ALLAN GROEN.

Public Archives and Records Office: POB 1000, Charlottetown, PE C1A 7M4; tel. (902) 368-4290; fax (902) 368-6327; e-mail archives@gov.pe.ca; internet www.gov.pe.ca/educ/archives/archives_index.asp; f. 1964; Provincial Archivist JILL MACMICKEN-WILSON.

Québec

Bibliothèque de l'Assemblée Nationale du Québec: Edifice Pamphile-Lemay, Québec, QC G1A 1A3; tel. (418) 643-4408; fax (418) 641-2635; e-mail bibliotheque@assnat.qc.ca; internet www.assnat.qc.ca; f. 1802; law and legislation, political science, parliamentary procedure, history, official publications of Quebec, newspapers; 955,000 vols; Chief Librarian PHILIPPE SAUVAGEAU; publs *Bulletin* (quarterly), *Journal des débats: index* (irregular), *Débats de l'Assemblée législative 1867–1962* (irregular), *Rapport Annuel* (annually).

Bibliothèque de la Compagnie de Jésus: Collège Jean-de-Brébeuf, L. B4–25, 3200 Chemin Côte-Ste-Catherine, Montréal, QC H3T 1C1; tel. (514) 342-9342; f. 1882; books from 16th–18th c., Canadiana; philosophy, scripture, theology; 195,000 vols; Dir C.-R. NADEAU.

Bibliothèque de l'Université Laval: Cité Universitaire, Québec, QC G1K 7P4; tel. (418) 656-3344; fax (418) 656-7897; internet www.bibl.ulaval.ca; f. 1852; 5,000,000 vols, 24,422 periodicals, 19,500 films, 140,000 maps; Dir Dr SYLVIE DELORME; publ. *Répertoire des vedettes-matière* (CD-ROM, 2 a year).

Bibliothèque de Montréal: 1210 Sherbrooke Est, Montréal, QC H2L 1L9; tel. (514) 872-5171; fax (514) 872-1626; internet www2.ville.montreal.qc.ca/biblio; f. 1902; 2,102,600 vols, of which 51,700 books, 20,757 pamphlets, 43,900 pictures and photographs, 1,547 maps, 3,035 slides and 99,200 microforms related to Canada and its history; 23 brs, 1 sound-recording library and 1 bookmobile; Dir JACQUES PANNETON.

Bibliothèque et Archives Nationales du Québec: 2275 rue Holt, Montréal, QC H2G 3H1; tel. (514) 873-1100; fax (514) 873-9312; e-mail info@banq.qc.ca; internet www.banq.qc.ca; f. 1967; merged with Archives Nationales du Québec (f. 1920) 2006; 4m. vols; Conservation Centre and Grande Bibliothèque in Montréal; 9 archive centres (Gatineau, Trois-Rivières, Montréal, Québec, Chicoutimi, Sherbrooke, Rouyn-Noranda, Rimouski, Sept-Iles); Chair and CEO LISE BISSONNETTE; publ. *À rayons ouverts* (4 a year).

Bibliothèques de l'Université de Montréal: CP 6128, Succursale Centre-ville, Montréal, QC H3C 3J7; tel. (514) 343-6905; fax (514) 343-6457; e-mail biblios@bib.umontreal.ca; internet www.bib.umontreal.ca; f. 1928; 3,106,971 vols, 21,087 current periodicals, 1,650,557 microforms, 189,164 audiovisual documents; Dir of Libraries JEAN-PIERRE CÔTÉ.

CAIJ – Montréal: Palais de Justice, 17e étage, 1 rue Notre-Dame est, local 17.50, Montréal, QC H2Y 1B6; tel. (514) 866-2057; fax (514) 879-8592; e-mail mlaforce@caij.qc.ca; f. 1828; 100,000 vols; Librarian MIREILLE LAFORCE.

Concordia University Libraries: 1455 de Maisonneuve Blvd West, Montréal, QC H3G 1M8; tel. (514) 848-2424; fax (514) 848-2882; e-mail judya@alcor.concordia.ca; internet library.concordia.ca; f. 1974; 2,730,000 vols; Dir WILLIAM CURRAN.

Fraser-Hickson Institute, Montréal: 4855 Kensington Ave, Montréal, QC H3X 3S6; tel. (514) 489-5301; fax (514) 489-5302; e-mail frances@fraserhickson.qc.ca; internet www.fraserhickson.qc.ca; f. 1870; 150,000 vols; collection and archives of Institut Canadien of Montréal, collection of archives of the Mercantile Library Association (Montréal); Chief Librarian FRANCES W. ACKERMAN; publs *Annual Report*, *Newsletter* (irregular).

McGill University Libraries: 3459 McTavish St, Montréal, QC H3A 1Y1; tel. (514) 398-4734; fax (514) 398-7356; e-mail doadmin.library@mcgill.ca; internet www.library.mcgill.ca; f. 1855; 14 libraries, 3.4m. vols, 13,876 current periodicals, 1,762,783 microtexts, 668,981 govt documents; Dir JANINE SCHMIDT.

Osler Library: McGill Univ., McIntyre Medical Sciences Bldg, 3655 Promenade Sir William Osler, 3rd Floor, Montréal, QC H3G 1Y6; tel. (514) 398-4475; fax (514) 398-5747; e-mail osler.library@mcgill.ca; internet www.mcgill.ca/osler-library; f. 1929; history of medicine and allied sciences; 61,201 vols; History of Medicine Librarian PAMELA MILLER; publ. *Newsletter*.

Saskatchewan

Regina Public Library: 2311 12th Ave, Regina, SK S4P 3Z5; tel. (306) 777-6000; fax (306) 949-7260; internet www.rpl.regina.sk.ca; f. 1908; 9 brs; 695,000 items; Library Dir A. A. CAMERON; publs *Community Information Catalogue*, *Regina Public Library Film Catalogue*.

Saskatchewan Legislative Library: 234-2405 Legislative Dr., Regina, SK S4S 0B3; tel. (306) 787-2276; fax (306) 787-1772; e-mail reference@legassembly.sk.ca; internet www.legassembly.sk.ca/leglibrary; f. 1878; 144,027 vols, 498,406 microforms, 1,082 other non-print items; social sciences, law and history; noted for its collection of government documents and Western Canadiana; Legislative Librarian (vacant); publ. *Checklist of Saskatchewan Government Publications* (monthly).

Saskatchewan Provincial Library: 1945 Hamilton St, Regina, SK S4P 2C8; tel. (306) 787-2972; fax (306) 787-2029; internet www.lib.sk.ca; f. 1953; co-ordinates library services in the province; 97,000 vols, specializing in library science, multilingual books and last copy fiction; Provincial Librarian JOYLENE CAMPBELL.

Saskatoon Public Library System: 311 23rd St East, Saskatoon, SK S7K 0J6; tel. (306) 975-7558; fax (306) 975-7542; internet www.publib.saskatoon.sk.ca; f. 1913; 7 brs, 1 booktrailer; 803,061 vols, 20,166 audio-cassettes, 39,291 videos, 44,278 compact discs, 904 current periodical titles; local history room; Dir of Libraries ZENON ZUZAK.

University of Saskatchewan Libraries: 3 Campus Drive, Saskatoon, SK S7N 5A4; tel. (306) 966-5927; fax (306) 966-5932; internet www.library.usask.ca; f. 1909; main library and 6 brs with 1,871,000 vols, 15,423 current journals, 3,054,000 items on microform, 427,902 govt documents and pamphlets, Russell Green music MSS, Adam Shortt collection of Canadiana, Conrad Aiken Collection of Published Works; Dir of Libraries F. WINTER.

Wapiti Regional Library: 145 12th St East, Prince Albert, SK S6V 1B7; tel. (306) 764-0712; fax (306) 922-1516; e-mail wapiti@panet.pa.sk.ca; f. 1950; 55 brs; 448,000 vols; Dir KEVIN PHILLIP.

Museums and Art Galleries

Alberta

Banff Park Museum: Box 900, Banff, AB T1L 1K2; tel. (403) 762-1558; fax (403) 762-1565; e-mail banff.vrc@pc.gc.ca; internet www.parkscanada.gc.ca/lnh-nhs/ab/banff/index-e.asp; f. 1895; natural and human history of the park; Historic Sites Supervisor STEVE MALINS.

Buffalo Nations Museum: 1 Birch Ave (Box 850), Banff, AB T1L 1A8; tel. (403) 762-2388; fax (403) 760-2803; e-mail buffalonations@telus.net; f. 1951 as Luxton Museum; promotes education and awareness of the Northern Plains and Canadian Rockies Indians; natural history exhibits; Pres. HAROLD HEALY.

Department of Earth and Atmospheric Sciences Museum, University of Alberta: Edmonton, AB T6G 2E3; tel. (780) 492-2518; fax (780) 492-2030; internet easweb.eas.ualberta.ca; f. 1912; geology, meteorites, mineralogy, invertebrate and vertebrate palaeontology, stratigraphy; Collections and Museums Administrator A. J. LOCOCK.

Edmonton Art Gallery: 2 Sir Winston Churchill Square, Edmonton, AB T5J 2C1; tel. (780) 422-6223; fax (780) 426-3105; e-mail info@edmontonartgallery.com; internet www.edmontonartgallery.com; f. 1924; Canadian and international drawing, painting, printmaking, sculpture and photography; Exec. Dir TONY LUPPINO.

Glenbow Museum: 130 9th Ave SE, Calgary, AB T2G 0P3; tel. (403) 268-4100; fax (403) 265-9769; e-mail glenbow@glenbow.org; internet www.glenbow.org; f. 1966; western Canadian and foreign cultural history, ethnology, military history, mineralogy and art; library of 100,000 vols, archives of 1,250,000 photos and negatives; Pres. Dr ROBERT R. JANES; Chair., Board of Governors ROBERT G. PETERS; publ. *Experience* (3 a year).

Medicine Hat Museum and Art Gallery: 1302 Bomford Crescent, Medicine Hat, AB T1A 5E6; tel. (403) 502-8580; fax (403) 502-8589; e-mail mhmag@medicinehat.ca; internet www.city.medicine-hat.ab.ca/cityservices/museum; f. 1967; cultural and natural history, palaeontology, and primitive peoples representative of south-east Alberta; art gallery; monthly exhibits by Canadian and international artists.

Provincial Museum of Alberta: 12845 102nd Ave, Edmonton, AB T5N 0M6; tel. (780) 453-9100; fax (780) 454-6629; e-mail pstepney@mcd.gov.ab.ca; internet www.pma.edmonton.ab.ca; f. 1963; Alberta history, geology, natural history; Dir Dr PHILIP H. R. STEPNEY.

Royal Tyrrell Museum of Palaeontology: Box 7500, Drumheller, AB T0J 0Y0; tel. (403) 823-7707; fax (403) 823-7131; e-mail tyrrell.info@gov.ab.ca; internet www.tyrrellmuseum.com; f. 1985; collection, research, display and interpretation of fossils as evidence for history of life, with emphasis on famous dinosaur fauna of Alberta; resource management, vertebrate and invertebrate palaeontology, taphonomy, palynology, sedimentology, stratigraphy, preparation, illustration, administration; library of 50,000 vols, special biographical collection on Joseph Burr Tyrrell; 110,000 catalogued fossil specimens; field station in Dinosaur Provincial Park; UNESCO World Heritage Site; Dir BRUCE G. NAYLOR.

British Columbia

H. R. MacMillan Space Centre: 1100 Chestnut St, Vancouver, BC V6J 3J9; tel. (604) 738-7827; fax (604) 736-5665; e-mail dlivingstone@hrmacmillanspacecentre.com; internet www.hrmacmillanspacecentre.com; f. 1988; administers the H. R. MacMillan Space Centre, H. R. MacMillan Planetarium and Gordon Southam Observatory; multimedia astronomy shows, laser shows, exhibitions, Observatory activities, lectures, etc.; 3,500 mems; Exec. Dir DONNA LIVINGSTONE; publ. *Starry Messenger* (quarterly).

Helmcken House Museum: c/o Royal BC Museum, 675 Belleville St, Victoria, BC V8W 9W2; tel. (250) 356-7226; fax (250) 356-8197; internet www.royalbcmuseum.bc.ca; located in house built in 1852 for the surgeon Dr J. S. Helmcken (1824–1920); historic medical collection; Curator of Human History, Royal BC Museum LORNE HAMMOND.

Museum of Northern British Columbia: 100 1st Ave West, Prince Rupert, BC V8J 1A8; tel. (250) 624-3207; fax (250) 627-8009; e-mail mnbc@citytel.net; internet www.museumofnorthernbc.com; f. 1924; exhibits cover 10,000 years of human habitation, incl. First Nations culture, local pioneer history and natural history; art gallery; library of 800 vols (50 rare); Dir ROBIN WEBER; Curator SUSAN MARSDEN.

Royal British Columbia Museum: 675 Belleville St, Victoria, BC V8W 9W2; tel. (250) 356-7226; fax (250) 356-8197; e-mail reception@royalbcmuseum.bc.ca; internet www.royalbcmuseum.bc.ca; f. 1886; contains reference collections and exhibits pertaining to natural history and human history of BC; CEO PAULINE RAFFERTY; publ. *Discovery* (newsletter, 3 a year).

Vancouver Art Gallery: 750 Hornby St, Vancouver, BC V6Z 2H7; tel. (604) 662-4700; fax (604) 682-1086; e-mail info@vanartgallery.bc.ca; internet www.vanartgallery.bc.ca; f. 1931; Canadian and foreign art by groundbreaking contemporary artists and major historical figures; library of 25,000 vols; Dir KATHLEEN BARTELS; publ. *Members' Newsletter* (3 a year).

Vancouver Maritime Museum: 1905 Ogden Ave, Vancouver, BC V6J 1A3; tel. (604) 257-8300; fax (604) 737-2621; e-mail genvmm@vmm.bc.ca; internet www.vmm.bc.ca; f. 1958; maritime history, local and international heritage vessels, RCMP *St Roch* Arctic patrol vessel, school programmes, lectures and summer festivals; library of 10,000 vols; Exec. Dir JAMES P. DELGADO; publ. *Signals* (quarterly).

Manitoba

Manitoba Museum of Man and Nature: 190 Rupert Ave, Winnipeg, MB R3B 0N2; tel. (204) 956-2830; fax (204) 942-3679; e-mail info@manitobamuseum.ca; f. 1965; human and natural history of Manitoba; planetarium; 'Touch the Universe' interactive science centre; library: *c.* 26,000 vols; Exec. Dir CLAUDETTE LECLERC; publ. *Happenings* (every 2 months).

Winnipeg Art Gallery: 300 Memorial Blvd, Winnipeg, MB R3C 1V1; tel. (204) 786-6641; fax (204) 788-4998; e-mail inquiries@wag.mb.ca; internet www.wag.mb.ca; f. 1912; exhibitions, lectures, films, performing arts, education programmes; library of 24,000 vols; Dir (vacant).

New Brunswick

Beaverbrook Art Gallery: POB 605, Fredericton, NB E3B 5A6; tel. (506) 458-8545; fax (506) 459-7450; e-mail emailbag@beaverbrookartgallery.org; internet www.beaverbrookartgallery.org; f. 1959; paintings; 18th-, 19th- and 20th-century English and continental paintings; 19th- and 20th-century Canadian paintings; 18th- and 19th-century English porcelain; English sculptures; medieval and Renaissance furniture, tapestries; Head, Programming and Communications LAURIE GLENN; publs *Tableau* (3 a year), *Annual Report*.

Fort Beauséjour – Fort Cumberland National Historic Site of Canada: 111 Fort Beauséjour Rd, Aulac, NB E4L 2W5; tel. (506) 364-5080; fax (506) 536-4399; e-mail fort.beausejour@pc.gc.ca; internet www.pc.gc.ca/beausejour; f. 1926; semi-restored ruins of a fort built by the French in 1751; barracks, underground casements and trenches overlooking the Bay of Fundy, the Tantramar marshes and extensive dykes; attached museum and visitor centre; Site Supervisor, Daily Operations JULIETTE MCLEOD.

Miramichi Natural History Museum: 149 Wellington St, Chatham NB E1N 1L7; fax (506) 773-6509; f. 1880; Curator KEN WEATHERBY.

New Brunswick Museum: 277 Douglas Ave, Saint John, NB E2K 1E5; tel. (506) 643-2300; fax (506) 643-2360; e-mail nbmuseum@nbm-mnb.ca; internet www.nbm-mnb.ca; f. 1842; archives, library, fine art, decorative art, natural science and history; Dir JANE FULLERTON.

York-Sunbury Historical Society Museum: POB 1312, Fredericton, NB E3B 5C8; tel. (506) 455-6041; fax (506) 458-8741; e-mail yorksun@nbnet.nb.ca; f. 1932; domestic and military exhibits of Fredericton and area; housed in British Officers' Quarters of about 1840; Exec. Dir KATE MOSSMAN.

Newfoundland and Labrador

The Rooms Corporation Provincial Museum and Art Gallery: POB 1800, Station C, St John's, NL A1C 5P9; located at: 9 Bonaventure Ave , St John's, NL A1C 5P9; tel. (709) 757-8020 (museum); tel. (709) 757-8040 (art gallery); fax (709) 757-8021 (museum); fax (709) 757-8041 (art gallery); e-mail information@therooms.ca; internet www.therooms.ca; f. 1887, refounded 1999; museum contains exhibits in the fields of archaeology, ethnology, marine, natural, human and military history; art gallery contains 7,000 works, both historical and contemporary, produced primarily by Newfoundland and Labrador artists, and significant works by Canadian and international artists; Dir of Provincial Museum PENNY HOLDEN; Dir of Provincial Art Gallery SHAUNA MCCABE.

Subsidiary museums:

Mary March Regional Museum and Loggers' Exhibit: Grand Falls–Windsor, NL; tel. (709) 292-4522; fax (709) 292-4526; e-mail pwells@nf.aibn.com; internet www.nfmuseum.com; Curator PENNY WELLS.

Southern Newfoundland Seamen's Museum: Grand Bank, NL; tel. (709) 832-1484; fax (709) 832-2053; e-mail gwcrews@nf.aibn.com; internet www.nfmuseum.com; Curator GERALD CREWS.

Nova Scotia

Art Gallery of Nova Scotia: 1723 Hollis St, POB 2262, Halifax, NS B3J 3C8; tel. (902) 424-7542; fax (902) 424-7359; internet www.agns.gov.ns.ca; f. 1975; paintings, drawings, sculpture, prints, collection of Nova Scotia folk art; Dir and Chief Curator JEFFREY SPALDING.

Fort Anne National Historic Site and Museum: POB 9, Annapolis Royal, NS B0S 1A0; tel. (902) 532-2321; fax (902) 532-2232; e-mail sandra_dares@pch.gc.ca; internet www.pc.gc.ca; f. 1917; Superintendent Operations THERESA BUNBURY.

Fortress of Louisbourg National Historic Site: 259 Park Service Rd, Louisbourg, NS B1C 2L2; tel. (902) 733-2280; fax (902) 733-2362; e-mail louisbourg_info@pch.gc.ca; internet fortress.uccb.ns.ca; f. 1963; reconstruction and restoration project, including 18th c. period rooms and museum complex; archives and library collections of 18th c. French and North American colonial material; District Dir CAROL WHITFIELD.

Maritime Museum of the Atlantic: 1675 Lower Water St, Halifax, NS B3J 1S3; tel. (902) 424-7890; fax (902) 424-0612; e-mail mmalibry@gov.ns.ca; internet museum.gov.ns.ca/mma/; f. 1982; naval and merchant shipping history; 'Titanic' and Halifax explosion exhibitions; small boat collection; collection of 20,000 photographs and 5,000 books; Dir MICHAEL MURRAY.

Nova Scotia Museum of Natural History: 1747 Summer St, Halifax, NS B3H 3A6; tel. (902) 424-7370; fax (902) 424-0560; e-mail museum-info@gov.ns.ca; internet nature.museum.gov.ns.ca; f. 1868; collections, research and exhibits relating to natural history of Nova Scotia; Dir D. L. BURLESON.

Ontario

Art Gallery of Hamilton: 123 King St West, Hamilton, ON L8P 4S8; tel. (905) 527-6610; fax (905) 577-6940; e-mail info@artgalleryofhamilton.com; internet www.artgalleryofhamilton.com; f. 1914; 8,500 works, mainly Canadian paintings, sculpture and graphics; also art from the USA, UK and other European countries; library of 3,000 vols; Pres. and CEO LOUISE DOMPIERRE; publ. *Insights* (members' magazine, 3 a year).

Art Gallery of Ontario: 317 Dundas St W, Toronto, ON M5T 1G4; tel. (416) 979-6648; fax (416) 204-2713; e-mail pa_assistant@ago.net; internet www.ago.net; f. 1900; European and North American art since 15th c.; Inuit art in all forms; Henry Moore; research; library of 100,000 vols; Dir MATTHEW TEITELBAUM; Chief Curator DENNIS REID; publs *Annual Report*, *Members' Journal* (4 a year).

Canada Science and Technology Museum Corporation: POB 9724, Station T, Ottawa, ON K1G 5A3; tel. (613) 991-6090; fax (613) 990-3636; e-mail info@technomuses.ca; internet technomuses.ca; f. 1967; shows Canada's role in science and technology through displays such as: steam locomotives, vintage cars, cycles, carriages, household appliances, computers, communications and space technology, model ships, and through experiments, demonstrations, special exhibitions and educational programmes and an evening astronomy programme; the Corporation also includes the Canada Aviation Museum and the Canada Agriculture Museum; Pres. and CEO CHRISTOPHER TERRY; publs *Material History Review* (2 a year), *Curator's Choice* (also in electronic edition, irregular), *Collection Profile* (also in electronic edition, 11 a year).

Canadian Museum of Nature: POB 3443 Station D, Ottawa, ON K1P 6P4; tel. (613) 566-4700; fax (613) 364-4763; e-mail questions@mus-nature.ca; internet www.nature.ca; f. 1912; research and collns in the areas of evolution, mineralogy, botany, zoology and palaeobiology; houses National Herbarium, the Canadian Centre for Biodiversity, the Biological Survey of Canada and the Centre for Traditional Knowledge; library of 36,000 vols, 2,000 periodical titles (200 active subscriptions); Pres. and CEO JOANNE DICOSIMO.

Collingwood Museum: POB 556, 45 St Paul St, Collingwood, ON L9Y 4B2; tel. (705) 445-4811; fax (705) 445-9004; e-mail museum@collingwood.ca; f. 1904; display, programming, research, special events; Supervisor SUSAN WARNER (acting).

Dundurn Castle: 610 York Blvd, Hamilton, ON L8R 3H1; tel. (905) 546-2872; fax (905) 546-2875; former home of Sir Allan MacNab, Prime Minister of United Province of Canada 1854–56, built 1834, restored 1967; guided tours, special exhibits, period demonstrations; Curator WILLIAM NESBITT.

Jordan Historical Museum of the Twenty: 3802 Main St, Jordan, ON L0R 1S0; tel. (905) 562-5242; fax (905) 562-7786; e-mail jhmtchin@vaxxine.com; f. 1953; a collection illustrating life in the Twenty Mile Creek area since 1776; Curator HELEN BOOTH.

Museum London: 421 Ridout St N, London, ON N6H 5H4; tel. (519) 661-0333; fax (519) 661-2559; e-mail ramurray@museumlondon.ca; internet www.museumlondon.ca; f. 1940; 25,000 historical artefacts, incl. paintings, prints, drawings and sculptures; undertakes collection and conservation of fine art and artefacts; exhibitions, lectures, films, workshops, tours and live performances; 900 mems; Exec. Dir BRIAN MEEHAN; publ. *At the Museum* (quarterly).

Marine Museum of Upper Canada: Exhibition Place, Toronto, ON M5T 1R5; tel. (416) 392-1765; fax (416) 392-1767; e-mail can-thb@immedia.ca; f. 1959; operated by the Toronto Historical Board; preserves and interprets the marine history of Toronto, Toronto Harbour and Lake Ontario; collections include 1932 steam tug *Ned Hanlan* in dry dock; Curator JOHN SUMMERS.

National Arts Centre: 53 Elgin St, Box 1534, Station B, Ottawa, ON K1P 5W1; tel. (613) 996-5051; fax (613) 996-9578; e-mail jmorris@nac-cna.ca; internet www.nac-cna.ca; opened 1969; opera, theatre, studio, workshops, restaurant and reception halls; 700 performances a year; resident 46-piece orchestra; produces theatre, dance and music performances in French and English; Chair. Dr DAVID S. R. LEIGHTON; Pres. and CEO PETER HERRNDORF; publs *Annual Report*, *Calendar* (monthly).

National Gallery of Canada: 380 Sussex Drive, POB 427 Station A, Ottawa, ON K1N 9N4; tel. (613) 990-1985; fax (613) 993-4385; e-mail info@gallery.ca; internet national.gallery.ca; f. 1880; largest collection of Canadian art in the world; collns incl. large and important prints and drawings colln; historical and contemporary Canadian and international photography colln; Canadian art colln; Inuit colln; European colln; large contemporary colln; site incl. Canadian Museum of Contemporary Photography; operates largest travelling exhibition program in North America; library of 275,000 vols; Dir PIERRE THÉBERGE; publs *National Gallery of Canada Review* (annually), *Vernissage* (4 a year).

Ontario Science Centre: 770 Don Mills Rd, Toronto, ON M3C 1T3; tel. (416) 696-1000; fax (416) 696-3124; e-mail webmaster@osc.on.ca; internet www.ontariosciencecentre.ca; f. 1969; more than 600 exhibits in all fields of science and technology; library of 11,000 vols; CEO LESLEY LEWIS; Dir, Visitor Experience JENNIFER MARTIN.

Queen's University Museums: Miller Hall, Union St, Kingston, ON K7L 3N6; geology dept, tel. (613) 533-6767, f. 1901, Curator M. H. BADHAM; biology dept, tel. (613) 533-6160, f. 1880, Curator A. A. CROWDER; anatomy dept, tel. (613) 533-2600, f. 1854, Curator Dr M. G. JONEJA.

Royal Ontario Museum: 100 Queen's Park, Toronto, ON M5S 2C6; tel. (416) 586-8000; fax (416) 586-5863; e-mail info@rom.on.ca; f. 1912; worldwide art, archaeology, geology and natural history, modern Canadian life; library of 150,000 vols; Far Eastern Library 20,000 vols; Dir WILLIAM THORSELL; publ. *Rotunda* (quarterly).

Attached institution:

George R. Gardiner Museum of Ceramic Art: 111 Queen's Park, Toronto, ON M5S 2C7; tel. (416) 586-8080; fax (416) 586-8085; e-mail mail@gardinermuseum.com; internet gardinermuseum.com; f. 1984.

Stephen Leacock Museum: Old Brewery Bay, 50 Museum Rd, Orillia, ON; tel. (705) 329-1908; fax (705) 326-5578; e-mail leacock@mail.transdata.ca; internet www.transdata.ca/~leacock; f. 1957; summer home, correspondence, manuscripts, personal effects of Stephen Butler Leacock 1869–1944; Curator DAPHNE MAINPRIZE.

Tom Thomson Memorial Art Gallery: 840 1st Ave West, Owen Sound, ON N4K 4K4; tel. (519) 376-1932; fax (519) 376-3037; e-mail sreid@e-owensound.com; internet www.tomthomson.org; f. 1967; Tom Thomson paintings, memorabilia; changing exhibitions of historic and contemporary art; Dir and Curator STUART REID; publ. *Newsletter* (4 a year).

Upper Canada Village: R.R. 1, Morrisburg, ON K0C 1X0; tel. (613) 543-3704; fax (613) 543-2847; internet www.uppercanadavillage.com; f. 1961; living historical site; 45 restored buildings portraying a rural community *c.* 1866; library of 5,000 vols; special collection of 19th c. archival materials including family and business records, photographs and social history documents from the region of eastern Ontario; Man. DAVE DOBBIE (acting).

Prince Edward Island

Confederation Centre Art Gallery and Museum: 145 Richmond St, Charlottetown, PE C1A 1J1; tel. (902) 628-6111; fax (902) 566-4648; e-mail artgallery@confederationcentre.com; internet www.confederationcentre.com; f. 1964; nat. colln of 15,000 works of Canadian art since 19th century: paintings, drawings, prints, sculpture and photography; Harris Colln (paintings, drawings, MSS and records of Robert Harris, 1849–1919); temporary exhibitions on historical research and the contemporary artist; Dir JON TUPPER; Registrar and Curatorial Man. KEVIN RICE.

Québec

Canadian Centre for Architecture: 1920 rue Baile, Montréal, QC H3H 2S6; tel. (514) 939-7000; fax (514) 939-7020; e-mail ref@cca.qc.ca; internet www.cca.qc.ca; f. 1979 as a non-profit organization, recognized as a museum in 1989; research centre and museum; aims to advance knowledge and promote public understanding of architecture, its history, theory, practice, and role in society, through study programmes, exhibitions, publications, seminars, lectures and internships; library of 200,000 printed monographs, approx. 4,500 runs of periodicals, a number of architecture-related artifacts (including toys) and ephemera; Founding Dir and Pres. of the Board PHYLLIS LAMBERT.

Canadian Museum of Civilization: 100 Laurier St, POB 3100, Station B, Gatineau, QC J8X 4H2; tel. (819) 776-7173; fax (819) 776-7152; e-mail library@civilization.ca; internet www.civilization.ca; f. 1856; archaeology, physical anthropology, ethnology, linguistics, folk culture studies, history of Canada; study collections open to qualified researchers and general public; incl. Archaeological Survey of Canada, Canadian Centre for Folk Culture Studies, Canadian War Museum, Canadian Ethnology Service, Canadian Postal Museum, Canadian Children's Museum and other elements; library of 200,000 vols, of which 70,000 accessible to public; Pres. and CEO Dr VICTOR RABINOVITCH.

Insectarium de Montréal: 4581 rue Sherbrooke Est, Montréal, QC H1X 2B2; tel. (514) 872-1400; fax (514) 872-0662; e-mail insectarium@ville.montreal.qc.ca; internet www.ville.montreal.qc.ca/insectarium; f. 1990; collection of 150,000 insects; Dir GUY BÉLAIR.

McCord Museum of Canadian History: 690 Sherbrooke St West, Montréal, QC H3A 1E9; tel. (514) 398-7100; fax (514) 398-5045; e-mail info@mccord.mcgill.ca; internet www.musee-mccord.qc.ca; f. 1921; museum of Canadian social history with collections of Canadian ethnology, paintings, drawings, prints, costumes, decorative arts, toys, documents; Notman Photographic Archives containing 800,000 glass plates and prints; Exec. Dir Dr VICTORIA DICKENSON.

Montréal Biodôme: 4777 ave Pierre-de-Coubertin, Montréal, QC H1V 1B3; tel. (514) 868-3000; fax (514) 868-3065; e-mail biodome@ville.montreal.qc.ca; internet www.biodome.qc.ca; f. ; museum of the environment; live collns, containing more than 4,800 animals of 230 species, and 750 plants species in four recreated ecosystems found in the Americas; housed in the velodrome used for the 1976 Olympic Games; Dir RACHEL LÉGER.

Montreal Museum of Fine Arts: 1379 and 1380 Sherbrooke St West, Montréal, QC H3G 2T9; tel. (514) 285-1600; fax (514) 844-6042; e-mail webmaster@mbamtl.org; internet www.mmfa.qc.ca; f. 1860; permanent collection of paintings (European and Canadian), sculptures, decorative arts and drawings; art from Asia, Africa and Oceania; library: over 90,000 vols and slide library; Pres. BERNARD LAMARRE; Dir GUY COGEVAL; publ. *Collage* (3 a year).

Musée d'Art Contemporain de Montréal: 185 St Catherine St West, Montréal, QC H2X 3X5; tel. (514) 847-6212; fax (514) 847-6291; internet www.macm.org; f. 1964; exhibits contemporary Québec and international art; organizes multimedia events, art videos, art workshops, lectures, etc.; library of 37,221 vols and exhibition catalogues, 713 periodicals, 42,913 slides, 36,514 microfiches, 483 videos, 285 audio cassettes, 11,193 document files on artists, styles, movements, etc., and complete archives of Paul-Emile Borduas; Dir-Gen. MARCEL BRISEBOIS; Chief Curator PAULETTE GAGNON.

Musée de l'Amérique Française (Museum of French North America): 9 rue de l'Université, CP 460, succ., Haute-Ville, QC G1R 4R7; tel. (418) 692-2843; fax (418) 692-5206; e-mail archives@mcq.org; internet www.mcq.org; f. 1983; art and history of French North America; Museum Dir CLAIRE SIMARD; Archives Dir DANIELLE AUBIN.

Musée du Québec/Musée National des Beaux-Arts du Québec: Parc des Champs de Bataille, Québec, QC G1R 5H3; tel. (418) 643-2150; fax (418) 646-3330; e-mail info@mnba.qc.ca; internet www.mnba.qc.ca; f. 1933; paintings, sculptures, drawings, prints, photographs, decorative art objects, interior design pieces; colln of 24,000 items (paintings, sculptures, drawings, prints, photographs, decorative art objects, interior design pieces) relating to Québecois art and artists; Exec. Dir Dr JOHN R. PORTER.

Planétarium de Montréal: 1000 rue Saint-Jacques Ouest, Montréal, QC H3C 1G7; tel. (514) 872-4530; fax (514) 872-8102; e-mail info@planetarium.montreal.qc.ca; internet www.planetarium.montreal.qc.ca; f. 1966; astronomy, meteorite collection, museum; Dir PIERRE LACOMBE.

Redpath Museum: 859 Sherbrooke St West, Montréal, QC H3A 2K6; tel. (514) 398-4086; fax (514) 398-3185; e-mail marie.laricca@mcgill.ca; internet www.mcgill.ca/redpath; f. 1882; natural history, geology, mineralogy, paleontology, anthropology, herpetology, vertebrate and invertebrate zoology; Dir GRAHAM BELL.

Saskatchewan

MacKenzie Art Gallery: 3475 Albert St, Regina, SK S4S 6X6; tel. (306) 522-4250; fax (306) 569-8191; e-mail mackenzie@uregina.ca; internet www.mackenzieartgallery.ca; f. 1954; permanent colln of Canadian historical and contemporary art, int. art since the 19th century, permanent colln displays and travelling exhibitions; public programmes; library: Resource Centre of 3,500 vols; Dir KATE DAVIS; Curator TIMOTHY LONG; publs *At the MacKenzie* (quarterly), *@ the MacKenzie* (ezine, monthly).

Mendel Art Gallery and Civic Conservatory (Saskatoon Gallery and Conservatory Corporation): 950 Spadina Crescent East, POB 569, Saskatoon, SK S7K 3L6; tel. (306) 975-7610; fax (306) 975-7670; e-mail mendel@mendel.saskatoon.sk.ca; internet www.mendel.ca; f. 1964; Canadian and international art, exhibitions, permanent collection; library of 10,000 vols; Dir TERRY GRAFF; publ. *Folio* (6 a year).

Musée Ukraina Museum: 202 Ave M South, Saskatoon, SK S7M 2K4; tel. and fax (306) 244-4212; e-mail info@mum.ca; internet www.mum.ca; f. 1953; ethnographic collections representing the spiritual, material and folkloric culture of Ukraine; Dir EMELIA PANAMAROFF.

Prince Albert Historical Museum: 10 River St East, Prince Albert, SK S6V 8A9; tel. (306) 764-2992; e-mail historypa@citypa.com; f. 1923; run by Prince Albert Historical Soc. (also operates the Diefenbaker House Museum; the Evolution of Education Museum; and the Rotary Museum of Police and Corrections); local historical exhibits, early settlement, pioneers, Indian life; archives and photographic colln available for research; Pres. H. S. MAY.

Royal Saskatchewan Museum: College Ave and Albert St, Regina, SK S4P 3V7; tel. (306) 787-2815; fax (306) 787-2820; e-mail dbaron@gov.sk.ca; internet www.gov.sk.ca/rsm; f. 1906; Earth Sciences Gallery depicts 2.5 billion years of Saskatchewan's geological history; First Nations Gallery traces 12,000 years of aboriginal history and culture; Paleo Pit interactive gallery; Megamunch, a roaring robotic Tyrannosaurus rex; Life Sciences Gallery features the flora, fauna and landscapes of Saskatchewan's diverse ecoregions; Dir DAVID BARON.

Saskatchewan Western Development Museum: 2935 Melville St, Saskatoon, SK S7J 5A6; tel. (306) 934-1400; fax (306) 934-4467; e-mail info@wdm.ca; internet www.wdm.ca; f. 1949; exhibit brs at North Battleford, Moose Jaw, Saskatoon, and Yorkton; collection associated with the settlement of the Canadian West; agricultural machinery, early transport and household items; annual summer shows; George Shepherd Library of 15,000 historical vols; Exec. Dir DAVID KLATT; publ. *Sparks off the Anvil* (6 a year).

Universities and Colleges

ACADIA UNIVERSITY

Wolfville, NS B4P 2 R6Telephone: (902) 542-2201
Fax: (902) 585-1072
E-mail: public.affairs@acadiau.ca
Internet: www.acadiau.ca

Founded 1838
Provincial control
Language of instruction: English
Academic year: September to April

Chancellor: ARTHUR IRVING
President and Vice-Chancellor: Dr GAIL DINTER-GOTTLIEB
Academic Vice-President: Dr CYRUS MACLATCHY (acting)
Vice-President, Finance and Transport: GARY DRAPER
Vice-President, Growth and Operations: DOV BERCOVICI
Senior Director of Communications and Public Affairs: SCOTT ROBERTS
Registrar: ROSEMARY JOTCHAM (acting)
Librarian: SARAH LOCHHEAD

Library: see Libraries and Archives
Number of teachers: 211 full-time, 37 part-time
Number of students: 3,894 full-time

DEANS

Faculty of Arts: Dr BRUCE MATTHEWS
Faculty of Professional Studies: Dr GARY NESS (acting)
Faculty of Pure and Applied Sciences: Dr PAUL CABILIO (acting)
Faculty of Theology: Dr LEE MCDONALD
Research and Graduate Studies: Dr TOM ELLIS

PROFESSORS

ARCHIBALD, T., Mathematics
ASH, S., Business Administration
ASHLEY, T. R.
BAILET, D., French
BALDWIN, D., History
BARR, S. M., Geology
BAWTREE, M., English
BEDINGFIELD, E. W., Recreation and Kinesiology
BEST, J., French
BISSIX, G., Recreation and Kinesiology
BOOTH, P., Classics
BOWEN, K., Sociology
CABILIO, P., Mathematics
CAMERON, B. W., Geology
CONRAD, M. R., History
DABORN, G. R., Biology
DADSWELL, M., Biology
DAVIES, J. E., Economics
DAVIES, R. A., English
FISHER, S. F., Music
GRIFFITH, B., Education
HERMAN, T. B., Biology
HOBSON, P., Economics
HORVATH, P., Psychology
JOHNSTON, E. M., Nutrition

LATTA, B., Physics
LEITER, M. P., Psychology
LOOKER, E. D., Sociology
MACLATCHY, C. S., Physics
MCLEOD, W., Kinesiology
MATTHEWS, B., History
MOODY, B. M., History
MOUSSA, H., Economics
MULDNER, T., Computer Science
NESS, G., Recreation and Kinesiology
OGILVIE, K. K., Chemistry
OLIVER, L., Computer Science
O'NEILL, P. T. H., Psychology
PARATTE, H. D., French
PIPER, D., Education
PYRCZ, G. E., Political Science
RAESIDE, R. P., Geology
RIDDLE, P. H., Music
ROSCOE, J. M., Chemistry
ROSCOE, S., Chemistry
SACOUMAN, R. J., Sociology
SPARKMAN, R., Business
STEWART, I., Political Science
STEWART, R., English
STILES, D. A., Chemistry
SUMARAH, J., Education
SYMON, S., Psychology
TOEWS, D. P., Biology
TOMEK, I., Computer Science
TOWNLEY, P., Economics
TRITES, A. A., Theology
TRUDEL, A., Computer Science
TUGWELL, M., Economics
VAN WAGONER, N. A., Geology
VERSTRAETE, B. C., Classics
WILSON, R. S., Theology

AFFILIATED COLLEGE

Acadia Divinity College: Wolfville; f. 1968; on campus; under direction of Atlantic United Baptist Convention; degrees granted by the University; Principal L. MCDONALD.

UNIVERSITY OF ALBERTA

Edmonton, AB T6G 2M7
Telephone: (780) 492-3113
Fax: (780) 492-7172
E-mail: info@ualberta.ca
Internet: www.ualberta.ca

Founded 1908
Provincial control
Language of instruction: English (Faculté Saint-Jean: French)
Academic year: September to August
Chancellor: JOHN FERGUSON
President and Vice-Chancellor: Dr R. D. FRASER
Vice-President (Academic) and Provost: Dr CARL G. AMRHEIN
Vice-President (External Affairs): SUSAN L. GREEN
Vice-President (Facilities and Operations): DON HICKEY
Vice-President (Finance and Administration): PHYLLIS CLARK
Vice-President (Research): Dr R. GARY
Associate Vice-President and Registrar: C. BYRNE (acting)
Associate Vice-President (Learning Support Systems) and Director of Libraries: E. INGLES
Library: see Libraries
Number of teachers: 1,500
Number of students: 37,000
Publications: *Calendar* (annually), *Folio* (2 a month), *Report of the Board of Governors of the University of Alberta* (annually), *The New Trail* (quarterly)

DEANS AND DIRECTORS

Faculty of Agriculture, Forestry and Home Economics: IAN N. MORRISON
Faculty of Arts: DANIEL WOOLF
Faculty of Business: M. PERCY
Faculty of Education: Dr FERN SNART (acting)
Faculty of Engineering: DAVID T. LYNCH
Faculty of Law: DAVID PERCY
Faculty of Medicine and Dentistry: D. L. J. TYRELL
Faculty of Nursing: Prof. GENEVIEVE I. GRAY
Faculty of Pharmacy and Pharmaceutical Sciences: FRANCO M. PASUTTO
Faculty of Physical Education and Recreation: Dr MICHAEL MAHON
Faculty of Rehabilitation Medicine: ALBERT M. COOK
Faculty of Science: GREGORY J. TAYLOR
Faculty of Extension: Dr CHERYL MCWATTERS
Faculty of Graduate Studies and Research: MARK R. T. DALE
Faculté St-Jean: M. ARNAL
Augustana Faculty: ROGER I. EPP
School of Library and Information Studies: A. ALTMAN
School of Native Studies: Dr ELLEN BIELAWSKI

AFFILIATED COLLEGES

North American Baptist College: 11525-23 Ave, Edmonton, AB T6J 4T3; affiliated since 1988; offers first-year courses in liberal arts; Pres. Dr M. DEWEY.

St Joseph's College: Edmonton, AB T6G 2J5; affiliated 1926; Roman Catholic; courses in philosophy and Christian theology; Pres T. SCOTT.

St Stephen's College: Edmonton, AB T6G 2J6; affiliated 1909; theological school of United Church of Canada; offers its own courses to degree level and certain courses open to students of the University; Principal G. ROGER.

UNIVERSITY RESEARCH INSTITUTES AND CENTRES

Alberta Centre for Gerontology: Project Co-ordinator MARNIE WOOD.

Alberta Law Reform Institute: Dir Prof. PETER J. M. LOWN.

Alberta Microelectronic Centre: Pres. and CEO C. LUMB.

Applied Mathematics Institute: Dir Dr T. BRYANT MOODIE.

Canadian Centre for the Development of Instructional Computing: Dir Dr M. W. PETRUK.

Canadian Circumpolar Institute (CCI): Dir Dr C. HICKEY.

Canadian Co-ordinating Centre for Cardiovascular Research and VIGOUR: Nat. Co-ordinator Dr P. W. ARMSTRONG.

Canadian Institute of Ukrainian Studies: Dir Dr Z. E. KOHUT.

Centre for Advanced Study in Theoretical Psychology: Dir Dr L. P. MOS.

Centre for Constitutional Studies: Dir B. P. ELMAN.

Centre for Criminological Research: Dir T. HARTNAGEL (acting).

Centre for the Cross-Cultural Study of Health and Healing: Co-Dirs Dr L. SPITZER, Dr E. WAUGH.

Centre for Ethnomusicology: Dir Dr R. QURESHI.

Centre for Experimental Sociology: Dir Dr W. DAVID PIERCE.

Centre for Health Promotion Studies: Dir Dr M. STEWART.

Centre for International Business Studies: Dir Dr R. MIRUS.

Centre for International Education and Development: Dir S. H. TOH.

Centre for Mathematics, Science and Technology Education: Dir Dr D. W. BLADES.

Centre for Research in Applied Measurement and Evaluation: Dir W. T. ROGERS.

Centre for Research in Child Development: Dir Dr G. BISANZ.

Centre for Research for Teacher Education and Development: Dir Dr J. D. CLANDININ.

Centre for Studies in Clinical Education: Dir Dr V. HOLLIS.

Centre for Subatomic Research: Dir Dr J. L. PINFOLD.

C-FER Technologies Inc.: Pres. and CEO Dr P. R. JAMIESON.

Developmental Disabilities Centre: Dir Dr R. SOBSEY.

Devonian Botanic Garden: Dir Dr D. VITT.

Health Law Institute: Chair. M. M. LITMAN.

Institute of Geophysics, Meteorology and Space Physics: Dir Dr F. W. JONES.

Institute of Health Economics: Board Chair. D. F. MAZANKOWSKI.

International Ombudsman Institute: Dir DIANE CALLLAN.

Peter Jacyk Centre for Ukrainian Historical Research: Dir Dr F. E. SYSYN.

Population Research Laboratory: Dir Dr A. MCKINNON.

Prairie Centre of Excellence for Research on Immigration and Integration: Dir Dr B. ABU-LABAN.

Rehabilitation Research Centre: Dir Dr S. WARREN.

Research Institute for Comparative Literature: Dir Prof. M. V. DIMIC.

Surgical-Medical Research Institute: Dir Dr R. V. RAJOTTE.

Telecommunications Research Laboratories (TRLabs): President and CEO H. G. RAINBIRD.

Telehealth Technology Research Institute: Dir M. MIAZAKI.

Theoretical Physics Institute: Dir W. ROZMUS.

Water Resources Centre: Dir Dr D. CHANASYK.

Western Centre for Economic Research: Dir Dr E. J. CHAMBERS.

ATHABASCA UNIVERSITY

1 University Drive, Athabasca, AB T9S 3A3
Telephone: (780) 675-6100
Fax: (780) 675-6145
Internet: www.athabascau.ca

Founded 1970
Provincial control
'Open' university providing undergraduate and masters-level courses for adult, non-residential students, with emphasis on distance and online education
Language of instruction: English

Chairman, Governing Council: DAVID BURNETT
President: Dr FRITS PANNEKOEK (acting)
Vice-President (Academic): Dr DIETMAR KENNEPOHL
Vice-President (Finance and Administration): PAT EAGAR
Executive Director, External Relations: Dr STEPHEN MURGATROYD
Registrar: GILBERT PERRAS
Librarian: S. SCHAFER

Library of 143,261
Number of teachers: 258
Number of students: 29,542
Publications: *Aurora* (interviews with leading thinkers and writers), *Electronic Jour-*

nal of Sociology, *Globalization*, *IRRODDL* (research for Open and Distance Learning), *Radical Pedagogy*, *Sport and the Human Animal*, *Theory and Science*, *Trumpeter*

DIRECTORS

Centre for Computing and Information Systems: Dr MOHAMED ALLY
Centre for Distance Education: Dr BOB SPENCER
Centre for Global and Social Analysis: Dr MARY RICHARDSON
Centre for Graduate Education in Applied Psychology: Dr SANDRA COLLINS
Centre for Innovative Management: Dr LINDSAY REDPATH
Centre for Language and Literature: Dr ANNE NOTHOF
Centre for Learning Accreditation: DIANNE CONRAD (acting)
Centre for Nursing and Health Studies: Dr DONNA ROMYN
Centre for Psychology: Dr BOB HELLER
Centre for Science: Dr BURT VORHEES
Centre for State and Legal Studies: Dr EVELYN ELLERMAN
Centre for Work and Community Studies: Dr SHEILA GREAVES
Centre for World and Indigenous Knowledge and Research: Assoc. Prof. TRACEY LINDBERG
School of Business: DAVID ANNAND

AUGUSTANA UNIVERSITY COLLEGE

4901–46 Ave, Camrose, AB T4V 2R3
Telephone: (403) 679-1100
Fax: (403) 679-1129
E-mail: admissions@augustana.ca
Internet: www.augustana.ab.ca

Founded 1910; independent status 1987 (fmrly Camrose Lutheran College)
Private (Evangelical Lutheran Church) liberal arts college
Language of instruction: English
Academic year: September to May

President: D. E. LANGFORD
Academic Dean: ROGER I. EPP
Registrar: JONATHAN D. HAWKINS (acting)
Librarian: NANCY E. GOEBEL

Number of teachers: 57
Number of students: 965

CHAIRPERSONS OF DIVISIONS

Biology, Chemistry and Geography: NEIL C. HAAVE
Fine Arts: KEITH B. HARDER
History, Sociology and Political Studies: PETR MIREJOVSKY
Humanities: PHILIP M. MERKLINGER
Modern Languages: KIM I. FORDHAM
Physical Education: YVONNE M. BECKER
Physics and Mathematical Sciences: JONATHAN J. J. MOHR
Psychology, Economics and Management: VARGHESE A. MANALOOR

BISHOP'S UNIVERSITY

Lennoxville, QC J1M 1Z7
Telephone: (819) 822-9600
Fax: (819) 822-9661
E-mail: liaison@ubishops.ca
Internet: www.ubishops.ca

Founded 1843, constituted a university by Royal Charter 1853
Language of instruction: English
Academic year: September to May

Chancellor: SCOTT GRIFFIN
Vice-Chancellor and Principal: ROBERT POUPART
Vice-Principal: JONATHAN RITTENHOUSE
Vice-Principal, Administration and Finance: MARK MCLAUGHLIN
Registrar and Secretary-General (vacant)
Librarian: WENDY DURRANT
Dean of Student Affairs: BRUCE STEVENSON

Number of teachers: 100 full-time
Number of students: 2,600

Publication: *Journal of Eastern Township Studies* (2 a year)

DEANS

Faculty of Business Administration: Prof. WILLIAM J. ROBSON
Faculty of Humanities: STEPHEN SHEERAN
Faculty of Natural Science and Mathematics: N. BRAD WILLMS
Faculty of Social Sciences: ANTON F. DE MAN
School of Education: CATHERINE BEAUCHAMP

BRANDON UNIVERSITY

270 18th St, Brandon, MB R7A 6A9
Telephone: (204) 728-9520
Fax: (204) 726-4573
E-mail: president@brandonu.ca
Internet: www.brandonu.ca

Founded 1899; gained full autonomy July 1967
Public control
Language of instruction: English
Academic year: September to April

Chancellor: K. KAVANAGH
President: Dr LOUIS P. VISENTIN
Vice-President, Academic and Research: JEFF WILLIAMS
Vice-President, Administration and Finance: SCOTT J. B. LAMONT
Registrar: D. BOWER
Librarian: R. FOLEY

Number of teachers: 170
Number of students: 2,800 (full- and part-time)

Publications: *Abstracts of Native Studies*, *Alumni News* (quarterly), *Annual Report*, *Canadian Journal of Native Studies*, *Cross Cultural Psychology Bulletin*, Calendars of several faculties

DEANS AND DIRECTORS

Faculty of Arts: Dr SCOTT GRILLS
Faculty of Education: THOMAS MACNEILL
Faculty of Science: JANET S. WRIGHT
School of Health Studies: Dr L. ROSS
School of Music: Dr G. CARRUTHERS
Department of Rural Development: DOUG RAMSAY (acting)
First Nations and Aboriginal Counselling Program: Dr FYRE JEAN GRAVELINE

HEADS OF DEPARTMENTS

Faculty of Arts:
- Business Administration: Prof. R. PLAYTER
- Drama: Prof. J. FORSYTHE
- Economics: Prof. J. DOLECKI
- English: Dr R. KRAMER
- Fine Arts: Prof. C. CUTSCHALL
- History: Dr J. NAYLOR
- Languages: Dr M. FINKE
- Native Studies: Dr S. CORRIGAN
- Philosophy: Prof. P. GOSSELIN
- Political Science: Dr L. LIU
- Religion: Dr E. MILTON
- Sociology and Anthropology: Dr W. DEHANEY

Faculty of Education:
- Administration and Education Services: Dr A. NOVAK
- Education in Humanities: Dr T. MACNEILL
- Education in Mathematics and Sciences: Dr G. NEUFELD
- Physical Education and Recreation: Dr N. STANLEY
- Psychology and Foundations of Education: Dr L. FROST

Faculty of Science:
- Botany: Dr W. PATON
- Chemistry: Dr C. BELKE
- Geography: Dr E. HAQUE
- Geology: Dr L. QUINN
- Mathematics and Computer Science: Dr J. WILLIAMS
- Physics and Astronomy: Dr R. DONG
- Psychology: Prof. D. OLESON
- Zoology: Dr J. HARE

School of Music:
- Applied Programme: Prof. A. EHNES
- General Programme: Dr A. BOWER
- Music and Education: Prof. S. PIMENTAL

UNIVERSITY OF BRITISH COLUMBIA

Vancouver, BC V6T 1Z1
Telephone: (604) 822-2211
Fax: (604) 822-5785
E-mail: presubc@interchange.ubc.ca
Internet: www.ubc.ca

Founded 1908
Academic year: September to August

Chancellor: ALLAN MCEACHERN
President and Vice-Chancellor: MARTHA C. PIPER
Vice-Presidents: LORNE A. WHITEHEAD (Academic and Provost), T. SUMNER (Administration and Finance), DENNIS PAVLICH (External and Legal Affairs), (VACANT) (Research), BRIAN SULLIVAN (Students)
Registrar: R. A. SPENCER
Librarian: CATHERINE QUINLAN

Number of teachers: 1,870
Number of students: 31,331

Publications: *BC Asian Review* (annually), *BC Studies* (4 a year), *BC Studies: The British Columbian Quarterly* (4 a year), *Canadian Journal of Botany* (4 a year), *Canadian Journal of Civil Engineering* (6 a year), *Canadian Journal of Woman and the Law* (annually), *Canadian Literature* (4 a year), *PRISM International* (4 a year), *University Calendar* (winter and summer), *Yearbook of International Law*

DEANS

Faculty of Agricultural Sciences: M. QUAYLE
Faculty of Applied Science: M. ISAACSON
Faculty of Arts: NANCY GALLINI
Faculty of Commerce and Business Administration: DANIEL F. MUZYKA
Faculty of Dentistry: E. H. K. YEN
Faculty of Education: ROB TIERNEY
Faculty of Forestry: JOHN N. SADDLER
Faculty of Graduate Studies: FRIEDA GRANOT
College of Health Disciplines: JOHN H. V. GILBERT (Principal)
Faculty of Law: MARY ANNE BOBINSKI
Faculty of Medicine: GAVIN STUART
Faculty of Pharmaceutical Sciences: ROBERT D. SINDELAR
Faculty of Science: JOHN W. HEPBURN

DIRECTORS OF SCHOOLS

School of Architecture: C. MACDONALD
School of Audiology and Speech Science: Prof. JUDITH R. JOHNSTON
School of Community and Regional Planning: Prof. W. E. REES
School of Family and Nutritional Sciences: Prof. A. MARTIN-MATTHEWS
School of Human Kinetics: PETER CROCKER (acting)
School of Journalism: DONNA LOGAN
School of Library, Archival and Information Studies: Prof. EDIE RASMUSSEN
School of Music: JESSE READ
School of Nursing: SALLY THORNE

School of Rehabilitation Sciences: LESLEY BAINBRIDGE
School of Social Work: GRAHAM RICHES

PROFESSORS

Faculty of Agricultural Sciences

Department of Agroecology:

BLACK, A.
CHANWAY, C.
CHENG, K.
CHIENG, S.-T.
COPEMAN, R.
CRONK, Q.
ELLIS, B.
ISMAN, M.
JOLLIFFE, P.
LAVKULICH, L.
MCKINLEY, S.
MYERS, J.
RAJAMAHENDRAN, R.
SCHREIER, H.
SHACKLETON, D.
TAYLOR, I.
UPADHYAYA, M.
WEARY, O.

Department of Community and the Environment:

CONDON, P.
PATERSON, D.
QUAYLE, M.

Department of Food, Nutrition and Health:

BARR, S.
CHENG, K.
DURANCE, T.
KITTS, D.
LI-CHAN, E.
RAJAMAHENDRAN, R.
THOMPSON, J.
VAN VUUREN, H.
VERCAMMEN, J.

Faculty of Applied Science

School of Architecture:

BROCK, L.
COLE, R.
CONDON, P.
MACDONALD, C.
PATKAU, P.
WAGNER, G.
WALKEY, R.
WOJTOWICZ, J.

Department of Chemical and Biological Engineering:

BERT, J.
BOWEN, B.
CHIENG, S.
DUFF, S.
ENGLEZOS, P.
GRACE, J.
HATZIKIRIAKOS, S.
JIM JIM, C.
KEREKES, R.
LO, K.
OLOMAN, C.
PIRET, J.
SMITH, K.
WATKINSON, P.

Department of Civil Engineering:

ADEBAR, P.
BANTHIA, N.
FANNIN, R.
FOSCHI, R.
HALL, E.
HALL, K. J.
ISSACSON, M.
LAWRENCE, G.
MAVINIC, D.
MINDESS, S.
NAVIN, F.
RUSSELL, A.
SEXSMITH, R.
STEIMER, S.

Department of Electrical and Computer Engineering:

DAVIES, M.
DUMONT, G.
IVANOV, A.
JAEGER, N.
KRISHNAMURTHY, V.
LAWRENCE, P.
LEUNG, C.
LEUNG, V.
PULFREY, D.
SALEH, R.
WARD, R.

Department of Mechanical Engineering:

ALTINTAS, Y.
CALISAL, S.
CHERCHAS, D.
DE SILVA, C.
EVANS, R.
GADALA, M.
GREEN, S.
HILL, P.
HODGSON, M.
HUTTON, S.
RAJAPAKSE, N.
SALCUDEAN, M.
SASSANI, F.
SCHAJER, G.
YELLOWLEY, I.

Department of Metals and Materials Engineering:

DREISINGER, D.
POURSARTIP, A.
REED, R.
TROCZYNSKI, T.
TROMANS, D.

Department of Mining Engineering:

MEECH, J.
SCOBLE, M.
WILSON, W.

School of Nursing:

ACORN, S.
ANDERSON, J.
BOTTORFF, D.
CARTY, E.
HILTON, A.
JOHNSON, J.
PATERSON, B.
THORNE, S.

Faculty of Arts

Department of Anthropology:

MATSON, R.
MILLER, B.

Department of Art History, Visual Art and Theory:

COHODAS, M.
EDER, R.
GUILBAUT, S.
O'BRIAN, J.
WATSON, S.
WINDSOR-LISCOMBE, R.
LUM, K.

Department of Asian Studies:

DUKE, M.
NOSCO, P.
OBEROI, H.
SCHMIDT, J.
TAKASHIMA, K.-I.

Department of Classical, Near Eastern and Religious Studies:

BARRETT, A. A.
HARDING, P.
SULLIVAN, S.
TODD, R.
WILLIAMS, E.

Department of Economics:

COPELAND, B.
DIEWERT, E.
ESWARAN, M.
EVANS, R.
GREEN, D.
KOTWAL, A.
LEMIEUX, T.
PATERSON, D.
REDISH, A.
RIDDELL, C.

Department of French, Hispanic and Italian Studies:

BOCCASSINI, D.
HODGSON, R.
MCEACHERN, J.
RAOUL, V.
SARKONAK, R.
TESTA, C.
URRELLO, A.

Department of Geography:

BARNES, T.
CHURCH, M.
GREGORY, D.
HIEBERT, D.
LEY, D.
MCCLUNG, D.
MCKENDRY, I.
OKE, T.
PRATT, G.
ROBINSON, J.
SLAYMAKER, O.
STEYN, D.
STULL, R.
WYNN, G.

Department of Germanic Studies:

MORNIN, E.
PETERSEN, K.
STENBERG, P.
PETRO, P.

Department of History:

FRIEDRICHS, C.
KRAUSE, P.
LARY, D.
NEWELL, D.
RAY, A.
UNGER, R.
WARD, P.

School of Journalism:

LOGAN, D.

School of Library, Archival and Information Studies:

DURANTI, L.
HAYCOCK, K.
RASMUSSEN, E.

Department of Linguistics:

PULLEYBLANK, D.
STEMBERGER, J.
VATIKIOTIS-BATESON, E.

School of Music:

BENJAMIN, W.
BERINAUM, M.
BUTLER, G.
CHATMAN, S.
COOP, J.
DAWES, A.
HAMEL, K.
READ, J.
SHARON, R.
TENZER, M.

Department of Philosophy:

BEATTY, J.
IRVINE, A.
RUSSELL, P.
SAVITT, S.
SCHABAS, M.
WILSON, C.

Department of Political Science:

JOB, B.
JOHNSTON, R.
LASELVA, S.
MARANTZ, P.
MAUZY, D.
RESNICK, P.
TUPPER, A.
TENNANT, P.
WALLACE, M.

Department of Psychology:

ALDEN, L.
CHANDLER, M.
COREN, S.
DUTTON, D.
ENNS, J.
GORZALKA, B.
GRAF, P.
HAKSTIAN, R.
LEHMAN, D.
LINDEN, W.
PINEL, J.
TEES, R.
WALKER, L.
WARD, L.
WERKER, J.

School of Social Work and Family Studies:

CHRISTENSEN, C.
MARTIN-MATHEWS, A.
PERLMAN, D.
RUSSELL, M.
WHITE, J.

Department of Sociology:

CRRESE, G.
CURRIE, D.
ELLIOTT, B.
ERICSON, R.
GUPPY, N.
JOHNSON, G.
JOPPKE, C.
MATTHEWS, D.

Department of Theatre, Film and Creative Writing:

ALDERSON, S.
DURBACH, E.
MAILLARD, K.
MCWHIRTER, G.
GARDINER, R.
WASSERMAN, J.

Faculty of Dentistry

Department of Oral Biological and Medical Sciences:

BRUNETTE, D.
DONALDSON, D.
LARJAVA, H.
UITTO, V.-J.
OVERALL, C.
CLARK, C.
DIEWERT, V.
HANNAM, A.
LOWE, A.
YEN, E.

Department of Oral Health Sciences:

CLARK, C.
DIEWERT, V.
HANNAM, A.
LOWE, A.
MCENTEE, M.

Faculty of Education

Faculty of Curriculum Studies:

CHALMERS, F. G.
ERICKSON, G.
GASKELL, P.
IRWIN, R.
KINDLER, A.
PETERAT, L.
PIRIE, S.

Department of Educational and Counselling Psychology, and Special Education:

AMUNDSON, N.
ARLIN, M.
BORGEN, W.
BUTLER, D.
DANILUK, J.
KAHN, S.
LONG, B.
PORATH, M.
SIEGEL, L.
WESTWOOD, M.
YOUNG, R.
ZUMBO, B.

Department of Educational Studies:

ADAM-MOODLEY, K.
BARMAN, J.
BOSHIER, R.
BROWN, D.
FISHER, D.
KELLY, D.
PRATT, D. D.
ROMAN, L.
RUBENSON, K.
SCHUETZE, H.
SHIELDS, C.
SORK, T.
STRONG-BOAG, V.
UNGERLEIDER, C. S.

School of Human Kinetics:

CROCKER, P.
FRANKS, I.
MCKENZIE, D.
RHODES, E.
TAUNTON, J.

Faculty of Forestry:

AVRAMIDIS, S.
BARKER, J.
BARRETT, D.
BUNNELL, F.
CHAFWAY, C.
EVANS, P.
FANNIN, J.
GUY, R.
HALEY, D.
HOBERG, G.
INNES, J.
EL-KASSABY, Y.
KIMMINS, J.
KLINKA, K.
MARTIN, K.
MCLEAN, J.
MURTHA, P.
RITLAND, K.
RUDDICK, J.
VAN DER KAMP, B.

Faculty of Law:

BAKAN, J.
BLACK, W.
BLOM, J.
BOYD, S.
BOYLE, C.
BURNS, P.
ELLIOT, R.
FARQUHAR, K.
GRANT, I.
JACKSON, M.
LEBARON, L. M.
MCDOUGALL, B.
PATERSON, R.
PAVLICH, D.
PUE, W.
SHEPPARD, A.
WEILER, J.
YOUNG, C.

Faculty of Medicine

Department of Anatomy:

BRESSLER, B.
CHURCH, J.
CRAWFORD, B.
EMERMAN, J.
NAUS, C.
OVALLE, W.
SLONECKER, C.
VOGL, A.
WEINBERG, J.

School of Audiology and Speech Sciences:

JOHNSTON, J.
STAPELLS, D.

Department of Biochemistry and Molecular Biology:

BRAYER, G.
BROWNSEY, R.
CULLIS, P.
DEDHAR, S.
FINLAY, B.
MACGILLIVRAY, R.
MACKIE, G.
MAUK, A.
MCINTOSH, L.
MOLDAY, R.
ROBERGE, M.
SADOWSKI, I.

Department of Family Practice:

BASSETT, K.
BATES, J.
CALAM, B.
DONNELLY, M.
GRAMS, G.
GRZYBOWSKI, S.
KHAN, K.
KLEIN, M.
KUHL, D.
LIVINGSTONE, V.
MCKENZIE, D.
SCOTT, I.
TAUNTON, J.
WHITESIDE, C.
WIEBE, C.
WOOLLARD, R.

Department of Healthcare and Epidemiology:

BARER, M.
BLACK, C.
HERTZMAN, C.
KAZANJIAN, A.
KENNEDY, S.
MATHIAS, R.
SINGER, J.
SCHECHTER, M.
SHEPS, S.
TESCHKE, K.

Faculty of Medical Genetics:

BURGESS, M.
EAVES, C.
FIELD, L.
FRIEDMAN, J.
HALL, J.
HIETER, P.
JEFFERIES, W.
JURILOFF, D.
KAY, R.
MAGER, D.
MCGILLIVRAY, B.
MCMASTER, W.
ROSE, A.
SADOVNICK, A.

Department of Medicine:

ABBOUD, R.
BAI, T.
BEATTIE, B.
BIRMINGHAM, C.
BOWIE, W.
BRUNHAM, R.
CAIRNS, J.
CALNE, D.
CHOW, A.
EAVES, A.
EISEN, A.
ESDAILE, J.
FLEETHAM, J.
FREEMAN, H.
HO, V.
HUMPHRIES, R.
KEOWN, P.
KERR, C.
LAM, S.
LUI, H.
MCLEAN, D.
MANCINI, G.
MONTANER, J.
OGER, J.
OSTROW, D.
PAGE, G.
PARÉ, P.
PATY, D.
PELECH, S.
PRIOR, J.
QUAMME, G.
RABKIN, S.

Reiner, N.
Rivers, J.
Road, J.
Russell, J.
Schellenberg, R.
Schrader, J.
Schulzer, M.
Steinbrecher, U.
Stein, H.
Stiver, H.
Stoessl, J.
Sutton, R.
Tsui, J.
Walley, K.
Wang, Y.
Wong, N.
Wright, J.
Yeung, M.

Department of Physiology:

Baimbridge, K.
Buchan, A.
Fedida, D.
Naus, C. C.
McIntosh, C.
Pearson, J

Department of Radiology:

Müller, N.
Cooperberg, P.
Culham, G.
Li, D.
Lyster, D.
MacKay, A.
Munk, P.

Department of Surgery:

Warnock, G.

Faculty of Science

Department of Botany:

DeWreede, R.
Douglas, C.
Ganders, F.
Glass, A.
Green, B.
Griffiths, A.
Maddison, W.
Taylor, F.
Taylor, I.
Towers, G.
Turkington, R.

Department of Chemistry:

Andersen, R.
Blades, M.
Brooks, D.
Burnell, E.
Comisarow, M.
Dolphin, D.
Douglas, D.
Fleming, D.
Fryzuk, M.
Fyfe, C.
Gerry, M.
Hepburn, J.
Herring, G.
Legzdins, P.
McIntosh, L.
Mitchell, K.
Orvig, C.
Patey, G.
Piers, E.
Sawatzky, G.
Scheffer, J.
Shapiro, M.
Sherman, J.
Shizgal, B.
Storr, A.
Tanner, M.
Withers, S.

Department of Computer Science:

Ascher, U.
Booth, K.
Condon, A.
Friedman, J.
Kiczales, G.
Kirkpatrick, D.
Klawe, M.
Lakshmanan, L.
Little, J.
Lowe, D.
Mackworth, A.
Ng, R.
Pai, D.
Pippenger, N.
Poole, D.
Rosenberg, R.
Woodham, R.

Department of Earth and Ocean Sciences:

Andersen, R.
Bostock, M.
Bustin, M.
Clarke, G.
Clowes, R.
Fletcher, K.
Groat, L.
Harrison, P.
Healey, M.
Hsieh, W.
Hungr, O.
Ingram, G.
Oldenburg, D.
Russell, K.
Smith, L.
Smith, P.
Steyn, D.
Stull, R.
Taylor, M.
Ulrych, T.
Weis, D.

Department of Mathematics:

Anstee, R.
Bluman, G.
Boyd, D.
Carrell, J.
Fournier, J.
Ghoussoub, N.
Lam, K.
Loewen, P.
MacDonald, J.
Marcus, B.
Peirce, A.
Perkins, E.
Seymour, B.
Sjerve, D.
Slade, G.
Ward, M.

Department of Microbiology and Immunology:

Smit, J.
Spiegelman, G.
Hancock, R. E. W.
Kronstad, J. W.
Jefferies, W. A.
Teh, H.-S.
Weeks, G.

Department of Statistics:

Heckman, N.
Harry, J.
Petkau, J.
Van Eeden, C.
Zamar, R.
Zidek, J.

Department of Zoology:

Adamson, M.
Berger, J.
Blake, R.
Brock, H.
Gass, C.
Gosline, J.
Grigliatti, T.
Jones, D.
Milsom, W.
Moerman, D.
Myers, J.
Pauly, D.
Pitcher, T.
Randall, D.
Schluter, D.
Sinclair, T.
Smith, J.
Snutch, T.
Steeves, J.
Tetzlaff, W.
Walters, C.

Sauder School of Business

Division of Accounting:

Feltham, G.
Simunic, D.

Division of Finance:

Giammarino, R.
Hamilton, S.
Heinkel, R.
Kraus, A.
Levi, M.

Division of Law:

Wand, Y.

Division of Marketing:

Griffin, D.
Weinberg, C.

Division of Operations and Logistics:

Atkins, D.
Granot, D.
Granot, F.
McCormick, T.
Oum, T.
Puterman, M.
Queyranne, M.
Zhang, A.
Ziemba, W.

Division of Strategy and Business Economics:

Antweiler, W.
Boardman, A.
Brander, J.
Frank, M.
Helsley, R.
Nakamura, M.
Nemetz, P.
Ross, T.
Spencer, B.
Vertinsky, I.
Winter, R.

THEOLOGICAL COLLEGES

Carey Hall and Carey Theological College: 5920 Iona Drive, Vancouver, BC V6T 1J6; tel. 224-4308; internet www.careytheologicalcollege.ca; Baptist; Principal Dr B. F. Stelck.

Regent College: 5800 University Boulevard, Vancouver, BC V6T 2E4; tel. 224-3245; internet www.regent-college.edu; trans-denominational; Pres. Rod Wilson.

St Andrew's Hall: 6040 Iona Drive, Vancouver, BC V6T 2E8; tel. (604) 822-9720; Presbyterian; Dean Rev. B. J. Fraser.

St Mark's College: 5935 Iona Drive, Vancouver, BC V6T 1J7; tel. 224-3311; internet www.stmarkscollege.ca; Roman Catholic; Principal Dr John D. Dennison.

Vancouver School of Theology: 6000 Iona Drive, Vancouver, BC V6T 1L4; tel. (604) 228-9031; fax (604) 228-0189; internet www.vst.edu; an ecumenical school of theology, incorporated 1971; continues work of the Anglican Theological College of BC and Union College of BC; provides theological education for laymen, for future clergy and for graduates in theology; Principal Dr Kenneth MacQueen.

BROCK UNIVERSITY

500 Glenridge Ave, St Catharines, ON L2S 3A1

Telephone: (905) 688-5550
Fax: (905) 688-2789
E-mail: regist@brocku.ca
Internet: www.brocku.ca

Founded 1964
Provincial control
Academic year: September to April
Language of instruction: English

Chancellor: NED GOODMAN
President and Vice-Chancellor: JACK LIGHTSTONE
Vice-President Administration: STEVEN PILLAR
Provost and Vice-President Academic: R. T. BOAK
Registrar: BARB DAVIS
Librarian: M. GROVE

Library: Library of 1,559,824 items
Number of teachers: 592
Number of students: 17,453
Publications: *Calendar* (annual), *Surgite* (quarterly)

depts of Applied language studies, Biological sciences, Biochemistry, Biophysics, Biotechnology, Business—accounting, Business—finance, operations and information systems, Business—marketing, international business and strategy, Business—organizational behaviour, human resource management, entrepreneurship and ethics, Business economics, Canadian studies, Chemistry, Child and youth studies, Classics, Communications, popular culture and film, Community health sciences, Computer science, Computing and business, Dramatic arts, Earth sciences, Economics, Education—adult education, Education—centre for continuing teacher education, Education—graduate and undergraduate studies, Education—pre-service education, English language and literature, Geography, Great books/liberal studies, History, Interactive arts and sciences, Intercultural studies, International political economy, Mathematics, Medieval and Renaissance studies, Modern languages, literatures and cultures, Music, Neuroscience, Nursing, Oenology and viticulture, Philosophy, Physical education and kinesiology, Physics, Political science, Psychology, Recreation and leisure studies, Sociology, Sport management, Studies in art and culture, Tourism and environment, Visual arts, Women's studies

DEANS

Faculty of Business: MARTIN KUSY
Faculty of Education: JAMES HEAP
Faculty of Humanities: ROSEMARY HALE
Faculty of Physical Education and Recreation: JOHN CORLETT
Faculty of Science and Mathematics: IAN BRINDLE
Faculty of Social Sciences: DAVID SIEGEL
Faculty of Graduate Studies: MARILYN ROSE

UNIVERSITY OF CALGARY

2500 University Drive NW, Calgary, AB T2N 1N4
Telephone: (403) 220-5110
Fax: (403) 282-7298
E-mail: reginfo@ucalgary.ca
Internet: www.ucalgary.ca

Founded 1945 as a br. of the University of Alberta; gained full autonomy 1966
Language of instruction: English
Academic year: July to June

Chancellor: W. J. WARREN
President and Vice-Chancellor: HARVEY WEINGARTEN
Provost and Vice-President (Academic): R. B. BOND
Vice-President (External Relations): R. COONEY
Vice-President (Finance and Services): M. W. MCADAM
Vice-President (Research and International): D. R. SALAHUB
Registrar: D. B. JOHNSTON
Director, Information Resources: A. DAVIS (acting)
Chief Information Officer (Information Technologies): H. A. ESCHE
Chief Development Officer: G. D. DURBENIUK

Number of teachers: 2,410 (1,569 full-time, 841 part-time)
Number of students: 27,928 (23,414 full-time, 4,514 part-time)
Publications: *Abstracts of English Studies*, *Annual Report*, *Arctic Journal* (Arctic Institute of North America), *Ariel: Review of International English Literature*, *Calgary Alumni*, *Canadian Energy Research Institute publs* (irregular), *Canadian Ethnic Studies*, *Canadian and International Education* (2 a year), *Canadian Journal of Law and Society* (both annually), *Canadian Journal of Philosophy* (all 4 a year), *Classical Views – Echos du monde classique*, *International Journal of Man-Machine Studies* (monthly), *Journal of Child and Youth Care*, *Journal of Comparative Family Studies*, *Journal of Educational Thought* (all 3 a year), *University Gazette* (every 2 weeks)

DEANS

Faculty of Communication and Culture: K. SCHERF
Faculty of Education: A. V. LAGRANGE
Faculty of Engineering: S. C. WIRASINGHE
Faculty of Environmental Design: B. R. SINCLAIR
Faculty of Fine Arts: A. CALVERT
Faculty of Graduate Studies: W. L. VEALE
Faculty of Humanities: R. J. SMITH
Faculty of Kinesiology: R. F. ZERNICKE
Faculty of Law: P. A. HUGHES
Faculty of Medicine: D. G. GALL
Faculty of Nursing: M. E. CLINTON
Faculty of Science: P. M. BOORMAN
Faculty of Social Sciences: S. J. RANDALL
Faculty of Social Work: G. ROGERS
Haskayne School of Business: M. A. GRANDIN
Continuing Education: J. W. HUMPHREY (Dir)

PROFESSORS

ADDICOTT, J. F., Biological Sciences
ADDINGTON, D. E. N., Psychiatry
AGOPIAN, E. E., Music
ANDREWS, J. W., Division of Applied Psychology
ARCHER, C. I., History
ARCHER, D. P., Anaesthesia and Clinical Neurosciences
ARCHER, K. A., Political Science
ARCHIBALD, J. A., Linguistics
ARMSTRONG, G. D., Microbiology and Infectious Diseases
ARTHUR, N. M., Division of Applied Psychology
ASTLE, W. F., Surgery
ATKINSON, M. H., Medicine
AUER, R. N., Clinical Neurosciences and Pathology and Laboratory Medicine
AUSTIN, C. D., Social Work
BACK, T. G., Chemistry
BANKES, N. D., Law
BARCLAY, R. M. R., Biological Sciences
BARKER, K. E., Computer Science
BARRY, D., Political Science
BAUWENS, L., Mechanical Engineering
BECH-HANSEN, N. T., Medical Genetics and Surgery
BECKER, W. J., Clinical Neurosciences and Medicine
BEHIE, L. A., Chemical and Petroleum Engineering
BELENKIE, I., Medicine
BELL, A. G., Music
BELL, D. M., Music
BELYEA, B., English
BENEDIKTSON, H., Pathology and Laboratory Medicine
BENNETT, S., English
BENTLEY, L. R., Geology and Geophysics
BERCUSON, D. J., History
BERSHAD, D. L., Art
BEZDEK, K., Mathematics and Statistics
BIDDLE, F. G., Paediatrics and Biochemistry and Molecular Biology and Medical Genetics
BINDING, P. A., Mathematics and Statistics
BIRSS, V. I., Chemistry
BISZTRICZKY, T., Mathematics and Statistics
BLAND, B. H., Psychology
BOND, R. B., English
BOS, L. P., Mathematics and Statistics
BOSETTI, B. L., Education
BOWAL, P. C., Haskayne School of Business
BOYCE, J. R., Economics
BRADLEY, J., Computer Science
BRANNIGAN, A., Sociology
BRANT, R. F., Community Health Sciences
BRAY, R. C., Surgery
BRENKEN, B. A., Mathematics and Statistics
BRENT, D. A., Communication and Culture
BROWDER, L. W., Biochemistry and Molecular Biology and Oncology
BROWN, C. A., Law
BROWN, C. B., Medicine, Oncology, Biochemistry and Molecular Biology
BROWN, J. L. S., Environmental Design
BROWN, J. S., Music
BROWN, K., French, Italian and Spanish
BROWN, R. J., Geology and Geophysics
BROWN, T. G., Civil Engineering
BROWNELL, A. K. W., Clinical Neurosciences and Medicine
BRUCE, C. J., Economics
BRUEN, A. A., Mathematics and Statistics
BRUTON, L. T., Electrical and Computer Engineering
BULLOCH, A. G. M., Physiology and Biophysics
BURET, A. G., Biological Sciences
BURGESS, E. D., Medicine
BURKE, M. D., Mathematics and Statistics
BUTZNER, J. D., Paediatrics
CAIRNCROSS, J. G., Clinical Neurosciences
CAIRNS, K. V., Division of Applied Psychology
CAMERON, E., Art
CAMPBELL, G. W., French, Italian and Spanish
CAMPBELL, N. R. C., Medicine
CANNON, M. E., Geomatics Engineering
CARTER, S. A., History
CAVEY, M. J., Biological Sciences
CERI, H., Biological Sciences
CHACONAS, G., Biochemistry, Molecular Biology, Microbiology and Infectious Diseases
CHADEE, K., Microbiology and Infectious Diseases
CHANG, K.-W., Mathematics and Statistics
CHEN, S. R. W., Physiology, Biophysics, Biochemistry and Molecular Biology
CHINNAPPA, C. C., Biological Sciences
CHIVERS, T., Chemistry
CHUA, J. H., Haskayne School of Business
CHURCH, D. L., Pathology and Laboratory Medicine and Medicine
CHURCH, J. R., Economics
CLARK, A. W., Pathology and Laboratory Medicine and Clinical Neurosciences
CLARK, P. D., Chemistry
CLARKE, M. E., Paediatrics and Psychiatry
CLEVE, R. E., Computer Science
COCKETT, J. R. B., Computer Science
COELHO, V. A., Music
COLE, W. C., Pharmacology and Therapeutics
COLEMAN, H. D. J., Social Work
COLIJN, A. W., Computer Science
COLLINS, D. G., Social Work
COLLINS, J. R., Mathematics and Statistics
CONLY, J. M., Pathology and Laboratory Medicine
COOK, F. A., Geology and Geophysics
COOPER, F. B., Political Science

COPPES, M. J., Oncology and Paediatrics
CORENBLUM, B., Medicine
COUCH, W. E., Mathematics and Statistics
COWIE, R. L., Medicine and Community Health Sciences
CROSS, J. C., Biochemistry, Molecular Biology, Obstetrics and Gynaecology
CURRY, B., Pathology and Laboratory Medicine and Clinical Neurosciences
DAIS, E. E., Law
DANSEREAU, E. D. M., French, Italian and Spanish
DAVIES, J. M., Anaesthesia
DAVIES, W. K. D., Geography
DAVIS, R. C., English
DAVISON, J. S., Physiology and Biophysics
DAY, R. L., Civil Engineering
DEACON, P. G., Art
DELONG, K. G., Music
DEWEY, D. M., Paediatrics
DICKIN, J. P., Faculty of Communication and Culture
DICKINSON, J. A., Family Medicine and Community Health Sciences
DOBSON, K. S., Psychology
DORT, J. C., Surgery
DOWTY, A., Political Science
DRAPER, D. L., Geography
DUCKWORTH, K., Geology and Geophysics
DUGAN, J. S., Drama
DUGGAN, M. A., Pathology, Laboratory Medicine, Obstetrics and Gynaecology
DUNN, J. F., Radiology, Physiology and Biophysics
DUNSCOMBE, P. B., Oncology
DYCK, R. H., Psychology
EAGLE, C. J., Anaesthesia
EATON, B. C., Economics
EBERLY, W. M., Computer Science
EDWARDS, M. V., Music
EGGERMONT, J. J., Physiology and Biophysics and Psychology
EINSIEDEL, E. F., Communications and Culture
EL-BADRY, M. M., Civil Engineering
EL-GUEBALY, M. A., Psychiatry
EL-SHEIMY, N. M., Geomatics Engineering
ELHAJJ, R. S., Computer Science
ELLIOTT, R. J., Haskayne School of Business
ELOFSON, W. M., History
EMES, C. G., Kinesiology
ENGLE, J. M., Music
ENNS, E. G., Mathematics and Statistics
EPSTEIN, M., Mechanical and Manufacturing Engineering
ERESHEFSKY, M. F., Philosophy
ESLINGER, L. M., Religious Studies
FACCHINI, P. J., Biological Sciences
FARFAN, P. C. M., Drama and English
FATTOUCHE, M. T., Electrical and Computer Engineering
FAUVEL, O. R., Mechanical and Manufacturing Engineering
FEDIGAN, L. M., Anthropology
FERRIS, J. R., History
FEWELL, J. E., Obstetrics and Gynaecology, Paediatrics and Physiology and Biophysics
FICK, G. H., Community Health Sciences
FLANAGAN, T. E., Political Science
FLETCHER, W. A., Clinical Neurosciences and Surgery
FONG, T. C., Radiology
FORD, G. T., Medicine
FOREMAN, C. L., Music
FOREMAN, K. J., Drama
FOUTS, G. T., Psychology
FRANCIS, R. D., History
FRANK, A. W., Sociology
FRANK, C. B., Surgery
FRENCH, R. J., Physiology and Biophysics
FRIDERES, J. S., Sociology
FRIESEN, J. W., Faculty of Education
FRITZLER, M. J., Medicine, Biochemistry and Molecular Biology
FUJITA, D. J., Biochemistry and Molecular Biology
GABOR, P. A., Social Work
GAISFORD, J. D., Economics
GEDAMU, L., Biological Sciences
GETZ, D. P., Haskayne School of Business
GHALI, W. A., Medicine and Community Health Sciences
GHANNOUCHI, F., Electrical and Computer Engineering
GHENT, E. D., Geology and Geophysics
GILES, W. R., Physiology and Biophysics and Medicine
GILL, B., French, Italian and Spanish
GILL, M. J., Medicine
GILLIS, A. M., Medicine
GORDON, D. V., Economics
GORDON, T. M., Geology and Geophysics
GOREN, H. J., Biochemistry and Molecular Biology
GORESKY, G. V., Anaesthesia and Paediatrics
GRAHAM, J. R., Social Work
GRAVEL, R. A., Cell Biology and Anatomy
GREEN, F. H. Y., Pathology and Laboratory Medicine
GREENBERG, S., Computer Science
GU, P., Mechanical and Manufacturing Engineering
GUPTA, A., Management
HABIBI, H. R., Biological Science
HAGEN, N. A., Oncology and Medicine
HAJI, I. H., Philosophy
HALL, B. L., Social Work
HANLEY, D. A., Medicine
HANLEY, P. J., Medicine
HARASYM, P. H., Office of Medical Education and Community Health Sciences
HARDER, L. D., Biological Sciences
HARDING, T. G., Chemical and Petroleum Engineering
HARPER, T. L., Environmental Design
HART, D. A., Microbiology and Infectious Diseases, Medicine
HARTMAN, F. T., Civil Engineering
HASLETT, J. W., Electrical and Computer Engineering
HAWE, H. P., Community Health Sciences
HAWKES, R. B., Cell Biology and Anatomy
HAWKINS, R. W., Communication and Culture
HEBERT, Y. M., Faculty of Education
HECKEL, W., Greek and Roman Studies
HELMER, J. W., Archaeology
HENDERSON, C. M., Geology and Geophysics
HERMAN, R. J., Medicine
HERWIG, H. H., History
HERZOG, W., Kinesiology
HETTIARATCHI, J. P. A., Civil Engineering
HEXHAM, I. R., Religious Studies
HEYMAN, R. D., Faculty of Education
HIEBERT, B. A., Division of Applied Psychology
HILLER, H. H., Sociology
HO, M., Microbiology, Infectious Diseases and Medicine
HODGINS, D. C., Psychology
HOGAN, D. B., Medicine and Clinical Neurosciences and Community Health Sciences
HOLLENBERG, M. D., Pharmacology and Therapeutics
HU, B., Clinical Neurosciences, Cell Biology and Anatomy
HUBER, R. E., Biological Sciences
HUGHES, M. E., Law
HULL, R. D., Medicine
HULLIGER, M., Clinical Neurosciences and Physiology and Biophysics
HUNT, J. D., Civil Engineering
HUSHLAK, G. M., Art
HYNES, M. F., Biological Sciences
IRVINE-HALLIDAY, D., Electrical and Computer Engineering
ISMAEL, J. S., Social Work
ISMAEL, T. Y., Political Science
JACOB, J. C., Faculty of Education
JADAVJI, T., Microbiology and Infectious Diseases and Paediatrics
JAMESON, E., History
JARDINE, D. W., Faculty of Education
JARRELL, J. F., Obstetrics and Gynaecology
JEJE, A. A., Chemical and Petroleum Engineering
JENNETT, P. A., Office of Medical Education and Community Health Sciences
JIRIK, F. R., Biochemistry and Molecular Biology
JOHNSON, E. A., Biological Sciences
JOHNSON, J. M., Obstetrics and Gynaecology
JOHNSTON, R. H., Electrical and Computer Engineering
JOHNSTON, R. N., Biochemistry and Molecular Biology
JOLDERSMA, H., Germanic, Slavic and East Asian Studies
JONES, A. R., Medicine and Oncology
JONES, D. C., Faculty of Education
JONES, V. J., Haskayne School of Business
JORDAN, W. S., Music
JOY, M. M., Religious Studies
JULLIEN, G. A., Electrical and Computer Engineering
KALBACH, M. H., Sociology
KALER, K. V. I., Electrical and Computer Engineering
KANTZAS, A., Chemical and Petroleum Engineering
KAPLAN, B. J., Paediatrics
KARGACIN, G. J., Physiology and Biophysics
KARIM, G. A., Mechanical and Manufacturing Engineering
KATZENBERG, M. A., Archaeology
KAUFFMAN, S. A., Biological Sciences, Physics and Astronomy
KAWAMURA, L. S., Religious Studies
KEAY, B. A., Chemistry
KEENAN, T. P., Environmental Design
KEITH, D. W., Chemical and Petroleum Engineering and Economics
KEITH, R. C., Political Science
KELLNER, J. D., Paediatrics, Microbiology and Infectious Diseases
KEREN, M., Communication and Culture and Political Science
KERTZER, A. E., English
KERTZER, J. M., English
KLASSEN, J., Pathology and Laboratory Medicine and Medicine
KLINE, D. W., Psychology
KLINE, T. J., Psychology
KNEEBONE, R. D., Economics
KNOLL, P. J., Law
KNOPFF, R., Political Science
KNUDTSON, M. L., Cardiac Sciences and Medicine
KOOPMANS, H. S., Physiology and Biophysics and Psychology
KOOYMAN, B. P., Archaeology
KOSTYNIUK, R. P., Art
KRAUSE, F. F., Geology and Geophysics
KREBES, E. S., Geology and Geophysics
KUBES, P., Physiology and Biophysics and Medicine
KURTZ, S. M., Education
LACHAPELLE, G. J., Geomatics Engineering
LAFLAMME, C., Mathematics and Statistics
LAFRENIÈRE, R., Surgery
LAI, D. W. L., Social Work
LAING, W. J. H., Art
LAMOUREUX, M. P., Mathematics and Statistics
LANGE, I. R., Obstetrics and Gynaecology
LARTER, S. R., Geology and Geophysics
LAU, D. C. W., Medicine
LAWTON, D. C., Geology and Geophysics
LEAHY, D. A., Physics and Astronomy
LEE, S. S., Medicine
LEE, T. G., Environmental Design
LEES-MILLER, S. P., Biochemistry and Molecular Biology
LEON, L. J., Electrical and Computer Engineering
LEUNG, H. K. Y., Electrical and Computer Engineering
LEVIN, G. J., Music
LEVY, J. C., Law

LEVY, R. M., Environmental Design
LEWKONIA, R. M., Medicine and Paediatrics and Medical Genetics
LINES, L. R., Geology and Geophysics
LOUIE, T. J., Medicine, Microbiology and Infectious Diseases
LOUTZENHISER, R. D., Pharmacology and Therapeutics
LOVE, J. A., Environmental Design
LUCAS, A. R., Law
LUKASIEWICZ, S. A., Mechanical and Manufacturing Engineering
LUKOWIAK, K., Physiology and Biophysics
LYTTON, J., Biochemistry, Molecular Biology, Physiology and Biophysics
MACDONALD, D. L., English
MACINTOSH, B. R., Kinesiology
MACINTOSH, J. J., Philosophy
MACNAUGHTON, W. K., Physiology and Biophysics
MAES, M. A., Civil Engineering
MAHER, P. M., Haskayne School of Business
MAHONEY, K. E., Law
MAINI, B. B., Chemical and Petroleum Engineering
MAINS, P. E., Biochemistry and Molecular Biology
MANDIN, H., Medicine
MARTIN, R. H., Paediatrics and Medical Genetics
MARTIN, S. L., Law
MARTINUZZI, R., Mechanical and Manufacturing Engineering
MASH, E. J., Psychology
MATO, D., Art
MAURER, F. O., Computer Science
MCCALLUM, P. M., English
MCCAULEY, F. E. R., Biological Sciences
MCCLELLAND, R. W., Social Work
MCCONNELL, C. S., Art
MCCREADY, W. O., Religious Studies
MCCULLOUGH, D. T., Drama
MCGHEE, J. D., Biochemistry and Molecular Biology
MCGILLIS, R. F., English
MCGILLIVRAY, M. D., English
MCKENZIE, K. J., Economics
MCKEOUGH, A. M., Division of Applied Psychology
MCKINNON, J. G., Surgery and Oncology
MCMORDIE, M. J., Environmental Design, Communication and Culture
MCMULLAN, W. E., Haskayne School of Business
MCRAE, R. N., Economics
MCWHIR, A. R., English
MEDDINGS, J. B., Medicine
MEEUWISSE, W. H., Kinesiology
MEHROTRA, A. K., Chemical and Petroleum Engineering
MEHTA, S. A., Chemical and Petroleum Engineering
MIDHA, R., Clinical Neurosciences
MILONE, E. F., Physics and Astronomy
MINTCHEV, M. P., Electrical and Computer Engineering
MITCHELL, D. B., Communication and Culture
MITCHELL, I., Paediatrics
MITCHELL, L. B., Cardiac Science and Medicine
MITCHELL, S. H., Education
MOAZZEN-AHMADI, N., Physics and Astronomy
MOCQUAIS, P. Y. A., French, Italian and Spanish
MODY, C. H., Medicine, Microbiology and Infectious Diseases
MOHAMAD, A. A., Mechanical and Maufacturing Engineering
MOLLIN, R. A., Mathematics and Statistics
MOORE, R. G., Chemical and Petroleum Engineering
MORCK, D. W., Biological Sciences
MORTON, F. L., Political Science
MUELLER, J. H., Division of Applied Psychology
MUNRO, M. C., Haskayne School of Business
MURPHREE, J. S., Physics and Astronomy
MURRAY, R. W., Linguistics
MURRAY, S. C., Kinesiology
MUZIK, I., Civil Engineering
MYLES, S. T., Surgery and Clinical Neurosciences
NATION, J. G., Obstetrics and Gynaecology and Oncology
NAULT, B. R., Haskayne School of Business
NEU, D. E., Haskayne School of Business
NEUFELDT, A. H., Faculty of Education
NEUFELDT, R. W., Religious Studies
NICHOLSON, W. K., Mathematics and Statistics
NIELSON, N., Haskayne School of Business
NIGG, B. M., Kinesiology
NKEMDIRIM, L. C., Geography
NORTON, P. G., Family Medicine
NOSAL, M., Mathematics and Statistics
NOSEWORTHY, T. W., Community Health Sciences
OETELAAR, G. A., Archaeology
OKONIEWSKI, M., Electrical and Computer Engineering
OSBORN, G. D., Geology and Geophysics
OSLER, M. J., History
PARKER, J. R., Computer Science
PATTISON, D. R. M., Geology and Geophysics
PAUL, R., Chemistry
PEREIRA ALMAO, P. R., Chemical and Petroleum Engineering
PERL, A. D., Political Science
PERREAULT, J. M., English
PIERS, W. E., Chemistry
PINEO, G. F., Medicine and Oncology
PITTMAN, Q. J., Physiology and Biophysics
POLLAK, P. T., Medicine, Cardiac Sciences, Pharmacology and Therapeutics
PONAK, A. M., Haskayne School of Business
PONTING, J. R., Sociology
POON, M.-C., Medicine and Paediatrics
POST, J. R., Biological Sciences
POWELL, D. G., Family Medicine
PRICE, G. D., Music
PROUD, D., Physiology and Biophysics
PRUSINKIEWICZ, P., Computer Science
PYRCH, T., Social Work
RABIN, H. R., Microbiology, Infectious Diseases and Medicine
RADTKE, H. L., Psychology
RAFFERTY, N. S., Law
RAMRAJ, V. J., English
RANGACHARI, P. K., Pharmacology and Therapeutics
RANGAYYAN, R. M., Electrical and Computer Engineering
RASPORICH, B. J., Communication and Culture
RATTNER, J. B., Cell Biology and Anatomy and Biochemistry and Molecular Biology and Oncology
RAY, D. I., Political Science
RAYMOND, S., Archaeology
REID, D. M., Biological Sciences
REMMERS, J. E., Medicine, Physiology and Biophysics
REVEL, R. D., Environmental Design
REYNOLDS, J. D., Physiology, Biophysics and Medicine
RIABOWOL, K. T., Biochemistry and Molecular Biology
RIEDIGER, C. L., Geology and Geophysics
RITCHIE, J. R. B., Haskayne School of Business
ROBERTSON, S. E., Division of Applied Psychology
ROHLEDER, T. R., Haskayne School of Business
ROKNE, J. G., Computer Science
RONSKY, J. L., Mechanical and Manufacturing Engineering
RORSTAD, O. P., Medicine
ROSS, W. A., Environmental Design
ROTH, S. H., Pharmacology and Therapeutics, and Anaesthesia
ROTHERY, M. A., Social Work
ROUNTHWAITE, H. I., Law
ROWNEY, J. I. A., Haskayne School of Business
ROWSE, J. G., Economics
RUDY, S. A., English
RUHE, G., Computer Science and Electrical and Computer Engineering
RUSSELL, A. P., Biological Sciences
SAINSBURY, R. S., Psychology
SAMUELS, M. T., Division of Applied Psychology
SANDERS, B. C., Physics and Astronomy
SANDS, G. W., Mathematics and Statistics
SANTAMARIA, P., Microbiology and Infectious Diseases
SARNAT, H. B., Paediatrics, Clinical Neurosciences Pathology and Laboratory Medicine
SAUER, N. W., Mathematics and Statistics
SAUNDERS, I. B., Law
SAUVE, R. S., Paediatrics and Community Health Sciences
SCHACHAR, N. S., Surgery
SCHNETKAMP, P. P. M., Biochemistry and Molecular Biology, and Physiology and Biophysics
SCHRYVERS, A. B., Microbiology and Infectious Diseases
SCHULZ, R. A., Haskayne School of Business
SCHWARZ, K.-P., Geomatics Engineering
SCIALFA, C. T., Psychology
SCOLLNIK, D. P. M., Mathematics and Statistics
SCOTT, R. B., Paediatrics
SEGAL, E. L., Religious Studies
SENSEN, C. W., Biochemistry and Molecular Biology
SERLETIS, A., Economics
SESAY, A. B., Electrical and Computer Engineering
SETTARI, A., Chemical and Petroleum Engineering
SEVERSON, D. L., Pharmacology and Therapeutics
SHAFFER, E. A., Medicine
SHANTZ, D. H., Religious Studies
SHAPIRO, B. L., Education
SHARKEY, K. A., Physiology and Biophysics
SHAW, W. J. D., Mechanical and Manufacturing Engineering
SHELDON, R. S., Medicine
SHIELL, A. M., Community Health Sciences
SHRIVE, N. G., Civil Engineering
SICK, G. A., Haskayne School of Business
SIDERIS, M. G., Geomatics Engineering
SIMMINS, G., Art
SINGHAL, N., Paediatrics
SMART, A., Anthropology
SMART, P. J., Anthropology
SMITH, D. D. B., History
SMITH, D. G., Geography
SMITH, D. J., Kinesiology
SMITH, F. R., Physiology and Biophysics
SMITH, G. B., Drama
SMITH, M. R., Electrical and Computer Engineering
SNIATYCKI, J. Z., Mathematics and Statistics
SNYDER, F. F., Paediatrics, Medical Biochemistry and Medical Biology
SOKOL, P. A., Microbiology and Infectious Diseases
SPENCER, R. J., Geology and Geophysics
SPRATT, D. A., Geology and Geophysics
STALKER, M. A., Law
STAM, H. J., Psychology
STAMP, R. M., Education
STAUM, M. S., History
STELL, W. K., Cell Biology and Anatomy and Surgery
STEWART, R. R., Geology and Geophysics
STOCKING, J. R., Art
STOREY, D. G., Biological Sciences

STOUGHTON, N. M., Haskayne School of Business
SUCHOWERSKY, O., Clinical Neurosciences
SUTHERLAND, C. T., Communication and Culture
SUTHERLAND, F. R., Surgery and Oncology
SUTHERLAND, G. R., Clinical Neurosciences
SUTHERLAND, L. R., Medicine and Community Health Sciences
SVRCEK, W. Y., Chemical and Petroleum Engineering
SWAIN, M. G., Medicine
SYED, N. I. S., Cell Biology, Anatomy, Physiology and Biophysics
TARAS, D., Communication and Culture
TARAS, D. G., Haskayne School of Business
TAY, R. S. T., Civil Engineering
TAYLOR, A. R., Physics and Astronomy
TAYLOR, M. S., Economics
TEMPLE, W. J., Surgery and Oncology
TER KEURS, H. E. D., Cardiac Sciences, Medicine, Physiology and Biophysics
TESKEY, G. C., Psychology
TESKEY, W. F., Geomatics Engineering
THOMAS, R. E., Family Medicine
THOMPSON, D. A. R., Environmental Design
THURSTON, W. E., Community Health Sciences
TIELEMAN, D. P., Biological Sciences
TOEWS, J. A., Psychiatry
TOMM, K. M., Psychiatry
TOOHEY, P. G., Greek and Roman Studies
TREBBLE, M. A., Chemical and Petroleum Engineering
TRIGGLE, C. R., Pharmacology and Therapeutics
TRUTE, B., Social Work and Nursing
TSENKOVA, S., Environmental Design
TURNER, L. E., Electrical and Computer Engineering
TURNER, R. W., Cell Biology, Anatomy, Physiology and Biophysics
TUTTY, L. M., Social Work
TYBERG, J. V., Cardiac Sciences, Medicine, Physiology and Biophysics
UNGER, B. W., Computer Science
URBANSKI, S. J., Pathology and Laboratory Medicine
VANBALKOM, W. D., Education
VAN DE SANDE, J. H., Biochemistry and Molecular Biology
VAN DER HOORN, F. A., Biochemistry and Molecular Biology
VANDERSPOEL, J., Greek and Roman Studies
VAN HERK, A., English
VAN ROSENDAAL, G. M. A., Medicine
VEALE, W. L., Physiology and Biophysics
VERBEKE, A. C. M., Haskayne School of Business
VERHOEF, M. J., Community Health Sciences and Medicine
VICKERS, J. N., Kinesiology
VINOGRADOV, O., Mechanical and Manufacturing Engineering
VIOLATO, C., Community Health Sciences
VIZE, P. D., Biological Sciences
VOGEL, H. J., Biological Sciences
VOORDOUW, G., Biological Sciences
VREDENBURG, H., Haskayne School of Business
WAISMAN, D. M., Biochemistry and Molecular Biology
WALKER, D. C., French, Italian and Spanish
WALKER, S., Environmental Design
WALL, A. J., French, Latin and Spanish
WALLACE, J. L., Physiology and Biophysics, and Pharmacology and Therapeutics and Medicine
WALLS, W. D., Economics
WALSH, M. P., Biochemistry and Molecular Biology
WAN, R. G., Civil Engineering
WANG, Y., Electrical and Computer Engineering
WANNER, R. A., Sociology
WARNICA, J. W., Cardiac Sciences and Medicine
WATERS, N. M., Geography
WEBBER, C. F., Education
WEISS, S., Cell Biology and Anatomy and Pharmacology and Therapeutics
WESTRA, H. J., Greek and Roman Studies
WHITE, T. H., Haskayne School of Business
WHITELAW, W. A., Medicine
WIEBE, S., Clinical Neurosciences, Paediatrics and Community Health Sciences
WIERZBA, I., Mechanical and Manufacturing Engineering
WILLIAMS, H. C., Mathematics and Statistics
WILLIAMSON, C. L., Computer Science
WILMAN, E. A., Economics
WILSON, M. G., Social Work
WINCHESTER, W. I. S., Education
WONG, N. C. W., Medicine
WONG, R. C. K., Civil Engineering
WONG, S. L., Biological Sciences
WOODROW, P., Art
WOODROW, R. E., Mathematics and Statistics
WOODS, D. E., Microbiology and Infectious Diseases
WRIGHT, L. M., Nursing
WU, P. P. C., Geology and Geophysics
WYVILL, B. L. M., Computer Science
YACOWAR, M., Art
YANG, X. J., Germanic, Slavic and East Asian Studies
YAU, A. W., Physics and Astronomy
YEUNG, E. C. J., Biological Sciences
YONG, V. W., Oncology and Clinical Neurosciences
YOON, J. W., Microbiology and Infectious Diseases and Paediatrics
YOUNG, D. B., Biochemistry, Molecular Biology and Oncology
ZAMPONI, G. W., Physiology, Biophysics, Pharmacology and Therapeutics
ZANZOTTO, L., Civil Engineering
ZAPF, M. K., Social Work
ZEKULIN, N. G. A., Germanic, Slavic and East Asian Studies
ZIEGLER, T., Chemistry
ZOCHODNE, D. W., Clinical Neurosciences
ZVENGROWSKI, P. D., Mathematics and Statistics

ATTACHED RESEARCH INSTITUTES

Arctic Institute of North America: see under Research Institutes.

Centre for Gifted Education.

Environmental Research Centre: Dir S. H. ROTH.

Humanities Institute: Dir W. O. MCCREADY (acting).

Institute for Advanced Policy Research: Dir K. J. MCKENZIE.

Institute of Health and Wellness: Dir R. F. ZERNICKE.

Institute for Space Research.

Institute for Sustainable Energy, Environment and Economy: Dir R. L. MANSELL.

Institute for Transportation Studies: Chair. N. M. WATERS.

CAPE BRETON UNIVERSITY

POB 5300, 1250 Grand Lake Rd, Sydney, NS B1P 6L2
Telephone: (902) 563-1330
Fax: (902) 563-1371
E-mail: registrar@capebretonu.ca
Internet: www.capebretonu.ca

Founded 1974
State control
Language of instruction: English
Academic year: September to April

Chancellor: ANNETTE VERSCHUREN
President and Vice-Chancellor: JOHN HARKER
Vice-President, Academic and Research: Dr ANTHONY SECCO
Vice-President, Finance and Operations: GORDON MACINNIS
Vice-President, Development: Dr KEITH BROWN
Vice-President, Student Services and Registrar: ALEXIS MANLEY
Dean of Research: Dr HARVEY JOHNSTONE

Library of 532,290 vols, 800 periodicals
Number of teachers: 153
Number of students: 3,600

depts of Education, Mathematics, physics and geology, Nutrition, Nursing, Psychology, Public health

DEANS

School of Arts and Community Studies: Dr J. ARTHUR TUCKER
School of Business Studies: JOHN MACKINNON
School of Science and Technology: Dr ALLEN BRITTEN
School of Education, Health, and Wellness: Dr JANE LEWIS

ATTACHED RESEARCH INSTITUTES

The mailing address is that of the University

Beaton Institute: repository of Cape Breton social, economic, political and cultural history; Dir WENDY ROBICHEAU.

Children's Rights Centre: f. 1996; conducts research and provides public education on children's rights; monitors implementation of UN Children's Rights Convention in Nova Scotia and Canada; Co-Dir Prof. KATHERINE COVELL; Co-Dir Prof. BRIAN HOWE.

Community Economic Development Institute: f. 1996 to provide support, training, policy advice and research in community economic development; Dir. Dr GERTRUDE MACINTYRE.

CARLETON UNIVERSITY

1125 Colonel By Drive, Ottawa, ON K1S 5B6
Telephone: (613) 520-2600
Fax: (613) 520-3847
E-mail: infocarleton@carleton.ca
Internet: www.carleton.ca

Founded 1942
Provincial control
Language of instruction: English
Academic year: September to May

Chancellor: MARC GARNEAU
President and Vice-Chancellor: Dr RICHARD VAN LOON
Vice-President (Academic and Provost): ALAN HARRISON
Vice-President (Advancement): LUCINDA BOUCHER
Vice-President (Finance and Administration): DUNCAN WATT
Vice-President (Research): FERIDUN HAMDULLAHPUR
Assistant Vice-President (Development and Alumni): SERGE ARPIN
Assistant Vice-President (Enrolment Management): SUSAN GOTTHEIL
Librarian: MARTIN FOSS

Library: see Libraries and Archives
Number of teachers: 786
Number of students: 22,535

Publications: *The President's Report* (annually), *Research and Works* (4 a year)

DEANS

Faculty of Arts and Social Science: MICHAEL SMITH
Faculty of Engineering: SAMI MAHMOUD
Faculty of Public Affairs and Management: KATHERINE GRAHAM
Faculty of Science: JEAN-GUY GODIN

Faculty of Graduate Studies and Research: ROGER BLOCKLEY

CHAIRS AND DIRECTORS

Faculty of Arts and Social Science (330 Paterson Hall, 1125 Colonel By Drive, Ottawa, ON K1S 5B6; tel. (613) 520-2355; fax (613) 520-4481; internet www.carleton.ca/fass):

Canadian Studies: F. ROCHER
English Language and Literature: R. HOLTON
Environmental Studies: N. DOUBLEDAY
French: C. DOUTRELEPONT
Geography: S. DALBY
History: E. P. FITZGERALD
Humanities: S. WILSON
Interdisciplinary Studies: K. ARNUP
Philosophy: J. DRYDYK
Psychology: J. LOGAN (acting)
Sociology and Anthropology: C. GORDON
Studies in Art and Culture: B. GILLIINGHAM (acting)
Women's Studies: P. RANKIN
Centre for Applied Language Studies: I. PRINGLE

Faculty of Engineering (3010 Minto Centre, 1125 Colonel By Drive, Ottawa, ON K1S 5B6; tel. (613) 520-5790; fax (613) 520-7481; internet www.carleton.ca/engineeringdesign):

Architecture: G. HAIDER
Civil and Environmental Engineering: G. HARTLEY (acting)
Electronics: L. ROY
Industrial Design: L. FRANKEL
Mechanical and Aerospace Engineering: R. BELL
Systems and Computer Engineering: R. GOUBRAN

Faculty of Public Affairs and Management (D391 Loeb Building, 1125 Colonel By Drive, Ottawa, ON K1S 5B6; tel. (613) 520-3741; fax (613) 520-3742; e-mail melanie_thompson@carleton.ca; internet www.carleton.ca/pam):

Business: V. KUMAR
Criminology and Criminal Justice: B. WRIGHT
Economics: A. RITTER
European and Russian Studies: P. DUTKIEWICZ
International Affairs: F. HAMPSON
Journalism and Communication: C. DORNAN
Law: C. SWAN
Political Economy: R. MAHON
Political Science: C. BROWN
Public Administration: L. PAL
Social Work: C. LUNDY

Faculty of Science (3239 Herzberg Laboratories, 1125 Colonel By Drive, Ottawa, ON K1S 5B6; tel. (613) 520-4388; fax (613) 520-4389; e-mail odscience@ccs.carleton.ca; internet www.carleton.ca/science):

Biochemistry: M. SMITH
Biology: J. CHEETHAM
Chemistry: G. BUCHANAN
Computational Sciences: L. COPLEY
Computer Science: D. HOWE
Earth Sciences: C. SCHROEDER-ADAMS
Environmental Science: D. WIGFIELD
Geography: S. DALBY
Integrated Science Studies: I. MUNRO
Mathematics and Statistics: C. GARNER
Physics: P. KALYNDAK
Psychology: J. LOGAN

CONCORDIA UNIVERSITY

Sir George Williams Campus, 1455 de Maisonneuve Blvd West, Montréal, QC H3G 1M8
Loyola Campus, 7141 Sherbrooke St West, Montréal, QC H4B 1R6
Telephone: (514) 848-2424
Fax: (514) 848-3494
Internet: www.concordia.ca

Founded 1974 by merger of Sir George Williams University (established 1948) and Loyola College (incorporated 1899)
Provincial control
Language of instruction: English
Academic year: May to April

Chancellor and University Secretariat: ERIC MOLSON
President and Vice-Chancellor: Prof. FREDERICK H. LOWY
Provost and Vice-President, Academic Affairs: MARTIN SINGER
Vice-President, Services: MICHAEL DI GRAPPA
Vice President and Secretary-General, External Affairs: MARCEL DANIS
Executive Director, Office of the President: GARY MILTON
Registrar: LINDA HEALEY
Director of Libraries: WILLIAM CURRAN

Library: see Libraries and Archives
Number of teachers: 1,837 (884 full-time, 953 part-time)
Number of students: 31,175

Publications: *Canadian Jewish Studies* (annually), *Canadian Journal of Irish Studies* (2 a year), *Canadian Journal of Research in Early Childhood Education* (2 a year), *Journal of Canadian Art History / Annales d'histoire de l'art canadien* (2 a year), *Journal of Religion and Culture* (annually), *Revue de l'Institut Simone de Beauvoir Institute Review* (annually)

DEANS

Faculty of Arts and Science: DAVID GRAHAM
Faculty of Engineering and Computer Science: NABIL ESMAIL
Faculty of Fine Arts: CATHERINE WILD
John Molson School of Business: JERRY TOMBERLIN
School of Graduate Studies and Research: ELIZABETH SACCA

HEADS OF DEPARTMENTS

Faculty of Arts and Science (Loyola Campus, 7141 Sherbrooke St West, Montréal, QC H4B 1R6; tel. (514) 848-2424, ext. 2080; fax (514) 848-4201; internet artsandscience.concordia.ca):

Applied Human Sciences: V. MANN-FEDER
Biology: L. VARIN
Chemistry and Biochemistry: M. LAWRENCE
Classics, Modern Languages and Linguistics: C. VALLEJO
Communication Studies: L. ROTH
Economics: W. SIMS
Education: E. JACOBS
English: T. BYRNES
Exercise Science: R. KILGOUR
French Studies: L. LEQUIN
Geography, Planning and Environment: J. ZACHARIAS
History: G. CARR
Journalism: E. RAUDSEPP
Mathematics and Statistics: H. KISILEVSKY
Philosophy: C. GRAY
Physics: M. FRANK
Political Science: R. TREMBLAY
Psychology: W. BUKOWSKI
Religion: N. JOSEPH
Sociology and Anthropology: C. JOURDAN
Teaching of English as a Second Language: E. JACOBS
Theological Studies: P. BRIGHT

Faculty of Engineering and Computer Science (1455 de Maisonneuve Blvd West, LB 1007–7, Montréal, QC H3G 1M8; tel. (514) 848-2424, ext. 3061; fax (514) 848-4509; internet www.encs.concordia.ca):

Building, Civil and Environmental Engineering: S. ALKASS
Computer Science and Software Engineering: C. LAM
Electrical and Computer Engineering: M. OMAIR AHMAD
Mechanical and Industrial Engineering: S. V. HOA

Faculty of Fine Arts (1455 de Maisonneuve Blvd West, VA–250, Montréal, QC H3G 1M8; tel. (514) 848-2424, ext. 2424; fax (514) 848-4599; internet fofa.concordia.ca):

Art Education: R. LACHAPELLE
Art History: L. LERNER
Art Therapy: S. SNOW
Cinema: R. KERR
Contemporary Dance: M. MONTANARO
Design Art: K. LANGSHAW
Music: R. MOUNTAIN
Studio Arts: D. ELLIOT
Theatre: A. CAPPELLUTTO

John Molson School of Business (1455 de Maisonneuve Blvd West, GM 403–11, Montréal, QC H3G 1M8; tel. (514) 848-2424, ext. 2779; fax (514) 848-4502; internet johnmolson.concordia.ca):

Accountancy: K. GHEYARA
Decision Sciences and Management Information Systems: D. KIRA
Finance: S. BETTON
Management: K. ARGHEYD
Marketing: M. BERGIER

HEADS OF UNITS WITHIN FACULTY OF ARTS AND SCIENCE

Interdisciplinary Studies: R. KILGOUR
Science and Human Affairs: A. WAYNE
Urban Studies: J. ZACHARIAS
Liberal Arts College: H. SHULMAN
Loyola International College: W. BUKOWSKI
School of Community and Public Affairs: D. SALEE
Science College: M. VON GRÜNAU
Simone de Beauvoir Institute and Women's Studies: L. ROBINSON

DIRECTORS

Applied Psychology Centre: M. DUGAS
Centre for the Arts in Human Development: P. ABRAMI
Centre for Building Studies: R. ZMEUREANU
Centre for Canadian-Irish Studies: M, KENNEALLY
Centre for Continuing Education: M. SANG
Centre for Community and Ethnic Studies: D. SALEE
Centre for Digital Arts: J. CEZAR
Centre for Human Relations and Community Studies: S. DINAN
Centre for Industrial Control: (vacant)
Centre for International Academic Cooperation: B. SAHNI
Centre for Mature Students: R. OPPENHEIMER
Centre for Native Education: M. TREMBLAY
Centre for Research in Human Development: L. SERBIN
Centre for Signal Processing and Communications: M. N. S. SWAMY
Centre for Structural and Functional Genomics: M. GUEST
Centre for Studies in Behavioural Neurobiology: B. WOODSIDE
Centre for the Study of Learning and Performance: (vacant)
Centre for Teaching and Learning Services: O. ROVINESCU
Concordia Centre for Broadcasting Studies: G. NIELSEN
Concordia Centre for Composites: S. V. HOA

Concordia Centre for Pattern Recognition and Machine Intelligence: C. Y. SUEN
Concordia Centre for Small Business and Entrepreneurial Studies: A. IBRAHIM
Concordia Computer-Aided Vehicle Engineering: I. STIHARU
Concordia Institute for Aerospace Design and Innovation: H. MOUSTAPHA
Concordia Institute for Information Systems Engineering: R. DSSOULI
Interuniversity Centre for Algebraic Computation: H. KISILEVSKY
Montreal Institute for Genocide and Human Rights Studies: F. CHALK, K. JONASSOHN

DALHOUSIE UNIVERSITY

Halifax, NS B3H 4H6
Telephone: (902) 494-2450
Fax: (902) 494-1630
E-mail: registrar@dal.ca
Internet: www.dal.ca

Founded 1818; merged with Technical University of Nova Scotia 1997
Private control
Language of instruction: English
Academic year: September to August

Chancellor: Dr RICHARD GOLDBLOOM
President and Vice-Chancellor: THOMAS D. TRAVES
Vice-Presidents: S. SCULLY (Academic and Provost), D. GODSOE (Development and Alumni Affairs), B. G. MASON (Finance and Administration), W. C. BRECKENRIDGE (Research), BONNIE NEUMAN (Student Services)
Registrar: ASA KACHAN
Librarian: W. MAES

Library: see Libraries
Number of teachers: 1,860 (full- and part-time)
Number of students: 13,514 full-time, 2,300 part-time, 1,328 international

DEANS

Faculty of Architecture: G. WANZEL
Faculty of Arts and Social Sciences: M. E. BINKLEY
Faculty of Computer Science: N. CERCONE
Faculty of Dentistry: D. PRECIOUS
Faculty of Engineering: W. CALEY
Faculty of Health Professions: WILLIAM WEBSTER
Faculty of Law: PHILLIP SAUNDERS
Faculty of Management: PHILIP ROSSON (acting)
Faculty of Medicine: H. COOK (acting)
Faculty of Science: K. TAYLOR
Faculty of Graduate Studies: J. C. T. KWAK

PROFESSORS

Faculty of Architecture and Planning (tel. (902) 494-3971; fax (902) 423-6672; e-mail arch.office@dal.ca; internet archplan.dal.ca):

CAVANAGH, E., Architecture
GRANT, J., Planning
KROEKER, R., Architecture
MACKAY-LYONS, B., Architecture
MACY, C., Architecture
PALERMO, F., Planning
POULTON, M., Planning
PROCOS, D., Architecture
WANZEL, J., Architecture

Faculty of Arts and Social Sciences (tel. (902) 494-1440; fax (902) 494-1957; e-mail fass@dal.ca):

APOSTLE, R., Sociology and Social Anthropology
AUCOIN, P. C., Political Science
BARKER, W., English
BAKVIS, H., Political Science
BARKOW, J. H., Sociology and Social Anthropology
BAXTER, J., English
BAYLIS, F., Philosophy
BEDNARSKI, H. E., French
BINKLEY, M. E., Sociology and Social Anthropology
BOARDMAN, R., Political Science
BURNS, S., Philosophy
CAMPBELL, R. M., Philosophy
CROWLEY, J. E., History
CURRAN, J. V., German (Chair.)
DAVIS, J., Political Science
DE MEO, P., French
DIEPEVEEN, L. P., English
FURROW, M. M., English
HANKEY, W., Classics (King's)
HANLON, G., History
HARVEY, F., Political Science
HUEBERT, R., English
KIRK, J. M., Spanish
LI, T. J., Sociology and Social Anthropology
LUCKYJ, C., English
MARTIN, R., Philosophy
MIDDLEMISS, D., Political Science
NEVILLE, C., History (Chair.)
OORE, I., French
OVERTON, D. R., Theatre
PARPART, J., International Development Studies
PEREIRA, N. G. O., History and Russian
PERINA, P., Theatre
RUNTE, H. R., French
SHAW, T. W., Political Science
SCHOTCH, P., Philosophy
SCHROEDER, D., Music
SCHWARZ, H. G., German
SCULLY, S., Classics
SERVANT, G. W., Music
SHERWIN, S., Philosophy
SMITH, J., Political Science (Chair.)
STARNES, C. J., Classics (King's)
STONE, M. I., English
TETREAULT, R., English
THIESSEN, V., Sociology and Social Anthropology
TRAVES, T., History
VINCI, T., Philosophy
WAINWRIGHT, J. A., English and Canadian Studies
WATERSON, K., French

Faculty of Computer Science (tel. (902) 494-2093; fax (902) 492-1517):

BODORIK, P.
BORWEIN, J.
BROWN, J. I.
COX, P.
FARRAG, A.
GENTLEMAN, M.
GRUNDKE, E.
HITCHCOCK, P.
JOST, A.
KEAST, P.
MACDONALD, N.
MILOS, E.
RAU-CHAPLIN, A.
RIORDAN, D.
SAMPALLI, S.
SCRIMGER, J. N.
SHEPHERD, M.
SLONIM, J.
WACH, G.
WATTERS, C. R.

Faculty of Dentistry (tel. (902) 494-2824; fax (902) 494-2527):

LEE, J. M., Applied Oral Sciences
LONEY, R., Dental Clinical Sciences
PRECIOUS, D. S., Oral and Maxillofacial Science
PRICE, R. B. T., Dental Clinical Science
RYDING, H. A., Applied Oral Sciences (Acting Chair.)
SUTOW, E. J., Applied Oral Sciences

Faculty of Engineering (tel. (902) 494-3267; fax (902) 429-3011; e-mail dean.engineering@dal.ca):

ALI, N. A., Civil Engineering
ALLEN, P., Mechanical Engineering
AL-TAWEEL, A., Chemical Engineering
AMYOTTE, P., Chemical Engineering
BASU, P., Mechanical Engineering
BEN-ABDALLAH, N., Biological Engineering (Head)
CADA, M., Electrical and Computer Engineering
CALEY, W. F., Mining and Metallurgical Engineering
CHEN, Z., Electrical and Computer Engineering
CHUANG, J. M., Mechanical Engineering
EL-HAWARY, M., Electrical and Computer Engineering
EL-MASRY, E., Electrical and Computer Engineering (Head)
FELS, M., Chemical Engineering
FENTON, G., Engineering Mathematics
GHALY, A., Biological Engineering
GILL, T., Food Science and Technology
GREGSON, P., Electrical and Computer Engineering
GUNN, E., Industrial Engineering
GUPTA, Y., Chemical Engineering (Head)
HUGHES, F. L., Electrical and Computer Engineering
ISLAM, M., Civil Engineering
KALAMKAROV, A., Mechanical Engineering
KEMBER, G., Engineering Mathematics
KIPOUROS, G., Mining and Metallurgical Engineering
KUJATH, M., Mechanical Engineering
MILITZER, J., Mechanical Engineering
PAULSON, A. T., Food Science and Technology
PEGG, M., Chemical Engineering
PHILLIPS, W., Engineering Mathematics (Head)
RAHMAN, M., Engineering Mathematics
ROBERTSON, W., Engineering Mathematics
ROCKWELL, M., Mining and Metallurgical Engineering
SANDBLOM, C., Industrial Engineering
SATISH, M., Civil Engineering
SPEERS, R. A., Food Science and Technology (Head)
TROTTIER, J.-F., Civil Engineering
UGURSAL, M., Mechanical Engineering
WATTS, K., Biological and Mechanical Engineering
YEMENIDJIAN, N., Mining and Metallurgical Engineering (Head)
ZOU, D. H., Mining and Metallurgical Engineering

Faculty of Health Professions (tel. (902) 494-3327; fax (902) 494-1966; internet healthprofessions.dal.ca):

School of Health and Human Performance:

HOLT, L. E.
LYONS, R. F.
MALONEY, T.
SINGLETON, J.
UNRUH, A.

School of Health Services Administration:

MCINTYRE, L.
NESTMAN, L.
RATHWELL, T. (Dir)

School of Nursing:

BUTLER, L. (Dir)
DOWNE-WAMBOLDT, B. (Dir)
KEDDY, B. A.

School of Occupational Therapy:

TOWNSEND, E. (Dir)

College of Pharmacy:

SKETRIS, I.
YEUNG, P. K. F.

School of Physiotherapy:

KOZEY, C. L.
MAKRIDES, L. (Dir)
TURNBULL, G. I.

Maritime School of Social Work:
DIVINE, D.
WIEN, F. C.

Faculty of Law (tel. (902) 494-3495; fax (902) 494-1316; e-mail lawinfo@dal.ca):
ARCHIBALD, B.
BLACK, V.
DEVLIN, R.
KAISER, H. A.
KINDRED, H. M.
MACKAY, A. W.
MCCONNELL, M. L.
POTHIER, D. L.
THOMAS, P.
THOMPSON, D. A. R.
THORNHILL, E. M. A.
VANDERZWAGG, D.
WOODMAN, F. L.
YOGIS, J. A.

Faculty of Medicine (tel. (902) 494-6592; fax (902) 494-7119; e-mail dean.medicine@dal.ca; internet www.medicine.dal.ca):
ALDA, H., Psychiatry
ALEXANDER, D., Surgery
ALLEN, A. C., Paediatrics, Obstetrics and Gynaecology
ANDERSON, D. R., Medicine, Community Health and Epidemiology
ANDERSON, P. A., Urology
ANDERSON, R., Microbiology and Immunology
ARMSON, A., Obstetrics and Gynaecology
ATTIA, E., Surgery
BARNES, S., Physiology and Biophysics, Ophthalmology
BASKETT, T., Obstetrics and Gynaecology
BAYLIS, F., Bioethics
BENSTED, T., Medicine
BITTER-SUERMANN, H., Surgery
BLAY, J., Pharmacology
BONJER, H. J., Surgery
BORTOLUSSI, R., Paediatrics
BRECKENRIDGE, W. C., Biochemistry
BROWN, M. G., Community Health and Epidemiology
BRYSON, S., Paediatrics
BYERS, D., Paediatrics
CAMERON, I., Family Medicine
CAMFIELD, C., Paediatrics
CAMFIELD, P. R., Paediatrics
CASSON, A., Surgery and Pathology
CHAUHAN, B., Ophthalmology Physiology and Biophysics
CLEMENTS, J. C., Biomedical Engineering
COHEN, M. M., Paediatrics
CONNOLLY, J., Medicine
COOK, H. W., Paediatrics
COONAN, T., Anaesthesia (Head)
COWDEN, E., Medicine (Head)
COX, J., Medicine
CRUESS, A. F., Ophthalmology (Chair.)
CROCKER, J. F. S., Paediatrics
CROLL, R. P., Physiology and Biophysics
CURRIE, R. W., Anatomy and Neurobiology
DANIELS, C., Diagnostic Radiology
DEVITT, H., Anaesthesia
DOANE, B. K., Psychiatry
DOOLEY, J., Paediatrics
DOOLITTLE, W. F., Biochemistry
DOWNIE, J. W., Pharmacology
DUCHARME, J., Emergency Medicine
DUNCAN, R., Microbiology and Immunology
DUNPHY, B., Obstetrics and Gynaecology
FARRELL, S., Obstetrics and Gynaecology
FERNANDEZ, L. A. V., Medicine
FERRIER, G. R., Pharmacology
FINE, A., Physiology and Biophysics
FINLEY, G. A., Anaesthesia
FINLEY, J. P., Paediatrics
FORWARD, K., Pathology, Medicine, Microbiology and Immunology
FOX, R. A., Medicine
FRANK, B. W., Division of Medical Education
FRENCH, A., Biomedical Engineering, Physiology and Biophysics
GARDNER, M. J., Medicine
GAJEWSKI, J., Urology
GASS, D. A., Family Medicine
GOLDBLOOM, R., Paediatrics
GRAVES, G., Obstetrics and Gynaecology (Head)
GRAY, M. W., Biochemistry (Head)
GREER, W., Pathology
GREGSON, P., Biomedical Engineering
GROSS, M., Surgery
GRUNFIELD, E., Medicine, Community Health and Epidemiology
GUERNSEY, D. L., Pathology, Physiology, Biophysics and Ophthalmology
HAASE, D. A., Medicine
HALL, R., Anaesthesia and Pharmacology
HALPERIN, S., Paediatrics
HANDA, S. P., Medicine
HANLY, J. G., Medicine
HAYES, V., Family Medicine
HEATHCOTE, J. G., Ophthalmology and Pathology (Head)
HIRSCH, D., Medicine and Psychiatry
HOLNESS, R. O., Surgery
HOPKINS, D. A., Anatomy and Neurobiology
HORACEK, B. M., Physiology, Biophysics and Biomedical Engineering
HORACKOVA, M., Physiology and Biophysics
HOSKIN, D. W., Microbiology, Immunology, and Pathology
HOWLETT, S., Pharmacology
HUGENHOLZ, H., Surgery
HUNG, O. R., Anaesthesia and Pharmacology
HYNDMAN, J. C., Surgery
IMRIE, D., Anaesthesia
ISA, N. N., Obstetrics and Gynaecology
ISSEKUTZ, A., Paediatrics and Pathology
ISSEKUTZ, T. B., Paediatrics, Microbiology, Immunology and Pathology
JAMIESON, C. G., Surgery
JOHNSTON, B. L., Medicine, Community Health and Epidemiology
JOHNSTON, G. C., Microbiology and Immunology (Head)
JOHNSTONE, D. E., Medicine
KAZIMIRSKI, J., Division of Medical Education
KELLS, C., Medicine
KELLY, M., Pharmacology
KELLY, M. E., Ophthalmology
KENNY, N. P., Paediatrics and Bioethics and Division of Medical Education
KHANNA, V. N., Medicine
KIBERD, B. A., Medicine
KIRBY, R. L., Medicine and Biomedical Engineering
KISELY, S. R., Community Health and Epidemiology, Psychiatry
KRONICK, J., Paediatrics (Head)
KUTCHER, S., Psychiatry
LAIDLAW, T., Division of Medical Education
LANGILLE, D. B., Community Health and Epidemiology
LANGLEY, G. R., Medicine
LAROCHE, G. R., Ophthalmology
LAWEN, J. G., Urology
LAZIER, C. B., Biochemistry
LEBLANC, R. P., Ophthalmology
LEBRON, G., Diagnostic Radiology
LEE, M., Applied Oral Sciences and Biomedical Engineering
LEE, P. W. K., Microbiology, Immunology and Pathology
LEE, T., Microbiology, Immunology and Pathology
LEIGHTON, A. H., Psychiatry
LESLIE, R. A., Anatomy, Neurobiology and Psychiatry (Head)
LO, C. D., Diagnostic Radiology
LUDMAN, H., Paediatrics
MACDONALD, A. S., Surgery
MACDONALD, N., Paediatrics
MCDONALD, T. F., Physiology and Biophysics
MCGRATH, P. J., Paediatrics, Psychiatry and Psychology
MACLACHLAN, R., Family Medicine (Head)
MACLEAN, L. D., Community Health and Epidemiology
MCMILLAN, D., Paediatrics
MACAULAY, R., Pathology
MAHONY, D. E., Microbiology and Immunology
MALATJALIAN, D. A., Pathology and Medicine
MANN, K. V., Division of Medical Education
MANN, O. E., Medicine
MARSHALL, J., Pathology, Microbiology and Immunology
MASSOUD, E., Surgery
MAXNER, C. E., Medicine and Opthalmology
MEINERTZHAGEN, I., Psychology, Physiology and Biophysics
MENDEZ, I., Surgery
MILLER, R. A., Medicine
MILLER, R. M., Diagnostic Radiology
MORRIS, I. R., Anaesthesia
MORRIS, S. F., Surgery
MOSHER, D., Medicine
MOSS, M. A., Pathology (Head)
MURPHY, P., Physiology and Biophysics (Head)
MURRAY, T. J., Medicine
NACHTIGAL, M., Pharmacology
NASHON, B. J., Surgery and Urology
NASSAR, B. A., Pathology, Medicine and Urology
NEUMANN, P. E., Anatomy and Neurobiology
NORMAN, R., Urology (Head)
O'NEILL, B., Medicine, Community Health and Epidemiology
PADMOS, M., Medicine
PALMER, F. B. ST. C., Biochemistry (Head)
PARKHILL, W. S., Surgery
PELZER, D., Physiology and Biophysicsand Division of Medical Education
PETERSON, T., Medicine and Pharmacology
PHILLIPS, S., Medicine
POLLAK, T., Medicine
POULIN, C., Community Health and Epidemiology
POWELL, C., Medicine
PURDY, R. A., Medicine
RAMSEY, M., Ophthalmology
RASMUSSON, D., Physiology and Biophysics
RENTON, K. W., Pharmacology
RO, H., Biochemistry
ROBERTSON, G. S., Pharmacology and Psychiatry
ROBERTSON, H. A., Pharmacology and Medicine (Head)
ROBINSON, K. S., Medicine
ROCKER, G., Medicine
ROCKWOOD, K., Medicine
ROWDEN, G., Pathology and Medicine
ROWE, R. C., Medicine
RUSAK, B., Psychiatry, Psychology and Pharmacology
RUTHERFORD, J., Anatomy and Neurobiology
SADLER, R. M., Medicine
SAWYNOK, J., Pharmacology
SCHLECH, W., Medicine
SEMBA, K., Anatomy and Neurobiology
SHUKLA, R. C., Anaesthesia
SIMPSON, D., Medicine
SINCLAIR, D., Emergency Medicine
SINGER, R. A., Biochemistry
STANISH, W. D., Surgery
STEWART, R. D., Anaesthesia, Emergency Medicine and Division of Medical Education
STEWART, S., Psychology
STOKES, A., Psychiatry (Acting Head)
STOLTZ, D. B., Microbiology and Immunology

STONE, R. M., Surgery (Head)
STROINK, G., Biomedical Engineering
STUTTARD, C., Microbiology and Immunology
SULLIVAN, J., Surgery
TURNBULL, G. K., Medicine
VAN DEN HOF, M., Obstetrics and Gynaecology
VANZANTEN, S., Medicine, Community Health and Epidemiology
VAUGHN, P., Division of Medical Education
WALLACE, C. J. A., Biochemistry
WALSH, N., Pathology
WARD, T., Paediatrics
WASSERSUG, R. J., Anatomy and Neurobiology
WEAVER, D., Medicine and Biomedical Engineering
WEST, M. L., Medicine
WILKINSON, M., Physiology, Biophysics, Obstetrics and Gynaecology
WOLF, H. K., Physiology and Biophysics
WRIGHT, J. R., Pathology, Surgery and Biomedical Engineering
YABSLEY, R. H., Surgery

Faculty of Management (tel. (902) 494-2582; fax (902) 494-1195; internet www.management.dal.ca):

School of Business Administration:

BROOKS, M. R.
CONRAD, J.
DUFFY, J.
FOOLADI, I.
MACLEAN, L. C.
MCNIVEN, J. D.
MEALIEA, L. W.
OPPONG, A.
ROSSON, P.
SANKAR, Y.
SCHELLINCK, D. A.

School of Public Administration:

AUCOIN, P. C.
BAKVIS, H.
BROWN, M. P.
MCNIVEN, J. D.
SIDDIQ, F.
SULLIVAN, K.
TRAVES, T.

School of Resource and Environmental Studies:

COHEN, F. G.
CÔTÉ, R.
DUINKER, P. (Dir)
WILLISON, J. H.

Henson College of Continuing Education (tel. (902) 494-2526; fax (902) 494-6875; e-mail henson-info@dal.ca):

BENOIT, J.
FRASER, L.
NOVACK, J.

Faculty of Science (tel. (902) 494-2373; fax (902) 494-1123; e-mail science@dal.ca; internet www.science.dal.ca):

BARRESI, J., Psychology
BEAUMONT, C., Oceanography
BENTZEN, P., Biology and Oceanography
BOUDREAU, B. P., Oceanography (Chair.)
BOWEN, A. J., Oceanography
BOYD, R. J., Chemistry (Chair.)
BRADFIELD, F. M., Economics
BROWN, J., Mathematics and Statistics
BROWN, R. E., Psychology
BRYSON, S. E., Psychology
BURFORD, N., Chemistry
BURNELL, D. J., Chemistry
BURTON, P., Economics
CAMERON, T. S., Chemistry
CAMFIELD, C., Psychology
CHATT, A., Chemistry
CLARKE, D. B., Earth Sciences
CLEMENTS, J., Mathematics and Statistics
COLEY, A., Mathematics and Statistics, Physics
CONNOLLY, J. F., Psychology
COXON, J. A., Chemistry
CROLL, R. P., Biology
CULLEN, J., Oceanography
DAHN, J. R., Chemistry and Physics
DARVESH, S., Chemistry
DASGUPTA, S., Economics
DILCHER, K., Mathematics and Statistics
DUNHAM, P. J., Psychology
DUNLAP, R., Physics
FENTRESS, J. C., Biology
FIELD, C. A., Mathematics and Statistics
FINLEY, G. A., Psychology
FOURNIER, R. O., Oceanography
FREEDMAN, W., Biology (Chair. – Biology)
GABOR, G., Mathematics and Statistics
GELDART, D. J., Physics
GIBLING, M. R., Earth Sciences (Chair.)
GRANT, J., Oceanography
GREATBATCH, R., Oceanography and Physics
GRINDLEY, B., Chemistry
GUPTA, R. P., Mathematics and Statistics
HALL, B. K., Biology
HAMILTON, D. C., Mathematics and Statistics
HAY, A., Oceanography
HILL, P. S., Oceanography
HILLS, E. L., Biology
HUTCHINGS, J. A., Biology
ISCAN, T., Economics
IVERSON, S. J., Biology
JAMIESON, R. A., Earth Sciences
JERICHO, M. H., Physics
JOHNSTON, M. O., Biology
KAY-RAINING BIRD, E., Psychology
KEAST, P., Mathematics and Statistics (Chair.)
KLEIN, R. M., Psychology
KREUZER, H. J., Physics
KUSALIK, P. G., Chemistry
KWAK, J. C., Chemistry
LANE, P. A., Biology
LEE, R., Biology
LEONARD, M. L., Biology
LESSER, B., Economics (Chair.)
LEWIS, M., Oceanography
LOLORDO, V. M., Psychology
LOUDEN, K. E., Oceanography
LYONS, R., Psychology
MACRAE, T., Biology
MCGRATH, P. J., Psychology
MCMULLEN, P., Psychology
MEINERTZHAGEN, I. A., Psychology
MITCHELL, D. E., Psychology
MOORE, C. L., Psychology
MOORE, R. M., Oceanography
MORIARTY, K., Mathematics and Statistics, and Physics
MYERS, R. A., Biology
NOWAKOWSKI, R., Mathematics and Statistics
O'DOR, R. K., Biology
OSBERG, L. S., Economics
PACEY, P. D., Chemistry
PARÉ, R., Mathematics and Statistics
PATON, B. E., Physics
PATRIQUIN, D. G., Biology
PHILLIPS, D., Psychology
PHIPPS, S. A., Economics
PINCOCK, J. A., Chemistry
POHAJDAK, B., Biology
RAJORA, O. P., Biology
REYNOLDS, P. H., Earth Sciences and Physics
ROBERTSON, H., Psychology
RUDDICK, B., Oceanography
RUSAK, B., Psychology and Psychiatry
SCHEIBLING, R., Biology
SCOTT, D., Earth Sciences
SEMBA, K., Psychology
SHAW, S., Psychology
STEWART, S., Psychology
STROINK, G., Physics (Chair.)
SUTHERLAND, W. R., Mathematics and Statistics
TAN, K. K., Mathematics and Statistics
TAYLOR, K., Mathematics and Statistics
THOMPSON, K., Mathematics and Statistics, and Oceanography
WACH, G. D., Earth Sciences
WALDE, S., Biology
WEAVER, D. F., Chemistry and Division of Neurology
WENTZELL, P. D., Chemistry
WHITE, M. A., Chemistry and Physics
WHITEHEAD, H., Biology
WILLISON, J. H. M., Biology and Resource, Environmental Studies
WOOD, R. J., Mathematics and Statistics
WRIGHT, J. M., Biology
XU, K., Economics
ZWANZIGER, J. W., Chemistry and Physics

ATTACHED INSTITUTES

Atlantic Centre for Excellence for Women's Health: Dir Dr B. CLOW.

Atlantic Health Promotion Research Centre: Dir Dr R. LYONS.

Atlantic Institute of Criminology: Dir Dr D. CLAIRMONT.

Atlantic Region Magnetic Resonance Centre: Dir Dr T. GRINDLEY.

Atlantic Research Centre: Dir Dr RENÉE LYONS.

Canadian Institute of Fisheries Technology: Dir Dr R. A. SPEERS.

Canadian Residential Energy End-use Data and Analysis Centre: Dir I. UGURSAL.

Centre for African Studies: Dir Dr REBECCA TIESSEN.

Centre for Foreign Policy Studies: Dir Dr FRANK HARVEY.

Centre for International Business Studies: Dir Dr D. CHERRY.

Centre for Marine Geology: Dir D. B. SCOTT.

Centre for Marine Vessel Development and Research: Dir Dr J. MILITZER.

Centre for Water Resource Studies: Dir Dr WILLIAM HART.

Dalhousie Health Law Institute: Dir J. DOWNIE.

Geographic Information System Centre: Dir Dr G. MUECKE.

Global Information Networking Institute: Dir Dr M. GENTLEMAN.

Institute for Research in Materials: Dir Dr M. A. WHITE.

Law and Technology Institute: Dir M. DETURBIDE.

Lester Pearson International Institute: Dir P. RODEE.

Minerals Engineering Centre: Dir Dr G. J. KIPOUROS.

Neuroscience Institute: Exec. Dir Dr SHELLEY ADAMO.

Norman Newman Centre for Entrepreneurship: Dir DAVE ROACH.

Nova Scotia CAD/CAM Centre: Dir Dr JEAN-FRANCOIS TROTTIER.

Oceans Institute of Canada: Pres. R. L. RACE.

RBC Centre for Risk Management: Dir Dr P. ROSSON.

Trace Analysis Research Centre: Dir Dr LOUIS RAMALEY.

Vehicle Safety Research Team: Dir Dr C. R. BAIRD.

COLLÈGE DOMINICAIN DE PHILOSOPHIE ET DE THÉOLOGIE

96 Empress Ave, Ottawa, ON K1R 7G3
Telephone: (613) 233-5696

Fax: (613) 233-6064
Internet: www.collegedominicain.com
Founded 1909 as 'Studium Generale' of Order of Friars Preachers in Canada; present name 1967
Private control
Languages of instruction: French, English
Academic year: September to April
Chancellor: Yvon Pomerleau
President and Regent of Studies: Gabor Csepregi
Vice-President and Vice-Regent of Studies (vacant)
Master of Studies and Registrar: Maxime Allard
Secretary-Treasurer: Sr. Estelle St-Arnaud
Librarian: Martin Lavoie
Library of 120,000 vols, 500 periodicals
Number of teachers: 25
Number of students: 635 (127 full-time, 508 part-time)

DEANS

Faculty of Theology: Marie-Thérèse Nadeau
Department of Philosophy: J.-F. Méthot
Institute of Pastoral Theology: Daniel Cadrin

UNIVERSITY OF GUELPH

Guelph, ON N1G 2W1
Telephone: (519) 824-4120
Fax: (519) 766-9481 (for undergraduate studies); (519) 766-0843 (for graduate studies)
Internet: www.uoguelph.ca
Founded 1964 from Ontario Agricultural College, Ontario Veterinary College and Macdonald Institute, formerly affiliated to the University of Toronto
Private/Provincial control
Language of instruction: English
Three semester system
Chancellor: L. M. Alexander
President and Vice-Chancellor: Alastair Summerlee
Provost and Vice-President (Academic): Maureen Mancuso (acting)
Vice-President (Alumni Affairs and Development): Pamella Healey (acting)
Vice-President (Finance and Administration): Nancy Sullivan
Vice-President (Research): Alan Wildeman
Vice-Provost and Chief Academic Officer: Michael Nightingale
Librarian: M. Ridley
Library: Library of over 2.5 m. vols
Number of teachers: 750
Number of students: 14,000
Publications: *Graduate Calendar*, *President's Report*, *Undergraduate Calendar*

DEANS

College of Arts: Jacqueline Murray
College of Biological Science: Michael Emes
College of Physical and Engineering Science: Peter Tremaine
College of Social and Applied Human Sciences: Alun Joseph
Ontario Agricultural College: Craig Pearson
Ontario Veterinary College: A. H. Meek
Faculty of Environmental Sciences: M. R. Moss
Faculty of Graduate Studies: Isobel Heathcote

CHAIRS AND DIRECTORS OF DEPARTMENTS AND SCHOOLS

Allen, O. B., Mathematics and Statistics
Balahura, R. J., Chemistry and Biochemistry
Bredahl, M., Agricultural Economics and Business
Butler, D. G. (acting), Clinical Studies
Calvert, B., Philosophy
Chouinard, D., Languages and Literatures
Dixon, M. (acting), Environmental Biology
Dobosiewicz, W., Computing and Information Science
Fitzgibbon, J. E., School of Rural Planning and Development
Gibbins, A. M., Animal and Poultry Science
Gillespie, T. J., Land Resource Science
Graham, T. E., Human Biology and Nutritional Sciences
Hinch, R. (acting), Sociology and Anthropology
Jeffrey, K. R., Physics
Kissick, J., Fine Art and Music
Kuhn, R., Geography
Leatherland, J., Biomedical Sciences
Livernois, J., Economics
Mancuso, M., Political Studies
Marmurek, H. H. C., Psychology
Otten, L., School of Engineering
Padanyi, P., Consumer Studies
Phillips, J., Molecular Biology and Genetics
Pletsch, D. (acting), Rural Extension Studies
Prescott, J. F., Pathobiology
Purslow, P., Food Science
Reader, R. (acting), Botany
Reiche, E. G., History
Ribble, C., Population Medicine
Shepard, A., English and Theatre Studies
Shute, J. C. M. (acting), Centre for International Programs
Sullivan, J. A., Horticultural Science
Taylor, J. R. (acting), Landscape Architecture
Tindale, J., Family Relations and Applied Nutrition
Van Der Kraak, G., Zoology
Walsh, J., School of Hospitality and Food Management
Whitfield, C. (acting), Microbiology

UNIVERSITY OF KING'S COLLEGE

Halifax, NS B3H 2A1
Telephone: (902) 422-1271
Fax: (902) 423-3357
E-mail: admissions@ukings.ns.ca
Internet: www.ukings.ns.ca
Founded 1789 by United Empire Loyalists; granted Royal Charter 1802; entered into association with Dalhousie University 1923
Language of instruction: English
Academic year: September to May
Chancellor: Michael Meighen
President and Vice-Chancellor: William Barker
Vice-President: Elizabeth Edwards
Registrar: E. Yeo
Bursar: G. G. Smith
Librarian: H. Drake Petersen
Number of teachers: 33
Number of students: 1,105
Publication: *The Hinge* (annually)

PROFESSORS

Barker, W., English
Bishop, M., French
Burns, S. A. M., Philosophy
Cobden, M., Journalism
Crowley, J., History
Hankey, W. J., Classics
Huebert, R., English
Kimber, S., Journalism
Starnes, C. J., Classics
Vinci, T., Philosophy

LAKEHEAD UNIVERSITY

Oliver Rd, Thunder Bay, ON P7B 5E1
Telephone: (807) 343-8110
Fax: (807) 343-8023
E-mail: communications@lakeheadu.ca
Internet: www.lakeheadu.ca
Founded 1965; previously established as Lakehead College of Arts, Science and Technology, 1956, and Lakehead Technical Institute, 1946
Academic year: September to April
Chancellor: Lorne G. Everett
President: Frederick F. Gilbert
Provost and Vice-President (Academic): Mary Louise Hill
Vice-President (Research and Development): Tim Buell
Vice-President (Administration and Finance): Michael Pawlowski
Registrar: Pentti A. Paularinne
Librarian: Anne Deighton
Number of teachers: 240
Number of students: 6,585 (5,308 full-time, 1,277 part-time)

DEANS

Arts and Science: James H. Gellert
Business Administration: Bahram Dadgostar
Education: Julia T. O'Sullivan
Engineering: Henri T. Saliba
Forestry: David Euler
Professional Schools: Ian Newhouse (acting)
Director of Graduate Studies and Research: Mark L. Howe

HEADS OF DEPARTMENTS

Anthropology: J. S. Hamilton
Biology: A. D. Macdonald
Chemistry: G. D. Martin
Economics: N. C. Bonsor
English: K. Fedderson
Geography: B. J. Lorch
Geology: S. A. Kissin
History: P. Jasen
Indigenous Learning: R. S. Robson
Kinesiology: W. J. Montelpare
Languages: A. Nabarra
Library and Information Studies: M. MacLean
Mathematical Sciences: C. T. Hoang
Music: A. Carastathis
Nursing: L. S. McDougall
Outdoor Recreation, Parks and Tourism: T. W. Stevens
Philosophy: R. E. Maundrell
Physics: W. J. Keeler
Political Science: D. A. West
Psychology: S. R. Goldstein
Social Work: S. Taylor
Sociology: T. Dunk
Visual Arts: M. Nisenholt

LAURENTIAN UNIVERSITY OF SUDBURY

935 Ramsey Lake Rd, Sudbury, ON P3E 2C6
Telephone: (705) 675-1151
Fax: (705) 675-4891
E-mail: admission@laurentian.ca
Internet: www.laurentian.ca
Founded 1960
Provincially assisted, non-denominational
Languages of instruction: French, English(-certain depts offer parallel courses in both languages)
Academic year: September to April
President: Judith Woodsworth
Vice-President for Administration: Robert F. Bourgeois
Academic Vice-President for Anglophone Affairs: Susan Silverton
Academic Vice-President for Francophone Affairs: Harley d'Entremont
Registrar: Ron Smith
Director of Library: Lionel Bonin
Director, Centre for Continuing Education: Denis Mayer

Director, Division of Physical Education: ROGER COUTURE
Director, Graduate Studies and Research: PAUL COLILLI

Number of teachers: 377 (full-time)
Number of students: 9,100

depts of Anthropology, Behavioural neuroscience, Biology, Classical studies, Commerce and administration, Earth science, English, Environmental earth science, Education (English), Education (French), Ethics studies, Film studies, Folklore, Geography, History, Liberal science, Mathematics and computer science, Midwifery, Modern languages and literatures, Music, Native human services, Native studies, Nursing, Philosophy, Physics and astronomy, Political science, Psychology, Radiation therapy, Religious studies, Social work, Sociology, Sport psychology, Sports administration

DEANS

Humanities and Social Sciences: JOHN ISBISTER
Sciences and Engineering: PATRICE SAWYER
Professional Schools: ANNE-MARIE MAWHINEY
Management: HUGUETTE BLANCO

CONSTITUENT INSTITUTIONS

Algoma University College: 1520 Queen St E, Sault Ste Marie, ON P6A 2G4; internet www.algomau.ca; Pres. C. ROSS; Registrar D. MARASCO.

Collège Universitaire de Hearst: Hearst, ON P0L 1N0; internet www.univhearst.eduf. 1952; Rector R. TREMBLAY; Registrar J. DOUCET.

FEDERATED UNIVERSITIES

University of Sudbury: Ramsey Lake Rd, Sudbury, ON P3E 2C6; f. 1957; conducted by the Jesuit Fathers; Pres. ANDRII KRAWCHUK; Registrar L. BEAUPRÉ.

Huntington University: Ramsey Lake Rd, Sudbury, ON P3E 2C6; f. 1960; related to United Church of Canada; Pres.-Principal KEVIN MCCORMICK; Registrar A. HOOD.

Thorneloe University: Ramsey Lake Rd, Sudbury, ON P3E 2C6; Provost S. ANDREWS; Registrar I. MACLENNAN.

UNIVERSITÉ LAVAL

Québec, QC G1K 7P4
Telephone: (418) 656-2131
Fax: (418) 656-5920
E-mail: acceuil@sg.ulaval.ca
Internet: www.ulaval.ca

Founded 1852; Royal Charter signed December 1852, Pontifical Charter 1876, Provincial Charter 1970
Language of instruction: French
Academic year: September to August

Rector: MICHEL PIGEON
Vice-Rector (Academic): CHRISTIANE PICHÉ
Vice-Rector (Administration and Executive): CLAUDE GODBOUT
Vice-Rector (Development and International Relations): DIANE LACHAPELLE
Vice-Rector (Human Resources): LISE DARVEAU-FOURNIER
Vice-Rector (Research): RAYMOND LEBLANC
Dean of Graduate Studies: MARC PELCHAT
Director of Undergraduate Studies: SERGE TALBOT
Director of Continuing Education: PIERRE DIONNE
Secretary-General: GILLES KIROUAC
Registrar: DANIELLE FLEURY
Librarian: CLAUDE BONNELLY

Library: see Libraries and Archives
Number of teachers: 1,490
Number of students: 38,829 (25,301 full-time, 13,528 part-time)

Publications: *Revue Scientifique* (education), *Cahiers de Droit* (law), *Anthropologie et Sociétés* (anthropology), *Recherches Féministes* (feminism), *Relations Industrielles* (industrial relations), *Visio* (history), *Ecoscience* (biology), *Communication* (mass communication), *Cahiers de Géographie du Québec* (geography), *Les Cahiers du Journalisme* (journalism), *Langues et Linguistique* (linguistics), *L'Année Francophone Internationale (L'AFI)* (literary), *Laval Théologique et Philosophique* (theology and philosophy), *Service Social* (online, social work), *Ethnologies* (annual journal of Canadian folklore studies), *Études Littérataires* (3 a year, literature), *Rédiger* (annually, technical writing), *Études Inuits* (2 a year, Inuit studies), *Recherches Sociographiques* (annually, Quebec studies), *Didaskalia* (2 a year, education), *Études Internationales* (4 a year, international studies), *Cahiers de Recherche* (annually, economics), *CRIRES* (education), *Revue d'Histoire Intellectuelle de l'Amérique Française* (monthly)

DEANS AND DIRECTORS

Faculty of Administrative Sciences: ROBERT W. MANTHA
Faculty of Agriculture and Food Sciences: JEAN-PAUL LAFOREST
Faculty of Architecture, Planning and Visual Arts: CLAUDE DUBÉ
Faculty of Dentistry: JEAN-PAUL GOULET
Faculty of Education: CLAUDE SIMARD
Faculty of Forestry and Geomatics: DENIS BRIÈRE
Faculty of Law: P. LEMIEUX
Faculty of Letters: JACQUES MATHIEU
Faculty of Medicine: PIERRE JACOB DURAND
Faculty of Music: GILLES SIMARD
Faculty of Nursing: LINDA LEPAGE
Faculty of Pharmacy: MONIQUE RICHER
Faculty of Philosophy: LUC LANGLOIS
Faculty of Sciences and Engineering: JEAN-BAPTISTE SÉRODES
Faculty of Social Sciences: MICHAEL LORENGER
Faculty of Theology and Religious Studies: MARCEL VIAU
Quebec Institute of Higher International Studies: LOUIS BÉLANGER

PROFESSORS

Faculty of Administrative Sciences (Pavillon Palasis-Prince, Bureau 1322, Québec, QC G1K 7P4; tel. (418) 656-2180; fax (418) 656-2624; e-mail fsa@fsa.ulaval.ca; internet www.fsa.ulaval.ca):

AUDET, M., Management
BANVILLE, C., Management Information Systems
BEAULIEU, M.-C., Finance and Insurance
BÉDARD, J., Accounting (Sciences)
BÉLIVEAU, D., Marketing
BELLEMARE, G., Finance and Insurance
BERGERON, F., Management Information Systems
BERNIER, G., Finance and Insurance
BHERER, H., Management
BLAIS, R., Management
BOCTOR, F. F., Operations and Decision Systems
BOIRAL, O., Management
BOULAIRE, C., Marketing
BOURDEAU, L., Management
BRUN, J.-P., Management
CARPENTIER, C., Accounting (School)
CAYER, M., Management
CORMIER, E., Accounting (School)
COULOMBE, D., Accounting (Sciences)
D'AVIGNON, G. R., Operations and Decision Systems
DES ROSIERS, F., Management
DIONNE, P., Management
FISCHER, P. K., Finance and Insurance
GARAND, D. J., Management
GARNIER, B., Management
GASCON, A., Operations and Decision Systems
GASSE, Y., Management
GAUTHIER, A., Operations and Decision Systems
GAUVIN, S., Marketing
GENDRON, M., Finance and Insurance
GOSSELIN, M., Accounting (School)
GRISÉ, J., Management
HASKELL, N., Marketing
KETTANI, O., Operations and Decision Systems
KISS, L. N., Operations and Decision Systems
LACASSE, N., Management
LAI, V. S., Finance and Insurance
LAMOND, B., Operations and Decision Systems
LANDRY, R., Management
LANG, P., Operations and Decision Systems
LEE-GOSSELIN, H., Management
LESCEUX, D., Marketing
LETARTE, P.-A., Management
MANTHA, R. W., Management Information Systems
MARTEL, A., Operations and Decision Systems
MOFFET, D., Finance and Insurance
MONTREUIL, B., Operations and Decision Systems
NADEAU, L., Accounting (School)
NADEAU, R., Operations and Decision Systems
PAQUETTE, S., Accounting (Sciences)
PARÉ, P.-V., Accounting (School)
PASCOT, D., Management Information Systems
POULIN, D., Management
PRÉMONT, P. E., Management Information Systems
RENAUD, J., Operations and Decision Systems
RIDJANOVIC, D., Management Information Systems
RIGAUX-BRICMONT, B., Marketing
ROY, M.-C., Management Information Systems
ROY, M.-J., Management
SAINT PIERRE, J., Finance and Insurance
SEROR, ANN C., Management
SU, Z., Management
SURET, J.-M., Accounting (School)
VERNA, G., Management
VÉZINA, R., Marketing
ZINS, M., Marketing

Faculty of Agriculture and Food Sciences (Pavillon Paul-Comtois, Bureau 1122, Québec, QC G1K 7P4; tel. (418) 656-3145; fax (418) 656-7806; e-mail fsaa@fsaa.ulaval.ca; internet www.fsaa.ulaval.ca):

ALLARD, G., Plant Science
AMIOT, J., Food Science and Nutrition
ANGERS, P., Food Science and Nutrition
ANTOUN, H., Soils and Agricultural Engineering
ARUL, J., Food Science and Nutrition
ASSELIN, A., Plant Science
BAILEY, J. L., Animal Sciences
BEAUCHAMP, C. J., Plant Science
BEAUDOIN, P., Agricultural Economics and Consumer Sciences
BEAUDRY, M., Food Science and Nutrition
BÉLANGER, R., Plant Science
BELZILE, F., Plant Science
BENHAMOU, N., Plant Science
BERGERON, R., Animal Sciences
BERNIER, J.-F., Animal Sciences
BLACKBURN, M., Soils and Agricultural Engineering
BRODEUR, J., Plant Science

CAILLIER, M., Soils and Agricultural Engineering
CALKINS, P., Agricultural Economics and Consumer Sciences
CAREL, M., Agricultural Economics and Consumer Sciences
CARON, J., Soils and Agricultural Engineering
CASTAIGNE, F., Food Science and Nutrition
CESCAS, M. P., Soils and Agricultural Engineering
CHALIFOUR, F. P., Plant Science
CHAREST, P.-M., Plant Science
CHOUINARD, Y., Animal Sciences
COLLIN, J., Plant Science
DANSEREAU, B., Plant Science
DEBAILLEUL, G., Agricultural Economics and Consumer Sciences
DESJARDINS, Y., Plant Science
DESPRES, J.-P., Food Science and Nutrition
DESROSIERS, T., Food Science and Nutrition
DION, P., Plant Science
DOSTALER, D., Plant Science
DOYEN, M., Agricultural Economics and Consumer Sciences
DUFOUR, J. C., Agricultural Economics and Consumer Sciences
EMOND, J.-P., Soils and Agricultural Engineering
FLISS, I., Food Science and Nutrition
FORTIN, J., Soils and Agricultural Engineering
GALIBOIS, I., Food Science and Nutrition
GALLICHAND, J., Soils and Agricultural Engineering
GAUTHIER, S., Food Science and Nutrition
GERVAIS, J.-P., Agricultural Economics and Consumer Services
GOSSELIN, A., Plant Science
GOUIN, D., Agricultural Economics and Consumer Sciences
GOULET, J., Food Science and Nutrition
JACQUES, H., Food Science and Nutrition
KARAM, A., Soils and Agricultural Engineering
LACHANCE, M. J., Agricultural Economics and Consumer Sciences
LAFOREST, J.-P., Animal Sciences
LAGACÉ, R., Soils and Agricultural Engineering
LAMARCHE, B., Food Science and Nutrition
LAMBERT, R., Agricultural Economics and Consumer Sciences
LAPOINTE, G., Food Science and Nutrition
LARUE, B., Agricultural Economics and Consumer Sciences
LAVERDIÈRE, M.-R., Soils and Agricultural Engineering
LEFRANÇOIS, M., Animal Sciences
LEMIEUX, S., Food Science and Nutrition
LEROUX, G., Plant Science
LEVALLOIS, R., Agricultural Economics and Consumer Sciences
LOCONG, A., Food Science and Nutrition
MAKHLOUF, J., Food Science and Nutrition
MARQUIS, A., Soils and Agricultural Engineering
MARTEL, R., Food Science and Nutrition
MARTIN, F., Agricultural Economics and Consumer Sciences
MICHAUD, D., Plant Science
MORISSET, M., Agricultural Economics and Consumer Sciences
OLIVIER, A., Plant Science
OUELLET, D., Food Science and Nutrition
PAQUIN, P., Food Science and Nutrition
PARENT, D., Animal Science
PARENT, L. E., Soils and Agricultural Engineering
PELLERIN, D., Animal Sciences
PERRIER, J.-P., Agricultural Economics and Consumer Sciences
PICARD, G., Food Science and Nutrition
POTHIER, F., Animal Science
POULIOT, Y., Food Science and Nutrition
RATTI, C., Soils and Agricultural Engineering
RIOUX, J.-A., Plant Science
ROBITAILLE, J., Agricultural Economics and Consumer Sciences
ROCHEFORT, L., Plant Science
ROMAIN, R., Agricultural Economics and Consumer Sciences
ROY, D., Food Science and Nutrition
SIRARD, M.-A., Animal Science
ST-LOUIS, R., Agricultural Economics and Consumer Sciences
SUBIRADE, M., Food Science and Nutrition
THÉRIAULT, R., Soils and Agricultural Engineering
TURGEON, S., Food Science and Nutrition
TURGEON-O'BRIEN, H., Food Science and Nutrition
VOHL, J.-C., Food Science and Nutrition
VUILLEMARD, J.-C., Food Science and Nutrition
WEST, E. G., Agricultural Economics and Consumer Sciences
ZEE, J., Food Science and Nutrition

Faculty of Architecture, Planning and Visual Arts (Édifice du Vieux-Séminaire de Québec, 1 Côte de la Fabrique, Bureau 2230, Québec, QC G1R 3V6; tel. (418) 656-2546; fax (418) 656-3325; e-mail faaav@faaav.ulaval.ca; internet www.faaav.ulaval.ca):

BLAIS, M., Architecture
CARRIER, M., Planning
CASAULT, A., Architecture
CHAINE, F., Visual Arts
CLOUTIER, L., Visual Arts
COSSETTE, M. A., Visual Arts
CÔTÉ, P., Architecture
DEMERS, C., Architecture
DESPRÉS, C., Architecture
DUBÉ, C., Planning
GIRARD, G., Visual Arts
JEAN, M., Visual Arts
LAVOIE, C., Planning
LEE-GOSSELIN, M., Planning
LEMIEUX, R., Visual Arts
MALENFANT, N., Visual Arts
MILL, R., Visual Arts
NAYLOR, D., Visual Arts
PICHÉ, D., Architecture
PLEAU, R., Architecture
POTVIN, A., Architecture
POULIOT, S., Visual Arts
ROCHON, A., Visual Arts
RODRIGUEZ-PINZON, M., Planning
TEYSSOT, G., Architecture
THÉRIAULT, M., Planning
TREMBLAY, G.-H., Architecture
VACHON, E., Architecture
VACHON, G., Architecture
VILLENEUVE, P., Planning
ZWIEJSKI, J., Architecture

Faculty of Dentistry (Pavillon de Médecine Dentaire, Bureau 1615, Québec, QC G1K 7P4; tel. (418) 656-2247; fax (418) 656-2720; e-mail fmd@fmd.ulaval.ca; internet www.ulaval.ca/fmd):

BASTIEN, R.
BERNARD, C.
CARON, C.
CHMIELEWSKI, W.
FOURNIER, A.
GAGNON, G.
GAGNON, P.
GAUCHEN, H.
GIASSON, L.
GOULET, J.-P.
GRENIER, D.
LACHAPELLE, D.
MORAND, M.-A.
MORIN, S.
NICHOLSON, L.
PAYANT, L.
PERUSSE, R.
PROULX, M.
ROBERT, D.
ROUABHIA, M.
ROY, S.
VALOIS, M.

Faculty of Education (Pavillon des Sciences de l'Éducation, Québec, QC G1K 7P4; tel. (418) 656-3062; fax (418) 656-7347; e-mail fse@fse.ulaval.ca; internet www.fse.ulaval.ca):

ARRIOLA-SOCOL, M., Foundations and Interventions in Education
BÉLANGER, J.-D., Teaching and Learning Studies
BOISCLAIR, A., Teaching and Learning Studies
BOIVIN, M.-D., Foundations and Interventions in Education
BOUCHARD, P., Foundations and Interventions in Education
BOURASSA, B., Foundations and Interventions in Education
CARDIN, J.-F., Teaching and Learning Studies
CARDU, H., Foundations and Interventions in Education
CLOUTIER, R., Foundations and Interventions in Education
DEBLOIS, L., Teaching and Learning Studies
DENIGER, M.-A., Foundations and Interventions in Education
DÉSAUTELS, J., Teaching and Learning Studies
DESGAGNÉ, S., Teaching and Learning Studies
DIAMBOMBA, M., Foundations and Interventions in Education
DIONNE, J., Teaching and Learning Studies
DRAPEAU, S., Foundations and Interventions in Education
DROLET, J.-L., Foundations and Interventions in Education
FOUNTAIN, R. M. B., Teaching and Learning Studies
FOURNIER, G., Foundations and Interventions in Education
FOURNIER, J.-P., Teaching and Learning Studies
GAGNON, J., Physical Education
GAGNON, R., Teaching and Learning Studies
GAULIN, C., Teaching and Learning Studies
GAUTHIER, C., Teaching and Learning Studies
GERVAIS, F., Teaching and Learning Studies
GIASSON, J., Teaching and Learning Studies
GUAY, F., Foundations and Interventions in Education
GUERETTE, C., Teaching and Learning Studies
GUILBERT, L., Teaching and Learning Studies
HAMEL, T., Foundations and Interventions in Education
JACQUES, M., Teaching and Learning Studies
JEANRIE, C., Foundations and Interventions in Educations
JEFFREY, D., Teaching and Learning Studies
KASZAP, M., Teaching and Learning Studies
LACHANCE, L., Foundations and Interventions in Education
LAFERRIÈRE, T., Teaching and Learning Studies
LANDRY, C., Foundations and Interventions in Education
LAPOINTE, C., Foundations and Interventions in Education
LAROCHELLE, M., Teaching and Learning Studies
LAROSE, S., Teaching and Learning Studies

LE BOSSE, Y., Foundations and Interventions in Education
LECLERC, C., Foundations and Interventions in Education
LEGAULT, M., Teaching and Learning Studies
MARANDA, M.-F., Foundations and Interventions in Education
MARCOUX, Y., Foundations and Interventions in Education
MARTEL, D., Physical Education
MASSOT, A., Foundations and Interventions in Education
MOISSET, J.-J., Foundations and Interventions in Education
MONETTE, M., Foundations and Interventions in Education
MURA, R., Teaching and Learning Studies
NADEAU, G.-A., Physical Education
PAGÉ, P., Teaching and Learning Skills
PELLETIER, P., Teaching and Learning Skills
PLANTE, J., Foundations and Interventions in Education
RATTE, J., Foundations and Interventions in Education
ROY-BUREAU, L., Teaching and Learning Skills
ROYER, E., Teaching and Learning Studies
ST-LAURENT, L., Teaching and Learning Studies
SAMSON, J., Physical Education
SAVARD, C., Physical Education
SIMARD, C., Teaching and Learning Studies
SIMARD, D., Teaching and Learning Skills
SPAIN, A., Foundations and Interventions in Education
TALBOT, S., Physical Education
THERIAULT, G., Physical Education
TROTTIER, C., Foundations and Interventions in Education
VALOIS, P., Foundations and Interventions in Education
VINCENT, S., Teaching and Learning Skills
ZIARKO, H., Teaching and Learning Skills

Faculty of Forestry and Geomatics (Pavillon Abitibi-Price, Bureau 1151, Québec, QC G1K 7P4; tel. (418) 656-3880; fax (418) 656-3177; e-mail ffg@ffg.ulaval.ca; internet www.ffg.ulaval.ca):

ALLARD, M., Geography
BAUCE, E., Wood and Forest Sciences
BEAUDOIN, M., Wood and Forest Sciences
BEAULIEU, B., Geomatics
BEAUREGARD, R., Wood and Forest Sciences
BÉDARD, Y., Geomatics
BÉGIN, J., Wood and Forest Sciences
BÉGIN, Y., Geography
BÉLANGER, L., Wood and Forest Sciences
BELLEFLEUR, P., Wood and Forest Sciences
BERNIER, L., Wood and Forest Sciences
BHIRY, N., Geography
BOULIANNE, M., Geomatics
BOUSQUET, J., Wood and Forest Sciences
BOUTHILLER, L., Wood and Forest Sciences
BRIÈRE, D., Wood and Forest Sciences
CAMIRÉ, C., Wood and Forest Sciences
CHEVALLIER, J.-J., Geomatics
CLOUTIER, A., Wood and Forest Sciences
CONDAL, A., Geomatics
DESROCHERS, A., Wood and Forest Sciences
DESSUREAULT, M., Wood and Forest Sciences
EDWARDS, G., Geomatics
FILION, L., Geography
FORTIN, Y., Wood and Forest Sciences
GODBOUT, C., Wood and Forest Sciences
HERNANDEZ PENA, R., Wood and Forest Sciences
LALONDE, M., Wood and Forest Sciences
LEBEL, L., Wood and Forest Sciences
LOWELL, K., Wood and Forest Sciences
MARGOLLIS, H., Wood and Forest Sciences
MERCIER, G., Geography
MUNSON, A., Wood and Forest Sciences
PICHÉ, Y., Wood and Forest Sciences
PIENITZ, R., Geography
PLAMONDON, A. P., Wood and Forest Sciences
PLANTE, F., Geomatics
POTHIER, D., Wood and Forest Sciences
RIEDL, B., Wood and Forest Sciences
RUEL, J.-C., Wood and Forest Sciences
ST-HILAIRE, M., Geography
SANTERRE, R., Geomatics
STEVANOVIC, J. T., Wood and Forest Sciences
THIBEAULT, J.-R., Wood and Forest Sciences
TREMBLAY, F., Wood and Forest Sciences
VIAU, A., Geomatics

Faculty of Law (Pavillon Charles-DeKoninck, Bureau 2407, Québec, QC G1K 7P4; tel. (418) 656-2131 ext. 6134; fax (418) 656-7230; e-mail fd@fd.ulaval.ca; internet www.ulaval.ca/fd):

ARBOUR, M.
BELLEAU, M.-C.
BOUCHARD, C.
BRETON, R.
BROCHU, F.
COTE-HARPER, G.
CRÊTE, R.
DELEURY, E.
DESLAURIERS, J.
DUPLE, N.
FERLAND, D.
GARDNER, D.
GIROUX, L.
GOUBAU, D.
HALLEY, P.
ISSALYS, P.
LANGEVIN, L.
LAQUERRE, P.
LAREAU, A.
LAUZIÈRE, L.
LEMIEUX, D.
LEMIEUX, P.
MANGANAS, A.
MELKEVILL, B.
NORMAND, S.
OTIS, G.
PRUJINER, A.
RAINVILLE, P.
ROUSSEAU, G.
TREMBLAY, G.
TURGEON, J.

Faculty of Letters (Pavillon Charles-De Koninck, Bureau 3254, Québec, QC G1K 7P4; tel. (418) 656-3460; fax (418) 656-2019; e-mail fl@fl.ulaval.ca; internet www.fl.ulaval.ca):

AUGER, P., Languages and Linguistics
AUGER, R., History
BACZ, B., Languages and Linguistics
BAKER, P., History
BAUDOU, A., Literature
BEAUCHAMP, M., Information and Communication
BEAUDET, M.-A., Literature
BEAUSOLEIL, P., Information and Communication
BELANGER, R., History
BELLEGUIC, T., Literature
BERNIER, J., History
BISAILLON, J., Languages and Linguistics
BOISVERT, L., Languages and Linguistics
BOIVIN, A., Literature
BORGONOVO, C., Languages and Linguistics
BOULANGER, J.-C., Languages and Linguistics
CARANI, M., History
CARDIN, M., History
CAULIER, B., History
CHARRON, J., Information and Communication
CLERC, I., Information and Communication
COSSETTE, J. C., Information and Communication
CUMMINS, S., Languages and Linguistics
DAGENAIS, B., Information and Communication
DAIGLE, J., History
DAVIAULT, A., Literature
DE BONVILLE, J., Information and Communication
DE KONINCK, Z., Languages and Linguistics
DE LA GARDE, R., Information and Communication
DEMERS, F., Information and Communication
DEMERS, G., Languages and Linguistics
DESDOUITS, A.-M., History
DESHAIES, D., Languages and Linguistics
DOLAN, C., History
DUBÉ, P., History
DUFFLEY, P., Languages and Linguistics
DUMONT, F., Literature
ESPANOL, E. M., Languages and Linguistics
FAITELSON-WEISER, S., Languages and Linguistics
FINETTE, L., Literature
FORTIER, A.-M., Literature
FORTIN, M., History
FYSON, D., History
GAGNÉ, M., Literature
GARON, L., Information and Communication
GAUTHIER, G., Information and Communication
GRENIER, D., History
GRIGNON, M., History
GUEVEL, Z., Languages and Linguistics
GUILBERT, L., History
HÉBERT, C., Literature
HERMON, E., History
HUMMEL, K., Languages and Linguistics
HUOT, D., Languages and Linguistics
HUOT-LEMONNIER, F., Languages and Linguistics
JOLICOEUR, L., Languages and Linguistics
JUNEAU, M., Languages and Linguistics
KAREL, D., History
KEGLE, C., Literature
KOSS, B. J., History
KUGLER, M., Information and Communication
LABERGE, A., History
LACHARITÉ, D. P., Languages and Linguistics
LADOUCEUR, J., Languages and Linguistics
LAPOINTE, M., History
LAVIGNE, A., Informatics and Communication
LEBEL, E., Information and Communication
LEMELIN, B., History
LEMIEUX, J., Information and Communication
LÉTOURNEAU, J., History
LOWE, R., Languages and Linguistics
LUKIC, R., History
MANNING, A., Languages and Linguistics
MARCHAND, J., Information and Communication
MARTIN, P., Languages and Linguistics
MATHIEU, J., History
MATHIEU, J., History
MERCIER, A., Literature
MOORE, E., History
MOSER VERREY, M., Literature
MOUSSETTE, M., History
NAKOS, D., Languages and Linguistics
NGUYEN-DUY, V., Information and Communication
NIQUETTE, M., Information and Communication
OUELLET, J., Languages and Linguistics
PAQUETTE, G., Information and Communication
PAQUOT, A., Languages and Linguistics
PARADIS, C., Languages and Linguistics
PARKS, S. E., Languages and Linguistics
PELLETIER, E., Literature
PERELLI-CONTOS, I., Literature

PERESTRELO, F., Languages and Linguistics
PICARD, J.-C., Information and Communication
PIETTE, C., History
POIRIER, C., Languages and Linguistics
PONTBRIAND, J.-N., Literature
PRÉVOST, P., Languages and Linguistics
RIVET, J., Information and Communication
ROY, L., Literature
SADETSKY, A., Languages and Linguistics
ST-GELAIS, R., Literature
SAINT JACQUES, D., Literature
SAUVAGEAU, F., Information and Communication
THENON, L., Literature
THÉRY, C., Literature
THOMAS, N. H., Literature
TREMBLAY, G., Geography
TURGEON, L., History
VALLIÈRES, M., History
VAN DER SCHWEREN, E., Literature
VERREAULT, C., Languages and Linguistics
VINCENT, D., Languages and Linguistics
WATINE, T., Information and Communication

Faculty of Medicine (Pavillon Ferdinand-Vandry, Bureau 1214, Québec, QC G1K 7P4; tel. (418) 656-5245; fax (418) 656-2501; e-mail fmed@fmed.ulaval.ca; internet www.fmed.ulaval.ca):

ABDOUS, B., Social and Preventive Medicine
AKOUM, A., Obstetrics and Gynaecology
ALARY, M., Social and Preventive Medicine
ALLEN, T., Family Medicine
AMZICA, F., Anatomy and Physiology
AUBIN, M., Family Medicine
AUDETTE, M., Medical Biology
AUGER, F., Surgery
AYOTTE, P., Social and Preventive Medicine
BACHELARD, H., Medicine
BACHVAROV, D., Medicine
BAIRATI, I., Surgery
BAIRAM, A., Paediatrics
BARDEN, N., Anatomy and Physiology
BASTIDE, A., Obstetrics and Gynaecology
BEAUCHAMP, D., Medical Biology
BEAUCHEMIN, J.-P., Family Medicine
BEAULIEU, A., Medicine
BEDARD, P., Medicine
BÉLANGER, A., Anatomy and Physiology
BÉLANGER, A. Y., Rehabilitation
BÉLANGER, L., Medical Biology
BERGERON, J., Medical Biology
BERGERON, J., Obstetrics and Gynaecology
BERGERON, M. G., Medical Biology
BERGERON, R., Family Medicine
BERNARD, P.-M., Social and Preventive Medicine
BERNATCHEZ, J.-P., Psychiatry
BERNIER, V., Medical Biology
BILODEAU, A., Family Medicine
BISSONNETTE, E., Medicine
BLANCHET, J., Obstetrics and Gynaecology
BLONDEAU, F., Family Medicine
BELONDEAU, L., Medicine
BOGATY, P., Medicine
BOIVIN, G., Medical Biology
BORGEAT, P., Anatomy and Physiology
BOUCHARD, J.-P., Medicine
BOUCHER, F., Paediatrics
BOULAY, M. R., Social and Preventive Medicine
BOULET, L.-P., Medicine
BOURBONNAIS, R., Rehabilitation
BOURGOIN, S.-G., Anatomy and Physiology
BRAILOVSKY, C. A., Family Medicine
BRASSARD, N., Obstetrics and Gynaecology
BRISSON, C., Social and Preventive Medicine
BRISSON, J., Social and Preventive Medicine
CABANAC, M., Anatomy and Physiology
CANDAS, B., Anatomy and Physiology
CAPADAY, C., Anatomy and Physiology
CARRIÈRE, M., Rehabilitation
CARUSO, M., Medical Biology
CHAHINE, M., Medicine
CHAKIR, J., Medicine
CHARRON, J., Medical Biology
CLOUTIER, A., Paediatrics
CORBEIL, J., Anatomy and Physiology
CORMIER, Y., Medicine
CÔTÉ, C., Rehabilitation
CÔTÉ, J., Anaesthesiology
CÔTÉ, J., Medical Biology
CÔTÉ, L., Medicine
COUET, J., Medicine
CUSAN, L., Anatomy and Physiology
DE KONINCK, M., Social and Preventive Medicine
DE KONINCK, Y., Psychiatry
DE SERRES, G., Medical Biology
DE WALS, P., Social and Preventive Medicine
DELAGE, R., Medicine
DERY, P., Paediatrics
DESCHÊNES, M., Anatomy and Physiology
DESHAIES, Y., Anatomy and Physiology
DESLAURIERS, J., Surgery
DESMEULES, M., Medicine
DEWAILLY, F., Social and Preventive Medicine
DIONNE, C., Rehabilitation
DIONNE, F. T., Social and Preventive Medicine
DODIN, S. D., Obstetrics and Gynaecology
DOILLON, C., Surgery
DORÉ, F. M., Medicine
DORVAL, J., Paediatrics
DOUVILLE, Y., Surgery
DROLET, G., Medicine
DUMESNIL, J.-G., Medicine
DURAND, P.-J., Social and Preventive Medicine
FAURE, R., Paediatrics
FLAMAND, L., Anatomy and Physiology
FOREST, J.-C., Medical Biology
FORTIER, M.-A., Obstetrics and Gynaecology
FORTIN, J.-P., Social and Preventive Medicine
FRADET, Y., Surgery
FRÉMONT, P., Rehabilitation
FRENETTE, J., Family Medicine
FRENETTE, J., Rehabilitation
GAGNON, F., Psychiatry
GAILIS, L., Medicine
GERMAIN, L., Surgery
GERVAIS, M., Rehabilitation
GIRARD, J. E., Social and Preventive Medicine
GLENN, J., Medical Biology
GOSSELIN, J., Anatomy and Physiology
GOVINDAN, M. J., Anatomy and Physiology
GRAVEL, C., Psychiatry
GUAY, G., Medicine
GUÉRIN, S., Anatomy and Physiology
GUIDOIN, R., Surgery
HANCOCK, R., Medical Biology
HUDON, C., Paediatrics
HUOT, J., Medicine
JEANNOTTE, L., Medical Biology
JOBIN, J., Medicine
JULIEN, J.-P., Anatomy and Physiology
JULIEN, P., Medicine
KHANDJIAN, E. W., Medical Biology
KINKEAD, R., Paediatrics
KINGMA, J. G., Medicine
L'ARRIÈRE, M., Rehabilitation
LABBÉ, J., Paediatrics
LABBÉ, R., Medical Biology
LABELLE, Y., Medical Biology
LABERGE, C., Medicine
LABRECQUE, M., Family Medicine
LABRIE, C., Anatomy and Physiology
LABRIE, F., Anatomy and Physiology
LACASSE, Y., Medicine
LAFRAMBOISE, R., Paediatrics
LAGACÉ, R., Medical Biology
LAGASSE, P.-P., Social and Preventive Medicine
LAJOIE, P., Social and Preventive Medicine
LALANNE, M., Medical Biology
LAMBERT, R. D., Obstetrics and Gynaecology
LAMONTAGNE, R., Family Medicine
LANDRY, J., Medicine
LANGELIER, M., Medicine
LANGLOIS, S., Medicine
LANIVIÈLE, R., Medicine
LAROCHELLE, L., Anatomy and Physiology
LATULIPPE, L., Medicine
LAVIOLETTE, M., Medicine
LAVOIE, J., Medical Biology
LEBEL, M., Medicine
LEBLANC, R., Social and Preventive Medicine
LEBLOND, P., Medicine
LECLERC, P., Medical Biology
LEDUC, Y., Family Medicine
LELIÈVRE, M., Paediatrics
LEMAY, A., Obstetrics and Gynaecology
LETARTE, R., Medical Biology
LEVALLOIS, P., Social and Preventive Medicine
LEVESQUE, D., Medicine
LÉVESQUE, R., Medical Biology
LIN, S.-X., Anatomy and Physiology
LUU, T. V., Anatomy and Physiology
MCFADYEN, B. J., Rehabilitation
MAHEUX, R., Obstetrics and Gynaecology
MALOUIN, F., Rehabilitation
MALTAIS, F., Medicine
MARCEAU, F., Medicine
MARCEAU, N., Medicine
MARCHAND, R., Anatomy and Physiology
MARCOUX, H., Family Medicine
MARCOUX, S., Social and Preventive Medicine
MARETTE, A., Anatomy and Physiology
MARTINEAU, R., Medical Biology
MAUNSELL, E., Social and Preventive Medicine
MAURIEGE, P., Social and Preventive Medicine
MAZIADE, M., Psychiatry
MERETTE, C., Psychiatry
MEYER, F., Social and Preventive Medicine
MIRAULT, M.-E., Medicine
MOFFET, H., Rehabilitation
MONTGRAIN, N., Psychiatry
MORISSETTE, J., Anatomy and Physiology
MOSS, T., Medical Biology
MOURAD, M. W., Medicine
MURTHY, M.-R.-V., Medical Biology
NACCACHE, P.-H., Medicine
NADEAU, A., Medicine
NADEAU, L., Medical Biology
NOREAU, L., Rehabilitation
OUELLETTE, M., Medical Biology
PAINCHAUD, G., Psychiatry
PAPADOPOULO, B., Medical Biology
PARENT, A., Anatomy and Physiology
PELLETIER, G.-H., Anatomy and Physiology
PERUSSE, L., Social and Preventive Medicine
PHILIPPE, E., Anatomy and Physiology
PIBAROT, P., Medicine
PIEDBOEUF, B., Paediatrics
POIRIER, D., Anatomy and Physiology
POIRIER, G., Medical Biology
POMERLEAU, G., Psychiatry
POUBELLE, P., Medicine
POULIN, R., Anatomy and Physiology
PUYMIRAT, J., Medicine
RATTÉ, C., Psychiatry
RAYMOND, V., Anatomy and Physiology
RICHARD, D., Anatomy and Physiology
RICHARDS, C. L., Rehabilitation
RIOUX, F., Medicine
RIVEST, S., Anatomy and Physiology
ROBERGE, C., Medical Biology
ROBICHAUD, L., Rehabilitation
ROUILLARD, C., Medicine
ROULEAU, J., Medicine

Rousseau, F., Medical Biology
Roy, M., Obstetrics and Gynaecology
Salesse, C., Otorhinolaryngology and Ophthalmology
Sato, M., Anatomy and Physiology
Sato, S., Medical Biology
Saucier, D., Family Medicine
Savard, P., Medicine
Seguin, C., Anatomy and Physiology
Series, F., Medicine
Shah, G., Medical Biology
Simard, J., Anatomy and Physiology
Steriade, M., Anatomy and Physiology
Sullivan, R., Obstetrics and Gynaecology
Talbot, J., Medical Biology
Tanguay, R., Medicine
Teasdale, N., Social and Preventive Medicine
Tessier, P., Medical Biology
Tetreault, S., Rehabilitation
Tetu, B., Medical Biology
Thivierge, J., Psychiatry
Tremblay, A., Social and Preventive Medicine
Tremblay, J.-P., Anatomy and Physiology
Tremblay, M. J., Medical Biology
Tremblay, Y., Obstetrics and Gynaecology
Trudel, L., Rehabilitation
Venrreault, R., Social and Preventive Medicine
Verret, S., Paediatrics
Vezina, M., Social and Preventive Medicine
Villeneuve, E., Psychiatry
Vincent, C., Rehabilitation
Vincent, M., Medicine

Faculty of Philosophy (Pavillon Félix-Antoine-Savard, Bureau 644, Québec, QC G1K 7P4; tel. (418) 656-2244; fax (418) 656-7267; e-mail fp@fp.ulaval.ca; internet www.fp.ulaval.ca):

Bégin, L.
Bilodeau, R.
Boss, G.
Cunningham, H.-P.
De Koninck, T.
Knee, P.
Lafleur, C.
Langlois, L.
Narbonne, J.-M.
Parizeau, M.-H.
Pelletier, Y.
Ricard, M.-A.
Sasseville, M.
Thibaudeau, V.
Tournier, F.

Faculty of Music (Pavillon Louis-Jacques-Casault, Bureau 3312, Québec, QC G1K 7P4; tel. (418) 656-7061; fax (418) 656-7365; e-mail mus@mus.ulaval.ca; internet www.ulaval.ca/mus):

Boulet, M.-M.
Cadrin, P.
Ducharme, M.
Laflamme, S.
Masson-Bourque, C.
Mathieu, L.
Papillon, A.
Parent, N.
Pinson, J.-P.
Ringuette, R.
Roberge, M.-A.
Stuber, U.
Terebesi, G.

Faculty of Nursing (Pavillon Paul-Comtois, Bureau 4106, Québec, QC G1K 7P4; tel. (418) 656-3356; fax (418) 656-7747; e-mail fsi@fsi.ulaval.ca; internet www.ulaval.ca/fsi):

Blondeau, D.
Côté, E.
Dallaire, C.
Ebacher, M.-F.
Fillion, L.
Godin, G.
Hagan, L.
Lepage, L.
Morin, D.
O'Neill, M.
Patenaude, L.
Pelletier, L.
Provencher, H.
Viens, C.

Faculty of Pharmacy (Pavillon Ferdinand-Vandry, Bureau 2241, Québec, QC G1K 7P4; tel. (418) 656-3211; fax (418) 656-2305; e-mail pha@pha.ulaval.ca; internet www.pha.ulaval.ca):

Beaulac-Baillargeon, L.
Belanger, P. M.
Castonguay, A.
Daleau, P.
Desgagné, M.
di Paolo-Chenevert, T.
Dionne, A.
Dorval, M.
Grégoire, J.-P.
Guillemette, C.
Juhasz, J.
Moisan, J.
Richer, M.
Tremblay, M.
Vézina, C.

Faculty of Sciences and Engineering (Pavillon Alexandre-Vachon, Bureau 1033, Québec, QC G1K 7P4; tel. (418) 656-2163; fax (418) 656-5902; e-mail fsg@fsg.ulaval.ca; internet www.fsg.ulaval.ca):

Adam, L., Actuarial Science
Ait-Kadi, D., Mechanical Engineering
Amiot, P. L., Physical Engineering and Optics
Anctil, F., Civil Engineering
Anderson, A., Biology
Auger, M., Chemistry
Barbeau, C., Chemistry
Baribeau, L., Mathematics and Statistics
Barrette, C., Biology
Bastien, J., Civil Engineering
Bazin, C., Mining, Metallurgical and Materials Engineering
Beaudoin, G., Geology and Geological Engineering
Beaulieu, D., Civil Engineering
Beaulieu, J.-M., Computer Science
Beaupré, D., Civil Engineering
Bédard, D., Actuarial Science
Bédard, G., Physical Engineering and Optics
Belisle, C., Mathematics and Statistics
Belkhiter, N., Computer Science
Bergevin, R., Electrical and Computer Engineering
Bernatchez, L., Biology
Borra, E. F., Physical Engineering and Optics
Bouchard, C., Civil Engineering
Boudreau, D., Chemistry
Boukouvalas, J., Chemistry
Bourbonnais, Y., Biochemistry and Microbiology
Bousmina, M. M., Chemical Engineering
Brisson, J., Chemistry
Bui, M. D., Computer Science
Cardou, A., Mechanical Engineering
Carmichael, J.-P., Mathematics and Statistics
Cassidy, C., Mathematics and Statistics
Cassidy, D. P., Geology and Geological Engineering
Chaib-Draa, B., Computer Science
Charlet, G., Chemistry
Chênevert, R., Chemistry
Chin, S. L., Physical Engineering and Optics
Chouinard, J.-Y., Electrical and Computer Engineering
Cloutier, C., Biology
Cossette, H., Actuarial Science
Cros, J., Electrical and Computer Engineering
Curodeau, A., Mechanical Engineering
D'Amours, S., Mechanical Engineering
Darveau, A., Biochemistry and Microbiology
De Champlain, A., Mechanical Engineering
De Koninck, J.-M., Mathematics and Statistics
Del Villar, R., Mining, Metallurgical and Materials Engineering
Desbiens, A., Electrical and Computer Engineering
Deschênes, C., Mechanical Engineering
Desharnais, J., Computer Science
Deslauriers, N., Biochemistry and Microbiology
Dodson, J., Biology
Doré, G., Civil Engineering
Dube, L. J., Physical Engineering and Optics
Dubé, D, Mining, Metallurgical and Materials Engineering
Duchesne, J., Geology and Geological Engineering
Duguay, M.-A., Electrical and Computer Engineering
Dumas, G., Mechanical Engineering
Dupuis, C., Computer Science
Dussault, P., Biochemistry and Microbiology
Fafard, M., Civil Engineering
Foriero, A., Civil Engineering
Fortier, L., Biology
Fortier, P., Electrical and Computer Engineering
Fortier, R., Geology and Geological Engineering
Fortin, A., Mathematics and Statistics
Frenette, M., Biochemistry and Microbiology
Fytas, K., Mining, Metallurgical and Materials Engineering
Gakwaya, A., Mechanical Engineering
Galstian, T., Physics, Physical Engineering and Optics
Galvez-Cloutier, R., Civil Engineering
Ganguly, U. S., Electrical and Computer Engineering
Garnier, A., Chemical Engineering
Gauthier, G., Biology
Gelinas, P. J., Geology and Geological Engineering
Gendron, G., Mechanical Engineering
Genest, C., Mathematics and Statistics
Gervais, J.-J., Mathematics and Statistics
Ghali, E., Mining, Metallurgical and Materials Engineering
Ghazzali, N., Mathematics and Statistics
Giguère, M., Actuarial Science
Glover, P., Geology and Geological Engineering
Gosselin, C., Mechanical Engineering
Goudreau, S., Mechanical Engineering
Goulet, V., Actuarial Science
Gourdeau, F., Mathematics and Statistics
Grandjean, B., Chemical Engineering
Grenier, D., Electrical and Computer Engineering
Guderley, H., Biology
Guenette, R., Mathematics and Statistics
Guertin, M., Biochemistry and Microbiology
Guillot, M., Mechanical Engineering
Hadjigeorgiou, J., Mining, Metallurgical and Materials Engineering
Hebert, R., Geology and Geological Engineering
Himmelman, J., Biology
Hodgson, B. R., Mathematics and Statistics
Hodouin, D., Mining, Metallurgical and Materials Engineering
Houle, G., Biology
Huot, J., Biology

Jacques, M., Actuarial Science
Johnson, L. E., Biology
Joncas, G., Physics, Physical Engineering and Optics
Kaliaguine, S., Chemical Engineering
Kirkwood, D., Geology and Geological Engineering
Knystautas, E., Physics, Physical Engineering and Optics
Konrad, J.-M., Civil Engineering
Kretschmer, D., Mechanical Engineering
Kroeger, H., Physics, Physical Engineering and Optics
Lacroix, R., Chemical Engineering
Lapointe, L., Biology
Larachi, F., Chemical Engineering
Laroche, G., Mining, Metallurgical and Materials Engineering
Larochelle, J., Biology
Larochelle, S., Electrical and Computer Engineering
Laurendeau, D., Electrical and Computer Engineering
Lavoie, M. C., Biochemistry and Microbiology
Leboeuf, D., Civil Engineering
Leclerc, M., Chemistry
Leduy, A., Chemical Engineering
Le Huy, H., Electrical and Computer Engineering
Lemay, J., Mechanical Engineering
Lemieux, C., Biochemistry and Microbiology
Lemieux, G., Biochemistry and Microbiology
Leroueil, S., Civil Engineering
Lessard, P., Civil Engineering
Lessard, R. A., Physics, Physical Engineering and Optics
Levasseur, M., Biology
Léveillé, G., Actuarial Science
Lévesque, B., Mechanical Engineering
Lévesque, C., Mathematics and Statistics
Locat, J., Geology and Geological Engineering
Luong, A., Actuarial Science
McBreen, P. H., Chemistry
McCarthy, N., Physics, Physical Engineering and Optics
Maciel, Y., Mechanical Engineering
Maldague, X., Electrical and Computer Engineering
Manouzi, H., Mathematics and Statistics
Marceau, E., Actuarial Science
Marchand, J., Civil Engineering
Marchand, M., Computer Science
Marchand, P., Computer Science
Marleau, L., Physics, Physical Engineering and Optics
Martel, H., Physics, Physical Engineering and Optics
Masse, J.-C., Mathematics and Statistics
Mathieu, P., Physics, Physical Engineering and Optics
Mineau, G., Computer Science
Moineau, S., Biochemistry and Microbiology
Morse, B., Civil Engineering
Moulin, B., Computer Sciences
Nguyen-Dang, T.-T., Chemistry
Pallotta, D., Biology
Paquette, N., Biology
Paraszczak, J., Mining, Metallurgical and Materials Engineering
Parizeau, M., Electrical and Computer Engineering
Payette, S., Biology
Pezolet, M., Chemistry
Philippin, G., Mathematics and Statistics
Picard, A., Civil Engineering
Piché, M., Physics, Physical Engineering and Optics
Pierre, R., Mathematics and Statistics
Pigeon, M., Civil Engineering
Pineault, S., Physics, Physical Engineering and Optics
Planeta, S., Mining, Metallurgical and Materials Engineering
Pomerleau, A., Electrical and Computer Engineering
Poulin, R., Mining, Metallurgical and Materials Engineering
Rancourt, D., Mechanical Engineering
Ransford, T.-J., Mathematics and Statistics
Richard, M. J., Mechanical Engineering
Ritcey, A.-M., Chemistry
Rivest, L.-P., Mathematics and Statistics
Robert, C., Physics, Physical Engineering and Optics
Robert, J.-L., Civil Engineering
Rocheleau, M., Geology and Geological Engineering
Rodrigue, D., Chemical Engineering
Roy, C., Chemical Engineering
Roy, D., Physics, Physical Engineering and Optics
Roy, P.-H., Biochemistry and Microbiology
Roy, R., Physics, Physical Engineering and Optics
Rusch, L. A., Electrical and Computer Engineering
Seguin, M. K., Geology and Geological Engineering
Serodes, J.-B., Civil Engineering
Sheng, Y., Physics, Physical Engineering and Optics
Tarasiewicz, R., Mechanical Engineering
Tawbi, N., Computer Science
Têtu, M., Electrical and Computer Engineering
Therrien, R., Geology and Geological Engineering
Tourigny, N., Computer Science
Tremblay, P., Electrical and Computer Engineering
Tremblay, R., Physics, Physical Engineering and Optics
Turcotte, J., Chemistry
Turmel, M., Biochemistry and Microbiology
Vadeboncoeur, C., Biochemistry and Microbiology
Vallée, R., Physics, Physical Engineering and Optics
Viarouge, P., Electrical and Computer Engineering
Vincent, W. F., Biology
Vo Van, T., Mining, Metallurgical and Materials Engineering
Voyer, N., Chemistry
Witzel, B., Physics, Physical Engineering and Optics
Zaccarin, A., Electrical and Computer Engineering

Faculty of Social Sciences (Pavillon Charles-DeKoninck, Bureau 3456, Québec, QC G1K 7P4; tel. (418) 656-2615; fax (418) 656-2114; e-mail fss@fss.ulaval.ca; internet www.fss.ulaval.ca):

Arcand, B., Anthropology
Audet, M., Industrial Relations
Baccigalupo, A., Political Science
Bakary, T., Political Science
Baribeau, J., Psychology
Bariteau, C., Anthropology
Barla, P., Economics
Barre, A., Industrial Relations
Beauchamp, C., Sociology
Beaudreau, B. C., Economics
Beaudry, M., Social Work
Bélanger, G., Economics
Bélanger, J., Industrial Relations
Bélanger, L., Political Science
Bernard, J.-T., Economics
Bernier, C., Industrial Relations
Bernier, J., Industrial Relations
Blais, F., Political Science
Blouin, R., Industrial Relations
Boisvert, J.-M., Psychology
Boivin, J., Industrial Relations
Boivin, M., Psychology
Bolduc, D., Economics
Boucher, N., Social Work
Bousquet, N., Sociology
Breton, G., Political Science
Carmichael, B., Economics
Chalifoux, J.-J., Anthropology
Clain, O., Sociology
Cloutier, R., Psychology
Comeau, Y., Social Work
Constantanos, C., Economics
Côté, P., Political Science
Couillard, M.-A., Anthropology
Crête, J., Political Science
Dagenais, H., Anthropology
Damant, D., Social Work
Darveau-Fournier, L., Social Work
Decaluwe, B., Economics
Delage, D., Sociology
Diguer, L., Psychology
Deom, E., Industrial Relations
Derriennic, J.-P., Political Science
Desève, M., Sociology
Desrochers, S., Psychology
Dessy, S. E., Economics
Dompierre, J., Industrial Relations
Dorais, L.-J., Anthropology
Dorais, M., Social Work
Doré, F.-Y., Psychology
Drainville, A., Political Science
Duclos, J.-Y., Economics
Dufort, F., Psychology
Duhaime, G., Sociology
Dumais, A., Sociology
Dumont, S., Social Work
Elbaz, M., Anthropology
Everett, J., Psychology
Forest, P. G., Political Science
Fortin, A., Sociology
Fortin, B., Economics
Fortin, C., Psychology
Fortin, D., Social Work
Gagné, G., Sociology
Gauthier, J., Psychology
Genest, S., Anthropology
Giles, A. J., Industrial Relations
Gingras, A.-M., Political Science
Gislain, J.-J., Industrial Relations
Gonzalez, P., Economics
Gordon, S. F., Economics
Gosselin, G., Political Science
Goulet, S., Psychology
Grondin, S., Psychology
Guay, L., Sociology
Hervouet, G., Political Science
Hudon, R., Political Science
Hung, N. M., Economics
Hurtubise, Y., Social Work
Imbeau, L., Political Science
Khalaf, L. A., Economics
Kirouac, G., Psychology
Labrecque, M.-F., Anthropology
Lacombe, S., Sociology
Lacouture, Y., Psychology
Lacroix, G., Economics
Ladouceur, R., Psychology
Laflamme, G., Industrial Relations
Lafleur, G.-A., Political Science
Laflamme, R., Industrial Relations
Laforest, G., Political Science
Lamonde, F., Industrial Relations
Lamoureux, D., Political Science
Landreville, P., Psychology
Langlois, L., Industrial Relations
Langlois, S., Sociology
Lapointe, P.-A., Industrial Relations
Laugrand, F. B., Anthropology
Lavallée, M., Psychology
Lavoie, F., Psychology
Leblanc, G., Economics
Lindsay, J., Social Work
Loranger, M., Psychology
Mace, G., Political Science
Marcoux, R., Sociology
Massé, R., Anthropology
Mercier, J., Political Science

MERCIER, J., Industrial Relations
MERCURE, D., Sociology
MONTREUIL, S., Industrial Relations
MOREL, S., Industrial Relations
MORIN, C.-M., Psychology
NORMANDIN, L., Psychology
PAQUIN, L., Economics
PELLETIER, R., Political Science
PEPIN, M., Psychology
PETRY, F., Political Science
PICHÉ, C., Psychology
POCREAU, J.-B., Psychology
POIRIER, S., Anthropology
ROLAND, M., Economics
SABOURIN, S., Psychology
SAILLANT, F., Anthropology
SAINT-ARNAUD, P., Sociology
SAINT-YVES, A., Psychology
SAMSON, L., Economics
SAVARD, J., Psychology
SENECAL, C., Psychology
SEXTON, J., Industrial Relations
SHEARER, B., Economics
SIMARD, J.-J., Sociology
SIMARD, M., Social Work
TESSIER, L., Social Work
TESSIER, R., Psychology
THWAITES, J., Industrial Relations
TRUCHON, M., Economics
TRUDEL, F., Anthropology
TURCOTTE, D., Social Work
TURMEL, A., Sociology
VAN AUDENRODE, M., Economics
VEILLETTE, D., Sociology
VEZINA, A., Social Work
VÉZINA, J., Psychology
VINET, A., Industrial Relations
ZYLBERBERG, J., Political Science

Faculty of Theology and Religious Studies (Pavillon Félix-Antoine-Savard, Bureau 832, Québec, QC G1K 7P4; tel. (418) 656-3576; fax (418) 656-3273; e-mail ftsr@ftsr.ulaval.ca; internet www.ftsr.ulaval.ca):

AUBERT, M.
BRODEUR, R.
CÔTÉ, L.
CÔTÉ, P.-R.
COUTURE, A.
FARRELL, S. E.
FAUCHER, A.
FORTIN, A.
HURLEY, R.
KEATING, B.
LEMIEUX, R.
MAGER, R.
PAINCHAUD, L.
PASQUIER, A.
PELCHAT, M.
POIRIER, P.-H.
RACINE, J.
ROBERGE, R. M.
ROUTHIER, G.
VIAU, M.

ATTACHED INSTITUTES

Institute on Aging and Social Participation of Elders: Dir JEAN VÉZINA.

Institute for Applied Ethics: Dir LUC BÉGIN.

Institute of Classical Studies: Dir PAUL-HUBERT POIRIER.

Institute for Cultural Heritage: Dir MARTINE CARDIN.

Institute for Electronic Business: Dir MICHEL AUDET.

Institut Québécois des Hautes Etudes Internationales (Institute of Higher International Studies): Dir LOUIS BÉLANGER.

ATTACHED RESEARCH CENTRES

Centre d'Etudes Nordiques (CEN): Dir YVES BÉGIN.

Centre Interdisciplinaire de Recherche sur les Activités Langagières: Dir FRANÇOIS MALTAIS.

Centre Interdisciplinaire de Recherche en Réadaptation et Intégration Sociale: Dir CAROL L. RICHARDS.

Centre Interuniversitaire en Calcul Mathématique Algébrique (CICMA): Dir CLAUDE LÉVESQUE.

Centre Interuniversitaire d'Etudes sur les Lettres, les Arts et les Traditions (CELAT): Dir MARCEL MOUSSETTE.

Centre Interuniversitaire d'Etudes Québécoises (CIEQ): Dir BRIGITTE CAULIER.

Centre Interuniversitaire d'Etudes et de Recherches Autochtones: Dir FRANÇOIS TRUDEL.

Centre Interuniversitaire sur le Risque, les Politiques Economiques el l'Emploi: Dir JEAN-YVES DUCLES.

Centre d'Optique, Photonique et Laser (COPL): Dir RÉAL VALLÉE.

Centre de Recherche sur l'Adaptation des Jeunes et des Familles à Risque: Dir DANIEL TURCOTTE.

Centre de Recherche en Aménagement et Développement (CRAD): Dir MARIUS THÉRIAULT.

Centre de Recherche en Biologie Forestière (CRBF): Dir ANDRÉ DESROCHERS.

Centre de Recherche en Biologie de la Reproduction (CRBR): Dir MARC-ANDRÉ SIRARD.

Centre de Recherche en Cancérologie (CRC): Dir LUC BÉLANGER.

Centre de Recherche sur le Cerveau, le Comportement et la Neuropsychiatrie (CRCN): Dir ANDRÉ PARENT.

Centre de Recherche en Endocrinologie Moléculaire et Oncologique (CREMO): Dir FERNAND LABRIE.

Centre de Recherche en Economie Agroalimentaire (CRÉA): Dir ROBERT ROMAIN.

Centre de Recherche sur la Fonction, la Structure et l'Ingénierie des Protéines (CREFSIP): Dir NORMAND VOYER.

Centre de Recherche en Géomatique (CRG): Dir GEOFFREY EDWARDS.

Centre de Recherche en Horticulture (CRH): Dir RUSSELL J. TWEDDELL.

Centre de Recherche en Infectologie (CRI): Dir MICHEL BERGERON.

Centre de Recherche sur les Infrastructures en Béton (CRIB): Dir JACQUES MARCHAND.

Centre de Recherche Interuniversitaire sur l'Education et la Vie au Travail (CRIÉVAT): Dir MARIE-FRANCE MARANDA.

Centre de Recherche Interuniversitaire sur la Formation et la Profession Enseignante (CRIFPE): Dir DENIS JEFFREY.

Centre de Recherche Interuniversitaire sur la Littérature et la Culture Québécoises (CRELIQ): Dir MARIE-ANDRÉE BEAUDET.

Centre de Recherche et d'Intervention sur la Réussite Scolaire (CRIRES): Dir MARC-ANDRÉ DENIGER.

Centre de Recherche sur le Métabolisme Energetique (CREME): Dir DENIS RICHARD.

Centre de Recherche sur les Propriétés des Interfaces et la Catalyse (CERPIC): Dir FAICAL LARACHI.

Centre de Recherche en Sciences et Ingénierie des Macromolécules (CERSIM): Dir ANNA-MARIE RITCEY.

Centre de Recherche en Sciences et Technologie du Lait (STELA): Dir YVES POULIOT.

Centre de Recherche sur les Technologies de l'Organisation Réseau (CENTOR): Dirs DIANE POULIN.

Groupe Interdisciplinaire de Recherche en Eléments Finis (GIREF): Dir ANDRÉ FORTIN.

Groupe Interinstitutional de Recherches Océanographiques du Québec (QUEBEC-OCEAN): Dir LOUIS FORTIER.

Groupe de Recherche en Ecologie Buccale (GREB): Dir DANIEL GRENIER.

Groupe de Recherche en Inadaptation Psychosociale chez l'Enfant (GRIP): Dir MICHEL BOIVIN.

Groupe de Recherche en Santé Respiratoire: Dir FRANÇOIS MALTAIS.

Institut Hydro-Québec en Environnement, Développement et Société: Dir JEAN-BAPTISTE SÉRODES.

Institute for Rural and Forest Environment: Dir LÉON-ÉTIENNE PARENT.

Neutraceuticals and Functional Foods Institute: Dir BENOÎT LAMARCHE.

Observatoire du Mont Mégantic (OMM): Dir GILLES JONCAS.

UNIVERSITY OF LETHBRIDGE

4401 University Drive, Lethbridge, AB T1K 3M4

Telephone: (403) 320-5700
Fax: (403) 329-5159
E-mail: inquiries@uleth.ca
Internet: www.uleth.ca

Founded 1967
Provincial control
Language of instruction: English
Academic year: September to April (2 semesters), also summer sessions

Chancellor: ROBERT HIRONAKA
President and Vice-Chancellor: WILLIAM HENRY CADE
Provost and Vice-President (Academic): SEAMUS O'SHEA
Vice President (Finance and Administration): NANCY WALKER
Registrar: LESLIE LAVERS
Chief Librarian: JUDY HEAD

Number of teachers: 248 full-time
Number of students: 5,361

Library of 498,000 vols

Publications: *Annual Calendar*, *Annual Report of the Board of Governors*

DEANS

Faculty of Arts and Science: CHRISTOPHER NICOL
Faculty of Education: Dr JANE O'DEA
Faculty of Management: Dr JOHN USHER
School of Fine Arts: C. SKINNER
School of Health Sciences: LYNN BASFORD
School of Graduate Studies: ALAM SHAMSUL

MC GILL UNIVERSITY

845 Sherbrooke St West, Montréal, QC H3A 2T5

Telephone: (514) 398-4455
Fax: (514) 398-3594
Internet: www.mcgill.ca

Founded 1821 by legacy of Hon. James McGill
Provincial control
Language of instruction: English
Academic year: September to May (two terms)

Chancellor: RICHARD W. POUND

Principal and Vice-Chancellor: HEATHER MUNROE-BLUM
Provost and Vice-Principal (Academic): LUC VINET
Deputy Provost and Chief Information Officer: ANTHONY C. MASI
Vice-Principal (Administration and Finance): Prof. MORTY YALOVSKY
Vice-Principal (Development and Alumni Relations): NANCY WELLS
Vice-Principal (Research): Dr LOUISE PROULX
Secretary-General: ROBIN GELLER
Registrar and Executive Director of Admissions, Recruitment and Registrar's Office: S. FRANKE
Director of Libraries: FRANCES GROEN

Library: see Libraries
Number of teachers: 5,428 (full-time and part-time)
Number of students: 30,580 (full-time and part-time)
Publications: *McGill Reporter* (every 2 months), *Annual Report*, *McGill Journal of Education* (3 a year), *McGill University Health Centre. Annual Report*, *McGill Journal of Medicine* (2 a year), *McGill Journal of Middle East Studies* (annually), *The McGill Journal of Political Economy* (annually), *The McGill Journal of Political Studies* (annually), *The McGill Law Journal* (quarterly), *MUHC Ensemble*

DEANS

Faculty of Agricultural and Environmental Sciences: Dr DEBORAH BUSZARD
Faculty of Arts: Prof. JOHN HALL
Faculty of Dentistry: Dr JAMES LUND
Faculty of Education: ROGER SLEE
Faculty of Engineering: JOHN E. GRUZLESKI
Faculty of Law: NICHOLAS KASIRER
Faculty of Management: GERALD H. B. ROSS
Faculty of Medicine: Dr ABRAHAM FUKS
Faculty of Music: DON MCLEAN
Faculty of Religious Studies: BARRY B. LEVY
Faculty of Science: ALAN SHAVER
Graduate and Postdoctoral Studies: MARTHA CRAGO
Continuing Education: ROBIN ELEY
Dean of Students: Dr BRUCE SHORE

DIRECTORS OF SCHOOLS

Architecture: D. COVO
Communication Sciences and Disorders: S. R. BAUM
Computer Science: D. THÉRIEN
Dietetics and Human Nutrition: K. GRAY-DONALD
Environment: N. ROULET
Graduate School of Library and Information Studies: J. BEHESHTI
Nursing: S. E. FRENCH
Physical and Occupational Therapy: R. DYKES
Social Work: (vacant)
Urban Planning: D. BROWN

CHAIRS OF DEPARTMENTS

Faculty of Agricultural and Environmental Sciences (including School of Dietetics and Human Nutrition) (21111 Lakeshore Rd, Ste Anne de Bellevue, QC H9X 3V9; tel. (514) 398-7928; fax (514) 398-7968; e-mail studentinfo@macdonald.mcgill.ca; internet www.mcgill.ca/macdonald):

Agricultural Economics: J. C. HENNING
Agricultural and Biosystems Engineering: G. S. V. RAGHAVAN
Animal Science: X. ZHAO
Biosource Engineering: R. KOK
Food Science and Agricultural Chemistry: W. D. MARSHALL
Natural Resource Sciences: B. CÔTÉ
Plant Science: M. FORTIN

Faculty of Arts (Dawson Hall, 853 Sherbrooke St W., Montréal, QC H3A 2T6; tel. (514) 398-4210; fax (514) 398-8102; e-mail adviser.artsci@mcgill.ca; internet www.mcgill.ca/arts):

Anthropology: M. BISSON
Art History and Communication Studies: W. STRAW
East Asian Studies: G. FONG
Economics: C. GREEN
English: M. KILGOUR
French Language and Literature: F. RICARD
German Studies: K. BAUER
Hispanic Studies: J. PÉREZ-MAGALLÓN
History: B. LEWIS
Italian: L. KROHA
Jewish Studies: E. ORENSTEIN
Linguistics: L. WHITE
Philosophy: R. P. BUCKLEY
Political Science: C. MANFREDI
Russian and Slavic Studies: P. M. AUSTIN
Sociology: S. STRAGGENBORG

Centre for Continuing Education (688 Sherbrooke St W., 11th Floor, Montréal, QC H3A 3R1; tel. (514) 398-6200; fax (514) 398-4448; e-mail info@conted.mcgill.ca; internet www.mcgill.ca/conted):

Career and Management Studies: P. MARTUCCI
Education: B. WALKER
General Studies: P. MARTUCCI (acting) (Director)
Translation Studies: J. ARCHIBALD

Faculty of Education (3700 McTavish St, Montréal, QC H3A 1Y2; tel. (514) 398-7042; fax (514) 398-4679; e-mail sao.education@mcgill.ca; internet www.education.mcgill.ca):

Educational and Counselling Psychology: S. P. LAJOIE (acting)
Integrated Studies: A. W. PARÉ
Kinesiology and Physical Education: H. PERRAULT

Faculty of Engineering (Macdonald Engineering Bldg, 3rd Floor, 817 Sherbrooke St, Montréal, QC H3A 2K6; tel. (514) 398-7257; fax (514) 398-7379; e-mail information@engineering.mcgill.ca; internet www.mcgill.ca/engineering):

Chemical Engineering: R. J. MUNZ
Civil Engineering and Applied Mechanics: D. MITCHELL
Electrical and Computer Engineering: D. LOWTHER
Mechanical Engineering: A. K. MISRA
Mining Metals and Materials Engineering: R. A. L. DREW

Faculty of Medicine (6th Floor, McIntyre Medical Bldg, Promenade Sir William Osler, Montréal, QC H3G 1Y6; tel. (514) 398-3515; fax (514) 398-3595; e-mail recep.med@mcgill.ca; internet www.medicine.mcgill.ca):

Anaesthesia: F. CARLI
Anatomy and Cell Biology: J. J. M. BERGERON
Biochemistry: D. Y. THOMAS
Biomedical Engineering: R. E. KEARNEY
Epidemiology and Biostatistics: R. FUHRER
Family Medicine: M. DAWES
Human Genetics: D. S. ROSENBLATT
Medicine: D. GOLTZMAN
Microbiology and Immunology: G. J. MATLASHEWSKI
Neurology and Neurosurgery: R. J. RIOPELLE
Obstetrics and Gynaecology: S. L. TAN
Oncology: G. BATIST
Ophthalmology: M. N. BURNIER, JR
Otolaryngology: M. D. SCHLOSS
Paediatrics: H. J. GUYDA
Pathology: C. COMPTON
Pharmacology and Therapeutics: H. ZINGG
Physiology: A. SHRIER
Psychiatry: J. PARIS
Radiation Oncology: C. R. FREEMAN
Surgery: J. L. MEAKINS

Faculty of Music (Strathcona Music Bldg, Room E203, 555 Sherbrooke St W., Montréal, QC H3A 1E3; tel. (514) 398-4535; fax (514) 398-8061; e-mail undergradadmissions.music@mcgill.ca; internet www.mcgill.ca/music):

Performance: G. FOOTE
Theory: W. WOSZCZYK

Faculty of Science (Dawson Hall, 853 Sherbrooke St W., Montréal, QC H3A 2T6; tel. (514) 398-4210; fax (514) 398-8102; e-mail adviser.artsci@mcgill.ca; internet www.mcgill.ca/science):

Anatomy and Cell Biology: J. J. M. BERGERON
Atmospheric and Oceanic Sciences: J. R. GYAKUM
Biochemistry: D. Y. THOMAS
Biology: P. F. LASKO
Chemistry: R. B. LENNOX
Earth and Planetary Sciences: A. MUCCI
Geography: G. O. EWING
Mathematics and Statistics: K. GOWRISANKAREN
Microbiology and Immunology: G. J. MATLASHEWSKI
Pharmacology and Therapeutics: H. ZINGG
Physics: M. GRANT
Physiology: A. SHRIER
Psychology: K. B. J. FRANKLIN

INCORPORATED COLLEGES AND CAMPUSES

Macdonald Campus: 21111 Lakeshore Rd, Ste Anne de Bellevue, QC H9X 3V9; site of the Faculty of Agricultural and Environmental Sciences, the School of Dietetics and Human Nutrition and the School of Environment.

Royal Victoria College: Montréal; non-teaching; provides residential accommodation for women students; Warden F. TRACY.

AFFILIATED BODIES

Montreal Diocesan Theological College: 3473 University St, Montréal, QC H3A 2A8; Principal J. M. SIMONS.

Presbyterian College: 3495 University St, Montréal, QC H3A 2A8; Principal J. VISSERS.

United Theological College: 3521 University St, Montréal, QC H3A 2A9; Principal P. JOUDREY.

ATTACHED RESEARCH INSTITUTES

Biological and Medical Sciences:

Aerospace Medical Research Unit: Dir D. WATT.

Anesthesia Research Unit: Dir F. CERVERO.

Applied Cognitive Science Research Group: Dir J. DONIN.

Artificial Cells and Organs Research Centre: Dir T. M. S. CHANG.

Avian Science and Conservation Centre: Dir D. M. BIRD.

Bellairs Research Institute, Barbados, W.I.: Dir B. R. DOWNEY.

Biomedical Ethics Unit: Dir K. GLASS.

Centre for Bone and Periodontal Research: Dir D. GOLTZMAN.

Centre for Indigenous Peoples' Nutrition and Environment: Dir T. JOHNS.

Centre for Medical Education: Co-Dirs P. MCLEOD, Y. STEINERT.

Centre for Research on Language, Mind and Brain: Dir S. R. BAUM.

Centre for Nonlinear Dynamics in Physiology and Medicine: Dir M. C. MACKEY.

Centre for Research in Neuroscience: Dir A. J. AGUAYO.

Centre for Research on Endocrine Mechanisms: Dir Y. C. PATEL.

Douglas Hospital Research Centre: Dir R. QUIRION.

Evolution Education Research Centre: Dir B. ALTERS.

Farm Management and Technology Program: Dir M. J. COUTURE.

Gault Nature Reserve: Dir M. LECHOWICZ.

Huntsman Marine Science Centre: Dir (vacant).

Institute of Parasitology: Dir T. SPITHILL.

International Centre for Youth Gambling Problems and High-Risk Behaviours: Dir J. DEREVENSKY.

Lady Davis Institute for Medical Research (Sir Mortimer B. Davis Jewish General Hospital): Dir S. O. FREEDMAN.

Lyman Entomological Museum and Research Laboratory: Dir T. A. WHEELER.

Macdonald Campus Farm: Dir P. LAVOIE.

McGill AIDS Centre: Dir M. WAINBERG.

McGill Cancer Centre: Dir M. TREMBLAY.

McGill Centre for Research on Pain: Dir C. BUSHNELL.

McGill Centre for Studies in Aging: Dir J. POIRIER.

McGill Centre for the Study of Host Resistance: Dir E. SKAMENE.

McGill Centre for Translational Research in Cancer: Dir G. BATIST.

McGill Centre for Tropical Diseases: Dir J. D. MACLEAN.

McGill Reproductive Centre: Dir S. L. TAN.

McGill Subarctic Research Station: Dir W. H. POLLARD.

McGill University Continuing Medical Education: Dir (vacant).

McGill University Health Centre Research Institute: Dir L. DÉRY CAPES.

McGill Vision Research Unit: Dir (vacant).

Molson Reserve: Dir J. FYLES.

Montreal Chest Institute Research Centre: Dir J. G. MARTIN.

Montreal Children's Hospital Research Institute: Dir R. ROZEN.

Montreal General Hospital Research Institute: Dir J. SHUSTER.

Montreal Neurological Institute: Dir D. COLMAN.

Morgan Arboretum: Dir C. IDZIAK.

Nutrition and Food Science Centre: Dir E. B. MARLISS.

Redpath Museum: Dir G. BELL.

Sheldon Biotechnology Centre: Dir (vacant).

Humanities and Social Sciences:

Anthropology of Development Program: Dir (vacant).

Business and Management Research Centre: Dir (vacant).

Centre for Applied Family Studies: Dir W. S. ROWE.

Centre for Developing Area Studies: Dir R. BOYD.

Centre for East Asian Research: Dir K. DEAN.

Centre for Educational Leadership: Dir L. BUTLER KISBUR.

Centre for Intellectual Property Policy (CIPP): Dir R. GOLD.

Centre for Interdisciplinary Research in Music, Media and Technology: Dir W. WOSZCZYK.

Centre for International Management Studies: Dir W. B. CROWSTON.

Centre for Strategy Studies in Organizations: Dir J. JORGENSEN.

Centre for the Study of Regulated Industries: Dir R. JAKHU.

Centre for the Study of Teaching and Writing: Dir C. PITTENGER.

Centre for University Teaching and Learning: Dir L. MCALPINE.

Dobson Centre for Entrepreneurial Studies: Dir P. JOHNSON.

English and French Language Centre: Dir H. RIEL-SALVATORE.

Institute of Air and Space Law: Dir P. S. DEMPSEY.

Institute of Comparative Law: Dir (vacant).

Institute of Islamic Studies: Dir E. ORMSBY.

McGill Centre for Medicine, Ethics and Law: Dir M. A. SOMERVILLE.

McGill Centre for Research and Teaching on Women: Dir S. MULAY.

McGill Centre for Society, Technology and Development: Dir J. G. GALATY.

McGill Conservatory of Music: Dir D. MCLEAN.

McGill Finance Research Centre: Dir V. R. ERRUNZA.

McGill Institute for the Study of Canada: Dir A. MAIONI.

McGill International Executive Institute: Dir (vacant).

Minimum Cost Housing Group: Dir V. BHATT.

Montreal Consortium for Human Rights Advocacy Training: Dir J. TORCZYNER.

Office of First Nations and Inuit Education: Dir H. V. KUHNLEIN.

Office of International Research: Dir F. CARRIER.

Office of Learning and Information Technologies: Dir (vacant).

Physical Sciences and Engineering:

Arctic Research Station (MARS): Dir W. H. POLLARD.

Biomedical Mass Spectrometry Unit: Dir (vacant).

Brace Centre for Water Resources Management: Dir C. A. MADRAMOOTOO.

Centre for Climate and Global Change Research: Dir W. POLLARD.

Centre for Intelligent Machines: Dir F. FERRIE.

Centre for the Physics of Materials: Dir M. GRANT.

Centre for Self-Assembled Chemical Structures: Dir L. REVEN.

J. Stewart Marshall Weather Radar Observatory: Dir I. ZAWADZKI.

McGill Centre for Bioinformatics Research: Dir M. HALLETT.

McGill High Energy Physics Group: Dir (vacant).

McGill Institute for Advanced Materials (MIAM): Dir M. GRANT.

McGill Metals Processing Centre: Dir R. I. L. GUTHRIE.

Office of Technology Transfer: Dir R. BRUNO.

Polymer McGill: Coordinator M. P. ANDREWS.

Pulp and Paper Research Centre: Dir T. G. M. VAN DE VEN.

McMASTER UNIVERSITY

Hamilton, ON L8S 4L8

Telephone: (905) 525-9140

Fax: (905) 527-0100

Internet: www.mcmaster.ca

Founded 1887 in Toronto; moved to Hamilton 1930

Private control

Language of instruction: English

Academic year: September to April

Chancellor: M. M. HAWKRIGG

President and Vice-Chancellor: Prof. PETER J. GEORGE

Provost and Vice-President (Academic): K. NORRIE

Vice-President (Research): M. SHOUKRI

Vice-President (Administration): K. BELAIRE

Vice-President (Health Sciences): J. KELTON

Registrar: L. ARIANO

Librarian: G. R. HILL

Library: see Libraries

Number of teachers: 1,025 full-time

Number of students: 17,775 full- and part-time

Publications: *Calendars* (annually), *The Courier* (every 2 weeks), *Journal of the Bertrand Russell Archives* (quarterly), *McMaster Times*, *McMaster University Library Research News*, *The Research Bulletin* (monthly), *Staff Directory* (annually), *Year I Handbook* (annually)

DEANS

Faculty of Engineering: M. ELBESTAWI

Faculty of Health Sciences: J. KELTON

Faculty of Humanities: N. RAHIMIEH

Faculty of Science: P. SUTHERLAND

Faculty of Social Sciences: S. J. ELLIOTT

School of Business: P. BATES

Graduate Studies: L. FINSTEN (acting)

Principal of the Divinity College: S. PORTER

CHAIRMEN OF SCHOOLS AND DEPARTMENTS

Accounting and Financial Management: K. NAINAR

Anaesthesia: N. BUCKLEY (acting)

Anthropology: M. COOPER

School of the Arts: H. MAGINNIS

Arts and Science Programme: G. WARNER

Biochemistry: G. D. WRIGHT

Biology: R. SINGH (acting)

Chemical Engineering: A. N. HRYMAK

Chemistry: B. MCCARRY

Civil Engineering: D. F. E. STOLLE

Classics: H. JONES

Clinical Epidemiology and Biostatistics: B. HAYNES

Computing and Software: P. A. TAYLOR

Economics: M. VEALL

Electrical and Computer Engineering: K. M. WONG

Engineering Physics: P. JESSOP

English: M. O'CONNOR

Family Medicine: C. A. LEVITT

Finance and Business Management: T. CHAMBERLAIN (acting)

French: M. KLIFFER

Geography and Geology: J. J. DRAKE

History: V. H. AKSAN

Human Resources and Management: W. WIESNER (acting)

Kinesiology: N. MCCARTNEY

Management Science and Information Systems: M. PARLAR (acting)

Marketing, Business Policy and International Business: K. DEAL

Materials Science and Engineering: G. A. IRONS

Mathematics and Statistics: M. VALERIOTE

Mechanical Engineering: S. ZIADA
Unit for Medical Physics and Applied Radiation Sciences: F. MCNEILL
Medicine: P. O'BYRNE
Modern Languages: R. H. MCNUTT (acting)
Nursing: Dr C. H. TOMPKINS
Obstetrics and Gynaecology: P. MOHIDE
Paediatrics: P. STEER
Pathology: F. SMAILL (acting)
Philosophy: R. ARTHUR
Physics: A. J. BERLINSKY
Political Science: A. PORTER
Psychiatry: R. SWINSON
Psychology: R. RACINE
Radiology: C. COBLENTZ (acting)
Rehabilitation Science: Dr M. LAW
Religious Studies: E. SCHULLER
Social Work: J. ARONSON
Sociology: C. J. CUNEO
Surgery: W. OROVAN

PROFESSORS

Faculty of Engineering:

BAETZ, B. W., Civil Engineering
BEREZIN, A. A., Engineering Physics
CAPSON, D. W., Electrical and Computer Engineering
CASSIDY, D. T., Engineering Physics
CHANG, J. S., Engineering Physics
DEEN, M. J., Electrical and Computer Engineering
DICKSON, J. M., Chemical Engineering
DRYSDALE, R. G., Civil Engineering
ELBESTAWI, M. A., Mechanical Engineering
FRANEK, F., Computing and Software
GARLAND, W. J., Engineering Physics
GERSHMAN, A. B., Electrical and Computer Engineering
GHOBARAH, A., Civil Engineering
HAUGEN, H., Engineering Physics
HRYMAK, A. N., Chemical Engineering
IRONS, G. A., Materials Science and Engineering
JANICKI, R., Computing and Software
JESSOP, P. E., Engineering Physics
JOHARI, G. P., Materials Science and Engineering
KITAI, A. H., Engineering Physics
KLEIMAN, R. N., Engineering Physics
KREYMAN, K., Computing and Software
LOUTFY, R., Chemical Engineering
LUO, Z.-Q., Electrical and Computing Engineering
LUXAT, J. C., Engineering Physics
MACGREGOR, J. F., Chemical Engineering
MAIBAUM, T., Computing and Software
MARLIN, T. E., Chemical Engineering
MASCHER, P., Engineering Physics
PARNAS, D. L., Computing and Software
PELTON, R. H., Chemical Engineering
PETRIC, A., Materials Science and Engineering
PIETRUSZCZAK, S., Civil Engineering
PRESTON, J. S., Engineering Physics
QIAO, S., Computing and Software
REILLY, J. P., Electrical and Computer Engineering
SIVAKUMARAN, K. S., Civil Engineering
SMITH, P. M., Electrical and Computer Engineering
STOLLE, D. F. E., Civil Engineering
SZABADOS, B., Electrical and Computer Engineering
SZYMANSKI, T. H., Electrical and Computer Engineering
TAYLOR, P. A., Computing and Software
TERLAKY, T., Computing and Software
THOMPSON, D. A., Engineering Physics
TODD, T. D., Electrical and Computer Engineering
TSANIS, I. K., Civil Engineering
VLACHOPOULOS, J. A., Chemical Engineering
WEAVER, D. S., Mechanical Engineering
WILKINSON, D. S., Materials Science and Engineering
WONG, K. M., Electrical and Computer Engineering
WOOD, P. E., Chemical Engineering
WU, X., Electrical and Computer Engineering
XU, G., Materials Science and Engineering
ZHU, S., Chemical Engineering
ZIADA, S., Mechanical Engineering
ZUCKER, J. I., Computing and Software

Faculty of Health Sciences:

ADACHI, R., Medicine
ANDREWS, D. W., Biochemistry
ANTONY, M., Psychiatry
ANVARI, M., Surgery
ARNOLD, A., Medicine
ARSENAULT, L., Pathology
ARTHUR, H. M., School of Nursing
ATKINSON, S. A., Paediatrics
BALL, A. K., Pathology
BARR, R. D., Paediatrics
BAUMANN, M. A., School of Nursing
BELBECK, L. W., Pathology
BIRCH, S., Clinical Epidemiology and Biostatistics
BLAJCHMAN, M, Pathology
BOYLE, M.H., Psychiatry
BROWNE, R. M., School of Nursing
BUCHANAN, M. R., Pathology
BUTLER, R. G., Pathology
CAPONE, J. P., Biochemistry
CHAMBERS, L. W., Clinical Epidemiology and Biostatistics
CHEN, V., Pathology
CHERNESKY, M., Paediatrics
CHIRAKAL, R., Radiology
CHURCHILL, D. N., Medicine
CILISKA, D. K., School of Nursing
COATES, G., Radiology
COBLENTZ, C., Radiology
COLLINS, S. M., Medicine
CONNOLLY, S. J., Medicine
COOK, D. J., Medicine
CRANKSHAW, D. J., Obstetrics and Gynaecology
CROITORU, K., Medicine
CUNNINGHAM, C., Psychiatry
DAYA, S., Obstetrics and Gynaecology
DENBURG, J. A., Medicine
DENBURG, S. D., Psychiatry
DICENSO, A., School of Nursing
FAHNESTOCK, M., Psychiatry
FARGAS-BABJAK, A., Anaesthesia
FERNANDES, C., Medicine
FIRNAU, G., Radiology
GAFNI, A. J., Clinical Epidemiology and Biostatistics
GAULDIE, J., Pathology
GERBER, G. E., Biochemistry
GERSTEIN, H. C., Medicine
GINSBERG, J. S., Medicine
GOLDSMITH, C. H., Clinical Epidemiology and Biostatistics
GROVES, D., Pathology
GROVER, A. K., Medicine
GUPTA, R. S., Biochemistry
GUYATT, G. H., Clinical Epidemiology and Biostatistics
HARNISH, D. G., Pathology
HARVEY, J. T., Surgery
HASSELL, J. A., Biochemistry
HATTON, M. W. C., Pathology
HAYNES, R. B., Clinical Epidemiology and Biostatistics
HENRY, J., Psychiatry
HEIGENHAUSER, G. J. F., Medicine
HOLDER, D. A., Medicine
HOLLAND, F. J., Paediatrics
HUCKER, S. J., Psychiatry
HUGHES, D., Obstetrics
HUIZINGA, J. D., Medicine
HUNT, R. H., Medicine
HUTCHISON, B. G., Family Medicine
ISSENMAN, R. M., Paediatrics
JORDANA, M., Pathology
KARMALI, M. A., Pathology
KATES, N., Psychiatry
KAUFMAN, K. J., Family Medicine
KEARON, C., Medicine
KELTON, J. G., Pathology
KILLIAN, K. J., Medicine
KIRBY, T., Medicine
KIRPALANI, H., Paediatrics
KWAN, C. Y., Medicine
LATIMER, E. J., Family Medicine
LAW, M. C., Rehabilitation Science
LEE, R. M. K. W., Anaesthesia
LEVINE, M., Clinical Epidemiology and Biostatistics
LEVITT, C. A., Family Medicine
LONN, E., Medicine
LUKKA, H., Medicine
LUDWIN, D., Medicine
MACMILLAN, H., Psychiatry
MACPHERSON, A., Medicine
MAHONY, J., Pathology
MAJUMDAR, B., School of Nursing
MAZUREK, M., Medicine
MANDELL, L., Medicine
MCDERMOTT, M. R., Pathology
MCKELVIE, R., Medicine
MCQUEEN, M., Pathology
MEYER, R., Medicine
MISHRA, R. K., Psychiatry
MOAYYEDI, P., Medicine
MOHIDE, P. T., Obstetrics and Gynaecology
MOLLOY, D. W., Medicine
MORILLO, C., Medicine
MUGGAH, H. F., Obstetrics and Gynaecology
NAHMIUS, C., Radiology
NEAME, P., Pathology
NEVILLE, A., Medicine
NIEBOER, E., Biochemistry
NILES, L. P., Psychiatry
NORMAN, G. R., Clinical Epidemiology and Biostatistics
O'BYRNE, P., Medicine
OFOSU, F., Pathology
OROVAN, W. L., Surgery
PAES, B. A., Paediatrics
PANJU, A., Medicine
PATTERSON, C. J. S., Medicine
PATTERSON, M., Radiology
PERDUE, M. H., Pathology
PINELLI, J. M., School of Nursing
RADHI, J., Pathology
RATHBONE, M. P., Medicine
RICHARDS, C. D., Pathology
RIDDELL, R., Radiology
RONEN, G. M., Paediatrics
ROSENBAUM, P. L., Paediatrics
ROSENFELD, J. M., Pathology
ROSENTHAL, K. L., Pathology
ROTSTEIN, C. M. F., Medicine
RUSTHOVEN, J., Medicine
RYAN, E., Psychiatry
SALAMAS, S., Pathology
SCHMIDT, B. K., Paediatrics
SCHULMAN, S., Medicine
SEARS, M. R., Medicine
SEGGIE, J., Psychiatry
SHANNON, H. S., Clinical Epidemiology and Biostatistics
SHARMA, A., Medicine
SMAILL, F., Pathology
SNIDER, D., Pathology
SOLOMON, P., School of Rehabilitation Science
SOMERS, S., Radiology
STEER, P., Paediatrics
STEINER, M., Psychiatry
STODDART, G. L., Clinical Epidemiology and Biostatistics
STRATFORD, P., School of Rehabilitation Science
SUR, R., Medicine
SWINSON, R. P., Psychiatry
SZATMARI, P., Psychiatry
SZECHTMAN, H., Psychiatry

TEO, K., Medicine
TOUGAS, G., Medicine
TURNBULL, J. D., Medicine
TURPIE, I. D., Medicine
UPTON, A. R. M., Medicine
VAN DER SPUY, R., Medicine
VERMA, D. K., Family Medicine
VICKERS, J. D., School of Nursing
WALKER, I. R., Medicine
WALTER, S. D., Clinical Epidemiology and Biostatistics
WARKENTIN, T., Pathology
WATTS, J. L., Paediatrics
WAYE, J., Pathology
WEBBER, C., Radiology
WEITZ, J., Medicine
WESSEL, J., Rehabilitation Science
WHELAN, D., Paediatrics
WHITTON, A., Medicine
WITELSON, S. F., Psychiatry
WRIGHT, G. D., Biochemistry
YANG, D. S. C., Biochemistry
YOUNG, E., Pathology
YOUNGLAI, E. V., Obstetrics and Gynaecology
YUSUF, S., Medicine
ZHOROV, B., Biochemistry

Faculty of Humanities:

ADAMSON, J., English
AHMED, A., French
ALLEN, B. G., Philosophy
ALSOP, J. D., History
ARTHUR, R. T. W., Philosophy
BAYARD, C. A., French
BOWERBANK, S., English
CLARK, D. L., English
CROSTA, S., French
DUNBABIN, K. M. D., Classics
FERNS, H. J., English
GAUVREAU, J. M., History
GIROUX, H., English and Communications Studies
GOELLNICHT, D. C., English
GRIFFIN, N. J., Philosophy
HITCHCOCK, D. L., Philosophy
JEAY, M. M., French
JONES, H., Classics
KACZYNSKI, B. M., History
KING, J., English
KOLESNIKOFF, N., Modern Languages and Linguistics
MAGINNIS, H. B. J., School of the Arts
MURGATROYD, P., Classics
NELLES, H. V., History
O'CONNOR, M. E., English
OSTOVICH, H. M., English
RAHIMIEH, N., English and Comparative Literature
RAPOPORT, P., School of the Arts
RENWICK, W., School of the Arts
SILCOX, M., English
STROINSKA, M., Modern Languages and Linguistics
WALMSLEY, P., English
WALUCHOW, W. J., Philosophy
WEAVER, J. C., History
YORK, L. M., English

Faculty of Science:

ALAMA, S., Mathematics and Statistics
ALLAN, L. G., Psychology
BAIN, A. D., Chemistry
BALAKRISHNAN, N., Mathematics and Statistics
BARBIER, J. R. H., Chemistry
BECKER, S., Psychology
BENNETT, P., Psychology
BERLINSKY, A. J., Physics and Astronomy
BRONSARD, L., Mathematics and Statistics
BROOK, M. A., Chemistry
CHETTLE, D. R., Physics and Astronomy
CHOUINARD, V. A., School of Geography and Geology
COUCHMAN, H. M., Physics and Astronomy
CRAIG, W., Mathematics and Statistics
DALY, M., Psychology
DE CATANZARO, D. A., Psychology
DICKIN, A. P., School of Geography and Geology
DRAKE, J. J., School of Geography and Geology
ELLIOTT, S. J., School of Geography and Geology
EYLES, C. H., School of Geography and Geology
EYLES, J. D., School of Geography and Geology
FENG, S., Mathematics
FINAN, T. M., Biology
GAULIN, B. D., Physics and Astronomy
GOLDING, B., Biology
GREEDAN, J. E., Chemistry
GUAN, P., Mathematics and Statistics
HALL, F. L., School of Geography and Geology
HAMBLETON, I., Mathematics and Statistics
HARRIS, R. S., School of Geography and Geology
HARRIS, W. E., Physics and Astronomy
HART, B. T., Mathematics and Statistics
HIGGS, P. G., Physics and Astronomy
HITCHCOCK, A. P., Chemistry
HOPPE, F. M., Mathematics and Statistics
HURD, T. R., Mathematics and Statistics
JACOBS, J. R., Biology
KALLIN, C., Physics and Astronomy
KANAROGLOU, P. S., School of Geography and Geology
KOLASA, J., Biology
KOLSTER, M., Mathematics and Statistics
LEIGH, W. J., Chemistry
LEVY, B. A., Psychology
LEWIS, T. L., Psychology
LIAW, K. L., School of Geography and Geology
LUKE, G. M., Physics and Astronomy
MACDONALD, P. D. M., Mathematics and Statistics
MAURER, D. M., Psychology
MCCARRY, B. E., Chemistry
MIN-OO, M., Mathematics and Statistics
MOORE, G. H., Mathematics and Statistics
MORRIS, W. A., School of Geography and Geology
MOTHERSILL, C. E., Medical Physics and Applied Radiological Science
MURPHY, K. M., Psychology
NICAS, A. J., Mathematics and Statistics
NURSE, C. A., Biology
O'DONNELL, M. J., Biology
PUDRITZ, R. E., Physics and Astronomy
RACINE, R. J., Psychology
RAINBOW, A. J., Biology
ROLLO, C. D., Biology
SAWYER, E. T., Mathematics and Statistics
SCHELLHORN, H., Biology
SCHROBILGEN, G. J., Chemistry
SEKULER, A., Psychology
SHI, A., Physics and Astronomy
SIEGEL, S., Psychology
SINGH, R. S., Biology
STOVER, H., Chemistry
SUTHERLAND, P., Physics and Astronomy
TERLOUW, J. K., Chemistry
TRAINOR, L. J., Psychology
VALERIOTE, M. A., Mathematics and Statistics
VENUS, D., Physics and Astronomy
VIVEROS-AGUILER, R., Mathematics and Statistics
WANG, M. Y. K., Mathematics and Statistics
WELCH, D. L., Physics and Astronomy
WERETILNYK, E. A., Biology
WERSTIUK, N. H., Chemistry
WILSON, C. D., Physics and Astronomy
WILSON, M. I., Psychology
WOLKOWICZ, G. S. K., Mathematics and Statistics
WOO, M. K., School of Geography and Geology
WOOD, C. M., Biology
YIP, P. C. Y., Mathematics and Statistics

Faculty of Social Sciences:

ARCHIBALD, W. P., Sociology
ARONSON, J. H., School of Social Work
BLIMKIE, C. J. R., Kinesiology
BROWN, R. A., Social Work
CAIN, R., Social Work
CANNON, A., Anthropology
CARROLL, B. A., Political Science
CHAN, K. S. Y., Economics
COLARUSSO, J. J., Anthropology
COLEMAN, W. D., Political Science
COOPER, M. O., Anthropology
CUNEO, C. J., Sociology
DENTON, M. A., Gerontology
DOOLEY, M. D., Economics
ELLIOTT, D., Kinesiology
FEIT, H. A., Anthropology
FINSTEN, L., Anthropology
FOX, J. D., Sociology
HERRING, D. A., Anthropology
HICKS, A. L., Kinesiology
HURLEY, J. E., Economics
JACEK, H. J., Political Science
JONES, S. R. G., Economics
KROEKER, P. T., Religious Studies
KUBURSI, A. A., Economics
LEACH, J. E., Economics
LEE, T. D., Kinesiology
LEVITT, C. H., Sociology
LEWCHUK, W., Economics
LEWIS, T. J., Political Science
MAGEE, L. J., Economics
MCCARTNEY, N., Kinesiology
MENDELSON, A., Religious Studies
MESTELMAN, S., Economics
MIALL, C., Sociology
MULLER, R. A., Economics
PORTER, T., Political Science
RACINE, J., Economics
RICE, J. J., School of Social Work
RODMAN, W. L., Anthropology
SALE, D. G., Kinesiology
SATZEWICH, V., Sociology
SAUNDERS, S. R., Anthropology
SCARTH, W. M., Economics
SCHULLER, E. M., Religious Studies
SHAFFIR, W. B., Sociology
SPENCER, B. G., Economics
SPROULE-JONES, M. H., Political Science
STARKES, J., Kinesiology
STEIN, M. B., Political Science
STUBBS, R. W., Political Science
VEALL, M. R., Economics
WATT, M. S., School of Social Work
WHITE, P. G., Kinesiology
YATES, C. A. B., Political Science

School of Business:

ABAD, P. L., Management Science and Information Systems
AGARWAL, N. C., Human Resources and Management
BABA, V., Business
BART, C. K., Marketing
CHAMBERLAIN, T. W., Finance and Business Economics
CHEUNG, C. S., Finance and Business Economics
COOPER, R. G., Marketing
DEAVES, R., Finance and Business Economics
HACKETT, R. D., Human Resources and Management
KLEINSCHMIDT, E. J., Marketing
KWAN, C. C. Y., Finance and Business Economics
MEDCOF, J. W., Human Resources and Management
MILTENBURG, J. G., Management Science and Information Systems
MOUNTAIN, D. C., Finance and Business Economics
PARLAR, M., Management Science and Information Systems

ROSE, J. B., Human Resources and Management
SHEHATA, M. M., Accounting
STEINER, G., Management Science and Information Systems
WESOLOWSKY, G. O., Management Science and Information Systems
YUAN, Y., Management Science and Information Systems
ZEYTINOGLU, F. I., Human Resources and Management

Divinity College (1280 Main St, W., Hamilton, ON L8S 4R1; tel. (905) 525-9140 ext. 24401; fax (905) 577-4782; internet www .macdiv.ca):

HORNSELL, M. J. A., Old Testament and Hebrew
LONGENECKER, R. N., New Testament
PORTER, S. E., New Testament

ATTACHED RESEARCH INSTITUTES

Centre for Electrophotonic Materials and Devices: Hamilton; research and development; Dir Dr D. A. THOMPSON.

R. Samuel McLaughlin Centre for Gerontological Health Research: Hamilton; research, training and promotion of health and preventive care for the elderly; organizes conferences; publishes reports; Dir Dr L. W. CHAMBERS.

Centre for Health Economics and Policy Analysis: Hamilton; research, consultation, education, liaison; organizes conferences, etc.; publishes health policy commentaries and research reports; Co-ordinator Dr J. HURLEY.

Centre for Peace Studies: Hamilton; research, graduate and undergraduate courses, seminars, lectures, conferences and other projects in the area of international peace; Dir Dr G. PURDY.

Gerontology Programme: Hamilton; f. 1979; a multidisciplinary unit to promote and develop research and educational programmes on aging; Dir Dr M. DENTON.

McMaster Institute for Energy Studies: Hamilton; f. 1980 to encourage communication between researchers in different fields of energy study; Dir Dr DEAN MOUNTAIN; publ. *Newsletter* (3 a year).

Institute of Environment and Health: Hamilton; research, health surveys and health assessments, identification and evaluation of hazards, development of preventive policies and strategies and of educational programmes; participation in community-based environment and health initiatives; conducts workshops and seminars; Dir Dr B. NEWBOLD (acting).

Brockhouse Institute for Materials Research: Hamilton; research in the chemistry, engineering, metallurgy and physics of solid materials is supplemented through this multidisciplinary unit; principal areas: lattice dynamics, kinetics and diffusion, mechanical properties, microelectric and electro-optic devices, optical materials, phase transformations, thermodynamics, radiation damage, structure determination, surfaces and catalysis; Dir Dr J. S. PRESTON.

Institute of Polymer Production Technology: Hamilton; provides a facility and environment in which University staff and technical personnel from industry can do research and development on process technology for polymer production; Dir (vacant).

Office of International Affairs: Hamilton; co-ordinates institutional international activities; provides leadership in international education and research, and in the provision of professional services by McMaster personnel to the global community; includes Centre for International Health; Dir Dr M. W. L. CHAN.

UNIVERSITY OF MANITOBA

Winnipeg, MB R3T 2N2
Telephone: (204) 474-8880
Fax: (204) 474-7536
E-mail: registrar@umanitoba.ca
Internet: www.umanitoba.ca

Founded 1877
Language of instruction: English
Academic year: September to April (two terms)

Chancellor: Dr WILLIAM NORRIE
President and Vice-Chancellor: Dr EMOKE SZATHMÁRY
Vice-President (Academic) and Provost: Dr ROBERT KERR
Vice-President (Administration): DEBORAH MCCALLUM
Vice-President (External): ELAINE GOLDIE
Vice-President (Research): Dr JOANNE KESELMAN
Director of Libraries: C. PRESSER

Library of 2,000,000 vols
Number of teachers: 1,142
Number of students: 24,981

DEANS

Faculty of Agricultural and Food Sciences: Dr H. BJARNASON
Faculty of Architecture: Dr DAVID R. WITTY
Faculty of Arts: ROBERT O'KELL
Faculty of Dentistry: J. DE VRIES
Faculty of Education: JOHN WIENS
Faculty of Engineering: DOUGLAS RUTH
Faculty of Graduate Studies: Dr TONY SECCO
Faculty of Environment: LESLIE KING
Faculty of Human Ecology: R. BIRD
Faculty of Law: HARVEY SECTER
Faculty of Management: J. L. GRAY
Faculty of Medicine: B. K. E. HENNEN
Faculty of Nursing: D. M. GREGORY
Faculty of Pharmacy: D. COLLINS
Faculty of Physical Education and Recreation Studies: D. W. HRYCAIKO
Faculty of Science: Dr MARK WHITMORE
Faculty of Social Work: BOB MULLALY

DIRECTORS

School of Agriculture: D. FLATEN
School of Art: D. AMUNDSON
School of Dental Hygiene: S. LAVIGNE
School of Medical Rehabilitation: J. COOPER (Overall Dir: E. ETCHEVERRY (Occupational Therapy: GISELE PEREIRA (Physical Therapy, acting)
School of Music: DALE LONIS
Continuing Education Division: A. PERCIVAL
Natural Resources Institute: C. EMDAD HAGUE

PROFESSORS

Faculty of Agricultural and Food Sciences:

BALLANCE, G. M., Plant Science
BJARNASON, H., Agribusiness and Agricultural Economics
BLANK, G., Food Science
BOYD, M. S., Agribusiness and Agricultural Economics
BRITTON, M. G., Biosystems Engineering
BRÛLÉ-BABEL, A. L., Plant Science
CAMPBELL, L. D., Animal Science
CENKOWSKI, S., Biosystems Engineering
CONNOR, M. L., Animal Science
DRONZEK, B. L., Plant Science
ENTZ, M., Plant Science
GALLOWAY, T. D., Entomology
GOH, T. B., Soil Science
GUENTER, W., Animal Science
HILL, R. D., Plant Science
HOLLEY, R. A., Food Science
HOLLIDAY, N. J., Entomology
JAYAS, D. S., Biosystems Engineering
KRAFT, D. F., Agribusiness and Agricultural Economics
MACKAY, P. A., Entomology
MACMILLAN, J. A., Agribusiness and Agricultural Economics
MCVETTY, P. B. E., Plant Science
MUIR, W. E., Biosystems Engineering
PRITCHARD, M. K., Plant Science
RACZ, G. J., Soil Science
REMPHREY, W. R., Plant Science
ROUGHLEY, R. E., Entomology
SCANLON, M. G., Food Science
SCARTH, R., Plant Science
VESSEY, J. K., Plant Science
WITTENBERG, K. M., Animal Science
ZHANG, Q., Biosystems Engineering

Faculty of Architecture:

COX, M. G., Interior Design
MACDONALD, R. I., Environmental Design
NELSON, C., Landscape Architecture
RATTRAY, A. E., Landscape Architecture
THOMSEN, C. H., Landscape Architecture

Faculty of Arts:

ALBAS, D. C., Sociology
ANNA, T. E., History
ARNASON, D. E., English
BAILEY, P. C., History
BARBER, D. G., Geograpy
BRIERLEY, J. S., Geography
BUMSTED, J. M., History
BUTEUX, P. E., Political Studies
CAMERON, N. E., Economics
CHERNOMAS, R., Economics
COMACK, A. E., Sociology
COOLEY, D. O., English
COSMOPOULOS, M. B., Classics
DEAN, J. M., Economics
DEBICKI, M., Political Studies
DELUCA, R., Psychology
EATON, W. O., Psychology
FERGUSON, B. G., History
FINLAY, J. L., History
FINNEGAN, R. E., English
FORTIER, P., French, Spanish and Italian
FRIESEN, G. A., History
GERUS, O. W., History
GONICK, C. W., Economics
GORDON, D. K., French, Spanish and Italian
GREENFIELD, H. J., Anthropology
GRISLIS, E., Religion
HALLI, S. S., Sociology
HELLER, H., History
HINZ, E. J., English
HUM, D., Economics
JOHNSON, C. G., English
JUDD, E. R., Anthropology
KENDLE, J. E., History
KESELMAN, H. J., Psychology
KESELMAN, J. C., Psychology
KINNEAR, E. M., History
KINNEAR, M. S. R., History
KULCHYSKI, P., Native Studies
KWONG, J., Sociology
LEBOW, M. D., Psychology
LEVENTHAL, L. Y., Psychology
LINDEN, E. W., Sociology
LOBDELL, R. A., Economics
LOXLEY, J., Economics
MCCANCE, D., Religion
MCCARTHY, D. J., Philosophy
MARTIN, D. G., Psychology
MARTIN, G. L., Psychology
MATHESON, C., Philosophy
NAHIR, M., Linguistics
NICHOLS, J. D., Linguistics
NICKELS, J. B., Psychology
NORTON, W., Geography
OAKES, J. E., Native Studies
O'KELL, R. P., English
PEAR, J. J., Psychology
PERRY, R. P., Psychology
PHILLIPS, P. A., Economics
RAMU, G. N., Sociology

REA, J. E., History
REMPEL, H., Economics
ROBERTS, L., Sociology
RUBENSTEIN, H., Anthropology
SCHAFER, A. M., Philosophy
SCHLUDERMANN, E. H., Psychology
SCHLUDERMANN, S., Psychology
SEGALL, A., Sociology
SHAVER, R. W., Philosophy
SHKANDRIJ, M., German and Slavic Studies
SIMPSON, W., Economics
SINGER, M., Psychology
SMIL, V., Geography
SMITH, G. C., Geography
SPRAGUE, D. N., History
STAMBROOK, F. G., History
STEIMAN, L. B., History
SZATHMÁRY, J. E., Anthropology
TAIT, R. W., Psychology
THOMAS, P. G., Political Studies
TODD, D., Geography
TOLES, G. E., English
WALZ, E. P., English
Rev. WATERMAN, A. M. C., Economics
WEIL, H. S., English
WIEST, R. E., Anthropology
WILLIAMS, D. L., English
WILSON, L. M., Psychology
WOLF, K., Icelandic
WOLFART, H. C., Linguistics
WORTLEY, J. T., History

Faculty of Dentistry:
BHULLAR, R. P.
BOWDEN, G. H. W.
DAWES, C.
DE VRIES, J.
FLEMING, N.
HAMILTON, I. R.
KARIM, A. C.
LAVELLE, C. L. B.
LOVE, W. B.
SCOTT, J. E.
SINGER, D. L.
SUZUKI, M.
WILTSHIRE, W.

Faculty of Education:
BARTELL, R., Educational Administration, Foundations and Psychology
CAP, O., Curriculum, Teaching and Learning
CHINIEN, C., Curriculum, Teaching and Learning
CLIFTON, R. A., Postsecondary Studies, Educational Administration, Foundations and Psychology
FREEZE, D. R., Educational Administration, Foundations and Psychology
GREGOR, A. D., Postsecondary Studies, Educational Administration, Foundations and Psychology
HARVEY, D. A., Curriculum, Teaching and Learning
HLYNKA, L. D., Curriculum, Teaching and Learning
JENKINSON, D. H., Curriculum, Teaching and Learning
KESELMAN, J. C., Educational Administration, Foundations and Psychology
KIRBY, D. M., Postsecondary Studies
LEVIN, B., Educational Administration, Foundations and Psychology
LONG, J. C., Educational Administration, Foundations and Psychology
MAGSINO, R., Educational Administration, Foundations and Psychology
MORPHY, D. R., Postsecondary Studies
PERRY, R. P., Postsecondary Studies
POROZNY, G. H. J., Curriculum, Teaching and Learning
ROBERTS, L. W., Postsecondary Studies
SCHULZ, W. E., Educational Administration, Foundations and Psychology
SEIFERT, K. L., Educational Administration, Foundations and Psychology
STAPLETON, J. J., Educational Administration, Foundations and Psychology
STINNER, A. O., Curriculum, Teaching and Learning
STRAW, S. B., Curriculum, Teaching and Learning
YOUNG, J. C., Educational Administration, Foundations and Psychology
ZAKALUK, B. L., Curriculum, Teaching and Learning

Faculty of Engineering:
BALAKRISHNAN, S., Mechanical and Industrial
BASSIM, M. N., Mechanical and Industrial
BRIDGES, G. E. J., Electrical and Computer
BURN, D. H., Civil and Geological
CAHOON, J. R., Mechanical and Industrial
CARD, H. C., Electrical and Computer
CHATURVEDI, M. C., Mechanical and Industrial
CIRIC, I. M. R., Electrical and Computer
CLAYTON, A., Civil and Geological
GOLE, A. M., Electrical and Computer
GRAHAM, J., Civil and Geological
KINSNER, W., Electrical and Computer
LAJTAI, E. Z., Civil and Geological
LEHN, W., Electrical and Computer
MARTENS, G. O., Electrical and Computer
MCLAREN, P. G., Electrical and Computer
MCLEOD, R. D., Electrical and Computer
MENZIES, R. W., Electrical and Computer
MUFTI, A. A., Civil and Geological
OLESZKIEWICZ, J. A., Civil and Geological
ONYSHKO, S., Electrical and Computer
PAWLAK, M., Electrical and Computer
POLYZOIS, D., Civil and Geological
POPPLEWELL, N., Mechanical and Industrial
RAGHUVEER, M. R., Electrical and Computer
RUTH, D. W., Mechanical and Industrial
SEBAK, A., Electrical and Computer
SEPEHRI, N., Mechanical and Industrial
SHAFAI, L., Electrical and Computer
SHAH, A. H., Civil and Geological
SHWEDYK, E., Electrical and Computer
SOLIMAN, H. M., Mechanical and Industrial
STIMPSON, B., Civil and Geological
STRONG, D., Mechanical and Industrial
THOMSON, D. J., Electrical and Computer
THORNTON-TRUMP, A. B., Mechanical and Industrial
WOODBURY, A. D., Civil

Faculty of Human Ecology:
BERRY, R. E., Family Studies
BIRD, R. P., Foods and Nutrition
BOND, J. B., Family Studies
ESKIN, N. A. M., Foods and Nutrition
HARVEY, C. D. H., Family Studies

Faculty of Law:
ANDERSON, D. T.
BUSBY, K.
DEUTSCHER, D.
ESAU, A.
GUTH, D. J.
HARVEY, D. A. C.
IRVINE, J. C.
MCGILLIVRAY, A.
NEMIROFF, G.
OSBORNE, P. H.
PENNER, R.
SECTER, H. L.
SNEIDERMAN, B.
STUESSER, L.
VINCENT, L.

Faculty of Management:
BARTELL, M., Business Administration
BECTOR, C. R., Business Administration
BHATT, S. K., Business Administration
BRUNING, E. R., Marketing
BRUNING, N. S., Business Administration
ELIAS, N. S., Accounting and Finance
FROHLICH, N., Business Administration
GODARD, J. H., Business Administration
GOOD, W. S., Marketing
GOULD, L. I., Accounting and Finance
GRAY, J. L., Business Administration
HILTON, M. W., Accounting and Finance
HOGAN, T. P., Business Administration
MCCALLUM, J. S., Accounting and Finance
NOTZ, W. W., Business Administration
OWEN, B. E., Business Administration
ROSENBLOOM, E. S.
STARKE, F. A., Business Administration

Faculty of Medicine:
ADAMSON, I. Y. R., Pathology
ANDERSON, J., Human Anatomy and Cell Science
ANGEL, A., Medicine and Physiology
AOKI, F. Y., Continuing Medical Education, Medical Microbiology, Medicine, Pharmacology and Therapeutics
ARNETT, J. L., Clinical Health Psychology and Continuing Medical Education
ARTHUR, G., Biochemistry and Medical Genetics
BAKER, S., Medicine
BARAGAR, F., Medicine
BARAKAT, S., Psychiatry
BARAL, E., Medicine, Radiology
BARWINSKY, J., Cardiothoracic Surgery
BEBCHUK, W., Psychiatry
BECKER, A., Paediatrics and Child Health
BEGLEITER, A., Medicine, Pharmacology and Therapeutics
BERCZI, I., Immunology
BLACK, G., Surgery
BLAKLEY, B., Otolaryngology
BOOTH, F., Paediatrics and Child Health
BORODITSY, R., Obstetrics, Gynaecology and Reproductive Sciences
BOSE, D., Anaesthesia, Medicine, Pharmacology and Therapeutics
BOSE, R., Pharmacology and Therapeutics
BOW, E., Medical Microbiology
BOWDEN, G. H., Medical Microbiology
BOWMAN, D. M., Medicine
BOWMAN, W. D., Paediatrics and Child Health
BRANDES, L. J., Medicine, Pharmacology and Therapeutics
BRISTOW, G. K., Anaesthesia
BRUNHAM, R. C., Medical Microbiology, Medicine, Obstetrics, Gynaecology and Reproductive Sciences
BRUNI, J. E., Human Anatomy and Cell Science
CARR, I., Pathology
CARTER, S. A., Medicine and Physiology
CASIRO, O., Paediatrics and Child Health
CATTINI, P., Physiology, Pharmacology and Therapeutics
CHERNICK, V., Paediatrics and Child Health
CHOY, P. C., Biochemistry and Molecular Biology
CHUDLEY, A. E., Continuing Medical Education, Human Genetics, Paediatrics and Child Health
COOMBS, C., Medical Microbiology
COOPER, J., Community Health Sciences
CRAIG, D. B., Anaesthesia
CRISTANTE, L., Surgery
CUMMING, G. R., Paediatrics and Child Health
DANZINGER, R. G., General Surgery
DAVIE, J. R., Biochemistry and Molecular Biology
DEAN, H., Paediatrics and Child Health
DUBO, H. I. C., Medicine
DUKE, P. C., Anaesthesia
EL-GABALAWY, H., Medicine
EVANS, J. A., Community Health Sciences, Human Genetics, Paediatrics and Child Health
FERGUSON, C. A., Paediatrics and Child Health
FINE, A., Medicine
FOERSTER, J., Medicine

FORGET, E., Community Health Sciences
GARTNER, J., Immunology, Pathology
GEIGER, J., Pharmacology and Therapeutics
GERRARD, J. M., Paediatrics and Child Health
GLAVIN, G., Pharmacology and Therapeutics
GORDON, R., Radiology
GREENBERG, C. R., Human Genetics, Paediatrics and Child Health
GREWAR, D. A. I., Family Medicine, Paediatrics and Child Health
GUIJON, F., Obstetrics, Gynaecology and Reproductive Sciences
HALL, P. F., Obstetrics, Gynaecology and Reproductive Sciences
HAMERTON, J. L., Paediatrics and Child Health
HAMMOND, G. W., Medical Microbiology, Medicine
HARDING, G. M., Medical Microbiology, Medicine
HARVEY, D. A., Community Health Sciences
HASSARD, T. H., Community Health Sciences
HAVENS, B., Community Health Sciences
HAYGLASS, K. T., Immunology
HELEWA, M., Obstetrics, Gynaecology and Reproductive Sciences
HERSHFIELD, E. A., Community Health Sciences
HERSHFIELD, E. S., Medicine
HOESCHEN, R., Medicine
HOGAN, T. P., Community Health Sciences
HORNE, J. M., Community Health Sciences
HOSKING, D., Surgery
HUDSON, R., Anaesthesia
HUGHES, K. R., Physiology
IRELAND, D. J., Otolaryngology
JAY, F. T., Medical Microbiology
JEFFERY, J., Medicine
JOHNSTON, J. B., Medicine
JORDAN, L. M., Physiology
KARDAMI, E., Human Anatomy and Cell Science
KATZ, P., Psychiatry
KAUFERT, J. M., Community Health Sciences
KAUFERT, P. A., Community Health Services
KAUFMAN, B. J., Medicine
KEPRON, M. W., Medicine
KIRK, P. J., Family Medicine
KIRKPATRICK, J. R., Continuing Medical Education, General Surgery
KREPART, G. V., Obstetrics, Gynaecology and Reproductive Sciences
KROEGER, E. A., Physiology
KRYGER, M., Medicine
LABELLA, F. S., Pharmacology and Therapeutics
LATTER, J., Medicine
LAUTT, W. W., Pharmacology and Therapeutics
LEJOHN, H. B., Human Genetics
LERTZMAN, M., Continuing Medical Education, Medicine
LEVI, C. S., Radiology
LEVITT, M., Medicine
LIGHT, B., Medicine
LIGHT, R. B., Medical Microbiology
LONGSTAFFE, S., Paediatrics and Child Health
LYONS, E. A., Radiology, Obstetrics, Gynaecology and Reproductive Sciences
MCCARTHY, D. S., Medicine
MCCLARTY, B., Radiology
MCCLARTY, G. A., Medical Microbiology
MCCOSHEN, J. A., Obstetrics, Gynaecology and Reproductive Sciences
MCCREA, D. A., Physiology
MCCULLOUGH, D. W., Continuing Medical Education, Otolaryngology
MACDOUGALL, B., Medicine
MCILWRAITH, R., Clinical Health Psychology
MCKENZIE, J. K., Community Health Sciences
MAKSYMIUK, A., Medicine
MINK, G., Medicine
MINUK, G. Y., Medicine, Pharmacology and Therapeutics
MOFFATT, M. E., Community Health Services, Paediatrics and Child Health
MOWAT, M., Biochemistry and Medical Genetics
MURPHY, L. C., Biochemistry and Molecular Biology, Medicine
MURPHY, L. J., Medicine and Physiology
MURRAY, R., Community Health Sciences
MUTCH, A., Anaesthesia
NAGY, J. I., Physiology
NAIMARK, A., Physiology
NANCE, D. M., Pathology
NICOLLE, L., Medicine, Medical Microbiology
OEN, K., Paediatrics and Child Health
OLWENY, C., Medicine
O'NEIL, J. D., Community Health Sciences
ONG, B. Y., Anaesthesia
OPPENHEIMER, L., General Surgery
ORR, F. W., Pathology
PANAGIA, V., Human Anatomy and Cell Science, Physiology
PARKINSON, D., Neurosurgery
PASTERKAMP, H., Paediatrics and Child Health
PATERSON, J. A., Human Anatomy and Cell Science
PEELING, J., Pharmacology and Therapeutics
PEELING, W. J., Radiology
PENNER, B., Medicine
PENNER, S. B., Pharmacology and Therapeutics
PETTIGREW, N., Pathology
PIERCE, G. N., Physiology
PLUMMER, F. A., Medical Microbiology, Medicine
POSTL, B., Community Health Sciences, Paediatrics and Child Health
POSTUMA, R., General Surgery
RAMSEY, E., Surgery
REED, M. H., Continuing Medical Education, Paediatrics and Child Health, Radiology
RENNIE, W., Orthopaedic Surgery
RHODES, R., Pathology
RIESE, K. T., General Surgery and Otolaryngology
RIGATTO, H., Paediatrics and Child Health, Obstetrics, Gynaecology and Reproductive Sciences
ROBERTS, D., Medicine
RONALD, A. R., Community Health Sciences, Medical Microbiology, Medicine
ROOS, L. L., Community Health Sciences
ROOS, N. P., Community Health Sciences
ROY, R., Clinical Health Psychology
RUSH, D., Medicine
SCHACTER, B., Medicine
SCHROEDER, M., Paediatrics and Child Health
SESHIA, M. M. K., Obstetrics, Gynaecology and Reproductive Sciences, Paediatrics and Child Health
SHEFCHY, S., Physiology
SHIU, R. P. C., Physiology
SHOJANIA, A. M., Medicine, Paediatrics and Child Health, Pathology
SIMONS, F. E. R., Immunology, Paediatrics and Child Health
SIMONS, K., Paediatrics and Child Health
SINGAL, P. K., Physiology
SITAR, D., Medicine, Pharmacology and Therapeutics
SMYTH, D. D., Continuing Medical Education, Pharmacology and Therapeutics
SMYTHE, D., Medicine
SNEIDERMAN, B. M., Community Health Sciences
STANWICK, R. S., Community Health Sciences
STEPHENS, N. L., Physiology
STRANC, M. F., Plastic Surgery
SZATHMÁRY, E. J. E., Human Genetics
TENENBEIN, M., Community Health Sciences, Medicine, Pharmacology and Therapeutics, Paediatrics and Child Health
THLIVERIS, J. A., Human Anatomy and Cell Science
THOMSON, I., Anaesthesia
UNRUH, H. W., Surgery
VRIEND, J., Human Anatomy and Cell Science
WALKER, J., Clinical Health Psychology
WARREN, C. P. W., Continuing Medical Education, Medicine
WARRINGTON, R. J., Immunology and Medicine
WEST, M., Surgery
WILKINS, J. A., Immunology, Medicine, Medical Microbiology
WILLIAMS, T., Medical Microbiology, Paediatrics and Child Health
WOODS, R. A., Human Genetics
WRIGHT, J. A., Biochemistry and Molecular Biology
WROGEMANN, K., Biochemistry and Molecular Biology, Human Genetics
YASSI, A., Community Health Sciences
YOUNES, M., Medicine
YOUNG, T. K., Community Health Sciences
ZELINSKI, T., Biochemistry and Medical Genetics

Natural Resources Institute:

BERKES, F.
HAQUE, C. EMDAD

Faculty of Nursing:

BEATON, J. I.
DEGNER, L. F.
GREGORY, D. M.

Faculty of Pharmacy:

BRIGGS, C. J.
COLLINS, D.
GRYMONPRE, R.
HASINOFF, B.
SIMONS, K. J.
TEMPLETON, J. F.
ZHANEL, G.

Faculty of Physical Education and Recreation Studies:

ALEXANDER, M. J. L.
DAHLGREN, W. J.
GIESBRECHT, G.
HARPER, J.
HRYCAIKO, D. W.
JANZEN, H. F.
READY, A. E.

Faculty of Science:

ABRAHAMS, M., Zoology
AITCHISON, P. W., Mathematics
ARNASON, A. N., Computer Science
AYRES, L. D., Geological Sciences
BALDWIN, W. G., Chemistry
BARBER, R. C., Physics and Astronomy
BELL, M. G., Mathematics
BERRY, T. G., Mathematics
BIRCHALL, J., Physics and Astronomy
BLUNDEN, P., Physics and Astronomy
BOOTH, J. T., Botany
BREWSTER, J. F., Statistics
BUTLER, M., Microbiology
CHARLTON, J. L., Chemistry
CHENG, S. W., Statistics
CHOW, A., Chemistry
CLARK, G. S., Geological Sciences
COLLENS, R. J., Computer Science
DAVISON, N. E., Physics and Astronomy
DICK, T. A., Zoology
DOOB, M., Mathematics

DUCKWORTH, H. W., Chemistry
EALES, J. G., Zoology
ELIAS, R. J., Geological Sciences
ENS, W., Physics and Astronomy
FALK, W., Physics and Astronomy
FU, J. C., Statistics
GERHARD, J. A., Mathematics
GHAHRAMANI, F., Mathematics
GRATZER, G., Mathematics
GUO, B., Mathematics
GUPTA, C. K., Mathematics
GUPTA, N. D., Mathematics
HALDEN, N. M., Geological Sciences
HAWTHORNE, F. C., Geological Sciences
HOSKINS, J. A., Computer Science
HOSKINS, W. D., Mathematics
HRUSKA, F. E., Chemistry
HUEBNER, E., Zoology
HUNTER, N. R., Chemistry
JAMIESON, J. C., Chemistry
JANZEN, A. F., Chemistry
KELLY, D., Mathematics
KENKEL, N. C., Botany
KING, P. R., Computer Science
KLASSEN, G. R., Microbiology
KOCAY, W. L., Computer Science
KRAUSE, G., Mathematics
LAKSER, H., Mathematics
LAST, W. M., Geological Sciences
LOEWEN, P. C., Microbiology
LOLY, P. D., Physics and Astronomy
MACARTHUR, R. A., Zoology
MCKINNON, D. M., Chemistry
MACPHERSON, B. D., Statistics
MAEBA, P. Y., Microbiology
MEEK, D. S., Computer Science
MENDELSOHN, N. S., Mathematics
MOON, W., Geological Sciences
MORRISH, A. H., Physics and Astronomy
O'NEIL, J. D. J., Chemistry
OSBORN, T. A., Physics and Astronomy
PADMANABHAN, R., Mathematics
PAGE, J. H., Physics and Astronomy
PAGE, S. A., Physics and Astronomy
PARAMESWARAN, M. R., Mathematics
PLATT, C., Mathematics
PUNTER, D., Botany
RIEWE, R. R., Zoology
ROBINSON, G. G. C., Botany, Environmental Science Program
ROSHKO, R. M., Physics and Astronomy
SAMANTA, M., Statistics
SCHAEFER, T., Chemistry
SCUSE, D. H., Computer Science
SEALY, S. G., Zoology
SECCO, A. S., Chemistry
SHARMA, K. S., Physics and Astronomy
SHERRIFF, B. L., Geological Sciences
SHIVAKUMAR, P. N., Mathematics
SICHLER, J., Mathematics
SOUTHERN, B. W., Physics and Astronomy
STANTON, R. G., Computer Science
STEWART, J. M., Botany
SUZUKI, I., Microbiology
SVENNE, J. P., Physics and Astronomy
TABISZ, G. C., Physics and Astronomy
TELLER, J. C., Geological Sciences
THOMAS, R. S. D., Mathematics
TRIM, D. W., Mathematics
VAN OERS, W. T. H., Physics and Astronomy
VAN REES, G. H. J., Computer Science
WALLACE, R., Chemistry
WALTON, D. J., Computer Science
WESTMORE, J. B., Chemistry
WIENS, T. J., Zoology
WILLIAMS, G., Physics and Astronomy
WILLIAMS, H. C., Computer Science
WILLIAMS, J. J., Mathematics
WOODS, R. G., Mathematics
WRIGHT, J. A., Microbiology
ZETNER, P. W., Physics and Astronomy

Faculty of Social Work:
FUCHS, D. M.
ROY, R.
TRUTE, B.

School of Art:
AMUNDSON, D. O.
BAKER, M. C.
FLYNN, R. K.
HIGGINS, S. B.
MCMILLAN, D. S.
PURA, W. P.
SAKOWSKI, R. C.
SCOTT, C. W.

School of Dental Hygiene:
BOWDEN, G. H. W.
DAWES, C.
FLEMING, N.
HAMILTON, I. R.
JAY, F.
KARIM, A. C.
LAVELLE, C. L. B.
SCOTT, J. E.
SINGER, D. L.

School of Medical Rehabilitation:
ANDERSON, J., Occupational Therapy
COOPER, J. E., Occupational Therapy
LOVERIDGE, B., Physical Therapy

School of Music:
ENGBRECHT, H.
JENSEN, K.
LONIS, D.
WEDGEWOOD, R.

Continuing Education Division:
PERCIVAL, A.

ATTACHED INSTITUTE

Natural Resources Institute: Dir Dr C. EMDAD HAQUE.

AFFILIATED COLLEGES

St Andrew's College: 29 Dysart Rd, Winnipeg, MB R3T 2M7; tel. (204) 474-8995; fax (204) 474-7624; f. 1964 (Ukrainian Orthodox Church); Principal V. OLENDER.

St Boniface College: 200 Cathedral Ave, St Boniface, MB R2H 0H7; tel. (204) 233-0210; fax (204) 237-3240; f. 1818 (Roman Catholic); Rector P. RUEST.

St John's College: 400 Dysart Rd, Winnipeg, MB R3T 2M5; tel. (204) 474-8531; fax (204) 474-7610; f. 1849 (Anglican); Warden and Vice-Chancellor Dr J. HOSKINS.

St Paul's College: 430 Dysart Rd, Winnipeg, MB R3T 2M6; tel. (204) 474-8575; fax (204) 474-7620; f. 1926 (Roman Catholic); Rector J. J. STAPLETON.

University College: 500 Dysart Rd, Winnipeg, MB R3T 2M8; tel. (204) 474-9522; fax (204) 474-7589; Provost G. WALZ.

MEMORIAL UNIVERSITY OF NEWFOUNDLAND

POB 4200, Elizabeth Ave, St John's, NL A1C 5S7
Telephone: (709) 737-8000
Fax: (709) 737-4569
Internet: www.mun.ca

Founded 1925 by Provincial Government as Memorial University College, university status 1949

Academic year: September to August (three terms)

Language of instruction: English

Chancellor: J. CROSBIE
President and Vice-Chancellor: A. MEISON
Vice-Presidents: E. SIMPSON (Academic and Pro Vice-Chancellor), W. W. THISTLE (Administration)
Research: K. KEOUGH
Principal, Sir Wilfred Grenfell College: A. FOWLER
Registrar: G. W. COLLINS
Librarian: R. ELLIS

Number of teachers: 1,367
Number of students: 16,000

Publications: *Canadian folklore canadien* (2 a year), *Communicator* (4 a year), *Culture and Tradition* (annually), *Échos du Monde Classique / Classical Views* (3 a year), *Gazette* (every 2 weeks), *Labour / Le Travail* (2 a year), *Luminus* (3 a year), *The Muse* (weekly), *Newfoundland Quarterly* (4 a year), *Regional Language Studies* (annually), *Research Matters* (3 a year)

DEANS AND DIRECTORS

Faculty of Arts: T. MURPHY
Faculty of Business Administration: GARY GORMAN
Faculty of Education: ALICE COLLINS
Faculty of Engineering and Applied Science: Dr M. R. HADDARA
Faculty of Human Kinetics: Dr COLIN HIGGS
Faculty of Medicine: (vacant)
Faculty of Science: W. DAVIDSON
School of Continuing Education: H. WEIR
School of Graduate Studies: G. KEALEY
School of Music: TOM GORDON
School of Nursing: M. BEATON
School of Pharmacy: C. LOOMIS (acting)
School of Social Work: E. DOW

PROFESSORS

Faculty of Arts:
ALLEN, T. J., Allen
BATH, A. J., Geography
BELL, D. N., Religious Studies
BELL, T. J., Physical Geography
BISHOP, N. B., French and Spanish
BORNSTEIN, C., Philosophy
BRADLEY, J., Linguistics
BRANIGAN, P., Linguistics
BROWN, S. C., Anthropology
BUBENIK, V., Linguistics
BUTLER, K., Physical Geography
BUTRICA, J., Classics
BYRNE, P., English
CATTO, N. R., Physical Geography
CHADWICK, A., French and Spanish
CHERWINSKI, W. J., History
CLARKE, S., Linguistics
CLOSE, D., Philosophy
CROCKER, S., Religious Studies
CULLUM, L., Religious Studies
DEAL, M., Anthropology
DEN OTTER, A. A., History
DEROCHE, M., Religious Studies
DYCK, C., Linguistics
EDINGER, E., Physical Geography
FEEHAN, J. P., Economics
FELT, L. F., Sociology
FISCHER, L., History
GRAHAM, D. E., French and Spanish
HARGER-GRINLING, V. A., French and Spanish
HARRIS, P. F., Linguistics
HART, P., History
HAWKIN, D. J., Religious Studies
HILL, R., Sociology
HILLER, J. K., History
HOUSE, J. D., Sociology
JACOBS, J. D., Geography
JOHNSTONE, F., Sociology
JONES, G. P., English
KENNEDY, J. C., Anthropology
LAI, T. T. L., Philosophy
LATUS, A., Philosophy
LEYTON, E. H., Anthropology
LYNDE, D., English
MCKENZIE, M., Linguistics
MANNION, J. J., Geography
MAXWELL, D. V., Philosophy
MAY, J. D., Economics
NARVAËZ, P., Folklore
NICHOL, D. W., English
NICHOL, K., Geography
NURSE, D., Linguistics
O'DEA, S., English

O'DWYER, B., English
PANJABI, R. K., History
PARKER, K. I., Religious Studies
PARKER, M., Classics
PETERS, H., English
POCIUS, G., Folklore
PORTER, J., Religious Studies
RAINEY, L., Religious Studies
RENOUF, P., Anthropology
ROLLMAN, H., Religious Studies
ROSENBERG, N., Folklore
ROY, N., Economics
RYAN, S., History
SCHRANK, B., English
SCHRANK, W. E., Economics
SHARPE, C., Geography
SHUTE, M., Religious Studies
SIMMS, A., Geography
SIMMS, E., Geography
SIMPSON, E., Philosophy
SHAWYER, A. J., Geography
SMITH, P., Folklore
STAFFORD, A., Philosophy
STAVELEY, M., Geography
SHORROKS, G., English Language and Literature
STOREY, C., Economic Geography
TANNER, A., Anthropology
THOMSPON, D., Philosophy
TSOA, E., Economics
TUCK, J. A., Anthropology
WHITE, R. W., Geography
WOOD, C., Geography

Faculty of Business Administration:
BARNES, J. G., Marketing
FASERUK, A. J., Business Administration
KUBIAK, W., Quantitative Methods
PARSONS, J., Information Systems
SAHA, S., Organizational Behaviour
SEXTY, R. W., Management and Policy
SKIPTON, M. D., Management and Policy
SOOKLAL, L. R., Human Resource Management and Organizational Theory
STEWART, D. B., Business Administration
WITHEY, M. J., Organizational Behaviour

Faculty of Education:
BARRELL, B., Education
BROWN, J., Education
BURNABY, B. J., Education
CAHILL, M., Education
CANNING, P., Education
CROCKER, R. K., Education
DOYLE, C. P., Education
GARLIE, N. W., Education
GLASSMAN, M. S., Education
HADLEY, N. H., Education
JEFFREY, G. H., Education
KELLEHER, R. R., Education
KELLY, U., Education
KENNEDY, W., Education
KIM, K. S., Education
MANN, B. L., Education
NESBIT, W. C., Education
OLDFORD-MATCHIM, J., Education
ROBERTS, B. A., Education
SHARPE, D. B., Education
SINGH, A., Education
STEVENS, K., Education
TRESLAN, D., Education

Faculty of Engineering:
ABDI, M., Mechanical Engineering
ADLURI, S., Civil Engineering
AHMED, M. H., Electrical and Computer Engineering
BASS, D. W., Mathematics and Statistics and Engineering
BOOTON, M., Mechanical Engineering
BOSE, N., Engineering
BRUCE-LOCKHART, M., Engineering
CLAUDE, D., Engineering
COLES, C., Civil Engineering
GEORGE, G., Electrical and Computer Engineering
GILL, E., Electrical and Computer Engineering
GOSINE, R., Electrical and Computer Engineering
HADDARA, M. M. R., Engineering
HAWBOLDT, K., Civil Engineering
HEYS, H., Electrical and Computer Engineering
HINCHEY, M., Mechanical Engineering
HUSAIN, T., Engineering
IQBAL, T., Electrical and Computer Engineering
JEYASURYA, B., Electrical and Computer Engineering
JORDAAN, I. J., Ocean Engineering
KHAN, F., Mechanical Engineering
KREIN, L., Mechanical Engineering
LI, C., Electrical and Computer Engineering
LYE, L., Engineering
MASEK, V., Electrical and Computer Engineering
MALONEY, C., Electrical and Computer Engineering
NIEFER, R., Engineering
NORVELL, T., Electrical and Computer Engineering
O'YOUNG, S., Electrical and Computer Engineering
QUAICOE, J., Electrical and Computer Engineering
PETERS, D., Electrical and Computer Engineering
POPESCU, R., Engineering
RAHMAN, M., Electrical and Computer Engineering
SABIN, G., Mechanical Engineering
SESHADRI, R., Mechanical Engineering
SHARAN, A., Mechanical Engineering
SHARP, J. J., Engineering
SHIROKOFF, J., Mechanical Engineering
SWAMIDAS, A. S. J., Engineering
VEITCH, B., Engineering
WILLIAMS, F., Engineering

Faculty of Medicine:
BEAR, J. C., Medicine (Genetics)
BROSNAN, J. T., Biochemistry and Medicine
BROSNAN, M. E., Biochemistry and Medicine
CARAYANNIOTIS, G., Medicine and Endocrinology
CORBETT, D. R., Medicine
GADAG, V., Biostatistics
GILLESPIE, L. L., Oncology
HANSEN, P. A., Medicine
HERZBERG, G. R., Biochemistry and Medicine
HOEKMAN, T., Biophysics
HOOVER, R., Biochemistry
HULAN, H., Biochemistry
KEOUGH, K., Biochemistry
LIEPINS, A., Medicine (Cell Sciences)
MARTIN, A. M., Biochemistry
MICHALAK, T. I., Medicine
MICHALSKI, C. J., Medicine (Molecular Biology)
MOODY-CORBETT, F., Physiology
NEUMAN, R. S., Medicine (Pharmacology)
PATER, A., Medicine (Molecular Biology)
PATERNO, G., Medicine (Oncology)
RAHIMTULA, A. D., Biochemistry and Medicine
SCOTT, T. M., Medicine (Anatomy)
VASDEV, S. C., Medicine (Biochemistry)
WEST, R., Pharmacy and Medicine

Faculty of Science:
ADAMEC, R. E., Psychology
ADAMS, R. J., Psychology
AFANASSIEV, I., Physics
AKSU, A. E., Earth Sciences
ANDERSON, R., Psychology
ANDREWS, E., Psychology
ANDREWS, T., Physics
ARLETT, C., Psychology
BARTHA, M., Computer Science
BARTLETT, R., Statistics
BODWELL, G. J., Chemistry
BOURGAULT, D., Physics
BRIDSON, J., Chemistry
BROWN, J. A., Psychology
BRUNNER, H., Mathematics and Statistics
BURRY, J. H., Mathematics
BURDEN, E., Earth Sciences
BURTON, D., Biology
BURTON, M., Biology
BUTTON, C., Psychology
HARLEY, C. A., Psychology
CALON, T. J., Earth Sciences
CHO, C. W., Physics
CLOUTER, M. J., Physics
CARR, S. M., Biology
COLBO, M. H., Biology
COLLINS, M., Biology
COURAGE, M., Psychology
CURNOE, S., Physics
DABINETT, P., Biology
DAVIDSON, W. S., Biochemistry, Molecular Biology
DEBRUYN, J. R., Physics
DEYOUNG, B., Physics
DRIEDZIC, W., Biochemistry, Molecular Biology
DUNBRACK, R. L., Biochemistry, Molecular Biology
DUNNING, G., Earth Sciences
EDDY, R. H., Mathematics and Statistics
EDINGER, E., Biology
EVANS, J., Psychology
FAHRAEUS-VAN RAE, G., Biology
FINNEY-CRAWLEY, J., Biology
FLETCHER, G. L., Ocean Sciences Centre (Biology)
GALE, J. E., Earth Sciences
GAMPERL, K., Biology
GARDNER, G., Biology
GASKILL, H. S., Mathematics
GEORGHIOU, P., Chemistry
GIEN, T. T., Physics
GILLARD, P., Computer Science
GOODAIRE, E. G., Mathematics and Statistics
GOSSE, V., Psychology
GOW, J., Biology
GRANT, M. J., Psychology
GREEN, J. M., Psychology
GREEN, J. M., Biology
HADDEN, K., Psychology
HAEDRICH, R. L., Ocean Sciences Centre (Biology)
HALL, J., Earth Sciences
HANNAH, E., Psychology
HANNAH, T. E., Psychology
HEATH, P. R., Mathematics and Statistics
HERMANUTZ, L., Biology
HISCOTT, R. N., Earth Sciences
HODYCH, J. P., Earth Sciences
HOOPER, R., Biology
HURICH, C. A., Earth Sciences
INDARES, A.-D., Earth Sciences
INNES, D., Biology
JABLONSKI, C. R., Chemistry
JENNER, G., Earth Sciences
JONES, I., Biology
JONES, I., Psychology
KNOECHEL, R., Biology
LAGOWSKI, J., Physics
LARSON, D. J., Biology
LEE, D., Biology
LEITCH, A. M., Earth Sciences
LEWIS, J. C., Physics
LIEN, J., Psychology
LOADER, C. E., Chemistry
LUCAS, C. R., Chemistry
MCKIM, W., Psychology
MADDIGAN, R., Psychology
MALSBURY, C., Psychology
MARTIN, G., Psychology
MASON, R. A., Earth Sciences
MEYER, R., Earth Sciences
MILLER, H. G., Earth Sciences
MILLER, E., Psychology

MILLER, T., Biology
MINIMIS, G., Computer Science
MOESER, S., Psychology
MONTEVECCHI, W. A., Psychology
MORROW, M. R., Physics
MURRIN, F., Biology
MYERS, J. S., Earth Sciences
NARAYANASWAMI, P. P., Mathematics and Statistics
PARMENTER, M. M., Mathematics and Statistics
PARSONS, J., Biology
PARSONS, J., Computer Science
PATEL, T. R., Biochemistry and Biology
PENNEY, C. G., Psychology
PETERSEN, C., Psychology
PICKUP, P. G., Chemistry
POIRIER, R., Chemistry
PODUSKA, K., Physics
QUINLAN, G. M., Earth Sciences
QUIRION, G., Physics
RABINOWITZ, F. M., Psychology
REVUSKY, B., Psychology
RICH, N. H., Physics
RIVERS, C. J. S., Earth Sciences
ROSE, B., Psychology
ROSE, G., Marine Institute
SCHNEIDER, D. C., Ocean Sciences Centre
SCOTT, P., Biology
SHAWYER, B. L. R., Mathematics and Statistics
SHERRICK, M., Psychology
SIWEI, L., Computer Science
SKINNER, D., Psychology
SMITH, F., Physics
SLAWINSKI, M., Earth Sciences
SNELGROVE, P., Biology
STAVELY, B. E., Biology
STEIN, A. R., Chemistry
STENSON, G. B., Psychology
STOREY, A. E., Psychology
SUMMERS, D., Mathematics and Statistics
SUTRADHAR, B. C., Mathematics and Statistics
SYLVESTER, P. J., Earth Sciences
TANG, J., Computer Science
THOMPSON, R. J., Ocean Sciences Centre
VOLKOFF, H., Biology
VIDYASANKAR, K., Computer Science
WADLEIGH, M., Earth Sciences
WALSH, D., Physics
WANG, C. A., Computer Science
WARKENTIN, I., Psychology
WHITEHEAD, J. P., Physics
WHITMORE, M. D., Physics
WHITTICK, A., Biology
WILSON, M., Earth Sciences
WILTON, D. H. C., Earth Sciences
WRIGHT, J. A., Earth Sciences
WROBLEWSKI, J. S., Ocean Sciences Centre (Physics)
ZUBEREK, W. M., Computer Science
ZEDEL, L., Physics

School of Nursing:

LARYEA, M., Nursing

School of Pharmacy:

WEST, R., Pharmacy

ATTACHED INSTITUTES

Art Gallery: Dir GAIL TUTTLE.

Botanical Garden: Dir W. NICHOLS.

Centre for Newfoundland Studies: Head JOHN SCOTT.

Harlow Campus: Director KAREN CRAKNELL.

Institut Frecker: Dir A. THAREAU.

Marine Institute: Exec. Dir L. O'REILLY.

Maritime History Archive: Curator W. HANDCOCK.

Queen's College: Provost Rev. Dr JOHN MELLIS.

Sir Wilfred Grenfell College: Principal A. FOWLER.

ATTACHED RESEARCH INSTITUTES

Archaeology Unit: Chair. J. A. TUCK.

Canadian Centre for Fisheries Innovation: Dir A. O'REILLY.

Canadian Centre for International Fisheries Training and Development: International Liaison Officer A. B. DICKINSON.

Cartographic Laboratory: Dir C. H. WOOD.

Centre for the Application of Developmental Science: Dirs M. HOWE, J. O'SULLIVAN.

Centre for Cold Ocean Resources Engineering: Pres/CEO J. WHITTICK.

Centre for Computer-Aided Engineering: Man. D. PRESS.

Centre for Earth Resources Research: Dir G. QUINLAN.

Centre for International Business: Dir B. WINSOR.

Centre for Management Development: Dir G. ROWE.

Centre for Material Culture Studies: Dirs S. O'DEA, G. POCIUS.

Centre for Offshore and Remote Medicine: Dir H. MANSON.

Continuing Engineering Education: Dir (vacant).

English Language Research Centre: Coordinator W. KIRWIN.

Folklore and Language Archive: Dir M. LOVELACE.

Geographical Information and Digital Analysis Laboratory: Dir A. SIMMS.

Health Research Unit: Dir J. SEGOVIA.

Institute for Folklore Studies in Britain and Canada: Dirs P. SMITH, J. WIDDOWSOR.

Institute of Social and Economic Research: Research Dir J. TUCK.

Labrador Institute of Northern Studies: Dir H. BEST.

Maritime Studies Research Unit: Chair. D. VICKERS.

Ocean Engineering Research Centre: Dir N. BOSE.

Ocean Sciences Centre: Dir W. KING.

P. J. Gardiner Institute for Small Business: Dir W. KING.

Seabright Corporation Ltd: Pres/CEO D. KING.

Telemedicine Centre: Dir JANICE COOPER (acting).

Telemedicine and Educational Technology Resources Agency: Co-Dir R. HYDE.

UNIVERSITÉ DE MONCTON

Moncton, NB E1A 3E9
Telephone: (506) 858-4000
Fax: (506) 858-4585
E-mail: info@umoncton.ca
Internet: www.umoncton.ca

Founded 1864 as St Joseph's University, name changed 1963
Language of instruction: French
Private control
Academic year: September to April
Campuses also in Edmundston and Shippagan
Chancellor: ROMÉO LEBLANC
Rector: YVON FONTAINE
Vice-Rector (Academic Research): NEIL BOUCHER
Vice-Rector (Edmundston Campus): PAUL ALBERT
Vice-Rector (Human Resources and Administration): NASSIR EL-JABI
Vice-Rector (Shippagan Campus): ARMAND CARON
Secretary-General: COLETTE LANDRY MARTIN (acting)
Librarian: PIERRE LAFRANCE
Number of teachers: 446 full-time
Number of students: 6,492 (5,027 full-time, 1,465 part-time)
Publication: *La Revue*

DEANS

Moncton Campus:

Faculty of Administration: GASTON LEBLANC
Faculty of Arts: ISABELLE MCKEE-ALLAIN
Faculty of Education: ANNE LOWE
Faculty of Engineering: GILLES CORMIER
Faculty of Higher Studies and Research: ANDREW BOGHEN
Faculty of Sciences: CHARLES BOURQUE
Faculty of Social Sciences: ISABELLE MCKEE-ALLAIN

DIRECTORS

Edmundston Campus:

Academic Services: ADIREN BÉRUBÉ
Arts and Letters: SAMIRA BELYAZID
Business Administration: GARY LONG
Education: CLAUDE CARRIER
Human Sciences: JACQUES PAUL COUTURIER
Sciences: DANIEL BÉLANGER
School of Forestry: LISE CARON
School of Nursing: FRANCE L. MARQUIS

Moncton Campus:

School of Kinesiology and Recreology: HERMEL J. COUTURIER
School of Law: S. ROUSELLE
School of Nursing: CYNTHIA BAKER
School of Nutrition and Home Economics: RÉGINA ROBICHAUD
School of Psychology: PAUL BOURQUE
School of Social Work: KATHERINE MARCOCCIO

Shippagan Campus:

Administration and Secretarial Sciences: R. DUGUAY
Arts and Human Sciences: G. D'SOUZA
Business Administration: MARTHE ROBICHAUD
Nursing: LIETTE CLÉMENT
Sciences: JACQUES ROBICHAUD

HEADS OF DEPARTMENTS AND SCHOOLS

Moncton Campus:

Faculty of Administration (Université de Moncton, Faculté d'Administration, Moncton, NB E1C 3E9; tel. (506) 858-4446; fax (506) 858-4093; e-mail fadmin@umoncton.ca; internet www.umoncton.ca/administration):

Accounting: E. MCGRAW
Administration: CLAUDE DES ROCHES

Faculty of Arts and Social Sciences (Université de Moncton, Faculté des Arts et des Sciences Sociales, Moncton, NB E1A 3E9; tel. (506) 858-4018; fax (506) 858-4166; e-mail arts-scsoc@umoncton.ca; internet www.umoncton.ca/facarts/arts.html):

Dramatic Art: A. ZAHARIA
English: P. CURTIS
French Studies: RAOUL BOUDREAU
History and Geography: GUY R. VINCENT
Music: M. WALTZ
Translation and Languages: F. GROGNIER
Visual Arts: F. COURTELLIER
Philosophy and Religions: IBRAHIM OUTTARA
Economics: RONALD C. LEBLANC
Political Science: CHEDLY BELKHODJA
Psychology: PAUL BOURQUE
Social Service: K. MARCOCCIO
Sociology: M. ALI-KHODJA
Public Administration: G. BOUCHARD

Faculty of Education (Université de Moncton, Faculté d'Education, Moncton, NB E1C

3E9; tel. (506) 858-4400; fax (506) 858-4317; e-mail landryro@umoncton.ca; internet www.umoncton.ca/educ/page.htm):

Learning and Teaching: T. LEBLANC
Physical Education: H. COUTURIER
School Guidance and Educational Administration: (vacant)

Faculty of Sciences (Université de Moncton, Faculté des Sciences, Moncton, NB E1C 3E9; tel. (506) 858-4301; fax (506) 858-4541; e-mail bourquch@umoncton.ca; internet www.sciences.umoncton.ca):

Biology: STÉPHAN REEBS
Chemistry and Biochemistry: LOUISE GIRARD
Mathematics and Statistics: JACQUES ALLARD
Physics and Astronomy: FRANCIS LEBLANC

ATTACHED RESEARCH INSTITUTES

Bureau de Soutien à l'Innovation: Dir RÉJEAN HALL.

Centre Assomption de Recherche de Développement en Entrepreneuriat: Dir GASTON LEBLANC.

Centre de Commercialisation Internationale: Dir J. LANDRY.

Centre de Conservation des Sols et de l'Eau de l'Est du Canada: Dir J.-L. DAIGLE.

Centre de Documentation et d'Etudes Madawaskayennes: Dir M. THÉRIAULT.

Centre d'Etudes du Vieillissement: Dir (vacant).

Centre d'Etudes Acadiennes: Dir MAURICE BASQUE.

Centre de Génie Eolien: Dir GÉRARD POITRAS.

Centre International d'Apprentissage du Français: Co-ordinator DAVID MACFARLANE.

Centre International de la Common Law en Français: Dir SERGE ROUSSELLE.

Centre International pour le Développement de l'Inforoute en Français: Dir ROGER GERVAIS.

Centre de Recherches sur les Aliments: Dir PASCAL AUDET.

Chaire de Recherche Clément-Cormier en Développement Economique: Dir D. SAVOIE.

Centre de Recherche en Conversion d'Energie: Dir S. SAMI.

Centre de Recherche et de Développement en Education: Dir CLAIRE LAPOINTE.

Centre de Recherche en Linguistique Appliquée: Dir GISÈLE CHEVALIER.

Centre de Recherche de Produit Marin: Dir SYLVAIN POIRIER.

Centre de Recherche en Sciences de l'Environnement: Dir CHARLES BOURQUE (acting).

Centre de Recherche de la Tourbe: Dir J.-Y. DAIGLE.

Centre de Ressources Pédagogiques: Dir YVAN PICARD.

Centre des Technologies de l'Information: Dir JEAN-PIERRE ANGERS.

Centre de Technologie Manufacturière: Dir SADEK EID.

Centre de Traduction et de Terminologie Juridiques: Dir G. SNOW.

Chaire des Caisses Populaires Acadiennes en Etudes Co-opératives: Dir (vacant).

Chaire d'Etudes K.-C.-Irving en Développement Durable: Dir LIETTE VASSEUR.

Chaire de Recherche du Canada en Analyse Littèraire Interculturelle: Dir JEAN MORENRY.

Chaire de Recherche du Canada en Conservation des Paysages: Dir MARC-ANDRÉ VILLARD.

Genieo Solutions Design: Dir GISÈLE LÉVESQUE.

Institut Canadien de Recherche sur le Développement Régional: Dir DONALD J. SAVOIE.

Institut Canadien de Recherche sur les Minorités Linguistiques: Dir RODRIGUE LANDRY.

Institut de Leadership: Dir HERMEL COUTURIER.

Institut de Recherche sur les Zones Côtières: Dir LISE OUELLETTE.

UNIVERSITÉ DE MONTRÉAL

CP 6128, Succursale Centre-ville, Montréal, QC H3C 3J7
Telephone: (514) 343-6111
Fax: (514) 343-5976
E-mail: international@umontreal.ca
Internet: www.umontreal.ca

Founded 1878
Public control
Language of instruction: French
Academic year: September to August

Chancellor: ANDRÉ BISSON
Rector: LUC VINET
Executive Vice-Rector: MICHEL TRAHAN
Vice-Rector (Human Resources): GISÉLE PAINCHAUD
Vice-Rector (Planning): FRANÇOIS DUCHESNEAU
Vice-Rector (Research): ALAIN CAILLÉ
Vice-Rector (Undergraduate Education and Continuing Education): MARYSE RINFRET-RAYNOR
General Secretary: MICHEL LESPÉRANCE
Registrar: FERNAND BOUCHER
Director of Finances: ANDRÉ RACETTE
Librarian: JEAN-PIERRE CÔTÉ

Library: see Libraries and Archives
Number of teachers: 6,150
Number of students: 54,465

Publications: *L'Actualité Economique*, *Criminologie*, *Cahiers du Centre d'études de l'Asie de l'Est*, *Cahiers d'Histoire*, *Cinémas*, *CIRCUIT* (North American modern music), *Collection Tiré à part* (School of Industrial Relations), *Études françaises*, *La Gazette des Sciences mathématiques du Québec*, *Géographie physique et Quaternaire*, *Gestion*, *Le Médecin vétérinaire du Québec*, *META*, *Journal des traducteurs*, *Paragraphes*, *Revue Juridique Thémis*, *Revue des Sciences de l'Education*, *Sociologie et sociétés*, *Surfaces*, *Théologiques*

DEANS

Faculty of Arts and Sciences: J. HUBERT
Faculty of Dental Medicine: CLAUDE LAMARCHE
Faculty of Education Sciences: M. CRESPO (acting)
Faculty of Environment Design: IRÉNE CINQ-MARS
Faculty of Law: J. FRÉMONT
Faculty of Medicine: P. VINAY
Faculty of Music: RÉJEAN POIRIER
Faculty of Nursing: CÉLINE GOULET
Faculty of Pharmacy: JACQUES TURGEON
Faculty of Theology: JEAN-MARC CHARRON
Faculty of Veterinary Medicine: RAYMOND S. ROY
Faculty of Continuing Education: J.-M. BOUDRIAS (Administrator)
Faculty of Graduate Studies: LOUIS MAHEU

PROFESSORS

Faculty of Arts and Sciences

Department of Anthropology:

BEAUCAGE, P.
BERNIER, B.
BIBEAU, G.
CHAPAIS, B.
CHAPDELAINE, C.
CLERMONT, N.
LEAVITT, J.
MEINTEL, D.
MULLER, J.-C.
PANDOLFI, M.
PARADIS, L. I.
SMITH, P.
THIBAULT, P.
TOLSTOY, P.
VERDON, M.

Department of Biology:

ANCTIL, M.
BOISCLAIR, D.
BOUCHARD, A.
BROUILLET, L.
CABANA, T.
CAPPADOCIA, M.
CARIGNAN, R.
HARPER, P.-P.
LEGENDRE, P.
MOLOTCHNIKOFF, S.
MORSE, D.
PINEL-ALLOUL, B.
SAINI, H. S.
SIMON, J.-P.

Department of Chemistry:

BEAUCHAMP, A. L.
BERTRAND, M.
BRISSE, F.
CARRINGTON, T.
CHARETTE, A.
D'AMBOISE, M.
DUGAS, H.
DUROCHER, G.
ELLIS, T. H.
HANESSIAN, S.
HUBERT, J.
LAFLEUR, M.
REBER, C.
ST-JACQUES, M.
WINNIK, F. M.
WUEST, J. D.
ZHU, J.

Department of Classical and Medieval Studies:

FASCIANO, D.

Department of Comparative Literature:

CHANADY, A.
GUÉDON, J.-C.
KRYSINSKI, W.
MOSER, W.

Department of Communication:

CARON, A. H.
GIROUX, L.
LAFRANCE, A. A.
RABOY, M.

Department of Computing Sciences and Operational Research:

ABOULHAMID, E. M.
BRASSARD, G.
CERNY, E.
DSSOULI, R.
FERLAND, J. A.
FLORIAN, M.
FRASSON, C.
GENDREAU, M.
JAUMARD, B.
LAPALME, G.
L'ÉCUYER, P.
MARCOTTE, P.
MCKENZIE, P.
MEUNIER, J.
NGUYEN, S.
POTVIN, J.-Y.

STEWART, N.
VAUCHER, J.

School of Criminology:

BROCHU, S.
BRODEUR, J.-P.
CUSSON, M.
LANDREVILLE, P.
OUIMET, M.
TREMBLAY, P.
TRÉPANIER, J.

Department of Demography:

LAPIERRE-ADAMCYK, E.
PICHÉ, V.

Department of Economics:

BOSSERT, W.
BOYER, M.
BRONSARD, C.
DUDLEY, L.
DUFOUR, J.-M.
GAUDET, G.
GAUDRY, M. J. I.
HOLLANDER, A.
LACROIX, R.
MARTENS, A.
MARTIN, F.
MONTMARQUETTE, C.
POITEVIN, M.
RENAULT, E.
VAILLANCOURT, F.

School of Educational Psychology:

CHARLEBOIS, P.
GAGNON, C.
LARIVÉE, S.
LEBLANC, M.
NORMANDEAU, S.
VAN GIJSEGHEM, H.
VITARO, F.

Department of English Studies:

MARTIN, R. K.

Department of French Studies:

BEAULIEU, J.-P.
CAMBRON, M.
GAUVIN, L.
HÉBERT, F.
LAFLÈCHE, G.
LAROSE, J.
MELANÇON, R.
MICHAUD, G.
NEPVEU, P.
PIERSSENS, M.
SOARE, A.
VACHON, S.

Department of Geography:

BRYANT, C. R.
CAVAYAS, F.
COFFEY, W.
COMTOIS, C.
COMTOIS, P.
COURCHESNE, F.
DE KONINCK, R.
FOGGIN, P. M.
GANGLOFF, P.
GRAY, J. T.
MANZAGOL, C.
MAROIS, C.
RICHARD, P. J. H.
ROY, A. G.
SINGH, B.
THOUEZ, J.-P.

Department of Geology:

BOUCHARD, M. A.
MARTIGNOLE, J.
TRZCIENSKI, W. E.

Department of History:

ANGERS, D.
BOGLIONI, P.
DICKINSON, J. A.
HUBERMAN, M.
KEEL, O.
LÉTOURNEAU, P.
LUSIGNAN, S.
MORIN, C.
PERREAULT, J. Y.
RABKIN, Y.
RAMIREZ, B.
ROUILLARD, J.
SUTTO, C.

Department of History of Art:

DE MOURA SOBRAL, L.
DUBREUIL, N.
GAUDREAULT, A.
KRAUSZ, P.
LAFRAMBOISE, A.
LAMOUREUX, J.
LAROUCHE, M.
LHOTE, J.-F.
MARSOLAIS, G.
NAUBERT-RISER, C.
TOUSIGNANT, S.
TRUDEL, J.

School of Industrial Relations:

BOURQUE, R.
BROSSARD, M.
CHICHA, M.-T.
COUSINEAU, J.-M.
DOLAN, S.
DURAND, P.
GUÉRIN, G.
MURRAY, G.
SIMARD, M.
TRUDEAU, G.

School of Library and Information Sciences:

BERTRAND-GASTALDY, S.
COUTURE, C.
DESCHATELETS, G.
LAJEUNESSE, M.
SAVARD, R.

Department of Linguistics and Translation:

CONNORS, K.
CORMIER, M. C.
FORD, A.
HOSINGTON, B.
JAREMA-ARVANITAKIS, G.
KITTREDGE, R.
MEL'ČUK, I. A.
MÉNARD, N.
MORIN, J.-Y.
MORIN, Y.-C.
NUSELOVICI NOUSS, A.
PATRY, R.
ST-PIERRE, P.
SCHULZE-BUSACKER, E.
SINGH, R.

Department of Literature and Modern Languages:

BOUCHARD, J.
PECK, J.
RÄKEL, H.-H.

Department of Mathematics and Statistics:

ARMINJON, P.
BÉLAIR, J.
BENABDALLAH, K.
BILODEAU, M.
BRUNET, R.
CLÉROUX, R.
DELFOUR, M.
DUFRESNE, D.
FRIGON, M.
GAUTHIER, P.
GIRI, N. C.
GIROUX, A.
HUSSIN, V.
JOFFE, A.
LALONDE, F.
LÉGER, C.
LEPAGE, Y.
LESSARD, S.
PATERA, J.
PERRON, F.
RAHMAN, Q. I.
REYES, G.
ROSENBERG, I.
ROUSSEAU, C.
ROY, R.
SABIDUSSI, G.
SAINT-AUBIN, Y.
SANKOFF, D.
SCHLOMIUK, D.
TURGEON, J.
WINTERNITZ, P.
ZAIDMAN, S.

Department of Philosophy:

BAKKER, E. J.
BODEÜS, R.
DUCHESNEAU, F.
GAUTHIER, Y.
GRONDIN, J.
LAGUEUX, M.
LAURIER, D.
LEPAGE, F.
LÉVESQUE, C.
PICHÉ, C.
ROY, J.
SEYMOUR, M.

Department of Physics:

BASTIEN, P.
CAILLÉ, A.
CARIGNAN, C.
COCHRANE, R. W.
DEMERS, S.
FONTAINE, G.
GOULARD, B.
LAPOINTE, J.-Y.
LAPRADE, R.
LEONELLI, R.
LÉPINE, Y.
LEROY, C.
LESSARD, L.
LEWIS, L. J.
LONDON, D.
MICHAUD, G.
MOFFAT, A.
MOISAN, M.
ROORDA, S.
TARAS, P.
TEICHMANN, J.
VINCENT, A.
WESEMAEL, F.
ZACEK, V.

Department of Politics:

BÉLANGER, A.-J.
BERNIER, G.
BLAIS, A.
BOISMENU, G.
CLOUTIER, E.
DION, S.
DUQUETTE, M.
ÉTHIER, D.
FAUCHER, P.
FORTMANN, M.
JENSON, J.
MONIÈRE, D.
NADEAU, R.
NOËL, A.
SOLDATOS, P.
THÉRIEN, J.-P.

Department of Psychology:

BERGERON, J.
BOUCHARD, M.-A.
BRUNET, L.
CLAES, M.
COMEAU, J.
COSSETTE-RICARD, M.
CYR, M.
DAVID, H.
DOYON, J.
DUBÉ, L.
FAVREAU, O.
FORTIN, A.
GRANGER, L.
HACCOUN, R.
HODGINS, S.
LASRY, J.-C.
LASSONDE, M.
LECOMTE, C.
LEPORE, F.
MATHIEU, M.
NADEAU, L.

Pagé, M.
Peretz, I.
Perron, J.
Robert, M.
Sabourin, M.
Savoie, A.
Stravynski, A.
Tremblay, R. E.
Wright, J.
Zavalloni, M.

Department of Sociology:

Bernard, P.
Fournier, M.
Hamel, J.
Hamel, P.
Houle, G.
Juteau, D.
Laurin, N.
Maheu, L.
McAll, C.
Racine, L.
Renaud, J.
Renaud, M.
Rocher, G.
Sales, A.
Vaillancourt, J.-G.

School of Social Work:

Bernier, D.
Chamberland, C.
Groulx, L. H.
Legault, G.
Mayer, R.
Panet-Raymond, J.
Rinfret-Raynor, M.
Rondeau, G.

Faculty of Dental Medicine

Department of Dental Prosthesis:

Baltajian, H.
Boudrias, P.
Lamarche, C.
Prévost, A.
Taché, R.

Department of Oral Health:

Charland, R.
Julien, M.
Kandelman, D.
Lavigne, G.
Masseredjian, V.
Remise, C.
Turgeon, J.
Wechsler, M.

Department of Stomatology:

Donohue, W. B.
Duncan, G.
Dupuis, R.
Duquette, P.
Forest, D.
Lemay, H.
Michaud, M.
Nanci, A.

Faculty of Education Sciences

Department of Curriculum and Instruction:

Beer-Toker, M.
Charland, J.-P.
Gagné, G.
Lemoyne, G.
Painchaud, G.
Paret, M.-C.
Pierre, R.
Retallack-Lambert, N.
Saint-Jacques, D.
Thérien, M.
Van Grunderbeeck, N.

Department of Education and Educational Administration Studies:

Ajar, D.
Bourgeault, G.
Brassard, A.
Chené, A.
Crespo, M.
Dupuis, P.
Joffe-Nicodème, A.
Lessard, C.
Pelletier, G.
Proulx, J.-P.
Tardif, M.
Trahan, M.
Van der Maren, J.-M.

Department of Psychopedagogy and Andragogy:

Comeau, M.
Dufresne-Tassé, C.
Gaudreau, J.
Langevin, J.
Lévesque, M.
Marchand, L.
Tremblay, N.

Faculty of Environmental Design

School of Architecture:

Adamczyk, G.
Dalibard, J.
Davidson, C. H.
Marsan, J.-C.

School of Industrial Design:

Camous, R. F.
Findeli, A.
Leclerc, A.

School of Landscape Architecture:

Cinq-Mars, I.
Jacobs, P.
Lafargue, B.
Poullaouec-Gonidec, P.

Institute of Urbanism:

Barcelo, A.-M.
Blanc, B.
Boisvert, M. A.
Cardinal, A.
Gariépy, M.
Lessard, M.
McNeil, J.
Parenteau, R.
Sokoloff, B.
Trépanier, M.-O.

Faculty of Law:

Benyekhlef, K.
Bich, M.-F.
Boisvert, A.-M.
Brisson, J.-M.
Chevrette, F.
Ciotola, P.
Côté, P.-A.
Côté, P. P.
Crépeau, F.
Deslauriers, P.
Dumont, H.
Fabien, C.
Frémont, J.
Gagnon, J. D.
Goldstein, G.
Gruning, D.
Hétu, J.
Knoppers, B. M.
Labrèche, D.
Lajoie, A.
Lamontagne, D.-C.
Lefebvre, G.
Leroux, T.
Lluelles, D.
Mackaay, E.
Molinari, P.
Neuwahi, N.
Pinard, D.
Popovici, A.
Rocher, G.
Talpis, J.
Tremblay, A.
Tremblay, L.
Trudel, P.
Turp, D.
Viau, L.
Woehrling, J.

Faculty of Medicine

Department of Anaesthesiology:

Blaise, G.
Donati, F.
Hardy, J.-F.

Department of Biochemistry:

Boileau, G.
Bouvier, M.
Brakier-Gingras, L.
Brisson, N.
Crine, P.
Daigneault, R.
DesGroseillers, L.
Lang, F. B.
Rokeach, L. A.
Skup, D.
Sygusch, J.

Department of Family Medicine:

Beaulieu, M.-D.
Millette, B.

Department of Health Administration:

Béland, F.
Blais, R.
Champagne, F.
Contandriopoulos, A.-P.
Denis, J.-L.
Dussault, G.
Lamarche, P.
Sicotte, C.
Tilquin, C.

Department of Medicine:

Ayoub, J.
Bichet, D.
Bradley, E.
Brazeau, P.
Butterworth, R. F.
Cardinal, J.
Chiasson, J.-L.
D'Amour, P.
Delespesse, G. J. T.
Duquette, P.
Gougoux, A.
Grassino, A.
Hallé, J.-P.
Hamet, P.
Huet, M.
Lacroix, A.
Laplante, L.
Lecours, A. R.
Le Lorier, J.
Malo, J.-L.
Marleau, D.
Martel-Pelletier, J.
Matte, R.
Mes-Masson, A.-M.
Nadeau, R.
Nattel, S.
Pelletier, J.-P.
Perreault, C.
Poitras, P.
Pomier-Layrargues, G.
Rasio, E.
Sarfati, M.
Sénécal, J.-L.
Tremblay, J.
Vinay, P.

Department of Microbiology and Immunology:

Auger, P.
Cohen, É.
De Repentigny, L.
Hallenbeck, P.
Lemay, G.
Menezes, J. P. C. A.
Montplaisir, S.
Morisset, R.
Sekaly, R.-P.

Department of Nutrition:

Delisle, H.
Des Rosiers, C.
Garrel, D.
Gavino, V.
Houde-Nadeau, M.
Lévy, E.
Poehlman, É.
Prentki, M.

SERRI, O.
SIMARD-MAVRIKAKIS, S.
VAN DE WERVE, G.

Department of Obstetrics and Gynaecology:
BÉLISLE, S.
DROUIN, P.

Department of Occupational and Environmental Health:
CARRIER, G.
CHAKRABARTI, S. K.
GÉRIN, M.
KRISHNAN, K.
VIAU, C.
ZAYED, J.

Department of Ophthalmology:
BOISJOLY, H.
LABELLE, P.

Department of Paediatrics:
ALVAREZ, F.
BARD, H.
CHEMTOB, S.
FOURON, J.-C.
FRAPPIER, J.-Y.
GAGNAN-BRUNETTE, M.
GAUTHIER-CHOUINARD, M.
LABUDA, D.
LACROIX, J.
LAMBERT, M.
LAPOINTE, N.
RASQUIN-WEBER, A.-M.
ROBITAILLE, P.
ROUSSEAU, É.
SEIDMAN, E.
TEASDALE, F.
VANASSE, M.
VAN VLIET, G.
WEBER, M.
WILKINS, J.

Department of Pathology and Cellular Biology:
BENDAYAN, M.
CHARTRAND, P.
DESCARRIES, L.
GIROUX, L.
KESSOUS, A.
LATOUR, J.-G.
SCHÜRCH, W.

Department of Pharmacology:
CARDINAL, R.
DE LÉAN, A.
DUMONT, L.
DU SOUICH, P.
ÉLIE, R.
GASCON-BARRÉ, M.
LAMBERT, C.
LAROCHELLE, P.
LAVOIE, P.-A.
MOMPARLER, R.
YOUSEF, I.

Department of Physiology:
ANAND-SRIVASTAVA, M.
BERGERON, M.
BERTELOOT, A.
BILLETTE, J.
CASTELLUCCI, V.
COUTURE, R.
DE CHAMPLAIN, J.
DREW, T. B.
FELDMAN, A. G.
GULRAJANI, R.
KALASKA, J. F.
LACAILLE, J.-C.
LAMARRE, Y.
LAVALLÉE, M.
LEBLANC, A.-R.
MAESTRACCI, D.
MALO, C.
READER, T. A.
ROBERGE, F.
ROSSIGNOL, S.
SAUVÉ, R.
SMITH, A.

Department of Preventive and Social Medicine:
BRODEUR, J.-M.
DASSA, C.
FOURNIER, P.
LABERGE-NADEAU, C.
LAMBERT, J.
MAHEUX, B.
PHILIPPE, P.
PINEAULT, R.
POTVIN, L.
SÉGUIN, L.
SIEMIATYCKI, J.

Department of Psychiatry:
AMYOT, A.
CHOUINARD, G.
LALONDE, P.
LEMAY, M.-L.
MONDAY, J.
MONTPLAISIR, J. Y.
SAUCIER, J.-F.
WEISSTUB, D. N.

Department of Radiology, Radio-Oncology and Nuclear Medicine:
BRETON, G.
LAFORTUNE, M.
SAMSON, L.

School of Rehabilitation:
ARSENAULT, B.
BOURBONNAIS, D.
CHAPMAN, C. E.
DUTIL, É.
FERLAND, F.
FORGET, R.
GAUTHIER-GAGNON, C.
GRAVEL, D.
WEISS-LAMBROU, R.

School of Speech Pathology and Audiology:
GAGNÉ, J.-P.
GETTY, L.
JOANETTE, Y.
LE DORZE, G.
SKA, B.

Department of Surgery:
BEAUCHAMP, G.
BERNARD, D.
CAOUETTE-LABERGE, L.
CARRIER, M.
CHARLIN, B.
DALOZE, P.
DUBÉ, S.
DURANCEAU, A.
LABELLE, H.
PAGÉ, P.
PAQUIN, J.-M.
RIVARD, C.-H.
ROBIDOUX, A.
SMEESTERS, C.
VALIQUETTE, L.
WASSEF, R.

Faculty of Music:
BELKIN, A.
DESROCHES, M.
DURAND, M.
EVANGELISTA, J.
GUERTIN, M.
LEFEBVRE, M.-T.
LEROUX, R.
LONGTIN, M.
NATTIEZ, J.-J.
PANNETON, I.
PICHÉ, J.
POIRIER, R.
RIVEST, J.-F.
SMOJE, D.
VAILLANCOURT, L.

Faculty of Nursing:
DUCHARME, F.
DUQUETTE, A.
GAGNON, L.
GOULET, C.
GRENIER, R.
KÉROUAC, S.
REIDY, M.
RICARD, N.

Faculty of Pharmacy:
ADAM, A.
BESNER, J.-G.
BISAILLON, S.
BRAZIER, J.-L.
CARTILIER, L.
GAGNÉ, J.
LAURIER, C.
MCMULLEN, J.-N.
MAILHOT, C.
ONG, H.
TURGEON, J.
VARIN, F.
WINNIK, F.
YAMAGUCHI, N.

Faculty of Theology:
DUHAIME, J.
NADEAU, J.-G.
PETIT, J.-C.

Faculty of Veterinary Medicine

Department of Clinical Sciences:
BLAIS, D.
BONNEAU, N. H.
BOUCHARD, É.
BRETON, L.
CARRIER, M.
CÉCYRE, A. J.
CHALIFOUX, A.
COUTURE, Y.
CUVELLIEZ, S.
D'ALLAIRE, S.
DI FRUSCIA, R.
DUBREUIL, P.
LAMOTHE, P. J.
LAROUCHE, Y.
LAVERTY, S.
LAVOIE, J.-P.
MARCOUX, M.
PARADIS, M.
VAILLANCOURT, D.
VRINS, A.

Department of Pathology and Microbiology:
BIGRAS-POULIN, M.
DROLET, R.
DUBREUIL, D.
ELAZHARY, Y.
FAIRBROTHER, J. M.
FONTAINE, M.
GIRARD, C.
GOTTSCHALK, M.
HAREL, J.
HIGGINS, R.
JACQUES, M.
LALLIER, R.
LARIVIÈRE, S.
MITTAL, K. R.
MORIN, M.
ROY, R. S.
SCHOLL, D. T.
SILIM, A. N.

Department of Veterinary Biomedicine:
BARRETTE, D.
BISAILLON, A.
DALLAIRE, A.
DEROTH, L.
GOFF, A. K.
LARIVIÈRE, N.
LUSSIER, J. G.
MURPHY, B. D.
SILVERSIDES, D. W.
SIROIS, J.
SMITH, L. C.
TREMBLAY, A. V.

Department of Kinesiology:
ALAIN, C.
ALLARD, P.
GAGNON, M.
GARDINER, P. F.
LABERGE, S.

LAVOIE, J.-M.
LÉGER, L.
PÉRONNET, F.
PROTEAU, L.

School of Optometry:
BEAULNE, C.
CASANOVA, C.
FAUBERT, J.
KERGOAT, H.
LOVASIK, J. V.
PTITO, M.
SIMONET, P.

AFFILIATED INSTITUTIONS

Ecole des Hautes Etudes Commerciales: 3000, chemin de la Côte-Sainte-Catherine, Montréal, QC H3T 2A7; tel. (514) 340-6000; f. 1907; Dir JEAN-MARIE TOULOUSE.

Ecole Polytechnique: 2500 ch. de Polytechnique, Montréal, QC H3T 1J4; tel. (514) 340-4711; f. 1873; Dir RÉJEAN PLAMONDON.

MOUNT ALLISON UNIVERSITY

Sackville, NB E4L 1E4
Telephone: (506) 364-2275
Fax: (506) 364-2216
E-mail: sas@mta.ca
Internet: www.mta.ca
Founded 1839
Private control
Language of instruction: English
Academic year: September to May
Chancellor: JAMES KEITH
President and Vice-Chancellor: KENNETH OZMON
Vice-President (Academic): MICHAEL FOX
Vice-President (Administration and Finance): D. J. STEWART
Registrar: CHRIS HUNTER
Librarian: BRUNO GNASSI
Library of 1,200,000 vols
Number of teachers: 150
Number of students: 2,250
Publications: *Mount Allison Newsletter*, *Mount Allison Record* (quarterly alumni production), *President's Report* (annually)

DEANS

Faculty of Arts: Dr CARRIE MACMILLAN
Faculty of Science: Dr MARGARET BEATTIE
Faculty of Social Sciences: Dr ROB SUMMERBY-MURRAY

PROFESSORS

AIKEN, R., Biology
BAERLOCHER, F. J., Biology
BAKER, C., Mathematics
BARCLAY, L., Chemistry
BEATTIE, M., Mathematics
BEATTIE, R., Mathematics
BOGAARD, P., Philosophy
BURKE, R., Fine Arts
CAMPBELL, B., Sociology
CODE, J., Music
CRAIG, T., English
DAWE, E., Music
DEKSTER, B., Mathematics
EDWARDS, P., French
ENNALS, P., Geography
FANCY, A. B., French
FLEMING, C. E. B., Sociology
GODFREY, W. G., History
GRANT, M. C., Religious Studies
HAWKES, R., Physics
HEMPEL, R., German
HOLOWNIA, T., Fine Arts
HUDSON, R., Commerce
HUNT, W., Political Science
IRELAND, R., Biology
IRWIN, A., Mathematics
JOERGER, T., German
LANGLER, R., Chemistry
MACMILLAN, C., English
MARK, J., Music
MILLER, B. A., Mathematics
MILLER, M., Music
POLEGATO, R., Commerce
READ, J. F., Chemistry
REINSBOROUGH, V. C., Chemistry
ROSEBRUGH, R., Mathematics
SEALY, R., Mathematics
STEWART, J. M., Biochemistry
STORM, C., Psychology
STRAIN, F., Economics
THOMPSON, R. G., Biology
TUCKER, M., Political Science
VARMA, P., Physics
VOGAN, N., Music
WEISS, J., Spanish

MOUNT SAINT VINCENT UNIVERSITY

Halifax, NS B3M 2J6
Telephone: (902) 457-6117
Fax: (902) 457-6498
E-mail: admissions@msvu.ca
Internet: www.msvu.ca
Founded 1925
Language of instruction: English
Academic year: September to April, two summer sessions
Chancellor: MARY LOUISE BRINK
President and Vice-Chancellor: Dr SHEILA A. BROWN
Academic Vice-President: Dr DONNA WOOLCOTT
Administrative Vice-President: AMANDA WHITEWOOD
Registrar: J. LYNNE THERIAULT
University Librarian: LILLIAN BELTAOS
Number of teachers: 232 (151 full-time, 81 part-time)
Number of students: 4,500
Publications: *Atlantis* (quarterly), *The Connection* (monthly), *Folia Montana*

DEANS

Arts and Sciences: Dr SHEVA MEDJUCK
Professional Studies: Dr MARY LYON
Student Affairs: Dr CAROL HILL

HEADS OF DEPARTMENTS

Applied Human Nutrition: LINDA MANN
Biology: Dr AMALIE FROHLICH
Business and Tourism: ANNE MACGILLIVARY
Chemistry: Dr KATHERINE DARVESH
Child and Youth Study: Dr KIM KIENAPPLE
Economics: Dr WENDY CORNWALL
Education: Dr ANDREW MANNING
English: Dr SUSAN DRAIN
Family Studies and Gerontology: Dr DEBORAH NORRIS
Fine Arts: Dr JOSETTE DELEAS (Co-ordinator)
History: Dr KENNETH DEWAR
Information Technology: PAULA CROUSE
Mathematics: Dr TINA HARRIOTT
Modern Languages: Dr LARRY STEELE
Philosophy/Religious Studies: Dr RANDI WARNE
Political Studies/Canadian Studies: Dr MICHAEL MACMILLAN
Psychology: Dr JENNIFER MCLAREN
Public Relations: BRENT KING
Sociology/Anthropology: Dr JOSEPH THARAMANGALAM
Speech and Drama: Dr WAYNE INGALLS (Co-ordinator)
Women's Studies: Dr MEREDITH RALSTON

UNIVERSITY OF NEW BRUNSWICK

POB 4400, Fredericton, NB E3B 5A3
Telephone: (506) 453-4666
Fax: (506) 453-4599
E-mail: qc2@unb.ca
Internet: www.unb.ca
Established 1785
Provincial control
Language of instruction: English
Academic year: September to May
Chancellor: RICHARD CURRIE
President: JOHN MCLAUGHLIN
Vice-President (Academic) (vacant)
Vice-President (Finance and Administration): DANIEL MURRAY
Vice-President (Research and International Co-operation): GREGORY KEALEY
Vice-President (Saint John Campus): KATHRYN HAMER
Comptroller: LARRY GUITARD
Secretary: STEPHEN STROPLE
Registrar: DAVID HINTON
Director (Development and Public Relations): SUSAN MESHEAU
Librarian: JOHN TESKEY
Number of teachers: 679
Number of students: 11,341 (9,730 full-time, 1,611 part-time)
Publications: *Acadiensis*, a historical journal of the Atlantic provinces (2 a year), *Experience UNB* (annually), *Fiddlehead* (short stories and poetry, quarterly), *Graduate Studies Calendar*, *International Fiction Review*, *Research Inventory* (annually), *Studies in Canadian Literature* (3 a year), *Summer School Calendar*, *Undergraduate Calendar*

DEANS

Faculty of Administration: DANIEL COLEMAN
Faculty of Arts: Dr PETER KENT (acting)
Faculty of Computer Science: VIRENDRA C. BHAVSAR
Faculty of Education: MARIAN SMALL (acting)
Faculty of Engineering: DAVID COLEMAN
Faculty of Forestry and Environmental Management: IAN SMITH (acting)
Faculty of Kinesiology: CHRIS STEVENSON
Faculty of Law: PHILIP BRYDEN
Faculty of Nursing: CHERYL GIBSON
Faculty of Science: ALLAN SHARP
School of Graduate Studies: GWEN DAVIES (acting)

Saint John Campus:

Faculty of Arts: Dr ROBERT MACKINNON
Faculty of Business: SHELLEY RINEHART (acting)
Faculty of Science, Applied Science and Engineering: Dr DEBORAH MACLATCHEY

PROFESSORS AND HEADS OF DEPARTMENT

Fredericton Campus:

Faculty of Administration:
ABEKAH, J.
ANGELES, R.
ARCELUS, F. J.
ASKANAS, W.
BETTS, N.
BOOTHMAN, B.
COLEMAN, D.
DU, D.
DUNNETT, J.
DUPLESSIS, D.
EISELT, H. A.
FLINT, D.
GAUDES, A.
GRANT, S.
HINTON, J.
KABADI, S.
LAUGHLAND, A. R.
LIM, W.
MAHER, E.
MAHER, R.
MITRA, D.
NAIR, K. P. K.
NASIEROWSKI, W.
NEVERS, R.
OTCHERE, I.
OTUTEYE, E.
OUYANG, M.
POST, P.

RAHIM, M. A.
RASHID, M.
RITCHIE, P.
ROY, J. A.
SHARMA, B.
SHEPPARD, R. G.
SIMYAR, F.
SRINIVASAN, G.
THOMAS, M. E.
TOLLIVER, J.
TRENHOLM, B.
WHALEN, H.
WIELMAKER, M.
ZULUAGA, L.

Faculty of Arts:
AHERN, D., Philosophy
ALLEN, J. G., Political Science
ALMEH, R., Sociology
ANDREWS, J., English
AUSTIN, D., English
BALL, J., International Development Studies
BALL, J. C., English
BEDFORD, D., Law and Society
BEDFORD, D., Women's Studies
BEDFORD, D. W., Political Science
BLACK, D., Anthropology
BONNETT, J., History
BOWDEN, G., Sociology
BRANDER, J. R. G., Economics
BROWN, A., French
BEDFORD, A., International Development Studies
BROWN, A., Women's Studies
BROWN, J. S., History
BYERS, E. S., Psychology
CAMPBELL, G., History
CANITZ, A. E., English
CARRIERE, M., French
CHARRON, D., French
CHARTERS, D., History
CICHOCKI, W., French
CLARK, D. A., Psychology
CONRAD, M., History
COOK, B. A., Economics
CULVER, K., Law in Society
CULVER, K., Philosophy
CUPPLES, B. W., Philosophy
DAVIES, G., English
D'ENTREMONT, B., Psychology
DICKSON, V., Economics
DOERKSEN, D., English
DONALDSON, A. W., Psychology
DUECK, C., Culture and Language Studies
DUPLESSIS, D., Law in Society
FALKENSTEIN, L., English
FARNWORTH, M., Economics
FERGUSON, B., Economics
FIELDS, D. L., Psychology
FRANK, D., History
GANTS, D. L., English
GEYSSEN, J. W., Classics and Ancient History
HAMLING, A., Women's Studies
HARRISON, D., Sociology
HIEW, C. C., Psychology
HORNE, C., Linguistics
HORNOSTY, J., Women's Studies
HORNOSTY, J. M., Sociology
HOWE, J. M., Sociology
JARMAN, M., English
KEALEY, G. S., History
KEALEY, L., History
KENNEDY, S., History
KERR, W., Classics and Ancient History
KERR, W., Law in Society
KLINCK, A., English
KUFELDT, K., Sociology
LACHAPELLE, D., Psychology
LANTZ, V., Economics
LARMER, R., Philosophy
LAUTARD, E. H., Sociology
LAW, S., Economics
LEBLANC, D., French
LECKIE, R., English
LEMIRE, B., History
LEMIRE, B. J., History
LEVINE, L., Economics
LINTON, M., Culture and Language Studies
LOREY, C., Culture and Language Studies
LOVELL, P. R., Anthropology
LOW, J., Sociology
MCDONALD, T., Economics
MCFARLAND, J., International Development Studies
MCGAW, R. L., Economics
MCTAVISH, L., Women's Studies
MARTIN, R., English
MIEDEMA, B., Sociology
MILLS, M. J., Classics and Ancient History
MILNER, M., History
MITRA, K., International Development Studies
MULLALY, E. J., English
MURRAY, J., Classics and Ancient History
MURRAY, J. S., Classics and Ancient History
MURRAY, K., Political Science
MURRELL, D., Economics
MYATT, A. E., Economics
NASON-CLARK, N., Sociology and Women's Studies
NEILL, W., Philosophy
NEILSON, L., Law in Society
PAPPONET-CANTAT, C., Anthropology and International Development Studies
PARENTEAU, W. M., History
PASSARIS, C. E., Economics
PIERCEY, D., Psychology
PLAICE, E., Anthropology
PLOUDE, R. J., English
POOL, G., International Development Studies
POOL, G. R., Anthropology
POULIN, C., Law in Society
POULIN, C., Psychology
POULIN, C., Women's Studies
RAHMANIAN, A., Philosophy
REHORICK, D. A., Sociology
REID, A., Culture and Language Studies
REZUN, M., Economics, International Development Studies and Political Science
RIDEOUT, V., Sociology
RIMMER, M. P., English
ROBBINS, W., Women's Studies
ROBBINS, W. J., English
ROBINSON, G. B., Psychology
ROWCROFT, J. E., Economics
SCHERF, K., English
SHANNON, C., Women's Studies
SIGURDSON, R., Political Science
SPINNER, B., Psychology
STOPPARD, J. M., Psychology
TASIC, V., Linguistics
THOMPSON, D. G., History
TRYPHONOPOULOS, D., English
TURNER, R. S., History
VAN DEN HOONAARD, W. C., Sociology
VIAU, R., French
VILLIARD, P., Linguistics
WAITE, G. K., History
WHITEFORD, G., International Development Studies
WIBER, M., Anthropology
WISNIEWSKI, L. J., Sociology
WORKMAN, T., Anthropology

Faculty of Computer Science:
BHAVSAR, V. C.
COOPER, R. H.
DEDOUREK, J. M.
DESLONGCHAMPS, G.
DU, W.
EVANS, P.
FRITZ, J.
GHORBANI, A. A.
HORTON, J. D.
KENT, K.
KURZ, B. J.
MACNEIL, D. G.
NICKERSON, B. G.
WASSON, W. D.
ZHANG, H.

Faculty of Education:
ALLEN, P., Adult and Vocational Education
BERRY, K., Educational Foundations
BEZEAU, L., Educational Foundations
BURGE, E., Adult and Vocational Education
CASHION, M., Educational Foundations
CLARKE, G. M., Curriculum and Instruction
COOPER, T. G., Curriculum and Instruction
EYRE, L., Health Education
GILL, B., Educational Administration
HUGHES, A. S., Curriculum and Instruction
LEAVITT, R., Curriculum and Instruction
MYERS, S., Health Education
NASON, P. N., Curriculum and Instruction
OTT, H. W., Educational Foundations
PAUL, L., Curriculum and Instruction
PAZIENZA, J., Curriculum and Instruction
RADFORD, K., Curriculum and Instruction
REHORICK, S., Curriculum and Instruction
SEARS, A., Curriculum and Instruction
SMALL, M. S., Curriculum and Instruction
SOUCY, D. A., Curriculum and Instruction
STEVENSON, M., Electrical and Computer Engineering
STEWART, J. (acting), Educational Foundations
SULLENGER, K., Science Education
WHITEFORD, G., Curriculum and Instruction
WILLMS, J. D., Educational Foundations

Faculty of Engineering:
BENDRICH, G., Chemical Engineering
BIDEN, E., Mechanical Engineering
BISCHOFF, P. H., Civil Engineering
BONHAM, D. J. (acting), Mechanical Engineering
CHANG, L., Electrical and Computer Engineering
CHAPLIN, R. A. (acting), Chemical Engineering
CHAPLIN, R., Chemical Engineering
COLEMAN, D. J. (acting), Geodesy and Geomatics
COLPITTS, B. (acting), Electrical and Computer Engineering
COUTURIER, M. (acting), Chemical Engineering
DARE, P., Geodesy and Geomatics (Chair)
DAWE, J. L. (acting), Civil Engineering
DIDUCH, C. (acting), Electrical Engineering
DORAISWAMI, R., Electrical Engineering
EIC, M., Chemical Engineering
HILL, E. F. (acting), Electrical Engineering
HUDGINS, B., Electrical and Computer Engineering
HUSSEIN, E. (acting), Mechanical Engineering
INNES, J. D., Civil Engineering
IRCHA, M. C., Civil Engineering
LANGLEY, R. B. (acting), Geodesy and Geomatics Engineering
LEE, Y. C., Geodesy and Geomatics
LEWIS, J. E., Electrical Engineering
LISTER, D., Chemical Engineering
LOVELY, D., Electical and Computer Engineering
LOWRY, B. (acting), Chemical Engineering
LUKE, D. M. (acting), Electrical Engineering
LYON, D., Mechanical Engineering
MAYER, L. (acting), Geodesy and Geomatics Engineering
MCLAUGHLIN, J. D., Geodesy and Geomatics Engineering
NI, Y., Chemical Engineering
NICHOLS, S. E. (acting), Geodesy and Geomatics
PARKER, P. A. (acting), Electrical Engineering
ROGERS, R. J., Mechanical Engineering
SHARAF, A. M. M., Electrical Engineering
SOUSA, A. C. M., Mechanical Engineering

SULLIVAN, P., Mechanical Engineering
TAYLOR, J. H. (acting), Electrical Engineering
TERVO, R., Electrical and Computer Engineering
THOMAS, M. D. A. (acting), Civil Engineering
VALSANGKAR, A. J. (acting), Civil Engineering
VANICEK, P., Geodesy and Geomatics Engineering
WAUGH, L. M., Civil Engineering

Faculty of Forestry and Environmental Management:

AFZAL, M. (acting)
ARP, P. A.
BECKLEY, T.
BOURQUE, C.
CHUI, Y.
CUNJAK, R.
CURRY, A.
DAUGHERTY, D.
DIAMOND, T.
ERDLE, T.
FORBES, G.
JAEGER, D.
JORDAN, G.
KEPPIE, D. M.
KERSHAW, J.
KRASOWSKI, M.
LANTZ, V.
LEBLON, B.
MACLEAN, D.
MENG, C.-H.
QUIRING, D. T. W.
ROBAK, E. W.
ROBERTS, M. R.
SAVIDGE, R.
SCHNEIDER, M. H.
SERGEANT, B.
SMITH, I.
ZUNDEL, P.

Faculty of Kinesiology:

BURKARD, J.
HAGGERTY, T. R.
PATON, G. A.
SEXSMITH, J.
STEVENSON, C. L.
WRIGHT, P. H.

Faculty of Law:

BELL, D. G.
BIRD, R. W.
BLADON, G. L.
CHATERJEE, A.
DORE, K. J.
FLEMING, D. J.
GOCHNAUER, M. L.
KUTTNER, T. S.
LAFOREST, A.
MCCALLUM, M. E.
MCEVOY, J. P.
MATHEN, C.
PEARLSTON, K.
PENNEY, S.
SIEBRASSE, N.
TOWNSEND, D.
VEITCH, E.
WILLIAMSON, J. R.

Faculty of Nursing:

ERICSON, P.
GETTY, G.
GIBSON, C.
GILBEY, V. J. U.
LEWIS, K.
OUELLET, L.
RUSH, K. L.
STORR, G.
WIGGINS, N.
WUEST, J.

Faculty of Science:

ADAM, A. G., Chemistry
BALCOLM, B., Chemistry
BANERJEE, P. K., Mathematics and Statistics
BARCLAY, D. W., Mathematics and Statistics
BROSTER, B., Geology
CASHION, P. J., Biology
CHERNOFF, W. W., Mathematics and Statistics
COOMBS, D. H., Biology
COOPER, R., Chemistry
CWYNAR, L., Biology
CULP, J., Biology
CUNJAK, R., Biology
DESLONGCHAMPS, G., Chemistry
DIAMOND, A., Biology
DILWORTH, T. G., Biology
FORBES, G., Biology
GEGENBERG, J., Mathematics and Statistics
HAMZA, A., Mathematics and Statistics
HUSAIN, V., Mathematics and Statistics
INGALLS, C., Mathematics and Statistics
JONES, C., Mathematics and Statistics
KEPPIE, D. M., Biology (also under Faculty of Forestry and Environmental Management)
LENTZ, D., Geology
LINTON, C., Physics
LYNCH, W. H., Biology
MAGEE, D., Chemistry
MARCHAND, E., Mathematics and Statistics
MASON, G. R., Mathematics and Statistics
MATTAR, S., Chemistry
MCKELLAR, R., Mathematics and Statistics
MONSON, B. R., Mathematics and Statistics
MUREIKA, R. A., Mathematics and Statistics
NEVILLE, J., Chemistry
NI, Y., Chemistry
PASSMORE, J., Chemistry
PICKERILL, R. K., Geology
RIDING, R. T., Biology
ROSS, W. R., Physics
SAUNDERS, G., Biology
SEABROOK, W. D., Biology
SHARP, A. R., Physics
SIVASUBRAMANIAN, P., Biology
SPRAY, J., Geology
THAKKAR, A., Chemistry
TIMOTHY, J. G., Physics
TINGLEY, D., Mathematics and Statistics
TUPPER, B. O. J., Mathematics and Statistics
TURNER, T. R., Mathematics and Statistics
VILLEMURE, G., Chemistry
WHITE, J. C., Geology
WHITTAKER, J. R., Biology
WILLIAMS, P. F., Geology
YOO, B. Y., Biology

Saint John Campus:

Faculty of Arts:

BEST, L., Psychology
BELANGER, L., French
BOTH, L., Psychology
BRADLEY, M. T., Psychology
CAMPBELL, M. A., Psychology
CAVALIERE, P. A., History
CHILDS, J., Economics
DARTNELL, M., Political Science
DESSERUD, D., Political Science
DITOMMASO, E., Psychology
DONNELLY, F., History and Politics
EVERITT, J., Political Science
GENDREAU, P., Psychology
GODDARD, M. J., Psychology
HILL, R., Economics
HILL, V., French
HYSON, S., Political Sciences
JEFFREY, L., Political Sciences
KABIR, M., Social Science
LINDSAY, D., History
MARQUIS, G., History
MOIR, R., Economics
MOSHIRI, S., Economics
NKUNZIMANA, O., French
PONS-RIDLER, S., Humanities and Languages
RIDLER, N. B., Social Science
SELIM, M., Economics
SNOOK, B., Psychology
TAUKULIS, H., Psychology
TONER, P., History and Politics
WILSON, A., Psychology
WHITNEY, R., History

Faculty of Business:

CHALYKOFF, J.
DAVIS, C. H.
DAVIS, G.
GILBERT, E.
MINER, F. C.
PIKE, E.
ROUMI, E.
STERNICZUK, H.
WANG, S.
WONG, J.

Faculty of Science, Applied Science and Engineering:

ALDERSON, H., Mathematical Sciences
ALDERSON, T., Mathematical Sciences
BECKETT, B. A., Physical Sciences
BOONE, C., Engineering
BUCHANAN, J., Nursing (non-professorial H, acting)
CHOPIN, T., Biology
CHRISTIE, J., Engineering
COTTER, G. T., Engineering (H)
DE'BELL, K., Mathematical Sciences
FEICHT, A., Chemistry (Chair)
GAREY, L. E., Mathematics, Statistics and Computer Science
GUPTA, R. D., Mathematics, Statistics and Computer Science
HALCROW, K., Biology
HAMDAN, M., Mathematics, Statistics and Computer Science
HUMPHRIES, R., Physical Sciences
KAMEL, M. T., Mathematics, Statistics and Computer Science
KAYSER, M., Physical Sciences
LEUNG, C.-H., Physical Sciences
LITVAK, M. K., Biology
LOGAN, A., Physical Sciences
MACDONALD, B., Biology
MACLATCHY, D., Biology
MCCULLUM, D., Engineering
MAHANTI, P., Computer Science and Applied Statistics
NUGENT, L., Nursing
PRASAD, R. C., Engineering
PUNNEN, A., Mathematical Sciences
RILEY, E., Engineering
ROCHETTE, R., Biology
SHAW, R., Computer Science and Applied Statistics
SOLLOWS, K., Engineering
STOICA, G., Mathematical Sciences
TERHUNE, J. M., Biology
THOMPSON, C., Computer Science and Applied Statistics (Chair)
WAGSTAFF, J., Physical Sciences
WALTON, B., Engineering
WILSON, L., Physical Sciences
XU, L.-H., Physical Sciences

ATTACHED COLLEGE

Renaissance College: Dean T. R. HAGGERTY.

FEDERATED UNIVERSITY

St Thomas University: Fredericton, NB; f. 1910; Pres DANIEL O'BRIEN.

NIPISSING UNIVERSITY

100 College Drive, Box 5002, North Bay, ON P1B 8L7
Telephone: (705) 474-3450
Fax: (705) 495-1772
E-mail: liaison@nipissingu.ca

Internet: www.nipissingu.ca
Founded 1967 as Nipissing College, affiliated to Laurentian University of Sudbury; merged with North Bay Teachers' College 1973; became independent, under current name, 1992
Academic year: September to August
Chancellor: DAVID B. LIDDLE
President: Dr DENNIS R. MOCK
Vice-President of Administration and Finance: MURRAY GREEN
Vice-President Academic and Research: Prof. ROBERT HAWKINS
Dean (Arts and Science): Dr ANDREW DEAN
Dean (Education): Dr RONALD COMMON
Registrar: DENIS LAWRENCE
Executive Director of Library Services: BRIAN NETTLEFOLD
Number of teachers: 194
Number of students: 5,556.

UNIVERSITY OF NORTHERN BRITISH COLUMBIA

3333 University Way, Prince George, BC V2N 4Z9
Telephone: (250) 960-5555
Fax: (250) 960-5543
E-mail: registrar-info@unbc.ca
Internet: www.unbc.ca
Founded 1990; full opening 1994
Language of instruction: English
Academic year: September to April (two semesters)
Chancellor: Dr K. GEORGE PEDERSEN
President/Vice-Chancellor: Dr CHARLES JAGO
Vice-President, Academic and Provost: Dr DEBORAH POFF
Vice-President, Administration and Finance: Dr COCHRAN
Vice-President, Research: Dr MAX BLOUW
Registrar: JOHN DEGRACE
University Librarian: ALISON NUSSBAUMER
Number of teachers: 176 (full-time)
Number of students: 3,500

DEANS

College of Arts, Social and Health Sciences: Dr JAMES RANDALL
College of Science and Management: Dr BILL MCGILL
Graduate Studies: Dr ROBERT TAIT

NOVA SCOTIA AGRICULTURAL COLLEGE

Truro, NS B2N 5E3
Telephone: (902) 893-6722
Fax: (902) 895-5529
E-mail: reg@nsac.ns.ca
Internet: www.nsac.ns.ca
Founded 1905
Under the direction of the Nova Scotia Department of Agriculture and Marketing
President: Dr PHILIP HICKS
Vice-President (Academic): Dr BRUCE GRAY
Vice-President (Administration): Dr BERNIE MACDONALD
Registrar: T. DOLHANTY
Librarian: B. R. WADDELL
Library: *c.* 19,000 vols
Number of teachers: 69
Number of students: 900
Publication: *NSAC College Calendar*

HEADS OF DEPARTMENTS

Business and Social Sciences: GARY GRANT
Engineering: KEVIN SIBLEY
Environmental Sciences: A.R. OLSON
Mathematics, Physics and Humanities: C. T. MADIGAN
Plant and Animal Sciences: Dr DEREK ANDERSON

NSCAD UNIVERSITY

5163 Duke St, Halifax, NS B3J 3J6
Telephone: (902) 422-7381
Fax: (902) 425-2420
E-mail: admissions@nscad.ca
Internet: www.nscad.ca
Founded 1887
Academic year: September to April
President: DAVID B. SMITH
Senior Vice-President for Academic Affairs and Research: KENN HONEYCHURCH
Vice-President for Finance and Administration: PETER FLEMMING
Registrar: LAURELLE LEVERT
Library Director: ILGA LEJA
Library of 50,000 vols, 220 art periodicals, 140,000 colour slides, large holding of films and video cassettes (incl. Canada Council Art Bank colln)
Number of teachers: 53
Number of students: 1,100 (800 full-time, 300 part-time)
depts of Craft, Design, Fine art, Foundation, Graduate studies, Historical and critical studies, Media art
Fine art studios in painting, sculpture, printmaking, ceramics, weaving, video, film, wood and metal working, textiles, fashion, jewellery, photography, digital media; undergraduate programmes include: Bachelor of Arts with major in art history; Bachelor of Design with majors in interdisciplinary design or international major in graphic design and Bachelor of Fine Arts with majors in interdisciplinary pre-teacher education, ceramics, film, fine art, intermedia, jewellery design and metalwork, photography and textiles; current graduate-level programmes: Master of Design, Master of Design International and Master of Fine Arts.

UNIVERSITY OF OTTAWA

550 Cumberland St, Ottawa, ON K1N 6N5
Telephone: (613) 562-5700
Fax: (613) 562-5103
Internet: www.uottawa.ca
Founded 1848
Independent, Provincially assisted
Language of instruction: French,
Language of instruction: English
Academic year: September to August (undergraduate 2 semesters, graduate 3 terms)
Chancellor: HUGUETTE LABELLE
Rector: GILLES G. PATRY (acting)
Vice-Rector (Academic): ROBERT MAJOR
Vice-Rector (Research): HOWARD ALPER
Vice-Rector (Resources): CAROLE WORKMAN
Vice-Rector (University Relations): DAVID MITCHELL
Assistant Vice-Rector (Strategic Enrolment Management) and Registrar: FRANÇOIS CHAPLEAU
Secretary-General: PIERRE-YVES BOUCHER
Librarian: LESLIE WEIR
Library: see under Libraries and Archives
Number of teachers: 1,737 (936 full-time, 801 part-time)
Number of students: 27,462 (20,500 full-time, 6,962 part-time)

DEANS

Faculty of Arts: TIBOR EGERVARI
Faculty of Education: MARIE JOSÉE BERGER
Faculty of Engineering: TYSEER ABOULNASR
Faculty of Health Sciences: DENIS PRUD'HOMME
Faculty of Law: LOUIS PERRET (Civil Law: BRUCE FELDTHUSEN (Common Law)
Faculty of Medicine: PETER WALKER
Faculty of Science: ANDRÉ DABROWSKI
Faculty of Social Sciences: CAROLINE ANDREW
Faculty of Graduate and Post-doctoral Studies: JOSEPH DE KONINCK
School of Management: MICHEÁL J. KELLY

HEADS OF FACULTY UNITS

Faculty of Arts:
- Classics and Religious Studies: PETER BEYER
- Communication: PATRICK BRUNET
- English: DAVID RAMPTON
- Geography: DANIEL LAGAREC
- History: EDA KRANAKIS
- Lettres françaises: PIERRE-MARIE KUNTSMANN
- Linguistics: ANDRÉ LAPIERRE
- Modern Languages and Literatures: JUAN RUANO DE LA HAZA
- Music: LORI BURNS
- Philosophy: DAVID RAYNOR
- Theatre: MARGARET CODERRE-WILLIAMS
- Visual Arts: PENNY COUSINEAU-LEVINE
- School of Translation and Interpretation: JEAN DELISLE
- Second Language Institute: MARIE-CLAUDE TREVILLE
- Institute of Canadian Studies: MARCEL OLSCAMP

Faculty of Education:
- Graduate Programs (Anglophone Sector): TIMOTHY STANLEY
- Graduate Programs (Francophone Sector): MARIELLE SIMON
- Teacher Education Section (Anglophone Sector): BARBARA GRAVES
- Teacher Education Section (Francophone Sector): FRANÇOIS DESJARDINS

Faculty of Engineering:
- Chemical Engineering: ANDRÉ Y. TREMLAY
- Civil Engineering: HIROSHI TANAKA
- School of Information Technology and Engineering: GILLES DESLISLE
- Mechanical Engineering: WILLIAM L. H. HALLETT

Faculty of Health Sciences:
- School of Human Kinetics: DIANE STE-MARIE
- School of Nursing: SYLVIE LAUZON
- School of Rehabilitation Sciences: CLAIRE-JEHANNE DUBOULOZ

Faculty of Management:
- EMBA Program: JEAN-LOUIS SCHAAN
- MBA Program: FRANÇOIS JULIEN
- MHA Program: WOJTEK MICHALOWSKI
- Undergraduate Programs: PETER KOPPEL

Faculty of Medicine:
- Anaesthesia: HOMER YANG
- Biochemistry, Microbiology and Immunology: ZEMIN YAO
- Cellular and Molecular Medicine: BERNARD JEAN JASMIN
- Epidemiology and Community Medicine: GEORGE WELLS
- Family Medicine: NICHOLAS BUSING
- Medicine: JEFF TURNBULL
- Obstetrics and Gynaecology: CARL NIMROD
- Ophthalmology: BRUCE JACKSON
- Oto-rhino-laryngology: JOSEPH GUERRINO MARSAN
- Paediatrics: JOHN REISMAN
- Pathology and Laboratory Medicine: JEAN MICHAUD
- Psychiatry: JACQUES BRADWEJN
- Radiology: REBECCA ANN PETERSON
- Surgery: ERIC POULIN

Faculty of Science:
- Biology: DAVID J. CURRIE
- Chemistry: ALAIN ST-AMANT
- Earth Sciences: KENNETH B. BENN
- Mathematics and Statistics: MAYER ALVO
- Physics: RICHARD HODGSON

Faculty of Social Sciences:
- Criminology: ROSS HASTINGS

Economics: ROSE ANNE DEVLIN
Political Science: PAUL-NORMAND DUSSAULT
School of Psychology: PIERRE MERCIER
School of Social Work: CÉCILE CODERRE
Sociology: RAYMOND MURPHY

PROFESSORS

Faculty of Arts (internet www.uottawa.ca/academic/arts):
BARBIER, J. A., History
BEHIELS, M. D., History
BERTHIAUME, P., French Literature
BRISSET, A., Translation and Interpretation
BURGESS, R., Classics
CARLSON, D., English
CASTILLO DURANTE, D., French Literature
CHILDS, D., English Literature
CHOQUETTE, R., Religious Studies
CLAYTON, J. D., Russian
CRAM, R., Music
DAIGLE, J.-G., History
DAVIS, D. F., History
DE BRUYN, F., English
DELISLE, J., Translation and Interpretation
DONSKOV, A., Russian
EGERVARI, T., Visual Arts
FERGUSON, S., Communication
FERRIS, I., English
FLOYD, C., Music
FORGET, D., French Literature
FRENCH, H. M., Geography
FROEHLICH, A. J. P., Theatre
GAFFIELD, C. M., History
GAJEWSKI, K., Geography
GELLMAN, S., Music
GEURTS, M.-A., Geography
GILBERT, A., Geography
GIROU-SWIDERSKI, M., French Literature
GOLDENBERG, N., Religious Studies
GOODLUCK, H., Linguistics
GRISE, Y., French Literature
HIRSCHBUHLER, P., Linguistics
HUNTER, D. G., Philosophy
IMBERT, P. L., French Literature
JARRAWAY, D., English Literature
JOHNSON, P. G., Geography
KILMER, M. F., Classics and Religious Studies
KUNSTMANN, P. M. F., French Literature
LABELLE, N., Music
LA BOSSIÈRE, C. R., English Literature
LACHANCE, P. F., History
LAFON, D., French Literature
LANGLOIS, A., Geography
LAPIERRE, A., Linguistics
LAURIOL, B., Geography
LEMELIN, S., Music
LEPAGE, Y. G., French Literature
LEVY, P., Communication
LEWKOWICZ, A. G., Geography
LONDON, A., English Literature
LUGG, A. M., Philosophy
LYNCH, G., English
MAKARYK, I. R., English
MANGANIELLO, D., English
MAYNE, S., English
MERKLEY, P., Music
MOSER, W., Modern Languages and Literature
MOSS, J., English
MUNOZ-LICERAS, J., Modern Languages and Literature
PIVA, M., History
POPLACK, S., Linguistics
PUMMER, R. E., Religious Studies
RADLOFF, B., English
RAMPTON, D. P., English
REID, L., Visual Arts
RIVERO, M. L., Linguistics
ROBERTS, R. P., Translation and Interpretation
RUANO DE LA HAZA, J., Modern Languages and Literature
SBROCCHI, L. G., Modern Languages and Literature
SEGUIN, H., Second Language Institute
STAINES, D., Arts
STICH, K. P., English
STOLARIK, M. M., History
VAILLANCOURT, P.-L., French Literature
VANDENDORPE, C., French Literature
VILLA, B. L., History
VON MALTZAHN, N., English
WELLAR, B. S., Geography
WESCHE, M. B., Centre for Second Language Learning
WILSON, K. G., English
YARDLEY, J. C., Classics

PROFESSORS

Faculty of Education (internet www.uottawa.ca/academic/education):
BÉLAIR, L.
BERGER, M.-J.
BOURDAGES, J. J.
COOK, S.
COUSINS, B.
FORGETTE-GIROUX, R.
FORTIN, J.-C.
GAGNE, E.
GIROUX, A.
HERRY, Y.
JEFFERSON, A. L.
LAVEAULT, D.
LEBLANC, R. N.
MACDONALD, C.
MASNY, D.
MICHAUD, J. P.
ST-GERMAIN, M.
TAYLOR, M.

Faculty of Engineering (internet www.eng.uottawa.ca):
ABOULNASR, T. T., Engineering
ADAMOWSKI, K., Civil Engineering
CHENG, S.-C., Mechanical Engineering
DHILLON, B. S., Engineering Management
DROSTE, R. L., Civil Engineering
EVGIN, E., Civil Engineering
FAHIM, A. E., Mechanical Engineering
GARDNER, N. J., Civil Engineering
GARGA, V. K., Civil Engineering
HADDAD, Y. M., Mechanical Engineering
HALLETT, W. L. H., Mechanical Engineering
KENNEDY, K. J., Civil Engineering
LIANG, M., Mechanical Engineering
MCLEAN, D. D., Chemical Engineering
MUNRO, M. B., Mechanical Engineering
NARBAITZ, R. M., Civil Engineering
NEALE, G. H., Chemical Engineering
NECSULESCU, D.-S., Engineering Management
REDEKOP, D., Mechanical Engineering
SAATCIOGLU, M., Civil Engineering
TANAKA, H., Engineering
TAVOULARIS, S., Mechanical Engineering
THIBAULT, J., Chemical Engineering
TOWNSEND, D. R., Civil Engineering

School of Information Technology and Engineering:
BOCHMANN, G. V.
CADA, M.
CHOUINARD, J.-Y.
DELISLE, G. Y.
DUBOIS, E.
GEORGANAS, N. D.
GIBBONS, D.-T.
HALL, T.
IONESCU, D.
KARMOUCH, A.
MATWIN, S. J.
MCNAMARA, D. A.
MOUFTAH, H. T.
OROZCO, B.-L.
PETRIU, E.
PROBERT, R. L.
RAYMOND, J.
SKUCE, D. R.
STOJMENOVIC, I.
SZPAKOWICZ, S.
URAL, H.
YANG, O. W.
YONGACOGLU, A. M.

Faculty of Health Sciences

School of Human Kinetics:
HARVEY, J.
LAMONTAGNE, M.
ORLICK, T. D.
RAIL, G.
ROBERTSON, G. E.
TRUDEL, P.

School of Nursing:
CRAGG, E. C.
EDWARDS, N.
FOTHERGILL-BOURBONNAIS, F.
O'CONNOR, A.

School of Rehabilitation Sciences:
DURIEUX-SMITH, A., Audiology and Speech-language Pathology

Faculty of Law (internet www.uottawa.ca/academic/droit-law):

Civil Law Section:
ARCHAMBAULT, J.-D.
BEAULNE, J.
BELLEAU, C.
BISSON, A.-F.
BOIVIN, M.
BOUDREAULT, M.
BRAEN, A.
DUPLESSIS, Y.
EMANUELLI, C.
GRONDIN, R.
JODOUIN, A.
LACASSE, J.-P.
MORIN, M.
PELLETIER, B.
PROULX, D.
VINCELETTE, D.

Common Law Section:
DES ROSIERS, N.
JACKMAN, M.
KRISHNA, V.
MAGNET, J. E.
MANWARING, J. A.
MCRAE, D. M.
MENDES, E. P.
MORSE, B. W.
PACIOCCO, D. M.
PERRET, L.
RATUSHNY, E. J.
RODGERS, S.
SHEEHY, E.
SULLIVAN, R.
ZWEIBEL, E.

Faculty of Management:
ADJAOUD, F.
CALVET, A. L.
CARO, D. H. J.
DE LA MOTHE, J.
DOUTRIAUX, J.
GANDHI, D. K.
GOH, S.
HENAULT, G. M.
HENIN, C. G.
JABES, J.
KELLY, M. J.
KERSTEN, G.
KINDRA, G. S.
LANE, D.
MANGA, P.
MICHALOWSKI, W.
NASH, J. C.
SIDNEY, J. B.
WRIGHT, D. J.
ZEGHAL, D.
ZUSSMAN, D.

Faculty of Medicine (internet www.uottawa.ca/academic/med):

ALTOSAAR, I., Biochemistry, Microbiology and Immunology
ANDERSON, P. J., Biochemistry, Microbiology and Immunology
BAENZIGER, J., Biochemistry, Microbiology and Immunology
BERNATCHEZ-LEMAIRE, I., Cellular and Molecular Medicine (Pharmacology)
BROWN, E., Biochemistry, Microbiology and Immunology
CHAN, A. C., Biochemistry, Microbiology and Immunology
CHEN, Y., Epidemiology and Community Medicine
CHEUNG, D. W., Cellular and Molecular Medicine (Pharmacology)
DE BOLD, A. J., Pathology and Laboratory Medicine
DILLON, J. R., Biochemistry, Microbiology and Immunology
DIMOCK, K. D., Biochemistry, Microbiology and Immunology
FRANKS, D., Pathology and Laboratory Medicine
FRYER, J. N., Cellular and Molecular Medicine (Anatomy)
GELFAND, T., History of Medicine
GIBB, W., Obstetrics and Gynaecology
HACHE, R. J. G., Medicine
HAKIM, A. M., Medicine
HÉBERT, R., Medicine
HINCKE, M., Cellular and Molecular Medicine (Anatomy)
JASMIN, B. J., Cellular and Molecular Medicine (Physiology)
KACEW, S., Cellular and Molecular Medicine (Pharmacology)
KRANTIS, A., Cellular and Molecular Medicine (Physiology)
KREWSKI, D., Medicine
LABOW, R., Surgery
LEMAIRE, S., Cellular and Molecular Medicine (Pharmacology)
MALER, LEONARD, Cellular and Molecular Medicine (Anatomy)
MARCEL, Y. L., Pathology and Laboratory Medicine
MARSHALL, K. C., Cellular and Molecular Medicine (Physiology)
MCBURNEY, M. W., Medicine
MCDOWELL, I. W., Epidemiology and Community Medicine
MILNE, R. W., Pathology and Laboratory Medicine
MUSSIVAND, T. F., Surgery
NAIR, R. C., Epidemiology and Community Medicine
PARRY, D. J., Cellular and Molecular Medicine (Physiology)
PETERSON, L. M., Cellular and Molecular Medicine (Physiology)
ROUSSEAUX, COLIN, Cellular and Molecular Medicine
SATTAR, S. A., Biochemistry, Microbiology and Immunology
SPASOFF, R. A., Epidemiology and Community Medicine
ST JOHN, R. K., Medicine
STAINES, W., Cellular and Molecular Medicine (Anatomy)
TANPHAICHITR, N., Obstetrics and Gynaecology
TSANG, B. K., Obstetrics and Gynaecology
TUANA, B. S., Cellular and Molecular Medicine (Pharmacology)
WALKER, P., Medicine
WELLS, G., Medicine
YAO, Z., Biochemistry, Microbiology and Immunology

Faculty of Science (internet www.science.uottawa.ca):

ALVO, M., Mathematics and Statistics
ARNASON, J. T., Biology
BAO, X., Physics
BRABEC, T., Physics
BONEN, L., Biology
BURGESS, W. D., Mathematics and Statistics
CASTONGUAY, C., Mathematics and Statistics
CHAPLEAU, F., Biology
CLARK, I. B., Earth Sciences
CURRIE, D. J., Biology
DABROWSKI, A. R., Mathematics and Statistics
DETELLIER, C. G., Chemistry
DURST, T., Chemistry
FALLIS, A. G., Chemistry
FENWICK, J. C., Biology
FOWLER, A., Earth Sciences
GAMBAROTTA, S., Chemistry
GIORDANO, T., Mathematics and Statistics
HANDELMAN, D. E., Mathematics and Statistics
HATTORI, K., Earth Sciences
HICKEY, D. A., Biology
HODGSON, R. J. W., Physics
IVANOFF, G. B., Mathematics and Statistics
JOOS, B., Physics
KAPLAN, H., Chemistry
LALONDE, A. E., Earth Sciences
LEAN, D. R., Biology
LONGTIN, A., Physics
MCDONALD, D. R., Mathematics and Statistics
MOON, T. W., Biology
MORIN, A., Biology
NEHER, E., Mathematics and Statistics
PERRY, S. F., Biology
PESTOV, V., Mathematics and Statistics
PHILOGÈNE, B. J. R., Biology
RACINE, M. L., Mathematics and Statistics
RANCOURT, D., Physics
RICHESON, D., Chemistry
ROSSMAN, W., Mathematics and Statistics
ROY, D., Mathematics and Statistics
SANKOFF, D., Mathematics and Statistics
SAYARI, A. H., Chemistry
SCAIANO, J. C., Chemistry
SCOTT, P. J., Mathematics and Statistics
STADNIK, Z., Physics
TEITELBAUM, H., Chemistry
VEIZER, J., Earth Sciences

Faculty of Social Sciences (internet www.uottawa.ca/academic/socsci):

ANDREW, C. P., Political Science
BEAUCHESNE, L., Criminology
CARDINAL, L., Political Science
CELLARD, A., Criminology
CHOSSUDOVSKY, M., Economics
COULOMBE, S., Economics
CRELINSTEN, R., Criminology
DA ROSA, V. M. P., Sociology
DENIS, A. B., Sociology
DENIS, S., Political Science
GABOR, T., Criminology
GRENIER, G., Economics
HASTINGS, J. R., Criminology
HAVET, J. L., Sociology
LACZKO, L., Sociology
LAUX, J. K., Political Science
LAVOIE, M., Economics
LOS, M. J., Criminology
MELLOS, K., Political Science
MOGGACH, D., Political Science
MURPHY, R. J., Sociology
PIRES, A., Criminology
POULIN, R., Sociology
ROBERTS, J., Criminology
SECCARECCIA, M., Economics
TAHON, M.-B., Sociology
THÉRIAULT, J. Y., Sociology
TREMBLAY, M., Political Science
WALLER, I., Criminology

School of Psychology:

BIELAJEW, C.
CAMPBELL, K. B.
CAPPELIEZ, P.
CLEMENT, R.
FIRESTONE, P.
FLYNN, R.
FOURIEZOS, G.
GIRODO, M.
HUNSLEY, J.
JOHNSON, S.
LEDINGHAM, J.
LEE, C.
LEMYRE, L.
MERALI, Z.
MESSIER, C.
MOOK, B.
PELLETIER, L.
RITCHIE, P.
SARRAZIN, G.
SCHNEIDER, B.
TOUGAS, F.
WHIFFEN, V.
YOUNGER, A.

School of Social Work:

CODERRE, C.
HOME, A. M.
TOUGAS, F.
ST-AMAND, N.

FEDERATED UNIVERSITY

Saint Paul University: 223 Main St, Ottawa, ON K1S 1C4; internet www.ustpaul.ca; Rector Rev. Prof. DALE SCHLITT

DEANS

Faculty of Canon Law: Rev. ROCH PAGÉ
Faculty of Human Sciences: JEAN-GUY GOULET
Faculty of Theology: Rev. DAVID PERRIN

PROFESSORS

Faculty of Canon Law:

HUELS, J.
MENDONÇA, REV. A.
MORRISEY, REV. F. G.
PAGE, R.

Faculty of Human Sciences:

BÉGIN, B.
DAVIAU, P.
GOULET, J.-G.
MEIER, A.
MOOREN, T.
RIGBY, P.

Faculty of Theology:

COYLE, J. K.
DUMAIS, REV. M.
MARTÍNEZ DE PISÓN, R.
MELCHIN, K.
PAMBRUN, J.
PEELMAN, REV. A.
PROVENCHER, REV. M. N.
SCHLITT, REV. D. M.
VAN DEN HENGEL, REV. J.
WALTERS, G.

UNIVERSITY OF PRINCE EDWARD ISLAND

550 University Ave, Charlottetown, PE C1A 4P3
Telephone: (902) 566-0439
Fax: (902) 566-0795
E-mail: registrar@upei.ca
Internet: www.upei.ca

Founded 1969 by merger of St Dunstan's University (f. 1855) and Prince of Wales College (f. 1834)
Academic year: September to May

Chancellor: NORMAN WEBSTER
President and Vice-Chancellor: H. WADE MACLAUCHLAN
Vice-President, Academic Development: VIANNE TIMMONS
Vice-President, Finance and Facilities: GARRY G. BRADSHAW
Registrar: KAREN SMYTHE

University Librarian: LYNN MURPHY
Library: see Libraries
Number of teachers: 192 full-time
Number of students: 2,800 full-time

DEANS

Faculty of Arts: RICHARD KURIAL
Faculty of Business Administration: Dr ROBERTA MACDONALD
Faculty of Education: Dr GRAHAM PIKE
Faculty of Nursing: Dr IRENE COULSON
Faculty of Science: Dr ROGER GORDON
Faculty of Veterinary Medicine: Dr TIMOTHY OGILVIE

DEPARTMENTAL HEADS

Anatomy/Physiology (Veterinary Medicine): LUIS BATE
Biology: CHRISTOPHER LACROIX
Business Administration: JACK BRIMBERG
Canadian Studies: JAMES SENTANCE
Chemistry: ROBERT HAINES
Classics: DAVID BUCK
Companion Animals (Veterinary Medicine): JAMES MILLER
Economics: MIAN ALI
Education: GERALD HOPKIRK
Engineering: DONALD GILLIS
English: GEOFFREY LINDSAY
Family and Nutritional Sciences: DEBBIE MACLELLAN
Fine Arts: JANOS FEDAK
Health Management (Veterinary Medicine): ELIZABETH SPANGLER
History: ANDREW ROBB
Mathematics and Computer Science: GORDON MACDONALD
Modern Languages: SCOTT LEE
Music: KAREN SIMON
Nursing: ROSEMARY HERBERT
Pathology/Microbiology (Veterinary Medicine): BASIL IKEDE
Philosophy: NEB KUJUNDZIC
Physics: DOUGLAS DAHN
Political Studies: BARRY BARTMANN
Psychology: CATHY RYAN
Radiography: CLARA MORRISON
Religious Studies: PHILIP DAVIS
Sociology/Anthropology: SATADAL DASGUPTA

UNIVERSITÉ DU QUÉBEC

475 rue de l'Eglise, Québec, QC G1K 9H7
Telephone: (418) 657-3551
Fax: (418) 657-2132
E-mail: info-uq@uqss.uquebec.ca
Internet: www.uquebec.ca

Founded 1968
Language of instruction: French

President: PIERRE MOREAU
Vice-President (Administration and Finance): LOUIS GENDREAU
Vice-President (Teaching and Research): DANIEL CODERRE
Secretary-General: MICHEL QUIMPER
Director of Public Relations (vacant)
Librarian (vacant)

Library: Library (network) of 2,340,000 vols
Number of teachers: 2,200
Number of students: 84,700

Publications: *Inventaire de la recherche subventionnée et commanditée* (annually), *Rapport annuel*, *Réseau* (4 a year).

CONSTITUENT INSTITUTIONS

Université du Québéc en Abitibi-Témiscamingue

445 blvd de l'Université, Rouyn-Noranda, QC J9X 5E4
Telephone: (819) 762-2922
Fax: (819) 797-4727
E-mail: registraire@uqat.ca
Internet: www.uqat.uquebec.ca

Founded 1981 as Centre d'etudes universitaires, name changed 1984

Rector: JULES ARSENAULT
Vice-Rectors: L. BERGERON (Resources), ROGER CLAUX (Teaching and Research)
Registrar: N. MURPHY
Director of Services: N. MURPHY
Secretary-General: J. TURGEON
Librarian: A. BÉLAND

Library: Library of 201,000 items
Number of teachers: 75
Number of students: 911 full-time
Number of students: 1,932 part-time

HEADS OF DEPARTMENTS

Applied Sciences: FRANÇOIS GODARD
Education: J.-P. MARQUIS
Human Behavioural Science: JEAN CARON
Management Sciences: JOHANNE JEAN
Social and Health Sciences: SARAH SHILDER

Université du Québec à Chicoutimi

555 blvd de l'Université, Chicoutimi, QC G7H 2B1
Telephone: (418) 545-5011
Fax: (418) 545-5049
E-mail: regist@uqac.ca
Internet: www.uqac.ca

Founded 1969
State control
Language of instruction: French
Academic year: September to April

Rector: MICHEL BELLEY
Secretary-General: MARTIN CÔTÉ
Registrar: CLAUDIO ZOCCASTELLO
Librarian: GILLES CARON

Library: Library of 250,000 print items
Number of teachers: 225
Number of students: 6,500 (3,200 full-time, 3,300 part-time)

Publication: *UQACtualité* (4 a year)

HEADS OF DEPARTMENTS

Applied Sciences: GILLES BOUCHARD
Arts and Letters: FRANCINE BELLE-ISLE
Basic Sciences: ANDRÉ LECLERC
Computer Science and Mathematics: JEAN ROUETTE
Economic and Administrative Sciences: GILLES BERGERON
Education Sciences: GUY OUELLET
Human Sciences: ANTOINE N'TETU
Religious Sciences and Ethics: NICOLE BOUCHARD

Université du Québec à Hull

CP 1250, Succursale 'B', Hull, QC J8X 3X7
Telephone: (819) 595-3900
Fax: (819) 595-3924
E-mail: registraire@uqah.uquebec.ca
Internet: www.uqah.ca

Founded 1970
Language of instruction: French
Academic year: September to June

Rector: FRANCIS R. WHYTE
Secretary-General: M. BONDU
Registrar: M. BÉRUBÉ
Librarian: M. TESSIER

Library: Library of 209,844 items
Number of teachers: 146
Number of students: 4,766 (2,037 full-time, 2,729 part-time)

Publication: *Savoir Outaouais* (3 a year)

DIRECTORS OF DEPARTMENTS

Accountancy: P. CHARRON
Administration: R. LEFEBVRE
Computer Science: W. J. BOCK
Education: G. FARID
Health Sciences: F. DE MONTIGNY
Industrial Relations: N. LAPLANTE
Psychoeducation: S. COUTU
Social Work: L. LACROIX

Université du Québec à Montréal

CP 8888, Succ. Centre-ville, Montréal, QC H3C 3P8
Telephone: (514) 987-3000
Fax: (514) 987-3009
E-mail: registrariat@uqam.ca
Internet: www.regis.uqam.ca

Founded 1969

Rector (vacant)
Vice-Rectors: LYNN DRAPEAU (Academics and Research), MICHEL ROBILLARD (Academic Services and Technological Development), ALAIN DUFOUR (Human Resources and Administrative Affairs), PAULE LEDUC (Partnership and External Affairs, acting), LOUISE DANDURAND (Strategic and Financial Planning and General Secretary)
Registrar: CLAUDETTE JODOIN
Librarian: JEAN-PIERRE CÔTÉ

Library of 2,388,000 vols
Number of teachers: 903
Number of students: 37,395 (18,406 full-time, 18,989 part-time)

HEADS OF DEPARTMENTS

Accountancy: A. NACIRI
Administration: D. DESBIENS
Biology: J. LAFOND
Chemistry: P. PICHET
Communications: E. CARONTINI
Computing: G. GAUTHIER
Dance: M. EPOQUE
Design: J. P. HARDENNE
Earth Sciences: M. LAMOTHE
Economics: Y. FAUVEL
Education: M. TURGEON
Geography: J. CARRIERE
History of Art: C. HOULD
History: J.-C. ROBERT
Kinanthropology: J. BOUCHER
Law: D. DESMARAIS
Linguistics: C. GERMAIN
Literature: M. NEVERT
Mathematics: R. V. ANDERSON
Music: C. DAUPHIN
Philosophy: R. NADEAU
Physics: E. BORIDI
Plastic Arts: C. MONGRAIN
Psychology: J. BELANGER
Political Sciences: T. HENTSCH
Religion: M.-A. ROY
Sexology: J.-J. LEVY
Social Work: H. DUVAL
Sociology: P. DROUILLY
Theatre: M. LAPORTE
Urban and Touristic Studies: L.-N. TELLIER

Université du Québec à Rimouski

300 Allée des Ursulines, Rimouski, QC G5L 3A1
Telephone: (418) 723-1986
Fax: (418) 724-1525
E-mail: uqar@uqar.uquebec.ca
Internet: wer.uqar.qc.ca

Founded 1969
State control
Academic year: September to April (2 semesters)

Rector: PIERRE COUTURE
Vice-Rectors: J.-N. THÉRIAULT (Administration and Human Resources), MICHEL RINGUET (Teaching and Research)
Secretary-General: M. BOURASSA
Librarian: GASTON DUMONT

Library: Library of 334,600 items
Number of teachers: 172
Number of students: 2,100 full-time
Number of students: 2,300 part-time

Publications: *Rapport annuel* (annually), *UQAR-Info* (6 a year)

HEADS OF DEPARTMENTS

Biology and Health Sciences: D. RAJOTTE
Economics and Business Studies: L. GOSSELIN
Education Sciences: P. CÔTÉ
Human Sciences: P. BRUNEAU
Letters: T. PAQUIN
Mathematics, Computer and Engineering: M. LAVOIE
Oceanography: S. DEMORA
Religion and Ethics: M. DUMAIS

ATTACHED CENTRE

Oceanography Centre: Dir V. KOUTITONSKY.

Université du Québec à Trois-Rivières

3351 blvd des Forges, CP 500, Trois-Rivières, QC G9A 5H7
Telephone: (819) 376-5045
Fax: (819) 376-5012
E-mail: crmultiservice@uqtr.ca
Internet: www.uqtr.ca
Founded 1969
Provincial control
Academic year: September to April
Rector: CLAIRE DE LA DURANTAYE
Vice-Rector: DANIEL MCMAHON (Administration and Finance)
Vice-Rector and Secretary-General: FRANÇOIS HÉROUX
Registrar: DENIS DE CARUFEL
Library: Library of 500,000 items
Number of teachers: 344
Number of students: 9,647 (5,680 full-time, 3,967 part-time)
Publication: *En Tête*

HEADS OF DEPARTMENTS

Accounting: RICHARD WILSON
Administration: VIVIANE GASCON, MICHEL POTVIN
Chemistry–Physics: HÉLÈNE-MARIE THÉRIEN, FRANÇOIS BOUCHER
Communication: YVON LAPLANTE
Education: JEAN-PIERRE ADAM
Engineering: RENÉ J. HARBEC DENIS LAGACÉ
French: LUC OSTIGUY
Art: MARIO ANCTIL
Biology: PIERRE MAGNAN
Chiropractic: ANDRÉ-MARIE GONTHIER
Geography: DENIS GRATTON
Health–Biology: CLAUDE GICQUAUD
History: GEORGES MASSÉ
Leisure Sciences: GILLES PRONOVOST
Mathematics and Computer Science: MARIE-FRANCE THIBAULT
Modern Languages: PIERRE DEMERS
Nursing Science: MICHÈLE CÔTÉ
Operational Research: FRANÇOIS BERGERON
Philosophy: SUZANNE FOISY
Physical Education: CLAUDE DUGAS
Psychology–Education: ANDRÉ PLANTE
Psychology: EMMANUEL HABIMANA
Theology: SUZANNE ROUSSEAU

Ecole Nationale d'Administration Publique

555 blvd Charest Est, Québec, QC G1K 9E5
Telephone: (418) 641-3000
Fax: (418) 641-3060
Founded 1969
Director-General: PIERRE DE CELLES
Library of 90,000 vols
Number of teachers: 59
Number of students: 1,143.

Ecole de Technologie Supérieure

1100 rue Notre-Dame Ouest, Montréal, QC H3C 1K3
Telephone: (514) 396-8800
Fax: (514) 396-8950
Founded 1974
Director-General: YVES BEAUCHAMP
Library of 30,000 vols
Number of teachers: 69.

Institut Armand-Frappier

531 blvd des Prairies, CP 100, Laval, QC H7V 1B7
Telephone: (514) 687-5010
Founded 1938
Director-General: PIERRE TALBOT
Library of 10,000 vols
Number of teachers: 36
Number of students: 126 (55 full-time, 71 part-time)
Microbiological research; graduate studies programme; production of vaccines and diagnostic products.

Institut National de la Recherche Scientifique

490 de la Couronne, Québec, QC G1K 9A9
Telephone: (418) 654-2500
Fax: (418) 654-2525
Internet: www.inrs.uquebec.ca
Founded 1969
Director-General: PIERRE LAPOINTE
Library of 65,500 vols
Number of teachers: 152
Number of students: 595 (489 full-time, 106 part-time).

Télé-université

Tour de la Cité, 2600 blvd Laurier, 7e étage, Québec, QC G1V 4V9
Telephone: (418) 657-2262
Founded 1972
Director-General: A. MARREC
Library of 12,000 vols
Number of teachers: 35
Number of students: 5,716 (258 full-time, 5458 part-time)
Distance-learning programmes.

QUEEN'S UNIVERSITY AT KINGSTON

Kingston, ON K7L 3N6
Telephone: (613) 545-2000
Fax: (613) 545-6300
E-mail: liaison@post.queensu.ca
Internet: www.queensu.ca
Founded 1841
Language of instruction: English
Academic year: September to May (two terms)
Chancellor: PETER LOUGHEED
Rector: MICHAEL KEALY
Vice-Chancellor and Principal: Dr W. C. LEGGETT
Vice-Principal (Academic): Dr S. FORTIER
Vice-Principal (Advancement): Dr G. N. HOOD
Vice-Principal (Health Sciences): Dr M. C. WALKER
Vice-Principal (Operations and Finance): Dr D. L. ANDERSON
Vice-Principal (Research): Dr B. J. HUTCHINSON
Registrar: JO-ANNE BECHTHOLD
Chief Librarian: PAUL WIENS
Number of teachers: 1,158
Number of students: 17,510
Publication: *Queen's Quarterly* (4 a year)

DEANS

Faculty of Applied Science: T. J. HARRIS
Faculty of Arts and Sciences: R. A. SILVERMAN
Faculty of Education: R. BRUNO-JOFRÉ
Faculty of Health Sciences: M. C. WALKER
Faculty of Law: A. HARVISON YOUNG
School of Business: DAVID SAUNDERS
School of Graduate Studies and Research: R. J. ANDERSON

PROFESSORS

Some staff teach in more than one faculty

Faculty of Applied Science (Ellis Hall, Kingston, ON K7L 3N6; tel. (613) 533-2055; fax (613) 533-6500; e-mail appsci@post.queensu.ca; internet appsci.queensu.ca):

AITKEN, G. J. M., Electrical and Computer Engineering
ANDERSON, R. J., Mechanical Engineering
ARCHIBALD, J. F., Mining Engineering
BEAULIEU, N. C., Electrical and Computer Engineering
BIRK, A. M., Mechanical Engineering
BOYD, J. D., Materials and Metallurgical Engineering
BRYANT, J. T., Mechanical Engineering
CAMERON, J., Materials and Metallurgical Engineering
CAMPBELL, T. I., Civil Engineering
CARTLEDGE, J. C., Electrical and Computer Engineering
DANESHMEND, L. K., Mining Engineering
DAUGULIS, A. J., Chemical Engineering
GRANDMAISON, E. W., Chemical Engineering
HALL, K., Civil Engineering
HAMACHER, V. C., Electrical and Computer Engineering
HARRIS, T. J., Chemical Engineering
JESWIET, J., Mechanical Engineering
JORDAN, M. P., Mechanical Engineering
KAMPHUIS, J. W., Civil Engineering
KORENBERG, M., Electrical and Computer Engineering
KRSTIC, V. D., Materials and Metallurgical Engineering
KUEPER, B., Civil Engineering
MCKINNON, S. D., Mining Engineering
MCLANE, P. J., Electrical and Computer Engineering
MITCHELL, R. J., Civil Engineering
MOUFTAH, H. T., Electrical and Computer Engineering
MULVENNA, C. A., Mechanical Engineering
NEUFELD, R. J., Chemical Engineering
OOSTHUIZEN, P. H., Mechanical Engineering
PICKLES, C. A., Materials and Metallurgical Engineering
POLLARD, A., Mechanical Engineering
ROSE, K., Civil Engineering
SAIMOTO, S., Materials and Metallurgical Engineering
SEN, P. C., Electrical and Computer Engineering
SMALL, C. F., Mechanical Engineering
SURGENOR, B. W., Mechanical Engineering
TAVARES, S. E., Electrical and Computer Engineering
TURCKE, D. J., Civil Engineering
VAN DALEN, K., Civil Engineering
WATT, W. E., Civil Engineering
WYSS, U. P., Mechanical Engineering
YEN, W.-T., Mining Engineering

Faculty of Arts and Science (Mackintosh-Corry Hall, Room F300, Kingston, ON K7L 3N6; tel. (613) 533-2470; fax (613) 533-2067; internet www.queensu.ca/artsci):

AARSSEN, L. W., Biology
AKENSON, D. H., History
AKL, S. G., Computing and Information Science
ATHERTON, D. L., Physics
BAIRD, M. C., Chemistry
BAKAN, A. B., Political Studies
BAKHURST, D., Philosophy
BANTING, K. G., Politics
BEACH, C. M., Economics
BECKE, A. D., Chemistry
BENINGER, R. J., Psychology

BERG, M., English
BERGIN, J., Economics
BERMAN, B. J., Politics
BERNHARDT, D., Economics
BICKENBACH, J. E., Philosophy
BLY, P. A., Spanish and Italian
BOADWAY, R. W., Economics
BOAG, P. T., Biology
BOGOYAVLENSKIJ, O. I., Mathematics and Statistics
BROWN, R. S., Chemistry
BURKE, F., Film
CALLE-GRUBER, M., French
CAMPBELL, H. E. A., Mathematics and Statistics
CARMICHAEL, D. M., Geological Sciences
CARMICHAEL, H. L., Economics
CASTEL, B., Physics
CHRISTIANSON, P., History
CLARK, A. H., Geology
CONAGHAN, C. M., Politics
CORDY, J. R., Computing and Information Science
CRAWFORD, R. G., Computing and Information Science
CRUSH, J., Geography
CUDDY, L. L., Psychology
DALRYMPLE, R. W., Geology
DAVIDSON, R., Economics
DE CAEN, D. J. P., Mathematics and Statistics
DIXON, J. M., Geology
DONALD, M. W., Psychology
DUNCAN, M. J., Physics
DU PREY, P. D., Art
ELTIS, D., History
ERDAHL, R. M., Mathematics and Statistics
ERRINGTON, E. J., History
FINLAYSON, J., English
FISHER, A., Music
FLATTERS, F. R., Economics
FLETCHER, R., Physics
FORTIER, S., Chemistry
FOX, M. A., Philosophy
FROST, B. J., Psychology
GEKOSKI, W. L., Psychology
GERAMITA, A. V., Mathematics and Statistics
GILBERT, R. E., Geography
GLASGOW, J., Computing and Information Science
GOHEEN, P. G., Geography
GREGORY, A. W., Economics
GREGORY, D. A., Mathematics and Statistics
GUNN, J. A. W., Politics
HAGEL, D. K., Classics
HAGLUND, D. G., Politics
HAMILTON, R., Sociology
HAMM, J.-J. N., French
HANES, D. A., Physics
HARRISON, J. P., Physics
HARTWICK, J. M., Economics
HELLAND, J., Art
HELMSTAEDT, H., Geology
HENRIKSEN, R. N., Physics
HERZBERG, A. M., Mathematics and Statistics
HEYWOOD, J. C., Art
HIRSCHORN, R. M., Mathematics and Statistics
HODSON, P. V., Biology
HOLDEN, R. R., Psychology
HOLMES, J., Geography
HUGHES, I., Mathematics and Statistics
HUNTER, B. K., Chemistry
JAMES, N. P., Geology
JEEVES, A. H., History
JIRAT-WASIVTYNSKI, V., Art
JOHNSTONE, I. P., Physics
JONKER, L. B., Mathematics and Statistics
KALIN, R., Psychology
KANI, E., Mathematics and Statistics
KILPATRICK, R. S., Classics
KNAPPER, C., Psychology
KNOX, V. J., Psychology
KOBAYASHI, A., Women's Studies
KYMLICKA, W., Philosophy
KYSTER, T. K., Geology
LAKE, K. W., Physics
LAYZELL, D. B., Biology
LEDERMAN, S., Psychology
LEGGETT, W. C., Biology
LEIGHTON, S. R., Philosophy
LELE, J. K., Politics
LESLIE, J. R., Physics
LESLIE, P. M., Politics
LEVISON, M., Computing and Information Science
LEWIS, F. D., Economics
LINDSAY, R. C. L., Psychology
LOBB, R. E., English
LOCK, F. P., English
LOGAN, G. M., English
LOVELL, W. G., Geography
LYON, D., Sociology
MACARTNEY, D. H., Chemistry
MCKAY, I. G., History
MACKINNON, J. G., Economics
MACLEAN, A. W., Psychology
MACLEOD, A. M., Philosophy
MALCOLMSON, R. W., History
MANUTH, V., Art
MARSHALL, W. L., Psychology
MCCAUGHEY, J. H., Geography
MCCOWAN, J. D., Chemistry
MCCREADY, W. D., History
MCDONALD, A. B., Physics
MCINNIS, R. M., Economics
MCLATCHIE, W., Physics
MCTAVISH, J. D., Art
MEWHORT, D., Psychology
MILNE, F., Economics
MINGO, J. A., Mathematics and Statistics
MONKMAN, L. G., English
MONTGOMERIE, R. D., Biology
MOORE, E. G., Geography
MORRIS, G. P., Biology
MUIR, D. W., Psychology
MURTY, M. R. P., Mathematics and Statistics
NARBONNE, G. M., Geology
NATANSOHN, A. L., Chemistry
O'NEILL, P. J., German
ORZECH, M., Mathematics and Statistics
OSBORNE, B. S., Geography
OVERALL, C. D., Philosophy
PAGE, S. C., Politics
PALMER, B. D., History
PEARCE, G. R. F., Sociology
PEARCE, T. H., Geology
PENTLAND, C. C., Politics
PERLIN, G. C., Politics
PETERS, R. D., Psychology
PIKE, R. M., Sociology
PLANT, R. L., Drama
PLAXTON, W. C., Biology
PRACHOWNY, M. F. J., Economics
PRADO, C. G., Philosophy
PRITCHARD, J., History
QUINSEY, V. L., Psychology
RASULA, J., English
RAY, A., Economics
REEVE, W. C., German
RIDDELL, J. B., Geography
ROBERTS, L. G., Mathematics and Statistics
ROBERTSON, B. C., Physics
ROBERTSON, R. J., Biology
ROBERTSON, R. M., Biology
ROSENBERG, M. W., Geography
SACCO, V. F., Sociology
SAYER, M., Physics
SCHROEDER, F. M., Classics
SHENTON, R. W., History
SILVERMAN, R. A., Sociology
SKILLICORN, D. B., Computing and Information Science
SMITH, G. S., History
SMITH, G. W., Economics
SMOL, J., Biology
SNIDER, D. L., Sociology
SNIECKUS, U. A., Chemistry
SPARKS, G. R., Economics
STAYER, J. M., History
STEVENSON, J. M., Physical and Health Education
STONE, J. A., Chemistry
STOTT, M. J., Physics
SYPNOWICH, C., Philosophy
SZAREK, W. A., Chemistry
TAYLOR, D. R., Physics
TAYLOR, P. D., Mathematics and Statistics
TENNENT, R. D., Computing and Information Science
THOMSON, C. J., Geology
TINLINE, R. R., Geography
VANLOON, G. W., Chemistry
VERNER, J. H., Mathematics and Statistics
WALKER, V. K., Biology
WANG, S., Chemistry
WARDLAW, D. M., Chemistry
WARE, R., Economics
WEISMAN, R. G., Psychology
WIEBE, M. G., English
WOLFE, L. A., Physical and Health Education
YOUNG, P. G., Biology
YUI, N., Mathematics and Statistics
ZAMBLE, E., Psychology
ZAREMBA, E., Physics
ZUK, I. B., Education
ZUREIK, E. T., Sociology

Faculty of Education (tel. (613) 533-6205; fax (613) 533-6203; e-mail regoff@educ.queensu.ca; internet educ.queensu.ca):

HUTCHINSON, N. L.
KIRBY, J. R.
MUNBY, A. H.
O'FARRELL, L.
RUSSELL, T.
UPITIS, R. B.
WILSON, R. J.

Faculty of Health Sciences (tel. (613) 533-2544; fax (613) 533-6884; e-mail jeb8@post.queensu.ca; internet meds.queensu.ca):

ADAMS, M. A., Pharmacology and Toxicology
ANASTASSIADES, T. P., Medicine
ANDREW, R. D., Anatomy and Cell Biology
ARBOLEDA-FLOREZ, J. E., Psychiatry
ASTON, W. P., Microbiology and Immunology
BENNETT, B. M., Pharmacology and Toxicology
BIRTWHISTLE, R. V., Family Medicine
BOEGMAN, R. J., Pharmacology and Toxicology
BRIEN, J. F., Pharmacology and Toxicology
BRUNET, D. G., Medicine
BURGGRAF, G. W., Medicine
BURKE, S. O., School of Nursing
CARSTENS, E. B., Microbiology and Immunology
CHAPLER, C. K., Physiology
CLARK, A. F., Biochemistry
COLE, S. P. C., Pathology
COTE, G. P., Biochemistry
CRUESS, A. F., Ophthalmology
DA COSTA, L. R., Medicine
DAGNONE, L. E., Emergency Medicine
DAVIES, P. L., Biochemistry
DEELEY, R. G., Pathology
DELISLE, G. J., Microbiology and Immunology
DEPEW, W. T., Medicine
DOW, K. E., Paediatrics
DUFFIN, J. M., Health Sciences
DWOSH, I. L., Medicine
EISENHAUER, E. A., Radoncology
ELCE, J. S., Biochemistry
ELLIOTT, B. E., Pathology
FERGUSON, A. V., Physiology
FISHER, J. T., Physiology
FLYNN, T. G., Biochemistry
FORD, P. M., Medicine
FORKERT, P. G., Anatomy and Cell Biology
FROESE, A. B., Anaesthesia

Gorwill, R. H., Obstetrics and Gynaecology
Hall, S. F., Otolaryngology
Heaton, J. P. W., Urology
Holden, J. J. A., Psychiatry
Hudson, R. W., Medicine
Jackson, A. C., Medicine
Jarrell, K. F. J., Microbiology and Immunology
Jhamandas, K., Pharmacology and Toxicology
Joneja, M. G., Anatomy and Cell Biology
Jones, G., Biochemistry
Kan, F. W. K., Anatomy and Cell Biology
Kisilevsky, R., Pathology
Kropinski, A. M., Microbiology and Immunology
Lamb, M. W., School of Nursing
Lawson, J. S., Psychiatry
Lillicrap, D. P., Pathology
Ludwin, S. K., Pathology
McCreary, B., Psychiatry
Mak, A. S., Biochemistry
Manley, P. N., Pathology
Massey, T. E., Pharmacology and Toxicology
Mercer, C. D., Surgery
Milne, B., Anaesthesia
Morales, A., Urology
Munt, P. W., Medicine
Nakatsu, K., Pharmacology and Toxicology
Nesheim, M. E., Biochemistry
Nickel, J. C., Urology
Nolan, R. L., Diagnostic Radiology
O'Connor, H. M., Emergency Medicine
O'Donnell, D. E., Medicine
Olney, S. J., Rehabilitation Therapy
Pang, S. C., Anatomy and Cell Biology
Pater, J. L., Community Health and Epidemiology
Paterson, W. G., Medicine
Pichora, D. R., Surgery
Poole, R. K., Microbiology and Immunology
Pross, H. F., Microbiology and Immunology
Racz, W. J., Pharmacology and Toxicology
Raptis, L. H., Microbiology and Immunology
Reid, R. L., Obstetrics and Gynaecology
Reifel, C., Anatomy and Cell Biology
Richmond, F. J., Physiology
Riopelle, R. J., Medicine
Rose, P. K., Physiology
Shanks, G. L., Rehabilitation Medicine
Shin, S. H., Physiology
Shortt, S. E. D., Community Health and Epidemiology
Simon, J. B., Medicine
Singer, M. A., Medicine
Smith, B. T., Paediatrics
Szewczuk, M. R., Microbiology and Immunology
Walker, D. M. C., Emergency Medicine
Weaver, D. F., Medicine
Wherrett, B. A., Paediatrics
Wigle, R. D., Medicine
Wilson, C. R., Family Medicine

Faculty of Law (Macdonald Hall, Kingston, ON K7L 3N6; tel. (613) 533-2220; fax (613) 533-6611; e-mail llb@gsilver.queensu.ca; internet gsilver.queensu.ca/law):

Adell, B. L.
Alexandrowicz, G. W.
Baer, M. G.
Bala, N. C.
Carter, D. D.
Delisle, R. J.
Easson, A. J.
Harvison Young, A.
Lahey, K. A.
Magnusson, D. N.
Manson, A. S.
Mullan, D. J.
Sadinsky, S.
Stuart, D. R.
Weisberg, M. A.

School of Business (Dunning Hall, Kingston, ON K7L 3N6; tel. (613) 533-2330; fax (613) 533-2013; e-mail info@business.queensu.ca; internet business.queensu.ca):

Anderson, D. L.
Arnold, S. J.
Barling, J. I.
Cooper, W. H.
Daub, M. A. C.
Gallupe, R. B.
Gordon, J. R. M.
Johnson, L. D.
McKeen, J. D.
Morgan, I. G.
Neave, E. H.
Nightingale, D. V.
Northey, M. E.
Petersen, E. R.
Richardson, A. J.
Richardson, P. R.
Rutenberg, D. P.
Taylor, A. J.
Thornton, D. B.

School of Policy Studies (tel. (613) 533-6555; fax (613) 533-6606; e-mail policy@policy.queensu.ca; internet gsilver.queensu.ca/sps):

Leiss, W.
Williams, T. R.

School of Urban and Regional Planning (tel. (613) 533-2188; fax (613) 533-6905; e-mail williamj@post.queensu.ca; internet info.queensu.ca/surp):

Leung, H. L.
Qadeer, M. A.
Skaburskis, A.

AFFILIATED COLLEGE

Queen's Theological College: Kingston, ON K7L 3N6; f. 1841; Principal Rev. H. E. Llewellyn.

REDEEMER UNIVERSITY COLLEGE

777 Garner Rd East, Ancaster, ON L9K 1J4
Telephone: (905) 648-2131
Fax: (905) 648-2134
E-mail: adm@redeemer.on.ca
Internet: www.redeemer.on.ca

Founded 1976; became Redeemer College 1980; university status 1982; present name 2000

Committed to the advancement of Reformed Christian education in all academic disciplines
Language of instruction: English
Private control
Academic year: September to May

President: Dr Justin Cooper
Vice-President (Academic): Dr Jacob Ellens
Vice-President (Administration and Finance): Bill van Staalduinen
Registrar: Richard Wikkerink
Librarian: Janny Eikelboom

Library: Library of 100,000 items
Number of teachers: 40
Number of students: 800

FACULTY DIVISION HEADS

Faculty of Arts and Foundations: Dr Douglas Loney
Faculty of Sciences and Social Sciences: Dr Douglas Needham

UNIVERSITY OF REGINA

3737 Wascana Pkwy, Regina, SK S4S 0A2
Telephone: (306) 585-4111
Fax: (306) 337-2525
E-mail: admissions.office@leroy.cc.uregina.ca
Internet: www.uregina.ca

Founded 1974 (previously Regina Campus, Univ. of Saskatchewan)
Provincial control
Language of instruction: English
Academic year: September to April (2 terms)

Chancellor: Dr William F. Ready
Vice-Chancellor and Pres.: Dr R. James Tomkins
Vice-Pres. for Academic Affairs: Dr George Maslany
Vice-Pres. for Admin.: David Button
Vice-Pres. for Research and Int. Affairs: Dr David Gauthier
Vice-Pres. for External Relations: Barbara Pollock
Univ. Sec.: Annette Revet
Registrar: Judy Chapman
Librarian: Carol Hixson

Library: 2.4m. items incl. 655,000 print and electronic vols and periodicals, c. 626,110 govt pbls (incl. 296000 in microform), 918,000 other items in microform; colln of recordings and materials in other media
Number of teachers: 468
Number of students: 11,057 (full-time 8209; part-time 2848)

Publications: *Carillon* (monthly), *Degrees* (2 a year), *Wascana Review* (2 a year)

DEANS

Faculty of Business Admin.: Garnet Garven
Faculty of Arts: Dr Thomas Chase
Faculty of Education: Dr Michael Tymchak
Faculty of Eng.: Dr Paitoon Tontiwachwuthikul
Faculty of Fine Arts: Dr Sheila Petty
Faculty of Kinesiology and Health Studies: Dr Craig Chamberlin
Faculty of Science: Dr Katherine Bergman
Faculty of Social Work: Dr David Schantz
Faculty of Graduate Studies and Research: Dr Rod Kelln
Centre for Continuing Education: Dr Harvey King (Dir)

PROFESSORS

Alfano, Dennis P., Psychology
Anderson, Leona, Religious Studies
Anderson, Robert, Business Admin.
Ashton, Neil W., Biology
Asmundson, Gordon, Kinesiology and Health Studies
Austin, Bryan J., Business Admin.
Bergman, Katherine, Geology
Blackstone, Mary, Theatre
Blake, Raymond, History
Brennan, William, History
Brigham, R. Mark, Biology
Broad, David, Social Work
Chan, Christine, Eng.
Channing, Lynn, Music
Chapco, William, Biology
Cherland, Meredith, Education
Chow, Sui, Psychology
Conway, John, Sociology and Social Studies
Cruikshank, Jane, Social Work
Dai, Liming, Eng.
Diaz, Harry, Sociology and Social Studies
Dolmage, Rod, Education
Dong, Mingzhe, Eng.
Drury, Shadia, Philosophy, Political Science
Durst, Doug, Social Work
Evans, Dennis, Visual Arts
Farenick, Douglas, Mathematics and Statistics
Fisher, J. C., Mathematics
Gauthier, David, Geography
Gilligan, Bruce, Mathematics
Gingrich, Paul, Sociology and Social Studies
Griffiths, John, Music
Gu, Yongan, Eng.
Hadjistavropoulos, Heather, Psychology
Hadjistavropoulos, Thomas, Psychology
Hamilton, Howard, Computer Science
Handerek, Kelly, Theatre

HANSEN, PHILLIP, Philosophy
HART, PAUL, Education
HAYFORD, ALISON, Sociology
HEINRICH, KATHERINE, Mathematics and Statistics
HOWARD, WILLIAM, English
HUANG, GUO, Eng.
HUBER, GARTH, Physics
IDEM, RAPHAEL, Eng.
ITO, JACK, Business Admin.
JEFFREY, BONNIE, Social Work
JIN, YEE-CHUNG, Eng.
JOHNSON, SHANTHI, English
KELLN, RODNEY, Chemistry and Biochemistry
KESTEN, CYRIL, Education
KIPLING BROWN, ANN, Education
KIRKLAND, STEPHEN, Mathematics and Statistics
KNUTTILA, K. MURRAY, Sociology and Social Studies
KORTÉ, HERBERT, Philosophy
LAVACK, ANNE, Business Admin.
LEAVITT, PETER, Biology
LEDREW, JUNE, Kinesiology and Health Studies
LEESON, HOWARD, Political Science
LENTON-YOUNG, GERALD, Theatre
LOLOS, GEORGE, Physics
LOUIS, CAMERON, English
MACLENNAN, RICHARD, Justice Studies
MAEERS, MHAIRI (VI), Education
MAGUIRE, BRIEN, Computer Science
MALLOY, DAVID, Kinesiology and Health Studies
MARCHILDON, GREGORY, Johnson-Shoyama graduate School of Public Policy
MASLANY, GEORGE, Social Work
MATHIE, EDWARD, Physics
MCINTOSH, RICHARD, Mathematics and Statistics
MISSKEY, WILLIAM, Systems Eng.
PALMER, RONALD, Electronic Systems Eng.
PAPANDREOU, ZISIS, Physics
PARANJAPE, RAMAN, Electronic Systems Eng.
PAUL, ALEXANDER, Geography
PETTY, SHEILA, Media Studies
PFEIFER, JEFFREY, Justice, Psychology
PICKARD, GARTH, Education
PITSULA, JAMES, History
QING, HAIRUO, Geology
RAUM, J. RICHARD, Music
RENNIE, MORINA, Business Admin.
ROBINSON, ANNABEL, Classics
RUDDICK, NICHOLAS, English
SAUCHYN, DAVID, Geography
SAXTON, LAWRENCE, Computer Science
SHAMI, JEANNE, English
SHARMA, SATISH, Systems Eng.
SMYTHE, WILLIAM, Psychology
SOIFER, ELDON, Philosophy
STARK, CANNIE, Psychology
STREIFLER, LEESA, Visual Arts
SZABADOS, BELA, Philosophy
TOMKINS, JAMES, Mathematics
TONTIWACHWUTHIKUL, PAITOON, Eng.
TYMCHAK, MICHAEL, Education
WALL, KATHLEEN, English
WATKINSON, AILSA, Social Work
WEE, ANDREW, Chemistry and Biochemistry
WIDDIS, RANDY, Geography
YAKEL, NORM, Education
YANG, XUE-DONG, Computer Science
YAO, YIYU, Computer Science
ZHANG, CHANG, Computer Science
ZIARKO, WOJCIECH, Computer Science

FEDERATED COLLEGES

Campion College: 3737 Wascana Parkway, Regina, SK S4S 0A2; tel. (306) 586-4242; fax (306) 359-1200; e-mail campion.college@uregina.ca; internet www.campioncollege.sk.caf. 1917; library of 50,000 vols; Pres. B. FIORE; Academic Dean Dr SAMIRA MCCARTHY.

First Nations University of Canada: 1 First Nations Way, Regina, SK S4S 7K2; tel. (306) 790-5950; fax (306) 790-5994; e-mail info@firstnationsuniversity.ca; internet www.firstnationsuniversity.caf. 1975; library of 55,200 vols, incl. the Eeniwuk Colln of 5,000 titles, supporting research in native studies; Pres. CHARLES PRATT (acting); Vice-Pres. for Academic Affairs Dr BERNIE SELINGER.

Luther College: Regina, SK S4S 0A2; tel. (306) 585-5444; fax (306) 585-5267; e-mail lutherreg@uregina.ca; internet www.luthercollege.eduf. 1913; Pres. Dr BRUCE PERLSON; Academic Dean Dr MARY VETTER.

ATTACHED INSTITUTES

Canadian Institute for Peace, Justice and Security: tel. (306) 585-4779; fax (306) 585-4815; internet www.uregina.ca/arts/cipjs; Dir Dr JEFFREY PFEIFER.

Canadian Plains Research Center: tel. (306) 585-4758; fax (306) 585-4699; e-mail canadian.plains@uregina.ca; internet www.cprc.caRegina; Exec. Dir Dr DAVID GAUTHIER.

Centre for Academic Technologies: tel. (306) 337-2400; fax (306) 337-2401; e-mail cat@uregina.ca; internet www.uregina.ca/cat/home.html; Dir Dr VI MAEERS.

Institut Français: Regina; tel. (306) 585-4828; fax (306) 585-5183; e-mail institut@uregina.ca; internet institutfrancais.uregina.ca/home.htm; Dir DOMINIQUE SARNY.

Organizational and Social Psychology Research Unit: tel. (306) 585-5268; fax (306) 585-4827; e-mail cannie.stark@uregina.ca; internet uregina.ca/~starkc; Dir CANNIE STARK.

Saskatchewan Institute of Public Policy: Univ. of Regina, College Avenue Campus, Regina, SK S4S 0A2; tel. (306) 585-5777; fax (306) 585-5780; e-mail sipp@uregina.ca; internet www.uregina.ca/sipp; Dir IAN PEACH.

Saskatchewan Instructional Development and Research Unit of the Faculty of Education: tel. (306) 585-4537; e-mail contactus@education.uregina.ca; internet education.uregina.ca/index.php?id=38f. 1985; Dir Dr MICHAEL TYMCHAK.

Saskatchewan Population Health and Evaluation Research Unit (SPHERU): tel. (306) 585-5674; fax (306) 585-5694; e-mail spheru@uregina.ca; internet www.spheru.ca; Dir Dr GEORGE MASLANY (acting).

Social Policy Research Unit: Faculty of Social Work, Univ. of Regina Regina, SK S4S 0A2; tel. (306) 585-5643; fax (306) 585-5408; e-mail social.policy@uregina.ca; Dir Dr GARSON HUNTER.

Teaching Development Centre: Dir J. MCNINCH.

ROYAL MILITARY COLLEGE OF CANADA

POB 17000 Stn Forces, Kingston, ON K7K 7B4Telephone: (613) 541-6000
Fax: (613) 542-3565
E-mail: liaison@rmc.ca
Internet: www.rmc.ca

Founded 1876
Languages of instruction: English, French
Academic year: September to May

Chancellor and President: The Minister of National Defence
Commandant: Brig. Gen. J. M. J. LECLERC
Principal and Director of Studies: Dr J. S. COWAN
Registrar: Cdr DEBORAH A. WILSON
Director of Cadets: Col W. N. PETERS
Chief Librarian: B. CAMERON
Library of 380,000 vols
Number of teachers: 174
Number of students: 865 (760 undergraduate, 105 graduate)

DEANS AND CHAIRMEN OF DIVISIONS

Arts: Dr J. J. SOKOLSKY
Engineering: Dr J. A. STEWART
Science: Dr R. F. MARSDEN
Continuing Studies: Dr M. F. BARDON
Graduate Studies and Research: Dr B. J. FUGERE

PROFESSORS

AKHRAS, G., Civil Engineering
AL-KHALILI, D., Electrical Engineering
ALLARD, P. E., Electrical Engineering
AMAMI, M., Business Administration
AMPHLETT, J. C., Chemistry
ANTAR, Y., Electrical Engineering
BARDON, M. F., Mechanical Engineering
BARRETT, A. J., Mathematics
BATALLA, E., Physics
BATHURST, R. J., Civil Engineering
BEATY, A., Civil Engineering
BENABDALLAH, H., Mechanical Engineering
BENESCH, R., Mathematics
BENNETT, L., Chemistry and Chemical Engineering
BENSON, M., French Studies
BONESS, R. J., Mechanical Engineering
BONIN, H. W., Chemical Engineering
BONNYCASTLE, S., English
BRADLEY, P., Military Psychology and Leadership
BUCKLEY, J., Physics
BUI, T., Chemistry and Chemical Engineering
BUSSIERES, P., Mechanical Engineering
CHAUDHRY, M. L., Mathematics
CHIKHANI, A. Y., Electrical Engineering
CONSTANTINEAU, P., Politics and Economics
CREBER, K., Chemistry and Chemical Engineering
DAVIES BOUCHARD, S., Continuing Studies
DEPLANCHE, D., Electrical and Computer Engineering
DREIZIGER, N. A. F., History
DUNNETT, P., Political and Economic Science
DUQUESNAY, D., Mechanical Engineering
EDER, W. E., Mechanical Engineering
ERKI, M., Civil Engineering
ERRINGTON, J., History
FAROOQ, M., Electrical Engineering
FINAN, J., Politics and Economics
FJARLIE, E. J., Mechanical Engineering
FUGERE, J., Mathematics and Computer Science
GAGNON, Y., Politics and Economics
GAUTHIER, N., Physics
GERVAIS, R., Mathematics
GODARD, R., Mathematics and Computer Science
GRAVEL, P., Mathematics and Computer Science
HADDAD, L., Mathematics and Computer Science
HASSAN-YARI, H., Politics and Economics
HAYCOCK, R. G., History
HEFNAWI, M., Electrical and Computer Engineering
HURLEY, W., Business Administration
ION, A., History
ISAC, G., Mathematics and Computer Science
JENKINS, A. L., Engineering Management
KLEPAK, H., History
LABBE, M., Mathematics and Computer Science
LABONTE, G., Mathematics
LACHAINE, A. R., Physics
LAGUEUX, P.-A., French Studies
LAPLANTE, J. P., Chemistry
LEWIS, B., Chemistry and Chemical Engineering
LUCIUK, L., Politics and Economics
MCDONOUGH, L., Politics and Economics
MCKERCHER, B., History

MALONEY, S., War Studies
MANN, R. F., Chemical Engineering
MOFFATT, W. C., Mechanical Engineering
MONGEAU, B., Electrical Engineering
MUKHERJEE, B. K., Physics
NEILSON, K. E., History
NOEL, J.-M., Physics
POTTIER, R. H., Chemistry
QUILLARD, G., French Studies
RACEY, T. J., Physics
RANGANATHAN, S., Mathematics
REIMER, K., Chemistry and Chemical Engineering
ROBERGE, P. R., Chemistry
ROCHON, P., Physics
SCHURER, C., Physics
SEGUIN, G., Electrical Engineering
SHEPARD, T., Electrical Engineering
SHOUCRI, R. M., Mathematics
SIMMS, B. W., Engineering Management
SOKOLSKY, J. J., Political Science
SRI, P. S., English
ST PIERRE, A., Business Administration
STACEY, M., Physics
STEWART, A., Civil Engineering
TARBOUCHI, M., Electrical and Computer Engineering
THOMPSON, W. T., Chemical Engineering
TORRIE, G. M., Mathematics
TREDDENICK, J. M., Economics
VINCENT, T. B., English
WEIR, R. D., Chemical Engineering
WHELAU, D., Mathematics and Computer Science
WHITEHORN, A. J., Political Science
WILSON, J. D., Electrical Engineering

ATTACHED INSTITUTES

Applied Military Science: Dir Col G. LINDSAY.

Language Centre (Second Languages): Dir M. SÉGUIN.

ROYAL ROADS UNIVERSITY

2005 Sooke Rd, Victoria, BC V9B 5Y2
Telephone: (250) 391-2511
Fax: (250) 391-2500
E-mail: learn.more@royalroads.ca
Internet: www.royalroads.ca

Founded 1995

President and Vice-Chancellor: RICHARD SKINNER
Vice-President, Learning: RON BORDESSA
Vice-President, Operations and Learning Support: DAN TULIP
Executive Assistant to the President: DEBORAH NYBERG
University Librarian: DANA MCFARLAND
Number of students: 2,300

DEANS

School of Business: ERIC WEST
Organizational Leadership and Learning Division: GERALD NIXON
Peace and Conflict Studies Division: JAMES BAYER
Science, Technology and Environment Division: STEVE GRUNDY

RYERSON UNIVERSITY

350 Victoria St, Toronto, ON M5B 2K3
Telephone: (416) 979-5000
Fax: (416) 979-5221
E-mail: info@ryerson.ca
Internet: www.ryerson.ca

Founded 1948 as Ryerson Institute of Technology; became Ryerson Polytechnical Institute 1964 and Ryerson Polytechnic University 1993; present name 2001
Provincial control
Language of instruction: English
Academic year: September to April

Chancellor: J. C. EATON
President and Vice-Chancellor: C. LAJEUNESSE
Provost and Vice-President (Academic): Dr ERROL ASPEVIG
Vice-President (Administration): L. GRAYSON
Vice-Provost (Faculty Affairs): MICHAEL DEWSON
Vice-President (University Advancement): A. KAHAN
Associate Vice-President (Academic): Dr JUDITH SANDYS
Registrar: KEITH ALNWICK
Chief Librarian: CATHY MATTHEWS

Number of teachers: 528
Number of students: 15,287 (full-time)

Publications: *Annual Report*, *Forum*, *The Ryerson Magazine*

DEANS

Faculty of Arts: Dr CARLA CASSIDY
Faculty of Business: TOM KNOWLTON
Faculty of Communication and Design: Dr IRA LEVINE (acting)
Faculty of Community Services: Dr SUE WILLIAMS
Faculty of Engineering and Applied Science: Dr STALIN BOCTOR
School of Continuing Education: M. BOOTH

HEADS OF DEPARTMENTS/SCHOOLS

Arts:
School of Arts and Contemporary Studies: MARK LOVEWELL
School of Business and Technical Communication: Dr S. CODY
School of Economics: Dr I. BRYAN
School of English: J. COOK
School of Fashion: LINDA LEWIS
School of French: K. KELLETT-BETSOS
School of Geographic Analysis: Dr P. COPPACK
School of Graphic Communications Management: M. BLACK
School of History: R. STAGG
School of Image Arts: B. DAMUDE
School of Interior Design: L. SCOTT-WEBBER
School of Journalism: V. CARLIN
School of Philosophy: A. HUNTER
School of Politics and Public Administration: Dr C. MOOERS
School of Psychology: G. SWEDE
School of Radio and Television Arts: R. TUCKER
School of Sociology: M. POMERANCE
Theatre School: P. SCHNEIDERMAN

Business:
School of Business Management: P. LUK
School of Hospitality and Tourism Management: K. PENNY
School of Information Technology Management: J. NORRIE
School of Retail Management: Dr R. MORLEY

Community Services:
School of Child and Youth Care: Dr C. STUART
School of Early Childhood Education: D. SHIPLEY
School of Environmental Health: Dr T. SLY
School of Health Services Management: W. ISAAC
School of Midwifery: J. ROGERS
School of Nutrition, Consumer and Family Studies: J. WELSH
School of Nursing: K. TUCKER-SCOTT
School of Social Work: Dr S. SILVER
School of Urban and Regional Planning: Dr J. MARS

Engineering and Applied Science:
School of Aerospace Engineering: Dr K. BEHDINAN
School of Applied Chemical and Biological Sciences: Dr C. EVANS
School of Architectural Science and Landscape Architecture: G. KOLIOS
School of Chemical Engineering: Dr A. LOHI
School of Civil Engineering: Dr S. EASA
School of Electrical Engineering: C. STOUTE
School of Industrial Engineering: Dr L. FANG
School of Mathematics, Physics and Computer Science: A. LAN
School of Mechanical Engineering: Dr L. FANG

ATTACHED INSTITUTIONS

Centre for Entrepreneurship Education and Research: Dir (vacant).

Centre for the Study of Commercial Activity: Dir Dr K. JONES.

ST FRANCIS XAVIER UNIVERSITY

POB 5000, Antigonish, NS B2G 2W5
Telephone: (902) 867-3931
Fax: (902) 867-5153
E-mail: pr@stfx.ca
Internet: www.stfx.ca

Founded 1853
Language of instruction: English
Academic year: September to May

Chancellor: Most Rev. RAYMOND LAHEY
President: Dr SEAN E. RILEY
Vice-President (Academic Affairs): Dr RON JOHNSON
Vice-President (Administration): RAMSAY DUFF
Vice-President (Student Services): JANA LUKER
Vice-President (University Advancement): PETER FARDY
Vice-President and Director of Coady International Institute: M. COYLE
Director of University Extension: R. WEHRELL
Registrar: J. STARK
Librarian: LYNNE MURPHY

Library: see Libraries and Archives
Number of teachers: 200
Number of students: 5,200 (4,200 full-time, 1,000 part-time)

Publications: *Antigonish Review* (literary), *Xavieran Annual*, *Xavieran Weekly*

DEANS

Faculty of Arts: M. MCGILLIVRAY
Faculty of Science: E. MCALDUFF

PROFESSORS

ANDERSON, A., Earth Sciences
AQUINO, M., Chemistry
ASPIN, M., Modern Languages
BALDNER, S., Philosophy
BELTRAMI, H., Earth Sciences
BECK, J., Chemistry
BERNARD, I., Education
BICKERTON, J., Political Science
BIGELOW, A., Psychology
BILEK, L., Human Kinetics
BROOKS, G. P., Psychology
BUCKLAND-NICKS, J., Biology
CALLAGHAN, T., Psychology
CLANCY, P., Political Science
DEMONT, E., Biology
DEN HEYER, K., Psychology
DOSSA, S. A., Political Science
DUNCAN, C. M., Business Administration
EDWARDS, J., Psychology
EL-SHEIKH, S., Economics
GALLANT, C. D., Mathematics, Statistics and Computer Science
GALLANT, L., Business Administration
GALLANT, M., Human Kinetics
GARBARY, D., Biology

GERGE, A., Music
GERRIETS, M., Economics
GILLIS, A., Nursing
GRANT, J., Education
GRENIER, Y., Political Science
HARRISON, J. F., Political Science
HENKE, P., Psychology
HOGAN, M. P., History
HOLLOWAY, S., Political Science
HUNTER, D., Physics
JACKSON, W., Sociology and Anthropology
JACONO, J., Nursing
JAN, N., Physics
JOHNSON, R. W., Psychology
KLAPSTEIN, D., Chemistry
KOCAY, V., Modern Languages
LANGILLE, E., Modern Languages
LIENGME, B., Chemistry
MCALDUFF, E., Chemistry
MACCAULL, W., Mathematics, Statistics and Computer Science
MACDONALD, B., Religious Studies
MACDONALD, M. Y., Religious Studies
MACEACHERN, A., Mathematics, Statistics and Computer Science
MACFARLANE, E., Nursing
MCGILLIVRAY, M., English
MACINNES, D., Sociology and Anthropology
MADDEN, R. F., Business Administration
MARAGONI, G., Chemistry
MARQUIS, P., English
MARSHALL, W. S., Biology
MELCHIN, M., Earth Sciences
MENSCH, J., Philosophy
MILNER, P., English
MURPHY, J. B., Earth Sciences
NACZK, M., Human Nutrition
NASH, R., Sociology and Anthropology
NEWSOME, G. E., Biology
NILSEN, K., Celtic Studies
NORRIS, J., Education
ORR, J., Education
PALEPU, R., Chemistry
PHILLIPS, P., History
PHYNE, J., Anthropology and Sociology
QUIGLEY, A., Adult Education
QUINN, J., Mathematics, Statistics and Computer Science
QUINN, W. R., Engineering
RASMUSSEN, R., Human Kinetics
SCHUEGRAF, E. J., Mathematics, Statistics and Computer Science
SEYMOUR, N., Biology
SMITH, D., English
SMITH, G., Music
SMITH-PALMER, T., Chemistry
STANLEY-BLACKWELL, L., History
STEINITZ, M. O., Physics
SWEET, W., Philosophy
TAYLOR, J., English
TRITES, G., Information Systems
WALLBANK, B., Physics
WANG, P., Mathematics, Statistics and Computer Science
WEHRELL, R., Extension
WILPUTTE, E., English
WOOD, D., English
WRIGHT, E., Psychology

ATTACHED INSTITUTE

Coady International Institute: POB 5000, Antigonish, NS B2G 2W5; tel. (902) 867-3960; f. 1959; runs leadership and organization development programs with peoples of Third World countries; diploma and certificate courses in Canada, also training courses and projects overseas; library of 7,000 vols, 90 periodicals; Dir M. COYLE; publ. *Newsletter* (2 a year).

UNIVERSITÉ SAINTE-ANNE

Church Point, NS B0W 1M0
Telephone: (902) 769-2114
Fax: (902) 769-2930
E-mail: admission@ustanne.ednet.ns.ca
Internet: www.usainteanne.ca

Founded 1890
Language of instruction: French
Academic year: September to April

Chancellor: JEAN-LOUIS ROY
President: Dr ANDRÉ ROBERGE
Vice-President (Academic): Dr NEIL BOUCHER
Registrar: MURIELLE COMEAU
Librarian: CÉCILE POTHIER-COMEAU

Library of 84,000 vols
Number of teachers: 37
Number of students: 400
Publication: *Port Acadie* (annually)

HEADS OF DEPARTMENTS

Commerce: CAROLINE THÉRIAULT
Education: Dr MIREILLE BAULU-MACWILLIE
English: Dr JAMES QUINLAN
Extension: Dr BETTY DUGAS
French: Dr MAURICE LAMOTHE
French Immersion: JOANNE BIRON
Humanities: ALBERT DUGAS
Science: ALAIN CHABOT

ATTACHED INSTITUTES

Acadian Research Center: Dir Dr GÉRALD BOUDREAU.

Provincial Resources Center: Dir JEAN-LOUIS ROBICHAUD.

Centre Yves Beauchênes: Dir CÉCILE POTHIER-COMEAU.

Centre Jodrey: Dir RONNIE ROBICHAUD.

SAINT MARY'S UNIVERSITY

923 Robie St, Halifax, NS B3H 3C3
Telephone: (902) 420-5400
E-mail: public.affairs@smu.ca
Internet: www.smu.ca

Founded 1802
Academic year: September to May

Chancellor: Archbishop TERRENCE PRENDERGAST
Vice-Chancellor: Rev. CLAUDE CHAMPAGNE
President: J. COLIN DODDS
Vice-President (Academic and Research): Dr TERRY MURPHY
Vice-President (Administration): GABRIELLE MORRISON
Vice President (Finance): LARRY CORRIGAN
Registrar: Dr ELIZABETH A. CHARD
Librarian: MADELEINE LEFEBVRE

Number of teachers: 525
Number of students: 8,535 (6,309 full-time, 2,230 part-time)

DEANS

Faculty of Arts: Dr ESTHER E. ENNS
Faculty of Science: Dr DAVID RICHARDSON
Faculty of Graduate Studies and Research: Dr KEVIN VESSEY (acting)
Sobey School of Business: Dr AL MICIAK

PROFESSORS

AMIRKHALKHAI, S., Economics
ARYA, P. L., Economics
BARRETT, G., Sociology
BOWLBY, P., Religious Studies
BOYLE, W. P., Engineering
CATANO, V. M., Psychology
CHAMARD, J. C., Management
CHARLES, A., Finance and Management Science
CHENG, T., Accounting
CHESLEY, G. R., Accounting
CHRISTIANSEN-RUFFMAN, L., Sociology and Women's Studies
CLARKE, D., Astronomy and Physics
CONE, D., Biology
DAR, A., Economics
DARLEY, J., Psychology
DAS, H., Management
DAVIS, S., Anthropology
DEUPREE, R., Astronomy and Physics
DIXON, P., Finance and Management Science
DOAK, E. J., Economics
DODDS, J. C., Finance and Management Science
DOSTAL, J., Geology
ELSON, C., Chemistry
EMMS, R., Modern Languages and Classics
ERICKSON, P. A., Anthropology
FARRELL, A., Modern Languages and Classics
FITZGERALD, P., Management
GORMAN, B., Accounting
GUENTHER, D., Astronomy and Physics
HAIGH, E., History
HARTNELL, B., Mathematics and Computing Science
HARVEY, A., Economics
HILL, K., Psychology
HOWELL, C. D., History and Atlantic Canada Studies
KATZ, W., English
KELLOWAY, K., Management and Psychology
KIANG, M.-J., Mathematics and Computing Science
KIM, C., Marketing
KONAPASKY, R., Psychology
LANDES, R., Political Science
LARSEN, M. J., English
LEE, E., Finance and Management Science
LINGRAR, P., Mathematics and Computing Science
MCCALLA, R., Geography
MACDONALD, M., Economics and Women's Studies
MACDONALD, R. A., English
MCGEE, H., Anthropology
MCMULLEN, J., Sociology
MICIAK, A., Marketing
MILLAR, H., Finance and Management Science
MILLS, A., Management
MILLWARD, H., Geography
MITCHELL, G., Astronomy and Physics
MORRISON, J. H., History and Asian Studies
MUIR, P., Mathematics
MUKHOPADHYAY, A. K., Economics
MURPHY, J., Religious Studies
OWEN, V., Geology
PARKER, R., English
PENDSE, S., Management
PE-PIPER, G., Geology
RAND, J., Biology
REID, J. G., History, Atlantic Canada Studies
RICHARDSON, D. H. S., Biology
SASTRY, V., Engineering
SEAMEN, A., English
SIDDIQUI, Q., Geology
STRONGMAN, D., Biology and Forensic Science
SWINGLER, D., Engineering
TARNAWSKI, V., Engineering
THOMAS, G., English
TURNER, D. G., Astronomy and Physics
TWOMEY, R. J., History
VAUGHAN, K., Chemistry
VELTMEYER, H., Sociology, International Development Studies
VESSEY, K., Biology
WAGAR, T., Management
WEIN, S., Philosophy
YOUNG, N., Accounting

UNIVERSITY OF SASKATCHEWAN

105 Administration Place, Saskatoon, SK S7N 5A2
Telephone: (306) 966-1212
Fax: (306) 966-6730
E-mail: askus@usask.ca
Internet: www.usask.ca

Founded 1907; two-campus institution 1967 (Saskatoon and Regina). Legislation was passed in 1974 creating two separate Universities
State control

Language of instruction: English
Academic year: September to August

President and Chancellor: R. P. MacKinnon
Provost and Vice-President (Academic): M. Atkinson
Vice-President (Finance and Resources): A. J. Whitworth
Vice-President (Research): S. E. Franklin
University Secretary: G. Barnhart
Registrar: K. McInnes
Librarian: F. Winter

Number of teachers: 1,091
Number of students: 20,113

Publication: *Calendar* (annually, online Calendar updated 2 a year)

DEANS

College of Agriculture: E. M. Barber
College of Arts and Science: J. R. Dillon
College of Commerce: G. E Isaac
College of Dentistry: G. S. Uswak (acting)
College of Education: C. Reynolds
College of Engineering: C. Laguë
College of Graduate Studies and Research: T. B. Wishart
College of Kinesiology: C. Rodgers
College of Law: B. Cotter
College of Medicine: W. L. Albritton
College of Nursing: J. Sawatzky (acting)
College of Pharmacy and Nutrition: D. K. Gorecki (acting)
College of Veterinary Medicine: C. S. Rhodes
College of Extension Studies: W. Archer

DIRECTOR

School of Physical Therapy: E. L. Harrison

PROFESSORS AND HEADS OF DEPARTMENT

Adams, G. P., Veterinary Biomedical Sciences
Akkerman, A., Geography
Albritton, W. L., Paediatrics
Allen, A. L., Veterinary Pathology
Altman, M., Economics (Head)
Anderson, A. B., Sociology
Anderson, D. W., Soil Science
Angel, J. F., Biochemistry
Ansdell, K. M., Geological Sciences (Head)
Archer, W., Extension
Archibold, O. W., Geography
Atkinson, M., Political Studies
Axworthy, C. S., Law
Babiuk, L. A., Veterinary Microbiology
Bailey, J. V., Large Animal Clinical Sciences
Baker, C. G., Dentistry
Baranski, A. S., Chemistry
Barber, E. M., Agricultural and Bioresource Engineering
Barber, S. M., Large Animal Clinical Sciences
Barbour, S. L., Civil Engineering (Head)
Barclay, R., Agricultural and Bioresource Engineering
Barth, A. D., Large Animal and Clinical Sciences
Basinger, J. F., Geological Sciences
Battiste, M., Educational Foundations
Bell, K. T. M., Art and Art History
Bell, L. S., Art and Art History
Berenbaum, S. L., Nutrition and Dietetics
Bergstrom, D. J., Mechanical Engineering
Bettany, J. R., Soil Science
Bickis, M. G., Mathematics and Statistics
Bidwell, P. M., English (Head)
Bilson, R. E., Law
Bingham, W., Paediatrics (Head)
Blackshaw, S. L., Psychiatry
Blakley, B. R., Veterinary Biomedical Sciences (Head)
Bolton, R. J., Electrical Engineering
Bond, D. J., Languages and Linguistics
Bonham-Smith, P. C., Biology
Borsa, J., Women's and Gender Studies (Head)
Bortolotti, G. R., Biology
Bowden, M. A., Law
Bowen, R. C., Psychiatry
Boyd, C. W., Management and Marketing (Head)
Brawley, L., Kinesiology
Bremner, M., Mathematics and Statistics
Brenna, D. S., Drama (Acting Head)
Bretscher, P. A., Microbiology and Immunology
Brooke, J. A., Mathematics and Statistics
Brown, F. B., Curriculum Studies
Brown, W. J., Agricultural Economics
Brown, Y. M. R., Nursing
Browne, P. J., Mathematics and Statistics
Buchanan, F. C., Animal and Poultry Science
Bunt, R. B., Computer Science
Burbridge, B., Medical Imaging (Head)
Burnell, P., History
Burton, R. T., Mechanical Engineering
Calder, R. L., English
Campbell, D. C., Anaesthesia (Head)
Campbell, J., Psychology
Campbell, J. R., Veterinary Large Animal Science
Card, C. E., Veterinary Large Animal Science
Card, R. T., Medicine
Carter, Jr, J. A., Computer Science
Caulkett, N. A., Small Animal Clinical Sciences
Chad, K., Kinesiology
Chapman, D., Anatomy and Cell Biology
Chartrand, P., Law
Chedrese, P. J., Obstetrics, Gynaecology and Reproductive Sciences
Chibbar, R. N., Plant Sciences
Chilton, N., Biology
Chirino-Trejo, J. M., Veterinary Microbiology
Chivers, D. P., Biology
Classen, H. L., Animal and Poultry Science
Cockcroft, D. W., Medicine
Collins, M., Educational Foundations
Cooley, R. W., English
Cooper-Stephenson, K. D., Law
Corcoran, M., Anatomy and Cell Biology
Cotter, W. B., Law
Cotton, D. J., Medicine
Coulman, B. E., Soil Science (Head)
Crone, L. A., Anaesthesia
Crossley, D. J., Philosophy
Crowe, T. G., Agricultural and Bioresource Engineering
Csapo, G., Music
Cuming, R. C. C., Law
Cushman, D. O., Economics
Dalai, A. K., Chemical Engineering
D'Arcy, C., Psychiatry
Davis, A. R., Biology
Davis, G. R., Physics and Engineering Physics
Dayton, E. B., Philosophy
de Boer, D. H., Geography
Delbaere, L. T. J., Biochemistry
Denham, W. P., English
Denis, W. B., Sociology
Desautels, M., Physiology
Deutscher, T. B., History
Devon, R. M., Anatomy and Cell Biology
Dick, R., Physics and Engineering Physics
Dickinson, H. D., Sociology (Head)
Dickson, G., Nursing
Dillon, J. R., Biology
Dodds, D. E., Electrical Engineering
Donat, J. R., Medicine
Dooley, P. C., Economics
Dosman, J. A., Medicine
Doucette, J. R., Anatomy and Cell Biology (Acting Head)
Dowling, P. M., Veterinary Biomedical Sciences
Duke, T., Small Animal Clinical Sciences
Dust, W., Surgery
Dwyer, P. M., Philosophy
Dyck, L. E., Psychiatry
Dyck, R. F., Medicine
Eager, D. L., Computer Science
Echevarria, E. C., Economics
Ellis, J. A., Veterinary Microbiology
England, G. J., Industrial Relations and Organization Behaviour
Ervin, A. M., Religious Studies and Anthropology
Fairbairn, B. T., History
Faried, S. O., Electrical Engineering
Farrow, C. S., Small Animal Clinical Sciences
Faulkner, R. A., Kinesiology
Ferguson, L. M., Nursing
Findlay, L. M., English
Flannigan, R. D., Law
Flynn, M., Educational Psychology and Special Education
Foldvari, M., Pharmacy
Forsyth, G. W., Veterinary Biomedical Sciences
Fowler, D. B., Plant Sciences
Fowler-Kerry, S. E., Nursing
Franklin, S., Geography
Fudge, J., Law
Fulton, M. E., Agricultural Economics
Furtan, W. H., Agricultural Economics
Gambell, T. J., Curriculum Studies
Gander, R. E., Electrical Engineering
George, G. N., Geological Sciences
Germida, J. J., Soil Science
Gingell, S. A., English
Goldie, H. A., Microbiology and Immunology
Gopalakrishnan, V., Pharmacology
Gordon, J. R., Veterinary Microbiology
Gorecki, D. K. J., Pharmacy
Graham, B. L., Medicine
Grahn, B. H., Small Animal Clinical Sciences
Grant, P. R., Psychology
Grassmann, W. K., Computer Science
Gray, R. S., Agricultural Economics (Head)
Greer, J. E., Computer Science
Griebel, R. W., Surgery
Gusta, L. V., Plant Sciences
Gusthart, J. L., Kinesiology
Gutwin, C., Computer Science
Haig Bartley, P. M., Drama
Haigh, J. C., Veterinary Large Animal Sciences
Haines, D. M., Veterinary Microbiology
Haines, L. P., Educational Psychology and Special Education
Hamilton, D. L., Veterinary Biomedical Sciences
Handy, J. R., History
Harding, A. J., English
Harris, D. I., Music
Harris, R. L., English
Harrison, E. L., Physical Therapy (Head)
Harvey, B. L., Plant Sciences
Haug, M. D., Civil and Geological Engineering
Hayes, S. J., Microbiology and Immunology
Hemmings, S. J., Medicine
Henderson, J. R., English
Hendry, M. J., Geological Sciences
Hertz, P. B., Mechanical Engineering
Hiebert, L. M., Veterinary Biomedical Sciences
Hill, G. A., Chemical Engineering
Hirose, A., Physics and Engineering Physics
Hobbs, J. E., Agricultural Economics
Hoeppner, V. H., Medicine
Holm, F. A., Plant Sciences
Hoover, J. N., Dentistry
Howard, S. P., Microbiology and Immunology
Howe, E. C., Economics
Hubbard, J. W., Pharmacy
Huci, P. J., Plant Sciences
Hull, P. R., Medicine
Hurst, T. S., Medicine
Ingledew, W. M., Applied Microbiology and Food Science
Irvine, D., Family Medicine
Ish, D., Law
Jackson, M. L., Veterinary Pathology

JELINSKI, M. D., Large Animal Clinical Sciences
JOHNSTON, G. H. F., Surgery
JUURLINK, B. H. J., Anatomy and Cell Biology
KALAGNANAM, S. S., Accounting (Head)
KALRA, J., Pathology
KASAP, S. O., Electrical Engineering
KASIAN, G. F., Paediatrics
KEIL, J. M., Computer Science
KEITH, R. G., Surgery (Head)
KELLY, I. W., Educational Psychology and Special Education
KENT, C. A., History (Acting Head)
KERR, W. A., Agricultural Economics
KERRICH, R. W., Geological Sciences
KHACHATOURIANS, G. G., Applied Microbiology and Food Science (Head)
KHANDELWAL, R. L., Medical Biochemistry (Head)
KIRK, A., Medicine
KOLB, N. R., Physics and Engineering Physics
KOLBINSON, D. A., Diagnostic and Surgical Sciences
KONCHAK, P. A., Dentistry
KORDAN, B., Political Studies
KORINEK, V. J., History
KOUSTOV, A. V., Physics and Engineering Physics
KREYSZIG, W. K., Music
KRONE, P. H., Anatomy and Cell Biology
KUHLMANN, F.-V., Mathematics and Statistics
KUHLMANN, S., Mathematics and Statistics
KULSHRESHTHA, S. N., Agricultural Economics
KULYK, W. M., Anatomy and Cell Biology
KUSALIK, A. J., Computer Science
KUSHWAHA, R. L., Agricultural and Bioresource Engineering
LAARVELD, B., Animal and Poultry Science (Head)
LAFERTÉ, S., Biochemistry
LAGUË, C., Agricultural and Bioresource Engineering
LEE, J. S., Biochemistry
LEHMKUHL, D. M., Biology
LEIGHTON, F. A., Veterinary Pathology (Head)
LEPNURM, R., Management and Marketing (Head)
LI, P. S., Sociology
LI, X. M., Psychiatry
LINDSAY, W. D., Accounting
LIVINGSTON, A., Veterinary Biomedical Sciences
LLEWELLYN, E. J., Physics and Engineering Physics
LOH, L. C., Medical Biochemistry
LONG, R. J., Industrial Relations and Organization Behaviour
LOW, N. H., Applied Microbiology and Food Science
LOWRY, N., Paediatrics
LUCAS, R. F., Economics
MAAKA, R., Native Studies (Head)
MCCALLA, G. I., Computer Science
MACDONALD, M. B., Nursing
MACDOUGALL, B., Native Studies
MACKINNON, J. C., History
MACKINNON, R. P., Law
MACLENNAN, J., Engineering
MCCROSKY, C., Electrical Engineering
MCKAY, G., Pharmacy (Head)
MACKINNON, R. P., Law
MCKINNON, J. J., Animal and Poultry Science
MCLENNAN, B. D., Biochemistry
MCMULLEN, L. M., Psychology (Head)
MCNEILL, D., Music (Head)
MAJEWSKI, M., Chemistry
MANSON, A. H., Physics and Engineering Physics
MAPLETOFT, R. J., Large Animal and Clinical Sciences
MARCINIUK, D. D., Medicine
MARKEN, R. N. G., English
MARSHALL, M., Mathematics and Statistics
MARTIN, J. R., Mathematics and Statistics
MARTZ, L. W., Geography
MATHESON, T. J., English
MAULÉ, C. P., Agricultural and Bioresource Engineering
MEHTA, M. D., Sociology
MERRIAM, J. B., Geological Sciences
MESSIER, F., Biology
MEYER, D. A., Archaeology
MICHELMANN, H. J., Political Studies
MIDDLETON, D., Veterinary Pathology (Head)
MIKET, M. J., Mathematics and Statistics
MILLER, J. R., History
MISRA, V., Veterinary Microbiology
MOEWES, A., Physics and Engineering Physics
MONTURE, P. A., Sociology
MOULDING, M. B., Restorative and Prosthetic Dentistry
MUIR, G. D., Veterinary Biomedical Sciences
MULLENS, J. G., Religious Studies and Anthropology (Head)
NEAL, B. R., Biology
NEUFELD, E. M., Computer Science
NOBLE, B. F., Geography
NORMAN, K. E., Law
OLATUNBOSUN, O. A., Obstetrics, Gynaecology and Reproductive Sciences (Head)
OVSENEK, N. C., Anatomy and Cell Biology
PACKOTA, G. V., Dentistry
PAN, Y., Geological Sciences
PARKINSON, D. J., English
PARTRIDGE, M. D., Agricultural Economics
PATERSON, P. G., Nutrition and Dietetics
PATTERSON, W., Geology
PATO, M. D., Medical Biochemistry
PATRICK, G. W., Mathematics and Statistics
PAWLOVICH, W. E., Educational Psychology and Special Education (Head)
PEDRAS, M. S. C., Chemistry
PENG, D.-Y., Chemical Engineering
PENNOCK, D. J., Soil Science
PETERNELJ-TAYLOR, C. A., Nursing
PETRIE, L., Veterinary Large Animal Sciences
PFEIFER, K., Philosophy
PHARR, J. W., Veterinary Anaesthesiology, Small Animal Clinical Sciences
PHILLIPS, B., Management and Marketing
PHILLIPS, F., Accounting
PHILLIPS, P. W. B., Political Studies
PIERSON, R. A., Obstetrics, Gynaecology and Reproductive Sciences
POLLEY, L. R., Veterinary Microbiology
POMEROY, J., Geography
POOLER, J. A., Geography
POPKIN, D. R., Obstetrics, Gynaecology and Reproductive Sciences
POST, K., Small Animal Clinical Sciences (Head)
PRATT, B. R., Geological Sciences
PROCTOR, L. F., Curriculum Studies
PUGSLEY, T. S., Chemical Engineering (Head)
PYWELL, R. E., Physics and Engineering Physics (Head)
QUALTIERE, L. F., Pathology
QUIGLEY, T. L., Law
RALPH, E. G., Curriculum Studies
RANGACHARYULU, C., Physics and Engineering Physics
RANK, G. H., Biology
RAWLINGS, N. C., Veterinary Biomedical Sciences
REED, M. G., Geography
REEDER, B. A., Community Health and Epidemiology (Head)
REEVES, M. J., Geological Sciences
REGNIER, R. H., Educational Foundations
RELKE, D., Women's and Gender Studies
REMILLARD, A. J., Pharmacy
RENAUT, R. W., Geological Sciences
RENIHAN, P. J., Educational Administration
REYNOLDS, C., Educational Administration
RHODES, C. S., Large Animal Clinical Sciences
RICHARDSON, J. S., Pharmacology
RINGNESS, C. O., Art and Art History (Acting Head)
ROESLER, W. J., Biochemistry
ROMANCHUK, K. G., Ophthalmology (Head)
ROMO, J. T., Plant Sciences
ROSAASEN, K. A., Agricultural Economics
ROSENBERG, A. M., Paediatrics
ROSSER, B. W. C., Anatomy and Cell Biology
ROSSNAGEL, B. G., Crop Development Centre
ROWLAND, G. G., Plant Sciences
RUDACHYK, L., Physical Medicine and Rehabilitation (Head)
RUTLEDGE HARDING, S., Pathology
SACKNEY, L. E., Educational Administration
ST LOUIS, L. V., Economics
SALT, J. E., Electrical Engineering
SANKARAN, K., Physical Medicine and Rehabilitation
SARKAR, A. K., Management and Marketing
SAWATZKY, J. E., Nursing
SAWHNEY, V. K., Biology
SAXENA, A., Microbiology
SCHISSEL, B., Sociology
SCHMUTZ, S. M., Animal and Poultry Science
SCHOENAU, G. J., Mechanical Engineering
SCHONEY, R. A., Agricultural Economics
SCHREYER, D., Anatomy and Cell Biology
SCHWIER, R. A., Curriculum Studies
SCOLES, G. J., Plant Sciences
SEMCHUK, K. M., Nursing
SHANTZ, S., Art and Art History
SHARMA, R. K., Pathology
SHERIDAN, D. P., Medicine
SHEVCHUK, Y. M., Pharmacy
SHMON, C. L., Small Animal Clinical Sciences
SHOKER, A., Medicine
SIBLEY, J. T., Medicine
SINGH, B., Veterinary Biomedical Sciences
SINGH, J., Veterinary Biomedical Sciences
SINHA, B. M., Religious Studies
SMART, M. E., Small Animal Clinical Sciences
SMITH, B. L., Nursing
SMITH, D. J., Curriculum Studies
SMOLYAKOV, A., Physics and Engineering Physics
SOFKO, G. J., Physics and Engineering Physics
SOKALSKI, A. A., Languages and Linguistics
SOTEROS, C. E., Mathematics and Statistics
SPARKS, G. A., Civil and Geological Engineering
SPINK, K. S., Kinesiology
SPRIGINGS, E. J. C., Kinesiology
SRINIVASON, R., Mathematics and Statistics
STEELE, T. G., Physics and Engineering Physics
STEER, R. P., Chemistry
STEEVES, J. S., Political Studies
STEPHANSON, R. A., English
STEPHENSON, J. W., Mathematics and Statistics
STEWART, L., History
STEWART, N. J., Nursing
STOICHEFF, R. P., English
STOOKEY, J. M., Veterinary Large Animal Sciences
STORY, D. C., Political Studies (Head)
SULAKHE, P. V., Physiology
SUTHERLAND, J. K., Restorative and Prosthetic Dentistry
SUVEGES, L. G., Pharmacy
SZMIGIELSKI, J., Mathematics and Statistics
SZYSZKOWSKI, W., Mechanical Engineering
TAKAYA, K., Electrical Engineering (Head)
TANNOUS, G. F., Finance and Management Science (Head)
TAYLOR, S. M., Small Animal Clinical Sciences
TEMPIER, R., Psychiatry (Head)
TEPLITSKY, P. E., Restorative and Prosthetic Dentistry
THACKER, P. A., Animal and Poultry Science
THOMLINSON, W., Physics and Engineering Physics
THOMPSON, D. G., Extension
THOMPSON, V. A., Psychology

THORNHILL, J. A., Physiology
THORPE, D. J., English (Head)
TOWNSEND, H. G. G., Veterinary Internal Medicine
TREMBLAY, J. P., Computer Science
TREMBLAY, M., Kinesiology
TYLER, R. T., Applied Microbiology and Food Science (Head)
TYMCHATYN, E. D., Mathematics and Statistics
VAN REES, K. C. J., Soil Science
VANDENBERG, A., Plant Sciences
VANDERVORT, L. A., Law
VERGE, V. M. K., Anatomy and Cell Biology
VON BAEYER, C. L., Psychology
WAISER, W. A., History
WALDRAM, J. B., Psychology
WALKER, E. G., Anthropology and Archaeology (Head)
WALKER, K. D., Educational Administration
WALLEY, F. L., Soil Science
WALTZ, W. L., Chemistry
WALZ, W., Physiology (Head)
WANG, R., Physiology
WARD, A., Curriculum Studies
WARD, D. E., Chemistry
WARRINGTON, R. C., Biochemistry
WASON-ELLAM, L., Curriculum Studies
WATSON, L. G., Mechanical Engineering
WAYGOOD, E. B., Biochemistry
WEST, N. H., Physiology
WETZEL, K. W., Industrial Relations and Organizational Behaviour
WHITE, G. N., Family Medicine
WHITING, S. J., Nutrition and Dietetics (Head)
WICKETT, R. E. Y., Educational Foundations
WILSON, D. G., Veterinary Large Animal Sciences (Head)
WILSON, T. W., Medicine (Head)
WISHART, T. B., Psychology
WOBESER, G. A., Veterinary Pathology
WONG, A. T., Extension
WOODHOUSE, H., Educational Foundations
WORMITH, J. S., Psychology
WOROBETZ, L. J., Medicine
WOTHERSPOON, T. L., Sociology
XIAO, C., Physics and Engineering Physics
XIAO, W., Microbiology and Immunology (Head)
YAGER, J. Y. Y., Paediatrics
YANNACOPOULOS, S., Mechanical Engineering
YONG-HING, K., Surgery
YU, P. H., Psychiatry
ZHANG, C., Mechanical Engineering
ZICHY, F. A., English
ZIOLA, B., Microbiology and Immunology

FEDERATED COLLEGE

St Thomas More College: 1437 College Drive, Saskatoon, SK. S7N 0W6; Pres. Rev G. SMITH.

AFFILIATED COLLEGES

Briercrest College: 510 College Dr., Caronport, SK S0H 0S0; Pres. Rev. D. UGLEM.

Central Pentecostal College: 1303 Jackson Ave, Saskatoon, SK S7H 2M9; Pres. Rev. D. STILLER.

College of Emmanuel and St Chad: 1337 College Drive, Saskatoon, SK S7N 0W6; Principal Rev. W. D. DELLER.

Gabriel Dumont College: Exec. Dir C. RACETTE.

Lutheran Theological Seminary: 114 Seminary Crescent, Saskatoon, SK S7N 0X3; Pres. D. E. BUCK.

St Andrew's College: 1121 College Drive, Saskatoon, SK S7N 0W3; Pres. T. FAULKER.

St Peter's College: Box 10, Muenster, SK S0K 2Y0; Pres. G. KOBUSSEN.

UNIVERSITÉ DE SHERBROOKE

2500 Blvd de l'Université, Sherbrooke, QC J1K 2R1
Telephone: (819) 821-7000
Fax: (819) 821-7966
E-mail: information@courrier.usherb.ca
Internet: www.usherbrooke.ca

Founded 1954
Private control
Language of instruction: French
Academic year: September to May

Chancellor: H. E. Mgr JEAN-MARIE FORTIER (Catholic Archbishop of Sherbrooke)
Rector: BRUNO-MARIE BÉCHARD
Vice-Rector (Administration): LUCE SAMOISETTE
Vice-Rector (Personnel and Students): JEAN DESCLOS
Vice-Rector (Research): EDWIN BOURGET
Vice-Rector (Studies): DENIS MARCEAU
Secretary-General: MARTIN BUTEAU
Registrar: FRANCE MYETTE
Librarian: SYLVIE BELZILE

Library of 1,676,000 vols
Number of teachers: 1,750 (650 full-time, 1,100 part-time)
Number of students: 22,272 (11,259 full-time, 11,013 part-time)

DEANS

Faculty of Administration: ROGER NOËL
Faculty of Applied Science: RICHARD J MARCEAU
Faculty of Education: CÉLINE GARANT
Faculty of Law: LOUIS MARQUIS
Faculty of Letters and Human Sciences: BERNARD CHAPUT
Faculty of Medicine: RÉJEAN HÉBERT
Faculty of Physical and Sport Education: PAUL DESHAIES
Faculty of Science: JEAN GOULET
Faculty of Theology, Ethics and Philosophy: MICHEL DION

PROFESSORS

Faculty of Administration

Accountancy:

BEAUCHESNE, A.
COMTOIS, J.
GODBOUT, R.
JOLIN, M.
LEMIEUX, P.
MENARD, P.
MORIN, R.
MORIN, R. J.
NOËL, R.

Finance:

BEN-AMOR, A.
GARANT, J.-P.
GARNIER, G.
GUÉRIN, F.
PAGE, J.
PRÉFONTAINE, J.
PREZEAU, C.

Management:

BERGERON, J.-L.
COUPAL, M.
LAFLAMME, M.
LEONARD, H.
PETIT, A.
PRÉVOST, P.
ROBIDOUX, J.
ROY, A. F.
TURCOTTE, P.

Marketing:

BOIVIN, Y.
D'ASTOUS, A.
VALENCE, G.

Quantitative Methods:

BASTIN, E.
BEAUDOIN, P.-H.
INGHAM, J.
MALTAIS, G.
THEORET, A.

Faculty of Applied Sciences

Chemical Engineering:

BOULOS, M.
BROADBENT, A. D.
CHORNET, E.
DEKEE, D.
GRAVELLE, D.
JONES, P.
THÉRIEN, N.

Civil Engineering:

AITCIN, P.-C.
BALLIVY, G.
BRUNELLE, P.-E.
GALLEZ, B.
JOHNS, K. C.
LAHOUD, A.
LEFEBVRE, D.
LEFEBVRE, G. A.
LEMIEUX, P.
LUPIEN, C.
MORIN, J.-P.
NARASIAH, S. K.
NEALE, K. W.
ROHAN, K.

Electrical Engineering and Computer Engineering:

ADOUL, J.-P.
AUBÉ, G.
BÉLAND, B.
BOUTIN, N.
DALLE, D.
DELISLE, J.
DENIS, G.
DUVAL, F.
GOULET, R.
LEROUX, A.
MORISSETTE, S.
RICHARD, S.
THIBAULT, R.

Mechanical Engineering:

BOURASSA, P.-A.
GALANIS, N.
LANEVILLE, A.
MASSOUD, M.
MERCADIER, Y.
NICOLAS, J.
PROULX, D.
ROY, C.
VAN HOENACKER, Y.

Faculty of Education

Counselling and School Administration:

DUPONT, P.
LAFLAMME, CL.
LIMOGES, J.
MARCEAU, D.
MASSE, D.
REID, A.

Pedagogy:

CORMIER, R. A.
HARVEY, V.
HIVON, R.
ROBIDAS, G.
SCHOLER, M.
SERRE, F.
STRINGER, G.

Pre-School and Primary Education:

LAFONTAINE, L.
MARTEL, G.
ROY, G.-R.
THÉRIEN, L.

Special Education:

HADE, D.
LEFEBVRE, R.
OTIS, R.
POULIN, G.
RHEAULT, M.
TARDIF, J.

Faculty of Law:

ANCTIL, J.

BERGERON, J.-G.
BLACHE, P.
BOISCLAIR, C L.
CHARRON, C.
CODÈRE, D.
DUBÉ, J.-L.
DUBÉ, M.
GAGNON, J.
KOURI, R.-P.
LAVOIE, J.-M.
MELANSON, J.
PATENAUDE, P.
PEPIN, R.
PHILIPS-NOOTENS, S.
POIRIER, M. Z.
RATTI, N.
TÉTRAULT, R.

Faculty of Letters and Human Sciences

Economics:

ASCAH, L.-G.
BASTIEN, R.
DAUPHIN, R.
HANEL, P.
LARIN, G.-N.
PELLETIER, G.-R.
ROY, G.
WENER, N.

Geography and Remote Sensing:

BONN, F.
CHOQUETTE, R.
DUBOIS, J.-M.
GAGNON, R.
GWYN, H.
MORIN, D.
NADEAU, R.
PAQUETTE, R.
POULIN, A.
POULIOT, M.

Human Sciences:

BLAIS, M.
CHAPUT, B.
CHOTARD, J.-R.
DE BUJANDA, J.-M.
DUMONT, M.
GAGNON, M.
GIROUX, L.
LACHANCE, A.-L.
LAPERRIÈRE, G.
LEGAULT, G.
LUC, L.
VALCKE, L.
VANDAL, G.

Letters and Communications:

BEAUCHEMIN, N.
BONENFANT, J.
DUPUIS, H.
FOREST, J.
GIGUÈRE, R.
GIROUX, R.
HÉBERT, P.
JONES, D.-G.
LÉARD, J.-M.
MALUS, A.
MARTEL, P.
MICHON, J.
PAINCHAUD, L.
SIROIS, A.
SUTHERLAND, R.
THEORET, M.
TREMBLAY, R.
VINET, M. T.

Psychology:

CHARBONNEAU, C L.
LECLERC, G.
L'ECUYER, R.
NORMANDEAU, A.
PAYETTE, M.
ST-ARNAUD, Y.

Social Service:

ALARY, J.
LEFRANÇOIS, R.
MALAVOY, M.

Faculty of Medicine

Anatomy and Cellular Biology:

BRIÈRE, N.
CALVERT, R.
MENARD, D.
NEMIROVSKY, M.-S.
NIGAM, V.-N.

Anaesthesia:

LAMARCHE, Y.
TÉTREAULT, J. P.

Biochemistry:

BASTIN, M.
DE MÉDICIS, M.-E.
DUPUIS, G.
GIBSON, D.
GRANT, A.
LEHOUX, J.-G.
TAN, L.

Biophysics and Physiology:

PAYET, M. D.
RUIZ-PETRICH, E.
SCHANNE, O.
SEUFERT, W. D.

Cardiovascular and Thoracic Surgery:

TEIJEIRA, F. J.

Community Health:

BÉLAND, R.
IGLESIAS, R.
VOBECKY, J.
VOBECKY, J. S.

Diagnostic Radiology:

BRAZEAU-LAMONTAGNE, L.
SCHMUTZ, G.

Family Medicine:

BERNIER, R.
CAUX, R.
GRAND'MAISON, P.

General Surgery:

DEVROEDE, G.
RIOUX, A.

Medicine:

BARON, M., Internal Medicine
BEAUDRY, R., Gastroenterology
BEGIN, R., Pneumology
BELLABARBA, D., Endocrinology
BÉNARD, B., Endocrinology
CÔTÉ, M., Cardiology
DUMAIS, B., Cardiology
HADDAD, H., Gastroenterology
LONGPRÉ, B., Haematology
LUSSIER, A., Rheumatology
MARCOUX, J.-A., Infectious Diseases
MÉNARD, D. B., Gastroenterology
MÉNARD, H., Rheumatology
MONTAMBAULT, P., Nephrology
NAWAR, T., Nephrology
PÉPIN, J.-M., Internal Medicine
PIGEON, G., Nephrology
PLANTE, A., Internal Medicine
PLANTE, G.-E., Nephrology
REIHER, J., Neurology
ROCHON, M., Haematology
ROULEAU, J. L., Cardiology
TÉTREAULT, L., Internal Medicine

Microbiology:

BOURGAUX, D.
BOURGAUX, P.
THIRION, J.-P.
WEBER, J.

Nuclear Medicine and Radiobiology:

JAY-GERIN, J.-P.
SANCHE, L.
VAN LIER, J.

Nursing Sciences:

CHARTIER, L.
LALANCETTE, D.

Obstetrics and Gynaecology:

AINMELK, Y.
BLOUIN, D.
GAGNER, R.

Ophthalmology:

BRUNETTE, J.-R.

Orthopaedic Surgery:

DES MARCHAIS, J. E.

Otorhinolaryngology:

CHARLIN, B.

Pathology:

COTÉ, R. A.
LAMARCHE, J.
MADARNAS, P.
MASSÉ, S.

Paediatrics:

BUREAU, M. A.
LANGLOIS, L.
LEMIEUX, B.
PARÉ, C.
ROLA-PLESZCZYNSKI, M.

Pharmacology:

ESCHER, E.
REGOLI, G.
SIROIS, P.

Faculty of Physical Education and Sport:

BISSONNETTE, R.
CUERRIER, J.-P.
DEMERS, P. J.
DESHAIES, P.
GAUTHIER, P.
LEMIEUX, G.-B.
NADEAU, M.
NADON, R.
OUELLET, J.-G.
QUENNEVILLE, G.
ROY, R.
ROYER, D.
THERRIEN, R.
VANDEN-ABEELE, J.

Faculty of Sciences

Biology:

BEAUDOIN, A.
BEAUMONT, G.
BÉCHARD, P.
BERGERON, J.-M.
CYR, A.
LEBEL, D.
MATTON, P.
MORISSET, J.-A.
O'NEIL, L.-C.
ROBIN, J.

Chemistry:

BANDRAUK, A. D.
BROWN, G. M.
CABANA, A.
DESLONGCHAMPS, P.
GIGUÈRE, J.
JERUMANIS, S.
JOLICOEUR, C.
LESSARD, J.
MÉNARD, H.
MICHEL, A.
PELLETIER, G.-E.
RUEST, L.

Mathematics and Computer Science:

ALLARD, J.
BAZINET, J.
BELLEY, J.-M.
BOUCHER, C.
BRISEBOIS, M.
COLIN, B.
CONSTANTIN, J.
COURTEAU, B.
CUSTEAU, G.
DUBEAU, F.
DUBOIS, J.
FOURNIER, G.
GIROUX, G.
HAGUEL, J.
KRELL, M.
LEDUC, P.-Y.
MORALES, P.

SAINT-DENIS, R.
SAMSON, J.-P.

Physics:

AUBIN, M.
BANVILLE, M.
CAILLÉ, A.
CARLONE, C.
CARON, L. G.
JANDL, S.
LEMIEUX, A.
SIMARD, P.-A.
TREMBLAY, A. M.

Faculty of Theology, Ethics and Philosophy:

BÉDARD, A.
BOISVERT, L.
MELANÇON, L.
OUELLET, F.
RACINE, L.
VACHON, L.
VAILLANCOURT, R.

SIMON FRASER UNIVERSITY

8888 University Drive, Burnaby, BC V5A 1S6
Telephone: (604) 291-3111
E-mail: sfumpr@sfu.ca
Internet: www.sfu.ca*SFU Vancouver*: 515 West Hastings St, Vancouver, BC V6B 5K3
Telephone: (604) 291-5000
Fax: (604) 291-5060
Internet: www.sfu.ca*SFU, Surrey*: 250, 13450 102 Ave, Surrey, BC V3T 2W1
Telephone: (778) 782-7500
Fax: (778) 782-7488
Internet: www.sfu.ca
Founded 1963
Provincial control
Language of instruction: English
Academic year: September to August (3 terms of 4 months each)
Chancellor: Dr BRANDT C. LOUIE
President and Vice-Chancellor: Dr MICHAEL STEVENSON
Academic Vice-President and Provost: Dr J. H. WATERHOUSE
Vice-President for Finance and Administration: P. HIBBITTS
Vice-President for Research: Dr B. M. PINTO
Vice-President for University Relations: Dr W. GILL
Registrar and Senior Director, Enrollment Services: K. ROSS
Dean of Library Services: L. COPELAND
Library of 1,000,000
Number of teachers: 730 (faculty status)
Number of students: 25,000
Publications: *Canadian Journal of Communication* (quarterly), *International History Review* (quarterly), *West Coast Line* (3 a year)

DEANS

Faculty of Applied Sciences: Dr B. S. LEWIS
Faculty of Arts: Dr J. T. PIERCE
Faculty of Business Administration: Dr C. E. LOVE
Faculty of Education: Dr P. SHAKER
Faculty of Science: Dr M. PLISCHKE (acting)
Continuing Studies: Dr J. C. YERBURY
Graduate Studies: Dr J. C. DRIVER

PROFESSORS AND DIRECTORS AND CHAIRMEN OF DEPARTMENT

Dir = Director of Dept, Chair. = Chairman of Dept

Faculty of Applied Sciences (9861 Applied Sciences Building, Burnaby; tel. (604) 291-4724; fax (604) 291-5802; internet fas.sfu.ca):

School of Communication:

ANDERSON, R. S.
GRUNEAU, R.
HACKETT, R. A.
HARASIM, L. M.
KLINE, S.
LABA, M. (Dir)
LEWIS, B. S.
LORIMER, R. M.
RICHARDS, W. D.
TRUAX, B. D.

School of Computing Science:

ATKINS, M. S.
BHATTACHARYA, B. K.
BURTON, F. W.
CAMERON, R. D.
DAHL, V.
DELGRANDE, J. P.
FUNT, B. V.
HADLEY, R. F.
HAN, J. W.
HELL, P.
HOBSON, R. F.
KAMEDA, T.
LI, Z. N. (Dir)
LIESTMAN, A. L.
LUK, W. S.
PETERS, J. G.
POPOWICH, F.
SHERMER, T. C.
YANG, Q.

School of Engineering Science:

BIRD, J. S.
BOLOGNESI, C. R.
CAVERS, J. K.
CHAPMAN, G. H.
DILL, J. C.
GRUVER, W. A.
GUPTA, K. K.
HARDY, R. H. S.
HO, P. K. M.
HOBSON, R. F.
JONES, J. D.
LEUNG, A. M.
PARAMESWARAN, M.
PAYANDEH, S.
RAWICZ, A. H.
SAIF, M. (Dir)
STAPLETON, S. P.
SYRZYCKI, M.

School of Kinesiology:

BAWA, P. N. S.
DICKINSON, J.
FINEGOOD, D. T.
GOODMAN, D.
HOFFER, J. A.
MACKENZIE, C. L.
MACLEAN, D. R.
MARTENIUK, R. G.
MORRISON, J. B. (Dir)
PARKHOUSE, W. S.
ROSIN, M.
TIBBITS, G.

School of Resource and Environmental Management Programme:

DE LA MERE, W. K.
GILL, A. M.
GOBAS, F. (Dir)
PETERMAN, R. M.
WILLIAMS, P. W.

Faculty of Arts (6168 Academic Quadrangle, Burnaby; tel. (604) 291-4414; fax (604) 291-3033; internet www.sfu.ca/arts):

Archaeology:

BURLEY, D. V. (Chair.)
DRIVER, J. C.
FLADMARK, K. R.
GALDIKAS, B. M. F.
HAYDEN, B. D.
NANCE, J. D.
NELSON, D. E.
SKINNER, M. F.

School for the Contemporary Arts:

ALOI, S. A.
DIAMOND, M.
GOTFRIT, M. S. (Dir)
MACINTYRE, D. K.
SNIDER, G.
TRUAX, B. D.
UNDERHILL, O.

School of Criminology:

BOYD, N. T.
BRANTINGHAM, P. J.
BRANTINGHAM, P. L.
BROCKMAN, J.
BURTCH, B.
CHUNN, D. E.
CORRADO, R. R.
FAITH, K.
GORDON, R. M. (Dir)
GRIFFITHS, C. T.
JACKSON, M. A.
LOWMAN, J.
MENZIES, R. J.
VERDUN-JONES, S. N.

Economics:

ALLEN, D. W.
BOLAND, L. A.
CHANT, J. F.
DEVORETZ, D. J.
DEAN, J. W.
DOW, G. (Chair.)
EASTON, S. T.
HARRIS, R. G.
JONES, R. A.
KENNEDY, P. E.
MAKI, D. R.
MUNRO, J. M.
OLEWILER, N. D.
SCHMITT, N.
SPINDLER, Z. A.

English:

COE, R. M.
DELANY, P.
DELANY, S. (Chair.)
DJWA, S.
GERSON, C.
MEZEI, K.
MIKI, R. A.
STOUCK, D.
STURROCK, J.

French:

DAVISON, R.
FAUQUENOY, M. C. (Chair.)
VISWANATHAN, J.

Geography:

BAILEY, W. G.
GILL, A. M.
HAYTER, R.
HICKIN, E. J.
PIERCE, J. T.
ROBERTS, A. C. B.
ROBERTS, M. C.

Gerontology Program:

GUTMAN, G. (Dir)
WISTER, A. V.

History:

BOYER, R. E.
CLEVELAND, W. L.
DEBO, R. K.
DUTTON, P. E.
FELLMAN, M. D.
GAGAN, D. P.
HUTCHINSON, J. F.
JOHNSTON, H. J. M.
LITTLE, J. I. (Chair.)
PARR, J.
STEWART, M. L.
STUBBS, J. O.

Humanities:

ANGUS, I.
DUGUID, S. (Chair.)
DUTTON, P. E.
MEZEI, K.
WALLS, J. W.

Latin American Studies:

BROHMAN, J. A C. (Dir)

Linguistics:

GERDTS, D. B.
ROBERTS, E. W.
MCFETRIDGE, P. (Chair)
SAUNDERS, R.

Philosophy:

HANSON, P. P. (Chair.)
JENNINGS, R. E.
ZIMMERMAN, D.

Political Science:

COHEN, L. J.
COHN, T. H.
COVELL, M. A.
ERICKSON, L. J. (Chair.)
GRIFFIN COHEN, M. G.
HOWLETT, M.
MCBRIDE, S.
MEYER, P.
ROSS, D. A.
SMITH, P. J.
STEVENSON, H. M.
WARWICK, P. V.

Psychology:

ALEXANDER, B. K.
BOWMAN, M. L.
HART, S. D.
KIMBALL, M.
KREBS, D. L.
MCFARLAND, C. G.
MISTLBERGER, R.
MORETTI, M. M.
ROESCH, R. M.
WHITTLESEA, B. W. A.

Sociology and Anthropology:

DYCK, N.
GEE, E. (Chair.)
HOWARD, M.
KENNY, M.
MACLEAN, D. R.

Women's Studies:

GRIFFIN COHEN, M. G.
KIMBALL, M. M. (Chair.)
STEWART, M. L.
WENDELL, S.

Faculty of Business Administration (3302 Lohn Building, Burnaby; tel. (604) 291-3708; fax (604) 291-4920; internet www.bus.sfu.ca):

CHOO, E. U.
CLARKSON, P. M.
FINLEY, D. R.
GRAUER, R. R.
LOVE, C. E.
MAUSER, G. A.
MEREDITH, L. N.
PINFIELD, L. T.
POITRAS, G.
RICHARDS, J. G.
SHAPIRO, D. M.
TUNG, R. L.
VINING, A. R.
WATERHOUSE, J. H.
WEDLEY, W. C.
WEXLER, M. N.
WYCKHAM, R. G.
ZAICHKOWSKY, J. L.

Faculty of Education (8622 Education Building, Burnaby; tel. (604) 291-3395; fax (604) 291-3203; internet www.educ.sfu.ca):

BAILIN, S.
BARROW, R.
CASE, R.
DE CASTELL, S. C.
EGAN, K.
GEVA-MAY, I.
GRIMMETT, P. P.
MAMCHUR, C. M.
MARTIN, J.
OBADIA, A. A.
RICHMOND, S.
TOOHEY, K
WINNE, P. H.
WONG, B. Y. L.
ZAZKIS, R.

Faculty of Science (P9451 Shrum Science Centre, Burnaby; tel. (604) 291-4590; fax (604) 291-3424; internet www.sfu.ca/~science):

Biological Sciences:

ALBRIGHT, L. J.
BECKENBACH, A. T.
BORDEN, J. H.
BRANDHORST, B. P.
CRESPI, B. J.
DILL, L. M.
FARRELL, A. P.
GRIES, G. J.
HAUNERLAND, N. H. (Chair.)
LAW, F. C. P.
MATHEWES, R. W.
PUNJA, Z. K.
RAHE, J. E.
ROITBERG, B. D.
WINSTON, M. L.
YDENBERG, R. C.

Chemistry:

BENNET, A. J.
CORNELL, R. B.
D'AURIA, J. D.
GAY, I. D.
HILL, R. H.
HOLDCROFT, S.
JONES, C. H. W.
MALLI, G. L.
PERCIVAL, P. W.
PINTO, B. M. (Chair.)
POMEROY, R. K.
RICHARDS, W. R.
SEN, D.
SLESSOR, K. N.

Earth Sciences:

HICKIN, E. J. (Chair.)
ROBERTS, M. C.

Mathematics:

BERGGREN, J. L.
BORWEIN, J. M.
BORWEIN, P. B.
BROWN, T. C.
GRAHAM, G. A. C.
HELL, P.
LACHLAN, A. H. (Chair.)
LEWIS, A. S.
REILLY, N. R.
RUSSELL, R. D.
SHEN, C. Y.

Molecular Biology and Biochemistry:

BAILLIE, D. L.
BRANDHORST, B. P.
CORNELL, R. B.
DAVIDSON, W. S.
HONDA, B. M.
RICHARDS, W. R.
SEN, D.
SMITH, M. J. (Chair.)

Physics:

BALLENTINE, L. E.
BECHHOEFER, J. L.
BOAL, D. H.
BOLOGNESI, C. R.
CLAYMAN, B. P.
CROZIER, E. D.
ENNS, R. H.
FRINDT, R. F.
HEINRICH, B.
KAVANAGH, K. L.
KIRCZENOW, G.
PLISCHKE, M. (Chair.)
SCHEINFEIN, M. R.
THEWALT, M. L. W.
TROTTIER, H. D.
VETTERLI, M.
WATKINS, S.

Statistics and Actuarial Science:

LOCKHART, R. A.
MACLEAN, D. R.
ROUTLEDGE, R. D.
SCHWARZ, C. J. (Chair.)
SITTER, R. R.
SWARTZ, T. B.

ATTACHED INSTITUTES

Behavioural Ecology Research Group: tel. (604) 291-3664; f. 1989; Dir Dr L. M. DILL.

Canadian Centre for Studies in Publishing: tel. (604) 291-5240; fax (604) 291-5239; f. 1987; Dir Dr R. M. LORIMER.

Centre for Coastal Studies: tel. (604) 291-4653; fax (604) 291-3851; Dir Dr P. GALLAGHER.

Centre for Education, Law and Society: tel. (604) 291-4484; fax (604) 291-3203; f. 1984; Dir Dr W. CASSIDY.

Centre d'Études Francophones Québec-Pacifique: tel. (604) 291-3544; fax (604) 291-5932; Dir Dr G. POIRIER.

Centre for Experimental and Constructive Mathematics: tel. (604) 291-5617; fax (604) 291-4947; f. 1993; Dir Dr J. BORWEIN.

Centre for Innovation in Management: tel. (604) 291-4183; fax (604) 291-5833; Dir Dr E. LOVE.

Centre for Labour Studies: tel. (604) 291-5827; fax (604) 291-3851; Dir Dr M. LEIER.

Centre for Policy Research on Science and Technology: tel. (604) 291-5116; fax (604) 291-5165; f. 1996; Dir R. SMITH.

Centre for Restorative Justice: fax (604) 291-4140; f. 2001; Dirs Dr R. M. GORDON, Dr E. ELLIOTT.

Centre for Scientific Computing: tel. (604) 291-4819; fax (604) 291-4947; Dir Dr R. RUSSELL.

Centre for Scottish Studies: tel. (604) 291-5515; fax (604) 291-4504; Dir Dr S. DUGUID.

Centre for the Study of Government and Business: fax (604) 291-5122; e-mail csgb@csgb.ubc.ca; internet www.csgb.ubc.ca; Co-Dirs Dr T. ROSS, Dr A. R. VINING.

Centre for Systems Science: tel. (604) 291-4588; fax (604) 291-4424; Dir Dr S. ATKINS.

Centre for Tourism Policy and Research: tel. (604) 291-3103; fax (604) 291-4968; f. 1989; Dir Dr P. W. WILLIAMS.

Chemical Ecology Research Group: tel. (604) 291-3646; fax (604) 291-3496; f. 1981; Dir Dr J. H. BORDEN.

Community Economic Development Centre: tel. (604) 291-5849; fax (604) 291-5473; e-mail cedc@sfu.ca; internet www.sfu.ca/cedcf. 1989; Dir Dr M. ROSELAND.

Co-operative Resource Management Institute: tel. (604) 291-4683; fax (604) 291-4986; f. 1998; Dir R. PETERMAN.

Criminology Research Centre: tel. (604) 291-4040; fax (604) 291-4140; f. 1978; Dir Dr W. GLACKMAN.

David Lam Centre for International Communication: tel. (604) 291-5021; fax (604) 291-5112; f. 1989; Dir Dr J. W. WALLS.

The Dialogue Institute.

Feminist Institute for Studies on Law and Society: f. 1990; Co-Dirs Dr D. CHUNN, Dr W. CHAN.

Gerontology Research Centre: tel. (604) 291-5062; fax (604) 291-5066; f. 1982; Dir Dr G. GUTMAN.

Institute for Canadian Urban Research Studies: tel. (604) 291-3515; fax (604) 291-4140; Dir Dr P. L. BRANTINGHAM.

Institute of Governance Studies: tel. (604) 291-4994; fax (604) 291-4786; Dir P. J. Smith.

Institute for the Humanities: tel. (604) 291-5516; fax (604) 291-5788; Dir Dr D. Grayston.

Institute of Micromachine and Microfabrication Research: tel. (604) 291-4971; fax (604) 291-4951; Dir Dr A. M. Parameswaran.

Institute for Studies in Criminal Justice Policy: tel. (604) 291-4040; fax (604) 291-4140; f. 1980; Dir Dr M. A. Jackson.

Institute for Studies in Teacher Education: fax (604) 291-3203; Co-Dirs P. Grimmett; tel. (604) 291-4937 Dr M. F. Wideen.

International Centre for Criminal Law Reform and Criminal Justice Policy: tel. (604) 822-9875; fax (604) 822-9317; f. 1991; Exec. Dir F. M. Gordon.

Logic and Functional Programming Group: tel. (604) 291-3426; fax (604) 291-3045; f. 1990; Dir Dr V. Dahl.

Mental Health, Law and Policy Institute: tel. (604) 291-3370; fax (604) 291-3427; f. 1991; Dir Dr R. Roesch.

Pacific Institute for the Mathematical Sciences: tel. (604) 291-4376; fax (604) 268-6657; f. 1996; Dir Dr P. Borwein.

Research Institute on South-eastern Europe: tel. (604) 291-5597; fax (604) 291-5837; Dir Dr A. Gerolymatos.

Tri-University Meson Facility (TRIUMF): tel. (604) 222-1047 ext. 6258; Dir Dr A. Shotter.

Western Canadian Universities Marine Biological Station (Bamfield): tel. (250) 728-3301; fax (250) 728-3452; f. 1969; Dir Dr A. N. Spencer.

W. J. VanDusen BC Business Studies Institute: tel. (604) 291-4183; fax (604) 291-5833; f. 1982; Dir Dr E. Love.

UNIVERSITY OF TORONTO

215 Huron St, Toronto, ON M5S 1A1Telephone: (416) 978-2011

Fax: (416) 978-5702

Internet: www.utoronto.ca

Founded 1827

Language of instruction: English

Provincially supported, assisted by private funds

Academic year: September to May (May to August, summer session)

Chancellor: Vivienne Poy

President: David Naylor

Vice-President and Provost: Shirley Neuman

Vice-President, Administration and Human Resources: Angela Hildyard

Vice-President and Chief Advancement Officer (vacant)

Vice-President, Research: John Challis

Chief Librarian: Carole Moore

Library: see Libraries and Archives

Number of teachers: 3,362

Number of students: 55,024 total

Publications: *Bulletin*, *Calendars*, *The Graduate*, *President's Report*, *Undergraduate Admission Handbook*

DEANS AND DIRECTORS

Faculty of Applied Science and Engineering: Tas Venetsanopoulos

Faculty of Architecture, Landscape and Design: Larry Wayne Richards

Faculty of Arts and Science: C. Amrhein (acting)

Faculty of Dentistry: David Mock

Faculty of Education: M. Fullan

Faculty of Forestry: R. B. Bryan

Faculty of Information Studies: Brian Cantwell Smith

Faculty of Law: R. J. Daniels

Faculty of Medicine: Catherine Whiteside

Faculty of Music: David Beach

Faculty of Nursing: Dyanne Affonso

Faculty of Pharmacy: K. Wayne Hindemarsh

Faculty of Physical Education and Health: B. Kidd

Faculty of Social Work: Jim Barber

School of Continuing Studies: M. C. Barrie

School of Graduate Studies: J. S. Cohen

Joseph L. Rothman School of Management: Prof. Roger Martin

PROFESSORS

N.B.—In the following list staff members of colleges are indicated thus: Erindale Coll. (E), New Coll. (N), St Michael's Coll. (M), Scarborough Coll. (S), Trinity Coll. (T), University Coll. (C), Victoria Univ. (V)

Faculty of Applied Science and Engineering:

Aarabi, P., Electrical and Computer Engineering
Abdelrahman, T., Electrical and Computer Engineering
Adams, B. J., Civil Engineering
Aitchison, J., Electrical and Computer Engineering
Allen, D., Chemical Engineering
Balke, S. T., Chemical Engineering
Bawden, W., Civil Engineering
Bidleman, T., Chemical Engineering
Birkemoe, P. C., Civil Engineering
Bonert, R., Electrical and Computer Engineering
Boocock, D. G. B., Chemical Engineering
Boulton, P. I. P., Electrical Engineering
Byer, P. H., Civil Engineering
Chaffey, C. E., Chemical Engineering
Charles, M. E., Chemical Engineering
Cheng, Y., Chemical Engineering
Chow, P., Electrical and Computer Engineering
Cluett, W., Chemical Engineering
Cobbold, R. S. C., Institute of Biomedical Engineering
Collins, M. P., Civil Engineering
Cormack, D. E., Chemical Engineering
Coyle, T., Chemical Engineering
Curran, J. H., Civil Engineering
Davies, S., Electrical and Computer Engineering
Davison, E. J. A., Electrical Engineering
Dawson, F., Electrical and Computer Engineering
Dewan, S. B., Electrical Engineering
Diamond, M., Chemical Engineering
Diosady, L. L., Chemical Engineering
Edwards, E., Chemical Engineering
Eizenman, M., Electrical and Computer Engineering
Erb, U., Materials Science
Evans, G., Chemical Engineering
Farnood, R., Chemical Engineering
Foulkes, F. R., Chemical Engineering
Fox, M. S., Industrial Engineering
Francis, B. A., Electrical Engineering
Frecker, R., Electrical and Computer Engineering
Fulthorpe, R., Chemical Engineering
Goldenberg, A. A., Mechanical Engineering
Gulack, P., Electrical and Computer Engineering
Hatzinakos, D., Electrical and Computer Engineering
Herman, P, Electrical and Computer Engineering
Hooton, R., Civil Engineering
Iravani, M. R., Electrical and Computer Engineering
Jacobsen, H.-A., Electrical and Computer Engineering
James, D. F., Mechanical Engineering
Jardine, A. K. S., Industrial Engineering
Jia, C., Chemical Engineering
Joy, M., Electrical and Computer Engineering
Karney, B., Civil Engineering
Kawaji, M., Chemical Engineering
Kirk, D. W., Chemical Engineering
Konrad, A., Electrical and Computer Engineering
Kortschot, M., Chemical Engineering
Kschischang, F., Electrical and Computer Engineering
Kuhn, D., Chemical Engineering
Kunov, H., Biomedical Engineering
Kwong, R. H., Electrical Engineering
Lavers, J. D., Electrical Engineering
Lehn, P., Electrical and Computer Engineering
Lee, E. S., Electrical Engineering
Leon-Garcia, A., Electrical Engineering
Li, D., Mechanical Engineering
Lo, H.-K., Electrical and Computer Engineering
Luus, R., Chemical Engineering
McKague, A., Chemical Engineering
Mandelis, A., Mechanical Engineering
Mann, S., Electrical and Computer Engineering
Martin, K., Electrical Engineering
Measures, R. M., Aerospace Studies
Meguid, S. A., Mechanical Engineering
Miller, E. J., Civil Engineering
Mims, C. A., Chemical Engineering
Mohanty, B., Civil Engineering
Ojha, M., Chemical Engineering
Packer, J. A., Civil Engineering
Paradi, J., Chemical Engineering
Park, C., Mechanical Engineering
Pasupathy, S. P., Electrical Engineering
Perovic, D., Materials Science
Reeve, D. W., Chemical Engineering
Rose, J., Electrical and Computer Engineering
Sain, M., Chemical Engineering
Salama, C. A. T., Electrical Engineering
Santerre, J., Chemical Engineering
Sargent, E., Electrical and Computer Engineering
Saville, B., Chemical Engineering
Sefton, M. V., Chemical Engineering
Semlyen, A., Electrical and Computer Engineering
Sevcik, K., Electrical and Computer Engineering
Sheikh, S. A., Civil Engineering
Shoichet, M., Chemical Engineering
Sleep, B., Civil Engineering
Smith, K. C., Electrical Engineering
Smith, P. W., Electrical Engineering
Sodhi, R., Engineering
Sousa, E., Electrical and Computer Engineering
Terzopoulos, D., Electrical and Computer Engineering
Tran, H. N., Chemical Engineering
Trass, O., Chemical Engineering
Turksen, I. B., Industrial Engineering
Vecchio, F. J., Civil Engineering
Venetsanopoulos, A. N., Electrical Engineering
Venter, R. D., Mechanical Engineering
Vranesic, Z. G., Electrical Engineering
Wallace, J. S., Mechanical Engineering
Wang, Z., Materials Science
Wania, F., Chemical Engineering
Ward, C. A., Mechanical Engineering
Wonham, W. M., Electrical Engineering
Woodhouse, K., Chemical Engineering
Wright, P. M., Civil Engineering
Yan, N., Chemical Engineering
Yip, C., Chemical Engineering
Young, R., Civil Engineering
Zaky, S. G., Electrical Engineering
Zandstra, P., Chemical Engineering
Zukotynski, S., Electrical Engineering

Faculty of Architecture, Landscape and Design:
CORNEIL, C. S.
EARDLEY, A.

Faculty of Arts and Science:
ABBATT, J., Chemistry
ABRAHAM, R. G., Astronomy and Astrophysics
ABOUHAIDAR, M. G., Botany
ACCINELLI, R. D., History
ADLER, E., Political Science
AIVAZIAN, V. A., Economics (E)
ALLOWAY, T. M., Psychology (E)
ANDERSON, G. M., Geology
ANDERSON, J. B., Botany (E)
ARNHEIM, C., Geography
ARTHUR, J. G., Mathematics
ASTER, S., History (E)
ASTINGTON, J., English
BACCHUS, F., Computer Science
BAILEY, D. C., Physics
BAILEY, R. C., Physics
BAIRD, J., English (C)
BAKER, M., Economics
BAKICH, O., Slavic Languages and Literature
BALDUS, B., Sociology
BARNES, C. J., Slavic Languages and Literature
BARRETT, F. M., Zoology
BARRETT, S. C. H., Botany
BARZDA, V., Physics
BASHKEVIN, S., Political Science
BEINER, R. S., Political Science (E)
BENJAMIN, D., Economics
BERGER, C. C., History
BERKOWITZ, M. K., Economics
BEWELL, A., English
BIERSTONE, E., Mathematics
BINNICK, R. I., Linguistics (S)
BIRGENEAU, R. J., Physics
BISZTRAY, G., Slavic Languages and Literature
BLAKE, T., Botany
BLANCHARD, P. H., History
BLAND, J. S., Mathematics (E)
BLISS, J. M., History
BLOOM, T., Mathematics
BODDY, J., Anthropology
BODEMANN, M., Sociology
BOLTON, C. T., Astronomy
BOND, J., Astronomy and Astrophysics
BOONSTRA, R., Life Sciences (S)
BORODIN, A. B., Computer Science
BOTHWELL, R., History
BOURNE, L. S., Geography
BOYD, M., Sociology
BRAUN, A., Political Science (E)
BRITTON, J., Geography
BROOK, T. J., History, East Asian Studies
BROOKS, D. R., Zoology
BROWN, I. R., Zoology (S)
BROWN, J. R., Philosophy
BROWN, R. M., Humanities (S)
BROWNLEE, J. S., East Asian Studies
BRUDNER, A., Political Science
BRUMER, P. W., Chemistry
BRYAN, R. B., Geography (S)
BRYANT, J., Sociology
BRYM, R. J., Sociology
BUCHWEITZ, R., Mathematics
BUNCE, M., Geography
BURKE, J. F., Spanish and Portuguese
BURTON, F. D., Anthropology (S)
CAMERON, D. R., Political Science
CANFIELD, J. V., Philosophy (E)
CAPOZZI, R., Italian Studies
CARLBERG, R. G., Physical Sciences (S)
CARR, J. L., Economics
CASAS, F. R., Economics
CHAMBERLIN, J. E., English
CHEETHAM, M., Fine Art
CHEN, J., Geography
CHIN, J., Chemistry
CHING, J. C., Religious Studies
CLARKE, W. H., Astronomy
CLIVIO, G. P., Italian Studies
CODE, R. F., Physics (E)
COOK, S. A., Computer Science
CORMAN, B., English Literature (E)
CORNEIL, D. G., Mathematics, Computer Science
CRAWFORD, G., Anthropology
CRUDEN, S., Geology (E)
CUMMINS, W. R., Botany (E)
CUNNINGHAM, F. A., Philosophy, Political Science
DANESI, M., Italian Studies
DAY, R. B., Political Economy (E)
DE KERCKHOVE, D., French
DE QUEHEN, A. H., English
DE SOUSA, R., Philosophy
DEL JUNCO, A., Mathematics
DENGLER, N. G., Botany
DENNY, M. G. S., Economics
DENT, J., History
DESAI, R. C., Physics
DEWAR, M., Classics
DEWEES, D. N., Political Economy
DIAMOND, M., Geography
DION, P.-E., Near Eastern Studies
DONALDSON, D., Chemistry
DONNELLY, M. W., Political Science, East Asian Studies
DRUMMOND, J. R., Physics
DUNLOP, D. J., Physics (E)
EDWARDS, E., Botany
EDWARDS, R. N., Physics
EISENBICHLER, K., Italian
ELLIOTT, G. A., Mathematics
ENRIGHT, W. H., Mathematics, Computer Science (S)
ERICKSON, B. H., Sociology
ESPIE, G., Botany
EVANS, M. J., Statistics
EYLES, N., Physical Sciences (S)
FAIG, M., Economics
FALKENHEIM, V. C., Political Science, East Asian Studies
FARRAR, D., Chemistry
FENNER, A., German
FIUME, E., Computer Science
FOOT, D. K., Economics
FORBES, H. D., Political Science
FORGUSON, L. W., University College
FRANCESCHETTI, A., Italian Studies (S)
FRIEDLANDER, J. B., Mathematics (S)
FRIEDMANN, H. B., Sociology (E)
FUSS, M. A., Economics
GAD, G. H. K., Geography
GALLOWAY, J. H., Geography
GARTNER, R. I., Sociology
GEORGES, M., Chemistry
GERTLER, M. S., Geography
GERVERS, M., History (S)
GILLIS, A. R., Sociology
GITTINS, J., Geology
GOERING, J., History
GOLDSTEIN, M., Mathematics
GOLDSTICK, D., Philosophy
GOTLIEB, C., Computer Science
GOURIEROUX, C., Economics
GRAHAM, I. R., Mathematics (E)
GREENWOOD, B., Geography (S)
GREENWOOD, B., Geology (S)
GREER, A. R., History
GREINER, P. C., Mathematics
GRIFFEN, P. A., Physics (S)
GROSS, M. R., Zoology
GUNDERSON, M. K., Economics
GWYNNE, D. T., Biology (E)
HAGAN, J. L., Sociology
HALLS, H. C., Geological Sciences (E)
HANNIGAN, J., Sociology
HANSELL, R. I. C., Zoology
HARVEY, D., Geography
HARVEY, E., Sociology
HARVEY, E. R., English (C)
HAYHOE, R., East Asian Studies
HEALEY, A., English
HEATH, M. C., Botany
HEHNER, E. C. R., Computer Science
HELMSTADTER, R. J., History
HIGGINS, V. J., Botany
HIGGS, D. C., History
HINTON, G. E., Computer Science
HIRST, G., Computer Science
HOLDOM, B., Physics
HORGEN, P. A., Botany (E)
HORI, K., Physics
HORTON, S., Economics
HOWARD, K., Geology (S)
HOWARD, P. J., English (S)
HOWELL, N., Sociology
HOWSON, S. K., Social Sciences (S)
HUTCHEON, L. A., English
INGHAM, J. N., History
INWOOD, B. C., Classics, Philosophy
ISRAEL, M., History
IVRII, V., Mathematics
JAAKSON, R., Geography
JACKSON, H., English
JACKSON, K. R., Computer Science
JACOBS, A. E., Physics (S)
JEFFREY, L., Mathematics
JELLINEK, M., Physics
JEPSON, A. D., Computer Science (E)
JOHN, S., Physics
JOHNSON, W. M. L. A., Fine Art
JOHNSTON, A., English (C)
JONES, A., Classics
JONES, C. L., Sociology
JUMP, G. V., Economics
JURDJEVIC, V., Mathematics
KAPRAL, R. E., Chemistry
KAPRANOV, M., Mathematics
KAY, L., Chemistry
KEE, H.-K., Physics
KEITH, W. J., English
KERVIN, J. B., Sociology (E)
KEY, A. W., Physics
KHESIN, B., Mathematics
KHOVANSKII, A., Mathematics
KIM, H., Mathematics
KIM, Y.-B., Physics
KLAUSNER, D. N., English
KLEIN, M. A., History
KLUGER, R. H., Chemistry
KOFMAN, L., Astronomy
KRAMER, C. E., Slavic Languages and Literature
KRIEGER, P., Physics
KRULL, U., Chemistry
KUKLA, A., Psychology, Philosophy (S)
LAMBEK, M. J., Anthropology (S)
LANCASHIRE, A. C., English
LANCASHIRE, D. I., English (E)
LANTZ, K. A., Slavic Languages and Literature
LAUTENS, M., Chemistry
LEDUC, L., Political Science
LEE, M. J., Physics (S)
LEE, R. B., Anthropology
LEGGATT, A. M., English
LEHMAN, A. B., Computer Science
LEVESQUE, H. J., Computer Science
LO, H.-K., Physics
LOGAN, R., Physics
LORIMER, J. W., Mathematics
LUKE, M., Physics
LUSTE, G. J., Physics
LUONG, H. V., Anthropology, East Asian Studies
LYNN, R., East Asian Studies
LYUBICH, M., Mathematics
MCCLELLAND, R. A., Chemistry (S)
MCDONALD, P., Chemistry
MCILWRAITH, T., Geography
MAGEE, J., Classics
MAGILL, D. W., Sociology
MAGNUSSON, L., English
MAGOCSI, P. R., Political Science
MALLOCH, D. W., Botany
MANNERS, I., Chemistry
MARGORIBANKS, R., Physics
MARTIN, J. F., Physics
MARTIN, P. G., Astronomy

MATHEWSON, G. F., Political Economy
MATUS, J., English
MATHON, R. A., Mathematics, Computer Science
MELINO, A., Economics
MENDELSOHN, E., Mathematics, Computer Science (S)
MENDELZON, A. O., Computer Science
MENZINGER, M., Chemistry
MERRILEES, B., French (C)
MIALL, A. D., Geology
MICHELSON, W., Sociology
MIKHALKIN, G., Mathematics
MILLER, R., Chemistry
MILKEREIT, B., Physics
MILLER, R., Physics
MILMAN, P., Mathematics
MIMS, C., Chemistry
MINTZ, J., Economics
MIRON, J. R., Geography (S)
MITROVICHA, J. X., Physics
MOCHNACKI, S., Astronomy
MOGGRIDGE, D. E., Economics
MOORE, G., Physics
MORGAN, K. P., Philosophy
MORRIS, G. K., Zoology (E)
MORRIS, R., Chemistry
MORRIS, S. W., Physics
MORRISON, J. C., Philosophy
MUNK, L., English
MUNRO, D. S., Geography (E)
MURNAGHAN, F., Mathematics
MURRAY, H., English
MURRAY, N., Astronomy
MURTY, V., Mathematics
MYLES, J., Sociology
MYLOPOULOS, J., Computer Science
NACHMAN, A., Mathematics
NEDELSKI, J., Political Science
NETTERFIELD, B., Physics
NEUMAN, S., English
NOYES, J. K., German
O'DAY, D., Zoology (E)
O'DONNELL, P. J., Physics (S)
OLIVER, W. A., French
ORCHARD, A., English
ORCHARD, I., Zoology
ORR, R. S., Physics
ORWIN, C. L., Political Science
OSBORNE, M., Economics
O'TOOLE, R., Sociology
OZIN, G. A., Chemistry
PANGLE, T. L., Political Science
PATERSON, J. M., French (E)
PAULY, P., Political Science, Economics
PEET, A., Physics
PELTIER, W. R., Physics
PERCY, J. R., Astronomy (E)
PERRON, P., French (C)
PIETROPAOLO, D., Italian
PITASSI, T., Computer Science
POLANYI, J. C., Chemistry
POPPITZ, E., Physics
POWELL, J., Chemistry
PRIESTLEY, L. C., East Asian Studies
PRUESSEN, R. W., History (E)
PUGLIESE, G., Italian
RACKOFF, C. W., Computer Science
RAYSIDE, D. M., Political Science
REDEKOP, M., English
REIBETANZ, J. H., English (C)
REID, D., Fine Art
REID, F. J., Economics (E)
REISZ, R. R., Zoology (E)
REITZ, J. G., Sociology
RELPH, T., Geography
REPKA, J. S., Mathematics
RICE, K. D., Linguistics
RICHARDSON, D. S., Fine Art
RISING, J. D., Zoology
ROBIN, P. Y., Geological Science (E)
ROSENTHAL, J., Mathematics
ROSENTHAL, P., Mathematics
ROSSOS, A., History
RUBINOFF, A., Political Science
RUTHERFORD, P., History
SALAFF, J. W., Sociology
SANDBROOK, K. R. J., Political Science
SANDERS, G., East Asian Studies
SAVARD, P., Physics
SCHWARTZ, D. V., Political Science
SCOTT, S. D., Geology
SEAGER, W. E., Philosophy (S)
SEAQUIST, E. R., Astronomy
SEARY, P. D., English
SECO, L., Mathematics
SELICK, P., Mathematics (S)
SELIGER, F., German
SEVCIK, K. C., Computer Science
SHAW, W. D., English (C)
SHEN, V., East Asian Studies
SHEPHERD, T., Physics
SHERK, A., Mathematics
SHERWOOD LOLLAR, B., Geology
SHI, S., Economics
SHUB, M., Mathematics
SIGMON, B. A., Anthropology (E)
SILCOX, P., Political Science (E)
SIMEON, R., Political Science, Law
SIOW, A., Economics
SIPE, J. E., Physics
SKOGSTAD, G. D., Political Science (S)
SMITH, J. J. B., Zoology
SMYTH, D., History
SOHM, P. L., Fine Art
SOECKI, S., English
SOLOMON, P. H., Political Science
SOLOMON, S., Political Science (S)
SPOONER, E. T., Geology
SPRULES, W. G., Zoology (E)
STATT, B., Physics
STEIN, J., Political Science
STEINBERG, A., Physics
STERNBERG, R., Spanish and Portugese
STEVENS, P., English
STREN, R. E., Political Science
STRONG, K., Physics
SULEM, C., Mathematics
SULLIVAN, R., English (E)
SUMNER, L. W., Philosophy
TAILLEFER, L., Physics
TALL, F. D., Mathematics
TANNER, J., Sociology (S)
TANNY, S., Mathematics
TEICHMAN, J., Political Science
TEPPERMAN, L. J., Sociology
TERZOPOLOUS, D., Computer Science
THOMPSON, J. C., Chemistry
THOMPSON, M., Chemistry
THOMPSON, R. P., Philosophy (S)
THOMSON, L., English
THYWISSEN, J., Physics
TRISCHUK, W., Physics
TOBE, S. S., Zoology
TOWNSEND, D., English
TROTT, D., French
TREBILCOCK, M., Economics
TREFLER, D., Economics
TUOHY, C., Political Science
TURNER, D. H., Anthropology
URQUHART, A. I. F., Philosophy
VAN DRIEL, H. M., Physics (E)
VIPOND, R., Political Science
VIRAG, B., Mathematics
WAGLE, N. K., History
WALKER, M. B., Physics
WATERHOUSE, D. B., East Asian Studies
WEI, J., Physics
WEINRIB, L., Political Science
WEISS, W. A., Mathematics (E)
WELLMAN, B. S., Sociology
WESTGATE, J. A., Geology
WHEATON, B., Sociology (E)
WHITE, G., Political Science
WHITE, R. R., Geography (E)
WHITTINGTON, S. G., Chemistry
WILLIAMS, D. D., Life Sciences (S)
WILSON, F. F., Philosophy
WOLFE, D., Political Science
WOOLDRIDGE, T. R., French
WORTMAN, D. B., Computer Science
YOUNG, R. P., Geology
YOUSON, J. H., Zoology (S)
YU, E., Computer Science
ZIMMERMAN, A. M., Zoology

Faculty of Dentistry:

BENNICK, A.
DAVIES, J.
DEPORTER, D. A.
ELLEN, R. P.
FERRIER, J. M.
FREEMAN, E.
HEERSCHE, J. N. M.
LEAKE, J. L.
LEVINE, N.
LEWIS, D. W., Community Dentistry
LOCKER, D.
MCCOMB, D.
MCCULLOCH, C. A.
MAIN, J. H. P., Oral Pathology
MAYHALL, J. T.
MELCHER, A. H.
MOCK, D.
PILLIAR, R. M.
SANDHAM, H. J.
SESSLE, B. J.
SODEK, J.
SYMINGTON, J. M.
TEN CATE, A. R.
TENENBAUM, H. C.
WATSON, P. A.
ZARB, G. A., Prosthodontics

Faculty of Law:

BEATTY, D. M.
BENSON, P.
BRUDNER, A.
BRUNÉE, J.
CHAPMAN, B.
COOK, R.
COSSMAN, B.
DANIELS, R.
DEWEES, D.
DICKENS, B.
DYZENHAUS, D.
FLOOD, C.
FRIEDLAND, M.
GREEN, A.
HAGAN, J.
JANISCH, H.
LANGILLE, B.
LEE, I.
MACKLEM, P.
NEDELSKY, J.
PHILLIPS, J.
RÉAUME, D.
RIPSTEIN, A.
ROACH, K.
ROGERSON, C.
SIMEON, R.
SOSSIN, R.
TREBILOCK, M.
WADDAMS, S.
WEINRIB, E.
WEINRIB, L.

Faculty of Medicine:

ABEL, S., Otolaryngology
ACKERMANN, U., Physiology
ADAMSON, S., Obstetrics and Gynaecology, Paediatrics
ADELI, K., Pathobiology
ANDERSON, G. H., Nutrition and Food Sciences
ANDREWS, B. J., Medical Genetics and Microbiology
ANDRULIS, I., Pathobiology, Microbiology
ARCHER, M. C., Nutritional Studies
ARROWSMITH, C., Immunology
ASA, S., Pathobiology
ATWOOD, H. L., Physiology
AUBIN, J., Medical Biophysics
AXELRAD, A. A., Medical Biophysics
BAINES, A. D., Clinical Biochemistry
BAKER, R. R., Medicine
BARKER, G., Anaesthesia
BAUMAL, R., Pathology
BAZETT-JONES, D., Biochemistry

BELIK, J., Paediatrics
BENCHIMOL, S., Medical Biophysics
BENSON, L., Paediatrics
BERGERON, C., Pathobiology
BEVAN, D., Anaesthesia
BHAVNANI, B., Obstetrics and Gynaecology
BIGGAR, W. D., Paediatrics
BISSONETEE, B., Anaesthesia
BLAKE, J., Obstetrics and Gynaecology
BLANCHETTE, V., Paediatrics
BLENCOWE, B., Medical Research, Microbiology
BLUMENTHAL, A., Pathobiology
BOCKING, A., Obstetrics and Gynaecology, Physiology
BOGGS, J., Pathobiology
BOGNAR, A., Microbiology
BOHN, D., Anaesthesia
BOONE, C., Medical Research
BOONSTRA, R., Zoology, Physiology
BOUFFET, E., Paediatrics
BOYD, N., Medical Biophysics
BRESLIN, C., Ophthalmology
BRET, P.
BRONSKILL, M., Immunology
BROWN, D., Otolaryngology
BRUBAKER, P., Physiology
BRUNTON, J., Pathobiology
BUNCIC, R., Ophthalmology
BURNHAM, W. M., Pharmacology
BURNS, P., Medical Biophysics
BUSTO, U., Pharmacology
BUTANY, J., Pathobiology
BUTLER, D., Physiology
BYRICK, R., Anaesthesia
CAMERMAN, N., Biochemistry
CAMPBELL, J. B., Microbiology
CARLEN, P. L., Medicine
CASPER, R. F., Obstetrics and Gynaecology
CHALLIS, J., Physiology and Obstetrics
CHAMBERLAIN, D., Pathobiology
CHAN, H. S., Biochemistry
CHAN, S. L., Paediatrics
CHAN, V. L., Microbiology
CHARLTON, M. P., Physiology
CHETTY, R., Pathobiology
CHIANG, L., Pathobiology
CHITAYAT, D., Paediatrics
CHUNG, F. F., Anaesthesia
CLARKE, D., Biochemistry
CLARKE, J. T. R., Paediatrics
COATES, A., Paediatrics, Physiology
COLE, D., Pathobiology
COLE, P., Otolaryngology
COLGAN, T., Pathobiology
COVENS, A., Obstetrics and Gynaecology
CRUZ, T., Pathobiology
CRYSDALE, W. S., Otolaryngology
CUNNANE, S., Nutritional Sciences
CUNNINGHAM, A., Medical Biophysics
DANEMAN, A., Medical Imaging
DANEMAN, D., Paediatrics
DANSKA, J., Medical Biophysics
DEBER, C. M., Medical Biophysics
DEBONI, U., Physiology
DENNIS, J., Pathobiology
DE PETRILLO, A. D., Obstetrics and Gynaecology
DIAMANDIS, E., Pathobiology
DIAMANT, N. E., Physiology
DICK, J. E., Microbiology
DIRKS, F., Medicine
DIRKS, P., Medicine
DIXON, W., Ophthalmology
DORIAN, P., Pharmacology
DOSCH, H., Paediatrics
DOSTROVSKY, J. O., Physiology
DRUCKER, D. J., Pathobiology
DRUTZ, H., Obstetrics and Gynaecology
DUBE, I., Pathobiology
DUFFIN, J., Anaesthesia
DULLIN, J., Medical Biophysics
DURIE, P., Paediatrics
EASTERBROOK, M., Ophthalmology
EDWARDS, A., Medical Research, Microbiology
ELLEN, R., Pathobiology
ELLIS, D., Otolaryngology
EMILI, A., Medical Research, Microbiology
FARINE, D., Obstetrics and Gynaecology
FELDMAN, B. M., Paediatrics
FELDMAN, F., Ophthalmology
FERNIE, G. R., Surgery
FISH, E., Medical Biophysics
FISHER, R. H. G., Family and Community Medicine
FONG, I., Pathobiology
FORNASIER, V., Pathobiology
FORSTNER, G. G., Paediatrics
FORSTNER, J., Biochemistry
FOSTER, F. S., Medical Biophysics
FOX, A., Medical Imaging
FOX, G., Anaesthesia
FREEDMAN, J., Pathobiology
FREEDOM, R., Pathobiology
FRIESEN, J., Medical Research
FROM, L., Medicine
FRECKER, R., Biomedical Engineering
FREEDMAN, M., Paediatrics
FREEDOM, R., Paediatrics
FREEMAN, J., Otolaryngology
FIEDBERG, J., Otolaryngology
GALLIE, B., Ophthalmology
GALLINGER, S., Pathobiology
GANOZA, M. C., Medical Research
GARE, D., Obstetrics and Gynaecology
GARIÉPY, J., Medical Biochemistry
GARVEY, M. B., Medicine
GEARY, D., Paediatrics
GEORGE, S., Pharmacology
GILDAY, D., Medical Imaging
GOLDMAN, B. S., Surgery
GOLDSTEIN, M. B., Medicine
GOTLIEB, A. I., Pathology
GRANT, D., Pharmacology
GREENBERG, G. R., Medicine
GREENBERG, M. L., Paediatrics
GREENBLATT, J. F., Medical Research
GREENWALD, M., Paediatrics
GREENWOOD, C., Nutritional Sciences
GRINSTEIN, S., Biochemistry
GRYNPAS, M., Pathobiology
GUHA, A., Medical Biochemistry
GULLANE, P. J., Otolaryngology
GURD, J., Biochemistry
HALLIDAY, W., Pathobiology
HAMPSON, D., Pharmacology
HANLEY, W., Paediatrics
HANNA, W., Pathobiology
HANNAH, M., Obstetrics and Gynaecology
HARRISON, R., Otolaryngology
HASLAM, R., Paediatrics
HAWKE, M., Pathobiology, Otolaryngology
HAY, J. B., Immunology
HEDLEY, D., Medical Biophysics
HEERSCH, J., Pharmacology
HELM, T., Paediatrics
HENKELMAN, R. M., Medical Biophysics
HERSCHORN, S., Urology
HILL, R., Medical Biophysics
HILLIARD, R., Paediatrics
HINEK, A., Pathobiology
HO PING KONG, Medicine
HOWELL, P., Biochemistry
HUGHES, T., Medical Research
HUNT, J. W., Medical Biophysics
HYDE, M., Otolaryngology
IKURA, M., Medical Biophysics
INABA, T., Pharmacology
INGLES, C. J., Medical Research
ISCOVE, N., Medical Biochemistry
ISENMAN, D. E., Biochemistry
JEEJEEBHOY, K. N., Medicine
JOHNSSTON, K. W., Vascular Surgery
JOHNSTON, M., Pathobiology
JORGENSEN, A. O., Anatomy and Cell Biology
JOTHY, S., Pathobiology
JULIUS, M., Medical Biophysics
KAHN, H. (acting), Pathobiology
KAIN, K., Pathobiology
KALNINS, V. I., Histology
KANDEL, R., Pathobiology
KAPLAN, D., Medical Genetics
KARMALI, M., Pathobiology
KAY, L., Biochemistry
KEELEY, F., Biochemistry, Pathobiology
KERBEL, R., Medical Biophysics, Pathobiology
KHANNA, J. M., Pharmacology
KHOKHA, R., Medical Biophysics, Pathobiology
KISH, S., Pharmacology
KLIP, A., Biochemistry, Paediatrics
KOREN, G., Paediatrics, Pharmacology
KOVACS, K., Pathobiology
KRAFT, S., Ophthalmology
KRAFTCHIK, B., Paediatrics
KRAICER, J., Physiology
KRAUSE, H., Medical Research
KUCHARCZYK, W., Radiology
KUKSIS, A., Medical Research
KUNOV, H., Otolaryngology
LANGER, B., Surgery
LANGILLE, B. L., Pathology
LAWEE, D. H., Family and Community Medicine
LEPOCK, J., Medical Biophysics
LETARTE, M., Medical Biophysics
LEVY, G. A., Medicine
LEWIS, P. N., Biochemistry
LI, R.-K., Pathobiology
LICKLEY, L., Physiology
LICKRISH, G., Obstetrics and Gynaecology
LIEBGOTT, B., Anatomy
LIEW, C. C., Clinical Biochemistry
LINGWOOD, C., Biochemistry
LIU, F.-F., Medical Biophysics, Physiology
LIVINGSTONE, R. A., Obstetrics and Gynaecology
LOGAN, W. J., Paediatrics
LOW, D., Pathobiology
LYE, S., Obstetrics and Gynaecology
MACDONALD, J. F., Physiology
MCGEER, A., Pathobiology
MCGRAIL, S., Otolaryngology
MCINNES, R. R., Paediatrics
MACKAY, M., Biomedical Communications
MCKEE, N., Plastic Surgery
MACLENNAN, D. H., Medical Research
MAHURAN, D., Pathobiology
MAK, T.-W., Medical Biophysics
MARKS, A., Neurobiology
MARSDEN, P., Medical Biophysics, Pathobiology
MARSHALL, V. W., Behavioural Science
MAZER, C. D., Anaesthesia
MESSNER, H., Medical Biophysics
MICKLE, D., Pathobiology
MICKLEBOROUGH, L., Cardiac Surgery
MILGRAM, N., Pharmacology
MILLER, F., Physiology
MINDEN, M., Medical Biophysics
MOCK, D., Pathobiology
MOSCARELLO, M., Pathobiology
MORAN, L., Biochemistry
MORAN, M. F., Medical Research
MORGAN, J. E., Obstetrics and Gynaecology
MORTIMER, C. B., Ophthalmology
MROSOVSKY, N., Physiology
NAG, S., Pathobiology
NAGY, A., Medical Genetics
NARANJO, C. A., Pharmacology
NEDZELSKI, J. M., Otolaryngology
NOBLE, W. H., Anaesthesia
NOYEK, A. M., Otolaryngology
O'BRIEN, P., Pharmacology
O'BRODOVICH, H., Paediatrics, Physiology
O'DOWD, B., Pharmacology
OHASHI, P., Medical Biophysics
OHLSSON, A., Paediatrics
OKEY, A. B., Pharmacology
OLIVIERI, N., Paediatrics
OPAS, M., Pathobiology
ORSER, B., Anaesthesia, Physiology
OSMOND, D. H., Physiology
OTTENSMEYER, F. P., Medical Biophysics
PACE-ASCIAK, C., Pharmacology

PAI, E., Biochemistry
PAIGE, C., Medical Biophysics
PANG, C., Physiology
PANG, K., Pharmacology
PANTALONY, D., Pathobiology
PAPPO, A., Paediatrics
PAPSIN, F. R., Obstetrics and Gynaecology
PARKER, J., Ophthalmology
PARKER, J. D., Pharmacology
PAVLIN, C., Ophthalmology
PENCHARZ, P., Paediatrics
PENN, L., Medical Biophysics
PENNINGER, J., Medical Biophysics
PERLMAN, M., Paediatrics
PETERS, W. J., Plastic Surgery
PINKERTON, P. H., Pathology
PLEWES, D., Medical Biophysics
POST, M., Pathobiology, Physiology
PRITZKER, K., Pathobiology
PRUD'HOMME, G., Pathobiology
PULLEYBLANK, D. E., Biochemistry
RABINOVITCH, M., Paediatrics
RACHLIS, A., Pathobiology
RAJALAKSHMI, S., Pathobiology
RAUTH, A., Medical Biophysics
READ, S. E., Paediatrics, Pathobiology
REGAN, M., Ophthalmology
REITHMEIER, R., Biochemistry
RENLUND, R., Physiology
REZNICK, R., General Surgery
RICHARDSON, C., Medical Biophysics
RIDDELL, R., Pathobiology
RITCHIE, J. W. K., Obstetrics and Gynaecology
ROBERTS, E., Paediatrics
ROBINSON, G., Psychiatry
ROIFMAN, C., Paediatrics
ROSE, D., Medical Biophysics
ROTSTEIN, O. D., Surgery
ROWLANDS, J. A., Medical Biophysics
RUTKA, J., Pathobiology
SADOWSKI, P. D., Medical Genetics, Pathobiology
SARMA, D., Pathobiology
SAUDER, D. N., Medicine
SCHATZKER, J., Surgery
SCHIMMER, B. P., Medical Research
SCHLICHTER, L., Physiology
SCHMITT-ULMS, G., Pathobiology
SCULLY, H., Cardiac Surgery
SEIDELMAN, W. E., Family and Community Medicine
SEGALL, J., Biochemistry, Medical Genetics
SELLERS, E. M., Pharmacology
SERMER, M., Obstetrics and Gynaecology
SESSLE, B., Dentistry
SETH, A., Pathobiology
SHAH, C. P., Preventive Medicine and Biostatistics
SHARPE, J. A., Otolaryngology
SHEAR, N., Pharmcology
SHEK, P., Pathobiology
SHERMAN, P., Paediatrics, Pathobiology
SHIER, R. M., Obstetrics and Gynaecology
SHIME, J., Obstetrics and Gynaecology
SHULMAN, H. S., Radiology
SHULMAN, M. J., Immunology, Medical Genetics
SILVERMAN, M., Medicine
SIMOR, A., Pathobiology
SIU, C. H., Medical Research
SLINGER, P., Anaesthesia
SNEAD III, O. C., Paediatrics
SODEK, J., Biochemistry
SOLE, M. J., Medicine
SONNENBERG, H., Physiology
SPEAKMAN, J., Ophthalmology
SQUARE, P., Speech-Language Pathology
SQUIRE, J., Pathobiology
STEIN, H., Ophthalmology
STEINER, G., Medicine
STEWART, D. J., Pathobiology
STEWART, P. A., Anatomy and Cell Biology
SUN, A., Physiology
TALLETT, S., Paediatrics
TANNOCK, I., Medical Biophysics
TANSWELL, A., Paediatrics
TATOR, C. H., Surgery
TAYLOR, G., Pathobiology
TAYLOR, I. M., Anatomy
TEMPLETON, D. M., Pathobiology
TENENBAUM, H., Pathobiology
TERBRUGGE, K., Medical Imaging
THOMPSON, L., Nutrition
THORNER, P., Pathobiology
TIMMER, V., Botany
TOMLINSON, D., Otolaryngology
TRIMBLE, W. S., Biochemistry
TRITCHLER, D., Medical Biophysics
TROPE, G., Ophthalmology
TSAO, M., Medical Biophysics, Pathobiology
TWEED, D., Physiology
UETECHT, J., Pharmacology
VAN DER KOOY, D. J., Anatomy and Cell Biology
VAN NOSTRAND, P., Otolaryngology
VAN TOL, H., Pharmacology
VAS, S., Pathobiology
VELLEND, H., Medicine
VRANIC, M., Physiology
WADDELL, J. P., Surgery
WALFISH, P. G., Otolaryngology
WANG, Y.-T., Pathobiology
WANLESS, I., Pathobiology
WARSH, J., Pharmacology
WEKSBERG, R., Paediatrics
WEISER, W., Medical Imaging
WEISBROD, G., Medical Imaging
WEITZMAN, S., Paediatrics
WELLS, J., Pharmacology
WELLS, P., Pharmacology
WILLIAMS, D., Biochemistry
WILLINSKY, R., Medical Imaging
WILSON, B., Medical Biophysics
WILSON, G., Pathobiology
WILSON, S., Medical Imaging
WILSON-PAUWELS, L., Biomedical Communications
WITTNICH, C., Cardiac Surgery
WOJTOWICZ, J., Physiology
WOLEVER, T., Nutritional Sciences
WOOLRIDGE, N., Biomedical Communications
WONG, P.-Y., Pathobiology
WONG, S., Medical Biophysics
WONG, J. T. F., Biochemistry
WOOD, M., Medical Imaging
WOOD, L., Medical Biophysics
WOODGETT, J., Medical Biophysics
WU, T. W., Clinical Biochemistry
YAFFE, M., Medical Biophysics
YIP, C. C., Medical Research
YOO, S.-J., Medical Imaging
ZAMEL, N., Otolaryngology
ZHOU, M., Physiology

Faculty of Music:

ARMENIAN, R., Director of Orchestral Activities
HARTENBERGER, R., Pecussion, Graduate Coordinator
HATZIS, C., Composition
HAWKINS, J., Theory and Composition
LAUFER, E. C., Music Theory
MACDONALD, L., Voice Studies
SHAND, P. M., Music Education

Faculty of Nursing:

GALLOP, R.
HILLAN, E.
HODNETT, E.
MCKEEVER, P.
O'BRIEN-PALLAS, L.
PRINGLE, D.
STEVENS, B.

Ontario Institute for Studies in Education:

ACKER, S., Sociology and Equity Studies in Education, Theory and Policy Studies in Education
ASTINGTON, J., Human Development
BECK, C., Curriculum, Teaching and Learning
BIEMILLER, A. J.
BOGDAN, D., Theory and Policy and Studies in Education
BOYD, D., Theory and Policy Studies in Education
COLE, A., Adult Education
CONNELLY, M., Curriculum, Teaching and Learning
CORTER, C. M.
CUMMING, A., Curriculum, Teaching and Learning
CUMMINS, J., Curriculum, Teaching and Learning
DARROCH-LOZOWSKI, V., Curriculum, Teaching and Learning
DAVIE, L., Curriculum, Teaching and Learning
DEI, G., Sociology and Equity Studies in Education
DIAMOND, P.
EICHLER, M., Sociology and Equity Studies in Education
FARRELL, J., Curriculum, Teaching and Learning, Theory and Policy Studies in Education
GASKELL, J., Sociology and Equity Studies in Education
GEVA, E., Curriculum, Teaching and Learning
GUTTMAN, M. A., Counselling Psychology
HANNAY, L., Curriculum, Teaching and Learning
HARVEY, E., Sociology and Equity Studies in Education
HAYHOE, R., Theory and Policy Studies in Education
HELLER, M., Sociology and Equity Studies in Education
HODSON, D., Curriculum, Teaching and Learning
JENKINS, J., Human Development
JORDAN, A., Curriculum, Teaching and Learning
KEATING, D., Human Development
KNOWLES, J. G., Adult Education
LABRIE, N., Curriculum, Teaching and Learning
LANG, D., Theory and Policy Studies in Education
LAPKIN, S., Curriculum, Teaching and Learning
LEITHWOOD, K., Theory and Policy Studies in Education
LENSKYJ, H., Sociology and Equity Studies in Education
LEVINE, D., Theory and Policy Studies in Education
LEWIS, M., Human Development
LIVINGSTONE, D., Sociology and Equity Studies in Education
MCLEAN, R., Curriculum, Teaching and Learning
MIEZITIS, S., Teacher Education
MILLER, J., Curriculum, Teaching and Learning
MISGELD, D., Theory and Policy Studies in Education
MOORE, C., Human Development
NG, R., Adult Education, Sociology and Equity Studies in Education
O'SULLIVAN, E., Adult Education
OATLEY, K., Human Development
OLSON, D., Human Development
PASCAL, C., Theory and Policy Studies in Education
PIERSON, R. R., Sociology and Equity Studies in Education
PIRAN, N., Counselling Psychology
PORTELLI, J., Theory and Policy Studies in Education
QUARTER, J., Adult Education
ROSS, J., Curriculum, Teaching and Learning

RYAN, J., Theory and Policy Studies in Education
SCARDAMALIA, J., Curriculum, Teaching and Learning
SIMON, R., Curriculum, Teaching and Learning
SKOLNIK, M., Theory and Policy Studies in Education
SPADA, N., Curriculum, Teaching and Learning
STANOVICH, K., Curriculum, Teaching and Learning
STERMAC, L., Counselling Psychology
SWAIN, M., Curriculum, Teaching and Learning
THIESSEN, D., Curriculum, Teaching and Learning
TROPER, H., Theory and Policy Studies in Education
VOLPE, R., Human Development
WIENER, J., Human Development
WILLOWS, D., Curriculum, Teaching and Learning
WILSON, D., Curriculum, Teaching and Learning, Theory and Policy Studies in Education

Faculty of Pharmacy:
O'BRIEN, P. J.
PANG, K. S.
PERRIER, D. G.
ROBINSON, J. B.
SEGAL, H.
STIEB, E. W., History of Pharmacy
THIESSEN, J. J.
UETRECHT, J. P.

Faculty of Social Work:
BARBER, J.
BOGO, M.
HULCHANSKI, D.
LIGHTMAN, E.
MCDONALD, L.
NEYSMITH, S.
SHERA, W.

School of Graduate Studies:
ANGENOT, M., Comparative Literature
BEATTIE, J. M., Criminology
BOND, R. J., Theoretical Astronomy
BRYDEN, R., Drama
COHEN, J. S., Graduate Studies
DOOB, A. N., Criminology
HACKING, I. M., History and Philosophy of Science and Technology
HARIANTO, F., International Studies
HEALEY, A. D., Medieval Studies
HERNANDEZ, C., International Studies
KAISER, N., Theoretical Astronomy
LEVERE, T. H., History and Philosophy of Science and Technology
MARKER, L. L., Drama
MARTIN, P. G., Theoretical Astronomy
NESSELROTH, P. W., Comparative Literature
PESANDO, J. E., Policy Analysis
RIGG, A. G., Medieval Studies
SHEARING, C. D., Criminology
STENNING, P. C., Criminology
STOCK, B. C., Comparative Literature
TREMAINE, S. D., Theoretical Astronomy
VALVERDE, M. V., Criminology
WINSOR, M. P., History and Philosophy of Science and Technology

Joseph L. Rothman School of Management:
AIVAZIAN, V., Finance
AMBURGEY, T. (acting), Strategic Management
AMERNIC, J. (acting), Accounting
BAUM, J. (acting), Strategic Management
BEATTY, D. (acting), Strategic Management
BERKOWITZ, M. (acting), Finance
BERMAN, O. (acting), Operations Management
BIRD, R. (acting), Economics
BOOTH, L. (acting), Finance
BORINS, S. (acting), Public Management
BREAN, D. (acting), Business Economics
BROOKS, L. (acting), Business Ethics and Accounting
CALLEN, J. (acting), Accounting
D'CRUZ, J. (acting), Strategic Management
DOBSON, W. (acting), International Business
DUAN, J.-C. (acting), Finance
EVANS, M. (acting), Organizational Behaviour
FELDMAN, M. (acting), Business Economics
FLECK, J. (acting), Business Government Relations
GOLDEN, B. (acting), Strategic Management
GUNZ, H. (acting), Organizational Behaviour
HALPERN, P. (acting), Finance
HORSTMANN, I. (acting), Business Economics
HUGHES, P. (acting), Strategic Management, Space Systems
HULL, J. (acting), Finance
HYATT, D. (acting), Business Economics
KIRZNER, E. (acting), Finance
KOLODNY, H. (acting), Organizational Behaviour
LATHAM, G. (acting), Organizational Effectiveness
MARTIN, R. (acting), Strategic Management
MCCURDY, T. (acting), Finance
MENZEFRICKE, U. (acting), Operations Management
MINTZ, J. (acting), Taxation
MITCHELL, A. (acting), Marketing
MOORTHY, S. (acting), Marketing
ONDRACK, D. (acting), Organizational Behaviour
PAULY, P. (acting), Economics
SMIELIAUSKAS, W. (acting), Accounting
SOMAN, D. (acting), Marketing
STARK, A. (acting), Strategic Management
STRANGE, W. (acting), Urban Economics
TOMBAK, M. (acting), Technology Management
TREFLER, D. (acting), Business Economics
WHITE, A. (acting), Finance
WHYTE, G. (acting), Organizational Behaviour
WILSON, T. (acting), Economics

School of Physical Education and Health:
COREY, P. (acting)
DONNELLY, P.
FERNIE, G.
GOODE, R.
JACOBS, I.
LEITH, L.
LENSKYJ, H.
MCCLELLAND, J.
MCKEE, N.
PLYLEY, M.
VOLPE, R.

UNIVERSITY COLLEGES

Erindale College/University of Toronto at Mississauga: 3359 Mississauga Rd North, Mississauga, ON L5L 1C6; tel. 828-5211; f. 1964; Principal IAN ORCHARD.

Innis College: 2 Sussex Ave, Toronto, ON M5S 1J5; tel. 978-7023; fax 978-5503; internet www.utoronto.ca/innisf. 1964; Principal F. CUNNINGHAM.

New College: 300 Huron St, Toronto, ON M5S 3JO; tel. 978-2461; fax 978-0554; internet http://utt2.library.utoronto.ca/www/new_college/index.htmf. 1962; President DAVID KLANDFIELD.

Scarborough College: 1265 Military Trail, Scarborough, ON M1C 1A4; tel. 287-8872; f. 1964; Principal R. P. THOMPSON.

University College: 15 King's College Circle, Toronto, ON M5S 3H7; tel. 978-3170; f. 1853; Principal PAUL J. PERRON.

Woodsworth College: 117–119 St George St, Toronto, ON M5S 1A9; tel. 978-2411; fax 978-6111; e-mail info@wdw.utoronto.caf. 1974; Principal N. M. MELTZ.

FEDERATED UNIVERSITIES

University of St Michael's College: 81 St Mary St, Toronto, ON M5S 1J4; tel. (416) 926-1300; f. 1958; conducted by the Basilian Fathers; Pres. Dr RICHARD ALWAY.

University of Trinity College: 6 Hoskin Ave, Toronto, ON M5S 1H8; tel. (416) 978-2522; f. 1851; Vice-Chancellor and Provost R. PAINTER.

Victoria University, Toronto: 73 Queen's Park Cres., Toronto, ON M5S 1K7; tel. (416) 585-4524; f. 1836; Pres. E. KUSHNER.

FEDERATED COLLEGES

Emmanuel College: 75 Queen's Park Cres., Toronto, ON M5S 1K7; tel. (416) 585-4540; f. 1928; United Church of Canada theological college; Principal JOHN HOFFMAN.

Knox College: 59 St George St, Toronto, ON M5S 2E5; tel. (416) 978-4500; Presbyterian theological college; Principal Rev. Dr RAYMOND HUMPHRYES (acting).

Regis College: 15 St Mary St, Toronto, ON M4Y 2R5; tel. (416) 922-5474; f. 1930; Roman Catholic theological college (Society of Jesus); Pres. Rev. JOHN E. COSTELLO.

Wycliffe College: 5 Hoskin Ave, Toronto, ON M5S 1H7; tel. (416) 979-2870; Anglican theological college; Principal Rev. H. S. HILCHEY (acting).

AFFILIATED INSTITUTES

Massey College: University of Toronto, Toronto, ON M5S 2E1; tel. (416) 978-2895; f. 1963; residential college for graduates and senior scholars engaged in research; Master J. S. DUPRE.

Pontifical Institute of Medieval Studies: 59 Queen's Park Cres. East, Toronto, ON M5S 2C4; affiliated to Univ. of St Michael's College; grants degrees in its own right, offering pontifical Licentiate in Medieval Studies (MSL) and Doctorate in Medieval Studies (MSD); Pres. Prof. M. DIMNIK.

TRENT UNIVERSITY

1600 West Bank Drive, Peterborough, ON K9J 7B8
Telephone: (705) 748-1332
Fax: (705) 748-1629
E-mail: liaison@trentu.ca
Internet: www.trentu.ca

Founded 1963
Language of instruction: English
Academic year: September to April (two semesters with reading periods intervening; summer sessions also available)

Chancellor: Dr ROBERTA BONDAR
President and Vice-Chancellor: BONNIE M. PATTERSON
Vice-President for Academic Affairs and Provost: SUSAN APOSTLE-CLARK
Vice-President for Administration: DON O'LEARY
Vice-President for External Relations and Advancement: DIANNE LISTER
Registrar: SUSAN SALUSBURY
Senior Director of Public Affairs: DON CUMMING
University Librarian: ROBERT F. CLARKE

Number of teachers: 467 (325 full-time, 142 part-time)
Number of students: 8,050 undergraduates (6,688 full-time, 1,362 part-time), 277 postgraduates

DEANS

Faculty of Arts and Science: CHRISTINE McKINNON
Faculty of Graduate Studies: DOUGLAS EVANS

PROFESSORS

ARVIN, M. C., Economics
BANDYOPADHYAY, P., Comparative Development Studies
BERRILL, D., School of Education
BERRILL, M., Biology
BISHOP, J., Business Administration
BRUNGER, A. G., Geography
BUTTLE, J., Geography
CHOUDRY, S., Economics
COGLEY, J. G., Geography
CONOLLY, L. W., English Literature
CURTIS, D. C. A., Economics
DAWSON, P. C., Physics
DELLAMORA, R. J., English Literature and Cultural Studies
DILLON, P., Environmental Studies, Chemistry
EVANS, D., Environmental Studies
EVANS, W., Environmental Studies, Physics
FEKETE, J. A., English Literature, Cultural Studies
FOX, M., Environmental Studies, Biology
HAGMAN, R. S., Anthropology
HEALY, P. F., Anthropology
HEITLINGER, A., Sociology
HURLEY, R., Computer Studies, Science
HUXLEY, C. V., Sociology and Comparative Development Studies
JAMIESON, S., Anthropology
JOHNSTON, G. A., English Literature
JONES, E. H., History
JURY, J. W., Physics and Computer Studies
KANE, S., English Literature, Cultural Studies
KATZ, S., Sociology
KEEFER, S., English Literature
KENNETT, D. J., Psychology
KINZL, K. H., Ancient History and Classics
KITCHEN, H. M., Economics
LAFLEUR, P., Geography
LASENBY, D. C., Biology
LEM, W., International Development Studies and Women's Studies
LEWARS, E. G., Chemistry
MAXWELL, E. A., Mathematics
MCCASKILL, D. N., Native Studies
MCKENNA-NEWMAN, C., Geography
MCKINNON, C., Philosophy
METCALFE, C., Environmental Studies
MILLOY, J., Native Studies and History
MITCHELL, O. S., English Literature
MORRISON, D. R., International Development Studies
NADER, G. A., Geography
NEUFELD, J. E., English Literature
NEUMANN, M., Philosophy
NOL, E., Biology
NORIEGA, T. A., Hispanic Studies
PAEHLKE, R. C., Political Studies, Environmental Studies
PALMER, B., Canadian Studies
PARNIS, M., Chemistry
PATTERSON, B., Business Administration
PETERMAN, M., English Literature
PICKEL, A., Political Studies
POLLOCK, Z., English Literature
POOLE, D. G., Mathematics
REKER, G. T., Psychology
SANGSTER, J., History and Women's Studies
SHEININ, D., History
SLAVIN, A. J., Physics
SMITH, C. T., Psychology
SO, J. K.-F., Anthropology
STANDEN, S. D., History
STOREY, I. C., Ancient History and Classics
STRUTHERS, J. E., Canadian Studies, History
SVISHCHEV, I., Chemistry
SUTCLIFFE, J., Biology
TAMPLIN, M., Anthropology
TAYLOR, C., Geography
TAYLOR, G., History
TINDALE, C., Philosophy
TOPIC, J. R., Anthropology
TORGERSON, D., Environmental and Resource Studies
TROMLY, F. B., English Literature
WADLAND, J. H., Canadian Studies
WALDEN, K., History
WERNICK, A. L., Cultural Studies
WHITE, B., Biology
WINOCUR, G., Psychology
ZHOU, B., Mathematics

TRINITY WESTERN UNIVERSITY

7600 Glover Rd, Langley, BC V2Y 1Y1
Telephone: (604) 888-7511
Fax: (604) 513-2061
E-mail: suderman@twu.ca
Internet: www.twu.ca

Founded 1962, university status 1985
Private control
Language of instruction: English
Academic year: September to April

President: Dr R. NEIL SNIDER
Executive Vice-President: Dr GUY SAFFOLD
Vice-President (Academic Affairs): Dr DENNIS JAMESON
Vice-President (Advancement): DORIS OLAFSON
Vice-President (Finance): JIM POULSON (acting)
Vice-President (Student Life): Dr KEN KUSH
Registrar: Dr LAWRENCE H. VANBEEK
Librarian: TED GOSHULAK

Library of 430,000 items
Number of teachers: 181 (96 full-time, 85 part-time)
Number of students: 3,500

DEANS

Faculty of Humanities and Social Sciences: Dr ROBERT BURKINSHAW
Faculty of Natural and Applied Sciences: Dr JOHN VAN DYKE
Faculty of Professional Studies and Performing Arts: Prof. LINDA SCHWARTZ
School of Business and Economics: KEVIN SAWATSKY

DEPARTMENT HEADS

Art: Prof. DORIS HUTTON AUXIER
Biology: Dr RICHARD PAULTON
Business: KEVIN SAWATSKY
Drama: Dr LLOYD ARNETT
Chemistry: Dr CRAIG MONTGOMERY
Communications: Dr WILLIAM STROM
English and Modern Languages: Dr BARBARA PELL
Geography, History and Political Science: Dr BRUCE SHELVEY
Linguistics: Dr MICHAEL WALROD
Music: LINDA SCHWARTZ
Mathematical Sciences: Dr JOHN BYL
Nursing: BARBARA PESUT
Philosophy: Dr PHILLIP WIEBE
Physical Education and Recreation: Dr BLAIR WHITMARSH
Psychology, Sociology and Anthropology: Dr RONALD PHILIPCHALK
Religious Studies: Dr MARTIN ABEGG
Teacher Education: Dr JOY MCCULLOUGH
Graduate Administrative Leadership: Dr DON PAGE
Graduate Biblical Studies: Dr PETER FLINT
Graduate Counselling Psychology: Dr MARVIN MCDONALD
Graduate Religion, Culture and Ethics: Dr PHILLIP WICKE

AFFILIATED COLLEGES

Canadian Baptist Seminary: Pres. Dr DARYL BUSBY.

Canadian Theological Seminary: Pres. Dr GEORGE DURANCE.

Northwest Baptist Seminary: Pres. Dr LARRY PERKINS.

Trinity Western Seminary: Pres. Dr R. NEIL SNIDER.

Western Pentecostal Bible College

UNIVERSITY OF VICTORIA

POB 1700, Victoria, BC V8W 2Y2
Telephone: (604) 721-7211
Fax: (604) 721-7212
E-mail: ucom@uvic.ca
Internet: www.uvic.ca

Founded 1963
Language of instruction: English
Provincial control
Academic year: September to April

Chancellor: NORMA I. MICKELSON
President and Vice-Chancellor: DAVID H. TURPIN
Vice-President (Academic) and Provost: JAMES L. CASSELS
Vice-President (External Relations): FAYE WIGHTMAN
Vice-President (Finance and Operations): JACK FALK
Vice-President (Research): Dr S. MARTIN TAYLOR
University Secretary: SHEILA SHELDON COLLYER
Administrative Registrar: D. CLEDWYN THOMAS
University Librarian: MARGARET C. SWANSON

Number of teachers: 701
Number of students: 18,415

Publications: *Calendar* (annually), *Malahat Review*

DEANS

Faculty of Business: ALI DASTMALCHIAN
Faculty of Education: BUDD HALL
Faculty of Engineering: MICHAEL MILLER
Faculty of Fine Arts: GILES HOGYA
Faculty of Graduate Studies: AARON DEVOR
Faculty of Human and Social Development: MICHAEL PRINCE (acting)
Faculty of Humanities: ANDREW RIPPIN
Faculty of Law: JOHN MCLAREN (acting)
Faculty of Science: THOMAS PEDERSON
Faculty of Social Sciences: JOHN A. SCHOFIELD

PROFESSORS

AGATHOKLIS, P., Electrical and Computer Engineering
ANDERSON, J., Educational Psychology and Leadership Studies
ANDRACHUK, G. P., Hispanic and Italian Studies
ANTONIOU, A., Electrical and Computer Engineering
ARMITAGE, A., Social Work
AUSIO, J., Biochemistry and Microbiology
AVIO, K. L., Economics
BACHOR, D. G., Psychological Foundations
BALFOUR, W. J., Chemistry
BARCLAY, J. A., Mechanical Engineering
BARNES, C., Earth and Ocean Sciences
BARNES, G. E., Child and Youth Care
BASKERVILLE, P. A., History
BAVELAS, J. B., Psychology
BEDESKI, R. E., Political Science
BENNETT, C., Political Science
BENOIT, C., Sociology
BERRY, E. I., English
BEST, M. R., English
BHARGAVA, V. K., Electrical and Computer Engineering
BHAT, A. K. S., Electrical and Computer Engineering
BLANK, K., English
BOAG, D. A., Faculty of Business

BOHNE, C., Chemistry
BORNEMANN, J., Electrical and Computer Engineering
BORROWS, J., Law
BRADLEY, K. R., Classics
BRENER, R., Visual Arts
BROWNING-MOORE, A., Music
BRUNT, H., Nursing
BRYANT, D., Pacific and Asian Studies
BUB, D., Psychology
BUCKLEY, J. T., Biochemistry and Microbiology
BURKE, R. D., Biology
CAMPBELL, M., Human and Social Development
CARROLL, W. K., Sociology
CASSELS, J. L., Law
CASSWELL, D. G., Law
CELONA, J., Music
CHAPMAN, R., Earth and Ocean Sciences
CHAPPELL, N. L., Sociology
COBLEY, E., English
COCKAYNE, E. J., Mathematics and Statistics
COOPERSTOCK, F. I., Physics and Astronomy
COWARD, H. G., History
CROIZIER, L., Writing
CROIZIER, R. C., History
CUNNINGHAM, J. B., Public Administration
CUTT, J., Public Administration
DEARDEN, P., Geography
DEVOR, H., Sociology
DIACU, F., Mathematics and Statistics
DIMOPOULOS, N., Electrical and Computer Engineering
DIPPIE, B. W., History
DIXON, R. A., Psychology
DJILALI, N., Mechanical Engineering
DOBELL, A. R., Public Administration
DOCHERTY, D., Physical Education
DONALD, L. H., Anthropology
DONG, Z., Mechanical Engineering
DOST, S., Mechanical Engineering
DYSON, L., Psychological Foundations
EDWARDS, A. S., English
EL GUIBALY, F. H., Electrical and Computer Engineering
ENGINEER, M., Economics
ESLING, J., Linguistics
FELLOWS, M., Computer Science
FERGUSON, G. A., Law
FLEMING, T., Education
FOSS, J., Philosophy
FOSTER, H., Law
FOSTER, H. D., Geography
FOWLER, R., Social and Natural Sciences
FRANCE, H., Psychological Foundations
FYLES, T. M., Chemistry
GALAMBOS, N., Psychology
GALLAGHER, Nursing
GALLOWAY, J., Law
GARTRELL, D., Sociology
GARRETT, C., Physics, Earth and Ocean Sciences
GIBSON-WOOD, C., History in Art
GIFFORD, R. D., Psychology
GILES, D. E., Economics
GILLIN, M., Law
GLICKMAN, B., Biology
GOOCH, B. N. S., English
GOUGH, T. E., Chemistry
GRANT, P. J., English
GREGORY, P. T., Biology
GULLIVER, A., Electrical and Computer Engineering
HALL, B., Curriculum and Instruction
HANLEY, B., Curriculum and Instruction
HARKER, W. J., Education
HARRINGTON, D., Chemistry
HARRIS, C., Communication and Social Foundations
HARTWICK, F. D. A., Physics and Astronomy
HARVEY, B., Psychological Foundations
HAWRYSHYN, C., Biology
HEDLEY, R. A., Sociology
HILLS, M., Nursing
HOCKING, M., Chemistry
HODGINS, J., Creative Writing
HOEFER, W. J. R., Electrical and Computer Engineering
HOGYA, G., Theatre
HORITA, R. E., Physics and Astronomy
HORSPOOL, R. N., Computer Science
HOWE, B. L., Physical Education
HOWELL, R. G., Law
HUENEMANN, R. W., Faculty of Business
HULTSCH, D. F., Psychology
ILLNER, R., Mathematics and Statistics
ISHIGURO, E. E., Biochemistry and Microbiology
JOHNSON, T. D., Education
JONES, J. C. H., Economics
KAMBOURELI, S., English
KAY, W. W., Biochemistry and Microbiology
KEELER, R., Physics and Astronomy
KELLER, A., English
KELLER, P., Geography
KERBY-FULTON, K., English
KESS, J. F., Linguistics
KINDERMAN, W., Music
KIRLIN, R. L., Electrical and Computer Engineering
KLUGE, E.-H., Philosophy
KOENIG, D., Sociology
KOOP, B., Biology
KREBS, H., Music
KUEHNE, V., Child and Youth Care
KWOK, H. H. L., Electrical and Computer Engineering
LAI, D. C.-Y., Geography
LANGFORD, J. W., Public Administration
LAPPRAND, M., French Language and Literature
LAZAREVICH, G., Music
LEADBEATER, B., Psychology
LEEMING, D. J., Mathematics and Statistics
LIDDELL, P., Germanic Studies
LIEDTKE, W. W., Education
LINDSAY, D., Psychology
LISCOMB, K., History in Art
LIVINGSTON, N., Biology
LONERGAN, S. C., Geography
LU, W.-S., Electrical and Computer Engineering
M'GONIGLE, R., Environmental Studies
MACGREGOR, J. N., Public Administration
MACPHERSON, G. R. I., History
MAGNUSSON, W., Political Science
MALONEY, M. A., Law
MANNING, E. G., Computer Science, Electrical and Computer Engineering
MARTIN-NEWCOMBE, Y., Communication and Social Foundations
MASSON, M. E. J., Psychology
MATEER, C., Psychology
MAYFIELD, M., Education
MAZUMDER, A., Biology
MCCANN, L., Geography
MCDAVID, J. C., Public Administration
MCDORMAN, T., Law
MCDOUGALL, I., Music
MCLAREN, A. G., History
MCLAREN, J. P. S., Law
MIERS, C. R., Mathematics and Statistics
MILLER, D., Computer Science
MISRA, S., Biochemistry and Microbiology
MITCHELL, D. H., Anthropology
MITCHELL, R. H., Chemistry
MOEHR, J. R., Health Information Service
MOLZAHN, A., Nursing
MORE, B. E., Music
MORGAN, C. G., Philosophy
MOSK, C. A., Economic Relations with Japan
MULLER, H., Computer Science
MURPHY, P., Communication and Social Foundations
MUZIO, J. C., Computer Science
MYRVOLD, W., Computer Science
NANO, F., Biochemistry and Microbiology
NEILSON, W. A. W., Law
NG, I., Business
NICHOLS, D., Physical Education
NIEMANN, O., Geography
OGMUNDSON, R., Sociology
OLAFSON, R. W., Biochemistry and Microbiology
OLESKY, D., Computer Science
OLESON, J. P., Classics
OSBORNE, J., History in Art
PAETKAU, V., Biochemistry
PEARSON, T. W., Biochemistry and Microbiology
PENCE, A. R., Child and Youth Care
PFAFFENBERGER, W. E., Mathematics and Statistics
PHILLIPS, J., Mathematics and Statistics
PICCIOTTO, C. E., Physics and Astronomy
PINDER, W. C., Business
PORTEOUS, J. D., Geography
PRINCE, M. J., Social Policy
PRITCHET, C. J., Physics
PROTTI, D. J., Health Information Science
PROVAN, J. W., Mechanical Engineering
PUTNAM, I., Mathematics and Statistics
RANGER, L., Music
REED, W. J., Mathematics and Statistics
REID, R. G. B., Biology
REITSMA-STREET, M., Child and Youth Care
RICKS, F. A. S., Child and Youth Care
RIEDEL, W. E., Germanic Studies
RING, R. A., Biology
ROMANIUK, P., Biochemistry and Microbiology
ROTH, E., Anthropology
ROTH, W.-M., Social and Natural Sciences
ROY, P., History
RUSKEY, F., Computer Science
RUTHERFORD, M., Economics
SAGER, E. W., History
ST PETER, C., Women's Studies
SCARFE, C. D., Physics and Astronomy
SCHAAFSMA, J., Economics
SCHAARSCHMIDT, G. H., Slavonic Studies
SCHOFIELD, J. A., Economics
SCHULER, R., English
SCHWANDT, E., Music
SCOBIE, S. A. C., English
SERRA, M., Computer Science
SHERWOOD, N., Biology
SHRIMPTON, G., Greek and Roman Studies
SMITH, D., Geography
SOUROUR, A. R., Mathematics and Statistics
SRIVASTAVA, H. M., Mathematics and Statistics
STEPANENKO, Y., Mechanical Engineering
STEPHENSON, P. H., Anthropology
STOBART, S. R., Chemistry
STORCH, J., Nursing
STOREY, V., Communication and Social Foundations
STRAUSS, E., Psychology
STRONG, D. F., Earth and Ocean Sciences
STUCHLY, M., Electrical and Computer Engineering
SYMINGTON, R. T. K., Germanic Studies
THALER, D., French Language and Literature
THATCHER, D. S., English
TUCKER, J., English
TULLER, S., Geography
TULLY, J., Political Science
TUNNICLIFFE, V. J., Earth and Ocean Sciences, Biology
TURNER, N., Environmental Studies
UHLEMANN, M. R., Education
VALGARDSON, W. D., Creative Writing
VAN DEN DRIESSCHE, R., Biology
VAN EMDEN, M., Computer Science
VAN GYN, G., Physical Education
VANCE, J. H., Education
VANDENBERG, D. A., Physics
VICKERS, G. W., Mechanical Engineering
VOGT, B., Music
VON ADERKAS, P., Biology
WADGE, W. W., Computer Science
WALDRON, M. A., Law
WALKER, R. B. J., Political Science
WALTER, G. R., Economics
WAN, P. C., Chemistry
WARBURTON, R., Sociology

WATTON, A., Physics and Astronomy
WEAVER, A., Earth and Ocean Sciences
WELCH, S. A., History in Art
WENGER, H. A., Physical Education
WHITICAR, M., Earth and Ocean Sciences
WILL, H. J., Public Administration
WILLIAMS, T., English
WILSON, J., Political Science
WOLFF, R., Business
WOON, YUEN-FONG, Pacific Asian Studies
WU, Z., Sociology
WYNAND, D., Creative Writing
YORE, L. D., Education
YOUDS, R., Visual Arts
YOUNG, J., Philosophy
ZIELINSKI, A., Electrical and Computer Engineering
ZIMMERMAN, D., History
ZUK, W., Arts in Education

UNIVERSITY OF WATERLOO

Waterloo, ON N2L 3G1
Telephone: (519) 888-4567 ext. 33614
Fax: (519) 746-8088
Internet: www.uwaterloo.ca

Founded 1957

Provincially supported
Language of instruction: English
Academic year: September to April (Co-operative programmes September to August, Summer Session July to August)

Chancellor: MIKE LAZARIDIS
President and Vice-Chancellor: DAVID L. JOHNSTON
Vice-President (Academic and Provost): AMIT CHAKMA
Vice-President (Administration and Finance): DENNIS E. HUBER
Vice-President (University Relations): LAURA TALBOT-ALLAN
Vice-President (University Research): ALAN GEORGE
Associate Provost (Academic and Student Affairs): BRUCE MITCHELL
Associate Provost (Human Resources and Student Services): CATHARINE SCOTT
Associate Provost (Information Systems and Technology): ALAN GEORGE
Registrar: KEN A. LAVIGNE
University Librarian: MARK HASLETT

Library of 2,006,887 vols
Number of teachers: 1,006 (full-time and part-time)
Number of students: 26,125
Publications: *Alternatives* (6 a year), *Environments Journal* (3 a year), *New Quarterly*

DEANS

Faculty of Applied Health Sciences: ROGER MANNELL
Faculty of Arts: KEN COATES
Faculty of Engineering: Prof. ADEL SEDRA
Faculty of Environmental Studies: Dr H. S. (DEEP) SAINI
Faculty of Mathematics: TOM COLEMAN
Faculty of Science: D. G. DIXON
Graduate Studies: Dr RANJANA P. BIRD

DEPARTMENT CHAIRMEN AND DIRECTORS OF PROGRAMMES AND SCHOOLS

Accounting: A. MASON
Anthropology: A. ZELLER
Applied Mathematics: J. WAINWRIGHT
Architecture: E. R. HALDENBY
Biology: B. GLICK
Canadian Studies: G. BROWN
Chemical Engineering: T. DKEVER
Chemistry: F. MCCOURT
Church Music and Worship: K. HULL
Civil Engineering: L. ROTHENBURG
Classical Studies: L. CURCHIN
Cognititve Science: P. THAGARD
Combinatorics and Optimization: P. SCHELLENBERG
Computer Science: J. WONG
Drama and Speech Communication: W. CHESNEY
Earth Sciences: M. CONIGLIO
East Asian Studies: J. CROSSLEY
Economics: J. BURBIDGE
Electrical and Computer Engineering: C. ROSENBERG
English Language and Literature: K. MCGUIRK
Environmental Economics: E. CARVALHO
Environmental Engineering: S. ANDREWS
Environment and Resource Studies: S. WISMER
Fine and Performing Arts: R. RYMAN
Fine Arts: J. BUYERS
French Studies: F. PARÉ
Geography: P. PARKER
Geological Engineering: M. KNIGHT
Germanic and Slavic Studies: M. BOEHRINGER
Health Studies and Gerontology: S. MCCOLL
History: P. J. HARRIGAN
Human Resources Management: P. ROWE
Independent Studies: R. HOLMES
International Studies: B. OREND
Italian: G. NICCOLI
Kinesiology: S. MCGILL
Legal Studies and Criminology: F. DESROCHES
Management Sciences: E. JEWKES
Management Studies: R. BODELL
Mechanical Engineering: G. E. SCHNEIDER
Mennonite Studies: M. EPP
Music: K. HULL
Optometry: W. BOBIER
Peace and Conflict Studies: L. EWERT
Philosophy: R. H. HOLMES
Physics: R. MANN
Planning: M. HAIGHT
Political Science: R. NUTBROWN
Psychology: M. DIXON
Pure Mathematics: F. ZORZITTO
Recreation and Leisure Studies: A. PEDLAR
Religious Studies: L. DAWSON
Social Development Studies: K. MOTT
Social Work: E. S. MESBUR
Society, Technology and Values: N. R. BALL
Sociology: J. GOYDER
Spanish and Latin American Studies: M. GUTIÉRREZ
Statistics and Actuarial Science: J. LAWLESS
Studies in Personality and Religion: J. GOLLNICK
Sexuality, Marriage and Family Studies: B. J. RYE
Systems Design Engineering: G. HEPPLER
Women's Studies: R. BURY

FEDERATED UNIVERSITY

St Jerome's University: Waterloo, ON N2L 3G3; f. 1864; federated 1960; Roman Catholic, conducted by the Congregation of the Resurrection; Pres. M. HIGGINS.

AFFILIATED COLLEGES

Conrad Grebel College: Waterloo, ON N2L 3G6; f. 1961; Mennonite; Pres. H. PAETKAU.

Renison College: Waterloo, ON N2L 3G4; f. 1959, affiliated 1960; Anglican; Principal J. CROSSLEY.

St Paul's United College: Waterloo, ON N2L 3G5; f. 1962; United Church of Canada; Principal G. BROWN.

UNIVERSITY OF WESTERN ONTARIO

1151 Richmond St, Suite 2, London, ON N6A 5B8
Telephone: (519) 661-2111
Fax: (519) 661-3710
E-mail: reg-admissions@uwo.ca
Internet: www.uwo.ca

Founded 1878

Academic year: September to April
Chancellor: ARTHUR S. LABATT
President and Vice-Chancellor: Dr PAUL DAVENPORT
Vice-President (Academic) and Provost: Dr GREG MORAN
Vice-President (Administration): GITTA KULCZYCKI
Vice-President (External): Dr TED GARRARD
Vice-President (Research): Dr TED HEWITT
Vice-Provost (Academic Programs and Students) and Registrar: Dr ROMA HARRIS
Vice-Provost (Policy, Planning and Faculty): Dr ALAN WEEDON
University Librarian: JOYCE GARNETT

Library of 3,085,319 vols
Number of teachers: 1,219 full-time
Number of students: 37,693 (33,329 full-time, 4,364 part-time)
Publications: *Alumni Gazette* (magazine, 3 a year), *The Business Quarterly*, *Dental Journal*, *Gazette* (student daily bulletin), *Mediations*, *Medical Journal*, *The President's Report*, *Reflections*, *The Science Terrapin*, *Western News* (weekly newspaper)

DEANS

Faculty of Arts and Humanities: Dr KATHLEEN OKRUHLIK
Faculty of Education: Dr A. T. PEARSON
Faculty of Engineering: Dr F. BERRUTI
Faculty of Health Sciences: Dr J. WEESE
Faculty of Information and Media Studies: Dr C. ROSS
Faculty of Law: Prof. I. HOLLOWAY
Schulich School of Medicine and Dentistry: Dr C. P. HERBERT
Don Wright Faculty of Music: Dr ROBERT WOOD
Faculty of Science: Dr R. A. HAINES (acting)
Faculty of Social Science: Dr B. TIMNEY
Faculty of Graduate Studies: Dr M. KREISWIRTH
Richard Ivey School of Business: C. STEPHENSON

PROFESSORS

Faculty of Arts and Humanities (tel. (519) 661-3043; fax (519) 661-3640; internet www.uwo.ca/arts):

ADAMS, S. J., English
BELL, J. L., Philosophy
BENTLEY, D. M. R., English
BRENNAN, S., Philosophy (Head)
BROWN, C. G., Classical Studies (Head)
BROWN, H., Philosophy
BRUSH, K., Visual Arts
CROWTHER, N. B., Classical Studies
DAVEY, F. W., English
DEMOPOULOS, W. G., Philosophy
ELLIOTT, B., Visual Arts
ESTERHAMMER, A., English, Modern Languages and Literatures
FALKENSTEIN, L., Philosophy
GEDALOF, A., Film Studies
GITTINGS, C., Film Studies (Head)
GOLDSCHLAGER, A. J., French
GRODEN, M. L., English
HARPER, W. L., Philosophy
HOFFMASTER, C. B., Philosophy
KNEALE, J. D., English (Head)
KREISWIRTH, M., English
LEE, A. M., Women's Studies (Head)
LENNON, T. M., Philosophy
LEONARD, J., English
LITTLEWOOD, A. R., Classical Studies
MAHON, P., Visual Arts (Head)
MARRAS, A., Philosophy
MAYNARD, P. L., Philosophy, Visual Arts
MURISON, L., Classical Studies
POOLE, R., English
PURDY, A., French
RAJAN, T., English
RANDALL, M., French

SOMERSET, J. A. B., English
TENNANT, J., French (Head)
THOMSON, C., French

Faculty of Education (tel. (519) 661-3182; internet www.uwo.ca/edu):

CUMMINGS, A.
DICKINSON, G. M.
LESCHIED, A.
MAJHANOVICH, S. E. W.
PEARSON, A. T.

Faculty of Engineering (tel. (519) 661-2128; internet www.eng.uwo.ca):

ADAMIAK, K., Electrical and Computer
BADDOUR, R. E., Civil and Environmental
BARTLETT, F. M. P., Civil and Environmental
BASSI, A., Chemical and Biochemical
BERRUTI, F., Dean's Office, Chemical and Biochemical
BRIENS, C. L., Chemical and Biochemical
DE LASA, H., Chemical and Biochemical
EL NAGGAR, H., Civil and Environmental
FLORYAN, J. M., Mechanical and Materials
GREASON, W. D., Electrical and Computer
HONG, H. P., Civil and Environmental
JIANG, J., Electrical and Computer
JOHNSON, J. A., Mechanical and Materials
JUTAN, A., Chemical and Biochemical
KARAMANEV, D., Chemical and Biochemical
KHAYAT, R. E., Mechanical and Materials
KNOPF, G. K., Mechanical and Materials
PATEL, R. V., Electrical and Computer
ROHANI, S., Chemical and Biochemical
SHANG, J. Q., Civil and Environmental
SHINOZAKI, D. M., Mechanical and Materials
SIDHU, T. S., Electrical and Computer
SIMONOVIC, S., Civil and Environmental
SINGH, A. V., Mechanical and Materials
VANFUL, E., Civil and Environmental
ZHU, J., Chemical and Biochemical

Faculty of Health Sciences (tel. (519) 661-4249; internet www.uwo.ca/fhs):

BAKA, R., Kinesiology
BELCASTRO, A. N., Kinesiology
BUCKOLZ, E., Kinesiology
CARRON, A. V., Kinesiology
DOYLE, P., Communication Sciences and Disorders
FORCHUK, C., Nursing
GARLAND, J., Physical Therapy
GOLDENBERG, D., Nursing
HALL, C. R., Kinesiology
IWASIW, C., Nursing
JAMIESON, D., Communication Sciences and Disorders
JOHNSON, C. S., Kinesiology
LASCHINGER, H., Nursing
LEMON, P., Kinesiology
MCWILLIAM, C., Nursing
MEIER, K. V., Kinesiology
MORROW, L. D., Kinesiology
MYERS, A. M., Kinesiology
NOBLE, E., Kinesiology
ORCHARD, C., Nursing (Head)
OVEREND, T., Physical Therapy (Head)
PATERSON, D. H., Kinesiology
PICHÉ, L. A., Kinesiology
SALMONI, A., Kinesiology (Head)
SEEWALD, R. C., Communication Sciences and Disorders
SEMOTIUK, D., Kinesiology
SUMSION, T., Occupational Therapy (Head)
TREVITHICK, J. R., Kinesiology
TRUJILLO, S., Health Sciences (Head)
VANDERVOORT, A. A., Physical Therapy
WATSON, R., Communication Sciences and Disorders (Head)
WEESE, W. J., Kinesiology

Faculty of Information and Media Studies (tel. (519) 661-3542; fax (519) 661-3506; internet www.fims.uwo.ca):

BABE, R. E.
CRAVEN, T. C.
HARRIS, R. M.
PARR, J.
ROSS, C. L.
SPENCER, D.
VAUGHAN, L. Q.
WILKINSON, M. A.

Faculty of Law (tel. (519) 661-3346; fax (519) 850-2412; internet www.law.uwo.ca):

BARTON, P. G.
BROWN, C.
EDGAR, T.
HOLLAND, W. H.
HOLLOWAY, I.
HOVIUS, B.
MCLAREN, R. H.
MERCER, P.
SOLOMON, R.
USPRICH, S. J.
WELLING, B.

Schulich School of Medicine and Dentistry (tel. (519) 661-3459; internet www.med.uwo.ca):

ADAMS, P. C., Medicine
ALBORES, A., Physiology and Pharmacology
ANG, L. C., Pathology
ARNOLD, J. M. O., Medicine
AVISON, W. R., Paediatrics; Epidemiology and Biostatistics
BAILEY, S. I., Surgery
BALL, E. H., Biochemistry
BANTING, D. W., Dentistry
BARR, R. M., Medicine
BATTISTA, J. J., Oncology
BAUMAN, G., Oncology (Head)
BELL, D. A., Medicine
BEND, J. R., Pathology
BERTRAND, M. A., Obstetrics and Gynaecology
BLAKE, P. G., Medicine
BOLLI, P., Medicine
BORRIE, M. J., Medicine
BOUGHNER, D. R., Medicine
BOURNE, R. B., Surgery
BRANDL, C. J., Biochemistry
BRIDGER, W. A., Biochemistry
BROWN, J. B., Family Medicine
BROWN, J. D., Clinical Neurological Sciences
BROWN, J. E., Medicine
CANHAM, P. B., Medical Biophysics
CECHETTO, D. F., Anatomy and Cell Biology
CERNOVSKY, Z. Z., Psychiatry
CHACONAS, G., Biochemistry
CHAMBERS, A. F., Oncology
CHAN, F. P., Anatomy and Cell Biology
CHANG, D. C. H., Anaesthesia and Perioperative Medicine (Head)
CHERIAN, G. M., Pathology
CHHEM, R. K., Diagnostic Radiology and Nuclear Medicine
CIRIELLO, J., Physiology and Pharmacology
CLARK, W. F., Medicine
COLCLEUGH, R. G., Surgery
COOK, M. A., Physiology and Pharmacology
COOK, R. A., Biochemistry
COOKE, J. D., Physiology and Pharmacology
CORDY, P. E., Medicine
CUNNINGHAM, I. A., Diagnostic Radiology and Nuclear Medicine
DALEY, T. D., Pathology
DEKABAN, G. A., Microbiology and Immunology
DELOVITCH, T. L., Microbiology and Immunology
DENSTEDT, J. D., Surgery (Head)
DIXON, S. J., Physiology and Pharmacology
DONNER, A. P., Epidemiology and Biostatics
DREYER, J. F., Medicine
DRIEDGER, A. A., Medicine
DROST, D. J., Diagnostic Radiology and Nuclear Medicine
DUNN, S. D., Biochemistry
EDMONDS, M. W., Medicine
ELLIS, C. G., Medical Biophysics
FEIGHTNER, J. W., Family Medicine
FELDMAN, R. D., Medicine
FENSTER, A., Diagnostic Radiology and Nuclear Medicine
FERGUSON, G. G., Clinical Neurological Sciences
FINNIE, K. J. C., Medicine
FISHER, W. A., Medicine
FISMAN, S. N., Psychiatry (Head)
FLINTOFF, W., Microbiology and Immunology
FLUMERFELT, B. A., Anatomy and Cell Biology
FOWLER, P.J., Surgery
FRAHER, L. J., Medicine
FREEMAN, T., Family Medicine (Head)
FREWEN, T. C., Paediatrics (Head)
GAGNON, R., Obstetrics and Gynaecology
GARCIA, B. M., Pathology (Head)
GEORGE, C. F. P., Medicine
GERACE, R. V., Medicine
GILBERT, J. J., Pathology
GIROTTI, M. J., Surgery
GIRVAN, D. P., Surgery
GLOOR, G. B., Biochemistry
GOODALE, M. A., Physiology and Pharmacology
GRANT, C. W., Biochemistry
GUENTHER, L. C., Medicine
GUPTA, M. A., Psychiatry
HAASE, P., Anatomy and Cell Biology
HACHINSKI, V., Clinical Neurological Sciences
HAHN, A. F. G., Clinical Neurological Sciences
HAMMOND, J. R., Physiology and Pharmacology
HAMPSON, E., Psychiatry
HAN, V. K. M., Paediatrics
HANIFORD, D. B., Biochemistry
HARRIS, K. A., Surgery
HAYES, K. C., Physical Medicine and Rehabilitation
HEGELE, R. A., Medicine
HENNING, J. L., Physiology and Pharmacology
HERBERT, C. P., Family Medicine
HILL, D. J., Medicine
HOBBS, B. B., Diagnostic Radiology and Nuclear Medicine
HODSMAN, A. B., Medicine
HOFFMASTER, C. B., Family Medicine
HOLLIDAY, R. L., Surgery
HOLLOMBY, D. J., Medicine (Head)
HOOPER, P., Ophthalmology (Head)
HORE, J., Physiology and Pharmacology
HOWARD, J. M., Paediatrics
HRAMIAK, I. M., Medicine
HRYCYSHYN, A. W., Anatomy and Cell Biology
HUANG, G., Physiology and Pharmacology
HUFF, M. W., Medicine
HUMEN, D. P., Medicine
HUNTER, G. K., Dentistry
HURST, L. N., Surgery
JAFFE, P. G., Psychiatry
JAIN, S. C., Psychiatry
JAMIESON, D. G., Medicine
JEVNIKAR, A. M., Medicine
JOHNSON, C., Medicine
JOHNSON, K. C., Epidemiology and Biostatics
JONES, D. L., Physiology and Pharmacology
JUNG, J. H., Paediatrics
KANG, C. Y., Microbiology and Immunology
KARLIK, S. J., Diagnostic Radiology and Nuclear Medicine
KARMAZYN, M., Physiology and Pharmacology
KENNEDY, T. G., Physiology and Pharmacology
KIDDER, G. M., Physiology and Pharmacology
KIERNAN, J. A., Anatomy and Cell Biology
KING, G. J., Surgery

KIRK, M. E., Pathology
KLEIN, G. J., Medicine
KOGON, S. L., Dentistry
KOREN, G., Paediatrics; Medicine
KOROPATNICK, D. J., Oncology
KOSTUK, W. J., Medicine
KRONICK, J. B., Medicine
KVIETYS, P. R., Physiology
LAIRD, D. W., Anatomy and Cell Biology
LAJOIE, G., Biochemistry
LAMPE, H. B., Otolaryngology
LANNIGAN, R., Microbiology and Immunology
LEASA, D. J., Medicine
LEE, D. H., Diagnostic Radiology and Nuclear Medicine
LEE, T. Y., Diagnostic Radiology and Nuclear Medicine
LEFCOE, M. S., Diagnostic Radiology and Nuclear Medicine
LELLA, J. W., History of Medicine
LEUNG, L. W. S., Clinical Neurological Sciences
LEWIS, J. F., Medicine
LINDSAY, R. M., Medicine
LO, T. C., Biochemistry
LOWNIE, S., Clinical Neurological Sciences (Joint Head)
McCARTHY, G. M., Dentistry
McCORMACK, D. G., Medicine
McDONALD, J. W., Medicine
McFADDEN, D. G., Microbiology and Immunology
McFADDEN, R. G., Medicine
McGRATH, P. A., Paediatrics
McKENZIE, F. N., Surgery
McLACHLAN, R. S., Clinical Neurological Sciences
MACRAE, D. L., Otolaryngology (Joint Head)
MAO, Y., Epidemiology and Biostatics
MAROTTA, J. T., Clinical Neurological Sciences
MENDONCA, J., Psychiatry
MENKIS, A. H., Surgery
MILLWARD, S. F., Diagnostic Radiology and Nuclear Medicine
MORRIS, V. L., Microbiology
MUIRHEAD, J. M., Medicine
MURKIN, J. M., Anaesthesia and Perioperative Medicine
NARAYANAN, N., Physiology and Pharmacology
NATALE, R., Obstetrics and Gynaecology
NEUFELD, R. W. J., Psychiatry
NICHOLSON, R. L., Diagnostic Radiology and Nuclear Medicine
NICOLLE, D. A., Opthalmology
NISKER, J. A., Obstetrics and Gynaecology
NORMAN, R. M. G., Psychiatry
NORRIS, J. W., Clinical Neurological Sciences
NOVICK, R. J., Surgery
PARNES, L. S., Otolaryngology
PATERSON, N. A. M., Medicine
PAYTON, K. B., Medicine
PERSAD, E., Psychiatry
PETERS, T. M., Diagnostic Radiology and Nuclear Medicine
PETERSEN, N. O., Biochemistry
POTTER, P. M. J., History of Medicine and Science
POZNANSKY, M. J., Biochemistry
PRABHAKARAN, V. M., Biochemistry
PRATO, F. S., Diagnostic Radiology and Nuclear Medicine
RALLEY, F. E., Anaesthesia and Perioperative Medicine
RALPH, E. D., Medicine
RANKIN, R. N., Diagnostic Radiology and Nuclear Medicine (Head)
REID, G., Microbiology and Immunology
REYNOLDS, R. P., Medicine
RICE, G. P. A., Clinical Neurological Sciences
RICHARDSON, B. S., Obstetrics and Gynaecology (Head)
RIEDER, M J., Paediatrics
RODGER, N. W., Medicine
RORABECK, C. H., Surgery
ROTH, J. H., Surgery
RUTLEDGE, F. S., Medicine
RUTT, B. K., Diagnostic Radiology and Nuclear Medicine
RYLETT, R. J., Physiology and Pharmacology
SANDHU, H. S., Dentistry (Head)
SANGSTER, J. F., Family Medicine
SHAW, G. S., Biochemistry
SHERAR, M. D., Oncology
SHKRUM, M. J., Pathology
SHOUKRI, M. M., Epidemiology and Biostatics
SHUM, D. T. W., Pathology
SILCOX, J. A., Obstetrics and Gynaecology
SIMS, S. M., Physiology and Pharmacology
SINGH, B., Microbiology and Immunology
SINGHAL, S. K., Microbiology and Immunology
SOLIMAN, G. L., Medicine
SPENCE, J. D., Clinical Neurological Sciences
STEWART, M. A., Family Medicine
STILLER, C. R., Medicine
STRONG, M. J., Clinical Neurological Sciences (Joint Head)
TAVES, D. H., Diagnostic Radiology and Nuclear Medicine
TEASELL, R. W., Physical Medicine and Rehabilitation (Head)
TEPPERMAN, B. L., Physiology and Pharmacology
THOMPSON, R. T., Diagnostic Radiology and Nuclear Medicine
TRICK, C. G., Microbiology and Immunology
TYML, K., Medical Biophysics
URBAIN, J. L. C. P., Diagnostic Radiology and Nuclear Medicine
VALVANO, M. A., Microbiology and Immunology
VAN DYK, J., Oncology
VILIS, T., Physiology and Pharmacology
VILOS, G., Obstetrics and Gynaecology
VINGILIS, E. R., Family Medicine
WALL, W. J., Surgery
WEAVER, L. C., Physiology and Pharmacology
WESTON, W., Family Medicine
WEXLER, D., Medicine
WHITE, D. J., Surgery
WILLIAMSON, P. C., Psychiatry
WILLIS, N. R., Ophthalmology
WILSON, J. X., Physiology and Pharmacology
WISENBERG, G., Medicine
WRIGHT, E., Otolaryngology (Joint Head)
WRIGHT, J. G., Epidemiology and Biostatistics
WYSOCKI, G. P., Pathology
YANG, K., Obstetrics and Gynaecology
YEE, R., Medicine
YOUNG, G. B., Clinical Neurological Sciences
ZAMIR, M., Medical Biophysics
ZHONG, Z., Surgery

Don Wright Faculty of Music (tel. (519) 661-2043; fax (519) 661-3531; e-mail music@uwo.ca; internet www.music.uwo.ca):

BRACEY, J. P., Music Performance Studies
FISKE, H., Music Education
GRIER, J., Music History
HEARD, A., Theory and Composition
KOPROWSKI, P. P., Theory and Composition
McKAY, J., Music Performance Studies (Head)
NOLAN, C., Theory and Composition (Head)
PARKS, R. S., Theory and Composition
TOFT, R. E., Music History (Head)
WOODFORD, P., Music Education (Head)

Faculty of Science (tel. (519) 661-3040; e-mail science@uwo.ca; internet www.uwo.ca/sci):

BAILEY, R., Biology
BAINES, K. M., Chemistry (Head)
BAIRD, N. C., Chemistry
BARRON, J. L., Computer Science
BATTISTA, J., Medical Biophysics (Head)
BAUER, M. A., Computer Science (Head)
BELLHOUSE, D. R., Statistical and Actuarial Sciences
BOIVIN, A., Mathematics
BRANDL, C., Biochemistry (Head)
CAMPBELL, K., Epidemiology and Biostatistics (Head)
CASS, F. P. A., Mathematics
CAVENEY, S., Biology
CORLESS, R. M., Applied Mathematics; Computer Science; Philosophy (Head, Applied Mathematics)
COTTAM, M. G., Physics and Astronomy
DAY, A. W., Biology
DEAN, P. A. W., Chemistry
DEBRUYN, J. R., Physics and Astronomy (Joint Head)
EATON, D. W. S., Earth Sciences
ELIAS, V. W., Applied Mathematics
ESSEX, G. C., Applied Mathematics
FENTON, M. B., Biology (Head)
FLORYAN, J. M., Applied Mathematics
GUTHRIE, J. P., Chemistry and Biochemistry
HEINICKE, A. G., Mathematics
HICOCK, S. R., Earth Sciences
HOCKING, W. K., Physics and Astronomy
HOLT, R. A., Physics and Astronomy
HUANG, Y., Chemistry
HUNER, N. P. A., Biology
JARDINE, J. F., Mathematics
JEFFREY, D. J., Applied Mathematics
JIN, J., Earth Sciences
JONES, B. L., Physics and Astronomy (Joint Head)
JÜRGENSEN, H., Computer Science
JUTAN, A., Applied Mathematics
KANE, R. M., Mathematics (Head)
KANG, C. Y., Biology
KERR, M. A., Chemistry
KHALKHALI, M., Mathematics
KOVAL, S. F., Earth Sciences, Microbiology and Immunology
KRISHNA, P., Biology
KULPERGER, R. J., Statistical and Actuarial Sciences
LACHANCE, M. A., Biology, Microbiology and Immunology
LAU, L. W. M., Physics and Astronomy
LEAIST, D. G., Chemistry
LEHMAN, M., Anatomy and Cell Biology (Head)
LENNARD, W. N., Physics and Astronomy
LIPSON, R. H., Chemistry
LONGSTAFFE, F. J., Earth Sciences
LUTFIYYA, H., Earth Sciences
MADHAVJI, J. W., Computer Science
MARTIN, R. R., Chemistry
McKEON, D. G. C., Applied Mathematics
McLEOD, A. I., Statistical and Actuarial Sciences
McNEIL, J. N., Biology
MERCER, R. E., Computer Science
MILLAR, J. S., Biology
MILNES, P., Mathematics
MINÀC, J., Mathematics
MIRANSKY, V. A., Applied Mathematics
MITTLER, S., Physics and Astronomy
NESBITT, H. W., Earth Sciences (Head)
NORTON, P. R., Chemistry
PAYNE, N. C., Chemistry
PLINT, A. G., Earth Sciences
PODESTA, R. B., Biology
POTTER, P., History of Medicine (Head)
PROVOST, S., Statistical and Actuarial Sciences
PUDDEPHATT, R. J., Chemistry
RAY, A. K., Applied Mathematics

RENNER, L. E., Mathematics
RILEY, D. M., Mathematics
ROHANI, S., Applied Mathematics
ROSNER, S. D., Physics and Astronomy
RYLETT, R. J., Physiology and Pharmacology (Head)
SECCO, R. A., Earth Sciences
SHAM, T. K., Chemistry
SHAW, G. S., Biochemistry and Chemistry
SHOESMITH, D. W., Chemistry
SICA, R. J., Physics and Astronomy
SINGH, M. R., Physics and Astronomy
SINGH, S. M., Biology
STANFORD, D. A., Statistical and Actuarial Sciences
STILLMAN, M. J., Chemistry
TRICK, C. G., Biology
USSELMAN, M. C., Chemistry
VALVANO, M., Microbiology and Immunology (Head)
WATT, S., Computer Science
WEEDON, A. C., Chemistry
WORKENTIN, M. S., Chemistry
WREN, J. C., Chemistry
YU, P., Applied Mathematics
YU, S., Computer Science
ZHANG, K., Computer Science
ZINKE-ALLMANG, M., Physics and Astronomy

Faculty of Social Science (tel. (519) 661-2053; fax (519) 661-3868; internet www.ssc.uwo.ca):

ABELSON, D., Political Science (Head)
ABELSON, D., American Studies (Joint Head)
ALLAHAR, A., Sociology
ALLEN, N., Psychology
ASHMORE, P. E., Geography
AVERY, D. H., History
AVISON, W. R., Sociology
BEAUJOT, R. P., Sociology
BHATIA, K. B., Economics
BOYER, R. S., Economics
BURGESS, D. F., Economics
CAIN, D. P., Psychology
CARROLL, M., Sociology
CHEN, X., Psychology
CHHEM, R. K., Anthropology
CLARK, S., Sociology
CODE, W. R., Geography
CONNIDIS, I. A., Sociology
CÔTE, J. E., Sociology
CREIDER, C., Linguistics (Joint Head)
CREIDER, C. A., Anthropology (Head)
CYBULSKI, J. S., Anthropology
DARNELL, R., First Nations Studies (Joint Head)
DAVENPORT, P., Economics
DAVIES, J. B., Economics
ELLIS, C., Anthropology
EMERY, G., History
ESSAS, V., Psychology
FISHER, W. A., Psychology
FLEMING, K., Management and Organizational Studies (Head)
FLEMING, M., Political Science
FORSTER, B., History (Head)
GARDINER, M., Sociology
GOODALE, M., Psychology
GRABB, E. G., Sociology
GREEN, M. B., Geography
HAMPSON, E., Psychology
HARSHMAN, R., Psychology
HEAP, D., Linguistics (Joint Head)
HELE, K., First Nations Studies (Joint Head)
HERNANDEZ-SAENZ, L. M., Latin American Studies (Head)
HEWITT, W. E., Sociology
JOHNSTON, A., American Studies (Joint Head)
KATZ, A. N., Psychology
KAVALIERS, M., Psychology
KELLOW, M., International Relations (Head)
KING, R. H., Geography
KNIGHT, J., Economics
KUIPER, N. A., Psychology
LUCKMAN, B. H., Geography
LUPKER, S. J., Psychology
MCBEAN, G., Geography, Political Science
MCDOUGALL, J. N., Political Science
MCQUILLAN, K., Sociology
MCRAE, K., Psychology
MARTIN, R. A., Psychology
MAXIM, P. S., Sociology
MEYER, J. P., Psychology
MOLTO, J. E., Anthropology
MORAN, G., Psychology
NEUFELD, R. W. J., Psychology
OLSON, J. M., Psychology
OSSENKOPP, K.-P., Psychology (Head)
PAUNONEN, S. V., Psychology
PEREZ, A., Political Science
RIDDELL-DIXON, E., Political Science
ROBINSON, C. M. G. F., Economics
ROLLMAN, G. B., Psychology
RUSHTON, J. P., Psychology
SANCTON, A. B., Political Science
SELIGMAN, C., Psychology
SHATZMILLER, M., History
SHERRY, D., Psychology
SHRUBSOLE, D., Geography (Head)
SLIVINSKI, A., Economics (Head)
SMART, C. C., Geography
SORRENTINO, R. M., Psychology
SPENCE, M. W., Anthropology
TIMNEY, B. N., Psychology
VERNON, P. A., Psychology
VERNON, R. A., Political Science
WANG, J., Geography
WHALLEY, J., Economics
WHITE, C., Anthropology
WHITE, J., Sociology (Head)
WHITEHEAD, P. C., Sociology
WINTROBE, R. S., Economics
YOUNG, R. A., Political Science

Richard Ivey School of Business (tel. (519) 661-3485; e-mail info@ivey.uwo.ca; internet www.ivey.uwo.ca):

ATHANASSAKOS, G.
BEAMISH, P. W.
BELL, P. C.
CONKLIN, D. W.
DAWAR, N.
DEUTSCHER, T. H.
FISHER, R. J.
FOERSTER, S. R.
GANDZ, J.
HARDY, K. G.
HATCH, J. E.
HENDRICKS, K. B.
HIGGINS, C. A.
HOWELL, J. M.
KALYMON, B.
KONRAD, A. M.
ROTHSTEIN, M. G.
SCHAAN, J. L.
SHACKEL, D. S. J.
VAN DEN BOSCH, M. B.
WHITE, R. W.
WILSON, J. G.
WYNANT, L.

AFFILIATED INSTITUTIONS

Brescia University College: 1285 Western Rd, London, ON N6G 1H2; internet www.uwo.ca/bresciaf. 1919; arts subjects; Principal T. TOPIC

PROFESSORS

SNYDER, J., Philosophy
TOPIC, T., Anthropology

Huron University College: 1349 Western Rd, London, ON N6G 1H3; internet www.huronuc.on.caf. 1863; arts and theological college; Principal Dr R. LUMPKIN

PROFESSORS

BLOCKER, J. S., History
CRIMMINS, J. E., Political Science
HAMILTON, G., Theology
HYLAND, P., English
MCCARTHY, D. R., English
READ, C., History
SCHACHTER, J. P., Philosophy
XU, D., Economics

King University College: 266 Epworth Ave, London, ON N6A 2M3; e-mail kings@uwo.ca; internet www.uwo.ca/kingsf. 1912 (Seminary), 1955 (College); seminary and college of arts; Principal Dr GERALD KILLAN

PROFESSORS

BAHCHELI, T., Political Science
BARUSS, I., Psychology
BROWN, H., Philosophy and Religious Studies
BROWN, J., Social Work
COMPTON-BROUWER, R., History
GORASSINI, D. R., Psychology
HARMAN, L., Sociology
IRVING, A., Social Work
KILLAN, G., History
KOPINAK, K., Sociology
LELLA, J. W., Sociology
MACGREGOR, D., Sociology
O'CONNOR, T., Religious Studies
PATERSON, G. H., English
PRIEUR, M. R., Religious Studies
SKINNER, N. F., Psychology
WERSTINE, P., English

WILFRID LAURIER UNIVERSITY

75 University Ave, Waterloo, ON N2L 3C5
Telephone: (519) 884-1970
Fax: (519) 886-9351
Internet: www.wlu.ca
Founded 1911; formerly Waterloo Lutheran University; name changed 1973
Language of instruction: English
State control
Academic year: September to April (two terms)

Chancellor: BOB RAE
President and Vice-Chancellor: Dr ROBERT ROSEHART
Vice-President (Academic): Dr SUSAN HORTON
Vice-President (Finance and Administration): JIM BUTLER
Registrar: Dr JOHN METCALFE
Librarian and Archivist: SHARON BROWN

Number of teachers: 838 (410 full-time, 428 part-time)
Number of students: 12,296 (10,097 full-time, 2,199 part-time)

Publications: *Anthropologica* (2 a year), *Canadian Bulletin of Medical History / Bulletin canadien d'histoire de la médecine* (2 a year), *Canadian Social Work Review / Revue canadienne de service social* (2 a year), *Dialogue: Canadian Philosophical Review / Revue canadienne de philosophie* (4 a year), *Leisure / Loisive* (4 a year), *Studies in Religion / Sciences Religieuses* (4 a year), *Toronto Journal of Theology* (4 a year), *Topia: A Canadian Journal of Cultural Studies* (2 a year)

DEANS

Faculty of Arts and Science: Dr ROBERT CAMPBELL
Faculty of Graduate Studies: Dr ADELE REINHARTZ
Faculty of Music: Dr CHARLES MORRISON
Faculty of Science: Dr ARTHUR SZABO
Faculty of Social Work: Prof. LUKE FUSCO
School of Business and Economics: Dr SCOTT CARSON
Waterloo Lutheran Seminary: Dr RICHARD CROSSMAN

DEPARTMENT CHAIRS

Anthropology: Dr ANDREW LYONS (acting)
Archaeology and Classical Studies: Dr JOANN FREED
Biology: Dr JANE RUTHERFORD
Business Administration: Dr M. DE
Chemistry: Dr IAN HAMILTON
Economics: Dr A. ROBERTSON
English: Dr ELEANOR TY
Geography and Environmental Studies: Dr M. L. BYRNE
History: Dr G. URBANIAK
Kinesiology and Physical Education: Dr PETER TIIDUS
Languages and Literatures: Dr IRA ASHCROFT
Mathematics: Dr DAVID VAUGHAN
Philosophy: Dr NEIL CAMPBELL
Physics and Computing: Dr S. CHAU
Political Science: Dr D. DOCHERTY
Psychology: Dr MICHAEL PRATT
Religion and Culture: Dr MICHEL DESJARDINS
Sociology: Dr GLENDA WALL

UNIVERSITY OF WINDSOR

Windsor, ON N9B 3P4
Telephone: (519) 253-4232
E-mail: registr@uwindsor.ca
Internet: www.uwindsor.ca

Founded 1857
Provincially assisted
Language of instruction: English
Academic year: September to May (2 semesters)

Chancellor: Dr FREDERIC L. R. JACKMAN
Vice-Chancellor and President: Dr ROSS H. PAUL
Vice-President (Administration and Finance): ERIC HARBOTTLE
Vice-President (University Advancement): AMANDA GELLMAN
Provost and Vice-President (Academic): Prof. NEIL GOLD
Vice-Provost (Students) and Registrar: Prof. BRIAN MAZER (acting)
Librarian: GWENDOLYN EBBETT

Number of teachers: 428 (full-time)
Number of students: 16,266 (full-time and part-time)

Publications: *The Lance* (weekly), *Review*, *Windsor University Magazine* (quarterly)

DEANS

Faculty of Arts and Social Science: Dr CECIL HOUSTON
Faculty of Education: Dr PAT ROGERS
Faculty of Engineering: Dr GRAHAM T. READER
Faculty of Human Kinetics: Dr JAMES WEESE
Faculty of Law: Prof. BRUCE ELMAN
Faculty of Nursing: Dr ELAINE DUFFY
Faculty of Science: Dr RICHARD J. CARON
Faculty of Graduate Studies and Research: Dr SHEILA CAMERON
Odette School of Business: Dr ROGER HUSSEY

PROFESSORS

Faculty of Arts:

AMORE, R. C., Political Sciences
ATKINSON, C. B., English
BABE, R. E., Communication Studies
BALANCE, W. D., Psychology
BAXTER, I., Visual Arts
BÉLANGER, S., Visual Arts
BERTMAN, S., Classical Studies
BIRD, H. W., Classical Studies
BLAIR, J. A., Philosophy
BROOKS, S., Political Science
BROWN-JOHN, C. L., Political Science
BUTLER, E. G., Music
CASSANO, P., French
COHEN, J. S., Psychology
DEANGELIS, J. R., Visual Arts
DEVILLERS, J. P., French
DILWORTH, T. R., English
DITSKY, J. M., English
GOLD/SMITH, S. B., Visual Arts
HANSON, J., Music
HAWKINS, F. R., Social Work
HOLOSKO, M. J., Social Work
HOUSEHOLDER, R., Music
KING, J. N., Religious Studies
KINGSTONE, B. D., French
KLINCK, D. M., History
LAKHAN, V. C., Geography
LINTON, J. M., Communication Studies
MCCRONE, K. E., History
MACKENDRICK, L. K., English
MADY KELLY, D., Dramatic Art
MURRAY, J., History
PAGE, J. S., Psychology
PALMER, D., Music
PHIPPS, A. G., Geography
PINNELL, W. H., Dramatic Art
REYNOLDS, D. V., Psychology
ROMSA, G. H., Geography
ROURKE, B. P., Psychology
SCHNEIDER, F. W., Psychology
SODERLUND, W. C., Political Science
STARETS, M., French
STEBELSKY, I., Geography
TRENHAILE, A. S., Geography
VAN DEN HOVEN, A., French
WARREN, B., Dramatic Art
WHITNEY, B., Religious Studies
WINTER, J. P., Communication Studies

Faculty of Business Administration:

ANDIAPPAN, P.
ANEJA, Y. P.
ARMSTRONG-STASSEN, M.
BRILL, P. H.
CHANDRA, R.
DICKINSON, J. R.
FARIA, A. J.
FIELDS, M.
HUSSEY, R.
KANTOR, J.
LAM, W. P.
MORGAN, A.
OKECHUKU, C.
PUNNETT, B. J.
SINGH, J.
TEMPLER, A.
THACKER, J. W.
WITHANE, S.

Faculty of Education:

CRAWFORD, W. J. I.
KUENDIGER, E.
LAING, D. A.
MORTON, L.
WILLIAMS, N. H.

Faculty of Engineering:

AHMADI, M., Electrical Engineering
ALFA, A. S., Industrial Engineering and Manufacturing Systems Engineering
ALPAS, A. T., Mechanical, Automotive and Materials Engineering
ASFOUR, A. A., Civil and Environmental Engineering
BEWTRA, J. K., Civil and Environmental Engineering
BISWAS, N., Civil and Environmental Engineering
BUDKOWSKA, B. B., Cultural and Environmental Engineering
DUTTA, S. P., Industrial Engineering and Manufacturing Systems Engineering
EL MARAGHY, H., Industrial Engineering and Manufacturing Systems Engineering
EL MARAGHY, W., Industrial Engineering and Manufacturing Systems Engineering
FRISE, P. R., Mechanical, Automotive and Materials Engineering
HEARN, N., Civil and Environmental Engineering
KWAN, H. K., Electrical Engineering
LASHKARI, R. S., Industrial Engineering and Manufacturing Systems Engineering
MADUGULA, M. K. S., Civil and Environmental Engineering
MILLER, W. C., Electrical Engineering
NORTH, W., Mechanical, Automotive and Materials Engineering
RAJU, G. R. G., Electrical Engineering
RANKIN, G. W., Mechanical, Automotive and Materials Engineering
READER, G. T., Mechanical, Automotive and Materials Engineering
SID-AHMED, M., Electrical Engineering
SOLTIS, J., Electrical Engineering
TABOUN, S., Industrial Engineering and Manufacturing Systems Engineering
WANG, H., Industrial Engineering and Manufacturing Systems Engineering
WATT, D. F., Mechanical, Automotive and Materials Engineering
WILSON, N. W., Mechanical, Automotive and Materials Engineering

Faculty of Human Kinetics:

BOUCHER, R. L., Athletics and Recreational Studies
MARINO, W., Kinesiology
OLAFSON, G. A., Kinesiology
SALTER, M. A., Kinesiology
WEESE, W. J., Kinesiology

Faculty of Law:

BERRYMAN, J.
BOGART, W. A.
BUSHNELL, I. S.
CARASCO, E. F.
CONKLIN, W.
ELMAN, B.
GOLD, N.
IRISH, M.
MAZER, B. M.
MENEZES, J. R.
MOON, R. J.
MURPHY, P. T.
STEWART, G. R.
WEST, J. L.
WILSON, L. C.
WYDRZYNSKI, C. J.

Faculty of Science

(Some professors are also attached to the Faculty of Engineering)

AL-AASM, I. S., Earth Sciences
ANGLIN, P., Economics
AROCA, R., Chemistry and Biochemistry
ATKINSON, J. B., Physics
BANDYOPADHYAY, S., Computer Science
BARRON, R. M., Mathematics and Statistics
BAYLIS, W. E., Physics
BRITTEN, D. J., Mathematics and Statistics
CAMERON, W. S., Nursing
CARON, R. J., Mathematics and Statistics
CARTY, L., Nursing
CHANDNA, O. P., Mathematics and Statistics
CIBOROWSKI, J. J. H., Biological Sciences
COTTER, D. A., Biological Sciences
DRAKE, G. W., Physics
DRAKE, J. E., Chemistry and Biochemistry
FACKRELL, H. B., Biological Sciences
FAN, Y., Economics
FORTUNE, J. N., Economics
FROST, R. A., Computer Science
FUNG, K. Y., Mathematics and Statistics
GENCAY, R., Economics
GILLEN, W. J., Economics
GLASS, E. N., Physics
HAFFNER, G. D., Biological Sciences
HUDEC, P. P., Earth Sciences
KALONI, P. N., Mathematics and Statistics
KENT, R. D., Computer Science
LEMIRE, F. W., Mathematics and Statistics
LOEB, S. J., Chemistry and Biochemistry
LOVETT DOUST, J. N., Biological Sciences

LOVETT DOUST, L., Biological Sciences
M'CLOSKEY, R. T., Biological Sciences
MCCONKEY, J. W., Physics
MCDONALD, J. F., Mathematics and Statistics
MCINTOSH, J. M., Chemistry and Biochemistry
MACISAAC, H. J., Biological Sciences
MAEV, R. G., Physics
MUTUS, B., Chemistry and Biochemistry
PAUL, S. R., Mathematics and Statistics
SALE, P. F., Biological Sciences
SIMPSON, F., Earth Sciences
SMITH, T. E., Earth Sciences
STEPHAN, D. W., Chemistry and Biochemistry
STRICK, J. C., Economics
SUH, S. C., Economics
TAYLOR, N. F., Chemistry and Biochemistry
THOMAS, B. C., Nursing
THOMAS, D., Biological Sciences
TRACY, D. S., Mathematics and Statistics
TUREK, A., Earth Sciences
WARNER, A., Biological Sciences
WONG, C. S., Mathematics and Statistics
ZAMANI, N. G., Mathematics and Statistics

FEDERATED UNIVERSITY

Assumption University: 400 Huron Church Rd, Windsor, ON; Pres. Rev. U. E. PARÉ.

AFFILIATED COLLEGES

Canterbury College: 172 Patricia Rd, Windsor, ON; Principal D. T. A. SYMONS.

Holy Redeemer College: Cousineau Rd, Windsor, ON; Principal Rev. R. CORRIVEAU.

Iona College: Sunset Ave, Windsor, ON; Principal Rev. D. G. GALSTON.

ATTACHED INSTITUTES

Fluid Dynamics Research Institute: Dir R. M. BARRON.

Great Lakes Institute: Dir G. D. HAFFNER.

International Compulsive Gambling Institute: Dir ROSE VAN ES.

UNIVERSITY OF WINNIPEG

515 Portage Ave, Winnipeg, MB R3B 2E9
Telephone: (204) 786-7811
Fax: (204) 786-8656
Internet: www.uwinnipeg.ca
Founded 1871; University status 1967
Controlled jointly by the Government of Manitoba and the United Church of Canada
Language of instruction: English
Academic year: September to April
Chancellor: H. SANDFORD RILEY
President: LLOYD AXWORTHY
Vice-President, Academic: PATRICK DEANE (acting)
Vice-President, Finance and Administration: STEPHEN WILLETTS
University Secretary: R. A. KINGSLEY
Director of Registrarial Services: N. LATOCKI
Librarian: W. R. CONVERSE
Number of teachers: 232
Number of students: 6,152

DEANS

Faculty of Arts and Science: M. N. ZAWOROTKO
Faculty of Theology: G. MACDERMID
Faculty of Continuing Education: C. NORDMAN
The Collegiate: ROBERT BEND

DEPARTMENT CHAIRMEN

Anthropology: C. MEIKLEJOHN (acting)
Biology: E. BYARD
Business Computing/Administrative Studies: S. RAMANNA
Chemistry: D. VANDERWEL
Classics: C. COOPER
Developmental Studies: E. POLYZOI
Economics: H. GRANT
Education: A. MAYS
English: N. BESNER
French Studies and German Studies: S. VISELLI
Geography: D. BLAIR
German and Canadian Studies: A. FREUND
German Studies: K. MEADWELL
History: D. BURLEY
Humanities: N. BESNER
Mathematics and Statistics: J. CURRIE
Philosophy: B. KEENAN
Physics: R. KOBES
Politics: A. MILLS
Psychology: H. BRADBURY
Physical Activity and Sport Studies: D. FITZPATRICK
Religious Studies: P. DAY
Sociology: S. KIRBY
Statistics: H. HOWLADER
Theatre and Drama: D. ARRELL

PROFESSORS

ABD-EL-AZIZ, Chemistry
ABIZADEH, S., Economics
BAILEY, D. A., History
BASILEVSKY, A., Statistics
BECKER, G., Psychology
BOTTERILL, C., Sport Psychology
BRADBURY, H., Psychology
BROWN, J., History
BROWN, W., Economics
BURLEY, D., History
CARLYLE, W. J., Geography
CARTER, T., Geography
CHAN, F. Y., Business Computing
CHEAL, D. J., Sociology
CLARK, J., Psychology
CLOUTIS, E., Geography
DANNEFAER, S., Physics
DAY, P., Religious Studies
DONG, X.-Y., Economics
EVANS, M., English
FEHR, B., Psychology
FORBES, S., Biology
FRIESEN, K., Chemistry
GINSBERG, J., Mathematics
GOLDEN, M., Classics
GRANT, H., Economics
GRANZBERG, G., Anthropology
GREENHILL, P., Women's Studies
HARVEY, C. J., French Studies
HATHOUT, S., Geography
HOWLADER, H., Statistics
HUEBNER, J., Biology
IZYDORCZYK, Z., English
KERR, D. P., Physics
KHAN, R. A., Political Science
KOBES, R., Physics
KUNSTATTER, G., Physics
KYDON, D. W., Physics
LEHR, J., Geography
LEO, C., Political Science
MCCORMACK, A. R., History
MCCORMACK, R., History
MCDOUGALL, I., Classics
MCINTYRE, M., Psychology
MAYS, A., Education
MEADWELL, K., French Studies
MEIKLEJOHN, C., Anthropology
MILLS, A., Political Science, Anthropology
MOODIE, G. E. E., Biology
NNADI, J., French Studies
NODELMAN, P. M., English
NORTON, R., Psychology
NOVEK, J., Sociology
PARAMESWARAN, U., English
PEELING, J., Chemistry
PIP, E., Biology
POLYZOI, E., Education
RANNIE, W., Geography
ROCKMAN, G., Psychology
RODRIGUEZ, L., French
SCHAEFER, E., Psychology
SCOTT, G., Geography
SELWOOD, J., Geography
SPIGELMAN, M., Psychology
STANIFORTH, R., Biology
STONE, D. Z., History
STRUB, H., Psychology
TOMCHUK, E., Physics
TOMLINSON, G., Chemistry
VISELLI, S., French Studies
WIEGAND, M., Biology
WRIGHT, C., Political Science
YOUNG, R. J., History

ATTACHED INSTITUTES

Institute of Urban Studies: 515 Portage Ave, Winnipeg; Dir T. CARTER.

Menno Simons College: 515 Portage Ave, Winnipeg; Pres. D. PEACHEY.

YORK UNIVERSITY

4700 Keele St, Toronto, ON M3J 1P3
Telephone: (416) 736-2100
Fax: (416) 736-5700
Internet: www.yorku.ca
Founded 1959, independent 1965
Public control
Language of instruction: English (Glendon College: English and French)
Academic year: September to April
Chancellor: A. J. BENNETT
President and Vice-Chancellor: L. R. MARSDEN
Vice-President (Academic): S. M. EMBLETON
Vice-President (Development): PAUL MARCUS
Vice-President (Finance and Administration): GARY BREWER
Vice-President (Research and Innovation): S. SHAPSON
Vice-President (Students and Alumni): BONNIE NEUMAN
University Secretary and General Counsel: HARRIET LEWIS
Number of teachers: 1,149 (full-time)
Number of students: 33,749
Publications: *Profiles* (quarterly), *York Gazette* (37 a year)

DEANS

Faculty of Arts: G. B. FALLIS
Faculty of Education: PAUL AXELROD
Faculty of Environmental Studies: DAVID MORLEY (acting)
Faculty of Fine Arts: P. SILVER
Faculty of Pure and Applied Science: GILLIAN E. WU
Faculty of Graduate Studies: J. LENNOX
Schulich School of Business: D. HORVATH
Osgoode Hall Law School: PATRICK J. MONAHAN
Joseph E. Atkinson College: R. BORDESSA
Glendon College: K. MCROBERTS (Principal)

PROFESSORS

Faculty of Arts:

ABRAMSON, M., Mathematics and Statistics
ANISEF, P., Sociology
APPELBAUM, E., Economics
ARMSTRONG, C., History
ARMSTRONG, P., Sociology
AXELROD, P., Social Science
BAYEFSKY, A. F., Political Science
BIALYSTOK, E., Psychology
BIRBALSINGH, F. M., English
BLUM, A. F., Sociology
BROWN, M. G., Humanities
BURNS, R. G., Mathematics and Statistics
BUTLER, G. R., Humanities
CARLEY, J., English
CHAMBERS, D., Physical Education
CODE, L. B., Philosophy

COHEN, D., English
COTNAM, J., French Studies
CUFF, R. D., History
CUMMINGS, M. J., English
DANZIGER, L., Economics
DARROCH, A. G. L., Sociology
DAVIES, D. I., Social Science and Sociology
DAVIS, C. A., Physical Education
DEWITT, D. B., Political Science
DONNENFELD, S., Economics
DOSMAN, E. J., Political Science
DOW, A. S., Mathematics and Statistics
EGNAL, M. M., History
EHRLICH, S. L., Languages, Literature and Linguistics
EMBLETON, S. M., Languages, Literatures and Linguistics
ENDLER, N. S., Psychology
FAAS, E., Humanities
FANCHER, R. E., Psychology
FICHMAN, M., Humanities
FLETCHER, F. J., Political Science
FLETT, G. L., Psychology
FOWLER, B. H., Physical Education
FREEMAN, D. B., Geography
FROLIC, M. B., Political Science
GILL, S., Political Science
GLEDHILL, N., Physical Education
GREEN, B. S., Sociology
GREEN, L. J. M., Philosophy
GREENBERG, L., Psychology
GREENGLASS, E. R., Psychology
GREER-WOOTTEN, B., Geography
GUIASU, S., Mathematics and Statistics
GUY, G. R., Languages, Literatures and Linguistics
HABERMAN, A., Humanities
HARRIES-JONES, P., Anthropology
HARRIS, L. R., Psychology
HATTIANGADI, J. N., Philosophy
HEIDENREICH, C., Geography
HELLMAN, J., Political Science and Social Science
HELLMAN, S., Political Science
HILL, A. R., Geography
HOBSON, D. B., Humanities
HOFFMAN, R. C., History
HRUSKA, K. C., Mathematics and Statistics
INNES, C., English
IRVINE, W. D., History
JARVIE, I. C., Philosophy
KANYA-FORSTNER, A. S., History
KAPLAN, H., Political Science and Social Science
KATZ, E., Economics
KING, R. E., Languages, Literatures and Linguistics
KLEINER, I., Mathematics and Statistics
KOCHMAN, S. O., Mathematics and Statistics
KOHN, P. M., Psychology
LANDA, J. T., Economics
LANPHIER, C. M., Sociology
LENNOX, J. W., English
LEYTON-BROWN, D., Political Science
LIGHTMAN, B. V., Humanities
LIPSIG-MUMMÉ, C., Social Science
LOVEJOY, P. E., History
MCROBERTS, K. H., Political Science
MADRAS, N. N., Mathematics and Statistics
MAIDMAN, M. P., History
MANN, S. N., History
MASON, S. N., Humanities
MASSAM, B. H., Geography
MASSAM, H., Mathematics and Statistics
MENDELSOHN, D. J., Languages, Literatures and Linguistics
MOUGEON, R., French Studies
MULDOON, M. E., Mathematics and Statistics
MURDIE, R. A., Geography
NAGATA, J., Anthropology
NELLES, H. V., History
NOBLE, D., Social Science
NORCLIFFE, G. B., Geography
NORTH, L., Political Science
O'BRIEN, G. L., Mathematics and Statistics
OLIN, P., Mathematics and Statistics
OLIVER, P. N., History
ONO, H., Psychology
PANITCH, L., Political Science
PELLETIER, J. M., Mathematics and Statistics
PEPLER, D. J., Psychology
PLOURDE, C., Economics
POLKA, B., Humanities
POPE, R. W. F., Languages, Literatures and Linguistics
PROMISLOW, S. D., Mathematics and Statistics
PYKE, S., Psychology
RADFORD, J. P., Geography
REGAN, D. M., Psychology
RENNIE, D. L., Psychology
ROBBINS, S. G., Physical Education
RODMAN, M. C., Anthropology
ROGERS, N. C. T., History
SALISBURY, T., Mathematics and Statistics
SHUBERT, A., History
SILVERMAN, M., Anthropology
SIMMONS, H., Political Science
SIMPSON-HOUSLEY, P., Geography
SMITHIN, J. N., Economics
SOLITAR, D., Mathematics and Statistics
STAGER, P., Psychology
STEPRANS, J., Mathematics and Statistics
SUBTELNY, O., History and Political Science
THOLEN, W., Mathematics and Statistics
VAN ESTERIK, P., Anthropology
WAKABAYASHI, B. T., History
WATSON, W. S., Mathematics and Statistics
WHITAKER, R., Political Science
WHITELEY, W. J., Mathematics and Statistics
WONG, M., Mathematics and Statistics
WU, J., Mathematics and Statistics

Faculty of Education:

BRITZMAN, D. P.
BUNCH, G.
EWOLDT, C.
HESHUSIUS, L.
PIPER, T. C.
ROGERS, P. K.
SHAPSON, S.

Faculty of Environmental Studies:

BELL, D. V. J.
DALY, G. P.
FOUND, W. C.
GREER-WOOTTEN, B.
HOMENUCK, H. P. M.
SPENCE, E. S.
VICTOR, P. A.
WEKERLE, G. R.
WILKINSON, P. F.

Faculty of Fine Arts:

BIELER, T., Visual Arts
MÉTRAUX, G. P. R., Visual Arts
MORRIS, P., Film and Video
RUBIN, D., Theatre
SANKARAN, T., Music
TENNEY, J., Music
THURLBY, M., Visual Arts
TOMCIK, A., Visual Arts
WHITEN, T., Visual Arts

Faculty of Pure and Applied Science:

ALDRIDGE, K. D., Earth and Atmospheric Science
ARJOMANDI, E., Computer Science
BARTEL, N. H., Physics and Astronomy
BOHME, D. K., Chemistry
CAFARELLI, E. D., Physical Education
CALDWELL, J. J., Natural Science, Physics and Astronomy
CANNON, W. H., Physics and Astronomy
COLMAN, B., Biology
COUKELL, M. B., Biology
DAREWYCH, J. W., Physics and Astronomy
DAVEY, K. G., Biology
DE ROBERTIS, M. M., Physics and Astronomy
DYMOND, P. W., Computer Science
FENTON, M. B., Biology and Environmental Science
FILSETH, S. V., Chemistry
FORER, A., Biology
FREEDHOFF, H. S., Physics and Astronomy
GLEDHILL, N., Physical Education
GOODINGS, J. M., Chemistry
HARRIS, G. W., Chemistry
HASTIE, D. R., Chemistry
HEATH, I. B., Biology
HEDDLE, J. A. M., Biology
HILLIKER, A. J., Biology
HOLLOWAY, C. E., Chemistry
HOOD, D. A., Physical Education
HOPKINSON, A. C., Chemistry
HORBATSCH, M., Physics and Astronomy
INNANEN, K. A., Physics and Astronomy
JARRELL, R. A., Natural Science
JARVIS, G. T., Earth and Atmospheric Science
KONIUK, R., Physics and Astronomy
LAFRAMBOISE, J. G., Physics and Astronomy
LEE-RUFF, E., Chemistry
LEVER, A. B. P., Chemistry
LEZNOFF, C. C., Chemistry
LICHT, L. E., Biology and Environmental Science
LIU, J. W. H., Computer Science
LOGAN, D. M., Biology and Natural Science
LOUGHTON, B. G., Biology
MALTMAN, K. R., Mathematics and Statistics
MCCALL, M., Physics and Astronomy
MCCONNELL, J. C., Earth and Atmospheric Science
MCQUEEN, D. J., Biology and Environmental Science
MILLER, J. R., Physics and Astronomy
PACKER, L. D. M., Biology
PEARLMAN, R. E., Biology
PRINCE, R. H., Physics and Astronomy
RUDOLPH, J., Chemistry
SALEUDDIN, A. S. M., Biology
SAPP, J. A., Biology
SHEPHERD, G. G., Earth and Atmospheric Science
SIU, K. W. M., Chemistry
SMYLIE, D. E., Earth and Atmospheric Science
STAUFFER, A. D., Mathematics and Statistics, Physics and Astronomy
STEEL, C. G., Biology
TAYLOR, P. A., Earth and Atmospheric Science
TOURLAKIS, G., Computer Science
TSOTSOS, J. K., Computer Science
WEBB, R. A., Biology

Schulich School of Business:

BURKE, R. J., Organizational Behaviour, Industrial Relations
BUZACOTT, J., Management Science
COOK, W. D., Management Science
CRAGG, A. W., Business Ethics
DERMER, J. D., Policy
FENWICK, I. D., Marketing
HEELER, R. M., Marketing
HORVATH, D., Policy
LITVAK, I. A., Policy
MCKELLAR, J., Real Property Development
MCMILLAN, C. J., Policy
MORGAN, G. H., Organizational Behaviour, Industrial Relations
OLIVER, C. E., Organizational Behaviour, Industrial Relations
PAN, Y., International Business
PETERSON, R., Policy
PRISMAN, E., Finance
ROBERTS, G. S., Finance
ROSEN, L. S., Accounting
THOMPSON, D. N., Marketing
TRYFOS, P., Management Science
WHEELER, D. C., Business and Sustainability

WILSON, H. T., Policy
WOLF, B. M., Economics

Osgoode Hall Law School:
ARTHURS, H. W.
BROOKS, W. N.
GEVA, B.
GRAY, R. J. S.
HASSON, R. A.
HATHAWAY, J. C.
HOGG, P. W.
HUTCHINSON, A. C.
MCCAMUS, J. D.
MANDEL, M. G.
MONAHAN, P. J.
MOSSMAN, M. J.
RAMSAY, I. D.
SALTER, R. L.
SLATTERY, B.
VAVER, D.
WATSON, G. D.
WILLIAMS, S. A.
ZEMANS, F. H.

Atkinson College:
ADELMAN, H., Philosophy
ARTHUR, R. G., Humanities
BARTEL, H., Administrative Studies
BEER, F. F., English
BORDESSA, R., Geography
CALLAGHAN, B., English
COWLES, M. P., Psychology
DRACHE, D., Political Science
DROST, H., Economics
ELLENWOOD, W. R., English
FLEMING, S. J., Psychology
GRAY, P. T., Humanities
GRAYSON, J. P., Sociology
HERREN, M., Classics and Humanities
KATER, M. H., History
LEVY, J., Nursing
LUXTON, M., Social Science
MAHANEY, W. C., Geography
MALLIN, S. B., Philosophy
OKADA, R., Psychology
SAUL, J. S., Social Science
SHANKER, S. G., Philosophy
SHTEIR, A. B., Humanities
STEINBACH, M. J., Psychology
UNRAU, J. P., English
WEISS, A. I., Computer Science and Mathematics
WILSON, B. A., Humanities
WOOD, J. D., Geography

Glendon College:
ABELLA, I. M., History
ALCOCK, J., Psychology
BAUDOT, A., French Studies
DOOB, P. B., English
GENTLES, I. J., History
HORN, M. S. D., History
KIRSCHBAUM, S. J., Political Science
KLEIN-LATAUD, C., Translation
MAHANT, E., Political Science
MORRIS, R. N., Sociology
MOYAL, G. J. D., Philosophy
OLSHEN, B. N., English and Multidisciplinary Studies
ONDAATJE, P. M., English
SHAND, G. B., English
TATILON, C., French Studies
TWEYMAN, S., Philosophy
WALLACE, R. S., English
WHITFIELD, A., Translation

ATTACHED INSTITUTES

Canadian Centre for German and European Studies: 230 York Lanes, York University, 4700 Keele St, Toronto, ON M3J 1P3; Dir J. PECK.

Centre for Atmospheric Chemistry: 006 Steacie Science, York University, 4700 Keele St, Toronto, ON M3J 1P3; Dir G. W. HARRIS.

Centre for Feminist Research: 228 York Lanes, York University, 4700 Keele St, Toronto, ON M3J 1P3; Dir D. KHAYATT.

Centre for Health Studies: 214 York Lanes, York University, Toronto, ON M3J 1P3; Dir G. D. FELDBERG.

Centre for International and Security Studies: 375 York Lanes, York University, 4700 Keele St, Toronto, ON M3J 1P3; Dir D. B. DEWITT.

Centre for Jewish Studies: 260 Vanier College, York University, 4700 Keele St, Toronto, ON M3J 1P3; Dir M. G. BROWN.

Centre for Practical Ethics: 102 McLaughlin, York University, 4700 Keele St, Toronto, ON M3J 1P3; Dir D. SHUGARMAN.

Centre for Public Law and Public Policy: 435 Osgoode, York University, 4700 Keele St, Toronto, ON M3J 1P3; Dir P. J. MONAHAN.

Centre for Refugee Studies: 322 York Lanes, York University, 4700 Keele St, Toronto, ON M3J 1P3; Dir P. PENZ.

Centre for Research in Earth and Space Science: 249 Petrie Science Building, York University, 4700 Keele St, Toronto, ON M3J 1P3; Dir G. SHEPHERD.

Centre for Research on Latin America and the Caribbean: 240 York Lanes, York University, Toronto, ON M3J 1P3; Dir V. PATRONI.

Centre for Research on Work and Society: 276 York Lanes, York University, Toronto, ON M3J 1P3; Dir C. LIPSIG-MUMMÉ.

Centre for the Study of Computers in Education: S869 Ross, York University, 4700 Keele St, Toronto, ON M3J 1P3; Dir R. D. OWSTON.

Centre for Vision Research: 103 Farquharson, York University, 4700 Keele St, Toronto, ON M3J 1P3; Dir J. TSOTSOS.

Joint Centre for Asia Pacific Studies: 270 York Lanes, York University, 4700 Keele St, Toronto, ON M3J 1P3; Dir B. FROLIC.

LaMarsh Centre for Research on Violence and Conflict Resolution: 217 York Lanes, York University, 4700 Keele St, Toronto, ON M3J 1P3; Dir D. J. PEPLER.

Nathanson Centre for the Study of Organized Crime and Corruption: 321A Osgoode, York University, 4700 Keele St, Toronto, ON M3J 1P3; Dir M. BEARE.

Robarts Centre for Canadian Studies: 227 York Lanes, York University, 4700 Keele St, Toronto, ON M3J 1P3; Dir D. DRACHE.

York Centre for Applied Sustainability: 355 Lumbers, York University, 4700 Keele St, Toronto, ON M3J 1P3; Dir D. BELL.

York Institute for Social Research: 242A Schulich School of Business, York University, 4700 Keele St, Toronto, ON M3J 1P3; Dir M. ORNSTEIN.

Schools of Art and Music

Alberta College of Art and Design: 1407 14th Ave NW, Calgary, AB T2N 4R3; tel. (403) 284-7600; fax (403) 289-6682; e-mail admissions@acad.ca; internet www.acad.ab.ca; f. 1926; 100 teachers; 1,000 students; library: 28,578 vols and collection of 124,845 slides, 75 periodical titles; 4-year Degree and Diploma programmes in Visual Arts and Design; Pres. LANCE CARLSON.

Banff Centre: POB 1020, Banff, AB T1L 1H5; tel. (403) 762-6100; fax (403) 762-6444; internet www.banffcentre.ca; f. 1933; offers programs in arts (Aboriginal Arts, Audio, Press, New Media, Creative Electronic Environment, Dance, Media and Visual Arts, Music, Opera, Theatre, Writing, Curatorial Practice), Leadership Development, Aboriginal Leadership and Management, Mountain Culture, Environmental Issues; Pres. and CEO MARY E. HOFSTETTER; Senior Vice-President, Programming JOANNE MORROW; Vice-President and CFO J. A NUTT.

Conservatoire de Musique de Montréal: 4750 ave Henri-Julien, Montréal, QC H2T 2C8; tel. (514) 873-4031; fax (514) 873-4601; e-mail CMM@mcc.gouv.qc.ca; internet www.mcc.gouv.qc.ca/conservatoire/montreal.htm; f. 1942; a government-controlled institution, largest of a network of seven in Quebec Province; 76 teachers; 340 students; library: 58,000 books and scores, 125 rare books, 20 MSS, 10,000 recordings and 80 periodicals; Dir ISOLDE LAGACÉ.

Conservatoire de Musique de Québec: 270 rue St-Amable, Québec, QC G1R 5G1; tel. (418) 643-2190; fax (418) 644-9658; e-mail cmq@mcc.gouv.qc.ca; internet www.mcc.gouv.gc.ca/conservatoire/quebec.htm; f. 1944; 50 teachers; 250 students; library: 68,000 vols, recordings, scores and periodicals; Dir GUY CARMICHAEL.

Maritime Conservatory of Performing Arts: 6199 Chebucto Rd, Halifax, NS B3L 1K7; tel. (902) 423-6995; fax (902) 423-6029; e-mail mconservatory@ns.sympatico.ca; f. 1887; Dir Dr IFAN WILLIAMS; 80 ; 1,200 .

Ontario College of Art and Design: 100 McCaul St, Toronto, ON M5T 1W1; tel. (416) 977-6000; fax (416) 977-6006; internet www.ocad.on.ca; f. 1876; library: 24,000 print vols, 225 periodical subscriptions, 44,000 pictures, 70,000 slides, etc.; post-secondary education in fine art and design; 200 teachers; 2,329 students; Pres. RON SHUEBROOK; Exec. Vice-Pres. PETER CALDWELL; Financial Aids and Awards Officer KELLY DICKINSON; Director of Library JILL PATRICK

DEANS

Faculty of Art: WENDY COBURN, PETER SRAMEK
Faculty of Design: LENORE RICHARDS
Faculty of Foundation Studies: CATHERINE WILD
Faculty of Liberal Studies: KATHRYN SHAILER

Royal Canadian College of Organists: 204 St George St, Suite 204, Toronto, ON M5R 2N5; tel. (416) 929-6400; fax (416) 929-2265; e-mail rcco@the-wire.com; internet www.rcco.ca; f. 1909; Pres. F. ALAN REESOR; Vice-Pres. PATRICIA WRIGHT; Treasurer DON TIMMINS; publs *Organ Canada* (quarterly), *The American Organist* (monthly, in asscn with American Guild of Organists).

Royal Conservatory of Music: 273 Bloor St West, Toronto ON M5S 1W2; tel. (416) 408-2824; fax (416) 408-3096; e-mail communityschool@rcmusic.ca; internet www.rcmusic.ca; f. 1886; 350 teachers; 10,000 students; Pres. PETER C. SIMON; Deans JEFF MELANSON, RENNIE REGEHR.

CAPE VERDE

The Higher Education System

Cape Verde has little history of higher education. During five centuries of colonial rule in the archipelago Portugal did not draft any known plans for the establishment of a university for Cape Verde. After independence the number of students enrolled in secondary education increased markedly, and the demand for higher education began to be addressed with the creation of several institutes of higher studies to train teachers and health workers. Most Cape Verdeans studied abroad; in 2002/03 there were 1,743 Cape Verdean students studying at overseas universities. However, the cost of foreign study was high. Thus, as domestic demand increased throughout the 1990s, more concrete plans were made for establishing a university. The Universidade Jean Piaget de Cabo Verde was founded in 2002; in 2003/04 there 3,036 students in higher education. There is also a higher institute of engineering and marine science.

Learned Society

LANGUAGE AND LITERATURE

Alliance Française: Rua de Santo Antonio, CP 37, Mindelo; tel. 232-11-49; fax 232-11-48; e-mail afmsvcapvert@cvtelecom.cv; internet www.afmindelo.n3.net; offers courses and exams in French language and culture and promotes cultural exchange with France.

Research Institute

ECONOMICS, LAW AND POLITICS

Instituto Nacional de Estatistica de Cabo Verde (Cape Verde National Statistical Institute): CP 116, Praia, Santiago; tel. 261-38-27; e-mail inecv@mail.telecom.cv; internet www.ine.cv; Pres. FRANCISCO FERNANDES TORRES.

Library

Praia

Biblioteca de Assembleia Nacional (National Assembly Library): Achada de Santo António, CP 20-A, Praia; tel. 262-32-90; fax 262-26-60; e-mail graca@cvtelecom.cv; internet www.parlamento.cv/biblioteca/index.htm; f. 1985; 5,000 vols, 100 periodicals; Dir ALBERTINA GRAÇA.

University

UNIVERSIDADE JEAN PIAGET DE CABO VERDE

Campus Universitário da Cidade da Praia, CP 775, Cidade de Praia

Telephone: 262-90-85

Fax: 262-90-89

E-mail: info@caboverde.ipiaget.cv

Internet: www.unipiaget.cv

Founded 2001; attached to Instituto Piaget, Portugal

Academic year: October to July

Rector: Prof. Dr ESTELA PINTO RIBEIRA LAMAS

Vice-Rector: Prof. Dr JORGE SOUSA BRITO

General Administrator: Prof. Dr DAVID RIBEIRO LAMAS

Number of teachers: 50

Number of students: 650

Courses: architecture, communications science, education science, pharmaceutical sciences, economics and management, professional education, nursing, civil construction engineering, information systems and engineering, chemistry and physics teaching, mathematics teaching, English language and literature teaching, Portuguese language and literature teaching, physiotherapy, hotel and tourism management, business information, psychology, sociology.

College

Instituto Superior de Engenharia e Ciências do Mar (ISECMAR) (Higher Institute of Engineering and Marine Science): CP 163, Ribeira de Julião, São Vicente; tel. 232-65-61; fax 232-65-63; e-mail info@isecmar.cv; internet www.isecmar.cv; f. 1984; Pres. ELISA FERREIRA SILVA

DEANS

Electrical and Mechanical Engineering: MANUEL EDUARDO FORTES TAVARES DE ALMEIDA

Electronic and Computer Engineering: ABEL FELISBERTO DE OLIVEIRA ALMADA

Marine Biology and Aquatic Research: JOSÉ MANUEL LIMA RAMOS

Natural and Human Sciences: EVA DUARTE SOULÉ

Nautical Sciences: DANIEL MARCOS SOUSA LOPES

CENTRAL AFRICAN REPUBLIC

The Higher Education System

Until the late 1960s higher education was closely linked to the former colonial power, France, from which the Central African Republic (CAR) had gained its independence in 1960. Students either travelled to France to study or attended the Foundation for Higher Education in Central Africa, established by the French to serve the CAR, Gabon, Chad and the Republic of Congo. The state-run Université de Bangui was founded in 1969 and remains the CAR's only university. The provision of state-funded higher education was severely disrupted during the 1990s and early 2000s, owing to the inadequacy of financial resources. The Ministry of Education oversees higher education. In 1999/2000 there were 6,323 students in higher education.

The University Council is the administrative and executive body of the Université de Bangui, and the Rector is the institutional head. All appointments and promotions are based on recommendations made to the Minister of Education by the University Council.

The secondary school Baccalauréat or Diplôme de Bachelier de l'Enseignement du Second Degré are the main criteria for admission to university. Higher education awards are divided into two cycles. The first cycle results in the award of a Diplôme for which two years of study in an area of specialization (general studies, literature, science, economics, law) are required. The second cycle lasts for a year following this and leads to the award of the Licence degree, after which an additional year of study results in award of a Maîtrise degree. The only doctoral qualification awarded by Université de Bangui is the Doctorat en Médecine, which requires six years of study. The Université de Bangui also offers vocational education.

The higher education system in the CAR is beset by numerous and complex challenges. For decades, various governments have failed to provide adequate funding for the education system or regular and decent pay for its workers. Strikes by students and professors have led to the shortening of academic years. The system suffers severe deficiencies in quality and does not satisfy real labour-market demand. It remains to be seen whether the National Plan for the Development of Education, to be implemented during 2000–10, will be adequately funded.

Learned Society

LANGUAGE AND LITERATURE

Alliance Française: cnr Rue de L'Industrie/Rue Du Poitou, BP 971, Bangui; tel. 61-49-41; fax 61-90-72; e-mail afbangui@yahoo.fr; offers courses and exams in French language and culture and promotes cultural exchange with France.

Research Institutes

GENERAL

Institut de Recherche pour le Développement (IRD): BP 893, Bangui; tel. 61-20-89; fax 61-68-29; f. 1949; soil science, geophysics, geology, medical entomology; library of 9,000 vols; Dir JEAN-YVES GAC; (see main entry under France).

AGRICULTURE, FISHERIES AND VETERINARY SCIENCE

Centre d'Etudes sur la Trypanosomiase Animale: BP 39, Bouar; stations at Bewiti, Sarki; annexe at Bambari.

Institut de Recherches Agronomiques de Boukoko (Agricultural Research Institute): BP 44, M'Baiki, Boukoko; f. 1948; research into tropical agriculture and plant diseases, fertilization and entomology; library of 2,740 vols; Dir M. GONDJIA.

Institut d'Etudes Agronomiques d'Afrique Centrale: Ecole Nationale des Adjoints Techniques d'Agriculture de Wakombo, BP 78, M'Baiki; affiliated to Université de Bangui; Dir R. ELIARD.

ECONOMICS, LAW AND POLITICS

Département des études de population à l'Union Douanière et Economique de l'Afrique Centrale: BP 1418, Bangui; tel. 61-45-77; f. 1964; Dir JEAN NKOUNKOU.

MEDICINE

Institut Pasteur: BP 923, Bangui; tel. 61-45-76; fax 61-08-66; f. 1961; research on viral haemorrhagic fevers, polio virus, tuberculosis, HIV/AIDS and simian retroviruses; WHO Regional Centre for poliomyelitis in Africa; Dir Dr ANTOINE TALARMIN; publ. *Rapport Annuel*.

NATURAL SCIENCES

Station Expérimentale de la Maboké: par M'Baiki; f. 1963 under the direction of the Muséum National d'Histoire Naturelle, Paris; studies in the protection of materials in tropical regions, mycology, entomology, virology, zoology, botany, anthropology, parasitology, protection of natural resources; Dir (vacant).

RELIGION, SOCIOLOGY AND ANTHROPOLOGY

Mission sociologique du Haut-Oubangui: BP 68, Bangassou; f. 1954; sociological and archaeological study of societies and cultures from the CAR, especially from the Gbaya, Nzakara and Zandé countries; historical maps and sociological documents; Head Prof. E. DE DAMPIERRE; publ. *Recherches oubanguiennes*.

TECHNOLOGY

Institut National de Recherches Textiles et Cultures Vivrières: BP 17, Bambari; Dir GABRIEL RAMADHANE-SAÏD.

Library

Bangui

Bibliothèque Universitaire de Bangui: BP 1450, Bangui; tel. 61-20-00; f. 1980; 26,000 vols, 600 periodicals (Central Library); 9,144 vols (Ecole Normale Supérieure); 5,240 vols, 168 periodicals (Faculty of Health Sciences); Dir JOSEPH GOMA-BOUANGA.

University

UNIVERSITÉ DE BANGUI

Ave des Martyrs, BP 1450, Bangui

Telephone: 61-20-00
Fax: 61-78-90
Internet: ww.univ-bangui.info

Founded 1969
Language of instruction: French
Academic year: October to June

Rector: FAUSTIN TOUADÉRA
Vice-Rector: JOSEPH MABINGUI
Secretary-General: GABRIEL NGOUANDJITANGA
Librarian: JOSEPH NGOMA-BOUANGA

Library: See Libraries and Archives
Number of teachers: 243
Number of students: 6,474

Publications: *Annales de l'Université de Bangui Wambesso*, *Espace francophone*, *Revue d'Histoire et d'Archéologie Centrafricaine*

DEANS

Faculty of Health Science: Prof. MAMADOU NESTOR NALI
Faculty of Law and Economics: DAMIENNE NANARE
Faculty of Letters and Humanities: GABRIEL NGOUANDJI-TANGA
Faculty of Science and Technology: Lic. MABOUA BARA

DIRECTORS

Department of Mathematics and Computer Studies: DANIEL SEGALEN
Institute of Applied Language Studies: FRANÇOIS LIM
Polytechnic Institute: JEAN BIANDJA
University Institute of Business Administration: MICHEL CREPON
University Institute for Research in Mathematics Teaching: JOSEPH DENAMGANAI
University Institute of Rural Development: GEORGES NGONDJO

Colleges

Ecole Centrale d'Agriculture: Boukoko.

Ecole Nationale d'Administration et de la Magistrature (ENAM) (National School of Administration and Judiciary): BP 1450, Bangui; tel. 61-04-88; state control under Sec.-Gen. of Govt; f. as school for future civil students and magistrates; curriculum now oriented to workshops for benefit of public-sector workers; Dir-Gen. ISAAC EDGAR BENAM.

Ecole Nationale des Arts: BP 349, Bangui; f. 1966; music, dance, dramatic art and plastic arts.

Ecole Territoriale d'Agriculture: Grimari.

CHAD

The Higher Education System

The main institution of higher education is the Université du N'Djamena, which was founded as the Université du Tchad in 1971 and adopted its current name in 1994. In addition, there are several technical colleges. Some 6,106 students were enrolled at higher education institutions in 2000/01.

Higher education in Chad is influenced by the French model, in which universities are under direct government supervision. The Ministry of Higher Education and Scientific Research oversees research activities through the National Committee of Scientific and Technical Research. The ministry has power over most education institutions in which teaching and research activities are performed. Some specialized institutions are supervised by other ministries. In 1990 the Government adopted a development strategy entitled Education-Formation-Emploi (EFE—Education-Training-Emploument). The strategy, made up of five programmes corresponding to five sectors of the education system, sought to improve the education system's efficiency and increase access to education. It focused on teacher training, curriculum design and the rationalization of management. The Government was committed to improving the management of public resources in an attempt to meet structural adjustment programmes, and directed its attention to investment and basic education. As a result, inadequate resources were allocated to higher education. EFE strategists decided to increase student enrolment, particularly to scientific and technological disciplines. The resulting growth served only to exacerbate existing imbalances. The implementation of EFE strategy has since stalled owing to a lack of resources, and the reforms have yet to yield satisfactory results.

The Baccalauréat is required for admission to university. University-level education consists of two cycles. The first cycle involves two years of study and leads to one of three diplomas, depending on the student's area of specialization: Diplôme Universitaire de Lettres Modernes (humanities), Diplôme Universitaire de Sciences (sciences) and Diplôme Universitaire de Sciences Juridiques, Economiques et de Gestion (social sciences). The second cycle leads to the award of the Licence after one of study following the award of the Diplôme, and the Maîtrise after a further one or two years of study. The Baccalauréat is also required for admission to non-university higher education and professional training courses.

Research Institutes

AGRICULTURE, FISHERIES AND VETERINARY SCIENCE

Institut de Recherches du Coton et des Textiles Exotiques (IRCT): BP 764, N'Djamena; f. 1939; cotton research (entomology, agronomy and genetics); Head of station at Bebedja M. Renou; Regional Dir M. Yehouessi.

Laboratoire de Recherches Vétérinaires et Zootechniques de Farcha: BP 433, N'Djamena; tel. 52-74-75; fax 52-83-02; f. 1952; veterinary and stockbreeding research and production of vaccines; training; library of 3,500 vols; Dir Dr Hassane Mahamat Hassane; publ. *Rapport annuel*.

EDUCATION

Centre de Recherche, des Archives et de Documentation, Commission nationale pour l'UNESCO: BP 731, N'Djamena; Sec.-Gen. Dr Khalil Alio; publ. *COMNAT: Bulletin d' Information*.

RELIGION, SOCIOLOGY AND ANTHROPOLOGY

Institut National des Sciences Humaines: BP 1117, N'Djamena; tel. 51-62-68; f. 1961; palaeontology, prehistory, proto-history, linguistics, sociolinguistics, history, ethno-sociology, sociology, anthropology, geography, social sciences, oral traditions; 6 researchers; library of 1,000 vols and 400 archive documents; Dir Moukthar Djibrine Mahamat; Gen. Sec. Djong-Yang Oüanlarbo; publ. *Revue de Tchad*.

Museum

N'Djamena

Musée National: BP 638, N'Djamena; tel. 51-33-75; fax 51-60-94; f. 1963; attached to Institut National des Sciences Humaines (see above); 100 collections; in process of reformation; depts of palaeontology, prehistory and archaeology, ethnography, scientific archives; Dir Djamil Moussa Nene.

University

UNIVERSITÉ DE N'DJAMENA

BP 1117, N'Djamena
Telephone: 51-44-44
Fax: 51-40-33
E-mail: rectorat@intnet.td

Founded 1971 as Université de Chad; present title 1994
State control
Languages of instruction: French, Arabic
Academic year: October to June

Rector: Mbaïlao Mbaïguinam
Secretary-General: Mahamat Barka
Librarian: Mahamat Saleh

Library of 30,000 vols
Number of teachers: 203
Number of students: 5,183
Publication: *Annuaire*

DEANS

Faculty of Arts and Human Sciences: Tchago Bouimon
Faculty of Exact and Applied Sciences: Tagui Guelbeye Tchang
Faculty of Health Sciences: Ivoulsou Douphang Phang
Faculty of Law and Economics: Enoch Nodjigoto (acting)

ATTACHED RESEARCH INSTITUTES

Institute of Humanities Research: Dir Mahamat Moukhtar.

Colleges

Ecole Nationale d'Administration: BP 768, N'Djamena; f. 1963; set up by the Government and controlled by an Administrative Council to train students as public servants; Dir N. Guelina.

Institut Supérieur des Sciences de l'Education: BP 473 N'Djamena; tel. 51-44-87; fax 51-45-50; f. 1992; Departments of Teacher Training for Primary Education, Teacher Training for Secondary Education and Teacher Training for Technical and Professional Education; Dir Mayore Karyo.

CHILE

The Higher Education System

There are three types of higher education institution in Chile: public and private universities (universidad publica and universidad privada), professional institutes (instituto profesional) and centres of technical training. In 2002 there were 521,609 students in higher education.

Students require the Licencia de Educación Media to be admitted to university, and state-funded universities must hold an entrance examination (Prueba de Aptitud Academica). There are three levels of university qualifications in Chile, one undergraduate and two postgraduate. Undergraduates study for three to five years for the Bachiller (Bachelors), Licenciado or a professional degree. Postgraduates study for two years following the Licenciado to receive the Magister, and then for a further three years for the Doctorado.

Technical and vocational training is coordinated by Instituto Nacional de Capitación Profesional, which administers and accredits qualifications and institutions. Entrance requirements are the same as those for university-level education. Centres of technical training award the title of Técnico Superior in fields of professional education; professional institutes offer training programmes of four to five years, leading to award of a professional title; and universities award the title of Ingeniero de Ejecucion after four years of full-time study in different fields. Two universities, Universidad de Santiago de Chile and Universidad Técnica 'Federico Santa Maria', offer courses requiring three years of full-time study and leading to the title of Técnico Universitario.

Learned Societies

GENERAL

Instituto de Chile: Almirante Montt 453, Clasificador 1349, Correo Central, 6500445 Santiago; tel. (2) 6382847; f. 1964; promotes cultural, humanistic and scientific studies; Pres. CARLOS RIESCO GREZ; Gen. Sec. ANTONIO DOUGNAC; publ. *Anales*.

Constituent academies:

Academia Chilena de la Lengua (Chilean Academy of Language): Clasificador 1349, Correo Central, Santiago; tel. (2) 382847; f. 1885; fmrly Academia Chilena; corresp. mem. of the Real Academia Española, Madrid; 36 mems; Dir ALFREDO MATUS OLIVIER; Sec. JOSÉ LUIS SAMANIEGO ALDAZÁBAL; publ. *Boletín de la Academia Chilena*.

Academia Chilena de la Historia (Chilean Academy of History): Almirante Montt 454, Santiago; tel. (2) 6399323; fax (2) 6399323; e-mail acchhist@ctcreuna.cl; internet www.uchile.cl/instituto; f. 1933; 36 mems; library of 2,500 vols; Pres. FERNANDO SILVA VARGAS; publs *Boletín de la Academia* (annually), *Archivo de D. Bernardo O'Higgins* (irregular).

Academia Chilena de Ciencias (Chilean Academy of Sciences): Clasificador 1349, Correo Central, Santiago; tel. 6382847; fax 6332129; f. 1964; 36 Academicians; 21 corresp.; 5 hon. Academicians; promotes research in pure and applied sciences; Pres. Dr JORGE E. ALLENDE; Sec. Dr JOSE CORVALÁN DÍAZ; publs *Boletín* (irregular), *Figuras señeras de la Ciencia en Chile* (irregular).

Academia Chilena de Ciencias Sociales, Políticas y Morales (Chilean Academy of Social, Political and Moral Sciences): Clasificador 1349, Correo Central, Santiago; tel. 382847; f. 1964; 36 mems; library of 7,000 vols; Pres. JUAN DE DIOS VIAL LARRAIN; Sec. HERNÁN GODOY URZÚA; publs *Boletín* (3 a year), *Anales* (annually), *Folletos*.

Academia Chilena de Medicina (Chilean Academy of Medicine): Almirante Montt 453, 6500445 Santiago; tel. (2) 6331902; fax (2) 6640775; f. 1964; 75 Academicians; 45 hon. foreign mems; library of 900 vols; Pres. Dr JAIME PÉREZ-OLEA; Sec. Dra SYLVIA SEGOVIA POLLA; publs *Boletín*, *Proceedings on the Chilean History of Medicine*, *monographs*, *annuals*.

Academia Chilena de Bellas Artes (Chilean Academy of Fine Arts): Clasificador 1349, Correo Central, 6500445 Santiago; tel. (2) 6331902; fax (2) 6337460; e-mail acchbear@ctcreuna.cl; internet www.uchile.cl/instituto; f. 1964; 40 mems (28 academicians, 11 corresp., 1 hon.); Pres. CARLOS RIESCO GREZ; Sec. SANTIAGO VERA; publ. *Boletín*.

UNESCO Office Santiago and Regional Bureau for Education in Latin America and the Caribbean/Oficina Regional de Educación de la Unesco para América Latina y el Caribe: Casilla de correo 3187, Santiago; located at: Calle Enrique Delpiano 2058, Santiago 3187; tel. (2) 6551050; fax (2) 6551046; e-mail santiago@unesco.org; internet www.unesco.cl; Dir ANA LUIZA MACHADO PINHEIRO.

AGRICULTURE, FISHERIES AND VETERINARY SCIENCE

Colegio de Ingenieros Forestales: San Isidro 22, Of. No. 503 Casilla 9686, Santiago; tel. 393289; f. 1972; 350 mems; Pres. JORGE I. CORREA DRUBI; Sec. LEONARDO ARAYA VALDEBENITO; publs *Actas de las Jornadas Forestales* (2 a year), *Renarres* (every 2 months).

Sociedad Agronómica de Chile (Agronomical Society of Chile): Casilla 4109, Calle Mac-Iver 120, Of. 36, Santiago; tel. 384881; f. 1910; 1,900 mems; library of 1,600 vols; Pres. Dr L. ANTONIO LIZANA M.; Sec. HECTOR E. NÚÑEZ; publ. *Simiente* (3 a year).

Sociedad Chilena de Producción Animal: Santa Rosa No. 11735, Casilla 2, Correo 15, La Granja, Santiago; tel. 5587042, ext. 307; f. 1979; 115 mems; Pres. Dr ALEJANDRO LÓPEZ V.; Sec./Treas. Dra MARÍA SOL MORALES S.

Sociedad Nacional de Agricultura (National Society of Agriculture): Casilla 40-D, Tenderini 187, Santiago; tel. (2) 6396710; fax (2) 6337771; e-mail gusrojas@entelchile.net; f. 1838; library of 3,500 vols; research in agricultural, social and economic problems; controls a plant genetics experimental station and a broadcasting chain with stations in several cities; register of pedigree cattle kept; technical assistance to farmers; annual international and agricultural show since 1869, and home show since 1980; Pres. RICARDO ARIZTÍA; Sec. LUIS QUIROGA; publs *Revista El Campesino*, *Boletín Económico y de Mercado*, *Vocero Agrícola*, *Informatoivo Frutícola*, *SNAFAX News*.

ARCHITECTURE AND TOWN PLANNING

Colegio de Arquitectos de Chile (Chilean College of Architects): Avda Libertador Bernardo O'Higgins 115, Casilla 13377, Santiago; tel. (2) 6398744; fax (2) 6398769; e-mail colegio@colegio-arquitectos.cl; f. 1942 for all Chilean and foreign architects working in Chile; 5,500 mems; library of 2,000 vols, 2,500 journals; Pres. RENÉ MORALES MORALES; Gen. Man. ERICO LUEBERT CID; publs *Revista CA* (quarterly), *Boletín* (monthly), *Bienal de Arquitectura* (every 2 years), *Congreso Nacional de Arquitectos* (every 2 years).

BIBLIOGRAPHY, LIBRARY SCIENCE AND MUSEOLOGY

Colegio de Bibliotecarios de Chile, AG: Diagonal Paraguay 383, Depto 122, Torre 11, Santiago; tel. (2) 2225652; fax (2) 6355023; e-mail cbc@uplink.cl; internet www.bibliotecarios.cl; f. 1969; 1,891 mems; Pres. MARCIA MARINOVIC SIMUNOVIC; Sec. ANA MARÍA PINO YÁÑEZ; publs *Eidisis* (4 a year), *Documento de Trabajo* (irregular).

ECONOMICS, LAW AND POLITICS

Servicio Médico Legal (Forensic Medicine Service): Avda La Paz 1012, Santiago; tel. 7371268; fax 7371323; f. 1915; advises tribunals on forensic medicine; 305 mems; library of 800 vols; Dir Dr MARCO ANTONIO MEDINA MOLINA; publs *Monografías Servicio Médico Legal* (3 a year), *Revista de Medicina Legal* (3 a year).

EDUCATION

Consejo de Rectores de las Universidades Chilenas (Council of Rectors of Chilean Universities): Alameda 1371 (4° piso), Casilla 14798, Santiago; tel. (2) 6964286; fax (2) 6988436; e-mail cruch@entelchile.net; internet www.consejoderectores.cl; f. 1954; co-ordinates the academic activities of its member institutions, develops policies aimed at enhancing higher-education activities, promotes changes in laws regulating university studies and student financial aid; 25 mem. univs; Pres. SERGIO BITAR CHACRA; Gen. Sec. CARLOS

Lorca Auger; publ. *Anuario Estadístico* (Statistical Yearbook, annually).

FINE AND PERFORMING ARTS

Asociación Plástica Latina Internacional de Chile (APLICH) (Chilean International Plastic Arts Association): Avda P. de Valdivia 1781, Casilla 177, Correo 29, Santiago; tel. and fax 2233444; e-mail raccor1@entelchile.net; internet www.mnba.cl; f. 1990; Pres. Alicia Argandoña R.; Sec.-Gen. Sergio Juzam Numan; publ. *APLICH al Día*.

HISTORY, GEOGRAPHY AND ARCHAEOLOGY

Instituto Geográfico Militar (Military Geographical Institute): Nueva Santa Isabel 1640, Santiago; tel. (2) 4606800; fax (2) 4606918; e-mail igm@igm.cl; f. 1922; 400 mems; library of 4,000 vols, 25,000 maps; Dir GDB Pablo Gran López; publ. *Revista Terra Australis* (annually).

Sociedad Chilena de Historia y Geografía (Chilean Society of History and Geography): Casilla 1386, Santiago; tel. 6382489; f. 1911; 304 mems; 13 hon.; 70 corresponding; library of 12,600 vols; Pres. Sergio Martínez Baeza; Sec.-Gen. Rene Artigas Moreira; publs *Revista Chilena de Historia y Geografía*, related works.

LANGUAGE AND LITERATURE

Alliance Française: Lycée Antoine de Saint Exupéry, Calle Louis Pasteur, 5418 Vitacura, Correo 10, Casilla 94 Las Condes, Santiago; tel. (2) 2185151; fax (2) 2183287; offers courses and exams in French language and culture and promotes cultural exchange with France; attached teaching offices in Concepción, Curico, Osorno, Renaca, Santiago, Valparaíso.

British Council: Eliodor Yáñez 832, 750-0651 Providencia, Casilla 115, Correo 55, Santiago; tel. (2) 410-6900; fax (2) 410 6929; e-mail info@britishcouncil.cl; internet www.britishcouncil.cl; offers courses and exams in English language and British culture and promotes cultural exchange with the UK; Dir John W. Knagg.

Goethe-Institut: Esmeralda 650, Santiago; tel. (2) 4621800; fax (2) 4621802; e-mail il@santiago.goethe.org; internet www.goethe.de/hs/sao/deindex.htm; offers courses and exams in German language and culture and promotes cultural exchange with Germany; library of 10,000 vols; Dir Dr Hartmut Becher.

Sociedad Chilena de Lingüística (Chilean Linguistics Society): La Verbena 3882, (Providencia) Santiago; f. 1971; over 100 mems; Pres. Ambrosio Rabanales; Sec. Mario Bernales; publ. *Actas*.

MEDICINE

Colegio de Químico-Farmacéuticos de Chile (College of Pharmacists): Casilla 1136, Santiago; tel. 392505; f. 1942; 2,500 regional councils in 12 main towns; Pres. Antonio Morris; publ. *Revista*.

Sociedad Chilena de Cancerología: Fundación Arturo López Pérez, Rancagua 878, Santiago; tel. (2) 2047919 ext. 304; fax (2) 2280705; f. 1964; 142 mems; Pres. José Manuel Ojeda; Sec. Jorge Gallardo; publ. *Revista Chilena de Cancerología* (3 a year).

Sociedad Chilena de Cardiología y Cirugía Cardiovascular: Esmeralda 678, 3° piso, Casilla 23-D, Santiago; tel. 30705; f. 1949; Pres. Dr Carlos Akel A.; Sec. Dr Jorge Carabantes C.; publ. *Revista*.

Sociedad Chilena de Dermatología y Venereología: Depto Dermatología, Hosp. J. J. Aguirre, Santos Dumont 999, Santiago; tel. 779484; f. 1938; Pres. Dra Julia Quiroz M.; Exec. Sec. Dra María Maira P..

Sociedad Chilena de Endocrinología y Metabolismo: Bernarda Morín 488, 2° piso, Providencia, Santiago; tel. (2) 2230386; fax (2) 7535556; e-mail sochem@sochem.cl; internet www.sochem.cl; f. 1961; Pres. Dr Gilberto Pérez Pacheco; Sec.-Gen. Dra Verónica Araya Quintanilla.

Sociedad Chilena de Enfermedades Respiratorias: Santa Magdalena 75, Oficina 701, Providencia, Santiago; tel. (2) 2316292; fax (2) 2443811; e-mail ser@serchile.cl; internet www.serchile.cl; f. 1930; 410 mems; Pres. Dr Manuel Barros; Sec. Dra Viviana Lezana; publs *Revista Chilena de Enfermedades Respiratorias* (4 a year), *Boletín Informativo* (monthly).

Sociedad Chilena de Gastroenterología: El Trovador 4280, of. 909, Las Condes, Santiago; tel. (2) 3425004; fax (2) 3425005; e-mail schgastr@netline.cl; internet www.socgastro.cl; f. 1938; Pres. Dr Juan Carlos Weitz Vattuone; Sec. Gen. Dr Marcela Miranda Corvalán; publs *Gastroenterologia Latinoamericana*, *Normas de Diagnóstico en Enfermedades Digestivas*.

Sociedad Chilena de Inmunología: Casilla 70061, Santiago 7; tel. 370081; f. 1972; 55 active mems; Pres. Dra Alicia Ramos; Sec. Dra Cecilia Sepúlveda.

Sociedad Chilena de Neurocirugía: Esmeralda 678 (2° piso int), Santiago; tel. (2) 6386839; fax (2) 6391085; e-mail neurocirugia@terra.cl; internet www.neurocirugia.cl; f. 1957; 100 mems; Pres. Dr Leonidas Quintana; Sec.-Gen./Treas. Dr Patricio Yokota; publ. *Revista Chilena de Neurocirugía* (2 a year).

Sociedad Chilena de Obstetricia y Ginecología: Román Díaz 205, Oficina 205, Providencia, Santiago; tel. (2) 2350133; fax (2) 2351294; e-mail sochog@entelchile.net; internet www.sochog.cl; f. 1935; 270 mems; Pres. Dr Enrique Oyarzun E.; Sec. Dr Eugenio Suarez P.; publ. *Revista Chilena de Obstetricia y Ginecología* (6 a year).

Sociedad Chilena de Oftalmología: Casilla 16197, Correo 9, Providencia, Santiago; tel. and fax (2) 2185950; e-mail sochioft@tie.cl; internet www.sochiof.cl; f. 1931; 500 mems; library of 500 vols; special collection of video tapes; Pres. Dr Patricio Meza R.; Sec. Dr Francisco Villaroel W.; publs *Archivos Chilenos de Oftalmología* (2 a year), *Boletín Informativo* (monthly).

Sociedad Chilena de Ortopedia y Traumatología: Evaristo Lillo 78, Ofic. 81, Las Condes, Santiago; tel. (2) 2072151; fax (2) 2069820; e-mail schot@schot.cl; internet www.schot.cl; f. 1949; 508 mems; library of 500 vols; Pres. Dr Ignacio Dockendorff B.; Sec.-Gen. Dr Jorge Vergara L.; publ. *Revista Chilena de Ortopedia y Traumatología* (4 a year).

Sociedad Chilena de Pediatría: CP 6841638, Casilla 593, Correo 11, Santiago; located at: Alcade Eduardo Castillo Velasco 1838, Ñuñoa, Santiago; tel. (2) 2371598; fax (2) 2380046; e-mail sochipe@terra.cl; internet www.sochipe.cl; f. 1922; 1,230 mems; Pres. Dra Alejandra Jara Gaete; Sec.-Gen. Dra Lidya Tellerías Castillo.

Sociedad Chilena de Reumatología: Bernarda Morin 488 (2° piso), Providencia, Santiago; tel. 3413113; e-mail sochire@entelchile.net; f. 1950; Pres. Dr Gonzalo Astorga P.; Sec. Dr Alberto Valdés S.; publ. *Boletín* (quarterly).

Sociedad de Farmacología de Chile: Casilla 70.000, Santiago 7; tel. (2) 6786050; fax (2) 7774216; f. 1979; 88 mems; Pres. Dra Lutske Tampier; Sec. Dra Teresa Pelissier.

Sociedad de Neurología, Psiquiatría y Neurocirugía de Chile: Calle Carlos Silva V 1292, Plaza Las Lilas, Providencia, Casilla 251, Correo 35, Santiago; tel. (2) 2329347; fax (2) 2319287; e-mail secretariagral@123.cl; internet www.sonepsyn.cl; f. 1932; Pres. Dr Enrique Jadresic; publ. *Revista Chilena de Neuro-Psiquiatría* (quarterly).

Sociedad Médica de Concepción (Medical Society): Casilla 60-C, Concepción; f. 1886; Pres. Dr Enrique Bellolioz; publ. *Anales Médicos de Concepción*.

Sociedad Médica de Santiago (Santiago Medical Society): Casilla 168, Correo Tajamar, Santiago; tel. (2) 2748985; fax (2) 3413068; e-mail smschile@smschile.cl; internet www.smschile.cl; f. 1869; 1,500 mems; library: 100 periodical titles; Pres. Dr Jaime Duclos; Sec. Dr Héctor Ugalde; publ. *Revista Médica de Chile* (monthly).

Sociedad Médica de Valparaíso (Medical Society of Valparaíso): Hontaneda 2653, Valparaíso; f. 1913; 271 mems; library of 3,500 vols; Pres. Dr Arturo Villagran Valdes; Sec. Dr Manuel Barros; publ. *Revista Médica de Valparaíso* (quarterly).

Sociedad Odontológica de Concepción: Casilla 2107, Concepción; f. 1924; 300 mems; Pres. Dr Eduardo Navarete; Sec. Dr Sergio Esquerré S.; publ. *Anuario*.

NATURAL SCIENCES

General

Academia Chilena de Ciencias Naturales (Chilean Academy of Natural Sciences): Almirante Montt 454, Santiago; tel. 6441030; fax 6332129; f. 1926; Pres. Dr Hugo Gunckel L.; Sec. Hans Niemeyer F.; publ. *Anales*.

Asociación Científica y Técnica de Chile (Scientific and Technical Association of Chile): Carlos Antúnez 1885, Dpto 205, Santiago; tel. 2354137; f. 1965; 22 mems; Pres. Héctor Cathalifaud Argandoña; Sec.-Gen. Elena Torres Seguel.

Corporación para el Desarrollo de la Ciencia: Marcoleta 250, Casilla 10332, Santiago; f. 1978; Pres. Fernando Díaz A.; Sec.-Gen. Héctor Cathalifaud A.; publ. *Revista CODECI*.

Sociedad Científica Chilena 'Claudio Gay' (Chilean Scientific Society): Casilla 2974, Santiago; tel. (2) 7455066; fax (2) 7455176; e-mail ugartepena@itn.cl; f. 1955; 45 mems; library of 5,000 vols; Dir Alfredo Ugarte-Peña.

Biological Sciences

Asociación Chilena de Microbiología: Casilla 59, Correo 22, Santiago; tel. (2) 2093503; fax (2) 2258427; f. 1964; 194 mems; Pres. Dr Eugenio Spencer; Sec. Dr Matilde Jashes; publ. *Acta Microbiológica* (2 a year).

Sociedad Chilena de Entomología (Entomological Society): POB 21132, Santiago 21; tel. (2) 6804635; fax (2) 6804602; internet www.insectachile.cl; f. 1922; 170 mems; library of 4,000 periodicals; Pres. Dra Fresia Ester Rosas A.; Sec. Ing. Agric. José Mondaca E.; publ. *Revista Chilena de Entomología* (annually).

Sociedad de Biología de Chile: Casilla 16164, Santiago 9; f. 1928; 565 mems; Pres. A. Cecilia Hidalgo T.; Sec. Dr Miguel Bronfman A.; publs *Biological Research*, *Revista Chilena de Historia Natural*.

Sociedad de Genética de Chile: Almirante Montt 454, Santiago; tel. and fax (2) 6387046; fax (2) 6387046; e-mail sochigen@adsl.tie.cl; internet www.sochigen.cl; f. 1964; 100 mems;

Pres. Dra LUCÍA CIFUENTES OVALLE; Sec.-Gen. Prof. PATRICIA PÉREZ-ALZOLA; publs *Biological Research*, *Revista Chilena de Historia Natural*.

Sociedad de Vida Silvestre de Chile (Chilean Wildlife Society): C/o Luis Fernando Leiva R., Manuel Montt 56, Temuco; tel. (45) 205409; internet www.imaginativa.cl/~dalakasane/translate.HTML; f. 1975; 300 mems; Pres. LUIS FERNANDO LEIVA R.; Sec. CRISTIAN PÉREZ APABLAZA; publs *Boletín de Vida Silvestre* (annually), *Enlace* (quarterly).

Mathematical Sciences

Sociedad de Matemática de Chile: Casilla 653, Santiago; tel. 2713882; fax 2713882; f. 1976; 250 mems; Pres. PATRICIO FELMER; Sec. OSCAR BARRIGA; publs *Gaceta*, *Notas*, *Revista del Profesor de Matemáticas*.

Physical Sciences

Asociación Chilena de Astronomía y Astronáutica: Casilla 3904, Santiago 1; tel. 6327556; f. 1957; union of amateur astronomers; arranges courses and lectures; astronomy, astrophotography, radioastronomy, telescope-making; owns the observatory of Mt Pochoco, near Santiago; 350 mems; library of 1,000 vols; Pres. JODY TAPIA NUÑEZ; Sec. BIANCA DINAMARCA FIERRO; publ. *Boletín ACHAYA* (monthly).

Asociación Chilena de Sismología e Ingeniería Antisísmica (Chilean Association of Seismology and Earthquake Engineering): Casilla 2796, Santiago; f. 1963; Pres. DR PATRICIO RUIZ.

Comisión Chilena de Energía Nuclear: Amunátegui 95, Casilla 188-D, Santiago; tel. (2) 4702500; fax (2) 4702570; e-mail oirs@cchen.cl; internet www.cchen.gov.cl; f. 1964; library of 9,000 vols, 200,000 reports; Pres. Dr ROBERTO HOJMAN GUIÑERMAN; Exec. Dir Ing. LORETO VILLANUEVA; publ. *Nucleotécnica* (annually).

Comité Oceanográfico Nacional (CONA): Casilla 324, Valparaíso; tel. (32) 266520; fax (32) 266522; e-mail cona@shoa.cl; internet www.shoa.cl/cona/conaweb.html; f. 1971; 29 mem. instns; coordinates oceanographic activities in the country; Pres. Capt. FERNANDO MINGRAM; Exec. Sec. ALEJANDRO CABEZAS; publ. *Ciencia y Tecnología del Mar* (annually).

Liga Marítima de Chile (Chilean Maritime League): Avda Errázuriz 471, 2° piso, Casilla 117-V, Valparaíso; f. 1914; runs course in nautical education; Pres. Rear Admiral ERI SOLIS OYARZÚN; Vice-Pres. RUBÉN LUZZI VILLANUEVA; Sec. JULIO ALLARD AGUIRRE; 1,350 mems; brs in Iquique, Tocopilla, Santiago, Concepción, Tomé, Valdivia, Puerto Montt and Punta Arenas; publ. *Mar* (annually).

Sociedad Chilena de Física: C/o Juan Carlos Retamal, Depto de Física, Universidad de Santiago de Chile, Alameda Libertador Bernardo O'Higgins 3363, Casilla 442, Correo 2, Santiago; e-mail jretamal@lauca.usach.cl; f. 1965; 250 mems; Pres. SERGIO HOJMAN.

Sociedad Chilena de Fotogrametría y Percepción Remota: Nueva Santa Isabel 1640, Santiago; tel. (2) 4606800; fax (2) 4606978; e-mail igm@igm.cl; library of 4,000 vols, 25,000 maps; Pres. Bgl SERGIO MATUS MARTÍNEZ-CONDE; Sec. Tcl. Crl JUAN GUTIÉRREZ PALACIOS.

Sociedad Chilena de Química: Casilla de Correo 2613, Concepción; tel. (41) 227815; fax (41) 235819; e-mail schq@surnet.cl; internet www.schq.cl; f. 1945; 1,000 mems; library of 1,500 vols and 400 periodicals; Pres. Dr GALO CÁRDENAS; Sec. Dr JUAN GODOY; publ. *Boletin* (4 a year).

Sociedad de Bioquímica de Concepción: Casilla 237, Escuela de Química y Farmacia y Bioquímica, Concepción; f. 1957; Pres. MARIO POZO LÓPEZ; Sec. FROILÁN HERNÁNDEZ CARTES.

Sociedad de Bioquímica y Biología Molecular de Chile: Casilla 16164, Santiago 9; tel. 209-3503; fax 225-8427; f. 1971; 130 mems; Pres. Dr RAFAEL VICUÑA; Sec. Dr OMAR ORELLANA.

Sociedad Geológica de Chile: Valentin Letelier 20, dpto 401, Casilla 13667, Correo 21, Santiago; tel. 6980481; f. 1962; 434 mems; Pres. ESTANISLAO GODOY; Sec.-Gen. WALDO VIVALLO; publs *Revista Geológica de Chile* (2 a year), *Comunicaciones* (annually).

TECHNOLOGY

Asociación Interamericana de Ingeniería Sanitaria y Ambiental: San Martín 352, Santiago; tel. 6984028; f. 1979; Pres. GUILLERMO RUIZ TRONCOSO; Sec. JULIO HEVIA MEDEL; publ. *Revista* (quarterly).

Colegio de Ingenieros de Chile, AG: Avda Santa María 0508, Casilla 13745, Santiago; tel. (2) 4221140; fax (2) 4221012; e-mail colegio@ingenieros.cl; internet www.ingenieros.cl; f. 1958; professional engineering assn; 22,000 mems; Pres. FERNANDO GARCÍA CASTRO; Gen. Man. PEDRO TORRES OJEDA; publs *Ingenieros* (4 a year), *C.I. Informa* (monthly).

Instituto de Ingenieros de Chile (Institute of Chilean Engineers): San Martín 352, Casilla 487, Santiago; tel. 6984028; fax 6971136; f. 1888; 800 mems; library of 2,100 vols; publs *Revista Chilena de Ingeniería*, *Anales*.

Instituto de Ingenieros de Minas de Chile: Encomenderos 260 Of. 31, Casilla 14668, Correo 21, Santiago; tel. (2) 2461615; fax (2) 2466387; e-mail iimch@entelchile.net; f. 1930; 1,200 mems; Pres. MARCO ANTONIO ALFARO; Sec. MANUEL VIERA; publ. *Minerales* (6 a year).

Sociedad Chilena de Tecnología en Alimentos (Chilean Society of Food Technology): Echaurren 149, Santiago; tel. (2) 6966236; fax (2) 6974780; e-mail sochital@lauca.usch.cl; internet www.geocities.com/sochital; f. 1963; publ. *Alimentos* (4 a year).

Sociedad Nacional de Minería (National Society of Mining): Avda Apoquindo 3000 (5° piso), Santiago; f. 1883; library of 1,500 vols, 15,000 documents on microfilm, 20,000 maps; Pres. HERNÁN HOCHSCHILD ALESSANDRI; Sec. Gen. JULIO ASCUÍ LATORRE; publ. *Boletín Minero*.

Research Institutes

AGRICULTURE, FISHERIES AND VETERINARY SCIENCE

Estación Experimental 'Las Vegas' de la Sociedad Nacional de Agricultura (National Agricultural Society Experimental Station): C/o Sociedad Nacional de Agricultura, Casilla 40-D, Tenderini 187, Santiago; f. 1924; library of 1,000 vols; Dir RAÚL MATTE VIAL; publ. *El Campesino* (monthly).

Instituto de Fomento Pesquero (Fishery Research Institute): Blanco 839, Valparaíso; tel. (32) 322000; fax (32) 322345; e-mail direccion@ifop.cl; internet www.ifop.cl; f. 1964 for research into fisheries and aquaculture, and to support the regulation of a sustainable marine environment; 400 mems; library of 9,000 vols; Dir GUILLERMO MORENO PAREDES; publ. *Boletín Bibliográfico* (monthly).

Instituto de Investigaciones Agropecuarias: Casilla 439, Correo 3, Santiago; tel. 5417223; fax 5417667; f. 1964; conducts research on plant and livestock production, horticulture, viticulture, oenology, field crops; 170 research workers; library: see Libraries; Pres. FERNANDO MUJICA CASTILLO; National Dir FRANCISCO GONZÁLEZ DEL RÍO; Dir of Intihuasi Agricultural Experiment Station ALFONSO OSORIO U.; Dir of Tamelaike Agricultural Experiment Station HERNÁN FELIPE ELIZALDE; Dir of La Platina Agricultural Experiment Station JORGE VALENZUELA BARNECH; Dir of Carillanca Agricultural Experiment Station ADRIÁN CATRILEO S.; Dir of Quilamapu Agricultural Experiment Station HERNÁN ACUÑA P.; Dir of Remehue Agricultural Experiment Station FRANCISCO LANUZA A.; Dir of Kampenaike Agricultural Experiment Station RAÚL LIRA F.; publs *Agricultura Técnica* (quarterly), *Memoria Anual*, *Bibliografía Agrícola Chilena* (annually), *Boletín Técnico* (irregular), *Tierra Adentro* (6 a year).

Instituto Forestal (Forestry Institute): Huérfanos 554, Casilla 3085, Santiago; tel. (2) 6930700; fax (2) 6381286; f. 1961; research and advice in all aspects of forestry; library of 4,500 vols; Dir GONZALO PAREDES VELOSO; publs *Informe Técnico*, *Boletín Estadístico*, *Ciencia e Investigación Forestal*.

ECONOMICS, LAW AND POLITICS

Instituto Latinoamericano y del Caribe de Planificación Económica y Social (ILPES) (Latin American and Caribbean Institute for Economic and Social Planning): Edif. Naciones Unidas, Avda Dag Hammarskjöld s/n, Vitacura, Casilla 1567, Santiago; tel. (2) 2102507; fax (2) 2066104; e-mail anaser@eclac.cl; internet www.ilpes.cl; f. 1962; a permanent body within the Economic Commission for Latin America and the Caribbean (ECLAC), which in turn forms part of the United Nations system; supports member countries in their strategic planning and management of public affairs, by providing training, advisory and research services; library of 60,000 vols, documents and periodicals; Dir FERNANDO SÁNCHEZ-ALBAVERA; publs *Cuadernos del ILPES*, *ILPES Bulletin*.

Instituto Nacional de Estadísticas (Statistical Office): Casilla 498, Correo 3, Santiago; Avda Pdte. Bulnes 418, Santiago; tel. (2) 3667777; fax (2) 6712169; e-mail ine@ine.cl; internet www.ine.cl; f. 1843; library of 16,104 vols; Dir Ing. MAXIMO AGUILERA REYES; publs *Compendio Estadístico* (annually), *Revista Estadística y Economía* (2 a year), *Indicadores Mensuales* (monthly), *Metodologías*.

EDUCATION

Centro de Investigación y Desarrollo de la Educación (CIDE): Erasmo Escala 1825, Casilla 13608, Santiago; tel. (2) 6987153; fax (2) 6718051; e-mail cide@reuna.cl; f. 1965; independent research centre; aims to provide education relevant to the basic needs of the people; research into education and the family, education and work, education and social values; library of 50,000 vols, 7,000 documents; Dir JOHN SWOPE.

Latin American Information and Documentation Network for Education (REDUC): Casilla 13608, Santiago; tel. 698-7153; fax 671-8051; e-mail reduc@cide.cl; internet www.reduc.cl; f. 1977; network of different educational research institutions; aims to disseminate information on education for research and policy making; 27 mems institutions; documentation centre of 20,000 research summaries; Dir GONZALO GUTIÉRREZ; publ. *Databases* (online).

HISTORY, GEOGRAPHY AND ARCHAEOLOGY

Instituto de Investigaciones Arqueológicas y Museo 'R.P. Gustavo Le Paige, S.J.': San Pedro de Atacama; tel. (55) 851002; fax (55) 851066; e-mail museospa@ucn.cl; f. 1985; affiliated to the Universidad Católica del Norte, Antofagasta; research in archaeology and anthropology; postgraduate courses (MA and PhD); library of books, 5,000 periodicals; Dir Dr AGUSTÍN LLAGOSTERA M.; publ. *Estudios Atacameños* (irregular).

MEDICINE

Instituto de Medicina Experimental del Servicio Nacional de Salud (Institute of Experimental Medicine of the National Health Service): Avda Irarrázaval 849, Casilla 3401, Santiago; tel. 49 79 30; f. 1937; affiliated to WHO; physiology, neuroendocrinology and cancer research; maintains tumour bank, available for use by other research centres; 15 mems; library of 6,800 vols; Dir Dr SERGIO YRARRÁZAVAL; Chief Sec. Mrs BERTA IRIBIRRA.

Instituto de Salud Pública de Chile (Chilean Public Health Institute): Avda Marathon 1000, Nuñoa, Casilla 48, Santiago; tel. 2391105; fax 2396960; f. 1980; centre for vaccine production, national control of pharmaceutical, food and cosmetic products, and for co-ordination of national network of health laboratories; 600 mems; library: central scientific 3,600 vols, Centre of Occupational Health and Air Pollution Library of 5,542 vols; Dir JORGE SÁNCHEZ VEGA; publs *Laboratorio al día*, *Boletín informativo de medicamentos*, *Manuales de Procedimiento de Laboratorio Clínico*, *Manual de Bioseguridad*.

NATURAL SCIENCES

General

Centro de Información de Recursos Naturales (CIREN) (Centre for Information on Natural Resources): Avda Manuel Montt 1164, Casilla 14995, Correo Central, Santiago; tel. 2236641; fax 2096407; e-mail ciren@reuna.cl; f. 1964; a privately run corporation; gathers data and provides a central information service in the areas of climate, soil, water, fruit production, afforestation, mining, agricultural resources; holds a land-owners register; library of 11,000 vols, 150 journals; Exec. Dir JOSÉ ANTONIO BUSTAMANTE GARRIDO.

Physical Sciences

Comité Nacional de Geografía, Geodesía y Geofísica (National Geographical, Geodetic and Geophysical Committee): Nueva Santa Isabel 1640, Santiago; tel. (2) 4606800; fax (2) 4606978; e-mail igm@igm.cl; f. 1935 to encourage and co-ordinate research in the fields mentioned; 119 mems; Dirs GDB PABLO GRAN LÓPEZ, TCL LUIS ALEGRÍA MATTA, Crl JUAN GUTTIÉRREZ PALACIOS.

Dirección Meteorológica de Chile (Meteorological Bureau): Casilla 63, Correo Aeropuerto Internacional, Santiago; tel. (2) 6763437; fax (2) 6019590; e-mail dimetche@meteochile.cl; f. 1884; library of 3,000 vols; Dir Col NATHAN MAKUC; publs *Boletín Climatologico* (monthly), *Boletín Agrometeorológico* (monthly), *Boletín de Radiación Ultravioleta*, *Anuario Meteorológico*, *Anuario Agrometeorológico*, *Informe Solarimetrico Semestral de Radiación e Insolación*.

European Southern Observatory (ESO): Casilla 19001, Correo 19, Avda Alonso de Córdova 3107, Vitacura, Santiago; tel. (2) 4633000; fax (2) 4633101; internet www.sc.eso.org/santiago/science; f. 1962; ESO is the European organization for astronomical research in the southern hemisphere; ESO operates three observational sites in the Chilean Atacama desert: the Very Large Telescope (VLT), is located on Paranal, a 2600-m high mountain south of Antofagasta; several medium-sized optical telescopes are operated at La Silla, 600 km north of Santiago, at 2400-m altitude; a new submillimetre telescope (APEX) is in operation at the 5000-m high Llano de Chajnantor, near San Pedro de Atacama; a large number of 12-m submillimetre antennas (ALMA) are currently under development; ESO Representative and Head of Science Office in Chile FELIX MIRABEL.

Instituto Antártico Chileno: Luis Thayer Ojeda 814, Casilla 16521, Correo 9, Santiago; tel. (2) 2310105; fax (2) 2320440; e-mail inach@inach.cl; internet www.inach.cl; f. 1963; a centre for technological and scientific development on matters relating to the Antarctic and adjacent ecosystems; 43 mems; library of 4,100 vols, 400 periodicals; Dir OSCAR PINOCHET DE LA BARRA; publs *Serie Científica* (annually), *Boletín Antártico Chileno* (2 a year).

Instituto Isaac Newton (Isaac Newton Institute): Casilla 8–9, Correo 9, Santiago; tel. (2) 2172013; fax (2) 2172352; e-mail inewton@terra.cl; internet www.ini.cl; f. 1978; promotes astronomy in nine Eastern European and Eurasian countries; Dir GONZALO ALCAINO; publs *Astronomical Journal* (10 a year), *Astronomy and Astrophysics* (70 a year), *Astrophysical Journal* (10 a year).

Observatorio Astronómico Nacional (National Astronomical Observatory): Universidad de Chile, Departamento de Astronomía, Biblioteca, Casilla 36-D, Santiago 1; tel. (2) 2294002; fax (2) 2294101; e-mail biblio@das.uchile.cl; internet www.das.uchile.cl; f. 1852; attached to the Universidad de Chile; Repsold Meridian circle, Transit instrument, Gauthier refractor astrograph, Heyde visual refractor, Danjon astrolabe and Zeiss transit instruments; astronomical station at Cerro El Roble; library of 7,247 vols; Dir MARÍA TERESA RUIZ.

Observatorio Interamericano de Cerro Tololo (Cerro Tololo Inter-American Observatory): Casilla 603, La Serena; tel. (51) 205200; fax (51) 205212; internet www.ctio.noao.edu; f. 1963; astronomical observation of stars only observable in the southern hemisphere; library of 21,405 vols; Dir Dr ALISTAIR R. WALKER.

Servicio Hidrográfico y Oceanográfico de la Armada de Chile (Hydrographic and Oceanographic Service of the Chilean Navy): Errazuriz 254, Playa Ancha, Valparaíso; tel. (32) 266666; fax (32) 266542; e-mail shoa@shoa.cl; internet www.shoa.cl; f. 1874; hydrographic surveys, nautical charts and publications, oceanography, maritime safety, national oceanographic data centre; library of 12,000 vols; Dir Capt. ROBERTO GARNHAM P.; publs *Anuario Hidrográfico* (annually), *Tablas de Marea de la Costa de Chile* (annually), *Noticias a los Navegantes* (monthly), *Derroteros de la Costa de Chile*.

Servicio Nacional de Geología y Minería: Casilla 10465, Santiago; tel. (2) 7375050; fax (2) 7372026; e-mail msuarez@sernageomin.cl; internet www.sernageomin.cl; f. 1981; geoscience and mining; library of 30,000 vols, 15,000 aerial photographs, 200 satellite photographs, 700 periodical titles, 6,000 maps; National Dir LUIS SOUGARRET SEITZ; publ. *Revista Geológica de Chile* (2 a year).

RELIGION, SOCIOLOGY AND ANTHROPOLOGY

Instituto Latinoamericano de Doctrina y Estudios Sociales: Almirante Barroso 6, Santiago, Casilla 14446, Correo 21; tel. 6714072; fax 6986873; f. 1965 for the study, dissemination and renewal of social thought within the Church; teaching and research in economics and social sciences; in-service courses for teachers and professionals; 54 mems; Exec. Vice-Dir R. P. GONZALO ARROYO; publs *DOCLA*, *Revista de Análisis Económico*, *Persona y Sociedad*.

TECHNOLOGY

Comisión Nacional de Investigación Científica y Tecnológica (CONICYT) (National Commission for Scientific and Technological Research): Casilla 297-V, Santiago; tel. (2) 3654400; fax (2) 6551396; e-mail info@conicyt.cl; internet www.conicyt.cl; f. 1969; government agency in charge of studying, planning and proposing national scientific and technological policy to the govt and developing, promoting and improving science and technology; mem. of ICSU; mem. of FID; library of 4,500 vols; Pres. Prof. MAURICIO SARRAZIN; Information Dir ANA MARIA PRAT; publs *Series Información y Documentación*, *Series Bibliografías*, *Series Directorios*, irregular study reports, documentation reports and annual reports, *C & T* (electronic edition only, monthly), *Panorama Científico* (monthly).

Instituto de Investigaciones y Ensayes de Materiales (IDIEM) Universidad de Chile (Institute for Materials Research and Testing): Plaza Ercilla 883, Casilla 1420, Santiago; fax (2) 6718979; f. 1898; library of 8,000 vols; Dir LUIS AYAYA R..

Instituto Nacional de Normalización (National Institute of Standardization): Casilla 995, Correo 1, Santiago; f. 1944; library: library of 160,000 technical standards; Dir LEE WARD.

Libraries and Archives

Concepción

Universidad de Concepción, Dirección de Bibliotecas: Barrio Universitario, Casilla 1807, 160-C, Correo 3, Concepción; tel. 234985; fax 244796; f. 1919; 425,250 vols, 6,315 periodicals; Dir DIETER OELKER LINK.

Santiago

Archivos Nacionales (National Archives): Clasificador 1400, Miraflores No. 50, Santiago; tel. (2) 6325735; fax (2) 6325735; e-mail archinac@oris.renib.cl; f. 1927; incl. historic and public administration collns; Dir MARÍA EUGENIA BARRIENTOS.

Biblioteca Central de la Universidad de Chile: Calle Arturo Prat 23, Casilla 10-D, Santiago; f. 1843, reorganized 1936; contains more than 200,000 vols, comprising donations from Canada, the UK, the USA and Spain, and from private collections, including those of Pedro Montt and Pablo Neruda; collection of periodicals comprising 14,500 titles, with over 500,000 issues; there are 40 other libraries in the University with an aggregate of 1,000,000 vols; Dir of Central Library Prof. HUMBERTO GIANNINI IÑIGUEZ.

Biblioteca Central, Instituto de Investigaciones Agropecuarias: Casilla 439 Correo 3, CP 7083150 Santiago; tel. (2) 7575223; fax (2) 5464668; e-mail selso@platina.inia.cl; internet alerce.inia.cl; f. 1947; 18,000 vols, 31,800 documents and papers incl. Chilean collection, 675 current periodicals, 9,764 Chilean university theses; Head Librarian

SONIA ELSO; publs *Agricultura Técnica* (quarterly, online), *Bibliografía Agrícola Chilena* (online only), *Boletín INIA* (irregular), *Collection Libros INIA* (irregular), *Serie Actas* (irregular), *Tierra Adentro* (every 2 months).

Biblioteca del Congreso Nacional (Congress Library): Huérfanos 1117, 2° piso, Clasificador Postal 1199, Santiago; tel. (2) 2701700; fax (2) 2701766; e-mail xfeliu@biblioteca.congreso.cl; internet www.congreso.cl/biblioteca; f. 1883; 1,000,000 vols and 5,600 periodicals on law, social sciences, politics and economics, human sciences and literature; 13,500 leaflets, 12,000 rare books, 1,353 maps and topographical charts, 4,000,000 Chilean press cuttings; official depository for international organizations, legal depository for national publs; open to the public; Dir XIMENA FELIÚ SILVA; Asst Dir ALICIA ROJAS ESTIBIL; publs *Serie Estudios, Alerta Informativa, Temas de Actualidad, Visión Semanal*.

Biblioteca Nacional de Chile (National Library): Avda B. O'Higgins 651, Clasificador 1105, Santiago; tel. (2) 3605200; fax (2) 6380461; f. 1813; 3,500,000 vols, 75,000 MSS., 83 incunabula; Dir MARTA CRUZ-COKE M.; publs *Bibliografía Chilena* (annually), *Mapocho* (2 a year), *Referencias Críticas sobre autores Chilenos*, bibliographies, catalogues.

Dirección de Bibliotecas de la Universidad de Santiago de Chile: Casilla 4637, Correo 2, Santiago; tel. 776-1220; fax 681-1422; f. 1979; 150,000 vols; Dir JORGE EDUARDO DEMANGEL RUÍZ.

Pontificia Universidad Católica de Chile, Sistema de Bibliotecas: Campus San Joaquín, Vicuña Mackenna 4860, Casilla 306, Correo 22, Santiago; tel. (2) 6864615; fax (2) 6865852; f. 1901; 10 university libraries; 1,587,518 vols; Dir MARÍA LUISA ARENAS FRANCO.

Valdivia

Sistema de Bibliotecas, Universidad Austral de Chile: Correo 2, Valdivia; tel. (63) 221290; fax (63) 221360; e-mail biblio@uach.cl; internet www.biblioteca.uach.cl; f. 1962; 147,000 vols, 1,600 periodicals; specializes in science; Dir LUIS VERA CARTES.

Valparaíso

Biblioteca Central de la Universidad Técnica 'Federico Santa María': Avda España 1680, CP 110-V, Valparaíso; tel. (32) 654147; fax (32) 797483; f. 1926; 110,000 vols, 2,400 periodicals; audiovisual material: cassettes, video cassettes, maps, microfilms, slides; specializes in science and technology; Dir MARÍA EUGENIA LAULIÉ; publs *Scientia: Serie A Mathematical Sciences, Gestión tecnológica* (quarterly), *USM Noticias* (monthly).

Biblioteca de la Pontificia Universidad Católica de Valparaíso: Avda Brasil 2950, Casilla 4059, Valparaíso; tel. (32) 273261; fax (32) 273183; e-mail abustos@ucv.cl; internet biblioteca.ucv.cl; f. 1928; 248,000 vols; Dir ATILIO BUSTOS GONZÁLEZ; publs *Biblioteca Agora, Electronic Journal of Biotechnology, Fondo de Etnomusicologia Margot Loyola Palacios*.

Biblioteca Publica No. 1 'Santiago Severin' de Valparaíso: Plaza Simón Bolívar, Valparaíso; tel. 213375; fax 213375; f. 1873; includes a collection of historical books on Chile and America and a collection of 17th- to 19th-century books; 94,149 vols, 166,814 periodicals; Dir YOLANDA SOTO VERGARA.

Museums and Art Galleries

Angol

Museo Dillman S. Bullock: Casilla 8-D, Angol; tel. 712395; fax 712395; f. 1946; general local flora and fauna; extensive local archaeological collection; library of 5,000 vols; undertakes research, scientific expeditions; Dir ALBERTO E. MONTERO.

Antofagasta

Museo Regional de Antofagasta: Bolívar No 188, Casilla 746, Antofagasta; tel. 227016; fax 221109; e-mail museoantof@terra.cl; f. 1984; archaeology, history, ethnography, geology; library: small library; Curator IVO KUZMANIĆ PIEROTIĆ.

Arica

Museo Arqueológico San Miguel de Azapa, Universidad de Tarapacá: Facultad de Ciencias Sociales Administrativas y Económicas, Depto de Arqueología y Museología, Casilla 6-D, Arica; tel. (58) 205555; fax (58) 205552; e-mail jcordova@uta.cl; internet www.uta.cl/masma; f. 1967; University museum, belonging to the Department of Anthropology; exhibits related to research on pre-Columbian, colonial and modern Andean people and anthropology; library of 3,000 vols; Dean JULIA CÓRDOVA GONZÁLEZ; publs *Chungara* (Chilean anthropology, 2 a year), *Cuadernos de Trabajo* (irregular).

Cañete

Museo Folklórico Araucano de Cañete 'Juan A. Ríos M.': Casilla 28, Cañete; f. 1968; to conserve, exhibit and research the Mapuche culture from its origins to contact with Spanish culture; to recreate the environment which Valdivia saw in 1552 when he built the Tucapel Fort (near the museum); anthropological research of the native Mapuche settlements which still exist; archaeological excavations in the surrounding area; library of 2,000 vols; Curator GLORIA CARDENAS TRONCOSO.

Concepción

Museo de Historia Natural de Concepción (Concepción Natural History Museum): Plaza Luis Acevedo, Concepción; tel. (41) 310932; fax (41) 310932; e-mail musconce@ctcreuna.cl; f. 1902; library of 6,732 vols; Curator MARCO SÁNCHEZ AGUILERA; publ. *Comunicaciones del Museo de Concepción*.

Museo de Hualpen (Hualpen Museum): Parque Pedro del Rio Zañartu, Casilla 2656, Concepción; tel. 227305; f. 1882; collections of Greek, Roman and Egyptian archaeology; Chilean arms and numismatic collections; Oriental art; Chilean and American folk arts; Chilean archaeology; eighteenth- and nineteenth-century furniture; Pres. VICTOR LOBOS LÁPERA.

Copiapó

Museo Regional de Atacama: Atacama 98, Casilla 134, Copiapó; tel. 212313; fax (52) 212313; f. 1973; archaeology, mineralogy, ecology and history; library of 15,000 vols; Dir MIGUEL CERVELLINO.

Iquique

Museo Antropológico de Iquique: Universidad Arturo Prat de Iquique, Casilla 121, Campus Pedro Lagos, Pedro Lagos y Grumete Bolados Sts, Iquique; f. 1987; attached to the Centro de Estudios del Desierto of the University; permanent exhibition showing the cultural development of the people of the region from 10,000 BC to 1900; research in archaeology, rural development of farming communities, history and ethnography; library: specialized library; Dir Arq. ALVARO CAREVIC RIVERA; publ. publ. research findings.

Museo Regional de Iquique: Baquedano 951, Iquique; tel. (57) 411034; fax (57) 413278; attached to the Dept of Social Development of the Municipality of Iquique; f. 1960; permanent exhibition of regional archaeology, ethnography and history; Dir CORA ROMY MORAGAS.

La Serena

Museo Arqueológico de La Serena (La Serena Archaeological Museum): Calle Cordovez esq. Cienfuegos, Casilla 617, La Serena; tel. 224492; fax 225398; f. 1943; sections on archaeology, pre-history, physical anthropology, colonial history, ethnology and palaeontology; library of 23,000 vols, 18,043 slides, 28,150 photographs; Dir GONZALO AMPUERO B.; library: specialized library; publ. *Boletín* (annually).

Linares

Museo de Arte y Artesanía de Linares: Casilla Postal 280, Linares; tel. (73) 210662; fax (73) 210662; e-mail mulin@ctcinternet.cl; internet www.dibam.renib.cl; f. 1966; arts and crafts from the Inca period to the present; valuable collections including unique clay miniatures; collection of Huaso implements; ceramics; exhibition of history and people of Linares; conferences, lectures, films; Dir PATRICIO ACEVEDO LAGOS.

Ovalle

Museo del Limari: Covarrubias esq. Antofagasta, Casilla 59, Ovalle; tel. (53) 620029; fax (53) 620029; e-mail mdlim@ctcinternet.net.cl; internet www.mdlim.cl; f. 1963; archaeology (esp. local); Curator DANIELA SERANI ELLIOTT.

Puerto Williams

Museo 'Martín Gusinde': Aragay 1, Puerto Williams, Isla Navarino, XII Región de Magallanes, Antártica Chilena; tel. and fax (61) 621043; e-mail pgrendi@yahoo.com; internet www.dibam.cl; f. 1975; situated on Navarino Island; history and geography of the southernmost archipelagos of the Americas; aboriginal culture, flora, fauna and minerals of the area; library of 500 vols; Curator PAOLA GRENDI ILHARREBORDE.

Punta Arenas

Museo Histórico Regional de Magallanes: Centro Cultural Braun-Menéndez, Hernando de Magallanes 949, Casilla 97, Punta Arenas; tel. (61) 244216; fax (61) 221387; f. 1983, fmrly Museo de la Patagonia, f. 1967; Patagonian history; library: specialized 3,500 vols; Curator Sra DESANKA URSIĆ V..

Museo Regional Salesiano 'Maggiorino Borgatello' (Salesian Regional Museum 'Maggiorino Borgatello'): Avda Bulnes 374, Casilla 347, Punta Arenas; f. 1893; scientific and ethnographical (notable relics of extreme South American and Tierra del Fuegan tribes), petroleum industry; Scientific Dir Prof. SERGIO LAUSIĆ GLASINOVIĆ.

Santiago

Museo Chileno de Arte Precolombino: Casilla 3687, Bandera 361, Santiago; tel. 6887348; fax 6972779; f. 1981 by the council of Santiago City and the Fundación Familia Larraín Echenique; 2,000 items of precolumbian art and 1,000 items in ethnographic collections from Mapuche and Aymara cultures; textiles, ceramics, metal work, stone sculptures; large collection of photographs, slides, video and audio cassettes; laboratory for textile and pottery conservation; laboratory for archaeological research; research on precolumbian music, rock art, Tiahuanaco, Aymara, Atacama and Araucanian cultures, prehistoric architecture, Andean textiles and symbolism; educational programmes; music archive; library of 6,000 vols, 500 periodicals; special collection of precolumbian art, conservation and archaeology; Dir CARLOS ALDUNATE DEL SOLAR; publs *Boletín* (annually), catalogue of exhibitions (irregular).

Museo de Arte Colonial de San Francisco: Alameda Bernardo O'Higgins 834, Santiago; tel. (2) 6398737; fax (2) 6398737; e-mail museosanfrancisco@museosanfrancisco.tie.cl; internet www.museosanfrancisco.cl; f. 1968 by the Franciscan Order; 16th–19th c. art (esp. 17th c. paintings); the life of St Francis depicted in 22 pictures; the life of San Diego de Alcalá depicted in 35 pictures; also other religious works of art, furniture, icons, embroidery, sculpture, carving, woodwork and metalwork; library: library; Dir ROSA PUGA D.

Museo de Arte Contemporáneo (Contemporary Art Museum): Parque Forestal frente a Calle Mosqueto, Santiago; tel. (2) 6395486; fax (2) 6394945; e-mail mac.uchile@entelchile.net; internet www.uchile.cl/mac; f. 1947; contemporary and fine arts; Dir FRANCISCO BRUGNOLI BAILONI.

Museo de Arte Popular Americano (Museum of American Folk Art): Parque Forestal s/n, Casilla 2100, Universidad de Chile, Santiago; tel. (2) 6821480; fax (2) 6821481; e-mail museopop@abello.dic.uchile.cl; f. 1943; objects of American folk art in pottery, basketware, wood and metal, Araucanian silverware; Dir SYLVIA RIOS MONTERO.

Museo de Historia Natural de San Pedro Nolasco (Natural History Museum): MacIver 341, Santiago; tel. 30691; f. 1922; library of 58,000 vols; special collections: Claudio Gay, G. Cuvier, A. E. Brehrm, Ch. Darwin.

Museo Histórico Nacional (National Historical Museum): Palacio de la Real Audiencia, Plaza de Armas, Casilla 9764, Santiago; tel. (2) 6381411; fax (2) 6331815; e-mail bdevose@oris.renib.cl; internet www.museohistoriconacional.cl; f. 1911; pre-Hispanic period to the present; costume, iconographic, arms, arts and crafts, and numismatic collections; dept of education; research in textile, paper and photographic restoration; library of 12,000 vols; Dir BARBARA DE VOS EYZAGUIRRE.

Museo Nacional de Bellas Artes (National Museum of Fine Arts): Parque Forestal, Casilla 3209, Santiago; tel. (2) 6330655; fax (2) 6393297; e-mail mivelic@oris.renib.cl; internet www.dibam.renib.cl; f. 1880; paintings, engravings, etchings and sculpture, Chilean and European paintings of 15th–20th centuries; library of 15,000 vols; Dir MILAN IVELIC.

Museo Nacional de Historia Natural (National Museum of Natural History): Casilla 787, Santiago; tel. (2) 6804603; fax (2) 6804602; e-mail webmaster@mnhn.cl; internet www.mnhn.cl; f. 1830; Departments: Zoology, Entomology, Hydrobiology, Botany, Mineralogy, Palaeontology, Anthropology, Museology, Education; Curator MARÍA ELIANA RAMÍREZ CASALI; publs *Boletín*, *Noticiario mensual*.

Museo de la Educación Gabriela Mistral: Chacabuco 365, Santiago Centro; tel. (2) 6818169; fax (2) 6822040; e-mail museodelaeducacion@gmail.com; internet www.museodelaeducacion.cl; f. 1941; permanent exhibition on Chilean educational history; photographic archive; organizes seminars, workshops and training in subjects such as education, culture and society; library of 40,000 vols; Dir Dr MARÍA ISABEL ORELLANA (acting).

Talca

Museo O'Higginiano y de Bellas Artes de Talca: 1 Norte No. 875, Casilla 189, Talca; tel. 227330; f. 1964; paintings, sculpture, Chilean history, archaeology, religious artefacts, antique furniture, arms; library of 430 vols; video tapes; Curator SERGIO ULLOA ROJOS; publ. *La Casona durante la Colonia*.

Temuco

Museo Regional de la Araucania (Araucania Museum): Avda Alemania 084, Casilla 481, Temuco; tel. (45) 730062; fax (45) 730064; f. 1940; opened to the public 1943; archaeological, artistic and ethnographic exhibits of the Araucanian, or Mapuche, Indians of South Chile, and others relating to the Conquest, Pacification and Colonization of Araucania as well as the history of Temuco city itself; maintains research section; library: specialized library of 886 vols about Mapuche culture and regional history; 1,400 reprints and maps of Mapuche reservations and foreign colonization; Dir HÉCTOR ZUMAETA ZÚÑIGA; publ. *Bulletin*.

Valdivia

Museo Histórico y Antropológico de la Universidad Austral de Chile: Casilla 586, Valdivia; tel. (63) 212872; fax (63) 212872; e-mail museo@entelchile.net; f. 1967; Centre for Conservation of Historical Monuments, Archaeology, Museums and Historical Archives; undertakes teaching, research, training of museum staff, conservation, museology; library of 3,000 vols, 4,000 photographs; Dir JORGE E. INOSTROZA SAAVEDRA.

Valparaíso

Museo de Historia Natural de Valparaíso (Natural History Museum): Calle Condell 1546, Casilla 3208, Correo 3, Valparaíso; tel. (32) 257441; fax (32) 220846; f. 1876; natural sciences and anthropology; library: *c.* 3,000 vols; Curator ANA AVALOS VALENZUELA; publ. *Anales*.

Vicuña

Museo Gabriela Mistral de Vicuña: Calle Gabriela Mistral 759, Casilla 50, Vicuña; tel. 411223; fax 412524; e-mail mgmistral@entelchile.net; f. 1971 to preserve the cultural legacy of the poet, Gabriela Mistral (Nobel prize for Literature 1945); documents, photographs and personal effects; replica of birthplace of poet, talks, films, music; library of 6,000 vols; Dir RODRIGO IRIBARREN AVILÉS; publ. *Boletín*.

Viña del Mar

Museo Comparativo de Biología Marina: Facultad de Ciencias del Mar y Recursos Naturales, Universidad de Valparaíso, Casilla 5080 Reñaca; tel. (32) 507820; fax (32) 507859; e-mail ricardo.bravo@uv.cl; f. 1955; echinoderms, molluscs and other invertebrates; algae and marine lichens from the coastal regions of the SE Pacific; library for the students of marine biology and oceanic engineering; Curator Dr RICARDO BRAVO; publ. *Revista de Biología Marina y Oceanografía*.

Universities and Technical Universities

UNIVERSIDAD DE ANTOFAGASTA

Avda Angamos 601, Casilla 170, Antofagasta
Telephone: (55) 637183
Fax: (55) 637102
E-mail: rectoria@uantof.cl
Internet: www.uantof.cl

Founded 1981
State control
Language of instruction: Spanish
Academic year: March to January

Rector: JAIME GODOY
Vice-Rector: MARCOS CRUTCHIT NORAMBUENA
Vice-Rector (Finance): RAÚL HENRÍQUEZ TOLEDO
Director-General of Administration: OSCAR MORALES CASTILLO
Director-General for Student Affairs: ALBERTO JAMETT
Director of Admissions: LUIS WITTWER
Director of Extension and Co-operation: EILEEN STOCKINS
Director of Planning and Research: RAUL IBARRA
Director of Research: OSCAR ZUÑIGA
Director of Teaching: VANESSA CHIANG
Secretary-General: MARIO BAEZA
Head of Rector's Office: SILVIA OLIVOS
Librarian: NORMA MONTERREY

Number of teachers: 320
Number of students: 6,067

Publications: *Estudios Oceanológicos*, *Hombre y Desierto*, *Innovación*

DEANS

Faculty of Basic Sciences: GUILLERMO MONDACA
Faculty of Education and Human Sciences: JUAN PANADES VARGAS
Faculty of Engineering: PEDRO CÓRDOVA
Faculty of Health Sciences: MARCOS CIKUTOVIC
Faculty of Law: DOMINGO CLAPS
Faculty of Marine Resources: HERNAN BAEZA

HEADS OF DEPARTMENTS

Aquaculture: ALBERTO OLIVARES
Biomedicine: ELVIRA MORENO
Chemical Engineering: SARA PAREDES
Chemistry: AMBROSIO RESTOVIC
Electrical Engineering: VICTOR FUENTES
Geomensural Engineering: HERNÁN TITICHOCA
Kinesiology: JORGE GÓMEZ
Mathematics: PEDRO HUERTA
Mechanical Engineering: HUGO CAYO
Medical Technology: HERNÁN SAGUA
Mining Engineering: JORGE CLUNES
Nursing: VERONICA ITURRA
Nutrition and Food Technology: RICARDO MURRAY
Obstetrics and Child Health: DIANA RUÍZ
Physics: MANUEL SANTANDER
Systems Engineering: GONZALO FLORES

ATTACHED INSTITUTES

Instituto del Desierto: research in energy and water resources of Atacama desert; agriculture and solar energy in the desert; Dir RENÉ CONTRERAS.

Instituto de Investigaciones Antropológicas: research in archaeology, anthropology, linguistics and literature of North Chile; Dir PATRICIO NÚÑEZ.

Instituto de Investigaciones Oceanológicas: research in marine life of northern coast of Chile; Dir LUIS RODRIGUEZ.

UNIVERSIDAD ARTURO PRAT

Avda Arturo Prat 2120, Iquique
Telephone: (57) 441208
Fax: (57) 394393
E-mail: j.torres@cec.unap.cl
Internet: www.unap.cl

Founded 1984
State control
Language of instruction: Spanish
Academic year: March to December

Rector: CARLOS MERINO PINOCHET
Vice-Rector (Academic): CÉSAR ARANCIBIA CÓRDOVA
Administrative Director: CARLOS LADRIX OSÉS
Librarian: ROBERTO JIMÉNEZ RAMÍREZ

Number of teachers: 500
Number of students: 5,300

HEADS OF DEPARTMENTS

Auditing and Information Systems: SERGIO ETCHEVERRY GUTIÉRREZ
Chemistry: ELIA SOTO SANHUEZA
Desert Farming: ALVARO CAREVIC RIVERA
Economics and Administration: ALDO CHIPOCO JORQUERA
Education and Humanities: MARÍA VERÓNICA FRÍAS PISTONO
Engineering: JAIME TAPIA QUEZADA
Marine Sciences: WINSTON PALMA SÁEZ
Physics and Mathematics: CARLOS ANCH CHANG
Social Sciences: JUAN PODESTÁ ARZUBIAGA
School of Architecture: JOSÉ MAIRA SOBRADO
School of Law: JORGE TAPIA VALDÉS
School of Nursing: XIMENA IBARRA MENDOZA
International Studies Institute: SERGIO GONZÁLEZ MIRANDA

UNIVERSIDAD DE ATACAMA

Casilla 240, Copiapó
Telephone: (52) 212005
Fax: (52) 212662
Internet: www.uda.cl

Founded 1981
State control
Language of instruction: Spanish
Academic year: March to December

Rector: MARIO MATURANA CLARO
Vice-Rector: ENRIQUE LILLO ANTÚNEZ
Director of Administration and Finance: NEYLÁN VALDIVIA ROJO
Librarian: MARIANELA VIVANCO CORTÉS

Number of teachers: 95
Number of students: 2,950

Publications: *Revista de Derecho de Aguas* (annually), *Revista de Derecho de Minas* (annually), *Revista de Ingeniería* (annually)

DEANS

Faculty of Engineering: MARIO MEZA MALDONADO
Faculty of Humanities and Education: JUAN IGLESIAS DÍAZ

DIRECTORS

Department of Education: ORLANDO ZULETA GONZÁLEZ
Department of Humanities: OSCAR PAINEAN BUSTAMANTE
Department of Mathematics and Computer Science: ELISEO MARTÍNEZ HERRERA
Department of Metallurgy: OSVALDO PAVEZ MIQUELES
Department of Mines: HUGO OLMOS NARANJO
Department of Natural Sciences: JUAN DÍAZ VARAS
Department of Physical Education, Sport and Recreation: ARMANDO OLIVA GONZÁLEZ
Language Institute: RICARDO VERA MARTÍNEZ

ATTACHED INSTITUTES

Instituto Asistencia a la Minería: Casilla 240, Copiapó; tel. (52) 212006; fax (52) 212662; Dir JUAN NAVEA DANTAGNAN.

Instituto Derecho de Minas y Aguas: Moneda 673, 8° piso, Santiago; tel. (2) 6328290; fax (2) 6383452; Dir ALEJANDRO VERGARA BLANCO.

Instituto de Investigaciones Científicas y Tecnológicas: Casilla 240, Copiapó; tel. (52) 218770; fax (52) 218770; Dir GERMÁN CÁCERES ARENAS.

Instituto Tecnológico: Casilla 240, Copiapó; tel. (52) 218018; fax (52) 218018; Dir TIMUR PADILLA BOCIC.

UNIVERSIDAD DEL BÍOBÍO

Avda Collao 1202, Casilla 5-C, Concepción
Telephone: (41) 261200
Fax: (41) 313897
E-mail: rector@ubiobio.cl
Internet: www.ubiobio.cl

Founded 1988
State control
Language of instruction: Spanish
Academic year: March to December
Campus also at Avda Andrés Bello s/n, Chillán

Rector: HILARIO HERNÁNDEZ GURRUCHAGA
Pro-Rector (Chillán): FELIX MARTÍNEZ RODRÍGUEZ
Vice-Rector (Academic): HÉCTOR GAETE FERES
Vice-Rector (Financial): CLAUDIO ROJAS MIÑO
Secretary-General: RICARDO PONCE SOTO
Director for International Liaison: ALDO A. BALLERINI

Number of teachers: 603
Number of students: 8,986

Publications: *Arquitecturas del Sur* (3 a year), *Cuadernos de Edificación en Madera* (3 a year), *Maderas: Ciencia y Tecnología* (2 a year), *Memoria Anual Institucional* (annually), *Mercado de suelo de Concepción* (3 a year), *Proyección UBB* (monthly), *Theoría* (annually), *Tiempo y Espacio* (annually)

DEANS

Faculty of Architecture, Construction and Design: RICARDO HEMPEL HOLZAPFEL
Faculty of Business Management: LUIS CONTRERAS VILLAR
Faculty of Education and Humanities (Chillán): MARCO AURELIO REYES COCA
Faculty of Engineering: PETER BACKHOUSE ERAZO
Faculty of Health and Food Sciences: NORA PLAZA CEBALLOS
Faculty of Sciences: JORGE PLAZA DE LOS REYES ZAPATA

DIRECTORS

Faculty of Architecture, Construction and Design:
- School of Architecture: RODRIGO VILLALOBOS PINO
- School of Civil Engineering: ANTONIO MOLINA CAMPOS
- School of Industrial Design: PATRICIO MORGADO URIBE
- Department of Arts and Technology of Design: MAGDA PEÑA FLORES
- Department of Building: CECILIA POBLETE ARREDONDO
- Department of Design and Theory of Architecture: RODRIGO GARCÍA ALVARADO
- Department of Graphic Design: HUGO CÁCERES JARA
- Department of Planning and Urban Design: MAGDA PEÑA FLORES
- Department of Visual Communication: NINÓN JEGÓ ARAYA

Faculty of Business Management:
- Department of Auditing and Computer Science: BENITO UMAÑA HERMOSILLA
- Department of Auditing and Management: MAURICIO GUTIÉRREZ URZÚA
- Department of Information Systems: EDUARDO JARA GOLDENBERG

Faculty of Education and Humanities:
- Department of Arts and Literature: JUAN GABRIEL ARAYA GRANDÓN
- Department of Educational Sciences: MARÍA ELENA CORREA ZAMORA
- Department of General Studies: ROBERTO CONTRERAS VACCARO
- Department of History, Geography and Social Sciences: JAIME REBOLLEDO VILLAGRA

Faculty of Engineering:
- School of Civil Engineering: JUAN MARCUS SCHWENK
- Department of Civil Industrial Engineering: FRANCISCO NÚÑEZ CERDA
- Department of Electrical Engineering: JORGE SALGADO SAGREDO
- Department of Mechanical Engineering: GASTÓN HERNÁNDEZ CAMPOS
- Department of Wood Engineering: LAURA REYES NÚÑEZ

Faculty of Health and Food Sciences:
- School of Food Engineering: Sr GRACIELA BUGUEÑO BUGUEÑO
- Department of Agroindustry: JORGE MORENO CUEVAS
- Department of Nursing: SILVIA ALARCÓN SANHUEZA
- Department of Nutrition and Public Health: PATRICIO OLIVA MORESCO

Faculty of Sciences:
- Department of Basic Sciences (Chillán): FERNANDO TOLEDO MONTIEL
- Department of Chemistry: CARMEN BREVIS AZÓCAR
- Department of Mathematics: GABRIEL SANHUEZA DAROCH
- Department of Physics: ELIANA MARTÍNEZ VILLARROEL

UNIVERSIDAD DE CHILE

Avda Bernardo O'Higgins 1058, Casilla 10-D, Santiago
Telephone: (2) 6781003
Fax: (2) 6781012
Internet: www.uchile.cl

Founded 1738 as Universidad Real de San Felipe; inaugurated 1843 as Universidad de Chile
State control
Academic year: March to December

Rector: LUIS A. RIVEROS C.
Pro-Rector: LUIS BAHAMONDE BRAVO
Academic Vice-Rector: MARIO SAPAG-HAGAR

Library: see Libraries and Archives
Number of teachers: 2,775 (including all branch institutions)
Number of students: 24,822

Publications: *Actualidad Universitaria* (monthly), *Anales de la Universidad de Chile* (annually), *Anuario Astronómico* (annually), *Bizantion Nea Hellas*, *Boletín Chileno de Parasitología* (4 a year), *Boletín de Filología* (2 a year), *Boletín Interamericano de Educación Musical* (annually), *Comentarios sobre la Situación Económica*, *Cuadernos de Ciencia Política* (4 a year), *Cuadernos de Historia* (annually), *Desarrollo Rural* (2 a year), *Estudios Internacionales* (4 a year), *Ocupación y Desocupación Encuesta Nacional* (2 a year), *Política* (2 a year), *Revista Chilena de Antropología* (annually), *Revista Chilena de Historia del Derecho*, *Revista Chilena de Humani-*

dades (annually), *Revista Comunicaciones en Geología* (annually), *Revista de Derecho Económico*, *Revista de Derecho Público*, *Revista Económica y Administración* (4 a year), *Revista de Filosofía* (annually), *Revista Musical Chilena* (2 a year), *Revista Psiquiátrica Clínica* (annually), *Terra Aridae* (2 a year), *U Noticias* (monthly)

DEANS

Faculty of Agriculture: MARIO SILVA G.
Faculty of Architecture and Town Planning: MANUEL FERNÁNDEZ HECHENLEITNER
Faculty of Chemical and Pharmaceutical Sciences: LUIS NÚÑEZ
Faculty of Dentistry: JOSÉ MATAS COLOM
Faculty of Economic and Administrative Sciences: NASSIR SAPAG
Faculty of Fine Arts: LUIS MERINO MONTERO
Faculty of Forestry: GUILLERMO JULIO A.
Faculty of Law: ANTONIO BASCUÑAN V.
Faculty of Medicine: Dr JORGE LAS HERAS
Faculty of Philosophy and Humanities: MARÍA ISABEL FLISHFISCH
Faculty of Physical and Mathematical Sciences: VÍCTOR PÉREZ VERA
Faculty of Sciences: CAMILO QUEZADA BOUEY
Faculty of Social Sciences: FERNANDO DURÁN
Faculty of Veterinary Sciences and Cattle Breeding: SANTIAGO URCELAY

ATTACHED INSTITUTES

Clinical Hospital of the University of Chile: Avda Santos Dumont 999, Santiago; Dir Dr ITALO BRAGHETTO.

Institute of International Studies: Condell 249, Santiago; Dir JEANETTE IRIGOIN.

Institute of Nutrition and Food Technology: Avda José Pedro Alessandri 5540, Santiago; Dir FERNANDO VIO.

Institute of Public Affairs: María Guerrero 940, Santiago; Dir OSVALDO SUNKEL.

UNIVERSIDAD DE LA FRONTERA

Avda Francisco Salazar 01145, Casilla 54-D, Temuco
Telephone: (45) 325000
Fax: (45) 325950
E-mail: ufro-tco@ufro.cl
Internet: www.ufro.cl

Founded 1981
State control
Academic year: March to December (two semesters)

Rector: SERGIO BRAVO ESCOBAR
Vice-Rector (Academic): MARÍA ELENA GONZÁLEZ PLITT
Vice-Rector (Administration and Finance): OSCAR ELTIT SPIELMANN
Secretary-General: REGINALDO ZURITA CHAVEZ
Library Director: WALTER LEBRECHT DÍAZ-PINTO

Number of teachers: 764
Number of students: 7,784

Publications: *Cubo* (annually), *Chilean Review of Biological Medical Sciences* (2 a year), *International Journal of Morphology* (quarterly), *Vertientes UFRO* (quarterly), *Revista Educación y Humanidades* (education and humanities, annually), *Revista Investigaciones en Educación* (educational research, annually), *Memoria Institucional* (annually), *Lengua y Literatura Mapuche* (2 a year), *Revista Médica del Sur* (medicine, 2 a year), *Revista Nuestra Muestra* (2 a year)

DEANS

Faculty of Agricultural and Forestry Sciences: HERNÁN PINILLA QUEZADA
Faculty of Education and Humanities: HUGO CARRASCO MUÑOZ
Faculty of Engineering and Administration: PLINIO DURÁN GARCIÁ
Faculty of Medicine: WILFRIED DIENER OJEDA

HEADS OF DEPARTMENTS

Faculty of Agricultural and Forestry Sciences (Francisco Salazar 01145, Tamuco; tel. (45) 325630; fax (45) 325634; e-mail hpin@ufro.cl):
- Agricultural Production: NÉSTOR SEPÚLVEDA BECKER
- Agricultural Sciences and Natural Resources: RUBÉN CARRILLO LÓPEZ
- Forestry Sciences: ZOIA NEIRA CEBALLOS

Faculty of Education and Humanities (Francisco Salazar 01145, Tamuco; tel. (45) 325370; fax (45) 325379; e-mail hcarrasc@ufro.cl; internet www.edu.ufro.cl):
- Education: IRMA LABRAÑA MÉNDEZ
- Physical Education, Sports and Recreation: LEOPOLDO MUÑOZ NIES
- Psychology: ALFREDO KÉLLER ALDUNATE
- Social SciencesLanguage, Literature and Communication: EUGENIA JOFRE RIBERA, RUBÉN LEAL RIQUELME
- Social Work: OLGA REBOLLEDO PIÑA

Faculty of Engineering and Administration (Arturo Prat 321, Temuco; tel. (45) 325800; fax (45) 325810; e-mail decing@ufro.cl):
- Administration and Economy: FERNANDO URRA JARA
- Chemical Engineering: VALERIO BIFANI COSENTINI
- Chemical Sciences: FERNANDO GALLARDO ARRIAGADA
- Civil Engineering: GUILLERMO JIMÉNEZ VON-BISCHOFFSHAUSEN
- Electrical Engineering: SERGIO CARTER FUENTEALBA
- Mathematics Engineering: JUAN A. GÓMEZ FERNÁNDEZ
- Mathematics and Statistics: ANTONIO SANHUEZA CAMPOS
- Mechanical Engineering: MARIO INOSTROZA DELGADO
- Physical Sciences: JUAN CARLOS PARRA ARAVENA
- Systems Engineering: SERGIO FIGUEROA SÁNCHEZ

Faculty of Medicine (Manuel Montt 112, Temuco; tel. (45) 325700; fax (45) 325710; e-mail decanmed@ufro.cl; internet www.med.ufro.cl):
- Basic Sciences: HORACIO NÚÑEZ STULZEL
- Integral Odontology: RAMÓN FUENTES FERNÁNDEZ
- Internal Medicine: JUAN PABLO RIEDEMANN GONZÁLEZ
- Medicine (specialized): JUAN ALBERTO HINOSTROZA FUSCHLOGER
- Mental Health and Psychiatry: LUIS SILVA FUENTES
- Obstetrics and Gynaecology: MIGUEL ANGEL PANTOJA MONSALVEZ
- Paediatrics and Infant Surgery: EDUARDO HEBEL WEISS
- Pathology: IVÁN ROA ESTERIO
- Pre-clinical Sciences: GLORIA RODRÍGUEZ MORETTI
- Public Health: JAIME SERRA CANALES
- Surgery and Traumatology: CARLOS MANTEROLA DELGADO

ATTACHED INSTITUTES

Centre of Reproductive Biotechnology: Dir RAÚL SÁNCHEZ GUTIÉRREZ.

Centre of Scientific Modelling: Dir CARLOS MUÑOZ POBLETE.

Evidence-Based Center for Training, Research and Management on Health: Dir SERGIO MUÑOZ NAVARRO.

Institute of Agroindustry: Dir GUSTAVO ARAVENA PAILLALEF.

Institute of Environment: Dir ITILIER SALAZAR QUINTANA.

Institute of Indigenous Studies: Dir ALEJANDRO HERRERA AGUAYO.

Institute of Information Science in Education: Dir ENRIQUE HINOSTROZA SCHEEL.

Institute for Local and Regional Development: Dir HEINRICH VON BAER VON LOCHOW.

UNIVERSIDAD DE LA SERENA

Avda Raúl Bitrán Nachary s/n, La Serena
Telephone: (51) 204000
Fax: (51) 204310
E-mail: uls@userena.cl
Internet: www.userena.cl

Founded 1981
State control
Academic year: March to December

Rector: JAIME POZO CISTERNAS
Vice-Rector (Academic): MARÍA LINA BERRÍOS SALAS
Vice-Rector (Administrative): JOSÉ AGUILERA MUÑOZ
General Director of Student Affairs: GLORIA LLAMBÍAS ABATTE
Secretary-General: EDGARDO ZELAYA CABALLERO
International Liaison Officer: JULIO PARADA PIZARRO
Librarian: MARÍA A. CALABACERO JIMÉNEZ

Number of teachers: 554
Number of students: 7,694

Publications: *Revista Actas de Logos* (annually), *Revista Crisalida* (annually), *Revista Humus* (annually), *Revista de Investigación y Desarrollo* (annually), *Revista Logos* (annually), *Revista Omnibus* (annually), *Revista Temas de Educación* (annually)

DEANS

Faculty of Economics and Social Sciences: GUIDO VÉLIZ CANTUARIAS
Faculty of Engineering: NIBALDO AVILÉS PIZARRO
Faculty of Humanities: CRISTIÁN NOEMI PADILLA
Faculty of Sciences: IVÁN FERNÁNDEZ ROJAS

HEADS OF DEPARTMENTS

Faculty of Economics and Social Sciences (Amunátegui s/n, La Serena; tel. (51) 204501; fax (51) 204509; e-mail gveliz@userena.cl; internet www.facse.uls.cl):
- Economics and Business: LUPERFINA ROJAS ESCOBAR
- History and Geography Teaching Programme: ROBERTO PÁEZ CONSTELLA
- Social Sciences: ENRIQUE NOVOA JEREZ

Faculty of Engineering (Benavente 980, La Serena; tel. (51) 204291; fax (51) 211775; e-mail fingeni@userena.cl):
- Architecture: PAZ WALKER FERNÁNDEZ
- Civil Engineering: LUÍS DÍAZ ZAMORA
- Civil Industrial Engineering: FEDERICO CAROZZI SALVATIERRA
- Food Engineering: HÉCTOR PAÉZ RIVERA
- Mining Engineering: FEDERICO BRUNNER MONTES DE OCA
- Mechanical Engineering: MARIO CÁCERES VALENZUELA

Faculty of Humanities (tel. (51) 204459; fax (51) 204386; e-mail cnoemi@userena.cl; internet www.fh.userena.cl):
- Arts and Letters: WALTERIO HOEFLER EBERS
- Education: BERNARDO JOPIA ALVAREZ
- Music: MARIO ARENAS NAVARRETE
- Psychology: MAURICIO GONZÁLEZ ARIAS

Faculty of Sciences (Benavente 920, La Serena; tel. (51) 204292; fax (51) 226662; e-mail ifernand@userena.cl):

Agronomy: CRISTIÁN GELDES GONZÁLEZ
Biology: SERGIO ZEPEDA MALUENDA
Chemistry: GUILLERMO SAÁ GAMBOA
Mathematics: GUSTAVO LABBÉ MORALES
Nursing: ANA MARÍA VÁSQUEZ AQUEVEQUE
Physics: PEDRO VEGA JORQUERA

HEADS OF SCHOOLS

Faculty of Economics and Social Sciences (Amunátegui s/n, La Serena; tel. (51) 204501; fax (51) 204509; e-mail gveliz@userena.cl):

School of Administration and Auditing: CALIXTO VEAS GAZ
School of Commercial Engineering: VICENTE TAPIA ALVAREZ
School of History and Geography Teaching Programme: FABIÁN ARAYA PALACIOS
School of Journalism: LLALILE LLARLLURI RAAD
School of Tourism Administration: LUZ ELENA CORNEJO GANGA

Faculty of Engineering (Benavente 980, La Serena; tel. (51) 204291; fax (51) 211775; e-mail fingeni@userena.cl):

School of Architecture: PAZ WALKER FERNÁNDEZ
School of Civil Construction: VICTOR AROS ARAYA
School of Civil Engineering: ALBERTO CORTÉS ALVAREZ
School of Food Engineering: FRANCISCO YAGNAM ABUFFÓN
School of Technical Engineering: JUAN CAMPOS FERREIRA

Faculty of Humanities (tel. (51) 204459; fax (51) 204386; e-mail cnoemi@userena.cl):

School of Design: LUÍS RICARDO BAEZA CORREA
School of Education: (vacant)
School of Psychology: MAURCIO GONZÁLEZ ARIAS
School of Teaching Humanities: ANA MARÍA CORTÉS ALCAYAGA
School of Teaching Music: OLIVIA CONCHA MOLINARI

Faculty of Sciences (Benavente 920, La Serena; tel. (51) 204292; fax (51) 211775; e-mail ifernand@userena.cl):

School of Agronomy: ADRIANA BENAVIDES LÓPEZ
School of Chemical Laboratories: LUIS ARANCIBIA LÓPEZ
School of Computation Engineering: ERIC JELTSCH FIGUEROA
School of Nursing: CARMEN RETAMAL VALENZUELA
School of Teaching Sciences: GERALDO BROWN GONZÁLEZ

UNIVERSIDAD DE LOS LAGOS

Casilla 933, Osorno
Telephone: (64) 230061
Fax: (64) 239517
E-mail: cvarela@puyehue.di.ulagos.cl
Internet: www.ulagos.cl

Founded 1993; fmrly Instituto Profesional de Osorno
State control
Academic year: March to December

Rector: RAÚL AGUILAR GATICA
Vice-Rector for Academic Affairs: MARÍA CECILIA PLANAS VERGARA
Vice-Rector for Administration and Finance: SERGIO HERMOSILLA PÉREZ
Librarian: EDUARDO BARROS BARROS

Number of teachers: 261 (143 full-time, 118 part-time)
Number of students: 3,635

Publications: *Alpha* (humanities), *Biota* (aquatic sciences), *Leader* (social sciences)

DIRECTORS

Department of Administration and Economics: ARNALDO DURÁN GRAU
Department of Aquaculture and Aquatic Resources: JUAN CARLOS URIBE BARICHIVICH
Department of Architecture: ROBERTO MARTÍNEZ KRAUHAAR
Department of Basic Sciences: JAIME ZAPATA BARRA
Department of Development: MARGARITA OYARCE IGOR
Department of Education: GLAUCO TORRES ROJAS
Department of Exact Sciences: JORGE WEVAR NEGRIER
Department of Food Science and Technology: ARNALDO CAQUEO CONTERAS
Department of Forest Resources: MARCOS CRUZ MELO
Department of Government and Business: NELSON DÍAZ PACHECO
Department of Humanities and Art: GONZALO BURGOS SOTOMAYOR
Department of Natural Resources and the Environment: LUIS FERREIRA OSSES
Department of Physical Education: HÉCTOR NEIRA MONJE
Department of Social Sciences: JUAN SÁNCHEZ ALVAREZ

UNIVERSIDAD DE MAGALLANES

Casilla 113-D, Punta Arenas
Telephone: 212945
Fax: 219276
Internet: www.umag.cl

Founded 1964 (previously branch of Universidad Técnica del Estado)
State control
Language of instruction: Spanish
Academic year: begins in March

Rector: Dr VÍCTOR FAJARDO MORALES
Vice-Rector (Academic): LUIS OVAL GONZÁLEZ
Secretary-General: FRANCISCO SOTO PIFFAULT
Librarian: ILUMINANDA ROJAS PALACIOS

Number of teachers: 168
Number of students: 3,200

Publications: *Anales del Instituto de la Patagonia, Austrouniversitaria*

DEANS

Faculty of Economics and Law: LUIS POBLETE DAVANZO
Faculty of Engineering: JUAN OYARZO PÉREZ
Faculty of Humanities, Social Sciences and Health Sciences: JUAN YUDIKIS PRELLER
Faculty of Sciences: OCTAVIO LECAROS PALMA

HEADS OF DEPARTMENTS

Administration and Economics: GUILLERMO GODOY SEVERINO
Agricultural and Aquacultural Resources Science and Technology: SERGIO KUSANOVIC MIMICA
Chemical Engineering: JOSÉ RETAMALES ESPINOZA
Civil Construction: RAÚL GALLARDO MORENO
Computer Science: CARLOS ARIAS MÉNDEZ
Education and Humanities: ANA MARÍA NAZAL MANZUR
Electrical Engineering: JORGE REYES MIRANDA
Health Sciences: ELIDE ALARCÓN BUSTOS
Mathematics and Physics: VÍCTOR DÍAZ HUENTELICÁN
Mechanical Engineering: HUMBERTO OYARZO PÉREZ
Science and Natural Resources: ANDRÉS MANSILLA MUÑOZ

ATTACHED INSTITUTE

Instituto de la Patagonia: Avda Bulnes 01890, Casilla 113-D, Punta Arenas; tel. 217173; fax 212973; f. 1969; scientific, cultural and social development of the South American region; Dir CLAUDIO VENEGAS CANELO.

UNIVERSIDAD METROPOLITANA DE CIENCIAS DE LA EDUCACIÓN

Casilla 147, Correo Central, Santiago
Telephone: 2257731
Internet: www.umce.cl

Founded 1889

Rector: JESÚS GONZÁLEZ
Vice-Rector: MAXIMINO FERNANDEZ FRAILE
Director of Administration: ROSANA SPROVERA MANRIQUEZ
Librarian: MARÍA ISABEL BRUCE

Number of teachers: 440
Number of students: 4,800

Publications: *Academia, Acta Entomológica chilena, Dimensión histórica de Chile, Educación Física*

DEANS

Faculty of Arts and Physical Education: MILTON COFRE ILUFFI
Faculty of Basic Sciences: MAFALDA SCHIAPPACASSE COSTA
Faculty of History, Geography and Literature: SILVIA VYHMEISTER TZSCHABRAN
Faculty of Philosophy and Education: JAIME ARAOS SAN MARTIN

UNIVERSIDAD DE PLAYA ANCHA DE CIENCIAS DE LA EDUCACIÓN

Avda Playa Ancha 850, Casilla 34-V, Valparaíso
Telephone: (32) 281758
Fax: (32) 285041
Internet: www.upa.cl

Founded 1948
Languages of instruction: Spanish, English
Languages of instruction: French, German
State control
Academic year: March to December

Rector: NORMAN CORTES LARRIEU
Pro-Rector: GERMÁN CAMPOS PARDO
Head of Administration and Finance: SERGIO INFANTE BARRA
Librarian: MARIA EUGENIA OLGUIN STEENBECKER

Number of teachers: 328
Number of students: 3,700

Publications: *Diálogos Educacionales, Diccionario Ejemplificado de Chilenismos, Nueva Revista del Pacífico, Notas Históricas y Geográficas, Proyección Universitaria, Revista de Orientación, Visiones Científicas*

DEANS

Faculty of Arts: BELFORT RUZ ESCUDERO
Faculty of Educational Sciences: RENE FLORES CASTILLO
Faculty of Humanities: DANIEL LAGOS ALTAMIRANO
Faculty of Natural and Exact Sciences: GUILLERMO RIVEROS GOMEZ
Faculty of Physical Education: ANTONIO MAURER FURST

HEADS OF DEPARTMENTS

Faculty of Arts:

Music: MARIA TERESA DEVIA LUBET
Visual Arts: ALBERTO MADRID LETELIER

Faculty of Educational Sciences:

Educational Sciences: GASTON AGUILAR PULIDO

Systematic Teaching: MARIA ISABEL MUÑOZ ROJO
Faculty of Humanities:
Languages and Information Sciences: LIDIA CONTARDO HOGTERT
Philosophy of Social Sciences: ENRIQUE MUÑOZ MICKLE
Faculty of Natural and Exact Sciences:
Biology and Chemistry: SERGIO ZAMORANO POZO
Mathematics and Physics: JOSE RUBIO VALENZUELA
Faculty of Physical Education:
Physical Education: ELIAS MARIN VALENZUELA
Sports and Recreation: PAMELA GALLEGUILLOS GUERRERO

UNIVERSIDAD DE SANTIAGO DE CHILE

Alameda Libertador Bernardo O'Higgins 3363, Casilla 442, Correo 2, Santiago
Telephone: (2) 6811100
Fax: (2) 6812663
Internet: www.usach.cl
Founded 1947 as Universidad Técnica del Estado; present name 1981
State control
Language of instruction: Spanish
Academic year: March to December

Rector: UBALDO ZUÑIGA QUINTANILLA
Vice-Rector (Academic): HÉCTOR MELO ARAYA
Vice-Rector (Research and Development): LUIS GAETE GARRETÓN
General Secretary: JAIME JIMÉNEZ CASTRO
Academic Registrar: BERNARDO CARRASCO REYES
Librarian: IRMA CARRASCO ALFARO

Number of teachers: 2,260
Number of students: 17,691

Publications: *Avances en Investigación y Desarrollo, Educación en Ingeniería, Mantención e Industria* (4 a year), *Boletín APYME* (6 a year), *Comunicación Universitaria, Contribuciones Científicas y Tecnológicas, Cuadernos de Humanidades*

DEANS
Faculty of Administration and Economics: JORGE PÉREZ BARBEITO
Faculty of Chemistry and Biology: JUAN COSTAMANGA MARTRA
Faculty of Engineering: RAMÓN BLASCO SÁNCHEZ
Faculty of Humanities: RAÚL LABBE OSSES
Faculty of Medicine: JOSÉ LUIS CÁRDENAS NÚÑEZ
Faculty of Sciences: RAFAEL LABARCA BRIONES
Faculty of Technology: ENRIQUE FALCONI CONCHA
School of Architecture: RODOLFO JIMÉNEZ CAVIERES (Dir)
School of Journalism: MARGARITA PASTENE VALLADARES (Dir)
School of Psychology: EMILIO MOYANO DÍAZ (Dir)
Undergraduate Programme: LEOPOLDO SÁEZ GODOY (Dir)

UNIVERSIDAD DE TALCA

2 Norte 685, Talca
Telephone: (71) 200101
Fax: (71) 228054
Internet: www.utalca.cl
Founded 1981
State control
Language of instruction: Spanish
Academic year: March to December

Rector: Dr ÁLVARO ROJAS MARÍN
Vice-Rector for Academic Affairs: JUAN ANTONIO ROCK TARUD
Vice-Rector for Cultural Affairs: PEDRO ZAMORANO PÉREZ
Vice-Rector for Development: JUAN PABLO PRIETO COX
Vice-Rector for Finance and Administration: PATRICIO ORTÚZAR RUIZ
Vice-Rector for Student Affairs: CARLOS HOJAS ALONSO
Secretary-General: CRISTIÁN SUÁREZ CROTHERS
Librarian: MARIA ANGÉLICA TEJOS MUÑOZ

Number of teachers: 400 (204 full-time, 196 part-time)
Number of students: 4,700

Publications: *Acontecer* (monthly), *Ius et Praxis* (2 a year), *Panorama Socio Económico* (annually), *Universum* (annually)

DEANS
Faculty of Agricultural Sciences: JORGE RETAMALES ARANDA
Faculty of Business Administration: ARCADIO CERDA URRUTIA
Faculty of Engineering: JORGE MARDONES ACEVEDO
Faculty of Forestry Sciences: IVAN CHACON CONTRERAS
Faculty of Health Sciences: CARLOS GIGOUX CASTELLÓN
Faculty of Juridical and Social Sciences: HUMBERTO NOGUEIRA ALCALÁ
School of Architecture: JUAN ROMÁN PÉREZ

DIRECTORS
Faculty of Agronomy (Avda Lircay s/n, Casilla 721, Talca; tel. (71) 200210; fax (71) 200362):
School of Agronomy: PAULA MANRÍQUEZ NOVOA
Faculty of Business Administration (Avda Lircay s/n, Casilla 721, Talca; tel. (71) 200310; fax (71) 200358):
School of Auditing: VICTOR HUGO RUIZ ROJAS
School of Commercial Engineering: MOISÉS FALCÓN ALVEAR
MBA Programme: GERMÁN ECHECOPAR KOECHLIN
Faculty of Engineering (Camino Los Niches s/n, Curico; tel. (75) 325955; fax (75) 325958):
School of Civil and Industrial Engineering: ALVARO COVARRUBIAS RISOPATRON
School of Mechanical Engineering: FELIPE TIRADO DÍAZ
Faculty of Forestry Sciences (Avda Lircay s/n, Casilla 721, Talca; tel. (71) 200442; fax (71) 200428):
School of Forestry Engineering: MAURICIO PONCE DONOSO
Faculty of Health Sciences (Avda Lircay s/n, Casilla 721, Talca; tel. (71) 200452; fax (71) 200439):
School of Medical Technology: SILVIA VIDAL FLORES
School of Odontology: (vacant)
Faculty of Juridical and Social Sciences (Avda Lircay s/n, Casilla 721, Talca; tel. (71) 200299; fax (71) 200410):
School of Law: MARÍA CECILIA RAMÍREZ GUZMÁN

ATTACHED INSTITUTES
Instituto de Biología Vegetal y Biotecnología: Dir ENRIQUE GONZÁLEZ VILLANUEVA.
Instituto de Estudios Humanísticos Abate Juan Ignacio Molina: Dir JAVIER PINEDO CASTRO.
Instituto de Investigación y Desarrollo Educacional: Dir GUSTAVO HAWES BARRIOS.
Instituto de Matemática y Física: Dir MANUEL O'RYAN LERMANDA.
Instituto de Química de Recursos Naturales: Dir IVAN RAZMILIC BONILLA.

UNIVERSIDAD DE TARAPACÁ

Gral Velásquez 1775, Casilla 7-D, Arica
Telephone: (58) 205100
Fax: (58) 232135
E-mail: rec@uta.cl
Internet: www.uta.cl
Founded 1981
State control
Language of instruction: Spanish
Academic year: March to December
Library of 80,242 vols, 499 periodicals

Rector: EMILIO RODRIGUEZ PONCE
Vice-Rector for Academic Affairs: ARTURO FLORES FRANULIC
Vice-Rector for Finance and Administration: MANUEL DOSONO MUÑOZ
Librarian: INÉS RODRÍGUEZ RIQUELME

Library of 73,300 vols, 622 periodicals
Number of teachers: 237
Number of students: 7,474

Publications: *Chungará* (2 a year), *Diálogo Andino* (2 a year), *Idesia* (2 a year), *Limite* (annually), *Revista Facultad de Ingeniería* (annually), *Revista de Fisica* (annually)

DEANS
Faculty of Agronomy: EUGENIO DOUSSOULIN ESCOBAR
Faculty of Education and Humanities: CARLOS HERRERA SAAVEDRA
Faculty of Engineering: JORGE BENAVIDES SILVA
Faculty of Sciences: HUGO BRAVO AZLAN
Faculty of Social Sciences, Business Administration and Economics: SERGIO PULIDO ROCCATAGLIATA

PROFESSORS
Faculty of Engineering:
ARACENA PIZARRO, D.
BARRAZA SOTOMAYOR, B.
BECK FERNÁNDEZ, H.
BENAVIDES SILVA, J.
BORJAS MONTERO, R.
BUSTOS ANDREU, H.
CAMPOS TRONCOSO, J.
COHEN HORNICKEL, W.
CORREA ARANEDA, E.
DÍAZ ROJAS, H.
DURÁN ARRIAGADA, R.
ESPINOZA VALLEDOR, J.
ESTUPIÑAN PULIDO, E.
FERNÁNDEZ MAGGI, M.
FIGUEROA PÉREZ, H.
FLORES CONDORI, C.
FUENTES HEINRICH, E.
FUENTES ROMERO, R.
GALLEGOS ARAYA, A.
GÁLVEZ SOTO, E.
GODOY RAMSAY, J.
GONZÁLEZ ARAYA, A.
GUÍRRIMAN CARRASCO, R.
HARNISCH VELOSO, I.
JERALDO CASTRO, A.
MARCHIONI CHOQUE, I.
MENDIZABAL JIMÉNEZ, H.
MUÑOZ ESPINOSA, J.
OSSANDON DÍAZ, H.
OSSANDON NUÑEZ, Y.
OVALLE CUBILLOS, R.
PAZ SEGURA, G.
PEDRAJA REJAS, L.
PONCE LÓPEZ, E.
RAMÍREZ VARAS, I.
RODRÍGUEZ ESTAY, A.
SANHUEZA HORMAZABAL, R.
SANZ CANTILLANA, T.
SAPIAÍN ARAYA, R.

TARQUE COSSIO, S.
TORRES ORTÍZ, E.
TORRES SILVA, H.
VALDÉS GONZÁLEZ, H.
VALDIVIA PINTO, R.
VERGARA DÍAZ, J.
VILLALOBOS ABARCA, J.
VILLANUEVA AGUILA, J.
VILLARROEL GONZÁLEZ, C.
ZAMORANO LUCERO, M.

Faculty of Science:

ALVAREZ INOSTROZA, L.
BARRIENTOS NUÑOZ, V.
BELTRAN BARRIOS, R.
BOGGIONI CASANOVA, S.
BÓRGUEZ BENITT, CELIA
BRAVO AZLÁN, H.
CABALLERO PETTERSEN, H.
CABELLO FERNÁNDEZ, G.
CALISTO PÉREZ, H.
CAMPOS ORTEGA, H.
CANDIA ANDRADE, M.
CARO ARAYA, M.
CASTRO SANTANDER, F.
CISTERNAS RIVEROS, M.
CORNEJO PONCE, L.
CORRALES MUÑOZ, J.
CORTÉS GAJARDO, W.
CRUZ MARINO, A.
ESPINOZA NAVARRO, O.
FERNÁNDEZ CARVAJAL, I.
FLORES ARAYA, J.
FLORES FRANCULIC, A.
GALAZ LEIVA, S.
GLASS SADIA, B.
GONZÁLEZ FLORES, M.
HERNÁNDEZ VILLASECA, L.
LAIME CONDORI, D.
LAVÍN BECERRA, L.
LAZO NÚÑEZ, E.
LEA RODRÍGUEZ, L.
LEIVA SAJURIA, C.
LOBATO ACOSTA, I.
LÓPEZ PERIC, H.
LORCA PIZARRO, S.
MARTÍN GARCÍA, E.
MEDINA DÍAZ, M.
MENESES VERA, C.
MONTALVO VILLALBA, M.
MOSCOSO ZÁRATE, D.
NARANJO GÁRATE, A. M.
OLIVARES TOLEDO, V.
O'NELL SEQUEIRA, M.
ORTEGA ARAYA, A.
ORTEGA ROJAS, A.
PACHÁ BUSTAMENTE, A.
PALLEROS SANTOS, H.
PEDREROS AVENDAÑO, M.
PÉREZ MORETTI, N.
QUELOPANA DEL VALLE, A.
QUIOZA PALOMINOS, S.
REY MAS, V.
REYES RUBILAR, T.
RIVAS AVILA, M.
ROJAS ESPINOZA, E.
ROJAS TRONCOSO, M.
ROMÁN FLORES, H.
SANHUEZA COLLINAO, M.
UBEDA DE LA CERDA, C.
VALENZUELA ESTRADA, M.
VASQUEZ ROJAS, M. I.
VILAXA OLCAY, A.
VILLANUEVA DÍAZ, H.
VILLEGAS BRAVO, J.
ZÚÑIGA AGUIRRE, J.
ZÚNIGA SALAS, P.

Faculty of Social Sciences:

ALBURQUENQUE ELIASH, M.
ALFONSO VARGAS, J.
ALFRED ALFARO, F.
ALVAREZ ROSALES, N.
BARRIENTOS BORDOLI, I.
BELMONTE SCHWARZBAUM, E.
BERNAL PERALTA, J.
BRIONES MORALES, L.
BUSSENIUS RISCO, J. C.
CABRALES GÓMEZ, F.
CAYO RIOS, G.
CHACAMA RODRÍGUEZ, J.
CHAIGNEAU ORFANOZ, S.
CISTERNAS ARAPIO, B.
CONTRERAS CORDANO, M.
CÓRDOVA GONZÁLEZ, J.
CUADRA PERALTA, A.
DONOSO MUÑOZ, M.
ESPINOZA VERDEJO, A.
FERREIRA REYES, R.
FIGUEROA GUACHALLA, M.
FLORES TAPIA, E.
GONZÁLEZ CORTÉS, H.
GUTIÉRREZ SAMOHOD, A.
HENRIQUEZ AGUILERA, A.
JIMÉNEZ QUÑONES, P.
KARMELIC PAVLOV, V.
LEAL SOTO, F.
LEBLANC VALENZUELA, L.
MUÑOZ ABELLA, G.
MUÑIZ OVALLE, I.
NAVARRETE ALVAREZ, M.
OCHOA DE LA MAZA, O.
PALMA QUIROZ, A.
PARRA SUAZO, O.
PERALTA MONTECINOS, J.
PULIDO ROCCATAGLIATA, S.
RAMÍREZ HUANCA, D.
RODRÍGUEZ PONCE, E.
ROMERO ROMERO, J.
RUÍZ LARRAL, C.
SALAS PALACIOS, R.
SANTORO VARGAS, C.
STANDEN RAMÍREZ, V.
STOREY MEZA, R.
ULLOA TORRES, H.
VIERA CASTILLO, D.

UNIVERSIDAD TECNOLÓGICA METROPOLITANA

Calle Dieciocho 161, Casilla 9845, Santiago
Telephone: 6981950
Internet: www.utem.cl

Founded 1981 as Instituto Profesional de Santiago; present name 1990s

Rector: MIGUEL AVENDAÑO BERRÍOS
Pro-Rector: MANUEL HEVIA SOTO
Vice-Rector for Academic Affairs: SERGIO GALLARDO E.
Vice-Rector for Administration: FÉLIX DURÁN FIERRO
Vice-Rector for Finance: VÍCTOR ROCHER FERRADA
Secretary (vacant)
Librarian: XIMENA SÁNCHEZ STAFORELLI

Number of teachers: 458
Number of students: 5,600

Publications: *Anuario Investigación del Departamento de Humanidades*, *Boletín Investigación del Departamento de Humanidades* (quarterly), *Trilogía*

DIRECTORS

Department of Basic Sciences and Mathematics: CLAUDIO VILA CEPPI (acting)
Department of Humanities: JUAN BERRUETA CASTRO (acting)
School of Accountancy: GUILLERMO ZÁRATE GIBERT
School of Administration: LUIS VALENZUELA SILVA
School of Civil Engineering: RENÉ ZORRILLA FUENZÁLIDA
School of Computer Studies: NINA VALDIVÍA ARENAS (acting)
School of Design: WALDO GONZÁLEZ HERVE
School of Librarianship: BRUNA BENZI BISTOLFI
School of Social Work: MARTA JALA RUBILAR
School of Technology: TOMÁS MASSARDO PÉREZ

UNIVERSIDAD DE VALPARAÍSO

Casilla 123-V, Valparaíso
Telephone: (32) 213071
Fax: (32) 220071
Internet: www.uv.cl

Founded 1981; previously branch of University of Chile
State control
Academic year: two terms, beginning March and August

Rector: AGUSTÍN SQUELLA NARDUCCI
Pro-Rector: JULIO CASTRO SEPÚLVEDA
Academic Director-General: OSVALDO BADENIER BUSTAMENTE
Secretary-General: ALDO VALLE ACEVEDO

Number of teachers: 760 (200 full-time, 560 part-time)
Number of students: 5,407

Publications: *Boletín Micológico*, *Revista de Biología Marina*, *Revista de Ciencias Sociales*

DEANS

Faculty of Architecture: JAIME FARÍAS CÓRDOVA
Faculty of Dentistry: Dr LUIS OLIVARES MELÉNDEZ
Faculty of Economics and Administration: JUAN RIQUELME ZUCCHET
Faculty of Law and Social Sciences: ITALO PAOLINELLI MONTI
Faculty of Marine Sciences: ROBERTO PRADO-FIEDLER
Faculty of Medicine: Dr DAVID SABAH JAIME
Faculty of Science: ANTONIO GLARÍA BENCOECHEA

Private Universities with Public Funding

PONTIFICIA UNIVERSIDAD CATÓLICA DE CHILE (Catholic University of Chile)

Casilla 114-D, Alameda 340, Santiago
Telephone: (2) 6862415
Fax: (2) 2223116
E-mail: soporte@puc.cl
Internet: www.puc.cl

Founded 1888
Private control
Academic year: March to December

Grand Chancellor: Exmo Rmo Mons. FRANCISCO JAVIER ERRÁZURIZ OSSA
Vice-Grand Chancellor: Pbro ANDRÉS ARTEAGA
Rector: PEDRO PABLO ROSSO
Pro-Rector: JUAN IGNACIO VARAS
Vice-Rector: NICOLÁS VELASCO
General Secretary: RAÚL MADRID
Director of Distance Education: RICHARD WARNER
Librarian: MARÍA LUISA ARENAS

Library: see Libraries and Archives
Number of teachers: 2,100 (1,300 full-time, 800 part-time)
Number of students: 18,000

Publications: *Revista Humanitas* (every 2 years), *Revista Universitaria* (4 a year)

ACADEMIC UNITS AND DEANS

Faculty of Agronomy: GUILLERMO DONOSO HARRIS
Faculty of Architecture and Fine Arts: JUAN JOSÉ UGARTE
Faculty of Biological Sciences: RENATO ALBERTINI BARTOLAMEOLLI
Faculty of Chemistry: LUIS HERNÁN TAGLE DOMÍNGUEZ

Faculty of Communication: Francisca Alessandri
Faculty of Economics and Management Sciences: Francisco Rosende Ramírez
Faculty of Education: Gonzalo Undurraga
Faculty of Engineering: Hernán de Solminihac
Faculty of History, Geography and Political Sciences: René Millar
Faculty of Law: Arturo Yirrazaval
Faculty of Mathematics: Guillermo Marshall
Faculty of Medicine: Gonzalo Grebe
Faculty of Philosophy: Luis Flores
Faculty of Physics: Ricardo Ramírez Leiva
Faculty of Social Sciences: Pedro Morandé Court
Faculty of Theology: R.-P. Samuel Fernández

BRANCH CAMPUS

Sede Regional de Villarrica: Casilla 111; Dir Mons. Paul Wevering Weidemann.

PONTIFICIA UNIVERSIDAD CATÓLICA DE VALPARAÍSO

Avda Brasil 2950, Casilla 4059, Valparaíso
Telephone: (32) 27-30-00
Fax: (32) 21-27-46
E-mail: rector@ucv.cl
Internet: www.ucv.cl

Founded 1928
Private control
Academic year: March to December

Chancellor: Mgr Gonzalo Duarte García de Cortázar
Rector: Prof. Alfonso Muga Naredo
Vice-Rectors: Enrique Montenegro Arcila (Academic and Student Affairs), Claudio Elórtegui Raffo (Administrative and Financial Affairs), Carlos Wörner Olavarría (Development Affairs), Gabriel Yany González (Research and Advanced Studies)
Secretary-General: Claudio Moltedo Castaño
Registrar: José Gaete Polanco
Librarian: Atilio Bustos González

Library: see Libraries and Archives
Number of teachers: 490
Number of students: 12,676

Publications: *Electronic Journal of Biotechnology* (online), *Revista de Derecho* (online), *Revista de Estudios Histórico-Jurídicos* (online), *Revista Geográfica de Valparaíso* (online), *Revista Investigaciones Marinas* (online), *Revista Perspectiva Educacional*, *Revista Philosophica*, *Revista Signos* (online)

DEANS

Faculty of Agronomy: Pedro Undurraga Martínez
Faculty of Architecture: Salvador Zahr Maluk
Faculty of Basic Sciences and Mathematics: Arturo Mena Lorca
Faculty of Economics and Administration: David Cademartori Rosso
Faculty of Engineering: Paulino Alonso Rivas
Faculty of Law and Social Sciences: Alejandro Guzmán Brito
Faculty of Natural Resources: Antonio Cifuentes de la Torre
Faculty of Philosophy and Education: Baldomero Estrada Turra
Institute of Religious Studies: María Inés Concha

UNIVERSIDAD AUSTRAL DE CHILE (Southern University of Chile)

Casilla 567, Valdivia
Telephone: (63) 221960
Fax: (63) 221765
Internet: www.uach.cl

Founded 1954
Private control
Language of instruction: Spanish
Academic year: March to December

Rector: Manfred Max Neef
Vice-Rector for Academic Affairs: Germán Campos P.
Vice-Rector for Economic and Administrative Affairs: Guillermo Urrutia S.
Secretary-General: Kain Exxs K.
Director of Extension: Juan Domingo Ramirez C.
Director of Postgraduate Studies: Alejandro Romero M.
Director of Public Relations: Viella Shipley
Director of Research: Ilona Concha G.
Director of Student Affairs: Enrique Salinas A.
Director of Undergraduate Studies: Angel Enzo Crovetto E.
Registrar: Maria C. Barriga Ramírez

Library: see Libraries and Archives
Number of teachers: 832
Number of students: 8,785

Publications: *Agro Sur*, *Archivos de Medicina Veterinaria*, *Bosque*, *English Notes*, *Estudios Filológicos*, *Estudios Pedagógicos* (annually), *Medio Ambiente*

DEANS

Faculty of Agriculture: René Anrique G.
Faculty of Economic and Administrative Sciences: Edmundo Borel Ch.
Faculty of Engineering Sciences: Fredy Ríos Martínez
Faculty of Fishery and Oceanography: Renato Westermeier H.
Faculty of Forestry Sciences: Andres Iroumé A.
Faculty of Juridical and Social Sciences: Juan Carlos Ferrada
Faculty of Medicine: Claus Grob B.
Faculty of Philosophy and Humanities: Carlos Amtmann M.
Faculty of Sciences: Eduardo Quiroz Reyes
Faculty of Veterinary Science: Fernando Wittwer M.

DIRECTORS

Faculty of Agriculture:
- Institute of Agricultural Economy: Juan Lerdón S.
- Institute of Agricultural Engineering and Soils: Roberto MacDonald H.
- Institute of Animal Production: Oscar Balocchi L.
- Institute of Food Science and Technology: Bernando Fraser
- Institute of Plant Production and Health: Roberto Carrillo Ll.

Faculty of Economic and Administrative Sciences:
- Institute of Administration: Horacio Sanhueza
- Institute of Economics: Angela Sáiz
- Institute of Statistics: Osvaldo Rojas Quintanilla
- Institute of Tourism: Silvia Costabel G.

Faculty of Engineering Sciences:
- Institute of Acoustics: Jorge Sommerhoff Hyde
- Institute of Civil Engineering: Heriberto Vivanco Bilbao
- Institute of Electricity and Electronics: Pedro Rey Clericus
- Institute of Industrial Design and Method: Roberto Cárdenas Parra
- Institute of Information Science and Quantitative Methods: Wladimir Ríos M.
- Institute of Nautical and Maritime Sciences: Raúl Navarro Arroyo
- Institute of Thermomechanics Materials and Methods: Ernesto Zumelzu Delgado

Faculty of Forestry Sciences:
- Institute of Forestry Management: Mario Niklistschek H.
- Institute of Silviculture: Antonio Lara A.
- Institute of Technology of Forestry Products: Roberto Juacida

Faculty of Juridical and Social Sciences:
- Institute of Juridical Sciences: Juan Omar Cofré
- Institute of Juridical Specialisms: Teodoro Croquevielle B.

Faculty of Medicine:
- Institute of Clinical Microbiology: Luis Zaror Cornejo
- Institute of Haematology: Alvaro León Rivera
- Institute of Histology and Pathology: Silvia Hein Galli
- Institute of Human Anatomy: Hugo Hernández Parada
- Institute of Immunology: Patricio Esquivel S.
- Institute of Locomotive Apparatus and Rehabilitation: Pedro Valdivia Carvajal
- Institute of Maternal Nursing: Liliana Martínez G.
- Institute of Medicine: Humberto Ibarra Vargas
- Institute of Neurology and Neurosurgery: Boris Flández Zbinden
- Institute of Nursing: Zoila Muñoz Jaramillo
- Institute of Obstetrics and Gynaecology: Raúl Puentes P.
- Institute of Paediatrics: Mario Calvo Gil
- Institute of Parasitology: Patricio Torres H.
- Institute of Physiology: Ricardo Castillo D.
- Institute of Psychiatry: Fernando Oyarzún Peña
- Institute of Public Health: Francisco Marín H.
- Institute of Specializations: Edgardo Robles Fernandez
- Institute of Surgery: Juan Pérez Pérez

Faculty of Philosophy and Humanities:
- Institute of Linguistics and Literature: Mauricio Pilleux D.
- Institute of Philosophy and Education: Gladys Jadue J.
- Institute of Social Communication: Gustavo Rodríguez B.
- Institute of Social Sciences: Freddy Fortoul V.

Faculty of Sciences:
- Institute of Biochemistry: Juan Carlos Slebe T.
- Institute of Botany: Carlos Ramirez G.
- Institute of Chemistry: Carlos Cabezas Cuevas
- Institute of Ecology and Evolution: Carlos Moreno M.
- Institute of Embryology: Oscar Goicoechea Bello
- Institute of Geosciences: Mario Pino Quivira
- Institute of Marine Biology: Jorge Navarro A.
- Institute of Mathematics: Manuel Bustos V.
- Institute of Microbiology: Germán Reinhardt Vater
- Institute of Physics: Diner Moraga O.
- Institute of Zoology: Germán Pequeño R.

Faculty of Veterinary Sciences:
- Institute of Animal Pathology: JORGE ULLOA H.
- Institute of Animal Reproduction: JORGE CORREA SOTO
- Institute of Clinical Veterinary Sciences: NÉSTOR TADICH B.
- Institute of Meat Sciences and Technology: JOSE A. DE LA VEGA MALINCONI
- Institute of Pharmacology: FREDERICK AHUMADA M.
- Institute of Stockbreeding: ROBERTO IHL B.
- Institute of Veterinary Anatomy: EDMUNDO BUTENDIECK B.
- Institute of Veterinary Preventive Medicine: RAFAEL TAMAYO C.
- Centre of Artificial Insemination: JORGE EHRENFELD VAN HASSELT

UNIVERSIDAD DE CONCEPCIÓN

Casilla 160-C, Correo 3, Concepción
Telephone: (41) 204000
Fax: (41) 227455
E-mail: foro@udec.cl
Internet: www.udec.cl

Founded 1919
Private control
Language of instruction: Spanish
Academic year: March to January

Rector: SERGIO LAVANCHY MERINO
Vice-Rector for Academic Affairs: ERNESTO FIGUEROA HUIDOBRO
Vice-Rector for Financial Affairs and Personnel: ALBERTO LARRAÍN PRAT
General Secretary: RODOLFO WALTER DÍAZ
Library Director: OLGA MORA MARDONES

Number of teachers: 1,410
Number of students: 16,800

Publications: *Acta Literaria*, *Agro-Ciencia* (2 a year), *Atenea* (monthly; science, art and literature), *Gayana*, *Informativo de Rectoría—PANORAMA* (public relations), *Revista de Derecho* (4 per year), *RLA—Revista de Lingüística Aplicada*

DEANS

Faculty of Agricultural Engineering: JOSÉ REYES AROCA
Faculty of Agriculture: ALFREDO VERA M.
Faculty of Architecture: RICARDO UTZ BARRIGA
Faculty of Biological Sciences: CARLOS GONZÁLEZ CORREA
Faculty of Chemical Sciences: BERNABÉ RIVAS QUIRÓZ
Faculty of Dentistry: FERNANDO ESCOBAR MUÑOZ
Faculty of Economic and Administrative Sciences: JUAN SAAVEDRA GONZÁLEZ
Faculty of Education: ABELARDO CASTRO HIDALGO
Faculty of Engineering: JOEL ZAMBRANO VALENCIA
Faculty of Forestry Sciences: FERNANDO DRAKE ARANDA
Faculty of Humanities and Art: EDUARDO NÚÑEZ CRISOSTO
Faculty of Law and Social Sciences: SERGIO CARRASCO DELGADO
Faculty of Medicine: OCTAVIO ENRÍQUEZ LORCA
Faculty of Natural Sciences and Oceanography: FRANKLIN CARRASCO VASQUEZ
Faculty of Pharmacy: CARLOS CALVO MONFIL
Faculty of Physical Sciences and Mathematics: JOSÉ SÁNCHEZ HENRÍQUEZ
Faculty of Social Sciences: EDUARDO AQUEVEDO SOTO
Faculty of Veterinary Medicine: RUBÉN PÉREZ FERNÁNDEZ

HEADS OF DEPARTMENTS

Faculty of Agricultural Engineering (Vicente Méndez 595, Chillán; tel. (42) 208797; fax (42) 275303; e-mail facagric@udec.cl; internet www.chillan.udec.cl/ingenieria):
- Energy and Mechanization: EDMUNDO HETZ HUENCHULLÁN
- Irrigation and Drainage: LUIS SALGADO SEGUEL
- Products and Structural Processes: JOSÉ CELIS HIDALGO

Faculty of Agriculture (Vicente Méndez 595, Chillán; tel. (42) 208817; fax (42) 275309; e-mail agronomi@chillan.udec.cl; internet www.chillan.udec.cl/agronomia):
- Animal Production: SILVIO TIMA PENDOLA
- Soils: ERICK ZAGAL NEVEGAS
- Vegetable Production: RUPERTO HEPP GALLO

Faculty of Biological Sciences (tel. (41) 204508; fax (41) 245975; e-mail cgonzalez@udec.cl; internet www.udec.cl/cbiologicas):
- Histology and Embryology: FRANCISCO NUALART SANTANDER
- Microbiology: MARÍA A. MONDACA JARA
- Molecular Biology: MARIO ALARCÓN ALVAREZ
- Pharmacology: MARCELO MEDINA VARGAS
- Physiological Science: M. ANTONIETA CRUZ RADOVAN
- Physiopathology: JUAN CARLOS VERA CÁRCAMO

Faculty of Chemical Sciences (Edmundo Larenas 129, Concepción; tel. (41) 204109; fax (41) 245974; e-mail brivas@udec.cl; internet www.udec.cl/facultades/fcq):
- Analytical and Inorganic Chemistry: CARLOS MILLÁN HERRERA
- Earth Sciences: ABRAHAM GONZÁLEZ MARTÍNEZ
- Organic Chemistry: JULIO BELMAR MELLADO
- Physical Chemistry: EDUARDO DELGADO RAMÍREZ
- Polymers: MARIO SUWALSKY WEINZIMER

Faculty of Dentistry (Roosevelt 1550, Concepción; tel. (41) 304386; fax (41) 243311; e-mail decaodont@udec.cl; internet www.udec.cl/odont):
- Oral Paediatrics: ALEJANDRO SAAVEDRA CRUZ
- Pathology and Diagnosis: ALEJANDRA MARTÍNEZ BELLO
- Public Health: ALEX BUSTOS LEAL
- Restorative Dentistry: OSCAR OCAMPO DÍAZ
- Surgical Stomatology: ANTONIO VILLAROEL MURIEL

Faculty of Economics and Administrative Sciences (Victoria 471, Concepción; tel. (41) 204186; fax (41) 229946; e-mail jsaavedr@udec.cl; internet www.udec.cl/economia):
- Accounting and Auditing: GUILLERMO ORTÍZ VALENZUELA
- Administration: CARLOS BAQUEDANO VENEGAS
- Economics: IVÁN ARAYA GÓMEZ

Faculty of Education (tel. (41) 204221; fax (41) 226187; e-mail acastro@udec.cl; internet www.udec.cl/educacion):
- Curricula and Instruction: BEATRIZ FIGUEROA SANDOVAL
- Educational Sciences: DECLER MARTÍNEZ CARRASCO
- Physical Education: HUGO ARANGUIZ ABURTO
- Research Methodology and Informatics in Education: SERGIO ROJAS DÍAZ

Faculty of Engineering (Edmundo Larenas s/n, Concepción; tel. (41) 204307; fax (41) 214294; e-mail jzambran@udec.cl; internet www.ing.udec.cl):
- Chemical Engineering: RODRIGO BÓRQUEZ YÁÑEZ
- Civil Engineering: MÓNICA WOYWOOD YOKOTA
- Electrical Engineering: LAUTARO SALAZAR SILVA
- Industrial Engineering: ALEJANDRO CONCHA ASTUDILLO
- Mechanical Engineering: LUIS QUIROZ LARREA
- Metallurgical Engineering: JAIME ALVAREZ MOISAN
- Systems Engineering: RICARDO CONTRERAS ARRIAGADA

Faculty of Forestry Sciences (Victoria 631, Concepción; tel. (41) 204848; fax (41) 246004; e-mail facfor@udec.cl; internet www.udec.cl/forsweb):
- Forestry Management and Environment: MANUEL LINEROS PARRA
- Silviculture: MANUEL SÁNCHEZ OLATE

Faculty of Humanities and Art (tel. (41) 204404; fax (41) 259108; e-mail enunez@udec.cl; internet www.udec.cl/facultades/humarte/index.html):
- Foreign Languages: MARY FUENTES MORRISON
- Historical and Social Sciences: LEONARDO MAZZEI DE GRAZIA
- Music: LIONEL SAAVEDRA PANTOJA
- Philosophy: CLAUDIO TRONCOSCO BARRÍA
- Plastic Arts: EILEEN KELLY MILLÁN
- Spanish: MAURICIO OSTRIA GONZÁLEZ

Faculty of Law and Social Sciences (tel. (41) 204549; fax (41) 259136; e-mail japinto@udec.cl; internet www.facjursoc.udec.cl):
- Economic Law: EDUARDO JURY SANTIBAÑEZ
- History and Philosophy of Law: JESÚS ESCANDÓN ÁLOMAR
- Labour Law: GABRIELA LANATA FUENZALIDA
- Penal Law: JUANA SANHUEZA ROMERO
- Political and Administrative Sciences: JUAN TOLEDO CARTES
- Private Law: HERNÁN TRONCOSO LARRONDE
- Procedural Law: HÉCTOR OBERG YÁÑEZ
- Public Law: HERNÁN MOLINA GUAITA

Faculty of Medicine (Chacabuco esquina Janequeo, Concepción; tel. (41) 204407; fax (41) 223933; e-mail oenrique@udec.cl):
- Internal Medicine: HERNÁN SOTOMAYOR LEÓN
- Medical Education: EDUARDO FASCE HENRY
- Normal and Pathological Anatomy and Legal Medicine: HORACIO OSORIO URBINA
- Nursing: PATRICIA JARA CONCHA
- Obstetrics and Gynaecology: JORGE CABRERA DITZEL
- Obstetrics and Paediatrics: PAULINA HAEMMERLI DÍAZ
- Paediatrics: SONIA FIGUEROA YASIN
- Psychiatry and Mental Health: BENJAMIN VICENTE PARADA
- Public Health: HEBERTO PÉREZ CASTRO
- Specialities: RAÚL GONZÁLEZ RAMOS
- Surgery: ALBERTO GYHRA SOTO

Faculty of Natural Sciences and Oceanography (tel. (41) 204704; fax (41) 244805; e-mail fcarrasc@udec.cl; internet www.natura.udec.cl):
- Botany: ROBERTO RODRÍGUEZ RUIZ
- Oceanography: CIRO OYARZÚN GONZÁLEZ
- Zoology: MARGARITA MARCHANT SAN MARTÍN

Faculty of Pharmacy (tel. (41) 204208; fax (41) 231903; e-mail farmaweb@udec.cl; internet www.udec.cl/farmacia):
- Applied Biochemistry: NATALIA ULLOA MUÑOZ
- Bromatology, Nutrition and Dietetics: CLAUDIO VILLEGAS FERRARI
- Instrumental Analysis: ALDO RODRÍGUEZ ESPINOZA
- Pharmacy: CARMEN GODOY MOSCIATTI

Faculty of Physical Sciences and Mathematics (tel. (41) 204103; fax (41) 251529; e-mail decanato@gauss.cfm.udec.cl; internet www.cfm.udec.cl):
- Atmospheric and Oceanographic Physics: DANTE FIGUEROA MARTÍNEZ
- Mathematical Engineering: GABRIEL GATICA PÉREZ
- Mathematical Methods: RENÉ LETELIER ALBORNOZ
- Physics: JAIME ARANEDA SEPÚLVEDA
- Statistics: MARÍA VALENZUELA HERNÁNDEZ

Faculty of Social Sciences (tel. (41) 204244; fax (41) 220810; e-mail osociales@udec.cl; internet www.udec.cl/csociales):
- Psychology: MARÍA VICTORIA PÉREZ VILLALOBOS
- Social Communication: HUGO OLEA MORALES
- Social Services: ISIS CHAMBLAS GARCÍA
- Sociology: MANUEL BAEZA RODRIGUEZ

Faculty of Veterinary Medicine (Vicente Méndez 595, Chillán; tel. (42) 208786; fax (42) 275302; e-mail rubperez@udec.cl; internet www.chillan.udec.cl/veterinaria):
- Animal Production and Reproduction: OSCAR SKEWES RAMM
- Clinical Sciences: ARMANDO ISLAS LETELIER
- Pathology and Preventive Medicine: JUANA LOPEZ MARTIN

ATTACHED CENTRES

Centro EULA Chile: environmental sciences; Dir OSCAR PARRA BARRIENTOS.

Institute GEA: applied and geological sciences; Dir MARÍA EUGENIA CISTERNAS SILVA.

UNIVERSIDAD CATÓLICA DEL MAULE

Avda San Miguel 3605, CP 617 Talca
Telephone: (71) 203-300
Fax: (71) 241-767
E-mail: webmaster@hualo.ucm.cl
Internet: www.ucm.cl
Founded 1991
Private control; financially supported by the State
Rector: Dr CLAUDIO ROJAS MIÑO
Vice-Rector (Academic): HERNÁN MAUREIRA PAREJA
Vice-Rector (Finance and Administration): MARIANO VARAS HERNÁNDEZ
Secretary-General: ORLANDO ARAVENA AGUILERA
Library of 46,700 vols, 227 periodicals
Number of teachers: 183
Number of students: 5,628

DEANS

Faculty of Agrarian and Forestry Sciences: CLAUDIO RODRÍGUEZ FIGUEROA
Faculty of Education: MARCELO ROMERO MÉNDEZ
Faculty of Engineering: GUSTAVO LEDEZMA MATURANA
Faculty of Health Sciences: HÉCTOR FIGUEROA MARÍN
Faculty of Religion and Philosophy: JAMES MORIN ST ONGE

DIRECTORS

Institute of Basic Sciences: SERGIO LILLO INOSTROZA
Institute of General Studies: CARLOS DÍAZ VALENZUELA
Institute of Social Sciences: JUANA ARIAS ROJAS

UNIVERSIDAD CATÓLICA DEL NORTE

Avda Angamos 0610, Casilla 1280, Antofagasta
Telephone: (55) 355002
Fax: (55) 355093
E-mail: mcamus@ucn.cl
Internet: www.ucn.cl
Founded 1956
Language of instruction: Spanish
Private control
Academic year: March to December
Chancellor: Most Rev. PABLO LIZAMA RIQUELME
Rector: MISAEL CAMUS IBACACHE
Vice-Rector (Academic Affairs): CARLOS MUJICA ROJAS
Vice-Rector (Coquimbo Campus): LUÍS MONCAYO MARTÍNEZ
Vice-Rector (Economic Affairs): MIRIAM ATIENZO SOTO
General Secretary: VICTORIA GONZÁLEZ STUARDO
Head of Admissions Office: VERONICA ALFARO NAVARRA
Librarian: DRAHOMÍRA SRÝTROVÁ TOMÁSOVÁ
Library of 152,033 vols
Number of teachers: 301
Number of students: 8,088
Publications: *Boletín de Educación*, *Cuadernos de Arquitectura*, *Estudios Atacameños*, *Norte: Revista divulgación de ciencias, tecnologia y cultura* (science, technology and culture), *Revista de Derecho*, *Revista Proyecciones*, *Revista Reflejos*, *Revista Vertiente*, *Tercer Milenio*

DEANS

Antofagasta Campus (tel. (55) 355000; fax (55) 355093):
- Faculty of Architecture, Civil Engineering and Construction: PABLO REYES FRANZANI
- Faculty of Economics: ULISES BACHO GAHONA
- Faculty of Engineering and Geological Sciences: TEODORO POLITIS JARAMIS
- Faculty of Humanities: GEORGINA MORA JIMÉNEZ
- Faculty of Sciences: SARA AGUILERA MORALES

Coquimbo Campus (Larrondo 1281, Coquimbo; tel. (51) 209701; fax (51) 209707):
- Faculty of Marine Sciences: EXEQUIEL GONZÁLEZ BALBONTÍN

ATTACHED INSTITUTES

Archaeological Research Institute and Museum 'R. P. Gustavo Le Paige': Dir AGUSTÍN LLAGOSTERA MARTÍNEZ.

Centre for Biotechnology.

Centre for Integral Construction Improvement.

Centre for Investigation of Company Technology Management.

Institute of Applied Regional Economics: Dir PATRICIO AROCA GONZÁLEZ.

Institute of Astronomy: Dir (vacant).

UNIVERSIDAD CATÓLICA DE LA SANTÍSIMA CONCEPCIÓN

Caupolicán 491, Concepción
Telephone: (41) 246-175
Fax: (41) 212-318
E-mail: ucsc@ucsc.cl
Internet: www.ucsc.cl
Founded 1991
Private control; financially supported by the State
Rector: FERNANDO JIMÉNEZ LARRAÍN
Secretary-General: ROLANDO GUTIÉRREZ GONZÁLEZ
Vice-Rector (Academic): EDUARDO SOUPER ESPINOSA
Vice-Rector (Financial and Administrative Affairs): GABRIEL HIDALGO AEDO
Library of 73,000 vols, 2,311 periodicals
Number of teachers: 263
Number of students: 5,979

DEANS

Faculty of Economics and Administration: JORGE ALAN CLEVELAND
Faculty of Education: FERNANDO SOTO SOTO
Faculty of Engineering: HUBERT MENNICKENT MENA
Faculty of Law: FERNANDO SAENGER GIANONI
Faculty of Medicine: Dr ALVARO LLANCAQUEO VALERI
Faculty of Science: Dr RAMÓN AHUMADA B.

DIRECTORS

School of Journalism: MARIO URZÚA ARACENA (Dir)
Theological Centre: Dr JUAN CARLOS INOSTROZA LANAS (Dir)

ATTACHED INSTITUTE

Instituto Tecnológico: Colón 2766, Talcahuano; tel. (41) 735-070; fax (41) 735-078; internet it.ucsc.cl; Rector FERNANDO JIMÉNEZ LARRAIN.

UNIVERSIDAD CATÓLICA DE TEMUCO

Manuel Montt 56, 15-D Temuco
Telephone: (45) 205-205
Fax: (45) 234-126
E-mail: dara@uct.cl
Internet: www.uct.cl
Founded 1991
Private control; financially supported by the State
Academic year: March to November
Rector: MÓNICA JIMÉNEZ DE LA JARA
Vice-Rector (Academic): ALIRO BÓRQUEZ RAMÍREZ
Vice-Rector (Finance and Administration): PEDRO BAKOVIC VIÑALS
Library of 43,560 vols, 4,100 periodicals
Number of teachers: 213
Number of students: 4,854

DEANS

Faculty of Agricultural and Forestry Sciences: MARCO ANTONIO FERNÁNDEZ NAVARRETE
Faculty of Agriculture and Veterinary Sciences: ROLANDO VEGA AGUAYO
Faculty of Arts, Humanities and Social Sciences: MARIO SAMANIEGO SASTRE
Faculty of Education: RENÉ MORGAN MELGOSA
Faculty of Science: OSVALDO RUBILAR ALARCÓN
School of Law: RODRIGO COLOMA CORREA (Dir)
Institute of Theological Studies: JUAN LEONELLI LEONELLI (Dir)

ATTACHED RESEARCH INSTITUTES

Centre of Sociocultural Studies: tel. (45) 205-626; fax (45) 205-626; e-mail tduran@uct.cl; Dir Dra TERESA DURÁN PÉREZ.

Centre of Sustainable Development: tel. (45) 205-629; fax (45) 205-626; e-mail cds@uct.cl; Dir Dr ANDRÉS YURJEVIC MARSCHAL.

Institute of Regional Studies: tel. (45) 205-685; fax (45) 205-626; e-mail artufilu@uct.cl; Dir ARTURO HERNANDEZ SALLÁS.

UNIVERSIDAD TÉCNICA 'FEDERICO SANTA MARÍA'

Avda España 1680, Casilla 110V, Valparaíso Telephone: (32) 654246
Fax: (32) 654443
E-mail: consultas@utfsm.cl
Internet: www.utfsm.cl

Founded 1926
Private control
Language of instruction: Spanish
Academic year: March to January

Rector: ADOLFO ARATA ANDREANI
Vice-Rectors: DANIEL ALKALAY LOWITT (Academic), GIOVANNI PESCE SANTANA (Economic and Administrative Affairs)
Secretary-General: FRANCISCO GHISOLFO ARAYA
Library Director: MARÍA EUGENIA LAULIÉ

Library: see Libraries and Archives
Number of teachers: 456 (237 full-time, 219 part-time)
Number of students: 9,311

Publications: *Gestión Tecnológica* (2 a year), *Revista Industrias* (4 a year), *Scientia* (annually).

BRANCH CAMPUSES

Campus Rancagua: Gamero 212, Rancagua; Dir SERGIO ESTAY VILLALÓN.

Campus Santiago: Avda Santa María 6400, Vitacura, Santiago; Dir SERGIO OLAVARRÍA SIMONSEN.

Sede José Miguel Carrera: Avda Federico Santa María 6090, Viña del Mar; Dir ROSENDO ESTAY MARTÍNEZ.

Sede Rey Balduino de Bélgica: Avda Alemparte 943, Talcahuano; Dir ALEX ERIZ SOTO.

Private Universities

UNIVERSIDAD ADOLFO IBAÑEZ

Balmaceda 1625, Casilla 17, Recreo, Viña del Mar
Telephone: (32) 503500
Fax: (32) 664006
E-mail: info@uai.cl
Internet: www.uai.cl

Founded 1953
Private control
Language of instruction: Spanish
Academic year: March to December

Chancellor: JUAN IGNACIO DOMÍNGUEZ COVARRUBIAS
Academic Vice-Chancellor: VICTOR KÜLLMER KIEKEBUSCH
Executive Director: JUAN ALBERTO PALAU GUZMÁN
Director of Administration and Finance: CONSTANZA AGUIRRE APARICIO
Librarian: MARÍA ZINA JIMÉNEZ

Number of teachers: 46 full-time
Number of students: 1,444

Publications: *Cuadernos Jurídicos* (3 a year), *Informe Económico* (4 a year), *INTUS LEGERE: Anuario de Filosofía, Historia y Letras* (annually)

DEANS

Faculty of Business and Economic Sciences: ANTONIO KOVACEVICH BISKUPOVIC
Faculty of Law: FERNANDO FARREN CORNEJO
School of Industrial Engineering: LUIS SECCATORE GÓMEZ
Institute of Humanities: GONZALO ROJAS SÁNCHEZ

UNIVERSIDAD CENTRAL

Toesca 1783, Casilla 285-V, Correo 21, Santiago
Telephone: 699-51-51
Fax: 672-29-28
Internet: www.ucentral.cl

Founded 1982
Private control
Language of instruction: Spanish
Academic year: March to January

Rector: HUGO GÁLVEZ GAJARDO
Vice-Rectors: GONZALO HERNANDEZ URIBE (Academic), ENRIQUE MARTIN DAVIS (Administration), PEDRO CRUZAT FUSCHLOCHER (Development), VICENTE KOVACEVIC POCKLEPOVIC (Planning and Finance)
Secretary-General: CARMEN HERMOSILLA VALENCIA
Librarian: NELLY CORNEJO MENESES

Number of teachers: 662
Number of students: 6,177

Publications: *Boletín Informativo*, *Parthenon* (2 a year), *Perspectiva*, *Revista de Arquitectura*, *Revista de Derecho*, *Revista de Psicología*, *Universidad y Sociedad*

DEANS

Faculty of Architecture and Fine Arts: RENÉ MARTÍNEZ LEMOINE
Faculty of Economics and Administration: FERNANDO ESCOBAR CERDA
Faculty of Law: RUBEN OYARZUN GALLEGOS
Faculty of Physical Sciences and Mathematics: LUIS LUCERO ALDAY
Faculty of Social Sciences: ARISTIDES GIAVELLI ITURRIAGA

DIRECTORS

School of Accounting: MARTÍN GARRIDO ARAYA
School of Architecture and Fine Arts: ELIANA ISRAEL JACARD
School of Business Administration: ROBERTO SZEDERKENYI DICKINSON
School of Civil Construction: ROBERTO PERALTA CARRASCO
School of Civil Engineering (Public Construction): FERNANDO BONHOME CERDA
School of Data Processing and Computer Sciences: SERGIO QUEZADA GONZÁLEZ
School of Economics and Administration: EUGENIO ARRATIA DUQUE
School of Engineering in Administration and Agrarian Business: BENJAMIN LABBE VERGARA
School of Environmental Studies, Ecology and Landscape Architecture: PABLO VODANOVIC VENEGAS
School of Law: VICTOR SERGIO MENA VERGARA
School of Political and Administrative Sciences: HECTOR AGUILERA SEGURA
School of Primary Education: SELMA SIMONSTEIN FUENTES
School of Psychology: LEONARDO VILLARROEL ILICH

ATTACHED RESEARCH CENTRES

Centre of Economic and Administrative Research: San Ignacio 414, Santiago; tel. 6954010; fax 6727377; Dir CARLOS RETAMAL UMPIERREZ.

Centre of Housing Research: José Joaquin Prieto 10001, Casilla 6D, San Bernardo; tel. 5585311; fax 5270323; Dir ALFONSO RAPOSO MOYANO.

Centre of Juridical Research: Lord Cochrane 417, Santiago; tel. 6957533; fax 6727377; Dir RUBEN CELIS RODRIGUEZ.

UNIVERSIDAD DIEGO PORTALES

Avda Manuel Rodríguez Sur 415, Santiago 8370179
Telephone: (2) 6762000
Fax: (2) 6762112
E-mail: admsion@udp.cl
Internet: www.udp.cl

Founded 1982

Rector: MANUEL MONTT
Provost: FRANCISCO JAVIER CUADRA
Vice-Rector (Academic and Research): CARLOS PEÑA
Vice-Rector (Administration, Finance and Development): HORACIO RÍOS
Director of Communications and Admission: BÁRBARA FASANI
Librarian: PAULINA GODOY

Number of teachers: 1,208
Number of students: 10,930

Publications: *El Portaliano*, *Noticias Académicas*

DEANS

Faculty of Architecture, Design and Art: MATHÍAS KLOTZ
Faculty of Business: MIGUEL LÉON
Faculty of Communication: ANDRÉS VELASCO
Faculty of Engineering: MIGUEL LÉON
Faculty of Health Sciences: FERNANDO MÖNCKEBERG
Faculty of Humanities: CARMEN FARIÑA
Faculty of Human Sciences and Education: JUAN PABLO TORO
Faculty of Industrial Engineering and Data Processing: LUIS COURT
Faculty of Law: ANDRÉS CUNEO

DIRECTORS

Pedro Maldonado School of Accounting and Auditing: PILAR TORRES
School of Advertising: CRISTIÁN LEPORATI
School of Architecture: RICARDO ABUAUAD
School of Business Administration: CRISTINA HUBE
School of Civil and Construction Engineering: MIGUEL MELLADO
School of Dentistry: MAXIMILIANO BENAVENTE
School of Design: FEDERICO SÁNCHEZ
School of Education: EDUARDO CABEZÓN
School of History: DIANA VENEROS
School of Industrial Engineering: GASTÓN CONCHA
School of Informatics for Management: LUIS ALBERTO GAETE
School of Informatics and Telecommunications Engineering: MIGUEL MELLADO
School of Journalism: ANDRÉS AZOCAR
School of Law: ESTER VALENZUELA
School of Literature: NICANOR PARRA
School of Medical Technology: MARÍA LILA VERA
School of Medicine: ALICIA VÁSQUEZ
School of Nursing: MARÍA ANGÉLICA PIWONKA
School of Political Sciences: MA. DE LOS ÁNGELES FERNÁANDEZ
Institute of Political Sciences and Sociology: CRISTÓBAL MARÍN
School of Psychology: PILAR TORRES
School of Sociology: CRISTÓBAL MARIN
School of Theatre: RAÚL OSORIO
School of Technical Engineering in Marketing and Finance: PEDRO MALDONADO
Associate Degree and Social Sciences Program: MA. ANTONIETA HUERTA

UNIVERSIDAD GABRIELA MISTRAL

Avda Ricardo Lyon 1177, Santiago
Telephone: 2734545
Internet: www.ugm.cl

Founded 1981
Academic year: March to January

Rector: ALICIA ROMO ROMÁN
Administrative Director: ESTANISLAO GALOFRÉ
Librarian: CARMEN BUSQUETS

Number of teachers: 450
Number of students: 3,500

DIRECTORS

Department of Economics and Business Administration: FRANCISCO JAVIER LABBÉ
Department of Education: SYLVIA SAILER
Department of Engineering: RODOLFO MARTÍNEZ
Department of Journalism: LURETO CAVIEDES
Department of Law: LISANDRO SERRANO
Department of Psychology: HERNÁN BERWART
Department of Social Sciences: RICARDO RIESCO

ATTACHED INSTITUTES

Centro de Estudios Económicos, Jurídicos, Administrativos y Sociales de la Empresa.
Centro de Estudios de la Mujer.
Instituto de Economía.
Instituto de Estudios del Pacífico.
Instituto de Lenguas.

UNIVERSIDAD PEREZ ROSALES

Brown Norte 290, Ñuñoa, Santiago Metropolitana
Telephone: (2) 7571300
Fax: (2) 2238825
E-mail: unitec@uvipro.cl
Internet: www.upper.cl
Founded 1992
Private control
Rector: KARIN RIEDEMANN H.
Secretary-General: ELISA CASTRO P.
Vice-Rector (Academic): CECILIA IBARRA M.
Vice-Rector (Teaching and Research): MÓNICA HERRERA P.
Director of Extension Studies and Humanities: PÍA MONTALVA D.
Head Librarian: CLAUDIA GILARDONI.

UNIVERSIDAD SAN SEBASTIÁN

Casilla 3427, Correo Concepción
Telephone: (41) 230116
Fax: (41) 244563
E-mail: uss@mater.uss.cl
Internet: www.uss.cl
Founded 1989
Private control
Academic year: March to December
Rector: GUIDO ALFREDO MELLER MAYR
Vice-Rector: SOLEDAD RAMÍREZ GATICA
Registrar: FERNANDO CANITROT MARTÍNEZ
Librarian: MARGARITA VALDERRAMA CÁCERES
Library of 6,000 vols
Number of teachers: 174
Number of students: 1,714

DEANS

School of Business Studies and Administration: JOSÉ LUIS PARRA ARIAS
School of Child Education: MAGDALENA BURMEISTER CAMPOS
School of Information Sciences: CRISTIÁN ANTOINE FAÚNDEZ
School of Law: MARCELO CONTRERAS HAUSER
School of Medicine: Dr ALEXIS LAMA TORO
School of Psychology: CARMEN BONNEFOY DIBARRART
School of Social Services: MARTA MONTORY TORRES

Colleges

Escuela Militar 'General Bernardo O'Higgins': Los Militares 4500, Las Condes, Santiago; fax 2082946; f. 1817 (by General O'Higgins); 90 military instructors and officials, 80 civilian instructors; 700 students; library: 25,000 vols; Dir Col OSCAR IZURIETA FERRER; Librarians OSCAR CORNEJO C., JUAN CARLOS MEDINA V.; publs *Revista 'Cien Aguilas'* (annually), *Memorial del Ejército, Armas y Servicio*.

Facultad Latinoamericana de Ciencias Sociales (FLACSO): Avda Dag Hammarskjold 3269, Vitacura, Santiago; tel. (2) 2900200; fax (2) 2900263; e-mail flacso@flacso.cl; internet www.flacso.cl; f. 1957; postgraduate training and research centre for Latin America; library: 30,000 vols, 710 periodicals; 16 teachers; 60 students; Dir CLAUDIO FUENTES SAAVEDRA; Librarian MARÍA INÉS BRAVO; publ. *Fuerzas Armadas y Sociedad* (3 a year).

Instituto Agrícola Metodista 'El Vergel' (Methodist Agricultural Institute): Casilla 2-D, Angol; tel. (45) 712103; fax (45) 711202; f. 1919; ornamental plant nursery, fruit nursery, fruit-garden, dairy, cattle ranch, apiculture, tourism, workshops, packing; museum; Administrator Rev. MARIO MAYER.

PEOPLE'S REPUBLIC OF CHINA

The Higher Education System

Some of the oldest institutions of higher education in the world are to be found in the People's Republic of China (for example, Hunan University dates back to the establishment of Yuelu Academy in 976). Higher education is dominated by state institutions, although some private universities have been established in recent years, and administration reflects the centralized nature of the State. During the 1950s a number of higher education establishments were designated 'key' institutions and received better staff, facilities and funding. The term 'key institution' is now officially defunct but is still used to denote the highest-rated institutions. The Cultural Revolution (1966–76) led to radical changes in the higher education system, as entrance examinations and continuous assessment were abolished; however, many of the changes were later reversed (the National University Entrance Examination was re-introduced in 1977). Following university unrest in 1989, including the Tianenman Square protests in Beijing, students were required to undergo a year of political 'training' prior to university. Further reforms were launched in 1992, under which institutions were given greater autonomy in decision-making. There was also a trend towards mergers that led to a decrease in the number of higher education institutions, from 1,984 in 1998 to 1,731 in 2004. In that year a total of 13.3m. students were enrolled in institutes of higher education. A new higher education reform programme was launched in early 2000, with the aim of modernizing courses and teaching materials and improving pedagogy.

Performance in the National University Entrance Examination, which was re-instated in 1977 following the Cultural Revolution, represents the main criteria for admission to higher education. Additionally, students may be required to undergo political education and perform some form of industrial or agricultural labour. The examination is conducted on a national basis and students are examined in five core subjects. A score in the range of 550–600 will gain admission to university. The university degree system consists of Xueshi (Bachelors), Shoshi (Masters) and Boshi (Doctorate). Bachelors degrees last four years and conform to one of the 249 programmes defined by the Ministry of Education. In 1989 it was announced that selection of postgraduate students would also be on the basis of 'moral' and physical fitness. A Masters degree requires two to three years of further study after the Bachelors, including research and submission of a thesis. The Doctorate is awarded after three years of study following the Masters and concludes with submission and defence of a thesis.

Diplomas from technical and vocational education at tertiary level are available from a number of different types of institution, and usually require two to three years of study. Institutions offering technical and vocational education include vocational technology colleges, vocational universities, radio and television universities (Dianda) and spare-time universities (Yeda). Vocational education is supervised by the Department of Education and Labour.

Learned Societies

GENERAL

Chinese Academy of Sciences: 52 San Li He Rd, Beijing 100864; tel. (10) 68597219; fax (10) 68511095; f. 1949; academic divisions of Mathematics and Physics (Dir Prof. WANG SHOUGUAN), Biological Science (Dir Prof. ZOU CHENGLU), Chemistry (Dir Prof. ZHANG CUNHAO), Earth Sciences (Dir Prof. TU GUANGZHI), Technological Sciences (Dir Prof. Prof. SHI CHANGXU); 633 mems; 13 foreign mems; attached research institutes: see Research Institutes; library: libraries: see Libraries and Archives; Pres. Prof. LU YONGXIANG; Sec.-Gen. Prof. ZHU XUAN.

Chinese Academy of Social Sciences: 5 Jianguomen Nei Da Jie, Beijing 100732; tel. 65137744; fax 65138154; internet www.cass.net.cn; f. 1977; attached research institutes: see Research Institutes; Pres. CHEN KUIYUAN; Sec.-Gen. ZHU JINCHANG.

UNESCO Office Beijing: Waijiaogongyu 5-13-3, Jianguomenwai Compound, Beijing 100600; tel. (10) 65322828; fax (10) 65324854; e-mail beijing@unesco.org; internet www.unescobeijing.org; designated Cluster Office for People's Republic of China, Democratic People's Republic of Korea, Japan, Mongolia and Republic of Korea; Dir YASUYUKI AOSHIMA.

AGRICULTURE, FISHERIES AND VETERINARY SCIENCE

China Society of Fisheries: 31 Minfeng Lane, Beijing 100032; tel. 66020794; fax 66062346; 15,000 mems; library of 12,000 vols; Pres. ZHANG YANXI; publs *Journal of Fisheries of China*, *Marine Fisheries*, *Freshwater Fisheries*, *Deep-sea Fisheries*, *Scientific Fish Farming*.

Chinese Academy of Agricultural Sciences: 30 Bai Shi Qiao Rd, Beijing 100081; tel. 62174433; fax 62174142; f. 1957; 40 attached research institutes; library of 650,000 vols, 7,000 periodicals; Pres. LU FEIJIE; publs *Acta Agronomica Sinica*, *Acta Horticulturae Sinica*, *Acta Phyliphulacica Sinica etc.*

Chinese Academy of Forestry: Wan Shou Shan, 100091 Beijing; tel. (10) 62582211; fax (10) 62584229; f. 1958; 4,700 mems; attached research institutes: see Research Institutes; library of 400,000 vols; Pres. JIANG ZEHUI; publs *Scientia Silvae Sinicae*, *Forestry Science and Technology*, *Chemistry and Industry of Forest Products*, *Forestry Research*, *Wood Industry*, *China Forestry Abstracts*, *Foreign Forestry Abstracts*, *Foreign Forest Product Industry Abstracts*, *World Forestry Research*.

Chinese Agricultural Economics Society: Agro-Exhibition, Beijing; Pres. CAI ZIWEI.

Chinese Association of Agricultural Science Societies: Ministry of Agriculture and Fisheries, 11 Nongzhanguan Nanli, Beijing 100026; f. 1917; Pres. HONG FUZENG; Sec.-Gen. LI HUAIZHI.

Chinese Sericulture Society: Sibaidu, Zhenjiang, Jiangsu 212018; tel. (511) 5616661; fax (511) 5622507; e-mail zjddsri@pulic.zj.js.cn; f. 1963; 10,000 mems; library of 50,000 vols; Pres. XIANG ZHONGHUAI; Sec.-Gen. ZHUANG DAHUAN; publ. *Sericultural Science* (quarterly).

Chinese Society for Horticultural Science: 12 Zhongguancun Nandajie, Beijing 100081; tel. (10) 68919528; fax (10) 62174123; e-mail ivfcaas@public3.bta.net.cn; f. 1930; 3,000 mems; Pres. ZHU DEWEI; publ. *Acta Horticulturae Sinica* (6 a year).

Chinese Society of Agricultural Machinery: 1 Beishatan, Deshengmen Wai, Beijing 100083; tel. (10) 64882231; fax (10) 64883508; e-mail bhmetecj@public3.bta.net.cn; f. 1963; 26,245 mems; library of 1,500,000 vols; Pres. LI SHOUREN; Sec.-Gen. GAO YUANEN; publs *Transactions of the Chinese Society of Agricultural Machinery* (quarterly), *Farm Machinery* (monthly), *Rural Mechanization* (6 a year), *China Agricultural Mechanization* (6 a year), *Tractor and Automobile Drivers* (6 a year).

Chinese Society of Forestry: Wanshoushan, Beijing 100091; tel. (10) 62889817; fax (10) 62888312; e-mail csf@csf.forestry.ac.cn; f. 1917; 75,000 mems; Pres. LIU YUHE; publ. *Scientia Silvae Sinicae* (6 a year).

Chinese Society of Tropical Crops: Baodao Xincun, Danzhou, Hainan; tel. (898) 23300157; fax (898) 23300157; e-mail scutafao@yahoo.com; f. 1978; 4,474 mems; library of 250,000 vols; Chair. ZENG YUZHUANG, YU RANGSHUI; Sec.-Gen. ZHENG WENRONG; publ. *Chinese Journal of Tropical Crops* (4 a year).

Crop Science Society of China: Institute of Crop Breeding and Cultivation, 30 Bai Shi Qiao Rd, Beijing 100081; tel. (10) 68918616; fax (10) 68975212; f. 1961; 22,000 mems; Pres. WANG LIANZHENG; Sec.-Gen. CHEN XINHUA; publs *Crops* (6 a year), *Acta Agronomica Sinica* (6 a year).

Soil Science Society of China: POB 821, Nanjing 210008; tel. (25) 86881532; fax (25)

86881000; e-mail jmzhou@issas.ac.cn; f. 1945; 15,000 mems; Pres. Prof. ZHOU JIANMIN; publs *Acta Pedologica Sinica* (6 a year), *Journal of Soil Science* (6 a year), *Pedosphere* (6 a year).

ARCHITECTURE AND TOWN PLANNING

Architectural Society of China: 9 Sanlihe Rd, Beijing 100835; tel. (10) 88082238; fax (10) 88082222; e-mail asc@mail.cin.gov.cn; f. 1953; 30,000 mems; library of 25,000 vols; Pres. SONG CHUNHUA; publs *Architectural Journal* (monthly), *Journal of Building Structure* (6 a year), *Architectural Knowledge* (monthly).

Chinese Society for Urban Studies: Bai Wanzhuang, Beijing 100835; tel. (10) 68393424; fax (10) 68313149; e-mail zhaibh@mail.cin.gov.cn; internet www.urbanstudies.org.cn; f. 1984; part of Min. of Construction; 30,000 mems; Pres. ZHOU GANSHI; Sec.-Gen. GU WENXUAN; publ. *Urban Studies* (6 a year).

BIBLIOGRAPHY, LIBRARY SCIENCE AND MUSEOLOGY

Chinese Archives Society: 21 Fengshen Hutong, Beijing; tel. (10) 66175130; fax (10) 66183636; e-mail cas@public.gb.com.cn; f. 1981; 74 institutional mems, 7,252 individual mems; Chair. SHEN ZHENGLE; publ. *Archive Science Study* (4 a year).

Chinese Association of Natural Science Museums: 126 Tian Qiao South St, Beijing 100050; tel. (10) 67024431; fax (10) 67021254; f. 1979; 1,200 individual mems; 320 group mems; Sec.-Gen. XIE YENGHUAN; publs *Newsletter* (quarterly), *China Nature* (6 a year, jointly with Beijing Natural History Museum and China Wildlife Conservation Association).

Chinese Society of Library Science: 39 Bai Shi Qiao Rd, Beijing 100081; tel. 68415566 ext. 5563; fax 68419271; f. 1979; 10,150 mems; Pres. LIU DEYOU; publ. *Journal of Library Science in China* (in Chinese, every 2 months).

ECONOMICS, LAW AND POLITICS

China Law Society: 6 Xizhi Men Nan Da Jie, Beijing 100035; tel. 66150114; fax 66182128; f. 1982; ind. academic instn for study of the Chinese socialist legal system; 523 corporate mems; 100,000 individual mems; library of 40,000 vols, incl. China Catalogue of Law Books; Pres. REN JIANXIN; Sec.-Gen. SONG SHUTAO; publs *Democracy and Law Journal*, *China Law Yearbook*, *Law of China*.

Chinese Association for European Studies: 5 Jiannei, Beijing 100732; tel. 65138428; f. 1981; 1,000 mems; Chair. Prof. QIU YUANLUN; publ. *European Studies* (every 2 months, co-edited with Inst. of West European Studies).

Chinese Association of Political Science: c/o Chinese Academy of Social Sciences, 5 Jianguomennei Ave, Beijing; tel. 65125048; f. 1980; asscn of workers in the field of political science; 1,025 mems; Pres. JIANG LIU; Sec.-Gen. ZHANG ZHIRONG; publs *Studies in Political Science* (every 2 months), *Political Science Abroad* (every 2 months).

Chinese Legal History Society: Law Dept, Beijing University, Haidian District, Beijing 100871; tel. 62561166; f. 1979; studies history of Chinese and foreign legal systems; 300 mems; Pres. Prof. ZHANG GUOHUA; Chief Sec. RAO XINXIAN; publs *Review of Legal History*, *Communications of Legal History*.

Chinese Research Society for the Modernization of Management: C/o China Association for Science and Technology, Sanlihe, Xijiao, Beijing; tel. 68318877 ext. 524; f. 1978; Pres. XIE SHAOMING; publ. *Modernization of Management*.

Chinese Society of the History of International Relations: 12 Poshangcun, Haidian District, Beijing; Pres. WANG SHENGZU.

EDUCATION

Chinese Education Society: 35 Damucang Lane, Beijing 100816; Pres. ZHANG CHENGXIAN.

HISTORY, GEOGRAPHY AND ARCHAEOLOGY

Chinese Historical Society: 5 Jianguomennei St, Beijing 100732.

Chinese Society for Future Studies: 32 Baishiqiao Rd, Haidian District, Beijing 100081; f. 1979; 1,000 mems; CEO DU DAGONG; publ. *Future and Development* (quarterly).

Chinese Society of Geodesy, Photogrammetry and Cartography: Baiwanzhuang, Beijing; tel. 68992229; f. 1959; 3,000 mems; Pres. Prof. WANG ZHIZHUO; Sec.-Gen. Prof. YANG KAI; publ. *Acta Geodetica et Cartographica Sinica*.

Chinese Society of Oceanography: 10 Fuxingmenwai, Beijing; Pres. PENG DEQING.

Geographical Society of China: No. A11, Datun Rd, Beijing 100101; tel. (10) 64870663; fax (10) 64889598; e-mail gsc@igsnrr.ac.cn; internet www.gsc.org.cn; f. 1909; 31 provincial divisions; special commissions: physical geog., climatology, hydrography, geomorphology and quaternary studies, marine geog., environmental geog. and chemical geog., medical geog., human geog., economic geog., sustained agriculture and rural development, urban geog., tourist geog., historical geog., world geog., quantative geog., cartography and geographical information systems; working commissions: geographical education, popularization of geographical knowledge, edition and publication, young geographers, academic affairs, international scientific and technical co-operation (China National Committee for International Geographical Union—IGU); branch societies: glaciology and geocryology, environmental remote sensing, desert research, coastal open region, mountain research, Changjang river research; geographical construction in the arid and semi-arid region; 18,900 mems; Pres. LU DADAO; Sec.-Gen. ZHANG GUOYOU; publs *Acta Geographica Sinica* (6 a year), *Economic Geography* (6 a year), *China National Geography* (monthly), *Journal of Glaciology and Geocryology* (6 a year), *Journal of Remote Sensing* (6 a year), *Human Geography* (6 a year), *Journal of Mountain Science* (6 a year), *World Regional Studies* (4 a year), *Journal of Geographical Sciences* (English edition, 4 a year), *Historical Geography* (4 a year).

LANGUAGE AND LITERATURE

Alliance Française: 6, Yangqiao Beili, Fengtai Qu, Beijing 100077; tel. (10) 65274157; fax (10) 67220943; e-mail afpek@163bj.com; internet www.alliancefrancaise.org.cn; offers courses and exams in French language and culture and promotes cultural exchange with France; attached teaching centres in Chengdu, Guangzhou, Nanjing, Shanghai and Wuhan.

British Council: Cultural and Education Section, British Embassy, 4th Fl., Landmark Bldg Tower 1, 8 North Dongsanhuan Rd, Chaoyang District, 100004 Beijing; tel. (10) 6590-6903; fax (10) 6590-0977; e-mail enquiry@britishcouncil.org.cn; internet www.britishcouncil.org/china; offers courses and exams in English language and British culture and promotes cultural exchange with the UK; attached offices in Shanghai, Guangzou and Chongqing; Dir and Cultural Counsellor MICHAEL O'SULLIVAN.

Chinese Writers' Association: 2 Shatanbeijie, Beijing 100720; 20,000 mems; Chair. BA JIN; publs include *People's Literature* (monthly), *Chinese Writers* (every 2 months), *Poetry* (monthly), *Minority Literature* (monthly), *Literature and Arts* (weekly newspaper).

Goethe-Institut: Cyber Tower, Bldg B, 17th Fl., No. 2, Zhong Guan Cun South Ave, Haidian District, Beijing 100086; tel. (10) 82512909; fax (10) 82512903; e-mail info@peking.goethe.org; internet www.goethe.de/os/pek/deindex.htm; offers courses and exams in German language and culture and promotes cultural exchange with Germany; attached centres in Shanghai; library of 10,000 vols; Dir DR ULRICH NOWAK.

MEDICINE

China Academy of Traditional Chinese Medicine: 18 Beixincang, Dongzhimennei, Beijing 100700; tel. (10) 64014411 ext. 2435; fax (10) 64016387; f. 1955; 12 attached research institutes; library of 300,000 vols; Pres. FU SHIYUAN; publs *Journal of Traditional Chinese Medicine*, *Chinese Acupuncture and Moxibustion*, *Chinese Journal of Integrated Traditional and Western Medicine*.

China Association of Traditional Chinese Medicine: A4 Yinghualu, Hepingli Dongjie, Beijing 100029; tel. 64212828; fax 64220867; f. 1979; 80,000 mems; Chair. CUI YULI; Gen. Sec. (vacant); publ. *China Journal of Traditional Chinese Medicine* (every 2 months).

China Association of Zhenjiu (Acupuncture and Moxibustion): 18 Beixincang Dongcheng Qu, Beijing 100700; tel. 64030611; f. 1979; 13,000 mems; Pres. HU XIMING; Sec.-Gen. LI WEIHENG; publ. *Chinese Acupuncture and Moxibustion*.

Chinese Academy of Medical Sciences and Peking Union Medical College: 9 Dongdan Santiao, Beijing 100730; tel. 553447; fax 5124876; f. 1917 (College), 1956 (Academy); the two instns have a single governing body; attached research institutes: see Research Institutes; Pres. Dr BA DENIAN; publ. *Chinese Medical Sciences Journal*.

Chinese Anti-Cancer Association: 52 Fucheng, Haidian District, Beijing 100036; tel. (10) 88140653; fax (10) 88140653; e-mail xuzhigang@caca.org.cn; internet www.caca.org.cn; f. 1985; 22,000 mems; Pres. Dr XU GUANGWEI; publs *Chinese Journal of Clinical Oncology* (monthly), *Chinese Journal of Cancer Biotherapy* (4 a year), *Chinese Journal of Cancer Research* (in English, 4 a year), *Journal of Practical Oncology* (6 a year), *Research on Prevention and Treatment of Cancer* (6 a year), *Cancer Rehabilitation* (6 a year).

Chinese Anti-Tuberculosis Society: 42 Dung-si-xi-da St, Beijing; tel. 553685; Pres. HUANG DINGCHEN; publ. *Bulletin* (quarterly).

Chinese Association for Mental Health: 5 An Kang Hutong, De Wai, Beijing 100088; tel. (10) 82085385; fax (10) 62359838; e-mail camh@163bj.com; internet www.camh.org.cn; f. 1985; 30,000 mems; Pres. CAI ZHUOJI; Sec.-Gen. LI ZHANJIANG; publs *Chinese Mental Health Journal* (12 a year), *Chinese Journal of Clinical Psychology* (4 a year), *Chinese Journal of Health Psychology* (6 a year).

Chinese Association of Integrated Traditional and Western Medicine: 18 Beixincang, Dongzhimennei, Beijing; tel. (10) 64010688; fax (10) 64010688; e-mail kjchen@mimi.cnc.ac.cn; f. 1981; 20,000 mems; Pres. CHEN KEJI; Sec.-Gen. CHEN SHIGUI; publ. *Chinese Journal of Integrated Traditional and Western Medicine* (monthly in Chinese, 4 a year in English).

Chinese Medical Association: 42 Dongsi Xidajie, Beijing; tel. 551943; tel. (10) 65265331; fax (10) 65265331; f. 1915; library of 80,000 vols; Pres. BAI XIQING; publs *Chinese Medical Journal* (English edition, monthly), *National Medical Journal of China* (monthly), *Chinese Journal of Internal Medicine* (monthly), *Chinese Journal of Surgery* (monthly).

Chinese Nursing Association: 42 Dongsi Xidajie, Beijing 100710; tel. (10) 65265331; fax (10) 65265331; f. 1909; Pres. ZENG XIYUAN; publ. *Chinese Journal of Nursing* (monthly).

Chinese Nutrition Society: 29 Nanwei Rd, Beijing 100050; tel. 63043472; fax 63041352; e-mail cnsoc@public3.bta.net.cn; internet www.cnsoc.org; f. 1981; 7,026 mems; Pres. GE KEYOU; publ. *Acta Nutrimenta* (Chinese and English, 4 a year).

Chinese Pharmaceutical Association: A38 Lishi Rd N., Beijing 100810; tel. 68316576; f. 1907; Pres. QI MAIJIA.

Chinese Pharmacological Society: 1 Xian Nong Tan St, Beijing 100050; tel. 63013366 ext. 404; fax 63017757; f. 1979; Pres. Prof. ZHANG JUNTIAN; Sec.-Gen. Prof. LIN ZHIBIN; publs *Acta Pharmacologica Sinica*, *Chinese Journal of Pharmacology and Toxicology*, *Chinese Pharmacological Bulletin*, *Pharmacology and Clinics of Chinese Materia Medica*.

NATURAL SCIENCES

General

China Association for Science and Technology (CAST): 3 Fuxing, Beijing 100863; tel. (10) 68571898; fax (10) 68571897; e-mail cast@public.bta.net.cn; internet www.cast.org.cn; f. 1958; almost all societies in China are affiliated members; organizes academic exchanges, int. conferences and in-service training for scientists, engineers and technicians; library of 50,000 vols; Pres. ZHOU GUANGZHAO.

Chinese Society for Oceanology and Limnology: 7 Nanhai Rd, Qingdao 266071; tel. (532) 2879062 ext. 3402; fax (532) 2870882; f. 1950; 7,000 mems; Pres. QIN YUNSHAN; Sec.-Gen. ZHOU MINGJIANG; publs *Oceanologia et Limnologia Sinica* (in Chinese, every 2 months), *Chinese Journal of Oceanology and Limnology* (quarterly, in English).

Chinese Society of the History of Science and Technology: 137 Chao Nei St, Beijing 100010; tel. (10) 64043989; fax (10) 64017637; f. 1980; 1,500 mems; Pres X. ZEZONG, LU YONGXIANG; publs *Studies in the History of Natural Sciences* (quarterly), *China Historical Materials of Science and Technology* (quarterly).

Biological Sciences

Biophysical Society of China: 15 Datun Rd, Chaoyang District, 100101 Beijing; tel. (10) 64889869; fax (10) 64871293; e-mail bscott@sun5.ibp.ac.cn; internet bsc.org.cn; f. 1980; 2,300 mems; Pres. Prof. ZHAO NANMING; Sec.-Gen. Prof. SHEN XUN; publs *Acta Biophysica Sinica* (4 a year), *Progress in Biochemistry and Biophysics* (6 a year).

Botanical Society of China: 20 Naxincun, Xiangshan, Beijing 100093; tel. (10) 62591431; fax (10) 62591431; e-mail bsco@public.bta.net.cn; 15,000 mems; Pres. KUANG TINGYUN; publs *Acta Botanica Sinica* (monthly), *Acta Phytotaxonomica* (6 a year), *Acta Phytoecologica et Geobotanica Sinica* (4 a year), *Chinese Bulletin of Botany* (4 a year), *Bulletin of Biology* (monthly), *Plants* (6 a year).

China Zoological Society: 19 Zhong Guan Cun Lu, Beijing; tel. 62552368; fax 62552368; e-mail czs@panda.ioz.ac.cn; f. 1934; 11,600 mems; Pres. CHEN DAYUAN; publs *Acta Zoologica Sinica* (6 a year), *Acta Zootaxonomica Sinica* (4 a year), *Acta Theriologica Sinica* (4 a year), *Acta Arachnologica Sinica* (2 a year), *Acta Parasitologica et Medica Entomologica Sinica* (4 a year), *Chinese Journal of Zoology* (6 a year).

Chinese Association for Physiological Sciences: 42 Dongsixidajie, Beijing 100710; Pres. CHEN MENGQIN.

Chinese Association of Animal Science and Veterinary Medicine: 33 Nongfengli, Dongdaqiao, Chao Yang District, Beijing 100020; tel. (10) 65005934; fax (10) 65005670; e-mail caavxshb@public.bta.net.cn; f. 1936; 50,000 mems; Pres. WU CHANGXIN; Sec.-Gen. YAN HANPING; publs *Chinese Journal of Animal and Veterinary Sciences*, *Chinese Journal of Animal Science*, *Chinese Journal of Veterinary Medicine*.

Chinese Society for Anatomical Sciences: 42 Dongsi Xidajie, Beijing 100710; tel. 65133311 ext. 247; fax 65123754; f. 1920; 3,000 mems; Pres. XU QUNYUAN; Sec.-Gen. LIU BIN; publs *Acta Anatomica Sinica* (4 a year), *Chinese Journal of Anatomy* (4 a year), *Chinese Journal of Clinical Anatomy* (4 a year), *Journal of Neuroanatomy* (4 a year), *Chinese Journal of Histochemistry and Cytochemistry* (4 a year), *Progress of Anatomical Sciences* (4 a year).

Chinese Society for Microbiology: Zhongguancun, Beijing 100080; tel. (10) 62554677; fax (10) 62554677; e-mail chenggs@sun.im.ac.cn; f. 1952; Pres. WEN YUNMEI; publs *Acta Microbiologica Sinica*, *Acta Mycologica Sinica*, *Chinese Journal of Biotechnology*, *Chinese Journal of Virology*, *Microbiology*, *Chinese Journal of Zoonoses*.

Chinese Society of Biochemistry and Molecular Biology: 15 Datun Rd, Chao Yang District, Beijing 100101; tel. (10) 64889859; fax (10) 64872026; e-mail csbmb@sun5.ibp.ac.cn; internet csbmb.ibp.ac.cn; f. 1979; 1,000 mems; Pres. C. L. TSOU; Sec.-Gen. J. M. ZHOU; publs *Chemistry of Life* (every 2 months), *Chinese Journal of Biochemistry and Molecular Biology* (every 2 months).

Chinese Society of Environmental Sciences: 115 Xizhimennei Nanxiaojie, Beijing; tel. 661006; f. 1979; 22,000 individual mems; 20 industrial/corporate mems; Pres. LI JINGZHAO; Sec.-Gen. QU GEPING; publs *China Environmental Science*, *China Environmental Management*, *Environmental Chemistry*, *Environmental Engineering*, *Environment*.

Chinese Society of Plant Physiology: 300 Fongling Rd, Shanghai; tel. 64042090; fax 64042385; f. 1963; 4,000 mems; Chair. Prof. TANG ZHANGCHENG; publs *Acta Phytophysiologica Sinica* (quarterly), *Plant Physiology Communications* (every 2 months).

Ecological Society of China: 19 Zhongguancun Lu, Beijing 100080; tel. (10) 62565694; fax (10) 62562775; f. 1979; 5,500 mems; Pres. Prof. WANG ZUWANG; Sec.-Gen. Prof. WANG RUSONG; publs *Journal of Ecology* (6 a year), *Acta Ecologica Sinica* (6 a year), *Journal of Applied Ecology* (4 a year).

Entomological Society of China: 19 Zhongguancun Lu, Haidian, Beijing 100080; tel. (10) 62565687; fax (10) 62630062; e-mail wangmm@panda.ioz.ac.cn; f. 1944; 11,000 mems; Pres. ZHANG GUANGXUE; Gen. Sec. LI DIANMO; publs *Acta Entomologica Sinica* (in Chinese), *Acta Zootaxonomia Sinica* (in Chinese), *Entomological Knowledge* (in Chinese), *Entomologia Sinica* (in Chinese), *Acta Parasitologica et Medica* (in Chinese).

Genetics Society of China: Bldg 917, Datun Rd, Andingmenwai, Beijing 100101; tel. 64919944; fax 64914896; f. 1978; 400 nat. mems, 6,600 mems of local socs; Pres. LI ZHENSHENG; Sec.-Gen. CHEN SHOUYI; publs *Acta Genetica Sinica*, *Hereditas* (every 2 months).

Palaeontological Society of China: 39 E. Beijing Rd, Nanjing 210008; tel. (25) 3612664; fax (25) 3357026; e-mail muxinan@public.1.ptt.js.cn; f. 1929; 1,230 mems; Pres. MU XINAN; Sec.-Gen. SUN GE; publ. *Acta Palaeontologica Sinica* (4 a year).

Mathematical Sciences

Chinese Mathematical Society: C/o Institute of Mathematics, Chinese Academy of Sciences, Beijing 100080; tel. (10) 62551022; fax (10) 62568356; e-mail cms@math08.math.ac.cn; f. 1935; Pres. K. C. CHANG; Sec.-Gen. LI WENLIN.

Physical Sciences

Acoustical Society of China: 17 Zhongguancun St, Beijing 100080; tel. (10) 62553765; fax (10) 62553898; f. 1985; 3,030 mems; Pres. CHEN TONG; Sec.-Gen. HOU CHADHUAN; publs *Acta Acustica* (every 2 months), *Applied Acoustics* (quarterly), *Chinese Journal of Acoustics* (quarterly, English version of *Acta Acustica*).

Chinese Academy of Meteorological Sciences: 7 Block 11, Hepingli, Beijing; tel. 64211631; fax 64218703; attached research institutes: see Research Institutes.

Chinese Aerodynamics Research Society: POB 2425, Beijing; Pres. ZHUANG GENGGAN.

Chinese Astronomical Society: Purple Mountain Observatory, Nanjing, Jiangsu 210008; tel. (25) 3302147; fax (25) 3301459; f. 1922; 1,611 mems; Pres. FANG CHENG; publs *Acta Astronomica Sinica* (4 a year), *Acta Astrophysica Sinica* (4 a year).

Chinese Chemical Society: POB 2709, Beijing 100080; tel. (10) 62564020; fax (10) 62568157; e-mail quixb@infoc3.icas.ac.cn; f. 1932; Pres. XI FU; publs *Chinese Journal of Chemistry* (6 a year), *Acta Chimica Sinica* (monthly).

Chinese Geological Society: 26 Baiwanzhuang, Beijing 100037; fax 68310894; f. 1922; 71,000 mems; Pres. ZHANG HONGREN; Sec.-Gen. ZHAO XUN; publs *Acta Geologica Sinica*, *Geological Review*.

Chinese Geological Survey: 24 Huangsi Dajie, Xicheng District, Beijing 100011; tel. (10) 51632963; fax (10) 51632907; e-mail netcenter@mail.cgs.gov.cn; internet www.cgs.gov.cn; f. 1959; attached to Ministry of Land and Resources; responsible for the centralized deployment and implementation of China's basic, public and strategic geological investigation and mineral exploration; provides basic geological information and data for the national economy; attached institutes: see Research Institutes; Dir-Gen. MENG XIANLAI; publs *Acta Geologic Sinica*, *Bulletin*, *Geological Review*.

Chinese Geophysical Society: Institute of Geophysics, POB 9701, Beijing 100101; tel. (10) 64889027; fax (10) 64871995; e-mail rxzhu@mail.c-geos.ac.cn; f. 1948; 4,000 mems; Pres. LIU GUANGDING; Sec.-Gen. ZHU

RIXIANG; publ. *Acta Geophisica Sinica* (every 2 months).

Chinese High-Energy Physics Society: POB 918, Beijing 100039; tel. 68235910; fax 68213374; e-mail zhouxb@alpha02.ihep.ac.cn; internet www.ihep.ac.cn; f. 1981; 962 mems; Chair. DAI YUANBEN; Sec.-Gen. HUANG TAO; publs *High Energy Physics and Nuclear Physics* (monthly), *Modern Physics* (6 a year).

Chinese Meteorological Society: 46 Baishiqiao Rd, Beijing 100081; f. 1924; 21,000 mems; Pres. ZHOU JINGMENG; Sec.-Gen. PENG GUANGYI; publs *Acta Meteorologica Sinica*, *Meteorological Knowledge*.

Chinese Nuclear Physics Society: POB 275-50, Beijing 102413; tel. 69358003; fax 69357787; e-mail zhusy@iris.czab.ac.cn; f. 1979; 1,300 mems; Pres. SHEN WENQING; Sec.-Gen. ZHU SHENGYUN; publ. *Nuclear Physics Review* (4 a year).

Chinese Nuclear Society: POB 2125, Beijing 100822; tel. (10) 68531473; fax (10) 68527188; e-mail cns@cnnc.com.cn; internet www.ns.org.cn; f. 1980; 8,894 mems; Pres. WANG NAIYAN; publ. *Chinese Journal of Nuclear Science and Technology*.

Chinese Physical Society: POB 603, Beijing 100080; tel. (10) 82649019; fax (10) 82649019; e-mail cps@aphy.iphy.ac.cn; internet www.cps-net.org; f. 1932; attached to Chinese Association for Science and Technology; 42,000 mems; Pres. YANG GUOZHEN; Sec.-Gen. WANG EN-GE; publs *Acta Physica Sinica* (in Chinese, monthly), *Chinese Physics Letters* (in English, monthly), *Progress in Physics* (in Chinese, 4 a year), *Wuli* (Physics, in Chinese, monthly), *Chinese Journal of Chemical Physics* (in Chinese, 6 a year), *Chinese Physics* (in English, monthly), *College Physics* (in Chinese, monthly), *Physics Teaching* (in Chinese, monthly), *Communications in Theoretical Physics* (in English, monthly).

Chinese Society for Mineralogy, Petrology and Geochemistry: 46 Guanshui Rd, Guiyang 550002, Guizhou Province; tel. and fax (851) 5895823; e-mail csmpg@vip.skleg.cn; internet www.gyig.ac.cn/society; f. 1978; 6,500 mems; library of 10,000 vols and periodicals; Pres. OUYANG ZIYUAN; publs *Acta Mineralogica Sinica* (4 a year), *Acta Petrologica Sinica* (4 a year), *Chinese Journal of Geochemistry* (in English, 4 a year), *Bulletin of Mineralogy, Petrology and Geochemistry* (4 a year), *Geochemica* (6 a year), *Journal of Paleography* (4 a year).

Chinese Society for Rock Mechanics: POB 9701, Jia No 11, Anwai Datun Lu, Beijing; tel. (10) 62011118; fax (10) 62031995; e-mail csrme@c-geos15.c-geos.ac.cn; f. 1985; 72 group mems; 12,250 individual mems; Pres. Prof. SUN JUN; Sec.-Gen. FU BINGJUN; publs *Chinese Journal of Rock Mechanics and Engineering* (6 a year in Chinese), *News of Rock Mechanics and Engineering* (4 a year in Chinese).

Chinese Society of Space Research: 1 Second Southern Ave, Zhongguancun, Beijing 100080; tel. (10) 62559882; f. 1980; Pres. Prof. WANG XIJI; publ. *Chinese Journal of Space Science* (quarterly).

Seismological Society of China: 5 Minzu Xueyuan Nanlu, Beijing 100081; tel. (10) 68417858; f. 1979; 1,233 mems; Pres. Prof. ZHANG GUOMIN; publ. *Acta Seismologica Sinica* (quarterly, in Chinese and English editions).

PHILOSOPHY AND PSYCHOLOGY

Chinese Psychological Society: Institute of Psychology, Chinese Academy of Sciences, Datun Rd, Jia 10 Hao, Chaoyang District, Beijing 100101; tel. and fax (10) 64855830; e-mail xuehui@psych.ac.cn; internet www.cpsbeijing.org; f. 1921; organizes annual conference on various topics by branch committees; National Congress of Psychology every two years; open lectures to public; promotion of psychological science through the internet; seminars organized for professionals in other fields; 2,000 mems; Pres. Prof. KAN ZHANG; Sec.-Gen. Prof. YUFANG YANG; publs *Acta Psychologica Sinica* (6 a year), *Psychological Science* (6 a year).

RELIGION, SOCIOLOGY AND ANTHROPOLOGY

Chinese Sociological Research Society: C/o Chinese Academy of Social Sciences, 5 Jianguomen Nei Da Jie, Beijing; f. 1979; Pres. FEI XIAOTONG; Exec. Sec. WANG KANG.

Chinese Study of Religion Society: Xi'anmen Ave, Beijing; Pres. REN JIYU.

TECHNOLOGY

Chemical Industry and Engineering Society of China: POB 911, Beijing; tel. 466025; f. 1922; 40,000 mems; Pres. YANG GUANGQI; Sec.-Gen. YIN DELIN; publs *Huagong Xuebao* (Journal of Chemical Engineering, quarterly), *Huagong Jinzhan* (Chemical Engineering Progress, every 2 months).

China Coal Society: Hepingli, Beijing 100013; tel. (10) 84262776; fax (10) 84261671; e-mail mtxbl@ccri.ac.cn; f. 1962; 53,000 mems; Pres. FAN WEITANG; Sec.-Gen. PAN HUIZHENG; publs *Journal* (irregular), *Modern Miners* (monthly).

China Computer Federation: POB 2704, Beijing 100080; tel. (10) 62562503; fax (10) 62567485; e-mail ccf@ns.ict.ac.cn; internet www.ccf.org.cn; f. 1962; fmrly Chinese Information Processing Soc.; 40,000 individual mems; Chair. ZHANG XIAOXIANG; Sec.-Gen. CHEN SHUKAI; publs *Chinese Journal of Computers*, *Journal of Computer Science and Technology* (in English), *Journal of Computer-aided Design and Computer Graphics*, *Journal of Software*, *Chinese Journal of Advanced Software Research*.

China Electrotechnical Society: 46 Sanlihe Rd, POB 2133, Beijing 100823; tel. (10) 68595358; fax (10) 68511242; e-mail cesintl@public.bta.net.cn; internet www.ces.org.cn; f. 1981; 50,000 mems; Pres. SHEN LIECHU; Sec.-Gen. LIU YUCHEN; publs *Transactions* (6 a year), *Electrotechnical Journal* (monthly), *Electricity Age* (monthly), *Early Youth Electrical World* (monthly).

China Energy Research Society: 54 San Li He Rd, Beijing 100863; tel. (10) 68511816; fax (10) 68511816; f. 1981; 18,000 mems; Pres. HUANG YICHENG; Sec.-Gen. BAO YUNQIAO; publs *Energy Policy Research Newsletter* (monthly), *Guide to World Energy* (every 2 weeks).

China Engineering Graphics Society: POB 85, Beijing 100083; tel. (10) 82317091; fax (10) 82326420; Pres. TANG RONGXI; publ. *Computer Aided Drafting, Design and Manufacturing* (2 a year).

China Fire Protection Association: 5th Floor, Fire Station, 19A Huawei XiLi, Chaoyang District, Beijing 100021; tel. (10) 87789260; fax (10) 87789785; e-mail cfpa-gjb@126.com; f. 1984; 30,000 mems; Pres. SUN LUN; publs *Fire Protection in China*, *Fire Science and Technology*, *Fire Technique and Products Information*.

Chinese Abacus Association: Sidaokou, Xizhimenwai, Shidaokou, Beijing; tel. 896275; f. 1979; 500,000 mems; Pres. ZHU XI-AN; Sec.-Gen. HU JING; publs *Chinese Abacus* (monthly), *Chinese Abacus News* (monthly).

Chinese Academy of Engineering (CAE): POB 3847, Beijing 100038; 3 Fuxing Rd, Beijing; tel. (10) 68530187; fax (10) 68519694; e-mail engacd@mail.cae.ac.cn; internet www.cae.ac.cn; f. 1994; 616 Academicians; Pres. XU KUANGDI; Sec. HE ZHONGWEI.

Chinese Academy of Space Technology: 31 Baishiqiao, POB 2417, Beijing 100081; tel. 68379439; fax 68378237; 4 mems; attached research institutes: see Research Institutes; Pres. QI FAREN.

Chinese Association of Automation: POB 2728, 100080 Beijing; tel. (10) 62544415; fax (10) 62620908; e-mail wangh@iamail.ia.ac.cn; internet www.gongkong.com; f. 1961; 40,000 mems; Pres Prof. CHEN HANFU, Prof. YANG JIACHI, Prof. DAI RUWAI; publs *Robot* (6 a year), *Pattern Recognition and Artificial Intelligence* (4 a year), *Automation Panorama* (6 a year), *Acta Automatica Sinica* (6 a year), *Information and Control* (6 a year).

Chinese Ceramic Society: Bai Wan Zhuang, Beijing 100831; tel. 68313364; fax 68313364; f. 1945; 30,000 mems; Pres. WANG YANMOU; Sec.-Gen. JIANG DONGHUA; publs *Journal of the Chinese Ceramic Society* (6 a year), *Bulletin of the Chinese Ceramic Society* (6 a year).

Chinese Civil Engineering Society: Bai Wan Zhuang, POB 2500, 100835 Beijing; tel. 68311313; fax 68313669; f. 1953; Pres. MAO YISHENG; Sec.-Gen. ZHAO XICHUN; publ. *Civil Engineering Journal*.

Chinese Hydraulic Engineering Society: 2-2 Baiguang Rd, Beijing 100053; tel. (10) 63202171; fax (10) 63202154; e-mail ches@mwr.gov.cn; internet www.hwcc.gov.cn; f. 1931; 93,309 mems; Pres. ZHU ERMING; Sec.-Gen. FENG GUANGZHI; publs *Journal of Hydraulic Engineering* (monthly), *Journal of Sediment Research* (monthly), *China Rural Water and Hydropower* (monthly).

Chinese Light Industry Society: B22 Fuchengmenwai Ave, Beijing 100037; tel. 894147; f. 1979; Pres. JI LONG.

Chinese Mechanical Engineering Society: 46 Sanlihe Rd, Beijing 100823; tel. (10) 68595319; fax (10) 68533613; e-mail headquarters@cmes.org; internet www.cmes.org; f. 1936; 180,000 mems; Pres. LU YONGXIANG; Gen. Sec. ZHANG YAN-MIN; publs *Chinese Journal of Mechanical Engineering* (6 a year, in English quarterly), *China Mechanical Engineering* (monthly).

Chinese Petroleum Society: POB 766, Liu Pu Kang, Beijing 100724; tel. (10) 62095615; fax (10) 62014787; f. 1979; academic assn of petroleum engineers; 60,000 mems; library: 20,000 books, 560 periodicals; Pres. JIN ZHONGCHAO; Sec.-Gen. LU JIMENG; publ. *Acta Petrolei Sinica* (Exploration and Development, and Refining and the Petrochemical Industry, each edition quarterly).

Chinese Railway Society: 10 Fuxing Rd, POB 2499, Beijing; f. 1978; railway transport, construction and rolling stock manufacture; Pres. LIU JIANZHANG; Sec.-Gen. ZHAO XICHUN; publs *Railway Journal*, *Railway Knowledge*.

Chinese Society for Metals: 46 Dongsi Xidajie, Beijing 100711; tel. (10) 65133925; fax (10) 65124122; e-mail csm@public.bta.net.cn; internet www.csm.org.cn; f. 1956; 100,000 mems; library of 50,000 vols, 20,000 serials, 1,270 periodicals; Pres. WENG YUQING; Sec.-Gen. LI WENXIU; publs *Iron and Steel* (monthly), *Acta Metallurgica Sinica* (in Chinese, monthly; in English, 6 a year), *China Metallurgy* (6 a year), *Journal of Materials Science & Technology* (6 a year).

Chinese Society for Scientific and Technical Information: 15 Fuxinglu, Beijing;

tel. 68014024; fax 68014025; e-mail cssti@istic.ac.cn; internet www.cssti.org.cn; f. 1964; organizes academic activities about information science and technology; 13,000 mems; Pres. WU HENG; publ. *Journal of the China Society for Scientific and Technical Information* (every 2 months).

Chinese Society of Aeronautics and Astronautics: 5 Liangguochang Rd, Dongcheng District, Beijing 100010; tel. (10) 84923943; fax (10) 84923942; e-mail mail@csaa.org.cn; internet www.csaa.org.cn; f. 1964; 21,800 mems; Pres. LIU GAOZHUO; Sec.-Gen. ZHANG JUEN; publs *Acta Aeronautica et Astronautica Sinica* (every 2 months), *Aerospace Knowledge* (monthly), *Chinese Journal of Aeronautics* (quarterly), *Journal of Aeronautical Materials* (every 2 months), *Journal of Aerospace Power* (every 2 months), *Model Airplane* (every 2 months).

Chinese Society of Astronautics (CSA): POB 838, Beijing 100830; located at: 2 Yue Tan Beixiao Tie, Beijing; tel. (10) 68768085; fax (10) 68051070; e-mail csaspace@163bj.com; f. 1979; 10,000 mems; Pres. LIU JIYUAN; Sec.-Gen. (vacant); publs *Space Exploration*, *Journal*.

Chinese Society of Electrical Engineering: 1 Lane 2, Baiguang Rd, Beijing 10076; Pres. ZHANG FENGXIANG.

Chinese Society of Engineering Thermophysics: POB 2706, Zhong Guan Cun, Beijing; f. 1978; 5,000 mems; Sec.-Gen. Prof. XU JIANZHONG; publ. *Journal of Engineering Thermophysics* (quarterly).

Chinese Society of Naval Architects and Marine Engineers: POB 817, Beijing; tel. 68340527; fax 68313380; f. 1943; Pres. WANG RONGSHENG; Sec.-Gen. WANG SHOUDAO; publs *Shipbuilding of China* (quarterly, contents and abstracts), *Ship Engineering* (every 2 months), *Naval and Merchant Ships* (monthly).

Chinese Society of Theoretical and Applied Mechanics (CSTAM): 15 Zhong-Guan-Cun, Beijing 100080; tel. (10) 62559588; fax (10) 62561284; e-mail cstam@sun.ihep.ac.cn; internet www.cstam.org.cn; f. 1957; 21,000 mems; Dir Prof. BAI YILONG; publs *Acta Mechanica Sinica* (6 a year, in English 4 a year), *Mechanics and Practice* (6 a year), *Journal of Experimental Mechanics* (4 a year), *Acta Mechanica Solida Sinica* (6 a year, in English 4 a year), *Journal of Computational Mechanics* (4 a year), *Explosion and Shock Waves* (4 a year), *Engineering Mechanics* (4 a year).

Chinese Textile Engineering Society: 3 Middle St, Yanjing Li, East Suburb, Beijing 100025; tel. (10) 65016537; fax (10) 65016538; f. 1930; 60,000 mems; Pres. JI GUOBIAO.

Nonferrous Metals Society of China: B12, Fuxing Rd, Beijing 100814; tel. (10) 63971451; fax (10) 63965399; e-mail nfsoc@public.bta.net.cn; internet www.nfsoc.org.cn; f. 1984; 39,000 mems; Pres. KANG YI; Sec.-Gen. NIU YINJIAN; publs *Journal of Nonferrous Metals* (quarterly, with English Abstracts), *Journal of Rare Metals* (quarterly, with English version), *Transactions of Nonferrous Metals Society of China* (quarterly, with English version).

Society of Automotive Engineers of China: 46 Fucheng Rd, Beijing 100036; tel. (10) 68121894; fax (10) 68125556; f. 1963; 1,520 mems; Pres. ZHANG XINGYE; publs *Automotive Engineering* (6 a year), *Auto Fan* (monthly).

Systems Engineering Society of China: Institute of Systems Science, Zhongguancun, Beijing 100080; tel. 62541827; fax 62568364; e-mail secs@iss.ac.cn; internet www.amss.iss.ac.cn.sesc; f. 1980; 3,000 individual mems; 150 collective mems; Pres. CHEN, GUANGYA; Sec.-Gen. WANG, SHOUYANG; publs *Systems Engineering* (quarterly), *Systems Engineering – Theory and Practice* (monthly), *Journal of Systems Science and Systems Engineering* (quarterly, in English), *Journal of Transportations Systems Engineering and Information Technology* (quarterly, in English).

Research Institutes

AGRICULTURE, FISHERIES AND VETERINARY SCIENCE

Chinese Research Institute of the Wood Industry: Wan Shou Shan, Beijing 100091; attached to Chinese Acad. of Forestry.

Forest Economics Research Institute: He Ping Li, Beijing; tel. 64210476; attached to Chinese Acad. of Forestry.

Forest Resource and Insect Research Institute: Kunming, Yunnan Province; attached to Chinese Acad. of Forestry.

Forestry Research Institute: Wan Shou Shan, Beijing 100091; tel. (10) 62888862; fax (10) 62872015; e-mail lumz@www.caf.ac.cn; internet nic6.forestry.ac.cn; f. 1953; attached to Chinese Acad. of Forestry; research into silviculture, tree cultivation, soil science, agroforestry, prevention of desertification, ornamental plants, biotechnology; 148 mems; Dir Prof. Dr LU MENG ZHU; publ. *Forest Research* (6 a year).

Institute of Agricultural Meteorology: 7 Block 11, Hepingli, Beijing; attached to Chinese Acad. of Meteorological Sciences.

Institute of Soil Science: POB 821, Nanjing 210008; tel. 7712572; fax 3353590; f. 1953; attached to Chinese Acad. of Sciences; library of 110,000 vols; Dir Prof. ZHAO QIGUO; publs *Soils*, *Advance of Soil Science*, *Acta Pedologica Sinica*, *Soil Science Research Report*, *Pedosphere*.

Sub-Tropical Forestry Research Institute: Fuyang, Zhejiang Province 311400; attached to Chinese Acad. of Forestry; Dir YANG PEISHOU.

Tropical Forestry Research Institute: Longdong, Guangzhou, Guandong Province 510520; attached to Chinese Acad. of Forestry.

BIBLIOGRAPHY, LIBRARY SCIENCE AND MUSEOLOGY

State Archives Bureau of China: 21 Feng Sheng Hutong, Beijing; tel. 665797; Dir FENG ZIZHI; publ. *Archival Work* (monthly).

ECONOMICS, LAW AND POLITICS

Economics Institute: 2 Yuetanxiaojie N., Fuchengmenurai, Beijing 100836; tel. 895323; attached to Chinese Acad. of Social Sciences; Dir ZHAO RENWEI.

Industrial Economics Institute: 2 Yuetanbeixiao Street, Fuchengmenwai, Beijing 100836; f. 1978; attached to Chinese Acad. of Social Sciences; Dir ZHOU SHULIAN.

Institute of American Studies: 3 Zhangzizhong Rd, Beijing 100007; tel. (10) 64039046; fax (10) 64000021; internet ias.cass.cn; f. 1981; attached to Chinese Acad. of Social Sciences; Dir HUANG PING; publ. *American Studies Quarterly*.

Institute of East European, Russian and Central Asian Studies: 3 Zhangzhizhong Rd, Beijing 100007; tel. 64014020; f. 1976; attached to Chinese Acad. of Social Sciences; library of 60,000 vols, 280 periodicals; Dir LI JINGJIE.

Institute of European Studies: 5 Jianguomennei Ave, Beijing 100732; tel. (10) 65138428; fax (10) 65125818; e-mail ies@cass.net.cn; internet europeanstudies.org; f. 1980; attached to Chinese Acad. of Social Sciences; Dir Prof. ZHOU HONG; publ. *Chinese Journal for European Studies* (6 a year).

Institute of Latin American Studies: POB 1113, Beijing; tel. (10) 64014009; fax (10) 64014011; e-mail latinlat@public.bta.net.cn; f. 1961; attached to Chinese Acad. of Social Sciences; Dir LI MINGDE.

Institute of West Asian and African Studies: 3 Zhangzhizhong Rd, Beijing 100007; f. 1961; attached to Chinese Acad. of Social Sciences; Dir-Gen Prof. YANG GUANG; publ. *West Asia and Africa* (6 a year).

Japanese Studies Institute: Dong Yuan, 3 Zhangzhizhong Rd, Beijing 100007; f. 1980; attached to Chinese Acad. of Social Sciences; Dir HE FANG.

Law Institute: 15 Shatan St N., Beijing 100720; tel. 64014045; f. 1958; attached to Chinese Acad. of Social Sciences; Dir WANG JIAFU.

Marxism-Leninism and Mao Zedong Thought Institute: Cegongzhuang, Beijing; f. 1980; attached to Chinese Acad. of Social Sciences; Dir SU SHAOZHI.

Political Science Institute: Shatan Bei Jie, Beijing 100720; f. 1981; attached to Chinese Acad. of Social Sciences; Dir YAN JIAQI.

Quantitative and Technical Economics Institute: 5 Jianguomennei Ave, Beijing 100732; tel. (10) 65137561; fax (10) 65125895; e-mail tswang@mx.cei.gov.cn; internet www.iqte-cass.org; f. 1982; attached to Chinese Acad. of Social Sciences; Dir WANG TONGSAN; publ. *Quantitative and Technical Economics* (monthly).

Rural Development Institute: Ritan Rd, Beijing; tel. (10) 65275067; fax (10) 65137559; e-mail keyanchu@cscrdi.cass.net.cn; internet www.cass.net.en/chinese/s04-nfs/s04-nfs.htm; f. 1978; attached to Chinese Acad. of Social Sciences; Dir Prof. ZHANG XIAOSHAN; publs *Chinese Rural Economy* (monthly), *Chinese Rural Survey* (6 a year).

Taiwan Studies Institute: 15 Poshangcun, Haidian District, Beijing 100091; tel. (10) 62883311; fax (10) 62880285; f. 1984; attached to Chinese Acad. of Social Sciences; Dir XU SHIQUAN; publ. *Taiwan Studies* (4 a year).

Trade, Finance and Material Supply Institute: 2 Yuetanbeixiao St, Beijing 100836; attached to Chinese Acad. of Social Sciences; Dir ZHANG ZHUOYUAN.

World Economy and Politics Institute: 5 Jianguomennei Ave, Beijing 100732; attached to Chinese Acad. of Social Sciences; Dir PU SHAN.

HISTORY, GEOGRAPHY AND ARCHAEOLOGY

Archaeology Institute: 27 Wangfujing Ave, Beijing 100710; f. 1950; attached to Chinese Acad. of Social Sciences; Dir WANG ZHONGSHU.

Changchun Institute of Geography: 16 Gongnong Rd, Changchun 130021, Jilin Province; tel. (431) 5652931; fax (431) 5652931; f. 1958; attached to Chinese Acad. of Sciences; Dir Prof. HE YAN.

Chinese Academy of Surveying and Mapping, National Bureau of Surveying and Mapping: 16 Bei Tai Ping Lu, Beijing 100039; tel. (10) 68212277; fax (10) 68218654; f. 1959; library of 50,000 vols; Dir LIU XIANLIN; publs *Remote Sensing*

Information, Trends in Science and Technology of Surveying and Mapping.

History (Chinese) Institute: 5 Jianguomennei Ave, Beijing 100732; attached to Chinese Acad. of Social Sciences; Dir LI XUEQIN.

History (Modern Chinese) Institute: 1 Dongcheng Lane, Wangfu Ave, Beijing 100006; tel. 555400; attached to Chinese Acad. of Social Sciences; Dir WANG QINGCHENG.

History (World) Institute: 1 Dongcheng Lane, Wangfu Ave, Beijing 100006; f. 1964; attached to Chinese Acad. of Social Sciences; Dir ZHANG CHUNNIAN.

Institute of Geography: Bldg 917, Datun Rd, Anwai, Beijing 100101; tel. (10) 64914841; fax (10) 64911844; f. 1940; attached to Chinese Acad. of Sciences; library of 90,000 vols; Dir Prof. ZHENG DU; publ. *Geographical Research* (quarterly).

LANGUAGE AND LITERATURE

Applied Linguistics Institute: 51 Nanxiao Street, Chaoyangmennei, Beijing 100010; tel. 557146; f. 1984; attached to Chinese Acad. of Social Sciences; Dir CHEN YUAN.

Chinese Literature Institute: 5 Jianguomennei Ave, Beijing 100732; attached to Chinese Acad. of Social Sciences; Dir LIU ZAIFU.

Foreign Literature Institute: 5 Jianguomennei Ave, Beijing 100732; attached to Chinese Acad. of Social Sciences; Dir ZHANG YU.

Institute of Ethnic Literature: 5 Jianguomennei Ave, Beijing 100732; tel. (10) 65138025; fax (10) 65134585; e-mail iel-scholarship@cass.org.cn; internet www.ilnm.cass.net.cn; f. 1981; attached to Chinese Acad. of Social Sciences; Dirs TANG XIAOGING, CHAO GEJIN; publ. *Studies of Ethnic Literature* (4 a year).

Institute of Linguistics: 5 Jianguomenmei Dajie, Beijing 100732; tel. (10) 65737403; fax (10) 65737403; f. 1950; attached to Chinese Acad. of Social Sciences; Dir SHEN JIAXUAN; publs *The Chinese Language and Writing, Dialects, Contemporary Linguistics*.

Journalism Institute: 2 Jintai Rd W., Chaoyang District, Beijing 100026; attached to Chinese Acad. of Social Sciences; Dir SUN XUPEI.

MEDICINE

Biomedical Engineering Institute: POB (25) 204, Tianjing 300192; fax (22) 361095; attached to Chinese Acad. of Medical Sciences; Deputy Dir WANG PENGYAN.

Blood Transfusion Institute: Renmin Rd N., Chengdu, Sichuan 61008; tel. (28) 332125; fax (28) 332125; attached to Chinese Acad. of Medical Sciences; Dir YANG CHENGMIN.

Cancer Institute and Hospital: Faculty of Oncology, Peking Union Medical College, Panjiayuan, Chaoyang District, Beijing 100021; tel. (10) 67781331; fax (10) 67713359; attached to Chinese Acad. of Medical Sciences; Dir DONG ZHIWEI.

Cardiovascular Diseases Institute: A167 Beilishi Rd, Beijing 100037; tel. 68314466; fax 68313012; e-mail fuwaih@public.bta.net.cn; attached to Chinese Acad. of Medical Sciences; Dir GAO RUNLIN.

Clinical Medicine Institute: 1 Shuaifuyuan Lane, Beijing 100730; tel. 65127733; fax 65124875; attached to Chinese Acad. of Medical Sciences; Dir LU ZHADLIN.

Dermatology Institute: 12 Jiangwangmiao St, Nanjing, Jiangsu 210042; tel. (25) 5411040; fax (25) 5414477; attached to Chinese Acad. of Medical Sciences; Dir YE SHUNZHANG.

Haematology Institute: 228 Nanjing Rd, Tianjing 300020; tel. (22) 707939; fax (22) 706542; attached to Chinese Acad. of Medical Sciences; Dir HAO YUSHU.

Health School: Badachu, Xishan, Beijing 100041; tel. 68862233; fax 68864137; attached to Chinese Acad. of Medical Sciences; Dir CHI XINGQIU.

Institute of Basic Medical Sciences: 5 Dongdan Santiao, Beijing 100005; tel. 65134466; fax 65124876; e-mail zheng@public3.bta.net.cn; attached to Chinese Acad. of Medical Sciences; Dir ZHENG DEXIAN.

Institute of Laboratory Animal Science: 5 Pan Jia Yuan Nan Li, Chao Yang District, Beijing 100021; fax 67780683; attached to Chinese Acad. of Medical Sciences; Dir LIU YINONG.

Institute of Microcirculation: 5 Dongdan Santiao, Beijing 100005; tel. (10) 65126407; fax (10) 62015012; f. 1984; attached to Chinese Acad. of Medical Sciences; Dir Prof. XIU RUIJUAN.

Institute of Plastic Surgery: Ba-Da-Chu, Beijing 100041; tel. (10) 68874826; fax (10) 68864137; e-mail yeguang@cdm.imicams.ac.cn; f. 1957; attached to Chinese Acad. of Medical Sciences; library of 20,000 vols; Dir Prof. SONG YEGUANG; publ. *Chinese Journal of Plastic Surgery and Burns*.

Materia Medica Institute: 1 Xiannongtan St, Beijing 100050; tel. 63013366; fax 63017757; attached to Chinese Acad. of Medical Sciences; Dir ZHANG JUNTIAN.

Medical Biology Institute: Huahongdong, Kunming, Yunnan 650160; f. 1959; attached to Chinese Acad. of Medical Sciences.

Medical Biotechnology Institute: 1 Tiantanxili, Beijing 100050; tel. 757315; fax 63017302; attached to Chinese Acad. of Medical Sciences; Dir ZHANG ZHIPING.

Medicinal Plant Development Institute: 151 Ma Lian Wa North Rd, Haidian District, Beijing 100094; tel. (10) 62896288; fax (10) 62899715; e-mail implad@implad.ac.cn; internet www.implad.ac.cn; f. 1983; attached to Chinese Acad. of Medical Sciences; library of 30,000 vols; Dir Prof. CHEN SHILIN.

Radiation Medicine Institute: POB 71, Tianjin 300192; attached to Chinese Acad. of Medical Sciences.

Shanghai Institute of Materia Medica: 294 Tai-Yuan Rd, Shanghai 200031; tel. (21) 64311833; fax (21) 64370269; f. 1932; attached to Chinese Acad. of Sciences; development of new drugs; library of 80,000 vols, 600 current periodicals; Dir CHEN KAIXIAN; publ. *Acta Pharmocologica Sinica*.

NATURAL SCIENCES

General

Fujian Institute of Research on the Structure of Matter: Xihe, Fuzhou, Fujian 350002; tel. (591) 3714517; fax (591) 3714946; e-mail fjirsm@ms.fjirsm.ac.cn; f. 1960; attached to Chinese Acad. of Sciences; library of 75,000 vols; Dir Prof. HUANG JINSHUN; publ. *Journal on Structural Chemistry* (6 a year).

Institute of Oceanology: 7 Nanhai Rd, Qingdao 266071; tel. (532) 2879062; fax (532) 2870882; e-mail iocas@ms.qdio.ac.cn; f. 1950; attached to Chinese Acad. of Sciences; library of 180,000 vols; Dir XIANG JIANHAI; publs *Studia Marina Sinica* (Chinese with English abstracts, annually), *Marine Sciences* (Chinese, 6 a year), *Chinese Journal of Oceanology and Limnology* (in English, 4 a year), *Oceanologia et Limnologia Sinica* (Chinese, 6 a year).

Institute of the History of Natural Sciences: 137 Chao Nei St, Beijing 100010; tel. (10) 64043989; fax (10) 64017637; e-mail webmaster@ihns.ac.cn; internet www.ihns.ac.cn; f. 1957; attached to Chinese Acad. of Sciences; library of 150,000 vols; Dir Prof. DUN LIU; publs *Studies in the History of Natural Sciences* (quarterly), *China Historical Materials of Science and Technology* (quarterly).

Qinghai Institute of Salt Lakes: 7 Xinning Rd, Xinning, Qinghai Province 810008; tel. 44306; fax 46002; f. 1965; attached to Chinese Acad. of Sciences; library of 85,000 vols; Dir LIU DEJIANG; publ. *Journal of Salt Lake Science*.

South China Sea Institute of Oceanology: 164 West Xingang Rd, Guangzhou 510301; tel. (20) 84452227; fax (20) 84451672; e-mail scsio@ns.scsio.ac.cn; internet www.scsio.ac.an; f. 1959; attached to Chinese Acad. of Sciences; library of 95,546 vols; Dir Dr SHI PING; publs *Journal of Tropical Oceanology* (6 a year), *Nanhai Studia Marina Sinica* (irregular, Chinese with English abstracts).

Biological Sciences

Institute of Applied Ecology: POB 417, Shenyang 110015; tel. (24) 3902096; fax (24) 3843313; f. 1954; attached to Chinese Acad. of Sciences; library of 95,000 vols; Dir SUN TIEHANG; publs *Chinese Journal of Ecology, Chinese Journal of Applied Ecology*.

Institute of Biophysics: 15 Datun Rd, Chaoyang District, Beijing 100101; tel. (10) 62022029; fax (10) 62027837; attached to Chinese Acad. of Sciences; Dir WANG SHURONG.

Institute of Botany: 141 Xizhimen Wai St, Beijing 100044; attached to Chinese Acad. of Sciences; Dir ZHANG XINSHI.

Institute of Developmental Biology: POB 2707, Beijing; fax 62561269; f. 1980; attached to Chinese Acad. of Sciences; specializes in biotechnology of fish and mammals; Dir YAN SHAOYI.

Institute of Genetics and Developmental Biology: Datun Rd, Andingmenwai, Beijing 100101; tel. (10) 64889331; fax (10) 64856610; e-mail genetics@genetics.ac.cn; internet www.genetics.ac.cn; attached to Chinese Acad. of Sciences; Dir Prof. JIAYANG LI.

Institute of Hydrobiology: Luojiashan, Wuhan 430072, Hubei Province; tel. (27) 68780789; fax (27) 68780123; e-mail zhh@ihb.ac.cn; internet www.ihb.ac.cn; f. 1930; attached to Chinese Acad. of Sciences; freshwater ecology, fisheries, biotechnology and molecular biology, aquatic environment protection; library of 70,000 vols; fish museum; Dir Dr. GUI JIANFANG; publ. *Acta Hydrobiologica Sinica* (every 2 months).

Institute of Microbiology: 13 Beiyitiao, Zhongguancun, Haidian District, Beijing 100080; tel. (10) 62552178; fax (10) 62560912; e-mail gaof@im.ac.cn; internet www.im.ac.cn; f. 1958; attached to Chinese Acad. of Sciences; 380 mems; Dir Prof. GEORGE F. GAO; publs *Acta Microbiologica Sinica* (every 2 months), *Chinese Journal of Biotechnology* (every 2 months), *Microbiology* (every 2 months), *Mycosystema* (quarterly).

Institute of Vertebrate Palaeontology and Palaeo-Anthropology: Academia Sinica, Beijing; f. 1929; attached to Chinese Acad. of Sciences; Dir QIU ZHANXIANG.

Institute of Zoology: Chinese Academy of Sciences, 19 Zhongguancun Rd, Haidian, Beijing 100080; tel. 62552219; fax

62565689; e-mail ioz@panda.ioz.ac.cn; internet panda.ioz.ac.cn; attached to Chinese Acad. of Sciences; Dir Prof. HUANG DAWEI; publs *Acta Zoologica Sinica* (6 a year), *Acta Entomologica Sinica* (4 a year), *Acta Zootaxonomica Sinica* (4 a year), *Chinese Journal of Zoology* (6 a year), *Chinese Journal of Entomology* (6 a year), *Entomologica Sinica* (in English, 4 a year).

Kunming Institute of Zoology: Kunming 650223, Yunnan Province; tel. (871) 5140390; fax (871) 5151823; f. 1959; attached to Chinese Acad. of Sciences; library of 180,000 vols; Dir SHI LIMING; publ. *Zoological Research* (quarterly).

Nanjing Institute of Geology and Palaeontology: 39 East Beijing Rd, Chi-Ming-Ssu, Nanjing 210008, Jiangsu Province; tel. (25) 7714437; fax (25) 3357026; f. 1951; attached to Chinese Acad. of Sciences; library of 26,000 vols; Dir MU XINAN; publs *Palaeontologia Sinica* (irregular), *Memoirs* (irregular), *Bulletin* (irregular), *Journal of Stratigraphy* (quarterly), *Acta Palaeontologica Sinica* (quarterly), *Palaeontologia Cathayana*, *Acta Micropalaeontologica Sinica* (quarterly), *Palaeontological Abstracts* (quarterly), *Palaeoworld* (irregular), *Acta Palaeobotanica et Palynologica Sinica* (irregular).

Research Centre for Environmental Sciences: POB 2871, Beijing 100085; tel. (10) 62923549; fax (10) 62923563; e-mail std@mail.rcees.ac.cn; internet www.rcees.ac.cn; f. 1975; attached to Chinese Acad. of Sciences; library of 30,000 vols; Dir Dr ZHAO JINGZHU; publs *Acta Scientiae Circumstantiae* (quarterly, with English abstracts), *Huanjing Kexue* (Environmental Sciences, 6 a year), *Huanjing Huaxue* (Environmental Chemistry, 6 a year), *Environmental Pollution Control Technology and Instruments* (6 a year), *Journal of Environmental Sciences* (in English, 4 a year), *Acta Ecologica Sinica* (12 a year).

Shanghai Institute of Biochemistry: Chinese Academy of Sciences, 320 Yue-Yang Rd, Shanghai 200031; tel. (21) 64374430; fax (21) 64338357; attached to Chinese Acad. of Sciences; Dir Prof. LI BOLIANG.

Shanghai Institute of Cell Biology: 320 Yue-Yang Rd, Shanghai; tel. (21) 64315030; fax (21) 64331090; e-mail jhc@sunm.shcnc.ac.cn; f. 1950; attached to Chinese Acad. of Sciences; Dir Dr GUO LI-HE; publs *Acta Biologiae Experimentalis Sinica*, *Chinese Journal of Cell Biology*, *Cell Research*.

Shanghai Institute of Entomology: 225 Chongqing S. Rd, Shanghai 200025; tel. 3282039; f. 1959; attached to Chinese Acad. of Sciences; Dir CHEN YUANGUANG.

Shanghai Institute of Physiology: 320 Yue-Yang Rd, Shanghai; tel. (21) 64370080; fax (21) 64332445; e-mail sls@fudan.ac.cn; f. 1944; attached to Chinese Acad. of Sciences; library of 150,000 vols; Dir XIONG-LI YANG; publ. *Acta Physiologica Sinica* (in Chinese with English abstract, every 2 months).

Shanghai Institute of Plant Physiology: 300 Fongling Rd, Shanghai 200032; tel. (21) 64042090; fax (21) 64042385; e-mail sipp@iris.sipp.ac.cn; f. 1944; attached to Chinese Acad. of Sciences; library of 150,000 vols; Dir Prof. Z. C. TANG.

South China Institute of Botany: Wushan, Guangzhou, 510650 Guangdong Province; tel. 87705626; f. 1929; attached to Chinese Acad. of Sciences; library of 59,000 vols; botanic garden, herbarium and arboretum; Dir LIANG CHENGYE; publs *Acta Botanica Austro Sinica*, *Journal of Tropical and Sub-tropical Botany* (4 a year).

Xishuangbanna Tropical Botanical Garden: Menglun, Mengla County, Yunnan 666303; tel. (Jinghong) 905; f. 1959; attached to Chinese Acad. of Sciences; library of 50,000 vols; Dir Prof. XU ZAIFU; publs *Tropical Plants Research* (quarterly), *Collected Research Papers on Tropical Botany* (annually).

Mathematical Sciences

Institute of Applied Mathematics: Academia Sinica, Box 2734, Beijing 100080; tel. 62562939; fax 62541689; f. 1979; attached to Chinese Acad. of Sciences; Dir ZHANG XIANGSUN.

Institute of Mathematics: Zhongguancun, Beijing 100080; attached to Chinese Acad. of Sciences; Dir YANG LE.

Physical Sciences

562 Comprehensive Geological Brigade: Yanqiaozhen 101601, Sanhe County, Hebei; attached to Chinese Acad. of Geological Sciences.

Beijing Observatory: Zhongguancun, Beijing 100080; attached to Chinese Acad. of Sciences; Dir WANG SHOUGUAN.

Changchun Institute of Applied Chemistry: 109 Stalin St, Changchun, Jilin Province; tel. 5682801; fax 5685653; f. 1948; attached to Chinese Acad. of Sciences; library of 120,000 vols; Dir Prof. WANG ERKANG; publs *Analysis Chemistry* (monthly), *Applied Chemistry* (every 2 months).

Changchun Institute of Physics: 1 Yan An Rd, Changchun 130021, Jilin Province; tel. (431) 5952215; fax (431) 5955378; f. 1958; attached to Chinese Acad. of Sciences; luminescence and its application, integrated optics; library of 69,800 vols; Dir JIN YIXIN; publs *Chinese Journal of Luminescence* (quarterly), *Chinese Journal of Liquid Crystal and Displays* (quarterly).

Chengdu Institute of Geology and Mineral Resources: 101 Renmin N. Rd, Chengdu 610082, Sichuan; attached to Chinese Acad. of Geological Sciences.

Chinese Institute of Atomic Energy: POB 275, Beijing; tel. 69357487; fax 69357008; f. 1958; attached to Chinese Acad. of Sciences; Dir Prof. SUN ZUXUN; publs *Annual Report*, *Chinese Journal of Nuclear Physics* (quarterly), *Journal of Nuclear and Radiochemistry* (quarterly), *Atomic Energy Science and Technology* (every 2 months), *Isotopes* (quarterly).

Cold and Arid Regions Environmental and Engineering Research Institute: 260 Donggang Rd W., Lanzhou 730000, Gansu Province; tel. (931) 8818203; fax (931) 8885241; e-mail dyj@ns.lzb.ac.cn; f. 1965; attached to Chinese Acad. of Sciences; library of 546,246 vols, 23,968 periodicals; Dir Prof. CHENG GUODONG; publs *Journal of Glaciology and Geocryology* (in Chinese, 4 a year), *Plateau Meteorology* (in Chinese, 4 a year), *Journal of Desert Research* (in Chinese, 4 a year).

Commission for the Integrated Survey of Natural Resources: POB 9717, Beijing 100101; tel. (10) 64889797; fax (10) 64914230; e-mail shkcheng@cisnar.ac.cn; f. 1956; attached to Chinese Acad. of Sciences; co-ordinates the integrated survey teams for the exploitation, utilization, conservation and evaluation of natural resources; multidisciplinary research; library of 40,096 vols; Dir Prof. CHENG SHENGKUI; publs *Journal of Natural Resources* (with English abstracts, 4 a year), *Resources Science* (6 a year).

Dalian Institute of Chemical Physics: 161 Zhongshan Rd, Dalian; tel. 3631841; fax 363426; f. 1949; attached to Chinese Acad. of Sciences; library of 70,000 vols; Dir YUAN QUAN; publs *Journal of Catalysis* (quarterly), *Chinese Journal of Chromatography* (every 2 months).

Guangzhou Institute of Chemistry: Academia Sinica, Guangzhou 510650; tel. (20) 85231815; fax (20) 85231119; e-mail cyha@gic.ac.cn; internet www.gic.ac.cn; f. 1958; attached to Chinese Acad. of Sciences; 270 mems; library of 80,000 vols; Dir CHENGYONG HA; publs *Guangzhou Chemistry* (quarterly), *Journal of Cellulose Science and Technology* (quarterly).

Institute for the Application of Remote Sensing Information: Changsha 410114, Hunan; attached to Chinese Acad. of Geological Sciences.

Institute of Acoustics: 17 Zhongguancun St, Beijing 100080; tel. (10) 62553765; fax (10) 62553898; e-mail lig@mail.ioa.ac.cn; internet www.ioa.ac.cn; f. 1964; attached to Chinese Acad. of Sciences; Dir LI QIHU.

Institute of Atmospheric Physics: Qijiahezi, Beijing 100029; tel. 64919693; fax 62028604; f. 1928; attached to Chinese Acad. of Sciences; library of 55,000 vols and periodicals; Dir Prof. ZENG QINGCUN; publs *Scientia Atmospherica Sinica* (in Chinese), *Chinese Journal of Atmospheric Sciences*, *Advances in Atmospheric Sciences* (all quarterly), *Collected Papers of the Institute of Atmospheric Physics* (in Chinese).

Institute of Atmospheric Sounding: 7 Block 11, Hepingli, Beijing; attached to Chinese Acad. of Meteorological Sciences.

Institute of Chemistry: Zhongguancun, Haidian District, Beijing; tel. 282281; fax 62569564; f. 1956; attached to Chinese Acad. of Sciences; library of 100,000 vols; Dir Prof. HU YADONG.

Institute of Climatology: 7 Block 11, Hepingli, Beijing; attached to Chinese Acad. of Meteorological Sciences.

Institute of Geochemistry: Chinese Academy of Sciences, 73 Guanshui Rd, Guiyang, Guizhou 550002; tel. (851) 5895095; fax (851) 5895574; f. 1966; attached to Chinese Acad. of Sciences; library of 150,000 vols; Dir LIU CONGQIANG; publs *Bulletin of Mineralogy, Petrology and Geochemistry* (quarterly), *Chinese Journal of Geochemistry* (in English, quarterly), *Acta Mineralogica Sinica* (quarterly), *Geology-Geochemistry* (4 a year).

Institute of Geology: 26 Baiwanzhuang Rd, Beijing 100037; attached to Chinese Acad. of Geological Sciences.

Institute of Geomechanics: Fahuasi, Beijing 100081; tel. (10) 68412303; fax (10) 68422326; f. 1956; attached to Chinese Acad. of Geological Sciences; Pres. Prof. WU GANGUO; publ. *Journal of Geomechanics* (quarterly).

Institute of Geophysics: A-11 Datun Rd, Chao Yang District, Beijing 100101; tel. (10) 64871497; attached to Chinese Acad. of Sciences; Dir ZHENG TIANYU.

Institute of Geotectonics: Academia Sinica, Changsha, Hunan Province 410013; tel. (731) 8859150; fax (731) 8859137; e-mail kikf@ms.csig.ac.cn; internet www.csig.ac.cn; f. 1961; attached to Chinese Acad. of Sciences; library of 36,000 vols; Dir CHEN GUODA; publ. *Geotectonica et Metallogenia* (quarterly).

Institute of High Energy Physics: POB 918, Beijing 100039; tel. (10) 68219643; fax (10) 68213374; e-mail mail@ihep.ac.cn; internet www.ihep.ac.cn; f. 1973; attached to Chinese Acad. of Sciences; Dir Prof. CHEN HESHENG; publs *Modern Physics* (6 a year), *High Energy Physics and Nuclear Physics* (monthly).

Institute of Karst Geology: 40 Seven Stars Rd, Guilin 541104, Guangxi; attached to Chinese Acad. of Geological Sciences.

Institute of Mesoscale Meteorology: 7 Block 11, Hepingli, Beijing; attached to Chinese Acad. of Meteorological Sciences.

Institute of Metal Research: Academia Sinica, 72 Wenhua Rd, Shenyang 110015; tel. (24) 3843531; fax (24) 3891320; f. 1953; attached to Chinese Acad. of Sciences; library of 85,000 vols, 2,300 periodicals; publs *Journal of Materials Science and Technology* (every 2 months), *Acta Metallurgica Sinica* (monthly), *Materials Science Progress* (every 2 months).

Institute of Mineral Deposits: 26 Baiwanzhuang Rd, Beijing 100037; attached to Chinese Acad. of Geological Sciences.

Institute of Photographic Chemistry: Academia Sinica, Bei Sha Tan, Beijing 100101; tel. (10) 62017061; fax (10) 62029375; f. 1975; attached to Chinese Acad. of Sciences; library of 32,000 vols; Dir CHEN-HO TUNG; publ. *Photographic Science and Photochemistry*.

Institute of Physics: Zhongguancun, Haidian District, Beijing 100080; fax 282271; attached to Chinese Acad. of Sciences; Dir YANG GUOZHEN.

Institute of Process Engineering: 1 Beiertiao, Zhongguancun, Beijing; fax (10) 62561822; e-mail office@home.icm.ac.cn; internet www.ipe.ac.cn; f. 1958; attached to Chinese Acad. of Sciences; library of 171,500 vols; Dir Prof. JINGHAI LI; publs *Chinese Journal of Process Engineering* (6 a year), *Computer and Applied Chemistry* (6 a year), *Chinese Journal of Spectroscopy Laboratory* (6 a year).

Institute of Rock and Mineral Analysis: 26 Baiwanzhuang Rd, Beijing 100037; tel. (10) 68311550; fax (10) 68320365; f. 1978; attached to Chinese Acad. of Geological Sciences.

Institute of Space Physics: Zhongguancun, Beijing 100080; tel. 288052; attached to Chinese Acad. of Sciences.

Institute of Synoptic and Dynamic Meteorology: 7 Block 11, Hepingli, Beijing; attached to Chinese Acad. of Meteorological Sciences.

Institute of the Corrosion and Protection of Metals: Academia Sinica, 62 Wencui Rd, Shenyang 110015; tel. 3894313; fax 3894149; f. 1982; attached to Chinese Acad. of Sciences; library of 7,000 vols, 500 journals; Dir Prof. WU WEITAO; publs *Annual Report*, *Corrosion Science and Protection Technology* (quarterly).

Institute of Theoretical Physics: Academia Sinica, POB 2735, Beijing 100080; tel. (10) 62555058; fax (10) 62562587; f. 1978; attached to Chinese Acad. of Sciences; library of 10,000 vols; Dir OU-YANG ZHONG CAN; publ. *Communications in Theoretical Physics* (in English, monthly).

Institute of Weather Modification: 7 Block 11, Hepingli, Beijing; attached to Chinese Acad. of Meteorological Sciences.

Lanzhou Institute of Physics: POB Lanzhou 94; attached to Chinese Acad. of Space Technology.

Nanjing Institute of Geology and Mineral Resources: 534 Zhongshan E. Rd, Nanjing 210016, Jiangsu; tel. (25) 84600446; e-mail njcgs@cgs.gov.cn; internet www.nanjing.cgs.gov.cn; f. 1962; 320 mems; attached to Chinese Geological Survey; publ. *Resources Survey and Environment*.

Purple Mountain Observatory: 2 West Beijing Rd, Nanjing 210008, Jiangsu; tel. (25) 3300818; fax (25) 3300818; f. 1934; attached to Chinese Acad. of Sciences; library of 36,000 vols; Dir LIU BENQUI; publs *Acta Astronomica Sinica* (quarterly), *Publications of Purple Mountain Observatory*.

Shaanxi Astronomical Observatory: POB 18, Lintong, Xian; tel. (29) 3890326; fax (29) 3890196; e-mail pub2@ms.sxso.ac.cn; f. 1966; attached to Chinese Acad. of Sciences; library of 3,500 vols; Dir Prof. LI ZHIGANG; publ. *Time and Frequency* (monthly).

Shanghai Astronomical Observatory: 80 Nandan Rd, Shanghai 200030; tel. (21) 64384522; fax (21) 64384618; e-mail office@center.shao.ac.cn; internet www.center.shao.ac.cn; f. 1872; attached to Chinese Acad. of Sciences; library of 80,000 vols; Dir Prof. ZHAO JUNLIANG; publs *Progress in Astronomy* (quarterly), *Annals of Shanghai Observatory*.

Shanghai Institute of Metallurgy: Chinese Academy of Sciences, 865 Changning Rd, Shanghai 200050; tel. 2511070; fax 2513510; f. 1928; attached to Chinese Acad. of Sciences; Dir ZOU SHICHANG.

Shanghai Institute of Nuclear Research: POB 800-204, Shanghai 201800; tel. (21) 59553998; fax (21) 59553021; f. 1959; attached to Chinese Acad. of Sciences; Dir Prof. YANG FUJIA; publs *Nuclear Science and Techniques* (quarterly), *Journal of Radiation Research and Radiation Processing* (quarterly), *Nuclear Technology* (in Chinese, monthly).

Shanghai Institute of Organic Chemistry: 345 Fenglin Lu, Shanghai 200032; tel. (21) 64163300; fax (21) 64166128; internet www.sioc.ac.cn; f. 1950; attached to Chinese Acad. of Sciences; library of 300,000 vols; Dir Prof. JIANG BIAO; publs *Acta Chimica Sinica* (in Chinese, monthly), *Chinese Journal of Chemistry* (in English, monthly), *Organic Chemistry* (in Chinese, monthly).

Shenyang Institute of Geology and Mineral Resources: Beiling Ave, Shenyang 110032, Liaoning; attached to Chinese Acad. of Geological Sciences.

Southwestern Institute of Physics: POB 15, Leshan, 614007 Sichuan; POB 432, Chengdu 610041, Sichuan; tel. (28) 2932304 (Chengdu); fax (28) 2932202 (Chengdu); e-mail wb@swip.ac.cn; f. 1965; attached to China National Nuclear Corporation; controlled nuclear fusion and application of intermediate technology; library of 150,000 vols, 630 periodicals; Dir Prof. PAN CHUANHONG; publ. *Nuclear Fusion and Plasma Physics* (quarterly).

Tianjin Institute of Geology and Mineral Resources: 4 8th Rd, Dazhigu, Tianjin, 300170; tel. (22) 24314386; fax (22) 24314292; e-mail tjigmr@public.tpt.tj.cn; f. 1962; attached to Chinese Acad. of Geological Sciences; Dir LU SONGNIAN; publ. *Progress in Precambrian Research* (4 a year).

Xi'an Institute of Geology and Mineral Resources: 160 Eastern to Youyi Rd, Xian 710054, Shaanxi; attached to Chinese Acad. of Geological Sciences.

Yichang Institute of Geology and Mineral Resources: POB 502, Yichang 443003, Hubei; attached to Chinese Acad. of Geological Sciences.

Yunnan Observatory: POB 110, Kunming 650011; fax (871) 3911845; e-mail ynao@public.km.yn.cn; f. 1972; attached to Chinese Acad. of Sciences; library of 35,000 vols; Dir Prof. TAN HUISONG; publ. *Publications of Yunnan Observatory* (quarterly).

PHILOSOPHY AND PSYCHOLOGY

Institute of Psychology: POB 1603, Beijing 100101; tel. 64919520; fax 64872070; e-mail yangyf@psych.ac.cn; f. 1951; attached to Chinese Acad. of Sciences; library of 145,000 vols, 1,500 periodicals; Dir Dr YANG YUFANG; publs *Acta Psychologica Sinica* (quarterly), *Journal of Developments in Psychology* (quarterly).

Philosophy Institute: 5 Jianguomennei Ave, Beijing 100732; f. 1977; attached to Chinese Acad. of Social Sciences; Dir XING FONSI.

RELIGION, SOCIOLOGY AND ANTHROPOLOGY

Institute of Population and Labour Economics: 5 Jianguo Mennei Ave, Beijing 100732; tel. (10) 85195417; fax (10) 85195427; e-mail iple@cass.org.cn; internet iple.cass.cn; f. 1980; attached to Chinese Acad. of Social Sciences; 48 mems; library of 10,000 vols; Dir Prof. CAI FANG; publs *China Labor Economics* (4 a year), *Population Science of China* (6 a year).

Institute of World Religions: 5 Jianguo Mennei St, Beijing 100732; tel. (10) 65138523; f. 1964; attached to Chinese Acad. of Social Sciences; Dir Prof. WU YUNGUI; publs *Studies on World Religions* (quarterly), *World Religious Culture* (quarterly).

Nationalities Studies Institute: Baishiqiao, Beijing; attached to Chinese Acad. of Social Sciences; Dir ZHAONA SITU.

Sociology Institute: 5 Jianguomennei Ave, Beijing 100732; f. 1979; attached to Chinese Acad. of Social Sciences; Dir HE JIANZHANG.

TECHNOLOGY

Beijing Institute of Control Engineering: POB 729, Beijing 100080; attached to Chinese Acad. of Space Technology.

Beijing Institute of Spacecraft Systems Engineering: POB 9628, Beijing 100086; attached to Chinese Acad. of Space Technology.

Changchun Institute of Optics and Fine Mechanics: 112 Stalin St, Changchun, Jilin Province; tel. 684692; fax 682346; f. 1950; attached to Chinese Acad. of Sciences; Dir WANG JIAQI; publ. *Optics and Precision Engineering* (every 2 months).

Chemical Processing and Forest Products Utilization Research Institute: Longpan Rd, Nanjing, Jiangsu Province; attached to Chinese Acad. of Forestry.

China Coal Research Institute: 5 Qingniangou Rd, Hepingli, Beijing 100013; tel. (10) 84262809; fax (10) 84261671; e-mail office@ccri.ac.cn; internet www.ccri.ac.cn; f. 1957; attached research institutes: see Research Institutes; Dir Prof. Dr ZHANG YUZHUO; publs *Coal Science and Technology* (in Chinese, monthly), *Journal of China Coal Society* (in Chinese, monthly; in English, 2 a year).

China National Space Administration: POB 2940, Beijing; 8 Fucheng Rd, Haidian District, Beijing 100037; tel. (10) 68516733; fax (10) 68516732; internet www.cnsa.gov.cn; co-ordinates and implements national space policy and development of space science, technology and industry, and arranges bilateral technical and scientific programmes, incl. launch of space probes; Administrator LUAN ENJIE.

China State Bureau of Technical Supervision (CSBTS): POB 8010, Beijing; tel. 62025835; fax 62031010; f. 1988; research and development for national standards and quality control; colln of nat. standards from 56 countries; Dir-Gen. ZHU YULI; publs *Standards Journal*, *Technical Supervision Journal*.

Institute of Automation: Zhong Guan Cun, Haidian District, Beijing; tel. (10) 62551397; fax (10) 62545229; f. 1956; attached to Chinese Acad. of Sciences; Dir HU FENGFENG; publs *Acta Automatica Sinica* (in Chinese, 6 a year), *Chinese Journal of Automation* (in English, quarterly).

Institute of Coal Chemistry: POB 165, Taiyuan 030001, Shanxi Province; tel. (351) 4041267; fax (351) 4041153; f. 1954; attached to Chinese Acad. of Sciences; Dir Prof. ZHONG BING; publ. *Journal of Fuel Chemistry and Technology* (quarterly).

Institute of Computer Technology: 6 Kexueyuan Nan Lu, Haidian District, Beijing 100080; tel. (10) 62565533; fax (10) 62567724; e-mail wgao@ict.ac.cn; internet www.ict.ac.cn; f. 1956; attached to Chinese Acad. of Sciences; Dir GAO WEN; publs *Journal of Computer Science and Technology*, *Computer Research and Development*, *Journal of Computer-aided Design and Graphics*.

Institute of Computer Technology: 24 Section 2, Sanhao St, Shenyang 110001, Liaoning; tel. 7705360; fax 7705319; attached to Chinese Acad. of Sciences; Dir CONG GUANGMIN.

Institute of Electronics: 17 Zhong Guan Cun Rd, POB 2702, Beijing 100080; tel. 62554424; fax 62567363; e-mail rooter@mail.ie.ac.cn; internet www.ie.ac.cn; f. 1956; attached to Chinese Acad. of Sciences; library of 35,000 vols; Dir Prof. YIN HEJUN; publs *Journal of Electronics and Information Technology* (in Chinese, monthly), *Journal of Electronics (China)* (in English, 6 a year).

Institute of Engineering Mechanics: 9 Xuefu Rd, Harbin 150080; tel. 6662901; fax 6664755; e-mail iem@public.hr.hl.cn; f. 1954; attached to China Seismological Bureau; earthquake and safety engineering; library of 110,000 vols; Dir QUIMIN FENG; publs *Earthquake Engineering and Engineering Vibration* (quarterly), *World Information on Earthquake Engineering* (quarterly), *Journal of Natural Disasters* (quarterly).

Institute of Engineering Thermophysics: 12B Zhongguancun Rd, Beijing; tel. 62554126; f. 1980; attached to Chinese Acad. of Sciences; Dir CAI RUIXIAN; publ. *Journal of Engineering Thermodynamics* (quarterly).

Institute of Hydrogeology and Engineering Geology: Zhengding County 050303, Hebei; attached to Chinese Acad. of Geological Sciences.

Institute of Mechanics: 15 Zhongguancun Rd, Beijing 100080; attached to Chinese Acad. of Sciences; Dir ZHENG ZHEMIN.

Institute of Meteorological Instrument Calibration: 7 Block 11, Hepingli, Beijing; attached to Chinese Acad. of Meteorological Sciences.

Institute of Optics and Electronics: POB 350, Shuangliu, Chengdu, Sichuan Province; tel. (28) 5180032; fax (28) 5180070; f. 1970; attached to Chinese Acad. of Sciences; library of 90,000 vols; Dir MA JIAGUANG; publ. *Opto-Electronics Engineering* (6 a year).

Institute of Semiconductors: POB 912, Beijing 100083; tel. (10) 288131; fax (10) 62562389; f. 1960; attached to Chinese Acad. of Sciences; Dir WANG QIMING.

Institute of Systems Science: 1A Nansi St, Zhongguancun, Beijing 100080; tel. (10) 62541830; fax (10) 62568364; e-mail issb@bamboo.iss.ac.cn; internet www.iss.ac.cn; f. 1979; attached to Chinese Acad. of Sciences; Dir Prof. XIAO-SHAN GAO; publs *Journal of Systems Science and Mathematics* (4 a year), *Journal of Systems Science and Systems Engineering* (6 a year), *Journal of Systems Science and Complexity*.

Science and Technology Development Corporation: 26 Baiwanghuang Rd, Beijing 100037; attached to Chinese Acad. of Geological Sciences.

Shanghai Institute of Ceramics: 1295 Ding Xi Rd, Shanghai 200050; tel. (21) 62512990; fax (21) 62513903; e-mail siccas@sunm.shcnc.ac.cn; internet www.sic.ac.cn; f. 1959; attached to Chinese Acad. of Sciences; library of 80,000 vols; Dir SHI ERWEI; publ. *Journal of Inorganic Materials* (6 a year).

Shanghai Institute of Optics and Fine Mechanics: POB 800-211, Shanghai, 201800; tel. (21) 69918000; fax (21) 69918800; internet www.siom.ac.cn; attached to Chinese Acad. of Sciences; laser science and technology; Dir Prof. ZHU JIANQING; publs *Acta Optica Sinica* (monthly, in Chinese), *Chinese Journal of Lasers* (monthly, in Chinese), *Chinese Optics Letters* (monthly, in English).

Shanghai Institute of Technical Physics: 500 Yutian Rd, Shanghai 200083; tel. (21) 65420850; fax (21) 63248028; e-mail sitp@mail.sitp.ac.cn; internet www.sitp.ac.cn; f. 1958; attached to Chinese Acad. of Sciences; infrared technology and physics, optoelectronics and remote sensing; library of 40,000 vols; Dir WANG JIANYU; publ. *Chinese Journal of Infrared and Millimetre Waves* (6 a year).

Xian Institute of Optics and Precision Mechanics: Xian, Shaanxi; tel. (29) 5261376; fax (29) 5261473; f. 1962; attached to Chinese Acad. of Sciences; library of 120,000 vols; Dir Prof. ZHAO BAOCHANG; publ. *Acta Photinica Sinica* (6 a year).

Xian Institute of Space Radio Technology: POB 165, Xian 710000; tel. (29) 5290500; fax (29) 5290588; f. 1965; attached to Chinese Acad. of Space Technology.

Zhengzhou Institute of the Multi-Purpose Utilization of Mineral Resources: 26 Funu Rd, Zhengzhou 450006, Henan Province; tel. (371) 8984974; fax (371) 8984942; f. 1956; attached to Chinese Acad. of Geological Sciences; library of 200,000 vols; Dir Prof. Dr ZHANG KEREN; publ. *Conservation and Utilization of Mineral Resources* (6 a year).

Libraries and Archives

Baoding

Hebei University Library: 2 Hezuo Rd, Baoding, Hebei Province; tel. (312) 5022922 ext. 417; fax (312) 5022648; f. 1921; 1,960,000 vols, 3,923 current periodicals, 3,000 back copies; special collection: 4,397 vols of Chinese ancient books, incl. local chronicles and family trees; Dir LOU CHENGZHAO; publ. *Journal of Hebei University*.

Beijing

Beijing Normal University Library: Xinjiekouwai Dajie St, Beijing 100875; tel. (10) 62208163; fax (10) 62200567; e-mail libli@bnu.cn; f. 1902; 2,700,000 vols, 14,436 periodicals; rich collection of thread-bound Chinese ancient books, incl. 1,500 titles of remarkable editions, 2,800 titles of local chronicles, 1,300 series; Dir YIU TIANCHI.

Capital Library: 15 Guozijian St, Dongcheng District, Beijing; tel. (10) 64040905; fax (10) 64040905; f. 1913; municipal library; 2,574,000 vols, 142,000 current periodicals; spec. collns incl. traditional opera, folk customs; Dir JIN PEILIN.

Central Archives of China: Wenquan, Haidian District, Beijing; tel. 62556611; f. 1959; revolutionary historical archives from the May 4th Movement of 1919 to the founding of the People's Republic in 1949, and archives of CPC and central government offices; 8,000,000 files; Curator WANG GANG; publs *CPC Documents*, *Central Archives of China Series*, *Collection of PCC Documents*, etc.

Centre for Documentation and Information, Chinese Academy of Social Sciences: 5 Jianguomennei Ave, Beijing 100732; tel. and fax (10) 65126393; e-mail kyc-tsg@cass.org.cn; internet www.lib.cass.org.cn; f. 1985; attached to Chinese Acad. of Social Sciences; administrates Chinese Society of Social Sciences Information; 2,400,000 vols; Dir YANG PEICHAO; publs *Social Sciences Abroad* (every 2 months), *Diogenes* (in Chinese, 2 a year).

First Historical Archives of China: Palace Museum inside Xihuamen, Beijing 100031; tel. (10) 63096487; fax (10) 63096489; f. 1925; 10,000,000 files; historical archives of Ming and Qing Dynasties; Curator XING YONGFU; publ. *Historical Archives* (quarterly).

Institute of Medical Information: 3 Yabaolu, Chaoyang District, Beijing 100020; tel. (10) 85630217; fax (10) 85625733; e-mail zlxu@library.imicams.ac.cn; internet www.library.imicams.ac.cn; f. 1958; attached to Chinese Acad. of Medical Sciences and Peking Union Medical Coll.; Dir Prof. XU ZENGLU.

Institute of Meteorological, Scientific and Technical Information: 7 Block 11, Hepingli, Beijing; attached to Chinese Acad. of Meteorological Sciences.

Institute of Scientific and Technical Information of China (ISTIC): 15 Fu Xing Lu, POB 3827, Beijing 100038; tel. (10) 68514020; fax (10) 68514025; f. 1956; 18,000,000 items from China and abroad, incl. research reports, conference proceedings, periodicals, patents, standards, catalogues and samples and audiovisual material; Dir-Gen. ZHU WEI; publs *Scientific and Technical Trends Abroad*, *Review of World Inventions*, *Journal of Scientific and Technical Information*, etc.

Institute of Scientific and Technological Information on Forestry: Wan Shou Shan, Beijing 100091; tel. (10) 62889713; fax (10) 62882317; e-mail wcli@isti.forestry.ac.cn; internet www.lknet.forestry.ac.cn; f. 1964; attached to Chinese Acad. of Forestry; Deputy Director LI WEIDONG.

Library of the Chinese Academy of Sciences: 33 Beisihuanxilu, Zhongguancun, Beijing 100080; tel. (10) 82626684; fax (10) 82626600; e-mail office@mail.las.ac.cn; internet www.las.ac.cn; f. 1950; 5,200,000 vols, 8,636 current periodicals, 51,000 reports of conference proceedings; spec. collns incl. local chronicles, collected works of the Ming and Qing Dynasties, 40,000 rubbings from stone tablets, 600,000 rare books, 28 web-based databases, 38 CD-rom databases; Chief Deputy Director ZHANG XIAOLIN; publs *Science and Technology International* (monthly), *Chinese Biotechnology* (monthly), *Chinese Physical Abstracts* (6 a year), *Chinese Mathematical Abstracts* (6 a year), *Library and Information Service* (monthly), *R&D Information* (monthly), *New Technology of Library and Information Service* (monthly), *High Technology and Industrialization* (monthly), *Progress in Chemistry* (6 a year).

Medical Library: 9 Dongdan Santiao, Beijing 100730; tel. 65127733; attached to Chinese Acad. of Medical Sciences; Dir LU RUSHAN.

National Library of China: 33 Zhongguancun Nandajie, Haidian District, Beijing

100081; tel. (10) 88545023; fax (10) 68419271; e-mail interco@publicf.nlc.gov.cn; internet www.nlc.gov.cn; f. 1909; 22,000,000 vols, 21,000 current periodicals, 1,100,000 microforms and audiovisual items; spec. collns incl. 291,696 vols of rare books of imperial libraries in the Southern Song, Ming and Qing dynasties; all kinds of Chinese publs incl. those in minority languages; foreign books, periodicals and newspapers, UN publs and govt publs of certain countries; blockprinted editions, books of rubbings, and other antique items; Dir Prof. REN JIYU; publs *Documents* (quarterly), *Journal of the National Library of China* (quarterly), *National Bibliography*.

Peking University Library: Haidian District, Beijing 100871; tel. (10) 62751051; fax (10) 62761008; e-mail office@lib.pku.edu.cn; internet www.lib.pku.edu.cn; f. 1902; 5,507,409 books, 708,717 vols of bound periodicals, spec. colln: 1,600,000 vols of thread-bound Chinese ancient books, incl. 200,000 vols of rare books, 70,000 rubbings, copy of *Complete Works of Shakespeare* (publ. 1623), Dante's *Divine Comedy* (publ. 1896), and plays by Schiller, etc.; Dir Prof. LONGJI DAI; publ. *Journal of Academic Libraries* (6 a year).

Renmin University of China Library: 175 Haidian Rd, Beijing; tel. 62511371; fax 62566374; f. 1937; 2,500,000 vols, 2,400 current periodical titles, 400,000 back copies; publs on philosophy, politics, law, economics, etc.; rich collection of philosophy of Marxism, law, economics, modern and contemporary history of China; special collection: Chinese revolutionary documents in liberated and base areas, ancient rare books of Song, Yuan, Ming and Qing Dynasties (2,400 titles); 154 staff; Dir Prof. YANG DONGLIANG; publs *Index to the Complete Works of Marx and Engels*, *Classification of the Renmin University of China Library*, *Index to the ancient rare books of RUC Library*.

Tsinghua University Library: Qinghuayuan, West Suburb, Beijing 100084; tel. 62782137; fax 62781758; e-mail tsg@mail.lib.tsinghua.edu.cn; internet www.lib.tsinghua.edu.cn; f. 1911; 2,500,000 vols, 15,495 periodicals (foreign 5,902); special collections: Chinese ancient books 30,000 titles (300,000 vols), including rare editions, only existing copies and handcopies, 3,000 titles (30,000 vols); rich collections of academic books and periodicals, conference literature, engineering historical data, local chronicles, collected papers on special subjects, major abstract journals, complete set of nearly 200 foreign periodicals; Dir XUE FANGYU; publs *Tsinghua Journal* (Natural Sciences and Social Sciences edns), *Tsinghua University Selections of Scientific Theses*, *Science Report*.

Changchun

Jilin Provincial Library: 10 Xinmin Ave, Changchun, Jilin Province; tel. 5643796; f. 1958; 2,700,000 vols; Dir JIN ENHUI; publ. *Research in Library Science* (every 2 months).

Jilin University Library: 117 Jiefang Rd, Changchun 130023, Jilin Province; tel. 8923189; f. 1946; 2,154,000 vols, 3,078 current periodicals, 299,808 back copies; special collection: local chronicles, clan trees, Asian Series, documents of Manchurian railways; Dir Prof. WANG TONGCHE.

Northeast Normal University Library: 138 Renmin St, Changchun, Jilin Province; tel. 5684174; f. 1946; 2,300,000 vols, 4,000 current periodicals, 11,600 back copies; publs from time of the War of Resistance Against Japan, rare Chinese ancient books; Dir SUN ZHONGTIAN; publ. *Jilin Libraries of Colleges and Universities* (quarterly).

Changsha

Hunan Provincial Library: 38 Shaoshan Rd, Changsha, Hunan Province; tel. 25653; f. 1904; 3,090,000 vols, 130,000 bound vols of periodicals, 900,000 ancient books.

Chengdu

Sichuan Provincial Library: 6 Lu Zongfu, Chengdu 610016, Sichuan Province; tel. (28) 6659219; f. 1940; 3,760,000 vols, 13,485 periodicals, historical material; Dir WANG ENLAI (acting); publ. *Librarian* (every 2 months).

Chongqing

Chongqing Library: 1 Changjiang Rd A, Chongqing, Sichuan Province; tel. 54832; f. 1947; 3,137,198 vols, 690,183 bound periodicals, 65,514 technical reports, 35,000 antique books, historical documents, UN publs; Dir LI PUJIE.

Dalian

Dalian City Library: 7 Changbai, Xigang District, Dalian, Liaoning Province; tel. (411) 3630033; fax (411) 3623796; f. 1907; 2,000,000 vols, 5,502 periodicals; 700 ancient books; Dir LIU ZHENWEI.

Fuzhou

Fujian Provincial Library: 37 Dongfanghong Dajie St, Fuzhou, Fujian Province; tel. 31604; f. 1913; 2,200,000 vols, 4,350 current periodicals, historical material; spec. collns incl. data on Taiwan and Southeast Asia.

Guangzhou

South China Teachers' University Library: Shipai, Tianhe District, Guangzhou, Guangdong Province; tel. 774911; 1,600,000 vols, over 3,000 current periodicals, 7,145 back copies; special collection: 180,000 vols of Chinese ancient books, incl. 1,025 titles of local chronicles; 106 staff; Deputy Dir YANG WEIPING.

Zhongshan Library of Guangdong Province: 211 Wenming Rd, Guangzhou, Guangdong Province; tel. 330676; f. 1912; 3,300,000 vols, 6,000 current periodicals, historical documents; spec. collns incl. research materials on Dr Sun Yat-sen; Dir HUANG JUNGUI; publs *Journal of Guangdong Libraries* (quarterly), *Library Tribune* (quarterly).

Guilin

Guilin Library of Guangxi Zhuang Autonomous Region: 15 North Ronghu Rd, Guilin, Guangxi Zhuang Autonomous Region; tel. 223494; f. 1909; 1,380,000 vols, 15,275 current periodicals, historical material; Deputy Dir YANG JIANHONG; publs *Catalogue of Guangxi Local Documents*, *Catalogue of Materials on Guangxi Minority Study* (vols 1–2).

Guiyang

Guizhou Provincial Library: 31 Beijing Rd, Guiyang, Guizhou Province; tel. 25562; f. 1937; 1,270,000 vols, 5,000 periodicals, historical material; publs *Journal* (quarterly), *Chronological Table of the Historical Calamities of Guizhou Province*, *Collected Papers on the Mineral Products of Guizhou Province*.

Hangzhou

Zhejiang Provincial Library: 38 Shuguang Rd, Hangzhou 310007, Zhejiang Province; tel. (571) 87999812; fax (571) 87995860; e-mail bgs@zjlib.net.cn; internet www.zjlib.net.cn; f. 1900; 4,210,000 vols, 7,526 current periodicals; Chief Officer CHENG XIAOLIAN; publ. *Library Science Research and Work* (quarterly).

Hankou

Wuhan Library: 86 Nanjing Rd, Hankou, Hubei Province; tel. 24334; f. 1953; 1,400,000 vols, 2,018 periodicals, 200,000 ancient books, historical material.

Harbin

Heilongjiang Provincial Library: 48 Wenchang St, Harbin 150008, Heilongjiang Province; tel. 2624581; fax 2627813; e-mail hljstsg@sina.com; f. 1958; 2,456,000 vols, 5,000 ancient books, historical material; spec. collns incl. Russian publs, 1920s–1940s Japanese publs; Dir WANG HAIQUAN; publ. *Library Development* (6 a year).

Hefei

Anhui Provincial Library: 38 Wuhu Rd, Hefei, Anhui Province; tel. 257602; f. 1913; 2,108,608 vols, 5,400 current periodicals, 30,000 antique books, historical documents; Dir WANG BAO SHENG; publs *Library Work* (quarterly), *Bulletin of Anhui Libraries* (quarterly).

Huhhot

Nei Monggol Autonomous Region Library (Inner Mongolia Autonomous Region Library): People's Park, Huhhot 010020, Nei Monggol Autonomous Region; tel. 27948; f. 1950; 1,260,000 vols, 2,131 current periodicals; spec. collns incl. Mongolia; Dir ZHANG XIANGTANG; publ. *Nei Monggol Library Work* (quarterly, in Mongolian and Chinese).

Jinan

Shandong Provincial Library: 275 Daminhu Rd, Jinan, Shandong Province; tel. 612338; f. 1908; 3,500,000 vols, 3,500 periodicals, ancient books, historical documents.

Shandong University Library: Jinan, Shandong Province; tel. 803861; f. 1901; 2,000,000 vols, 3,000 current periodicals, 260,000 back copies; 77% of holdings are on liberal arts; special collection: rare books, rubbings from stone inscriptions, calligraphy and paintings, revolutionary documents; 118 staff; Dir Prof. XU WEN-TIAN.

Kunming

Yunnan Provincial Library: 2 South Cuihu Rd, Kunming, Yunnan Province; tel. 5298; f. 1950; 2,150,000 vols, 7,172 periodicals, historical material.

Lanzhou

Gansu Provincial Library: 250 Binghedong Rd, Lanzhou, Gansu Province; tel. 28982; f. 1916; 2,400,000 vols, historical material; spec. collns incl. Imperial Library of Qianlong; Dir PAN YINSHENG; publ. *Library and Information* (quarterly).

Nanchang

Jiangxi Provincial Library: 160 North Hongdu Rd, Nanchang, Jiangxi Province; tel. (791) 8517065; f. 1920; 2,200,000 vols, 6,600 periodicals, historical material; publ. *Journal of the Jiangxi Society of Library Science* (quarterly).

Nanjing

Nanjing Library: 66 Chengxian St, Nanjing, Jiangsu Province; tel. (25) 57717619; fax (25) 83372163; e-mail ntbgs@sina.com; internet www.jslib.com.cn; f. 1907; 7,790,000 vols, 8,000 current periodicals, 1,700,000 ancient books; Exec. Dir MA NING; publ. *New Century Library* (every 2 months).

Nanjing University Library: 22 Hankou Rd, Nanjing 210093, Jiangsu Province; tel. (25) 3592943; fax (25) 3592943; internet lib.nju.edu.cn; f. 1902; 3,560,000 vols, 5,000 current periodicals, 566,400 bound vols of periodicals; systematic collection of literature, history, philosophy, economics, law, mathematics, physics, chemistry, astronomy, geology, geography, meteorology, environmental science, computer science, biology and medicine, in Chinese and foreign languages; fairly complete collection of reference books from most countries, rich collection of major retrieval serials; special collection: 1,452 titles of rare books (Song, Yuan, Ming and Qing Dynasties), 10,000 sheets of rubbings from stone inscriptions, many paintings, MSS and handcopies, 4,600 titles (40,000 vols) of local chronicles, mainly of Jiangsu and Sichuan Provinces, also books on orientalism, bibliography and archaeology; Dir Prof. ZHANG YIBING; publ. *Journal of Serials Management and Research* (2 a year).

Second Historical Archives of China: 309 East Zhongshan Rd, Nanjing, Jiangsu Province; tel. 4409996; f. 1951; archive material of the Republic of China (1912–1949); 1,740,000 files, 246,000 periodicals; Curator XU HAO; publs *Republican Archives* (quarterly), *Collected Archives Series of the History of the Republic of China*.

Nanning

Guangxi Zhuang Autonomous Region Library: 61 Minzu Dadao, Nanning, Guangxi Zhuang Autonomous Region; tel. 5860297; fax 5860297; e-mail gxlib@mail.nn.gx.cn; internet www.gxlib.org.cn; f. 1931; 2,050,000 vols, 4,575 current periodicals; Dir WANG XUEGUANG; publ. *Library World* (quarterly).

Shanghai

East China Normal University Library: 3663 North Zhongshan Rd, Shanghai; tel. (21) 62579196; f. 1951; 2,640,000 vols, 5,187 current periodicals, 237,000 back copies; notable collection on pedagogy, psychology, geography, classical philosophy, local histories and bibliography; the earliest editions of thread-bound Chinese ancient books are those of the Song Dynasty and of foreign books (publ. 1630); rubbings from stone inscriptions; Dir WANG XIJING; publ. *Library Information* (monthly).

Fudan University Library: 220 Handan Rd, Shanghai 200433; tel. 65643162; fax 65649814; e-mail zfqin@fudan.edu.cn; f. 1918; 3,500,000 vols, incl. remarkable editions of Chinese ancient books; special collections: 709 different editions of *The Books of Songs* and 3,000 titles of collected works of famous writers of Qing Dynasty; Dir Prof. QIN ZENG-FU.

Shanghai Library: Huaihai Rd, Shanghai; tel. (21) 3273176; fax (21) 3278493; f. 1952; 8,200,000 vols, 14,449 periodicals, 152,270 technical reports, early MSS, historical material, microforms, audio-visual material; Dir ZHU QING ZHO; publs *Catalog of Chinese Series* (1959), *Contents of Modern Chinese Journals*, *Catalog of Shanghai Library Collections of Local Histories*, *Catalog of Works and Translations by Guo Moruo*, *National Index of Newspapers and Periodicals*.

Shenyang

Liaoning Provincial Library: Shenyang, Liaoning Province; f. 1948; 1,923,366 vols, 13,307 periodicals.

Taiyuan

Shanxi Provincial Library: 1 Wenguan Lane, South Jiefang Rd, Taiyuan, Shanxi Province; f. 1918; 1,700,000 vols, 9,900 periodicals.

Tianjin

Nankai University Library: 94 Weijin Rd, Tianjin 300071; tel. (22) 23502410; fax (22) 23505633; e-mail tsg@nankai.edu.cn; internet www.lib.nankai.edu.cn; f. 1919; 3,145,805 vols, 3,349 current periodicals, 511,159 bound copies of periodicals; special collections: 2,000 titles of rare books, 4,000 titles of local chronicles, 10,000 reference books, complete set of 100 periodicals with back issues of more than 50 years, 5,946 audiovisual items, 1,689 multimedia CD-ROMs, 51 databases; Dir Prof. YAN SHIPING; publs *Catalog of Rare Books Held by Nankai University Library*, *Catalog of Thread-Bound Ancient Books Held by Nankai University Library*.

Tianjin Library: 12 Chengdedao Rd, Heping District, Tianjin; tel. 315171; f. 1907; 2,800,000 vols, 3,900 current periodicals, 500,000 ancient books; Dir DONG CHANGXU; publ. *Library Work and Research* (quarterly).

Urumqi

Xinjiang Library: 11 South Xinhua Rd, Urumqi, Xinjiang Uygur Autonomous Region; f. 1946; 546,800 vols, 3,723 periodicals, historical documents; spec. collns incl. books in Xinjiang nationality languages.

Wuhan

Central China Teachers' University Library: Mt Guizishan, Wuhan, Hubei Province; tel. 72631; f. 1951; 1,255,000 vols, 6,486 periodicals.

Hubei Provincial Library: 45 Wuluo Rd, Wuchang District, Wuhan 430060, Hubei Province; tel. 871284; f. 1904; 2,605,000 vols, 930,000 vols of periodicals, 50,000 antique books; Dir XIONG JINSHAN; publ. *Library & Information Science Tribune* (quarterly).

Wuhan University Library: Mt Luojiashan, Wuhan, Hubei Province; tel. 7872290; fax 7872290; e-mail jwshen@lib.whu.edu.cn; f. 1913; 2,900,000 vols, 6,000 current periodicals, 300,000 back copies; rich collection of works on basic theories, and newspapers and periodicals published before 1949; special collection: 180,000 vols of thread-bound local chronicles, over 500 titles of rare books of Yuan, Ming and Qing Dynasties; 141 staff; Dir SHEN JIWU.

Xiamen

Xiamen University Library: 422 Siming Nan Rd, Xiamen, Fujian Province; tel. (592) 2186127; fax (592) 2182360; e-mail xiaodh@xmu.edu.cn; internet library.xmu.edu.cn; f. 1921; 2,400,000 vols, 6,000 current periodicals, 90,000 back copies; publs on natural and social sciences, especially economics, biology, chemistry, and data on Southeast Asia and Taiwan; Dir CHEN MINGGUANG.

Xian

Shaanxi Provincial Library: 146 Xi Ave, Xian, Shaanxi Province; f. 1909; 2,300,000 vols.

Shaanxi Teachers' University Library: Wujiafen, South Suburb, Xian 710062, Shaanxi Province; tel. 711946, ext. 248; f. 1953; 1,884,487 vols, 2,628 current periodicals, 6,116 back copies; as one of the largest university libraries of Northwest China, it has a fairly rich collection of publications on philosophy, social sciences, literature, linguistics and philology, natural sciences, and thread-bound remarkable editions of Chinese ancient books, local chronicles, 7,000 sheets of rubbings from bronze and stone tablets of the Zhou, Qing, Han and Tang Dynasties, elhi textbooks and materials on pedagogy; 119 staff; Exec. Dir WANG KEJUN.

Xian Jiaotong University Library: Xianning Rd, Xian, Shaanxi Province 710049; tel. (29) 3268102; fax (29) 3237910; e-mail lib@xjtu.edu.cn; f. 1896; 1,840,000 vols, 4,373 current periodicals, 9,000 back copies; systematic collection of scientific and technical publs, complete sets of 15 world-famous sci-tech periodicals having a history of over 100 years; 143 staff; Dir Prof. LI RENHOU.

Xining

Qinghai Provincial Library: 44 Jiefang Rd, Xining, Qinghai Province; f. 1935; 1,354,000 vols, 2,819 periodicals; publ. *Libraries in Qinghai* (quarterly).

Yinchuan

Ningxia Library: Tongxin Rd N, Yinchuan, Ningxia Hui Autonomous Region; f. 1958; 1,300,000 vols.

Zhengzhou

Henan Provincial Library: 150 Song Shan Nan Rd, Zhengzhou, Henan Province; tel. (371) 7972396; f. 1909; 2,360,000 vols, 4,419 current periodicals, 700,000 antique books, historical material; Dir TONG JIYONG; publ. *Journal of Henan Libraries* (quarterly).

Museums and Art Galleries

Beijing

Arthur M. Sackler Museum of Art and Archaeology: Peking University, Dept of Archaeology, Beijing 100871; tel. (10) 62751667; fax (10) 62751667; f. 1993; attached to Peking University; Dir Prof. GAO CHONGWEN.

Beijing Lu Xun Museum: Ritiao, Gongmenkou, Beijing; Curator LI HELIN.

Beijing Natural History Museum: 126 Tianqiao South St, Beijing; tel. (10) 67024431; fax (10) 67021254; e-mail bnhm@public3.bta.net.cn; internet www.bnhm.org.cn; f. 1951; library of 50,000 vols; Dir AI CHUNCHU; publs *Memoirs* (with English abstract), *China Nature* (with English contents, jointly with the China Wildlife Conservation Assn, the Chinese Assn of Natural Science Museums and Beijing Natural History Museum).

China Art Gallery: 1 Wu Si St, East City District, Beijing; tel. (10) 64016234; f. 1958; traditional Chinese painting and sculpture; library of 13,700 vols; Dir LIU KAIQU.

Geological Museum of China: 15 Yangrouhutong, Xisi, Beijing 100034; tel. (10) 66557402; fax (10) 66557477; e-mail ngmc@public2.bta.net.cn; f. 1916; Dir CHENG LIWEI.

Military Museum of the Chinese People's Revolution: 9 Fuxing Rd, Beijing 100038; tel. 68014441; f. 1958; Curator QIN XINGHAN; publ. *Military History* (every 2 months).

National Museum of China: East Side of Tiananmen Square, Beijing 100006; tel. (10) 65129347; fax (10) 65128986; e-mail webmaster@nationalmuseum.cn; internet www.nationalmuseum.cn; f. 2003 by merger of National Museum of Chinese History (f. 1912) and National Museum of the Chinese Revolution (f. 1950); Chinese historical artefacts and documents since the Neolithic era; archeology, history and arts; Dir LU ZHANGSHEN; publs *Journal*, *Modern China and Cultural Relics*.

Palace Museum: 4 Jingshan Qian Jie, Beijing 100009; tel. (10) 65132255; fax (10)

65123119; e-mail gugong@dpm.org.cnt; internet www.dpm.org.cn; f. 1925; paintings, ceramics, bronzes, jades, applied arts, calligraphy, carvings, coins, furniture, arms, decorative arts, musical instruments, clocks, seals, toys; library of 700,000 vols; Dir ZHENG XINMIAO; publs *Palace Museum Journal* (6 a year), *Forbidden City* (6 a year).

Quanzhou

Quanzhou Museum for Overseas Communications History: Quanzhou City, Fujian Province; tel. (595) 226655; f. 1959; Chinese foreign trade and China's int. relations in the fields of culture, science and religion; Curator WANG LIANMAO; publ. *Research into Overseas Communications History* (published jointly with the China Society of Research on Overseas Communications History, 2 a year).

Shanghai

Shanghai Museum: 201 Ren Min Da Dao, Shanghai 200003; tel. 63723500; fax 63728522; e-mail webmaster@shanghaimuseum.net; internet www.shanghaimuseum.net; f. 1952; library of 200,000 vols; Dir CHEN XIEJUN.

Universities and Colleges

ANHUI UNIVERSITY

3 Fei Xi Rd, Hefei 230039, Anhui
Telephone: (551) 5106114
Fax: (551) 5107999
Internet: www.ahu.edu.cn
Founded 1928
Academic year: September to July
President: HUAN DEKUAN
Vice-Presidents: WEI SUI, YI YOU MIN, LAN XI JIE, WU LIANG
Heads of Graduate Dept: ZHU SHI QUN, WANG XING HAI
Librarian: XU JUN DA
Number of teachers: 1,100
Number of students: 26,787
Publications: *Anhui University Law Review* (2 a year), *Hui Study* (annually), *Journal of Anhui University* (natural sciences, 6 a year), *Journal of Anhui University* (philosophy and social science, 6 a year)

DEANS

Business Administration: ZHOU YA NA
Chinese: TAO XIN MIN
Economics: RONG ZHAO ZI
Electrical Science and Technology: CHEN JUN NING
Foreign Studies: HUANG QING LONG
History: WU CHUN MEI
Law: LI MING FA
Life Science: LI JIN HUA
Management: XIE YANG QUN
Mathematics and Computing Science: JIANG WEI
Philosophy: LI XIA
Physics and Material Science: SHI SHOU HUA

PROFESSORS

BA, ZHAO LIN, Chinese
CAO, ZHUO LIANG, Physics and Material Science
CHEN, DAO GUI, Chinese
CHEN, GUI JING, Mathematics and Computing Science
CHEN, HUA YOU, Mathematics and Computing Science
CHEN, JUN NING, Electrical Science and Technology
CHEN, QIN, Life Science
CHEN, SHENG QING, Law
CHEN, ZHANG JIN, Physics and Material Science
CHENG, JING RONG, Physics and Material Science
DOU, REN SHENG, Physics and Material Science
DU, XIAN NENG, Mathematics and Computing Science
DU, PENG CHENG, Business Administration
FAN, YI ZHENG, Mathematics and Computing Science
FANG, BIN, Electrical Science and Technology
FANG, QING QING, Physics and Material Science
FANG, XIANG ZHENG, Physics and Material Science
FENG, YI MING, Economics
GAO, QING WEI, Electrical Science and Technology
GE, CHUANG LI, Electrical Science and Technology
GE, LI FENG, Electrical Science and Technology
GU, RONG BAO, Mathematics and Computing Science
GU, ZU DAO, Chinese
GUAN, XIN LIN, Business Administration
GUO, JIAN YOU, Physics and Material Science
HAN, JIA HUA, Physics and Material Science
HE, JIA QING, Life Science
HU, GUO GUANG, Physics and Material Science
HU, MAO LIN, Mathematics and Computing Science
HU, SHU HE, Mathematics and Computing Science
HU, YAN JUN, Electrical Science and Technology
HUANG, PEI, Life Science
JIA, HAI JI, Economics
JIANG, WEI, Mathematics and Computing Science
KE, DAO MING, Electrical Science and Technology
KONG, FAN CHAO, Mathematics and Computing Science
LI, CAI FU, Management
LI, JIN HUA, Life Science
LI, MING FA, Law
LI, SHOU SHEN, Economics
LI, XIA, Philosophy
LI, XIAO HUI, Electrical Science and Technology
LI, XIU SONG, History
LI, YU CHENG, Life Science
LIU, XIN FANG, History
LOU, PING, Physics and Material Science
LU, QIN YI, History
LU, RONG SHAN, Economics
LU, YING BIN, Economics
MA, REN JIE, Management
MA, XIU SHUI, Electrical Science and Technology
MING, JUN, Electrical Science and Technology
REN, KAI, Philosophy
RONG, ZHAO ZI, Economics
SHENG, YE SHOU, Life Science
SHENG, ZHAO XUAN, Mathematics and Computing Science
SHI, FU YUAN, Electrical Science and Technology
SHI, SHOU HUA, Physics and Material Science
SHI, XIANG QIAN, Philosophy
SUN, YI KAI, Philosophy
SUN, YU FA, Electrical Science and Technology
SUN, ZHAO QI, Physics and Material Science
TANG, HUA QUAN, Chinese
TANG, QI XUE, History
TAO, XIN MIN, Chinese
WANG, DA MING, Chinese
WANG, DAO MING, Economics
WANG, DAO QING, Chinese
WANG, HUI, Management
WANG, LIANG LONG, Mathematics and Computing Science
WANG, RONG, Law
WANG, XIN YI, History
WANG, YI PING, Life Science
WANG, YIN HAI, Physics and Material Science
WANG, YONG DE, Chinese
WANG, YU, Life Science
WEI, WEI, Economics
WEN, CHUN RU, Philosophy
WU, CHUN MEI, History
WU, JIA RONG, Chinese
XIAO, JIAN, Mathematics and Computing Science
XIAO, YA ZHONG, Life Science
XIE, YANG QUN, Management
XIONG, XIAO QI, Economics
XU, CHANG QING, Mathematics and Computing Science
XU, CHENG ZHI, Chinese
XU, JIAN HUA, Mathematics and Computing Science
XU, JUN DA, Philosophy
XU, ZAI GUO, Chinese
XU, ZHANG CHENG, Physics and Material Science
YAN, PENG FEI, Mathematics and Computing Science
YANG, FANG ZHI, Economics
YANG, SHANG JUN, Mathematics and Computing Science
YANG, XIAO LI, Chinese
YAO, XUE BIAO, Physics and Material Science
YE, LIU, Physics and Material Science
YI, YOU MIN, Physics and Material Science
YONG, XI QI, Mathematics and Computing Science
YU, BEN LI, Physics and Material Science
YUE, FANG SUI, Chinese
YUE, JIE XIAN, Philosophy
ZENG, FAN YIN, Economics
ZHA, XIANG DONG, Life Science
ZHANG, BU CHANG, Life Science
ZHANG, JIAN FENG, Economics
ZHANG, JIN XI, History
ZHANG, LU GAO, Chinese
ZHANG, NENG WEI, Philosophy
ZHANG, QI YOU, Chinese
ZHANG, ZI XIA, History
ZHENG, MING ZHEN, Philosophy
ZHOU, HUAI YU, History
ZHOU, LI ZHI, Life Science
ZHOU, NAN, Law
ZHOU, SHENG MING, Physics and Material Science
ZHOU, YA NA, Business Administration
ZHOU, ZHI YUAN, History
ZHOU, ZHONG ZE, Life Science
ZHU, SHI QUN, Philosophy
ZHU, XUE SHAN, Law
ZHU, ZONG YAN, Economics

ATTACHED CENTRES

Centre for Hui Studies of Anhui University: Dir Prof. ZHU, WANG SHU.

Modern Education Technology Centre of Anhui University: Dir Prof. WANG, BIAO.

Modern Experiment Centre of Anhui University: Dir Prof. MENG, XIANG CHUN.

BEIJING BROADCASTING UNIVERSITY

Ding Fu Zhuang St, Chao Yang District, Beijing 10024
Telephone: (10) 65779319
Fax: (10) 65779134
Internet: www.cuc.edu.cn
Founded 1954
Ministry of Education control
Academic year: August to July
President: LIU JI NAN
Number of teachers: 772
Number of students: 28,000

Publications: *Asia Media and Communication Studies* (annually), *Journal of Beijing Broadcasting University* (modern communication, 4 a year), *Journal of Beijing Broadcasting University* (natural science, 4 a year), *Media Studies* (irregular)

DEANS

Advertising Studies: HUANG SHENG MIN
Animation: LU SHENG ZHAN
Film and Television Arts: LI XING GUO
Information Engineering and Science: LI JIAN ZENG
International Communication: XU QIN YUAN
Journalism and Communication: DING JUN JIE
Literature: MIAO DI
Media Management: ZAN YAN QUAN
Presentation Art: LI XIAO HUA
Social Sciences: GAO HUI RAN
Television: GAO XIAO HONG

PROFESSORS

BI, GEN HUI, Film and Television Arts
CAI, CHAO SHI, Information Engineering
CAI, GUO FEN, International Communication
CAI, WEN MEI, Journalism and Communication
CAO, LU, Journalism and Communication
CAO, QING RUI, Film and Television Arts
CHEN, BIAN ZHI, International Communication
CHEN, JING SHENG, Broadcasting
CHEN, WEI XING, International Communication
CHEN, YUAN MENG, International Communication
DING, JUN JIE, Journalism and Communication
DONG, HUA MIAO, Film and Television Arts
DU, HAN FENG, Literature
FENG, SONG CHE, Social Sciences
FU, JUN QING, Journalism and Communication
GAO, FU AN, Media Management
GAO, FU AN, Film and Television Arts
GAO, XIAO HONG, Television
GUAN, LING, Film and Television Arts
GUO, ZHEN ZHI, Television
HA, YAN QIU, Journalism and Communication
HE, LAN, International Communication
HE, SU LIU, Television
HE, XIAO BING, Film and Television Arts
HOU, MIN, Broadcasting
HUANG, JING HUA, Advertising Studies
HUANG, ZHI XUN, Information Engineering
HUO, WEN LI, Television
JIA, FOU, Animation
JIANG, XIU HUA, Information Engineering
JIN, GUI RONG, Film and Television Arts
KE, HUI XIN, Journalism and Communication
LEI, YUE JIE, Journalism and Communication
LI, DONG, Information Engineering
LI, JIAN ZENG, Information Engineering
LI, JIAN ZENG, Science
LI, SHENG LI, Film and Television Arts
LI, XING GUO, Film and Television Arts
LI, ZENG RUI, Information Engineering
LI, ZENG RUI, Science
LI, ZUO FENG, Literature
LIANG, MING, Film and Television Arts
LIANG, YI GAO, Journalism and Communication
LIANG, ZHENG LI, Media Management
LIN, ZHENG BAO, Information Engineering
LIU, JIAN BO, Information Engineering
LIU, JING LIN, Journalism and Communication
LIU, LI WEN, Literature
LIU, LI WEN, Film and Television Arts
LIU, SHU LIANG, Film and Television Arts
LIU, TING, Film and Television Arts
LIU, YE YUAN, Film and Television Arts
LU, GUI ZHEN, Information Engineering
LU, JIAN, Film and Television Arts
LU, SHENG ZHAN, Animation
LU, YING KUN, Film and Television Arts
LUO, LI, Broadcasting
MAO, ZHI JI, Information Engineering
MIAO, DI, Literature
NI, XUE LI, Film and Television Arts
PAN, YE, Film and Television Arts
PENG, HUI GUO, Animation
PU, ZHEN YUAN, Literature
QIN, YU MING, Television
REN, SU QIN, Social Sciences
REN, YUAN, Television
SHENG, QIN, Information Engineering
SHI, MIN YONG, Animation
SHI, XU SHENG, Film and Television Arts
SONG, PEI YI, Film and Television Arts
SONG, PEI YI, Media Management
WANG, CHUN ZHI, Information Engineering
WANG, HONG, Television
WANG, MING YA, Film and Television Arts
WANG, WEI, International Communication
WANG, WU LU, Journalism and Communication
WANG, XIAO HONG, Television
WANG, YA PING, Animation
WEI, YONG ZHENG, Social Sciences
WU, YIN, Television
WU, YU, Broadcasting
XING, XIN, Broadcasting
YANG, FENG JIAO, Television
YANG, LEI, Information Engineering
YANG, LU PING, Television
YANG, XIAO LU, Film and Television Arts
YAO, XIAO OU, Literature
YE, FENG YING, Television
YOU, FEI, Film and Television Arts
YUAN, QING FENG, Film and Television Arts
ZAN, YAN QUAN, Media Management
ZENG, XIANG MIN, Television
ZENG, ZHI HUA, Broadcasting
ZHANG, FEN ZHU, Film and Television Arts
ZHANG, GE DONG, Film and Television Arts
ZHANG, GUI ZHEN, International Communication
ZHANG, JING, Literature
ZHANG, JUN, Animation
ZHANG, QI, Information Engineering
ZHANG, SHU, Journalism and Communication
ZHANG, XIAO FENG, Social Sciences
ZHANG, YAN, Journalism and Communication
ZHANG, YAN, Film and Television Arts
ZHANG, YONG HUI, Information Engineering
ZHANG, YU HUA, Film and Television Arts
ZHAO, SHU PING, Television
ZHAO, XIAO GUANG, Literature
ZHAO, YU MING, Journalism and Communication
ZHONG, TAO, Literature
ZHONG, YI QIAN, Advertising Studies
ZHOU, HONG GUO, Media Management
ZHOU, HUA BIN, Film and Television Arts
ZHOU, JING BO, Film and Television Arts
ZHOU, YONG, Film and Television Arts
ZHOU, YUE LIANG, Film and Television Arts

ATTACHED CENTRES AND INSTITUTIONS

Asia Media Research Centre: Dir CHEN WEI XING.

Centre for Chinese Economic Studies: Dir ZAN YAN QUAN.

Centre for Radio and Television Studies: Dir HU ZHENG RONG.

Communication Acoustics Laboratory: Dir MENG ZI HOU.

Higher Education Research Institution: Dir YANG SHU YU.

Media Economy Research Institution: Dir ZHOU HONG GUO.

BEIJING UNIVERSITY OF AERONAUTICS AND ASTRONAUTICS

37 Xueyuan Rd, Beijing 100083
Telephone: 62017251
Fax: 62028356
Internet: www.buaa.edu.cn

Founded 1952

Controlled by the aviation industries of China

Languages of instruction: Chinese, English
Academic year: September to August

President: Prof. SHEN SHITUAN
Vice-Presidents: Prof. DENG XUEYING, XU CONGWEI, FEI BINJUN, WU ZHE
Director, International Academic Exchange: CUI DEYU
Librarian: Prof. JIN MAOZHONG

Library of 1,100,000 vols, 98,000 periodicals

Number of teaching and research staff: 2,300
Number of students: 12,600 (2,000 postgraduate)

Publications: *Journal* (quarterly), *Journal of Aerospace Power* (quarterly), *Acta Aeronautica et Astronautica Sinica* (monthly), *Journal of Engineering Graphics* (2 a year), *Acta Materiae Compositae Sinica* (quarterly), *Model World* (quarterly), *Aerospace Knowledge* (monthly), *College English* (every 2 months), *DADDM* (2 a year), *China Aeronautical Education* (quarterly)

DEPARTMENTAL DEANS

Materials Science and Engineering: Prof. XU HUIBIN
Electronic Engineering: Prof. ZHANG XIAOLIN
Automatic Control: Prof. LI XINGSHAN
Propulsion: Prof. LI QIHAN
Flying Vehicle Design and Applied Mechanics: Prof. WANG JINJUN
Computer Sciences and Engineering: Prof. JIN MAOZHONG
Manufacturing Engineering: Prof. TANG XIAOQING
Mechanical and Electrical Engineering: Prof. YANG ZONGXU
Foreign Languages: Prof. LI BAOKUN
Systems Engineering: Prof. YANG WEIMIN

PRINCIPALS

School of Continuing Education: Prof. WANG BAORAI
School of Management: Prof. JIANG XIESHENG
Graduate School: Prof. DENG XUEYING
School of Astronautics: Prof. ZHANG ZHENPENG
Flying College: Prof. WANG XIAOWAN (Exec. Dir)
School of Haidian Applied Technology: Prof. LIU TIANSHEN
School of Science: Prof. GUAN KEYING (Dean)
School of Humanities and Social Sciences: Prof. SHENG SHUREN (Dean)

ATTACHED RESEARCH INSTITUTES

Chinese Aeronautical Establishment BUAA Branch: Dir Prof. SHEN SHITUAN.

Research Institute of Higher Education: Dir Assoc. Prof. LEI QING.

Research Institute of Thermal Power Engineering: Dir Prof. ZHOU SHENG.

Research Institute of Fluid Mechanics: Dir Prof. LU ZHIYONG.

Research Institute of Solid Mechanics: Dir Prof. GAO ZHENTONG.

Research Institute of Unmanned Flight Vehicle Design: Prof. LI CHUNJIN.

Research Institute of Computer Software Engineering: Dir Prof. JIN MAOZHONG.

Research Institute of Manufacturing Engineering: Dir Prof. TANG XIAOQING.

Research Institute of Robotics: Dir Prof. WANG YINMIAO.

Research Institute of Reliability Engineering: Dir Prof. YANG WEIMIN.

BEIJING UNIVERSITY OF BUSINESS AND TECHNOLOGY

33 Fu-cheng Rd, Beijing 100037
Telephone: (10) 68904774
Fax: (10) 68417834

Founded 1950
Academic year: September to July
President: Prof. SU ZHIPING
Vice-Presidents: LI ZHONG, LIU XIUSHENG, LI DIANFU, WANG ZHONGDE, PAN BANGJIN, NI ZHIHENG
Librarian: GAO YUNZHI
Number of teachers: 700
Number of students: 14,000 (400 graduate)
Publications: *Journal* (every 2 months), *Commercial Economy Research* (monthly), *Correspondence Department Report* (quarterly)

HEADS OF DEPARTMENTS

Graduate Study: LI CHUN
Economics and Trade: LIU XIUSHENG
Business: LAN LING
Accounting: TANG GULIANG
Chemistry: SUN JIAYAO
Law: LI RENYU
Mechanical Automation: LIU XUAN
Information Engineering: HE WEI
Journalism: SHEN YI

BEIJING UNIVERSITY OF CHEMICAL TECHNOLOGY

15 Bei San Huan East Rd, Chao Yang District, Beijing 100029
Telephone: (10) 64434820
Fax: (10) 64423089
E-mail: office@buct.edu.cn
Internet: www.buct.edu.cn

Founded 1958
Academic year: September to July
President: WANG ZI GAO
Vice-Presidents: DING JU YUAN, WANG GUI, ZHAO SU ZHEN, ZUO YU
Head of Graduate Department: FU ZHI FENG CO
Librarian: ZHANG YU CHUAN
Number of teachers: 1,800
Number of students: 16,900
Publications: *Journal of Beijing University of Chemical Technology* (natural sciences, 6 a year), *Journal of Beijing University of Chemical Technology* (social science, 4 a year)

DEANS

College of Chemical Engineering: ZHANG ZE YAN
College of Economics and Management: YAO FEI
College of Information Science and Technology: ZHAO HENG YONG
College of Life Sciences and Technology: TAN TIAN WEI
College of Literature and Law: FU YU LONG
College of Machine Electricity Engineering: WANG KUI SHENG
College of Materials Science and Engineering: YU DING SHENG
College of Science: JIANG GUANG FENG
Professional Technology Institute: XU XI TANG

PROFESSORS

CAO, LIU LIN, Information Science and Technology
CAO, ZHI QING, Machine Electricity Engineering
CHEN, BIAO HUA, Chemical Engineering
CHEN, CHANG SHU, Literature and Law
CHEN, JIAN FENG, Chemical Engineering
CHEN, XIAO CHUN, Chemical Engineering
CHEN, YAO QI, Literature and Law
CHEN, ZHONG LI, Literature and Law
CUI, WEI QI, Literature and Law
DANG, ZHI MIN, Materials Science and Engineering
DUAN, XUE, Science
FENG, LIAN XUN, Machine Electricity Engineering
GAO, ZHENG MING, Chemical Engineering
GENG, XIAO ZHEN, Machine Electricity Engineering
GUO, FEN, Chemical Engineering
GUO, KAI, Chemical Engineering
HAI, RE TI, Chemical Engineering
HE, JING, Science
HUA, YOU QING, Materials Science and Engineering
HUANG, LI, Materials Science and Engineering
HUANG, MIN LI, Materials Science and Engineering
HUANG, MING ZHI, Materials Science and Engineering
HUANG, XIONG BIN, Chemical Engineering
JI, SHENG FU, Chemical Engineering
JIANG, BO, Machine Electricity Engineering
JIN, RI GUANG, Materials Science and Engineering
LI, CHANG JIANG, Science
LI, CHUN XI, Chemical Engineering
LI, DIAN QING, Science
LI, HANG QUAN, Materials Science and Engineering
LI, HONG GUANG, Information Science and Technology
LI, QI FANG, Materials Science and Engineering
LI, QUN SHENG, Chemical Engineering
LI, WU SI, Economics and Management
LI, XIAO YU, Materials Science and Engineering
LI, XIU JIN, Chemical Engineering
LI, YUE CHENG, Chemical Engineering
LI, ZHI LIN, Materials Science and Engineering
LIU, FENG XIN, Information Science and Technology
LIU, HUI, Chemical Engineering
LIU, JIE, Materials Science and Engineering
LIU, KUN YUAN, Chemical Engineering
LIU, WEI, Chemical Engineering
MA, YUN YU, Life Sciences and Technology
MAO, BING QUAN, Science
MO, DE JU, Information Science and Technology
PAN, LI DENG, Information Science and Technology
PANG, YAN BIN, Information Science and Technology
QIAN, CAI FU, Machine Electricity Engineering
QIAO, JIN LIANG, Materials Science and Engineering
QU, YI XIN, Chemical Engineering
SHENG, WEI YONG, Literature and Law
SONG, HUAI HE, Materials Science and Engineering
SU, HAI JIA, Life Sciences and Technology
SUN, JUN, Economics and Management
TAN, TIAN WEI, Life Sciences and Technology
WANG, FANG, Life Sciences and Technology
WANG, JIAN HONG, Chemical Engineering
WANG, JIAN LIN, Information Science and Technology
WANG, KUI SHENG, Machine Electricity Engineering
WANG, MING MING, Economics and Management
WANG, WEN CHUAN, Chemical Engineering
WANG, XUE WEI, Information Science and Technology
WANG, ZI GAO, Chemical Engineering
WEI, GANG, Materials Science and Engineering
WEI, JIE, Materials Science and Engineering
WU, CHONG GUANG, Information Science and Technology
WU, DE ZHEN, Materials Science and Engineering
WU, GANG, Materials Science and Engineering
WU, XIANG ZHI, Chemical Engineering
WU, YI XIAN, Materials Science and Engineering
XIONG, RONG CHUN, Materials Science and Engineering
XU, CHUN CHUN, Materials Science and Engineering
XU, GUANG JUN, Economics and Management
XU, HONG, Machine Electricity Engineering
XU, PENG HUA, Machine Electricity Engineering
YANG, QI, Science
YANG, RU, Materials Science and Engineering
YANG, WANG TAI, Materials Science and Engineering
YANG, WEN SHENG, Science
YANG, YUAN YI, Science
YANG, ZU RONG, Chemical Engineering
YAO, FEI, Economics and Management
YIN, DENG XIANG, Literature and Law
YU, DING SHENG, Materials Science and Engineering
YUAN, DE YU, Literature and Law
YUAN, QI PENG, Life Sciences and Technology
ZHANG, JING CHANG, Science
ZHANG, LI QUN, Materials Science and Engineering
ZHANG, MEI LING, Machine Electricity Engineering
ZHANG, MING GUO, Literature and Law
ZHANG, PENG, Life Sciences and Technology
ZHANG, WEI DONG, Chemical Engineering
ZHANG, XING YING, Materials Science and Engineering
ZHANG, YING KUI, Economics and Management
ZHANG, YU CHUAN, Materials Science and Engineering
ZHANG, ZE YAN, Chemical Engineering
ZHAO, BAO YUAN, Economics and Management
ZHAO, HENG YONG, Information Science and Technology
ZHAO, SHU QING, Information Science and Technology
ZHAO, SU HE, Materials Science and Engineering
ZHEN, DAN XING, Chemical Engineering
ZHONG, CHONG LI, Chemical Engineering
ZHOU, HENG JIN, Materials Science and Engineering
ZHU, QUN XIONG, Information Science and Technology

ATTACHED CENTRES AND INSTITUTES

Applied Chemistry Research Institute: Dir DUAN XUE.

Biology Resource and Biology Energy Research Institute: Dir TAN TIAN WEI.

Centre of Advanced Elastomer Materials: Dir ZHANG LI QUN.

Chemical Engineering and Technology Research Institute: Dir WANG WEN CHUAN.

Institute of Plastics Machinery and Engineering: Dir ZHU FU HUA.

Law and Intellectual Property Rights Research Institute: Dir GONG SAI HONG.

Politics and Administration Research Institute: Dir FU YU LONG.

Research Centre of the Ministry of Education for High Gravity Engineering and Technology: Dir CHEN JIAN FENG.

Technology And Social Research Institute: Dir YIN DENG XIANG.

BEIJING UNIVERSITY OF CHINESE MEDICINE

11 East Rd, Bei San Huan, Chao Yang District, Beijing 100029
Telephone: (10) 64213841
Fax: (10) 64213817
Internet: www.bjucmp.edu.cn

Founded 1956
Ministry of Education control
Academic year: September to July

President: ZHENG SHOU ZE
Vice-Presidents: QIAO WANG ZHONG, WANG QING GUO, WEI TIAO MAO, XU XIAO
Heads of Graduate Department: TU YA, WANG WEI
Librarian: ZHANG QI CHENG

Number of teachers: 2,705
Number of students: 9,925

Publications: *Chinese Medicine Education* (6 a year), *Journal of Beijing University of Chinese Medicine* (6 a year), *Journal of Beijing University of Chinese Medicine* (clinical studies, 4 a year)

DEANS

College of Acupuncture: GU SHI ZE
College of Basic Medicine: GUO XIA ZHEN
College of Chinese Traditional Medicine: LI JIA SHI
College of Nursing: ZHANG MEI
Network Education College: YU YONG JIE

PROFESSORS

BAI, LING MIN, Chinese and Western Medicine
CHEN, JIA XU, Chinese Medicine (Diagnostics)
CHEN, LI XIN, Chinese and Western Medicine
CHEN, MING, Basic Medicine
CHEN, SHU CHANG, Chinese Medicine (Surgery)
CHEN, XIN YI, Chinese and Western Medicine
FENG, QIAN JIN, Chinese and Western Medicine
FU, YAN LING, Basic Medicine
GAO, XUE MIN, Chinese Medicine (Clinical)
GAO, YAN BING, Chinese Medicine
GAO, YING, Chinese Medicine
GU, LI GANG, Chinese and Western Medicine
GU, SHI ZE, Acupuncture
GUO, WEI QIN, Chinese Medicine
GUO, XIA ZHEN, Basic Medicine
GUO, YA JIAN, Chinese Medicine (Traditional)
HAO, RUI FU, Chinese Medicine
HAO, WANG SHAN, Basic Medicine
HOU, JIA YU, Chinese Medicine (Traditional)
HU, LI SHENG, Chinese and Western Medicine
HUANG, QI FU, Chinese and Western Medicine
JI, SHAO LIANG, Chinese Medicine (Diagnostics)
JIANG, LI SHENG, Basic Medicine
JIANG, LIANG GUO, Chinese Medicine
JIN, GUANG LIANG, Basic Medicine
JIN, ZHE, Chinese and Western Medicine
LI, FENG, Chinese Medicine (Diagnostics)
LI, GUO ZHANG, Chinese and Western Medicine
LI, JIA SHI, Chinese Medicine (Traditional)
LI, JIN XIANG, Chinese Medicine
LI, NAI QING, Chinese and Western Medicine
LI, PENG TAO, Chinese and Western Medicine
LI, RI QING, Chinese Medicine (Surgery)
LI, SHI FAN, Basic Medicine
LI, XUE WU, Acupuncture
LI, YU HANG, Basic Medicine
LI, YUN GU, Chinese Medicine (Traditional)
LIANG, RONG, Chinese Medicine (Diagnostics)
LIN, QIAN, Chinese and Western Medicine
LIU, JIN MING, Chinese Medicine
LIU, TIAN JUN, Acupuncture
LIU, TONG HUA, Chinese Medicine
LIU, YAN CHI, Basic Medicine
LU, WEI XING, Chinese and Western Medicine
LU, YUN RU, Chinese Medicine (Traditional)
LU, ZHAO LIN, Basic Medicine
LV, REN HE, Chinese Medicine
MENG, QING GANG, Basic Medicine
NIU, JIAN ZHAO, Chinese and Western Medicine
NIU, XIN, Chinese and Western Medicine
QIAO, YAN JIANG, Chinese Medicine (Traditional)
QIU, QUAN YING, Chinese and Western Medicine
QU, SHUANG QING, Basic Medicine
REN, TIAN CHI, Chinese Medicine (Traditional)
SHI, REN BIN, Chinese Medicine (Traditional)
SONG, NAI GUANG, Basic Medicine
SU, JING, Basic Medicine
SUN, JIAN NING, Chinese Medicine (Traditional)
SUN, YING LI, Chinese and Western Medicine
TANG, QI SHENG, Chinese Medicine
TANG, YI PENG, Chinese and Western Medicine
TIAN, DE LU, Chinese Medicine
TIAN, JING ZHOU, Chinese Medicine
TU, YA, Acupuncture
WANG, HONG TU, Basic Medicine
WANG, JI FENG, Chinese and Western Medicine
WANG, QI, Basic Medicine
WANG, QING GUO, Basic Medicine
WANG, SHUO REN, Chinese and Western Medicine
WANG, TIAN FANG, Chinese Medicine (Diagnostics)
WANG, WEI, Chinese and Western Medicine
WANG, WEN QUAN, Chinese Medicine (Traditional)
WANG, XIN YUE, Chinese Medicine
WANG, YU LAI, Chinese Medicine
WEI, LU XUE, Chinese Medicine (Traditional)
WU, WEI PING, Chinese Medicine
XIAO, PEI GEN, Chinese Medicine (Traditional)
XU, LIN, Chinese and Western Medicine
XU, QIU PING, Chinese Medicine (Traditional)
YAN, JI LAN, Basic Medicine
YAN, JIAN HUA, Basic Medicine
YAN, YU NING, Chinese Medicine (Traditional)
YAN, ZHENG HUA, Chinese Medicine (Clinical)
YANG, JING XIANG, Chinese Medicine
YANG, SHU PENG, Chinese Medicine (Traditional)
YE, YONG AN, Chinese Medicine
ZHANG, BING, Chinese Medicine (Clinical)
ZHANG, QI CHENG, Basic Medicine
ZHANG, YAN SHENG, Chinese Medicine (Surgery)
ZHANG, YUN LING, Chinese Medicine
ZHAO, JI PING, Acupuncture
ZHAO, JIN XIN, Chinese Medicine
ZHOU, PING AN, Chinese Medicine
ZHOU, YI HUAI, Chinese Medicine

ATTACHED FACILITIES

Centre of Education Technical Training.

Dong Fang Hospital: Dir YANG JIN XIANG.

Dong Zhi Men Hospital Affiliated to the Beijing University of Chinese Medicine: Dir WANG YU LAI.

Pharmaceutical Factory of Beijing University of Chinese Medicine

BEIJING FILM ACADEMY

Xi Tu Cheng Lu 4, Hai Dian District, Beijing 100088
Telephone: 62012132
Internet: www.bfa.edu.cn

Founded 1950

President: SHEN SONGSHENG
Vice-Presidents: XIE FEI, MENG HAIFENG
Deputy Librarians: CHEN WENJING, LU SHIPING

Library of 150,000 vols
Number of teachers: 273
Number of students: 286 (29 postgraduate)

Publication: *Journal*

HEADS OF DEPARTMENTS

Film Direction: ZHENG DONGTIEN
Acting: CHIAN XIEGE
Cinematography: ZHENG GAOEN
Screen Script: WANG DI
Sound Recording: WANG JUNZHI
Design: LU ZHICHONG

BEIJING FOREIGN STUDIES UNIVERSITY

2 North Xisanhuan Ave, Haidian District, Beijing 100089
Telephone: (10) 68916215
Fax: (10) 68423144
E-mail: bwxzb@bfsu.edu.cn
Internet: bfsu.edu.cn

Founded 1941
Academic year: September to July

Chancellor: Prof. CHEN NAIFANG
Vice-Chancellors: Prof. YANG XUEYI, Prof. Dr HE QIXIN, Prof. ZHONG MEISUN, Prof. ZHOU LIE

Library of 600,000 vols
Number of teachers: 700
Number of students: 10,000

Publications: *Foreign Language Teaching and Research*, *Foreign Literatures*, *Soviet Art and Literature*, *International Forum*

HEADS OF DEPARTMENTS

English: DU XUEZENG
Russian: LI YINGNAN
French: TANG XINGYING
German: YUAN JIANHUA
Spanish: LIU YONGXIN
Afro-Asian Languages: ZHANG TIEYING
Eastern European Languages: GONG KUNYU
English Language Communication: GU YUEGUO
Arabic: GUO SHAOHUA
Japanese: WANG YULIN
Chinese: CHENG YUZHEN
Interpretation and Translation: ZHUANG YICHUAN
Adult Education: LOU GUANGQING
Social Science: TAO XIU'AO
International Business: PENG LONG
Diplomacy: LI YONGHUI
Occupational Education: ZHONG MEISUN
Beijing Centre of Japanese Studies: YUAN ANSHENG

BEIJING FORESTRY UNIVERSITY

Xiaozhuang, Haidan District, Beijing 100083
Telephone: 62338279
Fax: 62325071
Internet: www.bjfu.edu.cn

Founded 1952

Rector: Prof. HE QINGTANG
Registrar: Prof. ZHOU XINCHEN
Librarian: Prof. GAO RONGFU

Library of 560,000 vols
Number of teachers: 700
Number of students: 3,500

HEADS OF DEPARTMENTS

School of Adult Education: Assoc. Prof. YAN JINMING
School of Forest Engineering and Products: Prof. LU ZHENYOU
School of Forest Resources and Environment: Prof. XIU JURU
School of Forestry Economics and Management: Prof. REN HENGQI
School of Landscape Architecture: Prof. ZHANG QIXIAN
School of Plant Sciences: Prof. LI FENGLAN
School of Soil and Water Conservation: Prof. SUN BAOPING
Department of Foreign Languages: Prof. SHI BAOHUI
Department of Postgraduate Studies: Prof. XIE MINGSHU
Department of Social Science: Prof. BAN DAOMING

BEIJING JIAOTONG UNIVERSITY

Shang Yuan Cun, Xi Zhi Men Wai, Hai Ding District, Beijing 100044
Telephone: (10) 51688421
Fax: (10) 62245827
Internet: www.njtu.edu.cn

Founded 1921
Academic year: September to July

President: TAN ZHEN HUI
Vice-Presidents: CHEN FENG, LI XUE WEI, NING BIN, WANG JIA QIONG
Head of Graduate Department: WANG YONG SHENG
Librarian: SHA SHU LI

Number of teachers: 2,500
Number of students: 15,000

Publication: *Journal* (6 a year)

DEANS

School of Civil Engineering and Architecture: XU ZHAO YI
School of Computer and Information Technology: RUAN QIU QI
School of Economy and Management: WANG JIA QIONG
School of Electrical Engineering: ZHENG QIONG LIN
School of Electronics and Information Engineering: ZHANG SI DONG
School of Humanities and Social Science: GUO HAI YUN
School of Mechanical, Electronic and Control Engineering: SUN SHOU GUANG
School of Science: ZHANG PING ZHI
School of Traffic and Transportation: SUN QUAN XIN

PROFESSORS

BI, YING, Humanities and Social Science
CHANG, YAN XUN, Science
CHEN, CHANG JIA, Electronics and Information Engineering
CHEN, HOU JIN, Electronics and Information Engineering
CHEN, JING YAN, Economy and Management
CHEN, SHI RONG, Humanities and Social Science
CHEN, SHU MIN, Humanities and Social Science
CHEN, XI SHENG, Economy and Management
CHEN, YIN HANG, Electronics and Information Engineering
CHENG, ZHEN WEI, Science
DENG, ZHEN BO, Science
DING, HUI PING, Economy and Management
DONG, BAO TIAN, Traffic and Transportation
DU, YAN LIANG, Mechanical
FAN, YU, Electrical Engineering
FANG, YUE FA, Mechanical
FENG, QI BO, Science
FENG, YAN QUAN, Science
FENG, YU MIN, Electronics and Information Engineering
GAO, WEN, Humanities and Social Science
GAO, YU CHEN, Civil Engineering and Architecture
GAO, ZI YOU, Traffic and Transportation
GUAN, KE YING, Science
GUAN, ZHONG LIANG, Economy and Management
HAN, BAO MING, Traffic and Transportation
HAO, RONG TAI, Electrical Engineering
HE, QING FU, Mechanical
HE, SHI WEI, Traffic and Transportation
HOU, YAN BIN, Science
HOU, ZHONG SHENG, Electronics and Information Engineering
HU, SI JI, Traffic and Transportation
HUANG, LEI, Economy and Management
HUANG, MEI, Electrical Engineering
HUANG, SHI HUA, Science
JI, JIA LUN, Traffic and Transportation
JIA, LI, Mechanical
JIA, LI MIN, Traffic and Transportation
JIA, YUAN HUA, Traffic and Transportation
JIANG, JIU CHUN, Electrical Engineering
JIANG, ZHONG HAO, Science
JIN, XIN MIN, Electrical Engineering
JIN, ZONG ZE, Mechanical
JU, SONG DONG, Economy and Management
LI, CHENG SHU, Electronics and Information Engineering
LI, DE CAI, Mechanical
LI, PEI XUAN, Economy and Management
LI, QIANG, Mechanical
LI, SI ZE, Science
LI, WEN XING, Economy and Management
LI, XUE WEI, Economy and Management
LIN, BO LIANG, Traffic and Transportation
LIN, DAI DAI, Economy and Management
LIU, CHANG BIN, Economy and Management
LIU, JIAN KUN, Civil Engineering and Architecture
LIU, JUN, Traffic and Transportation
LIU, KAI, Traffic and Transportation
LIU, KUN HUI, Science
LIU, MING GUANG, Electrical Engineering
LIU, WEI NING, Civil Engineering and Architecture
LIU, YAN PEI, Science
LIU, YAN PING, Economy and Management
LIU, YI SHENG, Economy and Management
LIU, ZUO YI, Traffic and Transportation
LV, YONG BO, Traffic and Transportation
MA, JIAN JUN, Traffic and Transportation
MAO, BAO HUA, Traffic and Transportation
NIE, YU XIN, Science
NING, TI GANG, Electronics and Information Engineering
NU, YI HONG, Economy and Management
OU, GUO LI, Economy and Management
QIAO, CHUN SHENG, Civil Engineering and Architecture
QU, HONG XIANG, Mechanical
RONG, CHAO HE, Economy and Management
SHA, FEI, Electronics and Information Engineering
SHANG, PENG JIAN, Science
SHAO, CHUN FU, Traffic and Transportation
SHEN, JIN SHENG, Traffic and Transportation
SHENG, XIN ZHI, Science
SHI, DING HUAN, Traffic and Transportation
SHI, MEI XIA, Economy and Management
SHI, ZHI FEI, Civil Engineering and Architecture
SHI, ZHONG HENG, Civil Engineering and Architecture
SONG, SHOU XIN, Economy and Management
SUN, QUAN XIN, Traffic and Transportation
SUN, SHOU GUANG, Mechanical
TAN, ZHEN HUI, Electronics and Information Engineering
TANG, TAO, Electronics and Information Engineering
TANG, TAO, Electronics and Information Engineering
TANG, ZHEN MIN, Electronics and Information Engineering
WANG, JIA QIONG, Economy and Management
WANG, JUN HONG, Electronics and Information Engineering
WANG, LI DE, Electrical Engineering
WANG, LIAN JUN, Civil Engineering and Architecture
WANG, MENG SHU, Civil Engineering and Architecture
WANG, WEI, Electrical Engineering
WANG, XI SHI, Electronics and Information Engineering
WANG, YAN YONG, Traffic and Transportation
WANG, YAO QIU, Economy and Management
WANG, YI, Electrical Engineering
WANG, YONG SHENG, Science
WANG, YUAN FENG, Civil Engineering and Architecture
WANG, YUE SHENG, Civil Engineering and Architecture
WEI, QING CHAO, Civil Engineering and Architecture
WEI, QING CHAO, Civil Engineering and Architecture
WEI, XUE YE, Electronics and Information Engineering
WU, CHONG QING, Science
WU, LIU, Science
XIA, HE, Civil Engineering and Architecture
XIAO, GUI PING, Traffic and Transportation
XIE, JI LONG, Mechanical
XIN, SHU MING, Mechanical
XIU, NAI HUA, Science
XU, TAO BO, Economy and Management
XU, YU GONG, Mechanical
XU, ZHAO YI, Civil Engineering and Architecture
XU, ZHAO YI, Civil Engineering and Architecture
YAN, FENG PING, Electronics and Information Engineering
YAN, GUI PING, Civil Engineering and Architecture
YAN, HONG SEN, Mechanical
YANG, HAO, Traffic and Transportation
YANG, QIN SHAN, Civil Engineering and Architecture
YANG, QING SHAN, Civil Engineering and Architecture
YANG, QING XIN, Mechanical
YANG, SHAO PU, Mechanical
YANG, ZHAO XIA, Traffic and Transportation
YAO, BIN, Economy and Management
YAO, PEI JI, Economy and Management
YAO, QIAN FENG, Civil Engineering and Architecture
YE, SHU JUN, Economy and Management
YI, XIANG YONG, Traffic and Transportation
YU, LEI, Traffic and Transportation
YU, QING, Traffic and Transportation
YUAN, LU QU, Economy and Management
YUAN, ZHEN ZHOU, Traffic and Transportation
ZHA, JIAN ZHONG, Mechanical, Electronic and Control Engineering
ZHAN, HE SHENG, Economy and Management
ZHANG, CHAO, Traffic and Transportation
ZHANG, GUO WU, Traffic and Transportation
ZHANG, HONG KE, Electronics and Information Engineering
ZHANG, HONG RU, Civil Engineering and Architecture
ZHANG, LEI, Economy and Management
ZHANG, LI, Electrical Engineering
ZHANG, LIN CHANG, Electronics and Information Engineering
ZHANG, LU XIN, Civil Engineering and Architecture
ZHANG, MING YU, Economy and Management
ZHANG, QIU SHENG, Economy and Management
ZHANG, SI DONG, Electronics and Information Engineering
ZHANG, WEN JIE, Economy and Management
ZHANG, XI, Traffic and Transportation

ZHANG, XI QING, Science
ZHANG, XIAO DONG, Electrical Engineering
ZHANG, XIAO QING, Electrical Engineering
ZHANG, XING CHEN, Traffic and Transportation
ZHANG, YI HUANG, Electrical Engineering
ZHANG, YU XIN, Traffic and Transportation
ZHANG, YUN TONG, Economy and Management
ZHANG, ZHI WEN, Traffic and Transportation
ZHANG, ZHONG YI, Traffic and Transportation
ZHANG, ZI MAO, Civil Engineering and Architecture
ZHAO, CHENG GAN, Civil Engineering and Architecture
ZHAO, JIAN, Economy and Management
ZHENG, QIONG LIN, Electrical Engineering
ZHONG, YAN, Traffic and Transportation
ZHOU, LEI SHAN, Traffic and Transportation
ZHOU, XI DE, Electrical Engineering
ZHOU, YU HUI, Electrical Engineering
ZHU, HENG JUN, Mechanical
ZHU, HONG, Science
ZHU, JIA SHAN, Traffic and Transportation
ZHU, XI, Civil Engineering and Architecture
ZHU, XIAO NING, Traffic and Transportation

ATTACHED INSTITUTES

Advanced Manufacture Technology Laboratory: Dir ZHA JIAN ZHONG.

Dynamic Engineering Institute: Dir ZHANG XIN.

Electrical Laboratory Centre: Dir WANG WEI.

Institute of Chemistry: Dir ZHU HONG.

Institute of Optelectronic Technology: Dir XU SHU RONG.

Mechanical Foundation and Material Engineering Laboratory: Dir HONG JIAN PING.

National Teaching Centre of Electrotechnics and Electronics: Dir ZHANG XIAO DONG.

BEIJING LANGUAGE AND CULTURE UNIVERSITY

15 Xue Yuan Rd, Hai Ding District, Beijing 100083
Telephone: (10) 82303035
Fax: (10) 82303903
Internet: www.blcu.edu.cn

Founded 1962
State control
Academic year: September to July

President: QU DELIN
Vice-Presidents: HUO MINGJIE, LIN GUOLI
Head of Graduate Department: QU DE NING
Librarian: ZHANG YAN FENG

Number of teachers: 700
Number of students: 8,000

Publications: *Chinese Culture Research* (4 a year), *Learning Chinese* (monthly), *World Chinese Teaching* (4 a year)

DEANS

College of Chinese Language: LI LI CHENG
Financial Department: LIU KE
College of Foreign Languages: ZHU WEN JUN
College of Humanities and Social Sciences: CHEN JUAN
College of Information Sciences: SONG ROU

PROFESSORS

CHEN, JUAN, Humanities and Social Sciences
CUI, XI LIANG, Humanities and Social Sciences
DU, DAO MING, Humanities and Social Sciences
FAN, LI, Foreign Languages
FANG, MING, Humanities and Social Sciences
HAN, DE MIN, Humanities and Social Sciences
HAN, JING TAI, Humanities and Social Sciences
HU, YU LONG, Foreign Languages
HUANG, ZHUO YUE, Humanities and Social Sciences
JIAO, FENG, Information Sciences
LI, LI CHENG, Chinese Language
LI, YANG, Chinese Language
LI, YAN SHU, Foreign Languages
LI, TIE CHENG, Humanities and Social Sciences
LI, WEI, Finance
LIANG, XIAO SHENG, Humanities and Social Sciences
LIU, XUN, Humanities and Social Sciences
LIU, GUI LONG, Information Sciences
LIU, KE, Finance
LV, WEN HUA, Humanities and Social Sciences
MA, SHU DE, Chinese Language
MA, ZHEN SHENG, Humanities and Social Sciences
NING, YI ZHONG, Foreign Languages
QIU, MING, Foreign Languages
SHEN, ZHI JUN, Chinese Language
SHI, DING GUO, Humanities and Social Sciences
SONG, ROU, Information Sciences
WANG, YE XIN, Chinese Language
WANG, ZHEN YA, Foreign Languages
XU, SHU AN, Humanities and Social Sciences
YAN, CHUN DE, Humanities and Social Sciences
ZHENG, GUI YOU, Humanities and Social Sciences
ZHENG, WANG PENG, Humanities and Social Sciences
ZHU, WEN JUN, Foreign Languages

ATTACHED CENTRES AND INSTITUTES

Centre for Education Technical Training: Dir WANG DE LIN.

Centre for Studies of Chinese as a Second Language: Dir Prof. ZHAO JIN MING.

Contemporary Chinese Literature Research Institute: Dir WANG NING.

Chinese Proficiency Test (HSK) Centre.

International Education Centre: Dir WANG LU JIANG.

Language Research Institute: Dir CAO ZHI YUN.

BEIJING MEDICAL UNIVERSITY

38 Xue Yuan Lu, Northern Suburb, Beijing 100083
Telephone: (10) 62091334
Fax: (10) 62015681
E-mail: dxb@mail.bjmu.edu.cn
Internet: www.bjmu.edu.cn

Founded 1912
Languages of instruction: Chinese, English
Academic year: August to July (2 terms)

President: WANG DEBING
Vice-Presidents: CHENG BOJI, HAN QIDE, LIN JIUXIANG, LU ZHAOFENG, WEI LIHUI, WANG YU
Dean for Education (vacant)
Director of Libraries: LIAN ZHIJIAN

Library of 730,000 vols, 66,500 periodicals
Number of teachers: 3,721
Number of students: 6,274

Publication: *Journal* (6 a year)

DEANS

School of Basic Medicine: Prof. JIA HONGTI
First School of Medicine: Prof. ZHANG YOUKANG
Second School of Medicine: Prof. LU HOUSHAN
Third School of Medicine: HOU KUANYONG
School of Public Health: Prof. LI LIMING
School of Oral Medicine: Prof. YU GUANGYAN
School of Pharmacy: Prof. ZHANG LIHE
School of Nursing: Prof. ZHENG XIUXIA
School of Mental Health: Prof. CUI YUHUA

There are 19 research institutes, 11 research centres and six affiliated hospitals

BEIJING METALLURGICAL MANAGEMENT INSTITUTE

Guan Zhuang Chao Yang District, Beijing
Telephone: 65762934
Fax: 65762807

Founded 1984

President: MA DEQING
Vice-Presidents: HUANG ZHENGYU, LI YAN
Librarian: ZHAO ZONGDE

Library of 70,000 vols
Number of teachers: 126
Number of students: 1,700

HEADS OF DEPARTMENTS

Management Engineering: YAO GUANGYE
Economics: MA YIMIN
Foreign Languages: LIU YAMING
Information Engineering: LIU ZHENWU
Research Institute of Economic Management and Adult Education: SUN YU

BEIJING NORMAL UNIVERSITY

Xinjiekouwai St 19, Beijing 100875
Telephone: (10) 62207960
Fax: (10) 62200074
E-mail: ipo@bnu.edu.cn
Internet: www.bnu.edu.cn

Founded 1902
State control
Academic year: September to July

President: YUAN GUIREN
Vice-Presidents: SHI PEIJUN, DONG QI, ZHENG JUNLI, XIE WEIHE, DAI JIAGANG, ZHENG SHIQU
Librarian: Prof. JIANG LU

Library: see Libraries
Number of teachers: 1,900
Number of students: 16,400 (8,400 full-time, 8,000 part-time)

Publications: *Journal* (Natural Science edition, 4 a year; Social Science edition, 6 a year), *Comparative Education Review* (monthly), *Foreign Language Teaching in Schools* (monthly), *Journal of Historiography* (monthly)

There are 12 colleges.

BEIJING UNIVERSITY OF POSTS AND TELECOMMUNICATIONS

10 Xi Tu Cheng Rd, Haidian District, Beijing 100088
Telephone: (10) 62282628
Fax: (10) 62281774
E-mail: faoffice@bupt.edu.cn
Internet: www.bupt.edu.cn

Founded 1954

Under control of Ministry of Posts and Telecommunications
Academic year: September to July

President: ZHU XIANGHUA
Vice-Presidents: LIN JINTONG, ZHONG YIXIN, ANG XIUFEN, ZHANG YINGHAI, RENG XIAOMIN, MI JIANHU
Chief Administrative Officer: WANG CHENGCHU
Librarian: MA ZIWEI

Library of 700,000 vols
Number of teachers: 800
Number of students: 8,000

Publications: *Academic Journal of BUPT* (quarterly), *Journal of China University of Posts and Telecommunications*

DEANS

Correspondence College: ANG XIUFEN
Graduate School: SONG JUNDE
Telecommunications College: LIN JINTONG
Fuzhou Extension: ANG XIUFEN
Management Humanities College: TANG SHOULIAN

HEADS OF DEPARTMENTS

Mechanical Engineering: Prof. SHI LIANGPING
Computer Engineering: Prof. AI BO
Applied Science and Technology: Prof. LIU JIE
Information Engineering: Prof. ZHANG HUIMIN
Foreign Language: Prof. YING YASHU

ATTACHED RESEARCH INSTITUTES

BUPT-BNR (Nortel China) Advanced Telecommunications R&D Centre: 10 Xi Tu Cheng Rd, Beijing 100088; Dir (China) ZHU QILIANG.

Research Institute: 10 Xi Tu Cheng Rd, Beijing 100088; communications systems and networks, information theory and processing, signal processing, artificial intelligence, neural networks and applications; Dir WU WEILING.

Institute of Communications and Optoelectronic Information Processing: 10 Xi Tu Cheng Rd, Beijing 100088; optical fibres, optical wave guides, holography and optical information processing; Dir XU DAXIONG.

BEIJING SPORT UNIVERSITY

Zhong Guan Cun, Hai Ding District, Beijing 100084
Telephone: (10) 62989047
Fax: (10) 62989289
Internet: www.bupe.edu.cn

Founded 1953
State control
Academic year: September to July

President: YANG HUA
Vice-Presidents: ZHONG BIN SHU, HE ZHEN WEN, CHI JIAN
Head of Graduate Department: CHI JIAN
Librarian: LIU CAI XIA

Number of teachers: 5,000
Number of students: 540

Publications: *China Method of Body Mechanics* (2 a year), *China School Sport* (6 a year), *Journal* (4 a year)

DEANS

School of Gym Education: ZHOU DIAN MIN
School of Gym Management: QIN CHUN LIN
School of Human Sport: XIE MIN HAO
School of Sports Coaching: YUAN ZUO SHENG
School of Wu Shu: LIU BAO CAI

PROFESSORS

GUI, XIANG, Wu Shu
JIN, YING HUA, Gym Management
JIN, JI CHUN, Human Sport Science
LIU, DA QING, Sports Coaching
MEN, HUI FENG, Wu Shu
MENG, WEN DI, Gym Management
QI, GUO YING, Gym Education
QIN, CHUN LIN, Gym Management
SU, PI REN, Gym Education
SUN, BAO LI, Gym Management
WANG, QIAN, Gym Education
WANG, MIN XIANG, Gym Education
WANG, RUI YUAN, Human Sport Science
WANG, WEI, Sports Coaching
XIA, HUAN ZHEN, Gym Education
XIE, MIN HAO, Human Sport Science
XIONG, XIAO ZHENG, Gym Management
XU, SHENG HONG, Sports Coaching
YAO, XIA WEN, Gym Education
YUAN, DAN, Gym Management
YUAN, ZUO SHENG, Sports Coaching
ZHANG, GUANG DE, Wu Shu
ZHAO, LIAN JIA, Gym Education
ZHOU, DENG SONG, Gym Education
ZHU, RUI QI, Wu Shu

ATTACHED INSTITUTIONS

Adult Education Institute: Dir ZHANG MING YAN.

Beijing Sport University Attached Technical Secondary School: Dir ZHOU AI QIN.

BEIJING INSTITUTE OF TECHNOLOGY

7 Bai Shi Giao, Hai Ding District, Beijing 100081
Telephone: (10) 68914246
Fax: (10) 68468035
Internet: www.bit.edu.cn

Founded 1940
State control
Academic year: September to July

President: KUANG JINGMING
Vice-Presidents: HOU GUANGMING, LI ZHIXIANG, YANG BIN, ZHAO CHANGLU
Head of Graduate Department: KUANG JINGMING
Librarian: CAO SHU REN

Number of teachers: 3,000
Number of students: 31,000

Publications: *Journal of Beijing Institute of Technology* (natural sciences, 6 a year), *Journal of Beijing Institute of Technology* (social sciences, 6 a year)

DEANS

School of Chemical Engineering and Materials: ZHOU, TONG LAI
School of Computers and Control: HOU, CHAO ZHEN
School of Design Art: ZHANG, NAI REN
School of Humanities and Social Sciences: XI, QIAO JUAN
School of Information Engineering: WANG, YUE
School of Management and Economics: WANG, XIU CUN
School of Mechatronic Engineering: LIU, LI
School of Science and Technology: XU, WEN GUO
School of Software: WANG, SHU WU
School of Vehicle and Transport Engineering: XU, CHUN GUANG

PROFESSORS

AN, JIAN PING, Information and Communication Engineering
BA, YAN ZHU, Optics Engineering
BAI, CHUN HUA, Mechatronic Engineering
BI, SHI HUA, Mechatronic Engineering
CAI, HONG YAN, Material Science and Engineering
CAO, GEN RUI, Apparatus Science and Technology
CAO, YUAN DA, Computer Science and Technology
CHAI, RUI JIAO, Mechatronic Engineering
CHEN, DONG SHENG, Vehicle and Transport Engineering
CHEN, HUI YAN, Vehicle and Transport Engineering
CHEN, JIA BIN, Control Science and Engineering
CHEN, JIE, Control Science and Engineering
CHEN, SHU FENG, Electronic Science and Technology
CHEN, SI ZHONG, Vehicle and Transport Engineering
CHEN, XIANG GUANG, Control Science and Engineering
CUI, ZHAN ZHONG, Mechatronic Engineering
DA, YA PING, Control Science and Engineering
DING, HONG SHENG, Vehicle and Transport Engineering
DONG, YU PING, Material Science and Engineering
DOU, LI HUA, Control Science and Engineering
DU, ZHI MING, Mechatronic Engineering
FAN, NING JUN, Mechatronic Engineering
FAN, TIAN YOU, Applied Mathematics
FAN, XIAO ZHONG, Computer Science and Technology
FEI, YUAN CHUN, Electronic Science and Technology
FENG, CHANG GEN, Mechatronic Engineering
FENG, CHANG GEN, Mechatronic Engineering
FENG, SHUN SHAN, Mechatronic Engineering
FU, MENG YING, Control Science and Engineering
GAN, REN CHU, Management Science and Engineering
GAO, BEN QING, Electronic Science and Technology
GAO, CHUN QING, Electronic Science and Technology
GAO, MEI GUO, Information and Communication Engineering
GAO, SHI QIAO, Engineering Mechanics
GAO, ZHI YUN, Optics Engineering
GE, WEI GAO, Applied Mathematics
GE, YUN SHAN, Vehicle and Transport Engineering
GOU, BING CONG, Electronic Science and Technology
GU, LIANG, Vehicle and Transport Engineering
GU, ZHI MIN, Computer Science and Technology
GUO, QIAO, Control Science and Engineering
HAN, BAO LING, Vehicle and Transport Engineering
HAN, BO TANG, Management Science and Engineering
HAN, FENG, Mechatronic Engineering
HAN, YUE QIU, Information and Communication Engineering
HE, PEI KUN, Information and Communication Engineering
HOU, CHAO ZHEN, Control Science and Engineering
HOU, GUANG MING, Management Science and Engineering
HU, CHANG WEN, Chemistry
HU, GENG KAI, Solid Mechanics
HUANG, FENG LEI, Mechatronic Engineering
HUANG, RUO, Vehicle and Transport Engineering
JIA, YUN DE, Computer Science and Technology
JIAO, QING JIE, Mechatronic Engineering
JIAO, YONG HE, Vehicle and Transport Engineering
KANG, JING LI, Mechatronic Engineering
KONG, LING JIA, Vehicle and Transport Engineering
KONG, ZHAO JUN, Management Science and Engineering
KUANG, JING MING, Information and Communication Engineering
LI, JIA ZE, Electronic Science and Technology
LI, JIAN, Management Science and Engineering
LI, JIN LIN, Management Science and Engineering
LI, KE JIE, Mechatronic Engineering
LI, LIN, Apparatus Science and Technology
LI, PING, Mechatronic Engineering
LI, SHI YI, Apparatus Science and Technology
LI, SHI YI, Mechatronic Engineering
LI, XIAO LEI, Vehicle and Transport Engineering
LI, ZHI XIANG, Management Science and Engineering
LIAO, NING FANG, Optics Engineering
LIN, YI, Vehicle and Transport Engineering
LIU, LI, Mechatronic Engineering
LIU, YU SHU, Computer Science and Technology

LIU, ZAO ZHEN, Control Science and Engineering
LIU, ZAO ZHEN, Mechatronic Engineering
LIU, ZHAO DU, Vehicle and Transport Engineering
LIU, ZHI WEN, Information and Communication Engineering
LONG, TENG, Information and Communication Engineering
LONG, XIN PING, Mechatronic Engineering
LU, GUANG SHU, Material Science and Engineering
LU, XIN, Electronic Science and Technology
LUO, WEI XIONG, Information and Communication Engineering
LUO, YUN JUN, Material Science and Engineering
MA, BAO HUA, Mechatronic Engineering
MA, BIAO, Vehicle and Transport Engineering
MA, CHAO CHEN, Vehicle and Transport Engineering
MA, SHU YUAN, Apparatus Science and Technology
MAI, XIAO QING, Mechatronic Engineering
MAO, ER KE, Information and Communication Engineering
MEI, FENG XIANG, Applied Mathematics
NING, GUO QIANG, Optics Engineering
NING, JIAN GUO, Mechatronic Engineering
NING, JIAN GUO, Solid Mechanics
OU, YU XIANG, Material Science and Engineering
PENG, ZHENG GUANG, Control Science and Engineering
QI, ZAI KANG, Mechatronic Engineering
QUAN, WEI QI, Optics Engineering
REN, XUE MEI, Control Science and Engineering
SHA, DING GUO, Apparatus Science and Technology
SHAO, BIN, Chemistry
SHENG, TING ZHI, Information and Communication Engineering
SHI, FENG, Computer Science and Technology
SHI, FU GUI, Applied Mathematics
SONG, HAN TAO, Computer Science and Technology
SONG, ZHEN GUO, Mechatronic Engineering
SUI, SHU YUAN, Mechatronic Engineering
SUN, FENG CHUN, Vehicle and Transport Engineering
SUN, GUANG CHUAN, Information and Communication Engineering
SUN, LIANG, Applied Mathematics
SUN, YE BAO, Vehicle and Transport Engineering
SUN, YU NAN, Electronic Science and Technology
TAN, HUI MIN, Mechatronic Engineering
TAN, HUI MIN, Material Science and Engineering
TAO, RAN, Information and Communication Engineering
WANG, BO, Control Science and Engineering
WANG, FU CHI, Material Science and Engineering
WANG, GUO YU, Vehicle and Transport Engineering
WANG, JIAN ZHONG, Mechatronic Engineering
WANG, PEI LAN, Mechatronic Engineering
WANG, QING LIN, Control Science and Engineering
WANG, SHUN TING, Control Science and Engineering
WANG, XIAO LI, Vehicle and Transport Engineering
WANG, XIAO MO, Information and Communication Engineering
WANG, XING WEN, Mechatronic Engineering
WANG, YONG TIAN, Optics Engineering
WANG, YU, Control Science and Engineering
WANG, YUE, Information and Communication Engineering
WU, QI ZONG, Management Science and Engineering
WU, QING HE, Control Science and Engineering
WU, SI LIANG, Information and Communication Engineering
WU, WEN HUI, Material Science and Engineering
XIA, EN JUN, Management Science and Engineering
XIANG, CHANG LE, Vehicle and Transport Engineering
XIE, JING HUI, Optics Engineering
XING, JIAN GUO, Electronic Science and Technology
XU, GENG GUANG, Mechatronic Engineering
XU, XIAO WEN, Electronic Science and Technology
XU, XING ZHONG, Applied Mathematics
XUE, WEI, Optics Engineering
YAN, JI XIANG, Electronic Science and Technology
YANG, JUN, Engineering Mechanics
YANG, RONG JIE, Material Science and Engineering
YANG, SHU YIN, Mechatronic Engineering
YAO, XIAO XIAN, Mechatronic Engineering
YI, JIANG, Mechatronic Engineering
YU, XIN, Electronic Science and Technology
YUAN, SHI HUA, Vehicle and Transport Engineering
ZENG, FENG ZHANG, Management Science and Engineering
ZENG, QING XUAN, Mechatronic Engineering
ZHAN, SHOU YI, Computer Science and Technology
ZHANG, CHENG NING, Vehicle and Transport Engineering
ZHANG, CHUN LIN, Vehicle and Transport Engineering
ZHANG, FU JUN, Vehicle and Transport Engineering
ZHANG, JING LIN, Mechatronic Engineering
ZHANG, PING, Mechatronic Engineering
ZHANG, QI, Mechatronic Engineering
ZHANG, QIANG, Management Science and Engineering
ZHANG, QING MING, Engineering Mechanics
ZHANG, TONG ZHUANG, Vehicle and Transport Engineering
ZHANG, WEI ZHENG, Vehicle and Transport Engineering
ZHANG, YONG FA, Solid Mechanics
ZHANG, YOU TONG, Vehicle and Transport Engineering
ZHANG, YU HE, Control Science and Engineering
ZHANG, YUN HONG, Chemistry
ZHAO, CHANG LU, Vehicle and Transport Engineering
ZHAO, CHANG MING, Electronic Science and Technology
ZHAO, DA ZUN, Optics Engineering
ZHAO, HONG KANG, Electronic Science and Technology
ZHAO, XING QI, Material Science and Engineering
ZHAO, YUE JIN, Apparatus Science and Technology
ZHEN, LIAN, Mechatronic Engineering
ZHENG, HONG FEI, Vehicle and Transport Engineering
ZHENG, LIAN, Control Science and Engineering
ZHONG, QIU HAI, Control Science and Engineering
ZHOU, JIAN, Applied Mathematics
ZHOU, LI WEI, Optics Engineering
ZHOU, TONG LAI, Chemistry
ZHU, DONG HUA, Management Science and Engineering
ZUO, ZHEN XING, Vehicle and Transport Engineering

ATTACHED CENTRES

State Key Laboratory for Prevention and Control of Catastrophic Explosions: Dir BAI YI LONG.

BEIJING UNIVERSITY OF TECHNOLOGY

100 Ping Le Yuan, Chao Yang District, Beijing 100226
Telephone: (10) 67392239
Fax: (10) 67392675
Internet: www.bjpu.edu.cn

Founded 1960
Academic year: September to July
President: FAN, BO YUAN
Vice-President: HOU, YI BIN
Head of Graduate Department: JIANG, YI JIAN
Librarian: FEI, REN YUAN
Number of teachers: 1,100
Number of students: 26,000
Publication: *Journal* (4 a year)

DEANS

College of Applied Science: ZHANG, ZHONG ZHAN
College of Architecture Engineering: HUO, DA
College of Computer Science: ZHANG, SHU JIE
College of Economics and Management: LI, JING WEN
College of Electronic Information and Control Engineering: WANG, PU
College of Energy and Environmental Engineering: MA, CHONG FANG
College of Foreign Languages: WANG, FU XIANG
College of Humanities and Social Sciences: LU, XUE YI
College of Life Science and Bio-Engineering: ZENG, YI
College of Material Science and Engineering: NIE, ZHA REN
College of Mechanical Engineering and Applied Electronics Technology: YANG, JIAN WU
College of Software Engineering: HOU, YI BIN

PROFESSORS

BAO, CHANG CHUN, Electronic Information and Control Engineering
CAO, WANG LIN, Architecture Engineering
CHEN, GUANG HUA, Material Science and Engineering
CHEN, JIAN XIN, Electronic Information and Control Engineering
CHEN, YANG ZHOU, Electronic Information and Control Engineering
CHENG, CAO ZONG, Applied Science and Physics
CHENG, SHUI YUAN, Energy and Environmental Engineering
CUI, PING YUAN, Electronic Information and Control Engineering
DAI, HONG XING, Energy and Environmental Engineering
DI, RUI HUA, Computer Science
DU, XIU LI, Architecture Engineering
DUAN, JIAN MIN, Electronic Information and Control Engineering
FEI, REN YUAN, Mechanical Engineering and Applied Electronics Technology
GUO, BAI NING, Computer Science
HAN, FU RONG, Economics and Management
HE, CUN FU, Mechanical Engineering and Applied Electronics Technology
HE, HONG, Energy and Environmental Engineering
HE, RUO QUAN, Architecture Engineering
HE, ZI NIAN, Energy and Environmental Engineering
HOU, BI HUI, Applied Science and Physics
HOU, YI BIN, Computer Science
HUANG, LU CHENG, Economics and Management
HUANG, TI YUN, Economics and Management
HUO, DA, Architecture Engineering
JIANG, YI JIE, Applied Science and Physics

KANG, BAO WEI, Electronic Information and Control Engineering
KANG, TIAN FANG, Energy and Environmental Engineering
LEI, YONG PING, Material Science and Engineering
LI, DE SHENG, Mechanical Engineering and Applied Electronics Technology
LI, GANG, Laser Engineering
LI, HUI MING, Economics and Management
LI, JING WEN, Economics and Management
LI, SHOU MEI, Applied Science and Physics
LI, XIAO YAN, Material Science and Engineering
LI, ZHEN BAO, Architecture Engineering
LI, ZHI GUO, Electronic Information and Control Engineering
LIAO, HU SHENG, Computer Science
LIU, CHUN NIAN, Computer Science
LIU, XIAO MING, Architecture Engineering
LIU, YOU MING, Applied Science and Physics
LIU, ZHONG LIANG, Energy and Environmental Engineering
LU, XUE YI, Economics and Management
MA, CHONG FANG, Energy and Environmental Engineering
MA, GUO YUAN, Energy and Environmental Engineering
NIE, ZHA REN, Material Science and Engineering
PENG, YONG ZHEN, Energy and Environmental Engineering
REN, FU TIAN, Architecture Engineering
REN, ZHEN HAI, Energy and Environmental Engineering
RUAN, XIAO GANG, Electronic Information and Control Engineering
SHANG, DE GUANG, Mechanical Engineering and Applied Electronics Technology
SHE, YUAN BIN, Energy and Environmental Engineering
SHENG, GUANG DI, Electronic Information and Control Engineering
SHENG, LAN SUN, Electronic Information and Control Engineering
SHI, YAO WU, Material Science and Engineering
SONG, ROU, Computer Science
SUI, YUN KANG, Mechanical Engineering and Applied Electronics Technology
TAO, LIAN JIN, Architecture Engineering
TAO, SHI QUAN, Applied Science and Physics
WAN, SU CHUN, Architecture Engineering
WANG, DA YONG, Applied Science and Physics
WANG, DAO, Energy and Environmental Engineering
WANG, GUANG TAO, Architecture Engineering
WANG, LI, Applied Science and Physics
WANG, PU, Electronic Information and Control Engineering
WANG, SONG GUI, Applied Science and Physics
WU, BIN, Mechanical Engineering and Applied Electronics Technology
WU, GUO WEI, Economics and Management
WU, WU CHEN, Electronic Information and Control Engineering
WU, YONG LUN, Mechanical Engineering and Applied Electronics Technology
XIA, DING GUO, Energy and Environmental Engineering
XUE, LIU GEN, Applied Science and Physics
XUE, SU GUO, Architecture Engineering
YAN, HUI, Material Science and Engineering
YAN, WEI MING, Architecture Engineering
YANG, HONG RU, Applied Science and Physics
YAO, HAI LOU, Applied Science and Physics
YI, BAO CAI, Computer Science
YIN, SHU YAN, Mechanical Engineering and Applied Electronics Technology
YIN, SHU YAN, Material Science and Engineering
YU, JIAN, Energy and Environmental Engineering
YU, KUAN XIN, Applied Science and Physics
YU, YUE QING, Mechanical Engineering and Applied Electronics Technology
ZENG, YI, Energy and Environmental Engineering
ZHANG, AI LIN, Architecture Engineering
ZHANG, HONG BIN, Electronic Information and Control Engineering
ZHANG, HONG BIN, Computer Science
ZHANG, HUI HUI, Mechanical Engineering and Applied Electronics Technology
ZHANG, JIE, Energy and Environmental Engineering
ZHANG, JIU JIE, Material Science and Engineering
ZHANG, WANG RONG, Electronic Information and Control Engineering
ZHANG, WEI, Mechanical Engineering and Applied Electronics Technology
ZHANG, WEN XIONG, Material Science and Engineering
ZHANG, YI GANG, Architecture Engineering
ZHANG, ZE, Applied Science and Physics
ZHANG, ZHEN HAI, Applied Science and Physics
ZHANG, ZHI GANG, Applied Science and Physics
ZHANG, ZHONG ZHAN, Applied Science and Physics
ZHONG, NING, Computer Science
ZHONG, RU GANG, Energy and Environmental Engineering
ZHOU, DA SEN, Energy and Environmental Engineering
ZHOU, MEI LING, Material Science and Engineering
ZHOU, WEI, Architecture Engineering
ZHOU, XI YUAN, Architecture Engineering
ZHOU, YU WEN, Energy and Environmental Engineering
ZONG, GANG, Economics and Management
ZUO, TIE XUN, Applied Science and Physics
ZUO, TIE YONG, Material Science and Engineering

ATTACHED CENTRES

College of Adult Education: Dir LU, ZHEN YANG.

College of Higher Professional Education: Dir YAN, NIAN ZHU.

Institute of Laser Engineering: Dir ZUO, TIE CHUAN.

CAPITAL NORMAL UNIVERSITY

105 Xi San Huan, Beijing 100037
Telephone: (10) 68900974
Fax: (10) 68902539
Internet: www.cnu.edu.cn

Founded 1954
Bureau of Education of Beijing
Academic year: September to July
President: XIANG YUAN XU
Vice-Presidents: HUI LI GONG, JIAN CHENG LIU, JIAN SHE ZHOU, WAN LIANG WANG
Head of Graduate Dept: JING HE LIANG
Librarian: YUE HU

Number of teachers: 1,147
Number of students: 24,905 (12,786 full-time, 12,119 part-time)

Publications: *Education Art* (12 a year), *Journal of Capital Normal University (Natural Sciences Edition)* (4 a year), *Journal of Capital Normal University (Social Sciences Edition)* (6 a year), *Language Teaching in Middle School* (12 a year), *Middle School Math* (12 a year)

DEANS

College of Biology: HE YIKUN
College of Education: MEN FANHUA
College of Environmental Resources and Tourism: GONG HUILI
College of Fine Arts: SUN ZHIJUN
College of Foreign Languages: YANG YANG
College of Information Technology: WANG WANSEN
College of International Culture: LIU XIAOTIAN
College of Music: YANG QING
College of Political Sciences and Law: WANG SHUMENG
Department of Chemistry: ZHANG ZHUOYONG
Department of Educational Technology: AI LUN
Department of History: SONG JIE
Department of Mathematics: ZHENG CHONGYOU
Department of Physics: ZHANG CUNLIN
Elementary Education College: WANG ZHIQIU
Physical Teaching and Research Section: SUN JIANHUI
School of Literature: WU SHIJING
Teaching and Research Division of Marxism: LI SONGLIN
University English Teaching and Research Division: XIE FUZHI

PROFESSORS

AN, YUFENG, Political Sciences and Law
BI, LUO, Environmental Resources and Tourism
CAI, TUANYAO, Biology
CHANG, RUILUN, Fine Arts
CHEN, XINXIA, Political Sciences and Law
CHI, YUNFEI, History
DAI, LIN, Fine Arts
DIAO, YONGZHA, Marxism
DONG, ZHONGXUN, Fine Arts
DU, XIAOSHI, Music
DU, XIXIAN, Fine Arts
FAN, YANNING, Political Sciences and Law
FANG, PING, Education
FANG, YAN, Physics
FU, HUA, Environmental Resources and Tourism
GONG, HUILI, Environmental Resources and Tourism
GU, XUEXIN, Chemistry
HAO, CHUNWEN, History
HE, YIKUN, Biology
HUANG, MEIYING, Music
HUO, LONGGUANG, Mathematics
JIN, QIONGHUA, Chemistry
LAN, WEI, Political Sciences and Law
LEI, DA, Music
LI, AIGUO, Fine Arts
LI, FULI, Physics
LI, JIAYANG, Biology
LI, SHUPEI, Mathematics
LI, SONGLIN, Marxism
LI, XIA, Chemistry
LI, YARU, Marxism
LIAN, SHAOMING, History
LIANG, JINGHE, History
LIN, LI, Foreign Languages
LIU, DACHUN, Mathematics
LIU, LIMIN, Foreign Languages
LU, XIAOMING, Chemistry
MENG, FANHUA, Education
NIE, YUEYAN, Political Sciences and Law
NING, HONG, Education
NING, KE, History
QI, SHIRONG, History
QIU, YUNHUA, Literature
REN, DONG, Biology
SHAO, HUIBO, Chemistry
SHEN, JINGLING, Physics
SHI, SHENGMING, Mathematics
SHUI, SHUFENG, Political Sciences and Law
SONG, JIE, History
SUN, ZHIJUN, Fine Arts
TAN, FENGTAI, Education
TANG, CHONGQIN, Music
TAO, DONGFENG, Literature
TIAN, BAO, Education
WANG, ANGUO, Music
WANG, CHANGCHUN, Education
WANG, DESHENG, Literature
WANG, GUANGMING, Literature
WANG, JIANPING, Education

WANG, LU, Educational Technology
WANG, SHIPING, Physics
WANG, SHUMENG, Political Sciences and Law
WANG, SHUQIN, Political Sciences and Law
WANG, ZHIQIU, Elementary Education
WEI, GUANGQI, History
WEN, LISHU, Political Sciences and Law
WU, JIANGPING, Mathematics
WU, SHIJING, Literature
XIA, JIGUO, History
XIA, LIMIN, Political Sciences and Law
XIE, CHENGREN, History
XING, HONGJUN, Physics
XING, YONGFU, Education
XU, PEIJUN, Physics
XU, YUZHEN, Education
YANG, QING, Music
YANG, SHENGPING, Political Sciences and Law
YANG, YANG, Foreign Languages
YANG, YUE, Biology
YE, XIAOBING, History
YIN, LIPING, Biology
YIN, TIELIANG, Music
YIN, WEIPING, Mathematics
ZHAN, LIJUAN, Music
ZHANG, CUNLIN, Physics
ZHANG, GUOLI, Music
ZHANG, JUNDA, Education
ZHANG, YONGHUA, Chemistry
ZHANG, ZHUOYONG, Chemistry
ZHAO, XUEZHI, Mathematics

ATTACHED CENTRES

Chinese Poetry Research Centre of Capital Normal University: Dir ZHAO MINLI.

Course Research and Development Centre: Dir LIU XINCHENG.

Knowledge Engineering Research Centre: Dir HUANG RONGHUAI.

Research and Design Laboratory for New-type Functional Matters: Dir ZHANG ZHUOYONG.

State Scientific Research Base for Cultivation of History Talents: Dir SONG JIE.

CAPITAL UNIVERSITY OF MEDICAL SCIENCES

10 Xi Tou Tiao, You An Men, Beijing 100054
Telephone: (10) 63291983
Fax: (10) 63051130
Internet: www.cpums.edu.cn

Founded 1960
Academic year: September to July
President: LU ZHAOFENG
Vice-Presidents: FAN QI, WANG XIAOMIN, WANG YUHUI
Head of Graduate Department: LU ZHAOFENG
Librarian: WANG JIEZHEN

Number of teachers: 2,500

Publications: *Journal* (4 a year), *School of Public Health* (4 a year)

DEANS

School of Basic Medical Sciences: CHEN TIEJUN
Biomedical Engineering Institute: LIU ZHICHENG
School of Chemical Biology and Pharmaceutical Sciences: PENG SHIQI
School of Chinese Traditional Medicine: QI FANG
First Faculty of Clinical Medicine: ZHANG JIAN
Second Faculty of Clinical Medicine: GAO DONGCHEN
Third Faculty of Clinical Medicine: GAO JUZHONG
Fourth Faculty of Clinical Medicine: LIU HONGBO
Fifth Faculty of Clinical Medicine: DAI JIANPING
Sixth Faculty of Clinical Medicine: ZHANG GUANGZHAO
Eighth Faculty of Clinical Medicine: XI XIUMING
Ninth Faculty of Clinical Medicine: ZHAO CHUNHUI
School of Health Administration and Education: LIANG WANNIAN
Faculty of Mental Health: CAI ZHUOJI
Faculty of Nursing: LI SHUJIA
Faculty of Obstetrics and Gynaecology: CHEN BAOYING
Faculty of Paediatrics: LI ZHONGZHI
School of Public Health and Family Medical Science: WANG WEI
Faculty of Rehabilitation: YOU HONG
Faculty of Stomatology: ZHENG SUN

PROFESSORS

AN, WEI, School of Basic Medical Sciences
AN, YUNQING, School of Basic Medical Sciences
BAI, YUXING, Faculty of Stomatology
CAI, ZHUOJI, Faculty of Mental Health
CHANG, XHIWEN, Fourth Faculty of Clinical Medicine
CHE, NIANCONG, School of Chinese Traditional Medicine
CHEN, BAOTIAN, Sixth Faculty of Clinical Medicine
CHEN, BAOYING, Faculty of Obstetrics and Gynecology
CHEN, BIAO, First Faculty of Clinical Medicine
CHEN, HAIYING, School of Chinese Traditional Medicine
CHEN, HUIDE, Third Faculty of Clinical Medicine
CHEN, HUIRU, Fourth Faculty of Clinical Medicine
CHEN, JUN, School of Basic Medical Sciences
CHEN, SHAN, Fourth Faculty of Clinical Medicine
CHEN, TIEJUN, School of Basic Medical Sciences
CHEN, XUESHI, Faculty of Mental Health
CHEN, YILIN, First Faculty of Clinical Medicine
CHEN, YINGCHUN, Sixth Faculty of Clinical Medicine
CHEN, YUPING, Sixth Faculty of Clinical Medicine
CHEN, ZHAN, Sixth Faculty of Clinical Medicine
CUI, GUOHUI, School of Chemical Biology and Pharmaceutical Sciences
CUI, SHUQI, School of Public Health and Family Medical Science
DAI, JIANPING, Fifth Faculty of Clinical Medicine
DAI, XINGHUA, Faculty of Obstetrics and Gynecology
DAO, HONG, School of Public Health and Family Medical Science
DING, BOTAN, Faculty of Rehabilitation
DING, ZONGYI, Faculty of Paediatrics
DONG, PEIQING, Sixth Faculty of Clinical Medicine
DONG, ZONGJUN, First Faculty of Clinical Medicine
DU, FENGHE, Fifth Faculty of Clinical Medicine
DU, LINDONG, Second Faculty of Clinical Medicine
DUAN, YANPING, School of Chinese Traditional Medicine
DUAN, ZHONGPING, Ninth Faculty of Clinical Medicine
FAN, DONGPO, Fifth Faculty of Clinical Medicine
FAN, MING, School of Basic Medical Sciences
FAN, XUNMEI, Faculty of Paediatrics
FANG, DEYUN, First Faculty of Clinical Medicine
GAO, BAOQIN, Fifth Faculty of Clinical Medicine
GAO, CHUNJIN, Third Faculty of Clinical Medicine
GAO, DONGCHEN, Second Faculty of Clinical Medicine
GAO, FENG, Faculty of Obstetrics and Gynecology
GAO, JUZHONG, Third Faculty of Clinical Medicine
GAO, MINGZHE, Sixth Faculty of Clinical Medicine
GAO, PEIYI, Fifth Faculty of Clinical Medicine
GAO, WENZHU, Faculty of Rehabilitation
GAO, XIULAI, School of Basic Medical Sciences
GAO, YIMIN, School of Chinese Traditional Medicine
GUAN, DELIN, Third Faculty of Clinical Medicine
GUO, AIMIN, School of Public Health and Family Medical Science
GUO, SONG, Faculty of Mental Health
GUO, XIUHUA, School of Public Health and Family Medical Science
HAN, DEMIN, Fourth Faculty of Clinical Medicine
HAN, LING, Sixth Faculty of Clinical Medicine
HE, YAN, Fifth Faculty of Clinical Medicine
HU, DAYI, Third Faculty of Clinical Medicine
HU, YAMEI, Faculty of Paediatrics
HU, YINYUAN, Faculty of Rehabilitation
HUA, QI, First Faculty of Clinical Medicine
HUANG, JIEYING, Second Faculty of Clinical Medicine
HUANG, SHUZHEN, Faculty of Mental Health
JI, SHURONG, Faculty of Rehabilitation
JIA, HONGTI, School of Basic Medical Sciences
JIA, JIANPING, First Faculty of Clinical Medicine
JIA, JIDONG, Second Faculty of Clinical Medicine
JIANG, BING, School of Health Administration and Education
JIANG, TAO, Fifth Faculty of Clinical Medicine
JIANG, WENHUA, First Faculty of Clinical Medicine
JIANG, ZAIFANG, Faculty of Paediatrics
JIANG, ZUONING, Faculty of Mental Health
JIN, RUI, Ninth Faculty of Clinical Medicine
JU, LIRONG, School of Public Health and Family Medical Science
LI, BIN, Fourth Faculty of Clinical Medicine
LI, CUIYING, Faculty of Stomatology
LI, FEI, First Faculty of Clinical Medicine
LI, HONGPEI, Fifth Faculty of Clinical Medicine
LI, JIANPING, School of Health Administration and Education
LI, KUNCHENG, First Faculty of Clinical Medicine
LI, LIN, First Faculty of Clinical Medicine
LI, LIN, School of Health Administration and Education
LI, PING, Sixth Faculty of Clinical Medicine
LI, REN, Third Faculty of Clinical Medicine
LI, SHUJIA, Faculty of Nursing Ease
LI, SHUREN, Second Faculty of Clinical Medicine
LI, XIA, Biomedical Engineering Institute
LI, YONGJIE, First Faculty of Clinical Medicine
LI, YUJING, Faculty of Stomatology
LI, ZHI'AN, Sixth Faculty of Clinical Medicine
LI, ZHIZIA, Fourth Faculty of Clinical Medicine
LI, ZHONGZHI, Faculty of Paediatrics
LIAN, SHI, First Faculty of Clinical Medicine
LIANG, WANNIAN, School of Health Administration and Education
LING, FENG, First Faculty of Clinical Medicine
LIU, BIN, Fourth Faculty of Clinical Medicine
LIU, CHANGGUI, Second Faculty of Clinical Medicine
LIU, HONGBO, Fourth Faculty of Clinical Medicine
LIU, HONGGANG, Fourth Faculty of Clinical Medicine

LIU, JINGZHONG, Third Faculty of Clinical Medicine
LIU, LEI, Fourth Faculty of Clinical Medicine
LIU, NONG, School of Basic Medical Sciences
LIU, WEIZHEN, School of Basic Medical Sciences
LIU, XICHENG, Faculty of Paediatrics
LIU, YONGBIN, Faculty of Rehabilitation
LIU, ZHICHENG, Biomedical Engineering Institute
LONG, JIE, Fifth Faculty of Clinical Medicine
LU, HUIZHANG, First Faculty of Clinical Medicine
LU, SHIQI, School of Basic Medical Sciences
LUAN, GUOMING, Fifth Faculty of Clinical Medicine
LUO, SHIQI, Fifth Faculty of Clinical Medicine
LUO, SHUQIAN, Biomedical Engineering Institute
MA, BINRONG, Biomedical Engineering Institute
MA, CHANGSHENG, Sixth Faculty of Clinical Medicine
MA, DAQING, Second Faculty of Clinical Medicine
MA, DONGLI, Fourth Faculty of Clinical Medicine
MENG, XU, Sixth Faculty of Clinical Medicine
NI, JIAYI, First Faculty of Clinical Medicine
PAN, JULI, Faculty of Stomatology
PENG, SHIQI, School of Chemical Biology and Pharmaceutical Sciences
QI, FANG, School of Chinese Traditional Medicine
QI, YING, Fourth Faculty of Clinical Medicine
QIAN, YING, School of Chinese Traditional Medicine
QIAO, ZHIHENG, Faculty of Rehabilitation
QU, RENYOU, Third Faculty of Clinical Medicine
SHE, KUNLING, Faculty of Paediatrics
SHEN, LUHUA, Second Faculty of Clinical Medicine
SHEN, YIN, Faculty of Paediatrics
SHI, SHENGGEN, Faculty of Stomatology
SHI, XIAOLIN, School of Basic Medical Sciences
SHI, XIANG'EN, Fifth Faculty of Clinical Medicine
SHI, YUYING, Fourth Faculty of Clinical Medicine
SONG, MAOMIN, Fifth Faculty of Clinical Medicine
SONG, WEIXIAN, Fourth Faculty of Clinical Medicine
SUN, BAOZHEN, Fourth Faculty of Clinical Medicine
SUN, BO, Fifth Faculty of Clinical Medicine
SUN, JIANBANG, First Faculty of Clinical Medicine
SUN, YANQING, Sixth Faculty of Clinical Medicine
SUN, ZHENG, Faculty of Stomatology
TANG, XHAOQU, School of Basic Medical Sciences
TIAN, XHU'EN, Faculty of Mental Health
WANG, BANGKANG, Faculty of Stomatology
WANG, BAOGUO, Fifth Faculty of Clinical Medicine
WANG, CHEN, Third Faculty of Clinical Medicine
WANG, DEXIN, Second Faculty of Clinical Medicine
WANG, ENXHEN, Fifth Faculty of Clinical Medicine
WANG, HUILING, Sixth Faculty of Clinical Medicine
WANG, JIE, Fifth Faculty of Clinical Medicine
WANG, PEIYAN, Third Faculty of Clinical Medicine
WANG, SONGLING, Faculty of Stomatology
WANG, SUQIU, Fifth Faculty of Clinical Medicine
WANG, TIANYOU, Second Faculty of Clinical Medicine
WANG, XHONGCHENG, Fifth Faculty of Clinical Medicine
WANG, WEI, School of Public Health and Family Medical Science
WANG, WENWEI, Fourth Faculty of Clinical Medicine
WANG, XHENFU, Fourth Faculty of Clinical Medicine
WANG, XHIGANG, Second Faculty of Clinical Medicine
WANG, XIAOLIANG, School of Chemical Biology and Pharmaceutical Sciences
WANG, XIAOMIN, School of Basic Medical Sciences
WANG, XIAOYAN, School of Health Administration and Education
WANG, YADONG, School of Health Administration and Education
WANG, YIZHEN, Fifth Faculty of Clinical Medicine
WANG, YONGJUN, Fifth Faculty of Clinical Medicine
WANG, YU, Second Faculty of Clinical Medicine
WANG, ZHONGGAO, First Faculty of Clinical Medicine
WENG, XINAHI, Third Faculty of Clinical Medicine
WENG, YONGZHEN, Faculty of Mental Health
WU, AINGHUA, Sixth Faculty of Clinical Medicine
WU, FENGYI, Third Faculty of Clinical Medicine
WU, HAO, Ninth Faculty of Clinical Medicine
WU, MINYUAN, Faculty of Paediatrics
WU, SHUZENG, Sixth Faculty of Clinical Medicine
WU, XUESHI, Sixth Faculty of Clinical Medicine
WU, ZHAOSU, Sixth Faculty of Clinical Medicine
XI, XIUMING, Eighth Faculty of Clinical Medicine
XIANG, XIUKUN, Fourth Faculty of Clinical Medicine
XIAO, RONG, School of Public Health and Family Medical Science
XU, QUNYAN, School of Basic Medical Sciences
XUE, MING, School of Health Administration and Education
YANG, BAOQIN, School of Chinese Traditional Medicine
YANG, HUI, School of Basic Medical Sciences
YANG, JINKUI, Fourth Faculty of Clinical Medicine
YANG, SHAOXU, Fifth Faculty of Clinical Medicine
YANG, SHENGHUI, Faculty of Stomatology
YANG, YUNPING, Faculty of Mental Health
YAO, CHONGHUA, Sixth Faculty of Clinical Medicine
YAO, TIANQIAO, Sixth Faculty of Clinical Medicine
YOU, HONG, Faculty of Rehabilitation
YOU, KAITAO, Third Faculty of Clinical Medicine
YU, CHUNJIANG, First Faculty of Clinical Medicine
YU, ZELI, Fourth Faculty of Clinical Medicine
YUAN, ZHENGGUO, School of Chinese Traditional Medicine
YUE, YUN, Third Faculty of Clinical Medicine
ZHAGN, CHANGHUAI, Second Faculty of Clinical Medicine
ZHAN, ZHENTING, Faculty of Stomatology
ZHANG, BINXI, Fourth Faculty of Clinical Medicine
ZHANG, FENGXIAN, Third Faculty of Clinical Medicine
ZHANG, GUANGZHAO, Sixth Faculty of Clinical Medicine
ZHANG, HONGYU, Third Faculty of Clinical Medicine
ZHANG, JIAN, First Faculty of Clinical Medicine
ZHANG, JIGU, Faculty of Mental Health
ZHANG, JINCAI, Faculty of Stomatology
ZHANG, JINRONG, Sixth Faculty of Clinical Medicine
ZHANG, JINZHE, Faculty of Paediatrics
ZHANG, JIZHI, Faculty of Mental Health
ZHANG, PENGTIAN, Second Faculty of Clinical Medicine
ZHANG, QIUHAN, First Faculty of Clinical Medicine
ZHANG, SHIJI, Faculty of Mental Health
ZHANG, SHUMIN, School of Chinese Traditional Medicine
ZHANG, SHUWEN, Second Faculty of Clinical Medicine
ZHANG, YU, First Faculty of Clinical Medicine
ZHANG, YUHAI, Second Faculty of Clinical Medicine
ZHANG, ZHAOGUANG, Sixth Faculty of Clinical Medicine
ZHANG, ZHAOQI, Sixth Faculty of Clinical Medicine
ZHANG, ZHITAI, Sixth Faculty of Clinical Medicine
ZHAO, CHUNHUI, Ninth Faculty of Clinical Medicine
ZHAO, DONG, Sixth Faculty of Clinical Medicine
ZHAO, JIZONG, Fifth Faculty of Clinical Medicine
ZHAO, MING, School of Chemical Biology and Pharmaceutical Sciences
ZHAO, YADU, Fifth Faculty of Clinical Medicine
ZHAO, YI, Second Faculty of Clinical Medicine
ZHAO, YUANLI, Fifth Faculty of Clinical Medicine
ZHENG, BANGHE, Fourth Faculty of Clinical Medicine
ZHENG, JIE, School of Basic Medical Sciences
ZHENG, YI, Faculty of Mental Health
ZHOU, BING, Fourth Faculty of Clinical Medicine
ZHOU, QIWEN, Sixth Faculty of Clinical Medicine
ZHOU, YAOTING, School of Chinese Traditional Medicine
ZHOU, YUJIE, Sixth Faculty of Clinical Medicine
ZHU, XINPING, School of Basic Medical Sciences

ATTACHED RESEARCH CENTRES AND INSTITUTES

Beijing Institute for Neurosciences: Dir JIA JIANPING.

Institute of Urology: Dir GAO JUXHONG.

Laboratory of Liver Protection and Rebirth Regulation: Dir AN WEI.

Laboratory of Nerve Rebirth Repairs Research: Dir XU QUNYUAN.

Research Centre for Cardiopulmonary-Vascular Treatment: Dir YANG XINSHUN.

Research Centre for Geriatric Medicine: Dir TANG ZHE.

CENTRAL ACADEMY OF ARTS AND DESIGN

34 North Dong Huan Rd, Beijing 100020
Telephone: 65026391
Founded 1956
President: CHANG SHANA
Vice-Presidents: WANG MING ZHI, YANG YONG SHAN, WANG ZHONG XIN
Library Director: QIU CHENGDE
Library of 170,000 vols
Number of teachers: 240
Number of students: 900 (36 postgraduates)
Publications: *Decoration* (quarterly), *College Journal* (monthly), *Reference on Arts and Crafts* (monthly)

HEADS OF DEPARTMENTS

Textile Dyeing and Fashion Design: LIU YUAN FENG
Ceramics: CHENG JIN HAI
Commercial Fine Arts Design: WANG GUO LUN
Interior Design: ZHANG YIMAN
Industrial Design: LIU GUANZHONG
Special Arts and Crafts: ZHANG CHANG
History of Arts and Crafts: XI JING ZHI

CENTRAL UNIVERSITY OF FINANCE AND ECONOMICS

39 Xue Yuan Nan Rd, Beijing 100081
Telephone: (10) 62289132
Fax: (10) 62289132
E-mail: wlb@cufe.edu.cn
Internet: www.cufe.edu.cn

Founded 1949
Ministry of Education control
Academic year: September to July
President: WANG GUANGQIAN
Vice-Presidents: CHEN MING, LI JUNSHENG, WANG GUOHUA, YUAN DONG
Head of Graduate Department: QI LAN
Librarian: HAN ZHIPING
Number of teachers: 500
Number of students: 14,000 (6,800 full-time, 7,200 part-time)
Publication: *Journal of the Central University of Finance and Economics* (12 a year)

DEANS

School of Accountancy: MENG YAN
Department of Athletics Economy and Management: GAO HAN
Business School: SUN GUOHUI
College of Culture and Communication: WANG QIANG
Department of Economic Mathematics: CHEN WENDENG
School of Economics: JIN ZHESONG
School of Finance: SHI JIANPING
Department of Foreign Languages: WANG XIAOHONG
School of Information: WANG LUBIN
Department of Insurance: HAO YANSU
Department of Investment Economics: WANG YAOQI
School of Law: GAN GONGEN
School of Public Finance and Administration: MA HAITAO
Department of Sociology: LI ZHIJUN

PROFESSORS

BAO, XIAOGUANG, Culture and Communication
CHEN, WENDENG, Economic Mathematics
CUI, XINJIAN, Business
DONG, CHENGZHANG, Information
GAN, GONGEN, Law
HAN, FULING, Finance
HAO, YANSU, Insurance
HOU, RONGHUA, Economics
HUO, PEI, Finance
HUO, QIANG, Finance
JIANG, WEIZHUANG, Public Finance and Administration
JIANG, XIAN, Economics
JIN, ZHESONG, Economics
LAN, CUIPAI, Law
LI, BAOREN, Public Finance and Administration
LI, JIAN, Finance
LI, JIXIONG, Insurance
LI, JUNSHENG, Public Finance and Administration
LI, SHUANG, Accountancy
LI, XIAOLIN, Insurance
LI, YAN, Public Finance and Administration
LI, ZHIJUN, Sociology
LIAO, SIPING, Culture and Communication
LIU, HENG, Public Finance and Administration
LIU, HONGXIA, Accountancy
LIU, YANG, Economics
MA, HAITAO, Public Finance and Administration
MENG, YAN, Accountancy
MIAO, RUNSHENG, Accountancy
PAN, JINSHENG, Finance
PAN, SHENGCHU, Information
QI, HUAIJIN, Accountancy
QI, LAN, Economics
SHI, JIANPING, Finance
SHI, SHULIN, Law
SUN, BAOWEN, Information
SUN, GUOHUI, Business
WANG, GUOHUA, Public Finance and Administration
WANG, JINYING, Business
WANG, JUNCAI, Accountancy
WANG, KEJING, Economics
WANG, LUBIN, Information
WANG, PEIZHEN, Finance
WANG, QIANG, Culture and Communication
WANG, RUIHUA, Accountancy
WANG, YONGJUN, Public Finance and Administration
WANG, YONGPING, Accountancy
WEI, ZHENXIONG, Accountancy
WEN, QIAN, Economics
WU, ZHENZHI, Finance
XI, SHUQIN, Accountancy
XU, SHANHUI, Finance
XU, XIANGYU, Investment Economics
YANG, JINGUANG, Accountancy
YANG, ZHIQING, Public Finance and Administration
YAO, SUI, Finance
ZHANG, BIQIONG, Finance
ZHANG, LIQIN, Finance
ZHANG, SHUJUN, Business
ZHANG, TIEGANG, Economics
ZHAO, LIFENG, Economics
ZHAO, XUEHENG, Public Finance and Administration

ATTACHED CENTRES

Asset Evaluation Institute: Dir LIU YUPING.

Culture Communication Institute: Dir LIU SHUYONG.

Economic Mathematics Institute: Dir GE BINHUA.

Finance and Economics Institute: Dir WANG YONGJUN.

Insurance Precision Calculation Institute: Dir LI XIAOLIN.

Law of Financial Tax and Finance Institute: Dir LAN CUIPAI.

Macroscopic Economy Management Institute: Dir HOU RONGHUA.

Modern Business Enterprise System Institute: Dir JIANG XUAN.

Share Economy Institute: Dir YUE FUBIN.

Social Economy Development Institute: Dir BA TU.

Stock and Futures Institute: Dir HUO QIANG.

Taiwan Economy Institute: Dir TANG GONGLIANG.

CENTRAL ACADEMY OF FINE ARTS

8 Hua Jia Di Nan Jie, Chaoyang District, Beijing 100102
Telephone: (10) 64771018
Fax: (10) 64771136
Internet: www.cafa.com.cn

Founded 1950
Ministry of Education control
Academic year: September to July
President: PAN GONGKAI
Vice-President: FAN DIAN
Head of Graduate Department: CHU DI
Librarian: SHEN JIANDONG
Number of teachers: 141
Number of students: 1,000
Publications: *Art Research* (4 a year), *World Art* (4 a year)

DEANS

School of Architecture: LU PINJING
School of Design: WANG MIN
School of Humanities: YIN JINAN
Art Education Department: JIN JIAZHEN
Art History Department: YIN JINAN
Chinese Painting Department: TIAN LIMING
Mural Painting Department: SUN JINGBO
Oil Painting Department: DAI SHIHE
Printmaking Department: SU XINPING
Sculpture Department: SUI JIANGUO
First Year Foundation Programme: WEN GUOZHANG

PROFESSORS

CAO, LI, Mural Painting
CHAO, GE, Oil Painting
CHEN, WENYI, Mural Painting
DAI, SHIHE, Oil Painting
DING, YILIN, Oil Painting
FAN, DI'AN, Humanities
GAO, RONGSHENG, Printmaking
HONG, PENGSHENG, Humanities
HU, JIANCHENG, Oil Painting
HU, WEI, Chinese Painting
HU, YUE, Architecture
HUANG, WEI, Architecture
LI, LINZUO, Mural Painting
LU, SHENGZHONG, Oil Painting
LU, PINJING, Architecture
LUO, SHIPING, Humanities
MA, LU, Oil Painting
QIU, ZHENZHONG, Chinese Painting
SU, XINPING, Printmaking
SUI, JIANGUO, Sculpture
SUN, JIABO, Sculpture
SUN, JINGBO, Mural Painting
TAN, PING, Design
TANG, YONGLI, Chinese Painting
TIAN, LIMING, Chinese Painting
WANG, MIN, Design
WANG, YONG, Chinese Painting
WEN, GUOZHANG, First-year Foundation Program
WU, CHANGJIANG, Printmaking
YIN, JINAN, Art History
ZHOU, ZHIYU, Design

ATTACHED MUSEUM

Art museum: Dir TANG PEI.

CENTRAL CHINA NORMAL UNIVERSITY

152 Luoyu Rd, Wuhan 430079, Hubei
Telephone: (27) 67868133
E-mail: master@mail.ccnu.edu.cn
Internet: www.ccnu.edu.cn

Founded 1903
Ministry of Education control
Academic year: September to July
President: MA MING
Vice-Presidents: HUANG YONGLING, LE GUANGZHOU, LI ZONGKAI, PANG XIANGNONG, YANG ZHENGNONG
Librarian: ZUO BIN
Number of teachers: 1,200
Number of students: 20,000
Publications: *Foreign Literature Studies* (6 a year), *Journal of Central China Normal University* (humanities and social science, 6 a year), *Journal of Central China Normal University* (natural sciences, 6 a year)

DEANS

School of Chemistry: YANG GUANGFU
School of City and Environmental Science: ZENG JUXIN
Department of Computer Science: TAN LIANSHENG
School of Economics: CAO YANG
School of Foreign Language and Literature: ZHANG WEIYOU
School of History and Culture: WANG YUDE
Department of Information Management: WANG XUEDONG
Department of Information Technology: ZHANG GUOPING
School of Life Science: CHEN QICAI
School of Literature: LI XIANGNONG
School of Management: WU JINSHENG
School of Mathematics and Statistics: DENG YINBIN
School of Music: TIAN XIAOBAO
College of Networking Academy: ZHANG YOULIANG
School of Physics and Technology: WANG ENKE
School of Political Science and Law: LIN JIAN
Department of Sociology: JIANG LIHUA

PROFESSORS

BAI, GUOZHONG, Information Management
CAI, JINQUAN, History and Culture
CAI, XU, Physics and Technology
CAO, YANG, Economics
CHEN, CHUANLI, Mathematics and Statistics
CHEN, GUOSHENG, Life Science
CHEN, HONGWEI, Foreign Language and Literature
CHEN, JIANXIAN, Literature
CHEN, JISHENG, Physics and Technology
CHEN, QICAI, Life Science
CHEN, QUN, Mathematics and Statistics
CHEN, YIN'E, Sociology
CHEN, YOULIN, Foreign Language and Literature
CHU, ZEXIANG, Literature
DAI, JIANYE, Literature
DENG, HONGGUANG, History and Culture
DENG, XIANRUI, City and Environmental Science
DENG, YINBIN, Mathematics and Statistics
DING, MINGWU, Chemistry
DING, YIHUA, History and Culture
FENG, GANG, Computer Science
FU, HUIHUA, Life Science
GAO, HUAPING, Literature
GONG, SHENGSHENG, City and Environmental Science
GU, YONGXING, History and Culture
GU, ZHIHUA, History and Culture
GUO, JUN, Foreign Language and Literature
GUO, TUOYING, Mathematics and Statistics
HAN, KEFANG, Physics and Technology
HAN, XUNGUO, Music
HE, BAIGEN, City and Environmental Science
HE, HONGWU, Chemistry
HE, JIANMING, History and Culture
HE, SUI, Mathematics and Statistics
HE, TINGTING, Computer Science
HE, XUEFENG, Sociology
HONG, HUAZHU, Life Science
HOU, FUDE, Physics and Technology
HU, JINZHU, Computer Science
HU, XIANGMING, Physics and Technology
HU, YAMIN, Literature
HU, ZONGQIU, Chemistry
HUA, XIANFA, Foreign Language and Literature
HUANG, HUAWEN, History and Culture
HUANG, QINGYANG, Life Science
HUANG, WANHUI, Computer Science
HUANG, XIAOQUN, Foreign Language and Literature
HUANG, XINTANG, Physics and Technology
HUANG, YONGLIN, Literature
HUANG, ZHENGBO, History and Culture
HUANG, ZHONGLIAN, Foreign Language and Literature
JIA, YA, Physics and Technology
JIA, ZHIJIE, Physics and Technology
JIN, BOXIN, City and Environmental Science
JIN, CONG, Computer Science
JING, CAIRUI, City and Environmental Science
LI, BANGJI, Computer Science
LI, GAOXIANG, Physics and Technology
LI, JIALIN, Physics and Technology
LI, JIAQING, City and Environmental Science
LI, JIARONG, Physics and Technology
LI, QIRONG, History and Culture
LI, TAOSHENG, Mathematics and Statistics
LI, WENXIN, Life Science
LI, XIANGNONG, Literature
LI, XIAOYAN, Computer Science
LI, XINGRUN, Life Science
LI, XUEBAO, Life Science
LI, YADAN, Foreign Language and Literature
LI, ZHIYANG, Physics and Technology
LI, ZHONGHUA, Chemistry
LIANG, MIAOYUAN, Computer Science
LIAO, MEIZHEN, Foreign Language and Literature
LIAO, ZHANRU, Chemistry
LIN, DELI, Life Science
LIU, ANHAI, Literature
LIU, FENG, Physics and Technology
LIU, GUSHENG, History and Culture
LIU, LIANSHOU, Physics and Technology
LIU, SHAOJUN, History and Culture
LIU, SHENGHUA, Chemistry
LIU, SHENGJIA, City and Environmental Science
LIU, SHENGXIANG, Life Science
LIU, SHOUHUA, Literature
LIU, WEI, History and Culture
LIU, WU, Physics and Technology
LIU, XIANLONG, Mathematics and Statistics
LIU, YONGHONG, Foreign Language and Literature
LIU, ZHAOJIE, Chemistry
LOU, CEQUN, Information Management
LU, GUANGHAN, Chemistry
LU, WUQIANG, City and Environmental Science
LUO, BANGCHENG, Mathematics and Statistics
LUO, DEHUI, History and Culture
MA, CHENGWU, Literature
MA, MIN, History and Culture
MENG, DAZHONG, Physics and Technology
MOU, JIMEI, Physics and Technology
NIE, ZHENDAO, Foreign Language and Literature
PENG, CHANGZHENG, History and Culture
PENG, JIANXIN, Life Science
PENG, JIANXIN, Life Science
PENG, NANSHENG, History and Culture
QIU, BAOSHENG, Life Science
QIU, ZIHUA, Literature
SHAO, QINGYU, City and Environmental Science
SHEN, JIE, Sociology
SHEN, ZHENGYU, Literature
SU, BAIMEI, Foreign Language and Literature
SUN, WENXIAN, Literature
TAN, BANGHE, Literature
TAN, CHUANFENG, City and Environmental Science
TAN, HONG, Mathematics and Statistics
TAN, LIANSHENG, Computer Science
TANG, CHENGCHUN, Physics and Technology
TAO, JIAYUAN, City and Environmental Science
TIAN, SONGQING, City and Environmental Science
WAN, JIAN, Chemistry
WANG, ENKE, Physics and Technology
WANG, GUOSHENG, Literature
WANG, GUOXIU, Life Science
WANG, LIHUA, Sociology
WANG, MANJUN, Literature
WANG, QINGSHENG, Literature
WANG, QIZHOU, Literature
WANG, WEIJUN, Information Management
WANG, XIANPEI, Literature
WANG, XUEDONG, Information Management
WANG, YANGANG, Chemistry
WANG, YOUNIAN, Literature
WANG, YUDE, History and Culture
WANG, YUFENG, Life Science
WANG, ZELONG, Literature
WEI, CHANGHUA, Computer Science
WU, GANG, Life Science
WU, QI, History and Culture
WU, YI, Sociology
WU, YUANFANG, Physics and Technology
XIA, MINGYUAN, Mathematics and Statistics
XIA, XIAOBIN, Life Science
XIANG, JIQUAN, Sociology
XIAO, DEBAO, Computer Science
XIE, MINYU, Mathematics and Statistics
XIN, FUYI, Literature
XIN, LAISHUN, History and Culture
XIONG, TIEJI, History and Culture
XIU, DIAO, Literature
XU, QIAOLI, City and Environmental Science
XU, SENLIN, Mathematics and Statistics
XU, ZUHUA, Literature
YAN, CHANGHONG, History and Culture
YAN, GUOZHENG, Mathematics and Statistics
YAN, SHAOXIANG, History and Culture
YANG, BAOLIANG, City and Environmental Science
YANG, CHANG, History and Culture
YANG, CHUNBIN, Physics and Technology
YANG, GUANGFU, Chemistry
YANG, SHAO, Life Science
YANG, SHUANGHUA, Computer Science
YANG, XU, Life Science
YAO, WEIJUN, History and Culture
YI, HONGGEN, Foreign Language and Literature
YOU, LIRONG, Sociology
YU, GUANGMING, City and Environmental Science
YU, ZEHUA, Life Science
ZENG, JUXIN, City and Environmental Science
ZENG, LIANMAO, City and Environmental Science
ZENG, QINGQIANG, Foreign Language and Literature
ZHAN, CHANGGUO, Chemistry
ZHAN, ZHENGKUN, Chemistry
ZHANG, AIDONG, Chemistry
ZHANG, CHANGNIAN, Music
ZHANG, FAN, Information Management
ZHANG, GUOPING, Physics and Technology
ZHANG, KAIQUAN, History and Culture
ZHANG, LIDE, Physics and Technology
ZHANG, LONGSHENG, Foreign Language and Literature
ZHANG, QUANMING, History and Culture
ZHANG, SANXI, Literature
ZHANG, SHAOYAN, Economics
ZHANG, WEIYOU, Foreign Language and Literature
ZHANG, YINGLIN, Foreign Language and Literature
ZHANG, YONGJIAN, Literature
ZHANG, YUNENG, Literature
ZHANG, ZHENGMING, History and Culture
ZHAO, YIJUN, Life Science
ZHENG, QUAN, Mathematics and Statistics
ZHENG, XIAOPING, Physics and Technology
ZHOU, DAICUI, Physics and Technology
ZHOU, GUOLIN, History and Culture
ZHOU, JIYUAN, Life Science
ZHOU, XIAOMING, Literature
ZHOU, ZHENGRONG, Mathematics and Statistics
ZHOU, ZONGKUI, Sociology
ZHU, CHANGJIANG, Mathematics and Statistics
ZHU, CHUANFANG, Chemistry
ZHU, XINDE, Chemistry
ZHU, YING, History and Culture
ZOU, SHANGHUI, City and Environmental Science

ZUO, BIN, Sociology

ATTACHED CENTRES AND INSTITUTES

Centre for Language and Language Education: Dir XING FUYI.

Culture Education Development Centre: Dir ZOU XINSHENG.

Institute of Chinese Modern History: Dir ZHU YING.

Key Laboratory of High-Energy Physics.

Key Laboratory of Pesticide and Chemical Biology: Dir YANG GUANGFU.

Research Centre for Basic Education Courses: Dir MA MIN.

Research Centre for Chinese Rural Study: Dir XU YONG.

Research Centre for Education Information: Dir SHEN XUBANG.

CENTRAL CONSERVATORY OF MUSIC

43 Bao Jia St, Beijing 100031
Telephone: (10) 66425598
Fax: (10) 66413138
E-mail: ccom@ccom.edu.cn
Internet: www.ccom.edu.cn

Founded 1950
Ministry of Culture control
Academic year: September to July

President: WANG CIZHAO
Vice-Presidents: LI XU, LIU KANGHUA, XU CHANGJUN, ZHOU HAIHONG
Head of Graduate Department: WANG CIZHAO
Librarian: ZHOU HAIHONG
Number of teachers: 278
Number of students: 1,665
Publication: *Haihong Journal of the Central Conservatory of Music* (4 a year)

DEANS

Composition Department: TANG JIANPING
Conducting Department: YU FENG
General Education Department: LIANG JING
Music Education Department: GAO JIANJIN
Musicology Department: ZHANG BOYU
Orchestral Instruments Department: LIU PEIYAN
Piano Department: YANG MING
Traditional Instruments Department: ZHAO HANYANG
Voice and Opera Department: LIU DONG

PROFESSORS

BIAN, MENG, Piano
CAI, ZHOANGDE, Musicology
CHEN, BIGANG, Piano
CHEN, DANBU, Composition
CHEN, ZIMIN, Musicology
CHENG, DA, Voice and Opera
DU, MINGXIN, Composition
DU, TAIHANG, Piano
DUAN, PINGTAI, Composition
GAO, JIANJIN, Music Education
GUI, XILI, Traditional Instruments
GUO, SHUZHEN, Voice and Opera
GUO, WENJING, Composition
HAN, XIAOMING, Orchestral Instruments
HAN, ZHIHONG, Piano
HAN, ZHONGJIE, Conducting
HE, RONG, Orchestral Instruments
HEI, HAITAO, Voice and Opera
HU, SHIXI, Voice and Opera
HU, ZHIHOU, Traditional Instruments
HUANG, HE, Traditional Instruments
HUANG, XIAOHE, Musicology
HUANG, PEIYING, Piano
LI, GUANGHUA, Traditional Instruments
LI, HENG, Traditional Instruments
LI, JITI, Composition
LI, MENG, Traditional Instruments
LI, QIFENG, Piano
LI, XIANGTING, Traditional Instruments
LI, XINCHANG, Voice and Opera
LI, YINGHUA, Musicology
LI, ZHENGUI, Traditional Instruments
LIANG, DANA, Orchestral Instruments
LIANG, NING, Voice and Opera
LIN, SHICHENG, Traditional Instruments
LIN, YAXIONG, Musicology
LIU, CHANGFU, Traditional Instruments
LIU, DONG, Voice and Opera
LIU, LIN, Composition
LIU, PEIYAN, Orchestral Instruments
LIU, YUAN, Composition
LUO, ZHONGRONG, Composition
MA, HONGHAI, Voice and Opera
PAN, BIXIN, Musicology
PAN, CHUN, Piano
PENG, KANGLIANG, Voice and Opera
PINI, YAXUO, Voice and Opera
SHENG, LIHONG, Composition
SONG, JIN, Musicology
TAI, ER, Piano
TANG, JIANPING, Composition
TIAN, LIANTAO, Musicology
WANG, CIZHAO, Musicology
WANG, SHUHE, Musicology
WANG, XIANLIN, Voice and Opera
WANG, XIUFENG, Voice and Opera
WANG, YAOLING, Orchestral Instruments
WU, SHIKAI, Composition
WU, ZHUQIANG, Composition
XIE, HUAZHEN, Piano
XU, CHANGJUN, Composition
XU, XIN, Conducting
YANG, HONGNIAN, Conducting
YANG, JUN, Piano
YANG, MING, Piano
YAO, HENGLU, Composition
YE, XIAOGANG, Composition
YU, FENG, Conducting
YU, RUNYANG, Musicology
YU, SUXIAN, Composition
YU, ZHIGANG, Musicology
YUAN, JINGFANG, Musicology
ZHANG, BOYU, Musicology
ZHANG, JIANYI, Voice and Opera
ZHANG, LIPING, Voice and Opera
ZHANG, QIAN, Musicology
ZHANG, SHAO, Traditional Instruments
ZHAO, BIXUAN, Voice and Opera
ZHAO, DENGYING, Voice and Opera
ZHAO, HANYANG, Traditional Instruments
ZHAO, RUILIN, Orchestral Instruments
ZHENG, XIAOYING, Conducting
ZHENG, ZHUXIANG, Musicology
ZHONG, ZILIN, Musicology
ZHOU, GUANGREN, Piano
ZHOU, HAIHONG, Musicology
ZHOU, QINGQING, Musicology
ZHU, DUN, Orchestral Instruments
ZHU, YIBING, Orchestral Instruments

ATTACHED CENTRES

Centre of Chinese Electronic Music: Dir ZHANG XIAOFU.

Institute of Musicology of the Central Conservatory: Dir ZHANG QIAN.

Music Therapy Centre: Dir ZHANG HONGYI.

Research Centre of Violin Manufacture: Dir ZHENG QUAN.

CENTRAL UNIVERSITY FOR NATIONALITIES

27 Nan Da Rd, Zhong Guan Village, Hai Dian District, Beijing 100081
Telephone: (10) 68932544
Fax: (10) 68932544
E-mail: cunofficexz@sina.com
Internet: www.cun.edu.cn

Founded 1951
State Ethnic Affairs Commission control
Academic year: September to July

President: RONG SHIXIANG
Vice-Presidents: AI'BI BULA, CHEN LI, GUO WEIPING, HUANG FENGXIAN, JIN YASHENG, REN ZHONGXIA, YAN YUMING
Head of Graduate Dept: CHEN LI
Librarian: LI DELONG
Number of teachers: 700
Number of students: 13,000
Publications: *Journal of The Central University for Nationalities* (natural sciences, 4 a year), *Journal of The Central University for Nationalities* (philosophy and social sciences, 6 a year)

DEANS

School of Arts: YIN HUILI
School of Education: WANG JUN
School of Ethnology and Sociology: YANG SHENGMIN
School of Foreign Language: HE KEYONG
School of Law: ZHU JING'AN
School of Literature, Journalism and Communication: BAI WEI
School of Management: LI JUNQING
School of Music: MENG XINYANG
College of Dance: SU ZIHONG
College of Economics: LIU YONGJI
College of Life and Environment Science: FENG JINZHAO
College of National Minorities: LI JINFANG
College of Science and Engineering: FENG JINZHAO
Department of History: LI HONGBIN
Department of Philosophy and Religion: GONG YUKUAN
Department of Physics: WEI XIAOKANG
Preparatory Department: SONG TAICHENG
Research Institute of Tibet: BANBAN DUOJIE

PROFESSORS

BAI, RUNSHENG, Literature, Journalism and Communication
BAI, WEI, Literature, Journalism and Communication
BAI, YINTAI, National Minority Study
BANBAN, DUOJIE, Tibetan Studies
BI, MUXUN, Literature, Journalism and Communication
BU, ZHONGJIAN, Philosophy and Religion
CHEN, CHANGPING, Ethnology and Sociology
CHEN, FANGYING, Science and Engineering
CHEN, JIANJIAN, Tibetan Studies
CHEN, NAN, History
CUI, GUANZHI, Science and Engineering
DALI, ZHABU, History
DING, HONG, Ethnology and Sociology
DING, SHIQING, National Minority Study
FENG, JINZHAO, Life and Environment Science
FENG, JINZHAO, Science and Engineering
FU, CHENGZHOU, Literature, Journalism and Communication
FU, YIXIN, Education
GEN, SHIMIN, National Minority Study
GENG, YUFANG, Tibetan Studies
GESANG, DUNZHU, Tibetan Studies
GESANG, JUMIAN, Tibetan Studies
GONG, YUKUAN, Philosophy and Religion
HA, JINGXIONG, Education
HAMITI, TIEMUER, National Minority Study
HASHI, E'ERDUN, National Minority Study
HE, JINRUI, Philosophy and Religion
HE, KEYONG, Foreign Languages
HE, QIMIN, Philosophy and Religion
HE, WEI, Science and Engineering
HU, SHAOHUA, History
HU, ZHENHUA, National Minority Study
HUANG, KAI, Science and Engineering
HUOXIGE, TAOKETAO, National Minority Study
JI, YONGHAI, National Minority Study
JIAO, YUGUO, Life and Environment Science
JIN, RIGUANG, Music
LI, BINQUAN, Tibetan Studies
LI, GUIZHI, History
LI, HONGBIN, History

LI, JINFANG, National Minority Study
LI, JUNQING, Management
LI, KUI, Arts
LI, XINCHANG, Music
LI, YAN, National Minority Study
LI, YAN, Law
LIN, JING, Music
LIU, BINGJIANG, Arts
LIU, JIANMING, Literature, Journalism and Communication
LIU, JINZHEN, Science and Engineering
LIU, YONGJI, Economics
LIU, YONGZHOU, Literature, Journalism and Communication
LU, SHAO'EN, Music
MEN, DUHU, National Minority Study
MENG, XINYANG, Music
PIAO, CHANGTIAN, Music
SHANG, YANBIN, History
SHAO, XIANSHU, Ethnology and Sociology
SHEN, JIA, Music
SONG, RUBU, National Minority Study
SU, ZIHONG, Dance
TAO, LIPAN, Literature, Journalism and Communication
TENG, XING, Education
WANG, JUN, Education
WANG, RAO, Tibetan Studies
WANG, TIANJIN, Economics
WANG, YUANXIN, National Minority Study
WANG, ZHONGHAN, History
WANGMEN, TIEGA, National Minority Study
WEI, FENGRONG, Science and Engineering
WU, LIJI, National Minority Study
XIAO, XIURONG, Management
XING, FUCHON, Science and Engineering
XING, LI, Literature, Journalism and Communication
XU, LUYA, Foreign Languages
XU, SHOUCHUN, Science and Engineering
XU, WANBANG, Ethnology and Sociology
XU, YONGZHI, Management
XU, YONGZHI, History
YANG, CONG, Economics
YANG, ROOMING, Life and Environment Science
YANG, SHENGMIN, Ethnology and Sociology
YAO, NIANCI, History
YIN, HUILI, Arts
YU, KESEN, Literature, Journalism and Communication
YU, QIMING, Philosophy and Religion
ZENG, SHIQI, National Minority Study
ZHANG, GONGJIN, National Minority Study
ZHANG, GUANGHUA, Science and Engineering
ZHAO, KANG, Tibetan Studies
ZHAO, SHILIN, Philosophy and Religion
ZHOU, LI, Management
ZHOU, RUNNIAN, Tibetan Studies
ZHU, JING'AN, Law
ZHU, ZHENGYUAN, Science and Engineering

ATTACHED CENTRES

Chinese National Minority Research Centre: Dir QI QINGFU.

Ethnology and Anthropology Research Institute: Dir ZHUANG KONGSHAO.

Folk Theories Policy Research Institute: Dir JIN BINGGAO.

Language Culture Research Institute: Dir WANG LINXU.

National Minority Arts Research Institute: Dir ZHAO YI.

National Minority Economics Research Institute: Dir WANG TIANJIN.

Religion Research Institute: Dir DONG DEFU.

Tibetan Research Institute: Dir BANBAN DUOJIE.

CENTRAL SOUTH UNIVERSITY

Chang Sha 410083, Hunan
Telephone: (731) 8879225
Fax: (731) 8830308
E-mail: csuweb@mail.csu.edu.cn
Internet: www.csu.edu.cn

Founded 1952

Academic year: September to July

President: HUANG BOYUN
Vice-Presidents: CHEN QIYUAN, CHEN ZHIYA, HU TIEHUI, LI GUIYUAN, QIU GUANZHOU
Head of Graduate Department: LIU YILUN
Librarian: FANG ZHENG

Publications: *International Chinese Nursing Journal* (4 a year), *Journal of Central South University* (6 a year), *Journal of Central South University* (medical sciences, 6 a year), *Journal of Central South University* (social sciences, 6 a year), *Transactions of Nonferrous Metals Society of China* (6 a year)

DEANS

School of Basic Medical Sciences: WEN JIFANG
School of Business: CHEN XIAOHONG
School of Chemistry and Chemical Engineering: HUANG KELONG
School of Civil Engineering and Architecture: YU ZHIWU
School of Energy and Power Engineering: ZHOU DIAOMIN
School of Fine Arts: DAI DUAN
School of Foreign Languages: TU GUOYUAN
School of Geoscience and Environmental Engineering: DAI TAGEN
School of Info-Physics and Geomatics Engineering: TANG JINGTIAN
School of Information Science and Engineering: GUI WEIHUA
School of Law: QI DUOJUN
School of Literature: OU YANG YOUQUAN
School of Materials Science and Engineering: YI DANQING
School of Mathematical Sciences and Computing Technology: ZOU JIEZHONG
School of Mechanical and Electrical Engineering: WU YUNXIN
School of Medical Technology and Information: GUO QULIAN
School of Metallurgic Science and Engineering: LI JIE
School of Nursing: HE GUOPING
School of Pharmaceutical Sciences: LI YUANJIAN
School of Physics, Sciences and Technology: YANG BINGCHU
School of Politics and Public Administration: LI JIANHUA
School of Public Health: XIAO SHUIYUAN
School of Resources Processing and Bioengineering: HU YUEHUA
School of Resources and Safety Engineering: LI XIBING
School of Stomatology: JIAN XINCHUN
School of Traffic and Transportation Engineering: SHI FENG

PROFESSORS

CAI, HONGWEI, Medical Technology and Information
CAI, ZIXING, Information Science and Engineering
CAO, JIAN, Physics, Sciences and Technology
CAO, XING, Business
CHANG, YETIAN, Medical Technology and Information
CHEN, FANGPING, Medical Technology and Information
CHEN, FENG, Materials Science and Engineering
CHEN, HAIBO, Mathematical Sciences and Computing Technology
CHEN, HUANXIN, Energy and Power Engineering
CHEN, HUANXIN, Civil Engineering and Architecture
CHEN, JIAN'ER, Information Science and Engineering
CHEN, KANGHUA, Powder Metallurgy
CHEN, LIQUAN, Chemistry and Chemical engineering
CHEN, QIYUAN, Chemistry and Chemical engineering
CHEN, SHIZHU, Materials Science and Engineering
CHEN, SONGQIAO, Information Science and Engineering
CHEN, XIAOHONG, Business
CHEN, XIAOQING, Chemistry and Chemical engineering
CHEN, XIAOSONG, Mathematical Sciences and Computing Technology
CHEN, XIUFANG, Civil Engineering and Architecture
CHEN, YIZHUANG, Politics and Public Administration
CHEN, YUEWU, Foreign Languages
CHEN, YUXIANG, Bioscience and Technology
CHEN, ZHENXING, Chemistry and Chemical engineering
CHEN, ZHIGANG, Information Science and Engineering
CHEN, ZHONGWEN, Foreign Languages
DAI, BINXIANG, Mathematical Sciences and Computing Technology
DAI, DUAN, Fine Arts
DAI, GONGLIAN, Civil Engineering and Architecture
DENG, CHAO, Business
DENG, DEHUA, Civil Engineering and Architecture
DENG, FEIYAOI, Chemistry and Chemical engineering
DENG, HANWU, Pharmaceutical Sciences
DENG, RUIJIAO, Nursing
DENG, TIANSHENG, Business
DU, YONG, Powder Metallurgy
FAN, XIANGRU, Business
FAN, XIANLONG, Foreign Languages
FAN, XIAOHUI, Resources Processing and Bioengineering
FAN, XIAOPING, Information Science and Engineering
FANG, LIGANG, Civil Engineering and Architecture
FANG, PING, Medical Technology and Information
FANG, YUNXIANG, Pharmaceutical Sciences
FANG, ZHENG, Chemistry and Chemical engineering
FENG, QIMING, Resources Processing and Bioengineering
FU, HELIN, Civil Engineering and Architecture
GAN, SIQING, Mathematical Sciences and Computing Technology
GAN, WEIPING, Materials Science and Engineering
GAO, YANG, Business
GONG, FAN, Chemistry and Chemical engineering
GONG, YANPING, Business
GU, JINGHUA, Resources Processing and Bioengineering
GU, YINGYING, Chemistry and Chemical engineering
GUAN, LUXIONG, Chemistry and Chemical engineering
GUI, WEIHUA, Information Science and Engineering
GUO, GUANGHUA, Physics, Sciences and Technology
GUO, QULIAN, Medical Technology and Information
GUO, SHAOHUA, Civil Engineering and Architecture
GUO, XIANGRONG, Civil Engineering and Architecture
HAN, JINGQUAN, Foreign Languages
HAN, QINGLAN, Business
HAN, XULI, Mathematical Sciences and Computing Technology
HAN, XULI, Information Science and Engineering

HE, BOQUAN, Resources Processing and Bioengineering
HE, GUOPING, Nursing
HE, HONGBO, Physics, Sciences and Technology
HE, HONGQU, Business
HE, JISHAN, Business
HE, XUEWEI, Literature
HE, YUNBO, Foreign Languages
HOU, MANLING, Chemistry and Chemical engineering
HOU, ZHENTING, Mathematical Sciences and Computing Technology
HU, HUIPING, Chemistry and Chemical engineering
HU, HUOSHENG, Information Science and Engineering
HU, KAI, Politics and Public Administration
HU, WEIXIN, Bioscience and Technology
HU, YUEHUA, Resources Processing and Bioengineering
HU, ZHENHUA, Business
HUANG, BOYUN, Materials Science and Engineering
HUANG, FANGLIN, Civil Engineering and Architecture
HUANG, JIAN, Chemistry and Chemical engineering
HUANG, JIANBO, Business
HUANG, JIANREN, Foreign Languages
HUANG, KELONG, Chemistry and Chemical engineering
HUANG, LANFANG, Chemistry and Chemical engineering
HUANG, PEIYUN, Materials Science and Engineering
HUANG, PEIYUN, Powder Metallurgy
HUANG, QIZHONG, Powder Metallurgy
HUANG, SHENGSHENG, Resources Processing and Bioengineering
HUANG, YANPING, Politics and Public Administration
HUANG, YONG'AN, Foreign Languages
HUANG, ZHUCHENG, Resources Processing and Bioengineering
HUO, GUOJING, Civil Engineering and Architecture
HUO, YAOHUI, Powder Metallurgy
JIA, WEIJIA, Information Science and Engineering
JIAN, XINCHUN, Stomatology
JIANG, DONGJIU, Nursing
JIANG, DONGMEI, Nursing
JIANG, JINZHI, Chemistry and Chemical engineering
JIANG, SHAOJIAN, Energy and Power Engineering
JIANG, TAO, Resources Processing and Bioengineering
JIANG, XINHUA, Information Science and Engineering
JIANG, YIMIN, Physics, Sciences and Technology
JIANG, YUREN, Chemistry and Chemical engineering
JIN, ZHANPENG, Materials Science and Engineering
LAN, XIAOJUN, Medical Technology and Information
LENG, WUMING, Civil Engineering and Architecture
LI, BAIQING, Foreign Languages
LI, DENGQING, Medical Technology and Information
LI, HE, Energy and Power Engineering
LI, HONGJIAN, Physics, Sciences and Technology
LI, HUANDE, Pharmaceutical Sciences
LI, JIANHUA, Politics and Public Administration
LI, JIE, Chemistry and Chemical engineering
LI, JUNPING, Mathematical Sciences and Computing Technology
LI, LIANG, Civil Engineering and Architecture
LI, LIPING, Business
LI, MINGSHENG, Business
LI, SONGREN, Resources Processing and Bioengineering
LI, XIAOBIN, Energy and Power Engineering
LI, XIAORU, Chemistry and Chemical engineering
LI, XIBIN, Powder Metallurgy
LI, XUE, Mathematical Sciences and Computing Technology
LI, YANGCHENG, Mathematical Sciences and Computing Technology
LI, YANGSHENG, Fine Arts
LI, YANLIN, Foreign Languages
LI, YIBING, Physics, Sciences and Technology
LI, YIBING, Information Science and Engineering
LI, YIMIN, Powder Metallurgy
LI, YIZHI, Business
LI, YUANGAO, Chemistry and Chemical engineering
LI, YUANJIAN, Pharmaceutical Sciences
LI, ZIRU, Business
LIANG, HONG, Chemistry and Chemical engineering
LIANG, LAIYIN, Business
LIANG, XIMING, Information Science and Engineering
LIANG, YIZENG, Chemistry and Chemical engineering
LIAO, SHENGMING, Energy and Power Engineering
LIAO, SHENGMING, Civil Engineering and Architecture
LIU, AIDONG, Business
LIU, BAOCHEN, Civil Engineering and Architecture
LIU, CHANGQING, Chemistry and Chemical engineering
LIU, DONGRONG, Business
LIU, GUOPING, Information Science and Engineering
LIU, JIAJIA, Chemistry and Chemical engineering
LIU, JIANSHE, Resources Processing and Bioengineering
LIU, KAIYU, Chemistry and Chemical engineering
LIU, LIHANG, Politics and Public Administration
LIU, LIYING, Pharmaceutical Sciences
LIU, MINGJING, Foreign Languages
LIU, QINGTAN, Civil Engineering and Architecture
LIU, SHIJUN, Chemistry and Chemical engineering
LIU, SUQIN, Chemistry and Chemical engineering
LIU, WEIJUN, Mathematical Sciences and Computing Technology
LIU, XIAOCHUN, Medical Technology and Information
LIU, XINXING, Resources Processing and Bioengineering
LIU, XIONGFEI, Physics, Sciences and Technology
LIU, YANPING, Bioscience and Technology
LIU, YAZHENG, Business
LIU, YEXIANG, Energy and Power Engineering
LIU, YIRONG, Mathematical Sciences and Computing Technology
LIU, YONGHE, Medical Technology and Information
LIU, YONGMEI, Business
LIU, YOUNIAN, Chemistry and Chemical engineering
LIU, ZAIMING, Mathematical Sciences and Computing Technology
LIU, ZEMIN, Literature
LIU, ZHIYI, Materials Science and Engineering
LIU, ZHUMING, Materials Science and Engineering
LUO, AIJING, Medical Technology and Information
LUO, AN, Information Science and Engineering
LUO, DAYONG, Information Science and Engineering
LUO, JIAOWAN, Mathematical Sciences and Computing Technology
LUO, WENDONG, Physics, Sciences and Technology
LUO, XIAOLING, Business
LUO, XINXING, Business
LUO, XUEGANG, Basic Medical Sciences
LUO, YIMING, Chemistry and Chemical engineering
LUO, ZIQIANG, Basic Medical Sciences
LU, HAIBO, Powder Metallurgy
LU, XICHEN, Politics and Public Administration
LU, YAOHUAI, Politics and Public Administration
MA, CHENGYIN, Chemistry and Chemical engineering
MAN, RUILIN, Chemistry and Chemical engineering
MAO, XUANGUO, Literature
MEI, MEIZHI, Energy and Power Engineering
MENG, ZE, Foreign Languages
NIU, YINJIAN, Resources Processing and Bioengineering
OU YANG, YOUQUAN, Literature
PAN, QINGLIN, Materials Science and Engineering
PANG, CHUNYAO, Chemistry and Chemical engineering
PEN, JINDING, Foreign Languages
PENG, JIEYING, Stomatology
PENG, LIMIN, Civil Engineering and Architecture
PENG, PINGYI, Politics and Public Administration
PENG, XIAOQI, Physics, Sciences and Technology
PENG, XIAOQI, Energy and Power Engineering
PENG, YUELIN, Mathematical Sciences and Computing Technology
QIAN, DONG, Chemistry and Chemical engineering
QIN, XIAOQUN, Basic Medical Sciences
QIU, KEQIANG, Chemistry and Chemical engineering
QIU, YUNREN, Chemistry and Chemical engineering
QU, LONG, Chemistry and Chemical engineering
QU, XUANHUI, Powder Metallurgy
RAO, QIUHUA, Civil Engineering and Architecture
RAO, YUELEI, Business
REN, FENGLIAN, Chemistry and Chemical engineering
REN, JIFAN, Literature
RUAN, JIANMING, Powder Metallurgy
SHE, XIEBIN, Foreign Languages
SHEN, CHAOHONG, Business
SHEN, MEILAN, Mathematical Sciences and Computing Technology
SHEN, QUNTAI, Information Science and Engineering
SHI, RONGHUA, Information Science and Engineering
SHI, ZHANGMING, Energy and Power Engineering
SHU, WANGEN, Chemistry and Chemical engineering
SI, SHIHUI, Chemistry and Chemical engineering
SONG, HUIPING, Bioscience and Technology
SU, YUCHANG, Materials Science and Engineering
SUN, XIANGMING, Fine Arts
SUN, ZHENQIU, Mathematical Sciences and Computing Technology
TAN, DAREN, Medical Technology and Information
TAN, GUANZXHENG, Information Science and Engineering

TAN, MENGQUN, Basic Medical Sciences
TAN, XIPEI, Politics and Public Administration
TAN, YUNJIE, Foreign Languages
TANG, HONG'E, Civil Engineering and Architecture
TANG, RUIREN, Chemistry and Chemical engineering
TANG, XIANHUA, Mathematical Sciences and Computing Technology
TANG, YOUGEN, Chemistry and Chemical engineering
TANG, ZHANGUI, Stomatology
TAO, XINLU, Nursing
TU, GUOYUAN, Foreign Languages
TU, LING, Stomatology
WAN, ZHONG, Mathematical Sciences and Computing Technology
WANG, DIANZUO, Resources Processing and Bioengineering
WANG, GUOSHUN, Business
WANG, HANQING, Energy and Power Engineering
WANG, HUI, Chemistry and Chemical engineering
WANG, JIABAO, Mathematical Sciences and Computing Technology
WANG, JIANQIANG, Business
WANG, JIANXIU, Chemistry and Chemical engineering
WANG, JIGUI, Medical Technology and Information
WANG, LINGSEN, Powder Metallurgy
WANG, MENGJUN, Civil Engineering and Architecture
WANG, MING'AN, Medical Technology and Information
WANG, MINGMING, Nursing
WANG, MINGPU, Materials Science and Engineering
WANG, SHIPING, Basic Medical Sciences
WANG, SHUHUA, Resources Processing and Bioengineering
WANG, XIAOCHUN, Medical Technology and Information
WANG, XINGHUA, Civil Engineering and Architecture
WANG, YAN, Chemistry and Chemical engineering
WANG, YIJUN, Information Science and Engineering
WANG, YONGHE, Civil Engineering and Architecture
WANG, YUECHUAN, Literature
WANG, ZHANGHUA, Literature
WANG, ZHIFA, Materials Science and Engineering
WANG, ZHIZHONG, Mathematical Sciences and Computing Technology
WEI, RENYONG, Information Science and Engineering
WEN, JIFANG, Basic Medical Sciences
WEN, YUSONG, Civil Engineering and Architecture
WU, JINMING, Business
WU, KUN, Mathematical Sciences and Computing Technology
WU, LIANGGANG, Business
WU, LIXIANG, Basic Medical Sciences
WU, XIANCHENG, Politics and Public Administration
XIA, CHANGQING, Materials Science and Engineering
XIA, JIAHUI, Bioscience and Technology
XIA, JINLAN, Resources Processing and Bioengineering
XIANG, SHU, Mathematical Sciences and Computing Technology
XIAO, LIMING, Foreign Languages
XIAO, TIEJIAN, Politics and Public Administration
XIAO, XIANZHONG, Basic Medical Sciences
XIAO, XIAODAN, Medical Technology and Information
XIAO, XU, Business
XIAO, ZEQIANG, Energy and Power Engineering
XIE, RUHE, Energy and Power Engineering
XIE, XIAOLI, Stomatology
XIE, YOUJUN, Civil Engineering and Architecture
XIONG, LVMAO, Politics and Public Administration
XIONG, XIANG, Powder Metallurgy
XIONG, YAN, Pharmaceutical Sciences
XU, HUI, Physics, Sciences and Technology
XU, JICHENG, Materials Science and Engineering
XU, QINGSONG, Mathematical Sciences and Computing Technology
XU, ZHISHENG, Civil Engineering and Architecture
YAN, AIMIN, Business
YAN, ZHEN, Literature
YANG, BINGCHU, Physics, Sciences and Technology
YANG, CHANGXIN, Information Science and Engineering
YANG, CHANGYING, Foreign Languages
YANG, DONGLIANG, Chemistry and Chemical engineering
YANG, GUOLIN, Civil Engineering and Architecture
YANG, HUAMING, Resources Processing and Bioengineering
YANG, JUNSHENG, Civil Engineering and Architecture
YANG, SHOUKANG, Foreign Languages
YANG, WEIWEN, Business
YANG, XINRONG, Information Science and Engineering
YANG, ZHANHONG, Chemistry and Chemical engineering
YE, BOLONG, Civil Engineering and Architecture
YE, HONGQI, Chemistry and Chemical engineering
YE, MEIXIN, Civil Engineering and Architecture
YI, DANQING, Energy and Power Engineering
YI, JIANHONG, Powder Metallurgy
YI, MAOZHONG, Powder Metallurgy
YIN, ZHIMIN, Materials Science and Engineering
YIN, ZHOULAN, Chemistry and Chemical engineering
YU, DEQUAN, Literature
YU, PING, Basic Medical Sciences
YU, SHENGHUA, Mathematical Sciences and Computing Technology
YU, SHOUYI, Information Science and Engineering
YU, ZHIWU, Civil Engineering and Architecture
YUAN, DONGYUAN, Physics, Sciences and Technology
YUAN, JINGEN, Civil Engineering and Architecture
YUAN, LEPING, Business
YUAN, MINGLIANG, Resources Processing and Bioengineering
YUAN, XIUGUI, Mathematical Sciences and Computing Technology
YUE, YIDING, Business
ZENG, CHANGQIU, Politics and Public Administration
ZENG, DONGMING, Chemistry and Chemical engineering
ZENG, QINGFU, Basic Medical Sciences
ZENG, QINGREN, Basic Medical Sciences
ZENG, QINGYUAN, Civil Engineering and Architecture
ZENG, SUMIN, Materials Science and Engineering
ZENG, YUHUA, Nursing
ZENG, ZHICHENG, Basic Medical Sciences
ZHANG, CHENGPING, Foreign Languages
ZHANG, CONGYI, Foreign Languages
ZHANG, HANJUN, Mathematical Sciences and Computing Technology
ZHANG, HONGYAN, Mathematical Sciences and Computing Technology
ZHANG, HUAILIANG, Fine Arts
ZHANG, JIANXIANG, Basic Medical Sciences
ZHANG, JIASHENG, Civil Engineering and Architecture
ZHANG, JINGSHENG, Resources Processing and Bioengineering
ZHANG, JINRU, Chemistry and Chemical engineering
ZHANG, LONGKUAN, Foreign Languages
ZHANG, NAN, Civil Engineering and Architecture
ZHANG, PINGMIN, Chemistry and Chemical engineering
ZHANG, QINGJIN, Resources Processing and Bioengineering
ZHANG, QISEN, Civil Engineering and Architecture
ZHANG, QUAN, Energy and Power Engineering
ZHANG, SENKUAN, Foreign Languages
ZHANG, SHIMIN, Chemistry and Chemical engineering
ZHANG, SIQI, Materials Science and Engineering
ZHANG, TAIMING, Chemistry and Chemical engineering
ZHANG, TAISHAN, Information Science and Engineering
ZHANG, XINGXIAN, Foreign Languages
ZHANG, XINMIN, Materials Science and Engineering
ZHANG, XU, Foreign Languages
ZHANG, YAOJUN, Foreign Languages
ZHAO, WANGDA, Civil Engineering and Architecture
ZHAO, YAOLONG, Information Science and Engineering
ZHENG, ZHIQIAO, Materials Science and Engineering
ZHENG, ZHOUSHUN, Mathematical Sciences and Computing Technology
ZHON, HONG, Chemistry and Chemical engineering
ZHONG, MEIZUO, Medical Technology and Information
ZHONG, SHI'AN, Chemistry and Chemical engineering
ZHONG, YOUXUN, Literature
ZHOU, CHAOYANG, Civil Engineering and Architecture
ZHOU, CHUNSHAN, Chemistry and Chemical engineering
ZHOU, DEBI, Chemistry and Chemical engineering
ZHOU, DIAOMIN, Energy and Power Engineering
ZHOU, FEIMENG, Chemistry and Chemical engineering
ZHOU, JICHENG, Physics, Sciences and Technology
ZHOU, KECHAO, Powder Metallurgy
ZHOU, KESHENG, Physics, Sciences and Technology
ZHOU, LIUXI, Foreign Languages
ZHOU, MINGDA, Chemistry and Chemical engineering
ZHOU, NAIJUN, Energy and Power Engineering
ZHOU, PIN, Energy and Power Engineering
ZHOU, QIAN, Energy and Power Engineering
ZHOU, SHIQIONG, Civil Engineering and Architecture
ZHOU, TAO, Chemistry and Chemical engineering
ZHU, DEQING, Resources Processing and Bioengineering
ZHU, KAICHENG, Physics, Sciences and Technology
ZHU, NIANQIONG, Nursing
ZHUANG, JIANMING, Resources Processing and Bioengineering
ZOU, BEIJI, Information Science and Engineering

ZOU, JIEZHONG, Mathematical Sciences and Computing Technology
ZUO, TIEYONG, Materials Science and Engineering

ATTACHED INSTITUTES

National Engineering Research Centre for Powder Metallurgy: Dir HUANG BOYUN.

National Laboratory of Medical Genetics of China: Dir XIA JIAHUI.

National Teaching Base of Engineering Chemistry Foundation Course: Dir GUAN LUXIONG.

National Teaching Base of Engineering Physics Foundation Course: Dir YANG BINGCHU.

State Key Laboratory for Powder Metallurgy: Dir HUANG BOYUN.

CHANG'AN UNIVERSITY

Nan Er Huan Rd, Xian 710064, Shanxi
Telephone: (29) 82334104
Fax: (29) 85261532
Internet: www.xahu.edu.cn

Founded 2000
Ministry of Education control
Academic year: September to July
President: ZHOU XU HONG
Vice-Presidents: LI YUN JI, LIU BO QUAN, LIU JIAN CHAO, MA JIAN
Head of Graduate Department: LU PENG MIN
Librarian: SHA AI MIN

Number of teachers: 3,438
Number of students: 36,383

Publications: *Automobile Racing Driver* (monthly), *China Journal of Highway and Transport* (4 a year), *Journal of Chang'an University* (architecture and environmental sciences, 6 a year), *Journal of Chang'an University* (natural sciences, 6 a year), *Journal of Chang'an University* (philosophy and social sciences, 6 a year), *Journal of Traffic and Transportation Engineering* (4 a year), *Journal of Earth Sciences and Environment* (4 a year), *Road Machinery and Construction Mechanization* (monthly)

DEANS

School of Construction Machinery: FENG ZHONG XU
School of Economics and Management: ZHOU GUO GUANG
School of Humanities and Social Science: LIU JI FA
School of Science: FENG JIAN HU
College of Applied Technology: HU XUE MEI
College of Construction Engineering: WANG YI HONG
College of Earth Science and Land Resources Management: LI YONG
College of Environmental Science and Engineering: WANG WEN KE
College of Foreign Languages: LI MIN QUAN
College of Geology Engineering and Geomatics: PENG JIAN MIN
College of Highway Engineering: XU YUE
College of Information Engineering: HE YI QU

PROFESSORS

CHEN, DE CHUAN, Highway Management
CHEN, HONG, Traffic Engineering
CHEN, KUAN MIN, Traffic Engineering
CHEN, ZHI XIN, Geology Engineering and Geomatics
CHEN, ZHONG DA, Highways
DAI, JING LIANG, Highways
DONG, QIAN LI, Economics and Management
DOU, MING JIAN, Highway Disaster Prevention and Cure
DU, DONG JU, Geology Engineering and Geomatics
FAN, WEN, Geology Engineering and Geomatics
FENG, JIAN HU, Science
FENG, ZHEN YU, Science
FENG, ZHONG XU, Construction Machinery
GUAN, WEI XING, Environmental Science and Engineering
GUO, YUAN SHU, Information Engineering
HAN, SEN, Highways
HAO, PEI WEN, Highways
HAO, XIAN WU, Bridges
HE, AN MING, Science
HE, SHUANG HAI, Bridges
HE, YI QU, Information Engineering
HU, DA LIN, Bridges
HU, YONG BIAO, Construction Machinery
HU, YUE, Bridges
HU, ZHAO TONG, Bridges
HUANG, PING MIN, Bridges
JIANG, CHANG YI, Earth science and Land Resources Management
JIAO, SHENG JIE, Construction Machinery
JU, YONG FENG, Information Engineering
LEI, SHENG YOU, Geognosy and Tube Engineering
LI, PEI CHENG, Environmental Science and Engineering
LI, QING CHUN, Geology Engineering and Geomatics
LI, XIU, Geology Engineering and Geomatics
LI, YONG, Earth science and Land Resources Management
LI, YUN FENG, Environmental Science and Engineering
LI, ZI QING, Bridges
LIU, BAO JIAN, Geognosy and Tube Engineering
LIU, JI FA, Humanities and Social Science
LIU, JIAN XIN, Bridges
LIU, LAI JUN, Bridges
LIU, YONG JIAN, Bridges
LONG, SHUI GEN, Construction Machinery
LU, PENG MIN, Construction Machinery
LV, KANG CHENG, Geognosy and Tube Engineering
MA, JIANG MING, Science
MA, RONG GUO, Traffic Engineering
MA, TIAN SHAN, Economics and Management
MAO, YAN LONG, Geology Engineering and Geomatics
MEN, YU MING, Geology Engineering and Geomatics
NI, WANG KUI, Geology Engineering and Geomatics
PEI, XIAN ZHI, Earth science and Land Resources Management
PENG, JIAN MIN, Geology Engineering and Geomatics
QIAN, ZHUANG ZHI, Earth science and Land Resources Management
SHA, AI MIN, Highways
SHEN, AI QIN, Highways
SHI, YONG MIN, Highway Management
SONG, YI FAN, Bridges
SU, SHENG RUI, Geology Engineering and Geomatics
TAN, CHENG QIAN, Geology Engineering and Geomatics
TIAN, WEI PING, Highway Disaster Prevention and Cure
WANG, BIN GANG, Highways
WANG, HU, Science
WANG, WEN KE, Environmental Science and Engineering
WANG, XIAO MOU, Geognosy and Tube Engineering
WANG, XUAN CANG, Highway Management
WEI, GUANG SHENG, Science
WU, XIAO GUANG, Highway Management
XIA, YONG XU, Geognosy and Tube Engineering
XIE, YONG LI, Geognosy and Tube Engineering
XU, HAI CHENG, Economics and Management
XU, JING LIANG, Road Reconnaissance
XUE, CHUN JI, Earth science and Land Resources Management
YAN, BAO JIE, Traffic Engineering
YANG, BIN CHENG, Bridges
YANG, SHAO WEI, Road Reconnaissance
YANG, XIAO HUA, Geognosy and Tube Engineering
YANG, XING KE, Earth science and Land Resources Management
YI, GUAN SHENG, Science
ZHANG, CHAO, Highways
ZHANG, DENG LIANG, Highways
ZHANG, JUN, Geology Engineering and Geomatics
ZHANG, QIN, Geology Engineering and Geomatics
ZHANG, ZHI QIANG, Geology Engineering and Geomatics
ZHAO, FA SHUO, Geology Engineering and Geomatics
ZHE, XUE SEN, Geognosy and Tube Engineering
ZHENG, CHUAN CHAO, Highways
ZHENG, NAN XIANG, Highways
ZHOU, GUO GUANG, Economics and Management
ZHOU, WEI, Traffic Engineering
ZHOU, XU HONG, Bridges
ZHU, GUANG MING, Geology Engineering and Geomatics

ATTACHED CENTRES

Engineering Mechanics Research Institute: Dir YU KE PING.

Higher Education Research Institute: Dir FENG ZHEN NING.

Highway Disaster Prevention and Cure Research Institute: Dir DOU MING JIAN.

Road Reconnaissance Research Institute: Dir XU YA YA.

CHANGCHUN UNIVERSITY OF EARTH SCIENCES

6 Ximinzhu St, Changchun, 130026 Jilin
Telephone: (431) 822391

Founded 1952
Languages of instruction: Chinese, English
Languages of instruction: Russian, Japanese
Academic year: September to January, March to July
Chancellor: Prof. ZHANG YIXIA
Vice-Chancellors: MA ZHIHONG, LIU BAOREN, Prof. SHUN YUNSHENG
Librarian: XIANG TIANYUAN

Library of 800,000 vols
Number of teachers: 830
Number of students: 3,890

Publications: *Journal*, *Geology of the World*

HEADS OF DEPARTMENTS

Geology: SUN DEYU
Hydrogeology and Engineering Geology: YU GUOGUANG
Applied Geophysics: HE QIAODENG
Geological Instrumentation: CAO MUYI
Rock and Mineral Testing and Analysis and Geochemistry: DUAN GUOZHENG
Drilling Engineering: ZHANG ZUPEI
Energy Geology: YANG BINGZHONG
Industry Administration: YAN FENGZENG
Social Sciences: MAO JIAN
Basic Sciences: YANG TIANXING
Foreign Language: LI YINGDA

CHANGCHUN INSTITUTE OF POSTS AND TELECOMMUNICATIONS

20 Nanhu St, Changchun, Jilin Province 130012
Telephone: 5171220
Fax: 5176342

Founded 1947
Controlled by the Ministry of the Information Industry
Language of instruction: Chinese
Academic year: September to July
President: SUN MUQIAN
Registrar: LIU YAN
Librarian: YU JIE
Library of 380,000 vols
Number of teachers: 407
Number of students: 2,125 (and 2,005 corresponding students)
Publication: *Journal of Changchun Institute of Posts and Telecommunications*

HEADS OF DEPARTMENTS
Telecommunications Engineering: SHENG DESHEN
Computer Science: TANG JIQUN
Management: WANG ZHIXUE

CHENGDU UNIVERSITY OF TECHNOLOGY

1st East Third Rd, Chenghua, Erxianqiao, Chengdu 610059, Sichuan
Telephone: (28) 84078898
Internet: www.cdut.edu.cn
Founded 1956
Provincial control
Academic year: September to July
President: LIU JIADUO
Vice-Presidents: HUANG RUNQIU, NI SHIJUN, TAN SHUMIN, WANG YINGCHUAN
Librarian: LI YONG
Library of 1,170,000 vols
Number of teachers: 2,021
Number of students: 25,000
Publications: *Computing Techniques for Geophysical and Geophysical Exploration* (4 a year), *Journal* (6 a year), *Journal of Geological Hazards and Environment Preservation* (4 a year), *Journal of Mineralogy and Petrology* (4 a year), *Scientific and Technological Management of Land and Resources* (6 a year)

DEANS
College of Applied Techniques and Automation Engineering: GE LIANGQUAN
Commercial College: LI YUSHENG
College of Energy Resources: ZHANG SHAONAN
College of Environment and Civil Engineering: XU QIANG
College of Foreign Languages and Cultures: LUO YIJUN
College of Geosciences: SUN CHUANMIN
College of Humanities and Law: LI QUANHUI
College of Information Engineering: WANG XUBEN
College of Information Management: GUO KE
College of Materials and Bioengineering: WANG LING
Australian Institute of Tourism and Hospitality: LI YUSHENG

PROFESSORS
CAO, JINWEN, College of Information Management
CAO, JUNXING, College of Information Engineering
CHEN, BUKE, College of Energy Resources
CHEN, CHANGQUAN, College of Information Management
CHEN, HONGDE, Geosciences College
CHEN, JUNMING, Australian Institute of Tourism and Hospitality
CHEN, WANJIANG, Commercial College
CHENG, XIA, Commercial College
DENG, LIN, College of Information Engineering
DENG, TIANLONG, College of Materials and Bioengineering
DING, ZHAOYU, Network Education College
FAN, BIWEI, College of Materials and Bioengineering
FANG, FANG, College of Applied Techniques and Automation Engineering:
FENG, WENGUANG, College of Energy Resources
FU, GUANGHAI, Commercial College
FU, RONGHUA, College of Environment and Civil Engineering
FU, RULIN, College of Information Engineering
GE, LIANGQUAN, College of Applied Techniques and Automation Engineering:
GU, XUEXIANG, Geosciences College
GUO, JIANG, College of Information Engineering
GUO, KE, College of Information Management
HE, MINGSHENG, College of Applied Techniques and Automation Engineering:
HE, ZHENGWEI, Geosciences College
HE, ZHENHUA, College of Information Engineering
HONG, ZHIQUAN, College of Information Engineering
HU, GUANGMANG, College of Information Engineering
HU, YUANLAI, College of Information Management
HUANG, DILONG, College of Information Engineering
HUANG, JIJUN, Geosciences College
HUANG, RUNQIU, College of Environment and Civil Engineering
HUANG, SIJING, Geosciences College
JIA, SUYUAN, College of Environment and Civil Engineering
KONG, FANJING, College of Foreign Languages and Cultures
KUANG, JIANCHAO, College of Information Management
LI, HONGMU, College of Applied Techniques and Automation Engineering:
LI, JUCHU, College of Applied Techniques and Automation Engineering:
LI, LIANGMING, Commercial College
LI, LUMING, College of Information Engineering
LI, QUANHUI, College Of Humanities And Law
LI, RUI, College of Information Engineering
LI, SHUSHENG, College of Environment and Civil Engineering
LI, TIANBIN, College of Environment and Civil Engineering
LI, WUQUAN, College of Foreign Languages and Cultures
LI, YUSHENG, Commercial College
LI, ZHENGWEN, College of Information Engineering
LI, ZHEQIN, College of Environment and Civil Engineering
LI, ZHIQUAN, College of Information Engineering
LIE, DEXIN, College of Environment and Civil Engineering
LIN, LI, Geosciences College
LIU, DENGZHONG, Geosciences College
LIU, HANCHAO, College of Environment and Civil Engineering
LIU, HONGJUN, College of Information Management
LIU, JIADUO, Geosciences College
LIU, MAOCAI, College of Information Management
LIU, SHUGEN, College of Energy Resources
LIU, XIANFAN, Geosciences College
LU, KUN, College of Applied Techniques and Automation Engineering:
LU, ZHENGYUAN, College of Energy Resources
LUO, MEI, College of Applied Techniques and Automation Engineering:
LUO, RUNTIAN, College of Foreign Languages and Cultures
LUO, SHENGXIAN, College of Information Engineering
LUO, YIJUN, College of Foreign Languages and Cultures
MA, RUNZE, Geosciences College
MA, YUXIAO, College of Applied Techniques and Automation Engineering:
MIAO, FANG, College of Information Engineering
NI, SHIJUN, College of Applied Techniques and Automation Engineering:
PENG, DAJUN, College of Energy Resources
QIE, JINLING, College of Information Engineering
QIU, KEHUI, College of Materials and Bioengineering
REN, GUANGMING, College of Environment and Civil Engineering
SHA, JICHANG, College of Information Management
SHENG, ZHONGMING, College of Energy Resources
SHI, HE, Geosciences College
SHI, ZHEJIN, College of Energy Resources
SUN, CHUANMIN, Geosciences College
SUN, SHUXIA, Network Education College
TAN, JIANXIONG, Geosciences College
TANG, JUXING, Geosciences College
TIAN, JINGCHUN, Geosciences College
TONG, CHUNHAN, College of Applied Techniques and Automation Engineering:
TUO, XIANGUO, College of Information Engineering
WAN, XINNAN, College of Environment and Civil Engineering
WANG, CHENGSHAN, Geosciences College
WANG, HONGFENG, Geosciences College
WANG, HONGHUI, College of Energy Resources
WANG, HUIZHOU, College of Foreign Languages and Cultures
WANG, LANSHENG, College of Environment and Civil Engineering
WANG, LING, College of Materials and Bioengineering
WANG, MOHUI, College of Materials and Bioengineering
WANG, SHITIAN, College of Environment and Civil Engineering
WANG, XIAOCHUN, College of Environment and Civil Engineering
WANG, XINZHUANG, College of Information Management
WANG, XUBEN, College of Information Engineering
WANG, YUNCHENG, College of Energy Resources
WANG, YUNSHENG, College of Environment and Civil Engineering
WANG, ZAIQI, College of Foreign Languages and Cultures
WEI, GUIMING, College of Information Management
WEN, CHUNQI, Geosciences College
WU, SHAN, Geosciences College
XI, DASHUN, College of Information Engineering
XIAN, YUANFU, Geosciences College
XIANG, YANG, College of Energy Resources
XIAO, CIXUN, College of Information Engineering
XING, WENXIANG, College of Information Management
XU, GUOSHENG, College of Energy Resources
XU, MO, College of Environment and Civil Engineering
XU, QIANG, College of Environment and Civil Engineering
YAN, HELIN, Geosciences College
YANG, SHAOGUO, College of Information Engineering
YANG, WUNIAN, Geosciences College
YANG, ZHENGXI, Geosciences College
YI, GUAN, College of Applied Techniques and Automation Engineering:
YI, HAISHENG, Geosciences College

YIN, HUIAN, College of Materials and Bioengineering
ZHANG, CHENGJIANG, College of Applied Techniques and Automation Engineering:
ZHANG, QICHUN, College of Materials and Bioengineering
ZHANG, SHAONAN, College of Energy Resources
ZHANG, ZUOYUAN, College of Environment and Civil Engineering
ZHAO, BING, Geosciences College
ZHAO, QIHUA, College of Environment and Civil Engineering
ZHAO, XIAFEI, College of Energy Resources
ZHAO, XIGUI, College of Energy Resources
ZHAO, ZESONG, Commercial College
ZHEN, HUAN, College of Foreign Languages and Cultures
ZHEN, MINGHUA, Geosciences College
ZHEN, RONGCAI, Geosciences College
ZHONG, BENSHAN, College of Information Engineering
ZHONG, YONGJIAN, Commercial College
ZHOU, JIAJI, College of Information Engineering
ZHOU, RONGSHENG, College of Applied Techniques and Automation Engineering:
ZHOU, SICHUN, College of Applied Techniques and Automation Engineering:
ZHOU, XIXIANG, College of Information Engineering
ZHU, CHUANGYE, Geosciences College
ZHU, JIESHOU, College of Information Engineering

ATTACHED RESEARCH INSTITUTES

Continuing Training College.

Ministerial Key Laboratory of Continental Dynamics of the Qinghai-Tibet Plateau.

Ministerial Key Laboratory of Land and Resources Information and Applied Technology.

National Laboratory of Geological Hazard Prevention and Geological Environment Protection: Dir LIU GUANGRUN.

Network Education College: Dir XING XIAOYONG.

Provincial Key Laboratory of Applied Nuclear Techniques in Geosciences.

Provincial Key Laboratory of Geodetection and Information Technology.

State Key Laboratory of Oil Gas Reservoir Geology and Exploitation: Dir LUO PINGYA.

CHENGDU UNIVERSITY OF TRADITIONAL CHINESE MEDICINE

37 Shierqiao Rd, Chengdu 610075
Telephone: (28) 87784542
Fax: (28) 87784606
E-mail: wsc@cdutcm.edu.cn
Internet: www.cdutcm.edu.cn

Founded 1956
State Control
Languages of instruction: Chinese, English
Academic year: September to August
President: Prof. ZHU BIDE
Vice-Presidents: XIE KEQING LIANG FANRONG LUO CAIGUI, FU CHUNHUA
Chief Administrative Officer: XU, LIAN
Librarian: JIANG YONGGUANG
Library of 602,000 vols
Number of teachers: 1,678
Number of students: 10,095
Publications: *Academic Journal* (4 a year), *Higher Education Research into Traditional Chinese Medicine* (4 a year)

HEADS OF DEPARTMENTS

Acupuncture: LIU, XUGUANG
Adult Education: WANG, ZISHOU
Basic Chinese Medicine: CHENG, GANG
Chinese Medicine: LUO CAIGUI
Chinese Pharmacology: LI ZHUYUN
International Education College: YAO, HONGWU

CHINA AGRICULTURAL UNIVERSITY

2 West of Yuanmingyuan Rd, Haidian District, Beijing 100094
Telephone: (10) 62732394
Fax: (10) 62732872
Internet: www.cau.edu.cn

Founded 1905
Academic year: September to July
President: CHEN ZHANGLIANG
Vice-Presidents: FU ZETIAN, JIANG SHUREN, MA JIANSHENG, SUN QIXIN, TAN XIANGYONG, ZHANG DONGJUN
Head of Graduate Department: CHEN ZHANGLIANG
Librarian: ZHANG QUAN
Number of teachers: 1,170
Number of students: 18,425
Publications: *Chinese Journal of Veterinary Medicine*, *Journal* (natural sciences, 6 a year)

DEANS

College of Agronomy and Biotechnology: DAI JINGRUI
College of Animal Science and Technology: LI DEFA
College of Biology Science: WU WEIHUA
College of Economic Management: WANG XIUQING
College of Food Science and Nutritional Engineering: LUO YUNBO
College of Humanities and Development: LI XIAOYUN
College of Information and Electrical Engineering: YANG RENGANG
College of Resource and Environment: ZHANG FUSUO
College of Science: JIAO QUNYING
College of Veterinary Medicine: WANG MING
College of Water Conservation and Civil Engineering: WANG FUJUN
College of International Studies: MENG FANXI

PROFESSORS

AO, GUANGMING, Biological Sciences
CAI, WANZHI, Agronomy and Biotechnology
CAO, YIPING, Resources and the Environment
CAO, ZHIPING, Resources and the Environment
CHANG, JINSHI, Water Conservation and Civil Engineering
CHEN, BAOFENG, Economic Management
CHEN, BU, Agronomy and Biotechnology
CHEN, HUANWEI, Resources and the Environment
CHEN, JIA, Biological Sciences
CHEN, JIANPING, Resources and the Environment
CHEN, MIN, Food Science and Nutritional Engineering
CHEN, QINGYUN, Agronomy and Biotechnology
CHEN, SANFENG, Biological Sciences
CHEN, SHAOJIANG, Agronomy and Biotechnology
CHEN, WENXIN, Biological Sciences
CHEN, YONGFU, Biological Sciences
CHEN, ZHANGLIANG, Agronomy and Biotechnology
CHENG, XU, Agronomy and Biotechnology
CUI, JIANYUN, Food Science and Nutritional Engineering
CUI, SHENG, Biological Sciences
CUI, ZONGJUN, Agronomy and Biotechnology
DAI, JINGRUI, Agronomy and Biotechnology
DENG, NAIYANG, Science
DENG, XIMIN, Agronomy and Biotechnology
DUAN, CHANGQING, Food Science and Nutritional Engineering
FENG, GONG, Humanities and Development
FENG, GU, Resources and the Environment
FENG, KAIWEN, Economic Management
FENG, SHAOYUAN, Water Conservation and Civil Engineering
FU, ZHIYI, Science
GAO, JUNPING, Agronomy and Biotechnology
GAO, QIJIE, Humanities and Development
GAO, WANGSHENG, Agronomy and Biotechnology
GAO, XIWU, Agronomy and Biotechnology
GAO, YANXIANG, Food Science and Nutritional Engineering
GONG, LIMIN, Animal Science and Technology
GONG, YUANSHI, Resources and the Environment
GONG, ZHIZHONG, Biological Sciences
GUO, SHUNTANG, Food Science and Nutritional Engineering
GUO, XIQING, Information and Electrical Engineering
GUO, YANGDONG, Agronomy and Biotechnology
GUO, YUHAI, Agronomy and Biotechnology
GUO, YUYUAN, Agronomy and Biotechnology
GUO, ZEJIAN, Agronomy and Biotechnology
HAN, BEIZHONG, Food Science and Nutritional Engineering
HAN, CHENGGUI, Agronomy and Biotechnology
HAN, JIANGUO, Animal Science and Technology
HAN, YUZHEN, Biological Sciences
HAN, ZHENHAI, Agronomy and Biotechnology
HAO, JINMIN, Resources and the Environment
HE, GUANGWEN, Economic Management
HE, XIURONG, Economic Management
HOU, CAIYUN, Food Science and Nutritional Engineering
HU, XIAOSONG, Food Science and Nutritional Engineering
HU, YUEGAO, Agronomy and Biotechnology
HUANG, GUANHUA, Water Conservation and Civil Engineering
HUANG, WEIDONG, Food Science and Nutritional Engineering
HUANG, WENBIN, Science
HUANG, YUANFANG, Resources and the Environment
HUANG, ZHIYONG, Agronomy and Biotechnology
JI, BAOPING, Food Science and Nutritional Engineering
JI, CHENG, Animal Science and Technology
JI, HAIYAN, Information and Electrical Engineering
JIA, WENSUO, Agronomy and Biotechnology
JIA, ZHIHAI, Animal Science and Technology
JIAN, HENG, Agronomy and Biotechnology
JIANG, RONGFENG, Resources and the Environment
JIANG, SHUREN, Science
JIANG, WEIBO, Food Science and Nutritional Engineering
JIAO, QUNYING, Science
JIAO, SHIYAN, Animal Science and Technology
KANG, DINGMING, Agronomy and Biotechnology
KANG, SHAOZHONG, Water Conservation and Civil Engineering
KE, BINGSHENG, Economic Management
LEI, TINGWU, Water Conservation and Civil Engineering
LENG, PING, Agronomy and Biotechnology
LI, BAOGUO, Resources and the Environment
LI, BAOMING, Water Conservation and Civil Engineering
LI, CHONGJIU, Science
LI, CHUNJIAN, Resources and the Environment
LI, DAWEI, Biological Sciences
LI, DEFA, Animal Science and Technology
LI, GENGLONG, Economic Management

LI, GUANGYONG, Water Conservation and Civil Engineering
LI, GUOHUI, Science
LI, GUOXUE, Resources and the Environment
LI, HUAIFANG, Agronomy and Biotechnology
LI, JI, Resources and the Environment
LI, JIANMIN, Agronomy and Biotechnology
LI, JIANQIANG, Agronomy and Biotechnology
LI, JIANSHENG, Agronomy and Biotechnology
LI, JILUN, Biological Sciences
LI, LITE, Food Science and Nutritional Engineering
LI, LONG, Resources and the Environment
LI, MINZAN, Information and Electrical Engineering
LI, NAN, Science
LI, NING, Biological Sciences
LI, OU, Humanities and Development
LI, PING, Economic Management
LI, SHAOKUN, Agronomy and Biotechnology
LI, SHENGLI, Animal Science and Technology
LI, SHUHUA, Agronomy and Biotechnology
LI, WEIJIONG, Resources and the Environment
LI, XIAOLIN, Resources and the Environment
LI, XIAOYUN, Humanities and Development
LI, XUEFENG, Science
LI, YAN, Biological Sciences
LI, YING, Biological Sciences
LI, ZANDONG, Biological Sciences
LI, ZHAOHU, Agronomy and Biotechnology
LI, ZICHAO, Agronomy and Biotechnology
LIAN, LINSHENG, Animal Science and Technology
LIAN, ZHENGXING, Animal Science and Technology
LIN, CONG, Water Conservation and Civil Engineering
LIN, DEGUI, Veterinary Medicine
LIN, QIMEI, Resources and the Environment
LIN, SHAN, Resources and the Environment
LIU, GUOJIE, Agronomy and Biotechnology
LIU, GUOQIN, Biological Sciences
LIU, LIMING, Resources and the Environment
LIU, QINGCHANG, Agronomy and Biotechnology
LIU, YONGGONG, Humanities and Development
LIU, ZHIYONG, Agronomy and Biotechnology
LOU, CHENGHOU, Biological Sciences
LU, FENGJU, Economic Management
LU, JUAN, Economic Management
LU, YAHAI, Resources and the Environment
LU, ZHIGUANG, Resources and the Environment
LUO, YUNBO, Food Science and Nutritional Engineering
MA, CHANGWEI, Food Science and Nutritional Engineering
MA, CHENGWEI, Water Conservation and Civil Engineering
MAO, DARU, Resources and the Environment
MENG, FANXI, International College
MENG, QINGXIANG, Animal Science and Technology
MI, GUOHUA, Resources and the Environment
MIN, SHUNGENG, Science
NIU, TIANGUI, Food Science and Nutritional Engineering
PAN, SHENQUAN, Agronomy and Biotechnology
PAN, XUEBIAO, Resources and the Environment
PENG, YOULIANG, Agronomy and Biotechnology
QIAO, JUAN, Economic Management
QIAO, ZHONG, Economic Management
QIN, FU, Economic Management
QIN, YAODONG, Resources and the Environment
REN, DONGTAO, Biological Sciences
REN, FAZHENG, Food Science and Nutritional Engineering
REN, LI, Resources and the Environment
REN, SHUMEI, Water Conservation and Civil Engineering
SHEN, DEZHONG, Resources and the Environment
SHEN, JIANZHONG, Veterinary Medicine
SHEN, ZUORUI, Agronomy and Biotechnology
SHI, DAZHAO, Agronomy and Biotechnology
SHI, JIEPING, Food Science and Nutritional Engineering
SHI, YUANCHUN, Resources and the Environment
SONG, YUAN, Biological Sciences
SU, DECHUN, Resources and the Environment
SU, ZHEN, Biological Sciences
SUN, BAOQI, Agronomy and Biotechnology
SUN, CHUANQING, Agronomy and Biotechnology
SUN, JUNSHE, Food Science and Nutritional Engineering
SUN, QIXIN, Agronomy and Biotechnology
SUN, YURUI, Information and Electrical Engineering
SUN, ZHEN, Resources and the Environment
TAN, XIANGYONG, Economic Management
TENG, GUANGHUI, Water Conservation and Civil Engineering
TIAN, WEIMING, Economic Management
WANG, AIGUO, Animal Science and Technology
WANG, BIN, Biological Sciences
WANG, CHUDUAN, Animal Science and Technology
WANG, DEHAI, Humanities and Development
WANG, FANG, Animal Science and Technology
WANG, FUJUN, Water Conservation and Civil Engineering
WANG, GUOYING, Biological Sciences
WANG, HEXIANG, Biological Sciences
WANG, HONGGUANG, Agronomy and Biotechnology
WANG, HUANHUA, Information and Electrical Engineering
WANG, HUAQI, Agronomy and Biotechnology
WANG, HUIMIN, Agronomy and Biotechnology
WANG, JIANHUA, Agronomy and Biotechnology
WANG, JINGGUO, Resources and the Environment
WANG, KU, Information and Electrical Engineering
WANG, MAO, Biological Sciences
WANG, MING, Veterinary Medicine
WANG, PU, Agronomy and Biotechnology
WANG, SHIPING, Food Science and Nutritional Engineering
WANG, SHOUCAI, Agronomy and Biotechnology
WANG, TAO, Biological Sciences
WANG, XIUQING, Economic Management
WANG, XUECHEN, Biological Sciences
WANG, YIMING, Information and Electrical Engineering
WEN, BOYING, Information and Electrical Engineering
WO, YUMING, Animal Science and Technology
WU, PING, Information and Electrical Engineering
WU, WEIHUA, Biological Sciences
WU, WENLIANG, Resources and the Environment
XIA, GUOLIANG, Biological Sciences
XIAO, HAIFENG, Economic Management
XIAO, XINGGUO, Biological Sciences
XIE, GUANGHUI, Agronomy and Biotechnology
XIN, XIAN, Economic Management
XU, HUIYUAN, Economic Management
XU, MINGLIANG, Agronomy and Biotechnology
XU, XUEFENG, Agronomy and Biotechnology
XUE, WENTONG, Food Science and Nutritional Engineering
YAN, TAILAI, Information and Electrical Engineering
YANG, DING, Agronomy and Biotechnology
YANG, HANCHUN, Veterinary Medicine
YANG, JIANCHANG, Agronomy and Biotechnology
YANG, MINGHAO, Information and Electrical Engineering
YANG, NING, Animal Science and Technology
YANG, PEILING, Water Conservation and Civil Engineering
YANG, QIULIN, Economic Management
YANG, RENGANG, Information and Electrical Engineering
YANG, XIAOBING, Agronomy and Biotechnology
YANG, ZHIFU, Resources and the Environment
YE, JINGZHONG, Humanities and Development
YE, ZHIHUA, Agronomy and Biotechnology
YI, MINGFANG, Agronomy and Biotechnology
YU, HUAIJIANG, Humanities and Development
YU, JIALIN, Biological Sciences
YU, RUIPING, Veterinary Medicine
YU, ZHENRONG, Resources and the Environment
YUAN, MING, Biological Sciences
ZANG, RIHONG, Economic Management
ZENG, SHENMING, Animal Science and Technology
ZENG, SHIMAI, Agronomy and Biotechnology
ZHAI, ZHIXI, Agronomy and Biotechnology
ZHANG, BAOGUI, Resources and the Environment
ZHANG, CONG, Resources and the Environment
ZHANG, DAPENG, Biological Sciences
ZHANG, FENGRONG, Resources and the Environment
ZHANG, FUSUO, Resources and the Environment
ZHANG, KEJIA, Veterinary Medicine
ZHANG, LONG, Agronomy and Biotechnology
ZHANG, QIN, Animal Science and Technology
ZHANG, QINGWEN, Agronomy and Biotechnology
ZHANG, RUAN, Animal Science and Technology
ZHANG, SHAOYING, Food Science and Nutritional Engineering
ZHANG, SHUQIU, Biological Sciences
ZHANG, WEI, Information and Electrical Engineering
ZHANG, XIAOMING, Animal Science and Technology
ZHANG, ZHENGHE, Economic Management
ZHANG, ZHENXIAN, Agronomy and Biotechnology
ZHANG, ZHONGJUN, Agronomy and Biotechnology
ZHANG, ZHONGZHI, Veterinary Medicine
ZHAO, DEMING, Veterinary Medicine
ZHAO, GUANGYONG, Animal Science and Technology
ZHAO, LIANGJUN, Agronomy and Biotechnology
ZHAO, MING, Agronomy and Biotechnology
ZHENG, DAWEI, Resources and the Environment
ZHENG, HANG, Biological Sciences
ZHOU, HE, Animal Science and Technology
ZHU, DAOLIN, Resources and the Environment
ZHU, DEHAI, Information and Electrical Engineering
ZHU, DEJU, Resources and the Environment
ZHU, QIZHEN, Humanities and Development
ZHU, SHIEN, Animal Science and Technology
ZUO, QIANG, Resources and the Environment
ZUO, TING, Humanities and Development

ATTACHED RESEARCH INSTITUTES

Bio-Environmental Engineering Laboratory (Key Laboratory of the Ministry of Agriculture): Dir CUI YIN AN.

Laboratory Animal Institute.

Laboratory of Soil and Water of the Ministry of Agriculture: Dir SHI YUANCHUN.

Key Laboratory of Modern Precision Agriculture System Integration of the Ministry of Education: Dir HAN LUJIA.

National Animal TSE Laboratory: Dir WANG MING.

National Drug Safety Evaluation Centre.

National Forage Engineering Technology Centre: Dir LI DEFA.

National Plant Physiology and Biology Chemistry Laboratory: Dir KUANG TINGYUN.

Quality Testing Centre of Primary Products of the Ministry of Agriculture: Dir JIANG SHUREN.

CHINA CENTRAL INSTITUTE OF FINE ARTS

5 Xiaowei hutong, East District, Beijing 100730

Telephone: 65254731

Founded 1950 by merger of National Beijing College of Art and Fine Arts Department of North China United University

President: JIN SHANGYI
Deputy Presidents: DU JIAN, YE YUZHONG
Librarian: TANG CHI

Library: Library of over 170,000 vols (25,000 in foreign languages), 8,500 vols periodicals
Number of teachers: 164
Number of students: 519, including 28 postgraduates

HEADS OF DEPARTMENTS

Chinese traditional painting: YAO YOUDUO
Graphic arts: TAN QUANSHU
History of Fine Art: XUE YONGNIAN
Mural paintings: LING YUNGING
Oil painting: SUN WEIMIN
Sculpture: CAO CHUNSHENG
Sculpture Research Studio: WANG KEQING

CHINA FOREIGN AFFAIRS UNIVERSITY

24 Zhanlan Rd, Xicheng, Beijing 100037
Internet: www.cfau.edu.cn

Founded 1955
Academic year: September to July

President: WU JIANMING
Vice-Presidents: QIN YAQING, QU XING
Head of Graduate Department: ZHENG QIRONG
Vice-Librarian: JIAN LEYI

Library of 23,500
Number of teachers: 170
Number of students: 1,600
Publication: *Journal* (4 a year)

DEANS

English: FAN SHOUYI
Foreign Affairs: ZHANG LILI
International Economics: JIANG RUIPING
International Law: JIN KESHENG

PROFESSORS

CHU, GUANGYOU, English
FAN, SHOUYI, English
HUANG, JINQI, English
JIANG, RUIPING, International Economics
QIN, YAQING, English
QU, XING, Foreign Affairs
REN, XIAOPING, English
SU, HAO, Foreign Affairs
WANG, SHAOREN, English
XIONG, ZHIYONG, Foreign Affairs
YANG, XUEYAN, English
YUAN, SHIBING, English
ZHANG, LILI, Foreign Affairs
ZHANG, YITING, English
ZHENG, QIRONG, Foreign Affairs

ATTACHED INSTITUTE

Institute of International Relations: Dir ZHU LIQUN.

CHINA UNIVERSITY OF GEOSCIENCES (WUHAN)

Yujiashan, Wuhan, 430074 Hubei

Telephone: (27) 87481030
Fax: (27) 87481392
E-mail: xb@dns.cug.edu.cn
Internet: www.cug.edu.cn

Founded 1952
Academic year: September to July

President: ZHANG, JINGAO
Vice-Presidents: YAO SHUZHEN, XING XIANGQIN, WANG YANXIN, OUYANG JIANPING

Library of 1,167,000 vols, 3,852 periodicals
Number of teachers: 2,800
Number of students: 23,600

Publications: *Earth Science*, *Journal of China University of Geosciences* (in English and Chinese), *Geological Science and Technology Information*, *Journal of Geoscience Translations*, *Chinese Journal of Engineering Geophysics*

21 colleges which offer 49 bachelor's degree courses, 65 master's degree courses and 30 doctoral courses.

CHINA MEDICAL UNIVERSITY

Bei Er Rd, He Ping District, Shenyang 110001, Liaoning

Telephone: (24) 23265491
Fax: (24) 23261169
Internet: www.cmu.edu.cn

Founded 1931
Provincial Department of Education control
Academic year: September to July

President: ZHAO QUN
Vice-Presidents: HAN MINTAN, HE QINCHENG, SUN BAOZHI, ZHAO LIKUI
Head of Graduate Department: ZHAO QUN
Librarian: NENG DIZHI

Number of teachers: 6,126
Number of students: 19,602 (11,094 full-time, 8,508 part-time)

Publications: *Chinese Journal of Health Statistics* (6 a year), *Chinese Journal of Practical Ophthalmology* (12 a year), *Journal* (6 a year), *Journal of China Clinical Medical Imaging* (4 a year), *Progress of Anatomical Sciences* (4 a year), *Liaoning Journal of Pharmacy and Clinical Remedies* (4 a year), *Liaoning Journal of Practical Diabetology* (4 a year), *Paediatric Emergency Medicine* (4 a year), *Practical Journal for Rural Doctors* (6 a year), *Progress In Japanese Medicine* (12 a year)

DEANS

Faculty of Forensic Medicine: WANG BAOJIE
School of Pharmacy: JIN XIN
School of Stomatology and Affiliated Stomatological Hospital: AI HONGJUN
College of Basic Medical Sciences: BAI SHULING
College of Nursing: LI XIAOHAN
College of Public Health: SUN GUIFAN
First Clinical College and First Affiliated Hospital: LI JIGUANG
Second Clinical College and Second Affiliated Hospital: GUO QIYONG
Third Clinical College and Third Affiliated Hospital: XU JIANJUN
Fourth Clinical College and Fourth Affiliated Hospital: HAN JIANPING
Department of Information Management and Information Systems: ZHAO YUHONG
Department of Social Science: GUO SHUYING

PROFESSORS

AI, HONGJUN, Stomatology
AN, XHUNLI, Basic Medical Sciences
BAI, SHULING, Basic Medical Sciences
BAO, ZHONGXIAO, Basic Medical Sciences
CAI, JINGYUAN, First Clinical College
CAI, JIQUN, Basic Medical Sciences
CAI, YUAN, Public Health
CAI, ZHIDAO, First Clinical College
CAO, YAMING, Basic Medical Sciences
CHANG, TIANHUI, Basic Medical Sciences
CHEN, HONGDUO, First Clinical College
CHEN, JUNQING, First Clinical College
CHEN, LIANG, First Clinical College
CHEN, SHUZHENG, Second Clinical College
CHEN, YUHUA, Basic Medical Sciences
CHU, HANG, First Clinical College
CUI, JIANJUN, Second Clinical College
CUI, LEI, Information Management and Information Systems
DAI, XIANWEI, Second Clinical College
DENG, XIANGDONG, First Clinical College
DENG, YAN, Stomatology
DING, LUOLAN, First Clinical College
DING, MEI, Forensic Medicine
DONG, XIAOJIE, Basic Medical Sciences
DONG, YULAN, Basic Medical Sciences
DU, XUEBIN, Social Science
DUAN, ZHIQUAN, First Clinical College
FAN, GUANGYU, First Clinical College
FAN, SHUDUO, Basic Medical Sciences
FANG, JINWU, First Clinical College
FANG, XIUBIN, Basic Medical Sciences
FU, BAOYU, First Clinical College
GAO, DIANWEN, Second Clinical College
GU, CHUNJIU, First Clinical College
GUAN, DAWEI, Forensic Medicine
GUO, DUISHAN, Second Clinical College
GUO, SHUYING, Social Science
HAN, JIANPING, Fourth Clinical College
HAN, YUKUN, Second Clinical College
HE, AN'GUANG, First Clinical College
HE, QINCHENG, Information Management and Information Systems
HE, SANGUANG, First Clinical College
HE, XIUQIN, First Clinical College
HONG, JIAKANG, Basic Medical Sciences
HONG, YANG, Basic Medical Sciences
HOU, XIANGMING, First Clinical College
HUANG, JIANQUN, First Clinical College
JI, SHIJUN, Second Clinical College
JIA, XINSHAN, Basic Medical Sciences
JIANG, RUOLAN, First Clinical College
JIN, CHUNLIAN, Basic Medical Sciences
JIN, WANBAO, Basic Medical Sciences
JIN, XIN, Pharmacy
LI, FUCAO, Basic Medical Sciences
LI, HOUWEN, First Clinical College
LI, JIGUANG, First Clinical College
LI, JINMING, Basic Medical Sciences
LI, LIYUN, First Clinical College
LI, SHAOYING, First Clinical College
LI, SHUQIN, Second Clinical College
LI, XIAOHAN, Nursing
LI, XINGYUAN, Second Clinical College
LI, XIULLING, First Clinical College
LI, YAN, Second Clinical College
LI, YUQUAN, Second Clinical College
LI, ZHENCHUN, Stomatology
LI, ZHENG, Second Clinical College
LI, ZHI, Basic Medical Sciences
LI, ZHUQIN, First Clinical College
LIU, CHUNRONG, First Clinical College
LIU, ENJIE, Basic Medical Sciences
LIU, ENQING, Second Clinical College
LIU, GUOLIANG, First Clinical College
LIU, HONGQIN, Second Clinical College
LIU, JUHUI, Forensic Medicine
LIU, JUNTING, Forensic Medicine
LIU, JUNTING, Pharmacy
LIU, LANQING, Second Clinical College
LIU, LIMIN, Forensic Medicine
LIU, SHUJIE, Stomatology
LIU, XIUMEI, First Clinical College
LIU, YANG, Public Health
LIU, YINGMIN, Second Clinical College

LIU, ZHENLIN, Public Health
LU, CHANGLONG, Basic Medical Sciences
LU, JINGMING, Second Clinical College
LU, SHENGMIN, Second Clinical College
MENG, FANHAO, Pharmacy
MU, HUACHUN, Basic Medical Sciences
PAN, YAPING, Stomatology
PAN, ZHIMIN, First Clinical College
PANG, XINING, Basic Medical Sciences
PEI, ZHUGUO, Second Clinical College
PIAO, AIYING, Second Clinical College
QIU, XUESHAN, Basic Medical Sciences
QU, MING, First Clinical College
REN, CHONG, First Clinical College
SHEN, KUI, First Clinical College
SHI, LIDE, Basic Medical Sciences
SHI, YUXIU, Basic Medical Sciences
SONG, FANGJI, First Clinical College
SONG, JIJIE, Basic Medical Sciences
SONG, JINDAN, Basic Medical Sciences
SONG, MIN, Basic Medical Sciences
SUN, GUIFAN, Public Health
SUN, GUIYUAN, Basic Medical Sciences
SUN, JIANCHUN, Second Clinical College
SUN, KAILAI, Basic Medical Sciences
SUN, LIGUANG, Basic Medical Sciences
TANG, HAO, Basic Medical Sciences
TIAN, XUSHENG, Basic Medical Sciences
WANG, BAOJIE, Forensic Medicine
WANG, CHUN, Fourth Clinical College
WANG, DEWEN, Forensic Medicine
WANG, DEZHI, Second Clinical College
WANG, ENHUA, Basic Medical Sciences
WANG, GUIZHEN, Basic Medical Sciences
WANG, HAIPENG, Basic Medical Sciences
WANG, HAIYI, Second Clinical College
WANG, HE, Basic Medical Sciences
WANG, HONGDA, First Clinical College
WANG, HUAILIANG, Basic Medical Sciences
WANG, HUIZHEN, Second Clinical College
WANG, LIANYING, Second Clinical College
WANG, LIJUN, Second Clinical College
WANG, LIYU, Social Science
WANG, MINGQIAN, Second Clinical College
WANG, SHUBAO, First Clinical College
WANG, SHULAN, First Clinical College
WANG, TIE, Second Clinical College
WANG, WEILIN, Second Clinical College
WANG, XINGDUO, First Clinical College
WANG, XUEYING, Second Clinical College
WANG, YANFENG, Second Clinical College
WANG, YUXIN, Stomatology
WANG, ZHAOGUAN, Second Clinical College-
WANG, ZHAOYUAN, Stomatology
WEI, KELUN, Second Clinical College
WU, BAOMIN, Second Clinical College
WU, HUAZHANG, Social Science
WU, JINGTIAN, First Clinical College
WU, KEGUANG, Second Clinical College
WU, YIJIANG, Fourth Clinical College
WU, YINGYU, Second Clinical College
WU, ZHENHUA, Second Clinical College
XIE, HUIFANG, Second Clinical College
XU, ZHAOFA, Public Health
XU, ZHENXING, First Clinical College
XUE, XINDONG, Second Clinical College
XUE, YIXUE, Basic Medical Sciences
YANG, GUORUI, First Clinical College
YANG, JUN, Public Health
YANG, SHILIN, Second Clinical College
YANG, XIANGHONG, Basic Medical Sciences
YANG, XIAODONG, Stomatology
YANG, YUXIU, First Clinical College
YAO, XINGJIA, Public Health
YIN, HONGNIAN, First Clinical College
YIN, SHUGUO, Second Clinical College
YU, BINGXHI, Basic Medical Sciences
YU, RUNJIANG, First Clinical College
YUAN, ZHUANG, Second Clinical College
ZENG, DINGYIN, First Clinical College
ZHA, HONGYAN, Basic Medical Sciences
ZHANG, DAORONG, Basic Medical Sciences
ZHANG, GANZHONG, First Clinical College
ZHANG, HAIPENG, Basic Medical Sciences
ZHANG, HONG, Basic Medical Sciences
ZHANG, JIAXING, Second Clinical College
ZHANG, JINGRONG, First Clinical College
ZHANG, LIFENG, Basic Medical Sciences
ZHANG, SHULAN, Second Clinical College
ZHANG, XUE, Basic Medical Sciences
ZHAO, CHONGZHI, Second Clinical College
ZHAO, GUIZHEN, Second Clinical College
ZHAO, GUOGUI, Second Clinical College
ZHAO, LIJUAN, First Clinical College
ZHAO, SHUFENG, Basic Medical Sciences
ZHAO, SHUXIA, Second Clinical College
ZHAO, YKUN, Basic Medical Sciences
ZHAO, YUHONG, Information Management and Information Systems
ZHONG, MING, Stomatology
ZHOU, BAOSEN, Public Health
ZHOU, WEI, Social Science
ZHOU, XIJING, First Clinical College
ZHOU, YONGDE, Second Clinical College
ZHU, LIPING, Basic Medical Sciences

ATTACHED RESEARCH INSTITUTES

Biological Technology Research Institute: Dir ZHANG JISHAN.

Brain Research Institute: Dir HE WEIWEI.

Diabetes Research Centre: Dir LIU GUOLIANG.

Medical Molecular Biology Research Institute: Dir SONG JINDAN.

Ministry of Public Health Key Laboratory of Cell Biology: Dir SONG JINDAN.

Ministry of Public Health Key Laboratory of Child Birth Defects: Dir JI SHIJUN.

Ministry of Public Health Key Laboratory of Immunity Dermatology: Dir CHEN HONGFENG.

Organ Transplantation Research Institute: Dir LIU YONGFENG.

Paediatrics Research Institute: Dir LI SHUQIN.

Prevention and Treatment of Geriatric Disease Research Centre: Dir HAO WENXUE.

Preventive Medicine Research Institute: Dir SUN GUIFAN.

Respiratory Diseases Research Institute: Dir KANG JIAN.

Tumour Research Institute: Dir CHEN JUNQING.

CHINA UNIVERSITY OF MINING AND TECHNOLOGY

Xuzhou, 221008 Jiangsu
Telephone: (516) 3885745
Fax: (516) 3888682
Internet: www.cumt.edu.cn

Founded 1909
State control
Academic year: September to July

President: Prof. XIE HEPING
Vice-Presidents: Prof. SUNG XUEFENG, Prof. WANG YUEHAN, Prof. GE SHIRONG, Prof. WANG JIANPING, Prof. KE WENJIN, Prof. LUO CHENG XUAN
Registrar: Prof. XING YONGCHANG
Director of International Division: ZHENG ZHENKANG
Librarian: Prof. TANG YI

Library of 330,000 vols
Number of teachers: 3,817
Number of students: 30,942

Publication: *Journal* (4 a year in Chinese, 2 a year in English)

HEADS OF ACADEMIC DIVISIONS

School of Mineral and Energy Resources Engineering: CAI QINGXIANG
School of Architecture and Civil Engineering: ZHOU GUOQING
School of Mechatronic and Materials Engineering: DUAN XIONG
School of Information and Electrical Engineering: JIANG JIANGUO
School of Resources and Geoscience: LIN JIAN
School of Chemical Engineering: LIU JIONGTIAN
School of Environment and Spatial Informatics: HAN BAOPING
School of Management: NIE RUI
School of Politics, Literature and Law: WANG YAN
School of Foreign Studies: YANG SHU
School of Science: MIAO XIEXIN
School of Computer Science and Technology: XIA SHIXIONG
Department of Physical Education: CHI ZHONGJUN
College of Adult Education: ZHANG FUSHENG
College of Applied Science and Technology: FAN ZHONGQI

CHINA UNIVERSITY OF PETROLEUM

2 North Rd, Dongying 257061, Shandong
Telephone: (546) 8392241
Fax: (546) 7366374
Internet: www.hdpu.edu.cn

Founded 1953
State control
Academic year: September to July

President: TONG ZHAOQI
Vice-Presidents: SHAN HONGHONG, SUN HAIFENG, TONG XINHUA, WANG RUIHE, ZHA MING
Head of Graduate Department: WANG RUIHE
Librarian: ZHANG ZHONGXUE

Number of teachers: 1,000
Number of students: 23,500

Publication: *Journal of China University of Petroleum* (6 a year)

DEANS

College of Architecture, Transport and Storage Engineering: ZHANG GUOZHONG
College of Chemistry and Chemical Engineering: JIN YOUHAI
College of Computer and Communication Engineering: DUAN YOUXIANG
College of Economic Administration: ZHANG ZAIXU
College of Foreign Languages: LUAN SHUWEN
College of Geo-Resources and Information: YIN XINGYAO
College of Humanities and Social Science: XIA CHONGYA
College of Information and Control Engineering: TIAN XUEMING
College of Mathematics and Computer Science: LI WEIGUO
College of Mechanical and Electronic Engineering: QI MINGXIA
College of Petroleum Engineering: YAO JUN
College of Physical Education: WEI RULI
College of Physics Science and Technology: GUAN JITENG

PROFESSORS

BAI, LIANPING, Information and Control Engineering
CHAO, KE, Humanities and Social Science
CHEN, GANGHUA, Geo-Resources and Information
CHEN, JIANMIN, Petroleum Engineering
CHEN, SHIYUE, Geo-Resources and Information
CHEN, YUEMING, Petroleum Engineering
CHENG, YUANFANG, Petroleum Engineering
DAI, JUNSHENG, Geo-Resources and Information
DU, JINLIANG, Humanities and Social Science
FAN, YIREN, Geo-Resources and Information
FANG, JIANHUI, Physics, Science and Technology
GAO, YIFA, Petroleum Engineering
GUAN, ZHICHUAN, Petroleum Engineering

GUANG, JITENG, Physics, Science and Technology
HAN, ZHIYONG, Petroleum Engineering
HE, LIMIN, Architecture, Transport and Storage Engineering
JIA, RUIGAO, Physics, Science and Technology
JIANG, HUA, Humanities and Social Science
JIANG, YOULU, Geo-Resources and Information
JIANG, ZAIXING, Geo-Resources and Information
JIN, QIANG, Geo-Resources and Information
LI, GUOHUA, Physical Education
LI, HANLIN, Geo-Resources and Information
LI, MINGZHONG, Petroleum Engineering
LI, SHURONG, Information and Control Engineering
LI, WEIGUO, Mathematics and Computational Science
LI, YUANCHENG, Physics, Science and Technology
LI, YUXING, Architecture, Transport and Storage Engineering
LI, ZHAOMIN, Petroleum Engineering
LI, ZILI, Architecture, Transport and Storage Engineering
LIANG, JINGUO, Architecture, Transport and Storage Engineering
LIN, CHENGYAN, Geo-Resources and Information
LIU, HUIQING, Petroleum Engineering
LIU, RUNHUA, Information and Control Engineering
LIU, ZHAN, Geo-Resources and Information
LUAN, SHUWEN, Foreign Languages
MA, XIGENG, Information and Control Engineering
MEN, FUDIAN, Physics, Science and Technology
QIU, SHIWEI, Architecture, Transport and Storage Engineering
QIU, ZHENGSONG, Petroleum Engineering
SHAN, YIXIAN, Information and Control Engineering
SHEN, ZHONGHOU, Petroleum Engineering
SHU, HENGMU, Architecture, Transport and Storage Engineering
SONG, DESHENG, Foreign Languages
SUN, BAOJIANG, Petroleum Engineering
SUN, JIANMENG, Geo-Resources and Information
SUN, XIULI, Foreign Languages
TIAN, XUEMIN, Information and Control Engineering
WAN, JIANHUA, Geo-Resources and Information
WANG, HUAQIN, Foreign Languages
WANG, JIANJUN, Humanities and Social Science
WANG, QINGTING, Foreign Languages
WANG, RUIHE, Petroleum Engineering
WANG, SHUTING, Foreign Languages
WANG, WEIFENG, Geo-Resources and Information
WANG, YANJIANG, Information and Control Engineering
WANG, YONGGANG, Geo-Resources and Information
XIA, CHONGYA, Humanities and Social Science
XING, LIANJUN, Physical Education
XU, MINGHAI, Architecture, Transport and Storage Engineering
XU, YIJI, Petroleum Engineering
XUE, SHIFENG, Architecture, Transport and Storage Engineering
YAN, XIANGZHEN, Architecture, Transport and Storage Engineering
YANG, DEWEI, Architecture, Transport and Storage Engineering
YANG, SHAOCHUN, Geo-Resources and Information
YANG, WEI, Physics, Science and Technology
YAO, JUN, Petroleum Engineering
YIN, XINGYAO, Geo-Resources and Information
YU, RANGANG, Architecture, Transport and Storage Engineering
YU, ZHAOXIAN, Physics, Science and Technology
YUAN, HONGCHAN, Foreign Languages
ZHAN, YONGLIANG, Architecture, Transport and Storage Engineering
ZHANG, GUOZHONG, Architecture, Transport and Storage Engineering
ZHANG, JIASHENG, Information and Control Engineering
ZHANG, QI, Petroleum Engineering
ZHANG, RONGHUA, Humanities and Social Science
ZHANG, ZHAOHUI, Information and Control Engineering
ZHAO, FULIN, Petroleum Engineering
ZHAO, XIUTAI, Petroleum Engineering
ZHAO, XIYU, Humanities and Social Science
ZHAO, YONGJUN, Geo-Resources and Information
ZHENG, JINWU, Information and Control Engineering
ZHONG, JIANHUA, Geo-Resources and Information
ZHOU, DETIAN, Humanities and Social Science
ZHOU, XIAOJUN, Petroleum Engineering
ZHOU, YAOQI, Geo-Resources and Information

CHINA PHARMACEUTICAL UNIVERSITY

Xuan Wu Men, Yan Zi Ji, Nanjing 210009, Jiangsu
Telephone: (25) 3271319
Fax: (25) 3271101
Internet: www.cpu.edu.cn

Founded 1936
Ministry of Education Control
Academic year: September to July

President: WU XIAOMING
Vice-Presidents: LI FENGWEN, PAN YUJIAN, WANG GUANGJI, ZHANG XIAOLIAN
Head of Graduate Department: CHU MINZUO
Librarian: MA SHIPING

Library of 700,000 vols
Number of teachers: 610
Number of students: 8,880

Publications: *Journal of China Pharmaceutical University* (6 a year), *Medical Evolution* (6 a year), *Medicine Annual of China*, *Medicine Education* (quarterly)

DEANS

School of Biological Pharmacy: WANG WEN
School of Economics and Economic School of International Medicine: GU HAI
Schools of Medicine and Chinese Traditional Medicine: KONG LINGYI
Department of Foreign Languages: DU HUI
Basic Institute: TAO LU
Institute of Physical Education: WANG YONGTAO

PROFESSORS

DAI, DEZAI, Medicine
GAO, SHANLIN, Chinese Traditional Medicine
GAO, XIANGDONG, Biological Pharmacy
GU, HAI, Economic School of International Medicine
HU, YUZHU
HUA, WEIYI, Medicine
HUANG, WENLONG, Medicine
JI, HUI, Medicine
JI, MIN, Medicine
KONG, LINGYI, Chinese Traditional Medicine
LIANG, JINGYU, Chinese Traditional Medicine
LIU, JINGJING, Biological Pharmacy
LIU, WENYING, Medicine
LIU, XIAODONG, Medicine
LIU, XIAODONG, Chinese Traditional Medicine
MA, SHIPING, Chinese Traditional Medicine
NI, KUNYI
PENG, SIXUN, Medicine
PING, QINENG, Medicine
QIAN, ZHIYU, Medicine
SHAO, RONG, Economic School of International Medicine
SHEN, ZILONG, Biological Pharmacy
TU, SHUCI, Medicine
WANG, GUANGJI, Medicine
WANG, QIUJUAN, Medicine
WANG, WEN, Biological Pharmacy
WU, WUTONG, Biological Pharmacy
WU, XIAOMING, Medicine
XI, TAO, Biological Pharmacy
XIANG, BINGREN
YANG, ZHONGLIN, Chinese Traditional Medicine
YE, WENCAI, Chinese Traditional Medicine
YOU, QIDONG, Medicine
YU, BOYANG, Chinese Traditional Medicine
ZHANG, LUYONG, Medicine
ZHANG, YIHUA, Medicine
ZHANG, ZHENGHANG, Medicine
ZHOU, JIANPING, Medicine
ZHU, DANNI, Chinese Traditional Medicine
ZHU, JIABI, Medicine

ATTACHED RESEARCH INSTITUTES

Altitude Vocation School: Dir YANG JINGHUA.

Analysis Testing Centre.

Journalism Newsroom: Dir ZHOU JIAYIN.

Medicine Metabolism and Dynamics Centre: Dir WANG GUANGJI.

Modern Education Technology Centre: Dir HU ZHUOYI.

National Laboratory of New Drug Screening: Dir DU GUANHUA.

CHINA UNIVERSITY OF POLITICAL SCIENCE AND LAW

Yuanyuan Rd, Chang Ping, Beijing 102249
Telephone: (10) 69745577
Fax: (10) 82228531
Internet: www.cupl.edu.cn

Founded 1952
State control
Academic year: September to July

President: XU XIANMING
Vice-Presidents: JIE ZHANYUAN, MA KANGMEI, ZHANG BAOSHENG, ZHANG GUILIN, ZHANG LIUHUA
Head of Graduate Department: ZHU YONG
Librarian: ZENG ERSHU

Number of teachers: 1,400
Number of students: 21,325

Publications: *Journal of China University of Political Science and Law (Tribune of Political Science and Law)* (6 a year), *Journal of Comparative Law* (6 a year)

DEANS

School of American and Comparative Law: XU CHUANXI
Business School: SUN XUANZHONG
Criminal and Judicial School: WANG MU
School of Foreign Languages: LI LI
School of German and Comparative Law: MI JIAN
International Law School: WANG CHUANLI
Law School: MA HUAIDE
School of Political and Public Management: ZHU WEIJIU

PROFESSORS

CAI, DINGJIAN, Law
CAI, TUO, Political and Public Management
CHE, HU, American and Comparative Law
CHEN, GUANGZHONG, Procedural Law
CHEN, HONGTAI, Political and Public Management
CHEN, LIJUN, Law
CHENG, XIAOXIANG, International Law

CONG, RIYUN, Political and Public Management
CUI, YONGDONG, Law
DING, MEI, German and Comparative Law
DONG, SHUJUN, Criminal and Judicial Law
DU, XINLI, International Law
DUAN, DONGHUI, International Law
FAN, CHONGYI, Procedural Law
FENG, XIA, International Law
GAO, JIAWEI, German and Comparative Law
GU, YONGZHONG, Procedural Law
HAO, WEIHUA, American and Comparative Law
HE, JIAHONG, Procedural Law
HONG, DAODE, Criminal and Judicial Law
HOU, TINGZHI, Business School
HU, WENZHENG, Business School
HUANG, DAOXIU, Foreign Languages
HUANG, YISI, Foreign Languages
JIANG, RUJIAO, International Law
JIAO, HONGCHANG, Law
JIAO, MEIZHEN, Foreign Languages
LANG, PEIJUAN, Law
LE, GUOAN, Criminal and Judicial Law
LI, JUQIAN, International Law
LI, LI, Foreign Languages
LI, MING, Research of Legal Historiography
LI, WEI, International Law
LI, XIAO, Business School
LIN, QIAN, Research of Legal Historiography
LIU, BANGHUI, Criminal and Judicial Law
LIU, CHANGMIN, Political and Public Management
LIU, GENJU, Criminal and Judicial Law
LIU, GUANGAN, Research of Legal Historiography
LIU, HONGYING, Law
LIU, JINGUO, Law
LIU, JUNSHENG, Political and Public Management
LIU, LI, International Law
LIU, MU, Criminal and Judicial Law
LIU, SHANCHUN, Law
LIU, SHEN, Law
LONG, MENGHUI, Foreign Languages
MA, CHENGYUAN, International Law
MA, HUAIDE, Law
MA, ZHIBING, Research of Legal Historiography
MI, JIAN, German and Comparative Law
MO, SHIJIAN, International Law
PAN, QIN, Criminal and Judicial Law
PENG, YANAN, American and Comparative Law
QI, DONGXIANG, American and Comparative Law
QI, XIANGQUAN, International Law
QU, CHAOLI, Political and Public Management
QU, XINJIU, Criminal and Judicial Law
RUAN, QILIN, Criminal and Judicial Law
SHI, XIAOLI, International Law
SHI, YAJUN, Political and Public Management
SHU, GUOYING, German and Comparative Law
SONG, YINGHUI, Procedural Law
SUN, XUANZHONG, Business School
WANG, CHUANLI, International Law
WANG, JIANCHENG, Procedural Law
WANG, JIANXIN, Political and Public Management
WANG, JIE, Law
WANG, MU, Criminal and Judicial Law
WANG, RENBO, Law
WANG, SHUNAN, Criminal and Judicial Law
WU, MINGYANG, Business School
XIAO, JIANHUA, Procedural Law
XIN, CHONGYANG, International Law
XU, CHUANXI, American and Comparative Law
XU, HAIMING, International Law
XU, HAOMING, German and Comparative Law
XU, SHIHONG, Institute of Legal Ancient Books Arrangement
XUAN, ZENGYI, International Law
XUE, GANGLING, Law
YANG, FAN, International Law
YANG, FAN, Business School
YANG, RONGXIN, Procedural Law
YANG, YANG, Political and Public Management
YANG, YUGUAN, Procedural Law, German and Comparative Law
YUE, LILING, German and Comparative Law
ZHANG, GUILIN, Political and Public Management
ZHANG, GUOJUN, Business School
ZHANG, JINFAN, Research of Legal Historiography
ZHANG, LI, International Law
ZHANG, LIYING, International Law
ZHANG, SHENG, Law
ZHANG, SHUYI, Law
ZHANG, XIAOMU, International Law
ZHANG, ZHONGQIU, Research of Legal Historiography
ZHAO, BAOCHENG, Criminal and Judicial Law
ZHAO, WEI, International Law
ZHAO, XIANGLIN, International Law
ZHAO, YIMIN, International Law
ZHENG, XIANWEN, Institute of Legal Ancient Books Arrangement
ZHENG, YONGLIU, German and Comparative Law
ZHOU, JIANHAI, International Law
ZHOU, ZHONGHAI, International Law
ZHU, JIANGENG, International Law
ZHU, WEIJIU, Political and Public Management
ZHU, YONG, Research of Legal Historiography
ZHU, ZIQIN, International Law

ATTACHED RESEARCH INSTITUTES

Centre for Legal Assistance to Pollution Victims in China: Dir WANG CANFA.

Institute of Comparative Law: Dir MI JIAN.

Procedural Law Research Centre: Dir .

Research Centre of European Law: Dir ZHANG TONG.

Research Studies of Legal Ancient Books Arrangement: Dir XU SHIHONG.

Research Studies of Legal Historiography: Dir ZHU YONG.

School of Continuing Studies: Dir LI SHUZHONG.

School of International Studies: Dir XIA YINLAN.

Studies in Comparative Legal Science: Dir JIANG PING.

CHINA CENTRAL RADIO AND TELEVISION UNIVERSITY

160 Fuxing Men Nei St, Beijing 100031
Telephone: (10) 66412407
Fax: (10) 66419025
E-mail: fao@crtvu.edu.cn
Internet: www.crtvu.edu.cn

Founded 1979 on the 'open university' principle
State control
Academic year: September to July
Forty-four provincial campuses, 961 branch schools

President: ZHANG YAOXUE
Vice-Presidents: YU YUNXIU, SUN LUYI, RUAN ZHIYONG, YAN BING
Library Director: SUN LUYI

Library of 100,000 vols (CRTVU), 32,869,000 vols (provinces)
Number of teachers: 188 full-time
Number of teachers: 565 part-time (CRTVU)
Number of teachers: 42,500 full-time
Number of teachers: 31,500 part-time (provinces)
Number of students: 2,300,000

Publication: *Distance Education in China* (every 2 months)

HEADS OF DEPARTMENTS

Economics: LIU CHEN
Engineering: SHEN YAFEN
Humanities: XU CHANGWEI
Teacher Training: ZHANG RUILIN
China Liaoyuan Radio and Television School: ZHANG SHAOGANG

CHINESE TRADITIONAL OPERA COLLEGE

3 Li Ren St, Xuan Wu District, Beijing 100054
Telephone: 33-5156

Founded 1978

President: YU LIN
Vice-Presidents: ZHU WENXIANG, GE SHILIANG
Librarian: LIU SHIYUAN

Library of 150,000 vols
Number of teachers: 246
Number of students: 329

Publication: *Traditional Opera Art* (quarterly)

HEADS OF DEPARTMENTS

Stage Art: ZHAO YINGMIAN
Traditional Opera Literature: ZHOU CHUANJIA
Performance: SU YI
Directing: JING TONG
Music: GUAN YANONG

CHONGQING UNIVERSITY

Chongqing, Sichuan Province 630044
Telephone: (23) 65102449
Fax: (23) 65316656
E-mail: fao@cqu.edu.cn
Internet: www.cqu.edu.cn

Founded 1929
State control
Languages of instruction: Chinese, English
Academic year: February to January

President: LIN FEI
Vice-President: WU ZHONGFU
Chief Administrative Officer: CHEN DEWEN
Librarian: TANG YIKE

Number of teachers: 2,000
Number of students: 14,000

Publication: *Journal* (every 2 months)

DEANS

College of Resources and Environmental Engineering: LI XIAOHONG
College of Electronic Information Engineering: CAO ZEHAN
College of Business Administration: YANG XIUTAI
College of Chemical Engineering: GAN GUNANGZHONG
College of Foreign Languages: JIANG ZHIWEN
College of Trade and Law: HE RONGWEI

HEADS OF DEPARTMENTS

First Department of Mechanical Engineering: YOU LIHUA
Second Department of Mechanical Engineering: LI HUAJI
Department of Optical Electronic Precision Machinery: PAN YINGJUN
Department of Engineering Mechanics: ZHANG PEIYUAN
Department of Thermal Engineering: HE ZHUWEI
Department of Electrical Engineering: SUN CAIXIN
Department of Metallurgical Engineering and Materials: GAO JIACHENG

Department of Radio Engineering (in College of Electronic Information Engineering): SHU XIANSHU
Department of Computer Science (in College of Electronic Information Engineering): ZHU QINGSHENG
Department of Automation (in College of Electronic Information Engineering): HUANG XIYUE
Department of Applied Mathematics: YANG DADI
Department of Applied Physics: YUN ZHIQIANG
Institute of Bio-engineering: CAI SHAOXI

CHONGQING UNIVERSITY OF MEDICAL SCIENCES

1 Medicine Rd, Yu Zhong, Chongqing 400046
Telephone: (23) 68804034
Internet: www.cqums.edu.cn

Founded 1956
Academic year: September to July

President: LEI HAN
Vice-Presidents: DENG SHIXIONG, DONG ZHI, HUANG AILONG, WANG LIHUA, XIE PENG
Librarian: LU CHANGHONG

Library of 570,000 vols
Number of teachers: 4,374
Number of students: 8,923

Publications: *Chinese Journal of Hepatology* (6 a year), *Journal of Chongqing Medical University* (6 a year), *Journal of Paediatric Pharmacy* (6 a year), *Journal of Ultrasound in Clinical Medicine* (6 a year), *Research In Medical Education* (6 a year)

DEANS

College of Basic Medicine: WANG YAPING
Department of Biomedical Engineering: WANG ZHIBIAO
Department of Medical Examining: TU ZHIGUANG
Department of Medical Imaging: REN HONG
Department of Reproductive Medical Science: WANG YINGXIONG
Institute of Humanity and Social Science: FENG ZHEYONG

PROFESSORS

CHEN, SHOUTIAN, Medical Imaging
CONG, YULONG, Medical Examining
DAI, YONG, Medical Examining
DONG, ZHI, Pharmacy
FENG, ZHEYONG, Humanities and Social Science
HU, GUOHU, Basic Medicine
JIANG, JIKAI, Medical Examining
KANG, GEFEI, Medical Examining
LEI, PEIYING, Medical Imaging
LEI, XIAOKUN, Humanities and Social Science
LI, HUIZHI, Pharmacy
LI, QINGEN, Pharmacy
LI, SHAOLIN, Basic Medicine
LIU, DAWEI, Preventive Medicine
LUO, JIA, Medical Imaging
LUO, YUNPENG, Basic Medicine
LU, CHANGHONG, Basic Medicine
MI, CAN, Basic Medicine
NING, BAODONG, Basic Medicine
PENG, HUIMING, Basic Medicine
QIU, ZONGYING, Pharmacy
QUAN, XUEMO, Medical Imaging
REN, HONG, Medical Imaging
SONG, FANGZHOU, Basic Medicine
SUN, SHANQUAN, Basic Medicine
TANG, SIJIE, Basic Medicine
TANG, WEIXUE, Basic Medicine
TU, ZHIGUANG, Medical Examining
WANG, RUIHUA, Preventive Medicine
WANG, WEIWEI, Basic Medicine
WANG, YANG, Preventive Medicine
WANG, YAPING, Basic Medicine
WANG, YINGXIONG, Reproductive Medical Science
WANG, ZHIBIAO, Biomedical Engineering
WANG, ZHIGANG, Medical Imaging
WU, FENG, Biomedical Engineering
XIANG, LIKE, Basic Medicine
XIE, ZHENGXIANG, Basic Medicine
YANG, ZHENGWEI, Basic Medicine
YANG, ZHIBANG, Basic Medicine
YI, YONGFENG, Basic Medicine
YU, YU, Basic Medicine
ZHANG, NENG, Basic Medicine
ZHAO, JIANNONG, Medical Imaging
ZHENG, ZHAOCHUN, Basic Medicine
ZHOU, CHENGHE, Pharmacy
ZHOU, JIANZHONG, Medical Imaging
ZHOU, QIXIN, Basic Medicine
ZHU, DAOYIN, Basic Medicine

ATTACHED RESEARCH INSTITUTES

Adult Education College: Dir CHEN DEXIANG.

Affiliated Hospital of Stomatology

DALIAN MARITIME UNIVERSITY

1 Linghai Rd, Dalian 116026, Liaoning Province
Telephone: (411) 4727874
Fax: (411) 4727395
E-mail: faodmu@dlmu.edu.cn
Internet: www.dlmu.edu.cn

Founded 1909
State control
Academic year: September to July

President: Prof. WU ZHAOLIN
Vice-Presidents: Dr SUN LICHENG, Dr SUN PEITING, WEN XIAOQIN
Registrar: WANG YUEHUI
Librarian: PANG FUWEN

Number of teachers: 728
Number of students: 12,722

Publications: *World Shipping* (6 a year), *Liaoning Navigation* (4 a year), *Higher Education Research in Areas of Communications* (2 a year), *Journal* (6 a year)

DEANS

Adult Education College: DING YONG
Automation and Electrical Engineering College: WANG XINGCHEN
Business College: FAN HOUMING
Computer Science and Technology College: ZHANG WEISHI
Electronic Information College: ZHANG SHUFANG
Environmental Science and Engineering College: DING YONGSHENG
Humanities and Social Sciences College: FENG WENHUA
Law College: QU GUANGQING
Marine Engineering College: REN GUANG
Navigation College: DONG FANG
Shipping Management College: YANG ZHAN
International Co-operation College: ZHANG SHIPPING

ATTACHED INSTITUTES

Institute of Navigation Science and Technology: Dir JIA CHUANYING.

Institute of Marine Machine Repair and Metal Processes: Dir SUN JUNCAI.

Institute of Automation: Dir DONG XIAOYONG.

Institute of Traffic Engineering and Electronic Systems: Dir LIU XIAOMING.

Institute of Marine Engineering Science and Application: Dir SUN PEITING.

Institute of Information Systems Engineering: Dir AN JUBAI.

Institute of Port and Shipping Management: Dir SUN GUANGQI.

Institute of Environmental Engineering: Dir BAI XIYAO.

Institute of Higher Maritime Education: Dir PANG GUOBIN.

Institute of Artificial Intelligence Control: Dir QIN JIANCHUN.

DALIAN UNIVERSITY OF TECHNOLOGY (DUT)

2 Linggong Rd, Ganjingzi District, Dalian 116023, Liaoning
Telephone: (411) 4678300
Fax: (411) 4708116
E-mail: dut@dlut.edu.cn
Internet: www.dlut.edu.cn

Founded 1949 as Dalian Institute of Technology
State control
Academic year: September to July

President: Prof. CHENG GENGDONG
Vice-Presidents: Prof. XUE GUANG, Prof. SHEN HONGSHU, Prof. WANG LIANSHENG, Prof. KONG XIANJING, Prof. JIANG DEXUE
Librarian: XIE MAOZHAO

Library of 1,840,000 vols, 8,000 periodicals
Number of teachers: 1,297
Number of students: 22,344 (incl. 5,883 postgraduate)

Publications: *Journal* (6 a year), *Journal of Mathematical Research and Exposition* (4 a year), *Journal of Computational Mechanics* (4 a year), *Journal of Social Sciences* (4 a year)

Units include 14 schools, 50 research institutes and 4 National Key Laboratories.

DAQING PETROLEUM INSTITUTE

Daqing 151400, Heilongjiang
Telephone: (459) 4653232
Fax: (459) 7332415
Internet: www.dqpi.net

Founded 1960
State control
Academic year: September to July

President: LIU YANG
Vice-Presidents: LIU YONG JIAN, LU YAN FANG, SONG ZHI CHEN, YANG XIAO LONG

Number of teachers: 1,762
Number of students: 10,000

Publications: *Journal* (4 a year), *Petroleum Industry Technology* (4 a year)

DEANS

College of Building Construction Engineering: SUN JIAN GANG
College of Computing and Information Technology: MA RUI MIN
College of Continuing Education: ZHAO JIN LIN
College of Earth Sciences: SHI SHANG MING
College of Economics and Management: SHAO QIANG
College of Electricity and Information Engineering: DUAN YU BO
College of Electronic Engineering: WANG MING JI
College of Foreign Languages: QIU XUE HE
College of Humanities: KUAN JIN LIN
College of Mathematics: WANG SHOU TIAN
College of Mechanical Science and Engineering: WANG ZUN CE
College of Oil Engineering Institute: CUI HAI QING

PROFESSORS

AI, CHI, Oil Engineering
BAI, XING HUA, Earth Sciences
CAO, YU QUAN, Electricity and Information Engineering
CHANG, YU LIAN, Mechanical Science and Engineering

CHEN, TAO PING, Oil Engineering
CHEN, XUE MEI, Mechanical Science and Engineering
CUI, HAI QING, Oil Engineering
CUI, ZHEN HUA, Mechanical Science and Engineering
DAI, GUANG, Mechanical Science and Engineering
DU, HONG LIE, Earth Sciences
DUAN, YU BO, Electricity and Information Engineering
FAN, HONG FU, Oil Engineering
FU, GUANG, Earth Sciences
FU, GUANG JIE, Electricity and Information Engineering
GAO, BING KUN, Electricity and Information Engineering
GUO, YU FENG, Electronic engineering
HAN, GUO YOU, Mechanical Science and Engineering
HAN, HONG SHENG, Oil Engineering
HAO, WEN SEN, Mechanical Science and Engineering
JIA, WEN JU, Computing and Information Technology
JIA, ZHEN QI, Oil Engineering
JIANG, MING HU, Mechanical Science and Engineering
JIN, SHAO XIAN, Electronic engineering
KANG, WANG LI, Oil Engineering
KONG, LING BIN, Mathematics
LI, BAO YAN, Mechanical Science and Engineering
LI, CHUN SHENG, Computing and Information Technology
LI, CONG XIN, Computing and Information Technology
LI, JIE, Earth Sciences
LI, XIAO PING, Mathematics
LI, YAN JIE, Mathematics
LING, JING LONG, Earth Sciences
LIU, JU BAO, Mechanical Science and Engineering
LIU, SU LIN, Mechanical Science and Engineering
LIU, TIE NAN, Electricity and Information Engineering
LIU, XIAO YAN, Earth Sciences
LIU, YANG, Oil Engineering
LIU, YI KUN, Oil Engineering
LIU, YONG JIAN, Oil Engineering
LU, LING JIE, Computing and Information Technology
LU, SHUANG FANG, Earth Sciences
LU, YAN FANG, Earth Sciences
MA, RUI MIN, Computing and Information Technology
MA, SHI ZHONG, Earth Sciences
NUAN, QING DE, Mechanical Science and Engineering
REN, FU SHAN, Mechanical Science and Engineering
REN, WEI JIAN, Electricity and Information Engineering
SHAO, QIANG, Economics and Management
SHI, SHANG MING, Earth Sciences
SONG, KAO PING, Oil Engineering
SONG, YU LING, Humanities
SUN, BO TAO, Foreign Language
SUN, JIAN GANG, Building Construction Engineering
SUN, YAN BIN, Economics and Management
SUN, YU XUE, Oil Engineering
TANG, GUO WEI, Computing and Information Technology
WANG, DE MING, Oil Engineering
WANG, HENG JIU, Economics and Management
WANG, JING QI, Earth Sciences
WANG, MING JI, Electronic engineering
WANG, SHOU TIAN, Mathematics
WANG, WEN GUANG, Earth Sciences
WANG, XIU MING, Earth Sciences
WANG, ZUN CE, Mechanical Science and Engineering
WU, WEN XIANG, Oil Engineering
XIA, HUI FENG, Oil Engineering
XU, BU YUN, Mechanical Science and Engineering
XU, SHAO HUA, Computing and Information Technology
YAN, TIE, Oil Engineering
YI, ZHI AN, Computing and Information Technology
ZENG, ZHAO YING, Mathematics
ZHANG, CHANG HAI, Mathematics
ZHANG, DA WEI, Oil Engineering
ZHANG, JI HUA, Foreign Language
ZHANG, JING, Earth Sciences
ZHANG, YONG HONG, Mechanical Science and Engineering
ZHANG, YU BIN, Mechanical Science and Engineering
ZHAO, WEI MIN, Mechanical Science and Engineering
ZHAO, ZI GANG, Oil Engineering
ZHOU, QING LONG, Mechanical Science and Engineering
ZHOU, QING LONG, Mechanical Science and Engineering
ZHU, JUN, Mechanical Science and Engineering

ATTACHED RESEARCH INSTITUTES

Centre of Modern Education Technology: Dir LI JIE.

Institute of Energy Conservation in Petroleum Engineering: Dir WU ZHAO YUN.

Research Centre of Petroleum and Natural Gas: Dir SONG KAO PING.

DONGBEI UNIVERSITY OF FINANCE AND ECONOMICS

217 Jianshan St, Shahekou District, Dalian 116025
Telephone: (411) 4691503
Fax: (411) 4691862
E-mail: dufe1952@pub.dl.inpta.net.cn
Internet: www.dufe.edu.cn

Founded 1952
State control
Languages of instruction: Chinese, English
Academic year: September to July

President: Prof. YU YANG
Vice-Presidents: Prof. GUO CHANGLU, Assoc. Prof. LIU JIANMIN, Prof. QIU DONG
President's Assistant: Assoc. Prof. ZHOU LIANSHENG
Librarian: ZHANG LI

Library of 900,000 vols
Number of teachers: 561
Number of students: 11,815 (incl. 5,678 correspondence)

Publication: *Research on Finance and Economics Issues*

HEADS OF SCHOOL

School of Accountancy: Prof. LIU YONGZE
School of Finance and Taxation: Prof. MA GOUQIANG
School of Business Management: Prof. LIU QINGYUAN
School of Hotel Management: Assoc. Prof. LI LI
School of Adult Education: Prof. CONG JIZENG
School of International Chinese: Assoc. Prof. ZHANG WENFENG

HEADS OF DEPARTMENTS

Postgraduate: Prof. HE JIAN
MBA Centre: Prof. Dr YU LI
Banking: Prof. ZHANG GUILE
Planning and Statistics: Assoc. Prof. YU HONGPING
Foreign Trade Economics: Prof. LI ZIZHI
Investment: Prof. MA XIUYAN
Law: Prof. GUI LIYI
Economic Information Management: Prof. ZHANG BUTONG
International Foreign Languages for Business: Assoc. Prof. HU YINGKUN
Economics: Prof. Dr WANG XUN

ATTACHED RESEARCH INSTITUTES

Research Institute of Economics: Dir Prof. JIN FENGDE.

Research Institute of Quantitative Economics: Dir Prof. LIU XINGQUAN.

Research Institute of Industrial Economics: Dir Prof. WANG XIANGCHUN.

Research Institute of Population: Dir Prof. JIANG PING.

Institute for Artificial Intelligence: Dir Prof. CHEN YOUGANG.

Research Institute of Stocks: Dir Prof. DAI YULIN.

Research Institute of Finance and Taxation: Dir Prof. MA GUOQIANG.

Research Institute of Investment: Dir Prof. MA XIUYAN.

Research Institute of Historical Maps: Dir Prof. LI KE.

Research Institute of Law: Dir Prof. GUI LIYI.

Research Institute of Banking: Dir Prof. LIN JIKEN.

Research Institute of Financial Management: Dir Prof. DONG WENQUAN.

Research Institute of Insurance: Dir Prof. ZHANG GUILE.

Research Centre for Japan: Dir Prof. JIN FENGDE.

Research Institute of Chinese Economics: Dir Prof. GAO LIANGMOU.

Research Institute of Commercial Economics: Dir Prof. LIU QINGYUAN.

Research Centre for Hong Kong, Macau and Taiwan: Dir Prof. WANG TIEJUN.

Research Institute of Statistics: Dir Prof. WANG QINGSHI.

Sanyou Research Institute of Accountancy: Dir Prof. LIU YONGZE.

Research Institute of Tourism: Dir Prof. LI LI.

DONGHUA UNIVERSITY

1882 West Yan-An Rd, Shanghai 200051
Telephone: 62197533
Fax: 62194722
Internet: www.dhu.edu.cn

Founded 1951 as East China Textile Institute of Science and Technology, re-named China Textile University 1985, current name 1999
Academic year: September to July

President: Prof. SHAO SHIHUANG
Vice-Presidents: Prof. JIN JIAYOU, Prof. HU XUECHAO, Prof. XUE YOUYI, Prof. TAN DEZHONG, Prof. ZHU SHIGEN
Registrar: Prof. ZHANG JIAYU
Librarian: Prof. YU MING

Library of 810,000 vols and periodicals
Number of teachers: 903
Number of students: 12,081

Publications: *Journal* (every 2 months, English edn 2 a year), *Textile Technology Overseas* (every 2 months)

HEADS OF COLLEGES

Fashion Institute: Prof. ZHANG WEIYUAN
Glorious Sun School of Business Management: Prof. SUN JUNKANG
Art and Design Institute: Prof. HUANG YUANQING

College of Textile Science and Technology: Prof. ZHU SUKANG
College of Chemistry and Chemicals: Prof. DAI JINJIN
College of Mechanical Engineering: Prof. WANG SHENZE
College of Information Science and Technology: Prof. SONG LIQUN
College of Science: Prof. XIE HANKUN
College of Humanities: ZHANG YI
College of Environmental Science and Engineering: Prof. XI DANLI
College of Materials Science and Engineering: Prof. CHEN YANMO
College of Foreign Languages: Prof. SHEN BAIYAO

HEAD OF DEPARTMENT

Physical Education: Prof. LIN SHENGGEN

EAST CHINA NORMAL UNIVERSITY

3663 Zhongshan Rd North, Shanghai 200062
Telephone: (21) 62233333
Fax: (21) 62576217
E-mail: webmaster@ecnu.edu.cn
Internet: www.ecnu.edu.cn

Founded 1951
Controlled by the Ministry of Education
Academic year: September to July (two semesters)

President: WANG JIANPAN
Vice-Presidents: MA QINRONG, DU GONGZHUO, WANG TIEXIAN, TANG MINGJIAN, YU LIZHONG, YE JIANNONG
Librarian: HUANG XIUWEN

Library of 3,535,000 vols
Number of teachers: 1,647
Number of students: 19,108

Publications: *Journal of Philosophy and Social Sciences* (6 a year), *Journal of Natural Sciences* (4 a year), *Journal of Educational Science* (4 a year), *Applied Probability and Statistics* (4 a year), *Psychological Science* (6 a year), *East Europe and Central Asia Today* (6 a year), *World Geography Research* (2 a year), *Theoretical Studies in Literature and Art* (6 a year), *Research into the Theory of Ancient Literature* (irregular)

DEANS

School of Educational Science and Technology: DING GANG
School of Pre-School and Special Education: NIE YOULI
School of Humanities: FENG SHAOLEI
School of Literature and Art: HONG BENJIAN
School of Foreign Languages: ZHANG CHUNBO
School of Business: JIN RUNGUI
School of Science and Engineering: WANG ZUGENG
School of Chemistry and Life Science: XU HONGFA
School of Resources and Environmental Science: CHEN ZHONGYUAN
Graduate School: YU LIZHONG
International College of Chinese Culture: WANG TIEXIAN
College of Continuing Education: SUN JIANMING
College of Educational Administration: MA QINRONG

EAST CHINA UNIVERSITY OF SCIENCE AND TECHNOLOGY

130 Meilong Rd, Shanghai 200237
Telephone: 4775678
Fax: 4777138
Internet: www.ecust.edu.cn

Founded 1952 (until 1993, East China University of Chemical Technology)

President: Prof. WANG XINGYU
Vice-Presidents: Prof. DAI GANCE, LIN ZHUYUAN, Prof. ZHU ZIBIN, Prof. ZHANG DONGSHAN

Library of 1,240,000 vols, 4,500 periodicals in 11 languages
Number of teachers: 1,841
Number of students: 8,322

Publication: *Journal* (every 2 months)

Departments of applied mathematics, applied physics, automatic control and electronic engineering, biochemical engineering, business management, chemical engineering, chemistry, computer science, environmental engineering, English for business, fine chemicals technology, foreign languages, industrial design, inorganic materials, management engineering, mechanical engineering, petroleum processing, polymer materials, social science.

Research institutes of agrochemical bioregulators, applied chemistry, applied mathematics, biomedical engineering, bioreactors (national lab.) chemical engineering, chemical environmental engineering, chemical physics, chemical reaction engineering (joint lab.), culture, economic development, fine chemicals technology, heterogeneous reaction engineering (national lab.), higher education, industrial automation, industrial design, inorganic chemical technology, inorganic materials, Marxism and ideological education, materials science, petroleum processing, process equipment and pressure vessels, speciality chemicals, technical chemical physics.

FUDAN UNIVERSITY

220 Handan Rd, Shanghai 200433
Telephone: (21) 65642222
Internet: www.fudan.edu.cn

Founded 1905; present status 2000, following merger with Shanghai Medical University
State control
Languages of instruction: Chinese, English
Academic year: September to July (two semesters)

President: Prof. WANG, SHENGHONG
Vice-Presidents: YANG, YULIANG ZHANG, YIHUA WANG, WEIPING XUE, MINGYANG XU, ZHONG ZHENG, ZUKANG ZHOU, LUWEI CAI, DAFENG XU MINZHI
Librarian: Prof. QIN ZENGFU

Library of 4,330,000 vols
Number of teachers: 2,400
Number of students: 28,800 undergraduates and 1,620 postgraduates

Publications: *Mathematics Annals Acta* (6 a year), *Fudan Social Sciences Journal*, *Fudan Natural Sciences Journal*

DEANS

School of Cultural Relics and Museum Science: Prof. ZHUANG XICHANG
School of Economics: Prof. HONG YUANPENG
School of Journalism: Prof. DING GANLIN
School of Life Science: Prof. LI YUYANG
School of Management: Prof. ZHENG SHAOLIAN
School of Technological Science: Prof. YUAN QU

CHAIRMEN OF DEPARTMENTS

Chinese Language and Literature: Prof. CHEN YUNJI
Foreign Languages and Literature: Prof. LU GUOQIANG
Journalism: Prof. DING GANLIN
Sociology: Prof. PENG XIZHE
History: Prof. YANG LIQIANG
Economics: Prof. SHU YUAN
World Economy: Prof. HUA MIN
International Finance: Prof. HU QINGKANG
International Politics: Prof. WANG HUNING
Philosophy: Prof. HUANG SONGJIE
Law: Prof. LI CHANGDAO
Mathematics: Prof. JIANG ERXIONG
Statistics and Operational Research: Prof. GUAN MEIGU
Physics: Prof. WANG WENCHENG
Nuclear Science: Prof. ZHENG CHENGFA
Chemistry: Prof. XIANG YIFEI
Biochemistry: Prof. HUANG WEIDA
Microbiology and Microbiological Engineering: Prof. ZHOU DEQING
Physiology and Biophysics: Prof. XU SUJUAN
Environmental and Resources Biology: Prof. ZHENG SHIZHANG
Genetics and Genetic Engineering: Prof. MAO YUMIN
Electronic Engineering: Prof. SHAO XIANGYI
Computer Science: Prof. SHI BOLE
Materials Science: Prof. ZONG XIANGFU
Polymer Science: Prof. YANG YULIANG
Applied Mechanics: Prof. LIU ZHAORONG
Light Sources and Illumination Engineering: Prof. HE MINGGAO
Management Science: Prof. XUE HUACHENG
Enterprise Management: Prof. WANG FANGHUA
Finance: Prof. OUYANG GUANGZHONG
Accounting: Prof. QIANG SHIZHENG
International Business Management: Prof. XUE QIUHE
Cultural Relics and Museum Science: Prof. WU HAOKUN
Technology of Cultural Relics Protection: Prof. XU ZHIZHENG

There are research institutes attached to almost all departments

FUJIAN AGRICULTURAL AND FORESTRY UNIVERSITY

Jinshan, Fujian Province, 350002
Telephone: (591) 3741721
Fax: (591) 3741251
Internet: www.fjau.edu.cn

Founded 1936
State control
Language of instruction: Chinese

President: Prof. LU LIUXIN
Vice-Presidents: Prof. YE SHANGQING, PAN TINGGUO, YOU MINSHENG
Librarian: HU FANPING

Library of 560,000 vols
Number of teachers: 843
Number of students: 3,880

Publications: *Journal of Fujian Agricultural University*, *Overseas Agricultural Science: Sugarcane*, *Current Communications on Overseas Agricultural Science and Technology*, *Wuyi Science*, *Journal of Entomology in Eastern China*

HEADS OF COLLEGE

College of Crop Science: LIN YANQUAN
College of Animal Science: HUANG YIFAN
College of Economics and Trade: HUANG JIANCHENG
College of Adult Education: YE YICHUN

ATTACHED RESEARCH INSTITUTES

Biological Control Institute: Dir ZHAO JINGWEI.

Institute of Plant Virology: Dir XIE LIANHUI.

Synthetic Research Institute of Sugarcane: Dir CHEN RUKAI.

Research Institute of Genetics and Crop Breeding: Dir YANG RENCUI.

Institute of Subtropical Fruits: Dir LIN SHUNQUAN.

Biotechnology Centre: Dir GUAN XIONG.

Research Laboratory of Fungus-Grass: Dr LIN ZHANXI.

FUJIAN MEDICAL UNIVERSITY

88 Jiaotong Rd, Fuzhou, Fujian 350004
Telephone: (591) 3568821
Internet: www.fjmu.edu.cn

Founded 1937

President: Prof. WU ZHONGFU
Vice-Presidents: LUO GUEILIN, LIN KEHUA
Head of Postgraduate Department: KANG YUANYUAN
Librarian: HUANG HUISHANG

Library of 258,448 vols
Number of teachers: 398
Number of students: 2,306

Publications: *Journal*, *Medical Education Study*

HEADS OF DEPARTMENTS

Medicine: LAN YUFU
Public Health: FU MINGSHENG
Stomatology: FAN RUXIONG
Medical Laboratory Science: DAI GENGSHUEN

FUJIAN NORMAL UNIVERSITY

8 Shang San Rd, Cang Shan Section, Fuzhou 350007, Fujian
Telephone: (591) 83456156
Fax: (591) 83425154
Internet: www.fjtu.edu.cn

Founded 1907
Department of Education of Fujian control
Academic year: September to July

President: LI JIANPING
Vice-Presidents: HUANG HANSHENG, LI MIN, WANG ZHENGLU, WANG WENDING, ZHENG YISHU
Head of Graduate Department: LI JIANPING
Librarian: WAN BAOCHUAN

Number of teachers: 2,500
Number of students: 30,000

Publications: *Journal* (natural sciences, 6 a year), *Journal* (philosophy and social sciences, 6 a year), *Mathematics of Fujian Middle School* (6 a year)

DEANS

School of Bioengineering: LI MIN
School of Chemistry and Material Science: HU BINGHUAN
School of Economy: LI JIANJIAN
School of Educational Sciences and Technology: YU WENSEN
School of Foreign Languages: LIN DAJIN
School of Geographical Sciences: YANG YUSHENG
School of Humanities: CHEN QINGYUAN
School of Law: GUO TIEMIN
School of Media: YAN CHUNJUN
School of Mathematics and Computer Science: LI YONGQING
School of Music: ZHENG JINYANG
School of Physics and Optoelectronic Technology: XIE SHUSEN
School of Public Administration: HE YILUN
School of Society and History: LIN JINSHUI
School of Software: WENG ZUMAO
School of Tourism: ZHENG YAOXIN
College of Physical Education and Sports Science: MEI XUEXIONG

PROFESSORS

CAI, XIULING, Economics
CHAI, YUPING, Public Administration
CHEN, GUIRONG, Public Administration
CHEN, GUORUI, Physical Education and Sports Science
CHEN, HUOPING, Educational Sciences and Technology
CHEN, JUNQIN, Physical Education and Sports Science
CHEN, KAI, Foreign Languages
CHEN, LIANGYUAN, Humanities
CHEN, QINGYUAN, Humanities
CHEN, RONG, Physical Education and Sports Science
CHEN, SHAOHUI, Economics
CHEN, SHAOPING, Chemistry and Material Science
CHEN, TIECHENG, Physical Education and Sports Science
CHEN, WEIZHEN, Foreign Languages
CHEN, YIPING, Bioengineering
CHEN, YONGCHUN, Public Administration
CHEN, YOUQIANG, Bioengineering
CHEN, ZEPING, Humanities
CHEN, ZHENG, Economics
CHENG, LIGUO, Educational Sciences and Technology
DAI, CONGTENG, Foreign Languages
DAI, XIANQUN, Society and History
DU, CHANGZHONG, Foreign Languages
GANG, SONG, Bioengineering
GAO, JIANMIN, Bioengineering
GU, YEPING, Humanities
GUO, TIEMIN, Economics
HE, YILUN, Public Administration
HONG, MING, Educational Sciences and Technology
HONG, YANGUO, Bioengineering
HU, BINGHUAN, Chemistry and Material Science
HU, CANGZE, Society and History
HU, ZHIGANG, Chemistry and Material Science
HUANG, AILING, Educational Sciences and Technology
HUANG, GUANGYANG, Educational Sciences and Technology
HUANG, GUOSHENG, Society and History
HUANG, GUOXIONG, Public Administration
HUANG, HANSHENG, Physical Education and Sports Science
HUANG, JIANZHONG, Bioengineering
HUANG, JIAYE, Economics
HUANG, RENXIAN, Educational Sciences and Technology
HUANG, ZHIGAO, Physics and Optoelectronic Technology
LAN, XUEFEI, Music
LI, HONGCAI, Physics and Optoelectronic Technology
LI, JIANJIAN, Economics
LI, JIANPING, Economics
LI, MIN, Bioengineering
LI, RONGBAO, Foreign Languages
LI, SHUZHEN, Public Administration
LI, XIANGMIN, Public Administration
LIAN, CHENGYE, Society and History
LIAN, RONG, Educational Sciences and Technology
LIN, BENCHUN, Foreign Languages
LIN, DAJIN, Foreign Languages
LIN, GUOPING, Society and History
LIN, JING, Educational Sciences and Technology
LIN, JINHUO, Chemistry and Material Science
LIN, JINSHUI, Society and History
LIN, LIN, Bioengineering
LIN, QING, Economics
LIN, SHANLANG, Economics
LIN, XIUGUO, Public Administration
LIN, ZHANG, Foreign Languages
LIN, ZIHUA, Economics
LIU, HUIYU, Society and History
LIU, JIANQIU, Bioengineering
LIU, RONGFANG, Chemistry and Material Science
LIU, YAMENG, Foreign Languages
LIU, YONGGENG, Humanities
MAO, NING, Bioengineering
MEI, XUEXIONG, Physical Education and Sports Science
PAN, XINHE, Humanities
PAN, YUTENG, Public Administration
QIAO, JIANZHONG, Music
QIU, LING, Foreign Languages
QIU, YISHEN, Physics and Optoelectronic Technology
QIU, YONGQU, Educational Sciences and Technology
SHI, QIAOQIN, Bioengineering
SU, XIAOQING, Physical Education and Sports Science
SU, ZHENFANG, Public Administration
SUN, SHAOZHEN, Humanities
TAN, XUEXHUN, Humanities
TANG, WENJI, Society and History
WANG, GUOHONG, Bioengineering
WANG, HANMIN, Humanities
WANG, JIANDE, Society and History
WANG, KE, Humanities
WANG, YAOHUA, Music
WANG, ZHENGLU, Society and History
WANG, ZHIBO, Public Administration
WEN, RI, Society and History
WENG, JIABAO, Chemistry and Material Science
WENG, YINTAO, Humanities
WENG, ZUMAO, Computer Software
WU, YOUGEN, Economics
WU, ZONGHUA, Chemistry and Material Science
XI, YANG, Humanities
XIAO, HUASHAN, Bioengineering
XIE, BIZHEN, Society and History
XIE, SHUSEN, Physics and Optoelectronic Technology
XU, HONGFENG, Physical Education and Sports Science
XU, MING, Educational Sciences and Technology
XU, YONG, Physics and Optoelectronic Technology
YAN, CHUNJUN, Humanities
YAN, YOUWEI, Educational Sciences and Technology
YANG, KONGCHI, Educational Sciences and Technology
YANG, MINGRU, Bioengineering
YANG, XINHUA, Public Administration
YANG, YUSHENG, Geographical Sciences
YANG, ZHAOFENG, Bioengineering
YE, YIDUO, Educational Sciences and Technology
YOU, YONGLONG, Bioengineering
YU, GECHUN, Public Administration
YU, WENSEN, Educational Sciences and Technology
YUAN, SHUQI, Geographical Sciences
ZENG, CONGSHENG, Geographical Sciences
ZHAN, GUANQUN, Society and History
ZHANG, DINGHUA, Bioengineering
ZHANG, HANJIN, Physical Education and Sports Science
ZHANG, HUARONG, Economics
ZHANG, WENGONG, Chemistry and Material Science
ZHANG, YANDING, Bioengineering
ZHEN, XIAOHUA, Society and History
ZHENG, DAXIAN, Geographical Sciences
ZHENG, JINYANG, Music
ZHENG, YI, Bioengineering
ZHENG, YOUXIAN, Public Administration
ZHU, HEJIAN, Geographical Sciences
ZHU, JIAN, Economics
ZHU, JINZI, Bioengineering
ZHU, LING, Humanities
ZHUANG, HUIRU, Bioengineering
ZHUANG, TAO, Foreign Languages
ZUAN, ZHENGFANG, Public Administration

ATTACHED RESEARCH INSTITUTES

Key Laboratory for Semitropical Resources and Environment: Dir YANG YUSHENG.

Research Centre for Basic Educational Courses: Dir YU WENSEN.

Studies Centre of Fujian and Taiwan: Dir WANG YAOHUA.

FUZHOU UNIVERSITY

523 Industry Rd, Fuzhou 350002, Fujian
Telephone: (591) 3739513
Fax: (591) 3713866
Internet: www.fzu.edu.cn

Founded 1958
Academic year: September to July
President: WU MIN SHENG
Vice-Presidents: CHEN GUO NAN, FAN GENG HUA, FANG ZHEN ZHENG, FU XIAN ZHI
Heads of Graduate Department: LIN SHU WEN, LIU SONG QING
Librarian: ZHANG WEN DE
Number of teachers: 1,200
Number of students: 20,000
Publications: *Journal* (natural sciences, 6 a year), *Journal* (philosophy, 4 a year)

DEANS

School of Biological Science and Technology: RAO PING FAN
School of Civil Engineering and Architecture: CHEN BAO CHUN
School of Electric Engineering and Automation: CHEN BAO CHUN
School of Environment and Resources: XU HAN QIU
School of Foreign Languages: WU SONG JIANG
School of Humanities and Social Sciences: LIN YI
School of Law: CHEN QUAN SHENG
School of Management: CHEN GUO HONG
School of Materials Sciences and Engineering: CHEN XIAN SHENG
School of Mathematics and Computer Science: WANG XIAO DONG
School of Mechanical Engineering: GAO CHENG HUI
School of Physics and Information Engineering: YU LUN
School of Public Management: WANG JIAN
School of Software: FAN GENG HUA
School of Zhi Cheng: TANG YI ZHU
Napier College: XIE LIU HUI
Sunshine College: CHEN GONG LIN

PROFESSORS

CAI, JIN DING, Electrical Engineering and Automation
CHEN, BAO CHUN, Civil Engineering and Architecture
CHEN, CHONG, Electrical Engineering and Automation
CHEN, FU JI, Public Management
CHEN, GUO HONG, Management
CHEN, LE SHAN, Mechanical Engineering
CHEN, LI, Mechanical Engineering
CHEN, RONG SI, Management
CHEN, SEN, Civil Engineering and Architecture
CHEN, SHU MEI, Mechanical Engineering
CHEN, XIAN SHENG, Materials Science and Engineering
CHEN, XIAO WEI, Foreign Languages
CHEN, XIN, Physics and Information Engineering
CHEN, XIN SHU, Civil Engineering and Architecture
DU, MING, Electrical Engineering and Automation
FANG, ZHEN ZHENG, Civil Engineering and Architecture
GAO, CHENG HUI, Mechanical Engineering
GUO, ZONG REN, Electrical Engineering and Automation
HU, JI RONG, Management
HU, XIAO RONG, Civil Engineering and Architecture
HUANG, KE AN, Management
HUANG, SHU ZHANG, Management
HUANG, WEN XIN, Management
HUANG, YAO ZHI, Mechanical Engineering
HUANG, ZHI GANG, Management
JIAN, WEN BIN, Environment and Resources
LAN, ZHAO HUI, Mechanical Engineering
LEI, DE SEN, Public Management
LIN, GUO RONG, Mechanical Engineering
LIN, QIANG, Physics and Information Engineering
LIN, SHU WEN, Mechanical Engineering
LIN, TONG, Mechanical Engineering
LIN, YI, Humanities and Social Sciences
LIN, YING XING, Management
LIN, YOU WEN, Management
LIN, YUAN QING, Management
LIU, MING HUA, Environment and Resources
LIU, YAN BIN, Mechanical Engineering
PAN, YAN, Management
PENG, DA WEN, Civil Engineering and Architecture
QI, KAI, Civil Engineering and Architecture
QIAN, KUANG WU, Materials Science and Engineering
QIU, GONG WEI, Electrical Engineering and Automation
RAO, PING FAN, Biological Science and Technology
RUAN, YU ZHONG, Materials Science and Engineering
SHENG, FEI MIN, Environment and Resources
SU, KAI XIONG, Physics and Information Engineering
SUN, QIU BI, Management
TANG, DE PING, Materials Science and Engineering
TANG, DIAN, Materials Science and Engineering
TANG, LI HONG, Public Management
TANG, NING PING, Electrical Engineering and Automation
WANG, JIAN, Public Management
WANG, QIN MIN, Physics and Information Engineering
WANG, WEI YI, Management
WANG, YING MING, Public Management
WANG, ZHONG LAI, Biological Science and Technology
WU, HAN GUANG, Electrical Engineering and Automation
WU, SONG JIANG, Foreign Languages
WU, XING NAN, Humanities and Social Sciences
XI, YONG QIN, Public Management
XIE, ZHI XIN, Civil Engineering and Architecture
XU, DOU DOU, Humanities and Social Sciences
XU, HAN QIU, Environment and Resources
YANG, FU WEN, Electrical Engineering and Automation
YANG, XIAO XIANG, Mechanical Engineering
YE, ZHONG HE, Mechanical Engineering
YEA, ZHONG, Management
YU, LUN, Physics and Information Engineering
YUAN, BING LING, Humanities and Social Sciences
ZHANG, BAI, Management
ZHANG, BEI MIN, Electrical Engineering and Automation
ZHANG, MAO XUN, Mechanical Engineering
ZHANG, QI SHAN, Mechanical Engineering
ZHANG, QI SHAN, Management
ZHANG, QIONG, Materials Science and Engineering
ZHANG, YE, Management
ZHENG, JIAN LAN, Civil Engineering and Architecture
ZHENG, SHI BIAO, Physics and Information Engineering
ZHENG, ZHEN, Civil Engineering and Architecture
ZHENG, ZHEN FEI, Civil Engineering and Architecture
ZHOU, RUI ZHONG, Civil Engineering and Architecture
ZHOU, XIAO LIANG, Management
ZHU, YONG CHUN, Civil Engineering and Architecture
ZHU, ZU PING, Mechanical Engineering

ATTACHED RESEARCH INSTITUTES

Centre for Discrete Mathematics and Theoretical Computer Science: Dir FAN GENG HUA.
Fuzhou University Central Laboratory: Dir WANG YUAN SHENG.
Information Engineering Research Center: Dir WANG, GIN MIN.

GANSU AGRICULTURAL UNIVERSITY

1 Yingmencun, Nanning District, Lanzhou 730070, Gansu Province
Telephone: (931) 7631125
Fax: (931) 7631125
E-mail: wujp@public.lz.gs.cn
Internet: www.gsau.edu.cn

Founded 1958
Academic year: September to July
President: Prof. WANG DI
Vice-Presidents: Prof. LI ZHENXIAO, LU JIANHUA, LAN YUZHEN
Director of Foreign Affairs: Prof. WU JIANPING
Librarian: LIU XI
Library of 500,000 vols
Number of teachers: 600
Number of students: 5,000 (125 postgraduates)
Publications: *University Journal* (monthly), *Journal of Grassland and Turf* (4 a year)

DEANS

Animal Science: CUI XIAN
Veterinary Science: LIU YING
Grassland Science: CAO ZHIZHONG
Agronomy: LI WEI
Plant Protection: ZHANG XINGHU
Soil Chemistry: SHI YINGFU
Forest Science: JIANG ZHIRONG
Horticulture: YU JIHUA
Agricultural Machinery and Engineering: WU JIANMING
Water Conservation: CHENG ZIYONG
Agricultural Business and Trade: WANG CENGLIN
Food Science: YU QUNLI
Basic Courses: YUAN TONGSHENG
Social Science: SHANG ZHENHAI

ATTACHED INSTITUTES

Foodstuffs and Feeding Institute.
Wool Institute.
Melon Institute.
Turf Institute

GUANGDONG COLLEGE OF MEDICINE AND PHARMACY

40 Guang Han Zhi, Haizhu District, Guangzhou, Guangdong Province 510224
Telephone: 4429040

Founded 1978
President: Prof. DU QI ZHANG (acting)
Vice-Presidents: LI TINGJIE, CHENG SHENGHAO
Librarian: LIAO MING QING
Library of 160,000 vols
Number of teachers: 300
Number of students: 1,800
Publication: *Journal*

HEADS OF DEPARTMENTS

Preventive Medicine: Prof. WU ZHEN QIANG
Pharmacy: Prof. CHEN JIAN YU
Clinical Medicine: Prof. HE YIEXIONG
Basic Medical Sciences: Prof. LAI MUXIAN

PROFESSORS

FENGHE, H., Pharmacology
FENGMING, Z., Epidemiology
JINCHENG, H., Pharmaceutical Chemistry

JINGXIAN, J., Internal Medicine
JINGZHI, H., Human Parasitology
JIPENG, L., Pharmacognosy
MUXIAN, L., Biochemistry
PUSHENG, W., Traditional Chinese Medicine
QIHUA, W., Human Anatomy
QIYUN, Y., Phytochemistry
QIZHANG, D., Pharmacology
SHIDE, S., Statistics
YIYUAN, Z., Dermatology
ZHICHENG, C., Hygiene
ZHUHUA, L., Microbiology

GUANGXI NORMAL UNIVERSITY

Yan Shan, Gui Lin 541004, Guangxi
Telephone: (773) 5812081
Fax: (773) 5812383
Internet: www.gxnu.edu.cn
Founded 1932
Ministry of Education control
Academic year: September to July
President: LIANG HONG
Vice-Presidents: LAN CHANGZHOU, LIU JIANBING, LIU MUREN, WANG JIE, YI ZHONG, ZHONG RUITIAN
Librarian: YAO QIAN
Library of 2,060,000 vols
Number of teachers: 1,043
Number of students: 40,000
Publication: *Journal of Guangxi Normal University* (4 a year)

DEANS

School of Chemistry and Chemical Engineering: LIANG FUPEI
School of Culture and Tourism: ZHOU ZUOMING
School of Law and Business: LUO ZHISONG
School of Sports: LIANG ZHUPING
College of Life Science: QIN XINMING
College of Politics and Public Management: TAN PEIWEN
College of Physics and Information Technology: WANG QIANG
College of Foreign Studies: LIU ZHAOZHONG
Educational Science College: GAO JINLING
Department of Resources and Environmental Science: HE XINGCUN

PROFESSORS

CAI, CHANGZHUO, International Culture and Education
CHEN, HONGJIANG, Politics and Public Management
CHEN, JITANG, Foreign Studies
CHEN, QIN, Politics and Public Management
CHEN, XIONGZHANG, Culture and Tourism
CHEN, ZHAOBIN, Physical Education
CHEN, ZHENFENG, Chemistry and Chemical Engineering
CUI, TIANSHUN, Resources and Environmental Science
CUI, YAODONG, Mathematics and Computer Science
DENG, BIYANG, Chemistry and Chemical Engineering
DENG, PEIMING, Mathematics and Computer Science
DING, CHANGMING, Mathematics and Computer Science
FENG, CUNHUA, Mathematics and Computer Science
GUO, LILIANG, Physical Education
HE, LINXIA, Culture and Tourism
HE, XIANGLIN, Foreign Studies
HE, XINGCUN, Resources and Environmental Science
HU, DALEI, Chinese Studies
HUANG, BINLIAN, Physics and Information Technology
HUANG, CHENGMING, Life Science
HUANG, JIESHAN, Social Sciences
HUANG, RUIXIONG, Social Sciences
HUANG, SHEN, Physical Education
HUANG, WEILIN, Chinese Studies
HUANG, ZHUSHENG, Law and Business
JIANG, GUOCHENG, Life Science
JIANG, SHIHUI, Educational Science
JIANG, YIMING, Chemistry and Chemical Engineering
LEI, REI, Chinese Studies
LI, DUNXIANG, Law and Business
LI, FUBO, Chinese Studies
LI, HONGHAN, Educational Science
LI, JIANG, Chinese Studies
LI, LAILONG, Chinese Studies
LI, LU, Educational Science
LI, XIAO, Foreign Studies
LI, YI, Resources and Environmental Science
LI, ZHIQING, Physical Education
LIANG, FUPEI, Chemistry and Chemical Engineering
LIANG, HONG, Chemistry and Chemical Engineering
LIANG, ZHUPING, Physical Education
LIAO, GUOWEI, Chinese Studies
LIN, FENGMIN, Social Sciences
LIN, SHIMIN, Mathematics and Computer Science
LIU, MUREN, Physics and Information Technology
LIU, XIAOLIN, Culture and Tourism
LIU, XINGJUN, Chinese Studies
LIU, YING, International Culture and Education
LIU, ZHAOZHONG, Foreign Studies
LU, XIAO, Physics and Information Technology
LU, YUTAI, Foreign Studies
LUO, GUILIE, Mathematics and Computer Science
LUO, XIAOSHU, Physics and Information Technology
LUO, XINGKAI, Physics and Information Technology
LUO, ZHISONG, Law and Business
MAI, YONGXIONG, Chinese Studies
MO, DAOCAI, Chinese Studies
MO, QIXUN, Chinese Studies
PO, JINZE, Foreign Studies
QI, PEIFANG, Politics and Public Management
QIN, YONGSONG, Mathematics and Computer Science
QIN, ZIXIONG, Physics and Information Technology
QUE, ZHEN, Chinese Studies
REN, GUANWEN, Culture and Tourism
SHEN, JIAZHUANG, Chinese Studies
SHI, GUIYU, Life Science
SU, GUIFA, Chemistry and Chemical Engineering
SUN, JIANYUAN, Chinese Studies
TAN, DEQING, Chinese Studies
TAN, PEIWEN, Politics and Public Management
TAN, ZHAOYI, Culture and Tourism
TANG, DEHAI, Educational Science
TANG, FUCHENG, Mathematics and Computer Science
TANG, GAOYUAN, Foreign Studies
TANG, LING, Culture and Tourism
TANG, ZHAOQING, Life Science
TENG, DINGMING, Chinese Studies
TONG, GUANGZHENG, Law and Business
WANG, CHAOYUAN, Chinese Studies
WANG, CHENGMING, Mathematics and Computer Science
WANG, DEFU, Social Sciences
WANG, DEMING, Chinese Studies
WANG, JIE, Chinese Studies
WANG, QIANG, Physics and Information Technology
WANG, XIANGJUN, Politics and Public Management
WANG, ZHIYING, Chinese Studies
WEI, HAN, Foreign Studies
WENG, JIAQIANG, Physics and Information Technology
WU, DIANHUA, Mathematics and Computer Science
XIE, XIANG, Physical Education
XU, JIWANG, Foreign Studies
XU, XUEFU, Educational Science
XU, XUEYING, Educational Science
XUE, YUEGUI, Life Science
YAN, XIAOWEI, Mathematics and Computer Science
YANG, LIYAN, Law and Business
YANG, QIGUI, Mathematics and Computer Science
YANG, SHANCHAO, Mathematics and Computer Science
YANG, SHUJIE, Chinese Studies
YANG, YONGBING, Physics and Information Technology
YANG, YONGLIANG, Physical Education
YAO, DAILIANG, Chinese Studies
YE, YONGJI, Arts Department
YI, XING, Politics and Public Management
YI, ZHONG, Mathematics and Computer Science
YIN, LINGLING, Physical Education
YU, PING, Mathematics and Computer Science
YUAN, BINYE, Foreign Studies
ZHANG, LIQUN, Chinese Studies
ZHANG, MINGFEI, Chinese Studies
ZHANG, SHICHAO, Mathematics and Computer Science
ZHAO, SHULIN, Chemistry and Chemical Engineering
ZHONG, RUITIAN, Politics and Public Management
ZHOU, LIANGREN, Foreign Studies
ZHOU, QUANLIN, Foreign Studies
ZHOU, SHANYI, Life Science
ZHOU, SHIZHONG, Law and Business
ZHU, CONGBIN, Culture and Tourism
ZHU, JUNQIANG, Law and Business
ZHU, SHOUXING, Chinese Studies

ATTACHED RESEARCH INSTITUTES

College of International Culture and Education.

Continuing Training College: Dir WU GUOQUAN.

Institute of Physics: Dir LUO XINGKAI.

GUANGXI TRADITIONAL CHINESE MEDICAL UNIVERSITY

179 Mingxiudong Rd, Nanning, Guangxi
Telephone: (771) 3137577
Fax: (771) 317517
Internet: www.gxtcmu.edu.cn
Founded 1956
President: Prof. WEI GUIKANG
Vice-Presidents: Prof. LI WEITAI, Assoc. Prof. ZHU HUA, Assoc. Prof. DEN JIAGANG
Librarian: LI JIANGUANG
Library of 300,000 vols
Number of teachers: 296
Number of students: 1,849
Publications: *Guangxi Journal of Traditional Chinese Medicine*, *Study in Higher Education of Traditional Chinese Medicine*

HEADS OF DEPARTMENTS

Traditional Chinese Medical Science: Assoc. Prof. JIANG YINGSHI
Pharmaceutical and Chinese Materia Medica: Assoc. Prof. LIU HUAGANG
No. 1 Clinical Medicine: Assoc. Prof. LAN QINGQIANG
No. 2 Clinical Medicine: Prof. XU FUYE

ATTACHED RESEARCH INSTITUTES

Institute of Traditional Chinese Medical Treatment and Medicine: Dir Prof. WONG TAILAI.

Institute of TCM Orthopaedics and Traumatology: Dir Prof. WEI GUIKANG.

Zhuang Institute of Medical Science: Dir Prof. HUANG JINGMING.

Institute of Acupuncture and Moxibustion: Dir Assoc. Prof. XIE GANGONG.

Institute of Traditional Chinese Medicine: Dir Assoc. Prof. LUO WEISHENG.

Institute of the Combination of Traditional Chinese Medicine and Western Medicine: Dir Assoc. Prof. XIAO TINGGANG.

GUANGXI UNIVERSITY

10 Xixiangtang Rd, Nanning, Guangxi Zhuang Autonomous Region 530004

Telephone: (771) 3832391
Fax: (771) 3823743
E-mail: gxugjc@public.nn.gx.cn
Internet: www.gxu.edu.cn

Founded 1928
State control
Academic year: September to June

President: Prof. TANG JILIANG
Registrar: Prof. FU ZHENFANG
Librarian: Prof. CHEN DAGUANG

Library of 2,020,000 vols
Number of teachers: 1,735
Number of students: 17,290

Publication: *Guangxi University Journal*

DEANS

College of Forestry: Prof. JIN DAGANG (Exec. Vice-Dean)
College of Animal Science and Technology: Prof. YANG NIANSHENG
College of Agronomy: Prof. MO TIANYAN
College of Mechanical Engineering: Prof. LI SHANGPING
College of Electrical Engineering: Prof. LU ZUPEI
College of Chemistry and Chemical Engineering: Prof. TONG ZHANGFA
College of Computer Science and Information Technology: Prof. LI TAOSHEN
College of Civil Engineering: Prof. YAN LIUBIN
College of Biological Technology and Sugar Industrial Engineering: Prof. LU JIAJIONG
College of Natural Resources and the Environment: Prof. MA SHAOJIAN
College of Sciences: Prof. XI HONGJIAN
College of Business: Prof. LIU CHAOMING
College of Culture and Mass Communication: Prof. LIANG YANG
College of Foreign Languages: Prof. ZHOU YI
College of Social Sciences and Management: Prof. XIE SHUN
College of Law: Prof. MENG QINGUO
College of Adult Education: Prof. HE BAOCHONG
Department of Physical Education: Prof. XU MINGRONG
Department of Teacher-Training: Prof. WANG HAIYIN (Vice-Dean)

GUANGZHOU UNIVERSITY

248 Guang Yuan Zhong Rd, Guangzhou 510405

Telephone: (20) 86394493
Fax: (20) 86370350
E-mail: faogzu@21cn.com
Internet: www.gzhu.edu.cn

Founded 1983; merged with 8 other institutions of higher education 2000
Academic year: September to July

President: Prof. LIN WEIMING
Vice-Presidents: Prof. CHEN WANPENG, Prof. YU GUOYANG, Prof. LI XUNGUI, Prof. SHU YANG, Prof. XU CIRONG, Prof. LONG SHAOFENG
Director of the International Office: Prof. LI YI
Director of Academic Affairs: Prof. YU QICAI
Director of Academic Research: Prof. XIAN QIAOLING
Director of Postgraduate Affairs: Prof. YAO PO
Director of the Institute for Higher Education Research: Prof. HUANG JIAQUAN
Library Director: Prof. ZHANG BAIYING

Publication: *Journal* (monthly)

Library of 182,000 vols
Number of teachers: 2,372
Number of students: 31,333

HEADS OF DEPARTMENTS

School of Economics and Management: Prof. PAN SHUJIAN
School of Law: Prof. ZHANG SHUANGXI
School of Education: Prof. CAI XIAOYUE
School of Humanities and Social Sciences: Prof. HE DAJIN
School of Foreign Studies: Prof. CHENG SHILU
School of Art and Design: Prof. WANG XIAOSHU
School of Science: Prof. PEI DINGYI
School of Information and Electromechanical Engineering: Prof. LI BAOWEN
School of Biology and Chemical Engineering: Prof. ZHENG CHENG
School of Civil Engineering: Prof. ZHOU YUN
School of Architecture and Urban Planning: Prof. DONG LI
School of Tourism: Prof. PENG QING
School of Continuing Education: Prof. WANG ZHONGDE

ATTACHED RESEARCH INSTITUTES

Institute for Computer Science and Software Research: Dir Dr ZHANG JINGZHONG.

Earthquake Engineering Research Test Centre: Dir Prof. ZHOU FULIN.

Institute for Material Research: Dir Prof. ZHANG CHUANMEI.

International Exchange Centre of Mathematics and Artificial Intelligence: Dir Prof. YANG LU.

GUANGZHOU UNIVERSITY OF TRADITIONAL CHINESE MEDICINE

12 Airport Rd, Guangzhou 510405, Guangdong

Telephone: (20) 36588233
Fax: (20) 36585258
Internet: www.gzhtcm.edu.cn

Founded 1956
Department of Education of Guangdong control
Academic year: September to July

President: FENG XINSONG
Vice-Presidents: CHEN YINGHUA, LI JIANJUN, LIN PEICHENG, WANG NINGSHENG, XU ZHIWEI
Head of Graduate Department: QIU SHIJUN
Librarian: LI JIAN

Number of teachers: 1,025
Number of students: 3,000

Publications: *Journal* (6 a year), *New Journal of Traditional Chinese Medicine* (12 a year), *Traditional Chinese Drug Research and Clinical Pharmacology* (6 a year)

DEANS

School of Basic Medical Sciences: CHEN QUN
School of Acupuncture and Massage: CAI TIEQU
School of Chinese Traditional Medicine: CHEN WEIWEN
School of Economy and Administration: QIU HONGZHONG
School of Information Technology: CHEN SU
School of Nursing: HE YANPING
First School of Medicine: DENG TIETAO
Second School of Medicine: LU YUBO
Third School of Medicine: ZHUANG HONG

PROFESSORS

CAI, TIEQU, Acupuncture and Massage
CHEN, DACAN, Medicine
CHEN, JINGHE, Medicine
CHEN, JIPAN, Medicine
CHEN, QUN, Basic Medical Sciences
CHEN, SU, Information Technology
CHEN, WEIWEN, Chinese Traditional Medicine
CHEN, XHAOFENG, Basic Medical Sciences
CHEN, ZHIQIANG, Medicine
CHENG, YI, Chinese Traditional Medicine
DENG, TIETAO, Medicine
GAO, YOUHENG, Chinese Traditional Medicine
HUANG, SHAOYING, Medicine
I, JIEFEN, Basic Medical Sciences
JIN, RUI, Medicine
LAI, WEN, Basic Medical Sciences
LAI, XINSHENG, Acupuncture and Massage
LI, HANJIN, Basic Medical Sciences
LI, JINGBO, Basic Medical Sciences
LI, RENXIAN, Medicine
LI, RI, Chinese Traditional Medicine
LI, WANYAO, Acupuncture and Massage
LI, WEI, Chinese Traditional Medicine
LI, WEIMIN, Chinese Traditional Medicine
LI, YIWEI, Nursing
LIANG, SONGMIN, Chinese Traditional Medicine
LIN, LI, Chinese Traditional Medicine
LIU, HUANLAN, Basic Medical Sciences
LIU, JUN, Medicine
LIU, SHICHANG, Medicine
LIU, XIAOBIN, Basic Medical Sciences
LUO, RONGJING, Basic Medical Sciences
LUO, YUNJIAN, Medicine
LU, YUBO, Medicine
OU, YONGXIN, Basic Medical Sciences
OUYANG, HUIQING, Medicine
PAN, YI, Basic Medical Sciences
PENG, SHENGQUAN, Medicine
QIU, HEMING, Medicine
QIU, HONGZHONG, Economy and Administration
WANG, HONGQI, Basic Medical Sciences
WU, MIMAN, Basic Medical Sciences
WU, QINGHE, Chinese Traditional Medicine
XIONG, MANQI, Medicine
XU, HONGHUA, Chinese Traditional Medicine
XU, NENGGUI, Acupuncture and Massage
XU, ZHIWEI, Basic Medical Sciences
YANG, SHUNYI, Acupuncture and Massage
YANG, ZHIMIN, Medicine
YUAN, HAO, Medicine
ZHANG, HONG, Acupuncture and Massage
ZHANG, JIAWEI, Acupuncture and Massage
ZHOU, DAIHAN, Medicine
ZHOU, LILING, Chinese Traditional Medicine
ZHUANG, LIXING, Acupuncture and Massage

ATTACHED RESEARCH INSTITUTES

National Modern Engineering Technology Research Centre for Chinese Traditional Medicine: Dir FENG XINSONG.

National Clinical Trial Research Centre for New Medicine (Chinese Traditional Medicine): Dir LAI SHILONG.

Safe Evaluation Research Key Laboratory of New Medicine (Chinese Traditional Medicine): Dir WANG NINGSHENG.

GUIZHOU UNIVERSITY

Guiyang, Guizhou

Telephone: (851) 3851187
Fax: (851) 3851381

Founded 1958 as Guizhou University as successor to institution which had been disbanded in 1953; merged with Guizhou Renmin University (Guizhou People's University) 1993

Chancellor: XU CAODONG
Vice-Chancellor: LIU CHAOZHENG

Number of teachers: 2,800
Number of students: 10,000

Colleges: Science and Engineering; Agriculture; Humanities; Biotechnology; Arts; Vocational Training.

GUIZHOU UNIVERSITY OF TECHNOLOGY

Caijiaguan, Guiyang 550003, Guizhou Province
Telephone: (851) 4731641
Fax: (851) 4731649
E-mail: fao@gut.gy.gz.cn

Founded 1958
Academic year: September to July

President: HU GUOGEN
Registrar: WANG YI
Secretary-General: YUAN HUAJUN
Librarian: HE LIQUAN

Library of 520,000 vols, 1,500 periodicals
Number of teachers: 780
Number of students: 8,000

Publication: *Journal* (6 a year)

HEADS OF DEPARTMENTS

Resource Engineering: ZHU LIJUN
Mining Engineering: YANG HOUHUA
Metallurgical Engineering: WU XIANXI
Mechanical Engineering: NIU MINGQI
Electrical Engineering: WU RUSHAN
Chemical Engineering: ZENG XIANGQIN
Civil Engineering: ZHANG HUI
Light Industry: ZHANG YIMING
Architecture: BAI NAIPENG
Computer Science: FU JIAXIANG
Foreign Languages: ZHANG CAIFENG
Engineering Management: YE ZHUGUANG
Adult Education No. 1: LIU ZHAOJIAN
Adult Education No. 2: LU KUN
Basic Science Courses: ZHOU GUOLI
Liberal Arts and Social Sciences: WU JIALING
Science Research: XIE QINSHENG
Physical Culture: LIU WEI

HANGZHOU UNIVERSITY OF COMMERCE

29 Jiao Gong Rd, Hangzhou, Zhejiang 310035
Telephone: (571) 8071024
Fax: (571) 8053079
E-mail: huc1@zjpta.net.cn
Internet: www.hzic.edu.cn

Founded 1911

Under control of Ministry of Internal Trade
Academic year: February to July, September to January

President: Prof. HU ZUGUANG
Vice-Presidents: Prof. WANG GUANGMING, DING ZHENGZHONG, HU WEIMIN, ZHANG JIANPING, ZHOU DAJUN
Chief Administrative Officer: KE LI
Librarian: ZHU SHANGWU

Library of 620,000 vols
Number of teachers: 326
Number of students: 5,100 full-time
Number of students: 3,600 part-time

Publications: *Economics and Business Administration*, *Academic Periodical*

HEADS OF DEPARTMENTS

Accounting: LIU JIANCHANG
Applied Fine Arts: ZHANG JIANCHUN
Business Administration: ZHU MINGWEI
Computer and Information Engineering: JU CHUNHUA
Electronic Engineering: REN ZHIGUO
Food Science and Technology: ZHONG LIREN
Foreign Languages: HUANG ZHIHONG
International Economics: YANG SENLIN
Investment Economics: HAN DEZHONG
Law: RUAN ZANLIN
Social Sciences: CHEN RONGFU
Statistics: LI JINCHANG
Tourism Management: XU ZHIWEI
Trade Economics: WANG CHUANWEI

HARBIN INSTITUTE OF ELECTRICAL TECHNOLOGY

53 Daqing Rd, Harbin, Heilongjiang 150040
Telephone: 6221000
Fax: 51623

Founded 1950
Academic year: September to July

President: HE LIAN
Vice-Presidents: ZHOU SHICHANG, BAO SHAOXUAN, LIANG YUANHUA
Registrar: LU MINGJUAN
Librarian: BAO SHAOXUAN

Library of 270,000 vols
Number of teachers: 537
Number of students: 2,015 (incl. 95 postgraduates)

Publication: *Journal* (quarterly)

HEADS OF DEPARTMENTS

Electrical Machinery Engineering: LI ZHESHENG
Electromagnetic Measurement and Instrumentation: MA HUAIJIAN
Computer Engineering: SUN XINGRU
Electrical Material Engineering: YANG JIAXIANG
Mechanical Engineering: JIANG CHEN
Basic Courses: LU CIQING
Social Sciences: SONG DIANQING
Administration: GUAN ZHIYAO
Foreign Languages: XU XIANG

ATTACHED INSTITUTE

Adult Education Institute: Dir YANG QI.

HARBIN ENGINEERING UNIVERSITY

145 Nantong Street, Harbin, Heilongjiang 150001
Telephone: (451) 2519212
Fax: (451) 2533090
E-mail: heu@public.hr.hl.cn
Internet: www.hrbeu.edu.cn

Founded 1953
Academic year: September to July

President: Prof. QIU CHANGHUA
Secretary of the University Party Committee: LIU ZHIGANG

Library of 900,000 vols
Number of teachers: 2,200
Number of students: 23,000

Publications: *Journal of HEU*, *Applied Science and Technology*, *Overseas Science and Technology*

HEADS OF DEPARTMENTS

Shipping Engineering College: YAO XIONGLIANG
Architectural Engineering College: MA JINGJUN
Motive Power and Nuclear Energy Engineering College: ZHANG WENPING
Automation College: HAO YANLING
Marine Acoustical Engineering College: LIU GUOZHI
Computer Science and Technology College: GU GUOCHANG
Mechanical and Electronic Engineering College: LI QINGFEN
Electronic Engineering College: GUO LILI
Economic Management College: LI BAIZHOU
College of Science: SU JINGHUI
Humanities and Social Sciences College: JIANG XIANGZHI
Chemical Engineering Department: ZHANG MILIN
Foreign Language Department: OU YANGQUAN
Physical and Military Training Department: JI LIEWEI
Institute of Adult Education: ZHOU ZHENRONG

HARBIN MEDICAL UNIVERSITY

194 Nan Gang Section, Xue Fu Rd, Harbin 150086, Heilongjiang
Telephone: (451) 86671349
Fax: (451) 86671349
Internet: www.hrbmu.edu.cn

Founded 1926
Department of Education of Heilongjiang Province control
Academic year: September to July

President: YANG BAOFENG
Vice-Presidents: CAO DEPIN, LI YUKUI, LIU WENCHUAN, WO ZHENZHONG
Head of Graduate Department: ZHANG BAOXING
Librarian: YUE WEIPING

Number of teachers: 1,151
Number of students: 9,228 (6,414 full-time, 2,814 part-time)

Publications: *Chinese Journal of Endemiology* (6 a year), *Journal* (6 a year)

DEANS

School of Basic Medical Sciences: FU SONGBIN
School of Mouth Cavity Medical Science: ZHANG BIN
School of Nursing: LI JIANFENG
School of Pharmacy: ZHU DALING
School of Public Health: SUN CHANGHAO
First School of Medicine: ZHOU JIN
Second School of Medicine: ZHANG QIFAN
Branch of Harbin Medical University: ZHANG SHIXUE
Department of Bioinformatics: LI XIA

PROFESSORS

AI, MINGLI, Medicine
BAI, XINZHI, Medicine
BAO, XIUZENG, Pharmacy
BAO, YONGPING, Public Health
BI, WENSHU, Medicine
BI, ZHENGGANG, Medicine
CHEN, BINGQING, Public Health
CHEN, GENGXIN, Medicine
CHEN, LI, Public Health
CHEN, SHUXIANG, Medicine
CHEN, XIUJIE, Pharmacy
CHENG, DEQING, University Branch
CHENG, LIHA, Medicine
CHENG, ZHI, Basic Medical Sciences
CHI, ZIANG, Medicine
CUI, HAO, Medicine
CUI, HONGBIN, Public Health
CUI, LIANBIN, Medicine
CUI, SHI, Medicine
CUI, YUNPU, Medicine
DAI, HAIBIN, Medicine
DAI, QINSHUN, Medicine
DAI, ZE, University Branch
DU, XIUXHEN, Medicine
DU, ZHIMIN, Pharmacy
FAN, LIHUA, Public Health
FU, LU, Medicine
FU, SHIYING, Medicine
FU, SONGBIN, Basic Medical Sciences
GAO, GUANGMING, Dentistry
GAO, GUANGXIN, University Branch
GAO, RUIJU, Medicine
GAO, SHANLING, Medicine
GONG, LINGTAO, University Branch
GU, SUYI, Medicine
GUAN, JINGMING, Medicine
GUAN, YONGMEI, Medicine
GUAN, ZHENZHONG, Medicine
GUO, LUNSHU, University Branch
GUO, ZHENG, Bioinformatics
HAN, DE'EN, Medicine

HAN, DEWEN, University Branch
HAN, FENGPING, Medicine
HAN, MINGZI, Medicine
HAN, XIANGYANG, Medicine
HAO, LI, University Branch
HONG, FENGYANG, Medicine
HONG, WANQING, Medicine
HU, SHUANGJIU, Medicine
HU, XIAOCHEN, Medicine
HUANG, YONGLIN, Medicine
HUANG, ZHENGSONG, Medicine
JI, YUBIN, Pharmacy
JI, ZHUANZHEN, University Branch
JIA, GUODONG, Medicine
JIANG, GUIQIN, Medicine
JIANG, HONGCHI, Medicine
JIANG, LIJING, Medicine
JIANG, XUEHAI, Medicine
LI, BAIXIANG, Public Health
LI, BANQUAN, Medicine
LI, BAOJIE, Medicine
LI, BAOXIN, Pharmacy
LI, BIN, Medicine
LI, BO, Basic Medical Sciences
LI, CHANGXHUN, Medicine
LI, CHUNMING, Medicine
LI, HEYU, Medicine
LI, JIANFENG, Nursing
LI, JIXUE, Medicine
LI, KANG, Public Health
LI, PEILING, Medicine
LI, QIUJIE, Nursing
LI, SHULIN, Medicine
LI, WEIMIN, Medicine
LI, XIA, Bioinformatics
LI, XIA, Pharmacy
LI, XIAOYUN, Medicine
LI, XIULAN, Medicine
LI, YURONG, Basic Medical Sciences
LI, ZHIXU, Medicine
LI, ZUNYI, Medicine
LIN, XUESONG, University Branch
LIN, YIJIA, Medicine
LIU, BAOLIN, Public Health
LIU, BOSONG, Medicine
LIU, DEXIANG, University Branch
LIU, ENZHONG, Medicine
LIU, FENGJI, Medicine
LIU, FENGZHI, Pharmacy
LIU, HAITANG, Medicine
LIU, HONG, Dentistry
LIU, HONGYUAN, Public Health
LIU, JINJIE, University Branch
LIU, RUIHAI, Public Health
LIU, SHUDE, Medicine
LIU, TIEFU, Medicine
LIU, WENZHU, Medicine
LIU, XIANJUN, Medicine
LIU, YUFENG, Medicine
LIU, ZHICHENG, Public Health
LOU, GUIRONG, Medicine
LU, DAGUANG, Medicine
LU, LEI, Medicine
LU, MINGJUN, Public Health
MA, YINGJI, Medicine
MENG, FANCHAO, Medicine
MNG, HUANBIN, Medicine
QI, YOUCHENG, Medicine
QIAO, GUOFENG, Pharmacy
QIN, HUADONG, Medicine
QIU, FENGQIN, Medicine
QIU, ZHONGYI, Medicine
QU, RENHAI, Medicine
QU, XIUFEN, Medicine
QUAN, HUDE, Public Health
SANG, YIMIN, Medicine
SHENG, YUCHEN, Medicine
SHI, YUZHI, Medicine
SI, ZHUANG, Medicine
SONG, CHUNFANG, Medicine
SONG, CUIPING, Medicine
SONG, ZHIMIN, University Branch
SUN, AHIBO, Medicine
SUN, CHANGHAO, Public Health
SUN, GANG, University Branch
SUN, JIANPING, Pharmacy
SUN, KAOXIANG, Pharmacy
SUN, KEMIN, Medicine
SUN, XIANCHAO, Medicine
SUN, YUNQIAO, Medicine
TAN, TIEZHENG, Medicine
TAN, WENHUA, Medicine
TIAN, SULI, Medicine
WANG, BINYOU, Public Health
WANG, BOWEN, Medicine
WANG, CAIXIA, University Branch
WANG, CHUNXIANG, Medicine
WANG, FUJING, Medicine
WANG, GUIZHAO, Medicine
WANG, GUOQING, Medicine
WANG, HUIMIN, Medicine
WANG, JINGHUA, University Branch
WANG, JINGHUA, Medicine
WANG, JUNCHENG, Medicine
WANG, LI, University Branch
WANG, LING, Pharmacy
WANG, LINGSHAN, Medicine
WANG, MENGXUE, Medicine
WANG, MINGJUN, Medicine
WANG, NAIQIAN, Medicine
WANG, SHENGFA, Medicine
WANG, SHOUREN, Medicine
WANG, TAIHE, Medicine
WANG, XIAOFENG, Medicine
WANG, XIUFAN, Medicine
WANG, ZHIBANG, Medicine
WANG, ZHIGUO, Pharmacy
WEI, LINYU, Medicine
WU, DEQUAN, Medicine
WU, KUN, Public Health
WU, LIJIE, Public Health
WU, LINHUA, Pharmacy
WU, QUNHONG, Public Health
WU, YONGWEN, Medicine
XI, ZHENSHAN, Medicine
XNG, JIE, University Branch
XU, JUNRU, Medicine
XU, LINSHENG, Medicine
XU, XUGUANG, Medicine
YANG, BAOFENG, Pharmacy
YANG, FUMING, Medicine
YANG, SHIXHUN, Medicine
YANG, WEILIANG, Medicine
YANG, XUEWEI, Medicine
YAO, LI, Medicine
YE, YUANZHU, Medicine
YIN, HUIQING, Medicine
YIN, KESEN, University Branch
YIN, XIAOQIAN, Medicine
YU, BO, Medicine
YU, DANPING, Medicine
YU, JINGHAI, Pharmacy
YU, JINGYUAN, Medicine
YU, WEIGANG, Medicine
YU, WEIPING, Public Health
YU, XIUXIAN, University Branch
YU, ZHONGSHU, Medicine
YUAN, XIZHEN, University Branch
YUANL, FENG, Medicine
YUE, WU, Medicine
ZHAGN, SHUTAO, Medicine
ZHANG, BAOKU, Medicine
ZHANG, BIN, Dentistry
ZHANG, FENGMING, Basic Medical Sciences
ZHANG, JUN, University Branch
ZHANG, MINGWEN, Medicine
ZHANG, PENG, Medicine
ZHANG, QIFAN, Medicine
ZHANG, SHUQI, Basic Medical Sciences
ZHANG, TINGDONG, Medicine
ZHANG, XIANGLI, University Branch
ZHANG, XIAOXIAN, Medicine
ZHANG, XICHEN, University Branch
ZHANG, XINYING, Medicine
ZHANG, XIUQI, Medicine
ZHANG, XIYU, Medicine
ZHANG, YAN, Medicine
ZHANG, YINA, Medicine
ZHANG, YUCHENG, Medicine
ZHANG, YUCHUN, Medicine
ZHANG, ZHONGYI, Public Health
ZHAO, CHANGJI, Medicine
ZHAO, SHUZHEN, Medicine
ZHAO, YASHUANG, Public Health
ZHAO, ZHIHAI, Medicine
ZHONG, ZHENYU, Medicine
ZHOU, JIN, Medicine
ZHOU, WENXUE, Medicine
ZHOU, XIAOMING, Medicine
ZHOU, YUQOI, University Branch
ZHOU, ZHONGFANG, Medicine
ZHU, DALING, Pharmacy
ZHU, GUICHUN, Medicine
ZHU, QUAN, Medicine
ZHU, SHUYING, Medicine
ZHU, SIHE, Medicine
ZHU, XIUYING, Medicine
ZHU, YAN, Medicine

ATTACHED RESEARCH INSTITUTES

Centre for Endemic Disease Control: Dir YANG BAOFENG.

Heilongjiang Medical Science Institute: Dir JIN LIANHONG.

National Clinical Trial Research Centre for New Medicine (Cardiovascular Medicine): Dir YU BO.

National Science Research and Pedagogical Training Centre (Medicine and Pharmacology): Dir FU SONGBIN.

HARBIN NORMAL UNIVERSITY

1 Danan Rd, Liming District, Harbin 150080, Heilongjiang

Telephone: (451) 86376222
Internet: www.hrbnu.edu.cn

Founded 1951
Academic year: September to July

President: CHEN SHUTAO
Vice-Presidents: FU DAOBIN, FU JUNLONG, LU YUSUN, SUN FUGUANG, WANG ZHONGQIAO, WANG XUANZHANG
Librarian: GUO SHIMING

Library of 3,340,000 vols
Number of teachers: 3,695
Number of students: 31,835

Publications: *Continuing Education Research* (6 a year), *Heilongjiang Researches on Higher Education* (6 a year), *Natural Science Journal of Harbin Normal University* (6 a year), *Northern Forum* (6 a year)

DEANS

College of Arts: LU XUSUN
College of Computer Science and Mathematics: WANG YUWEN
College of Education Science and Technology: ZHAO HENIN
College of Life and Environment: ZHAO WENGE
College of Literature: GUO CONGLIN
College of Physics and Chemistry: LU SHUCHENG
College of Politics, Law and Economics Management: XU XIAOFENG
College of Sports Sciences: LIU ZHONGWU
Foreign Language Institute: JIANG TAO

PROFESSORS

CHEN, SHUTAO, Computer Science and Mathematics
DAI, BOQING, Physics and Chemistry
FENG, SUYUN, Literature
FU, DAOBIN, Literature
GAO, HUIMING, Arts
GE, YUNCHENG, Physics and Chemistry
GE, ZHIYI, Literature
GUO, CONGLIN, Literature
HUA, DEZUN, Life and Environment
LI, CHANGYU, Literature
LI, JILIN, Life and Environment
LU, YUSUN, Arts
LUO, ZHENYA, Literature
LU, SHUCHENG, Physics and Chemistry

SONG, WEN, Computer Science and Mathematics
SUN, MUTIAN, Literature
TAO, YABIN, Arts
TIAN, GUOWEI, Life and Environment
WANG, LISAN, Arts
WANG, TONGCHANG, Education Science and Technology
WANG, XUANZHANG, Physics and Chemistry
WANG, YUWEN, Computer Science and Mathematics
WANG, ZHONGQIAO, Literature
XU, GUOLIN, Physics and Chemistry
XU, HENGYONG, Physics and Chemistry
XU, XIANGLING, Life and Environment
XU, XIAOFENG, Literature
YU, LIJIE, Life and Environment
ZHANG, JINGCHI, Literature
ZHANG, JUNMING, Politics, Law and Economics Management
ZHANG, YONGZHENG, Computer Science and Mathematics
ZHAO, HENIN, Education Science and Technology
ZHAO, YUNLONG, Arts
ZHOU, JINXIAN, Literature

ATTACHED RESEARCH INSTITUTES

Adult Education College.

College of International Culture and Education: Dir ZHANG DAZHU.

Professional Technical College: Dir WANG FENGJUN.

Star College: Dir LIU SHUMING.

HARBIN UNIVERSITY OF SCIENCE AND TECHNOLOGY

57 Xuefu Rd, Nan Gang, Harbin 150080, Heilongjiang
Telephone: (451) 86390114
Internet: www.hrbust.edu.cn

Founded 1953
Academic year: September to July
President: ZHAO QI
Vice-Presidents: DU GUANGCUN, LI DAYONG, TENG CUNXIAN, WU JUNFENG, ZHAO HONG
Head of Graduate Department: ZHEN MINLI
Librarian: CHEN JIE
Library of 173,800 vols
Number of teachers: 2,379
Number of students: 19,907
Publications: *Electric Machines and Control* (4 a year), *Journal* (6 a year), *Science-Technology and Management* (6 a year)

DEANS

College of Applied Science: CUI YUNAN
College of Chemistry and Environmental Engineering: LIU BO
College of Computer and Control Science: QIAO PEILI
School of Economics and Management: XIU GUOYI
College of Electrical and Electronic Engineering: WEI XINLAO
College of International Culture Education: ZHAO DAWEI
School of Law: ZHANG YING
College of Material Science and Engineering: GUO ERJUN
School of Mechanical Engineering: SHAO JUNPENG
College of Observation Technology and Communications Engineering: YU XIAOYANG
Software College: LIU SHENGHUI
Foreign Language Institute: LUI LIQUN

PROFESSORS

CHEN, DEYUN, Computer and Control Science
CHEN, DONGYAN, Applied Science
CHEN, GUANGHAI, Applied Science
CHEN, RONGDUO, Economics and Management
CHEN, YUQUAN, Mechanical Engineering
CUI, YUNAN, Applied Science
DENG, CAIXIA, Applied Science
DU, DESHENG, Computer and Control Science
DU, KUNMEI, Electrical and Electronic Engineering
DUAN, TIEQUN, Mechanical Engineering
FAN, JINGYUN, Material Science and Engineering
FAN, YONG, Material Science and Engineering
GAO, ANBANG, Mechanical Engineering
GAO, CHANGYUAN, Economics and Management
GAO, ZHONGWEN, Computer and Control Science
GE, BAOJUN, Electrical and Electronic Engineering
GE, JIANGHUA, Mechanical Engineering
GUO, ERJUN, Material Science and Engineering
GUO, JIANYING, Observation Technology and Communications Engineering
HE, ZHONGXIAO, Computer and Control Science
HU, BAOXIA, Computer and Control Science
JI, DONGHAI, Applied Science
JI, ZHESHENG, Material Science and Engineering
JING, XU, Computer and Control Science
KONG, FANLIANG, Applied Science
LEI, QINGQUAN, Electrical and Electronic Engineering
LI, DAYONG, Material Science and Engineering
LI, DONGMEI, Applied Science
LI, FENGZHEN, Material Science and Engineering
LI, GECHENG, Computer and Control Science
LI, HONGXIA, Economics and Management
LI, LEI, Economics and Management
LI, QUANLI, Computer and Control Science
LI, WEILI, Electrical and Electronic Engineering
LI, YUMING, Chemistry and Envirnomental Engineering
LI, ZHENJIA, Mechanical Engineering
LI, ZHONGHUA, Electrical and Electronic Engineering
LIANG, JINGXI, Economics and Management
LIANG, YANPING, Electrical and Electronic Engineering
LIN, JIAQI, Applied Science
LIU, BO, Chemistry and Envirnomental Engineering
LIU, RUNTAO, Applied Science
LIU, SHENGHUI, Computer and Control Science
LIU, WEIJUN, Mechanical Engineering
LIU, WENLI, Electrical and Electronic Engineering
LIU, XIANLI, Mechanical Engineering
LIU, XINGJIA, Mechanical Engineering
LUO, XIAOGUANG, Economics and Management
MA, HONGFEI, Economics and Management
MA, HUAIJIAN, Observation Technology and Communications Engineering
MENG, DAWEI, Electrical and Electronic Engineering
PAN, ZHUANGYUAN, Applied Science
QI, LIANGQUN, Economics and Management
QIAO, PEILI, Computer and Control Science
REN, FUJUN, Mechanical Engineering
SHAO, JUNPENG, Mechanical Engineering
SHAO, TIEZHU, Economics and Management
SHI, LIANSHENG, Material Science and Engineering
SONG, JIASHENG, Economics and Management
SONG, RUNBIN, Material Science and Engineering
SUI, XIULING, Mechanical Engineering
SUN, FENGLIAN, Material Science and Engineering
SUN, LIJIONG, Computer and Control Science
SUN, MINGSONG, Computer and Control Science
SUN, QUANYING, Mechanical Engineering
SUN, XIAOJUN, Chemistry and Envirnomental Engineering
TAN, GUANGYU, Mechanical Engineering
TENG, CUNXIAN, Economics and Management
WAN, GUOQIN, Material Science and Engineering
WANG, HONGQI, Economics and Management
WANG, LIPING, Material Science and Engineering
WANG, MUKUN, Observation Technology and Communications Engineering
WANG, PEIDONG, Computer and Control Science
WANG, TONG, Mechanical Engineering
WANG, XUAN, Applied Science
WANG, XUDONG, Electrical and Electronic Engineering
WANG, YIJIE, Applied Science
WANG, YUDONG, Economics and Management
WEI, XINLAO, Electrical and Electronic Engineering
WEN, JIABIN, Electrical and Electronic Engineering
WU, HONGBO, Economics and Management
WU, JUNFENG, Computer and Control Science
WU, YUBIN, Material Science and Engineering
WU, ZHONGYANG, Computer and Control Science
XIAOXU, 0, Material Science and Engineering
XIU, GUOYI, Economics and Management
XU, LI, Mechanical Engineering
XU, XIAOCUN, Mechanical Engineering
YANG, JIAXIANG, Electrical and Electronic Engineering
YANG, MINGGUI, Mechanical Engineering
YIN, JINGHUA, Applied Science
YOU, BO, Mechanical Engineering
YU, HUILI, Mechanical Engineering
YU, LI, Economics and Management
YU, XIAOYANG, Observation Technology and Communications Engineering
YU, YANDONG, Material Science and Engineering
YUAN, JIANXIONG, Mechanical Engineering
ZHAI, LILI, Economics and Management
ZHANG, CUNXI, Electrical and Electronic Engineering
ZHANG, CUNYI, Mechanical Engineering
ZHANG, DECHENG, Economics and Management
ZHANG, GUOJIE, Economics and Management
ZHANG, JIAZHEN, Mechanical Engineering
ZHANG, LIYONG, Observation Technology and Communications Engineering
ZHANG, XIANYOU, Material Science and Engineering
ZHANG, XIAOHONG, Electrical and Electronic Engineering
ZHANG, YONGDE, Mechanical Engineering
ZHANG, YONGJUN, Mechanical Engineering
ZHANG, ZHONGMING, Mechanical Engineering
ZHAO, DAWEI, Economics and Management
ZHAO, HONG, Electrical and Electronic Engineering
ZHAO, XINLUO, Economics and Management
ZHEN, DIANCUN, Electrical and Electronic Engineering
ZHEN, MINLI, Mechanical Engineering

ATTACHED RESEARCH INSTITUTES

Adult Education College: Dir CHEN FENGLIN.

Institute of Science and Engineering: Dir CHANG YAPING.

HARBIN INSTITUTE OF TECHNOLOGY

92 West Dazhi St, Harbin 150001, Heilongjiang
Telephone: 6412114

Fax: 6221048
Internet: www.hit.edu.cn
Founded 1920
President: Prof. YANG SHIQIN
Vice-Presidents: LIU JIAQU, WANG SHUGUO, WANG ZUWEN, SHI GUANGJI, ZHANG DACHENG
Librarian: SHI HUILAI
Library of 1,000,000 vols
Number of teachers: 2,300
Number of students: 14,843 (incl. 2,652 postgraduates)
Publications: *Journal*, *Technology of Energy Conservation*, *Metal Science and Technology*, *Higher Engineering Education*, *Studying Computers*

DEANS

School of Astronautics: Prof. JIA SHILOU
School of Management: LI YIJUN
School of Energy Science and Engineering: Prof. WANG ZUWEN
School of Computer and Electrical Engineering: Prof. HONG WENXUE
School of Electric Mechanical Engineering: Prof. WANG SHUGUO
School of Materials Science and Engineering: Prof. ZHAO LIANCHENG
School of Science: Prof. GENG WANZHEN
School of Humanities and Social Sciences: Prof. JIANG ZHENHUA

HEBEI MEDICAL UNIVERSITY

361 Zhongshan East Rd, Shijiazhuang City, Hebei Province 050017
Telephone: (311) 6048177
Fax: (311) 6048177
E-mail: fad@hebmu.edu.cn
Internet: www.hebmu.edu.cn
Founded 1915
Academic year: September to July
President: WEN JINKUN
Vice-President: WANG YANTIAN
Vice-President: WANG RUNTIAN
Vice-President: WANG GENGXIN
Vice-President: DUAN HUIJUN
Vice-President: JI HAIJIN
Vice-President: ZHANG ZHANKUI
Head of Graduate School: CONG BIN
Librarian: MO ZHENYUN
Library of 541,000 vols
Number of teachers: 887
Number of students: 12,753
Publications: *Chinese Journal of Ultrasonography* (monthly), *Clinical Focus* (every 2 weeks), *Journal* (6 a year)

HEADS OF DEPARTMENTS

School of Basic Medicine: LI WENBIN
1st School of Clinical Medicine: WANG YANTIAN
2nd School of Clinical Medicine: CAI WENQING
3rd School of Clinical Medicine: ZHANG YINGZE
4th School of Clinical Medicine: WANG SHIJIE
School of Combined Traditional Chinese and Western Medicine: DU HUILAN
School of Nursing: ZHAO LING
School of Pharmaceutical Sciences: REN LEIMING
School of Public Health: LIU DIANWU
School of Stomatology: DONG FUSHENG
Adult Education College: YANG YAN
International Education College: FANG JIAYI
College of TCM: WANG YALI

HEBEI UNIVERSITY

1 Hezuo Rd, Baoding 071002, Heibei
Telephone: (312) 5079709
E-mail: hbu@mail.hbu.edu.cn
Internet: www.hbu.edu.cn
Founded 1921
Hebei Province control
Academic year: September to July
President: WANG HONGRUI
Vice-Presidents: HA MINGHU, LI SHUANGYIN, SUN HANWEN, SUN JINGYUAN, WEI SUI
Head of Graduate College: HA MINGHU
Librarian: LI ZHENGANG
Library of 3,170,000 vols
Number of teachers: 2,500
Number of students: 47,500
Publications: *Journal* (natural sciences, 6 a year), *Journal* (philosophy and social sciences, 6 a year)

DEANS

College of Arts: YANG WENHUI
College of Chemistry and Environment Science: MA FENGRU
College of Economics: GU LIUBAO
College of Education: HE GUOQIN
College of Electronic and Information Engineering: WANG PEIGUANG
College of Foreign Languages: LI ZUOWEN
College of Industry and Commerce: WANG HONGRUI
Faculty of Journalism & Communication: BAI GUI
College of Life Science: REN GUODONG
College of Literature: LI JINSHAN
College of Machinery and Civil Engineering: ZHANG JIANHUI
College of Management: SUN JIANFU
College of Mathematics and Computer Studies: WANG XIZHAO
College of Medicine: YANG GENGLIANG
College of Physics and Technology: HAN LI
College of Political Science and Law: LIU ZHIGANG
College of Quality and Technical Supervision: LI XIAOTING

PROFESSORS

BA, XINWU, Chemistry and Environmental Science
BAI, GUI, Journalism and Communication
BAI, SHUQIN, Political Science and Law
BI, WUQIN, Political Science and Law
BIAN, ZHAOLING, Management
CAI, HAIBO, Arts
CAO, MINGLUN, Foreign Languages
CAO, RU, Journalism and Communication
CAO, YUPING, Life Science
CHEN, JUNYING, Education
CHEN, SHUANGXIN, Arts
CHEN, ZHIGUO, Economics
CHENG, CHANGYU, Economics
CHENG, XINXUAN, Management
DING, JIHUI, Machinery and Civil Engineering
DING, XIAOZHENG, Journalism and Communication
DONG, LIFANG, Physics and Technology
DONG, ZHENGXIN, Economics
DU, HAO, Journalism and Communication
DU, YOUJUN, Journalism and Communication
FANG, BAOAN, Management
FANG, YOULIANG, Machinery and Civil Engineering
FENG, XIUQI, Education
FENG, YULONG, Life Science
FU, SONGTAO, Education
GAO, JUNGANG, Chemistry and Environmental Science
GAO, SHUJUN, Management
GU, LIUBAO, Economics
GU, XIAOHUA, Management
GU, ZHONGLIANG, Arts
GUO, BAOZENG, Electronics and Information Engineering
GUO, FULIANG, Literature
GUO, JIAN, Arts
GUO, JIAN, Industry and Commerce
GUO, SHIXIN, Economics
GUO, XUYUAN, Literature
HAN, CHENGWU, Literature
HAN, LI, Physics and Technology
HAN, PANGSHAN, Arts
HAN, PANSHAN, Literature
HAN, XIUJING, Economics
HE, GUOQIN, Education
HE, XUELI, Life Science
HE, ZHIPU, Arts
HOU, GUANYING, Journalism and Communication
HOU, YUHUA, Management
HU, NING, Arts
HU, YAN, Management
HUA, ZHUXIN, Industry and Commerce
HUANG, GENGZHUO, Arts
HUANG, PENGZHANG, Management
JIAN, MIN, Arts
JIANG, JIANYUN, Literature
JIANG, JIZHI, Life Science
JIANG, LIHUA, Economics
JIAO, GUOZHANG, Journalism and Communication
JIAO, MAOLIN, Literature
JIE, YONGJUN, Arts
KAN, ZHENRONG, Life Science
KANG, SHUSHENG, Economics
KANG, XIANJIANG, Life Science
KONG, LINGHONG, Political Science and Law
LI, FANGHUA, Electronics and Information Engineering
LI, GANSHUN, Economics
LI, GUOHUA, Literature
LI, HEPING, Political Science and Law
LI, HUARUI, Literature
LI, JINSHAN, Literature
LI, JINZHENG, Literature
LI, JITAI, Chemistry and Environmental Science
LI, LINJIE, Economics
LI, RENKAI, Literature
LI, SHU, Economics
LI, SHUANGJIE, Economics
LI, SHUQI, Machinery and Civil Engineering
LI, SUMIN, Education
LI, TONGSHUANG, Chemistry and Environmental Science
LI, WENCAI, Literature
LI, WENXIU, Machinery and Civil Engineering
LI, XIAOTING, Quality and Technical Supervision
LI, XIAOWEI, Physics and Technology
LI, YAHONG, Journalism and Communication
LI, YANAN, Journalism and Communication
LI, YANBIN, Arts
LI, ZUOWEN, Foreign Languages
LIANG, SUZHEN, Political Science and Law
LIAO, XIANGRU, Life Science
LIU, CUIYING, Management
LIU, HUIWEN, Journalism and Communication
LIU, JINZHONG, Literature
LIU, JINZHU, Arts
LIU, SIJIN, Literature
LIU, YONGRUI, Education
LIU, YUKAI, Literature
LIU, ZHIGANG, Political Science and Law
LIU, ZHIQIANG, Physics and Technology
LIU, ZHIQIANG, Electronics and Information Engineering
LU, HONGPING, Economics
LU, MINGFANG, Physics and Technology
LU, ZIZHENG, Journalism and Communication
MA, CHENGLIAN, Journalism and Communication
MA, YANLING, Management
MAO, ZHUOLIANG, Foreign Languages
MEI, BAOSHU, Arts
MENG, SHIEN, Management
PEI, GUIFEN, Economics
PENG, YINGCAI, Physics and Technology
PENG, YINGCAI, Electronics and Information Engineering
QI, YI, Arts

QIAO, YUNXIA, Journalism and Communication
REN, GUODONG, Life Science
RONG, XINFANG, Foreign Languages
SONG, DENGYUAN, Electronics and Information Engineering
SONG, RUITIAN, Physics and Technology
SONG, YAOWU, Education
SUN, HANWEN, Chemistry and Environmental Science
SUN, SHENGCUN, Journalism and Communication
SUN, ZHIZHONG, Economics
TAO, DAN, Journalism and Communication
TIAN, JIANMING, Literature
TIAN, JUNFENG, Mathematics and Computer Science
WANG, BAOXING, Education
WANG, HONGRUI, Electronics and Information Engineering
WANG, HONGRUI, Industry and Commerce
WANG, JINYING, Economics
WANG, JUNJIE, Journalism and Communication
WANG, JUNLI, Life Science
WANG, PEIGUANG, Electronics and Information Engineering
WANG, QIN, Economics
WANG, SHUHUI, Management
WANG, WENLI, Electronics and Information Engineering
WANG, XIZHAO, Mathematics and Computer Science
WANG, YANLING, Journalism and Communication
WANG, YINSHUN, Physics and Technology
WANG, ZHENCHAO, Electronics and Information Engineering
WU, GENGZHEN, Journalism and Communication
WU, HONGCHENG, Education
WU, YAQING, Economics
WU, YONGZHEN, Management
XIE, CHANGFA, Education
XIONG, RENWANG, Arts
XU, JINGZHI, Physics and Technology
XU, MING, Journalism and Communication
XUE, KEMIU, Literature
YANG, BAOZHONG, Literature
YANG, GENGLIANG, Chemistry and Environment Science
YANG, GENGLIANG, Medicine
YANG, WENHUI, Arts
YANG, XIUGUO, Journalism and Communication
YANG, XUEXIN, Industry and Commerce
YAO, ZIHUA, Chemistry and Environmental Science
ZHANG, DAOCHUAN, Life Science
ZHANG, DEQIANG, Chemistry and Environmental Science
ZHANG, JIANHUI, Machinery and Civil Engineering
ZHANG, LIPING, Life Science
ZHANG, LIXIN, Education
ZHANG, RISHENG, Education
ZHANG, SHUANGCAI, Management
ZHANG, WEI, Journalism and Communication
ZHANG, WENCHUAN, Arts
ZHANG, YANJING, Political Science and Law
ZHANG, YUKE, Economics
ZHAO, YANYAN, Medicine
ZHEN, SHUQING, Political Science and Law
ZHENG, YUNLONG, Physics and Technology
ZHENG, ZHITING, Literature
ZHU, BAOCHENG, Life Science
ZHU, MINGSHENG, Life Science

ATTACHED RESEARCH INSTITUTES

Adult Education College: Dir KANG, HEPING.

Centre for the History of Song: Dir JIANG, XIDONG.

HEBEI UNIVERSITY OF ECONOMICS AND TRADE

Wu Qi Rd, Shijiazhuang, Hebei Province 050061
Telephone: (311) 6039189
Fax: (311) 6039123
Internet: www.heuet.edu.cn

Founded 1982

President: YU RENGANG
Vice-Presidents: CUI YUANMIN, HU DONGYANG, YAO JINGGUAN, MAZHI ZHONG, WU SHENGCHEN, HU BAOZHONG
Librarian: MA KE

Library of 250,000 vols
Number of teachers: 900
Number of students: 10,000
Publication: *Economics and Management*

HEADS OF DEPARTMENTS

Industrial Economic Management: LU CHANGFU
Agricultural Economic Management: QIN WENBO
Planning and Statistical Economic Management: LIU YAOHUA
Financial and Accounting Management: FAN CHANGYING
Labour Economics and Management: HAO BING
Political Work in Business: LI SHUZENG
Economics and Trade: YIE JIANFENG

HEBEI NORMAL UNIVERSITY

265 Huadong Rd, Shijiazhuang 030002, Hebei
Internet: www.hebtu.edu.cn

Founded 1902

Academic year: September to July

President: SU BAORONG
Vice-Presidents: JIANG CHUNLAN, LI YOUCHENG, LU JUNHENG, WANG CHANGHUA, ZHEN SHIJUN
Librarian: JIAO ZHILAN

Number of teachers: 3,438
Number of students: 36,185
Publication: *Journal* (4 a year)

DEANS

College of Education Science: LU ZHONGYI
College of Foreign Languages: PAN BINXIN
College of Law and Political Science: ZHANG JILIANG
College of Life Science: DUANG XIANGLIN
College of Literature: XING JILIANG
College of Mathematics and Information: DENG MINGLI
College of Physics: LIU JIANJUN
College of Resources and the Environment: WANG WEI

PROFESSORS

BAI, ZIMING, Foreign Languages
CHANG, CONGQIAN, Foreign Languages
CHEN, CHAO, Literature
CHEN, HUI, Literature
CHENG, RUZHEN, Maths and Information
CUI, JIYIN, Literature
CUI, ZHIYUAN, Literature
DENG, MINGLI, Mathematics and Information
DI, ZHAOYING, Mathematics and Information
DING, REN, Mathematics and Information
DONG, JUNMIN, Foreign Languages
DU, JIANZHENG, Education Science
DUAN, XIAOYING, Foreign Languages
DUAN, ZHEREN, Foreign Languages
FAN, SHUCHENG, Law and Political Science
GAO, SHUNSHENG, Mathematics and Information
GAO, SUOGANG, Mathematics and Information
GAO, TING, Mathematics and Information
GAO, XINFA, Resouces and Environment Science
GAO, YUANXIANG, Resouces and Environment Science
GAO, ZHIHUAI, Foreign Languages
GE, JINGFENG, Resouces and Environment Science
GU, ZHONGQUAN, Foreign Languages
GUI, DINGKANG, Foreign Languages
GUO, BAOLIANG, Literature
GUO, QUNYING, Foreign Languages
HE, ANBAO, Foreign Languages
HE, LIANFA, Mathematics and Information
HU, WENLIANG, Resouces and Environment Science
HU, YINGTONG, Foreign Languages
HUANG, HONGQUAN, Foreign Languages
HUANG, HONGXU, Foreign Languages
HUANG, HUAFANG, Resouces and Environment Science
JIANG, CHUNLAN, Mathematics and Information
KANG, QINDE, Mathematics and Information
LEI, JIANGUO, Mathematics and Information
LI, SHIJU, Law and Political Science
LI, SUO, Literature
LI, TIANGUI, Law and Political Science
LI, XILONG, Literature
LI, YANNIAN, Literature
LI, ZHENGSHUAN, Foreign Languages
LIANG, YI, Foreign Languages
LIANG, ZHIHE, Mathematics and Information
LIE, WUJUN, Mathematics and Information
LIU, HONG, Education Science
LIU, HUANQUN, Foreign Languages
LIU, MING, Education Science
LIU, SHITIAN, Law and Political Science
LIU, YAN, Resouces and Environment Science
LIU, ZHONGMING, Law and Political Science
LU, ZHONGYI, Education Science
LU, ZI, Resouces and Environment Science
MA, HENGJUN, Literature
MA, RENHUI, Resouces and Environment Science
MA, YUN, Literature
MENG, GUOHUA, Foreign Languages
MI, JUSHENG, Mathematics and Information
NAN, YUESHENG, Resouces and Environment Science
PAN, BINXIN, Foreign Languages
QIAN, JINPING, Resouces and Environment Science
QIAO, YUYING, Mathematics and Information
SHI, GUOXING, Education Science
SHI, JINGXIU, Literature
SU, BAORONG, Literature
TANG, GUOZENG, Law and Political Science
TIAN, XIUYUN, Law and Political Science
WANG, CHANGHUA, Literature
WANG, DELIN, Education Science
WANG, FENGMIN, Law and Political Science
WANG, FUISHENG, Foreign Languages
WANG, JIANXUN, Foreign Languages
WANG, WEI, Resouces and Environment Science
WANG, XIN, Education Science
WANG, YANYING, Mathematics and Information
WANG, ZHENCHANG, Foreign Languages
WU, WEIREN, Foreign Languages
WU, XIUHUA, Literature
WU, ZHENGDE, Mathematics and Information
XIAO, GUIQING, Law and Political Science
XING, JIANCHANG, Literature
XU, JIANPING, Literature
XU, QINGHAI, Resouces and Environment Science
YAN, KELE, Education Science
YANG, CHUNHONG, Mathematics and Information
YANG, DONG, Literature
YANG, TONGYONG, Literature
YI, SHENGLEI, Foreign Languages
YI, WEI, Foreign Languages
ZHAI, HONGCHANG, Education Science

ZHAN, YUANJIE, Resouces and Environment Science
ZHANG, CHENGZONG, Resouces and Environment Science
ZHANG, GUOYING, Foreign Languages
ZHANG, JI, Law and Political Science
ZHANG, JILIANG, Law and Political Science
ZHANG, JUNCAI, Literature
ZHANG, JUNHAI, Resouces and Environment Science
ZHANG, WENXIANG, Law and Political Science
ZHANG, YIWEN, Resouces and Environment Science
ZHANG, YOUHUI, Mathematics and Information
ZHANG, ZHENGGUO, Mathematics and Information
ZHANG, ZILONG, Mathematics and Information
ZHENG, ZHENFENG, Literature
ZHUANG, BIAO, Literature

ATTACHED RESEARCH INSTITUTES

Professional Technical School: Dir DIAO ZHEJUN.

HEFEI UNIVERSITY OF TECHNOLOGY

59 Tunxi Rd, Hefei, Anhui Province 230009
Telephone: (551) 4655210
Fax: (551) 4651517
Internet: www.hfut.edu.cn
Founded 1945
President: CHEN XINZHAO
Vice-Presidents: XU HUIPENG, WANG DEZE, TANG JIAN, LIU GUANGFU, ZHENG ZHIXIANG
Registrar: ZHOU XU
Librarian: SUN XUANYIN
Number of teachers: 4,513
Number of students: 18,216
Publications: *Journal*, *Teaching and Study of Industrial Automation*, *Engineering Mathematics*, *Forecasting*, *Techniques Abroad*, *Tribology Abroad*
Fifteen departments.

HEILONGJIANG UNIVERSITY OF CHINESE MEDICINE

24 Dongli Section He Ping Rd, Harbin 150040, Heilongjiang
Telephone: (451) 82118254
Fax: (451) 82193031
Internet: www.hljucm.net
Founded 1959
Academic year: September to July
President: KUANG HAIXUE
Vice-Presidents: CHENG WEI, LI BINGZHI, LI JINGXIAO, WANG XIJUN
Head of Graduate Department: NING XIE
Librarian: YOU YANJUN
Number of teachers: 370
Number of students: 5,002 (4,817 full-time, 185 part-time)
Publications: *Acts of Chinese Medicine and Pharmacology* (6 a year), *Information on Traditional Chinese Medicine* (6 a year), *Journal of Clinical Acupuncture and Moxibustion* (monthly)

DEANS

School of Basic Medical Sciences: LI YI
School of Human Sciences: TONG ZILIN
School of Pharmacy: LI YONGJI
First School of Medicine: TIAN ZHENKUN
Second School of Medicine: SUN ZHONGREN

PROFESSORS

AN, LIWEN, Medicine
CHEN, HONGBIN, Basic Medical Sciences
CHENG, WEIPING, Medicine
DAI, TIECHENG, Medicine
DONG, QINGPING, Medicine
DU, XIAOWEI, Pharmacy
DUAN, FUJIN, Basic Medical Sciences
GAO, QUANGUO, Basic Medical Sciences
GONG, ZHANYUE, Medicine
GU, JIALE, Medicine
HAN, BO, Medicine
HOU, LIHUI, Medicine
HUI, XIULI, Medicine
JIA, GUIZHI, Pharmacy
JIANG, DEYOU, Basic Medical Sciences
JIN, SHUYING, Basic Medical Sciences
KANG, GUANGSHENG, Basic Medical Sciences
KUANG, HAIXUE, Pharmacy
LI, JINGXIA, Medicine
LI, LINGGEN, Medicine
LI, QIUHONG, Pharmacy
LI, TINGLI, Pharmacy
LI, YADONG, Basic Medical Sciences
LI, YAN, Medicine
LI, YANBING, Pharmacy
LI, YI, Basic Medical Sciences
LI, YONGJI, Pharmacy
LIU, HANDE, Human Sciences
LIU, HUASHENG, Basic Medical Sciences
LIU, JIANQIU, Medicine
LIU, JILI, Human Sciences
LIU, YUANZHANG, Medicine
LU, BINGWEN, Basic Medical Sciences
LUO, HONGSHI, Medicine
MA, YINGLI, Pharmacy
MENG, RI, Pharmacy
NIE, YUNAHENG, Medicine
QU, JIE, Human Sciences
QUAN, HONG, Pharmacy
SONG, LIQUN, Medicine
SU, LIANJIE, Pharmacy
SU, YUNMING, Basic Medical Sciences
SUN, HUI, Pharmacy
SUN, WEIZHENG, Medicine
SUN, ZHONGREN, Medicine
TIAN, ZHENKUN, Pharmacy
TIAN, ZHENKUN, Medicine
TONG, ZILIN, Human Sciences
WANG, DEMIN, Medicine
WANG, DONG, Pharmacy
WANG, FEI, Basic Medical Sciences
WANG, GANG, Medicine
WANG, HEPING, Pharmacy
WANG, JIANMING, Pharmacy
WANG, LI, Basic Medical Sciences
WANG, TIECE, Basic Medical Sciences
WANG, XIAXIAN, Basic Medical Sciences
WANG, XIJUN, Pharmacy
WANG, XING, Medicine
WANG, XUEHUA, Basic Medical Sciences
WANG, YUMEI, Medicine
WANG, YUXI, Medicine
WU, BOYAN, Basic Medical Sciences
XIE, JINGRI, Medicine
YAN, JING, Pharmacy
YU, JIABIN, Pharmacy
YU, XIAOHONG, Basic Medical Sciences
ZHANG, FULI, Basic Medical Sciences
ZHANG, YOUTANG, Basic Medical Sciences
ZHANG, ZHIMIN, Basic Medical Sciences
ZHAO, WENJING, Basic Medical Sciences
ZHOU, DECHEN, Basic Medical Sciences
ZHOU, LING, Medicine
ZHOU, MIN, Basic Medical Sciences
ZHOU, WI, Medicine
ZHOU, YABIN, Medicine
ZHU, YONGZHI, Medicine
ZHU, ZHIZHEN, Basic Medical Sciences

HENAN COLLEGE OF TRADITIONAL CHINESE MEDICINE

1 Jin-Shui Rd, Zhengzhou 450008, Henan
Telephone: and fax (371) 65962930
E-mail: haiwai@hactcm.edu.cn
Internet: www.henantcm.net
Founded 1958
State Control
Language of instruction: Chinese, English
Academic year: September to July
President: Prof. PENG BO
Vice-President: Prof. LI JIANSHENG
Librarian: LAI QIANKAI
Library of 800,000 vols
Number of teachers: 2,421
Number of students: 10,000
Publications: *Henan Traditional Chinese Medicine* (monthly), *Journal* (every 2 months)

HEADS OF DEPARTMENTS

Acupuncture and Moxibustion: Prof. LIN ZHANGPU
Traditional Chinese Medicine (TCM): Prof. FAN WEIHONG
Traditional Materia Medica (TMM): Prof. MIAO MINSAN

PROFESSORS

CAI, F. Y., TCM
CHEN, G. Z., Philosophy
CHEN, R. F., Internal Medicine
DONG, Y. S., Acupuncture
FENG, M. Q., TCM
GAO, T. S., TCM
HOU, S. L., TMM
JI, C. R., TMM
LI, X. W., TCM
LI, Y. L., Paediatrics
LI, Z. H., TCM
LI, Z. S., Internal Medicine
LOU, D. F., TCM Traumatology
LU, S. C., Qigong
MA, Z. H., TCM
SHANG, C. C., TCM
SHAO, J. M., Acupuncture
SHI, G. Q., TCM
SHUN, L. H., Acupuncture
SUN, C. Q., Physiology
SUN, H. B., Parasitology
SUN, J. Z., Internal Medicine
TANG, S., TCM
WANG, A. B., TCM History
WANG, R. K., Diagnostics
WANG, Y. M., Pharmaco-Chemistry
YANG, L. Y., Anatomy
YANG, Y. S., TMM
ZHANG, G. Q., TMM
ZHENG, J. M., TCM Paediatrics
ZHAO, M. Q., TCM
ZHOU, W. C., TCM

HENAN UNIVERSITY

Ming Lun Rd, Kaifeng 475001, Henan
Internet: www.henu.edu.cn
Founded 1912
Academic year: September to July
President: GUAN AIHE
Vice-Presidents: GUO TIANBANG, HUANG YABIN, LU KEPING, SHI QUANSHENG, WANG FAZENG, ZHAO GUOXIANG
Librarian: LI JINGWEN
Number of teachers: 3,600
Number of students: 240,000
Publications: *Chinese Quarterly Journal of Mathematics*, *Journal* (6 a year), *Journal of Henan University Chemical Research* (4 a year), *Quarterly Journal of Pure and Applied Mathematics*

DEANS

Faculty of History and Culture: ZHANG QIANHONG
College of Arts: ZHAO WEIMING
College of Civil Engineering: BAO PENG
College of Communication and Journalism: LI JIANWEI
College of Economics: DI MINGZAI
College of Environmental Planning: QIN YAOCHEN
College of Foreign Languages: ZHANG KEDING
College of Life Science: SONG CHUNPENG

College of Medicine: MA YUANFANG
School of Business Administration: WEI CHENGLONG
School of Chemistry Engineering: CUI YUANCHENG
School of Computer and Information Engineering: LIU XIANSHENG
School of Mathematics and Information Science: LI QISHENG
School of Physics and Information Optoelectronics: ZHANG WEIFENG

PROFESSORS

CHEN, CHANGYUAN, History and Culture
CHEN, JIAHAI, Arts
CHEN, SHOUXIN, Mathematics and Information Science
CHENG, MINGSHENG, History and Culture
DI, MINGZHAI, Economics
DING, SHENGYAN, Life Science
DING, SHENGYAN, Environmental Planning
DONG, FACAI, Life Science
GAO, HAILIN, History and Culture
GAO, JIANGUO, Economics
GAO, JIANHUA, Environmental Planning
GONG, LIUZHU, History and Culture
GU, YUZONG, Physics and Information Optoelectronics
HOU, XUN, Physics and Information Optoelectronics
HU, CHANGLIU, Mathematics and Information Science
HU, CONGE, Mathematics and Information Science
HU, YUXIN, Life Science
HUANG, YABIN, Physics and Information Optoelectronics
JIA, XINGQIN, Mathematics and Information Science
JIA, YUYING, History and Culture
JU, QINGLIN, Arts
LI, CHENGDE, History and Culture
LI, GUANGYI, History and Culture
LI, GUOQIANG, Mathematics and Information Science
LI, JIANWEI, Communication and Journalism
LI, JIE, Business Administration
LI, MING, History and Culture
LI, QISHENG, Mathematics and Information Science
LI, RUI, Mathematics and Information Science
LI, SUOPING, Life Science
LI, YONGWEN, Environmental Planning
LI, YUJIE, History and Culture
LI, ZHENHONG, History and Culture
LIN, JIAKUN, History and Culture
LIU, BINSHAN, Foreign Languages
LIU, HONG, Arts
LIU, JIANZHONG, Business Administration
LIU, KUNTAI, History and Culture
LU, ZHENGUANG, Communication and Journalism
MA, JIANHUA, Environmental Planning
MA, LING, Arts
MA, XIAOQUAN, History and Culture
MAO, HAITAO, Physics and Information Optoelectronics
MIAO, CHANGHONG, Environmental Planning
MIAO, CHENG, Life Science
MIAO, SHUMEI, History and Culture
MO, YUJUN, Physics and Information Optoelectronics
NIU, JIANQIANG, History and Culture
OU, ZHENGWEN, History and Culture
QI, LING, Economics
QIAN, HUAISUI, Environmental Planning
QIN, MINGZHOU, Environmental Planning
QIN, YAOZHEN, Environmental Planning
SANG, FUDE, Life Science
SHAN, LUN, Life Science
SONG, CHUNPENG, Life Science
SONG, YINGLI, Communication and Journalism
SU, KEWU, Economics
SUN, QIULIN, Environmental Planning
TAN, CHENGLIN, Environmental Planning
TANG, GUIQIN, Arts
WAN, SONGYU, History and Culture
WANG, CHANGSHUN, Physics and Information Optoelectronics
WANG, CHUMING, Economics
WANG, FAZHENG, Environmental Planning
WANG, JILIN, History and Culture
WANG, JINGYE, Communication and Journalism
WANG, JINXIAN, Business Administration
WANG, XINGYU, Business Administration
WANG, YANFA, Arts
WANG, ZHANGUO, Physics and Information Optoelectronics
WANG, ZHENDUO, Communication and Journalism
WEI, CHENGLONG, Economics
WEI, QIANZHI, History and Culture
WENG, YOUWEI, History and Culture
WU, TAO, History and Culture
WU, XUELI, Foreign Languages
XU, XINGYA, Economics
YAN, ZHAOXIANG, History and Culture
YANG, HAIJUN, Communication and Journalism
YANG, XUEZHI, Mathematics and Information Science
YAO, BOHUA, Mathematics and Information Science
YAO, YINGTING, History and Culture
YI, GUOSHENG, Physics and Information Optoelectronics
YI, QIXIANG, History and Culture
YU, BAOLONG, Physics and Information Optoelectronics
YU, JINFU, Economics
ZHANG, DEZONG, History and Culture
ZHANG, JIATAI, History and Culture
ZHANG, JIN, Foreign Languages
ZHANG, KUN, Economics
ZHANG, MINGLIANG, Mathematics and Information Science
ZHANG, QIANHONG, History and Culture
ZHANG, QIUZHOU, History and Culture
ZHANG, RUFA, Communication and Journalism
ZHANG, TAIHAI, Business Administration
ZHANG, TIANDING, Communication and Journalism
ZHANG, WEIFENG, Physics and Information Optoelectronics
ZHANG, XINGMAO, Economics
ZHANG, XIUYING, Business Administration
ZHANG, ZHONGLIANG, Communication and Journalism
ZHANG, ZHONGSUO, Physics and Information Optoelectronics
ZHAO, BINDONG, Environmental Planning
ZHAO, BUYUN, History and Culture
ZHAO, JIANGUO, Communication and Journalism
ZHAO, WEIMING, Arts
ZHAO, ZHENQIAN, Arts
ZHAO, ZHIFA, Economics
ZHENG, HUISHENG, History and Culture
ZHOU, BAOZHU, History and Culture
ZHU, SHAOHOU, History and Culture

ATTACHED RESEARCH INSTITUTES

Adult Education College: Dir JIAO FENG.

Key Research Institute of Yellow River Civilization and Sustainable Development: Dir LI XIAOJIAN.

Laboratory of Plant Stress Biology: Dir SUN DAYE.

Laboratory for Special Functional Materials: Dir ZHANG ZHIJUN.

HOHAI UNIVERSITY

1 Xikang Rd, Nanjing 210098
Telephone: (25) 3323777
Fax: (25) 3315375
Internet: www.hhu.edu.cn

Founded 1915 (fmrly East China Technical Univ. of Water Resources), name changed 1985
State control
Languages of instruction: Chinese, English
Academic year: September to July

President: Prof. JIANG HONGDAO
Vice-Presidents: Prof. LIU XINREN, Prof. JIN ZHONGQING, Prof. ZHANG CHANG
Librarian: DONG TINGSONG

Number of teachers: 1,343
Number of students: 8,000

Publications: *Journal, Advances in the Science and Technology of Water Resources, Economics of Water Resources, Water Resources Protection, Journal of Higher Education*

DEANS

College of Civil Engineering: Prof. ZHUO JIASHOU
College of Water Resources and Environment: Prof. WANG HUIMIN
College of Harbour, Waterway and Coastal Engineering: Prof. ZHANG CHANGKUAN
College of Water Conservancy and Hydropower Engineering: Prof. SUO LISHENG
College of Electrical Engineering: Prof. YANG JINTANG
College of Mechanical and Electrical Engineering: Prof. JIN YAHE
College of Computer and Information Engineering: Assoc. Prof. ZHU YAOLONG
College of International Industry and Commerce: Assoc. Prof. ZHANG YANG
College of Technical Economics: Prof. ZHENG CHUIYONG

HUAQIAO UNIVERSITY

Quanzhou 362011, Fujian
Telephone: (595) 2693630
Fax: (595) 2681940
E-mail: wsc@hqu.edu.cn
Internet: www.hqu.edu.cn

Founded 1960
State control
Academic year: starts September

President: Prof. WU CHENGYE
Vice-Presidents: Prof. GUO HENGQUN, Assoc. Prof. GUAN YIFAN, Assoc. Prof. LI JIMIN
Registrar: Prof. HONG SHANGREN
Librarian: Prof. ZHANG WEIBIN

Library of 775,449 vols, 16,235 periodicals
Number of teachers: 542 (full-time)
Number of students: 12,000

Publications: *Journal of Huaqiao University* (Natural Science and Social Science editions, 4 a year, in Chinese), *Research in Higher Education by Overseas Chinese* (2 a year, in Chinese)

DEANS

College of Teaching Chinese as a Foreign Language: Assoc. Prof. LI HONG
College of Foreign Languages: Assoc. Prof. WANG HUAIHUI
College of Economic Management: Prof. YE MINGQIANG
College of Information Science and Engineering: Prof. GUO HENGQUN
College of Electromechanical Engineering and Automation: Prof. XU XIPENG
College of Materials Science and Engineering: Prof. WU JIHUAI
Fujian Conservatory of Music: Prof. CAI JIKUN

HEADS OF DEPARTMENTS

Civil Engineering: Prof. WANG QUANFENG
Architecture: Prof. FANG YONG
Chinese Culture: Prof. WANG JIANSHE
Fine Arts: Assoc. Prof. SUN DEMING
Law: Prof. ZOU LIGANG

Mathematics: Prof. HUANG XINZHONG

ATTACHED INSTITUTES

Institute of Overseas Chinese Studies: Dir Assoc. Resident Fellow CAI ZHENXIANG.

Institute of Environmental Protection: Dir Resident Fellow YANG YUJIE.

Institute of Taiwanese Economy: Dir Prof. WU CHENGYE.

Institute of Stone-machining: Dir Assoc. Prof. XU XIPENG.

HUAZHONG AGRICULTURAL UNIVERSITY

Shizhishan, Wuhan 430070, Hubei
Telephone: (27) 87282026
Fax: (27) 87396057
E-mail: fao@mail.hzau.edu.cn/en.htm
Internet: www.hzau.edu.cn

Founded 1898, present name 1985
State control
Languages of instruction: Chinese, English
Academic year: September to July
President: ZHANG DUANPIN
Vice-Presidents: LI GUIFANG, WANG CHUANXIN, LI MINGJIA, LIU GUIYOU, CHEN HUANCHUN, XIE CONGHUA, GAO CHI
Librarian: WAN JIQIN
Library of 620,000 vols
Number of teachers: 2,215
Number of students: 15,000
Publication: *Journal* (quarterly)

DEANS

College of Adult Education: ZHANG DUANPIN
College of Animal Husbandry and Veterinary Science: BI DINGREN
College of Arts and Humanities and Social Science: LI CHONGGUANG
College of Basic Sciences: CHEN CHANGSHUI
College of Economics and Trade: WANG YAPENG
College of Engineering and Technology: ZHANG YANLIN
College of the Fishing Industry: XIE CONGXIN
College of Food Science and Technology: PAN SIYI
College of Horticulture and Forestry Science: BAO MANZHU
College of Land Management: WANG YAPENG
College of Life Sciences and Technology: ZHANG QIFA
College of Plant Science and Technology: ZHANG XIANLONG
College of Resources and Environment: CAI CHONGFA

HUAZHONG UNIVERSITY OF SCIENCE AND TECHNOLOGY

1037 Luoyu Rd, Wuhan 430074, Hubei
Telephone: (27) 87542157
Fax: (27) 87547063
E-mail: fao@hust.edu.cn
Internet: www.hust.edu.cn

Founded 1953
Academic year: September to July
President: Prof. FAN MINGWU
Vice-Presidents: Prof. HUANG GUANGYING, Prof. CAO SHUQIN, Prof. LIU XIANJUN, Prof. FENG XIANGDONG, Prof. DING LIEYUN, Prof. FENG YOUMEI, Prof. WANG CHENG, Prof. DING HANCHU, Prof. XIANG JIZHOU, Prof. LI PEIGEN
Librarian: Assoc. Prof. WU JINWEI
Library of 2,070,000 vols, 550,000 vols of periodicals in Chinese and foreign languages
Number of teachers: 4,000
Number of students: 50,000
Publications: *HUST Journal* (in separate natural sciences, social sciences and medical sciences editions), *New Architecture, Applied Mathematics, Hydroelectric Energy, Journal of Solid State Mechanics, Journal of Higher Education, Linguistics Study, Research in Higher Education of Engineering, Foreign Medicine and Molecular Biology, Clinic Emergency, Gastroenterology in Combined Traditional Chinese Medicine and Western Medicine, China's Organic Chemistry and Cellular Chemistry, Medicine and Society, Chinese Medicine Digest* (detection and clinical), *Radiant Diagnosis* (Chinese medical digest), *Foreign Medicine* (social medicine), *Practice of Radiology, Sino–German Tumour Clinic, Internal Emergency, Clinical Urology, Clinical Cardiology, Clinical Otolaryngology, Clinical Haematology, Clinical Gastroenterology, Nursing*

DEANS

School of Humanities: Prof. ZHANG SHUGUANG
School of Education: Prof. ZHANG YINGQIANG
School of Law: Prof. LUO YUZHONG
School of Public Administration: Prof. XIA SHUZHANG
School of Management: Prof. ZHANG JINLONG
School of Economics: Prof. XU CHANGSHENG
School of Journalism and Information Communication: Prof. WU TINGJUN
School of Mechanical Science and Engineering: Prof. SHAO XINYU
School of Materials Science and Engineering: Prof. LI DEQUN
School of Energy and Power Engineering: Prof. LIU WEI
School of Electrical and Electronics Engineering: Prof. GU CHENGLIN
School of Hydropower and Information Engineering: Prof. WU ZHONGRU
School of Traffic Science and Engineering: Prof. ZHAO YAO
School of Life Science and Technology: Prof. LUO QINGMING
School of Architecture and Urban Planning: Prof. YUAN PEIHUANG
School of Civil Engineering and Mechanics: Prof. CHEN CHUANYAO
School of Computer Science and Technology: Prof. LU ZHENGDIAN
School of Software Engineering: Prof. CHEN CHUANBO
School of Information Technology and Engineering: Prof. HUANG DEXIU
School of Environmental Science and Engineering: Prof. SHEN YUNFENG
School of Science: Prof. YE ZHAOHUI
Tongji Medical School: Prof. XIANG JIZHOU

HEADS OF DEPARTMENTS

Department of Sociology: Prof. LEI HONG
Department of Foreign Languages: Prof. FAN WEIWEI
Department of Physical Education: Prof. XIE BIN

HUBEI UNIVERSITY

11 Xueyuan Rd, Wuchang, Wuhan 430062, Hubei
Telephone: (27) 88663896
E-mail: xiaoban@hubu.edu.cn
Internet: www.hubu.edu.cn

Founded 1931
Hubei Province control
Academic year: September to July
President: WU CHUANXI
Vice-Presidents: GU HAOSHUANG, LI JINHE, YAN MINGMING, ZHOU JIMING
Librarian: ZHANG WEIHUA
Library of 1,520,000 vols
Number of teachers: 1,000
Number of students: 12,700
Publications: *Acta Arachnologica Sinica* (2 a year), *Chinese Journal of Colloids and Polymers* (4 a year), *Journal* (4 a year), *Journal of the Adult Education College of Hubei University* (6 a year)

DEANS

Faculty of Arts: LUN ZUNMING
School of Business: LIU JIANPING
Faculty of Chemistry and Materials Science: WANG SHIMIN
Faculty of Education: JIN GUOPING
Faculty of Foreign Studies: XU QIUMEI
Faculty of History and Culture: GUO YING
School of Life Science: CHEN JIAN
Faculty of Philosophy: DAI MAOTANG
School of Resources and the Environment: LI ZHAOHUA
Institute of Physics and Electronic Technology: WANG HAO

PROFESSORS

BIAN, XIANGYI, Arts
CAO, WANQIANG, Physics and Electronic Technology
CHAN, SHAOHUA, Physics and Electronic Technology
CHANG, SHIYUAN, Chemistry and Materials Science
CHEN, PEIZHI, Chemistry and Materials Science
CHEN, QIUHUI, Mathematics and Computer Science
CHEN, TIANYOU, Business
CHEN, YIHAN, Physics and Electronic Technology
CHEN, YOUQING, Education
CHEN, ZHIHUI, Physics and Electronic Technology
CHEN, ZHUXING, Chemistry and Materials Science
CHENG, CHONGZHEN, Business
CHENG, SIHUI, Education
CHENG, YUANFA, Physics and Electronic Technology
DAI, MAOTANG, Philosophy
FENG, CHUANQI, Chemistry and Materials Science
FENG, HAO, Business
GAO, LU, History and Culture
GONG, GUIFANG, Foreign Studies
GONG, QUN, Philosophy
GU, HAOSHUANG, Physics and Electronic Technology
GU, PEI, History and Culture
GUAN, RONG, Chemistry and Materials Science
GUO, KANGSONG, Arts
GUO, YING, History and Culture
HAN, HUA, Education
HE, PEIXIN, Chemistry and Materials Science
HU, SHUGUANG, Chemistry and Materials Science
HUANG, SHIQIANG, Chemistry and Materials Science
HUANG, YUEHUI, Arts
JIANG, CHANG, Philosophy
JIANG, TAO, Chemistry and Materials Science
JIN, CONG, Mathematics and Computer Science
JIN, KEZHONG, Arts
LEI, TINAN, Education
LI, JUANWEN, Business
LI, JUANWEN, Resources and the Environment
LI, LUOQING, Mathematics and Computer Science
LI, YAN, Chemistry and Materials Science
LI, ZHAOHUA, Resources and the Environment
LI, ZONGRONG, Mathematics and Computer Science
LIU, CHUANE, Arts
LIU, HEGUO, Mathematics and Computer Science
LIU, JIANPING, Business

LIU, SHENGWU, Arts
LIU, ZHUNMING, Arts
LOU, ZHAOWEN, Chemistry and Materials Science
LU, DEPING, Chemistry and Materials Science
LU, ZHILU, Foreign Studies
QIN, ZHAOGUI, History and Culture
SHAO, CHANGGUI, Physics and Electronic Technology
SHI, JINPING, Business
SHU, HUAI, Arts
SONG, KEFU, Arts
TAN, SHUKUI, Business
TIAN, FANJI, Mathematics and Computer Science
TU, HUAIZHANG, Arts
WAN, CHANGGAO, Mathematics and Computer Science
WANG, HAO, Physics and Electronic Technology
WANG, HONGLING, Business
WANG, JIAZHI, Foreign Studies
WANG, SHENGFU, Chemistry and Materials Science
WANG, SHIMIN, Chemistry and Materials Science
WANG, YANG, History and Culture
WANG, ZHENGXIANG, Resources and the Envirnoment
WU, CHUANXI, Mathematics and Computer Science
WU, MIN, Mathematics and Computer Science
XIA, QINGHUA, Chemistry and Materials Science
XIAN, KEN, Mathematics and Computer Science
XIANG, SONG, Foreign Studies
XIAO, DE, Business
XIAO, WEIDONG, Chemistry and Materials Science
XIE, FEIHOU, Education
XIE, JUFANG, Physics and Electronic Technology
XU, QIUMEI, Foreign Studies
XU, XUEJUN, Education
XU, ZHUSHUN, Chemistry and Materials Science
YAN, CUIE, Chemistry and Materials Science
YAN, MEIFU, Education
YAN, MINGMING, Education
YAN, XUEJUN, Business
YANG, JIANBO, Arts
YANG, YAOKUN, Philosophy
YE, YONG, Chemistry and Materials Science
YI, HONGCHUAN, Arts
YOU, WULI, Foreign Studies
ZHANG, BICHENG, Chemistry and Materials Science
ZHANG, HESHENG, Chemistry and Materials Science
ZHANG, JIANMING, Business
ZHANG, QINGZONG, Foreign Studies
ZHANG, TIANJIN, Physics and Electronic Technology
ZHAO, SHAOYI, Mathematics and Computer Science
ZHENG, YUMEI, Mathematics and Computer Science
ZHOU, DEJUN, History and Culture
ZHOU, HAO, Foreign Studies
ZHOU, TAOSHENG, Physics and Electronic Technology
ZHU, JIANZHEN, History and Culture
ZHU, WEIMING, Arts

ATTACHED RESEARCH INSTITUTES

School of Adult Education: Dir LI CHENFENG.

HUNAN AGRICULTURAL UNIVERSITY

Fu Rong District, Chang Sha 410128, Hunan
Telephone: (731) 4618001
Fax: (731) 4611473
Internet: www.hunau.net

Founded 1951
Academic year: September to July
President: ZHOU QINGMING
Vice-Presidents: BO LIANYANG, FU SHAOHUI, LU XIANGYANG, PENG KEQIN, ZHU YINGSHENG
Librarian: XIAO QIMING
Library of 909,600 vols
Number of teachers: 978
Number of students: 34,259
Publications: *Crop Research* (4 a year), *Journal* (4 a year)

DEANS

School of Agriculture: WANG GUOHUAI
College of Bio-Safety Science and Technology: GAO BIDA
Institute of Computing and Information Engineering: SHEN YUE
College of Economics Management: ZENG WEI
College of Engineering Technology: SUN SONGLIN
Faculty of Food Science and Technology: XIA YANBIN
School of Literature: QU LINYAN
College of Resources and the Environment: DUAN JIANNAN
College of Science: RAO LIQUN

PROFESSORS

BO, LIANYANG, Bio-Safety Science and Technology
CHEN, JINXIANG, Agriculture
CUI, GUOXIAN, Agriculture
DAI, LIANGYING, Bio-Safety Science and Technology
DENG, FANGMING, Food Science and Technology
DUAN, JIANNAN, Resources and the Environment
FANG, ZHI, Resources and the Environment
GAO, BIDA, Bio-Safety Science and Technology
GAO, YINGWU, Engineering Technology
GUAN, CHUNYUN, Agriculture
GUO, QINGQUAN, Agriculture
HUANG, HUANG, Agriculture
HUANG, YIHUAN, Food Science and Technology
HUANG, ZHENGQUAN, Literature
LAO, LIQUN, Science College
LI, FINGJUN, Bio-Safety Science and Technology
LI, XINGHUI, Food Science and Technology
LI, XUN, Agriculture
LIAO, BOHAN, Resources and the Environment
LIAO, XIAOLAN, Bio-Safety Science and Technology
LIU, DEHUA, Food Science and Technology
LIU, GUOHUA, Agriculture
LIU, QIANG, Resources and the Environment
LIU, ZHONGHUA, Food Science and Technology
LIU, ZHONGSONG, Agriculture
LUO, JUNWU, Food Science and Technology
LUO, KUAN, Bio-Safety Science and Technology
MA, MEIHU, Food Science and Technology
OU YANG, XIRONG, Agriculture
PENG, XILIN, Literature
QU, LINYAN, Literature
RONG, XIANGMING, Resources and the Environment
SHENG, XIAOBANG, Agriculture
SHI, ZHAOPENG, Food Science and Technology
SHUN, HUANLIANG, Agriculture
TAN, JICAI, Food Science and Technology
TAN, JICAI, Bio-Safety Science and Technology
TAN, XINGHE, Food Science and Technology
TANG, CHUYU, Engineering Technology
TANG, QIYUAN, Agriculture
TU, LIAOMEI, Agriculture
WANG, GUOHUAI, Agriculture
WANG, GUOLIANG, Agriculture
WANG, GUOPING, Bio-Safety Science and Technology
WEN, LIZHANG, Bio-Safety Science and Technology
WU, LIYOU, Bio-Safety Science and Technology
XI, YANBIN, Food Science and Technology
XIA, YANBIN, Food Science and Technology
XIAO, QIMING, Bio-Safety Science and Technology
XIAO, TIEGUANG, Bio-Safety Science and Technology
YAN, HEHONG, Agriculture
YANG, RENBIN, Resources and the Environment
YANG, WEILI, Food Science and Technology
YANG, ZHIJIAN, Agriculture
ZENG, FUSHENG, Economics Management
ZENG, QINGRU, Resources and the Environment
ZHANG, FUQUAN, Agriculture
ZHANG, XIWEI, Economics Management
ZHANG, YANGZHU, Resources and the Environment
ZHOU, DONGSHENG, Agriculture
ZHOU, JIHENG, Agriculture
ZHOU, MEILAN, Agriculture
ZHOU, QINGMING, Agriculture
ZHU, QI, Food Science and Technology

ATTACHED RESEARCH INSTITUTES

Adult Education College.

East Technology School: Dir ZHOU, QINGMING.

International School: Dir LI DINGJUN.

Professional Technology College: Dir NING YUN.

HUNAN UNIVERSITY

Yule, Changsha 410082
Telephone: (731) 8822745
Fax: (731) 8824525
Internet: www.hunu.edu.cn

Founded 976 as Yuelu Academy; became Hunan Institute of Higher Education 1903, Hunan University 1926, Hunan National University 1937, South-Central Institute of Civil Engineering 1953, Hunan Institute of Technology between 1953 and 1959, and Hunan University 1959; merged with Hunan College of Finance and Economics 2000
State control
President: WANG KEMING
Library of 2,380,000 vols
Number of teachers: 1,563
Number of students: 34,000.

HUNAN MEDICAL UNIVERSITY

88 Xiang Ya Rd, Changsha, 410078 Hunan
Telephone: (731) 4471347
Fax: (731) 4471339
Internet: hmu.hypermart.net

Founded 1914
Academic year: September to July
President: Prof. HU DONGXU
Vice-Presidents: Prof. SUN ZHENGQIU, Prof. WU ZHONGQI, Prof. ZHOU HONGHAO, Prof. HU TIEHUI, Prof. TIAN YONGQUAN, Prof. CHEN ZHUCHU
Librarian: Assoc. Prof. LIU XIACHUN
Library of 560,000 vols
Number of teachers: 652 (full-time)
Number of students: 3,846 (incl. 585 postgraduates)
Publications: *Bulletin* (6 a year), *Journal of Foreign Medicine—Psychiatry, Neurology and Neurosurgery, Physiology and Pathol-*

ogy Sections, *Journal of Modern Medicine* (monthly), *Chinese Journal of General Surgery* (every 2 weeks), *Journal of Medical Degree and Postgraduate Education* (4 a year), *Higher Medical Education Management* (4 a year), *Journal of Applied Uro-Surgery* (4 a year), *Chinese Journal of Otolaryngological and Craniosacral Surgery*, *Chinese Journal of Endoscopy* (4 a year), *Chinese Journal of Psychology* (4 a year)

DIRECTORS

Faculty of Basic Medical Sciences: WEN JIFANG
1st Affiliated Hospital (Clinical Medicine): TIAN YONGQUAN
2nd Affiliated Hospital (Clinical Medicine): LIAO ERYUAN
3rd Affiliated Hospital (Clinical Medicine): LIU XUNYANG
Faculty of Laboratroy Research: CHEN ZHENGYAN
Faculty of Stomatology: JIAN XINCHUN
Faculty of Mental Health: CHEN YUANGUANG
Faculty of Library and Information Sciences: LIU XIAOCHUN
Faculty of Nursing: ZHOU CHANGJU
Faculty of Pharmacology: TANG GUISHAN (Deputy Dir)
Faculty of Preventive Medicine: TANG HONGZHUAN (Deputy Dir)

PROFESSORS

LU GUANGXIU, Biology and Genetics
WEN JIFANG, Pathology
FAN JUNYUAN, Organic Chemistry
HUANG GANCHU, Physics and Chemistry
ZHANG YANXIAN, Pathology
CHENG RUIXUE, Pathology
YOU JIALU, Pathophysiology
ZENG XIANFANG, Parasitology
YI XINYUAN, Parasitology
DENG HANWU, Pharmacology
LI YUANJIAN, Pharmacology
GUO ZHAOGUI, Clinical Pharmacology
GUO SHISHI, Immunology
LIU LIHOU, Anatomy
LUO XUEGANG, Anatomy
SUN XIUHONG, Physiology
LI JUNCHENG, Physiology
MA CHUANTAO, Cardiovascular Physiology
SONG HUIPING, Biochemistry
HAN FENGXIA, Biology
CHEN SHUZHEN, Microbiology
ZHU JIMING, Histology and Embryology
XU YOUHENG, Haemophysiology
WANG QIRU, Haemophysiology
JIANG DEZHAO, Haemophysiology
YAO KAITAI, Experimental Oncology
LI GUIYUAN, Molecular Biology
HU WEIXIN, Tumour Molecular Biology
CAO YA, Tumour Molecular Biology
CHEN ZHUCHU, Tumour Cellular Biology
XIA JIAHUI, Biology and Medical Genetics
LI LUYUN, Medical Genetics
DENG HANXIANG, Biology and Medical Genetics
ZHAO SHUYING, Children's Health
TANG MINGDE, Environmental Health
HU MANLING, Health Chemistry
HUANG ZHENNAN, Health Statistics
SUN ZHENGQIU, Health Statistics
HUANG YIMING, Nutritious Food and Health
CHEN ZHENGYAN, Clinical Biochemistry
CHA GUOZHANG, Clinical Microbiology and Immunology
LIU XIAOCHUN, Library and Information Sciences
FANG PING, Library and Information Sciences
ZHOU HONGHAO, Pharmacology
HU DONGXU, Cardiac Surgery
HU TIEHUI, Cardiac Surgery
HU JIANGUO, Cardiac Surgery
YIN BANGLIAN, Cardiac Surgery
GONG GUANGFU, Cardiac Surgery
CHEN SHENGXI, Cardiac Surgery
LI XUERONG, Medical Psychology
CHEN YUANGUANG, Psychiatry
YANG DESEN, Psychiatry
LUO JIAN, Internal Medicine (Kidney Diseases)
CAO ZHIHAN, Internal Medicine (Kidney Diseases)
JI LONGZHEN, Internal Medicine (Kidney Diseases)
ZHAO SHUIPING, Internal Medicine (Cardiology)
WANG ZHONGLIN, Internal Medicine (Cardiology)
CHEN GANREN, Internal Medicine (Cardiology)
QI SHUSHAN, Internal Medicine (Cardiology)
ZHANG GUANGSEN, Internal Medicine (Haematology)
LU HANBO, Internal Medicine (Haematology)
LU YINZHU, Internal Medicine (Cardiovascular Diseases)
SUN MING, Internal Medicine (Cardiovascular Diseases)
YIN BENYI, Internal Medicine (Cardiology)
WU ESHENG, Internal Medicine (Respiratory Diseases)
ZHANG XICHUN, Internal Medicine (Digestive Diseases)
HAN XIUYUN, Internal Medicine (Endocrinology)
LIAO ERYUAN, Internal Medicine (Endocrinology)
CAO PING, Internal Medicine (Haematology)
CHEN FANGPING, Internal Medicine (Haematology)
QI ZHENHUA, Internal Medicine (Haematology)
XIE ZHAOXIA, Internal Medicine (Haematology)
LI HEJUN, Orthopaedic Surgery
ZHOU JIANGNAN, Orthopaedic Surgery
FU YINYU, Orthopaedic Surgery
LIU REN, Uro-Surgery
HUANG XUN, Uro-Surgery
JIANG XIANZHEN, Uro-Surgery
QI FAN, Uro-Surgery
SHEN PENGFEI, Uro-Surgery
HU FUZEN, General Surgery
LIU XUNYANG, General Surgery
CHEN DAOJING, General Surgery
ZHANG YANGDE, General Surgery
LU XINSHENG, General Surgery
LU WENNENG, General Surgery
OU YANG ZHITING, General Surgery
XU LILI, Gynaecology and Obstetrics
LIN QIUHUA, Gynaecology and Obstetrics
ZHOU CHANGJU, Gynaecology and Obstetrics
YI ZHUWEN, Paediatrics
YANG YUJIA, Paediatrics
YE YIYAN, Paediatrics
YU XIAOLIANG, Paediatrics
SU XIANSHI, Infectious Diseases
TANG DEMING, Infectious Diseases
OU YANG KE, Infectious Diseases
HU GUOLING, Infectious Diseases
JIANG YOUQIN, Ophthalmology
HUANG PEIGANG, Ophthalmology
LU YONGDE, Otorhinolaryngology
XIE DINGHUA, Otorhinolaryngology
TAO ZHENGDE, Otorhinolaryngology
XIAO JIANYUN, Otorhinolaryngology
TIAN YONGQUAN, Otorhinolaryngology
CHEN QIZHI, Anaesthesiology
LI DETAI, Radiology
BAI XIANXIN, Radiology
SU JIANZHI, Isotopes in Medicine
PAN AIYIN, Isotopes in Medicine
ZHU WEIGUANG, Chinese Traditional Medicine
LI XINGQUN, Chinese Traditional Medicine
LI JIABANG, Chinese Traditional Medicine
JIN YIQIANG, Chinese Traditional Medicine
HUANG ZHAOMIN, Rebabilitation
WANG LIZHUANG, Emergency Medicine
LUO XUEHONG, Emergency Medicine
GAO JIESHENG, Internal Medicine (Rheumatology)
LI RUIZHEN, Ultrasound Diagnosis
CHEN FUWEN, Dermatology
LIU ZHIRAN, Dermatology
MA ENQING, Burns Medicine
LU BINGQING, Neurology
YANG QIDONG, Neurology
LIU YUNSHENG, Neurosurgery
YUAN XIANRUI, Neurosurgery
SHEN ZIHUA, Stomatology
JIAN XINCHUN, Stomatology
XU XIUHUA, Infection
WU ZHONGQI, Medical Hyperbaric Oxygen

HUNAN NORMAL UNIVERSITY

36 Lu Shan Rd, He Xi, Changsha 410081, Hunan
Telephone: (731) 8883131
Fax: (731) 8851226
E-mail: webmaster@hunnu.edu.cn
Internet: www.hunnu.edu.cn

Founded 1938
Ministry of Education control
Academic year: September to July

President: LIU XIANG RONG
Vice-Presidents: GONG WEI ZHONG, JIANG JI CHENG, LIANG SONG PING, ZHOU JING MING
Heads of Graduate Department: SHI OU, CHEN JIAN CHU
Librarian: YAN ZHAO HUI

Number of teachers: 1,000
Number of students: 22,000

Publications: *Ancient Chinese Research* (4 a year), *Chinese Literature Research* (4 a year), *Consumer Economy* (4 a year), *Journal* (education science, 6 a year), *Journal* (medicine, irregular), *Journal* (social science, 6 a year), *Life Science Research* (4 a year), *Modern Law* (4 a year)

DEANS

School of Chemistry and Chemical Engineering: XIE QING JI
School of Education Science: ZHANG CHUAN SUI
School of Foreign Languages: HUANG ZHEN DING
School of International Chinese Culture: JI XUE FENG
School of Law: JIANG XIN MIAO
School of Life Science: WU XIU SHAN
School of Literature: TAN GUI LIN
School of Mathematics and Computer Science: DONG XIN HAN
School of Medicine: FU XIAO HUA
School of Physical Education: LI YAN LING
School of Tourism: XIE JUN GUI
College of Commerce: LIU MAO SONG
Department of Computer Education: WANG LU YA

PROFESSORS

CAI, XUE BING, Law
CHEN, BO, Chemistry and Chemical Engineering
CHEN, CHUAN MIAO, Mathematics and Computer Science
CHEN, HUAN GEN, Mathematics and Computer Science
CHEN, JIA QIN, Life Science
CHEN, LIANG BI, Life Science
CHEN, YUN LIANG, Law
CHEN, ZE, Life Science
CHEN, ZUO HONG, Life Science
CUI, ZHEN HUA, International Chinese Culture
DENG, HONG WEN, Life Science
DENG, LE, Life Science
DENG, LE, Chemistry and Chemical Engineering
DENG, XUE JIAN, Life Science

DONG, XIN HAN, Mathematics and Computer Science
DU, XUE TANG, Mathematics and Computer Science
FANG, KUI, Mathematics and Computer Science
FU, PENG, Life Science
FU, ZAI HUI, Chemistry and Chemical Engineering
GU, YONG GENG, Mathematics and Computer Science
GUO, JING YUN, Mathematics and Computer Science
HAO, SAN RU, Computer Education
HE, DING SHENG, Chemistry and Chemical Engineering
HOU, YAO PING, Mathematics and Computer Science
HUANG, JIAN PING, Computer Education
HUANG, YI NONG, Tourism
HUANG, YUAN QIU, Mathematics and Computer Science
JI, XUE FENG, International Chinese Culture
JIANG, XIAN FU, Law
JIANG, XIAO CHENG, Life Science
JIANG, XIN MIAO, Law
JIN, GUANG HUI, Physical Education
JIN, ZU JUN, Mathematics and Computer Science
LENG, GANG SONG, Mathematics and Computer Science
LI, AI NIAN, Law
LI, FANG CHENG, Life Science
LI, HAI TAO, Chemistry and Chemical Engineering
LI, JIAN ZONG, Life Science
LI, SHUANG YUAN, Law
LI, XIAN BO, Law
LI, YAN LING, Physical Education
LI, ZE LIN, Chemistry and Chemical Engineering
LIANG, SONG PING, Life Science
LIU, HONG, Mathematics and Computer Science
LIU, KE MING, Life Science
LIU, MING YAO, Life Science
LIU, SHAO JUN, Life Science
LIU, YING DI, Life Science
LIU, YUN, Life Science
LIU, ZHEN XIU, Mathematics and Computer Science
LUO, CHEN, Life Science
MA, MING, Chemistry and Chemical Engineering
MA, WEI PING, Physical Education
NUAN, SHENG, Life Science
PENG, XIAN JING, Life Science
QIAN, GUANG MING, Mathematics and Computer Science
QIN, ZHENG DI, Computer Education
QIU, MENG SHENG, Life Science
QIU, XI MIN, Chemistry and Chemical Engineering
QU, FU DONG, Tourism
QUAN, HUI YUN, Mathematics and Computer Science
REN, JI CUN, Chemistry and Chemical Engineering
SHEN, JIAN HUA, Mathematics and Computer Science
SHEN, WEN XUAN, Mathematics and Computer Science
SHI, SHAO RONG, Physical Education
SHI, XIAN LIANG, Mathematics and Computer Science
SHI, YING GUANG, Mathematics and Computer Science
SUN, HONG TAO, Physical Education
TAN, PING PING, Physical Education
WANG, BAO HE, Life Science
WANG, GUI GUO, Law
WANG, GUO QIU, Mathematics and Computer Science
WANG, HONG QUAN, Life Science
WANG, LU YA, Computer Education
WANG, XIAN TAO, Mathematics and Computer Science
WANG, XIAN CHUN, Life Science
WU, XIU SHAN, Life Science
XIA, LI QIU, Life Science
XIANG, KAI NAN, Mathematics and Computer Science
XIAO, BEI GENG, Law
XIAO, XIAO MING, Chemistry and Chemical Engineering
XIE, JING YUN, Life Science
XIE, JUN GUI, Tourism
XIE, QING JI, Chemistry and Chemical Engineering
XU, CHUN XIAO, Tourism
XU, DA, Mathematics and Computer Science
XU, FEI XIONG, Tourism
XU, MAN CAI, Chemistry and Chemical Engineering
XU, MENG LIANG, Life Science
YAN, HENG MEI, Life Science
YANG, XIANG QUN, Mathematics and Computer Science
YANG, XIN JIAN, Mathematics and Computer Science
YAO, SHOU ZHUO, Chemistry and Chemical Engineering
YI, CHANG MIN, Life Science
YIN, DA ZHONG, Life Science
YIN, DONG HONG, Chemistry and Chemical Engineering
YUAN, WU ZHOU, Life Science
ZENG, YUE, Chemistry and Chemical Engineering
ZHANG, BAI ZHEN, Physical Education
ZHANG, JIAN, Life Science
ZHANG, TIAN XIAO, Life Science
ZHANG, XUAN JIE, Life Science
ZHANG, YAO, Mathematics and Computer Science
ZHANG, ZHI GUANG, Life Science
ZHENG, YAN, Tourism
ZHENG, YUAN MIN, Law
ZHOU, GONG JIAN, Life Science
ZHOU, JIAN SHE, Physical Education
ZHOU, TIE JUN, Physical Education
ZHOU, XIN YI, Computer Education
ZHU, QI DING, Mathematics and Computer Science

ATTACHED RESEARCH INSTITUTES

Computer Technology Applied Research Centre.

Environmental Education Research Centre.

GIS Research Centre: Dir GUO REN ZHONG.

Image Recognition and Computer Visualization Research Institute: Dir WANG WEI XING.

INNER MONGOLIA UNIVERSITY

235 Daxue West Rd, Huhehaote 010021, Inner Mongolia
Telephone: (471) 4992241
Fax: (471) 4951761
Internet: www.imu.edu.cn

Founded 1957
Academic year: September to July

President: XU RIGAN
Vice-Presidents: CHEN GUOQING, HU GEJILETU, LIANG XIXIA, LI YANJUN, TONG GUOQING
Head of Graduate Department: LIANG XIXIA
Librarian: A LATANCANG

Number of teachers: 1,447
Number of students: 20,000

Publications: *Journal* (humanities and social sciences, 6 a year), *Journal* (natural sciences, 6 a year), *Journal* (philosophy and social sciences, 6 a year)

DEANS

College of Art: LI YULIN
College of Chemistry and Chemical Engineering: SU HAIQUAN
College of Computer Science: GAO GUANGLAI
College of Continuing Education: FU WENJUN
College of Economics and Management: GUO XIAOCHUAN
College of Foreign Languages: LI KANING
College of Humanities: QIAN JIANMEI
School of Law: DING WENYING
College of Life Science: YANG JIE
College of Physical Education: YU ZHIHAI
College of Public Administration: JIN HAIHE
College of Science and Technology: BAN SHILIANG
College of Vocational Technology: CHAI JINYI
Academy of Mongolian Studies: BAI YINMENDE

PROFESSORS

A, LATANCANG, Science and Technology
BAI, XUELIANG, Life Science
BAN, SHILIANG, Science and Technology
BAO, QINGDE, Humanities
BAO, WENHAN, Humanities
BO, YINHUI, Humanities
BU, LINBEILE, Mongolian Studies
BU, RENBATU, Mongolian Studies
CHEN, GUOQING, Science and Technology
CHEN, YOUZUN, Law
CONG, ZHIJIE, Public Administration
DU, LIKE, Humanities
EN, HE, Mongolian Studies
GE, RILETU, Mongolian Studies
GUO, XIAOCHUAN, Economics and Management
HAO, WEIMIN, Mongolian Studies
HE, JIANG, Life Science
HU, TINGMAO, Life Science
JIA, GUISHENG, Public Administration
JIN, HAIHE, Public Administration
LANG, BAORU, Humanities
LI, HONG, Science and Technology
LI, QIANZHONG, Science and Technology
LI, SHUXIN, Humanities
LI, XIAOCHUN, Humanities
LIAN, ZIXIN, Public Administration
LIANG, XIXIA, Science and Technology
LIU, AIHUA, Public Administration
LIU, CHENG, Mongolian Studies
LIU, LIHUA, Public Administration
LIU, XIN, Public Administration
LUO, LIAOFU, Science and Technology
MA, JI, Humanities
MA, ZHANXIN, Economics and Management
MENG, BIN, Economics and Management
MENG, HUIJUN, Economics and Management
MING, YUE, Public Administration
NIU, JIANMING, Life Science
NIU, JINGZHONG, Humanities
QING, GEERTAI, Mongolian Studies
QUAN, FU, Mongolian Studies
REN, WEIDE, Public Administration
REN, YUFENG, Humanities
SHI, ZHENGJI, Humanities
SUN, JIONG, Science and Technology
SUN, KAIMIN, Public Administration
TONG, CHUAN, Life Science
WANG, HONGYAN, Law
WANG, MEICUI, Economics and Management
WANG, YAN, Economics and Management
WANG, YINGCHUN, Life Science
WU, QILATU, Mongolian Studies
WU, YINGJI, Life Science
WU, YUNNA, Public Administration
XU, RIGAN, Life Science
YANG, CHI, Life Science
YANG, JIE, Life Science
YANG, XINMIN, Science and Technology
YU, ZHIHAI, Public Administration
YUN, GUOHONG, Science and Technology
ZHANG, CUIZHEN, Public Administration
ZHANG, FENGMING, Law
ZHANG, ZHIZHONG, Public Administration
ZHAO, MIN, Public Administration
ZHEN, XIUYU, Humanities
ZHOU, QINGSHU, Mongolian Studies

ATTACHED RESEARCH INSTITUTES

Centre for Mongolian Studies: Dir QIMUDE DAOERJI.

Inner-Mongolian Key Laboratory of Mongolian Medicine and Chemistry: Dir XU RIGAN.

Institute of Macromolecular Chemistry and Mongolian Medicine

INNER MONGOLIA AGRICULTURAL UNIVERSITY

Xinjian East Rd, Beyong Nanmen, Huhehaote 010018, Inner Mongolia
Telephone: (471) 4301576
Fax: (471) 4301530
Internet: www.imau.edu.cn

Founded 1952
Provincial control
Academic year: September to July

President: LI CHANGYOU
Vice-Presidents: HOU XIANZHI, LI JINQUAN, REN QIANG, WANG LINHE, ZHENG JUNBAO

Library of 750,000 vols
Number of teachers: 1,010
Number of students: 18,800

Publication: *Journal* (4 a year)

DEANS

College of Animal Science and Animal Medicine: LI JINQUAN
College of Agriculture: YU ZHUO
College of Biology Engineering: ZHOU HUANMIN
College of Computing and Information Engineering: PEI XICHUN
College of Ecology and the Environment: WANG MINQIU
College of Economics Management: XIU CHANGBO
College of Forestry: ZHANG QIULIANG
College of Forestry Engineering: WANG XIAOLIANG
College of Humanities and Social Sciences: GAO CHAO
College of Mechanical and Electrical Engineering: WANG CHUNGUANG
College of Water Conservancy and Civil Engineering: JI BAOLIN

PROFESSORS

AN, SHOUQIN, Forestry
AO, CHANGJIN, Animal Science and Medicine
AO, RIGELE, Animal Science and Medicine
BAI, SHULAN, Forestry
CAO, GUIFANG, Animal Science and Medicine
CHANG, JINBAO, Forestry
CHAO, LUNBAGEN, Water Conservancy and Civil Engineering
CHEN, YAXIN, Water Conservancy and Civil Engineering
CUI, ZHIGUO, Animal Science and Medicine
DAO, ERJI, Animal Science and Medicine
DE, LIGEERSANG, Food Science and Engineering
DOU, WEIGUO, Mechanical and Electrical Engineering
DU, WENLIANG, Mechanical and Electrical Engineering
FAN, MINGSHOU, Agriculture
FENG, LIN, Forestry
GA, ERDI, Animal Science and Medicine
GAO, CHAO, Humanities and Social Sciences
GE, RILE, Forestry
GUANG, PINGYUAN, Animal Science and Medicine
GUO, LIANSHENG, Ecology and the Environment
GUO, LIANSHENG, Forestry
HE, YINFENG, Food Science and Engineering
HOU, XIANZHI, Animal Science and Medicine
HU, HEBATEER, Animal Science and Medicine
JIN, SHUGUANG, Animal Science and Medicine
LI, CHANGYOU, Water Conservancy and Civil Engineering
LI, JINQUAN, Animal Science and Medicine
LI, LIANGUO, Agriculture
LI, PEIFENG, Animal Science and Medicine
LI, QINGFENG, Ecology and the Environment
LI, YUNZHANG, Animal Science and Medicine
LIU, DEFU, Ecology and the Environment
LIU, KELI, Agriculture
LIU, YONG, Economics Management
LIU, ZHENGYI, Animal Science and Medicine
MA, SHUOSHI, Mechanical and Electrical Engineering
MA, XUEEN, Animal Science and Medicine
MANG, LAI, Animal Science and Medicine
MO, LIGEN, Biology Engineering
PANG, BAOPING, Agriculture
PEI, XICHUN, Computer and Information Engineering
QI, TONGCHUN, Mechanical and Electrical Engineering
QIAO, CHEN, Agriculture
QIAO, GUANGHUA, Economics Management
QIAO, LING, Animal Science and Medicine
QIN, HUA, Food Science and Engineering
SAI, YINCHAOKETU, Biology Engineering
SHANG, SHIYOU, Mechanical and Electrical Engineering
SHENG, XIANGDONG, Water Conservancy and Civil Engineering
SHENG, ZHIYI, Animal Science and Medicine
SHI, HAIBIN, Water Conservancy and Civil Engineering
SI, YA, Humanities and Social Sciences
TAN, PENZHEN, Humanities and Social Sciences
TIAN, DE, Mechanical and Electrical Engineering
TIAN, ZIHUA, Agriculture
TONG, SHUMIN, Mechanical and Electrical Engineering
WAN, TAO, Biology Engineering
WANG, BINXIU, Economics Management
WANG, CHUNGUANG, Mechanical and Electrical Engineering
WANG, CHUNJIE, Animal Science and Medicine
WANG, HAOFU, Humanities and Social Sciences
WANG, LAI, Biology Engineering
WANG, LIMING, Forestry
WANG, LINHE, Ecology and the Environment
WEN, HENG, Water Conservancy and Civil Engineering
WU, NI, Animal Science and Medicine
WU, SHUQING, Animal Science and Medicine
XIU, CHANGBO, Economics Management
XU, ZHIXIN, Ecology and the Environment
XUE, HERU, Computer and Information Engineering
YAN, SUMEI, Animal Science and Medicine
YAN, WEI, Ecology and the Environment
YAN, WEI, Forestry
YANG, BAOSHOU, Animal Science and Medicine
YANG, MINGSHAO, Mechanical and Electrical Engineering
YANG, XIAOYE, Animal Science and Medicine
YAO, FENGTONG, Economics Management
YAO, YUNFENG, Ecology and the Environment
YU, ZHUO, Agriculture
YUAN, XIUYING, Forestry
YUN, JINGFENG, Ecology and the Environment
YUN, XINGFU, Agriculture
YUN, YUEHUA, Humanities and Social Sciences
ZHANG, DEMIAN, Mechanical and Electrical Engineering
ZHANG, HEPING, Food Science and Engineering
ZHANG, LILING, Animal Science and Medicine
ZHANG, QIULIANG, Forestry
ZHANG, SHAOYING, Agriculture
ZHANG, XINLING, Economics Management
ZHANG, ZHIYI, Mechanical and Electrical Engineering
ZHAO, GENBAO, Computer and Information Engineering
ZHAO, SHIJIE, Mechanical and Electrical Engineering
ZHAO, YUANFENG, Economics Management
ZHAO, ZHENHUA, Animal Science and Medicine
ZHAO, ZHIGONG, Animal Science and Medicine
ZHOU, HUANMIN, Animal Science and Medicine
ZHOU, HUANMIN, Biology Engineering

ATTACHED RESEARCH INSTITUTES

Adult Education College.

Agriculture and Forestry Engineering Design Research Institute.

Higher Education Research Office.

International Exchange Centre: Dir PEI XICHUN.

Laboratory for Conservation and Cultivation of Biological Resources in Sand.

Laboratory for Genetics and Breeding.

Modern Education Technology Centre.

Vocational and Technology College: Dir GE MAOYUE.

INNER MONGOLIA UNIVERSITY FOR NATIONALITIES

22 Huolinhe Rd, Tongliao 028043, Inner Mongolia
Telephone: (475) 8313292
Fax: (475) 8218937
Internet: www.imun.edu.cn

Founded 1960
Academic year: September to July

President: WANG DINGZHU
Vice-Presidents: LIU ZONGRUI, MA GUOWEN, PAN XIANG, XIAO JIANPING
Head of Graduate Department: XING PENGNIN
Librarian: DONG SHALI

Library of 700,000 vols
Number of teachers: 2,262
Number of students: 31,271

Publications: *Journal* (natural sciences; 6 a year in Chinese, 2 a year in Mongolian), *Journal* (social sciences, 6 a year)

DEANS

College of Arts: (vacant)
College of Education Science: (vacant)
College of Law and History: PU FANDA
College of Literature: XU WENHAI
College of Mathematics and Computer Science: (vacant)
College of Mongolian Medicine: BA GENNA
College of Mongolian Studies: (vacant)
College of Sports: (vacant)

PROFESSORS

A, GULA, Mongolian Medicine
AN, GUANBU, Mongolian Medicine
BA, GENNA, Mongolian Medicine
BA, RIGEQI, Mongolian Medicine
BAI, YANMANDULA, Mongolian Medicine
PU, FANDA, Law and History
XUN, WENHAI, Literature
YANG, AMING, Mongolian Medicine

ATTACHED RESEARCH INSTITUTES

Adult Education College: Vice-Dir REN JUN.

JIANGSU UNIVERSITY

301 Xuefu Rd, Zhenjiang 212013, Jiangsu
Telephone: (511) 8780048
Fax: (511) 8791785
Internet: www.ujs.edu.cn

Founded 2001
Academic year: September to July
President: YANG JICHANG
Vice-Presidents: CAO YOUQING, SONG JINGZHANG, SONG YUQING, SUN YUKUN, XU HUAXI, YUAN SHOUQI, YUAN YINNAN, ZHAO JIEWEN
Head of Graduate Department: MAO HANPING
Librarian: SONG SHUNLIN
Number of teachers: 900
Number of students: 26,320
Publication: *Journal* (6 a year, editions: higher education, medicine, natural sciences, social sciences)

DEANS

Faculty of Science: TIAN LIXIN
School of Art Education: ZHU ZHENGLUN
School of Automotive and Traffic Engineering: CAI YIXI
School of Biological and Environmental Engineering: WU CHUNDU
School of Chemistry and Chemical Engineering: XIE JIMIN
School of Computer Science and Telecommunications: JU SHIGUANG
School of Electrical and Information Engineering: LIU GUOHAI
School of Energy Resources and Power Engineering: YANG MINGUAN
School of Foreign Languages: LUO XINMIN
School of Humanities and Social Sciences: DA YUANYI
School of Industrial and Business Administration: MEI QIANG
School of Materials Science and Engineering: (vacant)
School of Mechanical Engineering: LI PINGPING
School of Medical Technology: XU WENRONG
School of Medicine: XU HUAXI
School of Normal Education: CHEN LIN
School of Pharmacy: XU XIMING
College of Adult Education: XIN JUNKANG

PROFESSORS

BAO, BINGHAO, Mechanical Engineering
CAI, LAN, Mechanical Engineering
CHEN, CUIYING, Mechanical Engineering
CHEN, GUOXIANG, Humanities and Social Science
CHEN, JIN, Mechanical Engineering
CHEN, LIZHEN, Business Administration
CHEN, ZHAOZHANG, Electrical and Information Engineering
CHEN, ZHIGANG, Materials Science and Engineering
CHENG, LI, Electrical and Information Engineering
CHENG, XIANYI, Computer Science and Telecommunications Engineering
CHENG, XIAONONG, Materials Science and Engineering
CHONG, KAI, Mechanical Engineering
DAI, QIXUN, Materials Science and Engineering
DING, GUILIN, Mechanical Engineering
DING, JIANNING, Mechanical Engineering
DONG, DEFU, Humanities and Social Science
FAN, MING, Business Administration
GE, XIAOLAN, Mechanical Engineering
GU, JINAN, Mechanical Engineering
HE, YOUSHI, Business Administration
HE, ZHIGUO, Art
HUANG, GENLIANG, Materials Science and Engineering
HUANG, XIQUAN, Medical Technology
JIN, LIFU, Humanities and Social Science
JU, SHIGUANG, Computer Science and Telecommunications Engineering
KONG, YUSHENG, Business Administration
LEI, YUCHENG, Materials Science and Engineering
LI, BOQUAN, Mechanical Engineering
LI, CHANGSHENG, Mechanical Engineering
LI, DETAO, Energy Resources and Power Engineering
LI, PINGPING, Mechanical Engineering
LI, XINCHENG, Mechanical Engineering
LI, YAOMING, Mechanical Engineering
LI, ZHENGMING, Electrical and Information Engineering
LIN, HONGYI, Energy Resources and Power Engineering
LIU, AIZHEN, Foreign Languages
LIU, FENGYING, Computer Science and Telecommunications Engineering
LIU, GUOHAI, Electrical and Information Engineering
LIU, JIANYI, Business Administration
LIU, QIUSHENG, Business Administration
LU, ZHANGPING, Mechanical Engineering
LU, ZHENGNAN, Business Administration
LUO, DEFU, Materials Science and Engineering
LUO, TIGAN, Energy Resources and Power Engineering
LUO, XINMIN, Materials Science and Engineering
LUO, ZHIGAO, Mechanical Engineering
MA, LVZHONG, Mechanical Engineering
MAO, HANPING, Mechanical Engineering
MEI, QIANG, Business Administration
QI, HONG, Energy Resources and Power Engineering
QIAO, ZHAOHUA, Humanities and Social Science
QIU, BAIJING, Mechanical Engineering
REN, NAIFEI, Mechanical Engineering
SHAO, HONGHONG, Materials Science and Engineering
SHAO, SHIHE, Medical Technology
SHEN, XIANGQIAN, Materials Science and Engineering
SHI, GUOHONG, Business Administration
SI, NAICHAO, Materials Science and Engineering
SONG, SHUNLIN, Computer Science and Telecommunications Engineering
SONG, XINNAN, Energy Resources and Power Engineering
SONG, YUQING, Computer Science and Telecommunications Engineering
SUN, JIAGUANG, Computer Science and Telecommunications Engineering
SUN, YUKUN, Electrical and Information Engineering
WANG, CUNTANG, Mechanical Engineering
WANG, GANG, Computer Science and Telecommunications Engineering
WANG, GUICHENG, Mechanical Engineering
WANG, QIAN, Energy Resources and Power Engineering
WANG, SHULIN, Mechanical Engineering
WANG, SHUQI, Materials Science and Engineering
WANG, ZE, Energy Resources and Power Engineering
WEI, QI, Energy Resources and Power Engineering
WEN, JIANLONG, Energy Resources and Power Engineering
WU, YANYOU, Mechanical Engineering
XIAO, TIEJUN, Computer Science and Telecommunications Engineering
XIE, GANG, Humanities and Social Science
XU, HUAXI, Medical Technology
XU, WENRONG, Medical Technology
XU, XIMING, Pharmacy
YANG, JICHANG, Mechanical Engineering
YANG, MINGUAN, Energy Resources and Power Engineering
YANG, PING, Mechanical Engineering
YAO, GUANXIN, Business Administration
ZHAN, YONGZHAO, Computer Science and Telecommunications Engineering
ZHANG, BINGSHENG, Humanities and Social Science
ZHANG, JIAN, Business Administration
ZHANG, RONGBIAO, Electrical and Information Engineering
ZHANG, YONGKANG, Mechanical Engineering
ZHANG, ZHUMEI, Humanities and Social Science
ZHAO, BUHUI, Electrical and Information Engineering
ZHAO, DEAN, Electrical and Information Engineering
ZHAO, JIN, Business Administration
ZHAO, XICANG, Business Administration
ZHAO, YANPING, Business Administration
ZHAO, YUTAO, Materials Science and Engineering
ZHOU, HONG, Medical Technology
ZHOU, JIANZHONG, Mechanical Engineering
ZHOU, JUN, Mechanical Engineering
ZHOU, TIANJIAN, Medical Technology
ZHOU, ZHICHU, Humanities and Social Science
ZHU, HUANGQIU, Electrical and Information Engineering
ZHU, WEIXING, Electrical and Information Engineering
ZUO, RAN, Energy Resources and Power Engineering

ATTACHED RESEARCH INSTITUTES

Jiangsu Fluid Machinery Engineering Research Centre: Dir SHI WEIDONG.

Jiangsu Key Laboratory for Automobile Research: Dir GAO XIANG.

Jiangsu Key Laboratory for Material Tribology: Dir CHENG XIAONONG.

Jiangsu Research Centre for Small- and Medium-Power Internal Combustion Engine Engineering

JIANGXI AGRICULTURAL UNIVERSITY

Meiling, Nanchang, Jianxi Province 330045
Internet: www.jxau.edu.cn
Founded 1980
President: Prof. LUO MING
Library: over 400,000 vols
Number of teachers: 530
Number of students: 2,900
Publication: *Journal*

Departments of agronomy, forestry, plant protection, horticulture, animal husbandry and veterinary science, farm engineering, agricultural economics.

ATTACHED INSTITUTES

Jiangxi Feed Science Research Institute.

Farm Animal Disease Prevention Research Institute.

Farm Crop Research Institute.

Insect Research Institute

JILIN UNIVERSITY

10 Qianwei Rd, Changchun 130012
Telephone: (431) 5166885
Fax: (431) 5166570
E-mail: fsc@jlu.edu.cn
Internet: www.jlu.edu.cn
Founded 1946; merged in 2001 with Jilin University of Technology (f. 1955), Norman Bethune University of Medical Sciences (f. 1939), Changchun University of Science and Technology (f. 1951) and Changchun Institute of Posts and Telecommunications (f. 1947), to form new Jilin University
Academic year: September to July (two semesters).
President: LIU ZHONGSHU
Head of Graduate School: QIU SHILUN
Librarian: BAO CHENGGUAN
Library of 2,510,000 vols
Publications: *Chemical Research in Chinese Universities* (Chinese and English edns),

Journal of Natural Science, Mathematics of Northeastern China, Northeast Asian Forum, Journal of Historical Studies, Higher Education Research and Practice, Legal Systems and Social Development, Modern Japanese Economy, Journal of Demography

Colleges: Philosophy and Sociology; Literature and Arts; Foreign Languages; Art; Physical Education; Economics; Law; Administration Studies; Management Studies; Economics and Information; Mathematics; Physics; Chemistry; Life Sciences; Machinery and Engineering; Motor Car Engineering; Materials Science and Engineering; Transport; Biology and Agricultural Engineering; Electronics and Engineering; Communications Engineering; Computer Science and Technology; Geological Sciences; Geological Exploration and Information Technology; Construction Engineering; Environment and Resources; Public Health Sciences; Clinical Medicine; Stomatology; Pharmacy; Nursing.

JINAN UNIVERSITY

601 Huangpu West Rd, Guangzhou 510632, Guangdong
Telephone: (20) 85220010
E-mail: officex@jnu.edu.cn
Internet: www.jnu.edu.cn

Founded 1906
Academic year: September to July

President: LIU RENHUAI
Vice-Presidents: HU JUN, JI ZONGAN, JIA YIMIN, JIANG SHUZHUO, LU DAXIANG, WANG HUA, YE QIN
Head of Graduate Department: GU WEIFANG
Librarian: ZHU LINA

Number of teachers: 1,477
Number of students: 22,000

Publications: *Chinese Journal of Pathophysiology* (6 a year), *Ecological Science* (quarterly), *Economic Front* (monthly), *Jinan Higher Education Research* (6 a year), *Journal* (6 a year), *Journal of the College of Chinese Language and Culture of Jinan University* (quarterly), *South-east Asian Studies* (6 a year)

DEANS

College of Chinese Language and Culture: BAO CHAO
College of Continuing Education: HAO ZHAOZHOU
College of Economics: LIU SHAOBO
College of Foreign Studies: LIANG DONGHUA
College of Information Science and Technology: BO YUANHUAI
College of Journalism and Communication: CAI MINGZE
College of Liberal Arts: SUN WEIMING
College of Life Science and Technology: ZHOU TIANHONG
College of Pharmacy: ZHANG RONGHUA
College of Science and Engineering: ZHANG YONGLIN
Shenzhen College of Tourism: LIU ZEPENG
Zhuhai Special Economic Zone College: HU JUN
International School: SUN BOHUA
School of Law: ZHOU XIANZHI
Management School: SUI GUANGJUN
Medical School: SU BAOGUI

PROFESSORS

AO, NINGJIAN, Life Science and Technology
CAI, JIYE, Life Science and Technology
CAI, MINGZE, Journalism and Communication
CAO, BAOLIN, Liberal Arts
CAO, YUNHUA, Law
CHEN, CHUSHENG, Liberal Arts
CHEN, EN, Economics
CHEN, QIAOZHI, Law
CHEN, WEIMING, Liberal Arts
CHEN, XIAOJIN, Liberal Arts
CHEN, XINGDAN, Science and Engineering
CHEN, XUEMEI, Economics
CHEN, YINYUAN, Life Science and Technology
CHEN, YONGLIANG, Economics
CHENG, GUOBIN, Liberal Arts
DENG, QIAOBIN, Chinese
DONG, JIANXIN, Management
DONG, TIANCE, Journalism and Communication
DU, JINMIN, Finance
DUAN, SHUNSHAN, Life Science and Technology
FEI, YONG, Liberal Arts
FENG, BANGYAN, Economics
FENG, XIAOYUN, Economics
GAO, WEINONG, Liberal Arts
GAO, YINGJUN, Science and Engineering
GONG, WEIPING, Economics
GU, GUOYAO, Finance
GUO, SHUHAO, Life Science and Technology
HAN, BOPING, Life Science and Technology
HAN, ZHAOZHOU, Statistics
HE, WENTAO, Finance
HONG, AN, Life Science and Technology
HU, JUN, Management
HU, JUN, Zhuhai SEZ College
HU, SHIZHEN, Economics
HUANG, DEHONG, Management
HUANG, YAOXIONG, Life Science and Technology
JI, MANHONG, Liberal Arts
JI, ZONG-AN, Liberal Arts
JIA, YIMIN, Liberal Arts
JIANG, DUXIAO, Life Science and Technology
JIANG, SHUZHUO, Chinese
JIN, LAHUA, Science and Engineering
LI, BOQIAO, Law
LI, GUISHENG, Life Science and Technology
LI, WEI, Life Science and Technology
LI, YIJUN, Life Science and Technology
LI, YUFANG, Economics
LIN, FUYONG, Zhuhai SEZ College
LIN, LIQIONG, Economics
LIN, RUPENG, Journalism and Communication
LING, WENQUAN, Management
LIU, DEXUE, International Economics and Trade
LIU, JIALIN, Journalism and Communication
LIU, JIANPING, Statistics
LIU, JIESHENG, Life Science and Technology
LIU, RENHUAI, Science and Engineering
LIU, SHAOBO, Finance
LIU, SHAOJIN, Chinese
LIU, YIN, Law
LIU, YINGLIANG, Life Science and Technology
LIU, ZHENGGANG, Liberal Arts
LIU, ZHENGWEN, Life Science and Technology
LU, JUNHUA, Pharmacy
MA, MINGDA, Liberal Arts
MA, QIUFENG, Journalism and Communication
MA, ZHIRONG, Zhuhai SEZ College
MEI, LINHAI, Economics
NIU, DESHENG, Economics
OUYANG, JIANMING, Life Science and Technology
PAN, SHANPEI, Life Science and Technology
PANG, QICHANG, Science and Engineering
QIU, SHUSEN, Liberal Arts
RAO, PENGZI, Chinese
SHAO, JINGMIN, Chinese
SU, BAOHE, Zhuhai SEZ College
SU, DONGWEI, Finance
SUI, GUANGJUN, Management
SUN, BOHUA, International School
SUN, DONGCHUAN, Zhuhai SEZ College
SUN, HANXIAO, Pharmacy
TAN, TIAN, Journalism and Communication
TAN, YUE, Finance
TANG, KAIJIAN, Liberal Arts
TANG, SHUNQING, Life Science and Technology
TANG, SHUZE, Science and Engineering
WANG, CONG, Finance
WANG, FUCHU, Economics
WANG, HUA, Management
WANG, LIEYAO, Liberal Arts
WANG, XIANGPING, Zhuhai SEZ College
WANG, XINMIN, Liberal Arts
WANG, YANKUN, Chinese
WANG, YIFEI, Pharmacy
WANG, YING, Life Science and Technology
WEI, ZHONGLIN, Liberal Arts
WEN, BEIYAN, Law
WU, CHAOBIAO, Statistics
WU, JIANG, Economics
WU, LIGUANG, International Economics and Trade
WU, XIANZHONG, Management
XIA, HONGSHENG, Management
XIANG, JUNJIAN, Life Science and Technology
XIE, QINAN, Statistics
XU, SHIHAI, Life Science and Technology
YANG, QIGUANG, Liberal Arts
YANG, XING, Finance
YANG, YING, Economics
YANG, YUFENG, Life Science and Technology
YAO, XINSHENG, Pharmacy
YE, CHUNLING, Pharmacy
YE, WENCAI, Pharmacy
YIN, HUA, Science and Engineering
YIN, PINGHE, Life Science and Technology
YU, DINGCHENG, Economics
YU, RONGMIN, Pharmacy
YU, YOULONG, Science and Engineering
ZENG, JIANXIONG, Journalism and Communication
ZENG, YAOYING, Life Science and Technology
ZHAN, BOHUI, Chinese
ZHANG, JIE, International Economics and Trade
ZHANG, QIFAN, Liberal Arts
ZHANG, QIZHONG, Life Science and Technology
ZHANG, RONGHUA, Pharmacy
ZHANG, SENWEN, Science and Engineering
ZHANG, SHIJUN, Liberal Arts
ZHANG, XIAOHUI, Liberal Arts
ZHANG, YAOHUI, Zhuhai SEZ College
ZHANG, YONGLIN, Science and Engineering
ZHANG, YUANMING, Life Science and Technology
ZHANG, YUCHUN, Liberal Arts
ZHANG, ZIYONG, Life Science and Technology
ZHAO, JIAMIN, Finance
ZHENG, WENJIE, Life Science and Technology
ZHONG, JINGANG, Science and Engineering
ZHOU, CHANGREN, Life Science and Technology
ZHOU, LIXIN, Life Science and Technology
ZHOU, TIANHONG, Life Science and Technology
ZHOU, XIANZH, Law
ZHU, CHENGPING, Liberal Arts
ZHU, WEIJIE, Life Science and Technology

ATTACHED RESEARCH INSTITUTES

Biological Material Key Laboratory.

Biotechnological Medicine Key Laboratory.

Genome Medicine Engineering Research Centre.

Modern Electronic Technology Experiment Centre.

Organ Transplant and Immunization Centre Laboratory.

Physiopathology Laboratory

KUNMING MEDICAL COLLEGE

84 Renmin Xilu, Kunming 650031, Yunnan
Telephone: (871) 5339224
Fax: (871) 5311542
Internet: www.kmmc.edu.cn

Founded 1956
Academic year: September to January, March to August

President: Prof. LIANG LIQUAN
Vice-Presidents: Prof. CHEN DECHANG, Prof. WANG ZICANG, ZHANG CHAO
Chief Administrative Officer: JIANG RUNSHENG
Library: *c.* 170,000 vols, 1,659 periodicals-over
Number of teachers: 1,200
Number of students: 2,789 (including 118 postgraduates)

HEADS OF DEPARTMENTS

Medicine (1): Prof. TANG JINQING
Medicine (2): Assoc. Prof. GUO YONGZHANG
Stomatology: Prof. LI JIE
Public Health: Prof. WANG TONGYING
Forensic Medicine: YAO FANGSHENG

KUNMING UNIVERSITY OF SCIENCE AND TECHNOLOGY

1 Wenchangxiang, Kunming 650093, Yunnan
Telephone: (871) 5144212
Fax: (871) 5158622
Internet: www.kmust.edu.cn
Founded 1954
Academic year: September to July
President: Prof. ZHANG WENBIN
Vice-Presidents: Prof. TAO HENGCHANG, Prof. XIANG NAIMING, Prof. HE TIANCHUN
Assistant President: Prof. SUN JIALIN
Registrar: Prof. ZHOU RONG
Librarian: Prof. LIU ZHONGHUA
Library of 1,100,000 vols
Number of teachers: 800
Number of students: 8,000
Publications: *Journal*, *Science and Technology in KUST*, *Research in Higher Education in KUST*

HEADS OF COLLEGE

College of Adult Education: Prof. XU BAOZHONG
College of Management and Economy: Prof. YANG BAOJIAN
College of Social Science and Art: LI XUEYOU

HEADS OF DEPARTMENTS

Geology and Survey Engineering: Prof. LIANG YONGNING
Mineral Processing and Mining: Prof. YANG SHIYONG
Metallurgy: Prof. WANG HUA
Mechanical Engineering: Prof. CHENG CHANGHUA
Automation: Prof. ZHANG YUNSHENG
Environmental Engineering and Chemistry: Prof. NING PING
Architectural Engineering and Mechanics: Prof. CHENG HEMING
Foreign Languages: Prof. HE YI
Basic Science: Prof. LI JIBIN
Computer Science: Prof. ZHANG HUAINING
Materials Engineering: Prof. SUN YONG
Physical Education: Assoc. Prof. WANG YUEZHOU
Graduate Study: Prof. XIE GANG

LANZHOU UNIVERSITY

298 Tianshui Rd, 730000 Lanzhou, Gansu Province
Telephone: 8828111
Fax: 8885076
Internet: www.lzu.edu.cn
Founded 1909
Academic year: September to July (2 semesters)
President: LI FASHEN
Vice-Presidents: YANG JUN, ZHAN XIU, ZHANG JIQING, LI LIAN, SHEN WEIGUO
Administrative Director: FENG YUYE
Librarian: ZHU ZISHENG
Number of teachers: 1,400
Number of students: 8,000
Publications: *Journal*, *Historical and Geographical Review of Northwest China*, *Collections of Articles on Dunhuang Studies*, etc

HEADS OF DEPARTMENTS

Chinese: ZHANG WENXUAN
History: YANG JIANXIN
Journalism: WANG ZUOREN
Philosophy: LIN LI
Economics: LI ZONGZHI
Law: LI GONGGUO
Library Science: WANG GUIZHONG
Foreign Languages and Literature: FENG JIANWEN
Mathematics: WANG MINLIANG
Marxist Studies: LIU JIASHENG
Physics: CHEN GUANGHUA
Modern Physics: LIU ZHENMING
Electronics and Information Science: LU ZHENSU
Mechanics: YU HUANRAN
Computer Science: XU DEQI
Material Science: WANG TIANMING
Chemistry: PAN XINFU
Geography: ZHOU SHANGHE
Geology: HAN WENFENG
Administration: HE HENGXIN
Atmospheric Science: CHOU JIFAN

LIAONING UNIVERSITY

66 Chongshan Middle Rd, Shenyang 110036, Liaoning
Telephone: (24) 86842756
Fax: (24) 62202013
E-mail: office@lnu.edu.cn
Internet: www.lnu.edu.cn
Founded 1948
Ministry of Education control
Academic year: September to July
President: CHENG WEI
Vice-Presidents: LIU ZHICHAO, MU HUAIZHONG, ZANG SHULIANG, ZHANG WEI
Head of Graduate Department: XU PING
Librarian: YANG XIAOJUN
Number of teachers: 1,200
Number of students: 23,000
Publications: *Journal* (natural sciences, quarterly), *Journal* (philosophy and social sciences, 6 a year), *Research of Japan* (quarterly)

DEANS

Faculty of Environmental Science: LI FAYUN
Faculty of History: DING HAIBIN
Faculty of Life Sciences: ZHOU RENQING
Faculty of Mathematics: DAI TIANMIN
Faculty of Physics: GUO YONGXIN
College of Adult Education: MA YONGJUN
Asia-Australia College of Business: ZHOU JIE
College of Business Management: GAO CHUANG
College of Chemistry and Engineering: SONG XIMING
College of Cultural Communication: GAO KAIZHENG
College of Economics: LIN MUXI
College of Foreign Languages: CHEN FENG
College of Higher Professional Techniques: YU ZHONGCHENG
College of Information Science and Technology: SHI XIANGBIN
College of Law: YANG SONG
College of Philosophy and Public Administration: SHAO XIAOGUANG
College of Radio, Film and Television: HU GUANGHUI
Sun Wah International Business School: CHENG WEI

PROFESSORS

BI, XIAOHUI, Philosophy and Public Administration
CHE, WEIYI, Mathematics
CHEN, CHUNGUANG, Information Science and Technology
CHEN, FENG, Foreign Languages
CHEN, XIN, Chemistry and Engineering
DAI, BOXUN, Business Management
DAI, TIANMIN, Mathematics
DING, HAIBIN, History
DING, NING, Information Science and Technology
DONG, SHOUYI, History
DONG, WENCHENG, Cultural Communication
FANG, BAOLIN, Business Management
GAO, CHUANG, Business Management
GAO, KAIZHENG, Cultural Communication
GAO, YANGKUI, Foreign Languages
GU, KUIXIANG, History
GUO, HUOXUN, Philosophy and Public Administration
GUO, JIE, Law
GUO, WENSHENG, Chemistry and Engineering
GUO, YONGXIN, Physics
HAO, JIANSHE, Law
HU, YUHAI, History
JIA, SHUFENG, Foreign Languages
JIAO, RUNMING, History
JIN, LISHUN, Business Management
LI, CHUNGUANG, History
LI, JUEXIAN, Mathematics
LI, LIPING, Information Science and Technology
LI, TIEMIN, Life Science
LI, YONGCHANG, History
LIN, MUXI, Economics
LIU, DUCAI, Law
LIU, FULIN, Mathematics
LIU, LIGANG, Business Management
LIU, WEIZHI, Cultural Communication
LIU, XINGZHI, Chemistry and Engineering
LU, JIERONG, Philosophy and Public Administration
LU, DIANZHEN, Chemistry and Engineering
LU, FANG, Mathematics
LU, GUOCHEN, Philosophy and Public Administration
LUO, JUNBO, Mathematics
MA, LIJUAN, Foreign Languages
NIU, BIN, Information Science and Technology
PENG, HAORONG, Business Management
QI, LIQUAN, Chemistry and Engineering
QI, ZHENGHUI, History
QIN, YONGLU, Information Science and Technology
QU, DELAI, Cultural Communication
REN, JI, Law
SHAO, XIAOGUANG, Philosophy and Public Administration
SHEN, GUIFENG, Physics
SHEN, HONGDA, Business Management
SHI, XIANGBIN, Information Science and Technology
SHI, YING, Law
SONG, XIMING, Chemistry and Engineering
SUN, HONGLIE, Mathematics
SUN, LI, Law
TANG, XIAOHUA, Business Management
TIAN, YUFENG, Information Science and Technology
TU, GUANGSHE, Cultural Communication
WANG, CHUNFEI, Cultural Communication
WANG, CHUNRONG, Cultural Communication
WANG, JUN, Chemistry and Engineering
WANG, QIUYU, Life Science
WANG, WEI, Cultural Communication
WANG, WEIFAN, Mathematics
WANG, WENCI, Foreign Languages
WANG, XIANGFENG, Cultural Communication
WU, CHUNYU, Physics
WU, WENZHONG, Foreign Languages

WU, XINJIE, Physics
XIAO, SHENG, Business Management
XING, ZHIREN, Law
XU, HAOGUANG, Cultural Communication
XU, ZHIGANG, Cultural Communication
XUE, JIANSHENG, Information Science and Technology
YANG, JIAZHEN, Chemistry and Engineering
YANG, LINRUI, Law
YANG, MING, Law
YANG, SONG, Law
YU, ZHONGZHUO, Business Management
ZANG, SHULIANG, Chemistry and Engineering
ZENG, XIAOFEI, Life Science
ZHANG, CHENGHUA, Physics
ZHANG, FENG, Chemistry and Engineering
ZHANG, JIE, History
ZHANG, LIZHEN, History
ZHANG, XIANGDONG, Chemistry and Engineering
ZHANG, YOUHUI, Information Science and Technology
ZHAO, BINGGUI, Law
ZHAO, DEZHI, Philosophy and Public Administration
ZHAO, GUOXING, Information Science and Technology
ZHAO, LINGHE, Cultural Communication
ZHENG, YONGFAN, Mathematics
ZHOU, FEI, Philosophy and Public Administration
ZHOU, RENQING, Life Science
ZHU, MINGLUN, Cultural Communication
ZUO, ZHICHENG, Foreign Languages

ATTACHED RESEARCH INSTITUTES

Ecosystem Environment Research Institute: Dir DONG HOUDE.

Institute of Japanese Studies: Dir CUI CHUNHE.

Population Research Institute: Dir MU HUAIZHONG.

Research Centre of Comparative Economics Systems: Dir CHENG WEI.

LIAONING NORMAL UNIVERSITY

Da Lian 116029, Liaoning
Telephone: (411) 2158235
Internet: www.lnnu.edu.cn

Founded 1951
Provincial control
Academic year: September to July

President: QU QINGBIAO
Vice-Presidents: HAN ZHENGLIN, QU WEI
Librarian: ZHAO YUNSHENG

Library of 1,330,000 vols
Number of teachers: 1,897
Number of students: 25,200

Publication: *Journal* (6 a year)

DEANS

Faculty of Chemistry and Chemical Engineering: JIAO QIANGZHU
College of the City and Environment: LIN XIANSENG
College of Education: FU WEILI
College of Film and Television Art: GAO GUANGFU
College of Foreign Languages: MA YANGGANG
College of History and Tourism: XIE JINGFANG
College of Law: YU PEILIN
College of Life Science: HOU HESHENG
College of Literature: WANG WEIPING
College of Management: ZHAO ZHONGWEN
College of Physics and Electronic Technology: PAN FENG
College of Politics: SHI YIJUN
College of Sports: HE MINXUE
School of Mathematics: HAN YOUFA

PROFESSORS

BI, ZHIGUO, Politics
CAI, MIN, Education
CHANG, JINCHANG, History and Tourism
CHANG, RUOSONG, Education
CHEN, DACHAO, Education
CHEN, LIU, Literature
CHEN, TUYUN, Mathematics
CHENG, XIAOGUANG, Foreign Languages
DIAO, YANBIN, Literature
DONG, GUANGCAI, Foreign Languages
DONG, XUEDONG, Mathematics
DU, LIN, Literature
DU, RUIZHI, Mathematics
DU, XINGZHI, History and Tourism
FAN, YINGHENG, Chemistry and Chemical Engineering
FANG, HONGXIAO, Life Science
FENG, CHUNLIANG, Chemistry and Chemical Engineering
FU, WEILI, Education
GAO, BO, Management
HAN, YOUFA, Mathematics
HAN, YUCHANG, Education
HE, MINXUE, Physical Education
HOU, HESHENG, Life Science
HOU, LIN, Life Science
HU, ZHENKAI, Education
HUANG, BIN, Physical Education
JIANG, HUA, Life Science
JIN, CHENGJI, Physical Education
JIN, HONGYUAN, Education
JIN, RENSHU, Management
LI, CHUNLIN, Literature
LI, JINXIANG, Chemistry and Chemical Engineering
LI, LAIZHI, Management
LI, RENXI, Life Science
LI, TIANJIAN, Mathematics
LI, XUGUANG, Foreign Languages
LI, YAOZHENG, City and Envirnoment Studies
LI, YINGJUN, Chemistry and Chemical Engineering
LIANG, GUIZHI, Literature
LIANG, SHUSHENG, Physics and Electronic Technology
LIN, HUA, Physical Education
LIN, XIANSHENG, City and Envirnoment Studies
LIU, FANFU, Foreign Languages
LIU, FUGENG, Foreign Languages
LIU, PEIHAN, Politics
LIU, WANQI, Law
LIU, WEN, Education
LIU, XIUCHUN, Politics
LIU, ZHEQING, Mathematics
LUAN, WEIXIN, City and Envirnoment Studies
LU, FENGYING, Law
LU, GUOFENG, Physical Education
MA, DONGYU, History and Tourism
MA, JIANSHENG, Education
MA, JUNSHAN, Literature
MA, YOUHUI, Life Science
MENG, DEXIU, Foreign Languages
MENG, ZHAOYUAN, Politics
NIU, SHUYUN, Chemistry and Chemical Engineering
PAN, FENG, Physics and Electronic Technology
QI, GUOYING, Physics and Electronic Technology
QU, GUANG, Literature
QU, JIANWU, Politics
QU, QINGBIAO, Politics
QU, WEI, Foreign Languages
SANG, DEJING, Life Science
SHI, LEI, Chemistry and Chemical Engineering
SHI, YIJUN, Politics
SHUN, RENAN, Chemistry and Chemical Engineering
SHUN, YUANGANG, Education
SONG, HUA, History and Tourism
TAO, YANG, Foreign Languages
TIAN, GUANGLIN, History and Tourism
WANG, BING, Foreign Languages
WANG, CHANGSHENG, Chemistry and Chemical Engineering
WANG, GUANLIN, Life Science
WANG, HONG, Physical Education
WANG, JIPENG, Literature
WANG, LI, Literature
WANG, QIHUA, Life Science
WANG, QINGJIAN, Mathematics
WANG, WEIPING, Literature
WANG, XIUWU, Life Science
WANG, XIUXIANG, Physical Education
WANG, YAOGUANG, Physical Education
WANG, YI, Literature
WANG, ZHIWEN, Physics and Electronic Technology
WEI, HUAZHONG, Education
WU, DESHENG, Literature
WU, ZHIHUA, Life Science
XIE, JINGFANG, History and Tourism
XIE, LIN, Mathematics
XIE, MINGJIE, Life Science
XU, YINGJUN, Foreign Languages
YAN, BANGYI, Literature
YAN, ZHILI, Physical Education
YANG, HONG, Life Science
YANG, LIZHU, Education
YANG, MING, Education
YANG, XIAO, Education
YANG, XIUXIANG, Politics
YANG, YINGJIE, History and Tourism
YANG, ZHONGZHI, Chemistry and Chemical Engineering
YI, HUAINING, City and Envirnoment Studies
YOU, WANSHENG, Chemistry and Chemical Engineering
YU, BING, Literature
YU, DAHUA, History and Tourism
YU, PEILING, Law
YU, WENQIAN, Physical Education
YUAN, XUEHAI, Mathematics
YUE, ZHONGXING, Physics and Electronic Technology
ZHANG, AIJUN, Politics
ZHANG, GUICHUN, Education
ZHANG, GUIREN, Politics
ZHANG, LIHUA, Education
ZHANG, NINGSHENG, Education
ZHANG, QI, Education
ZHANG, SHUMIN, Chemistry and Chemical Engineering
ZHANG, WEIDONG, Life Science
ZHANG, XIAONING, Foreign Languages
ZHANG, YAOGUANG, City and Envirnoment Studies
ZHAO, YI, History and Tourism
ZHAO, YUBAO, History and Tourism
ZHAO, ZHENYING, History and Tourism
ZHAO, ZHONGWEN, Management
ZHONG, GUIQING, City and Envirnoment Studies
ZHOU, DANHONG, Chemistry and Chemical Engineering
ZHOU, WEI, Life Science
ZHOU, XIAOYAN, Education
ZHOU, ZHIQIANG, Politics
ZHU, NINGBO, Education
ZHU, ZHIJUN, Politics

ATTACHED RESEARCH INSTITUTES

College of Continuing Education.

College of International Culture: Dir HE JINRONG.

LIAONING TECHNICAL UNIVERSITY

Fu Xin 3350461, Liaoning
Internet: www.lntu.edu.cn

Founded 1958
State control
Academic year: September to July

President: SHI JINFENG
Vice-Presidents: MA ZHUANG, PAN YISHAN, SHAO LIANGBIN, WANG JIREN, ZHANG ZUOGANG, ZHANG SHUSEN
Head of Graduate Department: LIANG BING
Librarian: LIE JIE

Number of teachers: 1,349

Number of students: 25,000

Publications: *Journal* (natural sciences, 6 a year), *Journal* (social sciences, 4 a year)

Constituent colleges and departments in the following areass: Resources and Environmental Engineering; Business Management; Mechanical Engineering; Architecture and Civil Engineering; Software; Technology and Economics; Geomatics Engineering; Mechanics and Engineering Sciences; Electrical Engineering; Electrical and Information Engineering; Materials Science and Engineering; Foreign Languages; Journalism and Communication; Politics and Law

PROFESSORS

FU, XINGWU, Electrical Engineering
GUO, FENGYI, Electrical Engineering
HUI, XIAOWEI, Electrical and Information Engineering
LI, WEIDONG, Electrical Engineering
LI, XIAOZHU, Electrical Engineering
LI, YIJIE, Electrical and Information Engineering
LI, ZHENGZHONG, Geomatics Engineering
LIU, JIANHUI, Electrical and Information Engineering
LU, SHIKUI, Electrical Engineering
MENG, QINGCHUN, Electrical Engineering
QIAO, YANGWEN, Geomatics Engineering
SONG, WEIDONG, Geomatics Engineering
SUN, JINGUANG, Electrical and Information Engineering
SUN, PENGYONG, Electrical and Information Engineering
WANG, JIAGUI, Geomatics Engineering
WANG, YUFENG, Electrical Engineering
XING, BAOJUN, Electrical Engineering
YE, JINGLOU, Electrical Engineering
YE, JINGLOU, Electrical and Information Engineering
ZHAO, GUOCAI, Electrical Engineering
ZHAO, GUOQIANG, Electrical Engineering
ZHU, HUA, Electrical Engineering

ATTACHED RESEARCH INSTITUTES

Institute of Project Demolition: Dir FEI HONGLU.

Institute of System Engineering: Dir SHAO LIANGBIN.

Laboratory of Geomatics Engineering: Dir SONG WEIDONG.

Laboratory of Security Engineering: Dir SONG QINGJIE.

NANCHANG UNIVERSITY

235 Nanjing East Rd, Nanchang 330047, Jiangxi

Telephone: (791) 8305499
Fax: (791) 8305835
Internet: www.ncu.edu.cn

Founded 1940
State control
Academic year: September to July

President: ZHOU WENBIN
Vice-Presidents: CHENG YANGGUO, FU MINGFU, GAN XIAOQING, LI JIANMIN, LIU SANQIU, SHAO HONG, XIE MINGYONG
Head of Graduate Department: LI MING
Librarian: HE XIAOPING

Number of teachers: 1,253
Number of students: 45,000

Publications: *Journal* (engineering and technology, quarterly), *Journal* (humanities and social sciences, 6 a year), *Journal* (natural sciences, quarterly)

DEANS

College of Architectural Engineering: GUI GUOQING
College of Arts and Design: XIONG MANLING
College of Information Engineering: CHEN KEN
College of Life Science: ZHU YOULIN
College of Mechanics and Engineering: LIU HESHENG
College of Natural Science: LIU NIANHUA
College of Science and Technology: HE JIESHAN
College of Software: LU XIAOYONG
School of Chemistry and Materials Science: ZHOU LANG
School of Economics and Management: YIN JIDONG
School of Environmental Science and Engineering: HU ZHAOJI
School of Foreign Languages: FANG KEPING
School of Humanities and Social Science: LI DONGNI
Centre for Public Administration Programmes: TAO XUERONG

PROFESSORS

BAO, ZHONGXU, Mechanics and Engineering
CAO, DEHE, Humanities and Social Sciencess
CAO, YUSHENG, Life Sciences
CHEN, DONGYOU, Humanities and Social Sciencess
CHEN, XINLING, Humanities and Social Sciencess
DENG, SHUILAN, Economics and Management
DENG, ZEYUAN, Life Sciences
FU, XIAOLONG, Art and Design
GAO, GUOZHEN, Mechanics and Engineering
GAO, YINYU, Life Sciences
GONG, LIANSHOU, Humanities and Social Sciencess
GU, XINGBIN, Humanities and Social Sciencess
GU, ZHENGSHI, Mechanics and Engineering
HE, CHENGHONG, Mechanics and Engineering
HE, YUN, Economics and Management
HU, PING, Humanities and Social Sciencess
HU, QING, Humanities and Social Sciencess
HU, ZHAOJI, Environmental Science and Engineering
HUANG, JIHUA, Mechanics and Engineering
HUANG, XIJIA, Economics and Management
HUANG, XINJIAN, Economics and Management
JIANG, BOQUAN, Environmental Science and Engineering
JIANG, SHUISHENG, Mechanics and Engineering
JIN, LAHUA, Environmental Science and Engineering
LI, CHENGGUI, Humanities and Social Sciencess
LI, DONGNI, Humanities and Social Sciencess
LI, SHENGMEI, Humanities and Social Sciences
LI, XIANTAN, Economics and Management
LIN, BO, Environmental Science and Engineering
LIU, HESHENG, Mechanics and Engineering
LIU, LUNXIN, Humanities and Social Sciences
LIU, NIANHUA, Natural Science
LIU, QIJING, Environmental Science and Engineering
LIU, RENSHENG, Humanities and Social Sciences
LIU, WEIDONG, Mechanics and Engineering
LIU, XIAOHONG, Environmental Science and Engineering
LIU, XIAOQIN, Art and Design
LIU, YING, Mechanics and Engineering
LU, BINGFU, Humanities and Social Sciences
LU, SHENGPING, Art and Design
LU, XIANFENG, Mechanics and Engineering
LU, XIAOYONG, Economics and Management
LU, XIXING, Humanities and Social Sciences
MA, WEI, Economics and Management
NI, YONGNIAN, Life Sciences
PENG, DIYUN, Economics and Management
QIU, ZUMIN, Environmental Science and Engineering
RUAN, RONGSHENG, Life Sciences
SUN, RISHENG, Environmental Science and Engineering
SUN, YONG, Art and Design
WAN, FANGZHEN, Humanities and Social Sciences
WAN, JINBAO, Environmental Science and Engineering
WANG, DEBAO, Humanities and Social Sciences
WANG, LIANGSHENG, Art and Design
WANG, XIANGYANG, Art and Design
WANG, ZHEPING, Humanities and Social Sciences
WEI, LI, Economics and Management
WEN, SHIHUA, Humanities and Social Sciences
WU, LUSHEN, Mechanics and Engineering
WU, XIAOWEI, Humanities and Social Sciences
XIAO, ANKUN, Mechanics and Engineering
XIE, MINGYONG, Life Sciences
XIE, YONG, Economics and Management
XIN, YONG, Mechanics and Engineering
XIONG, JIANXIN, Art and Design
XIONG, MANLING, Art and Design
XIONG, RUIWEN, Mechanics and Engineering
XIONG, XIANGHUI, Mechanics and Engineering
XU, YANG, Life Sciences
YANG, GUOTAI, Mechanics and Engineering
YANG, MINGLANG, Art and Design
YANG, XUECHUN, Mechanics and Engineering
YANG, XUEPIN, Humanities and Social Sciences
YAO, YAPING, Humanities and Social Sciences
YI, PING, Humanities and Social Sciences
YIN, JIDONG, Economics and Management
YIN, XINGFAN, Humanities and Social Sciences
YING, YULONG, Life Sciences
YU, RANGYAO, Humanities and Social Sciences
YUAN, LIHUA, Humanities and Social Sciences
ZHAN, ZHIYOU, Humanities and Social Sciences
ZHANG, HUA, Mechanics and Engineering
ZHANG, NING, Natural Science
ZHANG, RENMU, Humanities and Social Sciences
ZHANG, SHENGYANG, Humanities and Social Sciences
ZHANG, YUMING, Economics and Management
ZHANG, YUSHENG, Humanities and Social Sciences
ZHANG, ZHIYONG, Humanities and Social Sciences
ZHAO, LIQIU, Economics and Management
ZHENG, DIANMO, Environmental Science and Engineering
ZHENG, WEIXIAN, Life Sciences
ZHENG, XIANGQING, Economics and Management
ZHENG, XIAOJIANG, Humanities and Social Sciences
ZHOU, GUOFA, Environmental Science and Engineering
ZHOU, PINGYUAN, Humanities and Social Sciences
ZHOU, SHU, Art and Design
ZHOU, TIANRUI, Mechanics and Engineering
ZHOU, WENBIN, Environmental Science and Engineering
ZHOU, YAOWANG, Humanities and Social Sciences
ZHU, CHUANXI, Natural Science

ATTACHED RESEARCH INSTITUTES

Key Laboratory of Food Science: Dir XIE MINGYONG.

Key Laboratory of Robotics and Welding Automation: Dir ZHANG HUA.

Research Centre for Information Engineering Technology in Manufacture: Dir ZHANG HUA.

Research Centre for Irradiance Materials and Apparatus: Dir JIANG FENGYI.

Vocational Technology College: Dir ZHAO GUOJIE.

NANJING UNIVERSITY

22 Hankou Rd, Nanjing 210093, Jiangsu
Telephone: (25) 3593186
Fax: (25) 3302728
Internet: www.nju.edu.cn

Founded 1902
State control
Language of instruction: Chinese
Academic year: September to June

President: JIANG SHUSHENG
Vice-Presidents: HON YINXING, CHEN JUN, SHIN JIANJUN, MIN TIEJUN, ZHANG DALIANG, ZHANG YIBIN
Librarian: QIAN CHENGDAN

Number of teachers: 2,400
Number of students: 27,000

Publications: *Journal* (humanities and social sciences), *Journal* (natural sciences), *Journal of Computer Science, Journal of Inorganic Chemistry, Progress in Physics, Contemporary Foreign Literature, Approximation Theory and its Application, Mathematics in Higher Education, Geology in Higher Education, Research in Higher Education, Mathematics Review* (2 a year)

DEANS

Graduate School: CHEN CHONGQING
Medical School: HAN XIAODONG
International Business School: ZHAO SHUMING
Adult Education School: WANG JIANQIANG
School of Humanities: DONG JIAN
School of Law: SHAO JIANDONG (acting)
School of Foreign Studies: WANG SHOUREN
School of Natural Sciences: GONG CHANGDE
School of Chemistry and Chemical Engineering: PAM YI
School of Technology: SUN ZHONGXIU
School of Geoscience: WANG YING
School of Life Science: ZHANG HONGZU
School of Intensive Instruction in Sciences and Liberal Arts: LU DEXIN

HEADS OF DEPARTMENTS

Astronomy: TONG YUHUA
Atmospheric Science: TAN ZHEMIN
Basic Medicine: HAN XIAODONG
Biochemistry: LI GENXI
Biological Science and Technology: LI GENXI
Business Communications: (vacant)
Chemical Engineering: ZHANG ZHIBING
Chemistry: SHEN JIANYI
Chinese Language and Literature: ZHOU XIAN
Clinical Medicine: HAN XIAODONG
Computer Science and Technology: CHEN DAOXU
Earth Science: HU KAI
Economics: SHEN KUNRONG
Economic Law: SHAO JIANDONG
Electronic Science and Technology: WANG XINLONG
English: ZHU GANG
Environmental Science and Technology: YIN DAQIANG
Foreign Languages and Literatures: WANG SHOUREN
Urban and Resource Science: GU CHAOLIN
History: ZHU YINGQUAN
Information Management: SHEN GUO CHAO
International Accounting: YANG XIONGSHENG
International Economic Law: SUN NANSHENG
International Economy and Trade: ZHANG ERZHENG
International Enterprise Management: (vacant)
International Finance: PEI PING
Land and Ocean Science: WANG YING
Law: XU JIANG
Library Science: SHEN GUCHAO
Macromolecular Materials Science and Engineering: XUE QI
Mass Communication: DING BOQUAN
Materials Science and Technology: CHENG YANFENG
Mathematics: YOU JIANGONG
Philosophy: XU XIAOYUE
Physics: SHI YI
Political Science: ZHANG FENGYANG
Russian and Japanese Languages and Literature: YE LIN
Sociology: ZHOU XIAOHONG
French, Spanish and German: XU JUN
Audio-Visual Centre: FENG XIAOQING
Centre for Chinese and American Studies: CHEN YONGXIANG (Chinese Co-Dir)
Computer Centre: YE XIANFENG

NANJING UNIVERSITY OF AERONAUTICS AND ASTRONAUTICS

29 Yudao Rd, Nanjing 210016, Jiangsu
Telephone: (25) 4892424
Fax: (25) 4891512
E-mail: office@nuaa.edu.cn
Internet: www.njmu.edu.cn

Founded 1952
Academic year: September to July

President: HU HAIYAN
Vice-Presidents: CHEN XIACHU, LIANG DEWANG, NIE HONG, WANG GUINONG, WANG YONGLIANG, WU QINGXIAN, WU YIZHAO
Head of Graduate Department: HU HAIYAN
Librarian: HUANG YINHUI

Number of teachers: 1,300
Number of students: 22,725

Publication: *Journal* (6 a year)

DEANS

College of Advanced Vocational Education: JIANG WEI
College of Aerospace Engineering: XU XIWU
College of Art: LIU CANMING
College of Automation Engineering: LIU JIANYE
College of Civil Aviation: SHEN YUANKANG
College of Economics and Management: LIU SIFENG
College of Energy and Power Engineering: ZHANG JINGZHOU
College of Humanities and Social Sciences: WANG YAN
College of Information Science and Technology: BEN DE
College of Materials Science and Engineering: TAO JIE
College of Mechanical Engineering: ZHU DI
College of Natural Science: YAN XIAOHONG

PROFESSORS

AI, JUN, Aerospace Engineering
AN, YUKUN, Natural Sciences
ANG, HAISONG, Aerospace Engineering
BAO, MING, Aerospace Engineering
BAO, MINGBAO, Humanities and Social Sciences
CAI, QIMING, Economics and Management
CAO, YUNFENG, Automation Engineering
CHANG, HAIPING, Energy and Power Engineering
CHE, GUANGJI, Art
CHEN, DA, Material Science and Engineering
CHEN, DAOLIAN, Automation Engineering
CHEN, GUOPING, Aerospace Engineering
CHEN, HONGQUAN, Aerospace Engineering
CHEN, HUAIHAI, Aerospace Engineering
CHEN, QI, Economics and Management
CHEN, QIAN, Aerospace Engineering
CHEN, RENLIANG, Aerospace Engineering
CHEN, SONGCAN, Information Science and Technology
CHEN, WEI, Energy and Power Engineering
CHEN, XIN, Automation Engineering
CHEN, ZHILIANG, Aerospace Engineering
DANG, YAOGUO, Economics and Management
DENG, ZHIQUAN, Automation Engineering
DING, QIULIN, Information Science and Technology
DING, YUNLIANG, Aerospace Engineering
DU, JIDA, Aerospace Engineering
FAN, YINHE, Energy and Power Engineering
FANG, XIANDE, Aerospace Engineering
GAN, MINLIANG, Civil Aviation
GAO, DEPING, Energy and Power Engineering
GAO, DEPING, Civil Aviation
GAO, ZHENG, Aerospace Engineering
GE, NING, Energy and Power Engineering
GONG, CHUNYING, Automation Engineering
GU, HONGBIN, Civil Aviation
GU, ZHIMING, Natural Sciences
GU, ZHONGQUAN, Aerospace Engineering
GUAN, DE, Aerospace Engineering
GUO, RONGWEI, Energy and Power Engineering
GUO, WANLIN, Aerospace Engineering
HAN, JINGLONG, Aerospace Engineering
HE, JIANGSHENG, Humanities and Social Sciences
HE, JIANPING, Material Science and Engineering
HU, HAIYAN, Aerospace Engineering
HU, JUN, Energy and Power Engineering
HU, MINGHUA, Civil Aviation
HU, MINGMIN, Aerospace Engineering
HUANG, HULIN, Energy and Power Engineering
HUANG, JINQUAN, Energy and Power Engineering
HUANG, MINGGE, Aerospace Engineering
HUANG, SHENGGUO, Civil Aviation
HUANG, SHULA, Art
HUANG, ZAIXING, Aerospace Engineering
HUANG, ZHENGXIN, Humanities and Social Sciences
JI, HONGHU, Energy and Power Engineering
JIANG, BIN, Automation Engineering
JIANG, KESHEN, Economics and Management
LI, BANGYI, Economics and Management
LI, DONG, Humanities and Social Sciences
LI, NAN, Economics and Management
LI, PENGTONG, Natural Sciences
LI, SHUNMING, Energy and Power Engineering
LI, ZIQUAN, Material Science and Engineering
LI, ZONGZHI, Humanities and Social Sciences
LIAN, QIANGUI, Humanities and Social Sciences
LIANG, DAKAI, Aerospace Engineering
LIANG, DEWANG, Energy and Power Engineering
LIU, CANMING, Art
LIU, RENPEI, Material Science and Engineering
LIU, SIFENG, Economics and Management
LIU, WEIHUA, Aerospace Engineering
LIU, XIANBIN, Aerospace Engineering
LIU, YIPING, Economics and Management
LIU, YU, Information Science and Technology
LU, LIZHI, Humanities and Social Sciences
MA, JIE, Humanities and Social Sciences
MENG, FANCHAO, Humanities and Social Sciences
MIAO, JIANJUN, Humanities and Social Sciences
MING, XIAO, Aerospace Engineering
NIE, HONG, Aerospace Engineering
NING, XUANXI, Economics and Management
PENG, CAN, Economics and Management
QIAN, XIAOLIN, Information Science and Technology
RUAN, XINBO, Automation Engineering
SHENG, SONGBO, Natural Sciences
SHI, YUNLONG, Humanities and Social Sciences

SONG, BAOYIN, Aerospace Engineering
SONG, YINGDONG, Energy and Power Engineering
SUN, JIANGUO, Energy and Power Engineering
SUN, JIUHOU, Aerospace Engineering
SUN, LIANGXIN, Aerospace Engineering
TAN, QINGMEI, Humanities and Social Sciences
TANG, DENGBIN, Aerospace Engineering
TAO, JIE, Material Science and Engineering
TONG, MINGBO, Aerospace Engineering
WANG, CAIYONG, Art
WANG, HUAMING, Aerospace Engineering
WANG, JIANDONG, Information Science and Technology
WANG, KAIFU, Aerospace Engineering
WANG, LUJIE, Humanities and Social Sciences
WANG, XINWEI, Aerospace Engineering
WANG, YAN, Humanities and Social Sciences
WANG, YONGLIANG, Aerospace Engineering
WEI, MINXIANG, Energy and Power Engineering
WEN, WEIDONG, Energy and Power Engineering
WU, DAIZHAO, Aerospace Engineering
WU, DINGMIN, Humanities and Social Sciences
WU, WENLONG, Aerospace Engineering
XIA, HONGSHAN, Civil Aviation
XIA, PINQI, Aerospace Engineering
XIAO, JUN, Material Science and Engineering
XIAO, PING, Humanities and Social Sciences
XIE, SHAOJUN, Automation Engineering
XING, YAN, Automation Engineering
XIONG, KE, Aerospace Engineering
XU, DAZHUAN, Information Science and Technology
XU, GUOHUA, Aerospace Engineering
XU, JINFA, Aerospace Engineering
XU, QIANG, Humanities and Social Sciences
XU, ZONGZE, Information Science and Technology
YANG, LILI, Art
YAO, WEIXING, Aerospace Engineering
YE, ZHIFENG, Energy and Power Engineering
YIN, HONGYOU, Natural Sciences
YU, XIONGQING, Aerospace Engineering
YU, XIWU, Aerospace Engineering
YUAN, SHENFANG, Aerospace Engineering
YUE, QIN, Natural Sciences
ZHANG, BUREN, Humanities and Social Sciences
ZHANG, CHENGLIN, Aerospace Engineering
ZHANG, GUODAI, Natural Sciences
ZHANG, JINGZHOU, Energy and Power Engineering
ZHANG, KUNYUAN, Energy and Power Engineering
ZHANG, LINGMI, Aerospace Engineering
ZHANG, LUMING, Natural Sciences
ZHANG, ZENGCHANG, Aerospace Engineering
ZHAO, CHUNSHENG, Aerospace Engineering
ZHAO, JIANXING, Energy and Power Engineering
ZHAO, MIN, Automation Engineering
ZHAO, NING, Aerospace Engineering
ZHAO, YOUQUN, Energy and Power Engineering
ZHENG, QI, Art
ZHENG, SHIJIE, Aerospace Engineering
ZHOU, CHUANRONG, Aerospace Engineering
ZHOU, DEQUN, Economics and Management
ZHOU, JIANJIANG, Information Science and Technology
ZHOU, LI, Aerospace Engineering
ZHU, JIANYING, Civil Aviation
ZHU, JINDONG, Humanities and Social Sciences
ZHU, JINFU, Civil Aviation
ZHU, WUJIA, Information Science and Technology
ZHU, ZHAODA, Information Science and Technology
ZUO, HONGFU, Civil Aviation

ATTACHED RESEARCH INSTITUTES

Aerospace Power Science and Technology Centre: Dir ZHOU BO.

Jiangsu Engineering Technology Research Centre of Digital Design and Manufacture: Dir LIAO WENHE.

Key Laboratory of Intellectual Materials and Structure Aviation Technology: Dir TAO BAOQI.

Key Laboratory of Vibration Engineering: Dir HU HAIYAN.

Laboratory of Airpower Dynamics: Dir WU DAIZHAO.

Laboratory of Helicopter Technology: Dir ZHANG CHENGLIN.

Research Centre for CAD and CAM: Dir ZHOU RURONG.

Research Centre of Ultrasonic Motors: Dir ZHAO CHUNSHENG.

State Key Laboratory of Helicopter Rotor Dynamics: Dir GAO ZHENG.

NANJING AGRICULTURAL UNIVERSITY

1 Weigang Rd, Nanjing 210095, Jiangsu
Telephone: (8625) 84395366
Internet: www.njau.edu.cn

Founded 1952
Ministry of Education control
Academic year: September to July

President: ZHENG XIAOBO
Vice-Presidents: CAO WEIXING, QU FUTIAN, SUN JIAN, WANG YAONAN, XU XIANG, ZHOU GUANGHONG
Librarian: GAO RONGHUA

Number of teachers: 2,400
Number of students: 24,000

Publications: *Agricultural Education of China* (6 a year), *Agricultural History of China* (quarterly), *Animal Husbandry and Veterinary Science* (6 a year), *Chinese Animal Products and Food* (6 a year), *Journal* (natural sciences, quarterly), *Journal* (social sciences, quarterly)

DEANS

College of Adult Education: XU XIANG
College of Agronomy: WAN JIANMIN
College of Animal Science and Technology: WANG TIAN
College of Economics and Management: ZHONG FUNING
College of Engineering: DING WEIMIN
College of Food Sciences and Technology: LU ZHAOXIN
College of Foreign Studies: XU XIANG
College of Horticulture: XILIN HOU
College of Humanities and Social Sciences: WANG SIMING
College of Information Sciences and Technology: GAO RONGHUA
College of International Education: YAN ZHIMING
College of Life Sciences: XU LANGLAI
College of Plant Protection: HAN ZHAOJUN
College of Public Management (incorporating College of Land Management): (vacant)
College of Resources and Environmental Sciences: SHEN QIRONG
College of Science: YANG CHUNLONG
College of Veterinary Medicine: ZOU SIXIANG
Graduate School: ZHENG XIAOBO

PROFESSORS

BAO, ENDONG, Veterinary Medicine
BIAN, XINMIN, Agronomy
CAI, QINGSHENG, Agronomy
CAI, QINGSHENG, Life Sciences
CAO, WEIXING, Agronomy
CHEN, FUYAN, Veterinary Medicine
CHEN, JIE, Veterinary Medicine
CHEN, JINFENG, Horticulture
CHEN, MAO, Humanities and Social Sciences
CHEN, QIUSHENG, Veterinary Medicine
CHEN, WANMING, Economics and Management
CHEN, WEIHUA, Veterinary Medicine
CHEN, WENLIN, Humanities and Social Sciences
CHEN, XIAOMIN, Resources and Environmental Sciences
CHENG, CHUNYOU, Foreign Languages
CHU, BAOJIN, Economics and Management
DAI, HAOGUO, Plant Protection
DENG, ZHAOCHUN, Foreign Languages
DING, WEIMIN, Engineering
DONG, MINGSHENG, Food Science and Technology
DONG, SHUANGLIN, Plant Protection
GAI, JUNYI, Agronomy
GAO, GUANG, Land Science
GE, JIQI, Land Management
GONG, YIQIN, Horticulture
GU, HUANZHANG, Economics and Management
GU, ZHENXIN, Food Science and Technology
GUAN, HENGLU, Humanities and Social Sciences
GUO, JIANHUA, Plant Protection
GUO, QIAOSHENG, Horticulture
GUO, SHIRONG, Horticulture
GUO, WEIMING, Horticulture
HAN, ZHAOJUN, Plant Protection
HONG, XIAOYUE, Plant Protection
HOU, GUANGXU, Foreign Languages
HOU, HANQING, Information Science and Technology
HOU, JIAFA, Veterinary Medicine
HOU, XILIN, Horticulture
HU, FENG, Resources and Environmental Sciences
HU, JINBO, Humanities and Social Sciences
HU, QIUHUI, Food Science and Technology
HU, YUANLIANG, Veterinary Medicine
HUANG, KEHE, Veterinary Medicine
HUANG, SHUIQING, Information Science and Technology
HUANG, WEIYI, Resources and Environmental Sciences
HUANG, YAO, Resources and Environmental Sciences
HUI, FUPING, Humanities and Social Sciences
JI, CHANGYING, Engineering
JIANG, HANHU, Food Science and Technology
JIANG, MINGYI, Life Sciences
JIANG, PING, Veterinary Medicine
LAN, YEQING, Land Science
LEI, ZHIHAI, Veterinary Medicine
LI, BAOPING, Plant Protection
LI, SHUNPENG, Resources and Environmental Sciences
LI, XIANGRUI, Veterinary Medicine
LI, YANGHAN, Agronomy
LI, YUEYUN, Economics and Management
LIANG, YONGCHAO, Resources and Environmental Sciences
LIN, MAOSONG, Plant Protection
LIU, BAOJIN, Economics and Management
LIU, DAJUN, Agronomy
LIU, DEHUI, Resources and Environmental Sciences
LIU, HONGLIN, Animal Science and Technology
LIU, LEI, Information Science and Technology
LIU, YOULIANG, Agronomy
LIU, YOUZHAO, Land Management
LIU, ZHAOPU, Resources and Environmental Sciences
LU, CHENGPING, Veterinary Medicine
LU, DAXIN, Engineering
LU, ZHAOXIN, Food Science and Technology
LU, ZUOMEI, Agronomy
LUO, WEIHONG, Agronomy
MA, KAI, Horticulture
MENG, LING, Plant Protection
MENG, LINGJIE, Economics and Management

NIU, YOUQI, Information Science and Technology
OU, MINGHAO, Land Management
PAN, GENXIN, Resources and Environmental Sciences
PAN, JIANJUN, Resources and Environmental Sciences
PENG, JISHENG, Humanities and Social Sciences
PENG, ZENGQI, Food Science and Technology
QIANG, SHENG, Agronomy
QIANG, SHENG, Life Sciences
QIN, LIJUN, Foreign Languages
QU, FUTIAN, Land Management
SHEN, JINLIANG, Plant Protection
SHEN, QIRONG, Resources and Environmental Sciences
SHEN, YIXIN, Animal Science and Technology
SHEN, YONGLIN, Veterinary Medicine
SHEN, ZHENGUO, Agronomy
SHEN, ZHENGUO, Life Sciences
SHENG, BANGYUE, Humanities and Social Sciences
SUN, HANGSHENG, Economics and Management
SUN, JIN, Resources and Environmental Sciences
TANG, YIZU, Agronomy
TU, KANG, Food Science and Technology
WANG, GENLIN, Animal Science and Technology
WANG, GUOJIE, Veterinary Medicine
WANG, HUAIMING, Economics and Management
WANG, JIANMIN, Agronomy
WANG, JINSHENG, Plant Protection
WANG, KAI, Economics and Management
WANG, KERONG, Plant Protection
WANG, LINYUN, Animal Science and Technology
WANG, RONG, Economics and Management
WANG, SIMING, Humanities and Social Sciences
WANG, TIAN, Animal Science and Technology
WANG, WANMAO, Land Management
WANG, XIAOHUA, Engineering
WANG, XIAOLONG, Veterinary Medicine
WANG, YINQUAN, Foreign Languages
WANG, YUQUAN, Land Science
WHONG, ZHIWEI, Resources and Environmental Sciences
WU, QINSHENG, Horticulture
WU, YIDONG, Plant Protection
WU, YULIN, Economics and Management
XIE, ZHUANG, Animal Science and Technology
XU, JIANHUA, Plant Protection
XU, LIANGLAI, Life Sciences
XU, LIREN, Veterinary Medicine
XU, XIANG, Economics and Management
XU, YIWEN, Humanities and Social Sciences
YAN, HUOQI, Humanities and Social Sciences
YAN, PEISHI, Animal Science and Technology
YANG, HONG, Land Science
YANG, LIANFANG, Plant Protection
YANG, LIGUO, Animal Science and Technology
YANG, MINGMIN, Land Science
YANG, QIANG, Veterinary Medicine
YANG, QING, Life Sciences
YANG, SHIHU, Agronomy
YANG, ZHIMIN, Life Sciences
YE, YIGUANG, Economics and Management
YIN, WENQING, Engineering
YING, RUIYAO, Economics and Management
YU, DEYUE, Agronomy
ZHAI, BAOPING, Plant Protection
ZHANG, BING, Economics and Management
ZHANG, CHUNLAN, Resources and Environmental Sciences
ZHANG, FANG, Humanities and Social Sciences
ZHANG, GUOTAI, Agronomy
ZHANG, HAIBIN, Veterinary Medicine
ZHANG, HONGSHENG, Agronomy
ZHANG, JINGSHUN, Economics and Management
ZHANG, RONGXIAN, Agronomy
ZHANG, SHAOLING, Horticulture
ZHANG, SHUXIA, Veterinary Medicine
ZHANG, TIANZHEN, Agronomy
ZHANG, WEIQIANG, Engineering
ZHANG, ZHEN, Horticulture
ZHAO, RUQIAN, Veterinary Medicine
ZHENG, XIAOBO, Plant Protection
ZHENG, YONGHUA, Food Science and Technology
ZHONG, FUNING, Economics and Management
ZHOU, GUANGHONG, Food Science and Technology
ZHOU, LIXIANG, Resources and Environmental Sciences
ZHOU, MINGGUO, Plant Protection
ZHOU, SHUDONG, Economics and Management
ZHOU, YINGHENG, Economics and Management
ZHU, JUN, Life Sciences
ZHU, SIHONG, Engineering
ZHU, WEIYUN, Animal Science and Technology
ZHU, YUELIN, Horticulture
ZONG, LIANGGANG, Resources and Environmental Sciences
ZOU, SIXIANG, Veterinary Medicine

ATTACHED RESEARCH INSTITUTES

Agricultural Economics Research Institute: Dir ZHONG FUNING.

Agricultural Entomology Research Institute: Dir HAN ZHAOJUN.

Animal Infectious Diseases Laboratory: Dir HOU JIAFA.

Animal Physiology Laboratory: Dir ZHAO RUXI.

Animal Reproduction Laboratory: Dir SHI FANGXIONG.

Applied Microbiology Laboratory: Dir HUANG WEIYI.

Cytogenetics Research Institute: Dir LIU DAJUN.

Hi-Tech Key Laboratory of Information Agriculture of Jiangsu Province: Dir CAO WEIXING.

Institute of Agricultural History: Dir WANG SIMING.

Key Laboratory of Microbiological Engineering in the Agricultural Environment: Dir ZHU JUN.

Key Laboratory of Crop Growth Regulation: Dir CAO WEIXING.

Plant Pathogen Research Institute: Dir ZHENG XIAOBO.

Rice Laboratory: Dir WAN JIANMING.

Soybean Research Institute: Dir YU DEYUE.

State Key Laboratory of Crop Genetics and Germplasm Enhancement: Dir ZHANG TIANZHEN.

Vegetable Sciences Research Institute: Dir CHEN JINFENG.

Weed Laboratory: Dir QIAN SHENG.

NANJING UNIVERSITY OF ECONOMICS

128 Tielubeijie, Nanjing 210003
Telephone: (25) 3418207
Fax: (25) 3418207
Internet: www.njue.edu.cn

Founded 1956, present status 1981
State control
Academic year: September to July

President: Dr XU CONGCAI
Vice-Presidents: LI SHIHUA, WANG SUITING, GAO YADONG, ZHANG ZHENGGANG, WANG JIAXIN
Librarian: DING DAKE

Library: over 500,000 vols
Number of teachers: 565
Number of students: 5,600 (incl. correspondence courses 3,000)

Publication: *Journal of Nanjing University of Economics*

HEADS OF DEPARTMENTS

Trade and Economics: QIAO JUN
Accounting: WANG KAITIAN
Business Management: LI YAFEI
Finance: LING YINGBING
Tourism: LI YAFEI
Economics: LI QUANGEN
Law (incl. Political Science and Philosophy): CAO KE
Basic Courses: ZHU LINGMEI
Adult Education School: CUI XINYOU
China Training Centre for Grain Distribution Management: XU CONGCAI (Dir)

NANJING FORESTRY UNIVERSITY

9 Xinzhuang, Longpan Rd, Nanjing 210037, Jiangsu
Telephone: (25) 85427131
Fax: (25) 85412389
E-mail: interpro@njfu.edu.cn
Internet: www.njfu.edu.cn

Founded 1952

President: Prof. YU SHIYUAN
Vice-Presidents: Prof. CAI FULIANG, Prof. ZHANG SHUQAN, Prof. SHI JISEN
Librarian: LIU XIUHUA

Library of 600,000 vols
Number of teachers: 731
Number of students: 4,000 (incl. 274 postgraduates)

Publications: *Journal of Nanjing Forestry University*, *Bamboo Research*, *China Forestry Science and Technology*, *Interior Design and Construction*, *Forestry Energy Conservation*

HEADS OF COLLEGES AND DEPARTMENTS

Forest Resources and Environment: Prof. CAO FULIANG
Wood Science and Technology: Prof. TAN SHOUXIA
Chemical Engineering: Prof. AN XINNAN
Mechanical and Electronic Engineering: Prof. ZHOU YONGZHAO
Forest Economics and Management: Prof. CHEN GUOLIANG
Civil Engineering: Prof. ZHAO CHEN
Adult Education: Prof. GUAN SUQI
Graduate Studies: Prof. YE JIANREN
Basic Courses Division: Assoc. Prof. WEI SHUGUANG
Social Sciences Division: Assoc. Prof. WANG GUOPIN

PROFESSORS

XIONG WENYUE, Forest Ecology
ZHU ZHENGDE, Forest Botany
LI ZHONGZHENG, Chemical Processing of Forest Products
CHEN ZHI, Chemical Processing of Forest Products
HUA YUKUN, Wood Processing
SU JINYUN, Forest Engineering
CHEN GUOLIANG, Forest Economics
SHEN GUANFU, Forest Mechanics

NANJING MEDICAL UNIVERSITY

140 Hanzhong Rd, Nanjing 210029, Jiangsu
Telephone: (25) 6649141
Fax: (25) 6612696
E-mail: xiaoban@njmu.edu.cn
Internet: www.njmu.edu.cn

Founded 1934
Academic year: September to July

President: CHEN QI

Vice-Presidents: Hu Gang, Huang Jun, Qu Zhaomin, Xu Yaochu, Wang Xinru
Librarian: Zhang Zhenghui

Library of 1,040,330 vols
Number of teachers: 1,148
Number of students: 7,283

Publications: *Jiangsu Medical Journal* (monthly), *Journal* (6 a year), *Journal of Clinical Neurology* (6 a year)

DEANS

First Clinical Medical College: Huang Jun
Second Clinical Medical College: Liu Hui
Third Clinical Medical College: (vacant)
School of Basic Medical Science: Zhu Changliang
School of Health Policy and Management: Meng Guoxiang
School of Medicine: Zhu Dongya
School of Nursing: Cui Yan
School of Public Health: Zhou Jianwei

PROFESSORS

Bi, Zhigang, Clinical Medicine I
Bian, Jiayi, Medicine
Cai, Yi, Clinical Medicine II
Cao, Kejiang, Clinical Medicine I
Chang, Yi, Clinical Medicine II
Chen, Guangming, Clinical Medicine I
Chen, Guoyu, Clinical Medicine I
Chen, Ronghua, Clinical Medicine II
Chen, Xiwei, Basic Medical Science
Chen, Yijiang, Clinical Medicine I
Chen, Yulian, Public Health
Cheng, Yunlin, Clinical Medicine I
De, Wei, Basic Medical Science
Ding, Jiong, Basic Medical Science
Ding, Xinsheng, Clinical Medicine I
Fan, Qinhe, Clinical Medicine I
Fan, Weiming, Clinical Medicine I
Fu, Chengzhang, Clinical Medicine I
Fu, Zheng, Clinical Medicine I
Hu, Guang, Basic Medical Science
Hu, Qin, Medicine
Hu, Weixing, Clinical Medicine I
Huang, Jun, Clinical Medicine I
Huang, Zhuhu, Clinical Medicine I
Li, Guoping, Clinical Medicine I
Li, Jianan, Clinical Medicine I
Li, Jun, Clinical Medicine II
Li, Shengnan, Basic Medical Science
Li, Yuehua, Basic Medical Science
Li, Zuohan, Clinical Medicine II
Liu, Chao, Clinical Medicine I
Liu, Jiayin, Clinical Medicine I
Liu, Qizhan, Public Health
Liu, Xunliang, Clinical Medicine I
Lu, Fengxiang, Clinical Medicine I
Luo, Dan, Clinical Medicine I
Ma, Wenzhu, Clinical Medicine I
Meng, Guoxiang, Health Policy and Management
Miao, Yi, Clinical Medicine I
Ni, Chunhui, Public Health
Qi, Xiaohong, Basic Medical Science
Shun, Nanxiong, Clinical Medicine I
Shun, Yujie, Basic Medical Science
Tang, Lingfang, Public Health
Wang, Defang, Clinical Medicine I
Wang, Hemin, Basic Medical Science
Wang, Hong, Clinical Medicine I
Wang, Shoulin, Public Health
Wang, Xiaoyun, Clinical Medicine I
Wang, Xinru, Public Health
Wang, Xuehao, Clinical Medicine I
Wang, Yingwei, Basic Medical Science
Wang, Yong, Basic Medical Science
Wang, Yubin, Clinical Medicine I
Wei, Baiqi, Medicine
Wu, Haiwei, Basic Medical Science
Wu, Hongfei, Clinical Medicine I
Wu, Jinchang, Clinical Medicine I
Wu, Wenxi, Clinical Medicine I
Wu, Zhengyan, Clinical Medicine I
Xiao, Hang, Public Health
Xu, Qunwei, Medicine
Xu, Xinrong, Clinical Medicine I
Yin, Kaisheng, Clinical Medicine I
Zhang, Fumin, Clinical Medicine I
Zhang, Haidi, Clinical Medicine I
Zhang, Jinan, Clinical Medicine I
Zhang, Qi, Public Health
Zhang, Yidong, Clinical Medicine II
Zhang, Zhengdong, Public Health
Zhang, Zhongnan, Clinical Medicine I
Zhao, Zhiquan, Clinical Medicine I
Zhou, Jianwei, Public Health
Zhou, Xuemin, Medicine
Zhou, Zuoming, Basic Medical Science
Zhu, Changliang, Basic Medical Science
Zhu, Dongya, Medicine
Zhu, Guoqing, Basic Medical Science
Zhu, Wenyuan, Clinical Medicine I

ATTACHED RESEARCH INSTITUTES

Stomatology Hospital: Dir Wang Lin.
Vocational and Technology College

NANJING INSTITUTE OF METEOROLOGY

114 Pancheng New Street, Nanjing 210044, Jiangsu
Telephone: 8731102
Fax: 7792648
E-mail: nimemail@nim02.njim.edu.cn
Internet: www.njim.edu.cn

Founded 1960
State control
Languages of instruction: Chinese, English
Academic year: September to July

President: Sun Zhaobo
Vice-President: Lu Weisong
Dean: Zhao Xueyu
Chief Administrative Officer: Xu Kai
Librarian: Pang Xinguo

Library of 500,000 vols
Number of teachers: 450
Number of students: 8,000

Publications: *Journal* (4 a year), *Meteorological Education and Science and Technology* (4 a year)

CHAIRMEN OF DEPARTMENTS

Atmospheric Sciences: He Jinhai
Environmental Sciences: Miao Qilong
Electronics and Information Sciences: Wang Zhenhui
Foreign Languages: Xu Xianwen
Social Science: Cheng Jianjun
Computer Science and Technology: Xiao Dongrong
Adult Education: Sun Dongyuan
Mathmatics: Li Gang
Physics: Zhu Yufeng
Postgraduate School: Du Bingyu
WMO Regional Meteorological Training Centre: Ye Qihao

NANJING NORMAL UNIVERSITY

122 Ninghai Rd, Nanjing 210097, Jiangsu
Telephone: (25) 3720999
Fax: (25) 3706565
Internet: www.njnu.edu.cn

Founded 1902
Provincial govt control
Academic year: September to August

President: Prof. Gong Pixiang
Vice-Presidents: Prof. Lu Bingshou, Prof. Chen Guojun, Prof. Tu Guohua, Prof. Chen Lingfu, Prof. Wang Xiaopeng, Prof. Zhu Xiaoman, Prof. Huang Tao
Dean of Postgraduate Studies: Pan Baiqi
Librarian: Wu Jin

Library of 1,650,000 vols
Number of teachers: 1,100
Number of students: 7,000 (incl. 430 postgraduates)

Publications: *Periodicals of Nanjing Normal University* (social sciences, natural sciences), *References for Educational Research, Fine Arts Education in China*, text books

HEADS OF DEPARTMENTS AND COLLEGES

College of Economics and Law: Gong Tingtai
College of Journalism and Communication: Yue Binglong
Jinling Women's College: Huang Tao
Adult Education College: Zhang Qiyuan
Educational Science College: Yang Qiliang
International Culture and Education College: Lu Tongqun
Chinese Language and Literature: He Yongkang
History and Sociology: Yu Kunqi
Foreign Languages and Literature: Chen Aimin
Mathematics: Song Yongzhong
Physics: Huang Keliang
Chemistry: Zhou Zhihua
Biology: Shi Guoxin
Geography Science College: Sha Run
Music: Yu Zizheng
Fine Arts: Fan Yang
Physical Education: Fan Wenbin
Computer Science: Cai Shaoji
Physics and Chemistry Laboratory: Liu Guojin
Classical Books and Documents Institute: Yu Xianhao
Education Research Institute: Yang Qiliang
Chinese Literature Institute: Zhong Zhenzhen
Jiangsu Teachers' Training Centre for Institutions of Higher Learning: Zhu Xiaoman
Jiangsu Journalists' Training Centre: Chen Guojun
Jiangsu Teachers' Training Centre for Pre-School Education: Yang Jiujun
Jiangsu International Economic and Cultural Exchange Centre: Shen Zhengchai
Jiangsu Personnel Training Centre for Intellectual Property Rights Protection: Chen Lingfu
Audiovisual Education Centre: Zhen Ken

NANJING UNIVERSITY OF POSTS AND TELECOMMUNICATIONS

66 Xin Mofan Ma Lu, Nanjing 210003, Jiangsu
Telephone: (25) 3492038
Fax: (25) 3492349
E-mail: nupt@njupt.edu.cn
Internet: www.njupt.edu.cn

Founded 1942
Academic year: September to July

President: Xie Ling
Vice-Presidents: Zhang Xiaoqiang, Yie Zhangzhao, Zhang Shunyi, Tang Jintu
Librarian: Yang Zhuying

Library: over 600,000 vols
Number of teachers: 768
Number of students: 7,970 (4,300 undergraduates, 270 postgraduates, 3,400 correspondence)

Publications: *NIPT Periodical*, *Journal of Social Science*

HEADS OF DEPARTMENTS

Management Engineering: Wang Liangyuan
Communications Engineering: Feng Guangzeng
Information Engineering: Yu Zhaomin
Computer Science and Technology: Wang Shaoli
Electrical Engineering: Wang Shuoping
Basic Courses: Chen Heming
Social Science: Xu Rurong

Physical Education: WANG KUANZHENG
Foreign Languages: HUAN SHUXIAN
Optical Fibre Communication Research Institute: SHEN JIANHUA
Information Network Technology Institute: ZHANG SHUNYI
Image Processing and Image Communications Institute: BI HOUJIE
Postal Engineering: GAO BIN
Training: WU RUIPING

PROFESSORS

BI HOUJIE, Image Communications
CAO WEI, Microwave Communications
CHEN TINGBIAO, Information Engineering
CHEN XI SHENG, Telecommunications Engineering
FENG GUANGZENG, Satellite Communications
HU JIANZHANG, Information Engineering
JU TI, Computer Engineering Science
KAN JIAHAI, Mathematics
LI BIAOQING, Telecommunications Engineering
LUO CHANGLONG, Computer Science
MEI ZHUOCHUN, Communication and Electronic Systems
MI ZHENGKUN, Communications Engineering
QI YUSHENG, Mobile Communication
QIN TINGKAI, Electrical Engineering
SHEN JINLONG, Computer Communication
SHEN YUANLONG, Electrical Engineering
SUN JINLUN, Communications Engineering
TANG JIAYI, Computer Science
WANG SHAOLI, Computer Communication
WANG SHUOPING, Electrical Engineering
WU XINYU, Electrical Engineering
WU ZHIZHONG, Electrical Engineering
XU CHENGQI, Telecommunications Engineering
YANG ZHUYING, Electrical Engineering
YIE ZHANGZHAO, Mathematics
YU ZHAOMIN, Information Engineering
ZHANG LIJUN, Telecommunications Engineering
ZHANG SHUNYI, Computer Communications
ZHANG XIAOQIANG, Communication Systems
ZHANG ZHIYONG, Electrical Engineering
ZHANG ZONGCHENG, Information Engineering
ZHENG BAOYU, Telecommunications Engineering
ZHU XIUCHANG, Information Engineering

NANJING UNIVERSITY OF SCIENCE AND TECHNOLOGY

200 Xiao Lingwei, Nanjing 210094, Jiangsu
Telephone: (25) 84315567
Internet: www.njust.edu.cn
Founded 1953
Commission of Science, Technology and Industry for National Defence control
Academic year: September to July
President: XU FUMING
Vice-Presidents: LIU LIHUA, SONG WENYU, WANG XIAOFENG, WANG XIN, XUAN YIMIN, YANG SHANZHI
Head of Graduate Department: WANG XIN
Librarian: PANG HONGJUN
Number of teachers: 1,505
Number of students: 29,626
Publications: *Higher Education Digest* (monthly), *Journal* (natural sciences, 6 a year), *Journal* (social sciences, 6 a year), *Journal of Ballistics* (quarterly), *Journal of Explosive Materials* (6 a year), *Journal of Optoelectronic Information* (6 a year)

DEANS

School of Adult Education: ZHANG XINKE
School of Chemical Engineering: WANG DAJUN
School of Economics and Management: YU ANPING
School of Electronic Engineering and Optoelectronic Technology: LIU ZHONG
School of Humanities and Social Sciences: WANG DAYONG
School of International Education: WANG QINYOU
School of Mechanical Engineering: QIAN LINFANG
School of Power Engineering: WANG ZHONGYUAN
School of Science: YANG XIAOPING
Vocational and Technical College: ZHANG YUEXIN
Department of Automation Engineering: BO YUMING
Department of Computer Science: TANG ZHENMIN
Department of Materials Science and Engineering: CHEN GUANG

PROFESSORS

AN, LICHAO, Chemical Engineering
BO, LIANFA, Electronic Engineering and Optoelectronic Technology
BO, YUMING, Automation Engineering
CAI, CHUN, Chemical Engineering
CAO, CONGYONG, Mechanical Engineering
CHANG, BENKANG, Electronic Engineering and Optoelectronic Technology
CHEN, GUANG, Materials Science and Engineering
CHEN, GUOLIANG, Materials Science and Engineering
CHEN, HEJUAN, Mechanical Engineering
CHEN, LEI, Electronic Engineering and Optoelectronic Technology
CHEN, QIAN, Electronic Engineering and Optoelectronic Technology
CHEN, QINGWEI, Automation Engineering
CHEN, RUSHAN, Electronic Engineering and Optoelectronic Technology
CHEN, YANRU, Electronic Engineering and Optoelectronic Technology
CHENG, YI, Chemical Engineering
CUI, CHONG, Materials Science and Engineering
DAI, YUEWEI, Automation Engineering
DENG, KAIMING, Natural Science
DU, YULAN, Economics and Management
DUAN, QIJUN, Mechanical Engineering
FAN, BAOCHUN, Power Engineering
FAN, XINMIN, Materials Science and Engineering
FANG, DAGANG, Electronic Engineering and Optoelectronic Technology
FANG, ZHIJIE, Chemical Engineering
FANG, ZILIANG, Mechanical Engineering
FENG, JUNWEN, Economics and Management
GAN, LIREN, Economics and Management
GEN, JIHUI, Power Engineering
GONG, GUANGRONG, Mechanical Engineering
GU, KEQIU, Mechanical Engineering
GU, XIAOHUI, Mechanical Engineering
GUO, ZHI, Automation Engineering
HAN, YUQI, Economics and Management
HAN, ZHIJUN, Economics and Management
HAN, ZIPENG, Power Engineering
HAO, JIANCHU, Chemical Engineering
HE, ANZHI, Natural Science
HE, QIHUAN, Chemical Engineering
HE, YONG, Mechanical Engineering
HE, ZHAOJI, Humanities and Social Sciences
HOU, XIAOXIA, Automation Engineering
HOU, YUANLONG, Mechanical Engineering
HU, KAIJIE, Humanities and Social Sciences
HU, WEILI, Automation Engineering
HUANG, JIN-AN, Automation Engineering
HUANG, YINSHENG, Chemical Engineering
HUANG, ZHENGYA, Chemical Engineering
HUI, JUNMING, Chemical Engineering
HUI, XIAOHUA, Electronic Engineering and Optoelectronic Technology
JIANG, JIANFANG, Automation Engineering
JIANG, LIPING, Electronic Engineering and Optoelectronic Technology
JIANG, RENYUAN, Mechanical Engineering
JIN, ZHONG, Computer Science
KANG, XIAODONG, Economics and Management
LAN, SHAOHUA, Computer Science
LI, BAOMING, Power Engineering
LI, CHENGJUN, Chemical Engineering
LI, DONGBO, Mechanical Engineering
LI, FENGSHENG, Chemical Engineering
LI, HONGCHANG, Chemical Engineering
LI, HUIZHONG, Materials Science and Engineering
LI, XIANGYIN, Natural Science
LI, XIAONING, Mechanical Engineering
LI, XINGGUO, Electronic Engineering and Optoelectronic Technology
LI, YAJUN, Mechanical Engineering
LI, YING, Mechanical Engineering
LI, ZHENHUA, Natural Science
LIANG, RENJIE, Mechanical Engineering
LIU, DABIN, Chemical Engineering
LIU, FENGYU, Computer Science
LIU, HONGYING, Chemical Engineering
LIU, JIACONG, Chemical Engineering
LIU, KUI, Humanities and Social Sciences
LIU, ZHONG, Electronic Engineering and Optoelectronic Technology
LIU, ZULIANG, Chemical Engineering
LOU, LANGHONG, Materials Science and Engineering
LU, CHUNXU, Chemical Engineering
LU, JIAN, Natural Science
LU, JINHUI, Electronic Engineering and Optoelectronic Technology
LU, LUDE, Chemical Engineering
LU, MING, Chemical Engineering
LUO, GUOWEI, Electronic Engineering and Optoelectronic Technology
MA, DAWEI, Mechanical Engineering
MA, YIZHONG, Economics and Management
MENG, YINGJUN, Electronic Engineering and Optoelectronic Technology
MOU, SHANXIANG, Electronic Engineering and Optoelectronic Technology
NI, OUQI, Chemical Engineering
NI, XIAOWU, Natural Science
PAN, GONGPEI, Chemical Engineering
PAN, RENMING, Chemical Engineering
PAN, ZHENGWEI, Mechanical Engineering
PENG, JINHUA, Chemical Engineering
PENG, XINHUA, Chemical Engineering
PU, XIONGZHU, Mechanical Engineering
QIAN, JIANPING, Automation Engineering
QIAN, LINFANG, Mechanical Engineering
SHEN, PEIHUI, Mechanical Engineering
SHEN, RUIQI, Chemical Engineering
SHENG, ANDONG, Automation Engineering
SHI, LIANJIE, Materials Science and Engineering
SHI, TIANHUA, Economics and Management
SHI, XIANGQUAN, Electronic Engineering and Optoelectronic Technology
SONG, YAOLIANG, Electronic Engineering and Optoelectronic Technology
SUN, GUIXIANG, Humanities and Social Sciences
SUN, HUAIJIANG, Computer Science
SUN, JIANPING, Economics and Management
SUN, JINSHENG, Automation Engineering
SUN, JINTAO, Electronic Engineering and Optoelectronic Technology
SUN, YAMIN, Computer Science
SUN, YU, Mechanical Engineering
TAN, LEBIN, Mechanical Engineering
TANG, ZHENMIN, Computer Science
TAO, CHUNKAN, Electronic Engineering and Optoelectronic Technology
WANG, DAYONG, Humanities and Social Sciences
WANG, FENGYUN, Chemical Engineering
WANG, HUAKUN, Mechanical Engineering
WANG, JIANXIN, Electronic Engineering and Optoelectronic Technology
WANG, JIANYU, Automation Engineering
WANG, JINGTAO, Materials Science and Engineering
WANG, JUNDE, Chemical Engineering

WANG, KEHONG, Materials Science and Engineering
WANG, LIANGGUO, Natural Science
WANG, LIANGMING, Power Engineering
WANG, LIANGMO, Mechanical Engineering
WANG, LIANJUN, Chemical Engineering
WANG, NAIYAN, Chemical Engineering
WANG, SHUMEI, Computer Science
WANG, XIAOMING, Mechanical Engineering
WANG, XIN, Chemical Engineering
WANG, YUSHI, Mechanical Engineering
WANG, ZESHAN, Chemical Engineering
WANG, ZHIQUAN, Automation Engineering
WEI, YUNYANG, Chemical Engineering
WEI, ZHIHUI, Natural Science
WEN, CHUNSHENG, Power Engineering
WU, HUIZHONG, Computer Science
WU, JIANG, Materials Science and Engineering
WU, JUNJI, Power Engineering
WU, XIAOBEI, Automation Engineering
XIA, DESHEN, Computer Science
XIAO, HEMING, Chemical Engineering
XIONG, DANGSHENG, Materials Science and Engineering
XU, FUMING, Chemical Engineering
XU, HOUQIAN, Power Engineering
XU, JIANCHENG, Mechanical Engineering
XU, JIANZHONG, Electronic Engineering and Optoelectronic Technology
XU, MING, Chemical Engineering
XU, MINGYOU, Power Engineering
XU, SHENGYUAN, Automation Engineering
XU, WANHE, Mechanical Engineering
XU, ZHENXIANG, Chemical Engineering
XU, ZHILIANG, Automation Engineering
XUAN, YIMIN, Power Engineering
XUE, HENGXIN, Economics and Management
XUE, XIAOZHONG, Power Engineering
YAN, LIANHE, Chemical Engineering
YANG, CHENGWU, Power Engineering
YANG, DETONG, Materials Science and Engineering
YANG, SHUIYANG, Humanities and Social Sciences
YANG, SHULIN, Chemical Engineering
YANG, XIAOPING, Natural Science
YANG, XUJIE, Chemical Engineering
YANG, ZHENYU, Computer Science
YAO, JUN, Humanities and Social Sciences
YE, YOUPEI, Computer Science
YIN, XIAOCHUN, Natural Science
YIN, ZHENGZHOU, Mechanical Engineering
YU, ANPING, Economics and Management
YU, YONGGANG, Power Engineering
YUAN, JUNTANG, Mechanical Engineering
YUAN, YAXIONG, Power Engineering
ZHANG, BAOMIN, Electronic Engineering and Optoelectronic Technology
ZHANG, CHI, Chemical Engineering
ZHANG, FENG, Power Engineering
ZHANG, FUXIANG, Mechanical Engineering
ZHANG, GONGXUAN, Computer Science
ZHANG, HONG, Computer Science
ZHANG, MINGYAN, Economics and Management
ZHANG, SHAOFAN, Power Engineering
ZHANG, TIE, Mechanical Engineering
ZHANG, XI, Mechanical Engineering
ZHANG, XIAOBING, Power Engineering
ZHANG, YOULIANG, Mechanical Engineering
ZHANG, YUE, Mechanical Engineering
ZHANG, YUEJUN, Chemical Engineering
ZHANG, ZHONGLIN, Economics and Management
ZHANG, ZHONGXIONG, Electronic Engineering and Optoelectronic Technology
ZHAO, BAOCHANG, Chemical Engineering
ZHAO, CHUNXIA, Computer Science
ZHAO, HUICHANG, Electronic Engineering and Optoelectronic Technology
ZHENG, JIANGUO, Mechanical Engineering
ZHONG, QIN, Chemical Engineering
ZHOU, BOSEN, Materials Science and Engineering
ZHOU, KEDONG, Mechanical Engineering
ZHOU, SHUGE, Electronic Engineering and Optoelectronic Technology
ZHOU, WEILIANG, Chemical Engineering
ZHOU, XIANZHONG, Automation Engineering
ZHU, JINAN, Mechanical Engineering
ZHU, RIHONG, Electronic Engineering and Optoelectronic Technology
ZHU, XIANCHEN, Economics and Management
ZHU, XIAOHUA, Electronic Engineering and Optoelectronic Technology
ZOU, YUN, Automation Engineering

ATTACHED RESEARCH INSTITUTES

China Mechatronic Technology Research Development Centre.

National Key Laboratory of Transient Physics.

National Key Laboratory of Flexible Manufacturing Systems.

State Miniprotein Technology Research and Dissemination Centre.

State Super Fine Powder Engineering Technological Research Centre

NANJING UNIVERSITY OF TECHNOLOGY

Gu Lou Section, 5 New Model Rd, Nanjing 210009, Jiangsu

Telephone: (25) 83587018
Fax: (25) 83587636
E-mail: xiaoban@njut.edu.cn
Internet: www.njuct.edu.cn

Founded 1902

Department of Education of Jiangsu Province control

Academic year: September to July

President: OU YANG PINGKAI

Vice-Presidents: SHU FANG, SUN CHUANSONG, SUN WEIMIN SUN, WANG JINMING, XU NANPING, ZAI JINMIN, ZHU YAO

Head of Graduate Department: HAN PINGFANG

Librarian: ZHANG ZHENGHUI

Number of teachers: 1,000
Number of students: 23,000

Publications: *Journal* (natural sciences, 6 a year), *Journal* (social sciences, 4 a year)

DEANS

College of Architecture and Urban Planning: WU JILIANG
College of Artistic Design: LIU WEIQING
College of Automation: LIN JINGUO
College of Chemistry and Chemical Engineering: XU NANPING
College of Civil Engineering: CHEN GUOXING
College of Economics and Management: HE HONGJIN
College of Foreign Languages and International Exchange: YIN FULIN
College of Information Science and Engineering: YANG XIAOJIAN
College of Law and Politics: LI BIN
College of Life Science and Pharmaceutical Engineering: ZHOU HUA
College of Management Science and Engineering: NIE QIBO
College of Materials Science and Engineering: XU ZHONGZI
College of Mechanical and Power Engineering: TU SHANDONG
College of Sciences: YU BIN
College of Urban Construction, Safety and Environmental Engineering: JIANG JUNCHENG

PROFESSORS

CAI, RUIYING, Information Science and Engineering
CAI, ZHIFU, Mechanical and Power Engineering
CEI, CHENGJIAN, Information Science and Engineering
CHEN, BIAO, Mechanical and Power Engineering
CHEN, CHANGLIN, Chemistry and Chemical Engineering
CHEN, GUOXING, Civil Engineering
CHEN, HONGLING, Chemistry and Chemical Engineering
CHEN, SU, Chemistry and Chemical Engineering
CHEN, XIANYI, Materials Science and Engineering
CUI, KEQING, Mechanical and Power Engineering
CUI, QUN, Chemistry and Chemical Engineering
DAI, SHUHE, Mechanical and Power Engineering
DENG, MIN, Materials Science and Engineering
FAN, YIQUAN, Chemistry and Chemical Engineering
GONG, JIANMING, Mechanical and Power Engineering
GONG, YANFENG, Urban Construction, Safety and Environmental Engineering
GU, BOQIN, Mechanical and Power Engineering
GU, HEPING, Chemistry and Chemical Engineering
GUAN, GUOFENG, Chemistry and Chemical Engineering
GUO, LUCUN, Materials Science and Engineering
HE, HONGJIN, Economics and Management
HE, JIAPENG, Urban Construction, Safety and Environmental Engineering
HUANG, PEI, Chemistry and Chemical Engineering
HUANG, YOUDIAO, Mechanical and Power Engineering
HUANG, ZHENREN, Mechanical and Power Engineering
JIAN, MIAOFU, Materials Science and Engineering
JIANG, JUNCHENG, Urban Construction, Safety and Environmental Engineering
JIANG, JUNCHENG, Mechanical and Power Engineering
JIN, SUMIN, Mechanical and Power Engineering
JIN, WANQIN, Chemistry and Chemical Engineering
LI, BIN, Law and Politics
LI, DONGXU, Materials Science and Engineering
LI, LIQUAN, Materials Science and Engineering
LI, XIANGYING, Foreign Languages and International Exchange
LI, YONGSHENG, Mechanical and Power Engineering
LIN, JINGUO, Automation
LIN, XIAO, Chemistry and Chemical Engineering
LING, XIANG, Mechanical and Power Engineering
LIU, WEIQING, Artistic Design
LIU, XIAOQIN, Chemistry and Chemical Engineering
LIU, ZHONGWEN, Chemistry and Chemical Engineering
LU, JINGUI, Information Science and Engineering
LU, LEI, Materials Science and Engineering
LU, WEILIAN, Automation
LU, XIAOHUA, Chemistry and Chemical Engineering
LU, XIAOPING, Chemistry and Chemical Engineering
LU, YINONG, Materials Science and Engineering
MA, GONGXUN, Mechanical and Power Engineering

MA, ZHENGFEI, Chemistry and Chemical Engineering
PAN, YU, Management Science and Engineering
PAN, ZHIHUA, Materials Science and Engineering
QIAO, XU, Chemistry and Chemical Engineering
QIU, TAI, Materials Science and Engineering
SHEN, LINJIANG, Sciences
SHEN, SHIMING, Mechanical and Power Engineering
SHEN, XIAODONG, Materials Science and Engineering
SHI, JUN, Chemistry and Chemical Engineering
SHI, MEIREN, Chemistry and Chemical Engineering
SUN, WEIMIN, Civil Engineering
TANG, MINGSHU, Materials Science and Engineering
TU, SHANDONG, Mechanical and Power Engineering
WANG, HUI, Information Science and Engineering
WANG, JUN, Chemistry and Chemical Engineering
WANG, TINGWEI, Materials Science and Engineering
WANG, YANRU, Chemistry and Chemical Engineering
WANG, YONGPING, Architecture and Urban Planning
WANG, ZHUOJUN, Law and Politics
WEI, PING, Life Sciences and Pharmaceutical Engineering
WEI, WUJI, Materials Science and Engineering
WU, CHENGZHEN, Materials Science and Engineering
WU, JILIANG, Architecture and Urban Planning
XIAO, WANRU, Sciences
XU, NANPING, Chemistry and Chemical Engineering
XU, YANHUA, Urban Construction, Safety and Environmental Engineering
XU, ZHONGZI, Materials Science and Engineering
YAN, SHENG, Materials Science and Engineering
YANG, XIANNING, Chemistry and Chemical Engineering
YANG, XIAOJIAN, Information Science and Engineering
YAO, CHENG, Sciences
YAO, HUQING, Chemistry and Chemical Engineering
YAO, XIAO, Materials Science and Engineering
YEI, XUCHU, Materials Science and Engineering
YIN, CHENBO, Mechanical and Power Engineering
YIN, FULIN, Foreign Languages and International Exchange
YIN, XIA, Mechanical and Power Engineering
YU, BIN, Sciences
YUN, ZHI, Chemistry and Chemical Engineering
ZENG, CHONGYU, Chemistry and Chemical Engineering
ZENG, YANWEI, Materials Science and Engineering
ZHANG, GANDAO, Life Sciences and Pharmaceutical Engineering
ZHANG, HONG, Mechanical and Power Engineering
ZHANG, JUN, Materials Science and Engineering
ZHANG, LIJING, Urban Construction, Safety and Environmental Engineering
ZHANG, LIXIONG, Chemistry and Chemical Engineering
ZHANG, QITU, Materials Science and Engineering
ZHANG, SHAOMING, Materials Science and Engineering
ZHANG, WEI, Materials Science and Engineering
ZHANG, YAMING, Chemistry and Chemical Engineering
ZHAO, HESHENG, Architecture and Urban Planning
ZHAO, SHILIN, Materials Science and Engineering
ZHAO, YINGKAN, Automation
ZHENG, FENGQIN, Mechanical and Power Engineering
ZHOU, CHANGYU, Mechanical and Power Engineering
ZHOU, HUA, Life Sciences and Pharmaceutical Engineering
ZHU, DUNRU, Chemistry and Chemical Engineering
ZHU, HONG, Materials Science and Engineering
ZHU, XURONG, Chemistry and Chemical Engineering
ZHUANG, JUN, Mechanical and Power Engineering

ATTACHED RESEARCH INSTITUTES

National Bioengineering Technology Research Centre: Dir OU YANG PINGKAI.

National Technology Research and Diffusion Centre for Heating Pipes: Dir TU SHANDONG.

NANJING UNIVERSITY OF TRADITIONAL CHINESE MEDICINE

282 Hanzhong Rd, Nanjing 210029, Jiangsu
Telephone: (25) 86798005
Fax: (25) 86798009
Internet: www.njutcm.edu.cn

Founded 1954
Academic year: September to July
President: XIANG PING
Vice-Presidents: CHEN DIPING, LIU SHENLIN, WU MIANHUA
Librarian: JI WENHUI
Library of 4,320,000 vols
Number of teachers: 1,308
Number of students: 6,000
Publication: *Journal* (6 a year)

DEANS

College of Basic Medicine: ZHANG MINGQIN
College of Pharmacy: DING ANWEI
First Clinical Medical College: (vacant)
Second Clinical Medical College: LI ZHONGREN
School of Commercial Management and Trade: (vacant)
School of Foreign Languages: (vacant)

PROFESSORS

BIAN, HUIMIN, Pharmacy
CAI, BAOCHANG, Pharmacy
CHEN, JIANWEI, Pharmacy
DING, ANWEI, Pharmacy
DING, SHUHUA, Clinical Medicine
FANG, TAIHUI, Pharmacy
GUO, LIWEI, Pharmacy
HUANG, YAOZHOU, Pharmacy
LI, XIANG, Pharmacy
LIU, HANQING, Pharmacy
PENG, GUOPING, Pharmacy
QIN, MINGZHU, Pharmacy
WANG, SHOUCHUAN, Clinical Medicine
WU, DEKANG, Pharmacy
WU, HAO, Pharmacy
YAN, DAONAN, Clinical Medicine
YU, XIAOWEI, Clinical Medicine
ZHOU, FUYI, Clinical Medicine
ZHU, QUAN, Pharmacy

ATTACHED RESEARCH INSTITUTES

Adult Education College.

Botanical Refinement Engineering Research Centre: Dir GUO LIWEI.

College of International Education.

Jiangsu Province Research and Development Centre for Marine Pharmaceuticals: Dir WU HAO.

NANKAI UNIVERSITY

94 Weijin Rd, Tianjin 300071
Telephone: (22) 23508208
Fax: (22) 23502208
E-mail: xb@office.nankai.edu.cn
Internet: www.nankai.edu.cn

Founded 1919
Academic year: September to July
President: Prof. HOU ZIXIN
Vice-Presidents: CHEN HONG, CHEN XUEQI, CHEN YONGCHUAN, GENG YUNQI, PANG JINJU, ZHANG JING
Librarian: Prof. YAN SHIPING
Library of 2,900,000 vols
Number of teachers: 1,465
Number of students: 23,000
Publications: *Nankai Journal* (6 a year), *Journal* (4 a year), *Nankai Economics Studies* (6 a year), *Nankai Management Review* (6 a year)

DEANS

College of Literature: Prof. CHEN HONG
College of History: Prof. LI ZHIAN
College of Law and Political Science: Prof. ZHU GUANGLEI
College of Foreign Languages and Literature: Prof. WANG JIANYI
College of Ideological and Cultural Education: Prof. LI YI
College of Economics: Prof. ZHOU LIQUN
College of International Business: Prof. LI WEIAN
College of Mathematics: Prof. LONG YIMING
College of Physics: Prof. XU JINGJUN
College of Chemistry: Prof. GUAN NAIJIA
College of Life Sciences: Prof. GENG YUNQI
College of Medicine: Prof. ZHU TIANHUI
College of Information Science and Technology: Prof. WU GONGYI
College Environmental Science and Engineering: Prof. ZHU TAN
College of Chinese Language and Culture: Prof. SHI FENG
Software College: Prof. HUANG YALOU
College of Occupational Technology: Prof. SU LICHUN
College of Modern Distance Education: Prof. LEI ZONGBAO
College of Economics and Societal Development: Prof. HOU ZIXIN
Teda College: Prof. XIAN GUOMING
College of Adult Education: Prof. JING HONGGANG

CHAIRMEN OF DEPARTMENTS

Chinese Language and Literature: Prof. QIAO YIGANG
Mass Communication: Prof. ZHAO HANG
Eastern Art: Prof. HAN CHANGLI
Art Design: Prof. XUE YI
History: Prof. LI ZHIAN
Antiquities and Museum Studies: Prof. ZHU YANMIN
Philosophy: Prof. WANG NANSHI
Political Science: Prof. ZHU GUANGLEI
Sociology: Prof. GUAN XINPING
Law: Prof. FU SHICHENG
English Language and Literature: Prof. YAN QIGANG
Japanese Language and Literature: Prof. WANG JIANYI
Western Language and Literature: Prof. YAN GUODONG
General English: Prof. XUE CHEN
Economics: Prof. HE ZILI

Risk Management and Insurance: Prof. JIANG SHENGZHONG
International Economics and Trade: Prof. TONG JIADONG
Finance: Prof. MA JUNLU
International Business Management: Prof. ZHANG YULI
Marketing: Prof. HAN DECHANG
Library Science: Prof. WANG ZHIJIN
Information Systems and Management: Prof. YAN JIANYUAN
Human Resource Management: Prof. QIU LICHENG
Tourism Management: Prof. WANG JIAN
Accounting: Prof. LIU ZHIYUAN
Financial Management: Prof. WANG QUANXI
Mathematics: Prof. DENG SHAOQIANG
Scientific Computing and Applied Software: Prof. YANG QINGZHI
Statistics: Prof. WANG ZHAOJUN
Information and Probability: Prof. RUAN JISHOU
Financial Information and Technology: Prof. CHEN DIANFA
Physics: Prof. LI XUEQIAN
Optical and Electrical Science: Prof. LU KECHENG
Biophysical Science: Prof. YANG WENXIU
Chemistry: Prof. GUAN NAIJA
Materials Chemistry: Prof. YUAN HUATANG
Biology: Prof. LI HOUHUN
Microbiology: Prof. BAI GANG
Biochemistry: Prof. WANG YONG
Electronic Information Science and Technology: Prof. YAN SHAOLIN
Electronic Science and Technology: Prof. LI GUOFENG
Microelectronics: Prof. ZHANG FUHAI
Communications Engineering: Prof. WU YUE
Automation: Prof. CHEN ZENGQIANG
Computer Science and Technology: Prof. XU JINGDONG
Environmental Science: Prof. SUN HONGWEN
Environmental Engineering and Management: Prof. LIU MAO
Chinese Language and Culture: Prof. CUI JIANXIN

PROFESSORS

College of Literature (tel. (22) 23508247; fax (22) 23508247; e-mail chinese@wxy.nankai.edu.cn; internet www.nankai.chinese.edu.cn):

Department of Chinese Language and Literature:

CHEN HONG, Ancient Chinese Literature
HONG BO, Ancient Chinese
LI JIANGUO, Ancient Chinese Literature
LIU LILI, Literature and Art Science
LU SHENGJIANG, Ancient Chinese Literature
LUO ZONGQIANG, Ancient Chinese Literature
MA QINGZHU, Modern Chinese
MENG ZHAOLIAN, Ancient Chinese Literature
NING JIAYU, Ancient Chinese Literature
PENG XIUYIN, Literature and Art Science
QIAO YIGANG, Modern and Contemporary Chinese Literature
SHI FENG, Experimental Phonetics
SUN CHANGWU, Ancient Chinese Literature
TAO MUNING, Ancient Chinese Literature
WANG LIXIN, Comparative and World Literature
WANG ZHIGENG, Comparative and World Literature
XING KAI, Languages and Literature of Ethnic Minorities in China
XU XIANGLIN, Ancient Chinese Literature
ZENG XIAOYU, Languages and Literature of Ethnic Minorities in China
ZHANG YI, Ancient Chinese Literature
ZHOU JIAN, Modern Chinese

Department of Mass Communication:

LUO DERONG, Editorial and Publishing Science
ZHAO HANG, Editorial and Publishing Science

Department of Eastern Art:

CHEN YUPU, Chinese Painting
FAN ZENG, Chinese Painting
HAN CHANGLI, Chinese Painting
SHEN QUAN, Chinese Painting

Department of Art Design:

XUE YI, Art Design

Department of Basic Cultural Education:

NING JIAYU, Ancient Chinese Literature

College of History (tel. (22) 23508422; fax (22) 23501637; e-mail lizhian@nankai.edu.cn):

Department of History:

CHANG JIANHUA, Ancient Chinese History
CHEN ZHENJIANG, Modern and Contemporary Chinese History
CHEN ZHIQIANG, Ancient and Medieval World History
FENG ERKANG, Ancient Chinese History
HA QUAN'AN, Ancient and Medieval World History
HOU JIE, Modern and Contemporary Chinese History
JIANG PEI, Modern and Contemporary Chinese History
JIANG SHENGLI, Historiography
LI ZHI'AN, Ancient Chinese History
LI XISUO, Modern and Contemporary Chinese History
LIN HEKUN, Modern and Contemporary World History
LIU MIN, Ancient Chinese History
LIU ZEHUA, Ancient Chinese History
MA SHILI, Modern and Contemporary World History
SUN LIQUN, Ancient Chinese History
WANG DUNSHU, Ancient and Medieval World History
WANG XIANMING, Modern and Contemporary Chinese History
XU TAN, Ancient Chinese History
ZHANG FENTIAN, Ancient Chinese History
ZHANG GUOGANG, Ancient Chinese History

Department of Relics and Museum Studies:

LIU YI, Museology
ZHU FENGHAN, Ancient Chinese History

Department of Philosophy:

CHANG JIAN, Western Philosophy
CHEN YANQING, Marxist Philosophy
CUI QINGTIAN, Logical Philosophy
HAN QIANG, Chinese Philosophy
LI NA, Logical Philosophy
LI JIANSHANG, Scientific and Technological Philosophy
LI XIANGHAI, Chinese Philosophy
LIU WENYING, Chinese Philosophy
LU YANG, Aesthetics
REN XIAOMING, Logical Philosophy
WANG NANSHI, Marxist Philosophy
XUE FUXING, Aesthetics
YAN MENGWEI, Marxist Philosophy

College of Law and Political Science (tel. (22) 23501400; fax (22) 23500327; e-mail fzxy@nankai.edu.cn; internet nkfzxy.my163.com):

Department of Political Science:

CAI TUO, International Relations
GE QUAN, Political Science
SHEN YAPING, Public Administration
WANG ZHENGYI, International Relations
YANG LONG, Political Science
YIN YANJUN, International Relations
ZHANG RUIZHUANG, International Relations
ZHU GUANGLEI, Political Science

Department of Sociology:

GUAN XINPING, Social Policy
HOU JUNSHENG, Applied Sociology
LIU JUNJUN, Applied Sociology
PENG HUAMIN, Social Work
WANG CHUHUI, Applied Sociology
WANG XINJIAN, Social Psychology
YUE GUOAN, Social Psychology

Department of Law:

BAI HUA, Theory of Law
FU SCHICHENG, Administrative Law
HOU XINYI, Theory of Law
HU SHIKAI, Theory of Law
LI YUNWU, Forensic Medicine
QI DAOMENG, Environmental Law
ZHAO ZHENGQUN, Administrative Law
ZHU JINGAN, International Private Law

College of Foreign Languages and Literature (tel. (22) 23509292; fax (22) 23500497; e-mail wyxy@office.nankai.edu.cn):

Department of English Language and Literature:

CHANG YAOXIN, English Literature
CUI YONGLU, English Translation
GU QI'NAN, English Literature
JIANG HUASHANG, English Literature
LIU SHICONG, English Translation
SU LICHANG, English Linguistics
MA QIUWU, English Linguistics
WANG HONGYIN, English Translation
WANG WENHAN, English Literature
WEI RONGCHENG, English Literature
YAN QIGANG, English Literature
ZHANG MAIZENG, English Linguistics

Department of Japanese Language and Literature:

LIU GUIMIN, Japanese Literature and Linguistics
WANG JIANYI, Japanese Literature and Linguistics

Department of Western Languages and Literature:

CHEN XI, Comparative Linguistics
YAN GUODONG, Sino-Russian Cultural Relations, Comparative Culture
ZHANG ZHITING, French Literature

Department of General Literature:

LI JINGYU, English Language
SUO JUNMEI, English Language
WANG SHIBIN, English Language
XUE CHEN, English Language
ZHANG JUNZHI, English Language
ZHANG WENQI, English Language
ZHOU SHUJIE, English Language

College of Ideological and Cultural Education (tel. (22) 23507985; fax (22) 23507985; e-mail jyxy@office.nankai.edu):

CAO JIE, Marxist Theories and Ideological and Political Education
DING JUN, Political Economics
DOU AIZHI, History of the Chinese Communist Party
LI JIANSONG, Political Economics
LI YI, Marxist Philosophy
LIU JINGQUAN, History of the Chinese Communist Party
SHAO YUNRUI, History of the Chinese Communist Party
WANG YUANMING, Marxist Philosophy
WU DONGSHENG, Marxist Theories and Ideological and Political Education
YANG YONGZHI, Theoretical Thoughts of Deng Xiaopin
ZHANG HONGGUANG, Scientific and Technological Philosophy
ZHAO TIESUO, History of the Chinese Communist Party

College of Economics (tel. (22) 23508981; fax (22) 23500261; e-mail jjxy@office.nankai.edu.cn):

Department of Economics:

HE ZILI, Comparative Economics
JIA GENLIANG, Development Economics
JING WEIMIN, Transitional Economics
LIU CHUNBIN, Agro-economics

LIU JUNMIN, Macroeconomics and Virtual Economics
WANG SHUYING, Industrial Economics
WEN HAICHI, Labour Economics
ZHANG RENDE, Comparative Economics
ZHANG SHIQING, Macroeconomics and Microeconomics
ZHANG TONGYU (acting), Political Economy
ZHAO JIN, History of Economics
ZHU GUANGHUA, Political Economy

Department of International Economics and Trade:

GAO LEYONG, International Economic Theories, International Investment
LI KUNWANG, Theory and Policy of International Trade
LIU ZHONGLI, International Trade Management
TONG JIADONG, International Trade, Economics of International Integration
XUE JINGXIAO, International Economics, Japanese Economy
YANG CANYING, Open Economy
ZHANG ZHICHAO, Public Finance, Economics of Development

Department of Finance:

LI ZHIHUI, International Finance
LIU YUCAO, International Finance
MA JUNLU, International Finance

Department of Risk Management and Insurance:

JIANG SHENGZHONG, Research, Insurance Management
LIU MAOSHAN, Research, Insurance Economics
XIAO YUNRU, Research, Actuarial Mathematics

College of International Business (tel. (22) 23500603; fax (22) 23501039; e-mail alison41@eyou.com):

Department of Human Resource Management:

LI WINJIAN, Human Resource Management
WU GUOCUN, Human Resource Management, Human Resource Development
XIE JINYU, Human Resource Management, Strategic Human Resource Management

Department of Marketing:

FAN XIUCHENG, Service Marketing Management
HAN DECHANG, Marketing
WU XIAOYUN, Global Marketing Management

Department of Information Systems and Management:

YAN JIANYUAN, Management Information Systems, Logistics Management

Department of Accounting:

FENG YANQI, International Accounting
LIU ZHIYUAN, Managerial Accounting
ZHOU XIAOSU, Financial Accounting

Department of Tourism Management:

LI TIANYUAN, Tourism Marketing
QI SHANHONG, Tourism Business Management
WANG JIAN, Tourism Development

Department of International Business:

HAN JINGLUN, Management
JIA LANXIANG, Management
LI FEI, Management
LI GUOJING, Management
QI ANBANG, Management
WANG YINGJUN, Management
ZHANG YULI, Management

Department of Library Science:

LIU YUZHAO, Library Management
WANG ZHIJIN, Library Management

Department of Financial Management:

QI YINFENG, Corporate Finance
WANG QUANXI, Corporate Finance

College of Mathematics (tel. (22) 23501233; fax (22) 23506423; e-mail longym@nankai.edu.cn; internet www.math.nankai.edu.cn):

Department of Mathematics:

DENG SHAOQIANG, Lie Groups and Lie Algebras
DING GUANGGUI, Functional Analysis
GU PEI, Algebra, Group Metahomomorphisms
GUO JINGMEI, Differential Topology
HOU ZIXIN, Lie Groups and Lie Algebras
HUANG YUMIN, Partial Differential Equations
LIANG KE, Lie Groups and Lie Algebras
LIN JINKUN, Algebraic Topology
LIU CHUNGEN, Nonlinear Analysis
MENG DAOJI, Basic Mathematics, Algebra, Lie Therapy

Department of Scientific Computing and Applied Software:

HU JIANGWEI, Numerical Mathematics
TIAN CHUNSONG, Numerical Mathematics

Department of Statistics:

WANG ZHAOJUN, Experimental Design, Statistical Process Control
ZHANG RUNCHU, Experimental Design, Multivariate Analysis, Applied Statistics

Department of Information and Probability:

FU FANGWEI, Coding Theory, Bioinformation
GUO JUNYI, Stochastic Process, Risk Theory
LIANG PU, Coding Theory, Bioinformation
SHEN SHIYI, Coding Theory, Bioinformation
WANG YONGJIN, Probability, Stochastic Process
WU RONG, Probability, Stochastic Process
ZHOU XINGWEI, Harmonic Analysis, Wavelet Analysis

Department of Financial Information and Technology:

CHEN WANYI, Control Theory, Financial Mathematics
WANG GONGSHU, Applied Statistics
WANG HONG, Control Theory

College of Physics (tel. (22) 23501490; fax (22) 23501490; e-mail physics@nankai.edu.cn; internet www.physics.nankai.edu.cn):

Department of Physics:

CAI CHONGHAI, Evaluation of Nuclear Data
CHEN TIANLUN, Nonlinear Dynamics, Partial Physics Theory
DING DATONG, Nuclear Magnetic Resonance, Computational Materials, Mesoscopic Physics
GAO CHENGQUN, Nuclear Physics
HU BEILAI, Statistical Physics, Plasma Physics
HUANG WUQUN, Nonlinear Dynamics
LI BAOHUI, Nuclear Magnetic Resonance, Computational Physics
LI XUEQIAN, Phenomenology of High Energy Physics
LU ZHENQIU, Inverse Scattering Physics and Imaging Techniques
LUO MA, Perturbative Chromodynamic Power Electronics
MENG XINHE, Particle Physics and the Universe, Mesoscopic Physics
NING PINGZHI, Nuclear Physics
SHEN HONG, Nuclear Physics
WEN JINGSONG, Micro-atmospheric Science Suspension Mechanics
ZHOU WENZHUANG, Crystallology
ZHU YAPING, X-Ray Crystallology

Department of Optical and Electrical Science:

LÜ FUYUN, Photoelectron Laser and Modern Optical Communication
LÜ KECHENG, Photoelectron Laser and Modern Optical Communication
SHENG QIUQIN, Opto-electronics and Optical Fibre Communication, Optical Sensors

Department of Biophysical Science:

YANG WENXIU, Cellular and Molecular Informatics, Cellular and Membrane Biophysics

College of Chemistry (tel. (22) 23508470; fax (22) 23502458; e-mail hxx@office.nankai.edu.cn):

Department of Chemistry:

BU XIANHE, Inorganic Chemistry
CAI ZUNSHENG, Physical Chemistry
CAO YURONG, Organic Chemistry
CHENG JINPEI, Inorganic Chemistry
CHENG PENG, Inorganic Chemistry
DENG GUOCAI, Inorganic Chemistry
GUAN NAIJIA, Physical Chemistry
HE JIAQI, Inorganic Chemistry
HE XIWEN, Analytical Chemistry
HU QINGMEI, Organic Chemistry
HUANG JIAXIAN, Polymer Chemistry
HUANG WEIPING, Inorganic Chemistry
HUANG ZHIRONG, Analytical Chemistry
JIANG ZONGHUI, Inorganic Chemistry
LI FANGXING, Polymer Chemistry
LIAO DAIZHENG, Inorganic Chemistry
LIN HUAKUAN, Physical Chemistry
LIU YU, Physical Chemistry
MENG JIBEN, Organic Chemistry
SHEN HANXI, Inorganic Chemistry
SHEN PANWEN, Analytical Chemistry
SONG LICHENG, Organic Chemistry
WANG BAIQUAN, Organic Chemistry
WANG XINSHENG, Organic Chemistry
WANG YONGMEI, Organic Chemistry
WU SHIHUA, Inorganic Chemistry
XU SHANSHENG, Organic Chemistry
YAN SHIPING, Inorganic Chemistry
YAN XIUPING, Analytical Chemistry
YANG GUANGMING, Inorganic Chemistry
YANG XIULIN, Physical Chemistry
YIN LIHUA, Inorganic Chemistry
YOU YINGCAI, Polymer Chemistry
YUAN MANXUE, Physical Chemistry
ZHANG BAOLONG, Organic Chemistry
ZHANG BAOSHEN, Polymer Chemistry
ZHANG GUIZHU, Analytical Chemistry
ZHANG ZHIHUI, Physical Chemistry
ZHAO HONGXI, Physical Chemistry
ZHAO ZUEZHANG, Physical Chemistry
ZHU CHANGYING, Polymer Chemistry
ZHU SHOURONG, Physical Chemistry
ZHU XIAOQING, Organic Chemistry
ZHU ZHIANG, Physical Chemistry
ZUO JU, Polymer Chemistry
ZUO YUMIN, Organic Chemistry

Department of Materials Chemistry:

CHE YUNXIA, Inorganic Chemistry
CHEN JUN, Materials Chemistry
CHEN TIEHONG, Physical Chemistry
GAO XUEPING, Materials Chemistry
LIU SHUANGXI, Physical Chemistry
SONG DEYING, Materials Chemistry
SUN BO, Inorganic Chemistry
TAO KEYI, Physical Chemistry
XIANG SHOUHE, Physical Chemistry
YAN JIE, Materials Chemistry
YUAN HUATUNG, Materials Chemistry
ZHENG WENJUN, Physical Chemistry

College of Life Sciences (tel. (22) 23501846; fax (22) 23508800; e-mail sky@office.nankai.edu.cn):

Department of Biology:

BU WENJUN, Zoological Systematics
CHEN QIANG, Biosensors, Biophysical Chemistry
CHEN RUIYANG, Cytogenetics
GAO YUBAO, Botany and Plant Ecology
LI HOUHUN, Insect Taxonomy, Zoogeography
LIU ANXI, Animal Physiology and Biochemistry

QIU ZHAOZHI, Zootaxy and Parasitology
SONG WENQIN, Molecular Cytogenetics
WANG XINHUA, Systematic Zoology
ZHENG LEYI, Zoological Systematics

Department of Microbiology:

BAI GANG, Molecular Immunology
DIAO HUXIN, Study of Petroleum Microorganisms
LIU FANG, Microbiological Sources and Molecular Biology
LIU RULIN, Microbiology
REN GAIXIN, Insect Microbiology
WANG LEI, Bacterial Genetics and Evolution
YANG WENBO, Resource Bacteriology and Engineering
XING LAIJUN, Modern Mycology

Department of Biochemistry:

CHEN QIMIN, Microbiology and Molecular Genetics, Molecular Virology
DU RONGQIAN, Molecular Biology
GENG YUNQI, Molecular Virology
HUANG XITAI, Biochemistry and Molecular Biology, Structure of Nucleic Acids and Gene Chips
WANG NINGNING, Plant Molecular Biology
WANG SHUFANG, Plant Physiology
WANG YONG, Plant Molecular Biology
YE LIHONG, Protein Biochemistry
YU ZIRAN, Purification and Characterization of Human Growth Hormones Expressed in Insect Cells
YU XINDA, Gene Engineering in Eukaryotic Cells
CAO YOUJIA, Biochemistry and Molecular Biology, Signals Transduction and Apoptosis

College of Medicine (tel. (22) 23509842; fax (22) 23509842; e-mail zhuth@nankai.edu.cn):

LIU WEN, Anatomy
ZHU TIANHUI, Medical Genetics

College of Information Science and Technology (tel. (22) 23505705; fax (22) 23509054; e-mail xxxy@office.nankai.edu.cn):

CHANG SHENGJIANG, Optical Information Processing
CHEN WENJU, Nonlinear Optical Physics and Materials Optoelectronics for Optical Information
DONG YUANYI, Photonics Technology and Modern Optical Communication
FANG ZHILIANG, Optical Information Processing
FU RULIAN, Laser and Biomedical Optics
GENG XINHUA, Photo-electronic Technology and Applications
HAN WEIHENG, Computer Software
LIN MEIRONG, Nonlinear Optical Physics and Materials, Optoelectronics for Optical Information
LIU FULAI, Optical Information Processing
MU GUOGUANG, Optical Information Processing
SHEN JINYUAN, Optical Information Processing
SUN YUN, Photo-electronic Materials and Technology
SUN ZHONGLI, Photo-electronic Technology, Semiconductor Materials and Devices
TANG GUOQING, Molecular Electronic Spectroscopy and Biomedical Photomaps
WANG QINGREN, Pattern Recognition and Intelligent Systems
WANG ZHAOQI, Optical Information Processing
WANG ZONGPAN, Photo-electronic Technology and Applications
XIONG SHAOZHEN, Optoelectronic Devices and Technology, Display Electronics
YUAN SHUZHONG, Fibre Communication and Fibre Sensors
ZHAI HONGCHEN, Institute of Modern Optics
ZHANG GUILAN, Nonlinear Optical Physics and Materials
ZHANG YANXIN, Optical Information Processing, Neural Networks and Pattern Recognition
ZHAO QIDA, Fibre Communication and Fibre Sensor
ZHU XIAONONG, Applications of Femtosecond Laser Science and Technology

Department of Computer Science and Technology:

BAI GANG, Pattern Recognition
LI QINGCHENG, Embedded Operating Systems
LIU JING, Computer Architecture
LU ZHICAI, Intelligent Control and Communication Networks
SUN GUIRU, Software Engineering
WU GONGYI, Computer Networks
YANG YULU, Computer Architecture
YUAN XIAOJIE, Database Technology, Data Warehousing, Data Mining
ZHU YAOTING, Multimedia Technology and Network Teaching

Department of Automation:

CHEN QIUSHUANG, Job Shop Schedule Systems, DEDS System
CHEN ZENGQIANG, Adaptive, Predictive and Intelligent Control
SUN YONGHUA, Adaptive Control Systems
TU FENGSHENG, Integrated Computer Manufacturing Systems
WANG XIUFENG, Modelling and Identification, Financial Decision Support Systems
WANG ZHIBAO, Financial Decision Support Systems
YUAN ZHUZHI, Adaptive and Predictive Control, Intelligent Communication

Department of Communications Engineering:

LI WENCHEN, Radio Communications
WU YUE, Radio Communications

Department of Microelectronics:

JIA XIANGLUAN, VLSI and System Design
NIU XIUQING, VLSI and System Design
NIU WENCHENG, Transducer Technology and Systems
QIN SHICAI, VLSI and System Design

Department of Electronic Science and Technology:

FANG LAN, Superconductivity, Electronics
SHAO SHUMIN, Vacuum Science and Technology, Functional Materials and Devices

Department of Electronic Information Science and Technology:

LI WEIXIANG, Systems and System Design
YAN SHAOLIN, Superconductor Electronics, Communications Science and Technology
YANG WENXIA, Net Communication

College of Environmental Science and Engineering (tel. (22) 23508807; fax (22) 23508936; e-mail hjxy@office.nankai.edu.cn):

Department of Environmental Science:

CHEN FUHUA, Environmental Chemistry
DAI SHUGUI, Environmental Chemistry
FU XUEQI, Environmental Chemistry
HU GUOCHEN, Environmental Biology
HUANG GUOLAN, Environmental Chemistry
JIN ZHAOHUI, Environmental Chemistry
SUN HONGWEN, Environmental Chemistry, Environmental Pollution Control
ZHANG BAOGUI, Environmental Chemistry, Analytic Chemistry
ZHU LIN, Environmental Biology

Department of Environmental Engineering and Management:

BAI ZHIPENG, Air Pollution Chemistry, Environmental Risk Assessment
LIU MAO, Environmental Safety Assessment
WAN QISHAN, Water Pollution Control
ZHU TAN, Environmental Planning and Management
ZHUANG YUANYI, Environmental Engineering

College of Chinese Language and Culture (tel. (22) 23501687; fax (22) 23501687; e-mail hy@office.nankai.edu.cn):

CUI JIANXIN, Modern Chinese
GUO JIMAO, Modern Chinese
SHI FENG, Chinese Linguistics
SHI XIANGDONG, Ancient Chinese

Software College (tel. (22) 23500526; fax (22) 23500526; e-mail cs@nankai.edu.cn; internet www.cs.nankai.edu.cn):

HUANG YALOU, Intelligent Robot Systems, Intelligent Information Processes

Department of Physical Education (tel. (22) 23502801; e-mail tyb@office.nankai.edu.cn):

WANG YUZHU, Track and Field
XING CHUNGUI, Volleyball
YANG XIANGDONG, Basketball (Dir)
ZHAO SHIJIE, Track and Field

Institute of Ancient Chinese Culture Studies (tel. (22) 23509662; fax (22) 23508247; e-mail chinese@wxy.nankai.edu.cn; internet www.nankai.chinese.edu.cn):

YE JIAYING, Ancient Chinese Literature and Culture

Chinese Philology Research Centre (tel. (22) 23507855; fax (22) 23508247; e-mail chinese@wxy.nankai.edu.cn; internet www.nankai.chinese.edu.cn):

HE LEYUE, Chinese Philology
XIANG GUANGZHONG, Chinese Philology
ZHAO XIANCUO, Chinese Philology

Institute of History (tel. (22) 23508903; fax (22) 23508903; e-mail lg433@eyou.com):

BAI XINLIANG, Ancient Chinese History
DU JIAJI, Ancient Chinese History
LIN YANQING, Ancient Chinese History
NAN BINGWEN, Ancient Chinese History
WANG MAOHE, Ancient Chinese History

Institute of International Economic Law (tel. (22) 23500694; fax (22) 23500327; e-mail shixuey@fm365.com; internet www.nkfzxy.my163.com):

CHENG BAOKU, International Economic Law
SHI XUEYING, International Economic Law

Institute of Population and Development (tel. (22) 23508012; fax (22) 23501773; e-mail rks@office.nankai.edu.cn):

LI JIANMIN, Economics of Population and Labour
TAN LIN, Economics of Population and Labour
YUAN XIN, Economics of Population and Labour

APEC Study Centre (tel. (22) 23501573; fax (22) 23500035; e-mail apecnk@office.nankai.edu.cn):

GONG ZHANKUI, Regional Economic Co-operation, International Trade and Investment

Institute of International Economics (tel. (22) 23508291; fax (22) 23502437; e-mail iitnk@office.nankai.edu.cn):

CHEN LIGAO, Open Economy
DAI JINPING, International Finance
LI RONGLIN, International Trade
QIU LICHENG, International Investment and Business
TENG WEIZAO, International Investment and Business
XIANG GUOMING, International Investment and Business
ZHANG CHENG, International Investment and Business

ZHANG YANGUI, International Investment and Business
ZHANG XIAOTONG, Econometrics

Transnational Studies Centre (tel. (22) 23505235; fax (22) 23502437; e-mail ctsnk@office.nankai.edu.cn):

CHEN LIGAO, Open Economy
DAI JINPING, International Finance
QIU LICHENG, International Investment and Business
XIAN GUOMING, International Investment and Business
ZHANG CHENG, International Investment and Business
ZHANG YANGUI, International Investment and Business
ZHANG XIAOTONG, Econometrics

Institute of Economics (tel. (22) 23503997; fax (22) 23501254; e-mail zhoulq@public.tpt.tj.cn):

CAO ZHENLIANG, Regional Economic Theory
CHEN ZHONGSHENG, Socialist Economic Theory
LIU XIN, Capitalist Economic Theory
PANG JINJU, Socialist Economic Theory
WANG YURU, History of Modern Economic Development
ZHOU BING, Socialist Economic Theory
ZHOU LIQUN, Socialist Economic Theory

Institute of Modern Research Management (tel. (22) 23508439; fax (22) 23503690; e-mail nkimm@public.tpt.tj.cn):

LE WEIAN, Corporate Governance
ZHANG JINCHENG, Service Management and Strategic Management

Institute of Mathematics (tel. (22) 23501029; fax (22) 23501532; e-mail nim@nankai.edu.cn):

CHEN YONGCHUAN, Combinatorics
FANG FUQUAN, Geometric Topology
FU LEI, Algebraic Geometry
GE MOLIN, Theoretical Physics
LI XUELIANG, Theory of Graphs and Combinatorial Optimizations
LONG YIMING, Nonlinear Analysis
ZHANG WEIPING, Differential Geometry
ZHOU XINGWEI, Harmonic Analysis, Wavelet Analysis

Photonics Research Centre (tel. (22) 23503697; fax (22) 23501490; e-mail zhangcp@nankai.edu.cn; internet www.physics.nankai.edu.cn):

LIU SIMIN, Nonlinear Optics, Solid Spectrum
TIAN JIANGUO, Photonics
XU JINGJUN, Condensed Matter Physics and Photonic Devices
ZHANG CHUNPING, Photonics and Biomedical Photonics
ZHANG GUANGYIN, Solid Spectrum, Photonics and Laser Physics

Institute of Polymer Chemistry (tel. (22) 23501386; fax (22) 23503510; e-mail gfzs@office.nankai.edu.cn):

HE BINGLIN, Polymer Chemistry
HUANG WENQIANG, Polymer Chemistry
LI CHAOXING, Polymer Chemistry
LI CHENXI, Polymer Chemistry
LI HONG, Polymer Chemistry
MA JIANBIAO, Polymer Chemistry
MI HUAIFENG, Biochemistry
SHI LINQI, Polymer Chemistry
SHI ZUOQING, Polymer Chemistry
WANG GUOCHANG, Polymer Chemistry
WU QIANG, Polymer Chemistry
YAN HUSHENG, Polymer Chemistry
YUAN ZHI, Polymer Chemistry
ZHANG BANGHUA, Polymer Chemistry
ZHANG ZHENGPU, Polymer Chemistry

Institute of Elemento-Organic Chemistry (tel. (22) 23508629; fax (22) 23503438; e-mail yss@office.nankai.edu.cn):

CHEN RUYU, Organic Chemistry
CHENG JUNRAN, Organic Chemistry
FANG JIANXIN, Organic Chemistry
GAO RUYU, Organic Chemistry
HAN JIAXIANG, Organic Chemistry
HUANG RUNQIU, Organic Chemistry
LI JING, Organic Chemistry
LI JINSHAN, Organic Chemistry
LI SHUZHENG, Organic Chemistry
LI ZHENGMING, Organic Chemistry
LIAO RENAN, Organic Chemistry
LIU HUAYIN, Organic Chemistry
LIU LUNZU, Organic Chemistry
TANG CHUCHI, Organic Chemistry
WANG GUANGYUAN, Organic Chemistry
XIE QINGLAN, Organic Chemistry
YANG HUAZENG, Organic Chemistry
ZHANG ZHENGZHI, Organic Chemistry
ZHANG ZUXIN, Organic Chemistry
ZHENG JIANU, Organic Chemistry
ZHOU QILIN, Organic Chemistry

Institute of Molecular Biology (tel. (22) 23501846; fax (22) 23508800; e-mail sky@office.nankai.edu.cn):

CAI BAOLI, Biodegradation and Biotechnology
GAO CAICHANG, Biochemistry and Molecular Biology
LI MINGGANG, Plant Molecular Biology
QIAO MINGQIANG, Molecular Microbiology and Microbial Technology
ZHANG JU, Medical Genetics
YU YAOTING, Biomaterials and Enzyme Engineering
ZHANG JINHONG, Enzyme Engineering and Biomedical Materials
ZHANG XIAODONG, Tumour Molecular Biology
ZHENG JIANYU, Molecular Biology

Institute of Modern Optics (tel. (22) 23502275; fax (22) 23503690; e-mail xxxy@office.nankai.edu.cn):

CHANG SHENGJIANG, Optical Information Processing
CHEN WENJU, Nonlinear Optical Physics and Materials
DONG XIAOYI, Photonics Technology and Modern Optical Communication
FANG ZHILIANG, Optical Engineering
FU RULIAN, Laser and Biomedical Optics
KAI GUIYUN, Fibre Communications and Fibre Sensors
LIN MEIRONG, Nonlinear Optical Physics and Materials
LIU FULAI, Optical Engineering
MU GUOGUANG, Optical Information Processing
SHEN JINYUAN, Optical Information Processing
TANG GUOQING, Molecular Electronic Spectroscopy and Biomedicine Photomaps
WANG ZHAOQI, Optical Information Processing
YUAN ZHUZHONG, Fibre Communications and Fibre Sensors
ZHAI HONGCHEN, Optical Information Processing, Optics Engineering
ZHANG GUILAN, Nonlinear Optical Physics and Materials
ZHANG YANXIN, Optical Information Processing Neural Networks and Pattern Recognition
ZHAO QIDA, Fibre Communications and Fibre Sensors
ZHU XIAONONG, Applications of Femtosecond Laser Science and Technology

Institute of Photoelectronics (tel. (22) 23502778; fax (22) 23502778; e-mail xxxy@office.nankai.edu.cn):

GENG XINHUA, Photoelectronic Technology and Applications
SUN YAN, Photoelectronic Materials and Technology
SUN ZHONGLIN, Photoelectronic Technology, Semiconductor Materials and Devices
WANG ZONGPAN, Photoelectronic Technology and Applications
XIONG SHAOZHEN, Optoelectronic Devices and Technology, Display Electronics

ATTACHED RESEARCH INSTITUTES

Centre for Japanese Studies: Dir Prof. YANG DONGLIANG.

Centre for Latin American Studies: Dir Prof. HONG GUOQI.

Centre for American History and Culture: Dir Prof. LI JIANMING.

Centre for Classical Studies: Dir Prof. WANG DUNSHU.

Centre for Sino-German Cultural Studies: Dir Prof. WANG DUNSHU.

Centre for Byzantine Studies: Dir Prof. CHEN ZHIQIANG.

Centre for Zhou Enlai Studies: Dir Prof. MI ZHENBO.

Centre for Chinese Overseas Students Studies: Dir Prof. LI XISUO.

Centre for Ming and Qing Dynasties Studies: Dir Prof. NAN BINGWEN.

Institute of Ancient Chinese Books and Culture: Dir Prof. ZHAO BOXIONG.

Institute of Social Philosophy: Dir Prof. CHEN YANQING.

Centre for Chinese Philosophy Studies: Dir Prof. LIU WENYING.

Centre for Religious Cultural Studies: Dir Prof. WANG ZHONGTIAN.

Centre for Political Economy Studies: Dir Prof. PANG JINJU.

Institute of Transport Economics: Dir Prof. LUO ZETAO.

Institute of New Energies Material Chemistry: Dir Prof. YUAN HUATANG.

Institute of New Catalytic Material Science: Dir Prof. LIU SHUANGXI.

Centre for Pesticide Engineering Research: Dir Prof. LI ZHENGMING.

Institute of Machine Intelligence: Dir Prof. HAN WEIHUAN.

Institute of Robotics and Information Automatic Systems: Dir Prof. LU GUIZHANG.

Institute of Pollution Control and Green Chemistry: Dir Prof. SUN HONGWEN.

Centre of Water Resource Protection Research: Dir Prof. WANG QISHAN.

Prevention and Control of Ambient Air Pollution: Dir Prof. BAI ZHIPENG.

China Cities and Regional Economics Research Centre: Dir Prof. LIU BINGLIAN.

Centre for Logistics Research: Dir Prof. LIU BINGLIAN.

Enterprise Research Centre: Dir Prof. WANG QUANXI.

NINGXIA MEDICAL COLLEGE

Sheng Li South Rd, Yinchuan 750004, Ningxia
Telephone: (951) 4095934
Internet: www.nxmc.edu.cn

Founded 1958
Academic year: September to July

President: SHUN TAO
Vice-Presidents: CHEN SHENGCHUN, DAI XIUYING, LI ZHENGZHI, SHI WEIZHONG, ZHANG JIANZHONG
Head of Graduate Department: LI ZHENGZHI
Librarian: WANG HUIFANG

Library of 200,000 vols
Number of teachers: 811
Number of students: 7,500

Publication: *Journal* (6 a year)

DEANS

School of Nursing: ZHANG LIN
School of Pharmacy: ZHANG DONGNIN
Department of Basic Medicine: WANG YANRONG
Department of Chinese Medicine: NIU YANG
Department of Clinical Medicine: WANG HUIXING
Department of Dentistry: MA MING
Department of Public Safety: SONG QIRU

PROFESSORS

GAO, WENHUA, Public Health
HOU, LINGLING, Chinese Medicine
HU, SANGPING, Basic Medicine
JIANG, HOUWEN, Chinese Medicine
JIN, ZHIJUN, Public Health
LI, YUCHUN, Chinese Medicine
LI, ZHENGZHI, Public Health
LIU, XIUFANG, Public Health
QIAN, LIQUN, Public Health
SONG, QIRU, Public Health
WANG, YANRONG, Basic Medicine
WANG, ZHONGJIU, Chinese Medicine
WEN, RUNLING, Public Health
ZHANG, YUJIE, Chinese Medicine
ZHANG, ZHENXIANG, Public Health
ZHU, YUDONG, Chinese Medicine

NORMAN BETHUNE UNIVERSITY OF MEDICAL SCIENCES

8 Xinmin St, Changchun 130021, Jilin

Telephone: (431) 5645911
Fax: (431) 5644739

Founded 1939
State control

President: Prof. WU JIAXIANG
Vice-Presidents: Prof. ZHU XUN, Prof. FAN HONGXUE, Prof. LI YULIN, Prof. LI DIANFU, Assoc. Prof. CHANG ZHONGXIAN, Assoc. Prof. YOU HONG
Dean of Education Department: Prof. ZHOU XIAOYAN
Chief Librarian: Prof. CHEN QIAN

Library of 485,000 vols, 3,570 periodicals
Number of teachers: 2,099
Number of students: 4,400

Publications: *Journal* (every 2 months), *Foreign Medicine—Gerontology* (every 2 months), *Journal of Stroke and Neurological Diseases* (quarterly), *Clinical Journal of Liver and Biliary Diseases* (quarterly)

DEANS

Basic Medical Sciences: YU YONGLI
First Clinical College: YU DESHUN
Second Clinical College: MU DELIN
Third Clinical College: ZHAO JISHENG
Preventive Medicine: SHUN ZHIWEI
Endemic Diseases: LI CAI
Stomatology: GAO WENXIN

PROFESSORS

School of Basic Medical Sciences:

CHENG, Y. Y., Pathological Anatomy
DU, K. Q., Physiopathology
HONG, M., Biochemistry
JIN, B., Anatomy
LI, F., Anatomy
LI, Y. L., Pathological Anatomy
LI, Z. B., Electron Microscope
LIU, M., Physiology
LIU, Z. H., Immunology
LU, Z., Pharmacology
NIE, Y. X., Histology and Embryology
WANG, S., Physiology
WANG, S. L., Histology and Embryology
WEI, J. J., Organic Chemistry
WEI, Y. D., Organic Chemistry
WEN, Z. G., Biology
WU, D. C., Anatomy
WU, G. X., Inorganic Chemistry
WU, J. X., Pathological Anatomy
YANG, G. Z., Immunology
YANG, H. Y., Biochemistry
YANG, S. J., Pharmacology
YU, Y. L., Immunology
ZHAO, X. J., Physiopathology
ZHONG, G. G., Physiology
ZHONG, R. Y., Pharmacology
ZHOU, Z. Z., Histology and Embryology
ZHU, S., Physiopathology
ZHU, X., Immunology

School of Preventive Medicine:

FAN, H. X., Radiation Toxicology
GUO, S. P., Epidemiology
JIN, Y. K., Radiation Injuries
JU, G. Z., Radiation Biology
LI, X., Radiation Biology
LIU, J., Radiation Toxicology
LIU, S. Z., Radiation Biology
SHU, Q., Epidemiology
SU, S. J., Radiation Protection
SUI, Z. R., Nutriology
WAN, X. Z., Radiation Injuries
WEI, J., Radiation Biology
YU, H., Radiation Toxicology
ZHANG, M., Radiation Biology
ZHANG, Y. M., Labour Health
ZHAO, H., Biostatistics
ZHAO, Q., Nutriology

First Clinical College:

CAI, S., Otorhinolaryngology
CAO, L. N., General Surgery
DU, B. D., Otorhinolaryngology
FENG, W., Paediatrics
FU, W. Y., Paediatrics
GUO, X. F., Otorhinolaryngology
GUO, X. W., Cardiovascular Diseases
HAN, G. X., Laboratory Tests
HUO, S. F., Paediatrics
HU, K. H., Paediatrics
JI, Z. D., Chest Surgery
LE, J., Gynaecology and Obstetrics
LI, S., Haematology
LI, T. Y., Paediatrics
LI, X. C., Traditional Chinese Medicine
LIANG, B. Y., Psychology
LIANG, Z. X., Paediatrics
LIN, S. H., Neurology
LIU, D. M., Cardiovascular Diseases
LIU, F. C., Neurosurgery
LIU, G. J., Oncology
LU, J., Paediatrics
LU, M. D., Infectious Diseases
QIAO, R. J., Ophthalmology
RAO, M. L., Neurology
SONG, G. P., Diseases of the Digestive System
SUO, J. X., Neurosurgery
TAN, K. A., Respiratory Diseases
TAN, Y., Laboratory Tests
TAN, Y. Q., General Surgery
WANG, C. K., Neurosurgery
WANG, F., Anaesthesia
WANG, G. C., Internal Medicine
WANG, J., Diseases of the Digestive System
WANG, M., Neurology
WANG, Y., CAT Scanners
WANG, Y. D., General Surgery
XU, G. B., Electrodiagnosis
XU, J., Ophthalmology
XU, X., Infectious Diseases
XU, X., Internal Medicine
XU, X. X., Orthopaedics
YANG, J. W., Cardiovascular Diseases
YANG, J. Y., Paediatrics
YANG, Z. Q., Otorhinolaryngology
YI, Y. L., Haematology
YIN, G., Internal Medicine
YU, G. D., Electrodiagnosis
ZHAN, Q. Q., Infectious Diseases
ZHANG, J. B.
ZHANG, L., Dermatology
ZHANG, S. D., Internal Medicine
ZHANG, S. Q., Neurology
ZHANG, X., Orthopaedics
ZHANG, Y., Neurology
ZHAO, D. C., Cardiovascular Diseases
ZHAO, J., Neurology
ZHAO, W., General Surgery
ZHAO, Z., General Surgery
ZHENG, P. R., Internal Medicine
ZHOU, B., Oncology
ZHU, D., Radiotherapy

Second Clinical College:

AN, Q. Z., Gynaecology and Obstetrics
GAO, F., General Surgery
GUAN, W., General Surgery
HAN, G., Paediatrics
HE, G. Z., Respiratory Diseases
HUANG, D. H., General Surgery
JIN, X. Z., Dermatology
LI, H., Ophthalmology
LI, S. R., Gynaecology and Obstetrics
LI, Z., Traditional Chinese Medicine
LIN, S. Q., Internal Medicine
LIU, W. C., Internal Medicine
LIU, Y. R., Paediatrics
MA, Y. D., Otorhinolaryngology
QI, B., Orthopaedics
QIU, T. S., General Surgery
SONG, Y. F., Internal Medicine
TIAN, R. G., Chest Surgery
WANG, N., General Surgery
WANG, Z. D., Gynaecology and Obstetrics
WEI, S. L., General Surgery
WU, S. D., Traditional Chinese Medicine
XU, Y. H., Otorhinolaryngology
YANG, X. Q., Gynaecology and Obstetrics
ZHANG, M. F., Dermatology
ZHANG, W., Internal Medicine
ZHANG, W. Y., Gynaecology and Obstetrics
ZHANG, Y., Neurology
ZHANG, Z. D., General Surgery
ZHAO, Z. G., Child Health
ZHOU, J., Neurosurgery
ZHU, F. Q., Gynaecology and Obstetrics

Third Clinical College:

CHEN, Y., Internal Medicine
CHENG, L., Radiotherapy
CIU, Z. M., Cardiovascular Diseases
DUAN, D. S., Orthopaedics
FENG, J., Diseases of Digestive System
GAO, F., Nuclear Medicine
HE, E. S. T., General Surgery
HE, S. L., General Surgery
JANG, H. Z., Orthopaedics
KAN, X. X., Laboratory Tests
LI, Z., Orthopaedics
LIU, B. Y., General Surgery
LIU, Y., Orthopaedics
LIU, Y. H., Orthopaedics
LU, X., Urological Surgery
MENG, X. M., General Surgery
SONG, X. L., Chest Surgery
SUN, D., Orthopaedics
SUN, R. W., Laboratory Tests
SUN, X. D., Stomatology
WAN, L. Z., Radiotherapy
WAN, M., Electrodiagnosis
WANG, M. C., Neurosurgery
WANG, M. X., Internal Medicine
WANG, S. Q., Traditional Chinese Medicine
WANG, S. X., Paediatrics
WANG, W., General Surgery
WANG, W. Z., Laboratory Tests
XIAO, Y. L., Nuclear Medicine
YANG, H. S., Radiotherapy
YU, C., Paediatrics
YU, S. F., Physiotherapy
YU, W., Gynaecology and Obstetrics
ZHAN, X. M., Haematology
ZHANG, D., General Surgery
ZHANG, M., Internal Medicine
ZHAO, E. C., Paediatrics
ZHAO, F., Radiotherapy
ZHAO, H. X., Chest Surgery

ZHAO, L., Internal Medicine
ZHAO, S. H., Traditional Chinese Medicine
ZHEN, X., Otorhinolaryngology
ZHENG, Z. L., General Surgery
ZHOU, F., Internal Medicine

School of Dentistry:
CAI, J. J., Oral Paediatrics
LIANG, T., Orthodontics
LIU, J., Oral Surgery
LIU, Z., Oral X-Ray
OUYANG, J., Oral Pathology
WANG, G. Y., Oral Internal Medicine
XU, Y. Z., Oral Surgery

Research Institute of Endemic Diseases:
AN, R. G., Analytical Chemistry
HOU, L. Z., Biochemistry
JIANG, X. L., Analytical Chemistry
LI, C., Biochemistry
LI, G. S., Pathology
YAN, W. Q., Biochemistry
YANG, T. S., Biochemistry

NORTH CHINA ELECTRIC POWER UNIVERSITY

204 Qingnian Rd, Baoding 071003, Hebei
Telephone: (312) 5024952
Fax: (312) 5028483
Internet: www.ncepu.edu.cn

Founded 1958
State control

President: LIU JI ZHEN
Vice-Presidents: AN LIAN SUO, LEI YING QI, LI HE MING, PENG ZHEN ZHONG
Heads of Graduate Department: AN LIAN SUO, DING CHANG FU
Librarian: KONG ZHENGHUI

Number of teachers: 2,348
Number of students: 20,000

Publications: *Electric Power Higher Education* (4 a year), *Electric Power Information* (4 a year), *Electric Power Record* (4 a year), *Journal* (4 a year), *Modern Electric Power* (6 a year)

DEANS

School of Adult Education: AN LIAN SUO
School of Applied Mathematics: LU ZHAN HUI
School of Applied Physics: ZHANG XIAO HONG
School of Automation: (vacant)
School of Computer Science and Technology: ZHU YONG LI
School of Dynamical Engineering: YANG YONG PING
School of Economy Management: QI JIAN XUN
School of Electrical and Communications Engineering: (vacant)
School of Electrical Engineering: CUI XIANG
School of Environment Engineering: ZHAO YI
School of Humanity and Social Science: LI JU YING
School of Mechanical Engineering: (vacant)
School of Physical Education: YAN GUO QIANG
Department of English: DAI ZHONG XIN

PROFESSORS

AI, XIN, Electrical Engineering
BAO, HAI, Electrical Engineering
CAO, CHUN MEI, Applied Physics
CHEN, SHENG JIAN, Computer Science and Technology
CHEN, WU, Computer Science and Technology
CHEN, YING MIN, Environmental Engineering
CUI, XIANG, Electrical Engineering
DAI, ZHONG XIN, English Department
DONG, XING HUI, Computer Science and Technology
DU, JIAN GUO, Computer Science and Technology
FANG, LU GUANG, Physical Education
FENG, HUI, Environmental Engineering
GUAN, RONG HUA, Applied Physics
GUO, LEI, English Department
HE, YONG GUI, Economics and Management
HU, MAN YIN, Environmental Engineering
HU, ZHI GUANG, Environmental Engineering
HUANG, YUAN SHENG, Economics and Management
JIA, ZHENG YUAN, Economics and Management
JIANG, GEN SHAN, Applied Physics
LI, JU YING, Humanities and Social Sciences
LI, QI, Applied Physics
LI, QUAN HUA, Physical Education
LI, SHOU XIN, Environmental Engineering
LIN, BI YING, Computer Science and Technology
LIU, ZHI YUAN, Humanities and Social Sciences
LU, FANG CHENG, Electrical Engineering
LU, ZHAN HUI, Applied Mathematics
MA, XIN SHUN, Applied Mathematics
NIU, DONG XIAO, Economics and Management
QI, JIAN XUN, Economics and Management
SUN, JIAN GUO, Computer Science and Technology
SUN, WEI, Economics and Management
WAN, SHI WEI, Applied Physics
WANG, BAO YI, Computer Science and Technology
WANG, CUI RU, Computer Science and Technology
WANG, JING MIN, Economics and Management
WANG, MIN, Humanities and Social Sciences
WU, KE HE, Computer Science and Technology
XIAO, XIANG NING, Electrical Engineering
XING, MIAN, Applied Mathematics
YAN, GUO QIANG, Physical Education
YANG, QI XUN, Electrical Engineering
YI, LIAN QING, Environmental Engineering
YI, ZENG QIAN, Applied Physics
YUAN, YONG TAO, Environmental Engineering
ZHANG, SHENG HAN, Environmental Engineering
ZHANG, TIAN XIN, Humanities and Social Sciences
ZHANG, XIAO HONG, Applied Physics
ZHANG, XU ZHEN, Humanities and Social Sciences
ZHANG, ZHEN SHENG, Environmental Engineering
ZHAO, WEN XIA, Applied Mathematics
ZHAO, YI, Environmental Engineering
ZHENG, GU PING, Computer Science and Technology
ZHU, LING, Electrical Engineering
ZHU, YONG LI, Computer Science and Technology

ATTACHED RESEARCH INSTITUTES

Electrical Engineering Research Institute: Dir LI HE MING.

Electric Power Economy Management Research Institute: Dir XIU DONG XIAO.

Environment Engineering Technology Research Institute: Dir ZHAO YI.

Industry Process Simulation and Control Laboratory: Dir MA YONG GUANG.

Information Technology Research Institute: Dir GAO QIANG.

Mechanical Engineering and Automation: Dir TANG GUI JI.

Pyrology Research Institute: Dir HAN PU.

NORTHEAST FORESTRY UNIVERSITY

26 Hexing Rd, Harbin 150040, Heilongjiang
Telephone: (451) 2190015
Fax: (451) 2110146
E-mail: faob@public.hr.hl.cn
Internet: www.nefu.edu.cn

Founded 1952
Academic year: September to July

President: Prof. LI JIAN
Vice-Presidents: Prof. HUO JIANYU, Prof. YANG CHUANPING, Prof. CHAO JUN, Assoc. Prof. CHEN WENBIN, Assoc. Prof. HU WANYI
Dean of Graduate School: FAN DELIN
Librarian: LIN XISHENG

Library of 570,000 vols
Number of teachers: 846
Number of students: 5,482 (incl. 307 postgraduates)

Publications: *Bulletin of Botany Research* (4 a year), *Chinese Wildlife* (4 a year), *Forest Fire Protection* (4 a year), *Science of Logging Engineering* (6 a year), *Forestry Finance and Accounting* (monthly), *Journal of Northeast Forestry University* (in English, 4 a year), *Forestry Research in Northern China* (in English, 4 a year)

HEADS OF COLLEGES AND DEPARTMENTS

College of Forest Resources and Environment: Prof. WANG FENGYOU
College of Wildlife Resources: Prof. JIA JINGBO
College of Forest Products: Prof. WANG FENGHU
College of Economics and Management: Prof. WANG ZHAOJUN
College of Humanities: Prof. WANG YAOXIAN
College of Civil Engineering: Prof. ZHANG YINGE
College of Electromechanical Engineering: Prof. LI DONGSHENG
College of Landscape Architecture: Prof. ZHUO LIHUAN
Normal College: Prof. SONG YE
College of Transportation: Prof. WANG LIHAI
College of Information and Computer Engineering: WANG NIHONG
College of Foreign Languages: Prof. LIU MENLAN
Department of Physical Education: Prof. MO SHONGSHAN
Correspondence College: CAO XIAOGUANG

PROFESSORS

DING, B., Silviculture
GE, M., Wood Science, Wood Chemistry
HU, Y., Forest Entomology
HUANG, Q., Plan Statistics
JIANG, M., Forestry Economics
LI, G., Forest Resources
LI JIAN, Wood Science and Technology, Wood Surface Chemistry
LI JINGWEN, Ecosystems, Community Ecology
LIU, G., Financial Accounting
LU, R., Wood and Composites Technology and Manufacturing
MA, J., Wildlife Management, Natural Reserves
MA, L., Forest Machinery
NIE, S., Phytocommunity Ecology, Phytotaxonomy
SHAO, L., Forest Disease Epidemiology, Taxonomy of Pathogenic Fungi
SHI, J., Forest Engineering
WANG, F., Ecosystems, Community Ecology
WANG, Y., Ecosystems, Physical and Chemical Ecology
WANG, Z., High Yield Forests
XIAN, K., Forest Protection, Water and Soil Conservation
XIANG, C., Taxonomy of Pathogenic Fungi, Management of Forest Diseases
YUE, S., Pest Control
ZHOU, X., Ecosystems, Economic Ecology
ZHOU, Y., Phytocommunity Ecology, Phytotaxonomy
ZHU, G., Forestry Vehicles, Sawing Equipment
ZU, Y., Unlinear Phytoecology

NORTHEASTERN UNIVERSITY

No. 11, Lane 3, Wenhua Lu, Heping District, Shenyang, 110006 Liaoning
Telephone: (24) 3893000
Fax: (24) 3892454
E-mail: neu@ramm.neu.edu.cn
Internet: www.neu.edu.cn

Founded 1923 as Northeastern University; became Northeast University of Technology in 1950; reverted to former name in 1993

Controlled by Ministry of Metallurgical Industry
Academic year: September to July (two semesters)
President: HE JICHENG
Vice-Presidents: YANG PEIZHEN, WANG ZHI, WANG QIYI, ZHOU GUANGYOU, LIU JIREN, WANG WANSHAN
Provost: Prof. DUAN YUEHU
Dean of General Affairs: Assoc. Prof. MENG QINGXIAN
Librarian: Prof. YANG HUAI
Library of 1,650,000 vols
Number of teachers: 1,950
Number of students: 18,814 undergraduates, 1,807 postgraduates

Publications: *Journal*, *Economics and Management of Metallurgical Enterprise*, *China Engineer*, *Control and Decision*, *Basic Automation*

DEANS

Graduate School: Prof. HE JICHENG
Liaoning Branch: Prof. MAO TIANYU
Qinhuangdao Branch: Prof. WANG ZHENFAN
Adult Education School: Prof. ZHAO LIANGZHEN
College of Business Administration: Prof. BI MENGLIN
College of Humanities and Law: Prof. PENG DINGAN
College of Mechanical Engineering: Prof. WANG DEJUN
College of Resources and Civil Engineering: Prof. CHEN BAOZHI
College of Materials and Metallurgical Engineering: Prof. HAO SHIMING
College of Information Science and Engineering: Prof. GU SHUSHENG
College of Gold Metallurgy: Prof. YANG LI

ATTACHED RESEARCH INSTITUTES

Computer Software Research Centre: Dir Prof. LIU JIREN.

Automation Research Centre: Dir Prof. CAI TIANYOU.

National Laboratory of Automated Tandem Rolling: Dir Prof. WANG GUODONG.

NORTHWEST UNIVERSITY

Tai Bai Bei Lu, Xian 710069, Shaanxi
Telephone: (29) 8302344
Fax: (29) 7232733
Internet: www.nwu.edu.cn

Founded 1912
Academic year: September to August.
President: Prof. HAO KEGANG
Vice-Presidents: LIU SHUNKANG, WANG JIAN, WANG SHUANCAI, CHEN ZONGXING
Librarian: Prof. ZHOU TIANYOU
Library: Library of 1.6 million vols
Number of teachers: 1,135
Number of students: 10,466 (incl. 571 postgraduates)

Publications: *Journal* (Arts and Social Science, Natural Sciences, quarterly), *Annual Report of Lu Xun Studies*, *Literature of the Tang Dynasty*, *Middle East*, *Studies in the History of North Western China*, *Studies in Higher Education*

HEADS OF DEPARTMENTS

Chinese Language and Literature: Prof. YANG CHANGLONG
History: Prof. ZHOU WEIZHOU
Philosophy: Prof. SHEN ZHONGYING
Foreign Languages and Literature: Prof. ZHOU SHIZHONG
Mathematics: Prof. GAO ZHIMIN
Physics: Prof. LIU JUCHENG
Chemistry: Prof. WANG JIANHUA
Chemical Engineering: Prof. LI BAOZHANG
Biology: Prof. SUN LIANKUI
Geology: Prof. MEI ZHICHAO
Geography: Prof. YE SHUHUA
Computer Science: Prof. LIU DEAN
Law: Prof. ZHANG TIANJIE
Library and Information Science: Prof. ZHOU TIANYOU
Tourism: Prof. ZHANG HUI
Economic Management: Prof. HE LIANCHENG
Electronics: Prof. WANG DAKAI

NORTHWESTERN POLYTECHNICAL UNIVERSITY

Xi'an 710072, Shaanxi
Telephone: (29) 8493119
Fax: (29) 8491000
E-mail: office@nwpu.edu.cn
Internet: www.nwpu.edu.cn

Founded 1938
State control
Languages of instruction: Chinese, English
Academic year: September to July (2 semesters).

Honorary President: Prof. JI WENMEI
President: Prof. JIANG CHENGYU
Vice-Presidents: Prof. GAO DEYUAN, Prof. WANG WEI, Prof. WANG RUNXIAN, Prof. YUAN JIANPING
Dean of Studies: Prof. WAN XIANPENG
Director of Foreign Affairs: Prof. TANG HONG
Librarian: Prof. GOU WENXUAN

Number of teachers: 1,400
Number of students: 28,000, incl. 5,160 postgraduates

Publications: *University Journal* (4 a year), *Mechanical Science and Engineering* (4 a year), *Journal of Theoretical and Applied Mechanics* (4 a year)

DEANS

Graduate School: Prof. JIANG CHENGYU
College of Continuing Education: Prof. WEI SHENGMIN
College of Marine Engineering: SONG BAOWEI
College of Astronautics: Prof. ZHOU JUN
College of Civil Aviation Engineering: Prof. SUN QIN
College of Materials Science: Prof. LI HEJUN
College of Management: Prof. YE ZHENGYIN
School of Mechatronic Engineering: Prof. ZHANG DINGHUA

HEADS OF DEPARTMENTS

Applied Mathematics: Prof. XU WEI
Aircraft Engineering: Prof. YE ZHENGYIN
Electronic Engineering: Prof. XU JIADONG
Aero-Engine and Thermal Power Engineering: Prof. CAI YUANHU
Automatic Control: Prof. WANG XINGMIN
Computer Science and Engineering: Prof. ZHOU XINGSHE
Social Sciences: Prof. LI JIANZHONG
Foreign Languages: Prof. WANG JIAN
Architectural and Civil Engineering: Prof. ZHANG XUN'AN
Engineering Mechanics: Prof. YUE ZHUFENG
Applied Physics: Prof. WEI BINGBO
Chemistry Engineering: Prof. FAN XIAODONG

PROFESSORS

AI, J. L., Aircraft Design
AN, J. W., Aircraft Automatic Control
BAI, C. R., Aerodynamics
CAI, W. D., Computer Application
CAI, Y. H., Aero-engines
CAO, C. N., Physics
CHEN, C. L., Physics
CHEN, G. D., Mechanics
CHEN, K. A., Noise Control
CHEN, M., Gyroscope and Inertial Navigation
CHEN, S. L., Flight Mechanics
CHEN, Z., Metallic Materials and Heat Treatment
CHENG, G., Signal Measuring and Instruments
CHENG, L. F., Physical Metallurgy
CHU, W. L., Aero-engines
CUI, Y. Z., China Revolutionary History
DAI, G. Z., Theory and Application of Automatic Control
DANG, J. B., Solid Mechanics
DENG, Z. C., Mechanics
DING, X. Q., Applied Mathematics
DUAN, Z. M., Signal Circuit and Systems Engineering
FAN, D., Aero-engines
FAN, M. F., China Revolutionary History
FAN, X. D., High Polymer Material
FAN, X. Y., Computer Application
FANG, Q., Flight Mechanics
FANG, Z. D., Mechanical Engineering
FENG, D., Traditional Chinese Painting
FENG, J. L., Linguistics (Japanese)
FU, H. Z., Physical Metallurgy
FU, L. Z., Mathematics
GAN, X. Y., Linguistics (English)
GAO, D. Y., Computer Science and Engineering
GAO, M. T., Drafting
GAO, X. G., Command Systems Engineering
GAO, Z. H., Aerodynamics
GE, W. J., Machinery Design and Manufacturing
GOU, D. B., Track and Field Sports
GOU, W. X., Solid Mechanics
GU, L. X., Guided Missile Design
GUO, H. Z., Metal Forming
GUO, L., Intelligent Signal Processing
GUO, X. P., Physical Metallurgy
HAO, C. Y., Space Vehicle Design
HE, C. A., Theory and Application of Automatic Control
HE, E. M., Aircraft Control
HE, G. Q., Rocket Engine
HE, H. C., Computer and Artificial Intelligence
HE, M. Y., Signal Circuit and Systems Engineering
HE, W. P., Space Flight Manufacturing Engineering
HE, X. S., General Mechanics
HE, Y. Y., Automatic Control
HU, X. L., Physical Chemistry
HU, Z. G., Computer Software
HUANG, J. G., Applied Electronic Technology
HUANG, Q. Q., Structure Intensity
HUANG, W. D., Physical Metallurgy
JIANG, C. Y., Space Flight Manufacturing Engineering
JIANG, D. W., Applied Mathematics
JIANG, J. S., Structural Mechanics
JIANG, Z. J., Computer Software
JIAO, G. Q., Solid Mechanics
JIE, W. Q., Physical Metallurgy
JIN, B. S., Mechanics of Materials
JING, Z. R., Electronic Engineering
KANG, F. J., Automatic Control
KANG, R. K., Machinery Manufacturing
LAI, X. X., Dialectics of Nature
LEI, Y., Signal Processing
LI, B. X., Rocket Engines
LI, E. P., Physics
LI, F. G., Metal Plasticity Processing
LI, F. W., Aerodynamics
LI, H. J., Metallic Materials and Heat Treatment
LI, H. L., Physical Metallurgy
LI, H. X., Aerodynamics

LI, J. L., Mathematics
LI, J. Z., Political Economy
LI, K. Z., Metallic Materials and Heat Treatment
LI, M. Q., Metal Forming
LI, S. J., Magnetos
LI, S. P., Plasticity Processing
LI, T. H., Materials Processing
LI, W. H., Computer Applications
LI, W. J., Aircraft Design
LI, X. Q., Drafting
LI, Y. J., Guided Missile Automatic Control
LI, Y. L., Fracture Mechanics
LI, Y. Z., Applied Polymer Science
LI, Y., Space Flight Manufacturing Engineering
LI, Z. H., Computer Software
LI, Z. S., Underwater Technology
LIAN, B. W., Radio Communication
LIAN, X. C., Aero-engines
LIANG, G. Q., Space Flight Manufacturing Engineering
LIANG, G. Z., Physical and Chemistry Experiment
LIANG, S. X., Equipment Management
LIAO, M. F., Aero-engines Intensity
LIN, H., Electric Technology
LIU, B. M., Metal Plasticity Processing
LIU, B., Aero-engines
LIU, D., Solid Mechanics
LIU, G., Mechanical Design
LIU, J. H., Welding
LIU, L., Physical Metallurgy
LIU, W. G., Electrical Machinery and Control
LIU, X. L., Aircraft Automatic Control
LIU, Z. T., Metallic Materials and Heat Treatment
LU, C. D., Machinery Manufacturing
LU, J. C., Automatic Control
LU, S., Engine Structure Intensity
LUO, C. R., Physics
LUO, X. B., Mathematics
LV, B. T., Metallic Materials and Heat Treatment
LV, G. Z., Aircraft Structure Intensity
LV, Z. Z., Solid Mechanics
MA, R. Q., Electric Engineering
MA, X. Q., Space Flight Manufacturing Engineering
MA, Y. L, Underwater Acoustics Engineering
MAO, G. W., Rocket Engines
MENG, B. A., Track and Field Sports
MENG, J. M., Linguistics (English)
MO, R., Computer Design
MU, D. J., Theory and Application of Automatic Control
NING, R. C., High Polymer Material
NIV, P. C., Mathematics
OU, Y. J., Applied Mathematics
PAN, J. Y., Management Engineering
PAN, Q., Automatic Control
PEI, C. M., Signal Processing
QI, L. H., Metal Art
QI, S. H., High Polymer Material
QIAN, Z. B., Hot Motive Equipment of the Torpedo
QIAO, S. R., Metallic Materials and Heat Treatment
QIAO, Z. D., Computational Aerodynamics
QIN, X. S., Machinery Manufacturing
QIN, Y. Y., Gyroscope and Inertial Navigation
QING, H. Y., Chemistry
QU, S. R., Drafting
REN, X. M., Aero-engines
SHEN, J., Physical Metallurgy
SHI, H. S., Radio Communication
SHI, K. M., Linguistics (German)
SHI, X. F., Administration
SHI, X. H., Mechanical Engineering
SHI, X. Q., Linguistics (French)
SHI, Y. K., Electrical Equipment
SHI, Y. M., Applied Mathematics
SHI, Y. Y., Ergonomics
SHI, Z. K., Theory and Application of Automatic Control
SONG, B. F., Aircraft Design
SONG, B. W., Machinery Manufacturing
SONG, Z. M., Applied Physics
SU, C. W., Applied Mathematics
SU, K. H., Chemistry
SUN, C., Signal Processing
SUN, G. Z., Drafting
SUN, J. C., Applied Acoustics and Noise Control Engineering
SUN, Q., Aircraft Design
SUN, S. D., Machinery Manufacturing
TANG, G. P., Mathematics
TANG, H., Personnel Management
TANG, S., Flight Mechanics
TANG, Y. Z., Aircraft Automatic Control
TAO, H., Space Flight Manufacturing Engineering
TIAN, C. S., Metallic Materials and Heat Treatment
TIAN, Z., Mathematics
TONG, S. R., Equipment Management
TONG, X. Y., Aircraft Design
TU, Q. P., Signal Processing
WAN, X. P., Aircraft Design
WANG, B., Physics
WANG, J. B., Aircraft Manufacture Engineering
WANG, J. F., Financial Accounting
WANG, J., Linguistics (English)
WANG, L. D., Physics
WANG, L., Rocket Engines
WANG, R. M., Compound Materials
WANG, R. X., Numerically Controlled Machine Tools
WANG, S. M., Mechanics
WANG, S. M., Basic Electrical Training
WANG, W., Aircraft Automatic Control
WANG, X. M., Automatic Control and Computer Application
WANG, Y. C., Hot Motive Equipment of the Torpedo
WANG, Y. M., Underwater Acoustics Engineering
WANG, Y. S., Radio Technology
WANG, Z. S., Motive Equipment Control Engineering
WEI, B. B., Physical Metallurgy
WEI, F., Mechanics of Materials
WEI, S. M., Ergonomics
WENG, Z. Q., Navigation Systems
WU, D. Y., Heat Energy Engineering
WU, H., Aero-engines
WU, J. J., Space Flight Manufacturing Engineering
WU, J., Computer Software
WU, X. G., Torpedo Control
WU, Z. Y., Armoured Concrete Systems
XI, D. K., Aerodynamics
XI, S. M., Metallic Materials and Heat Transfer
XIAO, Y. L., Mathematics
XIE, F. Q., Metal Surface Corrosion
XIN, K., Linguistics (English)
XU, D. M., Torpedo Automatic Control
XU, J. D., Microwave and Antenna Technology
XU, M., Aerodynamics
XU, W., Applied Mathematics
XU, Y. D., Physical Metallurgy
XU, Z., Applied Mathematics
YAN, J. G., Automatic Control
YAN, J., Aircraft Navigation Control
YANG, G. C., Physical Metallurgy
YANG, H. C., Computer Design
YANG, H., Space Flight Technology
YANG, J., Aircraft Automatic Control
YANG, N. D., Systems Engineering
YANG, S. Q., Welding
YANG, Y. F., Linguistics (English)
YANG, Y. N., Aerodynamics
YANG, Y. Q., Metallic Materials and Heat Transfer
YANG, Y. S., Electrical Technology
YANG, Z. C., Solid Mechanics
YANG, Z. Y., Computer Applications
YAO, Z. K., Metal Forming
YE, Z. L., Applied Mathematics
YE, Z. Y., Aerodynamics
YU, H. X., Radio Communication
YUAN, J. P., Flight Mechanics
YUAN, W. Z., Machinery Manufacturing
YUAN, Z. K., Dialectics of Nature
YUE, Z. F., Aircraft Design
ZHANG, A., Command Systems Engineering
ZHANG, B. Q., Aerodynamics
ZHANG, D. H., Ergonomics
ZHANG, D. S., Structural Mechanics
ZHANG, D., Guided Missile Design
ZHANG, H. C., Theory and Application of Automatic Control
ZHANG, H. F., Thermal and Solar Energy Engineering
ZHANG, H. G., Linguistics (German)
ZHANG, H. S., Signal Circuit and Systems Engineering
ZHANG, K. S., Solid Mechanics
ZHANG, K. Y., Applied Mathematics
ZHANG, L. T., Physical Metallurgy
ZHANG, Q. X., Physical Metallurgy
ZHANG, Q. Y., High Polymer Material
ZHANG, S. S., Equipment Engineering
ZHANG, W. G., Aircraft Navigation Control
ZHANG, W. H., Space Flight Manufacturing Engineering
ZHANG, X. A., Building Structure
ZHANG, X. K., Space Flight Manufacturing Engineering
ZHANG, X. M., Detonator Technology
ZHANG, Y. M., Torpedo Design
ZHANG, Y. Y., Computer Software
ZHANG, Y. Z., Automatic Control
ZHAO, J. L., Modern Optics Application
ZHAO, J. W., Sound Electronic Engineering of Water
ZHAO, R. C., Signal and Graph Processing
ZHAO, S. Z., Machinery Manufacturing
ZHAO, X. A., Linguistics (English)
ZHAO, X. M., Mathematics
ZHAO, X. P., Solid Mechanics
ZHAO, Y. S., General Mechanics
ZHAO, Z. W., Computer Software
ZHI, B. S., Automatic Control
ZHI, X. Z., General Mechanics
ZHOU, D. Y., Command Systems Engineering
ZHOU, J., Aircraft Navigation Control
ZHOU, J. H., Analysis and Design of Control Systems
ZHOU, Q., Automatic Control
ZHOU, W. C., Physical Metallurgy
ZHOU, X. S., Computer Applications
ZHOU, Y. H., Physical Metallurgy
ZHOU, Z., Flight Mechanics
ZHU, H. R., Heat Energy Engineering
ZHU, J. Q., Aero-engines
ZHU, M. Q., Measurement Control in Mechanical Engineering
ZHU, X. P., Automatic Control
ZHU, Y. A., Computer Applications
ZOU, G. R., Materials Processing Engineering

ATTACHED RESEARCH INSTITUTES AND CENTRES

Institute of Applied Mathematics: Dir Prof. LUO XUEBO.

Institute of Mechanical Electronic Engineering: Dir Prof. FANG CHONGDE.

Centre for Automobile Engineering: Dir Prof. FANG CHONGDE.

Institute of Instrument Research: Dir Prof. QIU WEIPING.

Centre for Aero-Sonar Research and Development: Dir Prof. WANG YINGMIN.

Institute of Electric Power Projects and Electronic Engineering: Dir Prof. ZHOU JIHUA.

Institute of Underwater Vehicles: Dir Prof. XU DEMIN.

Marine Science and Information Technology Research Centre: Dir Prof. HUANG JIANGUO.

Institute of Environmental Engineering: Dir Prof. CHEN KEAN.

Institute of Pressure Welding Engineering: Dir Prof. QIN XIONGPU.

Thermal Composite Materials Laboratory: Dir Prof. CHENG LAIFEI.

Institute of Advanced Materials in Physical Metallurgy: Dir Prof. LIU LIN.

Institute of Photoelectricity for Materials with an Information-Based Function: Dir Prof. JIE WANQI.

Centre for Research and Development into High Technology Forging and Casting: Dir Prof. HUANG WEIDONG.

Institute of Airspace Management and Flow Control: Dir Prof. BAI CUNRU.

Institute of Dependability Engineering: Dir Prof. SONG BIFENG.

Centre for Air Blower Pump Engineering: Dir Prof. XI DEKE.

Institute of Air Blower New Technology: Dir Prof. XI DEKE.

Institute of Aircraft Survival Technology: Dir Prof. LV GUOZHI.

Institute of Aerodynamic Elasticity: Dir Prof. YE ZHENGYAN.

Institute of Fluid Dynamics Analysis and Design: Dir Prof. BAI JUNQIANG.

Centre for Aerofoil Research: Dir Prof. QIAO ZHIDE.

Centre for ATE Technology and Fluid Engineering Research and Development: Dir Prof. BAI JUNQIANG.

Institute of Biomedical Science Engineering: Dir Prof. QI MIN.

Centre for Electronics and Information Engineering: Dir Prof. HAO CHONGYANG.

Xi'an Institute of Friction Welding Engineering and Technology: Dir Prof. HAO CHONGYANG.

Institute of Modern Information and Electronic Systems: Dir Prof. HE MINGYI.

Institute of Signal Processing: Dir Prof. ZHAO RONGCHUN.

Institute of Communication and Electronic Systems: Dir Prof. LIAN BAOWANG.

Institute of Electronic Science and Technology: Dir Prof. ZHANG XIUYAN.

Institute of Multimedia Communication and Software Technology: Dir Prof. WU JIAN.

Institute of Mechanical Kinetics and Engineering: Dir Prof. QIAO WEIYANG.

Institute of Air-Conditioner Refrigeration and Solar Energy: Dir Prof. ZHANG HEFEI.

Institute of Environmental Engineering and New Energy Resources Utilization: Dir Prof. ZHANG HEFEI.

Institute of Micro Aero-Engines: Dir Prof. YANG XIANGREN.

Institute of Spin Machinery and Wind Energy Equipment Testing: Dir Prof. LIAO MINGFU.

Institute of Guided Missile Navigation and Control: Dir Prof. ZHOU JUN.

Institute of Test and Control: Dir Prof. LI JINXIAN.

Institute of Space Systems Engineering and Industrial Automation Technology: Dir Prof. YAN JIE.

Institute of Space Observation Technology: Dir Prof. WANG ZHIGANG.

Institute of Target Prediction: Dir Prof. PAN QUAN.

Institute of Rare Earth Permanent Magnetism Motors (REPM): Dir Prof. LIU WEIGUO.

Institute of Pattern Science and Technology: Dir Prof. GUO LEI.

Institute of Resources and Environmental Information Engineering: Dir Prof. XUE HUIFENG.

Institute of Link Technology: Dir Prof. TAO HUA.

Shaanxi Provincial CAD Engineering and Technology Centre: Dir Prof. ZHANG DINGHUA.

Institute of Hard Space Material Cutting: Dir Prof. KANG RENKE.

'Jiang' Foundation Industrial Design Training Centre: Dir Prof. LU CHANGDE.

Institute of Industrial Design: Dir Prof. LU CHANGDE.

Centre for Data Processing: Dir Prof. WEI SHENGMIN.

Aerospace History Research Centre: Dir Prof. HUANG YAOMIN.

CAD/CAM Centre: Dir Prof. ZHANG DINGHUA.

Institute of Automation Software and Information: Dir Prof. WANG RUNXIAO.

Model Research and Training Centre: Dir Prof. MA ZHEEN.

Software Development Centre, NPU: Dir Prof. ZHANG YANYUAN.

Institute of Computer Survey and Control and Emulation Technology: Dir Prof. ZHAI ZHENGJUN.

Institute of Construction and Architecture Science: Dir Prof. DENG ZICHEN.

Institute of Architectural Design: Dir Prof. LI JUAN.

Institute of Architectural Materials Science: Dir Prof. ZHANG DESI.

Institute of Dynamics, Vibration and Control: Dir Prof. HE XINGSUO.

Institute of Space Survey: Dir Prof. HE XINGSUO.

Centre for Vibration Engineering and Technology: Dir Prof. JIANG JIESHENG.

Dong Ying Bohai High Polymer Materials Research Institute: Dir Prof. FAN XIAODONG.

Centre for Composite Materials Research: Dir Prof. NING RONGCHANG.

Institute of the Environmental Chemical Industry: Dir Prof. NING RONGCHANG.

Centre for High Polymer Water Absorbent Engineering: Dir Prof. NING RONGCHANG.

Institute of Biomedical High Polymer Materials: Dir Prof. YANG QINGFANG.

Institute of Corrosion and Protection: Dir Prof. LIU DAOXIN.

Institute of Civil Aircraft Maintenance and Breakdown Diagnosis: Dir Prof. SONG DONG.

Institute of Higher Learning: Dir Prof. BAO GUOHUA.

Aeronautical Micro-Electronics Research and Training Centre: Dir Prof. GAO DEYUAN.

Institute of High Technology Training Centre: Dir Prof. DAI GUANZHONG.

Institute of Plastics Applications: Dir Prof. WANG RUMIN.

Institute of Pilotless Mini-Aircraft: Dir Prof. DANG JINBAO.

Institute of Broadband Network and Long Distance Education Technology: Dir Prof. WANG FUBAO.

Institute of Education Technology: Dir Prof. DUAN WEIJUN.

PEKING UNIVERSITY

5 Yiheyuan Rd, Hai Dian, Beijing 100871
Telephone: 62752114
Fax: 62751207
Internet: www.pku.edu.cn

Founded 1898
Languages of instruction: Chinese, English
Academic year: September to June

President: XU ZHIHONG
Vice-Presidents: MIN WEIFANG, CHI HUISHENG, HAN QIDE, CHEN ZHANGLIANG, HE FANGCHUAN, LIN JUNJING, LIN JIUXIANG, LII ZHAOFENG, HAO PING
Registrar: LI KE'AN
Librarian: DAI LONGJI

Library of 4,610,000 vols
Number of teachers: 4,537
Number of students: 55,000

Publication: *Peking University Academic Journal*

HEADS OF DEPARTMENTS

School of Mathematical Science: ZHANG JIPING
Department of Mechanics and Engineering Science: FANG JING
School of Physics: YE YANLIN
Department of Geophysics: HUANG JIAYOU
Department of Technical Physics: YE YANLIN
Department of Electronics: XIANG HAIGE
Department of Computer Science and Technology: LI XIAOMING
College of Molecular and Chemical Engineering: ZHAO XINSHENG
College of Life Sciences: ZHOU ZENGQUAN
Department of Geology: PAN MAO
Department of Urban and Environmental Sciences: YANG KAIZHONG
Department of Psychology: WANG LEI
Department of Chinese Language and Literature: WEN RUMIN
Department of History: WANG TIANYOU
Institute of Archaeology and Museums: GAO CHONGWEN
Department of Philosophy: YE LANG
School of International Studies: QIAN QICHEN
School of Economics: YAN ZHIJIE
Guanhua School of Management: LI YINING
School of Law: ZHU SULI
Department of Information Management: WU WEICI
Department of Political Science and Public Administration: WANG PUQU
Department of Sociology: MA RONG
College of Foreign Languages: HU JIALUAN
Department of Arts: YE LANG
School of Marxism: CHENG ZHANAN
Department of Astronomy: CHEN JIANSHENG
Department of Religious Studies: YE LANG
Graduate School of Education: MIN WEIFANG
College of Journalism and Mass Communication: GONG WENXIANG
School of Basic Medical Sciences: JIA HONGTI
School of Pharmaceutical Sciences: PENG SHIQI
School of Public Health: LI LIMING
School of Nursing: ZHENG XIUXIA

There are also 82 research institutes

PEKING UNION MEDICAL COLLEGE

9 Dong Dan San Tiao, Dongcheng District, Beijing 100730
Telephone: (10) 65295912
Fax: (10) 65133086
E-mail: liudp@pumc.edu.cn
Internet: www.pumc.edu.cn

Founded 1917
Academic year: September to July

President: LIU DEPEI
Vice-Presidents: HE WEI, LIU QIAN, LU CHONGMEI, QI KEMING, SONG XUEMIN
Head of Graduate Department: LIU DEPEI

Librarian: WANG ZHAOLING

Number of teachers: 3,328

Publications: *Acta Academiae Medicinae Sinicae* (6 a year), *Bilingual Journal of Medicine International* (6 a year), *Chinese Chemical Letters* (12 a year), *Journal of Asian Natural Products Research* (4 a year)

DEANS

School of Basic Medical Sciences: ZHENG DEXIAN
School of Nursing: SHEN NING
Institute of Materia Medica: WANG XIAOLIANG
Institute of Medical Biology Technology: JIANG JIANDONG
Cancer Hospital: ZHAO PING
Fu Wai Hospital: HU SHENGSHOU
Orthopedic Surgery Hospital: QI KEMING
Peking Union Medical College Hospital: LIU QIAN

PROFESSORS

BAO, XIULAN, Peking Union Medical College Hospital
CAI, BOQIANG, Peking Union Medical College Hospital
CAI, LIXING, Peking Union Medical College Hospital
CAI, WEIMING, Cancer Hospital
CAO, JIMIN, School of Basic Medical Sciences
CHEN, CUANXIA, Peking Union Medical College Hospital
CHEN, DECHANG, Peking Union Medical College Hospital
CHEN, GUOZHANG, Orthopaedic Surgery Hospital
CHEN, HONGSHAN, Institute of Medical Biology Technology
CHEN, JIE, Peking Union Medical College Hospital
CHEN, TINGYUAN, Peking Union Medical College Hospital
CHEN, XI, Fu Wai Hospital
CHU, DATONG, Cancer Hospital
DAI, JINGLEI, Cancer Hospital
DAI, YUHUA, Peking Union Medical College Hospital
DONG, JINGWU, Peking Union Medical College Hospital
DONG, YI, Peking Union Medical College Hospital
FAN, JINCAI, Orthopaedic Surgery Hospital
FANG, DEFU, School of Basic Medical Sciences
FANG, QI, Peking Union Medical College Hospital
GAO, JUZHEN, Cancer Hospital
GAO, RUNLIN, Fu Wai Hospital
GU, DAZHONG, Cancer Hospital
GU, DONGFENG, Fu Wai Hospital
GUAN, YAN, Peking Union Medical College Hospital
GUANG, YAO, Peking Union Medical College Hospital
GUI, LAI, Orthopaedic Surgery Hospital
GUO, HUIYUAN, Institute of Medical Biology Technology
GUO, YUZHEN, Peking Union Medical College Hospital
HA, XIANGWEN, Cancer Hospital
HAO, YUZHI, Cancer Hospital
HE, ZHAMA, Fu Wai Hospital
HE, ZHUGEN, Cancer Hospital
HONG, FENGYI, Cancer Hospital
HONG, WANJUN, Cancer Hospital
HU, JINGQUN, Cancer Hospital
HU, SHENGSHOU, Fu Wai Hospital
HUANG, GUOJUN, Cancer Hospital
HUANG, HANYUAN, Peking Union Medical College Hospital
HUANG, LIANG, Institute of Materia Medica
HUANG, XIZHEN, Peking Union Medical College Hospital
HUANG, YIRONG, Cancer Hospital
HUI, RUTAI, Fu Wai Hospital
JI, BAOHUA, Peking Union Medical College Hospital
JI, XIAOCHENG, Peking Union Medical College Hospital
JIANG, JIANDONG, Institute of Medical Biology Technology
JIANG, MING, Peking Union Medical College Hospital
JIANG, XIUFANG, Peking Union Medical College Hospital
JIANG, ZHUMING, Peking Union Medical College Hospital
JIAO, HAIYAN, Peking Union Medical College Hospital
JIN, LAN, Peking Union Medical College Hospital
LI, CHANGLING, Cancer Hospital
LI, DIANDONG, Institute of Medical Biology Technology
LI, HANHONG, Peking Union Medical College Hospital
LI, JIAXIU, Cancer Hospital
LI, KUI, Cancer Hospital
LI, LIHUAN, Fu Wai Hospital
LI, LING, Cancer Hospital
LI, LONGYU, Peking Union Medical College Hospital
LI, QINGHONG, Cancer Hospital
LI, SENKAI, Orthopaedic Surgery Hospital
LI, TAISHENG, Cancer Hospital
LI, ZEJIAN, Peking Union Medical College Hospital
LIANG, XIAOTIAN, Institute of Materia Medica
LIANG, ZHIQUAN, School of Basic Medical Sciences
LIU, DAWEI, Peking Union Medical College Hospital
LIU, DEPEI, School of Basic Medical Sciences
LIU, FUSHENG, Cancer Hospital
LIU, GENTAO, Institute of Materia Medica
LIU, JINGSHENG, School of Basic Medical Sciences
LIU, LIYING, Cancer Hospital
LIU, QIAN, Peking Union Medical College Hospital
LIU, RUIXUE, Peking Union Medical College Hospital
LIU, SHUFAN, Cancer Hospital
LIU, TONGHUA, Peking Union Medical College Hospital
LIU, XINFAN, Cancer Hospital
LIU, YULING, Institute of Materia Medica
LIU, YUQING, Fu Wai Hospital
LIU, ZHONGXUN, Institute of Medical Biology Technology
LOU, ZHIXIAN, Institute of Medical Biology Technology
LU, CHONGMEI, School of Nursing
LU, NING, Cancer Hospital
LU, WEIXUAN, Peking Union Medical College Hospital
LUO, HUIYUAN, Peking Union Medical College Hospital
LUO, WEICI, Peking Union Medical College Hospital
MIAO, YANJUN, Cancer Hospital
OU YANG, HAN, Cancer Hospital
PAN, QINJING, Cancer Hospital
PAN, YANRUO, Peking Union Medical College Hospital
PU, JIELIN, Fu Wai Hospital
QI, KEMING, Orthopaedic Surgery Hospital
QI, MEIFU, Peking Union Medical College Hospital
QI, YONGFA, Cancer Hospital
QIANG, TUNAN, Cancer Hospital
QIAO, SHUBIN, Fu Wai Hospital
QIN, DEXING, Cancer Hospital
QIU, GUIXING, Peking Union Medical College Hospital
QIU, HUIZHONG, Peking Union Medical College Hospital
REN, YUZHU, Peking Union Medical College Hospital
SHAO, YONGFU, Cancer Hospital
SHEN, NING, School of Nursing
SHI, MULAN, Cancer Hospital
SHI, YUANKAI, Cancer Hospital
SONG, ZONGLU, Peking Union Medical College Hospital
SU, XUEZENG, Cancer Hospital
SUN, GENGTIAN, Cancer Hospital
SUN, JIANHENG, Cancer Hospital
SUN, LI, Cancer Hospital
SUN, LIXHONG, Fu Wai Hospital
SUN, NIANGU, Peking Union Medical College Hospital
SUN, YAN, Cancer Hospital
SUN, YINGLONG, Fu Wai Hospital
TANG, BANGCI, Peking Union Medical College Hospital
TANG, PINGZHANG, Cancer Hospital
TANG, WEISONG, Peking Union Medical College Hospital
TU, GIYI, Cancer Hospital
WANG, DANHUA, Peking Union Medical College Hospital
WANG, JIAQI, Orthopaedic Surgery Hospital
WANG, JINWAN, Cancer Hospital
WANG, LIANGJUN, Cancer Hospital
WANG, LUHUA, Cancer Hospital
WANG, MEI, Cancer Hospital
WANG, QILU, Cancer Hospital
WANG, SHIZHEN, Peking Union Medical College Hospital
WANG, XHISHI, Peking Union Medical College Hospital
WANG, XIAOMING, School of Basic Medical Sciences
WANG, YIPENG, Peking Union Medical College Hospital
WEI, MIN, Peking Union Medical College Hospital
WU, AIRU, Cancer Hospital
WU, NING, Cancer Hospital
WU, NING, Peking Union Medical College Hospital
WU, YANGFENG, Fu Wai Hospital
XI, ZHI, Cancer Hospital
XU, BINGHE, Cancer Hospital
XU, BINGZE, Cancer Hospital
XU, CHENGSU, School of Basic Medical Sciences
XU, GUOZHEN, Cancer Hospital
XU, JINGQIN, Peking Union Medical College Hospital
XU, LETIAN, Peking Union Medical College Hospital
XU, ZHENGANG, Cancer Hospital
YANG, GONGHUAN, School of Basic Medical Sciences
YANG, LIN, Cancer Hospital
YANG, YAOJIN, Fu Wai Hospital
YANG, ZIBIN, School of Basic Medical Sciences
YE, QIBIN, Peking Union Medical College Hospital
YIN, WEIBO, Cancer Hospital
YOU, KAI, Peking Union Medical College Hospital
YU, DEQUAN, Institute of Materia Medica
YU, GAOZHI, Cancer Hospital
YU, GUORUI, Cancer Hospital
YU, HONGZHAO, Cancer Hospital
YU, MENGXUE, Peking Union Medical College Hospital
YU, XHIHAO, Cancer Hospital
YUE, JILIANG, Orthopaedic Surgery Hospital
ZENG, XIAOFENG, Peking Union Medical College Hospital
ZENG, XUAN, School of Basic Medical Sciences
ZHAN, RUGANG, Cancer Hospital
ZHANG, BAONING, Cancer Hospital
ZHANG, DAWEI, Cancer Hospital
ZHANG, DECHANG, School of Basic Medical Sciences
ZHANG, DECHAO, Cancer Hospital
ZHANG, DELI, Peking Union Medical College Hospital
ZHANG, FENCHUN, Peking Union Medical College Hospital
ZHANG, HONGXING, Cancer Hospital
ZHANG, HUILAN, Fu Wai Hospital

ZHANG, JIANXI, Peking Union Medical College Hospital
ZHANG, SHIYUAN, Peking Union Medical College Hospital
ZHANG, WENHUA, Cancer Hospital
ZHANG, XHIXIAN, Cancer Hospital
ZHANG, XIANGRU, Cancer Hospital
ZHANG, XUE, School of Basic Medical Sciences
ZHANG, YOUJU, Peking Union Medical College Hospital
ZHANG, ZHENHAN, Peking Union Medical College Hospital
ZHANG, ZHIPING, Institute of Medical Biology Technology
ZHAO, MIN, Orthopaedic Surgery Hospital
ZHAO, PING, Cancer Hospital
ZHAO, SHIHUA, Fu Wai Hospital
ZHAO, SHIMIN, Peking Union Medical College Hospital
ZHAO, YAN, Peking Union Medical College Hospital
ZHAO, YUPEI, Peking Union Medical College Hospital
ZHEN, YONGSU, Institute of Medical Biology Technology
ZHENG, DEXIAN, School of Basic Medical Sciences
ZHONG, SHOUGUANG, Peking Union Medical College Hospital
ZHOU, JICHANG, Cancer Hospital
ZHOU, QIAN, Peking Union Medical College Hospital
ZHOU, XHUNWU, Cancer Hospital
ZHOU, YANMIN, Peking Union Medical College Hospital
ZHU, CHUANQIU, Peking Union Medical College Hospital
ZHU, DAHIA, School of Basic Medical Sciences
ZHU, GUANGJI, School of Basic Medical Sciences
ZHU, JUN, Fu Wai Hospital
ZHU, LI, Peking Union Medical College Hospital
ZHU, WENLING, Peking Union Medical College Hospital
ZHU, XIAODONG, Fu Wai Hospital
ZHUANG, HONGXING, Orthopaedic Surgery Hospital
ZHUI, YUANYU, Peking Union Medical College Hospital

ATTACHED RESEARCH INSTITUTES

Epidemiology Laboratory: Dir QIAO YOULILN.

Institute of Animal Experimentation: Dir FANG FUDE.

Institute of Blood Transfusion: Dir WANG JINGXING.

Institute of Biology and Medical Science Engineering: Dir LENG XIGANG.

Institute of Dermatosis: Dir CHEN ZHIQIANG.

Institute of Haematology: Dir HAN ZHONGCHAO.

Ministry of Public Health Key Laboratory of Biosynthesis of Natural Products: Dir ZHU PING.

Ministry of Public Health Laboratory of Endocrinology: Dir SHI TIEFAN.

National Centre for Pharmaceutical Screening: Dir DU GUANHUA.

National Engineering Research Centre for the Development of New Drugs: Dir WANG XIAOLIANG.

National Key Laboratory of Experimental Haematology: Dir HAN CHAOZHONG.

National Key Laboratory of Medical Science and Molecular Biology: Dir SHEN YAN.

National Key Laboratory of Numerator Tumour Science: Dir QIANG BOQIN.

National Research Centre for Analysis of Drugs and Metabolites: Dir ZHOU TONGHUI.

QINGHAI NATIONALITIES COLLEGE

25 Ba Yi Rd, Xining 810007, Qinghai
Telephone: 76803
Founded 1949
President: DUO JIE JIAN ZAN
Vice-Presidents: SHAO DESHAN, Assoc. Prof. YU DEYUAN, ZHUO MA CAI DAN
Librarian: YAO KERANG
Library of 550,000 vols
Number of teachers: 330
Number of students: 1,572
Publications: *Journal of Qinghai Nationalities Institute*, *Qinghai Nationalities Research*

HEADS OF DEPARTMENTS

Basic Courses: ZHANG WENKUI
Chinese: HU ANLIANG
Law: SUN XIANZHEN
Mathematics: NIAN KUN
Minority Nationalities Languages and Literature: GE MING DUO JIE
Physics and Chemistry: WU QIXUN
Politics: MEI JINCAI
Preparatory Courses: QU TAI

PROFESSORS

FENG, Y., Theory of Arts
HU, A., Ancient Chinese
MI, Y., History of Chinese
ZHU, K., Modern Literature

QUFU NORMAL UNIVERSITY

57 Jingxuanxi Rd, Qufu 273165, Shandong
Telephone: (537) 4458831
Fax: (537) 4455669
Internet: www.qfnu.edu.cn
Founded 1955
Academic year: September to July
President: TIAN DEQUAN
Librarian: DU YU
Library of 1,880,000 vols
Number of teachers: 2,200
Number of students: 42,000
Publications: *Journal* (4 a year), *Qilu Journal* (6 a year)

DEANS

College of Literature: XUE YONGWU
College of Mathematics Science: (vacant)

PROFESSORS

CHEN, KESHOU, Literature
CHEN, QINGPING, Literature
DAN, CHENGBIN, Literature
GAO, SHANGQU, Literature
LIU, FENGGUANG, Literature
LIU, XINSHENG, Literature
LIU, YAOJIN, Literature
PU, ZHAOLIN, Literature
QIAN, JIAQING, Literature
TANG, XUENING, Literature
XU, ZHENGUI, Literature
XUE, YONGWU, Literature
ZHANG, LIANRANG, Literature
ZHANG, QUANZHI, Literature
ZHAO, DONGSHUAN, Literature
ZHAO, LIMING, Literature
ZHENG, JIEWEN, Literature

ATTACHED RESEARCH INSTITUTES

Adult Education College: Dir DU YIDE.

RENMIN UNIVERSITY OF CHINA

39 Haidian Rd, Haidian District, Beijing 100872
Telephone: (10) 62563399
Fax: (10) 62566374
Internet: www.ruc.edu.cn
Founded 1937
State control
Academic year: starts September
President: LI WENHAI
Vice-Presidents: DU HOUWEN, LI KANGTAI, LI SHAOGONG, LUO GUOJIE, MA SHAOMENG, YANG DEFU, ZHENG HANGSHENG, MA SHAOMENG
Librarian: DAI YI
Number of teachers: 1,595
Number of students: 14,289 (incl. 1,284 postgraduates)
Publications: *Teaching and Research*, *Economic Theory and Business Management*, *Information Service News*, *Population Research*, *Archival News* (every 2 months), *The History of Qing Dynasty Research Newsletter*, *International Journalism World* (quarterly), *Learned Journal of the People's University of China* (every 2 months)

HEADS OF DEPARTMENTS

Philosophy: CHEN XIANDA
International Politics: YIE ZONGKUI
Economics: YU XUEBEN
Economic Planning: LIU CHENGRUI
Statistics: YUAN WEI
Industrial Economics: DENG RONGLING
Agricultural Economics: ZHOU ZHIXIANG
Commercial Economics: LI JINXUAN
College of Labour and Personnel Administration: ZHAO LUKUAN
Finance and Banking: HAN YINGJIE
Economic Information Management: CHEN YU
Law: ZENG XIANYI
Journalism: HE ZIHUA
Population Studies: GUO ZHIGANG
Chinese Language and Literature: CHEN CHUANCAI
History: GU XUESHUN
Land Management: ZHOU ZHIXIANG
Accounting: ZHU XIAOPING
Investment Economics: LANG RONGSHEN
Commodity Studies: ZHANG DALI
International Economics: (vacant)
College of Archives: CAO XICHEN
Sociology: ZHENG HANGSHENG
Foreign Languages: JIANG CHUNYU
Centre of Physical Education: LI DEYIN
College of Correspondence Education: FANG JIA
Centre of Teaching Chinese as a Foreign Language: LIU JIN

ATTACHED INSTITUTES

Institute of Economic Studies: Dir HU NAIWU.

Institute of Foreign Economy and Management: Dir HUANG MENGFAN.

Institute of East European Studies: Dir ZHOU XINCHENG.

Institute of Sociology: Dir SHA LIANXIANG.

Institute of Population Theory: Dir GUO ZHIGANG.

Institute of Chinese Language and Writing: Dir HU RUICHANG.

Institute of the History of the Qing Dynasty: Dir LI WENHAI.

Institute of Legal Research: Dir WANG YIYING.

Institute of Public Administration: Dir QI MINGSHAN.

Institute of Soft Sciences: Dir LI ZHONGSHANG.

SHAANXI NORMAL UNIVERSITY

199 Chang'an South Rd, Xian 710062, Shaanxi
Telephone: (29) 85308992
Fax: (29) 85307025
Internet: www.snnu.edu.cn

Founded 1944
Ministry of Education control
Academic year: September to July

President: FANG YU
Vice-Presidents: XIAO ZHENGHONG, ZHANG JIANXIANG, ZHAO BIN, ZHOU DEMING
Head of Graduate Department: LI JIKAI
Librarian: YANG ENCHENG

Number of teachers: 2,600
Number of students: 40,000

Publications: *Journal* (natural sciences, quarterly), *Journal* (philosophy and social sciences, 6 a year)

DEANS

College of Arts: HU YUKANG
College of Chemistry and Materials Science: ZHANG CHENGXIAO
College of Chinese Language and Literature: LI XIJIAN
College of Computer Science: FENG DEMIN
College of Educational Science: YOU XUJUN
College of Food Engineering: CHEN JINPING
College of Foreign Languages: MA ZHENYI
College of Further Education: JIA WENXING
College of History and Civilization: JIA ERQIANG
College of International Business: LI ZHONGMIN
College of Life Sciences: WANG ZHEZHI
College of Mathematics and Information Science: WU JIANHUA
College of News and Media: LIU LU
College of Physical Education: LI ZHENBIN
College of Physics and Information Technology: ZHAO WEI
College of Political Economy: WANG ZHENYA
College of Teachers and Administrators: GONG JIANGUO
College of Tourism and the Environment: HUANG CHUNCHANG
e-College: LU JIURU

PROFESSORS

CAO, HAN, Computer Science
CAO, HUAIXIN, Mathematics and Information Science
CAO, WEIAN, History and Civilization
CHANG, JINCANG, History and Civilization
CHEN, FENG, History and Civilization
CHEN, JINPING, Life Science
CHEN, JINPING, Food Engineering
CHEN, XIAORUI, Educational Science
CHEN, YASHAO, Chemistry and Materials Science
DANG, HUAIXING, Chinese Language and Literature
DU, HONGKE, Mathematics and Information Science
DU, JIULIN, Physics and Information Technology
DU, WENYU, History and Civilization
DUAN, YUFENG, Food Engineering
FANG, YU, Chemistry and Materials Science
FENG, DEMING, Computer Science
FENG, WENLOU, Chinese Language and Literature
FU, SHAOLIANG, Chinese Language and Literature
GUO, MIN, Computer Science
GUO, QINNA, Chinese Language and Literature
HAO, WENWU, Educational Science
HE, JUHOU, Computer Science
HU, ANSHUN, Chinese Language and Literature
HU, DAODAO, Chemistry and Materials Science
HU, JI, History and Civilization
HU, MANCHENG, Chemistry and Materials Science
HUANG, QIN-AN, Mathematics and Information Science
HUANG, YUAN, Life Science
HUO, SONGLIN, Chinese Language and Literature
HUO, YOUMING, Chinese Language and Literature
JI, GUOXING, Mathematics and Information Science
JIA, ERQIANG, History and Civilization
LI, BAOLIN, Chemistry and Materials Science
LI, BAOXIN, Chemistry and Materials Science
LI, GUOQING, Educational Science
LI, HONGWU, Educational Science
LI, HUISHI, Mathematics and Information Science
LI, JIANFENG, Food Engineering
LI, JIKAI, Chinese Language and Literature
LI, QUANLU, Physics and Information Technology
LI, SHENGGANG, Mathematics and Information Science
LI, WANSHE, Mathematics and Information Science
LI, XIJIAN, Chinese Language and Literature
LI, YONGFANG, Physics and Information Technology
LI, YONGMING, Mathematics and Information Science
LI, YUMIN, History and Civilization
LI, ZHEN, Chinese Language and Literature
LIAN, ZHENMIN, Life Science
LIANG, DAOLI, Chinese Language and Literature
LIN, SHUYU, Physics and Information Technology
LIU, FENGDAO, Chinese Language and Literature
LIU, JING, Chinese Language and Literature
LIU, LU, News and Media
LIU, PENG, Physics and Information Technology
LIU, XINKE, Educational Science
LIU, XINPING, Mathematics and Information Science
LIU, ZHAOTIE, Chemistry and Materials Science
LIU, ZONGHUAI, Chemistry and Materials Science
LU, JIURU, Chemistry and Materials Science
LUO, ZENGRU, Mathematics and Information Science
MA, GEDONG, Chinese Language and Literature
MA, ZHENDUO, Foreign Languages
MIAO, RUNCAI, Physics and Information Technology
NIU, YONG, Physics and Information Technology
QIU, GUOYONG, Computer Science
QIU, NONGXUE, Food Engineering
QIU, XUENONG, Life Science
QU, YAJUN, Chinese Language and Literature
REN, YI, Life Science
RUN, QINGSHENG, Chinese Language and Literature
SHANG, ZHIYUAN, Physics and Information Technology
SHE, XIAOPING, Life Science
SUN, RUNGUANG, Physics and Information Technology
TANG, YIGONG, History and Civilization
TIAN, CHENRUI, Life Science
TIAN, JIANRONG, Educational Science
WANG, BO, Chemistry and Materials Science
WANG, CHENRUI, Food Engineering
WANG, GUOJUN, Mathematics and Information Science
WANG, HUI, History and Civilization
WANG, SHUANGHUAI, History and Civilization
WANG, WENLIANG, Chemistry and Materials Science
WANG, XIAOAN, Life Science
WANG, XIAOMING, Computer Science
WANG, XILI, Computer Science
WANG, XIN, Physics and Information Technology
WANG, YINGZONG, Physics and Information Technology
WANG, YINHUI, Computer Science
WANG, ZHEZHI, Life Science
WANG, ZHIWU, Chinese Language and Literature
WEI, GENGYUAN, Chinese Language and Literature
WEI, JIANGUO, Chinese Language and Literature
WEI, JUNFA, Chemistry and Materials Science
WU, BAOWEI, Mathematics and Information Science
WU, HONGBO, Mathematics and Information Science
WU, JIANHUA, Mathematics and Information Science
WU, YANSHENG, Chinese Language and Literature
WU, ZHENQIANG, Computer Science
XI, GENGSI, Life Science
XIAO, ZHENGHONG, History and Civilization
XING, XIANGDONG, Chinese Language and Literature
XUE, PINGSHUAN, History and Civilization
YANG, CUNTANG, History and Civilization
YANG, ENCHENG, Chinese Language and Literature
YANG, HEQING, Chemistry and Materials Science
YANG, HONGKE, Chinese Language and Literature
YANG, WANMIN, Physics and Information Technology
YANG, ZUPEI, Chemistry and Materials Science
YIN, SHENGPING, History and Civilization
YOU, XILIN, Chinese Language and Literature
YOU, XUQUN, Educational Science
YUAN, LIN, History and Civilization
ZANG, ZHEN, History and Civilization
ZHANG, CHENGXIAO, Chemistry and Materials Science
ZHANG, GUOJUN, Chinese Language and Literature
ZHANG, JIANHUA, Mathematics and Information Science
ZHANG, JIANMIN, Physics and Information Technology
ZHANG, JIANZHONG, Mathematics and Information Science
ZHANG, MAORONG, History and Civilization
ZHANG, XIAOLING, Chemistry and Materials Science
ZHANG, XINKE, Chinese Language and Literature
ZHANG, XUEZHONG, Chinese Language and Literature
ZHANG, YUHU, Chemistry and Materials Science
ZHANG, ZHIQI, Chemistry and Materials Science
ZHANG, ZHUJUN, Chemistry and Materials Science
ZHAO, BIN, Mathematics and Information Science
ZHAO, SHICHAO, History and Civilization
ZHAO, WANGQIN, Chinese Language and Literature
ZHENG, XINGWANG, Chemistry and Materials Science
ZHENG, ZHEMIN, Life Science
ZHOU, TIANYOU, History and Civilization

ATTACHED RESEARCH INSTITUTES

Ancient Books Cataloguing Institute: Dir HUANG YONGNIAN.

Classical Documents and Data Institute: Dir ZHANG XUEZHONG.

Education Management Institute.

Education Research Institute: Dir LU JIURU.

GAP Engineering and Technique Research Centre of Shaanxi Province: Dir SHE XIAOPING.

Humanities Study Institute: Dir HAN XING.

Institute of Biological Techniques and Biological Development.

Institute of Christian Culture Studies: Dir YOU XILIN.

Institute of Environmental Resources and Regional Development.

Institute of Historical Change in the North-west Environment and Development in Economic Society: Dir ZHU SHIGUANG.

Institute of Modern Optics: Dir MIAO RUNCAI.

Institute of the Tang Dynasty: Dir SHI NIANHAI.

Laboratory of Macromolecular Science: Dir FANG YU.

Lexicographical Work Institute: Dir BAI YULIN.

Mao Zedong Thought Research Institute.

Research Centre of Canadian Education.

Research Centre of Tourism Development

SHAANXI UNIVERSITY OF SCIENCE AND TECHNOLOGY

49 Renmin West Rd, Xianyang 712081, Shaanxi
Telephone: (910) 3579500
Fax: (910) 3579700
Internet: www.sust.edu.cn

Founded 1958
Academic year: September to July
President: LUO HONGJIE
Vice-Presidents: CAO JUJIANG, CUI JIHUA, SHEN YIDING, ZHANG MEIYUN
Head of Graduate Department: ZHANG XIAOLEI
Librarian: GAO DONGQIANG
Number of teachers: 900
Number of students: 18,000
Publications: *The Future* (6 a year), *Journal* (6 a year)

DEANS

College of Chemistry and Chemical Engineering: ZHANG GUANGHUA
College of Computer and Information Engineering: CHEN HUA
College of Design: YANG JUNSHUN
College of Electrical and Electronic Engineering: MENG YANJING
College of Electromechanical Engineering: DANG XINAN
College of Life Science and Engineering: CHEN HE
College of Management: YAN YUJIE
College of Materials Science and Engineering: WANG XIUFENG
College of Paper Manufacture Engineering: ZHANG MEIYUN
College of Resources and the Environment: MA JIANZHONG
College of Science: LIN XIAOLIN
College of Vocational Technology (Xian): LI WENHAN
College of Vocational Technology (Xianyan): ZHANG WEIPING
Department of Foreign Languages: LI XIAOHONG

PROFESSORS

CHEN, HE, Life Sciences and Engineering
CHEN, HUA, Computer and Information Engineering
CHEN, JUNZHI, Chemistry and Chemical Engineering
CHEN, MANRU, Design
CHEN, TAILUN, Science
CHENG, FENGXIA, Resources and the Environment
DANG, HONGSHE, Electrical and Electronic Engineering
DANG, SISHAN, Science
DANG, XIN-AN, Electromechanical Engineering
DONG, WENBIN, Life Sciences and Engineering
DU, RUIQING, Foreign Languages
GAN, JIANZHI, Design
GONG, TAISHENG, Resources and the Environment
HOU, ZAIEN, Science
LI, GUOXING, Science
LI, LINSHENG, Chemistry and Chemical Engineering
LI, XI, Electrical and Electronic Engineering
LI, XIAORUI, Chemistry and Chemical Engineering
LI, ZHONGJIN, Chemistry and Chemical Engineering
LIN, XIAOLIN, Computer and Information Engineering
LIU, SHUXING, Life Sciences and Engineering
LU, JIALI, Life Sciences and Engineering
LU, XINGFANG, Resources and the Environment
LUO, CANGXUE, Life Sciences and Engineering
LUO, HONGJIE, Materials Science and Engineering
MA, JIANZHONG, Resources and the Environment
MENG, YANJING, Electrical and Electronic Engineering
MIAO, HONGYAN, Materials Science and Engineering
NING, DUO, Electrical and Electronic Engineering
QI, XIANGJUN, Life Sciences and Engineering
QIANG, XIHUAI, Resources and the Environment
SHAN, JINGMIN, Design
SHEN, YIDING, Chemistry and Chemical Engineering
SONG, HONGXIN, Life Sciences and Engineering
SUN, YU, Electrical and Electronic Engineering
TIAN, SANDE, Life Sciences and Engineering
WANG, DEZHONG, Design
WANG, FENG, Materials Science and Engineering
WANG, HONGRU, Resources and the Environment
WANG, JIANGEN, Resources and the Environment
WANG, LIANJIE, Life Sciences and Engineering
WANG, MENGXIAO, Electrical and Electronic Engineering
WANG, QUANJIE, Resources and the Environment
WANG, XIUFENG, Materials Science and Engineering
WANG, XUECHUAN, Resources and the Environment
XU, JIANZHONG, Foreign Languages
XU, MUDAN, Life Sciences and Engineering
YANG, JIANZHOU, Chemistry and Chemical Engineering
YANG, JUNSHUN, Design
YU, CONGZHEN, Resources and the Environment
YU, DAYUAN, Electrical and Electronic Engineering
ZHANG, CHUANBO, Resources and the Environment
ZHANG, GUANGHUA, Chemistry and Chemical Engineering
ZHANG, XIAOLEI, Resources and the Environment
ZHANG, ZHENGXI, Computer and Information Engineering
ZHENG, ENRANG, Electrical and Electronic Engineering
ZHOU, LIAN, Materials Science and Engineering
ZHU, ZHENFENG, Materials Science and Engineering

SHANDONG UNIVERSITY

Shanda Nanlu, Shandong 250100, Jinan
Telephone: (531) 8364701
Fax: (531) 8565657
Internet: www.sdu.edu.cn

Founded 1901
Ministry of Education control
Academic year: September to July
President: ZHAN TAO
Vice-Presidents: FAN HONGJIAN, FANG HONGJIAN, HU JIACHEN, LI CHENGJUN, WANG QILONG, YU XIUPING, ZHANG YONGBING
Head of Graduate Department: WANG QILONG
Librarian: SU WEIZHI
Number of teachers: 3,154
Number of students: 50,000
Publications: *Young Thinker* (6 a year), *Journal of Shandong University* (editions: philosophy and social sciences; natural sciences; health science; engineering science, 6 a year), *Journal of Literature, History and Philosophy* (6 a year), *Folk Custom Research* (quarterly), *Studies of Zhouyi* (6 a year)

DEANS

School of Business Administration: XU XIANGYI
School of Chemistry and Chemical Engineering: JIANG JIANZHUANG
School of Civil Engineering: CAO SHENGLE
School of Computer Science and Technology: MENG XIANGXU
School of Continuing Education: ZHUANG PING
School of Control Science and Engineering: JIA LEI
School of Dentistry: YANG PISHAN
School of Economics: ZANG XUHENG
School of Electrical Engineering: ZHAO JIANGUO
School of Energy and Power Engineering: PAN JIHONG
School of Environmental Science and Engineering: GAO BAOYU
School of Fine Arts: LI XIAOFENG
School of Foreign Languages and Literature: WANG SHOUYUAN
School of History and Culture: WANG YUJI
School of Information Science and Engineering: YUAN DONGFENG
School of Law: CHEN JINZHAO
School of Life Science: QU YINBO
School of Literature and Journalism: CHEN YAN
School of Marxist Theory Education: ZHOU XIANGJUN
School of Materials Science and Engineering: JIANG MINHUA
School of Mathematics: LIU JIANYA
School of Mechanical Engineering: LI JIANFENG
School of Medicine: ZHANG YUN
School of Nursing: LOU FENGLAN
School of Pharmacy: LOU HONGXIANG

School of Philosophy and Social Development: FU YOUDE
School of Physics and Microelectronics: XIE SHIJIE
School of Political Science and Public Administration: LIU YUAN
School of Public Health: ZHAOS ZHONGTANG

PROFESSORS

BAI, ZENGLIANG, Life Sciences
BAO, SITAO, Literature and Journalism
BAO, XIAOMING, Life Sciences
BAO, YIFEI, Civil Engineering
BIAN, XIUFANG, Materials Science and Engineering
BU, YUXIANG, Chemistry and Chemical Engineering
CAI, LVZHONG, Information Science and Engineering
CAI, ZHENGTING, Chemistry and Chemical Engineering
CAO, CHENGBO, Chemistry and Chemical Engineering
CAO, QINGJIE, Mathematics
CAO, SHENGLE, Civil Engineering
CHAO, ZHONGCHEN, History and Culture
CHEN, CHUANZHONG, Materials Science and Engineering
CHEN, DAIRONG, Chemistry and Chemical Engineering
CHEN, GUANJUN, Life Sciences
CHEN, HONG, Foreign Languages and Literature
CHEN, JIGUANG, Civil Engineering
CHEN, KAOSHAN, Life Sciences
CHEN, LIANBI, Medicine
CHEN, QINGLAI, Civil Engineering
CHEN, SHANGSHENG, History and Culture
CHEN, SHAOZHU, Mathematics
CHEN, SHENHAO, Chemistry and Chemical Engineering
CHEN, XIAO, Chemistry and Chemical Engineering
CHEN, XISHEN, Materials Science and Engineering
CHEN, YAN, Literature and Journalism
CHEN, ZENGJING, Mathematics
CHEN, ZHIJUN, Business Administration
CHEN, ZIAN, History and Culture
CHENG, XINGKUI, Physics and Microelectronics
CHENG, ZHAOLIN, Mathematics
CHI, ZHENMING, Life Sciences
CONG, YAPING, Foreign Languages and Literature
CUI, DAYONG, History and Culture
CUI, XI, Public Health
CUI, XING, Medicine
CUI, ZHAOJIE, Environmental Science and Engineering
DING, RONGGUI, Business Administration
DING, SHILIANG, Physics and Microelectronics
DING, SHILIANG, Chemistry and Chemical Engineering
DING, YUANMING, Philosophy and Social Development
DUAN, QI, Mathematics
EHRLICH, M. A., Philosophy and Social Development
FAN, JINXUE, Law
FAN, XIULING, Business Administration
FANG, HUI, History and Culture
FANG, LEI, Political Science and Public Administration
FENG, DACHENG, Chemistry and Chemical Engineering
FENG, DIANMEI, Law
FENG, MEILI, Nursing
FENG, SHENGYU, Chemistry and Chemical Engineering
FU, YONGJUN, Philosophy and Social Development
FU, YOUDE, Philosophy and Social Development
GAN, YING, Business Administration
GAO, BAOYU, Chemistry and Chemical Engineering
GAO, BAOYU, Environmental Science and Engineering
GAO, JIANGUO, Philosophy and Social Development
GAO, PEIJI, Life Sciences
GAO, RUWEI, Physics and Microelectronics
GAO, YINGMAO, Medicine
GAO, ZHENMING, Information Science and Engineering
GE, BENYI, Literature and Journalism
GENG, HAORAN, Materials Science and Engineering
GENG, JIANHUA, Literature and Journalism
GENG, ZUNJING, Civil Engineering
GONG, YAOQIN, Medicine
GU, LUANZHAI, History and Culture
GU, QINGMIN, Medicine
GU, YUEZHU, Chemistry and Chemical Engineering
GUAN, SHAOJI, History and Culture
GUAN, XIAOJUN, Materials Science and Engineering
GUO, DAJUN, Mathematics
GUO, JIDE, Foreign Languages and Literature
GUO, YANLI, Literature and Journalism
HAN, SHENGHAO, Physics and Microelectronics
HAO, AIYOU, Chemistry and Chemical Engineering
HAO, JINGCHENG, Chemistry and Chemical Engineering
HE, MAO, Physics and Microelectronics
HE, ZHONGHUA, Philosophy and Social Development
HONG, XIAOGUANG, Computer Science and Technology
HOU, WANGUO, Chemistry and Chemical Engineering
HOU, XUEYUAN, Information Science and Engineering
HU, JIFAN, Physics and Microelectronics
HU, PEICHU, Mathematics
HU, WEICHENG, Medicine
HU, WEIQING, History and Culture
HU, WENRONG, Environmental Science and Engineering
HU, XINSHENG, History and Culture
HU, ZHENGMING, Business Administration
HUANG, FAYOU, Literature and Journalism
HUANG, FENG, Life Sciences
HUANG, QINGZHI, Political Science and Public Administration
HUANG, SHENG, Civil Engineering
HUANG, WANHUA, Literature and Journalism
HUANG, XIRONG, Chemistry and Chemical Engineering
JI, AIGUO, Pharmacy
JI, FAHAN, Literature and Journalism
JI, PEIRONG, Political Science and Public Administration
JI, YUNXIA, Foreign Languages and Literature
JIA, LEI, Control Science and Engineering
JIA, ZHIPING, Computer Science and Technology
JIANG, BAOFA, Public Health
JIANG, JIANZHUANG, Chemistry and Chemical Engineering
JIANG, MINHUA, Materials Science and Engineering
JIANG, QINGLI, Environmental Science and Engineering
JIANG, SHENG, History and Culture
JIANG, SHOULI, Mathematics
JIANG, YONG, Philosophy and Social Development
JIN, WENRUI, Chemistry and Chemical Engineering
KONG, FANJIN, Literature and Journalism
KONG, JIAN, Life Sciences
KONG, LINGREN, History and Culture
LI, CHUANLIN, Computer Science and Technology
LI, DAIBIN, Control Science and Engineering
LI, DAXING, Mathematics
LI, FENGXIAN, Environmental Science and Engineering
LI, GANZUO, Chemistry and Chemical Engineering
LI, GUOJUN, Mathematics
LI, HONGWEI, Life Sciences
LI, HUA, Physics and Microelectronics
LI, JIANFENG, Literature and Journalism
LI, JIE, Public Health
LI, JINGZHOU, Computer Science and Technology
LI, JINYU, Physics and Microelectronics
LI, JUN, Business Administration
LI, MUSEN, Materials Science and Engineering
LI, QIN, Philosophy and Social Development
LI, QINGZHONG, Computer Science and Technology
LI, QIQIANG, Control Science and Engineering
LI, SHAOMING, Foreign Languages and Literature
LI, SHUCAI, Civil Engineering
LI, WEI, History and Culture
LI, XIAO, History and Culture
LI, XIAOYAN, Chemistry and Chemical Engineering
LI, XUEQING, Computer Science and Technology
LI, XUEZHEN, Foreign Languages and Literature
LI, YAJIANG, Materials Science and Engineering
LI, YUCHEN, Computer Science and Technology
LI, YUEZHONG, Life Sciences
LI, ZHENZHONG, Medicine
LI, ZHONGYOU, Materials Science and Engineering
LIANG, HUIXING, Law
LIANG, ZUOTANG, Physics and Microelectronics
LIAO, QUN, Literature and Journalism
LIE, JIE, Philosophy and Social Development
LIE, JIE, Computer Science and Technology
LIN, JIANQIANG, Life Sciences
LIN, JUREN, Philosophy and Social Development
LIN, LU, Mathematics
LIN, MING, Law
LIN, XINYING, Public Health
LIU, BAOYU, Law
LIU, CHENGBO, Chemistry and Chemical Engineering
LIU, FENGJUN, History and Culture
LIU, GANG, Business Administration
LIU, GUIZHEN, Mathematics
LIU, HONGWEI, Business Administration
LIU, JIANYA, Mathematics
LIU, JIAZHUANG, Mathematics
LIU, JU, Information Science and Engineering
LIU, KAI, Medicine
LIU, LUPENG, Philosophy and Social Development
LIU, PING, History and Culture
LIU, RONGXING, Computer Science and Technology
LIU, SHIGUO, Law
LIU, SHUMEI, Foreign Languages and Literature
LIU, SHUTANG, Control Science and Engineering
LIU, SHUWEI, Medicine
LIU, TIANLU, History and Culture
LIU, XIANXI, Medicine
LIU, XINLI, Philosophy and Social Development
LIU, YIHUA, Physics and Microelectronics
LIU, YU-AN, Political Science and Public Administration
LIU, YUFENG, History and Culture
LIU, YUNGANG, Control Science and Engineering
LIU, YUTIAN, Electrical Engineering

LIU, ZHAOLI, Mathematics
LIU, ZHAOXU, Nursing
LIU, ZHENQIAN, Foreign Languages and Literature
LIU, ZHIYU, Medicine
LIU, ZONGLIN, Chemistry and Chemical Engineering
LOU, FENGLAN, Nursing
LOU, HONGXIANG, Pharmacy
LU, JUNWEI, History and Culture
LU, WEIZHONG, Foreign Languages and Literature
LU, YAO, History and Culture
LUAN, FENGSHI, History and Culture
LUO, FUTENG, Literature and Journalism
MA, FENGSHU, Political Science and Public Administration
MA, GUANGHAI, Philosophy and Social Development
MA, HONGLEI, Physics and Microelectronics
MA, JUN, Computer Science and Technology
MA, LIXIAN, Medicine
MA, LONGQIAN, Literature and Journalism
MA, RUIFANG, Literature and Journalism
MA, SHAOHAN, Mathematics
MEI, LIANGMO, Physics and Microelectronics
MENG, LIRONG, Computer Science and Technology
MENG, XIANGCAI, History and Culture
MENG, XIANGXU, Computer Science and Technology
MIAO, JUNYING, Life Sciences
MIAO, QINGHAI, Physics and Microelectronics
MIAO, RUNTIAN, Philosophy and Social Development
MIAO, XINGWEI, Foreign Languages and Literature
MIN, GUANGHUI, Materials Science and Engineering
MO, WENCHUAN, Business Administration
NING, FEI, Computer Science and Technology
NIU, YUNQING, Literature and Journalism
PAN, AILING, Business Administration
PANG, SHOUYING, Literature and Journalism
PENG, SHIGE, Mathematics
PENG, YUHUA, Information Science and Engineering
PENG, ZHIZHONG, Business Administration
QI, GUIJIE, Business Administration
QI, YANPING, Law
QIAN, ZENGYI, Literature and Journalism
QIAO, YIZHENG, Control Science and Engineering
QIAO, YOUMEI, History and Culture
QU, YINBO, Life Sciences
REN, DENGYI, Materials Science and Engineering
REN, QUAN, Information Science and Engineering
REN, XIANGHONG, History and Culture
RUI, HONGXING, Mathematics
SHANG, QINGSEN, Civil Engineering
SHANG, YU, Philosophy and Social Development
SHAO, LIHUA, Public Health
SHENG, YUQI, Literature and Journalism
SHI, BING, Computer Science and Technology
SHI, KAIQUAN, Mathematics
SHI, LIANYUN, Business Administration
SHI, YUMING, Mathematics
SONG, GANG, Medicine
SUI, QINGMEI, Control Science and Engineering
SUN, DEJUN, Chemistry and Chemical Engineering
SUN, HONGJIAN, Chemistry and Chemical Engineering
SUN, JILIN, Literature and Journalism
SUN, KANGNING, Materials Science and Engineering
SUN, NAZHENG, Mathematics
SUN, SIXIU, Chemistry and Chemical Engineering
SUN, TONGJING, Control Science and Engineering
SUN, WENSHENG, Medicine
SUN, XINQIANG, Law
SUN, YINGCHUN, Foreign Languages and Literature
SUN, ZIMEI, Literature and Journalism
TAN, HAOZHE, Literature and Journalism
TAN, SHIBAO, History and Culture
TAN, YEBANG, Chemistry and Chemical Engineering
TANG, ZIHENG, Literature and Journalism
TIAN, GUOHUI, Control Science and Engineering
TIAN, XUELEI, Materials Science and Engineering
WAN, JIANCHENG, Computer Science and Technology
WANG, CHENGRUI, Physics and Microelectronics
WANG, CHUNLEI, Physics and Microelectronics
WANG, DEGANG, Business Administration
WANG, FENGSHAN, Pharmacy
WANG, FUTAI, Business Administration
WANG, HAIYANG, Computer Science and Technology
WANG, HUAIJING, Medicine
WANG, JIANMIN, Political Science and Public Administration
WANG, JIANWU, Chemistry and Chemical Engineering
WANG, JIAYE, Mathematics
WANG, JIEZHEN, Public Health
WANG, JINFENG, Physics and Microelectronics
WANG, JINXING, Life Sciences
WANG, JIYANG, Materials Science and Engineering
WANG, JUNJU, Foreign Languages and Literature
WANG, KEMING, Physics and Microelectronics
WANG, KEMING, Materials Science and Engineering
WANG, LILI, Foreign Languages and Literature
WANG, LIPING, Law
WANG, PEIYUAN, Literature and Journalism
WANG, PENG, Life Sciences
WANG, PING, Literature and Journalism
WANG, QILONG, Chemistry and Chemical Engineering
WANG, QING, Civil Engineering
WANG, QINGYOU, Information Science and Engineering
WANG, QUANJUAN, Civil Engineering
WANG, RENQING, Life Sciences
WANG, RUBIN, Pharmacy
WANG, SHANBO, Philosophy and Social Development
WANG, SHAOXING, Political Science and Public Administration
WANG, SUMEI, Public Health
WANG, TIANHONG, Life Sciences
WANG, WEI, Mathematics
WANG, WENCHENG, Literature and Journalism
WANG, WENQIAO, Mathematics
WANG, XIAOSHU, Literature and Journalism
WANG, XIAOYI, History and Culture
WANG, XIAOYUN, Mathematics
WANG, XINCHUN, Philosophy and Social Development
WANG, XINGYUAN, Business Administration
WANG, XINNIAN, Physics and Microelectronics
WANG, XUEDIAN, History and Culture
WANG, YIMING, Business Administration
WANG, YOUZHI, Civil Engineering
WANG, YUJI, History and Culture
WANG, YUZHEN, Control Science and Engineering
WANG, ZHIFU, Materials Science and Engineering
WANG, ZHIYU, Public Health
WANG, ZHOUMING, Literature and Journalism
WANG, ZUNONG, Life Sciences
WANG, ZUOCHENG, Materials Science and Engineering
WEI, ZHONGLI, Mathematics
WEN, SHULIN, Materials Science and Engineering
WU, AIHUA, Business Administration
WU, JIAN, Chemistry and Chemical Engineering
WU, RUNTING, Literature and Journalism
WU, XIAOJUAN, Information Science and Engineering
WU, YAOHUA, Control Science and Engineering
WU, YOUSHI, Materials Science and Engineering
WU, ZHEN, Mathematics
XIA, GUANGMIN, Life Sciences
XIA, HAIRUI, Physics and Microelectronics
XIA, YUEYUAN, Physics and Microelectronics
XIANG, FENGNING, Life Sciences
XIAO, JINMING, Law
XIAO, MIN, Life Sciences
XIAO, XIA, Foreign Languages and Literature
XIE, HONGXIANG, Literature and Journalism
XIE, HUI, Law
XIE, KEQIN, Public Health
XIE, QUBING, Physics and Microelectronics
XIE, SHIJIE, Physics and Microelectronics
XIONG, ZHIPING, Civil Engineering
XU, BIN, Materials Science and Engineering
XU, CHAO, Literature and Journalism
XU, DONG, Materials Science and Engineering
XU, GUIFA, Public Health
XU, GUIYING, Chemistry and Chemical Engineering
XU, MINGYU, Mathematics
XU, PING, Life Sciences
XU, QIULIANG, Computer Science and Technology
XU, WENFANG, Pharmacy
XU, XIANGYI, Business Administration
XU, YANSHENG, Civil Engineering
YAN, BINGGANG, Philosophy and Social Development
YANG, DANPING, Mathematics
YANG, HUIXIN, Business Administration
YANG, JINGHE, Chemistry and Chemical Engineering
YANG, LIANZHONG, Mathematics
YANG, LUHUI, Political Science and Public Administration
YANG, RUIZHI, Literature and Journalism
YANG, XUEJIN, Business Administration
YANG, YANZHAO, Chemistry and Chemical Engineering
YI, HONGXUN, Mathematics
YIN, YANSHENG, Materials Science and Engineering
YU, GUANG, Business Administration
YU, GUANGHAI, History and Culture
YU, HONGXIA, Public Health
YU, XIUPING, Medicine
YUAN, DONGFENG, Information Science and Engineering
YUAN, SHISHUO, Literature and Journalism
YUAN, YIRANG, Mathematics
YUE, QINGYAN, Environmental Science and Engineering
ZENG, GUANGZHOU, Computer Science and Technology
ZENG, ZHENYU, History and Culture
ZHAN, TAO, Mathematics
ZHANG, CAIMING, Computer Science and Technology
ZHANG, CHANGKAI, Life Sciences
ZHANG, CHENGHUI, Control Science and Engineering
ZHANG, CHUNGUANG, Chemistry and Chemical Engineering
ZHANG, CHUNLING, Public Health
ZHANG, HENG, Medicine
ZHANG, HUAZHONG, Computer Science and Technology
ZHANG, JIANYE, Medicine
ZHANG, JINLONG, History and Culture
ZHANG, JUREN, Life Sciences
ZHANG, KELI, Literature and Journalism
ZHANG, LIHENG, History and Culture

ZHANG, LINING, Medicine
ZHANG, NAIJIAN, Physics and Microelectronics
ZHANG, PEILIN, Physics and Microelectronics
ZHANG, PEIZHONG, Civil Engineering
ZHANG, QINGFAN, Control Science and Engineering
ZHANG, QINGZHU, Pharmacy
ZHANG, RUILIN, Physical Education
ZHANG, SHUNHUA, Mathematics
ZHANG, SHUXUE, History and Culture
ZHANG, SHUZHENG, Literature and Journalism
ZHANG, TAO, History and Culture
ZHANG, TIQIN, Business Administration
ZHANG, XIEN, Political Science and Public Administration
ZHANG, XINGYU, Information Science and Engineering
ZHANG, XIUMEI, Medicine
ZHANG, XIWEI, History and Culture
ZHANG, XUEJUN, Literature and Journalism
ZHANG, XUEYAO, Physics and Microelectronics
ZHANG, YULIN, Control Science and Engineering
ZHANG, YUZHEN, Life Sciences
ZHANG, YUZHONG, Life Sciences
ZHAO, AIGUO, History and Culture
ZHAO, BINGXIN, Business Administration
ZHAO, GUOQUN, Materials Science and Engineering
ZHAO, JIANGUO, Electrical Engineering
ZHAO, JINGHUA, Business Administration
ZHAO, SHENGZI, Information Science and Engineering
ZHAO, WEIMIN, Medicine
ZHAO, XIAOFAN, Life Sciences
ZHAO, ZHONGTANG, Public Health
ZHENG, CHUN, Literature and Journalism
ZHENG, FENGLAN, Literature and Journalism
ZHENG, LIQIANG, Chemistry and Chemical Engineering
ZHENG, LIQIANG, Chemistry and Chemical Engineering
ZHENG, PEIXIN, History and Culture
ZHENG, XUNZUO, Literature and Journalism
ZHONG, MAIYING, Control Science and Engineering
ZHONG, WEILIE, Physics and Microelectronics
ZHOU, GENYAN, Medicine
ZHOU, GUANGYUAN, History and Culture
ZHOU, HONGXING, Mathematics
ZHOU, LAIXIANG, Literature and Journalism
ZHOU, XIAOYU, History and Culture
ZHU, DAMING, Computer Science and Technology
ZHU, RUIFU, Materials Science and Engineering
ZHU, WEISHEN, Civil Engineering

SHANDONG AGRICULTURAL UNIVERSITY

61 Dai Zong St, Taian 271018, Shandong
Telephone: (538) 8242291
Fax: (538) 8226399
E-mail: xb@sdau.cdu.cn
Internet: www.sdau.edu.cn

Founded 1906
Department of Education of Shandong control
Academic year: September to July
President: WEN FUJIANG
Vice-Presidents: DONG SHUTING, YAO LAICHANG, ZHANG JINGHE, ZHANG XIANSHENG
Head of Graduate Department: WANG ZHENLIN
Librarian: ZHANG XIANIQI
Number of teachers: 1,151
Number of students: 20,000
Publications: *Journal* (natural sciences, 4 a year), *Journal* (social sciences, 4 a year), *Shandong Journal of Animal Husbandry and Veterinary Science* (6 a year)

DEANS

College of Agricultural Resources and Environment: SHI YANXI
College of Agronomy: WANG HONGGANG
College of Animal Technology: TAN JINGHE
College of Chemistry and Materials Science: ZHOU JIE
College of Economy and Management: HU JILIAN
College of Food Science and Engineering: DONG HAIZHOU
College of Foreign Languages: LI ZHILING
College of Forestry: MU ZHIMEI
College of Horticulture: WANG XIUFENG
College of Humanities and Law: SUN YANQUAN
College of Hydrology and Civil Engineering: LIU FUSHENG
College of Information Science and Technology: WANG YUNCHENG
College of Life Science: ZHENG CHENGCHAO
College of Mechanical and Electronic Engineering: ZHENG WEI
College of Plant Protection: LI DUOCHUAN
College of Science: ZHOU JIE

PROFESSORS

AI, SHIYUN, Chemistry and Materials Science
CAI, TONGJIE, Animal Technology
CHANG, WEISHAN, Animal Technology
CHEN, XUESEN, Horticulture
CHENG, SHUHAN, Information Science and Technology
CUI, DECAI, Life Sciences
CUI, WEI, Humanities and Law
CUI, WEIZHENG, Forestry
CUI, YANSHUN, Animal Technology
CUI, ZHIZHONG, Animal Technology
DIAO, YOUXIANG, Animal Technology
DING, AIYUN, Plant Protection
DING, SHIFEI, Information Science and Technology
DONG, HAIZHOU, Food Science and Engineering
DONG, JINLING, Economy and Management
DONG, SHUTING, Agronomy
DU, SHOUJUN, Humanities and Law
FAN, WEIXING, Animal Technology
FAN, ZHICHENG, Horticulture
FENG, CHENGMING, Electromechanical Engineering
FENG, YONGJUN, Agricultural Resources and Environment
GAO, HUA, Information Science and Technology
GAO, HUA, Science
GAO, HUIYUAN, Life Sciences
GAO, QINGRONG, Agronomy
GAO, RONGQI, Agronomy
GUANGLIANG, DONGYE, Agricultural Resources and Environment
GUO, HUABEI, Information Science and Technology
GUO, HUABEI, Science
GUO, XINMIN, Electromechanical Engineering
HA, YIMING, Science
HE, MINGRONG, Agronomy
HU, CHANGHAO, Agronomy
HU, JILIAN, Economy and Management
HU, YANJI, Agronomy
JIANG, LIN, Chemistry and Materials Science
JIANG, YONGBIN, Economy and Management
JIN, XIANG, Chemistry and Materials Science
KANG, JINGFENG, Electromechanical Engineering
KONG, LINGRANG, Agronomy
LI, ANFEI, Agronomy
LI, DEQUAN, Life Sciences
LI, DUOCHUAN, Plant Protection
LI, FUCHANG, Animal Technology
LI, JIRONG, Horticulture
LI, JIYE, Hydrology and Civil Engineering
LI, QIANG, Plant Protection
LI, QINGQI, Agronomy
LI, RUXIN, Electromechanical Engineering
LI, TONGSHU, Animal Technology
LI, XIANGDONG, Agronomy
LI, XIANGDONG, Plant Protection
LI, XIANLI, Horticulture
LI, ZENGJIA, Agronomy
LI, ZHAOHUI, Plant Protection
LI, ZHENSHENG, Plant Protection
LIANG, XUETIAN, Hydrology and Civil Engineering
LIN, HAI, Animal Technology
LIN, HONGXIAO, Hydrology and Civil Engineering
LIN, QUANYE, Forestry
LING, CHENGHOU, Electromechanical Engineering
LIU, CHUANBAO, Hydrology and Civil Engineering
LIU, CHUNSHENG, Agricultural Resources and Environment
LIU, FUSHENG, Hydrology and Civil Engineering
LIU, KAIQI, Plant Protection
LIU, LIANWE, Science
LIU, LIANWEI, Chemistry and Materials Science
LIU, SHIDANG, Animal Technology
LIU, XIAOGUANG, Plant Protection
LIU, YAN, Foreign Languages
LIU, ZHONGXIANG, Animal Technology
LU, FUSUI, Chemistry and Materials Science
LU, FUSUI, Science
LUO, WANCHUN, Plant Protection
MA, SHUSHENG, Hydrology and Civil Engineering
MENG, QINGWEI, Life Sciences
MENG, XIANGDONG, Horticulture
MIAO, LIANG, Information Science and Technology
MU, LIYI, Plant Protection
MU, ZHIMEI, Forestry
NIE, JUNHUA, Agricultural Resources and Environment
PANG, QINGJIANG, Hydrology and Civil Engineering
PEIZHENG, ZHANG, Food Science and Engineering
QI, SHUJUN, Foreign Languages
QU, XIANGJIN, Science
SHAN, LUN, Agronomy
SHEN, XIANG, Horticulture
SHI, JIANMIN, Economy and Management
SHI, PEI, Agronomy
SHI, YANXI, Agricultural Resources and Environment
SHU, HUAIRUI, Horticulture
SHUHAN, CHENG, Science
SONG, JIANCHENG, Agronomy
SU, LANZHEN, Agronomy
SUN, MINGGAO, Forestry
SUN, XUGEN, Forestry
SUN, YANQUAN, Humanities and Law
SUN, ZHONGXU, Horticulture
TAN, JINGHE, Animal Technology
TIAN, BO, Plant Protection
TIAN, JICHUN, Agronomy
TIAN, QIZHUO, Agronomy
WAN, JIACHUAN, Economy and Management
WAN, YONGSHAN, Agronomy
WANG, DECHUN, Economy and Management
WANG, HANZHONG, Life Sciences
WANG, HONGGANG, Agronomy
WANG, HONGMO, Economy and Management
WANG, HUIMING, Electromechanical Engineering
WANG, KAIYUN, Plant Protection
WANG, LIQIN, Horticulture
WANG, SHUYING, Animal Technology
WANG, XIANZE, Life Sciences
WANG, XIUFENG, Horticulture
WANG, YUNCHENG, Information Science and Technology
WANG, YUNCHENG, Science
WANG, ZELI, Life Sciences
WANG, ZHENLIN, Agronomy
WANG, ZHONGHUA, Animal Technology
WEI, JIANGCHUN, Plant Protection

WEN, FUJIANG, Life Sciences
XING, SHIYAN, Forestry
XU, HONGFU, Plant Protection
XU, KUN, Horticulture
XU, WEIAN, Plant Protection
XUE, XINGLI, Economy and Management
XUESONG, HUANG, Food Science and Engineering
YAN, YANCHUN, Life Sciences
YAN, ZHENYUAN, Hydrology and Civil Engineering
YANG, DI, Humanities and Law
YANG, HONGQIANG, Horticulture
YANG, JIHUA, Forestry
YANG, QUANMING, Animal Technology
YANG, XUECHENG, Economy and Management
YANG, ZAIBIN, Animal Technology
YIN, XIANGCHU, Plant Protection
YIN, XUNHE, Animal Technology
YIN, YANPING, Agronomy
YU, SONGLIE, Agronomy
YU, XIANCHANG, Horticulture
YU, YIMIN, Hydrology and Civil Engineering
YU, YUANJIE, Agronomy
YU, ZHENWEN, Agronomy
YUE, YONGSHENG, Animal Technology
ZENG, YONGQING, Animal Technology
ZHAI, HENG, Horticulture
ZHANG, CHUNQING, Agronomy
ZHANG, GUANGMIN, Plant Protection
ZHANG, GUANGMIN, Plant Protection
ZHANG, LIANGCHENG, Hydrology and Civil Engineering
ZHANG, MIN, Agricultural Resources and Environment
ZHANG, TIANYU, Plant Protection
ZHANG, XIANSHENG, Life Sciences
ZHANG, XIAOHUI, Electromechanical Engineering
ZHANG, ZHIGUO, Agricultural Resources and Environment
ZHAO, GENGXING, Agricultural Resources and Environment
ZHAO, HONGKUN, Animal Technology
ZHAO, LANYONG, Forestry
ZHAO, TANFANG, Agronomy
ZHENG, CHENGCHAO, Life Sciences
ZHENG, GUOSHENG, Life Sciences
ZHOU, JIE, Chemistry and Materials Science
ZHOU, JIE, Science
ZHOU, YANPING, Economy and Management
ZHU, FENGGANG, Chemistry and Materials Science
ZHU, FENGGANG, Science
ZHU, LUSHENG, Agricultural Resources and Environment
ZHU, RUILIANG, Animal Technology
ZOU, QI, Life Sciences

SHANDONG INSTITUTE OF ECONOMICS

4 East Yanzishan Rd, Jinan 250014, Shandong
Telephone: (531) 8934161
Internet: www.china-sd.com/business/sdjjxy/home2e.htm
Founded 1958
President: Prof. HU JIJIAN
Vice-Presidents: Prof. LIU SHIFAN, Prof. REN HUI, LI RENQUAN
Librarian: LI ZIRUI
Number of teachers: 322
Number of students: 2,118
Publications: *Shandong Economy*, *Accountant*, *Statistics and Management*

HEADS OF DEPARTMENTS

Industrial and Commercial Economics: LONG ZENGRUI
Planning and Statistics: ZHANG XIAOFEI
Financial Accounting: LIU XUEYAN
Finance and Banking: TANG RUOYAN
International Trade: XIE HONGZHONG
Computer Science and Management: ZHAO XIQING

SHANDONG NORMAL UNIVERSITY

88 Wen Hua East Rd, Jinan 250014, Shandong
Telephone: (531) 6180018
Fax: (531) 6180017
E-mail: xiaoban@sdnu.edu.cn
Internet: www.sdnu.edu.cn
Founded 1950
Provincial control
Academic year: September to July
President: ZHAO YANXIU
Vice-Presidents: QI WANXUE, TANG BO, WANG ZHAOLIANG, WANG ZHIMIN, ZHANG QINGGANG
Head of Graduate Department: ZHANG WEIJUN
Librarian: SHEN DAGUANG
Number of teachers: 1,150
Number of students: 37,300 (24,300 full-time, 13,000 part-time)
Publications: *China Population, Resources and Environment* (6 a year), *Journal* (humanities and social sciences, 6 a year), *Journal* (natural sciences, 4 a year), *Journal of the School of Foreign Languages of Shandong Teachers' University* (4 a year), *Shandong Foreign Languages Journal* (6 a year)

DEANS

College of Broadcasting: MENG XIANGZENG
College of Chemistry, Chemical Engineering and Materials Science: DONG YUBIN
College of Chinese Language and Literature: ZHOU JUNPING
College of Educational Science: ZHANG WENXIN
College of Fine Arts: KONG XINMIAO
College of Foreign Languages: YANG MIN
College of History, Culture and Social Development: WANG WEI
College of Information and Management: LIU XIYU
College of Legal Science: HAN YUGUI
College of Life Science: AN LIGUO
College of Mathematics Science: FU XILIN
College of Music: ZHANG ZHUN
College of Physical Education: YU TAO
College of Physics and Electronics: WANG CHUANKUI
College of Population, Resources and the Environment: REN JIANLAN

PROFESSORS

AN, LIGUO, Life Sciences
BI, HUALIN, Chemistry, Chemical Engineering and Materials Science
CAI, JINLING, Chemistry, Chemical Engineering and Materials Science
CAO, CHUNCHUN, Foreign Languages
CAO, DAOPING, Life Sciences
CAO, MINGHAI, Chinese Language and Literature
CHEN, DEZHAN, Chemistry, Chemical Engineering and Materials Science
CHEN, HAIHONG, History, Culture and Social Development
CHEN, HUANZHEN, Mathematical Science
CHEN, QING, Broadcasting
CHEN, XIULAN, Physics and Electronics
CHEN, YIMING, Music
CHENG, DAOPING, Population, Resources and the Environment
CHENG, JIEMIN, Population, Resources and the Environment
CHENG, XHUANFU, Physics and Electronics
DAI, SHIJUN, Chinese Language and Literature
DENG, HONGMEI, Chinese Language and Literature
DIAO, PEIJUN, Legal Science
DONG, SHAOKE, Chinese Language and Literature
DONG, YUBIN, Chemistry, Chemical Engineering and Materials Science
DU, GUICHEN, Chinese Language and Literature
FAN, XIJUN, Physics and Electronics
FU, HAILUN, Mathematical Science
FU, RONGRU, Life Sciences
FU, XILIN, Mathematical Science
GAO, FENGQIANG, Educational Science
GAO, HUA, Foreign Languages
GAO, JINGZHEN, Mathematical Science
GAO, TIEJUN, Physics and Electronics
GAO, YIQING, Fine Arts
GUO, CHENGSHAN, Physics and Electronics
GUO, GENSHENG, Broadcasting
HAN, HONGFEI, Physical Education
HAN, MEI, Population, Resources and the Environment
HAN, YUGUI, Legal Science
HE, JIAMEI, Population, Resources and the Environment
HE, JINGLIANG, Physics and Electronics
HONG, XUEBIN, Broadcasting
HOU, FULIN, Life Sciences
HOU, KANGWEI, Music
HUANG, MINGSHUI, Music
JI, GUANGMAO, Chinese Language and Literature
JIANG, CHONGQIU, Chemistry, Chemical Engineering and Materials Science
JIANG, ZHENCHANG, Chinese Language and Literature
JIANG, ZHONGYING, Broadcasting
JIANG, ZIWEN, Mathematical Science
KONG, XINMIAO, Fine Arts
LI, AIHUA, Legal Science
LI, HONGRUI, Chemistry, Chemical Engineering and Materials Science
LI, HUAIXIANG, Chemistry, Chemical Engineering and Materials Science
LI, JIAN, Physics and Electronics
LI, LAIZHONG, Chemistry, Chemical Engineering and Materials Science
LI, PING, Population, Resources and the Environment
LI, QIAN, Mathematical Science
LI, SHIZHENG, Mathematical Science
LI, TAOXIN, Educational Science
LI, XIAOLIN, Chemistry, Chemical Engineering and Materials Science
LI, XUEMIN, Mathematical Science
LI, YANXHU, Chinese Language and Literature
LI, YUJIANG, Population, Resources and the Environment
LI, YUNLONG, Life Sciences
LI, ZHIHUA, Chemistry, Chemical Engineering and Materials Science
LIANG, FANZHEN, Chemistry, Chemical Engineering and Materials Science
LIN, SHENGLU, Physics and Electronics
LIU, CHUNYING, Foreign Languages
LIU, FANG'AI, Information and Management
LIU, FENGLING, Chemistry, Chemical Engineering and Materials Science
LIU, HAIYAN, Educational Science
LIU, HONG, Information and Management
LIU, PEIYU, Information and Management
LIU, TAO, Physical Education
LIU, WENXIAN, Physics and Electronics
LIU, XIAOLIAN, Physical Education
LIU, XIYU, Information and Management
LIU, YANSHENG, Mathematical Science
LIU, ZAISHENG, Music
LU, HONG, Broadcasting
MA, SHUNYE, Mathematical Science
MA, YONGQING, Legal Science
MAN, BAOYUAN, Physics and Electronics
MENG, XIANGZENG, Broadcasting
NIE, QINGXIANG, Physics and Electronics
QI, WANXUE, Educational Science
QU, MINGWEN, Foreign Languages
QU, WENGUANG, Mathematical Science

QUAN, CHAOLU, Educational Science
REN, JIANLAN, Population, Resources and the Environment
SHENG, DAZHONG, Chemistry, Chemical Engineering and Materials Science
SHI, JINGMIN, Chemistry, Chemical Engineering and Materials Science
SHI, ZHIQIANG, Chemistry, Chemical Engineering and Materials Science
SONG, FENGGUANG, Fine Arts
SONG, JIGUO, Fine Arts
SONG, LILI, Music
SUN, LEI, Mathematical Science
SUN, XIHUA, Population, Resources and the Environment
TANG, BO, Chemistry, Chemical Engineering and Materials Science
TANG, BO, Life Sciences
TANG, NING, Music
TIAN, JIANGUO, Mathematical Science
TIAN, SHUFENG, Broadcasting
TONG, DIANMIN, Physics and Electronics
WAN, GUANGXIA, Legal Science
WANG, BAOSHAN, Life Sciences
WANG, BING, Educational Science
WANG, CHUANKUI, Physics and Electronics
WANG, HONGJIAN, Chemistry, Chemical Engineering and Materials Science
WANG, HONGQI, Chinese Language and Literature
WANG, HUAIYOU, Chemistry, Chemical Engineering and Materials Science
WANG, HUAXUE, Chinese Language and Literature
WANG, KUIYONG, Information and Management
WANG, QINGXIN, Foreign Languages
WANG, SHENGHAI, Physical Education
WANG, WANSEN, Chinese Language and Literature
WANG, WEI, History, Culture and Social Development
WANG, YOUBANG, Population, Resources and the Environment
WANG, ZEXIN, Chemistry, Chemical Engineering and Materials Science
WANG, ZHIMING, Chinese Language and Literature
WEI, JIAN, Chinese Language and Literature
WEI, WEI, Educational Science
WU, QINGFENG, Chinese Language and Literature
WU, QUANYUAN, Population, Resources and the Environment
WU, YIQIN, Chinese Language and Literature
XIA, ZHIFANG, Chinese Language and Literature
XIANG, YANG, Music
XIAO, LONGFU, Foreign Languages
XU, CHANGJUN, Music
XU, QINGPU, Legal Science
XU, QINGRU, Music
XU, XINZHAI, Mathematical Science
XU, YAOTONG, Population, Resources and the Environment
YAN, BAOQIANG, Mathematical Science
YANG, GUOLIANG, Physical Education
YANG, MIN, Foreign Languages
YANG, SHOUSEN, Chinese Language and Literature
YU, JINJIANG, Foreign Languages
YU, QUANXUN, Physics and Electronics
YU, TAO, Physical Education
ZHANG, CONGSHAN, Broadcasting
ZHANG, ENYI, Broadcasting
ZHANG, FUJI, Legal Science
ZHANG, GUORONG, Chemistry, Chemical Engineering and Materials Science
ZHANG, HUI, Life Sciences
ZHANG, JINGHUAN, Educational Science
ZHANG, JINPING, Broadcasting
ZHANG, QINGGANG, Physics and Electronics
ZHANG, QINGHUA, Chinese Language and Literature
ZHANG, SHUFENG, Educational Science
ZHANG, SHUQIN, Foreign Languages
ZHANG, WENXIN, Educational Science
ZHANG, XIJIE, Fine Arts
ZHANG, YUFEN, Mathematical Science
ZHANG, YUHONG, Life Sciences
ZHANG, ZHIDE, Chemistry, Chemical Engineering and Materials Science
ZHANG, ZHULU, Population, Resources and the Environment
ZHANG, ZHUN, Music
ZHAO, CHENGFU, Educational Science
ZHAO, JIAN, Population, Resources and the Environment
ZHAO, JIE, Physics and Electronics
ZHAO, QINGUO, Fine Arts
ZHAO, QINGZHEN, Information and Management
ZHAO, YANXIU, Life Sciences
ZHENG, MINGCHUN, Information and Management
ZHENG, XINQI, Population, Resources and the Environment
ZHOU, BO, Chinese Language and Literature
ZHOU, JUNPING, Chinese Language and Literature
ZHOU, ZHICHEN, Chemistry, Chemical Engineering and Materials Science
ZHU, DEFA, Chinese Language and Literature
ZHU, JUNKONG, Physics and Electronics
ZHUANG, WAN, Mathematical Science
ZHUANG, WENZHONG, Life Sciences
ZHUO, ZHUANG, Physics and Electronics

SHANGHAI INTERNATIONAL STUDIES UNIVERSITY

550 Dalian Rd West, Shanghai 200083
Telephone: (21) 65360599
Fax: (21) 65313756
E-mail: oisasisu@mail.online.sh.cn
Internet: www.shisu.edu.cn

Founded 1949
Academic year: September to July
President: DAI WEIDONG
Vice-Presidents: SHENG YULIANG, TAN JINGHUA, WU YOUFU, ZHU JIANGUO
Head of Graduate Department: FENG QINGHUA
Librarian: ZHU LEI
Number of teachers: 300
Number of students: 8,300
Publications: *The Arab World* (6 a year), *Educational Technology for Foreign Language Teaching* (6 a year), *Journal* (6 a year)

DEANS

College of Eastern Languages: LU PEIYONG
College of the English Language: SHI ZHIKANG
College of International Business Administration: LIN XUNZI
College of International Cultural Exchange: XU BAOMEI
College of International Education: SHI HUILI
Graduate Institute of Interpretation and Translation: CHAI MINGJIONG
College of Japanese Culture and Economy: PI XIGENG
College of Journalism and Communication: HU SHUZHONG
School of Law: YU JIANHUA
College of the Russian Language: ZHENG TIWU
College of Western Language and Literature: WEI MAOPING

PROFESSORS

CAI, YOUSHENG, Western Language and Literature
CAO, DEMING, Western Language and Literature
CHAI, MINGJIONG, Graduate Institute of Interpretation and Translation
CHEN, HUIZHONG, International Cultural Exchange
CHEN, XIAOCHUN, Western Language and Literature
DAI, HUIPING, Graduate Institute of Interpretation and Translation
DAI, WEIDONG, English
DOU, HUI, Law
DU, YUNDE, Graduate Institute of Interpretation and Translation
FENG, QINGHUA, English
HE, ZHAOXIONG, English
HU, LONG, Journalism and Communication
HU, SHUZHONG, Journalism and Communication
LI, WEIPING, English
LU, JINGSHENG, Western Language and Literature
LU, LOUFA, Graduate Institute of Interpretation and Translation
LU, PEIYONG, Eastern Languages
LU, YONGCHANG, Russian
LU, GUANGDAN, English
MEI, DEMING, English
PI, XIGENG, Japanese Culture and Economy
QIAN, PEIXIN, Western Language and Literature
QIU, MAORU, English
SHEN, YUCHENG, Japanese Culture and Economy
SHI, HUILI, International Education
SHI, ZHIKANG, English
SHI, ZHIKANG, Graduate Institute of Interpretation and Translation
SHU, SHENGPENG, Western Language and Literature
TAN, JINGHUA, Japanese Culture and Economy
WEI, MAOPING, Western Language and Literature
WU, DAGANG, Japanese Culture and Economy
WU, DINGBO, English
XIE, TIANZHEN, Graduate Institute of Interpretation and Translation
XU, YULONG, English
YANG, JINHUA, International Cultural Exchange
YU, JIANHUA, Law
ZHANG, SHIHUA, Western Language and Literature
ZHANG, WEILIANG, English
ZHANG, YONGHUA, Journalism and Communication
ZHANG, ZHUXIN, Journalism and Communication
ZHENG, TIWU, Russian
ZHOU, PING, Japanese Culture and Economy
ZHOU, SHEN, English
ZHOU, WENJU, Eastern Languages

SHANGHAI JIAOTONG UNIVERSITY

1954 Hua Shan Rd, Shanghai 200030
Telephone: 62812444
Fax: 62821369
Internet: www.sajtu.edu.cn

Founded 1896
Academic year: September to July
President: XIE SHENGWU
Vice-Presidents: SHENG HUANYE, BAI TONGSHUO, YE QUYUAN, SHEN WEIPING, ZHANG SHENGKUN, XU XIAOMING
Director of President's Office: ZHANG WEI
Librarian: CHEN ZHAONEN
Library of 1,826,000 vols
Number of teachers: 2,889
Number of students: 13,882 (incl. 2,831 postgraduates)
Publication: *Journal* (also in English, every 2 months)

HEADS OF SCHOOL

School of Naval Architecture and Ocean Engineering: LI RUNPEI

School of Power and Energy Resources Engineering: XU JIJUN
School of Electronics and Information Technology: XI YUGENG
School of Electric Power Engineering: HOU ZHIJIAN
School of Materials Science and Engineering: WU JIANSHENG
School of Machinery Engineering: YAN JUNQI
School of Science: SHI ZHONGCI
School of Life Sciences and Technology: TANG ZHANGCHENG
School of Humanities and Social Sciences: YE DUNPING
School of Civil Engineering and Mechanics: LIU ZHENGXING
School of Chemistry and Chemical Engineering: TANG XIAOZHENG
School of Management: ZHANG XIANG
School of Foreign Languages: ZHENG SHUTANG
Department of Physical Education: SUN QILING
Department of Plasticity Technology: RUAN XUEYU

RESEARCH INSTITUTES

Structural Mechanics Institute of Naval Architecture and Ocean Engineering: Dir JIN XIANDING.

Hydromechanics Institute of Naval Architecture and Ocean Engineering: Dir WANG GUOQIANG.

Institute of Underwater Engineering: Dir ZHU JIMAO.

Institute of Harbour Engineering and Hydraulic Engineering: Dir SHI ZHONG.

National Key Ocean Engineering Laboratory: Dir LI RUNPEI.

Research Centre for Vibration, Shock and Noise (National Key Laboratory): Dir HAN ZHUSHUN.

Institute of Engineering Thermophysics and Energy Resources: Dir CHENG HUIER.

HDTV Institute: Dir HUANG BAOLIN.

Institute of Image Processing and Pattern Recognition: Dir SHI PENGFEI.

Institute of Optical Fibre Technology: Dir YE AILUN.

Institute of Large-Scale Integrated Circuits: Dir LIN ZHENGHUI.

Institute of Computer Networks: Dir YANG CHUANHOU.

Institute of Composite Materials: Dir SHUN KANG.

National Key Laboratory of Base Metals: Dir GU MINGZHI.

Institute of Manufacturing Technology and Automation: Dir HU DEJIN.

Institute of Production Systems and Control: Dir CHAI JIANGUO.

Institute of Computer Integrated Systems: Dir MA DENGZHE.

Institute of Motor Design and Manufacturing: Dir ZHANG JIANWU.

Institute of Electromechanical Control: Dir FENG ZHENGJIN.

Institute of Robotics: Dir LU TIANSHENG.

Institute of Mechanical Engineering Design and Automation: Dir YE QINGTAI.

Institute of Graphic Technology and Computer-Aided Design: Dir JIANG SHOUWEI.

Institute of Mechanics and Automated Design: Dir HUANG WENZHEN.

Institute of Mathematics, Science and Technology: Dir FANG AINONG.

Institute of Optics and Photonics: Dir CHEN YINGLI.

Institute of Condensed Material Physics: Dir ZHENG HANG.

Institute of Solar Energy: Dir GUO LIHUI.

Institute of Space and Astrophysics: Dir YOU JUNHAN.

Institute of Biomedical Instruments: Dir CHEN YAZHU.

Institute of Health Science and Technology: Dir ZHU ZHANGYU.

Institute of Ecology and the Environment: Dir XU DAQUAN.

Institute of Social Science and Engineering: Dir ZHANG YUYU.

Institute of Science, Technology and Social Development: Dir QIAN XUECHENG.

Institute of Ideological and Political Education and Ethics: Dir YU YAPING.

Institute of Philosophy and Public Policy: Dir LIU FENG.

Institute of Architectural Design: Dir LIU SHUOTAN.

Institute of Polymeric Materials: Dir XU XI.

Institute of Pure Chemical Industry: Dir HUANG DEYIN.

Institute of Environmental Chemical Industry: Dir JIA JINPING.

Institute of Systems Engineering: Dir WANG HUANCHEN.

Institute of Human Resources Management: Dir LI DE.

SHANGHAI NORMAL UNIVERSITY

100 Guilin Rd, Nanjing 200234, Jiangsu
Telephone: (21) 64322881
Fax: (21) 64360512
Internet: www.shtu.edu.cn

Founded 1954
Academic year: September to July

President: YU LIZHONG
Vice-Presidents: JIANG WEIYI, LIU ZHIGANG, LU JIANPING, XIANG JIAXIANG
Librarian: CAO XU
Library of 2,600,000 vols
Number of teachers: 1,181
Number of students: 40,000

Publications: *Chinese University Academic Abstracts* (6 a year), *Journal* (6 a year)

DEANS

Architecture Engineering College: LIU JIANXIN
Engineering College of Machinery and Electronics Information: LIN XIAOYUN
Fine Arts College: XU WANGYAO
Life and Environmental Science College: LI HEXING
Mathematics and Science College: ZHANG JIZHOU
Sports College: LU CHANGYA
School of Arts: XIE JING
School of Commerce: FU HONGCHUN
School of Education: LU JIAMEI
School of European Culture and Trade: MAO XUNCHENG
School of Foreign Languages: GU DAXIN
School of Law and Politics: SHANG HONGRI
School of Literature: SUN XUN
School of Music: DAI DINGCHENG

PROFESSORS

CAI, LONGQUAN, Foreign Languages
CAO, TONG, Life and Environmental Sciences
CAO, XU, Literature
CEN, GUOZHEN, Education
CHEN, KEJIAN, Law and Politics
CHEN, MINGZHENG, Arts
CHEN, WEI, Literature
CHEN, WEIPING, Law and Politics
CHENG, XINGHUA, Foreign Languages
CHENG, ZHEHUAN, Law and Politics
DAI, DINGCHENG, Music
DENG, MINGDE, Foreign Languages
FAN, KAITAI, Literature
FAN, WUYUN, Literature
FANG, GUANGCHANG, Law and Politics
FEI, HELIANG, Mathematics and Science
FU, HONGCHUN, Commerce
GAN, FENG, Law and Politics
GAO, HUIZHU, Law and Politics
GAO, JIANHUA, Mathematics and Science
GU, DAXI, Foreign Languages
GU, HAIGEN, Education
HE, YUNFENG, Law and Politics
HONG, XIAOXIA, Law and Politics
HUANG, BAOHUA, Literature
JIA, HUANZHEN, Arts
JIANG, CHUANGUANG, Law and Politics
KANG, AISHI, Arts
LI, HEXING, Life and Environmental Sciences
LI, JIAHOU, Arts
LI, SHENG, Law and Politics
LI, SHI, Literature
LI, WEIHUI, Commerce
LI, WEIMING, Sports
LI, XIAOYUN, Machinery and Electronics Information Engineering
LI, YIZHEN, Life and Environmental Sciences
LI, ZHIGUO, Commerce
LIU, DANQING, Literature
LIU, JIANXIN, Architecture
LIU, YANYAN, Law and Politics
LU, CHANGYA, Sports
LU, JIAMEI, Education
LU, RUOPING, Arts
LU, RUZHAN, Literature
MA, DELING, Law and Politics
MEI, ZIHAN, Literature
MI, ZHENG, Arts
QI, LUYANG, Literature
REN, ZHONGLUN, Literature
SHANG, HONGRI, Law and Politics
SHAO, YONG, Literature
SHEN, HEBO, Life and Environmental Sciences
SHI, YONGBING, Mathematics and Science
SHUN, XUN, Literature
SUN, JINGRAO, Literature
SUN, XUSHENG, Sports
SUN, YUWEI, Law and Politics
TAN, WEIGUO, Foreign Languages
TANG, LIXING, Literature
TAO, BENYI, Literature
WANG, CUIYING, Sports
WANG, GUORONG, Mathematics and Science
WANG, JIREN, Literature
WANG, TIANQU, Literature
WANG, XIAODUN, Literature
WANG, XINQIU, Foreign Languages
WANG, YANMING, Mathematics and Science
WEI, SHIXIAN, Arts
WENG, MINHUA, Literature
WU, HONGLIN, Arts
WU, JINGDONG, Law and Politics
WU, JUNMING, Life and Environmental Sciences
WU, QUANXI, Life and Environmental Sciences
WU, XIAQIN, Life and Environmental Sciences
XIA, HUIXIAN, Education
XIE, LIMIN, Education
XU, SHIYI, Literature
XU, WEIHONG, Arts
XUE, HESHENG, Commerce
XUE, SIJIA, Life and Environmental Sciences
YAN, GWENHU, Literature
YANG, DONG, Sports
YANG, JIANLONG, Literature
YANG, ZHONGHUA, Mathematics and Science
YANG, ZHONGNAN, Life and Environmental Sciences
YE, HUANIAN, Foreign Languages
YE, HUANIAN, Literature
YU, XIBING, Life and Environmental Sciences
YUAN, BING, Literature

YUAN, FENG, Law and Politics
YUE, RONGXIAN, Mathematics and Science
ZHANG, JIZHOU, Mathematics and Science
ZHANG, ZIQIANG, Machinery and Electronics Information Engineering
ZHAO, XIAONAN, Arts
ZHENG, KELU, Literature
ZHOU, GENYU, Life and Environmental Sciences
ZHOU, ZHONGZHI, Law and Politics
ZHU, SHUNQUAN, Mathematics and Science
ZHU, XIANSHENG, Literature

SHANGHAI SECOND MEDICAL UNIVERSITY

280 South Chongqing Rd, Shanghai 200025
Telephone: (21) 63846590
Fax: (21) 63842916
Internet: www.shsmu.edu.cn

Founded 1952
Languages of instruction: Chinese, English, French
Academic year: September to July

Chancellor: FAN GUANRONG
Vice-Chancellor: Prof. QIAN GUANXIANG
Vice-Chancellor: Assoc. Prof. ZHU ZHENGGANG
Vice-Chancellor: Prof. CHEN ZHIXING
Vice-Chancellor: Prof. ZHUANG MENGHU
Registrar: Prof. CAI WEI
Librarian: Assoc. Prof. ZHANG WENHAO

Library of 420,000 vols
Number of teachers: 3,379
Number of students: 5,000

Publications: *Journal of Shanghai Second Medical University* (in Chinese and English), *Journal of Clinical Paediatrics* (in Chinese), *Chinese Journal of Endocrinology and Metabolism* (in Chinese), *Shanghai Journal of Immunology* (in Chinese)

DEANS

College of Basic Medical Sciences: Prof. LU YANG
Faculty of Clinical Medicine in Rui Jin Hospital: Prof. LI HONGWEI
Faculty of Clinical Medicine in Ren Ji Hospital: Prof FAN GUANRONG
Faculty of Paediatrics and Clinical Medicine in Xin Hua Hospital: Prof. SHEN XIAOMIN
School of Stomatology: Prof. ZHANG ZHIYUAN
Faculty of Clinical Medicine in No. 6 People's Hospital: Prof. LIN FAXIONG
Department of Social Sciences: XIANG YANG
Junior Medical College in Bao Gang Hospital: JUN SHENGJI
Health School: Assoc. Prof. WU XIANGQIAN

ATTACHED INSTITUTES

Basic Medical Research Centre of SSMU.

Research and Training Centre for Reproductive Medicine of Shanghai.

Research Centre for Clinical Pharmacology of SSMU.

Research Centre for Traditional Chinese Medicine of SSMU.

Shanghai Biomaterial Research and Test Centre.

Shanghai Institute of Biomedical Engineering.

Shanghai Institute of Burns.

Shanghai Institute of Digestive Diseases.

Shanghai Institute of Endocrinology.

Shanghai Institute of Haematology.

Shanghai Institute of Hypertension.

Shanghai Institute of Immunology.

Shanghai Institute of Orthopaedics and Traumatology.

Shanghai Institute of Paediatrics.

Shanghai Institute of Plastic and Reconstructive Surgery.

Shanghai Institute of Stomatology.

Shanghai Municipal Key Laboratory of Medical Technology.

There are five affiliated hospitals

SHANGHAI TIEDAO UNIVERSITY

450 Zhennan Lu, Shanghai 200333
Telephone: (21) 2506812
Fax: (21) 2506812
Internet: www.shtdu.edu.cn

Founded 1995 by merger of Shanghai Institute of Railway Technology and Shanghai Railway Medical College
State control
Academic year: September to July (two terms)

President: Prof. CHEN GUANMAO
Vice-Presidents: Prof. ZHU GUANGJIE, Prof. LI MENG, Prof. MA WENZENG, Prof. MAO YONGJIANG, Prof. XU LONG, Assoc. Prof. SUN ZHANG
Registrar: Prof. MIAO RUNSHEN
Librarian: Prof. WU WENQI

Library of 850,000 vols, 2,900 periodicals
Number of teachers: 1,164
Number of students: 6,354

Publication: *Journal*

HEADS OF DEPARTMENTS

Mechanical and Electrical Engineering: Prof. QI WENXING
International Economics and Management: Prof. PEN YUNO
Medicine: Prof. XU LONG
Information Science and Technology: Prof. ZHANG SHUJING
Civil Engineering: Prof. CHAO XUQIN
Foreign Languages: Prof. HUA WEI

PROFESSORS

AI, Y., Hygienics
CAI, N., Physiology
CAI, T., Surgery
CHAO, X., Bridge, Tunnel and Structural Engineering
CHEN, D. L., Dermatology
CHEN, D. Y., Fluid Drive
CHEN, H., Mechanical Engineering
CHEN, J., Railway Locomotives and Rolling Stock
CHEN, S., Railway Locomotives and Rolling Stock
CHENG, S., Pathology
DENG, N., Internal Medicine
DU, Q., Electrification and Automation
FAN, P., Mechanical Engineering
FENG, Z. Q., Histology and Embryology
FENG, Z. Z., Railway Vehicles
GONG, J., Railway Locomotives and Rolling Stock
GUO, D. F., Railway Location and Construction
GUO, D. P., Orthopaedics
HOU, H., Neuropathology
HU, B., Anatomy
HU, K., Bridge, Tunnel and Structural Engineering
HU, M., Computer Communication
HUA, W., English
HUANG, S., Transport Management
JI, L., Transport Management
JIANG, E., Internal Combustion Engines
LE, S., Stomatology
LI, D., Surgery
LI, H., Mathematics
LI, J., Ophthalmology
LI, M., Applied Computer Technology
LI, S., Internal Medicine
LI, Y., Mechanics
LIN, Z., Ultrasonic Diagnosis
LIU, C., Internal Medicine
LIU, Q., Hydraulic Pressure Technology
LIU, X., Railway Automation
LIU, Y., Electrical Appliances
LIU, Z., Paediatrics
LU, G., Civil Engineering
LU, Y., Civil Engineering
NIE, C., Fluid Drive and Control
PAN, K., Stomatological Surgery
PENG, Y. O., Economics
QI, W., Internal Combustion Engines
QIU, W., Medical Genetics
REN, J., Transport Management
RUAN, Y., Computer Engineering
SHAO, B., Power Electronics Technology
SHEN, P., Railway Locomotives and Rolling Stock
SHEN, Z., Infectious Diseases
SHI, S., Stomatology
SONG, J., Anaesthesia
SUN, P., Surgery
SUN, Q., Railway Location and Construction
SUN, S., Parasitology
SUN, Y., Laboratory Testing
TAN, B., Mechanical Engineering
TAO, S., Computer Engineering
TAO, Z., Fluid Drive
TONG, D., Wheel-rail System
WANG, B., Applied Computer Technology
WANG, B., Surgery
WANG, D., Telecommunications
WANG, F., Railway Vehicles
WANG, Q., Railway Electrification and Automation
WANG, R., Mathematics
WANG, W., Railway Engineering
WANG, Y., Biochemistry
WU, F., Telecommunications
WU, J., Railway Location and Construction
WU, W. Q., Transport Signals and Control
WU, W. Y., Psychiatry
WU, X., Railway Location and Construction
WU, Z. K., Electrical Appliances
WU, Z. R., Civil Engineering
XIA, Y., Mechanics
XIONG, W., Mechanics
XU, T., Mechanics
YANG, G., Mechanics
YANG, H. C., Histology and Embryology
YANG, H. Y., Transport Management
YANG, X., Civil Engineering
YE, E., Hygienics
YIN, L., Mechanics
YU, W., Pharmacology
YUAN, S., Stomatology
ZHANG, D. X., Railway Locomotives and Rolling Stock
ZHANG, D. Z., Railway Locomotives and Rolling Stock
ZHANG, J., Gynaecology and Obstetrics
ZHANG, S. C., Stomatology
ZHANG, S. J., Telecommunications and Information Processing
ZHANG, W. C., Civil Engineering
ZHANG, X., Mechanics
ZHANG, Y. J., Electrical Technology
ZHANG, Y. Z., Internal Medicine
ZHANG, Z., Railway Locomotives and Rolling Stock
ZHAO, S., Politics
ZHENG, G., Stomatology
ZHENG, T., Power Electronics Technology
ZHOU, Z., Stomatological Surgery
ZHU, J., Railway Location and Construction
ZHU, M., Mechanics
ZHU, P., Theoretical Physics
ZHU, X., Mathematics
ZONG, G., Structural Engineering

SHANGHAI UNIVERSITY OF FINANCE AND ECONOMICS

777 Guoding Rd, Shanghai 200433
Telephone: (21) 65903505
Fax: (21) 65100561
Internet: www.shufe.edu.cn

Founded 1917
Ministry of Education control
Academic year: September to July
President: TAN MIN
Vice-Presidents: CONG SHUHAI, HUANG LINFANG, SUN ZHENG, WANG HONGWEI, ZHOU ZHONGFEI
Head of Graduate Department: FENG ZHENGQUAN
Librarian: LI XIAOYE
Number of students: 20,000
Publications: *Economics and Management of Foreign Countries* (monthly), *Higher Education of Finance and Economics* (quarterly), *Journal* (6 a year), *Journal of Finance and Economics* (monthly)

DEANS

School of Accountancy: CHEN XINYUAN
School of Applied Mathematics: CHEN QIHONG
School of Economics: TIAN GUOQIANG
School of Finance: DAI GUOQIANG
School of Humanities: ZHANG XIONG
School of International Business Management: SUN HAIMING
School of Law: ZHOU ZHONGFEI
School of MBA Programmes: LUO ZUWANG
School of Public Economy Administration: JIANG HONG
Department of Foreign Languages: WANG XIAOQUN
Department of Information Management: LIU LANJUAN
Department of Physical Education: CHEN XIAO
Department of Statistics: HAN XIAOLIANG

PROFESSORS

BIAN, ZUWU, Statistics
CHANG, NING, Statistics
CHAO, GANGLING, Marketing
CHE, WEIHAN, International Economics
CHEN, HUIQIN, Statistics
CHEN, QIHONG, Applied Mathematics
CHEN, QIJIE, Marketing
CHEN, WENHAO, Accountancy
CHEN, XIAO, Physical Education
CHEN, XINKANG, Marketing
CHEN, XINYUAN, Accountancy
CHEN, YUN, Public Economy Administration
CHENG, ENFU, Economics
CHU, MINWEI, Public Economy Administration
CHU, YIYUN, Accountancy
CONG, SHUHAI, Public Economy Administration
DAI, GUOQIANG, Banking
DING, BANGKAI, Law
DONG, FENGGU, Statistics
DOU, JIANMING, Statistics
DU, XUNCHENG, Economics
FEI, FANGYU, International Finance
GAN, CHUNHUI, Industry Economics
GU, GUIDING, Applied Mathematics
GU, GUOZHU, Humanities
GUO, SHIZHENG, Public Economy Administration
GUO, YUDAN, International Trade
HAN, QING, Economics
HAN, XIAOLIANG, Statistics
HE, JIANMIN, Tourism Management
HE, YUCHANG, Economics
HU, JINGBEI, Economics
HU, YIJIAN, Public Economy Administration
HU, YIMING, Accountancy
HU, YONGGANG, Economics
HUO, WENWEN, Finance
JIANG, HONG, Public Economy Administration
JIANG, YIHONG, Accountancy
JIN, DEHUAN, Finance
LAN, YISHENG, International Trade
LI, XIAOYE, Humanities
LI, XIAOYU, Statistics
LI, XIN, Economics
LIANG, ZHIAN, Applied Mathematics
LIAO, YINLIN, Statistics
LIN, JUE, International Economics
LIU, HANLIANG, Statistics
LIU, LIJUAN, Resource Management
LIU, YONGMING, Banking
LU, PINYUE, Humanities
LU, SHIMIN, Banking
LU, WANZHONG, Statistics
LUO, ZUWANG, Humanities
MA, GUOXIAN, Public Economy Administration
MI, WENZHAN, Humanities
PAN, FEI, Accountancy
PEI, YIRAN, Humanities
PENG, JIAQIANG, Humanities
QI, ZHIXIANG, Humanities
QU, WEIDONG, International Finance
SHAO, JIANLI, Statistics
SHENG, BANGHE, Humanities
SHI, BINGCHAO, Banking
SHI, XIQUAN, International Finance
SU, JUNHE, Statistics
SUN, HAIMING, Industry Economics
SUN, YUNWU, Statistics
SUN, ZHENG, Accountancy
TAN, MIN, Economics
TAN, ZHENG, Information Management
TAO, TINGFANG, Tourism Management
WANG, DEFA, Statistics
WANG, HONGWEI, Public Economy Administration
WANG, HUILING, Statistics
WANG, LIMING, Statistics
WANG, LIYA, Foreign Languages
WANG, SONGNIAN, Accountancy
WANG, XIAOMING, Statistics
WANG, XIAOQUN, Foreign Languages
WANG, XINXIN, Marketing
WANG, XUEMIN, Statistics
WANG, YU, Business Management
WU, LONGSHENG, Resource Management
XI, JUNYANG, International Finance
XIA, JIANMING, Business Management
XIE, ZHIGANG, Finance
XU, DAJIAN, Humanities
XU, GUOXIANG, Statistics
XU, JIANPING, Humanities
XU, JINLIANG, Finance
XU, ZHENDAN, Accountancy
XUE, HUACHENG, Information Management
YAN, GUANGHUA, Business Management
YANG, DAKAI, Public Economy Administration
YANG, GONGPU, Industry Economics
YANG, JUNCHANG, Public Economy Administration
YANG, NAN, Statistics
YIN, CHENGYUAN, Applied Mathematics
YING, SHICHANG, Finance
YOU, JIARONG, Accountancy
YU, DINGWEI, Statistics
YU, ZHIYOU, Finance
YUAN, HONGQI, Accountancy
YUE, YAOXING, International Trade
ZAN, TINGQUAN, Information Management
ZHANG, CHUN, Accountancy
ZHANG, JUE, Humanities
ZHANG, MIAO, Statistics
ZHANG, MING, Accountancy
ZHANG, MINGFANG, Statistics
ZHANG, XIONG, Humanities
ZHANG, YAN, Humanities
ZHANG, YAOTING, Economics
ZHANG, YINJIE, Economics
ZHAO, JIANYONG, Accountancy
ZHAO, XIAOJU, Banking
ZHAO, XIAOLEI, Economics
ZHAO, XIAOSHENG, Foreign Languages
ZHOU, ZHONGFEI, Law
ZHU, BAOHUA, Economics
ZHU, GUOHUA, Industry Economics
ZHU, JIANZHONG, Statistics
ZHU, MINGXIONG, Statistics
ZHU, PINGFANG, Economics
ZHU, RONGEN, Accountancy
ZHU, YINGPING, Humanities
ZHU, ZHONGDI, International Economics

SHANGHAI UNIVERSITY

1220 Xin Zha Rd, Shanghai 200041
Telephone: (21) 2553062
Fax: (21) 2154780
Internet: www.shu.edu.cn
Founded 1983
Chancellor: Prof. WANG SHENGHONG
Deputy Chancellor: Prof. LIN JIONGRU
Vice-Chancellors: Prof. CAO ZHONGXIAN, Prof. LI MINGZHONG
University Dean: Prof. WENG SHIRONG
University Co-ordinator for Foreign Affairs and International Programmes: ZHONG GUOXIANG
Number of teachers: 1,200, incl. 296 profs
Number of students: 7,500
Publications: *Journal*, *Sociology*, *Secretariat*

PRESIDENTS

College of Engineering: Prof. MA GUOLIN
College of Liberal Arts: Prof. WANG XIMEI
College of Business: Prof. JIANG JIAJUN
College of Fine Arts: Prof. LI TIANXIANG
College of International Business: Prof. LU GUANQUAN
College of Political Science: Prof. WANG XIMEI

HEADS OF DEPARTMENTS

College of Engineering:
- Machinery: Prof. SHEN JIMIN
- Computer Science and Microwave: Prof. YU SHIQUAN
- Radio Technology: Prof. FU XUANYING
- Electrical Technology: Prof. XIE SHEN
- Engineering Technology: Prof. ZHANG SONGSHAN

College of Liberal Arts:
- Chinese Language and Literature: Prof. WU HUANZHANG
- History: Prof. YUAN JUNQING
- Law: Prof. XU YIREN
- Sociology: Prof. SHEN GUANBAO
- Secretarial Science: Prof. WANG LIXIN
- Archive Science: Prof. ZHANG JUNYAN
- Information Science: Prof. LI QI

College of Business:
- Business Administration and Technology: Prof. WANG NAILIANG
- Trade and Economics: Prof. CHEN XINJIAN
- Accounting and Statistics: Prof. HONG JIAMIN
- Food: Prof. YANG ZHONGYI
- Applied Computer Science: Prof. WANG XILIN

College of International Business:
- English: Prof. ZHANG GUANPEI
- International Business and Economics: Prof. WANG GUOMING
- Japanese: Prof. SHEN SHOUZHEN

College of Fine Arts:
- Art Design: Prof. WANG YIXIAN
- Traditional Chinese Painting: Prof. GU BINGXIN
- Oil Painting: Prof. JIONG JIUNMO
- Sculpture: Prof. ZHANG YONGHAO

College of Political Science:
- Political Science: Prof. ZHANG ZHIFU

SHANTOU UNIVERSITY

243 University Rd, Shantou 515063, Guangdong
Telephone: (754) 2902350
Fax: (754) 2510509
Internet: www.stu.edu.cn
Founded 1981

Provincial Control
Academic year: September to July
President: XU XIAOHU
Vice-Presidents: LI YUGUANG, WU GUANGGUO, XIANG BING, XIAO ZELI, ZHENG YI
Head of Graduate Department: WANG ZHAN
Librarian: HUANG TING

Number of teachers: 630
Number of students: 12,880 (8,254 full-time, 4,614 part-time)

Publications: *Chinese Literature* (6 a year), *Journal* (4 a year), *Journal (Humanities and Social Sciences Edition)* (6 a year), *Journal (Natural Science Edition)* (4 a year)

DEANS

College of Business: XUE YUNKUI
College of Engineering: GONG LEIGUANG
College of Law: ZHOU WEI
College of Literature: FENG SHANG
College of Medicine: LI YUGUANG
College of Science: LI DAN
School of Art and Design: JIN DAIQIANG
School of Journalism and Communication: CHEN WANYING
Department of Physical Education: XU BIN
Department of Social Science: CHENG JIAMING

PROFESSORS

CAO, BINGYUAN, Science
CHEN, FANGJING, Literature
CHEN, GUOQIANG, Science
CHEN, HANWEN, Business
CHEN, HONGLIN, Science
CHEN, MAOHUAI, Medicine
CHEN, WANYING, Journalism and Communication
CHEN, YAN, Art and Design
CHENG, JIAMING, Social Science
DING, XIAOJUN, Medicine
DING, ZHAOKUN, Science
DU, DANMING, Business
DU, GANGJIAN, Law
DU, LUNLUN, Literature
DUAN, MINGKE, Medicine
FANG, JIE, Science
GAO, KUNSHAN, Science
GONG, LEIGUANG, Engineering
GUO, XIANGUO, Medicine
GUO, XISHEN, Science
HAN, YALI, Science
HANG, JIAN, Art and Design
HE, SHAOHENG, Medicine
HERFORD, P. M., Journalism and Communication
HU, XINGRONG, Journalism and Communication
HUANG, CHANGJIANG, Science
HUANG, DONGYANG, Medicine
HUANG, XUELAN, Law
HUANG, YAN, Business
HUANG, YUANMING, Science
HUO, XIA, Medicine
JIANG, XUEWU, Medicine
JIN, DAIQIANG, Art and Design
KONG, KANGMEI, Medicine
LAN, SHENG, Science
LI, DAN, Science
LI, ENMIN, Medicine
LI, GUICANG, Literature
LI, KANGSHENG, Medicine
LI, PING, Law
LI, QING, Art and Design
LI, SHENGPING, Engineering
LI, YUGUANG, Medicine
LIN, FURONG, Science
LIN, SHUNCHAO, Medicine
LIU, JIANBIN, Engineering
LIU, XIAOHUA, Science
LOU, ZENGJIAN, Science
LUO, WENHONG, Medicine
MA, WENHUI, Science
MAI, JIEHUA, Science
MO, YAN, Literature
NI, ZHENHUA, Engineering
QI, DAQING, Business
QI, WEILI, Medicine
QIAN, SHUANRU, Medicine
QIAN, ZHIQIANG, Art and Design
QIN, DANIAN, Medicine
QIU, HANYING, Medicine
QIU, QINGCHUN, Science
SHEN, MINFEN, Engineering
SHI, GANGGANG, Medicine
SU, MIN, Medicine
TIAN, DONGPING, Medicine
WANG, CHEN, Medicine
WANG, FUREN, Literature
WANG, HUIGE, Medicine
WANG, JUNMING, Science
WANG, SHOUZHI, Art and Design
WANG, YINHE, Science
WANG, ZIYUAN, Science
WU, GUANGFUO, Science
WU, JIANXHONG, Medicine
WU, RENHUA, Medicine
WULAN, HASHI, Science
XIANG, BING, Business
XIAO, TAN, Science
XIE, HUICAI, Engineering
XIE, ZHUANGNING, Engineering
XU, JIANHENG, Medicine
XU, LUHANG, Law
XU, XIAOHU, Medicine
XU, ZONGLING, Business
XUE, YUNKUI, Business
YANG, SHOUZHI, Science
YANG, ZHONGQIANG, Science
YE, RUISONG, Science
YIN, YEGAO, Science
YUAN, ZHOU, Journalism and Communication
ZHAO, XIAOHUA, Engineering
ZHENG, XHIPEI, Medicine
ZHENG, YI, Engineering
ZHOU, WEI, Law

SHANXI AGRICULTURAL UNIVERSITY

Taigu 030801, Shanxi
Telephone: (354) 6288211
Fax: (354) 6222942
E-mail: sxauxb@sxau.edu.cn
Internet: www.sxau.edu.cn

Founded 1950
Provincial control
Academic year: September to July
President: DONG CHANGSHENG
Vice-Presidents: CUI KEYONG, WANG JUNDONG, YUE WENBIN
Librarian: KANG CHENGYE

Number of teachers: 602
Number of students: 7,300

Publications: *Journal* (natural sciences, quarterly), *Journal* (social sciences, quarterly), *Study of Agriculture in Higher Education* (6 a year)

DEANS

College of Adult Education: REN JIAYAN
College of Agriculture: LI SHENGCAI
College of Animal Technology: LI HONGQUAN
College of Economics and Trade: (vacant)
College of Engineering Technology: (vacant)
College of Food Science and Engineering: HAO LIPING
College of Forestry: (vacant)
College of Horticulture: (vacant)
College of Horticulture: REN JIAYAN
College of Life Sciences: (vacant)
College of Resources and Environmental Science: SUN TAISEN
College of Social Science: (vacant)
Department of Modern Education and Technology: (vacant)

PROFESSORS

BAI, ZHONGKE, Resources and Environmental Science
CHANG, MINGCHANG, Food Science and Engineering
DONG, CHANGSHENG, Animal Technology
FAN, WENHUA, Resources and Environmental Science
HAN, JUCAI, Agriculture
HAO, JIANPING, Agriculture
HAO, LIN, Food Science and Engineering
HAO, LIPING, Food Science and Engineering
HE, YUNCHUN, Agriculture
HONG, JIANPING, Resources and Environmental Science
LI, BINGLIN, Agriculture
LI, HONGQUAN, Animal Technology
LI, SHENGCAI, Agriculture
LIN, DAYI, Resources and Environmental Science
LIU, HUIPING, Agriculture
LU, XIN, Resources and Environmental Science
MA, LIZHEN, Food Science and Engineering
PANG, QUANHAI, Animal Technology
SUN, TAISEN, Resources and Environmental Science
TANG, CHAOZHONG, Animal Technology
WANG, HONGFU, Agriculture
WANG, JUNDONG, Animal Technology
WANG, RUFU, Food Science and Engineering
WANG, SHENGUI, Resources and Environmental Science
WANG, YUGUO, Agriculture
WANG, ZHIRUI, Animal Technology
WANG, ZHIYA, Resources and Environmental Science
WEN, WEIYE, Animal Technology
WU, CAI-E, Food Science and Engineering
XIE, YINGHE, Resources and Environmental Science
YANG, JINZHONG, Agriculture
YANG, WUDE, Agriculture
ZHANG, HENG, Resources and Environmental Science
ZHAO, LIZHI, Agriculture

SHANXI UNIVERSITY

36 Wu Cheng Rd, Taiyuan 030006, Shanxi
Telephone: (351) 7010944
Fax: (351) 7011981
E-mail: xiaoban@sxu.edu.cn
Internet: www.sxu.edu.cn

Founded 1902
Provincial control
Academic year: September to July
President: GUICHUN GUI
Vice-Presidents: JIA SUOTANG, LIU WEIQI, LIU ZHENSHENG, QI FENG, XING LONG
Head of Graduate Department: GAO CE
Librarian: LI JIALIN

Number of teachers: 1,105
Number of students: 19,913 (11,905 full-time, 6,912 part-time)

Publications: *Acta Sinica Quantum Optica* (philosophy and social sciences, 4 a year), *Journal* (natural sciences, 4 a year), *Journal* (philosophy and social sciences, 4 a year), *Journal of Teachers College of Shanxi University* (4 a year), *Shanxi Library Journal* (6 a year)

DEANS

College of Fine Arts: WANG ERXI
College of Music: WANG LIANG
College of Physical Education: LI JIANYING
College of Physics and Electronics Engineering: LIANG JIUQING
School of Chemistry and Engineering: ZHAO YONGXIANG
School of Chinese Language and Literature: QIAO QUANSHENG

School of Computing and Information Technology: LIANG JIYE
School of Economics: LIU JIANSHENG
School of Education Science: HOU HUAIYIN
School of Environmental Science and Resources: GUO DONGSHENG
School of Foreign Languages: NIE JIANZHONG
School of Law: WANG JIJUN
School of Life Science and Technology: MA ENBO
School of Management: CAO LIJUN
School of Philosophy and Sociology: QIAO RUIJIN
School of Political Science and Public Administration: LI LUQU
Department of History: LI SHUJI
Department of Mathematics: LI SHENGJIA

PROFESSORS

AN, XIMENG, Philosophy and Sociology
BI, FUSHENG, Philosophy and Sociology
CAO, LIJUN, Management
CHEN, JINSHENG, Law
CHEN, SHIBIN, Music
CHEN, ZHAOBIN, Chemistry and Engineering
CHENG, RENGAN, History
DENG, BING, Chemistry and Engineering
DONG, CHUAN, Chemistry and Engineering
DONG, YUMING, Law
FAN, WENBIAO, Environmental Science and Resources
FAN, YINGFANG, Chemistry and Engineering
GAO, XING, Music
GONG, RONGDE, Fine Arts
GUO, DONGSHENG, Environmental Science and Resources
GUO, GUICHUN, Philosophy and Sociology
GUO, YUXIANG, Fine Arts
HAN, JIANRONG, Life Science and Technology
HAN, XIANGMING, Education Science
HAN, ZHIMO, Fine Arts
HAO, JIANGRUI, Physics and Electronics Engineering
HONG, LIANGZHEN, Chinese Language and Literature
HOU, HUAIYIN, Education Science
HU, JIANHUA, Physical Education
HU, MINGLIANG, Foreign Languages
HUANG, FENGCHUN, Chemistry and Engineering
HUANG, SHUPING, Chemistry and Engineering
HUANG, SHUPING, Chemistry and Engineering
JIA, LIANFENG, Physics and Electronics Engineering
JIA, SHUOTANG, Physics and Electronics Engineering
JIA, XINCHUN, Mathematics
JIA, XIUYING, Foreign Languages
JIN, WEIJUN, Chemistry and Engineering
KANG, JINSHENG, Chinese Language and Literature
LAI, YUNZHONG, Physics and Electronics Engineering
LAN, HUANG, Chinese Language and Literature
LI, DEREN, Fine Arts
LI, FUYI, Mathematics
LI, JIANYING, Physical Education
LI, JINLONG, Physical Education
LI, LUQU, Political Science and Public Administration
LI, RUINING, Physics and Electronics Engineering
LI, SHENGJIA, Mathematics
LI, SHUJI, History
LI, WENDE, Chemistry and Engineering
LI, YUE'E, Foreign Languages
LI, ZHENGMIN, Chinese Language and Literature
LI, ZHIQIANG, Economics
LI, ZHONGHAO, Physics and Electronics Engineering
LIANG, JIAHUA, Management
LIANG, JIUQING, Physics and Electronics Engineering
LIANG, JIYE, Computer Science and Information Technology
LIANG, LIPING, Political Science and Public Administration
LIANG, ZHANDONG, Mathematics
LIU, BO, Chemistry and Engineering
LIU, CHAO, Music
LIU, GUIHU, Chinese Language and Literature
LIU, HAILIANG, Foreign Languages
LIU, HONGBING, Music
LIU, JIANSHENG, Economics
LIU, SHUQING, Chinese Language and Literature
LIU, WENSEN, Physics and Electronics Engineering
LIU, XHENSHENG, Chemistry and Engineering
LIU, XIAOHUI, Life Science and Technology
LIU, XIAOLI, Physical Education
LIU, YEPING, Fine Arts
LIU, ZHENSHENG, Chemistry and Engineering
MA, AIPING, Law
MA, ENBO, Life Science and Technology
MA, GUIBIN, Chemistry and Engineering
MA, HAILIANG, Foreign Languages
MA, WEIHUA, Law
MA, YONGMING, Chemistry and Engineering
MA, YUSHAN, History
MENG, ZIQIANG, Life Science and Technology
MIAO, DUOQIAN, Mathematics
NIE, HONGYIN, Chinese Language and Literature
NIE, YIXIN, Physics and Electronics Engineering
PAN, JINGHAO, Chemistry and Engineering
PAN, QING, Physics and Electronics Engineering
PANG, RENJI, Foreign Languages
PEI, CHENGFA, Economics
PEI, CHENGFA, Management
PENG, KUIXI, Physics and Electronics Engineering
PENG, YUNYE, Law
QIAO, DECAI, Physical Education
QIAO, QUANSHENG, Chinese Language and Literature
QIAO, RUIJIN, Philosophy and Sociology
QIN, XUEMEI, Chemistry and Engineering
REN, JIANGUO, Chemistry and Engineering
SHI, YAN, Physical Education
SHUANG, SHAOMIN, Chemistry and Engineering
SONG, BINGYAN, Philosophy and Sociology
SU, CHUNSHENG, Chinese Language and Literature
TIAN, YANNI, Chemistry and Engineering
WANG, HAI, Physics and Electronics Engineering
WANG, JIJUN, Law
WANG, JUNMIN, Physics and Electronics Engineering
WANG, LAN, Life Science and Technology
WANG, LIANG, Music
WANG, RONGSHENG, History
WANG, SHIYING, Mathematics
WANG, XIANMING, History
WANG, YI, Law
WANG, YINTIAN, History
WANG, YUANZHI, Law
WANG, ZHENGREN, Foreign Languages
WEI, GUANHLAI, History
WU, GAOSHOU, Philosophy and Sociology
WU, MIN, Political Science and Public Administration
WU, MINZHONG, Political Science and Public Administration
XIA, XHIXHONG, Chemistry and Engineering
XIANG, LILING, Management
XIE, CHANGDE, Physics and Electronics Engineering
XIE, JIAOLIANG, Life Science and Technology
XIE, SHULIAN, Life Science and Technology
XIE, YINGPING, Life Science and Technology
XING, LONG, History
XU, BINGSHENG, Chinese Language and Literature
XU, GENQI, Mathematics
XU, YONGMIN, Philosophy and Sociology
YAN, FENGWU, Chinese Language and Literature
YAN, JURANG, Mathematics
YANG, BINSHENG, Chemistry and Engineering
YANG, JUPING, History
YANG, LIAN, Chinese Language and Literature
YANG, PIN, Chemistry and Engineering
YANG, SUPING, Life Science and Technology
YI, HUILAN, Life Science and Technology
YU, GUODONG, Foreign Languages
YUE, QIANHOU, History
ZHANG, CUIYING, Management
ZHANG, FENG, Life Science and Technology
ZHANG, HENG, Chinese Language and Literature
ZHANG, JINGSHI, Education Science
ZHANG, JINTUN, Environmental Science and Resources
ZHANG, KUANSHOU, Physics and Electronics Engineering
ZHANG, MIN, Chinese Language and Literature
ZHANG, MINGYUAN, Fine Arts
ZHANG, RU, Chinese Language and Literature
ZHANG, RUIRONG, Music
ZHANG, SHENGWAN, Chemistry and Engineering
ZHANG, TIANCAI, Physics and Electronics Engineering
ZHANG, XIAOGE, Music
ZHANG, XINWEI, Management
ZHANG, YIXIAN, Life Science and Technology
ZHANG, ZHAO, Chemistry and Engineering
ZHANG, ZHUANGHUA, Life Science and Technology
ZHAO, AIMIN, Mathematics
ZHAO, JIANGUO, Chinese Language and Literature
ZHAO, RUIMIN, History
ZHAO, XIAOJUN, Law
ZHAO, YONGXIANG, Chemistry and Engineering
ZHAO, YUXIA, Philosophy and Sociology
ZHAO, ZHAOMING, Life Science and Technology
ZHOU, GUOSHENG, Physics and Electronics Engineering

SHENYANG AGRICULTURAL UNIVERSITY

120 Dongling Rd, Shenyang 110161, Liaoning
Telephone: (24) 88421121
Fax: (24) 88417415
Internet: www.syau.edu.cn

Founded 1952
Academic year: September to July
President: ZHANG YULONG
Vice-Presidents: LI TIANLAI, LIU GUANGLIN, MENG QINGCHENG
Head of Graduate Department: JIN BAOLIAN
Librarian: DUAN YUXI
Number of teachers: 859
Number of students: 20,105
Publications: *Chinese Journal of Soil Science* (6 a year), *Higher Agricultural Education* (monthly), *Journal* (natural sciences, 6 a year), *Journal* (social sciences, quarterly), *Journal of Pig Rearing* (6 a year), *New Agriculture* (monthly)

DEANS

College of Agronomy: CAO MINJIAN
College of Biological Science and Technology: ZHANG LIJUN
College of Economics and Trade: FANG TIANKUN

College of Engineering: LI CHENGHUA
College of Food Science: LIU CHANGJIAN
College of Forestry: LIU MINGGUO
College of Horticulture: LI ZUOXUAN
College of Information and Electrical Engineering: PU ZAILIN
College of Land and the Environment: WANG QIUBING
College of Plant Protection: FU JUNFAN
College of Practical Technology: YANG YINSHAN
College of Science and Technology: (vacant)
College of Veterinary: HU JIANMING
College of Water Resources: WANG TIELIANG

PROFESSORS

BEI, NAXIN, Plant Protection
BIAN, QUANLIAN, Veterinary
CAO, MINJIAN, Agronomy
CAO, YUANYIN, Plant Protection
CAO, ZHIQIANG, Agronomy
CHEN, ENFENG, Land and the Environment
CHEN, JIE, Plant Protection
CHEN, WENFU, Agronomy
CHEN, XIAOFEI, Water Resources
CHEN, XISHI, Land and the Environment
CHEN, ZHENWU, Agronomy
CHENG, GUOHUA, Biological Science and Technology
CHENG, YULAI, Food Science
CHI, DAOCAI, Water Resources
CONG, BIN, Plant Protection
DAI, PENGJUN, Economics and Trade
DONG, WENXUAN, Horticulture
DU, GUANGMING, Horticulture
DU, SHAOFAN, Veterinary
DUAN, YUXI, Plant Protection
FANG, TIANKUN, Economics and Trade
FENG, HUI, Horticulture
FU, JUNFAN, Plant Protection
GAO, DESAN, Biological Science and Technology
GAO, GUOPING, Forestry
GAO, XINGLIAN, Engineering
GUAN, LIANZHU, Land and the Environment
GUO, XIUWU, Horticulture
GUO, YUHUA, Agronomy
HAN, XIAORI, Land and the Environment
HE, JUNSHI, Water Resources
HE, LILI, Horticulture
HOU, LIBAI, Agronomy
HU, JIANMIN, Veterinary
HUANG, RUIDONG, Agronomy
HUI, SHURONG, Basic Education
JI, JIANWEI, Information and Electrical Engineering
JI, MINGSHAN, Plant Protection
JI, MINGXI, Water Resources
JI, SHUJUAN, Food Science
JIANG, QILIANG, Plant Protection
LAN, QINGGAO, Economics and Trade
LI, BAOFA, Engineering
LI, BAOHUA, Basic Education
LI, BAOJIANG, Horticulture
LI, BINGCHAO, Basic Education
LI, CHENGHUA, Engineering
LI, GUOJIE, Insititute of Higher Education
LI, JIANNAN, Biological Science and Technology
LI, TIANLAI, Horticulture
LI, XINHUA, Food Science
LI, YONGKUI, Engineering
LI, YUXIA, Basic Education
LI, ZUOXUAN, Horticulture
LIANG, CHENGHUA, Land and the Environment
LIANG, JINGYI, Plant Protection
LIN, GUOLIN, Land and the Environment
LIU, CHANGJIANG, Food Science
LIU, MINGGUO, Forestry
LIU, RONGHOU, Engineering
LIU, ZHIHENG, Plant Protection
LIU, ZHONGQIN, Economics and Trade
LU, GUOZHONG, Plant Protection
LU, JIE, Economics and Trade
LU, SHUXIA, Biological Science and Technology
LUO, GUANGBIN, Veterinary
MAO, TAO, Food Science
MENG, XIANJUN, Food Science
MI, YONGNING, Water Resources
NIU, SHEN, Centre for Analysis and Testing
PU, ZAILIN, Information and Electrical Engineering
QIN, LI, Biological Science and Technology
QIU, LICHUN, Engineering
REN, WENTAO, Engineering
SHEN, XIANGQUN, Horticulture
SHI, ZHENSHENG, Agronomy
SI, LONGTING, Horticulture
SUN, JUNDE, Land and the Environment
TANG, YONG, Biological Science and Technology
WANG, BOLUN, Agronomy
WANG, CHUNPING, Economics and Trade
WANG, HONGPING, Plant Protection
WANG, HUICHENG, Engineering
WANG, JINGKUAN, Land and the Environment
WANG, JINMIN, Agronomy
WANG, LIXUE, Water Resources
WANG, QINGXIANG, Agronomy
WANG, QIUBING, Land and the Environment
WANG, SHAOBIN, Agronomy
WANG, XIAOQI, Plant Protection
WANG, XUEYING, Biological Science and Technology
WEI, YUTANG, Horticulture
WU, LUPING, Horticulture
WU, YUANHUA, Plant Protection
XIAO, SHENGAN, Social Science
XIE, FUTI, Agronomy
XU, XIAOMING, Physical Education
XU, ZHENGJIN, Agronomy
YAN, HONGWEI, Forestry
YANG, GUIQIN, Veterinary
YANG, SHOUREN, Agronomy
YANG, YONG, Information and Electrical Engineering
YI, YANLI, Land and the Environment
YIN, MINGFANG, Forestry
YU, ZHONGTAO, Social Science
ZHAI, YINLI, Economics and Trade
ZHANG, BAOSHI, Agronomy
ZHANG, KAIBIN, Horticulture
ZHANG, LIJUN, Biological Science and Technology
ZHANG, LONGBU, Agronomy
ZHANG, SHUSHEN, Plant Protection
ZHANG, XIURAN, Information and Electrical Engineering
ZHANG, YONGMING, Social Science
ZHANG, YULIN, Social Science
ZHANG, YULONG, Land and the Environment
ZHANG, ZHIHONG, Horticulture
ZHANG, ZULI, Engineering
ZHAO, YUJUN, Veterinary
ZHOU, BAOLI, Horticulture
ZHOU, HONGFEI, Agronomy
ZHOU, QILONG, Information and Electrical Engineering
ZHOU, YANMING, Centre for Analysis and Testing

SHENZHEN UNIVERSITY

Nantou, Shenzhen 518060, Guangdong
Telephone: (755) 6534940
Fax: (755) 6534662
E-mail: szufao@szu.edu.cn
Internet: www.szu.edu.cn

Founded 1983
State control
Academic year: September to July

President: XIE WIEXIN
Vice-Presidents: Prof. ZHANG BIGONG, Prof. ZHANG BAOQUAN, Prof. LIANG GUILIN, Prof. XING MIAO
Registrar: LIN QIGUANG
Librarian: MAO ZHUOMING

Library of 900,000 vols
Number of teachers: 659
Number of students: 12,000

Publications: *Shenzhen University Journal* (Social Sciences and Humanities), *Shenzhen University Journal* (Natural Sciences), *World Architecture Review*

HEADS OF FACULTIES

Faculty of Arts: Prof. YU LONGYU
Faculty of Economics: Prof. CAO LONGQI
Faculty of Science: Prof. SHU QIQING
Faculty of Information Engineering: Prof. YONG ZHENGZHENG
Faculty of Architecture and Civil Engineering: Prof. XU ANZHI
Faculty of Engineering Technology: Prof. ZHU QIN
Faculty of Art: Prof. LIAO XINGQIAO
Faculty of Golf Sport and Management: Prof. LIN ZUJI
Faculty of Adult Education: Prof. YANG ZHONGXIN
Teachers' College: Prof. ZHANG BIGONG
Department of English: Prof. CAO YIAJUN
Sports Department: Prof. CHEN XIAORONG

ATTACHED INSTITUTES

Joint Institute of Applied Nuclear Technology: Dir GUO CHENGZHAN.

SEZ Economic Studies Institute: Dir SU DONGBIN.

New Energy Research Institute: Dir WANG ENTANG.

Telecommunications Technology Research Institute: Dir JIN BINGRONG.

Advanced Technology Research Centre: Dir YANG SHUWEN.

Holographic Material Research Institute: Dir YE JINGDE.

SICHUAN AGRICULTURAL UNIVERSITY

12 Xinkang Rd, Yaan 625014, Sichuan
Telephone: (835) 2882233
Fax: (835) 2883166
Internet: www.sicau.edu.cn

Founded 1906
Academic year: September to July

President: WEN XINTIAN
Vice-Presidents: REN ZHENGLONG, YANG WENYU, ZHANG QIANG, ZHENG YOULIANG, ZHU QING
Librarian: XIA JIMING

Number of teachers: 1,700
Number of students: 21,500

Publication: *Journal* (quarterly)

Schools and Faculties: Agronomy, Plant Protection, Environmental Engineering, Land Resource Management, Animal Science, Veterinary Science, Forestry and Grass Science, Economical Management in Agriculture and Forestry, Information and Engineering Technology, Vocational Technology, Life Science, Humanities and Social Sciences; Further Education College.

SICHUAN UNION UNIVERSITY

Jiuyanqiao, Chengdu 610064, Sichuan
Telephone: (28) 5412233
Fax: (28) 5410187
E-mail: scuu@sun.scuu.cdnet.edu.cn

Founded 1994 by merger of Sichuan University and Chengdu University of Science and Technology
State control
Language of instruction: Chinese
Academic year: September to July

President: LU TIECHENG

Vice-Presidents: CHEN JUNKAI, LIU YINGMING, LONG WEI, LI ZHIQIANG, ZHANG YIZHENG, YANG JIRUI
Registrar: XIAO DINGQUAN
Librarians: LIU YINGMING, CAI SHUXIAN, FENG ZESI

Library of 3,650,000 vols
Number of teachers: 3,660
Number of students: 19,150

Publications: *South Asian Studies Quarterly, Religion Studies, Oil-field Chemistry, Journal of Atomic and Molecular Physics, Polymeric Material Science and Technology, Sichuan Union University Journal of Natural Science, Sichuan Union University Journal of Social Science, Sichuan Union University Journal of Engineering Science*

DEANS

College of Humanities: CAO SHUNQING
College of Law: TANG LEI
College of Foreign Languages: (vacant)
College of Journalism: QIU PEIHUANG
College of Economics and Management: CHEN GAOLIN
College of Sciences: (vacant)
College of Life Sciences and Engineering: CHEN FANG
College of Information Science and Engineering: TAO FUZHOU
College of Materials Science and Engineering: GU YI
College of Manufacturing Science and Engineering: (vacant)
College of Energy Resources Science and Engineering: (vacant)
College of Urban and Rural Construction and Environmental Protection: LUO TEJUN
College of Chemical Science and Engineering: ZHU JIAHUA
College of Light Science and Engineering: WU DACHENG
College of Fine Art: DENG SHENGQING
School of Adult Education and Vocational Education: WANG ZHONGMING

HEADS OF DEPARTMENTS

College of Humanities:
- Chinese Languages and Literature: GONG HANXIONG
- History: WANG TINGZHI

College of Law:
- Philosophy: DENG SHENGQING
- Law: TANG LEI

College of Foreign Languages:
- Foreign Languages and Literature: SHI JIAN

College of Economics and Management:
- Economics: ZHAO HUAISHUN
- Economic Management: LIAO JUNPEI
- Foreign Economics and Trade: ZHAO CHANGWEN
- Commercial and Industrial Administration: YANG JIANG
- Finance, Tax and Investment: ZHAO YUHUA
- Management Engineering: LI SHIYAN

College of Science:
- Mathematics: XIONG HUAXIN
- Applied Mathematics: LIU GUANGZHONG
- Physics: XIE MAONONG
- Applied Physics: WANG ZHAOQING
- Chemistry: FU HEJIAN

College of Life Sciences and Engineering:
- Biology: JIA YONGJIONG
- Bioengineering: HU YONGSONG

College of Information Science and Engineering:
- Information Management: ZHANG XIAOLIN
- Secretaryship and Archiving: LIU CHENGZHI
- Radioelectronics: HUANG KAMA
- Optical Electronics: CHEN JIANGUO
- Automation: ZHAO YAO
- Applied Electronics: DONG BAOWEN
- Computer Science: LI ZHISHU

College of Materials Science and Engineering:
- Inorganic Materials: RAN JUNGUO
- Polymer Materials: (vacant)
- Plastics Engineering: FAN WUYI
- Materials Science: FEN LIANGHUAN

College of Manufacturing Science and Engineering:
- Mechanical Engineering: YIN GUOFU
- Metallic Materials: LI NING
- Testing Technology and Control Engineering: ZHAO SHIPING

College of Energy Resources Science and Engineering:
- Electric Power Engineering: LI XINGYUANG
- Hydraulic Engineering: LIANG CHUAN

College of Urban and Rural Construction and Environmental Protection:
- Architectural Engineering: LUO TEJUN
- Environmental Science and Engineering: SHI JIANFU
- Civil Engineering and Applied Mechanics: TIAN YONGQIAN

College of Chemical Science and Engineering:
- Chemical Mechanics: HUANG WEIXING
- Chemical Engineering: LIANG BIN
- Applied Chemistry: XIE CHUAN

College of Light Industry and Textile Engineering:
- Leather Technology and Engineering: CHEN WUYONG
- Food Science and Engineering: LU LIANTONG
- Textile Engineering: GU DAZHI

ATTACHED INSTITUTES

Institute of Humanities and Social Sciences: Dir (vacant).

Institute of Materials Science: Dir ZHANG XINGDONG.

Polymer Institute: Dir XU XI.

Institute of Classical Texts: Dir SHU DAGANG.

Institute of South Asian Studies: Dir (vacant).

Institute of Population Studies: Dir HE JINGXI.

Institute of Nuclear Physics: Dir SUN GUANQING.

Institute of High-temperature and High-pressure Atomic and Molecular Physics: Dir HONG SHIMING.

Institute of Religion: Dir LI GANG.

National Laboratory of Polymer Materials: Dir LI HUILIN.

National Laboratory of High-speed Hydraulics: Dir YANG YONGQUAN.

Analytical and Testing Centre: Dirs ZHANG XINGDONG, TU MINDUAN.

Open Laboratory of Radiation Physics and Application: Dir LIN LIBIN.

SICHUAN UNIVERSITY

24 South Section 1, Yihuan Rd, Chengdu 610065, Sichuan
Telephone: (28) 85402443
Fax: (28) 85403260
Internet: www.scu.edu.cn

Founded 1896
State control
Academic year: September to July
President: ZHAO YANXIU
Vice-Presidents: LI ZHIQIANG, LIU YINGMING, TANG DENGXUE, XIE HEPING, YANG JIRUI, ZHANG WEIGUO, ZHAO ZHAODA
Head of Graduate Department: LIU YINGMING
Librarian: LI BINGYAN

Library of 4,847,300 vols
Number of teachers: 1,035
Number of students: 44,003

Publication: *Journal* (editions: natural sciences, 6 a year; engineering, monthly; medicine, quarterly; philosophy and social sciences, quarterly)

DEANS

College of Art: (vacant)
College of Chemistry: HU CHANG WEI
College of Economics and Management: ZHOU GUANG YAN
College of Foreign Languages and Cultures: SHI JIAN
College of Literature and Journalism: CAO SHUNQING
College of Mathematics: LI AN MIN
College of Physical Science and Technology: GONG MIN
College of Politics: WANG GUO MIN
College of Polymer Science and Engineering: YANG MING BO
College of Software Engineering: ZHOU JI LIU
West China College of Stomatology: ZHOU XUE DONG
College of Water Resources and Hydropower: LIANG CHUAN
School of Architecture and the Environment: FAN YU BO
School of Chemistry and Engineering: ZHU JIA HUA
School of Community and Sanitation: MA XIAO
School of Computer Science and Engineering: (vacant)
School of Electricity and Electronic Information: ZHAO ZHUO YAO
School of History and Culture: WANG TING ZHI
School of Law: (vacant)
School of Life Science: CHEN FANG
School of Manufacturing Science and Engineering: YIN GUO FU
School of Materials Science and Engineering: (vacant)
West China School of Pharmacy: ZHANG ZHI RONG
School of Physical Education: TANG CHENG
School of Pre-Clinical and Forensic Medicine: HOU YI PING
School of Tourism: (vacant)

PROFESSORS

AI, NAN SHAN, Architecture and the Environment
AO, FAN, Foreign Languages and Cultures
CAO, GUANG FU, Mathematics
CAO, YI PING, Electronics and Information Engineering
CAO, YI, Life Sciences
CAO, YU RONG, Politics
CENG, ZONG YONG, Life Sciences
CHEN, DAO BANG, Pre-Clinical and Forensic Medicine
CHEN, DE BEN, Chemistry
CHEN, GAO LIN, Economics and Management
CHEN, GUO DI, Pre-Clinical and Forensic Medicine
CHEN, HONG CHAO, Chemistry
CHEN, JIAN KANG, Water Resources and Hydropower
CHEN, JUN KAI, Architecture and the Environment
CHEN, KANG YANG, Law
CHEN, QIAN DE, Architecture and the Environment
CHEN, QIAO, Pre-Clinical and Forensic Medicine
CHEN, TIAN LANG, Chemistry

CHEN, WEN JUN, Chemistry
CHEN, YONG GE, Law
CHEN, ZE FANG, Chemistry
CHEN, ZHONG RONG, Foreign Languages and Cultures
CHENG, LI, Tourism
CHENG, XI LIN, Foreign Languages and Cultures
DAI, ZONG KUN, Electronics and Information Engineering
DAN, DE ZHONG, Architecture and the Environment
DENG, XIAO KANG, Pre-Clinical and Forensic Medicine
DENG, ZHEN HUA, Pre-Clinical and Forensic Medicine
DOU, HOU SONG, Chemistry
FAN, HONG, Architecture and the Environment
FAN, YU BO, Architecture and the Environment
FANG, GUO ZHEN, Chemistry
FANG, SHU XIN, History and Culture
FENG, YI JUN, Chemistry
FENG, ZE HUI, Foreign Languages and Cultures
FU, HE JIAN, Chemistry
FU, HUA LONG, Life Sciences
GAO, CHUN HUA, Manufacturing Science and Engineering
GAO, RONG, Life Sciences
GU, BIN, Life Sciences
GU, ZHONG BI, Electronics and Information Engineering
GUAN, PENG, Pre-Clinical and Forensic Medicine
HE, CHANG RONG, Water Resources and Hydropower
HE, JIANG DA, Water Resources and Hydropower
HE, JING XU, Law
HE, PEI YU, Electronics and Information Engineering
HE, PING, Foreign Languages and Cultures
HE, QING, History and Culture
HE, XING JIN, Life Sciences
HE, YA PING, Pre-Clinical and Forensic Medicine
HE, YU EN, Chemistry
HOU, XIAN DENG, Chemistry
HU, HUO ZHEN, Life Sciences
HU, JIA YUAN, Chemistry
HU, JUN MEI, Pre-Clinical and Forensic Medicine
HUANG, DE CHANG, Economics and Management
HUANG, FA LUN, Mathematics
HUANG, GUANG LIN, Chemistry
HUANG, NAN JING, Mathematics
HUANG, NIAN CI, Electricity and Electronic Information
HUANG, NING, Pre-Clinical and Forensic Medicine
HUANG, SHAN, Electricity and Electronic Information
HUANG, YING, Pre-Clinical and Forensic Medicine
JIANG, BO, Chemistry
JIANG, CHENG FA, Chemistry and Engineering
JIANG, WEN JU, Architecture and the Environment
JIN, MING, Law
JING, DONG, Electricity and Electronic Information
JU, XIAO MING, Water Resources and Hydropower
KANG, ZHEN HUANG, Architecture and the Environment
KE, JI GUI, Foreign Languages and Cultures
LEI, YONG XUE, Politics
LI, AN MIN, Mathematics
LI, BO HUAI, Tourism
LI, DE YU, Architecture and the Environment
LI, FANG, Chemistry
LI, FU HAI, Economics and Management
LI, GUO CHENG, Electricity and Electronic Information
LI, HONG, Pre-Clinical and Forensic Medicine
LI, HUI, Chemistry and Engineering
LI, JIAN MING, Chemistry and Engineering
LI, JIAO, Foreign Languages and Cultures
LI, JIE, Politics
LI, JU CAI, Chemistry
LI, KE FENG, Water Resources and Hydropower
LI, LIANG, Pre-Clinical and Forensic Medicine
LI, MENG LONG, Chemistry
LI, PING, Law
LI, RUI XIANG, Chemistry
LI, SHI YAN, Economics and Management
LI, TAO, History and Culture
LI, XIAO SONG, Infrastructure and Sanitation
LI, YAO ZHONG, Chemistry
LI, YING BI, Pre-Clinical and Forensic Medicine
LI, YING, Chemistry
LI, ZAN, Law
LI, ZHANG ZHENG, Architecture and the Environment
LI, ZHI SHU, Computer Science and Engineering
LI, ZHONG FU, Mathematics
LI, ZHONG MING, Polymer Science and Engineering
LIANG, BING, Chemistry and Engineering
LIANG, JI HUA, Mathematics
LIANG, YUAN DI, Economics and Management
LIAO, LIN CHUAN, Pre-Clinical and Forensic Medicine
LIN, BI GUO, Foreign Languages and Cultures
LIN, DA QUAN, Manufacturing Science and Engineering
LIU, CHANG JUN, Electronics and Information Engineering
LIU, DONG QUAN, Software Engineering
LIU, FEI PENG, Electricity and Electronic Information
LIU, GUANG ZHONG, Economics and Management
LIU, JIA YONG, Electronics and Information Engineering
LIU, LI MIN, Foreign Languages and Cultures
LIU, MIN, Pre-Clinical and Forensic Medicine
LIU, NIAN, Electricity and Electronic Information
LIU, QI CHAO, Software Engineering
LIU, RONG ZHONG, Manufacturing Science and Engineering
LIU, SHAN JUN, Water Resources and Hydropower
LIU, SHENG QING, Manufacturing Science and Engineering
LIU, TIAN QI, Electricity and Electronic Information
LIU, TING HUA, Polymer Science and Engineering
LIU, YI FEI, History and Culture
LIU, YU SHENG, Electricity and Electronic Information
LONG, JIAN ZHONG, Electronics and Information Engineering
LONG, KUI, Foreign Languages and Cultures
LONG, WEI, Manufacturing Science and Engineering
LONG, YUN FANG, Infrastructure and Sanitation
LONG, ZONG ZHI, Law
LUO, DI LUN, Foreign Languages and Cultures
LUO, LIN, Water Resources and Hydropower
LUO, LIN, Architecture and the Environment
LUO, MAO KANG, Mathematics
LUO, MEI MING, Chemistry
LUO, SU QIONG, Infrastructure and Sanitation
LUO, TE JUN, Architecture and the Environment
LUO, WAN BO, Computer Science and Engineering
LUO, XIANG LIN, Polymer Science and Engineering
LV, GUANG HONG, Computer Science and Engineering
LV, TAO, Mathematics
MA, HONG, Mathematics
MA, LI TAI, Foreign Languages and Cultures
MENG, YAN FA, Life Sciences
MU, CHUN LAI, Mathematics
NIE, GANG, Politics
NING, YUAN ZHONG, Electricity and Electronic Information
PEI, JUE MIN, Architecture and the Environment
PENG, BANG BEN, History and Culture
PENG, LIAN GANG, Mathematics
QI, JIAN GUO, Pre-Clinical and Forensic Medicine
QIN, SHI LUN, Architecture and the Environment
QIU, WANG SHENG, Foreign Languages and Cultures
QU, ZHAO YANG, Pre-Clinical and Forensic Medicine
SHI, JIAN, Foreign Languages and Cultures
SHI, YING PING, Tourism
SHU, QIN, Electricity and Electronic Information
SONG, HANG, Chemistry and Engineering
SONG, WEI, Economics and Management
SUN, CHENG JUN, Infrastructure and Sanitation
SUN, JIN QUAN, History and Culture
SUN, QI, Mathematics
TAN, DA LU, Architecture and the Environment
TAN, XIAO PING, Architecture and the Environment
TAN, YANG, Pre-Clinical and Forensic Medicine
TANG, JIA LING, Polymer Science and Engineering
TANG, LEI, Law
TANG, NING JIU, Computer Science and Engineering
TANG, YA, Architecture and the Environment
TAO, LI, Economics and Management
TU, SHANG YIN, Foreign Languages and Cultures
TU, YUAN ZHAO, Electricity and Electronic Information
WAN, JIA YI, Chemistry
WANG, DAO HUI, Electricity and Electronic Information
WANG, FAN, Pre-Clinical and Forensic Medicine
WANG, GUO MIN, Politics
WANG, JIAN PING, Law
WANG, LEI, Pre-Clinical and Forensic Medicine
WANG, LI, Water Resources and Hydropower
WANG, LI, Life Sciences
WANG, QI ZHI, Architecture and the Environment
WANG, QING YUAN, Architecture and the Environment
WANG, SHU YU, Foreign Languages and Cultures
WANG, XIAO LU, Foreign Languages and Cultures
WANG, YA JING, Pre-Clinical and Forensic Medicine
WANG, YING HAN, Polymer Science and Engineering
WANG, ZHEN XUE, Electronics and Information Engineering
WEI, XIN PING, Water Resources and Hydropower
WEI, ZHONG HAI, Politics
WEN, CHU AN, Foreign Languages and Cultures
WU, JIANG, Chemistry
WU, JIN, Pre-Clinical and Forensic Medicine
WU, QING, Pre-Clinical and Forensic Medicine
WU, XIAN HONG, Foreign Languages and Cultures

WU, ZHI HUA, Polymer Science and Engineering
XIA, SU LAN, Chemistry and Engineering
XIANG, TAO, Pre-Clinical and Forensic Medicine
XIANG, ZHAO YANG, Law
XIAO, AN FU, Foreign Languages and Cultures
XIAO, SHEN XIU, Chemistry
XIAO, XU, Politics
XIE, BANG HU, Polymer Science and Engineering
XIONG, FENG, Architecture and the Environment
XU, DAO YI, Mathematics
XU, HENG, Life Sciences
XU, LAN, Electronics and Information Engineering
XUE, YING, Chemistry
YANG, FANG JU, Pre-Clinical and Forensic Medicine
YANG, GANG, Polymer Science and Engineering
YANG, HONG GENG, Electricity and Electronic Information
YANG, HONG YU, Computer Science and Engineering
YANG, JIANG, Economics and Management
YANG, JIE, Chemistry
YANG, JUN LIU, Architecture and the Environment
YANG, SHI WEN, History and Culture
YANG, SUI QUAN, Law
YANG, WAN QUAN, Electronics and Information Engineering
YANG, WU NENG, Foreign Languages and Cultures
YANG, YI, Manufacturing Science and Engineering
YANG, YI, Life Sciences
YANG, ZHEN ZHI, Tourism
YANG, ZHENG GUANG, Politics
YE, GUANG DOU, Polymer Science and Engineering
YI, DAN, Foreign Languages and Cultures
YI, XU FU, Pre-Clinical and Forensic Medicine
YIN, HUA QIANG, Architecture and the Environment
YIN, YONG XIANG, Chemistry and Engineering
YOU, XIAN GUI, Chemistry and Engineering
YU, JIAN HUA, Architecture and the Environment
YU, ZHONG DE, Software Engineering
YUAN, DAO HUA, Computer Science and Engineering
YUAN, DE CHENG, Foreign Languages and Cultures
YUAN, DE QI, Chemistry
YUAN, LI HUA, Chemistry
YUAN, PENG, Water Resources and Hydropower
YUAN, YONG MING, Chemistry
YUAN, ZHI RUN, Architecture and the Environment
YUE, LI MIN, Pre-Clinical and Forensic Medicine
ZENG, CHENG MING, Life Sciences
ZENG, LING FU, Infrastructure and Sanitation
ZHANG, CHAO, Electricity and Electronic Information
ZHANG, DAI RUN, Electricity and Electronic Information
ZHANG, DE XUE, Mathematics
ZHANG, GUANG KE, Water Resources and Hydropower
ZHANG, HONG WEI, Computer Science and Engineering
ZHANG, HUA, Electricity and Electronic Information
ZHANG, JIAN ZHOU, Computer Science and Engineering
ZHANG, KE RONG, Infrastructure and Sanitation
ZHANG, LIN, Water Resources and Hydropower
ZHANG, PIN, Pre-Clinical and Forensic Medicine
ZHANG, WEI NIAN, Mathematics
ZHANG, WEI, Pre-Clinical and Forensic Medicine
ZHANG, XIN PEI, Architecture and the Environment
ZHANG, XU, Mathematics
ZHANG, YI ZHONG, Electricity and Electronic Information
ZHANG, YONG KUI, Chemistry and Engineering
ZHAO, CHANG SHEN, Polymer Science and Engineering
ZHAO, CHENG YU, Life Sciences
ZHAO, SHI PING, Manufacturing Science and Engineering
ZHAO, YUN, Life Sciences
ZHENG, CHANG YI, Chemistry
ZHENG, HUA, Politics
ZHONG, SHU LIN, Chemistry
ZHONG, YIN PING, Polymer Science and Engineering
ZHOU, AN MIN, Electronics and Information Engineering
ZHOU, BO, Architecture and the Environment
ZHOU, BU XIANG, Electricity and Electronic Information
ZHOU, GUANG YA, Foreign Languages and Cultures
ZHOU, JI LIU, Software Engineering
ZHOU, JIAN LUE, Chemistry
ZHOU, LI MING, Pre-Clinical and Forensic Medicine
ZHOU, WEI, Law
ZHOU, XUE, Pre-Clinical and Forensic Medicine
ZHOU, YI, Tourism
ZHU, HUI, Foreign Languages and Cultures
ZHU, XIN MIN, Economics and Management
ZHU, YUN MIN, Mathematics
ZHUANG, CHENG SAN, Computer Science and Engineering
ZUO, WEI MIN, Law

SOOCHOW UNIVERSITY

1 Shi Xin St, Suzhou 215006, Jiangsu
Internet: www.suda.edu.cn

Founded 1900
Academic year: September to July
President: QIAN PEIDE
Vice-Presidents: BAI LUN, GE JIANYI, ZHANG XUEGUANG, ZHU XIULIN
Head of Graduate Department: ZHU SHIQUN
Librarian: WANG GUOPING

Library of 3,320,000 vols
Number of teachers: 1,200
Number of students: 32,300

Publication: *Journal of Suzhou University* (editions: engineering sciences, medical science, 6 a year; natural sciences, philosophy and social science, quarterly)

DEANS

College of Politics and Public Management: ZHOU KEZHEN
School of Agricultural Science and Technology: SHEN WEIDE
School of Chemistry and Chemical Engineering: JI SHUNJUN
School of Computer Science and Technology: ZHU QIAOMING
School of Electronic Information: ZHAO HEMING
School of Foreign Languages: WANG LABAO
School of Life Sciences: ZHANG XUEGUANG
School of Literature Department: LUO SHIJIN
School of Mathematical Sciences: WANG LABAO
School of Mechatronic Engineering: RUI YANNIAN
School of Medicine: WU AIQIN
School of Physical Education and Sports: WANG JIAHONG
School of Social Sciences: WANG LABAO
Material Engineering Institute: CHEN GUOQIANG
Institute of Pollution and Public Health: TONG JIAN

PROFESSORS

BAO, SHIQIAO, Medicine
CAO, YONGLUO, Mathematical Sciences
CAO, YONGLUO, Mechanical and Electronic Engineering
CHEN, LINSEN, Computer Science and Technology
CHEN, QINGGUAN, Mechanical and Electronic Engineering
CHEN, ZIXING, Medicine
CUI, ZHIMING, Mechanical and Electronic Engineering
FENG, ZHIHUA, Mechanical and Electronic Engineering
FU, GEYAN, Mechanical and Electronic Engineering
GAO, FANGYING, Social Science
GAO, QI, Medicine
GU, ZHENLUN, Medicine
GU, ZONGJIANG, Medicine
GUI, SHIHE, Mechanical and Electronic Engineering
HONG, FASHUI, Life Sciences
HU, HUACHENG, Medicine
HUA, RENDE, Art
HUANG, QIANG, Medicine
JIANG, WENKAI, Physical Education and Sports
JIANG, XINGHONG, Medicine
JIN, WEIXING, Social Science
LAN, QING, Medicine
LI, DECHUN, Medicine
LIANG, JUN, Art
LIAO, LIANGYUN, Art
LIU, CHUNFENG, Medicine
LIU, ZHIHUA, Medicine
LU, HUIMIN, Medicine
LU, JIAN, Social Science
MA, WEIZHONG, Literature
QIAN, HAIXIN, Medicine
QIN, ZHENGHONG, Medicine
RUI, YANNIAN, Mechanical and Electronic Engineering
SHEN, YULIANG, Mathematical Sciences
SHEN, ZHENYA, Medicine
SHI, GUANGYU, Mechanical and Electronic Engineering
SHI, SHIHONG, Mechanical and Electronic Engineering
SONG, HUICHUN, Life Sciences
SUN, JUNYING, Medicine
SUN, MINZHI, Physical Education and Sports
TANG, TIANSI, Medicine
TANG, ZHENGPEI, Social Science
TANG, ZHINGMING, Mathematical Sciences
TIAN, JIUMAI, Physical Education and Sports
TU, YIFENG, Chemstry and Chemical Engineering
WAN, JIEQIU, Commerce
WANG, GUANGWEI, Commerce
WANG, GUOPING, Social Science
WANG, JIAHONG, Physical Education and Sports
WANG, ZHAOYUE, Medicine
WEI, XIANGDONG, Social Science
WEN, DUANGAI, Medicine
WU, DEPEI, Medicine
WU, HAORONG, Medicine
WU, JINCHANG, Medicine
XIA, CHAOMING, Medicine
XIA, CHUNLIN, Medicine
XU, HAOWEN, Physical Education and Sports
XUE, YONGQUAN, Medicine
YAN, CHUNYIN, Medicine
YANG, JICHENG, Medicine
YANG, XIANGJUN, Medicine
YIN, YUNXING, Mechanical and Electronic Engineering
YU, HONGBING, Mathematical Sciences
YU, TONGYUAN, Social Science

YU, ZHENG, Social Science
ZANG, ZHIFEI, Social Science
ZHANG, LIN, Physical Education and Sports
ZHANG, MING, Social Science
ZHANG, PENGCHUAN, Art
ZHANG, RI, Medicine
ZHANG, SHIMING, Medicine
ZHANG, XIQING, Medicine
ZHANG, XUEGANG, Life Sciences
ZHANG, XUEGUANG, Medicine
ZHANG, ZHAOYU, Social Science
ZHAO, ZENGYAO, Commerce
ZHONG, KANGMIN, Mechanical and Electronic Engineering
ZHOU, DAI, Medicine
ZHOU, JIANPENG, Chemstry and Chemical Engineering
ZHU, CONGBING, Social Science
ZHU, JIANG, Life Sciences
ZHUGE, HONGXIANG, Medicine
ZHUGE, KAI, Art

SOUTH CHINA AGRICULTURAL UNIVERSITY

Wushan, Guangzhou 510642, Guangdong
Telephone: (20) 85280007
Fax: (20) 85282693
E-mail: office@scau.edu.cn
Internet: www.scau.edu.cn

Founded 1909
State (provincial) control
Academic year: September to July

President: Prof. LUO SHIMING
Vice-President: Prof. LUO XIWEN
Vice-President: Prof. CHEN BEIGUANG
Vice-President: Assoc. Prof. CHEN CHANGSHENG
Librarian: YE JINGHUA

Library of 700,000 vols
Number of teachers: 753
Number of students: 12,501

Publications: *Journal* (quarterly), *Poultry Husbandry and Disease Control* (monthly), *Guangdong Agricultural Sciences* (jointly published with Guangdong Acad. of Agricultural Science, monthly)

DEANS

College of Forestry: Prof. CHEN XIMU
College of Adult Education: Prof. NIU BAOJUN
Polytechnic College: Prof. OU YINGGANG
College of Economics and Trade: Prof. LI DASHENG
College of Biotechnology: Prof. PENG XINXIANG
College of Science: Prof. ZHANG GUOQUAN
College of Liberal Arts: Prof. ZHANG WENFANG
College of Resources and Environment: Prof. LI HUAXING
Department of Agronomy: Prof. ZHANG GUIQUAN
Department of Horticulture: Assoc. Prof. CHEN RIYUAN
Department of Sericulture: Assoc. Prof. XU XINGYAO
Department of Animal Science: Prof. FENG DINGYUAN
Department of Animal Medicine: Prof. ZENG ZHENLING
Department of Food Science: Assoc. Prof. LI BIN
Department of Physical Education: Assoc. Prof. WANG CHANGQING

PROFESSORS

BI, Y. Z., Animal Nutrition and Immunology
CAO, Y., Silkworm Biotechnology
CHEN, B.G., Forest Ecology
CHEN, D. C., Pomology
CHEN, W. K., Insect Toxicology
CHEN, W. X., Post-harvest Physiology of Fruit and Vegetables
CHEN, X. M., Plant Systematics and Evolution
CHEN, Y. S., Animal Genetics and Breeding
CHEN, Y. Q., Food Biochemistry
CHEN, Z. L., Veterinary Medicine
CHEN, Z. Q., Crop Genetics and Breeding
FAN, H. Z., Plant Pathology
FAN, X. L., Soil Chemistry
FENG, D. Y., Animal Nutrition and Feed Science
FENG, Q. H., Veterinary Medicine
FU, C., Economic Policy and Development
FU, W. L., Animal Physiology
GAO, X. B., Plant Pathology
GU, D. J., Insect Ecology
GUO, Z. F., Plant Physiology and Molecular Biology
HONG, T. S., Agricultural Mechanization
HUANG, B. Q., Insecticide
HUANG, H. B., Fruit Tree Physiology
HUANG, Q. Y., Veterinary Microbiology
HUANG, X. Y., Food Nutrition
HUANG, Z. L., Biochemistry
JI, Z. L., Agricultural Product Storage and Processing
JIAN, Y. Y., Plant Biotechnology
JIANG, H., Agricultural Economics and Management
JIANG, Z. D., Plant Pathology
KONG, X. M., Veterinary Pathology
LAN, S. F., Ecological Energy and Value of Energy
LI, B. T., Plant Taxonomy
LI, D. S., Economics of Agricultural Engineering
LI, G. Q., Veterinary Parasitology
LI, H. X., Soil Science
LI, J. P., Soil Chemistry
LI, K. F., Wood Science
LI, M. Q., Plant Physiology
LI, Z. L., Crop Cultivation
LIANG, G. W., Insect Ecology
LIANG, J. N., Crop Cultivation
LIAO, Z. W., Soil Science and the Environment
LIN, J. R., Silkworm Genetics and Breeding
LIN, S. Q., Pomology
LIN, Y. G., Genetic Engineering
LU, Y. G., Plant Genetics
LUO, B. L., Agricultural Economics and Management
LUO, F. H., Forest Management
LUO, S. M., Agroecology
LUO, X. W., Agricultural Mechanization
MEI, M. T., Plant Biotechnology
OU, Y. G., Agricultural Engineering
PAN, Q. H., Plant Pathology
PANG, X. F., Insect Ecology and Taxonomy
PENG, X. X., Plant Physiology and Molecular Biology
REN, S. X., Insect Ecology
SUN, Y. M., Food Chemistry
TAN, Z. W., Plant Genetics and Breeding
TIE, L. Y., Fashion Design
WAN, B. H., Plant Genetics and Breeding
WANG, D. L., Tea Science
WANG, J., Forest Pathology
WANG, S. Z., Landscape Gardening
WANG, Z. S., Animal Ecology
WANG, Z. Z., Plant Pathology
WEN, S. M., Agricultural Economics and Management
WU, H., Botany
WU, Q. T., Agricultural Environment Protection
XIAO, H. G., Plant Pathology
XIN, C. A., Poultry Disease
XU, F. C., Plant Physiology
XU, H. H., Insect Toxicology
XU, X. Y., Silkworm Pathology
YAN, X. L., Plant Nutrition
YANG, G. F., Animal Genetics and Breeding
YANG, Y. S., Genetic Engineering
ZENG, L., Insect Ecology
ZENG, Z. L., Veterinary Pharmacology
ZHANG, G. Q., Crop Genetics and Breeding
ZHANG, T. L., Agricultural Mechanization
ZHANG, W. F., Agricultural Economics and Management
ZHANG, X. Q., Animal Genetics and Breeding
ZHANG, Y. H., Agricultural Economics and Management

SOUTH CHINA NORMAL UNIVERSITY

Shipai, Guangzhou 510631, Guangdong
Telephone: (20) 85210169
Fax: (20) 85210991
Internet: www.scnu.edu.cn

Founded 1933
Academic year: September to July

President: WANG GUOJIAN
Vice-Presidents: HU SHEJUN, HUANG LIYA, LI YONGJIE, LIU MING, MO LEI, QIAN XIANBIN, WU YINGMIN
Head of Graduate Department: XIAO HUA
Librarian: ZHU JIANLIANG

Number of teachers: 2,400
Number of students: 60,600

Publications: *High School Physics Education* (monthly), *Journal* (6 a year), *Journal of Physical Education* (6 a year), *Oriental Culture* (6 a year)

DEANS

College of Economics and Management: LI YONGJIE
College of Educational Information Technology: XU FUYING
College of Foreign Languages: (vacant)
College of Humanities: KE HANLING
College of International Culture: LI SHENGBING
College of Life Science: MA GUANGZHI
College of Optoelectronic Technology: LIU SONGHAO
College of Physics and Telecommunications Engineering: LIU QIONGFA
College of Politics and Law: HU ZEHONG
College of Sports: ZHOU AIGUANG
School of Continuing Education: HUANG ZHIYING
School of Education Science: MO LEI
Department of Art: HUANG LIYA
Department of Chemistry: ZENG HEPING
Department of Computer Science: BAO SUSU
Department of Geography: XU XIANGJUN
Department of Mathematics: HUANG ZHIDA
Department of Music: CHENG JIANPING
Department of Tourism Management: GAN QIAOLIN

PROFESSORS

BAO, ZONGTI, Physics and Telecommunications Engineering
BIN, JINHUA, Life Sciences
CHANG, HONGSEN, Physics and Telecommunications Engineering
CHEN, HAO, Physics and Telecommunications Engineering
CHEN, HUOWANG, Computer Science
CHEN, JUNFANG, Physics and Telecommunications Engineering
CHEN, QI, Sports Science
CHEN, XIANGLIN, Life Sciences
CHEN, XINMIN, Economics and Management
CHEN, YAOSHENG, Economics and Management
CHEN, YONGSHAO, Mathematics
CHEN, YUQUN, Mathematics
CHEN, ZHANGHE, Life Sciences
DENG, SHUXUN, Sports Science
DING, SHIJIN, Mathematics
DING, XIN, Educational Information Technology
DONG, WULUN, Economics and Management
FANG, XINGQI, Economics and Management
FENG, YOUHE, Mathematics
GAN, QIAOLIN, Tourism Management
GAO, SHIAN, Mathematics

HAO, XUANMING, Sports Science
HE, ZHENGJIANG, Physics and Telecommunications Engineering
HU, LIAN, Physics and Telecommunications Engineering
HU, XIAOMING, Sports Science
HUANG, KUANROU, Sports Science
HUANG, LIREN, Mathematics
HUANG, WENFANG, Life Sciences
HUANG, YUSHAN, Sports Science
LI, DONGFENG, Life Sciences
LI, HONGQING, Life Sciences
LI, JIANYING, Economics and Management
LI, JIDONG, Economics and Management
LI, KEDONG, Educational Information Technology
LI, LING, Life Sciences
LI, SHAOSHAN, Life Sciences
LI, SHIJIE, Mathematics
LI, WEISHAN, Chemistry
LI, WEN, Mathematics
LI, YIJUN, Sports Science
LI, YONGJIE, Economics and Management
LI, YUNLIN, Educational Information Technology
LIN, CHANGHAO, Mathematics
LIN, YONG, Economics and Management
LING, JIANGHUAI, Economics and Management
LIU, BOLIAN, Mathematics
LIU, CHENGYI, Sports Science
LIU, QIONGFA, Physics and Telecommunications Engineering
LIU, SONGHAO, Optoelectronics
LIU, YUQIANG, Mathematics
LU, YUANZHEN, Sports Science
MO, LEI, Education Science
PAN, RUICHI, Life Sciences
PENG, BIYU, Economics and Management
SANG, XINMIN, Educational Information Technology
SHEN, WENHUAI, Mathematics
SUN, DAOCHUN, Mathematics
SUN, RUYONG, Life Sciences
TAN, HUA, Sports Science
TANG, SHANGYONG, Mathematics
TANG, ZAIXIN, Economics and Management
TANG, ZHILIE, Physics and Telecommunications Engineering
TONG, QINGXI, Geography
WANG, ANLI, Life Sciences
WANG, LINQUAN, Mathematics
WANG, QIAN, Sports Science
WANG, WEINA, Life Sciences
WANG, XIAOJING, Life Sciences
WENG, PEIXUAN, Mathematics
WU, CHAOLIN, Economics and Management
XIA, HUA, Physics and Telecommunications Engineering
XIAO, GUOQIANG, Sports Science
XIAO, PENG, Life Sciences
XIONG, JIANWEN, Physics and Telecommunications Engineering
XIONG, JINCHENG, Mathematics
XU, FUYING, Educational Information Technology
XU, JIE, Life Sciences
XU, XIAOYANG, Sports Science
XU, XUAN, Chemistry
YANG, WENXUAN, Sports Science
YANG, YONGHUA, Economics and Management
YE, QINGSHENG, Life Sciences
YI, FAHUAI, Mathematics
YU, YING, Chemistry
YUANG, GUANLING, Physics and Telecommunications Engineering
ZENG, HEPING, Chemistry
ZHENG, ZHI, Chemistry
ZHANG, JIANWU, Economics and Management
ZHANG, JUNPENG, Physics and Telecommunications Engineering
ZHANG, MOUCHENG, Mathematics
ZHANG, ZHIYONG, Sports Science
ZHAO, XUEZENG, Economics and Management
ZHOU, AIGUANG, Sports Science
ZHU, JIANJUN, Life Sciences
ZUO, ZAISHI, Mathematics

SOUTH CHINA UNIVERSITY OF TECHNOLOGY

Wushan, Guangzhou 510641, Guangdong
Telephone: (20) 87110000
Fax: (20) 85516386
Internet: www.scut.edu.cn

Founded 1952
State control
Academic year: September to July

President: LIU HUANBIN
Vice-Presidents: HAN DAJIAN, HUANG SHISHENG, JIA XINZHEN, LIU SHUDAO, CHEN NIANQIANG
Registrar: LIN YANGSU
Librarian: LI JIANBIN
Library of 1,350,000 vols
Number of teachers: 2,200
Number of students: 14,000

Publications: *Journal*, *Control Theory and Applications*

DEANS

School of Electric Power: WU JIE
School of Chemical Engineering: CHEN HUANQIN
School of Light Chemical Engineering and Food Engineering: GAO DAWEI
School of Business Administration: SUN DONGCHUAN
School of Materials Science and Engineering: JIA DEMIN
School of Electrical Communication: ZHU XUEFENG
School of Adult Education: WU MAN

HEADS OF DEPARTMENTS

School of Electric Power:
- Department of Power Engineering: YANG ZELIANG
- Department of Electrical Power Engineering: WU JIE

School of Chemical Engineering:
- Department of Chemical Engineering: LI ZAIZI
- Department of Applied Chemistry: ZHANG HANWEI

School of Light Chemical Engineering and Food Engineering:
- Department of Light Chemical Engineering: ZHANG HUAIYU
- Department of Food Engineering: LI TIANYI
- Department of Biological Engineering: GUO YONG

School of Business Administration:
- Department of International Business Administration: CAI GUOQIANG
- Department of International Trade: KUANG GUOLIANG
- Department of International Finance and Investment Economics: LAN HAILIN

School of Materials Science and Engineering:
- Department of Inorganic Materials Science and Technology: DENG ZAIDE
- Department of Polymer Materials Science and Technology: ZHAO YAOMING
- Department of Electrical Materials Science and Engineering: CHEN XUMING

School of Electrical Communication:
- Department of Radio Engineering: ZHANG LING
- Department of Automation: ZHU XUEFENG
- Department of Computer Science and Engineering: WANG ZUOXIN

Departments not attached to a School:
- Electric Machinery and Engineering: XIE CUNXI
- Architecture: WU QINGZOU
- Civil Engineering: CAI JIAN
- Automatic Control and Industrial Equipment Engineering: QU JINPING
- Applied Mathematics: WANG GUOQIANG
- Applied Physics: LI GUANQI
- Social Sciences: CHEN JIANXIN
- Foreign Languages: QIN XIUBAI

ATTACHED INSTITUTES

Institute of Architectural Design: Dir HE JINGTANG.

Institute of Chemical Engineering: Dir YANG XIAOXI.

Institute of Environmental Science: Dir WAN YINHUA.

Institute of Light Chemical Engineering: Dir YANG LIANSHENG.

National Key Laboratory of Pulp and Paper Engineering: Dir LU XIANHE.

SOUTH WESTERN UNIVERSITY OF FINANCE AND ECONOMICS

55 Guanghua St, Chengdu 610074, Sichuan
Telephone: (28) 7352937
Fax: (28) 7352355
Internet: www.swufe.edu.cn

Founded 1950
State control
Academic year: September to July

President: WANG YUGUO
Vice-Presidents: FENG XIDE, LIU CAN, ZHAO DEWU
Head of Graduate Department: ZHAO ZHENXIAN
Librarian: LIU FANGJIAN
Library of 1,000,000 vols
Number of teachers: 1,300
Number of students: 14,000

Publications: *The Economist*, *Finance and Economics* (6 a year)

DEANS

School of Accounting: PENG SHAOBING
School of e-Commerce: PU GUOQUAN
School of Economics: LI PING
School of Economic Information Engineering: SHAOBING SONG
School of Finance: YIN MENGBO
School of Insurance: AI SUNLIN
School of International Business: CHENG MINXUAN
School of Law: GAO JINKANG
School of Public Administration: YIN QINGSHUANG
School of Public Finance and Taxation: WANG GUOQING
School of Statistics: SHI DAIMIN
Department of Economical Mathematics: XIANG KAILI

PROFESSORS

AI, SUNLIN, Insurance
CAI, CHUN, Accounting
CAO, TINGGUI, Finance
CHEN, MINGLI, Law
CHEN, SUYU, Law
CHEN, YONGSHENG, Finance
CHEN, YUANHONG, Accounting
CHENG, MINXUAN, International Business
CHENG, QIAN, Public Finance and Taxation
DENG, GUANJUN, e-Commerce
DING, RENZHONG, Economics
DU, ZHIHAN, Economic Mathematics
FAN, XINGJIAN, Accounting
FENG, JIAN, Accounting
FENG, XIDE, Economics
FENG, YADONG, Law
FU, DAIGUO, Accounting
FU, HONGCHUN, Economics
GAO, JINKANG, Law
GUO, FUCHU, Accounting
HE, ZERONG, Finance

JIANG, LING, Economics
JIANG, YUMEI, Law
KUANG, SONG, Economic Information Engineering
LI, NANCHENG, Statistics
LI, PING, Economics
LI, SHI, Statistics
LIN, WANXIANG, Accounting
LIN, YI, Insurance
LIU, CAN, Economics
LIU, RONG, Public Finance and Taxation
LIU, SHIBAI, Economics
MA, XIAO, Public Finance and Taxation
MU, LIANGPING, Economics
NI, KEQIN, Finance
PAN, XUEMO, Accounting
PANG, HAO, Statistics
PENG, SHAOBING, Accounting
REN, ZHIJUN, Economics
SHEN, XIAOMEI, Public Administration
SHI, DAIMIN, Statistics
SUN, RONG, Insurance
TU, KAIYI, International Business
WANG, GUOQING, Public Finance and Taxation
WANG, XIANGXI, e-Commerce
WANG, YONGXI, Economics
WANG, YUGUO, Economics
WANG, ZHIAN, Accounting
XIANG, KAILI, Economic Mathematics
XIANG, RONGMEI, Statistics
XIE, JIANMIN, e-Commerce
XIE, SHENGZHI, Economic Information Engineering
XIE, ZHILONG, e-Commerce
XING, QIANGGUO, Public Administration
XU, LANG, Statistics
YIN, MENGBO, Finance
YIN, QINGSHUANG, Public Administration
YIN, YINPIN, Public Finance and Taxation
YIN, ZHONGMING, International Business
YUAN, WENPING, Economics
YUE, CAISHEN, Law
ZENG, KANGLIN, Finance
ZENG, XIAOLING, Accounting
ZHANG, HEJIN, Finance
ZHANG, KUANHAI, Economic Information Engineering
ZHANG, QIAOYUN, Finance
ZHANG, WEI, Economics
ZHANG, XINCAI, e-Commerce
ZHAO, DEWU, Accounting
ZHENG, JINGJI, Economics
ZHONG, CHENG, e-Commerce
ZHOU, GUANGDA, Statistics
ZHOU, HONGYUAN, Finance
ZHOU, QIHAI, Economic Information Engineering
ZHOU, XIAOLIN, Public Finance and Taxation
ZHU, MINGXI, Public Finance and Taxation
ZHUO, ZHI, Insurance

SOUTHEAST UNIVERSITY

Si Pai Lou 2, Nanjing 210096
Telephone: (25) 83792412
Fax: (25) 83615736
E-mail: oic@seu.edu.cn
Internet: www.seu.edu.cn
Founded 1902
State control
President: Prof. GU GUANQUN
Vice-Presidents: Prof. SUN ZAIYANG, Prof. ZOU CAIYONG, Prof. PU YUEPU, Prof. ZHAO QIMAN, Prof. ZUO WEI, Prof. YI HONG, Prof. LIU JINGNAN
Library: *c.* 1,500,000 vols
Number of teachers: 1,900
Number of students: 35,972
Publication: *Journal*

HEADS OF DEPARTMENTS

Architecture: Prof. WANG JIANGUO
Mechanical Engineering: Prof. SHI JINFEI
Power Engineering: Prof. XU ZHIGAO
Radio Engineering: Prof. YOU XIAOHU
Civil Engineering: Prof. LI AIQUN
Electronic Engineering: Prof. WANG BAOPING
Mathematics: Prof. CHEN JIANLONG
Automatic Control: Prof. LI QI
Computer Science: Prof. LUO JUNZOU
Physics: Prof. YANG YONGHONG
Biomedical Engineering: Prof. GU NING
Material Science and Engineering: Prof. JIANG JIANQING
Electrical Engineering: Prof. CHEN MING
Foreign Languages: Prof. LI XIAOXIANG
Physical Education: Prof. CHEN YU
Chemical Engineering: Prof. SUN YUEMING
Instrument Science and Engineering: Prof. ZHANG WEIGONG

DIRECTORS

Adult Education College: Prof. SUN ZAIYANG
Distance Education College: Prof. ZUO WEI
Institute of Software Engineering: Prof. WU JIEYI
Institute of Design: Prof. GE AIYONG
Institute of Planning: Prof. WANG JIANGUO
School of Economics and Management: Prof. XU KANGNING
School of Science Engineering: Prof. LU ZHUHONG
School of Communication and Transportance: Prof. WANG WEI
School of Basic Medical Science: Prof. XIE WEI
School of Clinical Medicine: Prof. LIU NAIFENG
School of Public Health: Prof. ZAI CHENKAI

ATTACHED INSTITUTES

Research Institute of Automatic Control: Dir Prof. CHEN WEINAN.
Architecture Design Institute: Dir Prof. SUN GUANGCHU.
Research Institute of Architecture: Dir Prof. QI KANG.
Centre of Material Analysis and Testing: Dir Prof. SHEN KECHENG.
Centre for Vibration Testing: Dir Prof. GAO WEI.
Research Institute of Higher Engineering Education: Dir Prof. CHEN MINGXI.
Audio and Visual Centre: Dir Prof. XU ZHIRUI.
Research Institute of Thermal Engineering: Dir Prof. ZHANG MINYAO.
State Key Laboratory for Millimetre Wave Research: Dir Prof. SUN ZHONGLIANG.
Mobile Radio and Point-to-Multipoint Communication Systems Research Laboratory (State Key Laboratory): Dir Prof. CHEN SHIXIN.
State Professional Laboratory for Computer-Aided Architectural Design: Dir Prof. QI KANG.
Laboratory of Molecular and Biomolecular Electronics: Dirs Prof. YU WEI, Prof. LU ZHUHONG.
CIMS Research Centre: Dir Prof. GU GUANQUN.
New and High Definition Display Tube Laboratory: Dir Prof. TONG LINSHU.
National Engineering Technology Centre: Dir SUN DAYOU.
Centre for Integrated Engineering: Dir Prof. CHEN DUXIN.
Oriental Culture Research Institute: Dir Dr TAO SIYAN.
Electric Light Research Centre: Dir Prof. LI GUANGAN.
Computer Network for Chinese Education and Research: .

Constituent Centres:

East China (Northern Region) Network Centre: Dir Prof. HE LIQUAN.
Jiangsu Education and Research Computer Network Centre: Dir Prof. HE LIQUAN.

SOUTHERN YANGTZE UNIVERSITY

170 Huihe Rd, Wuxi 214036, Jiangsu
Telephone: (510) 5804243
Fax: (510) 5807976
Internet: www.sytu.edu.cn
Founded 1902
State control
Academic year: September to July
President: TAO WENYI
Vice-Presidents: CHEN JIAN, FENG BIAO, JIANG ZHONGPING, LOU GUODONG, WANG WU, ZHU TUO
Head of Graduate Department: ZHANG HAO
Librarian: ZHANG YIXIN
Number of teachers: 1,504
Number of students: 19,600
Publication: *Journal of Southern Yangtze University* (editions: food and biotechnology, natural sciences, humanities and social science, 6 a year; beverage and frozen food industry, quarterly)

DEANS

School of Biotechnology: XU YAN
School of Chemical and Materials Engineering: CAO GUANGQUN
School of Commerce: FU XIANZHI
School of Communication and Control Engineering: JI ZHICHENG
School of Design: GUO WEIMIN
School of Education: CHEN MINGXUAN
School of Food Science and Technology: JIN ZHENGYU
School of Information Technology: XU WENBO
School of Law and Politics: ZHU TONGDAN
School of Literature: XU XINGHAI
School of Mechanical Engineering: ZHANG YUZHONG
School of Science: (vacant)
School of Textiles and Clothing: GAO WEIDONG
Department of Architecture: ZHU YOUGUO
Department of Art: (vacant)
Department of International Studies: GUO XIHUA
Department of Medical Science: (vacant)
Department of Physical Education: YANG RONGLIN

PROFESSORS

CAO, GUANGQUN, Chemical and Materials Engineering
CHEN, ANJUN, Mechanical Engineering
CHEN, JIAN, Biotechnology
CHEN, JIONG, Literature
CHEN, ZHENGXING, Food Science and Technology
DENG, ZIMEI, Law and Politics
DING, WEIGUO, Commerce
DING, XIAOLIN, Food Science and Technology
DONG, YUZI, Information Technology
DU, GUOCHENG, Biotechnology
FANG, HANWEN, Literature
FANG, KUANJUN, Textiles
FENG, BIAO, Food Science and Technology
GAO, WEIDONG, Textiles
GE, MINGQIAO, Textiles
GU, GUOXIAN, Biotechnology
GU, WENYING, Food Science and Technology
GU, YAOLIN, Information Technology
GU, YIFAN, Literature
GUO, SHIDONG, Food Science and Technology
HUANG, HUANCHU, Law and Politics

HUANG, WEINING, Food Science and Technology
HUANG, ZHIHAO, Literature
HUANG, ZHONGJING, Law and Politics
JIANG, BO, Food Science and Technology
JIANG, CHENGYONG, Literature
JIN, JIAN, Biotechnology
JIN, QIRONG, Biotechnology
JIN, ZHENGYU, Food Science and Technology
LE, GUOWEI, Food Science and Technology
LI, HUAZHONG, Biotechnology
LI, SHIGUO, Mechanical Engineering
LI, WEIJIANG, Biotechnology
LIU, HUANMING, Law and Politics
LUN, SHIYI, Biotechnology
MA, JIANGUO, Food Science and Technology
MA, QIFAN, Commerce
MAO, ZHONGGUI, Biotechnology
MENG, QING-EN, Law and Politics
PAN, BEILEI, Food Science and Technology
QIU, AIYONG, Food Science and Technology
QUAN, WENHAI, Biotechnology
SHAO, JIYONG, Commerce
SHI, YONGHUI, Food Science and Technology
SIMA, NAN, Literature
SUN, HONG, Literature
SUN, YANTANG, Information Technology
SUN, ZHIHAO, Biotechnology
SUN, ZHOUNIAN, Literature
TANG, JIAN, Food Science and Technology
TAO, BOHUA, Literature
TAO, WENYI, Biotechnology
WANG, SHITONG, Information Technology
WANG, WU, Biotechnology
WANG, YONGFENG, Literature
WANG, ZHANG, Food Science and Technology
WANG, ZHENGXIANG, Biotechnology
WANG, ZHIWEI, Mechanical Engineering
WU, GE, Commerce
WU, GEMING, Literature
WU, PEIZONG, Biotechnology
WU, XIANZHANG, Biotechnology
XIA, WENSHUI, Food Science and Technology
XIE, ZHENRONG, Law and Politics
XU, WENBO, Information Technology
XU, XINGHAI, Literature
XU, YAN, Biotechnology
XU, ZHENGYUAN, Information Technology
YAO, HUIYUAN, Food Science and Technology
YAO, JINMING, Literature
YU, SHIYING, Food Science and Technology
YUAN, HUIXIN, Mechanical Engineering
YUAN, ZHENHUI, Law and Politics
ZENG, YOUXIN, Commerce
ZHANG, GENYI, Food Science and Technology
ZHANG, HEGUAN, Commerce
ZHANG, JIWEN, Information Technology
ZHANG, KECHANG, Biotechnology
ZHANG, MIN, Food Science and Technology
ZHANG, QIUJU, Mechanical Engineering
ZHANG, XINCHANG, Mechanical Engineering
ZHANG, XINGYUAN, Biotechnology
ZHANG, XIQING, Mechanical Engineering
ZHANG, YIXIN, Information Technology
ZHANG, YONGXIN, Literature
ZHANG, YUZHONG, Mechanical Engineering
ZHAO, GUANGAO, Biotechnology
ZHAO, JIANGUO, Biotechnology
ZHAO, YONGWU, Mechanical Engineering
ZHOU, HUIMING, Food Science and Technology
ZHOU, QING, Biotechnology
ZHOU, WUCHUN, Literature
ZHU, TONGDAN, Law and Politics
ZHU, ZHIFENG, Textiles
ZHUGE, HONGYUN, Literature
ZHUGE, JIAN, Biotechnology

SOUTHWEST AGRICULTURAL UNIVERSITY

Beipei, Chongqing, 400716 Sichuan
Telephone: (23) 68251276
Fax: (23) 68250942
E-mail: headmaster@swau.edu.cn
Internet: www.swau.edu.cn

Founded 1950
Academic year: September to July

President: WANG XIAOJIA
Vice-Presidents: DING ZHONGMIN, WANG YONGCAI, XIANG ZHONGHUAI, ZHANG JIAYE
Head of Graduate Department: ZHOU LUWEI
Librarian: LUO YUNZHONG

Library of 1,290,000 vols
Number of teachers: 958
Number of students: 190,000

Publications: *Journal* (editions: natural sciences, philosophy and social sciences, 6 a year), *South China Fruits* (6 a year)

DEANS

College of Agriculture and Life Science: LI JIANA
College of Animal Science and Technology: NIE KUI
College of Basic Technology Science: XU DENGYI
College of Economics and Trade: WANG ZHAO
College of Engineering: CHEN JIAN
College of Fisheries Science: ZHENG SHUMING
College of Food Science: LI HONGJUN
College of Foreign Language: LI HANG
College of Horticulture and Landscape: YIN KELIN
College of Humanities and Social Science: (vacant)
College of Information: YU JIANQIAO
College of Plant Protection: XIAO CHONGGANG
College of Resources and the Environment: HUANG JIANGUO
College of Sericulture and Biotechnology: WU DAYANG

PROFESSORS

CHEN, BIN, Plant Protection
CHEN, JIAN, Horticulture and Landscape
CHEN, ZONGDAO, Food Science
DAI, SIRUI, Economics and Trade
DUAN, YUCHUAN, Economics and Trade
HE, RONG, Fisheries Science
HUANG, JIANGUO, Resources and the Environment
HUANG, TONGLING, Plant Protection
JIANG, SHUNAN, Plant Protection
KAN, JIANQUAN, Food Science
LI, HANG, Foreign Languages
LI, HONGJUN, Food Science
LI, JIANA, Agriculture and Life Sciences
LI, LONGSHU, Plant Protection
LI, MINGYANG, Horticulture and Landscape
LI, XIAOMIN, Animal Science and Technology
LI, YUEMIN, Animal Science and Technology
LI, YUNRUI, Plant Protection
LI, ZHENGGUO, Food Science
LIANG, GUOLU, Agriculture and Life Sciences
LIU, JIANHU, Fisheries Science
LIU, QINJIN, Food Science
LIU, YINGHONG, Plant Protection
LU, CHENG, Sericulture and Biotechnology
LUO, YONGHUANG, Animal Science and Technology
NIE, KUI, Animal Science and Technology
RAN, GUANGHE, Economics and Trade
TAN, WANZHONG, Resources and the Environment
TANG, WEISHENG, Foreign Languages
WANG, JINJUN, Plant Protection
WANG, XIAOJIA, Horticulture and Landscape
WANG, XITONG, Economics and Trade
WANG, YONGCAI, Animal Science and Technology
WANG, ZHAO, Economics and Trade
WU, DAYANG, Sericulture and Biotechnology
WU, MINGZHU, Horticulture and Landscape
WU, QING, Fisheries Science
WU, YINGLI, Animal Science and Technology
XIA, QINGYOU, Sericulture and Biotechnology
XIE, DETI, Agriculture and Life Sciences
XIE, HEFANG, Animal Science and Technology
XU, DENGYI, Basic Science and Technology
XU, MAODE, Sericulture and Biotechnology
YE, GONGQIANG, Economics and Trade
YIN, KELIN, Horticulture and Landscape
YU, JIANQIAO, Information Science
YU, QIU, Foreign Languages
YU, YONGXIONG, Animal Science and Technology
ZENG, FANKUN, Food Science
ZHANG, JIAYE, Animal Science and Technology
ZHANG, LIN, Fisheries Science
ZHANG, WEN, Horticulture and Landscape
ZHANG, XIAOYOU, Economics and Trade
ZHANG, XINGGUO, Horticulture and Landscape
ZHAO, ZHIMO, Agriculture and Life Sciences
ZHAO, ZHIMO, Plant Protection
ZHENG, SHUMING, Fisheries Science
ZHENG, YONGHUA, Fisheries Science
ZHOU, CHANGYONG, Horticulture and Landscape
ZHOU, ZEYANG, Sericulture and Biotechnology
ZHOU, ZHIQIN, Horticulture and Landscape
ZHU, LIQUAN, Horticulture and Landscape
ZHU, YONG, Sericulture and Biotechnology
ZUO, FUYUAN, Animal Science and Technology

SOUTHWEST CHINA NORMAL UNIVERSITY

Beibei, Chongqing 400715, Sichuan
Telephone: (23) 68252501
Fax: (23) 68863325
E-mail: headmaster@swnu.edu.cn
Internet: www.swnu.edu.cn

Founded 1950
Academic year: September to July

President: ZHAO YANXIU
Vice-Presidents: CHEN SHIJIAN, HE XIANGDONG, LI MING, LI XIAOLONG, SHI YAOCHU
Head of Graduate Department: CUI YANQIANG
Librarian: DUAN ZEYONG

Library of 1,400,000 vols
Number of teachers: 1,200
Number of students: 18,400

Publication: *Journal* (editions: humanities and social sciences, natural sciences, philosophy and social sciences, 6 a year)

DEANS

School of Administration: ZHANG YUEGUANG
School of Chemistry and Chemical Engineering: ZHOU GUANGMING
School of Computer and Information Science: ZHANG WEIQUN
School of Economics: ZHU ZESHAN
School of Educational Science: YANG SHANGQIU
School of Fine Arts: CHEN HANG
School of Foreign Languages: LI LI
School of History, Culture and Tourism: ZHANG MINGFU
School of Life Sciences: SUN MIN
School of Literature: LIU MINGHUA
School of Material Science and Engineering: ZENG SUMIN
School of Mathematics and Finance: CHEN GUIYUN
School of Physical Culture: XIA SIYONG
School of Physics and Electronic Information Engineering: CHEN HONG
School of Politics and Law: LUO HONGTIE
School of Psychology: ZHANG QINGLIN
School of Resources and Environmental Science: WANG JIANLI
School of Sociology, Public Administration and Management: QIN QIWEN
Conservatory of Music: DAI XIONG
Preparatory Course Department for Minority Students: HE JINYUAN

PROFESSORS

CHEN, DEMAO, Material Science and Engineering
CHEN, GUIYUN, Mathematics and Finance
CHEN, HONG, Physics and Electronic Information Engineering
CHEN, NIAN, Resources and Environmental Science
CHEN, PENG, Physics and Electronic Information Engineering
CHEN, SHIJIAN, Educational Science
CHEN, ZHIAN, Foreign Languages
CHEN, ZHIQIAN, Material Science and Engineering
CHENG, XIAOPING, Computer and Information Science
DAI, XIONG, Music
DAI, XUN, Literature
DENG, HUIWEN, Computer and Information Science
DENG, LEI, Mathematics and Finance
DENG, XIAOZHAO, Computer and Information Science
DIAO, CHENGTAI, Resources and Environmental Science
DONG, XIAOYU, Literature
DUAN, ZEYONG, Mathematics and Finance
FAN, WEI, Educational Science
FANG, YOUGUO, Literature
FENG, JIUCHAO, Physics and Electronic Information Engineering
FU, XIANGKAI, Chemistry and Chemical Engineering
GAO, FENG, Life Sciences
GUO, LIYA, Physical Culture
GUO, YUQI, Mathematics and Finance
HE, PING, Life Sciences
HE, ZONGMEI, Literature
HU, CHANGHUA, Life Sciences
HU, CHANGLIN, History, Culture and Tourism
HUANG, CHENGZHI, Chemistry and Chemical Engineering
HUANG, JINGHONG, Resources and Environmental Science
HUANG, RONGSHENG, Politics and Law
HUANG, XITING, Psychology
HUANG, YUMING, Chemistry and Chemical Engineering
JIA, ZHIGAO, Foreign Languages
JIANG, XIANQUAN, Material Science and Engineering
KUANG, MINGSHENG, Resources and Environmental Science
LAN, YONG, History, Culture and Tourism
LI, HONG, Psychology
LI, JIAN, Physics and Electronic Information Engineering
LI, JIANGUO, Computer and Information Science
LI, LI, Foreign Languages
LI, MAOKANG, Literature
LI, MING, Chemistry and Chemical Engineering
LI, NIANBING, Chemistry and Chemical Engineering
LI, QING, Material Science and Engineering
LI, RUISHAN, Material Science and Engineering
LI, SHANGWU, Foreign Languages
LI, XIAOLONG, History, Culture and Tourism
LI, YANGRONG, Mathematics and Finance
LI, YI, Literature
LIANG, JIANPING, Physical Culture
LIAO, BOQIN, Physics and Electronic Information Engineering
LIAO, ZHIHUA, Life Sciences
LIU, CUNYE, Physics and Electronic Information Engineering
LIU, DESEN, Physics and Electronic Information Engineering
LIU, DIANZHI, Psychology
LIU, FENG, Computer and Information Science
LIU, GUANGYUAN, Physics and Electronic Information Engineering
LIU, JIARONG, Foreign Languages
LIU, LIHUI, Foreign Languages
LIU, MINGHUA, Literature
LIU, SHAOPU, Chemistry and Chemical Engineering
LIU, YIBING, Administration
LIU, YUNYAN, Educational Science
LU, HUAYU, History, Culture and Tourism
LU, JINGHUA, Material Science and Engineering
LU, RUIHUA, Physics and Electronic Information Engineering
LUO, HONGQUN, Chemistry and Chemical Engineering
LUO, HUIDI, Computer and Information Science
LUO, LINGFEI, Life Sciences
LUO, YIMIN, Foreign Languages
LUO, YUEJIA, Psychology
NIE, CHAOYI, Material Science and Engineering
PENG, ZUOXIANG, Mathematics and Finance
QIN, QIWEN, Sociology, Public Administration and Management
QIN, ZHIHUI, Physical Culture
QIU, DAOCHI, Resources and Environmental Science
QIU, YUHUI, Computer and Information Science
RAN, YANGQIANG, Physics and Electronic Information Engineering
REN, QINGQUAN, Physical Culture
SHI, HUI, Resources and Environmental Science
SONG, NAIQING, Mathematics and Finance
SUN, MIN, Life Sciences
SUN, QIANG, Physics and Electronic Information Engineering
TAN, CHAOXIAN, Foreign Languages
TAN, FENG, Life Sciences
TANG, CHUNLEI, Mathematics and Finance
TANG, YUNMING, Life Sciences
WAN, BENQIANG, Chemistry and Chemical Engineering
WANG, BENCHAO, Literature
WANG, DEQING, Educational Science
WANG, DESHOU, Life Sciences
WANG, DONGZHE, Material Science and Engineering
WANG, JIA, Computer and Information Science
WANG, JIANLI, Resources and Environmental Science
WANG, LI, Resources and Environmental Science
WANG, QIAN, Physics and Electronic Information Engineering
WANG, WENDI, Mathematics and Finance
WANG, XIAOXUN, History, Culture and Tourism
WANG, YING, Chemistry and Chemical Engineering
WANG, ZHIPING, Physical Culture
WEI, GANG, Life Sciences
WEN, SILONG, Music
WEN, XU, Foreign Languages
WU, JIANHUA, History, Culture and Tourism
WU, ZHENGMAO, Physics and Electronic Information Engineering
XIA, CONGDE, Physical Culture
XIA, GUANGQIONG, Physics and Electronic Information Engineering
XIA, SIYONG, Physical Culture
XIAO, GUOQIANG, Computer and Information Science
XIAO, ZHEN, Computer and Information Science
XIE, JIANPING, Life Sciences
XIE, SHIYOU, Resources and Environmental Science
XIE, XIAOJUN, Life Sciences
XIONG, ZUHONG, Physics and Electronic Information Engineering
XU, DEJIN, Foreign Languages
XU, GANG, Resources and Environmental Science
XU, HONGQUAN, Literature
XU, HUI, Educational Science
XU, JIAFU, History, Culture and Tourism
XU, SHIDUAN, History, Culture and Tourism
XU, SONGYAN, History, Culture and Tourism
XU, ZENGHONG, History, Culture and Tourism
YANG, BINGJUN, Foreign Languages
YANG, CHANGYONG, Educational Science
YANG, QINGYUAN, Resources and Environmental Science
YANG, SHANGQIU, Educational Science
YANG, SICONG, Literature
YANG, XIAOPING, Educational Science
YANG, XINGLI, Resources and Environmental Science
YI, LIANYUN, Educational Science
YIN, MINGXIANG, Foreign Languages
YU, JI, Literature
YUAN, DAOXIAN, Resources and Environmental Science
YUAN, RUO, Chemistry and Chemical Engineering
YUAN, SUIHUA, Physics and Electronic Information Engineering
ZENG, BO, Life Sciences
ZENG, SUMIN, Material Science and Engineering
ZHANG, GUANGXIANG, Mathematics and Finance
ZHANG, JINFU, Psychology
ZHANG, MINGFU, History, Culture and Tourism
ZHANG, MINGJU, Resources and Environmental Science
ZHANG, PING, Material Science and Engineering
ZHANG, QINGLIN, Psychology
ZHANG, QITANG, Life Sciences
ZHANG, QIZHONG, Life Sciences
ZHANG, SHIYA, Educational Science
ZHANG, SHUFANG, Music
ZHANG, WEIQUN, Computer and Information Science
ZHANG, WEN, History, Culture and Tourism
ZHANG, XIANJUN, Chemistry and Chemical Engineering
ZHANG, YAOGUANG, Life Sciences
ZHANG, YOUGANG, Music
ZHANG, YUANLI, Mathematics and Finance
ZHANG, ZHUJUN, Chemistry and Chemical Engineering
ZHANG, ZILI, Computer and Information Science
ZHAO, LINGLI, Literature
ZHAO, YI, History, Culture and Tourism
ZHENG, RUILUN, Physics and Electronic Information Engineering
ZHENG, YONG, Psychology
ZHONG, ZHANGCHENG, Life Sciences
ZHOU, GUANGMING, Chemistry and Chemical Engineering
ZHOU, HONG, Educational Science
ZHOU, MINGMING, Chemistry and Chemical Engineering
ZHOU, YI, Educational Science
ZHU, CE, Computer and Information Science
ZHU, DEQUAN, Educational Science

SOUTHWEST JIAOTONG UNIVERSITY

111 North 1, Er Huan Rd, Chengdu 610031, Sichuan

Telephone: (28) 87600114
Fax: (28) 87600502
Internet: www.swjtu.edu.cn

Founded 1896
State control
Academic year: September to July

President: ZHOU BENKUAN
Vice-Presidents: CHEN ZHIJIAN, HUANG QING, JIANG GEFU, LIN ANLIN, PU DEZHANG, YANG LIZHONG
Head of Graduate Department: HUANG QING
Librarian: DONG DEZHEN
Number of teachers: 1,961

Number of students: 20,000
Publication: *Journal* (natural sciences, in Chinese and English, every 2 months)

DEANS

Faculty of Software: WU GUANG
College of Foreign Languages: XIA WEIRONG
College of Traffic and Transportation: ZHANG DIANYE
School of Art and Communication: WANG SHUNHONG
School of Architecture: QIU JIAN
School of Civil Engineering: LI QIAO
School of Computer and Communications Engineering: FAN PINGZHI
School of Economics and Management: JIA JIANMIN
School of Electrical Engineering: LI QUNZHEN
School of Environment Science and Engineering: LIU BAOJUN
School of Material Science and Engineering: HUANG NAN
School of Mechanical Engineering: XU MINGHENG

PROFESSORS

CAI, HUAI, Computer Science and Communications Engineering
CAI, YING, Civil Engineering
CEN, MINYI, Civil Engineering
CHE, HUIMIN, Civil Engineering
CHEN, JUNYING, Material Science and Engineering
CHEN, XIANGDONG, Computer Science and Communications Engineering
CHEN, XIAOCHUAN, Electrical Engineering
CHENG, QIANGONG, Civil Engineering
DAI, GUANGZE, Material Science and Engineering
DENG, RONGGUI, Civil Engineering
DENG, YOUQIANG, Economics and Management
DENG, YUCAI, Civil Engineering
DIAO, MINGBI, Economics and Management
FAN, HONG, Computer Software
FAN, LILI, Economics and Management
FAN, PINGZHI, Computer Science and Communications Engineering
FANG, XUMING, Computer Science and Communications Engineering
FENG, BO, Material Science and Engineering
FENG, QUANYUAN, Computer Science and Communications Engineering
FENG, XIAOYUN, Electrical Engineering
FU, YONGSHENG, Environmental Science and Engineering
GAO, BO, Civil Engineering
GAO, LONGCHANG, Economics and Management
GAO, SHIBIN, Electrical Engineering
GUAN, BAOSHU, Civil Engineering
GUO, JIN, Computer Science and Communications Engineering
GUO, YAOHUANG, Economics and Management
HE, CHUAN, Civil Engineering
HE, DAKE, Computer Science and Communications Engineering
HE, GUANGHAN, Civil Engineering
HU, HOUTIAN, Civil Engineering
HU, PEI, Economics and Management
HU, XIEWEN, Civil Engineering
HUANG, DENGSHI, Economics and Management
HUANG, DINGFU, Civil Engineering
HUANG, NAN, Material Science and Engineering
HUANG, ZEWEN, Material Science and Engineering
JIA, JIANMIN, Economics and Management
JIA, ZHIYONG, Economics and Management
JIANG, GUANLU, Civil Engineering
JIANG, QI, Material Science and Engineering
JIANG, SHIZHONG, Civil Engineering
JIN, WEIDONG, Electrical Engineering
LAO, YUANCHANG, Civil Engineering
LENG, YONGXIANG, Material Science and Engineering
LI, CHENGHUI, Civil Engineering
LI, CHENGZHONG, Computer Science and Communications Engineering
LI, JUN, Economics and Management
LI, QIAO, Civil Engineering
LI, QUNZHEN, Electrical Engineering
LI, XIAOHONG, Material Science and Engineering
LI, YADONG, Civil Engineering
LI, YONGSHU, Civil Engineering
LI, YUANFU, Civil Engineering
LI, ZHI, Electrical Engineering
LIAO, HAILI, Civil Engineering
LIU, DAN, Environmental Science and Engineering
LIU, HANWEI, Material Science and Engineering
LIU, XUEYI, Civil Engineering
LIU, ZHENGPING, Civil Engineering
LU, CHANGJIANG, 0
LU, HELIN, Civil Engineering
LU, YANG, Civil Engineering
LU, ZHENQIN, Civil Engineering
LUO, BIN, Computer Science and Communications Engineering
LUO, YUANLIANG, Economics and Management
MA, YONGQIANG, Computer Science and Communications Engineering
MOU, RUIFANG, Environmental Science and Engineering
PAN, WEI, Computer Science and Communications Engineering
PENG, DAIYUAN, Computer Science and Communications Engineering
PENG, QIYUAN, Traffic and Transportation
PU, JINHUI, Civil Engineering
QI, TAIYUE, Civil Engineering
QIAN, DONGSHENG, Civil Engineering
QIANG, YONGJIU, Civil Engineering
QIU, WENGE, Civil Engineering
QUE, YANJUN, Civil Engineering
SHI, BENSHAN, Economics and Management
SU, BIN, Computer Software
SUN, LINFU, Civil Engineering
TANG, XIAOHU, Computer Science and Communications Engineering
WAN, FUGUANG, Civil Engineering
WANG, BEN, Electrical Engineering
WANG, CHENGZHANG, Economics and Management
WANG, JIN, Material Science and Engineering
WANG, JUNSHI, Material Science and Engineering
WANG, MINGNIAN, Civil Engineering
WANG, PING, Civil Engineering
WANG, QIAN, Economics and Management
WANG, YONG, Material Science and Engineering
WONG, JIE, Material Science and Engineering
WU, GUANG, Civil Engineering
WU, GUANG, Environmental Science and Engineering
WU, GUANG, Computer Software
WU, GUANGNING, Electrical Engineering
WU, ZHENYE, Economics and Management
XIA, WEIRONG, Foreign Languages
XIAO, JIAN, Electrical Engineering
XIE, QIANG, Civil Engineering
XU, JIANPING, Electrical Engineering
YAN, CHUANPENG, Material Science and Engineering
YANG, BANGCHENG, Material Science and Engineering
YANG, CHUAN, Material Science and Engineering
YANG, JIMEI, Economics and Management
YANG, LIZHONG, Civil Engineering
YANG, LIZHONG, Environmental Science and Engineering
YANG, PING, Material Science and Engineering
YANG, SHUNSHENG, Environmental Science and Engineering
YANG, YONGGAO, Computer Software
YAO, LINGKAN, Civil Engineering
YE, ZIRONG, Economics and Management
YI, SIRONG, Civil Engineering
YIN, ZHIBEN, Computer Science and Communications Engineering
YIN, ZHIBEN, Computer Software
ZENG, HUASANG, Computer Science and Communications Engineering
ZHANG, CUIFANG, Computer Science and Communications Engineering
ZHANG, DIANYE, Traffic and Transportation
ZHANG, JIANQIANG, Environmental Science and Engineering
ZHANG, JIASHU, Computer Science and Communications Engineering
ZHANG, JICHUN, Civil Engineering
ZHANG, KUNLUN, Electrical Engineering
ZHANG, WEI, Economics and Management
ZHANG, XIYAN, Material Science and Engineering
ZHAO, LEI, Civil Engineering
ZHAO, RENDA, Civil Engineering
ZHAO, SHANRUI, Civil Engineering
ZHAO, YUGUANG, Civil Engineering
ZHENG, KAIFENG, Civil Engineering
ZHOU, DEPEI, Civil Engineering
ZHOU, GUOHUA, Economics and Management
ZHOU, RONGHUI, Computer Science and Communications Engineering
ZHOU, SHAOBING, Material Science and Engineering
ZHOU, ZHONGRONG, Material Science and Engineering
ZHOU, ZUOWAN, Material Science and Engineering
ZHU, BING, Civil Engineering
ZHU, CHANGJIN, Computer Science and Communications Engineering
ZHU, DEGUI, Material Science and Engineering
ZHU, FENG, Electrical Engineering
ZHU, WENHAO, Material Science and Engineering
ZHUANG, SHENGXIAN, Electrical Engineering

SOUTHWEST PETROLEUM INSTITUTE

Chengdu, Nanchong 637001, Sichuan
Telephone: (817) 2642301
Internet: www.swpi.edu.cn

Founded 1958
Provincial control
Academic year: September to July

President: LUO PINGYA
Vice-Presidents: DU ZHIMIN, LI YUN, LIU JIADUO, ZHANG BIN, ZHOU MAO
Librarian: REN HAO

Library of 1,473,000 vols
Number of teachers: 888
Number of students: 15,951

Publications: *Higher Petroleum Education* (4 a year), *Journal* (4 a year)

DEANS

College of Chemistry: (vacant)
College of Computer Science: (vacant)
College of Electronic Information: DU JIAN
College of Petroleum Engineering: CHEN PING
College of Resources and the Environment: SHEN ZHAOGUO
College of Software: (vacant)
School of Building Engineering: YAO ANLIN
School of Foreign Studies: (vacant)
School of Industrial and Commercial Administration: (vacant)
School of Literature: HE SHA
School of Mechanical and Electrical Engineering: (vacant)
School of NIIT Education: (vacant)

School of Resource Science and Engineering: LI CHUNFU

PROFESSORS

BENG, JUN, Resources and the Environment
CHEN, JINGSHAN, Petroleum Exploration
CHEN, PING, Petroleum Engineering
CHENG, SHIQI, Resources and the Environment
DENG, JIANMING, Petroleum Engineering
DU, ZHIMIN, Petroleum Engineering
DUAN, DARONG, Electronic Information
GUO, XIAOYANG, Petroleum Engineering
HONG, QINYU, Depositation
HU, XINGQI, Electronic Information
HUANG, BINGGUANG, Petroleum Engineering
HUANG, LINJI, Petroleum Engineering
HUANG, ZHIYU, Electronic Information
JIANG, PING, Resource Science and Engineering
KANG, YILI, Petroleum Engineering
LI, BINGYUAN, Petroleum Engineering
LI, CHANGJUN, Petroleum Engineering
LI, CHUANLIANG, Petroleum Engineering
LI, CHUNFU, Resource Science and Engineering
LI, QIAN, Petroleum Engineering
LI, SHILUN, Petroleum Engineering
LI, YINGCHUAN, Petroleum Engineering
LI, YUN, Petroleum Engineering
LI, ZHIPING, Petroleum Engineering
LIAN, ZHANGHUA, Petroleum Engineering
LIANG, ZHENG, Resource Science and Engineering
LIAO, XIMING, Resources and the Environment
LIEHUI, 0, Petroleum Engineering
LIU, CHONGJIAN, Petroleum Engineering
LUO, MINGGAO, Resources and the Environment
LUO, PINGYA, Petroleum Engineering
MA, DEKUN, Resource Science and Engineering
PU, XIAOLIN, Petroleum Engineering
QIN, QIRONG, Resources and the Environment
SHEN, ZHAOGUO, Survey and Exploration of Mineral Products
SHI, TAIHE, Petroleum Engineering
SUN, LIANGTIAN, Petroleum Engineering
WANG, TINDONG, Resources and the Environment
WANG, XINZHI, Resources and the Environment
WANG, YUAN, Petroleum Engineering
YAN, QIBIN, Survey and Exploration of Mineral Products
YANG, SHIGUANG, Electronic Information
YAO, ANLIN, Building Engineering
YUAN, ZONGMING, Petroleum Engineering
ZHANG, BAILIN, Resources and the Environment
ZHANG, FAN, Resources and the Environment
ZHANG, MINGHONG, Resource Science and Engineering
ZHANG, PENG, Resource Science and Engineering
ZHANG, TINSHAN, Resources and the Environment
ZHAO, JINZHOU, Petroleum Engineering
ZHAO, LIQIANG, Petroleum Engineering
ZHAO, LIZHI, Electronic Information
ZHOU, KAIJI, Petroleum Engineering

SOUTHWEST UNIVERSITY OF POLITICAL SCIENCE AND LAW

2 Zhuangzhi Rd, Shapingba, Chongqing 400031
Telephone: (23) 65382114
Fax: (23) 65383284
Internet: www.swupl.edu.cn

Founded 1953
Academic year: September to July

President: LONG ZONGZHI
Vice-Presidents: FU ZITANG, LI CHUNRU, LIU JUN, WANG JIANHUA
Head of Graduate Department: YANG SHUMING
Librarian: ZOU YULI

Library of 800,000 vols
Number of teachers: 1,000
Number of students: 20,000

Publications: *Contemporaneity Law School* (every 2 months), *Journal* (every 2 months)

DEANS

School of Administration: CAO DAYOU
School of Administrative Law: (vacant)
School of Applied Law: LI WEI
School of Civil and Business Law: ZHAO WANYI
School of Criminology: GUAN GUANGCHENG
School of Economic and Trade Law: TANG QINGYANG
School of Economics: LIU LUJI
School of Foreign Languages: SONG LEI
School of Law: CHEN ZHONGLIN
School of Media: ZHAO ZHONGJI
School of Politics and Public Affairs: RAN ZHI

PROFESSORS

BAI, SHENG, Administration
CAO, DAYOU, Administration
CHANG, YI, Law
CHEN, JINQUAN, Administrative Law
CHEN, WEI, Civil and Business Law
CHEN, ZHONGLIN, Law
DENG, RUIPING, Economic and Trade Law
FU, ZITANG, Economic and Trade Law
FU, ZITANG, Law
GAO, SHAOXIAN, Law
GUAN, GUANGCHENG, Criminology
HAN, TIANSEN, Economic and Trade Law
HU, GUANGZHI, Economic and Trade Law
HU, RUKUI, Politics and Public Affairs
HU, SHICHENG, Criminology
LAI, DAQING, Economic and Trade Law
LI, CHANGQI, Economic and Trade Law
LI, JINRONG, Economic and Trade Law
LI, KAIGUO, Civil and Business Law
LI, PEIZE, Law
LI, SHENGYU, Administrative Law
LI, WEI, Law Application
LI, YONGSHENG, Law
LI, ZUJUN, Law
LIAO, ZHONGHONG, Law
LIN, RUIYING, Politics and Public Affairs
LIU, LUJI, Economics
LIU, XIANGSHU, Economic and Trade Law
LONG, ZONGZHI, Law
LU, DAIFU, Economic and Trade Law
RAN, ZHI, Politics and Public Affairs
REN, ZUYAO, Economics
SHI, HUIRONG, Civil and Business Law
SONG, LEI, Foreign Languages
SONG, YUBO, Administration
SUN, CHANGYONG, Law
TIAN, PINGAN, Law
WAN, YINGZHONG, Economics
WANG, LIRONG, Law
WANG, SHIHU, Civil and Business Law
WANG, XUEHUI, Administrative Law
WEN, ZHENGBANG, Administrative Law
WU, YUE, Economic and Trade Law
XIAO, YUNSHU, Foreign Languages
XU, JINGCUN, Law
XU, MINGYUE, Economic and Trade Law
YANG, SHUMING, Economic and Trade Law
YU, RONGGEN, Law
ZENG, DAIWEI, Administrative Law
ZENG, FANYUE, Politics and Public Affairs
ZHANG, GENG, Civil and Business Law
ZHANG, QIAN, Administrative Law
ZHANG, SHIDI, Media
ZHANG, YUMIN, Civil and Business Law
ZHAO, MING, Administrative Law
ZHAO, WANYI, Civil and Business Law
ZHAO, XUEQING, Economic and Trade Law
ZHAO, ZHONGJI, Media
ZHENG, CHUANKUN, Administrative Law
ZHONG, MINGZHAO, Economic and Trade Law
ZHU, JIANHUA, Law
ZUO, KAIDA, Politics and Public Affairs

SUN YAT-SEN UNIVERSITY

135 Xingang Rd, Guangzhou 510275, Guangdong
Telephone: (20) 84111583
Fax: (20) 84039173
E-mail: adpo@sysu.edu.cn
Internet: www.sysu.edu.cn

Founded 1924
State control
Academic year: September to July

President: HUANG DAREN
Vice-Presidents: CHEN YUCHUAN, WANG JIANPING, CHEN WEILING, YAN GUANGMEI, XU YUANTONG, CHEN RUZHU, LI PING, XU JIARUI, XU NINGSHENG, LIANG QINGYIN, YU SHIYOU
Librarian: CHENG HUANWEN

Library of 4,170,000 vols
Number of teachers: 7,700
Number of students: 41,000

Publications: *Journal* (Social Sciences and Natural Sciences edns, each 4 a year), *Journal of the Graduates*, *South China Population*, *Pearl River Delta Economy*

HEADS OF SCHOOL

Graduate School: Prof. HUANG DAREN
College of Continuing Education: Prof. ZHAO GUODU
School of Humanities: Prof. CHEN CHUNSHENG
School of Chemistry and Chemical Engineering: Prof. CHEN XIAOMING
School of Environmental Science and Engineering: Prof. SUN XIAOMING
School of Foreign Languages: Prof. HUANG GUOWEN
School of Law and Political Science: Prof. REN JIANTAO
School of Life Sciences: Prof. XU ANLONG
School of Business: Prof. WEI MINGHAI
School of Information Science and Technology: Prof. HUANG JIWU
School of Physics and Engineering: Prof. XU NINGSHENG
School of Mathematics and Computational Science: Prof. ZHU XIPING
School of Geographical Science and Planning: Prof. BAO JIGANG
Lingnan (University) College: Prof. SHU YUAN
School of Pre-Clinical Medicine: Prof. XIE FUKANG
Guang Hua School of Stomatology: Prof. LING JUNQI
School of Nursing: Prof. YOU LIMING
School of Public Health: LING WENHUA
School of Overseas Educational Exchange: Prof. XU NINGSHENG

HEADS OF DEPARTMENTS

School of Humanities (tel. (20) 84113112; fax (20) 84112853; e-mail hsdcll@sysu.edu.cn; internet hera.sysu.edu.cn/chinese):

Chinese Language and Literature: Prof. OUYANG GUANG
History: Prof. LIU ZHIWEI
Anthropology: Assoc. Prof. ZHOU DAMING
Philosophy: Prof. LI HONGLEI

School of Chemistry and Chemical Engineering (tel. (20) 84113691; fax (20) 84112245; e-mail cep02@sysu.edu.cn; internet hera.sysu.edu.cn/chem/main.htm):

Chemistry: Prof. ZHU XIHAI
Applied Chemistry: Prof. DENG QINYING
Polymer and Material Science: Prof. MAI KANCHENG

School of Environmental Science and Engineering (tel. (20) 84112495; fax (20) 84113616; e-mail ee@susy.edu.cn; internet hera.sysu.edu.cn/gao/default.htm):

Atmospheric Science: Prof. FAN SHAOJIA
Environmental Science: Prof. WANG JINSAN

School of Foreign Languages (tel. (20) 84113603; fax (20) 84036782; e-mail fl04@sysu.edu.cn):

English: Prof. GAO WENPING
Foreign Languages: Prof. YANG LINGFEI
College English: Prof. FENG QIZHONG

School of Geographical Science and Planning (tel. (20) 84112486; fax (20) 84112834; e-mail ee04@sysu.edu.cn):

Urban and Regional Planning
Remote Sensing and Geographical Information Engineering
Natural Territorial Resource and Environment
Water Resources and Environment
Tourism and Recreation

School of Law (tel. (20) 84113151; fax (20) 84037920; e-mail lpdl@sysu.edu.cn; internet hera.sysu.edu.cn/pol/index.htm):

Law: Prof. HUANG JIANWU
Sociology: Prof. CAI HE

School of Life Sciences (tel. (20) 84110786; fax (20) 84036215; e-mail ls@sysu.edu.cn; internet ls.sysu.edu.cn):

Biology and Biotechnology: Prof. HUANG XUELIN
Biochemistry: Prof. ZHU SHINING
Pharmacy: Prof. YANG DEPO

School of Business (tel. (20) 84112697; fax (20) 84036924; e-mail mnh@sysu.edu.cn):

Management: Prof. LIU EPING
Accounting and Auditing: Prof. LIN BIN
Tourism and Hotel Management: Prof. ZHAN JUNCHUAN

School of Information Science and Technology (tel. (20) 84112522; fax (20) 84113673; e-mail is01@sysu.edu.cn):

Computer Science: Prof. LOU DINGJUN
Radio-electronics: Prof. LUO XIZHANG
Information Management: Prof. CHEN YONGSHENG

School of Physics and Engineering (tel. (20) 84113395; fax (20) 84113048; e-mail stdp@sysu.edu.cn; internet hera.sysu.edu.cn/physics/default.htm):

Physics: Prof. WU SHENSHANG
Applied Mechanics and Engineering: Prof. SUN MINGGUANG

School of Mathematics and Computational Science (tel. (20) 84110192; fax (20) 84037978; e-mail mcp@sysu.edu.cn; internet hera.zsu.edu.cn/math/maths.htm):

Mathematics: Prof. ZHOU XUEQIN
Scientific Computation and Computer Application: Prof. CHEN ZHONGYING

Lingnan (University) College (tel. (20) 84110198; fax (20) 84036547; e-mail ln@sysu.edu.cn):

Economics: Prof. LU JIALIU
International Business: Assoc. Prof. HUANG JINGBO
Public Finance and Taxation: Assoc. Prof. YANG WEIHUA
Finance: Assoc. Prof. LU JUN
Economic Management: Assoc. Prof. ZHANG JIANQI

School of Communication and Design (tel. and fax (20) 84112835; e-mail bdcheng@sysu.edu.cn):

New Media and Video Production
Mass Communication
Artistic Design

School of Overseas Educational Exchange (tel. (20) 84111589; fax (20) 84111587; e-mail adpohz@sysu.edu.cn):

Teaching Chinese

SUN YAT-SEN UNIVERSITY OF MEDICAL SCIENCES

74 Zhongshan Rd II, Guangzhou 510089, Guangdong
Telephone: 778223
Fax: (20) 765679
Internet: www.gzsums.edu.cn

Founded 1866
State control
Languages of instruction: Chinese, English

President: LU GUANGQI
Vice-Presidents: ZHUO DAHONG, ZHU JIAKAI, TAN XUCHANG, GU JIANHUI
Librarian: HUANG RUXUEN

Library of 545,900 vols
Number of teachers: 1,101
Number of students: 3,825 (incl. 489 postgraduates)

Publications: *Academic Journal*, *Chinese Journal of Neurology and Psychiatry*, *Chinese Journal of Nephrology*, *Chinese Journal of Microsurgery*, *New Chinese Medicine*, *Ophthalmic Science*, *Cancer*, *Family Doctor*

DEANS

School of Basic Sciences: LI GUIYUN
First School of Clinical Medicine: XIAO GUANHUI
Second School of Clinical Medicine: ZHANG XUMING
Third School of Clinical Medicine: GU CAIRAN
School of Public Health: CHENG CHENZHANG
Faculty of Stomatology: REN CAI-NIAN

There are eight research institutes, 30 research laboratories, an attached ophthalmic centre, four hospitals, and an affiliated school of nursing

TAIYUAN UNIVERSITY OF TECHNOLOGY

West Fen River Park, Taiyuan, Shanxi
Telephone: (351) 6010140
Fax: (351) 6041236
Internet: www.tyut.edu.cn

Founded 1902
Academic year: September to July

President: XIE KECHANG
Vice-Presidents: GUO MINTAI, HAO JIANGGONG, HU BOYAN, LU MING, LU ZHENGUANG, MA FUCHANG, XU BINGSHE
Head of Graduate Department: LING KAICHENG
Librarian: WANG SHENGKUN

Library of 1,830,000 vols
Number of teachers: 1,506
Number of students: 15,659

Publications: *Coal Transformation* (quarterly), *Journal* (natural sciences, 6 a year; social sciences, quarterly), *Journal of Social Science of Shanxi High Schools* (monthly), *Journal of Systemic Dialectics* (quarterly)

DEANS

College of Architecture and Environmental Engineering: (vacant)
College of Chemical Engineering and Technology: (vacant)
College of Economics Management: NIU CHONGHUAI
College of Electrical and Power Engineering: BU QINGHUA
College of Humanities: (vacant)
College of Information Engineering: XIE KEMING
College of Materials Science and Engineering: XU BINGSHE
College of Mechanical Engineering: (vacant)
College of Mining Engineering: KANG LIXUN
College of Science: (vacant)
College of Textile Engineering and Arts: (vacant)

PROFESSORS

BU, QINGHUA, Electrical and Power Engineering
CHEN, JUNJIE, Information Engineering
DUAN, FU, Information Engineering
DUAN, KANGLIAN, Mining Engineering
FANG, JINGHUA, Electrical and Power Engineering
GUO, YONGYI, Mining Engineering
HAN, FUCHUN, Electrical and Power Engineering
JIA, XIAOCHUAN, Electrical and Power Engineering
KANG, LIXUN, Mining Engineering
LI, XUEZHONG, Mining Engineering
NIU, CHONGHUAI, Economics Management
REN, PINGZHAO, Electrical and Power Engineering
SONG, JIANCHENG, Electrical and Power Engineering
TIAN, QUZHEN, Mining Engineering
WANG, HANBIN, Economics Management
ZHANG, JIANPING, Economics Management
ZHAO, YIFANG, Mining Engineering
ZHAO, YUHUAI, Electrical and Power Engineering

TIANJIN CONSERVATORY OF MUSIC

57 Eleventh Meridian Rd, Hedong District, Tianjin 300171
Telephone: 412882
Internet: www.tjcm.edu.cn

Founded 1958

President: Prof. YANG JINHAO (acting)
Vice-Presidents: Prof. CHEN JIXU, Assoc. Prof. XU YONGKUN, Assoc. Prof. SHI WEIZHENG
Librarian: Assoc. Prof. WANG ZHIJIAN

Library of 99,106 vols, 20,000 records
Number of teachers: 178
Number of students: 344 (incl. 9 postgraduates)

Publication: *Music Study and Research* (quarterly)

DEANS

Composition: Prof. CHEN ENGUANG
Vocal: Assoc. Prof. XIA ZHONGHENG
Chinese Traditional Music: Assoc. Prof. SONG GUOSHENG
Orchestra: Prof. YAN ZHENGPING
Education: Assoc. Prof. YANG LIZHONG

TIANJIN MEDICAL UNIVERSITY

22 Qi Xiang Tai Rd, Heping District, Tianjin 300070
Telephone: 341234
Fax: 319429
Internet: www.tijmu.edu.cn

Founded 1951

President: WU XIANZHONG
Vice-Presidents: CUI YITAI, FANG PEIHUA, XING KEHAO, LI JINGFU
Chief Librarian: BAI JINGWEN

Library: *c.* 284,000 vols
Number of teachers: 761
Number of students: 1,883

Publications: *Journal of Tianjin Medical College* (quarterly), *Foreign Medicine* (quarterly), *Medical Inquiry* (every 2 months), *Medical Translation* (quarterly), *Medical Education Research* (2 a year)

CHAIRMEN

Medicine: ZHANG NAIXIN
Stomatology: SHI SHUJUN
Public Health: LAI ZEMIN
Nursing: ZOU DAOHUI
Biomedical Engineering: LI YUANMING

HEADS OF DEPARTMENTS

Basic Courses of Internal Medicine: YU XIANWU
Microbiology: REN ZHONGYUAN
Pathology: ZHANG NAIXIN
Pathophysiology: TANG TE
Histology and Embryology: ZHANG YANCHENG
Parasitology: YANG SHUSEN
Physiology: ZHANG JI GUO
Biochemistry: TANG XINZHI
Pharmacology: ZHANG CAILI
Electron Microscopy: BAI JINGWEN
Immunology: PAN JUFEN
Anatomy: CHEN ZHONGXIN
Chemistry: YE QINGXIAN
Physics: SU GUANGJUN
Foreign Languages: YANG GUANGWU
Nutrition and Hygiene: WANG DUSHENG
Labour Hygiene: CHENG WEINAN
Epidemiology: GENG GUANYI

PROFESSORS

Internal Medicine:
- SHI YUSHU
- HUANG XIANGQIAN
- DU WENBIN
- ZHOU JINTAI
- YIN WEI
- HUANG TIGANG
- WANG PEIXIAN
- CHENG YUQIAN
- HUANG NAIXIA

Surgery:
- YU SONGTING
- GUO SHIFU
- LIU ZIKUAN
- WU XIANZHONG
- LI QINGRUI
- WANG PENGZHI
- DAI ZHIHUA
- DONG KEQUAN
- SHENG XIKUN

Obstetrics and Gynaecology:
- ZHAI ZHANCAN
- JIAO SHUZHU

Paediatrics:
- LIU YUJI
- HUANG HONGHAI

Ophthalmology:
- YUAN JIAQING
- WANG YANHUA
- SONG GUOXIANG
- ZHANG LIANJING
- YING SHIHAO

Oto-rhino-laryngology:
- YAN CHENGXIAN
- GUO QIXIN
- WANG YANYOU

Dermatology:
- FU ZHIYI
- SHEN JIANMING

Radiology:
- WU ENHUI
- YANG TIANEN
- LIAN ZHONGCHENG
- LI JINGXUE
- ZHAO CHANGJIANG
- HE NENGSHU

Neurology:
- XUE QINGCHENG
- CHEN SHIJUN
- JIANG DEHUA
- YANG LUCHUN
- PU PEIYU

Isotope:
- LU TIZHANG
- FANG PEIHUA
- ZHENG MIAORONG

Endocrinology:
- PANG ZHILING
- MA LIYUN
- LI LIANGE

Stomatology:
- SUN XUEMIN
- HOU ZHIYAN

ATTACHED INSTITUTE

Institute of Endocrinology: Dir GAO YUQI.

TIANJIN NORMAL UNIVERSITY

241 Weijing Rd, Tianjin 300074
Telephone: (22) 23540025
Fax: (22) 23541665
E-mail: msk@mail.tjnu.edu.cn
Internet: www.tjnu.edu.cn

Founded 1958
Academic year: September to July

President: JIN RUNCHENG
Vice-Presidents: WANG GUILIN, WANG YAOJIN, XU JIANDONG

Library of 2,140,000 vols
Number of teachers: 2,113
Number of students: 30,000

Publication: *Journal* (4 a year)

DEANS

College of Basic Education: WANG GONGLIANG
College of Biology and Chemistry: GU BINHONG
College of Chemistry and Environmental Science: (vacant)
College of Computer and Information Engineering: (vacant)
College of Economics: (vacant)
College of Education Science: GAO HENGLI
College of Foreign Languages: GU GANG
College of History and Culture: HOU JIANXIN
College of Literature: MENG ZHAOYI
College of Management: (vacant)
College of Mathematics: (vacant)
College of News and Communication: LIU WEIDONG
College of Physical Culture and Science: ZHANG JINNIAN
College of Physics and Electronic Information: CHANG XIANGRONG
College of Politics and Public Administration: GAO JIAN
Institute of Arts: SHUN GUANGJUN

PROFESSORS

BA, XINSHENG, History and Culture
BAO, YUANKAI, Arts
BI, GUANGJI, Physics and Electronic Information
CHANG, SHIYAN, Politics and Public Administration
CHEN, SHANGWEI, Politics and Public Administration
CHEN, XU, Biology and Chemistry
CHEN, YAN, Literature
CHEN, YUANLONG, Arts
CUI, FENGFU, Mathematics
DING, WEIMING, Economics
DONG, SIDAI, Politics and Public Administration
DUO, LIAN, Biology and Chemistry
FENG, JINCHENG, Biology and Chemistry
GAO, HENGWEN, Literature
GAO, JIAN, Politics and Public Administration
GAO, JIE, Management
GE, LUNHONG, Foreign Languages
GONG, ZUOMING, Chemistry and Environment Science
GU, BINHONG, Biology and Chemistry
GU, GANG, Foreign Languages
GU, WEIQING, Management
GUO, JIAN, Mathematics
GUO, QINGZHU, Foreign Languages
HAO, GUISHENG, Politics and Public Administration
HAO, JINKU, Biology and Chemistry
HE, CHENGQUAN, Chemistry and Environment Science
HONG, SONGLING, Economics
HOU, JIANXIN, History and Culture
HOU, RUNSHENG, Physical Culture and Science
LI, BAOYI, Mathematics
LI, DAPENG, Literature
LI, HUA, Literature
LI, JIECHUAN, History and Culture
LI, LONGZHU, Management
LI, PEIWU, Chemistry and Environment Science
LI, XUEZHI, History and Culture
LI, YI, Physics and Electronic Information
LI, YIJIN, Literature
LI, YUNXING, Foreign Languages
LI, ZHENGANG, Physics and Electronic Information
LIAO, QIBING, Physical Culture and Science
LIU, CHUNMAO, Management
LIU, DONGHUA, Biology and Chemistry
LIU, HONG, Economics
LIU, LILI, Biology and Chemistry
LIU, QIANG, Biology and Chemistry
LIU, SHIMING, Politics and Public Administration
LIU, WEIDONG, News and Communication
LIU, XIANGJUN, Biology and Chemistry
LIU, XIAOLAN, Biology and Chemistry
LIU, YUZHEN, Foreign Languages
LONG, XIUQING, History and Culture
LU, GUANGYUAN, Physics and Electronic Information
MA, DEPU, Politics and Public Administration
MA, JUNMING, History and Culture
MA, RUIJIANG, History and Culture
MA, YI, News and Communication
MAO, JIANYAO, Mathematics
MENG, ZHAOYI, Literature
MIU, FANGMING, Biology and Chemistry
PAN, RONG, History and Culture
PANG, ZHUOHENG, History and Culture
PENG, JINRONG, Economics
PENG, YONGKANG, Biology and Chemistry
PING, HUIYUAN, Literature
RONG, CHANGHAI, Politics and Public Administration
SHEN, LAIFAN, Arts
SHUN, HUIMIN, Economics
SHUN, QIFENG, Arts
SONG, CHANGLI, Literature
SONG, YI, Arts
TIAN, QINGJUN, Physics and Electronic Information
WAN, QUAN, Economics
WAN, TANGMING, Literature
WANG, FU, Arts
WANG, GUANGMING, Mathematics
WANG, GUOSHOU, Literature
WANG, JIANING, Foreign Languages
WANG, JINGAN, Biology and Chemistry
WANG, JINLING, Biology and Chemistry
WANG, TONGQI, Politics and Public Administration
WANG, XINHUA, Economics
WANG, XIUGE, Politics and Public Administration
WANG, YAN, Basic Education College
WANG, YAPING, History and Culture
WANG, YONGCHENG, Physics and Electronic Information
WANG, YUBEN, Mathematics
WANG, ZHENYING, Biology and Chemistry
WEI, WENYUAN, Mathematics
WEI, ZIGUANG, Biology and Chemistry
WU, CHUNHUA, Politics and Public Administration
XIA, XIAOYANG, Physics and Electronic Information

XIAO, LIJUN, History and Culture
XU, DATONG, Politics and Public Administration
XU, DELING, Economics
XU, LIMIAO, Chemistry and Environment Science
XU, RONGKUN, Arts
XU, YONGLONG, Management
XU, ZHELIN, Mathematics
YAN, YONGXIN, Management
YANG, JIALING, Biology and Chemistry
YANG, XIYUN, History and Culture
YOU, ZHEQING, Physics and Electronic Information
YU, JINCHENG, Politics and Public Administration
ZENG, YUEXIN, Physics and Electronic Information
ZHAI, CHANGMING, Politics and Public Administration
ZHANG, FUYE, Arts
ZHANG, JIER, Mathematics
ZHANG, JINGNIAN, Physical Culture and Science
ZHANG, LINJIE, Literature
ZHANG, QIYING, Economics
ZHANG, WENHUI, Biology and Chemistry
ZHANG, XIN, Biology and Chemistry
ZHANG, ZHIYONG, Physics and Electronic Information
ZHAO, DENGYING, Arts
ZHAO, JIE, Physics and Electronic Information
ZHAO, LIMING, Literature
ZHAO, LIZHU, Foreign Languages
ZHENG, LIANBING, Biology and Chemistry
ZHONG, YUXIU, Foreign Languages
ZHU, SHAOHONG, Mathematics

TIANJIN POLYTECHNIC UNIVERSITY

63 Chenglinzhuang Rd, Hedong District, Tianjin 300160
Telephone: (22) 24528000
Fax: (22) 24528001
E-mail: zxb@tjpu.edu.cn
Internet: www.tjpu.edu.cn

Founded 1958
Academic year: September to July

President: Prof. ZHANG, HONGWEI
Vice-Presidents: Prof. JIANG XIUMING, Assoc. Prof. YANG HONG, YANG JIDI, Prof. XIAO CHANGFA
Directors of International Office: Prof. CHENG, BOWENProf. LI YUXIANG
Librarian: HANG, GUANGFENG

Library of 700,000 vols, 2,100 periodicals
Number of teachers: 1,086
Number of students: 23,600

Publication: *Journal* (6 a year)

HEADS OF SCHOOLS AND COLLEGES

College of Adult Education: Prof. YANG XIULAN
College of Vocational Technology: Prof. YANG, XIULAN
School of Accounting: Prof. WEI, YAPING
School of Art Design: Prof. XU, DONG
School of Computer Technology and Automation: Prof. HANG, QUIRI
School of Economics: Prof. ZHAO, HONG
School of Foreign Languages: Assoc. Prof. YU, XIAODAN
School of Humanities and Law: Prof. ZHANG, CHUNHONG
School of Information and Communications Engineering: Prof. MIAO, CHANYUN
School of International Culture: Prof. LI YUXIANG
School of Management: Assoc. Prof. WU, ZHONGYUAN
School of Material Science and Chemical Engineering: Prof. CHENG, LI
School of Mechanical and Electronic Engineering: Prof. WU BAOLIN
School of Science: Prof. SUN MINGZHU
School of Textiles and Clothing: Prof. WANG, RUI
Institute of Function Fibre: Prof. MA, YAJING
Institute of Laser Processing: Prof. YANG, XICHEN
Institute of Membrane Technology: Prof. LI, XINMIN
Institute of Textile Composite Material: Prof. LI, JIALU

There are 38 research institutes and laboratories

TIANJIN UNIVERSITY

92 Weijin Rd, Tianjin 300072
Telephone: (22) 27406148
Fax: (22) 23358706
Internet: www.tju.edu.cn

Founded 1895
State control
Academic year: August/September to July (two semesters)

President: Prof. SHAN PING
Vice-Presidents: Prof. WANG YULIN, Prof. GAO WENXIN, Prof. YU DAOYIN, Prof. KOU JISONG, Prof. HU XIAOTANG
Secretary-General: Prof. SU QUANZHONG (Deputy)
Dean of Studies: Prof. CHEN RONGJIN
Chief for General Affairs: Prof. LI JINPU
Librarian: Prof. YANG JIACHENG

Library of 1,740,000 vols, 148,854 periodicals
Number of teachers: 2,438
Number of students: 18,000

Publications: *Journal* (quarterly), *Collection of Research Achievements*, various departmental publs

DEANS

School of Management: Prof. ZHANG SHIYING
School of Precision Instruments and Opto-Electronics Engineering: Prof. JIN SHIJIU
School of Electronic Information Engineering: RING RUNTAO
School of Architecture: Prof. ZHANG QI
School of Electrical Automation and Energy Resources Engineering: Prof. SUNG YUGENG
School of Sciences: JIANG ENYONG
School of Chemical Engineering: Prof. ZHAO XUEMING
School of Mechanical Engineering: Prof. ZHANG CE
School of Constructional Engineering: Prof. GU XIAOLU
School of Materials Science and Engineering: Prof. LI JIAJUN
School of Letters: Assoc. Prof. LIU YUSHAN
Graduate School: Prof. YU DAOYIN
School of Adult Education: Prof. CHEN RONGJIN
School of Petrochemical Engineering: Prof. CHEN HONGFANG (Dir)

DIRECTORS OF DEPARTMENTS

School of Management:
- Management Engineering: Assoc. Prof. WANG XUEQING
- Industrial Engineering: Assoc. Prof. SONG GUOFANG
- International Project Management: Assoc. Prof. LI CHANGYAN
- Engineering Economics: Assoc. Prof. FAN YICHANG
- International Enterprises Management: Prof. HE JINSHENG
- Management Information Systems: Assoc. Prof. LI MINQIANG

School of Precision Instruments and Opto-Electronics Engineering:
- Precision Instruments Engineering: Assoc. Prof. LIN YUCHI
- Opto-Electronics Information Engineering: Prof. CHEN CAIHE
- Biomedical Engineering and Scientific Instrumentation: Prof. FAN SHIFU

School of Electronic Information Engineering:
- Electronic Information Technology: ZHAO YAXING
- Computer Science and Technology: HE PILIAN
- Microelectronics: WU XIAWAN

School of Architecture:
- Architecture: Assoc Prof. ZHANG YUKUN
- Urban Planning: Assoc. Prof. YUN YINGXIA

School of Electrical Automation and Energy Resources Engineering:
- Electrical Power Engineering: Prof. CHEN CHAOYING
- Automation: Prof. XU ZHENLIN
- Thermoenergy and Refrigeration Engineering: Assoc. Prof. LI WEIYI

School of Sciences:
- Applied Mathematics: CAI GAOTING
- Applied Physics: LIN JIADI
- Applied Chemistry: TIAN YILING

School of Chemical Engineering:
- Chemical Engineering: Assoc. Prof. ZHANG FENGBAO
- Applied Chemistry and Pure Chemical Engineering: Assoc. Prof. LIU DONGZHI
- Biochemical Engineering: Prof. SUN YAN
- Chemical Engineering Equipment and Machinery: Prof. CHEN XU
- Organic Synthesis and Polymer Chemical Engineering: Assoc. Prof. HAN JINYU
- Catalysis Science and Engineering: Assoc. Prof. WANG RIJIE

School of Mechanical Engineering:
- Mechanics: Prof. KANG YILAN
- Mechanical and Electronics Engineering I: Prof. HUANG TIAN
- Mechanical and Electronics Engineering II: Prof. LI WUSHEN
- Automobile Engineering: Prof. SHU GEQUN
- Mechanical Design: DONG GANG

School of Constructional Engineering:
- Civil Engineering: Prof. JIANG XINLIANG
- Environmental Engineering: Assoc. Prof. JI MIN
- Construction Equipment Engineering: Assoc. Prof. ZHANG YUFENG
- Hydraulic and Hydroelectric Construction Engineering: Assoc. Prof. LIAN JIJIAN
- Naval Engineering: Assoc. Prof. HUANG YANSHUN
- Port Engineering: Prof. LI YANBAO
- Ocean Engineering: Prof. SHI QINGZENG
- Communications and Transport Engineering: Assoc. Prof. ZHANG ZHIQIANG

School of Materials Science and Engineering:
- Inorganic Non-Metallic Materials Science and Engineering: Prof. XU TINGXIAN
- Polymer Science and Engineering: Assoc. Prof. CHENG GUOXIANG
- Metal Materials Science and Engineering: Assoc. Prof. QU YUANFANG

School of Letters:
- English: Assoc. Prof. ZHOU KERONG
- Law: Assoc. Prof. SUN ZAIYOU
- Social Sciences: Prof. ZONG WENJU
- Chinese: Assoc. Prof. MENG XIANTANG
- Foreign Languages Teaching Section for Postgraduate Students: Prof. XIA YIHU
- Japanese Teaching Section: Assoc. Prof. ZHENG YUHE
- College English Teaching Section: Assoc. Prof. JI WEIWU

ATTACHED RESEARCH INSTITUTES

Institute of Systems Engineering: Dir Prof. ZHANG WEI.

Institute of Management Science: Dir Prof. WU YUHUA.

Institute of Information and Control: Dir Assoc. Prof. WANG YIZHI.

Institute of Opto-Electronics and Precision Engineering: Dir Prof. ZHANG YIMO.

Institute of Sensor Technology: Dir Prof. WANG MINGSHI.

Institute of Illumination Technology: Dir Prof. FA SHIFU.

Institute of Opto-Electronic Measuring and Control Technology: Dir Prof. HU XIAOTANG.

Institute of Lasers and Opto-Electronics: Dir Prof. YAO JIANQUAN.

Institute of Biomedical Engineering: Dir Prof. WANG MINGSHI.

Research Centre for Opto-Electronic Information: Dir Prof. ZHANG YIMO.

Centre for Precision Instruments: Dir Senior Eng. HAN RUCONG.

State Key Laboratory for Precision Measuring Technology and Instruments: Dir Prof. YE SHENGHUA.

Laboratory for Photoelectronics and Information Engineering (National Ministry of Education): Dir Prof. YU DAOYIN.

Institute of Television and Image Formation Processing: Dir YU SILE.

Electronics Practice and Experiment Centre: Dir LI TAN.

IBM New Technology Centre: Dir SUN JIZHOU.

Institute of Architectural Design and Theory: Dir Prof. ZOU DENONG.

Institute of Architectural Science and Technology: Dir Assoc. Prof. MA JIAN.

Institute of Architectural Environmental Art: Dir Assoc. Prof. DONG YA.

Wang Xuezhong Art Research Institute: Dir Prof. WANG XUEZHONG.

Institute of Electric Power and Automation Engineering: Dir Prof. HE JIALI.

Institute of Thermoenergy Engineering: Dir Prof. MA YITAI.

Institute of Electric Power and Electronics Application Technology: Dir Prof. SUN YUGENG.

Geothermal Research and Training Centre: Dir Prof. ZHANG QI.

Centre for Modern Electrical Engineering and Electronics: Dir Assoc. Prof. ZHOU SHUTANG.

Centre for Building Automation: Dir Assoc. Prof. WU AIGUO.

Electric Power Research and Training Centre: Dir Prof. HE JIALI.

Electrical Automation Engineering Technology Centre: Dir Assoc. Prof. QIAO JIANSHENG.

Institute of Chemical Engineering: Dir Prof. ZHOU MING.

Centre for Chemical Engineering Experimentation: Dir Assoc. Prof. GUO HONGYU.

ECL Chemical Engineering Laboratory: Dir Prof. XU XI'EN.

Key Laboratory for Distillation Technology: Dir Prof. YUAN XIGANG.

Institute of Engineering Mechanics and Measuring Techniques: Dir Prof. KANG YILAN.

Institute of Advanced Manufacturing Technology: Dir Prof. HUANG TIAN.

Institute of Mechanical and Electronics Engineering: Dir Assoc. Prof. ZHANG HAIGEN.

Institute of Vehicles and Motors: Dir Prof. SHU GEQUN.

Institute of Welding Engineering Technology: Dir Prof. LI WUSHEN.

Institute of New Materials for Welding: Dir Prof. CHEN BANGGU.

Experimental Centre for Mechanical Design: Dir Prof. DONG GANG.

National Key Laboratory for Combustion Engines: Dir Prof. SU WANHUA.

Institute of Structural Engineering: Dir Prof. JIANG XINLIANG.

Institute of Environmental Engineering: Dir Assoc. Prof. JI MIN.

Institute of Hydraulic Engineering: Dir Prof. CAO ZHIXIAN.

Institute of Ocean and Naval Engineering: Dir Prof. YU JIANXING.

Institute of Geotechnical Engineering: Dir Prof. YAN SHUWANG.

Testing Centre for Structural Engineering: Dir Prof. JIANG XINLIANG.

Centre for Hydraulic Engineering Experimentation: Eng. GENG JIUYUE.

Institute of Materials Science and Engineering: Dir Prof. SHENG JING.

Institute of Advanced Ceramics: Dir Prof. YUAN QIMING.

Institute of Polymer Materials Science and Engineering: Dir Prof. YAO KANGDE.

Institute and Experimental Base for a Military Project on Ceramic Materials and Appliances: Dir Prof. XU TINGXIAN.

Analysis Centre of Tianjin University: Dir Assoc. Prof. FAN GUOLIANG.

Research Centre for Form Memorization Alloy Engineering (State Education Commission): Dir Prof. LIU WENXI.

Institute of Traditional Culture and Humanities: Dir Prof. ZONG WENJU.

Institute of Taiwan: Dir Prof. CAI JIARUI.

Centre for Science and Technology and the Study of Society: Dir Prof. WANG SHUEN.

Institute of Architectural Design: Dir Prof. YANG CHANGMING.

Tianjin Internal Combustion Engine Research Institute: Dir Prof. LI DEKUAN.

TIANJIN UNIVERSITY OF COMMERCE

East Entrance of Jinba Road, Beichen District, Tianjin 300134

Telephone: (22) 26667666
Fax: (22) 26675789
Internet: www.tjuc.edu

Founded 1980

President: Prof. LIU SHUHAN

Library of 400,000 vols, 1,817 periodicals
Number of teachers: 839
Number of students: 15,000

Publication: *University Journal*

DEANS

College of Administration: ZHANG GUOWANG
College of Biological Technology and Food Science: PANG GUANGCHANG
College of Economy and Trade: BAI LING
College of Information Engineering: LIU DUO
College of International Exchange: KOU XIAOXUAN
College of Law and Politics: SHI RUIJIE
College of Mechanical Engineering: (vacant)
College of Science: YU YILIANG
College of Tourism Administration: WANG WENJUN
School of Foreign Languages: PAUL CHILTON

TIANJIN UNIVERSITY OF LIGHT INDUSTRY

1038 Dagu Nanlu, Tianjin 300222

Telephone: (22) 8340538
Fax: (22) 8341536
E-mail: tjili@tju.edu.cn

Founded 1958
State control
Languages of instruction: Chinese, English

President: TAN GUOMIN
Vice-Presidents: YANG SHUHUI, CHANG RUXIANG, XU MINLIANG, LI JUN
Chief Administrative Officer: LI ZHENG

Library of 450,000 vols
Number of teachers: 552
Number of students: 5,109

Publication: *Journal*

Divisions of mechanical and electrical engineering, chemistry and chemical engineering, biotechnology and food technology, industrial art engineering, management and systems engineering, applied liberal arts and sciences.

TIBET UNIVERSITY

Lhasa, Tibet Autonomous Region

Telephone: (891) 6324482
E-mail: master@utibet.edu.cn
Internet: www.utibet.edu.cn

Founded 1951, as Tibet Cadres School, current name and status 1985, based on Tibet Teachers' College
State control

Library of 22,000 vols
Number of teachers: 320
Number of students: 1,400

Main degree areas: Tibetan language, Chinese and English, politics and history, mathematics and physics, chemistry, biology and geography, Tibetan art and music, economics and management..

RESEARCH CENTERS

Cosmic Rays Research Center.

Population Research Center.

China–Korea Tibetan Cultural Arts Research Center.

TONGJI MEDICAL UNIVERSITY

13 Hang Kong Lu, Wuhan, Hubei 430030

Telephone: (27) 83692777
Fax: (27) 3643050
Internet: www.tjmu.edu.cn

Founded 1907
State control
Languages of instruction: Chinese, English, German
Academic year: September to July

Chancellor: Prof. LIU SHUMAO
President: Prof. XUE DELIN
Vice-Presidents: Prof. LIU SHENGYUAN, Prof. WANG CAIYUAN, Prof. WANG XIMING, Prof. WEN LIYANG, Prof. LI GUOCHENG, Prof. WANG ZUQIN
Registrar: Prof. LUO WUJIN
Librarian: Prof. XU FENGYING (Deputy Librarian)

Library of 400,000 vols
Number of teachers: 2,692
Number of students: 7,962

Publications: *Acta Universitatis Medicinae Tongji* (Chinese and English, every 2 months), *Journal* (Chinese, quarterly), *China Higher Medical Education* (Chinese, every 2 months), various departmental publs

DIRECTORS

College of Basic Medicine: Prof. SHI YOU'EN
College of Public Health: Prof. CHEN XUEMIN
College of Pharmacy: Prof. TIAN SHIXIONG
First College of Clinical Medicine: (vacant)
Second College of Clinical Medicine: Prof. HONG GUANG XIANG
College for Continuing Medical Education: Prof. XIANG CHUNTING
Faculty of Forensic Medicine: Prof. QIN QISHENG
Faculty of Medical Library and Information Sciences: Prof. LI DAOPING (Deputy Dir)
Faculty of Foreign Languages: Prof. ZHANG HONGQING
Faculty of Social Sciences: Prof. HU JICHUN
Faculty of Maternal and Child Health: Prof. LIU XIAOXIAN
Faculty of Paediatrics: Prof. HONG GUANG-XIANG

AFFILIATED HOSPITALS

Xiehe Hospital: Dir (vacant).

Tongji Hospital: Dir Prof. HONG GUANG-XIANG.

ATTACHED INSTITUTES

Institute of Reproductive Medicine: Dir Prof. XIA WENJIA.

Institute of Organ Transplantation: Dir Prof. XUE DELIN.

Institute of Cardiovascular Diseases: Dir Prof. YANG CHENYUAN.

Institute of Basic Medicine: Dir Prof. SHI YUO'EN.

Institute of Integration of Traditional Chinese Medicine and Western Medicine: Dir Prof. HUANG GUANG YING.

Institute of Environmental Medicine: Dir Prof. CHEN XUEMIN.

Institute of Social Medicine: Dir Prof. CHEN SHIRONG.

Institute of Occupational Medicine: Dir Prof. HE HANZHEN.

Institute of Haematology: Dir Prof. SONG SHANJUN.

Institute of Hepatopathy: Dir Prof. WANG JIALONG.

Institute of Medical Education: Dir Prof. ZHOU DAIYAN.

Institute of Medical Information Science: Deputy Dir Prof. QIN HUIJI.

TONGJI UNIVERSITY

1239 Siping Rd, Shanghai 200092
Telephone: 65982200
Fax: 65028965
Internet: www.tongji.edu.cn

Founded 1907

President: WU QIDI
Vice-Presidents: GU GUOWEI, ZHENG SHILING, ZHOU ZHEN, YU XINHUI, XU ZUOZHANG, DONG CONGQI
Librarian: MA ZAITIAN

Number of teachers: 2,300 (incl. 293 professors)
Number of students: 15,500 (incl. 2,100 postgraduates)

Publications: *Tongji Journal*, several technical publications

DEANS

Graduate School: WU QIDI
Professional Education and Correspondence School: WU QIDI
College of Economics and Management: HUANG YUXIANG
College of Architecture and Urban Planning: CHEN BINZHAO
College of Structural Engineering: FAN LICHU
College of Mechanical Engineering: MAO QINGXI
College of Environmental Engineering: LIU SUIQING
College of Computer Science: XUAN GUORONG
College of Humanities and Law: DENG WEIZHI
Sino-German School: WU QIDI

HEADS OF DEPARTMENTS

Management Engineering: LIN ZHIYAN
Business Administration: WU DONGMING
Architectural Engineering: ZHAO XIUHENG
Urban Planning: CHEN BINZHAO
Road and Traffic Engineering: SUN LIJUN
Industrial Design: YIN ZHENGSHENG
Landscape and Tourism: LIU BINYI
Art and Culture: SHI JIANWEI
Building Engineering: SHI MINHUA
Bridge Engineering: YUAN WANCHENG
Automobile Engineering: CHEN LIFAN
Heat Engineering: CHEN YI
Underground Building and Engineering: YANG LINDE
Real Estate and Surveying: ZHAO CAIFU
Mechanical Engineering: XU BAOFU
Environmental Engineering: YANG HAIZHEN
Computer Science and Engineering: ZHAO YIGUN
Marine Geology and Geophysics: WANG JIALIN
Applied Mathematics: SHAO JIAYU
Materials Science and Engineering: WANG XINYOU
Physics: CHEN HONG
Chemistry: SHI XIANFA
Engineering Mechanics and Technology: ZHANG RUOJING
Foreign Languages: WANG JIASHU
German: ZHU JIANHUA
Japanese: TAN JIANHAO
Social Science: SUN QIMING
Law: WANG WEIDA
Economics and Trade: DONG JINGHUAN
Electrical Engineering: XIAO YUNSHI
Preparatory School for German Language: HANG GUOSHENG

TSINGHUA UNIVERSITY

1 Qinghuayuan, Beijing 100084
Telephone: (10) 62782015
Fax: (10) 62770349
E-mail: lbzhz@mail.tsinghua.edu.cn
Internet: www.tsinghua.edu.cn

Founded 1911 as Tsinghua Xuetang; renamed Tsinghua School 1912; university section added 1925; became National Tsinghua University 1928; re-structured 1952
Academic year: September to July

President: Prof. GU BINGLIN
Vice-Presidents: Prof. GONG KE, Prof. CEN ZHANGZHI, Prof. KANG KEJUN, Prof. WANG JINSONG, Prof. ZHANG FENGCHANG
Provost: Prof. WANG JINSONG
Librarian: XUE FANGYU

Number of teachers: 2,877
Number of students: 26,312 (incl. 12,135 graduate)

Publication: *Tsinghua Science and Technology* (every 2 months)

DEANS

Academy of Art and Design: Prof. WANG MINGZHI
Graduate School: Prof. GU BINGLIN
Institute of Nuclear and New Energy Technology: Prof. ZHANG ZUOYIN
School of Aerospace: WANG YONGZHI
School of Architecture: Prof. QIN YOUGUO
School of Civil Engineering: Prof. YUAN SI
School of Economics and Management: Prof. ZHAO CHUNJUN
School of Humanities and Social Sciences: Prof. LI QIANG
School of Information Science and Technology: Prof. GONG KE
School of Journalism and Communication: Prof. FAN JINGYI
School of Law: Prof. WANG CHENGUANG
School of Mechanical Engineering: Prof. GUO ZENGYUAN
School of Medicine: Prof. WU JIEPING
School of Public Policy and Management: Prof. CHEN QINGTAI
School of Sciences: Prof. ZHOU GUANGZHAO
Teaching and Research Division of Physical Education: Prof. CHEN WEIQIANG

HEADS OF DEPARTMENTS

Architecture: Prof. LI DEXIANG
Urban Planning: Prof. ZENG GUANGZHONG
Civil Engineering: Prof. LIU XILA
Hydraulic Engineering: Prof. LEI ZHIDONG
Environmental Engineering: Prof. HAO JIEMING
Mechanical Engineering: Prof. LU ANLI
Automobile Engineering: Prof. CHENG QUANSHI
Thermal Engineering: Prof. WU ZANSONG
Precision Instruments and Mechanology: Prof. ZHOU ZHAOYING
Electrical Engineering: Prof. HAN YINGDUO
Information Electronics: Prof. DONG ZAIWANG
Computer Science and Technology: Prof. WANG DINGXIN
Automation: Prof. HU DONGCHENG
Engineering Physics: Prof. JING ZHAOXIONG
Engineering Mechanics: Prof. QIAN ZHANGZHI
Chemical Engineering: Prof. DAI YOUYUAN
Applied Mathematics: Prof. XIAO SHUTIE
Modern Applied Physics: Prof. GU BINGLIN
Chemistry: Prof. LIAO MUZHENG
Biological Science and Technology: Prof. SUI SENFANG
Economics: Prof. LI ZINAI
Management Engineering: Prof. XU GUOHUA
Management Information Systems: Prof. ZHAO CHUNJUN
International Trade and Finance: Prof. ZHAO JIAHE
Social Sciences: Prof. LI RENHAI
Foreign Languages: Prof. CHENG MUSHENG
Chinese Language and Literature: Prof. XU BAOGEN

UNIVERSITY OF ELECTRONIC SCIENCE AND TECHNOLOGY OF CHINA

4 North Jian She Rd, Chengdu 610054, Sichuan
Telephone: (28) 3202353
Fax: (28) 3202365
E-mail: whfu@uestc.edu.cn
Internet: www.uestc.edu.cn

Founded 1956
Academic year: September to July

President: Prof. LIU SHENGGANG
Director of the International Office: Prof. FU WENHAO
Librarian: Prof. WU WEIGONG

Library of 1,000,000 vols
Number of teachers: 1,380
Number of students: 20,000 (2,000 postgraduate)

Publication: *University Journal* (6 a year)

Eight colleges, sixteen departments, ten research institutes, and six centres.

UNIVERSITY OF INTERNATIONAL BUSINESS AND ECONOMICS

10 Hui Xin East St, Chao Yang District, Beijing, 100029
Telephone: (10) 64492001
E-mail: zhaoban@uibe.edu.cn
Internet: www.uibe.edu.cn

Founded 1951
State control
Academic year: September to July

President: CHEN ZHUN MIN
Vice-Presidents: HU FU YIN, LIU YA, WANG ZHENG FU, XU ZI JIAN
Heads of Graduate Department: YANG CHANG CHUN, YANG FENG HUA
Librarian: QIU XIAO HONG

Number of teachers: 1,600
Number of students: 20,000

Publications: *International Trade Problem Research* (quarterly), *Japanese Study and Research* (quarterly), *Journal* (6 a year), *Logistics World* (quarterly)

DEANS

International College of Excellence: CEHN SU DONG
Haier Business School: ZHANG XIN MIN
School of Continuing Education: XIE YI BIN
School of Finance: WU JUN
School of Foreign Studies: YANG YAN HONG
School of Higher Vocational Education: XIE WEI FANG
School of Humanities and Politic Administration: ZHENG JUN TIAN
School of Information Technology and Management Engineering: CHEN JIN
School of Insurance: CHEN XIN
School of International Business and Economics: ZHANG XIN MIN
School of International Education: (vacant)
School of International Studies: LI PING
School of International Trade and Economics: LIN GUI JUN
School of Law: SHENG SI BAO
School of Long-Distance Education: XIE YI BIN
School of Physical Education: LI FENG QIAO
Sino-American School of International Management: LIU BAO CHENG
Sino-French School of International Management: LIU BAO CHENG
Institute of Executive Development: XU ZI JIAN
Sino-German Institute: CHEN JIAN PING

PROFESSORS

BAI, SHU QIANG, International Trade and Economics
CHANG, LI, International Studies
CHANG, YU TIAN, International Studies
CHE, HONG BO, Humanities and Political Administration
CHEN, GONG HE, Information Technology and Management Engineering
CHEN, JIAN PING, Chinesisch-Deutsches Institut
CHEN, JIN, Information Technology and Management Engineering
CHEN, XIN, Insurance
DU, QI HUA, International Trade and Economics
FAN, LI BO, International Business and Economics
FENG, LI CHENG, International Trade and Economics
FU, HUI FEN, International Business and Economics
GE, TIE YING, Foreign Studies
GUO, FEI, International Trade and Economics
GUO, MING HUA, Chinesisch-Deutsches Institut
HAN, QI, International Trade and Economics
HUANG, JING YANG, Insurance
JIA, HUAI QIN, International Business and Economics
JIA, WEN HAO, International Studies
JIANG, PING, International Business and Economics
JIANG, XIAN JING, International Studies
JIN, BING YUN, Foreign Studies
KONG, SHU HONG, International Trade and Economics
LI, AI WEN, Foreign Studies
LI, BO JIE, Chinesisch-Deutsches Institut
LI, DA FENG, Information Technology and Management Engineering
LI, PING, International Studies
LI, QING, International Trade and Economics
LI, SHI, International Trade and Economics
LI, XIAO, Information Technology and Management Engineering
LIANG, PEI, International Trade and Economics
LIN, GUI JUN, International Trade and Economics
LIN, HAN QUAN, International Business and Economics
LIU, SHU LIN, International Trade and Economics
LIU, YUAN, International Trade and Economics
LIU, ZI AN, International Business and Economics
LU, JIN YONG, International Trade and Economics
LU, YONG, Foreign Studies
MA, CHUN GUANG, International Business and Economics
MEN, MING, International Trade and Economics
RONG, ZHEN, Humanities and Political Administration
SANG, BAI CHUAN, International Trade and Economics
SHENG, SI BAO, Law
SHENG, SU PING, International Studies
SHI, YAN PING, International Trade and Economics
TANG, YI HONG, International Trade and Economics
WANG, EN MIAN, International Studies
WANG, GUAN FU, International Studies
WANG, JIAN, International Trade and Economics
WANG, LIN SHENG, International Trade and Economics
WANG, SHAO XI, International Trade and Economics
WANG, TIAN QING, Foreign Studies
WANG, XIAO LIN, International Trade and Economics
WANG, XIU LI, International Business and Economics
WANG, ZHENG FU, Chinesisch-Deutsches Institut
WU, FEN, International Studies
WU, GE, International Business and Economics
WU, JUN, Finance
XI, NING HUA, Information Technology and Management Engineering
XU, YONG BIN, Foreign Studies
XU, ZI JIAN, International Business and Economics
XUE, RONG JIU, International Trade and Economics
YANG, CHANG CHUN, International Trade and Economics
YANG, YAN HONG, Foreign Studies
YAO, LI PING, Foreign Studies
YE, DONG YA, International Trade and Economics
YU, LI JUN, International Studies
YU, XU LIAN, International Business and Economics
ZHANG, JIAN PING, International Business and Economics
ZHANG, JIE, International Business and Economics
ZHANG, JING, Foreign Studies
ZHANG, MI, Foreign Studies
ZHANG, WEI, International Trade and Economics
ZHANG, XIN MIN, International Business and Economics
ZHANG, ZUO QI, Information Technology and Management Engineering
ZHAO, JUN, International Business and Economics
ZHAO, ZHONG XIU, International Trade and Economics
ZHENG, JUN TIAN, Humanities and Political Administration
ZHU, KAI, Foreign Studies
ZHU, MING XIA, International Trade and Economics

UNIVERSITY OF INTERNATIONAL RELATIONS

12 Po Shang Cun, Hai Ding District, Beijing 250014
Telephone: (10) 62861310
Fax: (10) 62861660
Internet: www.uir.edu.cn

Founded 1949
Academic year: September to July

Number of teachers: 1,000

Schools: Science and Technology Information, Culture and Communication, Law, National Politics, National Economy, English Language, Japanese and French Language, Marxism and Leninism and Continuing Education.

UNIVERSITY OF SCIENCE AND TECHNOLOGY BEIJING

30 Xueyuan Lu, Beijing 100083
Telephone: (10) 62332312
Fax: (10) 62327283
Internet: www.ustb.edu.cn

Founded 1952, present name 1988

President: Prof. YANG TIANJUN
Vice-President: Prof. XU JINWU
Head of Foreign Relations: LIU YONGCAI

Library of 837,000 vols
Number of teachers: 2,849
Number of students: 5,122 undergraduates, 1,424 graduates

Publications: *Journal of UST Beijing*, *Higher Education Research*.

UNIVERSITY OF SCIENCE AND TECHNOLOGY OF CHINA

96 Jinzhai Rd, Hefei 230026
Telephone: (551) 3601000
Fax: (551) 3631760
E-mail: iao@ustc.ac.cn
Internet: www.ustc.edu.cn

Founded 1958 by Chinese Academy of Sciences
Academic year: September to January, March to July

President: ZHU QINGSHI
Vice-Presidents: CHENG YI, HOU JIANGUO, LI DING, LI GUODONG, XU WU
Secretary-General: WANG KEQIANG
Director of Foreign Affairs: ZHANG MENGPING

Library of 1,620,000 vols, 230,000 periodicals
Number of teachers: 3,500
Number of students: 13,186

Publications: *Chinese Journal of Low Temperature Physics*, *Education and Modernization*, *Experimental Mechanics*, *Journal*, *Journal of Chemical Physics*

HEADS OF DEPARTMENTS

Astronomy and Applied Physics: DING ZEJUN
Automation: TAN TIENIU

Chemical Physics: BAO XINHE
Chemistry: HONG MAOCHUN
Computer Science and Technology: LI GUOJIE
Earth and Space Sciences: CHEN YU
Electronic Engineering and Information Science: LIU FALIN
Electronic Science and Technology: WANG JIANYU
Foreign Languages: CUI HANJIAN
History of Science and Technology and Archaeometry: ZHU QINGSHI
Information Management and Decision Science: LIANG LIANG
Life Sciences: LIN QISHUI
Management Science: CHEN XIAOJIAN
Material Science and Engineering: LU KE
Mathematics: CHEN FALAI
Modern Mechanics: HE LINGHUI
Physics: DING ZHEJUN
Polymer Science and Engineering: WANG LIXIANG
Precision Machinery and Precision Instrumentation: WANG KEYI
Science and Technology Policy and Communications: TANG SHUKUN
Statistics and Finance: FANG ZHAOBEN
Thermal Science and Energy Engineering: JI JIE

DIRECTORS OF ATTACHED RESEARCH INSTITUTES

Advanced Research Center of Geoscience and Astronomy of the Third World Academy of Sciences: ZHENG YONGFEI.

Anhui Province High School Key Laboratory of Advanced Functional Materials: CHEN CHUSHENG.

Anhui Province High School Key Laboratory of Physical Electronics: AN QI.

Anhui Province Key Laboratory of High Performance Computing and Application: CHEN GUOLIANG.

Anhui Province Key Laboratory of Molecular Medicine: TIAN ZHIGANG.

Anhui Province Key Laboratory of Optoelectronic Science and Technology: MING HAI.

Center of Astrophysics Research: WANG TINGGUI.

Center for Childhood Amblyopia and Strabismus Research: CHEN LINYI.

Center of Nonlinear Science: GU CHAOHAO.

Center of Petroleum and Natural Gas Research: LU DETANG.

Consultation and Training Center of Thermal Safety Technology: FAN WEICHENG.

Hefei National Laboratory for Physical Sciences at the Microscale: TANG SHUXIAN.

Huawei Information Technology Institute: YE GUOHUA.

Information Processing Center: YU NENGHAI.

Institute of Applied Mechanics: WU XIAOPING.

Institute of Biomedical Engineering: FENG HUANQING.

Institute of Brain Science Research: TANG XIAOWEI.

Institute of Communication and Information Systems: ZHU JINHUN.

Institute of High Precision Technology: ZHU JIARU.

Institute of Industrial Automation: WU GANG.

Institute of Information and Decision Science: CHEN HUAPING.

Institute of Intelligent Information Technology: ZHUANG ZHENQUAN.

Institute of International Development: FENG JIANGYUAN.

Institute of International Economics: SUN JIAN.

Institute of Mathematics: SHU QIWANG.

Institute of Natural Science History: HU HUAKAI.

Institute of Network and System Integration: WANG XUFA.

Institute of Photon Technology: MING HAI.

Institute of Quantum Chemistry: XIN HOUWEN.

Institute of Science and Technology Law: SONG WEI.

Institute of Solid State Chemistry and Inorganic Membranes: MENG GUANGYAO.

Institute of Statistics: YING ZHILIANG.

Institute of Strong Laser Technology: WANG SHENGBO.

Institute of Superconductivity: LI XIAOGUANG.

Institute of Theoretical Physics: YAN MULIN.

International Institute of the Environment of the Polar Region: SUN LIGUANG.

International Institute of Modern Eyeoptics: LIU GUANGJIN.

International Institute of Science and Technology Archaeology: WANG CHANGSUI.

Joint Institute of High Energy Physics: CHEN HONGFANG.

Key Laboratory of Basic Plasma Physics: LI DING.

Key Laboratory of Bond-Selective Chemistry: ZHU QINGSHI.

Key Laboratory of Crust-Mantle Materials and Environments: ZHENG YONGFEI.

Key Laboratory of Fire Science: FAN WEICHENG.

Key Laboratory of Quantum Information: GUO GUANGCAN.

Key Laboratory of Structure Research: HOU JIANGUO.

Laboratory of Atomic and Molecular Physics: XU KEZUN.

Laboratory of Chemistry Global Dynamics: ZHENG YONGFEI.

Laboratory of Mechanical Behaviour and Design of Materials: YU JILIN.

Laboratory for Plasma Physics Research: LI DING.

Lanfan Knowledge Management Institute: TANG SHUKUN.

Microsoft Key Laboratory of Multi-Media Computing and Communication: WEI GUO.

National High Performance Computing Center at Hefei: CHEN GUOLIANG.

National Synchrotron Radiation Laboratory: CHENG LIUSI.

Research Center of Comprehensive National Strength Information Monitoring Systems: FENG JIANGYUAN.

Research Center for Green Science and Technology: ZHU QINGSHI.

Research Center of Material Science: QIAN YITAI.

Research Center of Microwave and Millimetre Wave Engineering: WANG DONGJIN.

Research Center of Smoking and Health: SU QINGDE.

Research Center of Space Science and Technology: GONG HUIXING.

Research Center for Thermal Safety Engineering and Technology: FAN WEICHENG.

Research and Development Center of e-Commerce: HUA ZHONGSHENG.

Signal Statistical Processing Center: YE ZHONGFU.

WEST CHINA CENTRE OF MEDICAL SCIENCES

17 Renminnanlu 3 Duan, Chengdu, Sichuan 610044
Telephone: (28) 85501047
Fax: (28) 85502321
E-mail: dff@wcums.ecu.cn
Internet: www.wcums.edu.cn
Founded 1910
State control; attached to Sichuan Union University
Languages of instruction: Chinese, English
Academic year: September to January, February to July
President: XIE HEPING
Vice-Presidents: ZHANG ZHAODA, LI HONG, BAO LANG
Chief Administrative Officer: BU HONG
Librarian: LI BINYAN
Library of 650,000 vols
Number of teachers: 1,057
Number of students: 4,998
Publications: *West China Journal of Stomatology*, *Journal of West China University of Medical Sciences*, *West China Journal of Pharmaceutical Sciences*, *Chinese Journal of Medical Genetics*, *West China Medical Journal*, *Chinese Journal of Ocular Fundus Diseases*, *Chinese Journal of Reparative and Reconstructive Surgery*, *Modern Preventive Medicine*

DEANS

School of Medicine: Dr SHI YINGKANG
School of Stomatology: Dr ZHOU XUEDONG
School of Public Health: Dr MA XIAO
School of Pharmacy: WANG FENGPENG
School of Basic Medical Sciences: Dr HOU YIPING
School of Continued Education: Dr HUO TINGFU

DISTINGUISHED PROFESSORS

School of Basic Medical Sciences:
- BAO LANG, Pathophysiology
- CAI MEIYING, Immunology
- CHEN HUAIQING, Biomedical Engineering
- CHEN JUNJIE, Biochemistry
- CHEN MANLING, Biochemistry
- DAI BAOMIN, Pathophysiology
- FU MINGDE, Biochemistry
- HU XIAOSHU, Parasitology
- LI RUIXIANG, Anatomy
- LIU BINGWEN, Biochemistry
- LU ZHENSHAN, Histology and Embryology
- OU KEQUN, Histology and Embryology
- WANG BOYAO, Pathophysiology
- WU LIANGFANG, Histology and Embryology
- ZHU BIDE, Histology and Embryology

West China School of Medicine:
- CAO ZEYI, Obstetrics and Gynaecology
- CAO ZHONGLIANG, Infectious Diseases
- CHEN WENBIN, Internal Medicine
- DENG XIANZHAO, Genito-Urinary Surgery
- FANG QIANXUN, Ophthalmology
- GAO LIDA, Neural Surgery
- HU TINGZE, Paediatric Surgery
- HUANG DEJIA, Diagnostic Imaging
- HUANG MINGSHENG, Psychiatry and Mental Health
- LEI BINGJUN, Infectious Diseases
- LI GANDI, Pathology

Li Xiujun, Internal Medicine
Liao Qingkui, Paediatrics
Lin Daicheng, Otolaryngology
Liu Xiehe, Psychiatry and Mental Health
Luo Chengren, Ophthalmology
Luo Chunhua, Paediatrics
Min Pengqiu, Diagnostic Imaging
Ouyang Qin, Gastroenterology
Peng Zhilan, Obstetrics and Gynaecology
Shen Wenlu, General Surgery
Shi Yingkang, Cardiological Surgery
Tang Tianzhi, Nuclear Medicine
Tang Zeyuan, Paediatrics
Wang Shilang, Obstetrics and Gynaecology
Wang Zengli, Internal Medicine
Wei Fukang, Paediatric Surgery
Xiao Lujia, General Surgery
Yan Lunan, General Surgery
Yan Mi, Ophthalmology
Yang Guanghua, Pathology
Yang Yuru, Genito-Urinary Surgery
Yang Zhiming, Orthopaedics
Zhang Zizhong, Medical Genetics
Zhang Zhaoda, General Surgery
Zhao Liansan, Infectious Diseases

School of Pharmacy:

Li Tun, Pharmaceutics
Liao Gongtie, Pharmaceutics
Lu Bin, Pharmaceutics
Wang Fengpeng, Chemistry of Natural Medicinal Products
Wang Xiankai, Pharmaceutical Chemistry
Weng Lingling, Pharmaceutical Chemistry
Xu Mingxia, Pharmaceutical Chemistry
Zheng Hu, Pharmaceutical Chemistry
Zhong Yugong, Pharmaceutical Chemistry

School of Public Health:

Li Changji
Li xiaosong, Health Statistics
Ni Zongzan
Peng Shusheng, Nutrition and Food Hygiene
Sun Mianling, Environmental Health
Wang Ruishu, Nutrition and Hygiene
Wang Zhiming, Occupational Health and Occupational Diseases
Wu Desheng, Environmental Health
Yang Shuqin, Health Statistics
Zhang Chaowu
Zhang Chenlie, Occupational Health and Occupational Diseases

School of Stomatology:

Cao Yonglie, Orthodontics
Du Chuanshi, Prosthodontics
Li Bingqu, Oral Medicine
Li Shenwei, Maxillofacial Surgery
Liu Tianjia, Oral Medicine
Luo Songjiao, Orthodontics
Mao Zhuyi, Maxillofacial Surgery
Wang Dazhang, Maxillofacial Surgery
Wang Hanzhang, Maxillofacial Surgery
Wei Zhitong, Orthodontics
Wen Yuming, Maxillofacial Surgery
Yue Songling, Oral Medicine
Zhang Yunhui, Oral Medicine
Zhao Yunfeng, Orthodontics
Zhou Xiukun, Orthodontics

Faculty of Forensic Medicine:

Wu Meiyun, Forensic Medicine

WUHAN UNIVERSITY

Wuhan 430072, Hubei
Telephone: (27) 87882547
Fax: (27) 87882661
E-mail: wupo@whu.edu.cn
Internet: www.whu.edu.cn

Founded 1893

Academic year: September to July

President: Prof. Hou Jiechang
Vice-Presidents: Prof. Wu Junpei, Prof. Chen Zhaofang, Prof. Li Wenxin, Prof. Hu Dekun, Prof. Liu Jingnan, Prof. Li Qingquan, Prof. Long Xiaole, Prof. Huang Congxin
Secretary-General: Prof. Ren Xinnian
Director of Foreign Affairs Office: Assoc. Prof. Peng Yuanjie
Librarian: Prof. Yan Jinwei

Number of teachers: 5,000
Number of students: 40,000

Publications: *Writing* (monthly), *French Studies* (every 2 years), *Journal of Mathematics* (4 a year), *Law Review* (6 a year), *Knowledge of Library Information* (4 a year), *Journal of Mathematical Medicine* (6 a year), *Journal of Audiology and Speech Pathology* (4 a year), *Stroke and Nervous Diseases* (4 a year), *Economic Review* (6 a year), *Journal of Analytical Science* (6 a year), *Journal* (Humanities edn, in Chinese; Social Sciences edn, in Chinese; Natural Sciences edn, in English; Engineering edn, in Chinese; Information Sciences edn, in English and Chinese; Medical Science edn, in Chinese)

HEADS OF SCHOOLS

Law: Prof. Zeng Lingliang
Business: Prof. Zhou Maorong
Information Management (Library and Information Science): Prof. Ma Feicheng
Foreign Languages: Prof. Wang Xiuzhen
Humanities: Prof. Guo Qiyong
Journalism and Communications: Prof. Luo Yicheng
Political Science and Management: Prof. Tan Junjiu
Public Management: Prof. Deng Dasong
International Relations: (vacant)
Mathematics and Probability: Prof. Chen Hua
Physics: Prof. Shi Jing
Chemistry and Molecular Science: Prof. Pang Daiwen
Life Science: Prof. He Guangcun
Resources and Environmental Science: Prof. Liu Yaolin
Materials Science and Engineering: (vacant)
Water Resources and Hydropower Engineering: Prof. Tan Guangming
Electrical Engineering: Prof. Chen Yunping
Dynamics and Mechanics: Prof. Wu Qingming
Urban Studies: Prof. Zhao Bing
Civil Engineering: Prof. Zhu Yiwen
Computer Science: Prof. He Yanxiang
Photoelectronics and Information Service: Prof. Ke Hengyu
Remote Sensing and Information Engineering: Prof. Wang Youchuan
Geomatics: Prof. Li Jiancheng
Medicine: Prof. Fan Mingwen
Stomatology: Prof. Fan Mingwen
Pharmacy: (vacant)
Public Health: (vacant)

ATTACHED INSTITUTES

Research Institute of Chinese Studies (3rd to 9th centuries): Dir Zhu Lei.

Research Centre of American and Canadian Economic Studies: Dir Chen Jiyong.

Research Institute of World History: Dir Hu Dekun.

Institute of French Studies: Dir Wu Hongmiao.

Research Institute of International Law: Dir Huang Jing.

Research Institute of Library and Information Science: Dir Qiu Junping.

Hubei Provincial Institute of Medical Virology: (vacant).

National Research Centre of Multimedia Software Engineering: Dir (vacant).

Research Institute of Environmental Law: Dir Cai Shouqiu.

Social Welfare Research Centre: Dir Deng Dasong.

Information Resources Research Centre: Dir Ma Faicheng.

Economic Development Research Centre: Dir Guo Xibao.

Traditional Chinese Culture Research Centre: Dir Feng Tianyu.

Research Institute of International Relations: Dir Luo Zhigang.

Yangtze Development Research School: Dir Wang Mengkui.

Research Centre for Sustainable Development of the Yangtze River Basin: Dir Wu Xinmu.

Research Centre for European Studies: Dir Zeng Lingliang.

Haide Communications Research Institute: Dirs Luo Yicheng, Zhang Jinhai.

Tourism Plan and Design Institute: Dir Zhang Wei.

Research Institute of Marxism: Dir Tao Delin.

WTO Research Centre: Dir Yu Mingyuo.

Research Centre for the Cyber Economy and Law: Dir Huang Jing.

Soft Science Research Centre: Dir Li Guang.

Research Institute of Sociology: Dir Zhou Yunqing.

Research Institute of Social Development: Dir Luo Jiaojiang.

Research Centre for Comparative Studies on Institutional Law: Dir Zhou Yezhong.

Research Centre for Comparative Studies on Criminal Law: Dir Li Xihui.

Protection Centre for the Rights of Disadvantaged Citizens: Dir Mo Hongxian.

Economic Research Centre: Dir Gu Shengzhu.

Research Institute of Technology, Economics and Management: Dir Xu Xusong.

Research Institute of Business Strategy: Dir Tan Liwen.

Higher Education Research Institute: Dir Liu Guanglin.

Research Institute of the Economic and Social History of China: Dir Chen Feng.

Research Institute of Ancient Document Studies: Dir Zong Fubang.

Research Institute of Marxist Philosophy: Dir Wang Xinyan.

Research Institute of Journalism and Communications: Dir Qing Zhixi.

Research Institute for the Mass Media in Taiwan, Hong Kong and Macao: Dir Shan Bo.

Research Institute of the Digital Library and Electronic Archives: Dir Chen Chuanfu.

Research Institute of Publishing: Dir Fang Qing.

Research Institute of Philology: Dir Cao Zhi.

Research Centre for Comparative Studies in Politics and Culture: Dir Tan Junjiu.

Research Institute of Western Literature: Dir Ren Xiaojing.

Research Institute of Historical Geography: Dir XU SHAOHUA.

Research Institute of Religious Studies: Dir DUAN DEZHI.

National Research Centre for Satellite Positioning Systems: Dir (vacant).

ME Institute of Mathematics: Dir (vacant).

ME Institute of Computer Software Engineering: Dir (vacant).

China Research Centre for Antarctic Cartography: Dir (vacant).

National Pharmaceutical Clinical Research Base: Dir (vacant).

China Typical Culture Preservation Centre: Dir (vacant).

ME Research Centre for Organosilicon Compounds and Materials Engineering: Dir (vacant).

Hubei Provincial Research Centre for Amino Acid Engineering Technology: Dir (vacant).

Wuhan Municipal Research Centre for Electrochemistry Engineering Technology: Dir (vacant).

WUHAN UNIVERSITY OF TECHNOLOGY

122 Luoshi Rd, Wuhan 430070, Hubei

Telephone: (27) 87658253
Internet: www.whut.edu.cn

Founded 1945
State control
Academic year: September to July

President: ZHOU ZUDE
Vice-Presidents: CHEN DONGSHENG, LI HAIYING, TAO DEXIN, YAN XINGPING, ZHANG LIANMENG, ZHANG QINGJIE
Librarian: XIAO JINSHENG

Library of 2,720,000 vols
Number of teachers: 2,400
Number of students: 37,000

Publication: *Journal* (editions: Management and Information Engineering; Material Sciences (in English); Social Sciences; Transportation Science and Engineering)

Schools: Economics, Material Science and Engineering, Literature and Law, International Studies, Arts and Design, Natural Sciences, Resources and Environmental Engineering, Mechatronic Engineering, Automotive Engineering, Automation, Computer Science and Technology, Information Engineering, Civil Engineering and Architecture, Transportation, Navigation, Energy and Power Engineering, Management Sciences; Departments: Logistics Engineering, Humanities, Chemical Engineering, Physical Education, Institutes: Continuing Education, Network Education

PROFESSORS

CAI, CHANGXIU, Mechanical Design and Theory
CHANG, ZHIHUA, Automotive Engineering
CHEN, BINKANG, Ship-Building and Marine Structure Design
CHEN, DINGFANG, Manufacturing Engineering and Automation
CHEN, GONGYU, Management Science and Engineering
CHEN, GUOHONG, Management Science and Engineering
CHEN, MINGZHAO, Marine Engineering
CHEN, TIEQUN, Automotive Engineering
CHEN, WEN, Material Physics and Chemistry
CUI, KERUN, Marine Engineering
DENG, CHUNAN, Automotive Engineering
DENG, MINGRAN, Management Science and Engineering
FENG, ENDE, Ship-Building and Marine Structure Design
FU, ZHENGYI, Material Processing Engineering
GAO, XIAOHONG, Marine Engineering
GONG, WENQI, Mineralogy
GU, BICHONG, Mechanical Design and Theory
HU, RONGQIANG, Mechanical Design and Theory
HU, SHUGUANG, Material Science and Engineering
HU, SHUHUA, Management Science and Engineering
JIANG, CANGRU, Structural Engineering
JIANG, DESHENG, Material Science and Engineering
JIANG, ZHENGFENG, Mechanical Design and Theory
LI, BIQING, Management Science and Engineering
LI, GANGYAN, Mechanical Design and Theory
LI, HAIYING, Management Science and Engineering
LI, LAYUAN, Transportation Information Engineering and Control
LI, QIANG, Material Physics and Chemistry
LI, SHIPU, Material Science and Engineering
LI, ZHIMING, Mechanical Design and Theory
LI, ZHUOQIU, Structural Engineering
LIN, QITAI, Mineralogy
LIN, ZONGSHOU, Material Science and Engineering
LIU, GUOXIN, Management Science and Engineering
LIU, HANXING, Material Physics and Chemistry
LIU, ZUOMING, Mechanical Design and Theory
LIU, ZUYUAN, Fluid Mechanics
LU, KAISHENG, Marine Engineering
LU, LING, Transportation Information Engineering and Control
MEI, BINGCHU, Material Processing Engineering
MO, YIMIN, Mechanical Design and Theory
NAN, CEWEN, Material Physics and Chemistry
OU YANG, SHIXI, Material Science and Engineering
PAN, CHUNXU, Material Processing Engineering
PENG, SHAOMIN, Structural Engineering
QU, WEILIAN, Structural Engineering
SHEN, CHENWU, Ship-Building and Marine Structure Design
SUN, GUOZHENG, Mechanical Design and Theory
TAO, DEXIN, Manufacturing Engineering and Automation
WAN, JUNKANG, Management Science and Engineering
WANG, CENGFANG, Ship-Building and Marine Structure Design
WANG, DEXUN, Fluid Mechanics
WANG, JIEDE, Ship-Building and Marine Structure Design
WANG, LUNKANG, Fluid Mechanics
WANG, SHAOMEI, Mechanical Design and Theory
WANG, ZHONGFAN, Automotive Engineering
WU, BOLIN, Material Physics and Chemistry
WU, DAIHUA, Structural Engineering
XIA, YUANYOU, Structural Engineering
XIAO, HANLIANG, Application Engineering for Load-Carrying Equipment
XIAO, JINSHENG, Marine Engineering
XIE, KEFAN, Management Science and Engineering
XIONG, QIANXING, Transportation Information Engineering and Control
XUE, YIYU, Automotive Engineering
YAN, SHILIN, Structural Engineering
YAN, XINGPING, Application Engineering for Load-Carrying Equipment
YAN, YUHUA, Material Physics and Chemistry
YANG, MINGZHONG, Mechanical Design and Theory
YUAN, CHUXIONG, Mineralogy
YUAN, RUNZHANG, Material Science and Engineering
ZHANG, LEWEN, Fluid Mechanics
ZHANG, LIANMENG, Material Processing Engineering
ZHANG, QINGJIE, Material Science and Engineering
ZHANG, SHIXIONG, Mineralogy
ZHANG, YOULING, Automotive Engineering
ZHANG, ZHONGPU, Mechanical Design and Theory
ZHAO, XIUJIAN, Material Physics and Chemistry
ZHONG, LUO, Structural Engineering
ZHOU, YICHEN, Marine Engineering
ZHOU, ZAOJIAN, Ship-Building and Marine Structure Design
ZHOU, ZUDE, Manufacturing Engineering and Automation
ZHU, MEIQI, Ship-Building and Marine Structure Design
ZHU, RUIGENG, Mineralogy
ZHU, XICHAN, Automotive Engineering

XIAMEN UNIVERSITY

422 Siming Rd S, Xiamen 361005, Fujian
Telephone: (592) 2182229
Fax: (592) 2086526
E-mail: xmupo@xmu.edu.cn
Internet: www.xmu.edu.cn

Founded 1921
Academic year: September to July

President: CHEN CHUANHONG
Vice-Presidents: ZHU CONGSHI, WU SHUIPENG, SUN SHIGANG, PAN SHIMO
Foreign Affairs Office: SU ZIXING
Registrar: YANG BING
Librarian: CHEN MINGGUANG

Library of 2,180,000 vols
Number of teachers: 2,589
Number of students: 12,125

Publications: *Xiamen University Journal* (philosophy and social sciences edn and natural sciences edn, both quarterly), *China's Social Economics* (quarterly)

DEANS

College of Humanities: CHEN ZHIPING
College of Foreign Languages and Cultures: LIAN SHUNENG
College of Economics: QIU HUABING
School of Management: WU SHILONG
School of Law: LIAO YIXIN
College of Art Education: WU PEIWEN
School of Chemistry and Chemical Engineering: WAN HUILIN
School of Computer and Information Engineering: CHEN HUIHUANG
School of Physics and Machinery Electronic Engineering: CHEN JINCAN
School of Oceanography and Environment: YAN DONGXING
Medical College: LIN YANLIN
College of Life Science: PEN XUANXIAN
Overseas Education College: ZHAN XINLI
Adult Education College: YANG YOUTING
Vocational Technical College: YANG SHENYUN

HEADS OF DEPARTMENTS AND INSTITUTES

College of Humanities (tel. (592) 2181932):
- Sociology: ZHANG YOUQIN
- Chinese: ZHU SHUIYONG
- History: DAI YIFENG
- Philosophy: CHEN XICHENG
- Journalism and Communication: ZHU JIANQIANG

College of Foreign Languages and Cultures (tel. (592) 2186380; fax (592) 2182476):
- Asian and European Language and Literature: FENG SHOULONG
- Foreign Languages: ZHANG LILONG
- Foreign Language Teaching: GUO YONGHUI

College of Economics (tel. (592) 2181387):
- Economics: CHEN YONGZHI
- Planning and Statistics: DAI YIYI
- Finance and Banking: LEI GENGQIANG
- International Trade: ZHANG DINGZHONG

School of Management (tel. (592) 2182873):
- Business Administration: SHEN WEITAO
- Accounting: CHEN HANWEN

School of Law (tel. (592) 2186653):
- Law: XU CONGLI
- Politics: ZHU RENXIAN

College of Art Education (tel. (592) 2182404; fax (592) 2181499):
- Music: YANG ZHEN
- Fine Arts: HE SHIYANG

School of Chemistry and Chemical Engineering (tel. (592) 2182430):
- Chemical Engineering: LI QINGBIAO
- Chemistry: ZHU YAXIAN
- Materials: FENG ZUDE

School of Computer and Information Engineering (tel. (592) 2183127):
- Computing: LU WEI
- Automation: CAI JIANLI
- Electronic Engineering: XIE TINGGUI
- Architecture: LING SHIDE

School of Physics and Machinery Electronic Engineering (tel. (592) 2182454; fax (592) 2189426):
- Physics: LIN GUOXING
- Electronic Engineering for Machinery: ZHU LIMIAO

School of Oceanography and Environment (tel. (592) 2183064):
- Oceanography: PAN WEIRAN

College of Life Science (tel. (592) 2185360; fax (592) 2186392):
- Biology: HUANG HEQING

XIAN INTERNATIONAL STUDIES UNIVERSITY

437 South Changan Rd, Xian 710061, Shanxi
Telephone: (29) 85309274
Fax: (29) 85261350
Internet: www.xisu.edu.cn

Founded 1952
Provincial control
Academic year: September to July
President: DU RUIQING
Vice-Presidents: CHU CHU, HU XISHE, LIU YUELIAN
Head of Graduate Department: YANG XIWEN
Librarian: YANG YONGCAI
Library of 901,000 vols
Publications: *Foreign Language Education* (6 a year), *Human Geography* (6 a year), *Journal of Xian Foreign Languages Institute* (4 a year)

DEANS

School of Audiovisual Communication: QIN YAMING
School of Culture and Communication: HU RUIHUA
School of Eastern Languages and Culture: ZHANG SEHNGYU
School of Economics: PAN HUIXIA
School of Tourism: DANG JINXUE
Department of French: ZHANG PING
Department of German: WEN RENBAI

PROFESSORS

DANG, JINXUE, Tourism
FENG, GUANG, Audiovisual Communication
GAO, YAOTING, German Studies
HU, RUIHUA, Culture and Communication
LI, QIUQUAN, Tourism
LIN, KAI, Audiovisual Communication
LIU, JIANQIANG, Eastern Languages and Culture
MA, YONGPING, Eastern Languages and Culture
WANG, XINGZHONG, Tourism
WANG, XINRONG, Eastern Languages and Culture
WEI, GENYUAN, Audiovisual Communication
WEN, RENBAI, German Studies
YAO, BAORONG, Tourism
YUAN, JIANPING, Russian Studies
ZHANG, BAONING, Culture and Communication
ZHANG, CONG, Culture and Communication
ZHANG, SHENGYU, Eastern Languages and Culture
ZHENG, MINGJIANG, Culture and Communication

XIAN JIAOTONG UNIVERSITY

28 West Xianning Rd, Xian 710049
Telephone: (29) 2668234
Fax: (29) 3234781
E-mail: mailxjtu@xjtu.edu.cn
Internet: www.xjtu.edu.cn

Founded 1896
State control
Academic year: September to July (two semesters)
President (vacant)
Registrar: LI NENGGUI
Administrative Officer: LIU BIN
Librarian: ZHOU JINGEN
Number of teachers: 3,241
Number of students: 26,410 (incl. 5,504 postgraduate)
Publications: *Journal* (monthly), *Applied Mechanics* (4 a year), *Engineering Mathematics* (4 a year), *Journal of Social Sciences* (4 a year), *Journal of Medical Sciences* (4 a year), *Journal of Economic Sciences* (4 a year)

DEANS

Graduate School: XU TONGMO
School of Management: XI YOUMIN
School of Mechanical Engineering: XING JIANDONG
School of Energy and Power Engineering: HUI SHEN
School of Electrical Engineering: WANG ZHAOAN
School of Electrical and Communications Engineering: ZHU SHIHUA
School of Architectural Engineering and Mechanics: CHEN YIHENG
School of Environmental and Chemical Engineering: CHENG GUANGXU
School of Materials Science and Engineering: XU KEWEI
School of Science: XU ZONGBEN
School of Humanities and Social Science: LIU YONGFU
School of Continuing Education: SUN BI
School of Life Sciences and Technology: WAN MINGXI
School of Network Education: YU DEHONG
School of Economics and Finance: XUE MOUHONG
School of Accountancy: XHANG TIANXI
School of Medical Science: YAN JIANQUN
School of Pharmacy: (vacant)
School of Stomatology: (vacant)
School of Foreign Languages: BAI YONGQUAN

There are 64 research institutes and 126 research laboratories

XIAN MEDICAL UNIVERSITY

205 Zhuquedajie, Nanjiao, Xian 710061, Shaanxi
Telephone: (29) 5261609
Fax: (29) 5267364
E-mail: mail1@irix.xamu.edu.cn

Founded 1937
Controlled by Ministry of Health
Language of instruction: Chinese
Academic year: September to January, March to July (3-year, 4-year, 5-year and 7-year courses)
President: Prof. REN HUIMIN
Vice-Presidents: Prof. FAN XIAOLI, Prof. CHEN HENGYUAN
Library Director: MA XINGFU
Number of teachers: 4,972
Number of students: 4,000
Publications: *Journal*, *Abstracts of Medicine, P.R. China* (Dermatology), *Journal of Audio-Visual Medical Education*, *Journal of Chinese Medical Ethics*, *Journal of Medical Geography Overseas*, *Journal of Medical Education in Northwest China*, *Journal of Modern TCM* (Traditional Chinese Medicine), *Journal of Maternity and Child Health Overseas*, *Journal of Pharmacy in Northwest China*, *Journal of Children's Health*, *Academic Journal of Xian Medical University* (Chinese and English editions)

DEANS

First Clinical Medical School: PAN CHENGEN
Second Clinical Medical School: CHEN JUNCHANG
Pre-clinical Medical School: GAO HONGDE
Secondary Health School: NI KAI
School of Stomatology: HU YONGSHENG
School of Pharmacy: YANG SHIMI
School of Forensic Medicine: LI SHENGBIN
School of Public Health: YAN HONG
School of Social Medicine: LI JINSUO
School of Adult Training: FENG XINZHOU
Faculty of Biomedical Engineering: JIN JIE
Faculty of Health Administration: GAO JIANMIN
Faculty of Foreign Languages: BAI YONGQUAN
Faculty of Maternal and Child Care: ZHANG MINGHUI
Faculty of Nursing: SHAO WEIWEI

PROFESSORS

BAI YONGQUAN, English
CHEN JUNCHANG, Surgery
CUI CHANGZONG, Internal Medicine
DENG YUNSHAN, Dermatology
DIAO GUIXIANG, Pathology
DING DONGNING, Chemistry
DING HUIWEN, Cardiology
DONG LEI, Digestive Medicine
FANG XIAOLI, Physiology
FENG XUELIANG, Internal Medicine
FENG YINQUN, Orthopaedics
GU JIANZHANG, Paediatrics
GUO YINGCHUN, Cardiology
HE LANGCHONG, Pharmaceutical Analysis
HU GUOYING, Isotopes
HU HAOBO, Health Administration
HU YONGSHENG, Stomatology
JI ZONGZHENG, Surgery
JIN JIE, Physics
KONG XIANGZHEN, Pathophysiology
LEI LIQUAN, Pathophysiology
LEI XIAOYING, Ultrasonic
LI GUOWEI, Surgery
LI RONG, Oncology
LI SHUXI, Digestive Medicine
LI YIMING, Surgery
LI YINGLI, Pharmacognosy
LI ZHE, Parasitology
LI ZHONGMIN, Internal Medicine
LIU HONGTAO, English
LIU HUIXI, Gynaecology and Obstetrics
LIU JINYAN, Internal Medicine
LIU SHANXI, Internal Medicine
LIU XIAOGONG, Surgery
LIU ZHIQUAN, Internal Medicine

LU GUILIN, Gynaecology and Obstetrics
LU ZHUOREN, Cardiology
MA AIQUN, Internal Medicine
MA XIUPING, Endocrine Medicine
MEI JUN, Physiology
MEN BOYUAN, Epidemics
NAN XUNYI, Urology
PAN CHENGEN, Surgery
PANG ZHIGONG, Analytical Chemistry
PIAN JANPING, Health Care of Children
QIN ZHAOYIN, Surgery
QIU SHUDONG, Histology and Embryology
QU XINZHONG, Gynaecology and Obstetrics
REN HUIMIN, Anatomy
RUAN MEISHENG, Stomatology
SHI JINGSEN, Surgery
SHI WEI, Neurology
SONG TIANBAO, Histology and Embryology
SU MIN, Pathological Anatomy
SUN NAIXUE, Ophthalmology
TAN SHENGSHUN, Dermatology
TAN TINGHUA, Physical Chemistry
WANG BAOQI, Inorganic Chemistry
WANG BINGWEN, Pharmacology
WANG HUI, History of the Communist Party
WANG JINGUI, Physical Education
WANG KUNZHENG, Orthopaedics
WANG QIANG, Stomatology
WANG SHICHEN, Internal Medicine
WANG SHIYING, Stomatology
WANG XUELIANG, Epidemics
WANG ZEZHONG, Radiology
WANG ZIMING, Urology
WU YINGYUN, Respiratory Medicine
XU WENYOU, Pharmacology
YANG DINGYI, Internal Medicine
YANG GUANGFU, Radiological Diagnosis
YE PINGAN, Anaesthesiology
YU BOLANG, Medical Image Diagnosis
YUAN BINGXIANG, Pharmacology
YUE JINSHENG, Infectious Diseases
ZHANG AHUI, Chemistry
ZHANG HUAAN, Pharmacology
ZHANG MINGHUI, Gynaecology and Obstetrics
ZHANG QUANFA, Cardiology
ZHANG SHULIN, Infectious Diseases
ZHANG YONGHAO, Parasitology
ZHANG ZHEFANG, Radiology
ZHAO GENRAN, Anatomy
ZHAO JUNYONG, Biochemistry
ZHAO ZHONGRONG, Radiology
ZHU HONGLIANG, Otorhinolaryngology
ZHU JIAQING, Cardiology

XIAN PETROLEUM INSTITUTE

18 Dian Zi Er Lu, Xian 710061, Shaanxi
Telephone: (29) 5253253
Fax: (29) 5263449

Founded 1958
Controlled by National Petroleum Corporation
Language of instruction: English
President: LIN RENZI
Vice-Presidents: XIN XIXIAN, XUE ZHONGTIAN, YANG ZHENGYI
Registrar: WANG XIAOQUAN
Librarian: XIE KUN

Library of 280,000 vols, 2,000 periodicals
Number of teachers: 558
Number of students: 4,000

Publications: *Journal* (natural science and social science editions), *Petroleum Library and Information*, *Supervision of Petroleum Industry Technology*

HEADS OF DEPARTMENTS

Petroleum Engineering: ZHONG ZONGMING
Mechanical Engineering: CHEN CHAODA
Chemical Engineering: CHEN MAOTAO
Petroleum Exploration Instruments and Automation: ZHANG LIWEI
Business Management: HU JIAN
Computer Science: WANG JIAHUA

PROFESSORS

CHEN XIAOZHENG, Petroleum Economics
FU XINGSHENG, Earth Strata Slope Angles, Well-Logging Methods and Instruments
GAO CHENGTAI, Well-testing
GAO JINIAN, Applied Electric-Hydraulic Control Technology
HU QI, Petroleum Instruments
LI DANG, Mechanism of High-Energy Gas Fracturing
LU JIAO, Petroleum Instruments
PANG JUFENG, Physics and Nuclear Well Logging
SHENG DICHENG, Walking Beam Pumping Units
WANG JIAHUA, Computers
WANG SHIQING, Mechanical Engineering
WANG YIGONG, Management Systems of Petroleum Machinery
WU KUN
WU YIJIONG, Pumping Wells
ZHANG SHAOHUAI, Drilling
ZHANG ZONGMING, Petroleum Tectonics of China
ZHAO GUANGCHANG, Economics and Management

XIAN UNIVERSITY OF ARCHITECTURE AND TECHNOLOGY

13 Yanta Rd, Xian 710055, Shaanxi
Telephone: (29) 2202121
Fax: (29) 5522471
E-mail: jianda@webmail.xauat.edu.cn
Internet: www.xauat.edu.cn

Founded 1956
Academic year: September to July

President: Prof. XU DELONG
Vice-Presidents: Prof. DUAN ZHISHAN, Prof. GAN ANSHENG, Prof. WANG XIAOCHANG, Assoc. Prof. MA JIANHUA
Head of the Graduate School: Assoc. Prof. YUAN SHOUQIAN
Librarian: Prof. LIU JIAPING

Library of 1,000,800 vols
Number of teachers: 2,100
Number of students: 22,518

Publications: *Journal* (quarterly), *Study of Higher Education, Science and Technology of Xian University of Architecture and Technology* (quarterly)

HEADS OF COLLEGES AND DEPARTMENTS

College of Architecture: Prof. LIU KECHENG
College of Civil Engineering: Prof. BAO GUOLIANG
College of Environmental and Municipal Engineering: Prof. WANG XIAOCHANG
College of Management: Prof. LUO FUZHOU
College of Metallurgy Engineering: Prof. LAN XINZHE
College of Information and Auto-control Engineering: Prof. ZHAO WENJING
College of Mechanical and Electrical Engineering: Prof. ZHANG XIAOLONG
College of Materials Science and Engineering: Prof. XU QIMING
College of Humanities and Chinese Literature: Prof. ZHANG TONGLE
College of Science: Prof. LI DONGLIANG
College of Environmental Arts: Prof. YANG HAOZHONG
College of Vocational Technology: Prof. LI HUIMIN
Department of Foreign Studies: Assoc. Prof. TANG YIFAN

XIAN UNIVERSITY OF SCIENCE AND TECHNOLOGY

58 Yanta Rd, Mid Sector, Xian 710054, Shaanxi
Telephone: (29) 5583033
Fax: (29) 5583719
E-mail: iecc@xust.sn.cn
Internet: www.xust.sn.cn

Founded 1958
Academic year: September to July

President: Prof. CHANG XINTAN
Vice-Presidents: Prof. LU JIANJUN, Prof. HAN JIANGSHUI, Prof. YANG GENGSHE, Prof. MA HONGWEI
Librarian: Prof. WANG TINGMAN

Library of 580,000 vols
Number of teachers: 750
Number of students: 14,200

Publications: *Journal* (monthly), *Higher Education Research* (every 2 months), *Scientech Talent Market* (every 2 months)

HEADS OF DEPARTMENTS

Science of Energy Resources and Engineering: Prof. XU JINGCAI
Civil Engineering: Prof. GU SHUANCHENG
Mechanical Engineering: Prof. GUO WEI
Communications Engineering: Prof. LU JIANJUN
Computer Engineering: Prof. GONG SHANGFU
Automation Engineering: Prof. WEI LI
Geological and Environmental Engineering: Prof. HOU ENKE
Basic Courses: Prof. LI YONG
Society and Science: Prof. TIAN XIAOQUAN
Materials Engineering: Prof. ZHOU ANNING
Surveying Engineering: Prof. LIANG MING
Management: Prof. ZHANG JINSUO
Foreign Languages and Literatures: Prof. YANG MEIZHONG
Physical Education: Prof. SUN QINGSHAN

XIAN UNIVERSITY OF TECHNOLOGY

5 Jinhua Rd (South), Xian 710048, Shaanxi
Telephone: (29) 82312541
Fax: (29) 83230026
E-mail: xzb@mail.xaut.edu.cn
Internet: www.xaut.edu.cn

Founded 1949; until 1993, Shaanxi Institute of Mechanical Engineering
Joint Ministry of Education and Provincial control
Academic year: September to July

President: Prof. CHEN ZHIMING
Vice-Presidents: Prof. CUI DUWU, Prof. LIU DING, Prof. FU YOUMING, Prof. ZHANG MIAOFENG
Librarian: Prof. SHI JUNPING

Library of 800,000 vols
Number of teachers: 1,050
Number of students: 26,200

Publications: *Journal of Xi'an University of Technology* (4 a year), *Journal of Shaanxi Water Power* (4 a year), *Foundry Technology* (6 a year)

DEANS

Faculty of Automation Engineering and Information Science: Prof. GAO YONG
Faculty of Computer Science and Engineering: Prof. ZHANG YIKUN
Faculty of Humanities and Social Sciences: Prof. LI QINGMING
Faculty of Management: Prof. DANG XINHUA
Faculty of Materials Science and Engineering: Prof. FAN ZHIKANG
Faculty of Mechanical Engineering: Prof. LI YAN
Faculty of Printing and Packaging Engineering: Prof. WANG JIAMIN
Faculty of Science: Prof. HE QINXIANG
Faculty of Water Conservancy and Hydroelectric Power: Prof. LUO XINGQI
Polytechnic College: Prof. WANG HUI

ATTACHED INSTITUTES

Institute of Growth Equipment for Crystals: Dir XUE KANGMEI.

Institute of Urban Economic Development Strategy: Dir Prof. CHENG ANDONG.

XIANGTAN UNIVERSITY

Yanggutang, Xiangtan 411105, Hunan
Telephone: (732) 8292130
Fax: (732) 8292282
E-mail: ecc@xtu.edu.cn
Internet: www.xtu.edu.cn

Founded 1975
State control
Language of instruction: Chinese
President: Prof. LUO HE'AN
Number of teachers: 1,309
Number of students: 31,600
Publications: *Journal* (social science and natural science editions), *Journal* (Philosophy and Social Sciences series, every 2 months), *Journal* (Natural Science series, quarterly), *Transaction of Chinese Verse* (quarterly).

XIDIAN UNIVERSITY

2 South Tai Bai Rd, Xian 710071, Shanxi
Telephone: (29) 8202221
Fax: (29) 8201620
E-mail: master@xidian.edu.cn
Internet: www.xidian.edu.cn

Founded 1937
State control
Academic year: September to July
President: DUAN BAOYAN
Vice-Presidents: CAO TIANSHUN, CHEN YONG, HAO YUE, LI RUFENG, YU NANNAN
Librarian: FAN LAIYAO
Library of 860,000 vols
Number of teachers: 1,900
Number of students: 15,000
Publication: *Journal* (editions: physical and social sciences)

DEANS

School of Computer Science and Engineering: WU BO
School of Economics and Management: ZHAO PENGWEI
School of Electronic Engineering: JIAO LICHENG
School of Humanities: ZHAO BOFEI
School of Mechatronics: JIA JIANYUAN
School of Science: (vacant)
School of Software: CHEN PING
School of Technical Physics: (vacant)
School of Telecommunications Engineering: LI JIANDONG
Institute of Physical Education: (vacant)

PROFESSORS

BAI, BAOMING, Telecommunications Engineering
CAI, XIQIAO, Software Engineering
CHEN, BOXIAO, Electronic Engineering
CHEN, JIANJUN, Mechatronic Engineering
CHEN, PING, Computer Science and Engineering
DUAN, ZHENHUA, Computer Science and Engineering
FENG, DAZHENG, Electronic Engineering
FU, FENGLIN, Telecommunications Engineering
GAO, XINBO, Electronic Engineering
GAO, YOUXING, Computer Science and Engineering
GONG, JIEMIN, Software Engineering
GONG, SHUXI, Electronic Engineering
GUO, BAOLONG, Mechatronic Engineering
HU, QIYING, Economics and Management
HUANG, LIYU, Electronic Engineering
JI, HONGBING, Electronic Engineering
JIA, JIANYUAN, Mechatronic Engineering
JIANG, ZHEXIN, Economics and Management
JIAO, LICHENG, Electronic Engineering
JIAO, YONGCHANG, Electronic Engineering
LI, BINGBING, Telecommunications Engineering
LI, HUA, Economics and Management
LI, WEIYING, Telecommunications Engineering
LI, YUSHAN, Electronic Engineering
LI, ZHIWU, Mechatronic Engineering
LIANG, CHANGHONG, Electronic Engineering
LIU, FANG, Computer Science and Engineering
LIU, HONGWEI, Electronic Engineering
LIU, HONGWEI, Science
LIU, JIAN, Software Engineering
LIU, MING, Mechatronic Engineering
LIU, QIZHONG, Electronic Engineering
LIU, ZHIJING, Computer Science and Engineering
MA, JIANFENG, Computer Science and Engineering
MA, JINPING, Electronic Engineering
NIU, ZHONGQI, Electronic Engineering
QIU, YANG, Mechatronic Engineering
QIU, YUANYING, Mechatronic Engineering
REN, ZHICHUN, Economics and Management
SHI, GUANGMING, Electronic Engineering
SUN, XIAOZI, Electronic Engineering
WANG, ANMIN, Economics and Management
WANG, BAOSHU, Computer Science and Engineering
WANG, JIALI, Mechatronic Engineering
WANG, LI, Software Engineering
WEN, XIAONI, Economics and Management
WEN, YOUKUI, Economics and Management
WEN, ZHENGZHONG, Mechatronic Engineering
WU, SHUNJUN, Electronic Engineering
XIE, YONGJUN, Electronic Engineering
XING, MENGDAO, Electronic Engineering
XU, CHUNXIANG, Economics and Management
XU, GUOHUA, Economics and Management
XU, LUPING, Electronic Engineering
YANG, WANHAI, Electronic Engineering
ZENG, PING, Computer Science and Engineering
ZENG, XINGWEN, Telecommunications Engineering
ZHANG, FUSHUN, Electronic Engineering
ZHANG, HUI, Telecommunications Engineering
ZHANG, JUNYING, Computer Science and Engineering
ZHANG, PING, Mechatronic Engineering
ZHANG, SHIXUAN, Electronic Engineering
ZHANG, SHOUHONG, Electronic Engineering
ZHANG, YONGRUI, Mechatronic Engineering
ZHAO, GUOQING, Electronic Engineering
ZHAO, KE, Mechatronic Engineering
ZHAO, PENGWEI, Economics and Management
ZHAO, WEI, Economics and Management
ZHAO, WENPING, Economics and Management
ZHAO, YIGONG, Electronic Engineering
ZHI, BOQING, Mechatronic Engineering
ZHOU, WEI, Mechatronic Engineering

XINJIANG UNIVERSITY

E-mail: wsc@xju.edu.cn14 Sheng Li Rd, Urumqi 830046, Xinjiang Uygur Autonomous Region
Telephone: (991) 8582221
Fax: (991) 8581249
E-mail: wsc@xju.edu.cn

Founded 1924; merged with Xinjiang Engineering Institute 2000
Academic year: September to July
Rector: ANIWER AMUT
Vice-Rectors: AZHAT SULITAN, ZHANG XIAOFAN, TASHPLAT TYIP
Librarian: WANG KAIYUAN
Library of 1,330,000 vols
Number of teachers: 1,830
Number of students: 39,000 (incl. 784 postgraduate)
Publication: *Xinjiang University Journal* (Natural Sciences and Social Sciences versions)
Teaching units: School of Economics and Management; College of Liberal Arts; Institute of Mathematics and Systematic Science; Institute of Life Sciences and Technology; College of Information Science and Engineering; College of Electrical Engineering; College of Construction Engineering; College of Adult Education; Department of Textile Engineering; School of Law; College of Foreign Languages; College of Chemistry and Chemical Engineering; Institute of Resources and Environmental Science; College of Mechanical Engineering; Higher Vocational and Technical College; College of Science and Technology; Department of Physics.
Research Institutes: Institute of Economics; Institute of Arid Ecology; Institute of Mathematical Theory; Institute of Demography; Institute of Applied Chemistry; Institute of Central Asian Culture; Institute of Altaic Study; Institute of Architectural Design.

YANBIAN UNIVERSITY

88 977 Gongyuan Rd, Yanji 133002, Jilin
Telephone: (433) 2713167
Fax: (433) 2719618
Internet: www.ybu.edu.cn

Founded 1949
Provincial control
Academic year: September to July
President: JIN BINMIN
Vice-Presidents: GAI TONGXIANG, LI SHUIJIN, PIAO YONGHAO, YU YONGHE
Head of Graduate Department: CUI XIONGHAN
Librarian: HAN ZHE
Library of 1,400,000 vols
Number of teachers: 1,345
Number of students: 16,447
Publications: *Chinese Studies*, *Collection of Papers on Korean Issues*, *Collection of Papers on Korean Nationality*, *Collection of Papers on North and South Korean Studies*, *Journal* (editions: agricultural, medical, sciences and engineering and social science), *Dongjiang* ('Eastern Border'), *Oriental Philosophy Research*

DEANS

College of Agriculture: ZHANG SHOUFA
College of Art: JIANG GUANGXUN
College of Chinese Language and Culture: (vacant)
College of Economics and Management: XUAN DONGRI
College of Foreign Languages: (vacant)
College of Medicine: CUI JIONGMO
Normal College: CUI CHENGRI
College of Nursing: JIN DONGXU
College of Pharmacy: CUI JIONGMO
College of Physical Education: LIU QIXIAO
College of Science and Engineering: WU XUE
College of Science and Technology: WU XUE
School of Law: CHEN ZHENMING

PROFESSORS

AN, GUOFENG, Chinese Language and Culture
BAI, HONGAI, Foreign Languages
CAI, MEIHUA, Normal College
CAO, XIULING, Chinese Language and Culture
CHEN, YANQIU, Agriculture
CUI, CHENGXUE, Normal College
CUI, RONGYI, Science and Technology
CUI, SHENGYUN, Science and Technology
CUI, TAIJI, Chinese Language and Culture

CUI, YONGCHUN, Art
FANG, HAOFAN, Normal College
FANG, MEISHAN, Art
FANG, NANZHU, Agriculture
FEI, HONGGEN, Normal College
FU, WEIJIE, Agriculture
GU, GUANGRUI, Science and Technology
GUO, ZHENPING, Science and Technology
HE, YUNPENG, Law
HUANG, ZHENJI, Chinese Language and Culture
JIANG, HAISHUN, Law
JIANG, JIJIAN, Agriculture
JIANG, LONGFAN, Normal College
JIANG, RISHAN, Science, Technology and Engineering
JIANG, YONGZHE, Physical Education
JIANG, YUN, Normal College
JIN, BINGHUO, Normal College
JIN, BINGMIN, Normal College
JIN, CHENGGAO, Normal College
JIN, CHUNZHI, Physical Education
JIN, DONGRI, Science and Technology
JIN, HAIGUO, Agriculture
JIN, HELU, Law
JIN, HEWAN, Pharmacy and Nursing
JIN, HEYAN, Normal College
JIN, HUALIN, Economics and Management
JIN, HUXIONG, Normal College
JIN, JIANGLONG, Agriculture
JIN, JISHI, Normal College
JIN, JUNCHENG, Art
JIN, KUANXIONG, Normal College
JIN, LONGZHE, Physical Education
JIN, QIANGYI, Normal College
JIN, XIANGHUA, Chinese Language and Culture
JIN, XINGGUANG, Agriculture
JIN, XINGSAN, Art
JIN, XUECHUN, Law
JIN, YINGXIONG, Physical Education
JIN, YONGCHUN, Law
JIN, YONGHAO, Science and Technology
JIN, YONGSHOU, Foreign Languages
JIN, YUANZHE, Medicine
JIN, ZHEHUA, Normal College
JIN, ZHEHUI, Foreign Languages
JIN, ZHENGYI, Normal College
JIN, ZHEZHU, Normal College
LI, AISHUN, Art
LI, BAOQI, Law
LI, CHUNYU, Pharmacy and Nursing
LI, GUANFU, Normal College
LI, MINDE, Foreign Languages
LI, MINZI, Art
LI, SHANJI, Science and Technology
LI, SHENGLONG, Art
LI, WUJI, Foreign Languages
LI, YUNJUN, Science and Technology
LI, ZONGXUN, Normal College
LIAN, ZHEMAN, Science and Technology
LIN, CHENGHU, Foreign Languages
LIN, JINSHU, Economics and Management
LIU, XIANHU, Agriculture
LU, CHENG, Agriculture
LU, LONGSHI, Agriculture
MA, JINKE, Normal College
MENG, FANPING, Medicine
NAN, CHENGYU, Foreign Languages
PAN, CHANGHE, Normal College
PIAO, CHENGXIAN, Economics and Management
PIAO, XIUHAO, Economics and Management
PU, SHIZHEN, Law
PU, TAIZHU, Normal College
PU, XIANGFAN, Science and Technology
PU, YUMING, Normal College
PU, ZHE, Medicine
PU, ZHENGYANG, Normal College
QU, BOHONG, Agriculture
QUAN, LONGHUA, Foreign Languages
QUAN, XUEXI, Normal College
QUAN, YU, Foreign Languages
QUAN, ZONGXUE, Science and Technology
SHAO, JINGBO, Science and Technology
SUN, DEBIAO, Normal College
SUN, DONGZHI, Medicine
SUN, SHU, Medicine
TIAN, GUANRONG, Science, Technology and Engineering
WANG, GUIFEN, Science and Technology
WANG, KEPING, Chinese Language and Culture
WANG, XIAOBO, Normal College
WEI, ZHIFANG, Normal College
WEN, ZHAOHAI, Normal College
WU, MINGGEN, Agriculture
WU, XUE, Science, Technology and Engineering
XIANG, KIAMING, Art
XU, JI, Normal College
XU, MINGZHE, Normal College
XU, WENYI, Medicine
XU, YUANXIAN, Law
XUAN, DONGRI, Economics and Management
YAN, CHANGGUO, Agriculture
YIN, BINGZHU, Science, Technology and Engineering
YIN, TAISHUN, Law
YU, CHUNHAI, Normal College
YU, CHUNXI, Foreign Languages
YU, YANCUN, Normal College
ZHANG, JINGZHONG, Normal College
ZHANG, MIN, Agriculture
ZHANG, SHOU, Science and Technology
ZHANG, SHOUFA, Agriculture
ZHANG, ZHENAI, Foreign Languages
ZHAO, ENHUA, Physical Education
ZHAO, JINGCHUN, Foreign Languages
ZHAO, LIANHUA, Science and Technology
ZHENG, DAHAO, Agriculture
ZHENG, RINAN, Normal College
ZHENG, XIANRI, Foreign Languages
ZHENG, YONGZHEN, Normal College
ZHOU, ZHIYUAN, Normal College

YANGZHOU UNIVERSITY

88 Daxue Rd South, Yangzhou 225009, Jiangsu
Telephone: (514) 7971850
Fax: (514) 7352262
Internet: www.yzu.edu.cn

Founded 1902
Provincial control
Academic year: September to July

President: GUO RONG
Vice-Presidents: FANG HONGJIN, FENG CHAONIAN, HU JIAXING, LIU CHAO, YANG JIADONG, ZHOU XINGUO
Head of Graduate Department: YUAN JIANLI
Librarian: ZHANG ZHENGHUI

Number of teachers: 2,000
Number of students: 46,000 (30,000 full-time, 16,000 part-time)

Publications: *Journal* (editions: higher education study, humanities and social sciences, 6 a year; agricultural and life sciences, natural sciences, 4 a year), *Journal of Taxation College of Yangzhou University* (4 a year)

DEANS

School of Agriculture: WANG YULONG
School of Animal Science and Technology: CHEN GUOHONG
School of Architectural Science and Engineering: LIU PING
School of Arts: ZHANG MEILIN
School of Biological Sciences and Biotechnology: JIAO XIN'AN
School of Chemistry and Chemical Engineering: HU XIAOYA
School of Chinese Language and Literature: YAO WENFANG
School of Economics: JIANG NAIHUA
School of Educational Science and Technology: CHEN JIALILN
School of Environmental Science and Engineering: FENG KE
School of Foreign Languages: YU HONGLIANG
School of Information Engineering: CHEN LING
School of Law: JIAO FUMIN
School of Management: CHEN YAO
School of Mathematical Sciences: WANG HONGYU
School of Mechanical Engineering: ZHOU YIPING
School of Medicine: TANG YAO
School of Physical Education: TONG ZHAOGANG
School of Physical Science and Technology: CHEN XIAOBING
School of Social Development: ZHOU JIANCHAO
School of Tourism and Food Science: LU XINGUO
School of Veterinary Science: QIN AIJIAN
School of Water Conservation and Hydraulic Engineering: CHEN JIANKANG
Guangling College: LIU YANQING

PROFESSORS

BAN, JIQING, Chinese Language and Literature
BAO, ZHENQIANG, Information Engineering
BI, QIAO, Physical Science and Technology
CAI, CHUANREN, Mathematical Science
CAO, JINHUA, Social Development
CHANG, HONG, Animal Science and Technology
CHEN, GUOHONG, Animal Science and Technology
CHEN, JIALILN, Educational Science and Technology
CHEN, JIANKANG, Water Conservancy and Hydraulic Engineering
CHEN, JIANMIN, Biological Sciences and Biotechnology
CHEN, LING, Information Engineering
CHEN, RONGFA, Mechanical Engineering
CHEN, XIAOBING, Physical Science and Technology
CHEN, XIAOBING, Physical Science and Technology
CHEN, XIAOMING, Management
CHEN, YAO, Management
CHENG, JILIN, Water Conservancy and Hydraulic Engineering
CHENG, YONG, Veterinary Science
CHOU, BAOYUN, Water Conservancy and Hydraulic Engineering
CHOU, ZHIGANG, Physical Education
CHU, XUN, Water Conservancy and Hydraulic Engineering
DAI, XHIYI, Agriculture
DIAO, SHUREN, Social Development
DING, JIATONG, Animal Science and Technology
DING, LI, Medicine
DONG, GUOYAN, Chinese Language and Literature
ER, RONGBEN, Chinese Language and Literature
FAN, MING, Management
FANG, HONGYUAN, Water Conservancy and Hydraulic Engineering
FANG, WENLI, Foreign Languages
FEI, XUN, Social Development
FENG, KE, Environmental Science and Engineering
FENG, YONGSHAN, Medicine
GAO, HUIMING, Medicine
GAO, SONG, Veterinary Science
GE, XIAOQUN, Medicine
GU, FENG, Chinese Language and Literature
GU, NONG, Chinese Language and Literature
GU, RUIXIA, Tourism and Food Science
GU, SHILIANG, Agriculture
GUO, XIA, Chemistry and Chemical Engineering
HE, DAREN, Physical Science and Technology
HU, JINGGUO, Physical Science and Technology
HU, RONG, Medicine

HU, XIAOYA, Chemistry and Chemical Engineering
HU, XUENONG, Information Engineering
HU, XUEQIN, Economics
HUA, CHANGYOU, Social Development
HUANG, CHENG, Economics
HUANG, QIAN, Medicine
HUANG, QIANG, Chinese Language and Literature
HUANG, SHUCHENG, Economics
HUANG, SHUCHENG, Tourism and Food Science
HUO, WANLI, Arts
JI, MINGCHUN, Medicine
JI, SUYUE, Mathematical Science
JIANG, NAIHUA, Economics
JIAO, FUMIN, Law
JIAO, WENFENG, Social Development
JIAO, XIN'AN, Biological Sciences and Biotechnology
JIN, YINGEN, Biological Sciences and Biotechnology
JIN, YU, Physical Education
LI, BICHUN, Animal Science and Technology
LI, CHANGJI, Chinese Language and Literature
LI, CUNHUA, Information Engineering
LI, GUOLI, Medicine
LI, HOUDA, Veterinary Science
LI, JIANJI, Veterinary Science
LI, JINYU, Animal Science and Technology
LI, SHIHAO, Agriculture
LIANG, JIANSHENG, Biological Sciences and Biotechnology
LIN, ZHIGUI, Mathematical Science
LIU, CHAO, Water Conservancy and Hydraulic Engineering
LIU, CHENG, Social Development
LIU, GANG, Management
LIU, HONG, Chinese Language and Literature
LIU, MOXIANG, Medicine
LIU, PING, Architectural Science and Engineering
LIU, XIUFAN, Veterinary Science
LIU, YAN, Architectural Science and Engineering
LIU, YANQING, Medicine
LIU, YONGJUN, Physical Science and Technology
LIU, ZHUHAN, Mathematical Science
LIU, ZONGPING, Veterinary Science
LU, JIANFEI, Agriculture
LU, LINGUANG, Water Conservancy and Hydraulic Engineering
LU, XINGUO, Tourism and Food Science
MAO, YUYANG, Tourism and Food Science
MO, YUEPING, Information Engineering
PAN, XHAOWEI, Physical Education
PIAO, PING, Medicine
QIANG, JIANYA, Tourism and Food Science
QIANG, JING, Medicine
QIANG, ZHONGHAO, Economics
QIN, AIJIAN, Veterinary Science
QIN, XINGFANG, Economics
SHAO, YAOCHUN, Physical Science and Technology
SHEN, JIE, Information Engineering
SHI, MINGYI, Medicine
SHI, YONGFAN, Physical Education
SU, PEIQING, Medicine
SUN, GUORONG, Biological Sciences and Biotechnology
SUN, HUAICHANG, Veterinary Science
TIAN, HANYUN, Chinese Language and Literature
TONG, ZHAOGANG, Physical Education
WANG, BAO'AN, Veterinary Science
WANG, HANDONG, Veterinary Science
WANG, HONGRONG, Animal Science and Technology
WANG, HONGYU, Mathematical Science
WANG, JIANJUN, Medicine
WANG, JUN, Chinese Language and Literature
WANG, LINSUO, Water Conservancy and Hydraulic Engineering
WANG, LONGTAI, Mechanical Engineering
WANG, QINGREN, Social Development
WANG, XINGCHI, Management
WANG, XINGLONG, Animal Science and Technology
WANG, YEMING, Architectural Science and Engineering
WANG, YONGPING, Chinese Language and Literature
WANG, YONGPING, Social Development
WANG, YOUPING, Biological Sciences and Biotechnology
WANG, YULONG, Agriculture
WANG, ZHAOLONG, Biological Sciences and Biotechnology
WANG, ZONGYUAN, Veterinary Science
WEI, JUN, Physical Education
WEI, SHANHAO, Chinese Language and Literature
WEI, WANHONG, Biological Sciences and Biotechnology
WU, JIAN, Management
WU, SHANZHONG, Social Development
WU, YANTAO, Veterinary Science
WU, ZHOUWEN, Chinese Language and Literature
XIAO, SHUFENG, Chinese Language and Literature
XIONG, DEPING, Economics
XU, DEMING, Chinese Language and Literature
XU, JIANZHONG, Chinese Language and Literature
XU, LICHUN, Medicine
XU, MINGLIANG, Biological Sciences and Biotechnology
XU, WEIPING, Social Development
XU, YIMIN, Veterinary Science
YAN, JUN, Physical Education
YANG, BENHONG, Social Development
YANG, JIADONG, Economics
YANG, QIANPU, Social Development
YANG, SHUHE, Mechanical Engineering
YAO, WENFANG, Chinese Language and Literature
YIN, SHIXUE, Environmental Science and Engineering
YIN, XINCHUN, Information Engineering
YU, HAIPENG, Economics
YUAN, JIANLI, Architectural Science and Engineering
YUAN, XINMING, Water Conservancy and Hydraulic Engineering
ZENG, LI, Mechanical Engineering
ZHANG, HONGCHENG, Agriculture
ZHANG, HONGLIANG, Chinese Language and Literature
ZHANG, HONGQUAN, Medicine
ZHANG, JUN, Physical Education
ZHANG, MIANG, Chemistry and Chemical Engineering
ZHANG, MINLI, Architectural Science and Engineering
ZHANG, PEIJIAN, Medicine
ZHANG, QIJUN, Chinese Language and Literature
ZHANG, QING, Law
ZHANG, RUIHONG, Mechanical Engineering
ZHANG, TIANPING, Information Engineering
ZHANG, ZHENGANG, Medicine
ZHAO, GUOQI, Animal Science and Technology
ZHAO, ZONGFANG, Agriculture
ZHOU, JIANCHAO, Social Development
ZHOU, MINGYAO, Water Conservancy and Hydraulic Engineering
ZHOU, XIAOXIA, Medicine
ZHOU, XINTIAN, Social Development
ZHOU, YIPING, Social Development
ZHOU, YIPING, Mechanical Engineering
ZHU, XIASHI, Chemistry and Chemical Engineering
ZHU, YONGZE, Medicine
ZHUANG, LIN, Social Development

YANSHAN UNIVERSITY

438 Hebei Ave, Qinhuangdao 066004, Hebei
Telephone: (335) 8057100
Fax: (335) 8051148
E-mail: headmaster@ysu.edu.cn
Internet: www.ysu.edu.cn

Founded 1960
Provincial control
Academic year: September to July
President: LIU HONGMIN
Vice-Presidents: KONG XIANGDONG, LI QIANG, LIU BIN, WANG YONGCHANG, XING GUANGZHONG, YANG YULIN
Head of Graduate Department: ZHAO YONGSHENG
Librarian: ZHANG FUCHENG
Library of 600,000 vols
Number of teachers: 1,321
Number of students: 28,000
Publication: *Journal* (editions: natural science, philosophy and social sciences, quarterly)

DEANS

College of Civil Engineering and Mechanics: (vacant)
College of Economic Administration: YUAN YE
College of Electrical Engineering: GUAN XINPING
College of Environment and Chemical Engineering: BAI MINGHUA
College of Fine Art: ZHANG JIAXIN
College of Foreign Languages: (vacant)
College of Humanities and Law: WU YONG
College of Information Science and Engineering: KONG LINGFU
College of Material Science and Engineering: TIAN YONGJUN
College of Mechanical Engineering: ZHANG QING
College of Science: JIN XILI

PROFESSORS

AN, ZIJUN, Mechanical Engineering
BAI, MINGHUA, Environmental and Chemical Engineering
BI, WEIHONG, Information Science and Engineering
CHANG, DANHUA, Information Science and Engineering
CUI, YUNQI, Mechanical Engineering
DONG, HONGXUE, Foreign Languages
DONG, SHIMIN, Mechanical Engineering
DU, FENGSHAN, Mechanical Engineering
FANG, BAOGUO, Humanities and Law
GAO, DIANKUI, Mechanical Engineering
GAO, DIANRONG, Mechanical Engineering
GAO, FENG, Mechanical Engineering
GAO, SHIYOU, Mechanical Engineering
GAO, YINGJIE, Mechanical Engineering
GONG, JING'AN, Mechanical Engineering
GUO, BAOFENG, Mechanical Engineering
GUO, JINGFENG, Information Science and Engineering
GUO, XIJUAN, Information Science and Engineering
HAN, DECAI, Mechanical Engineering
HAN, PEIFU, Information Science and Engineering
HAN, XIAOJUAN, Mechanical Engineering
HOU, LANTIAN, Information Science and Engineering
HU, GUODONG, Mechanical Engineering
HU, ZHANQI, Mechanical Engineering
HUANG, ZHEN, Mechanical Engineering
HUI, JIXING, Humanities and Law
JIANG, SHIPING, Mechanical Engineering
JIANG, WANLU, Mechanical Engineering
JIN, ZHENLIN, Mechanical Engineering
JING, TIANFU, Material Science and Engineering
KONG, LINGFU, Information Science and Engineering
KONG, XIANGDONG, Mechanical Engineering
LI, BAODONG, Humanities and Law
LI, FULIANG, Humanities and Law
LI, JINLIANG, Mechanical Engineering

LI, JIUTONG, Mechanical Engineering
LI, KUIYING, Material Science and Engineering
LI, QIANG, Mechanical Engineering
LI, WEIMIN, Mechanical Engineering
LI, XIANKUI, Mechanical Engineering
LI, YUPENG, Mechanical Engineering
LIAN, JIACHUANG, Mechanical Engineering
LIU, GUOHUA, Information Science and Engineering
LIU, HONGMIN, Mechanical Engineering
LIU, RIPING, Material Science and Engineering
LIU, XIPING, Mechanical Engineering
LIU, YONGSHAN, Information Science and Engineering
LIU, ZEQUAN, Foreign Languages
LIU, ZHUBO, Mechanical Engineering
LU, XIUCHUN, Mechanical Engineering
LU, YI, Mechanical Engineering
NIE, SHAOMIN, Mechanical Engineering
PAN, MINGHAN, Information Science and Engineering
PENG, YAN, Mechanical Engineering
QIAO, CHANGSUO, Mechanical Engineering
QIN, SIJI, Mechanical Engineering
REN, YUNLAI, Mechanical Engineering
SHEN, GUANGXIAN, Mechanical Engineering
SHEN, LIMIN, Information Science and Engineering
SHEN, XIAOMEI, Humanities and Law
SHENG, YIPING, Environmental and Chemical Engineering
SHI, RONG, Mechanical Engineering
SONG, GUOSEN, Information Science and Engineering
SUN, HUIXUE, Mechanical Engineering
SUN, XUGUANG, Mechanical Engineering
TANG, JINGLIN, Mechanical Engineering
WANG, CHENGRU, Information Science and Engineering
WANG, FUSHENG, Foreign Languages
WANG, HAIRU, Mechanical Engineering
WANG, JUN, Mechanical Engineering
WANG, QINGXUE, Humanities and Law
WANG, XINSHENG, Information Science and Engineering
WANG, YIQUN, Mechanical Engineering
WANG, YONGCHANG, Mechanical Engineering
WEI, LIBO, Humanities and Law
WEN, DESHENG, Mechanical Engineering
WU, XIAOMING, Mechanical Engineering
WU, YONG, Humanities and Law
WU, YUEMING, Mechanical Engineering
XIAO, HONG, Mechanical Engineering
XU, CHENGQIAN, Information Science and Engineering
XU, HONGXIANG, Mechanical Engineering
XU, LIZHONG, Mechanical Engineering
XU, RUI, Material Science and Engineering
YANG, YULIN, Mechanical Engineering
YE, DEQIAN, Information Science and Engineering
YU, DESHENG, Information Science and Engineering
YU, DONGLI, Material Science and Engineering
YU, ENLIN, Mechanical Engineering
YU, JIANPING, Foreign Languages
YU, RONGJIN, Information Science and Engineering
YU, YUFENG, Information Science and Engineering
ZHANG, HAI, Mechanical Engineering
ZHANG, LIYING, Mechanical Engineering
ZHANG, QING, Mechanical Engineering
ZHANG, QISHENG, Mechanical Engineering
ZHANG, TAO, Mechanical Engineering
ZHANG, TONGYI, Mechanical Engineering
ZHANG, WEIDONG, Foreign Languages
ZHANG, WENZHI, Mechanical Engineering
ZHANG, ZHONGYI, Humanities and Law
ZHAO, JINGYI, Mechanical Engineering
ZHAO, JUN, Mechanical Engineering
ZHAO, TIESHI, Mechanical Engineering
ZHAO, YONGHE, Mechanical Engineering
ZHAO, YONGSHENG, Mechanical Engineering
ZHENG, SHENGXUAN, Information Science and Engineering
ZHOU, CHAO, Mechanical Engineering
ZHOU, QINGTIAN, Mechanical Engineering
ZHU, GUANGRONG, Humanities and Law
ZOU, MUCHANG, Information Science and Engineering

YANTAI UNIVERSITY

Yantai 264005, Shandong
Telephone: (535) 6888995
Fax: (535) 6888801
Internet: www.ytu.edu.cn

Founded 1984
State control
Languages of instruction: Chinese, English

President: ZHANG JIANYI
Registrar: LU XUEMING
Librarian: SUN JILIANG

Library of 40,000 vols
Number of teachers: 450
Number of students: 3,839

Publication: *Journal*

Degree programmes in Chinese language and literature, foreign languages and literature, law, electronics and computing, biochemical engineering, chemical engineering, machine design and manufacture, architecture, industrial and civil engineering, applied mathematics, applied physics, finance and economics and management, international business, fisheries industry, physical education.

YUNNAN FINANCE AND TRADE INSTITUTE

Shangmacun, North Suburb, Kunming 650221, Yunnan
Telephone: (871) 5122394
Fax: (871) 5163384

Founded 1981

President: Prof. WU JIANAN
Presidents: Assoc. Prof. MA GUANGBI, WU TANXUE, YANG LIZHI
Registrar: ZHOU ANFAN
Librarian: LIU SHUNDE

Library of 280,000 vols
Number of teachers: 289
Number of students: 2,620

Publications: *Journal*, *Foreign Economic Theory and Administration*

HEADS OF DEPARTMENTS

Banking: Assoc. Prof. ZHOU HAOWEN
Finance: Assoc. Prof. DING ZHI
Planning and Statistics: Assoc. Prof. XU SHULONG
Accounting: Assoc. Prof. MO GUOJIANG
Business Administrative Economics: Assoc. Prof. ZHAO GAN
Industrial Economics: WANG JIANG

YUNNAN INSTITUTE FOR THE NATIONALITIES

420 Huanchengbei Rd, Kunming 650031, Yunnan
Telephone: (871) 5154308
Fax: (871) 5154304
Internet: www.ynni.edu.cn

Founded 1951
State control
Languages of instruction: Chinese, English, Thai, Burmese and some minority languages
Academic year: September to July

President: ZHAO JIAWEN
Vice-Presidents: HUANG HUIKUN, PU TONGJIN, ZHAO JUNSHAN
Chief Administrative Officer: DI HUAYI
Librarian: DUAN SHENG'OU

Library of 430,000 vols, 28 special collections
Number of teachers: 385
Number of students: 4,969

Publication: *Journal* (Social Sciences edition and Science edition, quarterly)

HEADS OF DEPARTMENTS

Chinese Language and Literature: LI SHUREN
Minority Languages and Literature: LU YI
Foreign Languages and Literature: LI DANHE
History: XIE BINGKUN
Social Science: ZHANG JIANGUO
Economics and Management: SUN GUOCHANG
Mathematics: CHEN NAIXIN
Physics: TAO ZHIWEI
Chemistry: DONG XUECHANG
Ethnic Studies Centre: HUANG HUIKUN
In-Service Training: ZHANG YOUJING
Preparatory: MA QINGLIN
Minority Arts: YANG JUN

YUNNAN UNIVERSITY

2 North Cuihu Rd, Kunming 650091, Yunnan
Telephone: (871) 5148533
Fax: (871) 5153832
Internet: www.ynu.edu.cn

Founded 1923
State control
Academic year: September to July

President: Prof. WU SONG
Vice-Presidents: Prof. WANG RONG, Prof. HONG PINJIE, Prof. LIN CHAOMIN, Prof. NI HUIFANG, Prof. ZHANG KEQIN, Prof. CHEN SHIBO
Registrar: Prof. YANG JIAHE
Librarian: Prof. WANG WENGGUAN

Library of 1,170,000 vols
Number of teachers: 888
Number of students: 7,160

Publication: *The Ideological Front* (6 a year)

PROFESSORS

School of Humanities (tel. (871) 5033607):
- JIN DANYUAN, Aesthetics
- LI CONGZONG, Modern Literature
- LI JIABIN, Ancient World History
- LI YAN, History of the Chinese Feudal Economy
- LIN CHAOMIN, Ethnic History
- QIAO CHUANZAO, Writing
- SUN QINHUA, Literary Language
- TANG MIN, Modern World History
- WANG KAILIAN, Classical Chinese Language
- XU KANGMING, Modern World History
- YANG ZHENKUN, Modern Literature
- YOU ZHONG, History of Chinese Minorities
- ZHANG FUSAN, Ethnic and Folk Literature
- ZHANG GUOQING, Classical Chinese Writings
- ZHANG XINCHANG, History and Archives of Chinese Minorities
- ZHU HUIRONG, Historical Geography

School of Economics (tel. (871) 5033613):
- CHEN JIANBO, Economic Statistics
- GUO SHUHUA, Finance
- HONG HUAXI, Economics
- HU QIHUI, Economics
- JIN RONG, Economics
- LI DEPU, Economics
- LU ZHAOHE, Demology
- MA JUN, Accountancy
- PAN JIANXING, Mathematical Statistics
- SHI BENZHI, Investment
- SHI LEI, Economic Statistics
- SUN WENSHUANG, Mathematical Statistics
- WANG XUEREN, Economics
- XU GUANGYUAN, Economics

YENG XIANMING, Finance
ZHANG JIANHUA, Foreign Trade
ZHANG JIN, Economic Statistics
ZHU YINGGENG, Ideological History of Western Economics

School of Public Administration (tel. (871) 5033609):

CHEN GUOXING, Socialism
CUI YUNWU, Public Administration
GAO LI, Ethics
HOU YIHONG, Management Psychology
JIANG ZIHUA, Politics
JIN ZIQIANG, Current Chinese Politics
KUANG ZHIMING, Politics
LI BIN, Philosophy
LIU JIAZHI, Philosophy
LIU YUNHANG, Aesthetics
WANG YANBING, Sociology
XIONG SIYUAN, Economics
YANG JIQIONG, Current Chinese Politics
ZENG JIAN, Dialectics
ZHOU PING, Politics

School of Tourism and Business Administration (tel. (871) 5034561):

GUANG NINGSHEN, Tourism Administration
LI HAO, Tourism Administration
LIU XUEYU, Business Management
TIAN WEIMING, Tourism Administration
WANG JIANPIN, Econometrics
XUE QUNHUI, Tourism Administration
YANG GUIHUA, Tourism Administration
ZHANG MINGAN, Business Management
ZHANG XIAOPIN, English

School of Law (tel. (871) 5184816):

CHEN ZIGUO, Civil Law
XU ZHISHAN, Constitution

School of Foreign Languages (tel. (871) 5033629):

GONG NINGZHU, Lao, Vietnamese
LI JIGANG, English
XU FENG
ZHANG XINHE, English

School of Sciences (tel. (871) 5032012):

CAO KEFEI, Physics
CHEN ZHONGZHANG, Physics
CONG LIANLI, Earth Sciences
GUO SHICANG, Earth Sciences
GUO XIAOJIANG, Mathematics
GUO YUQI, Mathematics
HE DAMING, Earth Sciences
HE XIANGPANG, Mathematics
HU JIAFU, Earth Sciences
HU WENGUO, Physics
JU JIANHUA, Earth Sciences
LI JIANPIN, Mathematics
LI YAOTANG, Mathematics
LI YONGKUN, Mathematics
LIN LIZHONG, Physics
LIU ZHENGRONG, Mathematics
LUO YAOHUANG, Physics
MEI DONGCHENG, Physics
PENG KUANGDING, Physics
PENG SHOULI, Physics
TANG XINGHUA, Mathematics
TIEN XINSHI, Physics
WANG WEIGUO, Earth Sciences
WEN XIAOMIN, Physics
WU XINGHUI, Material Sciences
XIE YINGQI, Atmospheric Science, Mathematics
YAN GUANGXIONG, Mathematics
YAN HUASHENG, Earth Sciences
YANG DEQING, Physics
YANG HUAKANG, Mathematics
YANG XUESHENG, Earth Sciences
YANG YU, Material Sciences
ZHANG LI, Physics
ZHANG ZHONGMIN, Physics
ZHAO XIAOHUA, Mathematics
ZHENG BAOZHONG, Material Sciences
ZHENG XIYIN, Mathematics
ZHOU QING, Physics

School of Computer Science (tel. (871) 5031597):

LI TAILING, Electronic Circuits and Communication
LI TIANMU, Electronics and Information Systems
LIU WEIYI, Fuzzy Database Theory
TIAN ZHILIANG, Management Operating Systems
ZHENG WENXING, Correspondence

School of Life Sciences and Chemistry (tel. (871) 5031412):

DAI SHUSHAN, Physics and Chemistry
HE SENQUAN, Organic Chemistry
HONG PINJIE, Microwave Plasma
HU ZHIHAO, Botany
HUANG SUHUA, Botany
LI LIANG, Organic Chemistry
LI QIREN, Plant Cell Engineering
LIU FUCHU, Organic Chemistry
LIU SONGYU, Analytical Chemistry
LIU XINHUA, Soil Ecology
TAO YUANQI, Quantum Organic Chemistry
WANG CHANGYI, Organic Chemistry
XU QIHENG, Analytical Chemistry
YANG CHUNJIN, Inorganic Chemistry
YANG PIPENG, Organic Chemistry
YIN JIANGUO, Inorganic Chemistry
ZAN RUIGUANG, Cell Biology
ZHENG ZHUO, Microbiology
ZUO YANGXIAN, Invertebrates

School of Adult Education (tel. (871) 5147702):

DU CHAO, Analytical Chemistry
SHI PENGFEI, Ancient Chinese Literature
WANG JIALIN, Analytical Chemistry
WANG SHIDONG, Fluxional Dynamic Systems

School of Development Research (tel. (871) 5031453):

CHEN LIN, Systems Engineering
LIAO HONGZHI, Systems Engineering
MAO YUGONG, Management Science
XIAO XIAN, History of International Relations
YANG MANSU, History of International Relations
YANG SHOUCHUANG, Ethnic History

Dianchi School (tel. (871) 5172513):

WU JIANGUO, Chemistry

AFFILIATED RESEARCH INSTITUTES

Institute of Ecology and Botany.

Yunnan Institute of Microbiology.

Institute of Cosmogony.

Institute of Southeast Asian Studies.

Institute of Demography.

Institute of Electronic Information and Technology.

Institute of Applied Chemistry.

Institute of Bioresearch Development.

Yunnan Institute of Applied Mathematics.

Institute of Applied Statistics.

Transducer and Technology Research Centre.

Institute of Applied Physics.

Institute of Physics.

Institute of New Materials.

Institute of Synthesis Chemistry.

Institute of Economic Reform and Development.

Institute of Tourism.

Institute of Ethnic Law.

Institute of the History of Southwest Frontier Ethnic Groups.

Institute of Ancient Books of the Southwest.

East Asia Institute of Visual Anthropology

ZHEJIANG UNIVERSITY

38 Zheda Rd, Hangzhou 310027, Zhejiang
Telephone: (571) 87951846
Fax: (571) 87951358
E-mail: zupo@zju.edu.cn
Internet: www.zju.edu.cn

Founded 1897; merged with Hangzhou University, Zhejiang Agricultural University and Zhejiang Medical University 1998
State control
Languages of instruction: Chinese, English(-for foreign students)
Academic year: September to June

President: Prof. PAN YUNHE
Executive Vice-President: Prof. NI MINGJIANG
Vice-Presidents: Prof. BU FANXIAO, Prof. HU JIANMIAO, Prof. LAI MAODE, Prof. ZHU, JUNProf. CHU, JIANProf. SI, JIANMIN
Director of International Programmes Office: Prof. QIU JIZHEN
Librarian: ZHU HAIKANG

Number of teachers: 3,285
Number of students: 90,475 (43,222 full-time, 30,571 part-time, 16,682 distance learning)

Publications: *Journal of Zhejiang University (Sciences)* (in Chinese and English), *Journal of Zhejiang University (Natural Science)* (in Chinese), *Journal of Zhejiang University (Medicine)* (in Chinese), *Journal of Zhejiang University (Agricultural and Life Sciences)* (in Chinese), *Journal of Zhejiang University (Humanities and Social Science)* (in Chinese), *Applied Mathematics of Chinese Universities* (in Chinese and English), *Materials Science and Engineering* (in Chinese), *Management Engineering* (in Chinese), *Spatial Structures* (in Chinese), *Engineering Design* (in Chinese), *Practical Oncology* (in Chinese), *Applied Psychology* (in Chinese), *China Higher Medical Education* (in Chinese), *Population and Eugenics* (in Chinese)

School of Agriculture and Biotechnology (depts of Agronomy, Applied Biosciences, Horticulture, Plant Protection, Tea Science), School of Animal Sciences (depts of Animal Science, Special Animal Science, Veterinary Medicine), School of Biomedical Engineering and Instrument Science (depts of Biomedical Engineering, Instrumentation Science and Engineering), School of Biosystems Engineering and Food Science (depts of Biosystems Engineering, Food and Nutrition Science), School of Civil Engineering and Architecture (depts of Architecture, Civil Engineering, Regional and Urban Planning, Water Conservation and Ocean Engineering), School of Computer Science (also known as School of Software Technology—depts of Computer Science and Engineering, Digital Media and Network Technology, Industrial Design), School of Economics (depts of Economics, Finance and Banking, International Economics and Trade, Public Administration and Public Finance), School of Education (depts of Education, Physical Education), School of Electrical Engineering (Applied Electronics, Electrical Engineering, Systems Science and Engineering), School of Environmental and Resource Sciences (depts of Environmental Science, Environmental Engineering, , Land Management, Natural Resource Science), School of Humanities (depts of Arts, Philosophy, Chinese Language and Literature, Information Resources and Management, Journalism and Communication Studies, International Cultural Studies, History, Sociology), School of Information Science and Engineering (depts of Control

Science and Engineering, Optical Engineering, Information and Electronic Engineering), School of International Studies (depts of English Language and Literature, Eastern and Western Languages and Literatures, Linguistics), School of Law (depts of Law, Political Science and Public Administration, Ideological and Political Education), , School of Life Sciences (depts of Biological Sciences, Biotechnology), School of Management (depts of Management Science and Engineering, Business Administration, Tourism, Administration, Agricultural Economics and Management),School of Materials Science and Chemical Engineering (depts of Chemical and Biochemical Engineering, Materials Science and Engineering, Polymer Science and Engineering), School of Mechanical and Energy Engineering (depts of Mechanical Engineering, Energy Engineering, Mechanics), School of Medicine (depts of Basic Medical Sciences, 1st, 2nd and 3rd depts of Clinical Medicine, Nursing, Public Health and Preventive Medicine, Stomatology), School of Pharmaceutical Sciences (dept of Chinese Traditional Pharmacy, Pharmacy), School of Medicine (depts of Stomatology, Basic Medical Sciences, Public Health and Preventive Medicine, Nursing and 1st, 2nd and 3rd Depts of Clinical Medicine), School of Sciences (depts of Mathematics, Physics, Chemistry, Earth Sciences, Psychology and Behavioural Sciences), Graduate School, School of Adult Education, School of Vocational Technical Education, School of Advanced Studies, Distance Learning School, International College, Chu Kechen College.

ZHEJIANG UNIVERSITY OF TECHNOLOGY

District 6, Zhaohui Xincun, Hangzhou 310032, Zhejiang
Telephone: (571) 88320114
Fax: (571) 88320272
E-mail: webmaster@zjut.edu.cn
Internet: www.zjut.edu.cn

Founded 1953
Academic year: September to July

President: Prof. SHEN YINCHU
Vice-Presidents: Prof. ZHANG LIBIN, Prof. XUAN YONG, Prof. XIAO RUIFENG, Prof. MA CHUN'AN
Librarian: Prof. HE LIMIN

Library of 1,002,000 vols
Number of teachers: 2,600
Number of students: 18,000

Publication: *Journal* (separate editions for natural sciences and social sciences, each 6 a year)

DEANS

College of Chemical Engineering: Prof. JI JIANBING
College of Electrical and Mechanical Engineering: Prof. CHAI GUOZHONG
College of Architecture and Civil Engineering: Prof. ZHENG JIANJUN
College of Biological and Environmental Engineering: Prof. CHEN JIANMENG
College of Information Engineering: Prof. CAI JIAMEI
College of Business Administration: Prof. CHENG HUIFANG
College of Sciences: Prof. CHENG CHENG
College of Vocational and Technical Education: Prof. DU SHIGUI
College of Pharmaceutical Sciences: Prof. QIAN JUNQING
College of Foreign Languages: Prof. LIAO FEI
College of Arts and Humanities: Prof. SUN LIPING
College of Law: Prof. ZHANG XU

ZHENGZHOU UNIVERSITY

100 Kexue St, Zhengzhou 450001, Henan
Telephone: (371) 7763036
Fax: (371) 7763036
E-mail: headmaster@zzu.edu.cn
Internet: www.zzu.edu.cn

Founded 1956
Provincial control
Academic year: September to July

President: SHEN CHANGYU
Vice-Presidents: GAO DANYING, JIAO LIUCHENG, SONG MAOPING, XU ZHENLU, ZHENG YULING
Head of Graduate Department: ZHU CHENGSHEN
Librarian: ZHANG LEISHUN

Library of 3,900,000 vols
Number of teachers: 2,200
Number of students: 44,000

Publication: *Journal* (editions: science, natural sciences, quarterly; philosophy and social science, medical science, 6 a year)

DEANS

College of Nursing: (vacant)
College of Public Health: HU DONGSHENG
College of Chemical Engineering: WEI XINLI
School of Applied Technology: LI SHUXIN
School of Basic Medical Science: DONG ZIMING
School of Civil Engineering: LIU LIXIN
School of Economics: DU SHUYUN
School of Education: WANG ZONGMIN
School of Electrical Engineering: CHEN TIEJUN
School of Environment and Water Conservancy: WANG FUMING
School of Foreign Languages: SHEN NANA
School of Information Management: KE PING
School of Journalism and Communication: DONG GUANGAN
School of Law: TIAN TUCHENG
School of Liberal Arts: ZHANG HONGSHENG
School of Materials Science and Engineering: GUAN SHAOKANG
School of Mechanical Engineering: ZHANG LUOMING
School of Physical Education: WU LANYING
School of Pharmacy: RAO YAOGANG
School of Physical Science and Technology: LI YUXIAO
School of Public Administration: (vacant)
School of Tourism Management: MAO ANFU
Department of Bioengineering: KANG QIAOZHEN
Department of Chemistry: LIU HONGMIN
Department of History and Archaeology: JIANG JIANSHE
Department of Management Engineering: (vacant)
Department of Mathematics: CHEN SHAOCHUN
Department of Music: GONG WEI
Institute of Physical Science and Technology: WANG ZHONGYONG

PROFESSORS

AN, GUOLOU, History and Archaeology
AN, YUHUI, Basic Medical Science
CAO, SHAOKUI, Materials Science and Engineering
CEN, SHAOCHENG, Mechanical Engineering
CHAN, JIE, Basic Medical Science
CHEN, HUAI, Civil Engineering
CHEN, JINGBO, Materials Science and Engineering
CHEN, JINZHOU, Materials Science and Engineering
CHEN, TAN, Public Health
CHEN, TIEJUN, Electrical Engineering
CHEN, YILANG, Chemical Engineering
CHENG, BAOSHAN, Law
CUI, JING, Basic Medical Science
CUI, JINGBIN, Basic Medical Science
CUI, LIUXIN, Public Health
CUI, XIULING, Chemistry
DONG, GUANGAN, Journalism and Culture
DONG, MINGMIN, Bioengineering
DONG, QIWU, Chemical Engineering
DONG, ZIMING, Basic Medical Science
DU, CHENXIA, Chemistry
DU, SHUYUN, Economic School
DU, XIANTANG, Bioengineering
DUAN, GUANGCAI, Public Health
FAN, MING, Information Engineering
FAN, XIQING, Physical Science and Technology
FAN, YAOTING, Chemistry
FANG, WENJI, Chemical Engineering
FENG, DONGQING, Electrical Engineering
FENG, LIYUN, Public Health
FU, CHUNJING, Basic Medical Science
FU, RUNFANG, Basic Medical Science
GAO, JIANHUA, Chemistry
GAO, JINFENG, Electrical Engineering
GAO, XIAOQUN, Basic Medical Science
GAO, ZHENGYAO, Physical Science and Technology
GONG, JUNFANG, Chemistry
GUAN, HUILING, Mechanical Engineering
GUAN, SHAOKANG, Materials Science and Engineering
GUAN, XINXIN, Chemistry
GUO, SHILING, Chemical Engineering
GUO, XIANJI, Chemistry
GUO, YANCHUN, Chemistry
GUO, YINGJIAN, Foreign Languages
GUO, YIQUN, Chemistry
GUO, YUANCHENG, Civil Engineering
HAN, GUOHE, History and Archaeology
HAN, JIE, Mechanical Engineering
HAN, QIAO, Chemistry
HAN, WEICHENG, Chemistry
HE, ZHANHANG, Chemistry
HOU, HONGWEI, Chemistry
HOU, ZONGYUAN, Law
HU, DONGSHENG, Public Health
HU, JIANLI, Chemistry
HUA, SHAOJIE, Mechanical Engineering
HUO, YUPING, Physical Science and Technology
JIA, HANDONG, Chemistry
JIA, XIAOLIN, Materials Science and Engineering
JIANG, DENGGAO, Chemical Engineering
JIANG, JIANCHU, Law
JIANG, JIANSHE, History and Archaeology
JIANG, MAYUN, Education
JIANG, YUANLI, Chemical Engineering
KE, PING, Information Management
LI, DAWANG, Civil Engineering
LI, GANG, Chemistry
LI, HAIMEI, Materials Science and Engineering
LI, JIANJUN, Chemistry
LI, JIANKE, Bioengineering
LI, LIMIN, Chemistry
LI, TIAN, Civil Engineering
LI, WENJIE, Public Health
LI, XIAOWEN, Basic Medical Science
LI, XINFA, Materials Science and Engineering
LI, YINGDAN, Public Health
LI, YUEBAI, Basic Medical Science
LI, YUXIAO, Physical Science and Technology
LI, ZHIMIN, Public Health
LI, ZHONGJUN, Chemistry
LIANG, ERJUN, Physical Science and Technology
LIANG, FENGRONG, Law
LIAO, XINCHENG, Chemistry
LIN, LIN, Chemistry
LIU, DAZHUANG, Chemical Engineering
LIU, DEFA, Law
LIU, GUOJI, Chemical Engineering
LIU, HONGMIN, Chemistry
LIU, HONGXIA, Chemistry
LIU, HUALIAN, Public Health
LIU, JINDUN, Chemical Engineering
LIU, JINXIA, Chemistry
LIU, LIXIN, Civil Engineering
LIU, MINYING, Materials Science and Engineering

LIU, PU, Chemistry
LIU, SHOUCHANG, Chemistry
LIU, XIANGWEN, Law
LIU, XIANLIN, Electrical Engineering
LIU, XINTIAN, Materials Science and Engineering
LIU, YUNBO, Foreign Languages
LU, MEIYI, History and Archaeology
LU, SONGYUE, Law
LU, TAIFENG, Law
LU, WENGE, Public Health
LU, XINGUANG, Materials Science and Engineering
LU, ZUHUI, Physical Science and Technology
LUO, DAPENG, Public Health
MA, SHENGGANG, Mechanical Engineering
MA, XIAOJIAN, Chemical Engineering
MAO, LUYUAN, Materials Science and Engineering
MIAO, HUIQING, Economic School
MIAO, LIANYING, Law
NING, JINCHENG, Law
NING, ZHENHUAN, Physical Science and Technology
NIU, YUNYIN, Chemistry
PEI, BINGNAN, Information Engineering
PEI, YINGXIN, Public Health
QI, YUANMING, Bioengineering
QIAO, HAILING, Basic Medical Science
QIN, GUANGYONG, Physical Science and Technology
QU, CHUANZHI, Basic Medical Science
QU, LINGBO, Chemistry
RAO, YAOGANG, Pharmacy
REN, BAOZENG, Chemical Engineering
REN, CUIPING, Chemistry
SHEN, GUIMING, Law
SHEN, KAIJU, Law
SHEN, NANA, Foreign Languages
SHEN, NINGFU, Materials Science and Engineering
SHEN, XIANZHANG, Electrical Engineering
SHEN, XIAOCHENG, Bioengineering
SHI, JIE, Chemistry
SHI, MAOSHENG, Law
SHI, QIUZHI, Chemistry
SHI, XUEZHONG, Public Health
SHUI, TINGLIANG, Chemical Engineering
SONG, MAOPING, Chemistry
SU, JINGXIANG, Information Engineering
SU, YUNLAI, Chemistry
SUN, PEIQIN, Chemical Engineering
SUN, YUFU, Materials Science and Engineering
TAN, XINMIN, Education
TANG, KEYONG, Materials Science and Engineering
TANG, MINGSHENG, Chemistry
TAO, JINGCHAO, Chemistry
TIAN, TUCHENG, Law
TONG, LIPING, Civil Engineering
WANG, DONGWEI, Civil Engineering
WANG, FENG, Law
WANG, FUAN, Chemical Engineering
WANG, GUANGLONG, Chemical Engineering
WANG, GUOLING, Education
WANG, HONGXING, Chemistry
WANG, HONGYING, Materials Science and Engineering
WANG, JIE, Electrical Engineering
WANG, JINGWU, Materials Science and Engineering
WANG, LIANFENG, Law
WANG, LIDONG, Bioengineering
WANG, MINCAN, Chemistry
WANG, MINGCHEN, Basic Medical Science
WANG, XIANGYU, Chemistry
WANG, XIKE, Materials Science and Engineering
WANG, XINGGUANG, History and Archaeology
WANG, XINLING, Civil Engineering
WANG, YAN, Chemical Engineering
WANG, YUDONG, Materials Science and Engineering
WANG, YUNZHI, History and Archaeology
WANG, ZHONGQUAN, Basic Medical Science
WANG, ZHONGYONG, Information Engineering
WEI, XINLI, Chemical Engineering
WU, FENG, Basic Medical Science
WU, MIN, Public Health
WU, MINGJIAN, Chemical Engineering
WU, XIAOLING, Mechanical Engineering
WU, YANGJIE, Chemistry
WU, YIMING, Public Health
WU, YOULIN, Physical Science and Technology
XIAO, GUOXING, Law
XIAO, QIANGANG, Law
XU, HAISHENG, Chemical Engineering
XU, QILOU, Civil Engineering
XU, QUN, Materials Science and Engineering
XU, SHUN, Chemistry
XU, XIUCHENG, Chemical Engineering
XU, YAN, Chemistry
XU, YOULI, History and Archaeology
XUE, CHANGGUI, Basic Medical Science
XUE, LEXUN, Bioengineering
YAN, SUQING, Public Health
YANG, CHANGCHUN, Chemistry
YANG, GUANYU, Chemistry
YANG, JIUJUN, Materials Science and Engineering
YANG, SHENGLI, Basic Medical Science
YANG, TIANYU, History and Archaeology
YANG, YUANHUI, Electrical Engineering
YE, BAOXIAN, Chemistry
YE, YANGDONG, Information Engineering
YU, XIANGDONG, History and Archaeology
YU, YANGUANG, Information Engineering
YUAN, SIGUO, Chemical Engineering
YUAN, ZULIANG, History and Archaeology
ZENG, ZHIPING, Chemical Engineering
ZHANG, AFANG, Materials Science and Engineering
ZHANG, BAOLIN, Chemical Engineering
ZHANG, BINGLIN, Physical Science and Technology
ZHANG, GUOSHUO, History and Archaeology
ZHANG, HAOQIN, Chemical Engineering
ZHANG, HENG, Mechanical Engineering
ZHANG, HONGQUAN, Public Health
ZHANG, HONGYUN, Chemistry
ZHANG, JIANMIN, Chemistry
ZHANG, LINNA, Mechanical Engineering
ZHANG, MINFU, History and Archaeology
ZHANG, PING, Basic Medical Science
ZHANG, QIAN, Basic Medical Science
ZHANG, QINXIAN, Basic Medical Science
ZHANG, RUI, Materials Science and Engineering
ZHANG, RUIQIN, Chemistry
ZHANG, SHUSHENG, Chemistry
ZHANG, SHUYUAN, Chemistry
ZHANG, XIUQUAN, Law
ZHANG, XUHUA, History and Archaeology
ZHANG, YADONG, Chemical Engineering
ZHANG, ZHAO, Basic Medical Science
ZHANG, ZHIHONG, Information Engineering
ZHAO, JIANWEN, Law
ZHAO, QINGXIANG, Materials Science and Engineering
ZHAO, WENEN, Chemical Engineering
ZHAO, XINGTAI, Education
ZHAO, YUFEN, Chemistry
ZHENG, YONGFU, History and Archaeology
ZHOU, CAIRONG, Chemical Engineering
ZHOU, CHUXIAN, Chemistry
ZHOU, DAPENG, Chemistry
ZHOU, PENG, Information Engineering
ZHOU, QINGLEI, Information Engineering
ZHOU, YUANFANG, Public Health
ZHU, CHENGSHEN, Materials Science and Engineering
ZHUANG, LEI, Information Engineering
ZHUANG, YINFENG, Materials Science and Engineering

ZHONGNAN UNIVERSITY OF ECONOMICS AND LAW

114 Wu Luo Rd, Wuhan 430064, Hubei
Telephone: (27) 88044332
Fax: (27) 88044339
E-mail: xz@znufe.edu.cn
Internet: www.znufe.edu.cn

Founded 1948
Academic year: September to July
President: WU HANDONG
Vice-Presidents: LI HANCHANG, TAN YOUTU, ZHANG ZHONGHUA, ZHAO LINGYUN
Head of Graduate Department: ZHU YANFU
Librarian: HU YUANMIN
Number of teachers: 1,173
Number of students: 35,200
Publications: *Journal* (6 a year), *Studies in Law and Business* (6 a year)

DEANS

School of Accounting: LUO FEI
School of Banking and Insurance: ZU XINGRONG
School of Business Administration: ZHANG XINGUO
School of Economics: LU XIANXIANG
School of Finance and Public Administration: YANG CANMING
School of Foreign Languages: XIE QUN
School of Humanities: WANG YUCHEN
School of Information: YANG YUNYAN
School of Journalism and Mass Media: YIN XIULIN
School of Law: QI WENYUAN
School of Public Administration: ZHAO MAN
School of Public Security: YANG ZONGHUI

PROFESSORS

CAI, HONG, Law
CAI, LING, Economics
CAO, SHIQUAN, Law
CHAO, LONGQI, Banking and Insurance
CHEN, CHIBO, Business Administration
CHEN, DAJIE, Finance and Public Administration
CHEN, GUANGYAN, Finance and Public Administration
CHEN, JINLIANG, Law
CHEN, XIAOJUN, Law
CHENG, LIHUA, Humanities
CHENG, QIZHI, Economics
CHENG, QUANMING, Finance and Public Administration
CUI, MINGXIA, Law
DAI, WUTANG, Economics
DU, XINGCHAI, Economics
DUAN, NINGHUA, Information Science
FAN, ZHONGXI, Law
FANG, SHIRONG, Law
GU, YUANQING, Economics
GUO, DAOYANG, Accounting
HU, XIANSHUN, Information Science
HUANG, SHIPING, Humanities
JIA, QIYU, Information Science
JIANG, HAISU, Business Administration
KU, KEJIAN, Business Administration
LEI, XINGHU, Law
LI, CHANGQING, Banking and Insurance
LI, DAMING, Finance and Public Administration
LI, DAORONG, Humanities
LI, GEFEI, Banking and Insurance
LI, GUANGZHONG, Accounting
LI, JIANXUN, Public Security
LI, MAONIAN, Information Science
LI, NAINZHAO, Banking and Insurance
LI, QINGZHI, Public Security
LI, WEINING, Economics
LI, XIANPEI, Business Administration
LI, XUANJU, Information Science
LIANG, YUXIA, Law
LIN, HANCHUAN, Economics
LIU, DAHONG, Law
LIU, KEFENG, Humanities
LIU, LIELONG, Economics
LIU, LUANSHENG, Humanities
LIU, MAOLIN, Law
LIU, SIHUA, Economics
LIU, TENGHONG, Information Science

LIU, XIANFAN, Humanities
LU, XIANXIANG, Economics
LU, ZHONGMEI, Law
LUO, FEI, Accounting
LUO, SHENGBAO, Business Administration
MEI, ZIHUI, Banking and Insurance
MOU, BINGHUA, Information Science
NI, PINGSONG, Finance and Public Administration
NIE, HUAMING, Banking and Insurance
OUYANG, XUCHU, Business Administration
PANG, FENGXI, Finance and Public Administration
PENG, XINGLV, Business Administration
PENG, YONGXING, Information Science
PENG, ZHENGHUI, Law
QI, WENYUAN, Law
QIN, YOUTU, Law
QIU, JIAWU, Information Science
QU, GUANGQIN, Law
SHEN, BENZHU, Law
SHONG, QINGHUA, Banking and Insurance
SU, SHAOZHI, Economics
SUN, XIAOFU, Law
SUN, XIAOMEI, Humanities
TANG, GUOPING, Accounting
TANG, WEIBEN, Economics
TANG, WUYUN, Economics
TONG, ZHIWEI, Law
WAN, HOUFEN, Business Administration
WANG, FULIN, Humanities
WANG, JUNPING, Public Security
WANG, QUANXIN, Law
WANG, SHOU'AN, Information Science
WANG, XINGYUAN, Information Science
WU, GUANGBING, Economics
WU, HANGDONG, Law
WU, JUNPEI, Finance and Public Administration
WU, LIANLIAN, Humanities
WU, YIJUN, Business Administration
WU, ZHIZHONG, Law
XIA, CHENGCAI, Accounting
XIA, XINYUAN, Economics
XIA, YONG, Law
XIONG, SHENGXU, Business Administration
XU, DUNKAI, Economics
XU, GUOXIN, Economics
XU, JIANGUO, Finance and Public Administration
XU, RENZHANG, Finance and Public Administration
YAN, DEYU, Accounting
YAN, LIDONG, Business Administration
YAN, QIZHONG, Business Administration
YAN, RICHU, Information Science
YANG, CANMING, Finance and Public Administration
YANG, JIAZHI, Economics
YANG, KAIHAN, Information Science
YANG, YUNYAN, Economics
YANG, ZONGHUI, Public Security
YAO, HUIYUAN, Economics
YAO, LI, Law
YE, QING, Finance and Public Administration
YU, XIYAN, Business Administration
YU, ZONGQI, Humanities
YUAN, JICHENG, Humanities
ZENG, QINGWEI, Information Science
ZHAN, CAILI, Accounting
ZHANG, CHAOQUN, Finance and Public Administration
ZHANG, FULIN, Humanities
ZHANG, HUAIFU, Finance and Public Administration
ZHANG, LONGPING, Accounting
ZHANG, SHIJING, Humanities
ZHANG, SHUZHEN, Law
ZHANG, YU, Public Security
ZHANG, YUANHUANG, Public Security
ZHANG, ZHENGLING, Humanities
ZHAO, LINGYU, Economics
ZHAO, MAN, Finance and Public Administration
ZHENG, ZHUJUN, Law
ZHOU, JUN, Banking and Insurance
ZHU, HAIFANG, Accounting
ZHU, YANFU, Economics
ZOU, LIGANG, Law
ZU, XINGRONG, Banking and Insurance

HONG KONG

Learned Societies

GENERAL

Royal Asiatic Society, Hong Kong Branch: GPO Box 3864, Hong Kong; tel. and fax 2813-7500; e-mail info@royalasiaticsociety.org.hk; internet www.royalasiaticsociety.org.hk; f. 1847, re-established 1959; for the encouragement of history, the arts, science and literature in relation to Asia, particularly Hong Kong and China and their cultures; lectures and social activities; 720 mems (incl. 150 overseas mems); library of 6,100 vols; Hon. Pres. ROBERT NIELD; Hon. Sec. DAVID MCKELLAR; publ. *Journal* (annually).

BIBLIOGRAPHY, LIBRARY SCIENCE AND MUSEOLOGY

Hong Kong Library Association: GPO Box 10095, Hong Kong; e-mail hklib@hklib.org.hk; internet www.hklib.org.hk; f. 1958; 694 mems; Pres. ANTHONY W. FERGUSON; Hon. Secs LUCINDA WONG; publs *Journal* (irregular), *Newsletter* (3 a year).

ECONOMICS, LAW AND POLITICS

Hong Kong Institute of Certified Public Accountants: 4th Fl., Tower Two, Lippo Centre, 89 Queensway, Hong Kong; tel. 22877228; fax 28656603; e-mail hksa@hksa.org.hk; internet www.hkicpa.org.hk; f. 1973; 23,224 mems; Pres. EDWARD F. K. CHEW; Chief Exec. and Registrar WINNIE C. W. CHEUNG; publ. *The Hong Kong Accountant* (monthly).

Hong Kong Management Association: 14/F Fairmont House, 8 Cotton Tree Drive, Central, Hong Kong; tel. 25266516; fax 28684387; e-mail hkma@hkma.org.hk; internet www.hkma.org.uk; f. 1960; management training courses, management consultancy services, library information, seminars, forums, awards and competitions; Chair. Hon. DAVID K. P. LI; Dir-Gen. ELIZABETH SHING; publ. *The Hong Kong Manager* (4 a year).

The Law Society of Hong Kong: 3rd Floor, Wing On House, 71 Des Voeux Rd, Central, Hong Kong; tel. 28460500; fax 28450387; internet www.hklawsoc.org.hk; f. 1907; 6,122 mems; Pres. PETER C. L. LO; publ. *Hong Kong Lawyer*.

LANGUAGE AND LITERATURE

Alliance Française: 123 Hennessy Rd, Wanchai Hong Kong; tel. 25277825; fax 25653478; e-mail info@alliancefrancaise.com.hk; internet www.alliancefrancaise.com.hk; offers courses and exams in French language and culture and promotes cultural exchange with France; Dir FRANÇOIS GAUDEAU.

British Council: 3 Supreme Court Rd, Admiralty, Hong Kong; tel. 29135100; fax 29135102; e-mail info@britishcouncil.org.hk; internet www.britishcouncil.org.hk/index.asp; teaching centre; offers courses and exams in English language and British culture and promotes cultural exchange with the UK; Dir RUTH GEE; Deputy Dir, Teaching Centre GEORGINA PEARCE.

Goethe-Institut: 14th Fl., Hong Kong Arts Centre, 2 Harbour Rd, Wanchai, Hong Kong; tel. 28020088; fax 28024363; e-mail info@hongkong.goethe.org; internet www.goethe.de/hongkong; f. 1963; offers courses and exams in German language and culture and promotes cultural exchange with Germany; library of 7,400 vols, including audiovisual materials; Dir MICHAEL MÜLLER-VERWEYEN.

Hong Kong Chinese PEN Centre: Flat A, 22F Block 4, City 1, Sha Tin, Hong Kong; f. 1955; 92 mems; library of 1,600 vols; Pres. CHU CHIH-TAI; Sec. WILLIAM HSU; publ. *PEN News* (weekly in Chinese).

MEDICINE

Hong Kong Medical Association: 5/F, 15 Hennessy Rd, Hong Kong; tel. 28650943; fax 25278285; e-mail hkma@hkma.org; internet www.hkma.org; f. 1920 to promote the welfare and protect the lawful interests of the medical profession, to promote co-operation with national and international medical societies, and to work for the advancement of medical science; 6,200 mems; Pres. Dr LO WING LOK; Hon. Sec. Dr LI SIU LUNG; publs *HKMA News* (monthly), *Hong Kong Medical Journal* (6 a year), *HKMA CME Bulletin* (monthly).

Research Institute

NATURAL SCIENCES

Physical Sciences

Hong Kong Observatory: 134A Nathan Rd, Kowloon, Hong Kong; tel. 29268200; fax 23119448; e-mail mailbox@hko.gov.hk; internet www.hko.gov.hk; f. 1883; govt dept which operates weather forecasting, cyclone warning and other meteorological and geophysical services; library of 40,000 vols; Dir Dr H. K. LAM; publs *Hong Kong Observatory Almanac* (annually), *Hong Kong Observatory Calendar*, *Hong Kong Tide Tables* (annually), *Daily Weather Chart*, *Marine Climatological Summaries* (annually), *Summary of Meteorological Observations in Hong Kong* (annually), *Tropical Cyclones* (annually), *Summary Charts for the South China Seas* (annually), *Monthly Weather Summary*.

Libraries and Archives

Hong Kong

Chinese University of Hong Kong University Library System: Sha Tin, New Territories, Hong Kong; tel. 2609-7305; fax 2603-6952; e-mail library@cuhk.edu.hk; internet www.lib.cuhk.edu.hk; f. 1963; 7 branch libraries: Chung Chi College Library, f. 1951; New Asia College Library, f. 1949; United College Library, f. 1956; Li Ping Medical Library, f. 1980; American Studies Library, f. 1993; Architecture Library, f. 1994; Law Library, f. 2006; 1,881,385 vols in Oriental and Western languages, 13,940 current periodicals; special collns: Careers Colln; CUHK theses submitted since 1967; Chinese Overseas colln; History of Medicine of Hong Kong, China and the Asia-Pacific region; Hong Kong Government documents; Hong Kong Studies; Instructional Materials colln; Modern Chinese Drama colln; rare Chinese books from the Yuan to the Qing dynasties; University Librarian Dr COLIN STOREY; publ. *Annotated Bibliography of Rare Books in the CUHK Libraries*.

Hong Kong Central Library: 66 Causeway Rd, Causeway Bay, Hong Kong; internet www.hkpl.gov.hk/hkcl; f. 2001; depository library for publs of Asian Development Bank, European Union, International Labour Organization, International Maritime Organization, United Nations, United Nations Educational, Scientific and Cultural Organization, World Bank, World Trade Organization and World Food Programme.

Hong Kong Polytechnic University Pao Yue-kong Library: Hung Hom, Kowloon, Hong Kong; tel. 2766-6857; fax 2765-8274; e-mail lbinf@polyu.edu.hk; internet www.lib.polyu.edu.hk; f. 1972; 930,734 books, 240,314 bound periodical vols, 640 electronic databases, 30,204 full-text e-journal titles, 179,842 e-books and 157 e-learning programmes; spec. collns: Industrial Standards (online, 55,967 vols); Slide Colln (260,000 items); local TV programmes (22,442); digital images (online, 117,704); audiovisual material (65,359 items); 387,618 microfiches; 2,392 reels of microfilm; PolyU Examination Paper Database, PolyU Course Scheme Database, PolyU Electronic Theses, Hongkongiana Online, Video-on-Demand, Newspaper Clippings Image Database; interlibrary loan and document delivery services; reference and personal information consultancy services,; Univ Librarian STEVE O'CONNOR; publs *Directory of Professional Associations and Learned Societies in Hong Kong*, *Newsletter*.

Public Records Office of Hong Kong: 13 Tsui Ping Rd, Kowloon, Hong Kong; tel. 2195-7700; fax 2804-6413; e-mail proinfo@cso.gcn.gov.hk; internet www.info.gov.hk/pro; f. 1972; 22,000 Hong Kong Government publs; newspapers collection; photographs collection; map collection; Archivist SIMON F. K. CHU.

University of Hong Kong Libraries: Pokfulam Rd, Hong Kong; tel. 28597000; fax 28589420; e-mail libadmin@hkucc.hku.hk; internet www.lib.hku.hk; f. 1911; 2,060,000 vols in East Asian and Western languages, 14,800 current print periodicals, 16,950 electronic titles on subscription, 61,000 audiovisual items, 48,700 reels of microfilm, 1,362,500 microfiches; spec. collns incl. Hong Kong Collection, Morrison Collection, Hong Kong Tourist Association Collection, Republic of China Government Publications, Taiwan Studies University of Hong Kong Theses; depository library for ADB, EDC, UN, UNRISD, WHO WTO publs; Librarian Dr ANTHONY W. FERGUSON.

Museums and Art Galleries

Hong Kong

Hong Kong Museum of Art: 10 Salisbury Rd, Tsim Sha Tsui, Kowloon, Hong Kong; tel. 2734-2092; fax 2723-7666; e-mail enquiries@lcsd.gov.hk; internet www.lcsd.gov.hk/hkma; f. 1962; Chinese antiquities, incl. the Henry Yeung collection; historical paintings, prints and drawings of Hong Kong, Macao and China, incl. Chater, Sayer, Law and Ho Tung collections; contemporary works by local artists; Chinese paintings and calligraphy, incl. the Xubaizhai Collection; Chief Curator CHRISTINA CHU.

Hong Kong Museum of History: 100 Chatham Rd South, Tsimshatsui, Kowloon, Hong Kong; tel. 2724-9042; fax 2724-9099; e-mail hkmh@lcsd.gov.hk; internet hk.history.museum; f. 1975; archaeology, ethnography, natural history and history of Hong Kong; Chinese fishing junk models; historical photographs and documents; postal history and numismatics collection; branches at Lei Cheng Uk Han Tomb Museum, Law Uk Folk Museum and Hong Kong Museum of Coastal Defence; Permanent exhibition 'The Hong Kong Story'; Chief Curator JOSEPH S. P. TING; publ. *Newsletter* (4 a year).

Hong Kong Science Museum: 2 Science Museum Rd, Tsim Sha Tsui East, Kowloon, Hong Kong; tel. 2732-3232; fax 2311-2248; e-mail science@lcsd.gov.hk; internet hk.science.museum; f. 1991; permanent and special exhibitions, education and extension activities, lecture hall and special exhibition hall rental; Chief Curator CHEE-KUEN YIP; publ. *Newsletter* (4 a year).

Hong Kong Space Museum: 10 Salisbury Rd, Tsim Sha Tsui, Kowloon, Hong Kong; tel. 27210226; fax 23115804; f. 1980 to promote interest in astronomy and related sciences by exhibitions, lectures, film, Omnimax and sky shows; 100 staff; library of 1,700 vols, also films and videos; Curator CHOW KIM FUNG; publs *Astrocalendar* (annually), *Newsletter* (quarterly).

Universities

CHINESE UNIVERSITY OF HONG KONG

Sha Tin, New Territories, Hong Kong
Telephone: 2609-7000
Fax: 2603-5544
Internet: www.cuhk.edu.hk

Founded 1963
Languages of instruction: Chinese, English
Academic year: August to July

Chancellor: CHIEF EXECUTIVE OF THE HONG KONG SPECIAL ADMINISTRATIVE REGION
Chairman of Council: EDGAR W. K. CHENG
Vice-Chancellor: LAWRENCE J. LAU
Pro-Vice-Chancellors: JACK C. Y. CHENG PAK-WAI LIU, KENNETH YOUNG
University Dean of Students: PUAY-PENG HO
Treasurer: ROGER K. H. LUK
Secretary: JACOB S. K. LEUNG
Registrar: BILLY K. L. SO
Librarian: COLIN STOREY

Library: see Libraries and Archives
Number of teachers: 1,059
Number of students: 17,587 (11,708 full-time, 5,879 part-time)
Publications: *Annals of Contemporary Diagnostic Pathology* (annually), *Asian Anthropology* (annually), *Asian Economic Journal* (4 a year), *Asian Journal of Counselling* (2 a year), *Asian Journal of English Language Teaching* (annually), *Asian Journal of Mathematics* (4 a year), *The China Review* (2 a year), *Chinese Academic Journal* (every 2 years), *Chinese Language Newsletter* (4 a year), *Comparative Literature and Culture* (annually), *Communications in Information and Systems* (4 a year), *Crosslinks in English Language Teaching* (every 2 years), *Education Journal* (2 a year), *Educational Research Journal* (2 a year), *Geographic Information Sciences* (2 a year), *Global Chinese Journal on Computers in Education* (2 a year), *Journal of Basic Education* (2 a year), *Journal of Chinese Studies* (annually), *Journal of Contemporary Chinese Education* (2 a year), *Journal of Translation Studies* (2 a year), *Methods and Application of Analysis* (4 a year), *Phenomenology and the Human Sciences* (annually), *Renditions* (2 a year), *Southeast Asia Bulletin of Mathematics* (6 a year), *Twenty-first Century* (6 a year)

DEANS

Faculty of Arts: DANIEL P. L. LAW
Faculty of Business Administration: TIEN-SHENG LEE
Faculty of Education: JOHN C. K. LEE
Faculty of Engineering: PETER T. S. YUM
Faculty of Medicine: TAI-FAI FOK
Faculty of Science: LEO W. M. LAU
Faculty of Social Science: YEE LEUNG
Graduate School: W. S. WONG

PROFESSORS

BAKER, H. D. R., Humanities
BOND, M. H., Psychology
CHAN, K. M., Orthopaedics and Traumatology
CHAN, N. H., Statistics
CHAN, W. W., Music
CHEN, H. C., Psychology
CHENG, J. C. Y., Orthopaedics and Traumatology
CHEUNG, F. M. C., Psychology
CHEUNG, S. H. N., Chinese Language and Literature
CHING, P. C., Electronic Engineering
CHIU, H. F. K., Psychiatry
CHOW, M. S. S., Pharmacy
CHUNG, T. K. H., Obstetrics and Gynaecology
COCKRAM, C. S., Medicine and Therapeutics (Medicine)
FAURE, D., History
FOK, T. F., Paediatrics
FUNG, K. P., Biochemistry
GIN, T., Anaesthesia and Intensive Care
GRIFFITHS, S., Public Health
HAZLETT, C. B., Medical Education
HO, S. S., Community and Family Medicine
HO, W. K. K., Biochemistry
HUI, M. K. M., Marketing
JIN, S. S. H., Translation
KEMBER, D. R., Learning Enhancement
KUAN, H. C., Government and Public Administration
KUNG, H. F., Virology
LAM, D. S. C., Ophthalmology and Visual Sciences
LANG, L. H. P., Finance
LAU, J. W. Y., Surgery
LAU, K. S., Mathematics

LAU, L. J., Economics
LAU, L. W. M., Physics (Materials Science)
LAU, S. K., Sociology
LEE, K. H., Hotel and Tourism Management, Marketing
LEE, R. P. L., Sociology
LEE, S. S., Infectious Disesases
LEE, S. Y., Statistics
LEE, T. T., Information Engineering
LEO, L. O. F., Humanities
LEUNG, K. S., Computer Science and Engineering
LEUNG, K. S., Orthopaedics and Traumatology
LEUNG, P. C., Orthopaedics and Traumatology
LEUNG, Y., Geography and Resource Management (Geography)
LEUNG, Y. S., History
LI, A. K. C., Surgery
LI, R. S. Y., Information Engineering
LI, W. K., Chemistry
LIN, C., Information Engineering, Electronic Engineering (Photonics)
LIU, P. W., Economics
LO, D. Y. M., Chemical Pathology
LO, L. N. K., Educational Administration and Policy
MCNAUGHT, C. M., Learning Enhancement
MIRRLEES, J. A., Distinguished Professor-at-Large
NG, H. K., Anatomical and Cellular Pathology
NG, T. B., Biochemistry
NGAN, K. N., Electronic Engineering
NIOU, E. M. S., Government and Public Administration
PARKER, D. H., English
POON, W. S., Surgery
SO, J. F. S., Fine Arts
SUN, S. S. M., Biology
SUNG, J. J. Y., Medicine and Therapeutics
TANG, K. L., Social Work
THOMPSON, D. R., Nursing (Clinical Nursing)
VAN HASSELT, C. A., Surgery (Otorhinolaryngology)
WONG, H. N. C., Chemistry
WONG, P. Y. D., Physiology
WONG, T. J., Accountancy
WONG, W. S., Information Engineering
WOO, J., Medicine and Therapeutics (Medicine)
WOO, K. S., Medicine and Therapeutics
WU, C., Chemistry
XIN, Z. P., Mathematics
XU, L., Computer Science and Engineering
XU, Y., Automation and Computer-Aided Engineering
YANG, C. N., Distinguished Professor-at-Large
YAO, A. C. C., Distinguished Professor-at-Large
YAO, D. D. W., Systems Engineering and Engineering Management
YAU, S. T., Distinguished Professor-at-Large
YEUNG, C. K., Surgery
YEW, D. T. W., Anatomy
YIM, A. P. C., Surgery
YOUNG, K., Physics
YOUNG, L., Finance
YUM, P. T. S., Information Engineering
ZHANG, J., Economics

CONSTITUENT COLLEGES

Chung Chi College: Sha Tin, Hong Kong; f. 1951; 296 teachers (full-time); 2,372 students (full-time); College Head YUEN-SANG LEUNG.

New Asia College: Sha Tin, Hong Kong; f. 1949; 261 teachers (full-time); 2,382 students (full-time); College Head HENRY N. C. WONG.

Shaw College: Sha Tin, Hong Kong; f. 1986; 247 teachers (full-time); 2,324 students (full-time); College Head PAK-CHUNG CHING.

United College: Sha Tin, Hong Kong; f. 1956; 246 teachers (full-time); 2,356 students (full-time); College Head KWOK-PUI FUNG.

ATTACHED INSTITUTES

Asia-Pacific Institute of Business: f. 1990; Exec Dir LESLIE YOUNG.

Graduate School: f. 1966; 8,081 students; Dean W. S. WONG.

Hong Kong Cancer Institute: f. 1990; Dir ANTHONY T. C. CHAN.

Hong Kong Institute of Asia-Pacific Studies: f. 1990; Dir Y. M. YEUNG.

Hong Kong Institute of Diabetes and Obesity: f. 2005; Dir JULIANA C. N. CHAN.

Hong Kong Institute of Educational Research: f. 1993; Dir LESLIE N. K. LO.

Institute of Biotechnology: f. 2003; Dir WALTER K. K. HO.

Institute of Chinese Medicine: f. 2000; Chair. P. C. LEUNG.

Institute of Chinese Studies: f. 1967; Dir J. F. S. SO.

Institute of Economics: f. 2005; Co-Dirs M. K. Y. FUNG, Y. W. SUNG.

Institute of Health Sciences: f. 2005; Dir (vacant).

Institute of Human Communicative Research: f. 2004; Dir CHARLES A. VAN HASSELT.

Institute of Mathematical Sciences: f. 1993; Dir S. T. YAU.

Institute of Optical Science and Technology: f. 2002; Dir CHINLON LIN.

Institute of Science and Technology: f. 1965; Dir WU CHI.

New Asia Yale-in-China Chinese Language Centre: f. 1963; Dir WU WEIPING.

Research Institute for the Humanities: f. 1991; Dir W. C. WONG.

School of Continuing Studies: f. 1965; Dir VICTOR S. K. LEE.

Shun Hing Institute of Advanced Engineering: f. 2004; Dir P. C. CHING.

CITY UNIVERSITY OF HONG KONG

83 Tat Chee Ave, Kowloon, Hong Kong
Telephone: 27887654
Fax: 27881167
Internet: www.cityu.edu.hk
Founded 1984 as City Polytechnic of Hong Kong; present name 1995
Autonomous control, financed by the University Grants Committee
Language of instruction: English
Academic year: September to August
President: Prof. H. K. CHANG
Vice-Presidents: Prof. EDMOND KO, Prof. DAVID TONG, Prof. Y. S. WONG
Librarian: Prof. C. C. CHENG (acting)
Library of 730,462 books, 160,975 vols of bound serials
Number of teachers: 1,138 (923 full-time, 215 part-time)
Number of students: 15,111 (11,369 full-time, 3,742 part-time)
Publications: *Annual Report* (annually), *Bulletin* (3 a year), *CityU Today* (monthly), *Linkage* (monthly), *Research Report* (annually)

DEANS AND PRINCIPAL

Faculty of Business: Prof. L. K. CHAN
Faculty of Humanities and Social Sciences: Prof. MATTHEW Y. CHEN
Faculty of Science and Engineering: Prof. RODERICK S. C. L. WONG
College of Higher Vocational Studies: JOHN DOCKERILL
School of Creative Media: DAVID SMITH
School of Graduate Studies: Prof. Y. V. HUI
School of Law: Prof. MIKE MCCONVILLE

HEADS OF DEPARTMENTS/DIVISIONS

Faculty of Business (tel. 27888550; fax 27887182; e-mail fblkchan@cityu.edu.hk; internet www.cityu.edu.hk/fb/homepage/index.htm):
- Accountancy: Prof. FERDINAND GUL
- Economics and Finance: Prof. EDEN YU
- Information Systems: Prof. K. K. WEI
- Management: Prof. KWOK LEUNG
- Management Sciences: Dr H. P. LO
- Marketing: Dr JOE N. ZHOU

Faculty of Humanities and Social Sciences (tel. 27887472; fax 27887258; e-mail fhmychen@cityu.edu.hk; internet www.cityu.edu.hk/fhs):
- Applied Social Studies: Prof. NG SIK-HUNG
- Chinese, Translation and Linguistics: Dr JONATHAN WEBSTER
- English and Communication: Prof. LEE CHIN-CHUAN
- Public and Social Administration: Prof. IAN HOLLIDAY

Faculty of Science and Engineering (tel. 27888653; fax 27888462; e-mail mawong@cityu.edu.hk; internet www.cityu.edu.hk/fse):
- Biology and Chemistry: Prof. DAVID J. RANDALL
- Building and Construction: Prof. ANDREW LEUNG YEE-TAK
- Computer Engineering and Information Technology: Prof. YAN HONG
- Computer Science: Prof. HORACE HO-SHING IP
- Electronic Engineering: Prof. DAVID HILL
- Manufacturing Engineering and Engineering Management: Prof. MICHAEL HUNG YAU-YAN
- Mathematics: Prof. ZHANG QIANG
- Physics and Material Science: Prof. HAYDN CHEN HAI-DUNG

College of Higher Vocational Studies (tel. 34426628; fax 27889315; e-mail opjohn@cityu.edu.hk; internet www.cityu.edu.hk/col):
- Building Science and Technology: JULIE KWOK-WAH MO
- Commerce: Dr KO SAI-HONG
- Computer Studies: Dr CHARLIE CHOI YIU-KUEN
- Language Studies: WANDA LAU WOON-YEE
- Social Studies: Dr WONG CHAN PIK-YUEN

ATTACHED INSTITUTES

Centre for Coastal Pollution and Conservation: Dir Prof. RUDOLF S. S. WU.

Centre of Electronic Packaging and Assemblies, Failure Analysis and Reliability Engineering: Dir Prof. Y. C. CHAN.

Centre for Innovative Applications of Internet and Multimedia Technologies: Dir Prof. HORACE H. S. IP.

Centre of Super-Diamond and Advanced Films: Dir Prof. S. T. LEE.

Chinese Civilisation Centre: Dir Prof. PEI KAI CHENG.

English Language Centre: Head JEAN YOUNG.

Institute of Chinese Linguistics: Dir Prof. C. C. CHENG.

Language Information Sciences Research Centre: Dir Prof. B. K. Y. T'SOU.

Liu Bie Ju Centre for Mathmatical Sciences: Dir Prof. RODERICK S. C. WONG.

Optoelectronics Research Centre: Dir Prof. P. L. CHU.

Quality Evaluation Centre: Dir Dr KWAN KWOK LEUNG.

School of Continuing and Professional Education: Dir CHARLES. K. H. WONG.
Wireless Communications Research Centre: Dir Prof. EDWARD YUNG KAI-NING.

HONG KONG BAPTIST UNIVERSITY

Kowloon Tong, Kowloon, Hong Kong
Telephone: 34117400
Fax: 23387644
E-mail: cpro@hkbu.edu.hk
Internet: www.hkbu.edu.hk

Founded 1956
Academic year: September to June
President and Vice-Chancellor: Prof. NG CHING-FAI
Vice-President (Academic): Prof. HERBERT H. TSANG
Vice-President (Administration) and Secretary: ANDY LEE
Vice-President (Development): Prof. FAN YIU KWAN
Vice-President (Special Projects): Prof. FRANK FU
Academic Registrar: Dr ROBERT LAM
Library of 927,232 vols, 3,565 current periodicals, 118,148 multimedia items, 57,477 e-book collections, 23,790 e-journals subscriptions, 160 databases
Number of teachers: 439 (full-time)
Number of students: 7,494
Publications: *Chinese and International Philosophy of Medicine Quarterly*, *Journal of the History of Christianity in Modern China*, *History and Culture*, *Sino Humanitas*

DEANS

Faculty of Arts: Prof. CHUNG LING
Faculty of Science: Prof. RICK WONG WAI KWOK
Faculty of Social Sciences: Prof. FRANK FU
School of Business: Prof. SIMON S. M. HO
School of Communication: Prof. GEORGETTE WANG
School of Continuing Education: Dr SIMON WONG
School of Chinese Medicine: Prof. LIU LIANG
Graduate School: Prof. TANG TAO
Academy of Visual Arts: Prof. WAN QINGLI

HONG KONG POLYTECHNIC UNIVERSITY

Yuk Choi Rd, Hung Hom, Kowloon, Hong Kong
Telephone: 27665111
Fax: 27643374
E-mail: polyu@polyu.edu.hk
Internet: www.polyu.edu.hk

Founded 1937 as Government Trade School; became Hong Kong Technical College 1947 and Hong Kong Polytechnic 1972; present name 1994
Autonomous control, financed by the University Grants Committee.
Language of instruction: English
Academic year: September to August
Chancellor: CHIEF EXECUTIVE OF THE HONG KONG SPECIAL ADMINISTRATIVE REGION OF THE PEOPLE'S REPUBLIC OF CHINA
President: Prof. POON CHUNG-KWONG
Deputy President: ALEXANDER H. C. TZANG
Vice-President (Academic Development): Prof. PHILIP K. W. YEUNG
Vice-President (Partnership and Development): Dr LUI SUN-WING
Vice-President (Research Development): Ir Prof. KO JAN-MING
Vice-President (Student Development): Prof. T. P. LEUNG
University Librarian: BARRY BURTON
Library: see Libraries and Archives
Number of teachers: 1,021 full-time
Number of students: 24,938
Publications: *Annual Report*, *University Calendar* (annually)

DEANS

Faculty of Applied Science and Textiles: Prof. ALBERT S. C. CHAN
Faculty of Business and Information Systems: Prof. JUDY TSUI
Faculty of Communication: Prof. T. P. LEUNG
Faculty of Construction and Land Use: Ir Prof. KO JAN-MING
Faculty of Engineering: Prof. SULEYMAN DEMOKAN
Faculty of Health and Social Sciences: Prof. THOMAS K. S. WONG

HEADS OF DEPARTMENTS

Faculty of Applied Science and Textiles (Rm A 407, Chung Sze Yuen Building, Hong Kong Polytechnic University, Hung Hom, Kowloon, Hong Kong; tel. 27665057; fax 23622578; e-mail scasteng@polyu.edu.hk; internet www.polyu.edu.hk/fast):

- Applied Biology and Chemical Technology: Prof. ALBERT S. C. CHAN
- Applied Mathematics: Prof. TEO KOK-LAY
- Applied Physics: Prof. C. L. CHOY
- Institute of Textiles and Clothing: Prof. TAO XIAOMING

Faculty of Business (Rm A 923, Li Ka Shing Tower, Hong Kong Polytechnic University, Hung Hom, Kowloon, Hong Kong; tel. 27665082; fax 23625773; e-mail fbenq@polyu.edu.hk; internet www.polyu.edu.hk/fb):

- Logistics: Prof. JOHN J. LIU
- Management and Marketing: Prof. EDWARD J. SNAPE
- School of Accounting and Finance: Prof. FERDINAND AKHTAR GUL

Faculty of Communication (Rm A 405, Chung Sze Yuen Building, Hong Kong Polytechnic University, Hung Hom, Kowloon, Hong Kong; tel. 27665066; fax 23638955; e-mail coquery@polyu.edu.hk; internet www.polyu.edu.hk/fcom):

- Chinese and Bilingual Studies: Dr CHAN SHUI-DUEN
- English: Prof. GRAHAME T. BILBOW
- School of Design: Prof. LORRAINE JUSTICE
- English Language Centre: Dr BRUCE MORRISON
- General Education Centre: Dr HO KOON-WAN (acting)

Faculty of Construction and Land Use (Rm AG 701, Chung Sze Yuen Building, Hong Kong Polytechnic University, Hung Hom, Kowloon, Hong Kong; tel. 27665038; fax 23622574; e-mail clfclu@polyu.edu.hk; internet www.polyu.edu.hk/~fclu):

- Building and Real Estate: Ir. Prof. ANDREW BALDWIN (acting)
- Building Services Engineering: Prof. JOHN GILLEARD
- Civil and Structural Engineering: Prof. Y. S. LI
- Land Surveying and Geo-Informatics: Prof. CHEN YONG-QI

Faculty of Engineering (Chung Sze Yuen Building, Hong Kong Polytechnic University, Hung Hom, Kowloon, Hong Kong; tel. 27665064; fax 21764563; e-mail denquiry@polyu.edu.hk; internet www.polyu.edu.hk/feng):

- Computing: Dr KEITH C. C. CHAN (acting)
- Electrical Engineering: Prof. KIT PO WONG
- Electronic and Information Engineering: Prof. ALEX WAI
- Industrial and Systems Engineering: Prof. W. B. LEE
- Mechanical Engineering: Prof. RONALD M. C. SO

Faculty of Health and Social Sciences (Rm A 408, Chung Sze Yuen Building, Hong Kong Polytechnic University, Hung Hom, Kowloon, Hong Kong; tel. 27665075; fax 23630146; e-mail fhss.email@polyu.edu.hk; internet www.polyu.edu.hk/fhss):

- Applied Social Sciences: Prof. ANGELINA W. K. YUEN TSANG
- Health Technology and Informatics: Prof. ARTHUR F. T. MAK
- Nursing: Prof. FRANCES WONG KAM-YUET
- Optometry: Prof. MAURICE K. H. YAP
- Rehabilitation Sciences: Prof. CHRISTINA HUI-CHAN

HONG KONG UNIVERSITY OF SCIENCE AND TECHNOLOGY

Clear Water Bay, Kowloon, Hong Kong
Telephone: 23586000
Fax: 23580545
Internet: www.ust.hk

Founded 1988; first student intake 1991
State control
Language of instruction: English
Academic year: September to June
Chancellor: CHIEF EXECUTIVE OF THE HONG KONG SPECIAL ADMINISTRATIVE REGION
President: PAUL C. W. CHU
Vice-President for Academic Affairs: Prof. YUK-SHEE CHAN
Vice-President for Administration and Business: PAUL BOLTON
Vice-President for Research and Development: Dr ROLAND T. CHIN
Director of Language Centre: Dr GREGORY C. A. JAMES
Director of Research Centre: Prof. ROLAND T. CHIN
Director of Library: SASMSON SOONG
Number of teachers: 458
Number of students: 6,290
Publications: *Academic Calendar*, *Annual Report*, *HKUST Newsletter*

DEANS

Business and Management: Prof. K. C. CHAN
Engineering: Prof. PHILLIP CHAN
Humanities and Social Science: Prof. WILLIAM TAY (acting)
Science: Prof. SHIU YUEN CHENG

PROFESSORS

BENLETAIEF, K., Electrical and Electronic Engineering
BIAN, Y. J., Social Science
BIDDLE, G. C., Accounting
CAO, X. R., Electrical and Electronic Engineering
CHAN, C. H., Electrical and Electronic Engineering
CHAN, C. M., Chemical Engineering
CHAN, C. T., Physics
CHAN, K. C., Finance
CHAN, K. K., Humanities
CHAN, K. L., Finance
CHAN, K. L., Mathematics
CHAN, Y. S., Finance
CHANG, C., Biology
CHANG, C. K., Chemistry
CHANSON, S., Computer Science
CHEN, C. W., Accounting
CHEN, S. N., Economics
CHENG, K. H., Economics
CHENG, S. Y., Mathematics
CHEUNG, M. S., Civil Engineering
CHEW, S. H., Economics
CHIN, T. H., Computer Science
CUE, N., Physics
DASGUPTA, S., Finance
DING, X. L., Social Science
EASTHAM, A. R., Civil Engineering

EASTHAM, T. R. L., Electrical and Electronic Engineering
FARH, L. J., Management of Organizations
FUNG, Y. M., Humanities
GE, W. K., Physics
GORN, G. J., Marketing
HA, A., Information and Systems Management
HAMDI, M., Computer Science
HAYNES, R. K., Chemistry
HSU, C. T., Mechanical Engineering
HU, I. C., Information and Systems Management
HUANG, J. C., Civil Engineering
HUANG, J. S., Mathematics
HUNG, C. T., Humanities
IP, N. Y., Biochemistry
KAO, S. Y., Humanities
KO, P. K., Electrical and Electronic Engineering
KWOK, C. S., Civil Engineering
KWOK, H. S., Electrical and Electronic Engineering
LAU, K. M., Electrical and Electronic Engineering
LAW, S. K., Management of Organizations
LEA, C. T., Electrical and Electronic Engineering
LEE, C. Y., Industrial Engineering and Engineering Management
LEE, D. L., Computer Science
LEE, Y. P., Biochemistry
LI, J. S., Mathematics
LI, X. Y., Chemistry
LI, Z. X., Electrical and Electronic Engineering
LIN, C. C., Industrial Engineering and Engineering Management
LIN, Y., Economics
LO, Y. L., Information and Systems Management
LOCHOVKY, F. H., Computer Science
LOY, M. T., Physics
LUI, T. M., Economics
LUNG, M., Biology
MOY, A., Mathematics
NG, K. M., Chemical Engineering
NG, T. K., Physics
NG, W. W., Civil Engineering
NI, M., Computer Science
PENG, H., Biology
PONG, T. C., Computer Science
QIAN, P. Y., Biology
RENNEBERG, R., Chemistry
SHEN, Y. S., Computer Science
SHENG, P., Physics
SIN, K. O., Electrical and Electronic Engineering
SO, Y. C., Social Science
TAM, K. Y., Information and Systems Management
TANG, H., Civil Engineering
TAY, W., Humanities
TONG, P., Physics
TSENG, M., Industrial Engineering and Engineering Management
TSUI, S. Y., Management of Organizations
TUNG, Y. K. R, Civil Engineering
VANHONACKER, W. R., Marketing
WEI, K. C., Finance
WESTLAND, J. C., Information and Systems Management
WONG, K. L., Physics
WOOD, D., Computer Science
WU, C. S., Biology
WU, Y. D., Chemistry
XU, K., Mathematics
YAN, Y. J., Chemistry
YANG, C. C., Mathematics
YANG, H., Civil Engineering
YU, K. R., Mathematics
YU, N. T., Chemistry
YU, T. X., Mechanical Engineering
YUE, P. L., Chemical Engineering
YUEN, M. F., Mechanical Engineering
ZHANG, G. C., Accounting
ZHANG, M. J., Biochemistry
ZHANG, T. Y., Mechanical Engineering
ZHANG, Z. Q., Physics
ZHOU, X. G., Management of Organizations
ZWEIG, D. S., Social Science
ZWICK, R., Marketing

ATTACHED INSTITUTES

Advanced Manufacturing Institute: Dir Prof. M. TSENG.

Biotechnology Research Institute: Dir Prof. Y. IP.

Europe Institute: Dir A. CHEUNG.

Hong Kong Telecom Institute of Information Technology: Dir Prof. K. BENLETAIEF.

Institute for the Environment and Sustainable Development: Dir Prof. M. FANG.

Institute for Integrated Microsystems: Dir Prof. T. X. YU.

Institute of Nano Science and Technology: Dir Prof. P. SHENG (acting).

Institute of Nanomaterials and Nanotechnology: Dir Prof. C. T. CHAN.

Logistics and Supply Chain Management Institute: Dir Prof. C. Y. LEE.

Shenzhen Institute: Dir Prof. Y. S. CHAN.

Sino Software Research Institute: Dir Prof. Y. S. SHEN.

ATTACHED RESEARCH CENTRES

Advanced Engineering Materials Facility: Dir Prof. K. Y. LEUNG.

Animal and Plant Care Facility: Dir Prof. S. C. WONG.

Applied Technology Center: Dir Dr K. K. YOUNG.

Center for Advanced Electronics System Packaging: Dir Prof. C. H. CHAN.

Center for Asian Financial Markets: Dir Prof. K. C. WEI.

Center for Chinese Linguistics: Dir Prof. M. ZHANG.

Center for Coastal and Atmosphere Research: Dir Prof. J. C. CHEN.

Center for Corporate Governance: Dir (vacant).

Center for Cultural Studies: Dir Prof. C. C. YEE.

Centre for Display Research: Dir Prof. H. S. KWOK.

Centre for Economic Development: Dir Prof. T. M. LUI.

Center for Energy and Thermal Systems: Dir Prof. C. T. HSU.

Center for Experimental Business Research: Dir Prof. R. ZWICK.

Center for Fund Management: Dir Prof. K. L. CHAN.

Center for Scientific Computation: Dir Prof. X. P. WANG.

Center for Wireless Information Technology: Dir Prof. K. BENLETAIEF.

CLP Power Wind/Wave Tunnel Facility: Dir Prof. C. S. KWOK.

Coastal Marine Laboratory: Dir Prof. P. Y. QIAN.

Consumer Media Center: Dir Prof. B. SHI.

Cooperative Nasopharyngeal Carcinoma Research Center: Dir Prof. L. LUNG.

Cyberspace Centre: Dir Prof. S. CHANSON.

Design and Manufacturing Services Facility: Dir Prof L. L. CAI.

Geotechnical Centrifuge Facility: Dir Prof W. W. NG.

Hainan Center: Dir Prof. Y. S. CHAN.

Hang Lung Center for Organizational Research: Dir Prof. S. Y. TSUI.

Infrastructure Research Center: Dir Prof. M. S. CHEUNG.

Materials Characterization and Preparation Facility: Dir Prof K. L. WONG.

Microelectronics Fabrication Facility: Dir Prof K. O. SIN.

Molecular Neuroscience Center: Co-Dirs Prof. Y. IP, Prof. Y. H. WONG.

Multimedia Technology Research Center: Dir Prof. C. L. AU.

Nansha Center: Dir Prof. T. H. CHIN.

Semiconductor Product Analysis and Design Enhancement Center: Dir Prof. K. O. SIN.

Shui On Center for China Business and Management: Dir Prof. K. C. CHAN (acting).

South China Research Center: Dir Prof. C. C. CHOI.

Survey Research Center: Dir Prof. Y. J. BIAN.

Technology Transfer Centre: Dir Dr Y. J. BIAN.

Traditional Chinese Medicine Safety Information Centre: Dir Dr C. T. CHE.

LINGNAN UNIVERSITY

Tuen Mun, Hong Kong
Telephone: 26168888
Fax: 24638363
Internet: www.ln.edu.uk

Founded 1967
Academic year: September to August
Pres.: Prof. EDWARD K. Y. CHEN
Vice-Pres.: Prof. MEE-KAU NYAW
Comptroller: HERDIP SINGH
Registrar: LOK-WOOD MUI
Library of 300,000 vols
Number of teachers: 142
Number of students: 2,141

DEANS

Business: Prof. TSANG-SING CHAN
Humanities and Social Sciences: Prof. STARR JOSEPH BARTON

HEADS OF DEPARTMENTS

Accounting and Finance: Prof. CHAN KOON-HUNG
Chinese: Prof. JOSEPH LAU
Cultural Studies: Dr CHAN CHING-KIU STEPHEN
Economics: Prof. HO LOK-SANG
English: Prof. DAVID BARRY D. ASKER
Information Systems: Prof. WONG BO-KAI (acting)
Language Institute: (vacant)
Management: Prof. DEAN WILLIAM TJOSVOLD
Marketing and International Business: Dr LUI HON-KWONG
Politics and Sociology: Prof. DAVID PHILLIPS
Philosophy: Prof. STEIN HAUGOM OLSEN
Translation: Prof. LAURENCE KWOK-PUN WONG

ATTACHED RESEARCH INSTITUTES

Asia-Pacific Institute of Ageing Studies: Dir Prof. DAVID PHILLIPS.

Centre for Asian Pacific Studies: Dir Prof. YAK-YEOW KUEH.

Centre for Literature and Translation: Dir Prof. CHING-CHIH LIU.

Centre for Public Policy Studies: Dir Prof. LOK-SANG HO.

Hong Kong Institute of Business Studies: Dir Prof. MEE-KAU NYAW.

Research Programme on Ethnicity and Overseas Chinese Economies: Dir Dr CHANG CHAK-YAN.

OPEN UNIVERSITY OF HONG KONG

30 Good Shepherd St, Homantin, Kowloon, Hong Kong

Telephone: 27112100

Fax: 27112100

E-mail: infoctr@ic.ouhk.edu.hk

Internet: www.ouhk.edu.hk

Founded 1989 as Open Learning Institute of Hong Kong; university status 1997.

President: Prof. JOHN CHI-YAN LEONG

Vice-President (Academic): Prof. DANNY WONG

Vice-President (Technology and Development): Prof. LEUNG CHUN-MING

Registrar: Dr R. T. ARMOUR

Librarian: WAI-MAN MOK

Number of teachers: 950

Number of students: 20,000

DEANS

Arts and Social Sciences: Prof. JOHN MINFORD (acting)

Business and Administration: Prof. Y. K. IP

Education and Languages: Prof. RONNIE CARR

Science and Technology: Prof. T. M. WONG

UNIVERSITY OF HONG KONG

Pokfulam Rd, Hong Kong

Telephone: 28592111

Fax: 28582549

Internet: www.hku.hk

Founded 1911

Academic year: September to June

Chancellor: CHIEF EXECUTIVE OF THE HONG KONG SPECIAL ADMINISTRATIVE REGION

Pro-Chancellor: Dr The Hon. DAVID K. P. LI

Vice-Chancellor: Prof. LAP-CHEE TSUI

Pro-Vice-Chancellors: Prof. C. F. LEE, Prof. J. G. MALPAS, Prof. J. A. SPINKS, Prof. P. K. H. TAM (acting), Prof. H. TONG

Treasurer: HENRY H. L. FAN

Registrar: H. W. K. WAI

Librarian: Dr A. W. FERGUSON

Number of teachers: 860 full-time

Number of students: 16,132

Publication: *Journal of Oriental Studies* (2 a year)

DEANS

Faculty of Architecture: Prof. K. W. CHAU

Faculty of Arts: Prof. J. G. MALPAS (acting)

Faculty of Business and Economics: Prof. R. Y. C. WONG (acting)

Faculty of Dentistry: Prof. L. P. SAMARANAYAKE

Faculty of Education: Prof. T. M BRAY

Faculty of Engineering: Prof. T. S. NG

Faculty of Law: Prof. J. M. M. CHAN

Faculty of Medicine: Prof. S. K. LAM

Faculty of Science: Dr F. C. C. LEUNG

Faculty of Social Sciences: Dr J. T. H. TANG

PROFESSORS

ABERNETHY, A. B., Human Performance

AU, T. K. F., Psychology

BRAY, T. M., Education

BURNS, J. P., Politics and Public Administration

CHAN, D. K. O., Zoology

CHAN, M. M. W., Medicine

CHAN, V. N. Y., Medicine

CHANG, E. C., Business

CHAU, K. W., Real Estate and Construction

CHE, C. M., Chemistry

CHEAH, K. S. E., Biochemistry

CHENG, K. M., Education

CHENG, K. S., Physics

CHIN, F. Y. L., Computer Science and Information Systems

CHO, C. H., Pharmacology

CHOW, N. W. S., Social Work and Social Administration

CHOW, S. P., Orthopaedic Surgery

CHWANG, A. T. Y., Mechanical Engineering

DUGGAN, B. J., Mechanical Engineering

FAN, S. T., Surgery

FANG, H. H. P., Civil Engineering

FREWER, R. J. B., Architecture

FUNG, P. C. W., Medicine

GHAI, Y. P., Law

GOLDSTEIN, L., Philosophy

HAGG, E. U. O., Dentistry

HANSEN, C., Philosophy

HEDLEY, A. J., Community Medicine

HO, P. C., Obstetrics and Gynaecology

IP, M. S. M., Medicine

JIM, C. Y., Geography

KO, R. C. C., Zoology

KUMANA, C. R., Medicine

KUNG, H., Molecular Biology

LAI, C. L., Medicine

LAI, K. N., Medicine

LAM, E., Botany

LAM, K. S. L., Medicine

LAM, S. K., Medicine

LAM, T. H., Community Medicine

LAM, W. K., Medicine

LAU, A. H. L., Business

LAU, C. P., Medicine

LAU, Y. L., Paediatrics and Adolescent Medicine

LEE, C. F., Civil Engineering

LEE, J. H. W., Civil Engineering

LI, V. O. K., Electrical and Electronic Engineering

LI, W. K., Statistics and Actuarial Science

LIANG, R. H. S., Medicine

LIE KEN JIE, M. S. F., Chemistry

LO, C. M., Surgery

LUK, K. D. K., Orthopaedic Surgery

MALPAS, J. G., Earth Sciences

MAN, R. Y. K., Mathematics

MOK, N., Mathematics

NG, T. S., Electrical and Electronic Engineering

NUNAN, D. C., English Centre

SAMARANAYAKE, L. P., Dentistry

SHERRIN, C. H., Professional Legal Education

TAM, P. K. H., Surgery

TAMBLING, J. C. R., Comparative Literature

TANG, S. W., Psychiatry

TIDEMAN, H., Dentistry

TONG, H., Statistics

TSE, D. K. C., Business

TSUI, A. B. M., Education

WEI, W. I., Surgery

WONG, J., Surgery

WONG, R. Y. C., Economics and Finance

WONG, S. L., Sociology

WU, F. F., Electrical and Electronic Engineering

YAM, V. W. W., Chemistry

YANG, E. S., Electrical and Electronic Engineering

YEH, A. G. O., Urban Planning and Environmental Management

YUEN, K. Y., Microbiology

ZHANG, F., Physics

Colleges

Hong Kong Academy for Performing Arts: 1 Gloucester Rd, Hong Kong; tel. 25848500; fax 28024372; e-mail aso@hkapa.edu; internet www.hkapa.edu; f. 1984; 3-year B.F.A. and B.Mus. programmes, 2-year diploma, 2-year advanced diploma, 1-year professional diploma programmes, 2-year advanced certificate, 2-year certificate, 1-year professional certificate programmes; library: 105,000 vols; 453 teachers (79 full-time, 374 part-time); 749 students; Dir Prof. KEVIN THOMPSON; Assoc. Dir (Administration) and Registrar Dr HERBERT HUEY; Assoc. Dir (Operations) PHILIP SODEN; Librarian LING WAI-KING; publs *Annual Report*, *Dramatic Arts* (annually)

DEANS

Dance: SUSAN STREET

Drama: DAVID JIANG

Film and Television: RICHARD WOOLLEY

Music: BENEDICT CRUFT

Technical Arts: JOHN WILLIAMS

Hong Kong Institute of Education: 10 Lo Ping Rd, Tai Po, New Territories, Hong Kong; tel. 29488888; fax 29486000; e-mail listen@its.ied.edu.hk; internet www.ied.edu.hk; f. 1994 by merger of five existing instns; provides full-time and part-time initial and professional development teacher education programmes at pre-primary, primary and secondary levels; offers 32 initial teacher education and 21 professional development programmes at sub-degree, degree and post-graduate diploma and masters degree levels; library: 605,914 vols; 381 teachers; 7,890 students; Pres. Prof. PAUL MORRIS.

Hong Kong Institute of Vocational Education, Morrison Hill Campus: 6 Oi Kwan Rd, Wanchai, Hong Kong; tel. 28358374; fax 28357413; internet www.vtc.edu.hk/ive/mh; f. 1969; courses in commercial studies, construction, electronic engineering, mechanical engineering, general studies, computing; library: 54,236 vols; 300 full-time teachers; 6,260 students; Principal MITZI LEUNG.

MACAO

Learned Societies

ECONOMICS, LAW AND POLITICS

Associação de Ciências Sociais de Macau (Macao Society of Social Sciences): Estrada Adolfo Loureiro 3A, Edificio Tak On, 3rd Floor A, POB 957, Macao; tel. 319880; fax 319880; f. 1985 to study society and serve Macao; 40 mems; Pres. HUANG WEI-WEN; Sec. CHEONG CHOK FU; publ. *Huo Keng* (Mirror of Macao, 2 a year).

FINE AND PERFORMING ARTS

Instituto Cultural de Macau: Av. da Amizade, Praceta Miramar 87-U, Ed. San On, Macao; tel. 700391; fax 700405; e-mail postoffice@icm.gov.mo; internet www.icm.gov.mo; f. 1982; cultural studies, classes for music, drama and ballet, promotion of cultural events; also oversees the Macao Historical Archives, the Macao Central Library and the Macao Museum (see below); Pres. Dra HEIDI HO; publ. *Revista de Cultura* (in English, Chinese and Portuguese, quarterly).

LANGUAGE AND LITERATURE

Alliance Française: Travessa Do Bom Jesus, 4th Fl, Macao; tel. 965342; fax 962697; e-mail allifran@macau.ctm.net; internet alliancefrmacao.free.fr/; offers courses and exams in French language and culture and promotes cultural exchange with France.

Libraries and Archives

Macao

Arquivo Histórico de Macau: Av. Conselheiro Ferreira de Almeida 91–93, Macao; tel. 330913; fax 561495; e-mail info.ah@icm.gov.mo; f. 1952; parent instn Instituto Cultural de Macau since 1986; 7,000 vols; Dir MARIA FATIMA LAU; publ. *Boletim do Arquivo Histórico de Macau*.

Biblioteca Central de Macau (Central Library of Macao): Av. Conselheiro Ferreira de Almeida 89A– B, Macao; tel. 371623; fax 318756; e-mail info@icm.gov.mo; f. 1895; 200,000 vols; general collection; Chinese Books (Sir Robert Ho Tung); parent instn Instituto Cultural de Macau since 1986; Dir TANG, MEI LIN; publs *Boletim Bibliográfico de Macau*, *Boletim de Literatura Infantil*, *Boletim Bibliográfico de Literatura Portuguesa*.

Biblioteca do Edificio do IACM (IACM Building Library): Av. Alm. Ribeiro 163, Edificio do IACM, Macao; tel. 572233; fax 312772; fmrly Biblioteca do Leal Senado; spec. collections incl. historical and scholarly works on China and Portuguese rule in the Far East and Africa; 30,000 vols, 20 periodicals.

Biblioteca Sir Robert Ho Tung (Sir Robert Ho Tung Library): Largo do Sto. Agostinho 3, Macao; tel. 377117; fax 314456; f. 1958; 17,592 vols; Librarian SAM CHAN FAI; publ. *Boletim Bibliográfico de Macau*.

Museums and Art Galleries

Macao

Museu de Arte de Macau (Macao Museum of Art): Centro Cultural de Macau, Av. Xian Xing Hai s/n Nape, Macao; tel. 7919800; fax 751317; e-mail artmuseum@iacm.gov.mo; internet www.artmuseum.gov.mo; f. 1999; collections include Shi Wan Ceramics, Chinese painting and calligraphy; historical pictures, Macao contemporary art; Dir UNG VAI MENG.

Museu de Macau (Macao Museum): Praceta do Museu de Macau 112, Macao; tel. 357911; fax 358503; e-mail macmuseu@macau.ctm.net; internet www.macaumuseum.gov.mo; f. 1998; history of Macao; administered by the Cultural Affairs Bureau of the Macao SAR Govt; library of 3,000 vols; Dir IOK LAN FU CHAN.

University

UNIVERSIDADE DE MACAU
(University of Macau)

Av. Padre Tomás Pereira SJ, Taipa, Macao
Telephone: 831622
Fax: 831694
E-mail: webmaster@umac.mo
Internet: www.umac.mo

Founded 1981 as University of East Asia; present name 1991
State control
Languages of instruction: Chinese, Portuguese, English
Academic year: September to June

Chancellor: CHIEF EXECUTIVE OF MACAO SPECIAL ADMINISTRATIVE REGION
Rector: Prof. IU VAI PAN
Vice-Rectors: Prof. RUI MARTINS HUANG YAJUN
Administrator: ALEX LAI IAT LONG
Librarian: Prof. CHARLES YEN

Library of 140,000 vols, 1,200 periodicals
Number of teachers: 343
Number of students: 5,020

Publications: *Boletim da Faculdade de Direito* (in Chinese and Portuguese, 2 a year), *Journal of Macau Studies* (3 a year)

DEANS

Faculty of Business Administration: Dr HUANG YAJUN
Faculty of Education: Dr DOMINICA SO CHIU-HO
Faculty of Law: Prof. MANUEL MARCELINO ESCOVAR TRIGO
Faculty of Science and Technology: Prof. LI YIPING
Faculty of Social Sciences and Humanities: Prof. LIU BOLONG

CHINA (TAIWAN)

The Higher Education System

Until 1947 Taiwan was governed from the mainland China; however, in 1947 the Chinese communists came to power in Beijing, and the National Government was forced to remove itself to Taipei, the capital of Taiwan, where it established the 'Republic of China'. The population is mainly Chinese in origin, and the official language is Mandarin (Guoyu); Taiwanese, Hakka and English are also spoken. Most universities have been founded since the establishment of the Republic of China, but some were formerly mainland institutions that either relocated during the Communist takeover or were refounded; these include Fu-Jen Catholic University (founded in 1925 in Beijing), National Central University (originally based in Nanking), National Chiao Tung University (founded in 1896 in Shanghai), National Tsing Hua University (founded in 1911 in Beijing), and Soochow University (founded in 1900 in the mainland province of Jiangsu). In 2005/06 there were 162 universities, junior colleges and independent colleges; total enrolment in higher education in that year was 1,296,558 students. In 1987 the nine teachers' junior colleges were upgraded to teachers' colleges. These admit senior secondary graduates for a four-year course. High school teachers are trained at normal universities. Higher education is highly centralized and the Constitution places great emphasis on the importance of education. The higher education system is based on the US model.

The Ministry of Education supervises the Universities and Colleges Joint Entrance Examination, which is required for admission to higher education. Students, however, may also gain admission through two other methods, either by applying directly to the institution in question and meeting that institution's entry requirements, or through recommendation on grounds of academic excellence.

Junior colleges, which provide two- or five-year Junior College Diploma programmes, are the first level of higher education. Two-year junior colleges admit graduates from Senior and Senior Vocational High Schools, while five-year junior colleges accept students from Junior High Schools. The majority of junior colleges are privately-run. Institutes of technology operate on a similar basis: two-year institutes admit junior college graduates and four-year institutes admit senior vocational school graduates. There are also 'Open' universities which specialize in adult education.

The Bachelors degree is the main university undergraduate qualification, and usually lasts four years, although specialist programmes such as dentistry and medicine may take six or seven years. At postgraduate level, the Masters degree requires one to four years' study, while the final qualification, the Doctorate, requires two to seven years' study following the Masters. Technical and vocational education and training is provided by senior vocational schools and junior colleges. Periods of study vary between two to five years.

Learned Societies

GENERAL

Academia Sinica: 128 Academia Rd, Section 2, Nankang, Taipei 115; tel. (2) 27822120; fax (2) 27853847; internet www.sinica.edu.tw; f. 1928; 220 mems; attached research institutes: see Research Institutes; library of 2,236,000 vols; Pres. Dr YUAN-TSEH LEE; Dir-Gen. Dr YIH-HSIUNG YEH; Chief of Secretariat Dr CHI-CHIUNG LO; publs *Bulletin of the Institute of Mathematics*, *Botanical Bulletin* (quarterly), *Zoological Studies* (quarterly), *Bulletin of the Institute of History and Philosophy*, *Taiwan Journal of Anthropology* (2 a year), *Bulletin of the Institute of Modern History* (4 a year), *Academia Economic* (papers), *EurAmerica Quarterly*, *Journal of Social Sciences and Philosophy*, *Taiwanese Sociological Review* (2 a year), *Taiwan Historical Research* (2 a year), *Language and Linguistics* (quarterly), *Asia-Major* (2 a year), *Bulletin of the Institute of Ethnology*, *Academia Sinica* (2 a year), *Mathmedia* (quarterly), *Newsletter for Modern Chinese History* (2 a year), *Statistica Sinica* (quarterly), *Research on Women in Chinese History* (annually), *Asia-Pacific Forum* (quarterly), *Disquisitions of the Past and Present* (2 a year), *Taiwan Economic Forecasts and Plicies Academia Economic Papers*.

China Academy: Hwa Kang, Yang Ming Shan; f. 1966; private instn for sinological studies, consisting of 20 academic asscns and research institutions and Chinese and foreign mems; 591 acads, 312 hon. acads, 1,815 fellows; library of 450,000 vols; Pres. CHANG CHI-YUN; Sec.-Gen. PAN WEI-HO; publs *Sino-American Relations* (quarterly in English), *Beautiful China Pictorial Monthly* (bilingual Chinese and English), *Sinological Monthly* (Chinese), *Sinological Quarterly* (Chinese), *Renaissance Monthly* (Chinese), *Chinese Culture* (quarterly in English).

China National Association of Literature and the Arts: 4 Lane 22, Nuigpo St W, Taipei.

China Society: 7 Lane 52, Wenchow St, Taipei; f. 1960; centre for Chinese studies; 100 mems; Pres. Dr CHEN CHI-LU; publ. *Journal* (annually).

AGRICULTURE, FISHERIES AND VETERINARY SCIENCE

Agricultural Association of China: 14 Wenchow St, Taipei; tel. (2) 23636681; f. 1917; mems: 159 instns, 2,554 individuals; Pres. TSONG-SHIEN WU; publ. *Journal* (quarterly).

Chinese Forestry Association: 2 Sec. 1, Hang-chow South Rd, Taipei 100; tel. (2) 33221299; fax (2) 33221099; e-mail cfa@forest.gov.tw; internet www.forestry.org.tw; f. 1967; 1,219 mems; Chair. JEN-TEH YEN; publ. *Quarterly Journal of Chinese Forestry*.

BIBLIOGRAPHY, LIBRARY SCIENCE AND MUSEOLOGY

Library Association of China: C/o National Central Library, 20 Chungshan S. Rd, Taipei; tel. (2) 23312475; fax (2) 23700899; e-mail lac@msg.ncl.edu.tw; internet lac.ncl.edu.tw; f. 1953; 2,800 mems; Pres. FANG-RUNG JUANG; Sec.-Gen. CHAO-CHEN CHEN; publs *Bulletin* (2 a year), *Newsletter* (4 a year).

ECONOMICS, LAW AND POLITICS

Chinese National Foreign Relations Association: 3rd Floor, 94 Nanchang St, Sec. 1, Taipei; Pres. HUANG KUO-SHU.

National Bar Association: 124 Chungking South Rd, Sec. 1, Taipei.

HISTORY, GEOGRAPHY AND ARCHAEOLOGY

Academia Historica (Academy of History): 406 Sec. 2, Pei Yi Rd, Hsintien, Taipei; tel. (2) 22175500; fax (2) 22170317; e-mail nha@academia.drnh.gov.tw; internet www.drnh.gov.tw; f. 1947; responsible for researching and compiling material on Taiwanese national history; 175 mems; library of 10,000,000 items (nat. archives, books, documents); Pres. CHANG YEN HSIEN; Sec.-Gen. Prof. LI CHUNG KUANG; publs *Bulletin* (2 a year), *Journal* (2 a year).

LANGUAGE AND LITERATURE

British Council: 2F-1, 106 XinYi Rd, Sec. 5, Taipei 110; tel. (2) 87221000; fax (2) 87860985; e-mail enquiries@britishcouncil.org.tw; internet www.britishcouncil.org/taiwan; teaching centre; offers courses and exams in English language and British culture and promotes cultural exchange with the UK; attached office in Kaohsiung; Dir GORDON SLAVEN.

Chinese Language Society: c/o Taiwan Normal University, Hoping East Rd, Taipei; f. 1953; Dir MAO TZU-SHUI; publ. *Chinese Language Monthly*.

MEDICINE

Chinese Medical Association: 201 Shih-Pai Rd, Sec. II, Taipei; f. 1915; 1,672 mems; Pres. Dr KWANG-JUEI LO; Sec.-Gen. Dr YANG-TE TSAI; publ. *Chinese Medical Journal* (monthly).

NATURAL SCIENCES

Mathematical Sciences

Chinese Statistical Association: 1 Nan Chung Rd, Sec. 1, Taipei; f. 1941; 1,082 mems; Pres. C. C. LEE; publ. *Chinese Statistical Journal*.

Mathematical Society of the Republic of China: Dept of Mathematics, National Cheng Kung University, Tainan 70101; fax (6) 2743191; Pres. LEE YUH-JIA; Sec. HUANG YOUNG-YE.

Physical Sciences

Chemical Society: POB 1-18, Nankang, Taipei; tel. (2) 26530323; fax (2) 26530440; e-mail ccswww@gate.sinica.edu.tw; internet www.ccs.sinica.edu.tw; f. 1932; 3,200 mems; Sec.-Gen. TASHIN J CHOW; publs *Journal* (6 a year in English), *Hua Hsueh* (4 a year in Chinese).

Committee on the Promotion of the Peaceful Uses of Atomic Energy: 110 Yenping South Rd, Taipei; Pres. MILTON J. T. SHIEH.

Physical Society of China: POB 23-30, Taipei.

PHILOSOPHY AND PSYCHOLOGY

Confucius-Mencius Society of the Republic of China: 45 Nanhai Rd, Taipei; f. 1960; spreads knowledge about Confucius and Mencius, seeks the improvement of public morals and the creation of a better society; 3,900 mems; Chair. Dr CHEN LI-FU; Sec. HUA CHUNG-LIN; publ. publs include *Confucius-Mencius Monthly*, *Journal of Confucius-Mencius Society*.

RELIGION, SOCIOLOGY AND ANTHROPOLOGY

Chinese Association for Folklore: 422 Fulin Rd, POB 68-1292, Shihlin, Taipei; f. 1932; Chinese and Asian folklore; 47 mems; library of 1,000 vols and MSS; Chair. Prof. LOU TSU-KUANG; Sec. AMY LOU.

TECHNOLOGY

Chinese Institute of Civil and Hydraulic Engineering: 4th Fl., 1 Jen Ai Rd, 2 Taipei; tel. (2) 23926325; fax (2) 23964260; e-mail ciche@ciche.org.tw; internet www.ciche.org.tw; f. 1973; 7,500 mems; Pres. YU CHENG; publs *Journal of Civil and Hydraulic Engineering* (quarterly), *Journal of the Chinese Institute of Civil and Hydraulic Engineering* (quarterly).

Chinese Institute of Engineers: Fl. 3, No. 1 Ren-ai Rd, Sec. 2, Taipei 100; tel. (2) 23925128; fax (2) 23973003; e-mail secretariat@cie.org.tw; internet www.cie.org.tw; f. 1912; 11,501 mems; library of 7,334 vols, 60 periodicals; Sec. FENZA CHIANG; publs *Engineering Journal* (every 2 months), *Newsletter* (quarterly), *Transactions* (every 2 months).

Research Institutes

GENERAL

National Institute for Compilation and Translation: 247 Choushan Rd, Taipei; fax (2) 23629256; f. 1932; translates foreign books, examines and approves textbooks, standardizes scientific and technical terms; library of 60,000 vols; Dir NANCY CHAO LI-YUN; publs *The Journal*, periodicals (2 a year).

AGRICULTURE, FISHERIES AND VETERINARY SCIENCE

Council of Agriculture (COA): 37 Nanhai Rd, Taipei; tel. (2) 23812991; fax (2) 23310341; e-mail coa@mail.coa.gov.tw; internet www.coa.gov.tw; f. 1984; govt agency under the Exec. Yuan, with ministerial status; administers nat. agriculture, forestry, fisheries, livestock farming and food; library of 18,000 vols; Minister CHIA-CHUANG SU; publs *General Reports* (annually), technical papers, news releases (irregular).

Taiwan Agricultural Research Institute: 189 Chung-Cheng Rd, Wan-Feng, Wu-Feng, Taichung; tel. (4) 3302301; fax (4) 3338162; e-mail mwf-doc@wufeng.tari.gov.tw; internet www.tari.gov.tw; f. 1895; insect collection; Dir LIN CHIEN-YIH; publs *Journal of Agricultural Research of China* (quarterly), *Annual Report*.

Taiwan Fisheries Research Institute: 199 Hou-Ih Rd, Keelung 220; tel. (2) 24622101; fax (2) 24629388; f. 1933; library of 16,000 vols; Dir-Gen I-CHIU LIAO; publs *Journal*, research reports.

Taiwan Forestry Research Institute: 53 Nan-Hai Rd, Taipei, 10066; tel. (2) 23039978; fax (2) 23142234; e-mail service@serv.tfri.gov.tw; internet www.tfri.gov.tw; f. 1985; 376 mems; library of 33,000 vols; Dir HEN-BIAU KING; Sec.-Gen. KUO-CHUAN LIN; publ. *Journal of Forest Science* (quarterly).

Taiwan Sugar Research Institute: 54 Sheng Chan Rd, Tainan; tel. (6) 2671911; fax (6) 2685425; e-mail tsc02@taisugar.com.tw; f. 1902; supported by Taiwan Sugar Corpn; library of 46,800 vols; Dir LONG-HUEI WANG; publs *Report* (quarterly in Chinese, English summary), *Annual Report* (in English), *Technical Bulletin*, *Extension Bulletin*.

ECONOMICS, LAW AND POLITICS

Co-operative League of the Republic of China: 11-2 Fu Chow St, Taipei; tel. (2) 23219343; fax (2) 23517918; f. 1940; co-operative business research and education; Chair. YANG CHIA-LIN; Exec. Dir/Sec.-Gen. HSU WEN-FU; publs *CLC Co-operative News* (annually), *Co-operative Economics* (quarterly).

Institute of Economics: C/o Academia Sinica, Nankang, Taipei 11529; tel. (2) 27822791; fax (2) 27853946; internet www.sinica.edu.tw/~econ; attached to Academia Sinica; Dir Dr CHUNG-MING KUAN; f. 1962; publs *Academia Economic Papers* (4 a year), *Taiwan Economic Forecast and Policy* (2 a year).

FINE AND PERFORMING ARTS

National Taiwan Arts Education Center: 47 Nan Hai Rd, Taipei; tel. (2) 23110574; fax (2) 23122555; e-mail service@linux.arte.gov.tw; internet www.arte.gov.tw; f. 1957; in charge of the research, extension and guidance of art education in Taiwan; Dir JOSEPH TSU-SHENG WU; publs *Journal of Aesthetic Education* (every 2 months), *Newsletter of Arts Education* (monthly), *The International Journal of Arts Education* (2 a year).

HISTORY, GEOGRAPHY AND ARCHAEOLOGY

Institute of History and Philology: c/o Academia Sinica, Nankang, Taipei 11529; attached to Academia Sinica; Dir Prof. TUNG-KUEI KUAN.

Institute of Modern History: C/o Academia Sinica, Nankang, Taipei 11529; attached to Academia Sinica; Dir Prof. YU-FA CHANG.

MEDICINE

Institute of Biomedical Sciences, Preparatory Office: C/o Academia Sinica, Taipei 115; attached to Academia Sinica; Dir Dr CHENG-WEN WU.

NATURAL SCIENCES

General

National Science Council: 106 Ho-ping East Rd, Section 2, Taipei 106; tel. (2) 27377973; fax (2) 27377248; e-mail tjhsu@nsc.gov.tw; internet www.nsc.gov.tw; f. 1959; a branch of central government which promotes national science and technology development, supports academic research, and establishes industrial parks; Exec. Officer TSENG-JU HSU; publs *East Asian Science, Technology and Society* (4 a year in English), *Indicators of Science and Technology* (in Chinese and English, annually), *International Journal of Science and Mathematics Education* (4 a year in English), *Journal of Biomedical Science* (6 a year in English), *NSC Monthly* (in Chinese, monthly), *NSC Review* (annually, in English and Chinese), *Yearbook of Science and Technology* (in Chinese, annually).

Biological Sciences

Central Laboratory of Molecular Biology, Preparatory Office: C/o Academia Sinica, Nankang, Taipei 11529; attached to Academia Sinica; Dir Dr CHIEN HO.

Institute of Biological Chemistry: C/o Academia Sinica, Nankang, Taipei 11529; attached to Academia Sinica; Dir Dr WEN-CHANG CHANG (acting).

Institute of Botany: C/o Academia Sinica, Nankang, Taipei 11529; tel. (2) 27899590; fax (2) 27827954; e-mail boplshaw@ccvax.sinica.edu.tw; internet www.botany.sinica.edu.tw; f. 1929; attached to Academia Sinica; Dir Dr JEI-FU SHAW; publs *Botanical Bulletin of Academia Sinica* (4 a year), *Annual Report*.

Institute of Zoology: C/o Academia Sinica, Nankang, Taipei 11529; attached to Academia Sinica; Dir Dr JEN-LEIH WU.

Mathematical Sciences

Institute of Mathematics: C/o Academia Sinica, Nankang, Taipei 11529; attached to Academia Sinica; Dir Dr KO-WEI LIH.

Institute of Statistical Science: c/o Academia Sinica, 128 Academia Rd Sec. 2, Taipei 115; tel. (2) 27835611; fax (2) 27831523; e-mail hlwu@stat.sinica.edu.tw; internet www.stat.sinica.edu.tw; f. 1982; attached to Academia Sinica; 40 mems; Dir Dr KER-CHAU LI; publ. *Statistica Sinica* (quarterly).

Physical Sciences

Atomic Energy Council: 67 Lane 144, Keelung Rd, Sec. 4, Taipei 106; tel. (2) 23634180; fax (2) 23635377; f. 1955; govt agency for the peaceful application of atomic energy; library of 11,000 vols, deposit library at the National Tsing Hua Univ. of 36,000 vols and 424,000 microcards; Chair. Dr YIH-YUN HSU; Sec.-Gen. KUANG-CHI LIU; publs *Nuclear Science Journal* (every 2 months), *Nuclear Climate* (monthly).

Central Geological Survey: POB 968, Taipei 100; tel. (2) 29462793; fax (2) 29429291; e-mail cgs@linx.moeacgs.gov.tw; internet www.moeacgs.gov.tw; f. 1946; library of 50,000 vols and periodicals; Dir CHAO-CHUNG LIN; publs *Bulletin*, *Ti-Chih* (geology, 2 a year), *Annual Report*; maps.

Institute of Atomic and Molecular Sciences, Preparatory Office: C/o Academia Sinica, Nankang, Taipei 11529; attached to Academia Sinica; Dir Dr CHAO-TIN CHANG.

Institute of Chemistry: C/o Academia Sinica, Nankang, Taipei 11529; attached to Academia Sinica; Dir Dr SUNNEY I. CHAN.

Institute of Earth Sciences: C/o Academia Sinica, Nankang, Taipei 11529; tel. (2) 27839910; fax (2) 27839871; attached to Academia Sinica; Dir Dr YEH YIH-HSIUNG.

Institute of Information Science: C/o Academia Sinica, Nankang, Taipei 11529; attached to Academia Sinica; Dir Dr YUE-SUN KUO (acting).

Institute of Nuclear Energy Research: POB 3, Lung-Tan 32500; tel. (2) 3651717; fax (3) 4711064; f. 1968; research in peaceful uses of atomic energy; Dir Dr HSIA DER-YU (acting); publ. *INER report series*.

Institute of Physics: C/o Academia Sinica, Nankang, Taipei 11529; attached to Academia Sinica; Dir Dr TUNG-MIN HO (acting).

PHILOSOPHY AND PSYCHOLOGY

Sun Yat-sen Institute for Social Sciences and Philosophy: C/o Academia Sinica, Nankang, Taipei 11529; tel. (2) 27821693; fax (2) 27854160; e-mail issp@www.issp.sinica.edu.tw; internet www.issp.sinica.edu.tw; f. 1981; attached to Academia Sinica; Dir Dr ANGELA KI CHE LEUNG; publ. *Journal of Social Sciences and Philosophy* (4 a year).

RELIGION, SOCIOLOGY AND ANTHROPOLOGY

Institute of Ethnology: c/o Academia Sinica, 128 Yen-Chiu-Yuan Rd (Sec. 2), Nankang, Taipei 11529; tel. (2) 26523431; fax (2) 26523436; e-mail tja@gate.sinica.edu.tw; internet www.sinica.edu.tw/ioe; f. 1955; attached to Academia Sinica; main field of research: social and cultural anthropology; Dir Prof. HUANG SHU-MIN; publs *Field Materials*, *Taiwan Journal of Anthropology* (2 a year).

Institute of European and American Studies: Academia Sinica, Nankang, Taipei 11529; attached to Academia Sinica; Dir Dr WEN-CHING HO; publ. *EurAmerica* (4 a year).

TECHNOLOGY

Industrial Technology Research Institute: 195 Chung Hsing Rd, Sec. 4, Chu-Tung, Hsinchu; tel. (35) 820100; fax (35) 820045; f. 1973; library of 130,000 vols; Pres. Dr OTTO C. C. LIN; publs *Chemical Industry Notes*, *CFC Newsletter*, *Mechatronics Journal*, *Electro-optics Development Journal*, *UCL Chemical Information Digest*, *Materials and Society*, *Reports of Center for Measurement Standards* (all monthly, in Chinese), *Superconductor Applications News*, *Metrology Information* (both every 2 months, in Chinese), *Opto-Electronics and Systems*, *Mining Technology*, *Energy-Resources and Environment* (quarterly, in Chinese), *MRL Bulletin of Research and Development* (2 a year, in English).

Research laboratories:

Energy and Resources Laboratories: Hsinchu; Dir Dr ROBERT J. YANG.

Mechanical Industry Research Laboratories: Hsinchu; Dir Dr C. RICHARD LIU.

Electronics Research and Service Organization: Hsinchu; Dir Dr DAVID C. T. HSING.

Materials Research Laboratories: Hsinchu and Kaohsiung; Dir Dr LI-CHUNG LEE.

Union Chemical Laboratories: Hsinchu; Dir Dr JOHN-SEE LEE.

Opto-Electronics and Systems Laboratories: Hsinchu; Dir Dr MIN-SHYONG LIN.

Centre for Measurement Standards: Hsinchu; Dir Dr CHANG HSU.

Centre for Pollution Control Technology: Hsinchu; Dir Dr LING-YUAN CHEN.

Computer and Communication Research Laboratories: Hsinchu; Dir Dr STEVEN CHENG.

Centre for Industrial Safety and Health Technology: Hsinchu; Dir Dr ADA W. S. MA.

Centre for Aviation and Aerospace: Hsinchu; Dir Dr RICHARD Y. H. LIN.

National Bureau of Standards: Ministry of Economic Affairs, 3rd Floor, 185 Hsinhai Rd, Sec. 2, Taipei 106; tel. (2) 27380007; fax (2) 27352656; f. 1947; nat. standards, weights and measures, patents, trademarks; library of 20,000 vols, 500 periodicals; Dir-Gen. MING-BANG CHEN; publs *Official Gazette for Standards* (monthly), *Official Gazette for Patents* (3 a month), *Official Gazette for Trademarks* (2 a month), *Chinese National Standards* (irregular), *Catalogue of Chinese National Standards* (annually), *Standards and Metrology Yearbook* (annually), *Patents and Trademarks Yearbook* (annually).

Libraries and Archives

Tainan

National Cheng Kung University Library: 1 Ta Hsueh Rd, Tainan 70101; tel. (6) 2757575 ext. 65701; fax (6) 2378232; e-mail em65701@email.ncku.edu.tw; internet www.lib.ncku.edu.tw; f. 1927; 1,685,049 vols, 12,676 periodicals; Dir MING-TZONG YANG; publs *Bulletin* (quarterly), *Newsletter* (monthly).

Taipei

Agricultural Science Information Center: POB 7-636, Taipei 106; tel. (2) 23626222; f. 1977; 11,000 vols, 638 periodicals, databases; Dir WAN-JIUN WU.

Dr Sun Yat-sen Library: 2F, 505 Jen Ai Rd, Sec. 4, Taipei; tel. (2) 27297030; fax (2) 27582460; f. 1929; 299,345 vols on Dr Sun Yat-sen's writings and studies on San Min Chu Yih and modern Chinese history; Curator SHAW MING-HUANG; publ. *Modern China* (every 2 months).

Fu Ssu-Nien Library, Institute of History and Philology: 130 Yen Chiu Yuan Rd, Sec. 2, Nankang, Taipei 11521; tel. (2) 27829555 ext. 136; fax (2) 27868834; f. 1928; 420,000 vols, 3,000 periodicals; spec. collns incl. 33,889 stone and bronze rubbings, 13,100 folk plays, 310,000 cabinet records of Ming and Ch'ing dynasties; Dir JUEI-HSIU WU.

National Central Library: 20 Chung Shan South Rd, Taipei 100; tel. (2) 23619132; fax (2) 23110155; internet www.ncl.edu.tw; f. 1933; 2,555,069 items incl. 190,000 rare books, stone rubbings; historical material; maintains centre for Chinese studies; Dir Dr CHUANG FANG-JUNG; publs *Chinese National Bibliography* (monthly), *NCL Bulletin* (2 a year), *Index to Chinese Periodicals* (4 a year), *NCL Newsletter* (in English, 2 a year), *NCL News Bulletin* (4 a year).

Branch library:

Taiwan Branch Library, National Central Library: 1 Hsinshen South Rd, Sec. 1, Taipei; tel. (2) 27724724; internet www.ncltb.edu.tw; f. 1915; 592,023 vols; spec. collns incl. Taiwan and Southern Asia; Dir LIN WEI-JEI; publs *The Annotative Catalogue of Taiwan Documents*, *Index to Taiwan-Related Periodical Literature collected in NCL Taiwan Branch*, *Union Catalogue of Taiwan-Related Bibliographies*, *Catalogue on China in Western Languages*, *Catalogue on China in Japanese Languages*, *Catalogue of Materials for the Blind*, *Catalogue of NCL Taiwan Branch Collection on Southeast Asia*, *List of Non-Chinese Serials in NCL Taiwan Branch*.

National War College Library: Yangmingshan, Taipei; 156,639 vols on political subjects; Librarian LO MOU-PIN.

Parliamentary Library, Legislative Yuan: 1 Chung Shan S Rd, Taipei 10040; tel. (2) 23585278; fax (2) 23585290; internet www.ly.gov.tw; f. 1947; general reference, govt publs, legal documents; 113,000 vols; Dir SHOW-RONG WANG; publs *Newsletter of books and documentation* (quarterly), *Chinese legislative news review index* (monthly), *Code resource pathfinder* (every two months), *Code and reference book catalogue* (irregular), *Gazette, proceedings and serials catalogue* (irregular), *LEGISIS thesaurus* (irregular), *Chinese legislative news reviews series* (irregular), *Selective abstracts of US Congressional Records* (irregular), *Index to Legal Periodicals* (irregular), *Legislative Decision Support Service* (monthly), *Subject Guide to Chinese Code* (irregular), *Code Amendment Cyclopedia* (irregular), *Index to Chinese Legislative Literature* (every 2 months), *Selected Dissemination of Information Series* (every 2 months), *The Legislative Yuan Library Catalogue* (irregular), *Collection of Interpellation Records* (irregular), *Legislative Microform Catalog* (irregular), *Index of Legislative Records* (every 3 years).

Taipei City Library: 46 Chinan Rd, Sec. 2, Taipei; f. 1952; 125,000 vols; 4 brs; Dir CHIH-SHIH YANG; publ. *Taipei Municipal Library Annals*.

Museums and Art Galleries

Kaohsiung

Kaohsiung Museum of Fine Arts: 20 Meishukuan Rd, Kaohsiung; tel. (7) 5550331; fax (7) 5550307; internet www.kmfa.gov.tw; f. 1994.

Taichung

Taiwan Museum of Art: 2, Sec. 1, Wu Chuan West Rd, Taichung 403; tel. (4) 23723552; fax (4) 23721195; e-mail artnet@art.tmoa.gov.tw; internet www.tmoa.gov.tw; f. 1986; mostly works of Taiwan artists; library of 35,000 vols; Dir WUH-KUEN LEE; publs *Newsletter* (monthly), *Journal* (4 a year).

Taipei

Chinese Postal Museum: 45 Chungking South Rd, Sec. 2, Taipei 100; tel. (2) 23945185; fax (2) 23518773; e-mail musol@mail.post.gov.tw; internet www.post.gov.tw/museum.htm; f. 1966; library of 27,000 vols; Dir SUSAN TENG-KUEI YU.

Hwa Kang Museum: 55 Hwa Kang Rd, Chinese Culture University, Yang Ming Shan, Taipei 111; tel. (2) 28610511; fax (2) 28621918; e-mail cuch@staff.pccu.edu.tw; internet w3.pccu.edu.tw; f. 1971; Chinese folk arts, pottery, porcelain, calligraphy and paintings; Dir MARGARET CHEN LEE.

National Museum of History: 49 Nan Hai Rd, Taipei 10728; tel. (2) 23610270; fax (2) 23610171; e-mail janet@moe.nmh.gov.tw; internet www.nmh.gov.tw; f. 1955; Chinese and Taiwanese historical and archaeological artefacts; library of 20,000 vols; Dir HUANG KUANG-NAN; publ. *Bulletin*.

National Palace Museum: Wai-shuang-hsi, Shih-lin, Taipei; tel. (2) 28812021; fax (2) 28821440; e-mail service01@npm.gov.tw; internet www.npm.gov.tw; f. 1925; colln consists chiefly of historic and archaeological treasures brought from mainland China; library of 155,136 vols, 624 periodical titles, 200,907 rare books, 395,335 Ch'ing documents; Dir SHIH SHOU-CHIEN; publs *Research Quarterly* (4 a year), *National Palace Museum Monthly of Chinese Art* (monthly).

National Taiwan Museum: 2 Siang-yang Rd, Taipei 100; tel. (2) 23822699; fax (2) 23822684; e-mail ntmmail@ntm.gov.uk; internet www.ntm.gov.uk; f. 1908; anthropology, earth sciences, zoology and botany; Dir HSIAO TSUNG-HUANG; publs *Journal of Taiwan Museum* (in English), *Taiwan Natural Science*.

National Taiwan Science Education Center: 41 Nan Hai Rd, Taipei; tel. (2) 23116734; f. 1958; planetarium, science exhibitions, lectures and films; Dir SHIH-BEY CHEN; publ. *Science Study Monthly*.

Shung Ye Museum of Formosan Aborigines: 282 Chishan Rd Section 2, Taipei 111; tel. (2) 28412611; fax (2) 28412615; e-mail shungye@gate.sinica.edu.tw; internet www.museum.org.tw; f. 1994; holds a collection of artefacts of Taiwan's indigenous peoples; promotes understanding between ethnic groups and undertakes research and preservation of Aboriginal cultural works; Supervisor JASON OU.

Taipei Astronomical Museum: 363 Kee-Ho Rd, Taipei 111; tel. (2) 28314551; fax (2) 28314405; e-mail tam001@tam.gov.tw; internet www.tam.gov.tw; f. 1996; Pres. GUO-GUANG CIOU; Gen. Sec. CHING-HSIUNG WANG; publs *Taipei Skylight* (4 a year), *Astronomical Almanac* (annually), *Report on Sunspot Observations* (annually).

Taipei Fine Arts Museum: 181, Sec. 3, Zhong Shan N.. Rd, Taipei 10461; tel. (2) 25957656; fax (2) 25944104; e-mail info@tfam.gov.tw; internet www.tfam.gov.tw; f. 1983; modern art; Dir TSAI-LANG HSIAO (acting); publs *Modern Art* (every 2 months), *Journal* (2 a year).

Universities

CHINESE CULTURE UNIVERSITY

55 Hwa Kang Rd, Yang Ming Shan, Taipei
Telephone: (2) 28610511
Fax: (2) 28615031
Internet: www.pccu.edu.tw

Founded 1962
Private control

President: LIN TSAI-MEI

Library of 630,000 vols, 3,500 periodicals
Number of teachers: 531
Number of students: 20,013

Colleges of arts, journalism and mass communication, science, engineering, business, agriculture, liberal arts, law, foreign languages and literature; graduate and evening schools.

CHUNG YUAN CHRISTIAN UNIVERSITY

Chung Li
Telephone: (3) 4563171
Fax: (3) 4563160
Internet: www.cycu.edu.tw

Founded 1955
Private control

Academic year: August to July

President: Dr SAMUEL K. C. CHANG

Library of 250,000 vols
Number of teachers: 12,491
Number of students: 11,798

Publications: *CYCU News*, *Chung Yuan Journal*

Colleges of science, engineering, business, design; evening department.

FENG CHIA UNIVERSITY

100 Wenhwa Rd, Seatwen, Taichung 40724
Telephone: (4) 24517250
Fax: (4) 24514907
E-mail: linkages@fcu.edu.tw
Internet: www.fcu.edu.tw

Founded 1961
Private control

Languages of instruction: Chinese, English
Academic year: September to June

President: AN-CHI LIU
Vice-President: YUAN-TONG LEE
Secretary-General: HAI-PING HSIEH
Chief Librarian: HSIANG-HOO CHING

Library of 590,000 vols
Number of teachers: 1,107
Number of students: 19,124 (17,517 undergraduate, 1,607 postgraduate)

Publications: *Civil Engineering Journal*, *Architecture Quarterly*, *Textile Science*, *Mechanical Engineering*, *Industrial Engineering*, *Computer Science*, *Banking and Insurance*, *Co-operative Research*, *Statistics Journal*, *Accounting Journal*, *Finance Research*, *International Trade*, *FCU Weekly*

DEANS

College of Business: PAO-LONG CHANG
College of Construction and Development: BING-JEAN LEE
College of Continuing Education: YOU-REN SHIAU
College of Engineering: TONG-MIIN LIOU
College of Humanities and Social Studies: YEN CHU
College of Information and Electrical Engineering: CHUANG-CHIEN CHIU
College of Sciences: TAI-LEE HU

HEADS OF DEPARTMENTS

College of Business (tel. (4) 24517250 ext. 4001; fax (4) 24520530; e-mail cob@fcu.edu.tw):

- Accounting: YU-CHIH LIN
- Business Administration: MEI-YANE CHUNG
- Co-operative Economics: WEN-RONG LIU
- Economics: CHI-CHU CHOU
- Finance: CHE-PENG LIN
- Insurance: GOW-NING YUAN
- International Trade: TING-JI LIN
- Public Finance: HUI-KUANG YU
- Statistics: WOAN-SHU CHEN
- E-Commerce Research Institute: KUN-HUANG HUARGE

College of Construction and Development (tel. (4) 24517250 ext. 4501; fax (4) 24519607; e-mail ccd@fcu.edu.tw):

- Architecture: SU-HSIN LEE
- Civil Engineering: YU-MIN KANG
- Construction Research Center: TSE-SHAN HSU
- Hydraulic Engineering: CHANG-SHIAN CHEN
- Land Management: JING-CHZI HSIEH
- Research Center for Geographical Information Systems: TIEN-YIN CHOU
- Traffic and Transport Engineering and Management: TA-YIN HU
- Urban Planning: MEI-JUNG LAI

College of Engineering (tel. (4) 24517250 ext. 3001; fax (4) 24517110; e-mail coe@fcu.edu.tw):

- Aeronautical Engineering: WEN-SHYONG KOU
- Chemical Engineering: CHYI-TSONG CHEN
- Fibres and Composite Materials: TIEN-WEI SHYR
- Industrial Engineering: ANGUS JEANG
- Machine Workshop: KUO-CHENG TAI
- Mechanical and Computer-aided Engineering: JIN-HUANG HUANG

College of Humanities and Social Sciences (tel. (4) 24517250 ext. 5501; fax (4) 24513797; e-mail cohs@fcu.edu.tw):

- Art Center: TSAI-HSIN CHANG
- Chinese Literature: JIANN-HWA SONG
- Language Center: KRIS VICCA
- Teacher Education Center: SHUU-JANE YANG
- Teaching of Foreign Languages and Literature: YEN CHU
- Teaching of History and Humanities: CHIH-CHIA HU
- Teaching of Social Sciences: HWAI-TZONG LEE

College of Information and Electrical Engineering (tel. (4) 24517250 ext. 3991; fax (4) 24515701; e-mail ciee@fcu.edu.tw):

- Automatic Control Engineering: CHERN-SHENG LIN
- Communications Engineering: CHENG-HO HSIN
- Electrical Engineering: CHANG-CHOU HWANG
- Electronic Engineering: WEN-LUH YANG
- Information Engineering: DON-LIN YANG
- Honors Program of Information and Electrical Engineering: HO-EN LIAO

College of Sciences (tel. (4) 24517250 ext. 5001; fax (4) 24513700; e-mail science@fcu.edu.tw):

- Applied Mathematics: JIANN-CHERNG YANG
- Environmental Engineering and Science: JYA-JYUN YU
- Materials Science: HSIN-CHIH LIN
- Physics Teaching and Research Center: YING-TE LEE

DIRECTORS OF GRADUATE INSTITUTES

Accounting and Taxation: YU-CHI LIN
Aeronautical Engineering: WEN-SHYONG KOU
Applied Mathematics: JIANN-CHERNG YANG
Architecture and Urban Planning: MEI-JUNG LAI
Automatic Control Engineering: CHERN-SHENG LIN
Business Administration: MEI-YANE CHUNG
Chemical Engineering: CHYI-TSONG CHEN
Chinese Literature: JIANN-HWA SONG
Civil and Hydraulic Engineering: YU-MIN KANG
Communications Engineering: CHENG-HO HSIN
Economics: CHI-CHU CHOU
Electrical and Communications Engineering: CHUANG-CHIEN CHIU
Electrical Engineering: CHANG-CHOU HWANG
Electronic Engineering: WEN-LUH YANG
Environmental Science and Engineering: JYA-JYUN YU
Finance: CHE-PENG LIN
History and Cultural Heritage Management: CHIH-CHIA HU
Industrial Engineering: ANGUS JEANG
Information Engineering: DON-LIN YANG
Insurance: GOW-NING YUAN
International Trade: TING-JI LIN
Land Management: JING-CHZI HSIEH
Materials Science: HSIN-CHIH LIN
Mechanical Engineering: JIN-HUANG HUANG
Optical Physics: YING-TE LEE
Statistics and Actuarial Science: WOAN-SHU CHEN

Textiles Engineering: TIEN-WEI SHYR
Traffic and Transportation Engineering and Management: TA-YIN HU

FU-JEN CATHOLIC UNIVERSITY

510 Chungcheng Rd, Hsin-Chuang, Taipei
Telephone: (2) 29031111 ext. 3016
Fax: (2) 29017391
E-mail: fjuweb@mails.fju.edu.tw
Internet: www.fju.edu.tw

Founded 1925 in Beijing; re-opened in Taiwan 1961
Academic year: August to July
President: Dr JOHN NING-YUEAN LEE
Vice-Presidents: Dr PERRY C. CHIU, Dr PETER SHANG-SHING CHOU, Rev. LOUIS GENDRON
Secretary-General: JOHN SHIANG-YANG HWANG
Dean of Academic Affairs: Dr YIU-LUNG CHEN
Dean of General Affairs: Prof. ZERMAN HU
Dean of Research and Development: Dr SHIH-MING KO
Dean of Student Affairs: Dr HUNG YAN CHEN
Registrar: TZU-CHI LI
Librarian: Dr H. H. CHENG

Library of 828,000 vols
Number of teachers: 1,591
Number of students: 23,658

Publications: *Catholic Observer*, *Fu Jen Philosophical Studies*, *Fu Jen Studies* (quarterly)

DEANS

College of Fine Arts: Dr MING-JIAN FANG
College of Foreign Languages: Dr NICHOLAS KOSS
College of Human Ecology: Dr SHAU-YEN HUANG
College of Law: Dr AH-YEE LEE
College of Liberal Arts: Dr THOMAS FU-BEING CHEN
College of Management: Dr DENG-YUAN HUANG
College of Medicine: Dr VINCENT HAN-SUN CHIANG
College of Science and Engineering: Dr JOSEPH L. G. HWA
School of Continuing Education: Dr CAJUS CHI-CHI LIN
Holistic Education Center: Dr DAMIANUS JEN-LUNGKAO

NATIONAL CENTRAL UNIVERSITY

Chung-Li 320
Telephone: (3) 4227151
Fax: (3) 4226062
Internet: www.ncu.edu.tw

Founded 1968 as re-establishment of National Central University (Nanking)
Academic year: February to January
President: Prof. CHAO-HAN LIU
Vice-President: KUANG-FU CHENG
Dean of Academic Affairs: KUAN-CHING LEE
Dean of General Affairs: EDMOND LIU-WU HOURNG
Dean of Research and Development: WEI-LING CHIANG
Dean of Student Affairs: DYI-HWA TSENG
Director of Secretariat: JIEN-MING JUE
Librarian: CHIEU-YIUG WANG

Number of teachers: 450
Number of students: 7,813

Publications: *Bulletin of Geophysics* (2 a year), *Journal of Humanities East/West* (2 a year)

DEANS

College of Earth Sciences: YI-BEN TSAI
College of Engineering: KUO-SHONG WANG
College of Information Technology and Electrical Engineering: SHING-TSAAN HUANG
College of Liberal Arts: JEH-HANG LAI
College of Management: JING-TWEN CHEN
College of Science: WING-HUEN IP

HEADS OF GRADUATE INSTITUTES

Institute of Applied Geology: KUO-LIANG WEN
Institute of Art Studies: FANG-CHENG WU
Institute of Astronomy: WEN-PING CHEN
Institute of Atmospheric Sciences: CHING-YUANG HUANG
Institute of Business Administration: D. J. HORNG
Institute of Chemical Engineering: CHENG-TUNG CHOU
Institute of Chinese Literature: LAI-SHIN KONG
Institute of Civil Engineering: S. Y. YEN
Institute of Communication Engineering: CHAR-DIR CHUNG
Institute of Computer Science and Information Engineering: JONATHAN LEE
Institute of Electrical Engineering: YI-JEN CHAN
Institute of English Language and Literature: MING-CHUNG YAUG
Institute of Environmental Engineering: CHUNG-TE LEE
Institute of Finance Management: MING-CHENG WANG
Institute of French Language and Literature: DER-MING ONG
Institute of Geophysics: CHOU-SOU CHEN
Institute of History: CHENG-HAN WU
Institute of Human Resource Management: JIHN-CHANG JEHNG
Institute of Industrial Economics: MING-CHUNG JEHNG
Institute of Industrial Management: YING-CHIN HO
Institute of Information Management: JIM LIN
Institute of Mechanical Engineering: YU-TZU WANG
Institute of Optical Sciences: HON-FAI YAU
Institute of Philosophy: SHUI-CHUEN LEE
Institute of Space Science: LIN-NI HAU
Institute of Statistics: Y. I. CHEN

DEPARTMENT HEADS

Atmospheric Sciences: CHING-YUANG HUANG
Business Administration: D. J. HORNG
Chemistry: KWANG-HWA LII
Chemical Engineering: CHENG-TUNG CHOU
Chinese Literature: LAI-SHIN KANG
Civil Engineering: SHANG-YAO YAN
Computer Science and Information Engineering: JONATHAN LEE
Earth Sciences: CHOW-SON CHEN
Economics: MING-CHENG WANG
Electrical Engineering: YI-JEN CHAN
English Language and Literature: WEN-CHI LIN
Finance Management: JIE-HAUN LEE
French Language and Literature: DER-MING ONG
Information Management: JIM LIN
Life Science: EDWARD H. LEE
Mathematics: CHIN-CHENG LIN
Mechanical Engineering: YU-TZU WANG
Physics: MIN-SHENG WANG

NATIONAL CHENGCHI UNIVERSITY

64 Zhinan Rd Sec. 2, Wenshan 116, Taipei
Telephone: (2) 29379611
E-mail: zivhsu@ncu.edu.tw
Internet: www.nccu.edu.tw

Founded 1927, university status 1946; state-funded
Language of instruction: Chinese
Academic year: September to July (two semesters)
President: JEI-CHENG CHENG
Dean of Academic Affairs: CHIN-YUE TUNG
Dean of General Affairs: MICHAEL KWAN
Dean of Student Affairs: LING-TAI CHOU
Librarian: OU-LAN HU

Library of 2,289,000 vols
Number of teachers: 948 (full- and part-time)
Number of students: 11,554

DIRECTORS OF GRADUATE SCHOOLS

East Asia Studies: KUEN-HSUEN CHIU
Labour Research: HUI-LING WANG
Library and Information Sciences: MEI-HUA YANG
Linguistics: YI-LI YANG
Russian Studies: CHUEN-SHAN CHAO
Technology and Innovation Management: SE-HUA WU
Dr Sun Yat-Sen Graduate Institute for Interdisciplinary Studies: CHUEN-YUEN WANG

DEANS

College of Commerce: SE-HWA WU
College of Communication: VEN-HWEI LO
College of Foreign Languages: CHAO-MING CHEN
College of International Affairs: DENG-KER LEE
College of Law: HSIU-HSIUNG LIN
College of Liberal Arts: HSIN-CHUAN HO
College of Science: LONG-YI TSAI
College of Social Sciences: AN-PANG KAO

HEADS OF DEPARTMENTS

Accountancy: LING-TAI CHO
Advertising: TSU-LONG CHENG
Arabic Language and Literature: CHUAN-TIEN LI
Business Administration: CHUO-MIN YU
Chinese Literature: CHIN-YU DUNG
Computer Science: YAO-NAN LIEN
Diplomacy: DENG-KE LI
Economics: WEI-LING MAO
English Language and Literature: CHI-KUEI LO
Education: MENG-CHUIN CHIN
Ethnology: HSIU-CHE LIN
Finance: CHI-HUANG LIN
History: NENG-SHIH LIN
International Trade: LIEN-KUO HU
Journalism: WEN-HUI LO
Land Economics: SEN-TIEN LIN
Law: CHUNG-MIN DUAN
Management Information Systems: WO-TSUNG LIN
Mathematical Sciences: CHUAN-CHIN SUNG
Money and Banking: HAO-MIN CHU
Oriental Languages and Cultures: CHI-HUI HUANG
Philosophy: HSIN-CHUEN HO
Political Science: FU-SHENG HSIEH
Psychology: MEI-CHEN LIN
Public Administration: CHUNG-EN WU
Public Finance: CHU-WEI TSENG
Radio and Television: TSUEI-CHEN WU
Risk Management and Insurance: CHENG-TSUNG HUANG
Russian: HUNG-MEI CHUNG
Sociology: KAO-CHIAO HSIEH
Statistics: TIEN-TSO CHENG

NATIONAL CHENG KUNG UNIVERSITY

1 Ta-Hsueh Rd, Tainan 70101
Telephone: (6) 2757575
Fax: (6) 2368660
E-mail: em50000@mail.ncku.edu.tw
Internet: www.ncku.edu.tw

Founded 1931 as Tainan Technical College, renamed Taiwan Provincial College of Engineering 1946, present name 1971
State control
Language of instruction: Chinese, some English
Academic year: September to June
President: Dr CHIANG KAO

Dean of Academic Affairs: Dr YAN-KUIN SU
Registrar: SHIN-FU HUANG
Librarian: Dr JEN-FA MIN

Number of teachers: 1,200
Number of students: 19,000

Publications: *Journal of National Cheng Kung University* (annually), *Faculty Publication List* (annually), *Newsletter* (quarterly), *Bulletin of National Cheng Kung University* (annually)

DEANS

College of Design: Dr MING-FU HSU
College of Electrical Engineering and Computer Science: Dr CHING-TING LI
College of Engineering: Dr WEN-TENG WU
College of Liberal Arts: Dr KAO-PING CHANG
College of Management Science: Dr WANN-YIH WU
College of Medicine: Dr RUEY-JEN SUNG
College of Sciences: Dr SHU-CHENG YU
College of Social Sciences: Dr JENN-YEU CHEN

Graduate institutes are attached to the College of Liberal Arts, the College of Engineering, the College of Sciences, the College of Management Science, the College of Medicine and the College of Social Sciences

NATIONAL CHIAO TUNG UNIVERSITY

1001 Ta Hsueh Rd, Hsinchu
Telephone: (35) 712121
Fax: (35) 721500
Internet: www.nctu.edu.tw

Founded 1896, re-established in Hsinchu 1958
Languages of instruction: Chinese, English
Academic year: August to July (two semesters)

President: Dr CHI-FU DEN
Dean of Academic Affairs: Dr LONG-ING CHEN
Dean of General Affairs: Dr CHUNG-BIAU TSAY
Dean of the Research and Development Council: Dr CHUNG-YU WU
Dean of Student Affairs: Dr FU-WHA HAN
Chief Secretary: Prof. HSIN-SEN CHU
Registrar: Assoc. Prof. CHIN-SHYONG CHEN
Chief Librarian: Dr RUEI-CHUAN CHANG

Library of 170,329 vols, 2,373 periodicals
Number of teachers: 415 (full-time)
Number of students: 4,896

Publications: *Chiao Ta Management Review*, *List of Publications of Faculty Members*, abstracts of papers and research reports

DEANS

College of Electrical Engineering and Computer Science: Dr CHE-HO WEI
College of Engineering: Dr TAI-YAN KAM
College of Management: Dr PAO-LONG CHANG
College of Science: Dr DER-SAN CHUU

HEADS OF DEPARTMENTS

College of Electrical Engineering and Computer Science:
- Communication Engineering: Dr SONG-TSUEN PENG
- Computer and Information Science: Dr CHIA-HOANG LEE
- Computer Science and Information Engineering: Dr HSI-JIAN LEE
- Control Engineering: Dr CHING-CHENG TENG
- Electronics Engineering: Dr WEN-ZEN SHEN

College of Engineering:
- Civil Engineering: Dr CHUN-SUNG CHEN
- Mechanical Engineering: Dr HSIN-SEN CHU

College of Management:
- Industrial Engineering and Management: Dr FUH-HWA LIU
- Management Science: Dr HER-JIUN SHEU
- Transportation Engineering and Management: Dr HSIN-LI CHANG

College of Science:
- Applied Chemistry: Dr CHAIN-SHU HSU
- Applied Mathematics: Dr GERARD J. CHANG
- Electrophysics: Dr RU-PIN CHAO PAN

DIRECTORS OF GRADUATE INSTITUTES

Applied Arts (Design and Music): Dr MING-CHUEN CHUANG
Applied Chemistry: Dr CHAIN-SHU HSU
Applied Mathematics: Dr GERARD J. CHANG
Biological Science and Technology: Dr CHENG ALLEN CHANG
Civil Engineering: Dr YUNG-SHOW FANG
Communication Engineering: Dr CHUNG-JU CHANG
Communication Studies: Dr SHIN-MIN CHEN
Computer and Information Science: Dr RONG-HONG JAN
Computer Science and Information Engineering: Dr SHU-YUEN HWANG
Control Engineering: Dr DER-CHERNG LIAW
Electronics: Dr TAN-FU LEI
Electro-Optical Engineering: Dr CI-LING PAN
Electrophysics: Dr MING-CHIH LEE
Environmental Engineering: Dr JEHNG-JUNG KAO
Industrial Engineering: Dr CHAO-TON SU
Information Management: Dr CHI-CHUN LO
Management Science: Dr SOUSHAN WU
Management Technology: Dr SHANG-JYH LIU
Materials Science and Engineering: Dr TZENG-FENG LIU
Mechanical Engineering: Dr HSIN-SEN CHU
Physics: Dr JSIN-FU JIANG
Statistics: Dr CHAO-SHENG LEE
Traffic and Transportation: Dr YUAN-CHING HSU

DIRECTORS OF RESEARCH CENTRES

Center for Telecommunications Research: Dr SIN-HORNG CHEN
Computer Center: Dr RUEI-CHUAN CHANG
Microelectronics and Information Science and Technology Research Center: Dr MING SZE
National Nano Device Center: Dr CHUN-YEN CHANG
Semiconductor Research Center: (vacant)

NATIONAL CHUNG HSING UNIVERSITY

250 Kuokuang Rd, Taichung
Telephone: (4) 2872991
Fax: (4) 2853813
Internet: www.nchu.edu.tw

Founded 1961

President: Dr CHENG-CHANG LI
Secretary-General: MU-CHIOU HUANG
Librarian: WOEI LIN

Number of teachers: 980
Number of students: 17,625

DEANS

College of Agriculture: MING-TSAO CHEN
College of Engineering: SHIH-SHYN WU
College of Law and Commerce: SEN-TIAN WU
College of Liberal Arts: CHUNG-HSUAN TUNG
College of Life Science: SCHENG-MING TSCHEN
College of Science: TENG-KUEI YANG

HEADS OF DEPARTMENTS AND INSTITUTES

Accounting: SHIOU-CHIH WANG
Agricultural Biotechnology Laboratories: DER-SYH TZENG
Agricultural Economics: CHIEN-ZER LIU
Agricultural Machinery Engineering: JAR-MIIN LAUN
Agricultural Marketing: HWANG-JAW LEE
Agronomy: MAU-SHING YEH
Animal Science: JENN-CHUNG HSU
Applied Mathematics: KUO-HSIUNG WANG
Botany: JU-YING HSIAO
Business Administration: ING-SAN HWANG
Chemical Engineering: CHIEH MING J. CHANG
Chemistry: HAN-MOU GAU
Chinese Literature: JAW-HWA SHYU
Civil Engineering: CHIEN-HUNG LIN
Computer Centre: JINN-KE JAN
Co-operative Economics: HSIANG-HSI LIU
Economics: TO-FAR WANG
Electrical Engineering: DYE-JYUN MA
English Literature and Language: HSIN-FA WU
Entomology: CHIN-CHANG YEH
Environmental Engineering: CHIH-JEN LU
Food Science: HAU-YANG TSEN
Forestry: JOOU-SHIAN LEE
History: YING-NAN WANG
Horticulture: MENG-JIAU TSENG
Land Economics and Administration: SUNG-SAN WANG
Law: YIH-SHAN LIN
Mechanical Engineering: JUNG-YANG SAN
Physics: PING-CHENG LI
Plant Pathology: DER-SHY TZENG
Public Administration and Policy: MIN-CHIN CHIANG
Public Finance: SHIH-HSIN HUANG
Sociology and Social Work: MIN-CHANG TSAI
Soil and Water Conservation: SHIN-HWEI LIN
Soil Science: CHEN FANG LIN
Statistics: HONG-LONG WANG
Veterinary Medicine: TIEN-JYE CHANG
Zoology: SHENG-HAI WU
Institute of Agricultural Biotechnology: FENG-NAN HOU
Institute of Agricultural Extension and Education: CHING-YING HUANG
Institute of Biochemistry: JUNGYIE KAO
Institute of Computer Science: SYING-JYAN WANG
Institute of Library and Information Science: WOEI LIN
Institute of Materials Engineering: FUN-SHENG SHEIU
Institute of Molecular Biology: LIANG-JWU CHEN
Institute of Natural Resource Management: DAIGEE SHAW
Institute of Urban Planning: HSUEH-TAO CHIEN
Institute of Veterinary Microbiology: LONG-HUW LEE
Institute of Veterinary Pathology: CHENG-I LIU

NATIONAL OPEN UNIVERSITY

172 Chung Cheng Rd, Lu Chow, Taipei 24702
Telephone: (2) 22829355
Fax: (2) 22831721
E-mail: elec007@mail.nou.edu.tw
Internet: www.nou.edu.tw

Founded 1986
Language of instruction: Chinese
Academic year: September to June

President: Dr SHENG-SHIUNG HUANG
Registrar: LI-CHI HSIEH
Dean of Academic Affairs: Dr CHIA-SHING YANG

Number of teachers: 2,037 (88 full-time, 1,949 part-time)
Number of students: 40,000

Publication: *National Open University Learning Journal* (every 2 weeks)

CHAIRMEN OF DEPARTMENTS

Arts in Commerce: JIN-HO YUAN
General Affairs: TSAI HSIANG-HUEI
General Studies: SZE-LU NA
Instructional Media: DWO-YAN CHANG
Liberal Arts: YUAN-JEN FANG
Living Sciences: WEN-CHIN CHOU

Management and Information: SUNG-BO CHEN
Public Administration: SHIH-PEI LAI
Research and Development: JUDY HUANG
Social Sciences: JEHNG OUYANG
Student Affairs: JESSE C. CHOU

NATIONAL PINGTUNG UNIVERSITY OF SCIENCE AND TECHNOLOGY

1 Hseuh-Fu Rd, Nei Pu Hsiang, Pingtung Hsien 912

Telephone: (8) 7703660
Fax: (8) 7702226
E-mail: choumasa@mail.npust.edu.tw
Internet: www.npust.edu.tw

Founded 1954 as Taiwan Provincial Institute of Agriculture; became National Pingtung Institute of Agriculture 1981 and National Pingtung Polytechnic Institute 1991; present name and status 1997

Pres.: CHANG-HUNG CHOU

Library of 227,198 vols
Number of teachers: 324
Number of students: 9,000

Publication: *Bulletin* (annually)

Colleges of Agriculture, Engineering, Management and Humanities and Social Sciences.

NATIONAL TAIWAN NORMAL UNIVERSITY

162 East Ho Ping Rd, Sec. 1, Taipei 10610

Telephone: (2) 23625101
Fax: (2) 23922673
Internet: www.ntnu.edu.tw

Founded 1946
Language of instruction: Chinese
State control
Academic year: August to July (two semesters)

President: MAW-FA CHIEN
Vice-President: CHUNG-YANG TSAI
Secretary-General: HSI-PING WANG
Dean of General Affairs: DAR-CHIN RAU
Dean of Internship Supervision and Placement
Dean of Research and Development: LILLIAN MEEI-JIN HUANG
Dean of Students: HU-HSIUNG LI
Dean of Studies: C. H. GEORGE KAO
Registrar: AN-PAN LIN
Library Director: HARRY LIANG

Number of teachers: 1,131
Number of students: 9,716

Publications: *A-V Education* (every 2 months), *Bulletin*, *NTNU Alumni* (monthly), *Secondary Education* (every 2 months), graduate institutional and departmental journals

DEANS

College of Education: WU-TIEN WU
College of Fine and Applied Arts: CHING-LANG CHANG
College of Liberal Arts: WEN-HSING WU
College of Sciences: CHU-NAN CHANG
College of Sports and Recreation: YAO-HUI CHIEN
College of Technology: LUNG-SHERN LEE
Extension Division: SUZ-WEI YANG

NATIONAL TAIWAN OCEAN UNIVERSITY

2 Pei-Ning Rd, Keelung

Telephone: (2) 24622192
Fax: (2) 24623563
Internet: www.ntou.edu.tw

Founded 1953 (formerly National Taiwan College of Marine Science and Technology)
Academic year: August to July

President: ROBERT R. HWANG
Vice-President: KUO-TIEN LEE
Dean of Academic Affairs: CHING-FONG CHANG
Dean of General Affairs: YU-HSING CHAO
Dean of Research and Development: DENG-FWU HWANG
Dean of Student Affairs: JEUN-LEN WU
Librarian: CHIN-HWA HU

Library of 200,000 vols, 2,000 periodicals
Number of teachers: 325
Number of students: 7,731

Publication: *Journal of Marine Science and Technology* (4 a year)

DEANS OF COLLEGES

Engineering: YOUNG-ZEHR KEHR
Life and Resource Science: SHANN-TZONG JIANG
Maritime Science: YEN-HORNG TSUEI
Science: CHAO-SHING LEE
Technology Science: RONG-HUA YEH

HEADS OF DEPARTMENTS

Applied Economics: CHIN-HWA SUN
Applied Geophysics: MIN-TE CHEN
Aquaculture: SHYN-SHIN SHEEN
Bioscience and Biotechnology: SHYE-JYE TANG
Communication and Guidance Engineering: JOHN F. AN
Computer Science: TUN-WEN PAI
Education: BAO-QUEY HUANG
Electrical Engineering: HSIEN-SEN HUNG
Environmental Biology and Fisheries Science: I-HSUN NIO
Food Science: TZE-KUEI CHIOU
Harbour and River Engineering: BAO-SHI SHIAU
Law of the Sea: CHEN-YO CHOH
Marine Biology: TJN-YAM CHAN
Marine Engineering and Technology: WEN-JER CHANG
Marine Resource Management: KWANG-MING LIU
Materials Engineering: JINN P. CHU
Mechanical and Marine Engineering: SHUEI-HAN JUANG
Merchant Marine: CHEN-HSIU LAI
Oceanography: CHUNG-RU HO
Opto-Electronic Sciences: HAI-PANG CHIANG
Shipping and Transportation Management: HSUAN-SHIH LEE
System Engineering and Naval Architecture: JIAHN-HORNG CHEN
Transportation Technology: KUN-CHING LIAO

NATIONAL TAIWAN UNIVERSITY

1 Roosevelt Rd, Section 4, Taipei 106

Telephone: (2) 2363-0231
Fax: (2) 2362-0886
E-mail: secretor@ms.cc.ntu.edu.tw
Internet: www.ntu.edu.tw

Founded 1928 during the Japanese occupation as the Taihoku Imperial University; taken over and renamed by Chinese Government in 1945
Language of instruction: Chinese
Academic year: August to July (two semesters)

President: WEI-JAO CHEN
Vice-President: SHIE-MING PENG
Dean of Academic Affairs: SI-CHEN LEE
Dean of Business Affairs: YUNG-MAU CHAO
Dean of Student Affairs: CHI-PENG HO
Library Director: MING-DER WU

Library of 2,478,072 vols
Number of teachers: 3,037
Number of students: 26,212

Publications: *Acta Botanica Taiwania*, *Acta Geologica Taiwanica*, *Acta Oceanographica Taiwanica*

DEANS

College of Agriculture: WEN-SHI WU
College of Electrical Engineering: POW-EN HSU
College of Law: YIH-NAN LIAW
College of Engineering: YEONG-BIN YANG
College of Liberal Arts: TONG-HWA LEE
College of Management: CHEN-EN KO
College of Medicine: BOR-SHEN HSIEH
College of Public Health: CHIEN-JEN CHEN
College of Science: MING-CHANG KANG
College of Social Sciences: TZONG-HO BAU
Division of Continuing Education and Professional Development: MING-JE TANG

DIRECTORS OF GRADUATE INSTITUTES

Accounting: CHAN-JANE LIN
Agricultural Chemistry: MIN-HSIUNG LEE
Agricultural Economics: ALAN YUN LU
Agricultural Engineering: MING-HSI HSU
Agricultural Extension: SHU-KWEI KAO
Agronomy: HUU-SHENG LUR
Anatomy: SEU-MEI WANG
Animal Science: YAN-NIAN JIANG
Anthropology: JIH-CHANG HSIEH
Applied Mechanics: CHIN-CHOU CHU
Art History: PAO-CHEN CHEN
Atmospheric Science: JONG-DAO JOU
Biochemical Science: INN-HO TSAI
Biochemistry: TA-HSIU LIAO
Bio-Industrial Mechatronics Engineering: SEN-FUH CHANG
Biomedical Engineering: HWA-CHANG LIU
Botany: KUO-CHIEH HO
Building and Planning: FENG-TYAN LIN
Business Administration: CHIA-SHEN CHEN
Chemical Engineering: YAN-PING CHEN
Chemistry: SHIUH-TZUNG LIU
Chinese Literature: KUO-LIANG YEH
Civil Engineering: TSAN-HWEI HUANG
Clinical Dentistry: WAN-HONG LAN
Clinical Medicine: MING-YANG LAI
Clinical Pharmacy: MING-YANG LAI
Communications Engineering: MAO-CHAO LIN
Computer Science and Information Engineering: OUH-YOUNG MING
Drama and Theatre: YAW-HERNG HU
Economics: CHIEN-FU LIN
Electrical Engineering: WAY-SEEN WANG
Electro-optical Engineering: HEN-WAI TSAO
Entomology: WEN-JER WU
Environmental Engineering: SHANG-LIEN LO
Environmental Health: FUNG-CHANG SUNG
Epidemiology: WEI-JANE CHEN
Finance: CHAU-CHEN YANG
Fisheries Science: HUAI-JEN TSAI
Food Science and Technology: JAMES SWI-BEA WU
Foreign Languages and Literature: HAN-LIANG CHANG
Forestry: HSIN-HSIUNG CHEN
Geography: JIUN-CHUAN LIN
Geology: TSUNG-KWEI LIU
Health Care Organization Administration: MING-CHIN YANG
Health Policy and Management: LEE-LAN YEN
History: MING-SHIH KAO
Horticulture: PUNG-LING HUANG
Industrial Engineering: YON-CHUN CHOU
Immunology: BETTY A. WU-HSIEH
Information Management: SENG-CHO CHOU
International Business: YI-LONG JAW
Journalism: HOLIN LIN
Law: YIH-NAN LIAW
Library and Information Science: HSUEH-HUA CHEN
Linguistics: I-WEN SU
Materials Science and Engineering: WEI-HSING TUAN
Mathematics: I-LIANG CHERN
Mechanical Engineering: PING-HEI CHEN
Medical Technology: JAU-TSUEN KAO
Microbiology: JIN-TOWN WANG
Molecular Medicine: CHAI-LI YU
Musicology: TUNG SHEN
Naval Architecture and Ocean Engineering: HUEI-JENG LIN
Nursing: SHIOW-LI HWANG

Occupational Medicine and Industrial Hygiene: CHUAN-CHAN CHANG
Oceanography: NAI-KUANG LIANG
Oral Biology: YUH-YUAN SHIAU
Pathology: IH-JEN SU
Pharmaceutical Science: JI-WANG CHERN
Pharmacology: MING-JAI SU
Philosophy: YIH-JING LIN
Physical Therapy: WA-FONG LIAW
Physics: WOEI-YANN HWANG
Physiology: YIN-LOUNG LAI
Plant Pathology: CHAN-PIN LIN
Political Science: CHU-CHENG MING
Psychology: CHONG JEN CHUANG
San-Min-Chu-I (Philosophy of the Father of the Republic): CHUEN-SHENG CHEN
Sociology: DUNG-SHENG CHEN
Toxicology: MIN-LING KUO
Veterinary Medicine: KUANG-YANG CHEN
Zoology: TAI-SHENG CHIU

NATIONAL TAIWAN UNIVERSITY OF SCIENCE AND TECHNOLOGY

43 Keelung Rd, Sec. 4, Taipei
Telephone: (2) 27376101
Fax: (2) 27376107
E-mail: president@mail.ntust.edu.tw
Internet: www.ntust.edu.tw

Founded 1974
Academic year: August to July (two semesters)

President: SHUN-TYAN CHEN
Dean of Studies: CHENG-SEEN HO

Library of 279,326 vols
Number of teachers: 315
Number of students: 8,106

HEADS OF DEPARTMENTS

Applied Foreign Languages: CHAO-PING KO
Architecture: CHING-YUAN LIN
Business Administration: YEN-SHENG HUANG
Chemical Engineering: DAH-SHYANG TSAI
Computer Science and Information Engineering: HAHN-MING LEE
Construction Engineering: HUNG-JIUN LIAO
Electrical Engineering: TSAI-HSIANG CHEN
Electronic Engineering: CHING-WEN HSUE
General Education: FU-CHUAN HSU
Humanities: CHUN-YING CHEN
Industrial and Commercial Design: LIN-LIN CHEN
Industrial Management: SHUO-YAN CHOU
Information Management: TZONG-CHEN WU
Mechanical Engineering: YEONG-SHIN TARNG
Polymer Engineering: MING-CHIEN YANG
Graduate School of Design: LIN-LIN CHEN
Graduate School of Engineering: ZONE-CHING LIN
Graduate School of Finance: YEN-SHENG HUANG
Graduate School of Management: KUN-JEN CHUNG

NATIONAL TSING HUA UNIVERSITY

101, Sec. 2, Kuang Fu Rd, Hsinchu 30013
Telephone: (3) 5715131
Fax: (3) 5710582
E-mail: presid@my.nthu.edu.tw
Internet: www.nthu.edu.tw

Founded Re-founded 1956
Language of instruction: Chinese
Academic year: August to July

President: FRANK H. SHU
Librarian: SHEAU-CHYN SHIEH

Number of teachers: 523
Number of students: 10,265

Publications: *InterAsia Cultural Studies* (quarterly), *Tsing Hua Hsiao Yu T'ung Hsun* (Alumni News, 2 a year), *Tsing Hua Journal of Chinese Studies* (Chinese literature and community science, quarterly), *Tsing Hua Journal for General Education* (quarterly), *Tsing Hua Journal for History Education* (2 a year)

DEANS

College of Electrical Engineering and Computer Science: CHENG-WEN WU
College of Engineering: LIH-JEN CHEN
College of Humanities and Social Sciences: YI-LONG HUANG
College of Life Science: WEN-GUEY WU
College of Nuclear Science: SHIANG-HUEI JIANG
College of Science: SHIN-LIN CHANG
College of Technology Management: CHIN-TAY SHIH

HEADS OF DEPARTMENTS

College of Electrical Engineering and Computer Science (tel. (3) 5734762; fax (3) 5711484; e-mail eecs@my.nthu.edu.tw; internet www.eecs.nthu.edu.tw):
Computer Science: Prof. BIING-FENG WANG
Electrical Engineering: Prof. CHUNG-CHIN LU
Graduate Institute of Communications Engineering: Prof. CHONG-YUNG CHI
Graduate Institute of Electronics Engineering: Prof. CHENN-SHIN LIEN
Graduate Institute of Information Systems and Applications: Prof. LONG-WEN CHANG
Graduate Institute of Photonics Technologies: Prof. SHIUH CHAO

College of Engineering (tel. (3) 5710521; fax (3) 5712670; e-mail engineer@my.nthu.edu.tw; internet www.mse.nthu.edu.tw/~college):
Chemical Engineering: Prof. SINN-WEN CHEN
Industrial Engineering and Engineering Management: Prof. AMY J. C. TRAPPEY
Materials Science and Engineering: Prof. N. H. TAI
Power Mechanical Engineering: Prof. DIEN SHAW
Graduate Institute of Micro-Electrical Mechanical Systems: Prof. LONG-SHENG FAN

College of Humanities and Social Sciences (tel. (3) 5742779; fax (3) 5723684; e-mail humansos@my.nthu.edu.tw; internet www.hss.nthu.edu.tw):
Chinese Literature: Prof. SHERMAN CHU
Economics: Prof. HWEI-LIN CHUANG
Foreign Languages and Literature: Prof. SAI-HUA KUO
Humanities and Social Science: Prof. YING-CHUN TSAI
Graduate Institute of Anthropology: Prof. HSIANG-HSUI CHEN
Graduate Institute of History: Prof. MIN-CHIH HUANG
Graduate Institute of Linguistics: Prof. YUEH-CHIN CHANG
Graduate Institute of Philosophy: Prof. RUEY-YUAN WU
Graduate Institute of Sociology: Prof. CHYUAN-YUAN WU
Graduate Institute of Taiwanese Literature: Prof. WAN-CHUAN HU

College of Life Science (tel. (3) 5751008; fax (3) 5717237; e-mail life@my.nthu.edu.tw; internet life.nthu.edu.tw):
Life Science: Prof. PING-CHIANG LYU
Institute of Bioinformatics and Structural Biology: Prof. PING-CHIANG LYU
Institute of Molecular and Cellular Biology: Prof. LIH-YUAN LIN
Institute of Molecular Medicine: Prof. YEN-CHUNG CHUNG
Graduate Institute of Biotechnology: Prof. ANN-SHYN CHIANG

College of Nuclear Science (tel. (3) 5719773; fax (3) 5716526; e-mail nuclear@my.nthu.edu.tw; internet www.ess.nthu.edu.tw/~college):
Engineering and Systems Science: Prof. J. J. KAI
Nuclear Science: Prof. IAN C. HSU

College of Science (tel. (3) 5719039; fax (3) 5723762; e-mail science@my.nthu.edu.tw; internet my.nthu.edu.tw/~science):
Chemistry: Prof. BIING-JIUN UANG
Mathematics: Prof. SHU-CHENG CHANG
Physics: Prof. JOW-TSONG SHY
Graduate Institute of Astronomy: Prof. JOW-TSONG SHY
Graduate Institute of Statistics: Prof. LONGCHEEN HUANG

College of Technology Management (tel. (3) 5743944; fax (3) 5745530; e-mail ctm@my.nthu.edu.tw; internet www.ctm.nthu.edu.tw):
Quantitative Finance: Prof. KUO-PING CHANG
Graduate Institute of Law for Science and Technology: Prof. CHIEN-TE FAN
Graduate Institute of Technology Management: Prof. SHIH-CHANG HUNG

SOOCHOW UNIVERSITY

70 Linhsi Rd, Shihlin, Taipei 111
Telephone: (2) 28819471
Fax: (2) 28829310
E-mail: secretary@scu.edu.tw
Internet: www.scu.edu.tw

Founded 1900
Private control
Languages of instruction: Chinese, English
Academic year: September to June (two semesters)

President: CHAO-SHUIAN LIU
Vice-President: CHUN-MEI MA
Vice-President for Academic Affairs: MAO-TING CHIEN
Registrar: CHENG-TSUN LIN
Librarian: YUAN-JEE DING

Library of 692,767 vols
Number of teachers: 1,149 (including part-time teachers)
Number of students: 15,085

Publications: *Journal of Chinese Studies* (annually), *Journal of Economics and Business* (quarterly), *Journal of Foreign Languages and Cultures* (annually), *Journal of History* (annually), *Journal of Japanese Language Teaching* (annually), *Journal of Mathematics* (annually), *Journal of Philosophical Studies* (2 a years), *Journal of Political Science* (2 a year), *Journal of Sociology* (2 a year), *Law Review* (2 a year)

DIRECTORS

School of Arts and Social Sciences: SIU-KEUNG WONG
School of Business: YUNG-HO CHIU
School of Foreign Languages and Cultures: TSONG-MINN LIN
School of Law: WEI-DA PAN
School of Science: HIN-CHUNG WONG
Extension School: PING-WEN LIN

TAIPEI NATIONAL UNIVERSITY OF THE ARTS

1 Hsueh Yuan Rd, Kuan-Tu, Taipei 112
Telephone: (2) 28961000
Fax: (2) 28945124
E-mail: www@www.tnua.edu.tw
Internet: www.tnua.edu.tw

Founded 1982 as National Institute of the Arts; university status 2004

Library of 300,000 vols
Number of teachers: 127

Number of students: 1,726
Pres.: Dr KUN-LIANG CHIU
Publications: *Arts Review* (annually), *Guandu Music Journal* (2 a year), *Journal of Cultural Resources* (annually), *Taipei Theatre Journal* (2 a year)

DEANS

Faculty of Culture Resources: HUI-CHENG LIN
Faculty of Dance: CHUNG-SHIUAN CHANG
Faculty of Fine Art: CHANG-HU LIN
Faculty of Music: HWANG-LONG PAN
Faculty of Theatre: MING-TE CHUNG

TAMKANG UNIVERSITY

151 Ying-Chuan Rd, Tamsui, Taipei 25137
Telephone: (2) 26215656
Fax: (2) 26237384
Internet: www.tku.edu.tw
Founded 1950 (formerly Tamkang College of Arts and Sciences)
Private control
Languages of instruction: Chinese, English
Academic year: August to July
President: Dr HORNG-JINH CHANG
Vice-Presidents: Dr CHAO-KANG FENG (Academic), Dr FLORA CHIA-I CHANG (Administrative)
Secretary-General: Dr TUN-LI CHEN
Dean of Academic Affairs: Dr HIS-JEN FU
Dean of General Affairs: Prof. CHING-JEN HUNG
Dean of Student Affairs: Dr HUAN-CHAO KEH
Librarian: Prof. HONG-CHU HUANG
Library of 753,911 vols, 6,901 periodicals
Number of teachers: 2,033
Number of students: 26,600
Publications: *Educational Media and Library Science*, *International Journal of Information and Management Science*, *Journal of Future Studies*, *Tamkang Journal*, *Tamkang Journal of International Affairs*, *Tamkang Review*, *Tamkang Mathematics*

DEANS OF COLLEGES

Business: Dr JONG-RONG CHIOU
Engineering: Dr SHI-CHIH CHU
Foreign Languages and Literature: Dr YAOFU LIN
International Studies: Dr WOU WEI
Liberal Arts: Dr SHIH-HSION HUANG
Management: Dr LIANG-YU OUYANG
Science: Dr KAN-NAN CHEN
Technocracy: Prof. HSIN-FU TSAI
Extension Education Centre: Prof. YAO-LUNG HAN

DIRECTORS OF GRADUATE INSTITUTES

Accounting: Dr CHEN-LI HUANG
Aerospace Engineering: Dr TZENG-YUAN CHEN
American Studies: Dr I-HSIN CHEN
Applied Statistics: Dr JONG-WUU WU
Architecture: Prof. HOANG-ELL JENG
Chemical Engineering: Dr KUO-JEN HWANG
Chemistry: Dr HUEY-CHUEN KAO
Chinese Literature: Dr PO-YUAN KAO
China Studies: Dr ANDY W. Y. CHANG
Civil Engineering: Dr CHO-SEN WO
Educational Media Library Science: Dr JEONG-YEOU CHIU
Educational Technology: Dr CHIEN-HUA WANG
Electrical Engineering: Dr JEN-CHIUN CHIANG
European Studies: Dr TZUNG-JEN TSAI
History: Dr TZENG-CHYUAN LIOU
Industrial Economics: Dr JIUNN-RONG CHIOU
Information Engineering: Dr KUO-CHEN SHIH
Information Management: Dr CHEN-CHUNG HUANG
International Affairs and Strategic Studies: Dr MING-HSIEN WONG
International Business: Dr JYH-HORNG LIN
Japanese Studies: Dr CHANG-HUEI LIU
Latin-American Studies: Dr KWO-WEI KUNG
Management Science: Dr PEI-CHI LEE
Mass Communication: Dr SHU-HUA CHANG
Mathematics: Dr CHIN-MEI KAU
Mechanical Engineering: Dr FENG-HUI YEH
Money, Banking and Finance: Dr GIN-CHUNG LIN
Physics: Dr WAY-FAUNG PONG
Public Administration: Dr MING-SIANG CHEN
Slavic Studies: Dr ALEXANDER PISAREV
South-east Asian Studies: Dr JUO-YU LIN
Transportation Management: Dr HSIAO-HSIEN LUO
Water Resources and Environmental Engineering: Dr PO-CHIEN LU
Western Languages and Literature: Dr CHUN-CHUNG LIN

TUNGHAI UNIVERSITY

181 Taichung Harbour Rd, Sec. 3, Taichung 40704
Telephone: (4) 23590200
Fax: (4) 23590361
E-mail: kpwang@mail.thu.edu.tw
Internet: www.thu.edu.tw
Founded 1955 under the auspices of the United Board for Christian Higher Education in Asia
Languages of instruction: Chinese, English
Academic year: September to July (two semesters)
President: KANG-PEI WANG
Dean of Academic Affairs: CHENG-TUNG LIN
Dean of General Affairs: I-CHAO HSIAO
Dean of Student Affairs: HUNG-DER FU
Librarian: CHUNG-LIN LU
Number of teachers: 826
Number of students: 14,500
Publications: *The Vineyard*, *Tunghai Bulletin*, *Tunghai Journal*, *Tunghai News*

DEANS

College of Agriculture: TSUN-CHUNG TSAI
College of Arts: HAI-YUN HUANG
College of Engineering: JEN-TENG TSAI
College of Management: TSAI-DING LIN
College of Science: CHING-SHENG CHEN
College of Social Sciences: JENN-HWAN WANG

Colleges and Institutes

China Medical College: 91 Hseuh Shih Rd, Taichung 404; tel. (4) 2057153; f. 1958; private control; two campuses (in Taichung and Peikang), six graduate institutes, 12 undergraduate schools, Chiang Kai-shek Medical Center, two teaching hospitals; 625 staff; 4,666 students; Pres. MASON CHEN.

Kaohsiung Medical University: 100 Shih Chuan 1st Rd, Kaohsiung 807; tel. (7) 3117820; fax (7) 3212062; internet www.kmu.edu.tw; f. 1954; private control; 428 teachers; 6,106 students; library: 175,802 vols, 2,970 periodicals; colleges of medicine, dental medicine, pharmacy, nursing, health sciences, life sciences; undergraduate division of 19 schools; 12 postgraduate institutes; 7 research centres: health and social services, industrial hygiene, gender studies, tropical medicine, orthopaedics, genomics, proteomics; Pres. Dr GWO-JAW WANG; publ. *Kaohsiung Journal of Medical Sciences* (monthly).

National Kaohsiung University of Applied Sciences: 415 Chien-Kung Rd, Kaohsiung 807; tel. (7) 3814526; fax (7) 3838435; f. 1963; depts of chemical, civil, mechanical, electrical, electronic, mould- and die-making engineering, industrial management, accounting, business administration, finance, international trade, tourism, taxation and finance, applied foreign languages, cultural industries development, human resource development, information management; graduate institutes of civil engineering and disaster prevention, electrical energy and control, electronic and information engineering, mechanical and precision engineering, commerce, tourism management, finance and information; library: 171,674 vols; 415 teachers; 10,727 students; Pres. Dr REN-YIH LIN; publ. *Journal* (annually).

Taipei Institute of Technology: 3, Sec. 1, Shin-sheng South Rd, Taipei; f. 1912; 8,973 students; library: 112,000 vols; Pres. Dr CHIH TANG.

Taipei Medical College: 250 Wu Hsing St, Taipei; tel. (2) 27361661; fax (2) 27362824; f. 1960; private control; undergraduate and graduate programmes; 568 teachers; 4,208 students; library: 83,000 vols; Pres. CHUNG-HONG HU; Vice-Pres. MEEI-SHIOW LU; Dean of Studies KUANG-YANG HSU; publ. *Journal* (2 a year).

Tatung University: 40 Chungshan N Rd, Sec. 3, Taipei; tel. (2) 25925252; fax (2) 25941371; e-mail registrar@ttu.edu.tw; internet www.ttu.edu.tw; f. 1956; private control; depts of Mechanical Engineering, Chemical Engineering, Materials Engineering, Bioengineering, Electrical Engineering, Computer Science and Engineering, Applied Mathematics, Business Management, Industrial Design, Information Management; graduate institutes in Electro-Optical Engineering and Communications Engineering; 200 teachers; 2,500 students; library: 159,683 vols; Pres. T. S. LIN; Dean of Studies JAN-CHEN HONG.

School of Art and Music

National Taiwan College of Arts: Panchiao, Taipei; tel. (2) 22722181; fax (2) 29687563; internet www.ntca.edu.tw; f. 1955; cinema, drama, radio and television, fine arts, painting, graphic arts, industrial arts, Chinese music, dance, music, sculpture; 364 teachers; 2,300 students; library: 104,000 vols; Pres. MING-SHEAN WANG.

COLOMBIA

The Higher Education System

The Roman Catholic Church pioneered higher education in Colombia, with the establishment of the Pontificia Universidad Javeriana in 1622, and remained the driving force behind universities until the 1930s. In 1994 the Educational Law (No. 115) put the Ministry of National Education in charge of public and private education. In 2002 there were an estimated 321 higher education institutes (including universities) in Colombia. Other university-level institutions include centros, corporaciones, escuelas, fundaciones, institutos and colegios.

Admission to higher education is on the basis of the secondary school certificate (Bachillerato) and, from March 2000, a new version of the State Higher Education Entrance Examination. The basic university degree structure consists of Licenciado (equivalent to Bachelors), Magister (Masters) and Doctorado (Doctorate) degrees. Undergraduates study for four to five years for the Licenciado or professional title. At postgraduate level the Diploma de Especialización (Diploma of Specialization) requires one to four years of study, usually in a professional or applied discipline. The Magister is awarded after two years of study following Licenciado, while a Doctorado requires two to three years of study in an area of specialization.

Public and private institutos tecnológicas (technical institutes) offer post-secondary technical and vocational education. The title Técnico Profesional Intermedio is awarded after two years of study following the Bachillerato, and a Título de Tecnólogo or a Técnico de Alto Nivel is awarded by technical institutes and some universities after three years of study. Another qualification is the Tecnólogo Especializado, which requires two years of study.

Learned Societies

GENERAL

Academia Colombiana de la Lengua (Colombian Academy): Apdo Aereo 13922, Bogotá; f. 1871; corresp. of the Real Academia Española (Madrid); 29 mems; 50 corresp. and hon. mems; library of 40,000 vols; Dir (vacant); Exec. Sec. JAIME BERNAL LEONGÓMEZ; publ. *Boletín*.

Casa de la Cultura de la Costa (House of Caribbean Coast Culture): Carrera 3, No. 19–60, Of. 401, Bogotá; tel. 243-3898; f. 1981; study centre for development of the Colombian coastal regions and int. Caribbean studies; mems: 36 companies and individuals, 86 congressmen from the coast; library of 2,000 vols; Pres. MARCO ANTONIO CONTRERAS; Sec. GERARDO MORA MEDINA; publ. *Revista Caribe Internacional* (monthly).

AGRICULTURE, FISHERIES AND VETERINARY SCIENCE

Sociedad de Agricultores de Colombia (Colombian Farmers' Society): Carrera 7 No. 24–89, 44° piso, Apdo Aéreo 3638, Bogotá; tel. (1) 2821989; fax (1) 2844572; e-mail sac@col.net.co; internet www.sac.org.co; f. 1871; consultative body for the Government; 400 mems; library of 5,500 vols, 435 periodical titles; Pres. RAFAEL MEJIA LÓPEZ; Sec. RICARDO SÁNCHEZ LÓPEZ; publs *Revista Nacional de Agricultura* (quarterly), *El Editorial Agrario* (irregular), *Documentos Independientes*.

BIBLIOGRAPHY, LIBRARY SCIENCE AND MUSEOLOGY

Asociación Colombiana de Bibliotecarios (ASCOLBI) (Colombian Association of Librarians): Calle 10, No. 3–16, Apdo Aéreo 30883, Bogotá; tel. 269-4219; f. 1942; 1,200 mems; Pres. SAUL SANCHEZ TORO; Gen. Sec. B. N. CARDONA DE GIL; publ. *Boletín* (quarterly).

Centro Regional para el Fomento del Libro en América Latina y el Caribe (CERLALC) (Regional Centre for the Promotion of Books in Latin America and the Caribbean): Calle 70 No. 9–52, Apdo Aéreo 57348, Bogotá; tel. (1) 3217501; fax (1) 3217503; e-mail libro@cerlalc.com; internet www.cerlalc.com; f. 1972 by UNESCO and Colombian govt, later joined by most states in the area; promotes production and circulation of books, and development of libraries; provides training; promotes protection of copyright; 21 mem. countries; library of 5,600 documents, 100 periodicals; Dir ALMA BYINGTON DE ARBOLEDA; publs *El Libro en América Latina y el Caribe* (quarterly), *Boletín Informativo CERLALC* (4 a year).

Fundación para el Fomento de la Lectura—(FUNDALECTURA): Avda (calle) 40 No. 16-46, Apdo 48902, Bogotá; tel. 3201511; fax 2877071; e-mail contactenos@fundalectura.org.co; internet www.fundalectura.org; f. 1984; promotion of reading, and children's and juvenile literature; library of 4,500 vols; Dir CARMEN BARVO; publs *Nuevas Hojas de Lectura* (4 a year), *Revista Latinoamericana de Literatura Infantil y Juvenil* (online at www.relalij.com, 2 a year).

ECONOMICS, LAW AND POLITICS

Academia Colombiana de Jurisprudencia (Colombian Academy of Jurisprudence): Carrera 9 No. 74–08, Oficina 203, Bogotá; tel. (1) 2124315; f. 1894; 50 mems; Pres. HERNANDO MORALES M.; publs *Revista* (2 a year), *Anuario*.

Sociedad Colombiana de Economistas: Carrera 20 No. 36–41, Apdo Aéreo 8429, Bogotá; tel. 2459637; f. 1957; to promote the improvement of the teaching of economic sciences and economics as a profession, for the economic and social development of the country; 5,500 mems; library of 25,000 vols; Pres. Dr SERGIO ENTRENA LÓPEZ; publ. *Revista* (6 a year).

EDUCATION

Asociación Colombiana de Universidades (Colombian Universities Association): Apdo Aéreo 252367, Calle 93, No. 16–43, Bogotá; tel. (1) 6231580; fax (1) 2185098; e-mail rci@ascun.org.co; internet www.ascun.org.co; f. 1957; 70 mem univs; Pres. Dr GALO BURBANO LÓPEZ; Sec.-Gen. Dr CARLOS FORERO ROBAYO; publs *ASCUN*, *Mundo Universitario* (annually).

Instituto Colombiano de Crédito Educativo y Estudios Técnicos en el Exterior (ICETEX) (Colombian Institute for Educational Loans and Advanced Studies Abroad): Carrera 3A, No. 18–24, Apdo Aéreo 5735, Bogotá; tel. (1) 2867780; fax (1) 2843510; e-mail icetex3@gaitana.interred.net.co; f. 1950; provides undergraduate and postgraduate grants; selects Colombian students for foreign scholarships, and finances foreign postgraduate students in Colombia; information and documentation centres; library of 15,000 vols; Dir Dr CARLOS A. BURITICÁ GIRALDO; publ. *Boletín Interno*.

HISTORY, GEOGRAPHY AND ARCHAEOLOGY

Academia Antioqueña de Historia (Antioquia Academy of History): Carrera 43, Nos 53–37, Apdo Aéreo 7175, Medellín; tel. (942) 395576; f. 1903; 60 mems; Pres. JAIME SIERRA GARCIA; Sec. ALICIA GIRALDO GÓMEZ; publs *Repertorio Histórico* (3 a year), *Bolsilibros*.

Academia Boyacense de Historia (Boyaca Academy of History): Casa del Fundador, Tunja; tel. (9792) 3441; f. 1905; publication and encouragement of historical, literary and anthropological studies in Boyaca; 30 mems; library of 1,000 vols, 600 MSS from the period 1539–1860; Pres. JAVIER OCAMPO LOPEZ; Sec. RAMÓN CORREA; publ. *Repertorio Boyacense* (2 a year).

Academia Colombiana de Historia (Colombian Academy of History): Calle 10 No. 8–95, Apdo Aéreo 14428, Bogotá; f. 1902; 40 mems excluding Colombian and foreign corresp. mems; library of 45,000 vols; Pres. Dr GERMÁN ARCINIEGAS; Sec. ROBERTO VELANDIA; Library Dir Dr RAFAEL SERRANO CAMARGO; publ. *Boletín de Historia y Antigüedades*.

Academia de la Historia de Cartagena de Indias (Cartagena Academy of History): Casa de la Inquisición, Plaza Bolívar, Cartagena; tel. 645432; f. 1918; 24 mems, and 48 Colombian, and 48 foreign corresponding mems; library of 10,000 vols; special collections on the history of Cartagena and Colombia; Pres. DONALDO BOSSA HERAZO; Sec.-Gen. CELEDONIO PIÑERES DE LA ESPRIELLA; publ. *Boletín Historial* (quarterly).

Sociedad Bolivariana de Colombia: Calle 19A No 4–40 E, Apdo 11812, Bogotá; tel. 2431166; f. 1924; 20 hon. mems; library of 1,000 vols, specialized bibliography on Simón Bolívar; Pres. Col ALBERTO LOZANO; publ. *Revista Bolivariana* (3 a year).

Sociedad Geográfica de Colombia (Colombian Geographical Society): Observatorio Astronómico Nacional, Apdo 2584, Bogotá; tel. 2348893; f. 1903; 40 mems; Pres. CLEMENTE GARAVITO; Sec. RAFAEL CONVERS PINZON; publs *Boletín* (3 a year), *Cuadernos de Geografía Colombiana*; branch socs in Barranquilla, Pasto, Medellín, Tunja, Sibundoy.

LANGUAGE AND LITERATURE

Alliance Française: Carrera 7A 84–72, Bogotá; tel. (1) 2563197; fax (1) 6556045; e-mail alfradir@neutel.com.co; internet www.alianzafrancesa.org.co; offers courses and exams in French language and culture and promotes cultural exchange with France; attached teaching offices in Armenia, Barranquilla, Bogatá-Centro, Bucuramanga, Cali, Cartagena, Manizales, Medellín, Pereira, Popayán and Santa Marta.

British Council: Calle 87 No. 12–79, Bogotá DC; tel. (1) 6187680; fax (1) 2187754; e-mail info@britishcouncil.org.co; internet www.britishcouncil.org/colombia; offers courses and exams in English language and British culture and promotes cultural exchange with the UK; library of 7,500 vols, 60 periodicals; Dir JOE DOCHERTY.

Attached Centre:

Teaching Centre: Calle 91 No. 21–55, Bogotá DC; tel. (1) 6917125; fax (1) 6185308; Head, Corporate Training Services TONY HASTINGS.

Goethe-Institut: Carrera 7, No. 81–57, Bogotá; tel. (1) 2547600; fax (1) 2127167; e-mail vl@bogota.goethe.org; internet www.goethe.de/hn/bog/deindex.htm; offers courses and exams in German language and culture and promotes cultural exchange with Germany; Dir FOLCO NÄTHER.

Instituto Caro y Cuervo: Carrera 11 No. 64–37, Apdo Aéreo 51502, Bogotá; tel. (1) 3456004; fax (1) 2170243; e-mail direcciongeneral@caroycuervo.gov.co; f. 1942; Hispanic philology and literature; 20 mems; library of 102,491 vols, 102,000 vols of periodicals; Dir HERNANDO CABARCAS ANTEQUERA; Sec-Gen. LILIANA RIVERA ORJUELA; publs *Poesia Rescatada*, *Thesaurus* (3 a year), *Biblioteca de Publicaciones del Instituto*, *Clásicos Colombianos*, *Filólogos Colombianos*, *Anuario Bibliográfico Colombiano*, *Diccionario de Construcción y Régimen de la Lengua Castellana*, *Archivo Epistolar Colombiano*, *Biblioteca Colombiana*, *La Granada Entreabierta*, *Biblioteca 'Ezequiel Uricoechea'*, *Atlas Linguístico-Etnográfico de Colombia*, *Noticias Culturales* (every 2 months), *Cuadernos del Seminario Andrés Bello*, *Litterae*, *Poesía Rescatada*, *Aguas Vivas*.

PEN Internacional, Colombia: Calle 88, 11A-20, Apdo 302, Bogotá; tel. (1) 2846761; fax (1) 2184236; e-mail cbalcaza@uniandes.edu.co; internet www.pencolombia.org; f. 1983; 50 mems; library of 1,000 vols; Pres. Dr CECILIA BALCÁZAR; Sec. GLORIA GUARDIA; publ. *Pliegos* (4 a year).

MEDICINE

Academia Nacional de Medicina de Colombia (Colombian National Academy of Medicine): Carrera 7 No. 69–05, Bogotá; tel. (1) 3458890; fax (1) 2128670; e-mail acadmed@cable.net.co; internet www.fepafem.org/anm; f. 1873; 557 mems; library of 10,000 vols; Pres. Dr JUAN MENDOZA-VEGA; Perm. Sec. Dr HERNANDO GROOT; publs *Medicina* (4 a year), *Temas Médicos* (annually).

Asociación Colombiana de Facultades de Medicina (Colombian Association of Medical Faculties): Apdo 53751, Calle 39A No. 28–63, Bogotá; tel. 3686711; e-mail sascome@col1.telecom.com.co; f. 1959 to further higher education and research in medicine; divisions of Education, Evaluation, Health and Social Security, Information; membership: 24 medical faculties (institutional mems), 4,500 individuals, 7 affiliated mems; library of 3,500 vols, 100 periodicals and audiovisual materials; Pres. JOSE MARIA MAYA; Exec. Dir. JULIO ENRIQUE OSPINA; publs *Boletín de Medicamentos y Terapéutica* (quarterly), *Gaceta Médica*, *Revista de ASCOFAME*, *Cuadernos de Actualización Médica Permanente*, *Boletín del Centro de Etica Médica y Bioética*.

Asociación Colombiana de Fisioterapía: Carrera 23 No. 47–51, Of. 3N-06-A, Bogotá; tel. 2876106; f. 1953; 950 mems; library of 300 vols; Pres. ELISA JARAMILLO DE LOPEZ; Exec. Sec. CLARA INES DE AMAYA; publ. *Revista* (annually).

Asociación Colombiana de Psiquiatría: Carrera 18 No. 84–87, Oficina 403, Bogotá; tel. (1) 2561148; fax (1) 6162706; e-mail asocopsi@cable.net.co; internet www.psiquiatria.org.co; f. 1961; 350 mems; Pres. Dr CARLOS ALBERTO FELIZZOLA DONADO; Sec. Dr ALVARO FRANCO; publ. *Revista Colombiana de Psiquiatría* (quarterly).

Asociación Colombiana de Sociedades Científicas: Cra. 16A No. 77-11, Oficina 404, Santafé de Bogotá; tel. 531-12-26; fax 236-74-83; e-mail sociedadsc@col.net.co; internet www.sociedadescientificas.com; f. 1957, present name 1970; health sciences; 3,692 mems; Exec. Dir Dr FABIO LOAIZA D.; publ. *Boletín* (quarterly).

Capitolo Colombiano de las Federaciones Latinoamericanas de Asociaciones de Cancer (Colombian Chapter of Latin American Cancer Asscns): Clínica del Country, Carrera 15 No. 84–13, Bogotá; tel. 2361168; f. 1983; Pres. CALIXTO NOGUERA.

Federación Médica Colombiana: No. 6–44, 11° piso, Bogotá; tel. 2110208; e-mail federacionmedicacol@hotmail.com; f. 1935; Pres. Dr SERGIO ISAZA VILLA; Sec. SERGIO ROBLEDA RIAGA; publ. *Directorio Médico Asistencial* (annually).

Instituto Nacional de Medicina Legal y Ciencias Forenses (National Institute of Legal Medicine and Forensic Sciences): Calle 7A, A 12–61, Santafé de Bogotá; tel. (1) 233854; f. 1914; staff of 800; library of 30,000 vols; Dir RICARDO MORA IZQUIERDO; publ. *Revista*.

Sociedad Colombiana de Cardiología (Colombian Cardiological Society): Avda 19 No. 97-31 Of. 401, Apdo Aéreo 1875, Bogotá; tel. 6234603; fax 6234603; f. 1950; 245 mems; Pres. Dr RICARDO ROZO URIBE; Sec. Dra MARGARITA BLANCO DE ESCOBAR; publ. *Revista SCC* (4 a year).

Sociedad Colombiana de Cirugía Ortopédica y Traumatología: Calle 134 No.13-83, Oficina 201, Bogotá; tel. (1) 6257338; fax (1) 6257417; e-mail secretaria@sccot.org.co; internet www.sccot.org.co; f. 1946; 961 mems; Pres. Dr CELSO PEDRAZA; Gen. Sec. Dr JAVIER PÉREZ; publ. *Carta de Ortopédica* (monthly).

Sociedad Colombiana de Obstetricia y Ginecología: Carrera 23, No. 39–82, Apdo Aéreo 34188, Bogotá; tel. 2681485; f. 1943; 300 mems; library of 1,000 vols; Pres. Dr JAIME FERRO CAMARGO; Vice-Pres. Dra MARIA TERESA PERALTA ABELLO; Sec.-Gen. Dr PIO IVÁN GÓMEZ SÁNCHEZ; publ. *Revista Colombiana de Obstetricia y Ginecología* (quarterly).

Sociedad Colombiana de Patología: Dpto de Patología, Universidad del Valle, Calí; f. 1955; to improve all aspects of pathology studies; 155 mems; Pres. Dr EDGAR DUQUE; Sec. and Treas. Dr JOSÉ A. DORADO.

Sociedad Colombiana de Pediatría (Colombian Paediatrics Society): Avdo 4 Norte, No. 16–23, Apdo 3124, Calí; tel. 611407; fax 673614; f. 1917; 150 mems; library of 2,300 vols; Pres. CESAR A. VILLAMIZAR LUNA; Sec. ALBERTO LEVY F.; publs *Pediatría* (quarterly), *Acta Pedriatrica Colombiana*.

Sociedad Colombiana de Radiología (Radiological Society): Carrera 13A No. 90–18, Of. 208, Bogotá; tel. (1) 6183895; fax (1) 6183775; f. 1945; 400 mems; library of 3,000 vols, collections of journals; Pres. CAYO DUARTE; Sec. PATRICIA CASTRO S..

NATURAL SCIENCES

General

Academia Colombiana de Ciencias Exactas, Físicas y Naturales (Colombian Academy of Exact, Physical and Natural Sciences): Transv. 27, No. 39A–63, Apdo Aéreo 44763, Santafé de Bogotá 1, DC; tel. (1) 244-31-86; fax (1) 244-31-86; e-mail jlozano@accefyn.org.co; internet www.accefyn.org.co; f. 1929; 49 mems (40 ordinary, 9 hon.); Pres. MOISÉS WASSERMAN; Sec. JOSÉ A. LOZANO; publ. *Revista* (4 a year).

Biological Sciences

Sociedad Colombiana de Biología: Calle 73 No. 10–10, Apartamento 301, Bogotá; Pres Dr GONZALO MONTES; Sec. MARGARET ORDÓÑEZ SMITH.

Mathematical Sciences

Sociedad Colombiana de Matemáticas: Apdo Aéreo 2521, Bogotá 1; tel. 3165000 ext.13232; f. 1955; 800 mems; library of 7,000 vols; Pres LEONARDO RENDÓN ARBELÁEZ; publs *Revista Colombiana de Matemáticas*, *Lecturas Matemáticas*.

Physical Sciences

Sociedad Colombiana de Ciencias Químicas: Apdo Aéreo 10968, Bogotá; tel. 2216920; fax 3150751; f. 1941 to promote chemical research in Colombia, to uphold professional ethical standards, to serve as an advisory body for public and private organizations, to maintain relations with similar institutions at home and abroad; 350 mems; Pres. FABIO H. VELANDIA CASALLAS; Sec. GILMA DAZA CASILIMAS; publ. *Química e Industria* (2 a year).

TECHNOLOGY

Asociación Colombiana de Industrias Gráficas—ANDIGRAF (Graphic Industry National Association): Carrera 4A No. 25B–46, Apdo Aéreo 45243, Bogotá; tel. 2819611; f. 1975; 200 company mems; Pres. JOSE GRANADA RODRIGUEZ; publs *Boletín Informativo* (monthly), *Colombia Gráfica* (annually).

Asociación Colombiana de Informática y Comunicaciones (Colombian Association of Information Technology and Communication): Avda Estación 5B Norte, 73 Oficina 205, Santiago de Cali; tel. 6675595; e-mail acvcsurocci@telesat.com.co; internet www.acvc.org.co; f. 1970; 400 company mems; library of 1,500 documents; Pres. JOSE GUILLERMO JARAMILLO G.; Exec. Dir CESAR AUGUSTO SALAZAR U.; publs *ACUC Noticias* (every 2 months), *Boletín El Usuario* (monthly), *Catálogo Nacional de Software—Guía de Servicios Informáticos* (annually).

Sociedad Colombiana de Ingenieros (Colombian Society of Engineers): Carrera 4, No. 10–41, Apdo 340, Bogotá; tel. 2862200; fax 2816229; f. 1887; 2,000 mems; library of 5,000 vols; Pres. HERNANDO MONROY VALENCIA; Exec. Dir SANTIAGO HENAO PÉREZ; publ. *Anales de Ingeniería* (quarterly).

Research Institutes

GENERAL

Instituto Colombiano para el Desarrollo de la Ciencia y la Tecnología 'Francisco José de Caldas' (Colciencias): Transversal 9A No. 133–28, Apdo Aéreo 051580, Santafé de Bogotá; tel. 2169800; fax 6251788; f. 1968; to promote scientific and technical development; co-ordinates and finances projects; library of 15,000 vols, 225 periodicals, 10,000 databases; Dir LUIS FERNANDO CHAPARRO OSORIO; Sec.-Gen. JUAN RICARDO MORALES ESPINEL; publs serials: *Carta de Colciencias* (monthly), *Colombia Ciencia y Tecnología* (quarterly).

AGRICULTURE, FISHERIES AND VETERINARY SCIENCE

Instituto Colombiano Agropecuario (Colombian Agricultural and Livestock Institute): Apdo Aéreo 7984, Calle 37 No. 8–43 (4° y 5° pisos), Bogotá; tel. 2855520; fax 2884169; e-mail gereica@impsat.net.co; internet www.iica-saninet/ica/ica.htm; f. 1962 to promote, co-ordinate and carry out research, teaching and development in agriculture and animal husbandry; library: see Libraries and Archives; Dir-Gen. ALVARO JOSÉ ABISAMBRA ABISAMBRA; publ. *Informe Anual*.

ECONOMICS, LAW AND POLITICS

Centro de Estudios sobre Desarrollo Económico (Centre for Economic Development Studies): Universidad de los Andes, Carrera 1E No. 18A–10, Apdo Aéreo 4976, Bogotá; tel. (1) 3412240; fax (1) 2815771; e-mail infcede@uniandes.edu.co; internet economia.uniandes.edu.co; f. 1958; library of 35,000 vols; Dir ROBERTO STEINER; publ. *Desarrollo y Sociedad* (2 a year).

Departamento Administrativo Nacional de Estadística (National Statistics Department): Transversal 45 # 26–70 Interior 1 CAN, Apdo Aéreo 80043, Bogotá; tel. 5978300; fax 5978384; e-mail dane@dane.gov.co; internet www.dane.gov.co; f. 1953; library of 12,000 vols, 850 periodicals received; Dir CÉSAR AUGUSTO CABALLERO REINOSO; publs *Boletín Mensual de Estadística* (monthly), *Anuario de Industria Manufacturera* (annually), *Anuario de Comercio Exterior* (annually), *Cuentas Nacionales de Colombia*, *Colombia Estadística*, *Bases de Contabilidad*, *Indicadores de Coyuntura*, *Estudios Censales*, *Metodología Cuentas Departamentales*, *DIVIPOLA*, *Plan Estadístico de Cundinamarca*, *Mujeres con Hijos Habitantes de la Calle*, *Atlas Sociodemigráfico de Colombia*.

EDUCATION

Centro de Investigación y Educación Popular: Carrera 5 No 33A-08, Apdo 25916, Bogotá; tel. 2858977; fax 2879089; f. 1962; private, non-profit org. specializing in social sciences education, and analysis of the Colombian system; library of 23,000 vols; Dir FERNAN GONZALEZ G.; publs *Cien Días* (quarterly), *Controversia* (irregular).

Instituto Colombiano para el Fomento de la Educación Superior: Apdo Aéreo 6319, Calle 17, No. 3–40, Bogotá; tel. 2819311; fax 286-80-45; e-mail snies@icfes.gov.co; f. 1968; branch of the Ministry of Education; govt body supervizing the running of higher education; co-ordinates the country's distance education system; library: documentation centre specializing in higher, distance and 'open' education, and national film collection: 9,200 vols, 2,500 documents, 2,527 periodicals, 1,015 films, a/v items and videocassettes; Dir LUIS CARLOS MUÑOZ URIBE; publs *Revista ICFES* (irregular), *Memorias de Eventos Científicos*, *Estadísticas de la Educación Superior*.

HISTORY, GEOGRAPHY AND ARCHAEOLOGY

Instituto Colombiano de Antropología e Historia (Colombian Institute of Anthropology and History): Calle 12 No. 2–41, Apdo Aéreo 407, Bogotá; tel. 3418849; fax 2811051; f. 1941; research in fields of history, archaeology and anthropology; oversees cultural, archaeological and anthropological patrimony of Colombia, and administers national archaeological parks; publishes editions of 'Flora of the Botanic Expedition' of the New Kingdom of Granada; library of 30,000 vols (open to public); Dir MARÍA VICTORIA URIBE-ALARCÓN; publs *Revista Colombiana de Antropología* (annually), *Fronteras de la Historia* (annually).

Instituto Geográfico 'Agustín Codazzi': Apdo 6721, Carrera 30 No. 48–51, Santafé de Bogotá; tel. (1) 369-40-53; fax (1) 369-40-99; e-mail webpage@igac.gov.co; internet www.igac.gov.co; f. 1935; prepares topographical, cadastral, sectional, national, and agricultural maps of the country, and geophysical, cadastral and geodetic surveys; prepares geographical studies of Colombia; library of 10,000 vols; Dir IVAN DARIO GOMEZ GUZMÁN.

MEDICINE

Instituto Nacional de Cancerología: Calle 1, No. 9–85, Bogotá 1; tel. (1) 3342474; fax (1) 3341844; e-mail biblioteca@incancerologia.gov.co; internet www.incancerologia.gov.co; f. 1934; diagnosis, therapy, control, teaching and research in cancer; advisor instn to Min. of Health, designs and implements national policies and programmes to control the spread of cancer; library of 26,000 vols; Dir-Gen. CARLOS VICENTE RADA ESCOBAR; publ. *Revista Colombiana de Cancerología*.

Instituto Nacional de Salud INPES (National Institute of Health): Avda el Dorado Carrera 50, Apdo Aéreo 80334, Bogotá; tel. 2221059; fax 2220194; f. 1968; library of 10,000 vols, 500 periodicals; Dir Dr MOISES WASSERMAN; publs *Biomédica*, *Informe Quincenal de Casos y Brotes de Enfermedades* (every 2 weeks), *Boletín Epidemiológico*.

NATURAL SCIENCES

Biological Sciences

Instituto de Ciencias Naturales (Institute of Natural Sciences): Universidad Nacional de Colombia, Apdo 7495, Bogotá; tel. (1) 3165305; fax (1) 3165365; e-mail inscien_bog@unal.edu.co; internet www.icn.unal.edu.co; f. 1936 to conduct scientific research; three main sections: botany, zoology and archaeology; library of 8,000 vols; Dir GLORIA GALEANO; publs *Caldasia*, *Flora de Colombia*, *Fauna de Colombia*, *Biblioteca José Jerónimo Triana*.

Instituto de Investigaciones Marinas de Punta de Betín 'José Benito Vives de Andreis' (INVEMAR): Apdo Aéreo 1016, Santa Marta; tel. 211380; fax 211377; f. 1963; institute of COLCIENCIAS; aims to study and preserve the marine wildlife of the Colombian Caribbean; library of 10,000 vols; Dir Dra LEONOR BOTERO; publ. *Anales*.

Physical Sciences

Observatorio Astronómico Nacional (National Astronomical Observatory): Carrera 8, Calle 8, Apdo Aéreo 2584, Bogotá; tel. 2423786; f. 1803; library of 3,000 vols; Dir JORGE ARRAS DE GREIFF; publs *Anuario del Observatorio*, occasional publications.

TECHNOLOGY

Instituto Colombiano de Geologia y Mineria (INGEOMINAS) (Institute for Research and Information in the Geosciences, Mining, the Environment and Nuclear Physics): Diagonal 53, No. 34–53, Apdo Aéreo 4865, Bogotá; tel. (1) 2221811; fax (1) 2220797; e-mail cliente@ingeomin.gov.co; internet www.ingeominas.gov.co; f. 1940 as National Geological Survey, name changed 1969; library of 6,000 books, 104 current periodicals, 2,400 technical reports; Dir Dr JULIAN VILLARRUEL TORO; publs *Boletín de Actividad Sismica*, *Boletín Geológico* (3 vols, annually), *Boletin de Vocanes Colombianos*, *Informe de Actividades Anuales*, *Revista Ingeominas*.

Instituto Colombiano de Normas Técnicas y Certificación (ICONTEC): Carrera 37, No. 52–95, Santafé de Bogotá; tel. 6078888; fax 2221435; e-mail cliente@calidad.icontec.org.co; internet www.icontec.org.co; f. 1963; 1,200 mems; library of 800,000 vols; Exec. Dir Ing. FABIO TOBON; Admin. Dir ALVARO PERDOMO B.; publs *Boletín Informativo* (monthly), *Normas y Calidad* (4 a year).

Instituto Colombiano del Petróleo (Colombian Petroleum Institute): Autopista Piedecuesta Km 7, Apdo Aereo 4185, Bucaramanga; tel. (57) 76445420; fax (57) 76445444; internet www.icp.ecopetrol.com.co; exploration and development of oil reserves; library of 19,000 vols, 500 periodicals and newspapers, 1,000 audiovisual items, 8,000 ICP documents; Dir JAIME CADAVID CALVO; publ. *GT & F Magazine*.

Instituto de Ciencias Nucleares y Energías Alternativas (Institute for Nuclear Sciences and Alternative Energy): Avda Eldorado, Carrera 50, Apdo Aéreo 8595, Santafé de Bogotá, DC; tel. 2220071; fax 2220173; f. 1959 to study the application of atomic and nuclear energy for peaceful uses, the development of alternative energy sources and the efficient use of energy; library of 18,000 vols, 60 periodicals, 70,000 reprints, 120,000 microforms; Dir Dr CESAR HUMBERTO ARIAS PABON; publs scientific reports, annual report.

Libraries and Archives

Barranquilla

Biblioteca Pública Departamental: Carrera 38 -B, No. 38–21, Barranquilla; tel. (95) 312015; f. 1923; 32,000 vols; Dir OLGA CHAMS.

Bello

Biblioteca del Marco Fidel Suárez: Avda Suárez, Bello, Antioquia; tel. (942) 750774; f. 1957; public library and regional centre; 2,615 vols; Dir WALTER GIL.

Bogotá

Archivo Nacional de Colombia: Archivo General de la Nación, Calle 24 No. 5–60, 4° piso, Bogotá; tel. 416015; f. 1868; *c.* 40,600 vols and 3,135 metres of documents; Dir JORGE PALACIOS PRECIADO; publs *Revista*, *Catálogos, and series of historic documents*.

Biblioteca Agropecuaria de Colombia: Inst. Colombiano Agropecuario, Apdo Aéreo 240142, Santafé de Bogotá; tel. (1) 344-30-00 ext. 1253; fax (1) 344-30-00 ext. 1248; e-mail fsalazar@corpoica.org.co; internet www.corpoica.org.co; f. 1954; 46,000 vols devoted to agriculture and livestock, 46,300 pamphlets, 1,900 journals, 29,560 documents, 170 maps, 150 audiovisual titles, 497 tapes; Dir FRANCISCO SALAZAR ALONSO.

Biblioteca Central de la Pontificia Universidad Javeriana: Carrera 7A, No. 41–

00, Bogotá; tel. 3208320 ext. 2132; fax 2850973; e-mail lmcabarc@javercol.javeriana.edu.co; f. 1931; 287,000 vols; Dir LUZ MARIA CABARCAS SANTOYA.

Biblioteca 'Luis-Angel Arango' del Banco de la República (Bank of the Republic Library): Carrera 5 No. 11–68, Apdo Aéreo 3531, Bogotá; tel. (1) 3431202; fax (1) 2863551; e-mail wbiblio@banrep.gov.co; internet www.lablaa.org; f. 1932; includes Museo Botero and Museo de Artes del Banco de la Republica; 1,050,000 vols, 23,000 periodicals, 14,000 maps, 102,000 slides, 4,000 original works of art, 25,000 sound recordings, 9,000 video recordings; Dir JORGE ORLANDO MELO; publ. *Boletín Cultural y Bibliográfico* (3 a year).

Biblioteca Nacional de Colombia (National Library): Calle 24, No. 5–60, Apdo 27600, Bogotá; tel. 3414029; fax 3414030; f. 1777; 800,000 vols, 22,000 periodicals; rare book section (*c.* 28,000 vols); Dir CARLOS JOSÉ REYES POSADA; publ. *Revista Senderos*.

Biblioteca Seminario Conciliar de San José (Library of the San José Seminary): Carrera 7 No.. 94–80, Bogotá 8; tel. (1) 6440405; fax (1) 2181096; e-mail biblioteca@seminariobogota.org; internet www.seminariobogota.org; f. 1581; 40,000 vols specializing in philosophy and theology; Dir Rev. JAIME MANCERA CASAS.

Departamento de Bibliotecas, Universidad Nacional de Colombia: Ciudad Universitaria, Apdo Aéreo 14490, Santafé de Bogotá; tel. 2691743; f. 1867; 230,000 vols; Dir VÍCTOR ALBIS.

División de Documentación e Información Educativa, Ministerio de Educación Nacional (Educational Documentation and Information Division, Ministry of Education): Avda El Dorado, CAN, Bogotá; tel. 222800; co-ordinates the Educational Documentation and Information Sub-system, the School Libraries National Programme and runs the National Educational Documentation Centre; 10,000 vols, 300 pamphlets, 6,000 documents, 300 periodicals; Dir MARY LUZ ISAZA; publs *Memorias del Ministro de Educación al Congreso Nacional* (annually), *Correo Educativo*.

Calí

Biblioteca Centenario: Avda Colombia Cl. 4 Oeste, Calí; tel. (2) 8932908; f. 1910; 22,000 vols; Dir ORIETTA LOZANO.

Biblioteca Departamental de Cali: Calle 14 Norte No 9N-45, Calí; tel. (2) 6613018; fax (2) 6618214; 54,000 vols; Dir ELISA INÉS ARBOLEDA MAYORK.

Cartagena

Centro de Información y Documentación Biblioteca Fernández de Madrid, Universidad de Cartagena: Centro Cra. 6 No.36–100, Cartagena; tel. (95) 6646182; fax (95) 6697778; e-mail unicart@Cartagena.cetcol.net.co; f. 1827; 50,000 vols; Librarian LUIS EDUARDO ESPINAL A.

Manizales

Biblioteca Central, Universidad de Caldas: Apdo Aéreo 275, Calle 65 No. 26-10, Manizales, Caldas; tel. (968) 861250 ext. 115; fax (968) 862520; e-mail biblio@ucaldas.edu.co; internet biblio.ucaldas.edu.co; f. 1958; 53,000 vols, 5,500 documents, 1,300 periodicals; Librarian SAUL SANCHEZ TORO; publs *Revista de la Universidad de Caldas* (2 a year), *Revista de Agronomía* (4 a year), *Revista de Medicina Veterinaria y Zootecnia* (2 a year), *HIPSIPILA – Revista Cultural de la Universidad* (2 a year), *Revista de Educación Física y Recreación* (2 a year).

Biblioteca Pública Municipal: Calle 23 No. 20–30, Manizales; tel. (9688) 31697; f. 1931; 8,100 vols; Librarian NELLY AGUIRRE DE FIGUEROA.

Medellín

Biblioteca de la Universidad Pontificia Bolivariana: Apdo Aéreo 56006, Medellín; tel. 4159075; fax 4118513; e-mail biblios@logos.upb.edu.co; internet biblio.upb.edu.co; f. 1936; 139,000 vols, 3,000 periodicals, 12,779 pamphlets, 150,000 audioivisual records; Librarian Lic. OLGA BEATRIZ BERNAL LONDOÑO; publs *Revista Universidad Pontificia Bolivariana*, *Revista de la Facultad de Filosofía*, *Cuestiones Teológicas*, *Revista de la Facultad de Derecho y Ciencias Políticas*, *Revista de la Facultad de Medicina*, *Revista de la Facultad de Trabajo Social*, *Comunicación UPB*.

Biblioteca Pública Piloto de Medellín (Pilot Public Library of Medellín): Carrera 64 con Calle 50 No. 50–32, Apdo Aéreo 1797, Medellín; tel. 230-24-22; fax 230-53-89; f. 1954 under the auspices of UNESCO; 85,000 vols; special collections: Antioquia and Antioquian authors, UNESCO depository; Dir GLORIA INES PALOMINO L..

Departamento de Bibliotecas, Universidad de Antioquia: Apdo Aéreo 1226, Medellín; tel. (4) 2105140; fax (4) 2116939; e-mail bcentral@biblioteca.udea.edu.co; internet biblioteca.udea.edu.co; f. 1935; 13 br. libraries; 662,000 vols, 7,000 periodicals; Dir NORA HELENA LÓPEZ CALLE; publs *Leer y Releer* (quarterly), *Ex-Libris* (quarterly).

Popayán

Departamento de Bibliotecas, Universidad del Cauca: Apdo Nacional 113, Calle 5 No 4–70, Popayán; tel. 233032; f. 1827; 70,000 vols; Dir JOSÉ MARÍA SERRANO PRADA; publs *Catálogo del Archivo Central del Cauca*, *Boletín Bibliográfico*, *Boletín Informativo*, *Cuadernos de Medicina*, *Boletín del Comité de Investigaciones Científicas*, *Revista Cátedra*.

Tunja

Universidad Pedagógica y Tecnológica de Colombia, Biblioteca Central, Tunja: Apdo Aéreo 1234, Tunja; tel. 400668; f. 1932; 68,000 vols; 1,800 periodical titles; special collections: theses, Fondo E. Posada, rare books, learned works; Dir BARBARA MARTIN MARTIN; publs *Lista de Canje*, *Apuntes del CENES*, *Educación y Ciencia*, *Cuadernos de Linguística hispánica-UPTC*, *Agricultura y Ciencia*, *Perspectiva Proceso Salud-Enfermedad*, *Inquietud Empresarial*, *Revista Facultad de Ingeniería*, *Revista de Ciencias Sociales*.

Museums and Art Galleries

Bogotá

Casa-Museo 'Jorge Eliécer Gaitán': Calle 42, No. 15–23, Bogotá; tel. (1) 2450368; fax (1) 2879093; f. 1948; collection relating to the history of Bogotá; run by the Centro Jorge Eliécer Gaitán; Dir GLORIA GAITÁN.

Casa Museo Quinta de Bolívar (Bolívar Museum): Calle 20, No. 2–91 Este, Bogotá; tel. 3366419; fax 3366410; e-mail quintadebolivar@excite.com; f. 1919 in the country house occupied by Simón Bolívar from 1820 to 1830, where relics of the Liberator and his epoch are exhibited; is administered by the Ministry of Culture and the Sociedad de Mejoras y Ornato de Bogotá; Dir DANIEL CASTRO BENÍTEZ.

Jardín Botánico de Bogotá 'José Celestino Mutis': Avda 57 No. 61–13, Bogotá; tel. (1) 4377060; fax (1) 6305075; e-mail bogotanico@jbb.gov.co; internet www.jbb.gov.co; f. 1955; research and conservation of biodiversity in the Andean ecosystem; library of 4,000 vols; Dir MARTHA LILIANA PERDOMO RAMIREZ; Gen-Sec ANGELA DIAZ ORTIZ; publ. *Pérez-Arbelaezia* (2 a year).

Museo Colonial (Museum of the Colonial Period): Carrera 6, No. 9–77, Bogotá; tel. (1) 3416017; fax (1) 2866768; e-mail colonial@mincultura.gov.co; f. 1942; paintings, sculpture, furniture, gold and silver work, drawings, etc., of the Spanish colonial period (16th, 17th and 18th c.); library of 1,000 vols in education dept; it is installed in a building erected by the Jesuits in 1604 to house the first Javeriana University; Dir CONSTANZA TOQUICA CLAVIJO; publ. *Cuadernos de Estudio* (annually).

Museo del Oro (Gold Museum): Calle 16 No. 5–41, Parque de Santander, Bogotá; tel. (1) 3348748; fax (1) 2847450; e-mail wmuseo@banrep.gov.co; internet www.banrep.gov.co/museo/home.htm; f. 1939; 36,000 pre-Columbian gold objects representing the gods, myths, and customs of the Quimbaya, Muisca, Tairona and other native Indian cultures; Dir CLARA ISABEL BOTERO CUERVO.

Museo Nacional (National Museum): Carrera 7, No. 28–66, Bogotá; tel. (1) 3342129; fax (1) 3347447; e-mail info@museonacional.gov.co; internet www.museonacional.gov.co; f. 1823; archaeology, ethnology, history since Spanish conquest; collections of portraits, arms, banners, medals, coins, ceramics, fine arts; theatre; exhibition gallery; Dir ELVIRA CUERVO DE JARAMILLO.

Museo Nacional de Antropología (National Museum of Anthropology): Calle 8, No. 8-87, Bogotá; tel. 2462481; fax 2330960; f. 1941; ceramics, stone carvings, gold objects, textiles, etc., from all districts of Colombia; is a department of the Instituto Colombiano de Antropología; Dir MYRIAM JIMENO SANTOYO; publs *Revista Colombiana de Antropología*, *Informes Antropológicos*.

Medellín

Museo de Ciencias Naturales del Colegio de San José (Natural Science Museum): Apdo Aéreo 1180, Medellín; f. 1913; natural history in general, zoology, botany, mineralogy, anthropology; library of 500 vols and 1,000 magazines; Dir H. MARCO A. SERNA D.; publs *Avancemos* (monthly), *El Colombiano* (daily), *Boletín Cultural* (quarterly), catalogues.

Museo Filatélico del Banco de la República: Edif. Banco de la República, Parque de Berrió, Medellín; tel. 515579; f. 1977; collections of Colombian postage stamps, and stamps from other countries; Dir HERNÁN GIL PANTOJA; publ. *Revista*.

Museo Universitario: Universidad de Antioquia, Apdo Aéreo 1226, Medellín; tel. 2105180; fax 2638282; e-mail museo@quimbaya.udea.edu.co; internet quimbaya.udea.edu.co/~museo; f. 1942; sections: anthropology, university history, natural sciences, visual arts, the human being, interactive exhibition; Dir ROBERTO L. OJALVO PRIETO; publ. *Códice* (scientific and cultural journal).

Roldanillo

Museo Omar Rayo: Calle 8a, 8–53, Roldanillo, Valle del Cauca; tel. 2229-8623; f. 1976, opened 1981; run by Fundación Museo Rayo; specializes in modern works on or with paper, fundamentally graphic art and design, by Latin American artists or those working in Latin America; a large collection has been donated by the artist Omar Rayo; library of 2,003 vols; Pres. of Foundation and Dir-Gen. OMAR RAYO REYES; publ. *Ediciones Embalaje*.

National Universities

POLITÉCNICO COLOMBIANO JAIME ISAZA CADAVID

Apdo aéreo 4932, Carrera 48 No. 7–151, El Poblado, Medellín, Antioquia
Telephone: (94) 310-5133
Fax: (94) 310-5174
E-mail: rectoria@elpoli.edu.co
Internet: www.politecnicojic.edu.co
Founded 1964
State control
Rector: Dr JUAN CAMILO RUIZ PÉREZ
Secretary-General: IVÁN ECHEVERRI VALENCIA
Vice-Rector (Administration): JUAN GUILLERMO VILLADA ARANGO
Vice-Rector (Teaching and Research): GIOVANI OROZCO ARBELÁEZ
Vice-Rector (Extension): GILBERTO GIRALDO BUITRAGO
Number of teachers: 880
Number of students: 13,500
Regional campus in Rionegro

DEANS
Faculty of Administration: FABIO TORRES LOZANO
Faculty of Basic, Social and Human Sciences: ELMER JOSÉ RAMÍREZ MACHADO
Faculty of Engineering: JAIRO MIGUEL VERGARA ÁVILA

DIRECTORS
School of Agriculture: JAIME LEÓN BOTERO AGUDELO
School of Audiovisual Communication: JOSÉ SAMUEL ARANGO MARTÍNEZ
School of Physical Education, Recreation and Sport: GONZALO JARAMILLO HERNÁNDEZ

UNIVERSIDAD DE LA AMAZONIA

Avda Circunvalación Barrio El Porvenir, Florencia, Caquetá
Telephone: (98) 434-0851
Fax: (98) 435-8231
E-mail: rectoria@uniamazonia.edu.co
Internet: www.uniamazonia.edu.co
Founded 1971 as Instituto Tecnológico Universidad Surcolombiana; curreent name and status 1982
State control
Rector: Dr OSCAR VILLANUEVA ROJAS
Secretary-General: MEYER HURTADO PARRA
Number of students: 4,000

DEANS
Faculty of Engineering: Ing. JULIO CESAR LUNA
Faculty of Agricultural Sciences: Mgr OSCAR ALFREDO MORELES GAMBOA
Faculty of Accountancy
Faculty of Basic Sciences: JOSE ANTONIO MARÍN PEÑA
Faculty of Education
Faculty of Law: LUIS FERNANDO URREGO CARVAJAL

UNIVERSIDAD DE ANTIOQUIA

Apdo Aéreo 1226, Ciudad Universitaria, Medellín, Antioquia
Telephone: (4) 2105020
Fax: (4) 2638282
E-mail: wwwmgr@www.udea.edu.co
Internet: www.udea.edu.co
Founded 1822
State control
Academic year: January to November
Rector: ALBERTO URIBE CORREA
Vice-Rector (General): MARTINIANO JAIME CONTRERAS
Vice-Rector (Academic): GUILLERMO LONDOÑO RESTREPO
Vice-Rector (Administrative): ALVARO PÉREZ ROLDÁN
Vice-Rector (Research): Dr GUSTAVO VALENCIA RESTREPO
Vice-Rector (Extension): MARGARITA BERRÍO DE RAMOS
Secretary-General: ANA LUCÍA HERRERA GÓMEZ
Librarian: NORA ELENA LÓPEZ
Library: see Libraries and Archives
Number of teachers: 1,043 (full-time)
Number of students: 21,337
Publications: *Revista Universidad de Antioquia* (4 a year), *Revista Iatreia* (4 a year), *Revista Estudias de Derecho* (2 a year), *Revista Lecturas de Economia* (2 a year)

DEANS
Faculty of Social and Human Sciences: LUZ STELLA CORREO BOTERO
Faculty of Exact and Natural Sciences: NÉSTOR LÓPEZ ARISTIZÁBAL
Faculty of Arts: CLARA MÓNICA ZAPATA JARAMILLO
Faculty of Education: CARLOS ARTURO SOTO LOMBANA
Faculty of Economics: MAURICIO ALVIAR RAMÍREZ
Faculty of Law and Political Science: MARTA NUBIA VELÁSQUEZ RICO
Faculty of Communications: EDISON DARÍO NEIRA PALACIO
Faculty of Engineering: CARLOS ARROYAVE POSADA
Faculty of Medicine: LUIS JAVIER CASTRO NARANJO
Faculty of Veterinary Medicine and Animal Husbandry: LUIS JAVIER ARROYAVE MORALES
Faculty of Dentistry: CARLOS MARIO URIBE SOTO
Faculty of Pharmaceutical Chemistry: AMANDA INÉS MEJÍA GALLÓN
National Faculty of Public Health: OSCAR SIERRA RODRÍGUEZ
Faculty of Nursing: ASTRID ELENA VALLEJO RICO

DIRECTORS
School of Bacteriology and Clinical Laboratory: ANGELA MARÍA ARANGO RAVE
School of Nutrition and Dietetics: DORA NICOLASA GÓMEZ CIFUENTES
Institute of Physical Education and Sports: ALAIN PEDRO BUSTAMANTE SIMÓN
Institute of Philosophy: ALFONSO MONSALVE SOLÓRZANO
School of Languages: ADRIANA GONZÁLEZ MONCADA
Institute of Political Sciences: MANUEL ALBERTO ALONSO ESPINAL
Institute of Regional Studies: DIEGO HERRERA GÓMEZ

ATTACHED INSTITUTE
Escuela Interamericana de Bibliotecología (Interamerican School of Librarianship): Apdo Aéreo 1307, Medellín; f. 1956; training in librarianship to postgraduate level; technical assistance on administration and organization of information centres and libraries; 10 full-time, 5 part-time staff; 292 students; library of 16,000 vols; Dir MARÍA TERESA MÚNERA TÓRRES; publ. *Revista Interamericana de Bibliotecología*.

UNIVERSIDAD DEL ATLÁNTICO

Carrera 43, No. 50–53, Apdo Aéreo 1890, Barranquilla, Atlántico
Telephone: 313-513
Founded 1941
Undergraduate courses
Rector: CRISTIAN UJUETA TOSCANO
Secretary-General: PABLO ARTETA MANRIQUE
Librarian: CARMEN VASQUEZ ARRIETA
Number of teachers: 592
Number of students: 8,798
Publication: *Economía*

DEANS
Faculty of Fine Arts: Dr HUGO VASQUEZ
Faculty of Economics: ROBERTO PERSAND BARNES
Faculty of Pharmacy and Chemistry: JOSE LLANOS AMARIS
Faculty of Law and Political Science: GUSTAVO DE SILVESTRI
Faculty of Chemical Engineering: AGUSTIN QUINTERO
Faculty of Architecture: RAFAEL RUIZ ZAPATA
Faculty of Education: ESTEBAN RODRIGUEZ
Faculty of Nutrition and Dietetics: LORIS JABBA DE TRUJILLO

UNIVERSIDAD DE CALDAS

Apdo Aéreo 275, Calle 65 No. 26-10, Manizales, Caldas
Telephone: (68) 861250 ext. 114
Fax: (68) 8862732
E-mail: biblio@ucaldas.edu.co
Internet: biblio.ucaldas.edu.co
Founded 1943
State control
Language of instruction: Spanish
Academic year: February to December (two semesters)
Rector: CARLOS-ENRIQUE RUIZ RESTREPO
Academic Vice-Rector: PEDRO NEL GARCÍA QUICENO
Registrar: CARLOS ALBERTO RUIZ VILLA
Librarian: SAUL SÁNCHEZ TORO
Library: see Libraries
Number of teachers: 488
Number of students: 3,620
Publications: *Revista Luna Azul* (ecology, 2 a year), *Altamira* (fine arts, annually), *IDEE Revista* (education, 2 a year), *Cuadernos Filósofos Literarios* (annually), *Boletín Científico Museo de Historia* (annually)

DEANS
Faculty of Agriculture: Dr GERMÁN GÓMEZ LONDOÑO
Faculty of Arts and Humanities: Dr JUAN CARLOS YEPES OCAMPO
Faculty of Exact and Natural Sciences: Dr MARCO TULIO JARAMILLO S.
Faculty of Juridical and Social Sciences: Dra MARÍA ROCÍO CIFUENTES PATIÑO
Faculty of Health Sciences: Dr LUIS FERNANDO URIBE VARGAS
Faculty of Engineering: Dra ADELA MARÍA CEBALLOS PEÑALOZA

UNIVERSIDAD DE CARTAGENA

Apdo Aéreo 1382, Cartagena, Bolívar
Telephone: 65-44-80
Fax: 65-04-26
Internet: www.unicartagena.edu.co
Founded 1827
State control
Academic year: February to December
President of the Council: Dr GUILLERMO PANIZA RICARDO
Rector: Dra BEATRIZ BECHARA DE BORGE

Academic Vice-Rector: Dr JAIME BARRIOS AMAYA
Administrative Director: Dr CLARET BERMUDEZ CORONEL
Chief Administrative Officer: Dr EDGAR REY SINNING
Librarian: PERLA ECHEVERRI LEMA
Library: see Libraries
Number of teachers: 560
Number of students: 4,310
Publications: *Prospecto Universidad*, *Revista Facultad de Economía*, *Revista Facultad de Medicina*, *Boletín Informativo*, *Revista Ciencia, Tecnología y Educación*

DEANS

Faculty of Law: Dr ALCIDES ANGULO PASSOS
Faculty of Medicine: Dr ROBERTO GUERRERO FIGUEROA
Faculty of Dentistry: Dr LUIS ALVAREZ GARCIA
Faculty of Pharmaceutical Chemistry: Dra THELMA DEL CASTILLO DE SALAZAR
Faculty of Engineering: Dr ALVARO CUBAS MONTES
Faculty of Economics: Dr GUILLERMO QUINTANA SOSSA
Faculty of Nursing: Lic. YADIRA FERREIRA DE SIERRA
Faculty of Social Work: Lic. NATACHA MORILLO DE RODRIGUEZ

UNIVERSIDAD DEL CAUCA

Apdo Nacional 113, Calle 5 No. 4–70, Popayán, Cauca
Telephone: 243020
Fax: 244851
E-mail: rectoria@ucauca.edu.co
Internet: www.ucauca.edu.co

Founded 1827
State control
Language of instruction: Spanish
Academic year: January to December

Rector: RAFAEL EDUARDO VIVAS LINDO
Vice-Rector (Academic): KONNY ELIZABETH CAMPO SARZOSA
Vice-Rector (Research): JUAN MARTÍN VELASCO M.
Vice-Rector (Culture and Welfare): EVIALRA CASTRILLÓN
President of Supreme Council: TEMISTOCLES ORTEGA
General Secretary: GUILLERMO MUÑOZ VELÁSQUEZ
Administrative Director: JOSÉ MARÍA ARBOLEDA CASTRILLÓN
Planning Head: CÉSAR OSORIO VERA
Library Director: AMPARO PRADO
Library: see Libraries
Number of teachers: 600
Number of students: 7,000

DEANS

Faculty of Law, Political and Social Sciences: Dr ALVARO HURTADO TEJADA
Faculty of Civil Engineering: Ing. MARGARITA POLANCO
Faculty of Electronic Engineering: Ing. FRANCISCO J. TERÁN CUARAN
Faculty of Health Sciences: Md. JAIME A. NATES BURBANO
Faculty of Accountancy, Administration and Economics: Dr ENRIQUE PEÑA FORERO
Faculty of Education Sciences: Dr GERARDO NAUNDORF SAEZ
Faculty of Humanities: Dr HÉCTOR ORTEGA BURBANO
Faculty of Arts: Lic. MATILDE CHÁVEZ DE TOBA

DIRECTORS OF POSTGRADUATE INSTITUTES

Civil Engineering: Ing. FERNANDO HURTADO
Electronics and Telecommunications: Ing. PEDRO VERA VERA
Law: CARLOS IGNACIO MOSQUERA U.
Accounting: LUIS A. COLVO
Health Sciences: ALONSO RUIZ PEREA
Human Sciences: LUCIANO RIVERA

UNIVERSIDAD POPULAR DEL CÉSAR

Apdo Aéreo 590, Sede Balneario Hurtado, Valledupar, César
Telephone: (95) 573-6203
Fax: (95) 573-5877
E-mail: univer@teleupar.net.co
Internet: www.unicesar.edu.co

Founded 1973 as Instituto Tecnológico del César; present name and status 1976
State control
Language of instruction: Spanish
Academic year: February to December (two semesters)

Rector: Dr OSCAR PACHECO HERNANDEZ
Library of 17,000 vols
Faculties of Business Administration, Economics and Accountancy, Engineering and Technology, Health Sciences, Education, and Law, Politics and Social Sciences.

UNIVERSIDAD DE CÓRDOBA

Apdo Aéreo 354, Carretera a Cereté, Km. 5, Montería, Córdoba
Telephone: 33-81
Internet: www.unicordoba.edu.co

Founded 1964
Academic year: April to March

Rector: Dr LAUREANO MESTRA DÍAZ (acting)
Academic Vice-Rector: Dr EFRAIN PASTOR NIEVES
Administrative Director: Dr ALVARO VIDAL OROZCO
Library Director: CARLOS HENAO TORO
Number of teachers: 270
Number of students: 2,493
Publications: *Revista*, *Trabajos de Grado presentados en la Universidad*

DEANS

Faculty of Veterinary Medicine and Animal Husbandry: Dr FRANCISCO AGUILAR MADERA
Faculty of Agricultural Engineering: Dr MAXIMILIANO ESPINOSA PERALTA
Faculty of Education: Dr JOSÉ MORALES MANCHEGO
Faculty of Nursing: Dra GISELLE FERRER FERRER
Faculty of Science: Dr AQUILES GONZÁLEZ SALAZAR

UNIVERSIDAD DE CUNDINAMARCA

Diagonal 18 No. 20–29, Fusagasugá, Cundinamarca
Telephone: (91) 867-2144
Fax: (91) 867-7898
E-mail: rectoria@udecund.edu.co
Internet: www.udecund.edu.co

Founded 1969
State control
Language of instruction: Spanish

Rector: Dr ALFONSO SANTOS MONTERO.

UNIVERSIDAD DE LA GUAJIRA

Apdo Aéreo 172, Riohacha
Telephone: 273856
Fax: 273856

Founded 1976
State control
Language of instruction: Spanish
Academic year: February to July, August to November

Rector: FRANCISCO JUSTO PÉREZ VAN-LEENDEN
Vice-Rector: ROSALBA CUESTA LÓPEZ
Chief Administrative Officer: CRISTÓBAL VEGA GUTIÉRREZ
Librarian: MARINELA MENGUAL MEZA
Number of teachers: 107
Number of students: 1,258
Publications: *WOUMMAINPA*, *Revista Universidad de La Guajira*, *Anuario Estadístico*

DEANS

Faculty of Business Administration: ISIDORO OSPINO MERIÑO
Faculty of Industrial Engineering: JAIRO SALCEDO DAVILA
Faculty of Education: JOSÉ CLEMENTE MARTÍNEZ

HEADS OF DEPARTMENTS

Faculty of Business Administration:
- Introduction to Law: HERNAN REINA
- Industrial Psychology, Professional Ethics: EFRAIN DELUQUE
- Principles of Administration: ERUNDINA ILLIDGE
- Development and Management Control: ALBERTO BRITTO
- Sport: SEGISMUNDO BERMUDEZ
- Tax Legislation: OSCAR PACHECO
- Administration III: WILLIAM GOMEZ
- Humanities II: ALVARO CUELLO
- Administration I: CRISTOBAL VEGA G.
- Macroeconomics: ABIMAEL SANCHEZ R.
- Principles of Administration: HERNANDO BEDOYA
- Introduction to Economics: WILMER ZUBIRIA
- Introduction to Law: NIDIA RESTREPO
- Mathematics I: CARLOS GUTIERREZ
- Spanish: RAFAEL CUENTAS FIGUEROA

Faculty of Industrial Engineering:
- Marketing: HERNANDO BEDOYA
- Industrial Psychology: EFRAIN DELUQUE
- Production: MIGUEL MURGAS
- Labour Legislation: ALAN PEREZ
- General Mechanics, Resistance of Materials: MIGUEL PITRE
- Electrical Engineering: JOSE F. PIRAQUIVE
- Engineering Materials: GONZALO CASTRO
- Electrical Engineering Laboratory: JONNYS ORTEGA
- Process Laboratory: MIGUEL PEÑA
- Plant Distribution, Mathematics I: ROLLAND PINEDO
- Humanities II: CESAR ARISMENDY
- English II: LUZ MARINA BOHADA DE P.

UNIVERSIDAD DISTRITAL 'FRANCISCO JOSÉ DE CALDAS'

Carrera 7, No. 40–53, Bogotá
Telephone: 3239300
Fax: 3239300 ext. 2002
E-mail: spral@udistrital.edu.co
Internet: www.udistrital.edu.co

Founded 1950
Number of teachers: 600
Number of students: 7,200

Rector: LUIS CARLOS MOLINA MARIÑO
Faculties: Engineering; Education and Science; Environment and Natural Resources; Technology.

UNIVERSIDAD FRANCISCO DE PAULA SANTANDER

Avda Gran Colombia 12E–96, Barrio Colsag, Apdo Aéreo 1055, Cúcuta, Norte de Santander
Telephone: (75) 753172
Internet: www.ufps.edu.co

Founded 1962
State control
Affiliated to the Universidad Nacional

Undergraduate courses
Chancellor: PATROCINIO ARARAT DÍAZ
Secretary-General: ALVARO ORLANDO PEDROZA ROAJS
Administrative Director: HÉCTOR MIGUEL PARRA LÓPEZ
Academic Vice-Chancellor: JOSÉ LUIS TOLOSA CHACÓN
Librarian: GLORIA MATILDE MELO SALCEDO
Library of 5,000 vols
Number of teachers: 350
Number of students: 6,500

DEANS

Faculty of Engineering: HUGO ALBERTO PORTILLA DUARTE
Faculty of Basic Sciences: JOSÉ LUIS MALDONADO
Faculty of Business Studies: JOSÉ RAMÓN VARGAS TOLOSA
Faculty of Education, Arts, Humanities and Sciences: RICARDO GARCIA
Faculty of Health Sciences: FANNY MARTINEZ
Faculty of Environmental Sciences: CIRO ESPINOSA

UNIVERSIDAD MILITAR NUEVA GRANADA

Carrera 11 No. 101-80, Bogotá
Telephone: (1) 275-7300
Fax: (1) 215-9689
E-mail: rectoria@santander.umng.edu.co
Internet: www.umng.edu.co
Founded 1982
State control
Language of instruction: Spanish
Rector: Brig. Gen. ADOLFO CLAVIJO ARDILA
Vice-Rector (General): Maj. Gen. JAIME HUMBERTO CORTES P.
Vice-Rector (Academic): Dra BLANCA PATRICIA BARRERO DE RIVERA
Vice-Rector (Administration): Col WLADISLAO REINOSO MARIN
Vice-Rector (Research): Dr GUILLERMO MONSALVO.

UNIVERSIDAD NACIONAL ABIERTA Y A DISTANCIA

Calle 14 sur No. 14–23, Bogotá
Telephone: (1) 344-3700
Fax: (1) 344-4120
E-mail: sgeneral@unad.edu.co
Internet: www.unad.edu.co
Founded 1981 as Unidad Universitaria del Sur de Bogotá; current name and status 1997
State control
Language of instruction: Spanish
Academic year: February to December
Rector: Dra JAIME LEAL AFANADOR
Vice-Rector (Academic): LETICIA ESCOBAR CEDANO
Vice-Rector (Finance and Administration): SEHIFAR BALLESTEROS MORENO
Secretary-General: ROBERTO SALAZAR RAMOS

DEANS

Faculty of Social, Human and Educational Sciences: CARLOS BERNAL GRANADOS
Faculty of Administrative Sciences: ROQUE JULIO RODRIGUEZ PARRA
Faculty of Agricultural Sciences: DOMINGO ALIRIO MONTAÑO ARIAS
Faculty of Basic Sciences and Engineering: JOSE HUMBERTO GUERRERO RODRIGUEZ

UNIVERSIDAD NACIONAL DE COLOMBIA

Ciudad Universitaria, Apdo Aéreo 14490, Bogotá
Telephone: (1) 316-50-00
Fax: (1) 221-98-91
E-mail: secgener@unal.edu.co
Internet: www.unal.edu.co
Founded 1867
Academic year: February to December
Campuses in Manizales, Medellín, Palmira, Arauca, San Andrés and Leticia
Rector: MARCO PALACIOS
Vice-Rector for Manizales Campus: GERMAN PALACIO CASTAÑEDA
Vice-Rector for Medellín Campus: JORGE EDUARDO HURTADO GÓMEZ
Vice-Rector for Palmira Campus: ARGEMIRO ECHEVERRY CANO
Vice-Rector for Arauca Campus: MARÍA SARA MEJÍA DE TAFUR
Vice-Rector for San Andrés Campus: ALEXIS DE GREIFF
Vice-Rector for Leticia Campus: ADRIANA SANTOS MARTÍNEZ
Library: see Libraries
Number of teachers: 3,055 (full-time)
Number of students: 43,159
Publications: *Acta Bibliográfica*, *Agronomía Colombiana*, *Alimentos*, *Anuario Colombiano de Historia*, *Anuario del Observatorio Astronómico Nacional*, *Boletín de Matemáticas*, *Caldasia* (natural science), *Cuadernos de Economía*, *Forma y Función* (philology and languages), *Geografía Geología Colombiana*, *Ideas y Valores*, *Ingeniería e Investigación*, *Lozania* (natural science), *Maguaré* (anthropology), *Mutisia* (natural science), *Revistas* (Faculty publications)

DEANS

Faculty of Arts: FERNANDO MONTENEGRO LIZARRALDE
Faculty of Science: MOISES WASSERMAN LERNER
Faculty of Agronomy: FABIO LEYVA BARÓN
Faculty of Humanities: GERMAN MELENDEZ ACUÑA
Faculty of Medicine: JAIME GALLEGO ARBELÁEZ
Faculty of Law and Political and Social Sciences: ADOLFO SALAMANCA CORREA
Faculty of Economics: LUIS IGNACIO AGUILAR
Faculty of Engineering: JULIO COMENARES MONTAÑEZ
Faculty of Nursing: CLARA BEATRIZ SÁNCHEZ HERRERA
Faculty of Dentistry: GLADYS NÚÑEZ BARRERA
Faculty of Veterinary Science and Animal Husbandry: RAMÓN FAYAD NAFAH

OTHER CAMPUSES

Medellín Campus: Apdo Aéreo 568, Medellín

DEANS

Faculty of Architecture: OCTAVIO URIBE TORO
Faculty of Stockbreeding: DIEGO HOYOS DUQUE
Faculty of Sciences: MARIO ARIAS ZABALA
Faculty of Humanities: CATALINA REYES CÁRDENAS
Faculty of Mining: GONZALO JIMÉNEZ CALAD

Manizales Campus: Carrera 27 No. 64-60, Manizales

DEANS

Faculty of Architecture and Engineering: JOSÉ JAIRO BOTERO ANGEL
Faculty of Science and Administration: GONZALO DE JESÚS SÁNCHEZ

Palmira Campus: Apdo Aéreo 237, Palmira

DEANS

Faculty of Stockbreeding: EUGENIO ESCOBAR HANRIQUE

ATTACHED RESEARCH INSTITUTES

Institute of Aesthetics Research: Head AMPARO VEGA.
Comunication and Cultural Studies: Head NEYLA GRACIELA PARDO.
Biotechnology: Head DOLLY MONTOYA CASTAÑO.
Educational Research: Head ORLANDO ACOSTA LOZADA.
Immunology: Head GONZALO ANDRADE.
Political Studies and International Relations: Head ALVARO CAMACHO GUIZADO.

UNIVERSIDAD DE NARIÑO

Ciudad Universitaria Torobajo, Pasto, Nariño
Telephone: (27) 7313605
Fax: (27) 7313605
Internet: www.udenar.edu.co
Founded 1827 as Colegio Provincial by General Francisco de Paula Santander; later named Colegio Académico; university status 1964
First degree courses
Rector: JAIRO MUÑOZ HOYOS
Vice-Rector: JAMIE HERNAN CABRERA
Vice-Rector (Administration): VICENTE PARRA
Vice-Rector (Research, Postgraduates and International Relations): CARLOS CORDOBA
Director of Planning: ARMANDO MUÑOZ
General Secretary: JUAN ANDRES VILLOTA RAMOS
Librarian: SEGUNDO BURBANO L.
Library: central library of 10,000 vols; agronomy library of 15,000 vols
Number of teachers: 700
Number of students: 8,000
Publications: *Awarca*, *Foro Universitario*, *Revista de Ciencias Agrícolas Meridiano*, *Revista de Investigaciones*, *Revista de Zootecnia*

DEANS

Faculty of Agroindustrial Engineering: NELSON ARTURO
Faculty of Agronomy: GERMÁN ARTEAGA MENESES
Faculty of Arts: ALVARO ZAMBRANO
Faculty of Economics and Administration: LUIS ALBERTO ARCOS
Faculty of Education: ALVARO TORRES
Faculty of Engineering: JAIRO GUERRERO GARCÍA
Faculty of Human Sciences: CARLOS SANTAMARIA
Faculty of Law: MANUEL CORAL PABON
Faculty of Natural Sciences and Mathematics: ARSENI HIDALGO TROYA
Faculty of Stockbreeding: HECTOR FABIO VALENCIA

UNIVERSIDAD DEL PACÍFICO

Avda Simón Bolívar 54 A-10, Buenaventura
E-mail: info@unipacifico.edu.co
Telephone: (92) 243-9789
Fax: (92) 243-1461
Internet: www.unipacifico.edu.co
Founded 1988
State control
Language of instruction: Spanish
Rector: Dr OMAR BARONA MURILLO
Secretary-General: Dra MARIA CARMELA QUIÑONEZ

HEADS OF DEPARTMENTS

Tropical Agronomy: Dr ARNULFO GOMEZ CARABALI
Sociology: Dr JOSE FELIX RIASCOS BENAVIDES
Architecture: Arq. HOLVER SANCLEMENTE CANIZALES

Information Technology: Ing. ROMMEL EDGARDO CELIS D'EVER
Aquaculture Technology: Dr EUDES EMILIO SANCHEZ MORALES

UNIVERSIDAD DE PAMPLONA

Ciudad Universitaria 'El Buque', Pamplona, Santander del Norte
Telephone: (7) 5685303
Fax: (7) 5682750
E-mail: rectoria@unipamplona.edu.co
Internet: www.unipamplona.edu.co
Founded 1960, university status 1970
State control
Language of instruction: Spanish
Academic year: February to December
Rector: ÁLVARO GONZÁLEZ JOVES
Vice-Rectors: LUIS ALBERTO GUALDRÓN SÁNCHEZ (Academic), YOLANDA ALBARRACÍN CONTRERAS (Research), LUIS GUSTAVO ARAQUE (Social Development)
Administrative Director: JAIRO AGUSTÍN ACEVEDO BAUTISTA
Secretary-General: ROSALBA OMAÑA BONILLA
Number of teachers: 215 (145 full-time, 70 part-time)
Number of students: 4,560
Publications: *Bistua* (natural and technological sciences, 2 a year), *Zulima* (business and economics, 2 a year), *Faria* (arts and humanities, 2 a year)

DEANS

Arts and Humanities: FLOR DELIA PÚLIDO C.
Natural and Technological Sciences: JAIRO ALONSO MENDOZA SUÁREZ
Education: INÉS ROMERO MARTÍNEZ
Business and Economics: JAIRO DEL CARMEN OLMOS S.
Health: PEDRO LEON PEÑARANDA L.

DEPARTMENTAL CHAIRPERSONS

Business: HENRY MAURICIO DIEZ S.
Food Technology: HENRY MORALES O.
Biology: CLAUDIA CLAVIJO OLMOS
Mathematics and Computer Sciences: AMPARO LAMUS
Physical Education, Recreation and Sports: TITO SEGUNDO BONILLA M.
Special Education: OLGA BELÉN CASTILLO
Education and Psychology: INÉS ROMERO M.
Social Communication: GILBERTO GONZÁLEZ H.
Spanish Language and Communication: YOLANDA VILLAMIZAR
Social Sciences: JOEL SILVA CARRILLO
Psychology: DIANA VILLAMIZAR C.
Rural Education: JOSUE NORBERTO RAMÓN S.
Language and Literature: CARLOS ALBERTO JAIMES G.
Distance Education: MANUEL A. JAIMES G.
Music: EDGAR CONTRERAS S.
Administrative Sciences and Systems: JORGE ENRIQUE TELLEZ P.
Natural Sciences and Environmental Education: CARLOS A. ROMERO R.
Sanitary Engineering: JANUARIO RESTREPO T.

UNIVERSIDAD PEDAGÓGICA NACIONAL

Apdo Aéreo 75144, Calle 73, No. 11–73, Santafé de Bogotá
Telephone: 3473562
Fax: 3473535
Internet: www.pedagogica.edu.co
Founded 1955
State control
Languages of instruction: Spanish, English
Academic year: January to December (two semesters)
Rector: Dr ADOLFO RODRÍGUEZ BERNAL
Administrative Vice-Rector: Dr HERNÁN VÁSQUEZ ROCHA
Academic Vice-Rector: Dr MANUEL ERAZO PARGA
Librarian: Dr CAMILO ROJAS LEÓN
Number of teachers: 660
Number of students: 4,190
Publications: *Revista Colombiana de Educación, Pedagogia y Saberes*

DEANS

Faculty of Humanities: Dra GLORIA RINCÓN CUBIDES
Faculty of Science and Technology: Dr RAFAEL HUMBERTO RAMÍREZ GIL
Faculty of Education: Dra MYRIAM PARDO TORRES

HEADS OF DEPARTMENTS

Fine Arts: FRANÇOIS KHOURY
Biology: JUDITH ARTETA DE MOLINA
Chemistry: FIDEL ANTONIO CÁRDENAS
Physics: JULIAN URREA BELTRÁN (acting)
Mathematics: MARGARITA ROJAS DE ROA
Social Sciences: LUIS ENRIQUE SUÁREZ QUEVEDO
Physical Education: LUIS ALFONSO GARZÓN
Languages: NOHORA PATRICIA MORENO GARCÍA
Technology: CARLOS JULIO ROMERO CASTRO
Educational Psychology: BLANCA AZUCENA S. DE OSORIO
Postgraduate School: LIBIA STELLA NIÑO ZAFRA

ATTACHED INSTITUTE

Instituto Pedagógico Nacional: Calle 127 No. 12A-20, Santafé de Bogotá; 2,178 students; Dir LUIS ERNESTO OJEDA SUÁREZ.

UNIVERSIDAD PEDAGÓGICA Y TECNOLÓGICA DE COLOMBIA

Apdo Aéreo 1094 y 1234, Carretera Central del Norte, Tunja, Boyacá
Telephone: 422175
Fax: 424311
Internet: www.uptc.edu.co
Founded 1953
State control
Language of instruction: Spanish
Academic year: February to December
Rector: OLMEDA VARGAS HERNÁNDEZ
Vice-Rector for Administration: FRANCISCO MANOSALVA CERON
Vice-Rector for Academic Affairs: MANUEL FRANCISCO CAICEDO RUIZ
Secretary-General: NUBIA ELENA PEDRAZA VARGAS
Librarian: BARBARÁ MARTÍN MARTÍN
Number of teachers: 520
Number of students: 15,850
Publications: *Acción Pedagógica* (education, 2 a year), *Agenda P & G* (planning and management, 2 a year), *Agrodesarrollo* (agriculture, 2 a year), *Anuario de Investigaciones* (research, annually), *Apuntes del Cenes* (economics and business administration, 2 a year), *Boletín de Acuerdos* (2 a year), *Boletín UPTC en Cifras* (university statistics, annually), *Ciencia en Desarrollo* (science, 2 a year), *Ciencia y Agricultura* (2 a year), *Cuadernos de Lingüística* (Hispanic linguistics, annually), *EPG Geografía* (2 a year), *Matemáticas & Educación* (2 a year), *Observatorio Urbano* (project management, 3 a year), *Pensamiento y Acción* (2 a year), *Perspectiva Geográfica* (2 a year), *Perspectiva Salud y Enfermedad* (health sciences, 2 a year), *Revista Metalurgia y Ciencia de Materiales* (2 a year), *Terra Nostra* (project management, 4 a year)

DEANS AND DIRECTORS

Faculty of Education: ANA MARGARITA SANTAFÉ CALDERÓN
Faculty of Sciences: CARLOS NORBERTO GÓMEZ GÓMEZ
Faculty of Engineering: LUIS EDUARDO VARGAS CARMONA
Faculty of Health Sciences: CARLOS ALBERTO JIMÉNEZ ESPINEL
Faculty of Agricultural Sciences: MAGNOLIA DEL PILAR CANO ORTIZ
Faculty of Law and Social Sciences: GERMÁN BERNAL CAMACHO
Faculty of Economics and Business Administration: VÍCTOR HERMES BARRERA GODOY
Sectional Faculty, Duitama: ALVARO CALVACHE ARCHILA
Sectional Faculty, Sogamoso: RAFAEL BALCAZAR COLLO
Sectional Faculty, Chiquinquirá: MANUEL HUMBERTO RESTREPO DOMÍNGUEZ
Institute of Open Learning and Correspondence Courses: FAUSTO RENAN MASTRODOMENICO CORREDOR
Centre of Educational Research: MARÍA NUBIA ROMERO BALLEN

UNIVERSIDAD DEL QUINDÍO

Cra. 15, Cl. 12N, Avda Bolívar, Apdo Aéreo 460, Armenia, Quindío
Telephone: (67) 450099
Fax: (67) 462563
Internet: www.uniquindio.edu.co
Founded 1960
State control
Language of instruction: Spanish
Academic year: January to June, July to December
Rector: HECTOR POLANIA RIVERA
Vice-Rector (Academic): MARCO AURELIO ARISTIZABAL OSORIO
Vice-Rector (Administrative): MARTHA MARIA MARIN MEJIA
Secretary-General: BERNARDO VELASQUEZ MAHECHA
Dean of Research Committee: AMPARO AGUDELO DE ARANGO
Registrar: NELLY RESTREPO SÁNCHEZ
Librarian: Lic. LUZ MARINA PATIÑO ZULUAGA
Library of 26,250 vols
Number of teachers: 697
Number of students: 16,626
Publications: *Revista Facultad de Formación Avanzada e Investigaciones*, *Revista de la Universidad del Quindío*

DEANS

Faculty of Open and Distance Learning: ROBERTO GIRALDO VIGOYA
Faculty of Health Sciences: DIEGO GUTIÉRREZ MEJÍA
Faculty of Civil Engineering: DIEGO GUERRERO CASTRO
Faculty of Public Accounting: CONSTANZA LORETH FAJARDO
Faculty of Basic and Technological Sciences: MARCO AURELIO CERON MUÑOZ
Faculty of Human Sciences: NELSON JOSÉ MURILLO VENEZ

UNIVERSIDAD INDUSTRIAL DE SANTANDER

Apdo Aéreo 678, Bucaramanga, Santander
Telephone: 343656
Fax: 976-451136
Internet: www.uis.edu.co
Founded 1947
Academic year: February to June, August to December
Rector: JORGE GÓMEZ DUARTE
Administrative Vice-Rector: HUMBERTO PRADILLA ARDILA

Academic Vice-Rector: GERMÁN OLIVEROS VILLAMIZAR
Secretary-General: Dra LILIA AMANDA PATIÑO DE CRUZ
Research Director: LUIS ALFONSO MALDONADO CERÓN
Librarian: ESPERANZA MÉNDEZ BRAVO

Number of teachers: 455
Number of students: 9,684

DEANS

Sciences: AUGUSTO LÓPEZ ZAGARRA
Physical/Mechanical Sciences: ROBERTO MARTÍNEZ ANGEL
Physical/Chemical Sciences: CARLOS JULIO MONSALVE MORENO
Health: GERMAN GAMARRA HERNÁNDEZ
Human Sciences: EMILIA ACEVEDO DE ROMERO
Distance Education: GLORIA INÉS MARÍN MUÑOZ

HEADS OF DEPARTMENTS

Sciences:
- Biology: ROSA AURA GAVILÁN DÍAZ
- Physics: MILTON FLÓREZ SERRANO
- Mathematics: ROSALBA OSORIO AGUILLÓN
- Chemistry: VICTOR GABRIEL OTERO GIL

Physical/Mechanical Sciences:
- Electrical Engineering: FRANCISCO A. RUEDA PATIÑO
- Civil Engineering: EDUARDO A. CASTAÑEDA PINZÓN
- Mechanical Engineering: ALFONSO GARCÍA CASTRO
- Industrial Engineering: FRANCISCO JAVIER MOSQUERA ROBBIN
- Systems Engineering: ELBERTO CARRILLO RINCÓN
- Design and Graphic Analysis: HÉCTOR JULIO PARRA MORENO

Physical/Chemical Sciences:
- Geology: JORGE ENRIQUE ZAMBRANO ARENAS
- Metallurgy: ORLANDO JOSÉ GÓMEZ MORENO
- Chemical Engineering: LEONARDO ACEVEDO DUARTE
- Petroleum Engineering: JOSÉ GREGORIO OCANDO RODRÍGUEZ

Human Sciences:
- Literature: MARIELA GÓMEZ DE OSSMA
- Arts: JESÚS ALBERTO REY MARIÑO
- Economics and Administration: SUSANA VALDIVIESO CANAL
- Social Sciences: BLANCA INÉS PRADA MÁRQUEZ
- Physical Education: JUAN JOSÉ MAYORGA CABALLERO
- Education: CONSTANZA VILLAMIZAR DE SUÁREZ
- History: AMADO ANTONIO GUERRERO RINCÓN

Health:
- Morphology and Pathology: ALFREDO ACEVEDO SARMIENTO
- Physiological Sciences: ÁLVARO GÓMEZ TORRADO
- Microbiological Sciences: GLADYS ORTEGA VANEGAS
- Nursing: MARÍA ANTONIETA FORERO DE LEÓN
- Internal Medicine: MARÍA EUGENIA RAMÍREZ QUINTERO
- Paediatrics: JAIRO RODRÍGUEZ HERNÁNDEZ
- Gynaecology and Obstetrics: MARTHA AGUDELO GARCÍA
- Surgery: HERNANDO CALA RUEDA
- Nutrition and Physical Rehabilitation: ESPERANZA CRUZ SOLANO
- Preventive Medicine and Public Health: ALBERTO ZÁRATE MARTÍNEZ
- Psychiatry: RODOLFO REY NUNCIRA

Distance Education:
- Professional Courses: LUZ EMILIA REYES ENCISO
- Advanced Training: GILBERTO GÓMEZ MANCILLA
- Continuing Education: LUCILA GUALDRÓN DE ACEROS

UNIVERSIDAD DE SUCRE

Apdo Aéreo 406, Cra. 28 No. 5-267, Sincelejo, Sucre
Telephone: (52) 821240
Fax: (52) 821240
Internet: www.unisucre.edu.co

Founded 1977
State control
Academic year: February to December

Rector: GUSTAVO VERGARA ARRÁZOLA
Chief Administrative Officer: VICTOR RAÚL CASTILLO JIMÉNEZ
Secretary-General: AMIRA VALDÉS ALTAMAR
Librarian: IRMA OCHOA DE FONSECA

Library of 12,000 vols
Number of teachers: 65
Number of students: 910

DEANS

Faculty of Engineering: PABLO ALFONSO CARO RETTIZ
Faculty of Sciences and Humanities: CARMEN PAYARES PAYARES
Faculty of Stockbreeding: JULIO ALEJANDRO HERNÁNDEZ
Faculty of Health Sciences: CARMEN CECILIA ALVIS DE PUENTES

UNIVERSIDAD SURCOLOMBIANA

Avda Pastrana Borrero con Carrera 1A, Neiva, Huila
Telephone: (88) 745444
Internet: www.usurcolombia.com

Founded 1970
State control
Language of instruction: Spanish
Academic year: February to December

Rector: ALVARO LOZANO OSORIO
Academic Vice-Rector: CARLOS BOLIVAR BONILLA
Administrative Vice-Rector: MARIA BEATRIZ PAVA MARÍN
Chief Administrative Officer: EFRAÍN POLANÍA VIVAS
Secretary: JOSÉ PIAR IRIARTE VELILLA
Librarian: LUIS ALFREDO PINTO

Number of teachers: 450
Number of students: 4,500

DEANS

Accountancy and Administration: ALFONSO MANRIQUE MEDINA
Educational Science: FABIO LOSADA PÉREZ
Engineering: ALFONSO ORTÍZ
Medicine and Health: ANTONIO ACEVEDO A.

HEADS OF DEPARTMENTS

Accountancy: HUMBERTO RUEDA
Business Administration: ORLANDO RODRIGUEZ
Mathematics and Physics: HERNANDO GONZALEZ S.
Pre-school Education: BEATRIZ PERDOMO DE G.
Educational Administration: GRACE ALVAREZ
Linguistics and Literature: MAGDALENA ARIAS B.
Agricultural Engineering: EDUARDO PASTRANA
Petroleum Engineering: ROBERTO VARGAS C.
Physical Education: ALVARO MOTTA MILLÁN
Nursing: MARIA ESNEDA BARRERA
Open University: NOHORA ELENA ROJAS
Post-Degrees Centre: AURA ELENA BERNAL

UNIVERSIDAD DEL TOLIMA

Apdo Aéreo No. 546, Santa Elena, Ibagué, Tolima
Telephone: (98) 2649219
Fax: (98) 2644869
E-mail: ut@ut.edu.co
Internet: www.ut.edu.co

Founded 1945
State control
Academic year: January to December

Rector: JESÚS RAMÓN RIVERA BULLA
Academic Vice-Rector: JOSÉ HERMAN MUÑOZ ÑUNGO
Administrative Vice-Rector: LUIS EVELIO GUZMÁN DIAZ
Vice-Rector for Development and Educational Resources: FABIO ALFONSO SANDOVAL PATARROYO
Registrar: LUZ ANGELA CALLE BARRERO
Librarian: CIELO URUEÑA LOZANO

Number of teachers: 201
Number of students: 10,130

Publication: *Revista Panorama Universitario*

DEANS

Faculty of Agricultural Engineering: CARLOS ANTONIO RIVERA BARRERO
Faculty of Business Administration: GERMÁN RUBIO GUERRERO
Faculty of Educational Science: LUIS ALBERTO MALAGÓN PLATA
Faculty of Forestry Engineering: RAFAEL VARGAS RÍOS
Faculty of Health Sciences: FRANCIA HELENA DE BETANCOURTH
Faculty of Science: RAMIRO URIBE KAFFURE
Faculty of Technology: ALBERTO MEJÍA RENGIFO
Faculty of Veterinary Medicine and Zootechnics: FRANCISCO SEGURA CANIZALES
Institute of Distance Education: LUCÍA DURÁN PINILLA

HEADS OF DEPARTMENTS

Faculty of Agricultural Engineering:
- Agricultural Expansion: HÉCTOR PENAGOS
- Soils and Water: ALBERTO GONZÁLEZ RUBIO
- Vegetable Health and Production: JAVIER FERNANDO OSORIO SARAVIA

Faculty of Business Administration:
- Administration, Marketing and Law: JÉSUS ALFONSO ARAQUE ACEVEDO
- Economics and Finance: JOSÉ RAMIRO GALVEZ ALDANA

Faculty of Education:
- Educational Psychology: RUBEN DARIO GUEVARA GONZÁLEZ
- Social Studies: ELSA BONILLA PIRATOVA
- Spanish and English: MARÍA JAZMIN SOTO ALVARADO

Faculty of Forestry Engineering (fax (98) 2666160; e-mail forestal@ut.edu.co):
- Engineering: VALERIO PEÑUELA CAICEDO
- Forest Science: OMAR AURELIO MELO CRUZ

Faculty of Health Science:
- Clinical Sciences: GUSTAVO MONTEALEGRE LYNETT
- CommunityHealth: PATRICIA ALENA DUEÑAS GRANADOS

Faculty of Science:
- Biology: ANTONIO JOSÉ GUIO DUQUE
- Chemistry: ENRIQUE ALIRIO ORTIZ
- Mathematics and Statistics: LUIS CECILIO GALVEZ
- Physics: JAIRO ARMANDO CARDONA BEDOYA

Faculty of Technology:
- Drawing: SAMUEL APARICIO ALBARÁN
- Topography: YESID SALAZAR BEDOYA

Faculty of Veterinary Medicine and Zootechnics:
- Animal Health: NORA BEATRIZ ANDRADE DE SABOGAL
- Cattle Breeding: RAMIRO MEJÍA GALLEGO

UNIVERSIDAD DEL VALLE

Ciudad Universitaria, Meléndez, Apdo Aéreo 25360, Apdo Nacional 439, Calí, Valle del Cauca

Telephone: (2) 392310
Fax: (2) 398484
Internet: www.univalle.edu.co

Founded 1945
State control
Language of instruction: Spanish
Academic year: January to June, August to December

Rector: JAIME E. GALARZA SANCLEMENTE
Vice-Rectors: CARLOS E. DULCEY BONILLA (Academic Affairs), Dr ALBERTO LOPEZ SANCHEZ (Administration), Dr HUMBERTO REY VARGAS (Research), Dr CECILIA MADRIÑAN POLO (University Welfare)
Library Director: Lic. ISABEL ROMERO DE DULCEY

Library of 267,656 vols
Number of teachers: 962
Number of students: 9,640 full-time
Number of students: 5,000 part-time

Publications: *Revista Universidad del Valle, Poligramas, Boletín Socioeconómico, Humboltia, Heurística, Colombia Médica, Revista de Ciencias, Fin de Siglo, Praxis Filosófica, Historia y Espacio, Cuadernos de Administración, Pliegos Administrativos, La Palabra, Planta Libre, Revista Estomatología, Lenguaje*

DEANS

Faculty of Architecture: Dr CARLOS ENRIQUE DULCEY BONILLA E.
Faculty of Engineering: Dr SILVIO DELVASTO
Faculty of Health: Dr HECTOR RAUL ECHAVARRIA ABAD
Faculty of Economics and Social Sciences: Dr LUGARDO ALVAREZ AGUDELO
Faculty of Humanities: Dr HUMBERTO VÉLEZ RAMÍREZ
Faculty of Education: Dr MARIO DIAZ
Faculty of Science: Dr LUIS FERNANDO CASTRO
Faculty of Administrative Science: Dr BERNARDO BARONA

HEADS OF DEPARTMENTS

Faculty of Engineering:
- Department of Mechanical Engineering: Dr RICARDO RAMÍREZ
- Department of Electrical Engineering: Dr HÉCTOR CADAVID
- Department of Information and Systems: Dra MARTHA CECILIA GÓMEZ
- Department of Fluid and Heat Sciences: Dr DIEGO MONTAÑA PALACIOS
- Department of Chemical and Biological Processes: Dr CARLOS VELEZ

Faculty of Health:
- Department of Morphology: Dr CAROLINA ISAZA DE LOURIDO E.
- Department of Physiology: Dr FELIX EDUARDO MELO GONZALEZ
- Department of Pathology: Dr EDWIN CARRASCAL
- Department of Anaesthesiology: Dr MARIO VELÁSQUEZ
- Department of Internal Medicine: Dr ALVARO MERCADO
- Department of Surgery: Dr JAIME ROBERTO ARIAS
- Department of Paediatrics: Dr FABIO PEREIRA
- Department of Obstetrics and Gynaecology: Dr EDGAR IVAN ORTIZ
- Department of Psychiatry: Dr CARLOS CLIMENT
- Department of Social and Preventive Medicine: Dr ALFREDO AGUIRRE
- Department of Microbiology: Dr SILVIO ARANGO
- Department of Stomatology: Dr JOSÉ DOMINGO GARCÍA
- Department of Nursing: Dr BLANCA AGUIRRE DE CABAL
- Department of Physical Medicine and Rehabilitation: Dr ORLANDO QUINTERO FLOREZ E.
- Department of Internal Medicine: (Resident Staff): Dr JOSÉ FRANCISCO DIAZ

Faculty of Architecture:
- Department of Environmental Technology and Construction: Dr OTTO VALDERRUTEN
- Department of Environmental Planning: Dr CARLOS ENRIQUE BOTERO
- Department of Design: Dr RICARDO AGUILERA

Faculty of Science:
- Department of Mathematics: Dr CARLOS RODRIGUEZ
- Department of Physics: Dr CARLOS JULIO URIBE
- Department of Chemistry: Dr ALONSO JARAMILLO
- Department of Biology: Dr HÉCTOR ARMANDO VÁRGAS

Faculty of Social and Economic Sciences:
- Department of Economics: Dr MAX ENRIQUE NIETO
- Department of Social Sciences: Dr RENAN JOSÉ SILVA

Faculty of Humanities:
- Department of Languages: Dra BLANCA DE ESCOCIA
- Department of History: Dr JORGE ELIECER SALCEDO SAAVEDRA
- Department of Music: Dra MARTHA LUCIA CALDERON
- Department of Philosophy: Dr JEAN PAUL MARGOT
- Department of Communications: Dr ALEJANDRO ULLO SANMIGUEL
- Department of Social Work: Dr VICTOR MARIO ESTRADA
- Department of Letters: Dr CARLOS ENRIQUE RESTREPO ACUÑA

Faculty of Education:
- Department of Teacher Training: Dra MARIELA DE BRAND
- Department of Psychology: Dr MIRALBA CORREA DE ROBLEDO
- Department of Curriculum: Dr HUMBERTO QUICENO
- Department of Educational Administration and Planning: Dr GUILLERMO SALAZAR
- Department of Physical Education and Sports: Dr GILDARDO PEREZ

Faculty of Administrative Science:
- Department of Business Administration: Dr MARÍA PAOLA CROCE DI PETTA
- Department of Information, Accounting and Finance: Dr LUIS ENRIQUE POLANCO

UNIVERSIDAD TECNOLÓGICA DEL CHOCÓ 'DIEGO LUIS CÓRDOBA'

Carrera 2A, Nro., 25–22, Quibdó, Chocó

Telephone: (57) 711589
Internet: www.utch.edu.co

Founded 1972
State control
Language of instruction: Spanish
Academic year: February to June, July to November

Rector: HECTOR D. MOSQUERA BENITEZ
Academic Vice-Rector: ALVARO GIRALDO GOMEZ
Administrative Vice-Rector: VICTOR RAUL MOSQUERA BENITEZ
Registrar: LEONILA BLANDÓN ASPRILLA
Librarian: ZAHILY SARRAZOLA MARTINEZ

Number of teachers: 125
Number of students: 1,500

Publications: *Libros Tecnicos en diferentes areas del Conocimieto, Obras Literarias*

DEANS

Faculty of Education: EFRAIN MORENO RODRIGUEZ
Faculty of Health and Social Security: MELIDA MORENO MURILLO
Faculty of Technology: LORENZO PORTOCARRERO SIERRA

HEADS OF DEPARTMENTS

Faculty of Education:
- Mathematics and Physics: FRANCIA A. BEJARANO
- Languages: CÉSAR E. RIVAS LARA
- Social Science: JORGE E. PEREA PEÑA
- Chemistry and Biology: JUAN MORENO TEHERAN
- Psycho-pedagogy and Educational Administration: MANUEL GREGORIO RAMIREZ
- Social Work: BERTHA CONTO GARCIA

Faculty of Technology:
- Civil Works: ROSA OROZCO ABADIA
- Mining: ALBERTO ERIK MARTINEZ HERRERA
- Fishing: ALBEIRO VELEZ GOMEZ
- Farming: FREDDY PINO MOSQUERA
- Industrial Administration: JESUS LOZANO ASPRILLA

UNIVERSIDAD DE LOS LLANOS

Km 11 Vía Puerto López, Villavicencio, Meta

Telephone: (98) 6698000
Fax: (98) 6698602
E-mail: rectoria@unillanos.edu.co
Internet: www.unillanos.edu.co

Founded 1974 as Universidad Tecnológica de Los Llanos Orientales; present name and status 1992
State control
Academic year: February to December

Rector: CARLOS ENRIQUE GARZÓN GONZÁLEZ
Secretary-General: RUTH CHAVEZ A.

Library of 10,000 vols
Number of teachers: 120
Number of students: 1,345

Publications: *Boletín, Boletín Estadístico, Catálogo*

Faculties of Animal Husbandry and Natural Resources, Basic Sciences, Health Sciences and Humanities.

UNIVERSIDAD DEL MAGDALENA

Carrera 32 No. 22-08, Santa Marta, Magdalena

Telephone: (95) 4301692
Fax: (95) 4302050
E-mail: rectoria@unimag.edu.co
Internet: www.unimag.edu.co

Founded 1958
State control
Language of instruction: Spanish
Academic year: February to December (two semesters)

Rector: Dr CARLOS EDUARDO CAICEDO OMAR

Library of 14,000 vols
Number of teachers: 156
Number of students: 2,009

Publications: *Revista Agronómica, Revista Económica, Revista Facultad Ingeniería Pesquera*

Faculties of Engineering, Basic Sciences, Education, Humanities, Health Sciences, Economics and Business and General Studies.

UNIVERSIDAD TECNOLÓGICA DE PEREIRA

Apdo Aéreo 97, Pereira, Risaralda
Telephone: (6) 63213292
Fax: (6) 63215839
E-mail: relint@utp.edu.co
Internet: www.utp.edu.co

Founded 1958
State control
Academic year: February to December

Rector: LUIS ENRIQUE ARANGO JIMÉNEZ
Academic Vice-Rector: GERMÁN LÓPEZ QUINTERO
Administrative Vice-Rector: FERNANDO NOREÑA JARAMILLO
Registrar: DIEGO OSORIO
General Secretary: CARLOS ALFONSO ZULUAGA ARANGO
Librarian: MARGARITA FAJARDO

Library of 30,000 vols, 1,400 periodicals
Number of teachers: 526

Publications: *Scientia et Technica* (2 a year), *Revista de Ciencias Humanas* (3 a year), *Revista Médica de Risaralda*

DEANS

Faculty of Basic Sciences: Fis. JOSÉ GÓMEZ ESPÍNDOLA
Faculty of Education: Lic. MARÍA TERESA ZAPATA SALDARRIAGA
Faculty of Electrical Engineering and Computer Science: Ing. OMAR IVÁN TREJOS BURITICÁ
Faculty of Environmental Sciences: Dr SAMUEL DARIO GUZMÁN LÓPEZ
Faculty of Fine Arts and Humanities: Mtro JUAN HUMBERTO GALLEGO RAMÍREZ
Faculty of Industrial Engineering: Ing. WILSON ARENAS VALENCIA
Faculty of Mechanical Engineering: Ing. WALDO LIZCANO ARIAS
Faculty of Medicine: Dr SAMUEL EDUARDO TRUJILLO HENAO
Faculty of Technology: Ing. JOSÉ REINALDO MARÍN BETANCOURTH

ESCUELA SUPERIOR DE ADMINISTRACIÓN PÚBLICA

Apdo Aéreo 29745, Diagonal 40 No. 46A–37, Santafé de Bogotá
Telephone: (1) 2224700
Fax: (1) 2224356
Internet: www.esap.edu.co

Founded 1958
State control
Language of instruction: Spanish
Academic year: February to November

Director-General: SAMUEL OSPINA MARÍN
Administrative Deputy Director: GUILLERMO LEÓN REY
Academic Deputy Director: TITO ANTONIO HUERTAS PORRAS
Secretary-General: GERMÁN PUENTES GONZÁLEZ
Librarian: MARÍA CRISTINA ESCOBAR DE ARANGO

Library of 27,000 vols
Number of teachers: 91
Number of students: 905

Publications: *Administración y Desarrollo* (2 a year), *Documentos ESAP*

DEANS

Faculty of Advanced Studies: OCTAVIO BARBOSA CARDONA
Faculty of Political and Administrative Sciences: TITO ANTONIO HUERTAS PORRAS

ATTACHED INSTITUTES

Institute of Human Rights 'Guillermo Cano': Dir GUILLERMO GONZÁLEZ RAMÍREZ.
Institute of International Studies: Dir HERNANDO ROA SUÁREZ.

Private Universities

UNIVERSIDAD CATÓLICA DE MANIZALES

Apdo 357, Carrera 23 No. 60–63, Manizales
Telephone: (68) 860019
Fax: (68) 860575
E-mail: sucatomz@col2.telecom.co
Internet: www.ucatolicamz.edu.co

Founded 1954
Private control
Language of instruction: Spanish
Academic year: February to June, July to November

Rector: JUDITH LEON GUEVARA
Vice-Rectors: GLORIA ARRIETA DE PLATA (Professional Teaching), Sr CECILIA GOMEZ JARAMILLO (Administrative), Sr BEATRIZ PATINO GARCIA (University Environment), MARCO FIDEL CHICA LASSO (Research), SILVIO CARDONA GONZALEZ (Higher Teaching), JORGE OSWALDO SANCHEZ BUITRAGO (Planning and Development)
Registrar: FANNY CASTELLANOS TORO
Librarian: GABRIEL DEL ROSARIO

Number of teachers: 248
Number of students: 2,567

Publications: *Boletín Informativo*, *Revista de Investigaciones*, *Protocolo*

HEADS OF STUDIES

Undergraduate Course in Bacteriology: Mag. LUZ ESTELLA RAMIREZ ARISTIZÁBAL
Undergraduate Course in Audiology: Esp. MARIA CONSTANZA MONTOYA NARANJO
Undergraduate Course in Nutrition and Diet: Nut. PIEDAD ROLDÁN JARAMILLO
Undergraduate Course in Respiratory Therapy: Mag. MARTHA LUCÍA CUJIÑO QUINTERO
Undergraduate Course in Advertising: Esp. ARMANDO SÁNCHEZ SUÁREZ
Undergraduate Course in Tourism Administration: Esp. MIRIAM ASTRID VELÁSQUEZ HENAO
Undergraduate Course in Education: Esp. MARIA LUCIEL MONTOYA GÓMEZ
Undergraduate Course in Architecture, Town Planning and Construction: Arq. ORLANDO CASTRO M.
Undergraduate Course in Telematic Engineering: Ing. MARCELO LOPEZ TRUJILLO
Undergraduate Course in Technology and Computer Science: Ing. CARLOS CUESTA IGLESIAS
Postgraduate Studies in University Teaching: Esp. ALEYDA HENAO DE NARANJO
Postgraduate Studies in Educational Planning: Esp. ALDEMAR GIRALDO DE DIAZ
Postgraduate Studies in Human Rights: Esp. FRANCISCO JAVIER JARAMILLO O.
Postgraduate Studies in Speech Therapy: Esp. OLGA LUCIA OCAMPO GÓMEZ
Postgraduate Studies in Curriculum Management: Esp. GLADYS ESTELLA GÍRALDO DE DÍAZ
Postgraduate Studies in Audioprosthesis: Mag. CARMEN CECILIA GALLEGO GÓMEZ
Masters Course in Microbiology: Mag. MARTHA EVA BURITICÁ DE MONSALVE

ATTACHED INSTITUTES

Centro de Estudios de la Comunicacíon Humana (CECH): Dir L. T. SULAY ROCÍO ECHEVERRY DE F..
Institute of Food-farming Quality Management (INGECAL): Dir PIEDAD CIRO BASTO.

UNIVERSIDAD AUTÓNOMA DE BUCARAMANGA

Calle 48, 39-234, Apdo Aéreo 1642, Bucaramanga
Telephone: (97) 6436261
Fax: (97) 6433958
Internet: www.unab.edu.co

Founded 1952
Private control
Language of instruction: Spanish
Academic year: January to November

Rector: Dr GABRIEL BURGOS MANTILLA
Administrative Vice-Rector: Dr JORGE HUMBERTO GALVIS COTE
Academic Vice-Rector: Dra GRACIELA MORENO URIBE
Librarian: ELENA UVAROVA

Number of teachers: 491
Number of students: 7,601

Publications: *Revista Reflexiones*, *Revista Prospectiva*, *Revista Cuestiones*, *Revista Temas Socio-Jurídicos*, *Revista Facultad de Contaduría*, *Periódico Zeta*, *Revista Medunab*

DEANS

Faculty of Accountancy: ELIZABETH MARTÍNEZ DE GUALDRÓN
Faculty of Business Administration: JUAN CARLOS HEDERICH MARTÍNEZ
Faculty of Business Psychology: LILIANA STELLA QUIÑONEZ TORRES
Faculty of Communication: LUZ AMALIA CAMACHO VELÁSQUEZ
Faculty of Economics: CATHERINNE GIOHANNA MÉDINA ARÉVALO
Faculty of Education: ALBA ROSA AROCHA HERNÁNDEZ
Faculty of Energy Engineering: ALVARO JOSÉ REY AMAYA
Faculty of Finance Engineering: JORGE RAÚL SERRANO DÍAZ
Faculty of Hospitality and Tourism Administration: LUIS GUSTAVO ALVAREZ RUEDA
Faculty of Law: JUAN CARLOS ACUÑA GUTIÉRREZ
Faculty of Marketing Engineering: ADRIANA SANTARELLI FRANCO
Faculty of Mechanical Engineering: EDUARDO CALDERÓN PORRAS
Faculty of Medicine: LUIS CAMACHO MÁRQUEZ
Faculty of Music: JESÚS ALBERTO REY MARIÑO
Faculty of Systems Engineering: WILSON BRICEÑO PINEDA
Faculty of Visual Arts Production: HERNAN HUMBERTO RESTREPO BOTERO

FUNDACIÓN UNIVERSIDAD DE BOGOTÁ 'JORGE TADEO LOZANO'

Apdo Aéreo 34185, Carrera 4, No. 22–61, Bogotá
Telephone: (1) 3341777
Fax: (1) 2826197
E-mail: btadeo12@andinet.lat.net
Internet: www.utadeo.edu.co

Founded 1954
Private control
Academic year: February to December (two semesters)

President: GUILLERMO RUEDA MONTAÑA
Rector: EVARISTO OBREGON GARCES
Vice-Rector (Academic): JUAN MANUEL CABALLERO PRIETO

Vice-Rector (Postgraduate Studies): MIGUEL BERMUDEZ PORTOCARRERO
Vice-Rector (Administrative): FANNY MESTRE DE GUTIERREZ
Secretary-General: OSCAR AZUERO RUIZ
Librarian: MARIA CONSUELO MONCADA CAMACHO

Number of teachers: 1,020
Number of students: 11,500

Publications: *Ecotropica*, *La Tadeo*, *Agenda cultural*, *Tadeísta*

DEANS

Faculty of Business Administration: Dra CONSUELO VIDAL DE BRUGGEMAN
Faculty of Agriculture and Stockbreeding Administration: INES ELVIRA TAMARA
Faculty of Agrology: Dr TOMAS LEON SICARD
Faculty of Fine Arts: NATALIA GUTIERREZ E.
Faculty of Marine Biology: IVAN REY CARRASCO
Faculty of International Commerce: HUGO VILLAMIL P.
Faculty of Social Communication: Dr MARGOTH RICCI DE GOSSAIN
Faculty of Public Accountancy: Dr GENOVEVA CAMACHO DE CONSTAIN
Faculty of Interior Design: Dr DICKEN CASTRO DUQUE
Faculty of Graphic Design: Dra PASTORA CORREA DE AMAYA
Faculty of Industrial Design: Dr FERNANDO CORREA MUÑOZ
Faculty of International Relations: ESTHER LOZANO DE REY
Faculty of Economic Sciences: JOAQUIN FLOREZ TRUJILLO
Faculty of Food Technology: JANETH LUNA
Faculty of Geographic Engineering: Dr JAIME VILLAREAL MORALES
Faculty of Marketing: JESUS ANTONIO POVEDA
Faculty of Publicity: Dr CHRISTIAN SCHRADER
Faculty of Computer Science: JUAN ORLANDO LIZCANO
Faculty of Law: CAMILO NOGUERA
Health Services Management: ALFONSO LEON CANCINO
Workers' Health: LEONARDO CAÑON ORTEGON
International Business Management: CIRO AREVALO Y.
Food Business Management: PEDRO LUIS JIMENEZ

DIRECTORS

Agro-industrial Marketing: ISMAEL PEÑA DIAZ
Marketing Management: ALEJANDRO SCHNARCH KIRBERG
Regional Development Planning: CARLOS A. GONZALEZ PARRA
International Relations: DIEGO URIBE VARGAS
Commercial Logistics: JORGE URIBE ROLDAN
History and Fine-Art Criticism: FRANCISCO GIL TOVAR

FUNDACIÓN UNIVERSIDAD CENTRAL

Carrera 5A No. 21–38, Bogotá
North Bogotá branch: Calle 75 No. 15–91, Bogotá
Telephone: (1) 3134537
Fax: (1) 3134720
E-mail: webpage@ucentral.edu.co
Internet: www.ucentral.edu.co

Founded 1966
Academic year: January to December

Rector: Dr RUBÉN AMAYA REYES
Vice Rector (Academic): Dra GLORIA RINCÓN CUBIDES
Vice Rector (Administration and Finance): Dr FERNANDO ALVAREZ MORALES
Secretary-General: Dr BILLY ESCOBAR PÉREZ

Number of teachers: 700
Number of students: 12,000

Publications: *Cuadernos del Cine Club* (2 a year), *Hojas Universitarias* (2 a year), *Magazin Mercadológico* (2 a year), *Nómadas* (2 a year), *NotiCentral* (4 a year)

Faculties of business administration, economics, accounting, social communication and journalism, musical studies, electronic engineering, mechanical engineering, systems engineering, water resources and environmental engineering, industrial engineering, marketing and advertising. Also postgraduate programmes.

UNIVERSIDAD EXTERNADO DE COLOMBIA

Calle 12, No. 1–17 Este, Bogotá
Telephone: (1) 3420288
Fax: (1) 2843769
E-mail: uextpub3@impsat.net.co
Internet: www.uexternado.edu.co

Founded 1886
Private control
Language of instruction: Spanish
Academic year: February to December

Rector: Dr FERNANDO HINESTROSA
Secretary-General: Dr HERNANDO PARRA NIETO
Administrative Director (vacant)
Librarian: Dra LINA ESPITALETA DE VILLEGAS

Number of teachers: 639
Number of students: 7,000

Publications: *Derecho del Estado* (2 a year), *Temas de Derecho Público* (4 a year), *Documentos para la Historia del Constitucionalismo Colombiano* (2 a year), *Derecho Penal y Criminología* (3 a year), *Revista de Derecho Privado* (2 a year), *Colección de Estudios en Derecho Penal – Cuadernos de Conferencias y Artículos* (3 a year), *Filosofía del Derecho* (4 a year), *Contexto* (4 a year), *Derecho Económico*, *Derecho y Vida*, *Revista Zero*, *Oasis – Observatorio de Análisis de los Sistemas Internacionales*, *Revista de Economía Institucional*, *Notas de Coyuntura Económica*, *Boletín Tiempo y Turismo*, *Lúdica* (social communication)

DEANS

Faculty of Business Administration: Dra DIANA CABRERA
Faculty of Economics: Dr MAURICIO PÉREZ
Faculty of Education: Dra MIRYAM OCHOA PIEDRAHITA
Faculty of Finance, Government and International Relations: Dr ROBERTO HINESTROSA
Faculty of Furniture Restoration: Dra HELENA WIESNER
Faculty of Hotel Management and Tourism: Dr LUIS CARLOS CRUZ CORTÉS
Faculty of Law: Dr FERNANDO HINESTROSA
Faculty of Public Finance: Dr HERNANDO PÉREZ DURÁN
Faculty of Social Communication and Journalism: Dr MIGUEL MÉNDEZ CAMACHO
Faculty of Social Sciences and Humanities: Dra LUCERO ZAMUDIO

UNIVERSIDAD ICESI

Calle 18 122–135, Calí, Valle del Cauca

Telephone: (2) 5552334
Fax: (2) 5552345
E-mail: wwwmgr@icesi.edu.co
Internet: www.icesi.edu.co

Founded 1979
Private control
Language of instruction: Spanish

President: FRANCISCO PIEDRAHITA
Secretary-General: MARÍA CRISTINA NAVIA K.
Librarian: MARTA CECILIA LORA

Number of teachers: 260
Number of students: 2,580 (2,124 undergraduates, 456 graduates)

Publications: *Revista Interacción* (termly), *Estudios Gerenciales* (termly), *Precedente* (termly), *Sistemas y Telemática* (weekly), *Innovando* (weekly)

DEANS

Faculty of Economics and Administration: Dr HÉCTOR OCHOA DÍAZ
Faculty of Engineering: Dr HENRY ARANGO
Faculty of Law and Social Sciences: Dr LELIO FERNANDEZ

PONTIFICIA UNIVERSIDAD JAVERIANA

Carrera 7 No. 40–76, Apdo Aéreo 56710, Bogotá
Telephone: (1) 3208320
Fax: (1) 2853348
E-mail: puj@javeriana.edu.co
Internet: www.javeriana.edu.co

Founded 1622 by the Jesuit Fathers; re-established 1931, present status 1937
Academic year: January to November (two semesters)

Grand Chancellor: R. P. P.-H. KOLVENBACH
Vice-Grand Chancellor: P. GABRIEL IGNACIO RODRÍGUEZ
Rector: P. GERARDO REMOLINA
Vice-Rector (Academic): Dr JAIRO H. CIFUENTES
Vice-Rector (Administrative): Ing. ROBERTO ENRIQUE MONTOYA
Vice-Rector (University Affairs): P. MIGUEL ROZO
Rector (Calí Section): P. JOAQUÍN SÁNCHEZ
Secretary-General: P. JAIME BERNAL
Library: see Libraries and Archives

Number of teachers: 3,958
Number of students: 28,611

Publications: *Theologica Xaveriana*, *Universitas Médica* (4 per year), *Universitas Jurídica*, *Universitas Humanistica*, *Universitas Economica*, *Universitas Canonica*, *Universitas Odontologica*, *Universitas Philosophica*, *Signo y Pensamiento* (2 a year), *Cuadernos de Agroindustria y Economía Rural*, *Ingeniería y Universidad*, *Revista Ibero-Latinoamericana de Seguros*, *Memoria y Sociedad*, *Universitas Scientiarum*, *Universitas Psychologica* (2 a year), *Papel Político*, *Cuadernos de Administración*

DEANS

Faculty of Architecture: Arq. ALVARO BOTERO
Faculty of Arts: M. JUAN ANTONIO CUÉLLAR
Faculty of Canon Law: Dr RAFAEL GÓMEZ
Faculty of Communication and Language: Dr JÜRGEN HORLBECK
Faculty of Dentistry: Dr ALEJANDRO ZAPATA
Faculty of Economic and Administrative Sciences: Dr GUILLERMO GALÁN
Faculty of Education: Dr JOSÉ BERNARDO TORO
Faculty of Engineering: Ing. FRANCISCO JAVIER REBOLLEDO
Faculty of Economic and Administrative Sciences (in Calí): Dr BERNARDO BARONA
Faculty of Environmental and Rural Studies: Dr LUIS MIGUEL RENJIFO
Faculty of Engineering (in Calí): Dr JORGE FRANCISCO ESTELA
Faculty of Humanities and Social Sciences (in Calí): Dr ESTEBAN OCAMPO
Faculty of Law: P. LUIS FERNANDO ALVAREZ
Faculty of Medicine: Dr IVAN SOLARTE
Faculty of Nursing: Dra ROSAURA CORTÉS DE TÉLLEZ
Faculty of Philosophy: Dr ALFONSO FLÓREZ

Faculty of Psychology: Dra ANGELA MARÍA ROBLEDO
Faculty of Political Sciences and International Relations: Dra CLAUDIA DANGOND
Faculty of Sciences: Dra ANGELA UMAÑA
Faculty of Social Sciences: Dra CONSUELO URIBE
Faculty of Theology: P. VÍCTOR MARTÍNEZ
Department of Languages: Dra NELLY ESPERANZA TORRES

AFFILIATED INSTITUTES

Instituto Geofísico—Universidad Javeriana (Geophysical Institute): Bogotá; f. 1941; Dir Ing. JORGE ALONSO PRIETO.

San Ignacio University Hospital: Dir Dr HERNÁN JIMÉNEZ.

Institute for Architectural Patrimony: Dir Arq. LUIS ISAZA LONDOÑO.

Institute for Human Genetics: Dir Dr JAIME EDUARDO BERNAL VILLEGAS.

Institute of Rural Studies: Dir Dr RICARDO DÁVILA.

Institute of Environmental Studies for Development: Dir Dr BENJAMÍN HERAZO C.

Institute of Human Development: Dir Dra ROSA MARGARITA VARGAS.

Javeriana Institute for Housing and Urban Planning: Dir Arq. OLGA LUCÍA CEBALLOS.

Institute for the Study of Inborn Errors of Metabolism: Dir Dr LUIS ALEJANDRO BARRERA.

Institute of Development Politics: Dir Dr ALEJANDRO VIVAS.

Institute of Health Promotion: Dir Dra AMELIA FERNÁNDEZ.

Institute of Bioethics: Dir Dr GERMÁN CALDERÓN LEGARDA.

Institute of Human Rights and International Relations: Dir Dr ROBERTO EDUARDO MORA.

Institute for Social and Cultural Studies 'PENSAR': Dir Dr GUILLERMO HOYOS VÁSQUEZ.

Aging Institute: Dr CARLOS ALBERTO CANO.

UNIVERSIDAD AUTÓNOMA LATINOAMERICANA

Carrera 55 (Tenerife) No. 49–51, Apdo 3455, Medellín
Telephone: (4) 5112199
Fax: (4) 5123418
E-mail: info@unaula.edu.co
Internet: www.unaula.edu.co

Founded 1966
Private control with state supervision
Language of instruction: Spanish
Academic year: February to November

President: Dr LUCIANO SANÍN ARROYAVE
Rector: Dr JAIRO URIBE ARANGO
Vice-Rector (Academic): Dr ANÍBAL VÉLEZ MUÑOZ
Vice-Rector (Administrative): Dr JOSÉ RAÚL JARAMILLO RESTREPO
Secretary-General: Dr ÁLVARO OCHOA MORALES
Registrar: Dr VICENTE IGLESIAS ESCORCE
Librarian: Dr ALONSO GUILLERMO MERINO G.

Number of teachers: 250
Number of students: 2,000

Publications: *Boletín Informativo* (monthly), *Revista Unaula* (annually), *Sociología* (annually), *Visión Autónoma* (2 a year), *Actividad Contable* (annually), *Apuntes de Economía* (annually), *Círculo de Humanidades* (4 a year), *Ratio Juris* (2 a year)

DEANS

Faculty of Accountancy: Dr JORGE ALBERTO SÁNCHEZ GIRALDO
Faculty of Economics: Dr ÁLVARO JAVIER CORREA VÉLEZ
Faculty of Education and Social Sciences: Dr FERNANDO CORTÉS GUTIÉRREZ
Faculty of Industrial Engineering: Dr ANÍBAL VÉLEZ MUÑOZ
Faculty of Law: Dr FERNANDO SALAZAR MEJÍA
Faculty of Sociology: Dr FRANCISCO MÚNERA DUQUE
Faculty of Postgraduate Studies: Dr HÉCTOR ORTIZ CAÑAS

UNIVERSIDAD CATÓLICA POPULAR DEL RISARALDA

Avda de las Américas, Frente al Parque Metropolitano del Café, Apdo Aéreo 2435, Pereira
Telephone: (96) 3127722
Fax: (96) 3127613
E-mail: ucpr@ucpr.edu.co
Internet: www.ucpr.edu.co

Founded 1975
Private control
Academic year: January to November

Grand Chancellor: Mons. FABIO SUESCÚN MUTIS
Rector: Fr ALVARO EDUARDO BETANCUR JIMÉNEZ
Vice-Rector: Dr JAIME MONTOYA FERRER
Administrative Director: Dr HÉCTOR FABIO LONDOÑO PARRA
Librarian: Dra JUDITH GÓMEZ GÓMEZ

Number of teachers: 250
Number of students: 1,850

Publication: *Páginas de la UCPR* (5 a year)

DEANS

Faculty of Industrial Economics: Dr HEDMAN ALBERTO SIERRA SIERRA
Faculty of Business Administration: Dr ARIEL GALVIS GONZÁLEZ
Faculty of Religious Studies: Dr HÉCTOR CÓRDOBA VARGAS
Faculty of Industrial Design: Dra CARMEN ADRIANA PÉREZ CARDONA
Faculty of Architecture: Dr EDGAR SALOMÓN CRUZ MORENO
Faculty of Social Communication and Journalism: Dra CRISTINA BOTERO SALAZAR
Faculty of Psychology: Dra BEATRIZ MARÍN LONDOÑO

UNIVERSIDAD EAFIT

Apdo Aéreo 3300, Avda Las Vegas, Carrera 49 No. 7 Sur-50, Medellín, Antioquia
Telephone: (4) 2619600
Fax: (4) 2664284
E-mail: webmaster@eafit.edu.co
Internet: www.eafit.edu.co

Founded 1960
Private control
Language of instruction: Spanish
Academic year: January to December

Rector: JUAN LUIS MEJÍA ARANGO
Registrar: MARÍA EUGENIA HOYOS
Academic Provost: MAURICIO VÉLEZ U.
Librarian: MARÍA CRISTINA RESTREPO LÓPEZ

Library of 40,000 vols
Number of teachers: 759
Number of students: 8,000

Publications: *Revista Universidad Eafit* (4 a year), *Eafitense* (monthly), *Ecos de Economía* (2 a year), *AD Minister* (2 a year), *Yesca y Pedernal* (4 a year), *Ruido Blanco* (2 a year), *Nuevo Foro Penal* (3 a year), *Cuadernos de Investigación*

DEANS

School of Engineering: ALBERTO RODRÍGUEZ G.
School of Administration and Accountancy: FRANCISCO LÓPEZ G.
School of Sciences and Humanities: LUCIANO ANGEL T.
School of Law: HUGO ALBERTO CASTAÑO Z.

UNIVERSIDAD INCCA DE COLOMBIA

Apdo Aéreo 14817, Bogotá
Telephone: (2) 865200
Fax: (2) 824932
Internet: www.unincca.edu.co

Founded 1955
Private control
Academic year: January to December

Rector: Dra LEONOR GARCIA DE ANDRADE
Vice-Rector: Dra MARUJA GARCIA DE CORDOBA
Administrative Vice-Rector: Dr JORGE ROJAS ALARCON
Academic Registrar: Dr MOISES NAJAR SANABRIA
General Secretary: Dr JOSE LUIS ROBAYO LEON
Librarian: MARTHA ISABEL ANGEL GIRALDO

Number of teachers: 520
Number of students: 6,700

DEANS

Faculty of Postgraduate Studies: Mg. CC. Biol. GERMAN PACHON OVALLE
Faculty of Basic and Natural Sciences: Bio. Mg. OVER QUINTERO CASTILLO
Faculty of Technical and Engineering Sciences: Ing. Sis. MARIO MARTINEZ ROJAS
Faculty of Human and Social Sciences: Mg. Mat. MESTOR BRAVO SALINAS
Faculty of Economic and Management Sciences: Sc. Oec. JULIO SILVA COLMENARES
Faculty of Judicial and State Sciences: Ab. Doc. OSCAR DUEÑAS RUIZ

UNIVERSIDAD LA GRAN COLOMBIA

Carrera 6A, No. 13–40, Apdo Aéreo 7909, Bogotá
Telephone: (1) 2868200
Fax: (1) 2828386
E-mail: rectorjg@colomsat.net.co
Internet: www.ugrancolombia.edu.co

Founded 1953
Private control
Academic year: January to November (two semesters)

Rector: JOSÉ GALAT NOUMER
Vice-Rector: RAFAEL BELTRAN BAJARANO
Gen-Sec.: RAÚL PACHECO BLANCO
Librarian: CONSTANZA GOMEZ DE NOVOA

Number of teachers: 661
Number of students: 9,650

DEANS

Faculty of Law: CARLOS FREDY NAVIA PALACIOS
Faculty of Architecture: LUIS ALFREDO QUIÑONES SARMIENTO
Faculty of Postgraduate Courses and Continuing Education: SERAFIN CRISANTO PEÑA MURCIA
Faculty of Accountancy: JOSE DONADO UCROS
Faculty of Economics: VICTOR MANUEL PEREZ ARGUELLEZ
Faculty of Civil Engineering: MANUEL RICARDO RUIZ ROMERO
Faculty of Sciences: AURA FELISA PEÑA

UNIVERSIDAD DE LA SABANA

Km 21, Autopista Norte de Bogotá D.C., Apdo Aéreo 140013, Bogotá
Telephone: (1) 8615555

Fax: (1) 8614220
E-mail: universidad.de.la.sabana@unisabana.edu.co
Internet: www.unisabana.edu.co

Founded 1979
Private control
Languages of instruction: Spanish, English
Academic year: February to November

Chancellor: JAVIER ECHEVARRÍA RODRÍGUEZ
Rector: Dr ALVARO MENDOZA RAMIREZ
Vice-Rectors: Dra LILIANA OSPINA DE GUERRERO (Academic), Dra MERCEDES SINISTERRA POMBO (University Welfare), Dra LAURA ELVIRA POSADA NÚÑEZ (Institutional Development)
Registrar: LUZ ANGELA VANEGAS
Secretary-General: Dr JAVIER MOJICA SÁNCHEZ
Head of Administration: Dr MAURICIO ROJAS PÉREZ
Academic Secretary: Dra LUZ ANGELA VANEGAS DE SÁNCHEZ
Librarian: Dra NELLY VÉLEZ SIERRA

Number of teachers: 491
Number of students: 8,872

Publications: *Pensamiento y Cultura* (annually), *Persona y Bioética* (annually)

DEANS

Faculty of Economic and Business Sciences: Dr HERNÁN DARÍO SIERRA ARANGO
Faculty of Social Communication and Journalism: Dr CESAR MAURICIO VELÁSQUEZ OSSA
Faculty of Law: Dr OBDULIO VELÁSQUEZ OSADA
Faculty of Education: Dra JULIA GALOFRE CANO
Faculty of Nursing: Dra LEONOR PARDO NOVOA
Faculty of Medicine: Dr EDUARDO BORDA CAMACHO
Faculty of Psychology: Dra MARÍA EUGENIA DE BERMÚDEZ
Faculty of Engineering: Dra GLORIA GONZÁLEZ MARIÑO

UNIVERSIDAD LIBRE DE COLOMBIA (Colombia Free University)

Calle 8 No. 5–80, Bogotá
Telephone: (1) 2820389
Fax: (1) 2823580
Internet: www.unilibre.edu.co

Founded 1923

Rector: FERNANDO DJANON RODRIGUEZ

Number of teachers: 2,500
Number of students: 32,000

Faculties of accountancy, law, engineering, medicine, economics, business administration, and education. Campuses in Calí, Pereira, Socorro, Cúcuta, Barranquilla, Cartagena.

UNIVERSIDAD LIBRE, SECCIONAL DE PEREIRA

Apdo Aéreo 1330, Calle 40 No. 7–30, Pereira
Telephone: (63) 366025
Internet: www.ulibrepei.edu.co

Founded 1971
Academic year: February to December

Rector: JAIME ARIAS LOPEZ
Librarian: LUZ MARIA HINCAPIE

Number of teachers: 121
Number of students: 1,311

Publication: *Boletín del Centro de Investigaciones* (quarterly)

DEANS

Faculty of Law: RODRIGO RIVERA CORREA
Faculty of Economics: BERNARDO VÁSQUEZ CORREA

UNIVERSIDAD DE LOS ANDES

Carrera 1, No. 18A-70, Bogotá
Telephone: (1) 3394949
Fax: (1) 3324448
E-mail: uniandes@uniandes.edu.co
Internet: www.uniandes.edu.co

Founded 1948
Private control
Languages of instruction: Spanish, English
Academic year: January to December

President: ALBERTO GUTIÉRREZ
Rector: CARLOS ANGULO
Vice-Rector (Academic): JOSÉ RAFAEL TORO
Vice-Rector (Administrative): CONSUELO CARRILLO
Secretary-General: MARGARITA GÓMEZ
Registrar: ALEJANDRO RICO RESTREPO
Librarian: ANGELA MARÍA MEJÍA DE RESTREPO

Library of 235,000 vols
Number of teachers: 1,094 (full- and part-time)
Number of students: 12,000

Publications: *Colombia Internacional* (4 a year), *Historia Crítica* (2 a year), *Nota Uniandina* (2 a year), *Revista de Estudios Sociales* (2 a year), *Revista de Ingeniería* (2 a year)

DEANS

Faculty of Administration: MARÍA LORENA GUTIÉRREZ
Faculty of Architecture and Design: WILLIE DREWS
Faculty of Arts and Humanities: CLAUDIA WMONTILLA
Faculty of Economics: JUAN CARLOS ECHEVERRY
Faculty of Engineering: ALAIN GAUTHIER
Faculty of Law: EDUARDO CIFUENTES
Faculty of Medicine: MARIO BERNAL
Faculty of Sciences: JOSÉ ROLANDO ROLDÁN
Faculty of Social Sciences: CARL LANGEBAEK

UNIVERSIDAD DE MEDELLÍN

Apdo Aéreo 1983, Carrera 87 No. 30–65, Belén Los Alpes, Medellín, Antioquia
Telephone: (4) 3414455
Fax: (4) 3414913
Telephone: udem@guayacan.udem.edu.co
Internet: www.udem.edu.co

Founded 1950
Academic year: February to December

Rector: NÉSTOR HINCAPIÉ VARGAS
Secretary-General: RAFAEL SOSA
Administrative Director: MARIA TRINIDAD PINEDA CUERVO
Academic Director: VICENTE ALBÉNIZ LACLAUSTRA
Director of Postgraduate Studies: CARLOS TULIO MONTOYA HERRERA
Librarian: MARTA LUZ TAMAYO PALACIO

Number of teachers: 623
Number of students: 8,801

Publications: *Revista Con-Textos* (2 a year), *Revista Universidad de Medellín* (2 a year)

DEANS

Faculty of Administrative Sciences: JORGE LEÓN JARAMILLO MOLINA
Faculty of Civil Engineering: ARTURO ALBERTO ARISMENDY JARAMILLO
Faculty of Communication and Corporate Relations: LUIS MARIANO GONZALEZ AGUDELO
Faculty of Educational Sciences: JAIRO PÉREZ ARROYAVE
Faculty of Environmental Engineering: JUAN CARLOS BUITRAGO BOTERO
Faculty of Industrial Economy: JAIRO PÉREZ ARROYAVE
Faculty of Law: JUAN CARLOS VASQUEZ RIVERA
Faculty of Public Accountancy: ESTELLA SABA LOPEZ
Faculty of Statistics and Informatics: MARTA CECILIA MEZA PELÁEZ
Faculty of Systems Engineering: MARTA CECILIA MESA

AFFILIATED INSTITUTE

Instituto de Derecho Penal y Criminología: Apdo Aéreo 1983, Medellín; Dir (vacant).

UNIVERSIDAD DEL NORTE

Apdo Aéreo 1569–51820, Km 5 Via Puerto Colombia, Barranquilla, Atlántico
Telephone: (5) 3509509
Fax: (5) 3598852
E-mail: webmaster@uninorte.edu.co
Internet: www.uninorte.edu.co

Founded 1966
Languages of instruction: Spanish, English
Academic year: January to December

Rector: JESÚS FERRO BAYONA
Vice-Rector: ALBERTO ROA VARELO (Academic)
Vice-Rector: ALMA LUCÍA DIAZGRANADOS (Administrative)
Dean of Students: GINA PEZZANO
Academic Secretary: CARMEN H. JIMENEZ DE PEÑA
Librarian: MARJORIE ELJACH AMADOR

Library of 46,664 vols, 728 periodicals
Number of teachers: 763
Number of students: 8,495

Publications: *Boletín Academia al Día* (6 a year), *Boletín Uninorte* (4 a year), *Revista Psicología desde el Caribe* (2 a year), *Revista Ingeniería y Desarrollo* (2 a year), *Revista Derecho* (2 a year), *Revista Salud Uninorte* (2 a year), *Revista Huellas* (4 a year), *Investigacion y Desarrollo* (4 a year), *Revista Pensamiento y Gestión* (2 a year), *Catalogo de Investigaciones* (2 a year)

DEANS

Division of Administrative Sciences: MIGUEL PACHECO SILVA
Division of Humanities and Social Sciences: JOSE AMA AMAR
Division of Engineering: JAVIER PAEZ SAAVEDRA
Division of Health Sciences: CARLOS MALABET SANTORO
Division of Law: LUIS ALBERTO GOMEZ
Field of Economics: JOSÉ MORENO CUELLO
Field of Basic Sciences: JOACHIM HAHN

UNIVERSIDAD PONTIFICIA BOLIVARIANA

Apdo Aéreo 56006, Circular 1A No. 70–01, Medellín, Antioquia
Telephone: (4) 4159015
Fax: (4) 2502080
E-mail: secretaria@logos.upb.edu.co
Internet: www.upb.edu.co

Founded 1936
Private control
Academic year: January to December

Chancellor: Mgr ALBERTO GIRALDO JARAMILLO
Rector: Mgr GONZALO RESTREPO RESTREPO
Vice-Rector (Academic): Pbro JORGE IVÁN RAMÍREZ AGUIRRE
Vice-Rector (Administration and Finance): Econ. OSCAR VELÁSQUEZ URIBE
Vice-Rector (Pastoral): Mgr CARLOS LUQUE AGUILERA
Secretary-General: Abog. CARMEN HELENA CASTAÑO CARDONA
Library Director: OLGA BEATRIZ BERNAL LONDOÑO

Library: see under Libraries
Number of teachers: 1,746
Number of students: 7,462
Publications: *Revista Universidad Pontificia Bolivariana* (2 a year), *Boletín de Programación de Radio Bolivariana* (every 2 months), *Revista Contaminación Ambiental* (2 a year), *Escritos* (philosophy, irregular), *Administración UPB* (annually), *Comunicación Social UPB* (annually), *Cuestiones Teológicas y Filosóficas* (2 a year), *Revista de Medicina UPB* (2 a year), *Revista de la Facultad de Derecho y Ciencias* (annually), *Revista de la Facultad de Trabajo Social UPB* (annually), *Pensamiento Humanista* (annually)

DEANS

School of Business Administration: Admor. ÁLVARO GÓMEZ FERNÁNDEZ
School of Architecture: Arq. CARLOS MARIO RODRÍGUEZ
School of Communications: C.S. JORGE ALBERTO VELÁSQUEZ BETANCUR
School of Law: Abog. JOSÉ ALFREDO TAMAYO JARAMILLO
School of Design, Philosophy and Humanities: Dis. RESTREPO POSADA CLEMENCIA
School of Divinity: Pbro GUILLERMO LEÓN ZULETA SALAS
School of Education: Mg. OLGA OSORIO RAMÍREZ
School of Humanities: Mons. CARLOS LUQUE AGUILERA
School of Electrical Engineering: Ing. MARISOL OSORIO CÁRDENAS
School of Electronic Engineering: Ing. MARISOL OSORIO CÁRDENAS
School of Mechanical Engineering: Ing. JORGE MANRIQUE HENAO
School of Chemical Engineering: Ing. MARÍA ELENA SIERRA VÉLEZ
School of Medicine: Méd. MARTA BETANCUR GÓMEZ
School of Social Work: T.S. OLGA CECILIA OSPINA DE GIRALDO
School of Basic Science: Ing. BERNARDO LOPERA VILLA
School of Economics: Econ. ROBERTO ZAPATA VILLEGAS
School of Psychology: Psic. JAIRO RESTREPO RINCÓN
School of Nursing: Enf. GLORIA ANGEL JIMÉNEZ
School of Textile Engineering: Ing. JORGE MANIQUE HENAO
School of Advertising: Dis. MARÍA PATRICIA VÉLEZ BERNAL
School of Philosophy: Pbro. ALVARO MURILLO CASTAÑO
Graduate School: Ing. AUGUSTO URIBE MONTOYA

UNIVERSIDAD DEL ROSARIO – COLEGIO MAYOR DE NUESTRA SEÑORA DEL ROSARIO

Calle 14, No. 6-25, Bogotá
Telephone: (1) 2970200
Fax: (1) 2818583
E-mail: orelaint@claustro.urosario.edu.co
Internet: www.urosario.edu.co

Founded 1653
Private control
Languages of instruction: Spanish, English
Academic year: February to November

Rector: Dr HANS-PETER KNUDSEN QUEVEDO
Vice-Rector: Dr JOSÉ MANUEL RESTREPO ABONDANO
Secretary-General: Dr LUIS ENRIQUE NIETO A.
Librarian: Dra MARGARITA LISOWSKA

Number of teachers: 692 (130 full-time, 138 half-time, 424 part-time)
Number of students: 6,066 (4,227 undergraduates, 1,839 graduates)
Publications: *Revista Desafíos*, *Revista de Economía del Rosario*, *Revista Estudios Sociojurídicos*, *Revista Universidad – Empresa* (2 a year)

DEANS

Faculty of Business Administration: Dr LUIS FERNANDO RESTREPO
Faculty of Continuing Education: Dra TERESITA CARDONA
Faculty of Economics: Dr HERNÁN JARAMILLO SALAZAR
Faculty of Hearing and Speech Therapy: Dr JAVIER SUÁREZ CASALLAS
Faculty of International Business: Dr LUIS FERNANDO RESTREPO
Faculty of International Finance and Commerce: Dr HERNAN JARAMILLO
Faculty of International Relations: Dr EDUARDO BARAJAS S.
Faculty of Journalism and Public Opinion: Dr CHRISTIAN SCHUMACHER GAGELMANN
Faculty of Law: Dr ALEJANDRO VENEGAS FRANCO
Faculty of Medicine: Dr LEONARDO PALACIOS
Faculty of Occupational Therapy: Dr JAVIER SUÁREZ CASALLAS
Faculty of Philosophy: Dr CHRISTIAN SCHUMACHER G.
Faculty of Physical Therapy: Dr JAVIER SUÁREZ CASALLAS
Faculty of Political Science: Dr EDUARDO BARAJAS S.
Faculty of Sociology: Dr CHRISTIAN SCHUMACHER GAGELMANN

UNIVERSIDAD SANTIAGO DE CALÍ

Apdo Aéreo 4102, Calle 5 No. 62-00 (Pampalinda), Calí, Valle del Cauca
Telephone: (2) 5183000
Fax: (2) 5516567
E-mail: secgener@usaca.edu.co
Internet: www.usaca.edu.co

Founded 1958
Private control
Languages of instruction: Spanish, English
Academic year: January to December

Rector: HEBERT CELÍN NAVAS
Vice-Rector: JOSÉ IGNACIO ZAMUDIO FRANCO
Administrative Director: CARLOS JULIO BARRERO SANMIGUEL
Director for University Welfare: WILSON LÓPEZ ARAGÓN
General Secretary: JORGE ELIÉCER TAMAYO MARULANDA
Academic Registrar: LUZ MARIA CANO ARIAS
Library Director: JAVIER SALDARRIAGA ARANGO

Number of teachers: 1,368
Number of students: 13,469

DIRECTORS OF PROGRAMMES

Undergraduate Programmes:
- Law and Political Sciences: MARTHA CECILIA FERNÁNDEZ CHÁVEZ
- Business Administration: KADIR ENRIQUEZ ECHEVERRY
- Public Accountancy: JAIRO CAMPAZ
- Industrial Engineering (Daytime Course): DANILO CÁRDENAS ERAZO
- Business Education, Industrial Engineering (Evening Course): ALEXANDER CIFUENTES ALARCÓN
- Electronic Engineering: CARLOS ORLANDO SAENZ BLANCO
- Business Administration and Management: DIEGO GARCÍA ZAPATA
- Professionalization: DIEGO GARCÍA ZAPATA
- Administration of Coastal and Marine Resources: DIEGO GARCÍA ZAPATA
- Commercial Engineering: FABIO GRISALES MORENO
- International Business and Finance: ROBERTO LEÓN ZAPATA NAVARRO
- Technology in International Business and Finance: ROBERTO LEÓN ZAPATA NAVARRO
- Continuing Education: UBERNEY MARULANDA GIRALDO
- Economics: GENTIL ROJAS LIBREROS
- Social Communication: ARTURO HERNÁN ARENAS FERNÁNDEZ
- Medicine: OSCAR ANTONIO BOLAÑOS MANRIQUE
- Odontology and Dental Machinery: CARLOS EMIRO TASAMÁ MEJÍA
- Surgical Instruments: GONZALO MARTÍNEZ ARANGO
- Radiology and Diagnostic Imaging: ALBERTO NICOLÁS DURÁN S.
- Respiratory Therapy: LOUIS WOOLLEY GASPARD
- Bioengineering: LIBARDO SÁNCHEZ AGREDO
- First-aid Equipment: ERNESTO DUEÑAS VANÍN
- Physiotherapy: FRANCESCA OCAMPO VALERO
- Nursing: OLGA OSORIO MURILLO
- Audiology: LILIANA ALVAREZ BOTERO
- Psychology: ALONSO GIRALDO MARULANDA
- Telematics and Systems Engineering: MARCO ANTONIO RODRÍGUEZ
- Systems Engineering Technology: MARCO ANTONIO RODRÍGUEZ
- Advertising: LEONARDO PEÑA CALDERÓN
- Biology and Chemistry: ESPERANZA GALARZA DE BECERRA
- Pre-school Education: OMAIRA HURTADO MARTÍNEZ
- Modern Languages: LILIANA GÓMEZ DÍAZ
- Business Administration (Scheme B): MILTON FLÓREZ HURTADO

Postgraduate Programmes:
- Administrative Law, Penal Law, Family Law, Environmental Law: MARINO GUTIÉRREZ OSORIO
- Teaching in Higher Education, Intellectual Development, Environmental Education, Social Sciences, Geography, History: ARMANDO ZAMBRANO LEAL
- Management Control and Auditing in Health Services, Occupational Health Management, Business Management, Strategic Management of Information Systems, Global Marketing, Environmental Management and Sustainable Development: RICARDO ASTUDILLO VELLEGAS
- Policy Management: LIBARDO OREJUELA DÍAZ
- Management in Pharmaceutical Sciences: EDUARDO CASTRO FERNÁNDEZ
- Criminology, Penology: GONZALO RODRIGO PAZ MAHECHA

ATTACHED INSTITUTES

Institute of Criminology: Dir GONZALO RODRIGO PAZ MAHECHA.

Language Institute: Dir MARILYN MOLANO MELO.

Centre for Legal Studies and Research: Dir (vacant).

Centre for Engineering Studies and Research: Dir (vacant).

Centre for Studies and Research in Social Communication and Advertising: Dir (vacant).

Antonio Llanos Cultural Centre: Dir (vacant).

UNIVERSIDAD DE SAN BUENAVENTURA

Trans. 26, No. 172-08, Apdo Aéreo 50679, Bogotá, D.C.
Telephone: (1) 6671090

Fax: (1) 6773003
Internet: www.usbbog.edu.co
Founded 1708, University status 1961
Private control
Language of instruction: Spanish
Academic year: February to November
Rector General: Fr LUIS JAVIER URIBE MUÑOZ
Secretary-General: Fr LUIS ARMANDO ROMERO GAONA.

CAMPUSES

Bogotá, D.C. Campus

Transversal 26, No. 172–08, Apdo Aéreo 75010, Bogotá
Telephone: (1) 6671090
Fax: (1) 6773003
Internet: www.usbbog.edu.co
Rector: Fr PABLO CASTILLO NOVA
Academic Director: Dr BLANCA DE PINILLA
Administrative Director: Dr RENÁN RODRIGUEZ CÁRDENAS
Librarian: Lic. JOSÉ BUELVAS
Number of teachers: 400
Number of students: 4,000
Publications: *Itinerario Educativo* (3 a year), *Franciscanum* (3 a year), *Management* (2 a year), *Ingenium* (2 a year)

DEANS
Faculty of Business Sciences: Dr JORGE GALEANO
Faculty of Education: Dr LUIS JAVIER CLARO
Faculty of Engineering: Ing. JAIME LEAL
Faculty of Gerontology: Dr OMAR PEÑA
Faculty of Philosophy: Fr MIGUEL ANGEL BUILES
Faculty of Psychology: Dr CLEMENCIA RAMÍREZ
Faculty of Theology: Fr FERNANDO GARZÓN

Calí Campus

La Umbría, Carretera a Pance, Apdo Aérero 25162, Calí
Telephone: (23) 552007
Fax: (23) 552006
Internet: www.usb.edu.co
Rector: Fr LUIS JAVIER URIBE MUÑOZ
Academic Director: Dr DELIO MERINO ESCOBAR
Administrative Director: Dr FRANCISCO VELASCO VELEZ
Librarian: CICILIA LIBREROS
Number of teachers: 360
Number of students: 5,041
Publications: *Economia* (2 a year), *Contaduria* (2 a year), *Ingeniería de Sistemas* (2 a year), *Educacion* (2 a year), *Derecho* (2 a year), *Boletín Institucional* (every 2 weeks), *Architectura*

DEANS
Faculty of Accountancy: Dr JUAN GUILLERMO OCAMPO
Faculty of Agroindustrial Engineering: Dr RAÚL SALAZAR
Faculty of Architecture: Dr JUAN MARCO ANGEL
Faculty of Business Administration: Dr DIDIER NAVARRO
Faculty of Economics: Dr FRANCISCO JOSÉ RIZO
Faculty of Education: Dr OCTAVIO CALVACHES
Faculty of Electronic Engineering: Dr HAROLD PEDROZA
Faculty of Industrial Engineering: Dr ARTURO HERNÁNDEZ
Faculty of Law: Dr JORGE LUIS ROMERO
Faculty of Pyschology: Dr JOEL OTERO
Faculty of Systems Engineering: Dr RICARDO LLANO

Cartagena Campus

Calle Real de Ternera, Apdo Aéreo 7833, Cartagena
Telephone: (53) 610465
Fax: (53) 630943
Internet: www.usbctg.edu.co
Rector: Fr ALBERTO MONTEALEGRE GONZÁLEZ
Academic Director: Dr NICANOR ESPINOSA
Administrative Director: Dr SILVIO MONTIEL
Secretary-General: Fr MARIO RAMOS
Number of teachers: 68
Number of students: 961

DEANS
Faculty of Accountancy: Dr DEMÓSTENES BARRIOS
Faculty of Architecture: Dr GUSTAVO LEMAITRE
Faculty of Bacteriology: Dr LOURDES BENITEZ
Faculty of Business Administration: Dr LUIS MOSQUERA
Faculty of Chemical Engineering: Dr IGNACIO BURGOS
Faculty of Food Engineering: Dr MAYRA AYUZ
Faculty of Law: Dr HERNANDO URIBE
Faculty of Physical Therapy: Dr SANDRA DÍAZ
Faculty of Psychology: Dr BERTHA NUÑEZ
Faculty of Systems Engineering: Dr JORGE BUSTOS

Medellín Campus

Carrera 56c No. 51–90, Apdo Aéreo 5222-7370, Medellín
Telephone: (4) 5113600
Fax: (4) 2316191
Internet: www.usb-med.edu.co
Rector: Fr HERNANDO ARIAS RODRÍGUEZ
Administrative Director: Dr EDGAR HINCAPIÉ
Secretary-General: Fr ANDRÉS BOTERO
Number of teachers: 249
Number of students: 2,640

DEANS
Faculty of Architecture: Dr MARCO BAQUERO
Faculty of Business Science: Dr HERNÁN ARIAS
Faculty of Education: Dr LUIS ALBERTO RADA
Faculty of Engineering: Dr JESÚS LONDOÑO
Faculty of Law: Dr JUAN SÁNCHEZ
Faculty of Psychology: Dr ENRIQUE ARBELÁEZ
Faculty of Sociology: Dr GUILLERMO RIVERA

UNIVERSIDAD SANTO TOMÁS

Carrera 9A, No. 51–23, POB 75032, Bogotá
Telephone: (1) 3484141
Fax: (1) 5740383
E-mail: sistemas@usta.edu.co
Internet: www.usta.edu.co
Founded 1580; restored 1965
Academic year: February to December
Rector: P. EDUARDO GONZÁLEZ GIL
Vice-Rector (Academic): P. FAUSTINO CORCHUELO ALFARO
Vice-Rector (Administrative): P. VICENTE BECERRA REYES
Secretary-General: HÉCTOR FABIO JARAMILLO SANTAMARIA
Librarian: P. ADALBERTO CARDONA GÓMEZ
Library of 69,800 vols
Number of teachers: 660
Number of students: 12,961
Publications: *Análisis*, *Cuadernos de Filosofía Latinoamericana*, *Revista Interamericana de Investigación, Educación y Pedagogía* (research and education, 2 a year), *Revista Ciencia, Tecnología y Ambiente* (science, technology and the environment, 2 a year), *Revista de Psicología*, *Revista CIFE*, *Revista Activos*

DEANS
Faculty of Civil Engineering: Ing. CARLOS ALBA MENDOZA
Faculty of Economics: Dr GILBERTO ENRIQUE HERAZO CUETO
Faculty of Electronic Engineering: Ing. CLAUDIA PATRICIA PÉREZ ROMERO
Faculty of Law: Dra LUZ AMPARO SERRANO QUINTERO
Faculty of Mechanical Engineering: JORGE ENRIQUE HERRERA FLAUTERO
Faculty of Philosophy: ALBERTO CÁRDENAS PATIÑO
Faculty of Physical Culture, Entertainment and Sports: PATRICIA CASALLAS REYES
Faculty of Psychology: EMILIO ESPEJO MOLANO
Faculty of Public Accounting: FERNANDO ARTURO RODRÍGUEZ MARTÍNEZ
Faculty of Social Communication: P. ADALMIRO ARIAS AGUDELO
Faculty of Sociology: RICARDO ARTURO ARIZA LÓPEZ
Faculty of Telecommunications Engineering: MAURICIO SAMUDIO LIZCANO

POSTGRADUATE INSTITUTES
Administration: Dir HERNÁN BOJACÁ MARTÍN.
Administration and Management of Quality Systems: Dir GERMÁN DARÍO MARÍN SEGURA.
Health Auditing: Dir Dr CARLOS IVÁN RODRÍGUEZ MELO.
Tax Auditing: Dir TAYRON ROA VARGAS.
Public Accounting: Dir TAYRON ROA VARGAS.
Administrative Law: Dir MARIA EUGENIA SAMPER.
Business and Commercial Law: Dir HERNANDO ACOSTA RODRÍGUEZ.
Family Law: Dir LUZ AMPARO SERRANO QUINTERO.
Penal Law: Dir YESID REYES ALVARADO.
Clinical and Family Psychology: Dir JAIRO ESTUPIÑAN MOJICA.
Economics: Dir DANILO TORRES REINA.
Finance: Dir HERNÁN BOJACÁ MARTÍN.
Management of Health and Social Security Institutions: Dir Dr CARLOS IVÁN RODRÍGUEZ MELO.
International Business Management: Dir Dr JAVIER OSWALDO GUECHA MARIÑO.
Strategic Management of Financial Institutions: Dir DANILO TORRES REINA.
Technical Management of Electronic Engineering Projects: Dir LUIS ALFONSO INFANTE.
Electronic Instrumentation: Dir LUIS ALFONSO INFANTE.
Systematic Family Supervision: Dir JAIRO ESTUPIÑAN MOJICA.
Juridical Psychology: Dir FERNANDO DÍAZ COLORADO.
Political Sociology and Governmental Administration: Dir Dra ANA MEDINA DE RUÍZ.
Socioeconomic Planning: Dir Dr DIEGO GIRALDO SAMPER.
Latin-American Philosophy: Dir CARMENZA NEIRA.
Systems Auditing: Dir Dr JAVIER OSWALDO GUECHA MARIÑO.

OTHER CAMPUSES

Bucaramanga Campus

Carrera 18, No. 9–27, Apdo Aéreo 75010, Bucaramanga
Telephone: (976) 712970
Fax: (976) 717067
E-mail: ustabuca@coll.telecom.com.co
Internet: www.usta.edu.co
Academic year: February to December
Sectional Rector: P. CARLOS ARTURO DÍAZ RODRÍGUEZ
Administrative Vice-Rector: P. JESÚS ANTONIO CEBALLOS GIRALDO
Academic Vice-Rector: P. PEDRO JOSÉ DÍAZ CAMACHO
General Secretary: Dr JOSÉ PABLO SANTAMARÍA
Library of 46,887 vols
Number of teachers: 423
Number of students: 4,500
Publications: *Temas* (humanities, 2 a year), *Iusticia* (law, 2 a year)

Tunja Campus

Calle 1 No. 11–64, Apdo Aéreo, Tunja
Telephone: (8) 7445847
Fax: (8) 7445851
E-mail: rectoria@ustatunja.edu.co
Internet: www.usta.edu.co
Academic year: January to December
Sectional Rector: P. JOSÉ ANTONIO BALAGUERA CEPEDA
Administrative Vice-Rector: P. CARLOS ARIEL BETANCOURT OSPINA
Academic Vice-Rector: P. SAMUEL ELIAS FORERO BUITRAGO
General Secretary (vacant)
Library of 6,800 vols
Number of teachers: 114
Number of students: 1,500
Publications: *Principia Iuris* (2 a year), *Iter Veritatis* (2 a year), *Colecciones Investigando* (annually).

UNIVERSIDAD DE LA SALLE

Apdo Aéreo 28638, Bogotá
Telephone: 2842606
Fax: 2815064
Internet: www.lasalle.edu.co
Founded 1964
Academic year: February to May, July to October
Rector: Bro. JOSE VICENTE HENRY VALBUENA
Academic Vice-Rector: Bro. LUIS HUMBERTO BOLÍVAR RODRÍGUEZ
Administrative Vice-Rector: Dr ORLANDO ORTIZ PEÑA
Vice-Rector for Promotion and Human Development: Bro. JOSE ANTONIO RODRÍGUEZ OTERO
Secretary-General: Dr JUAN GUILLERMO DURÁN MANTILLA
Librarian: Dr NAPOLEÓN MUÑOZ NEDA
Number of teachers: 1,000
Number of students: 11,300
Publications: *Revista de la Universidad*, *Ensayo en Administración*, *Reflejos*

DEANS

Faculty of Architecture: Dr TOMÁS FERNANDO URIBE
Faculty of Civil Engineering: Dr MIGUEL ORTEGA RESTREPO
Faculty of Economics: Dr SEBASTIÁN ARANGO FONNEGRA
Faculty of Education: Dra LUZ AMPARO MARTÍNEZ R.
Faculty of Philosophy and Letters: Dr LUIS ENRIQUE RUÍZ LÓPEZ
Faculty of Optometry: Dr CARLOS HERNANDO MENDOZA
Faculty of Library Science and Archives: Dr HUGO NOEL PARRA FLÓREZ
Faculty of Agricultural Administration: Dr CARLOS ARTURO GONZÁLEZ
Faculty of Accountancy: Dr JESÚS MARÍA PEÑA BERMÚDEZ
Faculty of Sanitary Engineering: Dr CAMILO H. GUÁQUETA R.
Faculty of Veterinary Medicine: Dr GONZALO LUQUE FORERO
Faculty of Social Work: Dra ROSA MARGARITA VARGAS
Faculty of Stockbreeding: Dr GERMÁN SERRANO QUINTERO
Faculty of Food Engineering: LUIS FELIPE MAZUERA
Faculty of Business Administration: Dr JESÚS SANTOS AMAYA
Division of Advanced Training: Dr FELIPE REYES DE LA VEGA

Schools of Art and Music

Conservatorio Nacional de Música (National Conservatory of Music): Dpto de Música, Facultad de Artes, Universidad Nacional, Bogotá; fax (1) 3681551; f. 1882 as Academia Nacional de Música, present name 1910; basic and university-level courses; 60 teachers; 900 students; library: 11,000 vols, scores and records; Dir LUIS E. AGUDELO.

Conservatorio de Música de la Universidad del Atlántico: Calle 68, No. 53–45, Apdo Aéreo 1890, Barranquilla; f. 1939; 21 teachers; 400 students; Dir Prof. GUNTER RENZ.

Conservatorio del Tolima: Calle 9, No. 1–18, Apdo Aéreo 615, Ibagué; tel. (82) 639139; fax (82) 615378; internet www.bundenet.com/umusical; f. 1906; 121 teachers; 1,295 students; library: 3,216 vols; Rector IVETTE JOSEFINA GARDEAZABAL MICOLTA.

Escuela de Música: Universidad de Nariño, Calle 21 No. 23-90, Pasto, Nariño; Dir FAUSTO MARTINEZ.

Escuela de Pintura y Artes Plásticas: Universidad del Atlántico, Calle 68, No. 53–54, Barranquilla; f. 1961; teaching of plastic arts; staff of 11; library: 1,900 vols; Dir Dr EDUARDO VIDES CELIS.

Instituto Musical de Cartagena: Apdo Aéreo No. 17–67, Cartagena, Bolívar; f. 1890; 12 teachers; 340 students; library: 1,500 vols; Dir Prof. JIRI PITRO M..

COMOROS

The Higher Education System

The Comoros declared their independence from France in 1975. French is one of the official languages, along with Comorian and Arabic. For many years higher education in the Comoros was limited to a number of programmes in teacher training, agriculture and health sciences at colleges and schools. Many students left the Comoros to study abroad; the World Bank estimated that 1,000 students did so in 1995. The Government provided scholarships for these students, but relied on funds from international donors to do so. The islands' first university, the Université des Comores, opened in December 2003. There was an enrolment of 2,187 students in 2004/05.

Illiteracy, especially among females, poses serious difficulties for the Comoros (as in many African countries). The development of higher education is hampered by the absence of a viable primary and secondary education system. In the Comoros more than one-third of school-age children have no access to six-year formal education; of those who do have access only one-tenth continue to lower-secondary education. Enrolment levels at primary, secondary and post-secondary education are estimated at 64%, 11% and just 2%, respectively.

Research Institute

AGRICULTURE, FISHERIES AND VETERINARY SCIENCE

Institut National de la Recherche pour L'Agriculture, La Pêche et l'Environment (INRAPE): Moroni; tel. 736688; fax 736357; agricultural and environmental research; Dir-Gen ABOUBACAR ALLAOUI.

Library

Moroni

Centre National de Documentation et de Recherche Scientifique (CNDRS): BP 169, Moroni; tel. 744187; fax 744189; f. 1979; incorporates the national library and archives, national museum and research centre (human and natural sciences); Dir Dr DJAFFAR MMADI.

University

UNIVERSITÉ DES COMORES

Route de la corniche BP 2585, Moroni
Telephone: 734227
E-mail: univ_com@snpt.km
Internet: www.univ-comores.com

Founded 2003
State control
Pres.: MOHAMED RACHADI.

DEMOCRATIC REPUBLIC OF THE CONGO

The Higher Education System

Prior to independence from Belgium in 1960, the country was known as Belgian Congo. Following independence it became the Democratic Republic of the Congo, and then Zaire in 1971; in 1997 the name reverted to Democratic Republic of the Congo. The oldest university is the Université de Kinshasa (formerly Université Lovanium), which was founded in 1954 by the Université Catholique de Louvain (Belgium). Between 1971 and 1981 the Université de Kinshasa was merged with the Université de Kisangani (formerly the Protestant-run Université Libre du Congo, founded 1963) and the Université de Lubumbashi (founded 1955) to form the National University of Zaire (UNAZA). Since 1981 these three state-run universities have reverted to autonomous institutions. There are also private universities at Kinshasa, Bas-Congo, Bakavu, Butembo and Goma. Other institutions of higher education include technical institutes and teaching institutes. In 1998/99 there were an estimated 60,341 students in tertiary education.

In 1997 the former ministries of primary, secondary, technical and higher education were merged into a supra-Ministry of National Education. As a result of the prolonged civil conflict, government funding for education was effectively suspended, contributing to a decline in enrolment. In 2002 an emergency programme for education, with an estimated cost of US $101m., was introduced to restore access to basic education. Administration of higher education is split between government ministries: the Ministry of Finance controls budget allocation; the Ministry of the Civil Service controls personnel; and the Ministry of Planning oversees the use of human resources. Senior administrative and academic figures, such as the Rector and heads of department, are appointed by the President and/or the Minister of National Education.

The Diplôme d'Etat d'Etudes Secondaires du Cycle Long is required for admission to university education. University degree programmes are divided into three cycles. The first cycle lasts three years and leads to the award of Graduat; the second cycle lasts two to three years and results in the award of the Licence, though some programmes, such as medicine and veterinary medicine, may require longer; and the third cycle is a two- to four-year programme of postgraduate study resulting in either Diplôme d'Études Spéciales (DES) or Diplôme de Spécialiste. Doctorates in agriculture are also available.

Technological and teaching-training institutes attached to universities provide three-year courses of higher vocational education, leading to the award of the Gradué.

Learned Societies

GENERAL

UNESCO Office Kinshasa: Immeuble Losonia, Blvd du 30 juin, POB 7248, Kinshasa; tel. 8848253; fax 8848252; e-mail kinshasa@unesco.org; Head of Office CATHERINE OKAI.

BIBLIOGRAPHY, LIBRARY SCIENCE AND MUSEOLOGY

Association des Archivistes, Bibliothécaires et Documentalistes: BP 805, Kinshasa 11; f. 1973, to assist the Government in the planning and organization of archives, libraries and documentation centres; professional training and seminars.

HISTORY, GEOGRAPHY AND ARCHAEOLOGY

Société des Historiens: BP 7246, Lubumbashi; f. 1974; attached to Min. of Higher Education and Scientific Research; aims to bring about a better understanding of the nation's past; to organize meetings, etc. for historians; to preserve the national archives, works of art, and archaeological remains; Pres. Prof. NDAYWEL È NZIEM; Sec.-Gen. Prof. Dr TSHIBANGU MUSAS KABET; publs *Likundoli* (2 a year), *Etudes d'Histoire Africaine* (annually).

LANGUAGE AND LITERATURE

Alliance Française: 11, Ave Lubefu, Commune de la Gombe, BP 5404, Kinshasa 10; tel. 8803221; fax 8804707; e-mail alliancefrancaise.kinshasa@ic.cd; offers courses and exams in French language and culture and promotes cultural exchange with France; attached teaching centres in Boma, Bukavu, Kananga, Kikwit, Kisangani, Lubumbashi and Matadi.

Research Institutes

GENERAL

Centre de Recherche en Sciences Humaines (CRSH): BP 3474, Kinshasa/Gombe; f. 1985 by fusion of IRS and ONRD; economics, law, administration, philosophy, linguistics, literature, sociology, social sciences, education, psychology, history; 94 research mems; library of 4,000 vols and 12,000 periodicals; Dir-Gen. MAKWALA MA MAVAMBU YE BEDA; publs *Cahier Zaïrois de Recherche en Sciences Humaines* (quarterly), *IRS—Information*.

AGRICULTURE, FISHERIES AND VETERINARY SCIENCE

Institut National pour l'Etude et la Recherche Agronomique (INERA): BP 2037, Kinshasa 1; tel. 32332; f. 1933; agronomical study and research; 2,250 staff; library of 38,428 vols; Pres. Dr Ir. MASIMANGO NDYANABO; publs *Rapport Annuel*, *Programme d'Activités* (annually), *Bulletin Agroclimatologique* (annually), *Bulletin Agricole du Zaïre* (2 a year), *Info-INERA* (monthly).

HISTORY, GEOGRAPHY AND ARCHAEOLOGY

Institut Géographique: 106 blvd du 30 Juin, BP 3086, Kinshasa-Gombe; f. 1949; geodetic, topographical, photogrammetric and cartographic studies; small library; Dir-Gen. Major LUBIKU LUSIENSE BELANI.

MEDICINE

Institut de Médecine Tropicale: BP 1697, Kinshasa; f. 1899; clinical laboratory serving Hôpital Mama Yemo with reference laboratory functions for other medical services in Kinshasa; Dir Dr DARLY JEANTY.

NATURAL SCIENCES

Biological Sciences

Institut Congolais pour la Conservation de la Nature: BP 868, Kinshasa 1; tel. 31401; f. 1925; 2,295 staff; library of 2,500 vols; Man. Dir EULALIE BASHIGE; publ. *Revue Leopard*.

TECHNOLOGY

Bureau de Recherches Géologiques et Minières (BRGM): BP 1974, Kinshasa 1; copper mining; Dir G. VINCENT; (see main entry under France).

Centre de Recherches Géologiques et Minières: 44 ave des Huileries, BP 898, Kinshasa 1; tel. 99-28-982; e-mail crgm@cedesurk.refer.org; f. 1939; staff of 120 undertake mineral exploration and geological mapping; library of 7,305 vols; Dir-Gen. Prof. NTOMBI MUEN KABEYA; publ. *Revue* (weekly).

Commissariat Général à l'Energie Atomique: BP 868-184, Kinshasa XI; f. 1959; scientific research in peaceful applications of atomic energy; 140 staff; library of 3,000 vols; Commissary Gen. Prof. MALU WA KALENGA; publs *Rapport de Recherche* (annually), *Bulletin d'Information Scientifique et Technique* (quarterly).

Libraries and Archives

Kinshasa

Archives Nationales: BP 3428, 42A ave de la Justice, Kinshasa-Gombe; tel. 31083; f. 1947; *c.* 3,000 vols; Curator KIOBE LUMENGA-NESO.

Bibliothèque Centrale de l'Université de Kinshasa: BP 125, Kinshasa 11; f. 1954; 300,000 vols; Chief Librarian (vacant); publs *Liste des Acquisitions*, *Nouvelles du Mont Amba* (weekly).

Bibliothèque Publique: BP 410, Kinshasa; f. 1932; 24,000 vols; Librarian B. MONGU.

Kisangani

Bibliothèque Centrale de l'Université de Kisangani: BP 2012, Kisangani; tel. 2948; f. 1963; 90,000 vols; Chief Librarian MUZILA LABEL KAKES.

Lubumbashi

Bibliothèque Centrale de l'Université de Lubumbashi: POB 2896, Lubumbashi; f. 1955; 300,000 vols, 1,000 periodicals, 500,000 microfiches and microfilms; Librarian MUBADI SULE MWANANSUKA; publs *Séries A, Lettres*, *Cahiers Philosophiques Africains* (every 2 months), *Likundoli* (irregular).

Museums and Art Galleries

Kananga

Musée National de Kananga: 160 Ave Kinkole, BP 612, Kananga.

Kinshasa

Musée National de Kinshasa: BP 4249, Kinshasa.

Lubumbashi

Musée National de Lubumbashi: BP 2375, Lubumbashi.

Universities

UNIVERSITÉ DE KINSHASA

BP 127, Kinshasa 11

Telephone: 30123

Founded 1954 as the Université Lovanium by the Université Catholique de Louvain in collaboration with the Government; reorganized 1971 and 1981

Language of instruction: French

Academic year: October to July

Rector: BOGUO MAKELI

Secretary-General: KAPETA NZOVU

Library: see Libraries and Archives

Number of teachers: 536

Number of students: 5,800

Publications: *Annales* (faculty publs, 2 a year), *Cahiers Economiques et Sociaux* (quarterly)

DEANS

Faculty of Economics: KINTAMBO MAFUKU

Faculty of Law: KISAKA KIA KOY

Faculty of Medicine: Dr NGALA KENDA

Faculty of Pharmacy: MULUMBA BIPI

Faculty of Sciences: MUKANA WA MURANA

Polytechnic Faculty: ANDRE DE BOECK

ATTACHED RESEARCH INSTITUTES

Centre de Cardiologie.

Centre Interdisciplinaire pour le Développement et l'Education Permanente (CIDEP): BP 2307, Kinshasa 1; training courses in management; branches at Kisangani, Lubumbashi and Karanga; politics and administration, commerce, social sciences, applied education, applied technology; 1,785 students; Sec.-Gen. MBULAMOKO ZENGE MOVOAMBE.

Centre Interdisciplinaire d'Etudes et de Documentation Politiques (CIE-DOP).

Centre de Recherches pour le Développement.

Centre de Recherche pour l'Exploitation de l'Energie Renouvelable (CREER).

Centre de Recherche Interdisciplinaire pour le Droit de l'Homme.

Institut d'Etudes et de Recherche Historique du Temps Présent.

Institut de Recherches Economiques et Sociales (IRES): BP 257, Kinshasa 11; Dir ILUNGA ILUKAMBA.

Institut des Sciences et Techniques de l'Information (ISTI): BP 14.998, Kinshasa 1; first degrees and doctorates; 15 staff; 103 students; Dir-Gen. MALEMBE TAMANDIAK.

Institut Supérieur des Bâtiments et Travaux Publics (IBTP): BP 4.731, Kinshasa 2; 83 staff; 916 students; Dir-Gen. BUTASNA BU NIANGA.

Institut Supérieur d'Arts et Métiers (ISAM): BP 15.198, Kinshasa 1; f. 1968; management training for the clothing industry; 18 staff, 101 students; Dir OMONGA OKAKO DENEWADE.

Institut Supérieur de Commerce, Kinshasa: BP 16.596, Kinshasa 1; 37 staff; 600 students; Dir-Gen. PANUKA D'ZENTEMA.

Institut Supérieur de Techniques Appliquées (ISTA): BP 6593, Kinshasa 31; tel. 20727; f. 1971; technical training; 513 staff; 5,814 students; library of 3,443 vols, 2,486 periodicals, 2,789 dissertations; Dir-Gen. Prof. MUKANA WA MUANDA (acting).

Institut Supérieur des Techniques Médicales (ISTM): BP 774, Kinshasa 11; tel. 22113; f. 1981; 80 staff, 1,005 students; Dir-Gen. Dr PHAKA MBUMBA.

Laboratoire d'Analyses des Médicaments et des Aliments

UNIVERSITÉ DE KISANGANI

BP 2012, Kisangani

Telephone: 2152

Founded 1963; present name 1981

State control

Language of instruction: French

Academic year: October to July (three terms)

Rector: MWABILA MADELA

Administrative Secretary: GUDIJIGA A GIKAPA

Academic Secretary: BOKULA MOISO

Budget Administrator: LINDONGA TEMELE-ZEMAKA

Library: see Libraries and Archives

Number of teachers: 216

Number of students: 2,439

Publication: *Le Cahier du CRIDE*

Faculties of science, medicine, social sciences, political science, administration..

ATTACHED RESEARCH INSTITUTES

Bureau Africain des Sciences de l'Education (BASE): BP 14, Kisangani; Dir A. S. MUNGALA.

Centre de Recherche Interdisciplinaire pour le Développement de l'Education (CRIDE): BP 1386, Kisangani; Dir KALALA NKUDI.

Institut Facultaire des Sciences Agronomiques (IFA): BP 1232, Kisangani; f. 1973; first degrees and doctorates in agriculture; 38 teachers; 683 students; library of 7,141 vols, 14,574 periodicals; Rector Dr Ir Prof. MAMBANI BANDA; publ. *Annales*.

Institut Supérieur de Commerce, Kisangani: BP 2.012, Kisangani; Dir KABAMBI MULAMBA.

Institut Supérieur d'Etudes Agronomiques de Bengamisa: BP 202, Kisangani; 31 staff; 328 students; Dir-Gen. LUMPUNGU KABAMBA.

UNIVERSITÉ KONGO

BP 202, Mbanza-Ngungu, Bas-Congo

Telephone: 232132

Founded 1990 as University de Bas-Zaïre

Private Control

Language of instruction: French

Rector: Prof. B. LUTULALA MUMPHASI

Secretary-General (Academic Affairs): Prof. PHUKU PHUATI

Secretary-General (Administration): F. KITUBA MAKUNSA

Number of teachers: 154

Number of students: 816

DEANS

Faculty of Agronomy: Prof. K. MAFWILA

Faculty of Economics and Management: Prof. KAMIANTAKO MIYAMWENI

Faculty of Law: Prof. K. BUKA

Faculty of Literature and Social Communication: (vacant)

Faculty of Medicine: Prof. Dr MBANZULU PITA

Polytechnic Faculty: Prof. PHUKU PHUATI

UNIVERSITÉ DE LUBUMBASHI

BP 1825, Lubumbashi

Telephone: 225285

E-mail: unilu@unilu.net

Internet: www.unilu.net/

Founded 1955; reorganized 1971 and 1981

Language of instruction: French

State control

Academic year: October to July (October–February, March–July)

Rector: Prof. KAUMBA LUFUNDA

Secretary-General (Academic): Prof. HUIT MULONGO

Secretary-General (Administrative): CHABU MUMBA

Chief Librarian: SUKA MUBADI

Number of teachers: 442

Number of students: 13,158

Publications: *Cahiers Philosophiques Africains*, various faculty publs, *Cahiers d'Études Politiques et Sociales* (2 a year), *Études d'Histoire Africaine* (2 a year), *Likundoli* (2 a year), *Mitunda* (African cultures, 2 a year), *Prospective et Perspective* (2 a year), *Recherches Linguistiques et Littéraires* (2 a year)

DEANS

Faculty of Agricultural Science: Prof. MICHEL NGONGO LUHEMBWE

Faculty of Economics: Prof. KASANGANA MWALABA

Faculty of Law: Prof. MALEMBA M. N'SAKILA

Faculty of Letters: Prof. KASHALA KAPALOWA

Faculty of Medicine: Prof. MUTETA WA PA MANDA

Polytechnic Faculty: Prof. KALENGA NGOY

Faculty of Psychology and Pedagogy: (vacant)

Faculty of Sciences: Prof. BYAMUNGU BIN RUSANGIZA

Faculty of Social, Administrative and Political Sciences: Prof. ELENGESA NDUNGUNA

Faculty of Veterinary Medicine: Prof. KASHALA KAPAWOLA

AFFILIATED RESEARCH INSTITUTES

École Supérieure de Commerce (ESC): ; Dir Prof. KIZOBO O'OBWENG O.

École Supérieure d'Ingénieur (ESI): ; Dir Prof. NGOIE NSENGA.

Institut Supérieur d'Etudes Sociales de Lubumbashi: BP 825, Lubumbashi 1; tel. 4315; f. 1956; 18 full-time staff, 785 students; Dir KITENGE YA.

Institut Supérieur de Statistique (ISS): BP 2471, Lubumbashi (Shaba); tel. 3905; f.

1967; 72 staff, 700 students; library of 3,000 vols, 10 periodicals; Dir-Gen. Prof. Dr MBAYA KAZADI; Academic Sec.-Gen. Prof. Dr ANYENYOLA WELO; Administrative Sec.-Gen. Lic. BIHINI YANKA; publ. *Annales*.

Institut Supérieur des Techniques Médicales: Dir Prof. MALONGA KAJ.

UNIVERSITY OF MBUJI-MAYI

BP 225 Ave de l'Université, Campus de Tshikama, Dibindi, Mbuji-Mayi, Kasaï Oriental

Telephone: 8854890
Fax: 8854111
E-mail: univmayi@yahoo.fr
Internet: www.fundp.ac.be/~itshiman/um/html/

Founded 1990
Private Control (Catholic Church)
Language of instruction: French
Academic year: November to July
Rector: RAPHAËL MBOWA KALENGAYI
Library of 14,000 , 75 periodicals
Number of teachers: 134
Number of students: 904

Faculties of Applied Science, Economics, Human Medicine and Law.

Colleges

Académie des Beaux-Arts (ABA): BP 8.349, Kinshasa 1; 44 staff; 248 students; Dir BEMBIKA NKUNKU.

Institut National des Arts (INA): BP 8332, 1 ave du Commerce, Zone en Gombé, Kinshasa 1; 72 staff; 147 students; Dir Prof. BAKOMBA KATIK DIONG.

REPUBLIC OF CONGO

The Higher Education System

Higher education was established while the Republic of Congo was under French administration (it was then part of French Equatorial Africa), through the foundation of an Institute for Advanced Studies and a Centre for Advanced Administrative and Technical Studies. Following independence in 1960 the Fondation de l'Enseignement Supérieur en Afrique Centrale was created, which comprised several centres and schools. It was dissolved in 1971 and in the same year the Université de Brazzaville was inaugurated; in 1977 it adopted its current name, Université Marien-Ngouabi. In 2000 there were some 20,000 students enrolled at the Université Marien-Ngouabi, which is the only state university. Public education exists at two levels: university and non-university. Private initiatives are also increasingly moving into the higher education system, providing mainly technical and professional training in subjects such as business management. Some Congolese students also attend further education establishments abroad. In September 2004 the World Bank approved a grant of US $20m. to assist with the reconstruction of the country's educational sector, which had been severely damaged by years of civil conflict.

The four types of higher educational establishment—public and private universities, training schools and institutions of continuing education—are stipulated in the 1990 law related to education, which was modified by the November 1995 law (008/90) defining the organizational structures of the Congolese educational system. This law also stipulates a number of depositions, among them equality in access, free public education, the Government's responsibility for the organization of education and the recognition of the private sector.

Admissions to the Université Marien-Ngouabi are determined by ministerial decree. Generally, the university accepts candidates of Congolese nationality and foreigners holding a high school degree (baccalauréat) or its equivalent in return for an application fee. University-level qualifications are divided into two cycles: first, either the Diplôme Universitaire d'Etudes Littéraires (DUEL) in arts and humanities or the Diplôme Universitaire d'Etudes Scientifiques (DUES) in the sciences is awarded after two years of study; second, the Licence is awarded after an additional two years of study after DUEL/DUES, with an option of studying a further two years for the Diplôme des Etudes Supérieures (DES). There are no Masters or doctoral programmes. There are also professional institutes and schools which award the DES, usually after two-year courses of study.

Learned Societies

GENERAL

Union Panafricaine de la Science et de la Technologie (UPST): Ave E. P. Lumumba, BP 2339, Brazzaville; tel. 83-65-35; fax 83-21-85; f. 1987; co-ordinates research into scientific and technological development; mems: *c.* 409 associations, academies, societies and research institutes; Pres. Prof. EDWARD S. AYENSU; publ. *Nouvelles de l'UPST* (quarterly).

LANGUAGE AND LITERATURE

PEN Centre of Congo: BP 2181, Brazzaville; tel. 81-36-01; fax 81-36-01; Pres. E. B. DONGALA.

Research Institutes

GENERAL

Direction Générale de la Recherche Scientifique et Technique: BP 2499, Brazzaville; tel. 81-06-07; f. 1966; special commissions for medical science, natural sciences, industrial and technological sciences, social sciences and agricultural sciences; library of 4,500 vols; Dir-Gen. Prof. MAURICE ONANGA; publ. *Sciences et Technologies*.

Institut de Recherche pour le Développement (IRD): BP 1286, Zone Industrielle, Pointe-Noire; tel. 94-02-38; fax 94-39-81; e-mail ird-pnr.dir@cg.celrelplus.com; f. 1950; biological and physical oceanography, pedology, nematology, botany, plant ecology, plant physiology; library; (see main entry under France); Dir LAURENT VEYSSEYRE.

Institut de Recherche pour le Développement (IRD–DGRST): BP 181, Brazzaville; tel. 83-26-80; fax 83-29-77; f. 1947; bioclimatology, hydrology, soil science, botany, entomology, medical epidemiology, phytopathology, nutrition, microbiology, demography and sociology; library of 16,000 vols; Dir C. REICHENFELD; (see main entry under France).

AGRICULTURE, FISHERIES AND VETERINARY SCIENCE

Centre de Recherche Forestière du Littoral: BP 764, Pointe-Noire; tel. and fax 94-39-12; f. 1992; forestry research; Dir Dr MAURICE DIABANGOUAYA.

Centre d'Etudes sur les Ressources Végétales (CERVE): BP 1249, Brazzaville; tel. 81-21-83; f. 1985; attached to Min. of Scientific Research; catalogues plant species of the Congo; promotes traditional phytotherapy; develops indigenous and exotic fodder plants; library of 100 vols; Dir Prof. LAURENT TCHISSAMBOU.

Station Fruitière du Congo: BP 27, Loudima; f. 1963; Dir C. MAKAY.

HISTORY, GEOGRAPHY AND ARCHAEOLOGY

Centre de Recherche Géographique et de Production Cartographique: Ave de l'OUA, BP 125, Brazzaville; tel. 81-07-80; e-mail cergec@hotmail.com; f. 1945; attached to Min. of Scientific Research; library of 2,786 vols; Dir F. ELONGO.

MEDICINE

Direction de la Médecine Préventive: BP 236, Brazzaville; tel. 81-43-51; f. 1978; attached to Ministry of Health and Social Affairs; responsible for carrying out policy on endemo-epidemic illnesses; 98 staff; Dir Dr RÉNÉ CODDY-ZITSAMELE; publ. publs various reports and research papers.

TECHNOLOGY

Centre de Recherche et d'Initiation des Projets de Technologie (CRIPT): BP 97, Brazzaville; tel. 51-44-95; fax 81-03-30; f. 1986; under the Ministry of Scientific Research; aims to develop farming and forestry, to promote the creation of industry, to set up projects concerned with industrial science and technology, and to adapt imported technology for local requirements; Dir Dr GASTON GABRIEL ELLALY.

Libraries and Archives

Brazzaville

Bibliothèque Nationale Populaire: BP 1489, Brazzaville; tel. 83-34-85; f. 1971; 15,000 vols (7,000 in branches); Dir PIERRE MAYOLA.

Bibliothèque des Sciences de la Santé et Centre de Documentation/AFRO Health Sciences Library and Documentation Centre: BP 6, Brazzaville; tel. 241-39425; fax 241-39673; f. 1952; 7,000 vols; Librarian MARIE-PAULE KABORE.

Bibliothèque Universitaire, Université Marien Ngouabi: BP 2025, Brazzaville; tel. 83-14-30; f. 1992; 78,000 vols; Chief Librarian INNOCENT MABIALA; publs *Cahiers congolais d'anthropologie et d'histoire*, *Cahiers de la Jurisprudence*, *Congolaise de Droit*, *Revue*.

Centre d'Information des Nations Unies: BP 1018, Ave Foch, Brazzaville; tel. 83-50-90; fax 83-61-40; f. 1983; affiliated to UN Dept of Information in New York; 4,378 vols (mostly NGO publs); Dir ISMAEL A. DIALLO; publs *Notes d'Information, monthly list of acquisitions*.

Museums and Art Galleries

Brazzaville

Musée National: BP 994, Brazzaville; tel. 81-03-30; f. 1965; ethnographic collection and national history; library of 285 vols; Dir JEAN GILBERT JULES KOULOUFOUA.

Kinkala

Musée Régional André Grenard Matsoua: BP 85, Kinkala; tel. 85-20-14; f. 1978; under the Min. of Culture and the Arts; ethnography; 5 staff; library; Curator BIVINGOU-NZEINGUI.

Pointe Noire

Musée Régional Ma-Loango Diosso: BP 1225, Pointe-Noire; tel. 94-15-79; f. 1982; attached to Min. of Culture and Arts; collects historical, ethnographical, scientific, artistic materials as a source of information on Congolese culture; Curator JOSEPH KIMFOKO-MADOUNGOU; publ. guide.

University

UNIVERSITÉ MARIEN-NGOUABI

BP 69, Brazzaville

Telephone: 81-01-41
Fax: 81-01-41

Founded 1961 as Centre d'Etudes Administratives et Techniques Supérieur; became University de Brazzaville 1971; present name 1977
State control
Language of instruction: French

Rector: CHARLES MBALAWA GOMBE

Library: see Libraries and Archives
Number of teachers: 550
Number of students: 15,844

Publications: *Sango* (every 2 months), *Annales, DIMI, Revue médicale du Congo, Mélanges*

DEANS

Faculty of Arts and Humanities: PAUL NZETE
Faculty of Economics: HERVÉ DIATA
Faculty of Health Sciences: GEORGES MOYEN
Faculty of Law: BERNARD TCHICAYA
Faculty of Science: JEAN MOALI

DIRECTORS OF SCHOOLS

Ecole Normale d'Administration et de Magistrature (ENAM): CYRIAQUE AYON-BOUE
Ecole Normale Supérieur (ENS): ROSALIE KAMA NIAMAYOUA
Ecole Normale Supérieure de l'Enseignement Technique (ENSET): BERNARD MABIALA

ATTACHED INSTITUTES

Institut de Développement Rural (IDR): BP 69, Brazzaville; f. 1976; Dir PAUL YOKA.

Institut Supérieur d'Education Physique et Sportive (ISEPS): BP 1100, Brazzaville; f. 1976; Dir BERNARD PACKA TCHISSAMBOU.

Institut Supérieur de Gestion: BP 2469, Brazzaville; f. 1976; Dir FRANÇOIS SITA.

Colleges

Collège d'Enseignement Technique Agricole: BP 30, Sibiti; f. 1943; Dir JEAN BOUNGOU.

Collège Technique, Commercial et Industriel de Brazzaville (et Centre d'Apprentissage): Brazzaville; f. 1959; Dir HUBERT CUOPPEY.

Ecole Supérieure Africaine des Cadres des Chemins de Fer (Higher School for Railway Engineers): Brazzaville; f. 1977; management and technical courses.

COSTA RICA

The Higher Education System

The Universidad de Costa Rica is the oldest institution of higher education in Costa Rica. It was founded in 1843 by the Roman Catholic Church as Universidad de Santo Tomás, closed in the 1880s and refounded under its current name in 1940. The Ministry of Education controls the formal education system through the aegis of the Consejo Superior de Educación (Higher Council of Education). The supervisory body of public universities is the Consejo Nacional de Rectores (National Council of Rectors). Private universities are under the control of the Consejo Nacional de Educación Superior de Universidades Privadas (National Council of Higher Education for Private Universities).

The administrative structure of a university consists of an Asamblea General (legislative body), Concejo Universitario (board of directors), Rectoría (president) and Vicerrectorías (vice-presidents). Faculties are the top academic divisions, and are sub-divided into departments. There are also attached research centres and institutes.

The Bachiller or Bachillerato is the main undergraduate qualification, for which a student is required to accrue 120–144 credits over four to five years; an additional 30–36 credits lead to the award of the Licenciado. At postgraduate level, following Bachiller or Bachillerato, a Maestría is awarded after two years of study or 60–72 credits. Finally, the Doctorado requires three-and-a-half years of study or 100–120 credits (including those accrued for the Maestría).

Technical and vocational education is offered by public and private 'para-universities'. Courses last for two to three years and lead to the award of the Diplomado or Técnico Superior.

Learned Societies

GENERAL

UNESCO Office San José: Apdo 220-2120, San Francisco de Guadalupe, San José; Paseo Colon, Avda 1 bis, Calle 28, Casa Esquinera 2810, San José; tel. 258-76-25; fax 258-74-58; e-mail san-jose@unesco.org; designated Cluster Office for Costa Rica, El Salvador, Guatemala, Honduras, Mexico, Nicaragua and Panama; Dir ALEJANDRO ALFONZO (acting).

HISTORY, GEOGRAPHY AND ARCHAEOLOGY

Academia de Geografía e Historia de Costa Rica (Costa Rican Academy of Geography and History): Apdo 4499-1000, San José; tel. 234-76-29; fax 234-76-29; f. 1940; 32 mems; Pres. Dra MARÍA EUGENIA BOZZOLI; Sec. EUGENIA IBARRA; publ. *Anales*.

LANGUAGE AND LITERATURE

Academia Costarricense de la Lengua (Costa Rican Academy of Language): Apdo 157, 1002 Paseo de los Estudiantes, San José; e-mail academia@acl.ucr.ac.cr; internet www.acl.ucr.ac.cr; f. 1923; corresp. of the Real Academia Española (Madrid); 18 mems; Dir ALBERTO F. CAÑAS ESCALANTE; Sec. FERNANDO DURÁN AYANEGUI; publ. *Boletín*.

Alliance Française: Avda 7, Calle 5, Apdo 10195, 1000 San José; tel. 222-2283; fax 233-5819; e-mail alcultfr@racsa.co.cr; internet www.alianzafr.ac.cr; offers courses and exams in French language and culture and promotes cultural exchange with France; Dir PATRICK LACOMBE.

MEDICINE

Colegio de Médicos y Cirujanos de Costa Rica: Sabana Sur, San José; tel. 232-34-33; fax 232-24-06; e-mail info@medicos.sa.cr; internet www.medicos.sa.cr; f. 1857 to promote the development of the medical profession through medical research, interchange between member assocs and co-operation with nat. and int medical authorities; 45 mem. assocs; Pres. Dr ARTURO ROBLES ARIAS; Sec. Dr ABDÓN CASTRO BERMÚDEZ; publs *Acta Médica Costarricense* (quarterly), *Medicine, Vida y Salud*.

Member Associations:

Asociación Costarricense de Cirugía (Costa Rican Surgery Association): POB 548, 1000 San José; tel. 231-03-01; fax 233-41-65; f. 1954; 150 mems; Pres. Dr EDUARDO FLORES MONTERO; Sec. Dr LUIS MORALES ALFARO.

Asociación Costarricense de Pediatría (Costa Rican Paediatrics Association): Apdo 1654, 1000 San José; tel. 221-68-21; fax 221-68-21; e-mail acope@hnn.sa.cr; f. 1951; organizes national conference annually in October; 370 mems; Pres. Dr EFRAÍN ARTAVIA LORÍA; Sec. Dra JULIA FERNÁNDEZ MONGE; publ. *Acta Pediátrica Costarricense*.

Asociación Costarricense de Cardiología (Costa Rican Cardiology Association): Apdo 527, Pavas, San José; tel. 253-88-68; fax 272-42-14; f. 1978; 36 mems; library of 50 vols; Pres. Dr ANDRES BENAVIDES SANTOS.

Asociación Costarricense de Medicina Interna (Association of Internal Medicine): Hospital San Juan de Díos, San José; tel. 257-52-52; fax 235-13-08; Pres. Dr RODOLFO LEAL VEGA.

Asociación de Obstetricia y Ginecología de Costa Rica (Obstetrics and Gynaecology Association): 580-1000 San José; tel. 232-34-33; fax 231-20-84; e-mail rmontiel@racsa.co.cr; Pres. Dr GERARDO MONTIEL LARIOS.

Research Institutes

GENERAL

Consejo Nacional para Investigaciones Científicas y Tecnológicas (CONICIT): Apdo postal 10318-1000 San José; tel. 224-41-72; fax 225-26-73; e-mail conicit@www.conicit.go.cr; internet www.conicit.go.cr; f. 1973; promotes development of science and technology; makes available funds for research; works in co-operation with the Min. of National Planning and Min. of Science and Technology; library of 3,500 vols; special collection: UNISIST program; Pres. Dr RONALD MELÉNDEZ; Exec. Sec. Lic. ALVARO BORBÓN; publ. *Memoria Anual CONICIT*.

AGRICULTURE, FISHERIES AND VETERINARY SCIENCE

Centro Agronómico Tropical de Investigación y Enseñanza (CATIE): 7170 Turrialba; tel. 556-64-31; fax 556-15-33; e-mail comunicacion@catie.ac.cr; internet www.catie.ac.cr; f. 1973 by the IICA and the Costa Rican Government as a non-profit-making scientific and educational assn for research and graduate education in development, conservation and the sustainable use of natural resources in Belize, Colombia, Costa Rica, Dominican Republic, El Salvador, Guatemala, Honduras, Mexico, Nicaragua, Panama and Venezuela; library of 92,000 vols, 5,000 current periodicals; Dir Dr PEDRO FERREIRA ROSSI; publs *Informe Anual*, *Revista Manejo Integrado de Plagas* (plant protection and public health, 4 a year), *Revista Agroforestería en las Américas*, *Revista Forestal Centroamericana*.

ECONOMICS, LAW AND POLITICS

Instituto Centroamericano de Administración Pública (ICAP) (Central American Institute of Public Administration): Apdo 10025, 1000 San José; tel. 234-10-11; fax 225-20-49; e-mail icapcr@racsa.co.cr; internet www.icap.ac.cr; f. 1954; master's degree programmes in public management; training courses for managers and technical personnel; advisory services; Center for Information Technology; mem. countries: Costa Rica, El Salvador, Guatemala, Honduras, Nicaragua, Panama; library of 30,800 vols; Dir Dr HUGO ZELAYA CÁLIX; publ. *Revista* (2 a year).

Instituto Latinoamericano de las Naciones Unidas para la Prevención del Delito y Tratamiento del Delincuente (UN Latin American Institute for Crime Prevention and Treatment of Offenders): Apdo 10071, 1000 San José; tel. 225-37-84; fax 233-71-75; e-mail aldaf@expreso.co.cr; internet www.ilanud.or.cr; f. 1975 as a UN regional agency; training, advice and research in the fields of law and criminology, crime prevention and treatment of offenders; specialized library and data bank for international use; arranges symposia, ministerial meetings; projects include standardization of criminal statistics, human rights in the administration of justice, female and juvenile crime, 'white-collar' crime; Dir Dr RODRIGO

PARÍS STEFFENS; publs *ILANUD* (2 a year), *Research Reports*, *Bulletin* (quarterly).

Instituto Nacional de Estadística y Censos: Apdo 10163, 1000 San José; de la Rotonda de La Bandera, 450 metros oeste, Calle Los Negritos, Edificio Ana Lorena, Mercedes de Montes de Oca, San José; tel. 253-75-79; fax 224-22-21; e-mail informacion@inec.go.cr; internet www.inec.go.cr; f. 1883; 250 mems; library of 8,500 items; Dir Licda MARÍA ELENA GONZÁLEZ QUESADA; publs *Indice de Precios al Consumidor* (monthly), *Costo de la Canasta Básica de Alimentos* (monthly), *Indicadores Demográficos* (annually), *Costa Rica: Cálculo de Población por Provincia, Cantón y Distrito* (2 a year), *Anuarío Estadístico de Costa Rica* (annually), *Encuesta de Hogares de Propósitos Múltiples, Módulo de Empleo* (annually), *Indices de Precios de los Insumos Básicos de la Industria de la Construcción* (monthly), *Estadísticas de la Construcción* (2 a year), *Estadísticas de Comercio Exterior* (2 a year), *Estadísticas Vitales: Población, Nacimientos, Defunciones, Matrimonios* (annually), *Mortalidad Infantil y Evolución Reciente* (2 a year), *Cifras Básicas sobre Fuerza de Trabajo* (annually), *Cifras Básicas sobre Pobreza e Ingresos* (annually).

EDUCATION

Fundación Omar Dengo: Apdo 1032-2050, 1000 San José; tel. 257-62-63; fax 222-16-54; e-mail info@fod.ac.cr; internet www.fod.ac.cr; f. 1987 to promote the economic, social and human development of Costa Rica, implementing innovative programs to improve the quality of education; Pres. ALFONSO GUTIÉRREZ; publ. *Estado de la Nación* (irregular).

HISTORY, GEOGRAPHY AND ARCHAEOLOGY

Instituto Geográfico Nacional: Apdo 2272, 1000 San José; Avda 20, Calle 5/7, San José; tel. 257-74-18; fax 257-52-46; e-mail igncr@ns.casapres.go.cr; f. 1944; library of 3,000 vols; Dir Geog. EDUARDO BEDOYA BENÍTEZ.

MEDICINE

Centro Internacional de Investigación y Adiestramiento Médico de la Universidad del Estado de Louisiana (Louisiana State University International Center for Medical Research and Training): Apdo 10155, San José; tel. 280-51-49; fax 224-72-36; e-mail icmrtlsu@sol.racsa.co.cr; f. 1962; research on viral diseases; library: *c.* 4,000 vols; Dir Dr RONALD B. LUFTIG.

Instituto Costarricense de Investigación y Enseñanza en Nutrición y Salud (INCIENSA) (Institute of Research and Teaching in Nutrition and Health): Apdo 4, Tres Ríos, Cartago; La Unión, Cartago; tel. 279-99-11; fax 279-55-46; e-mail lisnavas@ns.casapres.go.cr; internet www.inciensa.sa.cr; f. 1977; attached to Min. of Health and affiliated to the University of Costa Rica; library of 4,500 vols; Dir LISSETTE NAVAS ALVARADO; publ. *Boletín INCIENSA* (3 a year).

NATURAL SCIENCES

Biological Sciences

Organization for Tropical Studies: Apdo 676-2050, San Pedro; tel. 524-06-07; fax 524-06-08; e-mail cro@ots.ac.cr; internet www.ots.ac.cr; f. 1963; promotes education, research and the responsible use of natural resources in the tropics; operates three biological stations: Las Cruces, incorporating Wilson Botanical Garden (premontane forest), Palo Verde (dry forest) and La Selva (tropical wet forest); consortium of 58 univs and research instns in the USA, Latin America and Australia; library of 10,000 vols, 50 current periodicals; Dir JORGE JIMÉNEZ; publs *Liana* (in Spanish and English versions, each 2 a year), *Amigos Newsletter* (2 a year), *Annual Report*.

Tropical Science Centre: Apdo 8-3870-1000, San José; tel. 253-32-67; fax 253-49-63; e-mail cct@cct.or.cr; internet www.cct.or.cr; f. 1962; private non-profit asscn; research and training in tropical science; consultation on tropical ecology, land use capability and planning, environmental assessments; biological reserve and field station at Monteverde Cloud Forest; library of 7,000 vols; Exec. Dir JULIO CALVO ALVARADO; publ. *Occasional Paper Series* (irregular).

Physical Sciences

Instituto Meteorológico Nacional: Apdo 5583, 1000 San José; Frente a Antiguo Emergencias del Hospital Calderón Guardia, Barrio Aranjuez, San José; tel. 222-56-16; fax 223-18-37; e-mail imn@imn.ac.cr; internet www.imn.ac.cr; f. 1888; climatology, hydrometeorology, agrometeorology, synoptic and aeronautical meteorology; Dir PAULO MANSO SAYAO; publ. *Boletín Meteorológico* (monthly).

TECHNOLOGY

Comisión de Energía Atómica de Costa Rica (National Atomic Energy Commission): Edif. Galerías del Este (3° piso), Apdo 6681-1000, San José; tel. 224-15-91; fax 224-12-93; e-mail coatom@racsa.co.cr; internet sibdi.bldt.ucr.ac.cr/cea; f. 1969; Pres. PATRICIA MORA RODRÍGUEZ; Dir LILLIANA SOLÍS DÍAZ.

Libraries and Archives

San José

Archivo Nacional de Costa Rica: Apdo 41-2020, Zapote (San José); 900 metros sur y 150 oeste de Plaza del Sol Curridabat, San José; tel. 234-72-23; fax 234-73-12; e-mail archivonacional@racsa.co.cr; internet www.archivonacional.go.cr; f. 1881; 5,000 vols, 8.5 shelf-km of documents; Dir-Gen. Lic. VIRGINIA CHACÓN ARIAS; publs *Revista del Archivo Nacional* (annually), *Cuadernillos del Archivo Nacional* (irregular), *Archívese* (bulletin, 4 a year).

Biblioteca Instituto Diplomático: POB 10-027, 1000 San José; tel. 257-85-29; fax 257-84-01; e-mail bmmp@rree.go.cr; internet www.rree.go.cr; f. 1991; attached to the Ministry of Foreign Affairs; international affairs, diplomacy, foreign policy; 4,000 vols; Librarian LUIS GONZÁLEZ CALVO.

Biblioteca 'Mark Twain'–Centro Cultural Costarricense-Norteamericano: Apdo 1489-1000, San José; tel. 207-75-74; fax 224-14-80; e-mail bibmarktwain@cccncr.com; internet www.cccncr.com; f. 1945; 16,000 vols and documents; Librarian GUISELLA RUIZ; publ. *CCCNoticias* (6 a year).

Biblioteca Nacional Miguel Obregón Lizano: Apdo 10.008, 1000 San José; Calles 15 y 17, Ave. 3 y 3B, San José; tel. 221-24-36; fax 223-55-10; e-mail dibinacr@racsa.co.cr; internet www.mcjdcr.go.cr/sistema_bibliotecas/biblioteca_nac.html; f. 1888; 270,000 vols; Dir GUADALUPE RODRIGUEZ MÉNDEN; publ. *Bibliografia Nacional*.

Centro de Información 'Alvaro Castro Jenkins': Avda Central y Primera, Calles 2 y 4, San José; tel. 243-44-60; fax 243-45-83; e-mail centroinf@bccr.fi.cr; internet www.bccr.fi.cr/ci; f. 1950; attached to the Central Bank; specializes in economics; 43,028 vols; Librarian DEYANIRA VARGAS DE BONILLA.

Departamento de Servicios Bibliotecarios, Documentación e Información de la Asamblea Legislativa: Apdo 75-1013, San José; tel. 243-23-94; fax 243-24-00; e-mail jvolio@congreso.aleg.go.cr; internet www.asamblea.go.cr; f. 1953; social sciences; 40,000 vols, 800 periodicals; Dir Lic. JULIETA VOLIO GUEVARA; publs *C. R. Leyes, decretos* (index of Costa Rican legislation, monthly), *Revista Parliamentaria* (4 a year).

Sistema de Bibliotecas, Documentación e Información: Ciudad Universitaria Rodrigo Facio, 2060 San Pedro de Montes de Oca, San José; tel. 253-61-52; fax 207-41-63; e-mail mbriceno@sibdi.ucr.ac.cr; internet sibdi.bldt.ucr.ac.cr; f. 1946; 443,853 vols, 13,425 periodicals, 48,059 theses, 23,212 audiovisual items, 5,615 maps and atlases; Dir Licda MA. EUGENIA BRICEÑO MEZA.

Museums and Art Galleries

Alajuela

Museo Histórico Cultural Juan Santamaría: Apdo 785-4050, Alajuela; tel. 441-47-75; fax 441-69-26; e-mail mhcjscr@ice.co.cr; internet www.museojuansantamaria.go.cr; f. 1974; attached to Ministry of Culture, Youth and Sports; 19th c. collection; library: *c.* 2,000 vols; Dir Prof. RAÚL AGUILAR PIEDRA; publ. *11 de Abril: Cuadernos de Cultura*.

San José

Museo de Arte Costarricense: Apdo 378, Fecosa 1009, San José; Parque Metropolitano de La Sabana, San José; tel. 222-71-55; fax 222-72-47; e-mail info@musarco.go.cr; internet www.musarco.go.cr; attached to Ministry of Culture, Youth and Sport; f. 1977; collects and exhibits representative works of Costa Rican art; promotes artistic work through workshops and grants; supervision and preservation of state art collections; library of 5,000 vols; Dir ELIZABETH BARQUERO.

Museo Indígeno (Native Museum): Seminario Central, San José; f. 1890; library of 40,000 vols; Dir Rev. WALTER E. JOVEL CASTRO.

Museo Nacional de Costa Rica: Apdo 749-1000, San José; Calle 17, Avda Central y 2, San José; tel. 221-44-29; fax 233-74-27; e-mail museonac@sol.racsa.co.cr; internet www.cr/arte/museonac/museonac.htm; f. 1887; general museum: pre-Columbian art, colonial and republican history, national herbarium, natural history, culture; library of 70,000 vols; Dir MELANIA ORTIZ VOLIO; publs *Brenesia* (natural sciences), *Trees and Seeds from the Neotropics*, *Vínculos* (anthropology, 2 a year).

Affiliated museums:

Museo de Entomología: Faculty of Music, Univ. de Costa Rica, San Pedro, San José; tel. 225-55-55; f. 1962; more than 1m. specimens of butterflies and other insects.

Museo de Zoología: Dpto de Biología, Univ. de Costa Rica, San José; mammals, herpetology, fish; small library.

Universities

ESCUELA DE AGRICULTURA DE LA REGION TROPICAL HÚMEDA (UNIVERSIDAD EARTH)

Apdo Postal 4442 SJ, San José

Telephone: 713-00-00

Fax: 713-00-01
E-mail: admision@earth.ac.cr
Internet: www.earth.ac.cr

Founded 1986
Private control
Academic year: January to December

President and Rector: Dr JOSÉ A. ZAGLUL SLON
Provost: Dr JAMES B. FRENCH
Rector: Dr JOSÉ A. ZAGLUL SLON
Vice-President (Administration and Finance): Ing. ALEX MATA
Librarian: JOSÉ RUPERTO ARCE

Library of 35,000 vols
Number of teachers: 40
Number of students: 400

Courses in agricultural engineering.

UNIVERSIDAD AUTÓNOMA DE CENTRO AMERICA

Apdo 7637-1000, San José
located at: Campus Los Cipreses, 1 km al Norte del Servicentro La Galera, Curridabat, San José

Telephone: 272-91-00
Fax: 271-20-46
E-mail: info@uaca.ac.cr
Internet: www.uaca.ac.cr

Founded 1976
Private control
Language of instruction: Spanish
Academic year: January to December (3 terms)

Rector: Lic. GUILLERMO MALAVASSI VARGAS
Chancellor: GONZALO GALLEGOS J.
Vice-Chancellor: LISETTE MARTÍNEZ L.
Registrar: PABLO ARCE
Librarian: JULISSA MÉNDEZ M.

Number of teachers: 2,500
Number of students: 5,000

Publications: *Ordenanzas y Anuario Universitario*, *Acta Académica* (2 a year).

CONSTITUENT COLLEGES

Colegio Andrés Bello: Apdo 2393-2050, San Pedro, San José; tel. 272-91-02; fax 271-38-39; e-mail abello@uaca.ac.cr; Dean Lic. HERBERTH SASSO.

Colegio de Ciencias Clorito Picado: 2393-2050, San Pedro, San José; tel. 272-91-00; fax 271-38-39; e-mail ccp@uaca.ac.cr.

Colegio Iñigo de Loyola: Apdo 12345-1000, San José; tel. 225-54-13; fax 225-54-13; Dean ELIO BURGOS.

Colegio Leonardo da Vinci: Apdo 44-1009, San José; tel. 290-25-52; fax 290-27-28; e-mail davinci@racsa.co.cr; Dean TERESITA BONILLA.

Collegium Academicum: Apdo 2393-2050, San Pedro, San José; tel. 272-91-02; fax 271-38-39; e-mail academicvm@uaca.ac.cr; Dean GASTÓN CERTAD.

Studium Generale Costarricense: Apdo 7651-1000 San José; tel. 271-21-00; fax 271-20-15; e-mail stvdivm@uaca.ac.cr; Dean Lic. MARIO GRANADOS.

UNIVERSIDAD DE COSTA RICA

Ciudad Universitaria 'Rodrigo Facio', San Pedro de Montes de Oca, San José

Telephone: 253-53-23
Fax: 234-04-52
E-mail: erojasa@cariari.ucr.ac.cr
Internet: www.ucr.ac.cr

Founded 1843, re-founded 1940
Autonomous control
Language of instruction: Spanish
Academic year: March to November

Rector: Dra YAMILETH GONZÁLEZ GARCÍA
Vice-Rector (Administration): Dr HERMANN HESS
Vice-Rector (Research): Dr HENNING JENSEN PENNINGTON
Vice-Rector (Student Life): MSc ALEJANDRINA MATA
Vice-Rector (Teaching): Dra LIBIA HERRERO URIBE
Registrar: Sr JORGE RECOBA VARGAS (acting)
Librarian: Lic. AURORA ZAMORA GONZÁLEZ (acting)

Library: see Libraries and Archives

Number of teachers: 3,800
Number of students: 28,986

DEANS

Faculty of Agronomy: Dr MANUEL ZELEDÓN
Faculty of Dentistry: Dr FERNANDO SAÉNZ FORERO
Faculty of Economics: Dr JUSTO AGUILAR FONG
Faculty of Education: ALEJANDRINA MATA SEGREDA
Faculty of Engineering: Ing. FERNANDO SILESKY GUEVARA
Faculty of Fine Arts: Dr LUIS DIEGO HERRA RODRÍGUEZ
Faculty of Law: Dr RAFAEL GONZÁLEZ BALLAR
Faculty of Letters: M. L. ENRIQUE MARGERY PEÑA
Faculty of Medicine: Dr GUIDO ULATE
Faculty of Microbiology: Dr MARIO CHAVES VILLALOBOS
Faculty of Pharmacy: Dra LIDIETTE FONSECA GONZÁLEZ
Faculty of Science: Dr OLDEMAR RODRÍGUEZ ROJAS
Faculty of Social Sciences: Dr ROBERTO SALOM ECHEVERRIA (acting)
Graduate Studies: Dra MAIA PÉREZ YGLESIAS

There are 21 research institutes attached to the various faculties.

REGIONAL CENTRES

Centro Regional del Atlántico: Dir Ing. CARLOS CALVO PINEDA.

Centro Regional de Guanacaste: Dir Ing. RAFAEL MONTERO ROJAS.

Centro Regional de Limón: Dir Dr ENRIQUE ZAPATA DUARTE.

Centro Regional del Occidente: Dir Dr ELIAM CAMPOS BARRANTES.

Centro Regional del Pacífico: Dir MARIANA CHAVES ARAYA (acting).

UNIVERSIDAD EMPRESARIAL DE COSTA RICA

Apdo 12640-1000, San José

Telephone: 253-59-52
Fax: 225-51-41
E-mail: info@unem.edu
Internet: www.unem.edu

Founded 1992 as International Postgraduate School affiliated with Universidad de San Jose; became independent and adopted present name 1997
Private control
Languages of instruction: Spanish, English
Academic year: January to December

Rector: Dr RAFAEL ANGEL PÉREZ CORDOVA
Registrar: ELAINE PÉREZ
Librarian: RODOLFO MARTÍNEZ

Number of teachers: 62
Number of students: 895

Publication: *Gazetta Empresarial*

Faculties of Administrative Sciences, Biological Sciences, Education and Humanities, Psychology and Behavioural Sciences, Social Sciences, Postgraduate Studies; School of Languages.

UNIVERSIDAD FIDELITAS

Apdo 8063-1000, San José

Telephone: 253-02-62
Fax: 253-21-86
E-mail: informacion@ufidelitas.ac.cr
Internet: www.ufidelitas.ac.cr

Founded 1980 as Collegium Fidélitas; present name 1994
Private control

Rector: JESÚS MERINO SERNA
General Manager: MIGUEL MARÍN VALENCIANO

Courses in: industrial engineering, electromechanical engineering, electrical engineering, civil engineering, computer systems engineering, public finance, business administration, law, pre-school education, teaching of English, university teaching in the first and second years, psychology, advertising design.

UNIVERSIDAD INTERNACIONAL DE LAS AMERICAS

Apdo 1447-1002 San José
Barrio Aranjuez, Calle 23 (Avenidas 7 y 7bis), El Carmen, San José

Telephone: 258-02-20
Fax: 222-32-16
E-mail: correo@uia.ac.cr
Internet: www.uia.ac.cr

Founded 1986
Private control
Library of 25,000 vols

Schools of Administration, International Business, Public Finance, Pharmacy, Electromechanical Engineering, Industrial Engineering, Computer Engineering, Dentistry, Journalism, Advertising, International Relations, Tourism, Law, Education, Languages, Medicine.

UNIVERSIDAD LATINA DE COSTA RICA

Apdo 1561-2050, San Pedro, San José

Telephone: 283-26-11
Fax: 225-28-01
E-mail: academico@ulatina.ac.cr
Internet: www.ulatina.ac.cr

Founded 1981
Private control

Campuses in Cañas, Grecia, Guápiles, Limón, Palmares, Paso Canoas, Puntarenas, San Isidro del General, Santa Cruz and Turrialba

Rector: ARTURO JOFRÉ VARTANIÁN
Vice-Rector (Academic): M.Sc. LUIS ALBERTO CHAVES MONGE

Courses in health sciences, engineering and architecture, economics and business administration, social sciences, education, tourism and environmental science.

UNIVERSIDAD ESTATAL A DISTANCIA (Open University)

Apdo 474, 2050 San Pedro de Montes de Oca, San José

Telephone: 527-20-00
Fax: 253-49-90
Internet: www.uned.ac.cr

Founded 1977
State control
Language of instruction: Spanish
Academic year: March to November

Rector: RODRIGO ARIAS CAMACHO
Academic Vice-Rector: JOSÉ LUIS TORRES
Executive Vice-Rector: LUIS GUILLERMO CARPIO MALAVASSI

Vice-Rector for Planning: SILVIA ABDELNOUR ESQUIVEL
Director of Information Technology, and Communications: MSc VIGNY ALVARADO CASTILLO
Librarian: RITA LEDEZMA

Number of teachers: 235
Number of students: 12,000

DIRECTORS

School of Business Administration: RODOLFO TACSAN CHEN
School of Education: (vacant)
School of Exact and Natural Sciences: Ing. OLMAN DÍAZ SÁNCHEZ
School of Social Sciences and Humanities: GERARDO ESQUIVEL MONGE

There are 28 regional centres where students can register, receive instruction, sit examinations and use library facilities

UNIVERSIDAD LATINOAMERICANA DE CIENCIA Y TECNOLOGIA (ULACIT)

Apdo 10235, 1000 San José
Telephone: 257-57-67
Fax: 233-97-39
E-mail: info@ulacit.ac.cr
Internet: www.ulacit.ac.cr
Founded 1987
Private control
Academic year: January to December
Campuses in San José and in Panama City (Panama)

President: SYLVIA CASTRO
Academic Vice-President: JOHN BROWN
Administrative Vice-President: JUSTO PARDO
Student Affairs Vice-President: ALEJANDRA QUIRÓS
Registrar: FLORY SOLANO
Librarian: LIGIA GONZALEZ

Library of 25,000 vols
Number of teachers: 275
Number of students: 4,500

DEANS

School of Business Administration: JUAN RICARDO WONG
School of Computer Sciences: WILBERTH MOLINA
School of Dentistry: Dr RAFAEL PORRAS
School of Education: Lic. NIDIA GUTIÉRREZ
School of Law: Lic. MARIANELA NÚÑEZ PIEDRA
School of Industrial Engineering: ORLANDO TORRES
School of Psychology: Lic. MARJORIE BARQUERO
Graduate School: ROSMERY HERNÁNDEZ

UNIVERSIDAD NACIONAL

Apdo 86-3000, Heredia
Telephone: 261-01-01
Fax: 237-75-93
E-mail: jmora@una.ac.cr
Internet: www.una.ac.cr
Founded 1973
State control
Language of instruction: Spanish
Academic year: February to November

Rector: Dra SONIA MARTA MORA ESCALANTE
Vice-Rector (Academic Affairs): Dr CARLOS LÉPIZ JIMÉNEZ
Vice-Rector (Development): MARCO TULIO FALLAS DÍAZ
Vice-Rector (Student Affairs): HERIBERTO VALVERDE CASTRO
Library Director: Lic. MARGARITA GARÇÍA

Number of teachers: 1,200
Number of students: 12,000

Publications: *Vida Silvestre Neotropical* (2 a year), *Repertorio Americano* (2 a year), *Revista Ciencias Ambientales, ABRA* (2 a year), *Relaciones Internacionales* (4 a year), *Uniciencia* (2 a year), *Revista de Historia* (2 a year)

DEANS

Faculty of Earth and Sea Sciences: Dr MARÍA DE LOS ANGELES ALVAREZ FERNÁNDEZ
Faculty of Exact and Natural Sciences: Dr LUIS MANUEL SIERRA SIERRA
Faculty of Health Sciences: Dr PEDRO UREÑA BONILLA
Faculty of Philosophy and Letters: M.A. JORGE ALFARO PERÉZ
Faculty of Social Sciences: M.Sc. JOSÉ CARLOS CHINCHILLA COTO
Centre of General Studies: Dr CARLOS ARAYA GUILLÉN
Centre for Research and Teaching in Education: M.Sc. IRMA ZÚÑIGA LEÓN
Centre for Research, Teaching and Extension in Fine Arts: M.A. ELSA FLORES MONTERO
Brunca Regional Centre: Lic. JUAN RAFAEL MORA CAMACHO

ATTACHED RESEARCH INSTITUTES

Centro de Investigaciones Apícolas Tropicales (CINAT): Dir M.Sc. HENRY ARCE ARCE.

Estación de Biología Marina.

Estación Nacional de Ciencias Marino-Costera.

Instituto de Estudios Latinoamericanos: Dir Lic. MARIO GERARDO VÍQUEZ VARGAS.

Instituto de Estudios de la Mujer: Dir ZAIRA CARVAJAL ORLICH.

Instituto de Estudios Sociales en Población.

Instituto Internacional del Oceáno.

Instituto de Investigación y Servicios Forestales (INISEFOR): Dir M.Sc. ELADIO CHAVES SALAS.

Instituto Regional de Estudios en Sustancias Tóxicas (IRET): Dir Ph.D. ELBA DE LA CRUZ MALAVASSI.

Observatorio Vulcanológico y Sismológico de Costa Rica (OVSICORI).

Programa Regional en Manejo de Vida Silvestre para Mesoamérica y el Caribe (PRMVS): Dir M.Sc. JORGE FALLAS GAMBOA.

UNIVERSIDAD DE SAN JOSE

Apdo 7446, 1000 San José
Telephone: 224-81-00
Fax: 224-39-80
E-mail: usjinfo@usj.edu
Internet: www.usj.ac.cr
Founded 1976 as Colegio Académicum; present name and status 1992
Private control
Language of instruction: Spanish
Academic year: January to December (3 terms)

Rector: MANUEL SANDI MURILLO
Registrar: Lic. RÓGER SEGNINI ESQUIVEL
Librarian: JOSÉ SEGNINI

Number of teachers: 175
Number of students: 1,800

Publication: *Revista Universitaria*

Schools of Law, Business Administration, Computer Science, International Trade, Education and Psychology, Humanities, Social Science, and International Post-Graduate School.

UNIVERSIDAD VERITAS

Apdo 1380–1000, San José
Telephone: 283-47-47
Fax: 225-29-07
E-mail: info@uveritas.ac.cr
Internet: www.uveritas.ac.cr
Private control
Academic year: January to December (three semesters)

Rector: Ing. JOSÉ JOAQUIN SECO

Number of teachers: 95
Number of students: 1,100

Faculties of Art, Design and Architecture.

INSTITUTO TECNOLÓGICO DE COSTA RICA

Apdo 159-7050 Cartago
Telephone: 552-53-33
Fax: 551-53-48
E-mail: archivo@itcr.ac.cr
Internet: www.itcr.ac.cr
Founded 1971
State control
Language of instruction: Spanish
Academic year: February to December

Rector: EUGENIO TREJOS
Vice-Rector (Academic): Dr LUIS GERARDO MEZA CASCANTE
Vice-Rector for Academic Services and Students: JEANNETTE BARRANTES M.
Vice-Rector for Administration: JOSÉ RAFAEL HIDALGO
Vice-Rector for Research and Extension: Dr JUAN FERNANDO ALVAREZ CASTRO
Registrar: WILLIAM VIVES BRENES
Librarian: CRISTINA GÓMEZ MOLINA

Library of 54,000 vols
Number of teachers: 455
Number of students: 6,000

Publications: *Tecnología en Marcha* (3 a year), *Comunicación* (2 a year), *Kurú: Revista Forestal*, *Revista Virtual Matemática Educación e Internet*, *Espacio Virtual de la Física*

Departments of Agricultural Management Engineering, Agricultural Engineering, Agronomy, Architecture and Town Planning, Forestry Engineering, Safety and Hygiene at Work, Construction Engineering, Materials Science and Engineering, , Electromechanical Engineering, Industrial Production Engineering, Industrial Design, Electronic Engineering, Computer Science, Business Administration, Biology, Mathematics, Social Sciences, Communication, Culture and Sport, Physics, and Chemistry.

ATTACHED RESEARCH CENTRES

Centre for Research and Development in Sustainable Agriculture for the Humid Tropics.

Research Centre in Agroindustrial Management.

Research Centre in Biotechnology: Dir D. FLORES MORA.

Research Centre in Computer Science: Dir L. SANCHO CH..

Research Centre in Environmental Protection: Dir H. QUESADA CARVAJAL.

Research Centre in Evaluation and Modern Technology Transfer in Manufacture: Dir R. BOLAÑOS MAROTO.

Research Centre for Forestry-Industry Integration: Dir Ing. A. MEZA MONTOYA.

Research Centre for Housing and Building: Dir Ing. R. VEGA GUZMÁN R..

Colleges

Instituto Centroamericano de Administración de Empresas (INCAE): Apdo 960, 4050 Alajuela; tel. 437-22-00; fax 433-91-01; e-mail library@mail.incae.ac.cr; internet www.incae.ac.cr; f. 1964 in Nicaragua with technical assistance from Harvard Univ.; Costa Rica campus opened 1983; (See also under Nicaragua); 2-year master's courses in business administration, managerial economics, natural resources, industrial administration and technological administration; executive training programmes; management research and consultation; library: 50,000 vols in fields of business administration, economic development, natural resources and Latin American economic and social conditions; Rector Dr ROBERTO ARTAVIA; Librarian Lic. THOMAS BLOCH.

Instituto Centroamericano de Administración Pública (ICAP): Apdo 10025-1000, 100 sur, 75 oste de la Heldería Pop's, Curridabat, San José; tel. 234-10-11; fax 225-20-49; e-mail icapcr@racsa.co.cr; internet www.icap.ac.cr; f. 1954 as Escuela Superior de Administración Pública (ESAPAC) by a jt project of the govts of Costa Rica, El Salvador, Guatemala, Honduras and Nicaragua (Panama incorporated 1961); master's degree programmes in public management; training courses for managers and technical personnel; advisory services; Center for Information Technology; Dir Dr HUGO ZELAYA CÁLIX; publ. *Revista Centroamerica de Administración Pública* (2 a year).

CÔTE D'IVOIRE

The Higher Education System

Côte d'Ivoire was a province in French West Africa before gaining its independence in 1960. The Université de Cocody in Abidjan is the oldest university, founded in 1958 as Centre d'Enseignement Supérieur d'Abidjan; in 1964 it became the Université Nationale de Côte d'Ivoire, and it acquired its current name in 1995. There are also two other universities, at Abodo-Adjamé (also in Abidjan) and at Bouaké. Some 47,187 students were enrolled at university-level institutions in 1997/98. Education in the north of the country was badly disrupted following the failed coup in 2002. The Ministry of Higher Education and Scientific Research oversees the universities. There are also two administrative bodies, the Council of Higher Education Teaching and the Standing Board of Higher Education Teaching. The universities are run by Councils.

The Baccalauréat is the secondary school qualification required for admission to university. After the first two years of undergraduate studies, a diploma is awarded based on the academic path being followed: arts and humanities (Diplôme Universitaire d'Etudes Littéraires—DUEL), sciences (Diplôme Universitaire d'Etudes Scientifiques—DUES), law (Diplôme Universitaire d'Etudes Juridiques—DUEJ), economics (Diplôme Universitaire d'Etudes Economiques Générales—DUEEG) or general studies (Diplôme d'Etudes Universitaires Générales—DEUG). After the Diplôme, a further year of study leads to the Licence. However, five years of study is required for the Diplôme d'Ingénieur. At postgraduate level, the Maîtrise is awarded following one year of study after the Licence. A further year of study leads to the Diplôme d'Etudes Approfondies (DEA). A final year of postgraduate study results in the award of either the Diplôme d'Etudes Supérieures or the Doctorat de Spécialité de Troisième Cycle. Vocational and technical education is provided by several schools and institutes.

Learned Societies

LANGUAGE AND LITERATURE

Alliance Française: AFI N'Gokro, BP 1899, Yamoussoukro; tel. and fax 30-64-25-30; e-mail afi_yakro@yahoo.fr; offers courses and exams in French language and culture and promotes cultural exchange with France; attached teaching offices in Abengourou, Korhogo and San Pedro.

Goethe-Institut: Cocody, Rue C27, par Ave C16 Jean Mermoz prolongée, BP 982, Abidjan; tel. 22-44-14-22; fax 22-44-96-89; e-mail verw@abidjan.goethe.org; internet www.goethe.de/af/abi/deindex.htm; offers courses and exams in German language and culture and promotes cultural exchange with Germany; library of 7,750 vols; Dir FRIEDRICH ENGELHARDT.

ECONOMICS, LAW AND POLITICS

Centre Ivoirien de Recherches et d'Etudes Juridiques: Blvd Latrille, opp. Eglise St Jean, Cocody 01, BP 3811, Abidjan; tel. 22-44-60-54; f. 1973; strategic research into problems affecting the judiciary in Côte d'Ivoire; Dir KOMENAN ZAPKA.

Centre de Recherche et d'Action pour la Paix (CERAP): 08 BP 2088, Abidjan 08; tel. 22-44-15-94; fax 22-44-84-38; e-mail info@cerap-inades.org; internet www.cerap-inades.org; f. 1962 by the Society of Jesus to promote the development of newly independent countries; research in development planning, economics, sociology, ethnology; library of 50,000 vols, 230 periodicals; Dir DENIS MAUGENEST; publs *Débats: Courrier d'Afrique de l'Ouest* (every 2 months), *Bulletin sur les droits de l'homme en Afrique de l'Ouest*.

Research Institutes

GENERAL

Institut de Recherche pour le Développement (IRD): Rue du Chevalier de Clieu, Zone 4, 15 BP 917, Abidjan 15; tel. 21-24-37-79; fax 21-24-65-04; e-mail rep@ird.ci; internet www.ird.ci; f. 1946; health education, economic development, environmental management; Rep. ALAIN MORLIÈRE; (see main entry under France).

AGRICULTURE, FISHERIES AND VETERINARY SCIENCE

Centre de Co-opération Internationale en Recherche Agronomique pour le Développement (CIRAD): see entry in Burkina Faso:.

Centre National de Recherche Agronomique (CNRA) (National Centre for Agricultural Research): Adiopodoumé, KM17 Route de Dabou, 01 POB 1740, Abidjan 01; tel. 23-47-24-24; fax 23-47-24-11; e-mail info@cnra.ci; internet www.cnra.ci; f. 1998; 140 mems; Dir-Gen. Dr KOFFI SIE; publ. *CNRA-Info* (quarterly).

MEDICINE

Institut Pasteur de Côte d'Ivoire: 01 BP 490, Abidjan 01; tel. 23-45-33-92; fax 23-45-76-23; e-mail pasteur@pasteur.ci; f. 1972; research laboratories for the study of viral diseases, including yellow fever, poliomyelitis, rabies, influenza, hepatitis, HIV/AIDS; clinical analysis laboratories used by the Centre Hospitalier Universitaire, Cocody; small library in process of formation; Dir Pr MIREILLE DOSSO.

Institut Pierre Richet: BP1500, Bouaké; tel. 30-63-37-46; fax 30-63-27-38; e-mail ipr@ird.ci; f. 1973; research into tropical endemic diseases, including malaria, sleeping sickness, dengue fever and yellow fever; part of l'Organisation de Co-opération et de Coordination de la Lutte contre les Grandes Endémies en Afrique de l'Ouest (OCCGE); training on 2 levels: technician in medical entomology, and medical entomologist; missions and field studies carried out as required by member countries of OCCGE; library containing special collection and field data; Dir P. CARNEVALE.

NATURAL SCIENCES

General

Centre de Recherches Océanographiques: 29 rue des Pêcheurs, BP V18, Abidjan; tel. 21-35-50-14; fax 21-35-11-55; e-mail abe@cro.ird.ci; internet www.refer.ci/ivoir_ct/rec/cdr/cro/accueil.htm; f. 1958; biological oceanography, physics and chemistry, hydrobiology; 40 staff; library of 30,000 vols; Dir Dr JACQUES ABE; publs *Archives Scientifiques*, *Journal Ivoirien d'Océanologie et de Limnologie*.

Physical Sciences

Station Géophysique de Lamto: BP 31, N'Douci; tel. 31-62-90-95; fax 31-62-92-20; e-mail lamtogeo@aviso.ci; f. 1962; seismological, infrared, atmospherical and climatological studies; Dir Prof. MAMADOU FOFANA; publ. *Bulletin of Teleseisms* (weekly).

RELIGION, SOCIOLOGY AND ANTHROPOLOGY

Centre des Sciences Humaines: BP 1600, Abidjan; f. 1960; ethnological and sociological research, especially in the cultural and religious field; museology, conservation, exhibitions; Dir Dr B. HOLAS; see also Musée de la Côte d'Ivoire.

TECHNOLOGY

Bureau de Recherches Géologiques et Minières (BRGM): 01 BP 1335, Abidjan 01; gold-mining stations at Ity, Bondoukou, Fetekio, Yaouré, Toulepleu.

Société pour le Développement Minier de la Côte d'Ivoire (SODEMI): 01 BP 2816, 31 blvd Latrille Abidjan 01; tel. 22-44-29-95; fax 22-44-08-21; e-mail sodemi@aviso.ci; f. 1962; carries out a programme of geological and geophysical minerals prospecting; mineral mining; library of 5,435 vols, 28 current periodicals, 2,556 geological or prospecting reports, 3,500 topographic and geological maps; Dir-Gen. J. N'ZI; publ. *Rapport annuel*.

Libraries and Archives

Abidjan

Archives de Côte d'Ivoire: BP V126, Abidjan; tel. 20-32-41-58; f. 1913; Dir (vacant).

Bibliothèque Centrale de la Côte d'Ivoire: BP 6243, Abidjan-Treichville; f. 1963; a service of the Ministry of National Education; public lecture service; 14,000 vols; founded with help of UNESCO; Librarian P. ZELLI ANY-GRAH.

Bibliothèque Centrale de l'Université de Cocody: BP V34, Abidjan 01; tel. 22-44-08-47; f. 1963; 95,000 vols, 1,650 periodicals; Librarian FRANÇOISE N'GORAN.

Bibliothèque du Centre Culturel Français: 01 BP 3995, 01 Abidjan; tel. 20-22-56-28; fax 20-22-71-32; 32,014 vols (adult library), 6,352 vols (children's library), and 5,000 vols in African Documentation section; 197 periodicals and reviews; Dir MICHEL JANNIN; Librarian GÉRARD AUDOUIN.

Bibliothèque Nationale: BPV 180, Abidjan; tel. 20-21-38-72; f. 1968; scientific library of 75,000 vols and 135 current periodicals; part of the former centre of the Institut Français d'Afrique Noire; Dir COFFIE TIBURCE; publ. *Bibliographie de la Côte d'Ivoire* (annually).

Museum

Abidjan

Musée des Civilisations: BP 1600, Abidjan 01; fmrly Musée de la Côte d'Ivoire; exhibits of ethnographical, sociological, artistic and scientific nature; attached to the Centre des Sciences Humaines; Dir MEMEL SILVIE KASSI.

Universities

UNIVERSITÉ D'ABOBO-ADJAMÉ

BP 801, Abidjan 02
Telephone: 22-37-81-22
Fax: 22-37-81-18
E-mail: abobo-adj@abobo.edu.ci
Internet: www.abobo.edu.ci

Founded 1957 as Centre d'Enseignement Supérieur; became part of Université Nationale de Côte-d'Ivoire 1964; independent status and present name 1992
State control
President: ETIENNE EHOUAN EHILÉ

Library of 14,000
Number of teachers: 50
Number of students: 5,000

Units of Basic Sciences, Food Technology and Higher Education; School of Health Sciences; Centres for Advanced Training and Ecology.

UNIVERSITÉ DE BOUAKÉ

BP V 18, Bouaké 01
Telephone: 30-63-48-57
Fax: 30-63-59-84
Internet: www.refer.ci/ivoir_ct/edu/sup/uni/bke/accueil.htm

Founded 1960; became part of Université Nationale de Côte-d'Ivoire 1964; independent status 1994
State control

President: FRANÇOIS KOUAKOU N'GUESSAN
Secretary-General: GERMAIN ADJA-DIBY

Units of Communication, Environment and Society, Economics and Development, Higher Education, Law, Administration and Development and Medical Sciences; Centres for Development Research and Lifelong Education.

UNIVERSITÉ DE COCODY

BP V34, Abidjan 01
Telephone: 22-44-90-00
Fax: 22-44-14-07
E-mail: acceuil@ucocody.ci
Internet: www.ucocody.ci

Founded 1958 as the Centre d'Enseignement Supérieur d'Abidjan; became part of Université Nationale de Côte d'Ivoire 1964; present name 1995
State control
Language of instruction: French
Academic year: September to July

President: CÉLESTIN TÉA GOKOU
General Secretary: JÉRÔME TOTO BALOUBI
Librarian: FRANÇOISE N'GORAN

Number of teachers: 1,081
Number of students: 37,500

Publications: *En-Quête* (Humanities), *Repères* (Humanities), *Revues Médicales* (quarterly), *Revues Sociales* (2 a year)

DEANS

Faculty of Biosciences: VALENTIN N'DOUBA
Faculty of Construction Engineering and Technology: MARIE-CHANTAL KOUASSI-GOFFRI
Faculty of Criminology: ZÉPHIRIN BOLIGA
Faculty of Earth Sciences and Mining Resources: JEAN BIENI
Faculty of Economics and Management: GILBERT-MARIE AKE NGBO
Faculty of Human and Social Sciences: IGNACE ZASSELI BIAKA
Faculty of Information, Art and Communication: AUGUSTE AGHI BAHI
Faculty of Languages, Literature and Civilization: FRANÇOIS ASSI ADOPO
Faculty of Law, Administration and Political Science: DJEDRO MELEDJE
Faculty of Mathematics and Computer Science: KONIN KOUA
Faculty of Medicine: ISIDORE MOHÉNOU DIOMANDE
Faculty of Odontostomatology: SIAKA TOURÉ
Faculty of Pharmaceutical Sciences: ANGLADE KLA MALAN

PROFESSORS

Faculty of Biosciences:

ACHY SEKA, A., Atmospheric Physics
AIDARA, D.
ASSA, A.
BOKRA, Y.
DEGNY, E.
DJAKOURE, A. L.
EBBY, N.
EHILE, E. E.
HONENOU, P.
KAMENAN, A.
KOPOH, K.
KOUAKOU, G.
KOUASSI, N., Zoology
KRA, G.
LOROUGNON, G.
N'DIAYE, A. S., Cell Biology
NEZIT, P., Mathematics
N'GUESSAN, Y. T., Organic Chemistry
OFFOUMOU, A. M.
SERI, B.
TOURE, S., Mathematics
TOURE, S.
TOURE, V., Organic Chemistry

Faculty of Economic Sciences:

ATSAIN, A.
ALLECHI, M.
KOULIBALY, M.

Faculty of Language, Literature and Civilization:

ANO, N., Oral Literature
BOKA, M., The African Novel in French
DIBI, K., Metaphysical Philosophy
HAUHOUOT, A., Geography
KODJO, N., History
KOMENAN, A. L., Philosophy
KONATE, Y., Philosophy
KONE BONI, T., Philosophy
LEZOU, D. G., The Francophone African Novel South of the Sahara, Semiotics
M'BRA, E., History
N'DA, P., The Francophone Novel
NIAMKET, K., Philosophy
NIANGORAN, B., Ethnology
SEMI-BI, Z., History
TANO, J., Differential Psychology

Faculty of Law:

BLEOU, D. M., Public Law
DEGNI-SEGUI, R., Public Law
ISSA, S., Private Law
SARASSORO, H., Private Law
WODIE, V. F., Public Law
YAO-N'DRE, P., Public Law

Faculty of Medicine:

ANDOH, J.
ATTIA, Y. R.
BAMBA, M.
BEDA, Y. B.
BOUHOUSSOU, K. M.
COULIBALY, O. A.
DAGO, A. B. A.
DJEDJE, M.
DOSSO, B. M.
EHOUMAN, A.
GADEGBEKU, A. S.
KADIO, A.
KANGA, J. M.
KANGA, M.
KEITA, A. K.
KONE, N.
KOUAKOU, N. M.
KOUAME, K. J.
LAMBIN, Y.
MOBIOT, M. L.
N'DORI, R.
N'DRI, K. D.
N'GUESSAN, K. G.
NIAMKET, E. K.
ODEHOURI, K. P.
ODI, A. M.
ROUX, C.
SANGARE, A.
SANGARE, I. S.
SOMBO, M. F.
TIMITE ADJOUA, M.
WAOTA, C.
WELFFENS-EKRA, C.

Faculty of Odontostomatology:

ANGOA, Y.
BAKAYOKO, L. R.
BROU, K. E.
EGNANKOU, K.
ROUX, H.
TOURE, S.

Faculty of Pharmacy:

BAMBA, M.
KONE, M.
MARCY, R.
OUATTARA, L.
YAPO, A. E.

DIRECTORS

Institute of African History of Art and Archaeology: ZAN SEMI-BI
Institute of African Literature and Aesthetics: (vacant)
Institute of Applied Linguistics: ASSY ADOPO
Institute of Ethnosociology: (vacant)
Institute of Teacher-Training and Teaching Research: ADOU AKA
Centre for Architectural and Urban Research: (vacant)
Centre for Communication Teaching and Research: REGINA SERIE TRAORE
University Centre for French Studies: N'GUESSAN KOUASSI

Colleges

Académie Régionale des Sciences et Techniques de la Mer: BP V 158, Abidjan; tel. 20-37-18-23; f. 1975 by 17 African countries; merchant shipping, training for radio officers, marine management; library; Dir-Gen. AKA ADOU.

Ecole Nationale d'Administration: BP V 20, Abidjan; tel. 22-41-52-25; fax 22-41-49-63; e-mail ena@globe.access.net; f. 1960; 954 students; library: 11,676 vols, 15 periodicals; Dir GUILLAUME KOUACOU DJAH.

Ecole Nationale des Postes et Télécommunications: BP 1501, Abidjan; tel. 21-25-54-94; fax 21-25-99-05.

Ecole Nationale Supérieure de Statistique et d'Economie Appliquée: Cnr Blvd François Mitterand and Blvd des Grandes Ecoles, Campus Universitaire de Cocody, 08 BP3, Abidjan 08; tel. 22-44-08-40; fax 22-44-39-88; e-mail ensea@ensea.ed.ci; internet www.ensea.refer.ci; f. 1961; 20 teachers; 120 students; library: 13,268 vols; Dir KOFFI N'GUESSAN.

Ecole Nationale Supérieure des Travaux Publics: BP 1083, Yamoussoukro; tel. 30-64-01-00; fax 30-64-03-06; f. 1963; comprises l'Ecole Préparatoire, l'Ecole Nationale Supérieure des Ingénieurs, le Centre de Formation Continue, Ecole Nationale des Techniciens Supérieurs; library: 60,000 vols; 97 teachers; 567 students; Dir SYLVAIN KACOU.

Ecole Supérieure d'Agronomie: BP 1313, Yamoussoukro; tel. 30-64-07-70; fax 30-64-17-49; e-mail esayakro@africaonline.ci; f. 1965; training of agricultural managers; research into agricultural production; 75 teachers; 600 students; library: 6,000 vols; Dir Dr KAMA BERTÉ.

Ecole Supérieure Interafricaine de l'Electricité/Interafrican Electrical Engineering College: BP 311, Bingerville; tel. 22-40-33-12; fax 22-40-35-07; f. 1979; bilingual (English and French) training to graduate level in electrical engineering for students sponsored by power-supply authorities or private companies from all over Africa; Dir-Gen. ABDOU KARIM DIAGNE.

Institut National Polytechnique Félix Houphouët-Boigny: BP 1093, Yamoussoukro; tel. 30-64-05-41; fax 30-64-04-06; f. 1975; technical and vocational training; comprises Ecole Supérieure d'Industrie, Ecole Supérieure de Commerce et d'Administration d'Entreprises, Ecole Supérieure d'Agronomie, Ecole Supérieure des Travaux Publics, Ecole de Formation Continue et de Perfectionnement des Cadres; library: 20,000 vols; 350 teachers; 3,500 students; Dir-Gen. ADO GOSSAN; publs *Akounda* (annually), *Leader* (quarterly).

CROATIA

The Higher Education System

Before gaining independence in 1991 Croatia was a federal republic of the former Yugoslavia. The oldest university is Sveučilište u Zagreb (University of Zagreb), which was founded in 1669. Higher education is administered according to the Higher Education Law of 1996, and is the responsibility of the Ministry of Science, Education and Sport. In 2004/05 a total of 126,322 students were enrolled at 103 institutions of higher education, and in 2006 there were six universities.

Higher education institutions set their own admissions requirements, with the approval of the Ministry of Science, Education and Sport. Students are usually required to possess the requisite secondary school qualifications and sit an entrance exam. In 2001 Croatia signed-up to the Bologna Agreement; the traditional undergraduate degrees, the Vise Obraazovanje (two to three years' study) and Visoko Obrazovanja (four to six years' study), have been phased out in favour of the Bachelors (four years). Study for a Magistar (Masters degree) in either arts or science subjects includes a magistarski rad (Masters thesis). The Doctorate is the highest postgraduate qualification, study for which includes the research and defence of a doktorski rad (doctoral thesis).

Tertiary-level technical and vocational education consists of one- to four-year programmes in industrial, trade, and craft occupations. Students who complete a postgraduate course in art at a polytechnic may attain the professional title of Master of Arts in accordance with a separate law.

Learned Societies

GENERAL

Društvo za Proučavanje i Unapredenje Pomorstva (Society for Research and Promotion of Maritime Sciences): Riva 16/V, POB 301, 51000 Rijeka; tel. (51) 334-210; fax (51) 334-210; e-mail dpuprh@inet.hr; f. 1962; research divided into 9 sections: economics, history, law, technology, natural sciences, nautical sciences, literature, ethnology, medicine; 323 elected mems; Pres. Prof. Dr BLANKA KESIĆ; Sec. Dr DUŠAN VRUS; publ. *Pomorski Zbornik* (Maritime Annals, annually).

Hrvatska Akademija Znanosti i Umjetnosti (Croatian Academy of Sciences and Arts): Zrinski trg 11, 10000 Zagreb; tel. (1) 4819-983; fax (1) 4819-979; e-mail kabpred@hazu.hr; internet www.hazu.hr; f. 1861; depts of Social Sciences, of Mathematical, Physical and Chemical Sciences, of Natural Sciences, of Medical Sciences, of Philology, of Literature, of Fine Arts, of Music, of Technical Sciences; 146 mems; 21 attached research institutes; library: see Libraries and Archives; Pres. MILAN MOGUŠ; Gen. Sec. SLAVKO CVETNIĆ; publs *Ljetopis*, *Rad* (Memoirs).

BIBLIOGRAPHY, LIBRARY SCIENCE AND MUSEOLOGY

Hrvatsko Knjižničarsko Društvo (Croatian Library Association): Hrvatske bratske zajednice 4, 10000 Zagreb; tel. and fax (1) 6159-320; e-mail hkd@nsk.hr; internet www.hkdrustvo.hr; f. 1940; 1,200 mems; Pres. ALENKA BELAN-SIMIĆ; Sec. ANA BARBARIĆ; publs *Novosti* (4 a year), *Vjesnik bibliotekara Hrvatske* (2 a year).

Hrvatsko Muzejsko Društvo (Croatian Museums Association): Habdelićeva 2, 10000 Zagreb; tel. (1) 4851-808; fax (1) 4851-977; e-mail msu@msu.tel.hr; internet www.hrmud.hr; f. 1945; 500 mems; Pres. NADA VRKLJAN-KRIŽIĆ; publ. *News of Museum Custodians and Conservators of Croatia* (quarterly).

EDUCATION

Hrvatski pedagoško-književni zbor (Pedagogical and Literary Association of Croatia): Trg Maršala Tita 4, 10000 Zagreb; tel. (1) 4855-713; fax (1) 4810-396; f. 1871; 3,000 mems in 17 socs; Pres. HRVOJE VRGOČ; Sec. KRISTINA ŠNIDARŠIĆ-VLAŠIĆ; publ. *Napredak* (4 a year).

HISTORY, GEOGRAPHY AND ARCHAEOLOGY

Croatian Geographic Society: Marulićev trg 19, PP 595 10000 Zagreb; tel. (1) 4895-402; fax 4895-451; e-mail geografija@geografija.hr; internet www.geografija.hr; f. 1897; 600 mems; library of 6,550 vols, 9,570 in special collections; Pres. ALEKSANDAR LUKIĆ; publs *Geografski glasnik* (annually), *Geografski horizont* (quarterly).

Hrvatsko numizmatičko društvo (Croatian Numismatic Society): Habdelićeva 2, POB 181, 10000 Zagreb; tel. (1) 431-426; f. 1928; *c.* 500 mems; library of 1,600 vols; Pres. EDGAR FABRY; Secs Prof. BORIS PRISTER, BERISLAV KOPAC; publs *Numizmatičke vijesti* (annually), *Numizmatika*, *Obol* (annually).

LANGUAGE AND LITERATURE

Alliance Française: 10000 Zagreb, Ante Kovačića 4; tel. and fax (1) 4818-292; e-mail alliance-francaise@zg.htnet.hr; internet www.alliance-francaise.hr; offers courses and exams in French language and culture and promotes cultural exchange with France; attached offices in Dubrovnik and Split.

British Council: Illica 12, PP55, 10001 Zagreb; tel. (1) 4899-500; fax (1) 4833-955; e-mail zagreb.info@britishcouncil.hr; internet www.britishcouncil.hr; offers courses and exams in English language and British culture and promotes cultural exchange with the UK; library of 7,500 vols, 60 periodicals; Dir ROY CROSS.

Goethe-Institut: Ul. grada Vukovara 64, 10000 Zagreb; tel. (1) 6195-000; fax (1) 6195-025; e-mail prog@zagreb.goethe.org; internet www.goethe.de/ms/zag/deindex.htm; offers courses and exams in German language and culture and promotes cultural exchange with Germany; library of 10,000 vols, 20 periodicals; Dir DR RUDOLF BARTSCH.

MEDICINE

Croatian Medical Association: Šubićeva ul. 9, 10000 Zagreb; tel. (1) 4693-300; fax (41) 4655-446; f. 1874; 29 regional brs, 88 mem. socs, 8,500 individual mems; Pres. Prof. Dr DUBRAVKO ORLIĆ; Gen. Sec. Prof. Dr IVAN BAKRAN; publs *Acta Stomatologica Croatica*, *Liječničke novine* (Medical News), *Liječnički Vjesnik* (Medical Journal).

Croatian Pharmaceutical Society: Masarykova 2, 10000 Zagreb; tel. (1) 4872-849; fax (1) 4872-853; e-mail hfd-fg-ap@zg.tel.hr; f. 1945; 1,040 mems; library of 2,000 vols; Chair. KREŠIMIR RUKAVINA; publs *Acta Pharmaceutica* (quarterly), *Farmaceutski glasnik* (monthly).

NATURAL SCIENCES

General

Hrvatsko Prirodoslovno Društvo (Croatian Society of Natural Sciences): Ilica 16/III, Zagreb; tel. (1) 425-288; fax (1) 425-288; e-mail periodicumbiologorum@public.srce.hr; f. 1885; Pres. Prof. Dr VELIMI PRAVDIĆ; Sec. Dr DAMIR KRALJ; publs *Periodicum Biologorum* (scientific journal with papers on biomedicine and biochemistry, 4 a year), *Priroda* (Nature, monthly).

TECHNOLOGY

Union of the Societies of Engineers and Technicians of Croatia: Berislavićeva 6, 10000 Zagreb; f. 1970; 3,017 mems; library of 5,000 vols; Chief Officer Prof. Dr Ing. ERVIN NONVEILLER; publ *Gradevinar*.

Research Institutes

GENERAL

Zavod za povijest i filozofiju znanosti Hrvatske akademije znanosti i umjetnosti (Institute for the History and Philosophy of Sciences of Croatian Academy of Sciences and Arts): Medical Sciences: Demetrova 18, 10000 Zagreb; Natural and Mathematical Sciences: Ante Kovačicá 5, 10000 Zagreb; Philosophy: Ante Kovačicá 5, 10000 Zagreb; f. 1960; incorporates Institute of the History of Pharmacy of the Croatian Pharmaceutical Society, Institute for the History of Medicine, Medical Faculty, University of Zagreb, Cabinet for the History of Veterinary Medicine, Museum of the Society of Physicians of Croatia and Institute for the Philosophy of Sciences; scientific institution to foster research into the history of science, especially that of the Croats; plans to study problems of methodology, to organize at Zagreb higher education for the study of the history of science, to collaborate with analogous institutes at home and abroad; library of 8,000 vols; Dir Prof. Dr ŽARKO DADIĆ; publ.

Rasprave i Gradja za Povijest Nauka (annually).

Zavod za Znanstveni i Umjetnički rad Hrvatske Akademije Znanosti i Umjetnosti (Institute for Science and Art of the Croatian Academy of Sciences and Arts): Trg Braće Radića 7, POB 100, 21000 Split; f. 1925 as Maritime Museum, re-constituted 1985 as Institute for Science and Art; library of 6,000 vols; Dir Prof. Dr VLADIMIR IBLER; publ. *Adrias*.

AGRICULTURE, FISHERIES AND VETERINARY SCIENCE

Institut za oceanografiju i ribarstvo (Institute of Oceanography and Fisheries): Šetalište Ivana Meštrovića 63, Split; tel. (21) 358-688; fax (21) 358-650; f. 1930; research in oceanography, hydrography, geology, marine biology, marine fisheries, ichthyology, mariculture and fishery technology; postgraduate study in fisheries; has a hatchery, a research vessel and a staff of 55 naturalists; library of 15,000 vols; Dir Dr IVONA MARASOVIĆ; publs *Acta Adriatica*, *Notes*.

Poljoprivredni Institut Osijek (Osijek Agricultural Institute): Južno Predgrade 17, POB 334, 31001 Osijek; tel. (31) 515-501; fax (31) 515-509; e-mail institut@poljinos.hr; internet www.poljinos.hr; f. 1916; agricultural and scientific research in breeding of wheat, barley, corn, soybeans, sunflowers and alfalfa; 160 mems; library of 5,380 vols; Dir Dr JOSIP KOVAČEVIĆ; publ. *Poljoprivreda* (Agriculture, 2 a year).

ARCHITECTURE AND TOWN PLANNING

Zavod za Arhitekturu i Urbanizam (Institute of Architecture and Town Planning): Ulica bracé Kavurića 1, 10000 Zagreb; tel. (1) 449-897; f. 1952 for the scientific study of the history of architecture and town planning and of methods of protection, conservation and presentation of monuments; 5 mems; library of 2,000 vols, 30 periodicals; Dir ANA DEANOVIĆ; publs *Bulletin Razreda za likovne umjetnosti* (2 a year), *Monographs* (irregular), *Rad JAZU* (irregular).

BIBLIOGRAPHY, LIBRARY SCIENCE AND MUSEOLOGY

Department for the Protection of the Cultural Heritage: Ilica 44, 10000 Zagreb; tel. (1) 4849-444; fax (1) 4849-445; f. 1910; attached to Min. of Culture; library of 12,050 vols, photo collection of 54,000 negatives, 10,000 charts; Dir BIANKA PERČINIĆ-KAVUR; publ. *Godišnjak zaštite spomenika kulture Hrvatske* (Yearbook of Protection of Croatian Cultural Monuments).

Hrvatski restauratorski zavod (Croatian Conservation Institute): Nike Grskovica 23, 10000 Zagreb; tel. (1) 4684-599; fax (1) 4683-289; e-mail uprava@h-r-z.hr; internet www.h-r-z.hr; f. 1948; restoration of and research into the conservation of paintings, historic architecture, wooden sculpture, furniture, stucco, stone, mosaics, wall paintings, architectural monuments, paper and leather, textiles, metal and other archaeological finds; underwater archaeological research; 150 mems; Dir Prof. FERDINAND MEDER.

Regionalni zavod za zaštitu spomenika kulture (Regional Institute for the Protection of Historic Monuments): Poljudsko šetalište 15, p.p. 191, 21000 Split; tel. (21) 342-327; f. 1854; library of 12,000 vols and periodicals, 130,000 photographs and negatives; Dir Dr JOŠKO BELAMARIĆ; Sec. NEIRA STOJANAC; publ. *Prilozi povijesti umjetnosti u Dalmaciji*.

ECONOMICS, LAW AND POLITICS

Institute for International Relations – IMO: POB 303, Ul. Lj. Farkaša Vukotinovića 2/II, 10000 Zagreb; tel. (1) 4826-522; fax (1) 4828-361; e-mail ured@irmo.hr; internet www.imo.hr; f. 1963; attached to Ministry of Science and Technology; interdisciplinary study of development processes and economic and international relations, and co-operation in the field of economics, culture, science, environmental protection and politics; organizes seminars, international conferences and specialist training programmes; library of 9,000 vols, 400 periodicals; Dir Prof. Dr MLADEN STANIČIĆ; publs *Croatian International Relations Review* (quarterly, in English), *Culturelink* (3 a year and special issue in English), *Euroscope* (6 a year, in Croatian).

Jadranski zavod Hrvatske akademije znanosti i umjetnosti (Adriatic Institute of the Croatian Academy of Sciences and Arts): Frane Petrića 4, 10000 Zagreb; tel. and fax (1) 4812-703; e-mail jz@hazu.hr; internet www.hazu.hr/jzavod; f. 1945; research in maritime law; library of 25,000 vols; Dir Prof. Dr VLADIMIR-DJURO DEGAN; publ. *Poredbeno pomorsko pravo* (Comparative Maritime Law, annually).

LANGUAGE AND LITERATURE

Leksikografski Zavod 'Miroslav Krleža' ('Miroslav Krleža' Lexicographic Institute): Frankopanska 26, 10000 Zagreb; tel. (1) 4800-398; fax (1) 4800-399; e-mail lzmk@lzmk.hr; internet www.lzmk.hr; f. 1951; collects and processes MSS for encyclopaedic, lexicographic, bibliographic, monographic and other scientific editions; publishes results of research and co-operates with similar institutions abroad; 10,000 contributors, specialists in all fields; library: specialized library of 35,000 vols; Dir Prof. TOMISLAV LADAN.

Staroslavenski institut (Old Church Slavonic Institute): Demetrova 11, 10000 Zagreb; tel. (1) 4851-377; fax (1) 4851-380; internet public.srce.hr/staroslavenski-institut; f. 1952; research in Croatian Church Slavonic language, literature and culture; library of 20,000 vols; Dir. Dr MARICA CUNČIĆ; Sec. MARINA ŠANTIĆ; publ. *Slovo* (annually).

MEDICINE

Institute for Medical Research and Occupational Health: Ksaverska cesta 2, POB 291, 10000 Zagreb; tel. (1) 4673-188; fax (1) 4673-303; e-mail uprava@imi.hr; internet mimi.imi.hr; f. 1949 to study the influence of ecological factors upon health; 149 mems; library of 8,500 vols; Dir Dr SANJA MILKOVIĆ-KRAUS; publ. *Arhiv za higijenu rada i toksilologiju* (Archives of Industrial Hygiene and Toxicology, in English and Croatian, 4 a year).

NATURAL SCIENCES

General

Institut 'Rudjer Bošković' (Rudjer Bošković Institute): Bijenička cesta 54, POB 1016, 10001 Zagreb; tel. (1) 4561-111; fax (1) 4680-084; f. 1950; library of 35,000 books and 400 current periodicals; attached to the University of Osijek, University of Rijeka and University of Zagreb; research in physics (theoretical, nuclear and atomic, medical, biophysics), chemistry (physical, organic, and biochemistry), biology (molecular biology, biomedicine), electronics; marine research centres in Rovinj and Zagreb; Dir Gen. Dr NIKOLA ZOVKO.

Biological Sciences

Bureau for Nature Conservation: Ilica 44/II, 10000 Zagreb; tel. (1) 432-022; fax (1) 431-515; f. 1961; 16 mems; library of 5,400 vols; photo collection of 12,200 negatives, 12,000 photos and 1,240 colour slides; Dir Prof. Dr MIHO MILJANIĆ.

Physical Sciences

Hidrometeorološki Zavod Hrvatske (Meteorological and Hydrological Institute of Croatia): Grič 3, 10000 Zagreb; tel. (1) 4565-693; fax (1) 4851-901; e-mail dhmz@cirus.dhz.hr; internet http://meteo.hr; f. 1947; meteorology, climatology, ecological studies, hydrology; library of 7,000 vols, 45 periodicals; Dir IVAN CACIĆ; publs *Bilten* (meteorological and hydrological bulletin, monthly), *Croatian Meteorological Journal* (annually).

PHILOSOPHY AND PSYCHOLOGY

Institute for the Philosophy of Science and Peace: A. Kovačića 5, 10000 Zagreb; tel. (1) 4818-280; fax (1) 4856-211; f. 1965; researches and promotes the synthesis and social ethics of sciences and arts; 5 mems; Pres. IVAN SUPEK.

RELIGION, SOCIOLOGY AND ANTHROPOLOGY

Institut za Društvena Istraživanja (Institute for Social Research): POB 280, Amruševa 8/3, 10002 Zagreb,; f. 1964; attached to Univ. of Zagreb; research in all fields of sociology, social anthropology, psychology; library of 16,400 vols and periodicals; Dir. RUŽA FIRST-DILIĆ; publs *Sociologija Sela* (Rural Sociology, quarterly), *Revija za Sociologiju* (Sociology Review).

Institute of Ethnology and Folklore Research: Zvonimirova 17, Zagreb; tel. (1) 4553-632; fax (1) 4553-649; e-mail institut@ief.hr; internet maief.ief.hr; f. 1948; library of 30,000 vols; 185,000 items of archives and documentation; Dir IVAN LOZICA; publ. *Narodna Umjetnost* (2 a year).

TECHNOLOGY

Končar–Institut za elektrotehniku d.d.: Baštijanova ul. b.b., 10001 Zagreb; tel. (1) 3667-315; fax (1) 3667-317; e-mail info@koncar-institut.hr; internet www.koncar-institut.hr; f. 1991; research and development division within Končar Group of companies; research and development in all fields of electrical engineering; library of 30,000 vols, 350 periodicals; Dir Dr STJEPAN CAR.

Libraries and Archives

Dubrovnik

Znanstvena knjižnica Dubrovnik (Scientific Library of Dubrovnik): Cvijete Zuzorić 6, 20000 Dubrovnik; tel. and fax (20) 432-986; e-mail dubrovacke-knjiznice@du.tel.hr; f. 1936; 267,000 vols, 7,000 vols of periodicals, 77 incunabula, 1,400 MSS, 13,490 books belonging to the Republic of Dubrovnik up to 1808 (Old Ragusina), collection of 14,000 vols (New Ragusina); Chief Officer MIRJANA URBAN.

Pula

Sveučilišna knjiznica u Puli (University Library of Pula): Herkulov prolaz 1, 52000 Pula; tel. (52) 213-888; fax (52) 214-603; e-mail skpu@knjiga.skpu.hr; f. 1861; 2,730 mems; copyright and lending library attached to Rijeka University; 300,000 vols; special collections: the Istrian area, Austro-

Hungarian Naval Library (20,000 vols); Dir BRUNO DOBRIĆ; publ. *Nova Istra* (literary review, 4 a year).

Rijeka

Sveučilišna knjižnica Rijeka (Rijeka University Library): Dolac 1, POB 132, 51000 Rijeka; tel. (51) 336-911; fax (51) 332-006; e-mail ravnatelj@svkri.hr; internet www.svkri.hr; f. 1627; legal deposit library; special collns of material on the Primorsko-Goranska region and on the Glagolitic script; repository of Univ. of Rijeka publs and dissertations; 375,000 vols, 23 incunabula, 71,000 vols of periodicals; Dir Dr SENKA TOMJANOVIĆ.

Split

Sveučilišna knjižnica u Splitu (Split University Library): Zagrebačka 3, 21000 Split; tel. (21) 361-231; fax (21) 361-474; e-mail svkst@svkst.hr; internet www.svkst.hr; f. 1903; 3,000 mems; 400,000 vols, 20,000 periodicals, 700 manuscripts, 5,000 rare books; Dir Prof. PETAR KROLO.

Varaždin

Gradska knjižnica i čitaonica 'Metel Ožegović' (Public Library): Trg Slobode 8A, 42000 Varaždin; tel. and fax (42) 212-767; e-mail gknjizmo@vz.htnet.hr; internet library.foi.hr/metel; f. 1838; 190,000 vols; Dir Prof. MARIJAN KRAŠ.

Zadar

Znanstvena Knjižnica Zadar (Zadar Research Library): Ante Kuzmanića b.b., 23000 Zadar; tel. (23) 211-365; fax (23) 312-129; e-mail zkzd@zkzd.hr; internet www.zkzd.hr; f. 1855; deposit library; special colln: Dalmatica; 800,000 vols; Dir MILENKA BUKVIĆ; publ. *Knjižno blago*.

Zagreb

Gradska knjižnica (Municipal Library): Starčevićev trg 6, 10000 Zagreb; tel. (1) 4572-081; fax (1) 4572-089; e-mail kgz@kgz.hr; internet www.kgz.hr; f. 1907; 367,517 vols, 14,115 periodicals; Dir LILIAN SABLJAK.

Hrvatski državni arhiv (Croatian State Archives): Marulićev trg 21, 10000 Zagreb; tel. (1) 4801-999; fax (1) 4829-000; e-mail knjiznica@arhiv.hr; internet www.arhiv.hr; f. 1643; 20,000 linear metres of records since 10th c., concerning the history of Croatia; 18,000,000 metres of film; 150,000 vols, 600,000 photographs; Dir Dr STJEPAN ĆOSIĆ; publs *Arhivski vjesnik* (Archives Bulletin), *Bulletin – Hrvatski drzavni arhiv* (Bulletin – Croatian State Archives), *Fontes – HDS* (Sources – CSA).

Knjižnica Hrvatske akademije znanosti i umjetnosti (Library of the Croatian Academy of Sciences and Arts): Trg Nikole Šubića Zrinskog 11, 10000 Zagreb; tel. (1) 4895-114; fax (1) 4895-134; e-mail library@hazu.hr; internet www.hazu.hr; f. 1867; 500,000 vols, 1,250 current periodicals; Dir VEDRANA JURICIC.

Nacionalna i sveučilišna knjižnica (National and University Library): Ul. Hrvatske bratske zajednice b.b., POB 550, 10000 Zagreb; tel. (1) 6164-009; fax (1) 6164-186; f. 17th c.; 1,840,000 vols; 187 incunabula; 67,000 rare and precious books; 165,595 vols of newspapers; 328,992 vols of periodicals; 16,300 prints and drawings; 27,906 maps; 18,737 scores; 29,793 records; 8,500 microfilms; 125,000 posters and leaflets; copyright and deposit library; Chief Librarian Dr JOSIP STIPANOV; publ. *Hrvatska bibliografija* (monthly and annually).

Radnička biblioteka 'Božidar Adžija' Zagreb (Workers' Library): Trg Kralja Petra Krešimira IV, 2, Zagreb; tel. (1) 4655-025; fax (1) 4655-039; e-mail knjiznica.bozidara.adzije@kgz.hr; internet www.kgz.hr/adzija/default.asp; f. 1927; 171,240 vols; Dir Prof. DRAGICA PREVIŠIĆ.

Museums and Art Galleries

Dubrovnik

Muzej Srpske Pravoslavne Crkve (Museum of the Serbian Orthodox Church): Od Puća 2, 20000 Dubrovnik; f. 1953; collection of portraits, and over 170 icons from Serbia, Crete, Corfu, Venice, Russia, Greece, Dubrovnik, Boka-Kotorska; the palace which houses the collection is also of historical interest; library of 25,000 vols.

Pomorski Muzej (Maritime Museum): St John's Fortress, 20000 Dubrovnik; tel. (20) 426-465; fax (20) 322-096; internet www.mdc.hr; f. 1872; Dubrovnik's maritime past; library of 10,027 vols; Curator Prof. ĐIVO BAŠIĆ.

Umjetnička Galerija Dubrovnik (Dubrovnik Museum of Modern Art): Frana Supila 23, 20000 Dubrovnik; tel. (20) 426-590; fax (20) 432-119; internet www.ugdubrovnik.hr; f. 1945; modern and contemporary works of art; library of 2,418 vols; Dir ANTUN MARAČIC.

Rijeka

Muzej Moderne i Suvremente Umjetnosti (Museum of Modern and Contemporary Art): Dolac 1, 51000 Rijeka; tel. (51) 334-280; fax (51) 330-982; e-mail mmsu-rijeka@ri.htnet.hrr; internet www.mgr.hr; f. 1948; paintings, sculpture and graphics from Croatia and other countries; library of 20,000 books and catalogues; Dir BRANKO FRANCESCHI; publs catalogues.

Prirodoslovni muzej (Natural History Museum): Lorenzov Prolaz 1, 51000 Rijeka; tel. and fax (51) 334-988; e-mail primuzri@ri.tel.hr; f. 1946; library of 4,024 vols; Dir MILVANA ARKO-PIJEVAC.

Slavonski Brod

Brlić House (Ivana Brlić-Mažuranić Memorial): Titov trg 8, 55000 Slavonski Brod; f. 1933; private family house containing archives, furniture, library (8,000 vols) showing the evolution over 300 years of a Croatian middle-class family; Ivana Brlić (1874–1938) was a writer and first woman mem. of the Yugoslav Acad. of Sciences and Arts; Curator VIKTOR RUŽIĆ.

Split

Arheološki muzej u Splitu (Archaeological Museum): Zrinjsko-Frankopanska 25, 21000 Split; tel. and fax (21) 318-714; e-mail arheoloski-muzej-st@st.tel.hr; internet www.mdc.hr/split-arheoloski/eng/index.html; f. 1820; prehistoric collections, relics from the Greek colonies on the east shore of the Adriatic Sea, Roman and Christian relics from Salonae and Dalmatia; Croatian medieval monuments from 9th to 13th century; numismatic collection; library of 30,000 vols, special collection: Dalmatica; Dir Prof. EMILIO MARIN; publ. *Vjesnik zu arheologiju i historiju dalmatinsku* (Bulletin of Dalmatian Archaeology and History, annually).

Etnografski muzej Split (Ethnographical Museum): Iza Lože 1, 21000 Split; tel. and fax (21) 344-164; e-mail etnografski-muzej-st@st.tel.hr; f. 1910; 19,500 items; national costumes, jewels, weapons, and traditional technological objects from Dalmatia, Dinaric Alps area and other neighbouring regions; illustrations section and textbook library (3,000 vols); Dir SILVIO BRAICA.

Galerija umjetnina (Art Gallery): Lovretska 11, 21000 Split; f. 1931; 2,300 paintings and sculptures (ancient and modern); library of 10,000 vols; Dir Prof. MILAN IVANIŠEVIĆ.

Ivan Meštrović Foundation: Mletačka 8, 10000 Zagreb; tel. (1) 4851-123; fax (1) 4851-126; e-mail fim@fim.hr; internet www.mdc.hr/mestrovic; f. 1991; permanent exhibition of sculptures of Ivan Meštrović (1883–1962); Dir IGOR MARDEVIĆ.

Muzej grada Splita (City Museum of Split): Papalićeva 1, 21000 Split; tel. and fax (21) 341-240; e-mail muzej-grada-st@st.tel.hr; f. 1946; political and cultural history of Split; library of 10,000 vols; Dir Prof. GORAN BORČIĆ; publ. *Editions*.

Prirodoslovni muzej (Museum of Natural Sciences): 21000 Split; f. 1924; contains more than 100,000 exhibits of mineralogical, palaeontological and zoological specimens from Dalmatia and the Adriatic Sea; collections of coleoptera, shells and birds (mostly Dalmatian); library of 3,500 vols; zoological garden (Vrh Marjana 1); Dir Prof. ANTUN CVITANIĆ.

Zagreb

Arheološki muzej u Zagrebu (Archaeological Museum of Zagreb): Nikola Subic Zrinski trg 19, 10000 Zagreb; tel. (1) 4873-101; fax (1) 4873 102; e-mail amz@amz.hr; internet www.amz.hr; f. 1846; museum of archaeological finds from neolithic times to 13th c., including pre-historic colln, Egyptian colln, Greek, Roman and medieval collns, numismatic colln; Lapidarium in courtyard, featuring stone monuments from Roman era; library of 45,000 vols; Dir Prof. ANTE RENDIĆ-MIOČEVIĆ; publ. *Vjesnik Arheološkog Muzeja u Zagrebu* (annually).

Etnografski muzej (Ethnographical Museum): Mažuranićev trg 14, 10000 Zagreb; tel. (1) 4826-220; fax (1) 4826-221; e-mail emz@etnografski-musej.hr; internet www.etnografski-muzej.hr; f. 1919; cultural traditions of the three ethnographic regions of Croatia: Pannonic, Dinaric, Adriatic; dept of non-European collections; library of 80,000 vols; Dir DAMODAR FRLAN; publ. *Ethnographical Researches* (annually).

Glyptothèque HAZU: Medvedgradska 2, 10000 Zagreb; tel. (1) 4667-334; fax (1) 4666-628; e-mail gliptoteka@hazu.hr; internet www.hazu.hr; f. 1937; collection of medieval frescos and plaster casts of ancient, medieval and recent sculptures and architecture; originals of Croatian sculptures since 19th c.; Dir Prof. ARIANA KRALJ.

Hrvatski muzej naivne umjetnosti (Croatian Museum of Naïve Art): Cirilometodska 3, 10000 Zagreb; tel. (1) 4851-911; fax (1) 4852-125; e-mail info@hmnu.hr; internet hmnu.org; f. 1952; Dir Prof. VLADIMIR CRNKOVIĆ.

Hrvatski povijesni muzej (Croatian Historical Museum): Matoševa 9, 10000 Zagreb; tel. (1) 4851-900; fax (1) 4851-909; e-mail hismus@hismus.hr; internet www.hismus.hr; f. 1846; history of Croatia with collections of different historical objects, arms, paintings, prints, stone monuments; 140,000 artefacts in total; library of 43,000 vols; Dir Prof. ANKICA PANDŽIĆ; Librarian Prof. ZORA GAJSKY.

Hrvatski prirodoslovni muzej (Croatian Natural History Museum): Demetrova 1, 10000 Zagreb; tel. (1) 4851-700; fax (1) 4851-644; e-mail hpm@hpm.hr; internet www.hpm.hr; f. 1846; departments of zoology, mineralogy and petrography, geology and palaeontology, botany; library of 30,000 vols; Dir SREĆKO LEINER; publ. *Natura croatica* (quarterly).

Hrvatski školski muzej (Croatian School Museum): Trg m. Tita 4, 10000 Zagreb; tel. (1) 4855-716; fax (1) 4855-825; e-mail hrskmuz@zg.tel.hr; f. 1901; history of the school system and education in Croatia; library of 37,000 vols on the history of schools and education in general; Dir Prof. ELIZABETA SERDAR; publ. *Anali za povijest odgoja* (Annals of the History of Education, annually).

Kabinet Grafike (Print Room): Hebrangova 1, 10000 Zagreb; tel. and fax (1) 4922-374; e-mail kabgraf@hazu.hr; internet www.hazu.hr/kabinet_grafike.html; f. 1951; 12,000 prints, drawings, and 4,000 posters; Dir EDO MURTIĆ.

Moderna Galerija (Gallery of Modern Art): Andrije Hebranga 1, 10000 Zagreb; tel. and fax (1) 4922-368; e-mail moderna-galerija@zg.htnet.hr; f. 1905; Croatian arts since 19th c.; collections of painting, sculpture and graphic arts; 1,945 medals; library of 5,922 vols; Dir IGOR ZIDIĆ.

Muzej grada Zagreba (City Museum of Zagreb): Opatička 20–22, 10000 Zagreb; tel. (1) 4851-361; fax (1) 4851-359; e-mail muzej-grada-zagreba@mgz.tel.hr; internet www.mdc.hr; f. 1907; exhibits on Zagreb since pre-historic times; library of 11,000 vols; Dir Prof. VINKO IVIĆ; publ. *Iz starog i novog Zagreba* (from Old and New Zagreb, irregular).

Muzej Suvremene Umjetnosti (Museum of Contemporary Art): Habdelićeva 2, 10000 Zagreb; tel. (1) 4851-930; fax (1) 4851-931; e-mail msu@msu.hr; internet www.msu.hr; f. 1954; library of 12,500 vols; Dir SNJEŽANA PINTARIĆ; publ. *Dokumenti* (Documents).

Muzej za umjetnost i obrt (Museum of Arts and Crafts): Trg maršala Tita 10, 10000 Zagreb,; tel. (1) 4882-111; fax (1) 4828-088; e-mail muo@muo.hr; internet www.muo.hr; f. 1880; fine and applied arts since 14th c.; furniture, textiles, ceramics, glass, metalwork, sculpture, paintings, photography, costumes, clocks and watches, ivory, architecture, design and posters; library: art library of 60,000 vols; Dir Prof. MIROSLAV GAŠPAROVIĆ.

Strossmayerova galerija starih majstora (Strossmayers' Gallery of Old Masters): Trg Nikole Šubića Zrinskog 11, 10000 Zagreb; tel. (1) 4895-115; fax (1) 4819-979; e-mail sgallery@hazu.hr; internet www.mdc.hr/strossmayer; f. 1884; 14th–19th c. art; library of 4,000 vols; Dir Prof. DURO VANDURA; publs *Bulletin, HAZU, Razreda za likovne umjetnosti*.

Tehnički muzej Zagreb (Technical Museum Zagreb): Savska cesta 18, 10000 Zagreb; tel. (1) 4844-050; fax (1) 4843-568; e-mail tehnicki-muzej@tehnicki-muzej.htnet.hr; internet www.mdc.hr/tehnicki/; f. 1954; library of 4,600 vols; Dir BOŽICA ŠKULJ.

Universities

SVEUČILIŠTE JOSIPA JURJA STROSSMAYERA U OSIJEKU
(Josip Juraj Strossmayer University of Osijek)

Trg sv. Trojstva 3, 31000 Osijek
Telephone: (31) 224-102
Fax: (31) 207-015
E-mail: rektorat@unios.hr
Internet: www.unios.hr

Founded 1975
State control

Academic year: October to September

Rector: GORDANA KRALIK
Vice-Rectors: DRAŽENKA JURKOVIĆ DRAGOMIR KRUMES, ŽANETA UGARČIĆ-HARDI
Chief Administrative Officer: ZDENKA BARIŠIĆ
Librarian: DRAGUTIN KATALENAC

Number of teachers: 523
Number of students: 13,214

Publications: *Ekonomski vjesnik* (Economic Courier), *Medicinski vjesnik* (Medical Courier), *Poljoprivreda* (Agriculture), *Pravni vjesnik* (Law Courier), *Sveučilišni Glasnik* (University Newsletter), *Tehnički vjesnik* (Technical Courier)

DEANS

Faculty of Agriculture: RUDOLF EMERT
Faculty of Civil Engineering: VLADIMIR SIGMUND
Faculty of Economics: IVAN FERENČAK
Faculty of Electrical Engineering: ŽELJKO HOCENÇKI
Faculty of Food Technology: VLASTA PILIŽOTA
Faculty of Law: VLADIMIR LJUBANOVIĆ
Faculty of Mechanical Engineering: NIKO MAJDANDŽIĆ
Faculty of Medicine: KREŠIMIR GLAVINA
Faculty of Philosophy: ANA PINTARIĆ
Department of Mathematics: DRAGAN JUKIĆ
Teacher Training College: MARGITA PAVLEKOVIĆ

PROFESSORS

Faculty of Agriculture (tel. (31) 224-200; fax (31) 207-017; e-mail nastava@suncokret.pfos.hr; internet www.pfos.hr):

BERTIĆ, B., Agrochemistry, Fertilizers
BUKVIĆ, Ž., Mechanization in Livestock Farming and Crop Production
EMERT, R., Agricultural Machinery and Maintenance
GUBERAC, V., Plant Breeding, Seed Science
IVEZIĆ, M., Entomology with Phytopharmacy and Plant Protection, Nematology
JOVANOVAC, S., General Livestock, Genetics of Domestic Animals
JURIĆ, I., Principles of Agriculture, Tropical Agriculture
JURKOVIĆ, D., Plant Protection, Phytopharmacy
KALINOVIĆ, I., Storage and Technology of Agricultural Products
KNEŽEVIĆ, I., Cattle Breeding
KNEŽEVIĆ, M., Botany
KOVAČEVIĆ, V., Cereal Crop Production
KRALIK, G., Husbandry of Swine, Poultry and Fur-bearing Animals
KRISTEK, A., Industrial Crops
MADJAR, S., Agricultural Improvement, Irrigation
MILAKOVIĆ, Z., Microbiology
RASTIJA, T., General Cattle and Horse Raising
SENČIĆ, D., Pig Breeding, Livestock Breeding
STEINER, Z., Nutrition of Domestic Animals
STJEPANOVIĆ, M., Forage Crops
VUKADINOVIĆ, V., Plant Physiology, Agricultural Mechanization
ZIMMER, R., Mechanization in Farming, Processing Technology and Storing
ŽUGEC, I., General Crop Production, Alternative Agriculture

Faculty of Civil Engineering (Drinska 16A, 31000 Osijek; tel. (31) 274-377; fax (31) 274-444; internet www.gfos.hr):

ANIČIĆ, D., Surveying, Earthquake Engineering
MEDANIĆ, B., Construction Management
SIGMUND, V., Construction Stability and Dynamics, Resistance of Materials
TAKAČ, S., Wooden Buildings, Bricklaying

Faculty of Economics (Gajev trg 7, 31000 Osijek; tel. (31) 224-400; fax (31) 211-604; internet www.efos.hr):

BABAN, LJ., Theory of Marketing, International Economics
BARKOVIĆ, D., Operational Research
CRNJAC, M., Mathematics
JELINIĆ, S., Commercial Law
KARIĆ, M., Microeconomics, Cost Management, Accounting
LAMZA-MARONIĆ, M., Management and Information Systems
LAUC, A., Sociology of Management
MELER, M., Introduction to Marketing, Marketing Management
NOVAC, B., Finance Management, Financial Markets
PROKLIN, P., Accounting
SEGETLIJA, Z., Business Logistics, Branch Marketing
SINGER, S., Strategic Management
SRB, V., Finance, Public Finance, Banking
TURKALJ, Ž., Business Organization

Faculty of Electrical Engineering (Kneza Trpimira 2B, 31000 Osijek; tel. (31) 224-600; fax (31) 224-605; internet www.etfos.hr):

FLEGAR, I., Electronics, Networking Theory, Electrical Compatibility
GODEC, Z., Metrology, Monitoring
JOVIĆ, F., Information and Communications, Computers and Processes, Computer and Terminal Networks, Artificial Intelligence
ŠTEFANKO, S., Fundamentals of Electrical Engineering, Theoretical Electrical Engineering
ŠVEDEK, T., Electronic Components, Microelectronics, High-Frequency Electronics
VALTER, Z., Fundamentals of Electromechanical Engineering

Faculty of Food Technology (F. Kuhača 18, 31000 Osijek; tel. (31) 224-300; fax (31) 207-115; internet www.ptfos.hr):

MANDIĆ, M., Quality Control, Sensor Analyses, Fundamentals of Food Technology, Food Science
PILIŽOTA, V., Raw Materials in Food Industry, Technology of Fruit and Vegetable Preserving and Processing
ŠERUGA, M., Physical Chemistry, Packing Materials, Methods of Analysis by Instrument
UGARČIĆ-HARDI, Ž, Raw Materials in Food Industry, Flour Production and Processing

Faculty of Law (S. Radića 13, 31000 Osijek; tel. (31) 224-500; fax (31) 224-540; internet www.pravos.hr):

BABAC, B., Administrative Law, Administrative Science
BELAJ, V., Civil Law
JELINIĆ, S., Commercial Law, Social Law, Copyright
KLASIČEK, D., International Law
LAUC, Z., Constitutional Law
LJUBANOVIĆ, V., Criminal Procedural Law
MECANOVIĆ, I., Constitutional Law, Informatics for Lawyers
ROMŠTAJN, I., Transport Law, Insurance Law
SRB, V., Financial Law and Sciences, Banking and Credit

Faculty of Mechanical Engineering (Trg I. B. Mažuranić 18, 35000 Slavonski Brod; tel. (35) 446-188; fax (35) 446-446; internet www.sfsb.hr):

BUDIĆ, I., Foundry, Processing Technology, Assembling Technology, Design
GRIZELJ, B., Metal Forming, Technology, Tools
HNATKO, E., Heat Engines and Devices
KATALINIĆ, B., Automation, Flexible Systems

KLJAJIN, M., Machine Elements, Technical Drafting
KRUMES, D., Materials, Heat Processing, Tribology, Surface Engineering, Tools
MAJDANDŽIĆ, N., Computers and Information Systems, Production Process, Artificial Intelligence, Planning Methods
MATEJIČEK, F., Mechanics, Engine Dynamics
RAOS, P., Polymer Processing, Machine Maintenance
VITEZ, I., Materials, New Technologies

Faculty of Medicine (J. Huttlera 4, 31000 Osijek; tel. (31) 512-888; fax (31) 512-833; internet www.mefos.hr):

BELICZA, B., History of Medicine, Medical Ethics
KOSTOVIĆ-KNEŽEVIĆ, LJ., Histology, Embryology
SOLDO, I., Infectious Diseases
ŠESTO, M., Internal Medicine
TUCAK, A., Urology, Civil War Medicine

Faculty of Philosophy (L. Jägera 9, 31000 Osijek; tel. (31) 211-400; fax (31) 212-514; internet www.pedos.hr):

APARAC-JELUŠIĆ, T., Library Science, Informatics and Communication
BRLENIĆ-VUJIĆ, B., Comparative Literature
JERKOVIĆ, J., Conducting, Choir
MARIJANOVIĆ, S., Croatian Literature
MIKUSKA, J., Animal Ecology and Zoogeography, Special Zoology, Vertebrates
NIKČEVIĆ, M., Methodology of Scientific Work, Methodics of Literature Teaching
OBAD, V., German Literature
PLANINIĆ, J., Introduction to Physics
ŽIVKOVIĆ, P., Medieval History

Department of Mathematics (Gajev trg 6, 31000 Osijek; tel. (31) 224-800; fax (31) 224-801; e-mail math@mathos.hr; internet www.mathos.hr):

BUTKOVIĆ, D., Linear Algebra
SCITOVSKI, R., Numerical Mathematics, Computer Exercises II
SVRTAN, D., Theoretical Mechanics, Discrete Mathematics
VOLENEC, V., Geometry Models, Metric Geometry

Teacher Training College (L. Jägera 9, 31000 Osijek; tel. (31) 200-602; fax (31) 200-604; internet www.vusos.hr):

BABIĆ, N., Pre-School Education, Teaching Methods in Pre-School Education, Education Communication

SVEUČILIŠTE U RIJECI
(University of Rijeka)

Trg braće Mažuranića 10, 51000 Rijeka
Telephone: (51) 406-500
Fax: (51) 216-671
E-mail: ured@uniri.hr
Internet: www.uniri.hr

Founded 1973
State control
Language of instruction: Croatian (and some courses in Italian)
Academic year: October to July

Rector: Prof. Dr DANIEL RUKAVINA
Vice-Rectors: Prof. Dr GORAN KALOGJERA, Prof. Dr ZDRAVKO LENAC, Prof. Dr PERO LUČIN, Prof. Dr JOŽE PERIĆ
Secretary-General: ROBERTA HLAČA MLINAR
Librarians: BRUNO DOBRIĆ (Pula), SENKA TOMLJANOVIĆ (Rijeka)

Number of teachers: 997
Number of students: 18,099 (12,959 full-time, 5,140 part-time)

Publications: *Gaudeamus* (several a year), *Sveučilišni vodič* (guide to curriculums, annually)

DEANS

Faculty of Civil Engineering in Rijeka: Assoc. Prof. Dr NEVENKA OŽANIĆ
Faculty of Economics and Tourism 'Dr Mijo Mirković' in Pula: Assoc. Prof. Dr ALFIO BARBIERI
Faculty of Economics in Rijeka: Prof. Dr VINKO KANDŽIJA
Faculty of Engineering in Rijeka: Prof. Dr TONČI MIKAC
Faculty of Law in Rijeka: Prof. Dr MIOMIR MATULOVIĆ
Faculty of Maritime Studies: Prof. PAVAO KOMADINA
Faculty of Medicine in Rijeka: Prof. Dr MILJENKO KAPOVIĆ
Faculty of Philosophy in Pula: Assoc. Prof. Dr ROBERT MATIJAŠIĆ
Faculty of Philosophy in Rijeka: Prof. Dr BRANKO RAFAJAC
Faculty of Tourism and Hospitality Management in Opatija: Prof. Dr ZORAN IVANOVIĆ
Teacher-Training School of Professional Higher Education in Gospić: Prof. STIPE GOLAC
Teacher-Training School of Professional Higher Education in Pula: Asst Prof. Dr NEVENKA TATKOVIĆ
Teacher-Training School of Professional Higher Education in Rijeka: Assoc. Prof. Dr ALEKSANDRA PEJČIĆ

SVEUČILIŠTE U SPLITU
(University of Split)

Livanjska 5/I, 21000 Split
Telephone: (21) 558-200
Fax: (21) 348-163
E-mail: rektorat.office@unist.hr
Internet: www.unist.hr

Founded 1974
State control
Language of instruction: Croatian
Academic year: October to September

Rector: Prof. Dr IVAN PAVIĆ
Vice-Rectors: Prof. Dr IVAN BILIČ, Prof. Dr PAVAO MAROVIĆ
Secretary-General: JOSIP ALAJBEG

Library of 369,000 vols
Number of teachers: 1,500
Number of students: 17,000

Publication: *Sveučilišni godišnjak*

DEANS

Faculty of Arts (Zadar): Dr NIKICA KOLUMBIĆ
Faculty of Civil Engineering: Dr ANTE MIHANOVIĆ
Faculty of Economics: Dr DAVOR POJATINA
Faculty of Electrical, Mechanical and Naval Engineering: Dr IGOR ZANCHI
Faculty of Law: Dr IVO GRABOVAC
Maritime Faculty (Dubrovnik): Dr JOSIP LOVRIĆ
Faculty of Natural Sciences and Arts: Dr KOSTA UGRINOVIĆ
Faculty of Technology: Dr NJEGOMIR RADIĆ
Faculty of Tourism and Foreign Trade (Dubrovnik): Dr DJURO BENIĆ

PROFESSORS

Faculty of Arts (Zadar):

BATOVIĆ, Š., Prehistoric Archaeology
BELOŠEVIĆ, J., Medieval Archaeology
CAMBJ, N., Classical and Old Christian Archaeology
ĆOSIĆ, V., French Language
DUKAT, Z., Greek Language and Literature
FRANIĆ, A., Modern Croatian Literature
GERERSDORFER, V., French Language and Medieval Literature
GRGIN, T., General and Systematic Psychology
JURIĆ, B., Political Economy and National Economic History
KALENIĆ, A. S., Latin Language and Literature
KOLUMBIĆ, N., Old Croatian Literature
MANENICA, I., Systematic Psychology
MIKIĆ, P., German Language
OBAD, S., Modern History
PEDERIN, S., German Literature
PETRICIOLI, I., Art History
SKLEDAR, N., Sociology
ZELIĆ, I., Visual Arts, Teaching Methods
ŽIVKOVIĆ, P., Croatian History up to 1918

Faculty of Civil Engineering:

BONACCI, O., Hydrology
DAMJANIĆ, F., Technical Mechanics
JOVIĆ, V., Hydromechanics
MARGETA, J., Water Supply
MAROVIĆ, P., Strength of Materials, Testing of Structures
MIHANOVIĆ, A., Mechanics, Stability and Dynamics of Structures
MILIČIĆ, J., Construction and Construction Machines
STOJIĆ, P., Hydrotechnical Systems
ŠESTANOVIĆ, S., Geology and Petrology
ŠKOMRLJ, J., Technology and Organization of Construction
VOJNOVIĆ, J., Building Construction
VRDOLJAK, B., Mathematics

Faculty of Economics:

ANDRIJIĆ, S., Macroeconomics, Econometrics
BUBLE, M., Organization Design, Job Evaluation
DOMANČIĆ, P., International Finance
DULČIĆ, A., Economics of Trade and Tourism
JELAVIĆ, A., Business Economics
LUKŠIĆ, B., Business Economics
ŠTAMBUK, D., Regional Economics

Faculty of Electrical, Mechanical and Naval Engineering:

DEŽELIĆ, R., Materials Technology
GRISOGONO, P., Industrial Furnaces and Fuels, Industrial Transportation
JADRIĆ, M., Electromagnetic Theory and Electrical Machinery
KURTOVIĆ, M., Asynchronous Machines, Electric Motor Plants, General Theory of Electric Machines
PILIĆ, L., Fluid Mechanics
SLAPNIČAR, P., Circuits

Faculty of Law:

BILIĆ, I., Political Economy
BORKOVIĆ, I., Administrative Law
BOSNIĆ, P., International Private Law
CARIĆ, A., Criminal Law
CVITAN, O., Administrative Sciences
DUJIĆ, A., Modern Political Systems
GRABOVAC, I., Maritime and Transport Law
PETRIĆ, I., Economic Politics
PETRINOVIĆ, I., History of Political Theories
RUDOLF, D., International Public Law
ŠMID, V., Civil Law
VISKOVIĆ, N., Theory of State and Law

Maritime Faculty:

FABRIS, O., Thermodynamics; Ships' Refrigerating Plants
LOVRIĆ, J., Ship Maintenance
SJEKAVICA, I., Terrestrial Navigation

Faculty of Natural Sciences and Arts:

JAKELIĆ, P., Graphic Design
KALOGJERA, A., Methods of Education
KRSTULOVIĆ, I., Painting
MARASOVIĆ, T., Croatian and European Medieval Art
MIDŽOR, A., Sculpture
MILAT, J., General Pedagogy
OMAŠIĆ, V., History

Faculty of Technology:

KOVAČIĆ, T., Polymers
KRSTULOVIĆ, R., Chemistry and Technology of Non-Metals

MEKJAVIĆ, I., Physical Chemistry
PETRIĆ, N., Thermodynamics
ROJE, U., Organic Industry – Technological Processes; Catalysis; Polymerization
RADOŠEVIĆ, J., Electrochemistry
VOJNOVIĆ, I., Materials and Energy Balance
ŽANETIĆ, R., Measuring and Process Operation

Faculty of Tourism and Foreign Trade (Dubrovnik):

KONJHODŽIĆ, H., International Finance
MARKOVIĆ, M., Economics and Business Organization
REŠETAR, M., Travel Agency Management; Business Analysis
PAPARELA, I., International Finance and Business Finance
ŽABICA, T., Economic and Tourist Geography

SVEUČILIŠTE U ZADRU
(University of Zadar)

Mihovila Pavlinovića bb, 23000 Zadar
Telephone: (23) 200-501
Fax: (23) 200-605
E-mail: rektorat@unizd.hr
Internet: www.unizd.hr

Founded 2003
State control
Academic year: October to June

Rector: Prof. Dr DAMIR MAGAŠ
Pro-Rectors: Prof. Dr MIRKO JAKIĆ, Prof. Dr DANICA ŠKARA, Prof. Dr ANTE UGLEŠIĆ
Secretary-General: ANTONELLA LOVRIĆ
Librarian: JADRANKA PETRIČEVIC

Library of 80,000 vols, 420 periodicals, 600 MSS
Number of teachers: 230
Number of students: 5,000

HEADS OF DEPARTMENTS

Archaeology: Prof. Dr BRUNISLAV MARIJANOVIĆ
Classical Philology: Assist. Prof. Dr MILENKO LONČAR
Croatian and Slavic Studies: Associate Prof. Dr DIVNA MRDEŽA ANTONINA
English Language and Literature: Assist. Prof. Dr DAMIR ĆAVAR
French Language and Literature: Prof. Dr VJEKOSLAV COSIĆ
Geography: Associate Prof. Dr MARTIN GLAMUZINA
German Language and Literature: Prof. Dr PAVAO MIKIĆ
History: Prof. MITHAD KOZLIČIĆ
History of Art: Prof. Dr NIKOLA JAKŠIĆ
Information and Communication Studies: Prof. Dr JOSIP VIDAKOVIĆ
Italian Language and Literature: Prof. Dr ŽIVKO NIŽIĆ (Associate Head)
Pedagogy: Asst Prof. Dr DIJANA VICAN
Philosophy: Asst Prof. Dr BORISLAV DADIĆ
Sociology: Assoc. Prof. Dr INGA TOMIĆ KOLUDROVIĆ
Transport and Maritime Studies: Asst Prof. Dr LEONARDO MARUŠIĆ
Department of Economy: Assoc. Prof. Dr STIPE BELAK
Department of Ethnology: Asst Prof. Dr GORAN PAVEL ŠANTEK
Department of Librarianship: Assoc. Prof. Dr SREĆKO JELUŠIĆ, Department of Psychology: Prof. Dr ILIJA MANENICA, Department of Teachers and Pre-school Educators: Asst Prof. Dr ROBERT BACALJA

SVEUČILIŠTE U ZAGREBU
(University of Zagreb)

Trg maršala Tita 14, POB 815, 10000 Zagreb
Telephone: (1) 4564-233
Internet: www.unizg.hr

Founded 1669
Academic year: October to September
Language of instruction: Croatian

Rector: Dr JASNA HELENA MENCER
University Vice-Rectors: Dr ALEKSA BJELIŠ, Dr TIHOMIR HUNJAK, Dr VJEKOSLAV JEROLIMOV, Dr VLASTA VIZEK VIDOVIĆ
Chief Administrative Officer: ANA RUŽIČKA

Number of teachers: 4,800
Number of students: 53,000

Publication: *Sveučilišni vjesnik* (University Herald)

DEANS OF FACULTIES

Agriculture: Dr JASMINA HAVRANEK
Architecture: Dr IVAN JURAS
Catholic Theology: Dr JOSIP BALOBAN
Chemical Engineering and Technology: Dr JASENKA JELENČIĆ
Civil Engineering: Dr DUBRAVKA BJEGOVIĆ
Defectology: Dr BRANKO RADOVANČIĆ
Economic Sciences: Dr IVAN LOVRINOVIĆ
Electrical Engineering: Dr MLADEN KOS
Forestry: Dr ZVONKO SELETKOVIĆ
Geodesy: Dr TOMISLAV BAŠIĆ
Geotechnics (in Varaždin): Dr VLASTA SZAVITZ-NOSSAN
Graphics: Dr LUCIJA KAŠTELAN-KUNST
Mechanical Engineering and Shipbuilding: Dr TONKO ĆURKO
Mining Engineering, Geology and Petroleum: Dr ZDENKO KRIŠTAFOR
Law: Dr DAVOR KRAPAC
Medicine: Dr BORIS LABAR
Metallurgy (in Sisak): Dr JOSIP ČRNKO
Natural Sciences and Mathematics: Dr IVAN VICOKOVIĆ
Organization and Informatics (in Varaždin): Dr ŽELJKO HUTINSKI
Pedagogical Sciences: Dr MILE SILOV
Pharmacy and Biochemistry: Dr MLADEN BIRUŠ
Philosophy: Dr NEVEN BUDAK
Physical Education: Dr MATO BARTOLUCI
Political Sciences: Dr ZVONKO POSAVEC
Stomatology: Dr VLADO CAREK
Textiles Technology: Dr DUBRAVKO ROGALE
Traffic and Transport: Dr ALOJZ BRKIĆ
Veterinary Medicine: Dr ZDENKO MAKEK
Academy of Dramatic Arts: Dr VJERAN ZUPPA
Academy of Fine Arts: Dr ZLATKO KAUZLARIĆ ATAČ
Academy of Music: Prof. FRANE PARAĆ

College

Inter-University Centre Dubrovnik: Frana Bulića 4, 20000 Dubrovnik; tel. (20) 413-626; fax (20) 413-628; e-mail iuc@iuc.hr; internet www.iuc.hr; f. 1972; an independent institution for international co-operation in teaching and research; Dir-Gen. Prof. IVO BANAC (Yale University—see chapter on USA).

CUBA

The Higher Education System

The oldest university is the Universidad de la Habana, which was founded in 1728 while Cuba was governed by Spain. Control of the island was ceded to the USA in 1898 and independence was gained in 1902. Most universities have been founded since 1959, when guerrilla forces led by Dr Fidel Castro Ruz seized control of government. State education in Cuba is universal and free at all levels. Education is based on Marxist-Leninist principles and combines study with manual work. Higher education institutions include universities, centros universitarios (university centres), institutos superiores politécnicos (higher polytechnic institutes) and institutos superiores (higher institutes). Workers attending university courses receive a state subsidy to provide for their dependants. Courses at intermediate and higher levels lay an emphasis on technology, agriculture and teacher training. In 2004/05 there were an estimated 361,800 students enrolled in higher education.

Admission to higher education is based on completion of upper secondary education and results of the national competitive entrance examination. The main undergraduate qualification is the Licenciado, which is awarded after five years of study. Courses may also lead to a professional title, such as Ingeniero (Engineer), Contador (Accountant), Estomatólogo (Dentist) or Arquitecto (Architect). Between undergraduate and doctoral-level studies there is a Masters-level qualification, Título de Máster. The first doctoral-level qualification is the Doctor en Ciencias Específicas, which requires three to four years' study. The second (and final) doctoral-level degree is the Doctor en Ciencias, awarded after additional years of research, published and defended before a jury. Technical and vocational education is offered at the secondary level and higher.

Learned Societies

GENERAL

Academia de Ciencias de Cuba (Cuban Academy of Sciences): Capitolio Nacional, Havana 10200; tel. and fax (7) 867-0599; e-mail acc@ceniai.cu; f. 1962; attached research institutes: see Research Institutes; National Archive: see Libraries and Archives; Pres. Dr ROSA ELENA SIMEÓN; publs *Boletín del Archivo Nacional* (annually), *Estudios de Historia de la Ciencia y la Tecnología* (annually), *Estudios de Política Científica y Tecnología* (annually), *Boletín Señal* (weekly), *Boletín de Síntesis*, *Cablegráfica* (monthly), *Revista Ciencias Técnicas, Físicas y Matemáticas* (2 a year), *Revista Ciencias Biológicas* (2 a year), *Revista Ciencias de la Tierra y del Espacio* (2 a year), *Actas Botánicas Cubanas* (annually), *Poeyana* (annually), *Revista Cubana de Ciencias Sociales* (2 a year), *Datos Astronómicos para Cuba* (annually), *Datos Astronómicos para el Caribe* (2 a year), *Boletín Climática* (annually), *Boletín Meteorológico Marino* (3 a year), *Revista Cubana de Meteorología* (2 a year), *Resumen Climático de Cuba* (annually), *Boletín Oficial de la ONIITEM* (annually), *Revista Ciencia de la Información* (quarterly), *Directorio Biotec* (annually), *Anuario L L. sobre estudios Lingüísticos*, *Anuario L.L. sobre estudios Literarios*, *Tablas de Mareas* (annually).

Ateneo de La Habana (Havana Athenaeum): Avda 5 No. 608, Vedado, Havana; f. 1902; Pres. Dr JOSÉ M. CHACÓN Y CALVO; Sec. Dr JOSÉ ENRIQUE HEYMANN Y DE LA GÁNDARA.

Casa de las Américas (House of the Americas): Calle 3ra esquina a G, El Vedado, Havana 10400; tel. (7) 55-2706; fax (7) 33-4554; e-mail casa@artsoft.cult.cu; f. 1959; cultural instn supporting Latin American literature, art and science; organizes festivals, exhibitions, conferences; maintains the 'José A. Echeverría' public library; documentary centre; Pres. ROBERTO FERNÁNDEZ RETAMAR; publs *Casa de las Américas* (3 a year), *Conjunto* (quarterly), *Boletín de Música* (2 a year), *Anales del Caribe* (annually), *Criterios* (annually).

EDUCATION

Consejo Nacional de Universidades (National University Council): Ministerio de Educación Superior, Ciudad Libertad, Havana 1; f. 1960; co-ordinating body for educational and scientific activities and for the administration of the four nat. univs; Pres. JOSÉ RAMÓN FERNÁNDEZ; Sec. Ing. MIGUEL MARRERO VALLET.

UNESCO Office Havana and Regional Bureau for Culture in Latin America and the Caribbean: Calzada 551 – Esq. a D, Vedado, Havana; tel. (7) 32-2840; fax (7) 33-3144; e-mail habana@unesco.org; internet www.unesco.org.cu; f. 1950; designated Cluster Office for Cuba, Dominican Republic and Haiti; Dir FRANCISCO JOSÉ LACAYO PARAJON.

LANGUAGE AND LITERATURE

Academia Cubana de la Lengua (Cuban Academy of Language): Avda 19 No. 502, Esq. a E, Vedado, Havana 4; f. 1926; corresp. of the Real Academia Española (Madrid); Dir Dra DULCE M. LOYNAZ; Sec. Dr DELIO CARRERAS.

Alliance Française: Avda Los Presidentes 405, between 17 and 19 El Vedado, Havana; tel. (7) 33-3370; fax (7) 55-3470; e-mail dgafcuba@enet.cu; offers courses and exams in French language and culture and promotes cultural exchange with France; attached office in Santiago.

British Council: 7ma Avda, e/Calle 34 y 36, Miramar, Havana; tel. (7) 204-1771; fax (7) 204-9214; e-mail information@cu.britishcouncil.org; internet www.britishcouncil.org/cuba; offers courses and exams in English language and British culture and promotes cultural exchange with the UK; Dir WILLIAM EDMUNDSON.

Unión de Escritores y Artistas de Cuba (Writers' and Artists' Union of Cuba): Calle 17 No. 351, Vedado, Havana; tel. (7) 53-5081; fax (7) 33-3158; internet www.uneac.com; f. 1961; 4,589 mems; Pres. CARLOS MARTÍ BRENES; Exec. Sec. MARTIZA HERNANDEZ; publs. *Ediciones Unión*, *La Gaceta de Cuba* (monthly), *Unión* (quarterly), *Literatura Cubana* (2 a year).

MEDICINE

Sociedad Cubana de Historia de la Medicina (Cuban Society for the History of Medicine): Calle L No. 406 esq. 23 y 25, Vedado, Havana 4; e-mail amaro@abril.sld.cu; Pres. Dr RUBÉN RODRÍGUEZ GAVALDÁ; Sec. Dra MARÍA DEL CARMEN AMARO CANO; publ. *Cuadernos*.

Sociedad Cubana de Radiología (Cuban Radiology Society): Calle L 406 esq. 23 y 25, Vedado, Havana 10400; tel. (7) 77-6077; fax (7) 33-5036; e-mail jbanasco@infomed.sld.cu; f. 1968; 200 mems; Pres. Prof. Dr CARLOS UGARTE; Sec. Prof. Dr JORGE BANASCO.

TECHNOLOGY

Sociedad Cubana de Ingenieros (Cuban Engineers' Association): Avda de Bélgica 258, Havana; f. 1908; 500 mems; library of 9,000 vols; Pres. Ing. GUSTAVO STERLING; Sec. Ing. HONORATO COLETE; publ. *Revista* (every 2 months).

Research Institutes

AGRICULTURE, FISHERIES AND VETERINARY SCIENCE

Centro de Investigaciónes para el Mejoramiento Animal (Research Centre for the Improvement of Livestock): Carretera Central Km 21½, Loma de Tierra, Cotorro, Havana 14000; tel. and fax (7) 57-9408; e-mail igat@cima-minag.cu; f. 1970; library of 4,600 vols; Dir JOSÉ R. MORALES; publ. *Revista Cubana de Reproducción Animal* (2 a year).

Centro de Investigaciones Pesqueras (Fisheries Research Centre): Barlovento, Santa Fé, Playa, Havana; f. 1959; library of 4,230 vols, 1,500 periodicals; Dir Lic. ADELA PRIETO T.; publ. *Ciencia y Tecnología Pesquera* (quarterly).

Estación Experimental Apícola (Experimental Station for Beekeeping): Arroyo Arenas, El Cano, La Lisa, Havana 19190; tel. (7) 202-0027; fax (7) 202-0950; e-mail eeapi@ceniai.inf.cu; f. 1982; library of 2,443 vols; Dir MSc. ADOLFO M. PÉREZ PIÑEIRO; publs *Apiciencia* (research, 3 a year), *Boletín Apiciencia* (for beekeepers, 4 a year).

Instituto Cubano de Investigaciones de los Derivados de la Caña de Azúcar (ICIDCA) (Cuban Institute for Research on Sugar Cane By-Products): Vía Blanca y Carretera Central 804, Apdo 4026, San Miguel del Padrón, Havana; tel. (7) 55-7015; fax (7) 98-8653; e-mail icidca@ceniai.inf.cu; internet www.icidca.cu; f. 1963; library of 7,000 vols; Dir LUIS O. GÁLVEZ TAUPIER; publ. *Sobre los derivados de la Caña de Azúcar* (quarterly).

Instituto de Investigaciones Agropecuarias 'Jorge Dimitrov' (Jorge Dimitrov Livestock Research Institute): Carretera de Bayamo a Manzanillo, Km 17, Paralejo a Bayamo, Granma; tel. 5239; attached to Cuban Acad. of Sciences; Dir Dr ISMAEL LEONARD ACOSTA.

Instituto de Investigaciones Avícolas (Poultry Research Institute): Calle 15, No. 853 e/4 y 6, Vedado, Ciudad Havana.

Instituto de Investigaciones de Sanidad Vegetal (Plant Health Research Institute): Calle 110 No. 514 entre 5ta B y 5ta F, Miramar, Playa, Havana CP 11600; tel. (7) 202-2516; fax (7) 202-9366; e-mail administrador@inisav.cu; internet www.inisav.cu; f. 1970; Director Dr JORGE OVIES DIAZ; publ. *Fitosanidad* (4 a year).

Instituto de Investigaciones en Riego y Drenaje (Research Institute for Irrigation and Drainage): Avda Camilo Cienfuegos y calle 27, A. Naranjo, Havana.

Instituto de Investigaciones en Viandas Tropicales (Research Institute for Tropical Vegetables): Apdo 6, Santo Domingo 53000, Villa Clara; tel. (42) 40-3103; fax (42) 40-3689; e-mail inivit@ip.etecsa.cu; f. 1967; tropical root and tuber crops, bananas and plantains; library of 14,439 vols; Dir Dr SERGIO RODRIGUEZ MORALES; publ. *Agrotecnia de Cuba*.

Instituto de Investigaciones Forestales (Institute of Forestry Research): Calle 174 No 1723 e/ 17B y 17C, Siboney, Municipio Playa, Havana 16; f. 1969; library of 10,000 vols; Dir JUAN A. HERRERO ECHEVARRÍA; publ. *Revista Forestal Baracoa* (2 a year).

Instituto de Investigaciones Fundamentales en Agricultura Tropical 'Alejandro de Humboldt' (Alexander von Humboldt Institute of Basic Research in Tropical Agriculture): Calle 2, Esq. a 1, Santiago de las Vegas, Havana 17200; tel. (7) 57-9010; fax (7) 57-9014; e-mail yamiletrst@inifat.esihabana.cu; f. 1904; library of 2,600 vols; Dir Dr ADOLFO RODRÍGUEZ NODALS; publ. *Agrotecnia de Cuba*.

Instituto de Investigaciones para la Mecanización Agropecuaria (Research Institute for Mechanization in Livestock Farming): Avda de las 3 Palmas No. 13926, Capdevila, Havana.

Instituto de Investigaciones Porcinas (Pig Research Institute): Carretera del Guatao Km 1, Punta Brava, Bauta, Havana.

Instituto de Suelos y Agroquímica (Research Institute for Soils and Agrochemicals): Calle 150 y 21A, Siboney, Havana.

Instituto Tecnológico de la Caña de Azúcar 'Carlos M. de Cespedes' (Carlos M. de Cespedes Sugar-Cane Technology Institute): La Inagua, Apdo 164, Guantánamo, Oriente; Dir MIGDONIO CAUSSE.

ECONOMICS, LAW AND POLITICS

Instituto de Administración (Institute for Administration): Miguel E. Capote 351, Bayamo, Oriente; Dir AIDA RAMÍREZ.

EDUCATION

Instituto de Superación Educacional (ISE) (Institute of Educational Advancement): Ciudad Libertad, Marianao, Havana; Dir Dra MARÍA LUISA RODRÍGUEZ CÓLOMBIÉ.

HISTORY, GEOGRAPHY AND ARCHAEOLOGY

Instituto de Geografía Tropical (Institute of Tropical Geography): Calle 13 No. 409 esquina F. Vedado, Plaza de la Revolución, Havana 10400; tel. (7) 832-4295; fax (7) 836-3174; e-mail geotrop@ama.cu; internet www.geotech.cu; f. 1962; attached to Min. of Science, Technology and Environment; 122 mems; Dir Dra MARLEN MARTHA PALET RABAZA.

LANGUAGE AND LITERATURE

Instituto de Literatura y Lingüística (Institute of Literature and Linguistics): Salvador Allende No. 710 entre Soledad y Castillejo, Havana 10300; tel. (7) 78-6486; fax (7) 33-5718; f. 1965; attached to Min. of Science, Technology and the Environment; Dir Dra NURIA GREGORI TORADA; publs *Anuario* (linguistics edition, annually), *Anuario* (literature edition, annually).

MEDICINE

Centro Ingeniería Genética y Biotecnología de Cuba (Centre for Genetic Engineering and Biotechnology of Cuba): Ave 31e 160 y 190, Rpto Cubanacan, Playa, Havana; internet www.cigb.edu.cu; f. 1986; research, development, production and commercial applications of biotechnology; vaccine research; Dir-Gen. Dr LUIS HERRERA MARTINEZ; publ. *Biotecnología Aplicada*.

Centro Nacional de Información de Ciencias Médicas (National Centre for Information on Medical Science): E No. 454, Entre 19 y 21 Vedado, Havana; tel. (7) 32-2004; fax (7) 33-3063; e-mail ojito@infomed.sld.cu; internet www.sld.cu/cnicm.html; Dir Dr JEREMÍAS HERNÁNDEZ OJITO; publs *Revista Cubana de Medicina, and other specialized medical journals*.

Instituto Nacional de Higiene, Epidemiología y Microbiología (National Institute of Hygiene, Epidemiology and Microbiology): Infanta No. 1158/Llinás y Clavel, Havana 3; tel. (7) 870-5723; fax (7) 33-3063; f. 1943; library of 3,000 vols; Dir Dr PEDRO MÁS BERMEJO.

Instituto Nacional de Oncología y Radiobiología de La Habana (National Institute of Oncology and Radiobiology in Havana): 29 y F, Vedado, Havana; tel. (7) 32-7297; fax (7) 32-8480; f. 1961; library of 2,700 vols; Dir Prof. ROLANDO CAMACHO RODRÍGUEZ; publ. *Revista Cubana de Oncología*.

NATURAL SCIENCES

General

Centro de Estudios de Historia y Organización de la Ciencia 'Carlos J. Finlay' (Carlos J. Finlay Study Centre for the History and Organization of Science): POB 70, Cuba No. 460, Esquina Amargura y Fte. Rey, Havana; tel. (7) 63-4823; f. 1977; attached to Cuban Acad. of Sciences; Dir Dr FRANCISCO GARCÍA VALLS; publs *Estudios de Historia de la Ciencia y la Tecnología* (annually), *Estudio de Politica Científica y Tecnológica* (annually).

Centro Nacional de Investigaciones Científicas (National Centre for Scientific Research): Ave. 25 No. 15202 esq. 158, Reparto Cubanacán, Playa, Havana; tel. (7) 271-4453; fax (7) 208-0497; e-mail editorialcenic@biocnic.cneuro.edu.cu; f. 1969; natural, biomedical and technological sciences, development of medicines and medical equipment; postgraduate education; library of 100,000 vols; Dir Dr CARLOS GUTIERREZ CALZADO; publs *Revista CENIC Ciencias Biológicas* (3 a year), *Revista CENIC Ciencias Químicas* (3 a year).

Centro Nacional para la Divulgación de la Ciencia y la Técnica (CNDCT) (National Centre for the Popularization of Science and Technology): Calle B, 352 esquina a 15 Vedado, Plaza de la Revolución, Havana 10400; tel. (7) 30-1451; e-mail cips@ceniai.inf.cu; attached to Cuban Acad. of Sciences; Dir Lic. ROBERTO CARRASCO VILCHES; publs *Boletin Señal* (weekly), *Boletín de Síntesis Cablegráfica* (monthly).

Instituto de Oceanología (Institute of Oceanology): Calle 1ra. No. 18406 esquina 184 y 186, Rpto. Flores, Playa, Havana 12100; tel. (7) 21-6008; e-mail oceano@oceano.inf.cu; f. 1965; attached to Min. of Science, Technology and the Environment; Dir Lic. JUAN PÉREZ; publ. *Avicennia*.

Biological Sciences

Centro Nacional de Producción de Animales de Laboratorio (CENPALAB) (National Centre for the Breeding of Laboratory Animals): Finca Tinabeque, Carretera de Bejucal, Cacahual, Santiago de las Vegas, Bejucal, Havana; tel. 3566; attached to Cuban Acad. of Sciences; Dir Dr FERNANDO GONZÁLEZ BERMÚDEZ.

Instituto de Ecología y Sistemática (Institute of Ecology and Systemization): Carretera Varona Km 3½, Capdevila Boyeros, Apdo Postal 8029, Havana 10800; tel. (7) 57-8779; fax (7) 57-8266; e-mail ecologia@ceniai.inf.cu; internet www.cuba.cu/ciencia/citma/ama/ecologia; f. 1965; attached to Cuban Acad. of Sciences; terrestrial ecology; Dir Dr PEDRO PÉREZ ALVAREZ; publs *Acta Botánica Cubana* (3 a year), *Poeyana* (3 a year).

Mathematical Sciences

Instituto de Investigaciones Estadísticas (Institute for Statistical Research): Calle 28 No. 504 esq. 5a y 7a, Miramar, Municipio Playa, Havana; tel. (7) 2-3815; f. 1982; library of 5,000 vols; Dir Dr RAMÓN SABADÍ RODRÍGUEZ; publs *Temas Estadísticos*, *Revista Estadística*.

Physical Sciences

Centro Nacional de Investigaciones Sismológicas (National Centre for Seismological Investigation): Calle 17, No. 61 esquina 4 y 6, Rpto. Vista Alegre, Santiago de Cuba; tel. (226) 4-1623; attached to Cuban Acad. of Sciences; Dir Ing. LUIS SIERRA QUESADA.

Instituto Cubano de Investigaciones Mineras y Metalúrgicas (Cuban Institute of Mineral and Metallurgical Research): Aguiar 207 e/Empedrado y Tejadillo, Havana; Dir CARLOS COCA OLIVER.

Instituto de Cibernética, Matemática y Física (ICIMAF) (Institute of Cybernetics, Mathematics and Physics): 15 esquina C. Vedado, Plaza de la Revolución, Havana 10400; attached to Cuban Acad. of Sciences; Dir Ing. RAIMUNDO FRANCO PARELLADA.

Instituto de Geofísica y Astronomía (Institute of Geophysics and Astronomy): Calle 212 No. 2906 entre 29 y 31, La Coronela, La Lisa, Havana 11600; tel. (7) 21-4331; fax (7) 33-9497; e-mail iga@cidet.icmf.inf.cu; f. 1964; attached to Min. of Science, Technology and the Environment; library of 1,000 vols; Dir Dra LOURDES PALACIO SUÁREZ; publ. *Datos Astronómicos para Cuba* (annually).

Instituto de Meteorología (Institute of Meteorology): Loma de Casablanca, Apdo 17032, Havana 11700; tel. (7) 61-7500; fax (7) 33-8010; attached to Min. of Science, Technology and Environment; Dir Dr TOMÁS GUTIERREZ PÉREZ; publs *Revista Cubana de Meteorología* (2 a year), *Boletín Meteorológico Marino* (2 a year).

PHILOSOPHY AND PSYCHOLOGY

Instituto de Filosofía (Institute of Philosophy): Calzada No. 251 esq. J., Vedado, Havana 10400; tel. (7) 832-1887; e-mail instituto@filosofia.cu; internet www.filosofia.cu; f. 1966; attached to Cuban Acad. of Sciences; library of 3,000 vols; Dir Dra CONCEPCIÓN NIEVES AYÚS; publs *Revista Cubana de Ciencias Sociales* (2 a year), *Revista Cubana de Filosofía* (online, 3 a year).

RELIGION, SOCIOLOGY AND ANTHROPOLOGY

Centro de Antropología (Centre for Anthropology): Buenos Aires No. 111 esquina Agua Dulce y Diana, Cerro, Havana 13000; tel. (7) 70-8220; attached to Min. of Science, Technology and Environment; Dir Dra LOURDES SERRANO PERALTA.

Centro de Investigaciones Psicológicas y Sociológicas (CIPS) (Centre for Research in Psychology and Sociology): Calle 0 esquina 17 y 19 Vedado, Plaza de la Revolución, Havana 10400; tel. (7) 32-8945; attached to Cuban Acad. of Sciences; undertakes socio-psychological surveys which relate to social politics in Cuba and the means of ensuring the participation of workers in the different levels of social planning; Dir Lic. ANGELA CASAÑAS MATA.

TECHNOLOGY

Centro de Desarrollo Científico de Montañas (Centre for the Scientific Development of Mountainous Regions): Matazón, Sabaneta, El Salvador, Guantanamo; tel. (21) 9-9230; attached to Cuban Acad. of Sciences; Dir Ing. FRANCISCO VELÁZQUEZ RODRÍGUEZ.

Centro de Desarrollo de Equipos e Instrumentos Científicos (CEDIC) (Centre for the Development of Scientific Equipment and Instruments): Luz No. 375 esquina Compostela y Picota, Havana; tel. (7) 61-2846; attached to Cuban Acad. of Sciences; laser technology and its application in medicine, nutrition and electronics; Dir Ing. LUIS EMILIO GARCÍA MAGARINO.

Centro de Diseño de Sistemas Automatizados de Computación (CEDISAC) (Centre for the Design of Automated Computer Systems): Industria esquina Dragones y San Jose, Havana 12400; tel. (7) 62-6531; attached to Cuban Acad. of Sciences; Dir Lic. BEATRIZ ALONSO BECERRA.

Centro de Investigaciones de Energía Solar (Centre for Research into Solar Energy): Micro 3 Reparto 'Abel Santamaría', Santiago de Cuba 90800; tel. and fax (226) 7-1131; e-mail relinter@cies.ciges.inf.cu; f. 1986; attached to Min. of Science, Technology and the Environment; Dir Ing. ORLANDO LASTRES DANGUILLECOURT.

Centro de Investigaciones para la Industria Minero Metalúrgica (Research Centre of the Metal-Mining Industry): Finca 'La Luisa' Km. $1\frac{1}{2}$, Carretera Varona No. 12028, Apdo 8067, Boyeros, Havana; tel. and fax (7) 57-8082; e-mail cipimm@chab.minbas.cu; internet www.camaracuba.cu; f. 1967; library of 4,000 vols; Dir Dr EDUARDO ACEVEDO; publs *Revista Tecnológica* (3 a year), *Infomin* (bulletin, monthly), *Resenas*.

Instituto Tecnológico de Electrónica 'Fernando Aguado Rico' (Fernando Aguado Rico Technological Institute of Electronics): Belascoaín y Maloja, Havana; Dir Ing. GONZALO IGLESIAS Y RODRÍGUEZ-MENA.

Libraries and Archives

Havana

Archivo Nacional de Cuba (Cuban National Archive): Compostela 906 esq. a San Isidro, Havana 10100; tel. (7) 862-9436; fax (7) 33-8089; e-mail arnac@ceniai.inf.cu; internet www.ceniai.inf.cu/ciencia/citma/aid/archivo/index.htm; f. 1840; 25,000 linear metres of archive material; 12,834 vols, 675 periodicals; Dir Dra BERARDA SALABARRÍA ABRAHAM; publ. *Boletín* (annually).

Biblioteca Central 'Rubén Martínez Villena' de la Universidad de la Habana (Rubén Martínez Villena Central Library of the University of Havana): Vedado, Havana 10400; tel. (7) 78-1230; fax (7) 33-5774; e-mail susan@dict.uh.cu; internet www.uh.cu; f. 1728; 945,000 vols; Dir Lic. BÁRBARA SUSANA SÁNCHEZ VIGNAU; publs *Revista de Biología* (annually), *Revista Investigación Operacional* (3 a year), *Revista de Ciencias Matemáticas* (2 a year), *Revista de Investigaciones Marinas* (3 a year), *Revista del Jardín Botánico Nacional* (annually), *Revista Cubana de Educación Superior* (3 a year), *Revista Cubana de Física* (2 a year), *Revista Cubana de Psicología* (3 a year), *Revista Universidad de la Habana* (2 a year), *Revista Economía y Desarrollo* (2 a year), *Revista Debates Americanos* (2 a year).

Biblioteca del Instituto Pre-universitario de La Habana (Library of the Havana Pre-University Institute of Education): Zuleta y San José, Havana; f. 1894; 32,000 books, newspaper library; Dir JOSÉ MANUEL CASTELLANOS RODILES.

Biblioteca 'Fernando Ortiz' del Instituto de Literatura y Lingüística (Fernando Ortiz Library of the Institute of Literature and Linguistics): Salvador Allende 710 entre Soledad y Castillejo, Havana 10300; tel. (7) 878-5405; fax (7) 873-5718; e-mail ill@ceniai.inf.cu; f. 1793; 1,000,000 items; Librarian Lic. Ma. ELOISA DÍAZ FAURE.

Biblioteca Histórica Cubana y Americana (Cuban and American History Library): Municipio de La Habana, Oficina del Historiador de la Ciudad, Havana; f. 1938.

Biblioteca 'José Antonio Echeverría' (José Antonio Echeverría Library): Calle 3ra esquina a G, El Vedado, Havana 10400; tel. (7) 55-2705; fax (7) 33-4554; f. 1959; Caribbean and Latin American books; 150,000 vols, 8,500 journals; Dir ERNESTO SIERRA; publ. *Boletín* (monthly).

Biblioteca 'Manuel Sanguily' (Manuel Sanguily Library): Ministerio de Relaciones Exteriores, Calzada y G., Vedado, Havana; tel. (7) 32-4074; e-mail madeleine@minrex.gov.cu; f. 1960; 29,512 vols, 3,200 periodicals; Dir Dra MADELEINE TERÁN.

Biblioteca Nacional 'José Martí' (José Martí National Library): Apdo 6670, Avda de Independencia e/20 de Mayo y Aranguren, Plaza de la Revolución José Martí, Havana; tel. (537) 881-2428; e-mail direccion@bnjm.cu; internet www.bnjm.cu; f. 1901; 4,242,936 items; Dir ELIADES ACOSTA MATOS; publs *Bibliografía Cubana* (annually), *Bibliotecas: Anales de Investigación*, *Catálogo Cuba en Publicaciones Extranjeras*, *Indice General de Publicaciones Periódicas Cubanas*, *Revista de la Biblioteca Nacional José Martí*.

Biblioteca Provincial 'Rubén Martínez Villena' (Rubén Martínez Villena Provincial Library): Obispo 160, Entre Mercaderes y San Ignacio, Edif. MINED, Havana; tel. (7) 61-4895; f. 1960; 94,328 vols; spec. braille colln; Dir Lic. ELA RAMOS RODRÍGUEZ.

Centro de Información Bancaria y Económica, Banco Central de Cuba (Banking and Economic Information Center, Central Bank of Cuba): Cuba 410, Havana 10100; tel. (7) 62-8318; fax (7) 66-6661; f. 1950; 32,000 vols; Man. NUADIS PLANAS GARCÍA; Library Dept Chief JORGE FERNÁNDEZ PÉREZ; publs *Cuba: Half Yearly Economic Report*, *Economic Report* (annually), *Journal of the Central Bank of Cuba*.

Centro de Información y Documentación Agropecuario (Livestock Information and Documentation Centre): Gaveta postal 4149, Havana 4; tel. (7) 81-8808; fax (7) 33-5086; f. 1971; 20,000 vols, 1,400 journals; Dir Dr DAVID WILLIAMS CANTERO; publs numerous journals.

Instituto de Información Científica Tecnológica (IDICT) (Institute of Scientific and Technical Information): Capitolio Nacional, Apdo 2213, Havana 2; tel. (7) 62-6501; fax (7) 33-8237; f. 1963; attached to Min. of Science, Technology and Environment; 150,000 vols, 8,000 journals; Dir-Gen. NICOLAS GARRIGA; publs. incl. *Ciencias de la Información* (quarterly), *Ciencia, Innovación y Desarrollo* (quarterly), *Boletín FID/CLA*(quarterly), *Newsletter* (quarterly).

Santiago

Biblioteca Central de la Universidad de Oriente (Central Library of the University of Oriente): Avda Patricio Lumumba s/n, Santiago de Cuba; tel. (226) 3-1973; f. 1947; 42,000 vols; Librarian Lic. MAURA GONZÁLEZ PÉREZ; publs *Revista Santiago*, *Revista Cubana de Química*.

Biblioteca Provincial 'Elvira Cape' (Elvira Cape Provincial Library): Calle Heredia 259, Santiago de Cuba 90100, Oriente; tel. (226) 5-4836; f. 1899; 169,000 vols, 1,760 periodicals; Dir ROSA DIGNA GUTIÉRREZ CALZADO.

Museums and Art Galleries

Camagüey

Museo Ignacio Agramonte (Ignacio Agramonte Museum): Camagüey; tel. (32) 28-2425; e-mail cmqcppatrimonia@pprincips.cult.cu; f. 1955; paintings, furniture, textiles and relics from the colonial period; Dir YOLANDA GUTIÉRREZ CAMPOS.

Cárdenas

Museo Municipal Oscar M. de Rojas (Oscar M. de Rojas Muncipal Museum): Avda de José Martí, Cárdenas; f. 1903; exhibits relating to Martí; library; Curator OSCAR M. DE ROJAS Y CRUZAT.

Havana

Acuario Nacional de Cuba (National Aquarium of Cuba): Ave. 1ra y Calle 60, Miramar, Playa, Havana 11300; tel. (7) 203-6401; fax (7) 204-1442; e-mail comercial@acuarionacional.cu; internet www.acuarionacional.cu; f. 1960; attached to Min. of Science, Technology and the Environment; library of 3,000 vols; Dir Lic. GUILLERMO GARCÍA MONTERO.

Jardín Botánico Nacional de Cuba (National Botanical Garden of Cuba): Carretera del Rocío Km $3\frac{1}{2}$, CP 19230, Calabazar,

Boyeros, Havana; tel. (7) 44-5525; fax (7) 33-5350; f. 1968; administered by Universidad de la Habana; library of 3,800 vols, 1,225 periodicals; herbarium; Dir-Gen. Dra. ANGELA LEIVA; publs *Revista* (annually), *Index Seminum* (every 2 years), *Reporte Annual*.

Museo Agrícola (Agricultural Museum): Ministerio de Agricultura, Havana; Curator ARCHIBALD DURLAND Y NIETO.

Museo Antropológico Montané (Montané Anthropological Museum): Facultad de Biología, Universidad de La Habana, Havana 4; tel. (7) 32-9000; f. 1903; library of 5,000 vols; Dir Dr ANTONIO J. MARTÍNEZ FUENTES.

Museo Casa Natal José Martí (House Museum of José Martí): Leonor Pérez 314, Havana; relics of José Martí and his works; Curator MARIA DE LA LUZ RAMIREZ ESTRADA.

Museo de Arte Colonial de la Habana (Havana Museum of Colonial Art): Plaza de la Catedral, Havana; housed in mansion built 1720; Dir MARGARITA SUÁREZ.

Museo de Historia Natural 'Felipe Poey' (Felipe Poey Museum of Natural History): Departamento de Biología Animal y Humana, Facultad de Biología, Universidad de la Habana, Calle 25 e/J e I, Vedado, Havana 4; tel. (7) 32-9000; fax (7) 32-1321; f. 1842; zoology; library of 80,520 vols; Dir Lic. MARTÍN ACOSTA CRUZ.

Museo Ernest Hemingway (Ernest Hemingway Museum): Finca Vigía, San Francisco de Paula, Havana 19180; tel. (7) 91-0809; fax (7) 55-8090; f. 1962; house, library and personal items of Ernest Hemingway who lived at the address 1939–60; Dir DANILO M. ARRATE HERNÁNDEZ.

Museo Municipal de Guanabacoa (Guanabacoa Muncipal Museum): Martí 108, Esquina a Versalles, Guanabacoa 11, Havana; tel. (7) 97-9117; f. 1964; popular Cuban religions of African origin; Dir MARIA CRISTINA PEÑA REIGOSA.

Museo Nacional y Palacio de Bellas Artes (National Museum and Palace of Fine Arts): Animas entre Zulueta y Monserrate, Havana Vieja 10200; tel. (7) 63-9042; fax (7) 62-9626; e-mail musna@cubarte.cult.cu; internet www.museonacional.cult.cu; f. 1913; ancient Egyptian, Greek and Roman art, 16th- to 19th-century European art, Cuban art from the Colonial period to the present; Dir MORAIMA CLAVIJO COLOM.

Attached museums:

Museo de Artes Decorativas (Museum of Decorative Arts): Calle 17, No. 502 entre D y E, Vedado, Havana 10100; tel. (7) 32-0924; fax (7) 61-3857; f. 1964; European and oriental decorative art since 17th c.; Dir KATIA VARELA.

Castillo de la Real Fuerza de la Havana (Castle of the Royal Garrison of Havana): O'Reilly entre Avda del Puerto y Tacón, Plaza de Armas, Havana Vieja 10100; tel. (7) 61-6130; fax (7) 61-3857; f. 1977; modern ceramic exhibits housed in a 16th c. fortification; Dir ALEJANDRO G. ALONSO.

Museo Napoleónico (Napoleonic Museum): San Miguel y Ronda, Havana; f. 1961; historical objects and works of art of Revolutionary and Imperial France; specialized library.

Museo Numismático (Numismatic Museum): Banco Central de Cuba, Oficios 8, Havana 1; tel. (7) 61-5857; f. 1975; coins, banknotes, medals and decorations; library; Dir INÉS MORALES GARCÍA.

Museo y Archivo Histórico Municipal de la Ciudad de La Habana (Havana Muncipal Historical Museum and Archive): Oficina del Historiador, Palacio de los Capitanes Generales, Plaza Carlos Manuel Céspedes, Havana; f. 1947; historical items since 1550.

Parque Zoológico Nacional (National Zoological Garden): Carretera de Varona Km 3½, Capdevila, Boyeros, Apdo 8010, Havana 10800; tel. (7) 44-1870; fax (7) 33-0802; f. 1975; attached to Cuban Acad. of Sciences; library of 1,300 vols; Dir Lic. GILDA DEL CUETO JIMÉNEZ.

Mariel

Museo de Pesca de la Escuela Naval del Mariel (Museum of Marine Fauna of the Mariel Naval Academy): Naval Academy, Mariel, Pinar del Río; f. 1943; specimens of deep-sea fish; Dir LUIS HOWELL RIVERO.

Matanzas

Museo Provincial de Matanzas (Matanzas Provincial Museum): Palacio de Junco, Calle de Milanés y Magdalena, Plaza de la Vigía, Matanzas; tel. (52) 3195; f. 1959; history, natural history, decorative arts; library of 1,000 vols; Dir Lic. GONZALO DOMÍNGUEZ CABRERA; publ. *Museo* (2 a year).

Remedios

Museo de Remedios 'José Maria Espinosa' (José Maria Espinosa Museum in Remedios): Maceo 32, Remedios; f. 1933; history, science, art; Dir. ALBERTO VIGIL Y COLOMA.

Santiago

Museo 'Emilio Bacardi Moreau' (Emilio Bacardi Moreau Museum): Aguilera y Pio Rosado, Apdo 759, Santiago; tel. (226) 62-8402; f. 1899; history, art; Curators JOSÉ A. AROCHA ROVIRA, FIDELIA PÉREZ GONZÁLEZ.

Universities

UNIVERSIDAD DE CAMAGÜEY

Carretera de Circunvalación Norte, Km 5½, Camagüey 74650
Telephone: (32) 6-1019
Fax: (32) 6-1126
E-mail: root@reduc.cmw.edu.cu
Internet: www.reduc.edu.cu

Founded as a branch of University of Havana 1967, present name 1974

State control

Academic year: September to July

Rector: Dr ANGEL VEGA GARCÍA
Vice-Rectors: CARLOS BASULTO, Dr RAFAEL LARRUA, JOSÉ LEÓN
Registrar: Lic. RAÚL GARRIGA CORZO
Librarian: Lic. SARA ARTILES VISBAL

Number of teachers: 450
Number of students: 3,200

Publication: *Revista de Producción Animal*

DEANS

Faculty of Animal Sciences: Dr NELSON IZQUIERDO
Faculty of Chemistry and Pharmacology: Ing. LUIS RAMOS
Faculty of Construction: ANA ISABEL CARDOSO
Faculty of Economics: Lic. PEDRO LINO DEL POZO
Faculty of Electromechanics: Dr LUIS CORRALES BARRIOS
Faculty of Law: Lic. NATALIA CARO

HEADS OF DEPARTMENTS

Animal Sciences:
- Agriculture: Dr MANUEL HERNÁNDEZ VICTORIA
- Morphophysiology: NIRIAM NIETO MARTÍNEZ
- Veterinary Science: Dr MAGALY COLLANTES CÁNOVAS

Chemistry and Pharmacology:
- Chemical Engineering: Lic. NOELIA VARGAS
- Chemistry: MARLEN VILLALONGA
- English: Lic. ADDYS PALOMINO
- Pharmacy: Lic. GILBERTO PARDO ANDREU

Construction:
- Architecture: Arq. MARÍA ELENA GUTIÉRREZ
- Civil Engineering: Dr WILFREDO MARTÍNEZ LÓPEZ DEL CASTILLO
- Mathematics: Lic. JOSÉ MANUEL RUIZ SOCARRÁS

Economics:
- Accountancy: Dr ROLANDO LA TORRE GUIRCE
- Business and Public Administration: Lic. ANGELA PALACIOS
- Economics: Dr JOSÉ PANTOJA GUERRA
- Regional Development: Dr RAMÓN GONZÁLEZ FUENTES

Electromechanics:
- Computer Studies: Lic. BÁRBARA VALDEZ
- Electrical Engineering: Ing. DAVEL BORGES VASCONCELLOS
- Mechanical Engineering: Ing. DORIS VASCONCELLOS VILATÓ
- Physics: Lic. ELOY ORTIZ

ATTACHED INSTITUTES

Centre for Research on Animal Production: Dir Ing. REDIMIO PEDRAZA OLIVERA.

Centre for Research on the Conservation of Historic Monuments: Dir Dra LOURDES GÓMEZ.

Centre for Research in Education: Dir Dra MARÍA TERESA MORENO.

Centre for Research into the Repair of Equipment: Dir Ing. PABLO OÑOZ GUTIÉRREZ.

UNIVERSIDAD DE CIEGO DE AVILA

Km 9 Carretera de Ciego de Avila a Morón, Ciego de Avila 69450
Telephone: (33) 22-4544
Fax: (33) 26-6365
E-mail: webmaster@rect.unica.cu
Internet: www.unica.cu

Founded 1978 as Instituto Superior Agrícola de Ciego de Avila; current name and status since 1996

Rector: Dr MARIO ARES SÁNCHEZ
Library Director: JORGE ANTONIO GÓMEZ CORDERO

Library of 41,963 vols
Number of teachers: 1,451
Number of students: 6,061

Publication: *Fidelia* (quarterly)

Faculties of Agronomy, Economics, Humanities, Computer Science and Engineering.

ATTACHED RESEARCH INSTITUTES

Centro de Estudios Hidrotécnicos.

Centro de Estudios Pedagógicos.

Centro de Estudios Turísticos.

UNIVERSIDAD DE CIENFUEGOS 'CARLOS RAFAEL RODRÍGUEZ'

Carretera de Rodas Km 4, Cuatro Caminos, Cienfuegos 59430
Telephone: (432) 2-1521
Fax: (432) 2-2762
E-mail: rector@ucfinfo.ucf.edu.cu
Internet: www.ucf.edu.cu

Founded 1979 as Instituto Superior Técnico de Cienfuegos; university status 1994; current name since 1998

State control

Rector: Dr ANDRÉS OLIVERA RANERO
Vice-Rector (Academic): Dr ABEL QUIÑONEZ URQUIJO
Vice-Rector (Administration): MAGDIEL E. CHAVIANO DÍAZ
Vice-Rector (Research and Postgraduate): Dra MIRIAN IGLESIAS LEÓN
Vice-Rector (Standardization of Higher Education): LOURDES POMARES CASTELLÓN
Secretary-General: Lic. BLAS JUANES RAMÍREZ
Librarian: Dr LÁSARO S. DIBUT TOLEDO

Library of 50,000 vols
Number of teachers: 363
Number of students: 2,600

Publication: *Anuarios Científico* (annually)

DEANS

Faculty of Computer Science: Dr MARIO ALVAREZ GUERRA PLACENCIA
Faculty of Economics and Business: FRANCISCO BECERRA
Faculty of Humanities: Dr MARIANELA MORALES CALATAYUD
Faculty of Mechanics: Dr JUAN B. COGOLLOS MARTÍNEZ
Faculty of Physical Education: OSCAR MUÑOZ HERNÁNDEZ

ATTACHED RESEARCH INSTITUTES

Centro de Estudios y Desarrollo de la Oleohidráulica y la Neumática (CEDON): e-mail lmcglez@fmec.ucd.edu.cu; Dir Dr LUIS M. CASTELLANOS GONZÁLEZ.

Centre de Estudios de Didáctica y Dirección de la Educación Superior (CEDDES): e-mail mcaceres@rectorado.ucf.edu.cu; Dir Dra MARITZA CÁCERES MESA.

Centro de Estudios de Energía y Medio Ambiente (CEEMA): e-mail marmas@fmec.ucf.edu.cu; Dir Dr MARCOS DE ARMAS TEIRA.

Centro de Estudio Socioculturales de Cienfuegos (CESOC): e-mail lmartin@fmec.ucf.edu.cu; Dir Dra LILIAN MARTÍN BRITO.

Centro de Estudio Para la Transformación Agraria Sostenible (CETAS): e-mail asocorro@fmec.ucf.edu.cu; Dir Dr ALEJANDRO RAFAEL SOCORRO CASTRO.

UNIVERSIDAD DE GRANMA

Carretera de Manzanillo Km 17.5, Bayamo, Granma
Telephone: (23) 9-2130
Fax: (23) 9-2131
E-mail: antonia@udg.granma.inf.cu
Internet: www.udg.co.cu

Founded 1967
State control

Rector: Dra ANTONIA MARÍA CASTILLO RUÍZ

Number of teachers: 316
Number of students: 2,300

Faculties of Accountancy and Finance, Agriculture, Engineering, Social and Human Sciences and Veterinary Medicine.

UNIVERSIDAD AGRARIA DE LA HABANA

Autopista Nacional y Carretera de Tapaste San José de las Lajas, La Habana
Telephone: (64) 6-3014
Fax: (64) 6-3395
E-mail: rector@main.isch.edu.cu
Internet: www.isch.edu.cu

Founded 1976

Rector: Dr JULIÁN RODRÍGUEZ RODRÍGUEZ

Number of teachers: 447
Number of students: 2,300

Faculties of Agronomy, Mechanization of Agricultural Production and Veterinary Science; department of Marxism-Leninism; campus on Isla de la Juventud.

ATTACHED RESEARCH INSTITUTES

Centro de Mecanización Agropecuaria (CEMA).

UNIVERSIDAD DE LA HABANA

Calle San Lázaro esq. L, Vedado, Havana 4
Telephone: (7) 832-4245; (7) 33-4163
Internet: www.uh.cu

Founded 1728, reorganized 1976

Rector: Dr FERNANDO ROJAS AVALOS
Secretary-General: Lic. ISAURA S. SARMIENTO

Library: see Libraries and Archives
Number of teachers: 1,635
Number of students: 15,980

Publications: *Boletín Universitario*, *Universidad de la Habana*, various scientific and technical publs

DEANS

Faculty of Accounting and Finance: Lic. JORGE MÁRQUEZ BUENO
Faculty of Arts and Letters: Dra ELENA SERRANO PARDIÑAS
Faculty of Biology: Lic. MARIO L. RODRÍGUEZ SUÁREZ
Faculty of Chemistry: Dr JACQUES RIEUMONT BRIONES
Faculty of Foreign Languages: Lic. NURIA GARCÍA MENÉNDEZ
Faculty of Geography: Lic. ARTURO RÚA DE CABO
Faculty of Journalism: Dra LÁZARA PEÑONES
Faculty of Law: Dr LUIS SOLÁ VILA
Faculty of Mathematics: Dr FRANCISCO GUERRA VÁZQUEZ
Faculty of Nuclear Sciences and Technology: Dr EVELIO BELLO VARELA
Faculty of Pharmacology and Food: Dra RUTH DAYSI HENRÍQUEZ HERNÁNDEZ
Faculty of Philosophy and History: Dr OSCAR GUZMÁN BETANCOURT
Faculty of Physics: Dr CARLOS RODRÍGUEZ CASTELLANOS
Faculty of Planning for the National Economy: Lic. ALFONSO FARNÓS MOREJÓN
Faculty of Political Economy: Dra DELIA L. LÓPEZ GARCÍA
Faculty of Psychology: FERNANDO GONZALEZ

ATTACHED RESEARCH INSTITUTES

Centro de Estudios Demográficos: Dir Dr ERAMIS BUENO SÁNCHEZ.

Centro de Informática Aplicada a la Gestión: Dir Dra OLGA LODOS HERNÁNDEZ.

Centro de Investigaciones Marinas: Dir Dra MARÍA ELENA IBARRA MARTÍN.

Departamento de Estudios para el Perfeccionamiento de la Educación Superior: Dir Ing. JESÚS GARCÍA DEL PORTAL.

Departamento de Investigaciones Económicas en la Educación Superior: Dir Dra GRETA CRESPO GÓMEZ.

Departamento de Investigaciones sobre los Estados Unidos: Dir Lic. ESTEBAN MORALES DOMÍNGUEZ.

Jardín Botánico Nacional: Dir Dra ANGELA LEYVA SANCHEZ.

Laboratorio de Investigaciones en Electrónica del Estado Sólido: Dir Dr PEDRO DÍAZ ARENCIBIA.

UNIVERSIDAD DE HOLGUÍN 'OSCAR LUCERO MOYA'

Avda 20 Aniversario, Nuevo Holguín, Gaveta Postal 57, 80100 Holguín
Telephone: (24) 48-1302
Fax: (24) 48-1662
E-mail: acristina@ict.uho.edu.cu
Internet: www.uho.edu.cu

Founded 1976 as Centro Universitario de Holguín; became Instituto Superior Técnico de Holguín 1982; current name and status 1995

Rector: Dr SEGUNDO PACHECO TOLEDO
Librarian: MATILDE RIVERON HERNÁNDEZ

Library of 90,980 vols
Number of teachers: 376
Number of students: 3,276

Publications: *Ambito* (4 a year), *Diéresis* (annually).

UNIVERSIDAD CENTRAL 'MARTA ABREU' DE LAS VILLAS

Carretera a Camajuaní Km. 5½, CP 54830, Santa Clara, Villa Clara
Telephone: (422) 8-1178
Fax: (422) 8-1608
E-mail: uclvdri@ucentral.quantum.inf.cu

Founded: 1952
Academic year: September to July

Rector: Dr ANDRÉS OLIVERA RANERO
Vice-Rector: Dr FRANCISCO LEE TENORIO
Secretary-General: Lic. FERNANDO ECHERRI FERRANDIZ
Librarian: Ing. JOSÉ RIVERO DÍAZ

Library of 386,000 vols
Number of teachers: 962
Number of students: 5,436

Publications: *Centro Agrícola*, *Centro Azúcar*, *Construcción de Maquinaria*, *Islas* (quarterly)

DEANS

Faculty of Agricultural Sciences: Ing. PEDRO QUESADA
Faculty of Building: Dr MIGUEL PINO RODRÍGUEZ
Faculty of Chemistry and Pharmacy: SERAFÍN MACHADO
Faculty of Economics and Industrial Engineering: FELIPE GONZALEZ
Faculty of Electrical Engineering: Dr FRANCISCO HERRERA FERNÁNDEZ
Faculty of Mathematics, Computing and Physics: Dr RAFAEL BELLO PÉREZ
Faculty of Mechanical Engineering: Dr CARLOS RENÉ GÓMEZ
Faculty of Social Sciences and Humanities: Dr EDGARDO ROMERO FERNÁNDEZ

UNIVERSIDAD DE MATANZAS 'CAMILO CIENFUEGOS'

Carretera a Veradero Km 3, Matanzas
Telephone: (45) 26-1950
Fax: (45) 26-2222
E-mail: info@umcc.cu
Internet: www.umcc.cu

Founded 1972

Library of 80,000 vols
Number of teachers: 381
Number of students: 3,020

Rector: Ing. JORGE RODRÍGUEZ PÉREZ
Vice-Rectors: Ing. JOSÉ R. DÍAZ (Administration and Services), Dr ROBERTO VIZCÓN TOLEDO (Research and Postgraduate Studies), Ing. MIGUEL SARRAF GONZÁLEZ (Teaching)

Publications: *Revista de Investigaciones Turísticas*, *Revista Pastos y Forrajes*

DEANS

Faculty of Agronomy: Dr SERGIO RODRÍGUEZ JIMÉNEZ
Faculty of Chemistry and Mechanics: Dr ROBERTO VIZCÓN TOLEDO
Faculty of Computer Science: Dr JULIO TELOT GONZÁLEZ
Faculty of Economics and Industry: Lic. BENITA N. GARCÍA GUTIÉRREZ

Faculty of Physical Education: Lic. FÉLIX MOYA
Faculty of Social Sciences and Humanities: Lic. ZOE DOMINGUEZ GARCÍA

ATTACHED RESEARCH INSTITUTES

Centro de Estudios de Anticorrosión y Tensioactivos (CEAT): Dir CARLOS A. ECHEVERRÍA LAGE.

Centro de Estudios de Combustión y Energía (CECYEN): e-mail barroso@quimec.umcc.cu; Dir JORGE ÁNGEL BARROSO ESTÉBANEZ.

Centro de Estudio y Desarrollo Educacional (CEDE): e-mail gerardo.ramos@umcc.cu; Dir Dr GERARDO RAMOS SERPA.

Centro de Estudios de Medioambiente (CEMAN): Dir Dra JUANA ZOILA JUNCO HORTA.

UNIVERSIDAD DE ORIENTE

Avda Patricio Lumumba s/n, 90500 Santiago de Cuba
Telephone: (22) 63-1860
Fax: (22) 63-2689
E-mail: marcosc@rect.uo.edu.cu
Internet: www.uo.edu.cu

Founded 1947
Academic year: September to July

Rector: Dr MARCOS CORTINA VEGA
Vice-Rectors: MSc ELIO CASTELLANOS, Dra ZAIDA VALDÉS ESTRADA, Dr SERGIO CANO ORTIZ, Dr JUAN BORY REYES, Dr PEDRO A. BEATÓN SOLER
Secretary-General: Arq. SONIA QUESADA
Librarian: Dr BAYARDO DUPOTEY RIBAS

Library: see Libraries and Archives
Number of teachers: 842
Number of students: 24,500 (5,500 undergraduate, 19,000 postgraduate and continuing education)
Publications: *Revista Cubana de Química* (3 a year), *Revista Santiago* (every 6 months), *Tecnología Química* (3 a year)

DEANS

Faculty of Building Construction: MSc ALEJANDRO FAJARDO
Faculty of Chemical Engineering: Dra ANA SÁNCHEZ DEL CAMPO LAFFITA
Faculty of Computing Sciences and Mathematics: MSc ALEJANDRO GARCÉS CALVELO
Faculty of Distance Learning: Dra ROSARIO LEÓN ROBAINA
Faculty of Economics: MSc ULISES PACHECO FERIA
Faculty of Electrical Engineering: MSc EMILIO SOTO MORLÁ
Faculty of Humanities: Dra ETNA SANZ
Faculty of Law: Dra JOSEFINA MÉNDEZ
Faculty of Mechanical Engineering: Dr ROBERTO ZAGARÓ ZAMORA
Faculty of Natural Sciences: Dr PEDRO MUNÉ BANDERA
Faculty of Social Sciences: Dra MARÍA JULIA JIMÉNEZ FIOL

UNIVERSIDAD DE PINAR DEL RÍO

Calle J. Martí 270 esq. a 27 de Noviembre, Pinar del Río 20100
Telephone: (82) 77-9353
Fax: (82) 77-9353
E-mail: mfdez@vrect.upr.edu.cu
Internet: www.upr.edu.cu

Founded 1972
State control
Academic year: September to July

Rector: Dr ANDRÉS ERASMO ARES ROJAS
Vice-Rector (Administration): Ing. RENÉ PLASENCIA
Vice-Rector (Community Relations): Dra MARTHA ARROYO CARMONA
Vice-Rector (Research): Dra MARISELA GONZÁLEZ PÉREZ
Vice-Rector (Teaching): Dr ANTONIO DE LA FLOR SANTALLA
Secretary-General: Lic. MAGALYS GONZÁLEZ HERNÁNDEZ
Librarian: Lic. MABEL RODRÍGUEZ

Number of teachers: 370
Number of students: 5,876
Publication: *Anuario Científico*

DEANS

Faculty of Agronomy and Forestry: Lic. YOEL PACHECO ESCOBAR
Faculty of Economics: Dra MAYRA CARMONA GONZÁLEZ
Faculty of Geology and Mechanics: Lic. JORGE SÁNCHEZ
Faculty of Humanities: Dra ALINA MARTÍNEZ
Faculty of Mining: Lic. YORKY MAYOR
Faculty of Telecommunications and Informatics: Dra MAGDALENA MAZÓN HERNÁNDEZ

HEADS OF DEPARTMENTS

Faculty of Agronomy and Forestry:
- Agronomy: Dra MARIOL MOREJÓN
- Chemistry: Dr JUAN FRANCISCO PASTOR BUSTAMENTE
- Forestry: Dra MILAGROS COBAS

Faculty of Economics:
- Accounting and Finance: Dra LAURA E. GONZÁLEZ
- Universal and Sectorial Economy: Dr JOEL GÓMEZ

Faculty of Geology and Mechanics:
- Geology: Dr CARLOS COFIÑO
- Mechanics: Ing. ARÍSTIDES RIVERA
- Physics: Lic. ELIO CRESPO

Faculty of Humanities:
- Languages: Lic. FIDELINA CASTILLO
- Humanities: (vacant)
- Social Sciences: Dr EFRAÍN ECHEVERRÍA

Faculty of Mining:
- Mining: Lic. YORKY MAYOR

Faculty of Telecommunications and Informatics:
- Informatics: Lic. CARIDAD SALAZAR
- Mathematics: Dr JUAN PÉREZ
- Telecommunications: Dr JOSÉ RAÚL VENTO

AFFILIATED INSTITUTES

Centre of Agroecology: e-mail mariol@af.upr.edu.cu; Dir Dra MARIOL MOREJÓN.

Centre for Forestry Sciences: e-mail betancourt@af.upr.edu.cu; Dir Dr YNOCENTE BETANCOURT FIGUERAS.

Centre for Higher Education Research: e-mail tdiaz@vrect.upr.edu.cu; Dir Dra TERESA DE LA C. DÍAZ.

Centre for Management and Tourism Studies: e-mail clazo@eco.upr.edu.cu; Dir Dr CARLOS LAZO VENTO.

Centre of Natural Resources and the Environment: e-mail jaula@vrect.upr.edu.cu; Dir Dr JOSÉ A. JAULA BOTET.

Centre for the Study of Co-operatives: e-mail arivera@eco.upr.edu.cu; Dir Dr CLAUDIO A. RIVERA.

Colleges

Instituto Superior de Ciencas Médicas de Camagüey: Carretera Central Oeste y Madam Curie, Camagüey; tel. (32) 9-2100; f. 1981 from medical faculty of Univ. of Camagüey 70100; schools of dentistry, medicine, nursing; biomedical, clinical and sociomedical research; 587 teachers; 3,500 students; Rector Dr ALBERTO CLAVIJO CORTIELES; pubs. *Revista de Ciencias Médicas de Camagüey* (every 6 months).

Instituto Superior de Relaciones Internacionales 'Raul Roa García': Calle 22 111 e/1ra y 3ra, Miramar, Playa, Havana; tel. (7) 202-2571; internet www.isri.cu; f. 1971; library: 14,000 vols; special collection containing the personal library of Dr Raúl Roa García; 61 teachers; Rector Dr OSCAR GARCÍA FERNÁNDEZ; Sec.-Gen. Dr RAFAEL MORENO.

Instituto Superior Politecnico 'José Antonio Echeverría': Calle 114 No. 11901 entre 119 y 127, CUJAE, Marianao, CP 19390, Havana; tel. (7) 261-4932; fax (7) 267-2694; e-mail rosy@tesla.cujae.edu.cu; f. 1976, fmrly Faculty of Technology of University of Havana; library: 157,370 vols; 1,012 teachers; 5,299 students; Rector Dr GUSTAVO COBREIRO SUÁREZ; Sec. Ing. RAÚL CAPETILLO ALVAREZ; publs *Ingeniería Electrónica,Automática y Telecomunicaciones* (3 a year), *Ingeniería Industrial* (3 a year), *Ingeniería Hidráulica y Ambiente* (3 a year), *Ingeniería Energética* (3 a year), *Ingenieria Mecanica* (3 a year), *Arquitectura y Urbanismo* (3 a year)

DEANS

Architecture: Dra ADA PORTERO RICOL
Civil Engineering: Dr LUIS CORDOVA LOPEZ
Electrical Engineering: Dr ORESTES LLANES SANTIAGO
Mechanical Engineering: Dr LEONARDO GOYOS PEREZ
Chemical Engineering: Dr GUIDO RIERA GONZALEZ
Industrial Engineering: Dra ALICIA ALONSO BECERRA.

Research centres:

Advanced Education Centre: Dir Dra ELSA M. HERRERO TUNIS.

Biomedical Engineering Centre: Dir Dr ERNESTO RODRÍGUEZ DENIS.

Electroenergetic Test Research Centre: Dir Dr MARIO MORERA HERNÁNDEZ.

Hydraulic Research Centre: Dir Dr JOSÉ R. PARDO GÓMEZ.

Innovation and Maintenance Study Centre: Dir Dr JUAN CARLOS DÍAZ.

Management Techniques Study Centre: Dir Dra MARITZA HERNÁNDEZ TORRES.

Microelectronic Research Centre: Dir Dr JUAN CARLOS DÍAZ.

Renewable Energy Technology Study Centre: Dir Dr CONRADO MORENO FIGUEREDO.

Process Engineering Centre: Dir Dr DAVID TOLEDANO LAVIN.

Systems Engineering Study Centre: Dir Dr ROBERTO SEPÚLVEDA.

Tropical Architecture and Construction Centre: Dir Dr JORGE ACEVEDO CATÁ.

Schools of Art and Music

Conservatorio Alejandro García Caturla: Avda 31 y Calle 82, Marianao, Havana.

Conservatorio de Música Amadeo Roldán: Rastro y Lealtad, Havana.

Escuela Nacional de Bellas Artes 'San Alejandro' (National School of Fine Arts): Dragones 308, Havana; f. 1818 as Academia de San Alejandro; formerly Escuela de Pintura, organized by the French painter, Jean Baptiste Vermay; 800 students; Dir DOMINGO RAMOS ENRÍQUEZ.

CYPRUS

The Higher Education System

Cyprus was governed by the United Kingdom until it achieved independence in 1960, following a guerrilla campaign by Greek Cypriots seeking unification (Enosis) with Greece. Government was on the basis of a power-sharing agreement between the Greek and Turkish communities, but in 1963 the Turks withdrew from central government. In 1974, after Greek officers of the Cypriot National Guard had staged a coup, the Turkish army occupied the northern third of the island, where Turkish Cypriots subsequently established a *de facto* Government and, in 1975, declared a Turkish Federated State of Cyprus (TFSC). In 1983 the TFSC unilaterally declared an independent Turkish Republic of Northern Cyprus (TRNC). The Greek Cypriot administration, meanwhile, claims to be the Government of all Cyprus, and is generally recognized as such. Until 1965 each community in Cyprus managed its own schooling through a Communal Chamber. On 31 March of that year, however, the Greek Communal Chamber was dissolved and a Ministry of Education (now Ministry of Education and Culture) was established to take its place. Inter-communal education has been placed under this Ministry.

Cyprus

The University of Cyprus, in Nicosia, was founded in 1989. There were a total of 37 higher education institutions in 2004/05, including professional institutes and colleges for art, forestry and management. In that year 20,078 students were enrolled in tertiary education, and 19,400 students were studying at universities abroad.

Students must hold the main secondary school qualification (Apolytirion) and sit a competitive entrance examination to gain admission to the University of Cyprus. Cyprus became a signatory to the Bologna Process in 2001, and a two-tier Bachelors and Masters degree system has been implemented. Non-university higher education consists of one to four-year Certificate, Diploma and Higher Diploma programmes, offered by the University of Cyprus and private institutions in professional fields of study. Private higher education institutions are registered and accredited by the Ministry of Education and Culture, in accordance with Law 67(I)96, introduced in September 1997.

The first university degree-level is the undergraduate Bachelors degree, which is awarded after four years' study. Students must accumulate 120–180 credit units in eight semesters. Both the postgraduate degrees, Masters and Doctor of Philosophy (PhD) require 30 credit units.

Post-secondary technical and vocational education is offered by both public and private institutions.

Turkish Republic of North Cyprus

Cyprus's first university, the Eastern Mediterranean University, which is located near Gazi Mağusa (Famagusta), was opened in 1979 as the Higher Technological Institute and was elevated to full university status under its current name in 1986. The European University of Lefke was founded in 1990. In 2004/05 35,473 students were enrolled at higher education establishments in the TRNC. In 2004/05 1,900 students were pursuing higher education studies abroad. All schools and educational institutes are administered by the Ministry of National Education and Culture (with a few exceptions of professional institutes attached to the appropriate Ministry). Education in the Turkish Cypriot zone is divided into two sections, formal and adult education. Formal education covers nursery, primary, secondary and higher education. Adult (informal) education caters for special training outside the school system.

Completion of the Lise Bitirme Diplomasi or equivalent is required for entry to university. The organization of undergraduate degrees is based on the US-style 'credit' and grade-point average (GPA) system. The Bachelors degree lasts eight semesters (four years) and students require at least 120 credits and a GPA of 2.0 to graduate. A two-year Diploma course is also available. Masters programmes like the Master of Arts (MA), Master of Business Administration (MBA) and Master of Science (MSc) take 1–2 years' study following the Bachelors, and require between 21 (MSc) and 42 (MBA) credits. A Masters is required for admission onto the Doctor of Philosophy (PhD) programme, which is a combination of core coursework and original research; candidates for PhD must submit a research thesis.

Technical and vocational education is provided by several colleges and institutes, admission to which is dependent upon the Lise Bitirme Diplomasi.

Learned Societies

GENERAL

Etaireia Kypriakon Spoudon (Society of Cypriot Studies): POB 1436, Nicosia; tel. (22) 463205; f. 1936; aims: the collection, preservation and study of material concerning all periods of the history, dialect and folklore of Cyprus; the Society maintains a Museum of Cypriot Folk Art; 250 mems; library of Kypria; library of 4,000 vols; Pres. KYPROS CHRYSANTHIS; Sec. A. SPYRIDAKIS; publs *Demosievmata, Kypriakai Spoudai* (Cypriot Studies, annually).

BIBLIOGRAPHY, LIBRARY SCIENCE AND MUSEOLOGY

Library Association of Cyprus: POB 1039, Nicosia; f. 1962; promotes library science and professional activities; 45 mems; Pres. COSTAS D. STEPHANOU; Sec. PARIS G. ROSSOS.

HISTORY, GEOGRAPHY AND ARCHAEOLOGY

Cyprus Geographical Association: POB 3656, Nicosia; tel. (22) 463205; f. 1968; research and study of the geography of Cyprus; aims to improve the teaching of geography, and safeguard professional interests of geographers; 200 mems; library of 500 vols; Pres. Prof. PANAYIOTIS ARGYRIDES; publ. *The Geographical Chronicles* (annually).

LANGUAGE AND LITERATURE

Alliance Française: 10 Panagi Lappa, POB 56681, Limassol 3309; tel. (25) 339181; fax (25) 387143; e-mail aflima@spidernet.com.cy; offers courses and exams in French language and culture and promotes cultural exchange with France.

British Council: 3 Museum St, 1097 Nicosia; postal address: POB 25654, 1387 Nicosia; tel. (22) 585000; fax (22) 677257; e-mail enquiries@cy.britishcouncil.org; internet www.britishcouncil.org.cy; offers courses and exams in English language and British culture and promotes cultural exchange with the UK; Dir PETER SKELTON.

Research Institutes

GENERAL

Cyprus Research Centre (Kentron Epistemonikōn Erevnōn): Kimon and Thucydides Street, Nicosia 1434; tel. (2) 800788; fax (2) 305546; under the jurisdiction of the Ministry of Education and Culture; f. 1967; aims: the promotion of scientific research in Cyprus with special reference to the historico-philological disciplines and the social sciences; research library; sections: (a) Historical Section: editing and publication of the sources of the history of Cyprus; (b) Ethnographic Section: collection, preservation, and publication of materials relating to the local culture of the island; (c) Philological and Linguistic Section: collection of lexicographic materials, the preparation of a historical dictionary of the Cypriot dialect, and the editing of literary and dialect texts; (d) Oriental Section: promotion of oriental studies in Cyprus, with special reference to Ottoman studies; (e) Archives Section: collection and preservation of MSS. and documents relating to all aspects of the society of Cyprus; Dir (vacant); publs *Texts and Studies of the History of Cyprus*, *Publications*, *Epeteris* (annually).

HISTORY, GEOGRAPHY AND ARCHAEOLOGY

Cyprus American Archaeological Research Institute: 11 A. Demetriou St, Nicosia 1066; tel. (22) 456414; fax (22) 671147; e-mail director@caari.org.cy; internet caari.org; f. 1978; one of the American Schools of Oriental Research; promotes the study of archaeology and related disciplines in Cyprus; encourages communication among scholars interested in Cyprus and provides residence facilities; library of 7,100 books, 100 current periodicals; representative ceramic, geological, lithic, archaeometallurgical and faunal reference collections, slide archive; Dir Dr THOMAS W. DAVIS.

Libraries and Archives

Famagusta

Municipal Library: POB 41, Famagusta; f. 1954; reference and lending sections, including many books on Cyprus and in several languages; the Famagusta Municipal Art Gallery, with a historical maps section, is attached; 18,000 vols; Librarian and Curator CH. CHRISTOFIDES.

Limassol

Municipal Library: 352 St Andrew St, 3035 Limassol; tel. (25) 362153; f. 1945; 12,000 vols; Librarian A. KYRIAKIDES.

Nicosia

Cyprus Library: Eleftheria Square, Nicosia 1011; tel. (22) 303180; fax (22) 304532; e-mail library@cytanet.com.cy; f. 1987; 107,000 vols, 445 CDs and DVDs, 176 video cassettes, 500 microforms; special collection: Cypriot studies; Librarian ANTONIS MARATHEFTIS; publ. *Bulletin of the Cyprus Bibliography*.

Cyprus Museum Library: POB 2024, Nicosia; tel. (22) 865848; fax (22) 303148; e-mail roctarch@cytanet.com.cy; f. 1883; incorporated in Dept of Antiquities 1934; 18,328 vols (excluding bound periodicals), 220 periodicals, Pierides colln of 1,400 vols; Librarian MARIA DEMETRIOU-ECONOMIDOU.

Cyprus Turkish National Library: Kızılay Ave, Lefkoşa, Turkish Republic of Northern Cyprus, via Mersin 10, Turkey; tel. (22) 283257; f. 1961; 56,000 vols; Chief Librarian FATMA ÖNEN.

Library of the Archbishop Makarios III Foundation: POB 21269, Nicosia 1505; tel. (22) 430008; fax (22) 346753; f. 1983; research library of 55,000 vols relating mostly to Greek, Byzantine and post-Byzantine studies, Christian theology and recent political history of Cyprus; incorporates the library of Phaneromeni, the library of the Holy Archbishopric of Cyprus, the library of the Society of Cypriot Studies, and the Foundation library; Dir Dr M. STAVROU.

Library of the Institute of Education: Macedonia Avenue, Latsia, Nicosia 2250; tel. (22) 402300; fax (22) 480505; e-mail papandreou@cyearn.pi.ac.cy; internet athena .pi.ac.cy; f. 1972; 60,000 vols, mainly on education; Dir ANDREAS PAPANDREOU.

State Archives of the Republic of Cyprus: Ministry of Justice and Public Order, 1461 Nicosia; tel. (22) 302664; fax (22) 667680; e-mail statearchives@sa.mjpo .gov.cy; internet www.mjpo.gov.cy; f. 1978; place of deposit for public records received from govt depts and other bodies, subject to the State Archives Law; makes these records available for research by members of the public; 11,703 vols; 159,000 Secretariat Archives files, 6.22 km of linear shelving of archival holdings; State Archivist EFFY PARPARINOU.

Museums and Art Galleries

Limassol

Cyprus Medieval Museum: Limassol Castle; tel. (25) 330419; f. 1987; rich collection of local and imported pottery from the Early Christian, Byzantine and medieval periods; unique collections of medieval tombstones, coats of arms and architectural exhibits from palaces, castles and churches; coins, arms, cannons, etc.

Nicosia

Cyprus Folk Art Museum: POB 1436, Nicosia; tel. (22) 463205; f. 1950; Cyprus arts and crafts from early to recent times; mainly Cypriot Greek items; Dir Dr ELENI PAPADEMETRIOU.

Cyprus Historical Museum and Archives: Pentelis 50, Strovolos, Nicosia; f. 1975; a private enterprise to create a cultural centre; aims to tape-record accounts of historical events in Cyprus, to photocopy all existing historical material about Cyprus, to liaise with the Ministry of Culture and Greek historians, to find and publicize historical treasures in private collections; library of 3,000 vols; Pres. PETROS STYLIANOU; Gen. Sec. CLEITOS SYMEONIDES.

Cyprus Museum: POB 22024, Nicosia; tel. (22) 865888; fax (22) 303148; e-mail antiquitiesdept@da.mcw.gov.cy; f. 1882; incorporated in Dept of Antiquities 1934; collns: (1) pottery from the Neolithic and Chalcolithic periods to the Graeco-Roman Age; (2) terracotta figures of the Neolithic Age to Graeco-Roman times, including the Ayia Irini group; (3) limestone and marble sculpture from the Archaic to the Graeco-Roman Age; (4) jewellery from the Neolithic period, especially Mycenaean (1400–1200 BC), to early Byzantine times, and coins from the 6th century BC to Roman times; (5) misc. collens, incl. inscriptions (Cypro-Minoan, Phoenician, Cypro-syllabic, Latin, Greek), bronzes, glass, alabaster, bone, etc.; exhibitions of jewellery, seals, coins; reconstructed tombs; extensive reserve collns are available for students; an archaeological library (see above) is housed in the Cyprus Museum bldg and is open to all; Dir Dr PAVLOS FLOURENTZOS; publs *Annual Report of the Department of Antiquities Cyprus (ARDAC)*, *Report of the Department of Antiquities Cyprus (RDAC)* (annual).

Universities

UNIVERSITY OF CYPRUS

Kallipoleos 75, POB 537, 1678 Nicosia
Telephone: (22) 756186
Fax: (22) 756198
Internet: www.ucy.ac.cy

Founded 1989
State control
Languages of instruction: Greek, Turkish
Academic year: September to June

President: MICHALAKIS A. TRIANTAFYLLIDES
Vice-President: ANDREAS PATSALIDES
Rector: Prof. STAVROS ZENIOS
Vice-Rector (vacant)
Director of Administration and Finance: Dr NICOS VAKIS
Librarian (vacant)

Number of teachers: 139
Number of students: 2,234

DEANS

Faculty of Economics and Management: Prof. CHRISTAKIS CHARALAMBOUS
Faculty of Humanities and Social Sciences: Assoc. Prof. YIANNIS E. IOANNOU
Faculty of Letters: Prof. MICHAEL PIERIS
Faculty of Pure and Applied Sciences: Assoc. Prof. CHARIS R. THEOCHARIS

PROFESSORS

Faculty of Economics and Management:
- CHACHOLIADES, M., Economics
- CHARALAMBOUS, C., Public and Business Administration
- PASHIARDES, P., Economics
- SPANOS, A., Economics
- TRIGEORGIS, L., Public and Business Administration
- ZENIOS, ST., Public and Business Administration

Faculty of Humanities and Social Sciences:
- DAVY, J., Foreign Languages and Literature
- DEMETRIOU, A., Education
- HAZAI, GY., Turkish Studies
- NATSOPOULOS, D., Education

Faculty of Letters:
- CHRYSOS, E., History and Archaeology
- PIERIS, M., Byzantine and Modern Greek Studies

Faculty of Pure and Applied Sciences:
- KERAVNOU-PAPAILIOU, E., Computer Science
- PAPAMICHAEL, N., Mathematics

EASTERN MEDITERRANEAN UNIVERSITY

POB 95, Gazi Mağusa, Turkish Republic of Northern Cyprus(via Mersin 10, Turkey)
Telephone: (392) 630-1111
Fax: (392) 365-4479
E-mail: info@emu.edu.tr
Internet: www.emu.edu.tr

Founded 1979 as Higher Technological Institute; university status 1986
Language of instruction: English
State control
Academic year: September to June (two semesters)

Rector: Prof. Dr HALİL GÜVEN
Vice-Rectors: Prof. Dr AYHAN BİLSEL, Assoc. Prof. Dr HALİL NADİRİ, Assoc. Prof. Dr MUSTAFA DAĞBAŞI, Asst. Prof. Dr ŞAMİL ERDOĞAN
Secretary-General: GÜROL ÖZKAYA
Registrar: HÜSEYİN ÜNSAL YETİNER
Librarian: OSMAN SOYKAN

Library of 125,000 vols, 600 periodical subscriptions and 25 electronic networks
Number of teachers: 641 full-time

Number of teachers: 141 part-time
Number of students: 14,256

Publications: *Journal of Cyprus Studies* (in English), *EMU Tourism Research Journal* (in English), *Review of Social, Economic and Business Studies* (in English), *Woman 2000* (in English)

DEANS

Faculty of Architecture: Prof. Dr İBRAHİM NUMAN
Faculty of Arts and Sciences: Prof. Dr AHMET KONROT
Faculty of Business and Economics: Prof. Dr HASAN ALİBIÇAK
Faculty of Communication and Media Studies: Assoc. Prof. Dr SEVDA ALANKUŞ
Faculty of Education: Prof. Dr SABRİKOÇ
Faculty of Engineering: Prof. Dr İZZET KALE
Faculty of Law: Prof. Dr TURGUT TURHAN

DIRECTORS

School of Computing and Technology: Prof. Dr HASAN AMCA
School of Tourism and Hospitality Management: Prof. Dr MEHMET ALTINAY
Institute for Graduate Studies and Research: Prof. Dr AYHAN BİLSEL
Institute of Advanced Technology Research and Development: Prof. Dr ŞENER UYSAL
Distance Education Institute: Asst Prof. Dr IŞIK AYBAY
School of Foreign Languages: HÜSEYİN DEMİREL

ATTACHED INSTITUTES

Centre for Ataturk Studies and Applied Research: Dir Assoc. Prof. Dr HASAN CICIOĞLU.

Centre for Cultural Heritage Studies and Archaeological Research: Dir Prof. Dr COŞKUN ÖZGÜNEL.

Centre for Environmental Research and Policy: Dir METIN BAYTEKN.

EMU Centre of Cyprus Studies: Dir ISMAİL BOZKURT.

EMU European Research and Information Centre: Dir Assoc. Prof. Dr HASAN ALİBIÇAK.

Information Technologies Research and Development Centre: Dir Asst Prof. Dr DERVIŞ DENZ.

EUROPEAN UNIVERSITY OF LEFKE

Gemıkonağı, Lefke, Mersin 10, Turkey
Telephone: (392) 228-6037
Fax: (392) 228-6165
E-mail: international@lefke.edu.tr
Internet: www.lefke.edu.tr

Founded 1990 by Cyprus Science Foundation; accredited by Higher Education Council of Turkey
Languages of instruction: English, Turkish
Academic year: October to June

President: Prof. Dr YILDIRIM ÖNER
General Secretary: METİN BAYTEKİN
Registrar: MEHMET YALÇIN
Librarian: ELIF BILOKÇUOĞLU

Library of 30,000 vols, 70 periodicals
Number of teachers: 120
Number of students: 2,800

Publication: *Laü'nün Sesi Journal* (6 a year)

DEANS

Faculty of Agricultural Sciences: Assoc. Prof. Dr ULRICH KERSTING
Faculty of Architecture and Engineering: Prof. Dr K. BALASUBRAMANIAN
Faculty of Arts and Sciences: Prof. Dr GÜNAY KARAAĞAÇ
Faculty of Communication Sciences: Prof. Dr FARUK KALKAN
Faculty of Economics and Administrative Sciences: Assoc. Prof. Dr FIKRET KUTSAL (acting)

HEADS OF DEPARTMENTS

Faculty of Agricultural Sciences (European University of Lefke, Güzelyurt, Mersin 10, Turkey; tel. (Turkey 392) 714-6781; fax (Turkey 392) 714-6783):
- Horticultural Production and Marketing: Asst Prof. Dr İLHAMI TOZLU

Faculty of Architecture and Engineering:
- Architecture and Interior Architecture: Prof. Dr BOZOK ÖZERDIM
- Civil Engineering: Asst Prof. Dr KONSTANTIN SOBOLEV
- Computer Sciences: Prof. Dr K. BALASUBRAMANIAN (acting)
- Electrical and Electronic Engineering: (vacant)

Faculty of Arts and Sciences:
- English Language Teaching: Asst Prof. Dr SÜLEYMAN GÖKER
- History: Asst Prof. Dr MEHMET DEMIRYÜREK
- Turkish Language and Literature: Prof. Dr GÜNAY KARAAĞAÇ (acting)

Faculty of Communication Sciences:
- Journalism: Assoc. Prof. Dr FILIZ SEÇIM
- Public Relations and Advertising: Asst Prof. Dr FAIK KARTELLI
- Radio, Television and Cinema: Prof. Dr FARUK KALKAN (acting)

Faculty of Economics and Administrative Sciences:
- Business: Asst Prof. Dr SERDAR SAYDAM
- Economics: Assoc. Prof. Dr FIKRET KUTSAL
- International Relations: Asst Prof. Dr SUPHI GALIP

ATTACHED INSTITUTE

Institute of Marine Sciences and Fisheries: Dir Prof. Dr IŞIK K. ORAY.

Colleges

Cyprus College: POB 22006, Nicosia; tel. (22) 662062; fax (22) 662051; internet www.cycollege.ac.cy; f. 1961; 2-year associate degree courses, 3- and 4-year bachelor degree courses in social sciences, business administration and computer science, MBA programme; 51 teachers; 1,020 students; library: 35,000 vols; Dir ANDREAS ELEFTHERIADES; Dean of Admissions MARINA ALEXANDROU; publs *The Observer*, *Journal of Business & Society*.

Cyprus College of Art: Lempa, 8260 Paphos; tel. (26) 270557; fax (26) 964269 *UK Office* (all enquiries): POB 304, Leeds, LS6 3YN, UK; tel. (113) 274-3287; e-mail enquiries@artcyprus.org; internet www.geocities.com/artcyprus; f. 1969; one-year foundation courses in art and design; undergraduate degree programmes in association with partner organisations in the UK; postgraduate courses in fine art; 8 teachers; 40 students; Dir STASS PARASKOS.

Cyprus Forestry College: Prodromos, Limassol 4841; tel. (25) 813606; fax (25) 462646; e-mail forcollege@fc.moa.gov.cy; internet www.moa.gov.cy/fc; f. 1951; technical-level and advanced training in forestry; library: 2,000 vols, 7 periodicals; 7 teachers; 20 students; Principal CHR. ALEXANDROU.

Cyprus International Institute of Management: 21 Akademias Ave, Aglandjia, POB 378, Nicosia; tel. (22) 330052; fax (22) 331121; f. 1990; 1-year full-time and 2-year part-time courses leading to MBA and MPSM degrees and Advanced Diploma; library: 3,000 vols; Dir Dr JIM LEONTIADES.

Higher Technical Institute: POB 20423, Nicosia 2152; tel. (22) 406300; fax (22) 494953; e-mail htics@cytanet.com.cy; internet www.htc.ac.cy; f. 1968; 3-year courses in civil, electrical, mechanical and marine engineering, computer studies; 90 teachers; 312 students; library: 15,800 vols; Dir CONSTANTINOS LOIZOU; publ. *HTI Review* (annually).

Intercollege (International College): 46 Makedonitissa Ave, POB 24005, Nicosia 1700; tel. (22) 841500; fax (22) 357481; e-mail nicosia@intercollege.ac.cy; internet www.intercollege.ac.cy; f. 1980; private control; instruction in English; undergraduate and postgraduate courses lead to qualifying examinations for local, British and US degrees; also centres at Limassol and Larnaca; library: 70,000 vols; 203 teachers (112 full-time, 91 part-time); 5,000 students (incl. 613 at Limassol and 566 at Larnaca); Dean of Academic Affairs ANDREAS POLEMITIS; Executive Dean NICOS PERISTIANIS; publ. *Cyprus Review* (2 a year).

Mediterranean Institute of Management: POB 20536, 1679 Nicosia; tel. (22) 806000; fax (22) 376872; e-mail info@kepa.mlsi.com.cy; internet www.kepa.gov.cy; f. 1976; international component of Cyprus Productivity Centre (a dept of Min. of Social and Labour Insurance) postgraduate management diploma course; research and management consultancy projects; library: 8,000 vols; 30 teachers; 90 students; Dir Dr IOANNIS MODITIS.

CZECH REPUBLIC

The Higher Education System

Higher education institutions predate the foundation of the former Czechoslovakia in 1918, with the oldest being Univerzita Karlova, which was founded in 1348. In 1990, following the removal of the communist Government, which had been in power since 1948, Czechoslovakia was replaced by the Czech and Slovak Federative Republic (CzSFR). In turn, the CzSFR was dissolved in 1993 and the Czech Republic and Slovakia became independent, sovereign states. Higher education reforms in both states were initiated under Act 172, passed in 1990; the Higher Education Act of 1998 (amended 2001) and a new education law in 2005 have also come into force. In 2004/05 some 250,261 students attended 25 universities. Higher education is financed by the Ministry of Education, Youth and Sport.

The secondary school leaving certificate (Maturita) is the main requirement for admission to higher education. Precise entry requirements vary among institutions, and students may have to sit an entrance examination. Legislation passed in 1998, and amended in 2001, brought the Czech Republic into line with the Bologna Process. The Bakalár is the main undergraduate degree, and lasts for three to four years. The first postgraduate degree, Magistr, is awarded after two to three years' study following the Bakalár. Some disciplines involve integrated undergraduate and postgraduate programmes lasting five to six years, leading to professional qualifications; these include engineering, architecture and medicine. Finally, following Magistr, doctoral studies take three to four years and result in the award of the title Doktor.

Post-secondary technical and vocational education dates from the establishment of vyšší odborná škola (tertiary technical schools) in 1992. there are now about 150 such establishments offering education and training in vocational fields. The period of study is between two to three-and-a-half years, and students are awarded the Diplomovaný Specialista.

Learned Societies

GENERAL

Akademie věd České republiky (AV ČR) (Academy of Sciences of the Czech Republic): Národní tř. 3, 117 20 Prague 1; tel. 221403111; fax 224240512; e-mail info@cas.cz; internet www.cas.cz; f. 1992; the Academy is a network of 60 autonomous research institutes which conduct theoretical and applied research in three broad sections: Chemical and Life Sciences (Dir Prof. HELENA ILLNEROVÁ), Humanities and Social Sciences (Dir Dr VILÉM HEROLD), Mathematics, Physics and Earth Sciences (Dir Dr KAREL JUNGWIRTH); attached research institutes: see Research Institutes; library and archive: see Libraries and Archives; Pres. Prof. VÁCLAV PAČEK; Pres. of Scientific Council Prof. Dr FRANTIŠEK ŠMAHEL; publ. *Akademický bulletin* (newsletter, monthly).

Rada vědeckých společností České republiky (Council of Scientific Societies of the Czech Republic): Středisko společných činností Akademie věd ČR, Národní 3, 117 20 Prague; tel. and fax 221403478; e-mail rvs@kav.cas.cz; internet www.cas.cz/rvs; co-ordinates 70 scientific societies, representing natural science, medicine and the social, and technical sciences; 34,000 mems; Pres. Prof. MUDr IVO HÁNA.

AGRICULTURE, FISHERIES AND VETERINARY SCIENCE

Česká Akademie Zemědělských Věd (Czech Academy of Agricultural Sciences): Těšnov 17, 117 05 Prague 1; tel. 222320582; fax 222328898; e-mail cazv@cazv.cz; internet www.cazv.cz; f. 1924; sections of Agricultural Engineering, Energy and Development (Chair. Ing. ZDĚNEK PASTOREK), Animal Production (Chair. Doc. Ing. JOSEF BOUSK), Economics, Management, Sociology and Information Technology (Chair. Doc. Ing. JAN HRON), Food Technology and Engineering (Chair. Ing. JIŘÍ CELBA), Forestry (Chair. Ing. PETR ZAHRADNÍK), Human Nutrition and Food Quality (Chair. Ing. CTIBOR PERLÍN), Plant Production (Chair. Dr FRANTIŠEK KOCOUREK), Soil Science (Chair. Ing. KAREL B. BŘEZINA), Veterinary Medicine (Chair. Prof. MVDr MIROSLAV TOMAN), Water Management (Chair. Doc. Ing. MILOSLAV JANEČEK; 658 mems; Pres. Prof. Ing. JAN HRON; publs *Genetika a šlechtění* (Czech Journal of Genetics and Plant Breeding, 4 a year), *Journal of Forest Science* (monthly), *Ochrana rostlin* (Plant Protection Science, 4 a year), *Potravinářské vědy* (Czech Journal of Food Sciences, 6 a year), *Rostlinná výroba* (Plant Production, monthly), *Veterinární medicína* (Veterinary Medicine, monthly), *Zahradnictví* (Horticultural Science, 4 a year), *Zemědělská ekonomika* (Agricultural Economics, monthly), *Zemědělská technika* (Research in Agricultural Engineering, 4 a year), *Živočišná výroba* (Czech Journal of Animal Science, monthly).

ARCHITECTURE AND TOWN PLANNING

Obec architektů (Society of Architects): 1, Letenská 5, 118 00 Prague; tel. 257535025; fax 257535033; e-mail obecarch@volny.cz; internet www.architekt.cz; f. 1989; 1,000 mems; Pres. JIŘÍ MOJŽÍŠ; publ. *Architekt* (monthly).

ECONOMICS, LAW AND POLITICS

Česká společnost ekonomická (Czech Economic Association): Tř. Politických vězňů 11, 110 00 Prague 1; tel. 224210571; f. 1962; 650 mems; Pres. Dr TOMÁŠ HOLUB; publ. *Bulletin* (3 a year).

Česká společnost pro mezinárodní právo (Czech Society for International Law): Národní tř. 18, 116 91 Prague 1; tel. 224912258; fax 224910495; e-mail balas@ilaw.cas.cz; f. 1969; 96 mems; Pres. JUDr V. MIKULKA; Sec. JUDr Ing. J. ZEMÁNEK; publ. *Studie z mezinárodního práva* (Studies in International Law).

Česká společnost pro politické vědy (Czech Association for Political Sciences): Nám. W. Churchilla 4, 130 67 Prague 3; tel. 224095204; fax 224220657; e-mail dvorakv@vse.cz; internet www.cspv.cz; f. 1964; 200 mems; Pres. Prof. VLADIMIRA DVOŘÁKOVÁ; Sec. Dr LADISLAV CABADA; publ. *Politologická Revue* (2 a year).

EDUCATION

Česká komise pro UNESCO (Czech Commission for UNESCO): Skokanská 3, 169 00 Prague 6; tel. 220466700; fax 220466500; e-mail unesco@mzv.cz; internet www.mzv.cz/unesco; f. 1994.

Česká pedagogická společnost (Czech Pedagogical Association): Poříčí 31, 603 00 Brno; tel. and fax 543232722; e-mail sekretar@cpds.cz; internet www.cpds.cz; f. 1964; 240 mems; Pres. Doc. Prof. VLASTIMIL ŠVEC; Sec. Dr M. RYBIČKOVÁ; publ. *Pedagogická orientace* (quarterly).

FINE AND PERFORMING ARTS

Asociace hudebních umělců a vědců (Association of Musicians and Musicologists): Maltézské nám. 1, 118 01 Prague 1; tel. 251553996; e-mail ahuv@seznam.cz; internet www.ahuv.cz; f. 1990; 1,200 mems; Pres. Prof. JIŘÍ HLAVÁČ; Exec. Sec. MARCELA POSEJPALOVÁ; publ. *Hudební rozhledy* (monthly).

Česká hudební společnost (Czech Music Society): Radlická 99, 150 00 Prague 5; tel. and fax 251552453; e-mail mila.smetackova@volny.cz; f. 1973; 5,000 mems; Pres. MÍLA SMETÁČKOVÁ; Sec.-Gen. EVA STRAUSOVÁ; publs *ČHS News* (2 a year), *Josef Suk Society News* (2 a year), *Vítězslav Novák Society News* (annually).

Český filmový a televizní svaz (FITES) (Czech Film and Television Association): Pod Nuselskými schody 1721/3, 120 00 Prague 2; tel. 222562331; fax 222562331; e-mail info@fites.cz; internet www.fites.cz; f. 1966; 760 mems; Pres. JAN KRAUS; publ. *Synchron* (6 a year).

Český spolek pro komorní hudbu (Czech Society for Chamber Music): c/o Česká filharmonie Rudolfinum, 1, Alšovo nábřeží 12, 110 00 Prague; tel. 227059228; fax 227059238; e-mail cskh@cfmail.cz; internet www.ceskafilharmonie.cz; f. 1894; 3,500 mems; Chair. Ing. IVAN ENGLICH.

Divadelní ústav (Theatre Institute): Celetná 17, 110 00 Prague 1; tel. 224809132; fax 224810278; e-mail foreign.dpt@czech-theatre.cz; internet www.divadlo.cz; f. 1956; research and documentation on Czech theatre; Czech centre of the International Theatre Institute (ITI); library of 100,000 vols; Dir ONDŘEJ ČERNÝ; publs *Theatre Czech* (annually), *Ročenka českých divadel* (annually), *Informační servis Divadelního ústavu* (monthly), *Divadelní noviny* (2 a month), *Loutkář* (10 a year), *Divadelní revue* (quarterly).

Společnost pro estetiku (Society for Aesthetics): Department of Aesthetics, Faculty of Philosophy, Charles University, Celetná 20, 110 00 Prague 1; tel. 224491384; e-mail vlastimil.zuska@ff.cuni.cz; internet www.cas.cz/rvs/index_gb.html; f. 1969; 85 mems; Pres. PhDr ROMAN DYKAST; Sec. K. NOVOTNÁ.

Unie výtvarných umělců (Union of Creative Artists): Masarykovo nábř. 250, 110 00 Prague 1; tel. and fax 541213555; e-mail uvucr@uvucr.cz; internet www.uvucr.cz; f. 1990; supports the professional interests of visual artists; acts as an information centre and co-ordinates the activities of its members; keeps a register of professional visual artists working in the Czech Republic; 3,000 mems; Pres. VÁCLAV KUBÁT; Exec. Vice-Pres. VÍT WEBER; publs *Art Folia* (annually), *Atelier* (every 2 weeks), *Technologia Artis* (annually), *Výtvarné umění* (quarterly).

HISTORY, GEOGRAPHY AND ARCHAEOLOGY

Česká archeologická společnost (Czech Archaeological Society): Letenská 4, 118 01 Prague 1; tel. 224317913; fax 224491401; e-mail zuzana.sklenarova@ff.cuni.cz; internet www.archaeology.cz/cas; f. 1919; 550 mems; Pres. Dr KAREL SKLENÁŘ; Sec. Mgr ONDŘEJ CHVOJKA; publs *Archeologie Moravy a Slezska* (Archaeology of Moravia and Silesia, annually), *Studia Hercynia* (annually), *Zprávy* (Bulletin, irregular).

Česká demografická společnost (Czech Demographic Society): Albertov 6, 128 43 Prague 2; tel. 221951418; fax 224920657; e-mail demodept@natur.cuni.cz; internet www.natur.cuni.cz/~demodept/cds; f. 1964; 450 mems; Pres. JITKA RYCHTAŘÍKOVÁ; Sec. FELIX KOSCHIN.

Česká geografická společnost (Czech Geographical Society): Albertov 6, 128 43 Prague 2; tel. 221951383; fax 224920657; e-mail perlin@mail.natur.cuni.cz; internet www.natur.cuni.cz/~ksgrrsek/cgs.php; f. 1894; 805 mems; Pres. Assoc. Prof. IVAN BIČÍK; Sec. Dr RADIM PERLIN; publ. *Sborník* (journal, quarterly).

Matice moravská (Moravian Society of History and Literature): Arne Nováka 1, 602 00 Brno; tel. 549493552; fax 549491520; e-mail matice@phil.muni.cz; internet www.matice-moravska.cz; f. 1849; 560 mems; Pres. Prof. PhDr JAN JANÁK; Sec. PhDr BRONISLAV CHOCHOLÁČ; publ. *Časopis Matice moravské* (2 a year).

LANGUAGE AND LITERATURE

Alliance Française: c/o French Embassy in the Czech Republic, Štěpánská 35, 111 21 Prague 1; tel. 221401063; fax 222230576; e-mail michel.wattremez@diplomatie.gouv.fr; internet www.alliancefrancaise.cz; offers courses and exams in French language and culture and promotes cultural exchange with France; attached offices in Brno, České Budějovice, Hradec Králové, Kladno, Kroměříž, Liberec, Louny, Ostrava, Pardubice, Plzeň, Pribram, Ústí nad Labem and Zlín; General Co-ordinator MICHEL WATTREMEZ.

British Council: Bredovský dvůr, Politických vězňů 13, 110 00 Prague 1; tel. 221991160; fax 224933847; e-mail info.praha@britishcouncil.cz; internet www.britishcouncil.cz; teaching centre; offers courses and exams in English language and British culture and promotes cultural exchange with the UK; attached teaching centre in Pilsen; Dir and Cultural Counsellor MANDY JOHNSON; Asst Dir, Teaching Centre DUNCAN LAMBE.

Český esperantský svaz (Czech Union of Esperantists): c/o Pavel Polnicky, Na Vinici 110/10, 290 01 Podebrady; e-mail cea.polnicky@quick.cz; internet www.esperanto.cz; tel. 325615651; f. 1969; 1,100 mems; Pres. VĚRA PODHRADSKÁ; publ. *Starto* (4 a year).

Czech Centre of International PEN: 28 října 9, 110 00 Prague 1; tel. 224235546; fax 224221926; e-mail centrum@pen.cz; f. 1924; 207 mems; Pres. JIRI STRÁNSKÝ; Sec. Ing. L. LUDVIKOVÁ.

Goethe-Institut: Masarykovo nábřeží 32, 110 00 Prague 1; tel. 221962111; fax 221962250; e-mail info@prag.goethe.org; internet www.goethe.de/ins/cz/pra/; offers courses and exams in German language and culture and promotes cultural exchange with Germany; library of 14,000 vols; Dir Dr STEPHAN NOBBE.

Literárněvědná společnost (Literary Society): Valentinská 1, 110 00 Prague 1; f. 1934; 285 mems; Pres. Dr SLAVOMÍR WOLLMAN; Sec. JOSEF VLÁŠEK.

Obec spisovatelů (Association of Writers): POB 669, 111 21 Prague 1; Železná 18, 110 00 Prague 1; tel. 224234060; e-mail obecspis@volny.cz; internet www.obecspisovatelu.cz; f. 1989; 700 mems; Hon. Pres. VÁCLAV HAVEL; Pres. EVA KANTŮRKOVÁ; publ. *Dokořán* (4 a year).

MEDICINE

Česká imunologická společnost (Czech Society for Immunology): Vídeňská 1083, 142 20 Prague 4; e-mail cis@biomed.cas.cz; internet www.biomed.cas.cz/cis/; f. 1986; 600 mems; Pres. Prof. Dr ALEŠ MACELA; Sec. Dr MARTIN BILEJ; publ. *Imunologický zpravodaj* (3 a year).

Česká lékařská společnost J. E. Purkyně (J. E. Purkyně Czech Medical Association): Sokolská 31 120 26 Prague 2; tel. 224266201; fax 224266212; e-mail cls@cls.cz; internet www.cls.cz; f. 1947; 34,500 mems; Pres. Prof. MUDr JAROSLAV BLAHOŠ; Scientific Sec. Prof. MUDr JIŘÍ HOMOLKA; publs *Acta Chirurgiae Plasticae* (in English, 4 a year), *Anesteziologie a intenzivní medicína* (Anaesthesiology and Intensive Critical Care Medicine, 6 a year), *Časopis lékařů českých* (Journal of Czech Physicians, monthly), *Česká a slovenská farmacie* (Czech and Slovak Pharmacy, 6 a year), *Česká a slovenská gastroenterologie a hepatologie* (Czech and Slovak Gastroenterology and Hepatology, 6 a year), *Česká a slovenská neurologie a neurochirurgie* (Czech and Slovak Neurology and Neurosurgery, 6 a year), *Česká a slovenská oftalmologie* (Czech and Slovak Ophthalmology, 6 a year), *Česká a slovenská psychiatrie* (Czech and Slovak Psychiatry, 8 a year), *Česká gynekologie* (Czech Gynaecology, 6 a year), *Česká radiologie* (Czech Radiology, 6 a year), *Česká revmatologie* (Czech Rheumatology, 4 a year), *Česká stomatologie a Praktické zubní lékařství* (Czech Stomatology and Practical Dentistry, 6 a year), *Československá dermatologie* (Czech-Slovak Dermatology, 6 a year), *Česko-slovenská patologie a Soudní lékařství* (Czech-Slovak Pathology and Forensic Medicine, 4 a year), *Česko-slovenská pediatrie* (Czech-Slovak Paediatrics, monthly), *Československá fyziologie* (Czechoslovak Physiology, 4 a year), *Epidemiologie, mikrobiologie, imunologie* (Epidemiology, Microbiology, Immunology, 4 a year), *Hygiena* (Hygiene, 4 a year), *Klinická biochemie a metabolismus* (Clinical Biochemistry and Metabolism, 4 a year), *Klinická onkologie* (Clinical Oncology, 6 a year), *Lékař a technika* (Physician and Technology, 6 a year), *Otorinolaryngologie a foniatrie* (Otorhinolaryngology and Phoniatrics, 4 a year), *Pracovní lékařství* (Occupational Medicine, 4 a year), *Praktický lékař* (General Practitioner, monthly), *Rehabilitace a fyzikální lékařství* (Rehabilitation and Physical Medicine, 4 a year), *Rozhledy v chirurgii* (Surgical Review, monthly), *Vnitřní lékařství* (Internal Medicine, monthly), *Revizní a posudkové lékařství* (Health Insurance and Medical Revision, 4 a year), *Endoskopie* (Endoscopy, 4 a year), *Transfuze a hematologie dnes* (Transfusion and Haematology Today, 4 a year).

NATURAL SCIENCES

General

Český svaz vědeckotechnických společností (Czech Association of Scientific and Technical Societies): Novotného lávka 5, 116 68 Prague 1; tel. 221082295; fax 222221780; e-mail dah@csvts.cz; internet www.csvts.cz; f. 1990; 136,000 mems; Pres. Ing. DANIEL HANUS; Sec. Ing. ZDENKA DAHINTEROVÁ; publs *Bio Prospect* (irregular), *Chemical Papers (Prague)* (6 a year), *Glass Paper* (irregular), *Plant Physician* (4 a year), *Reporter* (4 a year), *Silicate Reporter* (irregular).

Společnost pro dějiny věd a techniky (Society of the History of Sciences and Technology): Kostelní 42, 170 78 Prague 7; tel. 220399208; fax 233371801; e-mail barvikova@archiv.cas.cz; internet dvt.hyperlink.cz; f. 1965; 350 mems; Pres. Dr MARTIN ŠOK; Sec. Dr MILADA SEKYRKOVÁ; publs *Acta historiae rerum naturalium necnon technicarum* (annually), *Dějiny věd a techniky* (4 a year), *Práce z dějin techniky a přívodních věd* (Treatise on the History of Technology and Sciences, irregular).

Biological Sciences

Česká botanická společnost (Czech Botanical Society): Benátská 2, 128 01 Prague 2; tel. 221951664; e-mail botspol@natur.cuni.cz; internet www.natur.cuni.cz/cbs; f. 1912; 787 mems; library of 3,000 vols, 1,400 periodicals; Chair. Dr LUBOMÍR HROUDA; Sec. Dr J. ŠTĚPÁNEK; publs *Preslia* (quarterly), *Zprávy ČBS* (irregular).

Česká parazitologická společnost (Czech Society for Parasitology): c/o Institute of Postgraduate Medical Education, 10, Ruská 85, 100 05 Prague; tel. 271019254; fax 272740458; e-mail fajfrlik@fnplzen.cz; internet www.parazitologie.cz; f. 1993; 199 mems; Pres. Dr LIBUSE KOLÁŘOVÁ; Sec. Dr KAREL FAJFRLÍK; publ. *Zprávy České parazitologické společnosti* (4 a year).

Česká společnost bioklimatologická (Czech Society for Bioclimatology): Boční II 1401, 141 31 Prague 4; tel. 267103321; fax 272761549; e-mail jstr@ig.cas.cz; internet www.chmi.cz/meteo/cbks/index.htm; f. 1965; 110 mems; Pres. Dr J. ROŽNOVSKÝ; Sec. Dr J. STŘEŠTIK; publ. *Digests of Science Reports* (2 a year).

Česká společnost entomologická (Czech Entomological Society): Viniěná 7, 128 00 Prague; tel. 224923535; e-mail klapagenda@centrum.cz; internet www.entospol.cz; f. 1904; 850 mems; library of 20,500 vols; Pres. Dr SVATOPLUK BÍLÝ; Sec. Dr JAN VITNER; publ. *Klapalekiana* (2 a year).

Česká společnost histo- a cytochemická (Czech Society for Histo- and Cytochemistry): Kamenice 3, 625 00 Brno; tel. 549493701; fax 549491320; e-mail pdubovy@med.muni.cz; internet www.med.muni.cz/hcspol; f. 1962; associated with the International Federation of Societies for Histochemistry and Cytochemistry; 120 mems; Pres. Prof. Dr PETR DUBOVÝ; Sec. Prof. Dr SVATOPLUK ČECH.

Česká společnost pro biomechaniku (Czech Society for Biomechanics): FTVS - Katedra anatomie a biomechaniky, J. Martiho 31, 160 00 Prague 6; tel. and fax 220560225; e-mail otahal@ftvs.cuni.cz; internet biomech.ftvs.cuni.cz/csb; f. 1990; 168 mems; Pres. Prof. STANISLAV OTÁHAL; Sec. Asst Prof. MIROSLAV SOCHOR; publ. *Bulletin* (2 a year).

Česká společnost zoologická (Czech Zoological Society): Viničná 7, 128 44 Prague 2; tel. 221951860; e-mail chalupsk@natur.cuni.cz; internet www.natur.cuni.cz/zoospol; f. 1927; 300 mems; library of 17,300 vols; Pres. Dr VÁCLAV PIŽL; Sec. Dr M. ŠVÁTORA; publ. *Acta Soc. Zool. Bohemicae* (4 a year).

Česká vědecká společnost pro mykologii (Czech Scientific Society for Mycology): POB 106, 111 21 Prague 1; tel. 224497259; internet www.natur.cuni.cz/cvsm; f. 1946; voluntary organization for professional and amateur mycologists; organises mycological lectures for the public, mycological excursions (mushroom-picking, micromycetes), seminar meetings; 220 mems; library of 700 books, 135 journal titles; Pres. Dr VLADIMÍR ANTONÍN; Sec. Dr ALENA KUBÁTOVÁ; publs *Czech Mycology* (in English, 4 a year), *Mykologické Listy* (in Czech, 4 a year).

Československá biologická společnost (Czechoslovak Biological Society): Tomešova 12, 602 00 Brno; tel. and fax 549492394; e-mail rjanisch@med.muni.cz; internet www.med.muni.cz/biolspol; f. 1922; 1,331 mems; Pres. Prof. Dr O. NEČAS; Sec. Prof. Dr R. JANISCH.

Československá společnost mikrobiologická (Czechoslovak Society for Microbiology): Vídeňská 1083, 142 20 Prague 4; tel. 296442494; fax 296442396; e-mail gabriel@biomed.cas.cz; internet www.cssm.info; f. 1928; 1,000 mems from Czech Republic and Slovakia; Pres. JAN ŠMARDA; Sec. JIRI GABRIEL; publs *Bulletin* (Czech, Slovak, quarterly), *Folia microbiologica* (English, every 2 months).

Mathematical Sciences

Jednota českých matematiků a fyziků (Union of Czech Mathematicians and Physicists): Žitná 25, 117 10 Prague 1; tel. 222211100; e-mail predseda@jcmf.cz; internet www.jcmf.cz; f. 1862; 2,500 mems; Pres. J. KURZWEIL; publs *Matematika-Fyzika-Informatika* (monthly), *Pokroky matematiky, fyziky a astronomie* (4 a year), *Rozhledy matematicko-fyzikální* (4 a year), *Učitel matematiky* (4 a year).

Physical Sciences

Česká astronomická společnost (Czech Astronomical Society): Královská obora 233, 170 00 Prague 7; tel. 233377204; e-mail borovic@asu.cas.cz; internet www.astro.cz; f. 1917; 700 mems; Pres. RNDr JIŘÍ BOROVIČKA; Sec. RNDr MILOSLAV ZEJDA; publ. *Kosmické rozhledy* (irregular).

Česká geologická společnost (Czech Geological Society): V Holešovičkách 41, 182 09 Prague 8; tel. 266009323; fax 266410649; e-mail budil@cgu.cz; internet www.geologickaspolecnost.cz; f. 1923; 500 mems; Pres. Dr PETR BUDIL; Sec. BLANKA ČIZKOVÁ; publ. *Journal* (quarterly).

Česká geologická služba (Czech Geological Survey): Klárov 3, 118 21 Prague 1; tel. 257089411; fax 257531376; internet www.cgu.cz; f. 1919 as the State Geological Survey of the Czechoslovak Republic; operates a research library; additional brs in Prague, Brno and Jeseník; archival store in Lužná u Rakovníka; Chair Dr MARTIN NOVAK.

Česká meteorologická společnost (Czech Meteorological Society): Na Šabatce 17, 143 06 Prague; tel. 221912548; fax 221912533; e-mail kmop@mff.cuni.cz; internet www.chmi.cz/poboc/br/metspol; f. 1958; provides information on meteorology and climatology, history of meteorology, and meteorological bibliography and terminology; 200 mems; Pres. Prof. RNDr JAN BEDNÁŘ; Sec. Doc. RNDr TOMÁŠ HALENKA.

Česká společnost chemická (Czech Chemical Society): Novotneho lavka 5, 116 68 Prague 1; tel. 221082383; fax 222220184; e-mail csch@csch.cz; internet www.csch.cz; f. 1866; 3,480 mems; Pres. Prof. RNDr JITKA ULRICHOVÁ; publs *Bulletin* (quarterly), *Chemické Listy* (monthly).

Spektroskopická společnost J. Marca Marci (J. Marcus Marci Spectroscopic Society): Thákurova 7, 166 29 Prague 6; tel. 233332343; e-mail immss@spektroskopie.cz; internet www.spektroskopie.cz; f. 1949; 970 mems; Chair. Prof. Dr VIKTOR KANICKÝ; Scientific Sec. JAN HÁLA.

Vědecká společnost pro nauku o kovech (Metals Society): Ke Karlovu 5, 121 16 Prague 2; tel. 221911362; fax 221911490; e-mail vsnk@met.mff.cuni.cz; f. 1966; 170 mems; Pres. Prof. VLADIMÍR ČÍHAL; Sec. Prof. VLADIMÍR ŠÍMA.

PHILOSOPHY AND PSYCHOLOGY

Filozofický ústav Akademie věd České republiky (Institute of Philosophy of the Czech Academy of Sciences): Jilská 1, 110 00 Prague 1; tel. 222220099; fax 222220108; e-mail flusekr@site.cas.cz; internet www.flu.cas.cz; f. 1990; 250 mems; Dir Dr PAVEL BARAN; publs *Acta Comeniana* (in English, French and German), *Filosofický časopis* (Philosophical Journal, summaries in English and German; 6 a year), *Teorie vedy* (Theory of Science, in Czech and English; quarterly).

RELIGION, SOCIOLOGY AND ANTHROPOLOGY

Česká společnost antropologická (Czech Anthropological Association): Salmovská 5, 120 00 Prague 2; f. 1964; 180 mems; Pres. RNDr J. JELÍNEK; Sec. Doc. Dr V. NOVOTNÝ; publ. *Zprávy* (quarterly).

Masarykova česká sociologická společnost (Masaryk Czech Sociological Association): Husova 4, 110 00 Prague 1; tel. and fax 222220631; e-mail mcss@seznam.cz; internet www.ceskasociologicka.org; f. 1964; 300 mems; Pres. JUDr MICHAL IILNER.

Národopisná společnost (Ethnographical Society): Národní třída 3, 117 20 Prague 1; e-mail valka@phil.muni.cz; f. 1893; 280 mems; Pres. Dr MIROSLAV VÁLKA; publs *Národopisný věstník* (annually), *Zpravodaj Národopisné Společnosti* (3 a year).

TECHNOLOGY

Česká společnost pro kybernetiku a informatiku (Czech Society for Cybernetics and Informatics): Pod Vodárenskou věží 2, 182 07 Prague 8; tel. 266053901; fax 286585789; e-mail cski@utia.cas.cz; internet www.cski.cz; f. 1966; 350 mems; Pres. OLGA ŠTĚPÁNKOVÁ; Sec. DAGMAR HARMANCOVÁ; publs *Kybernetika* (in English, every 2 months), *Zpravodaj* (monthly).

Česká společnost pro mechaniku (Czech Society for Mechanics): Dolejškova 5, 182 00 Prague 8; tel. 266053045; e-mail csm@it.cas.cz; internet www.csm.cz; f. 1966; 580 individual mems, 18 organizational mems; Pres. Prof. Ing. LADISLAV FRÝBA; Sec. Ing. JITKA HAVLÍNOVÁ; publ. *Bulletin* (3 a year).

Česká společnost pro vědeckou kinematografii (Czech Society for Scientific Cinematography): Zemědělská 1, 613 00 Brno; tel. 545135021; f. 1923; 150 mems; Pres. Ing. V. BOUČEK; Sec. Ing. L. RYGL; publ. *Bulletin* (annually).

Research Institutes

ARCHITECTURE AND TOWN PLANNING

Architecture and Building Foundation: Václavské nám. 31, 111 21 Prague 1; tel. 224225000; fax 224216004; e-mail fibiger@abf.cz; f. 1991; library of 10,000 vols; Dir Dr JAN FIBIGER; publs *ABF Forum* (quarterly), *Building Products Review* (annually), *Forum of Architecture and Building* (monthly).

ECONOMICS, LAW AND POLITICS

CERGE-EI: POB 882, Politických vězňů 7, 111 21 Prague 1; tel. 224005123; fax 224227143; e-mail office@cerge-ei.cz; internet www.cerge-ei.cz; f. 1991; attached to Acad. of Sciences of the Czech Republic and to Charles University; conducts American-style PhD program in Economics; library of 80,000 vols; depository for World Bank publs; Dir Dr LUBOMÍR LÍZAL; publs *Czech Republic* (annually), *Working Papers* (monthly).

Ústav státu práva AV ČR (Institute of State and Law AS CR): Národní 18, 116 91 Prague 1; tel. 221990711; fax 224933056; e-mail ilaw@ilaw.cas.cz; internet www.ilaw.cas.cz; attached to Acad. of Sciences of the Czech Republic; library of 40,000 vols, 100 periodicals; Dir Dr JAROSLAV ZACHARIÁŠ; publ. *Právnik* (monthly).

EDUCATION

Institut základů vzdělanosti Univerzity Karlovy (Charles University Institute of Fundamental Learning): Legerova 63, 120 00 Prague 2; tel. 290002617; attached to Acad. of Sciences of the Czech Republic and Charles University; Dir Doc. PhDr ZDENĚK PINC.

FINE AND PERFORMING ARTS

Ústav dějin umění AV ČR (Institute of Art History AS CR): Husova 4, 110 00 Prague 1; tel. 222222144; fax 222221654; e-mail arthist@site.cas.cz; internet www.udu.cas.cz; f. 1953; attached to Acad. of Sciences of the Czech Republic; Dir Dr ĽUBOMIR KONEČNÝ; publs *Estetika* (4 a year), *Fontes Historiae Artium* (book series, irregular), *Studia Rudolphina* (annually), *Umění* (6 a year).

Ústav pro hudební vědu AV ČR (Institute of Musicology AS CR): Puškinovo nám. 9, 160 00 Prague 6; tel. 224311212; fax 224324728; e-mail uhv@imus.cas.cz; internet www.cas.cz/en/pdf/uhv.pdf; attached to Acad. of Sciences of the Czech Republic; library of 25,000 vols; Dir Prof. Dr IVAN VOJTĚCH; publ. *Hudební věda* (4 a year).

HISTORY, GEOGRAPHY AND ARCHAEOLOGY

Archeologický ústav AV ČR, Brno (Archaeological Institute AS CR, Brno): Královopolská 147, 612 64 Brno; tel. 541514101; fax 541514123; e-mail archeo@iabrno.cz; internet www.iabrno.cz; attached to Acad. of Sciences of the Czech Republic; Dir Dr PAVEL KOUŘIL; publs *Fontes Archeologicae Moravicae* (irregular), *Studie Archeologického ústavu* (2 a year).

Archeologický ústav AV ČR, Praha (Archaeological Institute AS CR, Prague): Letenská 4, 118 01 Prague 1; tel. 257530922; fax 257532288; e-mail jiran@arup.cas.cz; internet www.arup.cas.cz; f. 1919; attached to Acad. of Sciences of the Czech Republic; Dir Dr LUBOŠ JIRÁŇ; publs *Archeologické rozhledy* (4 a year), *Památky archeologické* (2 a year).

Historický ústav AV ČR (Institute of History AS CR): Prosecká 76, 190 00 Prague 9; tel. 286887513; fax 286887513; e-mail bucharova@hiu.cas.cz; internet www.hiu.cas .cz; f. 1921; attached to Acad. of Sciences of the Czech Republic; Dir Dr MILOSLAV POLÍVKA; publs *Český časopis historický* (4 a year), *Historica* (Historical Sciences in the Czech Republic, annually), *Moderní dějiny* (annually), *Slovanský přehlad* (4 a year), *Mediaevalia Historica Bohemica* (annually), *Folia Historica Bohemica* (irregular), *Slovanské historické studie* (annually), *Historická geografie* (every 2 years), *Historia Europae Centralis* (annually).

Kabinet pro klasická studia FLÚ AV ČR (Institute for Classical Studies AS CR): Na Florenci 3, 110 00 Prague 1; tel. 222828303; fax 222828305; e-mail uks@ics.cas.cz; internet www.clavmon.cz; f. 1953; attached to Acad. of Sciences of the Czech Republic; Head Dr JIŘÍ BENEŠ; publs *Eirene* (on classical studies, annually), *Listy filologické* (Folia Philologica, 2 a year).

Orientální ústav AV ČR (Oriental Institute AS CR): Pod vodárenskou věží 4, 182 08 Prague 8; tel. 266053111; fax 286581897; e-mail orient@orient.cas.cz; internet www .orient.cas.cz; f. 1922; attached to Acad. of Sciences of the Czech Republic; Dir Dr STANISLAVA VAVROUŠKOVÁ; publ. *Archiv orientální* (4 a year).

Slovanský ústav AV ČR (Institute of Slavonic Studies AS CR): Valentinská 1, 110 00 Prague 1; tel. 224800251; fax 224800252; e-mail slu@slu.cas.cz; internet www.slu.cas.cz; f. 1922; attached to Acad. of Sciences of the Czech Republic; Dir Prof. VLADIMÍR VAVŘÍNEK; publs *Byzantinoslavica* (2 a year), *Germanoslavica* (2 a year), *Slavia* (4 a year).

Ústav pro soudobé dějiny AV ČR (Institute of Contemporary History AS CR): Vlašská 9, 118 40 Prague 1; tel. 257531122; fax 257531121; e-mail tuma@usd.cas.cz; internet www.usd.cas.cz; f. 1990; attached to Acad. of Sciences of the Czech Republic; Czech and Slovak history from 1938–2000; Dir Dr OLDŘICH TŮMA; publ. *Soudobé dějiny* (4 a year).

Výzkumný ústav geodetický, topografický a kartografický (VUGTK) (Research Institute of Geodesy, Topography and Cartography): 250 66 Zdiby 98; tel. 284890351; fax 284890056; e-mail vugtk@vugtk.cz; internet www.vugtk.cz; f. 1954; library of 70,000 vols; Dir Dr Ing. VÁCLAV SLABOCH; publ. *Proceedings of Research Works* (every 2 years).

LANGUAGE AND LITERATURE

Ústav pro českou literaturu AV ČR (Institute of Czech Literature AS CR): Na Florenci 3/1420, 110 00 Prague 1; tel. 234612111; fax 224818437; e-mail literatura@ucl.cas.cz; internet www.ucl.cas .cz; f. 1947; attached to Acad. of Sciences of the Czech Republic; library of 130,000 vols; Dir Dr PAVEL JANOUŠEK; publ. *Česká literatura* (6 a year).

Ústav pro jazyk český AV ČR (Czech Language Institute AS CR): Letenská 4, 118 51 Prague 1; tel. 257533756; fax 257531761; e-mail ujc@ujc.cas.cz; internet www.ujc.cas .cz; f. 1911; attached to Acad. of Sciences of the Czech Republic; Dir RNDr KAREL OLIVA; publs *Acta Onomastica* (annually), *Bibliografie české lingvistiky* (annually), *Časopis pro moderní filologii* (2 a year), *Linguistica Pragensia* (2 a year), *Naše řeč* (5 a year), *Slovo a slovestnost* (4 a year).

MEDICINE

Farmakologický ústav AV ČR (Institute of Pharmacology AS CR): 4 – Krč, Videňská 1083, 142 20 Prague; tel. 261710024; e-mail fku@cas.cz; attached to Acad. of Sciences of the Czech Republic; Dir Dr EVŽEN BUCHAR.

Ústav experimentální medicíny AV ČR (Institute of Experimental Medicine AS CR): Vídeňská 1083, 142 20 Prague 4; tel. 241062230; fax 241062782; e-mail uemavcr@biomed.cas.cz; internet uemweb .biomed.cas.cz; f. 1975; attached to Acad. of Sciences of the Czech Republic; Dir Prof. EVA SYKOVÁ.

NATURAL SCIENCES

General

Ústav geoniky AV ČR (Institute of Geonics AS CR): Poruba, Studentská 1768, 708 00 Ostrava; tel. 596979352; fax 596919452; e-mail geonics@ugn.cas.cz; internet www .ugn.cas.cz; f. 1982; attached to Acad. of Sciences of the Czech Republic; Dir Dr RICHARD ŠŇUPÁREK; publ. *Moravian Geographical Report* (2 a year).

Biological Sciences

Biofyzikální ústav AV ČR (Institute of Biophysics AS CR): Královopolská 135, 612 65 Brno; tel. 541517111; fax 541211293; e-mail ibp@ibp.cz; internet www.ibp.cz; f. 1955; attached to Acad. of Sciences of the Czech Republic; Dir RNDr STANISLAV KOZUBEK.

Botanický ústav AV ČR (Institute of Botany AS CR): 252 43 Průhonice; tel. 271015233; fax 267750031; e-mail ibot@ibot .cas.cz; internet www.ibot.cas.cz; attached to Acad. of Sciences of the Czech Republic; Dir Dr FRANTIŠEK KRAHULEC; publs *Folia Geobotanica* (4 a year), *Index Seminum et Plantarum* (annually).

Entomologický ústav AV ČR (Institute of Entomology AS CR): Branišovská 31, 370 05 Česke Budějovice; tel. 385310350; fax 385310354; e-mail entu@entu.cas.cz; internet www.entu.cas.cz; f. 1962; attached to Acad. of Sciences of the Czech Republic; Dir Prof. Dr FRANTIŠEK SEHNAL; publ. *European Journal of Entomology* (4 a year).

Fyziologický ústav AV ČR, v.v.i. (Institute of Physiology AS CR): Videňská 1083, 142 20 Prague 4; tel. 241062424; fax 241062488; e-mail fgu@biomed.cas.cz; internet www.biomed.cas.cz; f. 1954; attached to Acad. of Sciences of the Czech Republic; Dir Dr JAROSLAV KUNEŠ; publ. *Physiological Research* (6 a year).

Hydrobiologický ústav AV ČR (Hydrobiological Institute AS CR): Na sádkách 7, 370 05 České Budějovice; tel. 387775881; fax 385310248; e-mail hbu@hbu.cas.cz; internet www.hbu.cas.cz; attached to Acad. of Sciences of the Czech Republic; Dir Dr JOSEF MATĚNA.

Mikrobiologický ústav AV ČR (Institute of Microbiology AS CR): Vídeňská 1083, 142 20 Prague 4; tel. 244472272; fax 244471286; e-mail mbu@biomed.cas.cz; internet www .biomed.cas.cz/mbu; f. 1962; attached to Acad. of Sciences of the Czech Republic; Dir Prof. RNDr BLANKA ŘÍHOVÁ; publ. *Folia Microbiologica* (6 a year).

Parazitologický ústav AV ČR (Institute of Parasitology AS CR): Branišovská 31, 370 05 České Budějovice; tel. 387775403; fax 385310388; e-mail paru@paru.cas.cz; internet www.paru.cas.cz; f. 1962; attached to Acad. of Sciences of the Czech Republic; Dir Dr TOMÁŠ SCHOLZ; publ. *Folia Parasitologica* (4 a year).

Ústav biologie obratlorců AV ČR (Institute of Vertebrate Biology AS CR): Květná 8, 603 65 Brno; tel. 543422538; fax 543211346; internet www.ivb.cz; f. 1954; 50 mems; attached to Acad. of Sciences of the Czech Republic; Dir Dr JAN ZIMA; publ. *Folia Zoologica* (quarterly).

Ústav experimentální botaniky AV ČR (Institute of Experimental Botany AS CR): Rozvojová 135, 165 02 Prague 6; tel. 220390453; fax 220390456; e-mail machackova@ueb.cas.cz; internet www.ueb .cas.cz; f. 1962; attached to Acad. of Sciences of the Czech Republic; Dir Prof. IVANA MACHÁČKOVÁ; publs *Biologia Plantarum* (irregular), *Photosynthetica* (irregular).

Ústav fyziky plazmatu AV ČR (Institute of Plasma Physics AS CR): Za Slovankou 3, 182 21 Prague 8; tel. 266052052; fax 286586389; e-mail ipp@ipp.cas.cz; internet www.ipp.cas .cz; f. 1959; attached to Acad. of Sciences of the Czech Republic; Dir Prof. Dr Ing. PAVEL CHRÁSKA.

Ústav molekulární biologie rostlin AV ČR (Institute of Plant Molecular Biology AS CR): Branišovská 31, 370 05 České Budějovice; tel. 385310357; fax 385310356; e-mail umbr@umbr.cas.cz; internet www.umbr.cas .cz; f. 1991; attached to Acad. of Sciences of the Czech Republic; Dir Prof. Dr J. ŠPAK.

Ústav molekulární genetiky AV ČR (Institute of Molecular Genetics AS CR): Flemingovo nám. 2, 166 37 Prague 6; tel. 220183111; fax 224310955; e-mail office@img .cas.cz; internet www.img.cas.cz; f. 1962; attached to Acad. of Sciences of the Czech Republic; Dir Prof. VÁCLAV PAČES; publs *Folia Biologica* (6 a year), *Biologické listy* (4 a year).

Ústav organické chemie a biochemie AV ČR (Institute of Organic Chemistry and Biochemistry AS CR): Flemingovo nám. 2, 166 10 Prague 6; tel. 220183111; fax 224310090; e-mail uochb@uochb.cas.cz; internet www.uochb.cas.cz; f. 1950; attached to Acad. of Sciences of the Czech Republic; Dir RNDr ZDENĚK HAVLAS; publ. *Collection of Czechoslovak Chemical Communications* (monthly).

Ústav půdní biologie AV ČR (Institute of Soil Biology AS CR): Na sádkách 7, České Budějovice; tel. 385310134;; fax 385300133; e-mail upb@upb.cas.cz; internet www.upb .cas.cz; f. 1979; attached to Acad. of Sciences of the Czech Republic; Dir RNDr VÁCLAV PIŽL.

Ústav živočišné fyziologie a genetiky AV ČR (Institute of Animal Physiology and Genetics AS CR): Rumburská 89, 277 21 Liběchov; tel. 206639511; fax 206697186; e-mail uzfg@iapg.cas.cz; internet www.iapg .cas.cz/uzfg; attached to Acad. of Sciences of the Czech Republic; Dir Prof. MVDr IVAN MÍŠEK.

Mathematical Sciences

Český statistický úřad (Czech Statistical Office): Na padesátém 81, 100 82 Prague 10; tel. and fax 274054070; e-mail infoservis@ czso.cz; internet www.czso.cz; f. 1899; library of 27,500 vols; Pres. JAN FISCHER; publs *Statistical Yearbook of the Czech Republic*, *CZSO Monthly Statistics*, *Statistical Bulletin* (quarterly), *Selected Economic and Social Indicators of the Czech Republic* (quarterly).

Matematický ústav AV ČR (Mathematical Institute AS CR): Žitná 25, 115 67 Prague 1; tel. 222090711; fax 222211638; e-mail mathinst@math.cas.cz; internet www.math .cas.cz; f. 1947; attached to Acad. of Sciences of the Czech Republic; Dir Prof. ANTONIN SOCHOR; publs *Applications of Mathematics* (6 a year), *Czechoslovak Mathematical Journal* (4 a year), *Mathematica Bohemica* (4 a year).

Physical Sciences

Astronomický ústav AV ČR (Astronomical Institute AS CR): Fricova 298, 251 65 Ondřejov; tel. 323620113; fax 323620117; e-mail reditel@asu.cas.cz; internet www.asu .cas.cz; f. 1950; attached to Acad. of Sciences of the Czech Republic; Dir Dr PETR HEINZEL; publs *Scripta Astronomica* (irregular), *Time and Latitude* (4 a year).

Česká geologická služba (Czech Geological Survey): 118 21 Prague 1, Klárov 3; tel. 257089500; fax 257531376; e-mail secretar@ cgu.cz; internet www.geology.cz; f. 1919; library: see Libraries and Archives; Dir Mgr. ZDENĚK VENERA; publs *Bulletin of Geosciences* (quarterly), *Geological Bibliography of the Czech Republic* (annually), *Geoscience Research Reports* (annually), *Journal of Geological Sciences* (annually), *Special Papers* (annually).

Fyzikální ústav AV ČR (Institute of Physics AS CR): Na Slovance 2, 182 21 Prague 8; tel. 266053111; fax 286890527; e-mail secretary@fzu.cz; internet www.fzu.cz; f. 1954; attached to Acad. of Sciences of the Czech Republic; Dir Dr KAREL JUNGWIRTH; publs *Československý časopis pro fyziku* (6 a year), *Czechoslovak Journal of Physics* (monthly), *Jemná mechanika a optika* (Fine Mechanics and Optics, monthly).

Geofyzikální ústav AV ČR (Geophysical Institute AS CR): Boční II/1401, 141 31 Prague 4; tel. 267103327; fax 271761549; e-mail gfu@ig.cas.cz; f. 1953; attached to Acad. of Sciences of the Czech Republic; Dir Dr ALEŠ ŠPIČÁK; publs *Studia Geophysica et Geodaetica* (4 a year), *Travaux Géophysiques* (annually), *Bulletin of the Czechoslovak Seismological Stations* (annually).

Geologický ústav AV ČR (Institute of Geology AS CR): 6 – Lysolaje, Rozvojová 165, 165 02 Prague; tel. 233087111; fax 220922670; e-mail inst@gli.cas.cz; internet www.gli.cas.cz; f. 1957; attached to Acad. of Sciences of the Czech Republic; library of 10,000 vols; Dir Dr VACLAV CILEK; publ. *Geolines* (2 a year).

Společná laboratoř chemie pevných látek AV ČR a Univerzity Pardubice (Joint Laboratory of Solid State Chemistry of the Institute of Macromolecular Chemistry of AS CR and Pardubice University): Studentská 84, 532 10 Pardubice; tel. 406036150; fax 406036011; e-mail slchpl@ upce.cz; internet slchpl.upce.cz; f. 1986; attached to Acad. of Sciences of the Czech Republic; Head Dr LADISLAV TICHÝ.

Státní úřad pro jadernou bezpečnost (State Office for Nuclear Safety): Senovážné nám. 9, 110 00 Prague 1; tel. 221624111; fax 221624704; e-mail press@sujb.cz; internet www.sujb.cz; Pres. DANA DRÁBOVÁ.

Ústav analytické chemie AV ČR (Institute of Analytical Chemistry AS CR): Veveří 97, 611 42 Brno; tel. 532290182; fax 541212113; e-mail uach@iach.cz; internet www.iach.cz/uiach; f. 1956; attached to Acad. of Sciences of the Czech Republic; Head Dr JOSEF CHMELÍK; publ. *Research Activities and Future Trends* (irregular).

Ústav anorganické chemie AV ČR (Institute of Inorganic Chemistry AS CR): 250 68 Řež u Prahy; tel. 220940158; fax 220941502; e-mail sekretar@iic.cas.cz; internet www.iic .cas.cz; f. 1959; attached to Acad. of Sciences of the Czech Republic; attached laboratories of inorganic materials and low temperatures located in Prague; Dir Prof. LUBOMÍR NĚMEC; publs *Bulletin* (annually), *Ceramics–Silikáty* (6 a year).

Ústav chemických procesů AV ČR (Institute of Chemical Process Fundamentals AS CR): Rozvojová 135, 165 02 Prague 6; tel. 220390111; fax 220920661; e-mail icecas@ icpf.cas.cz; internet www.icpf.cas.cz; f. 1960; attached to Acad. of Sciences of the Czech Republic; Dir Prof. JIŘÍ DRAHOŠ.

Ústav fyzikální chemie Jaroslava Heyrovského AV ČR (Jaroslav Heyrovský Institute of Physical Chemistry AS CR): Dolejškova 3, 182 23 Prague 8; tel. 286583014; fax 286582307; e-mail director@ jh-inst.cas.cz; internet www.jh-inst.cas.cz; f. 1972; attached to Acad. of Sciences of the Czech Republic; library of 18,000 books and periodicals, 200 current periodical titles; Dir Prof. Dr PETR CÁRSKY.

Ústav fyziky atmosféry AV ČR (Institute of Atmospheric Physics AS CR): 4, Boční II/ 1401, 141 31 Prague; tel. 272016011; fax 272763745; e-mail iap@ufa.cas.cz; internet www.ufa.cas.cz; f. 1964; attached to Acad. of Sciences of the Czech Republic; monitors atmospheric pollution; carries out research in meteorology, climatology, and ionospheric and magnetospheric physics; library of 7,818 books, 39 periodicals; Dir Dr JAN LAŠTOVIČKA.

Ústav fyziky materiálů AV ČR (Institute of the Physics of Materials AS CR): Žižkova 22, 616 62 Brno; tel. 541212286; fax 541212301; e-mail secretar@ipm.cz; internet www.ipm.cz; f. 1956; attached to Acad. of Sciences of the Czech Republic; Dir Assoc. Prof. Dr PETR LUKÁŠ; publs *Engineering Mechanics* (6 a year), *Metallic Materials* (6 a year).

Ústav jaderné fyziky AV ČR (Nuclear Physics Institute AS CR): 250 68 Řež; tel. 220941147; fax 220941130; e-mail ujf@ujf.cas .cz; internet www.ujf.cas.cz; f. 1955; attached to Acad. of Sciences of the Czech Republic; Dir Dr JAN DOBEŠ.

Ústav jaderného výzkumu Řež a.s. (Nuclear Research Institute Řež plc): Husinec-Řež 130, 250 68 Řež; tel. 266172000; fax 220940840; e-mail paz@ujv.cz; internet www .ujv.cz; f. 1955; nuclear power and safety; fuel cycle chemistry; radiopharmaceuticals; library of 101,200 vols, 21,000 reports; Chair. FRANTIŠEK PAZDERA; publs *Annual Report*, *Nucleon* (quarterly).

Ústav makromolekulární chemie AV ČR (Institute of Macromolecular Chemistry AS CR): Heyrovský nám. 2, 162 06 Prague 6; tel. 296809111; fax 296809410; e-mail office@imc .cas.cz; internet www.imc.cas.cz; f. 1959; attached to Acad. of Sciences of the Czech Republic; Dir Prof. KAREL ULBRICH.

Ústav pro hydrodynamiku AV ČR, v.v.i. (Institute of Hydrodynamics AS CR): Pod Patankou 30/5, 166 12 Prague 6; tel. 233109011; fax 233324361; e-mail ih@ih.cas .cz; internet www.ih.cas.cz; f. 1953; attached to Acad. of Sciences of the Czech Republic; research in hydromechanics, rheology and hydrology; Dir Dr ZDENEK CHARA; publs *Engineering Mechanics* (6 a year), *Journal of Hydrology and Hydromechanics* (6 a year).

Ústav struktury a mechaniky hornin AV ČR (Institute of Rock Structure and Mechanics AS CR): V Holešovičkách 41, 182 09 Prague 8; tel. 266009111; fax 284680105; e-mail irsm@irsm.cas.cz; internet www.irsm .cas.cz; f. 1958; attached to Acad. of Sciences of the Czech Republic; library of 28,000 vols; Dir Ing. KAREL BALIK; publs *Acta Montana, Series A: Geodynamics* (in English, irregular), *Acta Montana, Series B: Fuel, Carbon, Mineral Processing* (in English, irregular), *Acta Montana, Series AB: Geodynamics, Fuel, Carbon, Mineral Processing* (in English and Czech, irregular).

Ústav termomechaniky AV ČR (Institute of Thermomechanics AS CR): Dolejškova 5, 182 00 Prague 8; tel. 286890383; fax 286584695; e-mail secr@it.cas.cz; internet www.it.cas.cz; f. 1954; attached to Acad. of Sciences of the Czech Republic; library of 12,000 vols; Dir Prof. ZBYNEK JANOUR; publs *Acta Technica CSAV* (4 a year), *Engineering Mechanics* (6 a year).

PHILOSOPHY AND PSYCHOLOGY

Centrum pro teoretická studia Univerzity Karlovy (Centre for Theoretical Study at Charles University): Jilská 1, 110 00 Prague 1; tel. 222220671; fax 222220653; e-mail office@cts.cuni.cz; internet www.cts.cuni.cz; attached to Acad. of Sciences of the Czech Republic; Dir Dr IVAN M. HAVEL.

Filozofický ústav AV ČR (Institute of Philosophy AS CR): Jilská 1, 110 00 Prague; tel. 222220124; fax 222220108; e-mail flusekr@site.cas.cz; internet www.flu.cas.cz; f. 1990; attached to Acad. of Sciences of the Czech Republic; Dir PhDr PAVEL BARAN; publs *Acta Comeniana* (irregular), *Filosofický časopis* (Philosophical Review, 6 a year), *Teorie vědy* (4 a year).

Psychologický ústav AV ČR (Institute of Psychology AS CR): Veveří 97, 602 00 Brno; tel. 532290270; e-mail cermak@psu.cas.cz; internet www.psu.cas.cz; f. 1967; attached to Acad. of Sciences of the Czech Republic; Dir Doc. PhDr IVO ČERMÁK; publs *Bulletin Psychologického ústavu* (irregular), *Československá psychologie* (6 a year), *Zprávy* (irregular).

RELIGION, SOCIOLOGY AND ANTHROPOLOGY

Etnologický ústav AV ČR (Institute of Ethnology AS CR): 1, Na Florenci 3, 110 00 Prague; tel. 222828503; fax 222828511; e-mail tyllner@eu.cas.cz; f. 1954; attached to Acad. of Sciences of the Czech Republic; Dir Dr LUBOMÍR TYLLNER; publ. *Český lid* (4 a year).

Sociologický ústav AV ČR (Institute of Sociology AS CR): Jilská 1, 110 00 Prague; tel. and fax 286840129; e-mail socmail@soc .cas.cz; internet www.soc.cas.cz; f. 1990; attached to Acad. of Sciences of the Czech Republic; Dir Dr MARIE ČERMÁKOVÁ; publs *Historická demografie* (annually), *Sociologický časopis* (Czech Sociological Review, 6 a year).

TECHNOLOGY

Laboratoř anorganických materiálů (Laboratory of Inorganic Materials): Technická 5, 166 28 Prague 6; tel. 224353783; fax 224310371; e-mail vaclava.majerova@vscht .cz; internet www.vscht.cz/sls; f. 1961; attached to Acad. of Sciences of the Czech Republic and Institute of Chemical Technology; Dir Prof. LUBOMÍR NĚMEC.

SVÚSS a.s. – Státní výzkumný ústav pro stavbu strojů (State Research Institute for Machine Design): Běchovice, 190 11 Prague; tel. 2743233; fax 2742078; f. 1946; library of 10,000 vols; Man. Dir Ing. PETR ŠTULC.

Ústav informatiky AV ČR, v.v.i. (Institute of Computer Science AS CR): Pod Vodárenskou věží 2, 182 07 Prague 8; tel. 266052083; fax 286585789; e-mail ics@cs.cas.cz; internet www.cs.cas.cz; attached to Acad. of Sciences of the Czech Republic; f. 1975; library of 8,000 vols; Dir Prof. Dr JIRI WIEDERMANN; publ. *Neural Network Word* (int. journal on neural and mass-parallel computing and information systems).

Ústav přístrojové techniky AV ČR (Institute of Scientific Instruments AS CR): Královopolská 147, 612 64 Brno; tel. 541514111; fax 541514402; e-mail institute@isibrno.cz; internet www.isibrno.cz; f. 1957; attached to Acad. of Sciences of the Czech Republic; Dir Dr LUDĚK FRANK.

Ústav pro elektrotechniku AV ČR (Institute of Electrical Engineering AS CR): 8, Dolejškova 5, 182 00 Prague; tel. 266051111; fax 286890433; e-mail institute@iee.cas.cz; internet www.iee.cas.cz; f. 1953; attached to Acad. of Sciences of the Czech Republic; Dir Prof. VIKTOR VALOUCH; publ. *Acta Technica* (4 a year).

Ústav radiotechniky a elektroniky AV ČR (Institute of Radio Engineering and Electronics AS CR): Chaberská 57, 182 51 Prague 8; tel. 284681804; fax 284680222; e-mail iree@ure.cas.cz; internet www.ure.cas.cz; f. 1955; attached to Acad. of Sciences of the Czech Republic; library of 16,500 vols, 390 periodicals; Dir Dr Ing. VLASTIMIL MATĚJEC.

Ústav teoretické a aplikované mechaniky AV ČR (Institute of Theoretical and Applied Mechanics AS CR): Prosecká 76, 190 00 Prague 9; tel. 286882121; fax 286884634; e-mail itam@itam.cas.cz; internet www.itam.cas.cz; attached to Acad. of Sciences of the Czech Republic; Dir Dr MILOŠ DRDÁCKÝ; publ. *Engineering Mechanics* (6 a year).

Ústav teorie informace a automatizace AV ČR (Institute of Information Theory and Automation AS CR): POB 18, 182 08 Prague 8; Pod Vodárenskou věží 4, 182 08 Prague 8; tel. 266053111; fax 286890378; e-mail utia@utia.cas.cz; internet www.utia.cas.cz; f. 1959; attached to Acad. of Sciences of the Czech Republic; Dir Prof. RNDr MILAN MAREŠ; publ. *Kybernetica* (6 a year).

VÚTS Liberec a.s. (Research Institute for Textile Machines, Liberec Co.): U jezu 4, 461 19 Liberec 4; tel. 485301111; fax 485302402; e-mail vuts@vuts.cz; internet www.vuts.cz; f. 1951; library of 10,000 vols; 154 mems; Gen. Dir Prof. Ing. MIROSLAV VÁCLAVÍK.

Libraries and Archives

Brno

Knihovna Moravské galerie v Brně (Library of the Moravian Gallery in Brno): Husova 18, 662 26 Brno; tel. 532169127; fax 532169180; e-mail knihovna@moravska-galerie.cz; internet www.moravska-galerie.cz; f. 1873; 110,000 vols; Dir Dr HANA KARKANOVÁ.

Moravská zemská knihovna (Moravian Library): Kounicova 65A, 601 87 Brno; tel. 541646111; fax 541646100; e-mail mzk@mzk.cz; internet www.mzk.cz; f. 1808; 3,850,000 vols, 4,300 periodicals; Dir Dr J. KUBÍČEK.

Ústřední knihovna a informační středisko Veterinární a farmaceutické univerzity (Central Library and Information Centre of the University of Veterinary and Pharmaceutical Sciences): Palackého 1–3, 612 42 Brno; tel. 541562080; e-mail gect@vfu.cz; internet sis.vfu.cz; f. 1919; 174,126 vols; Chief Librarian TOMÁŠ GEC; publ. *Acta veterinaria Brno* (quarterly).

České Budějovice

Státní vědecká knihovna (State Research Library): Na Sadech 26-27, Lidická 1, 370 59 České Budějovice; tel. 386111211; fax 386351901; e-mail library@cbvk.cz; internet www.cbvk.cz; f. 1885; 1,500,000 vols; Dir Dr KVETA CEMPIRKOVA.

Hradec Králové

Studijní a vědecká knihovna (Research Library): Pospíšilova 395, POB 7, 500 03 Hradec Králové; tel. 495514871; fax 495511781; e-mail knihovna@svkhk.cz; internet www.svkhk.cz; f. 1949; 1,189,172 vols; Dir Mgr. EVA SVOBODOVÁ.

Liberec

Krajská vědecká knihovna v Liberci (Research Library in Liberec): Rumjancevova 1362/1, 460 53 Liberec; tel. 482412111; fax 482412122; e-mail library@kvkli.cz; internet www.kvkli.cz; f. 1945; 760,000 books, 1,600 periodicals, 29,000 vols of standards, 380,000 vols of patents, 27,000 vols of printed music, 9,000 sound recordings, 3,500 vols of maps, 600 CD-ROMs; Dir PAVEL HARVÁNEK; publs *Světlík* (World of the Liberec Region Libraries, 6 a year), *Výroční zpráva* (annual report).

Olomouc

Vědecká knihovna v Olomouci (Research Library in Olomouc): Bezručova 2, 771 77 Olomouc; tel. 585223441; fax 585220615; e-mail is@vkol.cz; internet www.svkol.cz; f. 1566; 1,660,000 vols, 1,448 MSS, 1,800 incunabula, 70,000 old prints; Dir Dr MARIE NÁDVORNÍKOVÁ; publ. *Knihovní obzor* (quarterly).

Ostrava

Moravskoslezská vědecká knihovna v Ostravě (Moravian-Silesian Research Library in Ostrava): Prokešovo nám. 9, 728 00 Ostrava; tel. 596118881; fax 596138322; e-mail msvk@svkos.cz; internet www.svkos.cz; f. 1951; 987,604 vols; Dir Ing. LEA PRCHALOVÁ.

Ústřední knihovna Vysoké školy báňské-Technické univerzity Ostrava (Central Library of the VSB-Technical University of Ostrava): 17 listopadu 15, 708 33 Ostrava-Poruba; tel. 596991278; fax 596994598; e-mail knihovna@vsb.cz; internet www.knihovna.vsb.cz; f. 1849; 380,000 vols; Dir DANIELA TKAČÍKOVÁ; publ. *Sborník vědeckých prací Vysoké školy báňské – Technické univerzity Ostrava* (Transactions, irregular).

Plzeň

Studijní a vědecká knihovna Plzeňského kraje (Education and Research Library of Pilsener Region): Smetanovy sady 2, 305 48 Plzeň; tel. 377224249; fax 377325478; e-mail svk@svkpl.cz; internet www.svkpl.cz; f. 1950; 791,000 books, 1,700 current periodicals, 793,000 documents; Dir Dr JAROSLAV VYČICHLO; publs *Přírůstky zahraniční literatury* (foreign accessions, quarterly), *Západni Čechy v tisku* (West Bohemia in Print).

Prague

Archiv AV ČR (Archives AS CR): Gabčíkova 2362/10, 182 00 Prague 8; tel. and fax 286010111; e-mail sekretariat@archiv.cas.cz; internet www.archiv.cas.cz; f. 1953; attached to Acad. of Sciences of the Czech Republic; 80,000 vols; Dir Dr ALENA MÍŠKOVÁ; publs *Práce z dějin věd* (Studies on the History of Sciences and the Humanities, 2 a year), *Studia historiae academiae scientiarum – Práce z dějin akademie věd* (Studies on the History of the Academy of Sciences, annually), *Studie o rukopisech* (Codicological Studies, annually).

Knihovna Akademie Věd Česky republiky (Library of the Academy of Sciences of the Czech Republic): Národní 3, 115 22 Prague 1; tel. 224240524; fax 224240611; e-mail infoknav@lib.cas.cz; internet www.lib.cas.cz; f. 1952; 1,000,000 vols, 2,102 periodicals; headquarters of the network of information centres and special libraries of academic institutes; Dir IVANA KADLECOVÁ.

Knihovna Archeologického ústavu AV ČR (Library of the Archaeological Institute of the Academy of Sciences of the Czech Republic): Letenská 4, 118 01 Prague; tel. 257014318; fax 257532288; e-mail knihovna@arup.cas.cz; internet www.arup.cas.cz; f. 1919; 12,426 vols; collection severely affected by flooding in 2002, previously 67,200 vols; Chief Librarian EVA SOUFKOVÁ; publs *Archeologické rozhledy* (quarterly), *Castellologica bohemica* (irregular), *Castrum Pragense* (irregular), *Mediaevalia archaeologica* (irregular), *Památky archeologické* (annually), *Památky Archeologické–Supplementum* (irregular), *Výzkumy v Čechách* (irregular).

Knihovna České geologické služby (Library of the Czech Geological Survey): Klárov 3, 118 21 Prague 1; tel. 257089411; fax 257320438; e-mail breit@cgu.cz; internet www.cgu.cz; f. 1924; archive of 60,000 vols; 173,010 vols; Dir RNDr HANA BREITEROVÁ; publs *Geological Bibliography of the Czech Republic* (annually), *Library of the Geological Survey* (irregular).

Knihovna Evangelické teologické fakulty Univerzity Karlovy (Library of the Protestant Theological Faculty of the Charles University): Černá 9, 115 55 Prague 1; tel. 221988104; fax 221988215; e-mail library@etf.cuni.cz; internet www.etf.cuni.cz/~library; f. 1919; 190,000 vols, 185 current periodicals; Dir BARBORA DROBÍKOVÁ; publs *Communio Viatorum* (3 a year), *Teologická reflexe* (2 a year).

Knihovna Národní galerie (Library of the National Gallery): Národni galerie v Praze, Staroměstské nám. 12, 110 15 Prague; located at: Hradčanské nám. 15, 119 04 Prague 1; tel. 220515458; fax 220513180; e-mail library@ngprague.cz; internet www.ngprague.cz; f. 1887; 90,000 vols; Dir MARTINA HORÁKOVÁ.

Knihovna Národního muzea (Library of the National Museum): Václavské nám. 68, 115 79 Prague 1; tel. 224497111; fax 224226488; internet www.nm.cz; f. 1818; 3,600,000 vols; Dir Mgr MARIE ŠÍROVÁ; publ. *Acta Musei Nationalis Pragae, Series C – Historia Litterarum.*

Knihovna Národního technického muzea (Library of the National Museum of Technology): Kostelní 42, 170 78 Prague 7; tel. 220399233; fax 220399200; e-mail knihovna@ntm.cz; internet www.ntm.cz; f. 1833; 200,000 vols; Chief Librarian RICHARDA SVOBODOVÁ.

Knihovna Orientálního ústavu Akademie věd České republiky (Library of the Oriental Institute of the Academy of Sciences of the Czech Republic): Pod vodárenskou věží 4, 182 08 Prague 8; tel. 266053950; fax 286581835; e-mail oilib@orient.cas.cz; internet www.orient.cas.cz; f. 1922; general library of 190,000 vols; Chinese library of 67,000 vols; Korean library of 3,500 vols; Tibetan collection; Librarian OLGA STANKOVIČOVÁ; publs *Archiv orientální* (4 a year), *Nový Orient* (monthly).

Knihovna Uměleckoprůmyslového musea (Museum of Decorative Arts Library): 17 listopadu 2, 110 01 Prague 1; tel. 251093135; fax 251093296; e-mail knihovna@upm.cz; internet www.knihovna.upm.cz; f. 1885; 165,000 vols; Dir PhDr JARMILA OKROUHLÍKOVÁ; publ. *Acta UPM* (irreg.).

Městská knihovna v Praze (Municipal Library of Prague): Mariánské nám. 1, 115 72 Prague 1; tel. 222113303; fax 222328230;

e-mail informace@mlp.cz; internet www.mlp.cz; f. 1891; 2,247,000 vols; Central Library, 48 brs and 3 mobile libraries; Dir Dr TOMÁŠ ŘEHÁK.

Národní knihovna České republiky (National Library of the Czech Republic): Klementinum 190, 110 00 Prague 1; tel. 221663111; fax 221663277; e-mail sekret.ur@nkp.cz; internet www.nkp.cz; f. 1366; 6,197,320 vols, 14,905 MSS, 3,500 incunabula, 200,000 early printed books; Dir Dr VLASTIMIL JEŽEK; publs *Česká národní bibliografie ČR* (Czech National Bibliography, monthly), *Miscellanea oddělení rukopisů a starých tisků* (annually), *Národní knihovna* (4 a year).

Branch library:

Slovanská knihovna (Slavonic Library): Klementinum 190, 110 00 Prague; tel. 221663356; fax 221663176; e-mail lukas.babka@nkp.cz; internet www.nkp.cz/slk; f. 1924; 751,795 vols; Dir Dr LUKÁŠ BABKA.

Národní lékařská knihovna (National Medical Library): Nové Město, Sokolská 54, 121 32 Prague 2; tel. 296335911; fax 296335959; e-mail nml@nlk.cz; internet www.nlk.cz; f. 1949; 335,000 vols, 1,500 current periodicals, 6,000 doctoral theses; WHO documentation centre; oversees translation of MeSH into Czech; operates union catalogue of medical literature; Dir HELENA BOUZKOVA; publs *Bibliographia medica čechoslovaca* (monthly), *Referátový výběr* (series of 4 abstracts journals, 4 or 6 a year).

Národní pedagogická knihovna Komenského (Comenius National Library of Education): Mikulandská 5, 116 74 Prague 1; tel. 221966402; fax 224930550; e-mail library@npkk.cz; internet www.npkk.cz; f. 1919; 458,000 vols; youth br. (Suk Library) of 55,000 vols (since 1790); Dir LUDMILA ČUMPLOVÁ; publ. *Přehled pedagogické literatury* (survey of Czech pedagogic literature, every 2 months).

Státní technická knihovna (State Technical Library): Mariánské nám. 5, POB 206, 110 01 Prague 1; tel. 2221663111; fax 222221340; e-mail informace@stk.cz; internet www.stk.cz; f. 1718; 1,501,632 vols, 1,524 periodicals, 31 databases; Dir Ing. MARTIN SVOBODA.

Univerzita Karlova, Pedagogická fakulta, Ústřední knihovna (Charles University Faculty of Education, Central Library): Rettigova 4, 116 39 Prague 1; tel. and fax 296242420; e-mail knihovna@pedf.cuni.cz; internet beta.pedf.cuni.cz; f. 1948; 190,859 vols, 239 periodicals; Dir Mgr. JITKA BÍLKOVÁ.

Úřad Průmyslového Vlastnictví (Industrial Property Office): Antonína Čermáka 2A, 160 68 Prague 6-Bubeneč; tel. 220383111; fax 224324718; e-mail posta@upv.cz; internet www.upv.cz; 30,000,000 documents; Dir of Patent Information Dept Ing. MIROSLAV PACLÍK.

Ústav dějin Univerzity Karlovy a Archiv Univerzity Karlovy (History Institute and Archives of Charles University): Ovocný trh 5, 116 36 Prague 1; tel. 224228104; fax 224491670; e-mail jirina.urbanova@ruk.cuni.cz; internet udauk.cuni.cz; history of education and of universities; 41,000 vols, 106 periodicals; Librarians Dr MARIE ŠTEMBERKOVÁ, Dr JIŘINA URBANOVÁ.

Ústav vědeckých informací 1. lékařské fakulty, Univerzita Karlova (Institute of Scientific Information, First Medical Faculty, Charles University): Kateřinská 32, 121 08 Prague 2; tel. 224923169; e-mail knihovna@lf1.cuni.cz; internet uvi.lf1.cuni.cz; f. 1949; 450,512 vols, 712 current periodicals; Dir Mgr HANA SKÁLOVÁ; publs *Acta Universitatis Carolinae Medica*, *Bulletin*, *Monografia*, *Proceedings of the Scientific Conferences*, *Sborník lékařský*.

Ústav zemědělských a potravinářských informací (Institute of Agricultural and Food Information): Londýnská 55, 120 21 Prague 2; tel. 224256387; fax 224253938; e-mail knihovna@uzpi.cz; internet www.knihovna.uzpi.cz; f. 1993; 1,200,000 vols; Dir Ing. C. PERLÍN; publs *Genetika a šlechtění* (Genetics and Plant Breeding, 4 a year), *Lesnictví* (Forest Science, monthly), *Ochrana rostlin* (Plant Protection Science, 4 a year), *Potravinářské vědy* (Food Science, 6 a year), *Rostlinná výroba* (Plant Production, monthly), *Veterinární medicina* (Veterinary Medicine, monthly), *Zahradnictví* (Horticulture, 4 a year), *Zemědělská ekonomika* (Agricultural Economics, monthly), *Zemědělská technika* (Agricultural Engineering, 4 a year), *Živočišná výroba* (Journal of Animal Science, monthly).

Ústřední tělovýchovná knihovna (Central Library of Physical Training): José Martiho 31, 162 52 Prague 6; tel. 220172158; fax 220172018; e-mail utk@ftvs.cuni.cz; internet www.ftvs.cuni.cz/knihovna; f. 1927; 300,000 vols; Dir PhDr JANA BĚLÍKOVÁ; publ. *Acta Universitatis Carolinae Kinanthropologica*.

Ústřední zemědělská knihovna (Central Agricultural Library): Slezská 7, POB 39, 120 56 Prague 2; tel. 227010213; fax 227010115; e-mail ihoch@uzpi.cz; internet www.uzpi.cz; f. 1926; a section of the Institute of Agricultural and Food Information; 1,100,000 vols; Dir PhDr IVO HOCH; publ. *Seznam časopisů* (List of Periodicals, annually).

Ústí nad Labem

Severočeská vědecká knihovna (North Bohemian Research Library): POB 134, W. Churchilla 3, 401 34 Ústí nad Labem; tel. 475209126; fax 475200045; e-mail library@svkul.cz; internet www.svkul.cz; f. 1945; 750,000 vols; Dir ALEŠ BROŽEK; publ. *Výběr kulturních výročí* (every 6 months).

Museums and Art Galleries

Brno

Moravská galerie v Brně (Moravian Gallery in Brno): Husova 18, 662 26 Brno; tel. 532169111; fax 532169180; e-mail m-gal@moravska-galerie.cz; internet www.moravska-galerie.cz; f. 1873; mostly European fine and applied art of all periods; library of 120,000 vols; Dir MAREK POKORNÝ; publ. *Bulletin* (annually).

Moravské zemské muzeum (Moravian Provincial Museum): Zelný trh 6, 659 37 Brno; tel. 542321205; fax 542212792; e-mail mzm@mzm.cz; internet www.mzm.cz; f. 1817; history, natural history, geology, arts, anthropology, horticulture; library of 260,000 vols; Dir PhDr PETR ŠULEŘ; publs *Acta Musei Moraviae–Scientiae Biologicae* (annually), *Acta Musei Moraviae–Scientiae Geologicae* (annually), *Acta Musei Moraviae–Scientiae Sociales* (annually), *Anthropologie* (3 a year), *Folia Ethnografica* (annually), *Folia Mendeliana* (annually), *Folia Numismatica* (annually), *Krystalinikum* (annually).

Muzeum města Brna (Brno Municipal Museum): Špilberk 1, 662 24 Brno; tel. 542123611; fax 542123613; e-mail muzeum.brno@spilberk.cz; internet www.spilberk.cz; f. 1904; history of Brno and Špilberk Castle; art gallery; Dir PhDr PAVEL CIPRIAN.

Technické muzeum v Brně (Technical Museum in Brno): Purkyňova 105, 612 00 Brno; tel. 541421411; fax 541214418; e-mail info@technicalmuseum.cz; internet www.technicalmuseum.cz; f. 1961; library of 42,000 vols; Dir VLASTIMIL VYKYDAL; publs *Archeologia technica* (annually), *Muzejní noviny*, *Nožířské listy* (annually), *Sborník z konzervátorského a restaurátorského semináře* (annually).

České Budějovice

Jihočeské muzeum v Českých Budějovicích (South Bohemian Museum in České Budějovice): Dukelská 1, 370 51 České Budějovice; tel. 387929311; fax 386356447; e-mail muzeumcb@muzeumcb.cz; internet www.muzeumcb.cz; f. 1877; history, archaeology, natural history, arts; Dir PAVEL ŠAFR; publs *Archeologické výzkumy v jižních Čechách* (archaeology, annually), *Jihočeský sborník historický* (history, annually), *Sborník Přírodní vědy* (nature, annually), *Výběr Časopis pro historii a vlastivědu jižních Čech* (regional and cultural History, 4 a year).

Cheb

Krajské muzeum Cheb (Cheb Regional Museum): nám. Krále Jiřího z Poděbrad 493/4, 350 11 Cheb; tel. 354400620; fax 354422292; e-mail sekretariat@muzeumcheb.cz; internet www.muzeumcheb.cz; f. 1874; history, local ceramics; library of 15,000 vols; spec. colln: library of Franciscan order; Dir PhDr EVA DITTERTOVÁ; publ. *Sborník chebského muzea* (annually).

Chrudim

Muzeum loutkářských kultur (Museum of Puppetry): Břetislavova 74, 537 60 Chrudim; tel. 469620310; fax 469620650; e-mail puppets@cps.cz; internet www.puppets.cz; f. 1972; Dir ALENA EXNAROVÁ.

Harrachov

Muzeum skla (Glass Museum): Novosad a Syn, Sklárna, 512 46 Harrachov; tel. 481528141; fax 481528148; internet www.sklarnaharrachov.cz; f. 1972; Dir K. PIPEK.

Hluboká nad Vltavou

Alšova jihočeská galerie (Aleš South Bohemian Gallery): Zámak è. 144, 373 41 Hluboká nad Vltavou; tel. 387967041; fax 387965436; e-mail ajg@ajg.cz; internet www.ajg.cz; f. 1953; Czech art since 13th c., 16th–18th c. European art, Czech and world ceramics since early 20th c.; library of 12,950 vols; Dir PhDr HYNEK RULÍŠEK.

Hradec Králové

Muzeum východních Čech, Hradec Králové (Museum of East Bohemia, Hradec Králové): Eliščino nábřeží 465, 500 01 Hradec Králové; tel. 495512462; fax 495512899; e-mail info@muzeumhk.cz; internet www.muzeumhk.cz; f. 1879; natural sciences, history; library of 70,000 vols; Dir PhDr ZDENĚK ZAHRADNÍK; publs *Acta* (irreg.), *Fontes* (irreg.).

Hukvaldy

Památník Leoše Janáčka (Leoš Janáček Memorial Museum): Smetanova 14, 739 46 Hukvaldy; tel. 541212811; e-mail fmaly@mzm.cz; internet www.mzm.cz; f. 1933; life and work of the composer; Dir B. VOLNÝ.

Jablonec nad Nisou

Muzeum skla a bižuterie (Museum of Glass and Jewellery): Muzea 398/4, 466 01 Jablonec nad Nisou; tel. 483369011; fax 483369012; e-mail msbjbc@quick.cz; internet www.msb-jablonec.cz; f. 1961; Bohemian glass, Jablonec jewellery; library of 15,000 vols; Dir Ing. JAROSLAVA SLABÁ.

Karlovy Vary

Galerie umění Karlovy Vary (Karlovy Vary Art Gallery): Goethova stezka 6, 360 01 Karlovy Vary; tel. 353224387; fax 353224388; e-mail info@galeriekvary.cz; internet www.galeriekvary.cz; f. 1953; 20th-century Czech art; Dir MIROSLAV LEPŠÍ.

Karlovarské muzeum (Karlovy Vary Museum): Nová louka 23, 360 01 Karlovy Vary; e-mail sekretariat@kvmuz.cz; internet www.kvmuz.cz; f. 1870; history, natural history, arts; Dir JAN BATÍK.

Zlatý klíč muzeum (Golden Key Museum): Lázeňská 3, 360 01 Karlovy Vary; tel. 353223888; f. 1960; art nouveau paintings; Dir MARIE GULGOVÁ.

Kolín

Regionální muzeum v Kolíně (Kolín Regional Museum): Brandlova 35, 280 02 Kolín; tel. and fax 321719018; e-mail muzeum@kolin.cz; internet www.kolin.cz/muzeum; f. 1895; local history; open-air museum at Kouřim; library of 49,500 vols; Dir JARMILA VALENTOVÁ.

Kopřivnice

Technické muzeum Tatra (Tatra Museum of Technology): Záhumenní 369, 742 21 Kopřivnice; tel. 556871106; fax 556821415; e-mail info@tatramuseum.cz; internet www.tatra.infomorava.cz; f. 1947; Tatra cars, trucks, railway carriages, aircraft, engines and chassis; Dir LENKA HODSLAVSKÁ.

Kutná Hora

České muzeum stříba (Czech Silver Museum): Hrádek, Barborská 28, 284 01 Kutná Hora; tel. 327512159; fax 327513813; e-mail muzeum@kutnohorsko.cz; internet muzeum.kutnohorsko.cz; f. 1877; medieval castle, medieval silver mine, Gothic town house, town life in 17th–19th centuries; Dir S. HRABÁNKOVÁ.

Liberec

Oblastní galerie v Liberci (Liberec Regional Art Gallery): U Tiskárny 1, 460 01 Liberec 5; tel. 485106325; fax 485106321; e-mail oblgal@ogl.cz; internet www.ogl.cz; f. 1873; 16th to 18th c. Dutch and Flemish painting, 19th c. French landscapes, 20th c. Czech art; Dir PhDr VĚRA LAŠTOVKOVÁ.

Severočeské muzeum v Liberci (North Bohemian Museum in Liberec): 1, Masarykova tř. 11, 460 01 Liberec; tel. 485246111; fax 485108319; e-mail muzeumlb@muzeumlb.cz; internet www.muzeumlb.cz; f. 1873; European and Bohemian applied arts, regional history, natural history; collections of glass, ceramics, porcelain, textiles, tapestries, jewellery, metal objects, furniture, posters, archaeological artefacts; library of 35,000 vols; Dir ALOIS ČVANČARA; publ. *Sborník Severočeského musea* (one issue each on history and natural history, every 2 years).

Lidice

Památník Lidice (Lidice Memorial Museum): Kladno district, 273 54 Lidice; tel. and fax 312253063; e-mail lidice@lidice-memorial.cz; internet www.lidice-memorial.cz; f. 1948; attached to Ministry of Culture of the Czech Republic; history of the destruction of the village of Lidice in the Second World War; gallery of painting and sculptures devoted to Lidice; Dir MARIE TELUPILOVA.

Litoměřice

Severočeská galerie výtvarného umění v Litoměřicích (North Bohemian Gallery of Fine Art in Litoměřice): Michalská 7, 412 01 Litoměřice; tel. 416732382; fax 416732383; e-mail reditel@galerie-ltm.cz; internet www.galerie-ltm.cz; f. 1958; European art since the 12th century, spec. collns of naive art, Czech Gothic art, Czech to present time; library of 13,000 vols; Dir PhDr JAN ŠTÍBR.

Mariánské Lázně

Městské muzeum Mariánské Lázně (Mariánské Lázně Municipal Museum): Goethovo nám. 11, 353 01 Mariánské Lázně; tel. 354622740; e-mail muzeum@goethe-haus.cz; f. 1887; history, geology; open-air geological park; Dir Ing. JAROMÍR BARTOŠ.

Mladá Boleslav

Škoda Auto Museum (Škoda Auto Museum): Tř. Václava Klementa 294, 293 60 Mladá Boleslav; tel. 326831134; fax 326832039; e-mail museum@skoda-auto.cz; internet www.skoda-auto.com/cze/company/museum; f. 1974; Dir MARGIT ČERNÁ.

Opava

Slezské zemské muzeum (Silesian Provincial Museum): Tyršova 1, 746 01 Opava; tel. and fax 553622999; e-mail szmred@szmo.cz; internet www.szmo.cz; f. 1814; history, natural history, arts; arboretum at Nový Dvůr; library of 200,000 vols; Dir Dr JAROMÍR KALUS; publs *Index Seminum* (annually), *Vlastivědné listy Slezska a severní Moravy* (2 a year), *Časopis Slezského zemského muzea* (natural sciences and historical sciences series, each 3 a year).

Pardubice

Východočeské muzeum v Pardubicich (Museum of Eastern Bohemia): Zámek č. 2, 530 02 Pardubice; tel. 466799240; fax 466513056; e-mail vcm@vcm.cz; internet www.vcm.cz; f. 1880; history, natural history, arts; library of 40,000 vols; Dir Dr FRANTISEK ŠEBEK; publs *Panurus* (annually), *Východočeský sborník historický* (annually), *Východočeský sborník přírodovědný* (annually).

Plzeň

Západočeská galerie v Plzni (West Bohemian Gallery in Plzeň): Pražská 13, 301 00 Plzeň; tel. 377223759; fax 377322970; e-mail info@zpc-galerie.cz; internet www.zpc-galerie.cz; f. 1954; Czech art from the 14th century to the contemporary period; Dir JANA POTUŽÁKOVÁ.

Západočeské muzeum v Plzni (West Bohemian Museum in Plzeň): Frantiskanska 13, 301 50 Plzeň; tel. 377237311; fax 377237311; e-mail pladman@zcm.cz; internet www.zcm.cz; f. 1878; history, natural history, arts; Dir Dr FRANTIŠEK FRÝDA; publs *Folia Musei Rerum Naturalium Bohemiae Occidentalis* (separate series for zoology, geology and botany, each 2 a year), *Sborník* (*Příroda,* 5 a year; *Historie,* annually).

Prace u Brna

Mohyla míru (Peace Monument): 664 58 Prace u Brna; tel. and fax 544244724; f. 1910; battle of Slavkov (Austerlitz); Dir Mgr ANTONÍN REČEK.

Prague

České muzeum výtvarných umění v Praze (Czech Museum of Fine Arts in Prague): Husova 19/21, 110 00 Prague 1; tel. 222220218; fax 222221190; e-mail muzeum@cmvu.cz; internet www.cmvu.cz; f. 1963; temporary exhibitions of modern and contemporary art; Dir Dr IVAN NEUMANN.

Galerie hlavního města Prahy (City Gallery Prague): Mickiewiczova 3, 160 00 Prague 6; tel. 222314259; fax 222327683; e-mail office@citygalleryprague.cz; internet www.citygalleryprague.cz; f. 1963; Pragensia, works by Czech artists since 19th c.; library of 2,000 vols; Dir JAROSLAV FATKA.

Historický ústav Armády České republiky/Army Historical Institute of the Czech Republic: U Památníku 2, 130 05 Prague 3; tel. 220204900; fax 222541308; e-mail museum@army.cz; internet www.militarymuseum.cz; Dir Mgr ALEŠ KNÍŽEK.

Constituent museums:

Armádní muzeum Žižkov (Army Museum): U. Památníku 2, 130 05 Prague 3; tel. 220204924.

Letecké muzeum Kbely (Aviation Museum, Kbely): Kbely, Mladoboleslavská ul., 197 00 Prague 3; tel. 220207513; e-mail info@militarymuseum.cz.

Vojenské technické muzeum (Museum of Military Technology): Krhanice, Prague; tel. 317702130; fax 317702123.

Muzeum hlavního města Prahy (Central Museum of the City of Prague): Na Poříčí 52, 110 00 Prague 1; tel. 224223696; fax 224214306; e-mail muzeum@muzeumprahy.cz; internet www.muzeumprahy.cz; f. 1881; history of Prague, archaeology, fine art; library of 17,000 vols; Dir ZUZANA STRNADOVÁ; publ. *Archeologica pragensia* (annually).

Národní galerie v Praze (National Gallery in Prague): Staroměstské nám. 12, 110 15 Prague 1; tel. and fax 222329331; e-mail genreditel@ngprague.cz; internet www.ngprague.cz; f. 1796; art of all periods; library of 71,000 vols; Dir Prof. MILAN KNÍŽÁK; publ. *Bulletin* (irregular).

Národní muzeum (National Museum): Central Bldg, Václavské nám. 68, 115 79 Prague 1; tel. 224497111; fax 224226488; e-mail nm@nm.cz; internet www.nm.cz; f. 1818; library: see Libraries and Archives; Dir Dr MICHAL LUKEŠ; publs *Časopis Národního muzea* (2 a year), *Muzejní a vlastivědná práce* (4 a year), *Numismatické listy* (6 a year), *Sborník Národního muzea v Praze* (Acta Musei Nationalis Pragae, 2 a year).

Constituent museums:

Historické muzeum (Historical Museum): Václavské nám. 68, 115 79 Prague 1; tel. 224497111; fax 224226488; e-mail nm@nm.cz; internet www.nm.cz; f. 1964; history of Czech Republic, history of money, ethnography of the Czech Republic, sport, Czech theatre; Dir Dr VERA PRENOSILOVA; publs *Fontes archaeologici Pragenses* (irregular), *Shornik Národního Muzea* (irregular).

České muzeum hudby (Museum of Czech Music): Karmeliská 2, 118 00 Prague 1; tel. 257257757; fax 257322216; e-mail c_muzeum_hudby@nm.cz; internet www.nm.cz; f. 1936; incl. Dvořák (Prague 2, Ke Karlovu 20), Smetana (Prague 1, Novotného lávka 1), musical instruments (Prague 1, Karmeliská 2); library, sound archives; Dir Dr DAGMAR FIALOVÁ.

Náprstkovo muzeum asijských, afrických a amerických kultur (Náprstek Museum of Asian, African and American Cultures): Betlémské nám. 1, 110 01 Prague 1; tel. 222221416; fax 222221418; e-mail npm@aconet.cz; internet www.nm.cz; f. 1862; research into Asian, African, American, Australian and Oceanian cultural heritage; permanent and temporary exhibitions, public lectures and cultural events; library of 250,000 vols; Dir Dr JANA SOUČKOVÁ; publ. *Annals* (annually).

Přírodovědecké muzeum (Natural History Museum): Václavské nám. 68, 115 79 Prague; tel. 224497111; fax 224222550; e-mail jiri.litochleb@nm.cz; internet www.nm.cz; f. 1964; Dir RNDr JIŘÍ LITOCHLEB;

publs *Acta Entomologica* (all irreg.), *Lynx* (annual), *Sborník Národního muzea, řada B* (Acta Musei Nationalis Pragae, Series B), *Journal of the National Museum, Natural History Series* (annual).

Národní technické muzeum (National Technical Museum): Kostelní 42, 170 78 Prague 7; tel. 220399111; fax 233399200; e-mail info@ntm.cz; internet www.ntm.cz; f. 1908; library: see Libraries and Archives; Dir Ing. TOMÁŠ KUPEC; publs *Sborník Národního technického muzea v Praze*, *Rozpravy Národního technického muzea*, *Bibliografie a prameny Národního technického muzea*.

Národní zemědělské muzeum (National Museum of Agriculture): Kostelní 44, 170 00 Prague 7; tel. 233379025; fax 233372561; e-mail nzm.praha@nzm.cz; internet www.nzm.cz; f. 1891; exhibition of agriculture and food industry located in Kačina Castle near Kutná Hora; exhibition of agricultural machinery located in Čáslav; exhibition of forestry, hunting and fisheries in Ohrada Castle nr České Budějovice; exhibition of horticulture in Valtice near Břeclav; library of 120,000 vols, photographic archive; Dir Mgr. PŘEMYSL REIBL; publs *Vědecké práce ZM.* (Scientific Studies), *Acta Museorum agriculturae*, *Prameny a studie* (Sources and Studies).

Památník národního písemnictví (Museum of Czech Literature): Strahovské nádvoří 1/132, 118 38 Prague 1; tel. 220516695; fax 220517277; e-mail post@pamatniknarodnihopisemnictvi.cz; internet www.pamatniknarodnihopisemnictvi.cz; f. 1953; literary archives containing 6 m. objects; library of 600,000 vols; Dir EVA WOLFOVÁ; publ. *Literární archiv* (annually).

Pedagogické muzeum J. A. Komenského v Praze (J. A. Comenius Pedagogical Museum in Prague): Valdštejnská ul. 20, 118 00 Prague 1; tel. 257533455; fax 257530661; e-mail pedagog@pmjak.cz; internet www.pmjak.cz; f. 1892; documents illustrating the development of national education and the life and work of Comenius; library of 25,000 vols; Dir Dr MARKÉTA PÁNKOVÁ.

Poštovní muzeum (Postal Museum): Nové mlýny 2, 110 00 Prague 1; tel. 222312006; fax 222311930; e-mail museumcp@pha.pvtnet.cz; internet www.cpost.cz; f. 1918; Dir Dr PAVEL ČTVRTNÍK.

Uměleckoprůmyslové museum v Praze (Museum of Decorative Arts): 17. listopadu 2, 110 00 Prague 1; tel. 251093111; fax 251093296; e-mail info@upm.cz; internet www.upm.cz; f. 1885; applied art from ancient times to the present; library of 150,000 vols; Dir Dr HELENA KOENIGSMARKOVÁ.

Židovské muzeum v Praze (Jewish Museum in Prague): Staré školy 1, 3, 110 00 Prague 1; tel. 221711511; fax 221711584; e-mail office@jewishmuseum.cz; internet www.jewishmuseum.cz; f. 1906; consists of the Maisel Synagogue, the Spanish Synagogue, the Pinkas Synagogue, the Old Jewish Cemetery, the Klausen Synagogue and the Ceremonial Hall; provides detailed commentary on Judaism and Jewish history, as well as the history of the Jews in Bohemia and Moravia; Dir Dr LEO PAVLÁT; publ. *Judaica Bohemiae* (annually).

Rožnov pod Radhoštěm

Valašské muzeum v přírodě (Wallachian Open-Air Museum): Palackého 147, 756 61 Rožnov pod Radhoštěm; tel. 571757111; fax 571654494; e-mail muzeum@vmp.cz; internet www.vmp.cz; f. 1925; open-air museum consisting of a wooden town, Wallachian village and mill valley; methodological centre for open-air museums; library of 15,000 vols; Dir Ing. VÍTĚZSLAV KOUKAL.

Slavkov u Brna

Historické muzeum ve Slavkově u Brna (Museum of History in Austerlitz): Palackého nám. 1, 684 01 Slavkov u Brna; tel. 544221204; fax 544221685; e-mail info@zamek-slavkov.cz; internet www.zamek-slavkov.cz; f. 1949; Napoleonic wars (particularly the Battle of Austerlitz), 17th- and 18th c.paintings, chapel of the Holy Cross; library colln on Napoleon; Dir JANA OMAR.

Tábor

Husitské Muzeum (Hussite Museum): Nám. Mikuláše z Husi 44, 390 01 Tábor; tel. 381252242; fax 381252245; e-mail tabor@husmuzeum.cz; internet www.husmuzeum.cz; f. 1878; Hussite movement; library of 40,000 vols; Dir MILOŠ DRDA; publ. *Husitský Tábor* (annually).

Teplice

Regionální muzeum v Teplicích (Teplice Regional Museum): Zámecké nám. 14, 415 01 Teplice; tel. 417537869; fax 417572300; e-mail info@muzeum-teplice.cz; internet www.muzeum-teplice.cz; f. 1897; history, natural history, arts; library of 75,000 vols; Dir Dr DUŠAN ŠPIČKA; publs *Archeologický výzkum* (archaeological research, irregular), *Zprávy a studie* (local history and natural history, every 2 years).

Terezín

Památník Terezín (Terezín Memorial): Principova Alej 304, 411 55 Terezín; tel. 416782225; fax 416782245; e-mail pamatnik@pamatnik-terezin.cz; internet www.pamatnik-terezin.cz; f. 1947; museums of the Small Fortress (resistance and political persecution 1940–45) and the wartime Jewish ghetto of Terezín; Art Exhibition of the Terezín Memorial; Terezín 1780–1939; the Litoměřice concentration camp; library of 11,000 vols; Dir Dr JAN MUNK; publs *Newsletter* (quarterly), *Terezínské listy* (annual).

Uherské Hradiště

Slovácké muzeum v Uherském Hradišti (Slovácko Museum in Uherské Hradiště): Smetanovy sady 179, 686 01 Uherské Hradiště; tel. 572556556; fax 572554077; e-mail info@slovackemuzeum.cz; internet www.slovackemuzeum.cz; f. 1914; history, art; library of 30,000 vols; Dir Dr IVO FROLEC; publ. *Slovácko* (annually).

Uherský Brod

Muzeum J. A. Komenského v Uherském Brodě (Uherský Brod J. A. Comenius Museum): Ul. Přemysla Otakara II 37, 688 12 Uherský Brod; tel. 572632288; fax 572634078; e-mail muzeum@mjakub.cz; internet www.mjakub.cz; f. 1898; life, work and heritage of Protestant bishop and educational reformer, J. A. Comenius (1592–1670); history and ethnology of the Uherskobrodsko region; library of 40,000 vols; Dir Dr PAVEL POPELKA; publ. *Studia Comeniana et historica* (2 a year).

Zlín

Muzeum jihovýchodní Moravy (Museum of South-Eastern Moravia): Soudní 1, 762 57 Zlín; tel. 577004633; fax 577004632; e-mail info@muzeum.zlin.cz; internet www.muzeum.zlin.cz; f. 1953; social science (archaeology, history, ethnography), natural history (botany, entomology, geology), shoe museum; library of 24,120 vols; Dir Dr IVAN PLÁNKA; publ. *Acta Musealia*.

Obuvnické muzeum (Footwear Museum): Tř. Tomáše Bati 1970, POB 175, 762 57 Zlín; tel. 577213978; fax 577213978; e-mail m.stybrova@seznam.cz; internet www.muzeum.zlin.cz/obuvmuz.htm; f. 1959; library of 3,000 vols; Dir MIROSLAVA STÝBROVÁ.

Universities

ČESKÉ VYSOKÉ UČENÍ TECHNICKÉ V PRAZE

(Czech Technical University in Prague)

Zikova 4, 166 36 Prague 6

Telephone: 224351111

Fax: 224310783

Internet: www.cvut.cz

Founded 1707; reorganized 1806, 1863, 1920, 1960

State control

Languages of instruction: Czech, English

Academic year: October to June

Rector: Prof. Ing. J. WITZANY

Vice-Rector (Construction): Prof. Ing. arch. A. NAVRÁTIL

Vice-Rector (Development): Prof. Ing. J. MACHÁČEK

Vice-Rector (Education): Prof. Ing. V. STEJSKAL

Vice-Rector (External Relations): Prof. Ing. F. VEJRAŽKA

Vice-Rector (International Relations): Prof. RNDr M. VLČEK

Vice-Rector (Science and Research): Prof. Ing. L. MUSÍLEK

Chief Administrative Officer: Doc. Ing. Z. VOSPĚL

Number of teachers: 1,468

Number of students: 21,282

Publications: *Acta Polytechnica* (in English, 6 a year), *Pražská Technika* (in Czech, 6 a year)

DEANS

Faculty of Architecture: Prof. Ing. arch. V. ŠLAPETA

Faculty of Civil Engineering: Prof. Ing. Z. BITTNAR

Faculty of Electrical Engineering: Prof. Ing. VLADIMÍR KUČERA

Faculty of Mechanical Engineering: Prof. Ing. PETR ZUNA

Faculty of Nuclear Science and Physical Engineering: Prof. Ing. MIROSLAV HAVLÍČEK

Faculty of Transportation Sciences: Doc. Ing. JOSEF JÍRA

HEADS OF DEPARTMENTS

Faculty of Civil Engineering (6, Thákurova 7, 166 29 Prague; tel. 224354874; fax 224310774; internet www.fsv.cvut.cz):

Advanced Geodesy: KRPATA, F.
Applied Informatics: KLVAŇA, J.
Architecture: DVOŘÁK, V.
Building Materials: SVOBODA, L.
Building Structures: WITZANY, J.
Cartography: HUML, M.
Concrete Structures and Bridges: KŘÍSTEK, V.
Construction Engineering Equipment: PAPEŽ, K.
Construction Management and Economics: ANTON, P.
Construction Technology: SVOBODA, P.
Geodesy and Land Adjustments: BLAŽEK, R.
Geotechnics: LAMBOJ, J.
Hydraulics and Hydrology: MAREŠ, K.
Hydrotechnics: ČIHÁK, F.
Irrigation, Drainage and Landscape Engineering: VRÁNA, K.
Languages: KASÍKOVÁ, S.

Mathematics: Černý, J.
Physical Education: Drnek, J.
Physics: Vodák, F.
Railway Engineering: Krejčiříková, H.
Road Engineering: Lehovec, F.
Sanitary Engineering: Grünwald, A.
Social Sciences: Vaníček, V.
Special Geodesy: Procházka, J.
Steel Structures: Studnička, J.
Structural Mechanics: Bittnar, Z.
Town and Regional Planning: Mansfeldová, A.
Centre of Experimental Geotechnics: Pacovský, J.
Computing Centre: Hora, V.
Laboratory of Ecological Risks in Urban Drainage: Pollert, J.

Faculty of Mechanical Engineering (6, Technická 4, 166 07 Prague; tel. 224352889; internet www.fsid.cvut.cz):

Applied Physics: Sopko, B.
Automotive and Aerospace Engineering: Macek, J.
Environmental Engineering: Nový, R.
Fluid Dynamics and Power Engineering: Petr, V.
Instrumentation and Control Engineering: Zítek, P.
Languages: Kybicová, H.
Management and Economics: Macík, K.
Manufacturing Technology: Mádl, J.
Materials Engineering: Steidl, J.
Mechanics: Konvičková, S.
Physical Education: Schmid, J.
Process Engineering: Rieger, F.
Production Machines and Mechanisms: Talácko, J.
Social Sciences: Klimeš, F.
Technical Mathematics: Kozel, K.

Faculty of Electrical Engineering (6, Technická 2, 166 27 Prague; fax 224310784; internet www.fel.cvut.cz):

Circuit Theory: Uhlíř, J.
Computer Science: Kolář, J.
Control Engineering: Šebek, M.
Cybernetics: Mařík, V.
Economics, Management and Humanities: Tomek, G.
Electric Drives and Traction: Mindl, P.
Electroenergetics: Doležal, J.
Electromagnetic Field: Mazánek, M.
Electrotechnology: Urbánek, J.
Languages: Kindlová, H.
Mathematics: Demlová, M.
Measurements: Haasz, V.
Mechanics and Materials Science: Bouda,V.
Microelectronics: Husák, M.
Power Engineering: Tlustý, J.
Physics: Jiřiček, O
Radioelectronics: Vejražka, F.
Sports and Physical Education: Filandr, J.
Telecommunications Engineering: Šimák, B.

Faculty of Nuclear Science and Physical Engineering (1, Břehová 7, 115 19 Prague; internet www.fjfi.cvut.cz):

Dosimetry and Application of Ionizing Radiation: Čechák, T.
Languages: Bezusová, V.
Materials: Nedbal, I.
Mathematics: Mareš, J.
Microtron Laboratory: Vognar, M.
Nuclear Chemistry: Beneš, P.
Nuclear Reactors: Matějka, K.
Physical Electronics: Vrbová, M.
Physics: Tolar, J.
Solid State Engineering: Vratislav, A.

Faculty of Architecture (6, Thákurova 7, 166 34 Prague; tel. 224311086; fax 224310573; internet www.fa.cvut.cz):

Architectural Conservation: Fanta, B.
Architectural Modelling: Pospíšil, J.
Computer-Aided Design: Kučera, V.
Construction Engineering I: Pavlík, M.
Construction Engineering II: Pokorný, A.
Design I: Bočan, J.
Design II: Navrátil, A.
Design III: Lábus, L.
Design of Buildings: Štípek, J.
Fine Arts: Mojžíš, J.
History of Architecture and Fine Arts: Urlich, P.
Industrial and Agricultural Buildings: Hlaváček, M.
Interior and Exhibition Design: Bednář, P.
Languages: Caravanasová, L.
Load-bearing Structures: Lorenz, K.
Theory of Architecture and Social Sciences: Šlapeta, V.
Urban Design and Planning: Mužík, J.

Faculty of Transportation Sciences (1, Konviktská 20, 110 00 Prague; tel. 224221720; fax 224229201; internet www.fd.cvut.cz):

Applied Mathematics: Vlček, M.
Automation in Transport and Telecommunications: Moos, P.
Control and Telematics: Votruba, Z.
Economics and Management in Transport and Telecommunications: Duchoň, B.
Financing and Operational Economics: Skurovec, V.
Flight Training School: Kulčák, L.
Humanities: Kubišová, V.
Logistics and Transport Processes: Svoboda, V.
Mechanics and Materials Science: Jíra, J.
Transport Systems: Kubát, B.
Transport Technology: Kovanda, J.

ATTACHED INSTITUTES

Business Innovation Centre: Dir Ing. P. Komarek.

Centre for Radiochemistry and Radiation Chemistry: Dir Doc. Ing. J. John.

Computing and Information Centre: Dir Doc. Ing. L. Ohera.

Institute of Biomedical Engineering: Dir Prof. Ing. M. Vrbová.

Institute of Experimental and Applied Physics: Dir Ing. S. Pospíšil.

Klokner (Building) Institute: Dir Ing. T. Klečka.

Masaryk Institute of Advanced Studies: Dir Doc. Ing. J. Petr.

Research Institute for Industrial Heritage: Dir PhDr B. Fragner.

ČESKÁ ZEMĚDĚLSKÁ UNIVERZITA V PRAZE
(Czech University of Agriculture, Prague)

Suchdol, Kamýcká 129, 165 21 Prague 6
Telephone: 224381111
Fax: 220920431
Internet: www.czu.cz

Founded 1906
State control
Language of instruction: Czech
Academic year: September to August

Rector: Prof. Dr Josef Kozák
Pro-Rectors: Prof. Dr Jiří Balík, Prof. Dr Pavel Kovář, Prof. Dr Václav Slavík, Prof. Dr Miroslav Svatoš
Registrar: Dr Miloš Frýbort
Librarian: Dr Ivan Hauzner

Library of 225,000 vols
Number of teachers: 429
Number of students: 5,000

Publications: *Agricultura tropica et subtropica* (1 or 2 a year), *Scientia Agriculturae Bohemica* (quarterly), *Scientific Papers*

DEANS

Faculty of Agricultural Economics and Management: Prof. Dr Jan Hron
Faculty of Agronomy: Prof. Dr Karel Voříšek
Faculty of Forestry: Prof. Dr Josef Gross
Technical Faculty: Prof. Dr Karel Pokorný
Institute of Applied Ecology: RNDr Zdeněk Lipský (Vice-Dean)
Institute of Tropical and Subtropical Agriculture: Prof. Dr Bohumil Havrland

HEADS OF DEPARTMENTS

Faculty of Agricultural Economics and Management (tel. 220920322; fax 220920321):

Agricultural Economics: M. Svatoš
Computer Science: I. Vrana
General Economics: B. Kadeřábková
Languages: M. Dvořáková
Law: J. Homolková
Management: J. Hron
Operational Research: J. Získal
Philosophy and Sociology: V. Majerová
Psychology: Z. Pechačová
Statistics: B. Kába
Trade and Finance: A. Valder

Faculty of Agronomy (tel. 220921351; fax 220920312; e-mail vorisek@af.czu.cz):

Agrochemistry and Plant Nutrition: V. Vaněk
Animal Nutrition: Z. Mudřík
Botany and Plant Physiology: V. Hejnák
Cattle Breeding: F. Louda
Chemistry and Quality of Products: P. Mader
Forage Crops: J. Šantrůček
General Animal Husbandry: I. Majzlík
General Plant Production and Agrometeorology: J. Soukup
Genetics and Breeding: J. Černý
Horticulture: J. Sus
Microbiology and Biotechnology: L. Voříšek
Pig and Poultry Breeding: M. Pour
Plant Protection: J. Ryšánek
Soil Science and Geology: J. Kozák
Special Plant Production: V. Hosnedl
Veterinary Medicine: F. Jílek
Zoology and Fishery: M. Barták

Faculty of Forestry (tel. 220920319; fax 220920438; e-mail gross@lf.czu.cz):

Dendrology: V. Chalupa
Ecology: K. Stasný
Forest Economics and Management: K. Pulkrab
Forest Protection: V. Kalina
Forest Surveys and Management: V. Kouba
Landscape Management: P. Kovář
Logging Technology and Timber Processing: I. Roček
Silviculture: Z. Poleno
Water Management: F. Hrádek

Technical Faculty (tel. 220920311; e-mail pokorny@tf.czu.cz):

Agricultural Machines: A. Rybka
Electrical Engineering and Automation: K. Pokorný
Exploitation of Tractors and Machines: M. Kavka
Farmyard Mechanization: M. Přikryl
Materials and Technologies: M. Brožek
Mathematics: V. Slavik
Mechanics and Engineering: J. Scheller
Operational Reliability of Machines: J. Pošta
Physics: J. Pecen
Tractors and Automobiles: V. Křepelka

UNIVERZITA HRADEC KRÁLOVÉ
(University of Hradec Králové)

Rokitanského 62, 500 03 Hradec Králové
Telephone: 493331111
Fax: 495545911
Internet: www.uhk.cz

Founded 1959 as Institute of Education; university status 2000
State control

Rector: Dr RNDr JAROSLAVA MIKULECKÁ
Vice-Rectors: Dr IVA JEDLIČKOVÁ (Administration and External Relations), Prof. Ing. BOHUMIL VYBÍRAL (Faculty of Humanities), RNDr ANTONÍN SLABÝ (Internal Affairs), Dr MARTIN BÍLEK (Strategy and Development)
Librarian: Mgr ZDENKA JEŽKOVÁ

Number of teachers: 355
Number of students: 5,600

DEANS

Faculty of Education: Ing. MARKÉTA BEDNÁŘOVÁ
Faculty of Humanities: Ing. IVANA SVOBODOVÁ
Faculty of Informatics and Management: JOSEF HYNEK

UNIVERZITA JANA EVANGELISTY PURKYNĚ V ÚSTÍ NAD LABEM
(Jan Evangelista Purkyně University in Ústí nad Labem)

Hoření 13, 400 96 Ústí nad Labem
Telephone: 475282111
Fax: 472772781
E-mail: rektor@rek.ujep.cz
Internet: www.ujep.cz

Founded as Pedagogical Faculty in Ústí nad Labem; university status 1991
State control

Rector: Dr RNDr STANISLAV NOVÁK
Librarian: Dr IVO BROŽEK

Library of 250,000 vols
Number of teachers: 375
Number of students: 6,000

DEANS

Faculty of Art and Design: Dr VLADIMÍR ŠVEC
Faculty of Education: Dr ZDENĚK RADVANOVSKÝ
Faculty of Environmental Studies: Dr Ing. JOSEF SEJÁK
Faculty of Science: Dr RNDr STANISLAV NOVÁK
Faculty of Social and Economic Studies: Prof. Ing. PAVLIK

ATTACHED RESEARCH INSTITUTES

Institute of Health Studies: Dir Dr MUDr LADISLAV PYŠNÝ.

Institute of Humanities: Dir Dr MICHAELA HRUBÁ.

Institute of Production Technology and Management: Dir Assoc. Prof. Dr FRANTIŠEK HOLEŠOVSKÝ.

Institute of Slavonic-Germanic Studies: Dir Dr CTIRAD KUČERA.

JIHOČESKÁ UNIVERZITA V ČESKÝCH BUDĚJOVICÍCH
(University of South Bohemia in České Budějovice)

Branišovská 31, 370 05 České Budějovice
Telephone: 389032001
Fax: 385310348
E-mail: rektorat@jcu.cz
Internet: www.jcu.cz

Founded 1991
State control
Academic year: September to June

Rector: Prof. Ing. FRANTIŠEK STŘELEČEK
Vice-Rectors: Doc. RNDr MILAN STRAŠKRABA (Foreign Relations), Doc. Ing. MARTIN KŘÍŽEK (Science), Doc. PhDr JIŘÍ DIVÍŠEK (Study Programmes), Prof. Ing. VÁCLAV ŘEHOUT (University Development)

Number of teachers: 418
Number of students: 5,500

Publications: *Memorial Volume of the Faculty of Agriculture – Economics* (2 a year), *Memorial Volume of the Faculty of Agriculture – Phytotechnics* (2 a year), *Memorial Volume of the Faculty of Agriculture – Zootechnics* (2 a year), *Opera historica* (annually)

DEANS

Faculty of Agriculture: Prof. Ing. JAN FRELICH
Faculty of Biological Sciences: Doc. RNDr ZDENĚK BRANDL
Faculty of Education: Doc. RNDr FRANTIŠEK MRÁZ
Faculty of Health and Social Studies: Doc. MUDr VLADIMÍR VURM
Faculty of Theology: Prof. ThDr KAREL SKALICKÝ

UNIVERZITA KARLOVA
(Charles University)

Ovocný trh 5, 116 36 Prague 1
Telephone: 224491111
Fax: 224210695
E-mail: sekretariat@ruk.cuni.cz
Internet: www.cuni.cz

Founded 1348
State control
Language of instruction: Czech
Academic year: September to June

Rector: Prof. Ing. IVAN WILHELM
Vice-Rectors: Prof. MUDr PAVEL KLENER, Doc. RNDr EVA KVASNIČKOVA, Doc. PhDr MICHAL ŠOBR, Doc. PhDr STANISLAV STECH, Prof. MUDr JOSEF STINGL, Doc. RNDr JAROSLAVA SVOBODOVÁ
Quaestor: Ing. JOSEF KUBÍČEK
Chancellor: RNDr TOMÁŠ JELÍNEK

Library: see Libraries and Archives
Number of teachers: 4,048
Number of students: 42,475

Publications: *Acta Universitatis Carolinae—series: Mathematica et Physica, Biologica* (4 a year), *Environmentalica* (annually), *Folia Pharmaceutica Universitatis Carolinae, Geologica* (4 a year), *Geographica* (2 a year), *Historia Universitatis Carolinae Pragensis, Iuridica* (4 a year), *Kinanthropologica* (2 a year), *Medica* (annually), *Novitates Botanicae Universitatis Carolinae* (annually), *Oeconomica* (2 a year), *Philologica* (10 a year), *Philosophica et Historica* (10 a year), *Prague Bulletin of Mathematical Linguistics, Psychologie v ekonomické praxi* (2 a year), *Sborník lékařský* (4 a year)

DEANS

Faculty of Catholic Theology: Prof. PhDr LUDWIG ARMBRUSTER
Faculty of Education: Prof. RNDr PAVEL BENEŠ
Faculty of Gospel Theology: Prof. ThDr. PAVEL FILIPI
Faculty of Humanities: Prof. PhDr JAN SOKOL
Faculty of Hussite Theology: Prof. ThDr JÁN LIGUŠ
Faculty of Law: Doc. JUDr VLADIMÍR KINDL
Faculty of Mathematics and Physics: Prof. RNDr IVAN NETUKA
1st Faculty of Medicine: Doc. MUDr ŠTĚPÁN SVAČINA
2nd Faculty of Medicine: Prof. MUDr JOSEF KOUTECKÝ
3rd Faculty of Medicine: Doc. MUDr BOHUSLAV SVOBODA
Faculty of Medicine in Hradec Králové: Prof. MUDr VLADIMÍR PALIČKA
Faculty of Medicine in Plzeň: Doc. MUDr JAROSLAV KOUTENSKÝ
Faculty of Pharmacy in Hradec Králové: Doc. RNDr JAROSLAV DUŠEK
Faculty of Philosophy: Prof. PhDr JAROSLAV VACEK
Faculty of Physical Training and Sport: Prof. Ing. VÁCLAV BUNC
Faculty of Sciences: Prof. RNDr PAVEL KOVÁŘ
Faculty of Social Sciences: Doc. RNDr JAN ÁMOS VÍŠEK

PROFESSORS

Faculty of Catholic Theology (6, Thákurova 3, 160 00 Prague; tel. 220181600; fax 220181215; e-mail dekan@kft.cuni.cz; internet www.ktf.cuni.cz):

MATĚJKA, J., Practical Theology
POLC, J., Church History
SLABÝ, A., Pastoral Medicine
SOUSEDÍK, S., History of Philosophy
WOLF, V., Systematic Theology
ZEDNÍČEK, M., Canon Law

Faculty of Education (M. D. Rettigové 4, Prague; tel. 221900111; fax 224947156; e-mail pavel.vasak@pedf.cuni.cz; internet www.pedf.cuni.cz):

BENEŠ, P., Chemistry
BRABCOVÁ, R., Czech Language
ČORNES, P., History
HEJNÝ, M., Mathematics
HELUS, Z., Pedagogical Psychology
HERDEN, J., Music Education
JELÍNEK, S., Russian Language
KOMAN, M., Mathematics
KOTÁSEK, J., Education
PARIZEK, V., Education
PEŠKOVÁ, J., Philosophy
PITHA, P., Philosophy
POLEDŇÁK, K., Music Education
VULTERIN, J., Analytical Chemistry

Faculty of Evangelical Theology (1, Černá 9, 115 55 Prague; tel. 221988216; fax 221988200; e-mail filipi@ftf.cuni.cz; internet www.ftf.cuni.cz):

FILIPI, P., Practical Theology
POKORNÝ, P., New Testament
REJCHRTOVÁ, N., Church History
TROJAN, J., Social Ethics

Faculty of Humanities (5, V Kříže 10, 150 00 Prague; tel. 251080111; e-mail sokol@fhs.cuni.cz; internet www.fhs.cuni.cz):

BENYOVSZKY, L., Philosophy
BOUZEK, J., Archaeology, Classical Philology
BYSTŘICKÝ, J., Philosophy, Media
ČEŠKA, J., Philosophy, Literature
DOHNALOVÁ, M., Economics
GABRIŠKOVÁ, L., Languages
HALBICH, M., Anthropology
HAVELKA, M., Sociology, Social History
HAVELKOVÁ, H., Gender Studies
HAVLÍČEK, Anthropology, Ethnology
HAVRDOVÁ, Z., Social Psychology
HORSKÝ, J., History, Historical Anthropology
HOZÁKOVÁ, J., Sociology
HROCH, M., History
KAČÍREK, M., Law
KRUŽÍK, J., Philosophy
MATOUŠEK, V., Anthropology, Archaeology
MORAVCOVÁ, M., Ethnology
MULLER, K., Sociology
NOVÁK, A., Philosophy
PINC, Z., Philosophy
PRUDKÝ, L., Sociology
RYNDA, I., Human Ecology
SELIGOVÁ, M., History
SHANAHAN, D., Languages, Film
SKOVAJSA, M., Political Philosophy

ŠKVAŘILOVÁ, B., Anthropology
SOKOL, J., Anthropology, Philosophy
SOUKUPOVÁ, B., Social History
SVATOŇ, O., Sociology
SVOBODA, A., Art, Design
TURKOVÁ, M., Ethnology
VANČÁT, J., Theory of Art
VANČATOVÁ, M., Ethnology
VOPĚNKA, P., Logic, Mathematics
ZIMA, P., Languages, Sociolinguistics

Faculty of Hussite Theology (4, Pacovská 350/4, 140 21 Prague; tel. 241733131; e-mail jligus@htf.cuni.cz; internet www.htf.cuni.cz):

HAŠKOVCOVÁ, H., Medical Ethics
HOLETON, D. R., Liturgics
KUČERA, Z., Systematic Theology
LIGUŠ, J., Philosophy of Communication
SÁZAVA, Z., Biblical Theology

Faculty of Law (1, nám. Curieových 7, 116 40 Prague; tel. 221005111; e-mail dekan@ius.prf.cuni.cz; internet www.prf.cuni.cz):

BAKEŠ, M., Financial Law
BELINA, M., Labour Law
BOGUSZAK, J., Theory of State and Law
CÍSAŘOVÁ, D., Criminal Law
GERLOCH, A., Theory, Philosophy and Sociology of Law
HENDRYCH, D., Administrative Law
KŘÍŽ, J., Civil Law
KUČERA, Z., International Law
MALÝ, K., History of State and Law
NOVOTNÝ, O., Criminal Law
PAVLÍČEK, V., Constitutional Law and Civic Sciences
ŠVESTKA, J., Civil Law
TICHÝ, L., European Law
WINTEROVÁ, A., Civil Law
ZOULÍK, FR., Civil Law

Faculty of Mathematics and Physics (2, K. Karlovu 3, 121 16 Prague; tel. 221951111; fax 221911292; e-mail dekan@dekanat.mff.cuni.cz; internet www.mff.cuni.cz):

ANDĚL, J., Mathematics and Statistics
BARVÍK, I., Physics
BEDNÁŘ, J., Physics
BENEŠ, V., Mathematics
BIČÁK, J., Theoretical Physics
BICAN, L., Mathematics
BIEDERMAN, H., Macromolecular Physics
ČÁPEK, V., Theoretical Physics
CIPRA, T., Mathematics
DUPAČOVÁ, J., Mathematics and Statistics
FEISTAUER, M., Mathematics
FORMÁNEK, J., Theoretical Physics
HAJČOVÁ, E., Information Science
HÁLA, J., Physics
HASLINGER, J., Physics
HORÁČEK, J., Theoretical Physics
HOŘEJŠÍ, J., Nuclear Physics
HÖSCHL, P., Physics
HRACH, R., Electronic Physics
HUŠEK, M., Mathematics
HUŠKOVÁ, M., Mathematics
ILAVSKÝ, M., Macromolecular Physics
JUREČKOVÁ, J., Probability and Statistics
KAKGER, A., Mathematics
KEPKA, T., Mathematics
KOWALSKI, O., Mathematics
KVASIL, J., Experimental Physics
LUKEŠ, J., Mathematical Analysis
MARTINEC, Z., Physics and Geophysics
MATOLÍN, V., Electronic Physics
MATOUŠEK, J., Informatics
NEŠETŘIL, J., Mathematics
NETUKA, I., Mathematics
NOVÁK, B., Mathematics
PANEVOVÁ, J., Information Science
PLÁŠIL, F., Informatics
POKORNÝ, J., Informatics
PULTR, A., Mathematics
ROHN, J., Mathematics
SECHOVSKÝ, V., Physics
SIMON, P., Mathematics
SKÁLA, L., Physics
SOUČEK, V., Mathematics
ŠTĚPÁN, J., Mathematics
ŠTĚPÁNEK, P., Mathematics
SVOBODA, E., Theoretical Physics
TICHÝ, M., Physics
TROJANOVÁ, Z., Electronic Physics
VALVODA, V., Physics
VELICKÝ, B., Physics
VIŠŇOVSKÝ, S., Physics
ZAJÍČEK, L., Mathematics
ZIMMERMANN, K., Information Science

1st Faculty of Medicine (2, Kateřinská 32, 121 08 Prague; tel. 224961111; fax 224915413; e-mail stepan.svacina@lf1.cuni.cz; internet www.lf1.cuni.cz):

ASCHERMANN, M., Internal Medicine
BENCKO, V., Hygiene
BETKA, J., Oto-rhino-laryngology
BROULÍK, P., Internal Medicine
DVOŘÁČEK, J., Urology
ELIŠKA, O., Anatomy
ELLEDER, M., Pathology
FARGHALL, H. M., Pharmacology
FUČÍKOVÁ, T., Immunology and Allergology
HÁJEK, Z., Gynaecology
HORKÝ, K., Internal Medicine
HYNIE, S., Pharmacology
KLENER, P., Oncology
KRAML, J., Biochemistry
LAŠTOVKA, M., Oto-rhino-laryngology
MAREČEK, Z., Internal Medicine
MAREK, J., Internal Medicine
MARTÍNEK, J., Histology and Embryology
NEČAS, E., Normal and Pathological Physiology
NEVŠÍMALOVÁ, S., Neurology
PAFKO, P., Surgery
PETROVICKÝ, P., Anatomy
POKORNY, J., Physiology
POVÝŠIL, C., Pathological Anatomy
RABOCH, J., Psychiatry
RACEK, J., Stomatology
RYBKA, V., Orthopaedic Surgery
ŠKRHA, J., Internal Medicine
SOSNA, A., Surgery
ŠTĚPÁN, J., Biochemistry
ŠTÍPEK, S., Biochemistry
STREJC, P., Forensic Medicine
TERŠÍP, K., Surgery
TESAŘ, V., Internal Medicine
TOPINKOVÁ, E., Social Medicine
TROJAN, S., Medical Physiology
VANĚK, J., Surgery
VÍTEK, F., Biophysics
VYMĚTAL, J., Clinical Psychology
ZEMAN, J., Paediatrics
ZEMAN, M., Surgery
ZIMA, T., Medical Chemistry
ŽIVNÝ, J., Gynaecology and Obstetrics

2nd Faculty of Medicine (5, V úvalu 84, 150 06 Prague; tel. 224431111; fax 224435820; e-mail josef.koutecky@lfmotol.cuni.cz; internet www.lf2.cuni.cz):

BOUŠKA, I., Forensic Medicine
BROŽEK, G., Physiology
DRUGA, R., Anatomy
GOETZ, P., Biology
HERGET, J., Pathological Physiology
HOŘEJŠÍ, J., Gynaecology and Obstetrics
KODET, R., Pathological Anatomy
KONRÁDOVÁ, V., Histology and Embryology
KOUTECKY, J., Oncology
MATOUŠOVIC, K., Internal Medicine
PELOUCH, V., Medical Chemistry and Biochemistry
SEEMANOVÁ, E., Genetics
ŠNAJDAUF, J., Surgery
SVIHOVEC, J., Pharmacology
VÍZEK, M., Pathological Physiology
VOJÁČEK, J., Internal Medicine

3rd Faculty of Medicine (10, Ruská 87, 100 00 Prague; tel. 267102111; e-mail michal.andel@lf3.cuni.cz; internet www.lf3.cuni.cz):

ANDĚL, M., Internal Medicine
CIKRT, M., Hygiene
GREGOR, P., Internal Medicine
HORÁK, J., Internal Medicine
HÖSCHL, C., Psychiatry
JELÍNEK, R., Histology and Embryology, Anatomy
LENER, J., Hygiene
KRŠIAK, M., Pharmacology
KUCHYNKA, P., Ophthalmology
MALINA, L., Dermatology
PROVAZNÍK, K., Hygiene
RAŠKA, I., Medical Biology
ROKYTA, R., Pathological Physiology
SCHINDLER, J., Microbiology
STEFAN, J., Forensic Medicine
STINGL, J., Anatomy

Faculty of Medicine in Hradec Králové (Šimkova 870, 500 38 Hradec Králové; tel. 495816111; fax 495513597; e-mail dekan@lfhk.cuni.cz; internet www.lfhk.cuni.cz):

DOMINIK, J., Surgery
FIXA, B., Internal Medicine
HEJZLAR, M., Microbiology
HRNČÍŘ, Z., Internal Medicine
HYBÁŠEK, I., Oto-rhino-laryngology
KRÁL, B., Internal Medicine
KVASNIČKA, J., Internal Medicine
MALÝ, J., Internal Medicine
MARTÍNKOVÁ, J., Pharmacology
NĚMEČEK, S., Histology and Embryology
PIDRMAN, V., Internal Medicine
ROZSÍVAL, P., Ophthalmology
ŠPAČEK, J., Pathological Anatomy
SRB, V., Hygiene
ŠTEINER, I., Pathological Anatomy
STRANSKY, P., Biophysics
VOBOŘIL, Z., Surgery
VODIČKA, I., Biophysics
ZADÁK, Z., Internal Medicine

Faculty of Medicine in Plzeň (Husova 13, 306 05 Plzeň; tel. 377593400; fax 197221460; e-mail dekan@lfp.cuni.cz; internet www.lfp.cuni.cz):

AMBLER, Z., Neurology
FAKAN, F., Pathological Anatomy
MICHAL, M., Pathological Anatomy
OPATRNÝ, K., Internal Medicine
RACEK, J., Biochemistry
RESL, V., Dermatovenereology
SKÁLOVÁ, A., Pathology
TĚŠÍNSKÝ, P., Ophthalmology
TOPOLČAN, O., Internal Medicine
TŘEŠKA, V., Surgery

Faculty of Pharmacy in Hradec Králové (Heyrovskiho tř. 1203, 501 65 Hradec Králové; tel. 495067111; fax 495512656; e-mail dusek@faf.cuni.cz; internet www.faf.cuni.cz):

DRŠATA, J., Biochemistry
FENDRICH, Z., Pharmacology
JAHODÁŘ, L., Pharmacognosy
KARLÍČEK, R., Analytical Chemistry
KVASNIČKOVÁ, E., Biochemistry
LÁZNÍČEK, M., Radiopharmacy
VIŠŇOVSKÝ, P., Pharmacology
WAISSER, K., Organic Chemistry

Faculty of Philosophy (1, nám. J. Palacha 2, 116 38 Prague; tel. 221619111; e-mail dekan@ff.cuni.cz; internet www.ff.cuni.cz):

BLÁHOVÁ, M., Auxiliary Historical Sciences
BOUZEK, J., Classical Archaeology
ČERMÁK, F., Czech Language
DOHALSKÁ, M., Phonetics
HALÍK, T., Sociology
HILSKY, M., English Literature
HLEDÍKOVÁ, Z., Auxiliary Historical Sciences
HORYNA, M., History of Art
KÖNIGOVÁ, M., Information and Librarianship
KROPÁČEK, L., History and Culture of Africa and Asia
KUČERA, K., Czech Language
KUKLÍK, J., Czech History
MACUROVÁ, A., Czech Language

Maur, E., Czech History
Opatrný, J., General History
Palek, B., General Linguistics
Palková, Z., Phonetics and Phonology
Skřivan, A., General History
Sláma, J., Archaeology
Slavický, M., Music Studies
Stehlíková, E., History and Theory of Theatre
Uličný, O., Czech Language
Vacek, J., Sanskrit and Tamil Philosophy
Verner, M., Egyptology

Faculty of Physical Education and Sport (6, José Martiho 31, 162 52 Prague; tel. 220562459; fax 220172370; e-mail karger@ftvs.cuni.cz; internet www.ftvs.cuni.cz):

Blahuš, P., Kinanthropology
Bunc, V., Kinanthropology
Dylevský, I., Anatomy
Houdek, V., Theory of Physical Culture
Kovář, R., Kinanthropology
Otahal, S., Biomechanics and Bionics
Rychtecký, A., Kinanthropology
Slepička, P., Kinanthropology
Svoboda, B., Sports Education
Tepľy, Z., Human Movement

Faculty of Sciences (2, Albertov 6, 128 43 Prague; tel. 222112111; e-mail stulik@prfdec.natur.cuni.cz; internet www.natur.cuni.cz):

Boublík, T., Physical and Macromolecular Chemistry
Bouška, V., Geological Mineralogy
Buchar, J., Zoology
Čepek, P., Geology
Černý, M., Organic Chemistry
Chlupáč, I., Geology
Drobník, J., Biotechnology
Feltl, L., Analytical Chemistry
Gardavský, V., Regional Geography
Hampl, M., Regional Geography
Hůrka, K., Zoology
Kalvoda, J., Physical Geography
Klinot, J., Organic Chemistry
Kořínek, V., Biology
Marek, F., Geology
Mareš, S., Geophysics
Matolín, M., Geophysics
Mejsnar, J., Biology
Nátr, M., Plant Physiology
Neubauer, Z., Philosophy of Natural Sciences
Novotný, I., Biology and Physiology of Animals
Pavlík, Z., Demography
Pertold, Z., Geology
Pešek, J., Geology
Podlaha, J., Inorganic Chemistry
Rieder, M., Geology
Smolíková, L., Physical and Macromolecular Chemistry
Stehlík, E., Mathematics
Štemprok, M., Geology
Strunecká, A., Biology
Štulik, A., Analytical Chemistry
Štys, P., Entomology
Tichá, M., Biochemistry
Váňa, J., Botany
Vávra, J., Parasitology
Zadražil, S., Genetics and Microbiology

Faculty of Social Sciences (1, Smetanavo nábřezí 6, 110 00 Prague; tel. 222112111; fax 224235644; e-mail mlcoch@mbox.fsv.cuni.cz; internet www.fsv.cuni.cz):

Hlaváček, Economics
Kouba, K., Political Economy
Kraus, J., Mass Communication
Křen, J., Czechoslovak History
Messtřík, M., Economics
Mlčoch, L., Economics
Pešek, J., Modern History
Petrusek, M., Sociology
Potůček, M., Sociology
Reiman, M., History and Politics of Russia and Eastern Europe
Sojka, M., Economic Theory
Turnovec, F., Economics
Urban, L., Political Economy

MASARYKOVA UNIVERZITA V BRNĚ
(Masaryk University in Brno)

Žerotínovo nám. 9, 601 77 Brno
Telephone: 549491011
Fax: 549491070
E-mail: info@muni.cz
Internet: www.muni.cz

Founded 1919
State control
Language of instruction: Czech
Academic year: September to August

Rector: Prof. Dr Peter Fiala
Vice-Rector (Academic Affairs): Prof. Dr Zuzana Brázdová
Vice-Rector (Research and Development): Prof. Dr Jana Musilová
Vice-Rector (Social Affairs of Students and External Relations): Assoc. Prof. Ing. Antonín Slaný

Library of 1,544,000 vols
Number of teachers: 3,072
Number of students: 26,681

Publications: *Universitas* (4 a year), *Scripta Medica* (6 a year), *Archivum mathematicum* (8 a year), *MUNI.CZ* (monthly, except July and August)

DEANS

Faculty of Arts: Dr Jan Pavlík
Faculty of Economics and Administration: Assoc. Prof. Dr Ivan Malý
Faculty of Education: Assoc. Prof. Dr Vladislav Mužík
Faculty of Informatics: Prof. Dr Jiři Zlatuška
Faculty of Law: Assoc. Prof. Dr Jan Svatoň
Faculty of Medicine: Assoc. Prof. Dr Jan Žaloudík
Faculty of Science: Assoc. Prof. Dr Milan Gelnar
Faculty of Sports Studies: Dr Michal Charvát
School of Social Studies: Assoc. Prof. Dr Ladislav Rabušic

PROFESSORS

Faculty of Arts (Arna Nováka 1, 660 80 Brno; tel. 549491511; fax 549491520; e-mail dekan@phil.muni.cz; internet www.phil.muni.cz):

Bátora, J., Archaeology
Blažek, V., Comparative Indo-European Linguistics
Cejpek, J., Library Studies
Fiala, J., Czech Literature
Gajdoš, J., Theory and History of Theatre
Horák, P., Philosophy
Horyna, B., Study of Religion
Hroch, J., Philosophy
Karlík, P., Czech Language
Krčmová, M., Czech Language
Kroupa, J., History of Arts
Kurfürst, P., Musicology
Malíř, J., Czech History
Měřínský, Z., Archaeology
Munzar, J., German Literature
Nechutová, J., Classics
Nekuda, V., Slavonic Archaeology
Oslzlý, P., Theatre and Film Studies
Pleskalová, J., Czech Language
Pospíšil, I., History of Russian Literature
Rusínová, Z., Czech Language
Slavíček, L., History of Art
Stehlíková, E., Theatre and Film Studies
Střítecký, J., Philosophy
Svoboda, M., Psychology
Šmajs, J., Philosophy
Štědroň, M., Musicology
Zouhar, J., Philosophy

Faculty of Economics and Administration (Lipová 41A, 659 79 Brno; tel. 549491710; fax 549491720; e-mail dekan@econ.muni.cz; internet www.econ.muni.cz):

Blazek, L., Theory of Management
Ivánek, L., Economics
Lanča, J., Economics and Corporate Management
Máša, M., Management
Ondrčka, P., Finance
Sejbal, J., Finance
Žák, M., Economics

Faculty of Education (Poříčí 7, 603 00 Brno; tel. 549493050; fax 549491620; e-mail dekan@ped.muni.cz; internet www.ped.muni.cz):

Chalupa, P., Geography
Chvalina, J., Mathematics
Hladký, J., English Language
Horová, I., Mathematics
Košut, M., Teaching of Music
Maňák, J., Education
Marečková, M., History
Novák, V., Mathematics
Švec, V., Education
Vítková, M., Special Education

Faculty of Informatics (Botanická 68A, Brno; tel. 549491810; fax 549491820; e-mail dekan@fi.muni.cz; internet www.fi.muni.cz):

Buzek, V., Informatics
Dokulil, M., Philosophy
Gruska, J., Informatics
Hřebíček, J., Company Information Systems
Materna, P., Logic
Novotný, M., Mathematics and Informatics
Serba, I., Informatics
Zezula, P., Informatics
Zlatuška, J., Informatics

Faculty of Law (Veveří 70, 611 80 Brno; tel. 549491211; fax 541213162; e-mail dekan@law.muni.cz; internet www.law.muni.cz):

Bejček, J., Economic Law
Filip, J., Constitutional Law and Political Science
Hajn, P., Economic Law
Hrušáková, M., Civil Law
Hurdík, J., Civil Law
Jílek, D., International Public Law
Malenovský, J., International Public Law
Rozehnalová, N., International Private Law
Telec, I., Civil Law
Vágner, I., Economics
Vlček, E., History of State and Law

Faculty of Medicine (Komenského nám. 2, 662 43 Brno; tel. 549491111; fax 542213996; e-mail dekan@med.muni.cz; internet www.med.muni.cz):

Adam, Z., Internal Medicine
Bednařík, J., Neurology
Benda, K., Radiology
Brázdová, Z., Social Medicine
Brhel, P., Occupational Medicine
Brychta, P., Surgery
Buček, J., Pathology
Čech, S., Histology
Češková, E., Psychiatry
Dapeci, A., Stomatology
Dítě, P., Internal Medicine
Drtílková, I., Psychiatry
Dubový, P., Anatomy
Dvořák, K., Pathology
Fakan, F., Anatomy
Fišer, B., Pathology and Physiology
Gál, P., Surgery
Hadašová, E., Pharmacology
Hep, A., Internal Medicine
Holčík, J., Social Medicine
Honzíková, N., Pathology and Physiology
Horký, D., Histology
Hrubá, D., Social Medicine

JANISCH, R., Biology
KADAŇKA, Z., Neurology
KOSTŘICA, R., Otorhynolaryngology
KUBEŠOVÁ, H., Internal Medicine
KUKLETA, M., Medical Physiology
KUKLETOVA, M., Stomatology
LITZMAN, J., Immunology
LOKAJ, J., Immunology
LUKÁŠ, Z., Anatomy
MALÝ, Z., Gynaecology and Obstetrics
MAYER, J., Internal Medicine
MELUZÍN, J., Internal Medicine
MUNZAROVÁ, M., Internal Medicine
PÁČ, L., Anatomy
PAČÍK, D., Surgery
PENKA, M., Internal Medicine
PETŘEK, M., Immunology
ŘEHŮŘEK, J., Ophthalmology
REJTHAR, A., Pathology
REKTOR, I., Neurology
ROZTOČIL, A., Gynaecology and Obstetrics
SEMRÁD, B., Internal Medicine
SEMRÁDOVÁ, V., Dermatovenereology
ŠEVČÍK, P., Anaesthesiology
SIEGLOVÁ, J., Functional Diagnostics and Rehabilitation
ŠMRČKA, V., Surgery
ŠPINAR, J., Internal Medicine
ŠULCOVÁ, A., Pharmacology
ŠVESTKA, J., Psychiatry
SVOBODA, A., Biology
TOMAN, J., Internal Medicine
VÁCHA, J., Pathological Physiology
VÁLEK, V., Radiology
VANĚK, J., Stomatology
VAŠKŮ, A., Pathological Physiology
VENTRUBA, P., Gynaecology and Obstetrics
VESELÝ, J., Surgery
VÍTOVEC, J., Internal Medicine
VLKOVÁ, E., Ophthalmology
VOMELA, J., Surgery
VORLÍČEK, J., Internal Medicine
WECHSLER, J., Surgery
WENDSCHE, P., Surgery
ZÁHEJSKÝ, J., Dermatovenereology
ŽALOUDÍK, J., Surgery
ZEMAN, K., Internal Medicine

Faculty of Science (Kotlářská 2, 611 37 Brno; tel. 549491411; fax 541211214; e-mail dekan@sci.muni.cz; internet www.sci.muni.cz):

BARTŮSEK, M., Analytical Chemistry
BRÁZDIL, R., Physical Geography
BRZOBOHATÝ, R., Palaeontology
DOŠKAŘ, J., Molecular Biology and Genetics
DOŠLÁ, Z., Mathematics
DOŠLÝ, O., Mathematical Analysis
GAISLER, J., Zoology
GLOSER, J., Plant Physiology
HÁLA, J., Inorganic Chemistry
HAVEL, J., Analytical Chemistry
HOLÍK, M., Physical Chemistry
HOLOUBEK, I., Environmental Chemistry
HOLÝ, V., Physics of Condensed Materials
HORSKÝ, J., Theoretical Physics
HUMLÍČEK, J., Physics
JANČA, J., Physics
JONAS, J., Organic Chemistry
KANICKÝ, V., Analytical Chemistry
KAPIČKA, V., Physics
KNOZ, J., Biology
KOČA, J., Organic Chemistry
KOLÁŘ, I., Algebra and Geometry
KOMÁREK, J., Analytical Chemistry
KOTYK, A., Biochemistry
KUČERA, I., Biochemistry
LENC, M., General Physics and Mathematical Physics
MALINA, J., Archaeology
MUSILOVÁ, J., Physics
NOVÁK, M., Geology
NOVÁK, V., Mathematics
NOVOTNÝ, J., Physics
OHLÍDAL, I., Quantum Electronics and Optics
POTÁČEK, M., Organic Chemistry
PŘICHYSTAL, A., Geology
PROŠEK, P., Physical Geography
RELICHOVÁ, J., Genetics
ROSICKÝ, J., Mathematics
ROZKOŠNÝ, R., Entomology
SCHMIDT, E., Physics
ŠKLENÁŘ, V., Physical Chemistry
ŠIMEK, M., Animal Physiology
SKULA, L., Mathematics
SLOVÁK, J., Geometry
STANĚK, J., Mineralogy and Petrography
UNGER, J., Anthropology
VAŇHARA, J., Zoology
VELICKÝ, B., Theoretical Physics
VETTERL, J., Physical Electronics
VICHEREK, J., Botany
VŘEŠŤÁL, J., Physical Chemistry
ŽÁK, Z., Inorganic Chemistry
ZIMA, J., Zoology

School of Social Studies (Gorkého 7, 602 00 Brno; tel. 549491911; fax 549491920; e-mail dekan@fss.muni.cz; internet www.fss.muni.cz):

FIALA, P., Politology
KELLER, J., Sociology
LIBROVÁ, H., Sociology
MACEK, P., Social Psychology
MAREŠ, P., Sociology
MOŽNÝ, I., Sociology
RABUŠIC, L., Sociology
SIROVÁTKA, T., Social Policy and Social Work
ŠMAUSOVÁ, G., Sociology
SMÉKAL, V., Psychology
STRMISKA, M., Political Science

ATTACHED INSTITUTES

Institute of Computer Science: Dir Assoc. Prof. Dr VÁCLAV RAČANSKÝ.

International Institute for Political Studies: Dir Dr BŘATISLAV DANČÁK.

MENDELOVA ZEMĚDĚLSKÁ A LESNICKÁ UNIVERZITA V BRNĚ (Mendel University of Agriculture and Forestry, Brno)

Zemědělská 1, 613 00 Brno
Telephone: 545131111
Fax: 545211128
E-mail: rektor@mendelu.cz
Internet: www.mendelu.cz

Founded by State Law in 1919
State control
Language of instruction: Czech
Academic year: September to January, February to June

Rector: S. PROCHÁZKA
Pro-Rectors: M. JANKU, J. NERUDA, J. STÁVKOVÁ, L. ZEMAN
Chief Administrative Officer: V. SEDLÁŘOVÁ
Chief Librarian: V. PERLOVÁ

Library of 400,000 vols
Number of teachers: 350
Number of students: 6,100 full-time, 1,200 part-time
Number of students: 423 part-time

Publication: *Acta Universitatis Agriculturae et Silviculturae Mendelianae Brunensis* (6 a year)

DEANS

Faculty of Agronomy: J. HLUŠEK
Faculty of Economics: B. MINAŘÍK
Faculty of Forestry and Wood Technology: L. SLONEK
Faculty of Horticulture: P. KUČERA

HEADS OF DEPARTMENTS

Faculty of Agronomy (Zemědělská 1, 613 00 Brno; tel. 545133001; fax 545212044; e-mail dekanaf@mendelu.cz; internet www.af.mendelu.cz):

Agriculture, Food and Environmental Engineering: J. MAREČEK
Agrochemistry, Soil Science, Microbiology and Plant Nutrition: J. HLUŠEK
Agrosystems and Bioclimatology: J. KŘEN
Animal Breeding: L. MÁCHAL
Animal Nutrition and Forage Production: L. ZEMAN
Applied and Landscape Ecology: F. TOMAN
Chemistry and Biochemistry: P. HRDLIČKA
Crop Science, Breeding and Plant Medicine: O. CHLOUPEK
Engineering and Automobile Transport: M. HAVLÍČEK
Food Technology: T. KOMPRDA
Molecular Embryology and Radiobiology: P. DVOŘÁK
Morphology, Physiology and Animal Genetics: P. JELÍNEK
Physical Training: I. ŠTEFL
Plant Biology: S. PROCHÁZKA
Zoology, Fisheries, Hydrobiology and Apiculture: Z. LAŠTŮVKA

Faculty of Economics (Zemědělská 1, 613 00 Brno; tel. 545132701; e-mail dekan@pef.mendelu.cz; internet www.pef.mendelu.cz):

Accounting and Taxation: V. VYBÍHAL
Business Economics: L. GREGA
Economics: M. SOJKA
Finance: O. REJNUŠ
Informatics: A. MOTYČKA
Law: M. JANKŮ
Management: P. ŽUFAN
Marketing and Trade: J. STÁVKOVÁ
Social Sciences: S. HUBÍK
Statistics and Operational Analysis: B. MINAŘÍK

Faculty of Forestry and Wood Technology (Zemědělská 3, 613 00 Brno; tel. 545134000; fax 545134157; e-mail dekanldf@mendelu.cz; internet www.ldf.mendelu.cz):

Forest Botany, Dendrology and Biogeocenology: K. KOBLÍŽEK
Forest Ecology: J. KULHAVÝ
Forest Establishment and Silviculture: P. KANTOR
Forest Management: J. SIMON
Forest Protection and Game Management: E. KULA
Forest and Timber Industry Economics and Policy: F. KALOUSEK
Forest and Timber Industry Technology: M. SKOUPÝ
Furniture, Design and Habitation: P. BRUNECKÝ
Geoinformation Technologies: V. ŽIDEK
Geology and Pedology: K. REJŠEK
Landscape Design and Protection: I. VYSKOT
Mathematics: P. RADL
Wood Basic Processing: L. SLONEK
Wood Science: P. HORÁČEK

Faculty of Horticulture (Valtická 337, 691 44 Lednice; tel. 519367211; fax 519367222; e-mail info@zf.mendelu.cz; internet www.zf.mendelu.cz):

Horticultural Engineering: P. ZEMÁNEK
Horticultural Plant Breeding and Propagation: P. SALAŠ
Landscape Architecture: J. DAMEO
Mendeleum Department of Plant Genetics: M. PIDRA
Planting Design and Maintenance: P. RAJNOCH
Pomology: B. KRŠKA
Post-Harvest Technology for Horticultural Products: J. BALÍK
Vegetable and Flower Science: K. PETŘÍKOVÁ
Viticulture and Oenology: P. PAVLOUŠEK

All-University Departments:
Botanical Garden and Arboretum: T. KOLOUŠEK
Institute of Information and Communication Technology: M. BANZET
Institute of Life-long Education: P. MACHAL
Institute of Scientific Information: J. POTÁČEK
Language and Cultural Studies: J. BREŠOVÁ

OSTRAVSKÁ UNIVERZITA V OSTRAVĚ (Ostrava University)

Dvořákova 7, 701 03 Ostrava
Telephone: 596160111
Fax: 596118219
Internet: www.osu.cz
Founded 1991
State control
Rector: Dr RNDr VLADIMIR BAAR
Vice-Rector for Research, Artistic Activity and International Relations: Ing. MUDr MIROSLAV PŘÁDKA
Vice-Rector for Strategy, Organisation and Development: Dr RNDr DALIBOR DVOŘÁK
Vice-Rector for Study: Dr IVA MÁLKOVÁ
Library of 200,000 vols
Number of teachers: 397
Number of students: 5,590

DEANS
Faculty of Arts: Dr PhDr ZDENKA KALNICKÁ
Medico-Social Faculty: Dr MUDr JAROSLAV HORÁČEK
Pedagogical Faculty: Dr PhDr ZBYNĚK JANÁČEK
Faculty of Science: Dr RNDr PETR ŠINDLER

ATTACHED RESEARCH INSTITUTES
Institute for the Artistic Studies.
Institute for Regional Studies.
Institute for Research and Application of Fuzzy Modelling

UNIVERZITA PARDUBICE (University of Pardubice)

Studentská 95, 532 10 Pardubice
Telephone: 466036111
Fax: 466036361
E-mail: promotion@upce.cz
Internet: www.upce.cz
Founded 1950 as Vysoká Škola Chemicko-Technologická v Pardubicích; present name and status 1994
State control
Languages of instruction: Czech, English
Academic year: September to August
Rector: Prof. Ing. MIROSLAV LUDWIG
Vice-Rectors: Doc. Ing. JIŘÍ CAKL, Doc. Ing. JAROSLAV JANDA, Doc. Ing. JIŘÍ MÁLEK
Bursar: Ing. MILAN BUKAČ
Librarian: IVA PROCHÁSKOVÁ
Library of 180,000 vols
Number of teachers: 381
Number of students: 4,794
Publications: *Scientific Papers* (annually), *Zpravodaj Univerzity Pardubice* (4 a year)

DEANS
Faculty of Chemical Technology: Doc. Ing. PETR MIKULÁŠEK
Faculty of Economics and Administration: Doc. Ing. JAN ČAPEK
Faculty of Humanities: Prof. MILENA LENDEROVÁ
Jan Perner Faculty of Transport: Prof. Dr Ing. KAREL ŠOTEK

ATTACHED RESEARCH INSTITUTES
Institute of Health Studies: Průmyslová 395, 530 03 Pardubice; Dir Prof. Dr. ARNOŠT PELLANT.
Institute of Informatics: Studenská 95, 532 10 Pardubice; Dir Doc. Ing. SIMEON KARAMAZOV.

UNIVERZITA PALACKÉHO V OLOMOUCI (Palacký University)

Křížkovského 8, 771 47 Olomouc
Telephone: 585631001
Fax: 585631012
E-mail: rektor@upol.cz
Internet: www.upol.cz
Founded 1573; re-opened 1946
State control
Languages of instruction: Czech, English, German
Academic year: September to August
Rector: Prof. RNDr LUBOMÍR DVOŘÁK
Vice-Rector for Devt: Prof. MUDr EVŽEN WEIGL
Vice-Rector for Int. and Public Relations: Mgr JAKUB DÜRR
Vice-Rector for Organization: JUDr LUDMILA LOCHMANOVÁ
Vice-Rector for Scientific and Research Activities: Prof. RNDr JITKA ULRICHOVÁ
Vice-Rector for Student Affairs: Doc. PaedDr MIROSLAV CHRÁSKA
Registrar: Ing. JIŘÍ JIRKA
Librarian: RNDr DANA LOŠŤÁKOVÁ
Library of 521,000
Number of teachers: 1,800
Number of students: 20,000
Publication: *Acta Universitatis Palackianae* (quarterly)

DEANS
Faculty of Education: Prof. PaedDr. LIBUŠE LUDÍKOVÁ
Faculty of Law: Dr JUDr Mag. iur. MICHAL MALACKA
Faculty of Medicine: Prof. MUDr. ZDERNĚK KOLÁŘ
Faculty of Philosophy: Prof. PhDr IVO BARTEČEK
Faculty of Physical Culture: Doc. PhDr. DUŠAN TOMAJKO
Faculty of Science: Prof. RNDr. JURAJ ŠEVČÍK
Sts Cyril and Methodius Faculty of Theology: Dr RNDr IVANA GABRIELA VLKOVÁ

PROFESSORS
Faculty of Education (Žižkovo nám. 5, 771 40 Olomouc; tel. 585635088; fax 585231400; e-mail libuse.ludikova@upol.cz):
CHRÁSKA, M., Theory of Education
HLŮZA, B., Botany
KLAPIL, P., Music Theory and Pedagogy
KOVAŘÍČEK, V., Theory of Education
LUDÍKOVÁ, L., Pedagogy of Special Needs Education
MEZIHORÁK, F., Czechoslovak History
NELEŠOVSKÁ, A., Theory of Elementary School
SLÁMA, O., Forest Ergonomics
STEINMETZ, K., Music Theory and Pedagogy
STOFFA, J., Electrical Engineering

Faculty of Law (17. Listopadu 8, 771 00 Olomouc; tel. 585637509; fax 585223537; e-mail michal.malacka@upol.cz):
DAVID, V., International Law
MAREČKOVÁ, M., History
MEČL, J., Theory of Law
TELEC, I., Civic Law

Faculty of Medicine (Tř. Svobody 8, 771 26 Olomouc; tel. 585632010; fax 585223907; e-mail zdenek.kolar@upol.cz):
BOUČEK, J., Psychiatry
DLOUHÝ, M., Surgery
DUDA, M., Surgery
EBER, M., Stomatology
EHRMANN, J., Internal Diseases
GLADKIJ, J., Social Medicine
HÁLEK, J., Electronics and Medical Procedures
HOLIBKA, V., General Anatomy
HOUDEK, M., Neurosurgery
HŘEBÍČEK, J., Pathological Physiology
HUŠÁK, V., Applied Physics
INDRÁK, K., Internal Diseases
JANOUT, V., Epidemiology
JAROŠOVÁ, M., Medical Genetics
JEZDINSKÝ, J., Pharmacology
JIRAVA, E., Stomatology
KAMÍNEK, M., Stomatology
KLAČANSKÝ, J., Oto-Rhino-Laryngology
KOĎOUSEK, R., Pathological Anatomy
KOLÁŘ, Z., Pathology
KOLEK, V., Internal Diseases
KOMENDA, S., Education
KRÁL, V., Surgery
KRČ, I., Internal Medicine
KUDELA, M., Gynaecology
LENHART, K., General Biology
LICHNOVSKÝ, V., Histology and Embryology
LUKL, J., Internal Diseases
MAČÁK, J., Pathology
MAČÁKOVA, J., Pathological Physiology
MACHÁČEK, J., Radiology
MALÍNSKÝ, J., Histology and Embryology
MIHÁL, V., Paediatrics
NEKULA, J., Radiology
PAZDERA, J., Stomatology
PEŠÁK, J., Medical Biophysics
PETŘEK, J., Physiology
ŠANTAVÝ, J., Medical Genetics
ŠČUDLA, V., Internal Diseases
SIMÁNEK, V., Medical Chemistry
STAŘEK, I., Oto-Rhino-Laryngology
ULRICHKOVÁ, J., Medical Chemistry and Biochemistry
URBÁNEK, K., Neurology
VAVERKOVÁ, H., Internal Diseases
VESELÝ, J., Pathological Physiology

Faculty of Philosophy (Křížkovského 10, 771 80 Olomouc; tel. 585633036; fax 585229162; e-mail ivo.bartecek@upol.cz):
ANDERS, J., Slavonic Studies
BARTEČEK, I., History
BARTONĚK, A., Classical Philology
BLECHA, I., Philosophy
ČERNÝ, J., General Linguistics
DANIEL, L., History of Visual Art
FIALA, J., History of Czech Literature
FIALOVÁ, I., History of German Literature
FLÍDROVÁ, H., Russian Language
FLOSS, P., History of Philosophy
HLOBIL, I., Theory and History of Visual Art
HRABOVÁ, L., General History
JAŘAB, J., American Studies and American Literature
KOMÁREK, M., Slavonic Studies and Czech Language
KOŘENSKÝ, J., Slavonic Studies and Czech Language
KRATOCHVÍL, S., Clinical Psychology
LOTKO, E., Czech Language
MACHÁČEK, J., English Studies and English Language
MAREK, P., Czech History
PEPRNÍK, J., English Language
POLEDŇÁK, I., Theory and History of Music
SOBOTKOVÁ, M., History of Czech Literature
SPÁČILOVÁ, L., German Language
SVOBODA, M., Psychology
ŠMAUSOVÁ, G., Sociology
ŠRÁMEK, J., French Literature
ŠTĚPÁN, J., Philosophy
ŠTĚPÁNEK, P., History of Visual Arts
SVARNY, O., General Linguistics

TÁRNYIKOVÁ, J., English Studies and English Language
TOGNER, M., History of Fine Art
TRAPL, M., Czech and Slovak History
VÁCLAVEK, L., History of German Literature
VIČAR, J., Theory and History of Music
ZAHRÁDKA, M., Russian Literature

Faculty of Physical Culture (Tř. Míru 115, 771 11 Olomouc; tel. 585636009; fax 585412899; e-mail dusan.tomajko@upol.cz):

FRÖMEL, K., Kinanthropology
HODAŇ, B., Theory of Physical Culture
MĚKOTA, K., Anthropomotory
OPAVSKÝ, J., Neurology
OŠŤÁDAL, O., Internal Diseases
RIEGEROVÁ, J., Kinanthropology
VÁLKOVÁ, H., Kinanthropology
VAVERKA, F., Kinanthropology
VYKOPALOVÁ, H., Security Services

Faculty of Science (Tř. Svobody 26, 771 46 Olomouc; tel. 585634060; fax 585225737; e-mail juraj.sevcik@upol.cz):

ANDRES, J., Mathematical Analysis
BAJER, J., Optics and Optoelectronics
BIČÍK, V., Zoology
BĚLOHLÁVEL, Z., Information Science
BOUCHAL, Z., Optics and Optoelectronics
BUREŠ, S., Zoology
CHAJDA, I., Algebra and Geometry
DUŠEK, M., Quantum Optics
DVOŘÁK, L., Biophysics
FRÉBORT, I., Biochemistry
HOBZA, P., Physical Chemistry
HRADIL, Z., Optics and Optoelectronics
KAMENÍČEK, J., Inorganic Chemistry
KRUPKA, D., Mathematics
KRUPKOVA, O., General Physics and Mathematical Physics
KUBÁČEK, L., Mathematical Statistics
LASOVSKÝ, J., Physical Chemistry
LEBEDA, A., Botany
LEMR, K., Analytical Chemistry
MAJERNÍKOVÁ, E., Physics of Condensed Matter and Acoustics
MAŠLÁŇ, M., Applied Physics
MIKEŠ, J., Geometry and Topology
NAUŠ, J., Biophysics
NEZVALOVA, D., Pedagogy
OPATRNÝ, T., General and Mathematical Physics
PASTOREK, R., Inorganic Chemistry
PEŘINA, J., Optoelectronics
PĚRINOVÁ, V., General Physics and Mathematical Physics
POSPÍŠIL, J., Experimental Physics
RACHŮNEK, J., Algebra
RACHŮNKOVÁ, I., Mathematical Analysis
ŘYCHNOVSKÁ, M., Ecology
ŠARAPATKA, B., Landscape Engineering
SLOUKA, J., Organic Chemistry
STANĚK, S., Mathematical Analysis
ŠTRNAD, M., Plant Physiology
ŠEVČÍK, J., Analytical Chemistry
STĚRBA, O., Ecology
TKADLEC, E., Ecology
TRÁVNÍCEK, Z., Inorganic Chemistry
ZAPLETAL, J., Geology

Sts Cyril and Methodius Faculty of Theology (Univerzitní 22, 771 11 Olomouc; tel. 585637111; fax 585224174; e-mail petr.chalupa@upol.cz):

AMBROS, P., Theology
GÓRECKI, E., Religious Law
HALAS, F. X., History
KARFÍKOVÁ, L., Evangelical Theory
MUSIL, J., Clinical Psychology
POJSL, M., History of Christian Art
POSPÍŠIL, C. V., Systematic Theology
TICHÝ, L., Theology

SLEZSKÁ UNIVERZITA V OPAVĚ
(Silesian University of Opava)

Na Rybníčku 626/1, 746 01 Opava
Telephone: 553684621
Fax: 553718019
E-mail: rektorat@slu.cz
Internet: www.slu.cz

Founded 1991
State control

Rector: Doc. PhDr RUDOLF ŽÁČEK
Questor: Ing. JAROSLAV KANIA

Library of 77,000 vols, 256 periodicals
Number of teachers: 550
Number of students: 4,000

DEANS

Faculty of Business Administration: PhDr BOHUMIL FIALA
Faculty of Philosophy and Science: Prof. PhDr ZDENĚK JIRÁSEK

ATTACHED INSTITUTE

Mathematical Institute in Opava: Dir Prof. RNDr MIROSLAV ENGLIŠ.

TECHNICKÁ UNIVERZITA V LIBERCI
(Technical University of Liberec)

Hálkova 6, 461 17 Liberec
Telephone: 485351111
Fax: 485105882
E-mail: rektor@vslib.cz
Internet: www.vslib.cz

Founded 1953
State control
Languages of instruction: Czech, English
Academic year: September to June

Rector: Prof. VOJTĚCH KONOPA
Pro-Rectors: Prof. OLDŘICH JIRSÁK, Assoc. Prof. JIŘI KRAFT, Assoc. Prof. ZDENĚK KÜS
Registrar: VLADIMÍR STACH
Librarian: ADAM KRETSCHMER

Library of 162,000
Number of teachers: 489
Number of students: 7,600

Publications: *Economics and Management* (7 a year), *Sborník vědeckých prací Technické univerzity* (Annals of Scientific Research)

DEANS

Faculty of Architecture: Prof. BOŘEK ŠIPEK
Faculty of Economics and Business Administration: Assoc. Prof. OLGA HASPROVA
Faculty of Education: Prof. MILOŠ RABAN
Faculty of Mechanical Engineering: Assoc. Prof. PETR LOUDA
Faculty of Mechatronics: Assoc. Prof. JIŘÍ MARYŠKA
Faculty of Textile Engineering: Prof. JIŘÍ MILITKÝ

PROFESSORS

BAKULE, V., Finance and Credit
BENEŠ, Š., Construction of Machines and Appliances
BEROUN, S., Transport Machines
CYHELSKÝ, L., Statistics
DUCHOŇ, B., Management Technology in Transport
EHLEMAN, J., Information Management
EXNER, J., Mechanical Engineering Technology
FOUSEK, J., Electromechanical Properties of Dielectrics
HAJNIŠ, K., Physical Education
HANUŠ, B., Control Engineering
HES, L., Textile Valuation
HINDLS, R., Insurance, Statistics
HONCŮ, J., Machine Design
HÝČA, M., Applied Mechanics
IBRAHIM, S., Textile Technology
JANOVEC, V., Electromechanical Properties of Dielectrics
JIRSÁK, O., Textile Technology
KAŇOKOVÁ, J., Statistics
KARGER, A., Mathematics, Economics, Topology
KONOPA, V., Technical Cybernetics
KOPKA, J., Teaching of Mathematics
KOŠEK, M., Technical Cybernetics
KOVÁŘ, R., Textile Technology
KOVÁŘ, Z., Combustion Engines
KRAFT, J., Enterprise Economics, Management
KRATOCHVÍL, P., Materials Engineering
KRYŠTŮFEK, J., Textile Technology
KVAČEK, R., Czech History
LANDOROVÁ, A., Financing
LUKÁŠ, D., Textile Technology
MILITKÝ, J., Textile Technology
NECKÁŘ, B., Structure of Textiles
NOSEK, J., Physics
NOSEK, S., Textile Machines
NOUZA, J., Technical Cybernetics
NOVÁ, I., Engineering Metallurgy
NOVÁK, O., Technical Cybernetics
OLEHLA, J., Machines and Devices Construction
OLEHLA, M., Production Systems and Processes
PŘIVRATSKÁ, J., Physics
SKALLA, J., Servodrivers and Automation
SODOMKA, L., Applied Physics
STIBOR, I., Organic Chemistry
STRAKOŠ, Z., Technical Cybernetics
STŘÍŽ, B., Elasticity and Strength
ŠUCHOMEL, J., Architecture and Design
ŠKALOUD, M., Mechanics
ŠKLÍBA, J., Applied Mechanics
ŠPATENKA, P., Mechanical Engineering Technology
ULIČNÝ, O., Czech Language
URSÍNY, P., Textile Technology
VÁGNEROVÁ, M., Psychology
VAVERKA, J., Building Engineering
VĚCHET, V., Technical Cybernetics
VOKURKA, K., Applied Physics
VOSTATEK, J., Finance
ZELINKA, B., Mathematical Informatics and Theoretical Cybernetics

UNIVERZITA TOMÁŠE BATI VE ZLÍNĚ
(Tomas Bata University in Zlín)

Mostní 5139, 760 01 Zlín
Telephone: 576031111
Fax: 576032213
E-mail: kancler@utb.cz
Internet: www.utb.cz

Founded 2000
State control
Academic year: September to June

Rector: Prof. PETR SAHA
Vice-Rector for Science and Research: Doc. DRAHOMÍRA PAVELKOVA
Vice-Rector for Teaching: Prof. ROMAN PROKOP

Number of teachers: 299
Number of students: 7,388

DEANS

Faculty of Economics and Management: Doc. VNISLAV NOVAČEK
Faculty of Multimedia Communications: Prof. PAVEL SKARKA
Faculty of Technology: Prof. JOSEF SIMONIK

ATTACHED RESEARCH INSTITUTES

University Institute: e-mail info@uni.utb.cz; internet www.uni.utb.cz; Dir Ing. JITKA CHUDAROVÁ.

VETERINÁRNÍ A FARMACEUTICKÁ UNIVERZITA BRNO (University of Veterinary and Pharmaceutical Sciences Brno)

Palackého 1–3, 612 42 Brno
Telephone: 541562002
Fax: 549250478
E-mail: rektor@vfu.cz
Internet: www.vfu.cz

Founded 1918
State control
Languages of instruction: Czech, English
Academic year: September to August

Rector: Prof. MVDr VLADIMIR VEČEREK
Pro-Rector for Education and Vice-Rector: Prof. MVDr IVA STEINHAUSEROVÁ
Pro-Rector for Scientific Research and Foreign Relations: Prof. MVDr PhD ALOIS NEČAS
Pro-Rector for Univ. Devt: Prof. MVDr Ing. PAVEL SUCHÝ
Registrar: JUDr DANUŠE HLOŽKOVÁ
Librarian: Mgr TOMÁŠ GEC

Library: see Libraries and Archives
Number of teachers: 262
Number of students: 2,565
Publication: *Acta Veterinaria Brno* (quarterly)

DEANS

Faculty of Pharmacy: Doc. RNDr. CSc. MILAN ŽEMLIČKA
Faculty of Veterinary Hygiene and Ecology: Prof. MVDr PhD LENKA VORLOVÁ
Faculty of Veterinary Medicine: Doc MVDr PhD LEOŠ PAVLATA

PROFESSORS

Faculty of Pharmacy (tel. 541562801; fax 541219751; e-mail dekanfaf@vfu.cz; internet www.vfu.cz):

BENEŠ, L., Pharmaceutical Chemistry
CSÖLLEI, J., Pharmaceutical Chemistry
KVĚTINA, J., Pharmacology and Toxicology
SLADKÝ, Z., Botanics
SUBERT, V., Pharmaceutical Chemistry
SUCHÝ, J., Pharmacognosy

Faculty of Veterinary Hygiene and Ecology (tel. 541562795; fax 549243020; e-mail fvhe@vfu.cz; internet ww.vfu.cz):

ČERNÝ, H., Anatomy
LITERÁK, I., Diseases of Game, Fish and Bees, Biology and Zoology
MINKS, J., Tropical Veterinary Medicine
PAVLÍK, I., Tuberculosis, Paratuberculosis and Mycobacterioses
SMUTNÁ, M., Veterinary Chemistry and Biochemistry
STEINHAUSEROVÁ, I., Food Hygiene and Technology, Veterinary Public Health
SUCHÝ, P., Animal Nutrition and Dietetics
ŠUCMAN, E., Veterinary Chemistry and Biochemistry
SVOBODOVÁ, Z., Veterinary Toxicology and Ecotoxicology
VÁVROVÁ, M., Chemistry and Technology of Environment Protection
VEČEREK, VA., Veterinary Public Health

Faculty of Veterinary Medicine (tel. 541562440; fax 549248841; e-mail dekanfvl@vfu.cz; internet www.vfu.cz):

DVOŘÁK, R., Diseases of Farm Animals
HALOUZKA, J., Veterinary Morphology
HANÁK, J., Equine Diseases
HERA, A., Veterinary Pharmacology
HOŘÍN, P., Animal Genetics
KNOTEK, Z., Diseases of Small Animals
NEČAS, A., Veterinary Surgery and Orthopaedics
POSPÍŠIL, Z., Epizootiology
SMOLA, J., Microbiology
SVOBODA, M., Diseases of Small Animals
SVOBODOVÁ, V., Veterinary Parasitology
TICHÝ, F., Histology and Embryology
TOMAN, M., Veterinary Immunology
TREML, F., Epizootiology

VYSOKÁ ŠKOLA BÁŇSKÁ – TECHNICKÁ UNIVERZITA OSTRAVA (Technical University of Ostrava)

17 listopadu 15, 708 33 Ostrava-Poruba
Telephone: 596991111
Fax: 596918507
E-mail: vaclav.roubicek@vsb.cz
Internet: www.vsb.cz

Founded 1716
State control
Academic year: September to August

Rector: Prof. Ing. VÁCLAV ROUBÍČEK
Vice-Rector (Development): Prof. Ing. PETR WYSLYCH
Vice-Rector (Education): Prof. Ing. JAROMÍR POLÁK
Vice-Rector (Finance and Organization): Prof. Ing. MIROSLAV NEJEZCHLEBA
Vice-Rector (Research and Development and International Affairs): Prof. Ing. TOMÁŠ ČERMÁK
Registrar: Ing. STANISLAV DZIOB
Librarian: Mgr DANIELA TKAČÍKOVÁ

Number of teachers: 812
Number of students: 14,579

Publications: *Akademik* (6 a year), *Sborník vědeckých prací VŠB-TU Ostrava* (irregular)

DEANS

Faculty of Civil Engineering: Prof. Ing. JINDŘICH CIGÁNEK
Faculty of Economics: Prof. Ing. JIŘÍ KERN
Faculty of Electrical Engineering and Informatics: Doc. Ing. KAREL CHMELÍK
Faculty of Mechanical Engineering: Prof. Ing. PETR HORYL
Faculty of Metallurgy and Material Engineering: Prof. Ing. LUDOVIT DOBROVSKÝ
Faculty of Mining and Geology: Prof. Ing. JAROSLAV DVOŘÁČEK

PROFESSORS

Faculty of Civil Engineering (tel. 596991316; fax 596991356; e-mail dekan.fast@vsb.cz):

ALDORF, J., Mine Construction and Geotechnics
CIGANEK, J., Mine Construction and Geotechnics

Faculty of Economics (1, Sokolská tř. 33, 701 21 Ostrava; fax 596110026):

HALÁSEK, D., Macroeconomics
JUREČKA, V., General Economics
KALUŽA, J., Informatics in Economics
KERN, J., Macroeconomics
NEJEZCHLEBA, M., Finance
POLÁCH, J., Finance
SMOLÍK, D., Environmental Protection and Reclamation
ŠNAPKA, P., Mining Economics and Management

Faculty of Electrical Engineering and Informatics (tel. 596995252; fax 596919597):

BLAHETA, R., Applied Mathematics
BLUNÁR, K., Communications Technology
BRANDŠTETTER, P., Electrical Machines, Apparatus and Drives
ČERMÁK, T., Electrical Drives
DIVIŠ, Z., Transport and Infrastructure
DOSTÁL, Z., Applied Mathematics
HASLINGER, J., Applied Mathematics
HRADÍLEK, Z., Electrical Power Engineering
LITSCHMANN, J., Engineering Cybernetics
NEVŘIVA, P., Technical Cybernetics
PALEČEK, J., Electrical Power Engineering
POKORNÝ, M., Measurement and Control Technology
RUSEK, S., Electrical Power Engineering
SOKANSKÝ, K., Electrical Power Engineering
SANTARIUS, Electrical Power Engineering
VONDRÁK, I., Computer Science

Faculty of Mechanical Engineering (tel. 597321216; fax 596916490):

ANTONICKÝ, S., Transportation and Technology
BAILOTTI, K., Transportation and Preparation Equipment
DANĚK, A., Transportation and Technology
DANĚK, J., Transportation and Technology
DEJL, Z., Machine Parts and Mechanisms
FUXA, J., Applied Mechanics
GONDEK, H., Mining Machinery
JANALÍK, J., Hydraulic Machines and Mechanisms
KOLAT, P., Thermal and Nuclear Power Engineering
KOUKAL, J., Engineering Technology
LENERT, J., Mechanics
MAKURA, P., Applied Mechanics
NOSKIEVIČ, P., Power Engineering
ONDROUCH, J., Technical Mechanics
PETRUŽELKA, M., Mechanical Technology
POLÁK, J., Transportation and Manipulation Technology
TŮMA, J., Automation of Machines and Technological Processes
VÍTEČEK, A., Automation of Machines and Technological Processes

Faculty of Metallurgy and Material Engineering (tel. 596995374; fax 596918592; e-mail jiri.kliber@vsb.cz):

ADOLF, Z., Steel-making
BAŽAN, J., Steel-making
DOBROVSKÝ, L., Chemical Metallurgy
FILIP, P., Materials Engineering
HAŠEK, P., Thermal Engineering in Industry
HYSPECKÁ, L., Physical Metallurgy
JELÍNEK, P., Casting
JONŠTA, Z., Physical Metallurgy
KALOČ, M., Technology of Fuels
KLIBER, J., Materials Forming
KLIKA, Z., Geochemistry, Mineralogy and Technology
KRAUSOVÁ, E., Economics and Management of Metallurgy
KURSA, M., Metallurgical Technology
LEŠKO, J., Chemical Metallurgy
MICHALEK, K., Metallurgical Technology
NENADÁL, J., Quality Management
OBROUČKA, K., Thermal Engineering
PETŘÍKOVÁ, R., Quality and Safety of Technical Systems
PŘÍHODA, M., Thermal Engineering
ROUBÍČEK, V., Technology of Fuels
SCHINDLER, J., Metallurgical Technology
SOMMER, B., Metal Forming
STRNADEL, B., Materials Engineering
TOŠENOVSKÝ, J., Industrial Process
TVRDÝ, M., Materials Engineering
VROŽINA, M., Automation of Metallurgical Processes
WICHTERLE, K., Chemical Engineering

Faculty of Mining and Geology (tel. 596995456; fax 596918589):

DIRNER, V., Environmental Protection and Reclamation
DVOŘÁČEK, J., Economics of Mining
FIGALA, J., General Ecology, Chronobiology
GRYGÁREK, J., Underground Mining
KRYL, V., Mining
LÁNÍČEK, J., Mathematics
LEMBÁK, M., Geotechnics and Underground Civil Engineering
MÁDR, V., Physics
NOVÁČEK, J., Mineral Processing and Ecotechnology
PALAS, M., Economic Geology
PETROŠ, V., Underground Mining
PIŠTORA, J., Applied Physics

PROKOP, P., Mine Ventilation
SCHEJBAL, C., Economic Geology
SCHENK, J., Geodesy and Mine Surveying
SIVEK, M., Economic Geology
STRAKOŠ, V., Automation in Mining
VAŠÍČEK, Z., Geology
VIDLÁŘ, J., Mineral Processing
WYSLYCH, P., Applied Physics
ZAMARSKÝ, V., Geology and Mineralogy

VYSOKÁ ŠKOLA CHEMICKO-TECHNOLOGICKÁ V PRAZE
(Institute of Chemical Technology, Prague)

Technická 5, 166 28 Prague 6
Telephone: 220444144
Fax: 220445018
E-mail: rektorat@vscht.cz
Internet: www.vscht.cz

Founded 1807
State control
Language of instruction: Czech
Academic year: September to June

Rector: Prof. VLASTIMIL RŮŽIČKA
Vice-Rector (Development and Building): Assoc. Prof. VLADIMÍR SÝKORA
Vice-Rector (Education): Prof. STANISLAV LABÍK
Vice-Rector (International Relations): Assoc. Prof. BOHUMIL BERNAUER
Vice-Rector (Science and Research): Prof. JITKA MORAVCOVÁ
Registrar: Ing. TOMÁŠ KOPŘIVA
Librarian: Dr ANNA SOUČKOVÁ

Library of 225,000 vols
Number of teachers: 470
Number of students: 3,068

DEANS

Faculty of Chemical Engineering: Assoc. Prof. DANIEL TURZÍK
Faculty of Chemical Technology: Assoc. Prof. ALEŠ HELEBRANT
Faculty of Environmental Engineering: Prof. GUSTAV ŠEBOR
Faculty of Food and Biochemical Technology: Assoc. Prof. KAREL MELZOCH

PROFESSORS

BASAŘOVÁ, G., Fermentation Chemistry and Biotechnology
BENDA, V., Biochemistry and Microbiology
BENEŠ, P., Social Sciences
BUBNÍK, Z., Cereal Chemistry and Technology
BURYAN, P., Gas, Coke and Air Protection
ČERVENÝ, L., Organic Technology
ČURDA, D., Food Preservation
DAVÍDEK, J., Food Chemistry and Technology
DEMNEROVÁ, K., Biochemistry and Microbiology
DEYL, Z., Analytical Chemistry
DOHÁNYOS, M., Water Technology and Environmental Engineering
DUCHÁČEK, V., Polymers
ECKERT, E., Chemical Engineering
GROS, J., Economics and Management of the Chemical Industry
HAJŠLOVÁ, J., Food Chemistry and Analysis
HANIKA, J., Organic Technology
HLAVÁČ, J., Silicate Technology
HORÁK, J., Organic Technology
HUDEC, L., Technology of Materials for Electronics
JANDA, V., Water Technology and Environmental Engineering
JIRKŮ, V., Fermentation Chemistry and Biotechnology
JURSÍK, F., Inorganic Chemistry
KADLEC, P., Sugar Technology
KÁŠ, J., Biochemistry
KLÍČ, A., Mathematics
KODÍČEK, M., Biochemistry and Microbiology
KRÁLOVÁ, B., Biochemistry and Microbiology
KRATOCHVÍL, B., Solid-state Chemistry
KUBÍČEK, M., Mathematics
KURAŠ, M., Environmental Engineering
LABÍK, S., Physical Chemistry
LIŠKA, F., Organic Chemistry
MALIJEVSKÝ, A., Physical Chemistry
MAREK, M., Chemical Engineering
MATĚJKA, Z., Power Engine
MATOUŠEK, J., Silicate Technology
NĚMEC, L., Inorganic Materials Laboratory
NOVÁK, J., Physical Chemistry
NOVÁK, P., Chemical Metallurgy and Corrosion Engineering
PÁCA, J., Fermentation Chemistry and Biotechnology
PALEČEK, J., Organic Chemistry
PALETA, O., Organic Chemistry
PAŠEK, J., Organic Technology
PECKA, K., Petroleum Technology and Petrochemistry
PITTER, P., Water Technology and Environmental Engineering
POKORNÝ, J., Food Chemistry and Technology
PORUBSKÝ, Š., Mathematics
PROCHÁZKA, A., Computing and Control Engineering
RAUCH, P., Biochemistry
RODA, J., Polymers
RUML, T., Biochemistry and Microbiology
RŮŽIČKA, V., Physical Chemistry
RYCHTERA, M., Fermentation Chemistry and Biotechnology
SCHMIDT, O., Automated Control Systems
SLÁDEČKOVÁ, A., Water Technology and Environmental Engineering
STIBOR, I., Organic Chemistry
SUCHANEK, M., Analytical Chemistry
ŠEBOR, G., Petroleum Technology and Petrochemistry
ŠVOBODA, J., Organic Chemistry
ŠVORČÍK, V., Materials Science
VELÍŠEK, J., Food Chemistry and Technology
VOLKA, K., Analytical Chemistry
WANNER, J., Water Technology and Environmental Engineering
ZÁBRANSKÁ, J., Water Technology and Environmental Engineering

VYSOKÁ ŠKOLA EKONOMICKÁ V PRAZE
(University of Economics, Prague)

Nám. W. Churchilla 4, 130 67 Prague 3
Telephone: 224095799
Fax: 224095695
E-mail: brazdova@vse.cz
Internet: www.vse.cz

Founded 1919
State control
Languages of instruction: Czech, English
Academic year: September to May

Rector: Prof. JAROSLAVA DURČÁKOVÁ
Vice-Rectors: Prof. IGOR ČERMÁK, Prof. BRONISLAVA HOŘEJŠÍ, Prof. VOJTĚCH KREBS, Prof. JIŘÍ PATOČKA, Prof. ZBYNĚK REVENDA
Bursar: JIŘÍ KŘÍŽ
Number of students: 14,000

Publications: *Acta Economica Pragensia* (2 a year), *Politická Ekonomie* (6 a year), *Prague Economic Papers* (4 a year)

DEANS

Business Administration: Prof. JIŘÍ KLEIBL
Economics and Public Administration: Prof. JIŘÍ SCHWARZ
Finance and Accounting: Prof. BOJKA HAMERNÍKOVÁ
Informatics and Statistics: Prof. RICHARD HINDLS
International Relations: Prof. DANA ZADRAŽILOVÁ
Management: Prof. PAVEL PUDIL

VYSOKÉ UČENÍ TECHNICKÉ V BRNĚ
(Brno University of Technology)

Antonínská 1, 601 90 Brno
Telephone: 541145111
Fax: 541211309
E-mail: rektor@ro.vutbr.cz
Internet: www.vutbr.cz

Founded 1899
State control
Language of instruction: Czech
Academic year: September to July

Rector: Prof. RNDr Ing. JAN VRBKA
Pro-Rectors: Asst Prof. PETR DUB, Prof. RNDr JOSEF JANČÁŘ, Prof. Ing. JIŘÍ KAZELLE, Asst Prof. LADISLAV ŠTĚPÁNEK
Registrar: Ing. JAROMÍR PĚNČÍK
Director of Public Relations and Administration: Mgr JITKA VANÝSKOVÁ
Librarian: NATAŠA JURSOVÁ

Number of teachers: 1,026
Number of students: 15,090

Publication: *Události na VUT v Brně* (monthly)

DEANS

Faculty of Architecture: Asst Prof. Ing. JOSEF CHYBÍK
Faculty of Business and Management: Asst Prof. Ing. KAREL RAIS
Faculty of Chemistry: Prof. Ing. MILAN DRDÁK
Faculty of Civil Engineering: Asst Prof. Ing. JAROSLAV PUCHRÍK
Faculty of Electrical Engineering and Communication: Prof. Ing. RADIMÍR VRBA
Faculty of Fine Arts: Prof. Dr JAN SEDLÁK
Faculty of Information Technology: Prof. Ing. TOMÁŠ HRUŠKA
Faculty of Mechanical Engineering: Prof. Ing. JOSEF VAČKÁŘ

PROFESSORS

Faculty of Architecture (Poříčí 5, 639 00 Brno; tel. 541146600; fax 542142125; e-mail chybik@ucit.fa.vutbr.cz; internet www.fa.vutbr.cz):

GŘEGORČÍK, J., Urban Studies
RULLER, I., Public Constructions
VAVERKA, J., Building Construction
ZEMÁNKOVÁ, H., Industrial Architecture

Faculty of Business and Management (Technická 2, 616 69 Brno; tel. 541141111; fax 541142458; e-mail dean@fbm.vutbr.cz; internet www.fbm.vutbr.cz):

DVOŘÁK, J., Economy and Management
KONEČNÝ, M., Economy and Management
MEZNÍK, I., Mathematics
NĚMEČEK, P., Economy and Management

Faculty of Chemistry (Purkyňova 118, 612 00 Brno; tel. 541149111; fax 541211697; e-mail drdak@fch.vutbr.cz; internet www.fch.vutbr.cz):

BRANDŠTETR, J., Chemistry of Materials
DRDÁK, M., Food Science and Biotechnology
FRIEDL, Z., Chemistry and Technology of Environmental Protection
JANČA, J., Chemistry
JANČÁŘ, J., Chemistry of Materials
KUČERA, M., Chemistry of Materials
NEŠPŮREK, S., Chemistry
OMELKA, L., Chemistry
PELIKÁN, P., Chemistry
RYCHTERA, M., Food Science and Biotechnology
SCHAUER, F., Environmental Chemistry and Technology
SOMMER, L., Chemistry and Technology of Environmental Protection
WEIN, O., Chemistry

Faculty of Civil Engineering (Veveří 95, 662 37 Brno; tel. 541147111; fax 5745147; e-mail dekan@fce.vutbr.cz; internet www.fce.vutbr.cz):

ADÁMEK, J., Structural Materials and Testing Methods
DROCHYTKA, R., Technology of Building Materials and Components
FIXEL, J., Geodesy
KOČÍ, J., Building Construction
KOKTAVÝ, B., Physics
MELCHER, J., Metal and Timber Structures
MYSLÍN, J., Building Construction
NEVOSÁD, Z., Geodesy
ŠÁLEK, J., Water Resources Management
STRÁSKÝ, J., Concrete and Masonry Structures

Faculty of Electrical Engineering and Communication (Údolní 53, 602 00 Brno; tel. 541141111; fax 541146100; e-mail dekan@feec.vutbr.cz; internet www.feec.vutbr.cz):

AUTRATA, R., Electrical and Electronic Technology
BIOLEK, D., Telecommunications
BRZOBOHATÝ, J., Microelectronics
CHVALINA, J., Mathematics
DIBLÍK, J., Mathematics
DOSTÁL, T., Radioelectronics
HAVEL, V., Mathematics
HONZÍKOVÁ, N., Biomedical Engineering
HRUŠKA, K., Physics
JAN, J., Biomedical Engineering
KAZELLE, J., Electrical and Electronic Technology
MELKES, F., Mathematics
MUSIL, V., Microelectronics
PIVOŇKA, P., Automation
POSPÍŠIL, J., Radioelectronics
PROCHÁZKA, P., Electrical Engineering
ŘÍČNÝ, V., Radioelectronics
ŠEBESTA, V., Radioelectronics
SIKULA, J., Physics
SKALICKÝ, J., Power Electrical and Electronic Engineering
SMÉKAL, Z., Telecommunications
SVAČINA, J., Radioelectronics
TOMÁNEK, P., Physics
VALSA, J., Electrical Engineering
VAVŘÍN, P., Automation and Measurement Engineering
VOMELA, J., Biomedical Engineering
VRBA, K., Telecommunications
VRBA, R., Microelectronics

Faculty of Fine Arts (Rybářská 13, 603 00 Brno; tel. 543146850; fax 543212670; e-mail dekan@ffa.vutbr.cz; internet www.ffa.vutbr.cz):

NAČERADSKÝ, J., Painting
RONAI, P., Figure Painting
SEDLÁK, J., History of Art

Faculty of Information Technology (Božetěchova 2, 612 66 Brno; tel. 541141139; fax 541141270; e-mail info@fit.vutbr.cz; internet www.fit.vutbr.cz):

ČEŠKA, M., Intelligent Systems
DVOŘÁK, V., Computer Systems
HONZÍK, J., Information Systems
HRUŠKA, T., Information Systems
SERBA, I., Computer Graphics and Multimedia

Faculty of Mechanical Engineering (Technická 2, 616 00 Brno; tel. 541141111; fax 541142222; e-mail dekan@fme.vutbr.cz; internet www.fme.vutbr.cz):

BABINEC, F., Process Engineering
BOHÁČEK, F., Machine Design
BUMBÁLEK, B., Technology
CHMELA, P., Optics and Fine Mechanics
CIHLÁŘ, J., Ceramics
DRUCKMÜLLER, M., Stochastics, Teaching of Mathematics
FILAKOVSKÝ, K., Aircraft Design
FOREJT, M., Snagging Technology
HLAVENKA, B., Production Engineering
JANÍČEK, P., Mechanics of Solids
JÍCHA, M., Heat and Nuclear Power
KAČUR, J., Mathematics
KADRNOŽKA, J., Heat and Nuclear Power
KAVIČKA, F., Heat and Nuclear Power
KOCMAN, K., Production Engineering
KOHOUTEK, J., Process Engineering
KOMRSKÁ, J., Physics
KRATOCHVÍL, O., Mechanics of Solids
KULČÁK, L., Aerospace Engineering
LIŠKA, M., Physics
MATAL, O., Heat and Nuclear Power
MEDEK, J., Process Engineering
NOVÁK, V., Mathematics
PÍŠTĚK, A., Aerospace Engineering
PÍŠTĚK, V., Combustion Engines and Motor Vehicles
POCHYLÝ, F., Heat and Nuclear Power
POKLUDA, J., Physics
PTÁČEK, L., Materials Engineering
RUSÍN, K., Foundry Engineering
SCHNEIDER, P., Process Engineering
SEDLÁČEK, B., Aerospace Engineering
ŠLAPAL, J., Mathematics, Teaching of Mathematics
SLAVÍK, J., Mechanics of Solids
STEHLÍK, P., Process Engineering
ŠTĚPÁNEK, M., Automation and Computer Science
STRÁNSKÝ, K., Materials Engineering
ŠVEJCAR, J., Materials Engineering
VAČKÁŘ, J., Quality and Metrology
VLK, F., Combustion Engines and Motor Vehicles
VRBKA, J., Mechanics of Solids
ŽENÍŠEK, A., Mathematics

ZÁPADOČESKÁ UNIVERZITA
(University of West Bohemia)

Univerzitní 8, 306 14 Plzeň
Telephone: 377631111
Fax: 377631112
E-mail: rektor@rek.zcu.cz
Internet: www.zcu.cz

Founded 1949 as Plzeň Institute of Technology, present name 1991
State control
Language of instruction: Czech
Academic year: September to June

Rector: Doc. Ing. JOSEF PRŮŠA
Vice-Rectors: Prof. RNDr IVO BUDIL, Doc. RNDr FRANTIŠEK JEŽEK, PhDr EVA PASÁČKOVÁ, Dr Ing. JAN RYCHLÍK, Doc. Ing. JAN HOREJC
Chancellor: PhDr HELENA HEJDOVÁ
Registrar: Ing. ANTONÍN BULÍN
Librarians: PhDr MILOSLAVA FAITOVÁ, Mgr ALENA SCHOŘOVSKÁ

Library of 377,527 vols
Number of teachers: 1,192
Number of students: 17,270

Publications: *Stady* (univ. papers, monthly), *Trojúhelník* (univ. journal, quarterly)

DEANS

Faculty of Applied Sciences: Prof. Ing. JIŘÍ KŘEN
Faculty of Economics: Doc. PhDr MILAN HRDÝ
Faculty of Education: Doc. PaedDr JANA COUFALOVÁ
Faculty of Electrical Engineering: Doc. Ing. JIŘÍ KOTLAN
Faculty of Law: JUDr JAROSLAV COUFALOVÁ
Faculty of Mechanical Engineering: Doc. Ing. JIŘÍ STANĚK
Faculty of Philosophy and Arts: Doc. PhDr LADISLAV CABADA

PROFESSORS

Faculty of Applied Sciences (Univerzitní 22, 306 14 Plzeň; tel. 377632000; fax 377632002; internet www.fav.zcu.cz):

BALDA, M., Mechanics
DRÁBEK, P., Mathematics
KŘEN, J., Continuum Mechanics, Biomechanics
KUČERA, M., Mathematics
KUFNER, A., Mathematics
KUNEŠ, J., Applied Physics
MATOUŠEK, V., Man–Machine Communication
MÍKA, S., Mathematics
MUSIL, J., Applied Physics
PLÁNIČKA, F., Mechanics
PŘIKRYL, P., Mathematics
PSUTKA, J., Cybernetics
ROSENBERG, J., Mechanics
RYJÁČEK, Z., Mathematics
SCHLEGEL, M., Cybernetics
SKALA, V., Computer Graphics
ŠESTÁK, J., Mechanics
ŠIMANDL, M., Cybernetics
ŠŤASTNÝ, M., Mechanics
VLČEK, J., Applied Physics
ŽAMPA, P., Cybernetics
ZEMAN, V., Mechanics

Faculty of Economics (Husova 11, 306 14 Plzeň; tel. 377633000; fax 377633002; internet www.fek.zcu.cz):

KŘIKAČ, K., Organization and Management of Engineering Production
MACH, M., Business Economics
MACEK, J., Statistics in Economics
SEMENIUK, P., Marketing, Trade and Services

Faculty of Education (Sedláčkova 38, 306 14 Plzeň; tel. 377636000; fax 377636002; internet www.fpe.zcu.cz):

JÍLEK, T., Teaching of History
KRAITR, M., Teaching of Chemistry
KUMPERA, J., Teaching of History
MEHNERT, E., Teaching of German Language
NEUBERT, R., Teaching of German Language – Modern German Literature for Children and Young People
NOVÁK, J., Teaching of Chemistry
PILOUS, V., Materials Engineering
RYCHTECKÝ, A., Physical Training
VÁŇA, J., Biology
VIKTORA, V., Czech Language

Faculty of Electrical Engineering (Univerzitní 26, 306 14 Plzeň; tel. 377634000; fax 377634002; internet www.fel.zcu.cz):

BARTOŠ, V., Electrical Machines and Apparatus
BENEŠOVÁ, Z., Theory of Electrical Engineering
DOLEŽEL, I., Theory of Electrical Engineering
HALLER, R., Electric Power Engineering
JERHOT, J., Electronics and Vacuum Technology
KOŽENÝ, J., Electric Power Engineering
KŮS, V., Electrical Drives and Power Electronics
MAYER, D., Theory of Electrical Engineering
MENTLÍK, V., Electrical Technology
MÜHLBACHER, J., Electric Power Engineering
PINKER, J., Electronic Systems
RYBÁŘ, J., Electrical Machine Design, Cooling
VONDRÁŠEK, F., Electrical Drives and Power Electronics
VOSTRACKÝ, Z., Electric Power Engineering

Faculty of Law (Sady Pětatřicátníků 14, 306 14 Plzeň; tel. 377637000; fax 377637002; internet www.fpr.zcu.cz):

ADAMOVÁ, S., History of the State and Law
BALÍK, S., History of the State and Law
ELIÁŠ, K., Commercial Law
GERLOCH, A., Theory of Law
HRONCOVÁ, J., Social Pathology
KNAPPOVÁ, M., Civil Law
KOPAL, V., International Law

KOSOVÁ, B., Social Pathology
KUČERA, Z., International Law
NOVÁK, M., Sociology
PAUKNEROVÁ, M., International Law
RŮŽIČKA, K., International Law
RYBÁŘ, M., Criminology
ŠÁMAL, P., Criminal Law
VÁLKOVÁ, H., Criminal Law

Faculty of Mechanical Engineering (Univerzitní 22, 306 14 Plzeň; tel. 377638000; fax 377638002; internet www.fst.zcu.cz):

BASL, J., Computer Integrated Production Systems
HOSNEDL, S., Machine Design
LEEDER, E., Computer Integrated Production Systems
LINHART, J., Power System Engineering
MAREŠ, R., Thermomechanics
MAŠEK, B., Materials Science and Metallography
PFROGNER, F., Materials Science and Metallography
ŠKOPEK, J., Power System Engineering
SOVA, F., Machining Technology
STEINER, M., Machine Design
ZRNÍK, J., Materials Science and Metallography

Faculty of Philosophy and Arts (Sedláčkova 38, 306 14 Plzeň; tel. 377635000; fax 377635002; internet www.ff.zcu.cz):

BLAŽEK, V., Anthropology
BUDIL, I., Anthropology
DOUBRAVOVÁ, J., Philosophy
FUNDA, O., Philosophy
HELUS, Z., Psychology
HRUŠKA, B., History
NEÚSTUPNÝ, E., Archaeology
VESELÝ, R., Oriental Sciences
VOPĚNKA, P., Philosophy

ATTACHED RESEARCH INSTITUTES

Institute of Art and Design: tel. 377636700; fax 377636702; e-mail mistera@uud.zcu.cz; internet www.uud.zcu.cz; Dir Doc., Akad. mal. JOSEF MIŠTERA.

New Technologies Research Centre: tel. 377634700; fax 377634702; e-mail rosen@ntc.zcu.cz; internet www.ntc.zcu.cz; Dir Prof. Ing. JOSEF ROSENBERG.

Schools of Art and Music

AKADEMIE MÚZICKÝCH UMĚNÍ
(Academy of Performing Arts)

Malostranské nám. 12, 118 00 Prague 1Telephone: 257534205
Fax: 257530405
Internet: www.amu.cz
Founded 1945
Languages of instruction: Czech, English
Academic year: October to June
Rector: IVO MATHÉ
Vice-Rectors: ZDENĚK KIRSCHNER, MIROSLAV KLÍMA
Registrar: TAMARA ČUŘÍKOVÁ
Library of 161,374 vols
Number of teachers: 338
Number of students: 1,178
Publications: *Acta Academica Informatorium* (10 a year), *Disk* (4 a year)

DEANS

Faculty of Film and Television: MICHAL BREGANT
Faculty of Music: JIŘÍ HLAVÁČ
Faculty of Theatre: MARKÉTA KOČVAROVÁ-SCHARTOVÁ

AKADEMIE VÝTVARNÝCH UMĚNÍ
(Academy of Fine Arts)

U akademie 4, 170 22 Prague 7
Telephone: 220408200
Fax: 233381662
E-mail: avu@avu.cz
Internet: www.avu.cz
Founded 1799
Languages of instruction: Czech, English
Academic year: October to July
Rector: Prof. JIŘÍ SOPKO
Pro-Rectors: Prof. EMIL PŘIKRYL, Doc. JIŘÍ LINDOVSKÝ
Registrar: Ing. VLADIMÍR KALUGIN
Library of 75,000 vols
Number of teachers: 58
Number of students: 265
Publications: *Almanach*, *Exhibition Catalogues*.

JANÁČKOVA AKADEMIE MÚZICKÝCH UMĚNÍ V BRNĚ
(Janáček Academy of Music and Performing Art in Brno)

Beethovenova 2, 662 15 Brno
Telephone: 542591111
Fax: 542591140
E-mail: rektor@jamu.cz
Internet: www.jamu.cz
Founded 1947
Languages of instruction: Czech, English
Academic year: September to June
Rector: Prof. VÁCLAV CEJPEK
Vice-Rector: Prof. PhDr LEOŠ FALTUS
Vice-Rector: Doc. PhDr MIROSLAV PLEŠÁK
Registrar: JUDr LENKA VALOVÁ
Library of 100,000 vols; special collections of printed music and records
Number of teachers: 118
Number of students: 580.

VYSOKÁ ŠKOLA UMĚLECKOPRŮMYSLOVÁ
(Academy of Art, Architecture and Design)

nám. Jana Palacha 80, 116 93 Prague 2
Telephone: 251098111
Fax: 251098289
E-mail: pr@vsup.cz
Internet: www.vsup.cz
Founded 1885
Rector: Dr JIŘÍ PELCL
Vice-Rector for International and Public Relations: Dr MARTINA PACHMANOVÁ
Vice-Rector for Study: Dr PAVLA PEČINKOVÁ
Registrar: Ing. LUBOŠ KVAPIL
Number of teachers: 55
Number of students: 400.

Janáčkova konzervatoř v Ostravě: Českobratrská 40, 729 62 Moravská Ostrava; tel. 596112007; fax 596111443; internet www.volweb.cz/jko; f. 1953; 145 teachers; 376 students; library: 23,000 vols, 7,000 records; Dir MILAN BÁCHOREK.

Konzervatoř, Brno (Conservatoire in Brno): třída kpt. Jaroše 45, 662 54 Brno; tel. 545215568; fax 545215568; f. 1919; music and drama departments; 124 professors; 360 students; library: 7,000 vols, 29,900 scores, 1,600 records; Dir Mgr E. ZÁMEČNÍK.

Konzervatoř P. J. Vejvanovského, Kroměříž: Pilařova 7, 767 64 Kroměříž; tel. 573339501; fax 573343270; e-mail mus.cons-km@snt.cz; internet www.konzkm.cz; f. 1949; 55 teachers; 190 students; library: 16,000 vols, 4,600 records; Dir M. ŠIŠKA.

Konzervatoř, Pardubice: Sukova třída 1260, 530 02 Pardubice; tel. and fax 466513503; e-mail reditelstvi@konzervatorpardubice.cz; internet www.konzervatorpardubice.cz; f. 1978; 79 teachers; 172 students; library: 2,200 books, 7,500 vols of music, 1,100 records; Dir Mgr JAROMÍR HÖNIG.

Konzervatoř, Plzeň: Kopeckého sady 10, 301 00 Plzeň; tel. 377226325; fax 377226387; e-mail sekretariat@konzervatorplzen.cz; internet www.konzervatorplzen.cz; f. 1961; 78 teachers; 158 students; library: 1,500 books, 1,400 records and CDs, 7,000 scores; Dir MIROSLAV BREJCHA.

Konzervatoř, Teplice: Hudba a Zpěv, Českobratrská 15, 415 01 Teplice; tel. 417538425; fax 417532645; e-mail studijni@konzervatorteplice.cz; internet www.konzervatorteplice.cz; f. 1971; 80 teachers; 200 students; library: 10,000 vols, 800 records; Dir Mgr MILAN KUBÍK.

Pražská konzervatoř: Na Rejdišti 1, 110 00 Prague 1; tel. 222319102; fax 222326406; e-mail conserv@prgcons.cz; internet www.prgcons.cz; f. 1808254 professors; 600 students; library: 85,000 vols, 19,000 records; Dir Mgr PAVEL TROJAN; Chief of Library (Archives) MILOSLAV RICHTER.

Taneční konzervatoř Praha (Prague Conservatory of Dance): Křižovnická 7, 110 00 Prague 1; tel. 222319145; fax 222324977; e-mail taneckonzpr@volny.cz; internet www.balet.cz/tkpraha; f. 1945; small library; languages of instruction: Czech, English; 60 teachers; 200 students; Dir Mgr JAROSLAV SLAVICKÝ; publ. *Taneční listy* (Dance Review).

DENMARK

The Higher Education System

Københavens Universitet (founded 1479) is the oldest university in Denmark. There are 12 universities and technical universities and many other university-level institutions, such as professional schools and polytechnics, which offer short- and medium-cycle programmes. These university-level institutions are to be merged into supra-institutions under legislation enacted in 1998 and 2001. Short-cycle vocational colleges are being reorganized as erhvervsakademier (vocational academies) and medium-cycle colleges are being merged into Centres for Higher Education. There is also a university in the Faroe Islands, as well as colleges there and in Greenland.

The higher education system is financed by the State; since 2001 the Ministry of Science, Technology and Innovation has been responsible for higher education. (However, the Ministry of Cultural Affairs oversees arts and cultural education programmes, and the Ministry of Education is responsible for short- and medium-cycle higher education.) The Act on the Universities (1992) extended the traditional academic freedom and autonomy enjoyed by the universities, but the Ministries still dictate regulations on *inter alia* admissions, curricula, quality assurance and appointments of academic staff. Quality assurance in the public universities is overseen by the Danish Evaluation Institute, which has incorporated the former Centre for Quality Assurance and Evaluation of Higher Education. Private universities must submit to an accreditation process run by the Danish Educational Support Agency, a body of the Ministry of Education.

To attend university, students must possess one of the secondary school leaving certificates (or equivalent qualification), namely studentereksamen (Upper Secondary School Leaving Examination), højere forberedelseseksamen (Higher Preparatory Examination), højere handelseksamen eksamen (Higher Business Examination) or højere teknisk eksamen (Higher Technical Examination). The number of available places each year is stipulated by the Minister of Education. Since legislation of 1993, reform of the higher education system of qualifications has broadly brought Denmark into line with the Bologna Process, and the standard degree system consists of Bachelors, Masters (candidatus) and Doctorate. The Bachelors undergraduate degree takes three to three-and-a-half years, or longer for professional programmes such as engineering or medicine. The Masters degree (candidatus) requires two years of study following the Bachelors, and a Doctorate is awarded following at least eight years of higher education.

There are 15 short-cycle, professionally-orientated programmes (erhvervsakademiuddannelser) offered by the erhvervsakademier (vocational academies), which last two years, and 20 medium-cycle programmes offered by Centres for Higher Education, leading to the award of the title of professionsbachelor (Professional Bachelors). Adult and continuing education was reformed under Act No. 488 (2000), which created three levels of qualifications: Videregående voksenuddannelse (advanced adult education), Diplomuddannelse (Diploma programmes) and Masteruddannelse (Masters programmes). Programmes of study last two years (part-time).

Technical and vocational education consist of erhvervsuddannelser (training programmes), grundlæggende social- og sundhedsuddannelser (basic social and health education) and other programmes in different fields. These courses are offered by tekniske skoler (technical colleges), handelsskoler (business colleges), landbrugsskoler (agricultural colleges) and social- og sundhedsskoler (social and healthcare colleges). There are a total of 85 programmes of vocational education.

Regulatory and Representative Bodies

GOVERNMENT

Ministry of Culture: Nybrogade 2, POB 2140, 1015 Copenhagen K; tel. 33-92-33-70; fax 33-91-33-88; e-mail kum@kum.dk; internet www.kum.dk; Minister BRIAN MIKKELSEN.

Ministry of Education: Frederiksholms Kanal 21–25, 1220 Copenhagen K; tel. 33-92-50-00; fax 33-92-55-47; e-mail uvm@uvm.dk; internet www.uvm.dk; Minister BERTEL HAARDER.

Ministry of Science, Technology and Innovation: Bredgade 43, 1260 Copenhagen K; tel. 33-92-97-00; fax 33-32-35-01; e-mail vtu@vtu.dk; internet www.videnskabsministeriet.dk; Minister HELGE SANDER.

ACCREDITATION

Danmarks Evalueringsinstitut (EVA) (Danish Evaluation Institute): Østbanegade 55, 3. sal, 2100 Copenhagen Ø; tel. 35-55-01-01; fax 35-55-10-11; e-mail eva@eva.dk; internet www.eva.dk; f. initiates and conducts evaluations of teaching and learning, evaluations cover public educational establishments and private institutions in receipt of state subsidy; acts as centre of knowledge for educational evaluation: compiles, produces and communicates nat. and int. experiences in the field of educational evaluation; may initiate evaluations on request, these evaluations are conducted as revenue-generating activities and may be requested by the govt, ministries and advisory boards, local authorities and educational establishments; offers courses in methods of self-evaluation, gives presentations on quality issues, and acts as sparring partner should the need arise among e.g. educational institutions and local authorities; conducts accreditation of several courses and institutions incl. Univ. Colleges and private courses, determining whether students at private teaching establishments should receive the Danish state grant; organized in 3 educational units: nusery and pre-school, basic teaching and education, higher education; unit specialized in methodology focusing on internal and external quality assurance; unit specialized in communication and information work; administrative unit; ; Dir AGI CSONKA.

FUNDING

Styrelsen for Statens Uddannelsesstøtte (Danish Educational Support Agency): Danasvej 30, 1780 Copenhagen V; tel. 33-26-86-00; fax 33-26-86-11; e-mail sustyrelsen@su.dk; internet www.sustyrelsen.dk; attached to Min. of Education; administers the Statens Uddannelsesstøtte (State Education Grant and Loan Scheme); prepares amendments of the scheme, registers applications, pays out grants and loans, offers guidance and information to the educational institutions, deals with complaints and appeals (which are decided by a Board of Appeal), draws up budgets and collects statistics for the use of the Min.; Dir HANNA DAM.

NATIONAL BODIES

Folkeuniversitetet (University Extension Services in Denmark): c/o Syddansk Universitet, Campusvej 55, 5230 Odense M; tel. 65-50-27-27; e-mail sekr@fu.dk; internet www.folkeuniversitet.dk; f. 1898 to promote education among the Danish population, in particular those unable to gain access to univs; Chair. EVA MØLLER; Man. Dir Dr SØREN EIGAARD.

Rektorkollegiet (Danish Rectors' Conference): Fiolstraede 44, 1. th, 1171 Copenhagen K; tel. 33-92-54-05; fax 33-92-50-75; e-mail rks@rks.dk; internet www.rks.dk; f. 1967; asscn of 8 Danish research univs; promotes interests of the univ. sector in dealings with the Min. of Science, Technology and Innovation; Exec. Dir SUSANNE BJERREGAARD.

Learned Societies

GENERAL

Kongelige Danske Videnskabernes Selskab (Royal Danish Academy of Science and Letters): H. C. Andersens Blvd 35, 1553 Copenhagen V; tel. 33-43-53-00; fax 33-43-53-01; e-mail kdvs@royalacademy.dk; internet www.royalacademy.dk; f. 1742; arranges meetings, seminars, symposia, public lectures, publishes journals; sections of History and Philosophy (Chair. CARL HENRIK KOCH), Mathematics and Natural Sciences (Chair. CHRISTIAN BERG); 499 mems (250 Danish, 250 foreign); Pres. Prof. Dr phil. TOM FENCHEL; Gen. Sec. and Treasurer Prof. Dr scient. HENRIK BREUNING-MADSEN; Head of Secretariat PIA GRÜNER; publs *Historisk-filosofiske Meddelelser* (history, philosophy, philology, archaeology, art history, irreg.), *Historisk-filosofiske Skrifter* (history, philosophy, philology, archaeology, art history, irreg.), *Matematisk-fysiske Meddelelser* (history, philosophy, philology, archaeology, art history, irreg.), *Meddelelser* (botany, zoology, palaeontology, general biology, irreg.), *Oversigt/Yearbook* (annually).

AGRICULTURE, FISHERIES AND VETERINARY SCIENCE

Dansk Skovforening (Danish Forestry Society): Amalievej 20, 1875 Frederiksberg C; tel. 33-24-42-66; fax 33-24-02-42; e-mail info@skovforeningen.dk; internet www.skovforeningen.dk; f. 1888; attends to the commercial and professional interests of Danish forestry; Chair. NIELS IUEL REVENTLOW; Dir JAN SØNDERGAARD; publ. *Skoven* (monthly).

Dansk Veterinærhistorisk Samfund (Danish Veterinary History Society): Ejgaardsparken 6, st. th., 2920 Charlottenlund; tel. 97-97-10-01; e-mail anton-rosenbom@post.tele.dk; f. 1934; 320 mems; annual European tour and seminar on the history of veterinary medicine; Pres. Dr ANTON ROSENBOM; publ. *Dansk Veterinærhistorisk Årbog* (every 2 years).

Foreningen af Mejeriledere og Funktionærer (Association of Dairy Managers): Det gamle Mejeri, Landbrugsvej 65, 5260 Odense S; tel. 66-12-40-25; fax 66-14-40-26; e-mail fmf@Maelkeritidende.dk; internet www.maelkeritidende.dk; f. 1887; 823 mems; Technical Dir SØREN STEEN JENSEN; publ. *Maelkeritidende* (every 2 weeks).

Jordbrugsakademikernes Forbund (Danish Federation of Graduates in Agriculture, Horticulture, Forestry and Landscape Architecture): Emdrupvej 28A, 2100 Copenhagen Ø; tel. 33-21-28-00; fax 38-71-03-22; e-mail post@jordbrugsakademikerne.dk; internet www.jordbrugsakademikerne.dk; f. 1976; 5,500 mems; Dir OVE HÖILUND MORTENSEN; publs *Jord og Viden*, *moMentum*.

Kongelige Danske Landhusholdningsselskab (Royal Danish Agricultural Society): Jacob Gades Allé 12, 6000 Vejen; e-mail lhs@1769.dk; internet www.1769.dk; f. 1769; Pres. PER BACH LAURSEN.

ARCHITECTURE AND TOWN PLANNING

Akademisk Arkitektforening (Architects' Association of Denmark): Arkitekternes Hus, Strandgade 27A, 1401 Copenhagen K; tel. 32-83-69-00; fax 32-83-69-01; e-mail aa@aa-dk.dk; internet www.arkitektforeningen.dk; f. 1951; 6,700 mems; Pres. GØSTA KNUDSEN; Dir BENTE BEEDHOLM; publs *Arkitekten*, *Arkitektur*.

Dansk Byplanlaboratorium (Danish Town Planning Institute): Nørregade 36, 1 - 1165 Copenhagen K; tel. 33-13-72-81; fax 33-14-34-35; e-mail db@byplanlab.dk; internet www.byplanlab.dk; f. 1921; educational services and seminars; library of 17,000 vols; complete collection of public documents and reports concerning urban and regional planning in Denmark; Chair. FREDDY AVNBY; Sec. (vacant) ELLEN HØJGAARD JENSEN; publ. *Dansk Byplanlaboratorium*.

BIBLIOGRAPHY, LIBRARY SCIENCE AND MUSEOLOGY

Biblioteksstyrelsen (National Library Authority): Nyhavn 31E, 1051 Copenhagen K; tel. 33-73-33-73; fax 33-73-33-72; e-mail bs@bs.dk; internet www.bs.dk; f. 1990 by merging of Rigsbibliotekarembedet and Bibliotekstilsynet; adviser to Govt on matters concerning academic and special libraries, public libraries, and information and documentation problems; administrator of development pools and grants, and of national Electronic Research Library; National Librarian JENS THORHAUGE; publ. *Nyt fra Nyhavn* (quarterly).

Danmarks Biblioteksforening (Danish Library Association): Vesterbrogade 20/5, 1620 Copenhagen 5; tel. 33-25-09-35; fax 33-25-79-00; e-mail dbf@dbf.dk; internet www.dbf.dk; f. 1905 to advance the development of the public library system; Pres. FINN VESTER; Dir WINNIE VITZANSKY; publs *Biblioteksvejviser* (Directory, annually), *Danmarks Biblioteker* (Newsletter, 10 a year).

Danmarks Forskningsbiblioteksforening (Danish Research Library Association): DF Secretariat, Statsbiblioteket, Universitetsparken, 8000 Århus C; tel. 89-46-22-07; fax 89-46-22-20; e-mail df@statsbiblioteket.dk; f. 1978; 700 personal, 145 institutional mems; Pres. CLAUS VESTERAGER PEDERSEN; publ. *DF-Revy* (8 a year).

Dansk Biblioteks Center AS: Tempovej 7–11, 2750 Ballerup; tel. 44-86-77-77; fax 44-86-78-91; e-mail dbc@dbc.dk; internet www.dbc.dk; f. 1991; provides Danish libraries with bibliographic data, a union catalogue, databases and online products; Man. Dir MOGENS BRABAND JENSEN; publ. *DBC Avisen* (4 a year).

Organisationen Danske Museer: Gl. Strandvej 2, 2990 Nivå; tel. 49-14-39-66; fax 49-14-39-67; e-mail info@mussek.dk; internet www.dkm-mus.dk; f. 2005 by merger of Foreningen af Danske Kunstmuseer and Dansk Kulturhistorisk Museums Forening; annual assemblies and study meetings; 200 institutional mems; Chair LENE FLORIS; Sec. KIRSTEN REX ANDERSEN.

ECONOMICS, LAW AND POLITICS

Danmarks Jurist- og Økonomforbund (Danish Lawyers and Economists Association): Gothersgade 133, POB 2126, 1015 Copenhagen K; tel. 33-95-97-00; fax 33-95-99-99; e-mail djoef@djoef.dk; internet www.djoef.dk; f. 1972; 47,503 mems; Pres. FINN BORCH ANDERSEN; Dir-Gen. MOGENS KRING RASMUSSEN; publs *DJØF Efteruddannelse* (2 a year), *Juristen* (law, 6 times a year), *Samfundsøkonomen* (societal economics, 6 times a year).

Dansk Selskab for Europaforskning (Danish Society for European Studies): c/o Centre for European Studies, University of Southern Denmark, Campusvej 55, 5230 Odense M; tel. 65-50-22-17; fax 65-50-22-80; e-mail ecsa-dk@sam.sdu.dk; internet www.ecsa.dk; f. 1975; aims to promote Danish academic study and teaching of the legal, economic, political and social aspects of European integration, by means of seminars and publications; 100 mems; Pres. Prof. FINN LAURSEN; Sec. STEN RYNNING.

International Law Association–Danish Branch: c/o Advocat Jan Erlund, Gorissen Federspiel Kierkegaard, H. C. Andersen Blvd 12, 1553 Copenhagen; fax 33-41-41-33; e-mail al@gfklaw.dk; f. 1925; Pres. ALEX LAUDRUP.

Nationalekonomisk Forening (Danish Economic Association): Danmarks Nationalbank, Havnegade 5, 1093 Copenhagen K; tel. 33-63-63-63; fax 33-63-71-15; internet www.econ.ku.dk/nf; f. 1873; 1,000 mems; Chair. Prof. MICHAEL MØLLER; Sec. SØREN STORMINGER-DALGAARD; publ. *Nationaloekonomisk Tidsskrift* (3 a year).

Udenrigspolitiske Selskab (Foreign Policy Society): Amaliegade 40A, 1256 Copenhagen K; tel. 33-14-88-86; fax 33-14-85-20; e-mail udenrigs@udenrigs.dk; internet www.udenrigs.dk; f. 1946; studies, debates, publs and conferences on int. affairs; library of 100 periodicals; 1,000 individual mems, 200 corporate mems; Dir KLAUS CARSTEN PEDERSEN; Sec. BRITA V. ANDERSEN; publ. *Udenrigs* (quarterly).

EDUCATION

Mellemfolkeligt Samvirke (Danish Association for International Co-operation): Borgergade 14, 1300 Copenhagen K; tel. 77-31-00-00; fax 77-31-01-01; e-mail ms@ms.dk; internet www.ms.dk; f. 1944; administration of Danish development workers and International Work Camps; public information service on the problems of developing countries and international co-operation; 6,300 mems; library of 40,000 vols on third world issues, immigrants and refugees in Denmark, 600 periodicals, 1,300 films; Gen. Sec. LARS UDSHOLT; publs *Etcetera* (8 a year), *FOCUS Kontakt* (6 a year), *Kontakt Globalt Magasin* (6 a year), *ZAPP Jorden Rundt* (6 a year).

FINE AND PERFORMING ARTS

Billedkunstnernes Forbund (Danish Association of Visual Artists): Vingårdstræde 21, 1070 Copenhagen K; tel. 33-12-81-70; fax 33-32-28-39; e-mail bkf@bkf.dk; internet www.bkf.dk; 1,200 mems; Chair. NANNA GRO HENNINGSEN; Sec. MOGENS HOLBØLL; publ. *Billedkunstneren*.

Dansk Billedhuggersamfund (Danish Sculptors' Society): c/o Mogens Lund 'Sundhuset', Clarasvej 2, 8700 Horsens; tel. 76-28-20-10; fax 75-65-76-60; e-mail mnl@billedhuggersamfundet.dk; internet www.skulptur.dk; f. 1905; 120 mems; Chair. KIT KJÆRBYE.

Dansk Komponistforening (Danish Composers' Society): Gråbrødretorv 16, 1, 1154 Copenhagen K; tel. 33-13-54-05; fax 33-14-32-19; e-mail dkf@komponistforeningen.dk; internet www.komponistforeningen.dk; f. 1913; 180 mems; Chair. JOHN FRANDSEN; Secs KIRSTEN WREM, TINA SCHELLE.

Dansk Korforening (Danish Choral Society): Absalonsgade 3, 4180 Sorø; f. 1911; mems: 27 choirs; Pres. ASGER LARSEN.

Danske Kunsthåndværkeres (Danish Arts and Crafts Association): Bredgade 66, 1260 Copenhagen K; tel. 33-15-29-40; fax 33-15-26-76; e-mail mail@danskekunsthaandaerkere.dk; internet www.danskekunsthaandvaerkere.dk; f. 1976; arranges exhibitions; professional advice for schools, museums, etc.; 450 mems; 8 regional groups of artist-craftsmen; Exec. Sec. NINA LINDE; publ. *KUNSTUFF–Danish Crafts and Design* (quarterly).

Kunstforeningen i København (Copenhagen Art Association): Gl. Strand 48, 1202 Copenhagen K; tel. 33-36-02-60; fax 33-36-02-66; e-mail info@glstrand.dk; internet www.kunstforeningen.dk; f. 1825; exhibitions of modern and contemporary art; Dir HELLE BEHRNDT; publ. *Nyhedsbrev* (newsletter, 1 or 2 a month).

Kunstnerforeningen af 18. November (Artists' Association of the 18th November): Frederiksgade 8, 1265 Copenhagen K; tel. 33-15-96-14; f. 1842; workshop, lectures, concerts, exhibitions, art collection; library of 300 vols; 165 mems; Pres. NIELS WAMBERG; Vice-Pres. POUL JENSEN.

Ny Carlsbergfondet (New Carlsberg Foundation): Brolæggerstræde 5, 1211 Copenhagen K; tel. 33-11-37-65; fax 33-14-36-46; e-mail sekretariatet@nycarlsbergfondet.dk; internet www.ny-carlsbergfondet.dk; f. 1902; supports the New Carlsberg Glyptotek (see Museums and Art Galleries, Copenhagen), and other Danish art museums; promotes the study of art and art history and develops and fulfils the appreciation of and need for art in Denmark; annual awards; Chair. H. E. NØRREGÅRD-NIELSEN; publ. *Årsskrift* (yearbook).

Samfundet til Udgivelse af Dansk Musik (Society for the Publication of Danish Music): Gråbrødrestræde 18, 1156 Copenhagen K; tel. 33-13-54-45; fax 33-93-30-44; e-mail sales@samfundet.dk; internet www.samfundet.dk; f. 1871; Chair. KLAUS IB JØRGENSEN.

Sammenslutningen af Danske Kunstforeninger (Association of Danish Art Societies): c/o Søren C. Olesen, Søbakkevej 4, 9500 Hobro Copenhagen K; tel. 98-52-20-32; internet www.sdkunst.dk; f. 1942; arranges touring art exhibitions with govt support; 15,000 mems; Dir SØREN C. OLESEN; Sec. FINN MIKELSEN; publ. *Nyhedsbrev* (newsletter, monthly).

HISTORY, GEOGRAPHY AND ARCHAEOLOGY

Arktisk Institut (Arctic Institute): Strandgade 100H, 1401 Copenhagen K; tel. 32-88-01-50; fax 32-88-01-51; e-mail arctic@dpc.dk; internet www.arktiskinstitut.dk; f. 1954; information, scientific and historic activities related to the Arctic; library of 14,000 vols, archives of Arctic expeditions, diaries, and more than 50,000 photographs, mainly of Greenland; Chair. PETER AUGUSTINUS; Dir JOHN JENSEN.

Dansk Selskab for Oldtids- og Middelalderforskning (Danish Society for Research of Ancient and Medieval Times): Nationalmuseet, 1220 Copenhagen K; e-mail else.rasmussen@natmus.dk; f. 1934; 130 mems; Pres. MICHAEL ANDERSEN; Sec. ELSE MATHORNE RASMUSSEN.

Danske Historiske Forening (Danish Historical Association): Njalsgade 102, 2300 Copenhagen S; tel. 35-32-82-44; fax 35-32-82-41; e-mail histtid@hum.ku.dk; internet www.historisktidsskrift.dk; f. 1839; 1,700 mems; Chair. Mag. CARSTEN DUE-NIELSEN; Secs Dr JAN PEDERSEN, Dr REGIN SCHMIDT; publ. *Historisk Tidsskrift* (2 a year).

Jysk Arkaeologisk Selskab (Jutland Archaeological Society): Moesgård, 8270 Højbjerg; tel. 89-42-45-04; fax 86-27-23-78; e-mail moesgaard@hum.au.dk; f. 1951; lectures and publication of primary archaeological and ethnological investigations; 1,500 mems; Pres. STEEN HVASS; Sec.-Gen. JAN SKARMBY MADSEN; publs *KUML* (annually), *Jysk Arkaeologisk Selskabs Skrifter* (monographs, irregular), *Handbooks* (irregular).

Jysk Selskab for Historie (Jutland Historical Society): Historisk Institut, Århus Universitet, 8000 Århus C; tel. 89-42-20-23; fax 89-42-20-47; f. 1866; 650 mems; Pres. HENRIK FODE; publs *Historie* (2 a year), *Nyt fra Historien* (2 a year).

Kongelige Danske Geografiske Selskab (Royal Danish Geographical Society): Øster Voldgade 10, 1350 Copenhagen K; tel. 35-32-25-00; fax 35-32-25-01; e-mail kh@geogr.ku.dk; internet www.geogr.ku.dk/dkgs; f. 1876; 450 mems; library of 100,000 vols; Protector HM Queen MARGRETHE II; Pres. HRH Crown Prince FREDERIK; Sec. OLE MERTZ; Head of Library PREBEN SONNE JØRGENSEN; publs *Geografisk Tidsskrift* (Danish Journal of Geography), *Folia Geographica Danica*, *Kulturgeografiske Skrifter*, *Atlas of Denmark*.

Kongelige Danske Selskab for Fædrelandets Historie (Royal Danish Society for National History): c/o Erik Nørr, Købmandsgården 2, 4130 Viby Sj; e-mail en@lak.sa.dk; internet www.danskemagazin.dk; f. 1745; 60 mems; 20 foreign corresps; Chair. NIELS-KNUD LIEBGOTT; Sec. ERIK NØRR; publ. *Danske Magazin*.

Kongelige Nordiske Oldskriftselskab (Royal Society of Northern Antiquaries): Prinsens Palais, Frederiksholms Kanal 12, 1220 Copenhagen K; f. 1825; 750 mems; library: library in the National Museum; Dir NIELS-KNUD LIEBGOTT; Sec. PETER VANG PETERSEN; publs *Aarbøger for Nordisk Oldkyndighed og Historie*, *Nordiske Fortidsminder*.

Samfundet for Dansk Genealogi og Personalhistorie (Danish Genealogical and Biographical Society): Groennevej 23, 2830 Virum; e-mail info@genealogi.dk; internet www.genealogi.dk; f. 1879; 1,100 mems; Chair. FINN ANDERSEN; Sec. POUL STEEN; publs *Hvem forsker Hvad* (yearly), *Personalhistorisk Tidsskrift* (2 a year).

Selskabet for Dansk Kulturhistorie (Society for the History of Danish Culture): Rosenborg Castle, Øster Voldgade 4A, 1350 Copenhagen K; tel. 33-15-32-86; fax 33-15-20-46; e-mail jh@dkks.dk; f. 1936; 35 mems; Pres. STEFFEN HEIBERG; Sec. JØRGEN HEIN.

LANGUAGE AND LITERATURE

Alliance Française: Christianshols Tværvej 19, 2930 Klampenborg, Copenhagen; tel. 39-64-04-28; e-mail internet@prebenhansen.dk; internet www.alliancefrancaise.dk; offers courses and exams in French language and culture and promotes cultural exchange with France; attached offices in Aarhus and Abyhoj; Dir PETER PREBEN HANSEN.

British Council: Gammel Mønt, 12.3, 1117 Copenhagen K; tel. 33-36-94-00; fax 33-36-94-06; e-mail british.council@britishcouncil.dk; internet www.britishcouncil.org/denmark; offers courses and exams in English language and British culture and promotes cultural exchange with the UK; Dir MICHAEL SØRENSEN-JONES.

Dansk Forfatterforening (Danish Writers' Association): Tordenskjolds Gård, Strandgade 6 st., 1401 Copenhagen K; tel. 32-95-51-00; fax 32-54-01-15; e-mail danskforfatterforening@danskforfatterforening.dk; internet www.danskforfatterforening.dk; f. 1894; professional org. representing fiction writers, non-fiction writers, poets, translators, writers and illustrators of books for children and young people; 1,300 mems; Pres. FRANTS IVER GUNDELACH; publ. *Forfatteren* (8 a year).

Danske Sprog- og Litteraturselskab (Society for Danish Language and Literature): Christians Brygge 1, 1219 Copenhagen; tel. 33-13-06-60; fax 33-14-06-08; e-mail sekretariat@dsl.dk; internet www.dsl.dk; f. 1911; 75 mems; Dir Prof. JØRN LUND; Sec. MARIA KROGH LANGNER; publ. *Nyhedsbrev* (newsletter, 2 a year).

Goethe-Institut: Nørre Voldgade 106, 1358 Copenhagen K; tel. 33-36-64-64; fax 33-36-64-61; e-mail info@kopenhagen.goethe.org; internet www.goethe.de/ne/kop/deindex.htm; offers courses and exams in German language and culture and promotes cultural exchange with Germany; Dir Dr CHRISTOPH BARTMANN.

MEDICINE

Den Almindelige Danske Lægeforening (Danish Medical Association): Trondhjemsgade 9, 2100 Copenhagen Ø; tel. 35-44-85-00; fax 35-44-85-05; e-mail dadl@dadl.dk; internet www.laeger.dk; f. 1857; to unite Danish doctors, to protect and promote the interests of the medical profession, and to serve as the body through which the influence of the medical profession may be exercised; 21,860 mems; Chair. BENTE HYLDAHL FOGH; Dir JØRGEN REEDTZ FUNDER; publs *Bibliotek for Læger* (history of medicine, quarterly), *Danish Medical Bulletin* (English, 6 a year), *DMA Directory (Vejviser)*, *Lægeforeningens Medicinfortegnelse (Physicians Desk Reference)* (every 2 years), *Ugeskrift for Laeger* (weekly).

Danmarks Farmaceutiske Selskab (Danish Pharmaceutical Society): Rygårds Allé 1, 2900 Hellerup; tel. 39-46-36-00; fax 39-46-36-39; e-mail info@farmaceutisk-selskab.dk; internet www.farmaceutisk-selskab.dk; f. 1912; to encourage the scientific and practical development of Danish pharmacy; 765 mems; Chair. Dr ALEJANDRA MØRK; Sec. Prof. Dr BENT HALLING-SØRENSEN.

Dansk Farmaceutforening (Association of Danish Pharmacists): Rygårds Alle 1, 2900 Hellerup; tel. 39-46-36-00; fax 39-46-36-39; e-mail df@pharmaceut.dk; internet www.farmaceutforeningen.dk; f. 1873; library of 16,000 vols; 3,205 mems; Pres. ARNE KURDAHL; publs *Fredag Formiddag* (weekly), *Farmaceuten* (every 2 weeks).

Dansk Medicinsk Selskab (Danish Medical Society): Esplanaden 8C, 3. sal, 1263 Copenhagen K; tel. 35-44-84-07; fax 35-44-84-08; e-mail cs@dadl.dk; internet www.dms.dk; f. 1919; an asscn of 100 socs and 18,000 individual mems, working in all aspects of medical science; awards the August Krogh Prize to a leading Danish scientist, annually; Chair. Prof. Dr JENS CHRISTIAN DJURHUUS; Sec. Prof. Dr J. MICHAEL HASENKAM.

Dansk Tandlægeforening (Danish Dental Association): Amaliegade 17, Postboks 143, 1004 Copenhagen K; tel. 70-25-77-11; fax 70-25-16-37; e-mail dtf@dtf-dk.dk; internet www.dtfnet.dk; f. 1873; 6,148 mems; Pres. SUSANNE ANDERSEN; publ. *Tandlaegebladet* (15 a year).

NATURAL SCIENCES

General

Selskabet for Naturlærens Udbredelse (Society for the Promotion of Natural Science): UNI-C, Vermundsgade 5, 2100 Copenhagen Ø; tel. 35-87-88-04; fax 35-82-40-76; e-mail snu@naturvidenskab.net; internet www.naturvidenskab.net; f. 1824; 200 mems; Pres. Prof. DORTE OLESEN; Sec. Dr JØRN JOHS. CHRISTIANSEN; publ. *KVANT / Fysisk Tidsskrift* (quarterly).

Biological Sciences

Danmarks Naturfredningsforening (Danish Society for the Conservation of Nature): Masnedøgade 20, 2100 Copenhagen Ø; tel. 39-17-40-00; fax 39-17-41-41; e-mail dn@dn.dk; internet www.dn.dk; f. 1911; 140,000 mems, 216 local cttees; Pres. ELLA MARIA BISSCHOP-LARSEN; Dir GUNVER BENNEKOU; publ. *Tidsskriftet natur og miljø* (quarterly).

Dansk Botanisk Forening (Danish Botanical Society): Sølvgade 83, 1307 Copenhagen K; tel. 33-14-17-03; e-mail dbotf@mail.tele.dk; internet www.botaniskforening.dk; f. 1840; 1,400 mems; Pres. WINNIE DANIELSEN; publ. *Urt* (popular botanical journal).

Dansk Naturhistorisk Forening (Danish Natural History Society): Universitetsparken

15, 2100 Copenhagen O; tel. 35-32-11-20; fax 35-32-10-10; e-mail dnf@zmuc.ku.dk; internet www.aki.ku.dk/dnf; f. 1833; 525 mems; Pres. DANNY EIBYE-JACOBSEN; publs *Årsskrift for Dansk Naturhistorisk Forening* (annually), *Danmarks Fauna* (irregular).

Dansk Ornithologisk Forening (Danish Ornithological Society): Vesterbrogade 138–140, 1620 Copenhagen V; tel. 33-28-38-00; e-mail dof@dof.dk; internet www.dof.dk; f. 1906; 12,000 mems; Dir JAN EJLSTED; publs *DOF-Nyt*(quarterly), *Fugle og Natur* (quarterly), *Tidsskrift* (quarterly).

Entomologisk Forening (Entomological Society): Zoological Museum, Universitetsparken 15, 2100 Copenhagen Ø; e-mail jfredskov@snm.ku.dk; internet www.zmuc.dk/entoWeb/entomologiskforening/; f. 1868; 360 mems; Pres. MICHAEL FIBIGER; Sec. JAN PEDERSEN; publ. *Entomologiske Meddelelser* (quarterly).

Physical Sciences

Astronomisk Selskab (Astronomical Society): Observatoriet, Juliane Maries Vej 30, 2100 Copenhagen Ø; tel. 36-72-36-34; fax 35-32-59-89; e-mail mq@spacecenter.dk; internet as.dsri.dk; f. 1916; 700 mems; Chair. MICHAEL QUAADE; publs *Knudepunktet* (4 a year), *Kvant* (jointly with Danish Physical Society, 4 a year).

Dansk Fysisk Selskab (Danish Physical Society): c/o Jørgen Schou, Afdelingen for Optik og Plasmaforskning, Forskningscenter Risø, 4000 Roskilde; tel. 46-77-47-55; fax 46-77-45-65; e-mail dorthe@ruc.dk; internet www.dfs.nbi.dk; f. 1972; arranges conferences; 700 mems; Pres. JØRGEN SCHOU; publ. *Kvant* (jointly with Danish Association for the Advancement of Science, quarterly).

Dansk Geologisk Forening (Geological Society of Denmark): c/o Geologisk Musem, Øster Voldgade 5-7, 1350 Copenhagen K; tel. 35-32-23-54; fax 35-32-23-25; e-mail sekretariat@2dgf.dk; internet www.2dgf.dk; f. 1893; promotes interest in geology and establishes a forum for geologists; lectures, discussions; excursions; administers two prizes; 600 mems; Chair. PETER FRYKMAN; Sec. GUNVER KRARUP PEDERSEN; publs *Bulletin* (2 a year), *Geologisk Tidsskrift* (2 a year).

Kemisk Forening (Danish Chemical Society): H. C. Ørsted Institutet, Universitetsparken 5, 2100 Copenhagen Ø; tel. 35-32-03-03; fax 35-35-06-09; e-mail president@chemsoc.dk; internet www.chemsoc.dk; f. 1879; 870 mems; Pres. MORTEN J. BJERRUM; Sec. MATTHEW S. JOHNSON; publ. *Dansk Kemi* (monthly).

PHILOSOPHY AND PSYCHOLOGY

Dansk Psykolog Forening (Danish Psychological Association): Stockholmsgade 27, 2100 Copenhagen Ø; tel. 35-26-99-55; fax 35-26-97-37; e-mail dp@dp.dk; internet www.dp.dk; f. 1947 for graduate psychologists and students; deals with questions of education and professional matters; works as a trade union to safeguard psychologists' interests; 7,800 mems; Dir MARIE ZELANDER; publ. *Psykolog Nyt* (fortnightly).

RELIGION, SOCIOLOGY AND ANTHROPOLOGY

Danske Bibelselskab (Danish Bible Society): Frederiksborggade 50, 1360 Copenhagen K; tel. 33-12-78-35; fax 33-93-21-50; e-mail bibelselskabet@bibelselskabet.dk; internet www.bibelselskabet.dk; f. 1814; editing and distributing Bibles and other biblical scriptures; Chair. CAI FRIMODT-MØLLER; Gen. Sec. Rev. TINE LINDHARDT; publs *Annual Report*, *News* (quarterly).

Grønlandske Selskab (Greenland Society): Kraemer Hus, L. E. Bruunsvej 10, 2920 Charlottenlund; tel. 39-63-57-33; fax 39-63-55-43; e-mail dgs@groenlandselskab.dk; internet www.groenlandselskab.dk; f. 1905; 1,500 mems with interest in Greenland and its people; Chair. H. C. GULLØV; publ. *Grønland* (8 a year).

TECHNOLOGY

Akademiet for de Tekniske Videnskaber (Danish Academy of Technical Sciences): 266 Lundtoftevej, 2800 Kgs. Lyngby; tel. 45-88-13-11; fax 45-88-13-51; e-mail atvmail@atv.dk; internet www.atv.dk; f. 1937; four divisions, covering fundamental and ancillary sciences, chemical science and engineering, mechanical engineering, civil engineering, electrical engineering, information technology, agricultural and food, industrial organization and economics, environmental issues, biology and technical hygiene; one thematic professional group on construction and town planning; undertakes professional meetings and projects within these fields; 640 mems; Chair. TORBEN GREVE; Man. Dir LASSE SKOVBY; publs *Årsrapport* (annual report, in Danish), *ATV NYT* (electronic newsletter, ad hoc, in Danish).

Byggecentrum (Building Centre): Hindsgavl Allé 2, 5500 Middelfart; tel. 70-12-36-00; fax 70-12-38-00; e-mail info@byggecentrum.dk; internet www.byggecentrum.dk; f. 1956; acts as centre for construction information; bookshop, database services, postgraduate training, exhibitions, training centre; Man. Dir JOERN VIBE ANDREASEN.

Dansk Husflidsselskab (Danish Society of Domestic Crafts): Tyrebakken 11, 5300 Kerteminde; tel. 63-32-20-96; fax 63-32-20-97; e-mail dansk@husflid.dk; internet www.husflid.dk; f. 1873; promotes domestic craftsmanship; 4,800 individual mems, 140 local orgs; Sec. BENTE SKOV MACHHOLM; publ. *Husflid* (every 2 months).

Elektroteknisk Forening (Society of Danish Electrotechnicians): Kronprinsensgade 28, 5000 Odense C; tel. 40-56-01-48; e-mail info@dkef.dk; internet www.dkef.dk; f. 1903; 1,400 mems; Sec.-Gen. ANDERS EBBESEN JENSEN; publ. *Elteknik* (10 a year).

Ingeniørforeningen i Danmark (IDA) (Society of Engineers of Denmark): Kalvebod Brygge 31–33, 1780 Copenhagen V; tel. 33-18-48-48; fax 33-18-48-99; e-mail ida@ida.dk; internet www.ida.dk; f. 1937; 61,000 mems; Pres. LARS BYTOFT OLSEN; Chief Exec. IB OUSTRUP; publ. *Ingeniøren* (weekly).

Research Institutes

GENERAL

Carlsberg Laboratorium: Gl. Carlsbergvej 10, 2500 Copenhagen Valby; e-mail carlslab@crc.dk; internet www.crc.dk/carls_lab.shtml; f. 1875; attached to Carlsberg Foundation; research in biomedicine, biotechnology and chemistry; library of 50,000 vols, 300 periodicals; Dir Dr KLAUS BOCK; Head of Research Laboratory Dr KLAUS BREDDAM.

Ministeriet for Videnskab, Teknologi og Udvikling (Ministry of Science, Technology and Innovation): Bredgade 43, 1260 Copenhagen K; tel. 33-92-97-00; fax 33-32-35-01; e-mail vtu@vtu.dk; internet www.videnskabsministeriet.dk; the Ministry has the political responsibility for research, universities, information technology and telecommunications; co-operates with the international research policy organizations of EC, OECD, Council of Europe, UNESCO and UN; provides comprehensive R & D statistics, planning and forecasts; Permanent Sec. UFFE TOUDAL PEDERSEN.

Attached bodies:

Danmarks Forskningspolitiske Råd (Danish Council for Research Policy): Bredgade 43, 1260 Copenhagen K; tel. 33-92-97-00; fax 33-32-35-01; e-mail fsk@fsk.dk; internet www.danmarksforskningsraad.dk; f. 1996; 9 mems appointed by the Minister of Research and Information Technology; advisory body to government in research policy matters; makes proposals on resources, structures, etc. required for the development and exploitation of Danish research; Chair. Dr BRUNO HANSEN; Head of Secretariat STEIN LARSEN.

Forskningsråd for Kultur og Kommunikation (Danish Research Council for Culture and Communication): Copenhagen; f. 1968; 15 mems appointed by the Minister of Research and Information Technology; advisory body to public authorities and institutions in the humanities; initiates and supports national and international research; awards grants and fellowships for scientific research.

Forskningsrådet for Natur og Univers (Danish Research Council for Natural Science and Space): Copenhagen; tel. 35-44-62-00; fax 35-44-62-01; e-mail fist@fist.dk; internet www.fist.dk; f. 1968; 15 mems appointed by the Minister of Science, Technology and Innovation; advisory body to public authorities and institutions in the natural sciences; initiates, supports and co-ordinates research, national and international; awards grants and fellowships for scientific research; Chair. Prof. Dr LARS STEMMERIK.

Forskningsråd for Samfund og Erhverv (Danish Social Science Research Council): Copenhagen; f. 1968; 15 mems appointed by the Minister of Research and Information Technology; advisory body to public authorities and institutions in the social sciences; initiates and supports national and international research; awards grants and fellowships for scientific research; Chair. Prof. BIRGITTE SLOTH.

Forskningsråd for Sundhed og Sygdom (Danish Research Council for Health and Sickness): Copenhagen; f. 1968; 15 mems appointed by the Minister of Research and Information Technology; advisory body to public authorities and institutions in medical sciences, including odontology and pharmacy; initiates and supports research, co-ordinates research, national and international; awards grants and fellowships to scientific research; Chair. Prof. Dr HENNING BECK-NIELSEN.

Forskningsråd for Teknologi og Produktion (Danish Research Council for Technology and Production): Copenhagen; f. 1973 to replace Danmarks teknisk-videnskabelige Forskningsrad and Statens Teknisk-Videnskabelige Forskningsråd; 15 mems appointed by the Minister of Education; advisory body to public authorities in the technical sciences; initiates and supports national and international research; awards grants and fellowships for scientific research; Chair. Prof. Dr STEEN URECK.

AGRICULTURE, FISHERIES AND VETERINARY SCIENCE

Danmarks Jordbrugs Forsknings (Danish Institute of Agricultural Sciences): Blichers Allé, POB 50, 8830 Tjele; tel. 89-99-19-00; fax 89-99-19-19; e-mail djf@agrsci.dk; internet www.agrsci.dk; f. 1882; research in agriculture and connected subjects; centres in Foulum, Bygholm, Aarslev, Flakkebjerg, and Sorgenfri; four experimental stations and the Department of Variety Testing in Tystofte; research group at the Royal Veterinary and Agricultural University in Copenhagen; 375 scientific staff; attached to Danish Ministry of Food, Agriculture and Fisheries; Chair. JENS KAMPMANN; Dir JUST JENSEN.

Hedeselskabet (Danish Land Development Service): Klostermarken 12, POB 110, 8800 Viborg; tel. 87-28-11-33; fax 87-28-10-01; e-mail hedeselskabet@hedeselskabet.dk; internet www.hedeselskabet.dk; f. 1866; forestry, forest nurseries, shelter belts, soil improvement, environmental protection, environmental engineering, land reclamation, drainage, irrigation, hydrology and research; specialists carry out practical assignments and research; technical projects designed and administered for farmers, foresters, industry, government authorities in Denmark and abroad; Man. Dir OVE KOCH; publs *Annual Report*, *Vækst* (every 2 months).

ECONOMICS, LAW AND POLITICS

Danmarks Statistik (Statistics Denmark): Sejrøgade 11, 2100 Copenhagen Ø; tel. 39-17-39-17; fax 39-17-39-99; e-mail dst@dst.dk; internet www.dst.dk; f. 1849; central institution for all Danish statistics; library: see Libraries and Archives; Dir JAN PLOVSING; publs *Nyt fra Danmarks Statistik* (daily bulletin), *Statistisk Årbog* (annually), *Statistisk Månedsoversigt* (monthly), *Statistisk Tiårsoversigt* (statistical 10-year survey, annually).

Dansk Center for Internationale Studier og Menneskerettigheder (Danish Centre for International Studies and Human Rights): Strandgade 56, 1401 Copenhagen K; tel. 32-69-86-86; fax 32-69-86-00; e-mail dcism@dcism.dk; internet www.dcism.dk; f. 2003; undertakes research and analysis concerning foreign security and development policy; conflict and genocide studies and human rights in Denmark and abroad; Head of the Board UFFE ELLEMANN-JENSEN.

Constituent institutes:

Dansk Institut for Internationale Studier (DIIS) (Danish Institute for International Studies (DIIS)): Strandgade 56, 1401 Copenhagen K; tel. 32-69-87-87; fax 32-69-87-00; e-mail diis@diis.dk; internet www.diis.dk; f. 2003; research departments: European Studies, Development Research, Globalisation and Governance Research, Holocaust and Genocide Studies, Conflict and Security Studies, Cold War Studies; library of 100,000 vols; Dir NANNA HVIDT; publ. *Den Ny Verden* (The New World, Danish); publ. *Den Ny Verden* (The New World, Danish).

Institut for Menneskerettigheder (Institute for Human Rights): Strandgade 56, 1401 Copenhagen K; tel. 32-69-88-88; fax 32-69-88-00; e-mail center@humanrights.dk; internet www.humanrights.dk; f. 2003; Programmes include: Universities and Research Partnership Programme, European Masters Programme, Civil Society and Networking, Access to Justice, Reform of Law and State Institutions, Human Rights and Business; Dir MORTEN KJÆRUM.

HISTORY, GEOGRAPHY AND ARCHAEOLOGY

Danske Komité for Historikernes Internationale Samarbejde (Danish Committee for International Historical Co-operation): Copenhagen University, 2300 Copenhagen S; f. 1926; 43 mems; Chair. Prof. NIELS STEENSGAARD.

MEDICINE

Finsen Center–Rigshospitalet: Blegdamsvej 9, 2100 Copenhagen; tel. 35-45-56-15; fax 35-38-54-50; e-mail finsenlab@finsenlab.dk; internet www.finsenlab.dk; f. 1896; cancer research; 24 scientific staff; Head of Laboratory Prof. Dr KELD DANO.

Institute of Cancer Biology: Strandboulevarden 49, 2100 Copenhagen; tel. 35-25-75-00; fax 35-25-77-21; e-mail bio@cancer.dk; internet www.cancer.dk/bio+research; f. 1949; experimental cancer research; Scientific Dir Prof. JULIO E. CELIS; Sec. DORTE HOLST PEDERSEN; publ. *Report* (every 2 years, in English).

NATURAL SCIENCES

General

Institut for Miljøvurdering (Institute for Environmental Assessment): Linnésgade 18, 1361 Copenhagen K; tel. 72-26-58-00; fax 72-26-58-39; e-mail imv@imv.dk; internet www.imv.dk; Chair. KNUD LARSEN; Dir PETER CALOW.

Biological Sciences

Arctic Station, University of Copenhagen: Arctic Station, POB 504, 3953 Qeqertarsuaq, Greenland; tel. (299) 92-13-84; fax (299) 92-13-85 correspondence to: Naturvidenskabelige Fakultet, Øster Voldgade 3, 1350 Copenhagen K; tel. 35-32-42-56; fax 35-32-42-20; e-mail as-science@greennet.gl; internet www.nat.ku.dk/as; f. 1906 for study of Arctic nature; laboratory; library; research ship 'Porsild'; Governors Assoc. Prof. KIRSTEN S. CHRISTOFFERSEN, Prof. BO ELBERLING, Prof. REINHARDT MØBJERG KRISTENSEN (Head), Dr POUL MØLLER PEDERSON; Chief Scientist HENRIK SULSBRÜCK; Sec. GITTE HENRIKSEN.

Danmarks Fiskeriundersøgelser (Danish Institute for Fisheries Research): Jægersborgvej 64–66, 2800 Lyngby; tel. 33-96-33-00; fax 33-96-33-49; e-mail dir@dfu.min.dk; internet www.difres.dk; f. 1995; fisheries, aquaculture, marine, freshwater and seafood research; large specialist library of fisheries and biology texts; Dir NIELS AXEL NIELSEN; publ. *Fisk og Hav*.

Statens Seruminstitut (State Serum Institute): Artillerivej 5, 2300 Copenhagen; tel. and fax 32-68-32-68; e-mail serum@ssi.dk; internet www.ssi.dk; f. 1902; microbiological and immunological research institute and centre for the prevention and control of infectious diseases and congenital disorders; 110 scientists; library: *c.* 19,000 vols; Pres. and Chief Exec. NILS STRANDBERG PEDERSEN; Dir of Research ERIK JUHL; publ. *Annual Report*.

Zoologisk Have (Copenhagen Zoo): Sdr. Fasanvej 79, 2000 Frederiksberg; tel. 72-20-02-00; fax 72-20-02-19; e-mail zoo@zoo.dk; internet www.zoo.dk; f. 1859; 3,300 animals of 264 species; participation in nature conservation projects worldwide; Man. Dir LARS LUNDING ANDERSEN; publ. *Zoo Nyt* (Zoo News, 4 a year).

Physical Sciences

Danmarks Meteorologiske Institut (Danish Meteorological Institute): Lyngbyvej 100, 2100 Copenhagen; tel. 39-15-75-00; fax 39-27-10-80; e-mail epost@dmi.dk; internet www.dmi.dk; f. 1872; meteorology and geophysics; library of 40,000 vols; 400 mems; Dir PETER AAKJÆR; publs *Magnetic Results* (Godhavn and Thule, Greenland), *Danmarks Klima* (annually).

Danmarks og Grønlands Geologiske Undersøgelse (Geological Survey of Denmark and Greenland): Ø. Voldgade 10, 1350 Copenhagen; tel. 38-14-20-00; fax 38-14-20-50; e-mail geus@geus.dk; internet www.geus.dk; f. 1995; library of 30,000 vols; Man. Dir MARTIN GHISLER; publs *Geological Survey of Denmark and Greenland Bulletin*, *Geological Survey of Denmark and Greenland Map Series*.

Kort & Matrikelstyrelsen (National Survey and Cadastre): Rentemestervej 8, 2400 Copenhagen NV; tel. 35-87-50-50; fax 35-87-50-51; e-mail kms@kms.dk; internet www.kms.dk; f. 1989, by amalgamation of former Geodetic Institute, Danish Cadastral Department and Hydrographic Division; responsible for geodetic survey of Denmark, Faroe Islands and Greenland; topographic survey and mapping of those areas, also nautical charting and issue of nautical publs; cadastral survey, registration, and mapping of Denmark; seismographic service in Denmark, Faroe Islands and Greenland; research and development within geodesy and seismology; development of digital maps and charts; Dir JESPER JARMBÆK.

Niels Bohr Institutet: Astronomisk Observatorium, Københavns Universitet, Juliane Maries Vej 30, 2100 Copenhagen Ø; tel. 35-32-59-99; fax 35-32-59-89; e-mail library@astro.ku.dk; internet www.astro.ku.dk; f. 1642; astronomy, physics and geophysics; library of 12,000 vols, 100 periodicals; Dir J. R. HANSEN.

NORDITA (Nordisk Institut for Teoretisk Fysik) (Nordic Institute for Theoretical Physics): Blegdamsvej 17, 2100 Copenhagen Ø; tel. 35-32-55-00; fax 35-38-91-57; e-mail nordita@nordita.dk; internet www.nordita.dk; f. 1957; member countries: Denmark, Finland, Iceland, Norway and Sweden; Dir PETTER MINNHAGEN.

RELIGION, SOCIOLOGY AND ANTHROPOLOGY

Instytut Polsko-Skandynawski/Polsk-Skandinavisk Forskningsinstitut: POB 2584, 2100 Copenhagen Ø; tel. 39-29-98-26; f. 1985; ind. research institute for Polish-Scandinavian studies; provides support for research in the field of history and biographical science; organizes lectures; 25 mems; library of 1,000 vols; 20 m of archives; Pres. Prof. Dr hab. E. S. KRUSZEWSKI; Dirs Prof. Dr hab. BOLESLAW HAJDUK, Prof. Dr Phil. BARBARA TÖRNQUIST-PLEWA.

Socialforskningsinstituttet (Danish National Institute of Social Research): Herluf Trolles Gade 11, 1052 Copenhagen K; tel. 33-48-08-00; fax 38-48-08-33; e-mail sfi@sfi.dk; internet www.sfi.dk; f. 1958; ind. research body under Min. of Social Affairs; library of 32,500 vols; Dir-in-Chief JØRGEN SØNDERGAARD; publ. *Social Forskning* (quarterly).

TECHNOLOGY

Forskningscenter Risø (Risø National Laboratory): POB 49, Frederiksborgvej 399, 4000 Roskilde; tel. 46-77-46-77; fax 46-77-56-88; e-mail risoe@risoe.dk; internet www.risoe.dk; f. 1958; research and development in fields of industrial materials, new functional materials, optics and sensor systems, plant production and ecology, systems analysis, wind energy and nuclear safety; library of 500,000 vols, 1,100 current periodicals; Dir JØRGEN KJEMS; publ. *Risø Report*.

Libraries and Archives

Ålborg

Aalborg Bibliotekerne (Central Library for the County of North Jutland): Rendsburggade 2, Postboks 839, 9100 Ålborg; tel. 99-31-43-00; fax 99-31-43-90; e-mail bibliotek@aalborg.dk; internet www.aalborgbibliotekerne.dk; f. 1895; 1,000,000 vols, 1,300 current periodicals; 15 brs and 3 mobile libraries; medical library; Chief Librarian BODIL HAVE.

Aalborg Universitetsbibliotek (Aalborg University Library): Langagervej 2, POB 8200, 9220 Ålborg Ø; tel. 96-35-94-00; fax 98-15-68-59; e-mail aub@aub.aau.dk; internet www.aub.aau.dk; f. 1973; open to the public; 650,000 vols; Chief Librarian NIELS-HENRIK GYLSTORFF.

Århus

Århus Kommunes Biblioteker (Århus Public Library): Møllegade 1, 8000 Århus C; tel. 89-40-92-00; fax 89-40-93-93; e-mail aakb@bib.aarhus.dk; internet www.aakb.dk; f. 1934; 1,124,228 vols (including audiovisual materials); Chief Librarian ROLF HAPEL.

Erhvervsarkivet. Statens Erhvervshistoriske Arkiv (Danish National Business History Archives): Vester Allé 12, 8000 Århus C; tel. 86-12-85-33; fax 86-12-85-60; e-mail mailbox@ea.sa.dk; internet www.sa.dk/ea; f. 1948; also a research institute for economic and social history; Chief Archivist CHR. R. JANSEN; publ. *Erhvervshistorisk Årbog* (Business History Yearbook).

Handelshøjskolens Bibliotek (Library of the Århus School of Business): Fuglesangs Allé 4, 8210 Århus V; tel. 89-48-66-88; fax 86-15-96-27; e-mail bibliotek@asb.dk; internet www.lib.asb.dk; f. 1939; 172,000 vols, 18,000 periodicals and electronic serials; spec. colln: European documentation centre for EU; Library Dir TOVE BANG.

Statsbiblioteket (State and University Library): Universitetsparken, 8000 Århus C; tel. 89-46-20-22; fax 89-46-22-20; e-mail sb@statsbiblioteket.dk; internet www.statsbiblioteket.dk; f. 1902; Legal Deposit Library, National Newspaper Collection, National Media Archive, Loan Center for Public Libraries; 4,850,022 vols; Chief Exec. SVEND LARSEN.

Copenhagen

Administrative Bibliotek: Slotsholmsgade 12, 1216 Copenhagen K; tel. 72-26-98-95; fax 72-26-98-99; e-mail dab@dab.dk; internet www.dab.dk; f. 1924; attached to Min. of Science, Technology and Innovation; central library and documentation centre for civil servants in central govt; 160,000 vols; spec. colln: Danish governmental publs; Head of Library NIELS H. JENSENIUS; publ. *Prima Vista* (quarterly).

Danmarks Biblioteksskoles Bibliotek (Library of the Royal School of Library and Information Science): Birketinget 6, 2300 Copenhagen S; tel. 32-58-60-66; fax 32-84-02-01; e-mail dbilaan@db.dk; internet www.db.dk/dbi/home_uk.htm; f. 1956; 182,000 vols; Librarian IVAR A. L. HOEL.

Danmarks Farmaceutiske Bibliotek, Københavns Universitet (Danish Pharmaceutical Library, Copenhagen University): Universitetsparken 2, 2100 Copenhagen; tel. 35-30-63-19; fax 35-30-60-60; e-mail bibliotek@farma.ku.dk; internet www.farma.ku.dk/bibliotek; f. 1892; 65,000 vols; Head of Library Service ALICE NØRHEDE.

Danmarks Kunstbibliotek (Royal Danish Academy of Fine Arts Library): Kgs Nytorv 1, Postboks 3053, 1021 Copenhagen K; tel. 33-74-48-00; fax 33-74-48-88; e-mail dkb@kunstbib.dk; internet www.kunstbib.dk; f. 1754; 150,000 vols on history of art and architecture, 205,000 architectural drawings, 364,000 photographs, 164,000 slides; Dir Dr PATRICK KRAGELUND.

Danmarks Paedagogiske Bibliotek (National Library of Education): Tuborgvej 164, POB 840, 2400 Copenhagen NV; tel. 88-88-93-00; fax 88-88-93-90; e-mail dpb@dpu.dk; internet www.dpb.dpu.dk; f. 1887; 895,000 vols, 3,057 current periodicals, 600,000 microfiches; Dir THØGER KRISTENSEN.

Danmarks Statistiks Bibliotek og Information (Statistics Denmark Library and Information): Sejrøgade 11, 2100 Copenhagen; tel. 39-17-30-30; fax 39-17-30-03; e-mail bib@dst.dk; internet www.dst.dk/omds/bib.aspx; f. 1849; attached to Danmarks Statistik (see Research Institutes: Economics, Law and Politics); 235,000 vols; Head of Div. PER KNUDSEN.

Danmarks Veterinaer- og Jordbrugsbibliotek (Danish Veterinary and Agricultural Library): Dyrlægevej 10, 1870 Frederiksberg C; tel. 35-28-21-45; fax 35-34-28-24; e-mail dvjb@kvl.dk; internet www.dvjb.kvl.dk; f. 1783; 586,000 vols; Chief Librarian FREDE MØRCH.

Frederiksberg Bibliotek (Frederiksberg Public Library): Falkoner Plads 3, 2000 Frederiksberg; tel. 38-21-18-00; fax 38-21-17-99; e-mail bib@fkb.dk; internet www.fkb.dk; f. 1887; 547,634 vols; 3 brs; also a music library and a special genealogy section; Chief Librarian ANNE MØLLER-RASMUSSEN.

Handelshøjskolens Bibliotek (Copenhagen Business School Library): Solbjerg Plads 3, 2000 Frederiksberg; tel. 38-15-38-15; fax 38-15-36-63; e-mail hbk.lib@cbs.dk; internet www.cbs.dk/library; f. 1922; 310,176 vols, 1,000 current print periodicals, 6,000 electronic periodicals; Dir MICHAEL COTTA-SCHØNBERG.

Københavns Biblioteker (Copenhagen Public Libraries): Fælles Service, Islands Brygge 37, 5, 2300 Copenhagen S; tel. 33-66-46-50; fax 33-66-71-20; e-mail bibliotek@kff.kk.dk; internet www.bibliotek.kk.dk; f. 1885; 2,240,881 vols; Library Dir JENS INGEMANN.

Københavns Stadsarkiv (Copenhagen City Archives): Rådhuset, 1599 Copenhagen V; tel. 33-66-23-70; fax 33-66-70-39; e-mail stadsarkiv@kff.kk.dk; f. before 1563; 37 linear km of archive material, 150,000 maps and drawings; Dir HENRIK GAUTIER; publ. *Historiske Meddelelser om København* (annually).

Kongelige Bibliotek, Nationalbibliotek og Københavns Universitetsbibliotek (Royal Library, National Library of Denmark and Cophagen University Library): POB 2149, 1016 Copenhagen K; tel. 33-47-47-47; fax 33-93-22-18; e-mail kb@kb.dk; internet www.kb.dk; f. 1482 as university library, 1648 as the King's Library, merged 1989; acts as the Danish National Library; principal research and university library for theology, the humanities, law and the social sciences, the natural and health sciences; nat. archive for MSS and archives of prominent Danes; incl. Danish Museum of Books and Printing, National Museum of Photography, Museum of Danish Cartoon Art; open to the public; 4,903,900 vols, 4,500 incunabula, 163,000 manuscripts and archives, 15,990,000 graphic documents, 279,000 maps and prints, 285,000 musical items; Dir-Gen. ERLAND KOLDING NIELSEN; publs *Fund og Forskning i Det Kongelige Biblioteks Samlinger* (annually), *Magasin fra Det Kongelige Bibliotek* (quarterly).

Kongelige Garnisonsbibliotek (Royal Danish Military Library): Kastellet 46, 2100 Copenhagen Ø; tel. 33-47-95-25; fax 33-47-95-36; e-mail is-kgb@fak.dk; internet www.kgbmil.dk; f. 1785; Army central research library; 130,000 vols on military development since medieval times; military strategy, operations, tactics, logistics and intelligence; regimental history, uniforms, weaponry and technology; military bibliographies; international relations, defence and security policy, international engagements and peacekeeping operations; 150 periodicals; 5,500 maps since 16th c.; Librarian Lt-Col SØREN HOEGENHAUG.

Kunstindustrimuseets Bibliotek (National Art and Design Library): Bredgade 68, 1260 Copenhagen K; tel. 33-18-56-56; fax 33-18-56-66; e-mail bib@dkim.dk; internet www.dkim.dk; f. 1890; 130,000 vols; Chief Librarian Dr MIRJAM GELFER-JØRGENSEN.

Marinens Bibliotek (Royal Danish Naval Library): Henrik Gerners Plads (bygn. 37), 1439 Copenhagen K; tel. 32-54-73-82; fax 32-96-31-71; e-mail is-mab@fak.dk; internet www.mab.dk; f. 1765; naval affairs and Greenland literature; 40,000 vols; Librarian Cdr s.g. KARSTEN PALLE HANSEN.

Patentdirektoratet Bibliotek (Library of the Danish Patent Office): Helgeshoj Allé 81, 2630 Taastrup; tel. 43-50-80-00; fax 43-50-80-01; e-mail bibliotek@dkpto.dk; internet www.dkpto.dk/bibliotek; f. 1894; 28,860 vols; 28,000,000 patent specifications; Heads of Library JON FINSEN, LIZZI VESTER; publs *Dansk Brugsmodeltidende* (Danish Utility Models Gazette, every 2 weeks), *Dansk Mønstertidende* (Danish Design Gazette, every 2 weeks), *Dansk Patenttidende* (Danish Patent Gazette, weekly), *Dansk Varemarketidende* (Danish Trademark Gazette, weekly).

Rigsarkivet (Danish National Archives): Rigsdagsgården 9, 1218 Copenhagen K; tel. 33-92-33-10; fax 33-15-32-39; e-mail mailbox@ra.sa.dk; internet www.sa.dk; f. 1582; the Danish National Archives in Copenhagen, together with four Provincial Archives (*Landsarkiver*), situated in Copenhagen, Odense, Viborg and Aabenraa, the National Business Archives in Aarhus and the Danish Data Archives in Odense make up the Danish State Archives; the Danish National Archives' central record office contains most of the medieval documents (1200–1559), the archives of the Central Administration, and the armed forces, and the papers of the Royal family and of famous statesmen; Dir JOHAN PETER NOACK; publs *Arkiv*, *Siden Saxo*.

Esbjerg

Centralbiblioteket i Esbjerg (Esbjerg Central Library): Nørregade 19, 6700 Esbjerg; tel. 76-16-20-00; fax 76-16-20-01; e-mail biblio@esbjergkommune.dk; internet www.esbbib.dk; f. 1897; 559,222 vols, 118,169 other items, incl. CD-ROMs and audiovisual material; Chief Librarian ANNETTE BRØCHNER LINDGAARD.

Hellerup

Gentofte Bibliotekerne (Public Library): Ahlmanns Allé 6, 2900 Hellerup; tel. 39-48-75-00; fax 39-48-75-07; e-mail bibliotek@gentofte.bibnet.dk; internet www.genbib.dk; f. 1918; 546,808 vols; 5 brs; Chief Librarian LONE GLADBO.

Lyngby

Danmarks Tekniske Videncenter (DTV) (Technical Knowledge Centre and Library of Denmark): PO 777, Anker Engelunds Vej 1, 2800 Kgs. Lyngby; tel. 45-25-72-00; fax 45-88-30-40; e-mail dtub@dtv.dk; internet www

.dtv.dk/dtub.aspx; f. 1942; centre for scientific information and library for the Technical Univ. of Denmark; 700,000 vols, 4,000 current periodicals, 11,000 e-journals; Dir ANNETTE WINKEL SCHWARZ.

Odense

Landsarkivet for Fyn (Provincial Archives of Funen): Jernbanegade 36A, 5000 Odense C; tel. 66-12-58-85; fax 66-14-70-71; e-mail mailbox@lao.sa.dk; internet www.sa.dk/lao; f. 1893; the archives include records of local administration of Funen and neighbouring islands, and collections of private papers; The Karen Brahe Library, the only nearly-complete private Danish library dating from the 17th c., with about 3,400 printed books and 1,153 MSS, is deposited in the Archives; Dir STEEN OUSAGER.

Odense Centralbibliotek (Odense Central Library): Østre Stationsvej 15, 5000 Odense C; tel. 65-51-43-01; fax 66-13-73-37; e-mail teleservice-bib@odense.dk; internet www.odensebib.dk; f. 1924; 1,010,000 vols, 145,000 CDs, audiobooks, video cassettes and DVDs; Library Dir LENE BYRIALSEN.

Syddansk Universitetsbibliotek (University Library of Southern Denmark): Campusvej 55, 5230 Odense M; tel. 65-50-10-00; fax 65-50-26-01; e-mail sdub@bib.sdu.dk; internet www.bib.sdu.dk; f. 1965; languages, literature, philosophy, religion, history, music, economics, social sciences, natural sciences, medicine; 1,400,000 vols, 18,300 periodicals (incl. 14,700 electronic); Dir AASE LINDAHL.

Roskilde

Roskilde Universitetsbibliotek (Roskilde University Library): Universitetsvej 1, POB 258, 4000 Roskilde; tel. 46-74-20-00; fax 46-74-30-90; e-mail rub@ruc.dk; internet www.rub.ruc.dk; f. 1971; open to general public; humanities, social sciences and natural sciences; 600,000 vols, 200,000 units of non-book material; Dir NIELS SENIUS CLAUSEN.

Silkeborg

Silkeborg Bibliotek (Public Library): Hostrupsgade 41A, 8600 Silkeborg; tel. 87-22-19-00; fax 87-22-19-01; e-mail biblioteket@silkeborg.bib.dk; internet www.silkeborg-bibliotek.dk; f. 1900; 216,000 vols, plus 128,000 in the Children's Dept, 50,000 records and cassettes; Chief Librarian PETER BIRK.

Vejle

Vejle Bibliotek (Vejle Library): Willy Sørensens Plads 1, 7100 Vejle; tel. 75-82-32-00; fax 75-82-32-13; e-mail vejlebib@vejlebib.dk; internet www.vejlebib.dk; f. 1895; 487,388 vols (including audio-books, CDs and DVDs), 3,922 periodicals; Chief Librarian LONE KNAKKERGAARD.

Viborg

Landsarkivet for Nørrejylland (Provincial Archives of Northern Jutland): 8800 Viborg; tel. 86-62-17-88; fax 86-60-10-06; e-mail mailbox@lav.sa.dk; internet www.sa.dk/lav; f. 1889, opened 1891; 44 km of shelving; Dir C. R. JANSEN.

Museums and Art Galleries

Ålborg

Ålborg Historiske Museum: Algade 48, 9000 Ålborg; tel. 99-31-74-00; fax 98-16-11-31; e-mail historiskmuseum@aalborg.dk; internet www.nordjyllandshistoriskemuseum.dk; f. 1863; archaeology, history, ethnology, glass, silver, tobacco industry; Dir LARS CHRISTIAN NØRBACH.

Nordjyllands Kunstmuseum (Museum of Contemporary Art): Kong Christians Allé 50, 9000 Ålborg; tel. 98-13-80-88; fax 98-16-28-20; e-mail nordjyllandskunstmuseum@aalborg.dk; internet www.nordjyllandskunstmuseum.dk; f. 1877, building inaugurated 1972; Fine Art Dept: Danish art since 1900 (painting, sculpture, graphics, sculpture park); Anna and Kresten Krestensen Colln: Danish and int. art 1920–1950; Kirsten and Axel P. Nielsen Colln (art of 1960s and 1970s); library of 11,000 vols; Dir NINA HOBOLTH.

Århus

ARoS Århus Kunstmuseum (Århus Art Museum): Aros Allé 2, 8000 Århus C; tel. 87-30-66-00; fax 87-30-66-01; e-mail info@aros.dk; internet www.aros.dk; f. 1859; Danish art since the 18th century and modern international art; library of 21,000 vols; Dir JENS ERIK SØRENSEN.

Naturhistorisk Museum (Natural History Museum): Universitetsparken, Bygning 210, 8000 Århus C; tel. 86-12-97-77; fax 86-13-08-82; e-mail nm@nathist.dk; internet www.naturhistoriskmuseum.dk; f. 1921; Denmark exhibition: natural history of Danish landscapes; Danish Animals exhibition; Animals of the World exhibition; African Savannah exhibition; permanent field laboratory: 'Molslaboratoriet', Femmöller, 8400 Ebeltoft; the museum laboratories are open to scientists, and specialize in terrestrial ecology, limnology, entomology, acarology, mammalogy, ornithology and bio-acoustics; the library contains 15,000 vols; Dir THOMAS SECHER JENSEN; publs *Natura Jutlandica* (in English), *Natur og Museum* (in Danish).

Auning

Dansk Landbrugsmuseum (Danish Agricultural Museum): Gl. Estrup, 8963 Auning, Jutland; tel. 86-48-34-44; fax 86-48-41-82; e-mail dansklandbrugsmuseum@gl-estrup.dk; internet www.gl-estrup.dk; f. 1889; exhibitions on the history of country life, agricultural technology and bee-keeping; Dir PETER BAVNSHØJ.

Charlottenlund

Ordrupgaard: Vilvordevej 110, 2920 Charlottenlund; tel. 39-64-11-83; fax 39-64-10-05; e-mail ordrupgaard@ordrupgaard.dk; internet www.ordrupgaard.dk; f. 1918; French and Danish 19th- and early 20th-c. paintings, including works by Degas, Delacroix, Gauguin, Hammershøi, Manet, Pissarro and Renoir; Danish arts and crafts of the 19th c.; Dir ANNE-BIRGITTE FONSMARK.

Copenhagen

Botanisk Have (Botanic Garden): Øster Farimagsgade 2B, 1353 Copenhagen K; tel. 35-32-22-22; fax 35-32-22-21; e-mail bothave@snm.ku.dk; internet www.botanic-garden.ku.dk; f. 1874; 25 acres of landscape garden, palm-house and green-houses; rare trees, plants (13,000 species); Dir Prof. OLE HAMANN.

Danske Filminstitut – Museum og Cinematek (Danish Film Institute – Archive and Cinematheque): Gothersgade 55, 1123 Copenhagen K; tel. 33-74-34-00; fax 33-74-34-03; e-mail museum@dfi.dk; internet www.dfi.dk; f. 1941; collns of films, books, posters, documentation; cinemas with daily screenings; library of 65,000 vols, 13,500 scripts, 370 periodicals; Dir DAN NISSEN; publ. *Kosmorama* (2 a year).

Geologisk Museum (Geological Museum): University of Copenhagen, Øster Voldgade 5–7, 1350 Copenhagen K; tel. 35-32-23-45; fax 35-32-23-25; e-mail rcp@savik.geomus.ku.dk; internet www.nathimus.ku.dk/geomus; f. 1772; minerals, rocks, meteorites and fossils; geology of Denmark and Greenland; Origin of Man; plate tectonics; volcanoes; salt in the subsoil; library; attached to University of Copenhagen; Chair Prof. MINIK ROSING.

Københavns Bymuseum (Museum of Copenhagen): Absalonsgade 3, 1658 Copenhagen V; located at: Vesterbrogade 59, 1620 Copenhagen V; tel. 33-21-07-72; fax 33-25-07-72; e-mail sekr@bymuseum.dk; internet www.bymuseum.dk; f. 1901; history of Copenhagen incl. pictures, architecture, models; houses the colln of Kierkegaard relics; Dir JØRGEN SELMER.

Kunstindustrimuseet (Danish Museum of Decorative Art): Bredgade 68, 1260 Copenhagen K; tel. 33-18-56-56; fax 33-18-56-66; e-mail info@kunstindustrimuseet.dk; internet www.kunstindustrimuseet.dk; f. 1890; European applied art from the Middle Ages to modern times, Chinese and Japanese art; library of 63,000 vols on applied art; Pres. OLAV GRUE; Dir BODIL BUSK LAURSEN.

Nationalmuseet (National Museum): Frederiksholms Kanal 12, 1220 Copenhagen K; tel. 33-13-44-11; fax 33-47-33-33; e-mail direktoeren@natmus.dk; internet www.natmus.dk; f. 1807 on basis of the older Royal Collns; consists of 5 divs; Dir CARSTEN U. LARSEN; Keepers of divs: Classical Antiquities BODIL BUNDGAARD RASMUSSEN, Danish Prehistory POUL OTTO NIELSEN, Denmark since 1660 ANNETTE VASSTRÖM, Ethnographic Colln PER KRISTIAN MADSEN, Middle Ages and Renaissance MICHAEL ANDERSEN; publs *Nationalmuseets Arbejdsmark* (annual), *Nyt fra Nationalmuseet* (quarterly), *Skrifter* (in 3 series), *catalogues*.

Attached museums:

Frilandsmuseet (Open Air Museum): Kongevejen 100, 2800 Lyngby; tel. 33-47-34-81; fax 33-47-33-97; e-mail frilandsmuseet@natmus.dk; f. 1897; examples of more than 50 farms, mills and houses from 1650 to 1950, representing virtually every region in Denmark and the Faroe Islands as well as the fmr Danish provinces of southern Sweden and northern Germany; displays of rural crafts; incorporates Brede Works factory community with workmen's and foremen's houses, eating house, orphanage and nursery garden; Dir INGER TOLSTRUP.

Frihedsmuseet (Museum of Danish Resistance): Churchillparken, 1263 Copenhagen K; tel. 33-47-39-21; fax 33-14-03-14; e-mail frihedsmuseet@natmus.dk; f. 1957; chronological devt of Danish resistance during the Nazi occupation 1940–45; Dir ESBEN KJELDBÆK.

Musikmuseet – Musikhistorisk Museum og Carl Claudius' Samling (Music Museum – Musical History Museum and Carl Claudius Collection): Åbenrå 30, 1124 Copenhagen K; tel. 33-11-27-26; fax 33-11-60-44; e-mail musik@natmus.dk; f. 1898; extensive colln of musical instruments from all over the world with special emphasis on European instruments from the Renaissance onwards; concerts, library, archives; Dir Dr LISBET TORP.

Ny Carlsberg Glyptotek: Dantes Plads 7, 1556 Copenhagen V; tel. 33-41-81-41; fax 33-91-20-58; internet www.glyptoteket.dk; f. 1888; Danish and French sculpture and painting since 19th c., Egyptian, Greek, Roman and Etruscan art, mainly sculpture;

Pres. KARSTEN OHRT; Dir FLEMMING FRIBORG; publ. *Meddelelser* (annually).

Orlogsmuseet (Royal Danish Naval Museum): Overgaden oven Vandet 58, 1415 Copenhagen K; tel. 33-11-60-37; fax 33-93-71-52; e-mail thm@thm.dk; internet www.orlogsmuseet.dk; f. 1957; 400 items depicting the Danish navy since the early 18th c., including models of ships, weapons, ships' decorations and maritime art; Curators STEEN SCHØN, JAKOB SEERUP.

Rosenborg Slot (Rosenborg Castle): Øster Voldgade 4A, 1350 Copenhagen K; tel. 33-15-76-19; fax 33-15-20-46; e-mail museum@dkks.dk; internet www.rosenborgslot.dk; f. 1833; contains 'The Chronological Collns of the Danish Kings'; the colln was founded by Frederik III in about 1660, and depicts the history of Danish kings from Frederik II in the mid-16th century to Frederik VII in the 19th century; consists of arms, apparel, jewellery, and furniture from 1470–1863; also houses the Royal Regalia and the Crown Jewels; Dir Chamberlain NIELS EILSCHOU HOLM; Museum Dir NIELS-KNUD LIEBGOTT.

Attached museum:

Amalienborgmuseet (Amalienborg Museum): Christian VIII's Palace, 1257 Copenhagen K; tel. 33-12-32-86; fax 33-93-32-03; e-mail amalienborgmuseet@dkks.dk; internet www.amalienborgmuseet.dk; f. 1994; exhibitions cover the reigns of Danish kings, from 1863–1972 (Christian IX, Frederik VIII, Christian X and Frederik IX); Curator GERDA PETRI.

Statens Museum for Kunst (Danish National Gallery): Sølvgade 48–50, 1307 Copenhagen K; tel. 33-74-84-94; fax 33-74-84-04; e-mail smk@smk.dk; internet www.smk.dk; contains the main collection of Danish paintings and sculpture; a number of works by other Scandinavian artists since 19th c.; J. Rump collection of modern French art; about 1,000 paintings by old masters of the Italian, Flemish, Dutch and German Schools (chiefly derived from the old royal collection, which was established as an art gallery in the 1760s); The Print Room includes about 300,000 Danish and foreign prints and drawings; library: about 130,000 vols; Dir ALLIS HELLELAND; publ. *Statens Museum for Kunst Journal*.

Teatermuseet: Christiansborg, Ridebane 10–18, 1218 Copenhagen K; tel. 33-11-51-76; fax 33-12-50-22; e-mail teatermuseet@teatermuseet.dk; internet www.teatermuseet.dk; f. 1912; situated in the old Court theatre, built in 1767; illustrates the development of the Danish theatre since 18th c.; Dir ULLA STRØMBERG.

Thorvaldsens Museum: Bertel Thorvaldsens Plads 2, 1213 Copenhagen K; tel. 33-32-15-32; fax 33-32-17-71; e-mail thm@thorvaldsensmuseum.dk; internet www.thorvaldsensmuseum.dk; f. 1839; sculptures and drawings by the Danish sculptor Bertel Thorvaldsen (1770–1844), his collections of contemporary European paintings, drawings and prints, and classical antiquities; and his library, archives relating to Thorvaldsen's studies and the museum's history; library of 8,000 vols; Dir STIG MISS.

Tøjhusmuseet (Royal Danish Arsenal Museum): Administration: Frederiksholms Kanal 29, 1220 Copenhagen K; main entrance: Tøjhusgade 3, Copenhagen; tel. 33-11-60-37; fax 33-93-71-52; e-mail thm@thm.dk; internet www.thm.dk; f. 1838; central state museum for the history of the Danish defence forces and for arms and armour; history of arms in Europe, since the introduction of gunpowder; history and development of international military materials; Dir OLE LOUIS FRANTZEN.

Zoologisk Museum (University of Copenhagen Zoological Museum): Universitetsparken 15, 2100 Copenhagen Ø; tel. 35-32-10-00; fax 35-32-10-10; e-mail tpape@zmuc.ku.dk; internet www.zmuc.dk; f. 1770; research is organized in three scientific departments: Vertebrates and Quaternary Zoology; Invertebrates (excl. insects, myriapods and arachnids); and Entomology; public education programmes and school service; attached to Faculty of Science, University of Copenhagen; Dir THOMAS PAPE; publ. *Steenstrupia* (2 a year).

Dronningmølle

Rudolph Tegners Museum og Statuepark (Rudolph Tegners Museum and Statue Park): Museumsvej 19, 3120 Dronningmølle; tel. 49-71-91-77; e-mail luise@rudolphtegner.dk; internet www.rudolphtegner.dk; f. 1938; devoted to the works and collections of the sculptor Rudolph Tegner (1873–1950); 200 works in plaster, clay, bronze and marble; Dir LUISE GOMARD.

Elsinore

Danmarks Tekniske Museum (Danish Museum of Science and Technology): Fabriksvej 25, 3000 Elsinore; tel. 49-22-26-11; fax 49-22-62-11; e-mail info@tekniskmuseum.dk; internet www.tekniskmuseum.dk; f. 1911; steam engines, electric appliances (including Valdemar Poulsen's telegraphone, the forerunner of modern tape recording), bicycles, cars and aircraft; authentic pewter workshop; library of 18,000 vols; Dir JENS BREINEGAARD; publ. *Arbog* (Yearbook).

Handels- og Søfartsmuseet (Danish Maritime Museum): Kronborg, 3000 Elsinore; tel. 49-21-06-85; fax 49-21-34-40; e-mail info@maritime-museum.dk; internet maritime-museum.pro.dir.dk; f. 1914; Danish shipping since 1400, including the Sound Dues, the Napoleonic Wars, trade with China and the former Danish colonies in India, navigation and the Lifeboat Service; maritime objects, model ships, paintings, photographs and text boards; depiction of the Danish sailor's life since 16th c.; regular temporary exhibitions; store rooms containing several thousand paintings and objects; administrative building in the castle grounds containing the museum's records; library of 28,000 vols; special collections of logbooks and photographs; Dir HANS JEPPESEN; Sec. ULLA-BRITTA HANSEN.

Kronborg: Kronborg 2c, 3000 Elsinore; tel. 49-21-30-78; fax 49-21-30-52; e-mail kronborg@ses.dk; internet www.ses.dk/kronborg; f. 1425; fortified royal castle dating from the late 16th c.; contains the Royal Apartments (furniture, tapestry, regalia), banqueting hall, chapel; known as 'Hamlet's castle'; Dir LARS HOLST.

Hillerød

Nationalhistoriske Museum paa Frederiksborg Slot (Museum of National History at Frederiksborg Castle): Frederiksborg Slot, 3400 Hillerød; tel. 48-26-04-39; fax 48-24-09-66; e-mail frederiksborgmuseet@frederiksborgmuseet.dk; internet www.frederiksborgmuseet.dk; castle built in 1560s, extended 1600–20, and established as museum in 1878; contains a chronological collection of portraits and paintings illustrating the history of Denmark, each era in a separate room, the furniture and appointments in keeping with the period of the paintings; 10,000 exhibits; library of 15,000 vols; Pres. NIELS EILSCHOU HOLM (Chamberlain); Dir METTE SKOUGAARD.

Højbjerg

Moesgård Museum: Moesgård, 8270 Højbjerg; tel. 89-42-11-00; fax 86-27-23-78; e-mail moesgaard@hum.au.dk; internet www.moesmus.dk; f. 1861; collections of Danish prehistoric antiquities; research organization in environmental, Danish and Oriental archaeology and ethnology; Dir JAN SKAMBY MADSEN.

Hørsholm

Jagt- og Skovbrugsmuseet (Danish Museum of Hunting and Forestry): Folehavevej 15–17, 2970 Hørsholm; tel. 45-86-05-72; fax 45-76-20-02; e-mail museum@jagtskov.dk; internet www.jagtskov.dk; f. 1942; Curator JETTE BAAGØE.

Humlebæk

Louisiana Museum for Moderne Kunst (Louisiana Museum of Modern Art): Gl. Strandvej 13, 3050 Humlebæk; tel. 49-19-07-19; fax 49-19-35-05; e-mail curator@louisiana.dk; internet www.louisiana.dk; f. 1958; neo-classic villa and estate transformed into a modern museum of art; collection of Danish and international art, including works by Arp, Francis Bacon, Calder, Dubuffet, Ernst, Sam Francis, Giacometti, Kiefer, Henry Moore, Picasso, Rauschenberg and Warhol; exhibitions of contemporary artists; cinema, concerts, theatre; Dir POUL ERIK TOEJNER; publ. *Louisiana Revy* (2 a year).

Odense

Odense Bys Museer (Odense City Museums): Overgade 48, 5000 Odense C; tel. 65-51-46-01; fax 65-90-86-00; e-mail museum@odense.dk; internet www.odmus.dk; f. 1860; Dir TORBEN GRØNGAARD JEPPESEN; publs *Anderseniana* (annually), *Fynske Fortællinger* (annually), *Fynske Minder* (annually), *Fynske Studier* (annually).

Selected museums:

Carl Nielsen Museet (Carl Nielsen Museum): Claus Bergs Gade, 5000 Odense C; tel. 65-51-46-01; fax 65-90-86-00; e-mail museum@odense.dk; internet www.museum.odense.dk/Carl_Nielsen.aspx; f. 1980; devoted to the composer's life (1865–1931) and work; Curator EJNAR ASKGAARD.

Fyns Kunstmuseum (Funen Art Museum): Jernbanegade 13, 5000 Odense C; e-mail museum@odense.dk; internet www.museum.odense.dk/Fyens_Kunstmuseum.aspx; f. 1880 as a smaller version of the Statens Museum for Kunst; art gallery; collection contains works since 1750; Curator ANNE CHRISTIANSEN.

Fynske Landsby (Funen Village): Sejerskovvej 20, 5260 Odense S; tel. 65-51-46-01; fax 65-90-86-00; e-mail museum@odense.dk; internet www.museum.odense.dk/Den_Fynske_Landsby.aspx; open-air museum recreating the time of the era of Hans Christian Andersen (1805–1875); Curator MYRTUE ANDERS.

Hans Christian Andersens Hus (Hans Christian Andersen Museum): Bangs Boder 29, 5000 Odense C; e-mail museum@odense.dk; internet www.museum.odense.dk/H_C_Andersen.aspx; f. 1905; devoted to the writer's life (1805–1875) and work; Curator EJNAR ASKGAARD.

Odense City Museum–Møntergården: Overgade 48, 5000 Odense C; tel. 65-51-46-01; fax 65-90-86-00; e-mail museum@odense.dk; internet www.museum.odense.dk/Bymuseet_Moentergaarden.aspx; local cultural history, coins and medals, archaeology; Curators KARSTEN KJER MICHAELSEN, ANDERS MYRTUE.

Roskilde

Vikingeskibsmuseet i Roskilde (Viking Ship Museum): Vindeboder 12, 4000 Roskilde; tel. 46-30-02-00; fax 46-30-02-01; e-mail museum@vikingeskibsmuseet.dk; internet www.vikingeskibsmuseet.dk; f. 1969; exhibits the five Viking ships found at Skuldelev in 1962, and aims to promote research in ship-building history in general; research on maritime subjects is carried out in co-operation with the National Museum of Denmark; Dir TINNA DAMGÅRD-SØRENSEN.

Universities and Technical Universities

AALBORG UNIVERSITET

POB 159, Fredrik Bajers Vej 5, 9100 Ålborg
Telephone: 96-35-80-80
Fax: 98-15-22-01
E-mail: aau@aau.dk
Internet: www.aau.dk

Founded 1974
State control
Academic year: September to July

Rector: JØRGEN ØSTERGAARD
Vice-Rector: ERIK LAURSEN
Administrative Officer: PETER PLENGE
Librarian: NIELS-HENRIK GYLSTORFF

Number of teachers: 1,000
Number of students: 12,000

Publications: *Biannual Report*, *Uglen* (10 a year), *Videnskabet* (2 a year)

DEANS

Faculty of Humanities: OLE PREHN
Faculty of Social Sciences: MARGRETHE NØRGAARD
Faculty of Technology and Science: FINN KJAERSDAM

ATTACHED RESEARCH DEPARTMENTS

Department of Acoustics: sub-department of Institute of Electronic Systems.

Department of Architecture and Design.

Department of Business Studies.

Department of Building Technology and Structural Engineering.

Department of Civil Engineering.

Department of Communication.

Department of Communication Technology (KOM): sub-department of Institute of Electronic Systems.

Department of Computer Science (IESD).

Department of Control Engineering (PROCES): sub-department of Institute of Electronic Systems.

Department of Economics, Politics and Public Administration.

Department of Education and Learning.

Department of Energy Technology.

Department of Health Science and Technology.

Department of History, International and Social Studies.

Department of Languages and Intercultural Studies.

Department of Life Science.

Department of Mathematical Sciences.

Department of Mechanical Engineering.

Department of Music and Music Therapy.

Department of Physics and Nanotechnology.

Department of Production.

Department of Social Studies and Organization.

Esbjerg Department of Engineering.

Institute of Electronic Systems

AARHUS UNIVERSITET

Nordre Ringgade 1, 8000 Aarhus C
Telephone: 89-42-11-11
Fax: 89-42-11-09
E-mail: au@au.dk
Internet: www.au.dk

Founded 1928
State controlled
Languages of instruction: Danish, English
Academic year: September to June

Rector: NIELS CHRISTIAN SIDENIUS
Pro-Rector: KATHERINE RICHARDSON
Director: STIG MØLLER

Number of teachers: 2,200
Number of students: 31,000

Publications: *CAMPUS* (22 a year), *AUgustus* (quarterly)

DEANS

Faculty of Agricultural Sciences: JUST JENSEN
Faculty of Arts: BODIL DUE
Faculty of Health Services: SØREN MOGENSEN
Faculty of Science: ERIK MEINECHE SCHMIDT
Faculty of Social Sciences: TOM LATRUP-PEDERSEN
Faculty of Theology: CARSTEN RIIS
Aarhus School of Business: BØRGE OBEL
National Environmental Research Institute: HENRIK SANDBECH (Director-General)
School of Education: LARS-HENRIK SCHMIDT

PROFESSORS

Faculty of Arts (Nordre Ringgade, Bygning 328, 8000 Aarhus C; tel. 89-42-11-11; fax 89-42-12-00; e-mail hum@au.dk; internet www.au.dk/hum):

ANDERSEN, P. B., Media Science
BACH, S., Latin Languages
BOHN, O.-S., English
BRANDT, P. A., Semiotics
DAY, A., English
ENGBERG, J., History
HANNESTAD, N., Classical Archaeology
JUUL JENSEN, U., Philosophy
KYNDRUP, M., Aesthetics and Culture
LANGSTED, J., Drama
LARSEN, S. E., History of Literature
MARSCHNER, B., Music
MCGREGOR, W. B., Linguistics
MØLLER, P. U., Slavonic Languages
MORTENSEN, F., Media Science
NØLKE, H., Latin Languages
OTTO, T., Ethnography
PADE, M., Classical Studies
POULSEN, B., History
ROESDAHL, E., Medieval Archaeology
SCHANZ, H.-J., History of Ideas
SØRENSEN, P. E., Scandinavian Studies
TOGEBY, O., Scandinavian Studies
VANDKILDE, H., Prehistoric Archaeology
WAMBERG, N. J., Art History
WEDELL-WEDELLSBORG, A., Chinese

Faculty of Health Sciences (Vennelyst Boulevard 9, 8000 Aarhus C; tel. 89-42-11-22; fax 86-12-83-16; e-mail sun@au.dk; internet www.au.dk.sun):

AALKJAER, C., General Physiology
ANDERSEN, J. P., Molecular Physiology
ASTRUP, J., Neurosurgery
AUTRUP, H. N., Environment and Occupational Medicine
BEK, T., Ophthalmology
BLACK, F. T., Medicine
BOLUND, L., Clinical Genetics
BONDE, J. P., Clinical Occupational Medicine
BÜNGER, C., Experimental Orthopaedic Surgery
CHRISTENSEN, B., General Medicine
CHRISTENSEN, E. I., Structural Cell Biology
CHRISTIANSEN, G., Medical Molecular Biology
CLAUSEN, T., Physiology
DAHL, R., Lung Diseases and Allergology
DANSCHER, G., Neurobiology
DJURHUUS, J. C., Surgery
EHLERS, N., Ophthalmology
ESMANN, M., Biophysics
FALK, E., Ischaemic Heart Disease
FOLDSPANG, A., Health Service Research
FRØKIER, J., Clinical Psychology and Nuclear Medicine
FUGLSANG-FREDERIKSEN, A., Neurophysiology
GJEDDE, A., Positron Tomography
GLIEMANN, J., Biochemistry
GREGERSEN, H., Gastrointestinal Sensory Motor Function
GREGERSEN, M., Forensic Medicine
GREGERSEN, N., Medical Molecular Biology
GUNDERSEN, H. J., Stereology
GYLDENSTED, C., X-ray Diagnostics
HAMILTON-DUTOIT, S., Pathology
HASENKAM, J. M., Heart Surgery
HOKLAND, P., Experimental Clinical Research
HÖLLSBERG, P., Virology
HVID, I., Experimental Orthopaedics
ISIDOR, F., Prosthetics
JAKOBSEN, J. K., Neurology
JENSEN, P. H., Medical Biochemistry
JENSEN, T. S., Pain Research
JENSENIUS, J. C. T., Immunology
JØRGENSEN, T. M., Urology
KARRING, T., Periodontology
KILIAN, M., Microbiology and Immunology
KIRKEVOLD, M., Clinical Nursing Science
KØLVRAA, S., Clinical Genetics
LAMBERT, J. D. C., Physiology
LARSEN, M. J., Endodontics
LAURBERG, P., Endocrinology
LAURITZEN, T., General Practice
LEDET, T., Biochemical Pathology
MAASE, H. VON DER, Oncology
MAUNSBACH, A., Anatomy
MELSEN, B., Orthodontics
MOESTRUP, S. K., Medical Biochemistry
MOGENSEN, C. E. S., Medicine
MOGENSEN, S. C., Virology and Immunology
MORS, N. P. O., Experimental Clinical Research
MOSEKILDE, L., Bone Diseases
MULVANY, M., Cardiovascular Pharmacology
MUNK-JØRGENSEN, P., Psychiatry
MØLLER, J. V., Biophysics
NEXOE, E., Clinical Biochemistry
NIELSEN, S., Structural Cell Biology and Pathophysiology
NIELSEN, T. T., Cardiology
NYGAARD, H., Biomedical Engineering
OLSEN, J., Social Medicine
OVERGAARD, J., Experimental Cancer Research
OVESEN, T., Experimental Clinical Research
PAASKE, W., Cardiovascular Surgery
PAKKENBERG, B., Neurostereology
PAULSEN, P. K., Surgery
PEDERSEN, F. S., Molecular Oncology
PEDERSEN, J. C. M., Microbiology and Immunology
POULSEN, S., Paediatric Dentistry
RICHELSEN, B., Clinical Nutrition
ROSENBERG, R., Psychiatry
SABROE, S., Health Sciences
SCHIØTZ, P. O., Paediatrics
SCHMITZ, O., Clinical Pharmacology
SCHØNHEYDER, H., Clinical Microbiology
SIGSGAARD, T., Occupational Medicine

SØBALLE, K., Experimental Orthopaedic Surgery
SØRENSEN, F. B., Pathology
SØRENSEN, H. T., Clinical Epidemiology
STENGARD-PEDERSEN, K., Rheumatology
SVENSSON, P., Oral Physiology
THOMSEN, P. H., Psychiatry for Children and Adolescents
TOENNESEN, E., Anaesthesiology
VESTERBY, C. A., Forensic Medicine
VESTERGAARD, P., Psychiatry
VÆTH, M., Biostatistics
VILSTRUP, H., Hepatology
WEEKE, J., Medical Endocrinology
WENZEL, A., Oral Radiology
ØRNTOFT, T. F., Molecular Cancer Diagnostics

Faculty of Science (Ny Munkegade, Bygning 520, 8000 Aarhus C; tel. 89-42-31-88; fax 89-42-35-96; e-mail nat@au.dk; internet au.dk/nat):

ANDERSEN, H. H., Mathematics
ANDERSEN, J. U., Experimental Physics
ASMUSSEN, S., Mathematics
BALSLEV, H., Biology
BESENBACHER, F., Experimental Solid State Physics
BOLS, M., Chemistry
BØDKER, S., Computer Science
BØTTIGER, J., Materials Science
CHRISTENSEN, K. R., Biological Oceanography
CHRISTENSEN, N. E., Theoretical Solid State Physics
CHRISTENSEN-DALSGAARD, J., Astronomy
CHRISTIANSEN, F. V. B., Population Biology
CLARK, B., Chemistry
FIELD, D., Experimental Molecular Physics
GRONBAK, K. G., Computer Science
HANSEN, T. I., Sports Medicine
IVERSEN, B., Materials Chemistry
JACOBSEN, H. J., Chemistry
JANTZEN, J. C., Mathematics
JENSEN, J. L., Mathematical Statistics
JENSEN, K., Computer Science
JØRGENSEN, K. A., Organic Chemistry
JØRGENSEN, P., Theoretical Chemistry
KJEMS, J., Molecular Biology
KORSTGÅRD, J. A., Structural Geology and Basin Tectonics
KRAGH, H., History of Science
KRISTENSEN, M., Nanophotonics
LOESCHKE, V., Biology
MACINTOSH, D. J., Biology
MADSEN, I. H., Mathematics
MADSEN, O. L., Computer Science
MØLMER, K., Physics
NIELSEN, J. A., Mathematical Finance
NIELSEN, M., Theoretical Computer Science
NIELSEN, N. C., Solid State NMR
ODGAARD, B. V., Palynology
OGILBY, P. R., Chemistry
PETERSEN, J. S., Chemistry
PIETROWSKI, J., Quaternary Geology
RATTAN, S. I. S., Molecular Biology
REVSBECH, N. P., Microbial Ecology
SKRYDSTRUP, T., Chemistry
STENSGAARD, I., Experimental Solid State Physics
VEDEL, E. B., Mathematical Statistics
WEBER, R. E., Zoophysiology

Faculty of Social Sciences (Bartholins Allé, Bygning 350 Universitetsparken, 8000 Aarhus C; tel. 89-42-11-33; fax 89-42-15-40; e-mail samfundsvidenskab@au.dk; internet www.socialsciences.au.dk):

AGERVOLD, M., Psychology
ANDERSEN, T. M., Economic Planning
BASSE, E. M., Jurisprudence
BLOM-HANSON, J., Political Science
CHRISTENSEN, B. J., Economic Planning
CHRISTENSEN, J. G., Political Science
CHRISTENSEN, J. P., Jurisprudence
DALBERG-LARSEN, J. V., Jurisprudence
DAMGAARD, E., Political Science
DANIELSEN, J. H., Jurisprudence
ELKLIT, A., Psychology
ELKLIT, J., Political Science
EVALD, J., Jurisprudence
GENEFKE, J., Economic Planning
GERMER, P., Jurisprudence
HALDRUP, N., National Economy
HOEGH-OLESEN, H., Psychology
HYLLEBERG, S. A. F., National Economy
IVERSEN, B. O., Jurisprudence
IVERSEN, T., Jurisprudence
JØRGENSEN, P. L., Economics
KRISTENSEN, L. H., Jurisprudence
KVALE, S., Psychology
MADSEN, O. Ø., Economic Planning
MADSEN, P. B., Jurisprudence
MAMMEN, J., Psychology
MOLS, N. P., Management
MORTENSEN, P. B., Register-based Research
NANNESTAD, P., Political Science
NIELSEN, G. T., Jurisprudence
NØRGAARD, I. M., Jurisprudence
NØRGAARD, O., Political Science
NYBORG, H., Psychology
OVERGAARD, P. B., Economic Planning
PALDAM, N. M., Economic Planning
PEDERSEN, J., Jurisprudence
PEDERSEN, P. J., Economics
REVSBECH, K., Jurisprudence
RISBJERG THOMSEN, S., Political Science
ROSHOLM, M., National Economy
SOERENSEN, G., Political Science
SOMMER, D., Psychology
SVENDSEN, G. T., Political Science
SVENSSON, P., Political Science
THOMSEN, H. H. B., Jurisprudence
TOGEBY, L., Political Science
VASTRUP, C., Economics
VEDSTED-HANSEN, J., Jurisprudence
ZACHARIAS, B., Psychology

Faculty of Theology (Tåsingegade 3, 8000 Aarhus C; tel. 89-42-10-24; fax 86-13-04-90; e-mail teo@au.dk; internet www.au.dk/teo):

ANDERSEN, S., Ethics and Philosophy of Religion
BILDE, P., History of Religions
DAVIDSEN, O., Biblical Studies
GEERTZ, A., History of Religions
HVIDBERG-HANSEN, F. O., Semitic Philology
INGESMAN, P., Cultural History of Christianity
JENSEN, H. J. L., Study of Religions
MORTENSEN, V., Missiology and Ecumenical Theology
NIELSEN, K., Old Testament Exegesis
SCHJØRRING, J. H., Church History
WIDMANN, P., Dogmatics

CONSTITUENT INSTITUTIONS

Handelshøjskolen i Aarhus (Aarhus School of Business): Fuglesangs Allé 4, 8210 Aarhus V; tel. 89-48-66-88; fax 86-15-01-88; e-mail asb@asb.dk; internet www.asb.dkf. 1939; 7,000 students; depts of Business studies, Economics, Language and business communication, Law, Management, Marketing and statistics.

Danmarks Miljøundersøgelser (National Environmental Research Institute): Box 358, Frederiksborgvej 399, 4000 Roskilde; tel. 46-30-12-00; fax 46-30-11-14; e-mail dmu@dmu.dk; internet www.dmu.dkf. 1989; 295 research and consultancy staff; depts of Arctic environment, Atmospheric environment, Environmental chemistry and microbiology, Freshwater ecology, Marine ecology, Policy analysis, Terrestrial ecology, Wildlife ecology and biodiversity.

Jordbrugsvidenskabelige Fakultet (Faculty of Agricultural Sciences): Blichers Allé 20, POB 50, 8830 Tjele; tel. 89-99-19-00; e-mail djf@agrsci.dk; internet www.agrsci.org; 375 research scientists; research depts of Agricultural engineering, Agroecology and environment, Animal health, welfare and nutrition, Food science, Genetics and biotechnology, Horticulture, Integrated pest management.

Danmarks Pædagogiske Universitetsskole (Danish School of Education): Tuborgvej 164, 2400 Copenhagen NV; tel. 88-88-90-00; fax 88-88-90-01; e-mail dpu@dpu.dk; internet www.dpu.dkf. 2000; library: see Libraries and Archives; 148 teachers; 4,000 students; depts of Curriculum research, Educational anthropology, Educational philosophy, Educational psychology, Educational sociology, Learning lab Denmark.

DANMARKS FARMACEUTISK UNIVERSITET/DANISH UNIVERSITY OF PHARMACEUTICAL SCIENCES

Telephone: 35-30-60-00
Fax: 35-30-60-01
E-mail: dfuni@dfuni.dk
Internet: www.dfuni.dk

Founded 1892

Academic year: September to July

departments: Medicinal Chemistry, Pharmacy, Pharmacology, Analytical Chemistry, Social Pharmacy

Rector: Prof. SVEN FRØKJAER
Head of Administration: JUDITH CHRISTIANSEN

Number of teachers: 150
Number of students: 1,200

Publication: *Lægemiddelforskning* (Drug Research, annually).

DANMARKS TEKNISKE UNIVERSITET (Technical University of Denmark)

Bygning 101A, 2800 Lyngby

Telephone: 45-25-25-25
Fax: 45-88-17-99
E-mail: dtu@adm.dtu.dk
Internet: www.dtu.dk

Founded 1829

President: LARS PALLESEN
Vice-President: Prof. KNUT CONRADSEN
University Director: JØRGEN HONORÉ

Number of professors: 67
Number of teachers: 1,491
Number of students: 5,949

DEANS OF FACULTY COMMITTEES

Chemistry, Chemical Engineering and Biotechnology: Prof. JOHN VILLADSEN
Civil and Environmental Engineering: Assoc. Prof. KNUD CHRISTENSEN
Electrical Engineering and Physics: Prof. STEEN MØRUP
Information Technology, Electronics and Mathematics: Prof. ERIK BRUUN
Mechanical Engineering, Energy and Production: Prof. P. TERNDRUP PEDERSEN

PROFESSORS

ADLER-NISSEN, J. L., Biotechnology
AHRING, B. K., Biotechnology
ALTING, L., Mechanical Engineering
ANDREANI, P., Analogue Integrated Systems
ANDERSEN, M. A. E., Power Electronics
ANDRAESEN, M. M., Product Development
ARVIN, E., Water Supply Engineering
BAY, N., Materials Processing
BENDSØE, M., Applied Functional Analysis
BJARKLEV, A. O., Optical Communication
BJERG, P. L., Environmental Geochemistry
BJERRUM, N., Chemical Engineering
BJØRNER, D., Computer Science
BLANKE, M.
BOHR, H., Biomolecular Structure and Function
BOHR, J., Physics

BOHR, T., Theoretical Physics
BRUNAK, S., Bio-informatics
BRUUN, K. E., Analogue Electronics
BRUUN, P., Industrial Management
BRØNS, M., Mathmematics
BUCHHAVE, P., Optics
CARLSEN, H., Energy Engineering
CHIFFRE, DE, L., Process Technology, Geometrical Metrology
CHORKENDORFF, I., Heterogeneous Catalysis
CHRISTENSEN, C. J. H., Heterogeneous Catalysis
CHRISTENSEN, E. L., Microwave Systems
CHRISTENSEN, TH. H., Environmental Engineering
CHRISTIANSEN, P. L., Non-linear Dynamics
CLAUSEN, J., Mathematic Optimization
CONRADSEN, K., Statistical Image Analysis
DAM-JOHANSEN, K., Combustion and Chemical Reaction Engineering
DAU, T., Hearing Aid Audiology and Acoustics
DITLEVSEN, O. D., Actions on Structures and Structural Reliability
EMMITT, S., Innovation and Management in Building
FANGER, P. O., Heating and Air Conditioning
FOGED, N., Geotechnical Engineering
FREDSØE, J., Marine Hydraulics
GAARSLEV, A., Construction Management
GANI, R., Systems Design
GIMSING, N. J., Structural Engineering
HAMMER, K., Microbiology
HANSEN, E. H., Analytical Chemistry
HANSEN, H. N., Microtechnical Production
HANSEN, L. K., Digital Signal Processing
HANSEN, P. C., Scientific Computing
HANSEN, P. F., Safety Assessment of Marine Systems
HANSEN, V. L., Mathematics
HASSAGER, O.
HEIN, L., Engineering Design Methodology
HENZE, M., Waste-water Engineering
HVAM, J. M., Optoelectronics
HVILSTED, S.
JACOBI, O. I., Geoinformatics and Photogrammetry
JACOBSEN, K. W., Physics
JAUHO, A.-P., Theoretical Nanotechnology
JENSEN, J. A., Biomedical Signal Processing
JENSEN, J. J., Marine Structures
JENSEN, O. M., Building Materials
JENSEN, P. L., Technology and Working Life – Working Environment
JEPPESEN, P., Optical Communication
JOHNSSON, J. E., Chemical Reaction Engineering
JUSTESEN, J., Error-Correcting Codes, Information Theory
JØRGENSEN, S. B., Technical Chemistry
KLEMM, P., Applied Microbiology
KLIT, P., Machine Elements and Lubrication Theory
KNUDSEN, L. R., Cryptology
KNUDSEN, S., Experimental and Computational Gene Expression Analysis
KRENK, S., Structural Mechanics
KRISTENSEN, M., Glass Components
KROZER, V., Microwave Electronics
LARSEN, P. S., Fluid Mechanics
LELEUR, S., Decision Support Systems and Planning
LIND, M., Control Systems
LUNDT, I.
LYNGAAE-JOERGENSEN, J., Polymer Technology
MADSEN, H.
MADSEN, J., Computer Systems
MADSEN, K., Numerical Analysis
MADSEN, O. G., Transport Optimization
MADSEN, P., Hydrodynamics
MADSEN, S. N.
MARKVORSEN, S., Differential Geometry
MENON, A., Microsystems Technology
MOLIN, S., Applied Microbiogenetics
MOLLERUP, J., Chromatography and Thermodynamics
MØLLER, P., Corrosion and Surface Technology
MØLTOFT, J., Reliability Engineering
MØRK, J., Active Semiconductor Components for Optical Communication Systems
MØRUP, S., Physics of Nanostructures
NIELSEN, J. B., Fermentation Physiology
NIELSEN, M. P., Structural Analysis
NIELSEN, O. A., Transport Planning
NIELSON, F., Computer Science
NIELSON, H. R., Programming Language Technology and Secure IT-Systems
NILSSON, J. F., Computer Science
NØRSKOV, J. K., Theoretical Physics
OLESEN, B. W., Indoor Environment and Energy
PAUL, J., Refrigeration
PEDERSEN, N. F.
PEDERSEN, P., Structural Mechanics
PEDERSEN, P. T., Strength of Materials
POLACK, J., Acoustics
QVALE, B., Mechanical Engineering
REITZEL, E., Form-finding of Minimal Structures
ROENNE-HANSEN, J., Electric Power Engineering
SKOU, N., Radar and Radiometer Systems
SKOUBY, K. E., Economy and Regulation of Telecommunication
SKRIVER, H. L.
SOMERS, M. A., Physical Metallurgy
SPLIID, H., Applied Statistics: Statistical Practice and Consulting
STENBY, H. E., Applied Thermodynamics and Separation Processes
STUBKJAER, K. E.
SUNDELL, J.
SVENDSEN, SV. AA. HØJGAARD, Energy Technology in Buildings
SVENSSON, B., Food Protein Biochemistry
TANNER, D., Organic Chemistry
TELLEMAN, P., Biochemical Microsystems
THOMASSEN, C., Mathematics
TROMBORG, B., Optoelectronics
TVERGAARD, V., Mechanics of Materials
TØNNESEN, O., Experimental High Voltage Technique
ULSTRUP, J., Inorganic Chemistry
VESTERAGER, J., Product Development
VILLADSEN, J., Biotechnology
VILLUMSEN, A., Geology
WANHEIM, T., Machine Engineering

HANDELSHØJSKOLEN I ÅRHUS
(Århus School of Business)

Fuglesangs Allé 4, 8210 Århus V
Telephone: 89-48-66-88
Fax: 86-15-01-88
Internet: www.asb.dk

Founded 1939

Rector: BØRGE OBEL
Secretary: JAN HALLE
Librarian: TOVE BANG

Number of teachers: 744 (266 full-time, 478 part-time)
Number of students: 7,150

PROFESSORS

ANDERSEN, K. A., Management Science
ANDERSEN, P., International Business
ANDERSEN, P. K., Company Law
BALLING, M., Finance
BERGENHOLTZ, H., Lexicography
BUKH, P. N., Financial Accounting
DREJER, A., Organization
ENGSTED, T., Finance
ERIKSSON, T., Economics
FRANDSEN, F., French
FREYTAG, P. V., Marketing
GROSEN, A., Finance
GRUNERT, K. G., Marketing
HASSELBALCH, O., Business Law
HILDEBRANDT, S., Organization Theory and Management
JENSEN, P., Economics
JUHL, H. J., Applied Statistics
KOCH, W., German
KRISTENSEN, K., Applied Statistics
MICHELSEN, A A., Tax Law
MØLLER, P. F., Financial Accounting
NEVILLE, M., Business Law
NØRREKLIT, H. S.-O., International Business
PILEGAARD, M., English
SKYTTE, H., Marketing
SMITH, N., Economics
STRANDSKOV, J., International Business
SØRENSEN, K. E., Business Law
TANGGAARD, C., Finance
THORSTENSON, A., Logistics
THRANE, T., English
THØGERSEN, J. C. B., Marketing
WESTERGÅRD-NIELSEN, N., Economics (Labour Economics)
ÖLANDER, F., Economic Psychology
ULHÖI, J. P., Organization Theory and Management

HANDELSHØJSKOLEN I KØBENHAVN
(Copenhagen Business School)

Solbjerg Plads 3, 2000 Frederiksberg
Telephone: 38-15-38-15
Fax: 38-15-20-15
E-mail: cbs@cbs.dk
Internet: www.cbs.dk

Founded 1917
State control
Academic year: September to July

President: FINN JUNGE-JENSEN
University Director: GERT BECHLUND
Executive Secretary: PERNILLE RISEGAARD

Library: see under Libraries and Archives
Number of teachers: 378
Number of students: 14,823

Publications: *ARK*, *CEBAL*, *SPRINT*, *Yearbook*

DEANS

Faculty of Economics and Business Administration: JENS AARIS THISTED
Faculty of Languages, Communication and Cultural Studies: SØREN BARLEBO RASMUSSEN

IT-UNIVERSITETET I KØBENHAVN
(IT University of Copenhagen)

Rued Langgaards Vej 7, 2300 Copenhagen S
Telephone: 72-18-50-00
Fax: 72-18-50-01
E-mail: itu@itu.dk
Internet: www1.itu.dk

Founded 1999; independent university status 2003
State-funded, autonomous control
Academic year: September to June

Vice-Chancellor: Dr MADS TOFTE
Chair of the Board: MOGENS MUNK RASMUSSEN

Number of teachers: 118
Number of students: 1,375

HEADS OF DEPARTMENTS

Department of Design and Use of Information Technology: ANNE LOTTE MØRK
Department of Digital Aesthetics and Communication: LISBETH KLASTRUP (acting)
Department of Innovation: CAMILLA JØRGENSEN HOLM
Department of Theoretical Computer Science: ANNETTE HJORT KNUDSEN

KØBENHAVNS UNIVERSITET
(University of Copenhagen)

Frue Plads/Noerregade 10, POB 2177, 1017 Copenhagen K
Telephone: 35-32-26-26
Fax: 35-32-26-28
E-mail: ku@ku.dk
Internet: www.ku.dk

Founded 1479
State control
Language of instruction: Danish
Academic year: September to August (2 terms)

Rector: RALF HEMMINGSEN
Pro-Rector: LYKKE FRIIS
University Director: ELSE SOMMER
Librarian: MICHAEL COTTA-SCHØNBERG

Number of teachers: 3,583
Number of students: 37,000

DEANS

Faculty of Health Science: ULLA WEWER
Faculty of Humanities: JOHN KUHLMANN MADSEN
Faculty of Law: VAGN GREVE
Faculty of Life Sciences: PER HOLTEN-ANDERSEN
Faculty of Science: NIELS O. ANDERSEN
Faculty of Social Sciences: TROELS OESTERGAARD SØRENSEN
Faculty of Theology: STEFFEN KJELDGAARD-PEDERSEN

PROFESSORS

Faculty of Health Sciences (Panum Instituttet, Blegdamsvej 3, 2200 Copenhagen N; tel. 35-32-79-00; fax 35-32-70-70; e-mail sund-fak@adm.ku.dk; internet www.sund.ku.dk):

- ASMUSSEN, E., Dental Materials
- BENDIXEN, G., Internal Medicine
- BOCK, E. M., Cellular Biology
- BOCK, J. E., Obstetrics and Gynaecology
- BOLWIG, T. G., Psychiatry
- BOYSEN, G., Neurology
- BRETLAU, P., Oto-rhino-laryngology
- BUUS, S., Basic Immunology
- CHRISTENSEN, N. J., Internal Medicine
- CHRISTOFFERSEN, P., Pathological Anatomy
- DABELSTEEN, S. E., Oral Diagnosis
- DEURS, B. G., Structural Cell Biology
- DIRKSEN, A., Internal Medicine
- GALBO, H., Physiopathology
- GJERRIS, F. O., Neurosurgery
- GYNTELBERG, F., Occupational Medicine
- HALD, T., Surgery
- HAUNSØ, S., Internal Medicine
- HEMMINGSEN, R. P., Psychiatry
- HENRIKSEN, J. H., Clinical Physiology
- HJØRTING-HANSEN, E., Oral and Maxillofacial Surgery
- HOLLNAGEL, H., General Practice
- HOLMSTRUP, P., Periodontology
- HOLST, J. J., Medical Physiology
- HORNSLET, A., Virology
- HULTBORN, H., Neurophysiology
- HØIBY, N., Microbiology
- KEHLET, N., Surgery
- KEIDING, N., Statistics
- KRASILNIKOFF, P. A., Paediatrics
- KRASNIK, A., Social Medicine
- KREIBORG, S., Paedodontics
- LARSEN, J. F., Obstetrics and Gynaecology
- LARSEN, S., Pathological Anatomy
- LORENZEN, I., Internal Medicine
- LUND, B., Surgery
- LUND-ANDERSEN, H., Eye Diseases
- MELLERGÅRD, M. J., Psychiatry
- MENNÉ, T., Dermatology
- MICHELSEN, N., Clinical Social Medicine
- MOGENSEN, J. V., Anaesthesiology
- MORLING, N., Forensic Genetics
- NIELSEN, J. O., Epidemic Diseases
- NORÉN, O., Biochemistry
- OLESEN, J., Neurology
- OTTESEN, B., Obstetrics and Gynaecology
- PAULSON, O. B., Neurology
- PETERSEN, P. E., Community Dentistry and Postgraduate Education
- PETTERSON, G., Thoraxsurgery
- PHILIP, J., Obstetrics and Gynaecology
- POULSEN, H. E., Clinical Pharmacology
- PRAUSE, J. U., Eye Diseases
- QUISTOR, F. F., Biochemistry
- REHFELD, J. F., Clinical Chemistry
- REIBEL, J., Oral Pathology and Oral Medicine
- ROSTGAARD, J., Normal Anatomy
- ROVSING, H. C., Radiology
- RØRTH, M., Clinical Oncology
- SCHOU, J., Pharmacology
- SCHROEDER, T. V., Surgery
- SCHROLL, M., Geriatrics
- SCHWARTZ, T. W., Molecular Pharmacology
- SIGGAARD-ANDERSEN, O., Clinical Chemistry and Laboratory Technique
- SIMONSEN, J., Forensic Pathology
- SJÖSTRÖM, H., Biochemistry
- SKAKKEBÆK, N., Paediatrics
- SKINHØJ, P., Epidemic Diseases
- SKOUBY, F., Paediatrics
- SOLOW, B., Orthodontics
- SØRENSEN, T. I. A., Clinical Epidemiology
- STADIL, F. W., Surgery
- SVEJGAARD, A., Clinical Immunology
- THYLSTRUP, A., Cardiology
- TOMMERUP, N., Medical Genetics
- TOS, M., Oto-rhino-laryngology
- VEJLSGAARD, G., Dermato-venereology
- WULF, H. C., Dermato-venereology
- WULFF, H. R., Clinical Decision Theory and Ethics
- ØLGAARD, K., Internal Medicine
- ÖWALL, B., Prosthodontics

Faculty of Humanities (Njalsgade 80, 2300 Copenhagen S; tel. 35-32-80-60; fax 35-32-80-52; e-mail hum-fak@fak.hum.ku.dk; internet www.hum.ku.dk):

- BOLVIG, A., History
- BONDEBJERG, I, Film Studies
- COLLIN, F., Philosophy
- DUNCAN, R., American Studies
- EKSELL, K., Semitic Philosophy
- ELBRO, C., Linguistics
- FLOTO, I., History
- FORTESQUE, M., Linguistics
- GABRIELSEN, V., Ancient History
- HARDER, P., English Literature
- HJARVARD, S., Film Studies
- HOV, L., Theatre
- HØJRUP, T., Ethnology
- JENSEN, K. B., Media Studies
- JØRGENSEN, J. N., Danish Language
- LIND, G., History
- LUND, N., History
- RANDSBORG, K., Archaeology
- RUUS, H., Danish Language
- SCHWAB, H., Music
- VILLAUME, P., History
- ZERLANG, M., Comparative Literature

Faculty of Law (Kannikestraede 11, 1169 Copenhagen K; tel. 35-32-26-26; fax 35-32-35-86; e-mail jurfak@jur.ku.dk; internet www.jur.ku.dk):

- BALVIG, F., Legal Sociology and Sociology of Law
- BLUME, P., Legal Informatics
- BONDESON, U., Criminology
- BRYDE ANDERSEN, M., Private Law, Computer Law
- DUE, O., European Union Law
- FOIGEL, I., Law of Taxation
- GREVE, V., Criminal Law
- KETSCHER, K., Social Law
- KOKTVEDGAARD, M., Law of Competition, Intellectual Property Law
- KRARUP, O., Public Law
- LOOKOFSKY, J., Law of Contracts and Torts, Private International Law
- NIELSEN, L., Family Law
- RASMUSSEN, H., International Law and European Union Law
- RØNSHOLDT, S., Administrative Law
- SMITH, E., Legal Procedure
- TAKSØE-JENSEN, F., Family Law, Law of Wills and Succession
- TAMM, D., History of Law
- VON EYBEN, B., Law of Property
- ZAHLE, H., Jurisprudence

Faculty of Life Science (Bülowsvej 17, 1870 Frederiksberg C; tel. 35-28-28-28; fax 35-28-26-64; e-mail life@life.dk; internet www.life.ku.dk):

- AASTED, B., Veterinary Microbiology
- ANKER, H., Economics and Natural Resources
- ASTRUP, A., Human Nutrition
- BAUER, R., Mathematics and Physics
- BISGAARD, M., Veterinary Microbiology
- BJERRUM, M., Chemistry
- BLIXENKRONE-MØLLER, M., Veterinary Microbiology
- BOGETOFT, P., Economics and Natural Resources
- BORGGÅRD, O., Chemistry
- CHRISTENSEN, L. P. G., Animal Sciences and Animal Health
- CHWALIBOG, A., Animal Science and Animal Health
- COLLINGE, D., Plant Biology
- ERIKSEN, E. N., Agricultural Sciences
- ESBJERG, P., Ecology and Molecular Biology
- FLAGSTAD, A., Clinical Sciences
- FLENSTED-JENSEN, M., Mathematics and Physics
- FRANDSEN, F., Ecology and Molecular Biology
- FREDHOLM, M., Animal Sciences and Animal Health
- FRIIS, C., Pharmacology and Pathobiology
- GIESE, H., Ecology and Molecular Biology
- GREVE, T., Clinical Sciences
- HANSEN, A. K., Pharmacology and Pathobiology
- HANSEN, H. C. B., Chemistry
- HAVE, H., Agricultural Sciences
- HELLES, F., Economics and Natural Resources
- HOVE, H., Animal Sciences and Animal Health
- HYLDGAARD-JENSEN, J., Anatomy and Physiology
- HYTTEL, P., Anatomy and Physiology
- JAKOBSEN, M., Agricultural Sciences
- JACOBSEN, N., Botany and Forest Genetics
- JENSEN, A. L., Clinical Sciences
- JENSEN, H. E., Agricultural Sciences
- KJELDSEN-KRAGH, S., Economics and Natural Sciences
- KÆRGAARD, N., Economics and Natural Resources
- LADEWIG, J., Animal Sciences and Animal Health
- LARSEN, J. B., Economics and Natural Resources
- LARSEN, J. L., Veterinary Microbiology
- LARSEN, L. E., General and Inorganic Chemistry
- LARSSON, L., Anatomy and Physiology
- MADSEN, J., Animal Sciences and Animal Health
- MARTENS, M., Dairy and Food Science
- MUNCK, L., Dairy and Food Sciences
- MØLLER, B. LINDBERG, Plant Biology
- NIELSEN, J., Chemistry
- NIELSEN, J. P., Clinical Sciences
- NIELSEN, N. E., Agricultural Sciences
- OLESEN, P. O., Agricultural Sciences
- OLSEN, I. A., Economics and Natural Resources
- OLSEN, J. E., Veterinary Microbiology
- PALMGREN, M., Plant Biology
- PORTER, J. R., Agricultural Sciences

PRIMDAHL, J., Economics and Natural Resources
QVIST, K. B., Dairy and Food Sciences
RUDEMO, M., Mathematics and Physics
SANDOE, P., Animal Sciences and Animal Health
SANDSTRÖM, B., Human Nutrition
SEBEK, M., Agricultural Sciences
SKADHAUGE, E., Anatomy and Physiology
SKIBSTED, L. H., Dairy and Food Sciences
SKOVGAARD, I. M., Mathematics and Physics
STAUN, H., Animal Sciences and Animal Health
STREIBIG, J. C., Agricultural Sciences
SVALASTOGA, E., Clinical Sciences
SVENDSEN, O., Pharmacology and Pathobiology
SØRENSEN, J., Ecology and Molecular Biology
THAMSBORG, S. M., Veterinary Microbiology
WEINER, J., Ecology and Molecular Biology

Faculty of Science (Øster Voldgade 3, 1350, Copenhagen K; tel. 35-32-42-12; fax 35-32-80-52; e-mail nat-fak@adm.ku.dk; internet www.nat.ku.dk):

ALS-NIELSEN, J., Experimental Condensed-Matter Physics
AMBJØRN, J., Physics
ANDERSEN, H. H., Physics
ANDERSEN, J. E. B., Human Physiology
ANDERSEN, N. O., Physics
ARCTANDER, P., Zoology
BATES, J. R., Meteorology
BERCHTOLD, M., Molecular Cell Biology
BERG, C., Mathematics
BJØRNHOLM, T., Chemistry
BONDE, H., Human Physiology
BOOMSMA, J., Zoology
BREUNING-MADSEN, H., Geography
CHRISTENSEN, S., Zoology
CHRISTIANSEN, C., Geography, Geomorphology
DAHL-JENSEN, D., Physics
EGEL, R., Genetics
ENGHOFF, H., Zoological Systematics and Zoological Geography
FENCHEL, T. M., Marine Biology
FJELDSÅ, J., Biodiversity
FREI, R. E., Geology
FRIIS, I., Systematic Botany and Plant Geography
GARRETT, R., Biology
GRIMMELIKHUIJZEN CORNELIS, J. P., Zoology
GRUBB, G., Mathematics
HAMANN, O., Botany
HAMMER, C. U., Geophysics
HANSEN, J., Physics
HANSEN, J. R., Physics
HARPER, D. A. T., Geology
HENGLEIN, F., Computer Science
JACKSON, A. O., Theoretical Nuclear Physics
JENSEN, K. H., Geology
JENSEN, K. S., Zoology
JENSEN, M. H., Physics
JOHANSEN, P., Computer Science
JOHANSEN, S., Mathematical Statistics
JONASSON, S. E., Ecological Botany
JONES, N. D., Computer Science
JUL, E., Computer Science
JØRGENSEN, H. E., Astronomy
KIMING, I., Mathematics
KRARUP, J. F., Computer Science
KRISTENSEN, N. P., Systematic Entomology
KRISTENSEN, R. M., Invertebrate Zoology
KROGH, A. S., Bioinformatics
KRÜGER, J., Geography
KÜHL, M., Zoology
LARSEN, E. H., Zoophysiological Laboratory
LARSEN, S. Y., Chemistry
LAURITSEN, F. R., Chemistry
LETH-JØRGENSEN, P., Cell Biology
MCGREGOR, P. K., Zoology
MAKOVICKY, E., Geology
MATTHIESSEN, C. W., Geography
MIKKELSEN, K. V., Chemistry
MIKOSCH, T., Mathematics
MOESTRUP, Ø., Spore Plants
MUNDY, J., Plant Physiology
NIELSEN, H. B., Theoretical Physics
NIELSEN, M. S., Freshwater Biology
NIELSEN, O. H., Molecular Biology
NIELSEN, O. J., Chemistry
NOVIKOV, I., Astronomy
OLESEN, P., Physics
PEDERSEN, G. K., Mathematics
PEDERSEN, P. A., Cell Biology
PEJRUP, M., Geography
PFISTER, G. U., Human Physiology
POLZIK, E., Physics
POULSEN, F. M., Molecular Biology
RAHBEK, C., Zoology
RICHTER, E. A., Exercise Physiology, Human Physiology
ROSENDAHL, S., Botany
ROSING, M. T., Geology
SCHMIDLI, H. P., Mathematics
SHAFFER, G., Geophysics
SKELBOE, S., Computer Science
SMITH, H., Physics
SOLOVEJ, J. P., Mathematics
SURLYK, F., Geology
SØRENSEN, M., Mathematics
THYBO, H., Geology
TIND, J., Mathematical Economics
TSCHERNING, C., Geophysics
WILLUMSEN, B. M., Molecular Biology
WINSLØW, C. E. B., Science Education
ØDUM, N. F., Molecular Biology

Faculty of Social Sciences (Kannikestraede 13, 1169 Copenhagen K; tel. 35-32-26-26; fax 35-32-35-32; e-mail samf-fak@samf.ku.dk; internet www.samf.ku.dk):

ANDERSEN, E., Economics
ANDERSEN, E. B., Theoretical Statistics
BERTILSSON, M., Sociology
ESTRUP, H., Economics
GRODAL, B. K., Economics
GUNDELACH, P., Sociology
GØRTZ, E., Social Description
HASTRUP, K., Anthropology
HEURLIN, B., Political Science
HJORTH-ANDERSEN, C., Economics
JUSELIUS, K., Economics
JØRGENSEN, T. B., Political Science
KEIDING, H., Economics
KNUDSEN, T., Political Science
PEDERSEN, O. K., International Politics
PEDERSEN, O. K., Political Science
SCHULTZ, C., Economics
SJØBLOM, B. G., Political Science
SØRENSEN, P. B., Economics
THYGESEN, N. C., Economics
VIND, K., Economic

Faculty of Theology (Købmagergade 44–46, ST, 1150 Copenhagen K; tel. 35-32-26-26; fax 35-32-26-26; e-mail dtf@fak.teol.ku.dk; internet www.teol.ku.dk):

GLEBE-MØLLER, J., Dogmatics
GRANE, L., Church History
GRØN, A., Ethics and Philosophy of Religion
HANSEN, H. B., Church History
HYLDAHL, N. C., New Testament Exegesis
JØRGENSEN, T., Dogmatics
KJELDGAARD-PEDERSEN, S., Church History, History of Dogma
LAUSTEN, M. S., Theology, Danish Church History
LEMCHE, N. P., Old Testament Exegesis
MÜLLER, M., New Testament Exegesis
THOMPSON, T. L., Old Testament Exegesis

ROSKILDE UNIVERSITETSCENTER

POB 260, Universitetsvej 1, 4000 Roskilde
Telephone: 46-74-20-00
Fax: 46-74-30-00
E-mail: ruc@ruc.dk
Internet: www.ruc.dk

Founded 1972
State control
Academic year: September to June (two semesters)

Rector: HENRIK TOFT JENSEN
Pro-Rector: INGER JENSEN
Administrative Officer: ERIK EBBE
Librarian: NIELS SENIUS CLAUSEN

Library of 500,000 vols
Number of teachers: 500
Number of students: 8,000

PROFESSORS

Humanities:

BRASK, P., Science of Texts, Theory and Methodology of Literary Analysis
BRYLD, C., History
DENCIK, L., Social Psychology
ELLE, B., Educational Psychology
HELTOFT, L., Danish
ILLERIS, K., Educational Research
KAMPMANN, J., Educational Research
KJØRUP, S., Philosophy and Communication
MCGUIRE, B. P., History
MORTENSEN, A. T., Philosophy and Communication
NISSEN, G., History
OLESEN, H. S., Educational Psychology
PEDERSEN, S., Philosophy
POULSEN, IB., Danish
POULSEN, J., Journalism
PREISLER, B., English
SCHRØDER, K. CHR., Communication
SIMONSEN, B., Educational Research
WEBER, K., Educational Research
WUCHERPHENNIG, W. P., German

Natural Sciences:

AGGER, P., Environmental Planning
ANDERSEN, O., Environmental Science
BRANDT, J., Geography
DYRE, J. C., Physics
FORBES, V. E., Environmental Biology
GALLAGHER, J. P., Computer Science
HANSEN, P. E., Chemistry
ILLERIS, S., Geography
LØBNER-OLESEN, A., Molecular Biology
NIELSEN, L. K., Transport and Environment
NISS, M., Mathematics
PRÆSTGAARD, E., Chemistry
SCHROLL, H., Environmental Assessment
SIMONSEN, K. F., Geography
SØRENSEN, B. E., Physics
THULSTRUP, E., Chemistry
WESTH-ANDERSEN, P., Chemistry

Social Sciences:

AAGE, H., Political Economy
ANDERSEN, J., Social Sciences
BOGASON, P., Public Administration
BOJE, TH. P., Social Sciences
DAVIS, J. D., Political Economy
FRAMKE, W., Tourism Planning
GREVE, B., Public Administration
JESPERSEN, J., Welfare State Studies
LAURIDSEN, L. S., International Development
MARCUSSEN, H. S., Institutional Aspect of Natural Resource Management
MATTSON, J., Business Administration
NIELSEN, K., Industrial Theory
NIELSEN, K. A., Technological and Organizational Development of Enterprises
OLSEN, O. J., Planning
SCHEUER, S., Social Sciences
SUNDBO, J., Business Administration
TORFING, J., Social Sciences
WHISTON, TH. G., Environmental Regulation

SYDDANSK UNIVERSITET
(University of Southern Denmark)

Campusvej 55, 5230 Odense M
Telephone: 65-50-10-00
Fax: 65-50-10-90
E-mail: sdu@sdu.dk
Internet: www.sdu.dk

Founded 1964 as Odense Universitet; present name 1998, following merger with Handelshøjskole Syd – Ingeniørhøjskole Syd and several other instns of higher education
State control
Languages of instruction: Danish, English
Academic year: September to June (two semesters)

Rector: JENS ODDERSHEDE
Pro-Rectors: FLEMMING JUST JØRN HENRIK PETERSEN
Chief Administrative Officer: PER OVERGAARD NIELSEN
Library: see under Libraries and Archives
Number of teachers: 747
Number of students: 16,500
Publication: *Ny Viden* (12 a year)

DEANS

Faculty of Arts: FLEMMING G. ANDERSEN
Faculty of Health Sciences: MOGENS HØRDER
Faculty of Science and Engineering: HENRIK PEDERSEN
Faculty of Social Sciences: BJARNE G. SØRENSEN

PROFESSORS

Faculty of Arts (tel. 65-50-29-31; fax 65-93-20-55; internet www.hum.sdu.dk):

BACHE, C., English Language and Literature
BASBØLL, H., Scandinavian Language
BORGNAKKE, K., General Pedagogy
DROTNER, K., Media Studies and Media Culture
HAMMER, O., Religious Studies and Comparative Religion
HOLM, P., Maritime and Regional History
JAKOBSEN, H. G., Scandinavian Language
JENSEN, B., Slavic Studies
JESPERSEN, K. J. V., History
JOHANSEN, J. D., Comparative Literature
JUST, F., History
KLAWONN, E. G., Philosophy
MAI, A.-M., Danish Literature
MORTENSEN, F. H., Scandinavian Language and Literature
NIELSEN, H. F., Historical and Comparative Germanic Linguistics
NYE, D., American Studies
QVORTRUP, L., Multimedia
ROBERING, K., Humanistic Information Science
SAUERBERG, L. O., English Language and Literature
SINHA, C. G., Language and Cognitive Linguistics

Faculty of Health Sciences (Winsløwparken 17/1, 5230 Odense; tel. 65-50-29-32; fax 65-91-89-14; e-mail fac@health-sci.sdu.dk; internet www.sdu.dk/health):

ANDERSEN, K. E., Dermato-venereology
BAKKETEIG, L., Epidemiology
BARINGTON, T., Clinical Immunology
BECK-NIELSEN, H., Medical Endocrinology
BENDIX, T., Biomechanics
BIE, P., Physiology
BINDSLEV-JENSEN, C., Dermatological Allergology
BRO, F., General Practice
BRØSEN, K., Clinical Pharmacology
CHRISTENSEN, K., Ageing and Longevity
DITZEL, H., Biomedicine
DOBBELSTEIN, M., Biomedicine
FENGER, C., Pathology
FINSEN, B., Biomedicine
GRANDJEAN, P. A., Environmental Medicine
GREEN, A., Clinical Epidemiology
HAGHFELT, T., Cardiology
HALLAS, J., Clinical Pharmacology
HOLMSKOV, U., Biomedicine
HUSBY, S., Paediatrics
HØILUND-CARLSEN, P., Clinical Physiology
HØRDER, M., Clinical Chemistry
JAKOBSON, A., Cancer Therapy
JENSEN, W. A., Biomedicine
JUNKER, P., Rheumatology
KASSEM, M., Biomedicine
KOLMOS, H. J., Microbiology
KRAGH-SØRENSEN, P., Psychiatry
LOUS, J., General Practice
MANNICHE, C., Biomechanics
OWENS, T., Biomedicine
PEDERSEN, C., Infectious Medicine
PETERSEN, S., Asthma and Allergy in Childhood
RASMUSSEN, J. Z., Anatomy
RITSKES-HOITINGA, M., Comparative Medicine and Laboratory Animal Science
SAHLIN, K., Exercise Physiology
SCHAFFALITZKY DE MUCKADELL, O. B., Medical Gastroenterology
SCHRØDER, H. D., Neuropathology and Neuromuscular Biology
SJØLIE, A. K., Ophthalmology
SKØTT, O., Physiology
SØRENSEN, T., Psychiatry
THOMSEN, J., Forensic Medicine
TOFT, P., Anaesthesiology
VACH, W., Medical Statistics
VAUPEL, J. W., Demographic Studies
WALTER, S., Surgery
WESTERGAARD, J. G., Obstetrics

Faculty of Natural and Engineering Sciences (tel. 65-50-20-82; fax 65-93-38-05; e-mail natfak@adm.sdu.dk; internet www.sdu.dk/nat):

ANGELOV, C. K., Software Engineering
BERNSEN, N. O., Natural Interactive Systems
BJERREGAARD, P., Biology
BUUR, J., User-oriented Product Development
CANFIELD, D., Biology
DOUTHWAITE, S. R., Molecular Biology
DYBKJÆR, L., Natural Interactive Systems
GERDES, K., Molecular Microbiology
HAAGERUP, U., Mathematics
ISSINGER, O., Biochemistry
JENSEN, J. B., Computer Science
JENSEN, O. N., Protein Mass Spectrometry
JØRGENSEN, B., Statistics
KNUDSEN, J., Biochemistry
KORNERUP, P., Computer Science
KRISTENSEN, B. B., Software Engineering
KRISTIANSEN, K., Eokaryotic Molecular Biology
LARSEN, K. S., Computer Science
LUND, H. H., Information Technology
MANN, M., Molecular Biology
MCKENZIE, C. J., Nanobioscience
MICHELSEN, A., Biology
MOURITSEN, O. G., Physics
NIELSEN, H. T., Chemistry
PEDERSEN, H., Mathematics
PERRAM, J. W., Applied Mathematics
PETERSEN, H. G., Applied Mathematics
ROEPSTORFF, P., Molecular Biology
RØRDAM, M., Mathematics
RUBAHN, H.-G., Physics and Technology
SIGMUND, H. P., Physics
TOWN, R. M., Chemistry
VALENTIN-HANSEN, P., Molecular Biology
WENGEL, J., Chemistry
WIIL, U. K., Software Engineering
WILLATZEN, H., Mathematical Modelling
ØSTERGARD, J. E., Physics and Technology

Faculty of Social Sciences (tel. 65-50-29-03; fax 65-93-56-92; e-mail office@sam.sdu.dk; internet www.sam.sdu.dk):

ASKEGAARD, S., Business Studies
BAGER, T., Business Studies
BOUCHET, D., Business Studies
CHRISTENSEN, J. A., Business Studies
CHRISTENSEN, L. T., Business Studies
CHRISTENSEN, P. M., Political Sciences
CHRISTENSEN, P. O., Business Studies
CHRISTENSEN, P. R., Business Studies
CHRISTIANSEN, T., Health Economics
CLAUSEN, N. J., Law
DAHLER-LARSEN, P., Political Sciences
ERIKSEN, B., Business Studies
FREYTAG, P. V., Business Studies
FRIMOR, H., Business Studies
GYRD-HANSEN, D., Health Economics
HANSEN, J. D., Business Studies
HANSEN, S. F., Law
JENSEN, S. E. H., National Economics
JØRGENSEN, N., Business Studies
JØRGENSEN, S., Business Studies
KAISER, V., National Economics
KLAUSEN, K. K., Public Organization Theory
KNUDSEN, T., Business Studies
LARSEN, P., Journalism
LAURSEN, F., Political Science
LUND, A., Journalism
MADSEN, T. K., Business Studies
MORTENSEN, B. O., Law
MOURITZEN, P. E., Political Sciences
MUNK, C., Business Studies
OBEL, B., Business Studies
PEDERSEN, K. M., Health Economics
PEDERSEN, M. N., Political Sciences
PETERSEN, H., Law
PETERSEN, J. H., Social Science
PETERSEN, N. C., Business Studies
SKYRUM-NIELSEN, P., Journalism
SLOTH, B., National Economics
SØRENSEN, C. J., National Economics
STEINICKE, M., Law
TETZSCHNER, H., Business Economics
VESTERGAARD, N., Business Economics

University-level Institutions

Arkitektskolen i Århus (Århus School of Architecture): Nørreport 20, 8000 Århus C; tel. 89-36-00-00; fax 86-13-06-45; e-mail a@aarch.dk; internet www.aarch.dk; f. 1965; architectural design, planning, furniture and industrial design; 100 teachers; 900 students; library: 44,000 vols; Rector PETER KRARUP KJÆR; publs *Skolehåndbogen* (annually), *Virksomhedsregnskab* (annually).

Danmarks Biblioteksskole (Royal School of Library and Information Science): Birketinget 6, 2300 Copenhagen S; tel. 32-58-60-66; fax 32-84-02-01; e-mail db@db.dk; internet www.db.dk; f. 1956; library: 182,000 vols; 65 teachers; 1,000 students; Rector LEIF LØRRING..

Attached institute:

Danmarks Biblioteksskole Aalborg (Royal School of Library and Information Science, Aalborg): Sohngårdsholmsvej 2, 9000 Aalborg; tel. 98-15-79-22; fax 98-15-10-42; e-mail dbaa@db.dk; internet www.db.dkf. 1973; Head LEIF EMEREK.

Danmarks Designskole (Danish School of Design): Strandboulevarden 47, 2100 Copenhagen Ø; tel. 35-27-75-00; fax 35-27-76-00; e-mail mail@dkds.dk; internet www.dkds.dk; f. 1875 as Tegne- og Kunstindustriskolen (School of Drawing and Art Industry); part of Danish National Centre for Design Research; space, furniture, scenography, fashion, textiles, pottery, glass, industrial design, graphic communication and digital design; 650 students; Pres. GØSTA KNUDSEN.

Designskolen Kolding (Kolding Design School): Ågade 10, 6000 Kolding; tel. 76-30-11-00; fax 76-30-11-12; e-mail dk@designskolenkolding.dk; internet www.designskolenkolding.dk; f. 1967; institute for form and theory, fashion and textiles, visual communication, industrial design and interactive media; department of ceramics; temporary exhibitions; 380 students; Rector BIRTE SANDORFF.

Fynske Musikkonservatorium (Carl Nielsen Academy of Music): Islandsgade 2, 5000 Odense C; tel. 66-11-06-63; fax 66-17-77-63; e-mail dfm@adm.dfm.dk; internet www.dfm.dk; f. 1929; 75 teachers; 150 students; library: 35,000 books and scores; Pres. BERTEL KRARUP.

Ingeniørhøjskolen i Århus (Engineering College of Århus): Dalgas Ave 2, 8000 Århus C; tel. 87-30-22-00; fax 87-30-22-01; e-mail iha@iha.dk; internet www.iha.dk; f. 1903; library: 18,000 vols; 110 teachers; 1,400 students; Rector OVE POULSEN

DIRECTORS

Civil and Constructional Engineering: POUL KRING JACOBSEN
Electronics and Information Technology: HENRIK OLSEN
Mechanical Engineering: ORLA K. ADAMSEN

Ingeniørhøjskolen i København (Engineering College of Copenhagen): Lautrupvang 15, 2750 Ballerup; tel. 44-80-50-88; fax 44-80-50-44; e-mail rector@ihk.dk; internet www.ihk.dk; f. 1879; applied sciences; awards BSc in engineering; library: 32,900 vols; 186 teachers; 2,100 students; Rector FLEMMING KROGH.

Ingeniørhøjskolen Odense Teknikum: Niels Bohrs Alle 1, 5230 Odense M; tel. 63-14-03-00; fax 63-14-03-04; e-mail iot@iot.dk; internet www.iot.dk; f. 1905; library: 30,000 vols; 130 teachers; 1,300 students; Rector HENNING ANDERSEN; Registrar KRISTINE LYNGBO.

Jyske Musikkonservatorium (Royal Academy of Music, Århus): Fuglesangs Allé 26, 8210 Århus V; tel. 89-48-33-88; fax 89-48-33-22; e-mail info@musik-kons.dk; internet www.musik-kons.dk; f. 1927; 150 teachers; 350 students; Principal FINN SCHUMACKER; Administrator KNUD AARUP.

Københavns tekniske Skole (Copenhagen Polytechnic): Rebslagervej 11, POB 899, 2400 Copenhagen NV; tel. 31-81-22-90; fax 31-81-35-90; 500 staff; 6,000 students; Dir MOGENS NIELSEN.

Kongelige Danske Kunstakademis Arkitektskole (School of Architecture of the Royal Danish Academy of Fine Arts): Philip de Langes Allé 10, 1435 Copenhagen K; tel. 32-68-60-00; fax 32-68-61-11; e-mail arkitektskolen@karch.dk; internet www.karch.dk; f. 1754; library: see Libraries and Archives; 1,100 students; Rector SVEN FELDING.

Kongelige Danske Kunstakademis Billedkunstskoler (School of Visual Arts of the Royal Danish Academy of Fine Arts): Kgs. Nytorv 1, Postboks 3014, 1021 Copenhagen K; tel. 33-74-46-00; fax 33-74-46-66; e-mail bk@kunstakademiet.dk; internet www.kunstakademiet.dk; f. 1754; library: see Libraries and Archives; Rector ELSE MARIE BUKDAHL.

Kongelige Danske Kunstakademi, Konservatorskolen (Royal Danish Academy of Fine Arts, School of Conservation): Esplanaden 34, 1263 Copenhagen K; tel. 33-74-47-00; fax 33-74-47-77; e-mail kons@kons.dk; internet www.kons.dk; f. 1973; library: 7,000 vols, 150 periodicals; 20 teachers; 100 students; Rector RENÉ LARSEN.

Kongelige Danske Musikkonservatorium (Royal Danish Academy of Music): Niels Brocksgade 1, 1574 Copenhagen V; tel. 33-69-22-69; fax 33-14-09-11; f. 1867; library: 50,000 vols; 170 teachers; c. 400 students; Principal STEEN PADE; Administrator BJARNE BACH ØSTERGAARD; Librarian TOVE KRAG.

Nordjysk Musikkonservatorium (Academy of Music, Ålborg): Ryesgade 52, 9000 Ålborg; tel. 98-12-77-44; fax 98-11-37-63; e-mail nordkons@nordkons.dk; internet www.nordkons.dk; f. 1930; 60 teachers; 115 students; Rector JENS-OLE BLAK.

Rytmisk Musikkonservatorium (Rhythmic Music Conservatory): Leo Mathisens Vej 1, Holmen, 1437 Copenhagen K; tel. 32-68-67-00; fax 32-68-67-66; e-mail rmc@rmc.dk; internet www.rmc.dk; f. 1986; state control; attached to Ministry of Culture; music teaching, music and movement, music performance, sound engineering, music management; 80 teachers; 200 students; Rector HENRIK SVEIDAHL.

Teknologisk Institut (Technological Institute): Gregersensvej, 2630 Tåstrup; tel. 72-20-20-00; fax 72-20-20-19; e-mail info@teknologisk.dk; internet www.teknologisk.dk and at Teknologiparken, 8000 Århus C; tel. 72-20-10-00; fax 72-20-10-19; f. 1906; building technology, energy, environment, industry, industrial and business development; 10,000 course participants; Pres. SØREN STJERNQVIST.

Vestjysk Musikkonservatorium (Academy of Music, Esbjerg): Kirkegade 61–63, 6700 Esbjerg; tel. 76-10-43-00; fax 76-10-43-10; e-mail info@vmk.dk; internet www.vmk.dk; f. 1946; 70 teachers; 120 students; Dir AXEL MOMME.

Vitus Bering Center for Videregående Uddannelse (Vitus Bering Centre for Higher Education): Strandpromenaden 4C, 8700 Horsens; tel. 76-25-50-00; fax 76-25-51-00; e-mail cvu@vitusbering.dk; internet www.vitusbering.dk; f. 1915; library: 27,000 vols; 260 teachers; 2,000 students; Dir SVEND TRØST; Pro-Rectors SUSAN DALUM, GUNNAR ERIKSEN, BENT BRUUN PEDERSEN; Dir of Studies HANS JØRN HANSEN

DEANS

Department of Civil Engineering: SØREN FISKER
Department of Export Engineering: ANKER STÆHR-JØRGENSEN
Department of Mechanical Engineering: AAGE PEDERSEN
Academic Division Architecture: JAN UWE WOLFF
Academic Division Building and Construction: KNUD ERIK GULDAGER
Academic Division of Continuing Education: FINN P. JENSEN
Academic Division of Higher Secondary Technical Education: WILLY SKOVGAARD
Academic Division Information Technology: HANS JØRN HANSEN
Academic Division Marketing and Economics: JANN SØNDERGAARD

FAROE ISLANDS

Learned Societies

GENERAL

Føroya Fróðskaparfelag/Societas Scientiarum Faeroensis (Faroese Society of Science and Letters): POB 209, 110 Tórshavn; tel. and fax 322074; e-mail fff@frodskaparfelag.fo; internet www.frodskaparfelag.fo; f. 1952; aims to procure scientific and scholarly literature and to promote research work; 170 mems; Pres. Dr ANDRAS MORTENSEN; publs *Fróðskaparrit* (Annals), *Supplementa*.

HISTORY, GEOGRAPHY AND ARCHAEOLOGY

Føroya Forngripafelag (Faroese Archaeological Society): POB 1173, 110 Tórshavn; tel. 312259; f. 1898; works in conjunction with the National Museum of Antiquities; 325 mems; Pres. MORTAN WINTHER POULSEN.

LANGUAGE AND LITERATURE

Rithøvundafelag Føroya (Faroese Writers Union): POB 1124, 110 Tórshavn; fax 310133; f. 1957; to promote the growth of Faroese literature and to protect authors' rights; 102 mems; Pres. HEDIN KLEIN.

TECHNOLOGY

Føroya Verkfrøðingafelag (Chartered Engineers Association): Tvørgøta 3, POB 2133, 165 Argir; tel. 314826; f. 1967; 140 mems; Pres. SÍMUN HAMMER; publ. *Verkfrøði* (3 a year).

Research Institutes

AGRICULTURE, FISHERIES AND VETERINARY SCIENCE

Fiskirannsóknarstovan (Faroese Fisheries Laboratory): Nóatún, Postboks 3051, 110 Tórshavn; tel. 353900; fax 353901; e-mail fishlab@frs.fo; internet www.frs.fo; f. 1951; fishery biology and oceanography; Dir HJALTI Í JÁKUPSSTOVU; publ. *Fiskirannsóknir* (1 or 2 a year).

Heilsufrøðiliga Starvsstovan (Food, Veterinary and Environmental Agency): Falkavegur 6, 100 Tórshavn; tel. 356400; fax 356401; e-mail hfs@hfs.fo; internet www.hfs.fo; f. 1975; research, services, quality control and inspection in the fish and food industry and in the environment; government dept; Dir BARÐUR ENNI; publ. *Ársfrágreiðing* (annual report).

Libraries and Archives

Tórshavn

Býarbókasavnid (Public Library): Niels Finsens gøtu 7, POB 358, 110 Tórshavn; tel. 302020; fax 302031; e-mail byarbok@byarbok.fo; internet www.byarbok.fo; f. 1969; 73,000 vols; City Librarian ANNA BRIMNES.

Føroya Landsbókasavn (National Library): J. C. Svabosgøtu 16, POB 61, Tórshavn; tel. 311626; fax 318895; e-mail utlan@flb.fo; internet www.flb.fo; f. 1828; 138,000 vols (20,000 scientific vols); open to the public; Dir MARTIN NÆS; publ. *Føroyskur Bókalisti* (annual list of Faeroese publs).

Føroya Landsskjalasavn (National Archives of the Faroe Islands): V. U. Hammershaimbsgøta 24, 100 Tórshavn; tel. 316677; fax 318677; e-mail fararch@lss.fo; internet www.lss.fo; f. 1932; medieval documents (1298–1599), archives of parliament and central and local administration (1615–1980); Dir SÁMAL T. F. JOHANSEN.

Museums and Art Galleries

Tórshavn

Føroya Fornminnissavn (National Museum): Kúrdalsvegur 2, POB 1155, 111 Tórshavn; tel. 310700; fax 312259; e-mail fornminn@natmus.fo; internet www.natmus.fo; f. 1898, taken over by State 1952; archaeology, ethnology, inspection of ancient monuments; Antiquary ARNE THORSTEINSSON.

Føroya Náttúrugripasavn (Natural History Museum): Debesartrøð, 100 Tórshavn; tel. 352300; fax 352301; e-mail ngs@ngs.fo; internet www.ngs.fo; f. 1955; depts of botany, zoology; Dir DORETE BLOCH.

Savnið 1940-45 (Faroe-British Museum): POB 362, 110 Tórshavn; tel. 312074; f. 1983; military and civilian artefacts from British occupation during Second World War (1939–1945).

University

FRÓDSKAPARSETUR FØROYA/ UNIVERSITAS FÆROENSIS (University of the Faroe Islands)

J. C. Svabos gøta 14, POB 272, 110 Tórshavn
Telephone: 352500
Fax: 352501
E-mail: setur@setur.fo
Internet: www.setur.fo

Founded 1965
Language of instruction: Faroese
Academic year: September to June

Rector: JÓAN PAULI JOENSEN
Sec.-Gen.: ANNIKA SØLVARÁ

Number of teachers: 22
Number of students: 150 full-time

DEANS

Faculty of Faroese Language and Literature: Prof. EIVIND WEYHE
Faculty of History and Social Sciences: ELIN SÚSANNA JACOBSEN
Faculty of Science and Technology: HANS PAULI JOENSEN

PROFESSORS

ANDREASSEN, E., Oral Literature
BLOCH, D., Zoology
BROWN, R. J., Geophysics
DANIELSEN, M., Electrical Engineering
HANSEN, B., Oceanography
JOENSEN, J. P., History and Ethnology
MARNERSDÓTTIR, M., Literature
SPARRE ANDERSEN, M., Geophysics

GREENLAND

Learned Societies

GENERAL

Grønlandske Selskab (The Greenland Society): see under Denmark.

Nunani Avannarlerni piorsarsimassutsikkut Attaveqaat (NAPA) (The Nordic Institute in Greenland): Imaneq 21, POB 770, 3900 Nuuk; tel. 324733; fax 325733; e-mail napa@napa.gl; internet www.napa.gl; f. 1987; financed by the 5 Nordic countries and 3 home rule areas within them; develops, supports and stimulates Greenlandic cultural life, prioritizing youth and children; advances inter-Nordic cultural relations; Chair. CLAUS NIELSEN; Man. ANDERS BERNDTSSON.

FINE AND PERFORMING ARTS

'Simerneq' (Artists' Society): POB 1009, 3900 Nuuk; f. 1978; arranges exhibitions of works of members and others; Sec. INGER HAUGE.

LANGUAGE AND LITERATURE

Kalaallit Atuakkiortut (Greenlandic Authors' Society): c/o ICC, POB 25, Dronning Ingridsvej 1, 3900 Nuuk; tel. 323632; fax 323001; internet forfatternet.katak.gl; f. 1975; copyrights for authors and translators; 83 mems; Pres. AQQALUK K. LYNGE; Sec. JUAANNA PETRUSSEN.

Research Institutes

AGRICULTURE, FISHERIES AND VETERINARY SCIENCE

Forsøgsstationen 'Upernaviarsuk' (Experimental Station 'Uper'): POB 152, 3920 Qaqortoq; tel. 648006; fax 648003; governmental institution carrying out experiments in sheep rearing, fodder crops, tree planting and gardening in a polar environment.

NATURAL SCIENCES

General

Kommissionen for Videnskabelige Undersøgelser i Grønland (Commission for Scientific Research in Greenland): Strandgade 100H, 1401 Copenhagen K, Denmark; tel. 32-88-01-00; fax 32-88-01-01; e-mail dpc@dpc.dk; internet www.kvug.dk; f. 1878; Greenlandic-Danish commission whose task is to propose new joint strategies for polar research; library of 24,000 vols, 9,000 pamphlets, 3,000 theses, 250 current periodicals; Chair. MINIK ROSING; Sec. CHARLOTTE SHANTI MUNCH.

Dansk Polarcenter (Danish Polar Center): Strandgade 100H, 1401 Copenhagen K, Denmark; tel. 32-88-01-00; fax 32-88-01-01; e-mail dpc@dpc.dk; internet www.dpc.dk; f. 1989; supports and co-ordinates Arctic and Antarctic research in Denmark and Greenland, and provides information on polar issues; library of 24,000 vols, 9,000 pamphlets, 3,000 theses, 250 current periodicals; Dir HANNE PETERSEN; publs *Meddelelser om Groenland, Bioscience* (Monographs on Greenland, Bioscience, irregular), *Meddelelser om Groenland, Geoscience* (Monographs on Greenland, Geoscience, irregular), *Meddelelser om Groenland, Man and Society* (Monographs on Greenland, Man and Society, irregular).

Biological Sciences

Arctic Station, University of Copenhagen: see under Denmark.

Danmarks Miljøundersøgelser, Afdeling for Arktisk Miljø (Danish Environmental Research Institute, Department of Arctic Environment): POB 358, Frederiksborgvej 399, 4000 Roskilde, Denmark; tel. 46-30-12-00; fax 46-30-19-14; e-mail jm@dmu.dk; internet www.dmu.dk; monitors esp. effects of mineral exploitation, climate change ecology in the Arctic, contaminants in Arctic ecosystems; marine mammal research and monitoring; Dir JESPER MADSEN.

Grønlands Naturinstitut (Greenland Institute of Natural Resources): Postboks 570, 3900 Nuuk; tel. 361200; fax 361212; e-mail info@natur.gl; internet www.natur.gl; applied research in natural resources, environmental protection and biodiversity; Dir KLAUS HOYER NYGAARD.

Physical Sciences

Dansk Meteorologisk Institut (Danish Meteorological Institute): see under Denmark.

Library

Nuuk

Nunatta Atuagaateqarfia/Grønlandske Landsbibliotek (National Library of Greenland): POB 1011, 3900 Nuuk; tel. 321156; fax 323943; e-mail nalib@katak.gl; internet www.katak.gl; 70,426 vols; Dir ELISA JEREMIASSEN.

Museum

Nuuk

Nunatta Katersugaasivia Allagaateqarfialu/Grønlands Nationalmuseum og Arkiv (Greenland National Museum and Archive): Hans Egedesvej 8, POB 145, 3900 Nuuk; tel. 322611; fax 322622; e-mail nka@natmus.gl; internet www.natmus.gl; f. 1966; research into archaeology, ethnology, art, history, public archival matters; Dir DANIEL THORLEIFSEN.

Colleges

Eqqumiitsuliornermik Ilinniarfik/Kunstskolen (School of Arts): POB 286, 3900 Nuuk; tel. 322644; e-mail kunst@greennet.gl; f. 1973; Dir ARNANNGUAQ HØEGH.

Ilinniarfissuaq/Grønlands Seminarium (Teacher Training School): POB 1026, 3900 Nuuk; tel. 321191; fax 322099; e-mail ilinnia@greennet.gl; internet www.ilinniarfissuaq.gl; f. 1849; pedagogical, social and administrative education and in-service training; 25 teachers; 130 students; Rector DORTHE KORNELIUSSEN.

Ilisimatusarfik/Grønlands Universitet (University of Greenland): POB 279, 3900 Nuuk; tel. 324566; fax 324711; e-mail email@ilisimatusarfik.gl; internet www.ilisimatusarfik.gl; f. 1984; Greenlandic language and literature, cultural and historical sciences, administration, theology; library: 18,000 vols, 150 periodicals; 14 teachers; 100 students; Rector OLE MARQUARDT; Pro-Vice-Chancellor KAREN LANGGÅRD; publ. *Grønlandsk Kultur- og Samfunds-Forskning* (annually).

Niuernermik Ilinniarfik/Grønlands Handelsskole (Business School): POB 1038, 3900 Nuuk; tel. 32-30-99; fax 32-32-55; e-mail ninuuk@ninuuk.gl; internet www.ninuuk.gl; f. 1980; courses and in-service training in journalism, interpreting and mercantile matters, also technical mercantile training; library: 6,500 vols; Dir BO NÓRRESLET.

DJIBOUTI

The Higher Education System

Higher education in Djibouti is modelled after the French system. The sole university in Djibouti, the Université de Djibouti, was founded in 2006 to replace the Pôle Universitaire de Djibouti, which was founded in 2000 and had over 1,700 students in 2004/05. Higher education is the responsibility of the Ministry of National Education and Higher Education.

The University offers undergraduate and postgraduate courses, and admission is on the basis of secondary school qualifications including the Baccalauréat de l'Enseignement Secondaire, the Baccalauréat Technologique or the Baccalauréat Professionnel. Higher education degrees are divided into three cycles: the Diplôme d'Etudes Universitaires Générales (DEUG) or Diplôme Universitaire de Technologie (DUT) is awarded after two years; the Licence requires one further year of study and the Maîtrise two; and finally the Diplôme Universitaire d'Études Approfondies (DEA) is awarded after a further two years of study.

Learned Society

LANGUAGE AND LITERATURE

Alliance Française: BP 56, Djibouti; tel. 353091; fax 355957; e-mail alliance-francaise@intnet.dj; offers courses and exams in French language and culture and promotes cultural exchange with France.

Research Institute

GENERAL

Institut Supérieur d'Etudes et de Recherches Scientifiques et Techniques (ISERT): BP 486, Djibouti; tel. 352795; fax 354812; Dir NABIL MOHAMED.

Library

Djibouti

Assemblée Nationale, Service de la Bibliothèque: BP 138, Djibouti; tel. 350172; fax 355503; f. 1977; 2,000 vols; Librarian ILTIREH DJAMA GUIREH.

University

UNIVERSITÉ DE DJIBOUTI

Ave Georges Clemenceau, BP 1904, Djibouti
Telephone: 250459
Fax: 250474
E-mail: ud@univ.edu.dj
Internet: www.univ.edu.dj

Founded 2000 as Pôle Universitaire de Djibouti, present name adopted 2006

Rector: AIDID ADEN GUEDI

Sec.-Gen.: PHILIPPE RIBIERE
Librarian: SAFIA ALI SAID

Number of teachers: 96
Number of students: 1,749

DIRECTORS

Faculty of Languages, Literature and Human Sciences: ABDOULMALIK IBRAHIM ZEID

Faculty of Law, Economics, Management and Tertiary Technological Procedures: Mag. TEEREY IBRAHIM

Faculty of Sciences and Industrial Technological Procedures: IBRAHIM SOULEIMAN GUILLEM

DOMINICA

The Higher Education System

Higher education is provided by a centre of the University of the West Indies, and the Ross University School of Medicine in Dominica (affiliated to Ross University School of Medicine, NJ, in the USA). There is also a teacher-training college and nursing school.

Admission to higher education is based on the Caribbean Examinations Council Secondary Education Certificate or GCE A-levels and O-levels. Students may also be required to sit an entrance examination. The University of the West Indies offers undergraduate Bachelors and postgraduate Masters degrees.

Learned Society

LANGUAGE AND LITERATURE

Alliance Française: Elmshall Rd, Bath Estate Bridge, POB 251, Roseau; tel. 4484557; fax 4486008; offers courses and exams in French language and culture and promotes cultural exchange with France.

Library

Roseau

Library of the House of Assembly: Victoria St, Roseau; tel. 4482401; fax 4498353; f. 1968; 300 vols of parliamentary reports, Proceedings of the House, speeches, ministerial statements, debates, legislation.

Museum

Roseau

Dominica Museum: Bay Front, Roseau; tel. 4488923; exhibits on Dominica's geology, history, archaeology, economy and culture, including its pre-Columbian population and the slave trade.

University

ROSS UNIVERSITY SCHOOL OF MEDICINE IN DOMINICA

POB 266, Portsmouth
Telephone: 4455355
Fax: 4455383

New York office: 460 West 34th St, 12th Floor, New York, NY 10001, USA
Telephone: (212) 279-5500 (New York)
Fax: (212) 629-3147 (New York)

Internet: www.rossmed.edu.dm; attached to Ross University School of Medicine, NJ (USA)

Library of 5,000 books, 190 current journals, 100 audiovisual items, 30 multimedia programmes.

College

University of the West Indies, Dominica Centre: Univ. Centre, POB 82, Roseau; tel. 4483182; fax 4488706; e-mail uwi@cwdom.dm; internet www.cavehill.uwi.edu/bnccde/dominica.

DOMINICAN REPUBLIC

The Higher Education System

The Universidad Autónoma de Santo Domingo, founded by Papal Bull in 1538, claims to be the oldest university in the Americas. Other universities in the Republic were all founded during the 20th century. There are 17 public and private universities, and higher education is also offered by colleges, institutes and schools of art and music. In 2003/04 there were an estimated 293,565 students enrolled in higher education. The Consejo Nacional de Educación Superior is the administrative body of higher education.

The secondary school qualification (Bachillerato) is the main requirement for admission to higher education. Undergraduate students are awarded the Licenciado or professional title after four years of study, and postgraduate students receive the Maestría after one- to three-years' study following the Licenciado. In some disciplines (law, medicine, dentistry, veterinary medicine) the Doctorado degree may be awarded. Both universities and technological institutes offer technical and vocational education. Courses last for two to three years and students gain the title Técnico.

Learned Societies

GENERAL

Instituto de Cultura Dominicana: Biblioteca Nacional, César Nicolás Penson, Santo Domingo; f. 1971; to promote the cultural tradition of the country, encourage artistic creation in general, and the expression of the spirit of the Dominican people; Pres. ENRIQUE APOLINAR HENRÍQUEZ; Sec. PEDRO GIL ITURBIDES.

BIBLIOGRAPHY, LIBRARY SCIENCE AND MUSEOLOGY

Asociación Dominicana de Bibliotecarios, Inc. (ASODOBI) (Librarians' Association): c/o Biblioteca Nacional, Plaza de la Cultura, César Nicolás Penson 91, Santo Domingo; tel. 688-4086; f. 1974 to develop library services in the Republic, increase the standing of the profession and encourage the training of its members; 90 mems; Pres. PRÓSPERO J. MELLA CHAVIER; Sec.-Gen. V. REGÚS; publ. *El Papiro* (quarterly).

Sociedad Dominicana de Bibliófilos Inc.: Las Damas 106, Santo Domingo; Pres. Lic. FRANK MOYA PONS.

EDUCATION

Asociación Dominicana de Rectores de Universidades (Dominican Association of University Presidents): Apdo 2465, Calle Luperón esq. Hostos (altos), Edif. Comisión de Monumentos, Zona Colonial, Santo Domingo; tel. 689-4931; fax 687-7401; f. 1981; 9 full mems; 8 regular mems; Exec. Dir Dra. GERTRUDYS MIESES.

HISTORY, GEOGRAPHY AND ARCHAEOLOGY

Academia Dominicana de la Historia (Dominican Academy of History): Calle Mercedes 204, Casa de las Academias, Santo Domingo; tel. 689-3446; fax 535-7891; f. 1931; 18 mems; 24 nat. corresp. mems; 60 foreign corresp. mems; Pres. Dr JULIO G. CAMPILLO PEREZ; Sec. Dr CARLZOS DOBAL; publ. *Clio* (quarterly).

LANGUAGE AND LITERATURE

Academia Dominicana de la Lengua (Dominican Academy): Avda Tiradentes 66, Ensanche La Fe, Santo Domingo; Corresp. of the Real Academia Española (Madrid); 13 mems; library of 50,000 vols; Pres. MARIANO LEBRÓN SAVIÑÓN; Sec. MANUEL GOICO CASTRO.

Alliance Française: Calle Horacio Vicioso 103, Centro De Los Heroes (La Feria), Santo Domingo; tel. 532-4300; fax 535-0533; e-mail dgaf@afsd.net; offers courses and exams in French language and culture and promotes cultural exchange with France; attached offices in Higuey, Mao, Monte Cristi, San Francisco de Macoris and Santiago de los Caballeros.

MEDICINE

Asociación Médica de Santiago (Santiago Medical Association): Apdo 445, Santiago de los Caballeros; f. 1941; library of 1,500 vols; 65 mems; Pres. Dr RAFAEL FERNÁNDEZ LAZALA; Sec. Dr JOSÉ COROMINAS P.; publ. *Boletín Médico* (quarterly).

Asociación Médica Dominicana (Dominican Medical Association): Apdo 1237, Santo Domingo; f. 1941; 1,551 mems; Pres. Dr ANGEL S. CHAN AQUINO; Sec. Dr CARLOS LAM ARCHE REY; publ. *Revista Médica Dominicana*.

Research Institutes

AGRICULTURE, FISHERIES AND VETERINARY SCIENCE

Instituto Azucarero Dominicano (Dominican Sugar Institute): Avda Jiménez Moya, Apdo 667, Santo Domingo; tel. 532-5571; Dir JIMMY GARCÍA SAVIÑÓN.

HISTORY, GEOGRAPHY AND ARCHAEOLOGY

Instituto Cartográfico Militar de las Fuerzas Armadas (Military Cartographic Institute): Base Naval 27 de Febrero, Santo Domingo; tel. 686-2954; f. 1950; photogrammetry, cartography, geodesy, hydrography, photographic laboratory; Dir Capt. DOMINGO GÓMEZ.

Libraries and Archives

Baní

Biblioteca 'Padre Billini': Calle Duarte No. 6, Baní; f. 1926; *c.* 38,000 vols; Dir Lic. FERNANDO HERRERA.

Moca

Biblioteca Municipal 'Gabriel Morillo': Calle Antonio de la Maza esq. Independencia, Moca; f. 1942; 6,422 vols; Dir Lic. ADRIANO MIGUEL TEJADA E..

San Pedro de Macorís

Biblioteca del Ateneo de Macorís (Library of the Athenaeum of Macorís): San Pedro de Macorís; f. 1890; 6,274 vols; Pres. Lic. JOSÉ A. CHEVALIER.

Santiago de los Caballeros

Biblioteca de la Sociedad Amantes de la Luz: España esq. Avda Central, Santiago de los Caballeros; f. 1874; public library of cultural society; 18,000 vols; Dir Lic. BERENI ESTRELLA DE INOA.

Santo Domingo

Archivo General de la Nación: Calle Modesto Diaz 2, Zona Universitaria, Santo Domingo; f. 1884; 16,000 vols; Dir ROBERTO CASSA; publ. *Boletín AGN* (quarterly).

Cámara de Comercio y Producción de Santo Domingo, Centro de Información y Documentación Comercial (Commercial Information and Documentation Centre of the Chamber of Commerce and Production of Santo Domingo): Arzobispo Nouel No. 206, Apdo 815, Santo Domingo; tel. (809) 682-2688; fax (809) 685-2228; e-mail camara.sto.dgo@verizon.net.do; internet www.camarasantodomingo.org.do; f. 1848; 13,500 vols, incl. books, journal, videos and CD-ROMs; Technician FRANCISCO A. DE LA ROSA A.; publs *Boletín Digital Camar@cción* (via email), *Camar@cción* (irregular).

Biblioteca de la Secretaría de Estado de Relaciones Exteriores (Library of the Secretariat of Foreign Affairs): Estancia Ramfis, Santo Domingo; special collections relating to international law; Dir Dr PRÓSPERO J. MELLA CHAVIER.

Biblioteca de la Universidad Autónoma de Santo Domingo (Library of Santo Domingo University): Ciudad Universitaria, Apdo 1355, Santo Domingo; 104,441 vols (Dominicana, historical archives, prints, maps, microfilms, etc.), 782,795 reviews (chiefly foreign, relating to the different faculties), microfilms, gramophone records; Dir Dra MARTHA MARÍA DE CASTRO COTES; publ. *Boletín de Adquisiciones*.

Biblioteca Dominicana: Santo Domingo; housed in a chapel of the Dominican Order dating from 1729; f. 1914; over 6,000 vols, of which Dominican authors comprise 700; collections of periodicals; also contains a students' reading-room, text-books, maps; Dir JOSÉ RIJO.

Biblioteca Municipal de Santo Domingo (Municipal Library of Santo Domingo): Padre Billini No. 18, Santo Domingo; Librarian LUZ DEL CARMEN RAPOZO.

Biblioteca Nacional: César Nicolás Penson, Santo Domingo; f. 1971; collects government publs; houses National Bibliography;

exhibitions, conferences, research and documentation; 153,955 vols; Dir Lic. ROBERTO DE SOTO.

Departamento de Documentación y Bibliotecas, Secretaría de Estado de Educación y Cultura (Library and Documentation Section): Santo Domingo; Dir Lic. ELIDA JIMÉNEZ.

Museums and Art Galleries

Santo Domingo

Galería Nacional de Bellas Artes (National Fine Arts Gallery): Santo Domingo; f. 1943; contains the later paintings and sculptures previously exhibited in the Museo Nacional; controlled by the Dirección General de Bellas Artes (Fine Arts Council); Dir Dr JOSÉ DE J. ALVAREZ VALVERDE.

Museo de Arte Moderno: Avda Pedro Henríquez Ureña, Plaza de la Cultura 'Juan Pablo Duarte', Santo Domingo; tel. 685-2153; fax 685-8280; e-mail museo_de_arte_moderno@yahoo.com; f. 1976; state controlled; modern art of national and foreign artists; permanent and exchange exhibitions; organizes lectures, conferences, films and children's workshops; library: art library of 2,047 vols; library: children's library of 2,050 vols; Dir Lic. MARÍA ELENA DITRÉN; publ. publs catalogue, guide, *Revista especializada, Boletín mensual de actividades*, monographs.

Museo de las Casas Reales (Museum of the Royal Houses): esq. Mercedes Las Damas, Apdo 2664, Santo Domingo; f. 1976; buildings used to be the headquarters of the colonial government; exhibition of items from that period (1492–1821); arms and armour, ceramics and items from shipwrecks; library of 17,700 vols; Dir Arq. EUGENIO PÉREZ MONTÁS; publ. *Casas Reales* (3 a year).

Museo del Hombre Dominicano (Museum of Dominican Man): Calle Pedro Henríquez Ureña, Plaza de la Cultura Juan Pablo Duarte, Santo Domingo; tel. 687-3622; fax 682-9112; e-mail museo_hd@hotmail.com; internet www.museodelhombredominicano.org; f. 1973 as Museo Nacional; 19,000 exhibits: *Pre-Columbian* (Indian archaeological; anthropological and ethnographical exhibits; ceramics, wooden objects, idols, amulets, charms, weapons and tools, pots, osseous remains); *Colonial* (weapons and armour, parts of ships, Spanish religious objects, ceramics, bells, etc.); library of 4,000 vols; Dir Dr CARLOS HERNÁNDEZ SOTO; publs *Boletín*, *Serie Investigaciones Antropológicas*, etc.

Museo Nacional de Historia Natural: Plaza de la Cultura, Santo Domingo; tel. 685-1580; fax 689-0100; e-mail jaragua@tricom.net; f. 1974; zoology, geology, palaeontology; library of 3,000 vols, 10 periodicals; Dr CARLOS ML. RODRÍGUEZ; publs *Hispaniolana* (journal, irregular), *Boletín Informativo* (4 a year).

Museo Nacional de Historia y Geografía: Calle Pedro Henríquez Ureña, Plaza de la Cultura, Santo Domingo; tel. 686-6677; fax 686-4943; f. 1982; history, geographical features and phenomena of the island of Santo Domingo; Dir Lic. VILMA BENZO DE FERRER; publ. *Revista de Historia y Geografía*.

Oficina de Patrimonio Cultural: Las Atarazanas 2, Santo Domingo; tel. 682-4750; f. 1967; Dir Arq. MANUEL E. DEL MONTE URRACA.

Controls:

Alcázar de Diego Colón (Columbus Palace):museum; f. 1957; the castle, built in 1510, was the residence of Don Diego Columbus, son of Christopher Columbus, and Viceroy of the island; period furniture and objects, paintings, musical instruments, ceramics, and the most important collection of tapestries in the Caribbean.

Casa-Fuerte de Ponce de León (Ponce de León's Fort): San Rafael del Yuma, Higüey; museum; f. 1972; the residence of Ponce de León who discovered Florida and Puerto Rico; authentic furniture and household items from a 16th-century house.

Fortaleza de San Felipe (St Philip's Fortress): Puerto Plata; museum; f. 1972; 16th-century fort; archaeological objects found during restoration.

Museo de la Familia Dominicana Siglo XIX (Museum of the Dominican Family):; f. 1973; a 16th-century house displaying household items for a noble family of the 19th century.

Sala de Arte Prehispánico: Apdo 723, Santo Domingo; f. 1973; run by the García Arévalo Foundation; studies and exhibits culture of pre-Hispanic times; library of 6,000 vols on anthropology and the history of Santo Domingo and the Caribbean; Dir MANUEL ANTONIO GARCÍA ARÉVALO; publs *Salida Semestral*, *Caney*.

Universities

PONTIFICIA UNIVERSIDAD CATÓLICA MADRE Y MAESTRA

Autopista Duarte, Santiago de los Caballeros

Telephone: 580-1962

Fax: 581-7750

E-mail: anunez@pucmmsti.edu.do

Internet: www.pucmmsti.edu.do

Founded 1962

Private control

Academic year: August to May (two semesters) and a session May to July

Rector: Mgr AGRIPINO NÚÑEZ COLLADO

Academic Vice-Rector: Ing. NELSON GIL

Executive Vice-Rector: Lic. SONIA GUZMÁN DE HERNÁNDEZ

Registrar: Lic. DULCE RODRÍGUEZ DE GRULLÓN

Librarian: Lic. ALTAGRACIA PEÑA

Number of teachers: 755

Number of students: 9,918

Publications: *Boletín de Noticias*, *Revista de Ciencias Jurídicas*

DEANS

Faculty of Engineering: Ing. VICTOR COLLADO

Faculty of Health Sciences: Dr RAFAEL FERNANDEZ LAZALA

Faculty of Humanities and Social Sciences: Lic. SARAH GONZÁLEZ

Campuses in Santo Domingo, Puerto Plata, Bonao

UNIVERSIDAD ABIERTA PARA ADULTOS

Apdo postal 1238, Avda Hispanoamérica, Urb. Thomén, Santiago

Telephone: 724-0266

Fax: 724-0329

E-mail: univ.adultos@uniabierta.edu.do

Internet: www.uniabierta.edu.do

Founded 1995

Rector: Dr ÁNGEL HERNÁNDEZ C.

UNIVERSIDAD APEC

Avda Máximo Gómez 72, esq. México, Apdo 2867, Santo Domingo

Telephone: 686-0021

Fax: 689-1060

E-mail: univ.apec@codetel.net.do

Internet: www.unapec.edu.do

Founded 1965

Academic year: July to June

President: Dr LUIS HEREDIA BONETTI

Rector: Lic. DENNIS R. SIMÓ

Vice-Rector (Academic): Lic. JUSTO PEDRO CASTELLANOS KHOURI

Vice-Rector (Administrative): Lic. CÉSAR REYNOSO

Vice-Rector (International): Lic. INMACULADA MADERA

Librarian: Lic. RAMÓN CEDANO

Library of 37,525 vols

Number of teachers: 658

Number of students: 9,000

Publications: *Investigación y Ciencia*, *Coloquios Jurídicos*, *Boletín Trimestral* (4 a year).

UNIVERSIDAD AUTÓNOMA DE SANTO DOMINGO

Ciudad Universitaria, Apdo 1355, Santo Domingo

Telephone: 533-1104

Fax: 533-1106

Founded 1538 by Papal Bull of Paul III, closed 1801–15; reopened as a lay institution in 1815, reorganized in 1914; oldest university in the Americas

Rector: Dr JULIO RAVELO ASTACIO

Vice-Rectors: Lic. RAMÓN CAMACHO JIMÉNEZ (Academic), Lic. JULIO URBÁEZ (Administrative)

Secretary-General: MARIO SURIEL

Personnel Director: Lic. JULIO CÉSAR RODRÍGUEZ

Number of teachers: 1,665

Number of students: 26,040

Publications: *Ciencia, Derecho y Política*

DEANS

Faculty of Agronomy and Veterinary Science: Ing. Agr. FRANK M. VALDÉZ L.

Faculty of Economic and Social Sciences: Dr EDILBERTO CABRAL

Faculty of Engineering and Architecture: Ing. MIGUEL ROSADO MONTES DE OCA

Faculty of Humanities: Lic. ANA DOLORES GUZMÁN DE CAMACHO

Faculty of Law and Politics: Lic. ROBERTO SANTANA

Faculty of Medicine: Dr CÉSAR MELLA MEJÍAS

Faculty of Sciences: Lic. PLÁCIDO CABRERA

UNIVERSIDAD CATÓLICA NORDESTANA

Restauración Esq. 27 de Febrero, 239 San Francisco de Macorís

Telephone: 588-3239

Fax: 244-1647

E-mail: rectoria@ucne.edu

Internet: www.ucne.edu

Founded 1978

Academic year: January to December (three semesters)

Rector: Mgr JESÚS MARÍA DE JESÚS MOYA

Vice-Rectors: Lic. PEDRO MANUEL LORA, Lic. JULIO CÉSAR PINEDA

Librarian: Lic. EMELDA RAMOS

Number of teachers: 210

Number of students: 4,300

Publications: *Ciencia y Humanismo* (every 2 years), *Gaceta Jurídica* (every 2 years)

DEANS

Faculty of Architecture: Arq. ZAMIRA ESTEVEZ
Faculty of Education: Lic. JOSEFINA PANTALEON
Faculty of Engineering: Ing. MARTIN PANTALEON
Faculty of Health Sciences: Dr ANGEL GARABOT
Faculty of Law: Lic. ANIBAL MEDRANO
Faculty of Modern Languages: Lic. RAFAEL SANZ
Faculty of Social Sciences and Economics: Lic. RAFAELA DE LA CRUZ
Faculty of Tourism: Lic. JAYME LÓPEZ
School of Computing and Systems: Ing. EVELYN VERAS (Dir)
School of Dentistry: DIGNA MARTE (Dir)
School of Medicine: Dr VINICIO BONILLA (Dir)

ATTACHED RESEARCH INSTITUTES

Fundación Loma Quita Espuela: Avda Libertad, San Francisco de Macorís.

UNIVERSIDAD CENTRAL DEL ESTE

Avda de Circunvalación, San Pedro de Macorís
Telephone: 529-3562
Fax: 529-5146
Internet: www.uce.edu.do
Founded 1970
Private control
Academic year: January to December (3 terms)
President and Rector: Dr JOSÉ E. HAZIM FRAPPIER
Vice-President: Dr JOSÉ A. HAZIM AZAR
Vice-Rector (Academic): Lic. RICHARD F. PEGUERO
Vice-Rector (Administration): Ing. MARILYN DÍAZ PÉREZ
Secretary General: Lic. PIEDAD L. NOBOA MEJÍA
Registrar: Lic. OLGA CHALAS
Librarian: Lic. ROSA DORIVAL
Library of 150,000 vols
Number of teachers: 677
Number of students: 6,700
Publications: *Anuario Científico, Publicaciones Periódicas, UCE*

DEANS

Faculty of Administration and Systems: Lic. SENCIÓN IVELISSE ZOROB
Faculty of Engineering and Natural Resources: Ing. OLGA BASORA
Faculty of Law: Dr ANTONIO LEÓN SASSO
Faculty of Medicine: Dr JUAN A. SILVA SANTOS
Faculty of Sciences and Humanities: Dr JOSÉ A. HAZIM AZAR

UNIVERSIDAD DE LA TERCERA EDAD

Calle Camila Henríquez Ureña, Esq. Jesús Maestro, Mirador Norte, Santo Domingo, Distrito Nacional
Telephone: 482-7093
Fax: 482-0109
E-mail: tercera.edad@codetel.net.do
Internet: www.ute.edu.do
Founded 1989; present status since 1992
State control
Academic year: January to December (two semesters)
Rector: Dr JOSÉ NICOLÁS ALMÁNZAR GARCÍA
Vice-Rector (Academic): Lic. ALTAGRACIA NÚÑEZ
Vice-Rector (Administration and Development): Dra FANNY POLANCO JORGE

SUBJECT CO-ORDINATORS

Design: Lic. ALICIA ARBAJE
Economics and Administration: Lic. RAFAEL OVIEDO JIMÉNEZ
Education: Lic. CARMEN PEÑA
Law: Lic. RHINA DE LOS SANTOS
Psychology: Lic. GERMANIA MORALES
Public Relations and Social Communication: Lic. RAFAEL PARADELL DÍAZ

UNIVERSIDAD DEL CARIBE

Apdo postal 67-2, Autopista 30 de Mayo Km 7½, POB 4765, Santo Domingo
Telephone: 535-8210
Fax: 535-0489
E-mail: inf@unicaribe.edu.do
Internet: www.universidaddelcaribe.edu.do
Founded 1995
Rector: MIGUEL ROSADO
Vice-Rector (Administration): ARTURO MENDÉZ.

UNIVERSIDAD DOMINICANA O&M

Apdo postal 509, Avda Independencia 200, Santo Domingo
Telephone: 533-7733
Fax: 535-0084
E-mail: info@udoym.edu.do
Internet: www.udoym.edu.do
Founded 1966
Rector: Dr JOSÉ RAFAEL ABINADER
Number of students: 28,000
Faculties of Engineering and Technology, Economics and Administration, Law, Humanities and Social Science and Continuing Education; campuses in Moca, Puerto Plata, Santiago, La Romana and San José de Ocoa.

UNIVERSIDAD EUGENIO MARÍA DE HOSTOS

Apdo Postal 2694, Santo Domingo
Telephone: 532-2495
Founded 1981
Private control
Rector: Lic. CARMEN MARÍA CASTILLO SILVA
Academic Vice-Rector: Lic. CARMEN ROSA MARTÍNEZ V.
Administrative Vice-Rector: Rev. RAFAEL MARCIAL SILVA
General Administrator: Dr JORGE DÍAZ VARGAS

DIRECTORS

Faculty of Health Sciences: Dr JOSÉ RODRÍGUEZ SOLDEVILLA
School of Computer Studies: Lic. SANDY SANTOS
School of Law: Lic. CECILIO GÓMEZ PÉREZ
School of Marketing Studies: Lic. PEDRO MELO
School of Medicine: Dr RAÚL ALVAREZ STURLA
School of Nursing: Lic. AMANDA PEÑA DE SANTANA
School of Oral Medicine: Dr CÉSAR LINARES IMBERT
School of Public Health: Dr MANUEL TEJADA BEATO
School of Veterinary Medicine: Dr TULIO S. CASTAÑOS VÉLEZ
Campus in Ozama: Lic. GUILLERMO DÍAZ
Campus in San Cristóbal: Lic. EMILIANO DE LA ROSA

UNIVERSIDAD EXPERIMENTAL 'FELIX ADAM'

Apdo postal 48-2 Feria, Calle Plaza de la Cultura 151, El Millón, Santo Domingo
Telephone: 683-3121
Fax: 683-3425
E-mail: universidadunefa@unefa.edu.do
Internet: www.unefa.edu.do
Founded 1991
Rector: Dr ANDRÉS MATOS SENA
Number of teachers: 36.

ATTACHED RESEARCH INSTITUTES

Centro de Investigación Científica.

UNIVERSIDAD IBEROAMERICANA

Apdo Postal 22-333, Avda Francia 129, Santo Domingo
Telephone: 689-4111
Fax: 686-5121
E-mail: unibe@codetel.net.do
Internet: www.unibe.edu.do
Founded 1982
Academic year: September to August
Rector: Dr GUSTAVO BATISTA VARGAS
Library of 20,000 vols
Publications: *Revista UNIBE de Ciencia y Cultura* (3 a year), *UNIBE Informe*

DEANS

Faculty of Health Sciences: Dr JULIO CASTAÑOS
Faculty of Law and Politics: Dr GUILLERMO MORENO

DIRECTORS

Faculty of Economics and Social Sciences:
- School of Business Administration: Lic. MIGUELINA FRANCO
- School of Hotel Management and Tourism: Lic. PILAR CONSTANZO
- School of Marketing: Lic. ZAYENKA MARTÍNEZ ROA

Faculty of Health Sciences:
- School of Dentistry: Dr CARLOS ALBERTO VALERA BISONÓ

Faculty of Human Sciences:
- School of Advertising and Communication: Lic. RAFAEL RINCÓN M.
- School of Architecture: Arq. VENCIAN BEN
- School of Design: SANDRA GÓMEZ
- School of Education: MARGARITA HEINSEN
- School of Psychology: Lic. FRANCESCA HERNÁNDEZ

UNIVERSIDAD INTERAMERICANA

Apdo postal 20687, Calle Dr Baez 2 y 4, Santo Domingo
Telephone: 685-6562
Fax: 689-8581
E-mail: unica@codetel.net.do
Founded 1982
Rector: ZORAIDA HEREDIA VDA. SUNCAR.

UNIVERSIDAD NACIONAL 'PEDRO HENRÍQUEZ UREÑA'

Autopista Duarte Km 6½, Santo Domingo
Telephone: 540-0422
Fax: 540-0425
E-mail: info@unphu.edu.do
Internet: www.unphu.edu.do
Founded 1966
Private control
Language of instruction: Spanish, English
Academic year: January to December
Rector: Arq. MIGUEL FIALLO
Vice-Rector for Academic Affairs: Lic. DANIELA FRANCO DE GUZMÁN
Vice-Rector for Administrative Affairs: Lic. JOSE RAFAEL ESPAILLAT
Vice-Rector for Development Affairs: Ing. VICTOR BERAS
Registrar: Dra SARI DUVERGÉ MEJÍA
Librarian: Dra CARMEN IRIS OLIVO
Library of 80,000 vols

Number of teachers: 759
Number of students: 8,000
Publications: *Aula*, *Biblionotas*, *Campus*, *Cuadernos de Filosofía*, *Cuadernos Jurídicos*, *Nuestra UNPHU*

DEANS
Faculty of Agronomy and Veterinary Science: Dr MIGUEL GONZALEZ
Faculty of Architecture and Arts: Arq. DIANA LAPAIX
Faculty of Economics and Social Sciences: Lic. LUIS MARTINEZ SILFA
Faculty of Engineering and Technology: Ing. CARLOS TRONCOSO
Faculty of Health Science: Dr CARLOS MONTERO
Faculty of Humanities: Lic. DIANA FRANCO DE GUZMAN
Faculty of Law and Politics: Dr MANUEL BERGÉS CHUPANI
Faculty of Science: Ing. CARLOS TRONCOSA
Faculty of Postgraduate Studies: Dr VICTOR BERAS

AFFILIATED INSTITUTES
Centro de Información de Drogas: Santo Domingo; Dir Dra ROSA RICOURT.
Centro de Investigación: Santo Domingo; Dir Dr LUCIANO SBRIZ.
Instituto de Estudios Biomédicos: Santo Domingo; Dir Dr SANTIAGO COLLADO CHASTEL.

UNIVERSIDAD TECNOLÓGICA DE SANTIAGO (UTESA)

Avda Estrella Sadhala (esq. Mirador del Yaque), Apdo 685, Santiago
Telephone: 582-7156
Fax: 582-7644
E-mail: utesa@codetel.net.do
Internet: www.utesa.edu
Founded 1974
Private control
Academic year: January to December
Rector: Dr PRIAMO RODRÍGUEZ CASTILLO
Vice-Rector (Academic): Mag. ARNALDO PEÑA VENTURA
Vice-Rector (Administration): Lic. MANUEL RODRÍGUEZ CASTILLO
Vice-Rector (Campus Premises): Mag. RAMÓN ANÍBAL CASTRO
Secretary-General: Mag. JOSEFINA CRUZ
Registrar: Lic. ANDRÉS VIVAS
Librarian: Mag. ILUMINADA DE LA HOZ
Library of 157,976 vols
Number of teachers: 1,027
Number of students: 35,742
Publications: *Ciencias y Tecnología*, *Revista Universitas*
Faculties of Social and Economic Sciences, Architecture and Engineering, Health Sciences, Science and Humanities and Secretarial Studies.

UNIVERSIDAD TECNOLÓGICA DEL CIBAO

Apdo postal 401, Atuopista Duarte Km 1½, Avda Universitaria, La Vega
Telephone: 573-1020
Fax: 573-6194
E-mail: uteci@codetel.net.do
Internet: www.uteci.edu.do
Founded 1983
Academic year: January to December
Rector: RAMÓN BENITO ANGELES FERNÁNDEZ.

UNIVERSIDAD TECNOLÓGICA DEL SUR

Apdo postal 194, Avda Enriquillo 01, Azua
Telephone: 521-3785
Fax: 521-4915
Founded 1984
Rector: ALTAGRACIA MILAGROS GARRIDO DE SÁNCHEZ
President: JUAN VALERIO SÁNCHEZ.

Colleges

Centros APEC de Educación a Distancia (CENAPEC): POB A-38, Santo Domingo; tel. 682-4648 ext. 235; fax 686-2277; e-mail cenapec@cenapec.edu.do; internet www.cenapec.edu.do; f. 1972; offer low-cost educational programmes by means of the distance education system; 525 teachers; 31,800 students; Pres. MIGUEL A. PUENTE H.; Exec. Dir MARIANO MELLA.

Instituto Superior de Agricultura (ISA) (Higher Institute of Agriculture): Apdo 166, Santiago; tel. 247-2000; fax 247-2626; f. 1962; independent institution but operates joint programme in agriculture with the Universidad Católica Madre y Maestra; training in agricultural sciences at high school and undergraduate level; subjects for degree course: horticulture, food technology, animal production, irrigation, agrarian reform, agricultural economics, administration; library: 14,000 vols; Pres. Dr FRANK JOSEPH THOMEN; Dir Ing. BENITO A. FERREIRAS; publ. publs occasional research papers.

Instituto Tecnológico de Santo Domingo: Avda de los Próceres, Galá, Apdo 342-9, Santo Domingo; tel. 567-9271; fax 566-3200; e-mail desarrollo@mail.intec.edu.do; f. 1972; undergraduate and postgraduate teaching and research; Rector Lic. RAFAEL TORIBIO; Academic Vice-Rector Lic. ALTAGRACIA LÓPEZ; Librarian Lic. LUCERO ARBOLEDA DE ROA; Library of 44,000 books, 1,400 periodicals; Number of students: 2,300; publs *Ciencia y Sociedad* (quarterly), *Documentos Intec* (annually), *Indice de Publicaciones de Universidades* (annually)

DIRECTORS
Basic and Environmental Sciences: Dr JOSÉ CONTRERAS
Business: Lic. AMARILIS GARCÍA
Civil Engineering: Ing. DANIEL COMARAZAMY
Health Sciences: Dr RAYMUNDO JIMÉNEZ
Humanities: Dr MANUEL MATOS MOQUETE
Industrial and Electromechanical Engineering: Ing. CARLOS CONDERO
Social Sciences: Lic. REINA ROSARIO

Schools of Art and Music

Dirección General de Bellas Artes (Fine Arts Council): Avda Máximo Gomez esq. Avda Independencia, Santo Domingo; tel. 682-1325; fax 689-1366; e-mail liricos@bellasartes.gov.do; internet www.bellasartes.gov.do; f. 1940; Dir Prof. RAFAEL VILLALONA..

Controls:

Academias de Música (Academies of Music): Villa Consuelo and Villa Francisca, Santo Domingo; also 19 provincial towns.

Conservatorio Nacional de Música (National Conservatoire of Music and Elocution): Santo Domingo.

Escuela de Arte Escénico (School of Scenic Art): Santo Domingo.

Escuela de Artes Plásticas (School of Plastic Arts): Santiago.

Escuela de Bellas Artes (School of Fine Arts): San Francisco de Macorís.

Escuela de Bellas Artes: San Juan de la Maguana.

Escuela Nacional de Bellas Artes (Fine Arts School): Santo Domingo.

ECUADOR

The Higher Education System

The Universidad Central del Ecuador, founded in 1586 as Universidad de San Fulgencio, is among the oldest universities in the Americas. Several universities were established in the 1860s, but most were founded during the 20th century. Higher education is administered by the Consejo Nacional de Educación Superior (National Council for Higher Education), and is governed by the Ley de Educación Superior (number 16 RO/77 of 15 May 2000).

Admission to higher education is on the basis of the Bachillerato, the main secondary school qualification; some universities also set entrance examinations. The main undergraduate degree is the Licenciado, which requires four years of study (a professional title can also be awarded). Following the Licenciado, the Masterado/Magister is a postgraduate degree that is awarded after two years of study. Finally, the Doctorado requires two to three years of study following the Licenciado. Not all institutions offer doctorate programmes. The Tecnólogo is the main qualification for technical and vocational education and is awarded after three-year 'short-cycle' courses.

Learned Societies

GENERAL

Casa de la Cultura Ecuatoriana 'Benjamín Carrión': Apdo 67, Avda 6 de Diciembre 794, Quito; tel. 223-391; fax 223-391; e-mail c.c.e@uio.satnet.net; f. 1944; covers all aspects of Ecuadorian culture; attached museums: see Museums and Art Galleries; library: attached library: see Libraries and Archives; 673 mems; Pres. Dr STALIN ALVEAR; Sec.-Gen. Dr MARCO PLACENCIA; publs *Letras de Ecuador* (2 a year), *Línea Imaginaria* (annually).

UNESCO Office Quito and Regional Bureau for Communication and Information: Foch #265 y de Diciembre, piso 2, Quito; tel. (2) 2529085; fax (2) 2504435; e-mail quito@unesco.org; designated Cluster Office for Bolivia, Colombia, Ecuador, Peru and Venezuela; Dir GUSTAVO LOPEZ OSPINA.

EDUCATION

Consejo Nacional de Educación Superior (CONESUP): Avda 9 de Octubre 624, y Carrión, Quito; tel. and fax 2506419; e-mail administrador@conesup.org.ec; internet www.conesup.net; f. 1982; responsible for approving new universities, technological institutes and academic programmes; Pres. Eng. VINICIO BAQUERO; Exec. Dir Lcdo DARIO MOREIRA; publs *Boletín Bimensual* (6 a year), *Planinformativo, Investigación Universitaria* (2 a year).

LANGUAGE AND LITERATURE

Academia Ecuatoriana de la Lengua (Academy of Ecuador): Apdo 17-07-9699, Quito; tel. (2) 543-234; fax (2) 901-518; f. 1875; 20 mems; Corresp. of the Real Academia Española (Madrid); library of 3,000 vols; Dir CARLOS JOAQUÍN CÓRDOVA; Sec. Emb. FILOTEO SAMANIÉGO; publs *Memorias* (annually), *Horizonte Cultural* (monthly).

Alliance Française: Eloy Alfaro 32–468, Casilla 17-11-6275, Quito; tel. (2) 245-2017; fax (2) 244-2293; e-mail afquito.dgaf@eolnet.net; internet www.afquito.org.ec; offers courses and exams in French language and culture and promotes cultural exchange with France; attached teaching offices in Cuenca, Guayaquil, Loja and Portoviejo; Dir MARCEL TAILLEFER.

MEDICINE

Academia Ecuatoriana de Medicina (Ecuadorian Academy of Medicine): Apdo postal 17-11-6202, Quito; tel. (2) 550-555; fax (2) 246-5557; e-mail jmalvear@accessinter.net; f. 1958; 120 mems.

Federación Médica Ecuatoriana (Medical Federation of Ecuador): Avda N. Unidas e Iñaquito, Quito; tel. 452-660; fax 456-812; f. 1942; 1,435 mems; Pres. Dr EDGAR MONTALVO MENDOZA; Sec. Dr ALBERTO CORDERO AROCA.

Sociedad Ecuatoriana de Pediatría (Paediatrics Society of Ecuador): C/o Dr Freddy Eskola Loyo (Secretary), Avda 13 # 13–14 y Calle 13, Quito; f. 1945; scientific extension courses and lectures; Pres. Dr AUGUSTO ANDRADE BARCIA; Sec. Dr FREDDY ESKOLA LOYO; publ. *Revista Ecuatoriana de Pediatría*.

Research Institutes

GENERAL

Institut de Recherche pour le Développement (IRD): Apdo 17-12-857, Quito; tel. (2) 565-336; fax (2) 504-020; f. 1974; geology, pedology, hydrology, botany and vegetal biology, agronomy, geography, human sciences, economics; library of 550 vols, 400 periodicals, 80 extracts; Dir Dr F. KAHN; (see main entry under France).

AGRICULTURE, FISHERIES AND VETERINARY SCIENCE

Instituto Interamericano Agricultural Experimental (Inter-American Experimental Agricultural Institute): Conocoto, Línea 63, Quito; part of OAS Interamerican Agricultural Institute.

Instituto Nacional Autónomo de Investigaciones Agropecuarias (Autonomous National Institute of Agricultural Research): Avda Amazonas y Eloy Alfaro, Edif. MAG (4° piso), Quito; tel. (2) 528-650; fax (2) 504-240; e-mail iniap@iniap-ecuador.gov.ec; f. 1959; Dir-Gen. Ing. VICENTE NOVOA; publ. *Revista* (4 a year).

Instituto Nacional de Pesca (National Fishery Institute): Letamendi 102 y La Ría, Casilla 5918, Guayaquil; f. 1960; fishing research and development; library of 20,000 vols; Dir Dr ROBERTO JIMÉNEZ S.; publs *Boletín Científico y Técnico, Revista Científica de Ciencias Marinas y Limnología, Boletín Informativo*.

ECONOMICS, LAW AND POLITICS

Instituto Latinoamericano de Investigaciones Sociales (ILDIS) (Latin American Social Sciences Research Institute): Casilla 17-03-367, Quito; tel. 562-103; fax 504337; f. 1974; affiliated to the Friedrich-Ebert Foundation; research in economics, sociology, political science and education; library of 15,000 vols; Dir Dr REINHART WETTMANN.

Instituto Nacional de Estadística y Censos (National Statistics and Census Institute): Juan Larrea N15-36 y José Riofrío, Quito; tel. (2) 255-6124; fax (2) 250-9836; e-mail inec1@ecnet.ec; internet www.inec.gov.ec; f. 1976; library of 6,500 vols; Dir-Gen. Ing. VÍCTOR MANUEL ESCOBAR BENAVIDES; publs *Indice de Precios al Consumidor Urbano* (monthly), *Indice de Precios de Materiales, Equipo y Maquinaria de la Construcción* (monthly), *Indice de Precios al Productor* (monthly).

HISTORY, GEOGRAPHY AND ARCHAEOLOGY

Centro de Investigaciones Históricas (Centre of Historical Research): Apdo 7,110, Guayaquil; f. 1930; library of 6,000 vols; Pres. Dr ABEL ROMEO CASTILLO; Sec.-Gen. JULIO ESTRADA YCAZA; publ. *Revista*.

Instituto Geográfico Militar (Military Geographical Institute): Casilla 17-01-2435, Quito; tel. (2) 522-148; fax (2) 569-097; e-mail igm1@igm.mil.ec; f. 1928; part of Ministry of Defence; main activity is preparation of national map series; undertakes projects for public and private organizations; provides cartographic and geographic documentation for national development and security; formulates disaster and land information systems; library of 10,500 vols; Dir Crnl E.M.C. FABIÁN MOSQUERA LÓPEZ; publs *Revista Geográfica* (2 a year), *Indices Toponímicos*.

MEDICINE

Instituto de Investigaciones para el Desarrollo de la Salud (Research Institute for Health Development): Calle Buenos Aires 340, 3 piso, Quito; tel. (2) 544-597; fax (2) 544-597; e-mail lopezjar@pi.pro.ec; f. 1988, by merger of Instituto Nacional de Investigaciones Nutricionales y Médico-Sociales and Instituto de Recursos Odontológicos del Area Andina; research on main aspects of public health; Dir PATRICIO LÓPEZ-JARAMILLO; publs *La Situación de la Salud en el Ecuador, La Situación de Salud en Areas Urbano Marginales, Control contra Bocio Endémico*, etc.

Instituto Nacional de Higiene y Medicina Tropical 'Leopoldo Izquieta Pérez' (National Institute of Hygiene): Julian Coronel 905 y Esmeraldas, Guayaquil; tel. (4) 281-542; fax (4) 394-189; f. 1941; 120 departments and sections; library of 5,600 vols; Dir Dr FRANCISCO HERNÁNDEZ MANRÍQUEZ; publ. *Revista Ecuatoriana de Higiene y Medicina Tropical*.

NATURAL SCIENCES

General

Instituto Oceanográfico de la Armada (Naval Oceanographic Institute): Avda 25 de Julio, Apdo 5940, Guayaquil; tel. (4) 248-4723; fax (4) 248-5166; e-mail inocar@inocar

.mil.ec; internet www.inocar.mil.ec; f. 1972 to study oceanography and hydrography; library of 2,500 vols; Dir CPNV-EM BYRON SANMIGUEL MARÍN (acting); publ. *Acta Oceanográfica del Pacífico* (annually).

Biological Sciences

Charles Darwin Research Station: Casilla 17-01-3891, Quito; location: Pto Ayora, Santa Cruz, Galapagos Islands; tel. (5) 526-146; fax (5) 526-651; e-mail director@fcdarwin.org.ec; internet www.darwinfoundation.org; f. 1964 under the auspices of the Ecuadorian Government, UNESCO and the Charles Darwin Foundation to study and preserve the flora and fauna of the Archipelago; maintains meteorological stations, a herbarium, a zoological museum and a marine laboratory; breeding programme for endangered reptiles; library of 4,000 vols, 12,000 separates, 105 current periodicals, slides, aerial photographs, maps; Dir Dr ROBERT BENSTED-SMITH; publs *Noticias de Galápagos* (2 a year), *Annual Report*, *Newsletter*.

Instituto Ecuatoriano de Ciencias Naturales (Ecuadorian Institute of Natural History): Apdo 408, Quito; tel. 215-497; f. 1940; research into natural resources and conservation; 46 mems, 24 foreign mems; library of 48,450 vols; Dir Prof. Dr MISAEL ACOSTA-SOLÍS; publ. *Flora* (official organ).

Physical Sciences

Instituto Nacional de Meteorología e Hidrología (Hydrometeorological Office): Iñaquito 700 y Corea, Quito; tel. (2) 265330; fax (2) 433934; f. 1961; library of 6,500 vols; Dir Ing. NELSON SALAZAR D.; publs. *Anuario Meteorológico*, *Anuario Hidrológico*, *Boletín Climatológico* (monthly).

Observatorio Astronómico de Quito (Quito Astronomical Observatory): Apdo 17-01-165, Parque La Alameda, Quito; tel. (2) 570-765; fax (2) 567-848; f. 1873; astronomy, astrophysics, seismology, meteorology and archaeoastronomy; library of 5,000 vols; Dir Dr ERICSON LÓPEZ IZURIETA; publs *Boletín Astronómico* (Series A, B), *Boletín Meteorológico*.

RELIGION, SOCIOLOGY AND ANTHROPOLOGY

Instituto Ecuatoriano de Antropología y Geografía (Ecuadorian Institute of Anthropology and Geography): POB 17-01-2258, Quito; premises at: Avda Orellana 557 y Coruña, Quito; tel. (2) 506-324; fax (2) 509-436; f. 1950; research in anthropology, folklore, history, social psychology and national questions; library of 5,000 vols; Dir Lcdo RODRIGO GRANIZO R.; publ. review *Llacta* (2 a year).

TECHNOLOGY

Comisión Ecuatoriana de Energía Atómica (Atomic Energy Commission of Ecuador): Avda González Suárez 2351 y Bosmediano, Casilla 17-01-2517, Quito; tel. (2) 458-013; fax (2) 253-097; f. 1958; 40 mems; research in nuclear physics, radioisotopes, radiobiology, chemistry, medicine; library of 5,000 vols; Exec. Dir Ing. CELIANO ALMEIDA; publ. *Noticias Trimestrales*.

Corporación de Desarrollo e Investigación Geológico-Minero-Metalúrgica (CODIGEM): Casilla 17-03-23, Avda 10 de Agosto 5844 y Pereira, Quito; tel. (2) 254-673; fax (2) 254-674; f. 1991 to replace Instituto Ecuatoriano de Minería; responsible for mineralogical research and prospecting in Ecuador, and for providing information to the public; produces national geological map; library of 1,205 vols, 22 periodicals; Exec. Pres. Ing. EFRÉN GALÁRRAGA SOTO; publs *Minería Ecuatoriana*, *Folleto Potencial Minero Ecuatoriano*.

Dirección General de Hidrocarburos (General Directorate of Hydrocarbons): Avda 10 de Agosto 321, Quito; f. 1969; supervises enforcement of laws relating to petroleum exploration and development, and sets standards for mining-petroleum industry; 210 mems; Dir Gen. Ing. GUILLERMO BIXBY; Sec. ERNESTO CORRAL; publs *Estadística Petrolera*, *Reporte Geológico de la Costa Ecuatoriana*, *Indice de Leyes y Decretos de la Industria Petrolera*.

Instituto de Ciencias Nucleares (Institute of Nuclear Science): Escuela Politécnica Nacional, Apdo 17-01-2759, Quito; tel. (2) 250-7126; fax (2) 256-7848; e-mail rmunoz@server.epn.edu.ec; f. 1957; library with department of microcards and microfilms; equipment for application of radioisotopes to chemistry, agriculture, medicine and radiation control; cobalt-60 pilot irradiator, batch type 40-10 kilocuries, linear electron accelerator 8 MeV with conveyor; 4 departments: Department of Applied Research, Head Prof. RICARDO MUÑOZ BURGOS; Department of Biomedical Applications, Dir RODRIGO FIERRO B.; Department of Industrial Applications, Head Ing. TRAJANO RAMÍREZ;Department of Radiation Control, Dir Ing. FREDDIE ORBE M.; Dir Dr FLORINELLA MUÑOZ BISESTI; publ. *Politécnica* (4 a year).

Libraries and Archives

Cuenca

Biblioteca de Autores Nacionales 'Fray Vicente Solano': Apdo 01-01-222, Cuenca; f. 1929; 43,000 vols; Dir JUAN CARLOS GONZALEZ V.

Biblioteca Hispano-Americana (Hispanic-American Library): Mariscal Sucre 338, Apdo 133, Cuenca; f. 1934; 54,700 vols; Dir CELIANO A. VINTIMILLA V..

Biblioteca 'Juan Bautista Vázquez' de la Universidad de Cuenca (Cuenca University Library): Apdo 168, Cuenca; f. 1882; 62,185 vols; Dir CELIANO A. VINTIMILLA V..

Biblioteca Panamericana (Pan-American Library): Apdo 57, Cuenca; tel. (593-7) 826130; f. 1912; 64,000 vols; Dir CLAUDIO ALBORNOZ V..

Biblioteca Pública Municipal (Public Municipal Library): Apdo 202, Cuenca; f. 1927; 50,000 vols; Dir JUAN TAMA MÁRQUEZ.

Guayaquil

Biblioteca 'Angel Andrés Garcia' de la Universidad 'Vicente Rocafuerte': Vélez 2203, Apdo 330, Guayaquil; f. 1847; 13,000 vols; Dir HERNÁN CABEZAS CANDEL; publ. publs *Revista de la Universidad 'Vicente Rocafuerte' and students' periodicals*.

Biblioteca de Autores Nacionales 'Carlos A. Rolando' (Library of Ecuadorian Writers): Palacio Municipal, Guayaquil; f. 1913; 12,000 vols, 15,000 pamphlets, 17,000 leaflets, 3,000 MSS relating to Ecuadorian authors and foreign works about Ecuador; Dir Dr CARLOS A. ROLANDO.

Biblioteca de la Casa de la Cultura Ecuatoriana: Núcleo de Guayas, 9 de Octubre y Pedro Moncayo, Apdo 3542, Guayaquil; f. 1945; 16,748 vols; Dir Lic. RUTH GARAICOA SORIA.

Biblioteca General, Universidad de Guayaquil: Casilla 3834, 09-01 Guayaquil; tel. 28-24-40; f. 1901; 50,000 vols; Dir Lic. LEONOR VILLAO DE SANTANDER; publs *Revista*, *El Universitario*.

Biblioteca Histórica y Archivo Colonial (Historical Library and Colonial Archives): Palacio de la Municipalidad, Apdo 75, Guayaquil; f. 1930; Dir Dr CARLOS A. ROLANDO; Sec. Prof. GUSTAVO MONROY GARAICOA.

Biblioteca Municipal 'Pedro Carbo' (Public Library): Avda 10 de Agosto, Calle Pedro Carbo, Guayaquil; f. 1862; 120,000 vols; Dir PATRICIA DE QUEVEDO; (see also under Museums).

Quito

Archivo-Biblioteca de la Función Legislativa: Palacio Legislativo, Quito; f. 1886; scientific and cultural; 27,000 vols; Dir Lic. RAFAEL A. PIEDRA SOLÍS; publs *Clave de la Legislación Ecuatoriana*, *Diario de Debates de la Legislatura*.

Archivo Nacional de Historia (National Historical Archives): Avda 6 de Diciembre 332, Apdo 67, Quito; f. 1938; 2,500 vols; colonial documents of the 16th to 19th centuries; Dir JORGE A. GARCÉS Y GARCÉS; Sec. JUAN R. FREKE-GRANIZO; publ. *Arnahis*.

Biblioteca de la Universidad Central del Ecuador (Central University Library): Quito; f. 1826; 170,000 vols; Dir ALONSO ALTAMIRANO; publs *Anales*, *Bibliografía Ecuatoriana*, *Anuario Bibliográfico*.

Biblioteca del Banco Central del Ecuador: Reina Victoria y Jorge Washington, Apdo 17-21-366 Eloy Alfaro, Quito; tel. 568957; fax 568973; f. 1938; 100,000 vols, 2,000 periodicals; specializes in economics, administration, banking and finance, social sciences; open to the public; Dir CARLOS LANDAZURI; publ. *Boletín Bibliográfico* (irregular).

Has attached:

Hemeroteca: Calle Arenas y 10 de Agosto Apdo 17-15-0029-C, Quito; tel. 561521; 5,000 periodicals; Dir JULIO OLEAS.

Musicoteca: Calles García Moreno y Sucre, Apdo 339, Quito; tel. 572784; music and video library; Dir ADRIANA ORTIZ.

Biblioteca Ecuatoriana 'Aurelio Espinosa Pólit': Apdo 17-01-160, Quito; f. 1928; Ecuadorian library, archive, Ecuadorian art and history museum; 300,000 vols; Librarian JULIAN G. BRAVO.

Biblioteca Municipal (Municipal Library): Casa de Montalvo, Apdo 75, Quito; f. 1886; 12,500 vols, 300 MSS, 4 incunabula.

Biblioteca Nacional del Ecuador (National Library): 12 de Octubre 555, Apdo 67, Quito; f. 1792; 70,000 vols of which 7,000 date from the 16th to 18th centuries; shares legal deposit with municipal libraries; Dir Dr EUGENIO ESPEJO.

Attached library:

Biblioteca de la Casa de la Cultura Ecuatoriana (Library of Ecuadorian Culture): Apdo 67, Avda Colombia, Quito; f. 1944; 12,000 vols and over 20,000 periodicals; includes the 'Laura de Crespo' Room of National Authors.

Museums and Art Galleries

Guayaquil

Museo Antropológico del Banco Central: Guayaquil; tel. (4) 327707; fax (4) 322792; f. 1974; archaeology of the Ecuadorian coast; gallery of contemporary Latin American art; research; library of 7,500 vols; Dir Arq. FREDDY OLMEDO R.; publ. *Miscelánea Antropológica Ecuatoriana*.

Museo Municipal (Municipal Museum): Avda 10 de Agosto, Calle Pedro Carbo,

Guayaquil; f. 1862; historical, ethnographical, palaeontological, geological exhibits; colonial period and modern paintings and numismatics (see also Libraries).

Quito

Museo Antropológico 'António Santiana': Universidad Central del Ecuador, Quito; f. 1925; sections of anthropology, archaeology, ethnography; library of 2,000 vols; Dir Dr HOLGUER JARA; publs *Humanitas, Boletín Ecuatoriano de Antropología* (irregular).

Museo de Arqueología y Etnología del Instituto Ecuatoriano de Antropología y Geografía (Museum of Archaeology and Ethnology): Casilla 2258, Quito; f. 1950; precious stones, ceramics, prehistoric sculptures.

Museo de Arte Colonial: Cuenca St and Mejía St, Quito; tel. 2212-297; f. 1914; attached to Casa de la Cultura Ecuatoriana 'Benjamín Carrión'; many examples of art from the Escuela Quiteña of the colonial epoch (17th and 18th centuries); Dir JUAN CARLOS FERNÁNDEZ-CATALÁN.

Museo de Artes Visuales e Instrumentos Musicales: Avda 12 de Octubre 555 y Patria, Quito; tel. (2) 2223-392; internet www.cultura.com.ec/martemoderno.htm; attached to Casa de la Cultura Ecuatoriana 'Benjamín Carrión'; art from Ecuador and Latin America since 19th c.

Museo de Ciencias Naturales de la Escuela Militar 'Eloy Alfaro': Avda Orellana, La Pradera 400, Quito; f. 1937; geological specimens and fauna from the Galapagos Islands; taxidermy and anatomy illustrated, especially of mammals and birds; Taxidermist LUIS ALFREDO PÉREZ VACA; publ. *Revista Anual del Plantel*.

Museo Jacinto Jijón Caamaño (Jacinto Jijón y Caamaño Museum): Pontifícia Universidad Católica, Avda 12 de Octubre y Carrión, Apdo 17-01-2184, Quito; tel. (2) 565-627; fax (2) 544-995; e-mail museo-jjc@puceuio.puce.edu.ec; f. 1969; archaeology, art; library of 2,000 vols; Dir ERNESTO SALAZAR.

Museo Municipal de Arte e Historia 'Alberto Mena Caamaño' (Civic Museum of Arts and History): Espejo 1147 y Benalcázar, Apdo 17-01-3346, Quito; tel. 584-326; fax 584362; e-mail dpc@hoy.net; f. 1959; archaeology, colonial art, 19th-century art, items of historical interest; history archive (1583–1980), information library; Dir ALFONSO ORTIZ CRESPO.

Museo Nacional de la Dirección Cultural del Banco Central del Ecuador: Reina Victoria y Jorge Washington (esquina), Edificio Aranjuez, Apdo 339, Quito; tel. 220547; fax 568972; e-mail jortiz@uio.bce.fin.ec; f. 1969; pre-historical archaeological exhibits; colonial and modern art (sculpture, paintings, etc.); library of 6,000 vols; Dir Lcdo JUAN ORTIZ GARCÍA.

Universities and Technical Universities

ESCUELA POLITÉCNICA DEL EJERCITO

Campus Politécnico, Avda El Progreso s/n, POB 171-5-231B, Sangolquí
Telephone: (2) 2334950
Fax: (2) 2334952
E-mail: espe@espe.edu.ec
Internet: www.espe.edu.ec
Founded 1922; current name since 1977
State control
Academic year: March to February (two semesters)
Rector: Ing. MARCO VERA RIOS
Vice-Rector (Academic): Ing. JORGE CHÁVEZ
Vice-Rector (Administration): Ing. DEMETRIO SANTANDER
Vice-Rector (Research): Ing. ROMMEL VINTIMILLA.

ESCUELA POLITÉCNICA NACIONAL (National Polytechnic School)

Ladrón de Guevara s/n, Apdo 17-01-2759, Quito
Telephone: (2) 256-2400
Fax: (2) 567-848
E-mail: postmaster@server.epn.edu.ec
Internet: www.epn.edu.ec
Founded 1869
Autonomous control
Language of instruction: Spanish
Academic year: October to February, March to July
Rector: Ing. MARCELO JARAMILLO
Vice-Rector: PdD STALIN SUÁREZ
Secretary Attorney: Ing. PATRICIO ESTUPIÑAN
Librarian: Tec. GERMANIA MERIZALDE
Number of teachers: 800
Number of students: 8,000
Publication: *Politécnica* (4 a year)

DIRECTORS

School of Engineering: Ing. JORGE MOLINA
School of Science: M.Ar. CARLOS ECHEVERRÍA
School of Technology: Ing. RODRIGO RUIZ

ESCUELA SUPERIOR POLITÉCNICA AGROPECUARIA DE MANABÍ

10 de Agosto 82 y Granda Centeno, Calceta
Telephone: (5) 2685134
Fax: (5) 2685156
E-mail: espam@espam.edu.ec
Internet: www.espam.edu.ec
Founded 1999
State control
Academic year: June to May (two semesters)
Rector: Ing. LEONARDO FÈLIX LÒPEZ
Secretary-General: Abog. LYA VILLAFUERTE VÈLEZ
Library of 800 vols

DIRECTORS

Agricultural Industry: Ing. SUSANA DUEÑAS DE LA TORRE
Agriculture: Ing. KLÉBER PALACIOS SALTOS
Cattle: Ing. KLÉBER PALACIOS SALTOS
Computer Science: Lic. VICENTE AVEIGA DE SANTANA
Environmental Science: Dr RONALDO MENDOZA VÉLEZ

ESCUELA SUPERIOR POLITÉCNICA DE CHIMBORAZO

Casilla 4703, Riobamba
Telephone: 96-1099
Founded 1972
Autonomous control
Language of instruction: Spanish
Academic year: from October
Rector: Ing. RODRIGO JARAMILLO G.
Vice-Rector: Dr. FERNANDO RODRÍGUEZ P.
Secretary-General: Dr PATRICIO PAZMIÑD F.
Librarian: Sr. CARLOS RODRÍGUEZ C.
Library of 35,000 vols, 80,000 periodicals
Number of teachers: 264
Number of students: 4,500 (excluding students from the Dept of Languages)
Publication: *GACETA* (every 3 months)

DEANS

Faculty of Agronomy: Ing. BAYARDO ULLOA E.
Faculty of Animal Husbandry: WILFRIDO CAPELO B.
Faculty of Business Administration: Econ. JORGE RÍOS CH.
Faculty of Mathematics and Physics: Ing. GUSTAVO MANCHENO T.
Faculty of Mechanical Engineering: Ing. PACÍFICO RIOFRÍO
Faculty of Nutrition and Dietetics: Lcda CARMEN PLAZA N.
Faculty of Sciences: Dr CARLOS DONOSO F.
Department of Chemistry: Dr JOSÉ MONTESINOS J.
Department of Physical Education: Lcdo RAÚL RODRÍGUEZ

ESCUELA SUPERIOR POLITÉCNICA DEL LITORAL

La Prosperina, Km $30^1/_2$ Vía Perimetral, Guayaquil
Telephone: (4) 269269
Fax: (4) 854629
E-mail: cee@ecua.net.ec
Internet: www.espol.edu.ec
Founded 1958
State control
Language of instruction: Spanish
Academic year: May to February
Rector: VICTOR BASTIDAS JIMÉNEZ
Provost and Vice-President (Academic Affairs): MARCOS VELARDE T.
Vice-President (Business Affairs and Finances): DANIEL TAPIA FALCONÍ
Vice-President (Student Affairs): ROBERT TOLEDO ECHEVERRÍA
Secretary-General: Lic. JAIME VÉLIZ LITARDO
Librarian: ELOÍSA PATIÑO LARA
Library of 47,000 vols
Number of teachers: 550
Number of students: 12,005
Publications: *Boletín Informativo Polipesca, Informes de Actividades, Tecnológica*

DIRECTORS

Department of Electrical Engineering and Computer Science: CARLOS VILLAFUERTE
Department of Geology, Mines and Petroleum Engineering: MIGUEL A. CHÁVEZ
Department of Maritime Engineering: EDUARDO CERVANTES
Department of Mechanical Engineering: EDUARDO RIVADENEIRA
Institute of Chemistry: JUSTO HUAYAMAVE
Institute of Humanities: OMAR MALUK
Institute of Mathematics: JORGE MEDINA
Institute of Physics: JAIME VÁSQUEZ
Agriculture School: HAYDÉE TORRES
Computer Science School: ALEXANDRA PALADINES
Electrical and Electronics School: CAMILO ARELLANO
Fisheries School: FRANCISCO PACHECO
Food Science School: MA. FERNANDA MORALES
Furniture and Cabinet School: VÍCTOR FERNÁNDEZ
Mechanics School: MIGUEL PISCO
Graduate School of Business: MOISÉS TACLE
Center for the Study of Foreign Languages: Lic. DENNIS MALONEY S.

UNIVERSIDAD AGRARIA DEL ECUADOR

Apdo 09-01-1248, Avda 25 de Julio y Avda Juan Pio Jaramillo, Via Puerto Maritimo, Guayaquil
Telephone: (4) 493441
Fax: (4) 493441
E-mail: info@uagraria.edu.ec
Internet: www.uagraria.edu.ec
Founded 1992

Rector: Ing. JACOBO BUCARAM ORTÍZ
Vice-Rector: Ing. GUILLERMO ROLANDO.

UNIVERSIDAD ANDINA SIMÓN BOLÍVAR ECUADOR

POB 17-12-569, Toledo N22-80 (Plaza Brasilia), Quito
Telephone: (2) 3228031
Fax: (2) 3228426
E-mail: uasb@uasb.edu.ec
Internet: www.uasb.edu.ec

Founded 1992
State control

Rector: ENRIQUE AYALA MORA
Secretary-General: VIRGINIA ALTA PERUGACHI
Librarian: ENRIQUE ABAD ROA

Publications: *Comentario Internacional: Revista del Centro Andino de Estudios Internacionales*, *Foro: Revista de Derecho*, *Kipus: Revista Andina de Letras*, *Procesos: Revista Ecuatoriana de Historia*

Campuses in Sucre (Bolivia) and Caracas (Venezuela); offices in Bogotá (Colombia) and La Paz (Bolivia)

DIRECTORS OF SUBJECT AREAS

Arts: FERNANDO BALSECA
Business: ALFONSO TROYA
Communication: JOSÉ LASO
Education: MARIO CIFUENTES
Health Studies: PLUTARCO NARANJO
History: GUILLERMO BUSTOS
Law: JOSÉ VICENTE TROYA
Social and Global Studies: CÉSAR MONTÚFAR

ATTACHED RESEARCH INSTITUTES

Centro Andino de Estudios Internacionales: tel. (4) 2560945; e-mail dctena@hoy.net; Pres. DIEGO CORDOVEZ.

Programa Andino de Derechos Humanos: tel. (4) 2556403; e-mail roque@uasb.edu.ec; Regional Co-ordinator ROQUE ESPINOSA.

UNIVERSIDAD CENTRAL DEL ECUADOR

Avda América y A. Pérez Guerrero, Casilla 1456, QuitoTelephone: (2) 226080
Fax: (2) 505860
E-mail: rectorado@ucentral.edu.ec
Internet: www.ucentral.edu.ec

Founded 1586 as Universidad de San Fulgencio; became Real y Pontificia Universidad de San Gregorio in 1622, Universidad de Santo Tomás de Aquino in 1688, then Universidad Central del Sur de la Gran Colombia; present name 1826.
State control
Language of instruction: Spanish
Academic year: September to July

Rector: Ing. VICTOR HUGO OLALLA PROAÑO
Vice-Rector: Ing. CARLOS ARROYO ALVAREZ
Registrar: Dra. LIDA FLORES CHACÓN
Librarian: Lic. JANETH CORNEJO

Number of teachers: 2,137
Number of students: 31,663

Publication: *Anales*

DEANS

Faculty of Administrative Sciences: Dr JOSÉ VILLAVICENCIO
Faculty of Agricultural Sciences: Ing. MIGUEL ARAQUE
Faculty of Architecture and Urbanism: Arq. PATRICIO AGUILAR VEINTIMILLA
Faculty of Arts: Prof. VICTORIA CARRASCO
Faculty of Chemistry: Dr ARTURO BASTIDAS
Faculty of Dentistry: Dr GUSTAVO RON
Faculty of Economics: Econ. JOSÉ VILLACÍS PAZ Y MIÑO
Faculty of Engineering, Physics and Mathematics: Ing. MARCO AYABACA CAZAR
Faculty of Geology, Mines, Petroleum and Environmental Studies: Ing. GUSTAVO PINTO ARTEAGA
Faculty of Law and Political and Social Sciences: Dr HOLGER CÓRDOVA
Faculty of Medical Sciences: Dr RICARDO CARRASCO
Faculty of Philosophy and Education: Mgs. GUILLERMO PÉREZ
Faculty of Psychology: Dr OSWALDO MONTENEGRO JIMÉNEZ
Faculty of Social Communication: Lic. PATRICIO MONCAYO
Faculty of Veterinary Medicine: Dr OSWALDO ALBORNÓZ

Campus at Riobamba offers courses in education, literature and philosophy

UNIVERSIDAD DE CUENCA

Avda 12 de Abril, Sector 16, Apdo 168, Cuenca
Telephone: 831-556
Fax: 835197
Internet: www.ucuenca.edu.ec

Founded 1868
Academic year: October to July

Rector: Dr GUSTAVO VEGA-DELGADO
Vice-Rector: Dr JAIME ASTUDILLO R.
Secretary-General: Dr WILSON ANDRADE R.
Administrative Director: MARGARITA GUTIERREZ
Librarian: MARGARITA GUTIERREZ

Number of teachers: 613
Number of students: 8,500

Publications: *Anales de la Universidad de Cuenca*, *Informe de Coyuntura-Facultad de Ciencias Económicas*, *IURIS—Revista de la Facultad de Jurisprudencia*, *Revista de la Facultad de Ciencias Agropecuarias*, *Revista de la Facultad de Ciencias Médicas*, *Revista del IDICSA*, *Revista del IDIS*, *Revista del IICT*, etc

DEANS

Faculty of Agriculture: Ing GERMÁN ARCOS
Faculty of Architecture: Arq. LEOPOLDO CORDERO O.
Faculty of Chemistry: Dr LUÍS TONÓN P.
Faculty of Dentistry: Dr RAÚL CORDERO R.
Faculty of Economics: Econ. LEONARDO ESPINOZA
Faculty of Engineering: Ing. FABIÁN CARRASCO C.
Faculty of Jurisprudence: PABLO ESTRELLA V.
Faculty of Medical Sciences: Dr RUBÉN DARÍO SOLÍS C.
Faculty of Philosophy and Letters: Dr JORGE VILLAVICENCIO V.

DIRECTORS

Institute of Computing and Information Science (ICEI): Ing. SALVADOR MONSALVE R.
Institute of Physical Education: Lcdo JULIO ABAD
Research Institute: Dr ALBERTO QUEZADA R.
Planning Unit: Ing. RAFAEL ESTRELLA A.

UNIVERSIDAD DE GUAYAQUIL

Casilla 09-001-471, Guayaquil
Telephone: (4) 329905
Fax: (4) 329905
Internet: www.ug.edu.ec

Founded 1867
Private control
Language of instruction: Spanish
Academic year: April to February (2 semesters)

Rector: Arq. JAIME POLIT ALCIVAR
Vice-Rectors: Ab. GUSTAVO ITURRALDE NÚÑEZ, Dr JOSÉ APOLO PINEDA (Academic), Ing. OSWALDO AYALA NÚÑEZ (acting) (Administrative)
Secretary-General: Dr ALBERTO SÁNCHEZ BALDA
Librarian: Lic. LEONOR V. DE SANTANDER

Number of teachers: 2,848
Number of students: 60,000

Publication: *Revista*

DEANS

Faculty of Administrative Sciences: Ing. Com. EDWARD FAGGIONI CAMACHO
Faculty of Agricultural Engineering: Ing. Agr. VICTOR VILLAO ROSALES (acting)
Faculty of Architecture: Arq. ALFONSO CORREA RODAS
Faculty of Chemical Engineering: Ing. LUIS PACTONG ASSAN
Faculty of Chemistry: Dr JULIO ALVAREZ CASTRO
Faculty of Economics: Eco. LEONARDO VICUÑA IZQUIERDO
Faculty of Industrial Engineering: Ing. ALFREDO ARÉVALO MOSCOSO
Faculty of Law, Social Sciences and Politics: Dr PUBLIO DAVILA ALAVA
Faculty of Mathematics and Physics: Ing. NESTOR LAYANA ROMERO (acting)
Faculty of Medicine: Dr SALOMON QUINTERO ESTRADA
Faculty of Natural Sciences: Bio. RAFAEL BECERRA SILVA
Faculty of Odontology: Dr JOSÉ APOLO PINEDA
Faculty of Philosophy, Literature and Education: Dr FRANCISCO MORÁN MÁRQUEZ
Faculty of Physical Education, Sport and Recreation: Dr CÉSAR HERMIDA BAQUERIZO
Faculty of Psychology: Dra LIDIA ANDRADE BORRERO
Faculty of Social Communication: Ab. ALBA CHÁVEZ DE ALVARADO
Faculty of Veterinary Medicine: Dr OMAR LOOR RISCO (acting)

ATTACHED INSTITUTE

Institute of Diplomacy and International Studies: Dir Ab. REYNALDO HUERTA ORTEGA.

Campuses in Milagro, Vinces and Guaranda

UNIVERSIDAD DEL AZUAY

Avda 24 de Mayo 7-77 y Hernán Malo, Cuenca, Azuay
Telephone: (7) 2881333
Fax: (7) 2815997
E-mail: webmaster@uazuay.edu.ec
Internet: www.uazuay.edu.ec

Founded 1968; present status 1990
Academic year: October to July

Rector: Dr MARIO JARAMILLO PAREDES
Vice-Rector: Ing. FRANCISCO SALGADO ARTEGA
Dean (Administration and Finance): Econ. CARLOS CORDERO DÍAZ
Dean (Research): Ing. JACINTO GUILLÉN GARCÍA

Library of 40,000 vols

Publication: *Marginalia* (2 a year)

DEANS

Faculty of Administration: Ing. MIGUEL MOSCOSO COBOS
Faculty of Design: Arq. PATRICIO LEÓN BUSTOS
Faculty of Law: Dr PATRICIO CORDERO ORDOÑEZ
Faculty of Medicine: Dr EDGAR RODAS ANDRADE
Faculty of Philosophy: JORGE QUINTUÑA ALVAREZ
Faculty of Science and Technology: Ing. MIRIAM BRIONES GARCÍA
Faculty of Theology: Fr ANTONIO ALONSO MARTÍNEZ

HEADS OF SCHOOLS

Faculty of Administration:
- Accountancy: Ing. LUÍS QUEZADAS SISALIMA
- Administration: Ing. HERNÁN COELLAR ESPINOZA
- Economics: Econ. ROBERTO MACHUCA COELLO
- Systems Engineering: Ing. FERNANDO BALAREZO RODRÍGUEZ

Faculty of Philosophy:
- Educational Sciences: CARLOS DELGADO ALVAREZ
- General and Clinical Psychology: ALBERTO ASTUDILLO PESANTEZ
- Professional Development: Lic. CARLOS DELGADO ALVAREZ
- Social Communication: CATALINA SERRANO CORDERO
- Special and Preschool Education: Dra ESPERANZA DURÁN DURÁN
- Therapeutic Educational Psychology: Dr MIGUEL MIRANDA VINTIMILLA
- Work and Organizational Psychology: CRISTINA CRESPO ANDRADE

Faculty of Science and Technology:
- Agricultural Engineering: Dr EDUARDO IDROVO MURILLO
- Electronic Engineering: Ing. GERMÁN ZUÑIGA
- Environmental Biology: Dr GUSTAVO CHACÓN
- Food Engineering: Dra DIANA CHALCO QUEZADA
- Mechanical Engineering: Ing. FERNANDO GUERRERO PALACIOS
- Production Engineering: Ing. IVAN ANDRADE DUEÑAS

ATTACHED RESEARCH INSTITUTES

Instituto de Estudios de Régimen Seccional de Ecuador (IERSE): Dir Dr PAUL GRANDA.

UNIVERSIDAD ESTATAL DE BOLÍVAR

Casilla 92, Guaranda
Telephone: (3) 980121
Fax: (3) 980123
Internet: reicyt.org.ec/ueb

Founded 1989
State control

Rector: Ing. GABRIEL AQUILES GALARZA LOPEZ
Vice-Rector: Lcdo PEDRO PABLO LUCIO GAIBOR
Registrar: Ing. GONZALO LOPEZ RIVADENEIRA
Librarian: Ing. RODRIGO SALTOS CHAVES

Number of teachers: 182
Number of students: 2,091

Publication: *Enlace Universitario*

DEANS

Faculty of Agriculture: Ing. MANUEL RODRIGO GAIBOR
Faculty of Administrative Sciences: Ing. DIÓMEDEZ NÚÑEZ MINAYA
Faculty of Education: Lcdo. MANUEL ALAVA MAGALLANES
Faculty of Health Sciences: Dr MANUEL ALBÁN LUCIO

UNIVERSIDAD ESTATAL DE MILAGRO

Km 1½, Vía Milagro Km 26, Los Rios, Milagro
Telephone: (4) 2970881
Fax: (4) 2974319
E-mail: unemi@hotmail.com

Founded 2001

Rector: Dr RÓMULO MINCHALA MURILLO
Secretary-General: AGUSTIN ARELLANO QUIROZ.

UNIVERSIDAD ESTATAL DEL SUR DE MANABÍ

Complejo Universitario, Ciudadela 10 de Agosto, Vía a Noboa, Jipijapa
Telephone: (5) 2600229
E-mail: unesum@hotmail.com

Founded 2001
State control

Rector: JORGE CLIMACO CAÑARTE MURILLO.

UNIVERSIDAD ESTATAL PENÍNSULA DE SANTA ELENA

Avda 9 de Octubre 515, Edificio Ching, 2 Piso, La Libertad
Telephone: (4) 2780018
Fax: (4) 2785398
E-mail: unipen@interactive.net.ec

Founded 1998
Academic year: September to April

Rector: XAVIER TOMALÁ
Vice-Rector: GEORGE CLEMENTE.

UNIVERSIDAD NACIONAL DE CHIMBORAZO

Avda Eloy Alfaro y 10 de Agosto, Riobamba
Telephone: (3) 2941999
Fax: (3) 2960343
E-mail: webmaster@unach.edu.ec
Internet: www.unach.edu.ec

Founded 1995
State control
Academic year: October to July (two semesters)

Rector: EDISON RIERA RODRÍGUEZ
Vice-Rector: ENRIQUE CRESPO

Faculties of Education, Humanities and Technology, Engineering, Physical Education and Health Sciences, and Political Science and Administration.

UNIVERSIDAD NACIONAL DE LOJA

Casilla Letra 'S', Ciudadela Universitaria, Loja
Telephone: (7) 561841
Internet: www.unl.edu.ec

Founded 1869 as the Junta Universitaria; university status 1943
State control
Language of instruction: Spanish
Academic year: October to July

Rector: Ing. GUILLERMO FALCONÍ ESPINOSA
Vice-Rectors: Dr REINALDO VALAREZO GARCÍA (Academic), Dr CÉSAR JARAMILLO CARRIÓN (Administrative), Dr REINALDO VALAREZO GARCÍA (Academic)
Secretary-General: Dr JAIME GUZMÁN REGALADO
Librarian: Dr ENITH COSTA MUÑOZ

Library of 3,500 vols
Number of teachers: 720
Number of students: 13,280

Publications: *Estudios Universitarios*, *Revista Científica*, and various faculty bulletins

DEANS

Faculty of Administrative Sciences: Dr FULVIO FERNANDEZ MACAS
Faculty of Agriculture: Ing. ALFREDO SAMANIEGO VÉLEZ
Faculty of Arts: Lic. OSWALDO MORA RIVAS
Faculty of Law, Political, Social and Economic Sciences: Dr CÉSAR MONTAÑO ORTEGA
Faculty of Medicine: Dr ALONSO ARMIJOS LUNA
Faculty of Philosophy, Literature and Education: Lic. HÉCTOR SILVA VILEMA
Faculty of Science and Technology: Ing. ERMEL LOAIZA
Faculty of Veterinary Science: Dr EDUARDO VÉLEZ RUIZ

ATTACHED INSTITUTES

Instituto de Ciencias Básicas: Dir Ing. WILMER MARINO A.

Instituto de Lenguas: Dir Lic. NUMA REINOSO LARREA.

Instituto Tecnológico, Alamor: Alamor; Dir Econ. GLADYS GARCÍA.

Instituto Tecnológico, Cariamanga: Cariamanga; Dir Lic. LUIS TORRES.

Instituto Tecnológico, Catacocha: Catacocha; Dir Ing. ALFREDO SILVA.

Instituto Tecnológico, Macará: Macará; Dir Lic. CARMEN CEVALLOS.

Instituto Tecnológico, Yanzatza: Yanzatza; Dir Ing. JOSÉ RAMÍREZ.

UNIVERSIDAD TÉCNICA DE AMBATO

Casilla 18-01-334, Ambato
Telephone: (3) 85-39-05
Fax: (3) 84-91-64
Internet: www.uta.edu.ec

Founded 1969

Rector: Ing. VÍCTOR HUGO JARAMILLO
Vice-Rector: Ing. ANÍBAL SALTOS SALTOS
Secretary-General: Dr PATRICIO POAQUIZA
Librarian: Lic. ELSA NARANJO

Number of teachers: 332
Number of students: 7,200

DEANS

Faculty of Accountancy: Econ. SANTIAGO BARRIGA
Faculty of Administration: Ing. JOSÉ SILVA
Faculty of Agricultural Engineering: Ing. NELLY CHERREZ
Faculty of Civil Engineering: Ing. MIGUEL MORA
Faculty of Education: Dr JULIO SALTOS
Faculty of Food Technology: Ing. ROMEL RIVERA
Faculty of Systems Engineering: Ing. VÍCTOR GUACHIMBOZA
Centro de Estudios a Distancia: Ing. GALO JARAMILLO
Centro de Estudios de Postgrado: Ing. FRANCISCO FERNÁNDEZ B.

UNIVERSIDAD TÉCNICA DE BABAHOYO

Apdo 66, Via Flores, Babahoyo, Los Ríos
Telephone: (4) 730208

Founded 1971

Rector: Dr BOLÍVAR LUPERA ICAZA
Vice-Rector: Ab. HUGOLINO ORELLANA VILLACRÉS
Secretary-General: ALBERTO BRAVO MEDINA
Librarian: Lic. MIGUEL BASTIDAS

Number of teachers: 450
Number of students: 5,000

DEANS

Faculty of Agriculture: Ing. Agr. WÁSHINGTON URQUIZA B.
Faculty of Education: Ab. AUSBERTO COLINO GONZALVO
Quevedo Campus (Director): Lic. ANGEL GUANOPATÍN
Research (Director): Ing. Agr. CARLOS MIÑAN FIALLOS

UNIVERSIDAD TÉCNICA DE COTOPAXI

Campus Universitario, Avda Simón Rodríguez s/n, Barrio El Ejido, Parroquia Eloy Alfaro, Latacunga, Cotopaxi
Telephone: (3) 2810296
Fax: (3) 2810295

E-mail: webmaster@utc.edu.ec
Internet: www.utc.edu.ec
Founded 1991
Rector: Francisco Ramiro Ulloa Enriquez
Vice-Rector: Hernán Yánez
Secretary-General: William Espinoza.

UNIVERSIDAD TÉCNICA DE ESMERALDAS

Avda Nuevo Horizonte, Apdo 179, Esmeraldas
Telephone: 711-851
Founded 1970
Rector: Lic. Antonio Preciado
Vice-Rector: Ing. Alfredo Arévalo
Secretary-General: Ab. Marco Reinoso Cañote
Librarian: Solanda Gobea
Number of teachers: c. 180
Number of students: c. 800

DEANS
Faculty of Administration: Dr Carlos Riofrío
Faculty of Education: Lic. Miguel Lara
Faculty of Mechanical Engineering: Ing. Leonardo Mera
Faculty of Sociology and Social Work: Lic. José Luna Ch.
Faculty of Stockbreeding: Ing. Raúl Tello

UNIVERSIDAD TÉCNICA DE MACHALA

Avda Panamerica Km 5 1/2 via a Pasaje, Machala
Telephone: (72) 934-633
E-mail: webmaster@utmachala.edu.ec
Internet: www.utmachala.edu.ec
Founded 1969
State control
Language of instruction: Spanish
Academic year: March to January
Rector: Ing. Víctor Hernán Cabrera Jaramillo
Vice-Rector: Ing. Alcides Espinoza Ramirez
Secretary-General: Ab. José Antonio Romero Tandazo
Librarian: María Unda Serrana de Barrezueta
Library of 5,000 vols
Number of teachers: 600
Number of students: 9,636
Publication: *Revista de la Facultad de Agronomía y Veterinaria*

DEANS
Faculty of Agronomy and Veterinary Science: Ing. Max Iñiguez
Faculty of Business Administration and Accountancy: Ing. Danilo Pico
Faculty of Chemical Sciences: Ing. Alberto Game
Faculty of Civil Engineering: Ing. Luis Ordóñez Jaramillo
Faculty of Sociology: Soc. Ramiro Ordoñez
School of Nursing: Lic. Daysi Espinoza de Ramírez
Institute of Languages: Laura León de Astudillo

UNIVERSIDAD TÉCNICA DE MANABÍ

Casilla 82, Portoviejo, Manabí
Telephone: 636-867
Internet: www.utm.edu.ec
Founded 1954
State control
Academic year: May to January (two semesters)
Rector: Dr Guido Alava Párraga
Secretary: Dr Plutarco García Saltos
Librarian: María Angela de Coronel
Number of teachers: 489
Number of students: 8,000
Publication: *Revista*

DEANS
Faculty of Administration and Economics: Econ. Segundo Zambrano
Faculty of Agricultural Engineering: Ing. Régulos Ceballos
Faculty of Agronomy: Ing. Marcos Medina Naranjo
Faculty of Chemistry, Mathematics and Physics: Ing. Eliécer Rodríguez Indarte
Faculty of Health Sciences: Dr Félix Mogro
Faculty of Social Sciences and Education: Dr Nilo Palma Palma
Faculty of Veterinary Sciences: Dr Ignacio Palacios Macías
Faculty of Zootechnology: Dr Mario Mata Moreira

UNIVERSIDAD TÉCNICA DEL NORTE

Ciudadela Universitaria 'El Olivo', Avda 17 de Julio, Ibarra
Telephone: (6) 2953461
Fax: (6) 2955833
E-mail: utn@utn.edu.ec
Internet: www.utn.edu.ec
Founded 1986
Rector: Dr Marco L. Muñoz Herreria
Faculties of Administration, Animal Husbandry and Environment, Applied Sciences, Educational Sciences and Health Sciences.

UNIVERSIDAD TÉCNICA ESTATAL DE QUEVEDO

Km 1 Vía a Quito, Casilla 73, Quevedo, Los Ríos
Telephone: (5) 751430
Fax: (5) 753300
E-mail: info@uteq.edu.ec
Internet: www.uteq.edu.ec
Founded 1984
State control
Rector: Ing. Manuel Haz Alvarez
Vice-Rector: Dr Tito Cabrera Vicuña
Librarian: Carmen Velasco López
Number of teachers: 144
Number of students: 2,900

DEANS
Faculty of Agrarian Science: Glen Mera Hallón
Faculty of Cattle Science: Roque Vivas Moreira
Faculty of Enterprise Science: Dr Ignacio Fuentes Cornejo
Faculty of Environmental Science: Antonio Véliz Mendoza
International Relations: Dr Joffre Rada Peralta

Private Universities

PONTIFICIA UNIVERSIDAD CATÓLICA DEL ECUADOR

Avda 12 de Octubre 1076 y Carrión, Apdo 17-012184, Quito
Telephone: (2) 529240
Fax: (2) 567117
E-mail: webmaster@puceuio.puce.edu.ec
Internet: www.puce.edu.ec
Founded 1946
Private control
Language of instruction: Spanish
Academic year: September to July
Grand Chancellor: Dr Antonio González Zumárraga
Vice-Chancellor: P. Allan Mendoza
Rector: Dr José Ribadeneira Espinosa
Vice-Rector: Dr Manuel Corrales Pascual
Librarian: Lic. Oswaldo Orbe
Number of teachers: 1,061
Number of students: 7,240
Publications: *Economía y Humanismo* (4 a year), *Revista PUCE* (2 a year)

DEANS
Faculty of Administrative Sciences: Dr Alfredo Paredes Santos
Faculty of Economics: Econ. René Báez Tobar
Faculty of Education: Dr Enrique Galarza
Faculty of Engineering: Ing. Diego Andrade Stacey
Faculty of Exact and Natural Sciences: Dr Alberto Padilla Abo-Mohor
Faculty of Humanities: Lic. Emilio Cerezo Alonso
Faculty of Jurisprudence: Dr Santiago Guarderas
Faculty of Linguistics and Languages: Dr Fernando Miño Garcés
Faculty of Nursing: Lic. Lourdes Carrera Sosa
Faculty of Psychology: Dr Jorge Flachier del Alcazier

DIRECTORS
School of Medical Technology: Lic. Letti García
School of Philosophy: Dr Hugo Reinoso Luna
School of Social Work: Mtr. Rafael García Silva

REGIONAL CAMPUSES
Ambato Campus: Parroquia Isamba, Apdo 124, Ambato; tel. 822050; courses in computer technology and English; Pro-Rector Dr César González Loor.
Esmeraldas Campus: Casilla 65, Esmeraldas; tel. 710-545; 391 students; courses in education, accountancy, nursing, English; Pro-Rector Dr Joaquín Zurutuza.
Ibarra Campus: Casilla 734, Ibarra; tel. 952-352; 741 students; courses in administration and accountancy, tourism and hotel management, design, civil engineering; Pro-Rector Dr Jesus Muñoz-Diez.

UNIVERSIDAD CATÓLICA DE CUENCA

POB 01-01-1937, Cuenca
Telephone: (7) 842606
Fax: (7) 831040
E-mail: uccsis@etapa.com.ec
Founded 1970
Private control
Academic year: October to July (3 terms)
Rector: Dr César Cordero Moscoso
Associate Rector: Dr Carlos Darquea López
Pro-Rector: Dr Marco Vicuña Domínguez
Academic Vice-Rector: Dr Eduardo Díaz
Administrative Vice-Rector: Dr Nelson Córdova Alvarez
Extension Vice-Rector: Dr Hugo Ortiz Segarra
Academic Director: Ing. Pablo Cisneros Quintanilla
Finance Director: Eco. Estuardo Rubio Auquilla
Chief Administrative Officer: Dr Enrique Campoverde Cajas
Secretary-General: Dr Rodrigo Cisneros Aguirre
Librarian: Prof. César Rivera Ochoa
Library of 7,000 vols
Number of teachers: 650
Number of students: 8,000

Publications: *Diálogo*, *Estudios*, *Panoramas*, *Presencia*, *Retama*

DEANS

Faculty of Agricultural Engineering, Mines and Veterinary Science: Dr EDUARDO CORONEL DIAZ
Faculty of Chemical and Industrial Engineering: Dr ALEJANDRO VÁSQUEZ CHICA
Faculty of Civil Engineering and Architecture: Ing. GERARDO AREVALO IDROVO
Faculty of Commercial Engineering: Eco. JULIO HERNÁNDEZ VINTIMILLA
Faculty of Distance Learning: Dr HUGO ORTIZ SEGARRA
Faculty of Economics: Dr HUGO ORTIZ SEGARRA
Faculty of Education and Psychology: Dr JOSÉ ESCANDÓN MEJÍA
Faculty of Electrical Engineering: Dr EDUARDO CORONEL DÍAZ
Faculty of Enterprise Engineering: Eco. MARCELO MENDIETA MÉNDEZ
Faculty of Informatics Systems: Dr EDUARDO CORONEL DIAZ
Faculty of Law and Social Sciences: Dr FRANCISCO PIEDRA LOJA
Faculty of Medicine and Health Sciences: Dr CARLOS DARQUEA LOPEZ
Faculty of Odontology: Dr OSWALDO VINTIMILLA MARCHÁN
Extension University at Azogues: Dr MARCO VICUÑA DOMÍNGUEZ
Extension University at Cañar: Dr HERNÁN CRESPO VERDUGO
Extension University at Macas: Lic. JOSÉ MERINO V.
Extension University at Méndez: Dr JORGE CÁRDENAS ESPINOZA
Extension University at San Pablo, Troncal: Eco. REMIGIO VÁZQUEZ LÓPEZ
School of Drama and Aerobics: Dr CARLOS EFRAÍN CRESPO
School of Journalism and Communications: Dra PRISCILA TAMAYO DE PALACIOS
School of Physical Education: Lodo TARQUINO SUQUINAGUA PATIÑO
School of Social Service: Dr CLAUDIO PEÑAHERRERA M.
Institute of Languages: Dr JOSÉ ESCANDÓN MEJÍA
Institute of Nursing: Dr OSWALDO VINTIMILLA MARCHÁN
Bilingual Secretarial School: Dra. GLADIS LEMARIE CAICEDO
Communications, Radio and Television Channel 2: Dr HUGO ORTIZ SEGARRA
Delegation in Europe: Prof. Dr FRANZ KANEHL (Germany)
Postgraduate Committee: Dr MARCO VICUNA DOMÍNGUEZ
University Hospital: Dr CARLOS DARQUEA LÓPEZ

UNIVERSIDAD CATÓLICA DE SANTIAGO DE GUAYAQUIL

Casilla 09-01-4671, Guayaquil
Telephone: (4) 200801
Fax: (4) 200071
Internet: www.ucsg.edu.ec

Founded 1962
Private control
Academic year: May to April

Rector: Dr GUSTAVO NOBOA BEJARANO
Vice-Rector: Dra NILA VELÁSQUEZ COELLO
Secretary-General and Registrar: Ab. GUILLERMO VILLACRES SMITH
Librarian: Lcda CLEMENCIA MITE DE SANTILLÁN

Library of 32,974 vols
Number of teachers: 612
Number of students: 6,249

Publications: *Revista Cuadernos*, *Revista Universidad*

DEANS

Faculty of Architecture: Arq. RAÚL CHIRIBOGA
Faculty of Economics: Econ. LUIS FERNANDO HIDALGO
Faculty of Engineering: Ing. ANTONIO BELTRÁN
Faculty of Law, Social and Political Sciences: Ab. VLADIMIRO ALVAREZ
Faculty of Medicine: Dr MICHAEL DOUMET
Faculty of Philosophy, Literature and Education: Dra OLGA AGUILAR
Faculty of Technical Education for Development: Ing. GONZALO-ARGUDO
Department of Theology: Fr JOSÉ CIFUENTES ROMERO

UNIVERSIDAD LAICA 'VICENTE ROCAFUERTE' DE GUAYAQUIL

Avda de las Américas, Apdo 11-33, Guayaquil
Telephone: (4) 287200
Fax: (4) 287431
E-mail: u.laica@impsat.net.ec
Internet: www.ulaicavr.com

Founded 1847; university status 1966
Private control
Language of instruction: Spanish
Academic year: April to January

Rector: Dra ELSA ALARCÓN SOTO
Vice-Rectors: Econ. ALFONSO SÁNCHEZ GUERRERO (Academic), Ing. ALFREDO AGUILAR ALAVA (General)
General Secretary: Ab. ALFONSO AGUILAR ALAVA
Librarian: Ab. CECILIA RODRÍGUEZ GRANDA

Library of 8,000 vols
Number of teachers: 307
Number of students: 9,317

Publications: *Boletín el Contador Laico*, *Boletín de Información Académica* (annually)

Faculties of Administrative Sciences, Jurisprudence, Agricultural Engineering, Journalism, Education, Civil Engineering, Economics, Architecture. Schools of Secretarial Administration, Social Work, English, Accountancy, Publicity and Marketing, Design.

UNIVERSIDAD TÉCNICA PARTICULAR DE LOJA

Casilla 11-01-608, Loja
Telephone: (7) 570204
Fax: (7) 584893
E-mail: utpl@accessinter.net
Internet: www.utpl.edu.ec

Founded 1971
Private control
Language of instruction: Spanish
Academic year: October to March, April to August

Chancellor: Pe Dr LUIS MIGUEL ROMERO FERNÁNDEZ
Rector: Ing. JAIME GERMAN GUAMÁN
Vice-Rector: Lic. FANNY AGUIRRE DE MOREIRA
Secretary-General: Dr CARLOS RAMÍREZ ROMERO
Director of Distance Education: Dra MARÍA JOSÉ RUBIO GÓMEZ
Librarian: Lic. AMADA JARAMILLO LOJÁN

Library of 25,000 vols
Number of teachers: 190190 full-time, 121 distance education
Number of students: 2,200 full-time, 7,218 distance education

Publications: *El Reloj* (monthly), *Universidad* (monthly), *Universidad Técnica Particular de Loja* (annually)

DEANS

Faculty of Agricultural Engineering: Ing. HÉCTOR RAMÍREZ
Faculty of Architecture: Arq. JORGE AUQUILLA
Faculty of Civil Engineering: Ing. JORGE HIDALGO TORRES
Faculty of Economics: Econ. FERNANDO MORA JIMÉNEZ
Faculty of Languages: Lic. GEOVANNY CASTILLO
Distance Education Faculty of Education: Lic. GERMÁN GONZÁLEZ

DIRECTORS

School of Accountancy and Auditing: Lic. ELSA CÁRDENAS
School of Fine Arts: Lic. FABIÁN FIGUEROA
School of Hotel Management and Tourism: Dr JAIME BUSTAMENTE
School of Industrial Mechanics: (vacant)
School of Mines: Ing. RUDY VALDIVIESO L.
Institute of Basic Sciences: Dr CONSTANTE RAMÍREZ
Institute of Computer Science: Ing. LILIANA ENCISO
Institute of Human Sciences and Religious Studies: Lic. ALONSO GUAMÁN
Executive Secretarial School: Lic. ENITH BRAVO L.
Graduate School: Dr LUIS VARELA E.
Cariamanga Campus: Lic. ANGEL J. CABRERA M.
Zamora Campus: Ing. ALFONSO OCHOA

Colleges

Colegio Nacional de Agricultura 'Luis A. Martínez': Casilla 286, Ambato; f. 1913; Dir Dr CÉSAR VÁSCONEZ S.; Sec. CÉSAR EDUARDO COBO N.; 500 students; publ. *Germinación*.

Colegio Nacional '24 de Mayo', Quito: Quito; f. 1934; an experimental institution for women's higher education; assisted by UNESCO; departments of modern humanities for students preparing for universities and commerce, administration and professional training; Rector Dra MARÍA A. CARRILLO DE MATA M.; number of teachers 122; number of students 3,388.

Centro Internacional de Estudios Superiores de Comunicación para América Latina (International Centre for Advanced Studies in Communications for Latin America): Diego de Almagro N32-113 y Andrade Marín, Apdo 17-01- 584, Quito; tel. (2) 544-624; fax (2) 502487; e-mail ejaramillo@ciespal.net; internet www.ciespal .net; f. 1959 with UNESCO aid; training, documentation and research in fields of information science, radio and television; library: 2,000 vols, 20,700 documents; Dir-Gen. Lic. EDGAR JARAMILLO SALAS; publ. *Chasqui* (4 a year).

Schools of Art and Music

Conservatorio de Música 'José María Rodríguez': Cuenca; teaching staff 11; Dir Prof. RAFAEL SOJOS JARAMILLO.

Conservatorio Nacional de Música (National Academy of Music): Madrid E12-120 y Andalucía, CP 17-01-3358, Quito; tel. (2) 564791; fax (2) 564792; e-mail conamusi@ uio.satnet.net; f. 1900; library: 14,000 vols; 120 teachers; 800 students; Dir LUCIANO CARRERA GALARZA; publ. *Conservatorio*.

EGYPT

The Higher Education System

The higher education system in Egypt consists of Islamic and secular sectors. The Islamic sector is based upon Al-Azhar University in Cairo, founded in AD 970 as an adjunct to Al-Azhar mosque. Cairo University, the first secular university, was founded in 1908, and in 1925 it became a public institution. The ministry of Higher Education and Scientific Research governs secular higher education through the aegis of the Supreme Council for Universities, while the Central Administration of Al-Azhar Institutes, a department of the Supreme Council of Al-Azhar Institutes, controls Islamic higher education. The Government is constitutionally required to provide free higher education to all, but students also pay enrolment fees. In 2003/04 there were an estimated 1,188,280 students enrolled at universities.

Students intending to attend university must hold the General Secondary School Certificate (or the Technical Secondary School Certificate); exact entry requirements vary between institutions. Islamic or Al-Azhar higher education requires the student to successfully complete Al-Azhar secondary school, otherwise applicants must take one year of Arabic and Koranic studies. The American University of Cairo, founded in 1919, is independent of the Egyptian higher education system but its degrees are recognised as equivalent to those awarded by Egyptian universities.

The main undergraduate degree is the Bachelors, which is usually awarded after four years, but in some disciplines may take five (architecture, dentistry, engineering, pharmacy, veterinary medicine) or six years (medicine). Instruction is in Arabic, except in dentistry, engineering, medicine, pharmacy, science and veterinary medicine, for which it is in English. The first postgraduate degree is the Diploma, which lasts for one year and leads to the award of the Diploma in Higher Studies, Diploma of Graduate Studies or simply the Diploma. The next postgraduate degree, the Masters, requires two years of study. Finally, the Doctor of Philosophy (PhD) is a three- to four-year course, based entirely on research.

Technical and vocational training is available at intermediate vocational institutes, higher technical institutes and as non-formal education. Intermediate technical institutes specialize in post-secondary, two-year diploma courses in the fields of commerce, health and industry; higher technical institutes focus on advanced courses in technical education across a wide range of subjects, leading to either the Diploma (two years) or Bachelors degree (four to five years). Non-formal education consists of refresher courses, evening classes and on-the-job training.

Learned Societies

GENERAL

Academy of the Arabic Language: 15 Aziz Abaza St, Zamalek, Cairo; tel. (2) 3405931; fax (2) 3412002; e-mail aal@idsc-gov.eg; f. 1932; 40 Egyptian active mems, also corresp. mems, hon. mems and foreign active mems; library of 60,000 vols; Pres. Prof. Dr AHMED SHAWKY DHEIF; Sec.-Gen. IBRAHIM ABDEL MEGEED; publ. *Review* (2 a year).

African Society: 5 Ahmed Hishmat St, Zamalik, Cairo; tel. (2) 3407658; f. 1972 to promote knowledge about Africa and national liberation movements in the Afro-Arab world and encourage research on Africa; organizes lectures, debates, seminars, symposia and conferences; participates in celebration of African national occasions; arranges cultural and scientific exchange with similar African societies; publishes bulletins and books in Arabic and English; 500 mems; library of 1,500 vols in Arabic; library of 2,000 vols in other languages; Sec.-Gen. M. FOUAD EL BIDEWY; publs *Africa Newsletter* (in Arabic), *African Studies* (irregular).

Institut d'Égypte (Egyptian Institute): 13 Sharia Sheikh Rihane, Cairo; f. 1798 by Napoleon Bonaparte; literature, arts and science relating to Egypt and neighbouring countries; 60 mems; 50 assoc. mems; 50 corresp. mems; library of 160,000 vols; Pres. Dr SILEMAN HAZIEN; Sec.-Gen. P. GHALIOUNGUI; publs *Bulletin* (annually), *Mémoires*.

AGRICULTURE, FISHERIES AND VETERINARY SCIENCE

Egyptian Society of Dairy Science: 1 Ouziris St, Garden City, Cairo; f. 1972; Pres. Dr ISMAEL YOUSRY; publ. *Egyptian Journal of Dairy Science*.

BIBLIOGRAPHY, LIBRARY SCIENCE AND MUSEOLOGY

Egyptian Association for Library and Information Science: c/o Dept of Archives, Librarianship and Information Science, Faculty of Arts, Univ. of Cairo, Cairo; tel. (2) 5676365; fax (2) 5729659; f. 1956; 4,000 mems; Pres. Dr S. KHALIFA; Sec. M. HOSAM EL-DIN.

Supreme Council of Antiquities: 3 Al-Adel Abou Bakr St., Zamalek, Cairo; tel. (2) 7365645; fax (2) 7357239; e-mail Hawass@sca.gov.eg; internet www.sca.gov.eg; f. 1859 to oversee the preservation of Egyptian cultural heritage; attached to Ministry of Culture of Egypt; Dir Dr GABBALLAH ALI GABBALLAH; Sec.-Gen. Dr ZAHI HAWASS.

ECONOMICS, LAW AND POLITICS

Egyptian Society of International Law: 16 Sharia Ramses, Cairo; tel. (2) 5743162; f. 1945; to promote the study of international law and to work for the establishment of international relations, based on law and justice; lectures; Pres. Dr MOUFEED CHEHAB; Sec.-Gen. Dr SALAH AMER; Admin. Dir A. EL MAHROUKY; 800 mems; library of 4,100 books, 120 periodicals, 100,000 documents; publ. *Revue Egyptienne de Droit International* (annually).

Egyptian Society of Political Economy, Statistics and Legislation: 16 Sharia Ramses, POB 732, Cairo; tel. (2) 5750797; fax (2) 5743491; e-mail espesl@hotmail.com; f. 1909; 3,018 mems; library of 45,000 vols; Pres. Dr ATIF SIDKY; Gen.-Sec. MUSTAFA EL-SAID; publ. *L'Egypte Contemporaine* (in Arabic, English and French, 4 a year).

EDUCATION

Supreme Council of Universities: Cairo University Buildings, 11511 Giza; tel. (2) 5728877; fax (2) 5728722; f. 1950; delineates general policy of university education and scientific research in order to attain national objectives in social, economic, cultural and scientific development plans; determines admission numbers, fields of specialization, equivalences, etc.; the Egyptian Universities Network (EUN) links university computer centres and research institutes throughout Egypt, and is the Egyptian gateway to the internet, and provides information services and online learning facilities; 18 mems; library of 3,300 vols (English and Arabic); Pres. THE MINISTER OF HIGHER EDUCATION AND MINISTER OF STATE FOR SCIENTIFIC RESEARCH; Sec.-Gen. Prof. Dr ABDELHAI EBAID.

FINE AND PERFORMING ARTS

Armenian Artistic Union: 3 Sharia Soliman, El-Halaby, POB 1060, Cairo; f. 1920; aims: promotion of Armenian and Arabic culture; 300 mems; Pres. VAHAG DEPOYAN.

L'Atelier: 6 Victor Bassili St, 6 Pharaana St, Azarita, Alexandria; tel. (3) 4820526; fax (3) 4837662; f. 1934; society of artists and writers; 350 mems; library of 5,500 vols; Hon. Pres. Prof. NAIMA EL-SHISHINY; Hon. Sec. D. FAROUK WAHBA; publ. *Bulletin*.

High Council of Arts and Literature: 9 Sharia Hassan Sabri, Zamalek, Cairo; f. 1956; publs books on literature, arts and social sciences.

Institute of Arab Music: 2 Sharia Tewfik, Alexandria; Pres. AHMED BEY HASSAN; Hon. Sec. ALY SAAD.

Institute of Arab Music: 22 Sharia Ramses, Cairo; tel. (2) 750702; f. 1924; promotion and teaching of Arab music; libraries of records, tapes and scores of Arab music; Chair. of Board HASSAN TAKER MOK; Sec.-Gen. FARZY RASHAD.

HISTORY, GEOGRAPHY AND ARCHAEOLOGY

Egyptian Geographical Society: 109 Qasr Al-Aini St, POB 422 Mohamed Farid, Cairo; tel. (2) 7945450; fax (2) 7956771; e-mail geoegypt@hotmail.com; internet www.egs-online.net; f. 1875, reorganized 1917; 1,500 mems; library of 50,000 vols; Pres. Prof. M. S. ABULEZZ; Sec.-Gen. Prof. YOUSEF A. FAYED; publs *Al-Majallah Al-Jugrafiyah Al-'Arabiyah* (2 a year), *Bulletin* (annual).

Hellenic Society of Ptolemaic Egypt: 20 Sharia Fouad I, Alexandria; f. 1908; Pres. Dr G. PARTHENIADIS; Sec. COSTA A. SANDI.

Société Archéologique d'Alexandrie: 6 Mahmoud, Moukhtar St, POB 815, Alexandria 21111; tel. (3) 4820650; f. 1893; 248 mems; Pres. Dr A. SADEK; Sec.-Gen. M. EL ABADI; publ. *Bulletin*.

Society for Coptic Archaeology: 222 Sharia Ramses, Cairo; tel. (2) 4824252; e-mail bgwassif@yahoo.com; f. 1934, for the study of Coptic archaeology, linguistics, papyrology, church history, liturgy and art; 360 mems; library of 15,650 vols; Pres. WASSIF BOUTROS-GHALI; Sec.-Gen. Dr ANTOINE KHATER; Librarian Father WADI ABULLIF; publ. *Bulletin* (annually).

LANGUAGE AND LITERATURE

Alliance Française: 4, Abou el Feda St, Port Saïd; tel. and fax (6) 6227431; e-mail allianceportsaid@suezcanal.net; internet www.allianceportsaid.com; offers courses and exams in French language and culture and promotes cultural exchange with France; library of 4,000 vols.

British Council: 192 El Nil St, Agouza, Cairo; tel. (2) 3031514; fax (2) 3443076; e-mail british.council@britishcouncil.org.eg; internet www.britishcouncil.org/egypt; teaching centre; offers courses and exams in English language and British culture and promotes cultural exchange with the UK; attached offices in Alexandria and Heliopolis (teaching centre); Dir Dr JOHN GROTE; Dir, English Language Services STEVEN MURRELL.

Goethe-Institut: 5, Sharia El-Bustan, 11518 Cairo; tel. (2) 5759877; fax (2) 5771140; e-mail info@cairo.goethe.org; internet www.goethe.de/ins/aegypten; offers courses and examinations in German language and culture and promotes cultural exchange with Germany; attached centre in Alexandria; Dir and Regional Man. HEIKO SIEVERS.

Instituto Cervantes: 20 Boulos Hann St, Dokki, Cairo; tel. (2) 7601746; fax (2) 7601743; e-mail cencai@cervantes.es; internet elcairo.cervantes.es; offers courses and exams in Spanish language and culture and promotes cultural exchange with Spain and Spanish-speaking Latin and Central America; library: library of 18,500 vols; Dir LUIS MORATINOS CUYAUBÉ.

MEDICINE

Alexandria Medical Association: 4 G. Carducci St, Alexandria; f. 1921; 1,200 mems; Pres. Prof. H. S. EL-BADAWI; Sec.-Gen. Prof. Dr TOUSSOUN ABOUL-AZI; publ. *The Alexandria Medical Journal* (English, French and Arabic, quarterly).

Cairo Odontological Society: 39 Kasr El-Nil, Cairo; Pres. Dr ABULNAGA M. ABDEL-AZIM; Sec. Dr J. ALCÉE.

Egyptian Medical Association: 42 Sharia Kasr El-Aini, Cairo; f. 1919; 2,142 mems; Pres. Prof. Dr A. EL-KATEB; Sec.-Gen. Prof. Dr A. H. SHAABAN; Vice-Pres. Prof. Dr M. IBRAHIM; publ. *Journal* (monthly, in Arabic and English).

Egyptian Orthopaedic Association: 16 Sharia Houda Shaarawi, Cairo 11111; tel. (2) 3930013; f. 1948; scientific and social activities in the field of orthopaedic surgery and traumatology; holds bi-annual scientific meetings, monthly clinical meetings; 1,700 mems; Pres. HASAN ELZAHER HASAN; Sec.-Gen. NABIL KHALIFA; publ. *Egyptian Orthopaedic Journal* (4 a year).

Ophthalmological Society of Egypt: Dar El Hekma, 42 Sharia Kasr El-Aini, Cairo; f. 1902; Pres. Prof. Dr EL-SAID KHALIL ABOU SHOUSA; Hon. Sec. Dr AHMAD EZ EL-DIN NAIM; 480 mems; publ. *Annual Bulletin*.

NATURAL SCIENCES

Biological Sciences

Egyptian Botanical Society: 1 Ozoris St, Tager Bldg, Garden City, Cairo; f. 1956 to encourage students of botany and links between workers in botany; organizes conferences, seminars, lectures, and field trips for collecting, preserving and identifying plants; 230 mems; Pres. Prof. Dr A. M. SALAMA; Sec. Dr MOHAMED FAWZY; publ. *Egyptian Journal of Botany* (3 a year).

Egyptian Society of Parasitology: 1 Ozoris St, Tager Bldg, Garden City, Cairo; f. 1967; holds scientific meetings, annual conference; covers subjects in the fields of helminthology, medical entomology, protozoology, molluscs, insect control, immunodiagnosis of parasitic diseases, treatment, etc.; 350 mems; Pres. Prof. MAHMOUD HAFEZ; Sec.-Gen. Prof. TOSSON A. MORSY; publ. *Journal* (2 a year).

Société Entomologique d'Egypte: 14 Sharia Ramses, POB 430, Cairo; f. 1907; 502 mems; library: publs bulletins and economic series, library of 28,000 vols; Pres. MAHMOUD HAFEZ; Vice-Pres. Dr ABDEL AZIZ HAFEZ SOLIMAN, Dr ABDEL AZIZ KAMEL; Sec.-Gen. Dr ABDEL HAKIM M. KAMEL.

Zoological Society of Egypt: Giza Zoo, Giza; f. 1927; aims to promote zoological studies and to foster good relations between zoologists in Egypt and abroad; field courses, lectures, etc; library of 2,500 vols; 260 mems; Pres. Dr HASSAN A. HAFEZ; Sec. MOHAMED H. AMER; publ. *Bulletin*.

PHILOSOPHY AND PSYCHOLOGY

Egyptian Association for Mental Health: 1 Sharia 'Ilhami, Qasr al-Doubara, Cairo; f. 1948; 630 mems.

Egyptian Association for Psychological Studies: 1 Osiris St, Tager Bldg, Garden City, Cairo; tel. (2) 3541857; f. 1948; 1,200 mems; Pres. Dr FOUAD A-L. H. ABOU-HATAB; publ. *Yearbook of Psychology*.

RELIGION, SOCIOLOGY AND ANTHROPOLOGY

Institut Dominicain d'Etudes Orientales: Priory of the Dominican Fathers, 1 Sharia Masna al-Tarabish, BP 18, Abbassiah 11381, Cairo; tel. (2) 4825509; fax (2) 6820682; e-mail ideo@link.com.eg; internet www.ideo-cairo.org; f. 1952; library of 100,000 vols; Dir Père R. MORELON; publ. *Mélanges* (every 2 years).

Social Sciences Association of Egypt: Cairo; f. 1957; 1,234 mems.

TECHNOLOGY

Egyptian Society of Engineers: 28 Sharia Ramses, Cairo; f. 1920; Pres. Prof. Dr IBRAHIM ADHAM EL-DEMIRDASH; Sec. Dr MOHAMED M. EL-HASHIMY.

Research Institutes

GENERAL

Academy of Scientific Research and Technology: 101 Kasr El-Eini St, Cairo; tel. (2) 3542714; fax (2) 356280; f. 1971; the national body responsible for science and technology, with many instns affiliated to it; library of 34,000 vols, 50,000 periodicals; Pres. Prof. Dr ALI A. HEBEISH.

Affiliated institutions:

Central Metallurgical Research and Development Institute

Egyptian National Scientific and Technological Information Network

General Directorate of Statistics on Science and Technology

Institute of Astronomy and Geophysics

Institute of Oceanography and Fisheries

National Information and Documentation Centre

National Institute for Standards

National Network for Technology and Development (UNTD)

National Research Centre

Petroleum Research Institute

Remote Sensing Centre

Scientific Instruments Centre

Science Museum

National Research Centre: Al-Tahrir St, Dokki, Cairo; tel. (2) 7617590; fax (2) 3370597; f. 1956; began functioning in 1947 and laboratory work started in 1956; fosters and carries out research in both pure and applied sciences; the 54 laboratories are divided into 13 sections: textile industries, food industries and nutrition, pharmaceutical industries, chemical industries, engineering, agriculture and biology, medical, applied organic and inorganic chemistry, physics, basic sciences, environment, genetic engineering and biotechnology; library of 12,000 vols; Pres. Prof. A. EL-SHERBEINY; publs *Bulletin*, *NRC News*.

AGRICULTURE, FISHERIES AND VETERINARY SCIENCE

Agricultural Research Centre, Ministry of Agriculture: Giza; Chair. H. E. Prof. Dr YOUSSEF WALLY.

Attached research institutes:

Agricultural Economics Research Institute: 7 Nadi El Said St, Dokki, Giza; tel. (2) 3372318; fax (2) 7607651; e-mail aeri@arc.sci.eg; f. 1973; Dir Dr AHLAM EL NAGAR; publ. *Classification of the Agricultural Land Resources According to the Yield of the Most Important Field Crops* (every 5 years).

Agricultural Engineering Research Institute: Nadi El Said St, Dokki, Giza; tel. (2) 7487212; fax (2) 3356867; e-mail aengri_gov@hotmail.com; Dir Dr AGMY EL-BERRY; publs *Egyptian Journal of Agricultural Research* (quarterly), *Misr Journal of Agricultural Engineering* (quarterly).

Agricultural Extension and Rural Development Research Institute: 8 El-Gamaa St, Giza; tel. (2) 5716301; fax (2) 5716303; e-mail aerdri@hotmail.com; f. 1977; Dir Dr MOHAMED HAMED SHAKER.

Animal Health Research Institute: Nadi El Said St, Dokki; tel. (2) 5703520; f. 1928; Dir Dr SAMIR AFRAM.

Animal Production Research Institute: Nadi El Said St, Dokki, Cairo; tel. (2) 5702934; f. 1938; Dir Dr MAMDOUH SHRAF ELDEEN.

Animal Reproduction Research Institute: Pyramids Rd, Giza; tel. (2) 8954325; Dir Dr MAHMOUD SABRI.

Central Laboratory for Agricultural Pesticides: 7 Nadi El-Said St, Dokki; tel. (2) 3373860; fax (2) 7602209; e-mail pesticide@arabia.com; Dir Prof. Dr SAID AHMED EMARA.

Central Laboratory for Food and Feed: Cairo University St, Giza; tel. (2) 5732280; Dir Dr AKILA SALEH.

Central Laboratory for Statistical Design and Analysis: Cairo University St, Giza; tel. (2) 5723000; Dir Dr AHMED ABDEL HALIM.

Cotton Research Institute: Cairo University St, Giza; tel. (2) 5725135; f. 1919; Dir Dr AHMED EL GOHARY.

Field Crops Research Institute: Cairo University St, Giza; tel. (2) 5736515; f. 1971; Dir RASHAD ABOU EL-ENIN.

Food Technology Research Institute: 7 Cairo University St, Giza; tel. (2) 5778324; fax (2) 5684669; e-mail nlftri@internet.egypt.com; f. 1991; Dir Dr SAID MANSOUR.

General Department of Agricultural Research Stations and Experiments: Cairo University St, Giza; tel. (2) 5721027; f. 1961; Dir Dr ISMAIL DARRAG.

Horticultural Research Institute: 9 Cairo University St, Giza; tel. (2) 5720617; fax (2) 5721628; e-mail hort_inst@hotmail.com; f. 1948; Dir. Dr ASSEM ASHALTOUT.

Plant Pathology Research Institute: Cairo University St, Giza; tel. (2) 5724893; f. 1919; research in various aspects of disease survey: ecology, biology, epidemiology and control measures; *c.* 170 research staff; library of 1,098 vols; Dir Dr MOKHTAR SATOUR; publs *Agricultural Research Review*, *Egyptian Phytopathology*, *Journal of Applied Microbiology*.

Plant Production Research Institute: Nadi El Said St, Dokki, Cairo; tel. (2) 5702193; Dir Dr MAGDY EL-HARIRY.

Plant Protection Research Institute: Nadi El Said St, Dokki, 12311 Giza; tel. and fax (2) 3372193; e-mail aahakaa@yahoo.com; f. 1912; Dir Dr MAHMOUD EL-SAID EL-NAGGAR.

Soil and Water Research Institute: Cairo University St, Giza; tel. (2) 5720608; f. 1969; Dir Dr NABIL EL MOWILHI.

Sugar Crops Research Institute: Cairo University St, Giza; tel. (2) 5731465; Dir AHMED HASAN NOUR.

Veterinary Serum and Vaccine Research Institute: Abbasia, Cairo; tel. (2) 4821009; fax (2) 6858321; e-mail svri@idsc.gov.eg; internet www.vsvri-eg.com; Dir Prof. Dr AHMED M. DAOUD.

Alexandria Institute of Oceanography and Fisheries: Kayet Bey, Alexandria; tel. (3) 4801499; fax (3) 4801174; f. 1931; library: see Libraries and Archives; Dir Prof. Dr ELHAM AMALY WASSEF; Sec. Sheik EL-ARAB SADEEK; publ. *Bulletin* (annually).

Institute of Freshwater Fishery Biology: 10 Hassan Sabry St (Fish Garden), PO Zamalik, Cairo; f. 1954; undertakes research in fish biology and culture; 7 scientists; Dir Prof. A. R. EL BOLOCK.

Institute of Oceanography and Fisheries: 101 Kasr El-Aini St, Cairo; tel. (202) 7921341; fax (202) 7921341; e-mail ruraiyan@rusys.eg.net; internet www.niof.sci.eg; f. 1931 in connection with the Faculty of Science, Cairo; undertakes oceanographical, environmental and fisheries research at Alexandria, the Red Sea, the Aqaba and Suez Gulfs at Attaka, inland waters and at Kanater (aquaculture); attached to the Academy of Scientific Research; Dir Prof. Dr EZZAT AWWAD IBRAHIM; publ. *Bulletin*.

ARCHITECTURE AND TOWN PLANNING

General Organization for Housing, Building and Planning Research: POB 1770, Cairo; tel. (2) 5711564; attached to the Ministry of Development, New Communities, Housing and Public Utilities; carries out basic and applied research work on building materials and means of construction; also provides technical information and acts as consultant to the different authorities concerned with building and construction materials; eight specialized laboratories; Chair. Prof. Dr H. F. EL-SAYED FAHMY; publs bulletins, reports.

ECONOMICS, LAW AND POLITICS

Centre d'Etudes et de Documentation Economiques, Juridiques et Sociales: 2 Sikkat al-Fadl, POB 392, Muhammad Farid, Cairo; tel. (2) 3928711; fax (2) 3928791; e-mail cedej@idsc.gov.eg; internet www.cedej.org.eg; f. 1969; attached to Sous-direction des Sciences Sociales et Humaines (MAE) and Centre National de la Recherche Scientifique (CNRS), Paris; co-operation, documentation and research on an exchange basis between Egypt and France; research on Egypt (19th and 20th century) and the Arab world; university exchanges in co-operation with Egyptian Govt; library of 30,000 vols; 8 documentalists scan and classify 40 Egyptian periodicals; Dir GHISLAINE ALLEAU; publs *Egypte – Monde Arabe* (2 a year), *Mutun* (in Arabic, 2 a year).

Institute of Arab Research and Studies: POB 229, 1 Tolombat St, Garden City, Cairo; tel. (2) 3551648; fax (2) 3562543; f. 1953; affiliated to the Arab League Educational, Cultural and Scientific Organization (ALECSO); library of 77,000 vols, 1,068 periodicals; studies in contemporary Arab affairs, economics, sociology, history, geography, law, literature, linguistics; Dir Prof. AHMED YOUSSEF AHMED; publ. *Bulletin of Arab Research and Studies* (annually).

Institute of National Planning: Salah Salem St, Nasr City, Cairo; tel. (2) 2627840; fax (2) 2631747; f. 1960; research, training, documentation and information; organized in 11 scientific and technical centres; library of 70,000 vols; Chief Board of Dirs Dr KAMAL EL GANZOURY; publs *Egyptian Review of Development and Planning*, *Issues in Planning and Development* (irregular).

EDUCATION

National Centre for Educational Research: Central Ministry of Education, 33 Sharia Falaky, Cairo; f. 1972; co-ordinates current educational policy with that of the National Specialized Councils; exchanges information with like institutions throughout the world; provides local and foreign documents on education; Dir Dr YOUSSEF KHALIL YOUSSEF; publs. *Contemporary Trends in Education* (2 a year), *Educational Information Bulletin* (monthly), and various works on education in Egypt and the Arab world.

HISTORY, GEOGRAPHY AND ARCHAEOLOGY

Deutsches Archäologisches Institut (German Institute of Archaeology): 31 Sharia Abu El-Feda, Cairo-Zamalek; tel. (2) 7351460; fax (2) 7370770; Dir Prof. Dr GÜNTER DREYER.

Institut Français d'Archéologie Orientale (French Institute of Oriental Archaeology): 37 rue Sheikh Ali Youssef, BP 11562, Cairo; tel. (2) 7971649; fax (2) 7944635; e-mail mgeorges@ifao.egnet.net; internet www.ifao.egnet.net; f. 1880; excavations, research, seminars and publications intended to widen knowledge of Egyptian history from the Pharaohs to the Islamic period; library of 80,000 books; Dir (vacant); Dir of Studies CHRISTIAN VELUD; publs *Annales Islamologiques* (annually), *Bulletin de la Céramique Egyptienne*, *Bulletin Critique des Annales Islamologiques*, *Bulletin de l'Institut Français d'Archéologie Orientale* (annually), *Cahiers des Annales Islamologiques*, *Cahiers de la Céramique Egyptienne*.

MEDICINE

Central Health Laboratories: Ministry of Health, 19 Sheikh Rehan, Cairo; f. 1885; Dir-Gen. Dr ABDEL MONEIM EL BEHAIRY; Bacteriology: Dr GUERGUIS EL MALEEH; Clinical Pathology: Dr NADIR MOHARRAM; Sanitary Chemistry: MOUNIR AYAD; Toxicology: DALAL ABDEL REHIM; Food Microbiology: Dr MAGDA RAKHA; library of 2,000 vols; publs *Bacteriology*, *Virology*, *Sera and Vaccines Production*.

Egyptian Holding Company for Biological Products and Vaccines: 51 Sharia Wezarat El-Zeraa, Agouza, Giza.

Memorial Institute for Ophthalmic Research: Sharia Al-Ahram, Giza, Cairo; f. 1925; library of 2,800 vols; Dir Dr ABDEL MEGID ABDEL RAHMAN; publ. *Report*.

National Nutrition Institute: Min. of Health and Population, 16 Kasr El-Aini St, Cairo; tel. (2) 3646413; fax (2) 3647476; e-mail nniegypt@nni.org.eg; internet www.nni.org.eg; f. 1955; research, analysis, training and education in nutrition science; 469 staff; Dir Dr AZZA GOHAR; publ. *Bulletin*.

National Organization for Drug Control and Research: 6 Abou Hazem St, Giza; f. 1976; 300 staff; Chair. Dr ALI HIGAZI.

Research Institute for Tropical Medicine: 10 Sharia Kasr El-Aini, Cairo; f. 1932; sections: clinical parasitology, helminthology, entomology, biochemistry, physiology and pharmacology, radiology, radiotherapy and radioisotopes, bacteriology, pathology, haematology, endoscopy, serology, immunology, malacology, animal house and field research units; library of 4,000 vols; Dir-Gen. M. HATHOUT.

Theodor Bilharz Research Institute: Warak El Hadar, Embaba, POB 30, Giza 12411; tel. (2) 5401019; fax (2) 5408125; e-mail info@tbri.sci.eg; internet www.tbri.sci.eg; f. 1979; for the control, diagnosis and treatment of endemic diseases, especially urinary and hepatic schistosomiasis; Dir Prof. Dr JEHAN G. EL-FENDI; publs *Egyptian Journal of Shistosomiosis*, *TBRI Biomedical Bulletin*, *TBRI Today*.

NATURAL SCIENCES

General

UNESCO Office Cairo and Regional Bureau for Science and Technology in the Arab States: 8 Abdel Rahman Fahmy St, Garden City, 11511 Cairo; tel. (2) 7945599; fax (2) 7945296; e-mail cairo@unesco.org; internet unesco-cairo.org; f. 1947; designated Cluster Office for Egypt, Sudan and Yemen; Dir Dr MOHAMED EL-DEEK; publ. *Newsletter* (2 a year).

Physical Sciences

Egyptian National Authority for Remote Sensing and Space Sciences: POB 1564, Alf Maskan, Cairo; tel. (2) 2964386; fax (2) 2964387; f. 1972; covers geology, mineral and energy resources, hydrogeology, agriculture, soils, geophysics, photogrammetry, engineering, physics and environment; operates advanced digital data processing facility for satellite and aircraft data, also Beechcraft King-Air aeroplane with most advanced remote sensing equipment; design and implementation of nat. space scientific and technical activities; library of 2,500 books; Chair. Prof. MOHAMED ADEL YEHIA.

Geological Survey and Mining Authority: Post Bag Ataba No. 11511, Cairo; fax (2) 4820128; f. 1896; regional geological mapping, mineral prospecting, evaluation of mineral deposits, and granting mineral exploration and exploitation rights; cartography laboratory; 763 research workers; library of 82,000 vols; Chair. Board GABER NAIM; publs occasional papers, maps.

National Research Institute of Astronomy and Geophysics: Helwan, Cairo; tel. (2) 5549780; fax (2) 5548020; f. 1903; comprises the Helwan Observatory, the Kottamyia Observatory, the Misallat geomagnetic observatory, seismic stations at Helwan, Aswan, Matrouh, and satellite tracking stations at Helwan and Abu Simbel; attached to the Academy of Scientific Research and Technology; library of 10,594 vols; Pres. Prof. ANAS MOHAMED IBRAHIM OSMAN; publs bulletins.

RELIGION, SOCIOLOGY AND ANTHROPOLOGY

Ibn Khaldun Center for Development Studies: 17, Street 12, POB 13, Mokatim, Cairo; tel. (2) 5080662; fax (2) 5081030; e-mail ibnkhaldun@ibnkhaldun.org; internet www.ibnkhaldun.org; f. 1988; advancement of applied social sciences with special emphasis on Egypt and the Arab and Third Worlds; the Center is an associated centre of the Arab Social Science Research network of the Arab Institute for Studies and Communication (ASSR–AISC); Dir Dr SAAD EDDIN IBRAHIM; publ. *Civil Society* (12 a year).

TECHNOLOGY

Central Metallurgical Research and Development Institute: POB 87, Helwan, 11421 Cairo; tel. (2) 5010642; fax (2) 5010639; e-mail rucmrdi@rusys.eg.net; internet www.cmrdi.sci.eg; f. 1972; attached to the Ministry of Scientific Research; extractive metallurgy, ore dressing, technical services, metal-forming and working, welding research; library of 4,000 vols; Chair. Prof. Dr BAHAA ZAGHLOUL.

Egyptian Atomic Energy Authority: 8 Ahmad Elzomor St, Nasr City, Children Village P.O., 11787 Cairo; tel. (3) 558264; fax (3) 540982; e-mail hisham_f@frcu.eun.eg; internet www.frcu.eun.eg/www/homepage/aea/aea.htm; f. 1957; maintains 22-MW open pool MultiPurpose Reactor at the Inshas site for production of radioisotopes for industrial and medical applications, research on neutron physics and personnel training; employs c. 850 academic scientists supported by c. 650 technical staff; Pres. Prof. ALY ISLAM M. ALY.

Attached research centres:

The Hot Laboratories and Waste Management Centre (HLWMC): POB 13975, Abu Zabal; tel. (4) 698155; fax (4) 698617; internet www.frcu.eun.eg/www/homepage/aea/cent3.htm; f. 1980; main facilities incl. low and intermediate level liquid waste station, radioisotope production laboratories, radwaste disposal site; organized in 3 divs: radioisotopes, fuel treatment, radwaste treatment.

National Centre for Radiation Research and Technology (NCRRT): 3 ahmed El-Zomor St, El-Zohoor District, POB 29, Nasr City, Cairo; tel. (2) 746791; fax (2) 749298; internet www.frcu.eun.eg/www/homepage/aea/cent2.htm; f. 1972; main facilities incl. a 400,000 Ci, Co-60 unit and an electron accelerator (under construction); organized in 3 divs: radiation research, industrial irradiation, biotechnology; Chair. Prof. Dr AMIN EL-BAHY.

The National Centre for Nuclear Safety and Radiation Control (NCNSRC): 3 Ahmed El-Zomor St, El-Zohoor District, POB 29, Nasr City, Cairo; tel. (2) 7403321; fax (2) 740308; internet www.frcu.eun.eg/www/homepage/aea/cent4.htm; f. 1982; organized in 3 divs: nuclear regulations and emergencies, radiation control, safety of nuclear installations.

Nuclear Research Centre (NRC): POB 13975, Abu Zabal; tel. (4) 698414; fax (4) 698899; internet www.frcu.eun.eg/www/homepage/aea/cent1.htm; main facilities incl. a 2-MW ET-RR-1 research reactor, a 2.5 Van de Graaff accelerator, a radioisotope production laboratory, nuclear fuel research and devt laboratory, laboratories for application of radio-isotopes, electronic instrumentation laboratory and radiation protection laboratory; organized in 4 divs: basic nuclear sciences, reactors, material and nuclear industry, radioisotope applications; Chair. Prof. Dr NASF CAMSAN.

Egyptian Petroleum Research Institute: 7th Region, Nasr City, Cairo; tel. (2) 2747847; fax (2) 2747433; f. 1976; organ of the Ministry for Scientific Research; joint Board with Egyptian General Petroleum Corporation; seven research sections, dealing with all aspects of petroleum and energy-related problems; contract research and commercial services to local oil companies; library of over 5,000 books and periodicals; 850 staff; Dir Dr FAROUK EZZAT; publ. *Egyptian Journal of Petroleum*.

Hydraulics Research Institute: Delta Barrage 13621; tel. (2) 2188268; fax (2) 2189539; e-mail draulics@intouch.com; f. 1949; Dir Prof. Dr M. B. A. SAAD.

National Institute for Standards: Tersa St, El-Matbaa, El Haram, POB 136, Giza 12211; fax (2) 3867451; internet www.nis-sci.eg; f. 1963; attached to the Ministry of Higher Education and Scientific Research; 190 staff; responsible for maintenance of national standards for physical units and their use for purposes of calibration; research on scientific metrology, to develop new techniques for measurements, calibrations, and development of new standards; constituent laboratories: electricity, photometry, frequency, thermometry, radiation, acoustics, mass, length metrology, engineering metrology, testing of materials, safety tests and textile testing, ultrasonics, polymer testing, and reference materials; Dir Prof. M. G. EL SHERBINY; publ. *The Egyptian Journal of Metrology*.

Textile Consolidation Fund: El-Syouf, Alexandria; incl. textiles quality control centre and textiles development centre; library of 5,000 vols; Gen. Man. MAGDI EL-AREF.

Libraries and Archives

Alexandria

Alexandria Municipal Library: 18 Sharia Menasha Moharrem Bey, Alexandria; f. 1892; 22,390 Arabic vols, 35,399 European vols, 4,086 MSS; Chief Librarian Sheikh BESHIR BESHIR EL-SHINDI.

Alexandria University Central Library: 136 Horiyah Rd, Shatby, Alexandria; f. 1942; 45,000 books, 1,000,000 microfiches and roll films, 1,200 periodicals, 2,500 MSS, 17,500 dissertations; Supervisor Prof. Dr SHAWKY SALEM.

Bibliotheca Alexandrina: El Shatby, Alexandria; tel. (3) 4878833; fax (3) 4830339; e-mail secretariat@bibalex.org; internet www.bibalex.org; f. 2001, built as successor to ancient Alexandria library; 4,000,000 vols, 100,000 MSS, 50,000 maps, 250,000 audio and audiovisual items; incl. collns from the Sidi Mursi Abul Abbas Mosque and the Al Azhar Religious Institute in Smouha; deposit library for UNESCO, WTO, Red Cross and Council of Europe; Dir-Gen. Dr ISMAIL SERAGELDIN.

Library of the Greek Orthodox Patriarchate of Alexandria: POB 2006, Alexandria; tel. (3) 4868595; fax (3) 4875684; e-mail patriarchate@greekorthodox-alexandria.org; internet www.greekorthodox-alexandria.org; f. AD43; 41,000 vols, 542 MSS, contains 2,241 rare editions; Librarian (vacant).

Assiut

Assiut University Library: Assiut; 250,000 vols; Dir S. M. SAYED.

Cairo

Al-Azhar University Library: Nasr City, Cairo; 80,000 vols, including 20,000 MSS; Librarian M. E. A. HADY.

American University in Cairo Library: 11 Youssef El Guindi St, POB 2511, Bab El Louk, Cairo; tel. (2) 7976904; fax (2) 7923824; e-mail selsawy@aucegypt.edu; internet library.aucegypt.edu; f. 1919; 275,000 vols; Dean, Libraries and Learning Technologies SHAHIRA EL-SAWY.

Arab League Information Centre (Library): Midan Al-Tahir, 11642 Cairo; tel. (2) 5750511; fax (2) 5740331; f. 1945; Sec.-Gen. Dr SAUD ABD AL-AZIZ EL-ZABIDI; 30,000 vols, 250 periodicals.

Cairo University Library: Orman, Giza; f. 1932; 1,407,000 vols, 10,000 periodicals; Gen. Dir FATMA IBRAHIM MAHMOUD.

Central Library of the Agricultural Research Centre: Gamaa St, Giza; tel. 723000, ext. 331; f. 1920; 25,000 vols; Dir ISMAIL ABDEL SAMIE; publ. *Agricultural Review*.

Centre of Documentation and Studies on Ancient Egypt: 3 Sharia El-Adel Abou Bakr, Zamalek, Cairo; f. 1956; scientific and documentary reference centre for all Egyptian Pharaonic monuments; 4,500 vols, 33,000 photographs; Dir-Gen. Dr MAHMOUD MAHER-TAHA; publs a wide range of specialist material on ancient Egypt.

Egyptian Library: Abdin Palace, Cairo; over 20,000 vols; Dir ABDEL HAMID HOSNI.

Egyptian National Library (Dar-ul-Kutub): Sharia Corniche El-Nil, Bulaq, Cairo; f. 1870; 1,500,000 vols (400,000 European); 11 brs with 250,000 vols, including fine arts library; deposit library; Dir Gen. ALI ABDUL-MOHSEN.

Library of the Central Bank of Egypt: 153 Mohamed Farid St, Cairo; tel. (2) 3905427; fax (2) 3904232; f. 1961; 15,430 vols; publs *Annual Report*, *Economic Review* (quarterly).

Library of the Ministry of Education: 16 Sharia El-Falaki, Cairo; tel. (2) 8544805; f. 1927; 55,966 vols (European and Arabic); Dir of Libraries HASSAN ABDEL SHAFI.

Library of the Ministry of Health: Sharia Magles esh-Shaab, Cairo; over 27,000 vols.

Library of the Ministry of Justice: Midan Lazoghli, Cairo; f. 1929; over 90,000 vols and periodicals in Arabic, French and English (law and social science); private library for the use of judges and members of the Parquet (public prosecution and criminal investigation authority); a centre attached to the library contains the latest texts of local and comparative legislature on Personal Status; Dir F. ABOU-EL-KHEIR.

Library of the Ministry of Supply and Internal Trade: 99 Sharia Kasr el-Aini, Cairo; over 20,000 vols.

Library of the Ministry of Waqfs: Sharia Sabri Alu Alam, Ean el-Luk, Cairo; f. 1942; 20,219 vols.

Library of the Monastery of St Catherine: 18 Midan El Daher, Cairo; f. 6th c.; over 4,000 Greek, Oriental and Slavonic MSS; contains the Codex Sinaiticus Syriacus; Librarians Monk DANIEL, Monk SYMEON.

Library of the National Research Institute of Astronomy and Geophysics: Helwan, Cairo; f. 1903; 11,000 vols; Dir Prof. R. M. KEBEASY; publ. *Bulletin*.

National Archives Central Administration: Corniche El Nil, Boulac, Cairo; tel. (2) 5752883; f. 1954; Dir IBRAHIM FAT'ALLAH AHMAD.

National Assembly Library: Palace of the National Assembly, Cairo; f. 1924; over 50,000 vols; Dir ANTOUN MATTA.

National Information and Documentation Centre: Al-Tahrir St, Dokki, Cairo; tel. (2) 3371696; fax (2) 3371696; e-mail nidoc@nrc.sci.eg; f. 1955; accumulates and disseminates information in all languages and in all branches of science and technology; 35,600 vols, 2,500 periodicals, UNESCO and WHO special collns; Dir WAGLAA MAHMOUD FAHMY; publ. 18 scientific journals.

Damanhour

Damanhour Municipal Library: Damanhour; 13,431 vols.

Mansoura

Mansoura Municipal Library: Mansoura; contains 17,984 vols (Arabic 13,036, European 4,948).

Zagazig

Sharkia Provincial Council Library: Zagazig; contains 12,238 vols (Arabic 7,861, European 4,377).

Museums and Art Galleries

Alexandria

Greco-Roman Museum: Museum St, Alexandria; f. 1892; exhibits from the Greek, Roman and Byzantine eras; library of 15,500 vols, Omar Tousson collection of 4,000 vols; Dir DOREYA SAID; publs *Annuaire du Musée Gréco-Romain, Guide to the Alexandrian Monuments*.

National Maritime Museum: Alexandria; Dir Dr MEHREZ EL HUSSEINI.

Aswan

Nubia Museum: Aswan; tel. (97) 319111; fax (97) 317998; f. 1997; history of Nubia since prehistoric times; Dir OSSAMA A. W. ABDEL MAGUID.

Cairo

Agricultural Museum: Dokki, Cairo; tel. (2) 5700063; f. 1938; exhibits of ancient and modern Egyptian agriculture and rural life, horticulture, irrigation; botanical and zoological sections; library of 8,885 vols; Dir SAMIR M. SULTAN.

Al-Gawhara Palace Museum: The Citadel, Cairo; f. 1954, refurnished 1956; built in 1811 in the Ottoman style, the Palace retains much of its original interior; contains Oriental and French furniture, including gilded throne, Turkish paintings, exhibitions of clocks, glass, 19th-century costumes.

Anderson Museum: Beit el-Kretlia, Cairo; f. 1936; private collections of Oriental art objects bequeathed to Egypt by R. G. Gayer Anderson Pasha in 1936; Curator YOUNES MAHRAN.

Cairo Geological Museum: POB Dawawin 11521, Cairo; premises at: Cornish El-Nil, Maadi Rd, Cairo; tel. (2) 3187056; fax (2) 3820128; a general dept of the Egyptian Geological Survey; f. 1904; 50,000 specimens, mostly Egyptian; depts: vertebrates, invertebrates, rocks and minerals; library of 4,200 vols and 6,000 periodicals; Dir-Gen. MOHAMMED AHMED EL-BEDAWI.

Cairo Museum of Hygiene: Midan-el-Sakakini, Daher, Cairo; Dir Dr FAWZI SWEHA.

Coptic Museum: Old Cairo, Cairo; f. 1910; sculpture and frescoes, MSS, textiles, icons, ivory and bone, carved wood, metalwork, pottery and glass; library of 6,587 vols; Dir Dr MAHAR SALIB.

Cotton Museum: Gezira, Cairo; f. 1923; established by the Egyptian Agricultural Society; all aspects of cotton growing, diseases, pests, and methods of spinning and weaving are shown; Dir M. EL-BAHTIMI.

Egyptian (National) Museum: Midan-el-Tahrir, Cairo; f. 1902; exhibits from prehistoric times until the 3rd century AD; excludes Coptic and Islamic periods; established by decree in 1835 to conserve antiquities; the Antiquities Department administers the archaeological museums and controls excavations; library of 40,000 vols; Dir Dr MOHAMED SALEH; publs *Annals of the Antiquities Service of Egypt*, etc.

Egyptian National Railways Museum: Cairo Station Buildings, Ramses Square, 11669 Cairo; tel. (2) 5763793; fax (2) 5740000; f. 1933; contains models of foreign and Egyptian railways, and technical information and statistics on the evolution and development of the Egyptian railway services; library of 5,595 vols (Arabic 2,694, European 2,901); Curator IBRAHIM SALEH ALY.

Museum of Islamic Art: Ahmed Maher Sq., Bab al-Khalq, Cairo 11638; f. 1881; collection of 86,000 items representing the evolution of Islamic art from the first quarter of 7th century up to 1900; Dir-Gen. Dr NIMAT M. ABU-BAKR; library of 15,000 vols; publs *Islamic Archaeological Studies* (annually), catalogues on Islamic decorative arts.

Museum of Modern Art: 4 Sharia Kasr El-Nil, Cairo; f. 1920; Curator SALAH E. TAHER.

War Museum: The Citadel, Cairo; library of 6,000 vols.

Universities

AIN SHAMS UNIVERSITY

Elkhalifa Elmaamoon St, Abbassia, Cairo
Telephone: (2) 6847818
Fax: (2) 6847824
E-mail: info@asunet.shams.edu.eg
Internet: www.asunet.shams.edu.eg
Founded 1950
Languages of instruction: Arabic, English and French
Academic year: October to June
President: Prof. Dr SALEH HASHEM MOSTAFA ABDEL RAZEK
Vice-President for Postgraduate Studies and Research: Prof. Dr ALI AHMED IBRAHIM YOUSSEF
Vice-President for Society and Environment: Prof. Dr MORAD-ABD EL KADER
Vice-President for Undergraduate Studies: Prof. Dr MOHAMED FAHIM TOLBA HASSAN
Secretary-General: MOKHTAR BADRAN
Chief Librarian: MOHAMED EMBABY
Number of teachers: 8,509
Number of students: 168,712

DEANS

Faculty of Agriculture: Prof. Dr ABDEL GHANY MOHAMED ABDEL GHANY ELGENDY
Faculty of Arts: Prof. Dr MOHAMED ABDEL LATIF HAREDE AMMAR
Faculty of Commerce: Prof. Dr EGLAL ABDEL MONIEM HAFEZ
Faculty of Computer Science and Information: Prof. Dr MOHAMED SAEED ABDEL WAHAB
Faculty of Dentistry: Prof. Dr HANY IBRAHIM EID
Faculty of Education: Prof. Dr MOSTAFA MAHMOUD RAMADAN
Faculty of Engineering: Prof. Dr MOHAMED ABDEL HAMIED MOHAMED SHAIERA
Faculty of Languages: Prof. Dr MAKAREM AHMED MOHAMED ELGHAMRY
Faculty of Law: Prof. Dr OMAR HELMI FAHMY MOHAMED ALI ESSIA
Faculty of Medicine: Prof. Dr FATHY MOHAMED ALI TASH
Faculty of Nursing: Prof. Dr ZEINAB ABDEL HAMIED ELSAYED LOTFY ELHAMADY
Faculty of Pharmacy: Prof. Dr MOHAMED MOHAMED MOSTAFA ELAZIZY
Faculty of Science: Prof. Dr MOSTAFA MOHAMED ISMAIEL
Faculty of Specific Education: Prof. Dr MAGDY FARIED ABDEL HAMIED BADAWY
Faculty of Women: Prof. Dr HAMDIA ABDEL HAMIED IBRAHIM
Institute of Childhood Studies: MOSTAFA MOHAMED HUSSIEN ELNASHAR
Institute of Environmental Studies and Research: ABDEL AZEEM MOHAMED MOSTAFA

ALEXANDRIA UNIVERSITY

22 El-Geish Ave, El-Shatby, Alexandria
Telephone: (3) 5960720
Fax: (3) 5960720
E-mail: info@alexeng.edu.eg
Internet: www.alex.edu.eg
Founded 1942
State control
Languages of instruction: Arabic, English, French
Academic year: October to June
President: Prof. Dr MOHAMED AHMED ABDALLA
Vice-President for Community Services and Environmental Affairs: Prof. Dr EZAT KHAMES AMIN MOSTAFA
Vice-President for Damanhour Branch: Prof. Dr MOHAMED AHMED BAUOMY
Vice-President for Postgraduate Studies and Research: Prof. Dr GOAD GOAD HAMADA
Vice-President for Undergraduate Studies: Prof. Dr OKASHA MOHAMED ABDEL AAL
Secretary-General: MOHAMED ROSHDY ABDEL GHANI
Chief Librarian: SOHER GAMAL

Library: see Libraries and Archives
Number of teachers: 3,979
Number of students: 144,707

DEANS

Faculty of Agriculture: Prof. Dr TAREK MAHMOUD ELKIEY
Faculty of Agriculture (in Damanhour): Prof. Dr ABDEL SALAM HELMY MOHAMED BELAL
Faculty of Agriculture (in Saba Basha): Prof. Dr ALY IBRAHIM ALY EBEDA
Faculty of Arts: Prof. Dr FATHY ABDEL AZIZ ABORADY
Faculty of Arts (in Damanhour): Prof. Dr MOHAMED ALY BAHGAT EL-FADLY
Faculty of Commerce: Prof. Dr MOHAMED ELFAUOMY MOHAMED IBRAHIM
Faculty of Commerce (in Damanhour): Prof. Dr KAMAL ELDIN MOSTAFA ELDAHRAWY
Faculty of Dentistry: Prof. Dr MOSTAFA MOHAMED EL-DEBANY
Faculty of Education (in Damanhour): Prof. Dr MAHMOUD FATHY OKASHA
Faculty of Education (in Marsa Matrouh): Prof. Dr MOHAMED YOUSEF HSSAN MOHAMED (acting)
Faculty of Engineering: Prof. Dr ABDEL LOTFY MOHAMADEEN
Faculty of Fine Arts: Prof. Dr MAGDY MOHAMED MOUSSA
Faculty of Kindergartens: Prof. Dr ELHAM MOSTAFA MOHAMED EBED
Faculty of Law: Prof. Dr MAGDY MAHMOUD MOHAMED SHEHAB
Faculty of Medicine: Prof. Dr ABDEL AZIZ BELAL
Faculty of Nursing: Prof. Dr NADIA TAHA MOHAMED AHMED
Faculty of Pharmacy: Prof. Dr NABIL AHMED MOHAMED ABDEL SALAM
Faculty of Physical Education (Females): Prof. Dr SADIA ABDEL GOAD MOHAMED SHEHA
Faculty of Physical Education (Males): Prof. Dr ABDEL MONIEM BADEER ELKOSIER
Faculty of Science: Prof. Dr MOSTAFA HUSSIEN FAHMY
Faculty of Specific Education: Prof. Dr ABDEL RAZEK MOHAMED ELSAYED
Faculty of Tourism and Hotels: Prof. Dr MAHER ABDEL KADER MOHAMED ALY
Faculty of Veterinary Medicine: Prof. Dr MOHAMED ALY EKELA TORKY
Higher Institute of Public Health: Prof. Dr HASSAN KAMEL BASSOUNY MOHAMED (see also under Colleges)
Institute of Medical Research: Prof. Dr AASSER ABDEL HAMIED HAFEZ (Dir)
Institute of Postgraduate Studies and Research: Prof. Dr MOHAMED EZZ ELDIN ELRAIE

AL-AZHAR UNIVERSITY

11751 Cairo
Telephone: (2) 2623278
Fax: (2) 2623284
E-mail: azhar@azhar.eun.eg
Internet: www.alazhar.org
Founded AD970; modernized and expanded 1961
Academic year: September to June
Rector: AHMAD AL-TAYIB
Vice-Rectors: Prof. SAMA GAD, Prof. TAHA ABU KREISHA
Library: see Libraries and Archives
Number of teachers: 9,000
Number of students: 185,000 (on several campuses)
Publication: *Annual Report*

DEANS

Faculty of Agriculture: Prof. AMIN YOUSSEF
Faculty of Arabic and Islamic Studies: Prof. MAHMOUD EL-SAIED SHAIKHOON
Faculty of Arabic Studies: Prof. ABDULLAH HELLAL
Faculty of Commerce: Prof. ABDEL-HAMID RABEE
Faculty of Education: MUHAMMAD ABDEL SAMEE OTHMAN
Faculty of Engineering: Prof. ABDEL-WAHID AHMAD
Faculty of Islamic Jurisprudence and Law: Prof. MOHAMMAD RAFAT OTHMAN
Faculty of Islamic Theology: Prof. ABDEL-MOUTI MOHAMMAD BAYOMI
Faculty of Language and Translation: Prof. AHMAD BASEM ABDEL-GHAFFAR
Faculty of Medicine: Prof. ISMAEEL KHALAF
Faculty of Science: Prof. ABDEL-WAHAB AL-SHARKAWI
Islamic Women's College: Prof. KAWTHAR KAMEL

AMERICAN UNIVERSITY IN CAIRO

POB 2511, 113 Sharia Kasr El-Aini, Cairo
American Office: 420 Fifth Ave, 3rd Fl., New York, NY 10018-2729, USA
Telephone: (2) 7942964
Fax: (2) 7957565
Internet: www.aucegypt.edu
Founded 1919
Private control
Language of instruction: English
Academic year: September to June
President: DAVID A. ARNOLD
Special Advisor to the President: Dr MOHAMMED ABDEL KHALEK ALLAM
Vice-Presidents: PAUL DONOGHUE, Dr ASHRAF EL-FIQI, Dr HUSSEIN EL-SHARKAWY, Dr LARRY FABIAN, KEN MANOTTI, ANDREW SNAITH
Provost: Dr EARL SULLIVAN
Library: see Libraries and Archives
Number of teachers: 303 (full-time)
Number of students: 5,294
Publications: *Alif* (English and Arabic Poetry), *Cairo Papers in Social Science*

DEANS

School of Business, Economics and Communications: Dr A. MORTAGY
School of Humanities and Social Sciences: Dr ANN M. LESCH
School of Sciences and Engineering: Dr F. ASSABGHY
Center for Adult and Continuing Education: Dr HARRY MILLER

HEADS OF DEPARTMENTS

Arabic Studies: Dr E. FERNANDES
Arabic Language Institute: Dr S. EL-BADAWI
Biology: Dr S. KAMAL ZADA
Chemistry: Dr J. RAGAI
Computer Science: Dr M. MIKHAIL
Construction Engineering: Dr S. KHEDR
Economics: Dr N. ESSAM RIZK
English and Comparative Literature: Dr W. D. MELONEY
English Language Institute: Dr Y. EL-EZABI
History: Dr D. R. BLANKS
Interdisciplinary Engineering: Dr E. FAHMY
Journalism and Mass Communication: Dr H. AMIN
Management: Dr I. ABDELAZIZ HEGAZY
Mathematics: Dr M. HERBERT
Mechanical Engineering: Dr M. SERAG EL-DIN
Performing and Visual Arts: Dr F. BRADLEY
Philosophy: Dr S. W. STELZER
Physics: Dr H. OMAR
Political Science: Dr E. HILL
Sociology, Anthropology, Psychology and Egyptology: Dr F. M. HAIKAL
Core Curriculum: Dr J. SWANSON

ATTACHED UNITS

Center for Adult and Continuing Education: non-credit study programme for 30,000 students a year; offers courses and post-secondary and post-graduate career programmes in Arabic/English, Arabic/French translation, English language, business and secretarial skills, and computing; Dean Dr HARRY MILLER.

Desert Development Center: research to improve the social and economic well-being of new desert settlers, integrating agriculture, renewable energy and community research; Dir Dr RICHARD TUTWILER (acting).

Social Research Center: current research projects on demography and human resettlement; Dir Dr HODA RASHAD.

ASSIUT UNIVERSITY

Assiut Governorate, Assiut
Telephone: (88) 324040
Fax: (88) 312064
E-mail: info@aun.eun.eg
Internet: www.aun.eun.eg
Founded 1957
Languages of instruction: Arabic, English, French
Academic year: October to June
President: Prof. Dr MOHAMED REFAAT MAHMOUD
Vice-President for Community Services and Environmental Affairs: Prof. Dr MOHAMED ABDEL SALAM ASHOUR
Vice-President for Postgraduate Studies and Research: Prof. Dr MAGDY ABBAS MOSTAFA EL-AKAD
Vice-President for Undergraduate Affairs: Prof. Dr MOHAMED IBRAHIM AHMED ABDEL KADER
Secretary-General: NABILA MAHMOUD ABDEL MAGIED
Chief Librarian: LAILA ABDALLA
Library of 387,180 vols, 614 current periodicals
Number of teachers: 1,634
Number of students: 62,596
Publication: *Faculty Bulletins* (quarterly)

DEANS

Faculty of Agriculture: Prof. Dr MOHAMED ATTIA ZAHRAN
Faculty of Arts: Prof. Dr ZEINAB ABDEEN MAHMOUD HASSAN ABO-KADRA
Faculty of Commerce: Prof. Dr ABDEL HADY ABDEL KADER SALEH SUOFY
Faculty of Computer and Information Sciences: Prof. Dr HOSSNY MOHAMED IBRAHIM (acting)
Faculty of Education: Prof. Dr ABDEL TAWAB ABDELLA ABDEL TAWAB DESSOUKY
Faculty of Education (New Valley Branch): Prof. Dr ABDALLA ELSAYED ABDEL GAWAD
Faculty of Engineering: Prof. Dr AHMED ABDEL MONIEM ALI ABOU ISMAIEL
Faculty of Law: Prof. Dr GABER ALI MAHRAN ALI
Faculty of Medicine: Prof. Dr MOHAMED ABDEL MONIEM EID
Faculty of Nursing: Prof. Dr SANNA SOLIMAN ABDEL HAMIED KAROUSH
Faculty of Pharmacy: Prof. Dr MOHAMED AHMED ABDEL RAHMAN ELSHANAWANY
Faculty of Physical Education: Prof. Dr MAHMOUD ABDEL HALIEM ABDEL KERIM
Faculty of Science: Prof. Dr EZZAT ABDALLA AHMED ABDEL KADER
Faculty of Social Work: Prof. Dr NABIL ABDEL RAHIEM
Faculty of Specific Education: Prof. Dr SAEED AHMED IBRAHIM
Faculty of Veterinary Medicine: Prof. Dr MOHAMED SALAH ELDIN MAHMOUD YOUSSEF

Institute of Cancer at South Egypt: Prof. Dr Mohamed Attef Abdel Aziz Mostafa
Institute of Sugar Studies and Technology: Prof. Dr Mohamed Ragab Bayoumy

CAIRO UNIVERSITY

POB 12611, Orman, Giza, Cairo
Telephone: (2) 5729584
Fax: (2) 5688884
E-mail: info@main-scc.cairo.edu.eg
Internet: www.cu.edu.eg

Founded 1908
State control
Languages of instruction: Arabic, English and French
Academic year: October to June

President: Dr Ali Abdel-Rahman
Vice-President for Beni-Suef Branch: Prof. Dr Mohamed Anas Kasem Gafar
Vice-President for Community Services and Environmental Affairs: Prof. Dr Abdalla Abdel Fattah Eltatawy
Vice-President for Fayoum Branch: Prof. Dr Galal Mostafa Saeed
Vice-President for Postgraduate Studies and Research: Prof. Dr Motaz Mohamed Hosny Khorshed
Vice-President for Undergraduate Studies: Prof. Dr Hamed Taher Hassaneen Foad
Secretary-General: Fayza Megahed
Librarian: Ahmed Shoab

Library: see Libraries and Archives
Number of teachers: 7,066
Number of students: 202,167

DEANS

Faculty of Agriculture: Prof. Dr Salwa Bayoumy Mohamed El-Maghouly
Faculty of Agriculture (in Fayoum): Prof. Dr Abdalla Mohamed Abdel Rahman Mousa
Faculty of Arabic and Islamic Studies (in Fayoum): Prof. Dr Mohamed Salah El-Deen Mostafa
Faculty of Archaeology: Prof. Dr Ola Mohamed Abd El-Aziz Elagezy
Faculty of Archaeology (in Fayoum): Prof. Dr Mohamed Abdel Halim Nour Eldin (acting)
Faculty of Arts: Prof. Dr Ahmed Magdy Hegazy
Faculty of Arts (in Beni-Suef): Prof. Dr Mohamed Mahran Rashwan (acting)
Faculty of Commerce: Prof. Dr Ahmed Farghaly Mohamed Hassan
Faculty of Commerce (in Beni-Suef): Prof. Dr Kawssar Abdel Fattah Mahamed Al-Abagy
Faculty of Computer and Information Science: Prof. Dr Aly Aly Mohamed Fahmy
Faculty of Dar El-Oloum: Prof. Dr Ahmed Mohamed Abd El-Aziz Keshk
Faculty of Dar El-Olum (in Fayoum): Prof. Dr Ibrahim Mohamed Ibrahim Sakr
Faculty of Dentistry: Prof. Dr Mahmoud Ibrahim Fahmy El-Refaay
Faculty of Economics and Political Science: Prof. Dr Kamal Mahmoud El-Menoufy
Faculty of Education (in Beni-Suef): Prof. Dr Mostafa Hassan Mohamed El-Nashar
Faculty of Education (in Fayoum): Prof. Dr Mohamed Abd El-Rahman El-Sharnoby
Faculty of Engineering: Aly Abdel Rahman Yousef
Faculty of Engineering (in Fayoum): Prof. Dr Samy El-Badawy Yehya
Faculty of Kindergartens: Prof. Dr Mona Mohamed Aly Gad
Faculty of Law: Prof. Dr Ahmed Elsayed Sawy
Faculty of Law (in Beni-Suef): Prof. Dr Reda Ibrahim Ebeid
Faculty of Mass Communication: Prof. Dr Magy El-Halawany
Faculty of Medicine: Prof. Dr Madiha Moahmoud Khatab
Faculty of Medicine (in Beni-Suef): Prof. Dr Mohamed Elsayed El-Batanouny
Faculty of Medicine (in Fayoum): Prof. Dr Kamal Elbasyouny
Faculty of Nursing: Prof. Dr Basamat Omar Ahmed
Faculty of Pharmacy: Prof. Dr Ahmed Atteia Mohamed Seada
Faculty of Pharmacy (in Beni-Suef): Prof. Dr Ahmed Abdel Bary Abdel Rahman
Faculty of Physiotherapy: Prof. Dr Kamal El-sayed Mohamed Shokry
Faculty of Science: Prof. Dr Hamdy Mahmoud Hassanen Elsayed
Faculty of Science (in Beni-Suef): Prof. Dr Ahmed Hafez Hussein El-Ghandour
Faculty of Science (in Fayoum): Prof. Dr Kamal Ahmed Mohamed Hassan Deeb
Faculty of Social Service (in Fayoum): Prof. Dr Ahmed Magdy Hegazy Mahmoud (acting)
Faculty of Specific Education: Prof. Dr Aly Mohamed Aly Elmelegy
Faculty of Specific Education (in Fayoum): Prof. Dr Ahmed Galal Ewies Elawa
Faculty of Tourism and Hotels (in Fayoum): Prof. Dr Awad Abbas Ragab
Faculty of Urban Planning: Prof. Dr Maher Moheb Isteno Afandy
Faculty of Veterinary Medicine: Prof. Dr Mohamed Ibrahim Mohamed Desouky
Faculty of Veterinary Medicine (in Beni-Suef): Prof. Dr Shawky Soliman Ibrahim Soliman
Institute of African Studies and Research: Prof. Dr El-Sayed Aly Fleefel
Institute of Educational Studies and Research: Prof. Dr Mostafa Abdel Samiaa
Institute of Statistical Studies and Research: Prof. Dr Abdel Ghani Mohamed Abdel Ghani Ibrahim
National Institute of Laser Science: Prof. Dr Hussien Mostafa Musa Khaled
National Institute of Tumours: Prof. Dr Mohamed Abdel Hareth Mohamed Abdel-rahman

HELWAN UNIVERSITY

Ain Helwan, Helwan, Cairo
Telephone: (2) 5569064
Fax: (2) 5555023
E-mail: info@helwan.edu.eg
Internet: www.helwan.edu.eg

Founded 1975, incorporating existing institutes of higher education
State control
Languages of instruction: Arabic, English
Academic year: September to June

President: Prof. Dr Amr Ezzat Salama
Vice-President (Community Service and Environmental Development): Abla Hanafy
Vice-President (Postgraduate Studies and Research): Prof. Dr Ahmad Abd El-Kareem Salama
Vice-President (Undergraduate Studies and Student Affairs): Mohammad Hazem Fathallah
Secretary-General: Sekina Hanafy Mahmoud Mohamed
Librarian: Mahmoud Qatr

Library of 34,795 vols, 425 journals, 9,379 theses
Number of teachers: 2,179
Number of students: 95,567

Publications: *Journal of Arts 2000*, *Journal of Economic and Legal Studies* (2 a year), *Journal of Educational and Social Studies*, *Journal of Engineering Research* (6 a year), *Journal of the Faculty of Arts* (2 a year), *Journal of Research on Art Education* (3 a year), *Journal of the Science and Art of Sport* (2 a year), *Journal of Studies on Social Work and Humanities*, *Science and Art of Music* (2 a year), *Scientific Journal of Commercial Studies and Research* (4 a year), *Scientific Journal of Physical Studies* (4 a year), *University Journal* (2 a year)

DEANS

Faculty of Applied Arts: Prof. Dr Adel Hefnawy
Faculty of Art Education: Prof. Dr Mohammad Labeeb Nada
Faculty of Arts: Prof. Dr Zebeda Ata
Faculty of Commerce and Business Administration: Prof. Dr Mohamed Amin Abdalla Amin Kaed
Faculty of Education: Prof. Dr Abd El-Motteleb Al-Korety
Faculty of Engineering (Mataria): Prof. Dr Tahany Youssef
Faculty of Engineering and Technology (Helwan): Prof. Dr Omar Hanafy
Faculty of Fine Arts: Prof. Dr Mohammad Tawfeek
Faculty of Home Economics: Prof. Dr Abd El-Rahman Atia
Faculty of Information and Computer Sciences: Prof. Dr Yehia Kamal HElmy
Faculty of Law: Prof. Dr Mohamed Elshahat Elgendy
Faculty of Music Education: Prof. Dr Amera Farag
Faculty of Pharmacy: Prof. Dr Mohamed Mohy Eldin Elmazar
Faculty of Physical Education (Men): Prof. Dr Sobhy Hasanein
Faculty of Physical Education (Women): Prof. Dr Hanan Roshdy
Faculty of Science: Prof. Dr Mohammad El-Sayyed
Faculty of Social Work: Prof. Dr Mohamed Refaat Kassem Abdel Rahman
Faculty of Tourism and Hotel Management: Prof. Dr Doha Moustafa

MANSOURA UNIVERSITY

60 Elgomhoria St, Mansoura
Telephone and fax: (50) 347900
E-mail: info@mans.edu.eg
Internet: www.mans.eun.eg

Founded 1973 from the Mansoura branch of Cairo University
State control
Languages of instruction: Arabic, English
Academic year: October to June

President: Prof. Dr Ahmed Gamal Eldin Abdel Fattah Mousa
Vice-President for Community Services and Environmental Affairs: Prof. Dr Mohamed Ahmed Gaballa Yossef
Vice-President for Postgraduate Studies and Research: Prof. Dr Magdy Mohamed Abou Rayaan
Vice-President for Undergraduate Studies: Prof. Dr Mohamed Suielm Mohamed Elbasuony
Secretary-General: Magdy Ahmed Mahmoud Saleh
Chief Librarian: Abdalla Hussien

Number of teachers: 2,230
Number of students: 107,022

Publications: *Egyptian Journal for Commercial Studies* (4 a year), *Journal of the Faculty of Arts* (2 a year), *Journal of Veterinary Medical Research* (annually), *Mansoura Dental Journal* (4 a year), *Mansoura Engineering Journal* (4 a year), *Mansoura Faculty of Education Journal* (3 a year), *Mansoura Journal of Forensic Medicine and Clinical Toxicology* (2 a year), *Mansoura Journal of Pharma-*

ceutical Sciences (2 a year), *Mansoura Medical Journal* (2 a year), *Mansoura Science Bulletin* (2 a year), *Mansoura University Journal of Agriculture* (12 a year), *Revue des Recherches Juridiques et Economiques* (2 a year)

DEANS

Faculty of Agriculture: Prof. Dr MAHER MOHAMED IBRAHIM ABDELAAL
Faculty of Arts: Prof. Dr ABDEL GHANY MAHMOUD ABDEL AATTY
Faculty of Commerce: Prof. Dr AHMED HAMED SAAD HAGAG
Faculty of Dentistry: Prof. Dr ALY ABDEL MEGIED ALY SAWAN
Faculty of Education: Prof. Dr TALAT HASSAN ABDEL REHIM
Faculty of Education (in Damiatta): Prof. Dr FAROUK ABDO HASSAN
Faculty of Engineering: Prof. Dr IBRAHIM GAR ELHELM RASHAD
Faculty of Information and Computer Science: AHMED ELSAEED TOULBA
Faculty of Law: Prof. Dr MAHMOUD MOHAMED MOHAMED HASSAN
Faculty of Medicine: Prof. Dr MEDHAT MOHAMED ALY
Faculty of Nursing: Prof. Dr SAMIA ABDEL AZIZ HAWAS
Faculty of Pharmacy: Prof. Dr MOHAMED HAMED ZAKI ELSHABOURY
Faculty of Physical Education (Male): MOSAAD ALY MAHMOUD ISMAIEL
Faculty of Science: Prof. Dr FATHY ABDEL KADER METWALLY AMER
Faculty of Science (in Damiatta): Prof. Dr SALAH KAMEL MOHAMED ELLABANY
Faculty of Specific Education: Prof. Dr FAROUK ELSAEED ELSAEED GIBREL
Faculty of Specific Education (in Damiatta): Prof. Dr MAHMOUD ELSAYED MOHAMED ELNAGH
Faculty of Specific Education (in Meniat El Nasr): AHMED ABDEL AZIZ ELREFAAI
Faculty of Specific Education (in Mitghamr): Prof. Dr MAMDOUH ABDEL MONIEM HASSNIEN
Faculty of Veterinary Medicine: ELSAIED ELSHERBINY ELSAIED

MENIA UNIVERSITY

Menia Governorate, Menia

Telephone: (86) 361443
Fax: (86) 342601
E-mail: info@minia.edu.eg
Internet: www.minia.edu.eg

Founded 1976, incorporating existing faculties of Assiut University
Languages of instruction: Arabic, English
Academic year: October to June

President: Prof. Dr ABD EL-MONIEM ABD EL-HAMID EL-BASSIOUNY
Vice-President for Community Services and Environmental Affairs: Prof. Dr ABD EL-GHAFAR FARIED ABD EL-GHAFAR
Vice-President for Postgraduate Studies and Research: Prof. Dr MOHAMED SAIED MOHAMED ALY
Vice-President for Undergraduate Studies: Prof. Dr MAHER GABER MOHAMED AHMED
Secretary-General: LAILA AHMED IBRAHIM SOROOR
Chief Librarian: NABELA EL-SAWY

Number of teachers: 1,288
Number of students: 36,906

DEANS

Faculty of Agriculture: Prof. Dr MOHAMED ATEF FAHMY AHMED KESHK
Faculty of Al Alsun (Languages): Prof. Dr AMAL MOSTAFA KAMAL MOHAMED
Faculty of Arts: Prof. Dr MOHAMED NAGEEB AHMED MOHAMED
Faculty of Computer and Information Science: (vacant)
Faculty of Dar Al Olum: Prof. Dr MOHY ELDIN OTHMAN RASHDAN
Faculty of Dentistry: Prof. Dr HANY HUSSIEN MOHAMED AMIN
Faculty of Education: Prof. Dr ATTA TAHA ZEDAN SHEHATA
Faculty of Engineering: Prof. Dr MOHAMED MONESS ALY AHMED
Faculty of Fine Arts: Prof. Dr WAFAA OMAR ABD ELHALEEM
Faculty of Medicine: Prof. Dr MOHAMED IBRAHIM BASUONY
Faculty of Nursing: Prof. Dr GALAL MOHAMED SHAWKY HAMED
Faculty of Pharmacy: Prof. Dr MOHAMED MONTASER ABD ELHAKIM
Faculty of Physical Education (Female): (vacant)
Faculty of Physical Education (Male): Prof. Dr BAHY ELDIN IBRAHIM SALAMA
Faculty of Science: Prof. Dr ABD ELRAHMAN ABD ELAZIZ AHMED
Faculty of Specific Education: Prof. Dr ABD ELAZEEM ABD ELSALAM ELFERGANY
Faculty of Tourism and Hotel Management: Prof. Dr ABD ELBARY AHMED ALY DAWOOD

MINUFIYA UNIVERSITY

Gamal Abd El-Nasser St, POB 32511, Shebeen El-Kam

Telephone: (48) 222170
Fax: (2) 5752777
E-mail: menofia@menofia.edu.eg
Internet: www.menofia.edu.eg

Founded 1976
State control
Languages of instruction: Arabic, English
Academic year: September to July

President: ABBAS ALI EL-HEFNAWY
Vice-President for Community and Environmental Development: SABRY ABD EL-LATIF MAHMOUD
Vice-President for Graduate Studies and Research: Prof. MOHAMMED NAZIM SAYED AHMED
Vice-President for Undergraduate Education: MOSTAFA ABD EL-RAHMAN
Secretary-General: MOSTAFA SADAK KHALIL
Librarian: HAMDY EL-SHAMY

Number of teachers: 2,928
Number of students: 71,225

Publications: *Minoufiya Journal of Electronic Engineering Research* (2 a year), *Minoufiya Medical Journal* (2 a year), *Scientific Journal of the Faculty of Science* (annually)

DEANS

Faculty of Agriculture: Prof. OSMAN ASAL
Faculty of Arts: Prof. ZEINAB AFIFI
Faculty of Commerce: Prof. THABET A. IDRIS
Faculty of Computers and Information: Prof. FAWZY A. TAWRKY
Faculty of Education: Prof. ABD EL-HADY ALI
Faculty of Electrical Engineering (in Menouf): Prof. HOSSAM EL-DIN HUSSEIN AHMED
Faculty of Engineering and Technology: Prof. ABD EL-MOHSIN FATHI KNAWY
Faculty of Home Economics: Prof. SAAD A. SALMAN
Faculty of Hotels and Tourism: Prof. MOHAMED M. ELBANNA
Faculty of Law: Prof. ABD EL-AZIM ABD EL-SALAM
Faculty of Medicine: Prof. MOHAMMED AHMED IBRAHIM
Faculty of Science: Prof. MAHMOUD A. EWAIDA
Faculty of Special Education: Prof. FARWUK OSMAN
Faculty of Sports: Prof. MOHAMED W. SOKAR
Faculty of Veterinary Medicine (Sadat City): Prof. AHMED A. ZAKLUL
Institute of Desert Environment Research: Prof. MOHAMMADY EL-SHANAWANY
Genetic Engineering and Biotechnology Research Institute: Prof. KHALIL EL-HALAFAWI
Higher Institute of Nursing: Prof. MAGDA M. MOHAMMED
Liver Institute: Prof. SALAH M. SALAH

MISR UNIVERSITY FOR SCIENCE AND TECHNOLOGY (MUST)

POB 77, Sixth of October City
Telephone: (11) 354703
Fax: (11) 354699
E-mail: info@must.edu
Internet: www.must.edu

Founded 1996
Private control
Language of instruction: English
Academic year: October to July

Chancellor: Prof. Dr SOUAD A. KAFAFI
President: Prof. Dr MAHMOUD S. SHERIF
Vice-President: Prof. Dr MOSTAFA S. TAWAKOL
Registrar: MAHMOUD ABDELRAHMAN
Librarian: ABDELSALAM MOSTAFA

Library of 4,000 vols
Number of teachers: 750 (500 full-time, 250 part-time)
Number of students: 3,000 (all undergraduate)

DEANS

College of Business and Economics: Prof. Dr HAMDIYA ZAHRAN
College of Dentistry: Prof. Dr ADEL ABDELHAKIM
College of Engineering: Prof. Dr IBRAHIM SHABAKA
College of Humanities: Prof. Dr ABDELAZIZ HAMOUDA
College of Medicine: Prof. Dr SALAH Z. EID
College of Pharmacy: Prof. Dr MOSTAFA S. TAWAKOL
College of Physiotherapy: Prof. Dr IBTESAM KHATAB

SOUTH VALLEY UNIVERSITY

Kena Governorate, Kena
Telephone: (96) 211717
Fax: (96) 211277
E-mail: info@svu.edu.eg
Internet: svu.edu.eg

Founded 1990
State control
Languages of instruction: Arabic, English
Academic year: October to June

President: Prof. Dr ABD ELMATION MOUSSA ABD ELLATIF
Vice-President (Aswan Branch): Prof. Dr MOHAMED HUSSIEN AMIN MOSTAFA
Vice-President (Community Services and Environmental Affairs): Prof. Dr HASSANEN MOHAMED HASSANEN ELKAMEL
Vice-President (Sohag Branch): Prof. Dr MAHMOUD REYAD MOTAMED KASSEM
Vice-President (Undergraduate Studies): Prof. Dr MOHAMED EZZ ELDIN RASHED HASSAN
Chief Librarian: AWATEF YASSIEN

Number of teachers: 851
Number of students: 51,730

DEANS

Faculty of Arts: Prof. Dr SAMED ABD ELRAHMAN FAHMY MOHAMED
Faculty of Education: Prof. Dr SABRY ELANSARY IBRAHIM ALY ABDALLA
Faculty of Education (Red Sea): Prof. Dr REFAAT MOHAMED BAHGAT MOHAMED

Faculty of Fine Arts (Luxor): Prof. Dr SALEH MOHAMED ABD ELMOATY
Faculty of Science: Prof. Dr HESHAM MANSOUR MAHMOUD RAGEH
Faculty of Specific Education: Prof. Dr ABD ELHAFEZ MAHMOUD HANAFY HAMAM
Faculty of Veterinary Medicine: Prof. Dr MOHAMED NOUR ELDIN ISMAIL SALAM

DEANS (ASWAN BRANCH)

Faculty of Arts: Prof. Dr AHMED SOKARNO ABD ELHAFEZ (acting)
Faculty of Education: Prof. Dr GAMAL MOHAMED SALEH
Faculty of Engineering: Prof. Dr MOHAMED THARWAT ABDEL RAHMAN
Faculty of Science: Prof. Dr MOHAMED TAWFEK ALY ELHATABY
Faculty of Social Science: Prof. Dr ABDEL REHEM MAHMOUD AHMED TAMAM

DEANS (SOHAG BRANCH)

Faculty of Agriculture: Prof. Dr ABOU ELMAREF MOHAMED DAMARANY
Faculty of Arts: Prof. Dr MOHAMED MONIER MOHAMED SABER HEGAB
Faculty of Commerce: Prof. Dr MOHAMED NASHAAT FOUAD
Faculty of Medicine: Prof. Dr ALY ABOU ELMAGD AHMED HANAFY
Faculty of Science: Prof. Dr HASSAN MOUSSA MOHAMED ELSHAROUNY

SUEZ CANAL UNIVERSITY

El-Shikh Zayed, Ismailia
Telephone: (64) 3297020
Fax: (64) 325208
E-mail: info@suez.edu.eg
Internet: www.suez.edu.eg

Founded 1976
State control
Languages of instruction: Arabic, English
Academic year: October to June

President: Prof. Dr FAROUK MAHMOUD ABD EL-KADER
Vice-Presidents: Prof. Dr ALY IBRAHIM ELSAYED IBRAHIM BADR (Community Services and Environmental Affairs), MOHAMED ELSAYED ALY RAHEEM (Port Said), Prof. Dr MOSTAFA KAMEL MOHAMED MOSBAH (Postgraduate Studies and Research), Prof. Dr IBRAHIM ASHOUR IBRAHIM BADR (Undergraduate Studies)
Secretary-General: NAINAA MOHAMED MOHAMED KHALIFA
Librarian: KAMILIA ALHOSARY

Number of teachers: 1,466
Number of students: 47,488

DEANS

El-Arish:
Faculty of Agricultural and Environmental Sciences: Prof. Dr MOHAMED RAGAB ABDO HUMOS
Faculty of Education: Prof. Dr NASSEF BEDEER IBRAHIM ELAASY

Ismailia:
Faculty of Agriculture: Prof. Dr MOHAMED SAMIR MOHAMED ATTEYA ELSHAZLY
Faculty of Commerce: Prof. Dr MOSTAFA ALY MAHMOUD ELBAZ
Faculty of Computers and Information Science: Prof. Dr MOHAMED HELMY MAHRAN
Faculty of Dentistry: Prof. Dr MOHAMED ELHUSSEINY MOHAMED MEKY
Faculty of Education: Prof. Dr MAHMOUD ABBASS MAHMOUD ABDEIN
Faculty of Medicine: Prof. Dr SOLIMAN HAMED SOLIMAN ELKAMASH
Faculty of Pharmacy: Prof. Dr SALAH ELDIN MOHAMED ABDALLA
Faculty of Science: Prof. Dr ELSAYED HUSSEIN MOSTAFA ELTAMNY
Faculty of Tourism and Hotels: Prof. Dr ABD EL-RAHMAN ABD EL-FATTAH MOHAMED
Faculty of Veterinary Medicine: Prof. Dr MOHAMED ELSAYED ANANY

Port Said:
Faculty of Commerce: Prof. Dr MOHAMED ABD EL-RAHMAN ELAADY
Faculty of Education: FAKRY IBRAHIM KHALIL KHALAF
Faculty of Engineering: Prof. Dr AHMAD KAMAL ABD-EL KHALEK
Faculty of Nursing: Prof. Dr HODA WADEEA TAWFEK
Faculty of Physical Education (Male): Prof. Dr SAYED ABDEL-GAWAD ELSAYED AHMED
Faculty of Specific Education: Prof. Dr MOHAMED SAYED AHMED SALEH

Suez:
Faculty of Commerce: Prof. Dr MAHMOUD SAYED AHMED SALEM
Faculty of Education: Prof. Dr BELAL AHMED SOLIMAN AHMED
Faculty of Industrial Education: Prof. Dr AHMED ESSA GAMEA ELNEKHILY
Faculty of Petroleum and Mining Engineering: Prof. Dr SHUHDY EL-MAGHRABY ELALFY SHALABY

TANTA UNIVERSITY

El-Geish St, Tanta
Telephone: (40) 331792
Fax: (40) 3302785
E-mail: info@dec1.tanta.edu.eg
Internet: www.tanta.edu.eg

Founded 1972
State control
Languages of instruction: Arabic, English
Academic year: October to June

President: Prof. Dr FOUAD KHALIFA HARRAS
Vice-President for Kafr El Sheikh Branch: Prof. Dr HASSAN IBRAHIM EID ALY
Vice-President for Postgraduate Studies and Research: Prof. Dr MOHAMED SHAFEEK SAEED
Vice-President for Undergraduate Studies: Prof. Dr SAMIR RAIYAD ABDEL BAREY HELAL
Secretary-General: RAWIA SOLIMAN GAD
Chief Librarian: ADEL YASSIEN

Number of teachers: 2,042
Number of students: 109,037

DEANS

Faculty of Agriculture: Prof. Dr IBRAHIM SAEED ELHAOUARY
Faculty of Agriculture (at Kafr El Sheikh): Prof. Dr AHMED HAFEZ ATTIA MASOUD
Faculty of Arts: Prof. Dr ELSAYED MOHAMED ABOU ELAZM DAWOOD
Faculty of Arts (at Kafr El Sheikh): (vacant)
Faculty of Commerce: Prof. Dr ELSAYED ALI MOHAMED LEBDA
Faculty of Commerce (at Kafr El Sheikh): (vacant)
Faculty of Dentistry: Prof. Dr MOHAMED MOHAMED MOSAAD NASSAR
Faculty of Education: Prof. Dr ABDEL WAHAB MOHAMED KAMEL ELSAYED
Faculty of Education (at Kafr El Sheikh): Prof. Dr RADWAN MOHAMED RADWAN ELBAROUDY
Faculty of Engineering: Prof. Dr MOHAMED ABDALLA ELKHAZENDAR
Faculty of Engineering (at Kafr El Sheikh): Prof. Dr OSSAMA AHMED IBRAHIM MASOUD (acting)
Faculty of Law: Prof. Dr MOSTAFA AHMED FOUAD
Faculty of Medicine: Prof. Dr OSAMA MOHAMED ABOU FARHA
Faculty of Pharmacy: Prof. Dr IBRAHIM ELKHALIL MANSOUR ELSHAMY
Faculty of Physical Education (Male): Prof. HASSAN IBRAHIM EID ALY
Faculty of Science: Prof. Dr MOHAMED EZZAT ABDEL MONSEF
Faculty of Specific Education: Prof. Dr MOHAMED ELANWAR HUSSEIN OSMAN (acting)
Faculty of Specific Education (at Kafr El Sheikh): Prof. Dr SAMIR MAHMOUD MOHAMED METWALLY
Faculty of Veterinary Science (at Kafr El Sheikh): Prof. Dr MAHMOUD ABDEL NABY OMAR (acting)

ZAGAZIG UNIVERSITY

Sharkia Governorate, Zagazig
Telephone: (55) 2310142
Fax: (55) 2345452
E-mail: info@zagziguniv.edu.eg
Internet: www.zu.edu.eg

Founded 1974, incorporating existing faculties of Ain-Shams University
State control
Languages of instruction: Arabic, English
Academic year: October to June

President: Prof. Dr ABDEL HAMIED BAHGAT FAYED
Vice-President for Undergraduate Affairs: Prof. Dr MAHER MOHAMED ALY ELDOMIATY
Vice-President for Community Service and Environmental Affairs: Prof. Dr LABEEB ISMAIL MOHAMED HASSAN MOAFY
Vice-President for Postgraduate Affairs and Research: Prof. Dr BAIOMY AOUD ALAA MOHAMED TARTOR
Vice-President for Banha Branch: Prof. Dr HOSSAN ELDIN MOHAMED ABEL AZIZ ELATTAR
Secretary-General: MOHAMED SAIED MORSY MOHAMED
Chief Librarian: RAMADAN ALY OTHMAN

Number of teachers: 4,250
Number of students: 151,091

DEANS

Faculty of Agriculture: Prof. Dr HASSAN AHMED HASSAN RABEEA
Faculty of Arts: Prof. Dr FAROUK KAMEL MOHAMED EZZ ELDIN
Faculty of Commerce: Prof. Dr OSAMA ABDEL HALEM MOSTAFA
Faculty of Computer and Information Science: Prof. Dr ISMAIL AMR ISMAIL MOHAMED
Faculty of Engineering: Prof. Dr MOHAMED KAMAL TOLBA EWADA
Faculty of Law: Prof. Dr NABIL AHMED HELMY MAHMOUD
Faculty of Medicine: Prof. Dr MOHAMED BAHGAT ELSAYED
Faculty of Nursing: Prof. Dr FATHY AHMED TANTAWY
Faculty of Pharmacy: Prof. Dr MOHAMED ABDALLA MOHAMED IBRAHIM
Faculty of Physical Education (Female): Prof. Dr NABILA ABDALLA MOHAMED OMRAN
Faculty of Physical Education (Male): Prof. Dr HAMED MAHMOUD AHMED ELKANWATY
Faculty of Science: Prof. Dr RAGAE ALSHEIK CHOWHAYIB ABDEL NASSER
Faculty of Specific Education: Prof. Dr BAHAA ELDIN ELSAYED ABDEL HALEM ELNAGAR
Faculty of Veterinary Medicine: Prof. Dr ALY ABDEL RASHED ALY SALAMA
Higher Institute of Ancient Near East Civilizations: Prof. Dr SOHAIR ELSAYED AHMED MONTASER
Higher Institute of Asian Research and Studies: Prof. Dr ATEF HASSAN MAHMOUD ELNOKALY
Higher Institute of Productive Efficiency: Prof. Dr MOURAD ALY NASHAT KHALED

DEANS (BANHA BRANCH)

Faculty of Agriculture: Prof. Dr MOHAMED BADER MOHAMED ALY SHAHEEN ELALFY
Faculty of Arts: Prof. Dr ELSAYED FADL FARAGALLA
Faculty of Commerce: Prof. Dr HAMED TOLBA MOHAMED ABOU HEEBA
Faculty of Education: Prof. Dr MOHAMED AOUDALLA SALEM
Faculty of Engineering: Prof. Dr SHABAN TAHA IBRAHIM
Faculty of Law: Prof. Dr OMAR FAROUK ELHUSSINEY
Faculty of Medicine: Prof. Dr ABDEL SHAFY MOHAMADY HASSAN TABL
Faculty of Nursing: Prof. Dr ABDEL REHEEM SAAD SHOULH
Faculty of Physical Education (Male): Prof. Dr MAHMOUD YEHYA MOHAMED SAAD
Faculty of Science: Prof. Dr SABRY SADEK AHMED ELSERFY
Faculty of Specific Education: Prof. Dr MAHMOUD AHMED MOUSSA
Faculty of Veterinary Medicine at Moshtohor: Prof. Dr HATEM HUSSEIN BAKRY

University-Level Institute

BENHA HIGHER INSTITUTE OF TECHNOLOGY

New Benha, El-Kaludia, Benha City 13512
Telephone: (13) 229293
Fax: (13) 230297
E-mail: ahuzayyin@gmx.net
Founded 1988
State control
Dean: AHMED SOLIMAN HUZAYYIN
Vice-Dean for Post-Graduates: ADEL ALAM EL DIN
Vice-Dean for Students: MAHMOUD FATHY M. HASSAN
Library of 8,100 vols
Number of teachers: 275
Number of students: 1,530
Departments of Basic Sciences, Civil Engineering, Electrical Engineering and Mechanical Engineering.

Colleges

Arab Academy for Science and Technology and Maritime Transport: Gamal Abdel Naser St, POB 1029, Miami, Alexandria; tel. (3) 5561497; fax (3) 5487786; internet www.aast.edu; f. 1972; Colleges of Engineering and Technology, Management and Technology and Maritime Transport; library: 36,000 vols, 350 periodicals; 490 teachers; 4,000 students; President Dr GAMAL MOKHTAR.

Cairo Polytechnic Institute: 108 Shoubra St, Shoubra, Cairo; f. 1961; engineering, agriculture, commerce; Dir H. H. MOHAMED.

Higher Industrial Institute: Aswan; f. 1962; state control; courses in mechanical, electrical and chemical engineering, mining and natural sciences.

Higher Institute of Public Health: 165 Sharia Gamal Abd El Nasser, El-Hadra PO, Alexandria; an autonomous unit of the Univ. of Alexandria; f. 1955; undertakes fundamental teaching and applied public health research; 81 staff mems and 50 instructors; departments of public health administration, biostatistics, nutrition, epidemiology, tropical health, microbiology, occupational and environmental health, family health; library: 10,000 vols; Dean Prof. YASSIN M. EL-SADEK; publ. *Bulletin*.

Mansoura Polytechnic Institute: Mit-Khamis St, Mansoura; f. 1957; 147 teachers; 2,290 students; library: 21,400 vols; Dir Dr ESAYED SELIM ELMOLLA.

Regional Centre for Adult Education (ASFEC): Sirs-el-Layyan, Menoufia; tel. (48) 351596; f. 1952 by UNESCO; training of specialists in fields of literacy, adult education and education for rural development; production of prototype educational material, research in community development problems; advisory service; Chair. F. A. GHONEIM; Dir SALAH SHARAKAM.

Sadat Academy for Management Sciences: Kernish el Nile el Maadi, POB 2222, Cairo; tel. (2) 3501033; fax (2) 3502901; f. 1981; principal governmental organization for management development in Egypt; activities carried out through ten academic depts: business administration, public administration, economics, production, administration law, personnel and organizational behaviour, accountancy, insurance and quantitative analysis, computer and information systems, languages; also consists of four professional centres: Training, Consultation, Research and Local Administration; and Faculty of Management (undergraduate) and National Institute of Management Development (postgraduate); library: 32,000 vols, 250 periodicals; 124 teachers; 4,948 students; Pres. Prof. Dr MOUSTAFA REDA ABD AL-RAHMAN; Sec.-Gen. MOHAMMED BAKRI; publ. *Magalet Al-Behouth Al Edaria* (Administrative Research Review, quarterly, in Arabic and English)..

Branches:

Alexandria Branch: 59 Mohandis Mahmoud Ismail St, Moharram Bey, POB 1176, Alexandria; tel. (3) 4227125; fax (3) 4220485.

Assyot Branch: 19 El-Nour St, Assyot; tel. (88) 322429.

Garden City Branch: 5 El Bergas St, Garden City, Cairo; tel. (2) 3551793.

Port Said Branch: Abdel-Salam Arif St, Port Said; tel. (6) 6235926.

Ramsis Branch (Faculty of Management): 14 Ramsis St, Cairo; tel. (2) 5753350; fax (2) 5777175.

Tanta Branch: 5 Quateni St, Tanta; tel. (40) 32083.

Schools of Art and Music

Academy of Arts: El-Afghany St, off Alharam Ave, Giza; tel. (2) 5850727; fax (2) 5611230; f. 1959; comprises eight institutes of university status; Pres. Prof. Dr FAWZY FAHMY AHMED; publ. *Alfann Almuasir* (quarterly)..

Constituent institutes:

Higher Institute of Arab Music: Cairo; tel. (2) 4851561; f. 1967; depts of instrumentation, singing, theory of composition; postgraduate studies; library of 11,000 vols; 125 teachers; 280 students; Dean Dr SAID HAIKUL.

Higher Institute of Art Criticism: Cairo; library of 2,500 vols; 8 teachers; 90 students; Dean Dr NAHIL RACHAB.

Higher Institute of Ballet: Cairo; tel. (2) 5853999; f. 1958; 2 branches in Alexandria and Ismailia; depts of classical ballet, choreography, post-graduate studies; library of 3,500 vols; 21 teachers; 21 students; Dean Dr MAGDA EZZ.

Higher Institute of Child Arts: Cairo; tel. (2) 5850727; f. 1990; postgraduate studies.

Higher Institute of Cinema: Cairo; tel. (2) 5850291; f. 1959; depts of scriptwriting, directing, editing, photography and camerawork, scenery design, sound production, animation and cartoons; postgraduate studies; library of 5,000 vols; 90 teachers; 450 students; Dean Dr SHAWKY ALY MOHAMED.

Higher Institute of Folklore: Cairo; tel. (2) 5851230; f. 1981; dept of postgraduate studies; library of 6,000 vols; 25 teachers; 60 students; Dean Dr ALYAA SHOUKRY.

Higher Institute of Music (Conservatoire): Cairo; tel. (2) 5853451; f. 1959; depts of composition and theory, piano, string instruments, wind instruments, percussion, singing, solfa and music education, musicology; postgraduate studies; library of 24,000 vols, 3,000 records; 90 teachers; 78 students; Dean Prof. Dr NIBAL MOUNIB.

Higher Institute of Theatre Arts: Cairo; tel. (2) 5853233; f. 1944; depts of acting and directing, drama and criticism, scenic and stage design; postgraduate studies; library of 15,500 vols; 90 teachers; 330 students; Dean Dr SANAA SHAFIE.

EL SALVADOR

The Higher Education System

The state-controlled Universidad de El Salvador, founded in 1841, was the only university until the mid-1960s, since when several private universities have been established. The Ministry of Education oversees higher education. Other institutions of higher education include colleges and technical institutes.

Entrance to higher education is achieved on the basis of obtaining the main secondary school qualification, the Bachillerato, and success in an entrance examination. The first undergraduate degree is the Diplomado, awarded after two to three years' study. Following this, the Licenciado can last from four to seven years and may also lead to a professional title. The Maestría is awarded after a further two years, and the Doctorado is available in some subjects.

Both universities and non-university institutions (colleges and technical institutes) offer technical and vocational qualifications. Courses last for two to three years and qualifications include Técnico (two years), Perito, Auxiliar and Técnico Superior (three-and-a-half years).

Learned Societies

GENERAL

Academia Salvadoreña (El Salvador Academy): Casa de las Academias, 9a Avda Norte y Alameda Juan Pablo II, San Salvador; fax 2222-9721; e-mail denysfuentesmyk@hotmail.com; f. 1876; corresp. of the Real Academia Española (Madrid); 22 mems; Dir ALFREDO MARTÍNEZ MORENO; Sec. RENÉ FORTÍN MAGAÑA.

HISTORY, GEOGRAPHY AND ARCHAEOLOGY

Academia Salvadoreña de la Historia (El Salvador Academy of History): Km. 10 Planes de Renderoz, Col. Los Angeles, Villa Lilia 13, San Salvador; f. 1925; Corresp. of the Real Academia de la Historia (Madrid); 18 mems; library of 9,000 vols; Dir JORGE LARDÉ Y LARÍN; Sec. PEDRO ESCALANTE MENA; publ. *Boletín* (irregular).

LANGUAGE AND LITERATURE

Alliance Française: 51 Avda Norte 152, Col. Escalon, Apdo 0175, San Salvador; tel. 2260-5807; fax 2260-5762; e-mail alliafrance@navegante.com.sv; offers courses and exams in French language and culture and promotes cultural exchange with France.

MEDICINE

Colegio Médico de El Salvador: Final Pasaje 10, Col Miramonte, San Salvador; tel. 2260-1111; fax 2260-0324; e-mail concolmed@telesal.net; f. 1943; 1,710 mems; promotes medical research and co-operation; Pres. Dr J. ASCENCIÓN MARINERO CÁCERES; publs *Archivos* (3 a year), *Revista Lealo* (every 2 months).

Sociedad de Ginecología y Obstetricia de El Salvador: Colegio Médico de El Salvador, Final Pasaje 10, Col. Miramonte, San Salvador; tel. 2235-3432; fax 2235-3432; f. 1947; 150 mems; library of 2,000 vols; Pres. Dr JORGE CRUZ GONZALEZ; Sec. Dr HENRY AGREDA RODRIGUEZ.

Research Institutes

AGRICULTURE, FISHERIES AND VETERINARY SCIENCE

Centro Nacional de Tecnología Agropecuaria y Forestal: Km. 33½, Carretera a Santa Ana, La Libertad; tel. 2302-0200; e-mail info@centa.gob.sv; internet www.centa.gob.sv; f. 1942; research and development of seeds; library of 11,000 vols, 134 current periodicals; Exec. Dir Lic. ERNESTO DAGLIO VAN SEVEREN; publs *Agricultura en El Salvador* (irregular), *Boletín Técnico* (occasional), *Circular* (occasional).

Instituto Salvadoreño de Investigaciones del Café: Ministerio de Agricultura, 23 Avda Norte No. 114, San Salvador; f. 1956; administered by the Ministry of Agriculture; publs monographs, *Boletín Informativo* (every 2 months).

ECONOMICS, LAW AND POLITICS

Dirección General de Estadística y Censos (Statistical Office): Avda Juan Bertis 79, Ciudad Delgado, Apdo postal 2670, San Salvador; tel. 2276-5900; fax 2286-2505; f. 1881; Dir-Gen. Lic. SALVADOR ARMANDO MELGAR; publs *Anuario Estadístico* (annually), *IPC* (monthly), *Encuesta de Hogares de Propósitos Múltiples* (annually), *Encuesta Económica* (annually).

NATURAL SCIENCES

Physical Sciences

Centro de Investigaciones Geotécnicas: Apdo 109, San Salvador; tel. 2293-1442; fax 2293-1462; e-mail cig@sal.gbm.net; reorganized 1964; departments of seismology, soil mechanics, building materials, geological surveys; 250 mems; library of 1,000 vols; Dir DOUGLAS HERNANDEZ; publs *Investigaciones Geológicas*, reports.

Servicio Meteorológico Nacional: Kilómetro 5½ Carretera a Nueva San Salvador, Calle las Mercedes frente a Círculo Militar y contiguo a Parque de Pelota, San Salvador; tel. 2223-7797; fax 2283-2269; e-mail meteorologia@snet.gob.sv; internet www.snet.gob.sv; f. 1889; library of 2,000 vols; Dir Lic. LUIS GARCÍA GUIROLA; publs *Almanaque Marino Costero*, *Almanaque Climatológico*, *Boletines Agroclimáticos* (online), *Boletines Climatológicos* (online), *Boletines El Niño* (online), *Weather Forecast, 24 hrs, 48 hrs, 7 days* (online).

TECHNOLOGY

Comisión Salvadoreña de Energía Nuclear (COSEN): c/o Ministerio de Economía, 1A Calle Poniente y 73 Avda Norte, San Salvador; f. 1961; to consider the applications in medicine, agriculture and industry of radioisotopes and nuclear energy.

Libraries and Archives

San Salvador

Archivo General de la Nación: Palacio Nacional, San Salvador; tel. 2222-9418; f. 1948; 2,000 vols; Dir ALBERTO ATILIO SALAZAR; publ. *Repositorio*.

Biblioteca del Ministerio de Relaciones Exteriores (Library of the Ministry of Foreign Affairs): Carretera a Santa Tecla, San Salvador; 10,000 vols; Librarian MANUEL ANTONIO LÓPEZ.

Biblioteca Nacional (National Library): 4ta Calle Oriente y Avda Mons. Oscar A. Romero # 124, San Salvador; tel. 2221-2099; fax 2221-8847; e-mail binaes@latinmail.com; internet www.binaes.gob.sv; f. 1870; 150,000 vols; special collections: old books, titles on int. organizations, Braille room; Dir Dr H. C. MANLIO ARGUETA.

Sistema Bibliotecario de la Universidad de El Salvador: Final 25 Avda Norte, Ciudad Universitaria, Apdo postal 2923, San Salvador; tel. 2225-0278; fax 2225-0278; e-mail sb@biblio.ues.edu.sv; internet www.ues.edu.sv/biblio.html; f. 1847; 44,000 vols; Dir MLIS CARLOS R. COLINDRES; publ. *Boletín Electrónico* (electronic newsletter, 4 a year).

Museums and Art Galleries

San Salvador

Museo de Historia Natural de El Salvador: Final Calle Los Viveros, Col. Nicaragua, San Salvador; tel. 2270-9228; fax 2221-4419; e-mail muhnes@telemovil.net; f. 1976; Dir DANIEL AGUILAR.

Museo Nacional 'David J. Guzmán' (National Museum): Avda la Revolución, Col. San Benito, San Salvador; f. 1883; specializes in history, archaeology, ethnology, library science and restoration; travelling exhibits programme; Dir MANUEL R. LÓPEZ; publs *Anales*, *Colección Antropología e Historia*, *El Xipe*, *La Cofradía*.

Also administers:

Museo de sitio San Andrés: Parque Arqueológico San Andrés, Km. 32, Carretera Panamericana, Ciudad Arce, Dpto de La Libertad; tel. 2505-5715; fax 2235-9453; e-mail fundar123@yahoo.com; internet www.fundar.org.sv; f. 1996; museum at major archaeological site, occupation of which spans c. 2,000 years.

Museo Tazumal: Chalchuapa, Dpto de Santa Ana; f. 1951; archaeological site museum.

Parque Zoológico Nacional: Final Calle Modelo, San Salvador; tel. 270-0828; fax 2274-3950; f. 1953; recreation, environmental education and research, conservation; library of 1,800 vols; Dir Arq. ELIZABETH DE QUANT.

Universities

UNIVERSIDAD CATÓLICA DE OCCIDENTE

25 Calle Oriente y 25 Avda Sur, Santa Ana
Telephone: 2447-8785
Fax: 2441-2655
E-mail: catolica@unico.edu.sv
Internet: www.unico.edu.sv

Founded 1983
Private control
Language of instruction: Spanish
Academic year: February to December

Rector: Monseñor ROMEO TOVAR ASTORGA
Vice-Rector: Lic. MOISÉS ANTONIO MARTINÉZ ZALDIVÁR LACALLE
Secretary-General: Lic. CÁSTULO AFRANIO HERNÁNDEZ ROBLES
Director of Administration: Lic. ROBERTO CHACÓN
Director of Communications: Lic. KAREN MÉNDEZ
Director of Public Relations: Lic JOSÉ JAIME DELEÓN
Director of University Welfare: Lic JOSÉ ARÍSTIDES MÉNDEZ
Director of Library: Lic. MAURICIO EDGARDO MENENDÉZ LEMUS

Number of teachers: 200
Number of students: 3,200

DEANS

Faculty of Economic Sciences: Lic. JOSÉ RICARDO RIVAS
Faculty of Engineering and Architecture: Arq. JULIO ENRIQUE NÁJERA
Faculty of Law and Social Sciences: Lic. ROBERTO ANTONIO SAYES
Faculty of Science and Humanities: Lic. JAIME OSMÍN TRIGUEROS FLORES

DIRECTORS

Department of Languages: Lic. JUAN FRANCISCO LINARES LINARES
Research Unit: Ing. NERY FRANCISCO HERRERA

ATTACHED INSTITUTES

Departamento de Educación a Distancia: promotes teacher training courses.

Instituto de Desarrollo Rural: promotes extra-curricular activities in the rural sphere, projects on agricultural development, training courses for the rural population, technical analysis for agricultural cooperatives and environmental health and hygiene projects.

Instituto de Promoción Humana: promotes courses in administration, administration for rural cooperatives, nutrition, administration for small businesses.

UNIVERSIDAD DE EL SALVADOR

Final 25 Avda, Ciudad Universitaria, Apdo 3110, San Salvador
Telephone: 2225-8826
Fax: 2225-8826
E-mail: mirsalva@navegante.com.sv
Internet: www.ues.edu.sv

Founded 1841
State control
Academic year: February to December
Branches in the Western, Eastern and Paracentral regions of El Salvador

Rector: Dra MARÍA ISABEL RODRÍGUEZ
Vice-Rector (Academic): Ing. Agr. JOAQUÍN ORLANDO MACHUCA
Vice-Rector (Administrative): Dra CARMEN RODRÍGUEZ DE RIVAS
Registrar: Licda ALICIA MARGARITA RIVAS
Library Dir: Licda JOSEFINA ROQUE

Number of teachers: 1,877
Number of students: 28,306

Publications: *El Universitario* (academic review, 4 a year), *Contacto Universitario* (bulletin of the Secretariat for National and International Relations, monthly), *Búho Dilecto* (science and humanities, 6 a year), *El Salvador: Coyuntura Económica* (economics, 4 a year), *Boletín Informativo de la Facultad de Ciencias Económicas* (monthly), *Revista Electrónica de la Facultad de Medicina* (2 a year), *El Quehacer Científico* (natural sciences and mathematics, 1 a year), *Enfoque Tecnológico* (nuclear research, 2 a year), *Aquí Odontología* (odontology, monthly), *Ventana Informativa* (bulletin of the Multidisciplinary Faculty of the Western Region, monthly)

DEANS

Faculty of Agriculture: Ing. Agr. JORGE ALBERTO ULLOA
Faculty of Chemistry and Pharmacy: Lic. SALVADOR CASTILLO ARÉVALO
Faculty of Dentistry: Dr OSCAR RUBÉN COTO DIMAS
Faculty of Economics: Lic. EMILIO RECINOS FUENTES
Faculty of Engineering and Architecture: Ing. MARIO ROBERTO NIETO
Faculty of Humanities: Licda ANA MARÍA GLOWER DE ALVARADO
Faculty of Jurisprudence and Social Sciences: Licda MORENA ELIZABETH NOCHEZ DE ALDANA
Faculty of Medicine: Dra ANA LETICIA ZAVALETA DE AMAYA
Faculty of Natural and Mathematical Sciences: Licda LETICIA NOEMÍ PÁUL DE FLORES
Multidisciplinary Faculty of the Eastern Region: JUAN FRANCISCO MÁRMOL CANJURA
Multidisciplinary Faculty of the Paracentral Region: Lic. JOSÉ NOEL ARGUETA
Multidisciplinary Faculty of the Western Region: JORGE MAURICIO RIVERA

ATTACHED RESEARCH INSTITUTES

Consejo de Investigaciones Científicas: Dir Dra ERLINDA HÁNDAL VEGA.

Instituto de Estudios Históricos, Antropológicos y Arqueológicos.

Instituto de Investigaciones Económicas: Dir Dr FERNANDO GUERRERO SÁNCHEZ.

UNIVERSIDAD CENTROAMERICANA 'JOSÉ SIMEÓN CAÑAS'

Apdo 01-168, San Salvador
located at: Blvd Los Próceres, San Salvador
Telephone: 2210-6600
Fax: 2210-6655
E-mail: correo@www.uca.edu.sv
Internet: www.uca.edu.sv

Founded 1965
Private control (Society of Jesus)
Language of instruction: Spanish
Academic year: March to December

Rector: Lic. JOSÉ MARÍA TOJEIRA
Vice-Rector (Academic): RODOLFO JOSÉ CARDENAL CHAMORRO
Vice-Rector (Finance): AXEL SODERBERG
Registrar: Lic. RENÉ ALBERTO ZELAYA
Librarian: Dra KATHERINE MILLER

Library of 195,000 vols
Number of teachers: 463
Number of students: 9,248

Publications: *Estudios Centroamericanos ECA* (online, 6 a year), *Revista de Administración y Empresas*, *Revista Realidad* (online, 6 a year), *Revista Proceso* (online, weekly), *Revista Carta a las Iglesias* (online, monthly), *Revista Latinoamericana de Teología*

DEANS

Faculty of Economics: Dr JOSÉ MANUEL RIVAS ZACATARES
Faculty of Engineering: Ing. CELINA PÉREZ
Faculty of Human and Natural Sciences: Dra SILVIA ELINOR AZUCENA DE FERNÁNDEZ

HEADS OF DEPARTMENTS

Faculty of Economics:
- Business Administration: Lic. FIDEL ERNESTO ZABLAH
- Economics: Licda ANA LILIÁN VEGA TREJO

Faculty of Engineering:
- Electronics and Information: Ing. CÉSAR VILLALTA
- Energy and Power Sciences: Ing. ISMAEL ANTONIO SÁNCHEZ FIGUEROA
- Spacial Planning: Arq. HERBERT ERNESTO GRANILLO
- Structural Mechanics: Ing. REYNALDO ZELAYA CERNA
- Systems and Processing Technology: Dr FRANCISCO ARMANDO CHÁVEZ

Faculty of Human and Natural Sciences:
- Education: Lic. AGUSTIN FERNÁNDEZ
- Law: Dr JOSÉ ENRIQUE ARGUMEDO
- Literature: Dr RICARDO ROQUE BALDOVINOS
- Mathematics: Ing. WILLIAM MENDOZA
- Philosophy: Dr HECTOR SAMOUR
- Psychology: Dr MAURICIO GABORIT
- Sociology: Lic. SERGIO RENÉ BRAN MOLINA
- Theology: Dr RAFAEL DE SIVATTE

Centre of Information, Documentation and Investigation Support (CIDAI): Lic. LUIS ARMANDO GONZÁLEZ
Institute of Human Rights: Dr BENJAMÍN CUÉLLAR
Master of Business Administration: Dra ESTELA CAÑAS

UNIVERSIDAD 'DR JOSÉ MATÍAS DELGADO'

Km $8\frac{1}{2}$ carretera a Santa Tecla, Ciudad Merliot
Telephone: 2212-9400
Fax: 2289-5314
E-mail: informacion@umjd.edu.sv
Internet: www.ujmd.edu.sv

Founded 1977
Private control
Language of instruction: Spanish
Academic year: January to June, July to December

Rector: Dr DAVID ESCOBAR GALINDO
Vice-Rector: Lic. CARLOS QUINTANILLA SCHMIDT
Academic Vice-Rector: Dr FERNANDO BASILIO CASTELLANOS
Registrar: Dr FERNANDO BASILIO CASTELLANOS
Library Dir: Lic. SARA ESCOBAR DE GONZÁLEZ

Library of 25,000 vols
Number of teachers: 380
Number of students: 4,000

DEANS AND DIRECTORS

Faculty of Agriculture and Agricultural Research: Lic. MARÍA GEORGIA GÓMEZ DE REYES

Faculty of Economics: Ing. ROBERTO ALEJANDRO SORTO FLETES
Faculty of Health Sciences: Dr JUAN JOSÉ FERNÁNDEZ
Faculty of Jurisprudence and Social Sciences: Dr HUMBERTO GUILLERMO CUESTAS
Faculty of Sciences and Arts: Arq. LUIS SALAZAR RETANA
School of Applied Arts: Arq. LUIS SALAZAR RETANA
School of Architecture: Arq. LUIS SALAZAR RETANA
School of Business Administration and Marketing: Lic. PATRICIA LINARES DE HERNÁNDEZ
School of Communications: Lic. RICARDO CHACÓN
School of Industrial Engineering: Ing. SILVIA BARRIOS DE FERREIRO
School of Psychology: Lic. ROXANA VIDES

UNIVERSIDAD DE ORIENTE

4a Calle Poniente 705, San Miguel
Telephone: 2661-1180
Fax: 2660-0879
E-mail: info@univo.edu.sv
Internet: www.univo.edu.sv

Founded 1981
Private control

Rector: Dr JOAQUÍN APARICIO ZELAYA
President: Prof. GREGORIO BALMORE IRAHETA
Secretary-General: ROGELIO CISNEROZ LAZO

DEANS

Faculty of Agriculture: Ing. ALVARO ARMANDO HERRERA COELLO
Faculty of Economics: Ing. LUIS ALONSO SILVA
Faculty of Engineering and Architecture: Ing. DAVID ARNOLDO FLORES GARAY
Faculty of Law: Dr GODOFREDO LAHUD
Faculty of Science and Humanities: Lic. JOSÉ DAVID DÍAZ REYES

UNIVERSIDAD PANAMERICANA DE EL SALVADOR

Calle Progreso 234 a 60m de Avda Bernal Colonia Miramonte Poniente, San Salvador
Telephone: 2260-1906
Fax: 2260-1859
E-mail: upaninfo@upan.edu.sv
Internet: www.upan.edu.sv

Founded 1989
Private control

Rector: Lic. OSCAR ARMANDO MORÁN FOLGAR
Vice-Rector: Lic. NUBIA ADALILA MENDOZA FIGUEROA
Secretary-General: Lic. CELINA DEL CARMEN LÓPEZ URÍAS
Registrar: Lic. ALMA ARACELY POZAS DE IBARRA
Librarian: RAQUEL HERNÁNDEZ

DEANS

Faculty of Economics: Lic. JOSUÉ ELÍAS MONTOYA
Faculty of Jurisprudence: Lic. ALEJANDRO GARCÍA GARAY
Faculty of Science and Humanities: Lic. NUBIA ADAILILA MENDOZA FIGUEROA

DIRECTORS

Institute of Research, Guidance and Assessment: Lic. VIRGINIA QUINTANA ESTRADA
School of Legal Sciences: Lic. MARGORI CAROLINA JUSTO
School of Library Science and Information Science: Lic. CARLOS FERRER

UNIVERSIDAD SALVADOREÑA ALBERTO MASFERRER

19 Avda Norte, entre 3a Calle Poniente y Alameda Juan Pablo II, Apdo postal 2053, San Salvador
Telephone: 2221-1136
Fax: 2222-8006
E-mail: informacion@mail.usam.edu.sv
Internet: www.usam.edu.sv
Founded 1979
State control
Language of instruction: Spanish
Academic year: January to December
Rector: Dr CÉSAR AUGUSTO CALDERÓN
ViceRector: Dr MIGUEL ANTONIO BARRIOS
Secretary-General: Lic. DAYSI C. M. DE GOMEZ
Registrar: Lic. ANA LORENA DE MELÉNDEZ
Librarian: Lic. XIMENA TIZNADO

Number of teachers: 283
Number of students: 2,000

Publication: *Revista Somos* (4 a year)

DEANS

Faculty of Dentistry: Dr ARMANDO RAFAEL MARTÍNEZ
Faculty of Law and Social Sciences: Lic. DELMER EDMUNDO CRUZ RODRÍGUEZ
Faculty of Medicine: Dra CARMEN J. CABEZAS DE SÁNCHEZ
Faculty of Pharmacy: Lic. SOCORRO VALDEZ
Faculty of Veterinary Medicine: Dra ANA EUGENIA VÉZQUEZ LIÉVANO

ATTACHED RESEARCH INSTITUTES

University Research Institute: Dir Dra YASMARA LÓPEZ MEARDI.

UNIVERSIDAD TECNOLÓGICA DE EL SALVADOR

Calle Arce 1120, San Salvador
Telephone: 2275-8888
Fax: 2275-8813
E-mail: infoutec@utec.edu.sv
Internet: www.utec.edu.sv

Founded 1981
Private control
Academic year: January to December

President and Rector: Lic. JOSÉ MAURICIO LOUCEL
Assistant Rector: Lic. CARLOS REYNALDO LÓPEZ NUILA
Vice-Rector (Academic Affairs and Strategic Development): Ing. NELSON ZÁRATE SÁNCHEZ
Vice-Rector (Administration): Ing. DANILO DÍAZ
Vice-Rector (Finance): Lic. MARÍA DE LOS ANGELES LOUCEL
Vice-Rector (Research and Extramural Studies): Lic. RAFAEL RODRÍGUEZ LOUCEL
Registrar: Dr JOSÉ ENRIQUE BURGOS
Librarian: Lic. MARÍA ELSA LÉMUS FLORES

Library of 16,000 vols
Number of teachers: 349
Number of students: 14,618

Publications: *Revista de Aniversario*, *Revista Entorno*, *Revista Redes*, *Boletín Comunica*

DIRECTORS

School of Architecture and Design: (vacant)
School of Art and Culture: Dr RAMÓN RIVAS
School of Business: Licda VILMA FLORES DE AVILA
School of Communications: (vacant)
School of Languages: (vacant)
School of Law: Lic. RENE ALFREDO PORTILLO CUADRA
School of Oceanography: Licda SUSAN LYN DE GUZMÁN
School of Science and Technology: Lic. RICARDO NAVARRETE

Colleges

Central American Technical Institute: Apdo 133, Santa Tecla, La Libertad; tel. 2228-0845; fax 2228-1277; f. 1969; courses in agricultural engineering, civil and construction engineering, architecture, electronics, mechanical engineering; library: 6,000 vols; Dir Ing. ROLANDO MARÍN COTO.

Escuela Nacional de Agricultura 'Roberto Quiñónez': Km $33\frac{1}{2}$ Carr. a Sta Ana, Apdo 2139, San Salvador; tel. 2228-2735; f. 1956; 350 students; 60 teachers; library: 7,000 vols; Dir Ing. MAURICIO ARÉVALO.

EQUATORIAL GUINEA

The Higher Education System

Equatorial Guinea has been independent for just over three decades, of which two were dominated by a brutal dictatorship. Its intellectual and cultural traditions were determined by colonial values rather than by its own cultural values, although it is slowly redressing this situation. The condition of general education (Equatorial Guinea has very limited resources) has an adverse affect on higher education, with students arriving having had very little access to books, and with an education based almost entirely on recitation. This naturally limits the level and type of coursework that may be offered. That the language of instruction is mainly Spanish while the majority of good jobs require English also presents difficulties. Many students elect to study abroad; this is supported by scholarships from foreign countries or agencies, administered by the Government. Equatorial Guinea has no national programme of scholarship for foreign study. In 1999/2000 there were 1,003 pupils in higher education. Since 1979, assistance in the development of the educational system has been provided by Spain. The Universidad Nacional de Guinea Equatorial (UNGE), founded in 1995, is Equatorial Guinea's only university. Two higher education centres, at Bata and Malabo, are administered by the Spanish Universidad Nacional de Educación a Distancia.

Learned Societies

LANGUAGE AND LITERATURE

Centro Cultural Hispano-Guineano: Malabo; f. 1982; maintains library; organizes cultural events; publs *Africa 2000* (3 a year), *Ediciones del Centro Cultural Hispano-Guineano*, series dedicated to Ecuatoguinean writers.

Institut Culturel d'Expression Française (ICEF): BP 936, Malabo; tel. 92660; fax 92985; internet www.chez.com/icefmalabo; f. 1984; offers courses and examinations in French language and culture and promotes cultural exchange with France; Dir VINCENT BRACK.

Research Institute

NATURAL SCIENCES

Biological Sciences

Bioko Biodiversity Protection Program: c/o Universidad Nacional de Guinea Ecuatorial, Carretera Luba s/n, Malabo; tel. 286768; e-mail butynski@bioko.org; internet www.bioko.org; part of academic partnership between Arcadia University (USA, *q.v.*) and Universidad Nacional de Guinea Ecuatorial (*q.v.*); conservation of Bioko Island's biodiversity, especially its critically endangered primates and nesting sea turtles, through devt of economically sustainable educational programs, research programs and conservation activities; maintains wildlife research centre at Moka; Co-Dirs GAIL HEARN, WAYNE MORRA; Project Dir JOSE MANUEL ESARA ECHUBE; Research Dir CLAUDIO POSA BOHOME.

Universities

UNIVERSIDAD NACIONAL DE EDUCACIÓN A DISTANCIA (UNED), EQUATORIAL GUINEA BRANCH

Edificio Poveda, C/ Amanecer de África s/n, Barrio de Ela Nguema, Malabo
Telephone: 92911
Fax: 92932
E-mail: unedmalabo@yahoo.es
Founded 1993
Language of instruction: Spanish
Dir: PILAR MONTES PALOMINO
Dir of Studies: Dr ANDRÉS ESONO ONDÓ
Library of 10,000 vols
part of Universidad Nacional de Educación a Distancia (Spain); br in Bata (tel. 82277).

UNIVERSIDAD NACIONAL DE GUINEA EQUATORIAL (UNGE)

Carretera Luba s/n, Malabo
Telephone: 91644
Fax: 94361
Founded 1995
State control
Languages of instruction: Spanish, French, English
Rector: CARLOS NSE NSUGA
Library: c. 7,500 vols
Number of teachers: 100
Number of students: 1,200
Schools of Agriculture, Fisheries and Forestry, Arts and Social Science (Malabo), Administration (Malabo), Teacher Training (Malabo, with br in Bata), Nursing (Bata), Medicine (Bata), Eng. and Technology (Bata).

ERITREA

The Higher Education System

From 1962 to 1993 Eritrea was a *de facto* province of Ethiopia. Independence was achieved in 1993 following a 33-year war of secession. Since independence Eritrea has begun to rebuild its infrastructure, economy and government. The University of Asmara (the only university) was founded by the Camboni Sisters Missionary Institute in 1958 and was originally known as the Holy Family University Institute. In 1960 the Institute was accredited by the Superior Council of the Institute of Italian Universities and in 1968 it achieved university-status under its current name; an English section was opened in the same year. In 2004/05 there were some 5,500 students enrolled on Bachelors degree courses at the University of Asmara. The Ministry of Education controls the university.

Admission to the university is on the basis of a degree-level pass in the Eritrean School Education Certificate Examinations and an entrance examination. The main undergraduate degree, the Bachelors, lasts four years. A Masters degree was launched in 2004. The University also offers diploma courses and evening classes.

Learned Societies

LANGUAGE AND LITERATURE

Alliance Française: POB 209, Asmara; tel. (1) 126599; fax (1) 121036; e-mail af@gemel.com.er; internet www.afasmara.org.er; offers courses and exams in French language and culture and promotes cultural exchange with France.

British Council: POB 997, 23 Lorenzo Tazas St, Asmara; tel. (1) 123415; fax (1) 127230; e-mail information@britishcouncil.org.er; internet www.britishcouncil.org/eritrea; offers courses and exams in English language and British culture and promotes cultural exchange with the UK; Dir Dr NEGUSSE ARAYA.

Libraries and Archives

Asmara

Asmara Public Library: 82 Felket Ave 173, Asmara; tel. (1) 118215; f. 1959; 32,400 vols; branch library with 11,000 vols in north Asmara; Dir MICHAEL BEYENE GHEBRE.

Massawa

Massawa Municipal Library: POB 17, Massawa; tel. (1) 552407; fax (1) 552249; f. 1997; 10,000 vols; Chief Librarian MUHAMMED NUR SAID.

Museum

Asmara

National Museum of Eritrea: Opp. Selam Hotel, Asmara; f. 1992; archaeology, ethnography and militaria; oversees excavations and preservation of the national archaeological heritage; Dir Dr YOSIEF LIBSEQAL.

University

UNIVERSITY OF ASMARA

POB 1220, Asmara
Telephone: (1) 161926
Fax: (1) 162236
E-mail: prcuoa@asmara.uoa.edu.er
Internet: www.uoa.edu.er
Founded 1958 (Italian section)1968 (English section)
State control
Language of instruction: English
Academic year: September to June (two semesters)

Chancellor: ISAYAS AFEWERKI
President: Dr WOLDE-AB YISAK
Director of Administration: TEWELDE ZEROM
Director of Academic Affairs: Dr TADESSE MEHARI
Director of Research and Human Resource Development: Dr ZEMENFES TSIGHE
Director of Student Affairs: Dr TEKIE ASEHUN
Librarian: ASSEFAW ABRAHA
Library of 60,000 vols
Number of teachers: 261
Number of students: 4,086
Publication: *Journal of Eritrean Studies* (2 a year)

DEANS AND DIRECTORS

College of Arts: Prof TEJ DHAR
College of Agriculture: Dr WOLDESELASSIE OGABZGHI
College of Business and Economics: Dr STIFANOS HAILEMARIAM
College of Education: LETTEDENGHIL OGBAMICAEL
College of Engineering: KAHSAI NEGUSSE
College of Health Sciences: Dr HIBRENEGUSS TEREFE
Faculty of Law: Dr MENGISTEAB NEGASH
College of Science: Dr TESFAMICAEL HAILE
College of Social Sciences: Dr GEBREMARIAM WOLDEMICHAEL
College of Social and Management Sciences: (vacant)
School of Graduate Studies: Dr BERAKI WOLDEHAIMANOT

HEADS OF DEPARTMENTS

Accounting: GHENET OGBE
Agricultural Engineering: SIRAK MEHARI
Agricultural Engineering: T. P. SINGH
Agricultural Extension: Prof. K. S. KRISHNAN
Animal Science: GOITOM ASGEDOM
Anthropology and Archaeology: Dr SENAIT BAHTA
Biology: Dr GHEBREHIWET MEDHANIE
Business Management: SAMUEL GHEBREAB
Chemistry: Dr BERHANE GHIRMAY
Civil Engineering: A. N. PATAL
Clinical Laboratory Science: GHIMJA FESSAHAYE
Computer Science: Dr MARKUS WALTER
Earth Sciences: Dr WOLDAI GHEBREAB
Economics: Dr MELAKE TEWOLDE
Educational Administration: Dr ALEX DUMBIA
Educational Psychology: Dr REZENE HABTEMARIAM
Electrical Engineering: Dr P. M. NAWGHARE
English: SARAH OGBAY
Geography: Dr BERHANE KELETA
History: HABTAI ZERAI
Journalism and Mass Communication: ROBEL TEKLAY
Land Resource and Environment: MEHRETEAB TESFAI
Law: MENGISTEAB NEGASH
Literature and Language Studies: Dr GHIRMAI NEGASH
Marine Science: YONATAN BOKRE
Mathematics: Dr ABREHAM ZEMUI
Mechanical Engineering: TEDROS KIFLE
Middle School Education Unit: SENAIT GHEBRU
Modern European Languages: ELISA SOLOMONE
Nursing: GHIDEY GHEREYOHANES
Pharmaceutical Sciences: Prof. SHARMA
Philosophy: Prof. G. S. RAMAIAH
Physics: Dr SERGEY KOTELNIKOV
Plant Sciences: Dr ADUGNA HAILE
Political Science: Dr SENAIT WOLDU
Public Administration: KIFLEMARIAM ABRAHAM
Science Education Unit: NEGASI GHEBREALFA
Social Science Education Unit: FETWI ADGOY
Sociology and Social Work: MUSSA SULTAN IDRIS
Statistics and Demography: Prof. J. C. PAUL

ESTONIA

The Higher Education System

From 1940 until 1991 Estonia was a Soviet Socialist Republic within the USSR. Higher education was based on the Soviet system, but following independence the Estonian Education Act of 1992 identified the development of Estonian language and culture as one of the main aims of education. Estonia implemented the Bologna process at undergraduate-level in 2002 and at postgraduate-level in 2005; this has led to the establishment of a two-tier Bachelors and Masters degree system (with exceptions in certain subjects). Institutions of higher education are either universities or applied higher education institutes. Universities provide academic education and applied higher education institutes provide vocational education. The Ministry of Education is responsible for higher education, with several organizations also involved in administrative and academic oversight; these include the Higher Education Advisory Chamber, the Research and Development Council, the Estonian Science Council, the Estonian Innovation Fund and the Higher Education Quality Assessment Council. The latter is responsible for quality assurance and accreditation.

The Ministry of Education sets requirements for admission to higher education, which generally consist of the Secondary Education Leaving Certificate (Gümnaasiumi lõputunnistus) and performance in national entrance examinations (Riigieksamitunnistus). Public universities admissions are determined by the State, which sets enrolment quotas, although universities may take additional paying students once the quotas have been met. Specialist institutions may also set specific admissions criteria. Under the Bologna process, higher education qualifications consist of Bachelors, Masters and Doctoral degrees. The Bakalaureusekraad (Bachelors) is the main undergraduate degree, consisting of three years of study. However, some degrees leading to professional qualifications require five years of study; this is particularly the case in medicine, veterinary medicine, pharmacy, architecture, engineering and teacher training. The first postgraduate degree is the Magistrikaad (Masters), which lasts two years and is dependent on attainment of the Bakalaureusekraad. The second level of postgraduate qualification (and final university degree) is the Doktorikraad; studies at this level last four years. Both the Magistrikaad and Doktorikraad may be either academic or professional qualifications. Since their introduction in 1999, the main institutions of post-secondary vocational and technical education are the rakenduskõrgkool (applied higher education institutes), which offer three- to four-year Diplom degrees.

Learned Societies

GENERAL

Estonian Academy of Sciences: Kohtu 6, 10130 Tallinn; tel. 644-21-29; fax 645-18-05; e-mail foreign@akadeemia.ee; internet www.akadeemia.ee; f. 1938 to advance scientific research and represent Estonian science nationally and internationally; promotes the adaptation of new knowledge for economic growth and improvement of the quality of life in Estonia; promotes the public appreciation of science and scientific methods of thought; encourages research co-operation at nat. and int. levels; divs of Astronomy and Physics (Head P. SAARI), Biology, Geology and Chemistry (Head I. KOPPEL), Humanities and Social Sciences (Head P. TULVISTE), Informatics and Technical Sciences (Head R. KÜTTNER); 75 mems (60 ordinary, 15 foreign); Pres. Prof. Dr RICHARD VILLEMS; Sec.-Gen. Prof. Dr LEO MÕTUS; publs *Acta Historica Tallinnensia*, *Linguistica Uralica*, *Oil Shale*, *Toimetised* (Proceedings: Physics and Mathematics, Engineering, Chemistry, Estonian Journal of Earth Sciences, Biology/Ecology), *Trames*.

HISTORY, GEOGRAPHY AND ARCHAEOLOGY

Estonian Geographical Society: Kohtu 6, 10130 Tallinn; Pres. JAAN-MATI PUNNING; Scientific Sec. LAINE MERIKALJU.

LANGUAGE AND LITERATURE

Alliance Française: Liivaluite 5, 11214 Tallinn; tel. 672-20-13; fax 672-11-98; e-mail hellemichelson@hot.ee; offers courses and exams in French language and culture and promotes cultural exchange with France.

British Council: Vana-Posti 7, 10146 Tallinn; tel. 625-77-88; fax 625-77-99; e-mail british.council@britishcouncil.ee; internet www.britishcouncil.org/estonia; offers exams in English; introduces British culture and promotes cultural exchange with the UK; library of 6,000 vols; Dir KYLLIKE TOHVER.

Estonian Mother Tongue Society: Roosikrantsi 6, 10119 Tallinn; tel. 644-93-31; e-mail es@eki.ee; internet www.emakeeleselts.ee; f. 1920; promotes and maintains interest in the Estonian language; co-ordinates language research and development; systematic research into Estonian dialects; language-planning and modern literary language research; arranges language days outside Estonia; also focuses on the modern literary language, loan-words in Estonian and the Estonian dialectal landscape; 346 mems (335 ordinary, 11 hon.); library of 5,735 vols; Chair. HELLE METSLANG; Scientific Sec. MARIA-MAREN SEPPER; publs *Emakeele Seltsi aastaraamat* (yearbook), *Oma Keel* (2 a year).

Goethe-Institut: Suurtüki 4B, 10133 Tallinn; tel. 627-69-60; fax 627-69-62; e-mail goethe@goethe.ee; internet www.goethe.de/ne/tal/deindex.htm; offers courses and exams in German language and culture and promotes cultural exchange with Germany; library of 9,000 vols, 25 periodicals; Dir MIKKO FRITZE.

NATURAL SCIENCES

General

Estonian Union of the History and Philosophy of Science: Ülikooli 18, 50090 Tartu; tel. 737-5500; f. 1967; attached to Estonian Academy of Sciences; 93 mems; Chair. JAAK AAVIKSOO; Scientific Sec. ERKI TAMMIKSAAR.

Biological Sciences

Estonian Naturalists' Society: Struve 2, 51003 Tartu; tel. 734-19-35; fax 742-70-11; e-mail struveelus@elus.tartu.ee; internet www.loodelus.ee/lus/english/indexi.html; f. 1853; 21 scientific and environmental subdivisions; library of 158,453 vols; Pres. Dr MAREK SAMMUL; Sec. Dr LINDA KONGO MONIKA PREDE.

Research Institutes

GENERAL

Institute for Islands Development: Losipargi 1, 93811 Kuressaare; tel. and fax (45) 39-145; e-mail marins@si.edu.ee; attached to Tallinn Technical University; Dir MARET PANK.

AGRICULTURE, FISHERIES AND VETERINARY SCIENCE

EAU Plant Biotechnological Research Centre EVIKA: Harjumaa, Teaduse 6A, 75501 Saku; tel. 604-14-84; fax 604-11-36; e-mail Hilja.Pihl@mail.ee; attached to Min. of Education, and Estonian Agricultural Univ.; Dir KATRIN KOTKAS.

Estonian Agrobiocentre: Rõõmu tee 10, 51013 Tartu; tel. and fax (7) 33-97-17; e-mail eabc@pb.uninet.ee; attached to Min. of Agriculture; veterinary research; Dir JÜRI KUMAR.

Estonian Institute of Agricultural Engineering: Harjumaa, Teaduse 13, 76609 Saku; tel. (2) 72-18-54; fax (2) 72-19-61; e-mail ergo@peak.edu.ee; attached to Min. of Agriculture; Dir ARVI KALLAS.

Estonian Research Institute of Agriculture: Teaduse 13, 75501 Saku; tel. 671-15-42; fax 671-15-40; e-mail info@eria.ee; internet www.eria.ee; Dir HINDREK OLDER.

Jõgeva Plant Breeding Institute: Aamisepa 1, 48309 Jõgeva; tel. and fax (77) 601-26; e-mail jogeva@jpbi.ee; attached to Min. of Agriculture; f. 1920; Dir MATI KOPPELL.

ARCHITECTURE AND TOWN PLANNING

OÜ ETUI BetonTEST - Ehitusinstituut (ETUI BetonTEST Ltd — Building Institute): Estonia pst. 7, 10143 Tallinn; tel. 645-41-58; fax 644-23-25; e-mail etui@betontest.ee; internet www.betontest.ee; Dir OLAV SAMMAL.

ECONOMICS, LAW AND POLITICS

Estonian Institute for Futures Studies: Lai 34, 10133 Tallinn; tel. 641-11-65; fax 641-17-59; e-mail eti@eti.online.ee; future scenarios for the development of Estonia and its neighbouring areas; Dir ERIK TERK.

Estonian Institute of Economic Research: Rävala puiestee 6, 19080 Tallinn; tel. 681-46-50; fax 667-83-99; e-mail eki@ki.ee; internet www.ki.ee; f. 1934; Dir MARJE JOSING; publs *Economic Indicators of Estonia* (10 a year), *Economic Survey of Baltic States* (4 a year), *Konjunktuur* (4 a year), *Baltic Facts* (annually).

Estonian Institute of Economics at Tallinn University of Technology: Estonia tee 7, 10143 Tallinn; tel. 644-45-70; fax 699-88-51; e-mail mail@tami.ee; internet www.tami.ee; f. 1947; attached to Tallinn University of Technology; 19 mems; Dir TIIA PÜSS; Research Dir ÜLO ENNUSTE.

HISTORY, GEOGRAPHY AND ARCHAEOLOGY

Institute of History: Rüütli 6, 10130 Tallinn; tel. 644-65-94; fax 644-37-14; e-mail ai@teleport.ee; f. 1947; Dir PRIIT RAUDKIVI; publs *Acta Historica Tallinnensia* (annually), *Eesti Arheoloogia Ajakiri* (annually).

LANGUAGE AND LITERATURE

Institute of the Estonian Language: Roosikrantsi 6, 10119 Tallinn; tel. and fax 641-14-43; e-mail eki@eki.ee; internet www.eki.ee; f. 1947; Dir Dr URMAS SUTROP; publ. *Eesti Keele Instituudi Toimetised* (irregular).

Under and Tuglas Literature Centre: Roosikrantsi 6, 10119 Tallinn; tel. 644-31-47; fax 644-01-77; e-mail utkk@utkk.ee; internet www.utkk.ee; f. 1993; attached to Estonian Acad. of Sciences; Dir Dr JAAN UNDUSK.

MEDICINE

Estonian Institute of Cardiology: Ravi 18, 10138 Tallinn; tel. 620-72-50; fax 620-70-02; e-mail jyri.kaik@mail.ee; f. 1984; attached to Min. of Social Affairs; Dir JÜRI KAIK.

National Institute for Health Development: Hiiu 42, 11619 Tallinn; tel. 659-39-00; fax 659-39-01; e-mail tai@tai.ee; internet www.tai.ee; f. 1947 as Estonian Institute of Experimental and Clinical Medicine; attached to Min. of Social Affairs; Dir MAARIKE HARRO.

Pärnu Institute of Health Resort Treatment and Medical Rehabilitation: Kuuse 4, 40012 Pärnu; tel. (44) 259-00; Dir ENDEL VEINPALU.

NATURAL SCIENCES

General

Estonian Marine Institute: Mäealuse 10A, 12618 Tallinn; tel. 626-74-10; fax 626-74-17; e-mail meri@sea.ee; internet www.sea.ee; f. 1992; Dir TOOMAS SAAT.

Biological Sciences

Estonian Biocentre: Riia 23, 51010 Tartu; tel. (7) 42-04-43; fax (7) 42-01-94; e-mail rvillems@ebc.ee; Dir RICHARD VILLEMS.

Institute of Ecology: Kevade 2, 10137 Tallinn; tel. 662-18-53; fax 662-22-83; e-mail eco@eco.edu.ee; internet www.eco.edu.ee; f. 1992; Dir J.-M. PUNNING; publs *Annual Report* (every 2 years), *Publications* (irregular).

Institute of Experimental Biology: Instituudi tee 11, 76902 Harku; tel. 656-06-05; fax 650-60-91; e-mail ebi@ebi.ee; f. 1957; attached to Estonian Agricultural Univ.; Dir. Prof. A. AAVIKSAAR.

Institute of Zoology and Botany: Riia 181, 51014 Tartu; tel. (7) 42-80-21; fax (7) 38-30-13; e-mail zbi@zbi.ee; internet www.zbi.ee; f. 1947; Dir URMAS TARTES.

International Centre for Environmental Biology: Mustamäe tee 4, 10621 Tallinn; tel. 611-58-04; fax 611-58-05; e-mail juri@iceb.ee; Dir JÜRI MARTIN.

Physical Sciences

Estonian Meteorological and Hydrological Institute: Rävala puiestee 8, 10143 Tallinn; tel. 646-15-63; e-mail jaan.saar@emhi.ee; internet www.emhi.ee; weather forecasts; environmental protection; collation, treatment and storage of results of meteorological and hydrological measurements; climatological survey of Estonia; attached to Min. of the Environment; Dir-Gen. JAAN SAAR.

Geological Survey of Estonia: Kadaka tee 80–82, 12618 Tallinn; tel. 672-00-94; fax 672-00-91; e-mail egk@egk.ee; internet www.egk.ee; attached to Min. of the Environment; Dir. VELLO KLEIN.

Institute of Geology: Estonia puiestee 7, 10143 Tallinn; tel. 644-41-89; fax 631-20-74; e-mail inst@gi.ee; internet www.gi.ee; f. 1947; attached to Tallinn University of Technology; Dir Dr ALVAR SOESOO; publ. *Proceedings* (4 a year).

Institute of Physics: Riia 142, 50411 Tartu; tel. (7) 42-81-02; fax (7) 38-30-33; e-mail dir@fi.tartu.ee; internet www.fi.tartu.ee; f. 1973; library of 27,000 vols, 50 periodicals; Dir ERGO NÕMMISTE.

National Institute of Chemical Physics and Biophysics: Akadeemia tee 23, 12618 Tallinn; tel. 639-83-00; fax 670-36-62; e-mail kbfi@kbfi.ee; internet www.kbfi.ee; f. 1979; Dir AGO SAMOSON.

Oil Shale Research Institute: Järveküla tee 12, 30328 Kohtla-Järve; tel. (33) 445-50; fax (33) 447-82; f. 1958; library of 100,000 vols; Dir RICHARD JOONAS.

Tartu Observatory: Tôravere, 61602 Tartu Maakond; tel. (7) 41-02-65; fax (7) 41-02-05; e-mail aai@aai.ee; internet www.aai.ee; f. 1808; library of 100,000 vols; Dir LAURITS LEEDJÄRV.

RELIGION, SOCIOLOGY AND ANTHROPOLOGY

Estonian Interuniversity Population Research Centre: POB 3012, 10504 Tallinn; tel. 645-41-25; fax 660-41-98; e-mail asta@ekdk.estnet.ee; Dir KALEV KATUS; publ. *EKDK RY* (series A, B, C and D, all irregular).

Institute of International and Social Studies: Estonia puiestee 7, 10143 Tallinn; tel. and fax 645-49-27; e-mail rasi@iiss.ee; internet www.iiss.ee; f. 1988; 25 mems; Dir RAIVO VETIK (acting).

TECHNOLOGY

Estonian Energy Research Institute: Paldiski maantee 1, 10137 Tallinn; tel. 662-20-28; fax 661-36-55; e-mail eeri@eeri.ee; internet www.eeri.ee; Dir ÜLO RUDI.

Institute of Cybernetics: Akadeemia tee 21, 12618 Tallinn; tel. 620-41-50; fax 620-41-51; e-mail dir@ioc.ee; internet www.ioc.ee; f. 1960; attached to Tallinn Technical Univ.; 50 mems; library of 8,000 vols; Dir JAAN PENJAM.

Libraries and Archives

Tallinn

Academic Library of Tallinn Pedagogical University: Rävala Ave 10, 15042 Tallinn; tel. 665-94-01; fax 665-94-00; e-mail ear@ear.eetlulib@tlulib.ee; internet www.ear.eewww.tlulib.ee; f. 1946; 2,445,165 vols, incunabula; Dir ANDRES KOLLIST.

National Library of Estonia: Tõnismägi 2, 15189 Tallinn; tel. 630-76-11; fax 631-14-10; e-mail nlib@nlib.ee; internet www.nlib.ee; f. 1918; nat. library status 1988; parliamentary library 1989; nat. and parliamentary library with public access; national ISBN, ISSN and ISMN agency; research library for the humanities and social sciences; professional development centre; cultural centre for book and art exhibitions, concerts, conferences; 3,408,238 vols; Dir-Gen. TIIU VALM; publs *Eesti Rahvusraamatukogu Toimetised* (Acta Bibliothecae Nationalis Estoniae, annually), *Raamatukogu* (The Library, 6 a year).

Tartu

Tartu University Library: Struve 1, 51003 Tartu; tel. (7) 37-57-02; fax (7) 37-57-01; e-mail library@utlib.ee; f. 1802; 3,751,000 vols, 504,000 theses, 28,000 MSS; Dir P. OLESK.

Museums and Art Galleries

Tallinn

Art Museum of Estonia: Kiriku Plats 1, 10130 Tallinn; tel. 644-93-40; fax 644-20-94; e-mail muuseum@ekm.ee; internet www.ekm.ee; f. 1919; collection of fine and applied art; art exhibitions; 55,135 items; Dir MARIKA VALK.

Estonian History Museum: Pikk 17, 10123 Tallinn; tel. 641-16-30; fax 644-34-46; e-mail post@eam.ee; internet www.eam.ee; f. 1842; library of 11,000 vols; Dir TOOMAS TAMLA.

Estonian Open Air Museum: Vabaõhumuuseumi tee 12, 13521 Tallinn; tel. 654-91-17; fax 654-91-27; e-mail evm@evm.ee; internet www.evm.ee; f. 1957; 18th- to 20th-century architectural and ethnographical objects; Dir M. LANG.

Estonian Theatre and Music Museum: Müürivahe 12, 10146 Tallinn; tel. 644-21-32; fax 641-81-66; e-mail info@tmm.ee; internet www.tmm.ee; f. 1924; library of 50,000 vols; Dir ÜLLE REIMETS; publ. *AegiKiri* (annually).

Tallinn City Museum: Vene 17, 10123 Tallinn; tel. 644-18-29; fax 644-15-74; e-mail info@linnamuuseum.ee; internet www.linnamuuseum.ee; f. 1937; library of 6,300 vols; Dir MARUTA VARRAK.

Tartu

Art Museum of Tartu University: Ülikooli 18, 50090 Tartu; tel. (7) 37-53-84; fax (7) 37-54-40; e-mail kmm@ut.ee; internet www.ut.ee/artmuseum; f. 1803; mainly plaster casts of ancient sculpture, gems and coins, 15th–19th c. graphic art, Russian icons, applied art, Greek and Roman antiquities; Dir INGE KUKK.

Estonian Literary Museum: Vanemuise 42, Box 368, 5100350002 Tartu; tel. (7) 37-77-

00; fax (7) 37-77-06; e-mail kirmus@kirmus.ee; internet www.kirmus.ee; f. 1909; comprises Archival Library (incl. Bibliography Dept), Estonian Folklore Archives, Estonian Cultural History Archives, Folklore Dept and Ethnomusicology Dept; Dir KRISTA ARU JANIKA KRONBERG; publs *Paar sammukest* (Some Small Steps, annually), *Folklore / Electronic Journal of Folklore* (print and electronic, 4 a yearquarterly), *Maetagused* (print and electronic, 4 a yearquarterly), *Pro Folkloristika: Estonian Folklore Archives* (annually).

Estonian National Museum: Veski 32, 51014 Tartu; tel. (7) 42-12-79; fax (7) 42-22-54; e-mail erm@erm.ee; internet www.erm.ee; f. 1909; ethnology and culture of the Estonian and Finno-Ugric people; library of 31,588 vols; Dir JAANUS PLAAT; publs *Eesti Rahva Muuseumi Aastaraamat* (annually), *Pro Ethnologia* (2 a year), *Eesti Rahva Muuseumi Sari* (annually).

Tartu Art Museum: Vallikraavi 14, 51003 Tartu; tel. and fax (7) 34-10-50; e-mail tartmus@tartmus.ee; internet www.tartmus.ee; f. 1940; Estonian and European art since 19th c.; library of 20,000 vols; Dir REET MARK.

Universities

ESTONIAN AGRICULTURAL UNIVERSITY

Kreutzwaldi 64, 51014 Tartu
Telephone: (7) 31-30-01
Fax: (7) 31-30-68
E-mail: info@eau.ee
Internet: www.eau.ee

Founded 1951

Rector: ALAR KARIS
Vice-Rector (Research): Dr ANDRES KOPPEL
Vice-Rector (Students): Dr HARDI TULLUS
Number of teachers: 380teachers
Number of students: 4,850students

Library of 500,000 vols

Publication: *Eesti Põllumajandusülikooli Teaduslike Tööde Kogumik*

Specialized areas: agronomy, horticulture, animal husbandry, veterinary medicine, meat and dairy technology, forestry, household economics, food production and marketing, agricultural engineering and energetics, agricultural economics and entrepreneurship, finance, land surveying, landscape architecture and management, water management, agricultural buildings, sustainable use of natural resources.

TALLINN TECHNICAL UNIVERSITY

Ehitajate tee 5, 19086 Tallinn
Telephone: 620-20-02
Fax: 620-20-20
E-mail: ttu@ttu.ee
Internet: www.ttu.ee
Founded 1918
Languages of instruction: Estonian, Russian
Academic year: September to June

Rector: Prof. PEEP SÜRJE
Vice-Rector (Academic Affairs): Prof. JAKOB KÜBARSEPP
Vice-Rector (Development): ANDRES KEEVALIK
Vice-Rector (Research): Prof. REIN VEIKMÄE
Librarian: JÜRI JÄRS

Library of 750,000 vols, 730 periodicals
Number of teachers: 1,600 (including affiliated institutions)
Number of students: 9,000

Publication: *Mente et Manu* (newsletter, weekly)

DEANS

Faculty of Chemistry and Materials Technology: Prof. ANDRES ÖPIK
Faculty of Civil Engineering: Prof. ROODE LIIAS
Faculty of Economics and Business Administration: Prof. ENN LISTRA
Faculty of Humanities: Prof. SULEV MÄELTSEMEES
Faculty of Information Technology: Prof. ENNU RÜSTERN
Faculty of Mechanical Engineering: Prof. PRIIT KULU
Faculty of Power Engineering: Prof. JUHAN VALTIN
Faculty of Science: Prof. MARGUS LOPP

PROFESSORS

Faculty of Chemistry and Materials Technology (tel. 620-27-96; fax 620-27-96; e-mail k@ttu.ee):

- CHRISTJANSON, P., Polymer Technology
- KALLAVUS, U., Materials Research
- KAPS, T., Woodworking
- MELLIKOV, E., Semiconductor Materials Technology
- MUNTER, R., Environmental Technology
- OJA, V., Chemical Engineering
- ÖPIK, A., Physical Chemistry
- PAALME, T., Food Science and Technology
- SOONE, J., Environmental Technology
- VIIKNA, A., Textile Technology
- VOKK, R., Food Science

Faculty of Civil Engineering (tel. 620-25-00; e-mail e@ttu.ee):

- ENGELBRECHT, J., Applied Mechanics
- HÄÄL, K., Heating and Ventilation
- IDNURM, S., Steel Structures
- KOPPEL, M., Road Construction
- KOPPEL, T., Hydrodynamics
- LAHE, A., Structural Mechanics
- LAVING, J., Traffic and Transportation Engineering
- LIIAS, R., Construction Economics and Management
- LOIGU, E., Environmental Protection
- LOORITS, K., Steel Structures
- OIGER, K., Timber and Plastic Structures
- PIHLAK, I., Architecture
- RAADO, L.-M., Building Materials
- SALUPERE, A., Solid Mechanics
- SUTT, J., Construction Economics and Management
- TÄRNO, Ü., Structural Mechanics

Faculty of Economics and Business Administration (Kopli tn. 101, 11712 Tallinn; tel. 620-41-01; fax 620-39-46; e-mail t@ttu.ee):

- AASMA, A., Economic Mathematics
- KALLAS, K., Financial Accounting
- KEREM, K., Economic Theory
- KILVITS, K., Economic Policy
- KOLBRE, E., Management Economics
- KUKRUS, A., Economic Law and Regulation
- LEIMANN, J., Organization and Management
- LISTRA, E., Finance and Banking
- PAVELSON, M., Economic Sociology
- PURJU, A., Public Economics
- SAAT, M., Business Administration
- TEDER, J., Small Businesses
- TINT, P., Working Environment and Safety
- VENSEL, V., Theory of Statistics and Econometrics

Faculty of Humanities (tel. 646-71-48; fax 646-71-48; e-mail h@ttu.ee):

- KAEVATS, Ü., Philosophy
- KATTEL, R., Public Administration and European Studies
- MÄELTSEMEES, S., Regional Policy
- RAJANGU, V., Educational Policy
- TEICHMANN, M., Psychology

Faculty of Information Technology (Raja tn. 15, 12618 Tallinn; tel. 620-22-51; fax 620-22-46; e-mail i@ttu.ee):

- ARRO, I., Signal Processing
- BULDAS, A., Information Security
- JÜRGENSON, R., Software Engineering
- KALJA, A., Systems Programming
- KUKK, V., Circuit and Systems Theory
- KUUSIK, R., Informatics
- LOSSMANN, E., Telecommunications
- MEISTER, A., Radio Engineering
- MIN, M., Electronic Measurement
- MÕTUS, L., Real Time Systems
- PENJAM, J., Theoretical Computer Science
- RANG, T., Electronics Design
- RÜSTERN, E., Automatic Control and Systems Analysis
- TAKLAJA, A., Microwave Engineering
- TAMMET, T., Network Software
- TEPANDI, J., Applied Artificial Intelligence
- UBAR, R.-J., Computer Engineering and Diagnostics
- VAIN, J., Formal Methods
- VELMRE, E., Applied Electronics

Faculty of Mechanical Engineering (tel. 620-33-50; fax 620-31-96; e-mail m@ttu.ee):

- AJAOTS, M., Fine Mechanics
- KIITAM, A., Quality Engineering
- KULU, P., Materials Science
- KÜTTNER, R., Computer-aided Design and Manufacturing
- LAANEOTS, R., Metrology and Measurement Techniques
- LAVRENTJEV, J., Automotive Engineering
- MELLIKOV, E., Semiconductor Materials Technology
- PAIST, A., Thermal Power Engineering
- PAPPEL, T., Machine Mechanics
- PAPSTEL, J., Production Engineering
- PÕDRA, P., Machine Elements
- ROOSIMÖLDER, L., Product Development
- SIIRDE, A., Thermal Power Equipment
- TAMRE, M., Mechatronics
- TIIKMA, T., Heat Engineering

Faculty of Power Engineering (Kopli tn. 82, 10412 Tallinn; tel. 620-35-48; fax 620-36-96; e-mail a@ttu.ee):

- ADAMSON, A., Rock Engineering
- JARVIK, J., Electrical Machines
- LAUGIS, J., Electrical Drives and Electricity Supply
- LEHTLA, T., Robotics
- LIIK, O., High Voltage Engineering
- MELDORF, M., Transfer in Power Systems
- VALDMA, M., Power Systems

Faculty of Science (tel. 620-29-95; fax 620-26-45; e-mail y@ttu.ee):

- JÄRVEKÜLG, L., Molecular Diagnostics
- KALJURAND, M., Analytical Chemistry
- LIPPING, T., Radiophysics
- LOIDE, R.-K., Theoretical Particle Physics
- LOPP, M., Organic Chemistry
- MEIGAS, K., Biomedical Technology
- PAAL, E., Algebra and Geometry
- PALUMAA, P., Genomics and Proteomics
- PUUSEMP, P., Algebra and Geometry
- SAMEL, N., Bio-organic and Natural Products Chemistry
- TAMM, T., Inorganic and General Chemistry
- TAMMERAID, L., Mathematical Analysis
- TIMMUSK, T., Molecular Biology
- TRUVE, E., Gene Technology
- VAARMANN, O., Applied Mathematics
- VILU, R., Biochemistry

TALLINN UNIVERSITY

Narva mnt 25, 10120 Tallinn
Telephone: (6) 40-91-01
Fax: (6) 40-91-16
E-mail: tlu@tlu.ee
Internet: www.tlu.ee

Founded 2005; through amalgamation of Tallinn Pedagogical University, Estonian Academic Library, Estonian Institute of Humanities and Institute of History
Language of instruction: Estonian
Rector: MATI HEIDMETS
Vice-Rector for Academic Affairs: HELI MATTISEN
Vice-Rector for Open University: MADIS LEPIK
Vice-Rector for Research and Development: PEETER NORMAK
Number of teachers: 844teachers
Number of students: 7,421students

DEANS
Faculty of Educational Sciences: Assoc. Prof. PRIIT REISKA
Faculty of Fine Arts: Prof. EHA RÜÜTEL
Faculty of Mathematics and Natural Sciences: Prof. ANDI KIVINUKK
Faculty of Philology: Prof. SULIKO LIIV
Faculty of Physical Education: Assoc. Prof. KRISTJAN PORT
Faculty of Social Sciences: Prof. ALEKSANDER PULVER

UNIVERSITY OF TARTU

Ülikooli 18, 50090 Tartu
Telephone: (7) 37-51-00
Fax: (7) 37-54-40
E-mail: proffice@ut.ee
Internet: www.ut.ee
Founded 1632
State control
Language of instruction: Estonian
Academic year: September to June
Rector: TONU LEHTSAAR (acting)
Pro-Rector (Academic Affairs): Prof. TÕNU LEHTSAAR
Pro-Rector (Research): Prof. AIN HEINARU
Academic Secretary: IVAR-IGOR SAARNIIT
Library Director: TOOMAS LIIVAMÄGI
Library: see Libraries and Archives
Number of teachers: 981
Number of students: 17,653
Publication: *Acta et Commentationes Universitatis Tartuensis* (44 series)

DEANS
Faculty of Biology and Geography: Prof. T. MEIDLA
Faculty of Economics and Business Administration: Prof. J. SEPP
Faculty of Education: Prof. T. TENNO
Faculty of Law: Prof. K. MERUSK
Faculty of Mathematics: Prof T. LEIGER
Faculty of Medicine: Prof. T. ASSER
Faculty of Philosophy: Prof. B. KLAAS
Faculty of Physical Education and Sports Sciences: Prof. V. ÖÖPIK
Faculty of Physics and Chemistry: Prof. J. JÄRV
Faculty of Social Sciences: Prof. J. ALLIK
Faculty of Theology: Prof. R. ALTNURME

Other Higher Educational Institutes

Estonian Academy of Arts: Tartu Maantee 1, 10145 Tallinn; tel. 626-73-09; fax 626-73-50; e-mail public@artun.ee; internet www.artun.ee; f. 1914; faculties of fine arts (painting, stage design, sculpture, graphics), applied art (textiles, fashion design, leather work, ceramics, glass and metal work), architecture (interior design, architecture), design (product design, graphic design), art history; 160 teachers; 523 students; library: 54,427 vols; Rector Prof. SIGNE KIVI.

Estonian Academy of Music: Rävala pst. 16, 10143 Tallinn; tel. 667-57-00; fax 667-58-00; e-mail ema@ema.edu.ee; internet www.ema.edu; f. 1919; departments: piano, strings, brass and woodwind, vocal, chamber music, conducting, composition, musicology; institute of music education; institute of teaching training in vocal and instrumental music; higher school of drama; 120 teachers; 560 students; library: 245,000 vols; Rector P. LASSMANN; publ. *Scripta Musicalia* (quarterly).

ETHIOPIA

The Higher Education System

The University of Addis Ababa is the oldest university in the country. It was originally founded in 1950 as University College of Addis Ababa, became known as Haile Selassie University in 1961 and adopted its current name in 1975. There have been efforts to establish higher education institutions in outlying areas of Ethiopia; however, most institutions are located in the central, north and north-western parts of the country (mostly Addis Ababa, Bahir Dar, Mekelle, Alemaya, Awassa and Jimma). There are currently six universities, all state-controlled. In 2003/04 172,111 students were enrolled at university level.

Higher education is financed by the Government, and the budget of each university is supervised by its Board. The University Senate is the managerial body of a University; the Academic Commission is the main academic body. The Academic Commission controls all aspects regarding the structure of degree programmes, certification and student issues. Heads of Department chair Department Councils, which are subordinate to the Academic Commission, and which make recommendations on matters of study, research, staff recruitment, pedagogy and examinations. The Ministry of Education appoints senior university officers, such as the President and Vice-Presidents. Heads of Department are either appointed by Deans of Faculty or elected by Department Councils.

The Ethiopian School Leaving Certificate Examination is the main requirement for admission to higher education. The primary undergraduate degree is the Bachelors, which takes four years, although some subjects require longer (five years for engineering, law and pharmacy; six years for medicine and veterinary medicine). The first postgraduate degree is the Masters, which lasts for two to three years, and the second postgraduate degree is the Doctor of Philosophy (PhD), which is awarded three years after the Masters.

A formal system of qualifications for technical and vocational education is still evolving, with the aim of creating a uniform structure based on courses of one to three years. Certificates are awarded following completion of Levels I (one year) and II (two years) and a Diploma is awarded after completion of Level III (three years).

Learned Societies

GENERAL

UNESCO Office Addis Ababa: POB 1177, Addis Ababa; located at: ECA Bldg, Menelik Ave, POB 1177 Addis Ababa; tel. (11) 5513953; fax (11) 5511414; e-mail ml.conde@unesco.org; designated Cluster Office for Djibouti, Eritrea and Ethiopia; Dir MAMDY CONDE.

AGRICULTURE, FISHERIES AND VETERINARY SCIENCE

Association for the Advancement of Agricultural Sciences in Africa: POB 30087, Addis Ababa; tel. (11) 5443536; f. 1968; aims to promote the development and application of agricultural sciences and the exchange of ideas, to encourage Africans to enter training and to hold seminars annually in different African countries; crop production and protection, animal health and production, soil and water management, agricultural mechanization, agricultural economics, agricultural education, extension and rural sociology, food science and technology; *c.* 1,200 mems (individual and institutional); library of 5,000 items; Admin. Sec.-Gen. Prof. M. EL-FOULY (acting); publs *AAASA Newsletter*, *African Journal of Agricultural Sciences*, *conferences*, *Proceedings of workshops*.

BIBLIOGRAPHY, LIBRARY SCIENCE AND MUSEOLOGY

Ethiopian Library and Information Association: POB 30530, Addis Ababa; tel. (11) 5518020; f. 1961; to promote the interests of libraries, archives, documentation centres, etc., and to serve those working in them; 200 mems; Pres. TAMIRAT MOTA; Sec. ZINABIE MEKONNEN; publs *Bulletin* (2 a year), *Directory of Ethiopian Libraries*, *Newsletter* (2 a year).

LANGUAGE AND LITERATURE

Alliance Française: Wavel St, POB 1733, Addis Ababa; tel. (11) 1550213; fax (11) 1553681; e-mail aef@allianceaddis.org; internet www.allianceaddis.org; offers courses and exams in French language and culture and promotes cultural exchange with France; attached teaching centre in Dire Dawa.

British Council: POB 1043, Artistic Bldg, Adwa Ave, Addis Ababa; tel. (11) 1550022; fax (11) 1552544; e-mail bc.addisababa@et.britishcouncil.org; internet www.britishcouncil.org/ethiopia; offers courses and exams in English language and British culture and promotes cultural exchange with the UK; library of 25,000 vols; Dir MICHAEL MOORE.

Goethe-Institut: POB 1193, Addis Ababa; tel. (11) 1552888; fax (11) 1551299; e-mail vl@telecom.net.et; internet www.goethe.de/af/add/enindex.htm; offers courses and exams in German language and culture and promotes cultural exchange with Germany; library of 1,500 vols, 24 periodicals; Dir Dr DIETER WERNER KLUCKE.

MEDICINE

Ethiopian Medical Association: POB 2179, Addis Ababa; e-mail ema.emj@telecom.net.et; tel. (11) 5533742; f. 1961; Pres. Dr TELAHUM TEKA; publ. *Ethiopian Medical Journal* (quarterly).

Ethiopian Public Health Association: POB 7117 Addis Ababa; tel. (11) 5509749; fax (11) 5514870; e-mail epha@ethionet.et; internet www.epha.ws; f. 1989; for the promotion of public health, prevention of diseases, timely treatment of the sick and rehabilitation of the disabled; Pres. Dr DAMEN HAILEMARIAM; Exec. Sec. Dr GETNET MITIKE; publ. *Ethiopian Journal of Health Development*.

NATURAL SCIENCES

Physical Sciences

Geophysical Observatory: Addis Ababa University, POB 1176, Addis Ababa; tel. (11) 1117253; fax (11) 1551863; e-mail observatory.aau@telecom.net.et; internet www.aau.edu.et/faculties/sc/geophysical/geophysical.htm; f. 1958; research in seismology, gravity, tectonics, crustal deformation, geomagnetic observation and geodesy; library of 100 vols and 10 periodicals; Sec. Assoc. Prof. LAIKE M. ASFAW; publ. *Seismological Bulletin* (2 a year).

Research Institutes

AGRICULTURE, FISHERIES AND VETERINARY SCIENCE

Awasa Agriculture Research Centre: c/o Awasa Agricultural College, POB 6, Awasa; tel. (46) 2200224; fax (46) 2204521; e-mail arc@padis.gn.apc.org; f. 1967; soil and water management, crop protection, horticulture, field crops, agronomy and crop physiology, agricultural economics and farming systems, livestock, forestry; library of 2,300 vols, 28 journals; Man. DANIEL DAURO.

Ethiopian Institute of Agricultural Research: POB 2003, Addis Ababa; tel. (11) 64626336460137; fax (11) 6461294; e-mail info_com@earo.org.etinfocom@eiar.gov.et; internet www.eiar.gov.et; f. 1966; agronomy and crop physiology, crop protection, animal production, animal feeds and nutrition, animal health, agricultural mechanization, horticulture, soil and water management, field crops, forestry, post-harvest technologies, biotechnology; financial aid provided by the Ethiopian government and other sources; 50 research centres and stations nationally; 2,915 mems; library of 150,000 vols; Deputy Dir-Gen. Dr ABATESOLOMON TSEDEKEASEFA; publs *Ethiopian Journal of Agricultural Economics*, *Ethiopian Journal of Agricultural Science*, *Ethiopian Journal of Animal Production*, *Pest Management Journal of Ethiopia*.

HISTORY, GEOGRAPHY AND ARCHAEOLOGY

Archeological Institute: POB 76, Addis Ababa; Dir Dr BERHANOU ABBÉBÉ; publ. *Annales d'Ethiopie*.

Ethiopian Mapping Authority: POB 597, Addis Ababa; tel. (11) 5518445; fax (11) 5515189; e-mail ema@telecom.net.et; internet www.telecom.net.et/~ema; f. 1955; under Min. of Economic Development and Co-operation; conducts land surveying, mapping, remote sensing and geographical research; 400 mems; library of 3,000 vols; Gen. Man. HADGU G. MEDHIN; publ. *Geo-Information Bulletin Ethiopia* (2 a year).

NATURAL SCIENCES

Biological Sciences

Desert Locust Control Organization for Eastern Africa (DLCO EA): POB 4255, Addis Ababa; tel. (11) 6461477; fax (11) 6460296; e-mail dlc@telecom.net.et; f. 1962; mems: Djibouti, Eritrea, Ethiopia, Kenya, Somalia, Sudan, Tanzania, Uganda; research into and control of desert locust and other pests, including armyworm, quelea, tsetse fly and mosquito; library of 2,000 vols; Dir PETER ONYANGO ODIYO; publ. *Annual Report*.

Institute of Biodiversity Conservation and Research: POB 30726, Addis Ababa; tel. (1) 6612244; fax (1) 6613722; e-mail bioresearch@telecom.net.et; internet www.telecom.net.et/~ibcr; f. 1998; promotes and carries out research into the development and sustainable use of the country's biodiversity; Gen. Man. Dr ABEBE DEMISSIE.

National Herbarium: Addis Ababa University, POB 3434, Addis Ababa; tel. (11) 1114323; fax (11) 1552350; e-mail nat.heb@telecom.net.et; f. 1959; Dir Prof. SEBSEBE DEMISSEW; Curator Dr ENSERMU KELBESSA; publ. *Flora of Ethiopia*.

Physical Sciences

Geological Survey of Ethiopia: POB 2302, Addis Ababa; tel. (11) 6464482; fax (11) 6463326; internet www.geology.gov.et; f. 1968 as a Department within the Ministry of Mines; as Ethiopian Institute of Geological Surveys 1984; 778 mems; library of 66,877 vols; Gen. Man. KETEMA TADESSE; Chief Geologist AMENTI ABRAHAM; Head of Geoscience Information Centre SISAY TESFAY; publs *Annual Report*, *Newsletter* (2 a year).

RELIGION, SOCIOLOGY AND ANTHROPOLOGY

Institute of Ethiopian Studies: Addis Ababa University, POB 1176, Addis Ababa; tel. (11) 1119469; fax (11) 1552688; e-mail ies.aau@telecom.net.et; internet www.ies-ethiopia.org; f. 1963; conducts, promotes and coordinates research and publication on Ethiopian Studies with special emphasis on the humanities and cultural studies; operates an advanced study and documentation centre and an ethnological-historical museum: see Museums and Art Galleries; library: see Libraries and Archives; Dir ELIZABETH W. GIORGIS (acting); publs *IES Bulletin* (4 a year), *Journal of Ethiopian Studies* (2 a year).

Libraries and Archives

Addis Ababa

Addis Ababa University Libraries: POB 1176, Addis Ababa; tel. (11) 1115673; fax (11) 1550655; e-mail kennedy.aau@telecom.net.et; internet www.aau.edu.et/libraries; f. 1950; 500,000 vols, 632 microfiches, 3,000 serial titles and an electronic journals database; colln includes; 90,000 vols on Ethiopia; consists of the main University library and six branch libraries: the Science Library, Technology North Library (Amist Kilo campus), Technology South Library (Lideta Campus), Faculty of Business and Economics Library, Central Medical Library and Law Library; Librarian Dr TAYE TADESSE.

British Council Knowledge and Learning Services: POB 1043, Artistic Bldg, Adwa Ave, Addis Ababa; tel. (11) 1550022; fax (11) 1552544; e-mail kls@et.britishcouncil.org; f. 1959; 51,000 vols, 137 periodicals; Librarian Ato MULUGETA HUNDE.

Institute of Ethiopian Studies Library: Addis Ababa University, POB 1176, Addis Ababa; tel. (11) 1550844; fax (11) 1123456; e-mail girmajem@ies.aau.edu.et; f. 1963; collection of printed and non-printed materials on Ethiopia, Somalia, Djibouti, Red Sea, Indian Ocean, Sudan; also materials on Middle East; 110,000 vols, 9,000 MSS; Librarian GIRMA JEMANEH; publ. *Journal of Ethiopian Studies*.

National Library and Archives of Ethiopia: POB 717, Addis Ababa; tel. (11) 5516532; fax (11) 5526411; e-mail nale@ethionet.et; internet www.nale.gov.et; f. 1944; 164,000 vols; consists of: Reference, Documentation and Periodical Division; Legal Deposit and Copyright Registration; Archives Repository and Research; Microfilm and Microfiche Library; Ethiopian Studies and MSS Division; Dir-Gen. ATIKILT ASSEFA.

Museums and Art Galleries

Addis Ababa

Museum of the Institute of Ethiopian Studies: University of Addis Ababa, POB 1176, Addis Ababa; tel. (11) 1550844; fax (11) 1552688; e-mail ies.aau@telecom.net.et; f. 1963; sections: exhibit of Haile Selassie's bedroom, material culture (household artefacts, clothing, handicrafts, etc.); ethno-musicology (all types of Ethiopian musical instruments, religious music and poetry, record archive of oral tradition and folklore); traditional art (church paintings and furnishings, icons, etc., Islamic calligraphy); stamps, coins and banknotes of Ethiopia; Curator AHMED ZEKARIA.

National Museum of Ethiopia: POB 76, Addis Ababa; tel. (11) 1119113; fax (11) 1553188; collns of early hominid fossils, incl. 'Lucy', a nearly complete skeleton of *Australopithecus afarensis*; Dir MAMITU YILMA.

Universities

ADDIS ABABA UNIVERSITY

POB 1176, Addis Ababa
Telephone: (11) 1550844
Fax: (11) 1550972
Internet: www.aau.edu.et

Founded 1950 as University College of Addis Ababa; became Haile Selassie University 1961; present name 1975
State control
Language of instruction: English
Academic year: September to July

President: Prof. ANDREAS ESHETÉ
Vice-President for Business and Development: Ato MOHAMMED HABIB
Associate Vice-President for Academic Affairs and External Relations Officer: Dr BUTTE GOTU
Associate Vice-President for Continuing and Distance Education Programmes: Dr MEKONEN DISASA
Associate Vice-President for Research and Graduate Programmes: Prof. ENDASHAW BEKELE
Registrar: Dr ZEMEDE ASFAW
Librarian: Dr TAYE TADESSE

Library of 493,000 vols
Number of teachers: 948
Number of students: 15,364

Publications: *Ethiopian Journal of Development Research*, *Ethiopian Journal of Education*, *Register of Current Research on Ethiopia and the Horn of Africa*, *SINET: An Ethiopian Journal of Science*

DEANS

Faculty of Business and Economics: Dr MULAT DEMEKE
Faculty of Education: Ato AKALU GETANEH
Faculty of Informatics: Ato GETACHEW JEMANEH
Faculty of Law: Ato GETACHEW ABERA
Faculty of Medicine: Dr ZUFAN LAKEW
Faculty of Science: Prof. GEZAHEGN YIRGU
Faculty of Technology: Dr ABEBE DINKU
Faculty of Veterinary Medicine: Dr MERGA BEKANA
College of Social Sciences: Dr BEKELE GUTEMA
School of Pharmacy: Dr TSIGE GEBREMARIAM
Institute of Language Studies: Dr GEREMEW LEMU

DIRECTORS

School of Fine Arts and Design: Dr MELAKU AYELE
School of Music: AKILU ZEWDIE
Institute of Development Research: Asst Prof. MULUGETA FISSEHA
Institute of Education: Ato DANIEL DESTA
Institute of Ethiopian Studies: ELIZABETH GEBREGIORGIS
Institute of Pathobiology: Prof. MOGESSIE ASHENAFI

ALEMAYA UNIVERSITY

POB 138, Dire Dawa
Telephone: (25) 6610705
Fax: (25) 6610717
E-mail: alemaya.univ@telecom.net.et
Internet: www.alemayau.edu.et

Founded 1952; university status 1985
State control
Language of instruction: English
Academic year: September to June

President: Prof. BELAY KASSA
Vice-President (Academic): Dr TENA ALAMIREW
Vice-President (Administrative): Dr BELAYNEH LEGESSE
Vice-President (Research and Development) (vacant)
Registrar: Dr FEKADU LEMESSA
Librarian: YARED MAMO

Number of teachers: 355
Number of students: 15,863 (9,790 full-time, 3,153 evening, 1,035 distance-education, 1,855 summer in-service)

Publications: *The Alemayan*, *Alemaya Annual Research Report*, *AUA News Letter*

DEANS

Faculty of Agriculture: Dr WAGAYEHU BEKELE
Faculty of Economics and Business: WORKENEH KASSA
Faculty of Education: Dr TESFAHUN KEBEDE
Faculty of Health Sciences: MELAKE DAMENA
Faculty of Law: ABDULMALIK ABUBEKER
Faculty of Technology: Dr KETEMA TILAHUN
Faculty of Veterinary Medicine: Dr MOHAMMED ABDELLA
Continuing Education Programme: Dr KEBEDE W/TSADIK

School of Graduate Studies: Dr CHEMEDA FININSSA

RESEARCH CENTRE

Alemaya Agricultural Research Centre: POB 138, Dire Dawa; Dir Dr TADELE TEFERA.

BAHIR DAR UNIVERSITY

POB 79, Bahir Dar
Telephone: (58) 2205943
Fax: (58) 2202025
Internet: www.ethionet.et/~bdu

Founded 2001 through merger of Bahir Dar Teachers' College and Bahir Dar Polytechnic Institute

President: Asst Prof. Dr TSEHAY JEMBERU
Vice-President (Academic and Research): YALEW ENDEWOKE
Vice-President (Adminstrative and Development): ZERIHUN MEKONNEN
Registrar: HAILEEYESUS WORKINEH

Faculties: Education; Engineering; Business and Economics, Law, Institute of Garment and Textile Support; due to open soon: Faculty of Agriculture and Environment, Faculty of Applied Science

Number of teachers: 250
Number of students: 17,000

Publication: *The Ethiopian Journal of Education, Science and Technology*

DEANS

Faculty of Business and Economics: Asst Prof. Dr ABEBE WALLE
Faculty of Education: Asst Prof. Dr MULUGETA KIBRET
Faculty of Engineering: Asst Prof. Dr MESFIN BELACHEW
Faculty of Law: Asst Prof. Dr TADESSE KASSA

DEBUB UNIVERSITY

POB 5, Awassa
Telephone: (46) 2200221
Fax: (46) 2205421
E-mail: aca@telecom.net.et
Internet: www.d-univ.edu.et

Founded 1999 by merger of Awassa College of Agriculture, Dilla College of Teachers' Education and Health Science and Wondo Genet College of Forestry
State control
President: ZINABU G. MARIAM
Library of 112,000 vols
Number of teachers: 386
Number of students: 8,366

Faculties of Natural Sciences, Social Sciences and Technology; Colleges of Agriculture, Health Sciences, Teachers' Education and Forestry.

JIMMA UNIVERSITY

Jimma
Telephone: (47) 1111340
Fax: (47) 1111458
E-mail: email-jihs@telecom.net.et
Internet: www.telecom.net.et/~junv.edu

Founded 1999 through merger of Jimma College of Agriculture (f. 1952) and Jimma Institute of Health Sciences (f. 1983)

President: Asst Prof. Dr DAMTEW MARIAM
Vice-President (Academic and Research): Asst Prof. Dr SOLOMON MOGUS
Vice-President (Administration and Development): KORA TUSHUNE
Vice-President (Training and Health Services): ABRAHAM AMLAK
Registrar: Dr SOLOMON GENET
Dean of Students: EWNETU SEID
Head of External Relations Office: Assoc. Prof. CHALLI JIRA
Head of Library and Documentation Service: GETACHEW BAYISA

Number of teachers: 370
Number of students: 16,279

DEANS

Faculty of Business: Asst Prof. SOLOMON ALEMU
Faculty of Education: ZELALEM TESHOME
Faculty of Medical Sciences: Asst Prof. Dr MINAS TSADIK
Faculty of Public Health: Asst Prof. KIFLE MIKAEL
Faculty of Science and Liberal Arts: TAREKEGN BIRHANU
Faculty of Technology: ADMASSU SHIMELES
College of Agriculture, Ambo: EYLACHEW ZEWDIE
College of Agriculture, Jimma: BERHANU BELAY
School of Graduate Studies: Prof. MEKONNEN ASSEFA

UNIVERSITY OF MEKELLE

POB 231, Mekelle, Tigray Region
Telephone: (34) 4400812
Fax: (34) 4400793
E-mail: mekelle.university@telecom.net.et
Internet: www.mu.edu.et
State control
Founded 2000
President: Dr MITUKU HAILE

Faculties of Agriculture, Business and Commerce and Engineering.

College

Yared Music School: POB 30097, Addis Ababa; tel. (11) 1550166; f. 1967; attached to Addis Ababa University; 130 students; Head TEKLE YOHANES ZIKE.

FIJI

The Higher Education System

The supra-national University of the South Pacific maintains one of its 11 campuses in Fiji. In 2004 there were 16,444 students at the University and its extension centres, of whom 200 held scholarships from the Fijian Government. There are also colleges and institutes of professional training and vocational education.

The Fiji School Leaving Certificate and Form Seven Examination are the main criteria for admission to higher education. The undergraduate Bachelors degree lasts for three years, the postgraduate Masters degree for one to two years and the Doctorate for two years following award of the Masters. Post-secondary vocational and technical training is offered by the University and colleges and institutes of professional training and vocational education. The main qualifications are the Certificate and Diploma.

Learned Societies

ECONOMICS, LAW AND POLITICS

Fiji Law Society: 100 Gordon St, POB 2389, Government Bldgs, Suva; tel. 3315690; fax 3314334; e-mail fls@kidanet.net.fj; internet www.fls.org.fj; f. 1956; Pres. DEVANESH SHARMA; Sec. and CEO AFRANA NISHA; publ. *Newsletter* (monthly).

LANGUAGE AND LITERATURE

Alliance Française: 14 MacGregor Rd, POB 14548, Suva; tel. 3313802; fax 3313803; e-mail allifra@is.com.fj; offers courses and exams in French language and culture and promotes cultural exchange with France.

MEDICINE

Fiji Medical Association: Ellery St, Box 1116, Suva; tel. and fax 3315388; e-mail fijimedassoc@connect.com.fj; f. 1953; 215 mems; Pres. Dr MARY SCHRAMM; publ. *Fiji Medical Journal* (4 a year).

Libraries and Archives

Lautoka

Western Regional Library: POB 150, Lautoka; tel. 6660091; f. 1964; books, periodicals, audio-visual cassette tapes.

Suva

Library Service of Fiji: Ministry of Education, POB 2526, Govt Bldgs, Suva; tel. 3315344; fax 3314994; f. 1964; public spec. and school library service; 12 e-Community Learning Centres, 1 mobile library, 28 school media centres, 40 govt dept libraries; 1,500,000 vols; Principal Librarian SOKOVETI TUIMOALA; publ. *Fiji National Bibliography* (publ. suspended until 2009).

National Archives of Fiji: POB 2125, Government Bldgs, Suva; Located at: 25 Carnarvon St, Suva; tel. 3304144; fax 3307006; f. 1954 as the Central Archives of Fiji and the Western Pacific High Commission; Govt records since 1871, Anglican and Methodist church records since 1835; 10,000 vols of monographs on the South Pacific, files on local newspapers since 1869, Fiji official publs since 1874, 2,800 reels of microfilm; Principal Archivist SETAREKI TALE.

Suva City Library: POB 176, Suva; tel. 3313433; fax 3302158; f. 1909, known as Carnegie Library, until 1953; public lending library; 77,000 vols (48,000 in children's library, 29,000 in adults' library), 25 periodicals; special collection: Fiji and the Pacific; mobile library service for schools; Chief Librarian HUMESH PRASAD.

Museums and Art Galleries

Suva

Fiji Museum: POB 2023, Government Buildings, Suva; tel. 3315944; fax 3305143; e-mail information@fijimuseum.org.fj; internet www.fijimuseum.org.fj; f. 1904; contains archaeological, ethnological and historical collections relating to Fiji; archives of Fijian oral traditions; photographic archives; Dir SAGALE BUADROMO; publs *Bulletin* (irregular), *Domodomo* (2 a year).

University

UNIVERSITY OF THE SOUTH PACIFIC

Private Mail Bag, Suva
Telephone: 3313900
Fax: 3301305
Internet: www.usp.ac.fj

Founded 1968
State control; regional university with 12 island State mems
Language of instruction: English
Academic year: February to November (two semesters)

Extension centres in the Cook Islands, Fiji, Kiribati, Marshall Islands, Nauru, Niue, Samoa, Solomon Islands, Tonga, Tuvalu, Vanuatu; link arrangements with Tokelau; the university's second campus is in Alafua, Samoa; third campus is in Vanuatu

Chancellor: FIAME NAOMI MATA'AFA
Vice-Chancellor (vacant)
Deputy Vice-Chancellor: Dr KONAIHOLEVA THAMAN (acting)
Pro-Vice Chancellors: Prof. ALBERT EBENEBE, Prof. JOHN LYNCH MERE PULEA
Registrar: WALTER FRASER
Librarian: ESTHER WININAMAORI WILLIAMS

Library of 830,000 vols
Number of teachers: 1,159
Number of students: 6,204 on campus, 9,109 extension students

Publications: *Alafua Agricultural Bulletin*, *Journal of Pacific Studies*, *Pacific Islands Communications Journal*, *SSED Review* (4 a year), *South Pacific Agricultural News* (every 2 weeks)

HEADS OF SCHOOLS

School of Agriculture: Prof. ALBERT EBENEBE (acting)
School of Humanities: Dr AKINISI KEDRAYATE
School of Law: Prof. ROBERT HUGHES
School of Pure and Applied Sciences: Dr ANJEELA JOKHAN
School of Social and Economic Development: Dr ROPATE QALO

PROFESSORS

BHASKARA, R., Economics
CAMPBELL, I., History and Politics
GASKELL, I., Literature and Language
HASSALL, G., Governance
HUGHES, R., Law
MEAKINS, R., Biology
NUNN, P., Oceanic Geoscience
OMLIN, C., Computer Science
ONWOBOLU, G., Engineering
PATHAK, R., Management
PETERSON, R., Banking
SHARMA, M. D., Banking
SOTHEESWARAN, S., Organic Chemistry
SUBRAMANI, Literature and Language
THAMAN, R., Pacific Island Biogeography
WHITE, M., Accounting and Financial Management
ZANN, L., Marine Studies

ATTACHED INSTITUTES

Centre for Development Studies: Dir Prof. ROBERT ROBERTSON.

Centre for the Enhancement of Learning and Teaching: Dir EILEEN TUIMALEALI'IFANO (acting).

Herbarium: Curator MARIKA TUIWAWA.

Institute of Applied Sciences: Dir WILLIAM AALBERSBORG.

Institute of Education: Dir Dr GEORGE TEESDALE.

Institute of Justice and Applied Legal Studies: Dir MERE PULEA.

Institute of Marine Resources: Dir AVINASH SINGH (acting).

Institute of Pacific Studies: Dir A. RAVUVU.

Institute for Research, Extension and Training in Agriculture: Dir MOHAMMED UMAR.

Oceania Centre for Arts and Culture: Dir Dr E. HAU'OFA.

Pacific Centre for Environmental and Sustainable Development: Curator MURARI LAL.

Pacific Institute of Advanced Studies in Development and Governance: Exec. Dir Dr RONALD DUNCAN.

Pacific Institute of Management: Dir Prof. Jan Nowak.

Colleges

Fiji College of Agriculture: POB 1544, Koronivia, Nausori; tel. 3479200; fax 3400275; e-mail elenibai@is.com.fj; f. 1954, reorganized 1962; three-year diploma course in tropical agriculture; library: library of 9,000 books, 450 periodicals; 10 teachers; 150 students; Principal Fiuwaki Waqalala; publs *Annual Report*, *Annual Research Report*, *Fiji Agricultural Journal* (2 a year), *Fiji Farmer*, *MAFF Newsletter* (12 a year), *MAFF Technical Bulletin* (12 a year).

Fiji Institute of Technology: POB 3722, Samabula, Suva; tel. 3381044; fax 3370375; e-mail webmaster@fit.ac.fj; internet www.fit.ac.fj; f. 1964 as Derrick Technical Institute; courses in building and civil engineering, business studies, electrical and electronic engineering, mechanical engineering, aeronautical engineering, maritime studies, printing, graphic design, hospitality and tourism, automobile engineering, applied computing, applied science, secretarial studies, agricultural engineering, environmental science, occupational health and safety, general studies; 210 full-time teachers; 6,000 students; library: 50,000 vols; Dir Kolino Meo.

Fiji School of Medicine: Private Mail Bag, Hoodless House, CWM Hospital Campus, Suva; tel. 3311700; fax 3303469; internet www.fsm.ac.fj; f. 1885 as Suva Medical School, reorganized as Central Medical School 1928; present name 1961; courses in medicine, dentistry, physiotherapy, environmental health, radiography, medical laboratory technology, dietetics and nutrition and pharmacy; 780 students; library: 16,000 vols; Dean Dr Wame Baravilala.

FINLAND

The Higher Education System

The higher education system consists of two parallel systems, universities and polytechnics: universities focus on academic teaching and research while polytechnics specialize on professional and vocational training. The structure of the degree system is the same in both sectors. There are 21 universities and 29 polytechnics. The oldest university is the Kuvataideakatemia (Academy of Fine Arts), which was founded in 1848.

All universities are state-owned and are administered by the Ministry of Education's Division for Higher Education and Science. University-level education is free but students may be required to pay extraneous services, such as healthcare and compulsory membership of the Student's Union. Under the Universities Act, universities are obliged to promote free research and provide free education. Universities enjoy relative autonomy in decision-making, based on three-year performance agreements with the Ministry of Education. Government funding accounts for about 64% of university budgets, with the rest coming from the Academy of Finland, the Technology Development Centre Tekes, business enterprises, the EU and other public bodies.

The current polytechnic system emerged during the 1990s and was in place by 2000. Like the universities, the polytechnics are controlled by the Division for Higher Education and Science within the Ministry of Education. The polytechnics are a mix of municipal and private ownership. Funding of public polytechnics is shared between central Government and local government. Polytechnics follow performance agreements made with the Ministry of Education.

Admission to both universities and polytechnics is on the basis of completed secondary education and entrance examination. University admissions are subjected to the Universities Decree (115/1998), and admission to polytechnics is governed by the Polytechnic Studies Act (351/2003). In 2005 a two-tier Bachelors and Masters degree system was implemented in both universities and polytechnics, in accordance with the Bologna Process. The award of degrees is based on a US-style academic 'credit' system. The university Bachelors degree lasts for three years and students must accrue 120 credits; the university Masters degree is a two-year course requiring 40–60 credits. The polytechnic Bachelors requires 120–160 credits over three-and-a-half to four years, and the polytechnic Masters 40–60 credits in one-and-a-half years. (Admission to the polytechnic Masters requires a polytechnic Bachelors and three years' professional experience.)

In some subject-areas the old-style degree system remains in place. For dentistry, medicine, and veterinary medicine, the first degree is the Lisensiaatti or Licentiate, which requires 200–250 credits and takes five to six years. The Lisensiaatti/Licentiate is a doctoral-level degree. Students who have received the Masters may take the Tohtori or Doctorate, which last four years. In addition to the technical and vocational education offered by polytechnics there is also an apprenticeship scheme combining workplace and classroom learning.

Regulatory and Representative Bodies

GOVERNMENT

Ministry of Education: POB 29, 00023 Government; Meritullinkatu 10, 00171 Helsinki; tel. (9) 16004; fax (9) 1359335; e-mail opmkirjaamo@minedu.fi; internet www.minedu.fi; Minister SARI SARKOMAA.

FUNDING

Suomen Akatemia (Academy of Finland): Vilhonvuorenkatu 6, POB 99, 00501 Helsinki; tel. (9) 774881; fax (9) 77488299; e-mail kirjaamo@aka.fi; internet www.aka.fi; funding org. for scientific research; works to advance the renewal and diversity of research, and supports the extensive application of research results for the benefit of welfare, culture, the economy and the environment; promotes equal opportunities in research; has wide range of funding instruments tailored to different purposes; funded research projects account for c. 3,000 researcher FTEs at univs and research institutes; operates within the administrative sector of Min. of Education and receives its funding through the state budget; Pres. MARKKU MATTILA; Vice-Pres RIITTA MUSTONEN, JUHA SARKIO.

Tekes/Teknologian ja Innovaatioiden Kehittämiskeskus (Finnish Funding Agency for Technology and Innovation): POB 69, Kyllikinportti 2, 00101 Helsinki; tel. (0) 10191480; fax (0) 106055050; e-mail tekes@tekes.fi; internet www.tekes.fi; f. 1983; funding org. for research and devt projects run by private enterprise, research institutes and univs; invested 465m. euros in research and innovation activity during 2006; encourages co-operation between differing fields of technology; assists companies to conduct meaningful and valuable research; does not derive any financial profit from its endeavours, nor does it claim any intellectual proprietary rights; has Technology Devt Depts at 14 regional Employment and Economic Devt Centres (known as the T&E Centres); maintains offices in Beijing, Brussels, Tokyo, San Jose, Silicon Valley, Shanghai and Washington, DC; Dir-Gen. Dr VELI-PEKKA SAARNIVAARA.

NATIONAL BODIES

Arene ry/Ammattikorkeoulujen rehtorineuvosto (Finnish Conference of Polytechnic Rectors): Rikhardinkatu 4 B 22, 00130 Helsinki; tel. (9) 6129920; fax (9) 61299230; e-mail timo.luopajarvi@arene.fi; internet www.arene.fi; Sec.-Gen. TIMO LUOPAJÄRVI.

Suomen yliopistojen rehtorien neuvosto (Finnish Council of University Rectors): POB 3 (Fabianinkatu 33), 00014 Univ. of Helsinki; tel. (9) 19122335; fax (9) 19122194; e-mail rectors-council@helsinki.fi; internet www.rectors-council.helsinki.fi; f. 1969; promotes and contributes to co-operation between univs and helps them to achieve their common strategic goals; works with political decision-makers, nat. authorities, ministries and central interest groups to advance research and higher education in Finland; strengthens the role of univs as key partners in social and political discussion; promotes int. co-operation between univs, especially in the Nordic countries, Europe and Asia; 21 mems; Sec.-Gen. Dr LIISA SAVUNEN.

Learned Societies

GENERAL

Finska Vetenskaps-Societeten/Suomen Tiedeseura (Finnish Society of Sciences and Letters): Hallituskatu 2B, 00170 Helsinki; tel. (9) 633005; fax (9) 661065; e-mail societas@scientiarum.fi; internet www.scientiarum.fi; f. 1838; 339 mems; Chair. Prof. LEIF C. ANDERSSON; Permanent Sec. Prof. CARL G. GAHMBERG; publs *Bidrag till kännedom av Finlands natur och folk*, *Commentationes Humanarum Litterarum*, *Commentationes Scientiarum Socialium*, *Sphinx-Årsbok-Vuosikirja* (Yearbook).

Suomalainen Tiedeakatemia (Finnish Academy of Science and Letters): Mariankatu 5, 00170 Helsinki; tel. (9) 636800; fax (9) 660117; e-mail acadsci@acadsci.fi; internet www.acadsci.fi; f. 1908; 571 ordinary mems, 210 foreign mems; Pres. SIMO KNUUTTILA; Sec.-Gen. MATTI SAARNISTO; publs *Annales Academiae Scientiarum Fennicae* (in 2 series: mathematics and humanities), *Folklore Fellows' Communications*, *Yearbook*.

Tieteellisten seurain valtuuskunta/Vetenskapliga samfundens delegation (Federation of Finnish Learned Societies): Mariankatu 5, 00170 Helsinki; tel. (9) 228691; fax (9) 22869291; e-mail tsv@tsv.fi; internet www.tsv.fi; f. 1899 to promote scholarly publishing, scientific information, scientific co-operation and science policy; houses the Exchange Centre for Scientific Literature and a meeting and conference centre; 231 mem. socs; Pres. Prof. ILKKA NIINILUOTO; Dir Dr AURA KORPPI-TOMMOLA; publs *Catalogue* (every 2 years), *Tieteessä tapahtuu* (journal, 8 a year).

AGRICULTURE, FISHERIES AND VETERINARY SCIENCE

Meijeritieteellinen Seura r.y. (Finnish Society for Dairy Science): Dept of Food Technology, POB 30, 00039 Valio; f. 1938 to promote research work and co-operation in the field of dairy science; 200 mems; Chair. Prof. TAPANI ALATOSSAVA; Sec. JANNE UUSI-RAUVA; publ. *Meijeritieteellinen Aikakauskirja* (Finnish Journal of Dairy Science).

Suomen Eläinlääkäriliitto (Finnish Veterinary Association): Makelankatu 2C, 00500 Helsinki; tel. (9) 77454810; fax (9) 77454818; internet www.sell.fi; f. 1892 to promote veterinary science and the practice of veterinary medicine; 1,976 mems; Chair. ANTTI NURMINEN; Chief Exec. MIKA LEPPINEN; publ. *Suomen Eläinlääkärilehti* (Finnish Veterinary Journal, monthly).

Suomen Maataloustieteellinen Seura r.y. (Scientific Agricultural Society of Finland): c/o MTT Agrifood Research Finland Economic Research, Luutnantintie 13, 00410 Jokioinen; tel. (9) 56080; fax (9) 5631164; e-mail maataloustieteenpaivat@smts.fi; internet www.smts.fi; f. 1909; 504 mems; Pres. Prof. JARI VALKONEN; Sec. KIRSI PARTANEN; publ. *Agricultural and Food Science* (4–6 a year).

Suomen Metsätieteellinen Seura (Finnish Society of Forestry Science): Unioninkatu 40A, 00170 Helsinki; tel. (9) 658707; fax (10) 2112102; e-mail sms@helsinki.fi; internet www.metla.fi/org/sms; f. 1909 to encourage forest research work in Finland; composed of persons devoting themselves to the study of forestry and its underlying theory; colln of vols held within the Viikki Science Library (see Libraries and Archives); 550 mems; Pres. Dr PEKKA SARANPÄÄ; Sec.-Gen. Dr EIJA JUUROLA; publs *Silva Fennica* (quarterly), *Metsätieteen aikakauskirja* (4 a year), *Silva Fennica Monographs* (irregular).

BIBLIOGRAPHY, LIBRARY SCIENCE AND MUSEOLOGY

Suomen Kirjastoseura (Finnish Library Association): Vuorikatu 22 A 18, 00100 Helsinki; tel. (9) 6221399; fax (9) 6221466; e-mail fla@fla.fi; internet kirjastoseura.kaapeli.fi; f. 1910; 2,000 mems; Pres. TARJA CRONBERG; Sec.-Gen. SINIKKA SIPILÄ; publ. *Kirjastolehti* (Bulletin, 7 a year).

Suomen Museoliitto/Finlands Museiförbund (Finnish Museums Association): Annankatu 16 B 50, 00120 Helsinki; tel. (9) 58411700; fax (9) 58411750; e-mail museoliitto@museoliitto.fi; internet www.museoliitto.fi; f. 1923; 191 mem. museums; library of 2,000 vols; Sec.-Gen ANJA-TUULIKKI HUOVINEN; publ. *Museo* (quarterly).

Suomen Tieteellinen Kirjastoseura (Finnish Research Library Association): POB 39, 00014 University of Helsinki; tel. (9) 61299240; fax (9) 61299230; e-mail meri.kuula-bruun@aka.fi; internet pro.tsv.fi/stks; f. 1929; 696 mems; Pres. TUULA RUHANEN; Sec. MERI KUULA-BRUUN; publ. *Signum* (Bulletin, 8 a year).

ECONOMICS, LAW AND POLITICS

Ekonomiska Samfundet i Finland (Economic Society of Finland): Swedish School of Economics and Business Administration, POB 479, 00101 Helsinki; tel. (9) 431331; fax (9) 43133333; f. 1894; 780 mems; Pres. HENRIK WINBERG; Sec. NIKOLAS ROKKANEN (acting); publ. *Ekonomiska Samfundets Tidskrift* (Journal, 3 a year).

Finnish Legal Society: Advokatbyrå Borenius & Kemppinen Ab, Georgsgatan 13A, 00120 Helsinki; tel. (9) 61533489; fax (9) 61533499; f. 1862; 794 mems; Pres. GUSTAF MÖLLER; Sec. JOHAN ROMAN; publ. *Tidskrift utgiven av Juridiska Föreningen i Finland*.

Hallinnon Tutkimuksen Seura r.y./Sällskapet för Förvaltningsforskning (Finnish Association for Administrative Studies): Dept of Political Science, POB 54, 00014 Univ. of Helsinki; tel. (9) 19124905; e-mail minna.tiili@helsinki.fi; internet www.uta.fi/jarjestot/hts; f. 1981; aims: to function as a common link for depts and researchers studying admin. questions, to co-ordinate the planning and surveillance of training in admin. sciences, to hold lectures and discussions, to take part in int. scientific co-operation; a mem. of the European Group of Public Admin.; 660 individual mems, 4 organizational mems; Pres. TURO VIRTANEN; Sec. MINNA TIILI; publ. *Hallinnon Tutkimus* (quarterly).

International Law Association, Finnish Branch: Regissorsvagen 22 A7, 00400 Helsingfors; e-mail finnish-ila@helsinki.fi; f. 1946; 105 mems; Pres. Prof. BENGT BROMS; Hon. Sec. MATTI TUPAMÄKI.

Ius Gentium (Finnish International Law Association): POB 208, 00171 Helsinki; tel. (9) 19122468; fax (9) 19123076; e-mail ius-gentium@helsinki.fi; internet www.helsinki.fi/jarj/iusgentium; f. 1983; research on int. law and legal theory; organizes seminars and lectures on topics relating to int. law and legal theory; 100 mems; Chair. ANJA LINDROOS; publs *Acta Societatis Fennicae Iuris Gentium, Finnish Yearbook of International Law, Kansainoikeus/Ius Gentium*, A, B and C Series.

Kansantaloudellinen Yhdistys (Finnish Economic Association): c/o Merja Kauhanen, Labour Institute for Economic Research, Pitkänsillanreta 3A, 00530 Helsinki; tel. (9) 25357345; e-mail yhdistys@ktyhdistys.net; internet www.ktyhdistys.net; f. 1884; 1,012 mems; Pres. JUHA TARKKA; Sec. and Treas. MERJA KAUHANEN; publs *Kansantaloudellinen Aikakauskirja* (Finnish Economic Journal), *Kansantaloudellisia Tutkimuksia* (Economic Studies).

Suomalainen Lakimiesyhdistys (Finnish Lawyers' Society): Kasarmikatu 23 A 17, 00130 Helsinki; tel. (9) 6120300; fax (9) 604668; e-mail sly@lakimies.org; internet www.lakimies.org; f. 1898; 3,000 mems; Pres. PEKKA VIHERVUORI; Sec. HANNELE KLEMETTINEN; publs *Lakimies-aikakauskirja* (8 a year), *Oikeustiede-Jurisprudentia* (annually), *Suomalaisen Lakimiesyhdistyksen Julkaisuja* (series A, B, C, D and E).

Suomen Tilastoseura/Statistiska Samfundet i Finland (Finnish Statistical Society): c/o Statistics Finland, POB 4A, 00022; tel. (9) 173412628; internet www.stat.fi/sts; f. 1920; aims to promote the development of theoretical and applied statistics, to unite statisticians working in various fields, to promote statistical education and research; 500 mems; Pres. LAURI TARKKONEN; Sec. MARIA VALASTE.

Suomen Väestötieteen Yhdistys (Finnish Demographic Society): c/o Hanna Remes, Dept of Sociology, POB 18, 00014 Univ. of Helsinki; tel. (9) 19123896; fax (9) 19123967; internet blogit.helsinki.fi/svy; f. 1973; fosters research and promotes interaction between scholars in the field of population studies; 101 mems; Chair. Prof. Dr KARI PITKÄNEN; Sec. HANNA REMES.

Suomen Ympäristöoikeustieteen Seura/Miljörättsliga Sällskapet i Finland (Finnish Society of Environmental Law): POB 1225, 00101 Helsinki; tel. (9) 27091890; fax (9) 6222293; e-mail sys@pro.tsv.fi; internet pro.tsv.fi/sys; f. 1980 to support and promote legal and administrative research of environmental problems, and to promote co-operation between researchers and authorities; 360 mems; Chair. Prof. ERKKI J. HOLLO; Sec. ROBERT UTTER; publ. *Ympäristöjuridiikka-Miljöjuridik* (Journal of Environmental Law).

Suomen Taloushistoriallinen Yhdistys (Economic History Society of Finland): Dept of History and Ethnology, University of Jyväskylä, POB 35 (H), 40014 Jyväskylä; tel. (14) 2601269; e-mail jaojala@campus.jyu.fi; f. 1952; studies economic and social history; 98 mems; Chair. Dr ILKKA NUMMELA; Hon. Sec. Prof. JARI OJALA; publ. *Scandinavian Economic History Review* (in co-operation with other Scandinavian societies for the advancement of the study of economic history).

FINE AND PERFORMING ARTS

Suomen Musiikkitieteellinen Seura r.y./Musikvetenskapliga Sällskapet i Finland r.f. (Finnish Musicological Society): Arwidssoninkatu 1, University of Turku, 20014 Turku; tel. (14) 2601348; fax (14) 2601331; e-mail sanqvi@cc.jyu.fi; internet www.jyu.fi/musica/mts; f. 1917; aims to encourage musicological research, develop international exchanges, and to function for the good of Finnish musical life by broadening knowledge of music and musical culture; 200 mems; Chair. Prof. ANNE SIVUOJA-GUNARATNAM; Sec.-Gen. SANNA QVICK; publs *Acta Musicologica Fennica, Musiikki* (4 a year).

Suomen Näytelmäkirjailjalitto (Finnish Dramatists' Society): Vironkatu 12B, 00170 Helsinki 17; f. 1921; Pres. ESKO SALERVO; Sec. PIRJO WESTMAN.

Suomen Säveltäjät r.y. (Society of Finnish Composers): Runeberginkatu 15A 11, 00100 Helsinki 10; tel. (9) 445589; fax (9) 440181; e-mail saveltajat@composers.fi; internet www.composers.fi; f. 1945; 151 mems; Pres. Prof. MIKKO HEINIÖ; Exec. Dir ANNU MIKKONEN.

Suomen Taideyhdistys (Fine Arts Society of Finland): Helsingin Taidehalli, Nervanderinkatu 3, 00100 Helsinki; tel. (9) 45420611; fax (9) 45420610; e-mail info@taidehalli.fi; internet www.suomentaideyhdistys.fi; f. 1846; arranges exhibitions, presents awards and scholarships; 3,000 mems; Pres. JAAKKO ILONIEMI; Sec. TIMO VALJAKKA.

Suomen Taiteilijaseura/Konstnärsgillet i Finland (Artists' Association of Finland): Nilsiänkatu 11-13 F 5, 00510 Helsinki; tel. (9) 61292120; fax (9) 61292160; e-mail suomen.taiteilijaseura@artists.fi; internet www.artists.fi; f. 1864; 2,300 mems; mem. socs consist of the Painters' Union of Finland, the Sculptors' Union of Finland, the Association of Graphic Artists in Finland, the Finnish Association of Artists in Photography and the Federation of the Fine Arts Associations in Finland; promotes professional interests of artists and holds an annual exhibition; Chair. KARI JYLHÄ; Sec.-Gen. PIIA RANTALA; publs *Taide* (Art), *Taiteilija-lenti* (4 a year).

Taidehistorian seura/Föreningen för konsthistoria r.y. (Society for Art History in Finland): PL 3, 00014 University of Helsinki; Unioninkatu 34, 00014 University of Helsinki; fax (9) 19122961; e-mail sihteeri@taidehistorianseura.fi; internet www.taidehistorianseura.fi; f. 1974 to promote research in art history in Finland; 483 mems; Pres. RENJA SUOMINEN-KOKKONEN; publ. *Taidehistoriallisia tutkimuksia/Konsthistoriska studier (Studies in Art History)*.

Turun Soitannollinen Seura (Musical Society of Turku): Sibelius Museum, Piispankatu 17, Turku; tel. (2) 2313789; fax (2) 518528; internet www.musisoi.net/yhteys .html; f. 1790; 655 mems; Pres. ALARIK REPO.

HISTORY, GEOGRAPHY AND ARCHAEOLOGY

Historian Ystäväin Liitto (Society of the Friends of History): Tieteiden talo, Kirkkokatu 6, 00170 Helsinki; tel. (9) 22869351; e-mail shs@histseura.fi; internet pro.tsv.fi/hyl; f. 1926; 1,500 mems; Sec. JULIA BURMAN; publs *Historiallinen Aikakauskirja* (Finnish Historical Review, quarterly), *Historiallinen Kirjasto* (both irregular), *Historian Aitta*.

Suomen Historiallinen Seura/Finska Historiska Samfundet (Finnish Historical Society): Tieteiden talo, Kirkkokatu 6, 00170 Helsinki; tel. (9) 22869351; fax (9) 22869266; e-mail shs@histseura.fi; internet www .histseura.fi; f. 1875; 900 mems; Chair. Dr Prof. KIMMO KATAJALA; Sec. JULIA BURMAN; publs *Bibliotheca Historica* (historical studies in Finnish, English and German), *Historiallinen Arkisto* (Historical Archives), *Historiallisia Tutkimuksia* (Historical Researches), *Suomen historian lähteitä* (Sources of the History of Finland), *Studia Fennica: Historica*, *Studia Historica* (historical studies in German, French and English).

Suomen Kirkkohistoriallinen Seura/ Finska Kyrkohistoriska Samfundet (Finnish Society of Church History): Dept of Church History, POB 33 (Aleksanterinkatu 7), 00014 Univ. of Helsinki; tel. (9) 19122055; fax (9) 19123033; e-mail jaakko.antila@ helsinki.fi; internet www.skhs.fi; f. 1891; 700 mems; Chair. Assoc. Prof. MIKKO KETOLA; Sec. JAAKKO ANTILA; publs *Toimituksia-Handlingar* (research papers, 3–6 a year), *Vuosikirja-Årsskrift* (Yearbook).

Suomen Maantieteellinen Seura/Geografiska Sällskapet i Finland (Geographical Society of Finland): c/o Dept of Geography, POB 64 (Kumpula campus), 00014 University of Helsinki; tel. (9) 19150763; fax (9) 19150760; internet www .helsinki.fi/ml/maant/geofi; f. 1888; 1,300 mems; library of 56,000 vols; Pres. Dr KATARIINA KOSONEN; Sec. P. HELLEMAA; publs *Fennia* (2 a year), *Terra* (quarterly).

Suomen Muinaismuistoyhdistys/Finska Fornminnesföreningen (Finnish Antiquarian Society): POB 913, 00101 Helsinki 10; tel. (9) 40501; fax (9) 40509400; e-mail sihteeri@muinaismuistoyhdistys.fi; internet www.muinaismuistoyhdistys.fi; f. 1870; 600 mems; Pres. HELENA EDGREN; Sec. HANNA FORSSELL; publs *Finskt Museum*, *Iskos*, *Kansatieteellinen Arkisto*, *Suomen Muinaismuistoyhdistyksen Aikakauskirja—Finska Fornminnesföreningens Tidskrift*, *Suomen Museo*.

Suomen Sukututkimusseura/Genealogiska Samfundet i Finland (Genealogical Society of Finland): Liisankatu 16A, 00170 Helsinki; tel. (9) 2781188; fax (9) 2781199; e-mail samfundet@genealogia.fi; internet www.genealogia.fi; f. 1917; 5,950 mems; library of 42,000 vols; Pres. JOHAN STÅHL; Exec. Dir P. T. KUUSILUOMA; publs *Genos* (quarterly), *Vuosikirja—Årsskrift* (Yearbook).

LANGUAGE AND LITERATURE

British Council: Urho Kekkosen katu 2C, 00100 Helsinki; tel. (9) 7743330; fax (9) 7018725; e-mail office@britishcouncil.fi; internet www.britishcouncil.fi; provides information about study opportunities in the United Kingdom; offers the IELTS English language exam and promotes cultural exchange with the United Kingdom; Dir TUIJA TALVITIE.

Finlands svenska författareförening (Society of Swedish Authors in Finland): Urho Kekkonens gata 8 B 14, 00100 Helsinki; tel. (9) 446266; e-mail forfattarna@ kaapeli.fi; internet www.forfattarna.fi; f. 1919; 191 mems; Pres. MIKAELA SUNDSTRÖM; Sec.-Gen. MERETE JENSEN.

Goethe-Institut: Mannerheimintie 20A, 00100 Helsinki; tel. (9) 6803550; fax (9) 604377; e-mail info@helsinki.goethe.org; internet www.goethe.de/ne/hel/deindex.htm; offers courses and exams in German language and culture and promotes cultural exchange with Germany; library of 2,800 vols, 30 periodicals; Dir EIKE FUHRMANN.

Klassillis-filologinen yhdistys (Society for Classical Philology): c/o Klassillisen filologian laitos, PL 4, 00014 University of Helsinki; fax (9) 19122161; internet www .helsinki.fi/hum/kla/kfy; f. 1882; promotes the study of classical philology and classical antiquity in general; 92 mems; Pres. ANNELI LUHTALA; Sec. MATIAS BUCHHOLZ; publ. *Arctos; Acta Philologica Fennica* (annual).

Kotikielen Seura (Society for the Study of Finnish): Castrenianum, PL 3, 00014 University of Helsinki; fax (9) 19123329; e-mail seura@kotikielenseura.fi; internet www .kotikielenseura.fi; f. 1876; Finnish linguistics; 792 mems; Pres. Prof. MARJA-LEENA SORJONEN; Sec. JOHANNA KOMPPA; publ. *Virittäjä* (quarterly).

Suomalais-Ugrilainen Seura (Finno-Ugrian Society): Mariankatu 7, POB 320, 00171 Helsinki; tel. (9) 662149; fax (9) 6988249; internet www.sgr.fi; f. 1883; Northern Eurasian linguistics and ethnography; 800 mems; Pres. Prof. Dr ULLA-MAIJA KULONEN; Sec. PAULA KOKKONEN; publs *Finnisch-Ugrische Forschungen* (every 2 years), *Journal* (every 2 years), *Mémoires* (2–5 a year).

Suomalaisen Kirjallisuuden Seura/ Finska Litteratursällskapet (Finnish Literature Society): Hallituskatu 1, POB 259, 00171 Helsinki 17; tel. (20) 1131231; fax (9) 13123220; e-mail sks@finlit.fi; internet www .finlit.fi; f. 1831 to promote study of folklore, ethnology, literature and Finnish language; 3,700 mems; Chair. Prof. PENTTI LEINO; Dir-Gen. and Sec. TUOMAS LEHTONEN; library: see Libraries and Archives; publs *Studia Fennica: Ethnologica*, *Studia Fennica: Folkloristica*, *Studia Fennica: Historica*, *Studia Fennica: Linguistica* (annually), *Studia Fennica: Litteraria*.

Suomen englanninopettajat r.y. (Association of Teachers of English in Finland): Rautatieläisenkatu 6A, 00520 Helsinki; tel. (9) 145414; fax (9) 2788100; e-mail english@ suomenenglanninopettajat.fi; internet www .suomenenglanninopettajat.fi; f. 1948; 2,900 mems; Pres. ANNE ONTERO; publ. *Tempus* (8 a year).

Suomen Kirjailijaliitto (The Union of Finnish Writers): Runeberginkatu 32, C28, 00100 Helsinki; tel. (9) 449752; e-mail info@ suomenkirjailijaliitto.fi; internet www .suomenkirjailijaliitto.fi; f. 1897; allied to the Scandinavian Authors' Council and European Writers' Congress; 520 mems; Gen. Sec. PÄIVI LIEDES; publs *Suomalaiset kertojat*, *Suomen Runotar*.

Svenska litteratursällskapet i Finland (Society of Swedish Literature in Finland): Riddareg. 5, 00170 Helsinki; tel. (9) 618777; fax (9) 61877377; e-mail info@sls.fi; internet www.sls.fi; f. 1885; 1,100 mems; library: see Libraries and Archives; Pres. Prof. HÅKAN ANDERSSON; Sec. Prof. ANN-MARIE IVARS; publ. *Skrifter* (10–15 a year).

Uusfilologinen Yhdistys (Modern Language Society): POB 24, 00014 University of Helsinki; tel. (9) 19123531; fax (9) 19122384; e-mail ufy-sihteeri@helsinki.fi; internet www .helsinki.fi/jarj/ufy; f. 1887; 244 mems; Pres. Prof. JUHANI HÄRMÄ; Hon. Sec. MARIANNA HINTIKKA; publs *Mémoires* (irreg.), *Neuphilologische Mitteilungen* (Bulletin, quarterly).

MEDICINE

Cancer Society of Finland: Liisankatu 21B, 00170 Helsinki; tel. (9) 135331; fax (9) 1351093; e-mail society@cancer.fi; internet www.cancer.fi; f. 1936; 140,000 ; Pres. HEIKKI JOENSUU; Sec.-Gen. HARRI VERTIO; publs *Syöpä – Cancer* (6 a year), *Focus Oncologie* (annually).

Finska Läkaresällskapet (Medical Society of Finland): Johannesbergsvägen 8, POB 82, 00251 Helsinki; tel. (9) 47768090; fax (9) 4362055; e-mail fls@fls.pp.fi; internet www .kulturfonden.fi/fls; f. 1835; 1,000 mems; library of 35,000 vols; Pres. Prof. LEIF ANDERSON; Sec. Dr MARIANNE GRIPENBERG; publ. *Finska Läkaresällskapets Handlingar*.

Suomalainen Lääkäriseura Duodecim (Finnish Medical Society Duodecim): Kalevankatu 11A, 00100 Helsinki; tel. (9) 618851; fax (9) 61885200; internet www.duodecim.fi; f. 1881; 18,100 mems; library of 17,000 vols; Pres. Prof. KIMMO KONTULA; Sec. Dr ILKKA RAURAMO; publ. *Duodecim* (24 a year).

Suomen Farmaseuttinen Yhdistys/ Farmaceutiska Föreningen i Finland (Finnish Pharmaceutical Society): Fredrikinkatu 61, 00100 Helsinki; internet pro.tsv.fi/finpharmsociety; f. 1887; 290 mems; Pres. TOM WIKBERG; Sec. LEENA PELTONEN.

Suomen Hammaslääkäriseura Apollonia (Finnish Dental Society Apollonia): Bulevardi 30 B 5, 00120 Helsinki; tel. (9) 6803120; fax (9) 646263; e-mail toimisto@ apollonia.fi; internet www.apollonia.fi; f. 1892; 5,900 mems; Pres. Prof. KYÖSTI OIKARINEN; Gen. Sec. Assoc. Prof. MAIJA T. LAINE-ALAVA.

NATURAL SCIENCES

Biological Sciences

Birdlife Finland: POB 1285, 00101 Helsinki; Annankatu 29A, 00101 Helsinki; tel. (9) 41353300; fax (9) 41353322; e-mail office@ birdlife.fi; internet www.birdlife.fi; f. 1973; promotes bird-watching, research and protection of birds, their habitats and biological diversity; 30 nat. assoc. orgs; affiliated to BirdLife International; 9,000 mems; Dir MIKA ASIKAINEN; publs *Linnut* (Birds, quarterly), *Ornis Fennica* (quarterly).

Kasvinsuojeluseura r.y. (Plant Protection Society): ARaitamaantie 8A (Kannelmäki), 00420 Helsinki; tel. (9) 4770790; fax (9) 47707920; internet www.kasvinsuojeluseura .fi; f. 1931; research on, and protection from, diseases, pests and weeds; arranges meetings and excursions, awards grants to researchers; 1,500 mems; Chair. HANNU SEPPANEN; Sec. MINNA-MARIA LINNA; publ. *Kasvinsuojelulehti*.

Societas Amicorum Naturae Ouluensis/ Oulun Luonnonystäväin Yhdistys r.y.: Dept of Biology (Botany), University of Oulu, 90570 Oulu; tel. (8) 5531546; fax (8) 5531500; f. 1925; 436 mems; Pres. Prof. P. LAHDESMAKI; Sec. S. KONTUNEN-SOPPELA; publs *Aquilo, Ser. Botanica*, *Ser. Zoologica*.

Societas Biochemica, Biophysica et Microbiologica Fenniae (Biochemical, Biophysical and Microbiological Society of Finland): c/o Dr Laura Seppä-Fagerhed, Viikki Biocenter, POB 56, 00014 University of Helsinki; tel. (9) 19159428; fax (9) 19159570; internet www.biobio.org; f. 1945;

900 mems; Pres. Dr MARC BAUMANN; Sec. Dr LAURA SEPPÄ-FAGERHED.

Societas Biologica Fennica Vanamo/ Suomen Biologian Seura Vanamo: POB 7, Latokartanonkaari 7, University of Helsinki, 00014 Helsinki; internet www.vanamo .fi; f. 1896; Pres. SEPPO TURUNEN; Sec. MARIA PIETILÄINEN; publs *Atlas Florae Europaeae*, *Luonnon Tutkija* (The Naturalist, 5 a year).

Societas Entomologica Fennica–Suomen Hyönteistieteellinen Seura (Entomological Society of Finland): Department for Applied Biology, POB 27, 00014 University of Helsinki; tel. (9) 19158662; fax (9) 19158663; internet www.sls.fi/entomolog; f. 1935; library; Pres. Dr ILKKA TERÄS; Sec. Dr LENA HULDÉN; publ. *Entomologica Fennica* (quarterly).

Societas pro Fauna et Flora Fennica: c/o R. Skytén, Finnish Museum of Natural History, Mycology Division, POB 7, Unionsgatan 44, 00014 University of Helsinki; tel. (9) 19124465; fax (9) 19124456; e-mail roland .skyten@helsinki.fi; internet www.societasfff .fi; f. 1821; discussion and research on all aspects of animals and plants in Finland; 1,025 mems; library of 44,000 vols; Pres. Prof. C.-A. HÆGGSTRÖM; Hon. Sec. R. SKYTÉN; publ. *Memoranda Societatis pro Fauna et Flora Fennica* (3 a year).

Physical Sciences

Geofysiikan Seura/Geofysiska Sällskapet (Geophysical Society of Finland): c/o Taija Huotari, Geological Survey of Finland, POB 96, 02151 Espoo; internet pro.tsv.fi/ geofysiikanseura; f. 1926; aims to promote geophysical research and provide links between researchers; 230 mems; Pres. Prof. MIKKO ALESTALO; Sec. TAIJA HUOTARI; publ. *Geophysica* (2 a year).

Suomen Geologinen Seura/Geologiska Sällskapet i Finland (Geological Society of Finland): POB 96, 02151 Espoo; tel. (9) 2055011; fax (9) 2055012; internet pro.tsv.fi/ sgs; f. 1886; 925 mems; Pres. KEIJO NENONEN; Sec. ANU KAAKINEN; publs *Bulletin* (1 or 2 a year), *Geologi* (10 a year).

Suomen Kemian Seura/Kemiska Sällskapet i Finland (Association of Finnish Chemical Societies): Urho Kekkosen katu 8 C 31, 00100 Helsinki; tel. (9) 4542040; fax (9) 45420440; e-mail toimisto@kemianseura.fi; internet www.kemianseura.fi/; f. 1970 to promote research in chemistry, chemical education, chemical industry; to organize the annual Finnish Chemical Congress; to act as a link between the three mem. socs, and to support and co-ordinate their activities; represents the mem. socs in common matters; 14 sections: wood and polymer chemistry, biotechnology, mass spectrometry, NMR spectroscopy, metal analysis, chromatography, chemometrics, explosives, optical spectroscopy, computational chemistry, catalysis, EURACHEM—Finland, synthetic chemistry, and NBC protection, rescue and safety; library of 800 vols; Chair. LEIF RAMM-SCHMIDT; publs *Kemia-Kemi*, *Acta Chemica Scandinavica*.

Constituent societies:

Finska Kemistsamfundet/Suomen Kemistiseura (Chemical Society of Finland): Hietaniemenkatu 2, 00100 Helsinki; f. 1891; 564 mems; Pres. PEKKA PYYKKÖ; Sec. URBAN WIIK.

Kemiallisteknillinen Yhdistys (Society of Chemical Engineers): Hietaniemenkatu 2, 00100 Helsinki; f. 1970; 816 mems; Pres. JAAKKO E. LAINE; Sec. JUHA VIRTANEN.

Suomalaisten Kemistien Seura (Finnish Chemical Society): Hietaniemenkatu 2, 00100 Helsinki; f. 1919; 3,480 mems; Pres. Dr TIMO NURMI; Sec. HELEENA KARRUS.

PHILOSOPHY AND PSYCHOLOGY

Suomen Filosofinen Yhdistys (Philosophical Society of Finland): Dept of Philosophy, POB 9 (Siltavuorenpenger 20A), 00014 Univ. of Helsinki; tel. (9) 77488232; fax (9) 19129229; e-mail risto.vilkko@helsinki.fi; internet www.helsinki.fi/filosofia/sfy.htm; f. 1873; promotes the study of philosophy and related disciplines in Finland; 480 mems; Pres. Prof. ILKKA NIINILUOTO; Sec. Dr RISTO VILKKO; publs *Acta Philosophica Fennica* (1–3 a year), *Ajatus* (annual).

Suomen Psykologinen Seura r.y. (Finnish Psychological Society): Liisankatu 16A, 00170 Helsinki; tel. (9) 2782122; fax (9) 2781300; e-mail psykologia@genealogia.fi; internet www.psykologienkustannus.fi/sps; f. 1952; 1,800 mems; small library; Pres. JARKKO HAUTAMÄKI; Sec. KATI HEINONEN; publs *Acta Psychologica Fennica* (series A, irregular and series B, annually), *Psykologia* (every 2 months).

RELIGION, SOCIOLOGY AND ANTHROPOLOGY

Suomalainen Teologinen Kirjallisuusseura (Finnish Theological Literature Society): POB 33 (Aleksanterinkatu 7), 00014 University of Helsinki, Helsinki; tel. (9) 19122076; fax (9) 19123033; e-mail stksj@ pro.tsv.fi; internet pro.tsv.fi/stksj; f. 1891; 850 mems; Chair. Prof. SIMO KNUUTTILA.

Suomen Antropologinen Seura/Antropologiska Sällskapet i Finland (Finnish Anthropological Society): Pl 59, 00014 University of Helsinki; tel. (9) 19123094; fax (9) 19123006; internet www.helsinki.fi/ antropologia/suomenantrologinenseura.htm; f. 1975 to promote co-operation between scholars from different fields of anthropology; organizes meetings and conferences; 600 mems; Pres. TIMO KAARTINEN; Sec. TIMO KALLINEN; publ. *Suomen Antropologi / Antropologi i Finland* (Journal of the Finnish Anthropological Society).

Suomen Itämainen Seura (Finnish Oriental Society): c/o Dept of Asian and African Studies, POB 59 (Unioninkatu 38B), 00014 University of Helsinki; fax (9) 19122094; e-mail hannu.juusola@helsinki.fi; internet www.helsinki.fi/hum/aakkl; f. 1917; 192 mems; Pres. Prof. TAPANI HARVIAINEN; Sec. Dr HANNU JUUSOLA; publ. *Studia Orientalia*.

TECHNOLOGY

Maanmittaustieteiden seura r.y. (Finnish Society of Surveying Sciences): Kellosilta 10, 00520 Helsinki; tel. (9) 1481900; fax (9) 1483580; internet mts.fgi.fi; f. 1926; 710 mems; Pres. PEKKA RAHKILA; Sec. MIKKO TAKALO; publ. *Nordic Journal of Surveying and Real Estate Research* (2 a year).

Rakenteiden Mekaniikan Seura (Finnish Association for Structural Mechanics): Dept of Civil and Environmental Engineering, Helsinki University of Technology, POB 2100, 02015 Helsinki University of Technology; tel. (9) 4513751; fax (9) 4513826; e-mail juha.paavola@hut.fi; internet rmseura.tkk.fi; f. 1970 for promoting research and exchange of knowledge on engineering materials, structural mechanics and design; 222 individual mems, 10 collective mems; Chair. JUHA PAAVOLA; Sec. SAMI PAJUNEN; publ. *Rakenteiden Mekaniikka* (Journal of Structural Mechanics, quarterly).

Suomen Atomiteknillinen Seura/Atomtekniska Sällskapet i Finland (Finnish Nuclear Society): c/o VTT, Lämpömiehenkuja 3A, POB 1000, 02044 VTT; tel. (20) 722-111; fax (20) 722-5000; e-mail sihteeri@ats-fns.fi; internet www.ats-fns.fi; f. 1966 to promote knowledge and devt of nuclear technology in Finland, and exchange information on an int. level; seminars and member meetings; 650 individual mems, 20 institutional mems; Chair. HARRIET KALLIO; Sec. JUHA POIKOLAINEN; publ. *ATS Ydintekniikka* (quarterly).

Svenska Tekniska Vetenskapsakademien i Finland (Swedish Academy of Engineering Sciences in Finland): Mariegaten 8 B 11, 00170 Helsinki; tel. (9) 2782400; fax (9) 2782177; e-mail stv@stvif.fi; internet www.stvif.fi; f. 1921; to promote research in engineering sciences; 175 mems; Pres. HENRIK WOLFF; Sec. Dr NIKLAS MEINANDER; publ. *Forhandlingar* (Proceedings).

Tekniikan Akateemisten Liitto TEK r.y. (Finnish Association of Graduate Engineers TEK): Ratavartijankatu 2, 00520 Helsinki; tel. (9) 229121; fax (9) 22912911; e-mail webmaster@tek.fi; internet www.tek.fi; f. 1896; serves as a link between engineers and architects, promotes technical sciences and industry, fosters Finnish economic life; regional offices in Espoo, Tampere, Oulu, Lappeenranta and Turku; 67,000 mems; Sec.-Gen. HEIKKI KAUPPI; publ. *TEK Member Magazine* (9 a year).

Tekniikan edistämissäätiö (Technological Foundation): c/o Kauppa-ja teollisuusministeriö, POB 32 (Aleksanterinkatu 4), 00023 Helsinki 17; internet www.kolumbus.fi/tes; f. 1949 to provide yearly fellowships for the advancement of technology; Pres. YRJÖ NEUVO; Sec. KARI MÄKINEN.

Teknillisten Tieteiden Akatemia/Akademin för Tekniska Vetenskaper r.y. (Finnish Academy of Technology): Mariankatu 8 B 11, 00170 Helsinki; tel. (9) 2782400; fax (9) 2782177; e-mail facte@facte.com; internet www.facte.com; f. 1957 to promote technical-scientific research; 440 mems; Pres. ASKO SAARELA; Sec. ANNELI ROSSI.

Tekniska Föreningen i Finland (Engineering Society in Finland—TFiF): Banvaktsg. 2, 00520 Helsinki; tel. (9) 4767718; fax (9) 4767333; e-mail helpdesk@tfif.fi; internet www.tfif.fi; f. 1880; 3,940 mems; Pres. UFFE CEDERQVIST; Man. Dir LARS ENGSTRÖM; publ. *Forum för ekonomi och teknik*.

Research Institutes

GENERAL

Suomen Akatemia (Academy of Finland): Vilhonvuorenkatu 6, POB 99, 00501 Helsinki; tel. (9) 774881; fax (9) 77488299; e-mail keskus@aka.fi; internet www.aka.fi/eng; f. 1969; promotes and provides funding for research in Finland; 37 acad. professorships; library of 25,000 vols; Pres. RAIMO VÄYRYNEN; Dir of Admin JUHA SARKIO; Dir of Research ANNELI PAULI.

AGRICULTURE, FISHERIES AND VETERINARY SCIENCE

Maa-ja elintarviketalouden tutkimuskeskus (Agrifood Research Finland): 31600 Jokioinen; tel. (3) 41881; fax (3) 41882222; internet www.mtt.fi; f. 1898; consists of 4 research units, 2 research programmes; Dir-Gen. Prof. ERKKI KEMPPAINEN; publs *Agricultural and Food Science* (Journal), *Koetoiminta ja Käytäntö* (Experimental Work and Practice).

Research units:

Kasvintuotannon tutkimus (Plant Production Research): 31600 Jokioinen; Dir Prof. AARNE KURPPA.

Kotieläintuotannon tutkimus (Animal Production Research): 31600 Jokioinen; Dir Prof. ASKO MÄKI-TANILA.

Maatalousteknologian tutkimus (Agricultural Engineering Research): Vakolantie 55, 03400 Vihti; tel. (9) 224251; fax (9) 2246210; Dir Prof. HANNU HAAPALA.

MTT Biotekniikka-ja elintarviketutkimus (MTT Agrifood Research Finland, Biotechnology and Food Research): 31600 Jokioinen; Dir EEVA-LIISA RYHÄNEN.

Taloustutkimus (Economic Research): Luutnantintie 13, 00411 Helsinki; tel. (9) 56080; fax (9) 5631164; Dir Prof. KYÖSTI PIETOLA.

Ympäristöntutkimus (Environmental Research): 31600 Jokioinen; Dir Prof. SIRPA KURPPA.

Metsäntutkimuslaitos (Finnish Forest Research Institute): Unioninkatu 40A, 00170 Helsinki; tel. (10) 2111; fax (10) 2112101; e-mail info@metla.fi; internet www.metla.fi; f. 1917; maintains 2 research centres and 7 stations; library of 43,000 vols; Dir-Gen. ELJAS POHTILA; publs *Acta Forestalia Fennica*, *Folia Forestalia*, *Silva Fennica*.

BIBLIOGRAPHY, LIBRARY SCIENCE AND MUSEOLOGY

Museovirasto (National Board of Antiquities): POB 913, 00101 Helsinki; tel. (9) 40501; fax (9) 40509300; internet www.nba.fi; f. 1884; directs and supervises Finland's admin. of antiquities, researches its cultural heritage, preserves artefacts, bldgs and sites of cultural and historical value; maintains the Nat. Museum and other museums; library of 180,000 vols with the Finnish Antiquarian Soc.; Dir-Gen. PAULA PURHONEN.

ECONOMICS, LAW AND POLITICS

Elinkeinoelämän Tutkimuslaitos, ETLA (Research Institute of the Finnish Economy): Lönnrotinkatu 4B, 00120 Helsinki; tel. (9) 609900; fax (9) 601753; e-mail info@etla.fi; internet www.etla.fi; f. 1946; research in economics, business economics and social policy; library of 20,000 vols; Man. Dir Dr SIXTEN KORKMAN; publ. *The Finnish Economy*.

LTT Tutkimus (LTT Research Ltd): Unioninkatu 18, 00130 Helsinki; tel. (9) 43138570; fax (9) 408417; e-mail ltt@hse.fi; internet www.ltt.fi; Chief Exec. TONI RIIPINEN; Dir MIKKO VALTAKARI.

Tilastokeskus (Statistics Finland): 00022 Statistics Finland; tel. (9) 17341; fax (9) 17342279; e-mail kirjaamo@stat.fi; internet www.stat.fi; f. 1865; library: library: see Libraries and Archives; Dir-Gen. HELI JESKANEN-SUNDSTRÖM; publs *Official Statistics of Finland* (statistical publs on 26 subjects), *Statistical Yearbook of Finland* (annually), *Bulletin of Statistics* (quarterly).

EDUCATION

Suomen Kasvatustieteellinen Seura/ Samfundet för Pedagogisk Forskning (Finnish Educational Research Association): Jyväskylän yliopisto/OKL, Seminaarinkatu 15, 40100 Jyväskylä; e-mail kt.paivat@oulu.fi; internet www.kasvatus.net; f. 1967; 245 mems; publ. *Kasvatus*.

MEDICINE

Minerva Foundation Institute for Medical Research: Biomedicum Helsinki, Haartmaninkatu 8, 00290 Helsinki; tel. (9) 4770040; fax (9) 47700425; e-mail dan.lindholm@helsinki.fi; internet www.helsinki.fi/minerva; f. 1959; non-profit organization owned by Minerva Foundation; basic and experimental biomedical, genetic and nutritional research; library of 4,000 vols; Chair. Prof. JIM SCHRÖDER; Head of Inst. Prof. DAN LINDHOLM.

NATURAL SCIENCES

Physical Sciences

Geodeettinen Laitos/Geodetiska institutet (Finnish Geodetic Institute): POB 15, 02431 Masala; tel. (9) 295550; fax (9) 29555200; e-mail kirjasto@fgi.fi; internet www.fgi.fi; f. 1918; 45 mems; library of 23,000 vols; Dir Prof. Dr RISTO KUITTINEN; publs *Suomen geodeettisen laitoksen julkaisuja* (Publications of the Finnish Geodetic Institute), *Suomen geodeettisen laitoksen tiedonantoja* (Reports of the Finnish Geodetic Institute), *Tiedote*.

Geologian Tutkimuskeskus/Geologiska Forskningscentralen (Geological Survey of Finland): POB 96, 02151 Espoo; Betonimiehenkuja 4, 02151 Espoo; tel. 2055011; fax 2055012; e-mail gtk@gtk.fi; internet www.gtk.fi/en; f. 1885; library of 152,000 vols; Dir-Gen. Prof. RAIMO MATIKAINEN; publs *Bulletin*, *Tutkimusraportti* (Research Report), *Vuosikertomus* (Annual Report).

Ilmatieteen laitos/Meteorologiska institutet (Finnish Meteorological Institute): POB 503, Erik Palménin aukio 1, 00101 Helsinki; tel. (9) 19291; fax (9) 179581; internet www.fmi.fi; f. 1838; library of 37,000 vols; 10,000 offprints; Pres. Dr PEKKA PLATHAN; publ. *Suomen meteorologinen vuosikirja* (Meteorological Yearbook of Finland, in Finnish and English).

Merentutkimuslaitos (Finnish Institute of Marine Research): Erik Palmenin aukio 1, 00560 Helsinki; tel. (9) 613941; fax (9) 3236728; e-mail info@fimr.fi; internet www.fimr.fi; f. 1918; physical, chemical and biological oceanography, polar studies, Baltic Sea research; library of 55,000 vols; Dir-Gen. Prof. EEVA-LIISA POUTANEN (acting); publs *Contributions* (dissertations), *Meri* (report series).

Säteilyturvakeskus (STUK)/Strålsäkerhetscentralen (Radiation and Nuclear Safety Authority): POB 14, 00881 Helsinki; tel. (9) 759881; fax (9) 75988500; e-mail stuk@stuk.fi; internet www.stuk.fi; f. 1958; government authority for radiation protection and nuclear safety, including inspection and research in the field; library of 30,000 vols; Dir-Gen. Prof. JUKKA LAAKSONEN; publs *Alara* (quarterly), *STUK-A Reports* (irregular).

RELIGION, SOCIOLOGY AND ANTHROPOLOGY

Donnerska institutet för religionshistorisk- och kulturhistoriskforskning / Steinerbiblioteket (Donner Institute for Research in Religious and Cultural History / Steiner Memorial Library): POB 70, Biskopsgatan 13, 20501 Åbo; tel. (2) 2154313; fax (2) 2311290; e-mail donner.institute@abo.fi; internet www.abo.fi/instut/di; f. 1959 to promote research in comparative religion; organizes Nordic conference on comparative religion every three years; library of 80,000 vols; Chair. Prof. NILS G. HOLM; Sec. Dr TORE AHLBÄCK; publ. *Scripta Instituti Donneriani Aboensis* (conference papers, 5 a year).

TECHNOLOGY

KCL, Oy Keskuslaboratorio – Centrallaboratorium Ab (Finnish Pulp and Paper Research Institute): POB 70, 02151 Espoo; tel. (9) 43711; fax (9) 464305; e-mail kcl@kcl.fi; internet www.kcl.fi; f. 1916; technical and scientific research in the pulp, paper and board industry; library of 60,000 vols; Pres. JUKKA KILPELÄINEN; publ. *Annual Report*.

VTT Technical Research Centre of Finland: Vuorimiehentie 5, POB 1000, 02044 VTT Espoo; tel. (20) 722111; fax (20) 7227001; e-mail kirjaamo@vtt.fi; internet www.vtt.fi; f. 1942; provides research, development, testing and information services to the public sector, companies and int. orgs; technological focus areas are applied materials, biotechnology and chemistry processes, energy, information and communication technologies, industrial systems management, microtechnologies and electronics, and technology in the community; Chair. (vacant); publs *VTT Review*, *VTT Symposium*, *VTT Innozone* (technology magazine).

Libraries and Archives

Åbo

Åbo Akademis Bibliotek (Åbo Akademi University Library): Domkyrkogatan 2–4, 20500 Åbo; tel. (2) 21531; fax (2) 2154795; e-mail anders.ekberg@abo.fi; internet www.abo.fi/library; f. 1918; 1,995,747 vols (excluding pamphlets and MSS); Chief Librarian Dr TORE AHLBÄCK; publ. *Skrifter utgivna av Åbo Akademis bibliotek*.

Espoo

Espoon kaupunginkirjasto–maakuntakirjasto (Espoo City Library–Regional Central Library): Vanha maantie 11, 02600 Espoo; tel. (9) 517022; fax (9) 513036; f. 1869; 1,000,000 vols; special collections: Uusimaa-Nylandica (provincial collection), Norwegian collection; 14 br. libraries, 2 in hospitals and institutions, 2 mobile units; Chief Librarian ULLA PACKALÉN.

Teknillisen Korkeakoulun Kirjasto (TKK) (Library of Helsinki University of Technology): POB 7000, 02015 Helsinki; located at: Otaniementie 9, 02150 Espoo; tel. (9) 4514112; fax (9) 4514132; e-mail infolib@tkk.fi; internet lib.tkk.fi; f. 1849; nat. resource library for technology; 1,000,000 vols, 5,000 periodicals on engineering and allied sciences, mathematics, environmental sciences, architecture, urban planning and industrial economy; online databases: index to Finnish technical periodical articles, Masters' theses in engineering and architecture, TKK Research Register, TKK Publications Register, TKK Expert Register; Dir. Lic. Tech. ARI MUHONEN.

Helsinki

Eduskunnan Kirjasto (Library of Parliament): 00102 Eduskunta, Helsinki; tel. (9) 4321; fax (9) 4323495; e-mail library@eduskunta.fi; internet lib.eduskunta.fi; f. 1872; 590,000 vols on administration, law, political and social sciences; the library is open to the public; Dir SARI PAJULA; publs *Bibliographia Iuridica Fennica 1982–1993* (online at https://selma.linneanet.fi/cgi-bin/Pwebrecon.cgi), *Eduskunnan kirjaston julkaisuja* (Library of Parliament Publications 1–6), *Eduskunnan kirjaston tutkimuksia ja selvityksiä* (Library of Parliament. Studies and reports 1–6), *Valtion virallisjulkaisut* (Government publications in Finland 1961–1996).

Helsingin Kauppakorkeakoulun Kirjasto (Library of the Helsinki School of Economics): Leppäsuonkatu 9E, 00100 Helsinki; tel. (9) 43138425; fax (9) 43138539; e-mail library@hse.fi; internet helecon.lib.hse.fi; f. 1911; 100,000 vols; several online databases; Librarian EEVA-LIISA LEHTONEN.

Helsingin Kaupunginkirjasto (Helsinki City Library): POB 4100, 00520 Helsinki;

located at: Rautatieläisenkatu 8, 00520 Helsinki; tel. (9) 3108511; fax (9) 31085517; e-mail city.library@hel.fi; internet www.lib.hel.fi; f. 1860; 35 br. libraries, 2 mobile libraries; total 1,645,183 vols (1,290,605 Finnish, 162,959 Swedish, 191,619 foreign), 203,152 sound recordings, 1,229 newspaper and journal titles; Dir MAIJA BERNDTSON.

Helsingin Yliopiston Humanistisen Tiedekunnan Kirjasto (University of Helsinki Arts Faculty Library): Unioninkatu 40B, POB 24 , 00014 University of Helsinki; tel. (9) 19123905; fax (9) 19121725; e-mail hh-kirjasto@helsinki.fi; internet www.helsinki.fi/hum/kirjasto/english; f. 1904; fmrly Helsingin Yliopiston Historiallis-Kielitieteellinen Kirjasto-Helsinki (University History and Philology Library); *c.* 180,000 vols; Chief Librarian PÄLVI KAIPONEN.

Helsingin Yliopiston Kirjasto–Suomen Kansalliskirjasto (Helsinki University Library–National Library of Finland): POB 15 (Unioninkatu 36), 00014 University of Helsinki; tel. (9) 19122709; fax (9) 19122719; e-mail hyk-palvelu@helsinki.fi; internet www.lib.helsinki.fi; f. 1640 in Turku (Åbo), moved to Helsinki 1828; national library of Finland and research library of arts and humanities; comprehensive collection of books printed in Finland, large foreign collection, incl. the Slavonic Library and the American Resource Center; Nordenskiöld collection (cartography), Finnish Historical Newspaper Library; 3,000,000 vols, 600,000 MSS, and 400 incunabula; Librarian KAI EKHOLM.

Helsingin Yliopiston Oikeustieteellisen Tiedekunnan Kirjasto (Faculty of Law Library of the University of Helsinki): POB 4 (Fabianinkatu 24A), 00014 University of Helsinki; tel. (9) 19122003; fax (9) 19122174; e-mail oik-kirjasto@helsinki.fi; internet www.helsinki.fi/oik/kirjasto; f. 1910; 60,000 vols; Librarian EEVA LAURILA; the library is open to all.

Helsingin Yliopiston Teologisen Tiedekunnan Kirjasto (Theology Library, University of Helsinki): POB 33 (Aleksanterinkatu 7), 00014 University of Helsinki; tel. (9) 1911; fax (9) 19123879; e-mail teol-kirjasto@helsinki.fi; internet www.helsinki.fi/teol/kirjasto/index.html; f. 1902; 90,000 vols, 450 periodicals, 7,200 microforms; Dir LIISA RAJAMÄKI.

Helsingin yliopiston Valtiotieteellisen tiedekunnan kirjasto (Social Science Library, University of Helsinki): POB 18 (Unioninkatu 35), 00014 Univ. of Helsinki; tel. (9) 19122547; fax (9) 19122048; e-mail valt-kirjasto@helsinki.fi; internet www.valt.helsinki.fi/kirjasto/library.htm; f. 1950; 80,000 vols; Chief Librarian Dr MARIA FORSMAN.

Kansallisarkisto (National Archives of Finland): POB 258, 00171 Helsinki 17; tel. (9) 228521; fax (9) 176302; e-mail kansallisarkisto@narc.fi; internet www.narc.fi; f. 1869; 84,650 vols, 45,125 metres of documents, 964,850 cartographic items, 26,135 reels of reading copies, 218,500 microfiches; central office for public archives; controls seven Provincial Archives at Turku, Hämeenlinna, Mikkeli, Vaasa, Oulu, Jyväskylä and Joensuu; holds historical documents and archives of the Government, Supreme Court and other court records, and private papers of statesmen and politicians; the Provincial Archives contain documents relating to regional and local administration; Dir-Gen. ThDr JUSSI NUORTEVA.

Attached archive:

Helsingin Kaupunginarkisto (Helsinki City Archives): 00530 Helsinki 53, Eläintarhantie 3F; internet www.hel.fi/tietokeskus; f. 1945; central archive repository for City Administration; private archives; Dir EEVA MIETTINEN.

Sibelius-Akatemian Kirjasto/Sibelius-Akademins bibliotek (Sibelius Academy Library): Töölönkatu 28, 00260 Helsinki; POB 86, 00251 Helsinki; tel. (9) 4054539; fax (9) 4054542; e-mail sibakirjasto@siba.fi; internet lib.siba.fi/eng; f. 1882; 65,000 scores, 32,000 records, 13,000 books, 296 periodicals, 550 video cassettes; Librarian IRMELI KOSKIMIES.

Sota-arkisto (Military Archives): POB 54, 00581 Helsinki; Työpajankatu 6A, 00580 Helsinki; tel. (9) 18126544; fax (9) 18126505; e-mail sark@sota-arkisto.fi; internet www.sota-arkisto.fi; f. 1918; central archive repository of the Defence Forces; Dir JAANA KILKKI.

Suomalaisen Kirjallisuuden Seuran Kirjasto (Library of the Finnish Literature Society): Hallituskatu 1, POB 259, 00171 Helsinki; tel. (9) 13123260; fax (9) 13123220; e-mail kirjasto@finlit.fi; internet www.finlit.fi; f. 1831; 235,000 vols on folklore, ethnology, cultural anthropology and Finnish literature; Librarian CECILIA AF FORSELLES-RISKA.

Attached libraries:

Suomalaisen Kirjallisuuden Seuran Kirjallisuusarkisto (Literary Archives of the Finnish Literature Society): Hallituskatu 1, POB 259, 00171 Helsinki; fax (9) 13123268; e-mail kirjallisuusarkisto@finlit.fi; internet www.finlit.fi; f. 1831; 1,300 shelf metres of MSS, correspondence, recordings and photographs on Finnish literature, history and language; Archivist ANNA MAKKONEN.

Suomalaisen Kirjallisuuden Seuran Kansanrunousarkisto (Folklore Archives of the Finnish Literature Society): Hallituskatu 1, POB 259, 00171 Helsinki; fax (9) 13123220; e-mail kansanrunousarkisto@finlit.fi; internet www.finlit.fi; f. 1831; 1,000 shelf metres of MSS, recordings, video cassettes and photographs on Finnish folklore and oral history; Archivist LAURI HARVILAHTI.

Svenska Handelshögskolans Bibliotek (Library of the Swedish School of Economics and Business Administration): Arkadiagatan 22, POB 479, 00101 Helsinki; tel. (9) 43133360; fax (9) 43133425; e-mail biblioteket@hanken.fi; internet www.hanken.fi/biblioteket; f. 1909; 100,000 vols; Librarian MARIA SCHRÖDER.

Svenska litteratursällskapet i Finland Folkkultursarkivet (Folk Culture Archives): Riddaregatan 5, 00170 Helsinki; tel. (9) 618777; fax (9) 61877477; e-mail sls@mail.sls.fi; internet www.sls.fi; f. 1937; 1,800 collections, 300,000 photographs; publs *Folklivsstudier, Meddelanden från Folkkultursarkivet*.

Terveystieteiden keskuskirjasto (National Library of Health Sciences): Haartmaninkatu 4, 00290 Helsinki; tel. (9) 19126643; fax (9) 2410385; e-mail terkko-info@helsinki.fi; internet www.terkko.helsinki.fi; f. 1965; the national medical library; WHO Documentation Centre in Finland; 100,000 vols, 1,300 periodicals; Chair. MATTI J. TIKKANEN; publs MEDIC data base (on Finnish publications, and access to int. databases), *Virtual Journal of Helsinki Medical Research* (monthly).

Tilastokirjasto (Library of Statistics): POB 2B, Statistics Finland, 00022 Helsinki; Työpajankatu 13B, 2nd Floor, Helsinki; tel. (9) 17342220; fax (9) 17342279; e-mail library@stat.fi; internet www.stat.fi/library; f. 1865; 320,000 vols, 2,900 periodicals, 35,000 microfiches, 470 electronic publs; Chief Librarian MARJA HIRVIKALLIO.

Viikin tiedekirjasto/Vetenskapliga biblioteket i Vik (Viiki Science Library): POB 62, 00014 University of Helsinki; tel. (9) 19158040; fax (9) 19158011; e-mail viiki-lib@helsinki.fi; internet www.tiedekirjasto.helsinki.fi; f. 1999; bioscience and biotechnology, ecology, systematics and the environment, food, pharmaceutics, home economics, consumer research, agriculture, forestry and general science; 1,042,174 vols, 6,666 periodicals; Chief Librarian HELI MYLLYS.

Joensuu

Joensuun kaupunginkirjasto–Pohjois-Karjalan maakuntakirjasto (Joensuu City Library–Central Library of North Karelia): Box 114, Koskikatu 25, 80101 Joensuu; tel. (13) 2676201; fax (13) 2676210; e-mail kirjasto@jns.fi; internet www.jns.fi; f. 1862; 500,000 vols; special collection of N. Karelia; Librarian SIRPA PESONEN.

Joensuun yliopiston kirjasto (Joensuu University Library): Yliopistokatu 4, POB 107, 80101 Joensuu; tel. (13) 2512690; fax (13) 2512691; e-mail joyk@joensuu.fi; internet www.joensuu.fi/library; f. 1970; deposit library; European Documentation Centre; 800,000 vols, 9,000 electronic journals; spec. colln on Kalevala; Chief Librarian HELENA HÄMYNEN.

Jokioinen

MTT (Maa- ja elintarviketalouden tutkimuskeskus) kirjasto (MTT Agrifood Research Finland Library): 31600 Jokioinen; tel. (3) 41881; fax (3) 41882339; e-mail kirjasto@mtt.fi; internet www.mtt.fi; f. 1935; 80,000 vols, 600 periodicals; Information Specialist SIRPA SUONPÄÄ.

Jyväskylä

Jyväskylän Yliopiston Kirjasto (Jyväskylä University Library): POB 35 (Seminaarinkatu 15), 40014 Jyväskylä Univ.; tel. (14) 2601211; fax (14) 2603371; e-mail jyk@library.jyu.fi; internet kirjasto.jyu.fi; f. 1912; deposit library for Finnish prints and audio-visual material; nat. resource library for education, physical education and psychology; 1,655,000 vols; Dir Ms. Dr PIRJO VATANEN.

Kuopio

Kuopion kaupunginkirjasto–Pohjois-Savon maakuntakirjasto (Kuopio City Library—Northern Savo Regional Library): Maaherrankatu 12, Box 157, 70101 Kuopio; tel. (17) 182111; fax (17) 182340; internet www.kuopio.fi/kirjasto; f. 1872; 700,000 vols; collections: letters of the author Minna Canth, Kuopio Lyceum collection, Iceland collection, North Saivo region collection; Chief Librarian HILKKA KOTILAINEN; publ. *Kuopion Kaupunginkirjaston toimintakertomus* (Annual Report).

Kuopion yliopiston kirjasto (Kuopio University Library): POB 1627, 70211 Kuopio; tel. (17) 163405; fax (17) 163410; e-mail kirjasto@uku.fi; internet www.uku.fi/kirjasto; f. 1972; 200,000 vols; Dir JARMO SAARTI.

Oulu

Oulun yliopiston kirjasto (Oulu University Library): POB 7500, 90014 University of Oulu; tel. (8) 5531011; fax (8) 5533572; e-mail kirjasto@oulu.fi; internet www.library.oulu.fi; f. 1959; 1,700,000 vols; depository library; European Documentation Centre; spec. collns incl. material concerning Northern and Arctic research; Chief Librarian PÄIVI KYTÖMÄKI; publ. *Acta Universitatis Ouluensis*.

Pori

Porin kaupunginkirjasto–Satakunnan maakuntakirjasto (Pori City Library–Satakunta County Library): Gallen-Kallelankatu 12, POB 200, 28101 Pori; tel. (2) 6215800; fax (2) 6332582; e-mail kirjasto@pori.fi; internet www.pori.fi/kirjasto; f. 1858; 623,000 vols; centre of Hungarian literature; Librarian MARJAANA KARJALAINEN.

Tampere

Tampereen kaupunginkirjasto–Pirkanmaan maakuntakirjasto (Tampere City Library–Pirkanmaa Regional Library): Pirkankatu 2, PL 152, 33101 Tampere; tel. (3) 314614; fax (3) 31464100; e-mail tampereen.kaupunginkirjasto@tt.tampere.fi; internet www.tampere.fi/kirjasto; f. 1861; 1,100,000 vols, 300 newspapers, 2,700 periodicals, 120,000 items of audiovisual material, 20,000 microfilms; special collections: Poland, Pirkanmaa region; Chief Librarian TUULA YLISALMI.

Tampereen teknillisen yliopiston kirjasto (Tampere University of Technology Library): POB 537, 33101 Tampere; located at: Korkeakoulunkatu 10, 33101 Tampere; tel. (3) 31153155; fax (3) 31152907; e-mail kirjasto@tut.fi; internet www.tut.fi/library; f. 1956; 210,000 vols, 700 printed periodicals, 10,000 electronic journals; Library Director ARJA-RIITTA HAARALA.

Tampereen yliopistollisen sairaalan lääketieteellinen kirjasto (Medical Library of Tampere University Hospital): Box 2000, 33521 Tampere; fax (3) 2474364; e-mail kirjasto@pshp.fi; internet www.pshp.fi/kirjasto; f. 1962; 70,000 vols, 900 periodicals, 3,000 electronic journals; Librarian MERVI AHOLA.

Tampereen yliopiston kirjasto (Tampere University Library): POB 617, 33014 Tampere Univ.; tel. (3) 35516443; fax (3) 35517493; e-mail kirjasto@uta.fi; internet www.uta.fi/kirjasto/lib; f. 1925; 550,000 monograph titles, 1,500 current periodicals, 15,000 electronic periodical titles; Chief Librarian Dr MIRJA IIVONEN; publ. *Bulletini* (electronic journal).

Turku

Turun kauppakorkeakoulun kirjastotietopalvelu (Turku School of Economics, Library and Information Services): Rehtorinpellonkatu 3, 20500 Turku; tel. (2) 481481; fax (2) 4814640; e-mail kirjasto@tse.fi; internet www.tse.fi/kirjasto; f. 1950; 100,000 vols; Dir ULLA NYGRÉN.

Turun Yliopiston Kirjasto (Turku University Library): 20014 Turun Yliopisto; tel. (2) 3336177; fax (2) 3335050; e-mail kirjasto@utu.fi; internet kirjasto.utu.fi; f. 1922; 2,800,000 vols; large collection of old Finnish literature; European Documentation Centre; Chief Librarian TUULIKKI NURMINEN; publ. *Annales Universitatis Turkuensis*.

Museums and Art Galleries

Helsinki

Helsingin Kaupunginmuseoon/Helsingfors Stadsmuseum (Helsinki City Museum): Sofiankatu 4, 00170 Helsinki; tel. (9) 1693933; fax (9) 667665; e-mail kaupunginmuseo@hel.fi; internet www.hel.fi/kaumuseo; f. 1911; cultural history museum; main exhibition on the history of Helsinki; special exhibitions to highlight various features of the city's past; collection of 200,000 objects; documentation and inventory pertaining to different eras; Helsinki landscape paintings and graphics; library of 15,000 vols; photo archive of 650,000 photos from 1860s to the present; Dir TIINA MERISALO; publs *Memoria*, *Narinkka*.

Kiasma–Museum of Contemporary Art: Mannerheiminaukio 2, 00100 Helsinki; tel. (9) 17336501; fax (9) 17336503; e-mail info@kiasma.fi; internet www.kiasma.fi; f. 1990; Finnish and international art since 1960s; Dir TUULA KARJALAINEN.

Luonnontieteellinen Keskusmuseo/Naturhistoriska Centralmuseet (Finnish Museum of Natural History): P. Rautatiekatu 13, POB 17, 00014 University of Helsinki; tel. (9) 1917484; fax (9) 1917488; e-mail luonnontieteellinenmuseo@helsinki.fi; internet www.fmnh.helsinki.fi/english; Dir. J. LOKKI.

Constituent museums:

Eläinmuseo/Zoologiska Museet (Zoological Museum): P. Rautatiekatu 13, POB 17, 00014 University of Helsinki; tel. (9) 1917430; fax (9) 1917443; e-mail luonnontieteellinenmuseo@helsinki.fi; Dir OLAF BISTRÖM.

Geologian Museo/Geologiska Museet (Geological Museum): Snellmaninkatu 3, POB 11, 00014 University of Helsinki; tel. (9) 19123424; fax (9) 19123466; e-mail luonnontieteellinenmuseo@helsinki.fi; Dir MARTTI LEHTINEN.

Kasvimuseo/Botaniska Museet (Botanical Museum): Unioninkatu 44, POB 7, 00014 University of Helsinki; tel. (9) 19124420; fax (9) 19124456; e-mail luonnontieteellinenmuseo@helsinki.fi; Dir PERTTI UOTILA.

Mannerheim-museo/Mannerheim-museet (Mannerheim Museum): Kalliolinnantie 14, 00140 Helsinki; tel. (9) 635443; fax (9) 636736; e-mail info@mannerheim-museo.fi; internet www.mannerheim-museo.fi; f. 1951; fmr home of Baron C. G. E. Mannerheim (1867–1951), Marshal of Finland, and exhibitions relating to his life and to the history of Finland; Dir VERA VON FERSEN.

Suomen Kansallismuseo/Finlands Nationalmuseum (National Museum of Finland): POB 913, 00101 Helsinki; located at: Mannerheimintie 34, 00100 Helsinki; tel. (9) 40501; fax (9) 40509400; e-mail kansallismuseo@nba.fi; internet www.kansallismuseo.fi; f. 1893; archaeology, history, ethnography, ethnology, numismatics; open-air museum at Seurasaari; Cygnaeus Gallery at Kaivopuisto, and several historical buildings throughout Finland; Dir Dr RITVA WÄRE.

Designmuseo/Designmuseet (Design Museum): Korkeavuorenkatu 23, 00130 Helsinki; tel. (9) 6220540; fax (9) 62205455; e-mail ebba.brannback@designmuseum.fi; internet www.designmuseum.fi; f. 1873; exhibits of industrial design and handicrafts; library of 10,000 vols; Dir MARIANNE AAV.

Valtion Taidemuseo/Statens Konstmuseum (Finnish National Gallery): Kaivokatu 2, 00100 Helsinki; tel (9) 173361; fax (9) 17336248; e-mail info@fng.fi; internet www.fng.fi; f. 1887 as the Ateneum, re-organized as the Finnish National Gallery in 1990; comprises Ateneum Art Museum, Museum of Contemporary Art Kiasma, Sinebrychoff Art Museum, Central Art Archives; library of 34,000 vols, 80 periodicals, 13,000 catalogues; Dir-Gen. TUULA ARKIO; Dir, Ateneum Art Museum SOILI SINISALO; Dir, Central Art Archives ULLA VIHANTA; Dir, Kiasma Museum of Contemporary Art TUULA KARJALAINEN; Dir, Sinebrychoff Art Museum ULLA HUHTAMÄKI; Librarian IRMELI ISOMÄKI.

Oulu

Pohjois-Pohjanmaan Museo (Northern Ostrobothnia Museum): PL 26, 90015 Oulu n Kaupunki; tel. (8) 55847161; fax (8) 55847199; e-mail ppm@ouka.fi; internet www.ouka.fi/ppm; f. 1896; specializes in historical-ethnological research on northern Ostrobothnia; Dir ILSE JUNTIKKA.

Pori

Satakunta Museo (Satakunta Museum): Hallituskatu 11, 28100 Pori; tel. (2) 6211078; fax (2) 6211061; e-mail satakunnanmuseo@pori.fi; internet www.pori.fi/smu; f. 1888; more than 80,000 archaeological and historical exhibits and more than 220,000 photographs relating to the history of the province of Satakunta; library of 13,115 vols in reference library and 9,228 old books; Dir JUHANI RUOHONEN; publ. *Sarka* (annually).

Tampere

Sara Hildénin Taidemuseo (Sara Hildén Art Museum): Särkänniemi, 33230 Tampere; tel. (3) 7143500; e-mail sara.hilden@tampere.fi; internet www.tampere.fi/sarahilden; f. 1979; exhibition centre for the works of the Sara Hildén Foundation collection (Foundation f. 1962 when Sara Hildén donated all her art works to it); modern art, with emphasis on Finnish and foreign art of the 1960s and 1970s; library of 9,000 vols; Dir RIITTA VALORINTA.

Tampereen museot (Tampere Museums): POB 487, 33101 Tampere; tel. (3) 31466966; e-mail vapriikki@tampere.fi; internet www.tampere.fi/vapriikki; Dir TOIMI JAATINEN.

Component museums:

Amurin Työläismuseokortteli (Amuri Museum of Workers' Housing): Satakunnankatu 49, 33210 Tampere; f. 1974; the development of workers' housing 1880–1970, with authentic buildings; Dir TOIMI JAATINEN.

Hämeen Museo (Häme Museum): Näsilinna, 33210 Tampere; f. 1904; prehistory and folk art of the cultural district of Tampere and the old Häme province; closed for renovation until 2007.

Turku

Sibelius-museo/Sibeliusmuseum (Sibelius Museum): Biskopsgatan 17, 20500 Turku; tel. (2) 2154494; fax (2) 2518528; e-mail sibeliusmuseum@abo.fi; internet www.sibeliusmuseum.abo.fi; f. 1926; archive and library, instrument colln and an exhibition section; archives and library contain material related to Sibelius and to Finnish music; instrument colln includes 1,500 musical instruments; associated with the musicological research department of Åbo Akademi University; Dir and Curator Dr JOHANNES BRUSILA.

Turun Maakuntamuseo/Åbo Landskapsmuseum (Turku Provincial Museum): POB 286, 20101 Turku; tel. (2) 2620111; fax (2) 2620444; e-mail maakuntamuseo@turku.fi; internet www.turku.fi/museo; f. 1881; consists of the Castle of Turku with the collns of Turku Historical Museum, Luostarinmäki Handicrafts Museum, Pharmacy Museum and the Qwensel House, Kylämäki Village of living history, Turku Biological Museum, furniture, paintings, costumes, textiles, porcelain, glass, silver, copper, firearms, uniforms, weapons, coins and medals, etc.; Dir Dr JUHANI KOSTET; publs *Aboa* (yearbook), *Raportteja* (Studies).

Turun Taidemuseo/Åbo Konstmuseum (Turku Art Museum): Aurakatu 26, 20100 Turku; tel. (2) 2627100; fax (2) 2627090; e-mail info@turuntaidemuseo.fi; internet www.turuntaidemuseo.fi; f. 1891; paintings, sculpture, prints and drawings, mainly of Finnish and Scandinavian art since early 19th century; Pres. ROGER BROO; Dir MAIJA KOSKINEN.

Universities

ÅBO AKADEMI
(Åbo Akademi University)

Domkyrkotorget 3, 20500 Turku
Telephone: (2) 21531
Fax: (2) 2517553
Internet: www.abo.fi

Founded 1918
Language of instruction: Swedish
State control
Academic year: September to May

Chancellor: CHRISTOFFER TAXELL
Rector: GUSTAV BJÖRKSTRAND
Vice-Rectors: OLLE ANCKAR, SVEN-ERIK HANSÉN
Administrative Director: ROGER BROO
Chief Librarian: TORE AHLBÄCK

Number of teachers: 370
Number of students: 7,950

Publications: *Årsberättelse* (Annual Review), *Acta Academiae Aboensis*

DEANS

Faculty of Arts: Prof. ULRIKA WOLF-KNUTS
Faculty of Chemical Engineering: Prof. TAPIO SALMI
Faculty of Economics and Social Sciences: Prof. MARIAM GINMAN
Faculty of Education: Prof. ANNA-LENA ØSTERN
Faculty of Mathematics and Natural Sciences: Prof. J. MATTINEN
Faculty of Social and Caring Sciences: Prof. GUNBORG JAKOBSSON
Faculty of Theology: Prof. I. DAHLBACKA

PROFESSORS

Faculty of Arts:

ANDERSSON, E., Swedish Language
ÅSTROM, A.-M., Nordic Ethnology
ENGMAN, M., History
HERTZBERG, L. H., Philosophy
HOLM, N. G., Comparative Religion
KORKMAN, M., Child Neuropsychology
LAINE, M., Psychology
LÖNNQVIST, B., Russian Language and Literature
MOISALA, P., Musicology
NEUENDORFF, D., German Language
NIKANNE, U., Finnish Language and Literature
SANDNABBA, K., Psychology
SELL, R., English Language and Literature
VILLSTRAND, N. E., Nordic History
VIRTANEN-ULFHIELM, T., English Language
WOLF-KNUTS, U., Nordic Folklore
WOLLIN, L., Swedish Language
ZILLIACUS, C., Literature

Faculty of Chemical Engineering:

BACK, R.-J., Computer Science
FAGERVIK, K., Chemical Engineering
HÄGGBLOM, K.-E., Automatic Control
HUPA, M., Inorganic Chemistry
IVASKA, A., Analytical Chemistry
LEWENSTAM, A., Sensor Technology
LILIUS, J., Computer Science
LÖNNBERG, K. B., Pulping Technology
MURZIN, D., Chemical Technology
ÖHMAN, G., Heating Technology
SALMI, T., Chemical Technology
SAXÉN, H., Heating Technology
SERE, K., Computer Science
TOIVONEN, H., Automation and Computer Technology
WIKSTRÖM, K., Industrial Management
WILÉN, C.-E., Polymer Technology

Faculty of Economics and Social Sciences:

ANCKAR, D. B. B., Political Science
ANCKAR, O., Economics
BACK, B., Management Science
CARLSSON, C., Management Science
GINMAN, M., Library and Information Science
HASSEL, L., Accounting
HONKA, H., Commercial Law
JÄNTTI, M., Economics
KARVONEN, L., Political Science
NORDBERG, L. B., Statistics and Econometrics
ÖSTERMARK, R., Accounting
REHN, A., Business Administration
SCHEININ, M., Constitutional and International Law
SILIUS, H., Women's Studies
SUKSI, M., Public Law
TÖRNROOS, J.-Å., Management Science
WALDEN, P., Management Science
WETTERSTEIN, L. P. L., Civil Law and Jurisprudence
WILLNER, J., Economics

Faculty of Education:

BJÖRKQVIST, O., Teaching of Mathematical Subjects
GRÖNHOLM, M., Teaching of Finnish Language
HANSÉN, S.-E., Education, Teacher-Training
LAHTINEN, U., Special Education
LINDAHL, M., Education (Childhood)
ØSTERN, A.-L, Teaching of Native Language
SJÖHOLM, K., Teaching of Foreign Languages

Faculty of Mathematical and Natural Sciences:

BJÖRKLUND, A., Geology and Mineralogy
BONSDORFF, E., Marine Ecology
EHLERS, C. W., Geology and Mineralogy
HÖGNÄS, N. G., Mathematics
HOTOKKA, M., Quantum Chemistry
JOHNSON, M., Biochemistry
LEINO, R., Organic Chemistry
LEPPÄKOSKI, E., Ecotoxicology and Environmental Toxicology
LILJA, J., Social Pharmacy
LINDBERG, M., Physics
LUNDBERG, B, Pharmaceutical Chemistry
MATTINEN, J. T., Organic Chemistry
ROSENHOLM, J. B., Physical Chemistry
SALMINEN, P., Mathematics
SISTONEN, L., Cell and Molecular Biology
SLOTTE, J. P., Biochemistry
STAFFANS, O., Mathematics
STUBB, H., Experimental Physics
TÖRNQUIST, K., Biology
WRIGHT, J. VON, Computer Science

Faculty of Social and Caring Sciences:

BJÖRKQVIST, K., Developmental Psychology
DJUPSUND, G., Political Science
ERIKSSON, K., Caring Science
HURME, H., Educational Psychology
JAKOBSSON, G., Social Policy
LINDSTRÖM, U., Caring Science

Faculty of Theology:

DAHLBACKA, I., Church History
KURTÉN, T., Theological Ethics
KVIST, H.-O., Dogmatics
LAATO, A., Old Testament Exegesis and Jewish Studies
SANDELIN, K.-G., New Testament Exegesis

ATTACHED INSTITUTES

British Studies Centre: Dir R. SELL.
Centre for Biotechnology: Dir R. LAHESMAA.
Centres for Continuing Education: Co-Dirs PAULA LINDROOS C. ROSENGREN.
Combustion Chemistry Research Group: Dir M. HUPA.
Computing Centre: Dir S.-G. LINDQVIST.
Donner Institute for Research in Religious and Cultural History: Dir T. AHLBÄCK.
Institute for Advanced Management Systems Research: Dir C. CARLSSON.
Institute of Comparative Nordic Politics and Administration: Dir (vacant).
Institute of Ecumenics and Social Ethics: Dir H.-O. KVIST.
Institute for Human Rights: Dir M. SCHEININ.
Institutum Judaicum Aboense: Dir KARL-GUSTAV SANDELIN.
Institute of Local Life Studies: Dir A.-M. ÅSTRÖM.
Institute of Maritime and Commercial Law: Dir H. HONKA.
Institute of Medieval Studies: Dir Å. RINGBOM.
Institute for Social Research concerning Swedish Finland (Vasa): Dir F. FINNÄS.
Institute of Women's Studies: Dir H. SILIUS.
Laboratory of Aquatic Pathobiology: Dir Doc. TOM WIKLUND.
Language Centre: Dir JAN JYLHÄ.
National PET Centre: Dir JUHANI KNUUTI.
South-East Asian Studies Centre: Dir A. ANTIKAINEN-KOKKO.
Turku Centre for Computer Science: Dir Prof. HANNU TENHUNEN.

HELSINGIN KAUPPAKORKEAKOULU
(Helsinki School of Economics)

Runeberginkatu 14–16, 00100 Helsinki
Telephone: (9) 43131
Fax: (9) 43138707
E-mail: tiedotus@hkkk.fi
Internet: www.hse.fi

Founded 1911
State control
Language of instruction: Finnish
Academic year: September to May

Chancellor: AATTO PRIHTI
Rector: EERO KASANEN
Vice-Rectors: OLLI AHTOLA, JYRKI WALLENIUS
Head of Administration: ESA AHONEN
Librarian: EEVA-LIISA LEHTONEN

Number of teachers: 156
Number of students: 4,170

Publication: *Acta Academiae Oeconomicae Helsingiensis* (Series B, C, D, F, M)

PROFESSORS

AHTOLA, O., Marketing
ANTTILA, M., Marketing
CHARLES, M., Applied Linguistics
ERONEN, J., Economic Geography
HAAPARANTA, P., International Economics
ILMAKUNNAS, P., Industrial and Labour Economics
KALLIO, M., Management Systems
KANGASHARJU, H., Languages and Communication
KANTO, A., Statistics
KASANEN, E., Finance
KELOHARJU, M., Finance
KINNUNEN, J., Financial Accounting
KIVIJÄRVI, H., Information Systems
KORHONEN, P., Management Science
KYLÄKOSKI, K., Management Accounting
LAHTI, A., Entrepreneurship
LEPPINIEMI, J., Finance and Capital Markets
LILJA, K., Business Administration
LOVIO, R., Organization and Management

MIETTINEN, K., Mathematics
MÖLLER, K., Business Economics
NISKAKANGAS, H., Law
POHJOLA, M., Economics
PUTTONEN, V., Finance
RUDANKO, M., Law
RÄSÄNEN, K., Organization and Management
SAARINEN, T., Information Systems
SERISTÖ, H., European Union Affairs
SUOMINEN, M., Finance
SÄÄKSJÄRVI, M., Business Information Systems
TAINIO, R., Business Administration
TOIVANEN, O., Technology Management
TROBERG, P., International Management Accounting
UUSITALO, L., Marketing Communications and Consumer Theory
VEPSÄLÄINEN, A., Logistics
VIRTANEN, K., Management Accounting
VÄLIMÄKI, J., Economics
WALLENIUS, J., Decision Making and Planning

ATTACHED INSTITUTES

International Centre: Dir JYRKI WALLENIUS.

JOKO Executive Education Ltd: Dir STIINA VISTBACKA.

Small Business Centre: Dir PENTTI MUSTALAMPI.

HELSINGIN YLIOPISTO/ HELSINGFORS UNIVERSITET (University of Helsinki)

POB 33 (Yliopistonkatu 4), 00014 University of Helsinki
Telephone: (9) 1911
Fax: (9) 19123008
E-mail: tiedotus@helsinki.fi
Internet: www.helsinki.fi

Founded 1640 Turku (Åbo), 1828 Helsinki
Languages of instruction: Finnish, Swedish
State control
Academic year: September to May (two terms)

Chancellor: Prof. K. O. RAIVIO
Rector: Prof. I. M. O. NIINILUOTO
Vice-Rectors: Prof. M. E. KOSONEN, Prof. M. T. MAKAROW, Prof. H. M. NIEMI, Prof. T. J. K. WILHELMSSON
Director of Administration: K. J. SUOKKO
Librarian: K. R. EKHOLM

Number of teachers: 1,694
Number of students: 37,852

DEANS

Faculty of Agriculture and Forestry: Prof. J. T. S. KOLA
Faculty of Arts: Prof. A. A. NENOLA
Faculty of Behavioural Sciences: Prof. J. J. HAUTAMÄKI
Faculty of Biosciences: Prof. J. K. NIEMELÄ
Faculty of Law: Prof. J. K. KEKKONEN
Faculty of Medicine: Assoc. Prof. M. J. TIKKANEN
Faculty of Pharmacy: Prof. R. V. K. HILTUNEN
Faculty of Science: Prof. H. S. S. SAARINEN
Faculty of Social Sciences: Prof. H. O. NIEMI
Faculty of Theology: Prof. A. M. LAUHA
Faculty of Veterinary Medicine: Prof. H. SALONIEMI

PROFESSORS

Faculty of Agriculture and Forestry (POB 62 (Viikinkaari 11), 00014 University of Helsinki; fax (9) 19158575; internet www.honeybee.helsinki.fi):

AHOKAS, J. M., Agricultural Engineering
ALATOSSAVA, J. T., Dairy Technology
DAHLIN, S. B., Logistics
HARI, P. K. J., Forest Ecology
HARTIKAINEN, H. H., Soil and Environment Chemistry
HATAKKA, A., Environmental Biotechnology
HEINONEN, I. M., Functional Food
HELENIUS, J. P., Agroecology
HELIÖVAARA, K. T., Forest Zoology
HOKKANEN, H. M. T., Agricultural Zoology
HYVÖNEN, L. E. T., Food Technology
HYVÖNEN, S. M., Marketing
JAAKKOLA, A. O., Agricultural Chemistry and Physics
JUSLIN, H. J., Forest Products Marketing
KANGAS, A., Forest Mensuration and Management
KOLA, J. T. S., Agricultural Politics
KOSKELA, M. O., Food Economics
KUULUVAINEN, J. T. M., Social Economics of Forestry
LAASASENAHO, J. E., Forest Mensuration and Management
LUUKKANEN, M. O., Silviculture in Developing Countries
MAKAROW, M. T., Applied Biochemistry
MIKKONEN, E. U. A., Logging and Utilization of Forest Products
MUTANEN, M. L., Nutrition Physiology
MÄKELÄ, P. S. A., Crop Production
MÄKINEN, V.-P. J., Agricultural Entrepreneurship
NÄSI, J. M., Animal Nutrition
OJALA, M. J., Animal Breeding
OLLIKAINEN, M. M. O., Environmental Economics
PEHKONEN, A. I., Agricultural Engineering
PIIRONEN, V. I., Food Chemistry
PUOLANNE, T. E. J., Meat Technology
PUTTONEN, P. K., Silviculture
RÄSÄNEN, L. K., Nutrition
SALKINOSA-SALONEN, M. S., Microbiology
SALOVAARA, H. O., Cereal Technology
SARIS, P.-E. J., Food Microbiology
SIPI, M. H., Forest Technology
SJÖBERG, A.-M. K., Technology of Households and Institutions
SUMELIUS, J. H., Agricultural Economics
TEERI, T. H., Plant Production
TENKANEN, T. M., Chemistry of Bioproduction
TERVO, M. J., Forest Product Marketing
TOKOLA, T. E., Geoinformatics
TUORILA, H. M., Food Technology
VALKONEN, P. T., Plant Pathology
VALSTA, L., Business Economics of Forestry
VANHATALO, A. O., Animal Science
WESTERMARCK, H. E., Extension Education
WESTMAN, C. J. V., Forest Soil Science
YLÄTALO, E. M. O., Agricultural Economics

Faculty of Arts (POB 3 (Fabianinkatu 33), 00014 University of Helsinki; fax (9) 19123100; internet www.hum.helsinki.fi):

APO, S.-K., Folklore
BACON, G. H. A., Film and Television Research
BREUER, U. M., German Philology
CARLSON, L. H., Language Theory and Translation
CHESTERMAN, A. P. C., Multilingual Communication
CLARK, P. A., Urban History
GOTHONI, R. R., Study of Religions
HAAPALA, A. K., Aesthetics
HAKULINEN, A. T., Finnish Language
HARVIAINEN, J. M. T., Semitic Languages
HELKKULA, M., French Language
HENRIKSSON, M. J., American Studies
HIETARANTA, P. S., English Language
HURSKAINEN, A. J., African Languages and Cultures
HYVÄRINEN, I. K., German Philology
HÄMEEN-ANTTILA, J. M., Arabic Language and Islamic Research
HÄRMÄ, J., Romance Philology
JANHUNEN, J.-A., East Asian Languages and Cultures
KALLIOKOSKI, J. T., Finnish Language
KARLSSON, F. G., General Linguistics
KONTTINEN, K. P. R., Art History
KORHONEN, J. A., German Philology
KOSKENNIEMI, K. M., Computer Linguistics
KOSKI, P. K. M., Theatre Science and Drama Literature
KOURI, E. I., General History
KULONEN, U.-M., Finno-Ugrian Philology
LAITINEN, L. M., Finnish Language
LARJAVAARA, M. E. T., Finnish Philology
LAVENTO, M. T., Archaeology
LEHTINEN, A. T., Finnish Philology
LEHTONEN, J. U. E., Finno-Ugrian Ethnology
LEINO, P. A., Finnish Language
LINDSTEDT, J. S., Slavonic Philology
LYYTIKÄINEN, P. R., Finnish Literature
MAZZARELLA, S. M., Scandinavian Literature
MEINANDER, C. H., History
MUSTAJOKI, A. S., Russian Language and Literature
NENOLA, A. A., Women's Studies
NEVALAINEN, T. T. A., English Philology
NIINILUOTO, I. M. O., Theoretical Philosophy
NIKULA, R. K., Arts History
NUMMI, J. T., Finnish Literature
PARPOLA, S. K. A., Assyriology
PEKKILÄ, E. O., Musicology
PESONEN, P. J., Russian Literature
PETTERSSON, B. J. O., American Literature
PLATO, J. VON, Philosophy
PYRHÖNEN, H. M., General Literature and Aesthetics
RAUD, R., Japanese Languages and Culture
RIIHO, T. T., Iberian Languages and Romanian
RIIKONEN, H. K., General Literature
SAARI, M. H., Scandinavian Languages
SAARINEN, H. K., General History
SALOMIES, O. I., Latin Language and Roman Literature
SANDU, N.-G., Theoretical Philosophy
SIIKALA, A. A.-L., Folklore
SILTALA, J. H., Finnish History
SUOMELA-HÄRMÄ, M. E., Italian Philology
TAAVITSAINEN, I. A. J., English Philology
TARASTI, E. A. P., Musicology
VEHMAS-LEHTO, R. L. I., Russian Language
VENTOLA, E. M., English Philology
VIHAVAINEN, T. J., Russian Studies
ÖSTMAN, J.-O. I., English Philology

Faculty of Behavioural Sciences (POB 9 (Siltavuorenpenger 20R), 00014 University of Helsinki; fax (9) 19120616; internet www.helsinki.fi/behav):

ALHO, K. A., Psychology
BUCHBERGER, A.-I.V, Pedagogics of Mother Tongue Teaching
ENGESTRÖM, Y. H. M., Adult Education
HAUTAMÄKI, J. J., Special Pedagogics
HYTÖNEN, J. M. K., Pedagogics
IIVONEN, A. K., Phonetics
KALLIONIEMI, A. J. V., Theological Pedagogy
KAUKINEN, L. K., Crafts
KELTIKANGAS-JÄRVINEN, A.-L., Applied Psychology
KLIPPI, A. M. K., Logopaedics
KRAUSE, M. C., Cognitive Science
KROKFORS, L. M., Pedagogics
LAVONEN, J. M. J., Pedagogy of Physics and Chemistry
NIEMI, H. M., Pedagogics
NYMAN, G. S., Psychology
OJALA, M. O., Pre-school and Early Childhood Education
PEHKONEN, E. K., Pedagogy of Mathematics and Computer Science
SCHEININ, P. M., Pedagogics
SIMOLA, H. J., Pedagogics
SUMMALA, K. H. I., Psychology

TANI, S. H., Pedagogy of Geography and the Environment
TELLA, S. K., Pedagogics
TUOMI-GRÖHN, T. T., Home Economics
TURKKI, K. M., Home Economics
UUSIKYLÄ, K. T., Pedagogics
VIRKKUNEN, R. J. T., Developmental Work Research
VIRSU, V. V. E., Neuropsychology
VUORINEN, R. H. E., Applied Psychology
ÅHLBERG, M. K., Biology Pedagogics

Faculty of Biosciences (POB 56 (Viikinkaari 9), 00014 University of Helsinki; fax (9) 19157561; e-mail bio-sci@helsinki.fi; internet www.helsinki.fi/bio/english):

BAMFORD, D. H., General Microbiology
DONNER, K. K., Zoology
ELORANTA, P. V., Limnology
GAHMBERG, C.-G., Biochemistry
HANSKI, I. A., Morphology and Ecology
HOLM, L. U. T., Bioinformatics
HYVÖNEN, J. T., Botany
HÄNNINEN, H. J. P., Zoology
KAILA, K. K., Physiological Zoology
KAIRESALO, T. A., Freshwater Ecology
KANGASJÄRVI, J. S., Plant Biology
KAUPPI, P. E., Environmental Protection
KEINÄNEN, K. P., Molecular Biology
KOKKO, H. M., Veterinary Ecology
KORHOLA, A. A., Arctic Global Change
KORHONEN, T. K., General Microbiology
KUIKKA, O. S., Fisheries Biology
KUOSA, H. J., Baltic Sea Research
KUPARINEN, J. S., Marine Biology
LEHTONEN, H. V. T., Fisheries Science
MERILÄ, J. K. K., Population Biology
NIEMELÄ, J. K., Urban Ecology
PALVA, E. T., Genetics
RANTA, E. J., Zoology
RIKKINEN, J. K., Zoology
ROMANTSCHUK, M. L., Environmental Biotechnology
SCHRÖDER, J. P., Genetics
STRÖMMER, R. H., Soil Ecology
SUNDSTRÖM, L. B., Evolution Biology
VIHKO, P., Biochemistry
VOIPIO, J. T. I., Electrophysiology

Faculty of Law (POB 4 (Yliopistonkatu 5), 00014 University of Helsinki; fax (9) 19122152; internet www.helsinki.fi/oik/tdk):

AUREJÄRVI, E. I., Civil Law
FRÄNDE, D. G., Criminal Law and Judicial Procedure
HALILA, H. J., Sports Law
HAVANSI, E. E. T., Judicial Procedure
HEIMONEN, M. O., Economics
HEMMO, M. A., Insurance and Tort Law
HOLLO, E. J., Environmental Law
KALIMA, K.-E. K., Financial Law
KANGAS, U. P. A., Civil Law
KEKKONEN, J. T., Judicial History and Roman Law
KONSTARI, T. T., Administrative Law
KOSKENNIEMI, M. A., International Law
KOSKINEN, P. T., Criminal Law
LAHTI, R. O. K., Criminal Law
LAPPALAINEN, J. A., Judicial Procedure
MAJAMAA, V. V., Environmental Law
MAJANEN, M. I., Criminal Law
MÄENPÄÄ, O. I., Administrative Law
MIKKOLA, M. L. A., Labour Law
RISSANEN, K. K., Commercial Law
RYYNÄNEN, O. J., Public Law
SISULA-TULOKAS, L. M., Civil Law
TEPORA, J. K., Civil Law
TIITINEN, K.-P., Labour Law
TIKKA, K. S., Financial Law
TUORI, K. H., Administrative Law
WILHELMSSON, T. K. J., Private and Commercial Law

Faculty of Medicine (POB 20 (Tukholmankatu 8), 00014 University of Helsinki; fax (9) 19126629; internet www.med.helsinki.fi):

ALALUUSUA, A. S. K., Dentistry
ALMQVIST, S. F., Child Psychiatry
ANDERSSON, L. C. L., Pathological Anatomy
BROMMELS, M. H., Health Care Administration
HAAHTELA, T. M. K., Clinical Allergology
HARJULA, A. L. J., Surgery
HERNESNIEMI, J. A., Neurosurgery
HIETANEN, J. H. P., Dentistry
HOLMBERG, P. E., Physics
HUUSKONEN, M. S., Occupational Health
HÄYRY, P. J., Transplantation Surgery and Immunology
HÖCKERSTEDT, K. A. V., Surgery
IKONEN, E. M., Cell and Tissue Biology
JOENSUU, H. T., Radiotherapy and Oncology
JÄNNE, O. A., Physiology
KALIMO, H. O., Applied Neuropathology
KALSO, E. A., Internal Medicine
KAPRIO, J. A., Public Health Service
KARLSSON, H. E., Psychiatry
KARMA, P. H., Otorhinolaryngology
KARPPANEN, H. O., Pharmacology
KARVONEN, J. M., Applied Dermatology and Venereology
KASTE, K. A. M., Neurology
KEKKI, P. V., General Practice and Primary Health Care
KESKI-OJA, J. K., Cell Biology
KINNULA, V. L., Pulmonary Medicine
KINNUNEN, P. K. J., Chemistry
KIVILAAKSO, E. O., Surgery
KIVISAARI, M. L., Diagnostic Radiology
KLOCKARS, M. L. G., General Practice
KNIP, J. M., Paediatrics
KONTULA, K. K., Molecular Medicine
KORPI, E. R., Pharmacology
KORTTILA, K. T., Anaesthesiology and Intensive Care
KÖNÖNEN, M. H. O., Stomatognatic Physiology and Prosthetic Dentistry
KONTTINEN, Y. T., Oral Medicine
LAHELMA, E. T., Public Health Science
LAITINEN, L. A. I., Tuberculosis and Pulmonary Medicine
LEHTO, V. P., Pathological Anatomy
LEIRISALO-REPO, T. K. M., Rheumatology
LEPÄNTALO, M. J. A., Vascular Surgery
LINDQVIST, J. C., Oral and Maxillofacial Surgery
LÖNNQVIST, J. K., Psychiatry
MAURY, C. P. J., Internal Medicine
MERI, S. K., Immunology
MEURMAN, J. H., Dentistry
MURTOMAA, H. T., Oral Public Health
MÄKELÄ, T. P., Biochemistry and Cell Biology
NEUVONEN, P. J., Clinical Pharmacology
NIEMINEN, M. S., Cardiology
NILSSON, C.-G. D., Obstetrics and Gynaecology
PAAKKARI, A. T. I., Pharmacology
PAAVONEN, J. A., Obstetrics and Gynaecology
PANULA, P. A. J., Biomedicine
PELTOLA, H. O., Infectious Diseases
PELTOMÄKI, P. T., Medical Genetics
PELTONEN-PALOTIE, L. P. M., Medical Genetics
PERTOVAARA, A. Y., Physiology
RANKI, P. A., Dermatology and Venereology
REPO, H., Internal Medicine
RINTALA, R. J., Child Surgery
ROSENBERG, P. H., Anaesthesiology
RUUTU, M. L., Urology
SAJANTILA, A. J., Genetical Forensic Medicine
SALASPURO, M. P. J., Alcohol and Narcotics Medicine
SANTAVIRTA, S. S., Orthopaedics and Traumatology
SARNA, S. J., Biometry
SIIMES, M. A., Paediatrics
SINTONEN, H. P., Health Economics
SKURNIK, M., Bacteriology
SOVIJÄRVI, A. R. A., Clinical Physiology
STENMAN, U.-H. E., Clinical Chemistry
TASKINEN, M.-R., Internal Medicine
TERVO, T. M. T., Applied Ophthalmology
TIKKANEN, M. J., Internal Medicine
TILVIS, R. S., Geriatrics
TUOMILEHTO, J. O. J., Public Health Science
UITTO, V. V.-J., Oral Biology
VIRKKUNEN, M. E., Forensic Psychiatry
VIRTANEN, I. T., Anatomy
VON WENDT, L. O. W., Child Neurology
VUORI, E. O., Forensic Chemistry
WAHLBECK, K. L. R., Psychiatry
YKI-JÄRVINEN, H., Internal Medicine
YLIKORKALA, R. O., Obstetrics and Gynaecology

Faculty of Pharmacy (POB 56 (Viikinkaari 9), 00014 University of Helsinki; fax (9) 19159138; e-mail ftdk-hallinto@helsinki.fi; internet www.helsinki.fi/farmasia/english):

AIRAKSINEN, M. S. A., Social Pharmacy
ELO, H. O., Pharmacological Chemistry
HILTUNEN, R. V. K., Pharmacognosy
HIRVONEN, J. T., Pharmaceutical Technology
KOSTIAINEN, R. K., Pharmaceutical Chemistry
MÄNNISTÖ, P. T., Pharmacology and Drug Development
MARVOLA, M. L. A., Biopharmacy
TASKINEN, J. A. A., Pharmaceutical Chemistry
TUOMINEN, R. K., Pharmacology and Toxicology
VUORELA, H. J., Pharmacognosy
YLIRUUSI, J. K., Pharmaceutical Technology

Faculty of Science (POB 44 (Jyrängöntie 2), 00014 University of Helsinki; fax (9) 19150039; internet www.helsinki.fi/facultyofscience):

AHLGREN, T. J., Physics
AHONEN-MYKA, A. H., Computer Science
ANNILA, A. J., Biophysics
ARJAS, E., Biometry
ASTALA, K. O., Mathematics
BECKMANN, A. H.-T., Geophysics
CHAICHIAN, M., High Energy Physics
ENQVIST, K.-P., Cosmogony
ERONEN, M. J., Geology and Palaeontology
FORTELIUS, H. L. M., Evolution Palaeontology
GYLLENBERG, M. A. G., Applied Mathematics
HALONEN, L. O., Physical Chemistry
HOYER, P. G., Elementary Particle Physics
HÄMERI, K. J., Aerosol Physics
HÄMÄLÄINEN, K. J., Physics
ILLMAN, S. A., Mathematics
KAJANTIE, K. O., Theoretical Physics
KARHU, J. A., Geology and Mineralogy
KASKI, S. J. I., Computer Science
KEINONEN, J., Applied Physics
KILPELÄINEN, I. A., Organic Chemistry
KIVINEN, J. T., Computer Science
KOSKINEN, H. E. J., Space Physics
KOSONEN, M. E., Planning Geography
KOTIAHO, A. A. T., Environmental Chemistry and Analytics
KULMALA, M. T., Physics
KUPIAINEN, A. J., Mathematics
LAHTINEN, O. A., Applied Mathematics
LEPPÄRANTA, M. J., Geophysics
LESKELÄ, M. A., Inorganic Chemistry
LUMME, K. A., Astronomy
LÖYTÖNEN, M. K., Cultural Geography
MARTIO, O. T., Mathematics
MATTILA, P. E. J., Mathematics
MATTILA, V. A. K., Astronomy
MAUNU, S.-L., Polymer Chemistry
MICHELSSON, J. A., Mathematics
NORDLUND, K. H., Aerosol Physics
NUMMELIN, E., Applied Mathematics
OIVANEN, M. T., Organic Chemistry

ORAVA, R. O., Experimental Particle Physics
PAAKKI, J. P., Computer Science
PELLIKKA, P. K. E., Geoinformatics
PESONEN, L. J., Geophysics
PYYKKÖ, V. P., Chemistry
PÄIVÄRINTA, L. J., Applied Mathematics
RAATIKAINEN, K. E. E., Computer Science
RIEKKOLA, M.-L., Analytical Chemistry
RISKA, D.-O. W., Physics
RITALA, M. K., Inorganic Chemistry
RÄISÄNEN, J. A., Physics
RÄMØ, O. T., Geology and Mineralogy
RÄSÄNEN, M. O., Physical Chemistry
SAARIKKO, H. M. T., Physics
SAARINEN, H. S. S., Chemistry
SALONEN, V.-P., Environmental Geology
SAVIJÄRVI, H. I., Meteorology
SEPPÄLÄ, M. K., Computer-applied Mathematics
SEPPÄLÄ, M. K., Geography
SERIMAA, R. E., Physics
SIPPU, S. S., Computer Science
SUOMINEN, J. K., Mathematics
TALMAN, P. K., Geography
TENHU, H. J., Polymer Chemistry
TIKKANEN, M. J., Geography
TIRRI, H. R., Computer Science
TOIVONEN, H. T. T., Computer Science
TOPPILA, O. S., Mathematics
TUKIA, P. P., Mathematics
TÖRNROOS, R. F., Geology and Mineralogy
UKKONEN, E. J., Computer Science
VERKAMO, A. I., Software Engineering
VESALA, T. V., Meteorology
VIITALA, P. J., Planning Geography
WESTERHOLM, J. O., Geography
WÄHÄLÄ-HASE, K., Organic Chemistry
VÄÄNÄNEN, J. A., Mathematics

Faculty of Social Sciences (POB 54 (Unioninkatu 37), 00014 University of Helsinki; fax (9) 19124835; internet www.valt.helsinki.fi):
AIRAKSINEN, T., Practical Philosophy
ALAPURO, R. S., Sociology
ARMSTRONG, K. V., Cultural Anthropology
AULA, P. S., Communication
BLOMBERG-KROLL, H. K., Social Policy
ERÄSAARI, R. O., Social Policy
GYLLING, H. A., Applied Ethics
HAILA, A.-K. E., Social Policy
HAUTAMÄKI, A. A., Social Psychology and Psychology
HÄYRINEN-ALESTALO, M. G., Science and Technology and Research
HELKAMA, K. E., Social Psychology
HENTILÄ, S. J., Political History
HJERPPE, R. T., Economic History
HONKAPOHJA, S. M. S., Economics
HUOTARI, K. H., Social Work
JALLINOJA, R. I., Family Sociology
KANNIAINEN, V. L., Economics
KARISTO, A. O., Social Policy
KARVINEN-NIINIKOSKI, S. M. E., Social Policy
KETTUNEN, P. T., Political History
KIVIKURU, U., Journalism
KOPONEN, M. J., Development Studies
KOSKELA, E. A., Economics
KULTTI, K. K., Economics
LIEBKIND-ORMALA, K. R., Social Psychology
MASSA, J. K., Environmental Politics
MORING, T. A., Communication
NIEMI, H. O., Statistics
NYLUND, M., Social Work
PALOKANGAS, T. K., Economics
PATOMÄKI, H. O., Political Science
PEKONEN, K. J., Political Science
PELTONEN, M. T., Social History
PERÄKYLÄ, A. M., Sociology
PIRTTILÄ-BACKMAN, A.-M., Social Psychology
RISKA, E. K., Sociology
ROOS, J. P., Social Policy
SAIKKONEN, P. J., Statistics
SASSI, S. S., Communication
SATKA, M. E. A., Social Policy
SIIKALA, J. J. T., Sociology
SJÖBLOM, S. M., Municipal Administration
SULKUNEN, P. J., Sociology
SUNDBERG, J. H., Political Science
TARKKONEN, L. J., Statistics
TÖRRÖNEN, L. M., Social Work
TUOMELA, R. H., Practical Philosophy
VÄLIVERRONEN, E. T., Mass Communication
VALKONEN, Y. T., Sociology
VARTIA, Y. O., Economics
VIRTANEN, T. I., Political Science
ÅBERG, L. E. G., Communication

Faculty of Theology (POB 33 (Aleksanterinkatu 7), 00014 University of Helsinki; fax (9) 19122106; internet www.helsinki.fi/teol):
AEJMELAEUS, L. J. T., Exegetics
HALLAMAA, J. I., Social Ethics
HEIKKILÄ, M. K. J., Practical Theology
HEININEN, S. K. M., General Church History
HELANDER, E. M., Church Sociology
KNUUTTILA, S. J. I., Theological Ethics and Philosophy of Religion
KOTILA, H. T., Practical Theology
LAUHA, A. M., Church History
PENTIKÄINEN, J. Y., Study of Religions
RUOKANEN, M. M., Doctrinal Theology
RÄISÄNEN, H. M., New Testament Exegetics
SAARINEN, R. J., Ecumenics
SOLLAMO, R. T., Biblical Languages
TIRRI, K. A. H., Theological Pedagogy
TYÖRINOJA, R. J., Systematical Theology
VEIJOLA, T. K., Old Testament Exegetics

Faculty of Veterinary Medicine (POB 66 (Agnes Sjöbergin katu 2), 00014 University of Helsinki; fax (9) 19157161; internet www.vetmed.helsinki.fi):
ANDERSSON, C. M., Animal Breeding
BJÖRKROTH, K. J., Food Hygiene
HÄNNINEN, M. L., Veterinary Environmental Hygiene
JÄRVINEN, A.-K., Pet Diseases
KATILA, M. T. H., Animal Breeding
KORKEALA, H. J., Food Hygiene
LINDBERG, L.-A., Anatomy
PALVA, A., Veterinary Microbiology
POHJANVIRTA, R. K., Toxicology
PYÖRÄLÄ, S. H. K., Veterinary Medicine
PÖSÖ, A. R., Veterinary Physiology
SALONIEMI, H., Animal Hygiene
SNELLMAN, P. M., Diagnostic Radiology
SPILLMANN, T., Veterinary Internal Medicine
SUKUNA, A. K. K., Veterinary Pathology
TULAMO, R.-M., Veterinary Surgery
VAINIO-KIVINEN, O. M., Pharmacology
VAPAATALO, O. P., Virology

ATTACHED INSTITUTES

Alexander Institute: Dir Prof. M. J. KIVINEN.

Finnish Genome Centre: Dir Prof. A. V. PALOTIE.

Finnish Institute for the Verification of the Chemical Weapons Convention: Dir Dr P. VANNINEN.

Finnish Museum of Natural History: Dir Prof. O. J. LOKKI.

Helsinki Collegium for Advanced Studies: Dir Prof. J. S. K. SIHVOLA.

Helsinki Institute of Physics: Dir Prof. D.-O. RISKA.

Institute of Biotechnology: Dir Acad. Prof. M. SAARMA.

Institute for Rural Research and Training: Dir Prof. P. S. SIISKONEN.

Institute of Seismology: Dir P. HEIKKINEN.

Language Centre: Dir P. M. FORSMAN SVENSSON.

Palmenia Centre for Continuing Education: Dir K. HÄMÄLÄINEN.

JOENSUUN YLIOPISTO
(University of Joensuu)

POB 111, 80101 Joensuu
Telephone: (13) 251111
Fax: (13) 2512050
E-mail: intnl@joensuu.fi
Internet: www.joensuu.fi
Founded 1969
Languages of instruction: Finnish, English
State control
Academic year: September to May (two semesters)

Rector: Prof. PERTTU VARTIAINEN
Vice-Rector: Prof. TEUVO POHJOLAINEN
Director of Administration: PETRI LINTUNEN
Director of Communications: KARI HIPPI
Director of International Relations: OUTI SAVONLAHTI
Librarian: HELENA HÄMYNEN

Number of teachers: 371
Number of students: 7,700

Publications: *Ostiensis* (magazine), *Sanansaattaja Joensuusta* (newsletter)

DEANS

Faculty of Education: ANNELI NIIKKO
Faculty of Forestry: OLLI SAASTAMOINEN
Faculty of Humanities: MARKKU FILPPULA
Faculty of Science: PIRJO VAINIOTALO
Faculty of Social Sciences: HANNU PERHO
Faculty of Theology: LAURI THURÉN

PROFESSORS

AHLGREN, M., Chemistry
AHPONEN, PL., Social Sciences
ALHO, J., Statistics
ANTIKAINEN, A., Sociology of Education
ATJONEN, P., Education
AULASKARI, R., Mathematics
BASCHMAKOFF, N., Russian Language
COLPAERT, A., Geography
ENKENBERG, J., Education
ERKAMA, T., Mathematics
FILPPULA, M., English Language
FRÄNTI, P., Computer Science
HAAPASALO, L., Education
HALL, C., German Language
HARSTELA, P., Forest Technology
HEIKKINEN, K., Women's Studies
HIRVONEN, P., English Language
HOLOPAINEN, I., Biology
HOLOPAINEN, L., Special Education
HUSA, J., Constitutional Law
HÄLLSTRÖM, G. AF, Theology
HÄMYNEN, T., History of Finland
JULKUNEN, M.- L., Didactics
JULKUNEN-TIITTO, R., Plant Ecology
JÄÄSKELÄINEN, R., English Language
JÄÄSKELÄINEN, T., Physics
KALASNIEMI, M., Russian Language
KELLOMÄKI, S., Forestry
KETTUNEN, P., Practical Theology
KNUUTTILA, H., Materials Science
KNUUTTILA, S., Folklore
KOLEHMAINEN, O., Statistics
KORPELA, J., General History
KOSKI, L., Sociology
KOTIRANTA, M., Church History
KOUKI, J., Forest Ecology and Biodiversity
KUITTINEN, M., Physics
KUJAMÄKI, P., German Language
KUKKONEN, J., Biology
KÄRENLAMPI, P., Wood Technology
KÄRKKÄINEN, M., Wood Utilization and Industry
LAINE, I., Mathematics
LEHTINEN, A., Geography
LINDEN, M., Economics
MANNERKOSKI, H., Forest Soil Science
MARTIKAINEN, E., Systematic Theology

MUIKKU-WERNER, P., Finnish Language
MUSTAKALLIO, H., Church History
MYRSKY, M., Tax Law
MÄÄTTÄ, K., Law and Economics
MÄÄTTÄ, T., Environmental Law
NIEMELÄ, P., Forest Ecology
NIEMI, E.- J., Language
NIEMI, S., Swedish Language
NIIKKO, A., Education
NUUTINEN, P., Education
NYBLOM, J., Statistics
OKSANEN, E., Botany
PAKKANEN, T., Chemistry
PAKKANEN, T., Materials Science
PALANDER, M., Finnish Language
PARKKINEN, J., Computer Science
PEIPONEN, K.-E, Physics
PELKONEN, P., Production of Wood and Peat for Energy
PERHO, H., Psychology
PIIROINEN, P., Practical Theology
POHJOLAINEN, T., Public Law
PUKKALA, T., Forest Management Planning
PYYSIÄANEN, M., Pedagogy of Religion
PÄIVINEN, R., Forestry
RANNIKKO, P., Environmental Policy
RAUMA, A., Home Economics
ROININEN, H., Animal Ecology
ROUVINEN, J., Chemistry
RÄTY, H., Psychology
SAASTAMOINEN, O., Forestry
SABOUR, M., Sociology
SAJAMA, S., Philosophy
SAJANIEMI, J., Statistics
SAVOLAINEN, T., Management and Leadership
SEITAMAA-HAKKARAINEN, P., Craft Science
SEPPÄLÄ, H., Church Music
SEPÄNMAA, Y., Literature
SEVÄNEN, E., Literature
SIISKONEN, H., History
SINISALO, P., Psychology
SORVALI, T., Mathematics
SUORANTA, J., Adult Education
SUTINEN, E., Computer Science
SVIRKO, Y., Physics
SYVÄOJA, J., Biochemistry
THURÉN, L., Exegetics
TIRKKONEN-CONDIT, S., Linguistic Theory and Translation
TOLONEN, Y., Economics
TUOMELA, J., Mathematics
TURUNEN, J., Electronics
TYKKYLÄINEN, M., Rural Research
VAINIOTALO, P., Chemistry
VANHALA-ANISZEWSKI, Russian Language
VANHALAKKA-RUOHO, M., Education
VARTIAINEN, P., Human Geography
VORNANEN, M., Animal PhysiologyVÄISÄNEN, P., Education

ATTACHED INSTITUTES

Centre for Tourism Studies: Dir Prof. ARVO PELTONEN.

Computing Centre.

Continuing Education Centre: Dir ESKO PAAKKOLA.

Educational Technology Centre: Dir Dr MARJA KALLO-RÖNKKÖ.

Finnish-Russian Cross-Border University.

Karelian Institute: Dir Dr ILKKA LIIKANEN.

Language Centre: Dir Dr ILKKA LIIKANEN.

Mekrijärvi Research Station: Dir Dr TANELI KOLSTRÖM.

Savonlinna Centre for Continuing Education and Regional Development: Dir Dr PELLERVO KOKKONEN.

University Library.

JYVÄSKYLÄN YLIOPISTO
(University of Jyväskylä)

POB 35, 40014 Univ. of Jyväskylä
Telephone: (14) 2601211
Fax: (14) 2601021
E-mail: tiedotus@jyu.fi
Internet: www.jyu.fi

Founded as Teacher Training School 1863, became College of Education 1934, and Univ. 1966
Languages of instruction: Finnish, English
State control
Academic year: September to July (three terms)

Rector: Prof. AINO SALLINEN
First Vice-Rector: Prof. TIMO TIIHONEN
Second Vice-Rector: Prof. MATTI LEINO
Administrative Dir: ERKKI TUUNANEN
Chief Librarian: PIRJO VATANEN

Number of teachers: 900
Number of students: 16,500

Publications: *Jyväskylä Studies in the Arts, Jyväskylä Studies in Biological and Environmental Science, Jyväskylä Studies in Business and Economics, Jyväskylä Studies in Communication, Jyväskylä Studies in Computing, Jyväskylä Studies in Education, Psychology and Social Research, Jyväskylä Studies in Humanities, Jyväskylä Studies in Languages, Jyväskylä Studies in Sport, Physical Education and Health, Kasvatus* (Finnish Journal of Education), *Studia Historica Jyväskyläensia, Studia Philologica Jyväskyläensia*

DEANS

Faculty of Education (including Dept of Teacher Training): Prof. HELENA RASKU-PUTTONEN
Faculty of Humanities: Prof. MAARIT VALO
Faculty of Information Technology: Prof. JUKKA HEIKKILÄ
Faculty of Mathematics and Science: Prof. MATTI MANNINEN
Faculty of Social Sciences: Prof. JARL WAHLSTRÖM
Faculty of Sport and Health Sciences: Prof. LASSE KANNAS
School of Business and Economics: Prof. JAAKKO PEHKONEN

PROFESSORS

Faculty of Education (fax (14) 2601601; e-mail ktk.tdk@edu.jyu.fi; internet www.jyu.fi/tdk/kastdk):

ALANEN, L., Early Childhood Education
HAKALA, J., Education
HÄNNIKÄINEN, M., Early Childhood Education
KAIKKONEN, P., Foreign Language Education
KAUPPINEN, A., Finnish Language Education
KORPINEN, E., Education
LAURINEN, L., Education
MÄÄTTÄ, P., Special Education
POIKKEUS, A.-M., Early Childhood Education
PUOLIMATKA, T., Education
RASKU-PUTTONEN, H., Educational Psychology
SALOVIITA, T., Special Education
VIIRI, J., Pedagogy of Mathematics and Science

Faculty of Humanities (fax (14) 2601201; e-mail humtdk@campus.jyu.fi; internet www.jyu.fi/tdk/hum):

COLLIANDER, P., German Language and Culture
ERKKILÄ, J., Music Therapy
HANKA, H., Art History
KALAJA, P., English Language
KARONEN, P., History
KIRSTINÄ, L., Literature
KOSKIMAA, R., Digital Culture
KUNNAS, T., Literature
LAHDELMA, T., Hungarology
LEPPÄNEN, S., English Language
LOUHIVUORI, J., Musicology
LUUKKA, M.-R., Finnish Language
MARTIN, M., Finnish Language
MERISALO, O., Romance Philology
MIELIKÄINEN, A., Finnish Language
MUITTARI, V., Scandinavian Philology
NUMMELA, I., History
PAKKANEN KILPIÄ, K., German Language and Culture
PIETIKÄINEN, S., Discourse Analysis
PIIRAINEN-MARSH, A., English Philology
RAHKONEN, M., Scandinavian Philology
SALLINEN, A., Speech Communication
SALOKANGAS, R., Journalism
SALO-LEE, L., Intercultural Communication
SIHVOLA, J., History
STARK, L., Ethnology
TOIVIAINEN, P., Musicology
VAINIO, M., Musicology
VALO, M., Speech Communication
VANHALA-ANISZEWSKI, M., Russian Language and Literature
VESTERINEN, I., Cultural Anthropology
VON BONSDORFF, P., Art Education
VOS, M., Organizational Communication
WAENERBERG, A., Art History
ZETTERBERG, S., History

Faculty of Information Technology (fax (14) 2602209; internet www.infotech.jyu.fi):

HEIKKILÄ, J., Information Systems and Electronic Business
HÄMÄLÄINEN, T., Information Technology: Telecommunications
JOUTSENSALO, J., Information Technology: Telecommunications
KÄRKKÄINEN, T., Software Engineering
LYYTINEN, K., Information Systems
MÄKINEN, R. A. E., Applied Mathematics
MIETTINEN, K., Industrial Optimization
NEITTAANMÄKI, P., Mathematical Information Technology
PUURONEN, S., Information Systems
RISTANIEMI, T., Information Technology
ROSSI, T., Software Technology
SAARILUOMA, P., Cognitive Science
SAKKINEN, M., Software Production
SALMINEN, A., Information Technology
TIIHONEN, T., Mathematical Information Technology
TYRVÄINEN, P., Digital Media
VEIJALAINEN, J., Software Production

Faculty of Mathematics and Science (fax (14) 2602201; e-mail pylvanai@jyu.fi; internet www.science.jyu.fi):

AHLSKOG, M., Physics
ALATALO, R., Ecology
ALÉN, R., Applied Chemistry
BAMFORD, J., Molecular Biology
ESKOLA, K. J., Theoretical Physics
GEISS, S., Stochastics
HOIKKALA, A., Evolutionary Genetics
HÄKKINEN, H., Mathematical Nanoscience
JÄRVENPÄÄ, E., Mathematics
JONES, R. I., Limnology
JULIN, R., Physics
KARJALAINEN, J., Fish Biology and Fisheries
KATAJA, M., Physics
KILPELÄINEN, T., Mathematics
KNUUTINEN, J., Applied Chemistry
KOLEHMAINEN, E., Organic Chemistry
KORPPI-TOMMOLA, J., Chemistry
KOSKELA, P., Mathematics
KUITUNEN, M., Environmental Sciences
KUNTTU, H., Physical Chemistry
KUUSALO, T., Mathematics
LEINO, M., Physics
LESKINEN, E., Statistics
MAALAMPI, J., Physics

MANNINEN, M., Physics
MAPPES, J., Ecology and Environmental Management
MÖNKKÖNEN, M., Applied Ecology
NÄKKI, R., Mathematics
NYBLOM, J., Statistics
OIKARI, A., Environmental Sciences
OKER-BLOM, C., Biotechnology
PENTTINEN, A., Statistics
RINTALA, J., Environmental Sciences
RISSANEN, K., Chemistry
SAKSMAN, E., Mathematics
SILLANPÄÄ, R., Chemistry
TIMONEN, J., Applied Physics
TÖRMÄ, P., Physics
VALKONEN, J., Chemistry
VIRTANEN, J., Nanoscience
VUENTO, M., Biochemistry
WHITLOW, H., Physics
YLÄNNE, J., Cell Biology
ÄYSTÖ, J., Physics

Faculty of Social Sciences (fax (14) 2602801; internet www.jyu.fi/tdk/yht):

AHONEN, T., Psychology
HEISKALA, R., Social Policy
JÄRVELÄ, M., Social Policy
JYRKÄMÄ, J., Social Gerontology
KANGAS, A., Cultural Policy
KORHONEN, T., Psychology
LAPPALAINEN, R., Clinical Psychology and Psychotherapy
LYYTINEN, H., Developmental Neuropsychology
MÄNTYSAARI, M., Social Work
NURMI, J.-E., Psychology
PALONEN, K., Political Science
PIHLSTRÖM, S., Philosophy
PULKKINEN, T., Political Science and Women's Studies
SEIKKULA, J., Psychotherapy
SIISIÄINEN, M., Sociology
WAHLSTRÖM, J., Psychology

Faculty of Sport and Health Sciences (fax (14) 2602001; internet www.jyu.fi/liikunta):

AVELA, J., Kinesiology
HEIKINARO-JOHANSSON, P., Physical Education
HEINONEN, A., Physiotherapy
HÄKKINEN, K., Sport Coaching and Fitness Testing
ITKONEN, H., Sport Sociology
KAINULAINEN, H., Sport Physiology
KANNAS, L., Health Education
KUJALA, U., Sport Medicine
LAAKSO, L., Physical Education
LINTUNEN, T., Sports Psychology
MÄLKIÄ, E., Physiotherapy
RANTANEN, T., Gerontology and Public Health
RINTALA, P., Applied Physical Education
SILVENNOINEN, M., Physical Education
SUOMI, K., Sports Planning and Administration
SUOMINEN, H., Sports Gerontology

School of Business and Economics (fax (14) 2603331; e-mail econ-webmaster@econ.jyu.fi; internet www.jyu.fi/economics):

AALTIO, J., Management and Leadership
HEIMONEN, K., Economics
KOIRANEN, M., Entrepreneurship
NIITTYKANGAS, H., Entrepreneurship
PEHKONEN, J., Economics
PELLINEN, J., Accounting
PESONEN, H.-L., Corporate Environmental Management
TAKALA, T., Management and Leadership
TERVO, H., Economics
UUISTALO, O., Marketing
VIRTANEN, A., Accounting

ATTACHED INSTITUTES

Agora Center: Dir PEKKA NEITTAANMÄKI.
Chydenius-Institute: Dir MIKKO VIITASALO.
Koulutuksen tutkimuslaitos (Institute for Educational Research): Dir JOUNI VÄLIJÄRVI.
Open University: Dir SATU HELIN.
Täydennyskoulutuskeskus (Continuing Education Centre): Dir ANNA-LIISA RASSI.
Tietohallintokeskus (Information Management Centre): Dir ESA AURAMÄKI.
Yliopiston kielikeskus (University Language Centre): Dir MAIJA KALIN.
Yliopiston museo (University Museum): Dir JANNE VILKUNA.
Ympäristöntutkimuskeskus (Institute for Environmental Research): Dir JARMO MERILÄINEN.

KUOPION YLIOPISTO (University of Kuopio)

Box 1627, 70211 Kuopio
Telephone: (17) 162211
Fax: (17) 162131
Internet: www.uku.fi
Founded 1966
State control
Language of instruction: Finnish
Academic year: August to June

Rector: M. I. J. UUSITUPA
Vice-Rectors: P. J. KALLIOKOSKI, S. R. T. SUNTIOINEN
Administrative Director: P. NERG
Librarian: J. K. K. SAARTI

Number of teachers: 400
Number of students: 6,000 incl. 1,000 postgraduate

DEANS

Business and Information Technology: J. T. NISKANEN
Medicine: P. O. J. B. LEHTONEN
Natural and Environmental Sciences: A. A. RUUSKANEN
Pharmacy: J. T. MÖNKKÖNEN
Social Sciences: P. N. NIEMELÄ
A. I. Virtanen Institute: J. E. KOISTINAHO

PROFESSORS

Faculty of Business and Information Technology (fax (17) 162595; internet www.uku.fi/itka):

AHONEN, J. J., Computer Science
EEROLA, A. E., Computer Science
GRÖNFORS, T. K., Computer Science (Information Technology)
KILPELÄINEN, P. T., Computer Science
LAURONEN, J. A. T., Electronic Business
NIHTILÄ, M. T., Applied Mathematics
NISKANEN, J. T., Accounting and Finance
PENTTONEN, M. A., Computer Science

Faculty of Medicine (fax (17) 162139; internet www.uku.fi/hallinto/tdkkans/laakis/index.html):

ALHAVA, E., Surgery
DUNKEL, L., Paediatrics
ESKELINEN, M. J., Surgery
GYLLING, H.K., Clinical Nutrition
HANNONEN, P. J., Rheumatology
HARVIMA, I. T., Dermatology and Venereology
HEINONEN, S. T., Gynaecology and Obstetrics
HELMINEN, H., Anatomy
HUSMAN, K. R. H., Occupational Medicine
JOHANSSON, R. T., Radiotherapy and Oncology
JÄÄSKELÄINEN, J. E., Neurosurgery
KAUHANEN, J. H., Public Health
KOPONEN, H. G., Psychiatry
KOSMA, V. M., Pathology
KRÖGER, H. P. J., Orthopaedics and Traumatology
KUMPUSALO, E. A., General Practice
LAAKSO, M. H. S., Internal Medicine
LEHTONEN, P. O. J. B., Psychiatry
LOUHEVAARA, V. A., Ergonomics
MANNINEN, H. I., Clinical Radiology
MARTTUNEN, M. J., Youth Psychiatry
MYKKÄNEN, H. M., Nutrition
NISKANEN, L. K., Internal Medicine
NUUTINEN, V. J., Otorhinolaryngology
PALVIMO, J. J., Medical Biochemistry
PELKONEN, J. L. T., Clinical Microbiology
PEUHKURINEN, K. J., Molecular Cardiology
RAUNIO, H. A., Pharmacology
SAARIKOSKI, S. V., Gynaecology and Obstetrics
SALONEN, J. T., Community Health (Epidemiology)
SIVENIUS, J., Neurology (Epilepsy and Rehabilitation)
SOIMAKALLIO, S., Diagnostic Radiology
SOININEN, H. S., Neurology
SULKAVA, R., Geriatrics
TAKKUNEN, O. S., Anaesthesiology
TAMMI, M. I., Anatomy
TIIHONEN, A. J. T., Forensic Psychiatry
TUKIAINEN, H. O., Pulmonary Diseases
UUSITALO, H. M. T., Ophthalmology
VIINAMÄKI, H. T., Psychiatry
VOUTILAINEN, R. J., Paediatrics
WASKILAMPI, T. M., Sociology

Faculty of Natural and Environmental Sciences (fax (17) 162139; internet www.uku.fi/laake):

BANIAHMAD, A., Biochemistry
CARLBERG, C., Biochemistry
HALMEKYTÖ, M. K., Animal Biotechnology
HÄMÄLÄINEN, J. P. I., Modelling in Paper Making
HYNYNEN, K. H., Medical Physics
JOKINIEMI, J., Fine Particle Technology
JURVELIN, J. S., Medical Physics and Engineering
JUUTILAINEN, J. P., Radiation Biology and Radiation Epidemiology
KAIPIO, J. P., Computational Physics
KALLIOKOSKI, P. J., Environmental Sciences (Industrial Hygiene)
KAMCHILINE, A., Optical Sensor Technology
KÄRENLAMPI, S. O., Biotechnology
LAAKSONEN, A. J., Environmental Physics
LAATIKAINEN, R., Chemistry
LAPPALAINEN, R. T., Biomedical Technology
MARTIKAINEN, P., Environmental Microbiology
MONONEN, J. J. O., Applied Zoology
NEVALAINEN, T. O., Laboratory Animal Science
OLKKONEN, H. O., Physics (Electronics)
RUUSKANEN, J., Environmental Health (Air Protection)
VARTIAINEN, T., Environmental Health Chemistry
VEPSÄLÄINEN, J. J., Chemistry
WONG, G., Bioinformatics
VON WRIGHT, A. J., Nutritional Biotechnology

Faculty of Pharmacy (fax (17) 162456; internet www.uku.fi/farmasia):

AHONEN, S. R., Pharmacy Practice
AZHAYEV, A., Pharmaceutical Bio-organic Chemistry
ENLUND, K. H., Social Pharmacy
GYNTHER, J., Drug Design
HUUPPONEN, R. A., Clinical Pharmacology
JÄRVINEN, T. L., Pharmaceutical Technology
KETOLAINEN, J. A. J., Pharmaceutical Technology
LAPINJOKI, S. P., Pharmaceutical Chemistry
MÖNKKÖNEN, J. T., Biopharmacy
URTTI, A. O., Biopharmacy
VÄHÄKANGAS, K. H., Toxicology

Faculty of Social Sciences (fax (17) 162523; internet www.uku.fi/yhttdk):

GRÖNFORS, M., Sociology

HÄMÄLÄINEN, J. E. A., Social Work and Social Pedagogy
KINNUNEN, J. E., Health Care Administration
LAURINKARI, J., Social Policy
NIEMELÄ, P., Social Policy
NIIRANEN, V. A. A., Social Administration and Management
PIETILÄ, A. M. K., Nursing Science (Preventive)
PÖLKKI, P. L., Child Welfare (Psychological Basis)
TOSSAVAINEN, K. A., Nursing Science (Didactics)
TÖTTÖ, P. S., Methods in Social Study
VALTONEN, H. J., Health Economics
VEHVILÄINEN-JULKUNEN, K. M., Nursing Science
VUORI, J. J., Health Care Administration

A. I. Virtanen Institute (fax (17) 163030; e-mail aivi@uku.fi; internet www.uku.fi/aivi):
ALHONEN, L. I., Animal Biotechnology
JÄNNE, J. E., Biotechnology
KOISTINAHO, J. E., Molecular Brain Research
PITKÄNEN, A. S. L., Neurobiology
YLÄ-HERTTUALA, S., Molecular Medicine
ÅKERMAN, K. E. O., Cell Biology

ATTACHED INSTITUTES

Centre for Training and Development: Dir PÄIVI NERG.

Computing Centre: Dir A. PLANMAN.

Institute of Public Health: Dir M. K. NYYSSÖNEN.

Kuopio University Pharmacy: Dir J. P. GYNTHER.

Language Centre: Dir A. HILDÉN.

National Laboratory Animal Centre: Dir T. NEVALAINEN.

KUVATAIDEAKATEMIA
(Academy of Fine Arts)

Kaikukatu 4, 00530 Helsinki
Telephone: 680-3320
Fax: 680-33260
E-mail: kanslia@kuva.fi
Internet: www.kuva.fi
Founded 1848
Rector: MIKA HANNULA
Number of teachers: 14
Number of students: 240
degree courses in painting, sculpture, graphics and media arts.

LAPIN YLIOPISTO
(University of Lapland)

POB 122, 96101 Rovaniemi
Telephone: (16) 341341
Fax: (16) 3412205
E-mail: tiedotus@urova.fi
Internet: www.urova.fi
Founded 1979
Languages of instruction: Finnish, English
State funded
Academic year: August to July
Rector: Prof. ESKO RIEPULA
Vice-Rectors: Prof. JUHA KARHU, Dir JUKKA MÄKELÄ
Dir of Administration: JUHANI LILLBERG
Librarians: LEA KARHUMAA SUSANNA PARIKKA
Library of 210,000 vols
Number of teachers: 222
Number of students: 4,368
Publication: *KIDE* (monthly)

DEANS

Faculty of Arts and Design: Prof. MAURI YLÄ-KOTOLA
Faculty of Business and Tourism: Prof. JUHA PANULA
Faculty of Education: Prof. KAARINA MÄÄTTÄ
Faculty of Law: Prof. ARI HUHTAMÄKI
Faculty of Social Sciences: Prof. KYÖSTI URPONEN

DIRECTORS

Arctic Centre: Dr PAULA KANKAANPÄÄ
Centre for Continuing Education: Dr HELKA URPONEN
Language Centre: HEIDI STRENGELL
Meri-Lappi Institute: AARO TIILIKAINEN
Northern Institute for Environmental and Minority Law: TIMO KOIVUROVA
Teacher-Training School: EIJA VALANNE

PROFESSORS

Faculty of Art and Design (tel. (16) 3412350; fax (16) 3412361):
BRUSILA-RÄSÄNEN, R., Media Communication
HÄNNINEN, K., Clothing and Textile Design
HAUTALA-HIRVIOJA, T., Art History
JOKELA, T., Art Education
KAMUNEN, V., Industrial Design
KIVELÄ, P., Industrial Design
LAITINEN, S., Art Education
TAYLOR, J., Media Education
TUOMINEN, M., Cultural History
UOTILA, M., Clothing and Textile Design
YLÄ-KOTOLA, M., Media Studies

Faculty of Business and Tourism:
HAAHTI, A., Tourism Studies
PANULA, J., Marketing
TYRVAINEN, L., Nature-Based Tourism

Faculty of Education (tel. (16) 3412420; fax (16) 3412401):
KURTAKKO, K., Adult Education, Continuing Education
MÄÄTTÄ, K., Educational Psychology
NASKALI, P., Pedagogics
NURMI, K., Adult Education
PEKKALA, L., Teacher Education
POIKELA, S., Education
RAJALA, R., Pedagogics
RUOKAMO, H., Pedagogics, Media Education

Faculty of Law (tel. (16) 3412520; fax (16) 3412500):
ANDEM, M., Private International Law, Space Law
HAKAPÄÄ, K., International Law
HALTTUNEN, R., General Jurisprudence, Legal History
HOLMA, K., Environmental Law
HUHTAMÄKI, H., Private Law
KARHU, J., Civil Law, Law of Obligations
KOSKINEN, S., Labour Law
MATTILA, H., Legal Linguistics
NIEMIVUO, M., Administrative Law
SAARENPÄÄ, A., Family and Inheritance Law
SARAVIITA, I., Public Law
UTRIAINEN, T., Criminal Law
VIROLAINEN, J., Juridical Procedure

Faculty of Social Sciences (tel. (16) 3412620; fax (16) 3412600):
PAASO, I., Public Law
PERTTULA, J., Psychology
POHJOLA, A., Social Work
STENVALL, J., Public Administration
SUIKKANEN, A., Sociology, Social Security and Social Care
URPONEN, K., Social Policy

ATTACHED RESEARCH INSTITUTES

Arctic Centre: Dir Prof. Dr PAULA KANKAANPÄÄ.

Centre for Continuing Education: Dir Dr HELKA URPONEN.

Language Centre: Dir Dr HEIDI STRENGELL.

Meri-Lappi Institute: Dir AARO TIILIKAINEN.

Teacher Training School: Rector EIJA VALANNE.

LAPPEENRANNAN TEKNILLINEN KORKEAKOULU
(Lappeenranta University of Technology)

Box 20, 53851 Lappeenranta
Telephone: (5) 62111
Fax: (5) 6212350
Internet: www.lut.fi
Founded 1969
Languages of instruction: Finnish, English
State control
Academic year: August to July (two terms)
Rector: Prof. MARKKU LUKKA
Vice-Rector (Research): Prof. JARMO PARTANEN
Vice-Rector (Studies): Prof. ILKKA PÖYHÖNEN
Administrative Officer: ARTO OIKKONEN
Librarian: ANJA UKKOLA
Library of 145,000 vols
Number of teachers: 200
Number of students: 4,500

PROFESSORS

AALTIO, I., Management and Organization
HANDROOS, H., Machine Automation
KERTTULA, E., Telematics
KOSKELAINEN, L., Power Plant Engineering
KYLÄHEIKO, K., Economics
KÄLVIÄINEN, H., Information Processing
KÄSSI, T., Industrial Economics
LARJOLA, J., Heat Transfer and Fluid Dynamics
LEHTOMAA, A., Entrepreneurship in Technology
LINDSTRÖM, M., Physical Chemistry
LIUHTO, J., International Operations
LUKKA, A., Logistics (esp. Transport), Inventories, Purchasing
LUKKA, M., Applied Mathematics
LUUKKO, A., Physics
MANNER, H., Paper Technology
MARQUIS, G., Steel Structures
MARTIKAINEN, J., Welding Technology
MARTIKKA, H., Design of Machine Elements
MARTTILA, E., Environmental Engineering
MIKKOLA, A., Virtual Engineering
MINKKINEN, P., Inorganic and Analytical Chemistry
NAOUMOV, V., Data Communications
NIEMI, M., Civil Law
NYSTRÖM, L., Process Technology
NYSTRÖM, M., Membrane Technology
PAATERO, E., Chemical Technology
PARTANEN, J., Electrical Systems
PIRTTILÄ, T., Industrial Engineering and Management (esp. Logistics)
PITKÄNEN, S., Engineering and Technology Management
PORRAS, J., Data Communications
PÖYHÖNEN, I., Wood Technology
PYRHÖNEN, J., Electrical Machines and Drives
PYRHÖNEN, O., Control Engineering
RANTANEN, H., Industrial Engineering
SARKOMAA, P., Technical Thermodynamics
TARJANNE, R., Energy Management and Economics
TIUSANEN, T., International Operations of Industrial Firms
TOIVANEN, P., Information Processing
TUOMINEN, M., Industrial Engineering and Management
TURUNEN, I., Process Systems Engineering
VERHO, A., Structural Design of Machinery
VORACEK, J., Information Processing
ZAMANKHAN, P., Computational Heat and Fluid Dynamics

OULUN YLIOPISTO
(University of Oulu)

Pentti Kaiteran Katu 1, POB 8000, 90014 University of Oulu
Telephone: (8) 5531011
Fax: (8) 5534551
E-mail: kirjaamo@oulu.fi
Internet: www.oulu.fi

Founded 1958
Language of instruction: Finnish
State control
Academic year: September to May (two terms)

Rector: Prof. L. Lajunen
Vice-Rectors: Prof. L. Huhtala, Prof. J. Koiso-Kanttila, Prof. V. Myllylä
Administrative Director: H. Pietilä
Librarian: P. Kytömäki

Number of teachers: 962
Number of students: 16,500

DEANS

Faculty of Economics and Business Administration: Prof. R. Svento
Faculty of Education: Prof. P. Siljander
Faculty of Humanities: Prof. M. Lehtihalmes
Faculty of Medicine: Prof. H. Ruskoaho
Faculty of Science: Prof. V. Mustonen
Faculty of Technology: Prof. V. Lantto

PROFESSORS

Faculty of Economics and Business Administration (POB 4600, 90014 University of Oulu; tel. (8) 5532905; fax (8) 5532906; internet www.taloustieteet.oulu.fi):

Alajoutsijärvi, K., Marketing
Juga, J., Logistics
Kallunki, J. P., Accounting
Koivumäki, T., Electronic Commerce
Peltonen, T., Management and Organization
Perttunen, J., Finance
Puhakka, M., Economics
Rahiala, M., Econometrics
Svento, R., Economics

Faculty of Education (POB 2000, 90014 University of Oulu; fax (8) 5533600; e-mail ktk-opintoasiat@oulu.fi; internet wwwedu .oulu.fi):

Fredrikson, M., Music Education
Hakkarainen, P., Early Childhood Education
Järvelä, S., Education
Järvikoski, T., Social Science
Järvilehto, T., Psychology
Kalaoja, E., Didactics
Keranto, T., Mathematics and Science Education
Korkeamäki, R.-L., Education
Luukkonen, J., Education
Mäkinen, K., Didactics of Foreign Languages
Ruismäki, H., Music Education
Siljander, P., Education
Soini, H., Educational Psychology
Suortti, J., Education
Syrjälä, L., Education
Varis, M., Didactics of Finnish Language and Literature
Yli-Luoma, P., Education

Faculty of Humanities (POB 1000, 90014 University of Oulu; fax (8) 5533230; internet www.oulu.fi/hutk/index.html):

Bluhm, L., German Language and Literature
Fält, O. K., History
Huhtala, L., Literature
Johnson, A., English
Korpilahti, P., Logopedics
Lauttamus, T., English
Lehtihalmes, M., Logopedics
Lehtola, V.-P., Saami Culture
Manninen, J., History of Science and Ideas
Mantila, H., Finnish
Nuñes Garces, M., Archaeology
Pennanen, J., Cultural Anthropology
Rossi, P., Scandinavian Languages
Sammallahti, P., Saami (Lapp) Language and Culture
Sorvali, I., Scandinavian Languages
Sulkala, H., Finnish
Suomi, K., Phonetics
Vahtola, J., Finnish and Scandinavian History

Faculty of Medicine (POB 5000, 90014 University of Oulu; tel. (8) 5375011; fax (8) 5375111; internet www.medicine.oulu.fi):

Airaksinen, P. J., Ophthalmology
Alahuhta, S., Anaesthesiology
Ala-Kokko, L., Medical Biochemistry
Hallman, H., Paediatrics
Hausen, H., Dentistry
Hillbom, M., Neurology
Huikuri, H., Internal Medicine
Isohanni, M., Psychiatry
Isola, A., Nursing Science
Jaakkola, M., Pulmonary Disease
Jalovaara, P., Surgery
Janhonen, S., Nursing Didactics
Joukamaa, M., Psychiatry
Juvonen, T., Surgery
Jämsä, T., Medical Technology
Järvelin, M.-R., Public Health Science
Kaprio, J., Public Health Science
Keinänen-Kiukaanniemi, S., General Practice
Kesäniemi, A., Internal Medicine
Knuuttila, M., Dentistry
Koivukangas, J., Neurosurgery
Koponen, H., Psychiatry
Kortelainen, M., Forensic Medicine
Larmas, M., Dentistry
Moilanen, I., Child Psychiatry
Myllylä, V., Neurology
Mäkelä, J., Gastroenterological Surgery
Nikkilä, J., Health Administration
Oikarinen, A., Dermatology and Venereology
Oikarinen, K., Dentistry
Paavonen, T., Pathological Anatomy
Pelkonen, O., Pharmacology
Peltonen, J., Anatomy
Pihlajaniemi, T., Medical Biochemistry
Pyhtinen, J., Diagnostic Radiology
Rajaniemi, H., Anatomy
Raustia, A., Dentistry
Risteli, J., Clinical Chemistry
Ruokonen, A., Clinical Chemistry
Ruskoaho, H., Molecular Pharmacology
Ryynänen, M., Obstetrics and Gynaecology
Räsänen, P., Psychiatry
Salo, T., Oral Pathology
Savolainen, M., Internal Medicine
Sorri, M., Otorhinolaryngology
Stenbäck, F., Pathology
Suramo, I., Diagnostic Radiology
Tapanainen, J., Obstetrics and Gynaecology
Tuulonen, A., Ophthalmology
Uhari, M., Paediatrics
Vainio, O., Clinical Microbiology
Vainio, S., Developmental Biochemistry
Virokannas, H., Occupational Health
Vuolteenaho, O., Physiology

Faculty of Science (POB 3000, 90014 University of Oulu; fax (8) 5531060; internet www.oulu.fi/science/index.html):

Aksela, H., Physics
Aksela, S., Physics
Alapieti, T., Geology and Mineralogy
Hanski, E., Geochemistry
Heikkinen, O., Geography
Heiskanen, A., Information Processing Science
Hiltunen, K., Biochemistry
Hohtola, A., Plant Physiology
Hohtola, E., Zoology
Holmström, L., Applied Mathematics
Hormi, O., Chemistry
Huttunen, S., Botany
Häggman, H., Plant Physiology
Iivari, J., Information Processing Science
Jauhiainen, J., Applied Geography and Regional Planning
Jokisaari, J., Physics
Järvilehto, M., Animal Physiology
Kaikkonen, P., Geophysics
Kaitala, A., Zoology
Karjalainen, P. T., Geography
Kinnunen, J., Mathematics
Kuutti, K., Information Processing Science
Laajoki, K., Geology and Mineralogy
Laasonen, K., Chemistry
Laitinen, R., Chemistry
Lajunen, L., Inorganic Chemistry
Lunkka, J. P., Surficial Geology
Läärä, E., Statistics
Muotka, T., Zoology
Mursula, K., Physics
Mustonen, V., Mathematics
Myllylä, R., Biochemistry
Nordström, K., Statistics
Nygrén, T., Physics
Oinas-Kukkonen, H., Information Processing Science
Oivo, M., Information Processing Science
Oksanen, J., Plant Ecology
Orell, M., Zoology
Paasi, A., Geography
Pamilo, P., Genetics
Perämäki, P., Inorganic Chemistry
Peuraniemi, V., Surficial Geology
Poutanen, J., Astronomy
Pulli, P., Information Processing Science
Pursiainen, J., Chemistry
Rahiala, M., Econometrics
Ruddock, L., Protein Science
Rummukainen, K., Theoretical Physics
Rusanen, J., Geoinformatics
Saarinen, J., Geography
Saranen, J., Applied Mathematics
Saukkonen, S., Information Processing Science
Savolainen, O., Genetics
Seppänen, V., Information Processing Science
Similä, J., Information Processing Science
Tervonen, I., Information Processing Science
Thuneberg, E., Theoretical Physics
Tuomi, J., Botany
Väänänen, K., Mathematics
Weckström, M., Biophysics
Wierenga, R., Biochemistry

Faculty of Technology (POB 4000, 90014 University of Oulu; fax (8) 5532006; internet www.ttk.oulu.fi):

Broner-Bauer, K., Architecture
Glisic, S., Telecommunication
Haapasalo, H., Industrial Engineering and Management
Hentilä, H., Planning and Urban Design
Heusala, H., Electronics
Härkki, J., Metallurgy
Inatti, J., Telecommunications
Juntti, M., Telecommunications
Karhu, S., Radio Technology
Karhunen, J., Machine Design
Karjalainen, J., Production Engineering
Karjalainen, P., Physical Metallurgy
Keiski, R., Mass and Heat Transfer Processes
Kess, P., Industrial Engineering and Management
Kløve, B., Water Management
Koiso-Kanttila, J., Architecture
Kortela, U., Control and Systems Engineering
Kostamovaara, J., Electronics
Lahdelma, S., Machine Condition Diagnostics
Lakso, E., Environment Engineering
Lantto, V., Material Physics

LAPPALAINEN, K., Production Engineering
LATVA-AHO, M., Telecommunications
LEIVISKÄ, K., Process Engineering
LEPPÄNEN, P., Telecommunications
MAHLAMÄKI, R., Architecture
MYLLYLÄ, R., Optoelectronics and Electronic Measurement Technology
MÄÄTTÄ, K., Electronics
MÄNTYLÄ, P., Mechanical Metallurgy
NEUBAUER, P., Bioprocess Engineering
NEVALA, K., Mechatronics
NIINIMÄKI, J., Mechanical Process Engineering
NISKANEN, J., Machine Construction
OJALA, T., Computer Engineering
PIETIKÄINEN, M., Computer Technics
PRAMILA, A., Technical Mechanics
RAHKONEN, T., Electronics
RIEKKI, J., Software Architecture for Embedded Systems
RUOTSALAINEN, K., Mathematics
RÖNING, J., Embedded Systems
SALONEN, E., Radio Technology
SAUVOLA, J., Multimedia Systems
SEIKKALA, S., Applied Mathematics
SEPPÄNEN, T., Biomedical Technology
SILVÉN, O., Signal Processing
SJÖLIND, S., Engineering Mechanics
TARUMAA, A., Planning and Urban Design
TASA, J., Architecture
TUPPURAINEN, Y., Architecture
VÄHÄKANGAS, J., Electronics Production Technology
VÄYRYNEN, S., Work Science

ATTACHED INSTITUTES

Institute of Electron Optics: POB 7100, 90014 University of Oulu; Dir S. SIVONEN.

Kajaani University Consortium: POB 51, 87100 Kajaani; Dir J. SUORTTI.

Laboratory Animal Centre: POB 5000, 90014 University of Oulu; Dir H.-M. VOIPIO.

Language Centre: POB 7200, 90014 University of Oulu; Dir H. ANTTILA.

Learning and Research Services: POB 7910, 90014 University of Oulu; Dir A.-M. YLIMAULA.

Meri-Lappi Institute: 94600 Kemi; Dir A. TIILIKAINEN.

Sodankylä Geophysical Observatory: 99600 Sodankylä; Dir T. TURUNEN.

Thule Institute: POB 7300, 90014 University of Oulu; Dir K. LAINE.

SIBELIUS-AKATEMIA
(Sibelius Academy)

POB 86, 00251 Helsinki

Telephone: (0) 2075390
Fax: (0) 207539600
E-mail: info@siba.fi
Internet: www.siba.fi

Founded 1882
Languages of instruction: Finnish, Swedish
State control
Academic year: September to May

Univ. status

Rector: GUSTAV DJUPSJÖBACKA
Vice-Rector: HANNU APAJALAHTI
Administrative Director: SEPPO SUIHKO

Library: see Libraries and Archives
Number of teachers: 240
Number of students: 1,700

DEANS

Church Music: PETER PEITSALO
Church Music (in Kuopio): OLAVI HAUTSALO
Composition and Music Theory: RIITTA VALKEILA
Folk Music: HEIKKI LAITINEN
Jazz Music: JARI PERKIÖMÄKI
Music Education: SOILI PERKIÖ
Music Technology: ROBERT DE GODZINSKY
Orchestral Instruments: MERIT PALAS
Piano Music: HUI-YING TAWASTSTJERNA
Vocal Music: OUTI KÄHKÖNEN

PROFESSORS

CANTELL, T., Arts Management
CASTRÉN, M., Music Research
GOTHONI, R., Chamber Music
HELASVUO, M., Wind Instrument Music
JOKINEN, E., Composition
JUSSILA, K., Organ Music
KURKELA, K., Music Performance and Research
KURKELA, V., Popular Music
LAITINEN, H., Folk Music
LAITINEN, M., Music Education
LEE, M.-K., Violin
LEHTINEN, M., Operatic Training
MURTOMÄKI, V., History of Music
NORAS, A., Cello Music
ORAMO, I., Music Theory
PORTHAN, O., Organ Music
PUUMALA, V.-M., Composition
RAEKALLIO, M., Piano Music
ROUSI, M., Cello Music
RUOHONEN, S., Opera
SAARIKETTU, K., Violin Music
SALOMAA, P., Vocal Music
SEGERSTAM, L., Orchestral Conducting
SIVUOJA-GUNARATNAM, A., Music Performance and Research
SUURPÄÄ, L., Music Theory
SZILVAY, R., Violin Music
TAITTO, I., Church Music
TAWASTSTJERNA, E. T., Piano Music
TUPPURAINEN, E., Church Music
UOTILA, J., Jazz Music
WESTERLUND, H., Music Education

SVENSKA HANDELSHÖGSKOLAN
(Swedish School of Economics and Business Administration)

POB 479, 00101 Helsinki

Telephone: (9) 431331
Fax: (9) 431333
E-mail: postmaster@shh.fi
Internet: www.hanken.fi

Founded 1909
Languages of instruction: Swedish, English
State control
Academic year: September to May

Rector: M. STENIUS
Vice-Rectors: T. BERGLUND J. KNIF
Administrative Director: M. LINDROOS
Librarian: M. SCHRÖDER

Number of teachers: 116
Number of students: 2,341

PROFESSORS

AHONEN, G., Political Science
BERGLUND, T., Economics
BJÖRK, B.-C., Computer Science
BJÖRKMAN, I., Management and Organization
BLOMQVIST, H. C., Economics
BRUUN, N., Commercial Law
EKHOLM, B.-G., Accounting
GRÖNROOS, C., Marketing and Corporate Geography
HÖGHOLM, K., Finance
KNIF, J., Finance
KOCK, S., Entrepreneurship and Management (at Vaasa)
LERVIKS, A.-E., Marketing and Corporate Geography
LILJEBLOM, E., Finance
LINDELL, M., Management and Organization
LINDQVIST, L.-J., Marketing and Corporate Geography
LÖFLUND, A., Finance
MÄNTYSAARI, P., Commercial Law
ROSENQVIST, G., Statistics and Computer Science
RYYNÄNEN, O., Commercial Law
SOIKKELI, L., Commercial Law
SPENS, K., Corporate Geography
STENBACKA, R., Economics
STENIUS, M., Finance
STRANDVIK, T., Marketing and Corporate Geography
SUNDGREN, S., Accounting
SVEIBY, K.-E., Political Science
TALLBERG, A., Accounting
TANDEFELT, M., Languages and Communication
WALLIN, J., Accounting

Vasa Branch: POB 287, Rådhusgatan 33, 65100 Vasa; tel. (6) 3533700; fax. (6) 3533703

TAIDETEOLLINEN KORKEAKOULU
(University of Art and Design Helsinki)

Hämeentie 135C, 00560 Helsinki

Telephone: (9) 75631
Fax: (9) 75630223
E-mail: info@uiah.fi
Internet: www.uiah.fi

Founded 1871
State control
Languages of instruction: Finnish, English, Swedish
Academic year: September to May
Rector: YRJÖ SOTAMAA
Vice-Rectors: MERJA SALO, YRJÄNÄ LEVANTO
Director of Administration: PEKKA SAARELA
Librarian: MARITA TURPEINEN
Library of 65,000 vols
Number of teachers: 695 (106 full-time, 589 part-time)
Number of students: 1,792
Publications: *Arttu* (bulletin, 4 a year), *Vuosikertomus* (annual report)

HEADS OF SCHOOLS

School of Art Education: Prof. JUHA VARTO
School of Design: Prof. HELENA HYVÖNEN
School of Motion Picture, Television and Production Design: Prof. LAURI TÖRHÖNEN
School of Visual Culture: Prof. JAN-KENNETH WECKMAN
Medialab: Prof. PHILIP DEAN

ATTACHED INSTITUTES

Continuing Education and Development Centre: Dir ERKKI KUJANPÄÄ.

Designium – The New Centre of Innovation in Design: Dir Dr JUHA JÄRVINEN.

Finnish Design Management Institute: Dir Prof. PETER MCGRORY.

Future Home Institute: Dir KIMMO RÖNKÄ.

Pori School of Visual Culture: Dir Prof. ANNE KOSKINEN.

Research Institute: Dir Dr PÄIVI HOVI.

West Finland Design Centre (MUOVA), Vaasa: Dir Dr SATU LAUTAMÄKI.

TAMPEREEN TEKNILLINEN YLIOPISTO
(Tampere University of Technology)

Box 527, 33101 Tampere

Telephone: (3) 3652111
Fax: (3) 3652170
Internet: www.tut.fi

Founded 1965
Language of instruction: Finnish
State control
Academic year: September to May

Rector: Prof. JARL-THURE ERIKSSON
Vice-Rectors: Prof. MARKKU KIVIKOSKI, Prof. TUOMO TIAINEN
Director of Administration: TIINA ÄIJÄLÄ
Librarian: ARJA-RIITTA HAARALA

Number of teachers: 1,906
Number of students: 12,000

DEANS

Department of Architecture: Prof. JUHANI KATAINEN
Department of Automation: Assoc. Prof. PENTTI LAUTALA
Department of Civil Engineering: Prof. RALF LINDBERG
Department of Electrical Engineering: Prof. LAURI KETTUNEN
Department of Environment: Assoc. Prof. HELGE LEMMETYINEN
Department of Industrial Engineering and Management: Prof. MARKKU PIRJETÄ
Department of Information Technology: Prof. HANNU-MATTI JÄRVINEN
Department of Materials Science: Prof. TUOMO TIAINEN
Department of Mechanical Engineering: Prof. PAUL H. ANDERSSON
Department of Science and Engineering: Prof. ROLF HERNBERG

PROFESSORS

AITTOMÄKI, A., Refrigeration Technology
ASTOLA, J., Digital Signals Processing
AUMALA, O., Metrology
ERIKSSON, J.-T., Electrodynamics and Magnetism
GABBOUJ, M., Information Technology
HAIKALA, I., Computer Science
HARJU, J., Telecommunications
HARTIKAINEN, J., Soil Mechanics and Foundation Engineering
JAAKKOLA, H., Information Technology
JALLINOJA, R., Architectural Theory
JARSKE, P., Telecommunications
KALLBERG, H., Transport
KALLI, S., Information Technology
KARVINEN, R., Fluid Dynamics and Heat Transfer
KATAINEN, J., Architectural Design
KAUNONEN, A., Control Engineering
KIVIKOSKI, M., Industrial Electronics
KORPINEN, L., Electrical Power Engineering
KOSKI, J., Structural Mechanics
KURKI-SUONIO, R., Computer Science and Engineering
KÄRNÄ, J., Electrical Power Engineering
LAKSO, T., Production Engineering
LAUTALA, P., Control Engineering
LEMMITYINEN, H., Chemistry
LEPISTÖ, T., Mathematics
LINDBERG, R., Structural Engineering
MALMIVUO, J., Bioelectronics
MATTILA, M., Occupational Safety Engineering
MAULA, J., Urban Planning
MÄKILÄ, P., Automation Technology
NOUSIAINEN, P., Textile Technology
NYBERG, T., Paper Machine Automation
OTALA, M., Industrial Management
PESSA, M., Semiconductor Technology
PUHALKA, J., Environmental Biotechnology
RENFORS, M., Telecommunications Engineering
RIIHELÄ, S., Construction Economics and Management
RIITAHUHTA, A., Machine Design
RISTALAINEN, E., Electronics
SAARIKORPI, J., Industrial Management and Engineering
SAARINEN, J., Signal Processing Laboratory
SARAMAKI, T., Signal Processing
SAVOLAINEN, A., Process Engineering
SIEKKINEN, V., Maintenance Technology
SIIKANEN, U., Architectural Construction
TALLQVIST, T., History of Architecture
TIANEN, T., Materials Engineering
TOMBERG, J., Information Technology
TORVINEN, S., Production Automation
TUHKANEN, T., Environmental Engineering
TUOKKO, R., Automation Technology
TUOMALA, M., Structural Mechanics
TÖRMÄLÄ, P., Plastics Technology
UUSI-RAUVA, E., Industrial Management and Engineering
VANHARANTA, H., Industrial Management and Engineering
VILENIUS, M., Hydraulic Machines

ATTACHED INSTITUTES

Institute of Digital Media: Box 553, 33101 Tampere; f. 1994; Dir Prof. PAULI KUOSMANEN.

Optoelectronics Research Centre: Box 692, 33101 Tampere; f. 1999; Dir Prof. MARCUS PESSA.

TAMPEREEN YLIOPISTO (University of Tampere)

Kalevantie 4, 33014 University of Tampere

Telephone: (3) 355111
Fax: (3) 2134473
E-mail: kirjaamo@uta.fi
Internet: www.uta.fi

Founded 1925
Languages of instruction: Finnish, English
State control
Academic year: September to May

Chancellor: Dr J. SIPILÄ
Rector: Prof. K. VARANTOLA
Vice-Rectors: Prof. J. LEHTO, Prof. A. ROPO
Administrative Director: T. LAHTI
Librarian: M. IVONEN

Number of teachers: 698
Number of students: 15,360

Publication: *Acta Universitatis Tamperensis*

DEANS

Faculty of Economics and Administration: Prof. A. HAVERI
Faculty of Education: Prof. T. TAKALA
Faculty of Humanities: Prof. M.-L. PIITULAINEN
Faculty of Information Sciences: Prof. M. JUHOLA
Faculty of Medicine: Prof. P. KIRKINEN
Faculty of Social Sciences: Prof. P. SUHONEN

PROFESSORS

Faculty of Economics and Administration (Kanslerinrinne 1, 33014 University of Tampere; tel. (3) 35516506; fax (3) 35516905; e-mail talhall.tiedekunta@uta.fi; internet www.uta.fi/tiedekunnat/talh):

AHONEN, P., Financial Administration and Public Sector Accounting
HAILA, Y., Environmental Policy
HARISALO, R., Public Administration
HAVERI, A., Local Government
HIRVONEN, M., Economics
HUHTANEN, R., Public Law
HÄKLI, J., Regional Studies
JÄRVINEN, R., Insurance
KULTALAHTI, J., Public Law
KULTALAHTI, O., Regional Studies
KUUSELA, H., Marketing
LAAKSO, S., Public Law
LUMIJÄRVI, I., Security Administration
MEKLIN, P., Local Public Economics
MYLLYMÄKI, A., Public Law
NÄSI, S., Accounting and Finance
NUOLIMAA, R., Business
OULASVIRTA, L., Local Public Economics
PENTTILÄ, S., Tax Law
ROPO, A., Management and Organization
RYYNÄNEN, A., Local Public Law
SOTARAUTA, M., Regional Studies
TUOMALA, M., Economics
VAINIOMÄKI, J., Economics
VARTOLA, J., Public Administration
VEHMANEN, P., Accounting and Finance
YLÄ-LIEDENPOHJA, J., Economics

Faculty of Education (Ratapihankatu 55, 33014 University of Tampere; tel. (3) 35516297; fax (3) 35516620; internet www.uta.fi/tiedekunnat/kasv):

KOHONEN, V., Foreign Language Education
NUMMENMAA, A. R., Early Childhood Education
ROPO, E., Education
RUOHOTIE, P., Education (Vocational)
SYRJÄLÄINEN, E., Education
TAKALA, T., Education (Comparative)
TUOMISTO, J., Adult Education
VARIS, T., Media Education
VÄRRI, V.-M., Education

Faculty of Humanities (Kanslerinrinne 1, 33014 University of Tampere; tel. (3) 35516520; fax (3) 35517240; e-mail humanistinen.tiedekunta@uta.fi; internet www.uta.fi/tiedekunnat/hum):

HAAPALA, P., Finnish History
HARLING-KRANCK, G., Scandinavian Languages
HAVU, J., French Language
HIETALA, M., General History
KLEMOLA, J., English Philology
LAALO, K., Finnish Language
LAUKKANEN, A.-M., Speech Communication and Voice Research
LEHTONEN, M., Media Culture
LEINONEN, M., Slavonic Philology
LEISIÖ, T., Ethnomusicology
LUKKARINEN, V., Art History
MAURANEN, A., English Philology
NIEMI, J., Finnish Literature
NIKULA, K., Scandinavian Languages
PAJUNEN, A., Finnish Language
PIITULAINEN, M.-L., German Language and Culture
RENVALL, Y. J., Actor Training
REUTER, E., German Language and Culture
ROSENHOLM, A., Slavonic Philology
RUDANKO, J., English Philology
SULKUNEN, I., Finnish History
TAMMI, P., Comparative Literature
TIITTULA, L., Translation Studies (German)
TOMMOLA, H., Translation Studies (Russian)
VARANTOLA, K., Translation Studies (English)

Faculty of Information Sciences (Kanslerinrinne 1, 33014 University of Tampere; tel. (3) 35517078; fax (3) 35514002; e-mail informaatiotieteiden.tiedekunta@uta.fi; internet www.uta.fi/tiedekunnat/inf):

HAAPARANTA, L., Philosophy
HELLA, L., Mathematics
JUHOLA, M., Computer Science
JÄRVELIN, K., Information Studies
KANGASSALO, H., Computer Science
KEKÄLÄINEN, J., Information Studies
LISKI, E., Statistics
MÄKINEN, E., Computer Science
MANNINEN, P., Statistics
MERIKOSKI, J., Mathematics
NUMMENMAA, J., Computer Science
RAISAMO, R., Computer Science
RUOHONEN, M., Computer Science
RÄIHÄ, K., Computer Science
RAISAMO, R., Computer Science
SAVOLAINEN, R., Information Studies
SINTONEN, M., Philosophy
SORMUNEN, E., Information Studies
VAKKARI, P., Information Studies
VITELI, J., Hypermedia

Faculty of Medicine (Medisiinarinkatu 3, 33014 University of Tampere; tel. (3) 35516653; fax (3) 35517385; internet www.uta.fi/tiedekunnat/laak):

ELOVAARA, I., Neurology
HEINONEN, P., Obstetrics and Gynaecology
HOLLI, K., Palliative Medicine
HURME, M., Microbiology and Immunology
HYÖTY, H., Virology
JÄRVINEN, M., Surgery
KANNUS, P., Injury Prevention
KARHUNEN, P., Forensic Medicine

KELLOKUMPU-LEHTINEN, P., Radiotherapy and Oncology
KIRKINEN, P., Obstetrics and Gynaecology
KOSMA, V., Pathology
LAASONEN, E. M., Radiology
LEINONEN, E., Psychiatry
LINDGEN, L., Anaesthesiology
MATTILA, K., General Practice
MOILANEN, E., Pharmacology
MUSTONEN, J., Internal Medicine
MÄKI, M., Paediatrics
NIEMELÄ, O., Laboratory Medicine
PAAVILAINEN, E., Nursing
PELTO-HUIKKO, M., Developmental Biology
PUKANDER, J., Otorhinolaryngology
PYYKKÖ, J., Otorhinolaryngology
REUNALA, T., Dermatology and Venereology
SALMINEN, L., Ophthalmology
SARANSAARI, P., Physiology
SEPPÄ, K., General Practice
TAMMELA, T., Urology
TAMMINEN, T., Child Psychiatry
TUOHIMAA, P., Anatomy
TURJANMAA, V., Clinical Physiology
VESIKARI, T., Virology
VIRJO, J., General Practice
YLIKOMI, T., Cell Biology
YLITALO, P., Clinical Pharmacology and Toxicology
ÅSTEDT-KURKI, P., Nursing

Faculty of Social Sciences (Yliopistonkatu 38, 33014 University of Tampere; tel. (3) 35516224; fax (3) 35517386; internet www.uta.fi/tiedekunnat/yht):

ALASUUTARI, P., Sociology
ALESTALO, M., Sociology
ANTTONEN, A., Social Policy
BLOM, R., Sociology
ERÄSAARI, L., Social Work
HARLE, V., International Politics
HIETANEN, J., Psychology
HUJANEN, T., Journalism and Mass Communication
JOKINEN, A., Social Work
JUHILA, K., Social Work
KOISTINEN, P., Social Policy
KORVAJÄRVI, P., Women's Studies
KOSKI-JÄNNES, A., Social Psychology
KUNELIUS, R., Journalism
KÄKÖNEN, J., Jean Monnet Professor
LAHIKAINEN, A. R., Social Psychology
LEHTONEN, H., Social Policy
NORDENSTRENG, K., Journalism and Mass Communication
OJANEN, M., Psychology
PAASTELA, J., Political Science
PALOHEIMO, H., Political Science
PUNAMÄKI, R.-L., Psychology
PÖSÖ, T., Social Work
RAUNIO, K., Social Work
RAUNIO, T., Political Science
ROSTILA, I., Social and Health Services
RYTÖVUORI-APUNEN, H., International Politics
SCHIENSTOCK, G., Work Research
SIPILÄ, J., Social Work
SUHONEN, P., Journalism and Mass Communication
VUORELA, U., Social Anthropology

AFFILIATED INSTITUTES

International School of Social Sciences (ISSS): Tampere; f. 1990; language of instruction: English; Dir K. NORDENSTRENG.

Kielikeskus (Language Centre): Tampere; f. 1975; Dir U.-K. TUOMI.

Lääketieteellisen teknologian instituutti (Institute of Medical Technology): Tampere; f. 1995; Dir O. SILVENNOINEN.

Solu- and kudosteknologiakeskus Regea (Regea Institute for Regenerative Medicine): Tampere; f. 2005; Dir R. SURONEN.

Täydennyskoulutuskeskus (Institute for Extension Studies): Tampere; f. 1970; Dir M. LEPPÄALHO.

Terveystieteen laitos (Tampere School of Public Health): Tampere; f. 1995; Dir P. RISSANEN.

Tietokonekeskus (Computer Centre): Tampere; f. 1966; Dir S. VISALA.

Yhteiskuntatieteellinen tietoarkisto (Finnish Social Science Data Archive): f. 1999; Dir S. BORG.

Yhteiskuntatieteiden tutkimuslaitos (Research Institute for Social Sciences): Tampere; f. 1945; Dir P. ALASUUTARI.

TEATTRIKORKEAKOULU
(Theatre Academy)

POB 163, 00531 Helsinki
Located at: Haapaniemenkatu 6, 00530 Helsinki
Telephone: (9) 431361
Fax: (9) 43136200
E-mail: international@teak.fi
Internet: www.teak.fi

Founded 1979
State control
Languages of instruction: Finnish, Swedish
Rector: PAULA TUOVINEN
Vice-Rector: ERIK SÖDERBLOM
Head of Administration: MAARIT HILDÉN
Library of 40,000 vols, 200 periodicals

HEADS OF DEPARTMENTS

Acting: MARJA-LIISA KUURANNE-AUTELO
Acting (Swedish): Prof. ERIK SÖDERBLOM
Dance: Prof. MARJO KUUSELA
Dance and Theatre Pedagogics: EEVA ANTTILA
Directing and Dramaturgy: MARJA-LIISA KUURANNE-AUTELO
Lighting and Sound Design: Prof. MARKKU UIMONEN

PROFESSORS

ARLANDER, A., Performance and Theory
KUUSELA, M., Choreography
LIIMATAINEN, J., Sound Design
MALMIVAARA, J., Directing
OUTINEN, K., Acting (Finnish)
PAAVOLAINEN, P., Research
SIRÉN, E., Contemporary Dance
SÖDERBLOM, E., Acting (Swedish)
UIMONEN, M., Lighting Design
VIERIKKO, V., Acting (Finnish)
VIRTANEN, H., Dramaturgy

TEKNILLINEN KORKEAKOULU
(Helsinki University of Technology)

POB 1000, 02015 Helsinki University of Technology
Telephone: (9) 4511
Fax: (9) 4512017
Internet: www.hut.fi

Founded 1908
State control
Language of instruction: Finnish (with some lectures in Swedish and English)
Academic year: September to May
Rector: Prof. MATTI PURSULA
Vice-Rectors: Prof. M. AIRILA, Prof. O. NEVANLINNA
Administrative Director: E. LUOMALA
Number of teachers: 528 (full-time)
Number of students: 13,500

DEANS

Department of Architecture: Prof. SIMO PAAVILAINEN
Department of Automation and Systems Technology: Prof. AARNE HALME
Department of Chemical Technology: Prof. MATTI LEISOLA
Department of Civil and Environmental Engineering: Prof. PERTTI VAKKILAINEN
Department of Computer Science and Engineering: Prof. OLLI SIMULA
Department of Electrical and Communications Engineering: Prof. PEKKA WALLIN
Department of Engineering, Physics and Mathematics: Prof. PEKKA HAUTOJÄRVI
Department of Forest Products Technology: Prof. TERO PAAJANEN
Department of Industrial Management: Prof. PAUL LILLRANK
Department of Materials Science and Rock Engineering: Prof. KARI HEISKANEN
Department of Mechanical Engineering: Prof. MAURI MÄÄTTÄNEN
Department of Surveying: Prof. KAUKO VIITANEN

PROFESSORS

AALTO, J., Structural Engineering
AALTONEN, K., Production Engineering
AHTILA, P., Industrial Energy Technology
AIRILA, M., Machine Design
AITTAMAA, J., Chemical Engineering
ALA-NISSILÄ, T., Physics
ALKU, P., Speech Communication Technology
ARKKIO, A., Electrical Engineering
ARTTO, K., Industrial Management
AUTIO, E., Industrial Management
BENGS, C., Urban and Rural Planning
BOEHM, J., Physics
DAHL, O., Industrial Environmental Technology
EHROLA, E., Road Engineering
EHTAMO, H., Systems Analysis
EIROLA, T., Mathematics
EKMAN, K., Machine Design
EKROOS, A., Law
ELORANTA, E., Industrial Management
ERNVALL, T., Transport Engineering
ESKELINEN, P., Radio Engineering
FOGELHOLM, C.-J., Energy Engineering
FORSEN, O., Corrosion Science and Hydrometallurgy
GASIK, M., Materials Processing
GRIPENBERG, G., Mathematics
HAGGREN, H., Photogrammetry
HALLIKAINEN, M., Space Technology
HALME, A., Automation Engineering
HALONEN, K., Integrated Circuit Design, Microelectronics Design
HALONEN, L., Power Systems and Illumination Engineering
HANNULA, S., Material Science
HARRIS, T., Urban Design
HARTIMO, I., Computer Technology
HAUTOJÄRVI, P., Physics
HEISKANEN, K., Mechanical Process Engineering and Recycling
HELANDER, V., History of Architecture
HOFFREN, J., Aeronautical Engineering
HOLAPPA, L., Metallurgy, Theoretical Process Metallurgy
HUKKINEN, J., Environmental Management
HUOVINEN, S., Structural Design of Building and Rehabilitation of Structures
HURME, M., Plant Design
HYÖTYNIEMI, H., Automation Technology
HÄGGMAN, S.-G., Communications
HÄKKINEN, P., Naval Architecture and Marine Engineering
HÄMÄLÄINEN, R., Applied Mathematics
HÄNNINEN, H., Engineering Materials
IKKALA, O., Technical Physics
IKONEN, E., Quantitative Science and Technology
JALKANEN, H., Metallurgy
JOKELA, R., Chemistry
JOLMA, A., Geoinformatics
JORMAKKA, J., Communications Engineering
JUHALA, M., Automotive Engineering
JUTILA, A., Bridge Engineering

JÄMSÄ-JOUNELA, S.-L., Process Control and Automation
JÄÄSKELÄINEN, I., Cognitive Technology
JÄRVENPÄÄ, E., Work Psychology
KAIVOLA, M., Engineering Physics
KANERVA, P., Structural Engineering and Building Physics
KANKAINEN, J., Construction Economics and Management
KANTOLA, R., Communications Engineering
KARHUNEN, J., Information Science
KARI, H., Computer Science
KARJALAINEN, M., Acoustics, Audio and Speech Processing
KARVONEN, T., Hydraulic Engineering
KASKI, K., Computational Engineering
KATILA, T., Biomedical Engineering
KAUPPINEN, V., Production Technology
KAURANEN, I., Development and Management in Industry
KIIRAS, J., Construction Economy and Management
KIURU, H., Water and Waste Water Engineering
KIVILAHTI, J., Materials and Manufacturing Technology for Electronics
KIVIVUORI, S., Physical Metallurgy and Materials Science
KOIVO, H., Control Engineering
KOIVUNEN, V., Signal Processing
KOMONEN, M., Architecture
KONTIO, J., Software Business and Engineering
KONTTURI, K., Physical Chemistry
KORHONEN, A., Processing and Heat Treatment of Materials
KOSKINEN, A., Organic Chemistry
KOSKINEN, K., Information Technology in Automation
KRAUSE, O., Industrial Chemistry
KUIVALAINEN, P., Microelectronics
KULMALA, S., Analytical Chemistry
KUOSMANEN, P., Machine Design
KYYRÄ, J., Power Electronics
LAAKSO, S., Biochemistry
LAAKSO, T., Telecommunications
LAAMANEN, T., Technology Strategy
LAINE, J. E., Paper Technology
LAINE, J. K., Digital Economy
LAINE, U., Speech Technology
LAKERVI, E., Power Systems
LAMPINEN, J., Computational Engineering
LAMPINEN, M., Applied Thermodynamics
LAPINTIE, K., Urban and Regional Planning
LARMI, M., Internal Combustion Engine Technology
LASSAS, M., Mathematics
LEHTONEN, M., Information Technology in Electric Energy Automation
LEISOLA, M., Bioprocess Engineering
LEVÄINEN, K., Real Estate Management
LILLRANK, P., Quality Management
LINDELL, I., Electromagnetics
LIPSANEN, H, Nanotechnology
LONDÉN, S.-O., Computational Mathematics
LOUKOLA-RUSKEENIEMI, K., Geology
LUND, P., Engineering Physics
LUOMI, J., Electrical Engineering
MALMI, L., Computer Science, Basic Programming Methodology
MANNILA, H, Computer and Information Sciences
MATUSIAK, J., Naval Architecture and Marine Engineering
MERILÄINEN, P., Engineering Physics
MÄKELÄINEN, P., Steel Structures
MÄNTYLÄ, M., Information Technology
MÄÄTTANEN, M., Strength of Materials
NEVANLINNA, O., Mathematics
NIEMELÄ, I., Computer and Information Sciences
NIEMINEN, R., Physics
NIINISTÖ, L., Inorganic Chemistry
NIKOSKINEN, K., Electromagnetics
NORDSTRÖM, K., Biochemistry
OITTINEN, P., Graphic Arts
OJA, E., Computer and Information Sciences
ORKAS, J., Foundry Technology
ORPONEN, P., Theoretical Computer Science
OVASKA, S., Industrial Electronics
PAAVILAINEN, S., Architecture
PAAVOLA, J., Structural Mechanics
PAKANEN, J., Electrical Installations in Buildings
PAULAPURO, H., Paper Technology
PELTONIEMI, M., Geophysics
PENTTALA, V., Building Materials Technology
PIETOLA, M., Machine Design
PIRILÄ, P., Energy Economics
PITKÄRANTA, J., Mathematics
PULLIAINEN, V., Space Technology
PURSULA, M., Transport Engineering
PUSKA, M., Physics
RAUTAMÄKI, M., Landscape Architecture
RAVASKA, O., Foundation Engineering and Soil Mechanics
RISKA, K., Arctic Technology
RÄISÄNEN, A., Radio Engineering
SAARELA, O., Aeronautical Engineering
SAARINEN, E., Systems Thinking
SAARINEN, K., Physics
SAIKKONEN, H., Information Processing Science
SALO, A., Systems Analysis
SALOMAA, M., Engineering Physics
SALOMAA, R., Technical Physics
SAMS, M., Cognitive Technology
SARVAS, J., Electromagnetics
SAVIOJA, L., Virtual Technology
SÄRKKÄ, P., Rock Engineering
SEGERCRANTZ, J., Mathematics
SEPPONEN, R., Applied Electronics
SEPPÄLÄ, J., Polymer Technology
SEPPÄNEN, O., Heating, Ventilation and Air Conditioning Technology
SHARMA, A., Communications Systems
SIHVOLA, A., Electromagnetics
SIIKALA, A.-M., Building Technology
SIIKONEN, T., Applied Thermodynamics
SIITONEN, T., Housing Design
SIMULA, O., Computer and Information Sciences
SINKKONEN, J., Electron Physics
SIRÉN, K., Design of Heating, Ventilating and Air Conditioning Systems
SKYTTÄ, J., Computer Technology
SMEDS, R., Information Networks
SOISALON-SOININEN, E., Information Processing Science
SOMERSALO, E., Mathematics
STENBERG, R., Mechanics
SULONEN, R., Information Processing
SUTTON, A., Computational Engineering
SYRJÄNEN, M., Knowledge Engineering
TAKALA, T., Interactive Digital Media
TANSKANEN, K., Logistics in Industrial Enterprises
TARHIO, J., Computer and Information Sciences
TEIKARI, V., Industrial Psychology
TIKKA, P., Pulping Technology
TIKKANEN, T., Marketing
TITTONEN, I., Physics in Microtechnologies
TRETYAKOV, S., Radio Engineering
TUHKURI, J., Mechanics of Materials
TULKKI, J., Computational Engineering
TUOMINEN, J., Information Technology in Industry
VAINIKAINEN, P., Radio Engineering
VAKKILAINEN, P., Hydrology and Water Resources Management
VALTONEN, M., Circuit Theory
VARSTA, P., Naval Architecture and Marine Engineering
VARTIAINEN, M., Work Psychology
VEPSÄLÄINEN, P., Foundation Engineering and Soil Mechanics
VERMEER, M., Geodesy
VIITANEN, K., Real Estate Economics and Valuation
VILJANEN, M., Structural Design of Buildings
VIRRANTAUS, K., Cartography and Geoinformatics
VIRTAMO, J., Telecommunications Technology
VISALA, A., Automation Technology
VUORIMAA, P., Multimedia Technology
VUORINEN, T., Forest Products Chemistry
VÄLIMÄKI, V., Audio Signal Processing
WALLENIUS, H., Economics
WALLIN, P., Electrical Engineering
WECK, T.-U., Structural Engineering
WICHMAN, R., Signal Processing
YLÄ-JÄÄSKI, A., Telecommunications Software
ÖSTERGÅRD, P., Information Theory

ATTACHED INSTITUTES

BIT Research Centre: Dir H. YRJÖLÄ.

Centre for Urban and Regional Planning: Dir H. LEHTONEN.

Computing Centre: Dir J. MARKULA.

Helsinki Institute of Information Technology: jointly with University of Helsinki; Dir Prof. M. MÄNTYLÄ.

Helsinki Institute of Physics: jointly with Universities of Helsinki and Jyväskylä; Dir O.-O. RISKA.

Language and Communication Centre: Dir M. KATAJAMÄKI.

Lifelong Learning Institute: Dir M. MARKKULA.

Low Temperature Laboratory: Dir Prof. M. PAALANEN.

Metsähovi Radio Research Station: Dir M. TORNIKOSKI.

TURUN KAUPPAKORKEAKOULU
(Turku School of Economics and Business Administration)

Rehtorinpellonkatu 3, 20500 Turku
Telephone: (2) 481481
Fax: (2) 4814299
E-mail: international@tukkk.fi
Internet: www.tukkk.fi

Founded 1950
Languages of instruction: Finnish, English
State control
Academic year: August to July

Rector: TAPIO REPONEN
Vice-Rector: PAAVO OKKO
Chief Administrative Officer: TUULA LIND
Librarian: ULLA NYGRÉN

Number of teachers: 100
Number of students: 2,000

PROFESSORS

ALVAREZ, L., Economic Mathematics and Statistics
GRANLUND, M., Accounting and Finance
HALINEN-KAILA, A., Marketing
HELMINEN, M., Commercial Law
LIUHTO, K., International Economics
LUKKA, K., Accounting and Finance
LÄHTEENMÄKI, S., Management and Organization
MARJANEN, H., Economic Geography
MÄKINEN, E. H., Marketing
NUMMELA, N., International Marketing
NURMI, R. W., Management and Organization
OJALA, L., Logistics
OKKO, P., Economics
PAASIO, A., Business Administration (Entrepreneurship)
SALMELA, H., Information Systems Science
SCHADÉWITZ, H. (acting), Accounting and Finance
SILLANPÄÄ, M., Commercial Law
SUOMI, R. V., Information Systems Science
TAINA, J., Shipping Economics
TOIVONEN, T., Economic Sociology
WIDGREN, M., Economics

ATTACHED CENTRES

Business Research and Development Centre: Head Prof. ANTTI PAASIO.

Finland Futures Research Centre: Head MARKKU WILENIUS.

TURUN YLIOPISTO
(University of Turku)

20014 TURKU
Telephone: (2) 33351
Fax: (2) 3336363
E-mail: international@utu.fi
Internet: www.utu.fi

Founded 1920
State control
Languages of instruction: Finnish, English
Academic year: August to July (two semesters)

Chancellor: Prof. EERO VUORIO
Rector: Prof. KEIJO VIRTANEN
Vice-Rectors: Prof. HARRI ANDERSSON, Prof. ERNO LEHTINEN, Prof. MATTI K. VILJANEN
Director of Administration: KARI HYPPÖNEN
Chief Librarian: TUULIKKI NURMINEN

Number of teachers: 800
Number of students: 18,048

Publication: *Annales Universitatis Turkuensis*

DEANS

Faculty of Education: Prof. ERKKI OLKINUORA
Faculty of Humanities: Prof. KAISA HÄKKINEN
Faculty of Law: Prof. HEIKKI KULLA
Faculty of Mathematics and Natural Sciences: Prof. JARMO HIETARINTA
Faculty of Medicine: Prof. JOUKO SUONPÄÄ
Faculty of Social Sciences: Prof. OSMO KIVINEN

PROFESSORS

Faculty of Education (tel. (2) 3338803; fax (2) 3338500; e-mail education@utu.fi; internet www.edu.utu.fi):

ELORANTA, V., Teaching of Natural Sciences
KESKINEN, S., Education
KIVIRAUMA, J., Education
KOSKENSALO, A., Teaching of Foreign Languages
LAINE, K., Early Education
LEHTINEN, E., Teacher Training
LEHTONEN, K., Open University Education
NIEMI, P., Education
NIINISTÖ, K., Education (Teacher Training)
OLKINUORA, E., Education
PELTONEN, J., Education (Teaching of Handicrafts)
RINNE, R., Adult Education
SARMAVUORI, K., Teaching of Mother Tongue
SOININEN, M., Didactics
VAURAS, M., Education (Learning and Teaching)
VIRTA, A., Teaching of History and Social Sciences

Faculty of Humanities (tel. (2) 333 5202; fax (2) 333 5200; e-mail kv-hum@utu.fi; internet www.utu.fi/hum/tdk):

AALTONEN, OLLI, Phonetics
AHOKAS, P., Comparative Literature
ANTTONEN, V., Comparative Religion
CARCEDO, A., Spanish Language, Culture and Translation
DE ANNA, L., Italian Language, Culture and Translation
GAMBIER, Y., French Translation Studies
HILTUNEN, R., Finnish Language
HIRVONEN, I., Scandinavian Philology
HOVI, K., General History
HUUMO, T., Cultural History
HÄKKINEN, K.
HÄYRYNEN, M., Landscape Studies
IMMONEN, K., French Language and Culture
ITKONEN, E., General Linguistics
ITÄLÄ, M.-L., German Translation Studies
JOHANSSON, M., Art History
KEINÄSTÖ, K., Finnish Literature
KOSTIAINEN, A., Ethnology
KUUSAMO, A., Finnish History
LAPPALAINEN, P., German Language
LEIMU, P., Russian Language and Culture
MYLLYNTAUS, T., Media Studies
NIKULA, H., Finnish Literature
PYYKKÖ, R., Comparative Literature and Drama
RIDELL, S., Finno-Ugric Languages
ROJOLA, L., Cinema and Television Studies
SAARILUOMA, L., English Philology
SAARINEN, S., Scandinavian Philology
SIHVONEN, J., French Language
SKINNER, J., Archaeology
SUNDMAN, M., English Translation Studies
SUOMELA-SALMI, E., French Language and Culture
TAAVITSAINEN, J.-P., Cultural History

Faculty of Law (tel. (2) 333 6307; fax (2) 333 6570; e-mail tls@utu.fi; internet www.law.utu.fi):

TOMMOLA, J., International Commercial Law
VAINIO-KORHONEN, K., Criminal Law
VIRTANEN, K., Roman Law and Legal History
ÄMMÄLÄ, T., International Law
BACKMAN, E. V., Private Law
BJÖRNE, L., Procedural Law
HANNIKAINEN, L., Labour Law
HELIN, M., Administrative Law
JOKELA, A. T., Environmental Law
KAIRINEN, M., Criminology and Sociology of Law
KULLA, H., Civil Law
KUMPULA, A., Criminal Law
LAITINEN, A., European Law
MÄHÖNEN, J., Financial Law
NOUSIAINEN, K., Comparative and General Law
NUUTILA, A.-M., Civil Law
OJANEN, T., Legislative Research
OSSA, J., Jurisprudence
SAARNILEHTO, A., Civil Law
TALA, J., Financial Law
TOLONEN, H., Criminal and Procedural Law
TUOMISTO, J., Constitutional and International Law

Faculty of Mathematics and Natural Sciences (tel. (2) 3336275; fax (2) 3336575; e-mail intsci@utu.fi; internet www.sci.utu.fi):

ANDERSSON, H., Organic Chemistry
ARO, E.-M., Geology and Mineralogy
ARPALAHTI, J., Animal Physiology
ÄYRÄS, P., Analytical Chemistry
EKLUND, O., Biochemistry
ERIKSSON, J.
HAAPAKKA, K., Theoretical Physics
HEINO, J., Food Chemistry
Inorganic Chemistry
HIETARINTA, J., Electronics and Information Technology
HUOPALAHTI, R., Ecology
HÖLSÄ, J.
ISOAHO, J., Food Chemistry
JORMALAINEN, V., Analytical Chemistry
Mathematics
KALLIO, H., Information Systems Science
KANKARE, J., Physics
KARHUMÄKI, J., Geography
KARSTÉN, E., Ecology
KAUPPINEN, J. K., Physics
KÄYHKÖ, J., Information Systems Science
KORPIMÄKI, E., Biochemistry
KUKK, E., Physics
LAHDELMA, R., Applied Mathematics
LAHTI, R., Organic Chemistry
LAIHO, R., Biotechnology
LEIPÄLÄ, T., Physical Chemistry
LÖNNBERG, H., Animal Physiology
LÖVGREN, T., Information Systems Science
LUKKARI, J., Plant Ecology
NIKINMAA, M., Microelectronics
NURMINEN, M., Physical Chemistry
OKSANEN, LAURI, Genetics
PAASIO, A., Geology and Mineralogy
PIHLAJA, K., Food Development
PRIMMER, C., Biodiversity Research
SAARINEN, T., Ecology
SALMINEN, S., Radiochemistry
SALO, J., Geology and Mineralogy
SARVALA, J., Physics
SOLIN, O., Physics
SUNDBLAD, K., Astronomy
SUOMINEN, K.-A., Astronomy
TORSTI, J., Physics
VALTAOJA, E., Mathematics
VALTONEN, M., Human Geography
VÄYRYNEN, J., Mathematics
VIKSTRÖM, K. T., Human Geography
VILJANEN, P., Plant Physiology
VILJANEN, V.-P., Analytical and Inorganic Chemistry

Faculty of Medicine (Sirkkalankatu 1, 20520 Turku; tel. (2) 333 8408; fax (2) 333 8413; e-mail intmedi@utu.fi; internet www.med.utu.fi):

AARNIO, P., Pathology
ALANEN, P., Pathology
ARO, H., Diagnostic Radiology
CARPÉN, O., Obstetrics and Gynaecology
COLLAN, Y., Medical Biochemistry
DEAN, P., Otorhinolaryngology
ERKKOLA, R., Oral Surgery
FINNE, J., Clinical Physiology and Nuclear Medicine
GRÉNMAN, R., Psychiatry
HAPPONEN, R.-P., Physiology
HARTIALA, J., Virology
HIETALA, J., Paediatrics
HUHTANIEMI, I., Immunology
HYYPIÄ, T., Anaesthesiology
ISOLAURI, E., Dermatology and Venereal Diseases
JALKANEN, S., Medical Genetics
JALONEN, J., Synthetic Drug Chemistry
JANSÉN, C., General Practice
KÄÄRIÄINEN, H., Pharmacology
KANERVA, L., Public Health
KIVELÄ, S.-L., Immunobiology
KORPI, E., Nursing Science
KOSKENVUO, M., Neurology
LASSILA, O., Obstetrics and Gynaecology
LEINO-KILPI, H., Neurology
MAJAMAA, K., Clinical Chemistry
MÄKINEN, J., Rheumatology
MARTTILA, R., Surgery
MONONEN, I., Ophthalmology
MÖTTÖNEN, T., Internal Medicine
NIINIKOSKI, J. H. A., Internal Medicine
NIKOSKELAINEN, E., Anaesthesiology
NIKOSKELAINEN, J., Anatomy
NUUTILA, P., Electron Microscopy
OLKKOLA, K., Medical Biochemistry
PARVINEN, M., Physiology
PELLINIEMI, L., Child Psychiatry
PENTTINEN, R., Oncology and Radiotherapy
PERTOVAARA, A., Surgery
PIHA, J., Infectious Diseases
PYRHÖNEN, S., Internal Medicine
ROBERTS, P. J., Psychiatry
RUUSKANEN, O., Anaesthesiology
RÖNNEMAA, T., Psychiatry
SAARIJÄRVI, S., Anatomy
SALO, M., Forensic Medicine
SALOKANGAS, R., Positron Emission Tomography
SANTTI, M., Clinical Pharmacology
SAUKKO, P., Paediatric Neurology
SCHEININ, H., Paediatrics
SCHEININ, M., Biomaterial Technology
SILLANPÄÄ, M., Otorhynolaryngology
SIMELL, O. G., Oral Pathology

SÖDERGÅRD, O. G., Pharmacology
SUONPÄÄ, J., Cariology
SYRJÄNEN, S., Pulmonary Diseases and Clinical Allergology
SYVÄLAHTI, E., Physiology
TENOVUO, J. O., Nursing Science
TERHO, E. O., Cell Anatomy
TOPPARI, J., Oral Development and Orthodontics
VÄLIMÄKI, M., Internal Medicine
VÄÄNÄNEN, K., Geriatrics
VARRELA, J., Bacteriology and Serology
VIIKARI, J., Molecular Biology
VIITANEN, M., Occupational Health
VUORINEN, M., Surgery
YLI-JOKIPII, P., Community Dentistry
YLINEN, K., Surgery

Faculty of Social Sciences (tel. (2) 3335362; fax (2) 3336270; e-mail intsoc@utu.fi; internet www.soc.utu.fi):

ANTOLA, E., Psychology
FORSSÉN, K., Social Policy
HAKOVIRTA, H., Psychology
HÄMÄLÄINEN, H., Sociology of Education
KANGAS, O., Theoretical Philosophy
KESKINEN, E., Practical Philosophy
KIVINEN, O., Sociology
KOISTINEN, O., Contemporary Chinese History
LAGERSPETZ, E., Psychology
MELIN, H., Political Science
MÜHLHAHN, K., Sociology
NIEMI, P., Psychology
NURMI, H., Social Insurance
PÖNTINEN, S., Psychology
RÄIHÄ, H., Economics
RITAKALLIO, V.-M., Political History
SALMIVALLI, C., Biostatistics
SALONEN, H., Statistics
SOIKKANEN, T., Economics
TUOMINEN, J., Economics
UUSIPAIKKA, E., Political Science
VILJANEN, M., European Institutions and Civilizations
VUORIO, E., Social Work
WICKSTRÖM, G., Political Science, International Politics

ATTACHED INSTITUTES

Archipelago Research Institute: internet http://www.utu.fi/erill/saarmeri; Head Dr ILPPO VUORINEN.

Centre for Extension Studies: internet www.tkk.utu.fi; Head KARI SEPPÄLÄ.

Centre for Maritime Studies: internet http://mkk.utu.fi; Head Dr JUHANI VAINIO.

Functional Foods Forum: internet www.utu.fi/fff; Head Prof. SEPPO SALMINEN.

Kevo Subarctic Research Institute: internet www.utu.fi/erill/kevo; Head (vacant).

Language Centre: internet http://kielikeskus.utu.fi; Head VESA VÄÄTÄJÄ.

Satakunta Environmental Research Centre: internet www.utu.fi/erill/syke; Head Dr MIKKO OJANEN.

Tuorla Observatory: internet www.astro.utu.fi; Head Prof. ESKO VALTAOJA.

Turku Centre for Biotechnology: internet www.btk.fi; Head Dr RIITTA LAHESMAA.

Turku Centre for Computer Science: internet www.tucs.fi/about; Dir Prof. RALPH-JOHAN BACK.

Turku PET Centre: internet http://pet.utu.fi; Head Prof. JUHANI KNUUTI.

VAASAN YLIOPISTO
(University of Vaasa)

POB 700, 65200 Vaasa
located at: Puuvillakuja 8, 65200 Vaasa
Telephone: (6) 3248111
Fax: (6) 3248208
E-mail: kirjaamo@uwasa.fi
Internet: www.uwasa.fi

Founded 1966
Languages of instruction: Finnish, Swedish, English
State control
Academic year: September to May

Rector: MATTI JAKOBSSON
Vice-Rectors: MERJA KOSKELA JUKKA VESALAINEN
Administrative Director: ANITA NIEMI-IILAHTI
Librarian: Director VUOKKO PALONEN

Library of 120,000 vols; also see entry for the Tritonia Academic Library
Number of teachers: 220
Number of students: 5,100
Publication: *Acta Wasaensia*

DEANS

Faculty of Business Studies: Prof. MARTTI LAAKSONEN
Faculty of Humanities: Prof. MARIANN SKOG-SÖDERSVED
Faculty of Public Administration: Prof. ARI SALMINEN
Faculty of Technology: Prof. ILKKA VIRTANEN

PROFESSORS

Faculty of Business Studies (tel. (6) 3248111; fax (6) 3248171; internet www.uwasa.fi/ktt):

GAHMBERG, H., Management and Organization
LAAKSONEN, M., Marketing
LAAKSONEN, P., Marketing
LAITINEN, E. K., Accounting and Business Finance
LAITINEN, T., Accounting and Business Finance
LARIMO, J., International Marketing
LEHTONEN, A., Law
LUOMALA, H., Marketing
NIKKINEN, J., Accounting and Business and Finance
PIHKALA, T., Management and Organization
ROTHOVIUS, T., Accounting and Business Finance
ROUTAMAA, V., Management and Organization
ROTHIVIUS, T., Accounting and Business Finance
SALMI, T., Accounting and Business Finance
SUUTARI, V., Management and Organization
TOLONEN, J., Business Law
VATAJA, J., Economics
VESALAINEN, J., Management and Organization
VIITALA, R., Management and Organization

Faculty of Humanities (tel. (6) 3248111; fax (6) 3248131; internet www.uwasa.fi/hut):

AALTONEN, S., English Language, Literature and Culture
BJÖRKLUND, S., Language Immersion
KOSKELA, M., Applied Linguistics
LAURÉN, CH., Swedish
LEHTINEN, E., Modern Finnish
NORDMAN, M., Swedish
PARRY, CH., German Literature
PILKE, N., Swedish
ROMPPANEN, B., Modern Finnish
SKOG-SÖDERSVED, M., German Literature
SÖDERGÅRD, M., Swedish

Faculty of Public Administration (tel. (6) 3248111; fax (6) 3248465; internet www.uwasa.fi/ytt):

KATAJAMÄKI, H., Regional Studies
SALMINEN, A., Public Administration
VARTIAINEN, P., Public Administration

Faculty of Technology (tel. (6) 3248111; fax (6) 3248344; internet www.uwasa.fi/itt):

ALANDER, J., Production Automation
HASSI, S., Mathematics
HELO, P., Logistics
KAUHANIEMI, K., Electrical Engineering
KEKÄLE, T., Production Economics
LINNA, M., Information Technology
PYNNÖNEN, S., Statistics
SALMENJOKI, K., Information Technology
TAKALA, J., Production Economics
VEKARA, T., Electrical Engineering
VIRTANEN, I., Operations Research and Management Science
WANNE., M., Information Technology

ATTACHED INSTITUTES

Computer Centre: Dir M. TAANONEN.

Levón Institute: Dir J. HAVUNEN.

Tritonia Academic Library: Dir VUOKKO PALONEN.

University of Vaasa, Seinäjoki: Dir T. ROUHUNKOSKI.

Polytechnics

Diakonia-ammattikorkeakoulu (Diaconia University of Applied Sciences): Maistraatinportti 2A, 00240 Helsinki; tel. (20) 1606220; fax (20) 1606222; internet www.diak.fi; f. 1996; education, nursing, social welfare, sign language interpretation and media; library: 140,000 vols, periodicals and audiovisual items; 3,000 students; Rector Dr JORMA NIEMALÄ.

Etelä-Karjalan ammattikorkeakoulu (South Karelia Polytechnic): Pohjolankatu 23, 53101 Lappeenranta; tel. (20) 49600; fax (20) 4966688; e-mail info@scp.fi; internet www.scp.fi; faculties of business administration, fine arts and design, healthcare and social services, technology and tourism and hospitality; 260 teachers; 2,700 students; Rector ANNELI PIRTTILÄ.

EVTEK-ammattikorkeakoulu (Espoon-Vantaan teknillinen ammattikorkeakoulu) (Espoo-Vantaa Institute of Technology): Vanha maantie 6, 02650 Espoo; tel. (20) 7553500; fax (20) 7553929; e-mail education@evtek.fi; internet www.evtek.fi; three divisions: EVTEK Institute of Technology, EVTEK Mercuria Business School, EVTEK Institute of Art and Design; library: 30,600 vols, 320 periodicals; Pres. Dr PERTTI TÖRMÄLÄ.

Haaga ammattikorkeakoulu (Haaga Polytechnic): POB 8, 00321 Helsinki; tel. (9) 58078214; fax (9) 58078489; e-mail hakutoimisto@haaga.fi; internet www.haaga.fi; Haaga Institute School of Hotel, Restaurant and Tourism Management; Helsinki School of Business; Malmi School of Business and Vierumäki Sports Institute; Pres. ANTTI HALLI.

Hämeen ammattikorkeakoulu (Häme Polytechnic): Visamäentie 35, 13100 Hämeenlinna; tel. (3) 6461; fax (3) 6464200; e-mail HAMK@hamk.fi; internet www.hamk.fi; f. 1996; culture, natural resources and the environment, natural sciences, social sciences, business and administration, social services, health and sports technology, communication and transport tourism, catering and domestic services and vocational teacher education; library: 120,000 vols, 450 periodicals in Finnish, 350 in other languages; 7,500 teachers; 400 students; Rector VEIJO HINTSANEN.

Helsingin ammattikorkeakoulu Stadia (Helsinki Polytechnic Stadia): POB 4010, Bulevardi 31, 00099 Helsinki; tel. (9) 3108611; fax (9) 31080599; e-mail info@stadia.fi; internet www.stadia.fi; f. 2000; library: 120,000 vols; 551 teachers; 7,284 students; Rector TIMO LUOPAJÄRVI.

Helsingin liiketalouden ammattikorkeakoulu (Helsinki Business Polytechnic): Ratapihantie 13, 00520 Helsinki; tel. (9) 148901; fax (9) 14890453; internet www.helia.fi; business management, information technology, journalism, tourism, management assistant training; vocational teacher education programmes; 230 teachers; 5,500 students; Rector RITVA LAAKSO-MANNINEN.

HUMAK (Hakutoimistoon) (Humanities Polytechnic): Kivirannantie 13–15, 95410 Kiviranta; internet www.humak.edu; f. 1998; programmes in civic activities and youth work, cultural management and production and sign language interpretering; 120 teachers; 1,300 students; Pres. EEVA-LIISA ANTIKAINEN.

Jyväskylän ammattikorkeakoulu (Jyväskylä Polytechnic): Rajakatu 35, 40200 Jyväskylä; tel. (14) 4446611; fax (14) 4446600; internet www.jypoly.fi; School of Cultural Studies, School of Business, School of Engineering and Technology, School of Information Technology, School of Health and Social Care, School of Tourism and Services Management; Institute of Natural Resources; Vocational Teacher Education College; 600 teachers; 7,500 students; Rector MAURI PANHELAINEN.

Kajaanin ammattikorkeakoulu (Kajaani Polytechnic): POB 52, Ketunpolku 3, 87101 Kajaani; tel. (8) 618991; fax (8) 61899603; e-mail kajaanin.amk@kajak.fi; internet www.kajak.fi; f. 1992; business and administration, tourism and hospitality management, health and sports and engineering; library: 27,000 vols, 350 periodicals; 130 students; 1,500 students; Rector ARTO KARJALAINEN.

Kemi-Tornion ammattikorkeakoulu (Kemi-Tornio Polytechnic): POB 505, 94101 Kemi; tel. (16) 258400; fax (16) 258401; internet www.tokem.fi; f. 1992; business administration, business and data-processing, cultural and media arts, health care, social services, technology; library: 90,000 vols, 600 periodicals; 195 teachers; 2,400 students; Dean LEENA ALALÄÄKKÖLÄ.

Kymenlaakso ammattikorkeakoulu (Kymenlaakso Polytechnic): POB 13, Pääskysentie 1, 48231 Kotka; tel. (5) 2208111; fax (5) 2208209; internet www.kyamk.fi; f. 1992; business and administration, culture, forestry and wood technology, maritime studies, social and health care and technology; library: 100,000 vols, 500 periodicals; 500 teachers; 3,500 students; Rector RAGNAR LUNDQVIST.

Lahden ammattikorkeakoulu (Lahti Polytechnic): POB 214, Paasikivenkatu 7, 15101 Lahti; tel. (3) 82818; fax (3) 8282066; internet www.lamk.fi; f. 1991; business studies, design, fine arts, music, hospitality management, social and health care, sports, technology and engineering and visual communication; 200 teachers; 5,000 students; Dr RISTO ILOMÄKI.

Laurea ammattikorkeakoulu (Laurea Polytechnic): Lummetie 2B, 01300 Vantaa; tel. (9) 205787150; fax (9) 205787200; internet www.laurea.fi; culture, natural resources and the environment, natural sciences, social sciences, business and administration, social services, health and sports, tourism, catering and domestic services, hotel and restaurant studies and correctional services; 8,000 students; Rector PENTTI RAUHALA.

Mikkelin ammattikorkeakoulu (Mikkeli Polytechnic): Patteristonkatu 3, 50101 Mikkeli; tel. (15) 3556407; fax (15) 3556377; internet www.mikkeliamk.fi; Business School, School of Engineering, School of Social Work and Health Care, School of Culture and Youth Work, School of Hospitality Management, School of Forestry (Pieksämäki), School of Health Care, Tourism and Culture (Savonlinna); 200 teachers; 4,000 students; Rector ERKKI KARPPANEN.

Österbottens Yrkeshögskola (Central Ostrobothnia Polytechnic): Talonpojankatu 4, 67100 Kokkola; tel. (6) 8252012; fax (6) 8252075; internet www.cop.fi; f. 1998; languages of instruction: Finnish, Swedish, English; technology, communication and transport, social sciences, business and administration, social services, health and sports, natural sciences, culture, humanities and education, tourism, catering and domestic services; post-graduate programmes in business administration and technology; 246 teachers; 3,300 students; Rector MARJA-LIISA TENHUNEN.

Oulun Seudun ammattikorkeakoulu (Oulu Polytechnic): Albertinkuja 20, POB 222, 90101 Oulu; tel. (8) 3126011; fax (8) 3126009; e-mail international@oamk.fi; internet www.oamk.fi; f. 1992; culture, natural resources and the environment, natural sciences, social sciences, business and administration, social services, health and sports and technology, communication and transport; 7,700 students; Rector LAURI LANTTO.

Pirkanmaa ammattikorkeakoulu (Pirkanmaa Polytechnic): Kuntokatu 4, 33520 Tampere; tel. (3) 2452111; fax (3) 2452351; e-mail piramk@piramk.fi; internet www.piramk.fi; f. 1992; social services, health and sports, social sciences, business and administration, natural sciences, tourism, catering and domestic services, culture, technology, communication and transport; 4,000 students; Rector OLLI MIKKILÄ; publ. *Spirit*.

Pohjois-Karjalan ammattikorkeakoulu (North Karelia Polytechnic): Tikkarinne 9, 80200 Joensuu; tel. (13) 2606404; fax (13) 2606401; e-mail info@ncp.fi; internet www.ncp.fi; f. 1992; culture, social sciences, business and administration, natural sciences, natural resources and the environment, tourism, catering and domestic services, social services, health and sports, technology, communication and transport; adult education; 400 teachers; 4,000 students; Pres. PENTTI MALJOJOKI.

Rovaniemen ammattikorkeakoulu (Rovaniemi Polytechnic): Jokiväylä 13, 96300; tel. (16) 3313366; fax (16) 3313328; e-mail polytechnic@ramk.fi; internet www.ramk.fi; f. 1996; business and administration, forestry and rural industries, healthcare and social services, sports and leisure, technology, tourism and hospitality management; 3,000 students; Pres. PENTTI TIERANTA.

Satakunnan ammattikorkeakoulu (Satakunta Polytechnic): Tiedepuisto 3, 28600 Pori; tel. (2) 6203000; fax (2) 6203030; e-mail int.kesy@samk.fi; internet www.spt.fi; f. 1997; business, fine art and media studies, social services and healthcare, technology and maritime management and tourism; 530 teachers; 6,417 students.

Savonia-ammattikorkeakoulu (Pohjois-Savo Polytechnic): POB 6, 70201 Kuopio; tel. (17) 2555062; internet www.savonia-amk.fi; f. 1992; social sciences, business and administration, culture, natural resources and the environment, tourism, catering and domestic services, social services, health and sports technology, communication and transport and natural sciences; 350 teachers; 7,000 students.

Seinäjoen ammattikorkeakoulu (Seinäjoki Polytechnic): Keskuskatu 34, 60100 Seinäjoki; tel. (20) 1245000; fax (20) 1245001; e-mail seamk.toimisto@seamk.fi; internet www.seamk.fi; f. 1996; natural resources and the environment, natural sciences, social sciences, business and administration, technology and communication and transport, social services, health and sports, tourism, catering and domestic services and culture; 350 teachers; 4,600 students; Rector TAPIO VARMOLA.

Svenska yrkeshögskolan (Swedish Polytechnic, Finland): Fabriksgatan 1, POB 6, 65200 Vaasa; tel. (6) 3285000; fax (6) 3285110; internet www.syh.fi; language of instruction: Swedish; culture, healthcare and social welfare and technology and communications; Rector ÖRJAN ANDERSSON.

Tampereen ammattikorkeakoulu (Tampere Polytechnic): Teiskontie 33, PL 21 33521 Tampere; tel. (3) 20711011; e-mail international.office@tamk.fi; internet www.tpu.fi; f. 1996; languages of instruction: Finnish, English; bachelor-level degrees in art and media, business economics and technology, international business, environmental engineering; teacher education centre; 400 full-time teachers, 700 part-time; 5,000 students; Rector MARKKU LAHTINEN.

Turun ammattikorkeakoulu (Turku Polytechnic): Sepänkatu 3, 20700 Turku; tel. (10) 55350; fax (10) 5535791; internet www.turkuamk.fi; f. 1992; 460 teachers; 9,000 students; Rector Dr JUHA KETTUNEN.

Vaasa ammattikorkeakoulu (Vaasa Polytechnic): Raastuvankatu 29, 65100 Vaasa; tel. (6) 3263111; fax (6) 3263002; e-mail info@puv.fi; internet www.puv.fi; f. 1996; languages of instruction: Finnish, Swedish, English; faculties of business economics, tourism, health care and social services and technology and communication; 240 teachers; 3,500 students; PENTTI RUOTSALA; publ. *Scenario* (1 or 2 a year).

Yrkeshögskolan Arcada (Arcada Polytechnic): Jan-Magnus Janssons plats 1, 00550 Helsingfors; tel. (7) 699699; fax (7) 699622; internet www.arcada.fi; f. 1996; courses in culture, healthcare and social work, rehabilitation, business administration and tourism, technology; library: 23,500 vols; 90 teachers; 1,900 students; Rector HENRIK WOLFF.

Yrkeshögskolan Sydväst (Sydväst Polytechnic): Raseborgsvägen 9, 10600 Ekenäs; tel. (19) 2227200; fax (19) 2227499; e-mail office@sydvast.fi; internet www.sydvast.fi; language of instruction: Swedish; design, tourism management, culture production, sports and health promotion, social care, healthcare, church community work, business administration, engineering, maritime studies, forestry, agriculture, horticulture, landscape planning and environmental instruction; 1,350 students; Rector JAN NYBOM.

ÅLAND ISLANDS

Learned Society

GENERAL

Ålands kulturstiftelse (Åland Cultural Foundation): POB 172, 22101 Mariehamn; tel. (18) 19535; internet www.kultur.aland.fi/kulturstiftelsen; f. 1950; promotes research of Åland history and cultural life in the islands; Pres. HENRIK GUSTAFSSON; Sec. THÉRÈSE KÅHRE.

Library

Mariehamn

Mariehamns stadsbibliotek–Centralbibliotek för Åland (Mariehamn City Library–Central Library of Åland): POB 76, Strandgatan 29, 22100 Mariehamn; tel. (18) 531411; fax (18) 531619; e-mail biblioteket@mariehamn.aland.fi; internet www.mhbibl.aland.fi; 120,000 vols; Alandica collection (works relating to the islands); Chief Librarian TOM ECKERMAN.

Museums and Art Galleries

Lappo

Skärgårdsmuseet (Museum of the Archipelago): 22840 Lappo; tel. (18) 56689; internet www.kulturfonden.fi/skargardsmuseet/; traditional island and fishing culture; blacksmith's workshop.

Mariehamn

Ålands konstmuseum (Åland Art Museum): Stadshusparken, 22100 Mariehamn; tel. (18) 25000; fax (18) 17440; e-mail konst.info@aland-museum.aland.fi; internet www.aland-museum.aland.fi/konst; f. 1963; local artists since 19th c.; Curator SUSANNE PROCOPÉ ILMONEN.

Ålands museum: Stadshusparken, 22100 Mariehamn; tel. (18) 25000; fax (18) 17440; e-mail info@aland-museum.aland.fi; internet www.aland-museum.aland.fi; f. 1934; prehistoric, historic and ethnological material; library of 27,000 vols; Dir ANNIKA DAHLBLOM; publs *Ålands Folkminnesförbund*, *Åländsk Odling* (annually), *Bygdeserien*.

Ålands Sjöfartsmuseum (Åland Maritime Museum): Hamngatan 2, 22100 Mariehamn; tel. (18) 19930; fax (18) 19936; e-mail info@sjofartsmuseum.ax; internet www.sjofartsmuseum.ax; f. 1935; ships' documents, model ships and figureheads; Pres. JAN LIMNELL; Dir Dr HANNA HAGMARK-COOPER; publ. *Sjöhistorisk Årsskrift för Åland* (annual).

College

Högskolan på Åland (Åland University College): POB 1010, 22111 Mariehamn; tel. (18) 537000; fax (18) 16913; e-mail info@ha.aland.fi; internet www.ha.aland.fi; f. 1981, present name 2003; language of instruction: Swedish; faculties: business administration, electrical engineering, health and caring sciences, hospitality, information technology, mechanical engineering, navigation; Open Polytechnic in Mariehamn attached to the university college; 32 teachers; 380 students; Rector AGNETA ERIKSSON-GRANSKOG.

FRANCE

The Higher Education System

The French higher education system was restructured following the student-led unrest of 1968. The Loi de l'Orientation d'Education was enacted (it was reconfirmed 1989) and greater autonomy was granted to institutions. However, ultimate responsibility for determining the curricula and teaching methods remain with the Ministry of Education. France and the French Overseas Posssessions are divided into 35 educational districts, called Académies, each responsible for the administration of education, from primary to higher levels, in its area. There are 91 universities (a term which includes instituts universitaires de technologie—university institutes of technology) under the Ministry of Education, including universities in French Overseas Possessions; these institutions are: Université des Antilles et de la Guyane (French Guiana, Guadeloupe, Martinique), Université de la Polynésie Française (French Polynesia), Université de Nouvelle Calédonie (New Caledonia) and Université de la Réunion (Réunion).

Students must have achieved the baccalauréat, the main secondary school qualification, to gain admission to higher education. Some institutions may set additional entrance examinations, and the grandes écoles require students to undertake two- to three-years' additional study at a lycée. Since 2002 France has gradually implemented the Bologna Process and established a two-tier Bachelors and Masters degree system, completed by Doctoral studies. Some institutions may still offer professional qualifications or non-standard degrees. The standard undergraduate degree is now the three-year Licence (equivalent to Bachelors). Following the Licence, students may take the Masters, which is awarded after two years and replaces the range of pre-Bologna five-year degrees. There are two Masters tracks, Research or Professional. The Research Masters is required for entry to Doctoral studies, and the Doctorate is awarded after three years of study. Alternatively, medical students are required to study for a total of seven years for the Doctoral degree of Diplôme d'État de Docteur en Médecine.

In addition to universities and instituts universitaires de technologie, other public institutions offering higher education include instituts universitaires professionnalisés, grandes écoles and ecoles normales eupérieures. There are also professional schools for engineering, business and management, political sciences and veterinary sciences. Instituts universitaires de technologie were first established in 1966 and offer specialist two-year programmes leading to the award of Diplôme Universitaire de Technologie. Instituts universitaires professionnalisés have been established since 1992 and train senior executives for engineering, business and management, general administration, information and communication. Courses last for six years, including a six-month work placement, and culminate in the award of the Maîtrise degree. Grandes écoles are regarded as the most prestigious establishments for graduates wishing to enter high public service or business. The most prominent grandes écoles are the écoles normales supérieures; courses last for four years and students are awarded the Diplôme d'Études Appronfondies.

Technical and vocational education is broken down into five levels, Niveau V to Niveau I, and is offered by secondary and post-secondary institutions. Broadly speaking, Niveaux III–I cover the post-secondary level, and lead to the award of a title such as Brevet de Technicien Supérieur, Diplôme d'Etat de Technicien, or Diplôme Universitaire de Technologie.

Regulatory and Representative Bodies

GOVERNMENT

Ministry of Culture and Communication: 3 rue de Valois, 75001 Paris; tel. 1-40-15-80-00; fax 1-42-61-35-77; e-mail point.culture@culture.fr; internet www.culture.gouv.fr; Minister CHRISTINE ALBANEL.

Ministry of Higher Education and Research: 1 rue Descartes, 75231 Paris Cedex 05; tel. 1-55-55-90-90; e-mail secretariat-communication@recherche.gouv.fr; internet www.enseignementsup-recherche.gouv.fr; Minister VALÉRIE PÉCRESSE.

Ministry of National Education: 110 rue de Grenelle, 75357 Paris Cedex 07; tel. 1-55-55-10-10; fax 1-45-51-53-63; internet www.education.gouv.fr; Minister XAVIER DARCOS.

ACCREDITATION

Comité national d'évaluation (CNE): 43 rue de la Procession, 75015 Paris; tel. 1-55-55-60-97; fax 1-55-55-63-94; e-mail sgcne@cne-evaluation.fr; internet www.cne-evaluation.fr; f. 1984; government org. with authority over all institutions of higher education in France; evaluation of quality of main 'missions of public service' of each such institution; Pres. (vacant).

Commission des Titres d'Ingénieur (CTI): La Blonderie, 4 chemin du Plat, 69130 Ecully; tel. 6-61-32-99-70; internet www.cti-commission.fr; f. 1934; quality assurance and accreditation for engineers; Pres. BERNARD REMAUD.

NATIONAL BODIES

Conférence des Directeurs des Ecoles Françaises d'Ingénieurs (CDEFI): 151 blvd de l'Hôpital, 75013 Paris; tel. 1-44-24-64-49; fax 1-44-24-64-51; e-mail cdefi@cdefi.fr; internet www.cdefi.fr; f. 1976; Exec. Dir ALEXANDRE RIGAL.

Conférence des Présidents d'Université: 103 blvd Saint-Michel, 75005 Paris; tel. 1-44-32-90-00; fax 1-44-32-91-58; f. 1971; consultative body at the disposition of the Minister of Education; also studies questions of interest to all universities and co-ordinates the activities of various commissions on all aspects of education; mems: 103 pres of univs and state institutions; Pres. The Minister for Education; First Vice-Pres. YANNICK VALLÉE.

Conférence des Recteurs Français: Chancellerie des universités de Paris, 47 rue des Ecoles, 75005 Paris; f. 1987 to establish personal and permanent links between mems, to encourage the discussion of professional problems, and to establish relations with nat. and int. bodies concerned with education, science and culture; 31 mems; the Rectors are Chancellors of the State univs in their administrative area; Pres. Rector MICHEL LEROY (Acad. de Nancy-Metz); Sec. Gen./Treas. Rector WILLIAM MAROIS (Acad. de Bordeaux).

Fédération Interuniversitaire de l'Enseignement à Distance (FIED): 1 chemin du Fort Griffon, 25030 Besançon Cedex; tel. 3-81-66-58-65; fax 3-81-66-58-71; e-mail fied@up.univ-mrs.fr; internet telesup.univ-mrs.fr; f. 1987; promotes distance learning by encouraging co-operation between French and international universities and institutions; 35 mems; Pres. RONAN CHABAUTY; Sec. CHANTAL ACHERÉ.

Union des Professeurs de Spéciales (Mathématiques et Sciences Physiques): 3 rue de l'École Polytechnique, 75005 Paris; tel. 1-43-26-97-92; fax 1-43-26-97-92; e-mail ups@prepas.org; internet www.prepas.org; f. 1927; 2,500 mems; Pres. GERARD DEBEAUMARCHÉ; Sec. CHRISTINE METIVIER; publ. *Bulletin* (4 a year).

Learned Societies

GENERAL

Académie des Jeux Floraux: Hotel d'Assézat, 31000 Toulouse; tel. 5-61-21-22-85; e-mail jeux.floraux@free.fr; internet jeux.floraux.free.fr; f. 1323; human sciences; composed of 40 'mainteneurs' and 25 'Maîtres ès Jeux Floraux'; Permanent Sec. JEAN NAYRAL DE PUYBUSQUE; publ. *Recueil* (annually).

Académie des Sciences, Agriculture, Arts et Belles-Lettres d'Aix: 2A rue du 4-Septembre, 13100 Aix-en-Provence; tel. 4-42-38-38-95; e-mail musee.arbaud@free.fr; f. 1829; library of 60,000 journals and plates, 10,000 books, 5,000 biographical MSS, 2,000 MSS related to local history, 1,200 portraits and 60 paintings of the Aix-en-Provence region; collections of ceramics, paintings, sculptures; 40 fellows, 50 assoc. mems; Pres. XAVIER LAVAGNE D'ORTIGUE; Perm. Sec. GEORGES SOUVILLE; publ. *Bulletin*.

Académie des Sciences, Arts et Belles-Lettres de Dijon: 5 rue de l'Ecole de Droit, 21000 Dijon; f. 1740; 550 mems; library; Pres. MICHEL PAUTY; Sec. MARTINE CHAUNEY-BOUILLOT; publs *Mémoires de l'Académie* (every 2 years), *Mémoires de la Commission des Antiquités de la Côte d'Or* (every 2 years).

Académie des Sciences, Belles-Lettres et Arts de Lyon: Palais Saint-Jean, 4 ave Adolphe Max, 69005 Lyons; tel. 4-78-38-26-54; fax 4-72-77-90-56; internet academiedelyon.nexenservices.com; f. 1700; 52 elected mems; library of 60,000 vols; Pres. M. J. REMILLIEUX; Chancellor M. N. MONGEREAU; publ. *Mémoires* (annually).

Académie des Sciences d'Outre-mer: 15 rue Lapérouse, 75116 Paris; tel. 1-47-20-87-93; fax 1-47-20-89-72; e-mail academie .sciencesoutre-mer@wanadoo.fr; internet perso.wanadoo.fr/academiedessciencesdoutremer; f. 1922; 275 mems (incl. 100 corresp., 50 assoc., 25 free mems); library of 60,000 vols and 2,000 periodicals; sections on Geography, Politics and Administration, Law, Economics and Sociology, Science and Medicine, Education; Perm. Sec. GILBERT MANGIN; publ. *Mondes et Cultures* (annually).

Académie Goncourt: Société de Gens de Lettres, c/o Drouant, Place Gaillon, 75002 Paris; internet www.academie-goncourt.fr; f. 1896 by Edmond de Goncourt; comprises 10 writers in the French language; each year they compile a shortlist of the most noteworthy fiction written in French and award 'le prix Goncourt' to the author of the work judged the best; Pres. FRANÇOIS NOURISSIER; Sec.-Gen. DIDIER DECOIN.

Agence de la Francophonie: 28 rue de Bourgogne, 75007 Paris; tel. 1-44-11-12-50; fax 1-44-11-12-76; e-mail oif@francophonie .org; internet www.francophonie.org; f. 1970; an intergovernmental organization of French-speaking countries for co-operation in the fields of education, culture, science, technology, and in any other ways to bring the peoples of those countries closer together; 47 mems; Dir CHRISTIAN VALANTIN.

Alliance Française de Paris: 101 blvd Raspail, 75270 Paris Cedex 06; tel. 1-42-84-90-00; fax 1-42-84-90-91; e-mail info@ alliancefr.org; internet www.alliancefr.org; f. 1883; French language school for foreigners; independent institution; 20,000 students; Pres. JACQUES VIOT; Sec.-Gen. JEAN HARZIC; Dir of the School ANNIE MONNERIE-GOARIN.

Comité des Travaux Historiques et Scientifiques: 1 rue Descartes, 75005 Paris; tel. 1-55-55-97-57; fax 1-55-55-97-60; e-mail martine.francois@education.gouv.fr; internet www.cths.fr; f. 1834; attached to Min. of Education; research and publs in the fields of history, archaeology, geography, human sciences, natural sciences, life sciences; organizes annual national congress of learned societies; 255 mems; Vice-Pres. M. J.-R. GABORIT; Gen. Sec. MARTINE FRANÇOIS; publ. *Actes du Congrès national des Sociétés savantes*.

Euskaltzaindia/Académie de la Langue Basque: 18 rue Thiers, 64100 Bayonne; tel. 5-59-25-64-26; fax 5-59-59-45-59; e-mail euskalbai@wanadoo.fr; internet www .euskaltzaindia.net; See also Spain chapter, Learned Societies.

Institut de France: 23 quai de Conti, 75270 Paris Cedex 06; tel. 1-44-41-44-41; fax 1-44-41-43-41; e-mail com@institut-de-france.fr; internet www.institut-de-france.fr; f. 1795; 623 mems; Chancellor PIERRE MESSMER; Dir of Services ERIC PEUCHOT.

Constituent academies:

Académie Française: 23 quai Conti, 75270 Paris Cedex 06; tel. 1-44-41-43-00; fax 1-43-29-47-45; e-mail contact@ academie-francaise.fr; internet www .academie-francaise.fr; f. 1635; 40 mems; Permanent Sec. HÉLÈNE CARRÈRE D'ENCAUSSE.

Académie des Inscriptions et Belles-Lettres: 23 quai Conti, 75270 Paris Cedex 06; tel. 1-44-41-43-10; fax 1-44-41-43-11; e-mail j.leclant.aibl@dial.oleane.com; internet www.aibl.fr; f. 1663; 195 mems (55 academicians, 40 foreign assocs, 50 French and 50 foreign corresp.); Pres. JACQUES JOUANNA; Permanent Sec. JEAN LECLANT; publs *Comptes Rendus des Séances* (4 a year), *Journal des Savants* (2 a year), *Monuments et Mémoires de la Fondation Eugène Piot* (annually).

Académie des Sciences: 23 quai Conti, 75270 Paris Cedex 06; tel. 1-44-41-44-41; fax 1-44-41-43-63; internet www .academie-sciences.fr; f. 1666; sections of the first division: Mathematics, Physics, Mechanical Engineering and Informatics, Sciences of the Universe; sections of the second division: Chemistry, Molecular and Cellular Biology, Genomics, Integrative Biology, Human Biology and Medical Sciences; inter-section; 250 mems, at most 150 foreign assocs and 143 corresp. mems; Pres. EDOUARD BRÉZIN; Vice-Pres. JULES HOFFMANN; Permanent Secs JEAN DERCOURT (Sciences of the Universe and their Applications), NICOLE LE DOUARIN (Chemical, Biological and Medical Sciences and their Applications); publs *Comptes Rendus Mathématique* (24 a year), *Comptes Rendus Mécanique* (monthly), *Comptes Rendus Physique* (10 a year), *Comptes Rendus Geoscience* (16 a year), *Comptes Rendus Palevol* (palaeontology and evolution, 8 a year), *Comptes Rendus Chimie* (monthly), *Comptes Rendus Biologies* (monthly), *La Lettre de l'Académie des Sciences* (newsletter, 4 a year).

Académie des Technologies: 28 rue Saint-Dominique, 75007 Paris Cedex 06; tel. 1-53-85-44-44; fax 1-53-85-44-45; e-mail secretariat@academie-technologies .fr; internet www.academie-technologies .fr; f. 2000 to analyse and publicize academic studies on technology and its impact on society, to ensure that society benefits from technological progress; 218 mems; Pres. FRANÇOIS GUINOT; Dir ALAN RODNEY.

Académie des Beaux-Arts: 23 quai Conti, 75270 Paris Cedex 06; tel. 1-44-41-43-20; fax 1-44-41-44-99; internet academie-des-beaux-arts.fr; f. 1648; sections of Painting, Sculpture, Architecture, Engraving, Musical Composition, Free Members, Artistic Creation (Cinema and Audiovisual Arts); 126 mems (55 ordinary, 55 corresp., 16 foreign assocs); Pres. JEAN PRODROMIDRÈS; Permanent Sec. ARNAUD D'HAUTERIVES; publ. *La Lettre de l'Académie des Beaux-Arts* (4 a year).

Académie des Sciences Morales et Politiques: 23 quai Conti, 75270 Paris Cedex 06; tel. 1-44-41-43-26; fax 1-44-41-43-27; e-mail kerbrat@asmp.fr; internet www.asmp.fr; f. 1795; sections of Philosophy, of Moral and Sociological Sciences, of Legislation, Public Law and Jurisprudence, of Political Economy, Statistics and Finance, of History and Geography, of General Interest; 122 mems (50 ordinary, 60 corresp., 12 foreign assocs); Pres. JEAN TULARD; Permanent Sec. MICHEL ALBERT; publs *Notices biographiques et bibliographiques*, *Cahiers des sciences morales et politiques*.

AGRICULTURE, FISHERIES AND VETERINARY SCIENCE

Académie d'Agriculture de France: 18 rue de Bellechasse, 75007 Paris; tel. 1-47-05-10-37; fax 1-45-55-09-78; e-mail aaf@paris .inra.fr; internet www.academie-agriculture .fr; f. 1761; 120 mems; 60 foreign mems; 180 corresp. mems; 60 foreign corresp. mems; Pres. ANDRÉ FROUIN; Perm. Sec. GEORGES PÉDRO; library of 80,000 vols, 500 periodicals; publ. *Comptes rendus* (4 a year).

Académie Vétérinaire de France: 34 rue Bréguet, 75011 Paris; tel. 1-53-36-16-19; e-mail academie@veterinaire.fr; internet www.academie-veterinaire-france.fr; f. 1844; 44 mems; Pres. PIERRE LARVOR; Sec.-Gen. CLAUDE MILHAUD.

Association Centrale des Vétérinaires: 10 place Léon Blum, 75011 Paris; f. 1889; 3,000 mems; Pres. Dr J. P. MARTY.

Association Française pour l'Etude du Sol (French Soil Science Society): INRA, BP 20619, ave de la Pomme de Pin, 45166 Olivet; tel. 2-38-41-48-23; fax 2-38-41-78-69; e-mail afretsol@orleans.inra.fr; internet www.afes .fr; f. 1934; pedology, agronomy; 800 mems; Pres. Dr ROLAND POSS; publ. *Etude et Gestion des Sols* (quarterly).

Société Française d'Economie Rurale: INA-PG, 16 rue Claude Bernard, 75231 Paris Cedex 05; tel. 1-47-07-47-86; fax 1-44-08-18-42; e-mail sfer@inapg.inra.fr; internet www .sfer.asso.fr/sfer; f. 1949; two study sessions a year; 400 mems; Pres. LUCIEN BOURGEOIS; Sec.-Gen. DENIS HAIRY; publ. *Economie Rurale* (every 2 months).

Société Nationale d'Horticulture de France (SNHF): 84 rue de Grenelle, 75007 Paris; tel. 1-44-39-78-78; fax 1-45-44-76-57; e-mail info@snhf.org; internet www.snhf .asso.fr; f. 1827; 8,000 mems, 120,000 affiliated mems; library of 16,000 vols; Pres. JEAN PUECH; Gen. Sec. (vacant); publ. *Jardins de France* (10 a year).

Société Vétérinaire Pratique de France: 10 Pl. Léon Blum, 75011 Paris; f. 1879; 750 mems; Pres. JEAN-PIERRE BARDET; Sec.-Gen. JACQUES DOUCET; publ. *Bulletin* (5 a year).

ARCHITECTURE AND TOWN PLANNING

Académie d'Architecture: 9 place des Vosges, 75004 Paris; tel. 1-48-87-83-10; internet www.archi.fr/AA; f. 1840 as Société Centrale des Architectes, name changed 1953; 100 elected mems; Pres. AYMERIC ZUBLENA; Gen. Sec. JEAN-MARIE VALENTIN.

Association Nationale pour la Protection des Villes d'Art: 39 ave de La Motte-Picquet, 75007 Paris; tel. 1-47-05-37-71; f. 1963; an association of local societies in 85 cities for the protection and restoration of historic and artistic buildings; Pres. J. DE SACY.

Cité de l'Architecture et du Patrimoine: Palais de Chaillot, 1 pl. du Trocadéro, 75116 Paris; tel. 1-58-51-52-00; fax 1-58-51-52-50; e-mail info@citechaillot.org; internet www .citechaillot.org; f. 1980; funded by Min. of Culture; contemporary French architecture and architectural heritage; library of 10,000 vols, 70 periodicals; Pres. FRANÇOIS DE MAZIÈRES; publs *Archiscopie* (monthly), *Colonnes* (2 a year).

Compagnie des Experts-Architectes près la Cour d'Appel de Paris: 24 rue Bezout, 75014 Paris; tel. 1-43-27-59-69; fax 1-43-20-47-96; e-mail info@ceacap.org; internet www.ceacap.org; f. 1928; 125 mems; Pres. MICHEL AUSTRY; Gen. Sec. ROBERT LEGRAS.

Conseil National de l'Ordre des Architectes: 9 rue Borromé, 75015 Paris; tel. 1-56-58-67-00; fax 1-56-58-67-01; e-mail info@cnoa.com; internet www.architectes.org; f. 1977 as the official regulating body for the architectural profession; Pres. of Conseil YVES MAGNAN; Sec. ALAIN FABREGA; publ. *d'Architectures* (monthly).

Office Général du Bâtiment et des Travaux Publics: 55 ave Kléber, 75784 Paris Cedex 16; tel. 1-40-69-51-00; internet www.ogbtp.com; f. 1918; combines the majority of societies, unions and federations of architects and contractors; Pres. YVES TOULET.

Société Française des Architectes: 247 rue St Jacques, 75005 Paris; tel. 1-56-81-10-25; fax 1-56-81-10-26; e-mail contact @sfarchi.org; internet www.sfarchi.org; f. 1877; cultural association; 1,000 mems; Pres. LAURENT SALOMON; publs *Tribune d'Histoire et d'Actualité de l'Architecture* (20 a year), *Le Visiteur* (2 a year).

Société pour la Protection des Paysages, et de l'Esthétique de la France: 39 ave de la Motte-Picquet, 75007 Paris; e-mail sppef@wanadoo.fr; internet sppef.free.fr; f. 1901; 4,000 mems; Pres. P. ALBRECHT; publ. *Sites et Monuments* (quarterly).

BIBLIOGRAPHY, LIBRARY SCIENCE AND MUSEOLOGY

Association des Archivistes Français: 9 rue Montcalm, 75018 Paris Cedex 03; tel. 1-46-06-39-44; fax 1-46-06-39-52; e-mail secretariat@archivistes.org; internet www.archivistes.org; f. 1904; 700 mems; Pres. HENRI ZUBER; Sec. AGNÈS DEJOB; publ. *La Gazette des Archives* (quarterly).

Association des Bibliothécaires Français: 31 rue de Chabrol, 75010 Paris; tel. 1-55-33-10-30; fax 1-55-33-10-31; e-mail abf@abf.asso.fr; internet www.abf.asso.fr; f. 1906; 2,500 mems; Pres. GILLES EBOLI; Gen. Sec. DANIEL LE GOFF; publ. *ABF Bulletin d'Informations* (quarterly).

Association des Professionnels de l'Information et de la Documentation (ADBS): 25 rue Claude Tillier, 75012 Paris; tel. 1-43-72-25-25; fax 1-43-72-30-41; e-mail adbs@adbs.fr; internet www.adbs.fr; f. 1963; 5,000 mems; organizes annual congress with Groupement français de l'industrie de l'information; Pres. CAROLINE WIEGANDT; publ. *Documentaliste – sciences de l'information* (6 a year).

Association Générale des Conservateurs des Collections Publiques de France: 6 rue des Pyramides, 75041 Paris Cedex 01; tel. 1-40-15-36-49; fax 1-47-03-44-82; f. 1922 to promote and improve museums and museums' curatorship; 1,000 mems; Pres. JACQUES MAIGRET; publ. *Musées et Collections Publiques de France* (quarterly).

Centre d'Archives et de Documentation Politiques et Sociales: 86 blvd Haussmann, 75008 Paris; f. 1949; Dir Dr G. ALBERTINI; publs *Informations Politiques et Sociales* (weekly in France, Africa and Asia), *Est et Ouest* (monthly), *Le Monde des Conflits* (monthly).

ECONOMICS, LAW AND POLITICS

Association d'Etudes et d'Informations Politiques Internationales: 86 blvd Haussmann, 75008 Paris; f. 1949; Dir G. ALBERTINI; publs *Est & Ouest* (Paris, twice monthly), *Documenti sul Comunismo* (Rome), *Este y Oeste* (Caracas).

Fondation Nationale des Sciences Politiques: 27 rue Saint Guillaume, 75337 Paris Cedex 07; tel. 1-45-49-50-50; fax 1-42-22-31-26; internet www.sciences-po.fr; f. 1945; administers the Institut d'Etudes Politiques de Paris (*q.v.*), promotes research centres and social science studies, documentation service; library of 620,000 vols; Pres. RENÉ RÉMOND; Admin. R. DESCOINGS; publs *Revue Française de Science Politique* (every 2 months), *Critique Internationale*, *Mots* (4 a year), *Revue Economique* (every 2 months), *Revue de l'OFCE* (quarterly), *Vingtième Siècle*.

Institut des Actuaires Français: 4 rue Chauveau-Lagarde, 75008 Paris; tel. 1-44-51-72-72; fax 1-44-51-72-73; e-mail info@actuaires-paris.com; internet www.institutdesactuaires.com; f. 1890; 600 mems; library of 5,000 vols; Pres. DANIEL BLANCHARD; publ. *Bulletin* (quarterly).

Institut d'Histoire Sociale: 4 ave Benoît-Frachon, 92023 Nanterre Cedex; tel. 1-46-14-09-29; fax 1-46-14-09-25; e-mail Pierre.Rigoulot@histoire-sociale.asso.fr; internet www.histoire-sociale.asso.fr; f. 1935; study of Communist and Soviet activities; library of 70,000 vols specializing in political sciences and history of workers' movements since beginning of 19th century, trade union periodicals and political reviews; Pres. JEAN-FRANÇOIS REVEL; Librarian VIRGINIE HÉBRARD; publs *Cahiers d'Histoire Sociale* (2 a year), *Chronique Economique Syndicale et Sociale* (monthly).

Institut Français des Relations Internationales: 27 rue de la Procession, 75740 Paris Cedex 15; tel. 1-40-61-60-00; fax 1-40-61-60-60; e-mail ifri@ifri.org; internet www.ifri.org; f. 1979; studies foreign policy, economy, defence and strategy; 560 mems; library of 32,000 vols; Dir-Gen. THIERRY DE MONTBRIAL; Sec.-Gen. FLORENT BARAN; publs *Cahiers d'Asie*, *Notes du Cerfa* (monthly), *Notes du CFE*, *Notes de l'IFRI*, *Nouvelles de Chine* (monthly), *Policy Papers*, *Politique Etrangère* (quarterly), *RAMSES (Rapport Annuel sur le Système Economique et les Stratégies)* (annually), *Travaux et Recherches*.

Société de Législation Comparée: 28 rue St Guillaume, 75007 Paris; tel. 1-44-39-86-23; fax 1-44-39-86-28; e-mail slc@legiscompare.com; internet www.legiscompare.com; f. 1869; comparative law; publishes books on comparative and foreign law; library of 100,000 vols; 600 mems (400 French, 200 overseas); Pres. JEAN-LOUIS DEWOST; Gen. Sec. DAVID CAPITANT; publ. *Revue Internationale de Droit Comparé* (quarterly).

Société d'Economie et de Science Sociales: 80 rue Vaneau, 75007 Paris; f. 1856; concerned with social reforms and sociology; 300 mems; library of 3,000 vols, including collection 'La Réforme Sociale'; Pres. EDOUARD SECRETAN; Sec. Prof. ANTOINE SAVOYE; publ. *Les Etudes Sociales* (2 a year).

Société d'Etudes Jaurésiennes: 21 blvd Lefebvre, 75015 Paris; tel. 1-48-28-25-89; fax 1-48-28-25-89; f. 1959 to promote all aspects of the life and works of Jean Jaurès; promotes the publication or re-edition of his speeches and writings; 500 mems; Pres. MADELEINE REBERIOUX; Sec.-Gen. GILLES HEURÉ; publs *Cahiers Jean Jaurès* (quarterly), *Cahiers trimestriels* (quarterly).

Société d'Histoire du Droit: 158 rue Saint Jacques, 75005 Paris; f. 1913; 550 mems; Pres. Prof. OLIVIER GUILLOT; Sec. A. LEFEBVRE.

Société Française de Statistique: C/o Institut Henri Poincaré, 11 rue Pierre et Marie Curie, 75231 Paris Cedex 05; tel. 1-44-27-66-60; fax 1-44-07-04-74; e-mail sfds@ihp.jussieu.fr; internet www.sfds.asso.fr; f. 1997; 1,000 mems; library of 60,000 vols; Pres. MICHEL DELECROIX; Gen. Sec. CHRISTIAN DERQUENNE; publs *Journal de la Société Française de Statistique* (4 a year), *Revue de Statistique Appliquée* (4 a year).

EDUCATION

Association Francophone d'Education Comparée: 1 ave Léon Journault, 92310 Sèvres; tel. 1-45-07-60-00; f. 1973 to promote comparative education among francophone teachers and educationalists; organizes one seminar a year and participates in meetings of the Comparative Education Society in Europe and the World Council of Comparative Educational Societies; 100 mems; Pres. JEAN-MICHEL LECLERCQ; Sec.-Gen. ANTOINE BEVORT; publs *Bulletin de liaison et d'information* (3 a year), *Education comparée* (annually).

Centre Culturel Calouste Gulbenkian: 51 ave d'Iéna, 75116 Paris; tel. 1-53-23-93-93; fax 1-53-23-93-99; e-mail calouste@gulbenkian-paris.org; internet www.gulbenkian-paris.org; f. 1965; non-profit-making; exhibitions, lectures, seminars, concerts; awards grants in the fields of education, art, science and charity; attached to Calouste Gulbenkian Foundation in Lisbon; library of 70,000 vols; Dir FRANCISCO BETHENCOURT; publ. *Arquivos do Centro Cultural Calouste Gulbenkian* (3 a year).

Fondation Biermans-Lapôtre: 9A blvd Jourdan, 75690 Paris Cedex 14; tel. 1-40-78-72-00; fax 1-45-89-00-03; f. 1924; promotes academic and scientific exchanges between France and Belgium; offers grants, etc.; affiliated to Fondation Universitaire (see Belgium chapter); Pres. ALFRED CAHEN; Dir FERNAND MORAY.

Office National d'Information sur les Enseignements et les Professions: 12 mail B. Thimonnier, BP 86 Lognes, 77423 Marne la Vallée, Cedex 02; tel. 1-64-80-35-00; fax 1-64-80-35-01; internet www.onisep.fr; f. 1970; Dir MICHEL VALDIGUIÉ; publs *Avenirs*, *ONISEP Communiqué* (every 2 months), *Bulletin d'Information* (monthly), *Réadaptation* (monthly), *Les Cahiers de l'ONISEP*.

FINE AND PERFORMING ARTS

Association Française d'Action Artistique: 1 bis, ave de Villars, 75007 Paris; tel. 1-53-69-83-00; fax 1-53-69-33-00; e-mail info@afaa.asso.fr; internet www.afaa.asso.fr; f. 1922; offers international cultural exchanges; assists in the development of the performing arts, visual arts, architecture, heritage and cultural projects in France; Pres. ROBERT LION.

Association du Salon d'Automne: Grand Palais, Porte H, 75008 Paris; tel. 1-43-59-46-07; fax 1-53-76-00-60; e-mail contact@salon-automne-paris.com; internet www.salon-automne-paris.com; f. 1903; sections: painting, engraving, mural and decorative art, sculpture, photography; Pres. JEAN-FRANÇOIS LARRIEU.

Jeunesses Musicales de France: 20 rue Geoffroy l'Asnier, 75004 Paris; tel. 1-44-61-86-86; fax 1-44-61-86-88; e-mail info@lesjmf.org; internet www.lesjmf.org; f. 1944; encourages young audiences, promotes concerts, festivals; 320 delegates in 450 towns; Pres. J. L. TOURNIER; Dir BRUNO BOUTLEUX.

Société de l'Histoire de l'Art Français: 2 rue Vivienne, 75084 Paris Cedex 02; tel. 1-40-20-50-77; fax 1-40-20-51-17; f. 1873; 1,000 mems; Pres. DANIEL ALCOUFFE; Gen. Sec. ELIZABETH FOUCART-WALTER; publs *Bulletin*, *Archives de l'Art Français*, *Annuels*.

Société des Amis du Louvre: Palais du Louvre, 75058 Paris Cedex 01; tel. 1-40-20-53-34; fax 1-40-20-53-44; e-mail contact@amis-du-louvre.org; internet www.amis-du-louvre.org; f. 1897; 70,000 mems;

Pres. MARC FUMAROLI; Sec.-Gen. SERGE-ANTOINE TCHEKHOFF; publs *Chronique*, *Bulletin Trimestriel* (quarterly).

Société des Artistes Décorateurs (SAD): Grand Palais, Porte C, Ave Franklin Roosevelt, 75008 Paris; tel. 1-43-59-66-10; fax 1-49-53-07-89; e-mail sadexpo@easynet.fr; internet www.sad-expo.com; f. 1901 to promote modern art; 400 mems; Pres. CLAUDE MOLLARD.

Société des Artistes Français: Grand Palais, Porte C., ave Franklin Roosevelt, 75008 Paris; tel. 1-43-59-52-49; fax 1-45-62-85-97; internet www.lesalon-artistesfrancais.com; f. 1882; 5,000 members; organises the annual Salon des Artistes Français (open to French and foreign artists); Pres. CHRISTIAN BILLET; publ. *Bulletin*.

Société des Artistes Indépendants: Grand Palais porte C, Ave Franklin D. Roosevelt, 75008 Paris; tel. 1-45-63-39-15; fax 1-43-59-50-89; e-mail indep@club-internet.fr; internet www.artistes-independants.fr; f. 1884; 2,500 members; supports modern artists; annual exhibition of paintings, sculpture, engravings and decorative art; Pres. FRANCKIE TACQUE; Sec.-Gen. FRANÇOISE LE GOFF.

Société des Auteurs, Compositeurs et Editeurs de Musique: 225 ave Charles-de-Gaulle, 92528 Neuilly sur Seine Cedex; tel. 1-47-15-47-15; fax 1-47-45-12-94; e-mail communication@sacem.fr; internet www.sacem.fr; f. 1851; 100,000 mems; deals with collection and distribution of performing rights; Pres. CLAUDE LEMESLE; Chair. BERNARD MIYET.

Société d'Histoire du Théâtre: Bibliothèque Nationale de France, 58 rue de Richelieu, 75084 Paris Cedex 02; tel. 1-42-60-27-05; fax 1-42-60-27-65; e-mail info@sht.asso.fr; internet www.sht.asso.fr; f. 1948; 1,000 mems; library of 45,000 vols; Pres. PAUL-LOUIS MIGNON; Sec.-Gen. ROSE MARIE MOUDOUES; publ. *Revue d'Histoire du Théâtre* (quarterly).

Société Française de Musicologie: 2 rue Louvois, 75002 Paris; tel. 1-53-79-88-45; e-mail sfmusico@club-internet.fr; internet www.sfm.culture.fr; f. 1917; 650 mems; Pres. PAUL PRÉVOST; Sec.-Gen. ALEXANDRA LAEDERICH; publ. *Revue de Musicologie* (2 a year).

Société Française de Photographie: 71 rue de Richelieu, 75002 Paris; tel. 1-42-60-05-98; fax 1-47-03-75-39; e-mail sfp@wanadoo.fr; internet www.sfp.photographie.com; f. 1854; 430 mems; library of 10,000 vols, and 25,000 old photographs; Pres. MICHEL POIVERT; publs *Bulletin* (quarterly), *Etudes photographiques* (2 a year).

Société Nationale des Beaux-Arts: 11 rue Berryer, 75008 Paris; tel. 1-43-59-47-07; fax 1-43-59-47-07; e-mail snba.berryer@libertysurf.fr; f. 1890; organizes art exhibitions; 900 ; Pres. ETIENNE AUDFRAY; Gen. Sec. GUY PERRON.

HISTORY, GEOGRAPHY AND ARCHAEOLOGY

Association de Géographes Français: 191 rue Saint-Jacques, 75005 Paris; tel. 1-44-32-14-00; fax 1-45-29-13-40; e-mail assogeo@wanadoo.fr; f. 1920; 300 mems; Pres. R. POURTIER; Sec. G. HUGONIE; publs *Bulletin* (quarterly), *Bibliographie géographique annuelle* (annual).

Association des Amis de la Revue de Géographie de Lyon: 18 rue Chevreul, 69362 Lyons Cedex 07; tel. 4-78-78-75-44; fax 4-78-78-71-58; e-mail buisson@univ-lyon3.fr; internet www.geocarrefour.org; f. 1923; Pres. NICOLE COMMERÇON; publ. *Revue de Géographie de Lyon* (quarterly).

Centre International d'Etudes Romanes: 7 pl. des Arts, 71700 Tournus; tel. 3-85-32-54-45; fax 3-85-32-18-98; internet www.art-roman.org; f. 1952; 400 mems; Hon. Pres. HUBERT BLANC; Vice-Pres. and Sec.-Gen. MARGUÉRITE THIBERT; publ. *Bulletin* (every 2 or 3 years).

Comité National Français de Géographie: 191 rue Saint-Jacques, 75005 Paris; internet cnfg.univ-paris1.fr; co-ordinates French geographical activity and participates in the work of the International Geographical Union; 400 mems; Pres. ALAIN MIOSSEC; Sec.-Gen. P. ARNOULD; publ. *Bibliographie Géographique Internationale* (published jointly with the International Geographical Union).

Comité Scientifique du Club Alpin Français: 24 ave de Laumière, 75019 Paris; tel. 1-53-72-87-13; fax 1-42-03-55-60; internet www.clubalpin.com; f. 1874; 90,000 mems; Dir J. MALBOS.

Demeure Historique: Hôtel de Nesmond, 57 quai de la Tournelle, 75005 Paris; tel. 1-55-42-60-00; fax 1-43-29-36-44; internet www.demeure-historique.org; f. 1924; 3,000 members; study, research and conservation of historic buildings, châteaux, etc.; Pres. JEAN DE LAMBERTYE; publ. *La Demeure Historique* (quarterly).

Fédération Française de Spéléologie: 130 rue Saint-Maur, 75011 Paris; tel. 1-43-57-56-54; fax 1-49-23-00-95; e-mail adherents@ffspeleo.fr; internet www.ffspeleo.fr; f. 1963; speleology; 12,000 mems; library of 2,000 vols, 600 periodicals; Pres. P. VAUTIER; publs *Spelunca* (quarterly), *Karstologia* (2 a year), *Spelunca Mémoires*, *Karstologia Mémoires*, *Bulletin Bibliographique Spéléologique*.

Institut Français d'Etudes Byzantines: 21 rue d'Assas, 75006 Paris; tel. 1-44-39-52-24; fax 1-44-39-52-36; e-mail bibliotheque.vernon.ifeb@icp.fr; internet www.icp.fr; f. 1897; Byzantine research, particularly on sources of ecclesiastical history; library of 50,000 vols; publ. *Revue des Etudes Byzantines* (annually).

Institut Français d'Histoire Sociale: Centre de documentation et de recherche, Archives Nationales, 60 rue des Francs-Bourgeois, 75141 Paris Cedex 03; tel. 1-40-27-64-49; f. 1948; 57 mems; library of 11,000 vols, 50,000 pamphlets, large collection of periodicals, manuscripts and illustrated documents; Pres. JEAN-PIERRE CHALINE; Vice-Pres. ALAIN CORBIN.

Société de Biogéographie: 57 rue Cuvier, 75231 Paris Cedex 05; f. 1924; 350 mems; Pres. C. SASTRE; Sec.-Gen. M. SALOMON; publs *Biogeographica*, *Mémoires hors série*.

Société de Géographie: 184 blvd St-Germain, 75006 Paris; tel. 1-45-48-54-62; fax 1-42-22-40-93; e-mail socgeo@socgeo.org; internet www.socgeo.org; f. 1821; 850 mems; library of 40,000 vols, 120,000 photographs at Bibliothèque Nationale de France, 58 rue de Richelieu, 75084 Paris Cedex 02 (Librarian HÉLÈNE RICHARD); Pres. Prof. J. BASTIÉ; Sec.-Gen. M. FLORIN; publ. *La Géographie* (4 a year).

Société de Géographie Humaine de Paris: 8 rue Roquépine, 75008 Paris; f. 1873; Pres. JACQUES AUGARDE; library of 2,000 vols; publ. *Revue Economique Française* (quarterly).

Société de l'Histoire de France: Ecole des Chartes, 19 rue de la Sorbonne, 75005 Paris; fax 1-55-42-75-09; internet www.shfrance.org; f. 1834; publishes a series of French historical texts and documents; gives public lectures on French history; 250 mems; Pres. Prof. YVES-MARIE BERCÉ; Sec. Prof. MARC H. SMITH; publ. *Annuaire-Bulletin* (annually).

Société d'Emulation du Bourbonnais: 93 rue de Paris, 03000 Moulins; tel. and fax 4-70-34-08-13; f. 1846; 600 mems; activities in the fields of history, science, arts and literature; library of 30,000 vols; folklore museum; Pres. SYLVIE VILATTE; publ. *Bulletin* (quarterly).

Société des Océanistes: Musée de l'Homme, 1, place du Trocadéro, 75116 Paris; tel. 1-47-04-63-40; e-mail oceanist@mnhn.fr; internet cimbad.mnhn.fr/oceanist; f. 1945; 560 mems; Pres. JEAN-PAUL LATOUCHE; Sec.-Gen. ISABELLE LEBLIC; publs *Journal* (2 a year), *Publications*.

Société d'Ethnographie de Paris: 6 rue Champfleury, 75007 Paris; f. 1859; 400 mems; Dirs A.-M. D'ANS, R. LACOMBE; publ. *L'Ethnographie* (2 a year).

Société d'Ethnologie Française: 6 ave du Mahatma Gandhi, 75116 Paris; tel. 1-44-17-60-00; 500 mems; holds annual national conference and study sessions; Pres. F. LAUTMAN; Sec.-Gen. F. MAGUET; publ. *Ethnologie Française* (quarterly).

Société d'Etude du XVIIe Siècle: C/o Université de Paris-Sorbonne, Occident Moderne, 1 rue Victor-Cousin, 75230 Paris Cedex 05; e-mail jean-louis.quantin@histoire.ursq.fr; f. 1948; 1,250 mems; Pres. JEAN-ROBERT ARMOGATHE; Sec. JEAN-LOUIS QUANTIN; publ. *XVIIe Siècle* (quarterly).

Société d'Histoire Générale et d'Histoire Diplomatique: 13 rue Soufflot, 75005 Paris; tel. 1-43-54-05-97; fax 1-46-34-07-60; f. 1887; history and diplomatic relations; 400 mems; publ. *Revue d'Histoire Diplomatique*.

Société d'Histoire Moderne et Contemporaine: Bureau 110, 56 rue Jacob, 75006 Paris; tel. 1-45-45-11-11; fax 1-58-71-71-96; e-mail rhmc@ens.fr; f. 1901; 1,100 mems; early modern and modern French and foreign history; Presidents PIERRE MILZA, DANIEL ROCHE; Sec.-Gen. PHILIPPE MINARD; publ. *Bulletin-Revue d'Histoire Moderne et Contemporaine* (4 a year, and a supplementary Bulletin annually).

Société Française d'Archéologie: Musée National des Monuments Français, Palais de Chaillot, 1 place du Trocadéro, 75116 Paris; tel. 1-47-04-78-96; fax 1-44-05-94-25; e-mail sfa.sfa@wanadoo.fr; internet www.sfarcheologie.com; f. 1834; mem. of CSSF; 2,800 mems; Pres. JEAN MESQUI; publs *Bulletin Monumental* (quarterly), *Congrès Archéologiques de France* (annually).

Société Française de Numismatique: Bibliothèque Nationale de France, Département des Monnaies, Médailles et Antiques, 58 rue de Richelieu, 75002 Paris; tel. 1-53-79-86-26; fax 1-53-79-86-26; e-mail secretariat@sfnum.asso.fr; internet www.sfnum.asso.fr; f. 1865; 700 mems; Pres. GEORGES GAUTIER; Gen. Sec. ANDRÉ RONDE; publs *Bulletin de la S. F. N.* (monthly), *Revue Numismatique* (annually).

Société Française d'Egyptologie: Collège de France, Place Marcelin-Berthelot, 75231 Paris Cedex 05; tel. 1-40-46-94-31; fax 1-40-46-94-31; e-mail sfe@egypt.edu; internet www.egypt.edu; f. 1923; 850 mems; Pres. D. VALBELLE; Sec. MARIE-CLAIRE CUVILLIER; publs *Bulletin* (3 a year), *Revue d'Egyptologie* (annually).

Société Française d'Histoire d'Outre-Mer: 15 rue Catulienne, 93200 Saint Denis; tel. 6-07-30-04-22; fax 1-45-82-62-99; e-mail sfhom4@yahoo.fr; internet www.sfhom.com; f. 1913; 420 mems; Pres. HÉLÈNE D'ALMEIDA-TOPOR; Sec.-Gen. JOSETTE RIVALLAIN; publ. *Outre-Mers* (history, 2 a year).

Société Historique, Archéologique et Littéraire de Lyon: Archives Municipales de Lyon, 18 rue Dugas Montbel, 69002 Lyons; e-mail shallyon@cegetel.net; f. 1807; 78 mems; Pres. JEAN-CLAUDE BILLION; Sec. CHRISTIANNE DÉAUX; publ. *Bulletin* (annual).

Société Nationale des Antiquaires de France: Palais du Louvre, Pavillon Mollien, 75058 Paris Cedex 01; f. 1803; history, philology and archaeology of the Antiquity, Middle Ages and Renaissance; 500 ; publs *Bulletin de la Société nationale des Antiquaires de France* (annually), *Mémoires de la Société nationale des Antiquaires de France* (irregular).

Vieilles Maisons Françaises: 93 rue de l'Université, 75007 Paris; tel. 1-40-62-61-71; fax 1-45-51-12-26; internet www.vmf.net; f. 1958; the society seeks to bring together all those who own buildings of historical interest and those who help to preserve them; 16,000 mems; Pres. PHILIPPE TOUSSAINT; publ. *Vieilles Maisons Françaises*.

LANGUAGE AND LITERATURE

Association des Ecrivains de Langue Française (ADELF) (French Language Writers Association): 14 rue Broussais, 75014 Paris; tel. 1-43-21-95-99; fax 1-43-20-12-22; f. 1926 as 'Société des romanciers et auteurs coloniaux français' to bring together writers of all nationalities whose works are published in French; awards 11 literary prizes; 1,200 mems in 79 countries; library of 2,000 vols; Pres. ALAIN GUILLAUME; Sec.-Gen. SIMONE DREYFUS; publs *Annuaire*, *Collection des Colloques*, *Le Point au ...* (newsletter, 4 a year), *Lettres et Cultures de langue française* (2 a year).

Association Française des Professeurs de Langues Vivantes: 19 rue de la Glacière, 75013 Paris; f. 1902; 3,000 mems; Pres. SYLVESTRE VANUXEM; Gen. Sec. JEAN-YVES PETITGIRARD; publs *Les Langues Modernes* (quarterly), *Le Polyglotte* (quarterly).

Association Guillaume Budé: 95 blvd Raspail, 75006 Paris; e-mail info@bude.asso.fr; internet www.bude.asso.fr; f. 1917; 3,000 mems; edits ancient Greek, Latin and Byzantine, classical texts with French translations and studies on history, philology and archaeology, which are published by the Société d'éditions 'Les Belles Lettres' at the same address; Pres. JACQUES JOUANNA; Vice-Pres. BERNARD DEFORGE, ALAIN MICHEL; publ. *Bulletin* (2 a year).

British Council: 9 rue de Constantine, 75340 Paris Cedex 07; tel. (1) 49-55-73-00; fax (1) 47-05-77-02; e-mail information@britishcouncil.fr; internet www.britishcouncil.fr; teaching centre; offers courses and exams in English language and British culture and promotes cultural exchange with the UK; Dir JOHN TOD.

Centre National du Livre: 53 rue de Verneuil, 75343 Paris Cedex 07; tel. 1-49-54-68-68; fax 1-45-49-10-21; internet www.centrenationaldulivre.fr; f. 1946, present name 1993, to uphold and encourage the work of French writers; to give financial help to writers, editors and public libraries; to promote translation into French; Pres. ERIC GROSS; Sec.-Gen. ANNE MILLER; publ. *Lettres*.

Espéranto-Jeunes (JEFO): 4 bis rue de la Cerisaie, 75004 Paris; tel. 1-42-78-68-86; fax 1-42-78-08-47; e-mail jefo@esperanto.org; internet esperanto-jeunes.org; f. 1969; promotes Esperanto among young people; 145 mems; Pres. BERTRAND HUGON; publs *Koncize* (4 a year), *JEFO informas* (4 a year).

Fondation Saint-John Perse: Cité du Livre, 10 rue des Allumettes, 13098 Aix-en-Provence Cedex 2; tel. 4-42-91-98-85; fax 4-42-27-11-86; e-mail fondation.saint.john.perse@wanadoo.fr; internet www.up.univ-mrs.fr/~wperse; f. 1975; collection of 16,000 documents comprising all MSS, books, correspondence, private library and personal belongings of Saint-John Perse (Nobel Prize for literature 1960); organizes annual exhibition and symposium; 500 mems; Pres. YVES-ANDRÉ ISTEL; Dir BEATRICE COIGNET; publs *Cahiers Saint-John Perse* (irregular), *Souffle de Perse* (irregular).

Goethe-Institut: 17 Ave d'Iéna, 75116 Paris; tel. 1-44-43-92-30; fax 1-44-43-92-40; e-mail kallies@paris.goethe.org; internet www.goethe.de/fr/par/deindex.htm; offers courses and exams in German language and culture and promotes cultural exchange with Germany; attached centres in Bordeaux, Lille, Lyons, Nice and Toulouse; library of 25,000 vols; Dir MARION HAASE.

Instituto Cervantes: 7 rue Quentin Bauchart, 75008 Paris; tel. 1-40-70-92-92; fax 1-47-20-27-49; e-mail cenpar@cervantes.es; internet paris.cervantes.es; offers courses and exams in Spanish language and culture and promotes cultural exchange with Spain and Spanish-speaking Latin and Central America; attached centres in Bordeaux and Lyons; library: library of 42,000 vols, 100 periodicals; Dir AUGSTÍN VERA LUJÁN.

La France Latine: Université de Rennes II, 1 Place du Recteur le Moal, C524302, 35043 Rennes Cedex; f. 1957 to preserve Latin culture and civilization in all its forms, maintains regional traditions and the 'Langue d'Oc' (Occitan dialect); Literary Dirs PHILIPPE BLANCHET S. THIOLIER-MÉJEAN; publ. *Revue* (2 a year).

Maison de Poésie (Fondation Emile Blémont): 11 bis rue Ballu, 75009 Paris; tel. 1-40-23-45-99; f. 1928; library: over 16,000 vols; annual prizes: Grand Prix de la Maison de Poésie, Prix Paul Verlaine, Prix Edgar Poe, Prix Gabriel Vicaire, Prix Léon Riotor, Prix Van Lerberghe, Prix Fernand Dauphin; Pres. JACQUES CHARPENTREAU; Sec. BERNARD LORRAINE; publ. *Le Coin de Table* (4 a year).

PEN International (Centre français): 6 rue François-Miron, 75004 Paris; tel. 1-42-77-37-87; fax 1-42-78-64-87; e-mail penfrancais@aol.com; internet www.penclub.fr; f. 1921; 550 mems; Pres. SYLVESTRE CLANCIER; Sec.-Gen. PHILIPPE PUJAS; publ. *La Lettre du PEN Club français* (every 2 months).

Société de Linguistique de Paris: Ecole Pratique des Hautes Etudes, 4e section, Sorbonne, 47 rue des Ecoles, 75005 Paris; internet www.slp-paris.com; f. 1864; 800 mems; Pres. A. BORILLO; Sec. M. A. LEMARECHAL; publs *Collection Linguistique*, *Bulletin*, *Mémoires* (annually).

Société des Anciens Textes Français: 19 rue de la Sorbonne, 75005 Paris; f. 1875; 125 mems; Pres. Prof. G. BIANCIOTTO; Dir Prof. G. HASENOHR; Gen. Sec. Prof. F. VIELLIARD.

Société des Auteurs et Compositeurs Dramatiques: 11 bis rue Ballu, 75442 Paris Cedex 09; tel. 1-40-23-44-44; fax 1-45-26-74-28; e-mail infosacd@sacd.fr; internet www.sacd.fr; f. 1777; to protect the rights of authors of theatre, radio, cinema, television and multimedia; Pres. CHRISTINE MILLER; publ. *La Revue de la SACD*.

Société des Etudes Latines: 1 rue Victor-Cousin, 75230 Paris Cedex 05; f. 1923; Sec.-Gen. Prof. JACQUELINE CHAMPEAUX; Administrator Prof. ALAIN MICHEL; publs *Revue des Etudes Latines* (annually), *Collection d'études latines*.

Société des Gens de Lettres: Hôtel de Massa, 38 rue du Faubourg St Jacques, 75014 Paris; tel. 1-53-10-12-00; fax 1-53-10-12-12; e-mail sgdlf@wanadoo.fr; internet www.sgdl.org; f. 1838; Pres. ALAIN ABSIRE; Gen. Sec. JEAN-CLAUDE BOLOGNE; publ. *Feuilleton* (2 a year).

Société d'Histoire Littéraire de la France: 112 rue Monge, 75005 Paris; tel. 1-45-87-23-30; fax 1-45-87-23-30; f. 1894; 400 mems; Pres. M. FUMAROLI; Dir S. MENANT; publ. *Revue d'Histoire Littéraire de la France* (every 2 months).

MEDICINE

Académie Nationale de Chirurgie: 'Les Cordeliers', 15 rue de l'École de Médecine, 75006 Paris; tel. 1-43-54-02-32; fax 1-43-29-34-44; e-mail ac.chirurgie@bhdc.jussieu.fr; internet www.bium.univ-paris5.fr/acad-chirurgie; f. 1731; 500 mems; library of 5,000 vols; Pres. Prof. CHARLES PROYE; Sec.-Gen. JACQUES POILLEUX; publs *Annales de Chirurgie* (10 a year), *e-Memoires* (online, 5 a year).

Académie Nationale de Médecine: 16 rue Bonaparte, 75272 Paris Cedex 06; tel. 1-42-34-57-70; fax 1-40-46-87-55; internet www.academie-medecine.fr; f. 1820 by Louis XVIII; library of 400,000 vols; 130 mems attached to sections on medicine, surgery, hygiene, biological sciences, social sciences, veterinary medicine, and pharmacy; Pres. CLAUDE BOUDÈNE; Perm. Sec. JACQUES-LOUIS BINET; publ. *Bulletin de l'Académie nationale de médecine* (9 a year).

Académie Nationale de Pharmacie: 4 ave de l'Observatoire, 75006 Paris; tel. 1-43-25-54-49; fax 1-43-29-45-85; e-mail courriers@acadpharm.net; internet www.acadpharm.org; f. 1803; 325 mems; Pres. F. BOURILLET; Gen. Sec. J.-P. CHIRON; publ. *Annales Pharmaceutiques Françaises*.

Association des Morphologistes: BP 184, 54505 Vandoeuvre-lès-Nancy; e-mail grignon@facmed.u-nancy.fr; f. 1899; 1,005 mems; Chief Editor Prof. G. GRIGNON; publ. *Morphologie* (4 a year).

Association Française d'Urologie: c/o Colloquium, 12 rue de la Croix Faubin, 75557 Paris Cedex 11; tel. 1-44-64-15-15; fax 1-44-64-15-16; e-mail contact@urofrance.org; internet www.urofrance.org; f. 1896; 750 mems; Pres. C. COULANGE; Vice-Pres. J.-L. D'AVIN; Sec.-Gen. E. CHARTIER-KASTLER; publ. *Progrès en Urologie*.

Association Générale des Médecins de France: 34 blvd de Courcelles, 75809 Paris Cedex 17; tel. 1-40-54-54-54; fax 1-40-54-54-40; Pres. P. BAUDOUIN; Sec. Dr TOUCHARD; publ. *Bulletin*.

Association Scientifique des Médecins Acupuncteurs de France (ASMAF): 2 rue du Général de Larminat, 75015 Paris; tel. 1-42-73-37-26; f. 1945 as Société d'Acupuncture; 1,500 mems; Pres. Dr GEORGES CANTONI; Sec.-Gen. Dr H. OLIVO; publ. *Méridiens* (quarterly).

Centre d'Etude de l'Expression: Centre hospitalier Sainte-Anne, 100 rue de la Santé, 75014 Paris; tel. 1-45-89-21-51; e-mail cee@ch-sainte-anne.com; f. 1973 to develop psychopathological and psychological studies of various forms of expression: plastic, verbal, mimic, body-language, musical, theatrical; Pres. PIERRE DAUMARD; Sec.-Gen. Dr ANNE-MARIE DUBOIS.

Comité National contre les Maladies Respiratoires et la Tuberculose: 66 blvd Saint-Michel, 75006 Paris; tel. 1-46-34-58-80; fax 1-43-29-06-58; e-mail cnmrt@magic.fr; f. 1916; research, information, health education, assistance for the handicapped; Pres. FRANÇOIS BONNAUD; publ. *La Lettre du Souffle* (4 a year).

Confédération des Syndicats Médicaux Français: 79 rue de Tocqueville, 75017 Paris; tel. 1-43-18-88-00; fax 1-43-18-88-20; e-mail csmf@csmf.org; internet www.csmf.org; f. 1930; 16,000 mems; Pres. Dr MICHEL CHASSANG; Sec.-Gen. Dr WANNEPAIN.

Fédération des Gynécologues et Obstétriciens de Langue Française: Hôpital St-Antoine, 184 rue du Fg St-Antoine, 75012 Paris; tel. 1-49-28-28-76; fax 1-49-28-27-57; e-mail jmilliez@sat.ap-hop-paris.fr; f. 1950; 600 mems; Pres. Prof. ULYSSE GASPARD (Liège); Sec.-Gen. Prof. JACQUES MILLIEZ (Paris); publ. *Journal de Gynécologie Obstétrique et Biologie de la Reproduction* (8 a year).

Fédération Nationale des Médecins Radiologues: 62 blvd de Latour Maubourg, 75007 Paris Cedex 07; tel. 1-53-59-34-00; fax 1-45-51-83-15; e-mail fnmr@fnmr.org; internet www.fnmr.org; f. 1907; 4,800 mems; Pres. Dr DENIS AUCANT; Secs-Gen. Dr JACQUES NINEY, Dr LAURENT VERZAUX.

Société de Médecine de Strasbourg: Faculté de Médecine, 4 rue Kirschleger, 67085 Strasbourg Cedex; f. 1919; 450 mems; organizes medical conferences; Pres. Prof. J. MCWARTER; Sec.-Gen. Dr MOISE; publ. *Journal de Médecine de Strasbourg* (monthly).

Société de Médecine Légale et de Criminologie de France: 2 place Mazas, 75012 Paris; tel. 1-43-43-42-54; internet www.smlc.asso.fr; f. 1868; Pres. Prof. MICHEL PENNEAU; Sec. DIDIER GOSSET; publ. *Médecine légale-droit médical*.

Société de Neurophysiologie Clinique de Langue Française: Hôpital Sainte Anne, 1 rue Cabanis, 75674 Paris Cedex 14; tel. 1-40-48-82-03; f. 1948; 520 mems; Pres. Pr J. TOUCHON; Sec.-Gen. Dr B. GUEGUEN; publ. *Neurophysiologie Clinique* (every 2 months).

Société de Pathologie Exotique: 25 rue du Docteur-Roux, 75724 Paris Cedex 15; tel. 1-45-66-88-69; fax 1-45-66-44-85; e-mail socpatex@pasteur.fr; internet www.pasteur.fr/socpatex; f. 1908; 637 mems; library of 2,000 vols, 125 periodicals; Pres. P. SALIOU; Sec.-Gen. Y. BUISSON; publ. *Bulletin* (5 a year).

Société de Pneumologie de Langue Française: 66 blvd Saint-Michel, 75006 Paris; tel. 1-46-34-03-87; fax 1-46-34-58-27; e-mail splf@splf.org; internet www.splf.org; Pres. M. FOURNIER; Secs-Gen. J. F. CORDIER, J. P. GRIGNET, B. HOUSSET, E. LEMARIÉ; publ. *Revue des Maladies Respiratoires*.

Société d'Histoire de la Pharmacie: 4 ave de l'Observatoire, 75270 Paris Cedex 06; tel. and fax 1-53-73-97-37; f. 1913; 1,000 mems; Pres. Prof. OLIVIER LAFONT; Sec. B. BONNEMAIN; publ. *Revue d'Histoire de la Pharmacie* (quarterly).

Société d'Ophtalmologie de Paris: 108 rue du Bac, 75007 Paris; f. 1888; Sec. Gen. Dr JEAN-PAUL BOISSIN; publ. *Bulletin* (monthly).

Société Française d'Allergologie et d'Immuno-Allergie Clinique: Institut Pasteur, 25 rue du Dr Roux, 75015 Paris; tel. 1-45-68-82-41; fax 1-40-61-31-60; f. 1947; 860 mems; Pres. Prof. D. VERVLOET; publ. *Revue Française d'Allergologie et d'Immunologie clinique* (5 a year).

Société Française d'Anesthésie et de Réanimation: 74 rue Raynouard, 75016 Paris; tel. 1-45-25-82-25; fax 1-40-50-35-22; e-mail sfar@invivo.edu; internet www.sfar.org; f. 1934; 4,298 mems; Pres. JEAN MARTY; Sec.-Gen. LAURENT JOUFFROY; publ. *Annales françaises d'Anesthésie et de Réanimation* (monthly).

Société Française d'Angéiologie: 153 ave Berthelot, 69007 Lyons; tel. 4-78-72-38-98; internet www.sfa-online.com; f. 1947; 450 mems; Pres. Dr FRANÇOIS ANDRÉ ALLAERT; Sec.-Gen. Dr MICHÈLE CAZAUBON; publ. *La revue Angéiologie* (4 a year).

Société Française de Biologie Clinique: BP 403, 54001 Nancy Cedex; tel. 3-83-35-36-25; fax 3-83-32-75-13; internet www.sfbc.asso.fr; Presi. PHILIPPE GILLERY; Sec.-Gen. NELLY JACOB.

Société Française de Chirurgie Orthopédique et Traumatologique: Secrétariat: 56 rue Boissonade, 75014 Paris; tel. 1-43-22-47-54; fax 1-43-22-46-70; e-mail sofcot@sofcot.com.fr; internet www.sofcot.com.fr; 1,950 mems; Pres. J. M. THOMINE; publs *Revue de Chirurgie Orthopédique*, *Bulletin des Orthopédistes Francophones* (2 a year).

Société Française de Chirurgie Pédiatrique: Chirurgie Infantile, Hôpital Hautepierre, 67098 Strasbourg Cedex; tel. 3-88-12-73-02; fax 3-88-12-73-03; f. 1959; 350 mems; Pres. Prof. PAUL MITROFANOFF; Sec.-Gen. Prof. J. L. CLAVERT; publ. *European Journal of Paediatric Surgery* (every 2 months).

Société Française de Chirurgie Plastique, Reconstructive et Esthétique: 26 rue de Belfort, 92400 Courbevoie; tel. 1-46-67-74-85; fax 1-46-67-74-89; e-mail sofcpre@wanadoo.fr; internet www.plasticiens.org; f. 1953; 544 mems; Pres. Prof. J. BAUDET; Sec.-Gen. Prof. J. P. CHAVOIN; publ. *Annales de Chirurgie Plastique et Esthétique* (6 a year).

Société Française de Chirurgie Thoracique et Cardio-vasculaire (French Society for Thoracic and Cardiovascular Surgery): 1 rue Cabanis, 75014 Paris; tel. 1-53-62-91-19; fax 1-53-62-91-20; e-mail sfctcv@wanadoo.fr; internet www.fstcvs.org; f. 1948; 643 mems; studies problems linked with thoracic and cardiovascular surgery; Pres. ROGER GIUDICELLI; Sec.-Gen. Dr R. NOTTIN, A. PAVIE; publ. *Journal de chirurgie thoracique et cardiovasculaire* (4 a year).

Société Française de Gynécologie: 20 rue Clément Marot, 75008 Paris; 582 mems; Pres. J. P. WOLFF; Sec.-Gen. ANDRÉ GORINS; publ. *Gynécologie* (every 2 months).

Société Française de Médecine Aérospatiale: Laboratoire de Médecine Aérospatiale du Centre d'Essais en Vol, 91228 Brétigny sur Orge Cedex; tel. 1-69-88-23-80; fax 1-69-88-27-25; internet www.soframas.asso.fr; f. 1960; publishes papers on experimental and clinical studies; 1,100 mems; Pres. Dr M.-P. CHARETTEUR; Sec.-Gen. Prof. G. SOLIGNAC; publ. *Médecine Aérospatiale* (quarterly).

Société Française de Mycologie Médicale: 28 rue du Docteur-Roux, 75724 Paris Cedex 15; tel. 1-40-61-32-54; fax 1-40-61-34-42; e-mail sfmm@pasteur.fr; internet mycolmed.chez.tiscali.fr; f. 1956; 500 mems; Pres. ODILE MORIN; Sec.-Gen. Prof. BERTRAND DUPONT; publ. *Journal de Mycologie Médicale* (quarterly).

Société Française de Neurologie: Service de Neurologie 1, Clinique Paul Castaigne, Hôpital de la Salpêtrière, 47 blvd de l'Hôpital, 75651 Paris Cedex 13; tel. 1-42-16-18-28; fax 1-44-24-52-47; internet www.sf-neuro.org; f. 1899; 550 mems; library of 22,000 vols; Sec.-Gen. Prof. C. PIERROT-DESEILLIGNY; publ. *Revue Neurologique* (monthly).

Société Française de Pédiatrie: Hôpital Trousseau, 26 ave du Dr Arnold Netter, 75571 Paris Cedex 12; tel. 1-49-28-92-96; fax 1-49-28-92-96; e-mail societe.francaise.pediatrie@wanadoo.fr; internet www.sfpediatrie.com; f. 1929; 1,500 mems; Pres. Prof. DANIÈLE SOMMELET; Sec.-Gen. Prof. GUY LEVERGER; publ. *Archives de Pédiatrie* (monthly).

Société Française de Phlébologie: 46 rue Saint-Lambert, 75015 Paris; tel. 1-45-33-02-71; fax 1-42-50-75-18; e-mail sfphlebo@club-internet.fr; internet www.sf-phlebologie.org; f. 1947; 2,000 mems; Pres. M. PERRIN; Sec.-Gen. F. VIN; publ. *Phlébologie—Annales Vasculaires* (4 a year).

Société Française de Phytiatrie et de Phytopharmacie: CNRA, Route de Saint Cyr, 78000 Versailles; tel. 1-49-50-75-22; f. 1951; 1,000 mems.

Société Française de Radiologie: 20 ave Rapp, 75007 Paris; tel. 1-53-59-59-69; fax 1-53-59-59-60; e-mail sfr@sfradiologie.org; internet www.sfrnet.org; f. 1909; 6,785 mems; Pres. GÉRARD MORVAN; Gen. Sec. PHILIPE GRENIER; publ. *Journal de Radiology* (monthly).

Société Française de Santé Publique: BP 7, 2 rue Doyen Jacques-Parisot, 54501 Vandoeuvre lès Nancy Cedex; tel. 3-83-44-39-17; fax 3-83-44-37-76; e-mail acceuil@sfsp.info; internet www.sfsp.info; f. 1877; 750 mems; Pres. Dr LAURENT CHAMBAUD; publ. *Santé publique* (4 a year).

Société Française d'Endocrinologie: c/o Masson Edit., 120 blvd Saint-Germain, 75280 Paris Cedex 06; internet www.sf-endocrino.net; f. 1939; 1,000 mems; Sec.-Gen. Prof. BERNARD CONTE-DEVOLX; publ. *Annales d'Endocrinologie* (every 2 months).

Société Française d'Histoire de la Médecine: 38 bis rue de Courlancy, 51100 Reims; tel. 3-26-48-32-60; fax 3-26-48-32-71; f. 1902; 700 mems; library; Pres. Prof. GUY PALLARDY; Gen. Sec. Dr ALAIN SEGAL; publ. *Histoire des Sciences médicales* (quarterly).

Société Française d'Hydrologie et de Climatologie Médicales: 15 ave Charles de Gaulle, 73100 Aix-les-Bains; tel. 4-79-35-14-87; internet www.soc-hydrologie.org; f. 1853; 320 mems; Pres. Prof. MICHEL BOULANGÉ; Sec.-Gen. Dr ROMAIN FORESTIER; publ. *La Presse Thermale et Climatique* (annually).

Société Française d'Opthalmologie: Maison de l'Ophtalmologie, 17 Villa d'Alésia, 75014 Paris; tel. 1-44-12-60-50; fax 1-44-12-23-00; e-mail sfp@sfo.asso.fr; internet www.sfo.asso.fr; f. 1883; annual conference; 7,200 mems; Pres. Dr J. L. ARNÉ; Sec.-Gen. Dr J. P. RENARD; publs *Rapport* (annually), *Journal Français d'Ophtalmologie* (10 a year).

Société Française d'Oto-Rhino-Laryngologie et de Pathologie Cervico-Faciale: 9 rue Villebois-Mareuil, 75017 Paris; internet orl-france.org; f. 1880; 1,500 mems; Pres. Dr R. BATISSE; Sec. Prof. CHARLES FRECHE; publ. *Comptes Rendus and Rapports Discutés au Congrès*.

Société Française du Cancer: 34 rue d'Ulm, 75231 Paris Cedex 05; tel. 1-44-32-40-98; fax 1-46-33-20-09; e-mail info@sfc.asso.fr; internet www.sfc.asso.fr; f. 1906; 440 mems; quarterly meetings, annual symposium; offers grants to doctors from abroad or French doctors for work abroad; Pres. J. ROBERT; Sec.-Gen. F. LAVELLE; publ. *Bulletin du Cancer* (monthly).

Société Française d'Urologie: 6 ave Constant Coquelin, 75007 Paris; f. 1919; 50 mems; Pres. Dr BOISSONNAT; publ. *Journal d'Urologie*.

Société Médicale des Hôpitaux de Paris: 45 quai de la Tournelle, 75005 Paris; tel. 1-43-25-71-95; fax 1-43-25-40-92; Sec. LOÏC GUILLEVIN; publ. *Annales de Médecine Interne*.

Société Médico-Psychologique: 14/16 ave Robert Schuman, 92100 Boulogne; f. 1852; 675 mems; Pres. Dr CLAUDE-JACQUES BLANC; Sec.-Gen. Prof. JEAN-FRANÇOIS ALLILAIRE; publ. *Annales médico-psychologiques* (monthly).

Société Nationale Française de Gastro-Entérologie: CHU Reims, rue Serge Kochman, 51092 Reims Cedex; tel. 3-26-35-94-31; fax 3-26-35-95-91; e-mail snfge@snfge.org; internet www.snfge.org; f. 1947; 1,600 mems; Pres. Prof. PHILIPPE RUSZNIEWSKI; Sec.-Gen. Prof. GUILLAUME CADIOT; publ. *Gastroentérologie clinique et biologique*.

Société Odontologique de Paris (SOP): 239 rue du Faubourg Saint-Martin, 75010 Paris; tel. 1-42-09-29-13; fax 1-42-09-29-08; internet www.sop.asso.fr; 2,500 mems; Pres. PHILIPPE SAFAR; Dir PHILIPPE CHALANSET; publs *Revue d'Odonto-Stomatologie* (4 a year), *Journal de la Société Odontologique de Paris*.

Société Scientifique d'Hygiène Alimentaire: 16 rue de l'Estrapade, 75005 Paris; f. 1904; 1,182 mems; Pres. Dr GUY EBRARD.

NATURAL SCIENCES

General

Comité National Français des Recherches Arctiques et Antarctiques: C/o Expéditions Polaires Françaises, 47 ave du Maréchal Fayolle, 75016 Paris; tel. 1-40-79-37-56; fax 1-40-79-37-71; e-mail bureau@mnhn.fr; f. 1958; Pres. J.-C. HUREAU.

Fédération Française des Sociétés de Sciences Naturelles: 57 rue Cuvier, 75231 Paris Cedex 05; tel. 1-40-79-34-95; fax 1-40-79-34-88; f. 1919; groups 175 societies; natural sciences and nature conservation; Pres. J. LESCURE; Gen. Sec. J. FRETEY; publ. *Revue de la FFSSN* (annually).

Biological Sciences

Les Naturalistes Parisiens: 45 rue de Buffon, 75005 Paris; f. 1904 to undertake research in natural history and deepen the scientific knowledge of its members; 600 mems; Pres. C. DUPUIS; publs *Bulletin* (quarterly), *Cahiers des Naturalistes*.

Société Botanique de France: rue J. B. Clément, 92296 Châtenay-Malabry Cedex; tel. 1-46-83-55-20; fax 1-46-83-13-03; internet www.bium.univ-paris5.fr/sbf; f. 1854; 800 mems; President ANDRÉ CHARPIN; Sec. ELISABETH DODINET; publs *Acta Botanica Gallica* (6 or 7 a year), *Le Journal de Botanique* (4 a year).

Société de Biologie: Université Pierre et Marie Curie, CP 2, 7 quai St Bernard, 75252 Paris Cedex 05; tel. 1-44-27-35-50; e-mail societe.biologie@snv.jussieu.fr; internet www.societedebiologie.com; f. 1848; 140 hon. mems; 50 elected mems, 120 associates, 120 corresp; Pres. Prof. ANDRÉ CALAS; Sec. Dr FRANÇOISE DIETERLEN; publ. *Journal* (4 a year, online).

Société d'Etudes Ornithologiques de France: Muséum National d'Histoire Naturelle, 55 rue Buffon, CP 51, 75231 Paris Cedex 05; tel. 1-40-79-38-34; fax 1-40-79-30-63; e-mail seof@mnhn.fr; internet www.mnhn.fr/assoc/seof; f. 1993; scientific study of wild birds and their protection; publishes monographs, national and regional ornithological lists, atlases, CDs; 800 –1000 mems; library of 22,000 vols; Pres. P. NICOLAU-GUILLAUMET; Sec.-Gen. J. PERRIN DE BRICHAMBAUT; publ. *Alauda* (4 a year).

Société Entomologique de France: 45 rue Buffon, 75005 Paris; tel. 1-47-07-10-10; fax 1-47-07-10-10; e-mail secretaire-general@lasef.org; internet www.lasef.org; f. 1832; 660 mems; library of 12,000 vols, 80 periodicals; Gen. Sec. H. PIGUET; publs *Annales* (quarterly), *Bulletin* (5 a year), *L'Entomologiste* (6 a year).

Société Française de Biologie Végétale: 4 place Jussieu, 75252 Paris Cedex 05; tel. 1-44-27-59-18; fax 1-44-27-61-51; e-mail marie-france.laforge@snv.jussieu.fr; internet www.sfbv.org; f. 1955; 600 mems; Pres. P. MOREAU; Sec.-Gen. A. ZACHOWSKI; publ. *Plant Physiology and Biochemistry* (monthly).

Société Française d'Ichtyologie: 43 rue Cuvier, 75231 Paris Cedex 05; tel. 1-40-79-37-49; fax 1-40-79-37-71; e-mail keith@mnhn.fr; internet www.mnhn.fr/sfi; f. 1976; fish culture, biology and systematics of fish, sea and freshwater fisheries; 320 mems; library of 5,000 vols, 800 periodicals; Pres. M. GAYET; Sec. P. KEITH; publ. *Cybium* (quarterly).

Société Mycologique de France: 20 rue Rottembourg, 75012 Paris; tel. and fax 1-44-67-96-90; e-mail smf@mycofrance.org; internet mycofrance.org; f. 1884; 1,800 mems; Pres. M. BUYCK; Sec.-Gen. M. CHALANGE; publ. *Bulletin Trimestriel*.

Société Nationale de Protection de la Nature: 9 rue Cels, 75014 Paris; tel. 1-43-20-15-39; fax 1-43-20-15-71; e-mail snpn@wanadoo.fr; internet www.snpn.com; f. 1854; 4,000 mems; Pres. FRANÇOIS RAMADE; Gen. Sec. MICHEL ECHAUBARD; publs *La Terre et la Vie* (4 a year), *Le Courrier de la Nature* (7 a year), *Zones Humides Infos* (4 a year).

Société Zoologique de France: 195 rue St Jacques, 75005 Paris; tel. 1-40-79-31-10; fax 1-40-79-57-35; e-mail dhondt@mnhn.fr; internet www.snv.jussieu.fr/zoologie; f. 1876; zoology, evolution; 600 mems; Pres. Prof. J. DAGUZAN; Gen. Sec. Dr J. L. D'HONDT; publs *Bulletin* (quarterly), *Mémoires* (irregular).

Mathematical Sciences

Comité National Français de Mathématiciens: c/o S. Ferenczi, Institut de Mathématiques de Luminy, 163 ave de Luminy, Case 907, 13288 Marseilles Cedex 9; fax 4-91-26-96-55; e-mail ferenczi@iml.univ-mrs.fr; f. 1951; Pres. P. ARNOUX; Sec. S. FERENCZI.

Société Mathématique de France: Institut Henri Poincaré, 11 rue Pierre et Marie Curie, 75231 Paris Cedex 05; tel. 1-44-27-67-96; fax 1-40-46-90-96; e-mail smf@dma.ens.fr; internet smf.emath.fr; f. 1872; 1,950 mems; Pres. MARIE-FRANÇOISE ROY; publs *Bulletin* (4 a year), *Mémoires* (4 a year), *Officiel des Mathématiques* (9 a year), *Astérisque* (monthly), *Gazette des Mathématiciens* (quarterly), *Revue d'Histoire des Mathématiques* (2 a year), *Panoramas et Synthèses* (2 a year), *Cours Spécialisés* (2 a year).

Physical Sciences

Association Française d'Observateurs d'Etoiles Variables: Observatoire Astronomique, 11 rue de l'Université, 67000 Strasbourg; tel. 3-85-89-09-78; e-mail afoev@astro.u-strasbg.fr; internet www.astro.u-strasbg.fr/afoev; f. 1921; observations (visual, photographic, PEP, CCD) of variable stars; 110 mems; Pres. M. VERDENET; Secs-Gen. J. GUNTHER, D. PROUST; publ. *Bulletin de l'AFOEV* (quarterly).

Association Française pour l'Etude du Quaternaire: Maison de la Géologie, 79 rue Claude Bernard, 75005 Paris; e-mail pierre.antoine@cnrs-bellevue.fr; internet www.afeq.cnrs-bellevue.fr; f. 1962 to prepare scientific publications and exchange information on the Quaternary; 600 mems; Pres. Dr D. LEFÈVRE; Sec. Dr C. FERRIER; publ. *Quaternaire* (4 a year).

Association Scientifique et Technique pour l'Exploitation des Océans: Immeuble Ile de France, La Défense 9, 4 place de la Pyramide, 92070 Paris La Défense Cedex 33; tel. 1-47-67-25-32; f. 1967; oil technology and allied activities, pollution control, polymetallic nodules, sand and gravel workings, fishing technology and fish farming; 80 mem. industries; Chair. PIERRE JACQUARD; Man. Dir B. E. DIMONT; publ. *Annuaire Technique et Industriel*.

Société Astronomique de France: 3 rue Beethoven, 75016 Paris; tel. 1-42-24-13-74; fax 1-42-30-75-47; e-mail ste.astro.france@wanadoo.fr; internet www.saf-lastronomie.com; f. 1887; 2,200 mems; Pres. PATRICK GUIBERT; Sec.-Gen. JEAN-CLAUDE AMACHER; publs *L'Astronomie* (monthly), *Observations et Travaux* (4 a year), *Les Ephémérides* (annually).

Société de Chimie Industrielle: 28 rue Saint-Dominique, 75007 Paris; tel. 1-53-59-02-10; fax 1-45-55-40-33; e-mail sci.fr@wanadoo.fr; internet www.scifrance.org; f. 1917; 4,000 mems; Pres. P. TRIFAROL; Del.-Gen. G. MATTIODA; publs *l'Actualité chimique*, *Informations Chimie*, *Analusis*.

Société des Experts-Chimistes de France: 23 rue du Commandant Jean Duhail, 94120 Fontenay-sous-Bois; tel. 1-48-76-17-24; fax 1-48-76-60-15; e-mail expert-chim@wanadoo.fr; f. 1912; 300 mems; Pres. MICHEL DERBESY; Sec.-Gen. CLAUDE VERON; publ. *Annales des Falsifications de l'Expertise Chimique et Toxicologique*.

Société Française de Biochimie et Biologie Moléculaire: 45 Rue des Saints-Pères, 75270 Paris Cedex 06; tel. 1-42-86-33-77; fax 1-42-86-33-73; e-mail sfbbm@cep.u-psud.fr; internet coli.polytechnique.fr/sfbbm; f. 1914; 1,320 mems; Pres. E. WESTHOF; Gen. Sec. P. DESSEN; publs *Biochimie*, *Regard sur la Biochimie*.

Société Française de Chimie: 250 rue St Jacques, 75005 Paris; tel. 1-40-46-71-60; fax 1-40-46-71-61; e-mail sfc@sfc.fr; internet www.sfc.fr; f. 1857; 4,600 mems; Pres. ARMAND LATTES; Sec.-Gen. JEAN-CLAUDE BRUNIE; publs *L'Actualité chimique* (monthly), *Analusis* (10 a year), *Journal de Chimie physique* (10 a year).

Société Française de Minéralogie et de Cristallographie: 4 place Jussieu, casier 83, 75252 Paris Cedex 05; tel. 1-44-27-60-24; fax 1-44-27-60-24; e-mail sfmc@ccr.jussieu.fr; internet www.sfmc-fr.org; f. 1878; 600 mems; Pres. JEAN-ROBERT KIENAST; Gen.-Sec. DANIEL NEUVILLE; publs *Bulletin de Liaison*, *European Journal of Mineralogy*.

Société Française de Physique: 33 rue Croulebarbe, 75013 Paris; tel. 1-44-08-67-10; fax 1-44-08-67-19; e-mail sfp@sfpnet.org; internet sfp.in2p3.fr; f. 1873; 2,500 mems; Pres. EDOUARD BREZIN; Gen. Sec. JEAN VANNIMENUS; publs *Bulletin*, *Catalogue de l'Exposition de Physique*, *Journal de Physique*, *Annales de Physique*, *Colloques*.

Société Géologique de France: 77 rue Claude-Bernard, 75005 Paris; tel. 1-43-31-77-35; fax 1-45-35-79-10; e-mail accueil@sgfr.com; internet sgfr.free.fr; f. 1830; 1,300 mems; library of 50,000 vols, 500 periodicals; Pres. PATRICK DE WEVER; Secs PHILIPPE AGARD, JEAN-YVES REYNAUD; publs *Bulletin* (6 a year), *Mémoires* (irreg.), *Géochronique* (quarterly), *Géologie de la France* (co-edited with BRGM), *Terra Nova* (co-edited with EUG and Sociétés géologiques européennes).

Union des Physiciens: 44 blvd Saint-Michel, 75270 Paris Cedex 06; tel. 1-43-25-61-53; fax 1-43-25-07-48; f. 1906; 8,000 mems; Pres. J. MAUREL; publ. *Bulletin* (monthly).

PHILOSOPHY AND PSYCHOLOGY

Association pour la Diffusion de la Pensée Français: 6 rue Ferrus, 75683 Paris Cedex 14; tel. 1-43-13-11-00; fax 1-43-13-11-25; f. 1946; aims to promote the French language and Francophone culture worldwide; 600 overseas mems; Pres. JACQUES BLOT.

Société Française de Philosophie: C/o 45 rue d'Ulm, 75320 Paris Cedex 005; e-mail inst.intern.philo@wandoo.fr; f. 1901; 180 mems; Pres. BERNARD BOURGEOIS; Sec.-Gen. CHRISTIANE MENASSEYRE; publs *Bulletin*, *Revue de Métaphysique et de Morale* (4 a year).

Société Française de Psychologie: 71 ave Edouard-Vaillant, 92774 Boulogne Cedex; tel. 1-55-20-58-32; fax 1-55-20-58-34; e-mail sfp@psycho.univ-paris5.fr; internet www.sfpsy.org; f. 1901; 1,000 mems; Pres. JACQUES PY; Sec.-Gen. ALAIN PAINEAU; publs *La Lettre de SFP*, *Psychologie Française*, *Pratiques Psychologiques*.

RELIGION, SOCIOLOGY AND ANTHROPOLOGY

Association Française des Arabisants: Collège de France, 52 rue du Cardinal Lemoine, 75005 Paris; e-mail afda@afda.asso.fr; internet www.afda.asso.fr.; f. 1973 to promote Arabic studies, to study questions of doctrine and practice relative to teaching and research in Arabic; to keep its members informed of ideas and activities of interest to teachers, researchers and students of Arabic; 450 mems; Pres. JEAN-YVES L'HOPITAL; Sec. ABDELLATIF IDRISSI; publs *L'Arabisant* (every 2 years), *Annuaire des Arabisants* (every 2 years), *Lettre d'Information* (2 a year), *Actes des journées d'études arabes* (irregular).

Société Asiatique: Palais de l'Institut, 23 quai de Conti, 75006 Paris; tel. 1-44-41-43-14; fax 1-44-41-43-14; internet www.aibl.fr/fr/asie/home.html; f. 1822; library of 90,000 vols; 725 mems; Pres. JEAN-PIERRE MAHÉ; publs *Journal Asiatique* (2 a year), *Cahiers*.

Société d'Anthropologie de Paris: Musée de l'Homme, place du Trocadéro, 75116 Paris; tel. 1-44-05-72-65; fax 1-44-05-72-41; f. 1859; biological anthropology; 310 mems; Pres. OLIVIER DUTOUR; Sec.-Gen. ALAIN FROMENT; publ. *Bulletins et Mémoires* (quarterly).

Société de l'Histoire du Protestantisme Français: 54 rue des Saints-Pères, 75007 Paris; tel. 1-45-48-62-07; fax 1-45-44-94-87; e-mail shpf@libertysurf.fr; f. 1852; library of 150,000 vols, 12,000 MSS in library, 2,000 periodical titles; Pres. LAURENT THEIS; Sec.-Gen. JEAN-HUGUES CARBONNIER; publs *Bulletin*, *Cahiers de Généalogie Protestante* (quarterly).

Société de Mythologie Française: 3 rue St-Laurent, 75010 Paris; tel. 1-42-05-30-57; e-mail phparrain@mythofrancaise.asso.fr; internet www.mythofrancaise.asso.fr; f. 1950; 200 mems; Pres. BERNARD SERGENT; publ. *Mythologie Française* (quarterly).

Société des Africanistes: Musée de l'Homme, 17 Place du Trocadéro, 75116 Paris; tel. 1-47-27-72-55; fax 1-47-04-63-40; e-mail africanistes@wanadoo.fr; internet www.mae.u-paris10.fr/africanistes; f. 1931; 400 mems; Pres. PHILIPPE LABURTHE-TOLRA; Sec. FRANÇOIS GAULME; publ. *Journal des Africanistes* (2 a year).

Société des Américanistes: Maison René Ginouvès, 21 allée de l'Université, 92023 Nanterre Cedex; tel. 1-46-69-26-34; e-mail jsa@mae.u-paris10.fr; f. 1895; 500 mems; Pres. PHILIPPE DESCOLA; Gen. Sec. DOMINIQUE MICHELET; publ. *Journal* (2 a year).

Société d'Histoire Religieuse de la France: 26 rue d'Assas, 75006 Paris; internet www.enc.sorbonne.fr/shrf; f. 1910; 600 mems; Pres. MARC VENARD; Sec.-Gen. OLIVIER PONCET; publ. *Revue d'Histoire de l'Eglise de France* (2 a year).

Société Française de Sociologie: 59/61 rue Pouchet, 75849 Paris Cedex 17; tel. 1-40-25-12-63; fax 1-42-28-95-44; e-mail afs@iresco.fr; internet www.iresco.fr/societes/afs; f. 1962; Pres. DANIEL BERTAUX; Sec. MICHÈLE VINAUGER.

TECHNOLOGY

Académie de Marine: BP 11, 00300 Armées, Paris; located at: 21 place Joffre, 75007 Paris; tel. 1-44-42-82-02; fax 1-44-42-82-04; e-mail academiedemarine@wanadoo.fr; internet www.academiedemarine.com; f. 1752; 66 mems and corresp. mems; attached to sections on History, Law, Naval Equipment, Navigation, Military Affairs, Economics, Yachting, Mercantile Marine; Pres. Contre-amiral FRANÇOIS BELLEC; Permanent Sec. Vice-amiral HENRI COCHET; publ. *Communications et Mémoires* (3 a year).

Association Aéronautique et Astronautique de France (AAAF): 61 Ave du Château, 78480 Verneuil-sur-Seine; tel. 1-39-79-75-15; fax 1-39-79-75-27; internet www.aaaf.asso.fr; f. 1972; 1,800 mems; formed by merger of Association Française des Ingénieurs de l'Aéronautique et de l'Espace and Société Française d'Astronautique; Pres. MICHEL SCHELLER; Sec.-Gen. GÉRARD LARUELLE; publ. *La Nouvelle Revue d'Aéronautique et d'Astronautique* (every 3 months).

Association des Anciens Elèves de l'Ecole Nationale Supérieure des Industries Agricoles et Alimentaires: 9–11 ave Franklin D. Roosevelt, 75008 Paris; tel. 1-42-25-92-48; 1,500 mems; Pres. JEAN-LOUIS TIXIER; Sec.-Gen. MICHEL MERY; publ. *Industries Alimentaires et Agricoles* (monthly).

Association Française des Sciences et Technologies de l'Information: 4 place Jussieu, 75252 Paris Cedex 05; tel. 3-83-59-20-51; e-mail asti.asso@lri.fr; internet www.asti.asso.fr; f. 1998; 25 mem. orgs; Pres. JEAN-PAUL HATON; Sec.-Gen. CLAUDE GIRAULT; publ. *Hebdo*.

Association Française du Froid: 17 rue Guillaume Apollinaire, 75006 Paris; tel. 1-45-44-52-52; fax 1-42-22-00-42; e-mail a.f.f@wanadoo.fr; internet www.aff.asso.fr; f. 1908; 1,000 mems; Pres. LOUIS LUCAS; Sec.-Gen. JEAN LETEINTURIER-LAPRISE; publs *Revue Générale du Froid* (10 a year), *Bulletin: Kryos*.

Association Nationale de la Recherche Technique: 41 Blvd des Capucines, 75002 Paris; tel. 1-55-35-25-50; fax 1-55-35-25-55; internet www.anrt.asso.fr; f. 1953 to promote technical research and organizations, and to foster contact with technical research institutions abroad; Pres. JEAN-FRANÇOIS DEHECQ; publ. *La lettre Européenne du Progrès Technique* (10 a year).

Conseil National des Ingénieurs et des Scientifiques de France: 7 rue Lamennais, 75008 Paris; tel. 1-44-13-66-88; fax 1-42-89-82-50; internet www.cnisf.org; f. 1848; Pres. NOËL CLAVELLOUX; Sec. MONIQUE MONIN; publ. *I.D.*.

Société de l'Electricité, de l'Electronique, et des Technologies de l'Information et de la Communication (SEE): 11–17 rue Hamelin, 75783 Paris Cedex 16; tel. 1-56-90-37-00; fax 1-56-90-37-19; e-mail see@see.asso.fr; internet www.see.asso.fr; f. 1883; Pres. JEAN-GABRIEL REMY; Sec. ANDRÉ COUSTÈRE; publs *Revue de l'Electricité et de l'Electronique* (10 a year), *3EI—Revue de l'Enseignement de l'Electrotechnique et de l'Electronique Industrielle* (4 a year), *e-STA—Revue des Sciences et Technologies de l'Automatique* (online), *Newsletter* (26 a year).

Société d'Encouragement pour l'Industrie Nationale: 4 place Saint-Germain-des-Prés, 75006 Paris; e-mail adm@industrienationale.fr; internet www.industrienationale.fr; f. 1801; Dir BERNARD MOUSSON; publ. *L'Industrie Nationale*.

Société Française de Métallurgie et de Matériaux (SF2M): 250 rue Saint Jacques, 75005 Paris; tel. 1-46-33-08-00; fax 1-46-33-08-80; internet www.sf2m.asso.fr; f. 1945; 1,200 mems; Pres. ANNICK PERCHERON-GUEGAN; Sec. PAUL V. RIBOUD.

Société Française de Photogrammétrie et de Télédétection: 2 ave Pasteur, 94165 St Mandé Cedex; tel. 1-64-15-32-86; fax 1-64-15-32-85; e-mail sfpt@ensg.ign.fr; internet www.ign.fr/sfpt; f. 1959; photogrammetry and remote sensing; 615 mems; Pres. G. BEGNI; Sec.-Gen. I. VEILLET; publ. *Bulletin* (quarterly).

Société Française des Microscopies: Case 243, Université Pierre et Marie Curie, 4 place Jussieu, 75252 Paris Cedex 05; tel. 1-44-27-26-21; fax 1-44-27-26-22; e-mail sfme@snv.jussieu.fr; internet www.sfmu.snv.jussieu.fr; f. 1959; to further all types of microscopy, electronic optics and electronic diffraction, spectroscopy, microprobe, cellular biology; 470 mems; Pres. ALAIN BRISSON; publs *Biology of the Cell* (9 a year), *European Physical Journal: Applied Physics* (6 a year).

Société Hydrotechnique de France: 25 rue des Favorites, 75015 Paris; tel. 1-42-50-91-03; fax 1-42-50-59-83; e-mail shf@shf.asso.fr; internet www.shf.asso.fr; f. 1912; fluid mechanics, applied hydraulics, geophysical hydraulics and water conservation; 600 mems; Pres. RENÉ COULOMB; Gen. Dir CHRISTIAN ORY; publs *La Houille Blanche Revue Internationale de l'Eau* (6 a year), *Proceedings*, *Journées de l'Hydraulique* (every 2 years), guides on hydroelectricity and flood forecasts, research documents.

Research Institutes

GENERAL

Centre National de la Recherche Scientifique (CNRS): 3 rue Michel-Ange, 75794 Paris Cedex 16; tel. 1-44-96-40-00; fax 1-44-96-49-65; internet www.cnrs.fr; f. 1939; coordinates and promotes scientific research, and proposes to the Govt means of doing research and how to allocate funds; makes grants-in-aid to scientific bodies and to individuals to enable them to carry out research work; subsidizes or sets up laboratories for scientific research; is split into 40 sections, covering all scientific fields; funds 11,600 researchers, 14,400 engineers and 4,000 technicians and admin. staff; depts of Mathematics, Physics, Planet and Universe (Scientific Dir MICHEL LANOO), Chemistry (Scientific Dir GILBERT CHAMBAUD), Life Sciences (Scientific Dir MICHEL VAN DER REST), Human and Social Sciences (Scientific Dir MARIE-FRANÇOISE COUREL), Environment and Sustainable Development (Scientific Dir BERNARD DELAY), Engineering (Scientific Dir PIERRE GUILLON); Pres. CATHÉRINE BRÉCHIGNAC; Dir-Gen. ARNOLD MIGUS; Sec.-Gen. JACQUES BERNARD.

I. Nuclear and Particle Physics:

Laboratoire souterrain de Modane (LSM): 90 rue Polset, 73500 Modane; tel. 4-79-05-22-57; fax 4-79-05-24-74; e-mail gilles.gerbier@lsm.in2p3.fr; internet www-lsm.in2p3.fr; Dir GILLES GERBIER.

Centre de spectrométrie nucléaire et de spectrométrie de masse (CSNSM): Université Paris XI, Bâtiment 104 et 108, 91400 Orsay; tel. 1-69-41-52-13; fax 1-69-41-50-08; e-mail direction@cnsnm.in2p3.fr; internet www-csnsm.in2p3.fr; f. 1946; Dir HUBERT FLOCARD.

Institut de Recherches Subatomiques: 23 rue du Loess, 67037 Strasbourg Cedex; tel. 3-88-10-62-14; fax 3-88-10-62-92; internet ireswww.in2p3.fr; f. 1960; Dir DANIEL HUSS.

Grand accélérateur national d'ions lourds (GANIL): blvd Henri Bacqueret, BP 55027, 14076 Caen Cedex 5; tel. 2-31-45-46-47; fax 2-31-45-46-65; e-mail gales@ganil.fr; internet ganinfo.in2p3.fr; Dir SYDNEY GALES.

Laboratoire d'Annecy-le-Vieux de physique des particules (LAPP): 9 chemin de Bellevue, BP 110, 74941 Annecy-le-Vieux Cedex; tel. 4-50-09-16-00; fax 4-50-27-94-95; e-mail colas@lapp.in2p3.fr; internet wwwlapp.in2p3.fr; f. 1975; Dir JACQUES COLACE.

Laboratoire de Physique Subatomique et de Cosmologie: Université Joseph Fourier Grenoble 1, CNRS/IN2P3, 53 ave des Martyrs, 38026 Grenoble Cedex; tel. 4-76-28-40-00; fax 4-76-28-40-04; internet lpsc.in2p3.fr; f. 1968; nuclear physics, particle physics, astrophysics; library of 10,000 vols; Dir JOHANN COLLOT.

Institut de physique nucléaire de Lyon (IPNL): Université Claude Bernard Lyon I, Bâtiment Paul Dirac, 4 rue Enrico Fermi, 69622 Villeurbanne Cedex; tel. 4-72-44-84-57; fax 4-72-43-15-40; e-mail b.ille@ipnl.in2p3.fr; internet lyoinfo.in2p3.fr; Dir BERNARD ILLE.

Laboratoire de l'accélérateur linéaire (LAL): Université Paris XI, Bâtiment 200, BP 34, 91898 Orsay Cedex; tel. 1-64-46-83-00; fax 1-69-86-98-63; e-mail direction@lal.in2p3.fr; internet www.lal.in2p3.fr; Dir GUY WORMSER.

Institut de physique nucléaire (IPN): Université Paris XI, Bâtiment 100, 91406 Orsay Cedex; tel. 1-69-15-67-50; fax 1-69-15-64-70; e-mail guillema@ipno.in2p3.fr; internet ipnweb.in2p3.fr; Dir DOMINIQUE MUELLER.

Laboratoire de physique nucléaire des hautes énergies (LPNHE): Université de Paris VI, Tour 33 RDC, 4 place Jussieu, 75252 Paris Cedex 05; tel. 1-44-27-63-13; fax 1-44-27-46-38; e-mail pascal.debu@lpnhep.in2p3.fr; internet www-lpnhep.in2p3.fr; Dir PASCAL DEBU.

Centre d'Etudes Nucléaires de Bordeaux-Gradignan (CENBG): Université Sciences et Technologies Bordeaux I, Chemin du Solarium, Le Haut-Vigneau, BP 120, 33175 Gradignan Cedex; tel. 5-57-12-08-04; fax 5-57-12-08-01; e-mail direction@cenbg.in2p3.fr; internet www.cenbg.in2p3.fr; Pres. BERNARD HAAS.

Laboratoire de physique corpusculaire de Clermont (LPC Clermont): Université Blaise Pascal Clermont Ferrand 2, 24 ave des Landais, 63177 Aubière Cedex; tel. 4-73-40-72-72; fax 4-73-26-45-98; e-mail baldit@clermont.in2p3.fr; internet clrwww.in2p3.fr; Dir ALAIN BALDIT.

Laboratoire de physique corpusculaire de Caen (LPC Caen): ENSI CAEN, Institut Sciences Matière Rayon, 6 blvd du Maréchal-Juin, 14050 Caen Cedex 4; tel. 2-31-45-29-90; fax 2-31-45-25-49; e-mail jean-claude.steckmeyer@in2p3.fr; internet caeinfo.in2p3.fr; Dir JEAN-CLAUDE STECKMEYER.

Physique corpusculaire et Cosmologie: Collège de France, 11 place Marcelin-Berthelot, 75231 Paris Cedex 05; tel. 1-44-27-14-39; fax 1-43-54-69-89; internet cdfinfo.in2p3.fr; Dir DANIEL VIGNAUD.

Centre de physique des particules de Marseille (CPPM): Université de la Méditerranée Aix-Marseille II, Case 902, 163 ave de Luminy, 13288 Marseille Cedex 09; tel. 4-91-82-72-00; fax 4-91-82-72-99; e-mail aleksan@cppm.in2p3.fr; internet marwww.in2p3.fr; Dir ROY ALEKSAN.

Laboratoire SUBATECH Nantes: Ecole des Mines, La Chantrerie, 4 rue Alfred Kastler, 44307 Nantes Cedex 3; tel. 2-51-85-81-00; fax 2-51-85-84-79; internet www-subatech.in2p3.fr; Dir J. MARTINO.

II. Mathematics and Physics:

Théorie des collisions atomiques: Université de Bordeaux 1, 351 cours de la Libération, 33405 Talence; tel. 5-56-84-61-81; fax 5-56-84-61-87; Dir ROBERT GAYET.

Laboratoire de physique théorique de l'ENS: École normale supérieure, 24 rue Lhomond, 75231 Paris Cedex 05; tel. 1-44-32-34-85; fax 1-43-36-76-66; internet www.lpt.ens.fr; f. 1974; Dir EUGENE CREMMER.

Laboratoire de photophysique moléculaire: Université Paris Sud, Bâtiment 210 et 350, 91405 Orsay Cedex; tel. 1-69-15-67-76; fax 1-69-15-67-77; internet www.ppm.u-psud.fr; f. 1972; Dir PHILIPPE BRÉCHIGNAC.

Centre de Physique Théorique: Centre de Luminy, Case 907, 13288 Marseille Cedex 9; tel. 4-91-26-95-07; fax 4-91-26-95-53; internet www.cpt.univ-mrs.fr; f. 1967; Dir MARC KNECHT.

Laboratoire Aimé Cotton: Campus d'Orsay Bâtiment 505, 91405 Orsay Cedex; tel. 1-69-82-40-50; fax 1-69-07-68-91; f. 1947; Sec. MARIE-THÉRÈSE DONEL.

Laboratoire des Champs Magnétiques Intenses (LCMI): 25 avenue des Martyrs, BP 166, 38042 Grenoble Cedex; tel. 4-76-88-10-00; fax 4-76-87-21-97; internet www.ujf-grenoble.fr/ujf/fr/recherche/labujf/lcmifran.phtml; f. 1971; Dir GÉRARD MARTINEZ.

Laboratoire d'optique quantique: École polytechnique, route de Saclay, 91128 Palaiseau Cedex; tel. 1-69-33-41-27; fax 1-69-33-30-17; f. 1971; Dir FRANÇOIS PRADÈRE.

Laboratoire de physique des solides: 1 place Aristide-Briand, 92190 Meudon; tel. 1-45-07-51-53; fax 1-45-07-58-99; f. 1970; Dir JACQUES CHEVALLIER.

Centre de Recherche sur l'Hétéro-Epitaxie et ses Applications: Parc de Valbonne Sophia-Antipolis, Rue Bernard Grégory, 06034 Valbonne; tel. 4-93-95-42-00; fax 4-93-95-83-61; Dir JEAN-YVES DUBOZ.

Laboratoire de magnétisme et matériaux magnétiques: 1 place Aristide-Briand, 92195 Meudon; tel. 1-45-07-53-18; fax 1-45-07-58-22; f. 1970; Dir VLADIMIR CAGAN.

Laboratoire de physique des matériaux: 1 place Aristide-Briand, 92195 Meudon; tel. 1-45-07-51-65; fax 1-45-07-58-99; f. 1948; Dir JACQUES CASTAING.

Centre de recherches sur les très basses températures: 25 avenue des Martyrs, BP 166X, 38042 Grenoble Cedex 9; tel. 4-76-88-10-00; fax 4-76-87-50-60; internet www.ujf-grenoble.fr/ujf/fr/recherche/labujf/crtbtfra.phtml; f. 1962; Dir HENRI GODFRIN.

Laboratoire de magnétisme Louis Néel: 25 avenue des Martyrs, BP 166X, 38042 Grenoble Cedex; tel. 4-76-88-10-89; fax 4-76-88-11-91; internet lab-neel.grenoble.cnrs.fr; f. 1971; Dir JOËL CIBERT.

Laboratoire des propriétés mécaniques et thermodynamiques des matériaux: Université de Paris 13, 99 Ave Jean-Baptiste Clément, 93430 Villetaneuse; tel. 1-49-40-35-01; fax 1-49-40-39-38; e-mail direction@lpmtm.univ-paris13.fr; internet www-lpmtm.univ-paris13.fr; f. 1973; Dir BRIGITTE BACROIX.

Centre de recherches sur les solides à organisation cristalline imparfaite (CRSOCI): 1B rue de la Férollerie, 45071 Orléans Cedex; tel. 2-38-63-39-37; f. 1969; Dir HENRI VAN DAMME.

Laboratoire de cristallographie: 25 avenue des Martyrs, BP 166, 38042 Grenoble Cedex 09; tel. 4-76-88-10-00; fax 4-76-88-10-38; e-mail secretariat_cristallo@grenoble.cnrs.fr; internet www-cristallo.polycnrs-gre.fr; f. 1971; Dir MICHEL ANNE.

Centre d'élaboration de matériaux et d'études structurales/Laboratoire d'optique électronique: 29 rue Jeanne-Marvig, BP 4347, 31055 Toulouse Cedex; tel. 5-62-25-78-00; fax 5-62-25-79-99; f. 1949; Dir JEAN GALY.

Centre de recherche sur les mécanismes de la croissance cristalline (CRMC2): Campus de Luminy, Case 913, 13288 Marseille Cedex 9; tel. 4-91-17-28-00; fax 4-91-41-89-16; e-mail direction@crmcn.univ-mrs.fr; internet www.crmc2.univ-mrs.fr; f. 1975; Dir SLAVA SAFAROV.

Laboratoire Léon Brillouin (LLB): Centre d'Etudes Nucléaires de Saclay, 91191 Gif-sur-Yvette Cedex; tel. 1-69-08-52-41; fax 1-69-08-82-61; internet www-llb.cea.fr; f. 1974; Dir MARIANNE LAMBERT.

Laboratoire de l'utilisation du rayonnement électromagnétique (LURE): Université de Paris 11, Bâtiment 209D, 91898 Orsay Cedex; tel. 1-64-46-80-00; internet www.lure.u-psud.fr; f. 1977; Dir A. TADJEDDINE.

Centre interdisciplinaire de recherches avec les ions lourds (CIRIL): BP 5133, 14040 Caen Cedex; tel. 2-31-45-46-01; fax 2-31-45-47-14; e-mail ciril@drecam.cea.fr; f. 1982; Dir JEAN-CLAUDE JOUSSET.

Laboratoire d'études des propriétés électroniques des solides: 25 ave des Martyrs, 38000 Grenoble Cedex; tel. 4-76-88-11-85; fax 4-76-88-79-88; internet lepes.polycnrs-gre.fr; f. 1983; Dir DIDIER MAYOU.

Centre de physique théorique: Ecole polytechnique, Route de Saclay, 91128 Palaiseau Cedex; tel. 1-69-33-40-87; fax 1-69-33-30-08; Dir GUY LAVAL.

Service des champs magnétiques intenses: 156 ave de Rangueil, 31077 Toulouse Cedex; tel. 5-61-55-95-15; fax 5-61-55-96-24; f. 1967; Dir SALOMON ASKENAZY.

Recherches mathématiques et documentation en vue de la recherche à l'IHP: Université de Paris 6, Institut Henri Poincaré, 11 rue Pierre-et-Marie-Curie, 75231 Paris Cedex 05; tel. 1-43-54-42-10; f. 1985; Dir NICOLE EL KAROUI.

Spectrométrie nucléaire et spectrométrie de masse: Campus d'Orsay, Bâtiment 104–108, BP 1, 91406 Orsay Campus; tel. 1-69-41-52-22; Dir HARRY BERNAS.

Microscopie électronique, analytique et quantitative: Université de Paris 11, Laboratoire de physique des solides, Bâtiment 510, 91405 Orsay Cedex; tel. 1-69-41-53-70; f. 1984; Dir CHRISTIAN COLLIEX.

Laboratoire de microstructures et microélectroniques (L2M): Centre national d'étude des télécommunications, Centre Paris B, 196 ave Henri Ravera, 92220 Bagneux; tel. 1-42-31-76-93; fax 1-45-31-73-78; f. 1984; Dir HUGUETTE LAUNOIS.

Laboratoire commun CNRS/Saint-Gobain: CRPAM, BP 109, 54704 Pont-à-

Mousson Cedex; tel. 1-83-83-24-24; fax 1-83-82-89-62; f. 1986; Dir ANDRÉ THOMY.

Laboratoire grenoblois de recherche sur les ions, les plasmas et la physique atomique (LAGRIPPA): CENG, BP 85X, 38041 Grenoble Cedex; tel. 4-76-88-40-01; fax 4-76-88-51-60; f. 1983; Dir JURGEN ANDRA.

Institut de physique et chimie des matériaux de Strasbourg (IPCM): Université de Strasbourg 1, 4 rue Blaise-Pascal, 67070 Strasbourg Cedex; tel. 3-88-41-60-00; fax 3-88-28-09-90; f. 1988; Dir FRANÇOIS GAUTIER.

Laboratoire d'étude des microstructures: O NERA, 20 ave de la Division-Leclerc, 92322 Châtillon Cedex; tel. 1-46-73-45-99; fax 1-46-73-41-55; internet www.lem.onera.fr/; f. 1988; Dir DENIS GRATIAS.

Spectroscopie en lumière polarisée: E SPCI, 10 rue Vauquelin, 75231 Paris Cedex 05; tel. 1-40-79-46-03; fax 1-43-31-42-22; f. 1967; Dir CLAUDE BOCCARA.

Magnétisme et optique des solides: 1 place Aristide-Briand, 92190 Meudon; tel. 1-45-34-75-50; fax 1-45-34-46-96; f. 1975; Dir HENRI LE GALL.

Structures organiques dissymétriques: Université de Paris 11, Centre Pharmaceutique, Laboratoire de Physique, Tour B, Avenue J.-B.-Clément, 92290 Châtenay-Malabry; tel. 1-46-83-56-23; fax 1-46-83-13-03; f. 1975; Dir COLETTE DE RANGO.

Problèmes d'interactions non-linéaires: Université Paris 7, Tour 33-43, 2 place Jussieu, 75251 Paris Cedex 05; tel. 1-43-36-25-25; f. 1975; Dir RAYMOND JANCEL.

Théorie des processus atomiques et moléculaires à basse énergie: Observatoire de Meudon, 5 place Jules Janssen, 92195 Meudon Cedex; tel. 1-45-07-75-30; fax 1-45-07-74-69; f. 1983; Dir MARYVONNE LE DOURNEUF.

Département d'astrophysique relativiste et de cosmologie (DARC): Observatoire de Meudon, 5 place Jules-Janssen, 92195 Meudon Principal Cedex; tel. 1-45-07-75-30; fax 1-45-07-79-71; internet luth2.obspm.fr/~darc/darc.html; f. 1975; Dir JEAN-PIERRE LASOTA.

Laboratoire de physique moléculaire et applications (LPMA): Université Paris 6, Case 76, 4 place Jussieu, 75252 Paris Cedex 05; tel. 1-44-27-44-77; fax 1-44-27-70-33; internet www.lpma.jussieu.fr; f. 1973; Dir CLAUDE CAMY-PEYRET.

Laboratoire de rhéologie: Université de Grenoble 1, 38041 Grenoble Cedex 9; tel. 4-76-82-51-64; e-mail rheologie @ ujf-grenoble.fr; internet rheologie.ujf-grenoble.fr; Dir JEAN-MICHEL PIAU.

III. Physical Sciences for Engineers:

Laboratoire d'aérothermique: 1C Avenue de la Recherche Scientifique, 45071 Orleans Cedex 2; tel. 2-38-25-77; fax 2-38-25-77-77; e-mail aero@cnrs-orleans.fr; internet web.cnrs-orleans.fr/~webaero; f. 1938; Dir JEAN-PIERRE MARTIN.

Laboratoire d'automatique et d'analyse des systèmes (LAAS): 7 ave du Colonel Roche, 31077 Toulouse Cedex 4; tel. 5-61-33-62-00; fax 5-61-55-35-77; e-mail laas-contact@laas.fr; internet www.laas.fr; f. 1967; Dir MALIK GHALLAB.

Institut de science et de génie des matériaux et des procédés: BP 5, Odeillo-Via, 66120 Font-Romeu; tel. 4-68-30-77-00; fax 4-68-30-29-40; f. 1950; Dir CLAUDE DUPUY.

Laboratoire de mécanique et d'acoustique (LMA): 31 chemin Joseph-Aiguier, 13402 Marseille Cedex 20; tel. 4-91-16-40-07; fax 4-91-71-28-66; e-mail mel.lma@lma.cnrs-mrs.fr; internet omicron.cnrs-mrs.fr/; f. 1941; Dir MICHEL RAOUS.

Laboratoire de physique et de métrologie des oscillateurs: 32 ave de l'Observatoire, 25044 Besançon Cedex; tel. 3-81-85-39-99; fax 3-81-85-39-98; e-mail lpmo@lpmo.edu; internet lpmo.univ-fcomte.fr; f. 1973; Dir DANIEL HAUDEN.

Laboratoire des signaux et systèmes (L2S): Supélec, 3 rue Joliot-Curie, 91190 Gif-sur-Yvette; tel. 1-69-85-17-12; fax 1-69-85-17-69; internet www.lss.supelec.fr; f. 1974; Dir ERIC WALTER.

Laboratoire d'électrostatique et de matériaux diélectriques: BP 166, 25 ave des Martyrs, 38042 Grenoble Cedex; tel. 4-76-88-10-76; fax 4-76-88-79-45; e-mail teisse@polycnrs-gre.fr; internet www-lemd.polycnrs-gre.fr; f. 1971; Dir ANDRÉ DENAT.

Laboratoire d'informatique pour la mécanique et les sciences pour l'ingénieur (LIMSI): Université de Paris Sud, Bâtiment 508 et 502bis, BP 133, 91403 Orsay; tel. 1-69-85-80-80; fax 1-69-85-80-88; e-mail dir@limsi.fr; internet www.limsi.fr; f. 1945; Dir PATRICK LE QUÉRÉ.

Laboratoire des sciences du génie chimique: BP 451, 1 rue Grandville, 54001 Nancy Cedex; tel. 3-83-35-21-21; fax 3-83-35-29-75; internet www.ensic.inpl-nancy.fr/LSGC; f. 1975; Dir MICHEL SARDIN.

Laboratoire de combustion et systèmes réactifs: 1C ave de la Recherche-Scientifique, 45071 Orléans Cedex 2; tel. 2-38-25-54-16; fax 2-38-25-78-75; internet web.cnrs-orleans.fr/~weblcsr; f. 1969; Dir ISKENDER GÖKALP.

Laboratoire d'ingénierie, des matériaux et des hautes pressions: Centre universitaire Paris Nord, 90 Ave Jean-Baptiste-Clément, 93430 Villetaneuse; tel. 1-49-40-34-37; fax 1-49-40-34-14; internet www-limhp-cnrs.univ-paris13.fr; Dir JEAN-FRANÇOIS BOCQUET.

Laboratoire EM2C Energétique Moléculaire et Macroscopique, Combustion: École centrale de Paris, gde-Voie des Vignes, 92295 Châtenay-Malabry Cedex; tel. 1-41-13-10-31; fax 1-47-02-80-35; e-mail secretariat@em2c.ecp.fr; internet www.em2c.ecp.fr; f. 1970; Dir NASSER DARABIHA.

Thermique de l'habitat (RAMSES): Université de Paris XI, bâtiment 508, 91405 Orsay Cedex; tel. 1-69-41-82-50; f. 1985; Dir LOUIS-MARIE CHOUNET.

Combinatoire et Optimisation: Université Pierre et Marie Curie (Paris 6), case 189, 4 place Jussieu, 75252 Paris Cedex 05; tel. 1-44-27-38-08; fax 1-44-27-40-01; internet www.ecp6.jussieu.fr; f. 1975; Dir JEAN FONLUPT.

Groupe de représentation et traitement des connaissances (GRTC): 31 chemin Joseph-Aiguier, 13402 Marseille Cedex 09; tel. 4-91-22-40-00; fax 4-91-71-08-08; f. 1984; Dir EUGÈNE CHOURAQUI.

Ingénierie électronique assistée par ordinateur: Institut méditerranéen de technologie, Technopile Château Combert, 13451 Marseille Cedex 13; fax 4-91-05-43-43; f. 1988; Dir JEAN MERMET.

Techniques de l'informatique, des mathématiques, de la microélectronique et de la microscopie quantitative: IMAG, 46 rue Félix-Viallet, 38031 Grenoble Cedex; tel. 4-76-57-46-22; fax 4-76-47-38-14; f. 1986; Dir BERNARD COURTOIS.

Laboratoire de physique des décharges: École supérieure d'électricité, plateau du Moulon, 91192 Gif-sur-Yvette; tel. 1-69-41-80-40; fax 1-69-41-30-60; f. 1972; Dir EMMANUEL MARODE.

Laboratoire de l'horloge atomique: Université de Paris XI, Bâtiment 221, 91405 Orsay Cedex; tel. 1-69-41-78-61; fax 1-69-41-08-80; f. 1973; Dir MICHEL DÉSAINTFUSCIEN.

Optique physiologique et fonctions visuelles: Muséum national d'histoire naturelle, 43 rue Cuvier, 75231 Paris Cedex 05; tel. 1-40-79-37-24; fax 1-40-79-37-16; f. 1983; Dir HANS BRETTEL.

Laboratoire de physique des interfaces et des couches minces: École polytechnique, plateau de Palaiseau, 91128 Palaiseau Cedex; tel. 1-69-33-40-09; fax 1-69-33-30-06; f. 1983; Dir BERNARD EQUER.

Laboratoire de physique des milieux ionisés: École polytechnique, plateau de Palaiseau, 91128 Palaiseau Cedex; tel. 1-65-33-41-15; fax 1-69-33-20-23; f. 1975; Dir JEAN VIRMONT.

Laboratoire de physique et applications des semi-conducteurs: Centre de recherches nucléaires, Université de Strasbourg II, 23 rue de Loess, BP 20, 67037 Strasbourg Cedex; tel. 3-88-28-65-43; fax 3-88-28-09-90; f. 1985; Dir PAUL SIFFERT.

Laboratoire pour l'utilisation des lasers intenses: École polytechnique, Route de Saclay, 91128 Palaiseau Cedex; tel. 1-69-33-41-12; fax 1-69-33-30-09; e-mail luli@greco2.polytechnique.fr; internet www.luli.polytechnique.fr; f. 1988; Dir FRANÇOIS AMIRANOFF.

Institut de mécanique statistique de la turbulence: Université d'Aix-Marseille II, 12 ave Général-Leclerc, 13003 Marseille; tel. 4-91-50-54-39; fax 4-91-08-16-37; f. 1969; Dir MICHEL COANTIC.

Institut de mécanique de Marseille: 60. rue Joliot Curie, 13453 Marseille; tel. 4-91-11-38-02; fax 4-91-11-38-38; f. 1966; Dir DANIEL DUFRESNE.

Laboratoire réacteurs catalytiques en milieu triphasique: Rhône-Poulenc Industrialisation, 24 ave Jean-Jaurès, BP 166, 69151 Décines-Charpieu Cedex; tel. 4-72-05-25-52; fax 4-72-05-20-45; f. 1987; Dir JEAN JENCK.

Laboratoire des matériaux et structures du génie civil: Cité Descartes, 2 allée Képler, 77420 Champs-sur-Marne; tel. 1-40-43-54-41; fax 1-40-43-54-50; tel. www.lcpc.fr; Dir PHILIPPE COUSSOT.

Laboratoire d'application des lasers de puissance: 16 bis ave du Prieur de la Côte d'Or, 94114 Arcueil; tel. 1-42-31-91-94; fax 1-42-31-99-92; Dir RÉMY FABBRO.

Action recherche et applications MATRA-IRIT en interface homme-système: Zone industrielle du Palays, 31 rue des Cosmonautes, 31077 Toulouse; tel. 5-61-39-66-25; fax 5-61-39-69-65; Dir JEAN-PAUL DENIER.

IV. Chemistry:

Laboratoire Interfaces et Systèmes Electrochimiques: Université de Paris 6, 4 place Jussieu, Tour 22–12, 75252 Paris Cedex 05; tel. 1-44-27-41-53; fax 1-44-27-40-74; e-mail lise@ccr.jussieu.fr; internet www.lise.jussieu.fr; Dir C. DESLOUIS.

Laboratoire de chimie quantique et modélisation moléculaire: Université Louis Pasteur, Institut Le Bel, 4 rue Blaise Pascal, 67000 Strasbourg; tel. 3-90-24-13-

04; fax 3-90-24-15-89; e-mail dir7551@quantix.u-strasbg.fr; internet quantique.u-strasbg.fr; Dir ALAIN DEDIEU.

Laboratoire de chimie métallurgique des terres rares: 2–8 rue Henri Dunant, 94320 Thiais; tel. 1-49-78-12-01; fax 1-49-78-12-03; internet ulysse.glvt-cnrs.fr/lcmtr; Dir ANNICK PERCHERON-GUEGAN.

Eléments de transition dans les solides: 1 place Aristide Briand, 92190 Meudon; tel. 1-45-34-75-50; fax 1-45-34-46-96; Dir GÉRARD SCHIFFMACHER.

Physicochimie des matériaux par techniques avancées: 1 place Aristide Briand, 92190 Meudon; tel. 1-45-34-75-50; fax 1-45-34-46-96; Dir BERNARD BLANZAT.

Laboratoire de dynamique et structure des matériaux moléculaires: UPRESA 8024, Bâtiment P5, Cité Scientifique, Université Lille 1, 59655 Villeneuve d'Ascq Cedex; tel. 3-20-43-69-47; fax 3-20-43-68-57; internet www-ldsmm.univ-lille1.fr; Dir MARC DESCAMPS.

Dynamique des interactions moléculaires: Université de Paris 6, Tour 22, 4 place Jussieu, 75252 Paris Cedex 05; tel. 1-43-26-09-82; Dir MARCEL ALLAVENA.

Chimie des interactions moléculaires: Collège de France, bâtiment C, 11 place Marcelin-Berthelot, 75231 Paris Cedex 05; tel. 1-44-27-12-11; Dir JEAN-MARIE LEHN.

Nouveaux procédés de synthèse organique: Ecole normale supérieure, Laboratoire de chimie, 24 rue Lhomond, 75231 Paris Cedex 05; tel. 1-43-29-12-25; Dir GERARD LINSTRUMELLE.

Centre de biophysique moléculaire: rue Charles Sadron, 45071 Orléans Cedex; tel. 2-38-51-55-88; fax 2-38-63-15-17; internet web.cnrs-orleans.fr/~webcbm; f. 1967; Dir JEAN-CLAUDE BELOEIL.

Institut de recherches sur la catalyse: 2 ave Einstein, 69626 Villeurbanne Cedex; tel. 4-72-44-53-00; fax 4-78-89-47-69; internet catalyse.univ-lyon1.fr; f. 1958; Dir THIERRY DES COURIÈRES.

Centre d'études de chimie métallurgique: 15 rue Georges-Urbain, 94407 Vitry-sur-Seine; tel. 1-56-70-30-30; fax 1-46-75-04-33; e-mail dircecm@glvt-cnrs.fr; internet www.cecm.cnrs.fr; f. 1936; Dir VASSILIS PONTIKIS.

Centre d'études et de recherches de chimie organique appliquée (CERCOA): 2–8 rue Henry-Dunant, BP 28, 94320 Thiais; tel. 1-46-87-33-55; fax 1-46-87-17-27; f. 1946; Dir MICHEL LANGLOIS.

Laboratoire de chimie du solide minéral: Université Henri Poincaré-Nancy I, Faculté des sciences BP 239 , 54506 Vandoeuvre-lès-Nancy Cedex; tel. 5-56-84-60-00; internet www.lcsm.uhp-nancy.fr; f. 1974; Dir PIERRE STEINMETZ.

Centre de recherches 'Paul Pascal': CNRS, Château Brivazac, ave A. Schweitzer, 33600 Pessac Cedex; tel. 5-56-84-56-56; fax 5-56-84-56-00; internet www.crpp.u-bordeaux.fr; f. 1963; Dir PHILIPPE BAROIS.

Institut de chimie des substances naturelles: Avenue de la Terrasse, BP 1, 91198 Gif-sur-Yvette Cedex; tel. 1-69-82-30-49; fax 1-60-07-72-47; e-mail suchen.fan@icsn.cnrs-gif.fr; internet www.icsn.cnrs-gif.fr; f. 1959; Dir JEAN-YVES LALLEMAND.

Laboratoire Maurice Letort: Route de Vandoeuvre, BP 104, 54600 Villers-lès-Nancy; tel. 3-83-27-60-10; f. 1963; Dir BOYAN MUTAFTSCHIEV.

Centre d'études et de recherches par irradiation: 3A rue de la Ferollerie, 45071 Orléans Cedex; tel. 2-38-25-54-26; fax 2-38-63-02-71; internet web.cnrs-orleans.fr/~ceri; f. 1974; Dir G. BLONDIAUX.

Laboratoire d'électrochimie interfaciale: 1 place Aristide-Briand, 92195 Meudon; tel. 1-45-34-75-50; fax 1-45-34-46-96; f. 1946; Dir MAX COSTA.

Centre de recherches sur les macromolécules végétales: BP 53, 38041 Grenoble Cedex; tel. 4-76-03-76-03; fax 4-76-54-72-03; internet www.cermav.cnrs.fr; f. 1967; Dir SERGE PEREZ.

Service central d'analyse: BP 22, Autoroute Lyon-Vienne, Echangeur de Solaize, 69390 Vernaison; tel. 4-78-02-22-22; fax 4-78-02-71-87; internet www.sca.cnrs.fr; f. 1958; Dir M. F. GRENIER-LOUSTALOT.

Laboratoire Thermodynamique, Propriétés Electriques, Contraintes et Structure aux Echelles Nanométriques (TECSEN): Faculté des Sciences et Techniques de St-Jérôme, 13997 Marseille Cedex 20; tel. 4-91-28-27-89; fax 4-91-28-27-93; internet www.umr-tecsen.com; f. 2000; Dir BERNARD PICHAUD.

Centre de recherches sur la physicochimie des surfaces solides: 24 ave du Président-Kennedy, 68200 Mulhouse; tel. 3-89-42-01-55; fax 3-89-32-09-96; f. 1967; Dir JACQUES SCHULTZ.

Laboratoire 'Pierre Sue': CEN-Saclay, Bâtiment 637, 91191 Gif-sur-Yvette Cedex; tel. 1-69-08-46-17; fax 1-69-08-69-23; internet www-drecam.cea.fr/lps; f. 1969; Dir STÉPHANE LEQUIEN.

Laboratoire de spectrochimie infrarouge et Raman (LASIR): 2 rue Henry Dunant, BP 28, 94320 Thiais; tel. 1-46-87-33-55; fax 1-20-43-49-95; internet lasir.univ-lille1.f; f. 1965; Dir JACQUES CORSET.

Laboratoire de chimie de coordination: CNRS, 205 route de Narbonne, 31077 Toulouse Cedex 4; tel. 5-61-33-31-00; fax 5-61-55-30-03; internet www.lcc-toulouse.fr; f. 1974; Dir JEAN-JACQUES BONNET.

Laboratoire Matériaux Organiques à Propriétés Spécifiques (LMOPS): BP 24, Autoroute Lyon-Vienne, Echangeur de Solaize, 69390 Vernaison; tel. 4-78-02-22-64; fax 4-78-02-77-38; f. 1977; Dir R. MERCIER.

Chimie du phosphore et des métaux de transition: DCPH-École Polytechnique, 91128 Palaiseau; tel. 1-69-41-82-00; fax 1-69-41-33-92; f. 1987; Dir FRANÇOIS MATHEY.

Centre de recherches sur la physique des hautes températures: 1D ave de la Recherche-Scientifique, 45071 Orléans Cedex; tel. 2-38-51-55-14; fax 2-38-64-26-70; f. 1968; Dir JEAN-PIERRE COUTURES.

Institut Charles Sadron: 6 rue Boussingault, 67083 Strasbourg Cedex; tel. 3-88-41-40-00; fax 3-88-41-40-99; internet www-ics.u-strasbg.fr/index.php3; f. 1947; Dir JEAN-FRANÇOIS LEGRAND.

Laboratoire CNRS Roussel-Uclaf: Roussel-Uclaf, BP 9, 102 route de Noisy, 93230 Romainville; tel. 1-48-91-52-80; f. 1984; Dir ROBERT LETT.

Physicochimie des biopolymères: BP 28, 94320 Thiais; tel. 1-46-87-33-55; fax 1-46-87-17-27; f. 1985; Dir BERNARD SEBILLE.

Laboratoire d'Electrochimie, catalyse et synthèse organique (LECSO): 2–8 rue Henri-Dunant, 94320 Thiais; tel. 1-49-78-11-43; fax 1-49-78-11-48; internet http://www.glvt-cnrs.fr/lecso; f. 1985; Dir Prof. JEAN-YVES NEDELEC.

Génie catalytique des réacteurs de raffinage: BP 22, 69360 St-Symphorien-d'Ozon; tel. 4-72-51-82-34; f. 1986; Dir JEAN-RENÉ BERNARD.

Génie de la fabrication des catalyseurs hétérogènes: Institut Français du Pétrole, BP 3, 69390 Vernaison; tel. 4-78-02-20-20; fax 4-78-02-10-51; f. 1986; Dir PIERRE TRAMBOUZE.

Précurseurs organométalliques de matériaux: Université de Montpellier II, 2 place E.-Bataillon, 34060 Montpellier Cedex; tel. 4-67-41-39-80; fax 4-67-54-30-79; f. 1986; Dir ROBERT CORRIU.

Laboratoire des composites thermostructuraux: 3 Allée de La Boétie, 33600 Pessac; tel. 5-56-84-47-00; fax 5-56-84-12-25; e-mail admin@lcts.u-bordeaux.fr; internet www.lcts.u-bordeaux1.fr; f. 1988; Dir ALAIN GUETTE.

Laboratoire de RMN et de modélisation moléculaire: Institut de Chimie, BP 296 R/8, 67008 Strasbourg; tel. 3-88-41-61-85; f. 1988; Dir PIERRE GRANGER.

Chimie et biochimie macromoléculaire: ENS, 46 allée d'Italie, 69364 Lyon Cedex 07; tel. 4-72-72-83-59; f. 1988; Dir BERNARD MANDRAND.

Polymères thermostables et leurs applications: IFP, BP 3, 69390 Vernaison; tel. 4-78-02-20-77; fax 4-78-02-10-51; f. 1988; Dir BERNARD SILLION.

Institut de Physique et Chimie des Matériaux de Strasbourg (IPCMS): 23, rue de Loess, BP 43, 67034 Strasbourg Cedex; tel. 3-88-10-71-41; fax 3-88-10-72-50; internet www-ipcms.u-strasbg.fr; f. 1988; Dir MARC DRILLON.

Conception d'analogues de biomolécules: application aux antiviraux: Université de Montpellier 2, UFR de Chimie, Place Eugène Bataillon, 34060 Montpellier Cedex; tel. 4-67-54-58-73; Dir JEAN-LOUIS IMBACH.

Stéréochimie et interactions moléculaires: ENS de Lyon, 46 allée d'Italie, 69364 Lyon Cedex 07; tel. 4-72-72-83-93; fax 4-72-72-84-83; internet www.ens-lyon.fr/STIM; Dir LYNDON EMSLEY.

V. Earth and Space Sciences:

Astrophysique nucléaire et nucléosynthèse: CEN-Saclay, DPHG, SAP Bât. 28, 91191 Gif-sur-Yvette Cedex; tel. 1-69-41-80-00; Dir HUBERT REEVES.

Magnétisme des roches et ses applications géologiques et géophysiques: Université de Paris 6, Laboratoire de géomagnétisme du parc St-Maur, 4 ave de Neptune, 94107 Saint-Maur-des-Fosses Cedex; tel. 1-48-86-32-72; fax 1-48-89-44-33; Dir LUCIEN DALY.

Ecologie et biochimie microbienne du milieu marin: Université d'Aix-Marseille 1, Laboratoire de microbiologie marine, Campus de Luminy, Case 907, 70 route Léon Lachamp, 13288 Marseille Cedex 9; tel. 4-91-26-90-51; Dir ARMAND BIANCHI.

Dynamique terrestre et planétaire: Universite Paul Sabatier, Observatoire Midi-Pyrenees, 14 avenue Edouard-Belin, 31400 Toulouse Cedex; tel. 5-61-33-29-69; fax 5-61-33-29-00; e-mail alexis.rigo@cnes.fr; Dir MARC SOURIAU.

Physique mathématique, modélisation et simulation: 3A ave de la Recherche Scientifique, 45071 Orléans Cedex 2; tel. 2-38-63-00-86; fax 2-38-63-01-48; Dir MARC FEIX.

Service d'aéronomie (SA): BP 3, 91371 Verrières-le-Buisson; tel. 1-64-47-42-45; fax 1-69-20-29-99; internet www.aero.jussieu.fr; f. 1958; Dir PIERRE BAUER.

Laboratoire d'Astronophysique de Marseille: Traverse du Siphon, les Trois Lucs, 13376 Marseille Cedex 12; tel. 4-01-05-59-00; fax 4-91-66-18-55; internet www.astrsp-mrs.fr/index_lam.html; f. 1965; Dir OLIVIER LE FÈVRE.

Institut d'Astrophysique de Paris (IAP): 98 bis blvd Arago, 75014 Paris; tel. 1-44-32-80-00; fax 1-44-32-80-01; internet www.iap.fr; f. 1936; Dir LAURENT VIGROUX.

Centre géologique et géophysique de Montpellier (CGGM): Université de Montpellier II, 2 Place Eugène Bataillon, 34060 Montpellier Cedex; tel. 4-67-14-30-30; fax 4-67-54-36-48; f. 1974; Dir MICHEL PRÉVOT.

Laboratoire de géologie du quaternaire (LGQ): Université d'Aix-Marseille 2, UER de Luminy, case 907, 13288 Marseille Cedex 9; tel. 4-91-26-96-50; f. 1958; Dir YVES LANCELOT.

Laboratoire de glaciologie et de géophysique de l'environnement (LGGE): rue Molière, BP 96, 38402 St Martin d'Hères Cedex; tel. 4-76-82-42-00; fax 3-76-82-42-01; internet www-lgge.ujf-grenoble.fr; f. 1947; Dir MICHEL FILY.

Centre de recherches en physique de l'environnement (CRPE): 38–40 rue du Général Leclerc, 92231 Issy-les-Moulineaux; tel. 1-45-29-44-44; fax 1-45-29-60-52; f. 1975; Dir GILLES SOMMERIA.

Laboratoire de météorologie dynamique: Ecole Polytechnique, Route départementale 36, 91128 Palaiseau Cedex; tel. 1-69-33-41-45; fax 1-69-33-30-05; internet www.lmd.jussieu.fr; f. 1939; Dir HERVÉ LE TREUT.

Observatoire de Haute-Provence (OHP): 04870 Saint-Michel-l'Observatoire; tel. 4-92-70-64-00; fax 4-92-76-62-95; internet www.obs-hp.fr; f. 1937; Dir MICHEL BOËR.

Centre de pédologie biologique (CPB): 17 rue Notre-Dame-des-Pauvres, BP 5, 54500 Vandoeuvre-lès-Nancy; tel. 3-83-51-08-60; f. 1961; Dir ADRIEN HERBILLON.

Centre de recherches pétrographiques et géochimiques (CRPG): 15 rue Notre-Dame-des-Pauvres, BP 20, 54501 Vandoeuvre-lès-Nancy Cedex; tel. 3-83-59-42-02; fax 3-83-51-17-98; internet www.crpg.cnrs-nancy.fr; f. 1953; Dir BERNARD MARTY.

Centre des faibles radioactivités (CFR): Ave de la Terrasse, 91190 Gif-sur-Yvette; tel. 1-69-82-30-30; f. 1961; Dir JEAN-CLAUDE DUPLESSY.

Centre de géochimie de la surface (CGS): 1 rue Blessig, 67084 Strasbourg Cedex; tel. 3-90-24-05-59; fax 3-90-24-04-02; e-mail dircgs@illite.u-strasbg.fr; internet cgs.u-strasbg.fr; f. 1963; Dir NORBERT CLAUER.

Centre armoricain d'études structurales des socles (CAESS): Institut de géologie, ave du Général-Leclerc, 35042 Rennes Cedex; tel. 2-99-28-61-10; f. 1974; Dir PIERRE CHOUKROUNE.

Centre de recherches sur la synthèse et la chimie des minéraux (CRSCM): 1A rue de la Férollerie, 45071 Orléans Cedex; tel. 2-38-51-53-96; fax 2-38-64-26-70; f. 1969; Dir MICHEL PICHAVANT.

Institut d'Astrophysique Spatiale: Université Paris-Sud, bâtiment 121, 91405 Orsay; tel. 1-69-85-85-00; fax 1-69-85-86-75; internet www.ias.u-psud.fr; f. 1979; Dir FABIENNE CASOLI.

Centre d'étude spatiale des rayonnements (CESR): Université de Toulouse III, 9 ave du Colonel Roche, BP 4346, 31028 Toulouse Cedex; tel. 5-61-55-66-49; fax 5-61-55-67-01; internet www.cesr.fr; f. 1979; Dir GILBERT VEDRENNE.

Laboratoire de physique et chimie de l'environnement (LPCE): 3A ave de la Recherche Scientifique, 45071 Orléans Cedex 2; tel. 2-38-25-52-60; fax 2-38-63-12-34; internet lpce.cnrs-orleans.fr; f. 1982; Dir P. L. BLELLY.

Laboratoire des écoulements géophysiques et industriels: Université de Grenoble, BP 53, 38041 Grenoble Cedex 9; tel. 4-76-82-50-28; fax 4-76-82-52-71; e-mail legi@hmg.inpg.fr; internet www.legi.hmg.inpg.fr; Dir VERRON JACQUES.

Laboratoire des sols, solides, structures et leurs interactions: Domaine Universitaire, 1025 rue de la piscine, BP 53, 38041 Grenoble Cedex 9; tel. 4-76-82-50-27; fax 4-76-82-70-43; e-mail lab3S@hmg.inpg.fr; internet http://www.3S.hmg.inpg.fr; Dir JACKY MAZARS.

Laboratoire d'Etude des Transferts en Hydrologie et Environnement (LTHE): ENSHMG, 1023 rue de la piscine, BP 53, , 38041 Grenoble; tel. 4-76-82-50-00; fax 4-76-82-50-01; e-mail lthelabo@hmg.inpg.fr; internet www.lthe.hmg.inpg.fr; Dir JEAN-DOMINIQUE CREUTIN.

VI. Life Sciences:

Laboratoire de neurobiologie cellulaire et fonctionnelle (LNCF): 31 chemin Joseph Aiguier, 13402 Marseille Cedex 20; tel. 4-91-16-41-28; fax 4-91-77-50-83; internet lncf.cnrs-mrs.fr; Dir Prof. ANDRÉ NIEOULLON.

Institut de biologie et chimie des protéines: 7, passage du Vercors, 69367 Lyon Cedex 07; tel. 4-72-72-26-00; fax 4-72-72-26-01; internet www.ibcp.fr; Dir ALAIN COZZONE.

Centre de Biochimie Structurale: 29 rue de Navacelles, 34090 Montpellier Cedex; tel. 4-67-41-79-05; fax 4-67-41-79-13; e-mail adm@cbs.cnrs.fr; internet www.cbs.cnrs.fr; Dir MICHEL KOCHOYAN.

Centre de recherches de biochimie macromoléculaire: Route de Mende, BP 5051, 34293 Montpellier Cedex; tel. 4-67-61-33-21; fax 4-67-52-15-59; internet www.crbm.cnrs-mop.fr; f. 1973; Dir PAUL MANGEAT.

Centre de service des animaux de laboratoire (SAL): 3 bis rue de la Férollerie, 45071 Orléans Cedex 02; tel. 2-38-63-29-48; f. 1953; Dir CLAUDE AUZANNEAU.

Centre d'Ecologie et Physiologie Energétique: Campus Cronenbourg, 23 rue Becquerel, 67087 Strasbourg Cedex 2; tel. 3-88-10-69-00; fax 3-88-10-69-06; e-mail web-cepe@c-strasbourg.fr; internet www.cepe.c-strasbourg.fr; Dir Y. DE MAHO.

Centre d'études biologiques des animaux sauvages (CEBAS): Villiers-en-Bois, BP 14, 79360 Beauvoir-sur-Niort; tel. 5-49-09-61-11; f. 1967; Dir PIERRE JOUVENTIN.

Institut Cochin: Département de Génétique et Pathologie Moléculaire, 24 rue du Faubourg St Jacques, 95014 Paris; tel. 1-44-41-24-24; fax 1-44-41-24-21; internet www.humangenetics.nl/euromrx/paris/paris4.html.

Laboratoire de recherche génétique sur les modèles animaux: CNRS, BP 8, 7 rue Guy Mocquet, 94801 Villejuif Cedex; tel. 1-47-26-46-58.

Laboratoire de biologie moléculaire eucaryote (LBME): 118 route de Narbonne, 31062 Toulouse Cedex; tel. 5-61-33-58-62; fax 5-61-33-58-86; e-mail weber@ibcg.biotoul.fr; internet www.iefg.biotoul.fr; Dir FRANÇOIS AMALRIC.

Laboratoire de microbiologie et génétique moléculaire: 118 route de Narbonne, 31062 Toulouse Cedex; tel. 5-61-33-58-00; fax 5-61-33-58-86; internet www.iefg.biotoul.fr; Dir JEAN-PIERRE CLAVERYS.

Institut d'Exploration Fonctionnelle des Génomes: 118 route de Narbonne, 31062 Toulouse Cedex; tel. 5-61-33-58-00; fax 5-61-33-58-86; internet www.iefg.biotoul.fr; Dir H. RICHARD FOY.

Centre de Biologie du Développement: 118 route de Narbonne, 31062 Toulouse Cedex; tel. 5-61-55-67-39; fax 5-61-55-65-07; internet www.iefg.biotoul.fr; Dir ALAIN VINCENT.

Laboratoire de Biologie Cellulaire et Moléculaire du contrôle de la Prolifération: 118 route de Narbonne, 31062 Toulouse Cedex; tel. 5-61-55-81-10; fax 5-61-55-81-09; internet www.iefg.biotoul.fr; Dir Prof. BERNARD DUCOMMUN.

Institut Jacques Monod: Université de Paris VII, 2 place Jussieu, tour 43, 75251 Paris Cedex 05; tel. 1-44-27-37-28; fax 1-44-27-78-70; internet www.ijm.jussieu.fr; f. 1966; molecular biology research institute; Dir JEAN-ANTOINE LEPESANT.

Institut de biologie moléculaire et cellulaire (IBMC): 15 rue René Descartes, 67084 Strasbourg Cedex; tel. 3-88-41-70-00; fax 3-88-60-22-36; internet www-ibmc.u-strasbg.fr; f. 1973.

Centre technique pour le soutien de la recherche sur le cancer: 16 ave Vaillant-Couturier, BP 3, 94801 Villejuif Cedex; tel. 1-46-78-57-57; fax 1-47-26-04-75; f. 1981; Dir JACQUES CROZEMARIE.

Laboratoire de chimie bactérienne: 31 chemin Joseph Aiguier, 13402 Marseille Cedex 20; tel. 4-91-16-40-77; fax 4-91-71-89-14; e-mail lcb-sec@ibsm.cnrs-mrs.fr; f. 1962; Dir MARC CHIPPAUX.

Institut d'embryologie cellulaire et moléculaire: 49 bis ave de la Belle-Gabrielle, 94736 Nogent-sur-Marne Cedex; tel. 1-48-73-60-90; fax 1-48-73-43-77; f. 1947; Dir NICOLE LE DOUARIN.

Laboratoire d'Enzymologie et Biochimie Structurales: Bâtiment 34, Avenue de la Terrasse, 91198 Gif-sur-Yvette Cedex; tel. 1-69-82-34-84; fax 1-69-82-31-29; internet www.lebs.cnrs-gif.fr; f. 1959; Dir JOËL JANIN.

Laboratoire de génétique des virus: Bât. 14, Avenue de la Terrase, 91198 Gif-sur-Yvette Cedex; tel. 1-69-82-30-30; f. 1946; Dir ANNE FLAMAND.

Laboratoire de neurobiologie moléculaire des interactions cellulaires: 5 rue Blaise Pascal, 67084 Strasbourg Cedex; tel. 3-88-61-48-48; f. 1965; Dir GUY VINCENDON.

Centre de recherches sur la nutrition: 9 rue Jules Hetzel, 92190 Meudon; tel. 1-45-07-52-18; f. 1946; Dir JEAN GIRARD.

Centre national de coordination des études et recherches sur la nutrition et l'alimentation (CNERNA): 11 rue Jean Nicot, 75007 Paris; tel. 1-42-75-93-24; f. 1945; Dir JACQUES FLANZY.

Laboratoire de pharmacologie et de toxicologie fondamentale: 205 route de Narbonne, 31077 Toulouse Cedex; tel. 5-61-17-59-00; f. 1960; Dir JEAN CROS.

Laboratoire de physiologie des organes végétaux après récolte: 4 ter route des Gardes, 92190 Meudon; tel. 1-45-34-75-50; f. 1942; Dir JEAN DAUSSANT.

Centre d'écologie et physiologie énergétiques (CEPE): CNRS, 23 rue Becquerel, 67087 Strasbourg; tel. 3-88-28-69-00; fax 3-88-10-69-06; internet www.cepe.c-strasbourg.fr; Dir YVON LE MAHO.

Institut Alfred Fessard: Avenue de la Terrasse, 91198 Gif-sur-Yvette Cedex; tel. 1-69-82-34-23; fax 1-69-07-05-38; internet www.cnrs-gif.fr/iaf; f. 1972; Dir JEAN-DIDIER VINCENT.

Centre d'écologie des ressources renouvelables: 29 rue Jeanne-Marvig, BP 4009, 31055 Toulouse Cedex; tel. 5-61-25-40-87; f. 1947; Dir HENRI DECAMPS.

Laboratoire de biologie et de génétique évolutives: Bât. 13, Avenue de la Terrasse, 91198 Gif-sur-Yvette Cedex; tel. 1-69-82-37-23; f. 1947; Dir JEAN DAVID.

Laboratoire de biologie et technologie des membranes et des systèmes intégrés: 43 blvd du 11 Novembre 1918, 69622 Villeurbanne Cedex; tel. 4-72-44-80-00; fax 4-78-89-47-69; f. 1976; Dir DANIÈLE GAUTHERON.

Centre d'immunologie de Marseille-Luminy: Case 906, Luminy, 13288 Marseille Cedex 09; tel. 4-91-26-94-00; fax 4-91-26-94-30; f. 1976; Dir BERNARD MALISSEN.

Laboratoire de génétique moléculaire des eucaryotes: 11 rue Humann, 67085 Strasbourg Cedex; tel. 3-88-37-12-55; f. 1977; Dir PIERRE CHAMBON.

Laboratoire de génétique et biologie cellulaires (LGBC): Centre Universitaire de Luminy, case 907, 13288 Marseille Cedex 9; tel. 4-91-26-96-00; f. 1981; Dir ROLAND ROSSET.

Laboratoire de physiologie neurosensorielle: 15 rue de l'Ecole de Médecine, 75006 Paris; tel. 1-43-29-61-54; f. 1981; Dir ALAIN BERTHOZ.

Centre de neurologie cellulaire et moléculaire: 67 rue Maurice-Günsbourg, 94205 Ivry-sur-Seine; tel. 1-46-72-18-00; f. 1969; Dir BERNARD PESSAC.

Centre d'études d'océanographie et de biologie marine: Station biologique, place Georges Teissier, 29211 Roscoff; tel. 2-98-69-72-30; fax 2-98-61-26-55; f. 1946; Dir PIERRE LASSERRE.

Laboratoire de physiologie et psychologie environnementales: 21 rue Becquerel, 67087 Strasbourg Cedex; tel. 3-88-28-67-83; fax 3-88-28-09-90; f. 1986; Dir ALAIN MUZET.

Laboratoire de neurobiologie: 31 chem. Joseph Aiguier, BP 71, 13402 Marseille Cedex 9; tel. 4-91-22-40-00; fax 4-91-22-08-75; f. 1986; Dir JEAN-LUC CLÉMENT.

Laboratoire des neurosciences fonctionnelles: 31 chem. Joseph Aiguier, BP 71, 13402 Marseille Cedex 09; tel. 4-91-22-40-00; fax 4-91-22-08-75; f. 1986; Dir JEAN MASSION.

Centre de recherches souterraines: 09200 Saint-Girons; tel. 5-61-66-31-26; f. 1948; Dir CHRISTIAN JUBERTHIE.

Institut de biochimie cellulaire: 1 rue Camille-Saint-Saëns, 33077 Bordeaux Cedex; tel. 5-56-98-24-22; f. 1980; Dir BERNARD GUÉRIN.

Centre CNRS-INSERM de pharmacologie, endocrinologie: rue de la Cardonille, 34094 Montpellier Cedex; tel. 4-67-14-29-51; fax 4-67-54-24-32; internet www.montp.inserm.fr/umr5101; f. 1982; Dir FRANÇOISE MOOS.

Laboratoire de biologie moléculaire des relations plantes-microorganismes: BP 27, 31326 Castanet-Tolosan; tel. 5-61-28-50-28; f. 1981; Dir PIERRE BOISTARD.

Institut de pharmacologie moléculaire et cellulaire: 660 Route des Lucioles, 06560 Valbonne Sophia-Antipolis; tel. 4-93-95-77-77; fax 4-93-95-77-08; internet www.ipmc.cnrs.fr; Dir PASCAL BARBRY.

Institut des sciences végétales: BP 1, 91198 Gif-sur-Yvette Cedex; tel. 1-69-82-36-36; fax 1-69-82-36-95; Dir ADAM KONDOROSI.

Relations structure-fonction des constituants membranaires: Université de Lille I, 59655 Villeneuve-d' Ascq Cedex; tel. 3-20-43-48-83; fax 3-20-43-49-95; Dir ANDRÉ VERBERT.

Biologie et génétique moléculaires: 7 rue Guy Môquet, BP 8, 94802 Villejuif; tel. 1-47-26-46-58; fax 1-47-26-88-36; Dirs DANIEL BLANGY, ANNE-MARIE DE RECONDO.

Oncologie virale: 7 rue Guy Môquet, BP 8, 94802 Villejuif; tel. 1-47-26-46-58; fax 1-47-26-76-02; Dir ION GRESSER.

Oncologie moléculaire: 7 rue Guy Môquet, BP 8, 94802 Villejuif; tel. 1-47-26-46-58; Dir PIERRE MAY.

Centres réactionnels photosynthétiques: BP 1, 91198 Gif-sur-Yvette; tel. 1-69-82-38-11; fax 1-69-82-35-62; Dir ANNE-LISE ETIENNE.

Centre d'écologie fonctionelle et évolutive Louis Emberger (CEFE): BP 5051, route de Mende, 34293 Montpellier Cedex 5; tel. 4-67-61-32-01; fax 4-67-41-21-38; e-mail direction@cefe.cnrs-mop.fr; internet www.cefe.cnrs-mop.fr/wwwsite; Dir BERNARD DELAY.

Centre de génétique moléculaire: Bât. 26, Avenue de la Terrasse, 91198 Gif-sur-Yvette; tel. 1-69-82-31-98; fax 1-69-82-31-60; e-mail cgmdir@cgm.cnrs-gif.fr; internet www.cgm.cnrs-gif.fr; Dir LAWRENCE AGGERBECK.

Centre de recherches sur le polymorphisme génétique des populations humaines: Hôpital Purpan, Ave de la Grande-Bretagne, 31300 Toulouse; tel. 5-61-49-60-80; Dir ANNE CAMBON-THOMSEN.

Rétrovirus et rétrotransposons des vertébrés: Université de Paris VII, Hôpital St-Louis, 12 bis rue Grange-aux-Belles, 75475 Paris Cedex 10; tel. 1-42-40-13-82; Dir GEORGES PERIES.

Laboratoire de génétique moléculaire: 7 rue Guy Môquet, 94802 Villejuif; tel. 1-47-26-46-58; fax 1-47-26-88-36; Dir ALAIN SARASIN.

Ontogénèse du comportement et vie sociale: 31 chemin Joseph-Aiguier, 13402 Marseille Cedex 09; tel. 4-91-22-40-00; Dir JACQUES GERVET.

Institut de biologie moléculaire des plantes (IBMP): 12 rue du Gén. Zimmer, 67084 Strasbourg; tel. 3-88-41-72-00; fax 3-88-61-44-42; internet ibmp.u-strasbg.fr; Dirs JACQUES-HENRI WEIL.

Régulation de l'expression des gènes eucaryotes: 7 rue Guy Môquet, BP 8, 94802 Villejuif; tel. 1-47-26-46-58; Dir JANINE DOLY.

Biochimie fonctionnelle des membranes végétales: Bât. 9, BP 1, 91190 Gif-sur-Yvette; tel. 1-69-82-38-57; fax 1-69-07-83-10; Dir ANTOINE TREMOLIÈRES.

Génétique moléculaire et cellulaire: Université de Lyon I, 43 blvd du 11 Novembre-1918, 69622 Villeurbanne Cedex; tel. 4-72-44-80-00; fax 4-72-44-05-55; Dir JACQUELINE GODET.

Immunovirologie moléculaire et cellulaire, virologie moléculaire: Université de Lyon I, rue Guillaume-Paradin, 69372 Lyon Cedex 08; tel. 4-78-77-86-00; fax 4-78-01-43-22; Dir LOUIS GAZZOLO.

Laboratoire des interactions plastes-cytoplasmes mitochondries: Centre d'Etudes nucléaires, BP 85X, 38041 Grenoble Cedex; tel. 4-76-88-37-85; fax 4-76-88-51-55; Dir JACQUES JOYARD.

Neuropharmacologie moléculaire: Université de Lyon I, rue Guillaume-Paradin, 69372 Lyon; tel. 4-78-77-86-32; fax 4-78-01-35-47; Dir JEAN-FRANÇOIS PUJOL.

Laboratoire de biologie moléculaire et cellulaire: ENS de Lyon, 46 all. d'Italie, 69364 Lyon Cedex 07; tel. 4-72-72-81-72; fax 4-72-72-80-80; internet www.ens-lyon.fr/LBMC; Dir ERIC GILSON.

Phytotron: Bât. 23, Avenue de la Terrasse, 91198 Gif-sur-Yvette; tel. 1-69-82-37-82; Dirs ROGER GUILLET, JACQUES TEMPE.

VII. Humanities and Social Sciences:

Centre de recherches archéologiques (CRA): Sophia-Antipolis, 06565 Valbonne Cedex; tel. 4-93-95-42-99; f. 1970; includes 14 research units; Dir FRANÇOISE AUDOUZE.

Institut de recherche et d'histoire des textes (IRHT): 40 ave d'Iéna, 75116 Paris; tel. 1-44-43-90-70; fax 1-47-23-89-39; internet www.irht.cnrs.fr; f. 1937; Dir ANNE-MARIE EDDÉ.

Laboratoire d'économie et de sociologie du travail (LEST): 35 ave Jules Ferry, 13626 Aix-en-Provence Cedex; tel. 4-42-37-85-00; fax 4-42-26-79-37; e-mail lest@univ-aix.fr; internet www.univ-aix.fr/lest; f. 1969; Dir JEAN-JACQUES SILVESTRE.

Institut national de la langue française (INALF): 52 blvd Magenta, 75010 Paris; tel. 1-42-45-00-77; f. 1960; includes nine units of linguistic research; Dir BERNARD QUEMADA.

Mission permanente à Karnak: Centre franco-égyptien des temples de Karnak, Service de la valise, Ministère des Relations extérieures, 37 quai d'Orsay, 75007 Paris; f. 1974; Dir FRANÇOIS LARCHÉ.

Institut de recherche en architecture antique: 28 place des Martyrs-de-la-Résistance, 13100 Aix-en-Provence; tel. 4-42-21-03-80; fax 4-42-96-31-75; e-mail iraa.aix@wanadoo.fr; internet www.univ-pau.fr/IRAA-CNRS; Dir PIERRE GROS.

Centre d'études de géographie tropicale (CEGET): Domaine Universitaire, 33405 Talence Cedex; tel. 5-56-84-68-30; f. 1968; Dir M. SINGARAVELOU.

Centre de géomorphologie: Rue des Tilleuls, 14000 Caen; tel. 2-31-86-48-00; f. 1963; Dir JEAN-PIERRE LAUTRIDOU.

Centre de recherche en droit comparé: 27 rue Paul-Bert, 94204 Ivry-sur-Seine Cedex; tel. 1-46-70-02-43; f. 1952; Dir JEAN HILAIRE.

Langues et civilisations à tradition orale (LACITO): Centre André-Georges Haudricourt, 7 rue Guy Môquet, Bât. D, 94801 Villejuif cedex; tel. 1-49-58-37-78; fax 1-49-58-37-79; e-mail lacito@vjf.cnrs.fr; internet lacito.vjf.cnrs.fr; f. 1976; Dir ZLATKA GUENTCHEVA.

IMAGEO: Centre de géographie, 191 rue St Jacques, 75005 Paris; tel. 1-43-29-31-39; f. 1976; Dir FERNAND VERGER.

Centre d'études et de recherches éco-géographiques (CEREG): Université de Strasbourg 1, 3 rue de l'Argonne, 67083 Strasbourg Cedex; tel. 3-88-35-43-00; f. 1976; Dir JEAN-LUC MERCIER.

Institut de recherche en pédagogie de l'économie et en audiovisuel pour la communication dans les sciences sociales (IRPEACS): 93 chemin des Mouilles, 69131 Ecully Cedex; tel. 4-72-29-30-30; f. 1975; Dir ANDRÉE TIBERGHIEN.

Centre de sociologie des organisations (CSO): 19 rue Amélie, 75007 Paris; tel. 1-40-62-65-70; fax 1-47-05-35-55; e-mail cso@cso.edu; internet www.cso.edu; f. 1975; Dir CATHERINE BALLE.

Institut d'histoire moderne et contemporaine (IHMC): Ecole normale supérieure, 45 rue d'Ulm, 75005 Paris; tel. 1-44-32-31-52; fax 1-44-32-30-44; e-mail Secretariat.ihmc@ens.fr; internet www.ihmc.ens.fr; f. 1979; Dir CHRISTOPHE CHARLE.

Institut d'histoire du temps présent (IHTP): 61, avenue du Président Wilson, 94235 Cachan Cedex; tel. 1-47-40-68-00; fax 1-47-40-68-03; e-mail ihtp@ihtp.cnrs.fr; internet www.ihtp.cnrs.fr; f. 1978; Dir HENRY ROUSSO.

Centre d'ethnologie française: 6 ave du Mahatma Gandhi, 75116 Paris; tel. 1-40-67-90-00; f. 1966; Dir MARTINE SEGALEN.

Institut des textes et manuscrits modernes (ITEM): 61 rue Richelieu, 75084 Paris Cedex 02; tel. 1-42-96-30-94; f. 1978; Dir ALMUTH GRÉSILLON.

Inventaire général des monuments et des richesses artistiques de la France: 10 rue du Parc-Royal, 75003 Paris; tel. 1-42-71-22-02; f. 1986; Dir PAUL-ALBERT FÉVRIER.

Centre de recherches sur la conservation des documents graphiques (CRCDG): 36 rue Geoffroy St Hilaire, 75005 Paris; tel. 1-44-08-69-90; fax 1-47-07-62-95; e-mail crcdg@mnhn.fr; internet www.crcdg.culture.fr; f. 1964; Dir BERTRAND LAVÉDRINE.

Centre de recherches historiques (CRH): 54 blvd Raspail, 75006 Paris; tel. 1-49-54-24-42; fax 1-49-54-23-99; internet www.ehess.fr/centres/crh; f. 1979; Dirs GÉRARD BÉAUR PAUL-ANDRÉ ROSENTAL.

Centre d'analyse et de mathématique sociale (CAMS): 54 blvd Raspail, 75270 Paris Cedex 06; tel. 1-49-54-20-41; fax 1-49-54-21-09; e-mail cams@ehess.fr; internet www.ehess.fr/centres/cams; f. 1967; Dir HENRI BERESTYCKI.

Laboratoire d'anthropologie sociale: 52 rue du Cardinal Lemoine, 75005 Paris; tel. 1-44-27-17-31; fax 1-44-27-17-66; internet www.ehess.fr/centres/las; f. 1980; Dir PHILIPPE DESCOLA.

Laboratoire de recherche économie appliquée (LAREA): Université de Paris X, 200 avenue de la République, 92001 Nanterre; tel. 1-40-97-72-00; f. 1985; Dir PHILIPPE HUGON.

Transformations de l'appareil productif et structuration de l'espace sociale (LATAPSES): Université de Nice, 34 avenue Robert Schuman, 06000 Nice; tel. 4-93-97-70-00; f. 1986; Dir RICHARD ARENA.

Centre de recherche médecine, maladie et sciences sociales (CERMES): 7 rue Guy-Môquet, 94801 Villejuif cedex; tel. 1-49-58-36-36; fax 1-49-58-34-38; e-mail cermes@vjf.cnrs; internet ifr69.vjf.inserm.fr/~webifr/CERMES; f. 1986; Dir MARTINE BUNGENER.

Institut de Recherches et d'Etudes sur le Monde Arabe et Musulman (IREMAM): 5 rue du Château de l'Horloge, BP 647, 13094 Aix-en-Provence Cedex 2; tel. 4-42-52-41-61; fax 4-42-52-49-80; e-mail secretariat.iremam@mmsh.univ-aix.fr; internet www.mmsh.univ-aix.fr/iremam; f. 1988; Dirs GHISLAINE ALLEAUME, EBERHARD KIENLE.

Laboratoire d'économie des transports (LET): 14 avenue Berthelot, 69363 Lyon Cedex 07; tel. 4-72-72-64-03; fax 4-72-72-64-48; e-mail let@let.ish-lyon.cnrs.fr; internet www.ish-lyon.cnrs.fr/let; f. 1988; Dir YVES CROZET.

Département et laboratoire d'économie théorique et appliquée (DELTA): ENS, 48 blvd Jourdan, 75014 Paris; tel. 1-43-13-63-00; fax 1-43-13-63-10; e-mail accueil@delta.ens.fr; internet www.delta.ens.fr; Dir THIERRY VERDIER.

Laboratoire de recherche sur les arts du spectacle: CNRS, 27 rue Paul-Bert, 94200 Ivry-sur-Seine; tel. 1-49-60-41-29; fax 1-46-71-84-98; e-mail laras@ivry.cnrs.fr; internet www.ivry.cnrs.fr/artsduspectacle; f. 1983; Dir ELIE KONIGSON.

Groupe de sociologie du travail: Université de Paris VII, Tour centrale, 2 place Jussieu, 75251 Paris Cedex 05; tel. 1-43-36-25-25; f. 1980; Dir CLAUDE DURAND.

Groupe de sociologie des religions et de la Laïcité: 59–61 rue Pouchet, 75849 Paris Cedex 17; tel. 1-40-25-10-94; fax 1-40-25-12-35; e-mail gsrl@iresco.fr; internet www.iresco.fr/labos/gsrl/accueil_f.htm; f. 1970; Dir JEAN PAUL WILLAIME.

Groupe de recherches sociologiques sur le droit et les institutions penales: Immeuble Edison, 43, Boulevard Vauban, 78280 Guyancourt; tel. 1-34-52-17-00; fax 1-34-52-17-17; f. 1970; Dir LAURENT MUCCHIELLI.

Institut d'économie et de politique de l'énergie (IEPE): Université de Grenoble II, BP 47, 38040 Grenoble Cedex 9; tel. 4-56-52-85-70; fax 4-56-52-85-71; e-mail lepii-epe@upmf-grenoble.fr; internet www.upmf-grenoble.fr/iepe; f. 1970; Dir PATRICK CRIQUI.

Laboratoire d'histoire des sciences et des techniques: 49 rue Mirabeau, 75016 Paris; tel. 1-45-27-66-30; f. 1968; Dir JEAN DHOMBRES.

Institut de recherche sur l'économie de l'education (IREDU): BP 26513, 21065 Dijon Cedex; tel. 3-80-39-54-50; fax 3-80-39-54-79; e-mail iredu@u-bourgogne.fr; internet www.u-bourgogne.fr/IREDU; f. 1986; Dir JEAN-JACQUES PAUL.

Laboratoire de sociologie du changement des institutions (LSCI): 59–61 rue Pouchet, 75849 Paris Cedex 17; tel. 1-40-25-10-67; fax 1-40-25-10-66; e-mail lsci@iresco.fr; internet www.iresco.fr/labos/lsci; f. 1986; Dir JEAN-LOUIS LAVILLE.

Laboratoire d'anthropologie urbaine: CNRS, 27 rue Paul-Bert, 94204 Ivry-sur-Seine; tel. 1-49-60-40-40; fax 1-45-15-01-66; internet www.ivry.cnrs.fr; f. 1988; Dir JACQUES GUTWIRTH.

Geste et Image: anthropologie de la gestuelle et didactique de la communication (GIAGEDIC): c/o AGI, BP 233, 75227 Paris Cedex 05; tel. 1-45-44-21-22; internet www.limsi.fr/Recherche/GI; f. 1988; Dir PATRICK BOURDOT.

Communication et politique: 27 rue Damesme, 75013 Paris; tel. 1-44-16-75-66; fax 1-44-16-75-69; e-mail lcp@damesme.cnrs.fr; internet www.lcp.cnrs.fr; f. 1988; Dir GEORGES VIGNAUX.

La préhistoire du Midi de la France et de la vallée du Rhône: Faculté St-Jérôme, 13397 Marseille Cedex 13; tel. 4-91-98-90-10; f. 1968; Dirs JEAN COMBIER, JEAN-LOUIS ROUDIL.

Institut des Traditions Textuelles: 7, rue Guy-Môquet, BP 8, 94801 Villejuif Cedex; tel. 1-49-58-36-07; fax 1-49-58-36-25; internet callimac.vjf.cnrs.fr/FR33.html; f. 1968; Dir MARIE-ODILE GOULET-CAZÉ.

Recherches philosophiques de la Renaissance aux Lumières: 156 ave Parmentier, 75010 Paris; tel. 1-42-03-06-35; f. 1969; Dir HENRY MECHOULAN.

Histoire des doctrines de la fin de l'Antiquité et du haut Moyen Age: 7, rue Guy-Môquet, BP 8, 94801 Villejuif Cedex; tel. 1-49-58-36-63; fax 1-49-58-36-64; e-mail mjmangin@vjf.cnrs.fr; internet upr_76.vjf.cnrs.fr; f. 1969; Dir MARIE-ODILE GOULET-CAZE.

Histoire et structure des orthographes et systèmes d'écritures (HESO): CNRS, 27 rue Paul-Bert, 94204 Ivry-sur-Seine Cedex; tel. 1-46-60-40-40; f. 1971; Dir CLAUDE GRUAZ.

Centre de recherche sur le droit des marchés et des investissements internationaux (CREDIMI): Université de Dijon, 4 blvd Gabriel, 2100 Dijon; tel. 3-80-39-53-90; fax 3-80-39-55-71; e-mail credimi.secretariat@u-bourgogne.fr; internet www.u-bourgogne.fr/CREDIMI; f. 1972; Dir ERIC LOQUIN.

Études d'ethnomusicologie: Musée de l'Homme, Département d'ethnomusicologie, 17 place du Trocadéro, 75116 Paris; tel. 1-47-04-58-63; Dir BERNARD LORTAT-JACOB.

Droits de propriété industrielle et intellectuelle: CUERPI, Université de Grenoble II, BP 47, 3840 Grenoble Cedex; tel. 4-76-82-56-58; f. 1974; Dir CHRISTIAN LE STANC.

Techniques et culture: CNRS, 27 rue Paul-Bert, 94204 Ivry-sur-Seine; tel. 1-46-60-40-40; f. 1975; Dir GENEVIÈVE BEDOUCHA.

Mouvements internationaux de capitaux: Service d'étude de l'activité économique, 4 rue Michelet, 75006 Paris; tel. 1-43-54-50-66; f. 1975; Dir PATRICK MESSERLIN.

Mari et le Proche-Orient ancien, travaux épigraphiques et archéologiques: 9 rue de la Perle, 75003 Paris; tel. 1-48-87-22-24; f. 1975; Dir JEAN-MARIE DURAND.

Centre de recherche sur le bien-être (CEREBE): 140 rue du Chevaleret, 75013 Paris; tel. 1-45-86-87-83; f. 1977; Dir PHILIPPE D' IRIBARNE.

Laboratoire d'économétrie de l'École polytechnique: École polytechnique, 1 rue Descartes, 75230 Paris Cedex 05; tel. 1-46-34-35-35; internet ceco.polytechnique.fr; f. 1977; Dir JEAN-PIERRE PONSSARD.

Nouvelle Gallia Judaica: Section des Sciences religieuses , 45 rue des Écoles, 75005 Paris; tel. 1-40-46-31-37; fax 1-56-80-23-55; internet www.ngj.ens.fr/ngj.html; f. 1977; Dir DANIÈLE IANCU-AGOU.

Dynamique bioculturelle: Pavillon Lenfant, 346 route des Alpes, 13100 Aix-en-Provence; tel. 4-42-23-57-94; f. 1978; Dir EMILE CROGNIER.

Géographie sociale et gérontologie: Université de Paris VII, Centre de géographie, 191 rue St-Jacques, 75005 Paris; tel. 1-46-34-51-96; f. 1982; Dir FRANÇOISE CRIBIER.

Sciences sociales du monde iranien contemporain: CNRS, 27 rue Paul-Bert, 94204 Ivry-sur-Seine Cedex; tel. 1-49-60-40-40; f. 1982; Dir MARIE LADIER-FOULADI.

Anthropologie alimentaire différentielle: Muséum national d'histoire naturelle, Laboratoire d'ethnobotanique, 57 rue Cuvier, 75231 Paris Cedex 05; tel. 1-47-07-36-25; f. 1983; Dir IGOR DE GARINE.

Fondements des sciences: Université de Strasbourg I, Institut de physique, 3 rue de l'Université, 67084 Strasbourg; tel. 3-88-36-35-32; f. 1983; Dir HERVÉ BARREAU.

Groupe d'étude sur la division sociale et sexuelle du travail (GEDISST): 59–61 rue Pouchet, 75849 Paris Cedex 17; tel. 1-40-25-12-06; fax 1-42-28-95-44; f. 1984; Dirs DANIÈLE CHABAUD-RYCHTER, GHISLAINE DONIOL-SHAW.

Centre de sociologie urbaine (CSU): 59–61 rue Pouchet, 75849 Paris Cedex 17; tel. 1-40-25-10-25; f. 1984; Dir CHRISTIAN TOPALOV.

Groupe d'analyse des politiques publiques (GAPP): Ecole Normale Supérieure de Cachan, 61 Avenue du Président Wilson, 94235 Cachan Cedex; tel. 1-47-40-59-57; fax 1-47-40-59-56; e-mail azzimon@gapp.ens-cachan.fr; internet www.gapp-cnrs.ens-cachan.fr; f. 1984; Dir JACQUES COMMAILLE.

Centre d'anthropologie des sociétés rurales Europe méditerranéenne: EHESS, 56 rue du Taur, 31000 Toulouse; tel. 5-61-23-29-53; f. 1979; Dir JEAN GUILAINE.

Civilisations protohistoriques de la France méditerranéenne: Centre archéologique, Mas Saint-Saveur, route de Perols, 34970 Lattes; tel. 4-67-65-31-67; f. 1983; Dir GUY BARRUOL.

Groupe de recherches sur l'Amérique Latine (GRAL): Université de Toulouse II, 5 allée Antonio-Machado, 31058 Toulouse Cedex; tel. 5-61-41-11-05; internet www.univ-tlse2.fr/amlat/gral; f. 1987; Dir CLAUDE BATAILLON.

Institut de Recherche sur le Sud-Est Asiatique (IRSEA): 3, place Victor Hugo, 75009 Paris; tel. 4-91-10-61-14; fax 4-91-10-61-15; e-mail irsea@newsup.univ-mrs.fr; internet www.up.univ-mrs.fr/wmap/IRSEA; f. 1993.

Milieux, société et culture en Himalaya: 7, rue Guy Môquet , 94801 Villejuif Cedex; tel. 1-49-58-37-36; internet www.vjf.cnrs.fr/himalaya; f. 1985; Dir GÉRARD TOFFIN.

Chypre et le Levant: Maison de l'Orient méditerranéen, 7 rue Raulin, 69007 Lyon; tel. 4-72-71-58-00; fax 4-78-58-12-57; internet www.mom.fr; f. 1986; Dir MARGUERITE YON.

Les pays grecs de la Méditerranée orientale: épigraphie, géographie, historique et sociétés: Maison de l'Orient, 7 rue Raulin, 69007 Lyon; tel. 4-72-71-58-00; fax 4-78-58-12-57; internet www.mom.fr; f. 1986; Dir BRUNO HELLY.

Laboratoire de recherches sur l'Afrique orientale: CNRS, Place Aristide-Briand, 92190 Meudon; tel. 1-45-34-75-50; f. 1986; Dirs GINETTE AUMASSIP, JEAN POLET.

Archéologie du Mexique et de l'Amérique centrale: Musée de l'homme, Palais de Chaillot, place du Trocadéro, 75116 Paris; tel. 1-47-04-63-11; f. 1986; Dir PIERRE BECQUELIN.

Centre Fustel de Coulanges: École normale supérieure, Laboratoire d'archéologie, 45 rue d'Ulm, 75230 Paris Cedex 05; tel. 1-43-29-12-25; f. 1986; Dir CHRISTIAN PEYRE.

Archéologies et Sciences de l'Antiquité: Maison René Ginouvès, 21 allée de l'Université, 92023 Nanterre Cedex; tel. 1-46-69-24-18; fax 1-46-69-24-92; e-mail arscan@mae.u-paris10.fr; internet web.mae.u-paris10.fr/recherche/armscan.htm; f. 1986; Dir ANNE-MARIE GUIMIER-SORBETS.

Maison de l'Archéologie et de l'Ethnologie: Maison René Ginouvès, 21, allée de l'Université, 92023 Nanterrre Cedex; tel. 1-46-69-24-00; fax 1-46-69-24-51; internet web.mae.u-paris10.fr; Dir PIERRE ROUILLARD.

Archéologies et Sciences de l'Antiquité: Maison René Ginouvès, 21, allée de l'Université, 92023 Nanterrre Cedex; tel. 1-46-69-24-18; fax 1-46-69-24-92; e-mail arscan@mae.u-paris10.fr; internet web.mae.u-paris10.fr/recherche/arscan.htm; Dir ANNE-MARIE GUIMIER-SORBETS.

Archéologie des Amériques: Maison René Ginouvès, 21, allée de l'Université, 92023 Nanterrre Cedex; tel. 1-46-69-25-09; fax 1-46-69-25-08; e-mail michelet@mae.u-paris10.fr; internet web.mae.u-paris10.fr/recherche/aapresenta.htm; Dir DOMINIQUE MICHELET.

Préhistoire et Technologie: Maison René Ginouvès, 21, allée de l'Université, 92023 Nanterrre Cedex; tel. 1-46-69-25-74; fax 1-46-69-25-69; e-mail roux@mae.u-paris10.fr; internet web.mae.u-paris10.fr/recherche/prehistoire.htm; Dir VALENTINE ROUX.

Textes Images et Monuments de l'Antiquité au Haut Moyen Age: Maison René Ginouvès, 21, allée de l'Université, 92023 Nanterrre Cedex; tel. 1-46-69-25-38; fax 1-46-69-25-42; e-mail jbf@mae.u-paris10.fr; internet web.mae.u-paris10.fr/recherche/tim.htm; Dir JEAN BOUFFARTIGUE.

Laboratoire d'ethnologie et de sociologie comparative: Maison René Ginouvès, 21, allée de l'Université, 92023 Nanterrre Cedex; internet web.mae.u-paris10.fr/recherche/ethnologie.htm; f. 1967; Dir LAURENCE CAILLET.

Lexicon Iconographicum Mythologiae Classicae: Maison René Ginouvès, 21, allée de l'Université, 92023 Nanterrre Cedex; tel. 1-46-69-25-11; fax 1-46-69-25-17; e-mail linant@mae.u-paris10.fr; internet web.mae.u-paris10.fr/recherche/limc.htm; Dir PASCALE LINANT DE BELLEFONDS.

Centre de Recherches Archéologiques Indus-Baluchistan: 19 ave d'Iéna, 75116 Paris; tel. 1-40-73-88-02; f. 1986; Dir JEAN-FRANÇOIS JARRIGE.

Recherches épistémologiques et historiques sur les sciences exactes et les institutions scientifiques (REHSEIS): Université PARIS 7 REHSEIS UMR 7596 59 rue Nationale, 75013 Paris; tel. 1-44-27-86-45; fax 1-44-27-86-47; internet www.diderotp7.jussieu.fr/rehseis/index.html; f. 1986; Dir KARINE CHEMLA.

Laboratoire d'analyse secondaire et de méthodes appliquées en sociologie (LASMAS): IRESCO, 59–61 rue Pouchet, 75849 Paris Cedex 17; tel. 1-40-25-10-03; fax 1-40-25-12-47; e-mail Lasmas@iresco.fr; internet www.iresco.fr/labos/lasmas/accueil_f.htm; f. 1986; Dir ANDRÉ GRELON.

Champ des activités surréalistes (CAS): 27 rue Paul-Bert, 94200 Ivry-sur-Seine; tel. 1-49-60-40-40; f. 1986; Dirs JACQUELINE CHENIEUX-GENDRON, MARIE-CLAIRE DUMAS.

Équipe de recherche en ethnologie amérindienne (EREA): IRESCO 59–61 rue Pouchet, 75017 Paris; tel. 1-40-25-11-73; fax 1-42-28-95-44; f. 1986; Dir FRANCE-MARIE CASEVITZ.

Civilisations Atlantiques et Archéosciences: Université de Rennes I, Laboratoire d'Anthropologie, Bât. 24–25, C. S. 74 205, 35042 Rennes Cedex; tel. 2-23-23-56-26; fax 2-23-23-69-34; e-mail archeosciences.accueil@univ-rennes1.fr; internet www.archeologie.univ-rennes1.fr; f. 1967; Dir GUEREC QUERRÉ.

Environnement climatique: statistique, modélisation, cartographie: Université de Grenoble 1, Laboratoire de biologie végétale, BP 53, 38041 Grenoble; tel. 4-76-51-46-00; f. 1967; Dir ANNICK DOUGUEDROIT.

Alimentation, cultures, espaces, sociétés: Faculté de médecine, BP 184, 54505 Vandoeuvre-lès-Nancy; tel. 3-83-56-56-56; f. 1988; Dir CLAUDE THOUVENOT.

Gallia et Gallia préhistoire: CNRS, 21, allée de l'Université, 92023 Paris; tel. 1-46-69-24-28; fax 1-46-69-24-30; e-mail gallia@mae.u-paris10.fr; internet www.revues-gallia.cnrs.fr; f. 1982; Dir PAUL VAN OSSEL.

Antiquités africaines: Université d'Aix-Marseille I, 29 ave Robert-Schuman, 13621 Aix-en-Provence; tel. 4-42-59-26-83; f. 1982; Dir GEORGES SOUVILLE.

Centre d'anthropologie de la Chine du sud et de la péninsule indochinoise (CACSPI): 27 rue Damesme, 75013 Paris; tel. 1-45-80-27-90; fax 1-45-88-01-84; Dir JACQUES LEMOINE.

Computer Centres:

Centre inter-régional de calcul électronique: Bâtiment 506, BP 167, 91403 Orsay Cedex; tel. 1-69-82-41-41; fax 1-69-28-52-73; f. 1969; Dir PHILIPPE SALZEDO.

Centre de calcul de Strasbourg: 23 rue de Loess, BP 20 CR, 67037 Strasbourg Cedex; tel. 3-88-28-68-66; f. 1968; Dir CLAUDE GAILLARD.

Centre de calcul, Antenne de Paris de l'IN2P3: 11 quai St Bernard, 75230 Paris Cedex 05; tel. 1-43-26-77-68; fax 1-43-26-82-76; f. 1966; Dir JACQUES COHEN-GANOUNA.

Centre de calcul de physique nucléaire de l'IN2P3: 27–29 blvd du 11 Novembre 1918, 69622 Villeurbanne Cedex; tel. 4-78-93-08-80; fax 78-94-30-54; Dir JACQUES COHEN-GANOUNA.

AGRICULTURE, FISHERIES AND VETERINARY SCIENCE

Centre de Co-opération Internationale en Recherche Agronomique pour le Développement (CIRAD): 42 rue Scheffer, 75116 Paris; tel. 1-53-70-20-00; fax 1-47-55-15-30; internet www.cirad.fr; (laboratories: BP 5035, 34032 Montpellier Cedex 1, tel 4-67-61-58-00); f. 1970, present name 1986; state-owned; research and development within the framework of French scientific and technical co-operation with developing countries; stations in over 50 countries; library of 134,000 vols, 3,300 scientific periodicals; Dir-Gen. GÉRARD MATHERON; Sec.-Gen. HERVÉ DEPERROIS; publ. *Annual Report*.

Research departments:

Département d'Élevage et de Médecine Vétérinaire (CIRAD-EMVT): Campus international de Baillarguet, BP 5035, 34398 Montpellier Cedex 5; tel. 4-67-59-37-10; fax 4-67-59-37-95; e-mail valo.emvt@cirad.fr; f. 1948; research and missions to countries of Africa, Asia and South America; Dir EMMANUEL CAMUS; publ. *Revue d'Elevage et de Médecine Vétérinaire des Pays Tropicaux* (quarterly).

Département des Cultures Annuelles (CIRAD-CA): 2477 ave Agropolis, BP

5035, 34398 Montpellier Cedex 5; tel. 4-67-61-58-00; fax 4-67-61-59-88; e-mail dirpersyst@cirad.fr; f. 1992; experts stationed in Benin, Brazil, Burkina Faso, Burundi, Cameroon, Chad, Colombia, Costa Rica, Côte d'Ivoire, Dominica, Gabon, Ghana, Guinea, Honduras, Laos, Madagascar, Mali, Niger, Paraguay, Philippines, Central African Republic, Senegal, Thailand, Togo, Turkey, Viet Nam; Dir MARCO WOPEREIS; publ. *Agriculture et développement* (quarterly, abstracts in French, English and Spanish).

Département des Cultures Pérennes (CIRAD-CP): Boulevard de la Lirondem, TA 80/PS3, 34398 Montpellier Cedex 5; tel. 4-67-61-58-00; fax 4-67-61-56-59; e-mail dircp@cirad.fr; f. 1992; research and technical assistance relating to cocoa, coconuts, coffee, oil palm and rubber; Dir DOMINIQUE BERRY; publ. *Plantations, recherche, développement* (in French and English or Spanish).

Département des Productions Fruitières et Horticoles (CIRAD-FLHOR): Blvd de la Lironde, TA 50/PS4, 34398 Montpellier Cedex 5; tel. 4-67-61-58-00; fax 4-67-61-58-71; e-mail flhor@cirad.fr; f. 1945; activities in the technical, scientific and economic aspects of horticulture (from product research to distribution) in tropical and Mediterranean zones and with respect to related agro-industries; many overseas brs; Dir HUBERT DE BON; publs *Fruits*, *FruiTrop*.

Département Forestier (CIRAD-Forêt): Campus international de Baillarguet, BP 5035, 34398 Montpellier Cedex 5; tel. 4-67-59-37-10; fax 4-67-59-37-55; e-mail forets@cirad.fr; forestry; Dir BERNARD MALLET; publ. *Bois et forêts des tropiques*.

Département des Territoires, Environnement et Acteurs (CIRAD-TERA): 73 rue Jean-François Breton, TA 60/15, 34398 Montpellier Cedex 5; tel. 4-67-61-58-00; fax 4-67-61-12-23; e-mail tera@cirad.fr; smallholder farming, land and resources, savannah and irrigated systems, humid tropics; Dir ROLLAND GUIS.

Département d'Amélioration des Méthodes pour l'Innovation Scientifique (CIRAD-AMIS): 2477 ave Agropolis, TA 40/02, 34398 Montpellier Cedex 5; tel. 4-67-61-58-00; fax 4-67-61-44-55; e-mail amis@cirad.fr; plant modelling, food production, agronomy, crop protection, biotechnology and plant genetic research, economics, policy and marketing; Dir JACQUES MEUNIER; publ. *Sésame bulletin*.

Centre de Recherches de Jouy: Domaine de Vilvert, 78352 Jouy-en-Josas Cedex; tel. 1-34-65-21-21; fax 1-34-65-20-51; e-mail communication@jouy.inra.fr; internet www.jouy.inra.fr; f. 1950; linked to Institut National de la Recherche Agronomique (*q.v.*); scientific research on livestock production and health, human nutrition, animal biology, microbiology, applied mathematics and bioinformatics, animal models for human and animal health; library of 6,000 vols, 2,200 periodicals.; Pres. Dr EMMANUEL JOLIVET.

Institut d'Immunologie Animale et Comparée (Institute of Animal and Comparative Immunology): Ecole Nationale Vétérinaire d'Alfort, 7 ave du Général de Gaulle, 94704 Maisons-Alfort Cedex; tel. 1-43-68-98-82; f. 1981; organizes courses; research in immunostimulation, clinical immunology, immunopathology; Dir Prof. CH. PILET.

Institut National de la Recherche Agronomique (INRA): 147 rue de l'Université, 75338 Paris Cedex 07; tel. 1-42-75-90-00; fax 1-47-05-99-66; internet www.inra.fr; f. 1946; agricultural research, including agricultural and food industries, rural economics and sociology, plant and animal production and forestry; administers and subsidizes a large number of centres, laboratories and experimental farms in France; Pres. and Dir-Gen. MARION GUILLOU; publs *Agronomy for Sustainable Development* (10 a year), *Animal Research* (6 a year), *Annales des Sciences Forestières* (every 2 months), *Apidologie* (every 2 months), *Genetics Selection Evolution* (every 2 months), *Le Lait* (every 2 months), *Reproduction Nutrition Development* (every 2 months), *Veterinary Research* (every 2 months), *Production Animales* (3 a year), *Cahiers d'Economie et Sociologie rurales* (every 3 months), *INRA Sciences Sociales* (every 2 months), *Bulletin des Technologies* (1 a year), *Courrier de l'Environnement* (online), *Archorales: Les Métiers de la Recherche* (online).

Laboratoire Central de Recherches Vétérinaires: BP 67, 22 rue Pierre Curie, 94703 Maisons-Alfort Cedex; tel. 1-49-77-13-00; fax 1-43-68-97-62; f. 1901; 140 mems; study of contagious diseases in domestic and wild animals; supervises sanitary regulations for import and export of livestock; Dir Dr ERIC PLATEAU.

ECONOMICS, LAW AND POLITICS

Centre d'Etudes de l'Emploi: Le Descartes I, 29 promenade Michel Simon, 93166 Noisy-le-Grand Cedex; tel. 1-45-92-68-00; fax 1-49-31-02-44; internet www.cee-recherche.fr; for the study and research of changes in the field of employment; research units: age and work, employment and social security, employment markets and institutions, workers and organizations; attached to min. of employment and min. of education; Dir PIERRE RALLE; publs *Connaisance de l'Emploi* (monthly), *CEE.INFO* (3 a year).

Centre d'Etudes Prospectives et d'Informations Internationales (Centre for International Prospective Studies and Information): 9 rue Georges Pitard, 75015 Paris; tel. 1-53-68-55-00; fax 1-53-68-55-03; e-mail postmaster@cepii.fr; internet www.cepii.fr; f. 1978 by the Government, under the aegis of Commissariat Général du Plan; aims to aid public and private decision-makers in the international economic field by conducting synthetic studies of the global economic environment in the mid-term (5–10 years), constructing economic models and data bases, and by providing a coherent statistical information system of the world economy and its major participants; 50 mems; library of 30,000 vols, 500 periodicals; Dir AGNÈS BÉNASSY-QUÉRÉ; publs incl. *Economie Internationale* (4 a year), *La Lettre du CEPII* (11 a year), *CEPII Newsletter* (electronic newsletter, 4 a year), *Rapport d'activité* (annually), *CEPII Working Papers* (monthly), *L'Economie mondiale* (annually), *CHELEM Data Bank: bilingual CD-ROM* (annually).

Institut de Recherches Economiques et Sociales: 16 blvd du Mont d'Est, 93192 Noisy-Le-Grand, Cedex; tel. (1) 48-15-18-93; fax (1) 48-15-19-18; e-mail info@ires-fr.org; internet www.ires-fr.org; f. 1982 by the main French trade unions in association with the French govt to meet the economic and social research needs of trade unions; central research areas: employment patterns, industrial relations, wage patterns, work patterns; Pres. PIERRETTE CROSEMARIE; Dir JACKY FAYOLLE; publs *La Revue de L'IRES* (3 a year), *La Chronique Internationale* (every 2 months), *La Lettre de l'IRES* (quarterly).

Institut de Sciences Mathématiques et Economiques Appliquées: 1 rue Maurice Arnoux, 92120 Montrouge; tel. 1-55-48-90-70; fax 1-55-48-90-71; e-mail perroux@univ-mlv.fr; internet www.ismea.org; f. 1944; int. co-operation and links with Third World univs; library of 14,500 vols; Chair. Prof. G. DESTANNE DE BERNIS; publs *Economies et Sociétés* (monthly), *Economie Appliquée* (quarterly).

Institut National de la Statistique et des Etudes Economiques: 18 blvd Adolphe Pinard, 75675 Paris Cedex 14; tel. 1-41-17-66-11; fax 1-41-17-66-66; e-mail renseignements@insee.fr; internet www.insee.fr; f. 1946; statistical research: population census, economic indices and forecasts; library: see Libraries; Dir-Gen. JEAN-MICHEL CHARPIN; publs *Annuaire Statistique* (annually), *Bulletin Mensuel de Statistique* (monthly), *Tableaux de l'économie française* (annually), *La France et ses régions* (every 3 years), *Insee Première* (60 a year), *Economie et Statistique* (monthly), *La société française – données sociales* (every 3 years), *Annales d'Economie et de Statistique* (quarterly), *Note de Conjoncture* (quarterly), *Tableau de bord hebdomadaire* (50 a year), *Courrier des Statistiques* (quarterly), *Insee Méthodes*, *Insee Résultats*, *La France des Services (Collection Références)* (annually), *Informations Rapides* (370 a year), *Synthèses*, *La Commerce en France (Collection Références)* (annually).

Institut National d'Etudes Démographiques: 133 Blvd Davout, 75980 Paris Cedex 20; tel. 1-56-06-20-00; fax 1-56-06-21-99; internet www.ined.fr; f. 1945; library of 40,000 vols; Dir FRANÇOIS HÉRAN; publs *Population* (quarterly), *Population et Sociétés* (monthly), *Les Cahiers de l'INED* (4–6 a year), *Classiques de l'Économie et de la Population* (2 or 3 a year).

EDUCATION

Centre International d'Etudes Pédagogiques de Sèvres: 1 ave Léon Journault, BP 75, 92318 Sèvres Cedex; tel. 1-45-07-60-00; fax 1-45-07-60-01; e-mail contact@ciep.fr; internet www.ciep.fr; f. 1945; research and studies in comparative education; training overseas teachers in French as a foreign language; 170 mems; Dir M. LÉOUTRE; publ. *Revue Internationale d'Education*.

Institut National de Recherche Pédagogique: 19 Mail de Fontenay, BP 17424, 69347 Lyons Cedex 07; tel. 4-72-76-61-71; fax 4-72-76-61-42; e-mail contact@inrp.fr; internet www.inrp.fr; f. 1879 to develop and promote research into teaching and education; 280 staff, 1652 assoc. mems; library: see Libraries and Archives; Dir EMMANUEL FRAISSE; publs *Revue Française de Pédagogie* (4 a year), *Repères* (2 a year), *Histoire de l'Education* (4 a year), *Etapes de la Recherche*, *Recherche et Formation* (3 a year), *Perspectives Documentaires* (3 a year), *Aster* (2 a year), *Didaskalia* (2 a year).

FINE AND PERFORMING ARTS

Institut de Recherche et Co-ordination Acoustique et de la Musique: Centre National d'Art et de Culture Georges-Pompidou, 1 place Igor-Stravinsky, 75004 Paris Cedex 04; tel. 1-44-78-48-43; fax 1-44-78-15-40; internet www.ircam.fr; attached to Centre National d'Art et de Culture Georges-Pompidou; interdisciplinary research centre for musicians and scientists; data processing, electroacoustics, instrumental and vocal research; Dir BERNARD STIEGLER.

Institut National d'Histoire de l'Art (INHA): 2 rue Vivienne, 75002 Paris; tel. 1-47-03-86-04; fax 1-47-03-86-36; e-mail inha@inha.fr; internet www.inha.fr; f. 2001; library: Institute library, to be opened in

2006, will include Bibliothèque d'art et d'archéologie Jacques Doucet, Bibliothèque centrale des musées nationaux, Bibliothèque de l'Ecole nationale supérieure des beaux arts, Bibliothèque de l'Ecole nationale des chartes; Dir-Gen. JEAN-MARC POINSOT.

HISTORY, GEOGRAPHY AND ARCHAEOLOGY

Centre de Recherches Historiques: Ecole des Hautes Etudes en Sciences Sociales, UMR 8558, 54 blvd Raspail, 75006 Paris; tel. 1-49-54-24-42; fax 1-49-54-23-99; e-mail crh@msh-paris.fr; internet www.ehess.fr; f. 1950; joint research in economic, social, cultural and political history; 126 mems; Dirs GÉRARD BÉAUR BERNARD VINCENT; publs *Annales* (history, social sciences, 6 a year), *Histoire et Mesure* (4 a year), *Cahiers* (2 a year), *1900* (annually), *Entreprises et Histoire* (4 a year).

Centre d'Études Supérieures de la Renaissance: 59 rue Néricault-Destouches, BP 11328, 37013 Tours Cedex 1; tel. 2-47-36-77-60; fax 2-47-36-77-62; e-mail cesr@univ-tours.fr; internet www.cesr.univ-tours.fr; f. 1956; library of 45,000 vols; Dir Prof. G. CHAIX; Sec. M. ANCELIN.

Fondation et Institut Charles de Gaulle: 5 rue de Solférino, 75007 Paris; tel. 1-44-18-66-77; fax 1-44-18-66-99; e-mail contact@charles-de-gaulle.org; internet www.charles-de-gaulle.org; f. Institute 1971, Foundation f. 1992; assembles material related to the life and work of Charles de Gaulle for the purpose of scholarship; library of 4,500 vols, periodicals, documents, cuttings, 4,000 photographs, recorded interviews, audiovisual material; Pres. YVES GUÉNA.

Institut Géographique National: 136 bis rue de Grenelle, 75700 Paris; tel. 1-43-98-80-00; fax 1-43-98-84-00; internet www.ign.fr; f. 1940; satellite-image, aerial and ground surveys, map printing; national map and aerial photograph library, scientific library; administers *Ecole Nat. des Sciences Géographiques*; Pres. MICHEL FRANC; Dir-Gen. JEAN POULIT; publ. *Bulletin d'Information* (quarterly).

Sous-Direction de l'Archéologie: 4 rue d'Aboukir, 75002 Paris; tel. 1-40-15-77-81; fax 1-40-15-77-00; e-mail jean-francois.texier@culture.gouv.fr; f. 1964; library of 4,500 vols, 47 periodicals; Dir JEAN-FRANÇOIS TEXIER.

MEDICINE

Institut Alfred-Fournier: 25 blvd Saint-Jacques, 75014 Paris; internet www.institutfournier.org; research into sexually transmitted diseases; f. 1923; Dir Dr P. BARBIER.

Institut Arthur-Vernes: 36 rue d'Assas, 75006 Paris; tel. 1-44-39-53-00; fax 1-42-84-26-09; internet www.institut-vernes.fr; f. 1981; Pres. J. C. SERVAN-SCHREIBER; Gen. Man CATHERINE RAUCHE.

Institut Gustave-Roussy: 39 rue Camille Desmoulins, 94805 Villejuif Cedex; tel. 1-42-11-42-11; fax 1-42-11-53-00; e-mail roussy@igr.fr; internet www.igr.fr; f. 1921; diagnosis and treatment of cancer, research, and training in oncology (affiliated with Univ. Paris-Sud for teaching purposes); library of 11,000 vols, with special collections on cancerology; Dir Prof. GILBERT LENOIR.

Institut National de la Santé et de la Recherche Médicale (INSERM): 101 rue de Tolbiac, 75654 Paris Cedex 13; tel. 1-44-23-60-00; fax 1-44-23-60-99; internet www.inserm.fr; f. 1941 as Institut National d'Hygiène, renamed 1964; assisted by scientific commissions and the Scientific Council; 270 research units throughout France; Pres. MONIQUE CAPRON; Dir-Gen. Prof. CHRISTIAN BRÉCHOT; publs *Annuaire des laboratoires, rapport d'activité, INSERM Actualités*, Collections, etc.

Institut Pasteur: 25–28 rue du Dr Roux, 75015 Paris; tel. 1-45-68-80-00; e-mail info@pasteur.fr; internet www.pasteur.fr; f. 1887; Pres. ALICE DAUTRY; Sec. AGNÈS LABIGNE; publs *Annales: Actualités, Annales Research in Virology, Bulletin* (quarterly), *Immunology and Microbiology* (16 a year).

NATURAL SCIENCES

General

Institut de Recherche pour le Développement (IRD): 213 rue La Fayette, 75480 Paris Cedex 10; tel. 1-48-03-77-77; fax 1-48-03-08-29; e-mail dic@paris.ird.fr; internet www.ird.fr; f. 1943; a public corporation charged to aid developing countries by means of research, both fundamental and applied, in the non-temperate regions, with special application to human environment problems, food production and tropical diseases; 35 centres in Africa, Asia, the Pacific, South America and French overseas territories; library and documentation centre; Pres. JEAN FRANÇOIS GIRARD; Dir-Gen. SERGE CALABRE; Gen.-Sec. CHRISTINE D'ARGOUGES; publ. *Sciences au Sud* (6 a year).

Maintains the following services:

Centre IRD de Bondy: 32 ave Henri Varagnat, 93143 Bondy Cedex; tel. 1-48-02-55-00; fax 1-48-47-30-88; e-mail bondy@ird.fr; internet www.bondy.ird.fr; geophysics, geodynamics, social sciences, entomology, applied computer science, scientific information (cartography, documentation, audiovisual); Dir JEAN FRANÇOIS GIRARD.

Flow Regimes from International Experimental and Network Data (FRIEND AMHY): BP 64501, 34394 Montpellier Cedex 5; tel. 4-67-41-61-00; internet armspark.msem.univ-montp2.fr/amhy; hydrology, hydrobiology and oceanography, soil biology, agrarian research, phytopathology, phytovirology, applied zoology, medical entomology, nutrition, geology, genetics; Gen. Co-ordinator ERIC SERVAT.

Centre IRD de Bretagne: BP 70, 29280 Plouzané Cedex; tel. 2-98-22-45-01; fax 2-98-22-45-14; e-mail irdbrest@ird.fr; internet www.brest.ird.fr; oceanography; Dir M. CLAUDE ROY.

Antenne IRD de Bouaké: BP 1434 , Bouaké, Côte d'Ivoire; tel. 31-63-95-43; fax 31-63-27-38; e-mail bouake@ird.ci; internet www.ird.ci/ird/bouake.html; jt research project with l'Institut des Savanes.

Institut Français de l'Environnement: 61 blvd Alexandre Martin, 45058 Orléans Cedex 1; tel. 2-38-79-78-78; fax 2-38-79-78-70; e-mail ifen@ifen.fr; internet www.ifen.fr; f. 1991; attached to Min. of Town and Country Planning and the Environment; collects and disseminates statistical information about the environment; focal point in France for European Environment Agency.

Biological Sciences

Institut de Biologie Physico-chimique: 13 rue Pierre et Marie Curie, 75005 Paris; tel. 1-58-41-50-00; fax 1-58-41-50-20; e-mail ifr550@ibpc.fr; internet www.ibpc.fr; f. 1927; Dir Dr J.-P. HENRY; Dirs of Laboratories R. LAVERY (Theoretical Biochemistry), J.-L. POPOT (Molecular Physical Chemistry of Biological Membranes), M. SPRINGER (Regulation of Microbial Gene Expression), J.-P. HENRY (Molecular and Cell Biology of Secretion), F.-A. WOLLMAN (Molecular and Membrane Physiology of the Chloroplast).

Institut de Biologie Structurale (IBS): 41 rue Jules Horowitz, 38027 Grenoble Cedex 1; tel. 4-38-78-95-50; fax 4-38-78-54-94; internet www.ibs.fr; jointly financed by the Commissariat à l'Energie Atomique (CEA) and the Centre National de la Recherche Scientifique (CNRS); Dir Prof. EVA PEBAY-PEYROULA.

Attached Laboratories:

Laboratoire de Biophysique Moléculaire (LBM): Dir JOSEPH ZACCAI.

Laboratoire de Cristallographie et Cristallogenèse des Protéines (LCCP): Dir JUAN-CARLOS FONTECILLA-CAMPS.

Laboratoire de Cristallographie Macromoléculaire (LCM): Dir OTTO DIDEBERG.

Laboratoire de Dynamique Moléculaire (LDM): Dir MARTIN FIELD.

Laboratoire d'Enzymologie Moléculaire (LEM): Dir GÉRARD ARLAUD.

Laboratoire d'Ingénierie des Macromolécules (LIM): Dir THIERRY VERNET.

Laboratoire de Microscopie Electronique Structurale (LMES): Dir JAMES CONWAY.

Laboratoire des Protéines du Cytosquelette (LPC): Dir ROBERT MARGOLIS.

Laboratoire des Protéines Membranaires (LPM): Dir EVA PEBAY-PEYROULA.

Laboratoire de Résonance Magnétique Nucléaire (LRMN): Dir JEAN-PIERRE SIMORRE.

Laboratoire de Spectrométrie de Masse des Protéines (LSMP): Dir ERIC FOREST.

Station Biologique de Roscoff: Place Georges-Teissier, BP 74, 29682 Roscoff Cedex; tel. 2-98-29-23-23; fax 2-98-29-23-24; e-mail postmaster@sb-roscoff.fr; internet www.sb-roscoff.fr; f. 1872; attached to Univ. Paris VI and CNRS; chemical and biological oceanography, plankton research, microbiology, biology of hydrothermal vent fauna, cell cycle and developmental biology, cell and molecular biology on macroalgae, population genetics, marine genomics; library of 5,000 vols, 1,000 periodicals; Dir Prof. ANDRÉ TOULMOND; publs *CBM-Cahiers de Biologie marine* (quarterly), *Travaux* (annually).

Physical Sciences

Association Nationale pour l'Etude de la Neige et des Avalanches (ANENA): 15 rue Ernest Calvat, 38000 Grenoble; tel. 4-76-51-39-39; fax 4-76-42-81-66; internet www.anena.org; f. 1971; to promote knowledge and give advice about avalanches and safety in snowy mountainous terrain; 700 mems; library of 2,000 vols; publ. *Neige et Avalanches* (quarterly).

Bureau de Recherches Géologiques et Minières (BRGM): 3 ave Claude Guillemin, BP 6009, 45060 Orléans Cedex 2; tel. 2-38-64-34-34; fax 2-38-64-35-18; internet www.brgm.fr; f. 1959; publicly owned industrial and trading organization; study and development of underground resources in France and abroad; library of 22,000 vols, 4,000 scientific journals, 55,000 maps; Dir-Gen. Y. LE BARS; publs *Géologie de la France* (quarterly), *Hydrogéologie* (quarterly), *Chronique de la Recherche minière* (quarterly), *Géochronique* (publ with Société géologique de France, quarterly), geological maps, bibliographies, SDI and retrospective searches.

Bureau des Longitudes: Palais de l'Institut, 3 rue Mazarine, 75006 Paris; tel. 1-43-26-59-02; fax 1-43-26-80-90; e-mail contact@bureau-des-longitudes.fr; internet www

.bureau-des-longitudes.fr; f. 1795 by Convention Nationale; 50 mems and corresp.; Pres. SUZANNE DÉBARBAT; Vice-Pres. FRANÇOIS BARLIER; Sec. PIERRE BAÜER; publs *Ephémérides Astronomiques*, *Connaissance des Temps*, *Ephémérides Nautiques*, *Cahier des Sciences de l'Univers*, and supplements to *Connaissance des Temps* (annually).

Centre de Recherches Atmosphériques: 8 route de Lannemezan, 65300 Campistrous; tel. 5-62-40-61-00; fax 5-62-40-61-01; e-mail campistrous@free.fr; internet campistrous.free.fr; f. 1960; cloud physics, atmospheric chemistry, planetary boundary layer; library of 2,000 vols; Dir R. DELMAS; publ. *Atmospheric Research* (quarterly).

Centre d'Etudes Marines Avancées: c/o Équipe Cousteau, 7 rue Amiral d'Estaing, 75116 Paris; tel. 1-53-67-77-77; fax 1-53-67-77-71; f. 1953; underwater exploration, study and research; Pres. (vacant); Sec.-Gen. HENRI JACQUIER; publ. *Calypso Log* (monthly).

Centre International pour la Formation et les Echanges en Géosciences (CIFEG): 3 ave Claude Guillemin, BP 36517, 45065 Orléans Cedex 2; tel. 2-38-64-33-67; fax 2-38-64-34-72; e-mail m.laval@cifeg.org; internet www.cifeg.org; f. 1981; geoscientific information networking; documentation centre on earth sciences of Africa and South-East Asia; exchanges between developed and developing countries; library of 3,500 vols, 65 periodicals, 400 maps; Pres. J. GIRI; Dir M. LAVAL; publ. *PANGEA* (2 a year).

Centre National de Recherches Météorologiques: 42 ave G. Coriolis, 31057 Toulouse Cedex; tel. 5-61-07-93-70; fax 5-61-07-96-00; internet www.cnrm.meteo.fr; f. 1946; meteorological research; 250 staff; Dir ERIC BRUN.

Commissariat à l'Energie Atomique (CEA): 31–33 rue de la Fédération, 75752 Paris Cedex 15; tel. 1-40-56-10-00; internet www.cea.fr; f. 1945; basic and applied nuclear research, energy generator studies; library; 5 affiliated civil research centres; Pres. of Atomic Energy Cttee The Prime Minister; Man. Dir YANNICK D'ESCATHA; publs *Les Défis du CEA*, *Rapport Annuel*, *Clefs CEA*, *CEA-Technologies*.

Attached research centres:

Centre CEA de Cadarache: 13108 St-Paul-lez-Durance Cedex; tel. 4-42-25-70-00; fax 4-42-25-45-45; f. 1960; reactor devt, nuclear safety and environmental protection, fundamental research; industrial innovation; Dir MARCEL DE LA GRAVIÈRE.

Centre CEA de Fontenay-aux-Roses: BP 6, 92265 Fontenay-aux-Roses Cedex; tel. 1-46-54-70-80; fax 1-42-53-98-51; f. 1945; first French reactor; Zoé natural uranium, heavy water moderated; work in life sciences; research in: radiobiology, environmental toxicology, neurovirology and emerging diseases; research and development in biomedical imaging and health technologies; cognitics, robotics for nuclear, industrial and medical needs; Dir ROGER GENET.

Centre CEA de Grenoble: 17 rue des Martyrs, 38054 Grenoble Cedex 9; tel. 4-76-78-44-00; fax 4-76-88-34-32; f. 1957; applied nuclear research on heat transfer studies and on behaviour of nuclear fuels; fundamental research on physics, chemistry, biology, materials science; advanced technologies: microelectronics, optronics, instrumentation, materials, heat exchangers, life sciences and tracer studies; library of 31,000 vols; Dir GEORGES CAROLA.

Centre CEA de Saclay: 91191 Gif-sur-Yvette Cedex; tel. 1-69-08-60-00; f. 1949; equipped with 2 high-flux experimental reactors, 6 particle accelerators and special laboratories: spent fuel study facility, isotope and labelled molecule production laboratories, activation analysis centre, ionizing radiations applications centre; laboratories specializing in research on reactors, nuclear metallurgy and chemistry, elementary particle physics, nuclear physics, astrophysics, condensed-matter physics, earth sciences, biology, radioactivity measurement and electronics; library of 48,000 vols, 400,000 reports; Dir ELIANE LOQUET.

Centre CEA de la Vallée du Rhône: BP 171, 30207 Bagnols-sur-Cèze Cedex; tel. 4-66-79-60-00; fax 4-66-90-14-35; f. 1982; fuel cycle research and development: uranium isotopic enrichment, spent fuel processing, waste conditioning, dismantling; fast reactors; Dir JEAN-YVES GUILLAMOT.

Centre CEA de Valduc: 21120 Is-sur-Tille; tel. 3-80-23-40-00; internet www-dam.cea.fr; f. 1996; nuclear materials used in arms production.

Centre CEA/Cesta (Gironde): BP 2, 33114 Le Barp; tel. 5-57-04-40-00; internet www-dam.cea.fr; production of nuclear arms.

Centre CEA/DAM Ile de France: BP 12, 91680 Bruyères-le-Châtel; tel. 1-69-26-40-00; internet www-dam.cea.fr; computerised research into nuclear explosions; monitoring of global seismic activity.

Institut Curie: 26 rue d'Ulm, 75248 Paris Cedex 05; tel. 1-44-32-40-00; fax 1-43-29-02-03; internet www.curie.fr; f. 1978 (fmrly Fondation Curie–Inst. du Radium); treatment, research and teaching in cancer; library of 7,000 vols; two sections: Research (Dir M. BORNENS), Medicine (Dir P. BEY); Pres. CLAUDE HURIET; Dir PHILIPPE KOURILSKY.

Institut Français de Recherche pour l'Exploitation de la Mer (IFREMER): 155 rue J. Jacques Rousseau, 92138 Issy-les-Moulineaux Cedex; tel. 1-46-48-21-00; fax 1-46-48-21-21; internet www.ifremer.fr; f. 1984; research in all fields of oceanography and ocean technology; Pres./Dir-Gen. JEAN-FRANÇOIS MINSTER; publs *Rapport Annuel*, *Aquatic Living Resources* (6 a year), *Oceanologica Acta* (6 a year).

Attached institutes:

Centre IFREMER de Brest: BP 70, 29280 Plouzane; tel. 2-98-22-40-40; fax 2-98-22-45-45; e-mail egiordma@ifremer.fr; internet www.ifremer.fr/brest; f. 1968; Dir FRANÇOIS LE VERGE.

Centre IFREMER de Toulon: BP 330, 83507 La Seyne sur Mer; tel. 4-94-30-48-00; internet www.ifremer.fr/toulon; Dir GUY HERROUIN.

Centre IFREMER Océanologique du Pacifique: BP 7004, 98719 Taravao, Tahiti; tel. 54-60-00; fax 54-60-99; internet www.ifremer.fr/cop/tahiti.htm; f. 1972; development of ocean resources: minerals, fishing and aquaculture in French South Pacific territories; 70 staff; library of 200 vols; Dir DOMINIQUE BUESTEL.

Centre IFREMER de Nantes: BP 21105, 44311 Nantes Cedex 03; tel. 2-40-37-40-43; fax 2-40-37-40-01; internet www.ifremer.fr/nantes; Dir ROBERT POGGI.

Institut Polaire Français Paul Emile: Technopôle Brest-Iroise, BP 75, 29280 Plouzané; tel. 2-98-05-65-00; fax 2-98-05-65-55; e-mail infoipev@ipev.fr; internet www.ipev.fr; f. 1992 by merger of Mission de Recherche des Terres Australes et Antarctiques Françaises and Expéditions Polaires Françaises; Dir GÉRARD JUGIE.

Laboratoire d'Astronomie de l'Université des Sciences et Techniques de Lille-Flandres-Artois: 1 impasse de l'Observatoire, 59000 Lille; tel. 3-20-52-44-24; f. 1934; astronomy, celestial mechanics; Dir L. DURIEZ.

Météo-France: 1 quai Branly, 75340 Paris Cedex 07; tel. 1-45-56-71-71; fax 1-45-56-70-05; internet www.meteofrance.com; f. 1945; Dir JEAN-PIERRE BEYSSON; publs *METEO-HEBDO* (weekly), *Atmospheriques* (3 a year), *Monographies*, *Bulletin Climatique* (monthly), *Données et Statistiques*, *Notes techniques*, *Bibliographies*, *La Météorologie* (3 a year), *Met Mar* (3 a year), *Cours et Manuels* (irregular), *Phénomènes Remarquables* (irregular).

Observatoire de Bordeaux: Université de Bordeaux I, CNRS, 2 rue de l'Observatoire, BP 89, 33270 Floirac; tel. 5-57-77-61-00; fax 5-57-77-61-10; internet www.obs.u-bordeaux1.fr; f. 1879; astrometry, astrodynamics, solar physics, radioastronomy, helioseismology, planetary atmosphere, radio aeronomy; library of 3,700 vols; Dir A. CASTETS; publ. *Rapport*.

Observatoire de la Côte d'Azur: BP 4229, 06304 Nice Cedex 4; tel. 4-99-00-30-11; fax 4-92-00-30-33; internet www.obs-nice.fr; f. 1881; astronomy and astrophysics; library of 12,000 vols, 250 periodicals; Dir JACQUES COLIN.

Observatoire de Lyon: 9 ave Charles-André, 69561 Saint-Genis-Laval Cedex; tel. 4-78-86-85-34; fax 4-78-86-83-86; e-mail accueil@obs.univ-lyon1.fr; internet www-obs.univ-lyon1.fr; f. 1880; specializes in two-dimensional photometry and infra-red imagery; library of 20,000 vols; Dir BRUNO GUIDERDONI.

Observatoire Astronomique de Marseille–Provence: 2 place Le Verrier, 13248 Marseilles Cedex 4; tel. 4-95-04-41-00; fax 4-91-62-11-90; e-mail Sylvie.Imbert@oamp.fr; internet www.oamp.fr; library of 5,000 vols; Dir MICHEL BLANC.

Observatoire de Paris: 61 ave de l'Observatoire, 75014 Paris; tel. 1-40-51-22-21; fax 1-43-54-18-04; internet www.obspm.fr; f. 1667; library of 60,000 vols; Pres. D. EGRET.

Attached stations:

Observatoire de Paris, Site de Meudon: 5 place Jules Janssen, 92195 Meudon Principal Cedex; tel. 1-45-07-75-30; fax 1-45-07-74-69; administered by the Observatoire de Paris; f. 1875; astrophysics; Dir M. COMBES.

Station de Radioastronomie de Nançay: 18330 Nançay; tel. 2-48-51-82-41; fax 2-48-51-83-18; administered by the Observatoire de Paris; f. 1953; study of the sun, comets, planets and radio sources; radio telescopes; Dir M. COMBES.

Observatoire de Physique du Globe de Clermont-Ferrand: 24 ave des Landais, 63177 Aubière Cedex; tel. 4-73-40-73-80; fax 4-73-40-73-82; e-mail A*Flossmann@opgc.univ-bpclermont.fr; internet www.obs.univ-bpclermont.fr; f. 1871; atmospheric physics, cloud systems, earth sciences, and geophysical surveillance; Dir Prof. ANDRÉA FLOSSMANN.

Observatoire Astronomique de Strasbourg: 11 rue de l'Université, 67000 Strasbourg; tel. 3-90-24-24-10; fax 90-24-24-32; internet astro.u-strasbg.fr; f. 1882; specializes in astronomical data and information, galactic evolution, cosmology, high-energy astrophysics; houses the Strasbourg Astronomical Data Centre (CDS); library of 16,000 vols; Dir JEAN-MARIE HAMEURY; publs *Publications de l'Observatoire* (irregular), *CDS Newsletter* (electronic, 3 a year).

Observatoire des Sciences de l'Univers de Besançon: BP 1615, 41 bis ave de l'Observatoire, 25010 Besançon Cedex; tel. 3-81-66-69-00; fax 3-81-66-69-44; e-mail direction@obs-besancon.fr; internet www.obs-besancon.fr; f. 1882; a research unit of the Université de Franche-Comté; library: *c.* 15,000 vols; Dir Prof. FRANÇOIS VERNOTTE.

Observatoire Midi-Pyrénées: Headquarters: 14 ave E. Belin, 31400 Toulouse; tel. 5-61-33-29-29; fax 5-61-33-28-88; internet www.omp.obs-mip.fr; library of 50,000 vols; solar, planetary, stellar, galactic and extragalactic astrophysics, atmospheric physics and chemistry, physical oceanography, surface sciences, earth sciences; Dir DOMINIQUE LE QUEAU.

RELIGION, SOCIOLOGY AND ANTHROPOLOGY

Centre Européen de Recherches sur les Congrégations et Ordres Religieux (CERCOR): Maison Rhône-Alpes des Sciences de l'Homme, 35 rue du 11 Novembre, 42023 Saint-Etienne Cedex 2; tel. 4-77-42-16-70; fax 4-77-42-16-84; e-mail nicole.bouter@univ-st-etienne.fr; f. 1981; a research group of CNRS (*q.v.*); studies the influence of monastic and religious orders on European life, from their origins to the present; 1,400 researchers in 35 countries; co-ordinates and promotes research (conferences, etc.), runs a specialized documentation service, publishes texts, etc.; library of 6,400 vols; Dir JEAN-FRANÇOIS COTTIER; publ. *Bulletin* (2 a year).

Institut d'Ethnologie du Muséum National d'Histoire Naturelle: Musée de l'Homme, Palais de Chaillot, Place du Trocadéro, 75116 Paris; tel. 1-44-05-73-45; fax 1-44-05-73-44; f. 1925; social anthropology, archaeology, linguistics; Dir M. PANOFF; publs *Collections Travaux et Mémoires*, *Mémoires*.

Institut d'Etudes Augustiniennes: 3 rue de l'Abbaye, 75006 Paris; tel. 1-43-54-80-25; fax 1-43-54-39-55; e-mail iea@wanadoo.fr; f. 1943; research into life, thought and times of St Augustine; library of 53,000 vols, 2,000 early printed books, 19 incunabula; Dir J.-C. FREDOUILLE; publs *Revue des Etudes Augustiniennes* (2 a year), *Recherches Augustiniennes* (irregular).

Institut du Monde Arabe: 1 rue des Fossés Saint Bernard, Place Mohammed-V, 75236 Paris Cedex 05; tel. 1-40-51-38-38; fax 1-43-54-76-45; e-mail ahull@imarabe.org; internet www.imarabe.org; f. 1980 by France and 21 Arab countries to promote knowledge of Arab culture and civilization; aims to encourage cultural exchanges, communication and co-operation between France and the Arab world, particularly in the fields of science and technology; international library and documentation centre of 60,000 vols, 1,200 periodicals; museum of Arab-Islamic civilization from 7th–19th c.; exhibitions of Arab contemporary art; audio-visual centre; Pres. YVES GUÉNA; Dir MOKHTAR TALEB-BENDIAB; publs *Qantara* (4 a year), *Al-Moukhtarat*.

Institut International d'Anthropologie: 1 place d'Iéna, 75116 Paris; tel. 1-47-93-09-73; fax 1-47-93-09-73; e-mail institutanthropologie@hotmail.fr; internet www.multimania.com/anthropa; f. 1920; 400 mems; affiliated to Ecole d'Anthropologie (*q.v.*); incorporates intercultural documentation centre; Pres. Dr A. PAJAULT; Sec.-Gen. Dr B. HUET; publ. *Nouvelle Revue Anthropologique* (irregular).

Institut Kurde de Paris (Kurdish Institute): 106 rue La Fayette, 75010 Paris; tel. 1-48-24-64-64; fax 1-48-24-64-66; e-mail info@filkp.org; internet www.institutkurde.org; f. 1983; research into Kurdish language, culture and history; Kurdish language teaching and publication of textbooks, maps, music cassettes, video films in Kurdish; library of 10,000 vols (accessible to the public); Pres. KENDAL NEZAN; publs *Information Bulletin* (monthly), *Kurmancî* (2 a year), *Etudes Kurdes* (2 a year).

Maison des Sciences de l'Homme: 54 blvd Raspail, 75270 Paris Cedex 06; tel. 1-49-54-20-00; fax 1-49-54-21-33; internet www.msh-paris.fr; f. 1963; supports research and int. co-operation in the social sciences; library of 120,000 vols, 2,000 current periodicals; Administrator M. AYMARD; publ. *MSH Informations* (quarterly).

Maison Rhône-Alpes de Sciences de l'Homme (MRASH): 14 ave Berthelot, 69363 Lyons Cedex 07; tel. 4-72-72-64-64; fax 4-72-80-00-08; f. 1988; supports research in the social sciences; Dir ALAIN BONNAFOUS.

TECHNOLOGY

Association Française pour la Protection des Eaux: 67 rue de Seine, 94140 Alfortville; tel. 1-43-75-84-84; fax 1-45-18-92-90; e-mail president@anpertos.org; internet www.anpertos.org; f. 1960; brings to public notice the necessity of protecting and preserving the quality and quantity of water-supplies, studies problems of water pollution and its prevention; 800 mems; Pres. P. L. TENAILLON; publ. *TOS*.

Centre National d'Etudes Spatiales (CNES): 2 place Maurice Quentin, 75001 Paris; internet www.cnes.fr; f. 1961; prepares national programmes of space research, provides information, promotes international co-operation; Pres. YANNICK D'ESCATHA; Dir-Gen. MICHEL LEFÈVRE.

France Telecom R & D: 38–40 rue du Général Leclerc, 92131 Issy les Moulineaux; tel. 1-45-29-44-44; internet www.rd.francetelecom.com; f. 1944; as the France Telecom research centre, is engaged in the development of future communications systems; as a technical centre, is responsible for according official approval for telecommunications equipment; 3,700 staff; library of 2,500 vols, 1,000 periodicals; CEO THIERRY BRETON; publs *L'Echo des Recherches* (quarterly), *Annales des Télécommunications* (every 2 months), *Bulletin Signalétique des Télécommunications* (monthly), *Annual Report*, *Innovation Telecom* (monthly), *Networks*.

Institut d'Hydrologie et de Climatologie: Faculté de Médecine, Pitié-Salpétrière, 91 blvd de l'Hôpital, 75013 Paris; tel. 1-45-83-69-92; 5 main laboratories in Paris, and further laboratories at the principal spas; Gen. Sec. Prof. G. OLIVE.

Institut Français du Pétrole: 1 et 4 ave de Bois-Préau, 92852 Rueil-Malmaison Cedex; tel. 1-47-52-60-00; fax 1-47-52-70-00; internet www.ifp.fr; f. 1945; scientific and technical organization for the purpose of research, development and industrialization, training specialists at the Ecole Nationale Supérieure du Pétrole et des Moteurs, information and documentation, international technical assistance in the different fields of the oil, gas and automotive engineering industries; library of 275,000 vols; Chair. and CEO O. APPERT; publs *Annual Report*, *Oil and Gas Science and Technology*.

Institut Laue-Langevin (ILL): BP 156, 38042 Grenoble Cedex 9; tel. 4-76-20-71-11; fax 4-76-48-39-06; e-mail welcome@ill.fr; internet www.ill.fr; f. 1967 by France and Fed. Repub. of Germany, UK became third equal partner in 1973; associated scientific members are Spain (1987), Switzerland (1988), Austria (1990), Russia (1996), Italy (1997) and Czech Republic (1999); research on fundamental and nuclear physics, solid state physics, metallurgy, chemistry and biology by using reactor neutrons; receives 1,500 guest scientists a year and carries out experiments on 25 ILL-funded instruments and several instruments funded by collaborating research groups; central facility is high flux beam reactor producing maximum flux of $1.5 \times 10^{15} n/cm^2/s$; library of 11,000 vols, 250 periodicals; Dir Dr C. CARLILE; publ. *Annual Report*.

Institut National de l'Audiovisuel: 4 ave de l'Europe, 94366 Bry-sur-Marne Cedex; tel. 1-49-83-23-67; fax 1-49-83-21-23; internet www.ina.fr; f. 1975; two research depts: *Recherche Prospective* (research combining telecommunications, computer science and audiovisual science); *Groupe de Recherches Musicales* (numerical development of synthesis and treatment of sound; psychoacoustics and musical perception, technology of electroacoustical instruments); library of 3,000 vols; Pres. EMMANUEL HOOG; publ. *Dossiers Audiovisuels* (every 2 months).

Institut National de l'Environnement Industriel et des Risques (INERIS) (National Institute for Environmental Technology and Hazards): Parc Technologique ALATA, BP 2, 60550 Verneuil-en-Halatte; tel. 3-44-55-66-77; fax 3-44-55-66-99; e-mail ineris@ineris.fr; internet www.ineris.fr; f. 1990; library of 28,000 vols; Dir-Gen. GEORGES LABROYE; publ. *INERIS Magazine* (5 a year).

Institut National de Recherche en Informatique et en Automatique (INRIA): Domaine de Voluceau, Rocquencourt, BP 105, 78153 Le Chesnay Cedex; tel. 1-39-63-55-11; fax 1-39-63-53-30; e-mail communication@inria.fr; internet www.inria.fr; f. 1967; five research units; library of 45,000 vols; Pres. and Dir-Gen. GILLES KAHN; publs *INédit* (newsletter), *Rapports de recherche et thèses*, *Rapports d'activités scientifiques*, *Les conférences et supports de cours INRIA*, *ERCIM News*.

Institut National des Sciences et Techniques Nucléaires (INSTN) (National Institute of Nuclear Science and Technology): CEA-Saclay, 91191 Gif-sur-Yvette Cedex; internet www-instn.cea.fr; f. 1956; provides courses in nuclear engineering, robotics and computer integrated manufacturing (CIM) and, in co-operation with the Universities, postgraduate courses in reactor physics, dynamics of structures, analytical chemistry, radiochemistry, metallurgy, data processing, robotics, radiobiology, energy management, the use of radioisotopes in medicine and pharmacy; Dir JEAN-PIERRE LE ROUX; Pres. BERNARD BIGOT.

Laboratoire de Biotechnologie de l'Environnement: Ave des Etangs, 11100 Narbonne; tel. 4-68-42-51-51; fax 4-68-42-51-60; internet www.montpellier.inra.fr/narbonne; f. 1895; attached to INRA; research in microbiological wastewater treatment; library of 5,000 vols; Dir JEAN-PHILIPPE DELGENÈS; publ. *Water Research*.

Office International de l'Eau: 21 rue de Madrid, 75008 Paris; tel. 1-44-90-88-60; fax 1-40-08-01-45; e-mail snide@oieau.fr; internet www.oieau.fr; f. 1991; documentation centre on water problems; library of 37,000 vols and 180,000 articles; Pres. M. RENARD; Dir D. PREUX; publ. *Information Eaux* (monthly).

Office National d'Etudes et de Recherches Aérospatiales (ONERA): 29 ave de la Division-Leclerc, 92322 Châtillon; tel. 1-46-73-40-40; fax 1-46-73-41-41; internet www.onera.fr; f. 1946 to develop, direct, and co-ordinate scientific and technical research in the field of aeronautics and space; library of 40,000 vols, 150,000 reports, 11,000 microfiches, 850 periodicals; Pres. MICHEL DE GLINIASTY; publ. *Aerospace Science and Technology* (English, 8 a year).

Libraries and Archives

Abbeville

Bibliothèque Municipale: Hôtel d'Emonville, place Clemenceau, BP 20010, 80101 Abbeville Cedex; tel. 3-22-24-95-16; fax 3-22-19-16-93; internet www.ville-abbeville.fr/Culture/biblio.html; f. 1643; 140,000 vols; Librarian P. HAZEBROUCK.

Aix-en-Provence

Bibliothèque Méjanes: 8–10 rue des Allumettes, 13090 Aix-en-Provence; tel. 4-42-91-98-88; fax 4-42-91-98-64; internet www.citedulivre-aix.com; f. 1810; 590,000 vols; Dir GILLES EBOLI.

Bibliothèque de l'Université d'Aix-Marseille III: 3 ave Robert-Schuman, 13626 Aix-en-Provence Cedex 1; tel. 4-42-17-24-40; fax 4-42-17-24-67; internet infobu.u-3mrs.fr; 156,000 vols, 273,000 periodicals, 86,000 theses; Librarian J. C. RODA.

Albi

Mediathèque Pierre Amalric: Ave Charles de Gaulle, 81000 Albi; tel. 5-63-38-56-10; fax 5-63-38-56-15; e-mail mediatheque@albi.fr; internet www.mairie-albi.fr/vivre/mediatheque.html; f. during the French Revolution; 300,000 vols; Librarian MATTHIEU DESACHY.

Amiens

Bibliothèque d'Amiens Métropole: 50 rue de la République, BP 542, 80005 Amiens Cedex 1; tel. 3-22-97-10-10; fax 3-22-97-10-70; internet www.bm-amiens.fr; f. 1826; 800,000 vols, 2,500 MSS, 300 incunabula; Chief Librarian JACQUELINE AYRAULT.

Bibliothèque de l'Université de Picardie Jules Verne: 15 placette Lafleur, BP 446, 80004 Amiens Cedex 01; tel. 3-22-82-71-65; fax 3-22-82-71-66; e-mail scd@-picardie.fr; internet www.bu.u-picardie.fr; f. 1966; 330,000 vols, 3,900 periodicals; Dirs F. MONTBRUN, B. LOCHER.

Angers

Bibliothèque Municipale: 49 rue Toussaint, 49100 Angers; tel. 2-41-24-25-50; fax 2-41-81-05-72; e-mail claudine.belayche@ville-angers.fr; internet www.bm.angers.fr; f. during the French Revolution; 400,000 vols, 2,120 MSS, 111 incunabula; Librarian CLAUDINE BELAYCHE.

Bibliothèque Universitaire d'Angers: 5 rue Le Nôtre, 49045 Angers Cedex; tel. 2-41-22-64-00; fax 2-41-22-64-05; e-mail bu@univ-angers.fr; internet bu.univ-angers.fr; f. 1970; Dir OLIVIER TACHEAU.

Avignon

Bibliothèque Municipale: 2 bis rue Laboureur, BP 349, 84025 Avignon Cedex 1; tel. 4-90-85-15-59; fax 4-90-14-65-61; e-mail bibliotheque.ceccano@wanadoo.fr; f. 1810; 300,000 vols, 7,000 MSS, 700 incunabula, 2,700 musical scores, 40,000 engravings and maps, 30,000 coins; Chief Librarian CÉCILE FRANC.

Bibliothèque Universitaire: 74 rue Louis Pasteur, 84018 Avignon Cedex 1; tel. 4-90-16-27-60; fax 4-90-16-27-70; e-mail bu@univ-avignon.fr; internet www.bu.univ-avignon.fr; f. 1968; 100,000 books, 1,200 periodicals, 3,000 electronic periodicals; Dir FRANÇOISE FEBVRE.

Besançon

Bibliothèques Municipales: 1 rue de la Bibliothèque, BP 09, 25012 Besançon Cedex; tel. 3-81-87-81-40; fax 3-81-61-98-77; e-mail marie-claire.waille@besancon.com; internet www.besancon.com/biblio/francais/bm1.htm; f. 1694; 350,000 vols, 3,800 MSS, 1,000 incunabula, etc.; Dir MARIE-CLAIRE WAILLE.

Bibliothèque de l'Université de Franche-Comté: 32 rue Mégevand, BP 1057, 25001 Besançon Cedex; tel. 3-81-66-53-50; fax 3-81-66-53-00; internet scd.univ-fcomte.fr; f. 1880; Dir SOPHIE DESSEIGNE.

Bordeaux

Bibliothèque Municipale: 85 cours du Maréchal Juin, 33075 Bordeaux Cedex; tel. 5-56-10-30-00; fax 5-56-10-30-90; e-mail bibli@mairie-bordeaux.fr; internet www.mairie-bordeaux.fr/bibliotheque/bibintro.htm; f. 1736; 900,000 vols, 4,200 MSS, 333 incunbula, 1,000 current periodicals; Chief Librarian PIERRE BOTINEAU.

Service Interétablissements de Coopération Documentaire des Universités de Bordeaux: 4 ave des Arts, 33607 Pessac Cedex; tel. 5-56-84-86-86; fax 5-56-84-86-96; e-mail sicod@bu.u-bordeaux.fr; internet www.montesquieu.u-bordeaux.fr/presentation/sicod.html; 3,200,000 vols; Dir GÉRARD BRIAND.

Brest

Service Commun de Documentation:; tel. 2-98-01-64-04; fax 2-98-47-75-25; e-mail scd@univ-brest.fr; internet www.univ-brest.fr; f. 1968; Dir ALAIN SAINSOT.

Caen

Bibliothèque de Caen: Place Louis-Guillouard, 14053 Caen Cedex; tel. 2-31-30-47-00; fax 2-31-30-47-01; e-mail bm@ville-caen.fr; internet www.bm.ville-caen.fr; f. 1809; 650,000 vols, 3,300 periodicals, 12,000 pre-1800 printed items, 40,000 slides, 4,900 video-cassettes, 70,000 compact discs, 7,500 talking books for the visually impaired, 1,815 software disks for micro-computer and CD-ROMs; special Normandy collection; Librarian NOËLLA DU PLESSIS.

Bibliothèque de l'Université de Caen: Esplanade de la Paix, BP 5186, 14032 Caen Cédex; tel. 2-31-56-58-70; fax 2-31-56-56-13; e-mail bibliotheque@unicaen.fr; internet www.unicaen.fr/menu_ucbn/menu-documentation.php; Dir FRANÇOISE BERMANN.

Cambrai

Bibliothèque Municipale Classée: 37 rue St Georges, BP 179, 59403 Cambrai Cedex; tel. 3-27-82-93-93; fax 3-27-82-93-94; e-mail admin@media-cambrai.com; f. 1791; 130,000 vols, 1,400 MSS, 600 incunabula; Librarian BÉNÉDICTE TÉROUANNE.

Carpentras

Bibliothèque Inguimbertine: 234 blvd Albin-Durand, 84200 Carpentras; tel. 4-90-63-04-92; fax 4-90-63-19-11; e-mail bib.inguimbertine@ville-carpentras.fr; f. 1745; 265,000 vols, 3,126 MSS; Librarian ISABELLE BATTEZ.

Châlons-sur-Marne

Bibliothèque Municipale à Vocation Régionale Georges Pompidou: 68 rue Léon-Bourgeois, 51038 Châlons-en-Champagne Cedex; tel. 3-26-26-94-30; fax 3-26-26-94-32; e-mail bibliotheque.mairie@chalons-en-champagne.net; internet www.chalons-en-champagne.net/bmvr; f. 1803; 330,000 vols, 2,000 MSS, 120 incunabula; Librarian RÉGIS DUTRÉMÉE.

Chambéry

Bibliothèque de l'Université de Savoie: route de l'Eglise, Jacob-Bellecombette BP 1104, 73011 Chambéry Cedex; tel. 4-79-75-85-64; fax 4-79-75-84-90; e-mail commanay@univ-savoie.fr; internet bib.univ-savoie.fr; f. 1962; 125,000 vols, 701 periodicals; Chief Librarian COLETTE COMMANAY.

Clermont-Ferrand

Bibliothèque Municipale et Interuniversitaire: 1 blvd Lafayette, BP 27, 63001 Clermont-Ferrand Cedex 01; tel. 4-73-40-62-40; fax 4-73-40-62-19; e-mail bmiu@univ-bpclermont.fr; internet bmiu.univ-bpclermont.fr; f. 1902; 682,437 vols, 2,587 current periodicals; Dir LIVIA RAPATEL.

Colmar

Bibliothèque de la Ville de Colmar: 1 place des Martyrs de la Résistance, BP 509, 68021 Colmar Cedex; tel. 3-89-24-48-18; fax 3-89-23-33-80; e-mail bibliotheque@ville-colmar.com; f. 1803; 400,000 vols, 1,300 MSS, 2,500 incunabula; Chief Librarian FRANCIS GUETH.

Dijon

Bibliothèque Municipale: 3–7 rue de l'Ecole-de-Droit, 21000 Dijon; tel. 3-80-44-94-14; fax 3-80-44-94-34; e-mail bmdijon@ville-dijon.fr; internet bm-dijon.fr; f. 1701; 460,000 vols; Chief Librarian ANDRÉ-PIERRE SYREN.

Bibliothèque de l'Université de Bourgogne: 6 rue Sully, 21000 Dijon; tel. 3-80-39-51-20; Dir F. HAGENE.

Douai

Bibliothèque Municipale: rue de la Fonderie, 59500 Douai; tel. 3-27-97-88-51; fax 3-27-99-71-80; e-mail bibliotheque@biblio.ville-douai.fr; internet www.ville-douai.fr/culture/bibliot/accueil.htm; f. 1770; 250,000 vols, 2,000 MSS, 300 incunabula, 200 periodicals; Librarian MICHELE DEMARCY.

Grenoble

Bibliothèque Municipale d'Etude et d'Information: 12 blvd Maréchal Lyautey, BP 1095, 38021 Grenoble Cedex 1; tel. 4-76-86-21-00; fax 4-76-86-21-19; e-mail info@bm-grenoble.fr; internet www.bm-grenoble.fr; f. 1772; 600,000 vols, 654 incunabula, 20,980 MSS, 81,000 prints, 2,575 maps; special collection: local history; Dir CATHERINE POUYET.

Service de Co-opération Documentaire Sciences-Médecine: BP 66, 38402 St Martin d'Hères; tel. 4-76-51-42-84; fax 4-76-51-98-51; internet www.ujf-grenoble.fr/BUS; linked with university science and medical libraries; Dir MARIE-FRANCE ROCHARD.

Service Interétablissements de Coopération Documentaire: Domaine universitaire BP 85, 38402 St Martin d'Hères Cedex; tel. 4-76-82-61-61; fax 4-76-82-61-68; e-mail sicd2admin@upmf-grenoble.fr; internet odyssee.upmf-grenoble.fr; f. 1880; Dir MARIE-NOËLLE ICARDO.

Haguenau

Musée Historique et Archives Municipales: 9 rue du Maréchal Foch, BP 40 261, 67504 Haguenau Cedex; tel. 3-88-93-79-22; fax 3-88-93-48-12; e-mail musees-archives@ville-hagenau.fr; f. 1899; 8,000 vols; Dir PIA WENDLING; publ. *Etudes Haguenoviennes* (annual).

La Rochelle

Médiathèque: Communauté de Villes, Ave Marillac, 17042 La Rochelle Cedex 1; tel. 5-46-45-71-71; fax 5-46-45-03-22; e-mail mediatheque@cda-larochelle.org; f. 1750; 360,000 vols; Librarian BRUNO CARBONE.

Le Havre

Bibliothèque Municipale: 17 rue Jules Lecesne, 76600 Le Havre; tel. 2-32-74-07-40; fax 2-32-74-07-50; e-mail biblio@ville-lehavre.fr; internet www.ville-lehavre.fr/quotidien/culture/bibliotheque/cadre.htm; f. 1796; public borrowing, reference, record library; 389,237 vols, 1,449 periodicals, 1,020 MSS; Librarian PATRICIA DOULERS.

Le Mans

Bibliothèque de l'Université du Maine: Avenue Olivier Messiaen, 72085 Le Mans Cedex 09; tel. 2-43-83-30-48; fax 2-43-83-35-37; e-mail bu@univ-lemans.fr; internet scd.univ-lemans.fr; 140,000 vols, 800 periodicals; Dir C. MENIL.

Lille

Bibliothèque Municipale: 34 rue Edouard Delesalle, 59043 Lille Cedex; tel. 3-20-15-97-20; fax 3-20-63-94-54; e-mail bmlille@mairie-lille.fr; f. 1726; 650,000 vols; Librarian DOMINIQUE AROT.

Bibliothèque de l'Université des Sciences et Technologies de Lille: Service commun de la documentation de Lille I: Ave Henri Poincaré, BP 155, 59653 Villeneuve d'Ascq Cedex; tel. 3-20-43-44-10; fax 3-20-33-71-04; e-mail jean-bernard.marino@univ-lille1.fr; internet www.univ-lille1.fr/bustl; 160,000 books, 60,000 theses; economics, humanities, technology, science; Chief Librarian JEAN-BERNARD MARINO.

Service Commun de la Documentation de Lille II: (Secteur Médecine/Pharmacie and Secteur Droit/Gestion): 1 place Déliot, BP 179, 59017 Lille Cedex; tel. 3-20-90-76-50; fax 3-20-90-76-54; internet wwwscd.univ-lille2.fr; f. 1993; Chief Librarian BRIGITTE MULETTE.

Service Commun de la Documentation de l'Université de Lille III — Charles de Gaulle: Domaine universitaire du Pont-de-bois, BP 99, 59652 Villeneuve d'Ascq Cedex; tel. 3-20-41-70-00; fax 3-20-91-46-50; internet www.univ-lille3.fr/portail/index.php?page=Scd; Dir JEAN-PAUL CHADOURNE.

Limoges

Bibliothèque Francophone Multimédia: 2 rue Louis Longequeue, 87032 Limoges Cedex; tel. 5-55-45-96-00; fax 5-55-45-96-96; e-mail francophonie@bm-limoges.fr; internet www.francophonie-limoges.com; f. 1804; 530,000 vols, 900 periodicals, 14,000 videos, 32,000 records; spec. collns incl. enamels, ceramics, porcelain; Librarian FRANÇOISE DIET-ESCARFAIL.

Bibliothèque de l'Université de Limoges: 39C rue Camille-Guérin, 87031 Limoges Cedex; tel. 5-55-43-57-00; fax 5-55-43-57-01; e-mail rohou@unilim.fr; internet www-scd.unilim.fr; f. 1965; 100,000 vols; Dir ODILE ROHOU.

Lyons

Bibliothèque Interuniversitaire de Lettres et Sciences Humaines: 5 parvis René-Descartes, BP 7000, 69342 Lyons; tel. 4-37-37-65-00; internet biu.ens-lsh.fr/biu; Dir CHARLES MICOL.

Bibliothèque Municipale: 30 blvd Vivier-Merle, 69431 Lyons Cedex 03; tel. 4-78-62-18-00; fax 4-78-62-19-49; e-mail bm@bm-lyon.fr; internet www.bm-lyon.fr; f. 1565; 2,350,000 vols, 12,449 MSS, 1,157 incunabula, 130,000 prints, 12,399 periodicals, 172,000 records, 59,883 photographs; Dir PATRICK BAZIN.

Marseilles

Bibliothèque et Centre de Documentation, Chambre de Commerce et d'Industrie Marseille-Provence: Palais de la Bourse, La Canebière, BP 1856, 13222 Marseilles Cedex 1; tel. 4-91-39-33-99; fax 4-91-91-42-25; f. 1872; economics, law, business, industry, commerce, agriculture, marine, Provence, overseas, history, geography; on-line information service; 60,000 vols, 60,000 brochures, 3,000 periodicals; Librarian FRANÇOIS NICOULAUD.

Bibliothèque Municipale: 23 rue de la providence, 13001 Marseilles; tel. 4-91-55-90-00; fax 4-91-55-23-44; internet www.bmvr.mairie-marseille.fr; f. 1800; 750,000 vols; Dir FRANÇOIS LARBRE.

Bibliothèque de l'Université de la Méditerranée (Aix-Marseille II): Campus Timone, 27 blvd Jean Moulin, 13385 Marseilles Cedex 05; tel. 4-91-32-45-37; fax 4-91-25-60-22; e-mail anne.dujol@bu2.univ-mrs.fr; internet bu2.timone.univ-mrs.fr; f. 1987; 7 academic libraries in Marseilles, Aix en Provence and Gap; medicine, pharmacy, dental sciences, sports econ.; rare books on medicine; Dir RONAN LAGADIC.

Metz

Bibliothèque Municipale: 1 cour Elie Fleur, 57000 Metz; tel. 3-87-55-53-33; fax 3-87-30-42-88; internet bm.mairie-metz.fr/metz; f. 1811; 400,000 vols, 1,195 MSS, 5,000 engravings, 463 incunabula; video cassettes, slides; Chief Librarian PIERRE LOUIS.

Service Commun de Documentation de l'Université Paul Verlaine–Metz: Ile du Saulcy, 57045 Metz Cedex 1; tel. 3-87-31-50-80; fax 3-87-33-22-90; e-mail colinmaire@scd.univ-metz.fr; internet www.scd.univ-metz.fr; f. 1972; 250,000 vols, 1,100 periodicals; Dir HERVÉ COLINMAIRE.

Montpellier

Bibliothèque Interuniversitaire: Administration: 60 rue des Etats généraux, 34965 Montpellier Cedex 2; tel. 4-67-13-43-50; fax 4-67-13-43-51; e-mail biu.secretariat@sc.univ-montp1.fr; internet www.biu.univ-montp1.fr; f. 1890; Chief Librarian PIERRE GAILLARD.

Bibliothèque Municipale: 240 rue de l'Acropole, 34000 Montpellier; tel. 4-67-34-87-00; fax 4-67-34-87-01; e-mail bm.secretariat@ville-montpellier.fr; internet sbib.bm.montpellier-agglo.com; f. during the French Revolution; 720,000 vols; Librarian M. G. GUDIN DE VALLERIN.

Mulhouse

Bibliothèque de l'Université et de la Société Industrielle de Mulhouse (Section Histoire des Sciences): 12 rue de la Bourse, 68100 Mulhouse; tel. 3-89-56-12-74; fax 3-89-33-63-79; e-mail f.pascal@uha.fr; internet www.scd.uha.fr; f. 1826; 30,000 vols, 700 (and 150 current) periodicals; Dir PHILIPPE RUSSELL.

Université de Haute Alsace, Service Commun de Documentation: 8 rue des Frères Lumière, 68093 Mulhouse; tel. 3-89-33-63-60; fax 3-89-33-63-79; e-mail scdmulhouse@uha.fr; internet www.scd.uha.fr; f. 1977; Dir. PHILIPPE RUSSELL.

Nancy

Bibliothèque Municipale: 43 rue Stanislas, 54042 Nancy Cedex; tel. 3-83-37-38-83; fax 3-83-37-63-29; e-mail bmnancy@mairie-nancy.fr; f. 1750; 500,000 vols; Chief Librarian ANDRÉ MARKIEWICZ.

Service Commun de Documentation: 30 rue Lionnois, 54000 Nancy; tel. 3-83-68-22-00; fax 3-83-68-22-03; e-mail Sebastien.Bogaert@scd.uhp-nancy.fr; internet scd.uhp-nancy.fr; 356,000 vols, 4,100 periodicals; Chief Librarian SEBASTIEN BOGAERT.

Nantes

Bibliothèque Municipale: 15 rue de l'Hermonnière, BP 44113, 44041 Nantes Cedex 01; tel. 2-40-41-95-95; fax 2-40-41-42-00; e-mail bm@mairie-nantes.fr; internet www.bm.nantes.fr; f. 1753; 900,000 vols; Chief Librarian AGNÈS MARCETTEAU.

Bibliothèque Universitaire de Nantes: Chemin de la Censive du Tertre, BP 32211, 44322 Nantes Cedex 03; tel. 2-40-14-12-30; internet www.bu.univ-nantes.fr; f. 1962; 260,000 vols, 5,000 periodicals; Chief Librarian MICHELLE GUIOT.

Nice

Bibliothèque Municipale à Vocation Régionale de Nice: 1 ave Saint-Jean-Baptiste, 06364 Nice Cedex 4; tel. 4-97-13-48-00; fax 4-97-13-48-05; e-mail direction@bmvr-nice.com.fr; internet www.bmvr-nice.com.fr/; f. 1802; 1m. vols, 208,700 compact discs, records and cassettes, 17,002 video cassettes, 519 CD-ROMs; network of 15 branch libraries; special collection on Michel Butor; Chief Librarian FRANÇOISE MICHELIZZA.

Bibliothèque de l'Université de Nice–Sophia Antipolis: Parc Valrose, BP 2053, 06101 Nice Cedex 02; tel. 4-92-07-60-00; fax 4-92-07-60-10; internet www.unice.fr/BU; f. 1963; 260,000 vols, 4,400 periodicals; Dir LOUIS KLEE.

Nîmes

Carré d'Art Bibliothèque: place de la Maison-Carrée, 30033 Nîmes Cedex; tel. 4-66-76-35-03; fax 4-66-76-35-10; e-mail bibiotheque.carre.art.de.nimes@wanadoo.fr; f. 1803; 323,000 vols, 590 periodicals, 800 MSS, 40,000 ancient books, 19,000 CDs; Chief Librarian J.-M. MASSADAU; publ. *Journal Carré d'Art* (3 a year).

Orléans

Médiathèque d'Orléans: 1 place Gambetta, 45043 Orléans Cedex 1; tel. 2-38-65-45-45; fax 2-38-65-45-40; e-mail bibliotheques@ville-orleans.fr; internet 81.80.204.170; f. 1714; 420,000 vols, 2,550 MSS; Librarian AGNÈS CHEVALIER.

Service Commun de la Documentation de l'Université d'Orléans: Domaine de la Source, 6 rue de Tours, 45072 Orléans Cedex 02; tel. 2-38-41-71-84; fax 2-38-41-71-87; e-mail secretariat.scd@univ-orleans.fr; internet www.univ-orleans.fr/SCD; f. 1965; 196,000 vols and theses, 1,100 periodicals; Dir CATHERINE MOREAU.

Paris

American Library in Paris: 10 rue du Général Camou, 75007 Paris; tel. 1-53-59-12-60; fax 1-45-50-25-83; e-mail alparis@noos.fr; internet americanlibraryinparis.org; f. 1920; private English-language lending and reference library open to all nationalities (subject to payment of fees); 115,000 vols, 450 periodicals; Chair. CHARMAINE DONNELLY; Dir SHIRLEY LAMBERT.

Archives de France: 56 rue des Francs-Bourgeois, 75141 Paris Cedex 03; tel. 1-40-27-60-00; fax 1-40-27-66-06; internet www.archivesdefrance.culture.gouv.fr; f. 1790; 480 km. documents; Dir-Gen. MARTINE DE BOISDEFFRE.

Attached units:

Centre des Archives Contemporaines: 2 rue des Archives, 77300 Fontainebleau; tel. 1-64-31-73-00; fax 1-64-31-73-03; Chief Curator CHRISTINE PETILLAT.

Centre des Archives du Monde du Travail: 78 blvd du Général Leclerc BP 405, 59057 Roubaix; tel. 3-20-65-38-00; fax 3-20-65-38-01; f. 1993; Chief Curator FRANÇOISE BOSMAN.

Centre des Archives d'Outre-Mer: 29 chemin du Moulin-Detesta, 13090 Aix-en-Provence; tel. 4-42-93-38-50; fax 4-42-93-38-89; f. 1962; Chief Curator MARTINE CORNEDE.

Centre Historique des Archives Nationales: 60 rue des Francs-Bourgeois, 75003 Paris; Chief Curator GÉRARD ERMISSE.

Centre National du Microfilm: Domaine d'Espeyran, 30800 St-Gilles-du-Gard; tel. 4-66-87-30-09; fax 4-66-87-03-44; Chief Curator ANNE DEBANT.

Bibliothèque Administrative de la Ville de Paris: Hôtel de Ville, 75196 Paris RP; tel. 1-42-76-48-87; fax 1-42-76-63-78; e-mail dac.bavp@mairie-paris.fr; f. 1872; 500,000 vols (reports, studies, statistics, official texts, budgets, etc.); 3,200 periodicals, 8,000 photographs, 1,800 MSS, 12,000 architectural designs, 40,000 microfiches, 2,000 microfilms; French and foreign local administration; French legislation; economic, political and social history; legislation of ex-French colonies; general biography; Chief Librarian PIERRE CASSELLE.

Bibliothèque Centrale et Archives des Musées Nationaux: 6 rue des Pyramides, 75041 Paris Cedex 01; tel. 1-40-20-52-66; fax 1-40-20-51-69; e-mail sbadg.dmf@culture.gouv.fr; internet www.inha.fr/bibliotheque/bcmn.html; f. 1871; 160,000 vols, 1,800 periodicals; books and MSS connected with the Louvre and the National Museums (Egyptology collection, Oriental antiquities, Greco-Roman antiquities, drawings, paintings and sculptures); open only to curators and authorized persons; Archivist and Librarian ISABELLE LE MASNE DE CHERMONT.

Bibliothèque Centrale de l'Ecole Polytechnique: Plateau de Saclay, 91128 Palaiseau Cedex; tel. 1-69-33-40-76; fax 1-69-33-28-33; internet www.bibliotheque.polytechnique.fr; f. 1794; 300,000 vols, 1,700 periodicals; Chief Librarian MADELEINE DE FUENTES.

Bibliothèque Centrale du Muséum National d'Histoire Naturelle: 38 rue Geoffroy-Saint-Hilaire, 75005 Paris; tel. 1-40-79-36-27; fax 1-40-79-36-56; e-mail mducreux@mnhn.fr; internet www.mnhn.fr/mnhn/bcm; f. 1635; 405,000 books, 7,050 MSS, 12,000 periodicals; Chief Librarian MICHELLE LENOIR.

Bibliothèque de Documentation Internationale Contemporaine: Centre Universitaire, 6 allée de l'Université, 92001 Nanterre Cedex; tel. 1-40-97-79-00; fax 1-40-97-79-40; e-mail courrier@bdic.fr; internet www.bdic.fr; f. 1914; over 1,000,000 vols, 90,000 series of periodicals, history of the two World Wars and international relations since beginning 20th c., social and revolutionary movements, political emigrations; Dir GENEVIÈVE DREYFUS-ARMAND; publs *Journal* (irregular), *Matériaux pour l'Histoire de Notre Temps* (3 a year).

Bibliothèque de Géographie: 191 rue Saint-Jacques, 75005 Paris; tel. 1-44-32-14-63; fax 1-44-32-14-67; e-mail bibgeo@univ-paris1.fr; 78,000 vols, 4,000 periodicals, 25,000 maps, 40,000 photographs; Librarian Mme JOSEPH.

Bibliothèque de la Cour des Comptes: 13 rue Cambon, 75100 Paris RP; tel. 1-42-98-97-12; fax 1-42-60-01-59; e-mail scda@courrier.cour-des-comptes-crc.fr; f. 1807 by Napoleon I; 50,000 vols on finance, law and economy; Librarian (vacant).

Bibliothèque de la Direction Générale de l'Institut National de la Statistique et des Etudes Economiques: 18 blvd Adolphe Pinard, 75675 Paris Cedex 14; tel. 1-41-17-53-43; fax 1-41-17-50-69; f. 1946; 100,000 vols, 5,000 periodicals; Head of Documentation Division GEORGES BORIE; Curator PIERRE-YVES RENARD.

Bibliothèque de la Sorbonne: 13 rue de la Sorbonne, 75257 Paris Cedex 05; tel. 1-40-46-30-27; fax 1-40-46-30-44; e-mail adminst@biu.sorbonne.fr; f. 1762; over 3 million vols, 13,000 periodicals; Chief Librarian CATHERINE GAILLARD; publ. *Mélanges de la Bibliothèque de la Sorbonne*.

Bibliothèque de l'Académie Nationale de Médecine: 16 rue Bonaparte, 75272 Paris Cedex 06; tel. 1-46-34-60-70; fax 1-43-25-84-14; e-mail bibliotheque@acadmed.univ-paris5.fr; f. 1820; 350,000 vols, 113 incunabula, 4000 periodicals (500 current); 7,000 biographical dossiers; Archives of the Académie Royale de Chirurgie (1731–93), Société Royale de Médecine (1776–93), Société de l'Ecole de Médecine (1800–21), Comité Central de Vaccine (1803–23) and Académie de Médecine (since 1820); also portraits, medals and sculptures; Librarian LAURENCE CAMOUS; publ. *Bulletin de l'Académie nationale de Médecine* (9 a year).

Bibliothèque de l'Arsenal: 1 rue de Sully, 75004 Paris; tel. 1-42-77-44-21; fax 1-42-77-01-63; internet www.bnf.fr/pages/connaitr/ars_site.htm; f. 1756 by the Marquess of Paulmy, public library in 1797; inc. with Bibliothèque Nationale 1934; specializes in literature; open to scholars; contains 100,000 vols; 15,000 MSS, many autographs; includes archives of the Bastille; 100,000 prints, 18th-century maps; houses the performing arts collection of the Bibliothèque Nationale (2,500,000 vols and other items); Dir (vacant).

Bibliothèque de l'Assemblée Nationale: Palais Bourbon, 75007 Paris; tel. 1-40-63-64-74; fax 1-40-63-52-53; e-mail bibliotheque@assemblee-nationale.fr; f. 1796; 690,000 vols, 1,870 MSS, and 80 incunabula, 2,800 periodicals, 50,000 microfiches, 2,500 microfilms, mainly on history, political science, law, economy; Dir FABRICE COSTA; publs *Sélection d'articles de périodiques*, *Sélection d'ouvrages récemment acquis* (8 a year).

Bibliothèque de l'Ecole Nationale Supérieure des Mines: 60 blvd Saint-Michel, 75272 Paris Cedex 06; tel. 1-40-51-90-56; fax 1-43-25-53-58; e-mail bib@bib.ensmp.fr; internet bib.ensmp.fr; f. 1783; 300,000 vols, 3,820 periodicals, 30,000 maps; Chief Librarian Mme F. MASSON.

Bibliothèque de l'Ecole Normale Supérieure: 45 rue d'Ulm, 75230 Paris Cedex 05; internet halley.ens.fr; f. 1810; 500,000 vols; Chief Librarian LAURE LÉVEILLÉ.

Bibliothèque de l'Institut de France: 23 quai Conti, 75006 Paris; tel. 1-44-41-44-10; fax 1-44-41-44-11; e-mail mireille.pastoureau@bif.univ-paris5.fr; internet www.bibliotheque-institutdefrance.fr; f. 1795; 1,000,000 vols, 8,000 periodicals, 8,000 MSS; Chief Curator Dr MIREILLE PASTOUREAU.

Bibliothèque de l'Institut National de Recherche Pédagogique: 5 parvis René Descartes, 69342 Lyons Cedex 07; tel. 1-37-37-66-10; fax 1-37-37-66-06; e-mail soula@inrp.fr; internet www.inrp.fr; f. 1879; 550,000 vols, 5,000 periodicals, 100,000 textbooks; educational research; Chief Librarian MARIE-LOUISE SOULA.

Bibliothèque de l'Institut National d'Histoire de l'Art–Collections Jacques Doucet: 2 rue Vivienne, 75002 Paris; 58 rue de Richelieu, 75083 Paris Cedex 02; tel. 1-47-03-76-23; fax 1-47-03-76-30; e-mail bibliotheque@inha.fr; internet www.inha.fr; f. 1918; 450,000 vols, 6,674 periodicals; Chief Librarian MARTINE POULAIN.

Bibliothèque des Avocats à la Cour d'Appel: Palais de Justice, 75001 Paris; f. 1708; confiscated during the Revolution, but refounded in 1810; 160,000 vols; not open to the public; Librarian MICHEL BRICHARD.

Bibliothèque du Conservatoire National des Arts et Métiers: 292 rue St-Martin, 75141 Paris Cedex 03; tel. 1-40-27-27-03; fax 1-40-27-29-87; f. 1794; 150,000 vols, 3,600 periodicals on science, technology, political economy; special collections: exhibition catalogues, Bartholdi, Organum; Librarian Mme BRIGITTE ROZET.

Bibliothèque du Ministère des Affaires Etrangères: 37 quai d'Orsay, 75351 Paris; tel. 1-43-17-42-61; fax 1-43-17-51-48; f. in 17th c.; over 500,000 vols; Librarian MARIE GALLUP.

Bibliothèque du Sénat: Palais du Luxembourg, 75291 Paris Cedex 06; tel. 1-42-34-35-39; fax 1-42-34-27-05; f. 1818; 450,000 vols, chiefly on history and law, 1,343 MSS and 45,000 prints; open to members of Parliament; Dir PHILIPPE MARTIAL.

Bibliothèque du Service Historique de la Marine: Château de Vincennes, BP 122, 00481 Armées; tel. 1-43-28-81-50; fax 1-43-28-31-60; e-mail contact@servicehistorique.marine.defense.gouv.fr; internet www.servicehistorique.marine.defense.gouv.fr; f. 1919; 300,000 vols on naval history; Chief Curator ALAIN MORGAT.

Bibliothèque du Service Historique de l'Armée de Terre: Château de Vincennes, BP 107, 00481 Armées; tel. 1-41-93-34-62; over 600,000 vols; f. *c.*1800; 16th- to 20th-century science and military history, French history, cartography; Librarian RAPHAËL MASSON.

Bibliothèque et Archives du Conseil d'Etat: Place du Palais-Royal, 75100 Paris 01 SP; tel. 1-40-20-81-31; fax 1-42-61-69-95; e-mail biblio.ce@wanadoo.fr; internet www.conseil-etat.fr; f. 1871; 100,000 vols on jurisprudence, administrative science, political science and legislation; Librarian SERGE BOUFFANGE.

Bibliothèque Forney: 1 rue du Figuier, 75004 Paris; tel. 1-42-78-14-60; fax 1-42-78-22-59; f. 1886; 135,000 vols, 20,000 periodicals, *c.* 250,000 other items, chiefly on arts and crafts; Librarian A.-C. LELIEUR.

Bibliothèque Georges Duhamel: Square Brieussel Bourgeois, 78200 Mantes-la-Jolie; tel. 1-34-78-80-73; f. 1797; encyclopaedic library; 88,882 vols; record library: 6,400 records, 1,500 compact discs; permanent exhibitions in Georges Duhamel picture gallery; Dir PAUL JOLAS; publ. *Rencontres Artistiques et Littéraires*.

Bibliothèque Gustav Mahler: 11 bis rue Vézelay, 75008 Paris; tel. 1-53-89-09-10; fax 1-43-59-70-22; internet www.bgm.org; f. 1986; reference collection for musicians, students, researchers; 30,000 vols, 35,000 musical scores, 6,000 reviews, 70,000 records; archives: MSS, letters, photos, etc. on Mahler's life and works; also 16,000 dossiers on contemporary composers, autographs and MSS of 19th- and 20th-century musicians; Pres. PIERRE BERGÉ; Librarian

ALAIN GALLIARI; publ. *Bulletin d'information de la BMGM* (annually).

Bibliothèque Historique de la Ville de Paris: 24 rue Pavée, 75004 Paris; tel. 1-44-59-29-40; fax 1-42-74-03-16; f. 1871; 650,000 vols, 15,000 MSS on history of Paris; Curator JEAN DERENS.

Bibliothèque Interuniversitaire Cujas de Droit et Sciences Economiques: 2 rue Cujas, 75005 Paris; tel. 1-44-07-79-87; fax 1-44-07-78-32; e-mail cujasdir@univ-paris1.fr; internet www-cujas.univ-paris1.fr; f. 1876; 1,000,000 vols; Chief Librarian DOMINIQUE ROCHE.

Bibliothèque Interuniversitaire de Médecine: 12 rue de l'Ecole-de-Médecine, 75270 Paris Cedex 06; tel. 1-40-46-19-51; fax 1-44-41-10-20; e-mail bium@bium.univ-paris5.fr; internet www.bium.univ-paris5.fr; f. 1733; 1,000,000 vols, 30,000 pre-1800 books and theses, 109 incunabula, 20,000 periodicals (2,300 current); Chief Librarian GUY COBOLET.

Bibliothèque Interuniversitaire de Pharmacie: 4 ave de l'Observatoire, 75270 Paris Cedex 06; tel. 1-53-73-95-23; fax 1-53-73-95-05; e-mail piketky@pharmacie.univ-paris5.fr; internet www.biup.univ-paris5.fr; f. 1570; centre for the acquisition and dispersion of scientific and technical information (CADIST) on beauty care; 280,000 vols, 945 periodicals, archives of Parisian apothecaries; Dir Mme FRANÇOISE MALET.

Bibliothèque Interuniversitaire des Langues Orientales: 4 rue de Lille, 75007 Paris; tel. 1-44-77-87-20; fax 1-44-77-87-30; e-mail biulo@idf.ext.jussieu.fr; internet www.univ-paris3.fr; f. 1868; languages and cultures of countries in Asia, Africa, Central and Eastern Europe, and Middle Eastern, Oceanian and Amerindian languages; 660,000 vols, 8,695 periodicals; Dir NELLY GUILLAUME.

Bibliothèque Mazarine: 23 quai de Conti, 75006 Paris; tel. 1-44-41-44-06; fax 1-44-41-44-07; e-mail webmaster@bibliotheque-mazarine.fr; internet www.bibliotheque-mazarine.fr; f. 1643 by Cardinal Mazarin, since 1945; attached to Institut de France; 500,000 vols, 4,600 MSS, 2,500 incunabula; Dir CHRISTIAN PÉLIGRY.

Bibliothèque-Musée de l'Opéra: 8 rue Scribe, 75009 Paris; tel. 1-53-79-37-40; fax 1-53-79-39-59; internet www.bnf.fr; f. 1875; a service of Bibliothèque Nationale, music dept; 200,000 vols, 30,000 scores, 80,000 libretti, 100,000 drawings, 40,000 lithographs, 100,000 photographs, 2,000 periodicals; Dir ODILE DUPONT; Curator ROMAIN FEIST.

Bibliothèque Nationale de France: quai François Mauriac, 75013 Paris; tel. 1-53-79-53-79; internet www.bnf.fr; f. 14th century; specialized depts: printed books (11,000,000 vols), periodicals (350,000 titles), maps and plans (890,000), prints and photographs (11m.), MSS (350,000 bound vols), coins, medals and antiques (580,000 items), music (incl. Bibliothèque-Musée de l'Opéra (q.v.)), sound archive and audiovisual aids (1m. discs and tape recordings, 20,000 films, 40,000 video materials), performing arts (3m. items), Bibliothèque de l'Arsenal (q.v.); Pres. JEAN-NOËL JEANNENEY; Dir-Gen. AGNÈS SAAL; publs *Chronique de la Bibliothèque Nationale de France* (6 a year), *Bibliographie nationale Française* (every 2 weeks).

Bibliothèque Polonaise: 6 quai d'Orléans, 75004 Paris; tel. 1-43-54-35-61; f. 1854; 200,000 vols, 25,000 drawings and engravings, sculptures, paintings, 8,000 maps (16th to 20th centuries), 5,000 photographs, archives of 19th- and 20th-century Polish emigration to France; Chopin memorabilia; also posters, medals and periodicals; Mickiewicz museum; specializes in 19th- and 20th-century history, literature and art; admin. by Société Historique et Littéraire Polonaise; Dir L. TALKO.

Bibliothèque Publique d'Information: Centre Georges-Pompidou, 75197 Paris Cedex 04; tel. 1-44-78-12-33; fax 1-44-78-12-15; e-mail bpi-info@bpi.fr; internet www.bpi.fr; f. 1977; 400,000 books, 2,722 periodicals, 2,425 films, 10,000 music records; Dir GÉRALD GRUNBERG.

Bibliothèque Sainte-Geneviève: 10 pl. du Panthéon, 75005 Paris; tel. 1-44-41-97-97; fax 1-44-41-97-96; e-mail bsgmail@univ-paris1.fr; internet www-bsg.univ-paris1.fr; f. 1624 by Cardinal F. de La Rochefoucauld; 1,300,000 vols, 14,000 periodicals, 120,000 early printed books, 1,500 incunabula and 4,200 MSS, 50,000 prints; encyclopedic library; special colln: Bibliothèque Nordique (160,000 vols, 3,500 periodicals), Estonian colln (1,000 vols); Dir YVES PEYRÉ.

Bibliothèque Thiers: 27 place Saint-Georges, 75009 Paris; tel. 1-48-78-14-33; fax 1-48-78-92-92; e-mail bibliotheque.thiers@free.fr; internet www.institut-de-france.fr; f. 1905; attached to Institut de France; 130,000 vols, 3,000 MSS and 30,000 engravings on 19th c. history; Dir DANUTA MONACHON.

Bibliothèques de l'Institut Catholique de Paris: c/o Bibliothèque de Fels, 21 rue d'Assas, 75270 Paris Cedex 06; tel. 1-44-39-52-30; fax 1-44-39-52-98; e-mail bibliotheque.de.fels@icp.fr; internet www.icp.fr; f. 1875; philosophy, theology, history, literature, psychology, pedagogy; 600,000 vols, incl. 450,000 vols, 623 current periodicals, 6,000 other periodicals; Dir of Libraries ODILE DUPONT.

CÉDIAS—Musée Social: 5 rue Las-Cases, 75007 Paris; tel. 1-45-51-66-10; fax 1-44-18-01-81; e-mail bibliotheque@cedias.org; internet www.cedias.org; f. 1894; social information and documentation; public library; 100,000 vols; Dir JEAN-YVES BARREYRE; publ. *Vie Sociale* (quarterly).

Centre de Documentation Contemporaine et Historique de l'Ecole Nationale des Ponts et Chaussées: 6 et 8 ave Blaise Pascal, Cité Descartes, Champs sur Marne, 77455 Marne-la-Vallée Cedex 2; tel. 1-64-15-34-70; fax 1-64-15-34-79; e-mail christiane.baudry@mail.enpc.fr; internet www.enpc.fr; f. 1747; over 200,000 vols on building, civil engineering, urban and regional planning, and transport, 3,200 MSS, 3,000 maps, 10,000 photographs 1850–1900; Dir CHRISTIANE BAUDRY.

Centre de Documentation Economique de la Chambre de Commerce et d'Industrie de Paris: 16 rue de Châteaubriand, 75008 Paris; tel. 1-55-65-72-72; fax 1-55-65-72-86; f. 1821; economics, business information, management, market surveys, companies; 300,000 vols, 750 periodicals; economic data bank (DELPHES); Dir GÉRARD FALCO.

Centre de Documentation et d'Information Scientifique pour le Développement (CEDID): 209 rue La Fayette, 75010 Paris; tel. 1-48-03-75-95; fax 1-48-03-08-29; f. 1985 by ORSTOM (*q.v.*); 70,000 documents on development and North-South co-operation, world environment, tropical agriculture, health, evolving societies, and women in third-world countries; 200 general and scientific reviews, press cuttings, database, etc.; open to the public.

Direction des Services d'Archives de Paris: 18 blvd Sérurier, 75019 Paris; tel. 1-53-72-41-23; fax 1-53-72-41-34; f. 1872; collns of various kinds of documents relating to the history of Paris, urbanisation and architecture; 34,000 vols specializing in history of Paris and admin. publs, 1,200 periodicals; Dir AGNÈS MASSON.

Institut François-Mitterrand: 10 rue Charlot, 75003 Paris; tel. 1-44-54-53-93; fax 1-44-54-53-99; e-mail ifm@mitterrand.org; internet www.mitterrand.org; f. 1996; archives documents relevant to the history of the second half of the 20th century.

UNESCO Library: UNESCO, 7 place de Fontenoy, 75352 Paris 07 SP; tel. 1-45-68-03-56; fax 1-45-68-56-98; e-mail library@unesco.org; internet www.unesco.org/library; f. 1946; UNESCO documents, publs and periodicals; 150,000 vols, 800 periodicals; Dir JOHN MILLER.

Pau

Bibliothèque Municipale: Square Paul-Lafond, BP 1621, 64016 Pau Cedex; tel. 5-59-27-15-72; fax 5-59-83-94-47; f. 1803; 350,000 vols; includes municipal archives; special collections on Henri IV and Béarn; Librarian OLIVIER CAUDRON.

Bibliothèque de l'Université de Pau et des Pays de l'Adour: Campus universitaire, 64000 Pau; tel. 5-59-92-33-60; fax 5-59-92-33-62; internet www.univ-pau.fr/SCD; f. 1962; 142,000 vols, 2,067 periodicals; Dir SYLVAINE FREULON.

Périgueux

Bibliothèque Municipale: 12 ave Georges Pompidou, 24000 Périgueux; tel. 5-53-53-32-51; fax 5-53-53-17-85; e-mail bm-perigueux@manadoo.fr; f. 1809; 170,000 vols; Librarian J. L. GLÉNISSON.

Perpignan

Bibliothèque Universitaire: BP 59939, Moulin à Vent, 52 ave Paul Alduy, 66962 Perpignan Cedex 9; tel. 4-68-66-22-99; fax 4-68-50-37-72; e-mail bu-perp@univ-perp.fr; internet www.univ-perp.fr/scms/bu/buweb.htm; f. 1962; 155,000 vols and 100,000 theses; special collections: Catalan, Mexican studies, history of Languedoc-Roussillon, renewable energy, materials science, geology of north Africa; Dir JOËL MARTRES.

Poitiers

Bibliothèque Universitaire de Poitiers: BP 605, 86022 Poitiers Cedex; tel. 5-49-45-33-11; fax 5-49-45-33-56; e-mail bu@univ-poitiers.fr; internet www.scd.univ-poitiers.fr; f. 1879; 452,000 vols, 5,830 periodicals; spec. collns: 30,000 early printed vols, Fonds Dubois (16th–19th c., economics, politics, social history), Argenson family archives; Dir STÉPHANE BASSINET.

Médiathèque François-Mitterrand: 4 rue de l'Université, BP 619, 86022 Poitier s Cedex; tel. 5-49-52-31-51; fax 5-49-52-31-60; e-mail mediatheque@mairie-poitiers.fr; internet www.bm-poitiers.fr; f. 1803; 750,000 books, 550 current periodicals; Dir JEAN-MARIE COMPTE; publ. *Les Carnets de la Médiathèque* (6 a year).

Reims

Bibliothèque Municipale: 2 rue des Fuseliers, 51095 Reims cedex; tel. 3-26-35-68-00; fax 3-26-35-68-34; e-mail cathedrale@bm-reims.fr; internet www.bm-reims.fr; f. 1809; 800,000 vols, 3,000 MSS; Librarian DELPHINE QUÉREUX-SBAÏ; publ. *Ouvrez les guillemets* (monthly).

Bibliothèque de l'Université de Reims: Ave François Mauriac, 51095 Reims Cedex; tel. 3-26-91-39-28; fax 3-26-91-39-30; e-mail carine.elbekri@univ-reims.fr; internet www.univ-reims.fr/bu; f. 1970; 362,751 vols, 4,278 periodicals; Dir CARINE EL BEKRI.

Rennes

Bibliothèque Municipale: 1 rue de La Borderie, 35042 Rennes Cedex; tel. 2-99-87-98-98; fax 2-99-87-98-99; e-mail contact@bm-rennes.fr; internet www.bm-rennes.fr; f. 1803; 650,000 vols; Chief Librarian MARIE-THÉRÈSE POUILLIAS.

Bibliothèque de l'Université de Rennes I:; tel. 2-23-23-34-18; fax 2-23-23-34-19; e-mail jean-yves.roux@univ-rennes1.fr; internet www.scd.univ-rennes1.fr; f. 1855; 550,000 vols; Dir GHYSLAINE DUONG-VINH.

Bibliothèque de l'Université de Rennes II: Place du Recteur Henri Le Moal, 35043 Rennes Cedex; tel. 2-99-14-12-55; fax 2-99-14-12-85; internet www.uhb.fr/scd; Librarian E. LEMAU.

Rouen

Bibliothèque Municipale: 3 rue Jacques-Villon, 76043 Rouen Cedex 1; tel. 2-35-71-28-82; fax 2-35-70-01-56; e-mail bibliotheque@rouen.fr; f. 1791; 500,000 vols incl. 600 incunabula, 6,000 MSS; Chief Librarian F. LEGENDRE.

Bibliothèque de l'Université de Rouen: Anneau central, rue Lavoisier, 76821 Mont-Saint-Aignan Cedex; tel. 2-35-14-60-41; fax 2-35-14-69-05; internet www.univ-rouen.fr; 400,000 ; Dir YANNICK VALIN.

St-Etienne

Bibliothèque de l'Université Jean-Monnet: 1 rue Tréfilerie, 42023 St-Etienne Cedex 2; tel. 4-77-42-16-99; fax 4-77-42-16-20; e-mail achard@univ-st-etienne.fr; internet www.univ-st-etienne.fr/scdoc; Dir MARIE-CLAUDE ACHARD.

Strasbourg

Bibliothèque Nationale et Universitaire de Strasbourg: 6 place de la République, BP 1029/F, 67070 Strasbourg Cedex; tel. 3-88-25-28-00; fax 3-88-25-28-03; e-mail bnus@bnus.u-strasbg.fr; internet www-bnus.u-strasbg.fr; f. 1871; 3,000,000 vols; Dir BERNARD FALGA.

Toulon

Bibliothèque de l'Université de Toulon et du Var: BP 10122, 83957 La Garde Cedex; tel. 4-94-14-23-26; fax 4-94-14-21-38; e-mail scd@univ-tln.fr; internet bu.univ-tln.fr; f. 1971; general library; Dir J. KERIGUY.

Toulouse

Bibliothèque Municipale: 1 rue de Périgord, BP 7092, 31070 Toulouse Cedex 7; tel. 5-61-22-21-78; fax 5-61-22-34-30; internet www.bibliothequedetoulouse.fr; f. 1782; 20 brs; 914,000 vols, 3,700 periodicals; Chief Librarian PIERRE JULLIEN (acting).

Bibliothèque Universitaire de l'Arsenal (Toulouse 1): 11 rue des Puits-Creusés, BP 7093, 31070 Toulouse Cedex 7; tel. 5-34-45-61-11; fax 5-34-45-61-30; internet www.univ-tlse1.fr/scd; f. 1879; 900,000 vols; spec. collns: Fonds Pifteau (books printed in Toulouse, books on regional history and geography), Fonds Chabaneau (18th-century books), Fonds Liguge (Spanish history), Fonds Claude Perroud (French Revolution), Fonds Montauban (History of Protestantism); Chief Librarian M. VAN DOOREN.

Tours

Bibliothèque Municipale Classée de Tours: 2 bis, ave André Malraux, 37042 Tours Cedex; tel. 2-47-05-47-33; fax 2-47-61-93-26; e-mail webmestre@bm-tours.fr; internet www.bm-tours.fr; f. 1791; original library destroyed in 1940; 501,000 vols, 3,000 periodicals; Librarian FRANÇOIS VIGNALE.

Service Commun de la Documentation de l'Université de Tours: 5 rue des Tanneurs, 37041 Tours Cedex (Letters); tel. 2-47-36-64-86; fax 2-47-36-67-99 Parc de Grandmont, 37200 Tours (Sciences and Pharmacy); 2 *bis* blvd Tonnellé, 37032 Tours Cedex (Medicine); 50 ave Portalis, 37206 Tours Cedex 3 (Law); tel. 2-47-36-11-24 6 place Jean-Jaurès, 41000 Blois (Blois section); internet www.scd.univ-tours.fr; Dir GIL-FRANÇOIS EUVRARD.

Troyes

Médiathèque de l'Agglomération Troyenne: 7 rue des Filles-Dieu, BP 602, 10088 Troyes Cedex; tel. 3-25-43-56-20; fax 3-25-43-56-21; e-mail contact@mediatheque-agglo-troyes.fr; internet www.mediatheque-agglo-troyes.fr; f. 1651; 400,000 vols; Librarian THIERRY DELCOURT.

Valence

Médiathèque Publique et Universitaire: Place Charles Huguenel, 26000 Valence; tel. 4-75-79-23-70; fax 4-75-79-23-82; e-mail medieval@wanadoo.fr; internet sicd2.upmf-grenoble.fr/bu/valence; f. 1775; 100,000 vols, 650 periodicals; Librarian JOHANN BERTI.

Valenciennes

Bibliothèque Municipale: 2–6 rue Ferrand, BP 281, 59300 Valenciennes Cedex; tel. 3-27-22-57-00; fax 3-27-22-57-01; e-mail mpdion@ville-valenciennes.fr; internet www.valenciennes.fr; f. 1598; 300,000 vols; Librarian MARIE-PIERRE DION-TURKOVICS.

Vandoeuvre-lès-Nancy

Institut de l'Information Scientifique et Technique (INIST-CNRS): 2 allée du Parc de Brabois, 54514 Vandoeuvre-lès-Nancy Cedex; tel. 3-83-50-46-00; fax 3-83-50-46-50; e-mail infoclient@inist.fr; internet www.inist.fr; f. 1988; collects, processes and distributes international research findings; produces two databases: PASCAL (Sciences, Technology, Medicine) and FRANCIS (Humanities, Social Sciences, Economics); 10,000 vols, 26,000 serial titles, 60,000 scientific reports, 62,000 conference proceedings, 110,000 doctoral theses; Dir-Gen. RAYMOND DUVAL.

Versailles

Bibliothèque Municipale: 5 rue de l'Indépendance Américaine, 78000 Versailles; tel. 2-39-07-13-20; fax 2-39-07-13-22; e-mail bibliotheque@mairie-versailles.fr; internet www.mairie-versailles.fr; f. 1803; 700,000 vols, 900 periodicals; Chief Librarian MARIE-FRANÇOISE ROSE.

Museums and Art Galleries

Agen

Musée des Beaux-Arts: Place du Docteur Esquirol, 47916 Agen Cedex 9; tel. 5-53-69-47-23; fax 5-53-69-47-77; e-mail musee@ville-agen.fr; internet www.ville-agen.fr/musee; f. 1876; local, Roman and medieval archaeology; paintings by Corneille de Lyon, de Troy, Drouais, Nattier, Goya, the Impressionists, Roger Bissière and François-Xavier Lalanne; ceramics; Chinese art; Curator MARIE-DOMINIQUE NIVIÈRE.

Aix-en-Provence

Musée Granet: Place St Jean de Malte, 13100 Aix-en-Provence; tel. 4-42-38-14-70; fax 4-42-26-84-55; f. 1765; Egyptian, Greek, Celto-Ligurian, Roman and Gallo-Roman archaeology; pictures of Cézanne and the French Schools, with special emphasis on Provence; Italian, Spanish, Flemish, Dutch and German Schools; modern painting; sculpture; modern painting; furniture of 16th, 17th and 18th centuries; Curator DENIS COUTAGNE.

Alençon

Musée des Beaux-Arts et de la Dentelle: Cour Carrée de la Dentelle, 61000 Alençon; tel. 2-33-32-40-07; fax 2-33-26-51-66; e-mail musee@ville-alencon.fr; internet www.ville-alencon.fr/musee.htm; f. 1857; 17th–19th c. French, Dutch and Flemish paintings, 16th–19th c. French, Italian and Dutch drawings, French, Flemish, Italian and Eastern European lace since 16th c.; 16th–19th c. French and British prints; ethnological items from Cambodia; Curator AUDE PESSEY-LUX.

Amboise

Musée de l'Hôtel de Ville: rue François I, BP 247, 37402 Amboise; tel. 2-47-23-47-42; fax 2-47-23-19-80; colln incl. tapestries, statues and paintings relating to the history of Amboise; Curator AGATHE GUENAND.

Musée de la Poste: 6 rue Joyeuse, 37400 Amboise; tel. 2-47-57-00-11; fax 2-47-23-19-80; f. 1971; collection includes material on historic postal services and transport; Curator CLAUDE CHAPPE.

Amiens

Musée de Picardie: 48 rue de la République, 80000 Amiens; tel. 3-22-97-14-00; fax 3-22-97-14-26; e-mail musees-amiens@amiens-metropole.com; internet w2.amiens.com/museedepicardie; f. 1854; fine collection of paintings of Northern and French Schools; murals by Puvis de Chavannes and Sol Le Witt; Egyptian, Greek and Roman antiquities; prehistoric, Iron and Bronze age collections; objets d'art of Middle Ages and Renaissance; 19th-century sculpture; 20th-century paintings; Chief Curator MATTHIEU PINETTE.

Angers

Musée des Beaux-Arts: 14 rue du Musée, 49100 Angers; tel. 2-41-05-38-00; fax 2-41-86-06-38; e-mail musees@ville.angers.fr; internet www.angers.fr/mba; f. 1797; housed in 15th-century 'logis Barrault'; paintings of 18th-century French School and 17th-century Dutch and Flemish Schools; sculpture, including busts by Houdon; Dir PATRICK LE NOUËNE.

Affiliated museums:

Galerie David d'Angers: 33 bis rue Toussaint, 49100 Angers; tel. 2-41-87-21-03; fax 2-41-86-06-38; f. 1984; sited in restored gothic church; almost all the sculptor's work.

Musée Jean Lurçat et de la Tapisserie Contemporaine: 4 blvd Arago, 49100 Angers; tel. 2-41-24-18-45 (Musée Jean Lurçat); tel. 2-41-24-18-48 (Musée de la Tapisserie Contemporaine); fax 2-41-86-06-38; occupies 12th-century Hôpital Saint-Jean; paintings of Jean Lurçat and tapestry.

Musée Pincé: 32 bis rue Lenepveu, 49100 Angers; tel. 2-41-88-94-27; fax 2-41-86-06-38; f. 1889; Greek, Roman, Etruscan and Egyptian antiquities; Chinese and Japanese art.

Antibes

Musée Picasso: Château Grimaldi, 06600 Antibes; tel. 4-92-90-54-20; fax 4-92-90-54-21; f. 1948; 230 works by Picasso; collection of modern and contemporary art: Atlan, Miró, Calder, Richier, Ernst, Hartung and others; Nicolas de Staël room with works from

Antibes period; sculpture garden; Dir MAURICE FRÉCHURET; publ. catalogues.

Arras

Musée des Beaux-Arts d'Arras: Ancienne Abbaye Saint-Vaast, 22 rue Paul Doumer, 62000 Arras; tel. 3-21-71-26-43; fax 3-21-23-19-26; e-mail musee.arras@ville-arras.fr; internet www.musenor.com/gm/gmarras.htm; f. 1825; medieval sculpture, 17th- and 19th-century paintings, porcelain, Gallo-Roman archaeology; Chief Curator STEPHANIE DESCHAMPS.

Arromanches

Exposition Permanente du Débarquement (Permanent Exhibition of the Landings): Place du 6 Juin, 14117 Arromanches; tel. 2-31-22-34-31; fax 2-31-92-68-83; e-mail info.arromanches@normandy1944.com; internet www.normandy1944.com; f. 1954; exhibition of the Normandy landings of D-Day, 6th June 1944; comprises artificial port and museum of relief maps, working models, photographs, diorama and films.

Avignon

Musée Calvet: 65 rue Joseph Vernet, 84000 Avignon; tel. 4-90-86-33-84; fax 4-90-14-62-45; e-mail musee.calvet@wanadoo.fr; internet www.avignon.fr/fr/culture/musees/calvet.php; f. 1810; fine art since 16th c.; Curator (vacant).

Musée Lapidaire: 27 rue de la République, 84000 Avignon; tel. 4-90-85-75-38; internet www.avignon.fr/fr/culture/musees/lapidaire.php; f. 1933; ancient Egyptian, Greek and Gallo-Roman sculpture; Curator ODILE CAVALIER.

Musée du Petit Palais: Place du Palais des papes, 84000 Avignon; tel. 4-90-86-44-58; fax 4-90-82-18-72; e-mail musee.petitpalais@mairie-avignon.com; internet www.avignon.fr/fr/culture/musees/petipal.php; f. 1976; in the old archbishop's palace (14th–15th century); medieval and Renaissance paintings of the Avignon and Italian Schools, medieval sculpture from Avignon; Curator DOMINIQUE VINGTAIN.

Bayonne

Musée Basque de Bayonne: Château-Neuf/Maison Dagourette, 64100 Bayonne; tel. 5-59-46-61-85; fax 5-59-59-03-71; internet www.musee-basque.com; f. 1922; 4 sections covering the history and folklore of the town of Bayonne, the French Basque country, the Spanish Basque country, and the Basques in the New World; library of 30,000 vols; Curator O. RIBETON; Curator R. ZULAIKA; publ. *Bulletin* (2 a year).

Besançon

Musée des Beaux-Arts et d'Archéologie: 1 place de la Révolution–place du Marché, 25000 Besançon; tel. 3-81-81-44-47; f. 1694, moved to present buildings 1843; Danish (pre- and protohistoric), Egyptian, Greek, Etruscan and Roman antiquities; regional (pre- and protohistoric, Gallo-Roman, early medieval) antiquities; medieval objets d'art; 15th–20th-century European paintings (especially French 18th–19th-century), sculpture, ceramics and objets d'art; 15th–20th century drawings in temporary exhibitions; Curators F. SOULIER-FRANÇOIS, P. LAGRANGE, F. THOMAS-MAURIN.

Biot

Musée National Fernand Léger: Chemin du Val de Pome, 06410 Biot; tel. 4-92-91-50-30; fax 4-92-91-50-31; internet www.musee-fernandleger.fr; permanent exhibition of paintings, drawings, ceramics.

Blérancourt

Musée National de la Co-opération Franco-Américaine: Château de Blérancourt, 02300 Blérancourt; tel. 3-23-39-60-16; f. 1924 to contain collections presented to the State by Mrs Anna Murray Dike, Miss Anne Morgan, and other French and American benefactors, relating to the history of Franco-American relations; the castle, formerly the ancestral home of the Ducs de Gesvres, is classed as an historical monument; library of 3,500 vols; Curator PHILIPPE GRUNCHEC.

Bordeaux

Musée d'Aquitaine: 20 cours Pasteur, 33000 Bordeaux; tel. 5-56-01-51-00; fax 5-56-44-24-36; e-mail musaq@mairie-bordeaux.fr; internet www.mairie-bordeaux.fr; f. 1987; regional prehistory, history and ethnology; ethnographical collection of pieces from Africa and Oceania; library of 20,000 vols; Curator HÉLÈNE LAFONT-COUTURIER.

Musée d'Art Contemporain de Bordeaux: Entrepôt Lainé, 7 rue Ferrère, 33000 Bordeaux; tel. 5-56-00-81-50; fax 5-56-44-12-07; e-mail capc@mairie-bordeaux.fr; internet www.mairie-bordeaux.fr/musees/capc/capc.htm; f. 1984 by 'Capc' asscn (f. 1974), financed by Direction des Musées de France and Bordeaux town; temporary exhibitions; permanent collection; library of 25,000 vols, mostly catalogues; photos, slides, videos; education service for schools; publs *Catalogue* (quarterly), *Calendrier* (5 a year).

Musée des Beaux-Arts: Jardin de la Mairie, 20 cours d'Albret, 33000 Bordeaux; tel. 5-56-10-20-56; fax 5-56-10-25-13; e-mail musbxa@mairie-bordeaux.fr; internet www.culture.fr/culture/bordeaux; f. 1801; 2,300 paintings, 504 sculptures, 2,370 drawings; Curator FRANÇOISE GARCIA.

Caen

Musée de Normandie: Château de Caen, 14000 Caen; tel. 2-31-30-47-60; fax 2-31-30-47-69; e-mail mdn@ville-caen.fr; internet www.ville-caen.fr/mdn; f. 1946; history, archaeology and ethnology of Normandy; Dir J.-Y. MARIN; publs *Annales de Normandie* (quarterly), *Publications* (irregular).

Carnac

Musée de Préhistoire: 10 place de la Chapelle, BP 80, 56340 Carnac; tel. 2-97-52-22-04; fax 2-97-52-64-04; e-mail info@museedecarnac.com; internet www.museedecarnac.com; municipal museum; f. 1881; local prehistory and archaeology; most important museum in the world for collections from megalithic period; research library; photographic archive (3,000 items); Dir ANNE-ELISABETH RISKINE.

Chantilly

Musée et Château de Chantilly (Musée Condé): BP 70243, 60631 Chantilly Cedex; tel. 3-44-62-62-62; fax 3-44-62-62-61; e-mail ngarnier@chateaudechantilly.com; internet www.chateaudechantilly.com; f. 1898; paintings, miniatures, furniture, drawings, 70,000 books, 3,000 MSS, etc.; Curator NICOLE GARNIER; publ. *Le Musée Condé* (annually).

Compiègne

Musée National du Château de Compiègne: 60200 Compiègne; tel. 3-44-38-47-02; fax 3-44-38-47-01; e-mail chateau.compiegne@culture.gouv.fr; internet www.musee-chateau-compiegne.fr; royal palace of the first kings of France, reconstructed under Louis XV and Louis XVI and partly redecorated under the 1st Empire; furniture of 18th and 19th centuries, mostly 1st Empire period; tapestries of 18th century; collns from the 2nd Empire period; souvenirs of the Empress Eugénie; Chief Curator EMMANUEL STARCKY.

Affiliated museum:

Musée National de la Voiture et du Tourisme: Château de Compiègne, 60200 Compiègne; tel. 3-44-38-47-00; fax 3-44-38-47-01; e-mail chateau.compiegne@culture.gouv.fr; internet www.musee-chateau-compiegne.fr; f. 1927 with the co-operation of the Touring Club de France; old carriages, sedan chairs, survey of devt of the bicycle and the automobile; 180 vehicles; Chief Curator JACQUES PEROT.

Dijon

Musée des Beaux-Arts: Palais des Etats, Cour de Bar, 21000 Dijon; tel. 3-80-74-52-70; fax 3-80-74-53-44; e-mail museedesbeauxarts@ville-dijon.fr; internet www.ville-dijon.fr; f. 1787 and housed in the Palace of the Dukes of Burgundy and the Palace of the States of Burgundy; Swiss primitives; paintings of Franco-Flemish School of 15th c. and of other French and foreign schools; prints and drawings; sculptures from tombs of the Dukes of Burgundy; marble, ivory, armour; modern art; Granville collection; Chief Curator EMMANUEL STARCKY.

Musée Magnin: 4 rue des Bons-Enfants, 21000 Dijon; tel. 3-80-67-11-10; fax 3-80-66-43-75; internet www.musee-magnin.fr; Italian and French paintings from 16th–19th c.; Curator RÉMI CARIEL.

Fontainebleau

Musée National du Château de Fontainebleau: 77300 Château de Fontainebleau; tel. 1-60-71-50-70; fax 1-60-71-50-71; e-mail contact.chateau-de-fontainebleau@culture.fr; internet www.musee-chateau-fontainebleau.fr; bldgs from 12th–19th centuries; paintings, interior decoration and furniture of the Renaissance, 17th and 18th centuries, 1st and 2nd Empires and 19th century; Dir BERNARD NOTARI.

Giverny

Claude Monet Foundation: 84 rue Claude Monet, 27620 Giverny; tel. 2-32-51-28-21; fax 2-32-51-54-18; e-mail contact@fondation-monet.com; internet www.fondation-monet.com; f. 1980 after restoration; consists of Monet's house and garden where he lived from 1883 to 1926; it was left by his son in 1966 to the Académie des Beaux-Arts; the house contains Monet's collection of Japanese engravings; Curator GERALD VAN DER KEMP; Sec.-Gen. Mme C. LINDSEY.

Grenoble

Musée de Grenoble: 5 pl. Lavalette, BP 326, 38010 Grenoble Cedex 01; tel. 4-76-63-44-44; fax 4-76-63-44-10; internet www.museedegrenoble.fr; f. 1796; art and antiquities; library of 50,000 vols; Dir GUY TOSATTO.

Langeais

Château de Langeais: 37130 Langeais; tel. 2-47-96-72-60; fax 2-47-96-54-44; e-mail chateau-langeais @wanadoo.fr; internet www.institut-de-france.fr/patrimoine; built in 15th c. and given to the Institut de France in 1904; furniture and tapestries from the 13th–15th c. and 15th c. architecture.

Le Havre

Musée des Beaux-Arts 'André Malraux': Blvd J. F. Kennedy, 76600 Le Havre; tel. 2-35-19-62-62; fax 2-35-19-93-01; internet www.ville-lehavre.fr; f. 1845; permanent collection from 14th–20th c. (Boudin, Impressionists, Dufy); Dir ANNETTE HAUDIQUET.

Affiliated museums:

Musée du Prieuré de Graville: Rue Elisée Reclus, 76600 Le Havre; tel. 2-35-47-14-01; f. 1926; sculpture from the 12th–18th c.; models of old houses; Dir CH. MAUBANT.

Musée de l'Ancien Havre: Rue Jérôme Bellarmato, 76600 Le Havre; tel. 2-35-42-27-90; f. 1955; drawings and documents on the history of Le Havre from 1517 to the present; naval models; Dir CH. MAUBANT.

Espace Maritime et Portuaire du Havre: Quai Frissard, 76600 Le Havre; tel. 2-35-24-51-00; fax 2-35-26-76-69; Le Havre maritime and port history since 1830; Dir CH. MAUBANT.

Le Mans

Musée Automobile de la Sarthe: Circuit des 24 Heures du Mans, BP 29254, 72009 Le Mans Cedex 1; tel. 2-43-72-72-24; fax 2-43-85-38-96; e-mail musee.automobile.lemans@wanadoo.fr; internet www.sarthe.com/sport/museeauto.htm; f. 1961; cars, cycles and motorcycles; Dir. FRANCIS PIQUERA.

Musée de la Reine Bérengère: 9–13 rue de la Reine Bérengère, 72000 Le Mans; tel. 2-43-47-38-51; fax 2-43-47-49-93; e-mail musees@ville-lemans.fr; 16th-century architecture, folklore, ceramics, local history; Curator FRANÇOISE CHASERANT.

Musée de Tessé: 2 ave de Paderborn, 72000 Le Mans; tel. 2-43-47-38-51; fax 2-43-47-49-93; fine arts, paintings and sculpture, archaeology, Egyptology; Curator FRANÇOISE CHASERANT.

Les Eyzies de Tayac

Musée National de Préhistoire: BP 7, 24620 Les Eyzies de Tayac; tel. (5) 53-06-45-45; fax (5) 53-06-45-55; e-mail mnp.eyzies@culture.gouv.fr; internet www.arachnis.asso.fr/DORDOGNE/viecult/musees/eyzies/msnpreh0.htm; f. 2004; clln of 18,000 objects, including prehistoric carvings; permanent exhibitions on human evolution and the prehistoric peoples of the Périgord region; Deputy Curator ALAIN TURQ.

Lille

Musée des Beaux-Arts: 18 *bis* rue de Valmy, 59800 Lille; tel. 3-20-06-78-00; fax 3-20-06-78-15; f. 1801; paintings of Flemish, Italian, Spanish, German, French and Dutch Schools; exceptional collection of drawings; sculpture, ceramics and archaeological exhibits; Chief Curator ARNAULD BREJON DE LAVERGNÉE.

Limoges

Musée Municipal de l'Evêché: Place de la Cathédrale, 87000 Limoges; tel. 5-55-45-98-10; fax 5-55-34-44-14; e-mail museveche@ville-limoges.fr; internet www.ville-limoges.fr; f. 1912; paintings, drawings, engravings, sculptures, Limoges enamels, metalwork; Egyptian collection; archaeological and lapidary collection; enamels research centre; library of 7,000 vols; Curator VÉRONIQUE NOTIN.

Musée National Adrien Dubouché: Place Winston Churchill, 87000 Limoges; tel. 5-55-33-08-50; fax 5-55-33-08-55; e-mail contact.musee-adriendubouche@culture.gouv.fr; internet www.musee-adriendubouche.fr; f. 1900; ceramics and glass; Curator CHANTAL MESLIN-PERRIER.

Lyons

Musée des Beaux-Arts: 20 place des Terreaux, 69001 Lyons; tel. 4-72-10-17-40; fax 4-78-28-12-45; e-mail mbal@mba-lyon.fr; f. 1801 and housed in the former Benedictine Abbey of the Dames de Saint-Pierre, built in 1659; the important collection contains paintings of French, Flemish, Dutch, Italian and Spanish Schools, and sections devoted to local painters, modern art, and murals by Puvis de Chavannes; ancient, medieval and modern sculpture; French, Italian, Oriental and Hispano-Moorish ceramics; drawings, prints, furniture, numismatic collection; Egyptian, Greek, Roman and Near and Middle Eastern antiquities; library of 50,000 vols; Chief Curator SYLVIE RAMOND; publs *Cahiers du Musée des Beaux-Arts de Lyon* (annually), illustrated guides.

Magny-les-Hameaux

Musée National des Granges de Port-Royal: 78114 Magny-les-Hameaux; tel. 1-30-43-73-05; f. 1952; history of Port-Royal and Jansenism; presented in the house of 'Petites Ecoles' where Racine studied; Curator VÉRONIQUE ALEMANY.

Maisons-Laffitte

Château de Maisons-Laffitte: 78600 Maisons-Laffitte; tel. 1-39-62-01-49; fax 1-39-12-34-37; internet www.maisonslaffitte.net; château dates from 1642; contains paintings, sculptures, tapestries; Curator FLORENCE DE LA RONCIÈRE.

Marseilles

Musée d'Archéologie Méditerranéenne: 2 rue de la Charité, 13002 Marseilles; tel. 4-91-14-58-80; fax 4-91-14-58-81; e-mail adurand@mairie-marseille.fr; internet www.mairie-marseille.fr/vivre/culture/musees/archeo.htm; f. 1863; Egyptian, Greek, Cypriot, Celto-Ligurian, Etruscan, Roman and Gallo-Roman antiquities; library of 4,500 vols; Curators AGNÈS DURAND, BRIGITTE LESCURE.

Affiliated museum:

Musée des Docks Romains: 28 place Vivaux, 13002 Marseilles; tel. 4-91-91-24-62; internet www.culture.gouv.fr/culture/archeosm/fr/fr-act-mus4.htm; f. 1963; ancient commerce; exhibits include amphorae, ingots and marine archaeology; Curator AGNÈS DURAND.

Musée des Beaux-Arts: Palais Longchamp, Aile Gauche, 7 rue Edouard Stephan, 13004 Marseilles; tel. 4-91-14-59-30; fax 4-91-14-59-31; e-mail dgac-musee-beauxarts@mairie-marseille.fr; internet www.mairie-marseille.fr/vivre/culture/musees/boart.htm; f. 1802; paintings (French, Italian, Flemish and German schools); murals by French artists, including Courbet, Corot, Daubigny, Millet, Daumier and Puvis de Chavannes; collection of paintings and sculptures by Puget; sculptures by Daumier and Rodin; Curator MARIE-PAULE VIAL.

Musée Cantini: 19 rue Grignan, 13006 Marseilles; tel. 4-91-54-77-75; fax 4-91-55-03-61; internet www.mairie-marseille.fr/vivre/culture/musees/cantini.htm; f. 1936; modern art (1900–60); library of 20,000 vols on 20th c. art; Curators NICOLAS CENDO, OLIVIER COUSINOU.

Musée de la Marine et de l'Economie de Marseille: Chambre de Commerce et d'Industrie Marseille-Provence, Palais de la Bourse, La Canebière, BP 21856, 13221 Marseilles Cedex 1; tel. 4-91-39-33-21; fax 4-91-39-56-15; e-mail patrick.boulanger@ccimp.com; internet www.ccimp.com/patrimoine; f. 1932; history of Marseilles and Mediterranean shipping; models of ships, paintings, drawings, plans; 25,000 tape recordings; Nossof, Cantelar and Grimard collns (history of steam ships); Archivist, Chief of Cultural Heritage Dept PATRICK BOULANGER.

Metz

Metz, Musées de La Cour d'Or: 2 rue du Haut Poirier, 57000 Metz; tel. 3-87-68-25-00; fax 3-87-36-51-14; e-mail musees@ca2m.com; internet www.mairie-metz.fr:8080; f. 1839; prehistory, protohistory, arts and popular traditions of northern Lorraine, and natural history collections (not open to public); architecture; fine arts (since 15th c.); archaeology and history; military collections (not open to public); library of 5,000 vols, 100 periodicals; Dir CLAUDE VALENTIN.

Montpellier

Musée Atger: Faculté de Médecine, 2 rue de l'Ecole de Médecine, 34000 Montpellier; tel. 4-67-66-27-77; fax 4-67-66-19-24; e-mail bu.medecine@univ_montp1.fr; internet www.biu.univ-montp1.fr/bu_sante/medecine/atger.php; f. 1813; drawings and paintings of French, Italian and Flemish schools, 16th–18th c. (Fragonard, Natoire, Tiepolo); Curator H. LORBLANCHET.

Musée Fabre: 13 rue Montpelliéret, 34000 Montpellier; tel. 4-67-14-83-00; fax 4-67-66-09-20; e-mail musee.fabre@montpellier-agglo.com; f. 1825 by the painter François-Xavier Fabre; paintings of French (Greuze, Delacroix, Courbet, Bazille, Géricault), Italian, Spanish, Dutch and Flemish Schools; drawings, sculpture (Houdon), furniture, tapestries, porcelain, silver; Dir MICHEL HILAIRE.

Mulhouse

Cité de l'Automobile–Musée National, Collection Schlumpf: 192 ave de Colmar, BP 1096, 68051 Mulhouse; tel. 3-89-33-23-23; fax 3-89-32-08-09; internet www.collection-schlumpf.com/schlumpf; f. 1982; history of the motor car since 1878; 424 vehicles on display, incl. an important colln of Bugattis; library of 4,500 vols; Dir EMANUEL BACQUET.

Musée de l'Impression sur Etoffes: 14 rue Jean-Jacques Henner, BP 1468, 68072 Mulhouse; tel. 3-89-46-83-00; fax 3-89-46-83-10; e-mail accueil@musee-impression.com; internet www.musee-impression.com; f. 1955; 18th–20th c. printed textiles; Curator JAQUELINE JACQUÉ; publ. *L'Imprimé* (2 a year).

Nancray

Musée de Plein Air des Maisons Comtoises: 25360 Nancray; tel. 3-81-55-29-77; fax 3-81-55-23-97; e-mail musee@maisons-comtoises.org; internet www.maisons-comtoises.org; f. 1984; folklore of Franche-Comté; 60,000 illustrations of rural architecture; Dir CATHERINE LOUVRIER; publs *Barbizier*, *Revue Régionale d'Ethnologie Comtoise* (annually).

Nancy

Musée des Beaux-Arts: Place Stanislas, 54000 Nancy; tel. 3-83-85-30-72; fax 3-83-85-30-76; e-mail mbanancy@mairie-nancy.fr; internet www.mairie-nancy.fr; f. 1793; paintings, sculpture, drawings, prints and glass from 15th–20th century; temporary exhibitions; Curator BLANDINE CHAVANNE.

Nantes

Musée des Beaux-Arts: 10 rue Georges-Clemenceau, 44000 Nantes; tel. 2-40-51-17-45-00; fax 2-40-41-67-90; e-mail musees@mairie-nantes.fr; internet www.nantes.fr; f. 1800; 2,200 paintings; library of 10,000 vols; Curator JEAN AUBERT.

Nice

Direction des Musées de Nice: Palais Masséna, 65 rue de France, 06050 Nice Cedex 1; tel. 4-93-88-11-34; fax 4-93-82-39-79; f. 1935; Dir JEAN FRANÇOIS MOZZICONACCI.

Comprises:

Galerie de la Marine: 59 quai des Etats-Unis, 06300 Nice; tel. 4-93-62-37-11; Curator ANNE-MARIE VILLERI.

Galerie des Ponchettes: 77 quai des Etats-Unis, 06300 Nice; tel. 4-93-62-31-24; Curator ANNE-MARIE VILLERI.

Musée d'Art et d'Histoire: Palais Masséna, 65 rue de France, 06050 Nice Cedex 1; tel. 4-93-88-11-34; fax 4-93-82-39-79; f. 1921; art and history; Dir LUC THEVENON.

Musée d'Archéologie: 160 Ave des Arènes de Cimiez, 06000 Nice; tel. 4-93-81-59-57; fax 4-93-81-08-00; f. 1989; Curator Mlle D. MOUCHOT.

Musée d'Art Moderne et d'Art Contemporain: Promenade des Arts, 06300 Nice; tel. 4-93-62-61-62; fax 4-93-13-09-01; e-mail mamac@ville-nice.fr; internet www.mamac-nice.org; f. 1990; collection 'Nice à partir des années 60'; nouveaux réalistes, pop art, fluxus, color field painting; Dir GILBERT PERLEIN.

Musée des Beaux-Arts: 33 ave des Baumettes, 06000 Nice; tel. 4-93-44-50-72; fax 4-93-97-67-07; internet www.musee-beaux-arts-nice.org; f. 1928; painting and sculpture 18th and 19th c., (Impressionists, Van Dongen); works of Jules Chéret; Dir BÉATRICE DEBRABANDÈRE–DESCAMPS.

Muséum d'Histoire Naturelle: 60 *bis* blvd Risso, 06300 Nice; tel. 4-97-13-46-80; fax 4-97-13-46-85; f. 1823; Curator ALAIN BIDAR.

Musée International d'Art Naïf Anatole Jakovsky: Château Ste Hélène-ave Val-Marie, 06200 Nice; tel. 4-93-71-78-33; fax 4-93-72-34-10; f. 1982; Dir ANNE DEVROYE-STILZ.

Musée Matisse: 164 ave des Arènes de Cimiez, 06000 Nice; tel. 4-93-81-08-08; fax 4-93-53-00-22; e-mail matisse@nice-coteazur.org; internet www.musee-matisse-nice.org; f. 1963; collections of paintings and sculptures by Henri Matisse; Curator MARIE-THÉRÈSE PULVÉNIS DE SELIGNY.

Musée Naval: Tour Bellanda, Colline du Château, 06300 Nice; tel. 4-93-80-47-61; Curator JEAN WURSTHORN.

Musée de Paléontologie–Terra Amata: 25 blvd Carnot, 06300 Nice; tel. 4-93-55-59-93; fax 4-93-89-91-31; f. 1976; Curator Mme M. GOUDET.

Musée du Vieux-Logis: 59 ave Saint Barthélémy, 06100 Nice; tel. 4-93-84-44-74; f. 1937; medieval furniture and sculpture; Curator LUC THEVENON.

Palais Lascaris: 15 rue Droite, 06300 Nice; tel. 4-93-62-72-40; fax 4-93-92-04-19; f. 1970; 17th and 18th.c. frescoes, furniture and art; Curator CH. ASTRO.

Musée National Message Biblique Marc Chagall: Ave du Dr Ménard, 06000 Nice; tel. 4-93-53-87-20; fax 4-93-53-87-39; e-mail museecie@rmn.fr; internet www.musee-chagall.fr; f. 1973; permanent collection of the artist's biblical works; temporary exhibitions; library of 3,000 vols; Curator JEAN LACAMBRE.

Nîmes

Musée Archéologique: 13 blvd Amiral-Courbet, 30000 Nîmes; tel. 4-66-76-74-80; fax 4-66-76-74-94; internet musees.nimes.fr; f. 1823; protohistoric and Gallic and Roman archaeology; library of 6,000 vols; Curator DOMINIQUE DARDE.

Musée d'Art Contemporain: Carré d'Art, place de la Maison Carrée, 30031 Nîmes Cedex 1; tel. 4-66-76-35-70; fax 4-66-76-35-85; e-mail carreart@mnet.fr; internet musees.nimes.fr; f. 1993; Dir FRANÇOISE COHEN.

Musée d'Histoire Naturelle: 13 blvd Amiral-Courbet, 30033 Nîmes Cedex 9; tel. 4-66-76-73-45; fax 4-66-76-73-46; e-mail museum@ville-nimes.fr; internet musees.nimes.fr; f. 1892; library of 3,000 vols; Dir LUC GOMEL.

Musée du Vieux Nîmes: Place aux Herbes, 30000 Nîmes Cedex; located at: Place aux Herbes, 30000 Nîmes; tel. 4-66-76-73-70; fax 4-66-76-73-71; e-mail musee.vieux-nimes@ville-nimes.fr; internet musees.nimes.fr; f. 1921; local history, folklore and traditional crafts; Curator MARTINE NOUGARÈDE.

Orléans

Musée des Beaux-Arts: 1 rue Fernand Rabier, 45000 Orléans; tel. 2-38-79-21-55; fax 2-38-79-20-08; e-mail vgalliot-rateau@ville-orleans.fr; internet www.ville-orleans.fr; f. 1823; sculpture since 16th c.; French, Flemish, Italian, Dutch, German and Spanish paintings and pastels (especially of 18th c.); Max Jacob and Gaudier-Brzeska room; Curator ISABELLE KLINKA.

Attached museum:

Musée Historique et Archéologique de l'Orléanais: Hôtel Cabu, Place Abbé Desnoyers, 45000 Orléans; tel. 2-38-79-21-55; fax 2-38-79-20-08; e-mail vgalliot-rateau@ville-orleans.fr; internet www.ville-orleans.fr; f. 1855; Gallo-Roman bronzes from Neuvy-en-Sullias; 17th–19th c. Orléans arts and crafts; the old port and river traffic; glassware and ceramics; Curator ISABELLE KLINKA.

Paris

Centre des Monuments Nationaux (Monum): Hôtel Béthune-Sully, 62 rue Saint-Antoine, 75004 Paris; tel. 1-44-61-21-54; fax 1-44-61-20-36; e-mail courrier@monuments-nat.fr; internet www.monum.fr; Dir CHRISTOPHE VALLET.

Cité des Sciences et de l'Industrie: 30 ave Corentin Cariou, 75930 Paris Cedex 19; tel. 1-40-05-70-00; fax 1-40-05-73-44; internet www.cite-sciences.fr; f. 1986; located in La Villette complex; permanent exhibitions: the universe, the earth, the environment, space, life, communication, etc.; multimedia public library (300,000 vols, 2,700 periodicals, 4,000 films, 1,300 educational software discs), history of science multimedia library, the Louis Braille room for the visually handicapped, Science Newsroom; Pres. GÉRARD THÉRY.

Galerie Nationale du Jeu de Paume: 1 Place de la Concorde, 75008 Paris; tel. 1-47-03-12-50; fax 1-47-03-12-51; re-f. 1991; devoted to temporary exhibitions of contemporary art; Dir DANIEL ABADIE.

Galeries Nationales du Panthéon Bouddhique: 19 ave d'Iéna, 75116 Paris; tel. 1-40-73-88-00; Chinese and Japanese art; Curator JEAN-FRANÇOIS JARRIGE.

Les Arts Décoratifs: 107 rue de Rivoli, 75001 Paris; tel. 1-44-55-57-50; fax 1-44-55-57-84; e-mail webmaster@lesartsdecoratifs.fr; internet www.lesartsdecoratifs.fr; f. 1864; library of 120,000 vols, 2,000 periodicals, 40,000 sale catalogues since 18th c.; Pres. HÉLÈNE DAVID-WEILL; Gen. Man. SOPHIE DURRLEMAN; Dir of Museums BÉATRICE SALMON.

Affiliated museums:

Musée des Arts Décoratifs: Les Arts Décoratifs, 107 rue de Rivoli, 75001 Paris; tel. 1-44-55-57-50; fax 1-44-55-57-84; e-mail webmaster@lesartsdecoratifs.fr; internet www.lesartsdecoratifs.fr; f. 1883; collection from Middle Ages to the present: woodwork, sculpture, tapestries, textiles, jewels, ceramics, furniture, painting, gold and silver work, glass; library of 100,000 vols, 1,500 periodicals; Dir BÉATRICE SALMON.

Musée de la Mode et du Textile: Les Arts Décoratifs, 107 rue de Rivoli, 75001 Paris; tel. 1-44-55-57-50; fax 1-44-55-57-84; e-mail webmaster@lesartsdecoratifs.fr; internet www.lesartsdecoratifs.fr; f. 1985; fashion, textiles and accessories; Dir BÉATRICE SALMON.

Musée Nissim de Camondo: Les Arts Décoratifs, 63 rue de Monceau, 75008 Paris; tel. 1-53-89-06-40; fax 1-53-89-06-42; e-mail webmaster@lesartsdecoratifs.fr; internet www.lesartsdecoratifs.fr; bequeathed by Count Moïse de Camondo who collected unique 18th c. objects in his Hôtel Parc Monceau; Dir BÉATRICE SALMON.

Musée de la Publicité: Les Arts Décoratifs, 107 rue de Rivoli, 75001 Paris; tel. 1-44-55-57-50; fax 1-44-55-57-84; e-mail webmaster@lesartsdecoratifs.fr; internet www.lesartsdecoratifs.fr; non-permanent exhibitions of posters, television, film and radio commercials; interactive multimedia library; Dir BÉATRICE SALMON.

Maison de Balzac: 47 rue Raynouard, 75016 Paris; tel. 1-55-74-41-80; fax 1-45-25-19-22; internet www.paris.fr/musees/balzac; f. 1961; museum and library of 15,000 books and periodicals; documents relating to life and work of Honoré de Balzac; first editions and autographed letters; comprehensive range of work from the romantic period; Curator YVES GAGNEUX.

Maison de Victor Hugo: 6 place des Vosges, 75004 Paris; tel. 1-42-72-10-16; fax 1-42-72-06-64; e-mail maisonsvictorhugo@mairie-paris.fr; internet www.paris.fr/musees/maison_de_victor_hugo; f. 1903; personal belongings, correspondence, first editions, drawings by Victor Hugo; library of 10,000 vols, 6,000 pamphlets; Curator DANIELLE MOLINARI.

Musée Astronomique de l'Observatoire de Paris: 61 ave de l'Observatoire, 75014 Paris; f. 1667; astronomical instruments of the 16th, 17th, 18th and 19th centuries; statues and pictures of celebrated astronomers.

Musée Carnavalet–Histoire de Paris: 23 rue de Sévigné, 75003 Paris; tel. 1-44-59-58-58; fax 1-44-59-58-11; internet www.carnavalet.paris.fr; f. 1880; Paris and its history from prehistoric times; depts include: archaeology, graphic arts, furniture, numismatics, painting, architectural models, sculpture; Chief Curator JEAN-MARC LÉRI.

Musée Cernuschi: 7 ave Vélasquez, 75008 Paris; tel. 1-53-96-21-50; fax 1-53-96-21-96; internet www.paris.fr/musees/cernuschi; f. 1896; Chinese art; Dir GILLES BEGUIN; publ. catalogues.

Musée Cognacq-Jay: 8 rue Elzévir, 75003 Paris; tel. 1-40-27-07-21; fax 1-40-27-89-44; internet www.paris.fr/musees/cognacq_jay; f. 1929; 18th c. works of art, French and English paintings, pastels, sculptures, porcelain, furniture, etc.; Curator GEORGES BRUNEL.

Musée d'Art Moderne de la Ville de Paris: 9 rue Gaston de Saint-Paul, 75116 Paris; located at: 11 ave du Président Wilson, 75116 Paris; tel. 1-53-67-40-00; fax 1-47-23-35-98; internet www.mam.paris.fr; f. 1961; modern and contemporary art; Curator FABRICE HERGOTT.

Musée de la Marine: Palais de Chaillot, 17 place du Trocadéro, 75116 Paris; tel. 1-53-65-69-69 ext. 120; fax 1-53-65-69-42; internet www.musee-marine.fr; f. 1827; collection of models and paintings of the navy; oceanographic research; library: 50,000 documents, 190,000 photographs; Dir Rear-Adm. GEORGES PRUD'HOMME; publs *Neptunia* (quarterly), catalogues.

Musée de la Monnaie: Monnaie de Paris, 11 quai de Conti, 75270 Paris Cedex 06; tel. 1-40-46-56-66; fax 1-40-46-57-00; e-mail musee@monnaiedeparis.fr; internet www.monnaiedeparis.fr; f. 1771; collections of coins, medals, drawings, paintings, old machines, engravings and stained glass windows; Dir EVELYNE COHEN.

Musée de l'Air et de l'Espace: BP 173, Aéroport du Bourget, 4 93352 Le Bourget Cedex; tel. 1-49-92-71-99; fax 1-49-92-70-95; e-mail musee.air@mae.org; internet www.mae.org; f. 1919; aeronautics, representative colln of aircraft; library of 40,000 vols; Dir Gen. GERARD FELDZER; publ. *Pégase* (quarterly).

Musée de l'Armée: Hôtel des Invalides, 129, rue de Grenelle, 75007 Paris; tel. 1-44-42-37-72; fax 1-44-42-38-44; e-mail comm-ma@invalides.org; internet www.invalides.org; f. 1905; collections of artillery, arms, armour, uniforms, flags; history of French Army from its origin to present day; Napoleon's tomb; Second World War; library of 50,000 vols, 60,000 prints, 74,400 photographs; Dir B. DEVAUX; publ. *Revue de la Société des Amis du Musée de l'Armée* (2 a year).

Musée de l'Histoire de France: Centre historique des Archives nationales, 60 rue des Francs-Bourgeois, 75141 Paris Cedex 03; tel. 1-40-27-60-96; fax 1-40-27-66-45; f. 1867; frequent exhibitions showing original documents from the National Archives tracing the principal events in the history of France; also historical objects and iconography; Dir DENIS GRISEL; Curator ARIANE JAMES SARAZIN.

Musée de l'Homme: Palais de Chaillot, place du Trocadéro, 75116 Paris; tel. 1-44-05-72-03; fax 1-44-05-72-12; e-mail bmhweb@mnhn.fr; internet www.mnhn.fr/mnhn/bmh; f. 1878; library of 400,000 vols, 5,000 periodicals, 1,000 microfiches; ethnography, anthropology, prehistory; attached to the Muséum National d'Histoire Naturelle (*q.v.*); also a research and education centre; Profs BERNARD DUPAIGNE, ANDRÉ LANGANEY, HENRY DE LUMLEY.

Musée de l'Orangerie: Jardin des Tuileries, 75001 Paris; tel. 1-40-20-67-70; fax 1-42-61-30-82; e-mail musee.orangerie@culture.gouv.fr; internet www.musee-orangerie.fr; f. 1927; permanent exhibition of the 'Nymphéas' (Water Lilies) murals by Claude Monet, and Jean Walter et Guillaume collection (Cézanne, Renoir, Rousseau, Picasso, Matisse, Derain, Modigliani, Soutine, Utrillo); Dir PIERRE GEORGEL.

Musée d'Ennery: 59 ave Foch, 75116 Paris; tel. 1-45-53-57-96; fax 1-45-05-02-66; f. 1903; 17th- to 19th-century Far East decorative arts; Curator JEAN-FRANÇOIS JARRIGE.

Musée des Arts et Métiers: 60 rue Réaumur, 75003 Paris; 292 rue St Martin, 75141 Paris Cedex 03; tel. 1-53-01-82-00; fax 1-53-01-82-01; e-mail musee@cnam.fr; internet www.arts-et-metiers.net; f. 1794; evolution of industrial technology from 16th c. to the present; Dir DANIEL THOULOUZE.

Musée des Monuments Français: Palais de Chaillot, Place du Trocadéro, 75116 Paris; tel. 1-44-05-39-10; fax 1-47-55-40-13; f. 1882; casts of portions of monuments and sculptures from beginning of Christianity to 20th century; architectural models; library of 10,000 works on history of art, 200,000 photographs, collection of scale reproductions of murals of the Middle Ages and materials connected with building and decoration; Dir GUY COGEVAL; publ. *Guides*.

Musée des Plans en Reliefs: Hôtel National des Invalides, 75007 Paris; tel. 1-45-51-95-05; fax 1-47-05-11-07; f. 1668.

Musée d'Histoire Contemporaine: Hôtel National des Invalides, 75007 Paris; tel. 1-45-51-93-02; f. 1914; attached to Bibliothèque de Documentation Internationale Contemporaine; 400,000 documents (paintings, engravings, posters, cartoons, etc.); 800,000 photographs and postcards; Curator LAURENT GERVEREAU.

Musée d'Orsay: 62 rue de Lille, 75343 Paris; tel. 1-40-49-48-00; fax 1-45-44-63-82; internet www.musee-orsay.fr; f. 1986; works from the second half of the 19th c. and early 20th c.: paintings and pastels, sculptures, art objects, photographs, also plans, sketches, etc.; audiovisual information, database, cultural service, exhibitions and dossier-exhibitions, cinema, lectures, concerts; Pres. SERGE LEMOINE.

Musée du Louvre: 75058 Paris Cedex 01; tel. 1-40-20-50-50; fax 1-40-20-54-42; e-mail info@louvre.fr; internet www.louvre.fr; f. 1793; Gen.-Dir HENRI LOYRETTE; depts and curators: Oriental Antiquities (ANNIE CAUBET), Egyptian Antiquities (CHRISTIANE ZIEGLER), Greek, Etruscan and Roman Antiquities (ALAIN PASQUIER), Islamic Art (FRANÇIS RICHARD), Sculpture (JEAN-RENÉ GABORIT), *Objets d'art* (DANIEL ALCOUFFE), Paintings (VINCENT POMAREDE), Drawings and Prints (FRANÇOISE VIATTE).

Musée du Luxembourg: 19 rue de Vaugirard, 75006 Paris; tel. 1-43-54-87-71; fax 1-43-25-20-33; e-mail info@museeduluxembourg.fr; internet www.museeduluxembourg.fr; f. 1750; hosts temporary exhibitions, according to a programme decided by the Min. of Culture and the Senate; Pres. of Senate CHRISTIAN PONCELET.

Musée du Petit Palais: Ave Winston Churchill, 75008 Paris; tel. 1-42-65-12-73; fax 1-42-65-24-60; municipal museum, f. 1900; paintings, sculptures and works of art from antiquity to 1925; Dir Mlle THÉRÈSE BUROLLET.

Musée Galliera: 10 ave Pierre Ier de Serbie, 75116 Paris; tel. 1-56-52-86-00; fax 1-47-23-38-37; e-mail bibliothequegalliera@free.fr; internet www.paris-france.org/musees; f. 1977; temporary exhibitions of French costumes and accessories from 1725 to the present day; library: library; Dir CATHERINE JOIN-DIETERLE.

Musée Gustave Moreau: 14 rue de la Rochefoucauld, 75009 Paris; tel. 1-48-74-38-50; fax 1-48-74-18-71; e-mail info@musee-moreau.fr; internet www.musee-moreau.fr; f. 1903 from a bequest by the painter Gustave Moreau of his house and contents, including paintings, watercolours, sketches, wax sculptures and designs; Curator GENEVIÈVE LACAMBRE.

Musée Jacquemart-André: 158 blvd Haussmann, 75008 Paris; tel. 1-45-62-11-59; fax 1-45-62-16-36; e-mail message@musee-jacquemart-andre.com; internet www.musee-jacquemart-andre.com; f. 1912; painting, sculpture, ceramics, tapestry and furniture from Renaissance to 18th century; Dir ALAIN SCHIEDÉ.

Musée Marmottan: 2 rue Louis Boilly, 75016 Paris; tel. 1-44-96-50-33; fax 1-40-50-65-84; e-mail marmottan@marmottan.com; internet www.marmottan.com; f. 1932; Primitives, Renaissance, Empire and Impressionists; Wildenstein Collection of medieval miniatures; permanent exhibition 'Monet et ses Amis'; affiliated to the *Académie des Beaux-Arts – Fondation Rouart*; Dir JEAN-MARIE GRANIER.

Musée National d'Art Moderne: 75191 Paris Cedex 04; tel. 1-44-78-12-33; internet www.centrepompidou.fr; attached to Centre National d'Art et de Culture Georges-Pompidou; painting since beginning of 20th c., sculpture, architecture, design, new media, drawings, photographs, art films; Dir ALFRED PACQUEMENT.

Musée National de la Légion d'Honneur et des Ordres de Chevalerie: Hôtel de Salm, 2 rue de la Légion d'Honneur, 75007 Paris; tel. 1-40-62-84-25; e-mail musee.gclh@free.fr; internet www.legiondhonneur.fr; f. 1925; contains histories of National Orders from the Middle Ages until the present and Awards of all countries: unique collection of decorations, costumes, arms, documents, etc.; also collection and documents relating to Napoleon I; Centre de Documentation International de l'Histoire des Ordres et des Décorations; Dir-Curator ANNE DE CHEFDEBIEN.

Musée National des Arts Asiatiques Guimet: 6 place d'Iéna, 75116 Paris; tel. 1-56-52-53-00; fax 1-56-52-53-54; internet www.museeguimet.fr; f. 1889; Asiatic Dept of Nat. Museums; library of 100,000 vols; art, archaeology, religions, history and music of India, Central Asia, Tibet, Afghanistan, China, Korea and Japan, Khmer, Thailand and Indonesia; Chief Curator JEAN-FRANÇOIS JARRIGE; Librarian FRANCIS MACOUIN; publs *Annales*, *Arts Asiatiques*.

Musée National des Arts d'Afrique et d'Océanie: 293 ave Daumesnil, 75012 Paris; tel. 1-44-74-84-80; f. 1931 as Musée des Colonies, 1935 Musée de la France d'Outre-Mer, present name 1960; exhibits from Maghreb, Africa and the Pacific Islands; tropical aquarium; temporary exhibitions; library: *c.* 5,000 vols, 160 periodicals; Dir GERMAIN VIATTE.

Musée National des Arts et Traditions Populaires: 6 ave du Mahatma Gandhi, 75116 Paris; tel. 1-44-17-60-00; fax 1-44-17-60-60; f. 1937; 142,000 objects; library: 90,000 books, 2,000 periodicals; 281,000 photographic documents, 70,000 tape records; Curator MICHEL COLARDELLE; publs *Architecture rurale française*, *Mobilier traditionnel français*, *Récits et contes populaires*, *Archives d'Ethnologie Française*, *Guides Ethnologiques*, *Catalogues des Expositions*, *Ethnologie française* (4 a year).

Musée National du Moyen Âge: Thermes et Hôtel de Cluny, 6 place Paul Painlevé, 75005 Paris; tel. 1-53-73-78-00; fax 1-43-25-85-27; e-mail lettreinfo.musee-moyenage@culture.gouv.fr; internet www.musee-moyenage.fr; f. 1843; everyday life and fine and decorative arts of the Middle Ages; Dir ELISABETH DELAHAYE.

Musée Picasso: 5 rue de Thorigny, 75003 Paris; tel. 1-42-71-25-21; fax 1-48-04-75-46; internet www.musee-picasso.fr; f. 1985 from a collection begun in 1979; traces the evolution of Picasso's art; 251 paintings, 160 sculptures, 107 ceramics, 1,500 drawings and engravings; library: *c.* 2,000 vols on Picasso and his world; Dir ANNE BALDASSARI; Chief Curator GÉRARD RÉGNIER; publs catalogues, guides.

Musée Rodin: Hôtel Biron, 77 rue de Varenne, 75007 Paris; tel. 1-44-18-61-10; fax 1-45-51-17-52; e-mail penseur@musee-rodin.fr; internet www.musee-rodin.fr; f. 1919; sculpture and drawings by Rodin and objects from his collections; annexe in Meudon; Dir JACQUES VILAIN.

Muséum National d'Histoire Naturelle: see under State Colleges.

Palais du Cinéma: Palais de Tokyo, 24 rue Hamelin, 75116 Paris; tel. 1-45-53-74-74; fax 1-45-53-74-76; exhibitions concerning motion pictures; motion picture theatres; library and film archive; Dir XAVIER NORTH.

Palais de la Découverte: Ave Franklin D. Roosevelt, 75008 Paris; tel. 1-56-43-20-20; fax 1-56-43-20-29; internet www.palais-decouverte.fr; f. 1937 as a scientific centre for the popularization of science; experiments explained to the public; departments of mathematics, astronomy, physics, chemistry, biology, medicine, earth sciences; also includes a Planetarium and cinema; library of 7,000 vols; Dir MICHEL DEMAZURE; publs *Revue*, *Monographies*.

Pavillon de l'Arsenal: 21 blvd Morland, 75004 Paris; tel. 1-42-76-33-97; fax 1-42-76-26-32; internet www.pavillon-arsenal.com; f. 1988; information and documentation centre on urban planning and architecture; permanent exhibition on Paris; temporary exhibitions, photo library, educational facilities, etc.; Dir Mme DOMINIQUE ALBA; publ. catalogues.

Pavillon des Arts: 101 rue Rambuteau, 75001 Paris; tel. 1-42-33-82-50; fax 1-40-28-93-22; f. 1983; municipal art gallery for temporary exhibitions; Dir BÉATRICE RIOTTOT EL-HABIB.

Pau

Musée Bernadotte: 8 rue Tran, 64000 Pau; tel. 5-59-27-48-42; internet musee.ville-pau.fr/InfosPratiques/Liens/Bernadotte; f. 1935; pictures and documents tracing the career of Jean Baptiste Bernadotte, Marshal under Napoleon, later King of Sweden; Swedish pictures; Curator PH. COMTE; publ. *Bulletin* (annually).

Musée des Beaux-Arts: rue Mathieu Lalanne, 64000 Pau; tel. 5-59-27-33-02; fax 5-59-98-70-10; e-mail museedesbeauxarts.pau@laposte.net; internet musee.ville-pau.fr; f. 1864; pictures from French, Flemish, Dutch, English, Italian and Spanish schools; contemporary artists; sculptures, engravings and drawings; numismatic collections; Curator GUILLAUME AMBROISE.

Musée National du Château de Pau: 64000 Pau; tel. 5-59-82-38-02; fax 5-59-82-38-18; e-mail olivier.pouvreau@culture.gouv.fr; internet www.musee-chateau-pau.fr; f. 1927; 16th and 17th c. collection of tapestries; state apartments of Louis-Philippe I and Napoleon III; exhibition on the reign of King Henry IV; engravings, drawings; library and research facility (Centre Jacques de Laprade) for students of history, literature and history of art; Curator PAUL MIRONNEAU; publ. *Bulletin* (quarterly).

Musée Régional Béarnais: 64000 Pau; tel. 5-59-27-07-36; a collection relating to the Bearnese country.

Perpignan

Casa Pairal, Musée Catalan des Arts et Traditions Populaires: Mairie de Perpignan, BP 931, 66931 Perpignan Cedex; located at: Le Castillet, Place de Verdun, 66000 Perpignan; tel. 4-68-35-42-05; fax 4-68-66-32-80; internet www.mairie-perpignan.fr; f. 1963; ethnography, folklore and anthropology of the Catalan region; Curator JACQUES-GASPARD DELONCLE.

Poitiers

Conservation des Musées de Poitiers: 3 bis rue Jean-Jaurès, 86000 Poitiers; tel. 5-49-41-07-53; fax 5-49-88-61-63; e-mail musees.poitiers@alienor.org; internet www.musees-poitiers.org; f. 1794; library of 10,000 vols, 50 periodicals; Curators MICHEL REROLLE, MARIE-CHRISTINE PLANCHARD, MARYSE REDIEN, PHILIPPE BATA.

Attached museums:

Baptistère Saint-Jean: Rue Jean-Jaurès, 86000 Poitiers; f. 1836; Merovingian archaeology.

Hypogée des Dunes: 101 rue du Père de la Croix, 86000 Poitiers; f. 1909; 7th–8th-c. Merovingian archaeology.

Musée Rupert de Chièvres: 9 rue Victor Hugo, 86000 Poitiers; tel. 5-49-41-07-53; f. 1887; reconstruction of a 19th c. collector's private house; pre-1800 paintings, furniture, objets d'art.

Musée Sainte-Croix: 3 bis rue Jean-Jaurès, 86000 Poitiers; tel. 5-49-41-07-53; f. 1974; fine arts, history of Poitou (archaeological, ethnographical collections, sculpture and paintings post 1800).

Reims

Musée des Beaux-Arts: 8 rue Chanzy, 51100 Reims; tel. 3-26-47-28-44; fax 3-26-86-87-75; e-mail cecile.leroux@mairie-reims.fr; f. 1795; paintings (especially French School, 17th c. Le Nain, and 19th c. Corot–Delacroix), and Cranach drawings; 15th and 16th c. 'Toiles Peintes'; collection of ceramics; Curator DAVID LIOT.

Musée Saint-Remi: 53 rue Simon, 51100 Reims; tel. 3-26-85-23-36; fax 3-26-82-07-99; the old Abbey of St Remi (12th to 18th centuries); Prehistoric, Celtic, Gallo-Roman, Romanesque and Gothic antiquities and sculptures; tapestries of St-Remi life (1530); old weapons; Chief Curator MARC BOUXIN.

Rennes

Musée des Beaux-Arts: 20 quai Emile Zola, 35000 Rennes; tel. 2-99-28-55-85; fax 2-99-28-55-99; e-mail museebeauxarts@ville-rennes.fr; internet www.mbar.org; f. 1799; paintings, drawings, engravings, sculpture of French and foreign Schools from the 15th c.; archaeology; library of 35,000 vols; Curator FRANCIS RIBEMONT.

Musée de Bretagne: 20 quai Emile Zola, 35000 Rennes; tel. 2-99-28-55-84; fax 2-99-28-40-17; e-mail museebzh@agglo-rennesmetropole.fr; internet www.musee-bretagne.fr; f. 1960; geology, prehistory, Armorica at the Roman period, medieval art, historical documents, popular art, furniture, 19th c. costumes, contemporary regional art and history; Dir FRANÇOIS HUBERT.

Rouen

Musées de la Ville de Rouen: 1 place Restout, 76000 Rouen; tel. 2-35-52-00-62; fax 2-35-15-43-23; internet www.rouen-musees.com.

Attached museums:

Musée des Beaux-Arts: Square Verdrel, 76000 Rouen; tel. 2-35-71-28-40; fax 2-35-15-43-23; f. 1801; paintings, drawings, sculpture, decorative art; Dir CLAUDE PÉTRY.

Musée de la Céramique: 1 rue Faucon, 76000 Rouen; tel. 2-35-07-31-74; fax 2-35-15-43-23; f. 1983; 16th–19th c. ceramics.

Musée de la Ferronnerie: Rue Jacques Villon, 76000 Rouen; tel. 2-35-88-42-92; fax 2-35-15-43-23; f. 1922; 3rd–19th c. ironwork; Curator MARIE PESSIOT.

Rueil-Malmaison

Musée National des Châteaux de Malmaison et de Bois-Préau: 92500 Rueil-Malmaison; tel. 1-41-29-05-55; fax 1-41-29-05-56; internet www.chateau-malmaison.fr; f. 1906; historical colln of Napoleon I and Joséphine; Curator BERNARD CHEVALLIER.

St-Denis

Musée d'Art et d'Histoire: 22 bis rue Gabriel Péri, 93200 St-Denis; tel. 1-42-43-05-10; fax 1-48-20-07-60; e-mail musee@ville-saint-denis.fr; internet www.musee-saint-denis.fr; f. 1901; located in a disused 17th-century Carmelite monastery; collns: medieval archaeology and ceramics; history and memorabilia from the monastery and Madame Louise; the Paris Commune; paintings by Albert André; Paul Eluard and Francis Jourdain collns; remains of the old hospital; documentation room for researchers and students; Curator SYLVIE GONZALEZ.

St-Etienne

Musée d'Art et d'Industrie: Place Louis Comte, 42000 St-Etienne; tel. 4-77-49-73-00; fax 4-77-49-73-05; e-mail museemai@mairie-st-etienne.fr; internet www.mairie-st-etienne.fr; f. 1833, at Palais des Arts since 1850; armaments, fabrics, bicycles; Curator NADINE BESSE.

Attached museums:

Musée d'Art Moderne: La Terrasse, 42000 St-Etienne; tel. 4-77-79-52-52; fax 4-77-79-52-50; e-mail mam@agglo-st-etienne.fr; f. 1987; collection of modern and contemporary art; library: library; Curator BERNARD CEYSSON.

Musée de la Mine: 3 blvd Franchet d'Esperey, 42000 St-Etienne; tel. 4-77-43-83-23; fax 4-77-43-83-29; e-mail museemin@mairie-st-etienne.fr; mining and industrial museum on the site of a former working mine.

St-Germain-en-Laye

Musée des Antiquités Nationales: Château, BP 3030, 78103 St-Germain-en-Laye Cedex; tel. 1-39-10-13-00; fax 1-34-51-73-93; e-mail germain@culture.fr; internet www.musee-antiquitesnationales.fr; f. 1862; Prehistoric, Bronze Age, Celtic, Gallo-Roman and Merovingian antiquities, comparative archaeology; library of 25,000 vols; Dir PATRICK PÉRIN; publ. *Antiquités nationales* (annually).

St-Malo

Musée de St-Malo: Château de St-Malo, 35400 St-Malo; tel. 2-99-40-71-57; fax 2-99-40-71-56; e-mail musee@ville-saint-malo.fr; f. 1950; history of Saint-Malo and temporary exhibitions; Curator PH. PETOUT.

Attached museum:

Musée International du Long Cours Cap-Hornier: Tour Solidor, St-Servan, 35400 St-Malo; tel. 2-99-40-71-58; e-mail musee@ville-saint-malo.fr; f. 1969; international history of sailing around the world since 16th c.; Curator PH. PETOUT.

St-Paul-de-Vence

Fondation Maeght: 06570 St-Paul-de-Vence; tel. 4-93-32-81-63; fax 4-93-32-53-22; e-mail contact@fondation-maeght.com; internet www.fondation-maeght.com; f. 1964; modern paintings and sculpture incl. Bonnard, Braque, Giacometti, Miró and Calder; work by contemporary artists; library of 23,000 vols on modern arts and daily films on art and artists; Curator JEAN-LOUIS PRAT.

St-Tropez

Annonciade, Musée de St-Tropez: Place Georges Grammont, 83990 St-Tropez; tel. 4-94-97-04-01; fax 4-94-97-87-24; internet www.saint-tropez.tv; f. 1955; French paintings 1890–1950; Curator JEAN-PAUL MONERY.

Saumur

Château Musée: Le Château, 49400 Saumur; tel. 2-41-40-24-40; fax 2-41-40-24-49; e-mail chateau.musee@ville-saumur.fr; internet www.ville-saumur.fr; f. 1829 and reorganized 1960; local archaeology, the collection of Comte Charles Lair of decorative arts, including tapestries, furniture, wood carvings, liturgical ornaments; fine porcelain of 16th-18th c.; Curator Mlle JACQUELINE MONGELLAZ.

Sceaux

Musée de l'Ile de France: Château de Sceaux, 92330 Sceaux; tel. 1-46-61-06-71; fax 1-46-61-00-88; f. 1935; old and modern paintings, sculpture, engravings, furniture, decorative art, tapestries, history and drawings of the environs of Paris; documentation centre on the Paris region; educational services; documentation centre; annexes: Orangerie and Pavillon de l'Aurore (Parc de Sceaux); Dir CECILE DUPONT-LOGIÉ.

Sèvres

Musée National de Céramique: Place de la Manufacture, 92310 Sèvres; tel. 1-41-14-04-20; fax 1-45-34-67-88; e-mail musee .sevres@culture.gouv.fr; f. 1824; ancient and modern ceramic art; Curator ANTOINETTE HALLÉ; publ. *Revue de la Société des Amis du Musée National de Céramique* (annual).

Soissons

Musée Municipal: 2 rue de la Congrégation, 02200 Soissons; tel. 3-23-93-30-50; fax 3-23-93-30-51; internet www.musee-soissons .org; f. 1857; antiquities, medieval sculpture, paintings since 17th century, local history and protohistory; archaeology of the Aisne Valley from Neolithic to Middle Ages; Curator DOMINIQUE ROUSSEL.

Attached museum:

Musée Arsenal: Site de l'abbaye Saint-Jean-des-Vignes, rue Saint Jean, 02200 Soissons; tel. 3-23-53-42-40; fax 3-23-93-30-51; internet www.musee-soissons.org; temporary exhibition space in the Arsenal; Dir DOMINIQUE ROUSSEL.

Strasbourg

Palais Rohan: 2 place du Château, 67000 Strasbourg; tel. 3-88-52-50-00; fax 3-88-52-50-09; internet www.musees-strasbourg.org.

Attached museums:

Musée Archéologique: C/o Palais Rohan, 2 place du Château, 67000 Strasbourg; tel. 3-88-52-50-00; fax 3-88-52-50-09; f. 1856; prehistoric, Celtic, Gallo-Roman and Merovingian collns; results of excavations in Alsace; Curator BERNADETTE SCHNITZLER.

Musée des Arts Décoratifs et Appartements Historiques: C/o Palais Rohan, 2 place du Château, 67000 Strasbourg; tel. 3-88-52-50-00; fax 3-88-52-50-09; f. 1883; furniture from 18th and 19th centuries; French paintings; ceramics; silver objects; musical instruments; wrought-iron and tin; Curator ETIENNE MARTIN.

Musée des Beaux-Arts: C/o Palais Rohan, 2 place du Château, 67000 Strasbourg; tel. 3-88-52-50-00; fax 3-88-52-50-09; f. 1801; French and foreign paintings: Old Masters, art from 14th–19th centuries, Italian, Spanish, Flemish, Dutch and French schools; Curator DOMINIQUE JACQUOT.

Toulouse

Musée des Augustins: 21 rue de Metz, 31000 Toulouse; tel. 5-61-22-21-82; fax 5-61-22-34-69; e-mail augustins@mairie-toulouse .fr; internet www.augustins.org; f. 1793 and housed in the former Augustine Convent, of which parts date from the 14th and 15th c.; Roman and Gothic sculptures, 16th–19th c. local and foreign paintings; Curator ALAIN DAGUERRE DE HUREAUX.

Tours

Musée des Beaux-Arts: 18 place François-Sicard, 37000 Tours; tel. 2-47-05-68-73; fax 2-47-05-38-91; e-mail musee-beauxarts@ ville-tours.fr; internet www.musees .regioncentre.fr; f. 1793 and moved in 1910 to the former Archbishop's palace; paintings by Mantegna, Rembrandt, Rubens, Vignon, Lancret, Boucher, Delacroix, Degas, Debré; sculpture by Le Moyne, Houdon, Bourdelle, Davidson, Calder; furniture, tapestries and objets d'art; library of 15,000 ; Curator PHILIPPE LE LEYZOUR.

Affiliated museums:

Château d'Azay-le-Ferron: 36290 Azay-le-Ferron; tel. 2-54-39-20-06; buildings, objets d'art and furniture of the 15th to 19th centuries; Curator PHILIPPE LE LEYZOUR.

Musée Saint-Martin: 3 rue Rapin, 37000 Tours; tel. 2-47-64-48-87; fax 2-47-05-38-91; f. 1990; contains collection of souvenirs of St Martin; Curator PHILIPPE LE LEYZOUR.

Musée du Compagnonnage: 8 rue Nationale, 37000 Tours; tel. 2-47-61-07-93; fax 2-47-21-68-90; e-mail museecompagnonnage@ ville-tours.fr; f. 1968; archives and historical masterpieces; Curator LAURENT BASTARD.

Musée de la Société Archéologique de Touraine: Hôtel Gouin, 25 rue du Commerce, 37000 Tours; tel. 2-47-66-22-32; Gallic and Roman archaeology, medieval and 16th c. sculptures, prehistoric artefacts; iconography of Tours, 18th and 19th c. pottery.

Musée des Vins de Touraine: 16 rue Nationale (parvis Saint-Julien), 37000 Tours; tel. 2-47-61-07-93; fax 2-47-21-68-90; f. 1975; Curator LAURENT BASTARD.

Ungersheim

Ecomusée d'Alsace: BP 71, 68190 Ungersheim; tel. 3-89-74-44-74; fax 3-89-74-44-65; e-mail contact@ecoparcs.com; internet www .ecomusee-alsace.com; f. 1984 by the Asscn Maisons Paysannes d'Alsace to safeguard the rural architecture of Alsace; an open-air museum comprising a reconstituted village of 70 cottages, showing life in olden days with a baker, an oil-mill, a blacksmith, a clog-maker, a sawmill working on site; nature walks, seminars; library of 950 vols, 4,000 drawings and reliefs, 25,000 photographs, videos; Pres. MARC GRODWOHL.

Vaison-la-Romaine

Musée Archéologique Théo Desplans: Colline de Puymin, 84110 Vaison-la-Romaine; tel. 4-90-36-50-00; fax 4-90-36-50-29; f. 1920, present site 1975; archaeological colln from excavations at Vaison; Curator CHRISTINE BEZIN.

Valenciennes

Musée des Beaux-Arts: blvd Watteau, 59300 Valenciennes; tel. 3-27-22-57-20; fax 3-27-22-57-22; e-mail mba@ ville-valenciennes.fr; internet www .valenciennes.fr; painting, sculpture, archaeology, etc.; Dir P. RAMADE.

Vallauris

Musée National Picasso 'La Guerre et la Paix': Place de la Libération, 06220 Vallauris; tel. 4-93-64-71-83; fax 4-93-64-50-32; internet www.musee-picasso-vallauris.fr; f. 1959; works by Picasso including *La Guerre et la Paix* in 12th c. chapel; Curator JEAN-MICHEL FORAY.

Verdun

Centre Mondial de la Paix, des Libertés et des Droits de l'Homme: Palais Episcopal BP 183, 55100 Verdun; tel. 3-29-86-55-00; fax 3-29-86-15-14; e-mail cmpaix@wanadoo .fr; f. 1994; exhibition on the First World War; and 'From War to Peace', an interactive exhibition which depicts the origins of war in Europe, attempts at peacekeeping and punishment of war crimes, the history of European co-operation and the EU, the UN, and the nature and application of human rights; meetings, conferences and roleplay situations for students; Dir JEAN-LUC DEMANDRE.

Versailles

Musée National du Château de Versailles: 78000 Versailles; tel. 1-30-84-74-00; fax 1-30-84-76-48; f. 1837 by Louis-Philippe; historical painting and sculpture, furniture of the 17th to 19th centuries; Grand Trianon, Petit Trianon châteaux, Hameau de la Reine, park; Pres. HUBERT ASTIER.

Vizille

Musée de la Révolution Française: Château de Vizille, 38220 Vizille; tel. 4-76-68-07-35; fax 4-76-68-08-53; e-mail musee .revolution@cg38.fr; internet www .musee-revolution-francaise.fr; f. 1984; relics, art and library connected with the French Revolution of 1789; library of 20,000 vols, 25,000 microfiches; Dir ALAIN CHEVALIER.

State Universities

UNIVERSITÉ DE PROVENCE (AIX-MARSEILLE I)

3 place Victor Hugo, 13331 Marseilles Cedex 3

Telephone: 4-91-10-60-00
Fax: 4-91-10-60-06
E-mail: webup@up.univ-mrs.fr
Internet: www.up.univ-mrs.fr

Universities of Aix en Provence consist of three universities based in Aix en Provence and Marseille; Arts, History, Geography and Modern Languages are principal subjects of instruction here

Founded 1970

President: YVES MATHIEU
Vice-Presidents: ROBERT CHENORKIAN, JEAN-MARC FABRE, JIMMY ELHADAD JULIEN CHATELAIN
Secretary-General: GÉRARD BARBERAN
Librarian: Mme GACHON

Library: see Libraries
Number of students: 26,000

Publication: *Guide de l'Etudiant*

TEACHING AND RESEARCH UNITS

Civilisations and Humanities: Dir: JEAN-MARIE GUILLON
Psychology and Educational Sciences: Dir: JEAN-LOUIS PAOUR
Roman, Latin-American, Oriental and Slavic Studies: Dir: BERNARD MARTOCQ
Anglo-Saxon and Germanic Languages: Dir: DOMINIQUE BATOUX
Letters, Arts, Communication and Linguistics: Dir: DENIS COLLOMP
Mathematics, Computing, Mechanics: Dir: BERNARD COUPET
Material Sciences: Dir: JEAN-MARC LAYET
Life, Earth and Environmental Sciences: Dir: JEAN-PIERRE ROLL
Geographical Sciences: Dir: SYLVIE DAVIET

ATTACHED INSTITUTES

Centre de Formation des Musiciens Intervenants (CFMI): tel. 4-42-96-32-40; Dir SERGE BOURDON.

Centre Interuniversitaire de Mécanique (UNIMECA): 60 rue Joliot-Curie, 13453 Marseilles Cedex 13; tel. 4-91-11-38-00; fax 4-91-11-38-38; Dir DANIEL DUFRESNE.

Département Environnement Technologie et Société (DENTES): tel. 4-91-10-63-28; Dir MAX CARBONEL.

École Polytechnique Universitaire de Marseille: 13451 Marseilles Cedex 20; tel. 4-91-05-44-36; fax 4-91-05-43-76; e-mail direction@polytech.univ-mrs.fr; Dir MICHEL TROQUET.

Institut de la Francophonie: tel. 4-42-95-35-53; Dir ROBERT CHAUDENSON.

IUP Génie de l'environnement: 3 Place Victor Hugo, 13331 Marseilles Cedex 03; tel. 4-91-10-63-28; fax 4-91-10-62-85; Dir MAX CARBONEL.

IUP Génie des Matériaux: 3 Place Victor Hugo, 13331 Marseilles Cedex 03; tel. 4-91-28-27-48; e-mail iup2m@up.univ-mrs.fr; Dir DENIS BERTIN.

IUP Métiers de l'Image et du Son (SATIS): 9 blvd Lakanal, 13400 Aubagne; tel. 4-42-82-41-91; Dir JACQUES SAPIEGA.

Maison Méditerranéenne des Sciences de l'Homme (MMSH): 5 rue du Château de l'Horloge, BP 647, 13094 Aix en Provence Cedex 2; tel. 4-42-52-40-00; Dir ROBERT ILBERT.

Observatoire Astronomique de Marseille-Provence (OAMP): Dir MICHEL BLANC.

UNIVERSITÉ DE LA MÉDITERRANÉE AIX-MARSEILLE II

Jardin du Pharo, 58 blvd Charles Livon, 13284 Marseilles Cedex 07Telephone: 4-91-39-65-00

Fax: 4-91-31-31-36

Internet: www.mediterranee.univ-mrs.fr

Founded 1973

Language of instruction: French

Academic year: October to June

Universities of Aix en Provence consist of three universities in Aix en Provence; Economic Science and Information Technology are the principal subjects of instruction here

President: YVON BERLAND

Vice-Presidents: DIDIER LAUSSEL (Administrative Council), DANIEL DUFRESNE (Council of Studies and University Life), JACQUES DERRIEN (Scientific Council), JOSÉ SAMPOL (Communications), MICHEL KASBARIAN (International Relations), NATHALIE ARNOUX (Students)

Secretary-General: DAMIEN VERHAEGHE

Number of teachers: 660

Number of students: 24,186.

TEACHING AND RESEARCH UNITS

Faculty of Medicine: 27, blvd Jean Moulin, 13385 Marseilles Cedex 5; tel. 4-91-32-43-00; fax 4-91-32-44-96; internet www.timone .univ-mrs.fr/medecine; Dean YVON BERLAND.

Faculty of Pharmacy: 27, blvd Jean Moulin, 13385 Marseilles Cedex 5; tel. 4-91-83-55-00; fax 4-91-80-26-12; internet www .pharmacie.univ-mrs.fr; Dean PATRICE VANELLE.

Faculty of Odontology: 27, blvd Jean Moulin, 13385 Marseilles Cedex 5; tel. 4-91-78-46-70; fax 4-91-78-23-43; internet www .molaire.timone.univ-mrs.fr; Dean ANDRE SALVADORI.

Oceanological Centre: Campus de Luminy, 163 ave de Luminy, 13288 Marseilles Cedex 9; tel. 4-91-82-93-00; fax 4-91-82-93-03; internet www.com.univ-mrs.fr; Dean M. IVAN DEKEYSER.

Faculty of Sciences at Luminy: 163, ave de Luminy, 13288 Marseilles Cedex 09; tel. 4-91-82-90-00; fax 4-91-26-92-00; internet www .luminy.univ-mrs.fr; Dean JACQUES BARATTI.

Faculty of Sports Sciences: 163 ave de Luminy, Case 910, 13288 Marseilles Cedex 9; tel. 4-91-17-04-12; fax 4-91-17-04-15; internet www.staps.univ-mrs.fr; Dean LAURENT GRELOT.

School of Engineeering: 163 ave de Luminy, Case 925, 13288 Marseilles Cedex 9; tel. 4-91-82-85-00; fax 4-91-82-85-91; internet www.esil.univ-mrs.fr; Dir JACQUES DERRIEN.

Institute of Mechanics: 60 rue Joliot Curie, 13453 Marseilles; tel. 4-91-11-38-02; fax 4-91-11-38-38; internet www.artemmis .univ-mrs.fr; Dir DANIEL DUFRESNE.

Faculty of Economic Science and Management: 14 rue Puvis de Chavannes, 13001 Marseilles; tel. 4-91-13-96-00; fax 4-91-90-58-29; internet www.sceco.univ-aix.fr; Dean THIERRY PAUL.

School of Journalism and Communication: 21 rue Virgile Marron, 13392 Marseilles Cedex 05; tel. 4-91-24-32-00; fax 4-91-24-32-07; internet www.ejcm.univ-mrs.fr; Dir PATRICK-YVES BADILLO.

Institute of Technology: Ave Gaston Berger, 13625 Aix en Provence Cedex 1; tel. 4-42-93-90-00; fax 4-42-93-90-90; internet www .iut.univ-aix.fr; Dir ROLAND KAZAN.

Institute of Labour: 12 traverse St Pierre, 13100 Aix en Provence; tel. 4-42-17-43-11; fax 4-42-21-20-12; e-mail irt@romarin .univ-aix.fr; Dir PATRICK BARRAU..

ATTACHED INSTITUTES

Centre de Recherche pour l'Enseignement des Mathématiques (IREM): Faculté des Sciences de Luminy, 163 ave de Luminy, 13288 Marseilles Cedex 9; tel. 4-91-26-90-91; fax 4-91-26-93-43; research into the teaching of mathematics; Dir ROBERT ROLLAND.

Centre International de Formation et de Recherche en Didactique (CIFORD): Faculté des Sciences de Luminy, 163 ave de Luminy, 13288 Marseilles Cedex 9; tel. 4-91-26-90-30; fax 4-91-26-93-55; Dir PAUL ALLARD.

Centre Universitaire Régional d'Etudes Municipales (CURET): 191 rue Breteuil, 13006 Marseilles; tel. 4-91-37-61-62; fax 4-91-37-61-63; courses in local government administration; Dir M. FOUCHET.

Institut Universitaire Professionnalisé (IUP) Affaires et Finances: Faculté des Sciences Economiques, 14 ave Jules Ferry, 13621 Aix-en-Provence Cedex; tel. 4-42-33-48-70; fax 4-42-33-48-72; course on business and finance.

UNIVERSITÉ PAUL CEZANNE–AIX-MARSEILLE III

3 ave Robert Schuman, 13628 Aix-en-Provence Cedex 1

Telephone: 4-42-17-28-00

E-mail: info.scuio@univ.u-3mrs.fr

Internet: www.univ.u-3mrs.fr

Founded 1973 as Université d'Aix-Marseille III (Université de Droit, d'Economie et des Sciences)

Academic year: September to June

Universities of Aix en Provence consist of three universities in Aix and Provence; Law, Economics and Foundation Science are the principal subjects of instruction here

President: J. BOURDON

Vice-Presidents: P. DJONDANG G. MILLE J. MESTRE A. CAR, P. ROUSSEAU

Secretary-General: C. BRAY

Librarian: J.-C. RODA

Number of teachers: 760

Number of students: 22,500

Publications: *L'Inter Cours* (monthly), *Interface* (monthly), annual research reports

DEANS

Faculty of Law and Political Science: J. MESTRE

Faculty of Applied Economics: J.-P. CENTI

Faculty of Science and Technology: A. CHARAI

TEACHING AND RESEARCH UNITS

Aix-en-Provence (Social Sciences):

Institute of Business Administration: Blvd des Camus, 13540 Puyricard; tel. 4-42-28-08-08; fax 4-42-28-08-00; internet www .iae-aix.com; Dir A. GED.

Institute of Penal Sciences and Criminology: Ave Henri Poncet, 13628 Aix en Provence Cedex 1; Dir J.-Y. LASSALLE.

Institute of Business Law: 3 Ave Robert Schuman, 13628 Aix en Provence Cedex 1; fax 4-42-17-29-51; internet www .ida-aixmarseille.com; Dir M. BUY.

Institute of Legal Research: Dir J.-M. PONTIER.

Institute of Regional Development: 2 Ave Henri Poncet, 13628 Aix en Provence Cedex 1; tel. 4-42-64-61-90; fax 4-42-64-61-91; internet www.iar.u-3mrs.fr; Dir D. PINSON.

Institute of Business Management: Dir A. GED.

Institute of Political Studies: 23 rue Gaston de Saporta, 13628 Aix en Provence; tel. 4-42-17-01-63; internet www.iep-aix.fr; Dir J. C. RICCI.

Institute of French Studies for Foreign Students: 23 rue Gaston de Saporta, 13628 Aix en Provence; tel. 4-42-21-70-90; fax 4-42-23-02-64; internet www.iefee.com; Dir R. GHEVONTIAN.

Institute of Public Management and Regional Government: 23 rue Gaston de Saporta, 13100 Aix en Provence; tel. 4-42-17-05-54; fax 4-42-17-05-56; internet www .managementpublic.u-3mrs.fr; Dir R. FOUCHET.

Institute of Higher Economic Study: 2 rue Jean Andréani, 13084 Aix en Provence Cedex 2; tel. 4-42-91-31-20; fax 4-42-91-31-29; e-mail secretariat.isec@wanadoo.fr; internet www.isec-u3.com; Dir P. BELTRAME.

Professional Training Unit: 10 rue de la fourane, 13090 Aix en Provence Cedex 1; tel. 4-42-93-65-80; fax 4-42-26-66-11; e-mail mission.formation-continue@univ.u-3mrs.fr; internet www.fcuniv.u-3mrs.fr; Dir B. SIRCOGLOU.

Marseille (Sciences and Technology):

Institut Universitaire de Technologie: 142 Traverse Charles Susini, 13388 Marseilles Cedex 13; tel. 4-91-28-93-00; fax 4-91-28-94-94; internet iutmrs.u-3mrs.fr; Dir R. OCCELLI.

UNIVERSITÉ D'ANGERS

40 rue de Rennes, BP 73532, 49035 Angers Cedex

Telephone: 2-41-96-23-23

Fax: 2-41-96-23-00

E-mail: presidence@univ-angers.fr
Internet: www.univ-angers.fr

Founded 1971; formerly Centre Universitaire d'Angers

President: ALAIN BARREAU
Vice-President: PHILIPPE VIOLIER
Secretary-General: HENRI-MARC PAPAVOINE
Librarian: OLIVIER TACHEAU

Number of teachers: 861
Number of students: 16,000

Publications: *Plantes médicinales et phytothérapie*, *Journal of the Short Story in English*, *Publications du Centre de Recherche en Littérature et Linguistique de l'Anjou et des Bocages*

DEANS

Faculty of Medicine: J.-P. ANDRE
Faculty of Science: G. MOGUEDET
Faculty of Law, Economic Sciences and Business Sciences: D. MARTINA
Faculty of Letters and Human Sciences: D. LE GALL
Faculty of Pharmacy: H. GUINAUDEAU

ATTACHED INSTITUTES

Etudes Supérieures de Tourisme et Hôtellerie d'Angers (ESTHUA): 7 allée François Mitterrand, BP 40455, 49004 Angers; tel. 2-41-96-21-99; fax 2-41-96-22-00; Dir M. BONNEAU.

Institut des Sciences et Techniques de l'Ingénieur d'Angers (ISTIA): 62 ave Notre-Dame du Lac, 49000 Angers; tel. 2-41-22-65-00; fax 2-41-22-65-01; Dir C. ROBLEDO.

Institut Universitaire de Technologie (IUT): 4 blvd Lavoisier, BP 42018, 49016 Angers, Cedex; tel. 2-41-73-52-52; fax 2-41-73-53-30; Dir Y. MEIGNEN.

UNIVERSITÉ D'ARTOIS

9 rue du Temple, BP 665, 62030 Arra s Cedex
Telephone: 3-21-60-37-00
Fax: 3-21-60-37-37
Internet: www.univ-artois.fr

Founded 1991

President: JEAN-JACQUES POLLET (acting)
Secretary-General: MARIE-PAULE DEJONGHE
Vice-President: MANUEL GROS
Librarians: CORINNE LEBLOND (Arras), ALEXANDRE ALLAIN (Béthune), FRÉDÉRIC WATRELOT (Douai), GHISLAINE HEYER (Lens), JULIE ROUSSEL (Liévin)

Number of teachers: 432 (incl. University Institutes of Technology)
Number of students: 12,000 (incl. University Institutes of Technology)

Publication: *Interpôles Artois* (8 a year)

TEACHING AND RESEARCH UNITS

Arras:

Faculty of Arts: Dir: JEAN-MARC VERCRUYSSE
Faculty of Languages: Dir: JACQUES SYS
Faculty of Economic and Social Administration: Dir: GILLES FIEVET
Faculty of History and Geography: Dir: GILLES DEREGNAUCOURT
Professional University Institute of Heritage and Tourism: Dir: CHARLES GIRY-DELOISON
Laboratoire Des Anciens Pays-Bas à l'Eurorégion: Dir: GILLES DEREGNAUCOURT
Centres de Recherche Histoire Economique Contemporaine: Dir: DENIS VARASCHIN
Centre de Recherche en Histoire Ancienne: Dir: JEAN-NICOLAS CORVISIER
Laboratoire 'Dynamique des réseaux et territoires': Dir: JEAN-PIERRE RENARD
CERACI (Centre d'Etudes et de Recherches de l'Artois sur les Cultures et les Intertextualités): Dir: JEAN-JACQUES POLLET
CERTA (Centre d'Etudes et de Recherche en Traductologie de l'Artois): Dir: MICHEL BALLARD
Grammatica (French Linguistics)
CRELID (Centre de Recherches Littéraires 'Imaginaire et Didactique'): Dir: FRANCIS MARCOIN
CERTEL (Centre d'Etudes et de Recherches sur les Textes Electroniques Littéraires)

Béthune:

Faculty of Economic Sciences: Dir: AHMED HENNI
Faculty of Applied Sciences: Dir: FRANCIS NOTELET
LSEE (Laboratoire des Systèmes Electrotechniques et Environnement): Dir: JEAN-FRANÇOIS BRUDNY
LGI2A (Laboratoire de Génie Informatique et d'Automatique de l'Artois): Dir: DANIEL JOLLY
EREIA (Equipe de recherche en économie internationale de l'Artois): Dir: THIERRY GRANGER
Laboratoire de Chimie Physique Appliquée: Dir: RODOLPHE MINETTI

Douai:

Faculty of Law: Dir: ALEXIS DE TOCQUEVILLE
Legal Research: Dir: MANUEL GROS

Lens:

Faculty of Science: Dir: BRAHIM KHELIFA
Mathematics Laboratory: Dir: DANIEL LI
LPCIA (Laboratoire de Physico-Chimie des Interfaces et Applications): Dir: MARC WARENGHEM
Centre IT Research: Dir: ERIC GRÉGOIRE
LBHE (Laboratoire de la barrière hémato-encéphalique): Dir: ROMÉO CECCHELLI

Liévin:

Faculty of Sports Science
LAMAPS (Laboratoire d'Analyse Multidisciplinaire des Pratiques Sportives): Dirs: OLIVIER CHOVAUX, VALÉRIE FAYT

UNIVERSITÉ D'AVIGNON ET DES PAYS DE VAUCLUSE

74 rue Louis Pasteur, 84029 Avignon Cedex 1
Telephone: 4-90-16-25-00
Fax: 4-90-16-25-10
Internet: www.univ-avignon.fr

Founded 1973; formerly UER Lettres et Sciences at the University of Provence

President: MICHEL VOLLE
Secretary-General: MARIE-BERNADETTE SUDAC
Librarian: Mlle FRANÇOISE FEBVRE

Number of teachers: 313
Number of students: 7,514

TEACHING AND RESEARCH UNITS

Exact and Natural Sciences: Dir: YVAN COTTA
Arts and Humanities: Dir: JACQUES MABY
Applied Sciences: Dir: ANDRÉ ULPAT
Law, Politics and Economics: Dir: MARTINE LE FRIANT

PROFESSORS

Sciences:

BENOIT, Computer Science
BLAVOUX, Geology
COULOMB, P., Cellular Biology
DE MORI BAJOLIN, Computer Science
DELORME, C., Physics
DUMOLIE, Communication
EL BEZE, M., Computer Science
ESPAGNAC, H., Plant Biology
GUIRAUD, R., Geology
LACOMBE, Chemistry
LAGANIER, Economics
LAMIZET, Communication
MAHÉ, J., Geology
MEDINA, Mathematics
MICHEL, R., Mathematics
PLANQUE, Economics
PUCCI, Chemistry
REIDENBACH, J.-M., Animal Biology
ROGGERO, J.-P., Chemistry
ROUX, B., Mathematics
SEEGER, Mathematics
VIVES, C., Physics
VOLLE, Mathematics
WILLIAMSON, Mathematics

Arts:

ABITEBOUL, English
AGOSTINI, English
AURIAC, F., Geography
BOUVIER-CAVORET, French
BRASSEUR, French
CHARRE, J., Geography
CHEYMOL, G., Literature
CHIFFOLEAU, Medieval History
FERRIÈRES, History
LUYAT, American
PROVOST, Roman History
REY-FLAUD, B., French
RISER, J., Geography
STRUBEL, French
ULPAT, A., English
VELASCO, Spanish

Law:

D'HAUTEVILLE, Law
PASQUALINI, Law
SCOFFONI, G., Law
VIRET, Public Law

ATTACHED INSTITUTES

Institut Universitaire Professionnalisé (IUP) en Génie Informatique et Mathématique: Technopôle d'Agroparc, BP 1228, 84911 Mont Favet; tel. 4-90-84-35-00; fax 4-90-84-35-01; e-mail secretariat@iup.univ-avignon.fr; internet www.iup.univ-avignon.fr; Dir PATRICK ISOARDI.

Institut Universitaire de Technologie (IUT): 337 Chemin des Meinajaries , BP 1207, 84911 Avignon Cedex 9; tel. 4-90-84-14-00; fax 4-90-84-00-77; internet www.iut.univ-avignon.fr; Dir J. SOUMILLE.

UNIVERSITÉ DE TECHNOLOGIE DE BELFORT-MONTBÉLIARD

90010 Belfort Cedex
Telephone: 3-84-58-30-00
Fax: 3-84-58-30-30
E-mail: contact@utbm.fr
Internet: www.utbm.fr

Founded 1999 as a result of merger of Ecole Nationale d'Ingénieurs de Belfort and Institut Polytechnique de Sévenans
State control

Director: Dr PASCAL FOURNIER

HEADS OF DEPARTMENTS

Information Technology: GRUER, PABLO
Mechanical Engineering: KLEIN, DIDIER
Control Systems Engineering: MIRAOUI, ABDELLATIF
Production Systems Engineering: LAGARD, CHRISTIAN
Humanities: LANDBECK, DOMINIQUE

UNIVERSITÉ DE BORDEAUX I

351 cours de la Libération, 33405 Talence Cedex
Telephone: 5-40-00-60-00
Fax: 5-56-80-08-37
Internet: www.u-bordeaux1.fr

President: FRANCIS HARDOUIN
Vice-Presidents: ROBERT CORI (Administration), PATRICK BUAT-MENARD (Science), YVES LEROYER (Curriculum and University Life)
Secretary-General: ANNE-MARIE BOISLIVEAU

Number of students: 14,000

TEACHING AND RESEARCH UNITS

Biology: Dir: DANIEL GALEY
Biosciences: Dir: PATRICK COTTIN
Chemistry: Dir: JEAN-BAPTISTE VERLHAC
Continued Professional Training: Dir: GÉRARD DEMAZEAU
Geology and Oceanology: Dir: JEAN-PIERRE PEYPOUQUET
Sciences: Dir: MARIE-LISE SANTUCCI
Earth and Marine Sciences: Dir: GÉRARD BLANC
Physics: Dir: JEAN LABARSOUQUE
Mathematics and Informatics: Dir: J. BOASEREZ
Technology: Dir: PIERRE LAFON

CONSTITUENT INSTITUTES AND SCHOOLS

Ecole Matmeca: tel. 5-40-00-60-53; fax 5-40-00-38-56; internet www.matmeca.u-bordeaux.fr; Dir PIERRE FABRIE.

Ecole Doctorale de Mathématiques et Informatique: tel. 5-40-00-69-39; fax 5-40-00-69-55; e-mail ecole@math.u-bordeaux1.fr; internet www.math.u-bordeaux.fr/Ecole_Doctorale; Dir THIERRY COLIN.

Ecole Doctorale du Vivant, Géosciences, Sciences de l'Environnement: tel. 5-40-00-33-01; fax 5-40-00-33-86; internet www.disvu.u-bordeaux1.fr/ecoles/edsvgse; Dirs ROBERT JAFFARD, JEAN-PIERRE PEYPOUQUET.

Ecole Doctorale des Sciences Chimiques: tel. 5-40-00-65-61; internet www.edsc.u-bordeaux.fr; Dir FRANÇOIS CARMONA.

Ecole Doctorale des Sciences Physiques et de l'Ingénieur: tel. 5-40-00-65-26; fax 5-40-00-65-25; e-mail edoc@ufr-phys.u-bordeaux.fr; internet www.disvu.u-bordeaux1.fr/ecoles/edsp; Dir NATHALIE LABAT.

Observatoire: 2 rue de l'Observatoire 33270 Floirac; tel. 5-57-77-61-63; fax 5-57-77-61-10; internet www.obs.u-bordeaux1.fr; Dir THIERRY JACQ.

Institut Universitaire de Technologie: Domaine Universitaire, 33405 Talence Cedex; tel. 5-56-84-57-02; internet www.iut.u-bordeaux1.fr; Dir PIERRE LAFON.

Institut de Chimie de la Matière Condensée de Bordeaux (ICMCB): tel. 5-40-00-62-96; fax 5-40-00-66-34; internet www.icmcb-bordeaux.cnrs.fr; Dir CLAUDE DELMAS.

Institut Européen de Chimie et Biologie (IECB): tel. 5-40-00-22-16; internet www.iecb-polytechnique.u-bordeaux.fr; Dir JEAN-JACQUES TOULMÉ.

Institut de Mathématiques de Bordeaux (IMCB): tel. 5-40-00-60-70; fax 5-40-00-21-23; e-mail institut@math.u-bordeaux1.fr; internet www.math.u-bordeaux.fr/maths; Dir PHILIPPE CASSOU-NOGUES.

Institut du Pin (IP): tel. 5-40-00-64-20; fax 5-40-00-64-22; e-mail ipin@ipin.u-bordeaux1.fr; internet www.u-bordeaux1.fr/ipin; Dir JEAN BARANGER.

Institut de Physique Fondamentale (IPF): tel. 5-40-00-83-13; internet www.u-bordeaux1.fr/ipf; Dir ERIC FREYS.

Institut de Recherche pour l'Enseignement des Mathématiques (IREM): tel. 5-40-00-89-74; Dir PIERRE DAMEY.

Institut des Sciences et Techniques d'Alimentation de Bordeaux (ISTAB): tel. 5-40-00-87-53; fax 5-56-37-03-36; e-mail scolarite@istab.u-bordeaux1.fr; internet www.u-bordeaux1.fr/istab; Dir FRANÇOIS RIBOULET.

UNIVERSITY PROFESSIONAL INSTITUTES

University Professional Institute of Electrical Engineering and Industrial Informatics: tel. 5-40-00-28-30; internet www.creea.u-bordeaux.fr; Dir YVES DANTO.

University Professional Institute of Mechanical Engineering: tel. 5-40-00-65-15; internet www.u-bordeaux1.fr/iup_gm; Dir MICHEL NOUILLANT.

University Professional Institute of Computer-Assisted Management: tel. 5-40-00-89-49; internet miage.u-bordeaux.fr; Dir NICOLE BIDOIT.

University Professional Institute of Industrial Systems Engineering – Aircraft Maintenance: tel. 5-56-13-31-58; internet www.u-bordeaux1.fr/ima; Dir CHRISTIAN BOUILLE.

ATTACHED INSTITUTES; (SEE UNDER COLLEGES AND INSTITUTES)

École Nationale Supérieure d'Électronique et de Radiocommunication de Bordeaux (ENSERB): 1 ave du Dr Albert Schweitzer 33402 Talence Cedex; tel. 5-56-84-65-00; fax 5-56-37-20-23; internet www.enserb.u-bordeaux.fr; Dir PHILIPPE MARCHEGAY.

École Nationale Supérieure de Chimie et de Physique de Bordeaux (ENSCPB): 16 ave Pey Berland, 33607 Pessac Cedex; tel. 5-40-00-65-65; fax 5-40-00-66-33; e-mail admin@enscpb.fr; internet www.enscpb.fr; Dir BERNARD CLIN.

UNIVERSITÉ VICTOR SEGALEN (BORDEAUX 2)

146 rue Léo-Saignat, 33076 Bordeaux Cedex
Telephone: 5-57-57-10-10
Fax: 5-56-99-03-80
E-mail: info@u-bordeaux2.fr
Internet: www.u-bordeaux2.fr
E-mail: info@u-bordeaux2.fr

Founded 1970
Academic year: September to July

President: BERNARD BÉGAUD
Secretary-General: CORINNE DUFFAU

Number of teachers: 1,012
Number of students: 17,005

Publication: *Anima* (4 a year)

TEACHING AND RESEARCH UNITS

Medical Sciences I Paul Broca: Dir: A. DURANDEAU
Medical Sciences II Hyacinthe Vincent: Dir: C. BÉBÉAR
Medical Sciences III Victor Pachon: Dir: P. MORLAT
Pharmacy: Dir: J. CAMBAR
Odontology: Dir: G. DORIGNAC
Public Health and Epidemiology: Dir: R. SALAMON
Biochemistry and Cellular Biology: Dir: C. SCHLICK
Social and Psychological Sciences: Dir: P. CLANCHÉ
Sports Science and Physical Education: Dir: S. FAUCHÉ
Institute of Oenology: Dir: Y. GLORIES
Sciences and Model Theory: Dir: C. SCHLICK
Bordeaux Higher Technical School of Biomolecular Science: Dir: C. CASSAGNE
Hydrothermal Therapy: Dir: C. NGUYEN BA
Institute of Cognitive Science: Dir: B. CLAVERIE

UNIVERSITÉ MICHEL DE MONTAIGNE (BORDEAUX III)

Domaine Universitaire, 33607 Pessac Cedex
Telephone: 5-57-12-44-44
Fax: 5-57-12-44-90
E-mail: accueil@u-bordeaux3.fr
Internet: www.montaigne.u-bordeaux.fr

President: Prof. SINGARAVELOU
Vice-Presidents: JEAN-PAUL CHARRIÉ, MICHEL PERROT, Prof. ADRIEN DELACROIX
Secretary-General: CLAUDE GAUDY
Chief Librarian: M. GUERIN

Number of teachers: 633
Number of students: 14,847

Publications: *Revue des études anciennes*, *Cahier d'outre-mer*, *Bulletin hispanique*, *Annales du Midi*, *Revue Géographique des Pyrénées et du Sud-Ouest*, *Aquitania*

TEACHING AND RESEARCH UNITS

Letters: PHILIPPE BAUDORRE
Philosophy: Dir: JEAN TERREL
History: Dir: BERNARD LACHAISE
Geography: Dir: JEAN-CLAUDE HINNEWINKEL
Language, Literature and Civilization of Anglophone Countries: Dir: B. RIGAL-CELLARD
Foreign Languages: Dir: ROGER BILLION
Germanic and Scandinavian Studies: Dir: NICOLE PELLETIER
Iberian and Latin American Studies: Dir: FRÉDÉRIC BRAVO
Institute of Information and Communication Sciences: Dir: HUGUES HOTIER
Science, Information, Communication and Arts: Dir: JEAN-PIERRE BERTIN-MAGHIT
University Institute of Information and Communication Sciences: Dir: PHILIPPE LOQUAY
University Institute of Technology: Dir: P. AUBRY
History of Art and Archaeology: Dir: DOMINIQUE JARASSE

PROFESSORS

ABECASSIS, A., Philosophy
AGOSTINO, M., Contemporary History
AGUILA, Y., Spanish
AUGUSTIN, J.-P., Geography
BARAT, J.-C., English
BART, F., Geography
BAUDRY, P., Sociology
BECHTEL, F., Physics applied to Archaeology
BERIAC, F., Medieval History
BERTIN-MAGHIT, J.-P., Cinema
BESSE, M. G., Portuguese Literature
BOHLER, D., Medieval Languages and Literature
BOST, J.-P., Ancient History
BOUCARUT, M., Petrography
BRAVO, F., Spanish
BRESSON, A., Medieval History
CABANES, J.-L., Contemporary French Literature
CAMBRONNE, P., Latin
CHAMPEAU, G., Spanish
CHARRIE, J.-P., Geography
COCULA, A.-M., Modern History
COCULA, B., French Language
CORZANI, J., Contemporary French Literature
COSTE, D., Comparative Literature
DEBORD, P., Ancient History
DE CARVALHO, P., Latin
DECOUDRAS, P. M., Land and Society in Tropical Environments
DEPRETTO, C., Russian
DESCAT, R., Greek History
DESCHAMPS, L., Latin
DES COURTILS, J., History of Art
DESVOIS, J.-M., Spanish
DI MÉO, G., Geography
DOTTIN ORSINI, M., Comparative Literature
DUBOIS, C., French
DUCASSE, R., Information Science
DURRUTY, S., English
DUTHEIL, F., Italian
DUVAL, G., English
FONDIN, H., Information and Communication Science
FOURTINA, H., English
FRANCHET D'ESPEREY, H., Latin
GARMENDIA, V., Spanish
GAUTHIER, M., American English

GILBERT, B., English
GORCEIX, P., German
GOZE, M., Urban Planning
GRANDJEAT, Y., North American Civilization
GUILLAUME, P., Modern History
GUILLAUME, S., Modern History
HOTIER, H., Information and Communication Science
HUMBERT, L., Geology
JARASSE, D., History of Modern Art
JOLY, M., Image Analysis
JOUVE, M., English
LACHAISE, B., Modern History
LACOSTE, J., History of Art
LAMORE, J., Spanish
LANGHADE, J., Arabic
LARRERE, C., Philosophy
LAVAUD, C., Philosophy
LAVEAU, P., German
LEBIGRE, J.-M., Physical Geography, Biogeography
LEPRUN-PIÉTON, S., Art, Plastic Arts
LERAT, C., English
LOPEZ, F., Spanish
LOUISE, G., Medieval History
LOUPES, P., History
LY, A., Spanish
MAILLARD, J.-C., Geography
MALEZIEUX, J.-M., Geology
MALLET, D., Arabic
MANTION, J.-R., 18th-century French Literature
MARIEU, J., Urban Planning and Projects
MARQUETTE, J.-B., History
MARTIN, D., French Language and Literature
MATHIEU, M., Contemporary Francophone Literature
MAZOUER, C., Contemporary French Literature
MONDOT, J., German
MORIN, S., Tropical Geography
MOULINE, L., Theatre
MULLER, C., General Linguistics
NAVARRI, R., French Language and Literature
NOTZ, M.-F., Medieval Language and Literature
OLLIER, N., English
ORPUSTAN, J.-B., Basque
PAILHE, J., Geography
PELLETIER, N., German
PERRIN-NAFFAKH, A.-M., Contemporary Language and Literature
PERROT, M., Information and Communications Science
PEYLET, G., Contemporary Language and Literature
PICCIONE, M.-L., Contemporary Language and Literature
PONCEAU, J.-P., Medieval Language and Literature
PONTET, J., Modern History
PORTINE, H., Teaching French as a Foreign Language
POUCHAN, P., Geology
RABATE, D., Contemporary French Literature
RAMOND, C., Philosophy
REYNIER-GIRARDIN, C., English
RIBEIRO, M., Portuguese
RICARD, M., Tropical Pacific Phytoplankton
RIGAL-CELLARD, B., English
RITZ, R., English
ROCHER, A., Japanese
RODDAZ, J.-M., Ancient History
ROSSI, G., Geography
ROUCH, M., Italian
ROUDIE, P., Geography
ROUYER, M.-C., English
ROUYER, P., Plastic Art
RUIZ, A., German
SALOMON, J.-N., Geography
SCHVOERER, M., Physics applied to Archaeology
SENTAURENS, J., Spanish
SEVESTRE, N., Music and History of Music
SHEN, J., Applied Mathematics
SHUSTERMAN, R., English
SINGARAVELOU, Geography
TAILLARD, C., History of Modern Art
TERREL, J., Philosophy
VADE, Y., Contemporary Language and Literature
VAGNE-LEBAS, M., Social Communication
VIGNE, M.-P., English
VITALIS, A., Information and Communication Science
VLES, V., Urban Planning
ZAVIALOFF, N., Russian

ATTACHED INSTITUTES

EGID Bordeaux: 1 Allée Daguin, 33607 Pessac Cedex; tel. 5-57-12-10-00; fax 5-57-12-10-01; e-mail secretariat@egid.u-bordeaux.fr; internet www.egid.u-bordeaux.fr; Dir M. RICARD.

UNIVERSITÉ MONTESQUIEU (BORDEAUX IV)

Ave Léon-Duguit, 33608 Pessac
Telephone: 5-56-84-85-86
Fax: 5-56-37-00-25
E-mail: umb4@montesquieu.u-bordeaux.fr
Internet: www.montesquieu.u-bordeaux.fr

Founded 1995 from units fmrly within the University of Bordeaux I
State control
President: GÉRARD HIRIGOYEN
Secretary-General: MARIE-FRANCE DUBERNET-BLANC
Librarian: D. MONTBRUN-ISRAËL
Number of teachers: 400
Number of students: 13,000

TEACHING AND RESEARCH UNITS

Juridical Studies (First Cycle): Dir: BERNARD GALLINATO-CONTINO
Private Law and History of Institutions: Dir: JEAN-PIERRE LABORDE
Public Law and Political Science: Dir: JEAN-PIERRE DUPRAT
Economics and Management Studies: Dir: MICHEL DUPUY
Intensive Curricula in Economics and Business Studies: Dir: JEAN-GUY DEGOS
Management of Economic and Social Institutions: Dir: GÉRARD BORDENAVE

CONSTITUENT INSTITUTE

Regional Institute of Management and Business Administration: Dir SERGE EVRAERT.

ATTACHED INSTITUTE

Institute of Political Studies: Dir ROBERT LAFORE.

UNIVERSITÉ DE BOURGOGNE

Maison de l'Université, Esplanade Erasme, BP 138, 21004 Dijon Cedex
Telephone: 3-80-39-50-11
Fax: 3-80-39-50-69
Internet: www.u-bourgogne.fr

Founded 1722 as Dijon Faculty of Law
President: JEAN-CLAUDE FORTIER
Secretary-General: PATRICE SERNICLAY
Librarian: F. HAGENE
Number of students: 24,879

Publications: *Annuaire, Journal d'Information, Publications de l'Université* (irregular series of monographs), *Livret de la recherche*

TEACHING AND RESEARCH UNITS

Law and Political Science: Dir: FRANCOISE FORTUNET
Economics and Business Studies: Dir: MARIE-CLAUDE PICHERY
Literature and Philosophy: Dir: NICOLE FICK
Languages and Communication: Dir: ANN PIROELLE
Human Sciences: Dir: MICHÈLE DION
Science and Technology: Dir: JEAN-PAUL DUFOUR
Life Sciences: Dir: YVES JASSEY
Medicine: Dir: MAURICE GIROUD
Pharmacy: Dir: SYLVETTE HUICHARD
Earth Sciences: Dir: JEAN-PIERRE GARCIA
Physical Education and Sport: Dir: BERNARD MEURGEY
University Institute of Technology (Dijon): Dir: ANDRÉ BERNARD
University Institute of Technology (Le Creusot): Dir: J.-L. GISCLON
University Institute of Technology (Chalon-sur-Saône): Dir: FRANCK HENDEL
Higher National School of Applied Biology: Dir: JEAN-PIERRE GRENOUILLET
Viticulture and Oenology Experimental Centre: Dir: JEAN-CLAUDE FOURNIOUX
Higher Institute of Transport and the Car: Dir: GEORGES VERCHERY
Preparatory Institute for General Administration: Dir: ALAIN WERNER
University Professional Institute in Burgundy for Industrial Engineering: Dir: B. BOBIN
Training of Research Engineers in Materials Science and Technology: Dir: ALEXIS STEINBRUNN

PROFESSORS

Arts Faculties:

ABDI, Psychology
ALI BOUACHA, French Linguistics
BASTIT, Philosophy
BAVOUX, Geography
BENONY, Psychology
Mme BERCOT, Modern Literature
CHAPUIS, Geography
CHARRIER, Geography
CHARUE, German
Mme CHARUE, German
CHEVIGNARD, American English
CHIFFRE, Geography
COMANZO, English
Mme COURTOIS, Comparative Literature
Mme DOBIAS, Classical Literature
DUCHENE, History
Mme DUCOS, Classical Literature
DURIX, English
Mme DURU, Education
Mme FAYARD, Modern History
FAYOL, Psychology
FERRARI, Philosophy
FOYARD, French Philology
GARNOT, Modern History
Mme HAAS, French Linguistics
IMBERTY, Italian
JACOBI, Information and Communication Science
Mlle JOLY, Latin
LAMARRE, Geography
LARRAZ, Romance Languages
Mme LAVAUD, Spanish
LAVAUD, Spanish
MCCARTHY, English
MORDANT, Protohistory
NOUHAUD, Spanish
Mlle PELLAN, English
Mme PERARD, Geography
Mme PERROT, Philosophy
Mme PIROELLE, English
PITAVY, English
Mme PITAVY, English
Mme POURKIER, Greek
QUILLIOT, Philosophy
RATIE, English
REFFET, German
RONSIN, Modern History
Mme SADRIN, English
SADRIN, French Literature
SAINT-DENIS, Medieval History
SAURON, Audiology

SOUILLER, Comparative Literature
SOUTET, Linguistics, Phonetics
TABBAGH, Medieval Archaeology
TAVERDET, French Philology
TUROWSLI, History of Art
Mme VINTER, Psychology
WOLIKOW, History and Civilization
WUNENBURGER, Philosophy
ZAGAR, Psychology

Science Faculties:
ANDREUX, Geochemistry
BELLEVILLE, J., Animal Physiology
BERGER, Physics
BERTRAND, Chemistry
BESANÇON, Chemistry
BOBIN, Physics
BONNARD, Mathematics
BOQUILLON, Physics
CAMPY, Geology
CEZILLY, Ecology
CHABRIER, Computer Sciences
CHAMPION, Physics
CLOUET, Animal Physiology
COLSON, Chemistry
CONNAT, Animal Biology
COQUET, Physics
CORTET, Mathematics
DEMARQUOY, Animal Physiology
DEREUX, Physics
DOLECKI, Mathematics
DORMOND, Chemistry
DULIEU, Animal Physiology
FANG, Mathematics
FLATO, Mathematics
FRANGE, Chemistry
FROCHOT, B., Ecology
GAUTHERON, B., Chemistry
GOUDONNET, Physics
GUILARD, R., Mathematics
GUIRAUD, Geology
JANNIN, Physics
JANNOT, Physics
JAUSLIN, Physics
JOUBERT, Mathematics
KUBICKI, Chemistry
LALLEMANT, Chemistry
LANG, J., Geology
LANGEVIN, Mathematics
LARPIN, Physical Chemistry
LASSALE, Mathematics
LATRUFFE, Biochemistry
LAURIN, Geology
LENOIR-ROUSSEAU, Zoology
LINES, Mathematics
LOETE, Physics
LOREAU, Geology
MARCUARD, Statistical Probability
MARNIER, Physics
MARTY, Plant Biology
MATVEEV, Mathematics
MAUME, B., Biochemistry
MEUNIER, Chemistry
Mme MICHELOT, Physics
MICHON, Mathematics
MILAN, Electronics
MILLOT, Physics
MOÏSE, C., Chemistry
MOUSSU, Mathematics
MUGNIER, Chemistry
NIEPCE, J.-CL., Chemistry
PAINDAVOINE, Automatics
PALLO, Informatics
PAUL, Plant Biology
PAUTY, Physics
PERRON, Mathematics
PIERRE, Physics
PINCZON, Mathematics
PRIBETICH, Electronics
PUGIN, Biochemistry
RACLIN, Mechanics
REMOISSENET, Physics
ROUSSARIE, Mathematics
SCHMITT, Mathematics
SEMENOV, Mathematics
SIEROFF, Neurophysiology
SIMON, Mathematics
STEINBRUNN, Chemistry
THIERRY, Geology
Mme TOURNEFIER, Biology
VALLADE, Plant Biology
WABNITZ, Physics
YETONGNON, Informatics

Faculties of Law and Economic Science:
BALESTRA, Economic Sciences
BART, Law, Roman Law
Mme BAUMONT, Economics
BODINEAU, History of Law
BOLARD, Private Law
BROUSSOLLE, Public Law
CASIMIR, Management
CHADEFAUX, Management
CHAPPEZ, Public Law
CHARREAUX, Management
CLERE, History of Law
COURVOISIER, Political Sciences
DE MESNARD, Economics
DESBRIÈRES, Economics
DOCKES, Private Law
DUBOIS, Public Law
FILSER, Management Sciences
Mme FORTUNET, History of Law
FRITZ, Political Sciences
Mme GADREAU, Economics
HURIOT, Economic Sciences
JACQUEMONT, Management
JOBERT, History of Law
KORNPROBST, Public Law
LOQUIN, Private Law
Mme MARTIN-SERF, Private Law
MATHIEU, Public Law
MICHELOT, Economics, Mathematics
PAUL, Economics of Education
PERREUR, Economic Sciences
PICHERY, M. C., Economics
PIERI, History of Law
Mme PIERI, Private Law
PIZZIO, Private Law
ROUGET, Economics
SALMON, Political Economy
SIMON, Public Law

Faculties of Medicine and Pharmacy:
ARTUR, Physical Biochemistry
AUTISSIER, Anatomy
Mme AUTISSIER, Physical Chemistry
BEDENNE, Gastroenterology
BELON, Pharmacology
BESANCENOT, Internal Medicine
BINNERT, Radiology
BLETTERY, Resuscitation
BONNIN, Parasitology
BRALET, Physiology
BRENOT, Vascular Surgery
BRON, Ophthalmology
BROSSIER, Physical Chemistry
BRUN, Endocrinology
BRUNOTTE, Biophysics
CAMUS, Pneumology
Mme CARLI, Haematology
CASILLAS, Rehabilitation
CHAILLOT, Pharmacy
CHAVANET, Infectious Diseases
COUGARD, Surgery
CUISENIER, Surgery
DAVID, Thoracic and Cardiac Surgery
DELCOURT, Pharmacy
DIDIER, Rehabilitation
Mme DUBOIS-LACAILLE, Pharmacognosy
Mme DUMAS, Pharmacology
DUMAS, Neurology
DUSSERRE, Biostatistics
ESCOUSSE, Clinical Pharmacology
FANTINO, Physiology
FAIVRE, Gastroenterology
FAVRE, General Surgery
FELDMAN, Gynaecology and Obstetrics
FREYSZ, Anaesthesiology
GAMBERT, Biochemistry
GIRARD, Anaesthesiology
GIROUD, Neurology
GISSELMANN, Epidemiology
GOUYON, Paediatrics
GRAMMONT, Orthopaedic Surgery and Traumatology
GUERRIN, Cancerology
HILLON, Hepatology, Gastroenterology
HORIOT, Radiotheraphy
Mme HUICHARD, Pharmaceutical Law
JEANNIN, Pneumology
Mlle JUSTRABO, Pathological Anatomy
KAZMIERCZAK, Bacteriology, Virology
KRAUSE, Radiology
LAMBERT, Dermatology
LORCERIE, Internal Medicine
LOUIS, Cardiology
MABILLE, S. P., Radiology
MACK, Biochemistry
MALKA, Stomatology and Maxillofacial Surgery
MARTIN, F., Immunology
MOURIER, Neurosurgery
NEEL, Biochemistry
NIVELON, Paediatrics
PADIEU, Biological Chemistry
PFITZEMEYER, Internal Medicine
Mme PIARD, Pathological Anatomy
PORTIER, Infectious and Tropical Diseases
POTHIER, Bacteriology
Mme POURCELOT, Pharmacy
RAT, General Surgery
RIFLE, Nephrology
Mme ROCHAT, Pharmacy
ROCHETTE, Pharmacy
ROMANET, Oto-rhino-laryngology
ROUSSET, Bacteriology
SAGOT, Gynaecology
SAUTREAUX, Neurosurgery
SCHREIBER, Pharmacy
SMOLIK, Occupational Medicine
SOLARY, Haematology
TAVERNIER, Rheumatology
TEYSSIER, Cytogenetic Histology
THEVENIN, Pharmacy
THIERRY, Neurosurgery
TRAPET, Adult Psychiatry
TROUILLOUD, Orthopaedic Surgery and Anatomy
VERGES, Endocrinology of Metabolic Diseases
WEILLER, Radiology
WILKENING, Anaesthesiology
WOLF, Cardiology
ZAHND, Embryology

University Institute of Technology:
BELEY, Biology, Applied Biochemistry
BERLIÈRE, Contemporary History
BESSIS, Botany
BERNARD, Physiology and Nutrition
BIZOUARD, M., Thermodynamics
BUGAUT, Biochemistry
CHANUSSOT, Physics
DIOU, Industrial Computer Science
GORRIA, Computer Engineering
GREVEY, Materials
POISSON, Biochemistry
SACILOTTI, Physics
TRUCHETET, Computer Engineering

Higher National School of Applied Biology:
BELIN, Alimentary Biotermology
BESNARD, Physiology of Nutrition
DIVIES, Microbiology
GERVAIS, Process Engineering
LE MESTE, Physical Chemistry of Food
L'HUGUENOT, Biochemistry
MOLIN, Mathematics
TAINTURIER, Organic Chemistry
Mme VOILLEY, Biology, Biochemistry

University Professional Institute of Management in Education, Training and Culture:
JAROUSSE, J.-P., Education
PATRIAT, C., Informatics and Communication
SOLAUX, A., Education

Physical Education and Sport:
MORLON, B., Biophysics

VANHOECKE, J., Physical Education and Sport

Viticulture and Oenology Experimental Centre:

CHARPENTIER, O., Oenology
FEUILLAT, M., Oenology

Higher Institute of Transport and the Car:

AIVAZZADEH, S., Mechanics
LESUEUR, Mechanics
VERCHERY, Mechanics

UNIVERSITÉ DE BRETAGNE OCCIDENTALE

Site 1–3, Rue des Archives, BP 808, 29285 Brest Cedex

Telephone: 2-98-01-60-20
Fax: 2-98-01-60-01
Internet: www.univ-brest.fr

President: JEAN-CLAUDE BODÉRÉ
Secretary-General: RENÉ FIRMIN
Librarian: ALAIN SAINSOT

Number of teaching staff: 820
Number of students: 19,090

TEACHING AND RESEARCH UNITS

Letters and Social Sciences: Dean: JEAN-CLAUDE GARDE
Law, Economics and Management: Dean: VÉRONIQUE LABROT
Medicine: Dean: YVES BIZAIS
Odontology: Dean: ALAIN ZERILLI
Science and Technology: Dean: PASCAL OLIVARD
Ecole Supérieure de Microbiologie et Sécurité Alimentaire de Brest (ESMISAB): Dir: YVES TIRILLY
Euro-Institut d'Actuariat (EURIA): Dir: HERVÉ LE BORGNE
Institut d'Administration des Entreprises: Dir: CHRISTIAN CADIOU
Institut de Préparation à l'Administration Générale: Dir: THIERRY SELLIN
Institut Universitaire Professionnalisé Métiers des Arts et de la Culture
Institut Universitaire Professionnalisé Innovation en Industrie Alimentaire: Dir: FABIENNE GUERARD
Institut Universitaire Ingénierie Informatique: Dir: YVON AUTRET
Institut Universitaire Génie Mécanique et Productique: Dir: BERNARD GINESTE
Institut Universitaire Télécommunications et Réseaux: Dir: PIERRE VILBE
University Institute of Technology (Brest): Dir: JOËL LE GUEN
University Institute of Technology (Quimper): Dir: ROGER PRAT

ATTACHED RESEARCH INSTITUTES

Institut de Synergie des Sciences de la Santé: Site CHU Morvan, 29609 Brest Cedex; tel. 2-98-01-81-30; fax 2-98-01-81-24; internet www.univ-brest.fr/i3s; Dir CLAUDE FEREC.

Institut des Sciences Agro-alimentaires et du Monde Rural: 2 rue de l'université, 29334 Quimper Cedex; tel. 2-98-90-85-48; Dir ADRIEN BINET.

Institut Universitaire Européen de la Mer (IUEM): place Nicolas Copernic, 29280 Plouzané; tel. 2-98-49-86-00; fax 2-98-49-86-09; e-mail direction.iuem@univ-brest.fr; internet www.univ-brest.fr/IUEM; Dir PAUL TREGUER.

Institut de Recherche sur l'Enseignement des Mathématiques (IREM): 6 Ave Victor Le Gorgeu, 29238 Brest Cedex 3; tel. 2-98-01-65-44; fax 2-98-01-64-41; e-mail irem@univ-brest.fr; Dir (vacant).

École Supérieure de Microbiologie et Sécurité Alimentaire de Brest (ESMISAB): Technopôle Brest-Iroise, 29280 Plouzané; tel. 2-98-05-61-00; fax 2-98-05-61-01; e-mail esmisab@univ-brest.fr; internet www.univ-brest.fr/esmisab; Dir YVES TIRILLY.

UNIVERSITÉ DE CAEN BASSE-NORMANDIE

Esplanade de la Paix, 14032 Caen Cedex

Telephone: 2-31-56-55-00
Fax: 2-31-56-56-00
Internet: www.unicaen.fr

Founded 1432; reorganized 1985

Rector: JEAN-BAPTISTE CARPENTIER
President: NICOLE LE QUERLER
Vice-Presidents: PATRICK DALLEMAGNE ROBERT FERRANDIER CÉLINE LECONTE
Secretary-General: FRANÇOIS RIOU
Librarian: FRANÇOISE BERMANN

Library: see Libraries
Number of teachers: 1,154
Number of students: 26,667

TEACHING AND RESEARCH UNITS

Law and Political Science: Dir: ANNICK BATTEUR
Geography: Dir: ANNE-MARIE FIXOT
Economics and Management Science: Dir: CÉCILE LE CORROLLER
Medicine: Dir: JEAN-LOUIS GERARD
Psychology: Dir: JOËLLE LEBREUILLY
Pharmaceutical Sciences: Dir: P. DALLEMAGNE
Science of Man: Dir: BERNARD DEFORGE
Modern Languages: Dir: ERIC GILBERT
History: Dir: JEAN QUELLIEN
Sciences: Dir: CHRISTIAN DUBUC
Sciences et Techniques des Activités Physiques et Sportives (STAPS): Dir: FRANCIS LESTIENNE
Institute of Fundamental and Applied Biology: Dir: ANDRÉ NOUVELOT
Business Administration: Dir: FABRICE LEVIGOUREUX
General Administration: Dir: FRANÇOISE EPINETTE
Institut universitaire professionnalisé Banque-Assurance: Dir: R. FERRANDIER
Institut universitaire professionnalisé: Agroalimentaire: Dir: JEAN-PAUL VERNOUX
Institut universitaire professionnalisé: Management du social et de la santé: Dir: DOMINIQUE BEYNIER
Institut universitaire de technologie de Cherbourg–Manche: Dir: PHILIPPE MAKANY
Institut universitaire de technologie d'Alencon: Dir: MOHAMED AYACHI
Institut universitaire de technologie de Caen: Dir: DENIS BLANCHON
Ecole d'Ingénieurs de Cherbourg: Dir: DOMINIQUE KERVADEC

ATTACHED INSTITUTES

Ecole Nationale Supérieure d'Ingénieurs de Caen: 6 Blvd Maréchal Juin, 14050 Caen Cedex; tel. 2-31-45-27-50; fax 2-31-45-27-60; internet www.ensicaen.fr; Dir D. GUERREAU.

Institut Universitaire de Formation des Maîtres: 186 rue de la Délivrande, 14053 Caen Cedex 04; tel. 2-31-46-70-80; fax 2-31-93-31-27; internet www.caen.iufm.fr; Dir JEAN MARC GUEGUENIAT.

UNIVERSITÉ DE CERGY-PONTOISE

8 Le Campus, 95033 Cergy-Pontoise Cedex

Telephone: 1-34-25-49-49
Fax: 1-34-25-49-04
Internet: www.u-cergy.fr

President: THIERRY COULHON
Secretary General: ERIC FRANÇOIS
Number of students: 11,225

HEADS OF DEPARTMENTS

Law: JEAN-PAUL CHAGNOLLAUD
Economics and Management: GABRIEL DESGRANGES
Finance: CONSTANTIN MELLIOS
Management Sciences: JOSEPH NGIJOL
Languages: BRIGITTE LESTRADE
Applied Foreign Languages: MARIE-PIERRE ARRIZABALAGA
English: ODILE BOUCHER-RIVALAN
Iberian and Latin American Studies: VICTOR BERGASA
Germanic Studies: MICHÈLE WEINACHTER
Humanities: PIERRE ZEMBRI
Modern Literature: DOMINIQUE FATTIER
Geography: FRANÇOIS PERNOT
History: FRANÇOIS PERNOT
Science and Technology: JACQUES AUGÉ
Biology: MARIE-FRANCE BRETON
Chemistry: Prof. CLAUDE CHEVROT
Computing: Prof. PHILIPPE GAUSSIER
Mathematics: Prof. H.-H. RUGH
Physics: Prof. HUNG THE DIEP
Earth and Environmental Sciences: RONAN HÉBERT
Civil Engineering: PATRICE COURDE
Electrical Engineering and Industrial Informatics: MARCEL GINDRE
Production Engineering: FRANÇOIS SCHAAL
Commerce (Saint Christophe): CLAUDE PATHERNAY
Commerce (Sarcelles): JOSEPH MARIE JULIE
Logistics Management and Transport: JACQUES QUINTALLET
Communication Sytems: BÉATRICE CORNIER

CONSTITUENT INSTITUTES

Institut Universitaire Professionel Génie Civil et Infrastructures: Dir Prof. RICHARD CABRILLAC.

Institut Universitaire Professionel Génie Electrique et Informatique Industrielle: Dir Prof. JEAN-YVES LE HUÉROU.

IPAG: Dir CLAUDINE VIARD.

Institut Universitaire de Technologie: Dir RICHARD POURRET.

UNIVERSITÉ D'AUVERGNE (CLERMONT-FERRAND I)

49 blvd F. Mitterrand, 63001 Clermont-Ferrand Cedex

Telephone: 4-73-34-77-77
Internet: www.u-clermont1.fr

Founded 1976; present status 1985

President: ANNIE VEYRE
Secretary-General: MICHÈLE MOSNIER
Librarian: Mlle SART

Number of teachers: 600
Number of students: 12,000.

TEACHING AND RESEARCH UNITS

Medicine: 28 place Henri Dunant, BP 38, 63001 Clermont-Ferrand; tel. 4-73-17-79-79; fax 4-73-17-79-13; internet medecine.u-clermont1.fr; Dean Prof. PATRICE DETEIX.

Pharmacy: 28 place Henri Dunant, BP 38, 63001 Clermont-Ferrand; tel. 4-73-17-79-79; fax 4-73-17-79-14; Dean Prof. M. MADESCLAIRE.

Law and Politics: 41 blvd F. Mitterrand, BP 38, 63002 Clermont-Ferrand; tel. 4-73-17-76-00; fax 4-73-17-75-75; e-mail UFR-Droit@droit.u-clermont1.fr; internet www-droit.u-clermont1.fr; Dean Prof. J.-P. MASSIAS.

Economic and Social Sciences: 41 blvd F. Mitterrand, BP 54, 63002 Clermont-Ferrand; tel. 4-73-43-42-00; fax 4-73-17-75-75; Dir CLAIRE GRELET.

University Institute of Technology (Clermont-Ferrand): Ensemble universitaire des Cézeaux, BP 86, 63172 Aubière;

tel. 4-73-17-70-00; fax 4-73-17-70-20; internet iutweb.u-clermont1.fr; Dir Prof. D. RICHARD.

Dentistry: 11 blvd Charles de Gaulle, 63000 Clermont-Ferrand Cedex; tel. 4-73-17-73-00; fax 4-73-17-73-09; internet webodonto .u-clermont1.fr; Dean Prof. THIERRY ORLIAGUET.

University Professional Institute of Business Management: Pôle Tertiaire et Technologique 26, Ave Léon-Blum , 63000 Clermont-Ferrand; tel. 4-73-17–77-00; fax 4-73-17-77-01; internet iup-management.net; Dir Prof. M. CHENEVOY.

IPAG: 26, Ave Léon-Blum, 63000 Clermont-Ferrand; tel. 4-73-17-77-50; fax 4-73-17-77-55; Dir Prof. M. DEYRA.

UNIVERSITÉ BLAISE PASCAL

34 ave Carnot, BP 185, 63006 Clermont-Ferrand Cedex 1

Telephone: 4-73-40-63-63
Fax: 4-73-40-64-31
Internet: www.univ-bpclermont.fr

Founded 1810; present status 1984 as Université de Clermont-Ferrand II–Université Blaise Pascal

President: ALBERT ODOUARD
Secretary-General: FRANÇOIS PAQUIS
Librarian: L. RAPATEL

Number of teachers: 800
Number of students: 16,000

Publications: *Journal de l'Université Blaise-Pascal* (3 a year), *Programme des Colloques* (annually).

TEACHING AND RESEARCH UNITS

Exact and Natural Sciences (Teaching): 24 ave des Landais, 63177 Aubière Cedex; tel. 4-73-40-70-02; fax 4-73-40-70-12; internet www.sciences.univ-bpclermont.fr; Dir G. BOURDIER.

Scientific and Technical Research: 24 ave des Landais, 63177 Aubière Cedex; tel. 4-73-40-70-03; fax 4-73-40-70-12; internet www .rst.univ-bpclermont.fr; Dir GILLES PETEL.

Literature, Languages and Human Sciences: 29 blvd Gergovia, 63037 Clermont-Ferrand Cedex; tel. 4-73-34-65-04; fax 4-73-34-65-44; internet www.lettres .univ-bpclermont.fr; Dir MICHELINE DECORPS.

Observatoire de Physique du Globe (OPGC): 24 ave des Landais, 63001 Clermont-Ferrand Cedex; tel. 4-73-40-73-80; fax 4-73-40-73-82; internet www.opgc .univ-bpclermont.fr; Dir ANDRÉA FLOSSMANN.

Physical Education and Sport: Complexe Scientifique des Cézeaux, BP 104, 63172 Aubière Cedex; tel. 4-73-40-75-40; fax 4-73-40-74-46; Dir HUGUETTE GONZALEZ.

University Institute of Technology (Montluçon): Ave Aristide Briand, BP 408, 03107 Montluçon Cedex; tel. 4-70-02-20-00; fax 4-70-02-20-78; internet www.moniut .univ-bpclermont.fr; Dir BERNARD GUILLEMET.

National Higher School of Chemistry: Ensemble scientifique des Cézeaux, BP 187, 63174 Aubière Cedex; tel. 4-73-40-71-45; fax 4-73-40-70-95; internet ensccf .univ-bpclermont.fr; Dir JACQUES LACOSTE.

Applied Language and Communication: 34 ave Carnot, 63037 Clermont-Ferrand Cedex; tel. 4-73-40-64-05; fax 4-73-40-64-24; internet www.lacc.univ-bpclermont.fr; Dir SUZAN GOUTET.

Psychology, Social Sciences and Educational Science: 34 ave Carnot, 63037 Clermont-Ferrand Cedex; tel. 4-73-40-64-63; fax 4-73-40-64-82; internet www.psycho .univ-bpclermont.fr; Dir P. CHAMBRES.

Computer Engineering (ISIMA): Complexe des Cézeaux, BP 125, 63173 Aubière Cedex; tel. 4-73-40-50-00; fax 4-73-40-50-01; internet www.isima.fr; Head A. QUILLIOT.

Centre Universitaire de Sciences et Techniques (CUST): Rue des Meuniers, BP 206, 63174 Aubière Cedex; tel. 4-73-40-75-00; fax 4-73-40-75-10; internet www.cust .univ-bpclermont.fr; Dir CLAUDE-GILLES DUSSAP.

UNIVERSITÉ DE TECHNOLOGIE DE COMPIÈGNE

Centre B. Franklin, BP 60319, Rue Roger Couttolenc, 60206 Compiègne Cedex

Telephone: 3-44-23-44-23
Fax: 3-44-23-43-00
E-mail: utc@utc.fr
Internet: www.utc.fr

Founded 1972

Academic year: September to August (2 semesters)

President: FRANÇOIS PECCOUD
Secretary-General: LUC ZIEGLER
Director of International Relations: P. WAGSTAFF
Librarian: ANNIE BERTRAND

Number of teachers: 313
Number of students: 3,200

Publication: *UTC-Infos* (6 a year)

DIRECTORS

Department of Mechanical Engineering: M. SIDAHMED
Department of Biological Engineering: N. COCHET
Department of Chemical Engineering: E. BRUNIER
Department of Computer Science: P. SIMARD
Department of Urban Engineering Systems: P. ORSERO
Department of Technology and Human Sciences: F. SEITZ
Department of Mechanical Engineering Systems: P. RAMOND

UNIVERSITÉ DE CORSE PASQUALE PAOLI/UNIVERSITÀ DI CORSICA

BP 52, 7 ave Jean-Nicoli, 20250 Corti

Telephone: 4-95-46-10-45
Internet: www.univ-corse.fr

Founded 1976; opened 1981

President: ANTOINE AIELLO
Secretary-General: FRANÇOIS-DOMINIQUE CIPRIANI
Chief Librarian: ROLAND RINALDI

DEANS

Faculty of Law and Economics: JEAN-YVES COPPOLANI
Faculty of Literature, Languages, Arts and Human Sciences: DOMINIQUE VERDONI
Faculty of Sciences: RAPHAEL PAPI
University Institute of Technology: CHRISTOPHE STORAI

ATTACHED RESEARCH INSTITUTES

Systèmes Physiques pour l'environnement (SPE): SPE UMA 6134, Quartier Grossetti, BP 52, 20250 Corte; tel. 4-95-45-01-65; fax 4-95-45-01-62; e-mail spe@ univ-corse.fr; internet spe.univ-corse.fr; Dir J. H. BALBI.

Centre de la Biodiversité Insulaire et Méditerranéenne (BIM): tel. 4-95-45-01-78; fax 4-95-45-01-66; Dir JEAN FRANÇOIS SANTUCCI.

Institut de Développement des Iles Mediterranéennes (IDIM): tel. 4-95-45-00-18; Dir JEAN YVES COPPOLANI.

Centre de Recherche Corse Méditerranée (CRCM): tel. 4-95-45-00-77; Dir PHILIPPE PESTEIL.

Institut d'Études Scientifiques de Cargèse: 20130 Cargèse; fax 4-95-26-80-45; internet cargese.univ-corse.fr; Dir ÉLISABETH DUBOIS-VIOLETTE.

UNIVERSITÉ D'ÉVRY-VAL D'ESSONNE

Boulevard des Coquibus, 91025 Évry Cedex-
Telephone: 1-69-47-70-10
Fax: 1-64-97-27-34
Internet: www.univ-evry.fr

President: DANIEL ANDRÉ
Sec.-Gen.: CHRISTOPHE MARMIN

Number of teachers: 462, incl. 127 at IUT
Number of students: 9,963, incl. 1652 at IUT

HEADS OF DEPARTMENTS

Fundamental and Applied Sciences: FRANÇOIS HIRSCH
Mathematics: MONIQUE JEANBLANC
Computing: PASCALE LE GALL
Physics: PIERRE NEDELLEC
Materials Science: THIERRY CARTAILLER
Biology: JAVIER PEREA
STAPS: FRANÇOIS COTTIN
Social and Management Sciences: JEAN-PIERRE DURAND
Economic and Social Administration: EMMANUEL QUENSON
Management: PASCAL LEFEBVRE
Sociology: SYLVIE CELERIER
History: JEAN-LOUIS LOUBET
Economic and Legal Sciences: FRANÇOIS COLLY
Economic Sciences: JEAN DE BEIR
Law: FRANÇOIS COLLY
Science and Technology: FRANÇOIS ARTIGUE
Basic Science Training: GÉRARD PORCHER
Electrical Engineering: SAID MAMMAR
Computer Engineering: MALIK MALLEM
Mechanical Engineering: OLIVIER DAUBE
Languages: MONIQUE PEARCE
Art: ISABELLE STARKIER
Applied Foreign Languages: STÉPHANIE GENTY
Arts and Music: YVETTE CHAPPER

UNIVERSITY INSTITUTE

Institut Universitaire de Technologie (IUT): 22 allée Jean Rostand, 91025 Évry Cedex; Dir PAUL DEMAREZ

HEADS OF DEPARTMENTS

Electrical Engineering and Industrial Informatics: HICHEM MAAREF
Production Engineering: CHRISTIAN NIERMONT
Mechanical Engineering: PAUL DEMAREZ
Thermonuclear Engineering: JEAN-FRANÇOIS MAILLARD
Commercialisation: CLAUDE BENSAID
Business Administration and Management: JEAN RENÉ VREVIN
Logistics and Transport: ROBERT RAKOTOMALALA
Commercial Technology: MONIQUE FOUTELET
Material Engineering Science: ALAIN ZOZIME

UNIVERSITÉ DE FRANCHE-COMTÉ

1 rue Claude Goudimel, 25030 Besançon Cedex

Telephone: 3-81-66-50-34
Fax: 3-81-66-50-36
E-mail: dri@univ-fcomte.fr
Internet: www.univ-fcomte.fr

Founded 1423 at Dôle, 1691 at Besançon

President: FRANÇOISE BÉVALOT

Vice-Presidents: DANIEL RONDOT, FRANCIS FARRUGIA, PIERRE-MARIE BADOT, ERIC PRÉDINE, NICOLAS CLERE
Secretary-General: LOUIS BÉRION
Library: see Libraries
Number of teachers: 1,244
Number of students: 20,718
Publications: *En Direct*, *Tout l'U*

TEACHING AND RESEARCH UNITS

Literature and Human Sciences: Dir: CLAUDE CONDÉ
Science and Technology: Dir: JOËL BERGER
Law, Economics and Politics: Dir: BERNARD LIME
Medicine and Pharmacy: Dir: HUGUES BITTARD
University Institute of Technology (Besançon-Vesoul): Dir: MICHEL TACHEZ
University Institute of Technology (Belfort-Montbéliard): Dir: PHILIPPE PRACHT
Besançon Observatory: Dir: FRANÇOIS VERNOTTE
Physical Education and Sport: Dir: JACQUELINE CALLIER
Industrial Science, Management and Technology: Dir: GABRIÈLE PADBERG
Higher Institute of Engineering: Dir: PHILIPPE PICART
Institute of Business Administration: Dir: BENOÎT PIGÉ
Center of Applied Linguistics: Dir: SERGE BORG

UNIVERSITÉ DE GRENOBLE I (UNIVERSITÉ JOSEPH FOURIER)

BP 53, 38041 Grenoble Cedex 9
Telephone: 4-76-51-46-00
Fax: 4-76-51-48-48
E-mail: secretariat.general@ujf-grenoble.fr
Internet: www.ujf-grenoble.fr
Founded 1339
Academic year: September to June
President: YANNICK VALLÉE
Vice-Presidents: CHRISTIANE KERIEL, PATRICE GADELLE, PIERRE BERARD JÉRÔME GUYONY JEAN-LUC DEBRU, BERNARD DOCHE, JOHN TUPPEN
Secretary-General: PHILIPPE WISLER
Number of teachers: 1,300
Number of students: 18,000
Publications: *Info-Hebdo* (weekly), *Papyrus* (2 a year), *La Pie* (monthly), *Le Gluon* (monthly)

TEACHING AND RESEARCH UNITS

Applied Mathematics and Computer Sciences: Dir: JEAN-PIERRE PEYRIN
Biology: Dir: JEAN-GABRIEL VALAY
Chemistry: Dir: GUY SERRATRICE
Geography: Dir: EMMANUEL ROUX
Mathematics: Dir: JACQUES GASQUI
Mechanical Engineering: Dir: JEAN-PIERRE CHOLLET
Medicine: Dir: BERNARD SÈLE
Pharmacy: Dir: PIERRE DEMENGE
Physical Education and Sport: Dir: MICHEL RASPAUD
Physics: Dir: LAURENT PUECH

ATTACHED INSTITUTES

Centre Scientifique Joseph Fourier Drôme-Ardèche: BP 2, 26901 Valence Cedex 9; tel. 4-45-82-11-11; fax 4-75-56-16-20; e-mail contact.valence@ujf-grenoble.fr; internet www-valence.ujf-grenoble.fr; Dir DANIEL ALIBERT.

Département Scientifique Universitaire (DSU): 480, ave centrale, 38400 Saint Martin d'Hères; tel. 4-76-51-42-62; fax 4-76-51-49-29; internet www.ujf-grenoble.fr/DSU; Dir CLAUDINE KAHANE.

Ecole de Physique des Houches: La Côte des Chavants, 74310 Les Houches; tel. 4-50-54-40-69; fax 4-50-55-53-29; e-mail secretariat.houches@ujf-grenoble.fr; internet www.ujf-grenoble.fr/HOUCHES; Dir JEAN DALIBARD.

Ecole Polytechnique: 28 ave Benoît Frachon, 38400 Saint Martin d'Hères; tel. 4-76-82-79-01; fax 4-76-82-79-01; internet polytech.ujf-grenoble.fr; Dir DANIEL CORDARY.

Collège Doctoral: tel. 4-76-51-45-69; fax 4-76-51-44-22; Dir PATRICK WITOMSKI.

Floralis–Filiale de la Valorisation de la Recherche de l'UJF: 2 ave de Vignate, 38610 Gières; tel. 4-56-52-03-03; fax 4-56-52-03-02; internet www.floralis.fr; Dir ERIC LARREY.

Formation Continue: 2 ave de Vignate, 38610 Gières; tel. 4-56-52-03-29; fax 4-56-52-03-32; e-mail formation-continue@ujf-grenoble.fr; Dir MICHEL VERGNOLLE.

Institut Universitaire de Technologie: 151 rue de la Papeterie, 38402 Saint Martin d'Hères; tel. 4-76-82-53-00; fax 4-76-82-53-26; e-mail administration.iut@ujf-grenoble.fr; internet www-iut.ujf-grenoble.fr; Dir JEAN-MICHEL TERRIEZ.

Observatoire des Sciences de l'Univers: 44 rue de la Piscine, 38400 Saint Martin d'Hères; tel. 4-76-51-49-81; fax 4-76-63-55-35; internet osug.obs.ujf-grenoble.fr; Dir JEAN-PIERRE GRATIER.

Service Commun des Enseignements Transversaux: Dir JEAN-PIERRE HENRY.

UNIVERSITÉ DE GRENOBLE II (UNIVERSITÉ PIERRE MENDÈS-FRANCE)

BP 47X, 38040 Grenoble CedexTelephone: 4-76-82-54-00
Fax: 4-76-82-56-54
Internet: www.upmf-grenoble.fr
Founded 1970
Academic year: September to June
President: CLAUDE COURLET
Vice-Presidents: THÉOPHILE OHLMANN (Scientific Council), ALAIN SPALANZANI (Executive Board), JACQUES FONTANEL (International Relations), ALAIN PESSIN (Education, Documentation and Culture), DAMIEN REUMAUX (Student Body)
Secretary-General: FRANCK LENOIR
Library: see Libraries
Number of teachers: 718
Number of students: 19,531
Publications: *Guide de l'Etudiant*, *Intercours*

TEACHING AND RESEARCH UNITS

School of Law: Dean: MARCEL-RENÉ TERCINET
School of Economy, Strategy and Enterprise: Dir: BERNARD GERBIER
School of Economics: Dir: ALBAN RICHARD
School of Human and Social Sciences: Dir: JACQUES BAILLE
School of Humanities: Dir: JEAN-LUC LAMBOLEY
Institute of Urban Studies: Dir: GILLES NOVARINA
School of Higher Business Studies: Dir: DIDIER RETOUR
University Technical Institute–Grenoble II: Dir: CLAUDE BENOÎT
University Technical Institute–Valence: Dir: GÉRARD JOUVE
Professional Institute of Business and Sales
Professional Institute of Economic Engineering: Dir: BERNARD DRUGMAN
Professional Institute of Arts and Culture: Dir: JEAN-MARC FRANCONY
Institute for Political Studies: Dir: PIERRE BRÉCHON
Médiat Rhône-Alpes: Dir: MARIE-MADELEINE SABY
Plate-forme Multimédia à Vigny Musset: Dir: GUY ROMIER

PROFESSORS

ALBOUY, M., Management
ANTONIADIS, A., Mathematics
ARNAUD, P., Sociology
BAILLE, J., Education
BARREYRE, P.-Y., Management
BELLISSANT, C., Computer Science
BERNARD, J.-P., Political Science
BIAYS, J. P., Political Science
BILLAUDOT, B., Economics
BORRELLY, R., Economics
BOUTOT, A., Philosophy
BRECHON, P., Political Science
CHATELUS, M., Economics
CHIANEA, G., History of Law
COURTIN, J., Informatics
COVIAUX, C., Private Law
CROISAT, M., Political Science
D'ARCY, F., Political Science
DESTANNE DE BERNIS, G., Economics
DIDIER, P., History of Law
DROUET D'AUBIGNY, G., Mathematics
EUZEBY, A., Economics and Management
EUZEBY, C., Economics
FOUCHARD, A., History
FRANCILLON, J., Private Law
GIROD, P., Management
GLEIZAL, J.-J., Public Law
GOUTAL, J.-L., Private Law
GRANGE, D., History
GRELLIERE, V., Law
GROC, B., Computer Science
GUILHAUDIS, M., Public Law
HOLLARD, M., Economics
JOLIBERT, A., Management
LARGUIER, J., Private Law
LESCA, H., Management
LE STANC, C., Law
MAISONNEUVE, B., Mathematics
MARIGNY, J., History
MARTIN, C., Management
N'GUYEN XUAN DANG, M.
OHLMANN, T., Psychology
PAGE, A., Management
PARAVY, P., History
PASCAL, G., Philosophy
PATUREL, R., Management
PECCOUD, F., Computer Science
PETIT, B., Private Law
PIETRA, R., Philosophy
POUSSIN, G., Psychology
POUYET, B., Public Law
RENARD, D., Political Science
RICHARD, A., Economics
ROMIER, G., Applied Mathematics
ROUSSET, M., Public Law
SALVAGE, PASCALE, Law
SALVAGE, PHILIPPE, Law
SCHNEIDER, C., Public Law
SEGRESTIN, D., Industrial Engineering
SIRONNEAU, J.-P., Sociology
SOLE, J., History
SOULAGE, B., Political Science
TERCINET, M., Public Law
TESTON, G.
TIBERGHIEN, G., Psychology
TRAHAND, J., Management
VALETTE-FLORENCE, P.
VERNANT, D., Philosophy

UNIVERSITÉ DE GRENOBLE III (UNIVERSITÉ STENDHAL)

BP 25, 38040 Grenoble Cedex 9
1180 ave Centrale, 38400
Telephone: 4-76-82-43-00
Fax: 4-76-82-41-85
Internet: www.u-grenoble3.fr
Founded 1970
President: PATRICK CHÉZAUD

Vice-Presidents: Odile Lagoacherie, Françoise Papa, Michel Lafon
Secretary-General: Gerard Lancian
Number of teachers: 330
Number of students: 7,500
Publication: *La Gazette de l'Université*

TEACHING AND RESEARCH UNITS
Languages: (vacant)
English: Dir: Susan Blattes
Literature: Dir: Roger Bellon
Communication Sciences: Dir: Luiz Busato
Linguistic Science: Dir: Christian Abry

DIRECTORS OF DEPARTMENTS
Languages, Literature and Foreign Civilizations:
German and Dutch Studies: Jean-François Marillier
Iberian and Spanish-American Studies: Anne Cayuela
Italian and Romanian Studies: Enzo Neppi
Russian and Slav Studies: Isabelle Despres
Oriental Studies: Rita Mazen
Trilingual Law and Economics: Suzan Berthier
Applied Foreign Languages: (vacant)
Modern and Classical Literature:
Languages, Literatures and French Civilization: Brigitte Combe
Classical Studies: Benoît Goin
Comparative Literature: Florence Goyet
Sciences of Language:
French as a Foreign Language: Violaine de Nuchèze, Jean Emmanuel le Bray

UNIVERSITÉ DE HAUTE-ALSACE

2 rue des Frères Lumière, 68093 Mulhouse Cedex
Telephone: 3-89-33-60-00
Fax: 3-89-33-63-19
Internet: www.univ-mulhouse.fr
Founded 1975
President: Guy Schultz
Secretary-General: Alain Collange
Librarian: Philippe Russell
Number of teachers: 473
Number of students: 8,000

TEACHING AND RESEARCH UNITS
Letters and Humanities: Dir: Yann Kerdiles
Sciences: Dir: Alain Brillard
Institute of Technology Colmar: Dir: Reiner Blaes
Institute of Technology Mulhouse: Dir: Francois Ott
Institute of Chemistry: Dir: Jacques Schultz
General Photochemistry: Dir: Daniel Joseph Lougnot
Mineralogy: Dir: Joël Patarin
Physics and Electronic Spectroscopy: Dir: Joël patarin
European centre for Accident Law: Dir: Claude Lienhard
Risk Assessment: Dir: Pierre Ehrburger
Group Security and Chemical Ecology: Dir: Serge Walter
Textile Research: Dir: Jean-yves Drean
Geometric Modelling and Algorithms: Dir: Jean-Claude Spehner
Applied Mathematics: Dir: Michel Goze
Intelligent Processing Systems: Dir: Pierre Ambs
Faculty of Economic and Social Sciences: Dir: Daniel Chassignet
Pluridisciplinaire d'Enseignement Professionnalisé Supérieur (PEPS): Dir: Saloua Bennaghmouch
Roman and Christian Antiquity: Dir: Marie-laure Freyburger
Science, Arts and Technology Research: Dir: Pierre Fluck
Institute of European Languages and Literature: Dir: Eric Lysoe
Organisational Research: Dir: Claude Nosol
Biology: Dir: Bernard Walter
Organic and Bio-organic Chemistry: Dir: Jacques Eustache
Technology: Dir: Marie- Hélène Tuilier
High Energy Physics: Dir: Rene blaes

UNIVERSITÉ DU HAVRE

25 rue Philippe Lebon, BP 1123, 76063 Le Havre Cedex
Telephone: 2-32-74-40-00
Fax: 2-35-21-49-59
E-mail: presidence@univ-lehavre.fr
Internet: www.univ-lehavre.fr
Founded 1984
State control
Academic year: September to July
President: Pierre-Bruno Ruffini
Vice-Presidents: Thierry Derrey, Pascal Pareige, Madeleine Brocard, Camille Galap
Secretary-General: François Beaucarne
Librarian: Pierrette Portron
Number of teachers: 460
Number of students: 6,977

TEACHING AND RESEARCH UNITS
Faculty of Science and Technology: Dir: Alain Piel
Faculty of International Affairs: Dean: Jean-Paul Barbiche
Faculty of Letters and Human and Social Sciences: Dean: Benjamin Steck
University Institute of Technology: Dir: Jean-Pierre Sceaux
Higher Institute of Logistics and Engineering: Dir: Alain Portron

UNIVERSITÉ DE LILLE I (UNIVERSITÉ DES SCIENCES ET TECHNOLOGIES DE LILLE)

59655 Villeneuve d'Ascq Cedex
Telephone: 3-20-43-43-43
Fax: 3-20-43-49-95
Internet: www.univ-lille1.fr
Founded 1855 as Faculty of Sciences; present status 1971
President: Hervé Baussart
Vice-Presidents: Jean-Michel Robbe, Lucien Leclercq, Patrick Caron, Pierre Behague, Bruno Bogaert, Jacques Brocard, Martine Carette, Bertin de Bettignies, Valérie Deldevre, Jacques Dufresne, Nabi el Haggar, Michel Feutrie, Ludovic Legrand, Martine Switek, Bernard Toursel
Secretary-General: Yves Chaimbault
Number of teachers: 1,310
Number of students: 20,058

TEACHING AND RESEARCH UNITS
Pure and Applied Mathematics: Dir: Mostafa Mbekhta
Computer Science, Electronics; Electrical Engineering and Automation: Dir: Maouche Salah
Physics: Dir: Michel Foulon
Chemistry: Dir: Robert Hubaut
Biology: Dir: Jean-Claude Andries
Earth Sciences: Dir: Mme Delcambre
Geography and Spatial Development: Dir: Jean-Pierre Bondue
Economics and Social Sciences: Dir: Philippe Rollet
University Institute of Technology (Lille): Dir: Henri Bocquet
Polytech'Lille: Dir: Jean-Louis Bon
Institute of Business Studies: Dir: Pierre Louart
Agricultural Institute: Dir: Bruno Delbreil
Higher National School of Chemistry in Lille: Dir: Jean-Claude Boivin
University Centre for the Economics of Permanent Education: Dir: Jacques Claudel
Telecom Lille: Dir: Guy Marmet

PROFESSORS
Boilly, B., Biology
Bonnelle, J.-P., Chemistry
Brezinski, C., Computer Sciences
Bruyelle, P., Geography
Chamley, H., Geotechnics
Constant, E., Electronics
Cordonnier, V., Calculus and Information Science
Dauchet, M., Theoretical Computing
Debourse, J.-P., Management Science
Debrabant, P., Engineering
Degauque, P., Electronics
Dhainaut, A., Biology
Dormard, S., Economics
Doukhan, J.-C., Engineering
Dupouy, J.-P., Biology
Dyment, A., Mathematics
Escaig, B., Solid State Physics
Foct, J., Chemistry
Fouret, R., Physics
Frontier, S., Biology
Glorieux, P., Physics
Gosselin, G., Sociology
Goudmand, P., Energy Generation
Gruson, L., Pure and Applied Mathematics
Guilbault, Biology
Lablache-Combier, A., Organic Chemistry
Laveine, J.-P., Palaeobotany
Lehmann, D., Geometry
Mme Lenoble, Atmospheric Optics
Lombard, J., Sociology
Loucheux, C., Macromolecular Chemistry
Macke, B., Physics
Maillet, P., Economic and Social Sciences
Micheaux, P., Mechanical Engineering
Paquet, J., Applied Geology
Porchet, M., Biology
Prouvost, J., Mineralogy
Raczy, L., Computer Sciences
Salmer, G., Electronics
Schamps, J., Physics
Seguier, G., Electro-Technology
Simon, M., Economic and Social Sciences
Sliwa, H., Chemistry
Spik, G., Biology
Stankiewicz, F., Economic Sciences
Toulotte, J.-M., Computer Sciences
Turrel, G., Chemistry
Vernet, P., Biology of Populations and Ecosystems
Vidal, P., Automation
Zeytounian, R., Mechanics

UNIVERSITÉ DE LILLE II (DROIT ET SANTÉ)

42 rue Paul Duez, 59800 Lille
Telephone: 3-20-96-43-43
Fax: 3-20-88-24-32
E-mail: ri@hp-sc.univ_lille2.fr
Internet: www.univ-lille2.fr
Founded 1969
State control
Language of instruction: French
Academic year: October to June
President: Prof. Christian Sergheraert
Vice Presidents: Prof. Xavier Vandendriessche, Prof. Pierre Mathiot, Prof. Jean-Pierre Aubert, Prof. Salem Kacet, Claire Daval, Irene Lautier, Prof. Paul Frimat, Robin Semal
Secretary-General: Guy Baillieul
Number of teachers: 1,000
Number of students: 22,000

DEANS

Faculty of Medical Sciences: Prof. JEAN PAUL FRANCKE
Faculty of Biological and Pharmaceutical Sciences: Prof. DANIEL VION
Faculty of Dentistry: Prof. PIERRE LAFFORGUE
Faculty of Legal, Political and Social Sciences: Prof. CHRISTIAN MARIE WALLON LEDUCQ
Physical Education and Sport: Dir: IRENE LAUTIER

CONSTITUENT INSTITUTES

Institut Universitaire de Technologie: Dir JEAN PIERRE KRAWIEC.

Institut de Médecine Légale et Sociale: Dir Prof. DIDIER GOSSET.

Institut de Chimie Pharmaceutique Albert Lespagnol: Dir Prof. JEAN PIERRE HENICHART.

Institut de Préparation à l'Administration Générale: Dir Prof. VINCENT CATTOIR JONVILLE.

Institut des Sciences du Travail: Dir PHILIPPE ENGLAS.

Institut d'Etudes Politiques: Dir Prof. JEAN LOUIS THIEBAULT.

UNIVERSITÉ DE LILLE III, CHARLES DE GAULLE (SCIENCES HUMAINES, LETTRES ET ARTS)

rue du Barreau, BP 149, 59653 Villeneuve d'Ascq Cedex
Telephone: 3-20-41-60-00
Fax: 3-20-91-91-71
Internet: www.univ-lille3.fr

Founded 1560, present status 1985

President: PHILIPPE ROUSSEAU
Secretary-General: DANIÈLE SAVAGE
Librarian: JEAN-PAUL CHADOURNE

Number of teachers: 821
Number of students: 22,000

Publications: *Revue du Nord* (history, 5 a year), *Revue des Sciences Humaines* (quarterly), *Etudes Irlandaises* (every 6 months), *Cahiers de Recherches de l'institut de Papyrologie et d'Egyptologie*, *Germanica* (1 or 2 a year), *Lexique* (annually), *Roman 20–50* (every 6 months), *Bien dire, bien apprendre*, *Uranie*, *Graphé*

TEACHING AND RESEARCH UNITS

History, Art and Politics: Dir: STÉPHANE LEBECQ
English Language, Literature and Civilization: Dir: THOMAS FRASER
German and Scandinavian Studies: Dir: MARTINE-SOPHIE BENOÎT-ROUBINOWITZ
Romance, Slav and Oriental Studies: Dir: NORAH DEI CAS
Classical Languages and Culture: Dir: ALAIN DEREMETZ
Mathematics, Economics and Social Sciences: Dir: PIERRE COURONNE
Philosophy: Dir: MICHEL CRUBELLIER
Psychology: Dir: DANIEL BEAUNE
Modern Literature: Dir: MARIE-MADELEINE CASTELLANI
Applied Foreign Languages: Dir: BERNARD BACH
Education: Dir: ALAIN DUBUS
Information, Documentation and Scientific and Technical Information: Dir: MARIE DESPRES-LONNET
Arts and Culture: Dir: CHRISTIAN HAUER
INFOCOM: Dir: BERNARD DELFORCE
University Institute of Technology B: Dir: MICHEL BUGHIN
Training Centre for Accompanying Musicians: Dir: PASCAL HAMEAUX
IUP–Information Communication: Dir: OLIVIER CHANTRAINE
IUP–Artistic and Cultural Professions: Dir: PIERRE DELCAMBRE

PROFESSORS (1ST CLASS AND EXCEPTIONAL)

History, Art and Politics:
CHADEAU, E., Contemporary History
DELMAIRE, B., Medieval History
DELMAIRE, R., Ancient Roman History
GUIGNET, PH., Modern History
ROSSELLE, D., Modern Economic and Social History
VALBELLE, D., Egyptology

English Studies:
BECQUEMONT, D., History of Ideas, Phonetics and Phonology
DUPAS, J. C., Anglo-Saxon Language and Literature
DURAND, R., North American Literature and Civilization
ESCARBELT, B., Anglo-Saxon Language and Literature
GOURNAY, J.-F., 19th-century Literature and Civilization
SYS, J., British Civilization, History of Ideas

German Studies:
COLONGE, P., 19th- and 20th-century Literature and Civilization
ROUSSEAU, A., Dutch Linguistics
VAN DE LOUW, G., Dutch
VAYDAT, P., Anglo-German Relations: 1870–1914

Romance, Slav, Semitic and Hungarian Studies:
ALLAIN, A., Russian

Classics:
BOULOGNE, J., Greek Language and Literature
DUMONT, J.-CHR., Social History of the Roman Republic

French Linguistics and Literature:
ALLUIN, B., Modern and Contemporary Language and Literature
BONNEFIS, PH., 19th-century Literature
BRASSEUR, A., Medieval Language and Literature
BUISIRE, A., French Language and Literature
CORBIN, D., French Language
GARY-PRIEUR, M. N., French Language
GUILLERM, J.-P., 19th-century Literature
GUILLERM-CURUTCHET, L., French Language and Literature
HORVILLE, R., 17th-century Literature
LESTRINGANT, FR., 16th-century Literature
MALANDAIN, P., Modern and Contemporary Language and Literature

Mathematics, Economics, Social Sciences:
CELEYRETTE, J., Mathematics

Philosophy:
KINTZLER, C., General Philosophy and Aesthetics
KIRSCHER, G., Modern and Contemporary Philosophy
MACHEREY, P., Aesthetics and History of Philosophy

Psychology:
LECONTE, P., Experimental Psychology
VERQUERRE, R., Psychology

Other Professors:
LOSFELD, G., Information Science
REUTER, Y., Teaching of French

ATTACHED INSTITUTE

University Institute of Technology B: 35 rue Sainte Barbe, BP 460, 59208 Tourcoing Cedex.

UNIVERSITÉ DE LIMOGES

33 rue François Mitterand, BP 23204 87032 Limoges Cedex 01
Telephone: 5-55-14-91-00
Fax: 5-55-45-76-34
Internet: www.unilim.fr

Founded 1808, closed 1840, reopened 1965
Academic year: October to June

President: ANTONIN NOUAILLES
Secretary-General: DANIEL POUMEROULY
Librarian: ODILE ROHOU

Library: see Libraries
Number of teachers: 742
Number of students: 14,186

TEACHING AND RESEARCH UNITS

Law and Economic Sciences: Dean: ALAIN SAUVIAT
Medicine: Dean: JEAN-CLAUDE VANDROUX
Pharmacy: Dean: GÉRARD HABRIOUX
Science and Technology: Dean: ALAIN CELERIER
Letters and Social Sciences: Dean: JACQUES MIGOZZI

PROFESSORS

Medicine:
ADENIS, J.-P., Ophthalmology
ALAIN, L., Infantile Surgery
ALDIGIER, J.-C., Cardiology
ARCHAMBEAUD, F., Clinical Medicine
ARNAUD, J. P., Orthopaedics, Traumatology, Plastic Surgery
BARTHE, D., Histology, Embryology
BAUDET, J., Obstetrics and Gynaecology
BENSAID, J., Clinical Cardiology
BERTIN, P., Therapeutics
BESSEDE, J.-P., Oto-rhino-laryngology
BONNAUD, F., Pneumo-Phthisiology
BONNETBLANC, J.-M., Dermatology, Venereology
BOULESTEIX, J., Paediatrics and Medical Genetics
BOUQUIER, J.-J., Clinical Paediatrics
BOUTROS, T. F., Epidemiology
BRETON, J.-C., Biochemistry
CATANZANO, G., Pathological Anatomy
COLOMBEAU, P., Urology
CUBERTAFOND, P., Digestive Surgery
DARDE, M. L., Parasitology
DE LUMLEY-WOODYEAR, L., Paediatrics
DENIS, F., Bacteriology, Virology
DENIZOT, N., Anaesthesiology
DESCOTTES, B., Anatomy
DUDOGNON, P., Occupational Therapy
DUMAS, J. PH., Urology
DUMAS, M., Neurology
DUMONT, D., Occupational Medicines
DUPUY, J.-P., Radiology
FEISS, P., Anaesthesiology
GAINANT, A., Digestive Surgery
GAROUX, R., Child Psychiatry
GASTINNE, H., Resuscitation
HUGON, J., Histology, Embryology
LABROUSSE, C., Occupational Therapy
LASKAR, M., Thoracic and Cardiovascular Surgery
LAUBIE, B., Endocrinology, Metabolism, Nutrition
LEGER, J.-M., Adult Psychiatry
LEROUX-ROBERT, C., Nephrology
MENIER, R., Physiology
MERLE, L., Pharmacology
MOREAU, J.-J., Neurosurgery
MOULIES, D., Infantile Surgery
PECOUT, C., Orthopaedics, Traumatology, Plastic Surgery
PICHON BOURDESSOULE, D., Haematology
PILLEGAND, B., Hepato-gastro-enterology
PIVA, C., Forensic Medicine and Toxicology
PRA LORAN, V., Haematology
RAVON, R., Neurosurgery
RIGAUD, M., Biochemistry
ROUSSEAU, J., Radiology

Sauvage, J.-P., Oto-rhino-laryngology
Tabaste, J.-L., Gynaecology, Obstetrics
Treves, R., Rheumatology
Vallat, J.-M., Neurology
Valleix, D., Anatomy
Vandroux, J.-C., Biophysics
Weinbreck, P., Tropical Medicine

Faculty of Law and Economics:

Alaphilippe, F., Private Law and Criminology
Archer, R., Economics
Cavagnac, M., Economics
Darreau, P., Economics
Flandin-Blety, P., Legal and Institutional History
Karaquillo, J.-P., Private Law and Criminology
Lenclos, J.-L., Public Law
Marguenaud, J.-P., Private Law
Mouly, J., Private Law
Pauliat, H., Public Law
Prieur, M., Public Law
Sauviat, A., Economics
Tarazi, A., Economics
Texier, P., Legal and Institutional History
Vareille, B., Private Law

Faculty of Pharmacy:

Bernard, M., Physical Chemistry and Pharmaceutical Technology
Bosgiraud, C., Biology
Brossard, C., Physical Chemistry and Pharmaceutical Technology
Buxeraud, J., Pharmacology
Cardot, Ph., Physical Chemistry and Pharmaceutical Technology
Chulia, A., Pharmacology
Clement-Chulia, D., Physical Chemistry and Pharmaceutical Technology
Delage, C., Physical and Mineral Chemistry
Ghestem, A., Botany
Habrioux, G., Biochemistry
Oudart, N., Pharmacology

Faculty of Sciences:

Baronnet, J.-M., Energetics
Catherinot, A., Energetics
Colombeau, B., Optics
Coudert, J. F., Methodology, Plasma and Automation
Decossas, J. L., E.E.A.
Deschaux, P., Physiology
Desmaison, J., Mineral Chemistry
Duval, D., Mathematics
Fauchais, P., Energetics
Frit, B., Mineral Chemistry
Gaudreau, B., Mineral Chemistry
Goursat, P., Mineral Chemistry
Guillon, P., Electronics, Electrotechnology and Automation
Julien, R., Biochemistry
Krausz, P., Organic, Analytical and Industrial Chemistry
Laubie, F., Mathematics
Marcou, J., Electronics, Electrotechnology and Automation
Martin, C., Energetics
Mazet, M., Organic, Analytical and Industrial Chemistry
Mercurio, D., Mineral Chemistry
Mercurio, J.-P., Mineral Chemistry
Moliton, A., Optics
Moliton, J. P., E.E.A.
Morvan, H., Biology
Obregon, J., Electronics, Electrotechnology and Automatics
Sabourdy, G., Geology
Thera, M., Mathematics

Faculty of Letters and Humanities:

Balabanian, O., Geography and Development
Barrière, B., Medieval Archaeological History
Bedon, R., Ancient Language and Literature
Behar, P., Germanic and Scandinavian Language and Literature
Capdeboscq, A. M., Romance Language and Literature
Caron, P., Modern and Contemporary French Language and Literature
Chandes, G., Middle Age to Renaissance French Language and Literature
Dumont, J., Ancient World Archaeological History
El Gammal, J. M., World Medieval Archaeological History
Filteau, C., Modern and Contemporary French Language and Literature
Fontanille, J., Language Sciences
Gendreau-Massaloux, Romance Language and Literature
Grassin, J.-M., Comparative Literature
Grassin, M., Anglo-Saxon English Language and Literature
Leclanche, J.-L., Middle Age to Renaissance French Language and Literature
Lemoine, B., Anglo-Saxon English Language and Literature
Levet, J.-P., Ancient Language and Literature
Moreau, J.-P., Anglo-Saxon English Language and Literature
Nouhaud, M., Ancient Language and Literature
Rambaux, C., Ancient Language and Literature
Valadas, B., Economic and Regional Geography
Verdon, J., World Medieval Archaeological History

University Institute of Technology:

Berland, R., Electronics, Electrotechnology and Automatics
Besson, J.-L., Dense Media and Materials
Caperaa, S., Civil Engineering
Caron, A., Information Processing
Fray, C., Electronics, Electrotechnology and Automatics
Glandus, J.-C., Mechanics, Mechanical Engineering and Civil Engineering
Jecko, B., Electronics, Electrotechnology and Automatics
Jecko, F., Electronics, Electrotechnology and Automatics
Labbe, J.-C., Chemistry of Materials
Malaise, M., Mechanics, Mechanical Engineering and Civil Engineering
Nardou, F., Physical Chemistry
Platon, F., Mechanics, Mechanical Engineering and Civil Engineering
Quere, R., Electronics, Electrotechnology and Automation
Quintard, P., Dense Media and Materials
Ratinaud, M. M., Biochemistry and Biology

AFFILIATED INSTITUTES

Higher National School for Engineers (Limoges): 16, Rue d'Atlantis, parc ESTER, 87068 Limoges Cedex; tel. 5-55-42-36-70; fax 5-55-42-36-80; e-mail direction@ensil.unilim.fr; internet www.ensil.unilim.fr; Dir Claude Fray.

University Institute of Technology (Limousin): Allée Andrés Maurois, 87065 Limoges Cedex; tel. 5-55-43-43-55; fax 5-55-43-43-56; e-mail dir.iut@unilim.fr; Dir Gilles Broussaud.

Institut de Préparation à l'Administration Générale: BP 1727, 87025 Limoges Cedex; tel. 5-55-43-56-48; fax 5-55-43-56-49; e-mail mfr.ipag@unilim.fr; Dir Jean Devaud.

University Professional Institute: 2 Rue du Docteur Marcland, 87025 Limoges Cedex; tel. 5-55-43-59-15; fax 5-55-43-59-36; e-mail iup@unilim.fr; Dir Jean-François Nys.

Higher National School of Industrial Ceramics: 47–73 ave Albert Thomas, 87065 Limoges Cedex; tel. 5-55-45-22-22; fax 5-55-79-09-98; e-mail directin@ensci.fr; internet www.ensci.fr; Dir Christian Gault.

Science, Technology, Health: 13 Rue de Genève, 87065 Limoges Cedex; tel. 5-55-45-76-74; fax 5-55-45-76-73; e-mail ed-sts@unilim.fr; internet www.unilim.fr/edsts; Dir Abbas Chazad Movahhedi.

Human and Social Sciences: 13 Rue de Genève, 87065 Limoges Cedex; tel. 5-55-45-76-36; fax 5-55-45-76-73; Dir Bertrand Westphal.

Institute of Material Sciences: 123 ave Albert Thomas, 87060 Limoges Cedex; tel. 5-55-43-56-36; Dir Jean-Claude Champarnaud.

Pôle Limousin des Sciences et Technologies de l'Information et de la Communication: 123 ave Albert Thomas, 87060 Limoges Cedex; tel. 5-55-45-72-50; fax 5-55-45-72-01; Dir Pierre-Yves Guillon.

Institute of Life and Health Sciences: 123 ave Albert Thomas, 87060 Limoges Cedex; tel. 5-55-45-76-76; fax 5-55-45-72-01; Dir Raymond Julien.

Social Health and Environment: 2 rue du Docteur Marcland, 87025 Limoges Cedex; tel. 5-55-43-58-20; fax 5-55-45-72-01; Dir Pierre-Marie Preux.

Institute of the Environment and Water: 123 ave Albert Thomas, 87060 Limoges Cedex; tel. 5-55-45-74-69; fax 5-55-45-74-59; Dir Jean-Claude Bollinger.

UNIVERSITÉ DU LITTORAL CÔTE D'OPALE

Services Centraux, 1 place de l'Yser, B.P. 1022, Général-De-Gaulle, 59375 Dunkerque Cedex 1

Telephone: 3-28-23-73-73
Fax: 3-28-23-73-13
Internet: www.univ-littoral.fr

Founded 1991

Campuses in Boulogne, Calais, Dunkerque and St-Omer

President: Daniel Boucher
Director of Library Services: Mireille Chazal

Library of 100,000 vols, 900 periodical subscriptions; CD-ROM databases; special collections: Centre de Documentation Européenne, Relais INSEE (statistics), science fiction, cartoons, theses

Number of students: 11,000

Areas of study: law, economics, management, literature, languages, fine and performing arts, humanities, social sciences, natural sciences, technology, sport.

UNIVERSITÉ LYON I (UNIVERSITÉ CLAUDE-BERNARD)

43 blvd du 11 Novembre 1918, 69622 Villeurbanne Cedex

Telephone: 4-72-44-80-00
Fax: 4-72-43-10-20
Internet: www.univ-lyon1.fr

Founded 1970
State control
Language of instruction: French
Academic year: October to June

President: Domitien Debouzie
Vice-Presidents: Robert Garrone (Administration), Guy Annat (Studies), Jean-François Mornex (Sciences)
Secretary-General: Jean-Pascal Bonhotal

Number of teachers: 1,900
Number of students: 27,000

Publications: *Lettre FLASH/INFO (quarterly)*, *Livret de l'Etudiant* (annually), *Annuaire sur la Recherche* (annually)

DIRECTORS OF TEACHING AND RESEARCH UNITS

Medicine:

Medicine 'Grange-Blanche': XAVIER MARTIN
Medicine 'Rth Laennec': DENIS VITAL-DURAND
Medicine 'Lyon-Nord': FRANÇOIS MAUGUIÈRE
Medicine 'Sud': FRANÇOIS-NOËL GILLY
Pharmaceutical and Biological Sciences: FRANÇOIS LOCHER
Rehabilitation: LIONEL COLLET
Human Biology: PIERRE FARGE
Dentistry: J. OLIVIER ROBIN

Sciences:

Institute of Financial and Actuarial Sciences: JEAN-CLAUDE AUGROS
Lyon Institute of Science and Engineering Technology: JEAN-PIERRE PUAUX
Chemistry and Biochemistry: JEAN-PIERRE SCHARFF
Biology: HUBERT PINON
Electrical Engineering: ANDRÉ BRIGUET
Computer Science: MARCEL EGEA
Mechanical Engineering: HAMDA BEN HADID
Mathematics: MARC CHAMARIE
Physics: JEAN-LOUIS VIALLE
Earth Sciences: PIERRE HANTZPERGUE
Science and Technology of Physical Education and Sport: RAPHAEL MASSAREL
University Institute of Technology 'A': MICHEL ODIN
University Institute of Technology 'B': GILBERT MAREST
Observatory: ROLAND BACON

ATTACHED INSTITUTES

Institut de Pharmacie Industrielle: 8 ave Rockefeller, 69373 Lyons Cedex 08; Dir ANNICK ROBIN.

Institut d'Audiophonologie: Hôpital Edouard-Herriot, Pavillon U, 5 place d'Arsonval, 69003 Lyons; Dir M. COLLET.

Institut de Médecine du Travail: 8 ave Rockefeller, 69373 Lyons Cedex 08; Dir Prof. GUY PROST.

Institut de Médecine et d'Hygiène Tropicales: 8 ave Rockefeller, 69373 Lyons Cedex 08; Dir S. PICOT.

Institut Michel-Pacha: Laboratoire Maritime de Physiologie, 83500 Tamaris-sur-Mer; Dir GÉRARD BRICHON.

Institut de Recherche sur l'Enseignement des Mathématiques (IREM): 43 blvd du 11 Novembre 1918, 69622 Villeurbanne; Dir MICHEL MISONY.

Institut de Médecine Légale et Criminologie Clinique 'Alexandre Lacassagne': 12 ave Rockefeller, 69373 Lyons Cedex 08; Dir Prof. M. P. MALICIER.

Institut de Recherches Chirurgicales: 8 rue Guillaume-Paradin, 69008 Lyons; Dir Dr JEAN-LOUIS PEIX.

Institut d'Histoire de la Médicine: 68 cours Gambetta, 69007 Lyons; Dir Prof. CHARVET.

UNIVERSITÉ LUMIÈRE LYON 2

86 rue Pasteur, 69365 Lyons Cedex 07
Telephone: 4-78-69-70-00
Fax: 4-78-69-56-01
Internet: www.univ-lyon2.fr

President: GILBERT PUECH
First Vice-President (Human Resources and Administration): HENRI BÉJOINT
Vice-President (Training): ISABELLE BONGARÇIN
Vice-President (International Relations): ISABELLE GUINAMARD
Vice-President (University Life, Culture and Sport): ALEXIS CHVETZOFF
Vice-President (Communication): ALEXANDRE BONUCCI
Vice-President (Resources and Budget): YVES CROZET
Vice-President (Research): YVES GRAFMEYER
Vice-President (Studies): FRANÇOISE DURIEUX
Secretary-General: BERNARD FRADIN

Number of teachers: 567
Number of students: 27,197

Publication: *Le Rayon Vert* (10 a year)

DEANS

Faculty of Literature, Science of Language and Arts: DENIS REYNAUD
Faculty of Modern Languages: FABRICE MALKANI
Faculty of Geography, History, History of Art and Tourism: JEAN-MICHEL DEWAILLY
Faculty of Law and Political Science: CLAUDE JOURNÈS
Faculty of Anthropology and Sociology: JACQUES BONNIEL
Faculty of Economics and Business Studies: ANDRÉ TIRAN

DIRECTORS

Institute of Psychology: JEAN-MARIE BESSE
Institute of Teacher Training: CHARLES GARDOU
Institute of Communication: DOMINIQUE BOURGAIN
Institute of Labour: ALAIN BOUILLOUX
Institute of Trade Union Training: FLORENCE DEBORD
Institut Universitaire de Technologie Lumière: MICHEL LE NIR
Institute of Political Studies: DANIEL DUFOURT

UNIVERSITÉ LYON 3 (UNIVERSITÉ JEAN MOULIN)

1 rue de l'Université, BP 0638, 69239 Lyons Cedex 02

Telephone: 4-78-78-78-78
Fax: 4-78-78-79-79
Internet: www.univ-lyon3.fr

Founded 1973

President: GUY LAVOREL
Vice-Presidents: IONNA SCHMIDT, JEAN-JACQUES WUNENBURGER, JACQUES BONNET, LAID BOUZIDI
Secretary-General: CLAUDE MARSOT

Number of teachers: 500
Number of students: 20,000

Publication: *Lyon 3 Infos* (monthly)

DEANS

Faculty of Law: J. SAID
Faculty of Languages: JEAN-LOUIS CHAUZIT
Faculty of Letters and Civilizations: NICOLE GONTHIER
Faculty of Philosophy: JEAN-JACQUES WUNENBURGER
Institute of Business Administration and Management: GILLES GUYOT
Institut Universitaire de Technologie

UNIVERSITÉ DU MAINE

Ave Olivier Messiaen, 72085 Le Mans Cedex 9

Telephone: 2-43-83-30-00
Fax: 2-43-83-30-77
Internet: www.univ-lemans.fr

Founded 1977

President: MAURICE HENRY
Secretary-General: PHILIPPE WISLER

Number of teachers: 395
Number of students: 10,308

Publication: *Livret de l'Etudiant* (annually)

DEANS

Faculty of Sciences: MICHEL PEZERIL
Faculty of Letters and Human Sciences: ABDELOUAHADE MOUBARIK
Faculty of Law and Social Sciences: O. BIENCOURT

ATTACHED INSTITUTES

University Institute of Technology (Laval): 52 rue des docteurs Calmette et Guérin, BP 2045, 53000 Laval Cedex 09; tel. 2-43-59-49-05; fax 2-43-59-49-08; internet www.iut-laval.univ-lemans.fr.

University Institute of Technology (Le Mans): Ave Olivier Messiaen, 72085 Le Mans Cedex 09; tel. 2-43-83-34-01; fax 2-43-83-30-88; internet iut.univ-lemans.fr.

Higher National School of Engineering: Rue Aristote, 72085 Le Mans Cedex 09; tel. 2-43-83-35-93; fax 2-43-83-37-94; e-mail ensim@univ-lemans.fr; internet ensim.univ-lemans.fr.

UNIVERSITÉ DE MARNE-LA-VALLÉE

5 blvd Descartes, Champs/Marne, 77454 Marne la Vallée Cedex 2

Telephone: 1-60-95-75-00
Fax: 1-60-95-75-75
Internet: www.univ-mlv.fr

Founded 1991

President: YVES LICHTENBERGER
Secretary-General: DENIS GUILLAUMIN
Librarian: EDWIGE ARCHIER

Number of teachers: 400
Number of students: 11,000

TEACHING AND RESEARCH UNITS

Languages and Civilisation: GILLES ROBEL
Letters, Arts and Communication: GISÈLE SEGINGER
Engineering: DOMINIQUE PERRIN
Human and Social Sciences: FREDÉRIC MORET
Economic Sciences: MANON DOS SANTOS
Mathematics: MATHIEU MEYER
Material Sciences: ROBERTO MARQUARDT
Science and Technology: PATRICK FAUCONNIER
Sports Science: ERIC LEVET-LABRY
Arts and Technologies: GISÈLE SEGINGER
University Institute of Technology: DOMINIQUE PRÉSENT
Institute of Computing and Electronics: JACQUES DÉSARMÉNIEN
Geosciences Engineering Institute: MICHEL MADON
Institute of Engineering Services: DANIEL LAURENT

UNIVERSITÉ PAUL VERLAINE–METZ

Ile du Saulcy, BP 80794, 57012 Metz Cedex 1

Telephone: 3-87-31-50-50
Fax: 3-87-31-50-55
E-mail: com@univ-metz.fr
Internet: www.univ-metz.fr

Founded 1970

President: RICHARD LIOGER
Vice-Presidents: G. RHIN, M. POTIER-FERRY, G. GINTER
Secretary-General: MICHEL CLEMENS
Librarian: SIMONE LAMARCHE

Number of teachers: 623
Number of students: 15,729

DEANS

Letters and Languages: ALAIN CULLIERE
Arts and Human Sciences: ERIC PEDON
Higher Management Studies: ETIENNE BAUMGARTNER

Mathematics, Computer Science, Mechanics: ABDERRAHIM ZEGHLOUL
Fundamental and Applied Sciences: JEAN-GEORGES GASSER
University Institute of Technology: BERNARD HEULLUY
Law, Economics and Administration: YAHN MANGEMATIN
University Institute of Technology at Thionville/Yutz: FRANÇOIS-XAVIER ROYER
Higher Franco-German Institute of Technology, Economy and Sciences: GABRIEL MICHEL

HEADS OF DEPARTMENTS

Letters and Human Sciences:
- Psychology: M. L. COSTANTINI
- Language Science: J. F. HALTE
- English: R. SPRINGER
- German: M. GRUNEWALD
- Spanish: A. CANSECO-JEREZ
- Classics: E. AUBRION
- Modern Languages: A. CULLIÈRE
- History: M. SEVE
- Geography: E. GILLE
- Philosophy: J. P. RESWEBER
- Religious Education: Y. LEDURE
- Communication Sciences: N. NEL
- Applied Foreign Languages: K. BIRAT
- International Exchange: P. SCHAEFFER
- Music: P. PREVOST
- Plastic Arts: P.-D. HUYGHE
- Sociology: S. GUTH
- Dramatic Arts: L. JULLIER

Law and Economics:
- Law: P. SCHAEFER
- Management and Business Administration: B. SIBAUD
- Environmental Sciences: Mlle VASSEUR

Mathematics, Computing and Mechanics:
- Mathematics and Computer Science: A. ZEGHLOUL
- Mechanics, Materials, Technology: J.-C. VÉRONIE

Fundamental and Applied Sciences:
- Natural Sciences: J. C. PIHAN
- Chemistry: J. C. MORETEAU
- Physics and Electronics: M. F. CHARLIER

There are 33 attached research centres and laboratories

UNIVERSITÉ DE MONTPELLIER I

BP 1017, 34006 Montpellier Cedex
Telephone: 4-67-41-20-90
Fax: 4-67-41-02-46
Internet: www.univ-montp1.fr

Founded 1970
State control
Language of instruction: French
Academic year: September to June

President: YVES LOUBATIÈRES
General Secretary: SYLVAIN SALTIEL
Librarian: BENOÎT LECOQ

Number of teachers: 829
Number of students: 18,538

Publications: *L'Economie Méridionale*, *Revue de la Société d'Histoire du Droit*, *Journal de Médecine*, *Le Ligament*, *Cadran*

TEACHING AND RESEARCH UNITS

Law: Dir: O. DUGRIP
Science and Economics: Dir: J. PERCEBOIS
Economic and Social Administration: Dir: YVES CHIROUZE
Medicine: Dir: C. SOLASSOL
Pharmacy: Dir: J.-L. CHANAL
Industrial Pharmacy: Dir: H. DELONCA
Odontology: Dir: P. PARGUEL
Alimentary, Oenological and Environmental Studies: Dir: J. C. CABANIS
Physical Education and Sport: Dir: L. BELEN

ATTACHED INSTITUTES

Montpellier Higher Institute for Business: Dir D. GATUMEL.

Research Institute for the Study of Juridical Information: Dir J.-L. BILON.

Regional Institute for Economic Study: Dir J.-M. BOISSON.

Institute for Preparation for General Administration: Dir P. DI MALTA.

UNIVERSITÉ DE MONTPELLIER II (SCIENCES ET TECHNIQUES DU LANGUEDOC)

Place Eugène Bataillon, 34095 Montpellier Cedex 5
Telephone: 4-67-14-30-30
Fax: 4-67-14-30-31
E-mail: presidence@univ-montp2.fr
Internet: www.univ-montp2.fr

President: JACQUES BONNAFE
Vice-President (Council of Administration): ALAIN SZAFARCZYK
Vice-President (Scientific Council): JEAN-LOUIS CUQ
Vice-President (Council of Studies and University Life): PIERRE MERLE
Secretary-General: NOELLE AVARD-CARDONA
Librarian: MIREILLE GALCERAN

Number of teachers: 745
Number of students: 13,450

Publications: *Naturalia Monspelianesia*, *Paléobiologie Continentale—Paléovertebrata*, *Cahiers de Mathématiques*.

TEACHING AND RESEARCH UNITS

Centre de Formation d'Apprentis: 8 Rue Jules Raimu, 30907 Nîmes Cedex; tel. 4-66-62-85-92; fax 4-66-62-85-91; e-mail cfaum2@univ-montp2.fr; internet www.cfa.iut-nimes.fr; Dir DANIEL MIGLIORINI.

Continued Professional Training: 99 ave d'Occitanie, 34096 Montpellier Cedex 5; tel. 4-99-58-52-72; fax 4-99-58-52-81; e-mail formperm@univ-montp2.fr; Dir JOSEPH CALAS.

Faculty of Sciences: Place Eugène Bataillon, 34095 Montpellier Cedex 5; tel. 4-67-14-30-34; fax 4-67-14-47-00; internet www.ufr.univ-montp2.fr; Dir JEAN-LOUIS VIDAL.

Institute of Business Management: tel. 4-67-14-38-65; fax 4-67-14-42-42; e-mail courrier@iae.univ-montp2.fr; internet www.iae.univ-montp2.fr; Dir ALAIN BRIOLE.

Polytech' Montpellier: tel. 4-67-14-31-60; fax 4-67-14-45-14; e-mail scola@polytech.univ-montp2.fr; internet www.polytech.univ-montp2.fr; Dir MICHEL DESBORDES.

University Institute of Technology of Montpellier: 99 ave d'Occitanie, 34296 Montpellier Cedex 5; tel. 4-67-14-40-40; fax 4-99-58-50-41; Dir ALAIN ROUSSET.

University Institute of Technology of Nîmes: 8 Rue Jules Raimu, 30907 Nîmes Cedex; tel. 4-66-62-85-00; fax 4-66-62-85-01; internet www.iut-nimes.fr; Dir SALAM CHARAR.

UNIVERSITÉ DE MONTPELLIER III (UNIVERSITÉ PAUL VALÉRY)

Route de Mende, BP 5043, 34199 Montpellier Cedex 5Telephone: 4-67-14-20-00
Fax: 4-67-14-20-52
Internet: www.univ-montp3.fr

Founded 1970
State control
Language of instruction: French
Academic year: September to July

President: JEAN-MARIE MIOSSEC
Vice-Presidents: CATHERINE BERTHET-CAHUZAC, YVES PEYRE, DOMINIQUE TRIAIRE
Secretary-General: JACQUES-ANTOINE MARTINI
Librarian: HUGUETTE BRELAZ

Number of teachers: 630
Number of students: 21,000

Publication: 68 research periodicals

TEACHING AND RESEARCH UNITS

Anglo-American, Germanic, Slav, Neo-Hellenic and Oriental Studies: Dir: JEAN-FRANÇOIS VERGNAUD
Applied Foreign Languages: Dir: PABLO NERIN
Economic, Mathematical and Social Sciences: Dir: ZEINEDDINE KHELFAOUI
Human and Environmental Sciences: Dir: DAVID LEFÈVRE
Letters, Arts, Philosophy and Linguistics: Dir: ANNE FRAÏSSE
Mediterranean Romance Languages: Dir: MICHEL BOURRET
Science of Society: Dir: PATRICK TACUSSEL

UNIVERSITÉ DE NANCY I (HENRI POINCARÉ)

24 rue Lionnois, BP 60120, 54003 Nancy Cedex
Telephone: 3-83-68-20-00
Fax: 3-83-68-21-00
E-mail: claire.bergerot@uhp.u-nancy.fr
Internet: www.uhp-nancy.fr

Founded 1970

President: JEAN-PIERRE FINANCE
Vice-President (Administration): HENRY COUDANE
Vice-President (Scientific): PATRICK ALNOT
Vice-President (Studies and University Life): CHRISTINE ATKINSON
Secretary-General: JEAN DÉROCHE

Number of teachers: 1,434
Number of students: 16,764

Publications: *Bulletin d'Information* (10 a year), *Transversales* (3 a year)

TEACHING AND RESEARCH UNITS

Medicine: Dir: PATRICK NETTER
Pharmacy: Dir: CHANTAL FINANCE
Dental Surgery: Dir: JEAN-PAUL LOUIS
Sciences: PIERRE GUILMIN
Biological Sciences: Dir: CHRISTIAN DOURNON
Mathematics, Computing and Automation: Dir: MARIE-CHRISTINE HATON
Materials Science and Processes: Dir: PIERRE GUILMIN
Sport and Physical Education: Dir: JEAN HUOT
University Institute of Technology (Nancy-Brabois): Dir: JEAN-MARIE HORNUT
University Institute of Technology (Longwy): Dir: PHILIPPE PIERROT
University Institute of Technology (Saint Dié): Dir: THIERRY CECCHIN
Higher School of the Science and Technology of Engineering: Dir: MICHEL ROBERT
Higher School of the Science and Technology of the Wood Industry: Dir: PASCAL TRIBOULOT
Higher School of Computing and its Applications: Dir: ANDRÉ SCHAFF

UNIVERSITÉ DE NANCY II

25 rue Baron Louis, BP 454, 54001 Nancy Cedex
Telephone: 3-83-34-46-00
Fax: 3-83-30-05-65
Internet: www.univ-nancy2.fr

Founded 1970
State control
Language of instruction: French
Academic year: October to May

President: HERBERT NERY

Vice-President, Administration Council: CHRISTIAN DUGAS DE LA BOISONNY
Vice-President, Scientific Council: BRUNO DEFFAINS
Vice-President, Council for Study and University Life: PASCALE FADE
Secretary-General: ODILE THIBIER
Librarian: J. B. MARINO

Library: see Libraries
Number of teachers: 531
Number of students: 22,000

Publications: *Les Annales de l'Est*, *Verbum*, *Revue Géographique de l'Est*, *Autrement dire*, *Etudes d'archéologie classique*, *La Revue française d'études américaines*

TEACHING AND RESEARCH UNITS

Law, Economic Sciences and Management: Dir: ETIENNE CRIQUI
Social and Economic Administration: Dir: MARTIAL DELIGNON
Training Institute in General Administration: Dir: HUBERT GERARDIN
Regional Institute of Labour: Dir: DANIEL BOULMIER
European University Centre: Dir: JEAN DENIS MOUTON
Literature: Dir: MARCEL PAUL-CAVALLIER
Foreign Languages and Literature: Dir: NICOLE FOURTANE
Historical and Geographical Sciences and Musicology: Dir: PATRICK CORBET
Human Sciences: Dir: NICOLE DUBOIS
Science of Languages: Dir: RICHARD DUDA
University Institute of Technology (at Nancy): Dir: HERVÉ COILLAND
University Institute of Technology (at Epinal): Dir: JEAN LEPAGE (acting)
Institute of Cinematographic Studies: Dir: RÉGIS LATOUCHE
Business Management (Lorraine): Dir: CHRISTIAN BOURION

UNIVERSITÉ DE NANTES

1 quai de Tourville, BP 13522, 44035 Nantes Cedex 01

Telephone: 2-40-99-83-83
Fax: 2-40-93-83-00
E-mail: president@president.univ-nantes.fr
Internet: www.univ-nantes.fr

Founded 1962
State control

President: FRANÇOIS RESCHE
Vice-Presidents: OLGA GALATANU (International Relations), JOSEPH SAILLARD (Scientific Council), YVON LE GALL (Culture), SOPHIE BINET (Students), JACQUES MARCHAND (Studies and University Life), SOPHIE VAN GOETHEM (Administration)
Librarian: MICHÈLE GUIOT

Number of teachers: 1,354
Number of students: 33,278

Publication: *Prisme* (6 a year)

TEACHING AND RESEARCH UNITS

Law and Political Sciences: M. HELIN
Economic Science and Business Studies: BRUNO HENRIET
Medicine: M. GROLLEAU
Pharmacology: ALAIN PINEAU
Dentistry: BERNARD GIUMELLI
Psychology: MOHAMMED BERNOUSSI
Sociology: CHARLES SUAUD
Science and Technology: DANIEL ARDOUIN
Institute of Business Administration: BERNARD FIOLEAU
Institute of Technology (Nantes): G. COEURDEUIL
Institute of Technology (Roche-sur-Yon): ALAIN DUBOUX
Institute of Technology (St-Nazaire): M. LEFEVRE
Human Sciences: Mme GANGLER
Sports Science: ARNAUD GUEVEL
International Language Centre
History, Art History and Archaeology: JACQUES WEBER
Letters and Languages: DOMINIQUE GANGLER
Institute of Geography: MARC ROBIN
Higher Institute of Electronics: M. REMAUD
Institute of Thermodynamics and Materials: M. SCHLEICH
Institute of Preparatory Administrative Studies: LIONEL PROUTEAU
Polytech' Nantes: l'Ecole d'ingénieurs de l'Université: BERNARD REMAUD

UNIVERSITÉ DE NICE SOPHIA ANTIPOLIS

Grand Château, 28 parc Valrose, BP 2135, 06103 Nice Cedex 2

Telephone: 4-92-07-60-60
Fax: 4-92-07-66-00
Internet: www.unice.fr

Founded 1965
State control
Language of instruction: French

President: ALBERT MAROUANI
Vice-Presidents: J. MAGNÉ A. CHIAVELLI, P. FERRAN, Y. HERVIER
Secretary-General: P. R. VERNISSE
Librarian: LOUIS KLEE

Number of teachers: 1,200
Number of students: 27,500

Publications: *Annuaire*, *Guide des formations de Recherche*.

TEACHING AND RESEARCH UNITS

Law, Politics, Economics and Management: Dir R. BERNARDINI.

Institute of Business Administration: Dir N. TOURNOIS.

Institute of Law, Peace and Development: 39 Ave Emile Henriot, 06050 Nice Cedex 1; tel. 4-92-15-71-94; fax 4-92-15-71-97; Dir L. BALMOND.

Medicine: Dir M. BENCHIMOL.

Odontology: Dir Prof. JASMIN.

Sciences: Parc Valrose, 06108 Nice Cedex 2; tel. 4-92-07-60-60; Dir R. NÉGREL.

Letters, Arts and Human Sciences: Dir A. ARNAUD.

Physical Education and Sports Sciences: 261 route de Grenoble, 06205 Nice Cedex 3; tel. 4-92-29-65-00; Dir I. MARGARITIS.

Culture and Space: Dir P. CARREGA.

Higher School of Information Sciences: 930 route des Colles, 06903 Sophia Antipolis Cedex; tel. 4-92-96-50-50; fax 4-92-96-50-55; e-mail essi@essi.fr; Dir A. GIULIERI.

University Institute of Technology: internet www.iut.unice.fr; Dir R. CHIGNOLI.

Higher School of Engineering: 1645 route des Lucioles, 06410 Biot; tel. 4-92-38-85-00; fax 4-92-38-85-02; internet www.esinsa.unice.fr; Dir A. CHAVE

PROFESSORS

Law, Politics, Economics and Management (7 ave Robert Schuman, 06050 Nice Cedex 1; tel. 4-92-15-70-00; fax 4-92-15-71-01):

Private Law:

AMBROISE CASTEROT, C.
ARRIGHI, J. P.
BERNARDINI, N.
BERNARDINI, R.
BOY, L.
COLLOMB, P.
LUCAS, F. X.
MARTIN, G.
RENUCCI, J. F.
VIDAL, D.

Public Law:

ASSO, B.
AUVRET-FINOK, J.
CHARVIN, R.
CRISTINI, R.
FERRARI, P.
LINOTTE, D.
NOËL, G.
PIQUEMAL, A.
QUIOT, G.
RAINAUD, J.-M.
RIDEAU, J.
SAUNIER, P.
TOUSCOZ, J.
VALLAR, CH.
WAGNER, F.
WECKEL, P.

History of Law:

BOTTIN, M.
CARLIN, M.-L.
ORTOLANI, M.
VERNIER, O.

Economics:

ARENA, R.
BERTHOMIEU, C.
BOMEL, P.
GAFFARD, J.-L.
GUICHARD, J.-P.
JOB, L.
MAROUANI, A.
RAINELLI, M.
RAVIX, J.
ROMANI, P.-M.
SPINDLER, J.
TORRE, D.

Management:

BARTHE, N.
BARTOLI, J. A.
BOYER, A.
CHIAVELLI, A.
GIORDANO, Y.
GUYON, C.
MARTIN, M.
MARTORY, B.
NOBRE, T.
TELLER, R.
TOURNOIS, N.
WEISL, R.

Politics:

BASSO, J.
BIDEGARAY, C.
BOUVET, L.
DABENE, O.
HEURTIN, J. P.

Letters, Arts and Human Sciences (98 blvd E. Henriot, BP 3209, 06204 Nice Cedex 3; tel. 4-93-37-53-53; fax 4-93-37-55-36):

Sociology and Ethnology:

DE VOS, C.
MANN, P.
ZIROTTI, J P.

Psychology:

BACCINO, T.
CARIOU, M.
FAURE, S.
GEFFROY, Y.
JURANVILLE, A.
LÉONARD, F.
MIOLLAN, C.
SCHADRON, G.
STEINER, D.

Philosophy:

DASTUR, F.
LARTHOMAS, J.-P.
MATTEÏ, J.-F.
ROBELIN, J.
TOSEL, A.

Comparative Literature:

CHEMAIN, A.
PUECH, S.

French Literature:

BONHOMME, B.
DOMENECH, J.
MARTINEAU, C.
PERIGOT, B.
RIEU, J.
SEILLAN, J. M
TASSEL, A.

French Philosophy:

GUEDJ, C.

History:

ARNAUD, P.
BOURSIER, J. Y.
CANDAU, J.
DEVEAU, J. M.
EL MECHAT, S.
JANSEN, P.
LAUWERS, M.
REBUFFAT, F.
SCHOR, R.

Geography:

CARREGA, P.
DAUPHINE, A.
ESCALLIER, R.
LABORDE, J.-P.
ROGNANT, L.
VOIRON, C.

Linguistics and Phonetics:

BOUCHET, R.
DALBERA, J.-PH.
GASIGLIA, R.
KOTLER, E.
MOLLO, E.
NICOLAI, R.
ZINGLE, H.

English:

BONIFAS, G.
GALLAGHER, M.
JUILLARD, M.
LAPRAZ, F.
LEMOSSE, M.
LLASERA, M.
MORGAN, G.
REMY, M.
SOUESME, J.-C.
TERREL, D.
VIOLA, A.
ZEENDER, M.

German:

DARMAUN, J.
FAURE, A.
VUILLAUME, M.
ZINGLE, H.

Latin:

BIRAUD, M.
DELBEY, E.
GUELFUCCI, M. R.
KIRCHER, C.
MUSTAPHA, M.

Romance Languages:

BARRACHINA, M. L.
BRAU, J.-L., Spanish
CASSAC, M.
FRESINA, C.
JAUBERT, A., French
MARTI, M.
MUSTAPHA, M.
SPIZZO, J., Italian

Music:

BONNET, A.
CARDUCCI, M.
LELEU, J.-L.

Information Science:

HILLAIRE, N.
RASSE, P.

Sciences (Parc Valrose, 06108 Nice Cedex 2; tel. 4-92-07-69-96; fax 4-92-07-69-76):

General:

PETIT, L.

Mathematics:

AUBERT, G.
BEAUVILLE, A.
BERNHARD, P.
BLUM, J.
BRIANCON, J.
CATHELINEAU, J.-L.
CHENAIS, D.
DIENER, F.
DIENER, M.
ELENCWAJG, G.
FABRE, S.
GALLIGO, A.
GIULIERI, A.
HIRSCHOWITZ, A.
LE BARZ, P.
LEBEAU, G.
LEMAIRE, J.
LEMAIRE, J.-M.
LE ROUX, J.
LOBRY, C.
MAISONOBE, P.
MARLIN, R.
MERLE, M.
MICHEL, O.
POPESCU, S.
POUPAUD, F.
RASCLE, M.
RIX, H.
ROUSSELET, B.
ROUVIÈRE, F.
SIMPSON, N.
THIELIGEN, A.
WALTER, C.
WOJTKOWIAK, Z.
XIOA, G.

Information Sciences:

BOND, I.
CAROMEL, D.
CAVARERO, A.
CAVARERO, J.-L.
COLLARD, P.
COSNARD, M.
FEDOU, J. M.
KOUNALIS, E.
LAFON, J. C.
LE CARME, O.
LE THANH, N.
LITOVSKY, I.
MIRANDA, S.
PEYRAT, CL.
PIERRE, L.
RUEHER, M.
SANDER, P.
RIGAULT, J.-P.

Physics:

AZEMA, A.
BATROUNI, G.
BROCH, H.
FARGES, J. P.
FEMENIAS, J. L.
GILLI, J. M.
JACQUEMOD, G.
KOFMAN, R.
KOSSIAVAS, G.
LAHEURTE, J.-P.
LAPRAZ, D.
LEGRAND, O.
LÉVY-LEBLOND, J.-M.
LEYCURAS, C.
LIPPI, G. L.
MALLET, G.
MEUNIER, J.-L.
OSTROWSKY, D.
OSTROWSKY, N.
PROVOST, J.-P.
ROMAGNON, J.-P.

Electronics and Industrial Computer Science:

ALENGRIN, G.
ANDRÉ, C.
BARCI, G.
CAMBIAGGIO, E.
CHAVE, A.
CHAZE, A. M.
CONDOM, R.
CUVELIER, L.
DUVAL, D.
GERIBALDI, S.
GINGRAS, M.
IACCONI, P.
LEGENDRE, J. J.
MARMIER, N.
MENEZ, J.
SBIRRAZZUOLI, N.

Astrophysics:

AIME, C.
BORGNINO, J.
LANTERI, H.
RICORT, G.
SCHOLL, M.

Geology:

BLANCHET, R.
CARUBA, R.
CHEMANDA, A.
DELTEIL, J.
LARDEAUX, J. M.
POPOFF, M.
PUPIN, J. P.
SCHARER, U.
STEPHAN, J.-F.
VIRIEUX, J.

General Chemistry:

CABROL BASS, D.
GUION, J.

Organic, Mineral and Analytical Chemistry:

GAL, F.
GAYMARD, F.
GUEDJ, R.
PASTOR, R.
ROUILLARD, M.

Biochemistry:

AILHAUD, G.
CHRISTEN, R.
CLERTANT, P.
COUSIN, J. L.
CUPPO, A.
CUZIN, F.
GLAICHENHAUS, N.
NEGREL, R.
VINCENT, J.-P.

Physiology and Biology:

ALLEMAND, D.
DELAUNAY, F.
EHRENFELD, J., Cellular and Comparative Physiology
FRANCOUR, P.
GARCIA, R.
GIRARD, J.-P., Cellular and Comparative Physiology
GOTTESMANN, C., Psychophysiology
HEROUART, D.
LE RUDULIER, D., Plant Biology and Microbiology
MARSAULT, R.
MEINESZ, A., Marine Ecology and Biology
MIENVILLE, J. M.
NICAISE, G., Applied Microscopy
PAYAN, P., Cellular and Comparative Physiology
PUPPO, A., Plant Biology and Microbiology
VIANI, R., Biophysics

Higher School of Information Sciences:

FRANCHI-ZANNETTACCI, P.
GIULIERI, A.
LAFON, J.-C.

Non-Linear Institute of Nice:

COULLET, P.
DEMAY, Y.
EHRENSTEIN, U.
IOOSS, G.
LE BELLAC, M.
ROCCA, F.

University Institute of Technology (41 blvd Napoleon III, 06141 Nice Cedex; tel. 4-97-25-82-00; fax 4-97-25-83-30):

BARLAUD, M.
DEMARTINI, J.
POMPEI, D.
TREDDICE, J.
TSCHAEGLE, A.

Physical Education and Sports Sciences (261 route de Grenoble, BP 3259, 06205 Nice Cedex 3; tel. 4-92-29-65-00; fax 4-92-29-65-49):

BRUANT, G.
LEGROS, P.
MARINI, J. F.

Medicine (Ave de Valombrose, 06107 Nice Cedex 2; tel. 4-93-37-77-77; fax 4-93-53-15-15):

ALBERTINI, M., Paediatrics
AMIEL, J., Urology
AYRAUD, N., Genetics
BALAS, D., Histology
BATT, M., Surgery
BAUDOUY, M., Cardiology
BENCHIMOL, D.
BERNARD, A., Immunology
BERNARD, E., Paediatrics
BERNARDIN, G., Resuscitation
BLAIVE, B., Pneumology
BOCQUET, J.-P., Hygiene
BOILEAU, P., Orthopaedic Surgery
BONGAIN, A., Obstetrics
BOQUET, P., Bacteriology
BOURGEON, A., Anatomy
BOUTTE, P., Paediatrics
BRUNETON, J.-N., Radiology
BUSSIÈRE, F., Biophysics
CAMOUS, J.-P., Therapeutics
CANIVET, B., Internal Medicine
CAREL, C., Histology
CASSUTO, J.-P., Haematology
CHATEL, M., Neurology
COUSSEMENT, A., Radiology
DARCOURT, G., Psychiatry
DELLAMONICA, P., Infectious Diseases
DEMARD, F., Otorhinolaryngology
DE PERETTI, F., Anatomy
DESNUELLE, C., Cellular Biology
FENICHEL, P.
FERRARI, E., Cardiology
FUZIBET, J.-G., Internal Medicine
GASTAUD, P., Ophthalmology
GIBELIN, P., Cardiology
GILLET, J.-Y., Gynaecology
GRELLIER, P., Neurosurgery
GRIMAUD, D., Anaesthesiology
GUGENHEIM, J., Digestive Surgery
HASSEN KHOOJA, R., Vascular Surgery
HERUTERNE, X., Nutrition
JAECHER, P., Nephrology
JCHAI, C., Anaesthesiology and Resuscitation
JOURDAN, J., Thoracic Surgery
LACOUR, J.-P., Dermatology
LAMBERT, J.-CL., Genetics
LAZOUNSKI, M., Molecular Biochemistry and Biology
LE FICHOUX, Y., Parasitology
LEBRETON, E., Surgery
LEFEBVRE, J.-C., Bacteriology
MATTEI, M., Resuscitation
MICHIELS, J.-F., Pathological Anatomy
MOUROUX, J., Cardiac and Thoracic Surgery
MOUIEL, J., Digestive Surgery
MYQUEL, M., Child Psychiatry
ORTONNE, J.-P., Dermatology
PADOVANI, B., Medical Radiological Imagery
PAQUIS, P., Neurosurgery
PAQUIS, V., Genetics
PESCE, A., Geriatric Internal Medicine
PRINGUEY, D., Psychiatry
QUATREHOMME, G., Regional Medicine and Health Law
RAMPAL, P., Hepatology
RAUCOULES, A. M., Anaesthesiology and Resuscitation
RAUNAUDNÉE CHINCHILLA, D., Blood Transfusion
ROBERT, P., Adult Psychiatry
SADOUL, J.-L., Metabolic Medicine
SANTINI, J., Otorhinolaryngology
TOUBOL, J., Urology
TRAN, D. K., Gynaecology
VAN OBBERGHEN, E., Molecular Biochemistry and Biology
ZIEGLER, L., Rheumatology

Odontology (24 ave des Diables Bleus, 06357 Nice Cedex 4; tel. 4-92-00-11-11; fax 4-92-00-12-63):

BOLLA, MARC
BOLLA, MICHÈLE
JASMIN, J.
MALHER, P.
MONTEIL, R.
ROCCA, J.-P.

UNIVERSITÉ D'ORLÉANS

Château de la Source, BP 6749, 45067 Orléans Cedex 2
Telephone: 2-38-41-71-71
Fax: 2-38-41-70-69
Internet: www.univ-orleans.fr

Founded 1961
Language of instruction: French
Academic year: September to June

Pres.: GÉRARD BESSON
Vice-Pres: MICHEL PERTUÉ, JACQUES CHARVET, JEAN-MARIE GINESTA
Sec.-Gen.: GÉRARD GASQUET
Librarian: Mme DESBORDES

Number of teachers: 832
Number of students: 17,500

Publications: *Bulletin d'informations de l'Université* (5 a year), *Plaquette en direction des entreprises* (annual), *1er contact* (annual), *Internships* (annual), research catalogue

TEACHING AND RESEARCH UNITS

Law, Economics and Management: Dir: JACQUES LEROY
Letters, Languages and Human Sciences: Dir: JEAN-MARIE GINESTA
Sciences and Sports Sciences: Dir: RÉGIS DE REYKE
Sciences: Dir: RENÉ ERRE
University Institute of Technology (Orléans): Dir: GÉRARD BAILLARGUET
University Institute of Technology (Bourges): Dir: JACQUES GUILLY
University Institute of Technology (Chartres): Dir: LEVI ALLAM
University Institute of Technology (Indre): Dir: CHRISTIAN ETIENNE
Ecole Polytechnique: Dir: JEAN-LOUIS BILLOËT

UNIVERSITÉ PARIS I (PANTHÉON-SORBONNE)

12 place du Panthéon, 75231 Paris Cedex 05
Telephone: 1-44-07-80-00
Internet: www.univ-paris1.fr

Founded 1971
State control
Language of instruction: French
Academic year: September to June

President: PIERRE-YVES HÉNIN
Vice-Presidents: CHRISTIANE PRIGENT, ANDRÉ HERVIER, NOÉ DISTEL
Secretary-General: SYLVIE NGUYEN
Librarian: GENEVIÈVE SIMONOT

Number of teachers: 1,024
Number of students: 43,256

TEACHING AND RESEARCH UNITS

General Economics, Business Administration: Dir: HUBERT DE LA BRUSLERIE
Economics: Dir: A. HERVIER
Public Administration and Public Law: Dir: Prof. B. CASTAGNEDE (acting)
Business Law: Dir: YVONNE FLOUR (acting)
International and European Studies: Dir: JEAN-CLAUDE MASCLET
Geography: Dir: Prof. P. BEKOUCHE (acting)
History: Dir: Prof. JEAN-MARIE BERTRAND (acting)
Philosophy: Dir: ANNICK JAULIN
Economic and Social Administration, Labour and Social Studies: Dir: Prof. R. LENOIR
Political Science: Dir: Prof. FR. DREYFUS (acting)
Legal Studies: Dir: Prof. FRANÇOIS GAUDU (acting)
Plastic Arts and Science of Art: Dir: JEAN DA SILVA (acting)
History of Art and Archaeology: Dir: Prof. CHR. PRIGENT
Mathematics and Informatics: Dir: Prof. J. BLOT (acting)

INSTITUTES

Institute of Business Administration: Dir: PIERRE-LOUIS DUBOIS
Institute of Demography: Dir: MARLÈNE LAMY (acting)
Institute of Economic and Social Development: Dir: Prof. BR. LAUTIER (acting)
Institute of Labour Social Sciences: Dir: JEAN-MARIE MONNIER

DEPARTMENTS

Applied Modern Languages, Economics and Law: Dir: L. THOMPSON (acting)
Applied Modern Languages, Humanities: Dir: A. HAKKAK (acting)
Social Sciences: Dir: Mme YOTTE

PROFESSORS

Public Administration and Public Internal Law (tel. 1-44-07-77-38; fax 1-44-07-17-75; e-mail ufr01@univ-paris1.fr):

BRECHON-MOULÈNES, C., Public Economic Law
CASTAGNEDE, B., Public Finance
DURUPTY, M., Public Law
FATOME, E., Administrative Law
FRIER, P., Public Law
GICQUEL, J., Public Law
JEGOUZO, Y., Administrative Law
LE MIRE, P., Public Law
MAISL, H., Administrative Law
MARCOU, G., Administrative Law
MATHIEU, B., Constitutional Law
MODERNE, F., Administrative Law
MORABITO, M., History of Law
MORAND-DEVILLER, J., Administrative Law
PFERS MANN, O., Comparative Public Law
PICARD, E., Administrative Law
RICHER, L., Administrative Law
TIMSIT, G., Public Law

Economic Analysis and Politics, Econometrics, Labour and Human Resources (Centre P.M.F., 90 rue de Tolbiac, 75013 Paris; tel. 1-44-07-88-88; fax 1-44-07-86-15; e-mail ufr02@univ-paris1.fr):

ANDREFF, W., Economy of the Transition
ARCHAMBAULT, E., Accountancy and Social Economics
BERTHELEMY, J. C., International Economics
BORDES, C., Money and Macroeconomics
CHAUVEAU, TH., Money and Finance
DE BOISSIEU, C., Monetary Economics
ENCAOUA, D., Industrial Economics
FARDEAU, M., Health Economics, Social Economics
FAU, J., Economic Analysis

FONTAGNE, L., International Economics
GARDES, F., Econometrics
GREFFE, X., Political Economy
HAIRAULT, J. O., Macroeconomics
HENIN, P., Macroeconomics
KEMPF, H., Macroeconomics
KOPP, P., Microeconomics
LAFAY, J. D., Public Economy
LAFFARGUE, J. P., International Economics
LANTNER, R., Economics and Industrial Politics
LAPIDUS, A., History of Economic Thought
LEVY-GARBOUA, L., Microeconomics
MASSON-D'AUTUME, A., Macroeconomics
MEIDINGER, C., Microeconomics
MENARD, C., Theory of Organization
PRADEL, J., Statistics
SCHUBERT, K., Macroeconomics
SOFER, C., Microeconomics
SOLLOGOUB, M., Microeconomics
VERNIÈRES, M., Economic Analysis
WIGNIOLLE, B., Macroeconomics
ZAGAME, P., Macroeconomics

History of Art and Archaeology (3 rue Michelet, 75006 Paris; tel. 1-53-73-71-00; fax 1-53-73-71-13; e-mail ufr03sec@univ-paris1.fr):

BURNOUF, J., Medieval Archaeology
CROISSANT, F., Greek Archaeology
DAGEN, P., Contemporary Art
DARRAGON, E., Contemporary Art
DEMOULE, J.-P., Protohistory
DENTZER, J. M., Oriental Archaeology
DUMASY, F., Classical Archaeology
GILI, J., Cinema
HUOT, J. L., Oriental Archaeology
LICHARDUS, M., Protohistory
MONNIER, G., History of Contemporary Art
MOREL, P., Modern Art
PIGEOT, N., Archaeology and Protohistory
POLET, J., African Art and Archaeology
PRESSOUYRE, L., Medieval Art and Archaeology
PRIGENT, C., Medieval Art
RABREAU, D., Modern Art
SCHNAPP, A., Greek Archaeology
SODINI, J. P., Byzantine Archaeology
TALADOIRE, E., Meso-American Archaeology
TREUIL, R. A., Archaeology and Protohistory
VANCI, M., Contemporary Art
VAN DER LEEUW, S., Archaeology and Protohistory
VOLFOVSKY, C., Preservation of Cultural Heritage

Plastic Arts (162 rue St Charles, 75015 Paris; tel. 1-44-25-04-01; fax 1-45-58-30-47; e-mail raufr04@univ-paris1.fr):

BAQUE, P., Visual Arts
CHATEAU, D., Aesthetics
CHIRON, E., Visual Arts
CLANCY, G., Aesthetics
CONTE, R., Visual Arts
DARRAS, B., Culture and Communication
DUGUET, A. N., Video and Media
FRENAULT-DERUELLE, P., Semiotics
HUYGHE, P. D., Visual Arts and Aesthetics
JIMENEZ, M., Aesthetics
LANCRI, J., Visual Arts
LEBENSZTEJN, J. C., History of Art
MIEREANU, C., Musicology
NOGUEZ, D., Cinema and Audiovisual Arts
SERCEAU, D., Cinema and Audiovisual Arts
SICARD, N., Visual Arts

Business Law (tel. 1-44-07-77-36; fax 1-43-54-97-54; e-mail ufr05@univ-paris1.fr):

AYNES, L., Private and Civil Law
BOULOC, B., Criminal Law
CADIET, L., Civil Procedure
CHAPUT, Y., Commercial Law – Insolvency
DAIGRE, J. J., Business Law
DAVID, C., Tax Law
DELEBECQUE, P., Civil Law
FLOUR, Y., Civil Law
GAUDU, F., Labour Law
GIUDICELLI, G., Criminal Law
GUTMANN, D., Insurance Law
HEUZE, V., Insurance Law
JOURDAIN, P., Civil Law
LABRUSSE, C., Civil Law
LE CANNU, P., Business Law
LE NABASQUE, H., Business Law
LIBCHABER, R., Civil Law
LUCAS DE LEYSSAC, C., Commercial Law
MENJUCQ, M., International Corporate Law
MUIR-WATT, H., Civil Law and International Civil Law
PARLEANI, G., Business Law
POLLAUD-DULIAN, F., Artistic and Literary Copyright Law
THIREAU, J. L., History of Law
VINEY, G., Civil Law

Managerial Economics and Business (17 rue de la Sorbonne, 75231 Paris Cedex 05; tel. 1-40-46-27-78; fax 1-40-46-31-77; e-mail raufr06@univ-paris1.fr):

AMADIEU, J. F., Human Resources Management
BAETCHE, A., Scientific Methods Applied to Marketing
DE LA BRUSLERIE, H., Finance
CHIROLEU-ASSOULINE, M., Macroeconomics
COT, A., Economics
COURET, A., Business Law
DESAIGUES, B., Environmental Economics
GOFFIN, R., Finance
GREGORY, P., Marketing
IPSOMER, I., Marketing
LAURENT, P., Business Law
MUCHIELLI, J.-L., Industrial Economics
PEYRARD, M., International and European Business
PONCET, P., Finance
RAIMBOURG, P., Finance
RAY, J.-E., Labour Law
ROJOT, J., Organization Theory and Human Resources Management
ROLLAND, C., Computer Science
ROURE, F., Finance
STEYER, A., Speculative Methods in Maketing

Development, International, European and Comparative Studies (tel. 1-44-07-77-33; fax 1-44-07-08-33; e-mail ufr07@univ-paris1.fr):

BARAV, A., European Community Law
BERLIN, D., European Community Law
BURDEAU, G., International Public Law
CARREAU, D., Economic Public Law
DAUDET, Y., International Public Law
DELMAS-MARTY, M., Penal Law
EISEMAN, P. M., International Public Law
HUDAULT, J., History of Law
IDOT, L., European Community Law
JUILLARD, P., International Economic Law
LAGARDE, P., International Private Law
LEGRAND, P., Comparative Law
LE ROY, E., Legal Anthropology
LOVISI, C., History of Law
MANIN, P., European Community Law
MASCLET, J. C., European Community Law
MAYER, P., International Private Law
RENOUX-ZAGAMÉ, M. F., History of Law
RUIZ FABRI, H., Constitutional Law
SIRINELLI, P., Private Law
SOREL, J. M., International Public Law
STERN, B., International Public Law

Geography (191 rue St Jacques, 75005 Paris; tel. 1-44-32-14-03; fax 1-44-32-14-54; e-mail raufr08@univ-paris1.fr):

BECKOUCHE, P., Ecconomic Geography
BOUINOT, J., Planning and Economic Geography
BRUN, J., Social Geography
CAZES, G., Geography of Tourism
CHALÉARD, J. L., Geography of Developing Countries
FRUIT, J. P., Rural Geography
KAISER, B., Geomorphology
LE COEUR, C., Natural Resources, Geomorphology
MALEZIEUX, J., Regional Geography, Land Use
MERLIN, P., Urban Geography
PECH, P., Environment
POURTIER, R., Tropical Geography
PREVELAKIS, G., Geopolitics
PUMAIN, D., Urban Geography
SAINT-JULIEN, TH., Human Geography, Statistics
SOPPELSA, J., Geopolitics
TABEAUD, M., Climatology

History (17 rue de la Sorbonne, 75231 Paris Cedex 05; tel. 1-40-46-27-88; fax 1-40-46-31-80; e-mail millot9@univ-paris1.fr):

BALARD, M., Mediterranean Medieval History
BENOÎT, P., Modern History
BERTRAND, J. M., Ancient History
BOULÈGUE, J.-M., History of Black Africa
BOURIN, M., Medieval History
CABANTOUS, A., Modern History
CHARLE, C., Contemporary History
CHARPIN, D., Near Eastern History
CHRISTOL, M., Roman History
CORBIN, A., Contemporary History
CORSI, P., Modern History
D'ALMEIDA-TOPOR, H., Contemporary History
DAVID, J. M., Ancient History
FRANK, R., Contemporary History
GAUVARD, C., Medieval History
GENET, J. P., Medieval History
GUERRA, F., History of Latin America
KAPLAN, M., Byzantine Medieval History
KASPI, A., History of North America
LEMAITRE, N., Modern History
MARSEILLE, J., Economic and Social History
MARTIN, J. C., Modern History
MICHAUD, C., Modern History
MICHEAU, F., Medieval History
MICHEL, B., History of Eastern Europe
ORY, P., Contemporary History
PARISSE, M., Medieval History
REY, M. P., Contemporary History
RIVET, D., Contemporary History
ROBERT, J. L., Contemporary History
SCHMITT, P., Ancient History
WORONOFF, D., Economic and Social History
ZYLBERBERG, M., Modern History

Philosophy (UFR Philosophie - Université Paris 1 Panthéon Sorbonne, 17 rue de la Sorbonne 75005 Paris; tel. 1-40-46-31-68; fax 1-40-46-31-57; e-mail philosec@univ-paris1.fr):

BLONDEL, E., Moral and Political Philosophy
BONARDEL, F., Philosophy of Religion
BRAGUE, R., History of Philosophy
CHAUVIRÉ, C., American Philosophy and Anthropology
CHEDIN, O., History of Philosophy
GRAS, A., Social Philosophy
KAMBOUCHNER, D., History of Philosophy
KERVEGAN, J. F., Philosophy of Law
MICHAUD, Y., Political Philosophy
MOEGLIN-DELCROIX, A., Aesthetics
MOSCONI, J., Philosophy of Mathematics
PINTO, E., Aesthetics
POLITIS, H., History of Philosophy
RIVENC, F., Philosophy of Logic
SALEM, J., History of Philosophy

Political Science (17 rue de la Sorbonne, 75231 Paris Cedex 05; tel. 1-40-46-28-04; fax 1-40-46-31-65; e-mail depscpo2@univ-paris1.fr):

BIRNBAUM, P., Political Sociology
BRAUD, P., Political Sociology
COLLIARD, J. C., Comparative Government
COTTERET, J.-M., Political Communication

DREYFUS, F., Constitutional Law
FRANÇOIS, B., Constitutional Law
GAXIE, D., Political Sociology
GRESLE, F., Sociology
KLEIN, J., International Relations
LAGROYE, J., Political Ideology
LESAGE, M., Theory of Organizations
PISIER, E., Political Philosophy
SFEZ, L., Communication
ZORGBIBE, C., International Relations

Economic and Social Administration, Labour and Social Studies (tel. 1-44-07-79-08; fax 1-44-07-79-08; e-mail raufr12@univ-paris.fr):

CHAPOULIE, Sociology
COUTURIER, G., Labour Law
GAZIER, B., Labour Economy
LENOIR, R., Sociology
PIGENET, Sociology
RODIÈRE, P., Labour Law
TSIKOUNAS, History

Mathematics, Statistics and Computer Science:

ABDOU, J., Game Theory
AUSLENDER, A., Optimization
BALASKO, Y., Mathematical Economics
BONNISSEAU, J.-M., Mathematics and Economics
CORNET, B., Mathematics and Economics
COTTRELL, M., Probability, Statistics and Neural Networks
GIRE, F., Computer Science
GUYON, X., Probability and Statistics
HADDAD, G., Differential Equations and Functional Analysis
JOUINI, E., Mathematics and Economics

Business Administration (21 rue Broca, 75005 Paris; tel. 1-53-55-28-00; fax 1-53-55-27-01; e-mail iae@univ-paris1.fr):

ALLOUCHE, J., Human Resources Management
GIARD, V., Operations Management
HELFER, J.-P., Marketing and Strategy
HOARAU, C., Finance and Control
LE FLOCH, P., Business Law
MAILLET, P., Finance
PAUCELLE, J. L., Information Systems
TRIOLAIRE, G., Management

Demography (i DUP, Centre PMF, 90 rue de Tolbiac, 75634 Paris Cedex 13; tel. 1-44-07-86-46; fax 1-44-07-86-47; e-mail cridup@univ-paris1.fr):

DITTGEN, A., Socio-Demography
GROSSAT, B., Socio-Demography
LAMY-FESTY, M., Social Demography
NORVEZ, A., Socio-Demography

Economic and Social Development (45 bis avenue de la Belle-Gabrielle, 94736 Nogent sur Marne Cedex; tel. 1-43-94-72-22; fax 1-43-94-72-44; e-mail iedes@univ.-paris1.fr):

GRELLET, G., Economic Development
HAUBERT, M., Social Development
LAUTIER, B., Economic and Social Development

Institute of Social Sciences (tel. 1-45-36-16-40; fax 1-46-65-70-80; e-mail patrick.diez@univ-paris1.fr):

FREYSSINET, J., Economics
OFFERLE, M., Political Science
PAULRE, B., Economics
PIOTEL, F., Sociology

Applied Modern Languages, Economics and Law (12 place du Panthéon, 75005 Paris; tel. 1-44-07-78-33; fax 1-44-07-78-33; e-mail seglas@univ-paris1.fr):

BULLIER, A.-J., Legal English Studies
KERSAUDY, F., English for Economists

UNIVERSITÉ DE PARIS II (UNIVERSITÉ PANTHÉON-ASSAS)

12 place du Panthéon, 75231 Paris Cedex 05
Telephone: 1-44-41-57-00
Fax: 1-44-41-55-13
Internet: www.u-paris2.fr

Founded 1970

President: JACQUELINE DUTHEIL DE LA ROCHÈRE
Secretary-General: THIÉRRY CRÉDEVILLE
Librarian: GENEVIÈVE SONNEVILLE

Number of teachers: 300
Number of students: 18,109

TEACHING AND RESEARCH UNITS

Law (First cycle): PIERRE CROCQ
Law (Second cycle) and Political Science: M. COMBACAU
Law (Third cycle) and Political Science: LAURENT LEVENEUR
Economics: ANTOINE BILLOT
Economic and Social Administration (First and Second cycles): MARTINE PELE
Information Sciences (French Press Institute): Dir: Prof. NADINE TOUSSAINT-DESMOULINS
Institute of Judicial Studies: Dir: Prof. S. GUINCHARD
Institute of Advanced International Studies: Dirs: C. LEBEN, P.-MARIE DUPUY
Institute of Comparative Law: Dir: Prof. LOUIS VOGEL
Institute for Administration Training: Dir: JEAN-MICHEL DE FORGES
Image and Communication Institute: Dir: Prof. C. TUAL
Institute of Business Law: Dir: Prof. MICHEL GERMAIN
Institute of Criminology: Dir: Prof. JACQUES-HENRI ROBERT
Higher Institute for Defence Studies: Dir: Prof. YVES CARO
Centre for Studies and Research in Construction and Housing: Dir: Prof. P. MALINVAUD
Centre for Human Resources Training: F. BOURNOIS
IUP–Management: Dir: Prof. RAYMOND TRÉMOLIÈRES

PROFESSORS

ALLAND, D., Public Law
ALPHANDERY, E., Economic Sciences
AMSELEK, P., Public Law
ANCEL, D., Private Law
AUBY, J. B., Public Law
AUDIT, B., Private Law
AVRIL, P., Political Science
BALLE, F., Political Science
BALLOT, G., Economic Sciences
BARRAT, J., Information Sciences
BÉAUD, O., Public Law
BENZONI, L., Economic Sciences
BERNARD, M., Education Sciences
BETBEZE, J.-P., Economic Sciences
BETTATI, M., Public Law
BIENVENU, J. J., Public Law
BILLOT, A., Economic Sciences
BLAISE, J.-B., Private Law
BLUMANN, C., Public Law
BOISIVON, J.-P., Management Science
BONET, G., Private Law
BONNEAU, T., Private Law
BOURNOIS, F., Management Science
BRESSON, G., Economic Sciences
BURDEAU, F., History of Law
BUREAU, D., Private Law
CARBASSE, J. M., History of Law
CARO, J.-Y., Economic Science
CARTIER, M.-E., Private Law
CASTALDO, A., History of Law
Mme CATALA, N., Private Law
CAZENAVE, P., Economic Sciences
CHAGNOLLAUD, D., Political Science
CHAMPENOIS, G., Private Law
CHARPIN, F., Economic Sciences
CHEVALLIER, J., Public Law
CHRISTIN, Y., Economic Sciences
COCATRE-ZILGIEN, P., History of Law
COHEN-JONATHAN, G., Public Law
COMBACAU, J., Public Law
CROCQ, P., Private Law
DECOCQ, A., Private Law
DELVOLVE, P., Public Law
DERIEUX, E., Information Science
DESNEUF, P., Economic Science
DESPLAS, M., Economic Sciences
DIBOUT, P., Public Law
DIDIER, P., Private Law
DISCHAMPS, J. C., Management Science
DONIO, J., Computing
DRAGO, G., Public Law
DUBOIS, P.-M., Public Law
DUPUY, G., Public Law
DURRY, G., Private Law
DUTHEIL DE LA ROCHÈRE, J., Public Law
FACCARELLO, G., Economic Sciences
FEYEL, G., History
FOUCHARD, P., Private Law
FOYER, J., Private Law
GAUDEMET, Y., Public Law
GAUDEMET-TALLON, H., Private Law
GAUTIER, P. Y., Private Law
GERMAIN, M., Private Law
GHOZI, A., Private Law
GJIDARA, M., Public Law
GOYARD, C., Public Law
GRIMALDI, M., Private Law
GUINCHARD, S., Private Law
HAROUEL, J.-L., History of Law
HUET, J., Private Law
HUMBERT, M., History of Law
JAHEL, S., Private Law
JARROSON, C., Private Law
JAUFFRET-SPINOSI, C., Private Law
JAVILLIER, J.-C., Private Law
JOUET, J., Information Science
LABROUSSE, C., Economic Sciences
LAFAY, G., Economic Sciences
LAINGUI, A., History of Law
LAMARQUE, J., Public Law
LARROUMET, C., Private Law
LEBEN, C., Public Law
LEFEBVRE-TEILLARD, A., History of Law
LE GALL, J.-P., Private Law
LEMENNICIER-BUCQUET, B., Economic Sciences
LEMOYNE DE FORGES, J. M., Public Law
LEQUETTE, Y., Private Law
LEVENEUR, L., Private Law
LOMBARD, M., Public Law
LOMBOIS, C., Private Law
LUBOCHINSKY, C., Economic Sciences
MALINVAUD, P., Private Law
MARTINEZ, J. C., Public Law
MAYAUD, Y., Private Law
MAZEAU, D., Private Law
MERLE, P., Private Law
MOLFESSIS, N., Private Law
MONCONDUIT, F., Political Science
MORANGE, J., Public Law
MOREAU, J., Public Law
Mme MOURGUES, M. DE, Economic Sciences
Mme NÊME, C., Economic Sciences
OLIVIER, J. M., Private Law
OTTAYJ, L., Private Law
PELÉ, M., Management Science
PERINET-MARQUET, H., Private Law
PONDAVEN, C., Economic Sciences
PORTELLI, H., Political Science
QUENET, M., History of Law
RAYNAUD, P., Political Science
REDSLOB, A., Economic Sciences
RIALS, S., Public Law
RIEFFEL, R., Information Sciences
RIGAUDIERE, A., History of Law
ROBERT, J.-H., Private Law
ROUGEMONT, M. DE, Computing
SCANNAVINO, A., Economic Sciences
SCHWARTZENBERG, R. G., Public Law
SUR, S., Public Law
SYNVET, H., Private Law
TERRÉ, F., Private Law
TEYSSIÉ, B., Private Law
THERY, P., Private Law

TOUSSAINT-DESMOULINS, N., Information Science
TREMOLIÈRES, R., Management Science
TRUCHET, D., Public Law
TUAL, C., English
VEDEL, C., Economic Sciences
VERPEAUX, M., Public Law
VITRY, D., Economic Sciences
VOGEL, L., Private Law
ZOLLER, E., Public Law

UNIVERSITÉ DE PARIS III (SORBONNE-NOUVELLE)

17 rue de la Sorbonne, 75230 Paris Cedex 05
Telephone: 1-40-46-28-84
Fax: 1-43-46-29-36
Internet: www.univ-paris3.fr

Founded 1970
State control
Language of instruction: French
Academic year: October to June

President: Prof. BERNARD BOSREDON
Vice-Presidents: MICHEL BERNARD (Administration), JEAN-FRANÇOIS TOURNADRE (Studies and University Life), GILLES DECLERQ (Science and Research), MARTINE AZUELOS (International Relations)
Secretary-General: BERNARD DEMASSIET

Number of teachers: 493
Number of students: 20,000

TEACHING AND RESEARCH UNITS

Theatre Studies: Dir: CATHERINE TREILHOU-BALAUDE
General and Comparative Literature: Dir: STÉPHANE MICHAUD
English-speaking World: Dir: ANDRÉ TOPIA
German: Dir: GÉRALD STIEG
General and Applied Linguistics and Phonetics: Dir: PATRICK RENAUD
Iberian and Latin American Studies: Dir: PIERRE CIVIL
French as a Foreign Language: Dir: GEORGES VÉRONIQUE
The East and the Arab World: Dir: HEIDEMARIE TOELLE
Higher School of Interpreters and Translators (ESIT): Dir: FORTUNATO ISRAËL
Interuniversity Centre of Hungarian Studies (CIEH): Dir: PATRICK RENAUD
French and Latin Literature and Linguistics: Dir: DOMINIQUE COMBE
Italian and Romanian Studies: Dir: MATHÉE GIACOMO
Institute of Latin-American Studies (IHEAL): Dir: POLYMMIA ZAGEFKA
Cinema and Audiovisual Studies: Dir: PHILIPPE DUBOIS
Department of Studies of Contemporary Society: Dir: JEAN-MARC DELAUNAY
Communication: Dir: FAYÇAL NAJAB
Cultural Mediation: Dir: CLAUDE AZIZA
Department of Applied Foreign Languages: Dir: GILBERT GUILLARD
Research Centre (CIR): Man.: GILLES DECLERCQ

UNIVERSITÉ DE PARIS IV (PARIS-SORBONNE)

1 rue Victor-Cousin, 75230 Paris Cedex 05
Telephone: 1-40-46-22-11
Fax: 1-40-46-25-88
Internet: www.paris4.sorbonne.fr

Founded 1970
State control
Language of instruction: French
Academic year: October to June

President: JEAN-ROBERT PITTE
Vice-Presidents: PIERRE BRUNEL, JEAN-PIERRE BARTOLI, MATTHIAS VINCENOT
Secretary-General: CATHERINE VIEILLARD
Librarian: B. VAN DOOREN

Number of teachers: 750
Number of students: 30,898

TEACHING AND RESEARCH UNITS

French and Comparative Literature: Dir: Prof. FRANÇOISE MÉLONIO
French Language: Dir: Prof. MIREILLE HUCHON
Latin Language and Literature: Dir: Prof. MICHÈLE FRUYT
Greek: Dir: Prof. PAUL DEMONT
Philosophy and Sociology: Dir: Prof. ALAIN RENAUT
History: Dir: Prof. JEAN-PIERRE CHALINE
Art and Archaeology: Dir: Prof. FRANÇOIS BARATTE
Geography: Dir: Prof. MICHELINE HOTYAT
English: Dir: Prof. PIERRE COTTE
Germanic Studies: Dir: Prof. YVON DESPORTES
Iberian and Latin-American Studies: Dir: Prof. ANNIE MOLINIÉ-BERTRAND
Italian and Romanian: Dir: Prof. FRANÇOIS LIVI
Slavonic Studies: Dir: Prof. FRANCIS CONTE
Applied Foreign Languages: Dir: Prof. BERNARD POLONI
Music and Musicology: Dir: Prof. NICOLAS MEEÙS
Institute of Applied Humanities: Dir: Prof. FRANÇOIS CHAZEL
Institute of Information and Communication: Dir: Prof. JEAN-BAPTISTE CARPENTIER
Institute of Eastern Studies: Dir: Prof. JEAN-PIERRE POUSSOU

DIRECTORS OF GRADUATE SCHOOLS

Sciences of Language and Communication: Prof. P. VALENTIN
French and Comparative Literatures: Prof. F. MOUREAU
Foreign Literatures and Cultures: Prof. J. M. VALENTIN
Philosophy and Social Sciences: Prof. R. BOUDON
Classical World and its Legacy: Prof. J. JOUANNA
Medieval Studies: Prof. PH. MÉNARD
History of Modern Civilizations: Prof. J. P. POUSSOU
Contemporary Societies: Prof. G. H. SOUTOU
History of Art and Archaeology: Prof. PH. BRUNEAU
Geography and Urban Studies: Prof. P. CLAVAL
Sciences of Religion and Religious Anthropology: Prof. J. C. FREDOUILLE
Music and Musicology: Prof. L. JAMBOU

UNIVERSITÉ RENÉ DESCARTES (PARIS V)

12 rue de l'École de Médecine, 75270 Paris Cedex 06
Telephone: 1-40-46-16-16
Fax: 1-40-46-16-15
E-mail: secretaire.general@univ-paris5.fr
Internet: www.univ-paris5.fr

Founded 1970
Academic year: October to July

President: JEAN-FRANÇOIS DHAINAUT
Vice-Presidents: D. HOUSSIN A. CARTRON S. IONESCU D. DURAND J. F. DHAINAUT H. MEAU-LAUTOUR S. GAYRAUD
Secretary-General: M. RONZEAU
Librarian: J. KALFON

Number of teachers: 1,950
Number of students: 29,300

Publications: *Dialogues de Descartes* (4 a year), *Recherche Descartes Valorisation* (monthly)

TEACHING AND RESEARCH UNITS

Human and Social Sciences: Dir: J. P. GOUDAILLIER
Institute of Psychology: Dir: J. D. BAGOT
Mathematics and Data Processing: Dir: D. SERET
Medicine: Cochin—Port-Royal: Dean: J. F. DHAINAUT
Medicine: Necker—Enfants Malades: Dean: PATRICK PERCHE
Biomedicine: Dir: D. JORE
Dentistry: Dean: B. PELLAT
Forensic Medicine and Medical Law: Dir: CHRISTIAN HERVÉ
Pharmaceutical and Biological Sciences: Dean: D. DURAND
University Institute of Technology: Dir: DOMINIQUE GASCON
Physical Education and Sports: Dir: PIERRE-FRANÇOIS RILHAC
Faculty of Law: Dean: M. DE GUILLENCHMIDT

UNIVERSITÉ DE PARIS VI (PIERRE ET MARIE CURIE)

4 place Jussieu, 75252 Paris Cedex 05
Telephone: 1-44-27-44-27
Fax: 1-44-27-38-66
E-mail: secretariat.general@upmc.fr
Internet: www.upmc.fr

Founded 1971

President: GILBERT BÉRÉZIAT
Secretary General: JEAN-YVES GACON

Number of teachers: 2,685
Number of students: 28,558

TEACHING AND RESEARCH UNIT DIRECTORS

Chemistry: JEAN-MARC VALERY
Computer Sciences: ANNE DERIEUX
Earth Sciences and the Evolution of Natural Environments: PHILIPPE D'ARCO
Electrical, Electronic and Automation, Applied Physics: PIERRE ENCRENAZ
Fundamental and Applied Physics: FRANÇOIS GENDRON
Life Sciences: DOMINIQUE DUNON
Mathematics: SYLVIE DELABRIERE
Mechanical and Robotic Engineering and Energy: PASCAL CHALLANDE
Medicine, Pitié-Salpétrière: GÉRARD SAILLANT
Medicine, Saint-Antoine: SERGE UZAN
Pure and Applied Mathematics: M. GAVEAU
Stomatology and Maxillofacial Surgery: JACQUES-CHARLES BERTRAND
Henri Poincaré Institute: MICHEL BROUE
Institute of Science and Technology: JEAN-MARIE CHESNEAUX
Oceanological Observatory, Banyuls: GILLES BOEUF
Oceanological Observatory, Roscoff: BERNARD KLOAREG
Oceanological Observatory, Villefranche-sur-Mer: MICHEL GLASS

UNIVERSITÉ DE PARIS VII (DENIS DIDEROT)

2 place Jussieu, 75251 Paris Cedex 05
Telephone: 1-44-27-44-27
Fax: 1-44-27-69-64
E-mail: mmtx@sigu7.jussieu.fr
Internet: www.diderotp7.jussieu.fr

Founded 1970

President: BENOÎT EURIN
Secretary-General: GEORGES ROQUEPLAN
Dirs: PATRICE PERRIN (Administration), ANNE JANIN (Science), MARIE-JEANNE ROSSIGNOL (Academic and University Life), LUCIENNE GERMAIN (International Relations)

Number of teachers: 1,800
Number of students: 26,000

TEACHING AND RESEARCH UNITS

Anthropology, Ethnology and Religious Studies: Dir: P. DESHAYES
Biochemistry: Dir: PATRICK VICART
Biology and Natural Sciences: Dir: CLAUDE LAMOUR-ISNARD
Chemistry: Dir: JEAN AUBARD
Dental Surgery: Dir: MARIE-LAURE BOY-LEFEVRE
Medicine (Lariboisière-Saint-Louis): Dir: ALAIN LE DUC
Medicine (Xavier-Bichat): Dir: J. M. DESMONTS
Geography, History and Social Sciences: Dir: JEAN-PIERRE VALLAT
Institute of Haematology: Dir: FRANÇOIS SIGAUX
Institute of English: Dir: PHILIPPE JAWORSKI
Eastern Asian Languages and Literature: Dir: CÉCILE SAKAI
Intercultural Studies in Applied Languages: Dir: JOHN HUMBLEY
Mathematics: Dir: PIERRE VOGEL
Computer Studies: Dir: GUY COUSINEAU
Physics: Dir: LUC VALENTIN
Linguistic Research: Dir: ALAIN ROUVERET
Clinical Human Sciences: Dir: PAUL-LAURENT ASSOUN
Earth and Physical Sciences: Dir: YVES GAUDEMER
Sciences of Texts and Documents: Dir: PIERRE CHARTIER
Social Sciences: Dir: ETIENNE TASSIN
Film, Communication and Information Studies: Dir: BAUDOIN JURDANT
University Institute of Technology: Dir: ALAIN JUNGMAN

UNIVERSITÉ DE PARIS VIII—VINCENNES À ST-DENIS

2 rue de la Liberté, 93526 St Denis Cedex 02
Telephone: 1-49-40-67-89
Fax: 1-48-21-04-46
Internet: www.univ-paris8.fr

Founded 1969
State control
Language of instruction: French

President: RENAUD FABRE
Vice-Presidents: DANIÈLE BUSSY-GENEVOIS (Administration), FRANÇOISE DECROISETTE (Scientific), DANIEL LEPAGE (Academic Studies and University Life)
Secretary-General: ALEXIS NAVROCORDATO
Librarian: MADELEINE JULLIEN

Number of teachers: 739
Number of students: 24,825

Publications: *Médiévales, Histoire, Epistémologie, Langage, Recherches linguistiques de Vincennes, Théorie, Littérature, Enseignement, Humoresques, Extrême-Orient, Extrême-Occident, Pratiques de Formation*

TEACHING AND RESEARCH UNITS

Arts, Philosophy and Aesthetics: Dir: S. VENDEVILLE
Power, Administration, Trade: Dir: F. ARPIN-GONNET
Territory, Economics and Society: Dir: D. GAZAGNADOU
History, Literature, Society: Dir: D. JEAN
Languages, Societies, Foreign Cultures: Dir: A. SARRABAYROOSE
Linguistics, Computer Studies, Technology: Dir: J. LOPEZ-KRAHE
Psychology, Clinical and Social Practices: Dir: T. NATHAN
Communication, Animation, Teaching: Dir: L. COLIN

ATTACHED INSTITUTES

Institut Français d'Urbanisme: Dir J.-P. DUCHEMIN.

Institut d'Etudes Européennes: Dir M. AZZOUG.

Institut Universitaire de Technologie de Tremblay 93: Dir PIERRE DAUMÉZON.

Institut Universitaire de Technologie de Montreuil 93: Dir T. BAFFOY.

Institut d'Enseignement à Distance: Dir T. NATHAN.

UNIVERSITÉ DE PARIS IX (PARIS-DAUPHINE)/UNIVERSITÉ PARIS DAUPHINE

Place du Maréchal de Lattre de Tassigny, 75775 Paris Cedex 16
Telephone: 1-44-05-44-05
Fax: 1-44-05-49-49
Internet: www.dauphine.fr

Founded 1968
State control
Language of instruction: French

President: BERNARD DE MONTMORILLON
Vice-Presidents of the Administrative Council: MICHEL POIX (Financial Affairs and Logistics), ALAIN-SERGE MESCHERIAKOFF (Legal Affairs)
Vice-President of the Scientific Council: VANGELIS PASCHOS
Vice-Presidents of Studies and University Life: FRANÇOISE PICQ, JULIEN JACOB (Students)
Head of Secretariat: LILIANE BEGAT

Library: General library of 150,000 vols, 2,000 current periodicals

Number of teachers: 1,446 (incl. 1000 part-time)
Number of students: 7,988

DIRECTORS

Teaching and Research Units:
- Applied Economics: RÉGIS BOURBONNAIS
- Business (I) and Applied Economics: PIERRE BEZBAKH
- Business (II): JAQUELINE DE LA BRUSLERIE
- Business Informatics: BERNARD GOLDFARB
- Decision Mathematics: (vacant)
- Science of Organizations: MARIE-EVE JOEL

University Professional Institutes:
- Applied Methods of Informatics and Business Enterprise: DANIÈLE MAILLES
- Mathematics and Informatics: GENEVIÈVE JOMIER
- Traditional Business (Banking, Finance and Insurance): LAURENT BATSCH

PROFESSORS

ALTER, N., Sociology
ARNOLD, V., Mathematics
AUBIN, J.-P., Mathematics
BENSOUSSAN, A., Applied Mathematics
BERLIOZ-HOUIN, B., Business Law
BERTHET, CH., Computer Studies
BIENAYME, A., Industrial Economics
BLONDEL, D., Economics
BOUQUIN, H., Finance
BRUNET, A., Civil Law
CAREY-ABRIOUX, C.
CAZES, P., Statistics
CHAITIN-CHATELIN, F., Mathematics
CHAVENT, G., Mathematics
CHEDIN, G., English Languages
CHEVALIER, J.-M., Economics
CLAASSEN, E., Economics
COHEN, E., Finance
COLASSE, B., Finance
COTTA, A., Business Organization
COUSOT, P., Computer Studies
DANA, R.
DE MONTMORILLON, B., Finance
DESMET, P.
DIDAY, E., Computer Studies
DOSS, H., Mathematics
EKELAND, I., Mathematics
ETNER, F., Economics
FLORENS, D., Mathematics
FRISON-ROCHE, M. A., Civil Law
GAUVIN, C., English Language
GEMAN, H., Finance
GHOZI, A., Civil Law
GIOVANNANGELI, J.-L., English Language and Literature
GOURIEROUX, C., Mathematics
GRELON, B., Civil Law
GUILLAUME, M., Economics
GUILLOCHON, B., Economics
HADDAD, S., Computer Studies
HAMON, J., Finance
HESS, C., Mathematics
JOMIER, G., Computer Studies
LARNAC, P.-M., Economics
LENA, H., Public Law
LE PEN, C., Economics
LE TALLEC, P., Mathematics
LEVY, E., Economics
LEVY, G., Computer Studies
LIONS, P.-L., Mathematics
LIU, M., Sociology
LOMBARD, M., Public Law
LORENZI, J.-H., Economics
MAILLES, D., Computer Studies
MANIN, A., Public Law
MARIET, F., Education
MATHIS, J., Finance
METAIS, J., Economics
MEYER, Y., Mathematics
MICHALET, C., Economics
MOREL, J.-M., Mathematics
NUSSENBAUM, M., Finance
PALMADE, J., Sociology
PARLY, J.-M., Economics
PASCHOS, V., Computer Studies
PIGANIOL, B., Management
PILISI, D., Economics
PINSON, S., Computer Studies
PIQUET, M., English Language and Literature
PRAS, B., Finance
RICHARD, J., Finance
RIGAL, J.-L., Computer Studies
RIVES-LANGE, J. L., Civil Law
ROMELAER, P., Finance
ROUX, D., Business Economics
ROY, B., Scientific Methods of Management
SALIN, P., Monetary Economics
SCHMIDT, C., Sociology
SIMON, Y., Finance
SIROEN, J.-M., Economics
SULZER, J.-R., Finance
TERNY, G., Public Economics
THIETART, R., Finance
TOLLA, P., Computer Studies
TRINH-HEBREARD, S., Sociology
VALLEE, C., Public Law

RESEARCH CENTRES

Business:

Centre de Recherche sur la Gestion (CEREG).

Centre de Recherche Européen en Finance et en Gestion (CREFIGE).

Centre de Recherche Economique Pure et Appliquée (CREPA).

Dauphine – Marketing – Stratégie – Prospective (DMSP).

Institute de Recherches Internationales – Groupe de Recherche Economique et Sociale (IRI–GRES.

Economics:

Centre de Recherche en Théorie Economique Jean-Baptiste Say.

Centre d'Etudes et de Recherches Prévisionnelles pour l'Industrie (CEPRI).

Groupe de Recherche en Economie Publique (GREP).

Centre d'Etudes et de Recherches sur les Processus de Management/Centre de

Recherche et d'Etudes sur le Financement de l'Economie et les Déséquilibres (CERPEM/CREFED).

Equipe Universitaire de Recherche – Institutions: Coordination, Organisation (EURIsCO).

Equipe Universitaire de Recherche sur les Institutions, les Organisations et la Coordination – Laboratoire d'Economie et de Gestion des Organisations de la Santé (EURIsCO–LEGOS).

Institut de Recherches Internationales – Centre de Géopolitique de l'Energie et des Matières Premières (IRI–CGEMP).

Centre de Recherche en Economie de l'Assurance (IRI–CREA).

Institut de Recherche Interdisciplinaire en Socioéconomie (IRIS).

Informatics:

Centre d'Etudes et de Recherches en Informatique Appliquée (CERIA).

Laboratoire d'Analyse et Modélisation de Systèmes pour l'Aide à la Décision (LAMSADE).

Languages:

Centre de Recherche Interdisciplinaire sur les Identités Culturelles et les Langues de Spécialités (CICLaS).

Law:

Institut de Droit Economique, Fiscal et Social (IDEFS).

Mathematics:

Centre de Recherche en Mathématiques de la Décision (CEREMADE).

Viabilité, Jeux, Contrôle (VJC).

Political Sciences:

Centre de Recherche et d'Etudes Politiques (CREDEP).

Sociology:

Centre d'Etude et de Recherche en Gestion et Sociologie des Organisations (CERSO).

Multi-disciplinary:

Laboratoire d'Economie et de Sociologie des Organisations de Défense (LESOD).

Groupe d'Etudes et de Recherche sur les Organisations Culturelles (GEROC).

INSTITUTES

Finance:

Institut Finance Dauphine (IFD).

Innovation:

Institut pour le Management de la Recherche et de l'Innovation.

DOCTORAL SCHOOLS

Ecole Doctorale Economie des Organisations (Concurrence, Innovation, Finance) (EDOCIF).

Ecole Doctorale de Gestion, Comptabilité, Finance (EDOGEST).

Ecole Doctorale des Sciences Sociales (Droit, Science politique, Sociologie) (EDOSSOC).

Ecole Doctorale Décision Informatique Mathématiques Organisation (EDDIMO).

UNIVERSITÉ DE PARIS X (PARIS-NANTERRE)

200 ave de la République, 92001 Nanterre Cedex

Telephone: 1-40-97-72-00
Fax: 1-40-97-75-71
Internet: www.u-paris10.fr

President: ANDRÉ LEGRAND
Secretary-General: GILLES GAI
Librarian: JEAN MALLET

Number of teachers: 1,500
Number of students: 34,000

TEACHING AND RESEARCH UNITS

Economic Sciences: Dir: M. GIBERT
Juridical Sciences: Dir: Mme TALLINEAU
Psychology and Education Sciences: Dir: M. SIROTA
History, Geography and Sociology: Dir: M. LEVILLAIN
Letters, Linguistics and Philosophy: Dir: Mme DELAVEAU
Anglo-American Studies: Dir: Mme FRISON
German, Romance Languages, Slav and Applied Foreign Languages: Dir: M. PHILLIPENKO
Institute of Technology (Ville d'Avray): Dir: M. PRIOU
Science and Techniques of Physical and Sporting Activities: Dir: M. PINARD

UNIVERSITÉ DE PARIS XI (PARIS-SUD)

15 rue G. Clémenceau, 91405 Orsay Cedex
Telephone: 1-69-41-67-50
Fax: 1-69-41-61-35
E-mail: secretariat@presidence.u-psud.fr
Internet: www.u-psud.fr

Founded 1970
State control
Language of instruction: French
Academic year: September to June

President: ANITA BERSELLINI
Secretary-General: DANIEL PERAULT
Librarian: ANNE-MARIE MOTAIS DE NARBONNE

Number of teachers: 1,720
Number of students: 28,000

Publications: *Aspects de la recherche* (annually), *Plein-Sud* (every 2 months).

TEACHING AND RESEARCH UNITS

Pharmacy (Châtenay-Malabry): 5 rue Jean Baptiste Clément, 92290 Châtenay-Malabry; tel. 1-46-83-57-89; fax 1-46-83-57-35; Dean ANNE-MARIE QUERDO.

Medicine (Kremlin-Bicêtre): 63 rue Gabriel Péri, 94276 Le Kremlin-Bicêtre Cedex; tel. 1-49-59-67-67; fax 1-49-59-67-00; Dean BERNARD CHARPENTIER.

Sciences (Orsay): 15 rue Georges Clémenceau, 91405 Orsay Cedex; tel. 1-69-41-67-50; fax 1-69-15-63-64; Dean JEAN-CLAUDE ROYNETTE.

Law and Economic Science (Sceaux): 54 blvd Desgranges, 92331 Sceaux Cedex; tel. 1-40-91-17-00; fax 1-46-60-92-62; Dean PIERRE SIRINELLI..

UNIVERSITY INSTITUTES

University Institute of Technology at Cachan: 9 ave de la Division Leclerc, 94230 Cachan; tel. 1-41-24-11-00; fax 1-46-64-62-18; Dir PIERRE DAUMEZON.

University Institute of Technology at Orsay: BP 127, 91403, Orsay Cedex; tel. 1-69-33-60-00; fax 1-60-19-33-18; Dir MICHEL PEDOUSSAUT.

University Institute of Technology at Sceaux: 8 ave Cauchy, 92330 Sceaux; tel. 1-40-91-24-99; fax 1-46-60-64-79; Dir RICHARD MILKOFF..

ATTACHED INSTITUTION

Ecole Supérieure d'Optique: see under Independent Institutes.

UNIVERSITÉ DE PARIS XII (PARIS-VAL-DE-MARNE)

61 ave du Général de Gaulle, 94010 Créteil Cedex

Telephone: 1-45-17-10-00
Fax: 1-42-07-70-12
Internet: www.univ-paris12.fr

Founded 1970
Academic year: October to July

President: PAUL MENGAL
Vice-Presidents: MARCEL PARIAT, FRANÇOISE BARTHELEMY, PHILIPPE GUERIN, J. F. DUFEU PATRICIA POL, VALERIO MOTTA
Secretary-General: GUY CAMUS
Librarian: PIERRE CARBONE

Number of teachers: 1,200
Number of students: 26,000.

TEACHING AND RESEARCH UNITS

Institute of Town Planning: Dir L. DAVEZIES.

Medicine: 8 rue du Gén. Sarrail, 94010 Créteil Cedex; Dir J. P. LE BOURGEOIS.

Law and Politics: 58 ave Didier, 94210 La Varenne-St Hilaire; Dir N. GUIMEZANES.

Economic Sciences: Dir D. THIEBAUT.

Letters and Humanities: Dir M. AQUIEN.

Science: Dir E. GARNIER ZARLI.

Public and Social Administration: Dir J. ATTUEL.

Education and Social Sciences: Dir C. DARDY.

Institute of Technology (Créteil-Vitry): Dir C. CUESTA.

Institute of General Administration: Dir J. C. ATTUEL.

Institute of Technology Sénart/Fontainebleau: Dir D. NICOLLE.

UNIVERSITÉ DE PARIS XIII (PARIS-NORD)

Ave J.-B. Clement, 93430 Villetaneuse
Telephone: 1-49-40-30-00
Fax: 1-49-40-33-33
E-mail: cab-pres@upn.univ-paris13.fr
Internet: www.univ-paris13.fr

Founded 1970
Academic year: September to June

President: M. POUCHAIN
Vice-President: A. NEUMAN
Secretary-General: M. RAUX
Librarian: A. TANE

Number of teachers: 1,000
Number of students: 21,500

Publications: *Psychologie clinique*, *Annales du CESER*, *Cahiers de Linguistique Hispanique Médiévale*

TEACHING AND RESEARCH UNITS

Scientific and Polytechnic Centre: Dir: N. LEBLANC
Law and Political Science: Dir: P. SUEUR
Letters and Humanities: Dir: J. BIARNES
University Institute of Technology (Saint-Denis): Dir: J. P. BERTHIER
University Institute of Technology (Villetaneuse): Dir: G. VICARD
Medicine and Human Biology Experimental Centre: Dir: D. BLADIER
Economic Sciences and Business Administration: Dir: P. GEOFFRON
Expression and Communications Sciences: Dir: D. CARRÉ
Institute of Town and Health: Dir: P. CORNILLOT

UNIVERSITÉ DE PAU ET DES PAYS DE L'ADOUR

Domaine Universitaire, Ave de l'Université, BP 576, 64012 Pau Université Cedex
Telephone: 5-59-92-30-00
Fax: 5-59-80-83-80
Internet: www.univ-pau.fr

Founded 1970
State control

President: JEAN-LOUIS GOUT
Vice-Presidents: J.-C. DOUENCE, J.-P. GACON, C. POUCHAN, J. P. MONTFORT, C. FIÉVET, M. UHALDEBORDE, E. POQUET, M. PARSONS
Secretary-General: JEAN RAVON
Librarian: SYLVAINE FREULON

Number of teachers: 600
Number of students: 14,100

TEACHING AND RESEARCH UNITS

Faculty of Law, Economics and Management: Dean: GÉRARD DENIS
Faculty of Exact Sciences: Dean: ALAIN GRACIA
Faculty of Literature, Languages and Human Sciences: Dean: CHRISTIAN MANSO
University Institute of Scientific Research: Dir: JEAN PEYRELASSE
Multidisciplinary Faculty (in Bayonne): Dean: HENRI LABAYLE
Institute of Business Administration: Dean: J.-J. RIGAL
Higher National School of Industrial Engineering: Dean: M. ROQUES
University Institute of Technology (in Bayonne): Dir: BERNARD CAUSSE
University Institute of Technology (in Pau): Dir: ROBERT HOO-PARIS

UNIVERSITÉ DE PERPIGNAN

Ave de Villeneuve, 66025 Perpignan Cedex
Telephone: 4-68-66-20-00
Internet: www.univ-perp.fr

Founded 1971

President: JEAN-MICHEL HOERNER
Secretary-General: JEAN-POL ISAMBERT
Librarian: FERNAND BELLEDENT

Number of teachers: 230
Number of students: 4,500

TEACHING AND RESEARCH UNITS

Humanities, Juridical, Economic and Social Sciences: Dir: JACQUELINE AMIEL DONAT
Exact and Experimental Sciences: Dir: NAGUI EL GHANDOUR
University Institute of Technology: Dir: CATHERINE SABATE

PROFESSORS

Humanities, Juridical, Economic and Social Sciences

Humanities:

ANDIOC, R., Romance Languages and Literature
AUBAILLY, J.-C., French
BELOT, A., Romance Languages and Literature
BROC, N., Geography
DAUGE, Y., Classics
DELEDALLE, G., Philosophy
DENJEAN, A., English Language and Anglo-Saxon Literature
HOLZ, J. M., Geography
HUGUET, L., Germanic and Scandinavian Languages and Literature
ISSOREL, J., Spanish
LEBLON, B., Romance Languages and Literature
MEYER, J., Contemporary History
RETHORE, J., Literature
SAGNES, J., History

Law and Economics:

BLANC, F. P., History of Law
BREJON DE LAVERGNEE, N., Economic Dynamics
CONSTANS, L., Public Law
Mme DONAT, J., Private Law and Criminology
DOUCHEZ, M.-H., Administrative Law
HUNTZINGER, J., International Law
PEROCHON, F., Law
RUDLOFF, M., Economics
SAINT-JOURS, Y., Private Law and Criminology
SERRA, Y., Private Law

Exact and Experimental Sciences:

AMOUROUX, M., Applied Physics and Computer Science
BAILLY, J. R., Biochemistry
BERÇOT, P., Applied Organic Synthesis
BLAISE, P., Chemistry
BODIOT, D., Mineral Chemistry and Thermochemistry
BOMBRE, F., Solid State Physics
BONNARD, M., Algebraic Topology
BOURGAT, R., General Biology
BRUNET, S., Applied Physics and Computer Science
BRUSLE, J., Marine Biology
CAUVET, A. M., Plant Biology and Physiology
CHOU, C. C., Functional Analysis
CODOMIER, L., Biology and Chemistry of Marine Plants (Research)
COMBES, C., Animal Biology
CROZAT, G., Physics
DAGUENET, M., Thermodynamics and Energetics
DUPOUY, J., General Biology
EL JAÏ, A., Computer Science
FABRE, B., Thermology
FOUGERES, A., Mathematics
GIRESSE, P., Marine Sedimentology Research Centre
GONZALEZ, E., Organic Chemistry
GOT, H., Sedimentology and Marine Geochemistry
HENRI-ROUSSEAU, O., Theoretical Chemistry
HILLEL, R., Chemistry
HORVATH, C., Mathematics
HUYNH, V. C., Atomic and Molecular Physics
JUPIN, H., Plant Biology
MARTY, R., Mathematics applied to Human Sciences
MEYNADIER, CHR., Thermodynamics and Energetics
PENON, P., Plant Physiology
SOULIER, J., Organic Chemistry
SOURNIA, A., Atomic and Molecular Physics
SPINNER, B., Mineral Chemistry and Thermochemistry
VIALLET, P., Physical Chemistry

University Institute of Technology:

AZE, D., Mathematics
BARRIOL, R., Mechanical Engineering
BARUSSEAU, J. P., Marine Sedimentology
COMBAUT, G., Marine Chemistry
FARINES, M., Organic Chemistry
COSTE, C., Industrial Chemistry
GRELLET, P., Biochemistry, Applied Biology
MASSE, J., Organic Chemistry
MASSON, PH., Animal Husbandry

UNIVERSITÉ DE PICARDIE JULES VERNE

Chemin du Thil, 80025 Amiens Cedex 01
Telephone: 3-22-82-72-72
Fax: 3-22-82-75-00
E-mail: dany.gryson@ca.u-picardie.fr
Internet: www.u-picardie.fr

Founded 1965
Academic year: October to June

President: GILLES DEMAILLY
Secretary-General: MICHEL DAUMIN
Librarian: FRANÇOISE MONTBRUN

Number of teachers: 800
Number of students: 23,000.

TEACHING AND RESEARCH UNITS

Law: Dir Prof. N. DECOOPMAN.
Economics: Dir Prof. P. MAURISSON.
Modern Languages: Dir Prof. P. SICARD.
Literature: Dir Prof. P. BERTHIER.
Philosophy and Human Sciences: Dir Prof. F. ROPEZ.
History and Geography: Dir Prof. N. CHALINE.
Medicine: 12 rue des Louvels, Amiens; Dir Prof. B. NEMITZ.
Pharmacy: 3 rue des Louvels, 80037 Amiens Cedex; Dir M. BRAZIER.
Sciences: 33 rue Saint-Leu, Amiens; Dir Prof. D. BEAUPÈRE.
Mathematics: 33 rue Saint Leu, 80039 Amiens Cedex; Dir M. MYOUPO.
University Institute of Technology: Ave des Facultés, Le Bailly, Amiens; Administrator M. LANGLET.
UER (Saint-Quentin): 48 rue Raspail, 02109 Saint-Quentin Cedex; Dir A. LEBRUN.

UNIVERSITÉ DE POITIERS

15 rue de l'Hôtel-Dieu, 86034 Poitiers Cedex
Telephone: 5-49-45-30-00
Fax: 5-49-45-30-50
E-mail: communication@univ-poitiers.fr
Internet: www.univ-poitiers.fr

Founded 1431

President: JEAN-PIERRE GESSON
Secretary-General: BERNARD CONTAL
Librarian: GENEVIÈVE FIROUZ-ABADIE

Number of teachers: 1,300
Number of students: 25,000

Publications: *Les Cahiers de Civilisation Médiévale, Les Cahiers Forell, La Licorne, Migrinter, Revue Norois*

TEACHING AND RESEARCH UNITS

Fundamental and Applied Sciences: Dir: GILLES RABY
Medicine and Pharmacy: Dir: ROGER GIL
Languages and Literatures: Dir: JOËL DALANÇON
Human Sciences: Dir: JEAN-MICHEL PASSERAULT
Law and Social Sciences: Dir: CHRISTIAN CHÊNE
Economics: Dir: JACQUES LÉONARD
Physical Education and Sport: Dir: PATRICK LEGROS
University Institute of Technology in Poitiers: Dir: CHRISTIAN BERRIER
University Institute of Technology in Angoulême: Dir: MICHEL PINÇON
University Institute of Business Administration: Dir: SERGE PERCHERON
National Higher School of Mechanical and Aero-engineering: Dir: FRANÇOIS ARMANET
Centre for Aerodynamic and Thermic Studies: Dir: MICHEL GUILBAUD
Poitiers Higher School for Engineering (ESIP): Dir: JEAN-HUGUES THOMASSIN
Preparatory Institute of General Administration: Dir: JEAN-LOUIS GOUSSEAU
Establishment for Research in Human Sciences and Society: Dir: CLAIRE GIRARD
Institute of Communication and New Technologies: Dir: JACQUES DEBORD

UNIVERSITÉ DE REIMS CHAMPAGNE-ARDENNE

Villa Douce, 9 boulevard de la Paix, 51097 Reims Cedex
Telephone: 3-26-05-30-00
Fax: 3-26-05-30-98
Internet: www.univ-reims.fr
Founded 1548, 1969
President: JACQUES MEYER
Vice-Presidents: JEAN-JACQUES ABNET, JACQUES BUR, MARCEL BAZIN
Secretary-General: MARTINE BEURTON
Library: see Libraries
Number of teachers: 1,000
Number of students: 26,000
Publications: *Flash-Infos* (weekly), *Livret de l'Université*, *Imaginaires*, *Etudes Champenoises* (annually), *Revue de l'Institut de Géographie* (termly), *Jurisprudence Cour d'appel* (quarterly), *Cahiers de l'Institut du Territoire et de l'Environnement de l'Université de Reims* (annually), *Cahiers du Centre de Recherches sur la Décentralisation Territoriale* (annually)

TEACHING AND RESEARCH UNITS

Exact and Natural Sciences: Dir: JACQUES PERRIN
Medicine: Dir: FRANÇOIS-XAVIER MAQUART
Pharmacy: Dir: JEAN LÉVY
Letters and Human Sciences: Dir: GÉRARD DUFOUR
Law and Political Sciences: Dir: GÉRARD CLÉMENT
Odontology: Dir: MICHEL MAQUIN
University Institute of Technology in Reims: Dir: GUY DELABRE
University Institute of Technology in Troyes: Dir: JOËL HAZOUARD
Economic Sciences and Management: Dir: GILLES RASSELET
University Institute of Technical Training in Charleville: Dir: JACQUES MALICET
Higher School of Packaging: Dir: JEAN-CLAUDE PRUDHOMME

UNIVERSITÉ DE RENNES I

2 rue du Thabor, 35065 Rennes Cedex
Telephone: 2-23-23-36-01
Fax: 2-99-38-22-92
E-mail: sai@univ-rennes1.fr
Internet: www.univ-rennes1.fr
Academic year: September to May
President: BERTRAND FORTIN
Secretary-General: ANNIE JULIEN
Number of teachers: 1,619
Number of students: 22,152.

TEACHING AND RESEARCH UNITS

Faculté de Droit et Science Politique: 9 rue Jean-Macé, 35042 Rennes Cedex; tel. 2-23-23-76-76; fax 2-23-23-76-55; Dean Prof. ETIENNE DOUAK.

Faculté de Médecine: Ave du Professeur Léon Bernard, 35043 Rennes Cedex CS 34317; tel. 2-23-23-44-20; fax 2-23-23-49-75; Dean Prof. FRANÇOIS GUILLÉ.

Faculté d'Odontologie: 2 Ave du Professeur Léon Bernard, 35043 Rennes; tel. 2-23-23-43-41; fax 2-23-23-43-04; Dean Prof. JEAN-CLAUDE ROBERT.

Faculté des Sciences Economiques: 7 place Hoche, 35065 Rennes Cedex CS 86514; tel. 2-23-23-35-45; fax 2-23-23-80-84; Dean Prof. PASCAL GAUDRON.

Faculté des Sciences Pharmaceutiques et Biologiques: Ave du Professeur Léon Bernard, 35043 Rennes Cedex CS 34317; tel. 2-23-23-44-30; fax 2-23-23-49-75; Dean Prof. JEAN-LOUIS BURGOT.

Faculté des Sciences de la Vie et de l'Environnement: Bât. 13, Campus Scientifique de Beaulieu, Ave du Général Leclerc, 35042 Rennes Cedex; tel. 2-23-23-61-12; fax 2-23-23-67-69; Prof. PATRICK JEGO.

UFR Mathématiques: Ave du Général Leclerc, 35042 Rennes Cedex CS 74205; tel. 2-23-23-66-67; fax 2-23-23-67-90; Dir Prof. LOUIS MAHÉ.

UFR Philosophie: 263 Ave du Général Leclerc, 35042 Rennes Cedex CS 74205; tel. 2-23-23-63-02; fax 2-23-23-51-51; Dir Prof. JACQUELINE DELIAU-LAGRÉE.

UFR Structure et Propriété de la Matière: 263 Ave du Général Leclerc, 35042 Rennes Cedex CS 74205; tel. 2-23-23-62-44; fax 2-23-23-69-85; Dir Prof. CHRISTIAN WILLAIME.

Ecole Nationale Supérieure des Sciences Appliquées et de Technologie: 6 rue de Kérampont, BP 80518, 22305 Lannion Cedex; tel. 2-96-46-50-30; fax 2-96-37-01-99; Dir Prof. JEAN SEGUIN.

Institut de Formation Supérieure en Informatique: Campus de Beaulieu, 35042 Rennes Cedex; tel. 2-99-84-71-00; fax 2-99-84-71-71; Dir Prof. YVES BEKKERS.

Institut de Gestion de Rennes: 11 rue Jean-Mace, CS 70803, 35708 Rennes Cedex 7; tel. 2-23-23-35-35; fax 2-23-23-78-00; Dir Prof. ARMEL LIGER.

Institut de Préparation à l'Administration Générale: 106 blvd de la Duchesse Anne, 35000 Rennes; tel. 2-23-23-78-93; fax 2-23-23-78-92; Dir MARIE-LIESSE HOUBÉ.

Institut Universitaire de Technologie de Lannion: Rue Edouard Branly, BP 30219, 22302 Lannion Cedex; tel. 2-96-48-43-34; fax 2-96-48-13-20; Dir Prof. JEAN-YVES LE BIHAN.

Institut Universitaire de Technologie de Rennes: Rue du Clos-Courtel, BP 90422, 35704 Rennes Cedex; tel. 2-23-23-40-00; fax 2-23-23-40-28; Dir Prof. BERTRAND FORTIN.

Institut Universitaire de Technologie de St Brieuc: 18 rue Henri Wallon, BP 406, 22004 St Brieuc Cedex; tel. 2-96-60-96-60; fax 2-96-60-96-12.

UNIVERSITÉ RENNES 2 – HAUTE BRETAGNE

Place du Recteur Henri Le Moal, CS 24307, 35043 Rennes Cedex
Telephone: 2-99-14-10-00
Internet: www.uhb.fr
Founded 1969
President: FRANÇOIS MOURET
First Vice-President: MARC GONTARD
Secretary-General: PHILIPPE GUY
Librarian: ELISABETH LEMAU
Number of teachers: 629
Number of students: 21,475.

TEACHING AND RESEARCH UNITS

Arts, Literature, Communications: Dir PIERRE BAZANTAY.

Humanities: Dir GÉRARD GUINGOUAIN.

Languages: Dir FRANÇOISE DUBOSQUET.

Physical Education and Sport: Dir PAUL DELAMARCHE.

Social Sciences: Dir MARC DAVID.

CIREFE (Teaching French to Foreign Students): Dir MARIE-FRANÇOISE BERTHU-COURTIVRON.

UNIVERSITÉ DE ROUEN

1 rue Thomas Becket, Secrétariat-Général, 76821 Mont-Saint-Aignan Cedex
Telephone: 2-35-14-60-00
Fax: 2-35-14-63-48
Internet: www.univ-rouen.fr
Founded 1966
Academic year: September to June
President: ERNEST GIBERT
Vice-Presidents: MOHAMED KETATA, BERNARD PROUST
Secretary-General (vacant)
Librarian: YANNICK VALIN
Number of teachers: 778
Number of students: 30,000.

TEACHING AND RESEARCH UNITS

Medicine and Pharmacy: BP 97, 76800 Saint-Etienne-du-Rouvray; Dir P. LAURET.

Sciences and Technology: Place Emile Blondel, 76821 Mont-Saint-Aignan Cedex; Dir M. LEREST.

Letters and Humanities: Rue Lavoisier, 76821 Mont-Saint-Aignan Cedex; Dir J. MAURICE.

Law and Economics: Blvd Siegfried, 76821 Mont-Saint-Aignan Cedex; Dir Y. SASSIER.

Behavioural and Educational Sciences: Rue Lavoisier, 76821 Mont-Saint-Aignan; Dir R. WEIL.

University Institute of Technology: Place Emile Blondel, 76821 Mont-Saint-Aignan; Dir P. MICHE.

Sport: Blvd Siegfried, 76821 Mont-Saint-Aignan Cedex; Dir J. P. LEFEVRE

PROFESSORS

Medicine and Pharmacy:

ANDRIEU-GUTTRANCOURT, J., Otorhinolaryngology
AUGUSTIN, P., Neurology
BACHY, B., Infantile Surgery
BENOZIO, E., Radiology
BERCOFF, E., Internal Medicine
BESANÇON, P., Chemistry
BESSOU, J. P., Surgery
BEURET, F., Rehabilitation
BIGA, N., Orthopaedics
BLANQUART, F., Rehabilitation
BONMARCHAND, G., Resuscitation
BONNET, J. J., Pharmacology
BRASSEUR, G., Ophthalmology
BRASSEUR, P. H., Bacteriology
CAILLARD, J.-F., Industrial Medicine
CAPRON, R., Biophysics
COLIN, R., Gastroenterology
COLONNA, L., Psychiatry
COMOY, D., Biochemistry
COSTENTIN, J., Pharmacology
COURTOIS, H., Internal Medicine
CRIBIER, A., Cardiology
CZERNICHOW, P., Epidemiology
DEHESDIN, D., Otorhinolaryngology
DENIS, P., Physiology
DUCROTTE, P., Hepatology
DUVAL, C., Clinical Obstetrics
FESSARD, C., Paediatrics
FILLASTRE, J. P., Nephrology
FREGER, P., Anatomy
GARNIER, J., Botany and Cryptogamy
GODIN, M., Nephrology
GRISE, PH., Urology
HECKETSWEILER, P., Hepatology
HEMET, J., Pathological Anatomy
HUMBERT, G., Tropical and Infectious Diseases
JANVRESSE, C., Hygiene
JOLY, P., Dermatology
JOUANY, M., Toxicology
KUHN, J. M., Endocrinology
LAFONT, O., Organic Chemistry
LAURET, P., Dermatology
LAVOINNE, D., Biochemistry
LECHEVALLIER, J., Infantile Surgery
LEDOSSEUR, P., Radiology
LEFUR, R., Cancerology
LELOET, X., Rheumatology
LEMELAND, J. F., Hygiene

LEMOINE, J. P., Gynaecology
LEREBOURS, E., Nutrition
LEROY, J., Therapeutics
LETAC, B., Cardiology
MACE, B., Histology
MAITROT, B., Biochemistry
MALLET, E., Biology
MARCHAND, J., Chemical Pharmacology
MATRAY, F., Medical Biochemistry
METAYER, J., Anatomy
MICHOT, F., Digestive Tract Surgery
MIHOUT, B., Neurology
MITROFANOFF, P., Infantile Surgery
MONCONDUIT, M., Haematology
MUIR, J. F., Pneumology
NOUVET, G., Pneumology
ORECCHIONI, A.-M., Pharmacology
PASQUIS, P., Physiology
PEILLON, C., Orthopaedic and Traumatological Surgery
PERON, J. M., Stomatology
PETIT, M., Psychiatry
PIGUET, H., Immuno-haematology
PROTAIS, P., Physiology
PROUST, B., Forensic Medicine
SAOUDI, N., Cardiology
SORIA, C., Pharmaceutical Biochemistry
SOYER, R., Thoracic Surgery
TADIE, M., Neurosurgery
TENIÈRE, P., General Surgery
TESTART, J., Clinical Surgery
THIEBOT, J., Radiology
THOMINE, M., Orthopaedic and Traumatological Surgery
TILLY, H., Haematology
THUILLIEZ, C., Therapeutics
TRON, F., Immunology
TRON, P., Paediatrics
VANNIER, J. P., Paediatrics
WATELET, J., General Surgery
WINCKLER, C., Anaesthesiology
WOLF, L., Therapeutic Internal Medicine

Sciences and Technology:

ANTHORE, R., Physics
ATTIAS, J., Biochemistry
AUGER, P., Physics
BALANGE, P., Biochemistry
BANEGE, A., Physics
BARBEY, G., Chemistry
BLANCHARD, D., Mechanics
BLAVETTE, D., Physics
BOISARD, J., Vegetal Biology
BORGHI, R., Mechanics
BOUAZIZ, R., Chemistry
BRISSET, J. L., Chemistry
CAGNON, M., Physics
CALBRIX, J., Mathematics
CARLES, D., Electronics
CARPENTIER, J. M., Chemistry
CASTON, J., Biology
CAZIN, L., Biology
CHAMPRANAUD, J. M., Computer Sciences
CHARPENTIER, J., Physiology
CHERON, B., Thermodynamics
COMBRET, C., Chemistry
COTTEREAU, M. J., Thermodynamics
DAVOUST, D., Chemistry
DEBRUCQ, D., Electronics
DERRIDJ, M., Mathematics
DE SAM LAZARO, J., Mathematics
DESBENE, A., Chemistry
DESBENE, P., Chemistry
DONATO, P., Mathematics
DOSS, H., Mathematics
DUHAMEL, P., Chemistry
DUVAL, J.-P., Computer Sciences
DUVAL, P., Physics
FOUCHER, B., Biochemistry
FRILEUX, P. N., Biology
GALLOT, J., Physics
GAYOSO, J., Chemistry
GORALCIK, P., Computer Sciences
GRENET, J., Physics
GUESPIN, J., Microbiology
HANNOYER, B., Physics
HANSEL, G., Mathematics
HUSSON, A., Biology
LAMBOY, M., Geology
LANERY, E., Mathematics
LANGE, C., Chemistry
LECOURTIER, Y., Electronics
LEDOUX, M., Thermodynamics
LENGLET, M., Chemistry
LOPITAUX, J., Chemistry
MAHEU, B., Thermodynamics
MENAND, A., Physics
METAYER, M., Chemistry
MEYER, R., Geology
MICHON, J. F., Computer Sciences
OZKUL, C., Physics
PAULMIER, C., Chemistry
PEREZ, G., Chemistry
PETIPAS, C., Physics
POIRIER, J. M., Chemistry
QUEGUINNER, G., Chemistry
RIPOLL, C., Biochemistry
SELEGNY, E., Chemistry
STRELCYN, J. M., Mathematics
SURIN, A., Mathematics
TEILLET, J., Physics
UNANUE, A., Chemistry
VAILLANT, R., Animal Physiology
VAUTIER, C., Physics
VERCHERE, J. F., Chemistry
VIGER, C., Electronics
VIGIER, P., Physics
WEILL, M., Thermodynamics

Letters and Humanities:

ARNAUD, J. C., Geography
BALAN, B., Epistemology
BENAY, J., German
BERGER, PH., Spanish
CAITUCOLI, C., Linguistics
CAPET, A., English
COIT, K., English
CORTES, J., Linguistics
CYMERMAN, C., Spanish
DELAMOTTE, R., Linguistics
GARDIN, B., Linguistics
GRANIER, J., Philosophy
GUERMOND, Y., Geography
HUSSON, G., Greek
LE BOHEC, S., Ancient History
LECLAIRE, J., English
LECLERC, Y., French
LEGUAY, J.-P., Medieval History
LEMARCHAND, G., Modern History
LESOURD, M., Geography
MAQUERLOT, J. P., English
MAURICE, J., French
MAZAURIC, C., Modern History
MERVAUD, C., French
MERVAUD, M., Russian
MILHOU, A., Spanish
MORTIER, D., Comparative Literature
NIDERST, A., French
NOISETTE DE CRAUZAT, CL., Musical History
PASTRE, J. M., German
PHILONENKO, A., Philosophy
PICHARDIE, J. P., English
PIERROT, J., Modern French Literature and Language
PIGENET, M., Contemporary History
POINSOTE, J. L., Classics
PUEL, M., English
RAVY, G., German
RETAILLE, B., Geography
ROUDAUT, F., French
SALAZAR, B., Spanish
SOHNA, R., Modern History
THELAMON, F., Ancient History
TREDE, M., Classics
VAN DER LYNDEN, A. M., Spanish
WALLE, M., German
WILLEMS, M., English
ZYLBERBER, G. M., Modern History

Law and Economics:

BADEVANT, B., Law
BRAS, J. P., Public Law
CAYLA, O., Public Law
CHRÉTIEN, P., Public Law
COURBE, P., Private Law
DAMMAME, D., Political Science
EPAULARD, A., Economics
GOY, R., Public Law
KULLMANN, J., Private Law
LEHMANN, P., Economics
MONNIER, L., Economics
PORTIER, F., Economics
RENOUX, M. F., Law
SASSIER, Y., Law
TAVERNIER, P., Public Law
TEBOUL, G., Public Law
TONNEL, M., Economics
VATTEVILLE, E., Administration and Management
VESPERINI, J.-P., Economics

Behavioural and Educational Sciences:

ABALLERA, F., Sociology
ASTOLFI, J. P., Educational Sciences
DURAND, J., Sociology
GATEAUX, J., Educational Sciences
HOUSSAYE, J., Educational Sciences
KOKOSOWSKI, A., Educational Sciences
LEMOINE, CL., Psychology
MALANDAIN, CL., Psychology
MARBEAUX-CLEIRENS, B., Psychology
MELLIER, D., Psychology

UNIVERSITÉ JEAN MONNET

34 rue Francis Baulier, 42023 Saint-Etienne Cedex

Telephone: 4-77-42-17-00

Fax: 4-77-42-17-99

Internet: www.univ-st-etienne.fr

Founded in 1969 as Université de Saint-Étienne; present name 1991

State control

Language of instruction: French

Academic year: October to June

President: MAURICE VINCENT

Vice-Presidents: YVES BOUVERET, JEAN-BAPTISTE ORSINI, ANDRÉ GEYSSANT

Secretary-General: P. BESSENAY

Librarian: Mme ACHARD

Number of teachers: 592

Number of students: 13,684

Publications: *L'Université communique* (weekly), and various institute bulletins

TEACHING AND RESEARCH UNITS

Law and Economics: Dir: P. ANCEL
Letters and Human Sciences: Dir: G. ARGOUD
Sciences: Dir: B. BUISSON
Medicine: Dir: P. QUENEAU
University Institute of Technology: Dir: J. MAZERAN
Arts, Communication, Pedagogy: Dir: CHRISTIANE LAUVERGNAT (acting)
Institute of Advanced Science and Technology (ISTA): Dir: ROBERT ROUGNY
Institute of Industrial Management: Dir: GÉRARD LABAURE

HEADS OF DEPARTMENTS

Law and Economics:

Law: P. ANCEL
Economics: M. VINCENT

Letters and Human Sciences:

Letters: M. SADOULET
English Studies: P. BADONNEL
German Studies: A. SAUTER
Spanish Studies: M. OTT
Italian Studies: J. ALEXANDRE
History: J. BAYON
Geography: RENÉ CONNERE
Plastic Arts: M. GILLES
Music: M. RANEAU

Sciences:

Biology: A. PERRIN
Chemistry: B. BOINON
Geology: A. GIRET

Mathematics: A. LARGILLIER
Physics: A. CACHARD

Medicine:
Anatomy: J.-G. BALIQUE
Pathological Anatomy: S. BOUCHERON
Anaesthesiology: C. AUBOYER, J.-C. BERTRAND
Bacteriology/Virology: O. GAUDIN
Biochemistry: A. CHAMSON
Biophysics and Medical Computer Science: J.-C. HEALY
Cancerology: T. SCHMITT
Cardiology: G. BARRAL
Child Psychiatry: D. SIBERTIN-BLANC
General Surgery: J.-G. BALIQUE
Paediatric Surgery: Y. CHAVRIER
Dermatology and Venerology: A. CAMBAZARD
Emergency Medicine: J.-C. BERTRAND
Endocrinology: H. ROUSSET
Medical Genetics, Paediatrics: F. FREYCON, B. LAURAS
Gynaecology and Obstetrics: P. SEFFERT
Haemobiology: C. BRIZARD, D. GUYOTAT
Hepatology, Gastroenterology: H. FRAISSE, J.-C. AUDIGIER
Histology and Embryology: J.-L. LAURENT
Immunology/Haematology: C. BRIZARD, D. GUYOTAT, M. LE PETIT
Forensic Medicine, Toxicology: M. DEBOUT
Preventive Medicine, Hygiene, Rheumatology: C. ALEXANDRE
Labour Medicine: C. CABAL
Nephrology: F. BERTHOUX
Neurology: D. MICHEL
Neurosurgery: J. BRUNON
Nutrition: H. ROUSSET
Ophthalmology: J. MAUGERY
Oto-Rhino-Laryngology: C. MARTIN
Orthopaedics and Traumatology: G. BOUSQUET, J.-L. RHENTER
Parasitology: R. TRAN MANH SUNG
Pathology of Infectious Diseases: O. GAUDIN, R. LUCHT
Pharmacology: M. OLLAGNIER
Pneumo-phthysiology: A. EMONOT
Physiology: A. GEYSSANT
Psychiatry: J. PELLET
Medical Psychology: J. PELLET
Radiology: G. BARRAL
Rehabilitation: P. MINAIRE
Rheumatology: G. RIFFAT, C. ALEXANDRE
Public Health: J.-M. RODRIGUES
Semeiology: H. ROUSSET
Stomatology: P. SEGUIN
Surgical Semeiology: J.-G. BALIQUE
Therapeutics: P. QUENEAU
Urology: A. GILLOZ

University Institute of Technology:
Electrical Engineering: B. FAURE
Mechanical Engineering: M. LAUVERNET
Business Administration: G. DISSARD
Commerce: D. MOREAU
Physics: C. GONNET
Industrial Maintenance: R. PHILIPPE

ATTACHED RESEARCH INSTITUTES

Centre de recherches économiques de l'Université de Saint-Etienne (CREUSET): Dir JOËL RAVIX.

Centre d'études et de recherches critiques sur le droit (CERCRID): Dir ANTOINE JEAMMAUD.

Centre d'études sociologiques appliquées à la Loire (CRESAL): Dir JACQUES ION.

Centre d'études et de recherches sur l'administration publique (CERAPSE): Dir STÉPHANE CAPORAL.

Institut de préparation aux études comptables: Dir JACQUES CAMUS.

Institut de la Renaissance et de l'âge classique: Dir ANTONY MACKENNA.

Centre Jean Palerme: Dir GILBERT ARGOUD.

Centre Jules Romains: Dirs PIERRE CHARRETON, BERNARD YON.

Centre d'études comparatistes: Dir STÉPHANE MICHAUD.

Centre de recherches sur l'environnement et l'aménagement (CRENAM): Dir THIERRY JOLIVEAU.

Centre Max Jacob: Dir LOUIS THEUBET.

Centre d'études du XVIIIe siècle: Dir HENRI DURANTON.

Centre interdisciplinaire et de recherches sur les structures régionales: Dir JEAN MERLEY.

Centre de recherche sur les pays ibériques et ibéro-américains: Dir JACQUES SOUBEYROUX.

Centre européen de recherches sur les congrégations et ordres religieux (CERCOR): Dir PIERRETTE PARAVY.

Centre d'etudes foréziennes: Dir FRANÇOIS TOMAS.

Institut du travail: Dir FRANÇOISE VENNIN.

Laboratoire de traitement et instrumentation: Dir JEAN-PIERRE GOURE.

Centre commun de physique et chimie des matériaux: Dir JEAN-MARIE VERGNIAUD.

Laboratoire de théorie des nombres: Dir FRANÇOIS GRAMAIN.

Laboratoire de rhéologie des matières plastiques: Dir JACQUES GUILLOT.

Equipe d'analyse numérique: Dir ALAIN BOURGEAT.

Laboratoire de recherche sur les capteurs à colloïdes et instrumentation: Dir JEAN MONIN.

Laboratoire de biologie végétale.

Equipe de géologie: Dir RENÉ-PIERRE MONOT.

Equipe de statistiques et modèles: Dir JACQUES BERRUYER.

Centre de ressources informatiques télécommunications et réseaux (CRITeR): Dir JEAN-LOUIS SUBTIL.

Centre international de langues et civilisation (CILEC): Dir YVES BOUVERET.

Groupe de recherches sur les gomérulonéphrites et transplantation rénales: Dir FRANÇOIS BERTHOUX.

Laboratoire de biophysique et information médicale: Dir JEAN-CLAUDE HEALY.

Laboratoire d'histologie-embryologie: Dir JEAN-LOUIS LAURENT.

Laboratoire de biochimie du collagène: Dir JACQUES FREY.

Laboratoire de physiologie: Dir ANDRÉ GEYSSANT.

Institut universitaire de réadaptation fonctionnelle: Dir PIERRE MINAIRE.

Laboratoire de biologie du tissu osseux: Dir CHRISTIAN ALEXANDRE.

Laboratoire d'immuno-dermatologie: Dirs GENIN, CAMBAZARD.

Groupe de recherches sur l'immunité des muqueuses: Dir ODETTE GAUDIN.

Laboratoire de pharmacologie médicale: Dir MICHEL OLLAGNIER.

Groupe de recherche en oncologie médicale: Dir JEAN-MICHEL VERGNON.

Equipe de neurologie réanimatrice hypoxie: Dir BERNARD LAURENT.

Laboratoire d'anatomie et de cytologie pathologique: Dir ALEXANDRE BAIL.

Institut de médecine du travail: Dir CHRISTIAN CABAL.

Laboratoire d'hématologie cellulaire et moléculaire: Dir DENIS GUYOTAT.

Service de psychiatrie: Dir JACQUES PELLET.

Laboratoire de parasitologie: Dir ROGER TRAN MANH SONG.

Groupe de recherches sur la thrombose: Dir HERVÉ DECOUSUS.

Laboratoire de neurologie: Dir DANIEL MICHEL.

Institut de biologie du sport de la Région Rhône-Alpes: Dir JEAN-RENÉ LACOUR.

Centre de microscopie électronique Médecine-Sciences: Dir CHRISTIAN ALEXANDRE.

Centre interdisciplinaire d'études et de recherches sur l'expression contemporaine (CIEREC): Dir LOUIS ROUX.

Centre de recherche en éducation: Dir DOMINIQUE GLASMAN.

Centre de recherche et études de management public: Dir JACQUES MAZERAN.

Groupe de recherches en techniques de commercialisation: Dir ODETTE DOMENACH.

UNIVERSITÉ DE SAVOIE (CHAMBÉRY)

BP 1104, 73011 Chambéry Cedex
27 rue Marcoz, 73000 Chambéry
Telephone: 4-79-75-85-85
Fax: 4-79-75-84-44
Internet: www.univ-savoie.fr

Founded 1970
Academic year: October to July

President: CLAUDE JAMEUX
Vice-Presidents: GILBERT ANGENIEUX (Administrative Council), ROMAN KOSSAKOWSKI (Scientific Council), MYRIAM DONSIMONI (Council of Studies and University Life), JAMES SHEPHERD (International Relations)
Secretary-General: JEAN-JACQUES PELLEGRIN
Director of Libraries: SIMONE LAMARCHE

Number of teachers: 600
Number of students: 12,368

Publications: *Annales* (annually), *Présences* (monthly)

TEACHING AND RESEARCH UNITS

Faculty of Language, Literature and Social Science: MICHÈLE PACHTER
Faculty of Law and Economics: Dir: GENEVIÈVE GONDOUIN
Interdisciplinary Centre for Mountain Sciences: Dir: PIERRE FAIVRE
Tertiary Management Studies: Dir: RENÉ THIEBLEMONT
Faculty of Fundamental and Applied Sciences: Dir: PIERRE BARAS

ATTACHED INSTITUTES

Annecy National College of Engineering: BP 806, 74016 Annecy Cedex;5 chemin de Bellevue, 74016 Annecy-Le-Vieux; tel. 4-50-09-66-00; fax 4-50-09-66-49; e-mail etudes@esia.univ-savoie.fr; internet www.esia.univ-savoie.fr; Dir LAURENT FOULLOY.

Chambéry National College of Engineering: 73376 Le Bourget du Lac Cedex; tel. 4-79-75-88-06; fax 4-79-75-87-72; internet www.esigec.univ-savoie.fr; Dir PIERRE BATTISTI.

Institute of Technology Annecy: 9 rue de l'Arc-en-ciel, BP 240, 74942 Annecy-le-vieux; tel. 4-50-09-22-22; fax 4-79-75-87-72; internet www.iut.univ-savoie.fr; Dir GILLES HEIDSIECK.

Institute of Technology Chambéry: Savoie Technolac, 73376 Le-Bourget-du-Lac

Cedex; tel. 4-79-75-81-75; fax 4-79-75-81-64; internet src-serveur2.univ-savoie.fr; Dir NICOLE ALBEROLA.

UNIVERSITÉ DE STRASBOURG I (UNIVERSITÉ LOUIS PASTEUR)

Institut Le Bel, 4 rue Blaise Pascal, 67070 Strasbourg Cedex

Telephone: 3-90-24-50-00

Fax: 3-90-24-50-01

Internet: www-ulp.u-strasbg.fr

Founded 1971

Academic year: September to June

Rector: GÉRALD CHAIX

President: Prof. BERNARD CARRIÈRE

Vice-Presidents: Prof. MICHEL GRANET (Research and Doctoral Education), Prof. ROLAND WIEST (Personnel), Prof. CHRISTIANE HEITZ (Initial and Continuing Education), YVETTE AGNUS (Development and Means), Prof. ALAIN BERETZ (Business Partnerships), Prof. RICHARD KLEINSCHMAGER (European Politics and International Policy)

Secretary-General: PASCAL AIMÉ

Librarian: IRIS REIBEL

Number of teachers: 1,452

Number of students: 18,055

Publication: *ULP Sciences* (univ. magazine, 4 a year).

TEACHING AND RESEARCH UNITS

Faculty of Medicine: 4 rue Kirschleger, 67085 Strasbourg Cedex; Dean BERTRAND LUDES.

Faculty of Dental Surgery: 4 rue Kirschleger, 67085 Strasbourg Cedex; Dean YOUSSEF HAIKEL.

Faculty of Pharmacy: 74 route du Rhin, BP 24, 67401 Illkirch Cedex; Dir CLAUDE HASSELMANN.

Faculty of Mathematics and Computer Science: 7 rue René Descartes, 67084 Strasbourg Cedex; Dir CATHERINE MONGENET.

Faculty of Chemistry: 1 rue Blaise Pascal, 67008 Strasbourg Cedex; Dir ANDRÉ FOUGEROUSSE.

Faculty of Physics: 3 rue de l'Université, 67084 Strasbourg Cedex; Dir JEAN-PIERRE MUNCH.

Faculty of Life Sciences: 28 rue Goethe, 67083 Strasbourg Cedex; Dir PIERRE POTIER.

Faculty of Behavioural and Educational Sciences: 12 rue Goethe, 67000 Strasbourg; Dir BRUNO WILL.

Faculty of Economics and Management: 61 ave de la Forêt-Noire, 67085 Strasbourg Cedex; Dean PATRICK ROGER.

Faculty of Geography: 3 rue de l'Argonne, 67083 Strasbourg Cedex; Dir JEAN-LUC MERCIER.

Faculty of the Observatory: 11 rue de l'Université, 67000 Strasbourg; Dir JEAN-MARIE HAMEURY.

European School for Chemistry, Polymers and Materials: 25 rue Becquerel, 67087 Strasbourg Cedex 2; Dir GUY SOLLADIÉ.

Earth Sciences School and Observatory: 5 rue René Descartes, 67084 Strasbourg Cedex; Dir MICHEL CARA.

Engineering School for Physics: Pôle API, Blvd Sébastien Brant, 67400 Illkirch-Graffenstaden; Dir JEAN-LOUIS BALLADORE.

University Institute of Technology Louis Pasteur: Allée d'Athènes, 67300 Schiltigheim; Dir PASCALE BERGMANN.

University School of Biotechnology: Blvd Sébastien Brant, 67400 Illkirch-Graffenstaden; Dir CLAUDE KEDINGER.

Professional Institute of Engineering Science: 15–17 rue du Maréchal Lefebvre, 67100 Strasbourg; Dir RALF PIXA.

University Institute of Technology of Haguenau: 30 rue du Marie André Traband, 67500 Haguenau; Dir FRANCIS BRAUN.

UNIVERSITÉ DE STRASBOURG II MARC BLOCH (SCIENCES HUMAINES)

22 rue Descartes, 67084 Strasbourg Cedex

Telephone: 3-88-41-73-00

Fax: 3-88-61-63-99

E-mail: payot@umb.u-strasbg.fr

Internet: umb.u-strasbg.fr

Founded 1538

State control

Academic year: October to June

President: DANIEL PAYOT

Vice-President: JEAN-JACQUES ALCANDRE

Secretary-General: CLAUDE PANARD

Number of teachers: 421

Number of students: 12,987

Publications: *Recherches anglaises et nord-américaines*, *Recherches ibériques et ibéro-américaines*, *Recherches germaniques*, *Bulletin analytique d'histoire romaine*, *Revue des sciences sociales de la France de l'Est*, *Travaux de l'Institut de Phonétique*, *KTEMA* (ancient Rome, Greece and the Orient), *Revue de Droit Canonique* (annually), *Revue des Sciences Religieuses* (quarterly)

DIRECTORS OF TEACHING AND RESEARCH UNITS

Classics: JEAN-CHRISTOPHE PELLAT

Modern Languages, Literature and Civilization: CHRISTIAN CIVARDI

Social Sciences, Social Work and Development: JUAN MATAS

Philosophy and Communication: MAURICE SACHOT

Languages and Applied Human Sciences: JEAN DEWITZ

History: JEAN-MICHEL MEHL

Arts: JEAN-LOUIS FLECNIAKOSKA

Sport Science: BERNARD MICHON

French and Comparative Linguistics and Literature: JEAN-PAUL SCHNEIDER

Catholic Theology (9 place de l'Université, 67084 Strasbourg Cedex): SIMON KNAEBEL

Protestant Theology (9 place de l'Université, 67084 Strasbourg Cedex): JEAN-FRANÇOIS COLLANGE

Music Teacher Training Centre (Ecole Normale 1, rue Froehlich, 67600 Selestat): JEAN-LOUIS FLECNIAKOSKA

HEADS OF DEPARTMENTS

Classics:

- Institute of South Asian Studies: BORIS OGUIBENINE
- Institute of Greek: BERNARD LAUROT
- Institute of Latin: FRANÇOIS HEIM
- Institute of Linguistics and French Language: MARTIN RIEGEL
- Institute of General and Comparative Literature: OLIVIER BONNEROT
- Institute of Phonetics: JEAN-PIERRE ZERLING
- Institute of Papyrology (9 place de l'Université): JEAN GASCOU

Modern Languages, Literature and Civilization:

- Department of English and North American Studies: BRIAN WALLIS
- Department of German Studies: HILDEGARD CHATELLIER
- Department of Alsatian and Mosellan Dialectology: ARLETTE BOTHOREL
- Department of Scandinavian Studies: SOPHIE GRIMAL
- Department of Dutch: CLAUDIA HUISMAN
- Department of Iberian and Ibero-American Studies: BRENDA LACA
- Department of Italian Studies: LUCA BADINI CONFALONIERI
- Department of Romanian Studies: Mme HÉLÈNE LENZ
- Department of Slavic and Soviet Studies: BELKIS-SONJA PHILONENKO
- Department of Modern Greek Studies: LAURENT PERNOT
- Department of Arab and Islamic Studies: GEORGES KHAIRALLAH
- Department of Hebrew and Jewish Studies: JOSEPH ELKOUBY
- Department of Turkish Studies: PAUL DUMONT
- Department of Persian Studies: HOSSEIN BEIKBAGHBAN
- Department of Japanese Studies: CHRISTIANE SEGUY
- Department of Hungarian Studies: ILDIKÓ SZTRAPKOVICS
- Department of Applied Linguistics and the Teaching of Living Languages: JÜRGEN OTT
- Department of Chinese Studies: CHRISTIAN CIVARDI

Sport:

- Institute of Physical Education and Sports Science: BERNARD MICHON

Social Sciences:

- Institute of Sociology: PASCAL HINTERMEYER
- Institute of Demography: ANNE-MARIE SAHLI
- Institute of Ethnology: ERIC NAVET
- Institute of Polemics: PATRICK WATIER
- Institute of Town Planning and Regional Administration: STEPHAN JONAS

Philosophy and Communication:

- Department of Philosophy: JEAN-CLAUDE CHIROLLET
- Department of General Linguistics: GEORGES KLEIBER
- Department of Computer Studies: MICHEL EYTAN
- Department of Education: MAURICE SACHOT

Languages and Applied Human Sciences:

- Department of Applied Modern Languages: JEAN DEWITZ

History:

- Institute of Art History: ROLAND RECHT
- Institute of Greek History: EDMOND LEVY
- Institute of Roman History: ALAIN CHAUVOT
- Institute of Medieval History: GEORGES BISCHOFF
- Institute of the History of Alsace: BERNARD VOGLER
- Institute of Modern History: JEAN-MICHEL BOEHLER
- Institute of Contemporary History: CHRISTIAN BAECHLER
- Institute of the History of Religions: FRANÇOIS BLANCHETIÈRE
- Institute of Byzantine Art and Archaeology: BERNARD BAVANT
- Institute of the History and Archaeology of the Ancient East: DOMINIQUE BEYER
- Institute of Classical Archaeology: GÉRARD SIEBERT
- Institute of Egyptology: CLAUDE TRAUNECKER
- Institute of National Antiquities: ANNE-MARIE ADAM
- Institute of Geography: CATHERINE SELIMANOVSKI

Arts:

- Department of Fine Art: JEAN-LOUIS FLECNIAKOSKA
- Department of Cinema and Audio-Visual: JEAN-FRANÇOIS MORIS

Department of Music: PIERRE MICHEL
Department of Plastic Arts: MICHEL DEMANGE, GUY GOULON
Catholic Theology:
Institute of Religious Education: GILBERT ADLER
Institute of Canon Law: MARCEL METZGER
Protestant Theology:
Centre of Pedagogical Study and Practice: BERNARD KAEMPF
Centre of Theological Training: JEAN-FRANÇOIS COLLANGE
Centre of Training in Church Music: ULRICH ASPER

UNIVERSITÉ DE STRASBOURG III (UNIVERSITÉ ROBERT SCHUMAN)

1 place d'Athènes, BP 66, 67045 Strasbourg Cedex
Telephone: 3-88-41-42-00
Fax: 3-88-61-30-37
E-mail: urs@urs.u-strasbg.fr
Internet: www-urs.u-strasbg.fr
Founded 1970
Academic year: October to July
President: FLORENCE BENOÎT-ROHMER
Vice-Presidents: DOMINIQUE D'AMBRA, SEBASTIEN COUDERT, XAVIER DELCOURT, CONSTANCE GREWE, MICHAEL HARTMEIER
Secretary-General: ERIC PIMMEL
Librarian: THEODORA BALMON
Number of teachers: 250
Number of students: 9,000
Publication: *Universcité* (5 a year)

DIRECTORS OF TEACHING AND RESEARCH UNITS

Law, Political Sciences and Management: WILLY ZIMMER
Law, Political and Social Research: CONSTANCE GREWE
Institute of Labour: (vacant)
Institute of Political Studies: Y. GAUTIER
Institute of Business Economics: P. IMBS
Centre for International Patent Rights: Y. REBOUL
University Centre for Journalistic Studies: A. CHANEL
European Institute for Advanced Commercial Studies: G. LAMBERT
University Institute of Technology: JOSEPH ROLLER
Institute of Advanced European Studies: M. DEVOLUY
Institute of Preparation for General Administration: Dr FRANCESCO DE PALMA
Adult Education Service: MARGUERITE JODER

PROFESSORS

ALEXANDRE, D., Private Law
ARROUS, J., General Economics and Statistics
BAUD, J. P., History of Law
BAUMERT, H., Management
BENOÎT-ROHMER, F., Public Law
BITSCH, M.-TH., History of Europe
BRILL, J. P., Private Law
CONSTANT, F., History
CONSTANTINESCO, V., Public Law
D'AMBRA, D., Private Law
DELCOURT, X., Journalism
DELOYE, Y., Political Science
DE QUENAUDON, R., Private Law
DEVOLUY, M., General Economics and Statistics
DIETSCH, M., General Economics and Statistics
EBER, N., Public Law
ECKERT, G., Public Law
FABREGUET, M., History
GARTNER, F., Public Law
GAUTIER, Y., Public Law
GIRAUDEAU, A., Physical Chemistry
GOYET, C., Private Law
GRANET, F., Private Law
GREWE, C., Public Law
GROSCLAUDE, J., Public Law
HERTZOG, R., Public Law
HINDERMANN, J.-P., Applied Chemistry
HOFNUNG, M., Public Law
JACOB, F., Private law
JEANCLOS, Y., History of Law
JOUANJAN, O., Public Law
KNAUB, G., Public Law
KOVAR, R., Public Law
LAMBERT, G., Management
LAVOINNE, Y., Journalism
LEMOINE, P., Chemistry
LIOUVILLE, J., Management
LLORENS, F., Public Law
MARCHESSOU, PH., Public Law
MATHIEN, M., Journalism
MESTRE, CH., Public Law
MUGUET, M.-P., Chemistry
MULLER, M.-P., Mathematics
OLSZAK, N., History of Law
PIETRI, N., History
POUGHON, J.-M., Legal History
PUECH, M., Private Law
REBOUL, Y., Private Law
ROMER, J.-C., History
RONTCHEVSKY, N., Private Law
SACHS-DURAND, C., Private Law
SCHEVIN, P., Management
SCHMIDT, D., Private Law
SIMLER, P., Private Law
SIMON, D., Public Law
STORCK, J.-P., Private Law
STORCK, M., Private Law
STRICKLER, Y., Private Law
WACHSMANN, P., Public Law
WIEDERKEHR, G., Private Law
WITZ, C., Private Law
ZIMMER, W., Public Law

UNIVERSITÉ DE TOULON ET DU VAR

Ave de l'Université, BP 132, 83957 La Garde Cedex
Telephone: 4-94-75-90-50
Fax: 4-94-08-14-32
Internet: www.univ-tln.fr
Founded 1970
Academic year: September to July
President: BRUNO RAVAZ
Vice-President (vacant)
Secretary-General: JEAN BESCOND
Librarian: JACQUES KERIGUY
Number of teachers: 380
Number of students: 10,000

TEACHING AND RESEARCH UNITS

Sciences and Technology: (vacant): Dir:
Law Sciences: (vacant): Dir:
Economic Sciences: Dir: JEAN BERNARD
Arts: Dir: PATRICK MENNETEAU
University Institute of Technology: Dir: BRUNO ROSSETO
Sports: Dir: JACQUES CRÉMIEUX
School of Engineering: Dir: FRANÇOIS RESCH

UNIVERSITÉ DE TOULOUSE I (SCIENCES SOCIALES)

Place Anatole France, 31042 Toulouse Cedex
Telephone: 5-61-63-35-00
Fax: 5-61-63-37-98
Internet: www.univ-tlse1.fr
Founded 1229
State control
President: BERNARD SAINT-GIRONS
Vice-President: JACQUES IGALENS
Secretary-General: DANIELE ROULLAND
Librarians: GERMAINE ROGÉ, MONIQUE PUZZO
Number of teachers: 411
Number of students: 19,027
Publications: *Livret de l'Etudiant*, *Annales*, *Livre de la Recherche*, *UT1 Magazine*

TEACHING AND RESEARCH UNITS

Law: Dir: H. ROUSSILLON
Economics: Dir: B. BELLOC
Economic and Social Administration: Dir: S. REGOURD
Information Science: Dir: C. ERNST

ATTACHED INSTITUTES

Ecole Supérieure Universitaire de Gestion: 2 rue Albert Lautmann, 31042 Toulouse Cedex; tel. 5-61-21-55-18; fax 5-61-23-84-33; Dir P. SPITERI.

Institut d'Etudes Politiques: 2 ter rue des Puits Creusés, 31042 Toulouse Cedex; tel. 5-61-11-02-60; fax 5-61-22-94-80; Dir C. HEN.

Institut Universitaire Technologique de Rodez: 33 ave du 8 mai 1945, 12000 Rodez; tel. 5-65-77-10-80; fax 5-65-77-10-81; Dir B. ALLAUX.

Centre Universitaire d'Albi: 2 ave Franchet d'Espérey, 81011 Albi Cedex 09; tel. 5-63-48-19-79; fax 5-63-48-19-71; Dir O. DEVAUX.

Centre Universitaire de Montauban: 116 blvd Montauriol, 82017 Montauban Cedex; tel. 5-63-63-32-71; fax 5-63-66-34-07; Dir B. MARIZ.

UNIVERSITÉ DE TOULOUSE II (LE MIRAIL)

5 allées Antonio Machado, 31058 Toulouse Cedex 1
Telephone: 5-61-50-42-50
Fax: 5-61-50-42-09
Internet: www.univ-tlse2.fr
President: RÉMY PECH
Secretary-General: JEAN-CLAUDE SELSIS
Number of teachers: 781
Number of students: 26,504
Publications: *Caravelle* (2 a year), *Criticón* (3 a year), *Homo* (annually), *Kairos* (2 a year), *Littératures* (2 a year), *Pallas* (2 a year), *Cinémas d'Amérique Latine* (annually), *Clio* (2 a year), *Science de la Société* (3 a year), *Anglophonia* (2 a year), *Sud/Ouest Européen*

TEACHING AND RESEARCH UNITS

Philosophy and Politics: Dir: L. SALA-MOLINS
Psychology: Dir: J.-R. HAÏT (acting)
Social Sciences: Dir: M. PERVANCHON (acting)
Behavioural Sciences, Education: Dir: S. ALAVA
Modern Languages, Foreign Literatures and Civilizations and General Linguistics: Dir: H. HOMBOURG
Studies of the English-Speaking World: Dir: J. L. BRETEAU
Ancient Literature and Languages: Dir: J.-P. MAUREL
French Literature, Languages and Music: Dir: F. GEVREY
History, Archaeology and History of Art: Dir: P. VAYSSIÈRE
Geography: Dir: D. WEISSBERG
Mathematics, Computer Science Statistics, Economics and Business Studies: Dir: P. CARBONNE
Hispanic and Hispano-American Studies: Dir: C. CHAUCHADIS
University Institute of Technology: Dir: J. J. MERCIER
Continuing Education: M. FOURNET
Audio-visual Studies: Dir: G. CHAPOUILLIE
Latin-American Studies (IPEALT): Dir: J. GILARD
Institut Universitaire de Formation de Musiciens Intervenant à l'Ecole Elémentaire et Pré-Elémentaire (IFMI): Dir: J. BROUSSAUDIER

UNIVERSITÉ PAUL SABATIER (TOULOUSE III)

118 route de Narbonne, 31062 Toulouse Cedex
Telephone: 5-61-55-66-11
Fax: 5-61-55-64-70
Internet: www.ups-tlse.fr

Founded 1969
State control
Academic year: September to June

President: RAYMOND BASTIDE
Vice-Presidents: R. CAUBET (Scientific Council), G. SOUM (Council of Studies and University Life)
Secretary-General: Mme A. VERDAGUER
Librarian: Mme HEUSSE

Number of teachers and researchers: 1,650
Number of students: 28,000

Publication: *Campus CONTACT Actualité* (monthly)

DEANS

Faculty of Medicine (Rangueil): G. LAZORTHES
Faculty of Medicine (Purpan): B. GUIRAUD CHAUMEIL
Faculty of Dental Surgery: J. PH. LODTER
Faculty of Pharmacy: P. COURRIÈRE

TEACHING AND RESEARCH UNITS

Mathematics, Information Science, Management: Dir: Prof. H. SENATEUR
Physics, Chemistry and Automation: Dir: Y. SALAMERO
Earth and Life Sciences: Dir: Prof. J. DERAMOND
Scientific Study of Physical and Sporting Activities: G. AUNEAU
University Institute of Technology: Dir: M. EYCHENE
Modern Languages: Dir: R. FAURE

UNIVERSITÉ DE TOURS (UNIVERSITÉ FRANÇOIS-RABELAIS)

3 rue des Tanneurs, BP 4103, 37041 Tours Cedex
Telephone: 2-47-36-66-00
Fax: 2-47-36-64-10
E-mail: scuio@univ-tours.fr
Internet: www.univ-tours.fr

Founded 1970
State control
Academic year: September to June

President: MICHEL LUSSAULT
Vice-Presidents: LOIC VAILLANT, ALAIN RONCIN, MARTINE PELLETIER, CORINE TOURET
Librarian: CORINNE TOUCHELAY

Number of teachers: 1,140
Number of students: 23,000

Publication: *François Rabelais Informations*

DIRECTORS OF TEACHING AND RESEARCH UNITS

Law, Economics and Social Sciences: CHRISTIAN GARBAR
Medicine: DOMINIQUE PERROTIN
Pharmacy: BERNARD YVONNET
University Institute of Technology: ROBERT COUDERT
Exact and Natural Sciences: ALAIN VERGER
Centre for Renaissance Studies: MARIE-LUCE DEMONET
Art and Humanities: FRANCOIS TESTU
Letters and Languages: HEINZ RASCHEL
University Institute of Technology (Blois): ISABELLE LAFFEZ
School of Engineering (Blois): JOEL LE MEUR
Polytechnic School (Tours): (vacant)

UNIVERSITÉ DE TECHNOLOGIE DE TROYES

12 rue Marie Curie, BP 2060, 10010 Troyes Cedex
Telephone: 3-25-71-76-00
Fax: 3-25-71-76-76
E-mail: info.utt@univ-troyes.fr
Internet: www.univ-troyes.fr

Founded 1994
State control
Academic year: September to June

President: Prof. PAUL GAILLARD
Director of Studies: Prof. PIERRE BAE
Head of Library: SABINE BARRAL

Library of 10,000 vols
Number of teachers: 90
Number of students: 1,150 (1,080 undergraduate, 70 postgraduate)

HEADS OF DEPARTMENTS

Mechanical Systems Engineering: Prof. JIAN LU
Industrial Systems Engineering: Prof. CHRISTIAN PRINS
Information Systems Engineering: Prof. PATRICK LALLEMENT
Technology and Human Sciences: Prof. DOMINIQUE BOURG

UNIVERSITÉ DE VALENCIENNES ET DU HAINAUT-CAMBRESIS

Le Mont Houy, BP 311, 59304 Valenciennes Cedex
Telephone: 3-27-14-12-34
Fax: 3-27-14-11-00
E-mail: uvhc@univ-valenciennes.fr
Internet: www.univ-valenciennes.fr

Founded 1964
State control
Language of instruction: French
Academic year: September to June

President: PASCAL LEVEL
Secretary-General: JEAN-PIERRE DARRAS
Librarian: A. STEINER

Library of 73,000 vols
Number of teachers: 485
Number of students: 12,000

Publications: *16 Lez Valenciennes* (annually), *Guide d'étudiant* (annually), *Rapport d'activité des laboratoires de recherche* (annually), *Lettre de l'Université* (monthly)

TEACHING AND RESEARCH UNITS

Institute of Science and Technology: Dir: P. LEVEL
Institute of Technology: Dir: J. M. DESRUMAUX
Literature, Modern Languages and Art: Dir: J. VAILLANT
Law, Economics and Management: Dir: M. DEFOSSEZ
Department of Administrative Studies: Dir: X. MOREAU
School of Mechanics and Energetics: Dir: YVES RAVALARD
School of Mechanics: Dir: J. P. BRICOUT
School of Data Processing and Production Technology: Dir: D. WILLAEYS

UNIVERSITÉ VERSAILLES/SAINT QUENTIN-EN-YVELINES

23 rue du Refuge, 78000 Versailles
Telephone: 1-39-25-41-03
Fax: 1-39-25-41-07
Internet: www.uvsq.fr

Founded 1991

President: DOMINIQUE GENTILE
Number of students: 9,300.

TEACHING AND RESEARCH UNITS

Unité de Formation et de Recherche St-Quentin-en-Yvelines: 47 blvd Vauban, 78280 Guyancourt; tel. 1-39-25-50-00; fax 1-39-25-53-55; courses in law, economics, social sciences, humanities; Dir JEAN-FRANÇOIS LEMETTRE.

Unité de Formation et de Recherche Versailles: 45 ave des Etats-Unis, 78000 Versailles; tel. 1-39-25-40-00; fax 1-39-25-40-19; courses in science; Dir JACQUES LAVERGNAT.

Polytechnic Institutes

INSTITUT NATIONAL POLYTECHNIQUE DE GRENOBLE

46 ave Félix Viallet, 38031 Grenoble Cedex 1
Telephone: 4-76-57-45-00
Fax: 4-76-57-45-01
Internet: www.inpg.fr

Founded 1907

President: YVES BRUNET
Vice-Presidents: ROGER MORET, BERNARD GUERIN, JEAN-MICHEL DION, JEAN-CLAUDE SABONNADIÈRE
Secretary-General: PIERRE BALME

Number of teachers: 350
Number of students: 4,300

Publication: *Ingénieurs INPG* (weekly, monthly and termly).

CONSTITUENT SCHOOLS

Ecole Nationale Supérieure d'Electricité et de Radioélectricité (ENSERG): 23 rue des Martyrs, BP 257, 38016 Grenoble Cedex; Dir MICHEL BARIBAUD.

Ecole Nationale Supérieure d'Electrochimie et d'Electrométallurgie de Grenoble (ENSEEG): 1130 rue de la Piscine, Domaine Universitaire, BP 75, 38402 Saint-Martin-d'Hères Cedex; Dir JEAN-CLAUDE POIGNET.

Ecole Nationale Supérieure de Génie Industriel (ENSGI): 46 ave Félix Viallet, 38031 Grenoble Cedex 1; Dir SERGE TICHKIEWITCH.

Ecole Nationale Supérieure d'Ingénieurs Electriciens de Grenoble (ENSIEG): Rue de la Houille Blanche, Domaine Universitaire, BP 46, 38402 Saint-Martin d'Hères; Dir ARLETTE CHERVY.

Ecole Nationale Supérieure d'Informatique et de Mathématiques Appliquées de Grenoble (ENSIMAG): Domaine Universitaire, BP 72, 38402 St Martin d'Hères; Dir GUY MAZARÉ.

Ecole Nationale Supérieure d'Hydraulique et de Mécanique de Grenoble (ENSHMG): 1025 rue de la Piscine, Domaine Universitaire, BP 95, 38402 Saint-Martin-d'Hères Cedex; Dir JEAN-MICHEL GRESILLON.

Ecole Nationale Supérieure de Physique de Grenoble (ENSPG): rue de la Houille Blanche, BP 46, 38402 Saint-Martin-d'Hères; Dir CLAIRE SCHLENKER.

Ecole Française de Papeterie et des Industries Graphiques (EFPG): 461 rue de la Papeterie, Domaine Universitaire, BP 65, 38402 Saint-Martin-d'Hères Cedex; Dir CHRISTIAN VOILLOT.

Ecole Supérieure d'Ingénieurs en Systèmes Industriels Avancés Rhône-Alpes (ESISAR): 50 rue Barthélémy de Laffemas, BP 54, 26902 Valence Cedex 9; Dir MICHEL DANG.

Collège Doctoral: 46 ave Félix Viallet, 38031 Grenoble Cedex 1; Dir PIERRE GENTIL..

AFFILIATED INSTITUTE

Centre Universitaire d'Education et de Formation des Adultes (CUEFA): 701 rue de la Piscine, Domaine Universitaire, 38402 Saint-Martin-d'Hères; Dir MAXIME VINCENT.

INSTITUT NATIONAL POLYTECHNIQUE DE LORRAINE

2 ave de la Forêt de Haye, BP 3, 54501 Vandoeuvre

Telephone: 3-83-59-59-59
Fax: 3-83-59-59-55
Internet: www.inpl-nancy.fr

Founded 1971
Language of instruction: French

President: MICHEL LUCIUS
Vice-Presidents: JEAN-CHARLES CHEVRIER, ANDRÉ LAURENT (Scientific Council), JEAN-PAUL TISOT (Council of Studies and University Life)
Secretary-General: NOËL GAND

Number of teachers: 400
Number of students: 4,000.

CONSTITUENT SCHOOLS

Ecole Nationale Supérieure d'Agronomie et des Industries Alimentaires: 2 ave de la Forêt de Haye, BP 172, 54505, Vandoeuvre Cedex; tel. 3-83-59-59-59; fax 3-83-59-59-55; f. 1970; 45 full-time staff, 417 students; library of 7,500 vols; Dir JÖEL HARDY; publ. *Bulletin Scientifique* (annually).

Ecole Nationale Supérieure d'Electricité et de Mécanique: 2 ave de la Forêt de Haye, 54500 Vandoeuvre; tel. 3-83-59-59-59; fax 3-83-59-59-55; 381 students; Dir Prof. JEAN-CLAUDE BRAUN.

Ecole Nationale Supérieure de Géologie: 94 ave de Lattre de Tassigny, BP 452, 54001 Nancy Cedex; tel. 3-83-32-85-86; fax 3-83-30-21-37; 247 students; Dir BERNARD DURAND.

Ecole Nationale Supérieure des Mines de Nancy: Parc de Saurupt, 54042 Nancy Cedex; tel. 3-83-58-42-32; fax 3-83-57-97-94; f. 1919; 361 students; library of 37,500 vols, 180 periodicals; Dir CLAUDE CREMET.

Ecole Nationale Supérieure des Industries Chimiques: 1 rue Grandville, 54042 Nancy Cedex; tel. 3-83-35-21-21; fax 3-83-35-08-11; 345 students; Dir Prof. A. STORCK.

Ecole Nationale Supérieure en Génie des Systèmes Industriels: 4 allée Pelletier Doisy, 54600 Villiers lès Nancy; tel. 3-83-44-38-38; fax 3-83-44-04-82; 45 students; Dir Prof. CLAUDINE GUIDAT.

Ecole Européenne d'Ingénieurs en Génie des Matériaux: 6 rue B. Lepage, 54010 Nancy Cedex; tel. 3-83-36-83-00; fax 3-83-36-83-36; 191 students; Dir Dr TORBJORN HEDBERG.

Ecole Supérieure d'Ingénieurs des Techniques de l'Industrie: 2 rue de la Citadelle, 54000 Nancy; tel. 3-83-35-82-82; 131 students; Dir FRANÇOIS MOLLEYRE (acting).

Ecole d'Architecture de Nancy: Rue Bastien Lepage, BP 435, 54000 Nancy; tel. 3-83-30-81-00; fax 3-83-30-81-30; 476 students; Dir DENIS GRANDJEAN.

INSTITUT NATIONAL POLYTECHNIQUE DE TOULOUSE

Place des Hauts-Murats, BP 354, 31006 Toulouse Cedex 6

Telephone: 5-62-25-54-00
Fax: 5-61-53-67-21
E-mail: inp@inp-toulouse.fr
Internet: www.inp-toulouse.fr

Founded 1970

President: ROLAND MORANCHO
Vice-Presidents: M. BABILE, BELLET, CANDAU, GOURDON, GRANDPIERRE, KALCK, METZ
Secretary-General: J. L. BOUZINAC

Number of teachers: 270
Number of students: 2,958.

CONSTITUENT SCHOOLS

Ecole Nationale Supérieure Agronomique: Ave de l'Agrobiopole, BP 107, Auzeville-Tolosane, 31326 Castanet-Tolosan Cedex; Dir M. CAMDAU.

Ecole Nationale Supérieure d'Electrotechnique, d'Electronique, d'Informatique et d'Hydraulique: 2 rue Camichel, 31071 Toulouse Cedex 7; Dir M. RODRIGUEZ.

Ecole Nationale Supérieure des Arts Chimiques et Technologiques (ENSIACET): Chemin de la Loge, 31078 Toulouse Cedex 4; Dir (vacant).

State Colleges and Institutes

Due to space limitations, we are restricted to giving a selection of colleges. Almost every one is a 'Grande Ecole' and awards a national degree.

GENERAL

COLLÈGE DE FRANCE

11 place Marcelin-Berthelot, 75231 Paris Cedex 05

Telephone: 1-44-27-12-11
Fax: 1-44-27-11-09
Internet: www.college-de-france.fr

Founded 1530 by François I

Administrator: JACQUES GLOWINSKI

Library of 85,000 vols54 professors

PROFESSORS

Science:

ARTAVANIS-TSAKONAS, Biology and Developmental Genetics
BERTHOZ, Physiology of Perception and Action
CHAMBON, Molecular Genetics
CHANGEUX, Cellular Communications
COHEN-TANNOUDJI, Atomic and Molecular Physics
CONNES, Analysis and Geometry
CORVOL, Experimental Medicine
FROISSART, Particle Physics
GENNES, DE, Solid State Physics
GLOWINSKI, Neuropharmacology
HAROCHE, Quantum Physics
JOLIOT, Cellular Bioenergetics
KOURILSKY, Molecular Immunology
LABEYRIE, Observational astrophysics
LE PICHON, Geodynamics
LEHN, Chemistry of Molecular Interaction
LIVAGE, Condensed Matter Chemistry
RICQLÈS, DE, Historical Biology and Evolutionism
YOCCOZ, Differential Equations and Dynamic Systems
ZAGIER, Number Theory

Letters:

BOUVERESSE, Philosophy of Language and Knowledge
BRIANT, Achaemenid History and Civilization, Alexander the Great
COPPENS, Palaeoanthropology and Prehistory
DESCOLA, Anthropology of Nature
DURAND, Assyriology
FAGOT-LARGEAULT, Philosopy of Biology and Medicine
FUMAROLI, Rhetoric and Society in Europe (16th–17th Centuries)
FUSSMAN, History of India
GOUDINEAU, National Antiquities
GRIMAL, Egyptian Civilization, Archaeology, Philology and History
GUESNERIE, Economic Theory and Social Organization
GUILAINE, Neolithic and Bronze Age Civilizations in Europe
HACKING, Philosophy and History of Scientific Concepts
HAGÈGE, Linguistic Theory
KELLENS, Indo-Iranian Languages and Religions
OSSOLA, Neo-Latin Modern Literature
RECHT, History of Medieval and Modern European Art
ROCHE, History of the French Enlightenment
SCHEID, Religion, Institutions and Society of Ancient Rome
TARDIEU, History of syncretisms from the end of antiquity
TOUBERT, History of the Western Mediterranean in the Middle Ages
VEINSTEIN, Turkish and Ottoman History
WACHTEL, History and Anthropology of Meso-American and South American Societies
WILL, History of Modern China
ZINK, French Medieval Literature

Ecole des Hautes Etudes en Sciences Sociales: 54 blvd Raspail, 75006 Paris; tel. 1-49-54-25-25; fax 1-45-44-93-11; internet www.ehess.fr; f. 1947; 270 teachers; 2,800 students; Pres. DANIÈLE HERVIEU-LÉGER.

Ecole Pratique des Hautes Etudes: 45–47 rue des Ecoles, 75005 Paris; tel. 1-40-46-33-97; fax 1-40-46-33-98; e-mail Valerie .Laffitte@ephe.sorbonne.fr; internet www .ephe.sorbonne.fr; f. 1868; library: 50,000 vols; 300 ; 4,000 ; Pres. JEAN BAUBÉROT; Chief Administrative Officer JEAN-CHARLES LINET.

Divisions:

Department of Life and Earth Science: 46 rue Saint-Jacques, 75005 Paris; tel. 1-40-46-31-30; fax 1-40-46-47-08; e-mail fbeauve@ephe.sorbonne.frf. 1868; Pres. JACQUES MICHAUX; publ. *Annuaire*.

Department of History and Philology: 45–47 rue des Ecoles, 75005 Paris; tel. 1-40-46-31-25; fax 1-40-46-31-39; f. 1868; Pres. LAURENT DUBOIS; publ. *Annuaire*.

Department of Religious Studies: 45–47 rue des Ecoles, 75005 Paris; tel. 1-40-46-31-37; fax 1-40-46-31-46; f. 1886; Pres. CLAUDE LANGLOIS; publ. *Annuaire*.

Pôle Universitaire Léonard de Vinci: 92916 Paris La Défense Cedex; located at: 2 ave Léonard de Vinci, Courbevoie, Hauts-de-Seine; tel. 1-41-16-70-00; fax 1-41-16-70-99; e-mail comm@devinci.fr; internet www .devinci.fr; f. 1995 by the General Council of the Hauts-de-Seine Département; departments: economics and social sciences, languages, general culture, personal development, sport; library: 40,000 books, reports, memoirs, market research reports, 800 journals, 800 CD-ROM titles, 600 international databases.

ADMINISTRATION

Ecole Nationale d'Administration: 13 rue de l'Université, 75007 Paris; tel. 1-49-26-45-45; fax 1-42-60-26-95; f. 1945 to provide training for the higher ranks of the Civil Service; 600 teachers; 400 students; library: 25,000 vols; Dir ANTOINE DURRLEMAN.

Groupe Ecole Supérieure de Commerce: 4 blvd Trudaine, 63037 Clermont-Ferrand; tel. 4-73-98-24-24; fax 4-73-98-24-49; f. 1919;

dependent on the Direction de l'Enseignement Supérieur du Ministre de l'Education; 200 teachers; 600 students; library: 9,000 vols; and Chamber of Commerce library of 12,000 vols; Dir L. HUA; publs *Point Zéro* (every 2 months), *Développements* (3 a year).

AGRICULTURE, FORESTRY, VETERINARY SCIENCE

Centre National d'Etudes Agronomiques des Régions Chaudes: 1101 ave Agropolis, BP 5098, 34033 Montpellier Cedex 1; tel. 4-67-61-70-00; fax 4-67-41-02-32; e-mail sauboa@cnearc.fr; internet www.cnearc.fr; f. 1902; library: 22,000 vols, 350 periodicals; Dir M. LATHAM; 20 teachers; 150 students.

Sections:

Cycle d'Etudes Supérieures d'Agronomie Tropicale.

Département de la Formation Continue.

Master Professionnel Natura 'Vulgarisation et Organisations Professionnelles Agricoles'.

Master of Science 'Développement Agricole Tropical'.

Ecole Nationale d'Ingénieurs des Travaux Agricoles de Clermont-Ferrand: Marmilhat, 63370 Lempdes; tel. 4-73-98-13-15; fax 4-73-98-13-98; e-mail gosset@gentiane.enitac.fr; internet www.enitac.fr; f. 1984; 45 teachers; 300 students; library: 10,000 vols; Dir GEORGES GOSSET.

Ecole Nationale du Génie Rural des Eaux et des Forêts: Centre de Nancy, 14 rue Girardet, 54042 Nancy Cedex; tel. 3-83-39-68-00; fax 3-83-30-22-54; internet www.engref.fr; f. 1965 by merger of the Ecole Nationale du Génie Rural and the Ecole Nationale des Eaux et Forêts; 15 teachers; 200 students; library: 50,000 vols, 1,600 periodicals; Dir DOMINIQUE DANGUY DES DÉSERTS; publ. *Revue Forestière Française* (every 2 months).

Ecole Nationale Supérieure Agronomique de Montpellier: Place Viala, 34060 Montpellier Cedex 1; tel. 4-99-61-24-44; fax 4-99-61-29-00; e-mail dep@ensam.inra.fr; internet www.agro-montpellier.fr; f. 1872; 70 teachers; 620 students; library: 100,000 vols, 1,400 periodicals; Dir ETIENNE LANDAIS.

Ecole Nationale Supérieure Agronomique de Rennes (ENSAR): 65 rue de Saint-Brieuc, 35042 Rennes Cedex; tel. 2-23-48-56-97; fax 2-23-48-56-80; e-mail dep@agrorennes.educagri.fr; internet www.agrorennes.educagri.fr; f. 1830; library: 10,000 vols; 90 teachers; 550 students; Dir P. THIVEND.

Ecole Nationale Supérieure des Industries Agricoles et Alimentaires (ENSIA): 1 ave des Olympiades, 91744 Massy Cedex; tel. 1-69-93-50-50; fax 1-69-20-02-30; e-mail ensia@ensia.fr; internet www.ensia.fr; f. 1893; library: 10,000 vols; 45 teachers; 450 students; Dir YVES DEMARNE; publs *Industries Alimentaires* (monthly), *Compte Rendu d'Activités* (annually), *Livret de l'Etudiant* (annually).

Ecole Nationale Supérieure du Paysage: 4 rue Hardy, RP 914, 78009 Versailles Cedex; tel. 1-39-24-62-00; fax 1-39-24-62-01; f. 1975; rural development, ecology, humanities, plastic arts, architecture, landscaping, town planning; library: 6,000 vols, 75 periodicals; Dir J. B. CUISINIER; publ. *Les Carnets du Paysage* (4 a year).

Ecole Nationale Vétérinaire d'Alfort: 7 ave Général de Gaulle, 94704 Maisons-Alfort Cedex; tel. 1-43-96-71-00; fax 1-43-96-71-25; f. 1765; 72 teachers; library: 150,000 vols; Dean Prof. ANDRÉ-LAURENT PARODI; publ. *Le Recueil de Médecine Vétérinaire*.

Ecole Nationale Vétérinaire de Lyon: 1 ave Bourgelat, BP 83, 69280 Marcy L'Etoile; tel. 4-78-87-25-00; fax 4-78-87-82-62; internet www.vet-lyon.fr; f. 1762; library: 10,000 vols; 73 teachers; Dir S. MARTINOT; publ. *Revue de Médecine Vétérinaire* (monthly).

Ecole Nationale Vétérinaire de Nantes: Atlanpole-La Chantrerie, BP 40706, 44307 Nantes Cedex 03; tel. 2-40-68-77-77; fax 2-40-68-77-78; e-mail direction@vet-nantes.fr; internet www.vet-nantes.fr; f. 1979; 73 teachers; 634 students; Dir (vacant).

Ecole Nationale Vétérinaire de Toulouse: 23 chemin des Capelles, 31076 Toulouse Cedex; tel. 5-61-19-38-02; fax 5-61-19-39-93; e-mail direction@envt.fr; f. 1828; library: 50,000 vols; 69 teachers; Dir Prof. P. BÉNARD; Sec.-Gen. J. G. MCCOOK; Librarian Prof. J. EUZEBY; publ. *Revue de Médecine Vétérinaire* (monthly).

Institut National Agronomique Paris-Grignon: Département Agronomie-Environnement, 16 rue Claude Bernard, 75231 Paris Cedex 05; tel. 1-43-37-15-50; f. 1972 with present title; teaching personnel 129; library: 50,000 vols and 1,700 periodicals; Dir (vacant).

Attached institute:

Département des Sols de l'INAP-G: 78850 Thiverval-Grignon; tel. 1-30-54-45-10; f. 1979; library: *c.* 1,000 vols; publ. *Sols* (3 or 4 a year).

Institut National d'Horticulture: 2 rue Le Notre, 49045 Angers Cedex 01; tel. 2-41-22-54-54; fax 2-41-73-15-57; e-mail inh@inh.fr; internet www.inh.fr; f. 1874; library: 19,000 vols; 50 teachers; 450 students; Dir F. COLSON.

Institut National Supérieur de Formation Agro-Alimentaire (INSFA): 65 rue de Saint-Brieuc, CS 84215, 35042 Rennes Cedex; tel. 2-23-48-50-00; fax 2-23-48-54-90; e-mail insfa@agrorennes.educagri.fr; internet www.agrorennes.educagri.fr; f. 1990; quality management, production management, marketing, research and development; library: 10,000 vols; 90 teachers; 238 students; Dir P. THIVEND.

ARCHITECTURE

Ecole d'Architecture de Lille et des Régions Nord: 2 rue Verte, quartier de l'Hôtel de Ville, 59650 Villeneuve d'Ascq; tel. 3-20-61-95-50; fax 3-20-61-95-51; internet www.lille.archi.fr; f. 1755 as Ecole d'Architecture, reorganized 1968; library: 15,000 vols; 100 teachers; 750 students; Dir BERNARD WELCOMME.

Ecole d'Architecture de Paris-La Villette: 144 rue de Flandre, 75019 Paris; tel. 1-44-65-23-00; fax 1-44-65-23-01; f. 1969, present name 1982; attached to Min. of Culture; 80 teachers; 2,300 students; library: 25,000 vols; Dir GERARD CATTALANO.

Ecole Spéciale d'Architecture: 254 blvd Raspail, 75014 Paris; tel. 1-40-47-40-47; fax 1-43-22-81-16; e-mail info@esa-paris.fr; internet www.esa-paris.fr; f. 1865; library: 7,000 vols; 450 students; 60 teachers; Dir OLIVIER LEBLOIS.

ECONOMICS, LAW AND POLITICS

Centre Français de Droit Comparé: 28 rue Saint-Guillaume, 75007 Paris; tel. 1-44-39-86-23; fax 1-44-39-86-28; e-mail cfdc@legiscompare.com; f. 1951; library: 100,000 vols; Pres. JACQUES ROBERT; Sec.-Gen. DIDIER LAMÈTHE; publ. *Revue Internationale de Droit Comparé* (4 a year).

Ecole Nationale de la Magistrature: 10 rue des Frères Bonic, 33080 Bordeaux; tel. 5-56-00-10-10; e-mail initiale@enm_magistrature.fr; f. 1958; 450 students; library: 50,000 vols; Dir DOMINIQUE MAIN; publs *Mémento de l'Instruction* (2 a year), *Instruction actualité* (every 2 months), *Revue* (annually).

Ecole Nationale de la Statistique et de l'Administration Economique (ENSAE): 3 ave Pierre Larousse, 92245 Malakoff Cedex; tel. 1-41-17-65-25; fax 1-41-17-38-53; e-mail info@ensae.fr; internet www.ensae.fr; f. 1942; attached to the Institut National de la Statistique et des Etudes Economiques (see Research Institutes); economics, statistics, finance; 330 students; Chair. A. TROGNON.

Ecole Nationale de la Statistique et de l'Analyse de l'Information (ENSAI): Campus de Ker Lann, rue Blaise Pascal, 35170 Bruz; tel. 2-99-05-32-32; fax 2-99-05-32-05; e-mail accueil@ensai.fr; internet www.ensai.com; f. 1942; attached to the Institut National de la Statistique et des Etudes Economiques (see Research Institutes); statistics and information processing at Masters level; 20 teachers; 310 students; Dir P. JOLY.

Institut d'Etudes Politiques: Ave Ausone, Domaine Universitaire, 33607 Pessac; tel. 5-56-84-42-52; fax 5-56-37-45-37; f. 1948; affiliated with Univ. Bordeaux IV; politics and administration, economics, management; library: 80,000 vols; 200 teachers and researchers; 1,200 students; Dir ROBERT LAFORVE.

Institut d'Etudes Politiques de Paris: 27 rue Saint-Guillaume, 75337 Paris Cedex 07; tel. 1-45-49-50-50; fax 1-42-22-31-26; f. 1945 as successor to l'Ecole Libre des Sciences Politiques; linked to Fondation Nationale des Sciences Politiques (*q.v.*); library: 700,000 vols; 4,000 students; Dir R. DESCOINGS.

EDUCATION

Ecole Normale Supérieure: 45 rue d'Ulm, 75230 Paris Cedex 05; tel. 1-44-32-30-00; fax 1-44-32-38-47; f. 1794 by the National Convention; library: see Libraries; 2,000 students; graduate and postgraduate studies in humanities, social sciences and science; Dir ETIENNE GUYON; Sec.-Gen. JEAN PASCAL BONHOTAL; Librarian PIERRE PETITMENGIN; publ. *Annales Scientifiques de l'Ecole Normale Supérieure*.

Ecole Normale Supérieure: 31 ave Lombart, 92260 Fontenay aux Roses; tel. 1-41-13-24-00; fax 1-41-13-24-09; f. 1880; library: 200,000 vols, 700 periodicals; 120 teachers; 450 students; Dir SYLVAIN AUROUX; Sec.-Gen. A. COURDAVAULT; Dir of Studies F. MAZIÈRE; publ. *Collections des Presses de l'ENS*.

Ecole Normale Supérieure de Cachan: 61 ave du Président Wilson, 94235 Cachan Cedex; tel. 1-47-40-20-00; fax 1-47-40-20-74; e-mail webmaster@ens-cachan.fr; internet www.ens-cachan.fr; f. 1912; library: 55,000 vols; 145 teachers; 1,150 students; Dir BERNARD DECOMPS.

HEADS OF DEPARTMENTS

Mathematics: JEAN-MICHEL MOREL
Physics: MIREILLE TADJEDINE
Chemistry: JEAN DELAIRE
Biology and Biochemistry: CHRISTIAN AUCLAIR
Civil Engineering: ALAIN COMBESCURE
Mechanical Engineering: JEAN-PIERRE PELLE
Industrial Design: Mme CLAIRE BRUNET
Economics and Business: BERTRAND MUNIER
Social Sciences: Mme CATHERINE PARADEISE
Foreign Languages: MICHEL PETIT

Ecole Normale Supérieure de Lyon: 46 allée d'Italie, 69364 Lyons Cedex 07; tel. 4-72-72-80-00; fax 4-72-72-80-80; e-mail webmaster@ens-lyon.fr; internet www.ens-lyon.fr; f. 1987; library: 48,400 vols, 830 periodicals; 225 teachers and researchers; 915 students; Dir BERNARD BIGOT; Sec.-Gen. FRANÇOISE GRANGER; Dean of Teaching Departments MARIE-CHRISTINE ARTRU; Librarian JACQUELINE DE CONDAPPA.

HEADS OF TEACHING DEPARTMENTS

Mathematics and Computer Science: JEAN-CLAUDE SIKORAV
Physics and Chemistry: PETER HOLDSWORTH
Life and Earth Sciences: VINCENT LAUDET

DIRECTORS OF RESEARCH LABORATORIES

Chemistry: P. SAUTET
Geology: Y. RICARD
Computing: J. M. MULLER
Biology: E. GILSON, J. L. DARLIX, C. DUMAS
Physics: S. CILIBERTO
Astrophysics: R. BACON
Mathematics: E. GRENIER

GEOGRAPHY

Ecole Nationale des Sciences Géographiques: 6 et 8 ave Blaise Pascal, Cité Descartes, Champs-sur-Marne, 77455 Marne-la-Vallée Cedex 2; tel. 1-64-15-30-01; fax 1-64-15-31-07; e-mail info@ensg.ign.fr; internet www.ensg.ign.fr; f. 1941; administered by Institut Géographique National; 30 teachers; 300 students, 2,000 trainees; library: specialized library of 36,000 books, 950,000 maps, 2,100,000 aerial photographs; Dir M. DENÈGRE.

PROFESSORS

BALABANE, M., Geometry, Mathematics
BEAUVILLAIN, E., Remote Sensing
BOTTON, S., Astronomy, Geodesy
BOUILLE, F., Programming
CHAPPART, G., Cartography
CHEDHOMME, J., Geomorphology
EGELS, Y., Photogrammetry
KASSER, M., Physics
LEAUTHAUD, J. M., Topography
MARMONIER, P., Geographical Information Systems
PELLE, S., Programming
SCHELSTRAETE, D., Photogrammetry
SILLARD, P., Numerical Analysis

HISTORY

Ecole Nationale des Chartes: 19 rue de la Sorbonne, 75005 Paris; tel. 1-55-42-75-00; fax 1-55-42-75-09; internet www.enc.sorbonne.fr; f. 1821, reorganized 1846; library: 150,000 vols; 170 students; Dir A. GUERREAU; Sec. J. BELMON; Chief Librarian I. DIU; publs *Bibliothèque de l'Ecole des Chartes*, *Mémoires et Documents*, *Matériaux pour l'Histoire*, *Etudes et Rencontres*, *Positions des thèses* (annually).

PROFESSORS

ARABEYRE, P., History of Law
BOURGAIN, P., Literary Manuscripts
CHARON, A., Bibliography and History of the Book
DELMAS, B., Modern Archival Sciences
GRIVEL, M., History of Art (16th–18th c.)
GUYOTJEANNIN, O., Diplomacy
LENIAUD, J. M., History of Art (since 19th c.)
NOYÉ, G., Archaeology
PARINET, E., History of Media (since 19th c.)
PLAGNIEUX, P., History of Art (Middle Ages)
PONCET, O., History of French Institutions
SMITH, M. H., Palaeography
VIELLIARD, F., Philology

Ecole Nationale du Patrimoine: 117 blvd St Germain, 75006 Paris; tel. 1-44-41-16-41; fax 1-44-41-16-76; f. 1990; trains curators of museums, archives and historical monuments; Dir JEAN-PIERRE BADY.

LANGUAGE AND LITERATURE

Institut National des Langues et Civilisations Orientales (INALCO): 2 rue de Lille, 75343 Paris Cedex 07; tel. 1-49-26-42-00; fax 1-49-26-42-99; e-mail secretariat.general@inalco.fr; internet www.inalco.fr; f. 1669; 228 teachers; 10,500 students; Pres. JACQUES LEGRAND; Sec.-Gen. JOSETTE LE CALVEZ.

DIRECTORS OF TEACHING AND RESEARCH DEPARTMENTS

Africa: JEAN-LUC VILLE
Central and Eastern Europe: CÉCILE ZERVUDACKI
China: FABIENNE MARC
Eurasia: HALKAWT ABDUL-HAKEM
Japan: EMMANUEL LOZERAND
Near and Middle East, North Africa: LUC DEHEUVELS
Russia: CHRISTINE BONNOT
South Asia: ANNIE MONTAUT
South-east and Northern Asia and the Pacific: JÉRÔME SAMUEL

Research centres:

Centre d'Etudes Balkaniques: INALCO, 73 rue Broca, 75013 Paris; tel. (1) 44-08-89-67; fax (1) 44-08-89-79; internet www.inalco.fr; Dir ODILE DANIEL.

Centre d'Etudes Chinoises: INALCO, 73 rue Broca, 75013 Paris; tel. (1) 44-08-89-72; fax (1) 44-08-89-79; internet www.inalco.fr; Dir ISABELLE RABOT.

Centre d'Etudes de l'Europe Médiane: INALCO, 104–106 quai de Clichy, 92110 Clichy-La Garenne; tel. 1-41-40-89-51; fax 1-41-40-89-21; Dir MARIA DE LA PERRIÈRE.

Centre d'Etudes Japonaises: INALCO, 73 rue Broca, 75013 Paris; tel. (1) 44-08-89-55; fax (1) 44-08-89-79; internet www.inalco.fr; Dir F. MACÉ.

Centre Georges Dumézil d'Etudes sur le Caucase: INALCO, 73 rue Broca, 75013 Paris Cedex 07; tel. (1) 44-08-89-57; fax (1) 44-08-89-79; internet www.inalco.fr; Dir ANAÏD DONABEDIAN.

Centre de Recherche Berbère: INALCO, 10 rue Riquet, 75019 Paris Cedex 07; tel. (1) 55-26-81-22; fax (1) 55-26-81-29; internet www.inalco.fr; Dir SALEM CHAKER.

Centre de Recherche sur l'Océan Indien Occidental: INALCO, 2 rue de Lille, 75343 Paris Cedex 07; tel. (1) 49-26-42-15; fax (1) 49-26-42-99; internet www.inalco.fr; Dir CLAUDE ALLIBERT.

Centre de Recherche sur l'Oralité: INALCO, 2 rue de Lille, 75343 Paris Cedex 07; tel. (1) 49-26-99-25; fax (1) 49-26-42-99; internet www.inalco.fr; Dir MICHÈLE THERRIEN.

Centre de Recherche Russe et Euro-Asiatique: INALCO, 104–106 quai de Clichy, 92110 Clichy-La Garenne; tel. 1-41-40-89-50; fax 1-41-40-89-21; Dir J. RADVANYI.

Cercle de Linguistique de L'INALCO: INALCO, 2 rue de Lille, 75343 Paris Cedex 07; tel. 1-49-26-42-31; fax 1-49-26-42-99; internet www.inalco.fr; Dir ANAÏD DONABEDIAN.

LIBRARIANSHIP

Ecole Nationale Supérieure des Sciences de l'Information et des Bibliothèques: 17/21 blvd du 11 Novembre 1918, 69623 Villeurbanne Cedex; tel. 4-72-44-43-07; fax 4-72-44-27-88; e-mail dupuigre@enssib.fr; f. 1963; 26 teachers; 300 students; library: 17,000 vols and 585 periodicals, also audio-visual items; Dir FRANÇOIS DUPUIGRENET DESROUSSILLES; publ. *Bulletin des Bibliothèques de France* (every 2 months).

MEDICINE

Ecole d'Application du Service de Santé des Armées: 1 place Alphonse Laveran, 75230 Paris Cedex 05; tel. 1-40-51-42-31; fax 1-40-51-47-74; f. 1850; mainly two-year graduate courses; library: 40,000 vols and 2,067 periodicals; Dir MGI DE SAINT-JULIEN; publ. *Médecine et Armées*.

Ecole Nationale de la Santé Publique: Ave du Professeur Léon Bernard, 35043 Rennes Cedex; tel. 2-99-02-22-00; fax 2-99-02-28-28; f. 1945; post-university courses; 60 full-time teachers; 500 full-time students; 4,000 part-time students; library: 15,000 vols; Dir PASCAL CHEVIT.

SCIENCES

Ecole Nationale de la Météorologie: 42 ave G. Coriolis, 31057 Toulouse Cedex 1; tel. 5-61-07-80-80; fax 5-61-07-96-30; e-mail enm.fr@meteo.fr; internet www.enm.meteo.fr; f. 1948; library: 4,000 vols; 35 teachers; 230 students; Dir JEAN-PIERRE CHALON.

Institut National des Sciences Appliquées de Lyon: 20 ave Albert Einstein, 69621 Villeurbanne Cedex; tel. 4-72-43-83-83; fax 4-72-43-85-00; e-mail dir@insa-lyon.fr; f. 1957; library: 80,000 vols; 450 teachers; 4,500 students; biochemistry, computer science, civil, electrical, energetics, production and mechanical engineering, material science; Dir JOËL ROCHAT.

Institut National des Sciences Appliquées de Rennes: 20 ave des Buttes de Coësmes, 35043 Rennes Cedex; f. 1961; physical and materials science, electronic engineering, civil engineering and town planning, computer science, communications systems, mechanical engineering and control; 130 teachers; 1,200 students; Dir DÉSIRÉ AMOROS.

Institut National des Sciences Appliquées de Rouen (INSA Rouen): Place Emile Blondel, BP 08, 76131 Mont-Saint-Aignan Cedex; tel. 2-35-52-83-00; fax 2-35-52-83-20; f. 1985; chemistry, mathematics, energy, mechanical engineering, technology and applied sciences; 109 teachers; 985 students; library: 15,000 vols, 200 periodicals; Dir Prof. GILBERT TOUZOT.

Muséum National d'Histoire Naturelle: 57 rue Cuvier, 75281 Paris Cedex 05; tel. 1-40-79-30-00; fax 1-40-79-34-84; internet www.mnhn.fr; f. 1635; teaching and research in natural history; administers the Zoological Garden, the Musée de l'Homme and several other natural history depts and institutions; Dir Prof. BERTRAND-PIERRE GALEY; Librarian MONIQUE DUCREUX.

PROFESSORS

BILLARD, R., Ichthyology
BLANDIN, P., Ecology
BODO, B., Applied Organic Chemistry
CAUSSANEL, C., Entomology
COINEAU, Y., Arthropods
COUDERC, H., Botany
COUTÉ, A., Cryptogamy
DEMENEIX, B., General and Comparative Physiology
DOUMENC, D., Biology of Marine Invertebrates and Malacology
DUBOIS, A., Zoology (Reptiles and Amphibians)
DUBOST, G., Conservation of Animal Species

DUPAIGNE, Ethnology
ERARD, C., Zoology
FABRIES, J., Mineralogy
GARESTIER, T., Biophysics
LANGANEY, A., Physical Anthropology
LEFEUVRE, J. C., Evolution of Natural Systems
LUMLEY, H. DE, Prehistory
MONNIER, Y., Ethnology-Biogeography
MORAT, P., Phanerogamy
REPERANT, J., Comparative Anatomy
REVAULT D'ALLONNES, M., Physical Oceanography
SANTUS, R., Photobiology
SCHREVEL, J., Parasitology
TAQUET, PH., Palaeontology
WEVER, P. DE, Geology

TECHNOLOGY

Conservatoire National des Arts et Métiers: 292 rue St Martin, 75141 Paris Cedex 03; tel. 1-40-27-20-00; f. 1794; 55 regional centres, diploma and doctorate courses; 470 teachers; 75,000 students (full- and part-time); library: see Libraries; Administrator LAURENCE PAYE-JEANNENEY

PROFESSORS

Department of Chemistry and Nuclear Science:
BOUCLY, P., Pharmaceutical Technology
CATONNE, J.-C., Industrial Electrochemistry
DELACROIX, A., Industrial Chemistry
DESCARSIN, M.-T., Industrial Electrochemistry
DESJEUX, J.-F., Applied Biology
DUCROCQ-BARDEZ, E., General Chemistry
FAUVARQUE, J.-F., Industrial Electrochemistry
FOOS, J., Isotopic Radiation and Applications
GUY, A., Applied Organic Chemistry
MORFIN, R., Biotechnology
NICOLAS, J., Industrial and Foodcrop Biochemistry
OLIVEROS, L., General Chemistry applied to Industry
VALEUR, B., General Chemistry applied to Industry

Department of Economics and Business Administration:
AIMETTI, J.-P., Business Strategy and Business Studies
BLOCH, J., Commercial Forecasting
BURLAUD, A., Management Accounting and Control
CANTAL-DUPART, M., Town Planning and Environment
CURIEN, N., Telecommunications Policy and Economics
DARMOIS-SCHMEDER, G., Economics of Technology and Innovation
DE KERVASDOUÉ, J., Health Services Economics and Management
DE MONTBRIAL, T., Applied Economic Analysis
DIDIER, M., Industrial Economics and Statistics
DREYFUS, B., Administration and Management of Local Collectives
EWALD, F., Insurance
GIGET, M., Economics of Technology and Innovation
GODET, M., Industrial Forecasting
GUILLERME, A., History of Technology
KLEIN, J., International Development of Business
LAFFOND, G., Economics and Industrial Statistics
LEBAN, R., Business Economics and Management
LECLERC, D., Finance and Accountancy
MARCHAN, D., Social Law
PETAUTON, P., Mathematical Theory of Insurance
PORTAIT, R., Financial Management of Business
REIGNÉ, P., Business Law
SCHEID, J. C., Finance and Accountancy
WISZNIAK, M., Mathematics of Business Dealing
ZIV, J.-C., Transport and Logistics

Department of Informatics:
ANCEAU, F., Principles of Informatics
ARNAUD, J.-P., Networks
AUTIN, A., Business Informatics
BERTHELOT, G., Business Informatics
BILLIONNET, A., Business Informatics
CABANES, A., Business Informatics
CARREZ, C., Business Informatics
CASTELLANI, X., Business Informatics
COSTA, M. H., Informatics
DEWEZ, L., Informatics, Programming
FACON, P., Business Informatics
FLORIN, G., Informatics, Programming
KAISER, C., Informatics, Programming
LEMAIRE, B., Operational Research
MAIQUES, L., Business Informatics
MEINADIER, J.-P., Systems Integration
NATKIN, S., Informatics, Programming
PRINTZ, J., Software Engineering
SCHOLL, M., Informatics, Programming
VIGUIE-DONZEAU-GOUGE, V., Informatics, Programming

Department of Mathematics:
DESTUYNDER, P., Scientific Calculus
HOCQUENGHEM, S., Applied Mathematics in Arts and Crafts
REINHARD, H., Mathematics in Engineering
SAPORTA, G., Applied Statistics
VELU, J., Applied Mathematics in Arts and Crafts

Department of Mechanical Engineering, Materials and Energetics:
BATHIAS, C., Metallurgy
BOURLES, H., Industrial Robotics
CHOMETON, F., Industrial Applications of Aerodynamics
COLOMBIE, P., Metallurgy
CORDEBOIS, J.-P., Mechanical Manufacturing
DEPREZ, D., Geological Engineering in Construction
JAUME, D., Industrial Robotics
KERN, F., Civil Engineering
LASSAU, G., Industrial Mechanics
LAVAUR, R., Civil Engineering
LEGER, D., Minerals
LEMASSON, P., Applied Physics in Industry
LUCAS, J., Heat Transfer in Industry
MEUNIER, F., Applied Physics in Cryogenics and Industrial Applications
OHAYON, R., Industrial Mechanics
PLUMELLE, C., Geological Engineering in Construction
PLUVIOSE, M., Turbomachinery
RENAUDAUX, J.-P., Mechanical Manufacturing
SURREL, Y., Instrumentation
VILLOUTREIX, G., Physical Chemistry and Applications of Macromolecular Materials
WOLFF, C., Physical Chemistry and Applications of Macromolecular Materials

Department of Physics and Electronics:
BELLANGER, M., Electronics
BONNET, J.-J., Applied Physics in Industry
CANIT, J.-C., Optics
CANRY, B., Industrial Robotics
FERNANDES, C., Physics of Electrical Components
FINO, B., Radiocommunications
GARCIA, A., Applied Accoustics
HIMBERT, M., Metrology
HINCELIN, G., Physics of Electrical Components
JOUHANEAU, J., Applied Acoustics
JUNCAR, P., Metrology
LATTUATTI, V., Industrial Robotics
LEPOUTRE, F., Physics of Captors and Measures
MANESSE, G., Electrotechnology
MISEREY, F., Physics of Electrical Components
RUMELHARD, C., Physics of Electrical Components
RIALLAND, J.-F., Electrotechnology
SOL, C., Electrotechnology
VIALLE, M., Applied Physics in Industry
VU THIEN, H., Signals and Systems

Department of Labour and Business Studies:
ADAM, G., Professional Relations
BARBIER, J. M., Training of Adults
CASPAR, P., Training of Adults
CLOT, Y., Psychology of Work
CUNY, X., Hygiene and Security
DEJOURS, C., Psychology of Work
FALZON, P., Ergonomics and Neurophysiology of Work
FARDEAU, M., Social integration of the Disabled
GERME, J. F., Human Resources Development
LE COADIC, Y., Scientific and Technological Information and Communication
MARCHAND, D., Labour Law and Social Security Law
PIOTET, F., Sociology of Work, Employment and Organizations
REYNAUD, J.-D., Sociology of Work and Professional Relations
ROUX-ROSSI, D., Labour Law and Social Security Law
SCHMITT, J.-P., Labour and Management Organization.

Attached institutes:

Institut d'Etudes Supérieures des Techniques d'Organisation: tel. 1-40-27-26-30; f. 1956; Dir M. SCHMITT.

Institut d'Informatique d'Entreprise: tel. 1-69-36-73-50; f. 1968; Dir M. CABANES.

Institut Français du Froid Industriel: tel. 1-40-27-27-20; Dir F. MEUNIER.

Institut National de Formation des Cadres Supérieurs de la Vente: tel. 1-40-27-27-21; f. 1956; Dir A. BLOCH.

Institut National des Techniques de la Documentation: tel. 1-40-27-26-73; f. 1950; Dir A. BOULOGNE.

Institut National des Techniques de la Mer: tel. 2-33-20-37-65; f. 1981; Dir J. C. GUARY.

Institut Scientifique et Technique de la Nutrition et de l'Alimentation: tel. 1-40-27-24-73; Dir S. HERCBERG.

Institut des Transports Internationaux et des Ports: tel. 2-35-19-58-17; f. 1980; Dir J.-C. ZIV.

Institut de la Construction et de l'Habitation: tel. 1-40-27-25-21; Dir J. CHAPUISAT.

Institut National des Techniques Economiques et Comptables: tel. 1-40-27-25-19; Dir J.-C. SCHEID.

Institut National d'Etude du Travail et d'Orientation Professionnelle: tel. 1-44-10-78-34; Dir J. GUICHARD.

Institut de Topométrie et Ecole Supérieure des Géomètres et Topographes: tel. 2-43-43-31-00; M. KASSER.

Centre d'Actualisation des Connaissances et de l'Etude des Matériaux Industriels: tel. 1-40-27-24-49; Dir C. WOLFF.

Ecole Nationale d'Assurances: tel. 1-44-63-58-47; Dir J. F. DE VULPILLIERES.

Centre pour la Maîtrise des Systèmes et du Logiciel: tel. 1-40-27-28-58; Dir J. PRINTZ.

Centre de Préparation au Diplôme d'Etat d'Audioprothésiste: tel. 1-53-01-80-51; Dir A. GARCIA.

Centre de Préparation de l'Ingénieur au Management: tel. 1-40-27-20-90; Dir R. LEBAN.

Centre de Recherche Technologie, Innovation et Société: tel. 1-40-27-24-73; Dir M. GIGET.

Institut National de Métrologie: tel. 1-40-27-21-55; Dir M. HIMBERT.

Institut Aérotechnique de St Cyr: tel. 1-30-45-00-09; Dir E. SZECHNYI.

Centre de Recherche sur les Marchés de Matières Premières: tel. 1-40-27-23-49; Dir J. KLEIN.

Centre de Documentation d'Histoire des Techniques: tel. 1-53-01-80-25; Dir A. GUILLERME.

Centre de Recherche et d'Expérimentation pour l'Enseignement des Mathématiques: tel. 1-40-27-22-94; Dir S. HOCQUENGHEM.

Centre de Sociologie du Travail et de l'Entreprise: tel. 1-40-27-26-46; Dir J.-M. BARBIER.

Centre de Formation de Formateurs de Branche: tel. 1-53-01-80-08; Dir L. VOLERY.

Institut de Technologie: tel. 1-53-01-80-21; Dir P. BOUCLY.

Ecole Supérieure de Conception et Production Industrielles: tel. 1-64-80-66-00; Dir J. P. CORDEBOIS.

Institut d'Hygiène Industrielle et de l'Environnement: tel. 1-40-27-25-65; Dir X. CUNY.

Ecole Centrale de Lille: Cité Scientifique, BP 48, 59651 Villeneuve d'Ascq Cedex; tel. 3-20-33-53-53; fax 3-20-33-54-99; internet www.ec-lille.fr; f. 1872; 7 research laboratories; library: 10,000 vols; 82 teachers; 1,040 students; Dir Prof. JEAN-CLAUDE GENTINA.

Ecole Centrale des Arts et Manufactures: Grande Voie des Vignes, 92295 Châtenay-Malabry Cedex; tel. 1-41-13-10-00; fax 1-41-13-10-10; e-mail webmaster@ads.ecp.fr; internet www.ecp.fr; f. 1829; higher degrees in multiple disciplines of engineering; library: 60,000 vols and 340 periodicals; 1,400 students; Dir HERVÉ BIAUSSER; publ. *Centraliens* (monthly).

Ecole des Mines de Douai: 941 rue Charles Bourseul, BP 838, 59508 Douai Cedex; tel. 3-27-71-22-22; fax 3-27-71-25-25; f. 1878; library: 15,000 vols; 250 teachers; 650 students; Dir PIERRE FRANCK CHEVET.

Ecole Nationale de l'Aviation Civile: BP 4005, 31055 Toulouse Cedex 4; tel. 5-62-17-40-00; fax 5-62-17-40-23; f. 1948; training of civil aviation personnel; advanced studies in engineering; library: 30,000 vols; 408 teachers and researchers; Dir M. SOUCHELEAU.

Ecole Nationale d'Ingénieurs de Metz (ENIM): Ile du Saulcy, 57045 Metz Cedex 1; tel. 3-87-34-69-03; fax 3-87-34-69-35; e-mail padilla@enim.fr; f. 1962; 1,000 students; Dir PIERRE PADILLA.

Ecole Nationale d'Ingénieurs de Tarbes (ENIT): 47 ave d'Azereix, BP 1629, 65016 Tarbes Cedex; tel. 5-62-44-27-00; fax 5-62-44-27-27; e-mail mugniery@enit.fr; f. 1963; mechanical, industrial and production engineering; 60 teachers; 850 students; library: 4,000 vols; Dir BERNARD MUGNIERY.

Ecole Nationale de la Photographie: 16 rue des Arènes, BP 149, 13631 Arles Cedex; tel. 4-90-99-33-33; fax 4-90-99-33-59; e-mail communication@enp-arles.com; internet www.enp-arles.com; f. 1982; under auspices of Ministry of Culture; 3-year course; 7 teachers; 75 students; library: 10,000 vols; Dir ALAIN LELOUP.

Ecole Nationale des Ponts et Chaussées: 6–8 ave Blaise Pascal, Cité Descartes, Champs-sur-Marne, 77455 Marne-la-Vallée Cedex 2; tel. 1-64-15-30-30; internet www.enpc.fr; f. 1747; civil and mechanical engineering, town and country planning, transport; library: 85,000 vols, 2,500 periodicals, 37,000 18th c. MSS, 900 maps, 30,000 photographs; 300 teachers; 1,300 students; Dir PHILIPPE CORTIER; Dep. Dir ALAIN NEVEU.

Ecole Nationale des Travaux Publics de l'Etat: Rue Maurice Audin, 69518 Vaulx en Velin Cedex; tel. 4-72-04-70-70; fax 4-72-04-62-54; e-mail webmaster@entpe.fr; internet www.entpe.fr; f. 1953 in Paris, moved 1975; 700 teachers (100 full-time, 600 part-time); 600 students; library: 14,000 vols; Dir PHILIPPE DHÉNEIN.

Ecole Nationale du Génie de l'Eau et de l'Environnement de Strasbourg: 1 quai Koch, BP 1039F, 67070 Strasbourg Cedex; tel. 3-88-24-82-82; fax 3-88-37-04-97; e-mail engees@engees.u-strasbg.fr; internet www-engees.u-strasbg.fr; f. 1960; 164 teachers (14 full-time, 150 part-time); 242 students; Dir D. LOUDIÈRE.

Ecole Nationale Supérieure de l'Aéronautique et de l'Espace: BP 4032, 31055 Toulouse Cedex 4; tel. 5-62-17-80-30; fax 5-62-17-83-33; e-mail panier@supaero.fr; f. 1909; 700 students; library: 15,000 vols; Dir J. KERBRAT.

Ecole Nationale Supérieure d'Electronique, Informatique et Radiocommunications de Bordeaux (ENSEIRB): 1 ave du Dr Albert Schweitzer, BP 99, 33402 Talence Cedex; tel. 5-56-84-65-00; fax 5-56-37-20-23; e-mail com@enseirb.fr; internet www.enseirb.fr; f. 1920; affiliated with Univ. Bordeaux I; 62 teachers; 716 students; Dir RICHARD CASTANET.

Ecole Nationale Supérieure de Chimie et de Physique de Bordeaux (ENSCPB): 16 Ave Pey Berland, 33607 Pessac Cedex; tel. 5-40-00-65-65; fax 5-40-00-66-33; e-mail admin@enscpb.fr; internet www.enscpb.fr; f. 1891; affiliated with Université de Bordeaux I; 400 students; Dir BERNARD CLIN.

Ecole Nationale Supérieure des Arts et Industries Textiles (ENSAIT): 9 rue de l'Ermitage, BP 30329, 59056 Roubaix Cedex 01; tel. 3-20-25-64-64; fax 3-20-24-84-06; e-mail jean-marie.castelain@ensait.fr; internet www.ensait.fr; f. 1883; library: 4,000 vols, 70 periodicals; 50 teachers; 210 students; Dir JEAN-MARIE CASTELAIN.

Ecole Nationale Supérieure des Arts et Industries de Strasbourg: 24 blvd de la Victoire, 67084 Strasbourg Cedex; tel. 3-88-14-47-00; f. 1875; 5-year diploma courses in mechanical, electrical, civil, building services and energetics, land surveying, polymer and composite materials, mecatronics and architecture; 948 students; Dir A. COLSON.

Ecole Nationale Supérieure d'Arts et Métiers: 8 blvd Louis XIV, 59046 Lille Cedex; tel. 3-20-62-22-10; fax 3-20-53-55-93; university-level courses with emphasis on mechanical engineering; f. 1881; 340 students; Dir Prof. J.-P. FRACHET; Librarian MICHÈLE DECORTE.

Ecole Nationale Supérieure d'Arts et Métiers (ENSAM): 151 blvd de l'Hôpital, 75013 Paris; tel. 1-44-24-62-99; fax 1-44-24-63-26; f. 1780; mechanical, computer, engineering and industrial sciences; 3,500 students; library: 20,000 vols; Dir-Gen. GUY GAUTHERIN; Librarian C. OLLENDORF.

Ecole Nationale Supérieure d'Ingénieurs de Constructions Aéronautiques: 1 place Emile Blouin, 31056 Toulouse Cedex 5; tel. 5-61-61-85-00; fax 5-61-61-85-85; e-mail mcastel@ensica.fr; f. 1946; aeronautics and space; library: 10,000 vols; 410 students; Dir JEAN-LOUIS FRESON.

Ecole Nationale Supérieure de Céramique Industrielle: 47–73 ave Albert Thomas, 87065 Limoges Cedex; tel. 5-55-45-22-22; fax 5-55-79-09-98; e-mail direction@ensci.fr; internet www.ensci.fr; f. 1893; library: 4,000 vols; 25 teachers; 150 students; Dir CHRISTIAN GAULT; publ. *Annuaire*.

Ecole Nationale Supérieure de l'Electronique et de ses Applications (ENSEA): 6 ave du Ponceau, 95014 Cergy Pontoise Cedex; tel. 1-30-73-66-66; fax 1-30-73-66-67; e-mail directeur@ensea.fr; internet www.ensea.fr; f. 1952; postgraduate courses in electrical engineering, computing and telecommunications; library: 6,000 vols, 150 periodicals; 80 teachers and researchers; 650 students; Dir PIERRE POUVIL.

Ecole Nationale Supérieure de Mécanique: see under University of Nantes.

Ecole Nationale Supérieure de Meunerie et des Industries Céréalières (ENSMIC): 16 rue Nicolas-Fortin, 75013 Paris; tel. 1-44-23-23-44; fax 1-45-85-50-27; f. 1924; courses in milling, baking, cereal food industry and feed technology; 260 students; affiliated with UPMC-Univ. Paris VI (training of engineers); Dir CHRISTIANE MAZEL; publs *Industries des Céréales* (every 2 months), *Les Journées de l'ENSMIC* (annually).

Ecole Nationale Supérieure des Mines de Paris: 60 blvd St Michel, 75272 Paris Cedex 06; tel. 1-40-51-90-00; fax 1-43-25-94-95; e-mail webmaster@paris.ensmp.fr; internet www.ensmp.fr; f. 1783; library: 500,000 vols and 2,500 periodicals; 290 teachers; 1,100 students; Pres. D. RANQUE; Dir B. LEGAIT; Sec.-Gen. PHILIPPE TOGNAZZONI; Librarian MASSON; publ. *Rapport* (annually).

Ecole Nationale Supérieure des Mines de Saint-Etienne: 158 cours Fauriel, 42023 Saint-Etienne Cedex 2; tel. 4-77-42-01-23; fax 4-77-42-00-00; e-mail tor@emse.fr; internet www.emse.fr; f. 1816; chemical process engineering, computer science, materials science, international project management, environmental science; library: 10,000 vols; 250 teachers and researchers; 600 students; Dir M. HIRTZMAN.

Ecole Nationale Supérieure du Pétrole et des Moteurs: 228–232 ave Napoléon Bonaparte, 92852 Rueil-Malmaison Cedex; tel. 1-47-52-64-57; fax 1-47-52-67-65; e-mail info-ifpschool@ifp.fr; internet www.ifp-school.com; f. 1954; 400 students; five centres: geological or geophysical exploration; petroleum engineering and project management; refining, petrochemicals, gas; internal combustion engines; economics and management; Dir J. L. KARNIK.

Ecole Nationale Supérieure de Techniques Avancées: 32 blvd Victor, 75015 Paris; tel. 1-45-52-44-08; fax 1-45-52-55-87; e-mail hoffmann@ensta.fr; internet www.ensta.fr; f. 1741, refounded 1970; systems engineering, naval architecture, oceanology, mechanics, nuclear techniques, chemical engineering, electronics, information technology; 3-year curriculum; 78 permanent teachers, 800 visiting; 170 students a year; undergraduate and postgraduate studies; library: 10,000 vols; Dir H. PASTEAU.

Ecole Nationale Supérieure des Télécommunications: 46 rue Barrault, 75634 Paris Cedex 13; tel. 1-45-81-77-77; fax 1-45-

89-79-06; f. 1878; attached to France Telecom; Dir JEAN HERR.

Ecole Nationale Supérieure des Télécommunications de Bretagne: BP 832, 29285 Brest Cedex; tel. 2-98-00-11-11; fax 2-98-45-51-33; f. 1977; attached to Ministry of Technology, Information and Posts; 108 full-time teachers; 764 students (207 postgraduate); Dir BERNARD AYRAULT.

Ecole Polytechnique: 91128 Palaiseau Cedex; tel. 1-69-33-47-36; f. 1794; 362 teachers; 859 students; library: 300,000 vols; Dir-Gen. JEAN NOVACQ; Librarian MADELEINE DE FUENTES.

Ecole Supérieure de Physique et de Chimie Industrielles de la Ville de Paris: 10 rue Vauquelin, 75005 Paris; tel. 1-40-79-44-00; fax 1-40-79-44-25; internet www.espci.fr; f. 1882; training of research engineers; 20 research laboratories; library: 5,000 vols; 65 teachers; 300 students; Dir JACQUES PROST.

Institut des Hautes Études Scientifiques: 35 route de Chartres, 91440 Bures-sur-Yvette; tel. 1-60-92-66-00; f. 1958; advanced research in mathematics, theoretical physics; library: 4,000 vols, 125 periodicals; Dir J.-P. BOURGUIGNON; publ. *Publications Mathématiques* (2 a year).

Institut National des Télécommunications: 9 rue Charles Fourier, 91011 Evry Cedex; tel. 1-60-76-40-40; fax 1-60-76-43-25; f. 1979; attached to Ministry of Finance, Industry and the Economy; mem. of Conférence des Grandes Ecoles; engineering and business schools; 150 full-time teachers; 1,000 students; Dir MICHEL LARTAIL.

ISMCM-CESTI Paris: 3 rue Fernand Hainaut, 93407 St Ouen Cedex; tel. 1-49-45-29-00; fax 1-49-45-29-91; f. 1948; 400 students; library: 3,000 vols; Dir HENRI VEYSSEYRE; publ. *La Lettre de l'ISMCM-CESTI* (2 a year).

CESTI-Toulon: Maison des Technologies, Place Georges Pompidou, Quartier Mayol, 83000 Toulon; tel. 4-94-03-88-00; fax 4-9403-88-04; e-mail information@toulon.ismcm-cesti.fr; internet www.toulon.ismcm-cesti.fr; f. 1994; training of engineers, applied research in automation and industrial engineering; 30 teachers; 150 students; Dir JEAN-MARC FAURE.

Catholic Colleges and Institutes

INSTITUT CATHOLIQUE DE PARIS

21 rue d'Assas, 75270 Paris Cedex 06
Telephone: 1-44-39-52-00
Fax: 1-45-44-27-14
E-mail: contact@icp.fr
Internet: www.icp.fr
Founded 1875
Academic year: October to June
Chancellor: Mgr ANDRÉ VINGT-TROIS
Rector: JOSEPH MAÏLA
Vice-Rector: Sr GENEVIÈVE MEDEVIELLE
General Secretary: FRANÇOIS ARDONCEAU
Director of Communication: FRANÇOISE GARDERE-CREAC'H
Librarian: ODILE DUPONT
Library: see Libraries
Number of teaching staff: 847, including 96 professors
Number of students: 15,000 (excluding affiliated schools)
Publications: *Transversalités: Revue de l'Institut Catholique de Paris* (quarterly), *Guide des Études* (annually)

DEANS AND DIRECTORS

Faculty of Canon Law: Père JEAN-PAUL DURAND
Faculty of Letters: NATHALIE NABERT
Faculty of Philosophy: Abbé P. CAPELLE
Faculty of Theology: Abbé HENRI-JÉRÔME GAGEY
Higher Institute of Ecumenical Studies: Abbé YVES-MARIE BLANCHARD
Higher Institute of Liturgy: Frère PATRICK PRÉTOT
Higher Institute of Pastoral Catechetics and University Extension: DENIS VILLEPELET
Higher Institute of Pedagogy: FRANÇOISE CHEBAUX
Institute for French Language and Culture and University Summer School: MURIEL CORDIER
Institute of Music and Liturgical Music: E. BELLANGER
Institute of Sacred Art: GENEVIÈVE HEBERT
Institute of Science and Theology of Religions: R. P. PAUL COULON
Institute of Social Sciences and Economics: JOSEPH MAÏLA
Biblical and Systematic Theology: Abbé JESUS ASURMENDI
Doctoral Studies: P. HERVÉ LEGRAND
School of Ancient Oriental Languages: FLORENCE MALBRAN-LABAT
University for Retired People: Dir: J. MENU

AFFILIATED SCHOOLS AND INSTITUTES

Ecole de Formation Psycho-Pédagogique: Paris; Dir M. C. DAVID.

Ecole de Bibliothécaires-Documentalistes: Paris; Dir D. VIGNAUD.

Institut Supérieur d'Interprétation et de Traduction: Paris; Dir M. MERIAUD.

Ecole Supérieure des Sciences Economiques et Commerciales: 95000 Cergy; Dir P. TAPIE.

Ecole de Psychologues-Praticiens: Paris; Dir J. P. CHARTIER.

Institut Supérieur d'Electronique de Paris: Dir M. CIAZYNSKI.

Centre de Formation Pédagogique Emmanuel Mounier: 78A rue de Sèvres, 75341 Paris Cedex 07; Dir R. MOREAU.

Institut Polytechnique Saint-Louis: 95000 Cergy.

Constituent schools:

- **Ecole de Biologie Industrielle:** 95000 Cergy; Dir F. DUFOUR.
- **Institut d'Agro-Développement International:** 95000 Cergy; Dir S. LAMY.
- **Ecole d'Electricité, de Production et des Méthodes Industrielles:** 95000 Cergy; Dir M. DARCHERIF.

Ecole Supérieure de Chimie Organique et Minérale: 95000 Cergy; Dir G. SANTINI.

Institut Géologique Albert-de-Lapparent: 95000 Cergy; Dir C. CHOMAT.

Institut Supérieur Agricole de Beauvais: Rue Pierre Waguet, 60000 Beauvais and 95000 Cergy; f. 1855; Dir M. P. CHOQUET.

Institut Libre d'Education Physique Supérieure: 95000 Cergy; Dir F. HELAINE.

UNIVERSITÉ CATHOLIQUE DE LILLE

60 blvd Vauban, BP 109, 59016 Lille Cedex
Telephone: 3-20-13-40-00
Fax: 3-20-13-40-01
Internet: www.etud.fupl.asso.fr
Founded 1875 as Faculty of Law, became university institution in 1877
Private (Roman Catholic) control
Rector: M. VANDECANDELAERE
Vice-Rector: Abbé J. BOULANGE
Administrative Officer: M. LABEY
Librarian: J.-CH. DESQUIENS
Library: nearly 500,000 volumes
Number of teachers: 1,300
Number of students: 15,000
Publications: *Mémoires et Travaux, Mélanges de Science Religieuse* (3 a year), *Vues d'ensemble, Encyclopédie Catholicisme, Repères, La Lettre de la Catho, Catho Actualités, Vie et Foi*

DEANS

Faculty of Theology: J. L. BLAQUART
Faculty of Economic Sciences: P. N'GAHANE
Faculty of Medicine: A. DUTOIT
Faculty of Letters and Human Sciences: J. HEUCLIN
Faculty of Science: B. MILHAU
Faculty of Law: H. LEFÈVRE

FEDERATED INSTITUTES

Ecole des Hautes Etudes Industrielles (HEI): 13 rue de Toul, 59046 Lille Cedex; tel. 3-28-38-48-58; f. 1885; civil engineering, chemistry and electrical engineering; 1,180 students; Dir M. VITTU.

Ecole Supérieure des Techniques Industrielles et des Textiles (ESTIT): GAFIT, 52 Allée Lakanal, BP 209, 59654 Villeneuve d'Ascq Cedex; tel. 3-20-79-90-10; f. 1895; textile, engineering; 260 students; Dir B. AVRIN.

Institut Supérieur d'Agriculture (ISA): 41 rue du Port, 59046 Lille Cedex; tel. 3-28-38-48-48; f. 1963; agricultural, agro-engineering; five-year course; 525 students; Dir P. CODRON.

Institut Supérieur d'Electronique du Nord (ISEN): 41 blvd Vauban, 59046 Lille Cedex; tel. 3-20-30-40-50; f. 1956; electronics engineering; 65 teachers; 554 students; Dir-Gen. PAUL ASTIER; Dir J. N. DECARPIGNY.

Institut Catholique d'Arts et Métiers (ICAM): 6 rue Auber, 59046 Lille Cedex; tel. 3-20-22-61-61; f. 1898; 490 students; Dir-Gen. G. CARPIER; Dir J. G. PRIEUR.

Institut Supérieur de Technologie du Nord (ISTN): 65 rue Roland, 59000 Lille; tel. 3-20-22-36-00; f. 1990; 177 students; Dir J. L. BIGOTTE.

IEFSI L'Ingénieur – Manager (Institut d'Economie, d'Entreprise et de Formation Sociale pour Ingénieurs): 41 rue du Port, 59000 Lille; tel. 3-20-15-44-87; f. 1962; 51 students; Dir P. RENSY.

Ecole de Hautes Etudes Commerciales du Nord (EDHEC): 58 rue du Port, 59046 Lille Cedex; tel. 3-20-15-45-00; f. 1920; 1,400 students; Dirs-Gén. O. OGER, J.-L. TURRIÈRE;.

Branch:

- **EDHEC Nice:** 393 Promenade des Anglais, BP 116, 06202 Nice Cedex; tel. 4-93-18-99-66; 400 students.

Institut d'Economie Scientifique et de Gestion (IESEG): 3 rue de la Digue, 59800 Lille; tel. 3-20-54-58-92; f. 1964; 510 students; Dir J. P. AMMEUX.

Centre de Recherches Economiques, Sociologiques et de Gestion (CRESGE): 1 rue Norbert Segard, 59000 Lille; tel. 3-20-13-40-60; f. 1964; Dir J.-CL. SAILLY.

Conseils et Recherches en Economie Agricole et Agro-alimentaire (CREA): 1 rue Norbert Segard, 59046 Lille; tel. 3-20-78-26-95; f. 1981; Dir (vacant).

Institut d'Expertise Comptable (IEC): 60 blvd Vauban, BP 109, 59016 Lille Cedex; tel. 3-20-54-86-44; 550 students; Dir P. POUJOL.

Ecole Supérieure de Traducteurs, Interprètes, et de Cadres du Commerce Extérieur (ESTICE): 60 blvd Vauban, BP

109, 59016 Lille Cedex; tel. 3-20-54-90-90; f. 1961; 100 students; Dir H. AMIOT CHANAL.

Institut Social Lille-Vauban (ISLV): 83 blvd Vauban, BP 12, 59004 Lille Cedex; tel. 3-20-21-93-93; f. 1932; 267 students; Dir E. PRIEUR.

Ecole de Formation d'Animateurs Sociaux (EFAS): 105 rue d'Artois, 59800 Lille; tel. 3-20-58-15-40; f. 1973; 193 students; Dir DIDIER LESAFFRE.

Ecole de Professeurs (EDP): 60 blvd Vauban, BP 109, 59016 Lille Cedex; tel. 3-20-13-41-20; f. 1962; 500 students; Dir L. DE BACKER.

Institut des Stratégies et Techniques de Communication (ISTC): 67 blvd Vauban, 59800 Lille; tel. 3-20-54-32-32; f. 1991; 62 students; Dir CLAUDE DOGNIN.

Institut de Formation en Soins Infirmiers (IFSI) et Ecole de Puéricultrices: 70 rue du Port, 59000 Lille; tel. 3-20-57-89-54; f. 1927; 424 students; Dir BERNADETTE MIROUX.

Ecole de Sages-Femmes (ESF): 115 rue du Grand But, 59160 Lomme; tel. 3-20-93-74-00; f. 1882; 61 students; Dirs M. DELCROIX, CHRISTIANE ROUX.

Institut de Formation en Kinésithérapie, Pédicurie et Podologie: 10 rue J. B. de la Salle, 59000 Lille; tel. 3-20-92-06-99; f. 1964; 325 students; Dirs M. PAPAREMBORDE, D. VENNIN.

Lycée Technologique OZANAM: 50 rue Saint Gabriel, 59000 Lille; tel. 3-20-21-96-50; 375 students; Dir R. LEHAMIEU.

Institut de Communication Médicale: 56 rue du Port, 59046 Lille Cedex; tel. 3-20-13-41-80; f. 1988; 59 students; Dir MARC DENEUCHE.

Lycée privé Notre-Dame de Grâce: Quai des Nerviens, BP 127, 59602 Maubeuge Cedex; tel. 3-27-53-00-66; 100 students; Dir JEAN-PIERRE LAMQUET.

Lycée privé commercial 'De la Salle': 2 rue Jean Le Vasseur, 59046 Lille Cedex; tel. 3-20-93-50-11; 251 students; Dir JEAN-LOUIS CARON.

Lycée privé Saint-Joseph: 26 route de Calais, 62200 Saint-Martin-lez-Boulogne; tel. 3-21-99-06-99; 307 students; Dir MICHEL DUFAY.

Ecole Supérieure de Management et l'Entreprise (ESPEME): 23 rue Delphin Petit, 59046 Lille Cedex; tel. 3-20-15-45-00; f. 1988; 420 students; Dir CHARLES TONDEUR..

Branch:

ESPEME Nice: 393 Promenade des Anglais, BP 116, 06202 Nice Cedex; tel. 4-93-18-99-66; 173 students; Dir BERNARD BOTTERO.

Ecole Supérieure Privée d'Application des Sciences (ESPAS): 83 blvd Vauban, 59800 Lille; tel. 3-20-57-58-71; f. 1988; 120 students; Dir O. TRANCHANT.

Institut de Formation d'Animateurs de Catéchèse pour Adultes (IFAC): 60 blvd Vauban, 59016 Lille Cedex; tel. 3-20-57-69-33; f. 1980; 25 students; Dir JACQUES BERNARD.

Institut Pratique d'Etudes Religieuses (IPER): 60 blvd Vauban, 59016 Lille Cedex; tel. 3-20-78-26-78; f. 1951; 100 students; Dir MARIE-HÉLÈNE LAVIANNE.

INSTITUT CATHOLIQUE DE TOULOUSE

31 rue de la Fonderie, BP 7012, 31068 Toulouse Cedex 7

Telephone: 5-61-36-81-00

Fax: 5-61-36-81-08

E-mail: documentation@ict-toulouse.asso.fr

Internet: www.ict-toulouse.asso.fr

Founded 1877 and administered by a Council of Bishops of the region

Academic year: October to June

Chancellor: HE Mgr EMILE MARCUS (Archbishop of Toulouse)

Rector: PÈRE PIERRE DEBERGÉ

Registrar: MONIQUE DELCROIX

Librarian (vacant)

Library: Library of over 250,000 vols

Number of teachers: 238

Number of students: 6,334

Publications: *Bulletin de Littérature ecclésiastique* (4 a year), *Revue Purpan* (4 a year)

DEANS

Faculty of Canon Law: P. DAVID

Faculty of Letters: B. BILLEREY

Faculty of Philosophy: M. HUBERT

Faculty of Theology: P. SOMME

INSTITUT DE SCIENCES ET THÉOLOGIE DES RELIGIONS

11 Impasse Flammarion, 13001 Marseilles

Telephone: 4-91-50-35-50

Fax: 4-91-50-35-55

E-mail: secretariat@istr-marseille.cef.fr

Internet: cathomed.cef.fr

Founded 1991 by the Diocese of Marseilles

Rector: CHRISTIAN SALENSON

Library of 500 vols

Number of teachers: 30

Number of students: 250

Publication: *Chemins de Dialogue* (every 2 years).

UNIVERSITÉ CATHOLIQUE DE L'OUEST

3 place André Leroy, BP 808, 49008 Angers Cedex 01

Telephone: 2-41-81-67-55

Fax: 2-41-81-66-45

E-mail: relint@uco.fr

Internet: www.uco.fr

Founded 1875, under the patronage of the Bishops of the western region of France

Academic year: September to June

Rector: Dr ROBERT ROUDDEAU

Vice-Rectors: LUC PASQUIER PATRICK GILLET

Secretary-General: BERNARD FLOURIOT

Librarian: Y. LE GALL

Library of 200,000 vols and periodicals

Number of students: 12,500

Publications: *Annuaire*, *Impacts* (quarterly)

DEANS

Faculty of Theology: LOUIS MICHEL RENIER

Teacher Training Institute: R. MARTIN

Modern Languages Institute: D. STAQUET

Institute of Applied Psychology and Sociology: PATRICK MARTIN

Applied Mathematics Institute: J. M. MARION

Basic and Applied Research Institute: J. P. BOUTINET

Literature and History Institute: B. HAM

Education and Communication Institute: CATHERINE NAFTI-MALHERBE

International Centre for French Studies (for Foreign Students): MARC RELIN

Applied Ecology Institute: P. GILLET

AFFILIATED SCHOOLS

Ecole Supérieure d'Electronique de l'Ouest: 4 rue Merlet de la Boulaye, 49000 Angers; f. 1956; Dir M. V. HAMON.

Ecole Supérieure des Sciences Commerciales d'Angers: 1 rue Lakanal, 49000 Angers; Dir M. POTE.

Ecole Technique Supérieure de Chimie de l'Ouest: 50 rue Michelet, 49000 Angers; Dir B. DAVID.

Institut Supérieur d'Action Internationale et de Production: 18 rue du 8 Mai 1945, 49124 St Barthélemy; Dir J. Y. BIGNONET.

Institut de Formation et de Recherche pour les Acteurs du Développement et de l'Entreprise: 1 place A. Leroy, 49008 Angers Cedex 01; Dir FASICURE LEBLOND.

Institut Supérieur des Métiers: 91 rue Haute Follio, 53000 Laval; Dir EMMANUEL ROUSSEAU.

Maison de L'Initiative: Campus de la Tour, d'Auvergne, 37 rue du Maréchal Foch, 22204 Guingamp Cedex; Dir C. NAFTI-MALHERBE.

Université Catholique de l'Ouest Bretagne Nord: Campus de la Tour, d'Auvergne, 37 rue du Maréchal Foch, 22204 Guingamp Cedex; Dir MICHEL DORVEAUX.

Université Catholique de l'Ouest Bretagne Sud: Le Vincin, BP 17, 56610 Arradon; Dir SYLVIE MURZEAU.

UNIVERSITÉ CATHOLIQUE DE LYON

25 rue du Plat, 69288 Lyons Cedex 02

Telephone: 4-72-32-50-12

Fax: 4-72-32-50-19

Internet: www.univ-catholyon.fr

Founded 1875

Rector: MICHEL QUESNEL

Vice-Rector: DENISE LE LOUP

Secretary-General: PATRICK BORDET

Librarian: Mlle BEHR

Library of 240,000 vols

Number of teachers: 300

Number of students: 7,422

Publications: *Bulletin*, *Cahiers*

DEANS

Faculty of Theology: JEAN-PIERRE LEMONON

Faculty of Philosophy: PIERRE GIRE

Faculty of Science: J. M. EXBRAYAT

Faculty of Letters: HENRI BRENDERS

Faculty of Law: PASCALE BOUCAUD

Independent Institutes

GENERAL

American University of Paris: 31 ave Bosquet, 75007 Paris; tel. 1-40-62-06-00; fax 1-47-05-34-32; e-mail admissions@aup.edu; internet www.aup.edu; f. 1962; language of instruction: English; mem. of Middle States Asscn of Colleges and Schools; 4-year arts and sciences undergraduate courses; two summer sessions; adult education programmes; large computer science laboratory; technical writing programme; library: over 100,000 vols; 100 teachers; 800 students; Pres. Dr MICHAEL K. SIMPSON.

Schiller International University – France:

(For general information, see entry for Schiller International University in Germany chapter)

Campuses:

Schiller International University – Paris Campus: 32 blvd de Vaugirard, 75015 Paris; tel. 1-45-38-56-01; fax 1-45-38-54-30; e-mail info-schiller@schillerparis.com; internet www.paris-schiller.com; Dir SOUHA AKIKI.

Schiller International University – Strasbourg Campus: Château du Pourtalès, 161 rue Mélanie, 67000 Strasbourg; tel. 3-88-45-84-64; fax 3-88-45-84-60; e-mail BlasiusH@aol.com; internet www.schillerstrasbourg.com.

AGRICULTURE

Ecole Supérieure d'Agriculture: 55 rue Rabelais, BP 748, 49007 Angers Cedex 1; tel. 2-41-23-55-55; fax 2-41-23-55-00; f. 1898; library: 45,000 vols, 520 periodicals; 600 students; Dir AYMARD HONORÉ; publs *Cahiers Agriscope* (3 a year), *Bibliographie Agricole et Rurale* (5 a year).

Ecole Supérieure d'Agriculture de Purpan: 75 voie du Toec, 31076 Toulouse Cedex 3; tel. 5-61-15-30-30; fax 5-61-15-30-00; e-mail malummer@esa_purpan.fr; internet www.esa_purpan.fr; f. 1919; 5-year diploma course; master's degrees in agriculture, management and technology in the food industry, agricultural economics and management, environment and regional development; library: 20,000 vols, 1,100 periodicals; 100 teachers (37 full-time); 700 students; Dir MICHEL ROUX; publ. *Purpan* (quarterly).

Ecole Supérieure d'Ingénieurs et de Techniciens pour l'Agriculture: BP 607, 27106 Val de Reuil Cedex; tel. 2-32-59-14-59; fax 2-32-59-87-32; f. 1919; 5-year diploma courses for agricultural engineers; Dir P. DENIEUL.

COMMERCE, BUSINESS ADMINISTRATION AND STATISTICS

Centre Européen d'Education Permanente (CEDEP) (European Centre for Executive Development): Blvd de Constance, 77305 Fontainebleau Cedex; f. 1971; management development courses in business administration for member companies (6 French, 2 Danish, 3 British, 1 Swedish, 2 Belgian, 1 Indian, 2 Dutch, 5 European); associated with the Institut Européen d'Administration des Affaires; Gen. Dir MITCHELL KOZA.

Ecole de Management de Normandie: 30 rue de Richelieu, 76087 Le Havre Cedex; tel. 2-32-92-59-99; e-mail info@ecole-management-normandie.fr; internet www.ecole-management-normandie.fr; f. 1871; campuses in Caen, Cherbourg and Deauville; courses in business administration, tourism and leisure management; library: 37,050 vols, 39 databases; 37 ; 1,302 ; Dir Gen. JEAN GUY BERNARD.

Ecole du Chef d'Entreprise (ECE): 24–26 rue Hamelin, 75116 Paris; f. 1944; business administration; 50 teachers; Pres. M. Y. CHOTARD; Dir C. GOURDAIN; Sec.-Gen. Mlle M. JANNOR.

Ecole Nouvelle d'Organisation Economique et Sociale (ENOES): 62 rue de Miromesnil, 75008 Paris; tel. 1-45-62-87-60; fax 1-45-63-55-44; f. 1937; courses in transport and logistics, business administration and accountancy; Pres. MICHEL FRYBOURG; Gen. Sec. MICHEL OHAYON.

Ecole Supérieure d'Economie, d'Art et de Communication – Groupe E.A.C.: 13 rue de la Grange Batelière, 75009 Paris; tel. 1-47-70-23-83; fax 1-47-70-17-83; f. 1987; library: 500 vols; 70 teachers; 350 students; Dir CLAUDE VIVIER.

Ecole Supérieure de Commerce de Lille: Ave Willy Brandt, 59777 Euralille; tel. 3-20-21-59-62; fax 3-20-21-59-59; f. 1892; library: 3,700 vols, 270 periodicals; 1,000 students; Dir JEAN-PIERRE DEBOURSE.

Ecole Supérieure de Commerce de Montpellier: 2300 ave des Moulins, 34185 Montpellier Cedex 4; tel. 4-67-10-25-00; fax 4-67-45-13-56; e-mail info@supco-montpellier.fr; internet www.supdeco-montpellier.com; f. 1897; 250 teachers; 1,750 students; three-year courses in business administration and management sciences; Dir Dr DIDIER JOURDAN.

Ecole Supérieure de Commerce de Pau: 3 rue Saint John Perse, Campus Universitaire, 64000 Pau; tel. 5-59-92-64-64; fax 5-59-92-64-55; f. 1970 by the Chamber of Commerce; library: *c.* 5,000 vols; 16 full-time; 120 part-time teachers; 500 students; Dir LAURENT HUA.

Ecole Supérieure des Sciences Economiques et Commerciales (ESSEC Business School – Paris): Ave Bernard Hirsch, BP 50105, 95021 Cergy-Pontoise Cedex; tel. 1-34-43-30-00; fax 1-34-43-30-01; e-mail indigo@essec.fr; internet www.essec.com; f. 1907; 4-year, 3-year, 2-year and 1-year degree courses; master's degree in business administration and management; M.Sc. in marketing, finance, logistics, information and decision systems, international law and management, agribusiness management, international supply management, urban management, and strategy and management of international business; M.B.A. programmes in hospitality, luxury-brand management; Executive M.B.A. and other executive education courses; doctoral and B.B.A. programmes; library: 49,000 vols, 1,500 periodicals; 370 teachers (100 full-time, 270 part-time); 3,700 students; President PIERRE TAPIE.

EM Lyon: BP 174, 23 ave Guy de Collongue, 69132 Ecully Cedex; tel. 4-78-33-78-00; fax 4-78-33-61-69; e-mail info@em-lyon.com; internet www.em-lyon.com; f. 1872; library: 12,927 vols; 80 teachers; 1,250 students; Dir PATRICK MOLLE.

Affiliated institutes:

Cesma MBA: Dir JUDITH RYDER.

Ecole Supérieure de Commerce de Lyon (ESC Lyon): 2-year master's course in management; Dir CHANTAL POTY.

Executive Education: Dir PAUL-ANDRÉ FAURE.

ESCP-EAP European School of Management: 79 ave de la République, 75543 Paris Cedex 11; tel. 1-49-23-20-00; fax 1-49-23-22-12; e-mail info@escp-eap.net; internet www.escp-eap.net; f. 1999 by merger of Groupe ESCP and Ecole Européenne des Affaires (EAP); 120 teachers in five countries; 3,000 students in five countries; campuses in Paris (France), London (UK), Berlin (Germany), Madrid (Spain) and Turin (Italy); postgraduate degree programmes, executive education; 5 research centres; Dean JEAN-LOUIS SCARINGELLA.

ESCP-EAP European School of Management: 79 ave de la République, 75543 Paris Cedex 11; tel. 1-49-23-20-00; fax 1-49-23-22-12; e-mail info@escp-eap.net; internet www.escp-eap.net; f. 1999 by merger of Groupe ESCP and Ecole Européenne des Affaires (EAP); 120 teachers in five countries; 3,000 students in five countries; campuses in Paris (France), London (UK), Berlin (Germany), Madrid (Spain) and Turin (Italy); postgraduate degree programmes, executive education; 5 research centres; Dean JEAN-LOUIS SCARINGELLA.

Groupe CERAM: BP 085, 06902 Sophia Antipolis Cedex; tel. 4-93-95-45-45; fax 4-93-65-45-24; f. 1978 by Nice Chamber of Commerce; library: 16,000 vols; 100 full-time; 120 part-time teachers; 750 students, plus 100 on MS course; Dir MAXIME CRENER.

Groupe CPA – Centre de Perfectionnement aux Affaires: 14 ave de la Porte de Champerret, 75017 Paris; tel. 1-44-09-34-00; fax 1-44-09-34-99; f. 1930 by the Paris Chamber of Commerce and Industry; general management courses for top executives; establishing close links with Groupe HEC (Hautes Etudes Commerciales); Dir JEAN-LOUIS SCARINGELLA.

Branches; see entry for HEC School of Management for details of branch institutions:

CPA Paris.

CPA Jouy en Josas.

CPA Lyon.

CPA Nord.

CPA Grand Sud-Ouest.

CPA Méditerranée.

CPA Madrid.

Groupe Ecole Supérieure de Commerce de Bordeaux: Domaine de Raba, 680 cours de la Libération, 33405 Talence Cedex; tel. 5-56-84-55-55; fax 5-56-84-55-00; e-mail groupe.esc@esc.bordeaux.fr; f. 1874 by Chamber of Commerce; library: 17,000 vols; 74 teachers; 1,800 students; Dir GEORGES VIALA.

Groupe Ecole Supérieure de Commerce et de Management (Groupe ESCEM): 1 Léo Delibes, BP 0535, 37205 Tours Cedex; tel. 2-47-71-71-71; fax 2-47-71-72-10; e-mail com@escem.fr; internet www.escem.fr; f. 1961; graduate management degree programme, master's and International M.B.A. degree programmes, continuing education and distance learning in management; courses in economics, marketing, finance, accountancy, management information systems, international business; master's degrees in business administration and information systems; 405 teachers (55 full-time, 350 part-time); 1,600 students; library: 13,000 vols; Dir GUY LE BOUCHER; publ. *Les Cahiers de Recherche de l'ESCEM* (2 a year).

Branch campus:

Groupe ESCEM Campus Poitiers: 11 rue de l'Ancienne Comédie, BP 5, 86001 Poitiers Cedex; tel. 5-49-60-58-00; fax 5-49-60-58-30; internet www.escem.fr.

Groupe ESC Brest: 2 ave de Provence, BP 7214, 29272 Brest Cedex; tel. 2-98-34-44-44; fax 2-98-34-44-69; f. 1962; library: 5,000 vols, 150 periodicals; 110 teachers; 533 students; Dir C. MONIQUE.

Groupe ESC Nantes Atlantique: 8 route de la Jonelière, BP 31222, 44312 Nantes Cedex 3; tel. 2-40-37-34-34; fax 2-40-37-34-07; f. 1900; library: 13,000 vols, 450 periodicals; 343 teachers (43 full-time, 300 part-time); 1,200 students; Pres. JEAN-FRANÇOIS MOULIN; Dir-Gen. and Dean AÏSSA DERMOUCHE.

Groupe ESIDEC: 3 place Edouard Branly, Technopôle Metz 2000, 57070 Metz; tel. 3-87-56-37-37; fax 3-87-56-37-99; e-mail vlebrun@gr_esidec_fr.edu; internet www.moselle.cci.fr/esidec/index.htm; f. 1988; run by the Moselle Chamber of Commerce and Industry; courses in management, logistics, marketing, finance, law, trade, purchasing; 40 teachers; 210 students; Dir THIERRY JEAN.

HEC School of Management: 78351 Jouy-en-Josas Cedex; tel. 1-39-67-70-00; fax 1-39-67-74-40; e-mail hecinfo@hec.fr; internet www.hec.edu; f. 1881; sponsored by the Paris Chamber of Commerce and Industry; incorporates CPA (Centre de Perfectionnement aux affaires); degree courses in fields of management; executive development programmes; library: 60,000 vols; 589 teachers (104 full-time, 450 part-time, 35 visiting); 2,500 students; Dean BERNARD RAMANANTSOA; Dir of CPA DEAN-MARC DE LEERSNYDER

DIRECTORS OF TEACHING UNITS

Ecole HEC: Michel Raimbault

M.S. HEC: Jean-Luc Neyraut

HEC Ph.D.: Bertrand Quélin

HEC Executive Development: Bertrand Moingeon

MBA (isa): Jean-Paul Mounier.

CPA Sites:

CPA Paris: 14 ave de la Porte de Champerret, 75017 Paris; tel. 1-44-09-34-00; fax 1-44-09-34-99.

CPA Lyon: 93 chemin des Mouilles, 69130 Ecully Cedex; tel. 4-78-33-52-12; fax 4-78-33-37-06; Dir Charles Ab-der-Halden.

CPA Nord: 551 rue Albert Bailly, 59700 Marcq-en-Baroeul; tel. 3-20-25-97-53; fax 3-20-27-12-94; Dir Jean-Claude Vacher.

CPA Grand Sud-Ouest: 20 blvd Lascrosses, 31000 Toulouse; tel. 5-61-29-49-91; fax 5-61-13-98-31; Dir Alain Mainguy.

CPA Méditerranée: c/o CERAM II, 60 rue Dostoïevski, 06902 Sophia Antipolis; tel. 4-92-96-96-95; fax 4-93-95-44-21; Dir Adrien Corbière-Médecin.

CPA Madrid: Calle Serrano 208, 28012 Madrid, Spain; tel. 91-538-37-59; fax 91-538-37-58; Dir Teodoro Aguado de los Ríos.

INSEAD: Blvd de Constance, 77305 Fontainebleau Cedex; tel. 1-60-72-40-00; fax 1-60-74-55-00; f. 1958; post-graduate MBA programme; PhD programme; executive development programmes; 100 professors; library: 40,000 vols; Chair. Board of Govs Claude Janssen; Dean Prof. Gabriel Hawawini.

Reims Management School: 59 rue Pierre-Taittinger, 51100 Reims Cedex; tel. 3-26-77-47-47; fax 3-26-04-69-63; e-mail service.com@reims-ms.fr; internet www.reims-ms.fr; f. 1928; schools and subject areas: Sup de Co (new economy), Cesem (International School of Management), Tema (management school with emphasis on technology), Sup TG (sales and administration), MBA (part- and full-time); 62 full-time teachers; 2,600 students; Dir Dominique Waquet.

Theseus International Management Institute: Rue Albert Einstein, BP 169, 06903 Sophia Antipolis Cedex; tel. 4-92-94-51-00; fax 4-93-65-38-37; e-mail info@theseus.fr; internet www.theseus.edu; f. 1989; MBA programmes; Dir-Gen. Prof. Ahmet Aykaç.

LAW AND POLITICAL SCIENCE

American Graduate School of International Relations and Diplomacy: 6 rue de Lubeck, 75116 Paris; tel. 1-47-20-00-94; fax 1-47-20-81-89; e-mail info@agsird.edu; internet www.agsird.edu; f. 1994; MA and PhD programs; 11 teachers; 90 students (50 full-time, 40 part-time); Dir Dr Marcia A. Grant.

Ecole des Hautes Etudes Internationales: 107 rue de Tolbiac, 75013 Paris; tel. 1-45-70-73-37; fax 1-45-70-99-33; e-mail contact@hep-hei-esj.net; internet www.hep-hei-esj.net; f. 1904; Pres. M. Schumann; Dir P. Chaigneau.

Ecole de Notariat d'Amiens: 7 rue Anne-Franck, 80136 Rivery; tel. 3-22-92-61-26; f. 1942; Dir M. Deschamps.

Ecole de Notariat de Paris: 9 rue Villaret-de-Joyeuse, 75017 Paris; f. 1896; Dir M. P. Mathieu.

Ecole Supérieure de Journalisme: 107 rue Tolbiac, 75013 Paris; tel. 1-45-70-73-37; fax 1-45-70-99-33; e-mail contact@hep-hei-esj.net; internet www.hep-hei-esj.net; f. 1899; Pres. M. Cazeneuve; Dir P. Chaigneau.

Institut International des Droits de l'Homme (International Institute of Human Rights): 2 Allée René Cassin, 67000 Strasbourg; tel. 3-88-45-84-45; fax 3-88-45-84-50; e-mail administration@iidh.org; internet www.iidh.org; f. 1969 by René Cassin; post-graduate teaching in international and comparative law of human rights; annual study session during July; annual two-week course in June on refugee law, organized in collaboration with the United Nations High Commissioner for Refugees (in French); 50 teachers; 350 students; Pres. Gérard Cohen-Jonathan; Sec.-Gen. Jean-François Flauss.

Attached centre:

International Centre for University Human Rights Teaching: Strasbourg; f. 1973 at the request of UNESCO; two-week courses for university teachers; 2 teachers; 40 students; Sec.-Gen. Prof. Jean-François Flauss.

MEDICINE

Ecole Dentaire Française: 3 rue de l'Est, 75020 Paris; tel. 1-47-97-77-81; Dir R. J. Cachia.

Institut et Centre d'Optométrie: 134 route de Chartres, 91440 Bures-sur-Yvette; tel. 1-64-86-12-13; fax 1-69-28-49-99; e-mail ico.direction@wanadoo.fr; internet www.ecole-optometrie.fr; f. 1917; 40 teachers; 350 students; Dir Jean-Paul Roosen.

RELIGION

Faculté Libre de Théologie Protestante de Paris: 83 blvd Arago, 75014 Paris; tel. 1-43-31-61-64; fax 1-47-07-67-87; e-mail iptparis@club-internet.fr; f. 1877; religious history, old and new testament, ecclesiastical history, systematic theology, philosophy, practical theology, Hebrew, Greek, German, English; library: 60,000 vols; 12 professors, 180 students; Dean Jacques-Noël Pérès.

Institut de Théologie Orthodoxe: 93 rue de Crimée, 75019 Paris; tel. 1-42-08-12-93; fax 1-42-08-00-09; f. 1925; 15 professors and 50 students; library: 30,000 vols; Dean Rev. Fr Boris Bobrinskoy; publ. *Pensée Orthodoxe* (every 2 years).

Institut Européen des Sciences Humaines: Centre Boutloin, 58120 Saint-Léger-de-Fougeret; tel. 3-86-79-40-62; fax 3-86-85-01-19; f. 1990; Muslim theology; library: 5,000 vols; 8 teachers; capacity for 200 students; Dir Zuhair Mahmood.

Institut Orthodoxe Français de Paris (Saint-Denis): 96 blvd Auguste-Blanqui, 75013 Paris; tel. 1-45-41-48-75; f. 1944; 20 professors and 125 students; library: 5,000 vols; faculties of theology and philosophy; Rector Bertrand-Hardy (Bishop Germain of Saint Denis); publ. *Présence Orthodoxe*.

Séminaire Israélite de France (Ecole Rabbinique): 9 rue Vauquelin, 75005 Paris; tel. 1-47-07-21-22; fax 1-43-37-75-92; f. 1829; Talmud, Bible, Jewish history and philosophy, Hebrew language and literature studies, rabbinical law; 6 teachers; 15 students; library: 60,000 vols; Dir Chief Rabbi Michel Gugenheim.

SCIENCES

Ecole d'Anthropologie: 1 place d'Iéna, 75116 Paris; tel. 1-47-93-09-73; fax 1-47-93-09-73; e-mail institutanthropologie@hotmail.fr; internet www.multimania.com/anthropa; f. 1876 by Prof. Broca; prehistory, physical anthropology, ethnology, biology, genetics, immunology, ethnography, demography, third world problems, psychology, criminology, anthropotechnics, biometeorology; Dir Prof. Bernard J. Huet; publ. *Nouvelle revue anthropologique* (irregular).

Institut de Paléontologie Humaine: 1 rue René Panhard, 75013 Paris; tel. 1-43-31-62-91; fax 1-43-31-22-79; e-mail iph@mnhn.fr; f. 1910 by Prince Albert I of Monaco; vertebrate palaeontology, palynology, palaeo-anthropology, prehistory, quaternary geology, sedimentology, geochronology; library: 25,000 vols; 107 students; Dir Henry de Lumley; publs *Archives*, *L'Anthropologie*, *Etudes Quaternaires*

PROFESSORS

De Lumley, H., Quaternary Geology

Heim, J. L., Anthropology

Simone, S., Statistical Analysis of Prehistoric Industries

Institut Edouard Toulouse: 1 rue Cabanis, 75014 Paris; tel. 1-45-65-81-38; f. 1983; teaching, training and research in psychiatry, seminars on psychoanalysis; Pres. Dr Jean Ayme; Sec. Dr Marcel Czermak; publ. *Cahiers de l'Hôpital Henri Rousselle*.

Institut Océanographique: 195 rue Saint Jacques, 75005 Paris; tel. 1-44-32-10-70; fax 1-40-51-73-16; e-mail institut@oceano.org; internet www.oceano.org; education, scientific research, museology, publishing; f. 1906 by Prince Albert I of Monaco; library: 30,000 vols; Pres. Jean Chapon; Dir Lucien Laubien; Sec. C. Beauverger; publ. *Oceanis* (4 a year).

Attached museum:

Musée Océanographique: see under Monaco.

SOCIAL AND ECONOMIC SCIENCES

CNOF – Management et Formation: Tour Manhattan, 6 place de l'Iris, 92400 Courbevoie; tel. 1-47-67-13-13; fax 1-47-78-82-24; f. 1926; provides executive, managerial and administrative training.

Collège Libre des Sciences Sociales et Economiques: 184 blvd Saint-Germain, 75006 Paris; f. 1895; composed of six sections: social, economic, international and public relations; evening and correspondence courses; diplomas conferred after two or three years' study, and submission of theses on some aspect of applied economics; Pres. J. Rueff; Dir L. de Sainte-Lorette.

Ecole de Hautes Etudes Sociales: 107 rue Tolbiac, 75013 Paris; tel. 1-45-70-73-37; fax 1-45-70-99-33; e-mail contact@hep-hei-esj.net; internet www.hep-hei-esj.net; f. 1899; Pres. M. Schumann; Dir P. Chaigneau.

Faculté des Lettres et Sciences Sociales: BP 800, 29200 Brest; tel. 2-98-80-19-87; f. 1960; library: 18,000 vols; 105 teachers; 2,752 students; President and Dean Prof. Michel Quesnel.

Institut Européen des Hautes Etudes Internationales (IEHEI): 10 ave des Fleurs, 06000 Nice; tel. 4-93-97-93-70; fax 4-93-97-93-71; e-mail iehei@wanadoo.fr; internet www.iehei.org; f. 1964; library: 4,000 vols; 20 teachers; 35 students; Pres. Vlad Constantinesco; Dir Claude Nigoul.

TECHNOLOGY

Ecole Catholique d'Arts et Métiers (ECAM): 40 montée Saint-Barthélemy, 69321 Lyons Cedex 05; tel. 4-72-77-06-00; fax 4-72-77-06-11; e-mail info@ecam.fr; internet www.ecam.fr; f. 1900; courses in mechanical engineering, materials science, electrical and electronic engineering, automation, information technology, production engineering; library: 5,000 vols; 525 students; Dir BERNARD PINATEL; publ. *Bulletin* (quarterly).

Ecole Centrale de Lyon: BP 163, 36 ave Guy de Collongue, 69131 Ecully Cedex; tel. 4-72-18-60-00; fax 4-78-43-39-62; f. 1857; cultural, scientific and technical training for engineers in all branches of industry; library: 15,000 vols; 900 students; Dir E. PASCAUD; Sec.-Gen. C. LACROIX.

Ecole de Thermique: 3 rue Henri Heine, 75016 Paris; tel. 1-44-30-41-00; fax 1-40-50-07-54; teaching centre for the Institut Français de l'Energie (IFE); Dir (vacant).

Ecole Française d'Electronique et d'Informatique: 10 rue Amyot, 75005 Paris; tel. 1-46-77-64-67; fax 1-46-77-65-77; e-mail admission@efrei.fr; internet www.efrai.fr; f. 1936; courses in telecommunications, electronic engineering and computer science; 50 teachers; 1,170 students; Dir H. MEUNIER.

Ecole Généraliste d'Ingénieurs de Marseille (EGIM): Technopôle de Château-Gombert, 38 rue Joliot Curie, 13451 Marseilles Cedex 20; tel. and fax 4-91-05-45-45; e-mail sdei@egim-mrs.fr; internet www.egim-mrs.fr; f. 1891; specialist courses in information and communications technology, mechatronics, systems engineering, marine engineering, thermal systems engineering, mechanical and materials engineering, microelectronics design, civil engineering; 70 teachers; 778 students; Dir JEAN-PAUL FABRE.

Ecole Spéciale de Mécanique et d'Electricité A.M. Ampère: 4 rue Blaise-Desgoffe, 75006 Paris; Dir P. DOCEUL.

Ecole Spéciale des Travaux Publics, du Bâtiment et de l'Industrie: 57 blvd Saint-Germain, 75005 Paris; tel. 1-44-41-11-18; fax 1-44-41-11-12; e-mail information@adm.estp.fr; internet www.estp.fr; f. 1891; civil engineering training programmes at undergraduate and graduate levels; continuing education courses; 700 teachers; 2,000 students; library: 10,000 vols; Dir S. EYROLLES.

Ecole Supérieure d'Electricité: Plateau de Moulon, 91192 Gif sur Yvette Cedex; tel. 1-69-85-12-12; fax 1-69-85-12-34; internet www.supelec.fr; campuses at Gif, Metz and Rennes; f. 1894; two- or three-year courses in electrical engineering, radio engineering, information science, electronics and computer science; 120 permanent teachers; 1,200 students; attached to Univ. Paris XI; Dir. Gen. J. J. DUBY; Dir of Studies F. MESA; Gen.-Sec. A. POTONNIER.

Ecole Supérieure d'Informatique: 94-98 rue Carnot, 93100 Montreuil; tel. 1-48-59-69-69; f. 1965; 90 teachers; 1,000 students; Dir LEO ROZENTALIS; publ. *Dossiers de l'Association pour la Promotion de l'Ecole Supérieure d'Informatique*.

Ecole Supérieure d'Ingénieurs en Electrotechnique et Electronique: Cité Descartes, BP 99, 93162 Noisy-le-Grand; tel. 1-45-92-65-10; fax 1-45-92-66-99; f. 1962; computer science, automation, telecommunications, signal processing, microelectronics; 1,000 students; 100 teachers; library: 18,000 vols; Dir ALAIN CADIX.

Ecole Supérieure d'Optique et Institut d'Optique: Centre Scientifique d'Orsay, Bât. 503, 91403 Orsay Cedex; tel. 1-69-35-88-88; fax 1-69-35-87-00; e-mail international@iota.u-psud.fr; internet www.institutoptique.fr; attached to Univ. Paris XI; f. 1920; optical engineering, optics and photonics at post-graduate level; 60 teachers (20 full-time, 40 assoc.); 240 students; Dir Prof. ANDRÉ DUCASSE.

Ecole Supérieure de Fonderie: Pôle Universitaire, 92916 Paris La Défense Cedex; tel. 1-41-16-12-30; fax 1-41-16-72-46; f. 1923; library: 2,150 vols; Dir G. CHAPPUIS.

Ecole Supérieure des Industries du Caoutchouc: 60 rue Auber, 94408 Vitry-sur-Seine Cedex; tel. 1-49-60-57-57; fax 1-49-60-70-66; e-mail info@ifoca.com; f. 1941; 8 teachers; 35 students; Dir GÉRARD GALLAS.

Ecole Supérieure des Industries du Vêtement: 73 blvd Saint-Marcel, 75013 Paris; tel. 1-40-79-92-60; fax 1-40-79-92-91; e-mail esiv@emi-ccip.fr; f. 1946; 14 teachers; 70 students; Dir ANNE STEFANINI.

Ecole Supérieure des Industries Textiles d'Epinal: 85 rue d'Alsace, 88025 Epinal Cedex; tel. 3-29-35-50-52; fax 3-29-35-39-21; e-mail esite@wanadoo.fr; f. 1905; training of industrial textile engineers; library: 1,500 vols; Dir J. TIERCET.

Ecole Supérieure des Techniques Aéronautiques et de Construction Automobile: 34 rue Victor Hugo, 92300 Levallois-Perret; tel. 1-41-27-37-00; fax 1-47-37-50-83; e-mail infos@estaca.fr; internet www.estaca.fr; f. 1925; private school offering 5-year courses in aeronautical, automotive, railway and space engineering; Masters course in Safety of Transportation Systems (taught in English); EUROMIND, European Masters in Design and Technology of Advanced Vehicle Systems (taught in English); 1,000 students; Dir ERIC PARLEBAS.

Ecole Supérieure du Bois: rue Christian Pauc, BP 10605, 44306 Nantes Cedex 3; tel. 2-40-18-12-12; fax 2-40-18-12-00; e-mail contact@ecolesuperieuredubois.com; internet www.ecolesuperieuredubois.com; f. 1934; training of engineers and management for wood industry; 13 full-time, 20 external; 250 students; Dir X. MARTIN.

Ecole Supérieure du Soudage et de ses Applications (Advanced Postgraduate Welding Engineering School): BP 50362, 95942 Roissy CDG Cedex; tel. 1-49-90-36-27; fax 1-49-90-36-50; e-mail m.d.jols@institutdesoudure.com; internet www.institutdesoudure.com; f. 1930; 55 teachers; 30 students; Dir MICHEL DIJOLS.

Ecole Technique Supérieure du Laboratoire: 93–95 rue du Dessous-des Berges, 75013 Paris; tel. 1-45-83-76-34; e-mail etsl.75@wanadoo.fr; f. 1934; Pres. J. CHOMIENNE; Dir. F. LAISSUS.

European Institute of Technology: 8 rue Saint Florentin, 75001 Paris; tel. 1-40-15-05-69; fax 1-49-27-98-11; f. 1988 to strengthen industrial research and development, and to increase the contribution of technological innovation to economic growth in Europe; Sec.-Gen. JOHN M. MARCUM.

Fondation EPF – Ecole d'Ingénieurs: 3 bis rue Lakanal, 92330 Sceaux; tel. 1-41-13-01-65; fax 1-46-60-39-94; e-mail jeneveau@epf.fr; f. 1925; engineering training; Pres. Dr ALAIN JENEVEAU.

Institut Français Textile–Habillement: Ave Guy de Collongue, 69134 Ecully Cedex; tel. 4-72-86-16-00; fax 4-72-86-16-50; e-mail information@ifth.org; internet www.ifth.org; f. 1946; library: 255 vols and documents; Dir M. BEDEAU.

Institut Textile et Chimique de Lyon (ITECH): 87 chemin des Mouilles, 69134 Ecully Cedex; tel. 4-72-18-04-80; fax 4-72-18-95-45; e-mail info@itech.fr; internet www.itech.fr; f. 1899; diploma courses in leather technology, painting and adhesives technology; plastics, textiles; 120 ; 360 ; Dir JEAN-PIERRE GALLET; Dean CHRISTIANE BASSET.

International Space University: Parc d'Innovation, 1 rue Jean Dominique Cassini, 67400 Illkirch-Graffenstaden; tel. 3-88-65-54-30; fax 3-88-65-54-47; e-mail info@isu.isunet.edu; internet www.isunet.edu; f. 1987; offers Master of Space Studies and Master of Space Management degree programmes, introductory space course and a summer session programme; 6 full-time, 6 part-time and 100 visiting teachers; 150 students; Pres Dr MICHAEL SIMPSON.

Schools of Art and Music

Conservatoire National de Région de Musique et de Danse de Lyon: 4 montée Cardinal Decourtray, 69005 Lyons; tel. 4-78-25-91-39; fax 4-72-38-77-08; e-mail communication@cnrlyon.fr; internet www.cnrlyon.fr; f. 1857; 160 teachers; 2,980 students; library: 2,600 vols, 40,000 scores, 4,500 records, 2,000 orchestral scores; Dir RENÉ CLÉMENT.

Conservatoire National de Région de Musique et de Danse de Boulogne-Billancourt: 22 rue de la Belle-Feuille, 92100 Boulogne-Billancourt; tel. 1-55-18-45-85; fax 1-55-18-45-86; e-mail cnr@cnrbb.org; internet www.cnrbb.org; f. 1953, present name 1978; library: 7,000 books, 40 periodicals, 20,000 scores, 6,000 records, 600 audio-visual and multimedia items.; 90 teachers; 1,650 students; Dir ALFRED HERZOG.

Conservatoire National Supérieur d'Art Dramatique: 2 bis rue du Conservatoire, 75009 Paris; tel. 1-42-46-12-91; fax 1-48-00-94-02; internet www.cnsad.fr; f. 1786; 55 ; 100 students; library: 10,100 vols; Dir CLAUDE STRATZ.

Conservatoire National Supérieur de Musique et de Danse: 209 ave Jean Jaurès, 75019 Paris; tel. 1-40-40-45-45; fax 1-40-40-45-00; e-mail cnsmdp@cnsmdp.fr; internet www.cnsmdp.fr; f. 1795; 386 teachers; 1,413 students; Dir ALAIN POIRIER.

Conservatoire National Supérieur Musique et Danse de Lyon: 3 quai Chauveau, CP 120, 69266 Lyons Cedex 09; tel. 4-72-19-26-26; fax 4-72-19-26-00; e-mail cnsmd@cnsmd-lyon.fr; internet www.cnsmd-lyon.fr; f. 1980; library: 42,000 vols; 170 teachers; 550 students; Dir HENRY FOURÈS.

Ecole d'Art de Marseille-Luminy: 184 ave de Luminy, 13288 Marseilles Cedex 9; tel. 4-91-41-01-44; fax 4-91-26-75-72; f. 1710; 420 students; library: 15,000 vols; Dir NORBERT DUFFORT; publs *Verba Volant* (2 a year), *Recherche et Création Artistiques* (monographs, 5 a year).

Ecole du Louvre: Palais du Louvre, Porte Jaujard, Place du Carrousel, 75038 Paris Cedex 01; tel. 1-55-35-18-00; fax 1-42-60-40-36; internet www.ecoledulouvre.fr; f. 1882; library: 40,000 vols; 1,700 students; Principal PH. DUREY; Sec.-Gen. M. C. DEVEVEY.

Ecole Nationale Supérieure des Arts Décoratifs (ENSAD): 31 rue d'Ulm, 75240 Paris Cedex 05; tel. 1-42-34-97-00; fax 1-42-34-97-85; e-mail info@ensad.fr; internet www.ensad.fr; f. 1766; visual arts and design; library: 15,000 vols and special collections; 164 teachers; 600 students; Dirs ELIZABETH FLEURY PATRICK RAYNAUD; publs *Catalogue des Projets de Fin d'Etudes* (2 a year), *Journal des Arts-Déco* (3 a year).

Ecole Nationale Supérieure des Beaux-Arts: 14 rue Bonaparte, 75272 Paris Cedex 06; tel. 1-47-03-50-00; fax 1-47-03-50-80; f. 1648 as Académie Royale de Peinture et de Sculpture, and in 1671 as Académie Royale d'Architecture; library: 120,000 vols; 75 teachers; 650 students; Dir (vacant); publs *Ecrits d'Artistes*, *Beaux-Arts Histoire*, *Espaces de l'art*.

Ecole Supérieure d'Art Clermont Communauté: 142 ave Jean Mermoz, 63100 Clermont-Ferrand; tel. 4-73-91-43-86; fax 4-73-90-27-80; e-mail erba@ville-clermont-ferrand.fr; internet www.ecoledart.ville-clermont-ferrand.fr; f. 1882; library: 7,000 vols and special collections; 17 teachers; 130 students; Dir SYLVAIN LIZON.

Schola Cantorum: 269 rue St Jacques, 75005 Paris; tel. 1-43-54-15-39; f. 1896 by Vincent d'Indy; music, dance and dramatic art; Dir MICHEL DENIS.

FRENCH GUIANA

Research Institutes

GENERAL

Institut de Recherche pour le Développement (IRD) Centre de Cayenne: 0,275 km Route de Montabo, BP 165, 97323 Cayenne Cedex; tel. 5-94-29-92-92; fax 5-94-31-98-55; e-mail direction@cayenne.ird.fr; internet www.cayenne.ird.fr; f. 1949; teledetection, pedology, hydrology, sedimentology, botany and vegetal biology; medical and agricultural entomology, ornithology, phytopharmacology, oceanography, sociology; 53 staff; library of 7,000 vols; Rep. PATRICK SÉCHET; publ. *L'Homme et la Nature en Guyane*; (see main entry under France).

MEDICINE

Institut Pasteur de la Guyane Française: 23 ave Pasteur, BP 6010, 97306 Cayenne Cedex; tel. 5-94-29-26-00; fax 5-94-30-94-16; internet www.pasteur-cayenne.fr; f. 1940; medical and biological research; Dir Dr ANDRÉ SPIEGEL.

Libraries and Archives

Cayenne

Archives Départementales de la Guyane: Place Léopold Héder, 97307 Cayenne Cedex; tel. 5-94-29-52-70; fax 5-94-29-52-89; f. 1983; history of French Guiana; Dir FRANÇOISE LEMAIRE-THABOUILLOT.

Bibliothèque A. Franconie: 1 ave du Général de Gaulle, BP 5011, 97305 Cayenne Cedex; tel. 5-94-29-59-16; fax 5-94-29-59-12; e-mail bibliotheque.franconie@cg973.fr; f. 1885; general lending library; 35,000 vols; Dir Mme MARIE-ANNICK ATTICOT.

Service Commun de la Documentation de l'Université des Antilles et de la Guyane (Section Guyane): Campus St-Denis, BP 1179, 97346 Cayenne Cedex; tel. 5-94-25-21-55; fax 5-94-30-96-68; e-mail nicole.clementmartin@guyane.univ-ag.fr; internet www.univ-ag.fr/buag; 26,213 vols, 415 periodicals; Dir of French Guiana Branch NICOLE CLÉMENT-MARTIN.

Museum

Cayenne

Musée Départemental (Musée de France): 1 ave Général de Gaulle, 97300 Cayenne; tel. 5-94-29-59-13; fax 5-94-29-59-11; e-mail musee.local.guyane@wanadoo.fr; f. 1901; flora and fauna of Guiana; historical documents; Dir JEAN-PASCAL STERVINOU.

University

Université des Antilles et de la Guyane: Ave d'Estrée, Campus Saint-Denis, BP 792, 97337 Cayenne Cedex; tel. 5-94-30-42-00; fax 5-94-30-79-53; e-mail charge.communication@guyane.univ-ag.fr; internet www.univ-ag.fr; 239 students; library: see Libraries and Archives; Pres. ALAIN ARCONTE; Vice-Pres. (French Guiana) HENRY CLERGEOT; (see also under Guadeloupe and Martinique).

TEACHING AND RESEARCH UNITS

Institute of Higher Education in Cayenne: Dir H. CLERGEOT

University Institute of Technology in Kourou: Dir C. MAILLE

FRENCH POLYNESIA

Learned Societies

GENERAL

Maison de la Culture Te Fare Tauhiti Nui: 646 Blvd Pomaré, BP 1709, Papeete; tel. 54-45-44; fax 42-85-69; e-mail secretariat@maisondelaculture.pf; internet www.maisondelaculture.pf; f. 1972; promotes culture locally and abroad; sponsors many public and private cultural events; library of 13,000 vols, children's library of 7,000 vols; Dir HEREMOANA MAAMAATUAIATAPU (acting).

NATURAL SCIENCES

General

Société des Etudes Océaniennes: BP 110, Papeete; tel. 41-96-03; e-mail contact@seo.pf; internet www.seo.pf; f. 1917; 450 mems; library; Pres. ROBERT KOENIG; publ. *Bulletin* (quarterly).

Research Institutes

GENERAL

Institut de Recherche pour le Développement (IRD) Centre de Tahiti: BP 529, Papeete 98713; tel. 50-62-00; fax 42-95-55; e-mail dirpapet@ird.pf; f. 1963; medical entomology, anthropology, oceanography; library of 7,000 vols; Rep. JACQUES ILTIS; (see main entry under France).

AGRICULTURE, FISHERIES AND VETERINARY SCIENCE

Centre Océanologique du Pacifique: BP 7004, Taravao, Tahiti 98709; tel. 54-60-00; fax 54-60-99; internet www.ifremer.fr/cop/; f. 1972; part of IFREMER (*q.v.*); research in aquaculture (crustacea, fish, shellfish); specialized library; Dir DOMINIQUE BUESTEL.

MEDICINE

Institut Territorial de Recherches Médicales 'Louis Malardé': BP 30, Papeete; tel. 41-64-64; fax 43-15-90; e-mail irm@malarde.pf; f. 1949; parasitology (particularly lymphatic filariasis), virology (dengue), microbiology, immunology, serology, biochemistry, pharmacotoxicology, bio-ecology and marine biochemistry, medical entomology; library of 1,000 vols, 9,185 periodicals; Dir Dr ELIANE CHUNGUE.

RELIGION, SOCIOLOGY AND ANTHROPOLOGY

Département des Traditions Orales, du Centre Polynésien des Sciences Humaines 'Te Anavaharau': Pointe de Pêcheurs, Punaauia Pk 15, Tahiti; tel. 58-34-76; fax 58-43-00; study of Polynesian oral tradition.

Museums and Art Galleries

Tamanu

Musée de Tahiti et des Iles—Te Fare Iamanaha: BP 380354 Tamanu, 98718 Punaauia; tel. 58-84-35; fax 58-43-00; e-mail musee@mail.pf; f. 1974; aims: the collection, conservation and appreciation of Polynesian cultural heritage; Dir HIRIATA MILLAUD.

Taravao

Musée Paul Gauguin: BP 7029, Taravao, Tahiti; tel. 57-10-58; fax 57-10-42; f. 1965; 1,000 documents on the life and work of the artist, Paul Gauguin (1848–1903), who spent the last part of his life in Tahiti and other parts of the South Pacific; library of unpublished documents; collection of paintings by Buffet, R. Delaunay, S. Delaunay and others; 20 original works by Gauguin (paintings, sculptures, watercolours); Curator G. ARTUR.

University

UNIVERSITÉ DE LA POLYNÉSIE FRANÇAISE (University of French Polynesia)

BP 6570, Aéroport de Faaa, Tahiti
Telephone: 80-38-03
Fax: 80-38-04
E-mail: courrier@ufp.pf
Internet: www.upf.pf

Founded 1999 from the French Polynesia centre of the former Université Française du Pacifique
State control
Academic year: September to June
Rector: LOUISE PELTZER
Library of 40,000 books, 260 periodicals, 400 audiovisual items
Number of teachers: 74
Number of students: 2,649
Departments of Arts and Humanities; Law, Economics and Management, Physical Activities and Sport; and Science, Medicine and Technology.

GUADELOUPE

Research Institutes

AGRICULTURE, FISHERIES AND VETERINARY SCIENCE

Département des Productions Fruitières et Horticoles–Centre de Co-opération Internationale en Recherche Agronomique pour le Développement (CIRAD-FLHOR): Station de Neufchâteau, Sainte-Marie, 97130 Capesterre-Belle-Eau; tel. 5-96-86-17-90; fax 5-96-86-17-91; cultivation of bananas and other fruits, sugar cane, flowers; animal parisitology and control; 31 research staff; Dir PATRICE GUILLAUME; (see main entry under France).

Institut National de la Recherche Agronomique (INRA), Centre Antilles-Guyane: Domaine Duclos, Prise d'Eau, 97170 Petit Bourg; tel. 5-96-25-59-00; fax 5-96-25-59-98; e-mail xande@antilles.inra.fr; internet www.antilles.inra.fr; f. 1948; (see main entry under France); soil science, animal science, forestry, plant science, rural economy and sociology, zoology and biological control, technology transfer; controls five research units, three experimental farms and a documentation service; Pres. JEAN-PIERRE POINSARD.

MEDICINE

Institut Pasteur de la Guadeloupe: BP 484, Abymes, 97183 Pointe-à-Pitre Cedex; tel. 5-90-89-69-40; fax 5-90-89-69-43; internet www.pasteur-guadeloupe.fr; f. 1948; medical and microbiological analysis laboratories; int. vaccination centre; Public Health Dept certified laboratories for water and food analysis (chemical and microbiological); mycobacteria research centre; 40 staff; small library; Dir Dr RONALD PERRAUT; publ. *Archives* (annual).

Libraries and Archives

Basse-Terre

Archives Départementales de la Guadeloupe: BP 74, 97102 Basse-Terre; tel. 5-90-81-13-02; fax 5-90-81-97-15; internet www.cg971.fr/archives/; f. 1951; 10,000 vols; Dir HÉLÈNE SERVANT; publ. *Bulletin de la Société d'Histoire de la Guadeloupe* (quarterly).

Pointe-à-Pitre

Bibliothèque Universitaire Antilles-Guyane (Section Guadeloupe): Campus de Fouillole, BP 32, 97159 Pointe-à-Pitre Cedex; tel. 5-96-48-90-01; fax 5-96-48-90-89; e-mail jacques.faule@univ-ag.fr; internet www.univ-ag.fr/buag; f. 1972; 65,000 vols, 750 periodicals, 2,200 electronic journals; Dir, Guadeloupe Branch JACQUES FAULE.

Museums and Art Galleries

Pointe-à-Pitre

Musée Schoelcher: 24 rue Peynier, 97110 Pointe-à-Pitre; tel. 5-96-82-08-04; f. 1883; collection assembled by Victor Schoelcher (1804–1893), local politician and campaigner against slavery; pictures of European monuments and historic sites, reproductions of antique sculptures from the Musée du Louvre, Paris; Egyptian antiquities, Senegalese ritual bell, Aztec and Greek pottery fragments; writing on travel and slavery by Schoelcher; Dir H. PETITJEAN ROGET.

Affiliated museums:

Ecomusée de Marie Galante: Habitation Murat, 97112 Grand Bourg, Marie Galante; tel. 5-96-97-94-41; f. 1980; local arts, history and traditions, and history of sugar cane; medicinal herb garden in the former animal enclosure; library of 400 vols; Dir C. MOMBRUN.

Fort Fleur d'Epée: Bas du Fort, Gosier 97190; tel. 5-96-90-94-61; f. 1759; military history, art gallery, coin collection.

Musée Edgar Clerc: Parc de la Rosette, 97160 Le Moule; tel. 5-96-23-57-57; fax 5-96-23-57-43; f. 1984; archaeological museum; library of 800 vols.

Parc Archéologique des Roches Gravées: Bord de mer, 97114 Trois-Rivières; tel. 5-96-92-91-88; f. 1970; 1 ha., containing tropical vegetation, volcanic rocks and stones bearing marks made by Arawak Indians, the original inhabitants of the island.

University

Université des Antilles et de la Guyane: BP 250, 97157 Pointe-à-Pitre Cedex; tel. 5-96-82-38-22; fax 5-96-91-06-57; internet www.univ-ag.fr; f. 1982; 444 teachers; 12,000 students; library: see Libraries and Archives; Pres. ALAIN ARCONTE; Vice-Pres. (Guadeloupe) DIDIER BERNARD; (see also under French Guiana and Martinique).

TEACHING AND RESEARCH UNITS

Exact and Natural Sciences: Dean OUSSEYNOU NAKOULIMA
Law and Economics: Dir GEORGES VIRASSAMY
Medicine: Dean EUSTASE JANKY
Sports: Dir CHRISTIAN ALIN

MARTINIQUE

Research Institutes

AGRICULTURE, FISHERIES AND VETERINARY SCIENCE

Centre de Co-opération Internationale en Recherche Agronomique pour le Développement (CIRAD): BP 214, 97285 Le Lementin Cedex 2; tel. 5-90-42-30-00; fax 5-90-42-31-00; e-mail thierry .goguey_muethon@cirad.fr; cultivation of bananas, pineapples, fruit-producing trees and intensive farming; Dir THIERRY GOGUEY MUETHON.

Institut de Recherche pour le Développement (IRD) Centre de la Martinique: BP 8006, 97259 Fort de France Cedex; tel. 5-90-39-77-39; fax 5-90-50-32-61; e-mail representant@ird-mq.fr; internet www.mq .ird.fr; f. 1958; soil science, nematology; library of 1,700 vols; Rep. DANIEL BARRETEAU; (see main entry under France).

MEDICINE

Laboratoire Départemental d'Hygiène de la Martinique: 35 blvd Pasteur, BP 628, 97261 Fort de France Cedex; tel. 5-90-71-34-52; fax 5-90-71-33-50; f. 1977; hygiene research and analysis of human blood and food and water; entomology; immunology of parasitic diseases; Dir Dr J. M. P. LAFAYE.

Libraries and Archives

Fort-de-France

Archives Départementales de la Martinique: BP 649, 19 rue Saint-John-Perse, Tartenson, 97263 Fort-de-France Cedex; e-mail archives@cg972.fr; internet www2 .cg972.fr/arch/html/index01.htm; f. 1949; 12,000 vols; Dir LILIANE CHAULEAU.

Bibliothèque Schoelcher: BP 640, Rue de la Liberté, Fort-de-France; tel. 5-90-70-26-67; fax 5-90-72-45-55; e-mail biblio-schoelcher-dep@cg972.fr; f. 1883; 226,000 vols; Dir ANIQUE SYLVESTRE.

Schoelcher

Service Commun de la Documentation de l'Université des Antilles et de la Guyane (SCUDAG—Section Martinique): BP 7210, 97275 Schoelcher Cedex; tel. 5-90-72-75-30; fax 5-90-72-75-27; e-mail m-f.bernabe@martinique.univ-ag.fr; internet www.univ-ag.fr/buag/main.php; f. 1972; administrative headquarters for the 3 branches of the univ. library (see also French Guiana and Guadeloupe); 100,000 vols, 738 periodicals; Dir of SCDUAG MARIE-FRANÇOISE BERNABÉ; Dir of Martinique Branch MARIE-FRANCE GROUVEL.

Museums and Art Galleries

Fort-de-France

Musée Départemental d'Archéologie Précolombienne et de Préhistoire de la Martinique: 9 rue de la Liberté, 97200 Fort-de-France; tel. 5-90-71-57-05; fax 5-90-73-03-80; e-mail musarc@cg972.fr; internet www2 .cg972.fr/mdap/default.htm; f. 1971; prehistory of Martinique; archaeological collections; Dir CÉCILE CELMA.

Musée Régional d'Histoire et d'Ethnographie: 10 Blvd Général de Gaulle, 97200 Fort de France; f. 1999; attached library specializing in works on slavery; Curator LYNE-ROSE BEUZE.

University

Université des Antilles et de la Guyane: Campus de Fouillole, 1st Fl., Bâtiment Mérault, , 97157 Pointe à Pitre Cedex; tel. 5-90-48-91-98; fax 5-90-48-92-78; e-mail vp-cur-gpe@univ-ag.fr; internet www .univ-ag.fr; library: see Libraries and Archives; Pres. ALAIN ARCONTE; Vice-Pres. (Martinique) DIDIER BERNARD; (see also under French Guiana and Guadeloupe).

TEACHING AND RESEARCH UNITS

Arts and Humanities: Dean JEAN-GEORGES CHALI

Law and Economics: Dean GEORGES VIRASSAMY

NEW CALEDONIA

Learned Societies

GENERAL

Groupe de Recherche en Histoire Océanienne Contemporaine (GRHOC): BP R4, 98845 Nouméa; tel. 26-58-58; e-mail angleviel@univ-nc.nc; f. 1996; historical and anthropological research; development of regional research; 10 mems; Pres. FRÉDÉRIC ANGLEVIEL; publs *101 Mots pour Comprendre* (annually), *Annales d'Histoire Calédonienne* (annually).

HISTORY, GEOGRAPHY AND ARCHAEOLOGY

Société d'Etudes Historiques de la Nouvelle-Calédonie: BP 63, 98845 Nouméa; f. 1968; research and study of the past; heritage conservation; publs books and periodicals on history, pre-history, Melanesian society, etc.; close contact with the univs of the Pacific area; 127 mems; archives; Pres. GABRIEL VALET; publ. *Bulletin* (quarterly).

LANGUAGE AND LITERATURE

Association des Ecrivains de Nouvelle-Calédonie: BP 712, 98845 Nouméa; e-mail jcb@jcbourdais.net; internet www .ecrivains-nc.org; f. 1996; 27 mems; Pres. NICOLAS KURTOVITCH; Sec. ARLETTE PEIRANO.

Research Institutes

GENERAL

Institut de Recherche pour le Développement (IRD) Centre de Nouméa: BP A5, 98848 Nouméa; tel. 26-10-00; fax 26-43-26; internet www.ird.nc; f. 1946; geology, geophysics, agropedology, hydrology, botany and plant ecology, pharmacology, phytopathology and applied zoology, physical and biological oceanography, archaeology, geography, microbiology; library: 12,500 vols, 150 periodicals; Rep. FABRICE COLIN; publs *Earth Sciences*, *Life Sciences*, *Sea Sciences*, *Social Sciences*; (see main entry under France).

EDUCATION

Centre Territorial de Recherche et de Documentation Pédagogiques de Nouvelle-Calédonie (New Caledonia Territorial Centre for Research and Pedagogic Documentation): BP 215, Nouméa; tel. 27-52-93; fax 28-31-13; f. 1978; research in education; library of 12,000 vols, 800 video tapes, 2,200 slide serials; Dir PHILIPPE BOYER.

MEDICINE

Institut Pasteur de Nouvelle Calédonie: BP 61, Nouméa; tel. 27-26-66; fax 27-33-90; e-mail direction@pasteur.nc; f. 1954; medical analysis laboratory; research laboratory: dengue fever, leptospirosis, tuberculosis; 80

staff; library of 1,080 vols; Dir Dr PAUL MARTIN; publ. *Rapport technique* (annually).

RELIGION, SOCIOLOGY AND ANTHROPOLOGY

Co-ordination pour l'Océanie des Recherches sur les Arts, les Idées et les Littératures (C.O.R.A.I.L.): BP 2448, 98846 Nouméa Cedex; fax 25-95-27; internet pages.univ-nc.nc/~vernaudo/index.html; f. 1987; for the study of francophone and anglophone literatures and civilizations of the South Pacific; annual themed conference; Pres. VÉRONIQUE FILLIOL; Sec. JACQUES VERNAUDON; publ. *Actes du Colloque* (annually).

Libraries and Archives

Nouméa

Bibliothèque Bernheim: BP G1, 98848 Nouméa Cedex; tel. 24-20-90; fax 27-65-88; e-mail bibbern@canl.nc; internet www.bernheim.nc; f. 1905; 141,000 vols, 28,500 vols of children's books, 85 periodicals; public library (adults and children), record library; historical, ethnological collections of 2,500 vols dealing with New Caledonia and the Pacific Islands; Librarian J. F. CARREZ-CORRAL.

Secretariat of the Pacific Community Library: BP D5, 98848 Nouméa Cedex; tel. 26-20-00; fax 26-38-18; e-mail library@spc.int; internet www.spc.int/library; f. 1947; reference library on health, women, youth, statistics, demography, cultural policy, agriculture, forestry, fisheries, and economic and social development in the Pacific Islands; 45,000 documents, 2,730 periodicals; br. library in Suva, Fiji; Librarian ELEANOR KLEIBER; publs *New Additions to the Library* (quarterly), *Select List of Publications* (annually).

Service Territorial des Archives de Nouvelle Calédonie: BP 525, Nouméa; tel. 28-59-42; fax 27-12-92; e-mail archives@gouv.nc; internet www.archives.nc; f. 1987; manages the historical and administrative archives of the territory; 5,196 linear m of archives; 7,000 vols; Dir JACQUES ANCEY (acting).

University

UNIVERSITÉ DE LA NOUVELLE-CALÉDONIE
(University of New Caledonia)

BPR 4, 98851 Nouméa Cedex
Telephone: 26-58-00
Fax: 25-48-29
E-mail: webadmin@univ-nc.nc
Internet: www.univ-nc.nc

Founded 1999 from the New Caledonia centre of the former Université Française du Pacifique
State control
Academic year: February to November

President: Prof. ALAIN FAGES
First Vice-President: JEAN-MARC BOYER
Second Vice-President: JEAN-MICHEL LEBIGRE
Secretary-General: PHILIPPE MARTIN
Registrar: THIERRY MABRU
Chief Librarian: GAËLLE GAUVRIT

Library of 34,000 books, 350 periodicals
Number of teachers: 70
Number of students: 2,300

Publication: *UNC-Info* (monthly)

Departments of Arts, Languages and Humanities; Law, Economics and Management; and Science and Technology.

Conservatoire National des Arts et Métiers: BP 3562, Nouméa Cedex; tel. 28-37-07; fax 27-79-96; e-mail noucnam@offratel.nc; f. 1971; attached to the Conservatoire National des Arts et Métiers in Paris; 12 staff, 500 students; Pres. JEAN BEGAUD; Dir BERNARD SCHALL.

RÉUNION

Learned Societies

GENERAL

Académie de l'Île de la Réunion: 142 rue Jean-Chatel, 97400 Saint-Denis; tel. 20-10-09; f. 1913; 25 mems; Pres. SERGE YCARD; Sec. YVES DROUHET; publ. *Bulletin*.

HISTORY, GEOGRAPHY AND ARCHAEOLOGY

Association Historique Internationale de l'Océan Indien: c/o Archives Départementales de la Réunion, 4 rue Marcel Regnol, 97490 Saint-Denis; f. 1960; 86 mems; Pres. CL. WANQUET; Sec.-Gen. B. JULLIEN; publ. *Bulletin de Liaison et d'Information* (2 a year).

Research Institutes

AGRICULTURE, FISHERIES AND VETERINARY SCIENCE

Centre de Co-opération Internationale en Recherche Agronomique pour le Développement (CIRAD): Station de la Bretagne, BP 20, 97408 Saint-Denis Cedex 9; tel. 52-80-10; fax 52-80-11; e-mail cirad-reunion@cirad.fr; f. 1962; library of 5,000 vols; agronomic research, mainly on sugar cane, fruit, vegetables, maize and fodder crops; water management and prevention of soil erosion; 49 research staff; Head JEAN-PIERRE GAY; publ. *Rapport Annuel*.

ECONOMICS, LAW AND POLITICS

Institut National de la Statistique et des Etudes Economiques–Direction Régionale de la Réunion: Parc Technologique, 10 rue Demarne, BP 13, 97408 Saint-Denis Cedex 9; tel. 48-89-00; fax 48-89-90; internet www.insee.fr/fr/insee_regions/reunion/home/home_page.asp; f. 1966; attached to INSEE, Paris (see main entry in chapter on France); produces statistical data, economic studies, etc.; database with 10,000 bibliographical references on the region, data bank with 2,000 chronological series; Dir JEAN GAILLARD; publs *L'Economie de la Réunion* (every 3 months), *Tableau Economique de la Réunion* (annually).

Libraries and Archives

St-Denis

Bibliothèque Centrale de Prêt: 1 place Joffre, 97400 St-Denis; tel. 21-03-24; fax 21-41-30; e-mail bdp@cg974.fr; f. 1956; 100,000 vols; Dir ELISABETH DÉGON.

Bibliothèque Départementale: 52 rue Roland Garros, 97400 St-Denis; tel. 21-13-96; e-mail bibliotheque.departementale@cg974.fr; f. 1855; 95,000 vols; Dir ALAIN VAUTHIER.

Service Commun de la Documentation (Bibliothèque Universitaire): Université de la Réunion, 15 ave René Cassin, BP 7152, 97715 St-Denis Cedex 9; tel. 93-83-79; fax 93-83-64; e-mail scd@univ-reunion.fr; internet www.univ-reunion.fr; f. 1971; arts, human sciences, law, economics, politics, social sciences, management, science, medicine; 171,252 vols, 1,495 current periodicals, 3,000 on-line periodicals; special collections on the Indian Ocean islands; Library Dir ANNE-MARIE BLANC.

St-Pierre

Médiathèque de Saint-Pierre: Rue du Collège Arthur, BP 396, 97458 St-Pierre Cedex; tel. 96-71-96; fax 25-74-10; e-mail ksl@mediatheque-saintpierre.fr; internet www.mediatheque-saintpierre.fr; f. 1967; 70,000 vols, 190 periodicals, 12,000 CDs, 2,500 videotapes; Dir LINDA KOO SEEN LIN.

Ste-Clotilde

Archives Départementales de La Réunion: 4 rue Marcel Pagnol, Champ-Fleuri, 97490 Ste-Clotilde; tel. 94-04-14; fax 94-04-21; e-mail archives@cg974.fr; f. 1946; specializes in the history of the Indian Ocean and information on Bourbon Island and Réunion; 5,000 vols, 100,000 other items in public and private archives; Dir NADINE ROUAYROUX.

Museums and Art Galleries

St-Denis

Muséum d'Histoire Naturelle: Jardin de l'Etat, 97400 St-Denis; tel. 20-02-19; fax 21-33-93; e-mail museum@cg.974.fr; internet www.cg974.fr/museum; f. 1854; library of

7,000 vols; zoology and mineralogy; Dir S. RIBES.

Musée Léon-Dierx: 28 rue de Paris, 97400 St-Denis; tel. 20-24-82; fax 21-82-87; e-mail musee.dierx@cg974.fr; f. 1911; fine arts; Curator LAURENCE LECIEUX.

St-Gilles-les-Hauts

Musée Historique de Villèle: Domaine Panon-Desbassayns, 97435 St-Gilles-les-Hauts; tel. 55-64-10; fax 55-51-91; e-mail musee.villele@cg974.fr; f. 1976; 18th c. plantation house and adjoining properties; French East India Co. furniture and china, prints, models, weapons, documents; Curator JEAN BARBIER.

University

UNIVERSITÉ DE LA RÉUNION (UNIVERSITÉ EUROPÉENNE DE L'OCÉAN INDIEN)

15 ave René Cassin, BP 7151, 97715 Saint-Denis Messag Cedex 9

Telephone: 93-80-80

Fax: 93-80-13

E-mail: ur.com@univ-reunion.fr

Internet: www.univ-reunion.fr

Founded 1970, university status 1982

President: Prof. SERGE SVIZZERO

Vice-Presidents: Prof. MOHAMED ROCHDI (Administration), Prof. GWENHAËL PONNAU, Prof. LAURENT SERMET (International Relations), Prof. PATRICK BACHELERY (Research Development), Prof. SERGE SVIZZERO (Science), BRUNO RASSABY (Students), Dr GILLES LAJOIE (Studies and University Life)

Director of South Campus: Prof. JEAN-CLAUDE GATINA

Librarian: ANNE-MARIE BLANC

Library: see Service Commun de la Documentation, Réunion

Number of teachers: 355

Number of students: 11,196

DEANS

Faculty of Arts and Humanities: MICHEL LATCHOUMANIN

Faculty of Law and Political and Economic Sciences: JEAN-BAPTISTE SEUBE

Faculty of Science and Technology: JACQUELINE SMADJA

ATTACHED INSTITUTES

Institut d'Administration des Entreprises: Dir MICHEL BOYER.

Institut Universitaire de Technologie: Dir DIDIER LENTREIN.

GABON

The Higher Education System

Gabon gained its independence from France 1960 and the higher education system still reflects its French heritage; many students also go to France to attend university or receive technical training. The first institutions of higher education were a polytechnic institute and law school associated with the Central African Higher Education Foundation, created in 1961 by the heads of state of the former French Equatorial Africa. Université Omar Bongo, the first university, was founded in 1970 and adopted its current name in 1978. The other two universities are Université des Sciences et techniques de Masuku (founded 1986) and Université des Sciences de la Santé (founded 2002). Higher education is highly centralized and controlled mostly by the State, which subsidizes each student for about 95% of the cost of education and provides financial aid equivalent to 40% of the total budget allocation for higher education. Student fees represent only 3% of income.

Admission to higher education is dependent upon award of the Baccalauréat, the main secondary school qualification. University-level degrees are divided into three cycles. The first cycle lasts for two years and leads to the award of Diplôme Universitaire d'Etudes Littéraires, Diplôme Universitaire d'Etudes Scientifiques, Diplôme Universitaire d'Etudes Juridiques, or Diplôme Universitaire d'Etudes Economiques. A further year of study (three in total) leads to the award of the Licence; a further two years (four in total) leads to the Maîtrise; these degrees comprise the second cycle. Some professional titles, such as Diplôme d'Ingénieur and the Doctorat en Médecine are awarded after five to six years of study. Finally, the third cycle consists of diploma programmes offered by professional institutions, admission to which is conditional on the Maîtrise. Higher vocational education is offered by professional schools and institutes.

Higher education has contributed significantly to Gabon's development. Graduates operate effectively at all levels of public and private administration. However, the recent increase in student numbers and the lack of sufficient funds are likely to have an adverse affect on the quality of both teaching and research. Despite this, higher education is still viewed as an investment which benefits all levels of society.

Learned Societies

GENERAL

UNESCO Office Libreville: BP 2183, Libreville; located at: Cité de la Démocratie, Bâtiment 6, B.P. 2183, Libreville; tel. (1) 762879; fax (1) 762814; e-mail unesclbv@inet.ga; designated Cluster Office for Republic of Congo, Democratic Republic of Congo, Equatorial Guinea, Gabon, São Tomé e Principé; Dir MAKHILY GASSAMA.

LANGUAGE AND LITERATURE

Alliance Française: BP 1371, Port Gentil; tel. and fax (2) 565941; e-mail alliance.francogab@inet.ga; offers courses and exams in French language and culture and promotes cultural exchange with France.

Research Institutes

GENERAL

Centre National de la Recherche Scientifique et Technologique (CENAREST): BP 13354, Libreville; tel. (1) 732578; internet www.cenarest.org; f. 1976; principal research body; designs and operates research programmes into human sciences, tropical ecology, agronomy, medicinal plants and plant biotechnology; consists of 5 research institutes: l'Institut de Pharmacopée et de Médecine Traditionnelles; l'Institut de Recherches Agronomiques et Forestières; l'Institut de Recherches en Ecologie Tropicale; l'Institut de Recherches en Sciences Humaines; and l'Institut des Recherches Technologiques; Dir SAMUEL MBADIGA.

AGRICULTURE, FISHERIES AND VETERINARY SCIENCE

Centre Technique Forestier Tropical, Section Gabon: BP 149, Libreville; f. 1958; silviculture, technology, genetic improvement; library of 500 vols; Dir J. LEROY DEVAL.

Institut de Recherches Agronomiques et Forestières (IRAF): BP 2246, Libreville; tel. (1) 732375; fax (1) 732378; e-mail angoye@assala.com; internet www.cenarest.org/instituts/iraf; f. 1977; attached to Centre National de la Recherche Scientifique et Technologique (CENAREST); research into agronomy, silviculture and forestry; Dir ALFRED NGOYE.

MEDICINE

Centre International de Recherches Médicales de Franceville: BP 769, Franceville; tel. (2) 677096; fax (2) 677295; e-mail faxcirmf@cirmf.sci.ga; f. 1979; undertakes basic and applied research in medical parasitology (e.g. malaria, filariosis, trypanosomiasis) and viral diseases (incl. HIV/AIDS, Ebola); library of 1,800 vols, 72 periodicals, 20,000 microfiches; Dir-Gen. Prof. PHILIPPE BLOT.

Institut de Pharmacopée et de Médecine Traditionnelle (IPHAMETRA): BP 1935, Libreville; tel. (1) 734786; fax (1) 732578; internet www.cenarest.org/instituts/iphametra; f. 1976; attached to Centre National de la Recherche Scientifique et Technologique (CENAREST); Dir Dr HENRI PAUL BOUROBOU.

NATURAL SCIENCES

Biological Sciences

Institut de Recherche en Ecologie Tropicale (IRET): BP 13354, Makokou; tel. (1) 443319; internet www.cenarest.org/instituts/iret; f. 1979; attached to Centre National de la Recherche Scientifique et Technologique (CENAREST); Dir PAUL POSSO.

RELIGION, SOCIOLOGY AND ANTHROPOLOGY

Institut de Recherches en Sciences Humaines (IRSH): BP 846, Libreville; tel. (1) 734719; internet www.cenarest.org/instituts/irsh; f. 1976; attached to Centre National de la Recherche Scientifique et Technologique (CENAREST); Dir Dr MAGLOIRE MOUNGANGAI.

TECHNOLOGY

Bureau de Recherches Géologiques et Minières (BRGM): BP 175, Libreville; f. 1960; Dir. M. BERTUCAT; (See main entry under France.).

Institut de Recherches Technologiques (IRT): BP 14070, Libreville; tel. (1) 733089; internet www.cenarest.org/instituts/irt; f. 1976; attached to Centre National de la Recherche Scientifique et Technologique (CENAREST); Dir Dr JEAN DANIEL MBEGAI.

Libraries and Archives

Libreville

Bibliothèque du Centre d'Information: BP 750, Libreville; f. 1960; 6,000 vols; 80 current periodicals.

Direction Générale des Archives Nationales, de la Bibliothèque Nationale et de la Documentation Gabonaise (DGABD): BP 1188, Libreville; tel. (1) 736310 (Archives Nationales); tel. (1) 730972 (Bibliothèque Nationale); tel. (1) 737247 (Documentation Gabonaise); f. 1969 (Nat. Archives and Nat. Library), 1980 (Gabonese Documentation); 36 mems; 29,000 vols, 2,000 periodical titles; 2 linear km archives, 639 microfilms, 666 maps and plans, 1,712 archive photographs; Archives Dir JÉRÔME ANGOUME-NGOGHE; Nat. Library Dir JEAN MICHEL NOUDODO; Documentation Dir JEAN PAUL MIFOUNA; Dir-Gen. RENÉ GEORGES SONNET-AZIZE.

Museum

Libreville

Musée National des Arts et Traditions du Gabon: BP 4018, Libreville; tel. (1) 761456; national museum; thematic exhibition on Gabonese masks; public library on arts from Gabon; Dir Prof. PAUL ABA'A NDONG.

Universities

UNIVERSITÉ OMAR BONGO

BP 13 131, Blvd Léon M'Ba, Libreville
Telephone: (1) 732045
E-mail: uob@internetgabon.com
Internet: www.uob.ga
Founded 1970, renamed 1978
State control
Language of instruction: French
Academic year: October to July

Rector: JEAN-ÉMILE MBOT
Vice-Rector for Academic Affairs and Research: JÉRÔME KWENZI-MAKALA
Vice-Rector for Administration and Inter-University Cooperation: JÉRÔME NDZOUNGOU
Secretary-General: GUY ROSSATANGA-RIGNAULT
Librarian: FERDINAND NGOUNGOULOU

Library of 12,000 vols
Number of teachers: 300
Number of students: 4,800

Publications: *Cahiers Gabonais d'Anthropologie, Cahiers d'Histoire et d'Archéologie, Exchorésis, Gabonica, Kilombo, Psychologie et Culture, Revue Gabonaise des Sciences de l'Homme, Revue Gabonaise des Sciences du Langage, Waves*

DEANS

Faculty of Law and Economics: Prof. JEAN JACQUES EKOMIE
Faculty of Letters and Sciences: GUY SERGE BIGNOUMBA

ATTACHED RESEARCH INSTITUTES

Centre d'Etudes en Littérature Gabonaise: Dir HÉMERY-HERVAIS SIMA EYI.

Centre d'Etudes et de Recherches d'Histoire Économique, Administrative et Financière (CERHEAF): Dir Prof. PIERRE NDOMBI.

Centre d'Etudes et de Recherches du Monde Anglophone (CERMA): Dir DANIEL RENÉ AKENDENGUE.

Centre d'Etudes et de Recherches Philosophiques (CERP): Dir GILBERT ZUE NGUEMA.

Centre de Recherches Afro-Hispaniques (CRAHI): Dir GISÈLE AVOME MBA.

Centre de Recherches et d'Etudes en Psychologie (CREP): Dir THÉODORE KOUMBA.

Groupe de Recherches en Langues et Cultures Orales (GRELACO): Dir Prof. JAMES DUPLESSIS EMEJULU.

Institut Cheikh Anta Diop (ICAD): Dir GRÉGOIRE BIYOGO NANG.

Laboratoire d'Analyse Spatiale et des Environnements Tropicaux (LANASPET): Dir GALLEY YAWO.

Laboratoire de Graphique et de Cartographie (LAGRAC): Dir Dr JULES DJEKI.

Laboratoire National d'Archéologie (LANA): Dir MICHEL ATHANASE LOCKO.

Laboratoire Universitaire de la Tradition Orale (LUTO): Dir Prof. FABIEN OKOUE-METOGO.

Politiques et Développement des Espaces et Sociétés de l'Afrique Subsaharienne (CERGEP): Dir MARC LOUIS ROPIVIA.

UNIVERSITÉ DES SCIENCES DE LA SANTÉ

BP 18231, Owendo, Libreville
Telephone: (1) 702028
Fax: (1) 702919
E-mail: rectorat@uss-univ.com
Founded 2002
State Control

Rector: ANDRÉ MOUSSAVOU-MOUYAMA

Courses in health sciences.

UNIVERSITÉ DES SCIENCES ET TECHNIQUES DE MASUKU

BP 901, Franceville
Telephone: (2) 677449
Fax: (2) 677520
Founded 1986
State control
Language of instruction: French

Rector: JACQUES LEBIBI
Vice-Rector for Academic Affairs and Research: BERTRAND M'BATCHI
Vice-Rector for Administrative Affairs and Inter-university Co-operation: Prof. AMBROISE EDOU MINKO
Secretary-General: Dr GEORGES AZZIBROUCK
Librarian: YVES NTOUTOUME

Library of 11,000 vols
Number of teachers and researchers: 110
Number of students: 800

DEAN

Faculty of Sciences: Dr LÉON NGADI

HEADS OF DEPARTMENTS

Biology: Dr IBRAHIM
Chemistry: Dr RAPHAËL BIKANGA
Geology: Dr MICHEL MBINA
Mathematics and Information Science: Dr MARTIAL NKIET
Physics: Dr ELOI BLAMPAIN

Colleges

Ecole Interprovinciale de Santé: BP 530, Mouila; tel. (2) 861177; f. 1981; 18 teachers; 76 students; Dir PIERRE FRANKLIN NGUEMA ONDO.

Institut Africain d'Informatique: BP 2263, Libreville; tel. (1) 720005; fax (1) 720011; e-mail info@iai.ga; internet www.iai.ga; f. 1971 by member states of OCAM to train computer programmers, computer science engineers and analysts; small library; 8 permanent teachers; 281 students; Dir FABIEN MBALLA.

GAMBIA

The Higher Education System

Higher education, in the sense of an institution offering Bachelors, Masters and Doctorate degrees, did not exist in Gambia until 1995. Prior to this Gambians wishing to pursue higher education could either study abroad or enrol at a post-secondary institution, the main such institutions being the Gambia College and the Gambia Technical Training Institute. A University Extension Programme was established in 1995 as a collaborative effort between the Government and the Nova Scotia Gambia Association (NSGA), a Canadian NGO, and Saint Mary's University (located in Halifax, Nova Scotia). The first university, the University of The Gambia, Banjul, was opened in 2000, with the assistance of Saint Mary's University. The higher education sector in Gambia is administered and funded by the Government.

Admission to university is on the basis of the West African Secondary School Certificate or equivalent qualification. The University of The Gambia offers Bachelors degrees, which are awarded following four years. There are no postgraduate degree courses. Technical and vocation education is offered by the Gambia Technical Training Institute and Gambia College. The main qualifications are the Diploma and Certificate.

Learned Society

LANGUAGE AND LITERATURE

Alliance Française: Kairaba Ave, Kanifing, POB 2930, Serrekunda, Banjul; tel. 4375418; fax 4374172; e-mail alliancefg@gamtel.gm; internet www.alliancefr-senegalgambie.org; offers courses and exams in French language and culture and promotes cultural exchange with France.

Research Institutes

MEDICINE

Medical Research Council Dunn Nutrition Unit, Keneba: Keneba, West Kiang; f. 1974; field station of the Dunn Nutrition Unit laboratory in Cambridge, UK; research on maternal undernutrition, including work on paediatric gastroenterology and nutrition, and the physiological adaptation of mothers to pregnancy and lactation; maternal vitamin and mineral requirements; research into long-term effects of ante-natal and early post-natal nutrition; research on growth deficiency and the role of economic status on malnutrition; calorimetry research on comparisons of energy expenditure between Gambians and Europeans; Supervisor Dr ELIZABETH POSKITT.

Medical Research Council: POB 273, Banjul; located at: Atlantic Blvd Fajara; tel. 4496715; fax 4494154; e-mail aoffong@mrc.gm; internet www.mrc.gm; f. 1947; laboratory research, field research and clinical studies aimed at reducing illness and death from tropical infectious diseases; research on viral diseases, bacterial diseases and malaria; a nutrition research group is based at the MRC Keneba Field Site; Unit Dir Prof. TUMANI CORRAH.

Library

Banjul

Gambia National Library: Department Mail Bag, Reg Pye Lane, Banjul; tel. 4228312; fax 4223776; e-mail national.library@ganet.gm; f. 1946 by British Ccl, taken over by Govt 1962, autonomous 1985; serves as a public and national library; national deposit library; 115,400 vols, 85 periodicals; special collection of Gambiana; Chief Librarian ABDOU WALLY MBYE; publs *National Bibliography*, *Wax Taani Xalel Yi* (children's magazine), *Annual Report*.

Museum

Banjul

Gambia National Museum: P.M.B. 151, Independence Drive, Banjul; tel. 4226244; fax 4227461; e-mail musmon@qanet.gm; library of 645 vols; f. 1982; Curator HASSOUM CESSAY.

University

UNIVERSITY OF THE GAMBIA

Administration Bldg, Kanifing, POB 3530, Serrekunda
Telephone: 4372213
Fax: 4395064
E-mail: unigambia@qanet.gm
Internet: www.unigambia.gm
Founded 1999
State control
Academic year: October to July (two semesters)
Vice-Chancellor: Prof. DONALD E. U. EKONG
Registrar: E. J. AKPAN
Student Affairs: LAMIN S. JAITEH
Senate: LANG SAJO MUSTAPHA JADAMA
Council: MOMODOU LAMIN TARRO
Number of teachers: 99 (78 full-time, 21 part-time)
Number of students: 1,356

DEANS

Faculty of Economics and Management Sciences: SULAYMAN M. B. FYE
Faculty of Humanities and Social Sciences: Prof. EDRIS MAKWARD
Faculty of Medicine and Allied Health Sciences: Prof. ETIM M. ESSIEN
Faculty of Science and Agriculture: Prof. FELIXTINA JONSYN-ELLIS (acting)

College

Gambia College: Brikama Campus, POB 144, Banjul; tel. 4484812; fax 4483224; e-mail gcollege@qanet.gm; f. 1978; library: 23,000 vols; 57 teachers; 400 students; Pres. A. B. SENGHORE; Registrar N. S. MANNEH

HEADS OF SCHOOLS

Agriculture: EBRIMA CHAM (acting)
Education: W. A. COLE
Nursing and Midwifery: F. SARR
Public Health: B. A. PHALL

GEORGIA

The Higher Education System

Georgia was formerly a constituent republic of the USSR, from which it gained its independence in 1999. Most institutions were founded during the Soviet period and consequently reflected Soviet practices, but since independence there have been numerous reforms and ongoing projects. The Law of Education (2004) laid out further plans for the reform of secondary and higher education, including implementation of the Bologna Process. In 2005/06 there were 144,313 students in higher education. Institutions of higher education are universities, institutes, academies and conservatories. Higher education is administered by the Ministry of Education and Science.

Higher education admissions are determined on the basis of performance in the Unified National University Entry Examinations, administered by the National Assessment and Examinations Centre. Students take a range of compulsory and voluntary subjects relevant to their intended path of study. In May 2005 Georgia signed up to the Bologna Process. It is intended that Georgia will have a new degree structure in place by 2007/08 consisting of Bachelors, Masters and Doctorate degrees, and that the European Credit Transfer System (ECTS) will be adopted to facilitate student transfers. The Bakalavris Diplomi (Bachelors) is the main undergraduate degree and is awarded after three to fours years' study. The older, Soviet-style Certified Specialist degree is still awarded in some (mainly) professional fields. A Masters degree is awarded after the Bachelors following two years of study. A new doctoral degree is being developed to replace the old-style Candidate of Science and Doctor of Science degrees.

Learned Societies

GENERAL

Georgian Academy of Sciences: 0108 Tbilisi, Pr. Rustaveli 52; tel. (32) 99-88-91; fax (32) 99-88-23; e-mail frg@gw.acnet.ge; internet www.acnet.ge; f. 1941; depts of Agricultural Science Problems (Academician-Sec. O. G. NATISHVILI), Applied Mechanics, Machine Building and Control Processes (Academician-Sec. M. E. SALIKVADZE), Biology (Academician-Sec. G. KVESITADZE), Chemistry and Chemical Technology (Academician-Sec. G. G. GVELESIANI), Earth Sciences (Academician-Sec. E. P. GAMKRELIDZE), Linguistics and Literature (Academician-Sec. T. GAMKRELIDZE), Mathematics and Physics (Academician-Sec. J. LOMINADZE), Physiology and Experimental Medicine (Academician-Sec. T. N. ONIANI), Social Sciences (Academician-Sec. G. B. TEVZADZE); 135 mems (66 academicians, 69 corresp.); attached research institutes: see Research Institutes; library: see Libraries and Archives; Pres. Acad. Prof. Dr THOMAS V. GAMKRELIDZE; publs *Metsnierba da Technika* (monthly), *Moambe* (Bulletin, in Georgian and English, monthly).

HISTORY, GEOGRAPHY AND ARCHAEOLOGY

Georgian Geographical Society: 0107 Tbilisi, Ketskhoveli 11; attached to Georgian Acad. of Sciences; Chair. V. SH. DZHAOSHVILI.

Georgian History Society: 0108 Tbilisi, Rustaveli 52; attached to Georgian Acad. of Sciences; Vice-Chair. A. M. APAKIDZE.

LANGUAGE AND LITERATURE

Amateur Society of Basque Language and Culture: 0108 Tbilisi, Pr. Rustaveli 52; attached to Georgian Acad. of Sciences; Chair. SH. V. DZIDZIGURI.

British Council: 0108 Tbilisi, Pr. Rustaveli 34; tel. (32) 25-04-07; fax (32) 98-95-91; e-mail office.bc@ge.britishcouncil.org; internet www.britishcouncil.org.ge; offers courses and examinations in English language and British culture and promotes cultural exchange with the UK; Dir JO BAKOWSKI; Librarian TAMUNA KVACHADZE.

Goethe-Institute: 0108 Tbilisi, ul. Sandukeli 16; tel. (32) 93-89-45; fax (32) 93-45-68; e-mail info@tbilissi.goethe.org; internet www.goethe.de/ins/ge/tif/deindex.htm; offers courses and examinations in German language and culture and promotes cultural exchange with Germany; library: 3500 vols; Dir UWE RIEKEN.

MEDICINE

Georgian Bio-Medico-Technical Society: 0103 Tbilisi, Telavi 51; attached to Georgian Acad. of Sciences; Chair. K. SH. NADAREISHVILI.

Georgian Neuroscience Association: c/o Beritashvili Institute of Physiology, 0160 Tbilisi, Gotua 14; tel. (32) 37-11-49; fax (32) 37-34-11; e-mail gena@geo.net.ge; internet www.itic.org.ge/gena; f. 1996; 105 mems; Pres. Prof. SIMON KHECHINASHVILI; Sec.-Gen. Prof. MERAB TSAGARELI.

Georgian Society of Patho-Anatomists: 0103 Tbilisi, V. Pshavela 27B; attached to Georgian Acad. of Sciences; Chair. T. I. DEKANOSIDZE.

NATURAL SCIENCES

Biological Sciences

Georgian Botanical Society: 0107 Tbilisi, Kodzhorskoe shosse; attached to Georgian Acad. of Sciences; Chair. G. SH. NAKHUTSRISHVILI.

Georgian Society of Biochemists: 0177 Tbilisi, Universitetis 2; tel. (32) 30-39-97; fax (32) 22-11-03; f. 1958; attached to Georgian Acad. of Sciences; 850 mems; Pres. Prof. NOUGZAR ALEKSIDZE; Sec. NANA ABASHIDZE.

Georgian Society of Geneticists and Selectionists: 0160 Tbilisi, ul L. Gotua 3; tel. (32) 37-42-27; attached to Georgian Acad. of Sciences; Chair. T. G. CHANISHVILI.

Georgian Society of Parasitologists: 0179 Tbilisi, Pr. Chavchavadze 31; tel. (32) 22-33-53; fax (32) 22-01-64; attached to Georgian Acad. of Sciences; f. 1958; 83 mems; Pres. Prof. B. E. KURASHVILI; Sec. K. G. NIKOLAISHVILI; publ. *Actual Problems of Parasitology in Georgia*.

Physical Sciences

Georgian Geological Society: 0108 Tbilisi, Pr. Rustaveli 52; tel. (32) 99-64-45; fax (32) 99-88-23; f. 1933; attached to Georgian Acad. of Sciences; 500 mems; Chair. IRAKLI P. GAMKRELIDZE.

Georgian National Speleological Society: 0193 Tbilisi, M. Aleksidze (Bl. 8); tel. (32) 33-74-49; fax (32) 33-14-17; f. 1980; attached to Georgian Acad. of Sciences; 75 mems; Chair. Z. K. TATASHIDZE; publ. *Caves of Georgia* (irreg.).

PHILOSOPHY AND PSYCHOLOGY

Georgian Philosophy Society: 0108 Tbilisi, Pr. Rustaveli 29; attached to Georgian Acad. of Sciences; Chair. N. Z. CHAVCHAVADZE.

Georgian Society of Psychologists: 0179 Tbilisi, Janashvili 22; attached to Georgian Acad. of Sciences; Chair. N. Z. NADIRASHVILI.

Research Institutes

GENERAL

Kutaisi Scientific Center: 4600 Kutaisi, Abashidze 22; tel. (331) 7-77-77; e-mail nkopa@sanetk.net.ge; attached to Georgian Acad. of Sciences; Dir R. ADAMAI.

AGRICULTURE, FISHERIES AND VETERINARY SCIENCE

Gulisashvili, V. Z., Institute of Mountain Forestry: 0186 Tbilisi, E. Mindeli 9; tel. (32) 30-34-66; e-mail postmaster@forest.acnet.ge; f. 1945; attached to Georgian Acad. of Sciences; Dir G. N. GIGAURI.

Institute of Water Management and Engineering Ecology: 0162 Tbilisi, Pr. Chavchavadze 60; tel. (32) 22-72-00; fax (32) 22-74-01; e-mail tsotnem@rambler.ru; f. 1929; attached to Georgian Acad. of Sciences; Dir T. MIRTSHOULAVA; publs *Proceedings*, *Recent Problems of Water Management*, *Transactions of International Conferences*.

Scientific Research Centre of the Biological Basis of Cattle-Breeding: 0162 Tbilisi, Paliashvili 87; tel. (32) 29-40-03; f. 1991; attached to Georgian Acad. of Sciences; Dir A. DOLMAZASHVILI.

ARCHITECTURE AND TOWN PLANNING

Zavriev, K. S., Institute of Construction Mechanics and Seismostability: 0193 Tbilisi, M. Aleksidze 8; tel. (32) 33-59-28; fax (32) 33-27-52; e-mail postmaster@seismo

.acnet.ge; f. 1947; attached to Georgian Acad. of Sciences; Dir Prof. G. K. GABRICHIDZE.

BIBLIOGRAPHY, LIBRARY SCIENCE AND MUSEOLOGY

Kekelidze, K. S., Institute of Manuscripts: 0193 Tbilisi, M. Aleksidze 1/3; tel. (32) 36-24-54; fax (32) 94-25-18; e-mail manuscript@iatp.org.ge; f. 1958; attached to Georgian Acad. of Sciences; Dir Z. ALEKSIDZE; publ. *Mravaltavi* (philology and history, annual).

ECONOMICS, LAW AND POLITICS

Gugushvili, P. V., Institute of Economics: 0105 Tbilisi, ul. Kikodze 22; tel. (32) 99-68-53; fax (32) 99-83-89; e-mail root@econom.acnet.ge; f. 1944; attached to Georgian Acad. of Sciences; Dir G. TSERETELI.

Institute of Political Science: 0162 Tbilisi, Paliashvili 87; tel. (32) 22-41-04; e-mail politic@gw.acnet.ge; f. 2000; attached to Georgian Acad. of Sciences; Dir V. KESHELAVA.

Institute of State and Law: 0105 Tbilisi, Kikodze 14; tel. (32) 98-32-45; e-mail root@stlow.acnet.ge; f. 1957; attached to Georgian Acad. of Sciences; Dir (vacant).

FINE AND PERFORMING ARTS

Chubinashvili, G. N., Institute of History of Georgian Art: 0108 Tbilisi, Pr. Rustaveli 52; tel. (32) 99-05-88; e-mail gahi@gas.hepi.edu.ge; f. 1941; attached to Georgian Acad. of Sciences; Dir T. SAKVARELIDZE; publ. *Ars Georgica*.

HISTORY, GEOGRAPHY AND ARCHAEOLOGY

Dzhavakhishvili, I. A., Institute of History and Ethnography: 0179 Tbilisi, ul. Melikishvili 10; tel. (32) 99-06-82; attached to Georgian Acad. of Sciences; Dir G. A. MELIKISHVILI.

Lordkipanidze Centre for Archaeological Studies: 0102 Tbilisi, D. Uznadze 14; tel. (32) 95-97-65; attached to Georgian Acad. of Sciences.

Mtskheta Institute of Archaeology: 3300 Mtskheta; f. 1994; attached to Georgian Acad. of Sciences; Dir A. APAKIDZE; publ. *Mtskheta*.

Vakhushti Bagrationi Institute of Geography: 0193 Tbilisi, M. Aleksidze 1 (Bl. 8); tel. (32) 33-74-49; fax (32) 33-14-07; e-mail geograf@gw.acnet.ge; f. 1933; attached to Georgian Acad. of Sciences; library of 68,000 vols; Dir ZURAB TATASHISZE; publ. *Caves of Georgia* (irreg.).

LANGUAGE AND LITERATURE

Chikobava, A. S., Institute of Linguistics: 0108 Tbilisi, ul. Ingorokva 8; tel. (32) 93-29-21; e-mail root@ike.acnet.ge; f. 1941; attached to Georgian Acad. of Sciences; Dir G. KVARATSKHELIA; publs *Iberian-Caucasian Linguistics*, *Problems of Georgian Literary Norms*, *Dialectological Studies*, *Etymological Studies*, *Problems of Georgian Language Structure*, *Problems of Modern General Linguistics*.

Shota Rustaveli Institute of Georgian Literature: 0108 Tbilisi, Kostava 5; tel. (32) 99-53-00; e-mail kli@literat.acnet.ge; f. 1932; attached to Georgian Acad. of Sciences; Dir G. D. BENASHVILI; publ. *Georgian Folklore*.

Tsereteli, G. V., Institute of Oriental Studies: 0103 Tbilisi, ul. G. Tsereteli 3; tel. (32) 23-23-72; fax (32) 23-30-08; e-mail root@orient.acnet.ge; f. 1960; attached to Georgian Acad. of Sciences; Dir T. GAMKRELIDZE.

MEDICINE

Beritashvili Institute of Physiology: 0160 Tbilisi, ul. Gotua 14; tel. (32) 37-12-31; fax (32) 37-34-11; e-mail info@biphysiol.ge; f. 1935; library of 48,000 vols; attached to Min. of Education and Science; Dir M. G. TSAGARELI.

Eliyava Institute of Bacteriophage, Microbiology and Virology: 0160 Tbilisi, ul. L. Gotua 3; tel. (32) 37-42-27; fax (32) 99-91-53; e-mail chanish@kheta.ge; f. 1923; attached to Georgian Acad. of Sciences; Dir T. CHANISHVILI.

Georgian Scientific Research Institute of Industrial Hygiene and Occupational Diseases: 0102 Tbilisi, D. Agmashenebeli 60; tel. (32) 95-65-94; f. 1927; library of 24,000 vols; Dir RUSUDAN DJAVAKHADZE; publ. periodicals on occupational hygiene and industrial diseases (annual).

Institute of Medical Biotechnology: 0159 Tbilisi, Chiaureli 2; tel. and fax (32) 52-99-16; e-mail medbio@gw.acnet.ge; f. 1991; attached to Georgian Acad. of Sciences; Dir V. I. BAKHUTASHVILI.

Institute of Pharmaceutical Chemistry: 0159 Tbilisi, P. Sarajishvili 36; tel. (32) 52-98-50; fax (32) 25-00-26; e-mail root@pharmac.acnet.ge; f. 1932; attached to Georgian Acad. of Sciences; library of 3,500 vols, 40 periodicals; Dir Prof. ETHER P. KEMERTELIDZE; publ. *Transactions*.

Institute of Radiology and Interventional Diagnostics: 0112 Tbilisi, ul. Tevdore Mgvdeli 13; tel. (32) 94-02-89; fax (32) 34-49-23; e-mail radiag@access.sanet.ge; f. 1991; Dir. Prof. FRIDON TODUA; publ. *Georgian Journal of Radiology* (quarterly).

Natishvili, A. N., Institute of Experimental Morphology: 0159 Tbilisi, Chiaureli 2; tel. (32) 52-09-06; f. 1946; attached to Georgian Acad. of Sciences; Dir N. A. JAVAKHISHVILI; publ. *Proceedings*.

Research and Teaching Clinical and Experimental Centre of Traumatology and Orthopaedics: 0102 Tbilisi, ul. Kalinina 51; tel. (32) 95-53-81; Dir B. TSERETELI.

Research Institute of Psychiatry: 0177 Tbilisi, ul. M. Asatiani 10; tel. (32) 39-47-65; fax (32) 94-36-73; e-mail georgia@gamh.kheta.ge; f. 1925; library of 8,000 vols, 7,000 periodicals..

Research Institute of Skin and Venereal Diseases: 0112 Tbilisi, ul. Ninoshvili 55; tel. (32) 95-35-64; fax (32) 96-48-02; e-mail dermat@nile.org.ge; f. 1935; library of 23,800 vols; Dir Dr BADZI CHLAIDZE; publ. *Trudy* (Proceedings, annual).

Scientific Research Centre for Radiobiology and Radiation Ecology: 0103 Tbilisi, Telavi 51; tel. (32) 94-20-17; fax (32) 93-61-26; e-mail kiazo@gw.acnet.ge; internet www.acnet.ge/radiobio; f. 1990; attached to Georgian Acad. of Sciences; Dir K. SH. NADAREISHVILI; publs *Radiation Studies* (2 a year), *Biomedical Techniques* (2 a year), *Problems of Ecology* (2 a year).

Virsaladze Institute of Medical Parasitology and Tropical Medicine: 0112 Tbilisi, D. Agmashenebeli 139; tel. (32) 95-92-26; e-mail medpar@geo.net.ge; internet geoparasitology.tripod.com; f. 1924; Dir G. CHUBABRIA.

Zhordania Institute of Human Reproduction: 0179 Tbilisi, Kostava 37; tel. (32) 99-61-97; fax (32) 99-81-08; Dir Prof A. KHOMASSURIDZE.

NATURAL SCIENCES

Biological Sciences

Batumi Botanical Gardens: 384533 Makhinjauri; f. 1912; attached to Georgian Acad. of Sciences; Dir V. PAPUNIDZE; publ. *Bulletin*.

Central Botanical Gardens: Botanikuri 1, 380005 Tbilisi; tel. and fax (32) 72-34-09; e-mail botbag@viam.hepi.edu.ge; f. 1636; attached to Georgian Acad,. of Sciences; Dir J. KERESELIDZE; publ. *Proceedings*.

Davitashvili, L. Sh., Institute of Palaeobiology: Niagvris 4, 380008 Tbilisi; tel. (32) 93-12-82; e-mail guram@paleobi.acnet.ge; f. 1957; attached to Georgian Acad. of Sciences; Dir G. A. MCHEDLIDZE.

Durmishidze Institute of Biochemistry and Biotechnology: D. Agmashenebeli 10 km, 380059 Tbilisi; tel. (32) 95-81-45; fax (32) 25-06-04; e-mail postmaster@biochem.acnet.ge; f. 1971; attached to Georgian Acad. of Sciences; library of 72,000 vols; Dir Prof. Dr G. I. KVESITADZE.

Institute of Molecular Biology and Biological Physics: Ul. L. Gotua 14, 380060 Tbilisi; tel. (32) 37-17-33; fax (32) 93-91-57; e-mail admin@biophys.org.ge; f. 1986; attached to Georgian Acad. of Sciences; Dir Dr M. M. ZAALISHVILI.

Institute of Zoology: Pr. Chavchavadze 31, 380079 Tbilisi; tel. (32) 22-01-64; f. 1941; attached to Georgian Acad. of Sciences; Dir I. ELIYAVA.

Ketskhoveli, N., Institute of Botany: Kojori 1, 0105 Tbilisi; tel. (32) 99-74-48; fax (32) 00-10-77; e-mail nakhutsrishvili@yahoo.com; f. 1933; attached to Georgian Acad. of Sciences; Dir G. NAKHUTSRISHVILI.

Mathematical Sciences

Muskhelishvili Institute of Computational Mathematics: Akuri 8, 380093 Tbilisi; tel. (32) 33-24-38; e-mail root@compmath.acnet.ge; f. 1956; attached to Georgian Acad. of Sciences; Dir Prof. N. VAKHANIYA; publs *Computational Mathematics and Programming*, *Mathematical and Technical Cybernetics*.

Razmadze, A., Mathematical Institute: M. Aleksidze 1, 0193 Tbilisi; tel. (32) 33-45-95; fax (32) 36-40-86; e-mail ninopa@rmi.acnet.ge; internet www.rmi.acnet.ge; f. 1935; attached to Min. of Education and Sciences; 69 mems; library of 95,690 vols; Dir Prof. NINO PARTSVANIA (acting); publs *Proceedings* (in English, 3 a year), *Memoirs on Differential Equations and Mathematical Physics* (in English, 3 a year), *Georgian Mathematical Journal* (in English, quarterly).

Physical Sciences

Abastumani Astrophysical Observatory: Kanobili Mountain, 383762 Abastumani; tel. (32) 95-53-67 Al. Kazbegi 2A, 380060 Tbilisi; tel. (32) 37-63-03; e-mail roki@gw.acnet.ge; f. 1941; attached to Georgian Acad. of Sciences; Dir R. KILADZE; publ. *Bulletin*.

Andronikashvili Institute of Physics: Ul. Tamarashvili 6, 380077 Tbilisi; e-mail postmaster@physics.acnet.ge; f. 1950; attached to Georgian Acad. of Sciences; Dir G. A. KHARADZE.

Dzanelidze, A. I., Geological Institute: M. Aleksidze 1 (bldg 9), 380093 Tbilisi; tel. (32) 29-39-41; e-mail geolog@gw.acnet.ge; f. 1925; attached to Georgian Acad. of Sciences; incorporates Scientific and Technical Centre of Physical Crystallography; Dir Prof. MIRIAN TOPCHISHVILI; publ. *Proceedings* (irregular).

Institute of Geophysics: M. Aleksidze 1, 380093 Tbilisi; tel. (32) 36-37-93; fax (32) 33-

28-67; e-mail seismo@ig.acnet.ge; f. 1933; attached to Georgian Acad. of Sciences; incorporates National Service of Seismic Defence; Dir T. L. CHELIDZE.

Institute of Hydrometeorology: David Agmashenebeli 150A, 380012 Tbilisi; tel. (32) 95-10-47; fax (32) 95-11-60; e-mail root@hydmet.acnet.ge; f. 1953; attached to Georgian Acad. of Sciences; Dir G. G. SVANIDZE; publ. *Transactions*.

Institute of Inorganic Chemistry and Electrical Chemistry: Mindeli 11, 380086 Tbilisi; tel. (32) 31-50-46; e-mail postmaster@elchem.acnet.ge; f. 1956; attached to Georgian Acad. of Sciences; Dir J. JONDO.

Melikishvili, P. G., Institute of Physical and Organic Chemistry: Jikia 5, 380086 Tbilisi; tel. (32) 99-88-23; f. 1929; attached to Georgian Acad. of Sciences; Dir T. ANDRONIKASHVILI.

Tavadze, F. N., Institute of Metallurgy and Materials Science: 15 Al. Kazbegi, Institute of Metallurgy, 1060 Tbilisi; tel. (32) 37-02-67; e-mail postmaster@metall.acnet.ge; f. 1945; attached to Georgian Acad. of Sciences; main fields of research: metallurgical processes, materials science and powder metallurgy; 280 mems; Dir ILIA B. BARATASHVILI.

Transcaucasian Hydrometeorological Research Institute: D. Agmashenebeli 150A, 380012 Tbilisi; tel. (32) 63-74-01; fax (32) 23-22-93.

PHILOSOPHY AND PSYCHOLOGY

Tsereteli Institute of Philosophy: Pr. Rustaveli 29, 380008 Tbilisi; tel. (32) 99-52-62; e-mail root@philos.acnet.ge; attached to Georgian Acad. of Sciences; f. 1946; Dir T. BUACHIDZE.

Uznadze, D. N., Institute of Psychology: Ul. Iashvili 22, 380007 Tbilisi; tel. (32) 93-24-54; e-mail root@psycho.acnet.ge; f. 1943; attached to Georgian Acad. of Sciences; Dir SH. NADIRASHVILI.

RELIGION, SOCIOLOGY AND ANTHROPOLOGY

Abuserisdze Tbeli Batumi Scientific Research Institute: Ninoshvili 23, 384516 Batumi; tel. (222) 3-29-01; fax (222) 7-58-17; e-mail isac@batumi.net; f. 1958; attached to Georgian Acad. of Sciences; Dir Dr IURI BIBILEISHVILI; publs *Monuments of South-Western Georgia* (annually), *Culture and Life in South-Western Georgia* (annually), *Folklore of South-Western Georgia* (annually), *Economic Problems in South-Western Georgia* (annually).

Institute of Demography and Sociological Studies: Ul. Pushkina 5, 380005 Tbilisi; tel. (32) 93-36-93; fax (32) 98-65-88; internet www.acnet.ge/demograph; f. 1990; attached to Georgian Acad. of Sciences; Dir Dr L. L. CHIKAVA; publ. *Demography* (4 a year).

TECHNOLOGY

Eliashvili Institute of Control Systems: K. Gamsakhurdia 34, 380060 Tbilisi; tel. (32) 37-20-44; e-mail postmaster@contsys.acnet.ge; f. 1956; attached to Georgian Acad. of Sciences; library of 10,000 vols; Dir M. SALUKVADZE; publs *Theory and Devices of Automatic Control* (annually), *Language Processors and Speech Recognition* (annually).

Institute of Cybernetics: Ul. S. Euli 5, 380086 Tbilisi; tel. (32) 30-30-49; e-mail inst@cybern.acnet.ge; f. 1960; attached to Georgian Acad. of Sciences; Dir G. KHARATISHVILI.

Institute of Engineering Geology and Hydrogeology: Pr. Rustaveli 31, 380008 Tbilisi; tel. (32) 52-72-19; fax (32) 00-11-53; e-mail bguram@gw.acnet.ge; f. 1958; attached to Georgian Acad. of Sciences; Dir G. BUACHIDZE; publ. *Problems of Hydrogeology and Engineering Geology*.

Institute of Machine Mechanics: Mindeli 10, 380086 Tbilisi; tel. (32) 32-39-56; fax (32) 31-52-05; e-mail imm@posta.ge; internet www.argosoft.com/imm; f. 1960; attached to Georgian Acad. of Sciences; Dir ROBERT ADAMIA.

Sukhumi I. N. Vekua Institute of Physics and Technology: Pr. Rustaveli 52, 0108 Tbilisi (relocated from Sukhumi due to conflict in Abkhazia); tel. and fax (32) 99-69-13; e-mail sipt@myoffice.ge; internet www.sipt.org.ge; f. 1945; attached to Georgian Acad. of Sciences; Dir V. KASHIA.

Tbilisi Scientific-Industrial Institute 'Analizkhelsatsko': Georgia Kakheti 36, 380090 Tbilisi; tel. (32) 74-08-29; e-mail web@gw.acnet.ge; f. 1956; attached to Georgian Acad. of Sciences.

Tsulukidze, G. A., Institute of Mining Mechanics: Mindelli 7, 380086 Tbilisi; tel. (32) 31-91-16; e-mail root@minig.acnet.ge; f. 1957; attached to Georgian Acad. of Sciences; Dir L. A. JAPARIDZE.

Libraries and Archives

Tbilisi

Central Library of the Georgian Academy of Sciences: 0193 Tbilisi, M. Aleksidze 1–4; tel. (32) 36-34-13; fax (32) 33-01-35; e-mail acadlibrary@gw.acnet.ge; f. 1941; 3,200,000 vols; Dir M. ZAALISHVILI.

Mikeladze, G. S., Scientific and Technical Library of Georgia: 0100 Tbilisi, ul. Dzneladze 27; 10,100,000 vols (without patents); Dir R. D. GORGILADZE.

National Library of Georgia: 0107 Tbilisi, Gulisashvili 5; tel. and fax (32) 99-80-95; f. 1846; 6,000,000 vols, 24,000 periodicals; Dir LEVAN BERDZENISHVILI.

Tbilisi Javakhishvili State University Library: 0128 Tbilisi, Pr. Chavchavadze 1; tel. (32) 22-10-32; internet www.tsu.edu.ge; f. 1918; 3,000,000 vols; Dir S. APAKIDZE.

Museums and Art Galleries

Kutaisi

Berdzenishvili, N. A., Kutaisi State Museum of History and Ethnography: 4600 Kutaisi, ul. Tbilisi 1; tel. (331) 5-56-76; f. 1912; attached to Georgian Acad. of Sciences; library of 25,000 vols; Dir Dr M. V. NIKOLEISHVILI.

Sokhumi

State Museum of the Abkhazian Autonomous Republic: 6600 Sokhumi, Ul. Lenina 22; f. 1915; history of the Abkhazian people; Dir A. A. ARGUN.

Sokhumi Botanical Garden: 6600 Sokhumi, ul. Chavchavadze 20; tel. (122) 2-44-58; attached to Georgian Acad. of Sciences; Dir (vacant).

Tbilisi

Georgian State Art Museum: 0107 Tbilisi, Ul. Gulisashvili 1; tel. (32) 99-66-35; f. 1920; Dir NODAR LOMOURI.

Georgian State Museum of Oriental Art: 0100 Tbilisi, ul. Azizbekova 3; Georgian fine and applied art; Dir G. M. GVISHIANI.

Janashia State Museum of Georgia: 0105 Tbilisi, Pr. Rustaveli 3; tel. (32) 99-80-22; fax (32) 98-21-29; e-mail root@stmus.acnet.ge; f. 1852; history, natural history; 3 brs: Samtskhe-Javakheti Museum of Iv. Javakhishvili, Zugdidi Historical Museum, Svaneti Historial-Ethnographic Museum; attached to Georgian Acad. of Sciences; library of 250,000 vols; Dir L. CHILASHVILI.

Modern Art Museum–National Picture Gallery: 0108 Tbilisi, Pr. Rustaveli 11; tel. (32) 93-16-52; f. 1920; Dir T. GOTSADZE.

State Museum of Georgian Literature: 0108 Tbilisi, Giorgi Chanturia 10; tel. (32) 99-86-67; f. 1930; Georgian literature since 19th century; library of 11,893 vols; Dir I. A. ORDZHONIKIDZE; publ. *Literary Chronicle*.

Tbilisi State Museum of Anthropology and Ethnography: 0100 Tbilisi, Pr. Komsomolskii 11; history and ethnography of Georgia; library of 150,000 vols; Dir A. V. TKESHELASHVILI.

Universities

ABKHAZIAN A. M. GORKII STATE UNIVERSITY

6600 Sokhumi, ul. Tsereteli 9
Telephone: (122) 2-25-98

Founded 1985
State control
Number of students: 3,800

Faculties of Physics and Mathematics, Economics, History and Law, Philology, Biology and Geography, Teacher Training.

BATUMI 'M. ABASHIDZE' STATE INSTITUTE OF CULTURE

6000 Batumi, Tamaris Dasaheba
Telephone: (222) 5-02-64

Founded 1992
State control

Rector: GAIOZ JORDANIA (acting)
Vice-Rector for Academic Affairs: NODAR VARSHANIDZE

Faculties of Art Research, Ballet, Cinema, Drama, Fine Arts, Musical Disciplines, TV-Radio Journalism.

BATUMI 'RUSTAVELI' STATE UNIVERSITY

6000 Batumi, Ninoshvili 35,
Telephone: (222) 7-17-80
Fax: (222) 7-17-86

Founded 1935
State control

Rector: NURI VERDZADZE
Rector: ROSTOM MUKHASHAVRIA

Faculties of Biology, Economics, Education, Foreign Languages, Geography, History, Initial Military Education and Physical Culture, Medicine, Philology, Physics and Mathematics.

GEORGIAN ACADEMY OF PHYSICAL EDUCATION

0179 Tbilisi, Pr. Chavchadze 49
Telephone: (32) 22-31-60
Fax: (32) 29-37-59

Founded 1938
State control

Rector: OMAR GOGIASHVILI.

GEORGIAN STATE ACADEMY OF ANIMAL HUSBANDRY AND VETERINARY MEDICINE

0114 Tbilisi, Krtsanisi
Telephone: (32) 72-04-49
Fax: (32) 99-50-91

Founded 1932
State control

Rector: JEMAL GUGUSHVILI
Vice-Rector: ROMAN TSAGAREISHVILI.

GEORGIAN TECHNICAL UNIVERSITY

0171 Tbilisi, ul. M. Kostava 77
Telephone: (32) 44-11-66
Fax: (32) 44-11-66
E-mail: intrelgu@yahoo.com
Internet: www.gtu.edu.ge

Founded 1990 (1922 as Georgia Polytechnic Institute)
State control
Languages of instruction: Georgian, Russian, English
Academic year: September to June

Rector: Prof. R. KHURODZE
Vice-Rector: Prof. ARCHIE PRANGISHVILI
Head of Foreign Affairs: TARIEL TAKTAKISHVILI
Head of Teaching and Methodology: O. ZUMBURIDZE
Librarian: V. PAPASKIRI

Number of teachers: 2,050
Number of students: 28,000

Publication: *Agmshenebeli* (newspaper)

DEANS

Faculty of Architecture: G. MIKIASHVILI
Faculty of Aviation: S. TEPNADZE
Faculty of Basic Sciences: T. DADIANI
Faculty of Chemical Engineering: N. KUTSLAVA
Faculty of Civil Engineering: C. LAGUNDARIDZE
Faculty of Communication: A. ROBITACHVILI
Faculty of Humanities: K. KOKRASHVILI
Faculty of Hydraulic Engineering: L. GOGELIANI
Faculty of Information Technology: Z. TSVERAIDZE
Faculty of Mechanics and Machine-Building: A. TAVKHELIDZE
Faculty of Metallurgy: N. TSERETELI
Faculty of Mining and Geology: A. ABSHILAVA
Faculty of Power Engineering: G. ARABIDZE
Faculty of Transport: O. GEBASHVILI

GORI STATE UNIVERSITY

1400 Gori, Chavchavadze 53
Telephone: (370) 7-29-97
Fax: (370) 7-32-13
E-mail: gori@ip.osgf.ge

Founded 1935
State control

Rector: GEDEVAN KHELAIA
Vice-Rector for Admin.: JEMALI DZIDZIGURI

Library of 200,000 vols

Depts of Auditing, accountancy and statistics, Correspondence learning, Finance and commerce, Foreign languages, History and law, International economic relations, business and management, Nature and philology, Pedagogics and medecine.

ILIA CHAVCHAVADZE STATE UNIVERSITY

0179 Tbilisi, Pr. I. Chavchavadze 32
Telephone: (32) 29-41-97
Fax: (32) 22-00-09
E-mail: uni@iliauni.edu.ge
Internet: www.iliauni.edu.ge

Founded 2006 by merger of Tbilisi Ilia Chavchavadze State Univ. of Language and Culture and Tbilisi Sulkhan-Saba Orbeliani State Pedagogical Univ.
State control

Rector: Prof. GIGI TEVZADZE
Admin. Dir: SERGO RATIANI

DEANS

Faculty of Education: IVANE KALADZE
Faculty of Humanities and Cultural Studies: SHUKIA APRIDONIDZE
Faculty of Life Sciences: GIORGI NAKHUTSRISHVILI
Faculty of Philology of Foreign Languages: MZIA BAKRADZE
Faculty of Philosophy and Social Sciences: Prof. GIGI TEVZADZE
Faculty of Physics and Mathematics: JUANSHER CHKAREULI

PROFESSORS

Faculty of Education (depts of Education psychology, correctional pedagogy and pre-School pedagogy, General pedagogy, Education economics and management, Specific methods):

IMEDADZE, NATELA
KALADZE, IVANE
KORINTELI, REVAZ
MALAZONIA, DAVID
MAQASHVILI, KETEVAN
SHAVERDASHVILI, EKATERINE

Faculty of Humanities and Cultural Studies (depts of Culture, History, Linguistics, Literary studies):

APRIDONIDZE, SHUKIA
GHAGHANIDZE, MERAB
KOBALAVA, IZABELA
KOCHLAMAZASHVILI, TAMAZ
LADARIA, NODAR
PITSKHELAURI, KONSTANTINE

Faculty of Life Sciences (dept of Biology):

BADRIDZE, IASON, Ecology of Behavior
GEGELASHVILI, GIORGI, Molecular and Cellular Biochemistry
KOPALIANI, NATIA, Zoology, Conservative Biology
NAKHUTSRISHVILI, GIORGI, Botany, Ecology
SHATIRISHVILI, AIVENGO, Genetics, Evolutionary Biology
SOLOMONIA, REVAZ, Biochemistry, Physiology
TARKHNISHVILI, DAVID, Ecology, Evolutionary Biology

Faculty of Philology of Foreign Languages (depts of English/American studies, Germanic studies, Romance studies, Slavic studies, Oriental studies, Comparative literary studies, Linguoculturology):

BAKRADZE, MZIA
DOKHTURISHVILI, MZAGHO
GAJIEV, VALEKH
GOGOLADZE, TEIMURAZ
GVENTSADZE, MZIA
JASHI, KETEVAN
MARSAGISHVILI, REZO
MIKADZE, MZIA
LEBANIDZE, GURAM (VAKHTANG)
PIRTSKHALAVA, NINO

Faculty of Philosophy and Social Sciences (depts of Philosophy, Sociology and demography, Psychology, Politology, international relations and security studies, Journalism, Economics):

BERIASHVILI, MAMUKA
DARCHIASHVILI, DAVID
IMEDADZE, IRAKLI
NODIA, GIORGI
SURGULADZE, REVAZ
TEVZADZE, GIGI
TEVZADZE, GURAM
TSULADZE, GIOGI

Faculty of Physics and Mathematics (depts of Mathematics, Physics):

CHKAREULI, JUANSHER
KHARAZISHVILI, ALEXANDRE
KHIMSHIASHVILI, GIORGI
JANGVELADZE, TEMUR
MURUSIDZE, IVANE
SVANADZE, MERAB
TSIBAKHASHVILI, NELI

KUTAISI 'AKAKI CERETELI' STATE UNIVERSITY

4600 Kutaisi, Tamar Mepe 55
Telephone: (331) 4-57-84
Fax: (331) 4-38-33
E-mail: admin@gateway.ge
Internet: ksu.gateway.ge

Founded 1933
State control

Rector: AVTANDIL NIKOLEISHIVILI

Number of teachers: 380
Number of students: 5,000

DEANS

Faculty of Economics: Asst Prof. E. BLIADZE
Faculty of Education: Asst Prof. T. GVINIANIDZE
Faculty of European Languages and Literature: Asst Prof. B. KOGUASHVILI
Faculty of History: Asst Prof. T. CHIGVARIYA
Faculty of Law: Asst Prof. R. GOLETIANI
Faculty of Medicine: Asst Prof. T. LOBZHANIDZE
Faculty of Natural Sciences: Asst Prof. R. JINJOLIYA
Faculty of Philology: Asst Prof. O. GVETADZE
Faculty of Physics and Mathematics: Asst Prof. G. TOMARADZE

TBILISI JAVAKHISHVILI STATE UNIVERSITY

0128 Tbilisi, Pr. Chavchavadze 1
Telephone: (32) 22-02-41
Fax: (32) 22-22-03
E-mail: usc@ictsu.tsu.edu.ge
Internet: www.tsu.edu.ge

Founded 1918
State control
Language of instruction: Georgian
Academic year: September to June

Rector: Prof. GIORGI KHUBUA
Vice-Rectors: Prof. ANZOR KELASHVILI (Academic), TSEZAR MOSIDZE (Economical and Admin. Affairs), Prof. AVTANDIL SILAGADZE (Economical Educational Affairs), Asst Prof. TEIMURAZ KHURODZE (Educational Programmes and Int. Relations), Asst Prof. PARMEN MARGVELASHVILI (Non-Budget Educational Affairs and Long-Term Planning)
Librarian: S. A. APAKIDZE

Library: see Libraries and Archives
Number of teachers: 1,659
Number of students: 16,000

Publications: *Proceedings* (quarterly, in two series), *Tbilisi University* (weekly)

DEANS

Faculty Economics and Business: MIKHEIL CHIKVILADZE
Faculty of Exact and Natural Sciences: ARCHIL UGULAVA
Faculty of Humanities: GOCHA JAPARIDZE
Faculty of Law: DAVID KERESELIDZE
Faculty of Medicine: IVANE BOKERIA
Faculty of Social and Political Sciences: DAVID APRASIDZE

ATTACHED INSTITUTES

Institute of Applied Mathematics: 0177 Tbilisi, ul. Universitetis 2.

Institute of Cosmic Rays.
Institute of Cybernetics.
Institute of the Ionosphere.
Institute of Low Temperatures.
Institute of Nuclear Physics.
Sarajishvili Institute of Neurology: Dir Prof. ROMAN SHAKARISHVILI.

TBILISI STATE INSTITUTE OF CULTURE

0102 Tbilisi, D. Agmashenebeli 40
Telephone: (32) 95-10-50
Fax: (32) 94-37-28
Founded 1992
State control
Rector: TEMUR ZHGENTI
Vice-Rector: VLADIMER KIRVALISHVILI
Faculties of Choreography, Fine and Applied Arts, Humanities and Musicology.

TBILISI STATE INSTITUTE OF ECONOMIC RELATIONS

0144 Tbilisi, Ketevan Tsamebuli 55
Telephone: (32) 93-50-45
Fax: (32) 94-31-60
E-mail: teusi@access.sanet.ge
Founded 1992
State control
Rector: GEURI TAVARTKILADZE
Vice-Rector: GELA ALADASHVILI.

TBILISI STATE MEDICAL UNIVERSITY

0177 Tbilisi, Vazha-Pshavela 33
Telephone: (32) 39-18-79
Fax: (32) 94-25-19
E-mail: iad@tsmu.edu
Internet: www.tsmu.edu
Founded 1918
State control
Academic year: September to June
Rector: Prof. ALEXANDER TELIA
Library of 500,000 vols
Number of teachers: 700
Number of students: 4,000
Publications: *Georgian Medical News* (monthly), *Research* (annual), *Annals of Biomedical Research and Education* (quarterly)

DEANS
Faculty of General Medicine: Prof. RAMAZ SHENGELIA
Faculty of Paediatrics: Prof. GURAM DAVITAIA
Faculty of Pharmacy: Prof. NIKOLOZ GONGADZE
Faculty of Psychotherapy and Psychosomatic Medicine: Prof. RAMZ SAKVARELIDZE
Faculty of Social Care and Management: Prof. BIDZINA ZURASHVILI
Faculty of Stomatology: Prof. GEORGE KIPIANI

TELAVI 'I. GOGEBASHVILI' STATE UNIVERSITY

2200 Telavi, Universitetis 1
Telephone: (250) 3-24-01
E-mail: telavi@hepi.edu.ge
Internet: teseu.iatp.org.ge
Founded 1939
State control
Academic year: September to June
Rector: ROIN CHIKADZE
Vice-Rector: SPIRIDON ROSTOMASHVILI
Library of 200,000 vols
Number of teachers: 224
Number of students: 2,980
Faculties of Basic Military Training and Physical Culture, History, Natural Sciences, Pedagogics and Methodology, Philology, Physics and Mathematics.

TSKHINVALI PEDAGOGICAL INSTITUTE–GEORGIAN SECTOR

Shida Qartli, 1400 Gori, Chavchavadze 57
Telephone: (370) 2-19-35
Founded 1932
State control
Rector: VAHTANG AHALAIA
Vice-Rector: V. BURCHULADZE
Faculties of Biology, Chemistry and Physical Training, Education, Teaching and Methods, Foreign Languages, Georgian language and Literature, History and Philology, Mathematics and Physics, Natural Sciences.

Other Higher Educational Institutes

Georgian S. Rustaveli State Institute of Theatre and Cinematography: 0108 Tbilisi, Pr. Rustaveli 17; tel. (32) 99-94-11; fax (32) 98-30-97; e-mail eliso@geo.net.ge; f. 1939; drama, film, television, stage management, archive management, art history; library: 50,000 vols; 150 teachers; 800 students; Rector Prof. GIGA LORDKIPHANIDZE.

Georgian State Agrarian University: 0131 Tbilisi, D. Agmashenebeli 13-km, Dighomi; tel. (32) 95-71-47; fax (32) 52-00-47; e-mail agrdig@geointer.net.ge; f. 1929 as Georgian Agricultural Institute; present name and status 1991; faculties of Agronomy, Technology and viticulture, Forestry, Agricultural mechanization, Agricultural electrification and automation, Hydromelioration and engineering ecology, Economics and humanities; library: 747,600 vols; 583 teachers; 7,500 students; Rector Prof. Dr NAPOLEON KARKASHADZE.

Georgian State Institute of Subtropical Agriculture: 4600 Kutaisi, Pr. Chavchavadze 13; tel. (331) 7-06-14; e-mail ssmsi@sanet.net.ge; faculties of Agri-business, Agricultural engineering, Agriculture and food technology, Economics; library: 90,000 vols; Rector GURAM KILASONIA.

Kutaisi N. I. Muskhelishvili Technical University: 4614 Kutaisi, Akhalgazrdobis Gamziri 98; tel. and fax (331) 2-06-90; e-mail vg@posta.ge; f. 1973; institutes: automobile and transport, cybernetics, electrical engineering, food and chemical industry, humanities and economics, mechanical engineering, technology and design; 360 teachers; 5,600 students; library: 250,000 vols, 300 periodicals; Rector AMIRAN HVADAGIANI.

Tbilisi State Academy of Arts: 0108 Tbilisi, ul. Griboedova 2; tel. and fax (32) 93-69-59; e-mail nanniashuili@posta.ge; f. 1922; faculties of Fine arts, Design, Architecture, Art history and theory; depts of Painting, Graphics, Sculpture, Ceramics, Glass, Graphic design, Metal and wood processing, Industrial design, Furniture, Fabric and tapestry fashion, Computer graphics, Architecture, Art history and theory, Restoration, Decorative arts; library: 42,000 vols; 355 ; 1,600 ; Rector Prof. IOSEB KOIAVA; publ. *Works* (annual).

Tbilisi V. Saradzhishvili State Conservatoire: 0108 Tbilisi, 8 Griboedova; tel. and fax (32) 99-91-44; e-mail tbil_conservatory@hotmail.com; f. 1917; courses: piano, singing, choral conducting, composition, orchestral instruments, musicology; 205 teachers; 700 students; library: 100,000 vols; Rector Prof. MANANA DOIJASHVILI.

GERMANY

The Higher Education System

During 1949–90 Germany was divided between the sovereign states of Federal Republic of Germany (FRG) and German Democratic Republic (GDR). Both states developed their own higher education systems. In the FRG the Grundgesetz (Basic Law) of 1949 stated that the majority of aspects of the administration and legislation of the education system were the responsibility of the Länder (States). Following re-unification in 1990, the former GDR was incorporated into the Federal structure, and adopted the higher education standards already implemented in the former FRG. Higher education thus remains the responsibility of the 16 Länder, and is overseen by the national Kultusministerkonferenz (Standing Conference of the Ministers of Education and Cultural Affairs of the Länder). Higher education is divided between Hochschulen and Fachhochschulen. Hochschulen encompass classical universities (Universität), technical universities (Technische Hochschule/Universität), combined Hochschulen-Fachhochschulen (Universität-Gesamthochschule), teacher-training institutes (Pädagogische Hochschule), theological universities (Theologische Hochschule), art universities (Kunsthochschule) and music universities (Musikhochschule). Fachhochschulen are universities of applied science specializing in technical vocation education and training.

Admission to Hochschulen is based on performance in Zeugnis der Allgemeinen Hochschulreife or Fachgebundene Hochschulreife, and admission to Fachochschulen depends on Fachhochschulreife, Zeugnis der Allgemeinen Hochschulreife or Fachgebundene Hochschulreife. Germany has implemented the Bologna Process and introduced a two-tier Bachelors and Masters degree system to replace the traditional German degrees in Hochschulen. The Bachelors lasts three to four years and the Masters a further one to two years. Doctoral studies follow the Masters. In Fachochschulen the traditional Fachhochschuldiplom (four years) has been retained as, unlike the Bachelors, it involves a large element of practical training; however, both the Bachelors and Masters degrees have been introduced in Fachochschulen.

Mixed academic and vocational training is also offered by Berufsakademien or Studienakademien, which were first established in Baden-Württemberg in 1974; they are not present in every Land. Students are awarded the Berufsakademien Diplom after a three year course. Technical and vocational education is offered by different types of institution in addition to the degree-level programmes offered by the Fachochschulen. An estimated two-thirds of German students of the relevant age attend Berufsschulen, which combine classroom-based instruction and practical experience in a three-year course. Berufsfachschulen specialize in two to three year occupational training courses, leading to the award of the titles Facharbeiterbrief (Skilled Worker Certificate), Kaufmannsgehilfenbrief (Clerical Assistant Certificate) and Gesellenbrief (Craftsman Certificate). Berufsobershulen are only available in some Länder and allow those who have completed secondary education and have acquired at least five years of professional experience to study for the Fachgebundende Hochschulreife, which confers eligibility to enter Hochschulen and Fachhochschulen. Fachschulen provide one- to three-year courses for those who already have previous vocational education and professional experience.

Regulatory and Representative Bodies

GOVERNMENT

Bund-Länder-Kommission für Bildungsplanung und Forschungsförderung (Bund-Länder Commission for Education Planning and Research Promotion): Friedrich-Ebert-Allee 38, 53113 Bonn; tel. (228) 5402-0; fax (228) 5402-150; e-mail blk@blk-bonn.de; internet www.blk-bonn.de; f. 1970 as Bund-Länder Commission for Educational Planning (Bund-Länder-Kommission für Bildungsplanung) by agreement between the Federal and Länder govts; granted additional functions in 1975 by the Skeleton Agreement on Research Promotion; adopted present name 1976; intergovernmental commission; permanent forum for discussion of all questions of education and research promotion which are of common interest to the Federal and Länder govts; makes recommendations to the Heads of the Federal and Länder govts on educational planning and research promotion; co-operates closely with the various Conferences of Länder Ministers; Chair. Prof. Dr E. Jürgen Zöllner; Dir. Jürgen Schlegel.

Federal Ministry of Education and Research: Hannoversche Str. 28–30, 10115 Berlin; tel. (30) 18570; fax (30) 185783601; e-mail bmbf@bmbf.bund.de; internet www.bmbf.de; Federal Minister Annette Schavan.

Kultusministerkonferenz/Die Ständige Konferenz der Kultusminister der Länder in der Bundesrepublik Deutschland (Standing Conference of the Ministers of Education and Cultural Affairs of the Länder): Postfach 2240, 53012 Bonn; Lennéstr. 6, 53113 Bonn; tel. (228) 5010; fax (228) 501777; e-mail poststelle@kmk.org; internet www.kmk.org; f. 1948; conference of ministers and senators of the 16 Länder whose portfolios encompass culture, education, research and training; maintains offices in Berlin; Pres. Prof. Dr E. Jürgen Zöllner; Gen.-Sec. Prof. Dr Erich Thies.

ACCREDITATION

Akkreditierungs-, Certifizierungs- und Qualitätssicherungs-Instituts (ACQUIN) (Accreditation, Certification and Quality Assurance Institute): c/o Universität Bayreuth, 95440 Bayreuth; Prieserstr. 2, 95444 Bayreuth; tel. (921) 55-4841; fax (921) 55-4842; e-mail sekr@acquin.org; internet www.acquin.org; f. 2001 as a consequence of the Bologna-process and the need for assuring the quality of newly introduced undergraduate and postgraduate degrees in Germany; member-based, non-profit org.; licensed by the Akkreditierungsrat (*q.v.*) to award its quality seal to study programmes which have successfully undergone accreditation; accreditation of German Bachelors and Masters study programmes in all subject fields based on the expertise of Standing Expert Cttee mems; evaluation and accreditation of selected int. study programmes; int. co-operation and networking; organizes projects and workshops with nat. and int. partners; develops new quality assurance methods; pilot project: 'Process Quality in Teaching and Learning'; Dir Prof. Dr Gerd Zimmermann.

Akkreditierungsrat (Accreditation Council): Adenauer Allee 73, 53113 Bonn; tel. 228 338 306 0; fax 228 338 306 79; e-mail akr@akkreditierungsrat.de; internet www.akkreditierungsrat.de; f. 1999 by Kultusministerkonferenz (*q.v.*) and Hochschulrektorenkonferenz (*q.v.*); attached to Stiftung zur Akkreditierung von Studiengängen in Deutschland (Foundation for the Accreditation of Study Programmes in Germany); acts on behalf of Länder to accredit accreditation agencies and degree programmes leading to Bakkalaureus/Bachelors and Magister/Masters degrees; financed by Stifterverband für die Deutsche Wissenschaft (*q.v.*); Man. Dir Dr Achim Hopbach.

Akkreditierungsagentur für Studiengänge im Bereich Heilpädagogik, Pflege, Gesundheit und Soziale Arbeit e.V. (AHPGS) (Accreditation Agency for Study Programmes in Special Education, Care, Health Sciences and Social Work): Hebelstr. 29, 79104 Freiburg; tel. (761) 203-5529; fax (761) 203-5516; e-mail sekretariat@ahpgs.de; internet www.ahpgs.de; promotes quality and transparency of German univ. study courses for health and social professionals; works to guarantee uniform and internationally comparable quality standards in the new Bachelors and Masters degrees through accreditation procedures; operates continual information exchange with other nat. and int. accreditation agencies as well as univ. representatives, practicioners' orgs and asscns; mems incl. the dean conference nursing science (33 univs), the assemblies of the depts social work (73 univs) and remedial education (8 univs) as well as the German Co-ordinating Agency for Public Health; accredited by the Akkreditierungsrat (*q.v.*); Dir Prof. Dr JÜRGEN VON TROSCHKE.

AQAS e.V./Agentur für Qualitätssicherung durch Akkreditierung von Studiengängen: In der Sürst 1, 53111 Bonn; tel. (228) 90960-10; fax (228) 90960-19; e-mail info@aqas.de; internet www.aqas.de; f. 2002; accredited by Akkreditierungsrat (*q.v.*); Chair. Prof. Dr DIETER TIMMERMANN; Man. EDNA HABEL.

ENIC/NARIC Germany: Central Office for Foreign Education, Secretariat of the Standing Conference of the Ministers of Education and Cultural Affairs, POB 2240, 53012 Bonn; tel. (228) 501-264; fax (228) 501-229; e-mail zab@kmk.org; internet www.kmk.org/zab/txt-eng.htm; attached to Kultusministerkonferenz (*q.v.*); Gen. Co-ordinator Dr PETER OBERSCHELP.

Fachakkreditierungsagentur für Studiengänge der Ingenieurwissenschaften, der Informatik, der Naturwissenschaften und der Mathematik e.V. (ASIIN): Postfach 10 11 39, 40002 Düsseldorf; Robert-Stolz-Str. 5, 40470 Düsseldorf; tel. (211) 6214-370; fax (211) 6214-125; e-mail info@asiin.de; internet www.asiin.de; f. 1999 as ASII, merged with Akkreditierungsagentur für die Studiengänge Chemie, Biochemie und Chemieingenieurwesen an Universitäten und Fachhochschulen (A-CBC) and adopted present name 2002; the only German accreditation agency to be explicitly specialized in accrediting degree programmes in engineering, informatics, natural sciences and mathematics; non-profit, registered asscn; accredited by Akkreditierungsrat (*q.v.*); represents competence in mechanical engineering, process engineering, civil engineering, surveying, architecture, city and spatial planning, physical technologies, materials and processes, agronomy, nutritional science, landscape architecture, life sciences, physics, electrical engineering, IT, informatics, computer science, business informatics, information systems, industrial engineering, chemistry, geosciences, mathematics; Man. Dir Dr IRING WASSER.

Foundation for International Business Administration Accreditation (FIBAA): Berliner Freiheit 20–24, 53111 Bonn; tel. (228) 280-3560; fax (228) 280-3569; e-mail info@fibaa.de; internet www.fibaa.de; accredits Bachelors, Masters and Diplom courses in fields such as business admin., economics, business computing, engineering and business admin., business psychology, business law, etc. in Germany, Austria and Switzerland; provides information and advice on Bachelors and Masters courses to univs, students and private enterprise; maintains offices in Zürich (Switzerland); Man. Dirs HANS-JÜRGEN BRACKMANN, Dr BIANKA LICHTENBERGER; Head of Accreditation Prof. Dr HEINER MÜLLER-MERBACH.

FUNDING

Deutscher Akademischer Austauschdienst e.V. (DAAD) (German Academic Exchange Service): Postfach 200404, 53134 Bonn; Located at: Kennedyallee 50, 53175 Bonn; tel. (228) 882-0; fax (228) 882-444; e-mail postmaster@daad.de; internet www.daad.de; br.anch offices: Markgrafenstr. 37, 10117 Berlin, Germany; 34 Belgrave Sq, London SW1X 8QB, England; 24 rue Marbeau, 75116 Paris, France; Maison Heinrich Heine, 27C blvd Jourdan, 75014 Paris, France; 11 Sharia Saleh Ayyoub, Cairo-Zamalek, Egypt; 176 Golf Links, New Delhi 110003, India; 871 United Nations Plaza, New York, NY 10017, USA; Rua Pres. Carlos de Campos 417, 22231-080 Rio de Janeiro, Brazil; POB 14050, Westlands 00800, Nairobi, Kenya; Akasaka 7-5-56, Minato-ku, Tokyo 107-0052, Japan; ul. Czeska 24, 03-902 Warsaw, Poland; Jl. Jend. Sudirman, Kav. 61–62, Summitmas I, Lt.19, Jakarta 12190, Indonesia; Leninski Prospekt 95A, 117313 Moscow, Russia; Xisanhuan Beilu 2, POB 8936-46, 100089 Beijing, People's Republic of China; f. 1925; awards scholarships and grants, largely funded from Federal budget, to promote academic and cultural exchange between German and foreign students and thereby encourage closer relations between Germany and other countries; exchange of professors, lecturers in German for foreign universities, IAESTE—student-trainees, scholarships for German and foreign students and graduates; 233 mem. univs; Pres. Prof. THEODOR BERCHEM; Pres. Prof. Dr THEODOR BERCHEM; Gen. Sec. Dr CHRISTIAN BODE, Dr CHRISTIAN BODE; publs *Annual Report*, *Newsletter* (4 a yearquarterly), *Postscript* (2 a year).

NATIONAL BODIES

Deutscher Volkshochschul-Verband eV (German Adult Education Association): Obere Wilhelmstr. 32, 53225 Bonn; tel. (228) 97569-0; fax (228) 97569-55; e-mail info@dvv-vhs.de; internet www.dvv-vhs.de; f. 1953; 16 regional associations of 1,000 Volkshochschulen with 4,000 brs; Pres. Prof. Dr RITA SÜSSMUTH; Chair. ERNST KÜCHLER; Dir ULRICH AENGENVOORT; publs *DVV magazin dis.kurs* (quarterly), *Adult Education and Development* (2 a year, in English, French and Spanish).

Hochschulrektorenkonferenz (German Rectors' and Presidents' Conference): Ahrstr. 39, 53175 Bonn; tel. (228) 887-0; fax (228) 887110; e-mail sekr@hrk.de; internet www.hrk.de; f. 1949; the central voluntary body representing the universities and higher education institutions; 261 mems; Pres. Prof. Dr MARGRET WINTERMANTEL; Sec.-Gen. Dr CHRISTIANE EBEL-GABRIEL.

Katholischer Akademischer Ausländer-Dienst: Hausdorffstr. 151, 53129 Bonn; tel. (228) 91758-0; fax (228) 9175858; e-mail zentrale@kaad.de; internet www.kaad.de; f. 1956; co-ordinates activities of Catholic organizations concerned with foreign students in Germany and grants scholarships; Pres. Prof. Dr JOSEF REITER; Dir Dr HERMANN WEBER; publs *Jahresakademie* (both annually), *Jahresbericht*.

Learned Societies

GENERAL

Akademie der Künste (Academy of Arts): Pariser Platz 4, 10117 Berlin-Mitte; tel. (30) 20057-0; e-mail info@adk.de; internet www.adk.de; f. 1696; sections of Fine Art, Architecture, Music, Literature, Performing Arts, Film and Media Arts; 365 mems; Pres. Prof. Dr ADOLF MUSCHG; publ. *Sinn und Form* (6 a year).

Akademie der Wissenschaften in Göttingen (Göttingen Academy of Sciences and Humanities): Theaterstr. 7, 37073 Göttingen; tel. (551) 395362; fax (551) 395365; e-mail udeppe@gwdg.de; internet www.adw-goettingen.gwdg.de; f. 1751; sections of Philology and History, Mathematics and Physics; 353 mems and corresp. mems; Pres. Prof. Dr HERBERT W. ROESKY; Sec. Prof. HEINZ GEORG WAGNER; publs *Nachrichten*, *Abhandlungen*, *Göttingische Gelehrte Anzeigen*, *Jahrbüch*.

Akademie der Wissenschaften und der Literatur Mainz (Mainz Academy of Sciences, Humanities and Literature): Geschwister Scholl-Str. 2, 55131 Mainz,; tel. (6131) 577-0; fax (6131) 577-111; e-mail generalsekretariat@adwmainz.de; internet www.adwmainz.de; f. 1949; sections of Mathematics and Natural Sciences (Vice-Pres. Prof. Dr ELKE LÜTJEN-DRECOLL), Philosophy and Social Sciences (Vice-Pres. Prof. Dr HELMUT HESSE), Literature (Vice-Pres. WALTER HELMUT FRITZ); 127 mems; Pres. Prof. Dr CLEMENS ZINTZEN; Sec.-Gen. Dr WULF THOMMEL; publs *Abhandlungen*, *Forschungsreihen*.

Bayerische Akademie der Wissenschaften (Bavarian Academy of Sciences and Humanities): Alfons-Goppel-Str. 11, 80539 Munich; tel. (89) 23031-0; fax (89) 23031-100; e-mail info@badw.de; internet www.badw.de; f. 1759; sections of Mathematics and Natural Sciences (Secs Prof. Dr GOTTFRIED SACHS., Prof. Dr ROLAND BULIRSCH) and Philosophy and History (Secs. Prof. Dr ARNOLD PICOT), Prof. Dr THOMAS O. HÖLLMANN; 150 mems; Pres. Prof. Dr DIETMAR WILLOWEIT; Gen. Sec. EVA REGENSCHEIDT-SPIES.

Berlin-Brandenburgische Akademie der Wissenschaften (Berlin-Brandenburg Academy of Sciences and Humanities): Jaegerstr. 22/23, 10117 Berlin; tel. (30) 20370-0; fax (30) 20370-600; e-mail bbaw@bbaw.de; internet www.bbaw.de; f. 1700, refounded 1992/93; sections of Humanities, of Social Sciences, of Mathematics and Natural Sciences, of Biological and Medical Sciences, of Engineering Sciences; 239 mems (144 ordinary, 64 extraordinary, 30 emeriti, 1 hon.); Pres. Prof. Dr GÜNTER STOCK; Sec.-Gen. ALMUTH ZIPPER; publs *Berichte und Abhandlungen* (irregular), *Gegenwork – Zeitschrift für den Disput über Wissen*, *Jahrbuch* (annually).

Deutsche Akademie der Naturforscher Leopoldina (German Academy of Natural Scientists Leopoldina): Emil-Abderhalden-Str. 37, 06108 Halle/Saale; tel. (345) 47239-0; fax (345) 47239-19; e-mail leopoldina@leopoldina-halle.de; internet www.leopoldina-halle.de; f. 1652; sections of Medicine (Sec. Prof. Dr INGO HANSMANN) and Natural Sciences (Sec. Prof. Dr GUNNER BERG); 1,050 mems; library: archive: see Libraries and Archives; Pres. Prof. Dr VOLKER TER MEULEN; Sec.-Gen. Prof. Dr JUTTA SCHNITZER-UNGEFUG; publs *Acta Historica Leopoldina*, *Jahrbuch* (annually), *Nova Acta Leopoldina*.

Goethe-Gesellschaft in Weimar eV: Burgpl. 4 99423 Weimar; Postfach 2251, 99403 Weimar; tel. (3643) 202050; fax (3643) 202061; internet www.goethe-gesellschaft.de; e-mail goetheges@aol.com; f. 1885; literature, art and history of Goethe's time; 3,500 mems; Pres. Dr JOCHEN GOLZ; Dir Dr PETRA OBERHAUSER; publs *Goethe-Jahrbuch*, *Schriften der G.G.* (irregular).

Goethe-Institut: Postfach 190419, 80604 Munich; premises at: Dachauer Str. 122 80637 Munich; tel. (89) 15921-0; fax (89) 15921-450; e-mail zv@goethe.de; internet www.goethe.de; f. 1951 to promote a wider knowledge abroad of the German language and to foster cultural co-operation with other countries; 143 institutes globally, 17 in Germany; Pres. Prof. Dr JUTTA LIMBACH; Sec.-Gen. Dr HANS-GEORG KNOPP; publs *Goethe-Institut aktuell* (quarterly), *Willkommen*.

Heidelberger Akademie der Wissenschaften (Heidelberg Academy of

Sciences and Humanities): Karlstr. 4, 69117 Heidelberg; tel. (6221) 543265; fax (6221) 543355; e-mail haw@urz.uni-heidelberg.de; internet www.haw.baden-wuerttemberg.de; f. 1909; sections of Mathematics and Natural Sciences (Sec. Prof. Dr HANS GÜNTER DOSCH), Philosophy and History (Sec. Prof. Dr VOLKER SELLIN); Pres. Prof. Dr PETER GRAF KIELMANSEGG; Man. Dir GUNTHER JOST.

Institut für Auslandsbeziehungen (Institute for Foreign Cultural Relations): Postfach 102463, 70020 Stuttgart; located at: Charlottenpl. 17, 70173 Stuttgart; tel. (711) 2225-0; fax (711) 2264346; e-mail info@ifa.de; internet www.ifa.de; f. 1917; library of 400,000 vols; Pres. ALOIS GRAF VON WALDBURG-ZEIL; Gen. Sec. DR KURT-JÜRGEN MAASS; publs *Ifa - Dokumente, Reihe Dokumentation, Zeitschrift für Kulturaustausch*.

Inter Nationes: Kennedyallee 91–103, 53175 Bonn; tel. (228) 880-0; fax (228) 880457; f. 1952; non-profit organization with the object of strengthening cultural relations between foreign countries and Germany; Chair. DR DIETER W. BENECKE; publs *Kulturchronik* (every 2 months), *Humboldt* (3 a year), *Fikrun wa fann* (2 a year), *Education and Science* (quarterly).

Nordrhein-Westfälische Akademie der Wissenschaften (Northrhine-Westphalia Academy of Sciences and Humanities): Palmenstr. 16, 40217 Düsseldorf; tel. (211) 61734-0; fax (211) 341475; e-mail akdw@akdw.nrw.de; internet www.akdw.nrw.de; f. 1950; sections of Natural, Engineering and Economic Sciences, Philosophy; 166 mems; Pres. Prof. Dr MANFRED J. M. NEUMANN; publs *Abhandlungen, Sitzungsberichte*.

Prinz-Albert-Gesellschaft eV (Prince Albert Society): c/o Silvia Böcking, Alte Schlossstr. 9, 96253 Untersiemau; tel. (921) 554190; fax (921) 55844188; e-mail Prinz-Albert-Gesellschaft@uni-bayreuth.de; internet www.prinz-albert-gesellschaft.uni-bayreuth.de; f. 1981; encourages research into Anglo-German relations in spheres of scholarship, culture and politics; Chair. Prof. Dr FRANZ BOSBACH; Sec. SILVIA BÖCKING; publ. *Prince Albert Studies* (Series).

Sächsische Akademie der Wissenschaften zu Leipzig (Saxon Academy of Sciences and Humanities in Leipzig): Postfach 100440, 04004 Leipzig,; tel. (341) 711530; fax (341) 7115344; e-mail saw@saw-leipzig.de; internet www.saw-leipzig.de; f. 1846; sections of Mathematics and Natural Sciences (Prof. Dr HEINER KADEN), Philology and History (Prof. Dr HEINER LÜCK), Technical Sciences (Prof. Dr DAGMAR HÜLSENBERG); 187 mems (115 ordinary, 72 corresp.); Pres. Prof. Dr med. UWE-FRITHJOF HAUSTEIN; Sec.-Gen. Dr phil. UTE ECKER; publs *Jahrbuch* (every 2 years), *Abhandlungen, Sitzungsberichte*.

Union der Deutschen Akademien der Wissenschaften (Union of the German Academies of Sciences and Humanities): Geschwister-Scholl-Str. 2, 55131 Mainz; tel. (6131) 218528-0; fax (6131) 218528-11; e-mail info@akademienunion.de; internet www.akademieunion.de; f. 1973; consists of academies of sciences and humanities in Berlin, Düsseldorf, Göttingen, Heidelberg, Leipzig, Mainz and Munich; deals with research projects common to the academies and co-ordinates the work of their mems; Pres. Prof. Dr GERHARD GOTTSCHALK; Gen. Sec. Dr DIETER HERRMANN; publ. *Newsletter*.

AGRICULTURE, FISHERIES AND VETERINARY SCIENCE

Agrarsoziale Gesellschaft eV (ASG): Postfach 1144, 37001 Göttingen; premises at: Kurze Geismarstr. 33, 37073 Göttingen; tel. (551) 497090; fax (551) 49709-16; e-mail info@asg-goe.de; internet www.asg-goe.de; f. 1947; 389 mems, plus 168 corporate mems; library of 6,000 vols; Chair. Dr HANS-HERMAN BENTRUP; Pres. HEINZ CHRISTIAN BÄR; publs *Arbeitsbericht der ASG, Kleine Reihe der ASG, Ländlicher Raum* (6 a year), *Materialsammlung der ASG, Schriftenreihe für ländliche Sozialfragen*.

Dachverband Wissenschaftlicher Gesellschaften der Agrar-, Forst-, Ernährungs-, Veterinär- und Umweltforschung eV: Eschbormer Landstr. 122, 60489 Frankfurt am Main; tel. (69) 24788306; fax (69) 24788114; internet daf.zadi.de; f. 1973; advancement and co-ordination of research; information; contacts; representation; 29 mems; Pres. Prof. Dr FOLKHARD ISERMEYER; Man. Dir LOTHAR HÖVELMANN.

Deutsche Landwirtschafts-Gesellschaft eV (German Agricultural Society): Eschborner Landstr. 122, 60489 Frankfurt; tel. (69) 24788-0; fax (69) 24788110; e-mail info@dlg-frankfurt.de; internet www.dlg.org; f. originally 1885, re-founded 1947; 16,000 mems; Pres. PHILIP VON DEM BUSSCHE; Dir Dr REINHARD GRANDKE; publs *Mitteilungen* (monthly), *Entwicklung und ländlicher Raum* (monthly, in German, English and French), *Zeitschrift für Agrargeschichte und Agrarsoziologie* (4 a year), *Journal of International Agriculture* (4 a year), *Agrifuture* (for European farmers, in English, 4 a year).

Deutsche Veterinärmedizinische Gesellschaft: Frankfurter Str. 89, 35392 Gießen; tel. (641) 24466; fax (641) 25375; e-mail media@dvg.net; internet www.dvg.net; f. 1949; 4,800 mems; Pres. Prof. Dr HOLGER MARTENS; Sec. Prof. Dr Dr h.c. KARSTEN FEHLHABER; publ. *Kongressbericht* (every 2 years).

Deutscher Forstwirtschaftsrat eV (German Forestry Council): Flerzheimer Allee 13, 53125 Bonn; tel. (228) 61963-0; fax (228) 61963-21; e-mail dfwr-rheinbach@t-online.de; internet www.dfwr.de; f. 1950; promotion of forestry; 67 mems; Pres. Bürgermeister HERMANN ILAENDER; Man. Dir STEPHAN SCHÜTTE.

Verband Deutscher Landwirtschaftlicher Untersuchungs- und Forschungsanstalten eV (VDLUFA) (Association of German Agricultural Analytical and Research Institutes): c/o LUFA Speyer, Obere Langgasse 40, 67346 Speyer; tel. (6232) 136-121; fax (6232) 136-122; e-mail info@vdlufa.de; internet www.vdlufa.de; f. 1888; 550 mems; Pres. Prof. Dr FRANZ WIESLER; Vice-Pres. (Animals) Prof. Dr HANS SCHENKEL; Vice-Pres. (Plants) Dr REINHOLD GUTSER; publs *Handbuch der landwirtschaftlichen Versuchs- und Untersuchungsmethodik (VDLUFA-Methodenbuch), VDLUFA-Mitteilungen, VDLUFA-Schriftenreihe*.

ARCHITECTURE AND TOWN PLANNING

Bauhaus Dessau Foundation: Gropiusallee 38, 06846 Dessau; tel. (340) 6508-0; fax (340) 6508-226; e-mail service@bauhaus-dessau.de; internet www.bauhaus-dessau.de; f. 1994 to preserve and convey the historic heritage of Bauhaus and contribute ideas and solutions to the problems of design in the contemporary environment; library: public research and reference library with particular reference to urban design, architecture and living; archive of 25,000 items from collections and legacies of Bauhaus teachers and students.

Attached college:

Bauhaus Kolleg: Gropiusallee 38, 06846 Dessau; tel. (340) 6508-403; fax (340) 6508-404; e-mail goegel@bauhaus-dessau.de; f. 1999; 1-year postgraduate programme; language of instruction: English; Dir OMAR AKBAR; Man. INA GOEGEL.

DAI–Verband Deutscher Architekten- und Ingenieurvereine eV: Keithstr. 2–4, 10787 Berlin; tel. (30) 21473174; fax (30) 21473182; e-mail dai@architekt.de; internet www.architekt.de; f. 1871; 5,500 mems; Chair. Prof. Dr-Ing. JÜRGEN FISSLER; publ. *DAI-Verbandszeitschrift BAUKULTUR*.

Deutscher Verband für Wohnungswesen, Städtebau und Raumordnung eV (German Federation for Housing and Planning): Georgenstr. 21, 10117 Berlin; tel. (30) 20613250; fax (30) 20613251; e-mail info@deutscher-verband.org; internet www.deutscher-verband.org; f. 1946; independent research in housing; urban and country planning; 700 mems; Chair. Dr IRENE WIESE-VON OFEN; Sec.-Gen. Dr HANS-MICHAEL BREY; publ. *Annual Report*; publ. *Newsletter*.

BIBLIOGRAPHY, LIBRARY SCIENCE AND MUSEOLOGY

Arbeitsgemeinschaft der Spezialbibliotheken eV: Geschaeftsstelle, c/o Ms. Jadwiga Warmbrunn, Herder Institut eV, Bibliothek, Gisonenweg 5–7, 35037 Marburg; tel. (6421) 184162; fax (6421) 184139; e-mail geschaeftsstelle@aspb.de; internet www.aspb.de; f. 1946; asscn of specialized libraries in the German-speaking countries; organizes conferences; acts as Section 5 (Spec.Libraries) of the German Libraries Asscn; c. 600 mems; Pres. Dr JÜRGEN WARMBRUNN; publ. *Conference proceedings (Tagungsband der Arbeits- und Fortbildungstagung)* (every 2 years).

Berufsverband Information Bibliothek e. V. (Association of Information and Library Professionals): POB 13 24, Gartenstr. 18, 72703 Reutlingen; tel. (7121) 34910; fax (7121) 300433; e-mail mail@bib-info.de; internet www.bib-info.de; f. 1949 as Verein der Bibliothekare und Assistentenen; present name 2000; 6,300 mems; Pres. Prof. Dr SUSANNE RIEDEL; Sec. MICHAEL REISSER; publ. *Buch und Bibliothek* (10 a year).

Deutsche Gesellschaft für Informationswissenschaft und Informationspraxis: Hanauer Landstr. 151–3, 60314 Frankfurt; tel. (69) 430313; fax (69) 4909096; e-mail mail@dgi-info.de; internet www.dgd.de; f. 1948 as Deutsche Gesellschaft für Dokumentation; present name 1999; promotion of information and documentation, information science and practice; 2,000 mems; Pres. Prof. Dr GABRIELE BEGER; publs *Deutscher Dokumentartag* (annually), *DGD-Online-Conference* (annually), *Information–Wissenschaft & Praxis* (7 a year), *Nachrichten für Dokumentation* (every 2 months).

Deutscher Museumsbund eV (German Museums Association): c/o Staatliche Museen Kassel, Schloss Wilhelmshöhe, 34131 Kassel; tel. (561) 31680-125; fax (561) 31680-111; e-mail office@museumbund.de; internet www.museumsbund.de; f. 1917; to promote museums, their development and museology; 1,270 mems; Pres. Dr MICHAEL EISSENHAUER; Vice-Pres. Prof. Dr WILLI ZYLANDER; publs *Bulletin* (quarterly), *Einkaufsführer für Museen* (annually), *Museumskunde* (2 a year).

Internationale Vereinigung der Musikbibliotheken, Musikarchive und Musikdokumentationszentren (IVMB) Gruppe Deutschland eV (International Association of Music Libraries, Archives and Documentation Centres—IAML): c/o Stadtbüchereien, Musikbibliothek, 40200 Dusseldorf; tel. (211) 89-92939; fax (211) 89-32939; e-mail sekretaer@aibm.info; internet www.aibm

.info; f. 1951; 210 mems; Pres. SUSANNE HEIN; Sec. THOMAS KALK; publs *Fontes Artis Musicae* (4 a year), *Forum Musikbibliothek* (4 a year).

Verein Deutscher Bibliothekare eV (Association of German Librarians): Universitätsbibliothek Augsburg, Universtätsstr 22, 86159 Augsburg; tel. (821) 5985361; fax (821) 5985407; internet www.vdb-online.org; f. 1900, ref. 1948; annual librarians' congress, workshops, seminars; 1,650 mems; Pres. Dr ULRICH HOHOFF; Sec. Dr THOMAS STÖBER; publs *Bibliotheksdienst* (monthly), *Buch und Bibliothek (BuB)* (10 a year), *Jahrbuch der Deutschen Bibliotheken* (every 2 years), *Zeitschrift für Bibliothekswesen und Bibliographie* (every 2 months), *VDB-Mitteilungen* (2 a year).

Württembergische Bibliotheksgesellschaft (Society of Friends of the Württemberg State Library): Postfach 105441, 70047 Stuttgart; tel. (711) 212-4428; fax (711) 212-4422; e-mail wbg@wlb-stuttgart.de; internet www.wlb-stuttgart.de; f. 1946 to support the reconstruction of the Württemberg State Library, to hold lectures, meetings, exhibitions, etc.; 500 mems; Pres. (vacant); Chair. Dr WULF D. VON LUCIUS; Sec. CHRISTINE DEMMLER.

ECONOMICS, LAW AND POLITICS

AFW Wirtschaftsakademie Bad Harzburg GmbH (Academy for Distance Study of Economics in Bad Harzburg): An den Weiden 15, 38667 Bad Harzburg; tel. (5322) 902034; fax (5322) 902040; e-mail bildung@afwbadharzburg.de; internet www.afwbadharzburg.de; until 1999 Akademie für Fernstudium (AfF); Dir DIETMAR BORSCH.

Deutsche Gesellschaft für Auswärtige Politik eV (German Council on Foreign Relations): Rauchstr. 17–18, 10787 Berlin; tel. (30) 2542310; fax (30) 25423116; e-mail info@dgap.org; internet www.dgap.org; f. 1955; 1,800 mems; library of 70,000 vols, 270 periodicals; discusses and promotes research on problems of international politics; operates one of the oldest specialised libraries on German foreign policy (open to the public); Pres. Dr AREND OETKER; Exec. Vice-Pres. FRITJOF VON NORDENSKJÖLD; Otto Wolff-Dir of the Research Institute EBERHARD SANDSCHNEIDER; publs *Die Internationale Politik* (yearbook), *Internationale Politik* (monthly, transatlantic edition 4 a year).

Deutsche Gesellschaft für Osteuropakunde eV (German Society for Eastern European Studies): Schaperstr. 30, 10719 Berlin; tel. (30) 21478412; fax (30) 21478414; e-mail info@dgo-online.org; internet www.dgo-online.org; f. 1913; 850 mems; Pres. Prof. Dr RITA SÜSSMUTH; Dir Dr FRANZ-LOTHAR ALTMANN; publs *Osteuropa* (monthly), *Osteuropa-Recht* (6 a year), *Osteuropa-Wirtschaft* (quarterly).

Deutsche Aktuarvereinigung eV: Hohenstaufenring 47–51, 50674 Cologne; tel. (221) 912554-0; fax (221) 912554-44; e-mail info@aktuar.de; internet www.aktuar.de; f. 1948; society for promotion of actuarial theory in collaboration with the universities; 838 mems; Pres. NORBERT HEINEN; Man. Dir MICHAEL STEINMETZ; publ. *Blätter* (2 a year).

Deutsche Statistische Gesellschaft: Albertus-Magnus-Pl., 50923 Cologne; tel. (221) 4704130; fax (221) 4705084; e-mail post@dstatg.de; internet www.dstatg.de; f. 1911; 800 mems; Pres. Prof. Dr KARL MOSLER; Man. Dir NANA DYCKERHOFF; publ. *Allgemeines Statistisches Archiv* (quarterly).

Deutsche Vereinigung für Politische Wissenschaft (German Political Science Association): c/o Osnabrück University FB1-Sozialwissenschaften, 49069 Osnabrück; tel. (541) 969-6264; fax (541) 969-6266; e-mail dvpw@uos.de; internet www.dvpw.de; f. 1951; 1,552 mems; Pres. Prof. Dr SUZANNE SCHÜTTEMEYER; Dir FELIX W. WURM; publ. *Politische Vierteljahresschrift* (quarterly).

Deutscher Juristentag eV: Postfach 1169, 53001 Bonn; tel. (228) 9839185; fax (228) 9839140; e-mail info@djt.de; internet www.djt.de; f. 1860; furthers discussion among jurists; 8,200 mems; Pres. Prof. Dr PAUL KIRCHHOF.

Gesellschaft für Öffentliche Wirtschaft (Society for Public Economy): Sponholzstr. 11, 12159 Berlin; tel. (30) 8521045; fax (30) 8525111; e-mail goew.dsceep@t-online.de; internet www.goew.de; f. 1951; 70 mems; research and information service and providers of public services; Pres. MICHAEL SCHÖNEICH; Dir WOLF LEETZ; publ. *Zeitschrift für öffentliche und gemeinwirtschaftliche Unternehmen* (quarterly).

Gesellschaft für Rechtsvergleichung (Society for Comparative Law): Belfortstr. 16, 79098 Freiburg; tel. (761) 2032126; fax (761) 2032127; e-mail gfr@uni-freiburg.de; internet www.wirtschaftsrecht.uni-freiburg.de/gfr; f. 1894; 1,400 mems; Chair. Prof. Dr UWE BLAUROCK; Sec.-Gen. Prof. Dr GERHARD HOHLOCH; publs *Arbeiten zur Rechtsvergleichung*, *Ausländische Aktiengesetze*.

Gesellschaft für Sozial- und Wirtschaftsgeschichte (Society for Social and Economic History): Friedrich-Schiller-Universität Jena, Lehrstuhl für Wirtschafts- und Sozialgeschichte, Carl Zeiss Str. 3, 07743 Jena; tel. (3641) 943320; fax (3641) 943322; internet www.gswg.net; f. 1961; 220 mems; Pres. Prof. Dr ROLF WALTER; Sec. Prof. Dr RAINER METZ.

Kommission für Geschichte des Parlamentarismus und der politischen Parteien (Commission for History of Parliamentarism and Political Parties): Colmantstr. 39, 53115 Bonn; tel. (228) 604830; fax (228) 6048323; e-mail info@kgparl.de; internet www.kgparl.de; f. 1951; 21 mems; Pres. Prof. Dr K. HILDEBRAND; Gen. Sec. Dr M. SCHUMACHER; publs *Beiträge zur Geschichte des Parlamentarismus und der politischen Parteien*, *Quellen zur Geschichte des Parlamentarismus und der politischen Parteien*.

EDUCATION

Humboldt Gesellschaft für Wissenschaft, Kunst und Bildung eV (Humboldt Society for Science, Art and Education): Finkenstr. 14, 37154 Northeim; tel. (5551) 8278; f. 1962; 650 mems; Pres. Dr MARIA VON NEREE-LOEBNITZ; publs *Abhandlungen* (every 2 years), *Mitteilungen* (every 2 years).

FINE AND PERFORMING ARTS

Bayerische Akademie der Schönen Künste: Max-Joseph-Pl. 3, 80539 Munich; tel. (89) 290077-0; fax (89) 290077-23; e-mail info@badsk.de; internet www.badsk.de; f. 1948; 242 mems; Pres. Prof. Dr DIETER BORCHMEYER; Gen. Sec. Dr KATJA SCHAEFER; publ. *Jahrbuch*.

Deutsche Gesellschaft für Photographie eV (German Society for Photography): Rheingasse 8–12, 50676 Cologne; tel. (221) 9232069; fax (221) 9232070; e-mail dgph@dgph.de; internet www.dgph.de; f. 1951; 1,000 mems; Chair. Dr SUSANNE LANGE; publ. *DGPh-Intern* (4 a year).

Deutsche Mozart-Gesellschaft e. V. (German Mozart Society): Frauentorstr. 30, 86152 Augsburg; tel. (821) 518588; fax (821) 157228; e-mail deutsche-mozart-gesellschaft@t-online.de; internet www.deutsche-mozart-gesellschaft.de; f. 1951; 3,000 mems; Pres. Dr DIRK HEWIG; publ. *Acta Mozartiana* (annually).

Deutscher Komponistenverband eV (German Composers' Association): Kadettenweg 80B, 12205 Berlin; tel. (30) 84310580; fax (30) 84310582; e-mail info@komponistenverband.org; internet www.komponistenverband.de; f. 1954; 1,300 mems; Pres. KARL HEINZ WAHRENJÖRG EVERS; Dir MANFRED TROJAHN.

Deutscher Verein für Kunstwissenschaft e. V. (German Society for Studies in Art History): Jebensstr. 2, 10623 Berlin; tel. (30) 3139932; fax (30) 32303824; e-mail dvfk@aol.com; internet www.dvfk-berlin.de; f. 1908; 1,000 mems; Chair. Prof. Dr RAINER KAHSNITZ; Sec. Dr JOSEF RIEDMAIER; publs *Zeitschrift des Deutschen Vereins für Kunstwissenschaft*, *Schrifttum zur Deutschen Kunst*.

IWF Wissen und Medien GmbH (IWF Knowledge and Media Ltd): Nonnenstieg 72, 37075 Göttingen; tel. (551) 5024-0; fax (551) 5024-400; e-mail iwf-goe@iwf.de; internet www.iwf.de; f. 1956; supports science and education through the development and transfer of audiovisual media, which it collects and customizes for use in teaching and research; offers media training and special courses, ranging from basic film-training to web design and video applications; 60 mems; library of 8,000 media items for higher education; Dir Dr H. U. FRHR VON SPIEGEL.

Kestner Gesellschaft: Goseriede 11, 30159 Hanover; tel. (511) 70120-0; fax (511) 70120-20; e-mail kestner@kestner.org; internet www.kestner.org; f. 1916; activities concerned with the promotion of modern art; 4,300 mems; Dir VEIT GOERNER.

Stiftung Preussischer Kulturbesitz (Prussian Cultural Foundation): Von-der-Heydt-Str. 16–18, 10785 Berlin; tel. (30) 25463-0; fax (30) 25463-268; e-mail info@hv.spk-berlin.de; internet www.preussischer-kulturbesitz.de; f. 1961 to preserve, augment and reunite the Prussian cultural heritage; comprises 16 State Museums, the State Library, the State Privy Archives, the Iberian-American Institute and the State Institute for Research in Music with the Museum for Musical Instruments; Pres. Prof. Dr phil. h.c. KLAUS-DIETER LEHMANN; publ. *Jahrbuch* (annually).

Verband Deutscher Kunsthistoriker eV (Association of German Art Historians): c/o Zentralinstitut für Kunstgeschichte, Meiserstr. 10, 80333 Munich,; tel. (89) 553488; fax (89) 54505221; e-mail info@kunsthistoriker.org; internet www.kunsthistoriker.org; f. 1948; 1,750 mems; Pres. Prof. Dr GEORG SATZINGER; Sec. Dr KATHARINA CORSEPINS; publ. *Kunstchronik* (monthly).

HISTORY, GEOGRAPHY AND ARCHAEOLOGY

Arbeitsgemeinschaft Historischer Kommissionen und Landesgeschichtlicher Institute (Association of Historic Councils and Regional History Institutes): Schückingstr. 36, 35037 Marburg; tel. (6421) 1840; f. 1898; controls 51 societies and institutes; Pres. Prof. Dr RODERICH SCHMIDT; Man. Dir Dr WINFRIED IRGANG.

Deutsche Akademie für Landeskunde eV (German Academy for Regional Geography of Germany): c/o Institut für Länderkunde, Schongauerstr. 9, 04329 Leipzig; tel. (6221) 544547; fax (6221) 545585; e-mail kontakt@deutsche-landeskunde.de; internet www.deutsche-landeskunde.de; f. 1882, re-f. 1946; study of German regional geography;

Chair. (Bonn) Prof. Dr WINFRIED SCHENK; Chair. (Heidelberg) Prof. Dr HANS GEBHARDT; publs *Berichte zur deutschen Landeskunde*, *Forschungen zur deutschen Landeskunde*, *Neues Schrifttum zur deutschen Landeskunde*.

Deutsche Gesellschaft für Geographie: c/o Geographisches Institut der Humboldt-Universität Berlin, Unter den Linden 6Rudower Chaussee 16, 1248910099 Berlin; tel. (30) 20936814; fax (30) 20936856; internet www.geographie.de; Pres. Prof. Dr ELMAR KULKE; Sec. Dr SEBASTIAN KINDER.

Deutsche Gesellschaft für Kartographie eV: Niedersächsisches Landesgesundheitsamt Gesundheitsberichterstattung, Roesebeckstr. 4–6, 30449 Hanover; tel. (511) 4505136; fax (511) 4505140; e-mail Sekretaer@dgfk.net; internet www.dgfk.net; f. 1950; promotes scientific and practical cartography; 2,530 mems; Pres. Dr PETER ASCHENBERNER; Sec. HOLGER SCHARLACH; publ. *Kartographische Nachrichten* (every 2 months).

Deutsche Gesellschaft für Ortung und Navigation eV (German Institute of Navigation): Kölnstr. 70, 53111 Bonn; tel. (228) 20197-0; fax (228) 20197-19; e-mail dgon.bonn@t-online.de; internet www.dgon.de; f. 1951 as Ausschuss für Funkortung, present name 1961; to promote research and development of methods and systems used for navigation; Pres. Prof Dr-Ing. PETER VÖRSMANN; publ. *European Journal of Navigation* (jt publication of various European navigation institutions, quarterly).

Deutscher Nautischer Verein von 1868 eV (German Nautical Association of 1868): Striepenweg 31, 21147 Hamburg; tel. (40) 79713401; fax (40) 79713402; e-mail dnv-ev@hansa-online.de; internet www.dnvev.de; f. 1868; 4,598 mems in 20 local Nautical Associations, 47 corporate mems; Pres. FRANK LEONHARDT; Sec. Capt. GARRIT LEEMREIJZE; publ. *Kalendar* (annually).

Fränkische Geographische Gesellschaft: Kochstr. 4/4, 91054 Erlangen; tel. (9131) 8522645; fax (9131) 8522013; e-mail fgg@geographie.uni-erlangen.de; internet www.fgg.uni-erlangen.de; f. 1954; 830 mems; library of 10,300 vols; Dir Prof. Dr HORST KOPP; Jt Gen. Secs Dr PETER LINDNER, Dr MANFRED SCHNEIDER; publs *Mitteilungen* (annually), *Erlanger Geographische Arbeiten* (annually), *Erlanger Geographische Arbeiten, Sonderband* (irregular).

Gesamtverein der Deutschen Geschichts- und Altertumsvereine (Union of German Historical and Archaeological Societies): Barer Str. 29, 80799 Munich; tel. (89) 23805-122; fax (89) 23805-197; e-mail treml@mpz.bayern.de; f. 1852; 238 affiliated asscns; Pres. Prof. Dr M. TREML; Treas. Prof. Dr WOLFGANG WÜST; publ. *Blätter für deutsche Landesgeschichte*.

Gesellschaft für Erdkunde zu Berlin (Berlin Geographical Society): Arno-Holz-Str. 14, 12165 Berlin; tel. (30) 790066-0; fax (30) 790066-12; e-mail mail@gfe-berlin.de; internet www.die-erde.de; f. 1828; 500 mems; library of 100,000 vols; Pres. Dr DIETER BIEWALD; Sec. Dr CHRISTOF ELLGER; publ. *Die Erde (Zeitschrift der Gesellschaft für Erdkunde zu Berlin)* (quarterly).

Monumenta Germaniae Historica: Ludwigstr. 16, Pf. 34 02 23, 80099 Munich; tel. (89) 286382384; fax (89) 281419; e-mail sekretariat@mgh.de; internet www.mgh.de; f. 1819; library of 120,000 vols; Pres. Prof. Dr RUDOLF SCHIEFFER; Sec. Prof. Dr GERHARD SCHMITZ; Librarian Priv. Doz. Dr ARNO MENTZEL-REUTERS; publ. *Deutsches Archiv für Erforschung des Mittelalters*.

Verband der Historiker und Historikerinnen Deutschlands (Union of German Historians): c/o Prof. Dr. Axel Schildt, Forschungsstelle für Zeitgeschichte in Hamburg (FZH), Schulterblatt 36, 20357 Hamburg; tel. (40) 43139720; fax (40) 43139740; e-mail vhhd@zeitgeschichte-hamburg.de; internet www.vhd.gwdg.de; f. 1893, re-f. 1949; 2,300 mems; Pres. Prof. Dr PETER FUNKE; Sec. Prof. Dr AXEL SCHILDT.

LANGUAGE AND LITERATURE

British Council: Hackescher Markt 1, 10178 Berlin; tel. (30) 3110990; fax (30) 31109920; e-mail info@britishcouncil.de; internet www.britishcouncil.de/e/; teaching centre; offers courses and exams in English language and British culture and promotes cultural exchange with the UK; attached offices in Düsseldorf, Leipzig and Munich; Dir KATHRYN BOARD; Teaching Centre Man. ZOË CHADWICK.

Deutsche Gesellschaft für Sprachwissenschaft (German Society for Linguistics): c/o Martin Neef, Seminar für Deutsche Sprache und LiteraturInstitut für Germanistik, Technische Universität Braunschweig, Bienroder Weg 80, 38106 Brunswick; tel. (531) 3918635; fax (531) 3918638; e-mail martin.neef@tu-bs.de; internet www.dgfs.de; f. 1978 for the advancement of the scientific investigation of language, and the support of linguists engaged in this; 1,050 mems; Pres. RICHARD WIESE; Sec. MARTIN NEEF; publ. *Zeitschrift für Sprachwissenschaft* (2 a year).

Gesellschaft für deutsche Sprache eV (Society for the German Language): Spiegelgasse 13, 65183 Wiesbaden; tel. (611) 99955-0; fax (611) 99955-30; e-mail sekr@gfds.de; internet www.gfds.de; f. 1947; 2,600 mems; library of 9,000 vols; Chair. Prof. Dr RUDOLF HOBERG; publs *Muttersprache* (quarterly), *Der Sprachdienst* (every 2 months).

Hölderlin-Gesellschaft eV: Hölderlinhaus, 72070 Tübingen; tel. (7071) 22040; fax (7071) 22948; e-mail info@hoelderlin-gesellschaft.de; internet www.hoelderlin-gesellschaft.info; f. 1943, reconstituted 1946; 1,300 mems; Pres. Prof.Dr PETER HÄRTLINGULRICH GAIER; Dir VALÉRIE LAWITSCHKA; publs *Hölderlin-Jahrbuch* (every 2 years), *Lyrik im Hölderlinturm*, *Schriften der Hölderlin-Gesellschaft* (irregular), *Turm-Vorträge*.

Instituto Cervantes: Rosenstr. 18–19, 10178 Berlin; tel. (30) 257618-0; fax (30) 257618-19; e-mail berlin@cervantes.de; internet www.cervantes.de; offers courses and exams in Spanish language and culture and promotes cultural exchange with Spain and Spanish-speaking Latin and Central America; attached centres in Bremen and Munich; library: library of 4,500 vols; Dir JOSÉ IGNACIO OLMOS SERRANO.

Mommsen-Gesellschaft: Institut für Geschichte 'Otto von Guericke', Universität Magdeburg, Zschokkestr. 32, 39014 Magdeburg; internet www.archaeologie.uni-freiburg.de/mommsen/; f. 1950; 600 mems; association of university teachers of classics, ancient history and archaeology, named after the classicist Theodor Mommsen (1817–1903); Pres. Prof. Dr MARTIN DREHER; Sec. Dr ECKART FREY.

PEN Zentrum Bundesrepublik Deutschland (German PEN Centre): Kasinostr. 3, 64293 Darmstadt; tel. (6151) 23120; fax (6151) 293414; e-mail PEN-Germany@t-online.de; f. 1951; 682 mems; Pres. JOHANN STRASSER; Sec.-Gen. WILFRIED F. SCHOELLER.

MEDICINE

Anatomische Gesellschaft (Anatomical Society): Institut für Anatomie, Universität zu Lübeck, Ratzeburger Allee 160, 23538 Lübeck; tel. (451) 500-4030; fax (451) 500-4034; e-mail kuehnel@anat.mu-luebeck.de; internet www.uni-luebeck.de/nc/anatges; f. 1886; 1,120 mems; Sec. Prof. Dr med. Dr h.c. mult. WOLFGANG KÜHNEL; publs *Annals of Anatomy* (6 a year), *Verhandlungen der Anatomischen Gesellschaft* (supplement, annually).

Deutsche Dermatologische Gesellschaft: Robert-Koch-Pl. 7, 10115 Berlin; tel. (30) 246253-0; fax (30) 246253-29; e-mail ddg@derma.de; internet www.derma.de; f. 1888; 2,500 mems; Pres. Prof. Dr HARALD GOLLNICK; Sec.-Gen. Prof. Dr THOMAS A. LUGER; publ. *Hautarzt* (monthly).

Deutsche Gesellschaft für Anästhesiologie und Intensivmedizin: Roritzerstr. 27, 90419 Nuremberg; tel. (911) 933780; fax (911) 3938195; e-mail dgai@dgai-ev.de; internet www.dgai.de; f. 1953; 10,000 mems; Dir HOLGER SORGATZ; Pres. Prof. Dr JOACHIM RADKE; Sec. Prof. Dr Dr h.c. K. VAN ACKERN; publ. *Anästhesiologie, Intensivmedizin, Notfallmedizin und Schmerztherapie (AINS)*.

Deutsche Gesellschaft für Angewandte Optik e. V. (German Society for Applied Optics): Str. 12 14, 15827 Dahlewitz; tel. (3641) 807440; fax (3641) 807600; e-mail dgao@iof.fhg.de; internet www.dgao.de; f. 1923; 680 mems; Pres. Dr F. MERKLE; Sec. Dr CHRISTEL BUDZINSKI; publ. *Optik* (monthly).

Deutsche Gesellschaft für Chirurgie (German Surgical Society): Luisenstrasse 58/59, 01117 Berlin; tel. (30) 28876290; fax (30) 28876299; e-mail DGChirurgie@t-online.de; internet www.dgch.de; f. 1872; 3,444 mems; Pres. H. D. SAEGER; Sec. H. BAUER; publ. *Langenbecks Archiv für Chirurgie*.

Deutsche Gesellschaft für Endokrinologie: c/o EndoScience, Endokrinologie Service GmbH, Thalkirchner Str. 1, 80337 Munich; tel. (89) 23237571; fax (89) 23237579; e-mail dge@endokrinologie.net; internet www.endokrinologie.net; f. 1953; 1,300 mems; Pres. Prof. Dr THOMAS GUDERMANN; Sec. Prof. Dr MARTIN GRUßENDORF; publ. *Endokrinologie-Informationen* (6 a year).

Deutsche Gesellschaft für Gynäkologie und Geburtshilfe (German Society for Gynaecology and Birth Support): Robert-Koch-Pl. 7, 10115 Berlin; tel. (30) 5148333; fax (30) 51488344; e-mail InfoDGGG@gmx.de; internet www.dggg.de; f. 1885; Pres. Prof. Dr K. DIEDRICH.

Deutsche Gesellschaft für Hals-Nasen-Ohren-Heilkunde, Kopf- und Hals-Chirurgie (German Society for Oto-rhino-laryngology and Head and Neck Surgery): Hittorfstr. 7, 53129 Bonn; tel. (228) 231770; fax (228) 239385; e-mail info@hno.org; internet www.hno.org; f. 1921; 10 European archives of oto-rhino-laryngology; 3,675 mems; Pres. Prof. Dr KARL HÖRMANN; Sec. Prof. Dr KARL-BERND HÜTTENBRINK; publ. *Laryngo-Rhino-Otologie*.

Deutsche Gesellschaft für Hygiene und Mikrobiologie: Institut für Hygiene und Mikrobiologie, Josef-Schneiderstr. 2, 97080 Würzberg; tel. (931) 20146936; fax (931) 20146445; internet www.dghm.org; f. 1906; 1,850 mems; Chair. Prof. Dr M. FROSCH; Sec. Prof. Dr Dr h.c. S. SUERBAUM.

Deutsche Gesellschaft für Innere Medizin (Internal Medicine): Schöne Aussicht 1, 65193 Wiesbaden; tel. (611) 2058040-0; fax (611) 2058040-46; e-mail info@dgim.de; internet www.dgim.de; f. 1882; 7,000 mems;

Chair. Prof. Dr WERNER SEEGER; Gen. Sec. Prof. Dr HANS-PETER SCHUSTER; publ. *Supplementum of Abstracts* (annually).

Deutsche Gesellschaft für Kinderheilkunde und Jugendmedizin (Paediatrics and Adolescent Medicine): Eichendorffstr. 13, 10115 Berlin; tel. (30) 3087779-0; fax (30) 3087779-99; e-mail info@dgkj.de; internet www.dgkj.de; f. 1883; 8,500 mems; Pres. Prof. Dr HANSJOSEF BÖHLES; Dir Dr GABRIELE OLBRISCH.

Deutsche Gesellschaft für Neurochirurgie: c/o Porstmann Kongresse GmbH, Alte Jakobstr. 77, 10179 Berlin; tel. (30) 284499-22; fax (30) 284499-11; e-mail gs@dgnc.de; internet www.dgnc.de; f. 1950; 244 mems; Pres. Prof. Dr med. DIETMAR STOLKE; Sec. Prof. Dr med. DIETER-KARSTEN BÖKER; publ. *Zentralblatt für Neurochirurgie* (4 a year).

Deutsche Gesellschaft für Orthopädie und Orthopädische Chirurgie eV: Kronprinzendamm 15, 10711 Berlin; tel. (30) 79744444; fax (30) 79744445; e-mail dgooc@bvonet.de; internet www.dgooc.de; f. 1901; Pres. Prof. Dr JOCHEN EULERT; Gen. Sec. Prof. Dr FRITZ UWE NIETHARD; publ. *Orthopädie Mitteilungen* (6 a year).

Deutsche Gesellschaft für Physikalische Medizin und Rehabilitation: Prof. Dr. med. Lothar Beyer, Westbahnhofstr. 2 , 07745 Jena; tel. and fax (3641) 622178; internet www.dgpmr.de; f. 1886; physical medicine and rehabilitation; 550 mems; Pres. Prof. Dr PETER KRÖLING; publs *Kurortmedizin* (every 2 months), *Physikalische Medizin*, *Rehabilitationsmedezin*.

Deutsche Gesellschaft für Plastische und Wiederherstellungschirurgie eV (German Society for Plastic and Reconstructive Surgery): Diakoniekrakenhaus, Elise-Averdieck-Str. 17, 27356 Rotenburg/Wümme; tel. (4261) 77-2126/7; fax (4261) 77-2128; e-mail info@dgpw.de; internet www.dgpw.de; f. 1962; 680 mems; Dir Dr V. STUDTMANN; Gen. Sec. Prof. Dr PETER M. VOGT; publ. *Journal* (2 a year).

Deutsche Gesellschaft für Psychiatrie, Psychotherapie und Nervenheilkunde (Psychiatry, Psychotherapy and Neurosciences): Reinhardtstr. 14, 10117 Berlin; tel. (30) 28096601; fax (30) 28093816; internet www.dgppn.de; f. 1842; 2,000 mems; Pres. Prof. Dr FRITZ HOHAGEN; Sec. Dr SEBASTIAN RUDOLF; publs *Nervenarzt*, *Spektrum*.

Deutsche Gesellschaft für Psychoanalyse, Psychotherapie, Psychosomatik und Tiefenpsychologie (DGPT) eV: Johannisbollwerk 20 III, 20459 Hamburg; tel. (40) 319-26-19; fax (40) 319-43-00; e-mail psa@dgpt.de; internet www.dgpt.de; f. 1949 to train psychotherapists; 2,900 mems; Pres. Dipl.-Psych. ANNE SPRINGER.

Deutsche Gesellschaft für Rechtsmedizin (German Society of Legal Medicine): Alberstr. 9, 79104 Freiburg; tel. (761) 2036854; fax (761) 2036858; e-mail legalmed@uniklinik-freiburg.de; internet www.dgrm.de; Pres. Prof. Dr STEFAN POLLAK.

Deutsche Gesellschaft für Sozialmedizin und Prävention (German Society for Social Medicine and Prevention): c/o Institut für Sozialmedizin und Gesundheitsökonomie, Leipziger Str. 44, 39120 Magdeburg; tel. (391) 5328043; fax (391) 5414258; internet www.dgsmp.de; f. 1964; 500 mems; Pres. Prof. Dr med. BERNT-PETER ROBRA; publ. *Das Gesundheitswesen* (monthly).

Deutsche Gesellschaft für Tropenmedizin und Internationale Gesundheit e. V.: Bernhard-Nocht-Str. 74, 20359 Hamburg; tel. (40) 42818-478; fax (40) 42818-512; e-mail dtg@bni-hamburg.de; internet www.dtg.org; f. 1907 to bring together persons interested in medical questions related to the tropics; 870 mems; Pres. Prof. E. REISINGER; Sec. Prof. Dr G. D. BURCHARD.

Deutsche Gesellschaft für Zahn-, Mund- und Kieferheilkunde (German Society for Dentistry and Oral Medicine): Liesegangstr. 17a, 40211 Düsseldorf; tel. (211) 610198-0; fax (211) 610198-11; e-mail dgzmk@t-online.de; internet www.dgzmk.de; f. 1859; 10,500 mems; Pres. Prof. Dr Dr GEORG MEYER; Sec. Dr KARL-RUDOLF STRATMANN; publs *APW DVD Journal*, *Clinical Oral Investigations*, *Deutsche Zahnärtztliche Zeitung* (monthly), *Oralprophylaxe*, *Zeitschrift für Zahnärztliche Implantologie*.

Deutsche Ophthalmologische Gesellschaft HeidelbergeV: c/o Augenklinik der Universität, Mathildenstr. Str. 8, 80336 Munich; tel. (89) 51603062896; fax (89) 516030344779; e-mail geschaeftsstelle@dog.org; internet www.dog.org; f. 1857; 5,300 mems; Pres. Prof. Dr NORBERTGERNOT PFEIFFERDUNCKER; Sec. Prof. Dr A. KAMPIK; publs *Der Ophthalmologe* (monthly), *Graefe's Archive for Clinical Research* (monthly).

Deutsche Physiologische Gesellschaft eV: Physiologisches Institut der Universität zu Kiel, Olshausenstr. 40, 24098 Kiel; tel. (431) 8802032; fax (431) 8804580; e-mail dgp@physiologie.uni-kiel.de; internet www.physiologische-gesellschaft.de; f. 1904; 890 mems; Pres. Prof. Dr GERHARD BURCKHARDT; Sec. Prof. Dr med. MICHAEL ILLERT; publ. *Zeitschrift: Physiologie* (2 a year).

Deutsche Psychoanalytische Gesellschaft: Arnimallee 12, 14195 Berlin; tel. (30) 84316152; fax (30) 84316153; e-mail geschaeftsstelle@dpg-psa.de; internet www.dpg-psa.de; f. 1910; psychoanalytic training, education and research; 500 mems; Pres. Prof. Dr FRANZ WELLENDORF; Dir Dr THILO EITH; publs *Forum der Psychoanalyse*, *Praxis der Kinderpsychologie und Kinderpsychiatrie*, *Zeitschrift für Psychosomatische Medizin und Psychoanalyse*.

Deutsche Psychoanalytische Vereinigung eV: Körnerstr. 11, 10777 Berlin; tel. (30) 26552504; fax (30) 26552505; e-mail geschaeftsstelle@dpv-psa.de; internet www.dpv-psa.de; br. of the International Psychoanalytical Association; Pres. Dr GERTRAUD SCHLESINGER-KIPP; Sec. Dr HELGA KREMP-OTTENHEYM.

NATURAL SCIENCES

General

Georg-Agricola Gesellschaft zur Förderung der Geschichte der Naturwissenschaften und der Technik e. V.: Institut für Wissenschafts- und Technikgeschichte, TU Bergakademie Freiberg, 09596 Freiberg; tel. (3731) 3950-41; fax (3731) 3950-13; internet www.georg-agricola-gesellschaft.de; f. 1926; promotes study of the history of science and technology, organises annual meetings; 230 mems; 23 mem. asscns; Pres. Prof. REINHARD SCHMIDT; Sec. Dr ROLAND LADWIG; Chairman of the Scientific Board Prof. Dr HANS-JOACHIM BRAUN; publ. *Die Technikgechichte als Vorbild der Modernen Technik*.

Gesellschaft Deutscher Naturforscher und Ärzte eV (Association of German Natural Scientists and Physicians): Hauptstr. 5, 53604 Bad Honnef; tel. (2224) 980713; fax (2224) 980789; e-mail gdnae@gdnae.de; internet www.gdnae.de; f. 1822; 5,000 mems; Pres. Prof. Dr HARALD FRITZSCH; Gen. Sec. Dr WOLFGANG T. DONNER; publ. *Verhandlungen der GDNAe* (every 2 years).

Görres-Gesellschaft zur Pflege der Wissenschaft: Adenauerallee 19, 53111 Bonn; tel. (228) 2674371; f. 1876; 3,000 mems; Pres. Prof. Dr Dr h.c. mult. PAUL MIKAT; Gen. Sec. Prof. Dr RUDOLF SCHIEFFER.

Joachim Jungius-Gesellschaft der Wissenschaften eV: Edmund-Siemers-Allee 1, 20146 Hamburg; tel. (40) 417444; fax (40) 4480752; e-mail jungiusges@uni-hamburg.de; internet www.jungius-gesellschaft.de; f. 1947; 145 mems (107 ordinary, 38 corresp.); Pres. Prof. Dr KURT PAWLIK; Vice-Pres. Prof. Dr JÖRN HENNING WOLF; publs *Veröffentlichungen* (annually), *Berichte aus den Sitzungen* (4 a year).

Naturwissenschaftlicher Verein für Bielefeld und Umgegend eV (Natural History Society for Bielefeld and the Region): Kreuzstr. 38, 33602 Bielefeld; tel. (521) 172434; fax (521) 5218810; e-mail info@nwv-bielefeld.de; internet www.nwv-bielefeld.de; f. 1908; 14 working groups, incl. astronomy, entomology and experimental archaeology; 600 mems; Pres. CLAUDIA QUIRINI; publ. *ILEX* (2 a year).

Wissenschaftsrat (Science Council): Brohlerstr. 11, 50968 Cologne; tel. (221) 3776-0; e-mail post@wrat.de; internet www.wissenschaftsrat.de; f. 1957 through co-operation of Länder and Federal Governments; advisory and co-ordinating body for science policy; makes recommendations on the structural and curricular development of the universities and on the organization and promotion of science and research; 54 nominated mems in two commissions (Scientific and Administrative); Chair. Prof. Dr KARL-MAX EINHÄUPL; Sec.-Gen. WEDIG VON HEYDEN; publ. *Empfehlungen und Stellungnahmen* (annually).

Biological Sciences

Bayerische Botanische Gesellschaft (Bavarian Botanical Society): Menzinger Str. 67, 80638 Munich; tel. (89) 17861-251; fax (89) 17861-193; e-mail bbg@lrz.uni-muenchen.de; internet www.bbgev.de; f. 1890; research into the flora of Bavaria and adjacent countries; preservation of species and plant communities; 900 mems; library of 10,000 vols; Pres. Dr W. LIPPERT; publ. *Berichte*.

Botanischer Informationsknoten Bayern (BIB) (Botanical Information Agency of Bavaria): Am Galgenberg 7, 93109 Wiesent; internet www.bayernflora.de; collects information and data on flora from regional research institutes; Pres. WOLFGANG AHLMER.

Deutsche Botanische Gesellschaft: Institut für Biologie, Humboldt-Universität zu Berlin, Invalidenstr. 42, 10115 Berlin; tel. (30) 20938816; fax (30) 20938445; e-mail info@deutsche-botanische-gesellschaft.de; internet www.deutsche-botanische-gesellschaft.de; f. 1882; 1,050 mems; Pres. Prof. Dr U.-I. FLÜGGE; publ. *Plant Biology*.

Deutsche Gesellschaft für Allgemeine und Angewandte Entomologie eV (German Society for General and Applied Entomology): Eberswalder Str. 84, 15374 Müncheberg; tel. (333432) 824730; fax (333432) 824706; e-mail dgaae@dgaae.de; internet www.dgaae.de; f. 1976; 870 mems; Pres. Prof. Dr GERALD BERND MORITZ; Sec.-Gen. Dr P. LÖSEL; publs *DGaaE Nachrichten* (3–4 a year), *Mitteilungen* (every 2 years).

Deutsche Gesellschaft für Züchtungskunde eV: Adenauerallee 174, 53113 Bonn; tel. (228) 213411; fax (228) 223497; e-mail info@dgfz-bonn.de; internet www.dgfz-bonn.de; f. 1905; livestock breeding, animal housing, reproduction, hygiene, nutrition; 650 mems; Pres. Dr E.-J. LODE; Man. Dr VOLKER SCHULZE; publ. *Züchtungskunde* (every 2 months).

Deutsche Malakozoologische Gesellschaft: Senckenberganlage 25, 60325 Frankfurt am Main; internet www.hausdernatur.de; f. 1868; study of Mollusca; 270 mems; library of 30,000 vols; Pres. Dr VOLLRATH WIESE; Sec. Dr RONALD JANSSEN; publs *Archiv für Molluskenkunde* (2 a year), *Mitteilungen* (1–2 a year).

Deutsche Ornithologen-Gesellschaft eV: c/o Institut f. Vogelforschung, An der Vogelwarte 21, 26386 Wilhelmshaven; tel. (44) 23914148; fax (44) 21968955; e-mail geschaeftsstelle@do-g.de; internet www.do-g.de; f. 1850; 2,500 mems; Pres. Prof. Dr BAIRLEIN; publs *Journal of Ornithology* (4 a year), *Vogelwarte* (4 a year).

Deutsche Phytomedizinische Gesellschaft eV (German Phytomedical Society): Messeweg 11–12, 38104 Brunswick; tel. (531) 2993213; fax (531) 2993019; e-mail geschaeftsstelle@dpg.phytomedizin.org; internet www.phytomedizin.org; f. 1949; 1,800 mems; Pres. Prof. Dr ANDREAS VON TIEDEMANN.

Deutsche Zoologische Gesellschaft eV (German Zoological Society): Corneliusstr. 12, 80469 München; tel. (89) 54806960; fax (89) 550387052; e-mail dzg@zi.biologie.uni-muenchen.de; internet www.dzg-ev.de; f. 1890; 1,650 mems; Pres. Prof. Dr DIETHARD TAUTZ (Cologne); Sec. Prof. Dr FRANZ PETER FISCHER (Munich); publ. *Frontiers in Zoology* (online only).

Gesellschaft für Biochemie und Molekularbiologie: Mörfelder Landstr. 125, 60598 Frankfurt; tel. (69) 660567-0; fax (69) 660567-22; e-mail info@gbm-online.de; internet www.gbm-online.de; f. 1947; 5,500 mems; Chair. Prof. Dr FRANZ-ULRICH HARTL; Sec. Prof. Dr U. BRANDT; publs *BIOspektrum* (6 a year), *Biological Chemistry* (monthly).

Gesellschaft für Naturkunde in Württemberg: Rosenstein 1, 70191 Stuttgart; tel. (711) 8936-201; fax (711) 8936-100; internet www.ges-naturkde-wuertt.de; f. 1844; 720 mems; Pres. Prof. Dr ULRICH KULL; publ. *Jahreshefte*.

Münchner Entomologische Gesellschaft eV (Munich Entomological Society): Münchhausenstr. 21, 81247 Munich; tel. (89) 81070; fax (89) 8107300; e-mail megmail@zsm.mwn.de; internet www.zsm.mwn.de; f. 1904; 550 mems; library of 10,000 vols, 728 periodicals; attached to library of the Zoological State Collection; Pres. Dr WALTER RUCKDESCHEL; publs *Mitteilungen* (annually), *Nachrichtenblatt der Bayerischen Entomologen* (quarterly).

Naturhistorische Gesellschaft Hannover (Hanover Society of Natural History): Willy-Brandt-Allee 5, 30169 Hanover; tel. (511) 9807871; fax (511) 9807879; internet www.N-G-H.org; f. 1797; 501 mems; Pres. Dr D. SCHULZ; publs *Beihefte*, *Berichte*.

Naturkundeverein Schwäbisch Gmünd eV (Natural History Society of Schwäbisch Gmünd): Im Prediger, Johannispl. 3, 73525 Schwäbisch Gmünd; tel. (7171) 6034130; e-mail vorstand@nkv-gd.de; internet www.nkv-gd.de; f. 1890; works to promote public awareness of and protection of the natural environment; oversees protected sites; Pres. WERNER K. MAYER; publ. *Unicornis*.

Naturwissenschaftlicher und Historischer Verein für das Land Lippe eV (Natural History and Historical Society for the Lippe Region): Willi-Hofmann-Str. 2, 32756 Detmold; tel. (5231) 766213; fax (5231) 766114; e-mail info@nhv-lippe.de; internet www.nhv-lippe.de; f. 1835; 800 ; four groups in Detmold, Bad Salzuflen, Lage and Lemgo; research into natural sciences, prehistory and local folk and art history; Pres. Prof. Dr JÜRGEN DÖHL; publs *Lippischen Geschichtsquellen*, *Lippische Mitteilungen aus Geschichte und Landeskunde* (annually).

Naturwissenschaftlicher Verein der Niederlausitz eV (Natural History Society of Lower Lusatia): Postfach 101005, 03010 Cottbus; e-mail info@nvn-cottbus.de; internet www.nvn-cottbus.de; f. 1990; research into local natural sciences and protection of nature and the environment; 90 mems; Pres. URSULA STRIEGLER.

Naturwissenschaftlicher Verein in Hamburg (Natural History Society of Hamburg): c/o Zoologisches Museum, Martin-Luther-King-Pl. 3, 20146 Hamburg; tel. (40) 428385635; fax (40) 428383937; e-mail nwv.zoologie@uni-hamburg.de; internet www.naturwissenschaftlicher-verein.de; f. 1837; 460 mems; Chair. Prof. Dr HARALD SCHLIEMANN.

Naturwissenschaftlicher Verein zu Bremen (Bremen Natural Science Association): c/o Übersee-Museum, Bahnhofspl. 13, 28195 Bremen; tel. (421) 16038153; fax (421) 1603899; e-mail info@nwv-bremen.de; internet www.bremen.de/info/nwv; f. 1864; 500 mems; Chair. HEINRICH KUHBIER; publ. *Abhandlungen* (annually).

Verein Naturschutzpark eV (Nature Reserves Federation): Niederhaverbeck 7, 29646 Bispingen; tel. (5198) 987030; fax (5198) 987039; e-mail vnp-info@t-online.de; internet www.verein-naturschutzpark.de; f. 1909; 4,500 mems; Dir Dr MATHIAS ZIMMERMANN; publ. *Naturschutz- und Naturparke*.

Vereinigung für Angewandte Botanik eV (Association for Applied Botany): Grisebachstr. 6, 37077 Göttingen; tel. (551) 39-3748; fax (551) 39-3759; e-mail hkoch@gwdg.de; internet www.uni-giessen.de/vab; f. 1902; 200 mems; Pres. Prof. Dr R. LIEBEREI; Sec. Prof. Dr H.-J. JÄGER; publ. *Angewandte Botanik* (Journal of Applied Botany, 3 a year).

Mathematical Sciences

Berliner Mathematische Gesellschaft eV (Berlin Mathematical Society): Str. des 17 Juni 136, 10623 Berlin; internet www.w-volk.de/BMG; f. 1901; Sec. Prof. Dr RUDOLF BAIERL; publ. *Sitzungsberichte*.

Deutsche Mathematiker Vereinigung e. V. (German Mathematical Association): Mohrenstr. 39, 10117 Berlin; tel. (30) 20372306; fax (30) 20372307; e-mail dmv@wias-berlin.de; internet www.mathematik.uni-bielefeld.de/dmv; f. 1890; 3,500 mems; Pres. Prof. Dr G. WILDENHAIN; Sec. Prof. Dr G. TÖRNER; publ. *Jahresbericht der DMV* (4 a year).

Gesellschaft für Angewandte Mathematik und Mechanik (Society for Applied Mathematics and Mechanics): GAMM–Geschäftsstelle, Technische Universität Dresden, c/o Prof. Dr-Ing. V. Ulbricht, Institut für Festkörpermechanik, 01062 Dresden; tel. (351) 463-34285; fax (351) 463-37061; e-mail gamm@mailbox.tu-dresden.de; internet gamm.ev.de; f. 1922; advancement of scientific work and international co-operation in applied mathematics, mechanics and physics; 2,300 mems; Pres. Prof. Dr R. JELTSCH; Sec. Prof. Dr-Ing V. ULBRICHT.

Gesellschaft für Operations Research eV (GOR) (German Society for Operations Research): Am Steinknapp 14B, 44795 Bochum; tel. (234) 462246; fax (234) 462245; e-mail gor@ruhr-uni-bochum.de; internet gor.uni-paderborn.de; f. 1998 by merger of *Deutsche Gesellschaft für Operations Research* and *Gesellschaft für Mathematik, Ökonomie und Operations Research*; promotes development of operations research and encourages co-ordination of theoretical and practical advances in the area; 1,060 mems; Pres. Prof. Dr GERHARD WÄSCHER; publs *Mathematical Methods of Operations Research* (6 a year), *OR News* (3 a year), *OR Spectrum* (quarterly).

Physical Sciences

Astronomische Gesellschaft: c/o Dr Siegfried Roeser, Zentrum für Astronomie, Universität Heidelberg, Moenchhofstr. 12–14, 69120 Heidelberg; tel. (6221) 541858; fax (6221) 541877; e-mail ag@ari.uni-heidelberg.de; internet www.astronomische-gesellschaft.org; f. 1863; 800 mems; Pres. Prof. Dr GERHARD HENSLER; Sec. Dr SIEGFRIED ROESER; publs *Reviews in Modern Astronomy* (annual), *Short Contributions* (annual).

Deutsche Bunsen-Gesellschaft für Physikalische Chemie eV: Theodor-Heuss Allee 25, 60486 Frankfurt; tel. (69) 7564620; fax (69) 7564622; e-mail h.behret@bunsen.de; internet www.bunsen.de; f. 1894; 1,700 mems; Chair. Prof. Dr MICHAEL DRÖSCHER; Dir Dr H. BEHRET; publs *Bunsen-Magazin* (6 a year), *Physical Chemistry Chemical Physics* (jtly with other learned socs, weekly).

Deutsche Geologische Gesellschaft (German Geological Society): Stilleweg 2, 30651 Hanover; tel. (511) 643-2507; fax (511) 643-2695; e-mail dgg@bgr.de; internet www.dgg.de; f. 1848; 3,000 mems; Pres. Dr WERNER STACKEBRANDT; publs *Geowissenschaftliche Mitteilungen* (4 a year), *Schriftenreihe* (irregular), *Zeitschrift* (4 a year).

Deutsche Geophysikalische Gesellschaft eV: c/o GFZ, Telegrafenberg, 14473 Potsdam; tel. (331) 288-1227; fax (331) 288-1228; internet www.dgg.tu-berlin.de; f. 1922; 950 mems; Chair. Prof. Dr HARRO SCHMELING; Man. Dir Dr MARCO BOHNHOFF; publs *Geophysical Journal International* (monthly), *Rote Blätter* (4 a year).

Deutsche Gesellschaft für Biophysik eV: c/o Prof. Dr Eberhard Neumann, Universität Bielefeld, Fakultät für Chemie und Biophysikalische Chemie, Universitätsstr., 33615 Bielefeld; tel. (521) 1062053; fax (521) 1062981; e-mail gallah@uni-muenster.de; internet www.dgfb.org; f. 1943; 450 mems; Pres. Prof. Dr EBERHARD NEUMANN; Sec. Prof. Dr HANS-JOACHIM GALLA.

Deutsche Gesellschaft für experimentelle und klinische Pharmakologie und Toxikologie eV: Institut für Pharmakologie und Toxikologie, Universität Bonn, Reuterstr. 2B, 53113 Bonn; tel. (228) 739558; fax (228) 735404; e-mail dgpt-online@uni-bonn.de; internet www.dgpt-online.de; f. 1920; 2,500 mems; Pres. Prof. Dr W. SCHMITZ.

Deutsche Meteorologische Gesellschaft eV (German Meteorological Society): c/o Freie Universität Berlin, Carl-Heinrich-Becker-Weg 6-10, 12165 Berlin; tel. (30) 79708324; fax (30) 7919002; e-mail sekretariat@dmg-ev.de; internet www.dmg-ev.de; f. 1883; 1,750 mems; Pres. Prof. Dr HERBERT FISCHER; Sec. Dr HERMANN OELHAF; publs *Beiträge zur Physik der Atmosphäre* (quarterly), *Meteorologische Zeitschrift* (every 2 months), *Mitteilungen DMG* (quarterly).

Deutsche Mineralogische Gesellschaft (German Mineralogical Society): Institut für Geologie, Mineralogie und Petrologie der Universität Tübingen, Wilhelmstr. 56, 72074 Tübingen; tel. (7071) 2972930; fax (7071) 293060; e-mail info@DMG-home.de; internet www.dmg-home.de; f. 1908; crystallography, petrology, geochemistry, ore minerals, applied mineralogy; 1,700 mems; Pres. Prof. Dr GREGOR MARKL; publs *Beihefte* (annually), *European Journal of Mineralogy (EJM)* (6 times a year).

Deutsche Physikalische Gesellschaft eV: Hauptstr. 5, 53604 Bad Honnef; tel. (2224) 9232-0; fax (2224) 9232-50; e-mail dpg@dpg-physik.de; internet www.dpg-physik.de; f. 1845; 49,000 mems; Pres. Prof. Dr K. W. URBAN; Sec. Dr V. HÄSELBARTH; publs *Physik Journal* (monthly), *Verhandlungen der DPG* (7 a year).

Deutscher Zentralausschuss für Chemie: Postfach 90 04 40, 60444 Frankfurt am Main; located at: Carl Bosch-Haus, Varrentrappstr. 40–42, 60486 Frankfurt am Main; tel. (69) 7917323; fax (69) 7917307; e-mail gdch@gdch.de; f. 1952; 7 mems; Sec. Prof. Dr WOLFRAM KOCH.

Deutsches Atomforum eV (German Forum on Nuclear Energy): Robert-Koch-Pl. 4, 10115 Berlin; tel. (30) 498555-0; fax (30) 498555-19; internet www.kernenergie.de; f. 1959; 620 mems; library of 1,100 vols; promotes the peaceful uses of atomic energy; Pres. Dr WALTER HOHLEFELDER; Dir DIETER H. MARX.

Geologische Vereinigung e. V. (Geological Association): Vulkanstr. 23, 56743 Mendig; tel. (2652) 989360; fax (2652) 989361; e-mail info@g-v.de; internet www.g-v.de; f. 1910; 1,700 mems; Chair. Prof. Dr GEROLD WEFER; publ. *Geologische Rundschau* (International Journal of Earth Sciences, 6 a year).

Gesellschaft Deutscher Chemiker: Postfach 90 04 40, 60444 Frankfurt am Main; located at: Carl Bosch-Haus, Varrentrappstr. 40–42, 60486 Frankfurt am Main; tel. (69) 7917320; fax (69) 7917307; e-mail gdch@gdch.de; internet www.gdch.de; f. 1946; 26,000 mems; Pres. Prof. Dr HENNING HOPF; Exec. Dir Prof. Dr WOLFRAM KOCH; publs *Angewandte Chemie* (weekly; international edition in English, weekly), *Chemie-Ingenieur-Technik* (monthly), *Chemie in unserer Zeit* (6 a year), *European Journal of Inorganic Chemistry* (2 a month), *European Journal of Organic Chemistry* (2 a month), *Chemischer Informationsdienst* (weekly), *Nachrichten aus der Chemie* (monthly), *Chemistry – A European Journal* (2 a month), *ChemPhysChem* (monthly), *ChemBioChem* (monthly), *Analytical and Bioanalytical Chemistry* (2 a month).

Paläontologische Gesellschaft (Palaeontological Society): Department für Geo- und Umweltwissenschaften (Sektion Paläontologie), Richard-Wagner-Str. 10, 80333 Munich; tel. (89) 2180-6603; e-mail b.reichenbacher@lrz.uni-muenchen.de; internet www.palaeontologische-gesellschaft.de; f. 1912; Pres. Prof. Dr BETTINA REICHENBACHER; publ. *Paläontologische Zeitschrift* (4 a year).

PHILOSOPHY AND PSYCHOLOGY

Deutsche Gesellschaft für Philosophie eV: c/o Prof. Dr Michael Quante, Philosophisches Seminar, Universität zu Köln, Albertus-Magnus-Pl., 50923 Cologne; tel. (221) 4702373; fax (221) 4705006; internet www.dgphil.de; f. 1948 as Allgemeine Gesellschaft für Philosophie in Deutschland eV; 760 mems; Pres. Prof. Dr CARL FRIEDRICH GETHMANN; Dir Prof. Dr MICHAEL QUANTE.

Deutsche Gesellschaft für Psychologie eV (German Psychology Society): Geschäftsstelle, Postfach 42 01 43, 48068 Münster; tel. (2533) 2811520; fax (2533) 281144; e-mail geschaeftsstelle@dgps.de; internet www.dgps.de; f. 1904; 2,500 mems; Pres. Prof. Dr MARCUS HASSELHORN; Sec. Prof. Dr THOMAS BLIESENER; publ. *Psychologische Rundschau* (quarterly).

Gesellschaft für Antike Philosophie eV (GANPH): c/o Prof. Dr Christoph Horn, Institut für PhilosophiePhilosophisches Seminar LFB I, Universität Bonn 53113 Bonn; internet www.ganph.de; f. 1999; to advance research into ancient philosophy; Pres. Prof. Dr DOROTHEA FREDE.

Gesellschaft für Geistesgeschichte eV (Society for the History of Ideas): c/o Universität Potsdam, Historisches Institut, Am Neuen Palais 10, Postfach 601553, 14415 Potsdam; tel. (331) 9771036; fax (331) 9771168; e-mail tgerber@rz.uni-potsdam.de; internet www.uni-potsdam.de/u/geschichte/neuere2/neuge2.htm; f. 1958; 150 mems; Pres. Prof. Dr JULIUS H. SCHOEPS; Sec. Dr THOMAS GERBER; publ. *Zeitschrift für Religions- und Geistesgeschichte*.

Gesellschaft für Wissenschaftliche Gerichts- und Rechtpsychologie (GWG) (Society for Forensic and Legal Science): Rablstr. 45, 81669 Munich; tel. (89) 4481282; fax (89) 44718018; e-mail info@gwg.info; internet www.gwg-institut.com; f. 1982; community of psychologists and doctors specialising in forensics; Dir Dr JOSEPH SALZGEBER.

Gottfried-Wilhelm-Leibniz-Gesellschaft eV: Waterloostr. 8 (Gottfried Wilhelm Leibniz Bibliothek – Niedersächsische Landesbibliothek), 30169 Hannover; tel. (511) 1267331; fax (511) 1267202; e-mail leibnizgesellschaft@gwlb.de; internet www.gwlb.de/leibniz/gesellschaft; f. 1966; 395 mems; Pres. Prof. ROLF WERNSTEDT; Gen. Sec. Dr WOLFGANG DITTRICH; publs *Studia Leibnitiana*, *Studia Leibnitiana Supplementa / Sonderhefte*.

RELIGION, SOCIOLOGY AND ANTHROPOLOGY

Albertus-Magnus-Institut: Adenauerallee 19, 53111 Bonn; tel. (228) 20146-0; fax (228) 20146-30; e-mail ami@albertus-magnus-institut.de; internet www.albertus-magnus-institut.de; f. 1931; critical publishing of the works of Albertus Magnus; 8 mems; Dir Prof. Dr L. HONNEFELDER; publ. *Editio Coloniensis*.

Berliner Gesellschaft für Anthropologie, Ethnologie und Urgeschichte (Berlin Society for Anthropology, Ethnology and Prehistory): Alix Hänsel Museum für Vor- und Frühgeschichte, Schloss Charlottenburg, Langhansbau Spandauer Damm 22, 14059 Berlin; tel. (30) 32674817; fax (30) 32674812; internet www.bgaeu.de; f. 1869; 350 mems; Pres. BERHNARD HÄNSEL; publ. *Mitteilungen*.

Deutsche Gesellschaft für Asienkunde eV (German Association for Asian Studies): Rothenbaumchaussee 32, 20148 Hamburg; tel. (40) 445891; fax (40) 4107945; e-mail post@asienkunde.de; internet www.asienkunde.de; f. 1967; promotion and coordination of contemporary Asian research; 700 mems; Pres. Dr THEO SOMMER; publ. *Asien* (quarterly).

Deutsche Gesellschaft für Soziologie: c/o Institut für Soziologie, Chemnitzer Str. 46a, 01062 Dresden; tel. (351) 46337404; fax (351) 46337113; e-mail dgs@mailbox.tu-dresden.de; internet www.soziologie.de; f. 1909; 1,350 mems; Pres. Prof. Dr KARL-SIEGBERT REHBERG; publ. *Soziologie–Forum der DGS*.

Deutsche Gesellschaft für Volkskunde eV (German Society for European Ethnology): Universität Hamburg, Institut für Volkskunde, Bogenallee 11, 24098 Kiel; tel. (40) 428385949; fax (40) 428386346; e-mail dgv@uni-hamburg.de; internet www.d-g-v.de; f. 1904; 1,200 mems; Pres. Prof. Dr THOMAS HENGARTNER; publs *Internationale Volkskundliche Bibliographie* (annually), *Mitteilungen der Deutschen Gesellschaft für Volkskunde* (4 a year), *Zeitschrift für Volkskunde* (2 a year).

Deutsche Morgenländische Gesellschaft (German Oriental Society): Südasien-Institut der Universität Heidelberg, Im Neuenheimer Feld 330, 69120 Heidelberg; tel. (6221) 548900; fax (6221) 544998; e-mail dmg@sai.uni-heidelberg.de; internet www.dmg-web.de; f. 1845; 698 mems; attached research institutes (Orient-Institut) in Beirut and Istanbul: see chapters on Lebanon and Turkey; library of 50,000 vols; Sec. Prof. Dr STEFAN LEDER; publs *Abhandlungen für die Kunde des Morgenlandes*, *Beiruter Texte und Studien*, *Bibliotheca Islamica*, *Journal of the Nepal Research Centre*, *Verzeichnis der orientalischen Handschriften in Deutschland*, *Zeitschrift der Deutschen Morgenländischen Gesellschaft*.

Deutsche Orient-Gesellschaft eV (German Oriental Society): Hüttenweg 7, Geschäftsstelle Altorientalisches Seminar der FU Berlin, 14195 Berlin; tel. (30) 83853601; fax (30) 83853600; e-mail dogva@mail.zedat.fu-berlin.de; internet www.orientgesellschaft.de; f. 1898; 976 mems; Pres. Prof. Dr HANS NEUMANN; Sec. Prof. Dr FELIX BLOCHER; publs *Abhandlungen*, *Alter Orient aktuell* (annually), *Mitteilungen der DOG* (annually), *Wissenschaftliche Veröffentlichungen*.

Deutsches Orient-Institut: Neuer Jungerfernstieg 21, 20354 Hamburg; tel. (40) 42825-514; fax (40) 42825-509; e-mail doi@doi.duei.de; internet www.duei.de; f. 1960 to study contemporary political, economic, and social developments in the countries of North Africa, the Middle East and Central Asia; 20 mems; library of 33,000 vols, 230 periodicals; Dir Prof. Dr UDO STEINBACH; Deputy Dir Dr HANSPETER MATTES; publs *Orient* (quarterly), *Mitteilungen* (irregular), *Schriften des Deutschen Orient-Instituts* (irregular), *Jahrbuch Nahost* (annually), *Hamburger Beiträge: Medien und politische Kommunikation – Naher Osten und islamische Welt* (irregular).

Gesellschaft für Anthropologie (Society for Anthropology): c/o Dr Mike Schweissing, Dept für Biologie der LMU München, Biodiversitätforschung/Anthropologie, Richard-Wagner-Str. 10, 8033 Munich; tel. (89) 21806716; e-mail m.schweissing@lmu.de; internet www.gfanet.de; f. 1992 by merger of Deutsche Anthropologische Gesellschaft und Gesellschaft für Anthropologie und Humangenetik; Chair. Prof. Dr GISELA GRUPE; Sec. Dr MIKE SCHWEISSING.

Institut für Asienkunde (Institute of Asian Affairs): Rothenbaumchaussee 32, 20148 Hamburg; tel. (40) 428874-0; fax (40) 4107945; e-mail ifa@ifa.duei.de; internet www.duei.de/ifa; f. 1956; research and documentation into all aspects of contemporary South, South-East and East Asia; 35 mems; library of 60,000 books; Pres. Dr W. RÖHL; Dir Prof. Dr M. SCHÄDLER; publs *China aktuell* (6 a year), *Südostasien aktuell* (6 a year), *China aktuell–Data Supplement* (6 a year), *Japan aktuell* (6 a year).

Rheinische Vereinigung für Volkskunde: Am Hofgarten 22, 53113 Bonn; tel. (228) 737618; fax (228) 739440; internet www.rvvb.uni-bonn.de; f. 1947; regional ethnology of the Rhineland; 300 mems; Pres. Prof. Dr H. L. COX; publs *Rheinisches Jahrbuch für Volkskunde*, *Bonner kleine Reihe zur Alltagskultur*.

Wissenschaftliche Gesellschaft für Theologie eV: Paulsenstr. 55-56, 121063 Berlin; tel. (30) 82097223; fax (30) 82097105; e-mail wgth.berlin@gmx.de; internet www.wgth.de; f. 1973; 629 mems in Germany, Switzerland, Austria, UK, Netherlands,

Romania, Czech Republic, Hungary and Scandinavia; six sections: Old Testament, New Testament, Church History, Systematic Theology, Practical Theology, Missions and Religion; Pres. Prof. Dr FRIEDRICH SCHWEITZER.

TECHNOLOGY

DECHEMA (Gesellschaft für Chemische Technik und Biotechnologie eV): Theodor-Heuss-Allee 25, 60486 Frankfurt am Main; tel. (69) 7564-0; fax (69) 7564-201; e-mail info@dechema.de; internet www.dechema.de; f. 1926; 5,000 mems; library of 25,000 vols; Pres. Prof. Dr rer. nat. ALFRED OBERHOLZ; Gen. Man. Prof. Dr rer. nat. Dr-Ing. E.h. GERHARD KREYSA; publs *Materialwissenschaft und Werkstofftechnik* (monthly), *Chemie – Ingenieur – Technik* (monthly), *Materials and Corrosion* (monthly), *WOICE of ACHEMA* (multimedia CD-rom on chemical engineering equipment, annually).

Deutsche Gemmologische Gesellschaft eV (German Gemmological Association): Postfach 12 22 60, 55714 Idar-Oberstein; tel. (6781) 50840; fax (6781) 508419; e-mail info@dgemg.com; internet www.dgemg.com; f. 1932; administers the German Gemmological Training Centre; 2,000 mems; library of 2,500 vols; Dir Dr U. HENN; publ. *Gemmologie* (4 a year).

Deutsche Gesellschaft für Luft- und Raumfahrt – Lilienthal-Oberth eV (DGLR) (German Society for Aeronautics and Astronautics): Godesberger Allee 70, 53175 Bonn; tel. (228) 30805-0; fax (228) 30805-24; f. 1912; support of aeronautics and astronautics for all scientific and technical purposes; 3,000 mems; Pres. Prof. Dr-Ing. JOACHIM SZODRUCH; Vice-Pres Dr-Ing. DETLEF MÜLLER-WIESNER, Dipl.-Ing. FRIEDER BEYER; Sec.-Gen. PETER BRANDT; publs *Aerospace Science and Technology* (8 a year), *Luft- und Raumfahrt* (6 a year), *Mitteilungen* (6 a year).

Deutsche Gesellschaft für Materialkunde eV (Materials Science and Engineering): Senckenberganlage 10, 60325 Frankfurt; tel. (69) 75306-750; fax (69) 75306-733; e-mail dgm@dgm.de; internet www.dgm.de; f. 1919; 2,700 mems; Pres. Prof. Dr GÜNTER GOTTSTEIN; Dir Dr P. P. SCHEPP; publs *Advanced Engineering Materials*, *Zeitschrift für Metallkunde*.

Deutsche Gesellschaft für Photogrammetrie, Fernerkundung und Geoinformation (DGPF): c/o EFTAS, Fernerkundung Technologietransfer GmbH, Oststr. 2-18, 48145 Münster; tel. (0251) 133070; fax (0251) 1330733; e-mail dgpf@fh-oldenburg.de; f. 1909; 850 mems; Pres. Prof. Dr Ing. THOMAS LUHMANN; Sec. Dr Ing. MANFRED WIGGENHAGEN; publ. *Photogrammetrie-Fernerkundung-Geoinformation* (every 2 months).

Deutsche Gesellschaft für Zerstörungsfreie Prüfung eV (DGZfP) (German Association for Non-Destructive Testing): Max-Planck-Str. 6, 13489 Berlin; tel. (30) 67807-0; fax (30) 67807-109; e-mail mail@dgzfp.de; internet www.dgzfp.de; f. 1933; conferences, training courses and personnel certification; 1,450 mems; Pres. JÖRG VÖLKER; Dir Dr RAINER LINK; publ. *ZfP-Zeitung* (monthly).

Deutsche Glastechnische Gesellschaft eV (German Society of Glass Technology):; tel. (69) 975861-0; fax (69) 975861-99; e-mail info@hvg-dgg.de; internet www.hvg-dgg.de; f. 1922; 1,460 mems; online retrieval service; library of 19,500 vols; Dir Dr ULRICH ROGER; publs *dgg Journal*, *Glass Science and Technology–Glastechnische Berichte* (monthly, in English and German).

Deutsche Keramische Gesellschaft eV (German Ceramic Society): Am Grott 7, 51147 Cologne; tel. (2203) 96648-0; fax (2203) 69301; e-mail info@dkg.de; internet www.dkg.de; f. 1919; 1,400 mems; Chair. Prof. Dr JÜRGEN G. HEINRICH; Dir Dr MARKUS BLUMENBERG; publ. *cfi-ceramic forum international/Fortscrittsberichte der DKG* (monthly).

Deutsche Lichttechnische Gesellschaft eV: Burggrafenstr. 6, 10787 Berlin; tel. (30) 2601-2439; fax (30) 2601-1255; e-mail litg@din.de; internet www.litg.de; f. 1912; 2,500 mems; Sec. REGINA VOIGT; publ. *Licht* (monthly).

Deutscher Beton- und Bautechnik-Verein eV (German Concrete Association): Kurfürstenstr. 129, 10785 Berlin; tel. (30) 236096-20; fax (30) 236096-23; internet www.betonverein.de; f. 1898; quality control, research, standardization and construction advice; 750 mems; Pres. Dr-Ing. HANS-ULRICH LITZNER; publs *Bemessungsbeispiele*, *Beton-Handbuch*, *Vorträge Betontag*.

Deutscher Kälte- und Klimatechnischer Verein eV (German Refrigeration Association): Pfaffenwaldring 10, 70569 Stuttgart; tel. (711) 6856-3200; fax (711) 6856-3242; e-mail info@dkv.org; internet www.dkv.org; f. 1909; 5 sections for production and industrial application of refrigeration, food science and technology, storage, transport and air conditioning; 1,300 mems; Pres. Dr-Ing. FRANK RINNE; Sec. IRENE REICHERT; publs *DKV-Aktuell* (quarterly), *DKV-Forschungsberichte* (irregular), *DKV-Statusberichte* (irregular), *DKV-Tagungsbericht* (annually).

Deutscher Markscheider Verein eV (Mining Surveyors): Shamrockring 1, 44623 Herne; tel. (2323) 154660; fax (2323) 154611; e-mail geschaeftsstelle@dmv-ev.de; internet www.dmv-ev.de; Pres. Dr-Ing. PETER GOERKE-MALLET.

Deutscher Verband für Materialforschung und -prüfung eV (DVM) (German Association for Materials Research and Testing): Unter den Eichen 87, 12205 Berlin; tel. (30) 811-30-66; fax (30) 811-93-59; e-mail office@dvm-berlin.de; internet www.dvm-berlin.de; f. 1896; organizes conferences, seminars and workshops; 350 mems; Pres. Dr Ing. HARALD ZENNER; Sec. KATHRIN LEERS; publs *Materialprüfung* (monthly), *DVM-Nachrichten* (news, quarterly).

Deutscher Verband für Schweissen und verwandte Verfahren eV (German Welding Society): Postfach 101965, 40010 Düsseldorf; Aachener Str. 172, 40223 Düsseldorf; tel. (0211) 1591-0; fax (0211) 1591-200; e-mail verwaltung@dvs-hg.de; internet www.die-verbindungs-spezialisten.de; f. 1947; welding and allied processes; 20,000 mems; Pres. Dr-Ing. A. GÄRTNER; Chair Dr-Ing. H. GEIS; publs *Aufbau und Verbindungstechnik in der Elektronic* (also English edition), *DVS-Berichte*, *DVS-Merkblätter*, *DVS-Richtlinien*, *DVS-Videos*, *Fachbibliographie Schweisstechnik*, *Fachbuchreihe Schweisstechnik*, *Fachwörterbücher*, *Forschungsberichte Humanisierung des Arbeitslebens der Schweisser*, *Der Praktiker*, *Referateorgan Schweissen und verwandte Verfahren*, *Schweissen und Schneiden* (also English language edition), *Schweisstechnische Forschungsberichte*, *Die Schweisstechnische Praxis*, *Schweisstechnische Software*.

Deutscher Verband Technisch-wissenschaftlicher Vereine (Union of Technical and Scientific Associations): Markgrafenstr. 37, 10117 Berlin; tel. (30) 93627871; fax (30) 93627869; e-mail info@dvt-net.de; internet www.dvt-net.de; f. 1916; comprises 80 technical and scientific associations; 82 mems; Chair. Prof. Dr HUBERTUS CHRIST; Dir JÖRG MAAS.

Deutscher Verein des Gas- und Wasserfaches eV (DVGW) (German Technical and Scientific Association on Gas and Water): Josef-Wirmer Str. 1–3, 53123 Bonn; tel. (228) 9188-5; fax (228) 9188-990; e-mail info@dvgw.de; internet www.dvgw.de; f. 1859; specifications and standardization, testing and certification, research and development, training, providing consultancy services and information; 6,700 mems; Pres. Prof. Dr-Ing. KLAUS HOMANN; publs *DVGW—Informationen*, *DVGW—Nachrichten*, *DVGW—Regelwerk*, *DVGW—Schriftenreihen*.

DIN Deutsches Institut für Normung eV (German Institute for Standardization): Burggrafenstr. 6, 10787 Berlin; tel. (4930) 2601-0; fax (4930) 2601-1231; e-mail postmaster@din.de; internet www2.din.de; f. 1917; 1,650 mems; Pres. Dr-Ing. GERD WEBER; Dir Dr-Ing. TORSTEN BAHKE; publs *DIN-Catalogue* (annually), *DIN-Mitteilungen* (monthly).

Fachgebiet Wasserwirtschaft und Hydroinformatik: Institut für Bauingenieurwesen, Technische Universität, Str. des 17 Juni 144, 10623 Berlin; tel. (30) 314-23961; fax (30) 313-22910; e-mail reinhard.hinkelmann@wahyd.tu-berlin.de; f. 1891, fmrly Deutscher Verband für Wasserwirtschaft und Kulturbau; hydromechanics, hydrology, hydraulic engineering, modelling and hydroinformatics; 118 mems; Dir Prof. Dr-Ing. REINHARD HINKELMANN.

Gesellschaft für Informatik eV: Wissenschaftszentrum, Ahrstr. 45, 53175 Bonn; tel. (228) 302-145; fax (228) 302-167; e-mail gs@gi-ev.de; internet www.gi-ev.de; f. 1969; promotion of informatics in research, education, applications; 24,500 mems; Pres. Prof. Dr MATTHIAS JARKE; Man. Dir Dr PETER FEDERER; publs *Informatik Spektrum*, *Künstliche Intelligenz*, *Wirtschaftsinformatik*.

Informationstechnische Gesellschaft im VDE (ITG) (Information Technology Society within VDE): Stresemannallee 15, 60596 Frankfurt; tel. (69) 6308360; fax (69) 6315233; e-mail itg@vde.com; internet www.vde.com; f. 1954; 33,000 mems; Chair. Prof. Dr-Ing. ALEXANDER RÖDER; Dir Dr-Ing. V. SCHANZ; publs *AEU International Journal of Electronics*, *Nachrichtentechnische Zeitschrift (NTZ)* (monthly).

Institut für gewerbliche Wasserwirtschaft und Luftreinhaltung GmbH (IWL) (Institute for Commercial Water Supply and the Prevention of Air Pollution): Chemiepark Knapsack, Industriestr., 50354 Hürth; tel. (2233) 482100; fax (2233) 482099; e-mail iwl-umweltinstitut@knapsack.de; internet www.iwl-umweltinstitut.de; f. 1956; Prof. Dr HORST-DIETER SCHÜDDEMAGE; publ. *IWL-Umweltbrief* (monthly).

Rationalisierungs-Kuratorium der Deutschen Wirtschaft eV (RKW) (German Productivity and Management Association): Düsseldorfer Str. 40, 65760 Eschborn; tel. (6196) 4952812; fax (6196) 4954801; e-mail rkw@rkw.de; internet www.rkw.de; f. 1921; 8,000 mems; Dirs Dr INGRID VOIGT, W. AXEL ZEHRFELD; publ. *RKW-Magazin* (monthly).

VDE Verband Deutscher Elektrotechniker eV (German Association of Electrical Engineers): Stresemannallee 15, 60596 Frankfurt am Main; tel. (69) 6308-0; fax (69) 6312925; e-mail service@vde.com; internet www.vde.com; f. 1893; 34,000 mems; Chair. ENNO LIESS; publs *dialog VDE-Mitglieder-Information*, *Elektrotechnische Zeitschrift*, *Nachrichtentechnische Zeitschrift*, *VDE-Buchreihe*, *VDE-Fachberichte*, *VDE-Schriftenreihe*, *VDE-Vorschriften*.

Verein der Zellstoff- und Papier-Chemiker und -Ingenieure eV (Association of Pulp and Paper Chemists and Engineers): Emilestrasse 21, 64293 Darmstadt; tel. (6151) 33264; fax (6151) 311076; e-mail info@zellcheming.de; internet www.zellcheming.com; f. 1905; 2,050 mems; Exec. Dir Dr Ing. WILHELM BUSSE; Chair. Dr CLEMENS BÜLOW; publ. *ipw–Das Papier*.

Stahlinstitut VDEh: Sohnstr. 65, 40237 Düsseldorf; tel. (211) 6707-0; fax (211) 6707-310; e-mail vdeh@vdeh.de; internet www.stahl-online.de; f. 1860 as Verein Deutscher Eisenhüttenleute; present name 2003; promotion of research, literature, documentation and information, education and training; 9,000 mems; library of 120,000 vols; Pres. and Exec. Dir Prof. Dr Ing. D. AMELING; publs *Literaturschau Stahl und Eisen* (every 2 weeks), *MPT Metallurgical Plant and Technology International* (6 a year), *Stahl* (6 a year), *Stahl und Eisen* (monthly), *Stahlmarkt* (monthly), *Steel Research (Archiv für das Eisenhüttenwesen)* (monthly).

Verein Deutscher Giessereifachleute (VDG) (German Foundrymen's Association): Postfach 105144, 40042 Düsseldorf; tel. (211) 6871-0; fax (211) 6871-364; e-mail info@vdg.de; internet www.vdg.de; f. 1909; 3,100 mems; library of 35,000 vols; Chair. Dr-Ing. GOTTHARD WOLF; publs *Casting Plant Technology International* (quarterly), *Giesserei* (monthly), *Giessereiforschung* (quarterly), seminars and courses.

Verein Deutscher Ingenieure (VDI) (Association of German Engineers): Postfach 101139, 40002 Düsseldorf; premises at: Graf-Recke-Str. 84, 40239 Düsseldorf,; tel. (211) 6214-0; fax (211) 6214-175; e-mail kundencenter@vdi.de; internet www.vdi.de; f. 1856; technical and scientific co-operation in 21 engineering sections concerning all fields of technology; training courses for professional engineers; documentation in various branches of engineering and prevention of air pollution and noise; 130,000 individual mems, 2000 corporate mems; Dir Prof. Dr-Ing. EIKE LEHMANN; publs *VDI-Verlag: Program: VDI-Nachrichten* (weekly newspaper), technical journals, books, etc.

Research Institutes

GENERAL

Max-Planck-Gesellschaft zur Förderung der Wissenschaften e. V. (Max Planck Society for the Advancement of Science): Postfach 101062, 80084 Munich; tel. (89) 2108-0; fax (89) 2108-1111; e-mail webmaster@gv.mpg.de; internet www.mpg.de; f. 1948; Pres. Prof. Dr PETER GRUSS; Sec.-Gen. Dr BARBARA BLUDAU; publ. *Max-PlanckResearch* (4 a year).

Attached research institutes:

Max-Planck-Institut für Sonnensystemforschung (Solar System Research): Max-Planck-Str. 2, 37191 Katlenburg-Lindau; tel. (5556) 979-0; fax (5556) 979-240; e-mail user@mps.mpg.de; internet www.mps.mpg.de; f. 1955; Man. Dir Prof. Dr ULRICH CHRISTENSEN.

Max-Planck-Institut für Evolutionäre Anthropologie (Evolutionary Anthropology): Deutscher Pl. 6, 04103 Leipzig; tel. (341) 3550-0; fax (341) 3550-119; e-mail info@eva.mpg.de; internet www.eva.mpg.de; f. 1997; Man. Dir Prof. Dr MICHAEL TOMASELLO.

Max-Planck-Institut für Astronomie (Astronomy): Königstuhl 17, 69117 Heidelberg; tel. (6221) 5280; fax (6221) 528246; e-mail user@mpia.de; internet www.mpia.de; f. 1967; Man. Dir Prof. Dr THOMAS HENNING; publ. *Sterne und Weltraum* (monthly).

Max-Planck-Institut für Astrophysik (Astrophysics): Karl-Schwarzschild-Str. 1, 85748 Garching; tel. (89) 30000-0; fax (89) 30000-2235; e-mail info@mpa-garching.mpg.de; internet www.mpa-garching.mpg.de; f. 1958; Man. Dir Prof. Dr RASHID SUNYAEV.

Bibliotheca Hertziana–Max-Planck-Institut für Kunstgeschichte (Bibliotheca Hertziana): Via Gregoriana 28, 00187 Rome, Italy; tel. 06-699931; fax 06-69993333; e-mail info@biblhertz.it; internet www.biblhertz.it; f. 1913; library of 260,000 vols; Man. Dir Prof. Dr SYBILLE EBERT-SCHIFFERER; publs *Römische Forschungen der Bibliotheca Hertziana*, *Römisches Jahrbuch der Bibliotheca Hertziana*, *Römische Studien der Bibliotheca Hertziana*, *Studi della Bibliotheca Hertziana*.

Max-Planck-Institut für Bildungsforschung (Human Development): Lentzeallee 94, 14195 Berlin; tel. (30) 82406-0; fax (30) 8249939; e-mail sekmayer@mpib-berlin.mpg.de; internet www.mpib-berlin.mpg.de; f. 1963; Man. Dir Prof. Dr JÜRGEN BAUMERT.

Max-Planck-Institut für Biochemie (Biochemistry): Am Klopferspitz 18A, 82152 Martinsried bei München; tel. (89) 85781; fax (89) 85783777; e-mail user@biochem.mpg.de; internet www.biochem.mpg.de; f. 1973; Man. Dir Prof. Dr DIETER OESTERHELT.

Max-Planck-Institut für Biogeochemie (Biogeochemistry): Hans-Knöll-Str. 10, 07745 Jena; tel. (3641) 57-60; fax (3641) 57-70; e-mail info@bgc-jena.mpg.de; internet www.bgc-jena.mpg.de; f. 1997; Man. Dir Prof. Dr MARTIN HEIMANN.

Max-Planck-Institut für Biophysik (Biophysics): Max-von-Laue-Str. 3, 60438 Frankfurt am Main; tel. (69) 6303-0; fax (69) 6303-4502; e-mail user@mpibp-frankfurt.mpg.de; internet www.mpibp-frankfurt.mpg.de; f. 1937; Man. Dir Prof. Dr WERNER KÜHLBRANDT.

Max-Planck-Institut für Chemie (Otto-Hahn-Institut) (Chemistry): Joh.-Joachim-Becher-Weg 27, 55128 Mainz; tel. (6131) 3050; fax (6131) 305388; e-mail gfd@mpch-mainz.mpg.de; internet www.mpch-mainz.mpg.de; f. 1912; Man. Dir Prof. Dr JOHANNES LELIEVELD.

Max-Planck-Institut für Biophysikalische Chemie (Karl-Friedrich-Bonhoeffer-Institut) (Biophysical Chemistry): Am Fassberg 11, 37077 Göttingen; tel. (551) 201-0; fax (551) 201-1222; e-mail ehoelsc@gwdg.de; internet www.mpibpc.gwdg.de; f. 1971; Man. Dir Prof. Dr REINHARD LÜHRMANN.

Max-Planck-Institut für Demografische Forschung (Demographic Research): Konrad-Zuse-Str. 1, 18057 Rostock; tel. (381) 2081-0; fax (381) 2081-202; e-mail webmaster@demogr.mpg.de; internet www.demogr.mpg.de; f. 1996; Man. Dir Prof. Dr JAMES W. VAUPEL.

Max-Planck-Institut für Dynamik Komplexer Technischer Systeme (Dynamics of Complex Technical Systems): Sandtorstr. 1, 39106 Magdeburg; tel. (391) 61100; fax (391) 6110500; e-mail secretary@mpi-magdeburg.mpg.de; internet www.mpi-magdeburg.mpg.de; f. 1996; Man. Dir Prof. Dr UDO REICHL.

Max-Planck-Institut für Eisenforschung GmbH (Iron Research): Postfach 140 444, 40074 Düsseldorf; premises at: Max-Planck-Str. 1, 40237 Düsseldorf; tel. (211) 67920; fax (211) 6792440; e-mail mpi@mpie.de; internet www.mpie.mpg.de; f. 1917; Man. Dir Prof. Dr MARTIN STRATMANN.

Max-Planck-Institut für experimentelle Endokrinologie (Experimental Endocrinology): Feodor-Lynen-Str. 7, 30625 Hanover; tel. (511) 5359-0; fax (511) 5359-148; e-mail gottschalk@vw.endo.mpg.de; internet www.endo.mpg.de; f. 1979; Man. Dir Prof. Dr GREGOR EICHELE.

Max-Planck-Forschungsstelle für Enzymologie der Proteinfaltung (Enzymology of Protein Folding): Weinbergweg 22, 06120 Halle (Saale); tel. (345) 5522801; fax (345) 5511972; e-mail user@enzyme-halle.mpg.de; internet www.enzyme-halle.mpg.de; f. 1997; Dir Prof. Dr GUNTER S. FISCHER.

Max-Planck-Institut für Entwicklungsbiologie (Developmental Biology): Spemannstr. 35, 72076 Tübingen; tel. (7071) 601350; fax (7071) 601300; e-mail mpi.entwicklungsbiologie@tuebingen.mpg.de; internet www.eb.tuebingen.mpg.de; f. 1937; Man. Dir Prof. Dr ANDREI N. LUPAS.

Max-Planck-Institut für Ethnologische Forschung (Social Anthropology): Advokatenweg 36, 06114 Halle (Saale); tel. (345) 2927-0; fax (345) 2927-502; e-mail hann@eth.mpg.de; internet www.eth.mpg.de; f. 1998; Man. Dir Prof. Dr GÜNTHER SCHLEE.

Max-Planck-Institut für Festkörperforschung (Solid State Research): Heisenbergstr. 1, 70569 Stuttgart; tel. (711) 6890; fax (711) 689-1010; e-mail gd@fkf.mpg.de; internet www.fkf.mpg.de; f. 1969; Man. Dir Prof. Dr BERNHARD KEIMER.

Friedrich-Miescher-Laboratorium für biologische Arbeitsgruppen in der Max-Planck-Gesellschaft (Biological Research Groups): Postfach 2109, 72011 Tübingen; located at: Spemannstr. 37–39, 72076 Tübingen; tel. (7071) 601-460; fax (7071) 601-455; internet www.fml.tuebingen.mpg.de; f. 1969; Man. of Spang Laboratory of Yeast and Worms Dr ANNE SPANG.

Fritz-Haber-Institut der Max-Planck-Gesellschaft: Faradayweg 4–6, 14195 Berlin; tel. (30) 8413-30; fax (30) 8413-3155; e-mail ertl@fhi-berlin.mpg.de; internet www.fhi-berlin.mpg.de; f. 1911; physical chemistry; Man. Dir Prof. Dr HANS-JOACHIM FREUND.

Max-Planck-Institut für Geistiges Eigentum, Wettbewerbs- und Steuerrecht (Intellectual Property, Competition and Tax Law): Marstallpl. 1, 80539 Munich; tel. (89) 24246-0; fax (89) 24246-501; internet www.ip.mpg.de; f. 1966; Man. Dir Prof. Dr RETO M. HILTY.

Max-Planck-Institut zur Erforschung von Gemeinschaftsgütern (Research into Collective Property): Kurt-Schumacher-Str. 10, 53113 Bonn; tel. (228) 91416-0; fax (228) 91416-55; internet www.mpp-rdg.mpg.de; f. 2003; Head Prof. Dr CHRISTOPH ENGEL.

Max-Planck-Institut für Molekulare Genetik (Molecular Genetics): Ihnestr. 63–73, 14195 Berlin; tel. (30) 8413-0; fax (30) 8413-1394; e-mail bould@molgen.mpg.de; internet www.molgen.mpg.de; f. 1965; Man. Dir Prof. Dr MARTIN VINGRON.

Max-Planck-Institut für Geschichte (History): Hermann-Föge-Weg 11, 37073 Göttingen; tel. (551) 4956-0; fax (551) 4956-170; e-mail lehmann@mpi-g.gwdg.de; internet www.geschichte.mpg.de; f. 1956;

library of 27,300 vols; Man. Dir Prof. Dr JÜRGEN BASEDOW.

Max-Planck-Institut für Gesellschaftsforschung (Study of Societies): Paulstr. 3, 50676 Cologne; tel. (221) 2767-0; fax (221) 2767-555; e-mail info@mpifg.de; internet www.mpifg.de; f. 1984; Man. Dir Prof. Dr JENS BECKERT.

Max-Planck-Institut für Gravitationsphysik (Albert-Einstein-Institut) (Gravitational Physics): Am Mühlenberg 1, 14476 Golm; tel. (331) 567-70; fax (331) 567-7298; e-mail office@aei-potsdam.mpg.de; internet www.aei-potsdam.mpg.de; f. 1994; Man. Dir Prof. Dr BERNARD FREDERICK SCHUTZ.

Max-Planck-Institut für Hirnforschung (Brain Research): Postfach 710 662, 60496 Frankfurt am Main; located at: Deutschordenstr. 46, 60528 Frankfurt am Main; tel. (69) 96769-0; fax (69) 96769-440; e-mail betz@mpih-frankfurt.mpg.de; internet www.mpih-frankfurt.mpg.de; f. 1914; Man. Dir Prof. Dr HEINRICH BETZ.

Max-Planck-Institut für Immunbiologie (Immunobiology): Stübeweg 51, 79108 Freiburg; tel. (761) 5108-100; fax (761) 5108-1358; internet www.immunbio.mpg.de; f. 1961.

Max-Planck-Institut für Infektionsbiologie (Infection Biology): Schumannstr. 21–22, 10117 Berlin; tel. (30) 28460-0; fax (30) 28460-111; e-mail sek@mpiib-berlin.mpg.de; internet www.mpiib-berlin.mpg.de; f. 1993; Man Dir Prof. Dr THOMAS F. MEYER.

Max-Planck-Institut für Informatik (Computer Science): Stuhlsatzenhausweg 85, 66123 Saarbrücken; tel. (681) 9325-0; fax (681) 9325-999; e-mail mpi@mpi-sb.mpg.de; internet www.mpi-sb.mpg.de; f. 1988; Man Dir Prof. Dr HANS-PETER SEIDEL.

Max-Planck-Institut für Kernphysik (Nuclear Physics): Saupfercheckweg 1, 69117 Heidelberg; tel. (6221) 516-0; fax (6221) 516-601; e-mail mpik@mpi-hd.mpg.de; internet www.mpi-hd.mpg.de; f. 1958; Man. Dir Prof. Dr JOACHIM ULLRICH.

Max-Planck-Institut für Kohlenforschung (Coal Research): Kaiser-Wilhelm-Pl. 1, 45470 Mülheim/Ruhr; tel. (208) 306-1; fax (208) 306-2980; e-mail oeffentlichkeitsarbeit@mpi-muelheim.mpg.de; internet www.mpi-muelheim.mpg.de; f. 1912; Man. Dir Prof. Dr FERDI SCHÜTH.

Max-Planck-Institut für Kolloid- und Grenzflächenforschung (Colloid and Interface Research): Am Mühlenberg 1, 14476 Golm; tel. (331) 5679-0; fax (331) 5679-102; e-mail info@mpikg-golm.mpg.de; internet www.mpikg-golm.mpg.de; f. 1992; Man. Dir Prof. Dr HELMUTH MÖHWALD.

Kunsthistorisches Institut in Florenz – Max-Planck-Institut (Art History Institute in Florence): Via Giuseppe Guisti 44, 50121 Florence, Italy; tel. 055-24911-1; fax 055-24911-55; internet www.khi.fi.it; f. 2002; Man. Dir Prof. Dr GERHARD WOLF.

Max-Planck-Institut für biologische Kybernetik (Biological Cybernetics): Spenmannstr. 38, 72076 Tübingen; tel. (7071) 601500; fax (7071) 601520; e-mail conchy.moya@tuebingen.mpg.de; internet www.kyb.tuebingen.mpg.de; f. 1968; Man. Dir Prof. Dr NIKOS K. LOGOTHETIS.

Max-Planck-Institut für Limnologie (Limnology): August-Thienemann-Str. 2, 24306 Plön; tel. (4522) 763-0; fax (4522) 763-310; e-mail lampert@mpil-ploen.mpg.de; internet www.mpil-ploen.mpg.de; f. 1891; Man. Dir Prof. Dr MANFRED MILINSKI.

Max-Planck-Institut für Mathematik (Mathematics): Vivatsgasse 7, 53111 Bonn; tel. (228) 402-0; fax (228) 402-277; e-mail director@mpim-bonn.mpg.de; internet www.mpim-bonn.mpg.de; f. 1981; Man. Dir Prof. Dr GÜNTER HARDER.

Max-Planck-Institut für Mathematik in den Naturwissenschaften (Mathematics in the Sciences): Inselstr. 22–26, 04103 Leipzig; tel. (341) 9959-50; fax (341) 9959-658; e-mail ezeidler@mis.mpg.de; internet www.mis.mpg.de; f. 1996; Man. Dir Prof. Dr EBERHARD ZEIDLER.

Max-Planck-Institut für Experimentelle Medizin (Experimental Medicine): Hermann-Rein-Str. 3, 37075 Göttingen; tel. (551) 3899-0; fax (551) 3899-389; e-mail noelle@vw.mpiem.gwdg.de; internet www.mpiem.gwdg.de; f. 1947; Man. Dir Prof. Dr KLAUS-ARMIN NAVE.

Max-Planck-Institut für medizinische Forschung (Medical Research): Jahnstr. 29, 69120 Heidelberg; tel. (6221) 4860; fax (6221) 486-351; e-mail sekr@mpimf-heidelberg.mpg.de; internet www.mpimf-heidelberg.mpg.de; f. 1927; Man. Dir Dr WINFRIED DENK.

Max-Planck-Institut für Metallforschung (Metals Research): Heisenbergstr. 3, 70569 Stuttgart; tel. (711) 689-0; fax (711) 689-1010; e-mail dosch@mf.mpg.de; internet www.mpi-stuttgart.mpg.de; f. 1921; Man. Dir Prof. Dr HELMUT DOSCH.

Max-Planck-Institut für Meteorologie (Meteorology): Bundesstr. 55, 20146 Hamburg; tel. (40) 41173-0; fax (40) 41173-298; e-mail grassl@dkrz.de; internet www.mpimet.mpg.de; f. 1975; Man. Dir Prof. Dr GUY P. BRASSEUR.

Max-Planck-Institut für marine Mikrobiologie (Marine Microbiology): Celsiusstr. 1, 28359 Bremen; tel. (421) 2028-50; fax (421) 2028-580; e-mail contact@mpi-bremen.de; internet www.mpi-bremen.de; f. 1992; Man. Dir Prof. Dr FRIEDRICH WIDDEL.

Max-Planck-Institut für terrestrische Mikrobiologie (Terrestrial Microbiology): Karl-von-Frisch-Str., 35043 Marburg; tel. (6421) 178-0; fax (6421) 178-999; e-mail mpi@mailer.uni-marburg.de; internet www.uni-marburg.de/mpi; f. 1990; Man. Dir Prof. Dr REGINE KAHMANN.

Max-Planck-Institut für Mikrostrukturphysik (Microstructure Physics): Weinberg 2, 06120 Halle am Saale; tel. (345) 558250; fax (345) 5511223; e-mail bruno@mpi-halle.de; internet www.mpi-halle.mpg.de; f. 1991; Man. Dir Prof. Dr JÜRGEN KIRSCHNER.

Max-Planck-Arbeitsgruppen für strukturelle Molekularbiologie am DESY (Structural Molecular Biology): c/o DESY, Notkestr. 85, Geb. 25B, 22607 Hamburg; tel. (40) 89-982801; fax (40) 89-716810; e-mail office@mpasmb.desy.de; internet www.mpasmb-hamburg.mpg.de; f. 1985; Heads Dr HANS-DIETER BARTUNIK, Prof. Dr ADA YONATH, Prof. Dr ECKHARD MANDELKOW.

Max-Planck-Institut für Molekulare Biomedizin (Molecular Biomedicine): Von-Esmarch-Str. 56, 48149 Münster; tel. (251) 83-58617; fax (251) 83-58616; e-mail info@mpi-muenster.mpg.de; internet www.mpi-muenster.mpg.de; f. 2001; Man. Dir Prof. Dr DIETMAR VESTWEBER.

Max-Planck-Institut für Neurobiologie (Neurobiology): Am Klopferspitz 18, 82152 Martinsried; tel. (89) 8578-3751; fax (89) 8995-0051; e-mail marget@neuro.mpg.de; internet www.neuro.mpg.de; f. 1917; Man. Dir Prof. Dr RÜDIGER KLEIN.

Max-Planck-Institut für Neurologische Forschung (Neurological Research): Gleueler Str. 50. 50931 Cologne; tel. (221) 4726-0; fax (221) 4726-298; e-mail wdh@pet.mpin-koeln.mpg.de; internet www.mpin-koeln.mpg.de; f. 1982; Man. Dir Prof. Dr WOLF-DIETER HEISS.

Max-Planck-Institut fur neuropsychologische Forschung (Cognitive Neuroscience): Stephanstr. 1A, 04103 Leipzig; tel. (341) 9940-00; fax (341) 9940-104; e-mail orendi@cns.mpg.de; internet www.cns.mpg.de; f. 1994; Dirs Prof. Dr ANGELA D. FRIEDERICI, Prof. Dr DETLEV YVES VON CRAMON.

Max-Planck-Institut für Chemische Ökologie (Chemical Ecology): Winzerlaer Str. 10, 07745 Jena; tel. (3641) 57-0; fax (3641) 57-2011; internet www.ice.mpg.de; f. 1996; Man. Dir Prof. Dr IAN BALDWIN.

Max-Planck-Forschungsstelle für Ornithologie (Ornithology): Schlossallee 2, 78315 Radolfzell; tel. (7732) 1501-0; fax (7732) 1501-69; e-mail berthold@vowa.ornithol.mpg.de; internet erl.ornithol.mpg.de; f. 1998; Man. Dir Prof. Dr PETER BERTHOLD.

Max-Planck-Institut für molekulare Pflanzenphysiologie (Molecular Plant Physiology): Am Mühlenberg 1, 14476 Golm; tel. (331) 56780; fax (331) 5678408; e-mail willmitzer@mpimp-golm.mpg.de; internet www.mpimp-golm.mpg.de; f. 1994; Man. Dir Prof. Dr MARK STITT.

Max-Planck-Institut für Physik (Werner-Heisenberg-Institut) (Physics): Föhringer Ring 6, 80805 Munich; tel. (89) 32354-0; fax (89) 3226704; e-mail bethke@mppmu.mpg.de; internet www.mppmu.mpg.de; f. 1917; Man. Dir Prof. Dr SIEGFRIED BETHKE.

Max-Planck-Institut für Physik komplexer Systeme (Physics of Complex Systems): Nöthnitzer Str. 38, 01187 Dresden; tel. (351) 871-0; fax (351) 8711999; e-mail gneisse@mpipks-dresden.mpg.de; internet www.mpipks-dresden.mpg.de; f. 1992; Dir Prof. Dr PETER FULDE.

Max-Planck-Institut für chemische Physik fester Stoffe (Chemical Physics of Solids): Nöthnitzer Str. 40, 01187 Dresden; tel. (351) 46460; fax (351) 464610; e-mail steglich@cpfs.mpg.de; internet www.cpfs.mpg.de; f. 1995; Man. Dir Prof. Dr RÜDIGER KNIEP.

Max-Planck-Institut für Extraterrestrische Physik (Extraterrestrial Physics): Giessenbachstr., 85748 Garching; tel. (89) 30000-0; fax (89) 30000-3569; e-mail mpe@mpe.mpg.de; internet www.mpe.mpg.de; f. 1963; Man. Dir Prof. Dr GÜNTHER HASINGER.

Max-Planck-Institut für molekulare Physiologie (Molecular Physiology): Otto-Hahn-Str. 11, 44227 Dortmund; tel. (231) 133-0; fax (231) 133-2699; e-mail acting.director@mpi-dortmund.mpg.de; internet www.mpi-dortmund.mpg.de; f. 1993; Man. Dir Prof. Dr HERBERT WALDMANN.

Max-Planck-Institut für physiologische und klinische Forschung – W. G. Kerchhoff-Institut (Physiological and Clinical Research): Parkstr. 1, 61231 Bad Nauheim; tel. (6032) 7051; fax (6032) 705211; e-mail w.schaper@kerchhoff.mpg.de; internet www.kerckhoff.mpg.de; f. 1931; Man. Dir Prof. Dr Dr h.c. WOLFGANG SCHAPER.

Max-Planck-Institut für Plasmaphysik (Plasma Physics): Boltzmannstr. 2, 85748 Garching; tel. (89) 3299-01; fax (89) 32992200; e-mail info@ipp.mpg.de; internet www.ipp.mpg.de; f. 1960; Scientific Dir Prof. Dr ALEXANDER M. BRADSHAW.

Max-Planck-Institut für Polymerforschung (Polymer Research): Ackermannweg 10, 55128 Mainz; tel. (6131) 379-0; fax (06131) 379-100; e-mail schwiesow@mpip-mainz.mpg.de; internet www.mpip-mainz.mpg.de; f. 1983; Man. Dir Prof. Dr KLAUS MÜLLEN.

Max-Planck-Institut für ausländisches und internationales Privatrecht (Foreign and International Private Law): Mittelweg 187, 20148 Hamburg; tel. (40) 41900-0; fax (40) 41900-288; e-mail hopt@mpipriv-hh.mpg.de; internet www.mpipriv-hh.mpg.de; f. 1926; Man. Dir Prof. Dr REINHARD ZIMMERMANN; publ. *Rabels Zeitschrift für ausländisches und internationales Privatrecht* (4 a year).

Max-Planck-Institut für Psychiatrie (Deutsche Forschungsanstalt für Psychiatrie) (Psychiatry): Kraepelinstr. 2–10, 80804 Munich; tel. (89) 30622-1; fax (89) 30622605; e-mail holsboer@mpipsykl.mpg.de; internet www.mpipsykl.mpg.de; f. 1917; Man. Dir Prof Dr Dr FLORIAN HOLSBOER.

Max-Planck-Institut für Psycholinguistik (Psycholinguistics): Wundtlaan 1, 6525 XD Nijmegen, Netherlands; tel. (Netherlands) (24) 3521911; fax (Netherlands) (24) 3521213; e-mail general@mpi.nl; internet www.mpi.nl; f. 1976; Man. Dir Prof. Dr ANNE CUTLER.

Max-Planck-Institut für psychologische Forschung (Psychological Research): Postfach 340 121, 80098 Munich; located at: Amalienstr. 33, 80799 Munich; tel. (89) 386020; fax (89) 38602199; internet www.mpipf-muenchen.mpg.de; f. 1981; Man. Dir Prof. Dr WOLFGANG PRINZ.

Max-Planck-Institut für Quantenoptik (Quantum Optics): Hans-Kopfermann-Str. 1, 85748 Garching; tel. (89) 32 905-0; fax (89) 32905-200; e-mail gerhard.rempe@mpq.mpg.de; internet www.mpq.mpg.de; f. 1981; Man. Dir Prof. Dr GERHARD REMPE.

Max-Planck-Institut für Radioastronomie (Radio Astronomy): Auf dem Hügel 69, 53121 Bonn; tel. (228) 525-0; fax (228) 525-229; e-mail postmaster@mpifr-bonn.mpg.de; internet www.mpifr-bonn.mpg.de; f. 1966; Man. Dir Dr J. ANTON ZENSUS.

Max-Planck-Institut für Europäische Rechtsgeschichte (European Legal History): Hausener Weg 120, 60489 Frankfurt am Main; tel. (69) 78978-0; fax (69) 78978169; e-mail user@mpier.uni-frankfurt.de; internet www.mpier.uni-frankfurt.de; f. 1964; Man. Dir Prof. Dr MARIE THERES FÖGEN; publ. *Jus Commune*.

Max-Planck-Institut für Ausländisches und Internationales Sozialrecht (Foreign and International Social Law): Amalienstr. 33, 80799 Munich; tel. (89) 386020; fax (89) 38602490; e-mail user@mpipf-muenchen.mpg.de; internet www.mpipf-muenchen.mpg.de/MPISR; f. 1980; Man. Dir Prof. Dr ULRICH BECKER; publ. *Zeitschrift für ausländisches und internationales Arbeits- und Sozialrecht* (4 a year).

Max-Planck-Institut für Ausländisches und Internationales Strafrecht (Foreign and International Criminal Law): Günterstalstr. 73, 79100 Freiburg im Breisgau; tel. (761) 70811; fax (761) 7081-294; e-mail webmaster@iuscrim.mpg.de; internet www.iuscrim.mpg.de; f. 1938; library of 64,000 vols; Man. Dir Prof. Dr HANS-JÖRG ALBRECHT; publs *Auslandsrundschau der Zeitschrift für die gesamte Strafrechtswissenschaft*, *European Journal of Crime, Criminal Law and Criminal Justice* (4 a year).

Max-Planck-Institut für Strahlenchemie (Radiation Chemistry): Stiftstr. 34–36, 45470 Mülheim/Ruhr; tel. (208) 306-4; fax (208) 306-3951; e-mail weber@mpi-muelheim.mpg.de; internet www.mpi-muelheim.mpg.de/mpistr_home.html; f. 1958; Man. Dir Prof. Dr KARL WIEGHARDT.

Max-Planck-Institut für Strömungsforschung (Flow Research): Bunsenstr. 10, 37073 Göttingen; tel. (551) 5176-0; fax (551) 5176-669; e-mail mpisf@gwdg.de; internet www.mpisf.mpg.de; f. 1925; Head Prof. Dr HERBERT WALTHER.

Max-Planck-Institut für Ausländisches Öffentliches Recht und Völkerrecht (Comparative Public Law and International Law): Im Neuenheimer Feld 535, 69120 Heidelberg; tel. (6221) 482-1; fax (6221) 482-288; e-mail information@mpiv-hd.mpg.de; internet www.mpiv-hd.mpg.de; f. 1924; Man. Dir Prof. Dr ARMIN VON BOGDANDY; publ. *Zeitschrift für ausländisches öffentliches Recht und Völkerrecht*.

Max-Planck-Institut zur Erforschung von Wirtschaftssystemen (Economic Systems): Kahlaische Str. 10, 07745 Jena; tel. (3641) 686-5; fax (3641) 686-990; e-mail witt@mpiew-jena.mpg.de; internet www.mpiew-jena.mpg.de; f. 1993; Dir Prof. Dr WERNER GÜTH.

Max-Planck-Institut für Wissenschaftsgeschichte (History of Science): Boltzmannstr. 22, 14195 Berlin; tel. (30) 22667-0; fax (30) 22667-299; e-mail zentrale@mpiwg-berlin.mpg.de; internet www.mpiwg-berlin.mpg.de; f. 1994; library of 60,000 vols; Exec. Dir Prof. Dr LORRAINE DASTON.

Max-Planck-Institut für Molekulare Zellbiologie und Genetik (Molecular Cell Biology and Genetics): Pfotenhauerstr. 108, 01307 Dresden; tel. (351) 210-0; fax (351) 210-2000; e-mail info@mpi-cbg.de; internet www.mpi-cbg.de; f. 1998; Man. Dir Prof. Dr WILLAND HUTTNER.

Max-Planck-Institut für Züchtungsforschung (Plant Breeding Research): Carl-von-Linné-Weg 10, 50829 Cologne; tel. (221) 5062-0; fax (221) 5062-513; e-mail user@mpiz-koeln.mpg.de; internet www.mpiz-koeln.mpg.de; f. 1927; Man. Dir Dr PAUL SCHULZE-LEFERT.

AGRICULTURE, FISHERIES AND VETERINARY SCIENCE

Bundesforschungsanstalt für Fischerei (Federal Research Centre for Fisheries): Palmaille 9, 22767 Hamburg; tel. (40) 389050; fax (40) 38905-200; e-mail info@iud.bfa-fisch.de; internet www.bfa-fisch.de; f. 1948; research into inland and sea fishing, aquaculture; library of 68,500 vols; Man. Dir CORNELIUS HAMMER; publs *Archive of Fishery and Marine Research*, *Informationen für die Fischwirtschaft*, *Schriften der Bundesforschungsanstalt für Fischerei*.

Attached research institutes:

Institut für Fischereiökologie: Palmaille 9, 22589 Hamburg; tel. (40) 38905-290; fax (40) 38905-261; e-mail info@ifo.bfa-fisch.de; Dir Prof. Dr HANS-STEPHAN JENKE.

Institut für Fischereitechnik und Fischereiökonomie: 22767 Hamburg; tel. (40) 38905-185; fax (40) 38905-264; e-mail info@ifh.bfa-fisch.de; internet www.bfa-fisch.de/iff; Dir Prof. Dr ERDMANN DAHM.

Institut für Ostseefischerei: Alter Hafen Süd 2, 18069 Rostock; tel. (381) 81161-00; fax (381) 81161-99; e-mail info@ior.bfa-fisch.de; Dir Dr CORNELIUS HAMMER.

Institut für Seefischerei: 22767 Hamburg; tel. (40) 38905-178; fax (40) 38905-263; e-mail info@ish.bfa-fisch.de; Dir Dr SIEGFRIED EHRICH.

Bundesforschungsanstalt für Landwirtschaft (FAL) (Federal Agricultural Research Centre): Bundesallee 50, 38116 Braunschweig; tel. (531) 596-0; fax (531) 596-1099; e-mail www.info@fal.de; internet www.fal.de; f. 1947; 12 institutes for specialized agricultural research; library of 133,000 vols; Pres. Prof. Dr KLAUS-DIETER VORLOP; publs *Annual Report*, *Landbauforschung Völkenrode* (3 or 4 a year), *Wissenschaft Erleben* (2 a year).

Deutsche Gesellschaft für Holzforschung eV (German Society for Wood Research): Bayerstr. 57–59, 5 Stock, 80335 Munich; tel. (89) 5161700; fax (89) 531657; e-mail mail@dgfh.de; internet www.dgfh.de; f. 1942; Pres. Dipl.-Ing. K. MOSER; Man. Dipl.-Ing. JOACHIM TEBBE; publs *DGfH aktuell* (4 a year), *Informationsdienst Holz der Entwicklungsgemeinschaft Holzbau*.

Forschungsgesellschaft für Agrarpolitik und Agrarsoziologie: Meckenheimer Allee 125, 53115 Bonn; tel. (228) 634781; fax (228) 634788; internet www.faa-bonn.de; f. 1952; study and scientific investigation of economic and social problems of agriculture and rural areas; 65 mems; Pres. Prof. Dr W. HENRICHSMEYER; Dir Dr HEINRICH BECKER.

Gesellschaft für Hopfenforschung (Society of Hops Research): 85283 Wolnzach-Hüll; tel. (8442) 3597; fax (8442) 2871; e-mail gfh@hopfenforschung.de; internet www.hopfenforschung.de; f. 1926; Pres. Dipl.-Ing. GEORG BALK; Dir Dr FRITZ LUDWIG SCHMUCKER; publ. *Jahresbericht Sonderkultur Hopfen* (annually).

ARCHITECTURE AND TOWN PLANNING

Akademie für Raumforschung und Landesplanung (Academy for Spatial Research and Planning): Hohenzollernstr. 11, 30161 Hannover; tel. (511) 34842-0; fax (511) 34842-41; e-mail arl@arl-net.de; internet www.arl-net.de; f. 1946; 550 mems (125 full, 425 corresp.); library of 20,000 vols; Pres. Prof. Dr-Ing. KLAUS BORCHARD; Gen. Sec. Prof. Dr-Ing. DIETMAR SCHOLICH; publ. *Raumforschung und Raumordnung* (Spatial Research and Planning, 6 a year, in German with summaries in English).

Deutsche Akademie für Städtebau und Landesplanung (Town and Country Planning Academy of Germany): Gubenerstr. 49, 10243 Berlin; tel. (30) 29362825; fax (30) 29362826; e-mail dasl-berlin@t-online.de; internet www.dasl.de; f. 1922; 600 mems; library of 5,000 vols; Pres. Prof. Dr-Ing. CHRISTIANE THALGOTT; publs *Almanach* (annually), *Vorbereitende Bericht* (1 or 2 a year).

BIBLIOGRAPHY, LIBRARY SCIENCE AND MUSEOLOGY

Gutenberg-Gesellschaft (Gutenberg Society): Liebfrauenpl. 5, 55116 Mainz; tel. (6131) 226420; fax (6131) 233530; e-mail gutenberg-gesellschaft@freenet.de; internet www.gutenberg-gesellschaft.uni-mainz.de; f. 1901 for the publication of research work on the art of printing and books from Gutenberg until the present day; 2,000 mems; Pres. THE MAYOR OF THE CITY OF MAINZ; Dir Dr CORNELIA FISCHER; Sec. KARL DELORME; publ. *Gutenberg-Jahrbuch* (annually).

ECONOMICS, LAW AND POLITICS

Arbeitsgemeinschaft Deutscher Wirtschaftswissenschaftlicher Forschungsinstitut eV (Asscn of German Economic Science Research Institutes): Königin-Luise-Str. 5, 14195 Berlin; f. 1949; 31 mem. institutes; co-ordinates programmes of the institutes and provides a permanent base for research exchange and co-operation; Chair. Prof. Dr KLAUS F. ZIMMERMANN; Sec.-Gen. RALF MESSER; publ. *Gemeinschaftsdiagnose* (2 a year).

Member institutes:

Abteilung Wirtschaftswissenschaft im Osteuropa Institut an der Freien Universität Berlin (Economics Department of the East European Institute at the Free University, Berlin): Garystr. 55, 14195 Berlin; tel. (30) 83854008; fax (30) 83852072; e-mail schrettl@wiwiss.fu-berlin.de; internet web.fu-berlin.de/wipol; f. 1950; economic research on East European countries; 10 mems; library of 85,000 vols and 95 periodicals; Dir Prof. Dr WOLFRAM SCHRETTL; publs *Berichte des Osteuropa Instituts/Reihe Wirtschaft und Recht*, *Wirtschaftswissenschaftliche Veröffentlichungen*.

BAW Institut für Wirtschaftsforschung GmbH (BAW Economic Research Institute Ltd): Wilhelm-Herbst-Str. 5, 28359 Bremen; tel. (421) 20699-0; fax (421) 20699-99; e-mail info@baw-bremen.de; internet www.baw.uni-bremen.de; f. 1947; library of 20,000 vols; Dir Prof. Dr FRANK HALLER; publs *BAW-Monatsbericht* (monthly), *Regionalwirtschaftliche Studien* (irregular).

Deutsches Institut für Wirtschaftsforschung (German Institute for Economic Research): 14195 Berlin, Königin-Luise-Str. 5; tel. (30) 897890; fax (30) 89789200; e-mail postmaster@diw.de; internet www.diw.de; f. 1925; Pres. Prof. Dr KLAUS F. ZIMMERMANN; publs *Economic Bulletin* (monthly), *Vierteljahrshefte zur Wirtschaftsforschung* (quarterly), *Wochenbericht* (weekly).

Deutsches Wirtschaftswissenschaftliches Institut für Fremdenverkehr an der Universität München (German Institute for Economic Research in Tourism and Travel, University of Munich): Sonnenstr. 27, 80331 Munich; tel. (89) 267091; fax (89) 267613; e-mail info@dwif.de; internet www.dwif.de; f. 1950; 6 staff; library: c.. 8,000 vols; Dir Dr J. MASCHKE; publ. *Jahrbuch für Fremdenverkehr*.

Energiewirtschaftliches Institut an der Universität zu Köln: Albertus Magnus Pl., 50923 Köln; tel. (221) 4702258; fax (221) 446537; internet www.ewi.uni-koeln.de; f. 1943; energy economics; 14 mems; library of 12,000 vols, 90 periodicals; Dir Prof. Dr AXEL OCKENFELS; publ. *Zeitschrift für Energiewirtschaft* (quarterly).

Forschunginstitut für Wirtschaftspolitik an der Universität Mainz: see under Johannes Gutenberg-Universität.

Forschungsstelle für Allgemeine und Textile Marktwirtschaft an der Universität Münster (Research Institute for General and Textile Economics): 48149 Münster, Fliednerstr. 21; e-mail 22fatm@wiwi.uni-muenster.de; tel. (0251) 22939; fax (0251) 83-31438; internet www.wiwi.uni-muenster.de; f. 1941; 25 mems; library of 15,000 vols; Dirs Prof. Dr DIETER AHLERT, Prof. Dr GUSTAV DIECKHEUER.

GfK-Nürnberg, Gesellschaft für Konsum-, Markt- und Absatzforschung eV (GfK Association): Nordwestring 101, 90319 Nuremberg; tel. (911) 395-0; fax (911) 395-2209; e-mail gfk_verein@gfk.com; internet www.gfk-verein.de; f. 1934; the not-for-profit section of the GfK Group for the Promotion of Market Research; carries out research and maintains close co-operation with scientific institutions, particularly Friedrich-Alexander University at Erlangen-Nuremberg; supports the education of market researchers, the ongoing training of leadership personnel and participation in commercial ventures; 600 mems; Pres. HAJO RIESENBECK; publ. *Yearbook of Marketing and Consumer Research*.

Hamburgisches Welt-Wirtschafts-Archiv (Hamburg Institute of International Economics): Neuer Jungfernstieg 21, 20347 Hamburg; tel. (40) 42834-0; fax (40) 42834-451; e-mail hwwa@hwwa.de; internet www.hwwa.de; f. 1908; research depts: int. macroeconomics, European integration, world economy; library of 1,200,000 vols, 7,500 periodicals; depository library for UN, EU; Pres. Prof. Dr THOMAS STRAUBHAAR; publs *HWWA Discussion Papers* (irreg.), *HWWA Report* (irreg.), *HWWA Studies* (irreg.), *Intereconomics* (every 2 months, in English), *Wirtschaftsdienst* (monthly).

Historisches Forschungszentrum der Friedrich-Ebert-Stiftung (Centre for Historical Research of the Friedrich-Ebert-Foundation): Godesberger Allee 149, 53175 Bonn; tel. (228) 883-0; fax (228) 3779606; e-mail Dieter.Dowe@fes.de; internet www.fes.de; f. 1925; Dir Prof. Dr DIETER DOWE; publ. *Archiv für Sozialgeschichte*.

ifo-Institut für Wirtschaftsforschung (ifo-Institute for Economic Research): Poschingerstr. 5, 81679 Munich; tel. (89) 9224-0; fax (89) 985369; e-mail ifo@ifo.de; internet www.ifo.de; f. 1949; empirical economic research; library of 90,000 vols; Pres. Dr Dr h.c HANS-WERNER SINN; publs *CESifo Forum* (in English, 4 a year), *ifo Dresden berichtet* (6 a year), *ifo Schnelldienst* (3 a month), *ifo Studien* (4 a year), *ifo Wirtschaftskonjunktur* (monthly).

Institut für Angewandte Wirtschaftsforschung Tübingen (Institute for Applied Economic Research): Ob dem Himmelreich 1, 72074 Tübingen; tel. (7071) 9896-0; fax (7071) 9896-99; e-mail iaw@iaw.edu; internet www.iaw.edu; f. 1957; analysis of issues in economic policy; research in economic theory; econometric macromodels; library of 12,500 vols; Dir Prof. Dr CLAUDIA M. BUCH; publ. *IAW-Mitteilungen* (quarterly).

Institut für Arbeitsmarkt- und Berufsforschung der Bundesanstalt für Arbeit: Regensburger Str. 104, 90478 Nürnberg; tel. (911) 179-0; fax (911) 179-3258; e-mail info@iab.de; internet www.iab.de; f. 1967; employment and labour market research; library of 55,000 vols; Dir Prof. Dr JUTTA ALLMENDINGER; publ. *Mitteilungen aus der Arbeitsmarkt- und Berufsforschung* (quarterly).

Institut der Deutschen Wirtschaft eV: Gustav-Heinemann-Ufer 84–88, 50968 Cologne; tel. (221) 4981-1; fax (221) 4981-533; e-mail welcome@iwkoeln.de; internet www.iwkoeln.de; f. 1951; education and labour market; economic and social policy; library of 200,000 vols; Pres. Dr HANS-DIETRICH WINKHAUS; Dir Prof. Dr MICHAEL HÜTHER; publ. *iw-trends* (4 a year).

Institut für Globale und Regionale Studien (German Institute of Global and Area Studies (GIGA)): Neuer Jungfernstieg 21, 20354 Hamburg; tel. (40) 42825-593; fax (40) 42825-547; e-mail duei@duei.de; internet www.duei.de; f. 1964; 40 mems; library of 9,000 vols and periodicals; Pres. Prof. Dr ROBERT KAPPEL; publs *Comparative Perspectives* (Journal of Transnational and Area Studies, 3 a year), *GIGA Focus* (60 a year), *NORD-SÜD aktuell* (quarterly).

Institut für Handelsforschung an der Universität zu Köln: Säckinger Str. 5, 50935 Cologne; tel. (221) 943607-0; fax (221) 943607-99; e-mail info@ifhkoeln.de; internet www.ifhkoeln.de; Dir Prof. Dr L. MÜLLER-HAGEDORN.

Institut für Marktanalyse und Agrarhandelspolitik der Bundesforschungsanstalt für Landwirtschaft Braunschweig-Völkenrode (FAL) (Institute for Market Analysis and Agricultural Trade Policy): Bundesallee 50, 38116 Braunschweig; tel. (531) 596-5301; fax (531) 596-5399; e-mail ma@fal.de; internet www.ma.fal.de; f. 1948; Dir Prof. Dr M. BROCKMEIER (acting); publ. *Agrarwirtschaft* (11 a year).

Institut für Seeverkehrswirtschaft und Logistik (Institute of Shipping Economics and Logistics): Universitätsallee GW 1 Block A, 28359 Bremen; tel. (421) 22096-0; fax (421) 22096-55; e-mail info@isl.org; internet www.isl.org; f. 1954; applied research and development projects in logistics systems, maritime economics and transport, information logistics/planning and simulation systems; library of 125,000 vols, 230 periodicals and newspapers; Exec. Dir Prof. Dr HANS-DIETRICH HAASIS; publs *Shipping Statistics and Market Review* (figures of shipping, shipbuilding, sea-ports and sea-borne trade, 10 a year and online at www.infoline.de), *Shipping Statistics Yearbook* (and online at www.infoline.de), *ISL Book Series*, *ISL Lectures, Contributions and Presentations*.

Institut für Weltwirtschaft an der Universität Kiel: see under Christian-Albrechts-Universität.

Institut für Wirtschaft und Gesellschaft Bonn eV (IWG BONN) (Bonn Institute for Economic and Social Research): Wissenschaftszentrum, Ahrstr. 45, 53175 Bonn; tel. (228) 372044; fax (228) 375869; e-mail kontakt@iwg-bonn.de; internet www.iwg-bonn.de; f. 1977; Dir STEFANIE WAHL; Scientific Dir MEINHARD MIEGEL.

Institut für Wirtschaftspolitik an der Universität zu Köln: Pohligstr. 1, 50969 Cologne; tel. (221) 470-5347; fax (221) 470-5350; e-mail iwp@wiso.uni-koeln.de; internet www.iwp.uni-koeln.de; economic policy, foreign trade policy, EU research; Dirs Prof. Dr JÜRGEN B. DONGES, Prof. Dr JOHANN EEKHOFF; publs *Untersuchungen zur Wirtschaftspolitik*, *Zeitschrift für Wirtschaftspolitik* (3 a year).

Osteuropa-Institut München: Scheinerstr. 11, 81679 Munich; tel. (89) 998396-0; fax (89) 9810110; e-mail oei@oei-muenchen.de; internet www.oei-muenchen.de; f. 1952; research into the history and economics of Eastern Europe and fmr USSR; library of 168,000 vols; Dir Prof. Dr JOACHIM MÖLLER; publs *Economic Systems* (4 a year), *Jahrbücher für Geschichte Osteuropas* (4 a year).

Rheinisch-Westfälisches Institut für Wirtschaftsforschung (Rhine-Westphalia Institute for Economic Research): Hohenzollernstr. 1–3, 45128 Essen; tel. (201) 8149-0; fax (201) 8149-200; e-mail rwi@rwi-essen.de; internet www.rwi-essen.de; f. 1943; study of the structure and development of the German (and int.) economy; special research facilities, advice on administration and economics for firms and students; 80 mems; library of 85,000 vols; Pres. Prof. Dr CHRISTOPH M. SCHMIDT; Dirs Prof. Dr THOMAS K. BAUER, Prof. Dr WIM KÖSTERS; publs *Discussion Papers* (irreg.), *Konjunkturberichte* (Economic Report, 2 a year), *Materialien* (surveys and extensive articles, irreg.), *Mitteilungen* (Bulletin, 4 a year), *News* (Newsletter, 6 a year), *Schriften* (articles on aspects of economic policy, irreg.).

Schmalenbach-Gesellschaft für Betriebswirtschaft eV: Bunzlauer Str. 1, 50858 Cologne, Nonnendammallee 101; tel. (2234) 480097; fax (2234) 480005; e-mail sg@schmalenbach.org; internet www.schmalenbach.org; f. 1978; economic research; 1,500 mems; Pres. Prof. Dr CLEMENS BÖRSIG; Man. Dr MARIA ENGELS; publ. *Schmalenbachs Zeitschrift für betriebswirtschaftliche Forschung (ZfbF)* (monthly).

Statistisches Bundesamt (Federal Statistical Office): Gustav-Streseman-Ring 11, 65189 Wiesbaden; tel. (611) 75-2405; fax (611) 75-3330; e-mail poststelle@destatis.de; internet www.destatis.de; f. 1950; library of 500,000 vols; Pres. JOHANN HAHLEN; publs *Statistisches Jahrbuch für die Bundesrepublik Deutschland* (Statistical Yearbook for the Federal Republic of Germany, annual), *Statistisches Jahrbuch für das Ausland* (Statistical Yearbook for Foreign Countries, annual), *Zahlenkompass—Statistisches Taschenbuch für Deutschland* (publ in English as *Key Data on Germany*, annual), *Glossar statistischer Fachbegriffe* (irreg.), *Wirtschaft und Statistik* (monthly), *Die Bundesländer: Strukturen und Entwicklungen* (2 a year), *Datenreport* (2 a year), *Statistik regional—Daten für die Kreise und kreisfreien Städte Deutschlands* (database, publ. in English as *Regional Statistics*, annual), *Statistik lokal—Daten für die Gemeinden, kreisfreien Städte und Kreise Deutschlands* (annual), *Kreiszahlen* (annual).

Wirtschafts- und Sozialwissenschaftliches Institut in der Hans-Böckler-Stiftung (Economic Research Institute of the Hans Böckler Foundation): Hans-Böckler-Str. 39, 40476 Düsseldorf; tel. (211) 7778-0; fax (211) 7778-120; e-mail zentrale@boeckler.de; internet www.boeckler.de; Dir Prof. Dr HEIDE PFARR; publ. *Mitteilungen* (monthly).

Arbeitsstelle Friedensforschung Bonn (Peace Research Information Unit Bonn): Beethovenallee 4, 53173 Bonn; tel. (228) 35-60-32; fax (228) 367-03-39; e-mail afb@priub.org; f. 1984; information and advice on research into peace; Dir Dr REGINE MEHL; publ. *AFB-Info* (2 a year, in German and English).

Arnold Bergstraesser Institut für kulturwissenschaftliche Forschung (ABI): Windausstr. 16, 79110 Freiburg im Breisgau; tel. (761) 88878-0; fax (761) 88878-78; e-mail info@arnold-bergstraesser.de; internet www.arnold-bergstraesser.de; f. 1960; socio-political research particularly on education, administration, political development and ethnic conflicts in Africa, Asia, Near East and Latin America; depts of overseas education and overseas admin; four regional depts: Africa, Asia, Latin America, Middle East/North Africa; 30 mems; library of 70,000 vols; Dirs Prof. Dr T. HANF, Prof. Dr J. RÜLAND; publ. *International Quarterly for Asian Studies* (2 a year).

Deutsches Übersee Institut–Übersee Dokumentation (German Overseas Institute–Overseas Documentation): Neuer Jungfernstieg 21, 20354 Hamburg; tel. (40) 42825-598; fax (40) 42825-512; e-mail dok@duei.de; internet www.duei.de/dok; f. 1966; sections on Africa, Asia and South Pacific, Latin America, Near and Middle East; database of 600,000 documentary units (references to research literature) available online from the database of the 'Fachinformationsverbund Internationale Beziehungen und Länderkunde'; Head Dr GOTTFRIED REINKNECHT; publs *Ausgewählte neuere Literatur* (selected bibliographies of recent literature, by regions, 4 a year), *Kompendium der deutsch-[ausländischen] Beziehungen* (directory on German relations with foreign countries, irregular), *Kurzbibliographien* (working/introductory bibliographies, irregular), *Spezialbibliographien* (specialized bibliographies, irregular).

Frobenius-Institut an der Johann Wolfgang Goethe-Universität: Grüneburgpl. 1, 60323 Frankfurt; tel. (69) 79833050; fax (69) 79833101; e-mail frobenius@em.uni-frankfurt.de; internet www.frobenius-institut.de; f. 1898; African, Indonesian and Melanesian cultures and history; library of 96,000 vols; Dir Prof. Dr KARL-HEINZ KOHL; publ. *Paideuma* (annually).

Gesellschaft für Deutschlandforschung eV (Society for Research on Germany): c/o Prof. Dr Karl Eckart, Horster Str. 51, 46236 Bottrop; tel. (2041) 61716; fax (2041) 24016; e-mail info@gfd-berlin.de; internet www.gfd-berlin.de; f. 1978; contemporary research on Germany; seminars and conferences; Pres. Prof. Dr KARL ECKART; Vice-Pres. Prof. Dr HANS-JÖRG BÜCKING (Berlin).

Herder-Institut eV: Gisonenweg 5–7, 35037 Marburg/Lahn; tel. (6421) 1840; fax (6421) 184139; e-mail herder@herder-institut.de; internet www.herder-institut.de; f. 1950; historical research on countries and peoples of Eastern Central Europe; library: library: see Libraries and Archives; Dir Dr PETER HASLINGER; publ. *Zeitschrift für Ostmitteleuropa-Forschung* (4 a year).

Institut Finanzen und Steuern eV (Finance and Taxation Institute): Postf. 7269, 53072 Bonn; located at: Markt 14, 53111 Bonn; tel. (228) 982210; fax (228) 9822150; e-mail info@ifst.de; internet www.ifst.de; f. 1949; Dir HANS-JÜRGEN MÜLLER-SEILS.

Institut für Afrika-Kunde (Institute of African Affairs): Neuer Jungfernstieg 21, 20354 Hamburg; tel. (40) 42825-523; fax (40) 42825-511; e-mail iak@iak.duei.de; internet www.duei.de/iak; f. 1963; contemporary social science research, documentation, discussion groups, international contact with organizations and individuals with specialized knowledge of African affairs; library of 46,000 vols and 400 periodicals; Dir Dr ANDREAS MEHLER; publs *Afrika im Blickpunkt* (irregular), *Afrika Spectrum* (3 a year), *Arbeiten aus dem Institut für Afrika-Kunde*, *Focus Afrika*, *Hamburg African Studies*, *Hamburger Beiträge zur Afrika-Kunde*.

Stiftung Wissenschaft und Politik (SWP). (German Institute for International and Security Affairs): Ludwigkirchpl. 3–4, 10719 Berlin; tel. (30) 88007-0; fax (30) 88007-100; e-mail swp@swp-berlin.org; internet www.swp-berlin.org; f. 1962; interdisciplinary research in int. affairs and security, computerized information system for the fields of int. relations and area studies (660,000 references), publicly available database 'World Affairs On-line'; library of 94,000 vols, 360 periodicals; Pres. U. HARTMANN; Dir Prof. Dr V. PERTHES; publs *SWP Research Papers*, *SWP Comments*.

Wissenschaftszentrum Berlin für Sozialforschung: Reichpietschufer 50, 10785 Berlin; tel. (30) 25491-0; fax (30) 25491684; e-mail wzb@wz-berlin.de; internet www.wz-berlin.de; f. 1969; a non-profit organization; aims to conduct international and interdisciplinary, empirical social science research and to communicate the results to the scientific and decision-making community; 4 research areas, 4 research groups; library of 100,000 vols, 600 periodicals, special collections on the themes of the research units; Pres. Prof. Dr JÜRGEN KOCKA; publs *WZB Abstracts* (annually), *WZB-Forschung* (3 a year), *WZB-Mitteilungen* (quarterly).

EDUCATION

Deutsches Institut für Internationale Pädagogische Forschung (German Institute for International Educational Research): Schloss-Str. 29, 60486 Frankfurt am Main; tel. (69) 24708-0; fax (69) 24708-444; e-mail dipf@dipf.de; internet www.dipf.de; f. 1951; educational information and research; library of 875,000 vols; libraries in Berlin and Frankfurt; Dir Prof. Dr ECKHARD KLIEME; Asst Dir Prof. Dr MARC RITTBERGER; publ. *DIPF informiert* (2 a year).

Gesellschaft für Pädagogik und Information eV: Pädagogisches Büro, Rathenaustr. 16, Postfach 2228, 33052 Paderborn; tel. (5251) 34024; f. 1964; 400 mems; to promote research and development in the field of educational technology and information science; Chair. Prof. Dr U. LEHNERT, Prof. Dr Dr G. E. ORTNER; publs *Pädagogik und Information*, *Schul Praxis—Wirtschaft und Weiterbildung*.

Gesellschaft zur Förderung Pädagogischer Forschung eV (Society for the Promotion of Educational Research): Postfach 900280, 60442 Frankfurt am Main; premises at: 60486 Frankfurt am Main, Schloss-Str. 29; tel. (69) 247080; fax (69) 24708444; f. 1950; dissemination of research results, organization of communication processes between educational research and school practice; 300 mems; Pres. BERND FROMMELT; Sec. P. DOEBRICH; publ. *Materialen zur Bildungsforschung* (book series, 2–3 a year).

FINE AND PERFORMING ARTS

Gesellschaft für Musikforschung: Heinrich-Schütz-Allee 35, 34131 Kassel-Wilhelmshöhe; tel. (561) 3105-255; fax (561) 3105-254; e-mail G.f.Musikforschung@T-Online.de; internet www.musikforschung.de; f. 1946; 1,800 mems; Pres. Prof. Dr DETLEF ALTENBURG; Treas. Dr GABRIELE BUSCHMEIER; publ. *Die Musikforschung* (quarterly).

Staatliches Institut für Musikforschung Preussischer Kulturbesitz mit Musikinstrumenten-Museum: Tiergartenstr. 1, 10785 Berlin; tel. (30) 25481-0; fax (30) 25481-172; e-mail sim@sim.spk-berlin.de; internet www.sim-berlin.de; f. 1935; collects musicological material, instruments, records, phonograms and tape recordings; conducts research into the development and history of musicology, inc. acoustics, musical instruments and the style and practice of executing music of the past; archival and documentary research and comparative musicological research; open to the public; lectures, concerts and exhibitions; library of 67,000 vols; Dir Dr THOMAS ERTELT; Dir of Museum Dr

CONNY RESTLE; publs *Studien zur Geschichte der Musiktheorie*, *Bibliographie des Musikschrifttums* (annually), *Jahrbuch* (annually), *Geschichte der Musiktheorie*, *Briefwechsel der Wiener Schule*, *Klang und Begriff: Perspektiven musikalischer Theorie und Praxis*.

Zentralinstitut für Kunstgeschichte (History of Art): Meiserstr. 10, 80333 Munich; tel. (89) 289-27556; fax (89) 289-27607; e-mail direktion@zikg.eu; internet www.zikg.eu; f. 1947; library of 450,000 vols; 800,000 photographs; Dir Prof. Dr WOLF TEGETHOFF; publs *Kunstchronik* (monthly), *Reallexikon zur Deutschen Kunstgeschichte*.

HISTORY, GEOGRAPHY AND ARCHAEOLOGY

Deutsches Archäologisches Institut (German Archaeological Institute): Podbielskiallee 69–71, 14195 Berlin; tel. (1888) 7711-0; fax (1888) 7711-191; e-mail info@dainst.de; internet www.dainst.org; f. 1829; brs in Rome (Prof. Dr DIETER MERTENS), Athens (Prof. Dr WOLF-DIETRICH NIEMEIER), Cairo (Prof. Dr GÜNTER DREYER), Istanbul (Prof. Dr ADOLF HOFFMANN), Madrid (Prof. Dr DIRCE MARZOLI), Middle East (Prof. Dr RICARDO EICHMANN), Sana'a (Dr IRIS GERLACH), Damascus (Dr KARIN BARTL), Eurasia (Prof. Dr SVEND HANSEN) and Tehran; also Römisch-Germanische Kommission, Frankfurt am Main (Prof. Dr SIEGMAR FREIHERR VON SCHNURBEIN), Kommission für Alte Geschichte und Epigraphik, München (Prof. Dr CHRISTOF SCHULER) and Kommission für Allgemeine und Vergleichende Archäologie, Bonn (Dr BURKHARDT VOGT); Pres. Prof. Dr HERMANN PARZINGER; Dir Dr ORTWIN DALLY; publs *Jahrbuch*, *Archäologischer Anzeiger*, *Berichte der Römisch-Germanischen-Kommission*, *Germania*, *Chiron*, *Athenische Mitteilungen*, *Römische Mitteilungen*, *Istanbuler Mitteilungen*, *Mitteilungen des DAI Kairo*, *Madrider Mitteilungen*, *Baghdader Mitteilungen*, *Teheraner Mitteilungen*, *Archäologische Berichte aus dem Yemen*, *Damaszener Mitteilungen*.

Institut für Europäische Geschichte (Institute of European History): Alte Universitätsstr. 19, 55116 Mainz; tel. (6131) 3939360; fax (6131) 3930154; e-mail ieg2@ieg-mainz.de; internet www.ieg-mainz.de; f. 1950; conducts and promotes research on the historical foundations of Europe; cross-cultural projects on European communication and transfer processes; projects on concepts and perceptions of Europe since 1450; research fellowship programme (research, training and international networking); library of 220,000 vols; Dir (History of Religion) Prof. Dr IRENE DINGEL; Dir (Universal History) Prof. Dr HEINZ DUCHHARDT; publs *Archiv für Reformationsgeschichte–Literaturbericht* (annually), *IEG-MAPS* (online), *Jahrbuch für Europäische Geschichte* (annually), *Veröffentlichungen des Instituts für Europäische Geschichte* (monographs and conference documentation).

Institut für Zeitgeschichte, München–Berlin (Institute of Contemporary History–Munich and Berlin): Leonrodstr. 46b, 80636 Munich; tel. (89) 126880; fax (89) 12688-191; e-mail ifz@ifz-muenchen.de; internet www.ifz-muenchen.de; f. 1949; German and European history research since 1918, particularly Weimar Republic, National Socialism and post-1945 history; library of 175,000 vols; Dir Prof. Dr Dr h.c. HORST MOELLER; publs *Quellen und Darstellungen zur Zeitgeschichte*, *Schriftenreihe der Vierteljahrshefte für Zeitgeschichte* (2 a year), *Studien zur Zeitgeschichte*, *Texte und Materialien zur Zeitgeschichte*, *Vierteljahrshefte für Zeitgeschichte* (quarterly).

Vereinigung zur Erforschung der Neueren Geschichte eV (Modern History Research Association): Argelanderstr. 59, 53115 Bonn; tel. (228) 216205; fax (228) 2426044; e-mail apw@uni-bonn.de; internet www.pax-westphalica.de; f. 1957; 17th-century to present-day history; Dir Prof. Dr MAXIMILIAN LANZINNER; Sec. Prof. Dr CHRISTOPH KAMPMANN; publ. *Acta Pacis Westphalicae* (Sources of the Westphalian Peace Conference).

LANGUAGE AND LITERATURE

Arbeitsstelle für Osterreichische Literatur und Kultur Robert-Musil-Forschung: Universität des Saarlandes, Gebäude 53/3. OG/323, Postfach 151150, 66041 Saarbrücken; tel. (681) 302-3334; fax (681) 302-3034; e-mail fzoelk@mx.uni-saarland.de; internet www.uni-saarland.de/fak4/fr41/afoelk; f. 1970; archives; study programmes, publications, symposia, bibliography; library of 5,000 vols; Dirs Prof. Dr PIERRE BÉHAR, Prof. Dr MARIE-LOUISE ROTH; publ. research reports; (See also International Robert Musil Society).

Institut für Deutsche Sprache: POB 101621, 68016 Mannheim; premises at: 68161 Mannheim, R5 6–13; tel. (621) 1581-0; fax (621) 1581-200; e-mail webmaster@ids-mannheim.de; internet www.ids-mannheim.de; f. 1964; scientific study of present-day and historical German; library of 80,000 vols, 300 journals; Dir Prof. Dr LUDWIG M. EICHINGER; publs *Amades-Arbeitspapiere und Materialien zur deutschen Sprache*, *Deutsch im Kontrast*, *Deutsche Sprache* (quarterly), *Jahrbuch*, *Phonai*, *Schriften*, *Sprachreport* (quarterly), *Studienbibliographien Sprachwissenschaft*, *Studien zur deutschen Sprache*.

MEDICINE

Bernhard-Nocht-Institut für Tropenmedizin (Tropical Medicine): Bernhard-Nocht-Str. 74 20359 Hamburg; tel. (40) 42818-0; fax (40) 42818400; e-mail bni@bni-hamburg.de; internet www.bni-hamburg.de; f. 1900; tropical medicine and parasitology; National Reference Centre for Tropical Infections; library of 41,000 vols and 47,500 reprints; Dir Prof. Dr BERNHARD FLEISCHER; publ. *Scientific Report* (annually).

C. & O. Vogt-Institut für Hirnforschung, Universität Düsseldorf (Brain Research): Postfach 101007, 40001 Düsseldorf; tel. (211) 8112777; fax (211) 8112336; f. 1937; morphometry, neuroanatomy; immunohistochemistry, psychopharmacology; neurochemistry; Dir Prof. Dr KARL ZILLES.

Chemotherapeutisches Forschungsinstitut Georg-Speyer-Haus: Paul-Ehrlich-Str. 42/44, 60596 Frankfurt am Main; tel. (69) 63395-0; fax (69) 63395297; e-mail Kost@em.uni-frankfurt.de; internet www.georg-speyer-haus.de; f. 1904; research into HIV/AIDS, tumours and allergies; library of 27,664 vols; Dir Prof. Dr BERND GRONER.

Deutsche Gesellschaft für Kardiologie, Herz- und Kreislaufforschung (German Cardiac Society): Achenbachstr. 43, 40237 Düsseldorf; tel. (211) 600692-0; fax (211) 600692-10; e-mail info@dgk.org; internet www.dgk.org; f. 1927; 5,140 mems; Dir and Gen. Sec. Prof. Dr GUNTHER ARNOLD; publs *Basic Research in Cardiology* (6 a year), *Clinical Research in Cardiology*, *Herzschrittmachertherapie und Elektrophysiologie*, *Intensiv- und Notfallmedizin*.

Deutsche Gesellschaft für Sexualforschung eV (German Association for Research into Sexuality): Universitätsklinikum Hamburg-Eppendorf, Zentrum für Psychosoziale Medizin, Institut und Poliklinik für Sexualforschung und Forensische Psychiatrie, Martinistr. 52, 20246 Hamburg; tel. (40) 42803-3214; fax (40) 42803-6406; e-mail hill@uke.uni-hamburg.de; internet www.dgfs.info; f. 1950; 220 mems; Pres. Prof. Dr WOLFGANG BERNER; Dir Dr ANDREAS HILL; publ. *Zeitschrift für Sexualforschung*.

Deutsche Krebsgesellschaft eV (German Cancer Society): Steinlestr. 6, 60596 Frankfurt am Main; tel. (69) 630096-0; fax (69) 630096-66; e-mail service@krebsgesellschaft.de; internet www.deutsche-krebsgesellschaft.de; f. 1900; promoting research, treatment and prevention of cancer; Pres. Prof. Dr M. BAMBERG; Sec.-Gen. Dr S. VON OESTERREICH; publs *Journal of Cancer Research and Clinical Oncology* (6 a year), *Der Onkologe*, *Forum* (German Cancer Society news, 8 a year).

Geomedizinische Forschungsstelle der Heidelberger Akademie der Wissenschaften (Geomedical Research Office of the Heidelberg Academy of Sciences): Karlstr. 4, 69117 Heidelberg; tel. (6221) 543265; fax (6221) 543355; e-mail haw@urz.uni-heidelberg.de; internet www.haw.baden-wuerttemberg.de; f. 1952; epidemiology of atherosclerotic diseases in Europe and Asia; 50 mems; library of 3,000 vols; Dir Prof. Dr G. SCHETTLER; publs *Geomedical Monographs Series* (6 vols), *World Atlas of Epidemic Diseases* (3 vols 1952–1961), *World Maps of Climatology*, geomedical studies.

GSF–Forschungszentrum für Umwelt und Gesundheit GmbH (National Research Centre for Environment and Health): Ingolstädter Landstr. 1, 85764 Neuherberg; tel. (89) 31870; internet www.gsf.de; f. 1964; controls 20 institutes; 1,500 mems; library: central library of 120,000 vols, 350 journals; Scientific and Technical Dir Prof. Dr Dr E.-G. AFTING; Administrative Dir Dr HANS JAHREISS.

Herz- und Diabeteszentrum NRW: Georgstr. 11, 32545 Bad Oeynhausen; tel. (5731) 97-0; fax (5731) 97-2300; e-mail info@hdz-nrw.de; internet www.hdz-nrw.de; f. 1985; cardiology, thoracic and cardiovascular surgery, paediatric cardiology, diabetology, gastroenterology, nuclear medicine, anaesthesiology, radiology, molecular biophysics, radiopharmacy, laboratory and transfusion medicine; library of 3,000 vols and 180 periodicals; Dir Dr O. FOIT.

Institut für Umweltmedizinische Forschung an der Heinrich-Heine-Universität Düsseldorf (Environmental Health Research Institute): Auf'm Hennekamp 50, 40225 Düsseldorf; tel. (211) 33890; fax (211) 3190910; internet www.iuf.uni-duesseldorf.de; f. 2001; molecular preventive medical research in the field of environmental health; evaluation of risks to human health that result from environmental factors, in order to develop preventive and therapeutic strategies; 110 mems; library of 15,000 vols; Dir Prof. Dr Med. JEAN KRUTMANN.

Institut für Wasser-, Boden- und Lufthygiene, Forschungsstelle Bad Elster (Institute for Water, Soil and Air Purity, Bad Elster Research Unit): Heinrich-Heine-Str. 12, 08645 Bad Elster; tel. (37437) 760; fax (37437) 76219; f. 1962; fed. govt instn; research in drinking water and bathing water, microbiology, toxicology, chemical analysis and ecology; library of 17,000 vols; Dir (Berlin) Prof. Dr H. LANGE-ASSCHENFELDT.

Institut für Wasserchemie und Chemische Balneologie der Technischen Universität München (Institute for Hydrochemistry and Chemical Balneology at the Technical University of Munich): Marchioninistr. 17, 81377 Munich; tel. (89) 2180-78231; fax (89) 2180-78255; internet www.ws.chemie.tu-muenchen.de; f. 1951; water chemistry, hydrogeology, environmental analytical chemistry; Dir Prof. Dr R. NIESSNER.

Max von Pettenkofer-Institut für Hygiene und Medizinische Mikrobiologie (Max von Pettenkofer Institute of Hygiene and Medical Microbiology): Pettenkoferstr. 9a, 80336 Munich; tel. (89) 5160-5201; fax (89) 5160-5202; internet www.mvp.uni-muenchen.de; Dirs Prof. Dr JÜRGEN HEESEMANN, Prof. Dr ULRICH KOSZINOWSKI.

Paul-Ehrlich-Institut, Bundesamt für Sera und Impfstoffe: Paul-Ehrlich-Str. 51-59, 63225 Langen; tel. (6103) 77-0; fax (6103) 77123; e-mail pei@pei.de; internet www.pei.de; f. 1896; depts of bacteriology, virology, immunology, veterinary medicine, allergology, medicinal biotechnology, haematology and transfusion medicine; research into safety of medicinal products and devices; library of 32,000 vols; Pres Prof. Dr. J. LÖWER; publ. *Arbeiten aus dem Paul-Ehrlich-Institut*.

Verein für Wasser-, Boden- und Lufthygiene eV (Society for Water, Soil and Air Purity): Rotthauser Str. 19, 45879 Gelsenkirchen; tel. (209) 9242-190; fax (209) 9242-199; e-mail verein@wabolu.de; internet www.wabolu.de; f. 1902; researches and subsidizes international studies into environmental water and air issues; Dir Prof. Dr LOTHAR DUNEMANN.

NATURAL SCIENCES

General

Forschungsinstitut und Naturmuseum Senckenberg (Research Institute and Natural History Museum): Senckenberganlage 25, 60325 Frankfurt am Main; tel. (69) 7542-0; fax (69) 746238; internet www.senckenberg.de; f. 1817; systematics, anatomy, distribution, ecology, evolution in zoology, botany, palaeozoology, palaeobotany, marine biology and geology, palaeoanthropology; Dir Prof. Dr DR V. MOSBRUGGER; publs *Senckenbergiana biologica*, *Senckenbergiana lethaea*, *Senckenbergiana maritima*, *Archiv für Molluskenkunde*, *Abhandlungen der Senckenbergischen Naturforschenden Gesellschaft*, *Natur und Museum* (6 a year), *Courier Forschungsinstitut Senckenberg*.

Biological Sciences

Alfred-Wegener-Institut für Polar- und Meeresforschung (Alfred Wegener Institute for Polar and Marine Research): Postfach 120161, 27515 Bremerhaven; tel. (471) 4831-0; fax (471) 4831-1149; e-mail awi-pr@awi-bremerhaven.de; internet www.awi-bremerhaven.de; f. 1980; Dir Prof. Dr JÖRN THIEDE; Admin. Dir Dr RAINER PAULENZ; publ. *Berichte zur Polar- und Meeresforschung* (Reports of Polar and Marine Research, irregular).

Constituent research units:

Biologische Anstalt Helgoland (Biological Institution Heligoland): 27483 Heligoland, Postfach 180; tel. (4725) 819-0; fax (4725) 819-283; internet www.awi-bremerhaven.de/BAH/index-d.html; f. 1892; research in marine ecology, esp. in the North Sea; library of 63,000 vols; Head Prof. Dr FRIEDRICH BUCHHOLZ; publ. *Helgoländer Meeresuntersuchungen* (Heligoland Marine Research, 4 a year).

Forschungsstelle Potsdam des Alfred-Wegener-Instituts für Polar und Meeresforschung (Potsdam Research Unit of the Alfred Wegener Institute for Polar and Marine Research): 14401 Potsdam, Postfach 600149; tel. (331) 288-2100; fax (331) 288-2137; internet www.awi-potsdam.de; f. 1992; terrestrial geoscientific research in the periglacial regions; research into atmospheric processes; Head Prof. Dr HANS-WOLFGANG HUBBERTEN.

Wadden Sea Station, List/Sylt: 25992 List/Sylt, Hafenstr. 43; tel. (4651) 956-0; fax (4651) 956-200; internet www.awi-bremerhaven.de/BAH/sylt-d.html; f. 1924; studies of coastal biological processes and ecosystems and monitoring of coastal changes and their long-term impact; Head Prof. Dr KARSTEN REISE.

Biozentrum Klein Flottbek: Ohnhorststr. 18, 22609 Hamburg; tel. (40) 42816-0; fax (40) 42816-254; e-mail sekretariat@botanik.uni-hamburg.de; internet www.biologie.uni-hamburg.de/bzf; f. 1821; research in plant physiology, cell biology, plant systematics, genetics and microbiology, applied plant molecular biology; botanical garden and herbarium comprising *c*. 800,000 specimens; *c*. 250 mems; library of 45,000 vols and 49,000 reprints; Man. Dir Prof. Dr MICHAEL BÖTTGER; publs *Institut für Allgemeine Botanik Hamburg*, *Mitteilungen*.

Deutsche Gesellschaft für Moor- und Torfkunde (German Society for Bog and Peat Research): Stilleweg 2, 30655 Hannover; tel. (511) 643-3612; fax (511) 643-3667; e-mail g.caspers@bgr.de; internet www.dgmtev.de; f. 1970; 325 mems; Pres. Dr G. CASPERS; publ. *TELMA* (annually).

Forschungszentrum Borstel–Zentrum für Medizin und Biowissenschaften (Borstel Research Centre for Medicine and Biological Sciences): Parkallee 1-40, 23845 Borstel; tel. (4537) 188-0; fax (4537) 188-244; internet www.fz-borstel.de; f. 1947; research in fields of immunology, pulmonology, microbiology, cell biology, allergy, chemistry and medicine; library of 50,000 vols; Dirs Prof. Dr TH. RIETSCHEL, Prof. Dr PETER ZABEL; Admin Man. Prof. Dr SILVIA BULFONE-PAUS.

Institut für Angewandte Botanik (Institute of Applied Botany at Hamburg University): Marseiller Str. 7, 20355 Hamburg; tel. (40) 42838-2331; fax (40) 42838-6593; e-mail iangebot@iangebot.uni-hamburg.de; internet www.physnet.uni-hamburg.de/botany; f. 1885; 140 mems; library of 130,000 vols; research on plant products, agriculture and horticulture; Dir Prof. Dr GÜNTER ADAM; publ. *Jahresberichte* (every 2 years).

Institut für Vogelforschung 'Vogelwarte Helgoland' (Institute of Avian Research): An der Vogelwarte 21, 26386 Wilhelmshaven; tel. (4421) 96890; fax (4421) 968955; e-mail ifv@ifv.terramare.de; internet www.vogelwarte-helgoland.de; f. 1910; Dir Prof. Dr FRANZ BAIRLEIN; publ. *Vogelwarte* (4 a year).

Naturforschende Gesellschaft Bamberg eV: Litzendorferstr. 17, 96129 Strullendorf; tel. (9505) 6356; fax (9505) 8305; internet www.stadt.bamberg.de; f. 1834; 250 mems; library of 18,000 vols; Dirs Dipl.-Biol. K. WEBER; publ. *Berichte*.

Naturforschende Gesellschaft Freiburg i. Br.: Albertstr. 23b. Freiburg, 79104; tel. (761) 2036484; fax (761) 2036483; e-mail naturforschende@geologie.uni-freiburg.de; internet www.naturforschende-gesellschaft.uni-freiburg.de; f. 1821; 300 mems; Pres. Prof. Dr R. MAECKEL; publ. *Berichte* (annually).

Mathematical Sciences

Mathematisches Forschungsinstitut Oberwolfach gGmbH (Mathematical Research Institute): Schwarzwaldstr. 9–11, 77709 Oberwolfach; tel. (7834) 979-0; fax (7834) 979-55; e-mail admin@mfo.de; internet www.mfo.de; f. 1944; library of 68,000 vols; Dir Prof. Dr GERT-MARTIN GREUEL; publ. *Oberwolfach Reports* (4 a year).

Physical Sciences

Astronomisches Institut der Universität Würzburg: Am Hubland, 97074 Würzburg; tel. (931) 888-5031; fax (931) 888-4603; internet www.astro.uni-wuerzburg.de; f. 1967; astronomy, theoretical astrophysics; library of 5,000 vols, 50 journals; Dir Prof. Dr KARL MANNHEIM.

Astronomisches Rechen-Institut (Astronomical Institute): Mönchhofstr. 12–14, 69120 Heidelberg; tel. (6221) 54-1845; fax (6221) 54-1888; internet www.ari.uni-heidelberg.de; f. 1700; attached to Zentrum für Astronomie der Universität Heidelberg; theoretical astronomy; 50 mems; library of 26,000 vols; Dir Prof. Dr JOACHIM WAMBSGANß; publs *Apparent Places of Fundamental Stars*, *Astronomische Grundlagen für den Kalender*, *Veröffentlichungen*.

Astrophysikalisches Institut und Universitäts-Sternwarte: Schillergässchen 2, 07745 Jena; tel. (3641) 947501; fax (3641) 947502; e-mail moni@astro.uni-jena.de; internet www.astro.uni-jena.de; f. 1813; Dir Prof. Dr RALPH NEUHÄUSER.

Bundesamt für Seeschiffahrt und Hydrographie (Federal Maritime and Hydrographic Agency): Bernhard-Nocht-Str. 78, 20359 Hamburg; tel. (40) 3190-0; fax (40) 3019-5000; e-mail posteingang@bsh.de; internet www.bsh.de; f. 1945; under the Federal Ministry of Transport; oceanography, tides and currents, geomagnetism, gravimetry, nautical technics, navigating methods, tonnage measurement, hydrographic surveying and nautical geodesy, bathymetry, sea-bed geology, pollution control, ice information service, nautical charts and publications; library of 153,000 vols; hydrographic information service; 900 mems; Pres. Prof. Dr PETER EHLERS; publs *Deutsche Hydrographische Zeitschrift* (quarterly), *Jahresbericht* (annually), *Nachrichten für Seefahrer* (weekly).

Bundesanstalt für Geowissenschaften und Rohstoffe (BGR) (Federal Institute for Geosciences and Natural Resources): Stilleweg 2, 30655 Hanover; tel. (511) 643-0; fax (511) 643-2304; e-mail poststelle@bgr.de; internet www.bgr.bund.de; f. 1958; geoscientific investigation, evaluation of mineral resources, environmental protection, geotechnology, seismology, marine and polar research; library of 296,000 vols; Pres. Prof Dr B. STRIBRNY; publs *Geologisches Jahrbuch*, *Zeitschrift fur angewandte Geologie*.

Deutsche Gemmologische Gesellschaft e. V. (German Gemmological Association): Prof.-Schlossmacher Str. 1, 55743 Idar-Oberstein; tel. (6781) 5084-0; fax (6781) 5084-19; e-mail info@dgemg.com; internet www.dgemg.com; f. 1932; educational training centre for gemmology, diamond grading, pearls and organic substances; Pres. Dr THOMAS LIND; Dir Dr ULRICH HENN; publ. *Gemmologie* (magazine, quarterly).

Deutscher Wetterdienst (German Meteorological Service): Postfach 100465, 63004 Offenbach am Main; premises at: Frankfurter Str. 135, 63067 Offenbach am Main; tel. (69) 8062-0; fax (69) 8062-4484; e-mail info@dwd.de; internet www.dwd.de; f. 1952; central office for the Federal Republic; library of 165,000 vols; Dir G. R. HOFFMANN; publs *Annalen der Meteorologie*, *Berichte des Deutschen Wetterdienstes*, *Deutsches Meteor-*

ologisches Jahrbuch (annually), *Europäischer Wetterbericht* (online), *Die Grosswetterlagen Europas* (monthly, online), *Jahresbericht* (Annual Report), *promet-Meteorologische Fortbildung* (4 a year), *Witterungsreport*.

Forschungszentrum Jülich GmbH (Jülich Research Centre): Wilhelm-Johnen-Str., 52425 Jülich; tel. (2461) 61-0; fax (2461) 61-8100; e-mail info@fz-juelich.de; internet www.fz-juelich.de; f. 1956; operated jointly by German federal govt (90%) and state of North Rhine-Westphalia (10%); research in information technology and physical basic research, energy (materials and technology), environmental life sciences; library of 600,000 vols, 250,000 microforms, 2,000 journal titles; CEO Prof. Dr JOACHIM TREUSCH.

Forschungszentrum Karlsruhe GmbH (Karlsruhe Research Centre): Hermann-von-Helmholtz-Pl. 1, 76344 Eggenstein-Leopoldshafen; tel. (7247) 82-0; fax (7247) 82-5070; e-mail info@fzk.de; internet www.fzk.de; f. 1956; environmental research, conversion of energy, climate modelling, nuclear fusion, nuclear safety, nuclear waste management, superconductivity, microsystems technology, medical technology; 4,000 mems; library of 253,000 vols, 1,600 periodical titles, 587,000 reports; Chair. Prof. Dr MANFRED POPP; publs *FZKA-Berichte*, *Hausmitteilungen*, *Nachrichten*.

Fraunhofer-Institut für Bauphysik: POB 800469, Nobelstr. 12, 70504 Stuttgart; tel. (711) 970-00; fax (711) 970-3395; e-mail info@ibp.fraunhofer.de; internet www.ibp.fraunhofer.de; f. 1929; research, development, testing, demonstration and consulting in the field of building physics; noise control, sound insulation, optimization of audibility conditions in lecture halls, measures for energy economy, lighting technology, new building materials, indoor climate, weathering protection, hygrothermics; Dirs Prof. Dr GERD HAUSER, Prof. Dr KLAUS SEDLBAUER; publ. *IBP Report* (building physics research results).

Geologisch-Paläontologisches Institut und Museum, Universität Hamburg (Geological and Palaeontological Institute and Museum): Bundesstr. 55, 20146 Hamburg; tel. (40) 428384999; fax (40) 428384007; internet www.geowiss.uni-hamburg.de/i-geolo/start.html; f. 1907; 12 scientific mems; library of 80,000 vols; Di Prof. Dr CHRISTIAN BETZLER; publ. *Mitteilungen aus dem Geologisch-Paläontologischen Institut der Universität Hamburg* (annually).

Hahn-Meitner-Institut Berlin GmbH: Glienicker Str. 100, 14109 Berlin; tel. (30) 80620; fax (30) 80622181; e-mail postmaster@hmi.de; f. 1957; solid state physics, atomic and molecular structures, solar energy (photovoltaic); library of 61,000 vols, 415,000 reports; Dirs Prof. Dr MICHAEL STEINER BIRGIT M. DÜPPE; Librarian (vacant).

Hamburger Sternwarte (Hamburg Observatory): Gojenbergsweg 112, 21029 Hamburg; tel. (40) 42891-4112; fax (40) 42891-4198; e-mail sternwarte@hs.uni-hamburg.de; internet www.hs.uni-hamburg.de; f. 1833; cosmology, quasars, stellar physics, interstellar medium, astrometry; library of 62,000 vols; Di Prof. D. REIMERS.

Institute for Analytical Sciences (ISAS): Bunsen-Kirchhoff-Str. 11, 44139 Dortmund; tel. (231) 1392-0; fax (231) 1392-120; e-mail info@ansci.de; internet www.isas-dortmund.de; f. 1952 as Institute of Spectrochemistry and Applied Spectroscopy; various aspects of fundamental and applied analytical spectrochemistry; Dir Prof. Dr ANDREAS MANZ.

Institut für Astronomie und Astrophysik Tübingen: Sand 1, 72076 Tübingen,; tel. (7071) 2972486; fax (7071) 293458; internet astro.uni-tuebingen.de; f. 1949; attached to Faculty for Mathematics and Physics of Eberhart-Karls Universität Tübingen; UV- and X-ray astronomy, optical astronomy, stellar atmospheres; library of 13,100 vols; Head Prof. KLAUS WERNER; Sec. and Librarian HEIDRUN OBERNDÖRFFER; publ. *Yearly Report*.

Institut für Astrophysik Göttingen (Institute of Astrophysics, Göttingen): Friedrich-Hund-Pl. 1, 37077 Göttingen; tel. (551) 394037; fax (551) 395043; e-mail sekr@astro.physik.uni-goettingen.de; internet www.uni-sw.gwdg.de; f. 1750; galactic and extragalactic astrophysics, high-energy astrophysics, solar physics, stellar spectroscopy and theoretical astrophysics; houses a modern Cassegrain reflecting telescope with 50 cm-mirror diameter and 5m focal length; Exec. Dir Prof. Dr W. KOLLATSCHNY.

Institut für Umwelt- und Zukunftsforschung (IUZ) an der Sternwarte Bochum: Blankensteiner Str. 200A, 44797 Bochum; tel. (234) 47711; fax (234) 5798958; e-mail info@iuz-bochum.de; internet www.sternwarte-bochum.de; development and testing of electronic equipment for tracking and reception of satellite data, development of display and reproduction systems for satellite imagery, photo-interpretation of satellite imagery for geo-scientific and environmental studies; remote sensing; Dir THILO ELSNER.

Attached institution:

Sternwarte Bochum-Grossplanetarium: 44791 Bochum, Castroper Str. 67; tel. (234) 9103691.

Kiepenheuer-Institut für Sonnenphysik: Schöneckstr. 6, 79104 Freiburg im Breisgau; tel. (761) 3198-0; fax (761) 3198-111; e-mail secr@kis.uni-freiburg.de; internet www.kis.uni-freiburg.de; f. 1942; optical investigation of the solar atmosphere, observatory at Tenerife (Canary Islands); 57 mems; Dir Prof. Dr OSKAR VON DER LÜHE.

Landessternwarte auf dem Königstuhl bei Heidelberg: Königstuhl, 69117 Heidelberg; tel. (6221) 5417-00; fax (6221) 5417-02; e-mail postmaster@lsw.uni-heidelberg.de; internet www.lsw.uni-heidelberg.de; f. 1897; astronomical scientific research; 50 mems; library of 25,000 vols; Dir Prof. Dr A. QUIRRENBACH.

Remeis-Sternwarte (Remeis Observatory): Sternwartstr. 7, 96049 Bamberg; tel. (951) 952220; fax (951) 952222; f. 1889; stellar astrophysics; attached to Erlangen—Nürnberg University; Chairs Prof. Dr IRMELA BUES, Prof. Dr ULRICH HEBER.

Universitäts-Sternwarte–Institut für Astronomie und Astrophysik und Observatorium Wendelstein: Scheinerstr. 1, 81679 Munich; tel. (89) 21806001; fax (89) 21806003; internet www.usm.uni-muenchen.de; f. 1816; extragalactic astronomy, plasma astrophysics, stellar atmospheres, stellar evolution, cosmochemistry; library of 18,000 vols; Dir Prof. Dr MANFRED HIRT.

UWG Gesellschaft für Umwelt- und Wirtschaftsgeologie mbH: Wolfener 36 (Aufg. K), 12681 Berlin; tel. (30) 23144-684; fax (30) 23144-700; geoscientific and environmental library (books, data, photographs (remote sensing), maps); Dir Dr KLAUS ERLER.

PHILOSOPHY AND PSYCHOLOGY

Institut für Forensische Psychiatrie: Charité–Universitätsmedizin Berlin, Campus Benjamin Franklin, Limonenstr. 27, 12203 Berlin; tel. (30) 8445-1411; fax (30) 8445-1440; e-mail info@forensik-berlin.de; internet www.forensik-berlin.de; f. 1970; studies and research in forensic psychiatry and psychology; weekly interdisciplinary colloquium; annual forensic science conference; library of 21,257 vols, 61 current periodicals, 1,476 special prints, 104 videos; Dir Prof. Dr HANS-LUDWIG KRÖBER.

Institut für Gerichtspsychologie (IfG) (Institute of Forensic Psychology): Gilsingstr. 5, 44789 Bochum; tel. (234) 34091; internet www.gerichtspsychologie-bochum.de; f. 1951; carries out reports on behalf of the courts and solicitors; 41 mems; Dir Dr FRIEDRICH ARNTZEN.

Institut für Philosophie Humboldt-Universität (Institute of Philosophy at Humboldt University): Unter den Linden 6, 10099 Berlin; tel. (30) 2093-2204; fax (30) 2093-2419; internet www2.hu-berlin.de/phil; offers open lectures; Kant archive; Dir Prof. Dr DOMINIK PERLER.

Institut für Philosophie Universität Leipzig (Institute of Philosophy at Leipzig University): Beethovenstr. 15, 04107 Leipzig; tel. (341) 9735820; fax (341) 9735849; internet www.uni-leipzig.de/~philos; organises conferences and weekly colloquia; Dir Prof. Dr GEORG MEGGLE; publ. *Leipziger Schriften zur Philosophie*.

Institut für Rechtspsychologie Halle (Institute of Forensic Psychology, Halle): Kleine Marktstr. 5, 06108 Halle/Salle; tel. (345) 2033566; fax (345) 6784703; e-mail institut@rechtspsychologie-halle.de; internet www.rechtspsychologie-halle.de; f. 1997; carries out studies in forensic psychology for law courts; Man. BÄRBEL GOLDHAMMER.

RELIGION, SOCIOLOGY AND ANTHROPOLOGY

Arbeitsgemeinschaft Sozialwissenschaftlicher Institute eV (Association of Social Science Institutes): Lennéstr. 30, 53113 Bonn; tel. (228) 2281-0; fax (228) 2281-120; e-mail sl@bonn.iz-soz.de; internet www.gesis.org/asi; f. 1949 to promote research in social sciences; 100 mems; Pres. Prof. Dr HEINER MEULEMANN; Man. Dir MATTHIAS STAHL; publ. *Soziale Welt* (quarterly).

Bundesinstitut für Bevölkerungsforschung (Federal Institute for Population Research): Postfach 5528, Friedrich-Ebert-Allee 4, 65180 Wiesbaden; tel. (0611) 752235; fax (0611) 753960; e-mail bib@destatis.de; internet www.bib-demographie.de; f. 1973 to promote all fields of demographic research and co-ordinate research work undertaken by demographers, incl. those in foreign countries; attached to Statistisches Bundesamt; Dir Prof. Dr CHARLOTTE HÖHN; publs *Demographie: Zeitschrift für Bevölkerungswissenschaft* (quarterly), *Mitteilungen* (quarterly).

Forschungsgruppe für Anthropologie und Religionsgeschichte eV (Research Group for Anthropology and History of Religion): Droste-Hülshoff-Str. 9B, 48341 Altenberge; tel. and fax 2505-1347; e-mail ugarit@uni-muenster.de; internet www.ugarit-verlag.de; f. 1970; research and documentation refer to all fields of religion including interconnections with anthropology, psychology, culture and environment; methodology of research; international co-operation and exchange; Pres. Prof. Dr M. L. G. DIETRICH; publs *Mitteilungen für Anthropologie und Religionsgeschichte* (annually), *Forschungen zur Anthropologie und Religionsgeschichte* (3 a year).

Gesellschaft Sozialwissenschaftlicher Infrastruktureinrichtungen eV (German

Social Science Infrastructure Services): POB 410960, 50869 Cologne; tel. (221) 47694-0; fax (221) 47694-77; e-mail gesis@za.uni-koeln.de; internet www.gesis.org; f. 1986; infrastructural services on numerical data, information bases and research methods for social scientists; Chair Prof. Dr ILONA OSTNER; Dirs Prof. Dr WOLFGANG JAGODZINSKI, Prof. Dr JÜRGEN KRAUSE, EKKEHARD MOCHMANN, Prof. Dr PETER PH. MOHLER; publs *ZA Information* (2 a year), *ZUMA Nachrichten* (2 a year), *ZUMA Nachrichten Spezial* (irregular), *IZ Telegramm* (4 a year), *HSR Historical Social Research* (3 or 4 a year), *Informationsdienst Soziale Indikatoren* (2 a year), *Newsletter Sozialwissenschaften in Osteuropa* (4 a year).

Informationszentrum Sozialwissenschaften (Social Sciences Information Centre): Lennéstr. 30, 53113 Bonn; tel. (228) 22810; fax (228) 2281120; e-mail iz@bonn.iz-soz.de; internet www.gesis.org/iz; f. 1969; colln and dissemination of information in the social sciences; Scientific Dir Prof. Dr JÜRGEN KRAUSE; publ. *Sozialwissenschaftlicher Fachinformationsdienst* (2 a year).

TECHNOLOGY

Arbeitsgemeinschaft Industrieller Forschungsvereinigungen 'Otto von Guericke' eV (AiF): Bayenthalgürtel 23, 50968 Köln; tel. (221) 376800; fax (221) 3768027; e-mail info@aif.de; internet www.aif.de; f. 1954; promotion of co-operative research for small and medium-sized industry; Pres. JOHANN WILHELM ARNTZ; Dir-Gen. Dr-Ing. MICHAEL MAURER.

Bundesanstalt für Materialforschung und -prüfung (Federal Institute for Materials Research and Testing): Unter den Eichen 87, 12205 Berlin; tel. (30) 8104-0; fax (30) 8112029; e-mail info@bam.de; internet www.bam.de; f. 1871; analytical chemistry; reference materials, chemical safety engineering, containment systems for dangerous goods, materials and the environment, materials engineering, materials protection and surface technologies, safety of structures, non-destructive testing, accreditation, quality in testing; library of 80,000 vols; Pres. Prof. Dr rer. nat. MANFRED HENNECKE; publs *Amtsblatt* (4 a year), *Jahresbericht* (Annual Report).

Bundesforschungsanstalt für Ernährung und Lebensmittel (Federal Research Centre for Nutrition and Food): Haid-und-Neustr. 9, 76131 Karlsruhe; tel. (721) 6625-0; fax (721) 6625-111; e-mail komm-al@bfe.uni-karlsruhe.de; internet www.bfel.de; f. 2004; incorporates: Institute for Hygiene and Toxicology: Dir Prof. Dr W. HOLZAPFEL; Institute for Chemistry and Biology: Dir Prof. Dr B. TAUSCHER; Institute for Nutrition Physiology: Acting Head Dr. W. WATZE; Institute for Economics and Sociology of Nutrition: Dir Dr U. OLTERSDORF; Institute for Process Engineering: Dir (Acting) Dr N. HOFFMANN; Centre for Molecular Biology: Dir Prof. Dr K.-D. JANY; Information Centre: Dir Dr T. STORCK; 176 mems; library of 30,000 vols.

Clausthaler Umwelttechnik-Institut GmbH (Clausthal Institute of Environmental Technology): Leibnizstr. 21–23, 38678 Clausthal-Zellerfeld; tel. (5323) 933-0; fax (5323) 933-100; e-mail cutec@cutec.de; internet www.cutec.de; f. 1990; wholly owned by state of Lower Saxony; research into waste avoidance, recycling and disposal; Man. Dir Prof. Dr-Ing OTTO CARLOWITZ.

Deutsche Forschungsanstalt für Lebensmittelchemie (German Research Institute for Food Chemistry): Lichtenbergstr. 4, 85748 Garching; tel. (89) 28914170; fax (89) 28914183; e-mail lebensmittelchemie@lrz.tum.de; internet dfa.leb.chemie.tu-muenchen.de; f. 1918; library: *c.* 3,000 vols; Dir Prof. Dr PETER SCHIEBERLE; publ. *Annual Research Report*.

Deutsche Zentrum für Luft- und Raumfahrt eV (DLR) (German Aerospace Centre): Linder Höhe, 51147 Cologne; tel. (2203) 601-0; fax (2203) 67310; e-mail redaktion@dlr.de; internet www.dlr.de; f. 1969; flight mechanics, guidance and control, fluid mechanics, structures and materials, space flight, telecommunication technology and remote sensing, energetics; library of 400,000 vols; Chair. Prof. Dr SIGMAR WITTIG; publs *DLR-Forschungsberichte*, *DLR-Mitteilungen* (both irregular), *DLR-Nachrichten* (quarterly).

Deutsche Montan Technologie GmbH (DMT): Am Technologiepark 1, 45307 Essen; tel. (201) 172-01; fax (201) 172-1462; e-mail dmt-info@dmt.de; internet www.dmt.de; f. 1990; specialists in mining; Pres. Dr MICHAEL KOPPITZ.

Deutsches Textilforschungszentrum Nord-West eV: Öffentliche Prüfstelle (ÖP), Adlerstr. 1, 47798 Krefeld; tel. (2151) 843-0; fax (2151) 843143; e-mail oeffentliche.pruefstelle@dtnw.de; internet www.dtnw.de; f. 1990; 100 mems; Dir Prof. Dr ECKHARD SCHOLLMEYER.

Forschungsinstitut Edelmetalle und Metallchemie (Reasearch Institute of Precious Metals and Metals Chemistry): Katharinenstr. 17, 73525 Schwäbisch Gmünd; tel. (7171) 10060; fax (7171) 100654; e-mail fem@fem-online.de; internet www.fem-online.de; f. 1922; basic and applied research into precious metals science and technology, electrochemical deposition, corrosion, light metals surface technology, plasma surface technology, physical metallurgy, environmental technology and analyses; library: library; Dir Dr A. ZIELONKA.

Forschungsinstitut für Wärmeschutz eV München (Thermal Insulation, Testing, Research): Lochhamer Schlag 4, 82166 Gräfelfing; tel. (89) 858000; fax (89) 8580040; e-mail info@fiw-muenchen.de; fax www.fiw-muenchen.de; f. 1918; 140 mems; Scientific Dirs Dr rer. nat. ROLAND GELLERT, Dr-Ing. MARTIN ZEITLER, Dr-Ing. MARTIN SPITZNER; publ. *Mitteilungen aus dem FIW München* (irregular).

Fraunhofer-Institut für Verfahrenstechnik und Verpackung (Process Engineering and Packaging): Giggenhauser Str. 35, 85354 Freising; tel. (8161) 491-100; fax (8161) 491-111; internet www.ivv.fraunhofer.de; f. 1942; food processing, environmental technology, preservation and packaging, general packaging; library of 6,000 vols; Dir HORST-CHRISTIAN LANGOWSKI.

Gesellschaft für Schwerionenforschung (GSI), mbH: Planckstr. 1, 64291 Darmstadt; tel. (6159) 71-0; fax (6159) 71-2785; e-mail info@gsi.de; internet www.gsi.de; f. 1969; carries out basic research with heavy ions in nuclear physics and chemistry, solid state and atomic physics, radiation biology, tumour therapy with ion beams, etc; heavy ion linear accelerator, synchrotron, storage ring and laboratory; library of 3,000 vols; Scientific Dir Prof. Dr WALTER F. HENNING; Exec. Dir Dr ALEXANDER KURZ; publs *GSI-Nachrichten*, *GSI-Scientific Report* (annually).

Institut für Bauforschung eV (Building Research): An der Markuskirche 1, 30163 Hanover; tel. (511) 96516-0; fax (511) 96516-26; e-mail office@bauforschung.de; internet www.bauforschung.org; f. 1946; Dir Prof. Dr-Ing. MARTIN PFEIFFER.

Institut für Erdöl- und Erdgasforschung (German Petroleum Institute): Walther-Nernst-Str. 7, 38678 Clausthal-Zellerfeld; tel. (5323) 711100; fax (5323) 711200; e-mail postmaster@ife-clausthal.de; f. 1943; oil and gas recovery, reservoir engineering, refinery technology, research in petroleum products, hydrocarbons and environment; 53 mems; library of 5,000 vols; Dir Prof. Dr D. G. KESSEL; publ. *Research Report* (annually).

Institut für Textil- und Verfahrenstechnik: Körschtalstr. 26, 73770 Denkendorf; tel. (711) 9340-0; fax (711) 9340-297; e-mail itv@itv-denkendorf.de; internet www.itv-denkendorf.de; f. 1921; 165 staff; library of 2,500 vols; Dir Prof. Dr-Ing. HEINRICH PLANK.

Landesumweltamt Nordrhein Westfalen: Wallneyer Str. 6, 45133 Essen; tel. (201) 7995-0; fax (201) 7995-1446; e-mail poststelle@lua.nrw.de; internet www.lua.nrw.de; f. 1994; research and advice in the fields of air pollution and noise control; prevention of accidental releases; water, wastewater, groundwater and waste management; library of 100,000 vols, 450 current periodicals, 20,000 microfilms; Pres. Dr HARALD IRMER.

Lehr- und Forschungsgebiet Internationale Wirtschaftsbeziehungen (Chair of International Economics): Templergraben 64 (Sammelbau, 6th Fl.), 52056 Aachen; tel. and fax (241) 80693931; internet www.iw.rwth-aachen.de; f. 1957; 36 mems; library of 100,000 vols; Dir Prof. Dr OLIVER LORZ; publs *Aachener Beiträge zur Internationalen Zusammenarbeit*, *Internationale Kooperation*, *intertechnik*.

Physikalisch-Technische Bundesanstalt (Federal Institute of Physics and Metrology): Bundesallee 100, 38116 Brunswick; tel. (531) 5923006; fax (531) 5923008; e-mail presse@ptb.de; internet www.ptb.de; f. 1887; divisions for mechanics and acoustics, electricity, thermodynamics and explosion protection, optics, precision engineering, ionising radiation, temperature and synchrotron radiation, and medical physics and information technology; library of 125,000 vols; Pres. Prof. Dr E. O. GÖBEL; publs *Jahresbericht* (annual report), *Maßstäbe* (2 a year), *PTB-Mitteilungen* (every 2 months).

Staatliche Materialprüfungsanstalt Darmstadt–Fachgebiet und Institut für Werkstoffkunde (State Material-Testing Foundation-Faculty and Institute of Material Science): Grafenstr. 2, 64283 Darmstadt; tel. (6151) 162351; fax (6151) 166118; internet www.mpa-ifw.tu-darmstadt.de; f. 1927; attached to Technical University of Darmstadt; Dir Prof. Dr-Ing. C. BERGER.

Libraries and Archives

Aachen

Hochschulbibliothek der RWTH Aachen: Templergraben 61, 52056 Aachen; tel. (241) 80-94445; fax (241) 8092273; e-mail bth@bth.rwth-aachen.de; internet www.bth.rwth-aachen.de; f. 1870; 2,100,000 vols; Dir Dr ULRIKE EIKE.

Offentliche Bibliothek Aachen (Aachen Public Library): Couvenstr. 15, 52058 Aachen; tel. (241) 4791-0; fax (241) 408007; e-mail bibliothek@mail.aachen.de; internet oeffentliche-bibliothek.aachen.de; f. 1831; general information about Aachen and the region, regional history; 585,000 vols; spec. collns incl. folklore, ethnology, archaeology, organ literature; Dir REINHARD KRAUSE.

Amberg

Staatsarchiv Amberg: Archivstr. 3, 92224 Amberg; tel. (9621) 307270; fax (9621) 307288; e-mail poststelle@staam.bayern.de; f. 1437, became state archive in 1921; 2.7m. items in archives; 32,500 vols; Co-Dir Dr MARIA RITA SAGSTETTER; Co-Dir R. FRITSCH.

Augsburg

Staats- und Stadtbibliothek: Stadt Augsburg, 86143 Augsburg; located at:Schaezlerstr. 25, 86152 Augsburg; tel. (821) 3242739; fax (821) 3242732; e-mail bibliothek.stadt@augsburg.de; internet www.augsburg.de/sustb.html; f. 1537; 480,000 vols, 3,662 MSS, 2,798 incunabula, 16,250 drawings and engravings; Dir Dr HELMUT GIER.

Staatsarchiv Augsburg: Salomon-Idler-Str. 2, 86159 Augsburg; tel. (821) 59963-30; fax (821) 59963-333; e-mail poststelle@staau.bayern.de; internet www.gda.bayern.de/augsb00.htm; f. 1830 in Neuburg; 2.4m. items; Dir Dr PETER FLEISCHMANN.

Universitätsbibliothek: Universitätsstr. 22, 86159 Augsburg; tel. (821) 5985300; fax (821) 5985354; e-mail dir@bibliothek.uni-augsburg.de; internet www.bibliothek.uni-augsburg.de; f. 1970; 2,005,427 vols, 103,285 theses, 58,622 maps, 383,544 items of audio-visual material and microforms, 1,267 incunabula, 1,544 MSS, 2,295 music MSS; Dir Dr ULRICH HOHOFF.

Aurich

Niedersächsisches Staatsarchiv Aurich: Oldersumer Str. 50, 26603 Aurich; tel. (4941) 176660; fax (4941) 176673; e-mail Aurich@nla.niedersachsen.de; internet www.staatsarchiv-aurich.niedersachsen.de; f. 1872; 20,000 vols; Dir Dr BERNHARD PARISIUS.

Bamberg

Staatsarchiv Bamberg: Hainstr. 39, 96047 Bamberg; tel. (951) 986220; fax (951) 98622-50; e-mail poststelle@staba.bayern.de; internet www.gda.bayern.de; f. 13th c., became Bavarian state archive in 1803; 27,500 vols; special collections: Frankish history, maps, plans, MSS, documents; Dir Dr RAINER HAMBRECHT.

Staatsbibliothek Bamberg: Neue Residenz, Dompl. 8, 96049 Bamberg; tel. (951) 95503-0; fax (951) 95503-145; e-mail info@staatsbibliothek-bamberg.de; internet www.staatsbibliothek-bamberg.de; f. 1803; 470,000 vols, incl. spec. colln of 6,000 old manuscripts, 3,400 incunabula and 80,000 prints and drawings; Chief Librarian Prof. Dr WERNER TAEGERT.

Universitätsbibliothek: Postfach 2705, 96018 Bamberg; located at: Feldkirchenstr. 21, 96052 Bamberg; tel. (951) 8631501; fax (951) 8631565; e-mail unibibliothek.bamberg@unibib.uni-bamberg.de; internet www.uni-bamberg.de/service_einrichtungen/unibib; f. 1973; 1,664,310 vols on theology, humanities and social sciences; Dir Dr FABIAN FRANKE; publ. *Schriften der Universitätsbibliothek Bamberg*.

Bayreuth

Universitätsbibliothek: Universitätsgelände, 95440 Bayreuth; tel. (921) 553420; fax (921) 553442; e-mail detlev.gassong@ub.uni-bayreuth.de; internet www.ub.uni-bayreuth.de; f. 1973 to serve the university and the public; 1,590,000 vols; Dir Dr KARL BABL.

Berlin

Akademiebibliothek der Berlin-Brandenburgischen Akademie der Wissenschaften: Unter den Linden 8, 10117 Berlin; tel. (30) 2661921; fax (30) 2082367; e-mail bibliothek@bbaw.de; internet bibliothek.bbaw.de; f. 1700; 650,000 vols, 890 periodicals; special collection of the publications of academies and learned societies; Dir HEIKE ANDERMANN.

Auswärtiges Amt, Referat Bibliothek und Informationsvermittlung: Werderscher Markt 1, 10117 Berlin; tel. (30) 172202; fax (30) 1752202; e-mail 116-s@auswaertiges-amt.de; 281,000 vols, 2,900 periodicals, 90,000 maps; Dir Dr WOLFGANG MOSER.

Bibliothek für Bildungsgeschichtliche Forschung: Postfach 171138, 10203 Berlin; premises at: 10243 Berlin, Warschauer Str. 34–38; tel. (30) 293360-0; fax (30) 293360-25; e-mail ritzi@bbf.dipf.de; internet www.bbf.dipf.de; f. 1876; holds conferences and exhibitions; 700,000 vols; Dir Dr CHRISTIAN RITZI; publs *Bestandsverzeichnisse zur Bildungsgeschichte* (directory of publications on the history of education, series), *Bibliographie Bildungsgeschichte* (history of education bibliography, annually), *Jahrbuch für Historische Bildungsforschung* (yearbook of education research history, annually), *Neuerwerbungsverzeichnis* (list of new acquisitions, monthly), *Tagungsbände* (conference papers), *Quellen und Dokumente zur Alltagsgeschichte der Erziehung* (sources and documents on the everyday history of education, series).

Bibliothek des Deutschen Bundestages: Pl. der Republik 1, 11011 Berlin; tel. (30) 22732626; fax (30) 22733073; e-mail bibliothek@bundestag.de; internet www.bundestag.de/htdocs_e/info/library; f. 1949; 1,300,000 vols, 9,000 periodicals, 38,000 maps; spec. collns of German and foreign official publs and parliamentary papers; depository library of 10 int. orgs; Dir URSULA FREYSCHMIDT; publs *Neue Bücher*, *Neue Aufsätze*, *Literaturtipps* (on topical economic and political subjects), *Schnellinformationen*.

Geheimes Staatsarchiv Preussischer Kulturbesitz (Secret Central Archives of the Prussian Cultural Possession): Dahlem, Archivstr. 12–14, 14195 Berlin; tel. (30) 83901-139; fax (30) 83901-180; e-mail gsta.pk@gsta.spk-berlin.de; internet www.gsta.spk-berlin.de; f. 1598; material and research on history of Prussia and the former Prussian territories from since 12th c.; 185,000 vols, 2,000 periodicals, 650,000 records and files, 120,000 maps; Dir Prof. Dr JÜRGEN KLOOSTERHUIS; publ. *Veröffentlichungen* (2–3 a year).

Ibero-Amerikanisches Institut Preussischer Kulturbesitz: Potsdamer Str. 37, 10785 Berlin; tel. (30) 2662500; fax (30) 2662503; e-mail iai@iai.spk-berlin.de; internet www.iai.spk-berlin.de; f. 1930; research institute and library dedicated to Latin America, Spain and Portugal; 800,000 vols, 4,500 current periodicals; Dir Dr BARBARA GÖBEL; publs *Bibliotheca Ibero-Americana*, *Biblioteca Luso-Brasileira*, *Iberoamericana*, *Indiana*, *Miscellanea Ibero-Americana*, *Monumenta Americana*, *Quellenwerke zur alten Geschichte Amerikas*, *Stimmen Indianischer Völker*.

Kunstbibliothek Staatliche Museen zu Berlin: Matthäikirchplatz 6, 10785 Berlin; tel. (30) 2662029; fax (30) 2662958; e-mail kb@smb.spk-berlin.de; internet www.smb.spk-berlin.de/kb; f. 1867; 400,000 vols; special collections: ornamental and architectural books, Lipperheidesche Kostumbibliothek, artists' books, posters, photographs, graphic design, drawings; Dir Prof. Dr BERND EVERS.

Landesarchiv Berlin (Berlin Regional Archive): Eichborndamm 115–121, 13403 Berlin; tel. (30) 90264-0; fax (30) 90264-250; e-mail info@landesarchiv-berlin.de; internet www.landesarchiv-berlin.de; f. 1948; legal documents, etc. for the Berlin area, and important material on the history of Berlin; 76,000 vols and 5,200 film rolls; Administrator MANFRED VELLGUTH.

Politisches Archiv des Auswärtigen Amts (Political Archive of the Foreign Office): Werderscher Markt 1, 10117 Berlin; tel. (30) 5000-0; fax (30) 5000-3402; e-mail 117-R@diplo.de; internet www.auswaertiges-amt.de/www/de/infoservice/politik/index_html; f. 1920; Foreign Office archives; documents since 1867; archives of former Foreign Ministry of the German Democratic Republic; Dir H. J. PRETSCH; publs *Akten zur auswärtigen Politik der Bundesrepublik Deutschland seit 1949* (series), *Akten zur deutschen auswärtigen Politik 1918–1945* (series).

Senatsbibliothek Berlin: Str. des 17 Juni 112, 10623 Berlin; tel. (30) 39987-324; fax (30) 39987-322; e-mail auskunft@senatsbibliothek.de; internet www.senatsbibliothek.de; f. 1949; central government library of Berlin and special library for urban and land planning and regional research; 501,034 vols, 892 periodicals; Dir MARION HECKER.

Staatsbibliothek zu Berlin–Preussischer Kulturbesitz: Unter den Linden 8, 10117 Berlin; also: 10785 Berlin, Potsdamer Str. 33 (Tiergarten); tel. (30) 266-0; tel. (30) 266-0; fax (30) 2015-1751; e-mail generaldir@sbb.spk-berlin.de; internet www.staatsbibliothek-berlin.de; f. 1661; 10,500,000 vols, 38,000 current periodicals and newspapers, 18,200 occidental MSS, 66,200 musical MSS, 439,000 music prints, 923,000 maps, 4,300 incunabula, 98,000 autographs, 12,400,000 pictures, 2m. microforms; Mendelssohn archive; Gen. Dir BARBARA SCHNEIDER-KEMPF; publs *Jahresbericht* (Annual Report), *Yearbook*.

Universitätsbibliothek der Freien Universität Berlin: Garystr. 39, 14195 Berlin; tel. 83854224; fax 83853738; e-mail auskunft@ub.fu-berlin.de; internet www.ub.fu-berlin.de; f. 1952; 2,200,000 vols, 2,800 periodicals, 12,000 e-journals, 429,000 theses; 6,600,000 vols in departmental libraries; Dir Prof. Dr rer. pol. ULRICH NAUMANN; publ. *Universitätsbibliographie*.

Universitätsbibliothek der Humboldt-Universität zu Berlin (University Library of Humboldt University, Berlin Branch): Hessische Str. 1–2, 10115 Berlin; tel. (30) 20933212; fax (30) 20933207; e-mail info@ub.hu-berlin.de; internet www.ub.hu-berlin.de; f. 1831; 6,000,000 vols, 10,000 current periodicals; Dir Dr MILAN BULATY; publ. *Schriftenreihe*.

Universitätsbibliothek der Technischen Universität Berlin: Universitätsbibliothek Fasanenstr. 88, im Volkswagen-Haus, 10623 Berlin; tel. (30) 31476101; fax (30) 31476104; e-mail info@ub.tu-berlin.de; internet www.ub.tu-berlin.de; f. 1879; 1,808,500 vols, 5,814 periodicals, 1,019 e-journals, 69,000 architectural drawings, complete German standards; Dir Dr W. ZICK.

Zentral- und Landesbibliothek Berlin (Berlin Central and Provincial Library): Breite Str. 30–36, 10178 Berlin; tel. (30) 90226-401; fax (30) 90226-163; e-mail info@zlb.de; internet www.zlb.de; f. 1901; central public library of Berlin; 3,200,000 vols, in print and online; Dir Dr CLAUDIA LUX.

Bochum

Stadtbücherei Bochum: Willy-Brandt-Pl. 2–6, 44777 Bochum; tel. (234) 910-2481; fax (234) 910-2437; e-mail stadtbue@bochum.de;

internet www.bochum.de/stadtbuecherei; f. 1905; 480,000 vols; Dir I. Mämecke.

Universitätsbibliothek: 44780 Bochum; tel. (234) 3222350; fax (234) 3214736; e-mail direktion-ub@ruhr-uni-bochum.de; internet www.ub.ruhr-uni-bochum.de; f. 1962; 1,942,000 vols, 371,000 theses; Dir Dr E. Lapp.

Bonn

Archiv der sozialen Demokratie (Friedrich-Ebert-Stiftung) (Archive of Social Democracy—Friedrich Ebert Foundation): Godesberger Allee 149, 53175 Bonn; tel. (228) 883-0; fax (228) 883-497; e-mail archiv.auskunft@fes.de; internet www.fes.de; f. 1969; contains material relating to the Sozialdemokratische Partei Deutschlands (SPD) and the German trade unions; history of German and international social movement, labour movement, labour problems; 600,000 vols, 3,000 periodicals; Dir of the Archive of Social Democracy Prof. Dr Michael Schneider; Dir of the Library of the Friedrich-Ebert-Foundation Dr Rüdiger Zimmermann.

Beethoven-Archiv (Beethoven Archive): Bonngasse 18–26, 53111 Bonn; tel. (228) 98175-0; fax (228) 98175-31; e-mail info@beethoven-haus-bonn.de; internet www.beethoven-haus-bonn.de; f. 1927; books, periodicals, documents on the work, life and times of Ludwig van Beethoven (1770–1827); Dir Dr Ernst Herttrich.

Bibliothek der Hochschulrektorenkonferenz (Library of the University Rectors' Conference): Ahrstr. 39, 53175 Bonn; tel. (228) 887-159; fax (228) 887-110; e-mail bibliothek@hrk.de; internet www.hrk.de/de/berichte_und_publikationen/130.php; f. 1954 (Westdeutsche Rektorenkonferenz); 67,000 vols, 800 periodicals, 95,000 records and acts; Head Dr Ulrich Meyer-Doerpinghaus.

Bibliothek der Hochschulrektorenkonferenz (Library of the University Rectors' Conference): Ahrstr. 39, 53175 Bonn; tel. (228) 887-159; fax (228) 887-110; e-mail bibliothek@hrk.de; internet www.hrk.de/de/berichte_und_publikationen/130.php; f. 1954 (Westdeutsche Rektorenkonferenz); 67,000 vols, 800 periodicals, 95,000 records and acts; Head Dr Ulrich Meyer-Doerpinghaus.

Bundesamts für Bauwesen und Raumordnung, Wissenschaftliche Bibliothek: Postfach 210150, 53156 Bonn; tel. (1888) 4012281; fax (1888) 4012249; e-mail karin.goebel@bbr.bund.de; internet www.bbr.bund.de; f. 1941; 150,000 vols, 450 periodicals; Dir Dr phil. Klaus Schliebe; publs *Informationen zur Raumentwicklung* (12 a year), *Raumforschung und Raumordnung* (5 or 6 issues a year), *Forschungen* (series, irregular), *Werkstatt: Praxis* (series, irregular).

Stadtarchiv und Stadthistorische Bibliothek Bonn (Bonn City Archive and Historical Library): Berliner Platz 2, 53103 Bonn; tel. (228) 772410; fax (228) 774301; e-mail stadtarchiv@bonn.de; internet www.archive.nrw.de/home.asp?stadta-bonn; f. 1899; 126,160 vols; Archivist and Librarian Dr Norbert Schlossmacher; publs *Bonner Geschichtsblätter* (annually), *Studien zur Heimatgeschichte des Stadtbezirkes Bonn-Beuel*, *Veröffentlichungen des Stadtarchivs Bonn*.

Universitäts- und Landesbibliothek: Postfach 2460, 53014 Bonn; located at: Adenauerallee 39–41, 53113 Bonn; tel. (228) 737350; fax (228) 737546; e-mail ulb@ulb.uni-bonn.de; internet www.ulb.uni-bonn.de; f. 1818; 1,975,000 vols, 130,000 micro materials, 6,800 current periodicals; Dir Dr Renate Vogt.

Bremen

Bibliothek/Informationszentrum des Instituts für Seeverkehrswirtschaft und Logistik (ISL): Universitätsallee GW1 Block A, 28359 Bremen; tel. (421) 22096-44; fax (421) 22096-55; e-mail infocenter@isl.org; internet www.isl.org; f. 1954; centre for maritime information and documentation offering professional services about industries, markets and companies within the areas of maritime industries, transport and logistics; 125,000 vols; Head Brigitte Ogiolda.

Staats- und Universitätsbibliothek: Postfach 330160, 28331 Bremen; tel. (421) 2182601; fax (421) 2182614; e-mail suub@uni-bremen.de; internet www.suub.uni-bremen.de; f. 1660; 3,100,000 vols, 8,800 current print periodicals, 3,900 online periodicals; Dir (vacant); publ. *Jahresbibliographie Massenkommunikation*.

Staatsarchiv: Am Staatsarchiv 1, 28203 Bremen; tel. (421) 361-6221; fax (421) 361-10247; e-mail zentrale@staatsarchiv.bremen.de; internet www.staatsarchiv-bremen.de; f. 1727; Dir Dr Konrad Elmshäuser (acting); publ. *Bremisches Jahrbuch*.

Brunswick

Bibliothek der Biologischen Bundesanstalt für Land- und Forstwirtschaft (Library of the Federal Biological Agency for Land and Forestry Economics): Messeweg 11/12, 38104 Braunschweig; tel. (531) 299-3397; fax (531) 299-3018; e-mail Bibliothek@bba.de; internet www.bba.de; f. 1950; plant protection and related fields; 59,000 vols, 1,200 periodicals, 44,000 reprints, 2,200 microfilms; Head A. Badke; publs *Amtliche Pflanzenschutzbestimmungen* (irregular), *BBA-Bekanntmachungen* (irregular), *Berichte aus der Biologischen Bundesanstalt für Land- und Forstwirtschaft*, *Nachrichtenblatt des Deutschen Pflanzenschutzdienstes* (monthly), *Pflanzenschutzmittel-Verzeichnis* (annually).

Stadtarchiv (City Archive): Löwenwall 18b, 38100 Braunschweig; tel. (531) 470-4711; fax (531) 470-4725; e-mail stadtarchiv@braunschweig.de; internet www.braunschweig.de/rat_verwaltung/verwaltung/fb41_4; f. 1860; 125,000 documents since 1031, municipal records, charters, maps and plans since 1228, special collections on the history of the town; special historical archive on prominent Brunswick women; Dir (vacant).

Universitätsbibliothek Braunschweig: Pockelsstr. 13, 38106 Braunschweig; tel. (531) 391-5018; fax (531) 391-5836; e-mail ub@tu-bs.de; internet www.biblio.tu-bs.de; f. 1748; 22,000 mems; 1,360,000 vols, 2,595 periodicals, 18,800 online journals, 120,000 standards, 168,000 dissertations; 48,000 microfiches; areas of specialization include: pharmacy (virtual library), DFG-Sondersammelgebiet, 15th–19th c. technology and natural history, children's books since 16th c., archive library of 6 publishing houses; Dir Prof Dr Dietmar Brandes.

Wissenschaftliche Stadtbibliothek: Steintorwall 15, 38100 Braunschweig; tel. (531) 470-4601; fax (531) 470-4640; e-mail stadtbibliothek@braunschweig.de; internet www.staedtische-bibliotheken.braunschweig.de; f. 1861; 370,000 vols, medieval MSS, 426 incunabula, 2,500 maps and plans up to 1850; special collection on the history of the town; Dir Dr Anette Haucap-Nass; publs *Braunschweiger Werkstücke*, *Kleine Schriften* (irregular).

Bückeburg

Niedersächsisches Landesarchiv, Staatsarchiv Bückeburg: Schloss, 31675 Bückeburg; tel. (5722) 9677-30; fax (5722) 1289; e-mail bueckeburg@nla.niedersachsen.de; internet www.staatsarchiv-bueckeburg.niedersachsen.de; f. 1961; archives of the old county, later principality, of Schaumburg-Lippe and the district of Schaumburg; central workshops for restoration and security filming for Lower Saxony; 4,000 documents, 35,000 vols, 20,000 maps; Dir Dr Hubert Höing; publs *Schaumburger Studien*, *Inventare und kleinere Schriften des Staatsarchivs Bückeburg*.

Chemnitz

Stadtbibliothek (City Library): Moritzstr. 20, 09111 Chemnitz; tel. (371) 4884222; fax (371) 4884299; e-mail info@stadtbibliothek-chemnitz.de; internet www.stadtbibliothek-chemnitz.de; f. 1869; 500,000 vols; special collection of literature on local government; Dir Elke Beer.

Universitätsbibliothek: Str. der Nationen 62, 09107 Chemnitz; tel. (371) 5311283; fax (371) 5311569; e-mail sekretariat@bibliothek.tu-chemnitz.de; internet www.bibliothek.tu-chemnitz.de; f. 1836; 1,185,000 vols, 97,000 theses, 2,580 periodicals, 12,068,000 patents; Dir Ingrid Thümer.

Clausthal-Zellerfeld

Universitätsbibliothek der Technischen Universität Clausthal (Library of the Technical University of Clausthal): Leibnizstr. 2, 38678 Clausthal-Zellerfeld; tel. (5323) 722301; fax (5323) 723639; e-mail ubclz@tu-clausthal.de; internet bibliothek.tu-clausthal.de; f. 1810; 459,000 vols, 805 periodicals, 5,000 geological maps; Dir Dr J. Schüling.

Coburg

Landesbibliothek (State Library): Schlosspl. 1, 96450 Coburg; tel. (9561) 8538-0; fax (9561) 8538-201; e-mail lco@bib-bvb.de; internet www.bib-bvb.de/landesbibliothek/home.htm; f. *c.*1550; 400,000 vols, 600 periodicals; Dir Dr Silvia Pfister.

Staatsarchiv Coburg (State Archive of Coburg): Herrngasse 11, 96450 Coburg; tel. (9561) 427070; fax (9561) 4270720; e-mail poststelle@staco.bayern.de; internet www.gda.bayern.de/cobix.htm; f. 13th c.; present title 1939; archives of the duchy and republic of Saxe-Coburg, since 1920 the rural district of Coburg; 295,000 documents; 8,000 vols; Dir Dr Stefan Nöth.

Cologne

Deutsche Zentralbibliothek für Medizin (German National Library of Medicine): Gleueler Str. 60, 50931 Cologne; tel. (221) 4785600; fax (221) 4785697; e-mail info@zbmed.de; internet www.zbmed.de; f. 1908; 1,300,000 vols and microforms, 8,000 current periodicals; virtual library in medicine (www.medpilot.de) and open access journal in medicine (www.egms.de); offers document delivery by post, fax and e-mail; Dir U. Korwitz.

Erzbischöfliche Diözesan- und Dombibliothek (Archbishop's Diocesean and Cathedral Library): Postfach 10-11-45, 50451 Cologne; located at: Kardinal-Frings-Str. 1–3, 50668 Cologne; tel. (221) 16423781; fax (221) 16423783; e-mail dombibliothek@erzbistum-koeln.de; internet www.dombibliothek-koeln.de; f. 1738; 446,000 vols; Dirs Prof. Dr Heinz Finger, K. Gross, Prof. Dr Siegfried Schmidt.

Historisches Archiv: Severinstr. 222–228, 50676 Cologne; tel. (221) 221-22327; fax (221)

221-22480; e-mail historichesarchiv@stadt-koeln.de; internet www.stadt-koeln.de/kulturstadt/historischesarchiv; f. 1322; records since 875 AD; 43,000 vols; Dir BETTINA SCHMIDT-CZAIA; publ. *Mitteilungen*.

Kunst- und Museumsbibliothek der Stadt Köln: Kattenbug 18–24, 50667 Cologne; tel. (221) 221-22388; fax (221) 221-22210; e-mail kmb@stadt-koeln.de; internet www.museenkoeln.de/kmb; f. 1957; 370,000 vols; Curator Dr E. PURPUS.

Rheinisches Archiv- und Museumsamt, Abteilung Archivberatung (Archive and Museums Office of the Rheinland, Department of Archive Services): Ehrenfriedstr. 19, 50259 Pulheim; tel. (2234) 98540; fax (2234) 9854285; e-mail rama@lvr.de; internet www.archivberatung.lvr.de; f. 1929; archive of the Landschaftsverband Rheinland with sources of the last 200 years; collections relating to local history; 16,500 vols; Dir Dr NORBERT KÜHN; publs *Archivhefte* (archival science in Rheinland), *Inventare nichtstaatlicher Archive* (inventories of non-state archives in Rheinland), *Rheinprovinz* (regional history of Rheinland).

Stiftung Rheinisch-Westfälisches Wirtschaftsarchiv zu Köln: Unter Sachsenhausen 10–26, 50667 Cologne; tel. (221) 1640-800; fax (221) 1640-829; e-mail rwwa@koeln.lhk.de; f. 1906; economic records of the region; research and publication of research results; lending and reference library of business documents; 35,000 vols; Dir Dr ULRICH S. SOÉNIUS; publ. *Schriften zur rheinisch-westfälischen Wirtschaftsgeschichte*.

Universitäts- und Stadtbibliothek: Universitätsstr. 33, 50931 Cologne; tel. (221) 4702260; fax (221) 4705166; e-mail sekretariat@ub.uni-koeln.de; internet www.ub.uni-koeln.de; f. 1920; 3,200,000 vols; Dir Prof. Dr W. SCHMITZ.

Darmstadt

Hessisches Staatsarchiv (State Archive of Hesse): Karolinenplatz 3, 64289 Darmstadt; tel. (6151) 165900; fax (6151) 165901; e-mail poststelle@stad.hessen.de; internet www.staatsarchiv-darmstadt.hessen.de; f. 1567; Dir Prof. Dr FRIEDRICH BATTENBERG; publs *Darmstädter Archivdokumente für den Unterricht*, *Darmstädter Archivenschriften*, *Geschichte im Archiv*.

Universitäts- und Landesbibliothek Darmstadt: Schloss, 64283 Darmstadt; tel. (6151) 165850; fax (6151) 165897; e-mail info@ulb.tu-darmstadt.de; internet www.ulb.tu-darmstadt.de; f. 1560; 1,900,000 vols, 4,090 MSS, 2,050 incunabula, 15,000 musicalia, 28,000 maps, 4,600,000 German and European patent documents; Dir Dr HANS-GEORG NOLTE-FISCHER.

Dessau

Anhaltische Landesbücherei Dessau: Zerbster Str. 10/35, 06844 Dessau; tel. (340) 213264; fax (340) 212501; e-mail bibliothek@dessau.de; internet www.bibliothek.dessau.de; f. 1898; 254,815 vols, 133 incunabula, 599 MSS, 342 current periodicals; Dir GABRIELE SCHNEIDER.

Detmold

Landesarchiv Nordrhein-Westfalen-Staats- und Personenstandarchiv Detmold: Willi-Hofmann-Str. 2, 32756 Detmold; tel. (5231) 7660; fax (5231) 766114; e-mail stadt@lav.nrw.de; internet www.archive.nrw.de; f. 1957 (formerly Lippisches Landesarchiv, f. 16th century); archives of former regions of Lippe (12th c. to 1947) and Minden (1815 to 1947), Dominion of Vianen (Netherlands), Detmold (since 1947); special collections: genealogy, French Citizens' Registers, Parish Registers, Jewish and Dissenters' Registers of Westphalia (1808 to 1874); copies of registers of births, deaths and marriages (1874–1938); 72,000 vols; Dir Dr JUTTA PRIEUR-POHL.

Lippische Landesbibliothek Detmold: Hornsche Str. 41, 32756 Detmold; tel. (5231) 926600; fax (5231) 92660-55; e-mail llbmail@llb-detmold.de; internet www.llb-detmold.de; f. 1614; 440,000 vols, 7,000 MSS; Dir DETLEV HELLFAIER.

Dortmund

Stadt- und Landesbibliothek Dortmund: Königswall 18, 44137 Dortmund; tel. (231) 50-23225; fax (231) 50-23199; e-mail stlb@stadtdo.de; internet www.stlb-dortmund.de; f. 1907; 1,200,000 vols; special collection of MSS and autographs and material on Westphalia; music dept; Dir ULRICH MOESKE; publs *Mitteilungen aus dem Literaturarchiv Kulturpreis der Stadt Dortmund* (every 2 years), *Mitteilungen* (irregular), *Autographeausstellungen* (irregular).

Stiftung Westfälisches Wirtschaftsarchiv (WWA) (Foundation of the Westfalian Economic Archive): Märkische Str. 120, 44141 Dortmund; tel. (231) 5417296; fax (231) 5417117; e-mail wwado@dortmund.ihk.de; internet www.archive.nrw.de; f. 1941; records of the economic, social and industrial history of Westphalia and the Ruhr; research; 4,000 shelf-metres of records; 50,000 vols; Dir Dr KARL-PETER ELLERBROCK.

Universitätsbibliothek Dortmund: Vogelpothsweg 76, 44227 Dortmund; tel. (231) 755-4001; fax (231) 755-4032; e-mail information@ub.uni-dortmund.de; internet www.ub.uni-dortmund.de; f. 1965; 1,700,000 vols, 7,500,000 patents; Dir MARLENE NAGELSMEIER-LINKE.

Dresden

Sächsische Landesbibliothek–Staats- und Universitätsbibliothek Dresden: Zellescher Weg 18, 01069 Dresden; tel. (351) 4677-379; fax (351) 4677-723; e-mail infverm@slub-dresden.de; internet www.slub-dresden.de; f. 1996; 4,101,000 vols, 147,000 theses, 131,000 maps, 178,000 tapes and records, 2,000,000 photographs, 131,000 standards, 12,850 current periodicals; Dir-Gen. (vacant) THOMAS BÜRGER; publs *Bibliographie Geschichte der Technik* (annually), *Sächsische Bibliographie* (annually), *SLUB-Kurier* (4 a year).

Sächsisches Hauptstaatsarchiv: Postfach 100 444, 01074 Dresden; premises at: 01097 Dresden, Archivstr. 14; tel. (351) 80060; fax (351) 802127; e-mail poststelle-d@sta.smi.sachsen.de; internet www.sachsen.de/de/bf/verwaltung/archivverwaltung; f. 1834; 71,000 vols; Dir Dr JÜRGEN RAINER WOLF; publs *Schriftenreihe des Sächsischen Hauptstaatsarchivs* (13 vols), *Einzelveröffentlichungen*.

Städtische Bibliotheken Dresden (City Libraries of Dresden): Freibergerstr. 33, 01067 Dresden; tel. (351) 8648101; fax (351) 8648102; e-mail mail@bibo-dresden.de; internet www.bibo-dresden.de; f. 1910; 751,490 vols; Dir Dr AREND FLEMMING.

Duisburg

Stadtarchiv Duisburg (City Archives of Duisburg): Karmelplatz 5 (Am Innenhafen), 47049 Duisburg; tel. (203) 283-2154; fax (203) 283-4330; e-mail stadtarchiv@stadt-duisburg.de; internet www.archive.nrw.de; f. 12th c.; administration, research into local and city history; reference library on local history and customs of Duisburg and Lower Rhine; 35,000 vols; Dir Dr HANS GEORG KRAUME; publs *Duisburger Forschungen*, *Duisburger Geschichtsquellen*.

Stadtbibliothek (City Library): Düsseldorfer Str. 5–7, 47049 Duisburg; tel. (203) 283-4218; fax (203) 283-4294; e-mail stadtbibliothek@stadt-duisburg.de; internet www.stadtbibliothek-duisburg.de; f. 1901; public library of 905,000 vols, 1300 periodicals; Dir Dr JAN-PIETER BARBIAN.

Düsseldorf

Bibliotek des Heinrich-Heine-Instituts (Heinrich Heine Institute Library): Bilker Str. 12–14, 40213 Düsseldorf; tel. (211) 8995574; fax (211) 8929044; e-mail heineinstitut@duesseldorf.de; internet www.duesseldorf.de/heineinstitut; f. 1970; 30,000 vols, 300 manuscripts, 35,000 autographs since the 18th c.; 130 bequests of literature, music, art and science and a special colln relating to the poet Heinrich Heine (1797–1856); Dir Prof. Dr J. A. KRUSE; publs *Archiv–Bibliothek–Museum* (4 a year), *Heine-Jahrbuch*, *Heine-Studien*.

Landesarchiv Nordrhein-Westfalen: Graf-Adolf-Str. 67, 40210 Düsseldorf; tel. (211) 159238-0; fax (211) 159238-111; e-mail poststelle@lav.nrw.de; internet www.lav.nrw.de; f. 2004; consists of Hauptstaatsarchiv Düsseldorf (f. 1832), the Staatsarchiv Münster (f. 1829), the Staats- und Personenstandsarchiv Detmold (f. 1955) and the Personenstandsarchiv Brühl (f. 1955); Pres. Prof. Dr WILFRIED REININGSHAUS; publ. *Der Archivar: Mitteilungsblatt für deutsches Archivwesen* (quarterly).

Universitäts- und Landesbibliothek Düsseldorf (University and State Library of Düsseldorf): Universitätsstr. 1, 40225 Düsseldorf; tel. (211) 81-12030; fax (211) 81-13054; e-mail ulb@ub.uni-duesseldorf.de; internet www.ub.uni-duesseldorf.de/home; f. 1970; 2,400,000 vols, 8,281 periodicals; Dir Dr IRMGARD SIEBERT.

Eichstätt

Universitätsbibliothek Eichstätt-Ingolstadt (University Library of Eichstätt-Ingolstadt): Universitätsallee 1, 85072 Eichstätt; tel. (8421) 93-1330; fax (8421) 93-1791; e-mail ub-direktion@ku-eichstaett.de; internet www.ku-eichstaett.de/Bibliothek.de; f. 16th c.; developed from former Library of Diocesan Seminary and State Library; special collections: theology, archives of Assn of German Catholic Press and of Assn of Catholic publishers and booksellers, Schlecht music library and MSS, Glossner Oriental and Judaistic library, German Institute of Pedagogics library, archives and library of the Inklings Society; 1,872,838 vols, 362,861 units of non-book materials, 2,424 MSS, 3,147 musical MSS, 1,094 incunabula, 3,282 periodicals; Dir Dr ANGELIKA REICH; publs *Aus den Beständen der Universitätsbibliothek Eichstätt*, *Bibliographien der Universitätsbibliothek Eichstätt*, *Kataloge der Universitätsbibliothek Eichstätt*, *Schriften der Universitätsbibliothek Eichstätt*.

Erfurt

Stadt- und Regionalbibliothek Erfurt: Postfach 100553, 99005 Erfurt; premises at: 99084 Erfurt, Domplatz 1; tel. (361) 6551590; fax (361) 6551599; internet www.erfurt.de; f. 1392; 547,739 vols (349,809 vols in scientific special collections), 471 periodicals; Dir HEIDEMARIE TRENKMANN.

Erlangen

Universitätsbibliothek Erlangen-Nürnberg (University Library of Erlangen-Nuremberg): Universitätsstr. 4, 91054 Erlangen; tel. (9131) 8523950; fax (9131) 8529309;

e-mail direktion@bib.uni-erlangen.de; internet www.ub.uni-erlangen.de; f. 1743; special collections on education, science and philosophy; 4,800,000 vols, 870,000 theses, 2,432 MSS, 140 papyri, 2,136 incunabula; Dir Dr H.-O. KEUNECKE.

Frankfurt am Main

Bibliothek des Freien Deutschen Hochstifts (Library of the Free German Literature Institute): Frankfurter Goethe-Museum, Grosser Hirschgraben 23–25, 60311 Frankfurt am Main; tel. (69) 13880-0; fax (69) 13880-222; e-mail info@goethehaus-frankfurt.de; internet www.goethehaus-frankfurt.de; f. 1859; 120,000 vols, 40,000 MSS and handwritten letters; 500 paintings and 16,000 prints on public display in the graphic art collection; Dir Dr CARL VON BOEHM-BEZING.

Deutsche Nationalbibliothek: Adickesallee 1, 60322 Frankfurt am Main; tel. (69) 15250; fax (69) 15251010; e-mail info-f@d-nb.de; internet www.d-nb.de; Deutsche Bibliothek (Frankfurt) and Deutsche Bücherei (Leipzig) unified 1990; acts as deposit library for Germany since 1913 and functions as national library and bibliographic information centre; special collections: Reichsbibliothek 1848, German exile literature 1933–1945, Anne-Frank-Shoah-Bibliothek; Dir-Gen. Dr ELISABETH NIGGEMANN; publ. *Deutsche Nationalbibliografie* (weekly, half-yearly and three-yearly issues).

Constituent libraries:

Deutsche Nationalbibliothek Deutsches Musikarchiv: Gärtnerstr. 25-32, 12207 Berlin; tel. (30) 77002-0; fax (30) 77002-299; e-mail info-b@d-nb.de; internet www.d-nb.de; f. 1970; 1,200,000 vols; Head of Dept Dr INGO KOLASA.

Deutsche Nationalbibliothek Frankfurt am Main: Adickesallee 1, 60322 Frankfurt am Main; tel. (69) 15250; fax (69) 15251010; e-mail info-f@d-nb.de; internet www.d-nb.de; f. 1947; 7,800,000 vols; Dir UTE SCHWENS.

Deutsche Nationalbibliothek Leipzig: Deutscher Platz 1, 04103 Leipzig; tel. (341) 22710; fax (341) 2271444; e-mail info-l@d-nb.de; internet www.d-nb.de; f. 1912; 13,621,814 vols; Dir BIRGIT SCHNEIDER.

Institut für Stadtgeschichte (Stadtarchiv) Frankfurt am Main: Münzgasse 9, 60311 Frankfurt am Main; tel. (69) 21237914; fax (69) 21230753; e-mail helmut.nordmeyer@stadt-frankfurt.de; internet www.stadtgeschichte-ffm.de; f. 1436; municipal records; documents since 9th c., registers since 13th c., deeds since 14th c.; records on Frankfurt from other archives; historical records in writings, pictures and sound; 50,000 vols, 750 current periodicals; Dir Dr EVELYN BROCKHOFF.

Universitätsbibliothek Johann Christian Senckenberg: Bockenheimer Landstr. 134–138, 60325 Frankfurt am Main; tel. (69) 798-39-230; fax (69)798-39-062; e-mail direktion@ub.uni-frankfurt.de; internet www.ub.uni-frankfurt.de; f. 1484; present name 2005 following merger of Stadt- und Universitätsbibliothek Frankfurt am Main (StUB) and the Senckenbergische Bibliothek (SeB) 2005; 4,200,000 vols; Dir BERNDT DUGALL.

Freiberg im Sachsen

Technische Universität Bergakademie Freiberg Universitätsbibliothek 'Georgius Agricola': Agricolastr. 10, 09596 Freiberg; tel. (3731) 392959; fax (3731) 393289; e-mail unibib@ub.tu-freiberg.de; internet www.tu-freiberg.de/~ub; f. 1765; 690,000 vols, 2,800 autographs, 26,000 standards, 3,690 cards, 70,000 university publications; special collections: mining and metallurgy, geosciences; Head KARIN MITTENZWEI; publ. *Veröffentlichungen der Bibliothek 'Georgius Agricola' der TU Bergakademie Freiberg* (irregular).

Freiburg im Breisgau

Deutsches Volksliedarchiv, Institut für internationale Popularliedforschung (German Folksong Archive and Research Centre for Song and Popular Culture): Silberbachstr. 13, 79100 Freiburg; tel. (761) 705030; fax (761) 70503-28; e-mail info@dva.uni-freiburg.de; internet www.dva.uni-freiburg.de; f. 1914; 70,000 vols; Head Prof. Dr MAX MATTER; publs *Lied und populäre Kultur/Song and Popular Culture* (annual), *Historisch-kritisches Liederlexikon* (annual), *Volksliedstudien*, *Deutsche Volkslieder mit ihren Melodien*, *Jahrbuch für Volksliedforschung*.

Stadtarchiv Freiburg im Breisgau (City Archive of Freiburg im Breisgau): Grünwälderstr. 15, 79098 Freiburg im Breisgau; tel. (761) 201-2701; fax (761) 201-2799; e-mail stadtarchiv@stadt.freiburg.de; internet www.freiburg.de; f. 1840; 75,000 vols; Dir Dr HANS SCHADEK; publs *Neue Reihe*, *Schau-ins-Land*, *Veröffentlichungen*.

Universitätsbibliothek: Werthmannplatz 2, Postfach 1629, 79016 Freiburg im Breisgau; tel. (761) 203-3900; fax (761) 203-3987; e-mail info@ub.uni-freiburg.de; internet www.ub.uni-freiburg.de; f. 1457; 3,556,218 vols, incl. dissertations; Dir BÄRBEL SCHUBEL.

Fulda

Hochschul- und Landesbibliothek: Heinrich-von-Bibra-Pl. 12, 36037 Fulda; tel. (661) 9640-970; fax (661) 9640-954; e-mail hlb@hlb.hs-fulda.de; internet www.hs-fulda.de/hlb; f. 1778; 613,000 vols, 840 MSS and 431 incunabula; Dir Dr MARIANNE RIETHMÜLLER.

Gießen

Universitätsbibliothek Gießen: Otto-Behaghel-Str. 8, 35394 Gießen; tel. (641) 9914032; fax (641) 9914009; e-mail auskunft@bibsys.uni-giessen.de; internet www.ub.uni-giessen.de; f. 1612; 3,790,146 vols, 396,468 dissertations; 2,694 MSS, 877 incunabula, 2,841 papyri; Dir Dr PETER REUTER.

Görlitz

Oberlausitzische Bibliothek der Wissenschaften bei den Städtischen Sammlungen für Geschichte und Kultur Görlitz (Upper Lusatian Library of Science, at the City Collection for History and Culture in Görlitz): Neiss Str. 30, Postfach 300131, 02826 Görlitz; tel. (3581) 671350; fax (3581) 671351; e-mail olb@goerlitz.de; f. 1950 (original library 1779); scientific, historical and general library including rare book collection; 126,000 vols; Librarian MATTHIAS WENZEL.

Gotha

Universitäts- und Forschungsbibliothek Erfurt/Gotha (University and Research Library of Erfurt/Gotha): Postfach 90 02 22, 99105 Erfurt; tel. (361) 7375500; fax (361) 7375509; e-mail bibliothek@uni-erfurt.de; internet www.bibliothek.uni-erfurt.de; f. 1647; 553,000 vols, 10,000 MSS; Dir CHRISTIANE SCHMIEDEKNECHT.

Göttingen

Niedersächsische Staats- und Universitätsbibliothek: Platz der Göttinger Sieben 1, 37073 Göttingen; tel. (551) 395231; fax (551) 395222; e-mail sekretariat@sub.uni-goettingen.de; internet www.sub.uni-goettingen.de; f. 1734; 4,000,000 vols, 19,000 electronic publs, 14,000 periodicals, 8,000 electronic periodicals, 13,300 MSS, 3,100 incunabula, 304,000 map sheets; Dir Dr N. LOSSAU.

Greifswald

Universitätsbibliothek (University Library): Friedrich-Ludwig-Jahn-Str. 14A, 17487 Greifswald; tel. (3834) 861515; fax (3834) 861501; e-mail ub@uni-greifswald.de; internet www.ub.uni-greifswald.de; f. 1604; 2,990,800 vols, including 4,100 periodicals, 2,081 autographs, 330 incunabula; Dir Dr PETER WOLFF.

Halle am Saale

Bibliothek der Deutschen Akademie der Naturforscher Leopoldina: Postfach 110543, 06019 Halle/Saale; located at: 06108 Halle/Saale, August-Bebel-Str. 50A; tel. (345) 4723947; fax (345) 4723949; e-mail biblio@leopoldina-halle.de; internet www.leopoldina-halle.de; f. 1732; 260,000 vols, 20,000 theses; Dir JOCHEN THAMM.

Universitäts- und Landesbibliothek Sachsen-Anhalt: August-Bebel-Str. 13 u. 50, 06098 Halle (Saale); tel. (345) 5522001; fax (345) 5527140; e-mail direktion@bibliothek.uni-halle.de; internet www.bibliothek.uni-halle.de; f. 1696; 4,840,000 vols, 7,200 print periodicals, 5,600 online journals. 115,300 MSS and autographs; spec. collns incl. Middle East and North Africa, regional studies and history of Saxony-Anhalt; Ponikau's library; Library of the Deutsche Morgenländische Gesellschaft; Dir Dr HEINER SCHNELLING; publs *Hercynia*, *Regionalbibliographie Sachsen-Anhalt* (online).

Hamburg

Bibliothek des Max-Planck-Institut für Ausländisches und Internationales Privatrecht (Max-Planck Institute Library for Foreign and International Private Law):e-mail knudsen@mpipriv-hh.mpg.de Mittelweg 187, 20148 Hamburg; tel. (40) 41900-0; fax (40) 41900-288; e-mail knudsen@mpipriv.de; internet www.mpipriv-hh.mpg.de; f. 1926; 450,000 vols, 4,000 periodicals, of which 1,950 current; Dir Prof. Dr HOLGER KNUDSEN.

Commerzbibliothek der Handelskammer Hamburg: Adolphspl. 1, 20457 Hamburg; tel. (40) 36138373; fax (40) 36138437; e-mail service@commerzbibliothek.de; internet www.commerzbibliothek.de; f. 1735 by the Commerzdeputation, later Hamburg Chamber of Commerce; historical map series; Hamburg newspapers 1721–1915; 174,000 vols on law, economics and social science; Librarian ULRIKE VERDIECK.

Deutsches Bibel-Archiv (German Bible Archive): Von Melle Park 6, 20146 Hamburg; tel. (40) 428384781; fax (40) 428384785; internet www.sub.uni-hamburg.de; f. 1931; biblical traditions in German literature and art; Bible translations; 8,000 vols; Dir Prof. Dr HEIMO REINITZER; publs *Abhandlungen und Vorträge*, *Bibel und deutsche Kultur*, *Naturalis historia bibliae*, *Vestigia bibliae*.

Staats- und Universitätsbibliothek Hamburg 'Carl von Ossietzky': Von-Melle-Park 3, 20146 Hamburg; tel. (40) 42838-2233; fax (40) 42838-3352; e-mail auskunft@sub.uni-hamburg.de; internet www.sub.uni-hamburg.de; f. 1479; deposit library for literature published in Hamburg; special collections: political science, administrative science, literature on American Indians and Eskimos, sea and coastal fishing, literature on Portugal and Spain; 3,166,000 vols, 20,1797 MSS (incl. 990 papyri); Dir Prof. Dr PETER RAU; publs *Kataloge der*

Handschriften, F. G. Klopstock: Werke und Briefe.

Staatsarchiv der Freien und Hansestadt Hamburg (State Archive of the Free and Hanseatic City of Hamburg): Kattunbleiche 19, 22041 Hamburg; tel. (40) 42831-3200; fax (40) 42831-3201; e-mail poststelle@staatsarchiv.hamburg.de; internet fhh.hamburg.de/stadt/Aktuell/behoerden/staatsarchiv/start.html; f. 13th century; history of Hamburg; 150,000 books; Dir Dr UDO SCHÄFER; publs *Hamburgisches Urkundenbuch, Veröffentlichungen.*

Hanover

Niedersächsische Landesbibliothek (State Library of Lower Saxony): Waterloostr. 8, 30169 Hanover; tel. (511) 12670; fax (511) 1267-202; e-mail information@gwlb.de; internet www.nlb-hannover.de; f. 1665; collection of coats of arms and seals; Leibniz archive; 1,600,000 vols, 8,000 periodicals, 4,320 MSS, 80,000 autographs, 375 incunabula, several thousand maps, etchings, woodcuts; Dir Dr GEORG RUPPELT.

Niedersächsisches Landesarchiv (Regional Archive of Lower Saxony): Am Archiv 1, 30169 Hanover; tel. (511) 120-6601; fax (511) 120-6699; e-mail poststelle@nla.niedersachsen.de; internet www.nla.niedersachsen.de; fmrly Hauptstaatsarchiv Hannover, 32,000 m shelf-space; Dir Dr BERND KAPPELHOFF.

Stadtbibliothek (City Library): Hildesheimer Str. 12, 30169 Hanover; tel. (511) 168-42169; fax (511) 168-46410; e-mail stadtbibliothek-hannover@hannover-stadt.de; internet www.stadtbibliothek-hannover.de; f. 1440; general information about the city and region; 680,000 vols, 2,000 periodicals; Dir CAROLA SCHELLE-WOLFF.

Technische Informationsbibliothek und Universitätsbibliothek Hannover (TIB/UB) (Technical Information Library and Hannover University Library): Welfengarten 1B, 30167 Hanover; tel. (511) 762-2268; fax (511) 762-4075; e-mail tibub@tib.uni-hannover.de; internet www.tib.uni-hannover.de; f. 1831; 8,200,000 items, 21,000 current periodicals; German research reports, patent specifications, standards; conference proceedings; doctoral dissertations and American reports (microforms); special emphasis on technical and scientific literature in Eastern and East Asian languages; acts as central technical library of the Federal Republic; Dir UWE ROSEMANN.

Heidelberg

Bibliothek des Max-Planck-Instituts für Ausländisches Öffentliches Recht und Völkerrecht (Library of the Max Planck Institute for Foreign Public and Civil Law): Im Neuenheimer Feld 535, 69120 Heidelberg; tel. (6221) 4821; fax (6221) 482288; e-mail library@mpil.de; internet www.mpil.de/ww/de/pub/bibliothek.cfm; f. 1924; 54,700 vols, 4,250 periodicals; Dir HARALD MÜLLER.

Universitätsbibliothek (University Library): Plöck 107–109, 69117 Heidelberg; tel. (6221) 542380; fax (6221) 542623; e-mail ub@uni-hd.de; internet www.ub.uni-heidelberg.de; f. 1386; 3,000,000 vols, 6,600 MSS, 1,800 incunabula, 4,500 non-book media, 12,000 e-journals; Dir Dr VEIT PROBST; publs *Heidelberger Dozentenbibliographie* (online), *Neuerwerbungslisten* (online), *Schriften der Universitätsbibliothek, Theke* (online).

Jena

Thüringer Universitäts- und Landesbibliothek: 07740 Jena, Postfach; Bibliotheksplatz 2, 07743 Jena; tel. (3641) 940000; fax (3641) 940002; e-mail thulb_auskunft@thulb.uni-jena.de; internet www.uni-jena.de/thulb; f. 1558; 160 mems; 2,700,000 vols, 772,000 pamphlets, 3,311 MSS, 11,040 current periodicals; Dir Dr SABINE WEFERS; publ. *Thüringen-Bibliographie* (online).

Karlsruhe

Badische Landesbibliothek: Erbprinzenstr. 15, 76133 Karlsruhe; tel. (721) 175-0; fax (721) 175-2333; internet www.blb-karlsruhe.de; f. 1500; 1,798,422 vols; 9,706 MSS; 1,361 incunabula; Dir Dr PETER MICHAEL EHRLE.

Bibliothek des Bundesgerichtshofs (Library of the Federal Court): Herrenstr. 45A, 76133 Karlsruhe; tel. (721) 1595000; fax (721) 1595612; e-mail bibliothek@bgh.bund.de; internet www.bundesgerichtshof.de; f. 1950; law library; 418,000 vols; Dir D. PANNIER.

Landesarchiv Baden-Württemberg—Generallandesarchiv Karlsruhe: Nördliche Hildapromenade 2, 76133 Karlsruhe; tel. (721) 9262206; fax (721) 9262231; e-mail glaKarlsruhe@la-bw.de; internet www.landesarchiv-bw.de/glak; f. 1803; 130,000 documents, 42,000 MSS, 3,500,000 report files; 76,000 vols on Baden history; Dir Prof. Dr VOLKER RÖDEL; publ. *Zeitschrift für die Geschichte des Oberrheins* (annually).

Universitätsbibliothek: Postfach 6920, 76049 Karlsruhe; tel. (721) 608-3101; fax (721) 608-4886; e-mail ub@ubka.uni-karlsruhe.de; internet www.ubka.uni-karlsruhe.de; f. 1840; 1,045,018 vols; Dir Dipl.-Ing. C.-H. SCHÜTTE.

Kassel

documenta Archiv: Untere Karlsstr. 4, 34117 Kassel; tel. (561) 787-4022; fax (561) 787-4028; e-mail bibliothek@documentaarchiv.de; internet www.documentaarchiv.de; f. 1961; 25,000 books, 50,000 exhibition catalogues, 120 current periodicals, all on modern art; files archive of 250,000 newspaper clippings, 150,000 art exhibition invitations, 1,383 folders of 'documenta' working papers; video and picture archive of 3,000 video titles, 25,000 slides, 1,000 Ektachromes, 7,500 black-and-white photographs, 2,000 artist portraits; also a research institute and administers the Arnold Bode Estate; Librarian PETRA HINCK.

Universitätsbibliothek Kassel–Landesbibliothek und Murhardsche Bibliothek der Stadt Kassel: Diagonale 10, 34111 Kassel; tel. (561) 804-2117; fax (561) 804-2125; e-mail direktion@bibliothek.uni-kassel.de; internet www.uni-kassel.de/bib; f. 1580; 1,762,856 vols, 10,112 MSS, 24,000 musical scores, 17,772 maps, 20,000 autographs, 5,036 print and 4,763 electronic periodicals; Dir Dr AXEL HALLE.

Kiel

Deutsche Zentralbibliothek für Wirtschaftswissenschaften (ZBW) (Central Library of Economics): Leibniz-Informationszentrum Wirtschaft, Düsternbrooker Weg 120, 24105 Kiel; tel. (431) 8814-555; fax (431) 8814-520; e-mail info@zbw.eu; internet www.zbw.eu; f. 1914; 4,000,000 vols; Dir HORST THOMSEN; publs *Wirtschaftsdienst – Journal for Economic Policy* (monthly), *Intereconomics – Review of European Economic Policy* (6 a year).

Schleswig-Holsteinische Landesbibliothek: 24103 Kiel, Wall 47–51; tel. (431) 6967710; fax (431) 6967711; e-mail landesbibliothek@shlb.de; internet www.shlb.de; f. 1895; culture, civilization, literature, musical scores and pictorial representations of topics concerning Schleswig-Holstein, editors of Schleswig-Holstein Bibliography and Dictionary of Schleswig-Holstein biography; special collection on chess; 200,000 vols and literary bequests of about 100 authors and scholars; Dir HARTWIG MOLZOW.

Universitätsbibliothek (University Library): Leibnizstr. 9, 24118 Kiel; tel. (431) 880; fax (431) 1596; e-mail sekretariat@ub.uni-kiel.de; internet www.uni-kiel.de/ub; f. 1665; 4,500,000 vols, 8,500 periodicals; 3 departments and 50 specialist libraries; special colln on Scandinavian languages, history and literature; Dir Dr ELSE WISCHERMANN.

Koblenz

Bundesarchiv: Postfach 56064 Koblenz; located at: Potsdamer Str. 1, 56075 Koblenz; tel. (261) 505-0; fax (261) 505-226; e-mail koblenz@barch.bund.de; internet www.bundesarchiv.de; f. 1952; central archives of the Federal Republic; 2,201,793 vols; 300,918 m of records of Reich, Federal and GDR Govts, agencies, political parties, private asscns; colln of private papers; 998,959 documentaries and newsreels (including 150,000 feature films), 12,274,141 photographs; 79,630 posters, 903,970 maps and technical drawings, 42,357 audio recordings, 624,832 files of machine-readable data held at various sites throughout Germany; Pres. Prof. Dr HARTMUT WEBER.

Landeshauptarchiv (Central State Archive): Postfach 201047, 56010 Koblenz; tel. (261) 9129-0; fax (261) 9129-112; e-mail post@landeshauptarchiv-ko.de; internet www.landeshauptarchiv.de; f. 1832; 87,000 vols, 43,000 linear m of archives; history of Rhineland Palatinate and former territories; Dir Dr HEINZ-GÜNTHER BORCK; publs *Blätter für deutsche Landesgeschichte* (annually), *Jahrbuch für westdeutsche Landesgeschichte* (annually).

Konstanz

Universitätsbibliothek: Universitätsstr. 10, 78457 Konstanz; tel. (7531) 88-2800; fax (7531) 883082; e-mail information.ub@uni-konstanz.de; internet www.ub.uni-konstanz.de; f. 1965; 2,000,000 1,800,000 vols, 110,000 theses; Dir P. HAETSCHER.

Landshut

Staatsarchiv Landshut: Burg Trausnitz, 84036 Landshut; tel. (871) 92328-0; fax (871) 92328-8; e-mail poststelle@stala.bayern.de; internet www.gda.bayern.de; f. 1753; 34,000 vols; Dir Dr M. RÜTH.

Leipzig

Institut für Länderkunde e.V. Geographische Zentralbibliothek und Archiv für Geographie (Central Library and Archive of the Institute for Geography): Schongauer Str. 9, 04329 Leipzig; tel. (341) 2556529; fax (341) 2556598; e-mail bibliothek@ifl-leipzig.de; internet www.ifl-leipzig.com; f. 1892; central geographical library containing 200,000 vols, special collection of maps and atlases of the 16th–18th c., geography archives; Dir Dr HEINZ-PETER BROGIATO; publs *Beiträge zur Regionalen Geographie* (2 a year), *Berichte zur Deutschen Landeskunde* (2 a year), *Daten, Fakten, Literatur zur Geographie Europas* (annually), *Europa regional* (4 a year).

Stadtarchiv: 04092 Leipzig; located at: 04318 Leipzig, Torgauer Str. 74; tel. (341) 2429-0; fax (341) 2429-121; e-mail stadtarchiv@leipzig.de; f. *c.*1100.

Stadtbibliothek Leipzig: Postfach 100927, 04009 Leipzig; premises at: Wilhelm-Leuschner-Platz 10–11, 04107 Leipzig; tel. (341) 1235343; fax (341) 1235305; e-mail stadtbib@

leipzig.de; internet www.leipzig.de/stadtbib.htm; f. 1677; 1,065,182 vols; Dir REINHARD STRIDDE.

Universitätsbibliothek (University Library): Beethovenstr. 6, 04107 Leipzig; tel. (341) 9730577; fax (341) 9730596; e-mail direktion@ub.uni-leipzig.de; internet www.ub.uni-leipzig.de; f. 1543; 5,000,000 vols, 7,200 periodicals; Hirzel colln contains books and material by and about Johann Wolfgang von Goethe (1749–1832); Dir Dr MONIKA LINDER.

Lübeck

Archiv der Hansestadt Lübeck: Mühlendamm 1–3, 23552 Lübeck; tel. (451) 1224150; fax (451) 1221517; e-mail archiv@luebeck.de; internet www.luebeck.de/kultur_bilding/archiv; f. 1298; municipal archives and documents of the churches, recognized public bodies, instns and private persons; 40,000 vols; Dir Prof. Dr A. GRASSMANN.

Bibliothek der Hansestadt Lübeck (Library of the Hanseatic City of Lübeck): Hundestr. 5–17, 23552 Lübeck; tel. (451) 1224114; fax (451) 1224112; e-mail stadtbibliothek@luebeck.de; internet www.luebeck.de/kultur_bildung/bibliothek; f. 1616; 1,158,000 vols, 3,275 maps, 41,000 vols of printed music, 1,423 MSS; Dir Dr J. FLIGGE.

Ludwigsburg

Staatsarchiv Ludwigsburg: Arsenalplatz 3, 71638 Ludwigsburg; tel. (7141) 18-6310; fax (7141) 18-6311; e-mail staludwigsburg@la-bw.de; internet www.la-bw.de/stal; f. 1868; archives for the administrative district of Stuttgart (Nordwürttemberg); 34,000 m of deeds; 43,000 vols; Dir Dr PETER MUELLER.

Magdeburg

Landeshauptarchiv Sachsen-Anhalt (State Archive of Saxony-Anhalt): Hegelstr. 25, 39104 Magdeburg; tel. (391) 56643; fax (391) 5664440; e-mail poststelle@lha.mi.lsa-net.de; f. 1823; 103,000 vols; 48,000 m of records, 158,000 maps; archives of state public record offices; Dir Dr ULRIKE HÖROLDT.

Stadtbibliothek Magdeburg: Breiter Weg 109, 39015 Magdeburg; tel. (391) 5404800; fax (391) 5404803; e-mail stadtbibliothek@magdeburg.de; internet www.magdeburg.de; f. 1525; 404,000 vols; Dir PETER PETSCH.

Mainz

Wissenschaftliche Stadtbibliothek: Rheinallee 3B, 55116 Mainz; tel. (6131) 12-26-49; fax (6131) 12-35-70; e-mail stb.direktion@stadt.mainz.de; internet www.bibliothek.mainz.de; f. 1477 as University Library, taken over by the City of Mainz in 1805; 614,509 vols, 2,364 incunabula, 1,288 MSS; Dir Dr STEPHAN FLIEDNER (acting); publs *Mainzer Zeitschrift*, *Beiträge zur Geschichte der Stadt Mainz*.

Universitätsbibliothek Mainz (University Library of Mainz): Jakob-Welder-Weg 6, 55128 Mainz; tel. (6131) 3922633; fax (6131) 393822; e-mail info@ub.uni-mainz.de; internet www.ub.uni-mainz.de; 1,815,143 vols, 814 MSS; Dir Dr A. ANDERHUB.

Mannheim

Universitätsbibliothek (University Library): Schloss, Ostflügel, 68131 Mannheim; tel. (621) 181-2941; fax (621) 181-2939; e-mail biblubma@bib.uni-mannheim.de; internet www.bib.uni-mannheim.de; 2,100,000 vols; Dir CHRISTIAN BENZ.

Marbach am Neckar

Schiller-Nationalmuseum und Deutsches Literaturarchiv Marbach: Schillerhöhe 8–10, 71672 Marbach; tel. (7144) 8480; fax (7144) 848299; e-mail info@dla-marbach.de; internet www.dla-marbach.de; f. 1895; German literature since 1750; large collection of autographs and documents, 1,100 legacies, 750,000 vols; Dir Prof. Dr ULRICH RAULFFOTT; publs *Marbacher Bibliothek* (annually), *Jahrbuch der Deutschen Schillergesellschaft* (annually), *Marbacher Magazin* (4 a year), *Marbacher Katalog* (annually).

Marburg

Bibliothek des Herder-Instituts: Gisonenweg 5–7, 35037 Marburg; tel. (6421) 184150; fax (6421) 184139; e-mail bibliothek.hi@mailer.uni-marburg.debibliothek@herder-institut.de; internet www.herder-institut.de; f. 1950; research library specializing in the history and culture of East Central Europe (Poland, Czech Republic, Slovakia, Estonia, Latvia, and Lithuania); East Central European library of 400,000 380,000 vols; Chief Librarian Dr JÜRGEN WARMBRUNN.

Deutsches Adelsarchiv (Germany Archive of the Nobility): Schwanallee 21, 35037 Marburg; tel. (6421) 26162; fax (6421) 27529; e-mail info@adelsarchiv.de; f. 1945; genealogy of German nobility; 15,000 vols; Dir Dr CHRISTOPH FRANKE; publ. *Genealogisches Handbuch des Adels*.

Hessisches Staatsarchiv Marburg: Friedrichspl. 15, 35037 Marburg; tel. (6421) 9250; fax (6421) 161125; e-mail poststelle@stama.hessen.de; internet www.staatsarchiv-marburg.hessen.de; f. 1870; 122,000 books, 115,000 charts; 220,000 maps and plans; 66 km of records of the Electorate of Hesse-Kassel, the abbeys of Fulda, Hersfeld, the principality of Waldeck; Dir Dr ANDREAS HEDWIG; publs *Repertorien*, *Schriften*.

Universitätsbibliothek: Postfach 1920, 35008 Marburg; located at: 35039 Marburg, Wilhelm-Röpke-Str. 4; tel. (6421) 2821319; fax (6421) 2826506; e-mail verwaltung@ub.uni-marburg.de; f. 1527; 1,923,911 vols, 736,519 theses, 3,020 MSS; Dir Dr D. BARTH.

Mönchengladbach

Bibliothek Wissenschaft und Weisheit (Library of Theology and Philosophy): Franziskanerstr. 30, 41063 Mönchengladbach; tel. (2161) 899135; fax (2161) 899171; f. 1929; attached to Zentralbibliothek der Kölnischen Franziskanerprovinz (fmrly Hochsculbibliothek); 70,000 vols; Dir Father O. GIMMNICH.

Stadtbibliothek (City Library): Blücherstr. 6, 41050 Mönchengladbach; tel. (2161) 256340; fax (2161) 256369; e-mail stadtbibliothek@moenchengladbach.de; internet www.stadtbibliothek-mg.de; f. 1904; 538,000 vols; special collection on social and political questions, library of the 'Volksverein für das katholische Deutschland 1890–1933'; Dir GUIDO WEYER.

Munich

Bayerische Staatsbibliothek: 80328 Munich; located at: Ludwigstr. 16, 80539 Munich; tel. (89) 28638-0; fax (89) 28638-2200; e-mail info@bsb-muenchen.de; internet www.bsb-muenchen.de; f. 1558; deposit library for Bavaria; 9,111,000 vols, 1,200,000 microforms, 91,100 MSS, 48,300 current periodicals, 389,000 maps, 355,000 scores, 88,000 audiovisual items, 2,202,000 single sheets and photographs; Dir Dr ROLF GRIEBEL; publs *Jahresbericht* (annually), *Bibliotheksforum Bayern* (4 a year), *Bibliotheksmagazin* (3 a year).

Bayerisches Hauptstaatsarchiv: Postfach 22 11 52, 80501 Munich; located at 80539 Munich, Schönfeldstr. 5; tel. (89) 28638-2596; fax (89) 28638-2954; e-mail poststelle@bayhsta.bayern.de; internet www.gda.bayern.de; f. 13th c., reorganized 1978; comprises five departments: (1) Ältere Bestände: 275,000 charters, 5726,000 documents and vols, 24,000 maps and plans; (2) Neuere Bestände (since 19th c.): 4,100 charters, 960,000 documents, 150,000 maps and plans; (3) Geheimes Hausarchiv: 10,000 charters, 22,000 documents and vols, 7,600 pictures; (4) Kriegsarchiv: 466,000 documents and vols, 130,000 maps and plans, 96,000 pictures; (5) Nachlässe und Sammlungen: collections of private papers, publications, posters, pictures, etc.; Dir Prof. Dr JOACHIM WILD; publs *Archivalische Zeitschrift*, *Bayerische Archivinventare*, *Archive in Bayern*.

Bibliothek des Deutschen Museums: Museumsinsel 1, 80538 Munich; tel. (89) 2179-224; fax (89) 2179-262; e-mail dm.bibliothek@deutsches-museum.debibliothek@deutsches-museum.de; internet www.deutsches-museum.de/bib/biblio/biblio.htmwww.deutsches-museum.de/bibliothek; f. 1903; 900,000 vols; Dir Dr HELMUT HILZ.

Deutsches Bucharchiv München (Institut für Buchwissenschaften): Bibliothek und Dokumentationsstelle, Literaturhaus München, Salvatorplatz 1, 80333 Munich; tel. (89) 291951-0; fax (89) 291951-95; e-mail kontakt@bucharchiv.de; internet www.bucharchiv.de; f. 1948; documentation, scientific and technical information about books and periodicals; special library for book research; 30,000 vols, 180 periodicals; Dir Prof. Dr LUDWIG DELP.

Deutsches Patentamt (German Patent Office): Abt. Informationsdienste (Bibliothek), 80297 Munich; tel. (89) 2195-0; fax (89) 2195-2221; e-mail info@dpma.de; internet www.dpma.de; f. 1877; industrial property; 1,116,000 vols, 37,000,000 patent specifications; Pres. JÜRGEN SCHADE.

Evangelischer Presseverband für Bayern eV (Evangelical Press Society of Bavaria): Birkerstr. 22, 80636 Munich; tel. (89) 12172-0; fax (89) 12172-138; e-mail redaktion@epv.de; internet www.epv.de; f. 1963; Pres. HARTMUT JOISTEN.

Münchner Stadtbibliothek (City Library of Munich): Rosenheimer Str. 5, 81667 Munich; tel. (89) 48098-3203; fax (89) 48098-3233; e-mail stb.zentraledienste.sekretariat.kult@muenchen.de; internet www.muenchner-stadtbibliothek.de; f. 1843; 3m. vols; Dir Dr WERNER SCHNEIDER.

Staatsarchiv (State Archive): Schönfeldstr. 3, 80539 Munich; tel. (89) 28638-2525; fax (89) 28638-2526; e-mail poststelle@stam.bayern.de; internet www.gda.bayern.de; f. 1814; 11,295,125 files (records), 9,157 documents (charts), 30,455 maps and plans, 25,000 vols (library); Dir RAINER BRAUN.

Stadtarchiv (City Archives): Winzererstr. 68, 80797 Munich; tel. (89) 2330308; fax (89) 23330830; e-mail stadtarchiv@muenchen.de; f. 1520; 65,000 vols, 78,000 documents, 16m. deeds, 22,000 maps and plans, 1,200,000 photos and postcards, 3,050 soundtracks, 1,500 films, 26,629 posters; Dir Dr R. BAUER.

Universitätsbibliothek: Geschw.-Scholl-Platz 1, 80539 Munich; tel. (89) 21802428; e-mail direktion@ub.uni-muenchen.de; internet www.ub.uni-muenchen.de; f. 1473; 2,698,396 vols, 3,284 MSS; Dir Dr GÜNTER HEISCHMANN.

Universitätsbibliothek der Technischen Universität (Technical University Library): Arcisstr. 21, 80333 Munich; tel. (89) 28928601; fax (89) 28928622; e-mail bibdir@ub.tum.de; internet www.ub.tum.de; f. 1868; 1,930,000 vols, 490,000 reports; Dir Dr REINER KALLENBORN; publ. *Jahrbuch*.

Münster

Landesarchiv Nordrhein-Westfalen, Staatsarchiv Münster: Bohlweg 2, 48147 Münster; tel. (251) 4885-0; fax (251) 4885-100; e-mail stams@lav.nrw.de; internet www.archive.nrw.de; f. 1829 as Provinzialarchiv for Westphalia, present title since 1946; 30,000 metres of documents and 100,000 charters, from 9th c. to the present; 150,000 vols; Dir Dr MECHTHILD BLACK-VELTRUP.

Universitäts- und Landesbibliothek: Postfach 8029, Krummer Timpen 3–5, 48043 Münster; tel. (251) 8324021; fax (251) 8328398; e-mail sekretariat.ulb@uni-muenster.de; internet www.uni-muenster.de/ulb; f. 1588, refounded 1902; 2,334,800 vols incl. 305,660 theses, 821 incunabula, 1,406 MSS, 7,258 print periodicals, 3,214 e-journals; Dir Dr BEATE TRÖGER.

Westfälisches Archivamt Münster im Landschaftsverband Westfalen-Lippe: Jahnstr. 26, 48133 Münster; tel. (251) 5913890; fax (251) 591269; e-mail westf.archivamt@lwl.org; internet www.archivamt-westfalen.de; f. 1927; non-state archives; training of archivists; 30,000 vols; Dir Dr NORBERT REIMANN; publs *Inventare der nichtstaatlichen Archive Westfalens, Westfälische Quellen und Archivpublikationen, Archivpflege in Westfalen-Lippe* (Journal), *Texte und Untersuchungen zur Archivpflege*.

Nuremberg

Bibliothek des Germanischen Nationalmuseums: Postfach 119580, 90105 Nuremberg; premises at: 90402 Nuremberg, Kornmarkt 1; tel. (911) 1331-151; fax (911) 1331-200; e-mail bibliothek@gnm.de; internet www.gnm.de; f. 1852; arts, history of civilization, German-speaking regions; special colln of art-history works since 800 AD; 615,223 vols, 3,380 MSS, 3,000 16th c. prints, 1,708 current periodicals; Dir Dr EBERHARD SLENCZKA; publs *Anzeiger des Germanischen Nationalmuseums* (annually), *Schrifttum zur Deutschen Kunst* (annually).

Landeskirchliches Archiv Nürnberg der Evangelisch-Lutherischen Kirche in Bayern: Veilhofstr. 28, 90489 Nuremberg; tel. (911) 588690; fax (911) 5886969; e-mail lkanuernberg@t-online.de; internet www.lkan-elkb.de; f. 1931; 170,000 vols; Dir Dr ANDREA SCHWARZ.

Staatsarchiv (State Archive): Archivstr. 17, 90408 Nuremberg; tel. (911) 93519-0; fax (911) 93519-99; e-mail poststelle@stanu.bayern.de; f. 1806; archives of middle Franconia since the middle ages; includes Nuremberg trial documents; 47,000 vols; Dir Dr RECHTER.

Stadtarchiv Nürnberg: Marientorgraben 8, 90402 Nuremberg; tel. (911) 231-2770; fax (911) 231-4091; e-mail stadtarchiv@stadt.nuernberg.de; internet www.stadtarchiv.nuernberg.de; f. 1865; reference library of 45,000 vols; Dir Dr MICHAEL DIEFENBACHER; publs *Quellen und Forschungen zur Geschichte und Kultur der Stadt Nürnberg, Nürnberger Werkstücke zur Stadt- und Landesgeschichte, Ausstellungskataloge*.

Stadtbibliothek Nürnberg: Egidienplatz 23, 90317 Nuremberg; tel. (911) 2312790; fax (911) 2315476; e-mail stb@stadt.nuernberg.de; internet www.stadtbibliothek.nuernberg.de; f. 1370; 980,000 vols, 3,132 MSS, 2,140 incunabula; Dir EVA HOMRIGHAUSEN.

Universitätsbibliothek Erlangen-Nürnberg, Wirtschafts- und Sozialwissenschaftliche Zweigbibliothek (University Library of Erlangen-Nuremberg, Economics and Social Studies Branch): Lange Gasse 20, 90403 Nuremberg; tel. (911) 5302-830; fax (911) 5302-852; e-mail bibliothek@wiso.uni-erlangen.de; internet www.ub.uni-erlangen.de/wisobib; f. 1919; 243,000 vols, 1,390 current periodicals; Dir JOACHIM HENNECKE.

Offenbach am Main

Deutscher Wetterdienst Deutsche Meteorologische Bibliothek (German Meteorological Service National Library for Meteorology): Postfach 100465, Kaiserleistr. 29/35, 63067 Offenbach am Main; tel. (69) 8062-4273; fax (69) 8062-4123; e-mail bibliothek@dwd.de; internet www.dwd.de; f. 1847; 170,000 vols (14,000 pre-1900), 1,000 current periodicals; the national library for meteorology, climatology; comprehensive records of data published by German and foreign instns; Librarian BRITTA BOLZMANN.

Oldenburg

Landesbibliothek: Pferdemarkt 15, Postfach 3480, 26024 Oldenburg; tel. (441) 799-2800; fax (441) 799-2865; e-mail lbo@lb-oldenburg.de; internet www.lb-oldenburg.de; f. 1792; 750,000 735,000 vols, 90,000 microforms, 1,071 MSS; regional library; Dir C. ROEDER; Librarians Dr R. FIETZ, M. KLINKOW, Dr K.-P. MÜLLER; publ. *Schriften*.

Niedersächsisches Staatsarchiv in Oldenburg (Archive of Lower Saxony in Oldenburg): Damm 43, 26135 Oldenburg; tel. (441) 9244100; fax (441) 9244292; e-mail oldenburg@nla.niedersachsen.de; internet www.staatsarchive.niedersachsen.de; f. before 1615; public record office for the former district of Oldenburg; record repository with 11,000 m of files; contributes to *Veröffentlichungen der Niedersächsischen Archivverwaltung*; 63,000 vols; Dir Dr GERD STEINWASCHER.

Osnabrück

Niedersächsisches Staatsarchiv (State Archive of Lower Saxony): Schloßstr. 29, 49074 Osnabrück, Schloss; tel. (541) 33162-0; fax (541) 33162-62; e-mail Osnabrueck@nla.niedersachsen.de; internet www.staatsarchive.niedersachsen.de; f. 1869; 80,300 vols; Dir Dr KEHNE.

Passau

Staatliche Bibliothek: Michaeligasse 11, 94032 Passau; tel. (851) 7564400; fax (851) 75644027; e-mail staatliche.bibliothek@uni-passau.de; f. 1612 as Jesuit library, refounded 1803 as nat. library; special collns: philosophy, theology, regional history and literature, emblematic, Jesuitica; 320,000 vols, 150 MSS, 322 incunabula; Dir Dr JÖRG KASTNER.

Universitätsbibliothek (University Library): Innstr. 29, 94032 Passau; tel. (851) 509-1630; fax (851) 509-1602; e-mail ubinfouni@passau.de; internet www.ub.uni-passau.de; f. 1976; 1,900,000 vols, 88,000 theses; Dir CAROLA RESCH.

Potsdam

Brandenburgisches Landeshauptarchiv Potsdam (Brandenburg State Central Archive, Potsdam): Postfach 60 04 49, 14404 Potsdam; An der Orangerie 3, 14469 Potsdam; tel. (331) 5674-120; fax (331) 5674-112; e-mail poststelle@blha.brandenburg.de; internet www.landeshauptarchiv-brandenburg.de; brs at Lübben (Spreewald) and Frankfurt an der Oder; f. 1949; 89,000 vols, 40,000 linear ft of files; Dir Dr KLAUS NEITMANN; publs *Brandenburgische Archive* (2 a year), *Jahrbuch für die Geschichte Mittel- und Ostdeutschlands*.

Stadt- und Landesbibliothek Potsdam: Am Kanal 47, 14467 Potsdam; tel. (331) 2896600; fax (331) 2896402; e-mail slb@slb.potsdam.org; internet slb.potsdam.org; f. 1969; Brandenburg collection, Gottfried Benn collection; 670,000 vols; Dir MARION MATTEKAT.

Regensburg

Bischöfliche Zentralbibliothek: St Petersweg 11–13, 93047 Regensburg; tel. (941) 59532-2513; fax (941) 59532-2521; e-mail bibliotek@bistum-regensburg.de; internet www.bistum-regensburg.de/bibliothek; f. 1972; 286,300 vols, 418 journals, with special collections on ascetics and sacred music; includes the library of St Jacob's Irish monastery and Proske's music library; Dir PAUL MAI.

Staatliche Bibliothek Regensburg: Gesandtenstr. 13, 93047 Regensburg; tel. (941) 630806-0; fax (941) 630806-28; e-mail sbr@bib-bvb.de; internet www.bib-bvb.de/sbr/sbr1.html; f. 1816; special collection of regional history; 278,991 vols, 12,932 maps, 16,077 microforms; Dir Dr MICHAEL DRUCKER.

Universitätsbibliothek: 93042 Regensburg; located at: 93053 Regensburg, Universitätsstr. 31; tel. (941) 943-3900; fax (941) 943-3285; e-mail friedrich.geisselmann@bibliothek.uni-regensburg.de; internet www.bibliothek.uni-regensburg.de; f. 1964; 3,470,000 vols, incl. 573,663 theses; Dir Dr FRIEDRICH GEISSELMANN.

Rostock

Universitätsbibliothek: Albert-Einstein-Str. 6, 18059 Rostock; tel. (381) 4988601; fax (381) 4988602; e-mail direktion.ub@uni-rostock.de; internet www.uni-rostock.de/ub; f. 1569; 2,200,000 vols, 330,000 theses, 3,422 periodicals, 3,350 MSS, 3,985,000 patents, 8,300 CD-ROMs, 37,360 standards; Dir Dr JÜRGEN HEEG.

Saarbrücken

Landesarchiv Saarbrücken (State Archive of Saarbrücken): Dudweilerstr. 1, 66133 Saarbrücken; tel. (681) 98039-0; fax (681) 98039-133; e-mail landesarchiv@landesarchiv.saarland.de; internet www.landesarchiv.saarland.de; f. 1948; 11,000 m of archives concerning the Saar, 25,000 vols; Dir Dr WOLFGANG LAUFER; 170 official publs.

Saarländische Universitäts- und Landesbibliothek (University and State Library of the Saarland): Postfach 151141, 66041 Saarbrücken; tel. (681) 302-2070; fax (681) 302-2796; e-mail sulb@sulb.uni-saarland.de; internet www.sulb.uni-saarland.de; Medical Library in Homburg, Saar; f. 1950; 1,705,000 vols incl. 375,000 theses; Dir Dr BERND HAGENAU.

Schleswig

Landesarchiv Schleswig-Holstein: Prinzenpalais, 24837 Schleswig; tel. (4621) 86-1800; fax (4621) 86-1801; e-mail landesarchiv@la.landsh.de; internet www.archive.schleswig-holstein.de/lash; f. 1870; 32,000 m of documents since 1059; 450,000 m of documentary film on Schleswig-Holstein; 110,000 vols; Dir Prof. Dr REIMER WITT.

Schwerin im Meckl

Landesbibliothek Mecklenburg-Vorpommern: Johannes-Stelling-Str. 29, 19053 Schwerin; tel. (385) 558440; fax (385) 5584424; e-mail lb@lbmv.de; internet www.lbmv.de; f. 1779; 650,000 vols; Dir Dr R.-J. WEGENER.

Sigmaringen

Landesarchiv Baden-Württemberg-Abteilung Staatsarchiv Sigmaringen: Postfach 1638, 72486 Sigmaringen; located at: Karlstr. 1–3, 72488 Sigmaringen; tel. (7571) 101551; fax (7571) 101552; e-mail staSigmaringen@la-bw.de; internet www.landesarchiv-bw.de/stas; f. 1865; archives of Regierungsbezirk Tübingen and Sigmaringen municipal archive; family archives of the princes of Hohenzollern, barons of Stauffenberg, etc.; 18,500 m of archives since 11th c.; 64,000 vols; Co-Dirs Dr O. H. BECKER, Dr V. TRUGENBERGER, Dr F.-J. ZIWES.

Speyer

Landesarchiv: Otto-Mayer-Str. 9, 67346 Speyer; tel. (6232) 9192-0; fax (6232) 9192-100; e-mail post@landesarchiv-speyer.de; internet www.landeshauptarchiv.de/speyer; f. 1817; historical archives of the Palatinate (878–1798), of the French administration until 1815 and the Bavarian administration until 1945; current accessions of administrations in the Palatinate and Rheinhesse; collection of maps; Dir Dr JOACHIM KERMANN.

Pfälzische Landesbibliothek (Regional Library of Pfalz): Otto-Mayer-Str. 9, 67343 Speyer; tel. (6232) 9006-224; fax (6232) 9006-200; e-mail info.plb@lbz-rlp.de; internet www.lbz-rlp.de; since 2004 part of the Landesbibliothekszentrums Rheinland-Pfalz; f. 1921; 963,830 vols on all subjects, with special reference to the Palatinate and the Saar; includes library of the Historischer Verein der Pfalz; Dir Dr JÜRGEN VORDERSTEMANN.

Stuttgart

Bibliothek der Staatlichen Hochschule für Musik und Darstellende Kunst: Urbanstr. 25, 70182 Stuttgart; tel. (711) 212-4664; fax (711) 212-4663; e-mail bibliothek@mh-stuttgart.de; internet www.mh-stuttgart.de; f. 1857; 18,820 vols, 81,203 musical scores, 3,624 records, 6,259 CDs, 243 videos, 163 DVDs; Librarians CATHERINA BECKER, CLAUDIA NIEBEL.

Bibliothek des Instituts für Auslandsbeziehungen (Institute for Foreign Relations, Library): Postfach 102463, 70020 Stuttgart; premises at: Charlottenpl. 17, 70173 Stuttgart; tel. (711) 2225147; fax (711) 2225-131; e-mail bibliothek@ifa.de; internet cms.ifa.de/info/bibliothek; f. 1917; 400,000 vols, 2,300 current periodicals, 11,000 microfilms; Pres. ALOIS VON WALDBURG-ZEIL; publ. *KulturAustausch* (online).

Bibliothek für Zeitgeschichte in der Württembergischen Landesbibliothek: Konrad Adenauer Str. 8, 70173 Stuttgart; tel. (711) 2124516; fax (711) 2124517; e-mail bfz@wlb-stuttgart.de; internet www.wlb-stuttgart.de/bfz; f. 1915; contemporary history, political sciences, military sciences, especially concerning World Wars I and II, and other conflicts since the beginning of 20th c.; 350,000 vols, 550 current periodicals, and special collections (photographs, maps, leaflets, posters, microfiches, etc.); Dir Prof. Dr GERHARD HIRSCHFELD; publs *Schriften der Bibliothek für Zeitgeschichte–Neue Folge*, *Stuttgarter Vorträge zur Zeitgeschichte*.

Fraunhofer-Informationszentrum Raum und Bau (IRB) (Fraunhofer Information Centre for Regional Planning and Building Construction): Nobelstr. 12, 70569 Stuttgart; tel. (711) 970-2500; fax (711) 970-2508; e-mail irb@irb.fhg.de; internet www.irb.fraunhofer.de; f. 1941; information centre for architecture and town and regional planning in Germany; 117,200 vols and 5,600 research reports, standards, test certificates and licences; Dir THOMAS H. MORSZECK; publs *ARCONIS Wissen zum Planen und Bauen und zum Baumarkt* (4 a year), *Kurzberichte aus der Bauforschung* (6 a year).

Hauptstaatsarchiv Stuttgart: Konrad-Adenauer-Str. 4, 70173 Stuttgart; tel. (711) 212-4335; fax (711) 212-4360; e-mail hstastuttgart@la-bw.de; internet www.landesarchiv-bw.de/hstas; history and regional studies of South-west Germany, with particular reference to Württemberg and Baden-Württemberg since 9th c.; archives of 107,000 charters, 18,000 m of files and vols, 40,000 maps and plans, 100,000 seals and arms; Dir (vacant).

Rathausbücherei der Landeshauptstadt Stuttgart (Town Hall Library of the State Capital of Stuttgart): Marktpl. 1, 70173 Stuttgart; tel. (711) 2163301; fax (711) 2163506; e-mail rathausbuecherei@stuttgart.de; internet www.stuttgart.de/stadtbuecherei/rathausbuecherei; f. archives 1730; history of Stuttgart and Württemberg, legal history, public administration; 127,383 vols; spec. collns incl. 18th.–19th c. first editions published in Stuttgart; Dir GABY VOLLMER.

Universitätsbibliothek (University Library): Postfach 104941, 70043 Stuttgart; Holzgartenstr. 16, 70174 Stuttgart; tel. (711) 6858-2222; fax (711) 6858-3502; e-mail ub@ub.uni-stuttgart.de; internet www.ub.uni-stuttgart.de; f. 1829; 1,236,371 books, including 212,135 theses, 2,357 print and 16,751 electronic periodicals, 186,489 standards, 107,373 micromaterials, 12,500 electronic documents; Dir WERNER STEPHAN.

Universitätsbibliothek Hohenheim: Garbenstr. 15, 70599 Stuttgart; tel. (711) 4592096; fax (711) 4593262; e-mail ubmail@uni-hohenheim.de; internet www.ub.uni-hohenheim.de; f. 1818; 500,000 vols; agriculture, sciences, economics; Dir KARL-WILHELM HORSTMANN.

Württembergische Landesbibliothek (State Library of Würtemberg): Postfach 105441, 70047 Stuttgart; Konrad Adenauerstr. 8, 70173 Stuttgart; tel. (711) 212-4424; fax (711) 212-4422; e-mail direktion@wlb-stuttgart.de; internet www.wlb-stuttgart.de; f. 1765; 3,389,586 vols, 7,062 incunabula; large collection of old Bibles; 15,248 MSS; Hölderlin archive and Stefan George archive; music and ballet colln; Dir Dr JÖRG ENNEN.

Trier

Bibliothek des Priesterseminars Trier: Postfach 1330, 54203 Trier; located at: 54290 Trier, Jesuitenstr. 13; tel. (651) 9484-141; fax (651) 9484-181; e-mail flohr@uni-trier.de; internet www.bps-trier.de; f. 1805; 440,000 vols on philosophy and theology, 542 theological manuscripts, and 122 incunabula; Librarian Dr MICHAEL EMBACH.

Stadtbibliothek Trier (Trier City Library): Weberbach 25, 54290 Trier; tel. (651) 718-1429; fax (651) 718-1428; e-mail stadtbibliothek@trier.de; internet www.trier.de; f. 1804; developed from the former Jesuit Library (f. 1560) and University Library; contains 403,000 books, 2,600 MSS and about 2,500 incunabula; scientific library; colln includes a Gutenberg Bible, and a page of the *Codex Egberti*; Chief Librarian Prof. Dr GUNTHER FRANZ; publs *Ausstellungskataloge Trierer Bibliotheken*, *Kurtrierisches Jahrbuch*, *Landeskundliche Vierteljahrsblätter*, *Ortschroniken des Trierer Landes*, *Rheinland-pfälzische Bibliographie*.

Universitätsbibliothek: Universitätsring 15, 54296 Trier; tel. (651) 201-2496; fax (651) 201-3977; e-mail bibliothek@ub.uni-trier.de; internet www.ub.uni-trier.de; f. 1970; open to the public; 1,610,000 vols; Dir Dr HILDEGARD MÜLLER.

Tübingen

Universitätsbibliothek: Wilhelmstr 32, 72016 Tübingen; tel. (7071) 2972577; fax (7071) 293123; e-mail sekretariat@ub.uni-tuebingen.de; internet www.ub.uni-tuebingen.de; f. in the last quarter of 15th c.; 3,400,000 books, journals, microfilms and microfiches, 2,800,000 vols and journals in faculty libraries, 2,100 incunabula, 8,863 MSS; Dir Dr U. SCHAPKA; publ. *Index theologicus (Ixtheo) Zeitschrifteninhaltsdienst Theologie* (on CD-ROM only, 4 a year).

Ulm

Stadtbibliothek Ulm (City Library of Ulm): Vestgasse 1, 89073 Ulm; tel. (731) 161-4100; fax (731) 161-1633; e-mail stadtbibliothek@ulm.de; internet www.stadtbibliothek.ulm.de; f. 1516; 491,432 vols, 518 current periodicals; special collections: the arts, regional history; Dir J. LANGE.

Weimar

Herzogin Anna Amalia Bibliothek: Platz der Demokratie 1, 99423 Weimar; tel. (3643) 545200; fax (3643) 545220; e-mail haab@swkk.de; internet www.swkk.de/haab; f. 1691; history of literature, art and music; special collections: German literature of the Classical Period (1750–1850), Faust, Liszt, Nietzsche, Shakespeare; 50,000 vols destroyed by fire September 2004; 1,000,000 vols; Dir Dr MICHAEL KNOCHE; publ. *Internationale Bibliographie zur deutschen Klassik* (annually).

Thüringisches Hauptstaatsarchiv Weimar (Central State Archive of Thuringia in Weimar): Postfach 2726, 99408 Weimar; Marstallstr. 2, 99423 Weimar; tel. (3643) 870-0; fax (3643) 870-100; e-mail weimar@staatsarchive.thueringen.de; internet www.thueringen.de/de/staatsarchive; f. 1547; Dir Prof. Dr habil. VOLKER WAHL.

Wiesbaden

Bibliothek des Statistischen Bundesamtes: Gustav-Stresemann-Ring 11, 65180 Wiesbaden; tel. (611) 754573; fax (611) 754433; e-mail bibliothek@destatis.de; internet www.destatis.de/bibliothek; f. 1948; collection of statistical records, esp. on the economic and demographic development of all countries; 500,000 vols, 1,200 journals; Dir Dr THOMAS HELMCKE.

Hessische Landesbibliothek Wiesbaden (State Library of Hesse in Wiesbaden): Rheinstr. 55–57, 65185 Wiesbaden; tel. (611) 334-2670; fax (611) 334-2694; e-mail information@hlb-wiesbaden.de; internet www.hlb-wiesbaden.de; f. 1813; 740,000 vols, 3,000 current periodicals, manuscripts and incunabula; Dir Dr MARIANNE DOERR.

Hessisches Hauptstaatsarchiv Wiesbaden (Central State Archive of Hesse in Wiesbaden): Mosbacher Str. 55, 65187 Wiesbaden; tel. (611) 881-0; fax (611) 881-145; e-mail poststelle@hhstaw.hessen.de; internet www.hauptstaatsarchiv.hessen.de; f. 1963; regional documents since 10th c.; Dir Dr KLAUS EILER; publ. *Nassauische Annalen* (annually).

Wolfenbüttel

Herzog August Bibliothek: Lessingplatz 1, Postfach 1364, 38299 Wolfenbüttel; tel. (5331) 8080; fax 808134; e-mail direktor@hab.de; internet www.hab.de; f. 1572; cultural history from the Middle Ages to the Enlightenment; 875,000 vols, 12,280 manuscripts, 3,500 incunabula, 3,000 artists' books; Dir Prof. Dr HELWIG SCHMIDT-GLINTZER; publs *Ausstellungskataloge*, *Kleine Schriften*, *Wolfenbütteler Beiträge*, *Wolfenbütteler Barocknachrichten*, *Wolfenbütteler Notizen zur Buchgeschichte*, *Wolfenbütteler Renaissance-*

Mitteilungen, *Wolfenbütteler Forschungen*, *Wolfenbütteler Hefte*, *Wolfenbütteler Bibliotheks-Informationen*, *Repertorien zur Erforschung der frühen Neuzeit*, *Malerbuch-Kataloge*.

Niedersächsisches Staatsarchiv (State Archive of Lower Saxony): Forstweg 2, 38302 Wolfenbüttel; tel. (5331) 935-0; fax (5331) 935-211; e-mail Wolfenbuettel@nla.niedersachsen.de; internet www.staatsarchive.niedersachsen.de; f. 16th c.; contains documents and records of the province of Brunswick; *c*. 60,000 vols; Dir Dr HORST-RÜDIGER JARCK.

Worms

Stadtarchiv im Raschi Haus: Hintere Judengasse 6, 67547 Worms; tel. (6241) 853-4700; fax (6241) 853-4710; e-mail stadtarchiv@worms.de; internet www.stadtarchiv.worms.de; Judaic museum; large collection of records, documents and maps; Head Archivist Dr GEROLD BOENNEN.

Stadtbibliothek (City Library): Marktpl. 10, 67547 Worms; tel. (6241) 853-4209; fax (6241) 853-4220; e-mail stadtbibliothek@worms.de; internet www.worms.de; f. 1881; 290,000 vols, 165 incunabula; special collections on Luther, Kant and the Nibelungenlied; Dir Dr BUSSO DIEKAMP; publ. *Der Wormsgau*.

Wuppertal

Stadtbibliothek (City Library): Kolpingstr. 8, 42103 Wuppertal; tel. (202) 563-2302; fax (202) 563-8489; e-mail stadtbibliothek@stadt.wuppertal.de; internet www.wuppertal.de/stadtbib; f. 1852; central library and 9 brs; special collections: theology, early Socialism; Else Lasker-Schüler-Archiv, Armin T. Wegner-Archiv; 750,000 vols; Dir UTE SCHARMANN.

Würzburg

Staatsarchiv Würzburg (State Archive of Würzburg): Residenz-Nordflügel, 97070 Würzburg; tel. (931) 35529-0; fax (931) 35529-70; e-mail poststelle@stawu.bayern.de; internet www.gda.bayern.de/staarin.htm; f. in Middle Ages; 36,000 vols, 6,850,000 documents; archives of Lower Franconia since Middle Ages; Dir Dr W. WAGENHÖFER.

Universitätsbibliothek: Am Hubland, 97074 Würzburg; tel. (931) 888-5943; fax (931) 888-5970; e-mail direktion@bibliothek.uni-wuerzburg.de; internet www.bibliothek.uni-wuerzburg.de; f. 1619; 3,324,306 vols, 225,063 theses, 2,949 incunabula, 2,258 manuscripts, 73 papyri; special Franconian collection; Dir Dr KARL SUEDEKUM.

Museums and Art Galleries

Aachen

Couven-Museum: Hühnermarkt 17, 52062 Aachen; tel. (241) 432-4421; fax (241) 37075; e-mail info@suermondt-ludwig-museum.de; internet www.couven-museum.de; f. 1958 in a house built in 1662; 20 rooms showing history of interior design during 18th–19th c., featuring the rococo, Louis XVI, Napoleon Empire and Biedermeier periods; includes reconstructed 'Adler-Apotheke', where chocolate was made for the first time in the city; colIns of porcelain and silverware; Dir BELINDA PETRI.

Internationales Zeitungsmuseum der Stadt Aachen (International Newspaper Museum): Pontstr. 13, 52062 Aachen; tel. (241) 4324508; fax (241) 4090656; e-mail izm@mail.aachen.de; internet www.izm.de; f. 1886; 165,000 newspapers; spec. library for press history; Dir PETER VAN DEN BRINK.

Ludwig Forum für Internationale Kunst (Ludwig Forum for International Art): Jülicher Str. 97–109, 52070 Aachen; tel. (241) 1807-104; fax (241) 1807-101; e-mail info@ludwigforum.de; internet www.ludwigforum.de; f. 1969; modern art since the 1960s; library: Modern art library of 35,000 vols, periodicals and video cassettes; special colIns of graffiti, light sculptures, American pop art and video art; Dir HARALD KUNDE.

Museum Burg Frankenberg (Burg Museum of Frankenberg): Bismarckstr. 68, 52066 Aachen; tel. (241) 432-4410; fax (241) 37075; e-mail info@suermondt-ludwig-museum.de; internet www.burgfrankenberg.de; f. 1961, castle dates from 13th c.; history of the city from Karl the Great to present; colIns of coins, local art; Dir Dr ADAM C. OELLERS.

Suermondt-Ludwig-Museum: Wilhelmstr. 18, 52070 Aachen; tel. (241) 47980-0; fax (241) 37075; e-mail info@suermondt-ludwig-museum.de; internet www.suermondt-ludwig-museum.de; f. 1882; Gothic art and sculptures; 17th c. paintings (Dutch and Flemish Schools in particular); 10,000 sketches and watercolours, incl. some by Dürer, Rembrandt and Goya; local art since 19th c.; library: history of art library of 50,000 vols; Dir ADAM C. OELLERS.

Zollmuseum Friedrichs (Customs Museum): Horbacher Str. 497, 52072 Aachen; tel. (241) 99706015; internet www.zollmuseum-friedrichs.de; 20 rooms and 3,000 exhibits documenting customs practice and history; colIns of confiscated materials and smugglers' devices; Dir KURT CREMER.

Baden-Baden

Museum Frieder Burda: Lichtentaler Allee 8b, 76530 Baden-Baden; tel. (7221) 39898-0; fax (7221) 39898-30; e-mail office@museum-frieder-burda.de; internet www.museum-frieder-burda.de; f. 2004; colln of modern art; 500 paintings, sculptures and objects; special colIns of German expressionism and later works by Picasso; Man. ANNETTE SMETANIG.

Staatliche Kunsthalle (State Art Museum): Lichtentaler Allee 8A, 76530 Baden-Baden; tel. (7221) 300763; fax (7221) 3859030076-500; e-mail info@kunsthalle-baden-baden.de; internet hosting.zkm.de/kbb; f. 1909; international exhibitions of classical and contemporary art; Dir Dr FRITZKAROLA EMSLANDERGRÄSSLIN (acting); publs catalogues.

Bayreuth

Deutsches Freimaurer Museum in Bayreuth (German Freemasons' Museum in Bayreuth): Im Hofgarten 1, 95444 Bayreuth; tel. (921) 69824; fax (921) 512850; e-mail museum.bayreuth@freimaurer.org; f. 1913; freemasonry history and practice; library of 25,000 membership records since 1933; includes sections on Rosicrucians, Illuminati, Templars; Dir ROLAND MARTIN HANKE.

Historisches Museum Bayreuth (Historical Museum of Bayreuth): Kirchpl. 6, 95444 Bayreuth; tel. (921) 764010; fax (921) 7640123; e-mail historischesmuseum@bayreuth.de; f. 1996; 1,200 square m, 34 exhibition rooms recording history of Bayreuth since 12th c.; Dir Dr SYLVIA HABERMANN.

Kunst Museum Bayreuth (Art Museum of Bayreuth): Altes Rathaus, Maximilianstr. 33, 95444 Bayreuth; tel. (921) 76453-10; fax (921) 76453-20; e-mail info@kunstmuseum-bayreuth.de; internet www.kunstmuseum-bayreuth.de; f. 1999; art since beginning of 20th c.; colIns include Dr Helmut und Constanze Meyer Kunststiftung, fantastic realism of Caspar Walter Rauh, British-American Tobacco colln on the history of the tobacco industry; Dir Dr MARINA VON ASSEL.

Richard-Wagner-Museum mit Nationalarchiv und Forschungsstätte der Richard-Wagner-Stiftung (Richard Wagner Museum, including National Archive and Research Office of the Richard Wagner Foundation): Richard-Wagner-Str. 48, 95444 Bayreuth; tel. (921) 757280; fax (921) 7572822; e-mail info@wagnermuseum.de; internet www.wagnermuseum.de; f. 1976; museum and archive of the life and works of Richard Wagner (1813–1883) and of the history of the Bayreuth festival; Dir Dr SVEN FRIEDRICH.

Bensheim-Auerbach

Grossherzogliche Porzellansammlung (Grand-Ducal Porcelain Collection): Schlossgartenstr. 10, Prinz-Georg-Palaïs, 64289 Darmstadt; e-mail info@porzellanmuseum-darmstadt.de; internet www.schlossmuseum-darmstadt.de; f. 1907; European porcelain, paintings, furniture, faïence; Dir BETTINA JOHN-WILLEKE.

Berlin

Berlinische Galerie: Alte Jakobstr. 124–28, 10969 Berlin; tel. (30) 78902600; fax (30) 78902700; e-mail bg@berlinischegalerie.de; internet www.berlinischegalerie.de; f. 1975; permanent colln of works since beginning of 20th c.: paintings and drawings (including works by Dix, Grosz and Kirchner), photographs, architectural drawings and models; temporary exhibitions of modern art; library of 65,000 vols, mainly on art since beginning of 20th c.; Dir Dr URSULA PRINZ (acting); Librarian SABINE SCHARDT.

Botanischer Garten und Botanisches Museum Berlin-Dahlem (Botanic Garden and Botanical Museum Berlin-Dahlem): Königin-Luise-Str. 6–8, 14191 Berlin; tel. (30) 83850-100; fax (30) 83850-186; e-mail zebgbm@bgbm.org; internet www.bgbm.org; f. 1679, Herbarium f. 1815, Museum f. 1879; attached to Freie Universität Berlin; plant taxonomy and phytogeography; library of 160,000 vols, 2,300 current periodicals, 3.5m. specimens; Dir Prof. Dr W. GREUTER; publs *Willdenowia* (2 a year), *Englera* (irregular).

Brücke-Museum: Bussardsteig 9, 14195 Berlin; tel. (30) 8312029; fax (30) 8315961; e-mail bruecke-museum@t-online.de; internet www.bruecke-museum.de; f. 1967; German expressionism, paintings, sculptures and graphic art of the Brücke group; Dir Prof. Dr MAGDALENA MOELLER; publ. *Brücke Archiv* (annually).

Deutsches Historisches Museum (German Historical Museum): Unter den Linden 2, 10117 Berlin; tel. (30) 203040; fax (30) 20304543; internet www.dhm.de; f. 1987; German and modern European history; library of 3,000 vols; Gen. Dir Dr HANS OTTOMEYER.

Haus der Wannsee-Konferenz, Gedenk- und Bildungsstätte (House of the Wannsee Conference, Memorial and Educational Site): Am Grossen Wannsee 56–58, 14109 Berlin; tel. (30) 8050010; fax (30) 80500127; e-mail info@ghwk.de; internet www.ghwk.de; f. 1992; memorial and educational site, with a permanent exhibition documenting the persecution and destruction of Jews in Europe 1933–1945; educational department; library; library of 39,000 vols; Dir Dr NORBERT KAMPE; publ. *Newsletter* (online).

Käthe-Kollwitz-Museum: Fasanenstr. 24, 10719 Berlin; tel. (30) 8825210; fax (30) 8811901; e-mail info@kaethe-kollwitz.de; internet www.kaethe-kollwitz.de; f. 1986; private museum (colln of Prof. Hans Pels-Leusden); permanent exhibition of Käthe Kollwitz's work; temporary exhibitions of artists related to Käthe Kollwitz; Dir MARTIN FRITSCH.

Museum für Naturkunde der Humboldt-Universität zu Berlin (Natural History Museum): Invalidenstr. 43, 10115 Berlin; tel. (30) 2093-8591; fax (30) 2093-8814; e-mail gesine.steiner@rz.hu-berlin.de; internet www.museum.hu-berlin.de; f. 1889; incl. research institutes of palaeontology, mineralogy and systematic zoology; Dir Prof. MICHAEL UNSCHEID.

Staatliche Museen zu Berlin–Preussischer Kulturbesitz: Stauffenbergstr. 41, 10785 Berlin; tel. (30) 2662610; fax (30) 2662992; internet www.smb.museum; f. 1957; supervises museums and collections at the following sites in Berlin: Berlin–Mitte (Museumsinsel), Tiergarten (Kulturforum), Dahlem, Charlottenburg, Köpenick; Gen. Dir Prof. Dr PETER-KLAUS SCHUSTER.

Museums:

Ägyptisches Museum und Papyrussammlung (Egyptian Museum and Papyrus Collection): Am Lustgarten, 10178 Berlin; e-mail aemp@smb.spk-berlin.de; internet www.smb.museum; f. 1828 as a section of the former Royal Art Collection, collections united 1991; Dir Prof. Dr DIETRICH WILDUNG.

Alte Nationalgalerie (Old National Gallery): Bodestr. 1–3, 10178 Berlin; tel. (30) 20905801; fax (30) 20905802; e-mail ang@smb.spk-berlin.de; internet www.smb.museum; f. 1861; 19th c. sculpture and painting; Dir Dr BERNHARD MAAZ.

Antikensammlung, Pergamonmuseum und Altes Museum (Collection of Classical Antiquties at the Pergamon Museum and the Old Museum): Berlin–Mitte; tel. (30) 20905201; fax (30) 20905202; e-mail ant@smb.spk-berlin.de; internet www.smb.museum; f. 1830; Dir Prof. Dr ANDREAS SCHOLL (Classical Antiquities).

Berggruen Museum (Berggruen Museum): Schlosstr., Berlin–Charlottenburg; tel. (30) 3269580; fax (30) 32695819; internet www.smb.museum; f. 1996 by the art dealer and collector Heinz Berggruen; private collection focusing on Picasso and his contemporaries, incl. Braque, Matisse, Klee, Laurens, Giacometti.

Ethnologisches Museum (Ethnological Museum): Berlin–Dahlem, Lansstr. 8; tel. (30) 8301-0; fax (30) 8301500; e-mail md@smb.spk-berlin.de; internet www.smb.museum; f. 1829 as the Ethnographic Collection, museum f. 1873; Dir Prof. Dr VIOLA KÖNIG.

Friedrich Christian Flick Collection: Invalidenstr. 50/51, 10557 Berlin; tel. and fax (30) 39783412; e-mail hbf@smb.spk-berlin.de; internet www.smb.museum; 2,000 works, mainly since 1990.

Friedrichswerdersche Kirche (Friedrichswerder Church): Berlin–Mitte, Werderscher Markt; tel. (30) 2081323; e-mail nng@smb.spk-berlin.de; internet www.smb.museum; early 19th c. sculpture.

Gemäldegalerie (Old Masters' Gallery): Berlin–Tiergarten, Matthäikirchplatz; tel. (30) 2662101; fax (30) 2662103; e-mail gg@smb.spk-berlin.de; internet www.smb.museum; f. 1830 from collections of The Great Elector (1620–1688) and Frederick the Great (1712–1786); Dir Prof. Dr BERND LINDEMANN.

Gipsformerei: Sophie-Charlotten-Str. 17-18, 14059 Berlin; tel. (30) 3267690; fax (30) 32676912; e-mail gf@smb.spk-berlin.de; internet www.smb.museum; f. 1819; replicas of 6,500 sculptures, from Germany and other European museums.

Hamburger Bahnhof–Museum für Gegenwart—Berlin (Museum of the Present): Berlin–Tiergarten, Invalidenstr. 50–51; tel. (30) 39783412; fax (30) 39783413; e-mail hbf@smb.spk-berlin.de; internet www.smb.museum; f. 1996; art since 1950.

Helmut Newton Stiftung (Helmut Newton Foundation): Jebensstr. 2, 10623 Berlin; tel. (30) 31864855; e-mail info@helmut-newton-stiftung.org; internet www.smb.museum; f. 2003 by the photographer Helmut Newton (1920–2004) to preserve and display his own works and those of his wife, June; temporary exhibitions of work by other photographers; Curator Dr MATTHIAS HARDER.

Kunstbibliothek: see Libraries and Archives.

Kunstgewerbemuseum (Museum of Decorative Arts): Berlin–Tiergarten, Matthäikirchplatz 4/6; tel. (30) 2662902; fax (30) 2662947; e-mail kgm@smb.spk-berlin.de; internet www.smb.museum; f. 1868; Dir Prof. Dr ANGELA SCHÖNBERGER.

Kupferstichkabinett–Sammlung der Zeichnung und Druckgraphik (Museum of Prints and Drawings): Berlin–Tiergarten, Matthäikirchplatz 8; tel. (30) 2662002; fax (30) 2662959; e-mail kk@smb.spk-berlin.de; internet www.smb.museum; f. 1831; collection covers Europe from the Middle Ages to the present and includes more recent items from America; 111,000 drawings, 550,000 prints, illuminated manuscripts, printed illustrated books etc.; works by Botticelli, Dürer, Bruegel the Elder, Rembrandt, Picasso, Giacometti; Dir Prof. Dr HEIN-TH. SCHULZE ALTCAPPENBERG.

Münzkabinett (Numismatic Collection): Bodestr., Berlin–Mitte; tel. (30) 20905701; fax (30) 20905702; e-mail mk@smb.spk-berlin.de; internet www.smb.museum; f. 1830 as Numismatic Collection, independent museum 1868; 500,000 coins, medals, paper money, seals–Greek, Roman, Middle Ages to present European, Oriental and Islamic; Bodemuseum currently undergoing renovation–temporary displays at Pergamon Museum, Altes Museum and Museum of Pre- and Early History; Dir Prof. Dr BERND KLUGE.

Museum Europäischer Kulturen (Museum of European Culture): Arnimallee 25, Berlin–Dahlem; tel. (30) 83901287; fax (30) 83901283; e-mail mek@smb.spk-berlin.de; internet www.smb.museum; f. 1999 following merger of the Museum für Volkskunde (Museum of Folklore) and European holdings from the Museum für Völkerkunde (Museum of Ethnology); Dir Prof. Dr KONRAD VANJA.

Museum für Fotografie (Museum of Ethnology): Berlin–Dahlem, Lansstr. 8; e-mail mv@smb.spk-berlin.de; internet www.smb.museum; f. 1829 as the Ethnographic Collection, museum f. 1873; Dir Prof. Dr KLAUS HELFRICH.

Museum für Indische Kunst (Museum of Indian Art): Lansstr. 8, Berlin–Dahlem; tel. (30) 8301361; fax (30) 8301502; e-mail mik@smb.spk-berlin.de; internet www.smb.museum; f. 1963; Dir Prof. Dr MARIANNE YALDIZ.

Museum für Islamische Kunst (Museum of Islamic Art): Pergamonmuseum, am Kupfergraben, Berlin–Mitte; tel. (30) 20905401; fax (30) 20905402; e-mail isl@smb.spk-berlin.de; internet www.smb.museum; f. 1904 as department of Kaiser Friedrich Museum (now Bodemuseum); Dir Prof. Dr CLAUS-PETER HAASE.

Museum für Ostasiatische Kunst (Museum of East Asian Art): Berlin–Dahlem, Lansstr. 8; tel. (30) 8301382; fax (30) 8301501; e-mail oak@smb.spk-berlin.de; internet www.smb.museum; f. 1992 following merger of collections from the Pergamon Museum and the Museum in Dahlem; Dir Prof. Dr WILLIBALD VEIT.

Museum für Vor- und Frügeschichte (Museum of Pre- and Early History): Berlin–Charlottenburg, Schloss Charlottenburg (Langhansbau); tel. (30) 32674811; fax (30) 32674812; e-mail mvf@smb.spk-berlin.de; internet www.smb.museum; f. 1931, collection made independent from the Museum for Ethnology; Dir Prof. Dr WILFRIED MENGHIN.

Neue National Galerie (New National Gallery): Berlin–Tiergarten, Potsdamer Str. 50; tel. (30) 2662651; fax (30) 2624715; e-mail nng@smb.spk-berlin.de; internet www.smb.museum; f. 1968 following merger of collections from the Alte Nationalgalerie and the Gallery of 20th Century Art; painting and sculpture since early 20th c.

Skulpturensammlung und Museum für Byzantische Kunst (Sculpture Collection and Museum of Byzantine Art): Berlin–Mitte, Am Kupfergraben, Bodemuseum; internet www.smb.museum; f. 2000 following unification of the Sculpture Collection and the Museum of Byzantine Art; Dir Prof. Dr ARNE EFFENBERGER.

Vorderasiatisches Museum (Museum of Ancient Near Eastern Antiquities): Berlin–Mitte, Am Kupfergraben; e-mail vam@smb.spk-berlin.de; internet www.smb.museum; f. 1899 as Collection of Western Asiatic Antiquities, museum f. 1953.

Stiftung Stadtmuseum Berlin, Landesmuseum für Kultur und Geschichte Berlins: Poststr. 13–14, 10178 Berlin; tel. (30) 24002-0; fax (30) 24002-187; e-mail info@stadtmuseum.de; internet www.stadtmuseum.de; f. 1874 as Märkisches Museum; illustrates history of Berlin, its culture and its art; library of 50,000 vols; Dir (vacant); publ. *Jahrbuch*.

Verwaltung der Staatlichen Schlösser und Gärten, West-Berlin (Administration of State Castles and Gardens): Charlottenburg Luisenpl., 10585 Berlin, Schloss; tel. (30) 32091-1; f. 1927; the administration controls Charlottenburg Castle, Grunewald Hunting Castle (with collection of paintings), Glienicke Castle and Peacock Island (Castle and Park); library of 5,000 vols; Chief Officers Prof. Dr WINFRIED BAER, Prof. Dr HELMUT BÖRSCH-SUPAN, Prof. Dr JÜRGEN JULIER.

Bonn

Beethoven-Haus: Bonngasse 18–26, 53111 Bonn; tel. (228) 98175-0; fax (228) 98175-31; e-mail info@beethoven-haus-bonn.de; internet www.beethoven-haus-bonn.de; f. 1889; birthplace of Ludwig van Beethoven (1770–1827); museum and research centre with Beethoven archive; 1,000 mems; library of 30,000 vols, 125 periodicals, 25,000 music scores (6,000 by Beethoven); Dir Dr MICHAEL LADENBURGER.

Kunstmuseum Bonn: Friedrich-Ebert-Allee 2, 53113 Bonn; tel. (228) 776260; fax (228) 776220; e-mail kunstmuseum@bonn.de; internet www.bonn.de/kunstmuseum; f. 1882, restored 1948, new building 1992; collection of 20th c. art; German expressionist painting, with important August Macke collection; contemporary international graphic art, contemporary German art, photos and videos; library: c. 47,000 vols; Dir Prof. Dr DIETER RONTE.

Rheinisches Landesmuseum Bonn (Rhineland Museum in Bonn): Colmantstr. 14–16, 53115 Bonn; tel. (228) 9881-0; fax (228) 9881-299; e-mail RLMB@lvr.de; internet www.lvr.de; f. 1820; prehistoric, Roman and Frankish antiquities of the Rhineland; Rhenish sculpture, painting and applied arts up to the 20th c.; Dutch paintings; library of 150,000 vols; Dir Prof. Dr FRANK GÜNTER ZEHNDER; publs *Bonner Jahrbücher des Rheinischen Landesmuseums und des Vereins von Altertumsfreunden im Rheinlande* (annually), *Das Rheinische Landesmuseum Bonn* (4 a year).

Zoologisches Forschungsinstitut und Museum Alexander Koenig (Alexander Koenig Zoological Research Institute and Museum): Adenauerallee 160, 53113 Bonn; tel. (228) 9122-0; fax (228) 9122-212; e-mail info.zfmk@uni-bonn.de; internet www.museumkoenig.de; f. 1912; zoology—vertebrates and insects; library of 150,000 vols; Dir Prof. Dr J. W. WÄGELE; publs *Bonner zoologische Beiträge* (4 a year), *Myotis: Mitteilungsblatt für Fledermauskundler* (annually).

Bremen

Focke-Museum (District Museum for Art and Culture): Schwachhauser Heerstr. 240, 28213 Bremen; tel. (421) 699600-0; fax (421) 6996099; e-mail post@focke-museum.bremen.de; internet www.focke-museum.de; f. 1900; exhibits from Middle Ages to 1900, pre- and early history, history of navigation, etc.; library of 40,000 vols; Dir Dr JÖRN CHRISTIANSEN; publ. *Hefte des Focke-Museums* (2 or 3 a year).

Kunsthalle Bremen (Bremen Art Museum): Am Wall 207, 28195 Bremen; tel. (421) 329080; fax (421) 3290847; e-mail office@kunsthalle-bremen.de; internet www.kunsthalle-bremen.de; f. 1823; European paintings since 15th c., prints and drawings; sculpture since 167th c.; Japanese drawings and books; library of 100,000 vols; Dir Dr WULF HERZOGENRATH.

Übersee-Museum Bremen (Museum of Overseas Culture, Bremen): Bahnhofsplatz 13, 28195 Bremen; tel. (421) 16038-101; fax (421) 16038-99; e-mail office@uebersee-museum.de; internet www.uebersee-museum.de; f. 1896; ethnology, history of commerce, natural history; library of 70,000 vols; Dir Dr WIEBKE AHRNDT; publ. *TenDenZen* (annually).

Brunswick

Herzog Anton Ulrich-Museum: Museumstr. 1, 38100 Braunschweig; tel. (531) 1225-0; fax (531) 1225-2408; e-mail info@museum-braunschweig.de; internet www.museum-braunschweig.de; f. 1754; collection includes old pictures, prints and drawings, medieval art, ceramics, 16th c. French enamels, carvings in ivory, bronzes, collection of lace, old clocks, etc.; library: art library of 60,000 vols; Dir Prof. Dr J. LUCKHARDT.

Städtisches Museum (City Musuem): Steintorwall 14 (Am Löwenwall), 38100 Brunswick; tel. (531) 4704505; fax (531) 4704555; e-mail staedtisches.museum@braunschweig.de; internet www.braunschweig.de/staedtisches_museum; f. 1861; collections illustrate topography, history and culture of the town; paintings since 19th c.; coins and medals (all periods and territories, with about 80,000 pieces); ethnographical collections; Dir Dr MARTIN EBERLE; publs *Arbeitsberichte*, *Braunschweiger Werkstücke*, *Miszellen*.

Museum Branch:

Zweigmuseum Altstadtrathaus: Altstadtmarkt 7, 38100 Brunswick; tel. (531) 4704551; fax (531) 4704555; e-mail staedtisches.museum@braunschweig.de; internet www.braunschweig.de/kultur/museen; f. 1991; building dates from late 13th c.; history of the city since 9th c.

Cologne

Agfa Foto-Historama (Agfa Museum of Photography): Bischofsgartenstr. 1, 50667 Cologne; tel. (221) 221-22411; fax (221) 221-24114; e-mail agfaphotohistorama@ml.museenkoeln.de; internet www.museenkoeln.de; history of photography; collection of cameras, photographs, caricatures and documents; Dir Dr BODO VON DEWITZ.

Josef-Haubrich-Kunsthalle (Josef Haubrich Museum): Josef-Haubrich-Hof, 50676 Cologne; tel. (221) 221-22335; fax (221) 221-24544; e-mail kunsthalle@netcologne.de; f. 1967; Dir (vacant).

Kölnisches Stadtmuseum: Zeughausstr. 1–3, 50667 Cologne; tel. (221) 221-25789; fax (221) 221-24154; e-mail ksm@museenkoeln.de; internet www.museenkoeln.de; f. 1888; history of Cologne from the Middle Ages to the present day; collns illustrate local culture, economy and everyday life, political history, craftsmen's and merchants' guilds, devotional objects, Judaica, transport, inventions made in the city, paintings by the Berckheyde brothers and Geldorp Gortzius, crafts, early globes, puppet theatre; library of 30,000 vols; Dir Dr WERNER SCHÄFKE.

Museum für Angewandte Kunst (Museum of Applied Art): An der Rechtschule, 50667 Cologne; tel. (221) 221-23860; fax (221) 221-23885; e-mail mfak@stadt-koeln.de; internet www.museenkoeln.de; f. 1888; library: see Libraries; applied art since Middle Ages; design colln since 1900; Dir Dr BIRGITT BORKOPP-RESTLE.

Museum für Ostasiatische Kunst (Museum for East Asian Art): Universitätsstr. 100, 50674 Cologne; tel. (221) 9405180; fax (221) 407290; e-mail mok@mok.museenkoeln.de; internet www.museenkoeln.de/mok; f. 1913; library of 12,000 vols; art from China (religious bronzes and ceramics), Korea (celadon objects of the 10th14th c. Koryo dynasty) and Japan (Buddhist painting and wood sculpture, Japanese screen painting); Dir Dr ADELE SCHLOMBS.

Museum Ludwig: Bischofsgartenstr. 1, 50667 Cologne; tel. (221) 221-26165; fax (221) 221-24114; e-mail info@museum-ludwig.de; internet www.museenkoeln.de; f. 1976; paintings, modern sculpture, prints, photos, videos; library; largest colln of Pop Art outside the USA; Russian avant-garde art; several hundred works by Picasso; Dir Prof. KASPER KÖNIG.

Rautenstrauch-Joest-Museum: Ubierring 45, 50678 Cologne; tel. (221) 33694-13; fax (221) 33694-10; e-mail rjm@rjm.museenkoeln.de; internet www.museenkoeln.de/rautenstrauch-joest-museum; f. 1901; ethnological museum; library of 40,000 vols; Dir Dr KLAUS SCHNEIDER; publ. *Ethnologica*.

Römisch-Germanisches Museum: Roncalliplatz 4, 50667 Cologne; tel. (221) 22122304; fax (221) 22124030; e-mail roemisch-germanisches-museum@stadt--koeln.de; internet www.museenkoeln.de/rgm; f. 1946; library of 14,000 vols; Dir Prof. Dr HANSGERD HELLENKEMPER; publs *Kölner Jahrbuch* (prehistory and early history, annually), *Kölner Forschungen*.

Schnütgen-Museum: Cäcilienstr. 29, 50667 Cologne; tel. (221) 22122310; fax (221) 22128489; e-mail schnutgen@netcologne.de; internet www.museenkoeln.de; f. 1906; library of 20,000 vols; 13,000 works of medieval art; houses 11th c. wooden crucifix; Dir Dr HILTRUD WESTERMANN-ANGERHAUSEN.

Wallraf-Richartz-Museum: Martinstr. 39, 50667 Cologne; tel. (221) 221-21119; fax (221) 221-22629; e-mail wrm@wrm.museenkoeln.de; internet www.museenkoeln.de/wrm; f. 1824; paintings, sculpture, prints, drawings dating from the Middle Ages, Baroque period, and 18th and 19th c.; library: see Libraries and Archives; Dir Dr RAINER BUDDE; publs *Wallraf-Richartz-Jahrbuch*, *Jahrbuch für Kunstgeschichte*.

Darmstadt

Hessisches Landesmuseum Darmstadt (State Museum of Hesse in Darmstadt): Friedenspl. 1, 64283 Darmstadt; tel. (6151) 165703; fax (6151) 28942; e-mail info@hlmd.de; internet www.hlmd.de; f. 1820; archaeology, prehistory, zoology, geology-palaeontology, mineralogy; art collections and cultural history since 9th c., incl. crafts, prints and drawings, stained glass, sculptures, painting, European art since 1945; library of 55,000 vols; Dir Dr INA BUSCH; publs *Kaupia–Darmstädter Beiträge zur Naturgeschichte* (2 a year), *Kunst in Hessen und am Mittelrhein* (annually).

Jagdmuseum Schloss Kranichstein: Kranichstein, 64289 Darmstadt, Schloss; tel. (6151) 718613; fax (6151) 732332; e-mail hessischer.jaegerhof@t-online.de; internet www.jagdschloss-kranichstein.de; f. 1918; pictures, hunting trophies and weapons, furnished rooms; owned by Stiftung Hessischer Jägerhof; Dir MONIKA KESSLER.

Schlossmuseum (Castle Museum): Residenzschloss, Marktpl. 15, 64283 Darmstadt; tel. (6151) 24035; fax (6151) 997457; e-mail info@schlossmuseum-darmstadt.de; internet www.schlossmuseum-darmstadt.de; f. 1920; Holbein Madonna, furnished rooms, ceremonial carriages and harness; Dir BETTINA JOHN-WILLEKE.

Dortmund

Museum für Kunst und Kulturgeschichte Dortmund (Dortmund Museum of Art and Cultural History): Hansastr. 3, 44137 Dortmund; tel. (231) 5025522; fax (231) 5025511; e-mail mkk@stadtdo.de; internet www.museendortmund.de/mkk; f. 1883; collections include medieval art and sculpture, furniture since 15th c., design, *objets d'art*, paintings, archaeology; library of 18,000 vols; Dir WOLFGANG E. WEICK; publ. catalogues.

Dresden

Landesamt für Archäologie mit Landesmuseum für Vorgeschichte (State Office of Archaeology and Museum of Prehistory): Japanisches Palais, Zur Wetterwarte 7, 01109 Dresden; tel. (351) 8926-0; fax (351) 8926-666; e-mail presse@archsax.smwk.sachsen.de; internet www.archsax.sachsen.de; f. 1993; preservation of ancient monuments, archaeological research and exhibitions; library of 40,000 vols specializing in prehistory; Dir Dr J. OEXLE; publs *Arbeits- und Forschungsberichte* (annually), *Archäologie aktuell im Freistaat Sachsen* (annually).

Mathematisch-Physikalischer Salon: Zwinger, 01067 Dresden; tel. (351) 4914660; fax (351) 4914666; e-mail mps@skd.smwk.sachsen.de; internet www.skd-dresden.de; f.

1560; historical watches and clocks, scientific instruments, etc.; library of 7,000 vols; Dir Dr PETER PLASSMEYER.

Militärhistorisches Museum der Bundeswehr (Militry-Historical Museum of the Federal Army): Olbrichtplatz 2, 01099 Dresden; tel. (351) 8232803; fax (351) 8232805; e-mail milhistmuseumbweingang@bwbbundeswehr.org; internet www.mhm.bunderswehr.de; f. 1990; German military history from the late Middle Ages to the present; exhibits include weapons, equipment, documents, uniforms and combat vehicles; cannons and caissons; also a mid-19th c. submarine, models, dioramas, paintings and sculptures; main focus of collns is post-1945 Germany; Dir Oberstleutnant FRANZ-JOSEFFERDINAND HEUSERFREIHERR VON RICHTHOFEN.

Museum für Tierkunde Dresden (Dresden Museum of Zoology): Königsbrücker Landstr. 159, 01109 Dresden; tel. (351) 8926326; fax (351) 8926327; e-mail birgit.walker@snsd.smwk.sachsen.de; internet globiz.sachsen.de/snsd/mtd_info.htm; f. 1728; library of 60,000 vols; Dir UWE FRITZ; publs *Entomologische Abhandlungen*, *Zoologische Abhandlungen*, *Malakologische Abhandlungen*, *Faunistische Abhandlungen*, *Reichenbachia Zeitschrift für entomolog. Taxonomie* (annually).

Museum Schloss Moritzburg (Museum of Moritzburg Castle): Schloss Moritzburg, 01468 Moritzburg bei Dresden; tel. (35207) 8730; fax (35207) 87311; e-mail schloss.moritzburg@schloesser.smf.sachsen.de; internet www.schloss-moritzburg.de; f. 1947; leather hangings, furniture, paintings, statues, porcelain, glasswork, principally of the 18th century; Dir INGRID MÖBIUS.

Staatliche Ethnographische Sammlungen Sachsen:see Staatliche Ethnographische Sammlungen Sachsen, Leipzig.

Staatliche Kunstsammlungen Dresden: Postfach 120551, 01006 Dresden;; tel. (351) 49142000; fax (351) 4914616; e-mail info@skd.smwk.sachsen.de; internet www.skd-dresden.de; f. 1560; library of 130,000 vols, housed in the Residenzschloss; Gen. Dir Dr MARTIN ROTH; publs *Dresdener Kunstblätter* (6 a year), *Jahrbuch* (annually).

Constituent institutions:

Gemäldegalerie Alte Meister (Picture Gallery of Old Masters): Semperbau am Zwinger, Theaterpl. 1, 01067 Dresden; tel. (351) 4914679; fax (351) 4914694; e-mail gam@skd.smwk.sachsen.de; internet www.skd-dresden.de; f. 16th c.; Italian Renaissance artists Raffael, Giorgione and Titian; 17th c.Flemish art, Rembrandt, Vermeer, Rubens; old German and Dutch, Jan van Eyck, Dürer, Cranach, Holbein; Spanish and French 17th c. artists Ribera , Murillo, Poussin, Lorrain; Dir Prof. Dr HARALD MARX.

Gemäldegalerie Neue Meister (Picture Gallery of New Masters): Albertinum, Brühlsche Terrasse, 01067 Dresden; tel. (351) 4914731; fax (351) 4914732; e-mail gnm@skd.smwk.sachsen.de; internet www.skd-dresden.de; f. 1960; art since 19th c.; collns of German Impressionism and Expressionism; Dir Dr ULRICH BISCHOFF.

Grünes Gewölbe (Green Vault): Residenzschloss, Taschenberg 2, 01067 Dresden; tel. (351) 4914591; fax (351) 4914599; e-mail gg@skd.smwk.sachsen.de; internet www.skd-dresden.de; Renaissance and Baroque artefacts; f. 1723; Dir Dr DIRK SYNDRAM.

Kunstgewerbemuseum (Museum of Decorative Arts): Schloss Pillnitz, August-Böckstiegel-Str. 2, 01326 Dresden; tel. (351) 26130; fax (351) 2613222; e-mail kgm@skd.smwk.sachsen.de; internet www.skd-dresden.de; f. 1876; courtly items incl. textiles and ceramics; Dir Drs ANDRÉ W. A. VAN DER GOES (acting).

Kupferstich-Kabinett (Cabinet of Prints and Drawings): Taschenberg 2, 01067 Dresden; tel. (351) 4914211; fax (351) 4914222; e-mail kk@skd.smwk.sachsen.de; internet www.skd-dresden.de; f. 1720; 50,000 paper works by 11,000 artists since 12th c.; Dir Dr WOLFGANG HOLLER.

Münzkabinett (Coin Cabinet): Schlossstr. 25, 01067 Dresden; tel. (351) 4914231; fax (351) 4914233; e-mail mk@skd.smwk.sachsen.de; internet www.skd-dresden.de; f. early 16th century; library of 30,000 specialist vols; 30,000 objects, incl. coins, medals, banknotes; Dir Dr RAINER GRUND (acting).

Museum für Sächsische Volkskunst mit Puppentheatersammlung (Museum of Saxon Folk Art with Puppet Theatre Collection): Jägerhof, Köpckestr. 1, 01097 Dresden; tel. (351) 8030817; fax (351) 8044963; e-mail info@skd.smwk.sachsen.de; internet www.skd-dresden.de; f. 1897; items of folk history; puppet collection; Dir Dr JOHANNES JUST.

Porzellansammlung (Porcelain Collection): Zwinger, Glockenspielpavillon, 01067 Dresden; tel. (351) 49146122000; fax (351) 49146292001; e-mail ps@skd.smwk.sachsen.debesucherservice@skd-dresden.de; internet www.skd-dresden.de; f. 1717; 20,000 pieces of Meissner, Japanese and Chinese porcelain; Dir Dr ULRICH PIETSCH.

Rüstkammer (Armoury): Semperbau am Zwinger, Theaterpl. 1, 01067 Dresden; tel. (351) 4914611; fax (351) 4914690; e-mail rk@skd.smwk.sachsen.de; internet www.skd-dresden.de; f. 1567; 10,000 chivalric objects, weapons and costumes; Dir Dr HEINZ-WERNER LEWERKEN.

Skulpturensammlung (Sculpture Collection): Albertinum, Brühlsche Terrasse, 01067 Dresden; tel. (351) 4914741; fax (351) 4914350; internet www.skd-dresden.de; sculptures since 3,000 BC; during restoration (March 2006–2009), a limited colln will be exhibited in the Dresden Zwinger; Dir Dr MORITZ WOELK.

Staatliches Museum für Mineralogie und Geologie (State Museum of Mineralogy and Geology): Königsbrücker Landstr. 159, 01109 Dresden; tel. (351) 8926403; fax (351) 8926404; internet globiz.sachsen.de/snsd; f. 1728; library of 35,000 vols; 400,000 minerals and fossils; Dir Dr ULF LINNEMANN; publs *Geologica Saxonica–Abhandlungen* (annually), *Schriften* (1–2 a year).

Stadtmuseum Dresden (Dresden City Museum): Wilsdruffer Str. 2, 01067 Dresden; tel. (351) 65648611; fax (351) 4951288; e-mail sekretariat@stmd.de; internet stadtmuseum.dresden.de; f. 1891; library of 7,500 vols, 22,500 pictures, 55,000 photographs; Dir Dr WERNER BARLMEYER; Dresden history and culture.

Attached Museums:

Kraszewski-Museum: Nordstr. 28, 01099 Dresden; tel. and fax (351) 8044450; fax (351) 8044450; exhibition on Polish history, in particular Józef Ignacy Kraszewski (1812–1887), who fought for Polish independence in the 19th c.; exhibitin German and Polish; JOANNA MAGACZ.

Kügelgenhaus–Museum der Dresdner Romantik (Museum of German Romanticism): Hauptstr. 13, 01097 Dresden; tel. (351) 8044760; fax (351) 8044760; f. 1981; home to the Museum der Dresdner Romantik; Dir MICHAELA HAUSDING.

Schillerhäuschen (The Schiller House): Schillerstr. 19, 01326 Dresden; tel. (351) 65648611; dedicated to the poet Friedrich Schiller (1759–1805).

Weber-Museum: Dresdner Str. 44, 01326 Dresden; tel. (351) 2618234; fax (351) 2618234; dedicated to the works of composer Carl Maria von Weber (1786–1826); concert venue; Dir DOROTHEA RENZ.

Verkehrsmuseum Dresden (Transport Museum Dresden): Augustusstr. 1, 01067 Dresden; tel. (351) 8644-0; fax (351) 8644-110; e-mail vmuseum.dresden@vmd.smwk.sachsen.de; internet www.verkehrsmuseum.sachsen.de; f. 1952; collection of automobiles, motorcycles, bicycles, streetcars, aircraft, model ships and railways; library of 59,000 vols (14,156 vols in special collection); Dir Dr MICHAEL DÜNNEBIER.

Düsseldorf

Aquazoo Löbbecke Museum: Kaiserswertherstr. 380, 40200 Düsseldorf; tel. (211) 899-6198; fax (211) 899-4493; e-mail aquazoo@stadt.dusseldorf.de; internet www.dusseldorf.de/aquazoo; f. 1904 (museum); 1876 (zoo); zoo and natural science museum; library of 600 vols; Dir Dr W. W. GETTMANN; publs *Westdeutscher Entomologentag Düsseldorf*, *Aquarius* (2 a year).

Kunsthalle Düsseldorf: Grabbeplatz 4, 40213 Düsseldorf; tel. (211) 899-6243; fax (211) 8929168; e-mail mail@kunsthalle-duesseldorf.de; internet www.kunsthalle-duesseldorf.de; f. 1967; contemporary art; Dir Dr ULRIKE GROOS.

Kunstsammlung Nordrhein-Westfalen (North Rhein-Westfalia Art Collection): Grabbepl. 5, 40213 Düsseldorf; tel. (211) 8381-130; fax (211) 8381-201; e-mail info@kunstsammlung.de; internet www.kunstsammlung.de; f. 1961; painting and sculpture since beginning of 20th c.; Dir Prof. ARMIN ZWEITE; publs *20_21* (2 a year), *K20K21 Programmbroschüre* (4 a year).

Museum Kunst Palast (mit Sammlung Kunstakademie and Glasmuseum Hentrich (Art Palace Museum (incorporating the Art Academy Collection and Hentrich Glass Museum): Ehrenhof 4–5, 40479 Düsseldorf; tel. (211) 89242460; fax (211) 8929307; e-mail info@museum-kunst-palast.de; internet www.museum-kunst-palast.de; f. 1913; European art and applied art from the Middle Ages–1800; collection of 19th c. German painting; early Iranian bronzes and ceramics; 6,500 textiles from late antiquity to the 19th c.; glass collection, mainly Art Nouveau, Jugendstil and Art Deco; collection of prints and drawings, including extensive collection of Italian Baroque drawings; contemporary art; design; museum for young visitors; library of 80,000 vols; Dir JEAN-HUBERT MARTIN.

Essen

Museum Folkwang: Goethestr. 41, 45128 Essen; tel. (201) 88-45002; fax (201) 88-45001; internet www.museum-folkwang.de; f. 1902; art since 19th c., including drawings, prints, posters and photographs; incl. German Poster Museum (Deutsches Plakat Museum) with 340,000 posters; library of 100,000 vols; Dir Dr HARTWIG FISCHER.

Flensburg

Museumsberg Flensburg: 24937 Flensburg; tel. (461) 852956; fax (461) 852993; e-mail museumsberg@flensburg.de; internet www.museumsberg.flensburg.de; f. 1876; contains about 26,000 exhibits, mainly arts and crafts, peasant art, and prehistory of

Schleswig; library: *c.* 12,000 vols; Dir Dr ULRICH SCHULTE-WÜLWER; publs *Beiträge zur Kunst- und Kulturgeschichte*, *Nordelbingen*.

Frankfurt am Main

Archäologisches Museum (Archaeological Museum): Karmelitergasse 1, 60311 Frankfurt am Main; tel. (69) 212-35896; fax (69) 212-30700; e-mail info.archaeolmus@stadt-frankfurt.de; internet www.archaeologisches-museum.frankfurt.de; f. 1937; prehistoric, Roman and early medieval objects from the Frankfurt area; Mediterranean and oriental archaeology; Dir Dr EGON WAMERS.

Deutsches Architektur-Museum (German Architecture Museum): Schaumainkai 43, 60596 Frankfurt am Main; tel. (69) 212-38844; fax (69) 212-36386; e-mail info.dam@stadt-frankfurt.de; internet www.dam-online.de; f. 1979, opened 1984; international collection of plans, sketches, paintings and models primarily of modern architecture; changing exhibitions, lectures, symposia; library and archive; library of 20,000 vols, 60 current periodicals and yearbooks; Dir PETER CACHOLA SCHMAL; publ. *Jahrbuch Architektur*.

Deutsches Filmmuseum (German Film Museum): Schaumainkai 41, 60596 Frankfurt am Main; tel. (69) 21238830; fax (69) 21237881; e-mail info@deutsches-filmmuseum.de; internet www.deutsches-filmmuseum.de; exhibits relating to the German film industry; library: library and archives shared with the Deutsches Filminstitut; Dir HANS-PETER REICHMANN.

Freies Deutsches Hochstift, Frankfurter Goethe-Museum (Goethe-Haus) (Free German Literature Institute, Frankfurt Goethe-Museum (Goethe House)): Gr. Hirschgraben 23–25, 60311 Frankfurt am Main; tel. (69) 13880-0; fax (69) 13880-222; e-mail info@goethehaus-frankfurt.de; internet www.goethehaus-frankfurt.de; f. 1859 L; birthplace of Johann Wolfgang von Goethe (1749–1832); German literature of the Romantic period and of Goethe's time; selected works since 19th c.; 30,000 MSS of German poetry principally from Goethe's time; 400 paintings, 16,000 etchings; library: see Libraries and Archives; Dir Prof. Dr ANNE BOHNENKAMP-RENKEN; publs *Jahrbuch*, *Reihe der Schriften*.

Historisches Museum Frankfurt: Saalgasse 19, 60311 Frankfurt am Main; tel. (69) 212-35599; fax (69) 212-30702; e-mail info.historisches-museum@stadt-frankfurt.de; internet www.historisches-museum.frankfurt.de; f. 1878; history of Frankfurt to the present; special collection: documents relating to elections of emperors 1562–1792, to the Assembly of Paulskirche 1848/49, and to trade fairs in the 16th–18th c.; Hoechst Porcelain 1746–1796; comic art and caricature; coin collection; children's museum; library of 50,000 vols; Dir Dr JAN GERCHOW.

Museum für Angewandte Kunst (Museum of Applied Art): Schaumainkai 17, 60594 Frankfurt am Main; tel. (69) 212-34037; fax (69) 212-30703; e-mail info.angewandte-kunst@stadt-frankfurt.de; internet www.museumfuerangewandtekunst.frankfurt.de; f. 1877; European applied art, Gothic to art nouveau and 20th-century art; Islamic and Far Eastern art; prints; Russian icons; digital applied art; library: *c.* 60,000 vols, 170 current periodicals and yearbooks; Dir Dr ULRICH SCHNEIDER.

Museum für Moderne Kunst (Museum of Contemporary Art): Domstr. 10, 60311 Frankfurt am Main; tel. (69) 212-30447; fax (69) 212-37882; e-mail mmk@stadt-frankfurt.de; internet www.mmk-frankfurt.de; f. 1991; art since the 1960s; library of 40,000 vols; Dir UDO KITTELMANN; Chief Curator Dr ANDREAS BEE.

Museum für Kommunikation: Schaumainkai 53, 60596 Frankfurt am Main; tel. (49) 696060-0; fax (49) 696060-666; e-mail mk.frankfurt@mspt.de; internet www.museumsstiftung.de; f. 1872; items on history of post and telecommunications; library of 13,000 vols; Dir Dr HELMUT GOLD.

Museum der Weltkulturen: Schaumainkai 29–37, 60594 Frankfurt am Main; tel. (69) 212-35391; fax (69) 212-30704; e-mail museum.weltkulturen@stadt-frankfurt.de; internet www.mdw.frankfurt.de; f. 1904; collections of art and ethnography from all continents, especially Oceania, South-east Asia, Africa, North and South America; special colln of contemporary art; library of 43,000 vols, 90 periodicals; Dir Dr ANETTE REIN; publ. *Journal-Ethnologie* (online, www.journal-ethnologie.de).

Städelsches Kunstinstitut und Städtische Galerie (Städel Art Museum and City Gallery): Dürerstr. 2, 60596 Frankfurt am Main; tel. (69) 605098-0; fax (69) 610163; e-mail info@staedelmuseum.de; internet www.staedelmuseum.de; f. 1816; 2,700 paintings, 100,000 drawings and prints, 600 sculptures spanning 700 years; library of 50,000 vols; Dir MAX HOLLEIN.

Freiburg im Breisgau

Adelhausermuseum: Gerberau 32, 79098 Freiburg im Breisgau; tel. (761) 2012561; fax (761) 2012563; e-mail adelhausermuseum@stadt.freiburg.de; internet www.museen.freiburg.de; f. 1895; native and exotic fauna; herb collection, mineralogy, precious stones, wood types, beekeeping, traditional arts and crafts from Africa, America, Asia and Oceania; social and cultural anthropology; library: ethnology: 4,700 vols, natural history: 5,000 vols; Dir Dr EVA GERHARDS.

Augustinermuseum: Augustinerplatz 1–3, 79098 Freiburg im Breisgau; tel. (761) 2012521; fax (761) 2012597; e-mail augustinermuseum@stadt.freiburg.de; internet www.augustinermuseum.de; f. 1923; art and culture of Upper Rhine area from Middle Ages to the 20th c.; library of 50,000 vols; Dir Dr DETLEF ZINKE.

Museum für Neue Kunst (Museum of Modern Art): Marienstr. 10A, 79098 Freiburg im Breisgau; tel. (761) 2012581; fax (761) 2012589; e-mail mnk@stadt.freiburg.de; internet www.mnk-freiburg.de; f. 1985; German art since 1910; Dir Dr JOCHEN LUDWIG.

Museum für Stadtgeschichte (Museum of City History): Münsterpl. 30, 79098 Freiburg im Breisgau; tel. (761) 2012515; fax (761) 2012598; e-mail msg@stadt.freiburg.de; internet www.museen.freiburg.de; city history since 1100; Dir PETER KALCHTHALER.

Museum für Ur- und Frühgeschichte (Museum of Prehistory and Early History): Colombischlössle, Rotteckring 5, 79098 Freiburg im Breisgau; tel. (761) 2012574; fax (761) 2012579; e-mail museumuf@stadt.freiburg.de; internet www.museen.freiburg.de; f. 1936; regional archaeology; library of 5,000 vols; Dir Dr HELENA PASTOR.

Gießen

Liebig Museum: Liebigstr. 12, 35390 Gießen; tel. (641) 76392; fax (641) 2502599; internet www.liebig-museum.de; exhibition of the life and work of Liebig through documents and pictures; pharmaceutical laboratory and display of chemical analysis since 19th c.; Chair. WOLFGANG BERGENTHUM.

Oberhessisches Museum und Gailsche Sammlungen der Stadt Gießen: Brandpl. 2, 35390 Gießen; tel. (0641) 3062477; fax (0641) 3012005; e-mail museum@giessen.de; internet www.giessen.de; f. 1879; palaeolithic collection, first Middle European flint tools; archaeological collections and treasures of Roman-German and Hessian Franconian culture; oil paintings, water-colours and modern copperplate engravings; Dir Dr FRIEDHELM HÄRING.

Comprises:

Altes Schloss: Brandpl. 2, 35390 Gießen; houses furniture and art in 14th c. building; collections of Gothic, Baroque, Renaissance, artefacts since 19th c.

Leib'sches Haus: Georg-Schlosser-Str. 2, 35390 Gießen; f. 1978; originally the seat of the Junkers of Rodenhausen; now museum of local history and culture; exhibits of material culture of Gießen and surrounding area; portraits, pictures, maps, engravings, textile manufacture and handicraft; furniture, farm implements, costumes, pottery; special exhibitions on the political thinkers Georg Büchner and Wilhelm Liebknecht (founder of the German Social Democratic Party).

Wallenfels'sches Haus: Kirchenpl. 6, Am Stadtkirchturm, 35390 Gießen; ethnological museum with artefacts dating from prehistoric times; examples from India, China, Japan, Ceylon, Java, East and West Africa, Egypt, New Guinea and Australia.

Gotha

Kommunale Galerien am Hauptmarkt: Hauptmarkt 44, 99867 Gotha; tel. (3621) 401101; fax (3621) 52669; Dir MARLIES MIKOLAJCZAK.

Münzkabinett (Coin Cabinet): Schloss Friedenstein, 99867 Gotha; tel. (3621) 53036; e-mail vorstand@stiftungfriedenstein.de; internet www.gotha.de/schloss_muenzen.htm; 130,000 numismatic objects; Dir UTA WALLENSTEIN.

Museum der Natur: Postfach 100319, 99853 Gotha; located at: 99867 Gotha, Parkallee 15; tel. (3621) 823010; fax (3621) 823020; e-mail mng@stiftungfriedenstein.de; internet www.stiftungfriedenstein.de; f. 1843; animal and fossil exhibitions, insects, local natural history; Dir RAINER SAMIETZ; publ. *Abhandlungen und Berichte*.

Museum für Kartographie (Museum of Cartography): Schloss Friedenstein, 99867 Gotha; tel. (3621) 854016; e-mail vorstand@stiftungfriedenstein.de; maps, atlases and globes; original copper engraving; Curator JUTTA SIEGERT.

Museum für Regionalgeschichte und Volkskunde (Museum of Regional History and Folklore): Schloss Friedenstein, 99867 Gotha; tel. (3621) 823415; fax (3621) 823419; e-mail mrv@stiftungfriedenstein.de; internet www.stiftungfriedenstein.de; f. 1928; exhibition of local history, with *Ekhof-Theater* (baroque theatre); Dir THOMAS HUCK; publ. *Gothaisches Museumsjahrbuch* (annually).

Schlossmuseum (Castle Museum): Schloss Friedenstein, 99867 Gotha; tel. (3621) 823414; fax (3621) 823419; e-mail schlossmuseum@stiftungfriedenstein.de; internet www.stiftungfriedenstein.de; art collections, historical rooms, coin collections, Egyptological exhibition; Dir Dr KATHARINA BECHLER.

Göttingen

Städtisches Museum (Municipal Museum): Ritterplan 7/8, 37073 Göttingen; tel. (551) 400-2843; fax (551) 400-2059; internet www.goettingen.de/kultur/museum; f. 1889; prehistory and early history, ecclesiastical art, history of Göttingen and the University, arts and crafts, etc.; library of 20,000 vols; Dir Dr JENS-UWE BRINKMANN.

Halle am Saale

Landesamt für Denkmalpflege und Archäologie Sachsen-Anhalt (Landesmuseum für Vorgeschichte) (Prehistory Museum): Richard-Wagner-Str. 9, 06114 Halle; tel. (345) 5247-30; fax (345) 5247-351; e-mail poststelle@lfa.mk.lsa-net.de; internet www.archlsa.de; f. 1882; pre- and medieval history; library of 73,000 vols; Dir Dr HARALD MELLER; publs *Jahresschrift für mitteldeutsche Vorgeschichte* (annually), *Veröffentlichungen* (annually), *Archäologie in Sachsen-Anhalt* (annually).

Hamburg

Altonaer Museum in Hamburg/Norddeutsches Landesmuseum (Altona Museum in Hamburg/North German Regional Museum): Postfach 500125, 22701 Hamburg; Museumstr. 23, 22765 Hamburg; tel. (40) 42811-3582; fax (40) 42811-2122; e-mail info@altonaermuseum.de; internet www.altonaer-museum.de; f. 1863; collections on art and cultural history, folk art, shipping and fishing; library of 70,000 vols; Dir Prof. Dr BÄRBEL HEDINGER; publs *Altonaer Museum in Hamburg, Jahrbuch* (Yearbook), catalogues of collections and exhibitions.

Hamburger Kunsthalle: Glockengiesserwall, 20095 Hamburg; tel. (40) 42813-1200; fax (40) 42854-2482; e-mail info@hamburger-kunsthalle.de; internet www.hamburger-kunsthalle.de; f. 1869; paintings since 14th c., sculpture since 19th c., drawings and engravings since 14th c., Greek and Roman coins, medals since 14th c.; library of 167,377 vols; Dir Prof. Dr UWE M. SCHNEEDEHUBERTUS GASSNER.

Museum für Hamburgische Geschichte: Holstenwall 24, 20355 Hamburg; tel. (40) 428132-2380; fax (40) 428132-3103; e-mail info@hamburgmuseum.de; internet www.hamburgmuseum.de; f. 1839; political history of Hamburg, library, coins, handicrafts, models, paintings, history of music, etc.; Dir Prof. Dr GISELA JAACKS; publs *Hamburger Beiträge zur Numismatik*, *Numismatische Studien*, *Beiträge zur deutschen Volks- und Altertumskunde*.

Museum für Kunst und Gewerbe Hamburg (Hamburg Museum of Art and Industry): Steintorpl. 1, 20099 Hamburg; tel. (40) 428134-2732; fax (40) 428134-2834; e-mail service@mkg-hamburg.de; internet www.mkg-hamburg.de; f. 1877; European sculpture and art since the Middle Ages, ancient art, art of the Near and Far East, European popular art, graphic, photographic and textile collections, contemporary design, historical keyboard instruments; library of 160,000 vols, 450 current periodicals; Dir Prof. Dr WILHELM HORNBOSTEL.

Museum für Völkerkunde Hamburg: Rothenbaumchaussee 64, 20148 Hamburg; tel. (1805) 308888; fax (40) 428879-242; e-mail marketing@voelkerkundemuseum.com; internet www.voelkerkundemuseum.com; f. 1879; ethnological collections from Africa, America, Asia, Australia, Europe and the Pacific; library of 130,000 vols; Dir Prof. Dr W. KÖPKE; publs *Beiträge zur Mittelamerikanischen Wegweiser zur Völkerkunde* (irregular), *Mitteilungen aus dem Museum für Völkerkunde, N.F.* (annually).

Hanover

Historisches Museum am Hohen Ufer (Historical Museum on the High Bank): Pferdestr. 6, 30159 Hanover; tel. (511) 16843052; fax (511) 16845003; f. 1903 as Vaterländisches Museum, 1937–50 Niedersächsisches Volkstumsmuseum, 1950–66 as Niedersächsisches Heimatmuseum; three sections: Lower Saxon Folklore, History of the City of Hanover, History of the Kingdom of Hanover up to 1866; library of 8,000 vols; Dir Dr T. SCHWARK.

Kestner-Museum: Trammplatz 3, 30159 Hanover; tel. (511) 16842120; fax (511) 16846530; e-mail kestner-museum@hannover-stadt.de; internet www.hannover.de; f. 1889; Egyptian, Greek, Etruscan and Roman art; illuminated MSS, incunabula, applied art and design since the Middle Ages; ancient, medieval and modern coins, medals; library of 30,000 vols, 200 current periodicals; Dir Dr WOLFGANG SCHEPERS; Curator Prof. Dr ROSEMARIE DRENKHAHN.

Niedersächsisches Landesmuseum Hannover (Regional Museum of Lower Saxony in Hanover): Willy-Brandt-Allee 5, 30169 Hanover; tel. (511) 9807-6865; fax (511) 9807-640; e-mail kommunikationinfo@nlm-h.niedersachsen.de; internet www.nlmhlandesmuseum-hannover.de; f. 1852; art dating from the Middle Ages to the early 20th century;, natural history, prehistoryarchaeology and ethnology sections; libraries attached to each section; Dir Dr HEIDE GRAPE-ALBERS; Dir (Ethnology) Dr ANNA SCHMID; Dir (Landesgalerie) Dr THOMAS ANDRATSCHKE; Dir (Natural History) ANDREA SPAUTZ; Dir (Prehistory) Prof. Dr DAGMAR-BEATRICE GAEDTKE-ECKARDT (acting).

Heidelberg

Kurpfälzisches Museum der Stadt Heidelberg: Hauptstr. 97, 69117 Heidelberg; tel. (6221) 5834020; fax (6221) 5834900; e-mail kurpfaelzischesmuseum@heidelberg.de; internet www.museum-heidelberg.de; f. 1879; Dir Dr FRIEDER HEPP.

Hildesheim

Roemer-und Pelizaeus Museum: Am Steine 1–2, 31134 Hildesheim; tel. (5121) 93690; fax (5121) 35283; e-mail info@rpmuseum.de; internet www.rpmuseum.de; f. 1845; natural history, applied art, prehistory, ethnography, Egyptian art; library of 35,000 vols; Dir Dr KATJA LEMBKE.

Jena

Goethe-Gedenkstätte (im Inspektorhaus des Botanischen Gartens): Friedrich Schiller Universität Jena, Fürstengraben 26, 07743 Jena; f. 1921; Curator Dr MICHAEL PLATEN.

Optisches Museum der Ernst-Abbe-Stiftung Jena (Optical Museum at the Ernst Abbe Foundation): Carl-Zeiss-Pl. 12, 07743 Jena; tel. (3641) 443165; fax (3641) 443224; e-mail info@optischesmuseum.de; internet www.optischesmuseum.de; f. 1922; history and development of optical instruments.

Romantikerhaus–Museum der deutschen Frühromantik (Romantikerhaus—Museum of Early German Romanticism): Unterm Markt 12A, 07743 Jena; tel. (3641) 443263; fax (3641) 228829; e-mail romantikerhaus@msn.com; internet www.jena.de/kultur/romantik.htm; f. 1981; Dir KLAUS SCHWARZ.

Stadtmuseum Göhre (Göhre City Museum): Markt 7, 07743 Jena; tel. (3641) 35980; fax (3641) 359820; e-mail goehre@stadtmuseum.jetzweb.de; internet www.jena.de/kultur/goehre_d.htm; f. 1903; library of 30,000 vols; Dir HOLGER NOWAK.

Karlsruhe

Badisches Landesmuseum: Schloss, 76131 Karlsruhe; tel. (721) 926-6514; fax (721) 926-6537; e-mail info@landesmuseum.de; internet www.landesmuseum.de; f. 1919; colln includes prehistoric, Egyptian, Greek and Roman antiquities, medieval, renaissance and baroque sculpture, works of art from the Middle Ages to the 20th century, weapons, folklore and coins, colln of Turkish trophies; library of 75,000 vols; Dir Prof. Dr HARALD SIEBENMORGEN.

Museum für Literatur am Oberrhein: Prinz-Max-Palais, Karlstr. 10, 76133 Karlsruhe; tel. (721) 133-4087; fax (721) 133-4089; e-mail info@literaturmuseum.de; internet www.karlsruhe.de/kultur/MLO/; f. 1965; exhibition of the works, manuscripts and pictures of various authors; library of 8,000 vols; Pres. Dr HANSGEORG SCHMIDT-BERGMANN; publs *Mitteilungen*, *Jahresgabe*.

Staatliche Kunsthalle: Hans-Thoma-Str. 2–6, 76133 Karlsruhe; tel. (721) 926-3355; fax (721) 926-6788; e-mail info@kunsthalle-karlsruhe.de; internet www.kunsthalle-karlsruhe.de; f. 1846; German, Dutch, Flemish, French and Italian paintings and sculpture, 14th–20th c.; print room; 90,000 prints and drawings; education service; library of 140,000 vols; Dir Prof. Dr KLAUS SCHRENK.

Staatliches Museum für Naturkunde Karlsruhe (State Museum of Natural History, Karlsruhe): Erbprinzenstr. 13, 76133 Karlsruhe; tel. (721) 1752111; fax (721) 1752110; e-mail museum@naturkundeka-bw.de; internet www.naturkundemuseum-karlsruhe.de; f. 1789; research and exhibitions in botany, zoology, mineralogy, geology, entomology, palaeontology, vivarium; library of 50,000 vols; Dir Prof. Dr VOLKMAR WIRTH; publs *Andrias*, *Carolinea*, *Exhibition Catalogues* (irregular).

Kassel

Brüder Grimm-Museum Kassel: Brüder Grimm-Platz 4A, 34117 Kassel; tel. (561) 103235; fax (561) 713299; e-mail grimm-museum@t-online.de; internet www.grimms.de; f. 1960; preservation of works of Jacob, Wilhelm and Ludwig Emil Grimm; collection of works by the brothers; original paintings, autographs, letters, drawings, etchings; Dir Dr BERNHARD LAUER.

Staatliche Museen Kassel (State Art Museums): 34131 Kassel, Schloss Wilhelmshöhe; tel. (561) 316800; fax (561) 31680111; e-mail info@museum-kassel.de; internet www.museum-kassel.de; f. 18th c.; Dir Dr MICHAEL EISSENHAUER.

Constituent museums:

Astronomisch-Physikalisches Kabinett: Kassel, Karlsaue 20C; tel. (561) 31680500; fax (561) 31680555; e-mail info@museum-kassel.de; internet www.museum-kassel.de; f. 1992; astronomy and physics collection with history of technology section; planetarium; Dir Dr MICHAEL EISSENHAUER.

Hessisches Landesmuseum: Kassel, Brüder-Grimm-Platz 5; tel. (561) 31680300; fax (561) 31680333; e-mail info@museum-kassel.de; internet www.museum-kassel.de; f. 1913; pre- and early history; arts-handicraft; folklore; wall papers; Dir Dr MICHAEL EISSENHAUER.

Neue Galerie: Schöne Aussicht 1, Kassel; tel. (561) 31680400; fax (561) 31680444; e-mail info@museum-kassel.de; internet www.museum-kassel.de; f. 1976; paintings and sculpture from 1750 to present; Dir Dr MICHAEL EISSENHAUER.

Schloss Friedrichstein Museum: Bad Wildungen; tel. (5621) 6577; fax (5621) 3650700; e-mail info@museum-kassel.de; internet www.museum-kassel.de; f. 1980;

15th–19th c. military and hunting exhibits; Dir Dr MICHAEL EISSENHAUER.

Schloss Wilhelmshöhe: 34131 Kassel; tel. (561) 316800; fax (561) 31680111; e-mail info@museum-kassel.de; internet www.museum-kassel.de; f. *c.*1800; department of classical antiquities, gallery of 15th–18th c. old master paintings, collection of drawings and engravings; library of 70,000 vols; Dir Dr MICHAEL EISSENHAUER.

Konstanz

Archäologisches Landesmuseum (Regional Archaeological Museum): Benediktinerpl. 5, 78467 Konstanz; tel. (7531) 9804-0; fax (7531) 68452; e-mail info@konstanz.alm-bw.de; internet www.konstanz.alm-bw.de; f. 1990; local archaeological artefacts; Dir JÖRG HEILIGMANN.

Bodensee-Naturmuseum (Lake Constance Natural History Museum): SeaLife Centre, Hafenstr. 9, 78462 Konstanz; tel. (7531) 128739-010; fax (7531) 128739-017; e-mail info@sealife.de; internet www.konstanz.de/kultur_freizeit/museen_galerien; f. 1967; geology, palaeontology, zoology and botany of Lake Constance; Curator Dr INGO SCHULZ-WEDDIGEN.

Hus-Museum: Hussenstr. 64, 78462 Konstanz; tel. (7531) 29042; e-mail hus-museum@t-online.de; internet www.konstanz.de/kultur_freizeit/museen_galerien; f. 1965; house of religious thinker, philosopher and reformer, Jan Hus (c. 1369–1415); display by Czech and Slovak artists depicting Hus' life, Council of Constance and the Hussite wars; Dir Dr LIBUSE RÖSCH.

Rosgarten Museum: Rosgartenstr. 3–5, 78462 Konstanz; tel. (7531) 900376; internet www.konstanz.de/kultur_freizeit/museen_-galerien; f. 1870; central museum for Lake Constance area; prehistoric, early historic collection; arts and crafts from the Middle Ages to 19th c.; library of 6,000 vols; Dir Dr BARBARA STARK.

Leipzig

Deutsches Buch- und Schriftmuseum der Deutschen Bücherei Leipzig (German Book Museum): Deutscher Platz 1, 04103 Leipzig; tel. (341) 2271-0; fax (341) 2271-444; e-mail dbsm@dbl.ddb.de; internet www.ddb.de; f. 1884; exhibits relate to history of books, writing and paper; library of 128,000 vols, 758 incunabula, 29,000 items of graphic art, 425,000 watermarks; Dir LOTHAR POETHE.

Museum der Bildenden Künste Leipzig (Leipzig Museum of Fine Arts): Katharinenstr. 10, 04109 Leipzig; tel. (341) 216999-20; fax (341) 216999-99; e-mail mdbk@leipzig.de; internet www.mdbk.de; f. 1837; 3,000 paintings; collns drawings and sculptures; Dir Dr HANS-WERNER SCHMIDT.

Museum für Kunsthandwerk Leipzig, Grassi-Museum (Museum of Applied Arts): Neumarkt 20, 04109 Leipzig; tel. (341) 2133719; fax (341) 2133715; e-mail grassimuseum@leipzig.de; internet www.grassimuseum.de; f. 1874; textiles, ceramics, glass, wood, and metal objects; prints and patterns relating to design; library: library; Dir Dr EVA M. HOYER.

Staatliche Ethnographische Sammlungen Sachsen (State Ethnographical Collection of Saxony): Postfach 100 955, 04009 Leipzig; Museum für Völkerkunde zu Leipzig/Grassimuseum, Johannispl. 5–11, 04103 Leipzig; tel. (341) 9731900; fax (341) 9731909; e-mail ses-sachsen@mvl.smwk.sachsen.de; internet www.ses-sachsen.de; f. 2003 by the merger of Museum für Völkerkunde zu Leipzig, Museum für Völkerkunde Dresden and Völkerkundemuseum Herrnhut; Dir Dr CLAUS DEIMEL.

Constituent Museums:

Museum für Völkerkunde Dresden (Ethnographical Museum Dresden): Königsbrücker Landstr. 159, 01109 Dresden; tel. (351) 8926202; fax (351) 8926203; e-mail info@mvd.smwk.sachsen.de; internet www.ses-sachsen.de; f. 1875; ethnography, physical anthropology; library of 60,000 vols; publs *Abhandlungen und Berichte* (Essays and Records), *Kleine Beiträge* (irreg.), *Dresdner Tagungsberichte* (irreg.), *Bibliographien Africa 1–3, Oceania 1–3* (irreg.).

Museum für Völkerkunde zu Leipzig (Ethnographical Museum in Leipzig): Museum für Völkerkunde zu Leipzig/Grassimuseum, Johannispl. 5–11, 04103 Leipzig; tel. (341) 9731900; fax (341) 9731909; e-mail mvl-grassimuseum@mvl.smwk.sachsen.de; internet www.ses-sachsen.de; f. 1869; ethnographical collns from Asia, Australia, Pacific Islands, Africa, America, Europe; library of 170,000 vols; publs *Jahrbuch* (Yearbook), *Abhandlungen und Berichte*.

Völkerkundemuseum Herrnhut (Ethnographical Museum Herrnhut): Goethestr. 1, 02747 Herrnhut; tel. (35873) 2403; fax (35873) 2403; e-mail voelkerkunde.herrnhut@mvd.smwk.sachsen.de; internet www.ses-sachsen.de; f. 1878; ethnography; contains colIns made by Moravian Church missionaries; Curator STEPHAN AUGUSTIN.

Stadtgeschichtliches Museum Leipzig: Neubau, Böttchergäßchen 3, 04109 Leipzig; tel. (341) 9651-30; fax (341) 9651-352; e-mail stadtmuseum@leipzig.de; internet www.stadtgeschichtliches-museum-leipzig.de; f. 1909; library and archive of 160,000 items; Dir Dr VOLKER RODEKAMP.

Lübeck

Museen für Kunst und Kulturgeschichte (Museums for Art and Cultural History): Düvekenstr. 21, 23552 Lübeck; tel. (451) 122-4134; fax (451) 122-4183; e-mail mkk@luebeck.de; internet www.museen.luebeck.de; library of 30,000 vols; Dir Dr THORSTEN RODIEK; publs *Kataloge des St Annen-Museums, Katalog des Behnhauses*.

Branch museums:

St Annen-Museum und Kunsthalle St Annen (St Annen Museum and Art Gallery): Lübeck, St Annenstr. 15; tel. (451) 122-4137; fax (451) 122-4183; e-mail mkk@luebeck.de; internet www.luebeck.de; f. 1915 (Museum); f. 2003 (Art Gallery); Late Gothic convent, built 1502–1515; medieval ecclesiastical art from Lübeck; domestic art from Lübeck, from Middle Ages to .18th c.; modern and contemporary art; Dir Dr THORSTEN RODIEK.

Museum Behnhaus/Drägerhaus: Lübeck, Königstr. 9–11; tel. (451) 122-4148; e-mail mkk@luebeck.de; internet www.museen.luebeck.de; f. 1921; museum of 19th c. art located in late 18th c. patrician house; art from Overbeck to Munch; Dir Dr THORSTEN RODIEK.

Museum Völkerkundesammlung: Lübeck, Parade 10 (Zeughaus am Dom); tel. (451) 122-4347; fax (451) 122-4348; e-mail vks@luebeck.de; internet www.vkhl.de; ethnology, art and culture of America, Africa, Oceania, East Asia, Judaica; Dir Dr THORSTEN RODIEK.

Museum Holstentor: Lübeck, Holstentorplatz; tel. (451) 122-4129; fax (451) 122-4183; e-mail mkk@luebeck.de; internet www.luebeck.de/museen; built 1464–1478; history of the city and the merchant of Lübeck; Dir Dr THORSTEN RODIEK.

Katharinenkirche: Lübeck, Königstrasse; tel. (451) 122-4134; fax (451) 122-4183; e-mail mkk@luebeck.de; internet www.luebeck.de/museen; 14th c.; fmrly Franciscan monasteries church; Dir Dr THORSTEN RODIEK.

Völkerkundesammlung (Ethnographic Collection): Grosser Bauhof 14, 23522 Lübeck; collection at: Parade 10, 23552 Lübeck; tel. (451) 1224342; fax (451) 1224348; e-mail vks@luebeck.de; internet www.luebeck.de; f. 1893; Dir BRIGITTE TEMPLIN.

Magdeburg

Magdeburger Museen: Otto-von-Guericke-Str. 68–73, 39104 Magdeburg; tel. (391) 5403501; fax (391) 5403510; e-mail museen@magdeburg.de; internet www.magdeburgermuseen.de; f. 1906; local history collection, art gallery, sculptures, handicrafts, graphics, bibliophilia, costumes, sociology, natural history and prehistory collection; Kulturhistorisches Museum, Kunstmuseum Kloster Unser Lieben Frauen, Museum für Naturkunde, Technikmuseum; library of 50,000 vols; Dir MATTHIAS PUHLE; publs *Abhandlungen und Berichte Naturkunde und Vorgeschichte*, *Magdeburger Museumshefte* (irregular), *Magdeburger Museumsschriften* (irregular).

Mainz

Gutenberg-Museum: Liebfrauenpl. 5, 55116 Mainz; tel. (6131) 122640; fax (6131) 123488; e-mail gutenberg-museum@stadt.mainz.de; internet www.gutenberg-museum.de; f. 1900; world museum of typography; library of 70,000 vols; Dir Dr EVA-MARIA HANEBUTT-BENZ.

Landesmuseum Mainz: Grosse Bleiche 49–51, 55116 Mainz; tel. (6131) 2857-0; fax (6131) 2857-88; internet www.landesmuseum-mainz.de; f. 1803; cultural history and art; Dir Dr ISABELLA FEHLE.

Münzsammlung (Coin Collection): Stadtarchiv Mainz, Rheinallee 3B, 55116 Mainz; tel. (6131) 122178; fax (6131) 123569; e-mail stadtarchiv@stadt.mainz.de; internet www.stadtarchiv.mainz.de; f. 1784; Dir Dr WOLFGANG DOBRAS.

Naturhistorisches Museum Mainz (Natural History Museum): Reichklarastr./Mitternachtspl., 55116 Mainz; tel. (6131) 122646; fax (6131) 122975; e-mail naturhistorisches.museum@stadt.mainz.de; internet www.uni-mainz.de/~lsnhmmz; collections; f. 1834, museum f. 1910; mineralogy, geology, palaeontology, zoology and botany of Rheinland-Pfalz and Rwanda; library of 40,000 vols, 15,000 pamphlets; Dir Dr rer. nat. ULRICH NORBERT SCHMIDTLENZ; publs *Beihefte*, *Mainzer Naturwissenschaftliches Archiv*, *Museumsführer*.

Römisch-Germanisches Zentralmuseum–Forschungsinstitut für Vor- und Frühgeschichte (Central Roman-German Museum–Research Museum for Prehistory and Early History): Ernst-Ludwig-Pl. 2, 55116 Mainz; tel. (6131) 91240; fax (6131) 9124199; e-mail info@rgzm.de; internet web.rgzm.de; f. 1852; studies in Old-world archaeology and prehistory, conservation of prehistoric, Roman and early medieval antiquities; library of 80,000 vols; Gen. Dir Dr FALKO DAIM; publs *Arbeitsblätter für Restauratoren*, *Archäologisches Korrespondenzblatt*, *Ausstellungskataloge*, *Corpus Signorum Imperii Romani*, *Führer durch die Ausstellungen*, *Jahrbuch*, *Kataloge*, *Studien zu den Anfängen der Metallurgie*, and various monographs, *Vulkanpark-Forschungen*.

Mannheim

Reiss-Engelhorn-Museen Mannheim: 68030 Mannheim, POB 103051; tel. (621) 293-3151; fax (621) 293-3099; e-mail reiss-engelhorn-museen@mannheim.de; internet reiss-engelhorn-museen.mannheim.de; f. 1957 as Reiss-Museum; museum of art, crafts and decorative arts, local theatre history, archaeology and prehistory, ethnology, local history and natural history; collection of historical European musical instruments; Forum Internationale Photgraphie (FIP); library of 120,000 vols; Dir Prof. Dr ALFRIED WIECZOREK.

Städtische Kunsthalle (City Art Museum): Moltkestr. 9, 68165 Mannheim; tel. (621) 293-6413; fax (621) 293-6412; e-mail kunsthalle@mannheim.de; internet www.kunsthalle-mannheim.com; f. 1907; 33,000 drawings, water colours and graphics, 1,700 paintings and 600 sculptures; Dir Dr ROLF LAUTER.

Marburg

Universitätsmuseum für Bildende Kunst: Lahn, Biegenstr. 11, im Ernst von Hülsen-Haus, 35032 Marburg; tel. (6421) 2822355; fax (6421) 2822166; e-mail museum@verwaltung.uni-marburg.de; internet www.uni-marburg.de/zv/news/uni-museum; f. 1927; Dir Dr JÜRGEN WITTSTOCK.

Universitätsmuseum für Kulturgeschichte: Landgrafenschloss, Wilhelmsbau, 35032 Marburg/Lahn; tel. (6421) 28225871; fax (6421) 2822166; e-mail museum@verwaltung.uni-marburg.de; internet www.uni-marburg.de/zv/news/museum; f. 1875; Dir Dr JÜRGEN WITTSTOCK.

Mettmann

Neanderthal-Museum: Talstr. 300, 40822 Mettmann; tel. (2104) 979797; fax (2104) 979796; e-mail museum@neanderthal.de; internet www.neanderthal.de; f. 1996; human evolution since earliest times; library of 4,000 vols; Dir Prof. Dr GERD-C. WENIGER.

Munich

Archäologische Staatssammlung München (State Archaeological Collection, Munich): Lerchenfeldstr. 2, 80538 Munich; tel. (89) 2112-402; fax (89)2112-4401; e-mail archaeologische.staatssammlung@extern.lrz-muenchen.de; internet www.archaeologie-bayern.de; f. 1885; prehistoric, Roman and early medieval antiquities from Southern Germany, prehistoric archaeology of Mediterranean and Near East; Dir Prof. Dr L. WAMSER; publ. *Kataloge* (irregular).

Bayerische Staatsgemäldesammlungen (Bavarian State Art Galleries): Barerstr. 29, 80799 Munich; tel. (89) 23805-195; fax (89) 23805-251; e-mail info@pinakothek.de; internet www.pinakothek.de; f. 1836; medieval to modern art, painting and sculpture; Gen. Dir Dr REINHOLD BAUMSTARK; Dir Doerner Institute Dr ANDREAS BURMESTER.

Bayerisches Nationalmuseum (National Bavarian Museum): Prinzregentenstr. 3, 80538 Munich; tel. (89) 21124-01; fax (89) 21124-201; e-mail bay.nationalmuseum@bnm.mwn.de; internet www.bayerisches-nationalmuseum.de; f. 1855; European fine arts, especially sculpture, decorative art and folk art; library of 75,000 vols; Dir Dr RENATE EIKELMANN; publs *Bayerische Blätter für Volkskunde*, *Bildführer*, *Forschungshefte*, *Kataloge*.

Deutsches Museum von Meisterwerken der Naturwissenschaft und Technik (German Museum of Scientific and Technological Masterpieces): 80306 Munich; premises at: Museumsinsel 1, 80538 Munich; tel. (89) 21791; fax (89) 2179324; e-mail information@deutsches-museum.de; internet www.deutsches-museum.de; f. 1903; history of science and technology from its origins to the present day; library of 815,000 vols; special collection of manuscripts and autographs, trade literature, plans, pictorial art, films, commemorative medals; research institute for the history of science and technology; 'Kerschensteiner Kolleg' for teacher in-service training; library of 90,000 vols, 3,500 current periodicals; Dir-Gen. Prof. Dr WOLFGANG M. HECKL; publ. *Kultur und Technik* (quarterly).

Affiliated museums:

Deutsches Museum Bonn (German Museum in Bonn): Ahrstr. 45, 53175 Bonn; tel. (228) 302255; fax (228) 302254; e-mail info@deutsches-museum-bonn.de; internet www.deutsches-museum-bonn.de; f. 1995; science and technology in Germany since 1945; Dir Dr ANDREA NIEHAUS.

Deutsches Museum Flugwerft Schleissheim (German Museum in Flugwerft Schleissheim): Effnerstr. 18, 85764 Oberschleissheim; tel. (89) 3157140; fax (89) 31571450; e-mail fws@deutsches-museum.de; f. 1992; aeronautical collection; Dir-Gen. Prof. Dr WOLF PETER FEHLHAMMER.

Deutsches Museum Verkehrszentrum (German Museum-Transport Centre): Theresienhöhe 14a, 80339 Munich; tel. (89) 2179-529; e-mail fws@deutsches-museum.de; internet verkehrszentrum.deutsches-museum.de; f. 2003; traffic museum; Dir SYLVIA HLADKY.

Generaldirektion der Staatlichen Naturwissenschaftlichen Sammlungen Bayerns, München (Bavarian Natural History Collections): Menzingerstr. 71, 80638 Munich; tel. (89) 17999240; fax (89) 17999255; e-mail generaldirektion@snsb.de; internet www.naturalhistorybavaria.de; f. 1827; Gen. Dir Prof. Dr REINHOLD LEINFELDER.

Subordinate institutions:

Staatssammlung für Anthropologie und Paläoanatomie: 80333 Munich, Karolinenpl. 2A; tel. (89) 5488438-0; fax (89) 5488438-17; e-mail asm.grupe@extern.lrz-muenchen.de; internet www.naturwissenschaftlichesammlungen-bayerns.de/Anthropologie/Anthro.html; f. 1886; Dirs Prof. Dr GISELA GRUPE, Prof. Dr JORIS PETERS.

Bayerische Staatssammlung für Paläontologie und Geologie: 80333 Munich, Richard-Wagner-Str. 10; tel. (89) 2180-6630; fax (89) 2180-6601; e-mail pal.sammlung@lrz.uni-muenchen.de; internet www.paleo.de/PSM_Home.htm; f. 1759; Dir Prof. Dr REINHOLD LEINFELDER; publ. *Zitteliana*.

Botanische Staatssammlung: 80638 Munich, Menzinger-Str. 67; tel. (89) 17861265; fax (89) 17861193; e-mail bsm@botanik.biologie.uni-muenchen.de; internet www.botanischestaatssammlung.de; f. 1813; Dir Prof. Dr SUSANNE RENNER; publs *Sendtnera*, *Arnoldia*.

Botanischer Garten München–Nymphenburg: 80638 Munich, Menzingerstr. 61–65; tel. (89) 17861310; fax (89) 17861340; e-mail botgart@botanik.biologie.uni-muenchen.de; internet www.botanik.biologie.uni-muenchen.de/botgart/home.html; f. 1914; Dir Prof. Dr SUSANNE RENNER.

Jura-Museum: 85072 Eichstätt, Willibaldsburg; tel. (8421) 2956; fax (8421) 89609; e-mail Jura-MuseumVF@altmuehlnet.de; internet www.jura-museum.de; f. 1976; natural history; Man. Dr MARTINA KÖLBL-EBERT; publ. *Archaeopteryx*.

Mineralogische Staatssammlung: 80333 Munich, Theresienstr. 41; tel. (89) 21804312; fax (89) 21804334; e-mail mineralogische.staatssammlung@lrz.uni-muenchen.de; internet www.lrz-muenchen.de/~Mineralogische.Staatssammlung; f. 1823; Dir Prof. Dr PETER GILLE.

Museum Mensch und Natur: 80638 Munich, Schloss Nymphenburg; tel. (89) 171382; fax (89) 1784380; e-mail museum@musmn.de; internet www.musmn.de; f. 1990; natural history; Man. Dr HANS-ALBERT TREFF.

Naturkunde-Museum Bamberg: 96047 Bamberg, Fleischstr. 2; tel. (951) 8631249; fax (951) 8631250; e-mail info@naturkundemuseum-bamberg.de; internet www.naturkundemuseum-bamberg.de; f. 1790; Man. Dr MATTHIAS MÄUSER.

Rieskrater-Museum Nördlingen: 86720 Nördlingen, Eugene-Shoemaker-Platz 1; tel. (9081) 2738220; fax (9081) 27382220; e-mail rieskratermuseum@noerdlingen.de; internet www.riescrater-museum.de; f. 1990; natural history; Man. Dr MICHAEL SCHIEBER.

Urwelt-Museum Oberfranken: 95444 Bayreuth, Kanzleistr. 1; tel. (921) 511211; fax (921) 511212; e-mail Urwelt-Museum-Oberfranken@t-online.de; internet www.Urwelt-Museum.de; f. 1997; natural history; Man. Dr JOACHIM RABOLD.

Zoologische Staatssammlung München: 81247 Munich, Münchhausenstr. 21; tel. (89) 81070; fax (89) 8107300; e-mail ZSM@zsm.mwn.de; internet www.zsm.mwn.de; f. 1807; Dir Prof. Dr GERHARD HASZPRUNAR; publ. *Spixiana*.

Neue Sammlung–Staatliches Museum für Angewandte Kunst (State Museum for Applied Arts): Türkenstr. 15 (Pinakothek der Moderne), 80333 Munich; tel. (89) 272725-0; fax (89) 272725-561; e-mail info@die-neue-sammlung.de; internet www.die-neue-sammlung.de; f. 1925; modern industrial arts and crafts, architecture, urban planning; industrial and graphic design; Dir Prof. Dr FLORIAN HUFNAGL.

Staatliche Antikensammlungen und Glyptothek (State Antique Collections): Königspl. 1, 80333 Munich; tel. (89) 286100; fax (89) 28927516; e-mail info@antike-am-koenigsplatz.mwn.de; internet www.antike-am-koenigsplatz.mwn.de; collections at: Königsplatz 1–3; Greek and Etruscan vases and bronzes, Greek and Roman sculpture, terracottas and bronzes, glass, jewellery.

Staatliche Graphische Sammlung München: Meiserstr. 10, 80333 Munich; tel. (89) 28927650; fax (89) 28927653; e-mail direktion@graphische-sammlung.mwn.de; internet www.pinakothek.de/pinakothek-der-moderne/graphik; f. 1758; German, Dutch, French and Italian prints and drawings since 15th c.; library of 40,000 vols; Dir Dr MICHAEL SEMFF.

Staatliche Münzsammlung (State Coin Collection): Residenzstr. 1, 80333 Munich; tel. (89) 227221; fax (89) 299859; e-mail smm.muenchen@t-online.de; internet www.stmwfk.bayern.de/kunst/museen/muenz.html; f. 16th c.; coins from different countries and centuries; special collections: Greek, Roman and Byzantine coins, German and Italian Renaissance medals, Bavarian coins, precious stones from antiquity, Middle

Ages and Renaissance; library of 20,000 vols; Dir Prof. Dr OVERBECK.

Staatliches Museum Ägyptischer Kunst (State Museum of Egyptian Art): Meiserstr. 10, 80333 Munich; premises at: Hofgartenstr., Munich; tel. (89) 28927-630; fax (89) 28927-638; e-mail info@aegyptisches-museum-muenchen.com; internet www.aegyptisches-museum-muenchen.de; f. 1966; library: small specialized library; Dir Dr SYLVIA SCHOSKE.

Staatliches Museum für Völkerkunde (State Museum of Ethnology): Maximilianstr. 42, 80538 Munich; tel. (89) 210136-100; fax (89) 210136-247; e-mail info@voelkerkundemuseum-muenchen.demuseum.voelkerkunde@extern.lrz-muenchen.de; internet www.voelkerkundemuseum-muenchen.de; f. 1868; collections on Asia, America, Africa and the Pacific Islands; library of 50,000 vols, 75 current periodicals; Dir Dr CLAUDIUS MÜLLER.

Städtische Galerie im Lenbachhaus: Luisenstr. 33, 80333 Munich; tel. (89) 233-32000; fax (89) 233-32003; e-mail lenbachhaus@muenchen.de; internet www.lenbachhaus.de; f. 1929; Munich artists including paintings by Kandinsky, Klee and the Blaue Reiter group; int. contemporary art; exhibitions, lectures, performances; Dir Dr HELMUT FRIEDEL.

Münster

Westfälisches Landesmuseum für Kunst und Kulturgeschichte (Westphalian Museum of Art and Cultural History): Domplatz 10, 48143 Münster; tel. (251) 590701; fax (251) 5907210; e-mail landesmuseum@lwl.org; internet www.lwl.org/landesmuseum; f. 1908; sculpture, painting, graphic art, goldsmith work since 9th c.; engraved portraits, history, numismatics; library of 121,000 vols; Dir Dr HERMANN ARNHOLD.

Nuremberg

Albrecht-Dürer-Haus: Albrecht-Dürer-Str. 39, 90317 Nuremberg; tel. (911) 2312568; fax (911) 2314971; e-mail museen@stadt.nuernberg.de; internet www.museen.nuernberg.de; f. 1828; life and work of the engraver Albrecht Dürer (1471–1528) presented in his home (inhabited 1509–28); Dir Dr JUTTA TSCHOEKE.

Germanisches Nationalmuseum: Kartäusergasse 1, 90402 Nuremberg; tel. (911) 1331-0; fax (911) 1331-200; e-mail info@gnm.de; internet www.gnm.de; f. 1852; German art and culture from prehistoric times to the present, fine art galleries, folk art, public library, archives, print room, musical instruments, arms, toys, etc.; library of 548,000 vols, 1,600 current periodicals; Chief Dir Prof. Dr G. ULRICH GROSSMANN.

Kunsthalle Nürnberg (Nuremberg Art Museum): Lorenzer Str. 32, 90402 Nuremberg; tel. (911) 231-2853; fax (911) 231-3721; e-mail kunsthalle@stadt.nuernberg.de; internet www.kunsthalle.nuernberg.de; f. 1967; changing exhibitions of international contemporary art; Dir ELLEN SEIFERMANN.

Stadtmuseum Fembohaus: Burgstr. 11, 90403 Nuremberg; tel. (911) 2315418; fax (911) 2315422; internet www.museen.nuernberg.de; f. 1958; art and cultural history of Nuremberg; Dir RUDOLF KÄS.

Offenbach am Main

Klingspor-Museum Offenbach: Herrnstr. 80, 63065 Offenbach am Main; tel. (69) 80652954; fax (69) 80652669; e-mail klingspormuseum@offenbach.de; internet www.klingspor-museum.de; f. 1953; collection and exhibition of calligraphy, typography, bookbinding, modern book art and private presses; library of 66,000 vols; special collection of 20th-century calligraphy; Dir Dr STEFAN SOLTEK; Librarian MARTINA WEISS.

Pforzheim

Schmuckmuseum Pforzheim im Reuchlinhaus: Jahnstr. 33, 75173 Pforzheim; located at: Jahnstr. 42, 75173 Pforzheim; tel. (7231) 392126; fax (7231) 391441; e-mail schmuckmuseum@stadt-pforzheim.de; internet www.schmuckmuseum.de; f. 1938; jewellery; Dir CORNELIE HOLZACH.

Potsdam

Brandenburgisches Landesmuseum für Ur- und Frühgeschichte (Pre- and Early History): Schloss Babelsberg, 14482, Potsdam; tel. (331) 708073; fax (331) 708074; f. 1953; Dir Prof. Dr J. KUNOW; publs *Veröffentlichungen des Brandenburgischen Landesmuseums für Ur- und Frühgeschichte* (annually), *Forschungen zur Archäologie im Land Brandenburg* (annually).

Stiftung Preussische Schlösser und Gärten Berlin-Brandenburg (Prussian Palaces and Gardens Foundation of Berlin-Brandenburg): Postfach 601462, 14414 Potsdam; premises at: 14471 Potsdam, Allee nach Sanssouci 5; tel. (331) 9694-0; fax (331) 9694-102; e-mail pressreferat@spsg.de; internet www.spsg.de; f. 1995; administers gardens and 150 palaces and other historic buildings in and around Berlin and Potsdam; Dir-Gen. Prof. Dr HARTMUT DORGERLOH; Admin. Dir Dr HEINZ BERG.

Recklinghausen

Museen der Stadt Recklinghausen (Recklinghausen City Museums): Grosse-Perdekamp-Str. 25–27, 45657 Recklinghausen; tel. (2361) 501935; fax (2361) 501932; e-mail kunst.re@t-online.de; internet www.kunst-in-recklinghausen.de; f. 1950; Dir Dr FERDINAND ULLRICH.

Attached museums:

Städtische Kunsthalle (City Art Gallery): Recklinghausen; tel. (2361) 501935; fax (2361) 501932; e-mail kunst.re@t-online.de; internet www.kunst-in-recklinghausen.de; f. 1950; paintings, drawings, prints and sculptures by contemporary artists; Dirs Dr FERDINAND ULLRICH, Dr HANS-JUERGEN SCHWALM.

Ikonen-Museum (Icon Museum): 45657 Recklinghausen, Kirchplatz 2A; tel. (2361) 501941; fax (2361) 501942; e-mail kunst.re@t-online.de; internet www.kunst-in-recklinghausen.de; f. 1956; Russian, Byzantine and Balkan icons, miniatures, metal work, Coptic sculpture and textiles; Dirs Dr FERDINAND ULLRICH, Dr EVA HAUSTEIN-BARTSCH.

Vestisches Museum: 45659 Recklinghausen, Hohenzollernstr. 12; tel. (2361) 501946; fax (2361) 501932; e-mail kunst.re@t-online.de; internet www.kunst-in-recklinghausen.de; f. 1987; Westphalian arts and crafts, local history, native art; Dirs Dr FERDINAND ULLRICH, Dr HANS-JUERGEN SCHWALM.

Schleswig

Stiftung Schleswig-Holsteinische Landesmuseen Schloss Gottorf (Foundation of Regional Museums in Schleswig-Holstein in Schloss Gottorf): Schloss Gottorf, 24837 Schleswig; tel. (4621) 813-0; fax (4621) 813535; e-mail info@schloss-gottorf.de; internet www.schloss-gottorf.de; f. 1835; houses Archaeological and Art and Culture Museums; library of 20,000 vols; Dir Prof. Dr CLAUS VON CARNAP-BORNHEIM; publs *Ausgrabungen in Haithabu* (irregular), *Ausgrabungen in Schleswig* (irregular), *Berichte über die Ausgrabungen in Haithabu* (irregular), *Die Funde der älteren Bronzezeit des nordischen Kreises* (irregular), *Offa* (annually), *Offa Bücher* (irregular), *Untersuchungen und Materialien zur Steinzeit in Schleswig-Holstein* (irregular).

Affiliated museums:

Archäologisches Landesmuseum (Provincial Museum of Archaeology):; f. 1985; archaeological and ethnological exhibits.

Eisenkunstgussmuseum Büdelsdorf (Ironwork Museum): Glück-Auf-Allee 4, 24782 Büdelsdorf; f. 1981; history of ironwork.

Jüdisches Museum Rendsburg (Jewish Museum): Prinzessinstr. 7–8, 24768 Rendsburg; tel. (4331) 25262; e-mail jmuseum@t-online.de; internet www.juedisches-museum-rendsburg.de; f. 1988.

Landesmuseum für Kunst und Kulturgeschichte (Museum Art and Culture):- artefacts from Middle Ages onwards; colln 19th c. paintings.

Volkskunde Museum Schleswig (Folklore Museum in Schleswig):tel. (4621) 96760; fax (4621) 967634; e-mail volkskunde@schloss-gottorf.de; f. 1993; history of local arts and crafts; Dir GUNTRAM TURKOWSKI.

Wikinger Museum Haithabu–Stiftung Schleswig-Holsteinische Landesmuseen Schloss Gottorf (Museum of the Viking age settlement Haithabu):; history of the archaeological dig; restored longship on port.

Stiftung Schleswig-Holsteinische Landesmuseen: Schloss Gottorf, 24837 Schleswig; tel. (4621) 813-0; fax (4621) 813-555; e-mail info@schloss-gottorf.de; internet www.schloss-gottorf.de; f. 1875; exhibits of art and culture of Schleswig-Holstein and surrounding area; library of 80,000 vols; Dir Prof. Dr HERWIG GURATZSCH; publs *Jahresberichte*, *Kataloge zu Sonderausstellungen*, *Neue Bilderhefte-Schloss Gottorf und seine Sammlungen*.

Schwerin

Archäologisches Landesmuseum und Landesamt für Bodendenkmalpflege Mecklenburg-Vorpommern: Domhof 4/5, 19055 Schwerin; tel. (385) 5214-0; fax (385) 5214-198; e-mail poststelle@kulturerbe-mv.de; internet www.kulturerbe-mv.de; f. 1953; library of 44,000 vols; Dir Dr FRIEDRICH LÜTH; publs *Bodendenkmalpflege in Mecklenburg-Vorpommern Jahrbuch*, *Beiträge zur Ur- und Frühgeschichte Mecklenburg-Vorpommerns*, *Museumskataloge*, *Materialhefte*, *Archäologie in Mecklenburg-Vorpommern*, *Archäologische Berichte aus Mecklenburg-Vorpommern*.

Speyer

Historisches Museum der Pfalz (Historical Museum of the Palatinate): Domplatz, 67324 Speyer; tel. (6232) 13250; fax (6232) 132540; e-mail info@museum.speyer.de; internet www.museum.speyer.de; f. 1869; art and cultural history of the Palatinate, includes wine museum and diocesan museum; library of 20,000 vols; Dir Dr ALEXANDER KOCH; publs *Mitteilungen des Historischen Vereins* (annually), *Pfälzer Heimat* (quarterly).

Stralsund

Kulturhistorisches Museum Stralsund (Cultural and Historical Museum of Stralsund): Mönchstr. 25–27, 18439 Stralsund; tel. (3831) 28790; fax (3831) 280060; e-mail khm@gmx.de; internet www.stralsund.abelnet.de/museen; f. 1858; prehistory, ecclesiastical art, folklore, local history, furniture, history of navigation and navy, modern art, handicrafts, 18th c. products; Dir Dr ANDREAS GRÜGER.

Stuttgart

Kunstmuseum Stuttgart (Stuttgart Art Museum): Kleiner Schlosspl. 2, 70173 Stuttgart; tel. (711) 2162188; fax (711) 216-7820; e-mail info@kunstmuseum-stuttgart.de; internet www.galerie-der-stadt-stuttgart.de; f. 1925; paintings, drawings, graphics and sculptures by German artists since 19th c.; Otto Dix collection; Curator Dr KARIN SCHICK.

Linden-Museum Stuttgart, Staatliches Museum für Völkerkunde (Linden Museum Stuttgart, State Museum for Ethnography): Hegelpl. 1, 70174 Stuttgart; tel. (711) 2022-3; fax (711) 2022-590; e-mail sekretariat@lindenmuseum.de; internet www.lindenmuseum.de; f. 1884; ethnographical museum; library of 40,000 vols, 270 current periodicals; Dir Prof. Dr THOMAS MICHEL; publ. *Tribus* (yearbook).

Staatliches Museum für Naturkunde Stuttgart: Rosenstein 1, 70191 Stuttgart; tel. (711) 89360; fax (711) 8936-100; e-mail museum.smns@naturkundemuseum-bw.de; internet www.naturkundemuseum-bw.de/stuttgart/start.html; f. 1791; botany, palaeontology, zoology; library of 75,000 vols; Dir Prof. Dr JOHANNA EDER; publs *Stuttgarter Beiträge zur Naturkunde, Serie A: Biologie* (irregular—up to 25 a year), *Stuttgarter Beiträge zur Naturkunde, Serie B: Geologie / Paläontologie* (irregular—up to 25 a year), *Stuttgarter Beiträge zur Naturkunde, Serie C: Wissen für Alle* (2 a year).

Staatsgalerie Stuttgart: Postfach 104342, 70038 Stuttgart; premises at: Konrad-Adenauerstr. 30–32, Stuttgart; tel. (711) 47040-0; fax (711) 2369983; e-mail info@staatsgalerie.de; internet www.staatsgalerie.de; f. 1843; art since the Middle Ages; collection of prints, drawings and photographs; Oskar Schlemmer Archive, Will Grohmann Archive, Sohm Archive; Dir Prof. Dr CHRISTIAN VON HOLST.

Württembergisches Landesmuseum Württemberg: Altes Schloss, 70173 Stuttgart; tel. (711) 279340098; fax (711) 27934909; e-mail info@landesmuseum-stuttgart.de; internet www.landesmuseum-stuttgart.de; f. 1862; archaeology from prehistoric to medieval times; , textiles and costumes, glass, furniture from the Middle Ages to the present, art and design of the 20th c., 4,000 years of glassmaking, Swabian sculpture, Renaissance clocks and watches, coins, musical instruments, Württemberg crown jewels; Roman lapidarium; Dir Prof. Dr CORNELIA EWIGLEBEN; Chief Curator Dr THOMAS BRUNE; publ. *Jahrbuch* (annually).

Trier

Rheinisches Landesmuseum Trier (Museum of the Rheinland in Trier): Weimarer Allee 1, 54290 Trier; tel. (651) 9774-0; fax (651) 9774-222; e-mail info@rlmtrier.de; internet www.rlmtrier.de; f. 1877; Roman and early medieval exhibits excavated in Trier and the local area; art history from the Middle Ages to the 19th c.; numismatic colln; restoration workshops; dendrochronological and archeobotanical analyses; municipal and regional archeological research; library of 70,000 vols; Dir Dr KARIN GOETHERT; publs *Funde und Ausgrabungen im Bezirk Trier* (annually), *Schriftenreihe des Rheinischen Landesmuseums Trier* (irregular), *Trierer Grabungen und Forschungen* (irregular), *Trierer Zeitschrift für Geschichte und Kunst* (annually).

Ulm

Ulmer Museum (Ulm Museum): Marktpl. 9, 89070 Ulm; tel. (731) 1614300; fax (731) 1611626; e-mail info.ulmer-museum@ulm.de; internet www.museum.ulm.de; f. 1924; collections of Ulm and Swabian art from 14th–19th c., international art since beginning of 20th c., archaeological collections, archives of the former Ulm School of Design (Hochschule für Gestaltung); Dir Dr BRIGITTE REINHARDT.

Weimar

Stiftung Weimarer Klassik und Kunstsammlungen: Burgplatz 4, 99423 Weimar; tel. (3643) 545-0; fax (3643) 202174; e-mail info@swkk.de; internet www.swkk.de; f. 1953; preserves and researches Weimar's artistic and cultural sites and collections, primarily the classical period in Weimar and modern art in Weimar; administers the Goethe-Nationalmuseum (comprises 23 museums and houses connected with Goethe and Schiller, and other buildings, incl. Liszt's house); also the Nietzsche-Archiv), the Schlossmuseum, the Bauhaus Museum, the Neues Museum, the Goethe- und Schiller-Archiv (800,000 MSS of German writers, artists, composers and scientists) and the Duchess Anna Amalia Bibliothek (850,000 vols); Pres. HELLMUT SEEMANN; Admin. Dir BEATE ALTMEYER.

Thüringisches Landesamt für Denkmalpflege und Archäologie (Thuringian Regional Office for the Preservation of Monuments and Archaeology): Humboldtstr. 11, 99423 Weimar; tel. (3643) 903324; fax (3643) 903328; e-mail post@tlad.de; internet www.tlad.de; f. 1888; library of 28,000 vols; publs *Ausgrabungen und Funde im Freistaat Thüringen*, *Jahresschrift 'Alt-Thüringen'*, *Restaurierung und Museumstechnik*, *Weimarer Monographien zur Ur- und Frühgeschichte*.

Attached museums:

Museum für Ur- und Frühgeschichte Thüringens (Thuringian Museum for Prehistory and Early History): Humboldtstr. 11, 99423 Weimar; tel. (3643) 818300; fax (3643) 818390; local history since 400,000 BC.

Steinsburgmuseum: Waldhaussiedlung 8, 98631 Römhild; tel. (36948) 20561; fax (36948) 82853; Celtic site and artefacts; Dir Dr M. SIEDEL.

Wittenberg

Lutherhaus, Reformationsgeschichtliches Museum (Museum of the History of the Reformation): Collegienstr. 54, 06886 Lutherstadt Wittenberg; tel. (3491) 42030; fax (3491) 4203270; e-mail info@martinluther.de; internet www.martinluther.de; f. 1883; portraits, MSS, pictures, woodcuts, copperplates, medallions and original works on the history of the Reformation; library of 60,000 vols; Dir Dr STEFAN RHEIN.

Worms

Museum der Stadt Worms im Andreasstift (Worms City Museum): Weckerlingpl. 7, 67547 Worms; tel. (6241) 9463914; fax (6241) 24068; e-mail museum@worms.de; internet www.worms.de/deutsch/tourismus/museen; f. 1881; archaeology, town history of Worms, spec. colln of glassware, Luther Room (diet of 1521); Dir (Administration) Dr THOMASGERALD SCHIWEKBOENNEN; publs *Der Wormsgau* (annually, also Beihefte), *Zeitschrift der Kulturinstitute der Stadt Worms und des Altertumsvereins Worms*.

Museum Heylshof: Stephansgasse 9, 67547 Worms; tel. and fax (6241) 22000; internet www.heylshof.de; f. 1923; 15th–19th c. paintings, sculptures, pottery, porcelains, glass; Curators CORNELIUS ADALBERT, F. V. HEYL.

Universities

FERNUNIVERSITÄT IN HAGEN (Distance-Learning University in Hagen)

58084 HagenTelephone: (2331) 98701
Fax: (2331) 987316
E-mail: postmaster@fernuni-hagen.de
Internet: www.fernuni-hagen.de

Founded 1974

68 Regional Study Centres
State control
Language of instruction: German
Academic year: October to September
Rector: Prof. Dr-Ing. HELMUT HOYER
Vice-Rectors: Prof. Dr SCHERM, Prof. Dr SCHIMANK, Prof. Dr SCHLAGETER
Chief Executive: REGINA ZDEBEL
Librarian: DIETER SCHMAUSS (acting)
Number of teachers: 510
Number of students: 44,000 (full- and part-time and associate)

Publications: *FernUni Perspektive*, *Informationen zum Studium*, *Anleitung zur Belegung*, *Forschungsbericht*, *Jahresberichte*, *Schriftenreihen*

DEANS

Department of Economics: Prof. Dr WEIBLER
Department of Culture and Social Sciences: Prof. Dr BENZ
Department of Electrical Engineering: Prof. Dr HALANG
Department of Law: Prof. Dr VORMBAUM
Department of Mathematics: Prof. Dr LOCHER
Department of Computer Sciences: Prof. Dr HAAKE

RHEINISCH-WESTFÄLISCHE TECHNISCHE HOCHSCHULE AACHEN

52056 Aachen
Telephone: (241) 801
Fax: (241) 8092312
E-mail: international@zhv.rwth-aachen.de
Internet: www.rwth-aachen.de

Founded 1870 as Polytechnikum, attained university status 1880
Academic year: October to September

Rector: Prof. Dr BURKHARD RAUHUT
Pro-Rectors: Prof. Dr KONSTANTIN MESKOURIS, Prof. Dr ROLF ROSSAINT, Prof. Dr REINHART POPRAWE
Deputy Director-General: Dr HEINZ-HERBERT KAUßEN
Librarian: Dr ULRIKE EICH

Library: see Libraries and Archives
Number of teachers: 4,248
Number of students: 29,598

Publication: *Alma Mater Aquensis* (annually)

DEANS

Faculty of Architecture: Prof. Dr PETER JOHN RUSSELL
Faculty of Arts and Humanities: Prof. Dr phil. CHRISTIAN STETTER
Faculty of Civil Engineering and Surveying: Prof. Dr WILHELM BENNING
Faculty of Economics: Prof. Dr HANS-JÜRGEN SEBASTIAN
Faculty of Electrical Engineering and Information Technology: Prof. Dr TOBIAS NOLL

Faculty of Geo-resources and Materials Engineering: Prof. Dr NICOLAI MARTENS
Faculty of Mathematics, Computer Science and Natural Sciences: Prof. Dr WOLFGANG THOMAS
Faculty of Mechanical Engineering: Prof. Dr KLAUS HENNING
Faculty of Medicine: Prof. Dr RUDOLF LÜTTICKEN

PROFESSORS

Faculty of Architecture (Schinkelstr. 1, 52056 Aachen; tel. (241) 8095000809; fax (241) 8092237; e-mail dekan@architektur.rwth-aachen.de; internet arch.rwth-aachen.de):

BAUM, M., Design Construction
BRUCHHAUS, G., District Planning and Design
COERSMEIER, U., Interior Design
HOFFMANN, H., Visual Form
HUMBLÉ, F., Building Planning and Design
JANSEN, M., History of Urban Development
KADA, K., Building Design and Function
KRAUSE, C., Landscape Ecology and Landscape Design
LAUENSTEIN, H., Open Space and Landscape Planning
MARKSCHIES, A., History of Art
NICOLIC, V., Building Construction and Design
PIEPER, J., History of Architecture and Conservation
RUOFF, J., Environment, Services and Design
RUSSELL, P., Computer-aided Design
SCHMIDT, H., Conservation
SCHNEIDER, H. N., Building Construction and Design
SCHULZE, M., Sculpture
SELLE, K., Planning Theory and Town Planning
TRAUTZ, M., Building Construction (Structural Design)
VAN DEN BERGH, W., Housing and Residential Development
VINKEN, G., Theory of Architecture
WACHTEN, K., Urban Design and Country Planning

Faculty of Arts and Humaities (Kármánstr. 17–19, 52056 Aachen; tel. (241) 8096002; fax (241) 8092334; e-mail adrian.leipold@fb7.rwth-aachen.de; internet www.rwth-aachen.de/fb7):

BEIER, R., Applied Linguistics
BEIN, T., Medieval German Language and Literature
DERINGER, L., English and American Language and Literature
ERTLER, K., Romance Languages and Literatures
ESSER, A., Philosophy
FICK, M., German Literature
GELLHAUS, A., German Literature
GILLMAYR-BUCHER, S., Biblical Studies
VON HAEHLING, R., History
HAMMERICH, K., Sociology
HEINEN, A., Modern and Contemporary History
HILL, P. B., Sociology
HORCH, H.-O., German and Jewish Literature
HÖRNING, K.-H., Sociology
HORNKE, L., Psychology
JÄGER, L., Linguistics and Media Theory
JAKOBS, E.-M., Communication Science
KEIL, G., Theoretical Philosophy
KELLERWESSEL, W., Philosophy
KERNER, M., Medieval and Modern History
KÖNIG, H., Political Science
LEWATER, D., Education Science
LIEDTKE, F., German Language
LUEKE, U., Theology
MEY, H., Sociology
MEYER, G., Theology
MEYER, P. G., English Linguistics (Synchronic)
MICHELSEN, U. A., Education
MOESSNER, L, English Linguistics and Medieval Studies
MÜSSELER, J., Work Psychology and Cognition
NEUSCHAEFER, A., Romance Languages and Literatures
NIEHR, T., German Language
PANGRITZ, A., Theology
RICHTER, E., Political Science
ROTTE, R., Political Science
SCHERBERICH, K., History
SCHMITZ, S., German Language
SPIJKERS, W., Psychology
STETTER, C., Germanic Linguistics
WENZEL, P., English Literature

Faculty of Civil Engineering (Mies-van-der-Rohe-Str. 1, 52074 Aachen; tel. (241) 8025075; fax (241) 8022201; e-mail dekanat@fb3.rwth-aachen.de; internet www.rwth-aachen.de/fb3):

BECKMANN, K. J., Urban and Transport Planning
BENNING, W., Geodesy
BRAMERSHUBER, W., Building Materials Research
BRUNK, M. F., Construction Management and Building Services
DOETSCH, P., Waste Management
FELDMANN, M., Steel and Light-Metal Construction
GÜLDENPFENNING, J., Mechanics and Building Construction
HEGGER, J., Structural Concrete
KÖNGETER, J., Hydraulic Engineering and Water Resources Management
MESKOURIS, K., Structural Statistics and Dynamics
NACKEN, H., Engineering Hydrology
OSEBOLD, R., Construction Management – Project Management
PINNEKAMP, J., Sanitary and Waste Engineering
RAUPACH, M., Building Materials Research
REICHMUTH, J., Airport and Air-Transportation Research
STEINAUER, B., Road Engineering, Earth Works and Tunneling
WENDLER, E., Transport Economics, Railway Engineering and Railway Operations
ZIEGLER, M., Geotechnics in Civil Engineering

Faculty of Economics (Kármánstr. 17–19, 52056 Aachen; tel. (241) 8096000; fax (241) 8092166; e-mail dekanat-fb8@rwth-aachen.de; internet www.wiwi.rwth-aachen.de):

BASTIAN, M., Business Information Systems and Operations
BRETTEL, M., Business Administration and Sciences for Engineers and Scientists (Centre for Entrepreneurship)
BREUER, W., Business Admininstration (Finance)
DYCKHOFF, H., Business Theory, Environmental Management and Industrial Controlling
FEESS, E., Economics (Microeconomics)
HARMS, P., Macroeconomics
HÖMBURG, R., Business Taxation and Auditing
HUBER, C., Civil Law, Business and Labour Law
LORZ, O., International Economics
MÖLLER, H. P., Business Administration, Accounting and Finance
REIMERS, K., Business Information Systems (Electronic Business)
SCHRÖDER, H.-H., Technology and Innovation Management
SEBASTIAN, H.-J., Optimization of Distribution Networks
STEFFENHAGEN, H., Corporate Policy and Marketing
THOMES, P., Economic and Social History
VON NITZSCH, R., Business Management
WOYWODE, M., International Management

Faculty of Electrical Engineering and Information Technology (Muffeter Weg 3, 52074 Aachen; tel. (241) 8027572; fax (241) 8022343; e-mail dekanat@fb6.rwth-aachen.de; internet www.fb6.rwth-aachen.de):

AACH, T., Image Processing
ASCHEID, G., Integrated Signal Processing Systems
BEMMERL, T., Operation Systems and Scalable Computing
DE DONCKER, R., Power Electronic and Electrical Drives
HAMEYER, K., Electrical Mechanics
HAUBRICH, H.-J., Power Systems and Power Economics
HEINEN, S., Integrated Analogue Circuits
JANSEN, R., Electromagnetic Theory
KAISER, W., History of Engineering and Technology
KRAISS, K.-F., Technical Informatics and Computer Science
KURZ, H., Semiconductor Technology
LEONHARDT, K. S., Medical Information Technology
LEUPERS, R., Software for Systems on Silicon
MAEHOENEN, P. H., Wireless Networks
MATHAR, R., Information Theory
MEYR, H., Integrated Signal Processing Systems
MOKWA, W., Materials in Electrical Engineering
NOLL, T. G., Electrical Engineering and Computer Systems
OHM, J.-R., Communications Engineering
SAUER, U., Electrochemical Energy Conversion
SCHNETTLER, A., High Voltage Technology
VARY, P., Communication Systems and Data Processing
VESCAN, A., GaN Device Technology
VORLÄNDER, M., Technical Acoustics
WALKE, B., Communications Networks
WASER, R., Materials in Electrical Materials

Faculty of Geo-resources and Materials Engineering (Intzestr. 1, 52056 Aachen; tel. (241) 8095665; fax (241) 8092370; e-mail dekanat-fb5@rwth-aachen.de; internet www.rwth-aachen.de):

Section of Geoscience:

AZZAM, R., Engineering Geology and Hydrogeology
BREUER, H., Geography, Economic and Applied Geography
CLAUSER, C., Applied Geophysics
FLAJS, G., Geology and Palaeontology
GRÄF, P., Geography, Physical Geography and Climatology
HAVLIK, G., Geography, Physical Geography and Climatology
HEGER, G., Crystallography
KRAMM, U., Mineralogy and Geochemistry
KUKLA, P., Geology and Palaeontology
LEHMKUHL, F., Geography, Physical Geography and Geoecology
LITTKE, R., Geology and Geochemistry of Petroleum and Coal
MEYER, M., Mineralogy and Economic Geology
ROTH, G., Applied Crystallography and Mineralogy
STANJEK, H., Clay Mineralogy
URAI, J. L., Structural Geology, Tectonics and Geomechanics

Section of Metallurgy and Materials Technology:

BLECK, W., Materials Science of Steels
BUERIG-POLACZ, A., Foundry Technology

CONRADT, R, Glass and Ceramic Composites
EMMERICH, H., Computational Materials Engineering
EPPLE, U., Process Control Engineering
FRIEDRICH, B., Process Metallurgy and Metal Recycling
GOTTSTEIN, G., Physical Metallurgy and Metal Physics
KAYSSER, W. A., Materials Science of Nonferrous Metals
KÖHNE, H., Heat and Mass Transfer
KOPP, R., Metal Forming
ODOJ, R., Materials Chemistry
PFEIFER, H., High Temperature Engineering
SCHNEIDER, J., Materials Chemistry
SENK, D. G., Metallurgy of Iron and Steel
TELLE, R., Ceramics and Refractories

Section of Mining Engineering:

FRENZ, W., Mining and Environment
HEIL, J., Coking, Briquetting and Thermal Waste Treatment
MARTENS, P. N., Mining Engineering
NIEHAUS, K., Excavation and Mining Equipment
NIEMANN-DELIUS, C., Surface Mining and Drilling
PRETZ, T., Processing and Recycling of Solid Waste Materials
PREUSSE, A., Mine Surveying, Mining Subsidence Engineering and Geophysics in Mining
SEELIGER, A., Mining and Metallurgical Machine Engineering
WOTRUBA, H., Mineral Processing

Faculty of Mathematics, Computer Science and Natural Sciences (Templergraben 64, 52064 Aachen; tel. (241) 8094500; fax (241) 8092124; e-mail dekan@fb1.rwth-aachen.de; internet www.fb1.rwth-aachen.de):

ALBRECHT, M., Organic Chemistry
BALLMANN, J., Mechanics
BAUMANN, H., Chemistry
BEGINN, U., Macromolecular and Supramolecular Chemistry
BEMELMANS, V., Mathematics
BENEKE, M., Theoretical Physics
BERGER, C., Experimental Physics
BERLAGE, T., Computer Science (Life Science Informatics)
BERNREUTNER, W., Theoretical Physics
BISCHOF, C., Computer Science (Scientific Computing)
BLUEMICH, B., Macromolecular Chemistry/NMR
BLÜGEL, S., Theoretical Physics
BOCK, H. H., Applied Statistics
BOEHM, A., Experimental Physics
BOHRMANN, J., Zoology and Human Biology
BOLM, C., Chemistry
BORCHERS, J., Computer Science (Media Computing)
BRAEUNIG, P.-M., Developmental Biology and Morphology of Animals
BRUECKEL, T., Experimental Physics
CAPELLMANN, H., Theoretical Physics
CONRATH, U., Plant Biochemistry
CRAMER, E., Applied Statistics
DAHMEN, W., Mathematics
DEDERICHS, P. H., Theoretical Physics
DOHM, V., Theoretical Physics
DRONSKOWSKI, R., Theoretical and Synthetic Solid-State Chemistry
ELLING, L., Biomaterial Sciences
ENDERS, D., Organic Chemistry
ENGLERT, U., Inorganic Chemistry
ENSS, V., Mathematics
ESSER, K.-H., Applied Mathematics
FELD, L., Experimental Physics
FISCHER, R., Molecular Biotechnology
FLEISCHHAUER, J., Theoretical Chemistry
FLÜGGE, G., Experimental Physics
FRENTZEN, M., Botany
GÄRTNER, F., Computer Science (Dependable Systems)
GAIS, H.-J., Organic Chemistry
GIESL, J., Computer Science
GRAEDEL, E., Mathematical Foundations of Computer Science
GÜNTHERODT, G., Experimental Physics
HARTMEIER, W., Biotechnology
HEINKE, H., Experimental Physics
HERMANN, P., Mathematics
HISS, G., Mathematics
HÖLDERICH, W., Fuel Chemistry
HROMKOVIC, J., Computer Science (Algorithms and Complexity)
IBACH, H., Experimental Physics
INDERMARK, K., Computer Science (Programming Languages)
JANK, G., Engineering Mathematics
JARKE, M., Computer Science (Information Systems)
JONGEN, H. TH., Mathematics
KAMPS, U., Statistics
KLEE, D., Biomaterials
KLEMRADT, U., Experimental Physics
KLINNER, U., Applied Microbiology
KOBBELT, L., Computer Science (Computer Graphics and Multimedia)
KÖLLE, U., Organometallic and Co-ordination Chemistry of the Transition Metals
KOWALEWSKI, S., Computer Science (Embedded Systems)
KREIBIG, U., Experimental Physics
KREUZALER, F., Botany/Molecular Genetics
KRIEG, A., Mathematics
KULL, H.-J., Theoretical Physics
LAKEMEYER, G., Computer Science (Knowledge-based Systems)
LEITNER, W., Technical Chemistry and Petrochemistry
LENGELER, B., Experimental Physics
LIAUW, M., Technical Chemistry and Reaction Engineering
LICHTER, H., Computer Science (Software Construction)
LÜCHOW, A., Theoretical and Computational Chemistry
LUEKEN, H., Inorganic Chemistry
LÜTH, H., Experimental Physics
LUKSCH, P., Computer Science
MAIER-PAAPE, S., Mathematics
MARTIN, M., Physical Chemistry
MERKE, I., Physical Chemistry
MÖLLER, M., Macromolecular Chemistry
MÜLLER-KRUMBHAAR, H., Theoretical Physics
NAGEL, M., Computer Science (Software Engineering)
NEY, H., Computer Science (Pattern Recognition)
NOELLE, S., Mathematics
OKUDA, J., Organometallic Chemistry
PAHLINGS, H., Mathematics
PLESKEN GEN. WIGGER, W., Mathematics
PRIEFER, U., Biology (Soil Ecology)
PRINZ, W., Computer Science (Cooperation Systems)
RAABE, G., Theoretical Chemistry
RAUHUT, B., Statistics and Mathematics of Economics
RICHTERING, W., Physical Chemistry
ROSSMANITH, P., Computer Science (Theoretical Computer Science)
SALZER, A., Organometallic Chemistry
SCHÄFFER, A., Environmental Biology and Chemodynamics
SCHAEL, S., Experimental Physics
SCHMITZ, D., Experimental Physics
SCHOELLER, H., Theoretical Physics
SCHOLLWOECK, U., Theoretical Physics
SCHROEDER, U., Computer Science (Computer-based Learning)
SCHUPHAN, I., Biology (Ecology, Ecotoxicology, Ecochemistry)
SCHWEIGERT, CH., Theoretical Physics
SEIDEL, T., Computer Science (Data Mining)
SELKE, W., Theoretical Physics
SIELING, D., Physics
SIMON, U., Inorganic Chemistry and Nanomaterials
SLUSARENKO, A., Plant Physiology
SPANIOL, O., Computer Science (Communication Systems)
STAHL, W., Physical Chemistry
STAPF, S., Macromolecular Chemistry
THOMAS, W., Computer Science (Logic and Discrete Systems
TRIESCH, E., Mathematics
URBAN, K., Experimental Physics
VON DER MOSEL, H., Mathematics
VON PLESSEN, G., Experimental Physics
WAGNER, H., Biology
WALCHER, S., Mathematics
WEINHOLD, E., Biorganic Chemistry
WENZL, H., Experimental Physics
WIEGNER, M., Mathematics
WOLF, K., Microbiology
WUTTIG, M., Experimental Physics
ZEIDLER, M., Physical Chemistry

Faculty of Mechanical Engineering (Eilfschornsteinstr. 18, 52062 Aachen; tel. (241) 8095305; fax (241) 8092144; e-mail dekanat-fb4@rwth-aachen.de; internet www.fb4.rwth-aachen.de):

ABEL, D., Automatic Control
ALLES, W., Flight Dynamics
BEHR, M. A., Computational Analysis of Technical Systems
BEISS, P., Materials Technology
BOBZIN, K., Surface Technology, Materials Science
BOHN, D., Steam and Gas Turbines
BRECHER, C., Machine Tools
BÜCHS, Z., Bioprocess Engineering
CORVES, B., Mechanism Theory and Dynamics of Machines
DELLMANN, T., Rail Vehicles and Materials-Handling Technology
DILTHEY, U., Welding Technology
EL-MAGD, E. A., Engineering Materials
FELDHUSEN, J., Engineering Design
GOLD, P. W., Machine Elements and Design
GRIES, T., Textile Engineering
GRUENEFELD, G., Laser Technology
HABERSTROH, E., Synthetic Rubber Technology
HENNING, K., Methods of Cybernetics in Engineering Sciences
ITSKOV, M., Continuum Machines
KLOCKE, F., Manufacturing Technology
KNEER, R., Heat and Mass Transfer
KUGELER, K., Reactor Safety and Reactor Technology
LOOSEN, P., Technology of Optical Systems
LUCAS, K., Technical Thermodynamics
MAIER, H.-R., Ceramic Components in Mechanical Engineering
MARQUARDT, W., Process Systems Engineering
MELIN, T., Chemical Engineering
MICHAELI, W., Plastics Processing
MODIGELL, M., Mechanical Unit Operations
MURRENHOFF, H., Fluid Power Drives and Control
NIEHUIS, R., Jet Propulsion and Turbo Machinery
OLIVIER, H., High-Temperature Gas Dynamics
PETERS, N., Technical Mechanics
PFENNING, A., Thermal Unit Operations
PISCHINGER, S., Internal Combustion Engines
PITZ-PAAL, R., Solar Technology
POPRAWE, R., Laser Technology
REIMERDES, H.-G., Aerospace and Lightweight Structures
SCHLICK, C., Industrial Engineering and Ergonomics
SCHMACHTENBERG, E., Plastics Materials Technology

SCHMITT, R., Metrology and Quality Management
SCHOMBURG, W. K., Construction and Development of Microsystems
SCHROEDER, W., Fluid Dynamics
SCHUH, G., Production Engineering
SCHULZ, W., Laser Production Processes
SINGHEISER, L., Materials for Energy Technology
STOLTEN, D., Fuel Cells
WALLENTOWITZ, H., Automotive Engineering
WEICHERT, D., General Mechanics

Faculty of Medicine (Pauwelstr.30, 52074 Aachen; tel. (241) 8089167; e-mail dekanat@ukaachen.de; internet www.ukaachen.de):

AMUNTS, K., Sturctural-Functional Brain Mapping
AUTSCHBACH, R., Thoracic and Cardiovascular Surgery
BEIER, H., Anatomy and Reproductive Biology
BERNHAGEN, J, Biochemistry
BÜLL, U., Nuclear Medicine
CONRADS, G., Medical Microbiology
DIEDRICH, P., Orthodontics
DOTT, W., Hygienics and Environmental Medicine
EBLE, M. J., Radiotherapy
ELLING, I., Biomaterial Science
ELLRICH, J., Neurosurgery
FAHLKE, C., Physiology
FINK, G., Cognitive Neurology
FLOEGE, J., Internal Medicine
GAUGGEL, G., Medical Psychology and Medical Sociology
GERZER, R., Aerospace Medicine
GILSBACH, J., Neurosurgery
GRESSNER, A. M., Clinical Chemistry and Pathobiochemistry
GREVEN, J., Pharmacology and Toxicology
GRÜNDER, G., Experimental Neuropsychiatry
GÜNTHER, R., Diagnostic Radiology
HANRATH, P., Internal Medicine
HEIMANN, G., Paediatrics
HEINRICH, P., Biochemistry
HERPERTZ-DAHLMANN, B., Child and Adolescent Psychiatry and Psychotherapy
HILGERS, R.-D., Medical Statistics
HÖRNCHEN, H., Paediatrics
HUBER, W., Neurolinguistics
JAHNEN-DECHENT, W., Cell and Molecular Biology at Interfaces
JAKSE, G., Urology
KAUFMANN, P., Anatomy
KNÜCHEL-CLARKE, C., Pathology
KORR, H., Anatomy
KRAUS, T., Occupational Medicine
KÜPPER, W., Laboratory Animal Science
KUHLEN, H., Anaesthesiology
LAMPERT, F., Conservative Dentistry, Periodontics and Preventive Dentistry
LENDLEIN, A., Technology and Development of Medical Products
LEONHARDT, S., Medical Informatics Technology
LUECKHOFF, A., Physiology
LUESCHER, B., Biochemistry and Molecular Biology
LUETTICKEN, R., Medical Microbiology
MARX, R., Dental Materials
MATERN, H., Internal Medicine
MATHIAK, K., Behavioural Psychobiology
MERK, H. F., Dermatology
MURKEN, A. H., History of Medicine and Hospitals
NEULEN, J., Gynaecological Endocrinology and Reproductive Medicine
NEUSCHAEFER-RUBE, C., Phoniatrics and Pedaudiology
NIENDORF, T., Experimental MR-Imaging
NIETHARD, F. U., Orthopaedics
NOTH, J., Neurology
OSIEKA, R., Internal Medicine
PAAR, O., Surgery
PALLUA, N., Plastic Surgery, Hand and Reconstructive Surgery
RATH, W., Gynaecology
RIEDIGER, D., Oral, Maxillo-facial and Plastic Facial Surgery
RINK, L., Immunology
RITTER, K., Virology
ROSSAINT, R., Anaesthesiology
SCHMALZIG, G., Pharmacology and Toxicology
SCHMITZ-RODE, T., Diagnostic Radiology
SCHNEIDER, F., Psychiatrics and Psychotherapy
SCHUMPELICK, V., Surgery
SEGHAYE, M.-C., Paediatric Cardiology
SPIEKERMANN, H., Prosthodontics
SPITZER, K., Medical Informatics
THRON, A., Neuroradiology
VÁSQUEZ-JIMÉNEZ, J., Paediatric Heart Surgery
WALTER, P., Opthalmology
WEBER, C., Cardiovascular Molecular Biology
WEIS, J., Neuropathology
WELLMANN, A., Pathology (Cytology)
WESTHOFEN, M., Otorhinolaryngology
WILLMES-VON HINCKELDEY, K., Neuropsychology
ZENKE, M., Biomedical Engineering and Cell Biology
ZERRES, K., Human Genetics

AFFILIATED INSTITUTIONS

Aachen Global Academy GmbH: Kármánstr. 17, 52056 Aachen; Dir Dr CHRISTOPH K. HEINEN.

Aachener Demonstrationslabor für integrierte Produktionstechnik GmbH: Seilbachstr. 25, 52062 Aachen; Dir Dr WERNER FISCHER.

ACCES e. V. – Materials + Processes: Intzestr. 5, 52072 Aachen; Dir ROBERT GUNTLIN.

Deutsches Wollforschungsinstitut e. V. (German Wool Research Institute): Veltmanplatz 8, 52062 Aachen; Dir Prof. Dr MARTIN MÖLLER.

Forschungsinstitut für Rationalisierung (Institute for Research in Rationalization): Pontdriesch 14–16, 52062 Aachen; Dir Prof. Dr HOLGER LUCZAK.

Forschungsinstitut für Wasser- und Abfallwirtschaft (Research Institute for Water and Waste Management): Mies-van-der-Rohe-Str. 17, 52062 Aachen; Dir FRIEDRICH-WILHELM BOLLE.

Forschungsstelle Technisch-Wirtschaftliche Unternehmensstrukturen der Stahlindustrie (Research Department for Technical and Economic Corporate Structures in the Steel Industry): Intzestr. 1, 52072 Aachen; Dir Prof. Dr WINFRIED DAHL.

Fraunhofer-Institut für Produktionstechnologie (Fraunhofer Institute for Production Technology): Steinbachstr. 17, 52074 Aachen; Dir Prof. Dr G. SCHUH.

Freunde und Förderer der RWTH Aachen: Wüllnerstr. 9, 52062 Aachen; em. Prof. ROLAND WALTER.

Institut für Kunststoffverarbeitung in Industrie und Handwerk (Institute of Plastics Technology): Ponstr. 49–55, 52062 Aachen; Dir Prof. Dr WALTER MICHAELI.

Institut für Prozess- und Anwendungstechnik Keramik (Institute for Process and Application Technology in Ceramics): Dir Prof. Dr HORST R. MAIER.

Prüf- und Entwicklungsinstitut für Abwassertechik: Mies-van-der-Rohe-Str. 1, 52074 Aachen; Dir Dr ELMAR DORGELOH.

Technische Akademie, Wuppertal e. V.: Hubertusallee 18, 42117 Wuppertal; Dir Dr MARTIN STACHOWSKE.

WZLfoum an der RWTH Aachen: Steinbachstr. 53, 52074 Wuppertal; Dir Dr TORSTEN KURR.

UNIVERSITÄT AUGSBURG

Universitätsstr. 2, 86159 Augsburg
Telephone: (821) 598-0
Fax: (821) 5985505
Internet: www.uni-augsburg.de

Founded 1970
State control
Language of instruction: German
Academic year: October to July

Rector: Prof. Dr WILFRIED BOTTKE
Vice-Rectors: Prof. Dr BERNHARD FLEISCHMANN, Prof. Dr ALOIS LOIDL, Prof. Dr THOMAS SCHEERER
Chancellor: ALOIS ZIMMERMAN
Registrar: HERMANN GOHL
Director of International Relations: Dr SABINE TAMM
Librarian: Dr ULRICH HOHOFF

Library: see Libraries and Archives
Number of teachers: 458
Number of students: 12,386

Publication: *Mitteilungen Institut fur Europaeische Kulturgeschichte*

DEANS

Faculty of Applied Computing: Prof. Dr WOLFGANG REIF
Faculty of Catholic Theology: Prof. Dr FRANZ SEDLMEIER
Faculty of Economics: Prof. Dr KLAUS TUROWSKI
Faculty of History and Philology: Prof. Dr HUBERT ZAPF
Faculty of Law: Prof. Dr MICHAEL KORT
Faculty of Mathematics and Natural Sciences: Prof. Dr SIEGFRIED HORN
Faculty of Philosophy and Social Science: Prof. Dr RAINER-OLAF SCHULTZE

PROFESSORS

Faculty of Applied Computing (86135 Augsburg; tel. (821) 5982174; fax (821) 5982175; e-mail reif@informatik.uni-augsburg.de; internet www.uni-augsburg.de/fakultaeten/fai):

ANDRÉ, ELISABETH, Multimedia Concepts and Applications
BAUER, BERNHARD, Software and Progamming Languages
FRIEDMANN, ARNE, Physical Geography
HAGERUP, TORBEN, Theoretical Computing
HILLENBRAND, HANS, Didactics
HILPERT, MARKUS, Human Geography
JACOBEIT, JUCUNDUS, Physical Geography
KIESSLING, WERNER, Databases and Information Systems
LIENHART, RAINER, Multimedia Computing
MÖLLER, BERNHARD, Databases and Information Systems
PEYKE, GERD, Human Geography
POSCHWATTA, WOLFGANG, Human Geography
REIF, WOLFGANG, Software and Progamming Languages
SCHNEIDER, THOMAS, Didactics
THIEME, KARIN, Human Geography
UNGERER, THEO, Information and Communication Systems
VOGLER, WALTER, Software and Progamming Languages
WIECZOREK, ULRICH, Didactics

Faculty of Catholic Theology (Universitätsstr. 10, 86159 Augsburg; tel. (821) 5985820; fax (821) 5985503; e-mail dekanat@kthf.uni-augsburg.de; internet www.kthf.uni-augsburg.de):

ARNTZ, KLAUS, Moral Theology
BALMER, H. P., Philosophy
GÜTHOFF, ELMAR, Church Law
HAUSMANNINGER, TH., Christian Ethics
KIENZLER, K., Basic Theology
KÜPPERS, K., Liturgy Science
RIEDL, GERDA, New Testament Exegesis
SCHEULE, RUPERT M. (acting), Christian Ethics
SEDLMEIER, F. (acting), Old Testament Exegesis
WURST, F., Church History

Faculty of Economics (Universitätsstr. 16, 86159 Augsburg; tel. (821) 5984015; fax (821) 5984212; e-mail dekanat@wiwi.uni-augsburg.de; internet www.wiwi.uni-augsburg.de):

BAMBERG, G., Statistics
BOEHLE, F., Socio-economics
BUHL, H. U., Business Administration
COENENBERG, A., Business Administration
FLEISCHMANN, B., Business Administration
GIEGLER, H., Sociology
GIERL, H., Business Administration
HANUSCH, H., Economics
HEINHOLD, M., Business Administration
KIFMANN, M., Sociology
KLEIN, R., Sociology
LAU, C., Sociology
LEHMANN, E., Business Management
MAUSSNER, A., Economics
MEIER, M., Economics
MICHAELIS, D., Economics
NEUBERGER, O., Psychology
PFAFF, A., Economics
SCHITTKO, U., Econometrics
STEINER, M., Business Administration
STENGEL, M., Psychology
TUMA, A., Business Administration
TUROWSKI, K., Business Informatics and Systems Engineering
WELZEL, P., Economics

Faculty of History and Philology (Universitätsstr. 10, 86159 Augsburg; tel. (821) 5982764; fax (821) 5985501; e-mail dekan.phil2@phil.uni-augsburg.de; internet www.philhist.uni-augsburg.de):

BICKENDORF, G., Art History
BUBLITZ, W., English Linguistics
BURKHARDT, J., History of Early Modern Times
DOERING-MANTEUFFEL, S., Folklore
ELSPASS, S., German Language
FÄCKE, C., French Didactics
GEPPERT, H. V., German and Comparative Literature
GÖTZ, D., Applied Linguistics
HERINGER, H.-J., German as a Foreign Language, German Philology
JACOB, J., Modern German
KAUFHOLD, M., Medieval History
KIESSLING, R., Bavarian and Swabian History
KOCKEL, V., Classical Archaeology
KRAUSS, H., Romance Literature
LAUSBERG, M., Classical Philology
LÖSER, F., German Language and Medieval History
MAYER, M., English Literature
MIDDEKE, M., English Literature
SCHEERER, T. M., Hispanic Studies
SCHRÖDER, K., Didactics of English
SCHWARZE, S., Romance Languages
TSCHOPP, S. S., History of European Culture
WEBER, G., Ancient History
WERNER, R., Applied Linguistics
WILLIAMS, W., German Language and Medieval Literature
WIRSCHING, A., Modern and Contemporary History
ZAPF, H., American Studies

Faculty of Law (Universitätsstr. 24, 86159 Augsburg; tel. (821) 598-4500; fax (821) 598-4503; e-mail dekan@jura.uni-augsburg.de; internet www.jura.uni-augsburg.de):

ALBERS, M., Civil Law
APPEL, I. (acting), Constitutional Law
BECKER, C., Civil Law, History of European Law
BEHR, V., Civil Law
BOTTKE, W., Penal Law
BUCHNER, H., Civil Law
GASSNER, U. M., Public Law
GSELL, B., Civil Law
JAKOB, W., Public Law
KORT, M., Civil Law
LEISTNER, M., Civil Law, Trade and Labour Law
MASING, J. (acting), Constitutional and Administrative Law
MÖLLERS, TH., Civil Law, Economic Law, European Law
NEUNER, J., Civil Law, Labour and Trade Law
ROSENAU, H., International Penal Law
ROTSCH, T., Penal Law
VEDDER, CH. (acting), Public Law

Faculty of Mathematics and Natural Sciences (Universitätsstr. 14, 86159 Augsburg; tel. (821) 5982250; fax (821) 5982300; e-mail dekan@mnf.uni-augsburg.de; internet www.uni-augsburg.de/einrichtungen/mnf):

BEHRINGER, K., Experimental Plasma Physics
BRÜTTING, W., Experimental Physics V
CLAESSEN, R., Experimental Physics II
COLONIUS, F., Applied Mathematics
DORFMEISTER, J, Analysis and Geometry
ECKERN, U. (acting), Theoretical Physics
ESCHENBURG, J., Differential Geometry
GIESL, P., Nonlinear Analysis
HAIDER, F., Experimental Physics
HÄNGGI, P., Theoretical Physics
HARTMANN, L., Chemistry, Physics and Material Sciences
HEINRICH, L., Applied Mathematics
HEINTZE, E., Pure Mathematics
HILSCHER, H., Didactics of Physics
HÖCK, K. H., Theoretical Physics II
HOPPE, R. H. W., Applied Mathematics
HORN, S., Experimental Physics
INGOLD, G.-L., Theoretical Physics
JUNGNICKEL, D., Applied Mathematics, Discrete Mathematics, Optimation, Operations Research
KAMPF, A., Theoretical Physics
KIELHÖFER, H.-J., Applied Analysis
KOPP, T., Physics
LOIDL, A., Experimental Physics
MANNHART, J., Experimental Physics
PUKELSHEIM, F., Applied Mathematics
RELLER, A., Solid State Chemistry
RITTER, J., Pure Mathematics
SCHERER, W., Chemistry, Physics and Material Sciences
SCHERTZ, R., Mathematics
SCHNEIDER, E., Didatics
SIEBERT, K. (acting), Applied Analytical Mathematics
STRITZKER, B., Experimental Physics
UNWIN, A., Computer-Oriented Statistics and Data Analysis
VOLLHARDT, D., Theoretical Physics
WIXFORTH, A., Experimental Physics
ZIEGLER, K., Theoretical Physics
ZIMMERMAN, R., Chemistry

Faculty of Philosophy and Social Sciences (Universitätsstr. 10, 86159 Augsburg; tel. (821) 5982605; fax (821) 5985504; e-mail dekan.phil1@phil.uni-augsburg.de; internet www.philso.uni-augsburg.de):

ALTENBERGER, H., Sports Education
ASBACH, O., Protestant Philosophy
ASCHENBRÜCKER, K., Didactics
BOEHLE, F., Sociology
BRUNOLD, A., Social Studies
EILDERS, C., Communications
GIEGLER, H., Sociology and Empirical Social Research
HERWARTZ-EMDEN, L., Pedagogics
HOYER, J., Music
KIRCHNER, C. (acting), Art Education
KRAEMER, R. D., Musical Training
LAMES, M., Movement and Training
LAEMMERMANN, G., Protestant Theology with Didactics of Religion
LAU, C., Sociology
MACHA, H., Pedagogics
MAINZER, K., Philosophy
MATTHES, E., Pedagogics
MÜHLEISEN, H.-O., Political Science
OBENDORFER, B., Protestant Theology
REINMANN, G., Media Education
SCHNEIDER, W., Sociology
SCHRÖER, C., Philosophie
SCHULTZE, R.-O., Political Science
STENGEL, M., Psychology
ULICH, D., Psychology
VON GEMÜNDEN, P., Protestant Theologie
WIATER, W., Pedagogics
WÜSTNER, K., Psychology

ATTACHED INSTITUTES

Institute of Business Administration: Dir Prof. Dr ADOLF G. COENENBERG (acting).

Institute of Economics: Dir Prof. Dr PETER WELZEL.

Institute for Social Economic Questions: Dir Prof. Dr HERBERT BUCHNER.

Institute of Statistics and Mathematical Theory of Economics: Dir Prof. Dr OTTO OPITZ.

Institute of Civil Law: Dir Prof. Dr TH. MÖLLERS.

Institute of Public Law: Dir Prof. Dr JOHANNES MUSING.

Institute of Penal Law: Dir Prof. Dr JOERG TENCKHOFF.

Institute of European Law: Dirs Prof. Dr VOLKER BEHR, Prof. Dr THOMAS M. J. MOELLERS.

Institute of Environmental Law: Dir Prof. Dr REINER SCHMIDT.

Institute of Informatics: Dir Prof. Dr WOLFGANG REIF.

Institute of Mathematics: Dir Prof. Dr JOACHIM LOHKAMP.

Institute of Physics: Dir Prof. Dr PETER HÄNGGI.

Institute of Philosophy: Dir Prof. Dr ARNO BARUZZI.

Institute of Spanish and Latin American Studies: Dirs Prof. Dr REINHOLD WERNER, Prof. Dr PETER WALDMANN, RENÉ STEINITZ.

Institute of Canadian Studies: Dir Prof. Dr RAINER-OLAF SCHULTZE.

Institute of European Cultural History: Dirs Prof. Dr JOHANNES BURKHARDT, Prof. Dr THEO STAMMEN, Prof. Dr TH. M. SCHEERER.

Institute of Interdisciplinary Informatics: Dir Prof. Dr KLAUS MAINZER.

Institute of Geography: Dir Prof. Dr FRANZ SCHAFFER.

Institute of Economic and Tax Law: Dirs Prof. Dr HERBERT BUCHNER, Prof. Dr WOLFGANG JAKOB.

Institute of Protestant Theology: Dir Prof. Dr GODWIN LÄMMERMAN.

Application Center for Materials and Environmental Research: Dir Prof. Dr WOLFGANG BIEGEL.

Environmental Science Center: Dir Dr JENS SOENTGEN.

IT Center: Dir Prof. Dr BERNHARD MÖLLER.

East Forum: Dir Prof. Dr WELLMANN.

OTTO-FRIEDRICH-UNIVERSITÄT BAMBERG

Kapuzinerstr. 16, 96045 Bamberg,
Telephone: (951) 863-0
Fax: (951) 863-1005
E-mail: post@uni-bamberg.de
Internet: www.uni-bamberg.de

Founded 1647
State control
Academic year: October to September (two semesters)

Rector: Prof. Dr Dr GODEHARD RUPPERT
Vice-Rectors: Prof. Dr RAINER DREWELLO, Prof. Dr REINHARD ZINTL
Chancellor: MARTINA PETERMANN
Librarian: Dr DIETER KARASEK

Number of teachers: 402
Number of students: 8,000

Publications: *Bamberger Universitätszeitung "uni.doc"* (7 a year), *Bamberger Geographische Schriften* (1–2 a year), *Bamberger Beiträge zur Englischen Sprachwissenschaft* (annually), *Gratia: Bamberger Schriften zur Renaissanceforschung* (2 a year), *Pressemitteilungen*, *Informationen* (irregular), *Personal- und Vorlesungsverzeichnis* (1 a term), *Bericht des Rektors*, *Forschungsforum* (annually), *Bamberger Editionen. Hg. v. H. Unger und H. Wentzlaff-Eggebert*, *uni.vers* (2 a year)

DEANS

Faculty of Catholic Theology: Prof. Dr HEINZ-GÜNTHER SCHÖTTLET
Faculty of Education, Philosophy and Psychology: Prof. Dr MAX PETER BAUMANN
Faculty of History and Geography: Prof. Dr INGOLF ERICSSON
Faculty of Information Systems and Applied Computer Science: Prof. Dr ELMAR J. SINZ
Faculty of Languages and Literature: Prof. Dr SEBASTIAN KEMPGEN
Faculty of Social and Economic Sciences: HEINZ-DIETER WENZEL
School of Social Work: Prof. Dr WILFRIED HOSEMANN

PROFESSORS

Faculty of Catholic Theology (An der Universität 2, 95045 Bamberg; tel. (951) 863-1701; fax (951) 863-1182; e-mail dekanat@ktheo.uni-bamberg.de; internet www.uni-bamberg.de/ktheo):

BIEBERSTEIN, K., Old Testament
BRUNS, P., Church History and Patrology
EID, V., Moral Theology
HEIMBACH-STEINS, M., Christian Social Theory
HERION, H., Religious Education
HIEROLD, A. E., Canon Law
KLAUSNITZER, W., Fundamental Theology and Theology of Ecumenical Movement
KRAUS, G., Dogmatics
SCHÖTTLER, H.-G., Pastoral Theology
WEHR, L., New Testament
WÜNSCHE, P., Liturgy

Faculty of History and Earth Sciences (Am Kranen 12, 96045 Bamberg; tel. (951) 863-2301; fax (951) 863-1193; e-mail dekanat@ggeo.uni-bamberg.de; internet www.uni-bamberg.de/ggeo/index.htm):

BRANDT, H., Ancient History
BRAUN, B., Geography I
BÜTTNER, F. O., Medieval Art History
DREWELLO, R., Monument Preservation and Restoration
ENZENSBERGER, H., History (Diplomatics and Palaeography)
ERICSSON, I., Medieval and Modern History, Archaeology
HABERLEIN, M., Modern History
HUBEL, A., Monument Preservation and Restoration
KERKHOFF-HADER, B., Local History and Folklore
KRINGS, W., Historical Geography
MATSCHE, F., Modern Art History
MÖCKL, K., Modern History
MÜLLER, J., Prehistory and Early History
PROTZNER, W., History Teaching
SCHELLMANN, G., Geography II
SCHULLER, M., Historical Architecture
TREUDE, E., Economic Geography

Faculty of Information Systems and Applied Computer Science:

FERSTL, O., Business Informatics
HEINRICH, A., Media Informatics
KRIEGER, U., Informatics
MENDLER, M., Foundation Economics
SCHLIEDER, C., Applied Informatics (Cultural, Historical and Geographical)
SCHMID, U., Applied Informatics (Cognitive Systems)
SINZ, E. J., Business Informatics
WIRTZ, G., Practical Informatics

Faculty of Languages and Literature (An der Universität 5, 96045 Bamberg; tel. (951) 863-2101; fax (951) 863-2102; e-mail dekanat@split.uni-bamberg.de; internet www.uni-bamberg.de/split):

BAIER, T., Classical Philology, Latin
BEISBART, O., German Language and Literary Instruction
BENNEWITZ, I., Medieval German Philology
BERGMANN, R., German Philology and Medieval Studies
BUS, H., American Studies
DE RENTIIS, D., Romance Philology
ECKER, H.-P., Diffusion Processes of Literature
FÖLLINGER, S., Classical Philology and Greek
FRAGNER, B., Iranian Studies
GIER, A., Romance Literature
GLÜCK, H., German Linguistics and German as a Foreign Language
GOCKEL, H., Modern German Literature
HAASE, M., Romance Philology
HOUSWITSCHKA, CH., English Literature
JAUSOHN, CH., British Culture
KEMPGEN, S., Slavic Linguistics
KORN, L., Islamic Art History and Archaeology
KREISER, K., Turkish Philology, History and Culture
MARX, F., Modern German Literature
MORALES SARAVIA, J., Romance Literature
RZEHAK, L., Iranian Studies
STÖBER, R., Communication Science
THEIS-BERGLMAIR, A.-M., Communication Science and Journalism
THIERGEN, P., Slavic Philology
ULRICH, M., Romance Linguistics
VIERECK, W., English Language and Medieval Studies
WIELANDT, R., Islamic Studies

Faculty of Pedagogy, Philosophy and Psychology (Markusplatz 3, 96045 Bamberg; tel. (951) 863-1801; fax (951) 863-1181; e-mail dekanat@ppp.uni-bamberg.de; internet www.uni-bamberg.de/ppp):

BAUMANN, M.-P., Folk Music
BEDFORD-STROHM, H., Protestant Theology
BERG, D., School Psychology
DÖRNER, D., Psychology
FAUST, G., Primary School Education
HÖRMANN, G., Pedagogics
HÖRMANN, S., Music Education
LACHMANN, R., Protestant Theology and Religious Instruction
LAUTENBACHER, S., Physiological Physiology
LAUX, L., Psychology IV
LIEBEL, H., Social Psychology
MÜHLFELD, C., Sociology of Social Work
RAEHLMANN, I., Labour Economics
RAHM, S., School Education
REINECKER, H., Clinical Psychology
REISCHMANN, J., Adult Education
ROSSBACK, H.-G., Family Education
SCHRÖER, CH., Philosophy I
SEUFERT, K.-K., Arts Education
SIMON-SHAEFER, R., Philosophy II
WEINERT, S., Psychology I
ZENCK, M., Historical Musicology

Faculty of Social and Economic Sciences (Feldkirchenstr. 21, 96052 Bamberg; tel. (951) 863-2501; fax (951) 863-1200; e-mail dekanat@sowi.uni-bamberg.de; internet www.uni-bamberg.de/sowi):

BECKER, W., Business Administration
BLOSSFELD, H.-P., Sociology
CREZELIUS, G., Tax Law
DAUSES, M. A., Public Law
DERLIEN, H.-U., Public Administration
DIRUF, G., Business Administration (Logistics)
ENGELHARD, J., European Management
GEHRING, T., International Policy
HECKMANN, F., Sociology
HEIDENREICH, M., Social Science (Europe)
HOFFMANN-LANGE, U., Political Science and Political Systems
KUPSCH, P., Business Administration (Auditing and Accounting)
MEINIG, W., Business Administration (Automobile Industry)
MEYER, U., Economics
MICKLITZ, H.-W., Private Law and Commercial Law
MÜNCH, R., Sociology II
OEHLER, A., Business Administration
PIEPER, R., Town and Social Planning
RATTINGER, H., Political Science II
SCHMID, M., Economics and International Economy
SCHULZE, G., Research Methods in Sociology
SCHWARZE, J., Social Policy
SEMBILL, D., Teaching of Economics
SIECKMANN, J.-R., Public Law
TRENK-HINTERBERGER, P., Labour and Social Law
VOGEL, F., Statistics
WENZEL, H.-D., Economics (Finance)
WIMMER, F., Business Administration (Marketing)
ZINTL, R., Political Science I
ZU KNYPHAUSEN-AUFSEß, D., Business Administration

School of Social Work (Kärntenstr. 7, 96052 Bamberg; tel. (951) 863-2001; fax (951) 863-1180; e-mail dekanat@sowes.uni-bamberg.de; internet www.uni-bamberg.de/sowes):

BIRK, U.-A., Law II
BOTT, W., Political Science
BROSCH, D., Law I
CYPRIAN, G., Sociology I
FREY, H.-P., Sociology II
FRÜCHTEL, F., Theory of Social Work
GROSER, M., Political Science
HAIDL, M., Education I
HOSEMANN, W., Social Work I
KLAPPROTT, J., Psychology I
MEHLICH, H., Informatics in Social Work
PLESSEN-RUDOLPH, H., Psychology I
PLOIL, E., Social Work II, Social Pedagogics
RIEMANN, G., Social Work III, Social Education
TRIPPMACHER, B., Pedagogics
WOLSTEIN, J., Social Medicine

UNIVERSITÄT BAYREUTH

95440 Bayreuth
Telephone: (921) 55-0
Fax: (921) 55-5290
E-mail: poststelle@uvw.uni-bayreuth.de
Internet: www.uni-bayreuth.de

Founded 1972
Academic year: October to September

President: Prof. Dr Dr h.c. HELMUT RUPPERT
Vice-Presidents: Prof. Dr GEORG KRAUSCH, Profin Dr WIEBKE PUTZ-OSTERLOH
Chancellor: Dr EKKEHARD BECK
Librarian: Dr KARL BABL

Number of teachers: 186
Number of students: 9,530

DEANS

Department of Applied Natural Sciences: Prof. Dr-Ing. ROLF STEINHILPER
Department of Biology, Chemistry and Geosciences: Prof. Dr ORTWIN MEYER
Department of Cultural Studies: Prof. Dr WOLFGANG SCHOBERTH
Department of Law and Economics: Prof. Dr Dr hc PETER OBERENDER
Department of Language and Literature: Prof. Dr DYMITR IBRISZIMOW
Department of Mathematics and Physics: Prof. LORENZ KRAMER

PROFESSORS

Department of Applied Natural Sciences (tel. (921) 55-7101; fax (921) 55-7106):

AKSEL, N., Applied Mechanics and Fluid Dynamics
ALTSTÄDT, V., Polymerics
BRÜGGEMANN, D., Technical Thermodynamics, Transport Processes
FISCHERAUER, G., Measurement Technology and Control Engineering
FREITAG, R., Bioprocess Technology
GLATZEL, U., Metallic Materials
JESS, A., Chemical Engineering
KRENKEL, W., Ceramic Materials
MOOS, R., Working Materials
RIEG, F., Engineering Design and CAD
STEINHILPER, R., Environmentally Compatible Production Technology
WILLERT-PORADA, M., Material Processing

Department of Biology, Chemistry and Geosciences (tel. (921) 55-2229; fax (921) 55-2351):

BACH, L., Urban and Regional Planning
BALLAUFF, M., Physical Chemistry I
BECK, E., Plant Physiology
BEIERKUHNLEIN, C., Biogeography
BITZER, K., Geology
BOGNER, F. X., Didactics of Biology
BREU, J., Inorganic Chemistry I
DETTNER, K., Animal Ecology II
DRAKE, H. L., Soil Microbiology
FOKEN, T., Micrometeorology
FRANK, H., Environmental Pollution
HAUHS, M., Ecological Modelling
HOFFMANN, K. H., Animal Ecology I
VON HOLST, D., Animal Physiology
HÜSER, K., Geomorphology
HUWE, B., Soil Science
KEMPE, R., Inorganic Chemistry II
KEPPLER, H., Experimental Geophysics
KOMOR, E., Plant Physiology
KRAUSCH, G., Physical Chemistry II
KRAUSS, G., Biochemistry
LEHNER, C., Genetics
LIEDE-SCHUMANN, S., Plant Systematics
LOHNERT, B., Geographical Development Research
MAIER, J., Economic Geography
MATZNER, E., Soil Sciences
MEYER, O., Microbiology
MONHEIM, R., Cultural Geography
MORYS, P., Inorganic Chemistry
MÜLLER, A., Macromolecular Chemistry II
MÜLLER-MAHN, D., Population and Social Geography
OBERMAIER, G., Didactics of Geography
PEIFFER, ST., Hydrology
PLATZ, G., Physical Chemistry I
POPP, H., Urban and Rural Geography
RAMBOLD, G., Plant Systematics
RÖSCH, P., Structure and Chemistry of Biopolymers
RUBIE, D., Structure and Dynamics of Earth Materials
SCHMID, F. X., Biochemistry
SCHMIDT, H.-W., Macromolecular Chemistry I
SCHOBERT, R., Organic Chemistry
SCHUMANN, W., Genetics
SEIFERT, F., Experimental Geosciences
SEIFERT, K., Organic Chemistry I/2
SENKER, J., Organic Chemistry I
SPRINZL, M., Biochemistry
STEUDLE, E., Plant Ecology
TENHUNEN, J., Plant Ecology
ULLMANN, M., Biocomputer Science
UNVERZAGT, C., Bio-organic Chemistry
WESTERMANN, B., Cell Biology
WRACKMEYER, B., Inorganic Chemistry II
ZECH, W., Soil Science and Soil Geography
ZÖLLER, L., Geomorphology

Department of Cultural Studies (tel. (921) 55-4101; fax (921) 55-844101):

BARGATZKY, T., Ethnology
BERNER, U., Religious Studies I
BETZWIESER, T., Musicology
BOCHINGER, CH., Religious Studies II
BORMANN, L., Evangelical Theory III
BOSBACH, F., History
BREHM, W., Sport Science and Physical Education
EBNER, R., Catholic Religious Teaching II
HAAG, L., School Education
HEGSELMANN, R., Philosophy I
HIERY, H., History
KLUTE, G., Ethnology (Africa)
KOCH, L., Education
KÜGLER, J., Catholic Theology I
LANGE, D., History (Africa)
LINDGREN, U., History of Science
NEUBERT, D., Developmental Sociology
PUTZ-OSTERLOH, W., Psychology
RITTER, W., Protestant Theology II
SCHEIT, H., Social Philosophy
SCHMIDT, W., Sports Medicine
SCHOBERTH, W., Evangelical Theology I
SCHORCH, G., Elementary School Education
SCHÜSSLER, R., Philosophy II
SPITTLER, G., Ethnology
UNGERER-RÖHRICH, U., Sports
WEISS, D., Bavarian Regional Geology
ZIESCHANG, K., Sport Science and Physical Education
ZINGERLE, A., Sociology
ZÖLLER, M., Sociology II

Department of Language and Literature (tel. (921) 55-3625; fax (921) 55-3641):

BEGEMANN, C., New German Literature
BENESCH, K., English Literature
BERGER, G., Romance Linguistics
DRESCHER, M., Roman and General Linguistics
HAUSENDORF, H., German Linguistics
IBISZIMOW, D., African Studies II
KHAMIS, S., Literatures in African Languages
KLOTZ, P., German Language and Literature
MIEHE, G., African Linguistics I
MÜLLER, J., Media Studies
MÜLLER-JACQUIER, B., Intercultural German Language and Literature
OSSWALD, R., Islamic Studies
OWENS, J., Arabic Studies
SCHMID, H.-J., English Linguistics
STEPPAT, M., English Literature
VILL, S., Theatre Studies
WOLF, G., Early German Philology

Department of Law and Economics (tel. (921) 55-2894; fax (921) 55-2985):

BERG, W., Public Law
BÖHLER, H., Economics III
BREHM, W., Civil Law
DANNECKER, G., Criminal Law
EMMERICH, V., Civil Law
EYMANN, T., Economics VIII
GÖRGENS, E., Economics II
GUNDEL, J., Public Law
HEERMANN, P., Civil Law
HERZ, B., Economics I
KAHL, W., Public Law
KLIPPEL, D., Civil Law, History of Law
KÜHLMANN, T., Economics IV
LEPSIUS, O., Public Law
LESCHKE, M., Economics V
LORITZ, K.-G., Civil Law II
MECKL, R., Economics IX
MICHALSKI, L., Civil Law
MÖSTL, M., Public Law and Constitutional History
NAGEL, E., Health Service Management and Health Sciences
OBERENDER, P., Economics IV
OHLY, A., Civil Law
REMER, A., Economics VI
SCHLÜCHTERMANN, J., Economics V
SCHMITZ, R., Criminal Law
SIGLOCH, J., Economics II
SPELLENBERG, U., Civil Law
ULRICH, V., Economics III
WORATSCHEK, H., Economics VIII

Department of Mathematics and Physics (tel. (921) 55-3196; fax (921) 55-2999):

BAPTIST, P., Mathematics and Didactics
BRAND, H., Theoretical Physics III
BRAUN, H., Experimental Physics V
BÜTTNER, H., Theoretical Physics I
CATANESE, F., Mathematics VIII
ESKA, G., Experimental Physics V
GRÜNE, L., Applied Mathematics
HENRICH, D., Applied Computer Science III
KERBER, A., Mathematics
KÖHLER, J., Experimental Physics IV
KÖHLER, W., Experimental Physics IV
KRAMER, L., Theoretical Physics II
KRÄMER, M., Mathematics
KÜPPERS, J., Experimental Physics III
LAUE, R., Computer Science
LEMPIO, F., Applied Mathematics
MERTENS, F.-G., Theoretical Physics I
MÜLLER, W., Mathematics
OTT, A., Experimental Physics I
PASCHER, H., Experimental Physics I
PESCH, H. J., Engineering Mathematics
PETERNELL, T., Mathematics
RAUBER, T., Applied Computer Science II
REHBERG, I., Experimental Physics V
REIN, G., Applied Mathematics
RIEDER, H., Applied Mathematics
ROESSLER, E., Experimental Physics II
SCHAMEL, H., Theoretical Physics
SCHITTKOWSKI, K., Computer Science
SCHWOERER, M., Experimental Physics II
SEILMEIER, A., Experimental Physics III
SIMADER, C. G., Mathematics
VAN SMAALEN, S., Crystallography
VON WAHL, W., Applied Mathematics
WESTFECHTEL, B., Applied Computer Science
ZIMMERMANN, W., Applied Computer Science

ATTACHED INSTITUTES

Forschungsinstitut für Musiktheater (FIMT) (Research Institute for Music Theatre): Dir (vacant).

Bayerisches Forschungsinstitut für Experimentelle Geochemie und Geophysik (Bayerisches Geoinstitut, IBGI) (Bavarian Research Institute for Experimental Geochemistry and Geophysics): Dir Prof. Dr D. RUBIE.

Institut für Materialforschung (Institute for Materials Research): Dir Prof. Dr G. ZIEGLER.

Bayreuther Institut für Makromolekülforschung (BIMF) (Bayreuth Institute for Macromolecular Research): Dir Prof. Dr H.-W. SCHMIDT.

Bayreuther Institut für Terrestrische Ökosystemforschung (BITÖK) (Bayreuth

Institute for Terrestrial Ecology Research): Dir Prof. Dr E. MATZNER.

Institut für Afrikastudien (IAS) (Institute for African Studies): Dir Prof. Dr H. POPP.

Afrikazentrum (IWALENA-Haus) (Africa Centre): Dir Dr T. WENDL.

Bayreuther Zentrum für Molekulare Biowissenschaften (BZMB) (Bayreuth Centre for Molecular Biosciences): Dir Prof. Dr O. MEYER.

Bayreuther Zentrum für Kolloide und Grenzflächen (BZKG) (Bayreuth Centre for Colloide and Border Areas): Dir Prof. Dr M. BALLAUFF.

Zentrum zur Förderung des Mathematisch- Naturwissenschaftlichen Unterrichts (Centre for Mathematical and Scientific Instruction): Dir Prof. Dr F. X. BOGNER.

Bayreuther Zentrum für Ökologie und Umweltforschung (Bayreuth Centre for Ecology and Environmental Research): Dir Prof. Dr E. MATZNER.

Bayreuther Institut für Europäisches Recht und Rechts Kultur, insbesondere Rechtsvergleichung und Wirtschaftsrecht (Bayreuth Institute for European Law and Legal Culture, Comparative Law and Economic Law): Dir Prof. Dr Dr h.c. mult. P. HÄBERLE.

FREIE UNIVERSITÄT BERLIN

Kaiserswerther Str. 16–18, 14195 Berlin (Dahlem)

Telephone: (30) 838-1
Fax: (30) 838-73217
E-mail: info@fu-berlin.de
Internet: www.fu-berlin.de

Founded 1948
Academic year: October to July

President (vacant)
Chancellor: PETER LANGE (acting)
Librarian: Dr ULRICH NAUMANN

Library: see Libraries and Archives
Number of teachers: 2,800
Number of students: 43,000

DIRECTORS OF DEPARTMENTS

Biology, Chemistry and Pharmacy: Prof. Dr HARTMUT H. HILGER
Economics and Business Administration: Prof. Dr MICHAEL KLEINALTENKAMP
Education and Psychology: Prof. Dr GERD R. HOFF
Geo-Sciences: Prof. Dr M. BÖSE
History and Culture: Prof. Dr MICHAEL BONGARDT
Humanities: Prof. Dr MARGOT. BÖSE
Law: Prof. Dr JOCHEM SCHMITT
Mathematics and Informatics: Prof. Dr J. SCHILLER
Medicine: Prof. Dr MARTIN PAUL
Philosophy and Humanities: Prof. Dr WIDU-WOLFGANG EHLERS
Physics: Prof. Dr NIKOLAUS SCHWENTNER
Political and Social Sciences: Prof. Dr UTE LUIG
Veterinary Medicine: Prof. Dr LEO BRUNNBERG

CENTRAL ATTACHED INSTITUTES

John F. Kennedy-Institut für Nordamerikastudien (J.F.K. Institute of North American Studies): Lanstr. 7, 14195 Berlin; tel. (30) 83852703; fax (30) 83852882; e-mail jfki@zedat.fu-berlin.de; internet web .fu-berlin.de/jfki; Chair. DETLEF BROSE.

Lateinamerika-Institut (Institute of Latin American Studies): Rüdesheimer Str. 54-56, 14197 Berlin; tel. (30) 83853073; fax (30) 83855464; e-mail ai@zedat.fu-berlin.de; internet web.fu-berlin.de/lai; Chair. Prof. Dr MARIANNE BRAIG.

Osteuropa-Institut (Institute of East European Studies): Garystr. 55, 14195 Berlin; tel. (30) 83853380; fax (30) 83853788; e-mail oei@zedat.fu-berlin.de; internet www.oei .fu-berlin.de; Chair. DETLEF BROSE.

HUMBOLDT-UNIVERSITÄT ZU BERLIN

Unter den Linden 6, 10099 Berlin

Telephone: (30) 2093-0
Fax: (30) 2093-2770
E-mail: hu-presse@uv.hu-berlin.de
Internet: www.hu-berlin.de

Founded 1810
State control
Academic year: October to September

President: Prof. Dr CHRISTOPH MARKSCHIES
Vice-Presidents: Prof. Dr SUSANNE BAER, Prof. Dr FRANK EVESLAGE, Prof. Dr HANS JÜRGEN PRÖMEL
Librarian: Dr M. BULATY

Library: see Libraries and Archives
Number of teachers: 2,633
Number of students: 39,000

Publications: *Humboldt-Spektrum* (4 a year), *Humboldt-Zeitung* (monthly during each semester)

DEANS

Faculty of Agriculture and Horticulture: Prof. Dr OTTO KAUFMANN
Faculty of Law: Prof. Dr INGOLF PERNICE
Faculty of Mathematics and Natural Sciences I: Prof. Dr MICHAEL LINSCHEID
Faculty of Mathematics and Natural Sciences II: Prof. Dr WOLFGANG COY
Faculty of Philosophy I: Prof. Dr MICHAEL BORGOLTE
Faculty of Philosophy II: Prof. Dr MICHAEL KÄMPER-VAN DEN BOOGAART
Faculty of Philosophy III: Prof. Dr THOMAS MACHO
Faculty of Philosophy IV: Prof. Dr ELK FRANKE
Faculty of Theology: Prof. Dr WILHELM GRÄB
School of Business and Economics: Prof. Dr OLIVER GÜNTHER
University Hospital 'Charité'–Faculty of Medicine: Prof. Dr MARTIN PAUL

UNIVERSITÄT DE KÜNSTE BERLIN (Berlin University of the Arts)

POB 120544, 10595 Berlin
premises at: Einsteinufer 43–53, 10587 Berlin

Telephone: (30) 3185-0
Fax: (30) 3185-2870
E-mail: presse@udk-berlin.de
Internet: www.udk-berlin.de

Founded 1975 by amalgamation of the Staatliche Hochschule für Bildende Künste (f. 1696) and the Staatliche Hochschule für Musik und Darstellende Kunst (f. 1869)

President: Prof. MARTIN RENNERT
Vice-Presidents: Prof. Dr PATRICK DINSLAGE, Prof. KIRSTEN LANGKILDE, Prof. CHRISTIANE MÖBUS, Prof. KARL-LUDWIG OTTO
Librarian: ANDREA ZEYNS

Library of 650,000 vols
Number of students: 4,300

Departments: fine arts; architecture; design; visual communication; publicity and communication; art education and art science; music; music education and science; performing arts and drama; educational and social sciences; aesthetic education; art and cultural sciences.

TECHNISCHE UNIVERSITÄT BERLIN

Str. des 17 Juni 135, 10623 Berlin

Telephone: (30) 314-0
Fax: (30) 314-23222
Internet: www.tu-berlin.de

The Bauakademie (Building Academy) of Berlin (f. 1799) and the Gewerbeakademie (f. 1821) were merged in 1879 as the Technische Hochschule Berlin, which was opened under its present name in 1946

President: Prof. Dr KURT KUTZLER
Vice-Pres.: Prof. Dr KLAUS PETERMANN, Prof. Dr JÖRG STEINBACH, ULRIKE STRATE
Chancellor: Dr ULRIKE GUTHEIL
Librarian: Dr WOLFGANG ZICK

Library: see Libraries and Archives
Number of professors: 500
Number of students: 31,700

Publications: *Mitteilungsblatt der TUB* (every 2 weeks), *TU intern* (9 a year), *TU International* (quarterly), *Universitätsführer* (every two years), *Vorlesungsverzeichnis* (2 a year)

DEANS

Architecture: Prof. Dr RUDOLF SCHÄFER
Economy and Management: Prof. Dr REINHARD BUSSE
Electrotechnology and Computing: Prof. Dr THOMAS SIKORA
Humanities: Prof. Dr ADRIAN VON BUTTLAR
Mathematics and Natural Sciences: Prof. Dr CHRISTIAN THOMSEN
Process Sciences and Engineering: Prof. Dr ULF STAHL
Transport and Machine Systems: Prof. Dr VOLKER SCHINDLER

UNIVERSITÄT BIELEFELD

Universitätsstr. 25, 33615 Bielefeld

Telephone: (521) 106-00
Fax: (521) 106-5844
E-mail: post@uni-bielefeld.de
Internet: www.uni-bielefeld.de

Founded 1969
State control
Academic year: April to March

Rector: Prof. Dr DIETER TIMMERMANN
Pro-Rector: Prof. Dr CHRISTOPH GUSY, Prof. Dr GERHARD SAGERER, Prof. Dr NORBERT SEEWALD, Prof. Dr ELKE WILD
Chancellor: HANS-JÜRGEN SIMM
Director of International Relations: Dr WERNER AUFDERLANDWEHR
Librarian: Dr NORBERT LOSSAU

Number of teachers: 758
Number of students: 17,521

Publications: *Forschungsbericht* (online), *Forschungsmagazin* (2 a year), *Pressedienst Forschung* (irregular), *Bielefelder Universitätszeitung* (4 a year), *Jahresbericht des Rektors und Statistisches Jahrbuch* (annually), *Bielefelder Universitätsgespräche* (irregular), *Personalverzeichnis/Lehrveranstaltungen* (2 a year)

DEANS

Faculty of Biology: Prof. Dr KARL-JOSEF DIETZ
Faculty of Chemistry: Prof. Dr GISELA LÜCK
Faculty of Economics: Prof. Dr ROLF KÖNIG
Faculty of Education: Prof. Dr KATHARINA GRÖNING-LIENKER
Faculty of Health Sciences: Prof. Dr KLAUS HURRELMANN
Faculty of History, Philosophy and Theology: Prof. Dr ANGSAR BECKERMANN
Faculty of Law: Prof. Dr DETLEF KLEINDIEK
Faculty of Linguistics and Literature: Prof. Dr LORE BENZ

Faculty of Mathematics: Prof. Dr WOLF-JÜRGEN BEYN
Faculty of Physics: Prof. Dr FRITHJOF KARSCH
Faculty of Psychology and Sport Science: Prof. Dr ULRICH SCHIEFELE
Faculty of Sociology: Prof. Dr LUTZ LEISERING
Faculty of Technology: Prof. Dr HELGE RITTER
Centre for Interdisciplinary Research: Prof. Dr IPKE WACHSMUTH

RUHR-UNIVERSITÄT BOCHUM

44801 Bochum, Postfach 102148
Located at: 44780 Bochum, Universitätsstr. 150
Telephone: (234) 32-201
Fax: (234) 32-14201
E-mail: B.Gremski@uv.ruhr-uni-bochum.de
Internet: www.ruhr-uni-bochum.de

Founded 1961
State control
Language of instruction: German
Academic year: April to March

Rector: Prof. Dr G. WAGNER
Pro-Rectors: Prof. Dr N. OTT, Prof. Dr E. W. WEILER, Prof. Dr J. WINTER
Chancellor: GERHARD MÖLLER
Librarian: Dr ERDMUTE LAPP

Number of teachers: 1,467
Number of students: 31,788

Publications: *RUBENS: Nachrichten, Berichte und Meinungen* (9 a year), *Rechenschaftsbericht des Rektorates* (annually), *RUBIN Wissenschaftsmagazin der Ruhr-Universität Bochum* (3 a year), *Universitätsreden* (irregular)

DEANS

Faculty of Biology: Prof. Dr STÜTZEL
Faculty of Catholic Theology: Prof. Dr GÖLLNER
Faculty of Chemistry: Prof. Dr HAVENITH-NEWEN
Faculty of Civil Engineering: Prof. Dr SCHERER
Faculty of East Asian Studies: Prof. Dr FINDEISEN
Faculty of Economics: Prof. Dr WERNERS
Faculty of Electrical Engineering: Prof. Dr BLINKMANN
Faculty of Geosciences: Prof. Dr ZEPP
Faculty of History: Prof. Dr BERGEMANN
Faculty of Law: Prof. Dr SEER
Faculty of Mathematics: Prof. Dr GERRITZEN
Faculty of Mechanical Engineering: Prof. Dr MESCHKE
Faculty of Medicine: Prof. Dr MUHR
Faculty of Philology: Prof. Dr LEBSANFT
Faculty of Philosophy, Pedagogy and Journalism: Prof. Dr W. JAESCHKE
Faculty of Physics and Astronomy: Prof. Dr MEYER
Faculty of Protestant Theology: Prof. Dr EBACH
Faculty of Psychology: Prof. Dr Dr SCHÖLMERICH
Faculty of Social Sciences: Prof. Dr VOSS
Faculty of Sport Science: Prof. Dr A. NEUMAIER

DIRECTORS OF CENTRAL ACADEMIC INSTITUTIONS

Centre of Further Education: Prof. Dr M. MUHLER
Institute for Social Movements: Prof. Dr K. TENFELDE
Institute for Neuro-Computing: Prof. Dr G. SCHÖNER
Institute for Development Research and Development Policy: Prof. Dr U. ANDERSEN
Institute for Energy and Natural Resources Law: Prof. Dr C. PIELOW
Institute for Industrial Science: Prof. Dr H. MINSSEN
Centre for Interdisciplinary Research in the Ruhr Area: Prof. Dr K. P. STROHMEIER
Institute for International Law of Peace and Human Rights: Prof. Dr J. WOLF
Institute for German Cultural Studies: Prof. Dr W. VOSS
Institute for Teacher Training: Prof. Dr R. FISCHER

PROFESSORS

Faculty of Biology (tel. (234) 322-4573; fax (234) 321-4237; internet www.biologie.ruhr-uni-bochum.de):

- BENNERT, W., Plant Taxonomy
- DENHARDT, G., General Zoology and Neurobiology
- DISTLER, C., General Zoology and Neurobiology
- FAISSNER, A., Cell Morphology and Molecular Neurobiology
- GERWERT, K., Biophysics
- HAEUPLER, H., Geobotany
- HAPPE, T., Plant Biochemistry, Photobiotechnology
- HATT, H., Cell Physiology
- HOFFMANN, K.-P., General Zoology and Neurobiology
- HOFMANN, E., Protein Crystallography, Biophysics
- JANCKE, D., Cognitive Neurobiology, general Zoology and Neurobiology
- KIRCHNER, W. H., Behavioural Biology and Teaching of Biology
- KÜCK, U., General and Molecular Botany
- LINK, G., Plant Cell Physiology and Molecular Biology, Plant Physiology
- LÜBBEN, M., Biophysics
- LÜBBERT, H., Animal Physiology
- NARBERHAUS, F., Biology of Micro-organisms
- NECKER, R., Animal Physiology
- NICKELSEN, J., Biology of Micro-organisms
- ÖTTMAYER, W., Plant Biochemistry
- PÖGGELER, S., General and Molecular Botany
- RAETHER, W., Special Zoology
- RÖGNER, M., Plant Biochemistry
- SCHAUB, G., Animal Taxonomy, Parasitology
- SCHLITTER, J., Biophysics
- SCHMIDT, M., General Zoology and Neurobiology
- SCHÜNEMANN, O., General and Molecular Botany
- SCHWENN, J.-D., Plant Biochemistry
- STÖRTKUHL, K., Cell Physiology, sensory Physiology
- STÜTZEL, T., Plant Taxonomy, Spermatophytes
- WAHLE, P., Developmental Neurobiology, General Zoology and Neurobiology
- WEILER, E., Plant Physiology
- WETZEL, C., Cell Physiology

Faculty of Catholic Theology (tel. (234) 32-22619; fax (234) 3214-410; e-mail kath-theol-fak@ruhr-uni-bochum.de):

- FREVEL, C., Old Testament Exegesis and Theology
- DAMBERG, W., Medieval and Modern Church History
- DSCHULNIGG, P., New Testament
- GEERLINGS, W., Church History, Patrology
- GÖLLNER, R., Practical Theology
- KNAPP, M., Fundamental Theology
- KNOCH, W., Dogmatics
- REINHARDT, H. J. F., Canon Law
- WIEMEYER, J., Christian Social Ethics
- ZELINKA, U., Moral Theology

Faculty of Chemistry (tel. (234) 32-24732; fax (234) 32-14108; e-mail chemie-dekanat@ruhr-uni-bochum.de; internet www.ruhr-uni-bochum.de/chemie):

- BENNECKE, G., Receptor Biochemistry
- DYKER, G., Organic Chemistry
- FEIGEL, M., Organic Chemistry
- FISCHER, R., Inorganic Chemistry
- GRÜNERT, W., Technical Chemistry
- HAVENITH-NEWEN, M., Physical Chemistry
- HERMANN, C., Physical Chemistry
- HEUMANN, R., Molecular Neurobiochemistry
- HOLLMANN, M., Receptor Biochemistry
- HOVEMANN, B., Molecular Cell Biochemistry
- VON KIEDROWSKI, G., Organic Chemistry
- MARX, D., Theoretical Chemistry
- MUHLER, M., Technical Chemistry
- MÜLLER, S., Organic Chemistry
- SANDER, W., Organic Chemistry
- SCHUHMANN, W., Analytical Chemistry
- SHELDRICK, W. S., Analytical Chemistry
- SOMMER, K., Didactics of Chemistry
- STAEMMLER, V., Theoretical Chemistry
- WEINGÄRTNER, H., Physical Chemistry
- WÖLL, C., Physical Chemistry

Faculty of Civil Engineering (tel. (234) 322-6124; fax (234) 3214-147; e-mail dekanat-bi@ruhr-uni-bochum.de; internet www.ruhr-uni-bochum.de/fbi):

- BREITENBÜCHER, R., Building Materials
- BRILON, W., Traffic Engineering
- BRUHNS, O. T., Mechanics
- HACKL, K., Mechanics
- HARTMANN, D., Applied Computer Science
- HÖFFER, R., Aerodynamics and Fluid Mechanics
- KINDMANN, R., Steel and Composite Constructions
- MESCHKE, G., Structural Mechanics
- ORTH, H., Environmental Engineering
- REESE, S., Computational Mechanics and Simulation
- SCHERER, M., Surveying and Geodesy
- SCHMID, G., Structural Mechanics and Computer Simulation
- SCHUMANN, A., Hydrology, Water Resources Management and Environmental Engineering
- STANGENBERG, F., Reinforced and Prestressed Concrete Structures
- STOLPE, H., Environmental Technology and Ecology
- TRIANTAFYLLIDIS, TH., Soil Mechanics
- WILLEMS, W., Structural Design and Building Physics

Faculty of East Asian Studies (tel. (234) 322-6189; e-mail anne.mueller@ruhr-uni-bochum.de; internet www.ruhr-uni-bochum.de/oaw):

- EGGERT, M., Korean Studies
- FINDEISEN, R., Chinese Language and Literature
- GU, X., East Asian Politics
- KLENNER, W., East Asian Economics
- MATHIAS, R., Japanese History
- RICKMEYER, J., Japanese Language and Literature
- ROETZ, H., Chinese History and Philosophy

Faculty of Economics (tel. (234) 32-22884; fax (234) 32-14140; e-mail wiwi-dekanat@ruhr-uni-bochum.de; internet www.wiwi.ruhr-uni-bochum.de):

- BAUER, T., Empirical Economics
- BENDER, D., International Economic Relations
- DIRRIGL, H., Controlling
- FOLKERS, C., Public Finance
- GABRIEL, R., Business Informatics
- HAMMANN, P., Management and Marketing
- HAUCUP, J., Economic Policy
- KARL, H., Economic Policy
- KÖSTERS, W., Monetary Economics
- LÖSCH, M., Statistics and Econometrics
- MAG, W., Theoretical Industrial Economics
- MANN, T., Law concerning the Economy
- NIENHAUS, V., Economic Policy
- PAUL, S., Banking and Finance
- PELLENS, B., International Accounting

SCHIMMELPFENNIG, J., Theoretical and Applied Microeconomics
SMOLNY, W., Applied Economics
STEVEN, M., Production and Operations
STREIM, H., Financial Accounting and Auditing
VOIGT, S., Economic Policy
WERNERS, B., Operations Research and Accounting

Faculty of Electrical Engineering and Information Sciences (tel. (234) 32-25666; fax (234) 3214-444; e-mail dekanat-ei@ruhr-uni-bochum.de; internet www.et.ruhr-uni-bochum.de):

AWAKOWICZ, P., General Electrical Engineering/Plasma Technology
BALZERT, H., Software Engineering
BRINKMANN, R. P., Theoretical Electrical Engineering/Plasma Technology
ERMERT, H., High-Frequency Engineering
FISCHER, H. D., Communications Engineering
GÖCKLER, H., Digital Signal Processing
HAUSNER, J., Integrated Systems
HOFMANN, M., Optoelectronic Devices and Materials
HUDDE, H., Sound and Vibration
KUNZE, U., Electronic Materials and Nanoelectronics
LANGMANN, U., Integrated Circuits
LUNZE, J., Automation
MARTIN, R., Information Technology and Communication Acoustics
MELBERT, J., Electronic Circuits and Measurement Techniques
OEHM, J., Circuit Design
PAAR, CH., Communication Security
SADIGHI, A.-R., Applied Data Security
SCHMILZ, G., Medical Engineering
SCHWENK, J., Network and Data Security
SOURKOUNIS, C., Power System Technology
STEIMEL, A., Power Engineering
TÜCHELMANN, Y., Integrated Information Systems

Faculty of Geosciences (tel. (234) 32-23505; fax (234) 3214-535; e-mail geodekanat@ruhr-uni-bochum.de; internet www.ruhr-uni-bochum.de/exogeol/geowiss.html):

ALBER, M., Engineering Geology
BUTZIN, B., Geography
CHAKRABORTY, S., Mineralogy and Petrology
FLEER, H., Climatology and Hydrogeology
FRIEDRICH, W., Geophysics
GIES, H., Mineralogy and Crystallography
HOHN, U., Economic and Social Geography
JÜRGENS, C., Geo-Remote Sensing
LÖTSCHER, L., Geography and Cultural Geography
MARESCH, W. V., Mineralogy
MÜLLER, J.-C., Cartography
MUTTERLOSE, J., Palaeontology and Geology
OTTO, K.-H., Didactics of Geography
RENNER, J., Seismology
SCHMITT, TH., Geography
STÖCKHERT, B., Geology
WOHNLICH, ST., Applied Geology
ZEPP, H., Physical Geography

Faculty of History (tel. (234) 32-22525; fax (234) 32-14240; e-mail dekan-gw@ruhr-uni-bochum.de; internet www.ruhr-uni-bochum.de/geschichtswissenschaft):

ADANIR, F., Southeast European History
BERGEMANN, J., Archaeology
BLEEK, W., Sociology, Political Science
BONWETSCH, B., East European History
BÜSING, H., Archaeology
EBEL-ZEPEZAUER, W., Pre- and Proto-History
EDER, W., Ancient History
ERBEN, D., History of Art
VON GRAEVE, V., Archaeology
GÜNTHER, L.-M., Ancient History
HÖLSCHER, L., Theory of History
HOPPE-SAILER, R., History of Art
MATHIAS, R., East Asian Studies
OBERWEIS, M., Auxiliary Sciences (Diplomacy, Palaeography, Numismatics)
SCHULTE, R., Modern and Contemporary History, Gender Studies
SÖNTGEN, B., History of Art
STEINHAUSER, M., History of Art
TENFELDE, K., Social History and Social Movement
WALA, M., History of North America
WALZ, R., Early Modern History
WEBER, W., Economic and Technical History
ZIEGLER, D., Economic and Business History

Faculty of Law (tel. (234) 32-26566; fax (234) 3214-530; e-mail Denise.Sablotny@jura.ruhr-uni-bochum.de; internet www.ruhr-uni-bochum.de/jura):

BERNSMANN, K., Criminal Law, Criminal Procedural Law
BORGES, G., Civil Law, Media Law and Law of Information Technology
BURGI, M., Public Law
FELTES, TH., Criminology
GREMER, W., Public Law, European Law
HÖRNLE, T., Criminal Law, Criminal Procedure Law
HUSTER, S., Public Law
KINDLER, P., Civil Law, Commercial Law, International Civil Law and Comparative Law
KRAMPE, CHR., Civil Law, Ancient Law and Roman Law
MUSCHELER, K., History of German Law, Civil Law, Church Law
POSCHER, R., Public Law, Sociology of Law
PUTTLER, A., Public Law
SCHILDT, B., History of Law, Civil Law
SCHREIBER, K., Procedural Law, Civil and Labour Law
SEER, R., Tax Law and Administrative Law
SIEKMANN, H., Public Law
WANK, R., Civil Law, Commercial and Labour Law
WINDEL, A., Procedural Law, Civil Law
WOLF, J., Public Law
WOLTERS, G., Criminal Law, Criminal Procedural Law

Faculty of Mathematics (tel. (234) 322-3476; fax (234) 3214-103; e-mail ffm@ruhr-uni-bochum.de; internet www.ruhr-uni-bochum.de/ffm):

ABRESCH, U., Mathematics
AVANZI, R., Mathematics
BARTENWERFER, W., Mathematics
BERTSCH, E., Computer Science
DEHLING, H., Mathematics
DETTE, H., Mathematics
DOBBERTIN, H., Mathematics, Cryptology
EICHELSBACHER, P., Mathematics
FLENNER, H., Mathematics
GERRITZEN, L., Mathematics
HEINZNER, P., Mathematics
HUCKLEBERRY, A. T., Mathematics
KIRSCH, W., Mathematical Physics
KNIEPER, G., Mathematics
KRIECHERBAUER, T., Mathematics
LAURES, G., Mathematics
MATTHIES, G., Mathematics
SIMON, H., Mathematics, Computer Science
STORCH, U., Mathematics
VERFÜRTH, R., Mathematics
WASSERMANN, G., Differential Topology

Faculty of Mechanical Engineering (tel. (234) 32-26191; fax (234) 32-14291; e-mail dekanmb@itm.ruhr-uni-bochum.de; internet www.ruhr-uni-bochum.de/maschinenbau):

ABRAMOVICI, M., Computer Science
EGGELER, G., Materials Science
MEIER, Production Systems
PAPENFUSS, H.-D., Applied Fluid Mechanics
POHL, M., Materials Testing
PREDKI, W., Mechanical Components – Industrial and Automotive Power Transmission
REINIG, G., Control Systems Engineering
ROGG, B., Fluid Mechanics
RÖHM, H.-J., Chemical and Environmental Engineering
SCHERER, V., Energy Plant Technology
SCHWEIGER, G., Applied Laser Technology and Measuring Systems
STOFF, H., Fluid Flow Machines
STÖVER, D. H. H., Materials Processing
STRATMANN, M., Materials Surfaces and Interfaces
SVEJDA, P., Thermodynamics of Mixtures
THEISEN, W., Materials Technology
WAGNER, G., Mechanical Components and Materials Handling
WAGNER, H.-J., Energy Systems and Energy Economics
WAGNER, W., Thermodynamics
WEIDNER, E., Process Engineering
WELP, E. G., Mechanical Components and Methodical Design

Faculty of Medicine (tel. (234) 32-24960; fax (234) 3214-190; e-mail medizin@rub.de; internet www.ruhr-uni-bochum.de/medizin):

ADAMIETZ, J. A., Radiology
ALTMEYER, P., Dermatology and Venereology
BRÜNING, TH., Industrial Medicine
BUFE, A., Paediatrics
BURCHERT, W., Radiology
DAZERT, S., Oto-Rhino-Laryngology
DERMIETZEL, R., Anatomy
VON DÜRING, M., Anatomy
ENGERT, J., Paediatric Surgery
EPPLEN, J., Genetics
ERDMANN, R., Biochemistry
EYSEL, U., Physiology
GATERMANN, S., Medical Microbiology
GOODY, R., Physiological Chemistry
GRONEMEYER, U., Ophthalmology
GUZMAN Y ROTAECHE, J., Pathology
HARDERS, A. G., Neurosurgery
HASENBRING, M., Medical Psychology
HERPERTZ, S., Psychosomatic Medicine and Psychotherapy
HEUSER, L., Radiology
HOHLBACH, G.-R., Surgery
HORSTKOTTE, D., Internal Medicine
INOUE, K., Anaesthesiology
JENSEN, A. W. O., Gynaecology and Obstetrics
KLEIN, H. H., Internal Medicine
KLEESIEK, K., Clinical Chemistry and Pathobiochemistry
KOESLING, D., Pharmacology and Toxicology
KÖRFER, R., Thoracic and Cardiovascular Surgery
KÖSTER, O., Radiology
KRÄMER, J., Orthopaedics
KRIEG, M., Clinical Chemistry
LACZKOVICS, A., Surgery, Thoracic and Cardiovascular Surgery
LAUBENTHAL, H., Anaesthesiology
LIERMANN, D., Radiology
MALIN, J.-P., Neurology
MANNHERZ, H. G., Anatomy and Cell Biology
MAYER, H., Paediatric Cardiology
MELLER, K., Experimental Cytology
MORGENROTH, K., Pathology
MÜGGE, A., Internal Medicine
MUHR, G., Surgery
MÜLLER, I., History of Medicine
MÜLLER, K.-M., Pathology
NICOLAS, V., Radiology
NOLDUS, J., Urologist

PESKAR, B., Clinical Experimental Medicine
PIENTKA, L., Geriatrics
POTT, L., Cellular Physiology
PRZUNTEK, H., Neurology
PUCHSTEIN, CH., Anaesthesiology
REUSCH, P., Pharmacology and Toxicology
RIEGER, CH., Paediatrics
RUMP, L. C., Nephrology
RUSCHE, H. H., General Medicine
SCHLEGEL, U., Neurology
SCHMIDT, W. E. W., Internal Medicine
SCHMIEGEL, W.-H., Internal Medicine
SCHULTZE-WERNINGHAUS, G., Internal Medicine
STEINAU, H.-U., Surgery
TRAMPISCH, H. J., Medical Informatics and Biomathematics
TRAPPE, H.-J., Internal Medicine
TSCHÖPE, D., Internal Medicine
ÜBERLA, K. T., Virology
UHE, W., Surgery
VIEBAHN, R., Surgery
WERNER, J., Biomedical Engineering
WILHELM, M., Hygiene
WOLFF, K.-D., Maxillofacial Surgery
ZENZ, M., Anaesthesiology

Faculty of Philology (tel. (234) 32-22623; fax (234) 32-14324; internet www.dekphil.ruhr-uni-bochum.de):

BASTERT, B., German Philology
BAUSCH, K.-R., Romance Philology
BEHRENS, R., Romance Philology
BEILENHOFF, W., Cinematography and Television Studies
BERNHARD, G., Romance Philology
BEYER, M., English Philology
BOETTCHER, W., Teaching of German Language and Literature
BOLLACHER, M., Modern German Literature
DEUBER-MANKOWSKI, A., Media Studies
EBEL, E., Scandinavian Studies
EFFE, B., Classical Philology
EIKELMANN, M., German Philology
ENDRESS, G., Arabic and Islamic Studies
FLUCK, H.-R., German Linguistics
FREITAG, K., American Studies
GLEI, R., Classical Philology/Latin
HASS, U., Theatre Studies
HEDIGER, V., Media Studies
HIMMELMANN, N., General Linguistics
HISS, G., Theatre Studies
HOUWEN, L., English Philology
KISS, T., General Linguistics
KLABUNDE, R., General Linguistics
KLODT, C., Classical Philology/Latin
KNAUTH, K. A., Romance Philology
KRENN, H., Romance Philology
LEBSANFT, F., Romance Philology
MENGE, H., German Linguistics
NIEDERHOFF, B., English
PITTNER, K., German Linguistics
PLUMPE, G., Modern German Literature
REICHMUTH, S., Islamic Studies
RUPP, G., Didactics of German Philology
SAPPOK, C., Slavonic Studies
SCHMID, U., Slavonic Studies
SCHMITZ-EMANS, M., General and Comparative Literature
SCHNEIDER, M., Modern German Literature
SCHÖNEFELD, D., English Philology
SIMONIS, L., General and Comparative Literature
SPANGENBERG, P., Media Sciences
STEINBRÜGGE, L., Romance Philology
THOMAS, B., Media Studies
TIETZ, M., Romance Philology
UHLENBRUCH, B., Russian and Soviet Culture
WARTH, E.-M., Cinematography and Television Studies
WEBER, I., English Philology
WEGERA, K.-P., History of German Language
WIEHL, P., Germanic Philology
ZELLE, C., Modern German Literature

Faculty of Philosophy, Education and Journalism (tel. (234) 32-22712; fax (234) 32-14505; e-mail Reinhild.Topp@ruhr-uni-bochum.de):

ADICK, C., Comparative Education
BELLENBERG, G., Educational Research Focus on Schools
DRIESCHNER, M., Natural Philosophy
HAARDT, A., Philosophy
HARNEY, K., Vocational Education and Lifelong Learning, Methods of Educational Research
HERZIG, B., Learning and Teaching Research
JAESCHKE, W., Classic German Philosophy
KEINER, E., History of Education
LESSING, H.-U., Philosophical Anthropology and Theory of the Humanities
MEYER-DRAWE, K., General Education
MOJSISCH, B., History of Philosophy
PARDEY, Logic and Philosophy of Language
PULTE, H., History and Philosophy of Science
ROSEMANN, B., Educational Psychology
SCHMIDT, K., Classic German Philosophy, Symbolic and Mathematical Logic
SCHOLTZ, G., History and Theory of the Humanities
SCHWEIDLER, Practical Philosophy
STEIGLEDER, K., Ethics in Medicine and Biosciences
WITTPOTH, J., Adult Education

Faculty of Physics and Astronomy (tel. (234) 322-3445; fax (234) 3214-447; e-mail dekanat@physik.ruhr-uni-bochum.de; internet physik.ruhr-uni-bochum.de):

CHINI, R., Astrophysics
CZARNETZKI, U., Experimental Physics
DETTMAR, R.-J., Astronomy
EFETOV, K., Theoretical Physics
FEUERBACHER, B., Experimental Physics
GERWERT, K., Biophysics
GOEKE, K., Theoretical Physics
GRAUER, R., Theoretical Physics
HERLACH, D., Experimental Physics
KEUDELL, A. VON, Experimental Physics
KOCH, H., Experimental Physics
KÖHLER, U., Experimental Physics
KÖNIG, J., Theoretical Physics
MALSBURG, C. VON DER, Neuroinformatics
MEYER, W., Experimental Physics
PELZL, J., Experimental Physics
POLYAKOV, U., Theoretical Physics
RITMAN, J., Experimental Physics
ROLFS, C., Experimental Physics
RUHL, H., Theoretical Physics
SCHLICKEISER, R., Theoretical Physics
SCHÖNER, G., Neuroinformatics
SOLTWISCH, H., Experimental Physics
WIECK, A., Experimental Physics
WINTER, J., Experimental Physics
WOLF, R., Experimental Physics
ZABEL, H., Experimental Physics

Faculty of Protestant Theology (tel. (234) 32-2250; fax (234) 3214-722; e-mail Ulrike.Burgner@ruhr-uni-bochum.de; internet www.ruhr-uni-bochum.de/ev-theol):

BEYER, F.-H., Practical Theology
EBACH, J., Old Testament
THOMAS, G., Systematic Theology
GELDBACH, E., Ecumenical and Denominational Studies
JÄHNICHEN, T., Christian Social Science
KARLE, J., Practical Theology
KRECH, V., Religious Science
STROHM, C., Church History (Reformation and Modern)
THIEL, W., Old Testament
WENGST, K., New Testament Exegesis and Theology
WICK, P., New Testament
WYRWA, D., Church History

Faculty of Psychology (tel. (234) 322-4606; fax (234) 3214-588; e-mail psy-dekanat@ruhr-uni-bochum.de; internet www.ruhr-uni-bochum.de/psy-dekanat):

BIERHOFF, H.-W., Social Psychology
BOCK, M., Psychology of Language and Communication
DAUM, I., Neuropsychology
GÜNTÜRKÜN, O., Biopsychology
GUSKI, R., Cognitive and Environmental Psychology
HASENBRING, M., Medical Psychology
REULECKE, W., Sport Psychology
ROSEMANN, B., Educational Psychology
SCHÖLMERICH, A., Development Psychology
SCHULTE, D., Clinical Psychology and Psychiatry
WOTTAWA, H., Methodology, Diagnostic and Evaluation
ZIMOLONG, B., Industrial and Organizational Psychology

Faculty of Social Sciences (tel. (234) 322-22967; fax (234) 3214-507; e-mail Christel.Maleszka@ruhr-uni-bochum.de; internet www.ruhr-uni-bochum.de/sowi):

ALTHAMMER, J., Social Politics
ANDERSEN, U., Political Science
BLEEK, W., Political Science
HEINZE, R. G., Sociology
LEHNER, F., Political Science
LENZ, I., Sociology
MINSSEN, H., Labour Organization
NOLTE, H., Social Psychology
OTT, N., Social Politics
PETZINA, D., Social and Economic History
PRIES, L., Participation and Organization
ROHWER, G., Methodology of Social Science and Social Statistics
SCHMIDT, G., Political Science
STROHMEIER, K. P., Sociology
TIEDE, M., Mathematical and Empirical Procedure in Social Sciences
VOSS, W., Mathematical and Empirical Procedure in Social Sciences
WIDMAIER, Political Science
WOLFF, J., Sociology of Developing Countries

Faculty of Sport Science (Gebäude UHW, Stiepelerstr. 129, 44801 Bochum; tel. (234) 322-7793; fax (234) 3214-246; e-mail Sportwiss-Dekanat@ruhr-uni-bochum.de; internet www.ruhr-uni-bochum.de/Spowiss):

BECKERS, E., Pedagogy of Sport
FERRANTI, A., Applied Training Science
HECK, H. J., Medicine in Sport
KELLMANN, M., Sports Psychology
KLEIN, M-L., Sociology of Sport, Sports Management
NEUMAIER, A., Theory of Movement, Biomechanics

Science of Music (tel. (234) 32-28394; internet www.ruhr-uni-bochum.de/muwi):

AHRENS, CHR., Music
LIEBSCHER, J., Music
WOITAS, M., Music

Centre for Further Education (Geb. LOTA, 44780 Bochum; tel. (234) 322-6466; fax (234) 321-4255; e-mail wbz@ruhr-uni-bochum.de; internet www.ruhr-uni-bochum.de/wbz; Dir: Prof. Dr M. MUHLER):

MUHLER, M.

Institute for Development Research and Development Policy (tel. (234) 322-2418; fax (234) 321-4294; e-mail ieeoffice@ruhr-uni-bochum.de; internet www.ruhr-uni-bochum.de/iee):

ANDERSEN, U., Society, Politics, Public Administration
BENDER, D., International Economic Relations
DÜRR, H., Social and Economic Geography
NIENHAUS, V., Economic Policy
VOSS, W., Statistics and Econometrics

WOLF, J., International Law
WOLFF, J. H., Society, Politics, Public Administration

Institute for Energy and Natural Resources Law (tel. (234) 322-7333; fax (234) 321-4292; e-mail TBE@ruhr-uni-bochum.de; internet www.ruhr-uni-bochum.de/ibe):

DRESEN, L., Seismology
HÜFFER, U., Civil Law, Commercial Law
IPSEN, K., Public Law
STEIN, D., Pipe Construction and Maintenance
TETTINGER, P. J., Public Law
UNGER, H., Nuclear and Modern Energy Systems
VON DANWITZ, T., Public Law, European Law

Institute for German Cultural Studies (tel. (234) 322-7863; fax (234) 321-4587; e-mail idf@ruhr-uni-bochum.de; internet www.ruhr-uni-bochum.de/deutschlandforschung):

ANDERSEN, U., Political Science
ANWEILER, D., Educational Research, Comparative Educational Research
BLEEK, W., Political Science
FAULENBACH, B., Modern History
KLUSSMANN, P. G., Modern German Literature
KROSS, E., Didactics of Geography
VOSS, W., Mathematical and Empirical Procedure in Social Sciences

Institute for Industrial Engineering (tel. (234) 322-7730; internet www.iaw.ruhr-uni-bochum.de/iaw):

MINNSSEN, H. (Dir)

Institute for Industrial Science (tel. (234) 322-3293; fax (234) 321-4118; internet www.iaw.ruhr-uni-bochum.de):

KAILER, N., Personnel and Qualifications
MINSSEN, H., Organization of Work
SCHNAUBER, H., Working Systems Design
STAUDT, E., Economics of Work

Institute for International Law of Peace and Armed Conflict (tel. (234) 322-7366; fax (234) 321-4208; internet www.ruhr-uni-bochum.de/ifhv):

WOLF, J., International Law

Institute for Neuro-Computing (tel. (234) 322-7965; fax (234) 321-4209; e-mail institut@neuroinformatik.ruhr-uni-bochum.de; internet www.neuroinformatik.ruhr-uni-bochum.de):

SCHÖNER, G., Theoretical Biology
VON DER MALSBURG, CH., Systems Biophysics

Institute for Social Movements (44789 Bochum, Clemensstr 17–19; tel. (234) 322-4687; fax (234) 321-4249; internet www.ruhr-uni-bochum.de/isb):

TENFELDE, K., Social History and Social Movements

Institute for Teacher Training (tel. (234) 321-1942; fax (234) 321-4647; e-mail zfl-kontakt@ruhr-uni-bochum.de; internet www.ruhr-uni-bochum.de/zfl):

BAUSCH, K-R., Romance Philology
BELLENBERG, G., Educational Science
KAMMERTÖNS, A., Didactics of Social Sciences
OTT, N., Social Politics
TIETZ, M., Romance Philology
WIECK, A., Experimental Physics

ATTACHED INSTITUTES

Berufsgenossenschaftliches Forschungsinstitut für Arbeitsmedizin (Research Institute for Occupational Medicine): Bürkle-de-la-Camp-Platz 1, 44789 Bochum; Dir Prof. Dr Dr H. BRÜNING.

Forschungsinstitut Arbeit, Bildung, Partizipation (Research Institute for Labour, Education and Participation): 45657 Recklinghausen, Münsterstr. 13–15; Dir Dr K. DÖRRE.

Institut für Angewandte Innovationsforschung (Institute for Applied Innovation Research): Buscheyplatz 13, 44801 Bochum; Chair. Prof. Dr B. KRIEGESMANN.

Institut für Diaspora- und Genozidforschung (Institute of Diaspora and Genocide Studies): Dir. Dr M. DABAG.

Institut für Gefährstoff-Forschung (Institute for Research into Dangerous Substances): Waldring 97, 44789 Bochum; e-mail igf@igf-bbg.de; Dir. Dr rer. nat. D. DAHMANN.

Institut für Umwelthygiene und Umweltmedizin des Hygiene-Instituts des Ruhrgebiets in Gelsenkirchen (Institute of Environmental Hygiene and Medicine): Rotthauserstr. 19, 45879 Gelsenkirchen; Dir Prof. Dr rer. nat. L. DUNEMANN.

Institut für Wohnungswesen, Immobilienwirtschaft, Stadt- und Regionalentwicklung GmbH (Institute of Housing, Real Estate, Urban and Regional Development Ltd): Springorumallee 20, 44795 Bochum; Dirs Prof. Dr V. EICHENER, Dipl. Volksw. M. SCHAUERTE.

KT-Institut für unterirdische Infrastruktur (KT-Institute for Underground Infrastructure): Exterbruch 1, 45886 Gelsenkirchen; Man. Dirs Dipl.-Ök. R. W. WANIEK, Dr-Ing. B. BOSSELER.

RHEINISCHE FRIEDRICH-WILHELMS-UNIVERSITÄT BONN

Regina-Pacis-Weg 3, 53113 Bonn
Telephone: (228) 73-0
Fax: (0228) 73-5579
E-mail: presse.info@uni-bonn.de
Internet: www.uni-bonn.de

Founded 1786, refounded 1818
State control
Academic year: October to September

Rector: Prof. Dr MATTHIAS WINIGER
Chancellor: Dr REINHARDT LUTZ
Librarian: Dr R. VOGT

Number of teachers: 530
Number of students: 31,000

Publications: *Bonner Akademische Reden*, *Politeia*, *Alma Mater*, *Academica Bonnensia*, *Bonner Universitäts-Nachrichten "Forsch"* (4 a year), *Studium Universale*, *Bonn University News International* (in English, annually)

DEANS

Faculty of Agriculture: Prof. Dr BERG
Faculty of Catholic Theology: Prof. Dr SCHÖLLGEN
Faculty of Evangelical Theology: Prof. Dr MEYER-BLANCK
Faculty of Law and Economics: Prof. Dr KRÄHEL
Faculty of Mathematics and Natural Sciences: Prof. Dr CREMERS
Faculty of Medicine: Prof. Dr Dr BIEBER
Faculty of Philosophy: Prof. Dr RUDINGER

PROFESSORS

Faculty of Agriculture (Meckenheimer Allee 174, 59115 Bonn; tel. (228) 722867; fax (228) 732140; e-mail landwirtschaftliche.fakultaet@uni-bonn.de; internet www.lwf.uni-bonn.de):

BERG, E., Agricultural Economics
DEHNE, H., Phytopathology
FÖRSTNER, W., Photogrammetry
GALENSA, R., Food Science and Food Chemistry
GOLDBACH, H., Plant Nutrition
HELFRICH, H.-P., Practical Mathematics
ILK, K. H., Satellite-assisted Physical Geodesy
KÖPKE, U., Ecological Agriculture
KÜHBAUCH, W., Plant Breeding
KUNZ, B., Food Technology and Food Biotechnology
KUTSCH, TH., Agricultural and Domestic Sociology
LÉON, J., Plant Production and Breeding
NOGA, G., Fruit and Vegetable Production
SCHELLANDER, K., Animal Breeding
SCHIEFER, G., Agricultural Economy
SCHNABL, H., Botany
STEHLE, P., Nutrition
WEIß, E., House and Town Planning
WITTMANN, D., Agricultural Zoology and Ecology

Faculty of Catholic Theology (Am Hof 1, 53113 Bonn; tel. (228) 73-7344; fax (228) 73-5985):

FABRY, H. J., Old Testament
FINDEIS, H.-J., New Testament
FÜRST, W., Pastoral Theology
GERHARDS, A., Liturgy
HOPPE, R., New Testament Science
HÖVER, G., Moral Theology
HOSSFELD, F.-L., Old Testament Science
LÜDECKE, N., Canon Law
MENKE, K.-H., Dogmatics, Theological Propaedeutics
MUSCHIOL, G., Church History
SCHÖLLGEN, G., Ancient Church History and Patrology
SCHULZ, M., Dogmatics
SONNEMANS, H., Fundamental Theology

Faculty of Evangelical Theology (Am Hof 1, 53113 Bonn; tel. (228) 73-7202):

BADER, G., Systematic Theology
HAUSCHILDT, E., Practical Theology
KINZIG, W., Church History
KREß, H., Systematic Theology, Social Ethics
MEYER-BLANCK, M., Theology Education
PANGRITZ, A., Systematic Theology
RÖHSER, G., New Testament
RÜTERSWÖRDEN, U., Old Testament
SCHMIDT-ROST, R., Practical Theology
STOCK, K., Systematic Theology
WOLTER, M., New Testament

Faculty of Law and Economics (Adenauerallee 24–42, 53113 Bonn; tel. (228) 73-9101; fax (228) 73-9100; e-mail dekanat@jura.uni-bonn.de; internet www.jura.uni-bonn.de):

BÖSE, D., Political Economy
BREITUNG, J., Economics
BREUER, R., Public Law
DI FABIO, U., Public Law
DOLZER, R., German and International Public Law
FLEISCHER, H., Civil Law
VON HAGEN, J., Economics
HERDEGEN, M., Public Law
HILLGRUBER, CHR., Public Law
KINDHÄUSER, U., Criminal Law
KNÜTEL, R., Roman and Civil Law
KÖNDGEN, J., Civil Law
KORTE, B., Operational Research
KRÄKEL, M., Business Administration
LÖWER, W., Public Law
MOLDOVANU, B., Economic Theory, Mathematical Theory of Economics
NEUMANN, M., Economic Policy
PAEFFGEN, H.-U., Criminal Law
PIETZCKER, J., Public Law
ROTH, W.-H., Civil Law, International Private Law, and Comparative Law
SANDMANN, K., Economic Policy
SCHILKEN, E., Civil Law
SCHMIDT-PREUß, M., Public Law
SCHWEIZER, U., Economic Policy
SHAKED, A., Economic Policy
THEISSEN, E., Business Administration
VERREL, T., Criminology

WAGNER, G., Civil Law
WALTERMANN, R., Civil Law
ZACZYK, R., Criminal Law, Philosophy of Law
ZIMMER, D., Commercial Law
ZIMMERMANN, K., Economic Policy

Faculty of Mathematics and Natural Sciences (Wegelerstr. 10, 53113 Bonn; tel. (228) 73-2233; fax (228) 73-3892; e-mail dekan@iam.uni-bonn.de; internet www.math-nat-fakultaet.uni-bonn.de):

ALBEVERIO, S., Mathematics
ALT, H. W., Mathematics
AUMANN, D., Chemistry
BALLMANN, W., Mathematics
BARGON, J., Physical Chemistry
BARTHLOTT, W., Botanics
BLECKMANN, H., Zoology
BRIESKORN, E., Mathematics
CREMERS, A. B., Informatics
DE BOER, K., Astronomy
DIETZ, K., Theoretical Physics
DIKAU, R., Geography
DÖTZ, K. H., Organic Chemistry
ECKMILLER, R., Informatics
EHLERS, E., Social and Economic Geography
FREHSE, J., Applied Mathematics
GLOMBITZA, K.-W., Pharmaceutical Biology
GRIEBEL, M., Scientific Computing
GROTZ, R., Geography
HAMENSTÄDT, U., Mathematics
HARDER, G., Mathematics
HERZOG, V., Cell Biology
HILDEBRANDT, S., Mathematics
HILGER, E., Experimental Physics
HUBER, M. G., Theoretical Atomic Physics
KARPINSKI, M., Informatics
KELLER, R., Zoology
KILIAN, K., Experimental Atomic Physics
KIRFEL, A., Mineralogy
KLEIN, F., Experimental Physics
KLEMPT, E., Experimental Physics
VON KOENIGSWALD, W., Palaeontology
LEISTNER, E., Pharmaceutical Biology
LIEB, I., Mathematics
MADER, W., Inorganic Chemistry
MAIER, K., Experimental Physics
MASCHUW, R., Atomic Physics
MEBOLD, U., Radio Astronomy
MENZ, G., Geography
MENZEL, D., Botany
MESCHEDE, D., Experimental Physics
MONIEN, H., Theoretical Physics
MÜLLER, W., Mathematics
NAHM, W., Mathematical Physics
NEUGEBAUER, H., Geophysics
NICKEL, P., Pharmaceutical Chemistry
NIECKE, E., Inorganic and Analytical Chemistry
NILLES, H. P., Theoretical Physics
PEYERIMHOFF, S., Theoretical Chemistry
RAITH, M., Geology and Petrology
SANDHAS, W., Theoretical Physics
SANDHOFF, K., Biochemistry
SAUER, K. P., Zoology and Ecological Studies
SCHOCH, B., Physics
SCHÖNHAGE, A., Informatics
SIMMER, C., Meteorology
SPETH, J., Theoretical Physics
STEFFENS, K. J., Pharmaceutical Technology
THEIN, J., Geology
TRÜPER, H. G., Microbiology
VÖGTLE, F., Chemistry
WANDELT, K., Physical Chemistry
WANDREY, CH., Biotechnology
WERMES, N., Experimental Physics
WILLECKE, K., Genetics
WINIGER, M., Geography

Faculty of Medicine (Sigmund-Freud-Str. 25, Haus 23, 53105 Bonn-Venusberg; tel. (228) 28-79201; fax (228) 28-79211; e-mail med-deha@ukb.uni-bonn.de; internet www.med.uni-bonn.de):

BAUR, M. P., Medical Statistics
BIDLINGMAIER, F., Clinical Biochemistry
BIEBER, TH., Dermatology and Venereology
BIERSACK, H.-J., Nuclear Medicine
ELGER, C. E., Epileptology
EXNER, M., Hygiene
FRANZ, TH., Anatomy
GÖTHERT, M., Pharmacology, Toxicology
GROTE, J., Physiology
HANFLAND, P., Experimental Haematology
HANSIS, M. L., Clinical Quality Management
HERBERHOLD, C., Oto-rhino-laryngology
HIRNER, A., Surgery
HOEFT, A., Anaesthesiology
JÄGER, A., Dentistry
KOECK, B., Dentistry
LENTZE, M. J., Paediatrics
LIEDTKE, R., Psychosomatic Medicine and Psychotherapy
LÜDERITZ, B., Internal Medicine, Cardiology
MADEA, B., Forensic Medicine
MAIER, W., Psychiatry
MÜLLER, ST., Urology
NOLDEN, R., Dentistry
PFEIFER, U., Pathology, Pathological Anatomy
PROPPING, P., Human Genetics
REICH, R., Oral and Maxillofacial Surgery
SAUERBRUCH, T., Internal Medicine
SCHAAL, K. P., Medical Microbiology
SCHILD, H. H., Radiology
SCHILLING, K., Anatomy
SCHMITT, O., Orthopaedics
SCHOTT, H., History of Medicine
SCHRAMM, J., Neurosurgery
SEITZ, H. M., Medical Parasitology
SPITZNAS, M., Ophthalmology
VETTER, H., Internal Medicine
WAHL, G., Oral Surgery
WIESTLER, O., Neuropathology

Faculty of Philosophy (Am Hof 1, 53113 Bonn; tel. (228) 73-7295; fax (228) 73-5986; internet www.philfak.uni-bonn.de):

BONNET, A.-M., History of Art
BREDENKAMP, J., Psychology
BRÜGGEN, E., Germanic Studies
COX, H. L., Folklore
DAHLMANN, D., East European History
DUMKE, D., Psychology
EHLERS, E., Social and Economic Geography
ESSER, J., English Philology
FEHN, K., Historical Geography
FISCHER, E., Musicology
FOHRMANN, J., Germanic Studies
GALSTERER, H., Ancient History
GROTZ, R., Geography
HESS, W., Communication and Phonetics
HILDEBRAND, K., Medieval and Modern History
HILGENHEGER, N., Education
HIRDT, W., Romance Philology
HOGREBE, W., Philosophy
HONNEFELDER, L., Philosophy
HÖNNIGHAUSEN, L., English Philology
KAISER, K., Political Science
KARSTEN, D., Political Science
KEIPERT, H., Slavonic Studies
KELZ, H., Phonetics
KLAUER, K. C., Psychology
KLEIN, TH., Germanic Studies
KLIMKEIT, H.-J., Comparative Religion
KOHRT, M., Germanic Studies
KÖLZER, T., Medieval and Modern History, Archival Science
KREINER, J., Japanology
KUBIN, W., Sinology
KUHN, A., History
KÜHNHARDT, L., Political Science
LADENTHIN, V., Education
LANGE, W. D., Romance Philology
LAUREYS, M., Philology
MECHLING, H., Sports
MIELSCH, H., Archaeology
NEUBAUER, W., Psychology
OEHLER, D., Comparative Science of Literature
PANTZER, P., Japanology
POHL, H., Constitutional History, Economics, Social History
POTTHOFF, W., Slavonic Studies
PREM, H. J., Ethnology
REICHL, K., English Philology
RÖßLER, U., Egyptology
ROSEN, K., Ancient History
SCHALLER, H.-J., Sports
SCHMITT, C., Roman Philology
SCHNEIDER, H., Germanic Studies
SCHOLZ, O. B., Psychology
SCHWARZ, H.-P., Political Science
SIMEK, R., Germanic Studies
STUHLMANN-LAEISZ, R., Logic and Foundations
WEEDE, E., Sociology
WILD, S., Semitic Philology
WINIGER, M., Geography
WOLF, H. J., Romance Philology
ZIMMER, ST., Linguistics
ZWIERLEIN, O., Classical Philology

ATTACHED INSTITUTES

Centre for Development Research: Dir Prof. Dr P. L. G. VLEK.

Centre for European Integration Research: Dir (vacant).

Franz Josef Dölger Institute: Dir Prof. Dr G. SCHÖLLGEN.

Institute for the Study of Labour: Dir Prof. Dr K. F. ZIMMERMANN.

Institute for Water Conservation Law and Waste Disposal Law: Dir Prof. Dr F. BREUER.

Max Planck Institute for Mathematics: Dir Prof. Dr D. ZAGIER.

Max Planck Institute for Radioastronomy: Dir Dr J. A. ZEUSUS.

Old Catholic Theology: Dir Prof. Dr G. EßER.

Research Institute for Discrete Mathematics: Dir Prof. Dr B. KORTE.

TECHNISCHE UNIVERSITÄT CAROLO WILHELMINA ZU BRAUNSCHWEIG

Pockelsstr. 14, 38106 Braunschweig
Telephone: (531) 391-0
Fax: (531) 391-4577
E-mail: president@tu-bs.de
Internet: www.tu-braunschweig.de

Founded 1745 as Collegium Carolinum; became Herzogliche Polytechnische Schule 1862 and Technische Hochschule 1877; present name 1968
State control
Academic year: October to September (two terms)

President: Prof. Dr-Ing. JÜRGEN HESSELBACH
Vice-Presidents: Prof. BERTHOLD BURKHARDT, Fr. Prof. BARBARA JÜRGENS, Prof. RAINER KOLSCH
Head of International Office: Dr ASTRID SEBASTIAN
Librarian: Prof. Dr rer. nat. habil. DIETMAR BRANDES

Library: see Libraries and Archives
Number of teachers: 230 full-time professors
Number of students: 13,366

Publications: *Mitteilungen der Carolo-Wilhelmina* (1 or 2 a year), *Personal- und Vorlesungsverzeichnis* (2 a year), *TU-aktuell* (6 a year), *Forschungsbericht* (every 5 years), *Veröffentlichung der Tech-*

nischen Universität Braunschweig (annually)

DEANS

Faculty of Architecture: Prof. Dr WERNER KAAG

Faculty of Biosciences and Psychology: Prof. Dr FRANK EGGERT

Faculty of Chemistry and Pharmacy: Prof. Dr KARL-HEINZ GERICKE

Faculty of Civil Engineering: Prof. Dr-Ing. DIETER DINKLER

Faculty of Economics and Social Sciences: Prof. Dr CHRISTIAN FLOTO

Faculty of Electronics and Information Technology: Prof. Dr-Ing. WOLFGANG KOWALSKY

Faculty of Humanities and Educational Sciences: Prof. Dr HERO JANßEN

Faculty of Mathematics and Computer Science: Prof. Dr LARS WOLF

Faculty of Mechanical Engineering: Prof. Dr-Ing. ROLF RADESPIEL

Faculty of Physics and Geosciences: Prof. Dr ANDREAS HANGLEITER

INTERNATIONAL UNIVERSITY BREMEN GMBH

Campus Ring 1, 28759 Bremen
Telephone: (421) 200-40
Fax: (421) 200-4113
E-mail: iub@iu-bremen.de
Internet: www.iu-bremen.de

Founded 1999
Private control
Language of instruction: English
Academic year: September to May

President: Prof. Dr JOACHIM TREUSCH
Director of Admissions: JON IKRAM
Director of Campus Activities and College Co-ordination: MARITA HARTNACK
Director of Corporate Communications and Media Relations: PETER WIEGAND
Director of Information Resources and Multimedia (IRC): HANS ROES
Director of Resource Development: ULF HANSEN
Director of Student Marketing: CHRISTINE SOUDERS
Vice-President, Science Park and Business Development: Dr ALEXANDER ZIEGLER-JOENS

DEANS

School of Engineering and Science: Prof. Dr BERNHARD KRAMER
School of Humanities and Social Sciences: Prof. Dr HENDRIK BIRUS
Jacobs Center for Lifelong Learning and Institutional Development: Prof. Dr URSULA STAUDINGER

UNIVERSITÄT BREMEN

Postfach 330440, 28334 Bremen
Located at: Bibliothekstr., 28359 Bremen
Telephone: (421) 218-1
Fax: (421) 218-4259
E-mail: presse@uni-bremen.de
Internet: www.uni-bremen.de

Founded 1971
State control
Academic year: October to September (two terms)

Rector: Prof. Dr WILFRIED MÜLLER
Chancellor: GERD-RÜDIGER KÜCK
Pro-Rectors: Prof. Dr ANGELIKA BUNSE-GERSTNER, Prof. Dr ILSE HELBRECHT
Librarian: ANNETTE RATH-BECKMANN

Number of teachers: 366
Number of students: 18,000

Publications: *Bremer Uni Schlüssel* (5 a year), *Impulse aus der Forschung* (2 a year), *Research Report* (every 2 years)

DEANS

Department of Biology and Chemistry: Prof. Dr G.-O. KIRST
Department of Cultural Sciences: Prof. Dr H. G. ARTUS
Department of Economics: Prof. Dr H.-D. HAASIS
Department of Geosciences: Prof. Dr H. VILLINGER
Department of Health and Human Studies: Prof. Dr A. KEIL
Department of Law: Prof. Dr L. BOELLINGER
Department of Literature and Language Studies: Prof. Dr. G. PASTERNACK
Department of Mathematics and Computer Science: Prof. Dr B. KRIEG-BRUECKNER
Department of Physics and Electrical Engineering: Prof. Dr JUERGEN GUTOWSKI
Department of Production Engineering, Economics for Engineering, and Commercial and Technical Science: Prof. Dr F.-J. HEEG
Department of Social and Educational Sciences: Prof. Dr A. KRETSCHMANN
Department of Social Sciences: Prof. Dr G. BAHRENBERG

PROFESSORS

Department 1 (Physics; Electrical Engineering)

Electrical Engineering:

ANHEIER, W., Microelectronics, Digital Systems
ARNDT, F., High Frequency Technology
BENECKE, W., Silicon-Micromechanics, Sensors and Actuators
BINDER, J., Micro- and Sensor-Systems, and Space Technology
GRÄSER, A., Automation Engineering
GRONWOLD, D., Electrical Technology
KAMMEYER, K.-D., Communications
LAUR, R., Electronics and Microelectronics
LOHMANN, B., Automatic Control
MARTE, G., Electronics
MEINERZHAGEN, B., Field Theory
MÜLLER, W., Analysis of the Engineering Professions
ORLIK, B., Electrical Drives and Power Electronics
RAUNER, F., Electrical Technology
SILBER, D. H., Power Electronics and Devices

Physics:

AUFSCHNAITER, S. VON, Teaching of Physics
AUGSTEIN, E., Meteorology and Physics of the Oceans
BLECK-NEUHAUS, J., Experimental and Environmental Physics
BOSECK, S., Experimental Physics
BURROWS, P., Environmental Physics
CZYCHOLL, G., Theoretical Physics
DIEHL, H., Biophysics
DREYBRODT, W., Experimental Physics, Molecular Spectroscopy
FALTA, J., Surface Science of Semiconductors
GUTOWSKI, J., Semiconductor Optics
HOMMEL, D., Epitaxy of Semiconductors
JÜPTNER, W., Laser Application
KÜNZI, K., Environmental Physics
LANGE, H., Sociology of Labour
NIEDDERER, H., Teaching of Physics
NOACK, C. C., Theoretical Physics
OLBERS, D., Theoretical Physics
PAWELZIK, K., Theoretical Biology
RICHTER, P., Theoretical Physics
ROETHER, W., Physical Oceanography in the Polar Regions
RYDER, P., Physics of Metals
SCHMITZ-FEUERHAKE, I., Experimental Physics
SCHWEDES, H., Teaching of Science
SCHWEGLER, H., Theoretical Physics, Theoretical Biophysics
STAUDE, W., Experimental Physics

Department 2 (Biology; Chemistry)

Biology:

ARNTZ, W., Ocean Ecology
BLOHM, D., Biotechology
ENTRICH, H., Theory and Practice of Education in the Natural Sciences
FAHLE, M., Neurobiology and Human Biology
FISCHER, H., Marine Microbiology
FLOHR, H., Biology
GRIMME, L. H., Biology, Biochemistry
HAGEN, W., Marine Zoology
HEYSER, W., Botany
HILDEBRANDT, A., Biology
KIRST, G.-O., Marine Botany
KOENIG, F., Botany
KREITER, A., Neurobiology
MOSSAKOWSKI, D., Evolutionary Biology
POERTNER, H.-O., Marine Biology
REINHOLD-HUREK, B., Microbiology
ROTH, G., Neurobiology
SAINT-PAUL, U., Marine Ecology
SCHLOOT, W., Genetics, Human Genetics
SMETACEK, V., Marine Biology
VALLBRACHT, A., Virology
WITTE, H., Zoology
WOLFF, M., Marine Ecology

Chemistry:

BALZER, W., Marine Chemistry
BEYERSMANN, D., Biochemistry
BREUNIG, H.-J., Inorganic Chemistry
GABEL, D., Organic Chemistry, Biochemistry
JAEGER, N., Physical Chemistry
JASTORFF, B., Organic Chemistry
JUST, E., Teaching of Chemistry
LEIBFRITZ, D., Organic Chemistry
MEWS, R., Inorganic Chemistry
MONTFORTS, F., Organic Chemistry
PLATH, P., Chemistry
RIEKENS, R., Teaching of Chemistry
RÖSCHENTHALER, G., Inorganic Chemistry
SCHREMS, O., Physical Chemistry
SCHROER, W., Physical Chemistry
SCHULZ-EKLOFF, G., Physical Chemistry
STOHRER, W.-D., Chemistry
THIEMANN, W., Physical Chemistry
WANCZEK, K., Inorganic Chemistry
WÖHRLE, D., Chemistry

Department 3 (Mathematics; Computer Science)

Computer Science:

BORMANN, U., Computer Networks
BRUNS, F.-W., Technology Design
FRIEDRICH, J., Computing and Society
GOGOLLA, M., Database Systems
HAEFNER, K., Education Technologies, Social Impacts and Transport Implications
HERZOG, O., Expert Systems and Foundations of Artificial Intelligence
KREOWSKI, H.-J., Theoretical Computer Science
KRIEG-BRÜCKNER, B., Programming Languages, Compilers and Software Engineering
KUBICEK, H., Information Management and Telecommunications
MAASS, S., Women's Studies and Technology
NAKE, F., Graphic Data Processing and Interactive Systems
PELESKA, J., Operating Systems, Distributed Systems
RÖDIGER, K.-H., Software Engineering and Ergonomics
SZCZERBICKA, H., Computer Architecture and Modelling

Mathematics:

ARNOLD, L., Random Dynamic Systems

BAENSCH, E., Numerical Methods for Partial Differential Equations
BECKER, G., Teacher Education
BOEHM, M., Modelling and Partial Differential Equations
BUNSE-GERSTNER, A., Numerical Linear Algebra
DENNEBERG, D., Non-additive Integration, Risk, Uncertainty and Insurance
DEUTSCH, M., Logic and Foundations of Mathematics
DOMBROWSKI, H.-D., Mathematical Foundations of Physics
FISCHER, H. W., Complex Analysis
GAMST, J., Algorithmic Algebra and Number Theory
HERRLICH, H., Topology, Category Theory
HINRICHSEN, D., Systems and Control Theory
HOFFMANN, R.-E., Topology, Categories and Lattices
HORNEFFER, K., Differential Geometry, Mathematical Foundations of Physics
HUPPERTZ, H., Teacher Education
KRAUSE, U., Positive Dynamic Systems
LINDENAU, V., Teacher Education
MAASS, P., Inverse Problems and Wavelets
MÜNZNER, H.-F., Differential Geometry, Dynamic Systems
OELJEKLAUS, E., Complex Algebraic Geometry
OSIUS, G., Statistics, Biometry
PEITGEN, H.-O., Complex Systems, Computer-aided Radiology
PORST, H.-E., Categorical Algebra
SCHÄFER, R., Numerical Hydrogeology
WISCHNEWSKY, M., Modelling, Neural Networks, Fuzzy Systems

Department 4 (Production Engineering; Economics for Engineering; Commercial and Technical Science):

BAUCKHAGE, K., Chemical and Process Engineering
BRINKSMEIER, E., Manufacturing Technology
GENTHNER, K., Technical Thermodynamics, Heat and Mass Transfer
GOCH, G., Metrology, Automation and Quality Science
GRATHWOHL, G., Ceramic Materials and Components
HARIG, H., Material Technology and Composites
HEEG, F.-J., Work Science
HENNEMANN, O. D., Bonding Technology and Polymers
HIRSCH, B. E., Production Resources, Logistics, Telematics
HOPPE, M., Vocational Teaching of Metal Engineering
KIENZLER, R., Applied Mechanics and Structural Mechanics
KUNZE, H.-D., Near Net Shape Production Technologies
MAYR, P., Material Science
MÜLLER, D. H., Engineering Design, CAE, CAD
RÄBIGER, N., Environmental Process Engineering
RATH, H. J., Technical Mechanics and Fluid Mechanics
SEPOLD, G., Laser and Plasma Technologies for Materials Processing
VISSER, A., Production Facilities
WITTKOWSKY, A., Design and Development of Technology

Department 5 (Geosciences):

BLEIL, U., Marine Geophysics
BROCKAMP, O., Mineralogy, Petrography, Clay Mineralogy
DEVEY, C., Petrology of the Ocean Crust
FISCHER, R. X., Crystallography
FÜTTERER, D., Geology
HENRICH, R., Sedimentology, Palaeo-oceanography
HERTERICH, K., Palaeo-oceanographic Modelling
JÖRGENSEN, B. B., Biogeochemistry
KUSS, H. J., Geology, Stratigraphy, Sedimentology
MILLER, H., Geophysics
OLESCH, M., Geology of the Polar Regions, Petrology
SCHULZ, H., Geochemistry, Hydrogeology
SPIESS, V., Marine Technology, Marine Environmental Geophysics
VILLINGER, H., Marine Technology, Geophysical Sensor Development
WEFER, G., Geology
WILLEMS, H., Historical Geology and Palaeontology

Department 6 (Law):

BÖLLINGER, L., Criminal Law
BRÜGGEMEIER, G., Civil and Economic Law
DÄUBLER, B., Labour, Commercial and Economic Law
DAMM, R., Civil Law, Economic Law
DERLEDER, P., Civil and Banking Law
DUBISCHAR, R., Civil Law
FEEST, J., Criminal Law and Criminology
FRANCKE, R., Legal Didactics
GESSNER, V., Comparative Law and Legal Sociology
HART, D., Economic Law
HINZ, M., Public Law and Political and Legal Sociology
HOFFMANN, R., Public Law, Labour Law and Political Science
JOERGES, C., Civil and Comparative Law
KNIEPER, R., Civil and Economic Law
LICHTENBERG, H., Labour and European Law
REICH, N., Civil and European Law
RINKEN, A., Public Law
RUEHE, U., Public Law
RUST, U., Gender Law
SCHEFOLD, D., Public Law
SCHMIDT, E., Civil Law and Procedure
SCHMINCK-GUSTAVUS, C., History of Law
SCHUMANN, K. F., Criminology
STUBY, G., Public Law and Political Science
THOSS, P., Criminal Law
WASHNER, R., Labour Law
WESSLAU, E., Criminal Law and Procedure
WINTER, G., Public and Environmental Law

Department 7 (Economics):

BAUER, E., Marketing of Research and Management
BIESECKER, A., Economic Theory
BRITSCH, K., Economic Statistics
DWORATSCHEK, S., Project Management
ECKSTEIN, W., Economics of Logistic Systems
ELSNER, W., Economic, Industrial and Regional Policy, Institutional Evolutionary Economics
FRANCKE, R., Economic Theory
GERSTENBERGER, H., Theory of State and Society
GRENZDÖRFFER, K., Economic Statistics, Labour Economics
HAASIS, H.-D., Production Management and Industrial Organization
HEIDE, H., Town and Country Planning
HICKEL, R., Public Finance
HUFFSCHMID, J., Political Economy, Economic Policy
KALMBACH, P., Economics
KOPFER, H., Economics of Logistics Systems
LEITHÄUSER, G., Economic Policy
LEMPER, A., Foreign Trade Theory and Politics
LIONVILLE, J., International Economics
MARX, F. J., Financial Accounting and Business Taxation
PODDIG, TH., Finance
SCHAEFER, H., Theory, Forecasting and Control
SCHMÄHL, W., Economics and Social Policy
SCHWIERING, D., Economics
SELL, A., International Economics
STEIGER, O., General Economic Theory and Monetary Economics
STUCHTEY, R. W., Economics of Marine Transport
VRING, TH. VON DER, Political Economy
WOHLMUTH, K., Comparative Economic Systems
ZACHCIAL, M., Transport Science and Transport Planning

Department 8 (Sociology; Geography; History; Politics)

Cultural History of Eastern Europe:

EICHWEDE, W., History and Politics of Socialist Countries
KRASNODEBSKY, Z., Polish Social and Cultural History
STÄDTKE, K., Cultural History of Eastern Europe

Geography:

BAHRENBERG, G., Social and Economic Geography
SCHRAMKE, W., Geography, Teaching of Geography
TAUBMANN, W., Cultural Geography
TIPPKÖTTER, R., Geography of Soils
VENZKE, J.-F., Physical Geography

History:

BARROW, L., Social and Political History of England
EICHWEDE, W., History and Politics of Socialist Countries
HACHTMANN, R., History of the 19th and 20th Centuries
HÄGERMANN, D., Medieval History
HAHN, M., History of Business, Political Theories
HOEDER, D., Social History of the USA
KLOFT, H., Ancient History
KOPITZSCH, F., History
KRAUSS, M., History of 19th- and 20th-century Social Economics
RECH, M., Prehistoric and Medieval History
SCHMIDT, J., Curricula in Economic and Social Studies
WAGNER, W., Politics, History of Political Education

Politics:

ALBERS, D., Labour Relations
EICHWEDE, W., History and Politics of Socialist Countries
KOOPMANN, K., Didactics of Social Science Education
LIEBERT, U., Comparative Politics, European Integration
LOTHAR, R., Politics, and Federal and Constitutional Law
PETERS, B., Political Theory and History of Ideas
SCHMIDT, M., Politics, Comparative Social Policies
WAGNER, W., Politics, History of Political Education
WIRTH, M., Parliamentary System of Federal Germany
ZOLL, R., History and Theory of Trade Unions
ZÜRN, M., Politics

Postgraduate Programme Development Policy with Focus on Non-Governmental Organizations:

FREYHOLD, M. VON, Development Policy and Sociology of Development

Sociology:

FREYHOLD, M. VON, Social Science
KRÄMER-BADONI, T., Town and Regional Planning
KRAUSE, D., Educational Planning
KRÜGER, M., Social Analysis

LAUTMANN, R., General Sociology and Sociology of Law
LUEDEMANN, CHR., Statistics and Empirical Research
PETER, L., Labour and Industrial Sociology
QUENSEL, S., Resocialization and Rehabilitation
REICHELT, H., Theory of Science and Society
SENGHAAS, D., Peace and Conflict Studies
WEYMANN, A., Social Theory, Educational Research

Department 9 (Cultural Sciences)

Art:

BUDDEMEIER, H., Communication, Mass Media
MÜLLER, M., Art History and Cultural Studies
PETERS, M., Art Education
SCHADE-THOLEN, S., Art History, Aesthetics

Cultural Science:

DRÖGE, F., Mass Communication Research
DUERR, H. P., Ethnology and Cultural History
NADIG, M., European Ethnology and Cultural Anthropology
RICHARD, J., Teaching of Drama
RICHTER, D., German Literature

Music:

BRECKOFF, W., Teaching of Music
KLEINEN, G., Teaching of Music, Musicology
RIEGER, E., Musicology

Philosophy:

MOHR, G., Practical Philosophy
SANDKÜHLER, H. J., Theoretical Philosophy
STÖCKLER, M., Philosophy of Natural Sciences

Religious Science:

KIPPENBERG, H.-G., Theory and History of Religions
LOTT, J., Religious Education
SCHULZ, H., Comparative Religion

Sport:

ARTUS, H. G., Teaching of Physical Education
BRAUN, H., History of Sport
FIKUS, M., Psychomotor Behaviour
SCHEELE, K., Sports Medicine

Department 10 (Literature and Language Studies)

Communication:

BACH, G., Teaching of English
BARROW, L., Social and Political History of England
BATEMANN, J. A., Applied Functional Linguistics, Natural Language Processing and Translation Science
DAHLE, W., German Language and Literature
EMMERICH, W., German Literature
FRANZBACH, M., Literature and Social History of Spain and Latin America
GALLAS, H., German Literature
JÄGER, H.-W., History of German Literature
KOCH, H. A., German and Comparative Literature
LIEBE-HARKORT, K., German as a Foreign Language
LIENERT, E., German Literature of the Middle Ages and the Early Modern Period
MENK, A.-K., Linguistics
PASTERNACK, G., Theory of Literature
PAUL, L., Applied Linguistics
SAUTERMEISTER, G., History of German Literature
STOLZ, TH., Linguistics
WAGNER, K.-H., Linguistics
WILDGEN, W., Linguistics
ZIMMERMANN, K., Spanish and Portuguese Linguistics

Department 11 (Health and Human Studies)

Psychology:

BAUMGÄRTL, F., Psychological Diagnosis
BERNDT, J., Physiology
GNIECH, G., Psychology
HEINZ, W.-R., Sociology and Social Psychology
HENNING, H.-J., Psychology
KIESELBACH, TH., Psychology
LEITHÄUSER, T., Development Psychology
PETERMANN, F., Clinical Psychology
REINKE, E., Clinical Psychology
STADLER, M., Psychology
VETTER, G., Theory of Learning
VOGT, R., Psychology
VOLMERG, B., Psychology

Public Health:

FRENTZEL-BEYME, R., Occupational and Environmental Epidemiology
GREISER, E., Occupational Health and Social Medicine
MÜLLER, R., Health Policy, Occupational Health and Social Medicine

Social Education:

AMENDT, G., Sub-Cultures
BAUER, R., Social Pedagogy
BLANDOW, J., Social Education
BROCKMANN, A.-D., Town and Regional Planning
HEINSON, G., Social Pedagogy
KEIL, A., General Education
LEIBFRIED, S., Social Planning
MERKEL, J., Pre-School Education

Teacher Training:

GOERRES, ST., Social Gerontology
HYAMS-PETER, H.-U., Social Education
KRÜGER-MÜLLER, H., Sociology
LITTEK, W., Education and Economics
MAANEN, H. VAN, Nursing Sciences
ORTMANN, H., Educational Sciences

Work Study:

MÜLLER, R., Health Policy, Occupational Health and Social Medicine
SENGHASS-KNOBLOCH, E., Humanization of Work
SPITZLEY, H., Technology and Society

Department 12 (Social and Educational Sciences)

Education Diploma:

DIETZE, L., Public Law
ROTH, L., Theory of Teaching
SCHÖNWÄLDER, H. G., Educational Planning and Economics
STRAKA, G., Extracurricular Education
ZIECHMANN, J., Psychology of Learning

Educational Science:

BECK, J., Educational Social Sciences
BOEHM, U., Structure and Development of Education
DRECHSEL, R., Education
DRECHSEL, W., Educational Social History
HUISKEN, F., Educational Political Economy
POLZIN, M., Aesthetic Education
PREUSS, O., Sociology of Education
UBBELOHDE, R., Educational Science
VINNAI, G., Analytical Social Psychology
VOIGT, B., Teacher Training

Further Education:

GERL, H., Adult Education
GÖRS, D., Distance Education
HOLZAPPFEL, G., Curricular Planning
KUHLENKAMP, D., Educational Planning
MADER, W., Adult Education
SCHLUTZ, E., Adult Education
WOLLENBERG, J., Adult Education in Political Science

Primary Education:

MILHOFFER, P., Sociology and Political Education
SCHMITT, R., Developmental Psychology
SPITTA, G., Beginning of German Language

Teaching the Handicapped:

DÖHNER, O., Medicine of Mental Illness
FEUSER, G., Education of Mentally Disturbed Children
HOMBURG, G., Educating People with Speech Defects
JANTZEN, W., History of Educating the Handicapped
KRETSCHMANN, R., Training of Educationally Handicapped
PIXA-KETTNER, U., Educating People with Speech Defects
REINCKE, W., Education for the Mentally Disturbed

Work Experience:

FISCHER, W. C., Consumer Economics
FRÖLEKE, H., Nutrition
HUISKEN, F., Educational Science
SCHRÖDER, A., Textile Technology

ATTACHED INSTITUTES

Academy for Labour and Politics: Dir Prof. Dr TH. LEITHÄUSER.

Alfred Wegener Institute for Polar and Marine Research: Dir Prof. Dr J. THIEDE.

ATB Institute for Applied Systems Technology Bremen GmbH: Dir Dr-Ing. U. KIRCHOFF.

Bremen Fibre Institute: Dir Prof. Dr-Ing. H. HARIG.

Bremen Institute for Applied Beam Technology: Dir Prof. Dr-Ing. G. SEPOLD.

Bremen Institute for Criminal Sciences: Dir Prof. Dr E. WESSLAU.

Bremen Institute for Drug Research: Prof. Dr ST. QUENSEL.

Bremen Institute for Prevention Research and Social Medicine: Dir Prof. Dr E. GREISER.

Bremen Institute of Industrial Technology and Applied Work Science at the University of Bremen: Dir Prof. Dr F.-J. HEEG.

Centre for Applied Information Technologies: Dir Prof. Dr M. B. WISCHNEWSKY.

Centre for Applied Space Technology and Microgravity: Dir Prof. Dr H. J. RATH.

Centre for Cognitive Sciences: Dir Prof. Dr G. ROTH.

Centre for Complex Systems and Visualization: Dir Prof. Dr H.-O. PEITGEN.

Centre for Continuing Education and Training: Dir Prof. Dr D. KUHLENKAMP.

Centre for European Law and Policy at the University of Bremen: Dirs Prof. Dr G. BRÜGGEMEIER, Prof. Dr M. ZUERN.

Centre for Human Genetics and Genetic Counselling: Dir Prof. Dr rer. nat. med. habil. W. SCHLOOT.

Centre for Medical Diagnostic Systems and Visualization: Dir Prof. Dr H.-O. PEITGEN.

Centre for Environmental Research and Technology: Dir Prof. Dr B. JASTORFF.

Centre for Networking and Distributed Data Processing: Dir Dr W.-D. SCHWILL.

Centre for the Philosophical Foundations of the Sciences: Dir Prof. Dr H. J. SANDKÜHLER.

Centre for Social Policy Research: Dir Prof. Dr R. MÜLLER.

Centre for Tropical Marine Ecology: Dir Prof. Dr G. HEMPEL.

Foundation Institute of Materials Science and Engineering: Dir. Prof. Dr-Ing. habil. P. MAYR.

Fraunhofer Institute for Applied Materials Research: Dir Prof. Dr-Ing. H.-D. KUNZE.

Computing Science Technology Centre: Dir Prof. Dr O. HERZOG.

German Press Research Institute: Dir Prof. Dr H.-W. JÄGER.

Institute for Honey Analysis: Dir Dr C. LÜLLMAN.

Institute for Municipal Energy Management and Policy at the University of Bremen: Dir Prof. Dr W. PFAFFENBERGER.

Institute for Science Transfer Through Further Education: Dir H.-J. ZAREMBA.

Institute for Shipping Economics and Logistics: Dir Prof. Dr W. ECKSTEIN.

Institute of Environmental Process Engineering: Dir Prof. Dr N. RÄBIGER.

Institute of Health Law and Law of Medicine: Dir Prof. Dr D. HART.

Institute of Technology and Education: Dir Prof. Dr F. RAUNER.

Max Planck Institute for Marine Microbiology: Dir Prof. Dr F. WIDDEL.

Research Centre for European Environmental Law: Dir Prof. Dr G. WINTER.

Research Centre for Work and Technology: Dirs Prof. Dr H. LANGE, Prof. Dr W. MÜLLER.

Research Institute for Independent Literature and Social Movements in Eastern Europe: Dir Prof. Dr W. EICHWEDE.

Research Institute for Labour and the Region: Dir Prof. Dr TH. KRÄMER-BADONI.

INTERNATIONAL UNIVERSITY IN GERMANY

Postfach 1550, 76605 Bruchsal
Telephone: (7251) 700110
Fax: (7251) 700150
E-mail: info@i-u.de
Internet: www.i-u.de

Founded 1998
Language of instruction: English
Academic year: September to July

President: Prof. Dr HEIDE ZIEGLER
Vice-President (vacant)
Number of teachers: 35
Number of students: 200

DEANS

School of Information Technology: Prof. Dr KEIICHI NAKATA
School of Business Administration: Prof. Dr FRANK MAIER

TECHNISCHE UNIVERSITÄT CHEMNITZ

09107 Chemnitz
Telephone: (371) 531-0
Fax: (371) 531-1684
E-mail: pressestelle@tu-chemnitz.de
Internet: www.tu-chemnitz.de

Founded 1836 as a royal trade school of Chemnitz; became Technische Universtät Chemnitz-Zwickau 1986; present name *c.* 1997
State control
Academic year: October to September

Rector: Prof. Dr KLAUS-JÜRGEN MATTHES
Vice-Rectors: Prof. Dr WOLFRAM DÖTZEL, Prof. Dr DIETER HAPPEL, Prof. Dr CORNELIA ZANGER
Chancellor: Dr EBERHARD ALLES
Librarian: ANGELA MALZ

Number of teachers: 158
Number of students: 1,032

Publication: *Spectrum* (4 a year)

DEANS

Faculty of Computer Science: Prof. Dr WOLFRAM HARDT
Faculty of Economics and Business Administration: Prof. Dr UWE GÖTZE
Faculty of Electrical Engineering and Information Technology: Prof. Dr THOMAS GEßNER
Faculty of Mathematics: Prof. Dr BERND HOFFMANN
Faculty of Engineering: Prof. Dr BERNHARD WIELAGE
Faculty of Natural Sciences: Prof. Dr KARL HEINZ HOFFMANN
School of Philosophy: Prof. Dr BERNHARD NAUCK

TECHNISCHE UNIVERSITÄT CLAUSTHAL

Adolph-Roemer-Str. 2A, 38678 Clausthal-Zellerfeld
Telephone: (5323) 720
Fax: 723500
E-mail: info@tu-clausthal.de
Internet: www.tu-clausthal.de

Founded 1775 as Bergakademie Clausthal; attained university status 1968
State control
Academic year: April to March

Rector: Prof. Dr-Ing. P. DIETZ
Chancellor: Dr Jur. PETER KICKARTZ
Vice-Chancellor: J. DRERUP
Librarian: Dr HELMUT CYNTHA

Number of teachers: 187, including 119 Ordinary Professors
Number of students: 2,900

Publications: *Lösestunde*, *Mitteilungsblatt*, *Vorlesungsverzeichnis* (annually)

DEANS

Faculty of Energy and Environment: Prof. Dr H. Y. SCHENK-MATHES
Faculty of Mathematics/Computing and Engineering: Prof. Dr N. MÜLLER
Faculty of Natural and Material Sciences: Prof. Dr W. SCHADE

HEADS OF DEPARTMENTS

Faculty of Energy and Environment

Economics
Prof. Dr M. ERLEI

Electrical Energy
Prof. Dr H.-P. BECK

Environmental Sciences
Prof. Dr O. CARLOWITZ

Fuel Technology
Prof. Dr R. WEBER

Geology and Palaeontology
Prof. Dr H.-J. GURSKY

Geophysics
Prof. Dr A. WELLER

Geotechnology
Prof. Dr W. BUSCH

Mineralogy
Prof. Dr K. MENGEL

Mining
Prof. Dr H. TUDESHKI

Mining and Energy Law
Prof. Dr G. KÜHNE

Oil and Gas Technology
Prof. Dr G. PUSCH

Preparation Technology
Prof. Dr K.-H. LUX

Faculty of Mathematics/Computing and Mechanical Engineering

Chemical Processes
Prof. Dr T. TUREK

Computing
Prof. Dr J. DIX

Electrical Processes
Prof. Dr M. VOSSIEK

Energy Conversion
Prof. Dr H. SCHWARZE

Machine Technology
Prof. Dr P. DIETZ

Mathematics
Prof. Dr L. ANGERMANN

Mechanical Engineering
Prof. Dr A. ESDERTS

Mechanical Processes
Prof. Dr A. WEBER

Process and Production Technology
Prof. Dr M. VOSSIEK

Technical Engineering
Prof. Dr G. BRENNER

Thermal Processes
Prof. Dr J. STRUBE

Welding Technology
Prof. Dr V. WESLING

Faculty of Natural and Material Sciences

Analytical Chemistry
Prof. Dr A. ADAM

Materials Technology
Prof. Dr L. WAGNER

Metallurgy
Prof. Dr K. H. SPITZER

Non-Metallic Materials
Prof. Dr A. WOLTER

Physical Chemistry
Prof. Dr D. JOHANNSMANN

Polymers and Synthetic Materials
Prof. Dr L. FROMANN

Organic Chemistry
Prof. Dr D. KAUFMANN

Physics
Prof. Dr D. KIP

Theoretical Physics
Prof. Dr P. BLÖCHL

BRANDENBURGISCHE TECHNISCHE UNIVERSITÄT COTTBUS

Postfach 101344, 03013 Cottbus
Premises at Konrad-Wachsmann-Allee 1, 03046 Cottbus
Telephone: (355) 69-0
Fax: (355) 69-2721
E-mail: intoff@tu-cottbus.de
Internet: www.tu-cottbus.de

Founded 1991
State control
Academic year: October to July

ChancellorDr WOLFGANG SCHRÖDER
PresidentProf. Dr rer. nat. habil. ERNST SIGMUND
Vice-President for Education and StudyPROF. DR-ING. BALLER
Vice-President for International RelationsProf. Dr-Ing. MICHAEL SCHMIDT
Vice-President for ResearchProf. Dr-Ing. GERHARD LAPPUS

Library of 400,000 vols, 2,000 periodicals, 80,000 technical standards
Number of teachers: 725
Number of students: 4,665

Publications: *Bodenschutz* (4 a year), *Bodenschutz und Rekultivierung* (10–12 a year), *Energie*, *Lehrstuhl Industriesoziologie* (2 a year)

DEANS

Faculty of Architecture and Civil Engineering: Prof. Dipl.-Ing. AXEL OESTREICH
Faculty of Environmental Sciences and Process Engineering: Prof. Dr BRIGITTE NIXDORF
Faculty of Mathematics, Physics and Information Sciences: Prof. Dr JÜRGEN REIF
Faculty of Mechanical Engineering, Electrical Engineering and Industrial Engineering: Prof. Dr ULRICH BERGER

TECHNISCHE UNIVERSITÄT DARMSTADT

Karolinenplatz 5, 64289 Darmstadt
Telephone: (6151) 1601
Fax: (6151) 165489
E-mail: praesident@pvw.tu-darmstadt.de
Internet: www.tu-darmstadt.de

Founded 1836 as Höhere Gewerbeschule, acquired university status in 1877
President: Prof. Dr-Ing. JOHANN-DIETRICH WÖRNER
Vice-Presidents: Prof. Dr REINER ANDERL, Prof. Dr JOHANNES BUCHMANN
Chancellor: Dr jur. HANNS SEIDLER
Number of professors: 295
Number of students: 16,000
Publication: *Thema Forschung* (2 a year)

DEANS

Architecture: Dipl.-Ing. JULIAN WÉKEL
Biology: Prof. Dr rer. nat. GERHARD THIEL
Chemistry: Prof. Dr MATTHIAS REHAHN
Computer Science: Prof. Dr ALEJANDRO BUCHMANN
Construction Engineering and Geodesy: Prof. Dr PETER CORNEL
Electrical Engineering and Information Technology: Prof. Dr PETER MEIßNER
History and Social Sciences: Prof. Dr HUBERT HEINELT
Human Sciences: Prof. Dr JOSEF WIEMEYER
Law and Economic Sciences: Prof. Dr AXEL WIRTH
Material Sciences and Geoscience: Prof. Dr HEINZ VON SEGGERN
Mathematics: Prof. Dr MATTHIAS HIEBER
Mechanical Engineering: Prof. Dr rer. nat. RALF LOTH
Mechanics: Prof. Dr-Ing. RICHARD MARKERT
Physics: Prof. Dr phil. nat. THEODOR TSCHUDI

PROFESSORS

ABELE, E., Mechanical Engineering
ABROMEIT, H., History and Social Sciences
ADAMY, J. H., Electrical Engineering and Information Technology
ALBE, K., Material Sciences and Geoscience
ALBER, H.-D., Mathematics
ALBER, G., Physics
ALBERT, B., Chemistry
ALEXA, M., Computing
ALFF, L., Material Sciences and Geoscience
ANDERL, R., Mechanical Engineering
ARICH-GERZ, B., History and Social Sciences
ARSLAN, U., Construction Engineering and Geodesy
BÄCHMANN, K., Chemistry
BALD, S., Construction Engineering and Geodesy
BALZER, G., Electrical Engineering and Information Technology
BARENS, I., Law and Economic Science
BAYREUTHER, F., Law and Economic Science
BECKER, M., Construction Engineering and Geodesy
BECKER, W., Mathematics
BERGER, C., Mechanical Engineering
BERGES, J., Physics
BERKING, H., History and Social Sciences
BETSCH, O., Law and Economic Science
BETTE, K. H., Human Sciences: Developmental Sciences, Psychology and Sport Science
BIBEL, W., Computing
BINDER, A., Electrical Engineering and Information Technology
BIRKHOFER, H., Mechanical Engineering
BIRKL, G., Physics
BÖHM, H. R., Construction Engineering and Geodesy
BOKOWSKI, J., Mathematics
BOLTZE, M., Construction Engineering and Geodesy
BORCHERDING, K., Human Sciences: Developmental Sciences, Psychology and Sport Science
BRAUN-MUNZINGER, P., Physics
BREUER, B. J., Mechanical Engineering
BRICKMANN, J., Chemistry
BRUDER, R., Mechanical Engineering
BRUDER, R., Mathematics
BUCHLER, J. W., Chemistry
BUCHMANN, A., Computing
BUCHMANN, J., Computing
BURMEISTER, P., Mathematics
BUSCH, M., Chemistry
BUSCHINGER, A., Biology
BUXMANN, P., Law and Economic Science
CASPARI, V., Law and Economic Science
CLAUS, P., Chemistry
CORNEL, P., Construction Engineering and Geodesy
CREUTZIG, J., Mathematics
DENCHER, N., Chemistry
DENINGER-POLZER, G., History and Social Sciences
DINSE, K. P., Chemistry
DIPPER, C., History and Social Sciences
DOMSCHKE, W., Law and Economic Science
DÖRSAM, E., Mechanical Engineering
DROSSEL, B., Physics
DÜR, M., Mathematics
ECKERT, C., Computing
ECKERT, J., Material Sciences and Geoscience
EGLOFF, G., History and Social Sciences
ELLERMEIER, W., Mathematics
ELSÄßER, W., Physics
ENCARNACAO, J., Computing
ENDERS, J., Physics
ENSINGER, W., Material Sciences and Geoscience
ENTORF, H., Law and Economic Science
EPPLE, B., Mechanical Engineering
EULER, P., Human Sciences: Developmental Sciences, Psychology and Sport Science
EVEKING, H., Electrical Engineering and Information Technology
EXNER, H. E., Material Sciences and Geoscience
FARWIG, R., Mathematics
FÄSSLER, T. F., Chemistry
FEILE, R., Physics
FERREIRO MÄHLMANN, R., Material Sciences and Geoscience
FESSNER, W.-D., Chemistry
FRIEDL, P., Chemistry
FRYDE-STROMER V. REICHENBACH, N., History and Social Sciences
FUEß, H., Material Sciences and Geoscience
FUJARA, F., Physics
FÜRNKRANZ, J., Computing
GALUSKE, R., Biology
GAMM, G., History and Social Sciences
GATERMANN, D., Architecture
GEHRING, P., History and Social Sciences
GERSHMAN, A., Electrical Engineering and Information Technology
GERSTENECKER, C., Construction Engineering and Geodesy
GIERSCH, C., Biology
GIVSAN, H., History and Social Sciences
GLESNER, M., Electrical Engineering and Information Technology
GÖPFERT, W., Construction Engineering and Geodesy
GÖRINGER, U., Biology
GÖTTSCHING, L., Mechanical Engineering
GRAUBNER, C.-A., Construction Engineering and Geodesy
GREWE, N., Physics
GRIEM, J., History and Social Sciences
GROCHE, P., Mechanical Engineering
GROSS, D., Mathematics
GROSSE-BRAUCKMANN, K., Mathematics
GRUBER, E., Chemistry
GRÜBL, P., Construction Engineering and Geodesy
GRUTTMANN, F., Construction Engineering and Geodesy
HAASE, W., Chemistry
HAGEDORN, P., Mathematics
HAHN, H., Material Sciences and Geoscience
HAMPE, M., Mechanical Engineering
HÄNSEL, F., Human Sciences: Developmental Sciences, Psychology and Sport Science
HANSELKA, H., Mechanical Engineering
HÄNSLER, E., Electrical Engineering and Information Technology
HARD, M., History and Social Sciences
HARTKOPF, T., Electrical Engineering and Information Technology
HARTMANN, M. L., History and Social Sciences
HARTMANN, H., Human Sciences: Developmental Sciences, Psychology and Sport Science
HARTMANN, E., Mathematics
HARTNAGEL, H. L., Electrical Engineering and Information Technology
HASSLER, U., Law and Economic Science
HAUSCHILD, M., Architecture
HEGGER, M., Architecture
HEIDER, J., Biology
HEIL, E., Mathematics
HEINELT, H., History and Social Sciences
HELM, C., Law and Economic Science
HERRMANN, C., Mathematics
HIEBER, M., Mathematics
HIMSTEDT, W., Biology
HINDERER, M., Material Sciences and Geoscience
HINRICHSEN, V., Electrical Engineering and Information Technology
HOFFMANN, H.-J., Computing
HOFFMANN, R., Computing
HOFFMANN, D. H. H., Physics
HOFMANN, K. H., Mathematics
HOFMANN, T., Computing
HOHENBERG, G., Mechanical Engineering
HOLSTEIN, T. W., Biology
HOPPE, A., Material Sciences and Geoscience
HUSS, S., Computing
HÜTT, M.-T., Biology
IHRINGER, T., Mathematics
ISERMANN, R., Electrical Engineering and Information Technology
JAEGERMANN, W., Material Sciences and Geoscience
JAGER, J., Construction Engineering and Geodesy
JAKOBY, R., Electrical Engineering and Information Technology
JANICH, N., History and Social Sciences
JANICKA, J., Mechanical Engineering
JANNIDIS, F., History and Social Sciences
JOSWIG, M., Mathematics
KAISER, W., Biology
KAISER, F., Physics
KALDENHOFF, R., Biology
KAMMERER, P., Computing
KANGASHARJU, J., Computing
KANKELEIT, E., Physics
KAST, W., Mechanical Engineering
KATZENBACH, R. H., Construction Engineering and Geodesy
KEIMEL, K., Mathematics
KEMPE, S., Material Sciences and Geoscience
KIEHL, M., Mathematics
KINDLER, J., Mathematics
KLEEBE, H.-J., Material Sciences and Geoscience
KLEIN, H.-F., Chemistry

KLEIN, A., Electrical Engineering and Information Technology
KLINGAUF, U., Mechanical Engineering
KNODT, M., History and Social Sciences
KOCH, A., Computing
KOHLENBACH, U., Mathematics
KOLMAR, H., Chemistry
KÖNIG, H. D., Electrical Engineering and Information Technology
KONIGORSKI, U., Electrical Engineering and Information Technology
KOOB, M., Architecture
KÖRDING, A., Physics
KOSTKA, A., Electrical Engineering and Information Technology
KRAIS, B., History and Social Sciences
KRAMER, L., Mathematics
KÜBLER, J., Physics
KÜHNE, T., Computing
KÜMMERER, B., Mathematics
LANDAU, K., Mechanical Engineering
LANG, J., Mathematics
LANGANKE, K., Physics
LANGE, J., Construction Engineering and Geodesy
LANGHEINRICH, W., Electrical Engineering and Information Technology
LANGNER, G., Biology
LAYER, PAUL G., Biology
LEHN, J., Mathematics
LEICHNER, R., Human Sciences: Developmental Sciences, Psychology and Sport Science
LICHTENTHALER, F., Chemistry
LIEBENWEIN, W., Architecture
LINKE, H.-J., Construction Engineering and Geodesy
LORCH, W., Architecture
LOTH, R., Mechanical Engineering
LÖW, M., History and Social Sciences
LUFT, G., Chemistry
LUSERKE, M., History and Social Sciences
LÜTTGE, U., Biology
MARKERT, R., Mathematics
MARLY, J., Law and Economic Science
MARTIN, A., Mathematics
MATHÉY, G. K., Architecture
MÄURER, H., Mathematics
MAY, H. D., Material Sciences and Geoscience
MAY, A., Mathematics
MEIßNER, P., Electrical Engineering and Information Technology
MEZINI, M., Computing
MOLEK, H., Material Sciences and Geoscience
MOTZKO, C., Construction Engineering and Geodesy
MÜHLHÄUSER, M. E., Computing
MÜLLER, W. F., Material Sciences and Geoscience
MÜLLER, R., Mathematics
MÜLLER-PLATHE, F., Chemistry
MULSER, P., Physics
MÜNK, H. D., Human Sciences: Developmental Sciences, Psychology and Sport Science
MUTSCHLER, P., Electrical Engineering and Information Technology
NEEB, K.-H., Mathematics
NESTLE, N., Physics
NEUHOLD, E., Computing
NEUNHOEFFER, H., Chemistry
NICKEL, E., Law and Economic Science
NOLTE, W., Mathematics
NORDMANN, A., History and Social Sciences
NORDMANN, R., Mechanical Engineering
OBERLACK, M., Mathematics
ORTNER, H., Material Sciences and Geoscience
ORTNER, E., Law and Economic Science
OSTERMANN, K., Computing
OSTROWSKI, M., Construction Engineering and Geodesy
OTTO, M., Mathematics
PAHL, G., Mechanical Engineering
PAULINYI, A., History and Social Sciences
PAUL-KOHLHOFF, A., Human Sciences: Developmental Sciences, Psychology and Sport Science
PAVLIDIS, D., Electrical Engineering and Information Technology
PETZINKA, K.-H., Architecture
PFEIFER, G., Architecture
PFEIFER, F., Biology
PFEIFFER, W., Electrical Engineering and Information Technology
PFLÜGER, M., Law and Economic Science
PFNÜR, A., Law and Economic Science
PFOHL, H.-C., Law and Economic Science
PINNAU, R., Mathematics
PLENIO, H. H., Chemistry
PONGRATZ, L., Human Sciences: Developmental Sciences, Psychology and Sport Science
PORTO, M., Physics
PUHANI, P., Law and Economic Science
QUICK, R., Law and Economic Science
RAUH, H., Material Sciences and Geoscience
REGGELIN, M., Chemistry
REHAHN, M., Chemistry
REIF, U., Mathematics
REISTER, D., Construction Engineering and Geodesy
RETZKO, H. G., Construction Engineering and Geodesy
RICHTER, A., Physics
RIEDEL, R., Material Sciences and Geoscience
RITTER, K., Mathematics
RÖDEL, J., Material Sciences and Geoscience
ROESNER, K., Mathematics
ROSE, H., Physics
ROTH, R., Physics
RÜPPEL, U., Construction Engineering and Geodesy
RÜRUP, H.-A., Law and Economic Science
RÜTZEL, J., Human Sciences: Developmental Sciences, Psychology and Sport Science
SASS, I., Material Sciences and Geoscience
SCHABEL, S., Mechanical Engineering
SCHÄFER, S. M., Construction Engineering and Geodesy
SCHÄFER, R., Chemistry
SCHÄFER, M., Mechanical Engineering
SCHAPPACHER, N., Mathematics
SCHEBEK, L., Construction Engineering and Geodesy
SCHEFFOLD, E., Mathematics
SCHEU, S., Biology
SCHIELE, B., Computing
SCHIFFER, H.-P., Mechanical Engineering
SCHLAAK, H., Electrical Engineering and Information Technology
SCHLEMMER, H., Construction Engineering and Geodesy
SCHMALZ-BRUNS, R., History and Social Sciences
SCHMID, V., Law and Economic Science
SCHMIDT, B., Chemistry
SCHMIDT, R., Human Sciences: Developmental Sciences, Psychology and Sport Science
SCHMIDT-CLAUSEN, H.-J., Electrical Engineering and Information Technology
SCHMIEDE, R., History and Social Sciences
SCHMITZ, B., Human Sciences: Developmental Sciences, Psychology and Sport Science
SCHNEIDER, J., Chemistry
SCHNEIDER, W. C., History and Social Sciences
SCHNEIDER, U. H., Law and Economic Science
SCHNELLENBACH-HELD, M., Construction Engineering and Geodesy
SCHOTT, D., History and Social Sciences
SCHUBERT, E., Construction Engineering and Geodesy
SCHULZ, H., Mechanical Engineering
SCHÜRMANN, H., Mechanical Engineering
SCHÜRR, A., Electrical Engineering and Information Technology
SCHUSTER, R., Chemistry
SCHÜTH, C., Material Sciences and Geoscience
SCHWABE-KRATOCHWIL, A., Biology
SCHWALKE, U., Electrical Engineering and Information Technology
SEELIG, W., Physics
SEILER, T. B., Human Sciences: Developmental Sciences, Psychology and Sport Science
SESINK, W., Human Sciences: Developmental Sciences, Psychology and Sport Science
SESSELMEIER, W., Law and Economic Science
SESSLER, G., Electrical Engineering and Information Technology
SIEKER, S., Law and Economic Science
SORGATZ, H., Human Sciences: Developmental Sciences, Psychology and Sport Science
SPECHT, G., Law and Economic Science
SPELLUCCI, P., Mathematics
STADTLER, H., Law and Economic Science
STAHL, M., History and Social Sciences
STEINMETZ, R., Electrical Engineering and Information Technology
STENZEL, J., Electrical Engineering and Information Technology
STEPHAN, P. C., Mechanical Engineering
STOFFEL, B., Mechanical Engineering
STREICHER, T., Mathematics
STÜHN, B., Physics
SURI, N., Computing
TEICH, E., History and Social Sciences
THIEL, G., Biology
TREBELS, W., Mathematics
TROPEA, C., Mechanical Engineering
TSAKMAKIS, C., Mathematics
TSCHUDI, T., Physics
ULLRICH-EBERIUS, C., Biology
URBAN, W., Construction Engineering and Geodesy
VIADA, E., Mathematics
VOGEL, H., Chemistry
VOGT, M., History and Social Sciences
VON NEUMANN-COSEL, P., Physics
VON SEGGERN, H., Material Sciences and Geoscience
VON STRYK, O., Computing
VORMWALD, M., Construction Engineering and Geodesy
VOß, H.-G., Human Sciences: Developmental Sciences, Psychology and Sport Science
WALDSCHMIDT, H., Computing
WALTER, H., Computing
WALTHER, C., Computing
WALTHER, T., Physics
WAMBACH, J., Physics
WEGMANN, H., Mathematics
WEIHE, K., Computing
WEILAND, T., Electrical Engineering and Information Technology
WEINBRUCH, S., Material Sciences and Geoscience
WEISCHEDE, D., Architecture
WEIßMANTEL, H., Electrical Engineering and Information Technology
WÉKÉL, J., Architecture
WERTHSCHÜTZKY, R., Electrical Engineering and Information Technology
WIEMEYER, J., Human Sciences: Developmental Sciences, Psychology and Sport Science
WILHELM, M., Mechanical Engineering
WILLE, R., Mathematics
WINNER, H., Mechanical Engineering
WIPF, H., Physics
WIRTH, A. E. H., Law and Economic Science
WOLF, K.-D., History and Social Sciences
WÖLFEL, H., Mechanical Engineering
WOLLENWEBER, E., Biology
WROBEL, B., Construction Engineering and Geodesy
WURL, H.-J., Law and Economic Science
ZANKE, U., Construction Engineering and Geodesy
ZILGES, A., Physics
ZOUBIR, A. M. D. E., Electrical Engineering and Information Technology

UNIVERSITÄT DORTMUND

44221 Dortmund
located at: Eichlinghofen, August-Schmidt-Str., 44227 Dortmund
Telephone: (231) 755-11
Fax: (231) 755-5145
Internet: www.uni-dortmund.de

Founded 1968
State control
Languages of instruction: German, English
Academic year: April to February

Rector: Prof. Dr EBERHARD BECKER
Vice-Rectors: Dr JOHANNES BOHLEN, Prof. Dr SEBASTIAN ENGELL, Prof. Dr UTA QUASTHOFF, Prof. Dr GÜNTHER RAGER
Chancellor: Dr ROLAND KISCHKEL
Librarian: MARLENE NAGELSMEIER-LINKE

Library of 1,920,000 vols
Number of students: 20,370

Publications: *Unizet* (10 a year), *Mundo* (2 a year)

DEANS

Faculty of Architecture and Civil Engineering: Prof. Dr UTA HASSLER
Department of Arts and Sports Studies: Prof. Dr MECHTHILD VON SCHOENEBECK
Department of Biochemical and Chemical Engineering: Prof. Dr PETER WALZEL
Department of Chemistry: Prof. Dr KLAUS JURKSCHAT
Department of Computer Science: Prof. Dr BERNHARD STEFFEN
Faculty of Cultural Studies: Prof. Dr GÜNTER NOLD
Faculty of Economics and Social Sciences: Prof. Dr WOLFGANG SCHÜNEMANN
Department of Education and Sociology: Prof. Dr PETER VOGEL
Faculty of Electrical Engineering and Information Technology: Prof. Dr RÜDIGER KAYS
Faculty of Human Sciences and Theology: Prof. Dr BERND GASCH
Department of Mathematics: Prof. Dr GERHARD ROSENBERGER
Faculty of Mechanical Engineering: Prof. Dr UWE CLAUSEN
Department of Physics: Prof. Dr METIN TOLAN
Faculty of Rehabilitation Sciences: Prof. Dr IRMGARD MERKT
Faculty of Spatial Planning: Prof. FRANZ-JOSEF BADE
Department of Statistics: Prof. Dr CLAUS WEIHS

PROFESSORS

Faculty of Architecture and Civil Engineering (tel. (231) 755-2074; fax (231) 755-5279; e-mail dekanat@busch.bauwesen.uni-dortmund.de; internet www.bauwesen.uni-dortmund.de):

BARTHOLD, F.-J., Numerical Methods and Information Processing
BLECKEN, U., Construction Management and Machines
BOFINGER, H., Design and Building Theory
HASSLER, U., Conservation and Building Research
HETTLER, A., Soil Mechanics and Foundation Engineering
MÄCKLER, C., Urban Design
MAURER, R., Concrete Engineering
MÜLLER, H., Environmental Architecture
NALBACH, G., Design, Spatial Design and the Fundamentals of Presentation
NEISECKE, J., Building Materials
NOEBEL, W., Design and Industrial Building
OBRECHT, H., Structural and Computational Mechanics
ÖTES, A., Structural Design
SCHIFFERS, K.-H., Organization of Building Planning and Site Management (OPS)
STANDKE, G. R., Design and Building Construction
UNGERMANN, D., Steel Construction

Department of Arts and Sports (tel. (231) 755-4153; fax (231) 755-4506; e-mail dek16ri@pop.uni-dortmund.de; internet www.uni-dortmund.de/FB16/index.html):

Institute of Art and Education:

BERTRAM-MÖBIUS, U.
BUSSE, K.-P.
VAN HAAREN, B.
WELZEL, B.

Institute of Geography and Education:

NUTZ, M.
SCHMIDT-KALLERT, E.

Institute of Music and Education:

ABEGG, W.
HOUBEN, E.
RÖTTER, G.
VON SCHOENEBECK, M.
STEGEMANN, M.

Institute of Sport and Education:

BRÄUTIGAM, M.
STARISCHKA, S.
THIELE, J.

Institute of Textile Design and Education/Comparative Textile Sciences:

MENTGES, G.

Department of Biochemical and Chemical Engineering (tel. (231) 755-2362; fax (231) 755-2361; e-mail dekanat@ct.uni-dortmund.de; internet www.chemietechnik.uni-dortmund.de):

AGAR, D., Technical Chemistry
BEHR, A., Technical Chemistry
ENGELL, S., Plant Control Technology
FAHLENKAMP, H., Environmental Technology
FRIEDRICH, C., Technical Microbiology
GÓRAK, A., Fluid Separation Processes
KÖSTER, U., Materials Science
SADOWSKI, G., Thermodynamics
SCHMID, A., Chemical Biotechnology
SCHMIDT-TRAUB, H., Plant Technology
STRAUß, K., Energy Processing and Fluid Mechanics
WALZEL, P., Mechanical Process Engineering
WEIß, E., Chemical Plant Technology
WICHMANN, R., Biological Engineering

Department of Chemistry (tel. (231) 755-3720; fax (231) 755-3771; e-mail dekan-chemie@chemie.uni-dortmund.de; internet www.chemie.uni-dortmund.de):

EILBRACHT, P., Organic Chemistry
GEIGER, A., Physical Chemistry
GRAF, D., Biology
HAAG, R., Organic Chemistry
JURKSCHAT, K., Inorganic Chemistry
KELLER, H.-L., Inorganic Chemistry
KRAUSE, N., Organic Chemistry
LIPPERT, B., Inorganic Chemistry
MELLE, I., Chemistry Teaching
MINKWITZ, R., Inorganic Chemistry
MITCHELL, T. N., Organic Chemistry
NIEMEYER, C. M., Biological and Chemical Microstructure Technology
REHAGE, H., Physical Chemistry
SANDMANN, A., Biology
SCHMUTZLER, R.-W., Physical Chemistry
VERBEEK, B., Biology
WALDMANN, H., Organic Chemistry
WINTER, R., Physical Chemistry

Department of Computer Science (tel. (231) 755-2121; fax (231) 755-2130; e-mail kossmann@dekanat.cs.uni-dortmund.de; internet www.informatik.uni-dortmund.de):

BISKUP, J., Information Systems
BUCHHOLZ, P., Modelling and Simulation
DITTRICH, G., Automata and Systems Theory
DOBERKAT, E.-E., Software Technology
KERN-ISBERNER, G., Information Engineering
KRUMM, H., Computer Networks and Distributed Systems
LINDEMANN, C., Computing Systems and Performance Analysis
MARWEDEL, P., Technical Computer Science, Embedded Systems
MORIK, K., Artificial Intelligence
MÜLLER, H., Computer Graphics
MÜTZEL, P., Algorithm Engineering
PADAWITZ, P., Compiler Construction
REUSCH, B., Automata and Sequential Logic Systems Theory
SCHWEFEL, H.-P., Systems Analysis
STEFFEN, B., Programming Systems
WEDDE, H., Operating Systems/Computer Architecture
WEGENER, I., Efficient Algorithms and Complexity Theory

Faculty of Cultural Studies (tel. (231) 755-2919; fax (231) 755-2894; e-mail zimmerma@mail.fb15.uni-dortmund.de; internet www.fb15.uni-dortmund.de):

Institute of English and American Studies:

BIMBERG, C.
GRÜNZWEIG, W.
KRAMER, J.
NOLD, G.
PETERS, H.

Institute of German Language and Literature:

BRÜNNER, G.
CONRADY, P.
DENNELER, I.
GERHARD, U.
HOFFMANN, L.
KÜHN, R.
LINK, J.
PARR, R.
QUASTHOFF, U.
RIEMENSCHNEIDER, H.
RISHOLM, E.
STORRER, A.

Institute of History:

HÖMIG, H.
SOLLBACH, G.
ZETTLER, A.

Institute of Journalism:

BOHRMANN, H.
BRANAHL, U.
EURICH, C.
HEINRICH, J.
KOPPER, G.
MACHILL, M.
PÄTZOLD, U.
PÖTTKER, H.
RAGER, G.

Faculty of Economics and Social Sciences (tel. (231) 755-3182; fax (231) 755-4375; e-mail elke.klika@wiso.uni-dortmund.de; internet www.wiso.uni-dortmund.de):

HIRSCH-KREINSEN, H., Technology and Society
HOLLÄNDER, H., Macroeconomic Theory
HOLZMÜLLER, H., Marketing
JEHLE, E., Operations Management and Logistics
KRAFT, K., Economics (Economic Policy)
LACKES, R., Business Information and Management Information Systems
LEININGER, W., Microeconomic Theory
LIENING, A., Teaching of Economics
NEUENDORFF, H., Sociology
RECHT, P., Operations Research and Economic Informatics
REICHMANN, T., Management Accounting
RICHTER, W., Public Economics
SCHÜNEMANN, W., Private Law
TEICHMANN, U., Money and Credit
WAHL, J., Investments and Finance
WELGE, M., Management
WEYER, J., Sociology

Department of Education and Sociology (tel. (231) 755-2194; fax (231) 755-5285; e-mail dekanat@fb12.uni-dortmund.de; internet www.fb12.uni-dortmund.de):

Institute of General and Vocational Education:

PÄTZOLD, G.
VOGEL, P.
WIGGER, L.

Institute of School Development Research:

BOS, W.
HOLTAPPELS, H.
SCHULZ-ZANDER, R.

Institute of Social and Elementary Education:

BIERFLEITER, C.
FRIED, L.
NOLDA, S.
UHLENDORFF, U.

Sociology:

BÜHRMANN, A. D.
GOLL, T.
HITZLER, R.
HORNBOSTEL, S.
KALBITZ, R.
NAEGELE, G.
REICHART, M.
REICHERT, M.
STALLBERG, E.

Institute of Teaching Science:

BEUTEL, S.-I.
KOCH-PRIEWE, B.
WIEDERHOLD, K.-A.
WILDT, J.

Faculty of Electrical Engineering and Information Technology (tel. (231) 755-2123; fax (231) 755-2051; e-mail info@dekanat.e-technik.uni-dortmund.de; internet www.e-technik.uni-dortmund.de):

FIEDLER, H., Integrated Systems
GÖTZE, J., Information Processing
HANDSCHIN, E., Electric Power Supply
KAYS, R., Communication Technology
KULIG, S., Electric Machines, Drive and Power Electronics
NEYER, A., Microstructure Technology
PEIER, D., High Voltage Engineering
SCHEHRER, R., Electronic Systems and Switching
SCHRÖDER, H., Circuits and Systems
SCHUMACHER, K., Microelectronics
SCHWIEGELSHOHN, U., Computer Engineering
VOGES, E., High Frequency Technology

Faculty of Human Sciences and Theology (tel. (231) 755-2886; fax (231) 755-5452; e-mail leschner@fb14.uni-dortmund.de; internet www.fb14.uni-dortmund.de):

Catholic Theology:

DORMEYER, D.
METTE, N.
MÖLLE, H.
RUSTER, T

Home Economics:

EISSING, G.

Organizational Psychology:

KASTNER, M.
KLEINBECK, U.

Philosophy:

FALKENBERG, B.
POST, W.
WINGERT, L.

Politics:

MEYER, T.

Protestant Theology:

BÜTTNER, G.
GREWEL, H.
MAURER, E.
MUNZEL, F.
POLA, T.
RIESNER, R.

Psychology:

GASCH, B.
KASTNER, M.
KLEINBECK, U.
LASOGGA, F.
METZ-GÖCKEL, H.
NEUMANN, R.
ROEDER, B.
ZIMMERMANN, P.

Department of Mathematics (tel. (231) 755-3051; fax (231) 755-3054; e-mail dekan@mathematik.uni-dortmund.de; internet www.mathematik.uni-dortmund.de):

ACHTZIGER, W., Applied Mathematics
BECKER, E., Algebra
BLUM, H., Applied Mathematics
HAZOD, W., Analysis and Stochastics
HENN, H.-W., Mathematics Teaching
KABALLO, W., Analysis
KOCH, H., Analysis
KREUZER, M., Algebra
KUZMIN, D., Applied Mathematics and Numerics
MENKE, K., Function Theory
MÖLLER, M., Approximation Theory
MÜLLER, G., Mathematics Teaching
ROSENBERGER, G., Algebra
SCHARLAU, R., Geometry and Algebra
SCHWACHTHÖFER, L., Differential Geometry
SELTER, C., Mathematics Teaching
SIBURG, F., Function Theory
SKUTELLA, M., Discrete Optimization
STEINMETZ, N., Function Theory
STÖCKLER, J., Approximation Theory
TUREK, S., Applied Mathematics and Numerics
VOIT, M., Analysis and Stochastics
ZAMFIRESCU, T., Geometry and Algebra

Faculty of Mechanical Engineering (tel. (231) 755-2723; fax (231) 755-2706; e-mail dekan@mb.uni-dortmund.de; internet www.mb.uni-dortmund.de):

CROSTACK, H.-A., Quality Control
CLAUSEN, U., Transport Systems and Logistics
DEUSE, J., Work and Production Systems
HOMPEL TEN, M., Transportation and Storage
JANSEN, R., Logistics
KAUDER, K., Fluid Energy Machines
KLEINER, M., Forming Technology and Lightweight Construction
KREIS, W., Machine Elements, Design and Handling Techniques
KUHN, A., Plant Organization
KÜNNE, B., Machine Elements
OTT, B., Technical Didactics
SVENDSEN, B., Mechanics
THERMANN, K., Machine Dynamics
TILLMANN, W., Materials Technology
UHLE, M., Measurement Technology
WEINERT, K., Machining Technology

Department of Physics (tel. (231) 755-3503; fax (231) 755-5027; e-mail dekanat@physik.uni-dortmund.de; internet www.physik.uni-dortmund.de):

BAACKE, J., Theoretical Physics
BAYER, M., Experimental Physics
BÖHMER, R., Experimental Physics
GERLACH, B., Theoretical Physics
GÖßLING, C., Experimental Physics
KEITER, H., Theoretical Physics
NIEMAX, K., Plasma and Laser Spectrochemistry
PASCHOS, E., Theoretical Physics
PFLUG, A., Physics Teaching
REYA, E., Theoretical Physics
RHODE, W., Experimental Physics
SPAAN, B., Experimental Physics
SUTER, D., Experimental Physics
TOLAN, M., Experimental Physics
WEBER, W., Theoretical Physics
WEISS, T., Acceleration Physics
WESTPHAL, C., Experimental Physics
WILLE, K., Accelerator Physics
WOGGON, U., Experimental Teaching

Faculty of Rehabilitation Sciences (tel. (231) 755-4541; fax (231) 755-4503; e-mail dekanat@nvl1.fb13.uni-dortmund.de; internet www.uni-dortmund.de/FB13/index.html):

Adapted Physical Activity and Movement Therapy:

HÖLTER, G.

Art Education and Art Therapy:

JÁDI, F.

Education for Individuals with Mental Disabilities:

DÖNHOFF, K.
HAVEMAN, M.
MEYER, H.

Gender Research in Special Needs Education:

SCHILDMANN, U.

Music Education and Music Therapy:

MERKT, I.

Rehabilitation for Individuals with Blindness and Visual Impairments:

CSOCSÁN, E.
WALTHES, R.

Rehabilitation for Individuals with Communication Disorders:

DUPUIS, G.
KATZ-BERNSTEIN, N.

Rehabilitation and Education for Individuals with Disabilities:

DEDERICH, M.

Rehabilitation for Individuals with Emotional and Behavioural Disorders:

PETERMANN, U.

Rehabilitation for Individuals with Learning Difficulties:

SCHMETZ, D.
WEMBER, F.

Rehabilitation for Individuals with Physical Disabilities:

LEYENDECKER, C.

Rehabilitation Psychology:

FRANKE, A.
FRÖSTER, H.

Rehabilitation Technology:

BÜHLER, C.

Sociology in Rehabilitation:

WACKER, E.

Vocational Education and Training:

BIERMANN, H.

Faculty of Spatial Planning (tel. (231) 755-2284; fax (231) 755-2620; e-mail dekanat@rp.uni-dortmund.de; internet www.raumplanung.uni-dortmund.de):

BADE, F.-J., Regional Economics
BAUMGART, S., Urban and Regional Planning
BECKER, R., Women's Studies and Housing in Spatial Planning
BLOTEVOGEL, H.-H., Regional and Federal Planning
DAVID, C.-H., Law and Spatial Planning
DAVY, B., Land Policy and Management
FINKE, L., Ecology and Landscape Planning
HENNINGS, G., Industrial and Commercial Development Planning
HOLZ-RAU, C., Transport Planning
KRAUSE, K.-J., Urban and Landscape Design
KREIBICH, V., Spring Centre, Urban and Regional Geography

KROES, G., Spring Centre, Urban and Regional Geography
KUNZMANN, K., Spatial Planning in Europe
REICHER, C., Urban Design and Land Use Planning
RÖDDING, W., Systems Theory and Systems Engineering
SCHMALS, K. M., Sociology and Spatial Planning
TIETZ, H.-P., Supply and Disposal Systems in Spatial Planning
VELSINGER, P., Political Economics, Regional Economics

Department of Statistics (tel. (231) 755-3113; fax (231) 755-3454; e-mail kunert@statistik.uni-dortmund.de; internet www.statistik.uni-dortmund.de):

GATHER, U., Mathematical Statistics and Industrial Application
HARTUNG, J., Statistics Applied in Engineering
ICKSTADT, K., Statistics in Biosciences
KRÄMER, W., Economic and Social Statistics
KUNERT, J., Mathematical Statistics and Scientific Application
TRENKLER, G., Statistics and Econometrics
URFER, W., Statistical Methods in Genetics and Ecology
WEIHS, K., Computer-Aided Statistics

ATTACHED INSTITUTES

Institut für Arbeitsphysiologie: Ardeystr. 67, 44139 Dortmund; Dir Prof. Dr HERMANN M. BOLD.

Institut für Gerontologie: Head Prof. Dr GERHARD NAEGELE.

Institut für Landes- und Stadtenwicklungsforschung des Landes NW.

Fraunhofer Institut für Materialfluss und Logistik: Heads Prof. Dr UWE CLAUSEN, Prof. Dr MICHAEL TEN HOMPEL, Prof. Dr AXEL KUHN.

Institut für Roboterforschung: Head Prof. Dr UWE SCHWIEGELSHOHN.

Fraunhofer-Institut für Software- und Systemtechnik (ISST): Joseph-von-Fraunhofer-Str. 20, 44227 Dortmund; Head Prof. Dr HERBERT WEBER.

Institut für Spektrochemie und Angewandte Spektroskopie: Heads Prof. Dr KAI NIEMAX, Prof. Dr A. MANZ.

Institut für Umweltschutz: Head Prof. Dr MICHAEL SPITELLER.

Landesinstitut Sozialforschungsstelle Dortmund.

Max-Planck-Institut für Molekulare Physiologie (MPI): Otto-Hahn-Str. 11, 44227 Dortmund; Head Prof. Dr HERBERT WALDMANN.

Technologie Zentrum Dortmund GmbH.

TECHNISCHE UNIVERSITÄT DRESDEN

Mommsenstr. 13, 01062 Dresden
Telephone: (351) 46335358
Fax: (351) 46337738
E-mail: auslandsamt@tu-dresden.de
Internet: www.tu-dresden.de

Founded 1828, University status 1961
State control
Academic year: October to September

Rector: Prof. Dr HERMANN KOKENGE
Vice-Rectors: Prof. WINFRIED KILLISCH, Prof. Dr HANG-GEORG MARQUARDT, Prof. Dr MONIKA MEDICK-KRAKAU
Chancellor: ALFRED POST

Number of teachers: 1,550
Number of students: 34,993, not incl. Faculty of Medicine

Publication: *Wissenschaftliche Zeitschrift* (6 a year)

DEANS

Faculty of Architecture: Prof. THOMAS WILL
Faculty of Civil Engineering: Prof. Dr RAIMUND HERZ
Faculty of Computer Science: Prof. Dr ALEXANDER SCHILL
Faculty of Economics and Business Management: Prof. Dr WOLFGANG UHR
Faculty of Education: Prof. Dr FRANK NESTMANN
Faculty of Electrical Engineering and Information Technology: Prof. Dr ADOLF FINGER
Faculty of Forestry, Geosciences and Hydrosciences: Prof. Dr PETER WERNER
Faculty of Law: Prof. Dr MARTIN SCHULTE
Faculty of Literature, Linguistics and Cultural Studies: Prof. Dr URSULA SCHAEFER
Faculty of Mathematics and Natural Sciences: Prof. Dr JÖRG WEBER
Faculty of Mechanical Engineering: Prof. Dr VOLKER ULBRICHT
'Carl Gustav Carus' Faculty of Medicine: Prof. Dr H. REICHMANN
Faculty of Philosophy: Prof. Dr KARL LENZ
'Friedrich List' Faculty of Transportation and Traffic Sciences: Prof. Dr GERD-AXEL AHRENS

UNIVERSITÄT DUISBURG-ESSEN

Campus Duisburg, Forsthausweg 2, 47057 Duisburg
Telephone: (203) 379-0
Fax: (203) 379-3333
E-mail: pressestelle@uni-due.deCampus Essen, Universitätsstr. 2, 45117 Essen
Telephone: (201) 183-1
Fax: (201) 183-2151
E-mail: pressestelle@uni-due.de
Internet: www.uni-duisburg-essen.de

Founded 2003 by merger of Gerhard-Mercator-Universität Duisburg (f. 1972) and Universität-Gesamthochschule-Essen (f. 1972)
Academic year: October to September (two semesters)

Rector: Prof. Dr LOTHAR ZECHLIN
Chancellor: Dr RAINER AMBROSY
Librarians: SIGURD PRAETORIUS (Duisburg), ALBERT BILO (Essen)

Library of 2,600,000
Number of teachers: 2,333
Number of students: 33,166

Publications: *Essener Unikate* (2 a year), *Forschungsbericht* (every 2 years), *Forum Forschung* (annually), *Results of Mathematics* (4 a year)

DEANS

Faculty of Art and Design: Prof. Dr KURT MEHNERT
Faculty of Business Economics: Prof. Dr PETER CHAMONI
Faculty of Business Studies: Prof. Dr HENDRIK SCHRÖDER
Faculty of Biology and Geography: Prof. Dr ULRICH SCHREIBER
Faculty of Chemistry: Prof. Dr ELKE SUMFLETH
Faculty of Construction Science: Prof. Dr RENATUS WIDMANN
Faculty of Education Sciences: Prof. Dr HORST BOSSONG
Faculty of Engineering Sciences: Prof. Dr ANDRÉS KECSKEMÉTHY
Faculty of Humanities: Prof. Dr ERHARD RECKWITZ
Faculty of Mathematics: Prof. Dr WERNER HAUßMANN
Faculty of Medicine and University Clinic: Prof. Dr KARL-HEINZ JÖCKEL
Faculty of Physics: Prof. Dr ROLF MÖLLER
Faculty of Social Sciences: Prof. Dr GERHARD BÄCKER

ATTACHED RESEARCH INSTITUTES

Deutsch-Französisches Institut für Automation und Robotik (IAR): Speaker Prof. Dr-Ing. STEVEN X. DING.

Rhein-Ruhr-Institut für Sozialforschung und Politikberatung e.V. (RISP): internet www.risp-duisburg.de; applied regional socio-economic research; promotes communication and co-operation between the academic world and public and private sector institutions in the Ruhrgebiet; Dir Prof Dr HERIBERT SCHATZ.

Deutsches Textilforschungszentrum Nord-West e.V.: Dir Prof. Dr ECKHARD SCHOLLMEYER.

Forschungsinstitut für wirtschaftliche Entwicklungen im Pazifikraum e.V. (FIP): Dir Prof. Dr GÜNTER HEIDUK.

Institut für Energie- und Umwelttechnik e.V. (IUTA): Dirs Prof. Dr-Ing. KLAUS GERHARD SCHMIDT, Dipl.-Volkswirt GÜNTER SCHÖPPE.

Essener Kolleg für Geschlechterforschung: Dir Prof. Dr DORIS JANSHEN.

Institut für Experimentelle Mathematik (IEM): internet www.exp-math.uni-essen.de; Dir Prof. Dr H. VINCK.

Instituts für niederrheinische Kulturgeschichte und Regionalenwicklung: Dir Prof. Dr DIETER GEUENICH.

IWW Rheinisch-Westfälisches Institut für Wasserforschung gemeinnützige GmbH: internet www.iww-online.de; Dirs Dr-Ing. WOLF MERKEL, KLAUS-DIETER NEUMANN.

Salomon Ludwig Steinheim Institut für deutsch-jüdische Geschichte e.V. (StI): internet sti1.uni-duisburg.de; research and adult education on Jewish history in Germany from the Renaissance to the present; Dir Prof. Dr MICHAEL BROCKE.

Entwicklungszentrum für Schiffstechnik und Transportsysteme e.V.: Dir Prof. Dr P. ENGELKAMP.

Institut für Mobil- und Satellitenfunktechnik GmbH (IMST GmbH): internet www.imst.de; Dirs Prof. Dr-Ing. INGO WOLFF, Dr-Ing. PETER WALDOW.

Foundation Centre of Turkish Studies: internet www.zft-online.de; Dir Prof. Dr FARUK SEN.

Institut für Energie- und Umwelttechnik eV (IUTA): internet www.iuta.de; Dir Prof. Dr K. G. SCHMIDT.

Institut für Prävention und Gesundheitsförderung: internet www.ipg-uni-essen.de; Dir Dr ALFONS SCHRÖER.

HEINRICH-HEINE-UNIVERSITÄT DÜSSELDORF

Universitätsstrasse 1, 40225 Düsseldorf
Telephone: (211) 81-00
Fax: (211) 342229
Internet: www.uni-duesseldorf.de

Founded 1965; formerly Medizinische Akademie, f. 1907
State control
Language of instruction: German
Academic year: October to September

Rector: Prof. Dr med. Dr phil. ALFONS LABISCH
Chancellor: ULF PALLME KÖNIG
Pro-Rectors: Prof. Dr rer. pol. RAIMUND SCHIRMEISTER, Dr HILDEGARD HAMMER, Prof. Dr phil. VITTORIA BORSÒ, Prof. Dr med. JÜRGEN SCHRADER

Head of Student Secretariat: K.-H. FEHR
Director of the International Office: Dr WERNER J. STÜBER
Librarian: Dr IRMGARD SIEBERT
Library: see Libraries and Archives
Number of teachers: 3,200
Number of students: 26,353

DEANS

Faculty of Economics: Prof. Dr HEINZ-DIETER SMEETS
Faculty of Mathematics and Natural Sciences: Prof. Dr GERD FISCHER
Faculty of Philosophy: Prof. Dr BERND WITTE
Faculty of Medicine: Prof. Dr WOLFGANG H. M. RAAB
Faculty of Law: Prof. Dr HORST SCHLEHOFER

PROFESSORS

Faculty of Economics (Universitätsstr. 1, Bld. 23.32.01.64, 40225 Düsseldorf; tel. (211) 81-13820; fax (211) 81-15353; e-mail wiwifak@uni-duesseldorf.de; internet www.uni-duesseldorf.de:7280/HHU/fakultaeten/wiwi):

BORNER, C., Business Administration and Finance
DEGEN, H., Statistics and Econometrics
FRANZ, K. P., Control and Taxation
GÜNTER, B., Business Administration and Marketing
HAMEL, W., Management and Business Administration
SCHIRMEISTER, R., Business Administration and Finance
SMEETS, H.-D., Economics
THIEME, H. J., Economics
WAGNER, G. R., Business Administration, Production Management and Environmental Economics

Faculty of Mathematics and Natural Sciences (Universitätsstr. 1, Bld. 25.32.00.30, 40225 Düsseldorf; tel. (211) 81-12235; fax (211) 81-15191; e-mail dekan.math-nat-fak@uni-duesseldorf.de; internet www.math-nat-fak.uni-duesseldorf.de):

ALFERMANN, A.-W., Botany
AURICH, V., Informatics
BOTT, M., Biochemistry
BRAUN, M., Organic Chemistry
BUCHNER, A., Psychology
BUELDT, G., Biological Structural Research
CONRAD, S., Informatics
DHONT, J.-K., Physics
EGGER, R., Theoretical Physics
ERNST, J. F., Microbiology
FISCHER, G., Mathematics
FRANK, W., Inorganic and Structural Chemistry
GANTER, CH., Inorganic and Structural Chemistry
GETZLAFF, M., Applied Physics
GÖRLITZ, A., Physics
GREVEN, H., Zoology
GRIESHABER, M., Zoophysiology
GRUNEWALD, F., Mathematics
HAESELER, A. VON, Bioinformatics
HEGEMANN, J., Microbiology
HEHL, F.-J., Psychology
HEIL, M., Psychology
HOCHBRUCK, M., Applied Mathematics
HÖLTJE, H.-D., Pharmacy
HOLLENBERG, C., Microbiology
HUSTON, J. P., Psychology
JAEGER, K.-E., Molecular Enzyme Technology
JAHNS, H. M., Botany
JANSSEN, A., Statistics and Documentation
JANSSEN, K., Mathematics
JARRE, F., Mathematics
JORDAN, E., Physical Geography
KERNER, O., Mathematics
KIRSCHBAUM, C., Psychology
KISKER, E., Applied Physics
KLÄUI, W., Inorganic Chemistry
KLEINEBUDDE, P., Pharmaceutical Technology
KLEINERMANNS, K., Physical Chemistry
KNUST, E., Genetics
KÖHLER, K., Mathematics
KÖHNEN, W., Teaching of Mathematics
KORNYSHEV, A., Physics
KOWALLIK, K. V., Botany
KRAUTH, J., Psychology
KUCKLÄNDER, U., Pharmaceutical Chemistry
KUNZ, W., Genetics
LIKOS, CH., Theoretical Physics
LÖSCH, R., Botany
LÖWEN, H., Theoretical Physics
LUNAU, K., Neurobiology
MARIAN, CH., Theoretical Chemistry
MAURE, M., Informatics
MEHLHORN, H., Zoology
MEISE, R., Mathematics
MEWIS, A., Inorganic and Structural Chemistry
PIETROWSKY, R., Psychology
PRETZLER, G., Experimental Physics
PROKSCH, P., Pharmaceutical Biology
PUKHOV, A., Theoretical Physics
RATSCHEK, H., Mathematics
REITER, D., Laser and Plasma Physics
RIESNER, D., Physical Biology
RITTER, H., Organic Chemistry
ROTHE, J., Informatics
RUETHER, U., Zoophysiology
SAHM, H., Biotechnology
SAMM, U., Plasma Physics
SCHIERBAUM, K., Raw Materials Science
SCHILLER, S., Experimental Physics
SCHLUE, W.-R., Neurobiology
SCHURR, U., Botany
SEIDEL, C., Physical Chemistry
SIMON, R., Genetics
SINGHOF, W., Mathematics
SPATSCHEK, K.-H., Theoretical Physics
STANDT-BICKEL, C., Organic Chemistry
STEFFEN, K., Mathematics
STOERIG, P., Psychology
STREHBLOW, H.-H., Physical Chemistry
VOLLMER, G., Teaching of Chemistry
WAGNER, R., Physical Biology
WANKE, E., Informatics
WEBER, H., Pharmacy
WEIN, N., Teaching Geography
WEINKAUF, R., Physical Chemistry
WEISS, H., Biochemistry
WENZENS, G., Geography
WESTHOFF, P., Botany
WILLBOLD, D., Physical Biology
WILLI, O., Experimental Physics
WISBAUER, R., Mathematics
WITSCH, K., Mathematics
WUNDERLICH, F., Parasitology

Faculty of Philosophy (Universitätsstr. 1, Bld. 23.21 Ebene 00 Raum 63 – Dekanatsbüro, 40225 Düsseldorf; tel. (211) 81-12936; fax (211) 81-12244; e-mail witte@phil-fak.uni-duesseldorf.de; internet www.phil-fak.uni-duesseldorf.de):

ALEMANN, U. VON, Politics
APTROOT, M., Yiddish Culture, Language and Literature
BARZ, H., Education
BAURMANN, M., Sociology
BEEH, V., Germanic Philology
BIRNBACHER, D., Philosophy
BLECKMANN, B., Ancient History
BÖHME-DÜRR, K., Media Sciences
BÖRNER-KLEIN, D., Yiddish Studies
BORSÒ, V., Romance Languages and Literature
BRANDES, D., Culture and History of Germans in Eastern Europe
BROCKE, M., Yiddish Studies
BÜHLER, A., Philosophy
BUSSE, D., Germanic Philosophy
BUSSE, W., English
FRIEDL, H., English
DIETZ, S., Philosophy
GEISLER, H., Romance Language and Literature
GLOGER-TIPPELT, G., Developmental and Educational Psychology
GOMILLE, M., English
GÖTZ VON OLENHUSEN, I., Modern History
HARTMANN, P., Sociology
HECKER, H., East European History
HERWIG, H., Germanic Philology
HÜLSEN-ESCH, A., Art History
HUMMEL, H., Politics
KANN, C., Philosophy
KELLER, R., Germanic Philology
KILBURY, J., Computer Linguistics
KÖRNER, H., Art History
KOUTEVA, T., English
KRUMEICH, G., Modern History
KÜPPERS, J., Classical Philology
LABISCH, A., History of Medicine
LAHIRI, A., Linguistics
LAUDAGE, J., Medieval History
LEINEN, F., Romance Philology
MAE, M., Modern Japan
MATUSSEK, P., Modern German
MILLER-KIPP, G., Education
MOLITOR, H., Modern History
NOUN, CH., Modern History
POTT, H.-G., Modern German
REICHEL, M., Classical Philology
RETTIG, W., Romance Philology
REUBAND, K. H., Sociology
ROHRBACHER, S., Yiddish Studies
SCHURZ, G., Philosophy
SCHWARZER, C., Education
SEIDEL, T., English
SIEPE, H., Romance Philology
STEIN, D., English
STIERSTORFER, K., English
STOCK, W. G., English
TIEGEL, G., Sport
WEBER, CH., Modern History
WITTE, B., Modern German
WUNDERLI, P., Romance Philology

Faculty of Medicine (Universitätsstr. 1, Bld. 23.11 Ebene 02 Raum 65, 40225 Düsseldorf; tel. (211) 81-12242; fax (211) 81-12285; e-mail nappm@uni-duesseldorf.de; internet www.uni-duesseldorf.de/HHU/Fak/NewMed):

ABHOLZ, H.-H., General Medicine
ACKERMANN, R., Urology
ALBERTI, L., Psychosocial Disturbances
ANGERSTEIN, W., Phoniatry and Audiology
BARZ, J., Forensic Medicine
BAYER, R., Physiology
BECKER, J., Dentistry
BENDER, H. G., Obstetrics and Gynaecology
BÖCKING, A., General Pathology and Pathological Anatomy
BOEGE, F., Clinical Chemistry and Laboratory Diagnostics
BOJAR, H., Physiological Chemistry
BORSCH-GALETKE, E., Industrial Medicine
BORNSTEIN, ST., Internal Medicine
DAHL, ST. VOM, Industrial Medicine
DALDRUP, T., Forensic Toxicology
DALL, P., Obstetrics and Gynaecology
DRESCHER, D., Dentistry
FISCHER, J. H., Pharmacology and Toxicology
FRANZ, M., Psychiatry, Clinical Psychology
FRITZEMEIER, C. U., Dentistry
FÜRST, G., Radiology
GABBERT, H. E., Pathology
GAEBEL, W., Psychiatry
GAMS, E., Cardiological Surgery
GANZER, U., Oto-rhino-laryngology
GERAEDTS, M., Health Sciences and Social Medicine
GERHARZ, C.-D., Pathology
GIANI, G., Diabetes Research, Biometry
GÖBEL, U., Paediatrics
GRABENSEE, B., Internal Medicine
HAAS, H., Neurophysiology

HAAS, R., Internal Medicine
HÄUSSINGER, D., Internal Medicine
HARTUNG, H.-P., Neurology
HARTWIG, H.-G., Anatomy
HEINZ, H.-P., Medical Microbiology
HERNER, B., Neurology
HERFORTH, A., Dentistry
HERING, P., Laser Medicine
HEUCK, C. C., Clinical Chemistry and Biochemistry
HEUGGE, U., Dermatology
HOHLFELD, T., Experimental Pharmacology
IDEL, H., Hygiene
KAHL, R., Toxicology
KELM, M., Internal Medicine
KNOEFEL, W., Internal Surgery
KRAUSPE, R., Orthopaedics
KRUTMANN, J., Dermatology and Venereology
KÜBLER, N., Dentistry and Plastic Surgery
LABISCH, A., History of Medicine
LINS, E. J. F., Neuroradiology
LUDWIG, S., Molecular Medicine
MAI, J. K., Neuroanatomy
MANNHOLD, R., Investigation of Molecular Active Substances
MAU, J., Statistics and Biomathematics in Medicine
MAYATEPEK, E., General Paediatrics
MÖDDER, U., Clinical Radiology
MORGENSTERN, J., Applied Biomedicine
MÜLLER-WIELAND, D., Clinical Biochemistry
MUELLER, H. W., Neurobiology
MUELLER, H. W., Nuclear Medicine
NOVOTNY, G. E. K., Anatomy
NÜRNBERG, B., Physiological Chemistry
PFEFFER, K. D., Medical Microbiology
POREMBA, C., Pathology
RAAB, W., Dentistry
REHKAEMPER, G., Brain Research
REIFFENBERGER, G., Neuropathology
ROSS, H.-G., Physiology
ROTH, S.
ROYER-POKORA, B., Human Genetics
RUZICKA, T., Dermatology and Venereology
SANDMANN, W., Surgery
SCHARF, R., Haematology
SCHERBAUM, W. A., Internal Medicine
SCHMIDT, K. G., Paediatrics
SCHMITT, G., Radio-oncology
SCHNEIDER, F., Psychiatry
SCHNEIDER, M., Internal Medicine
SCHRADER, J., Physiology
SCHRÖR, K., Pharmacology and Toxicology
SCHULZE-OSTHOFF, K., Molecular Medicine
SEITZ, R., Neurology
SIEGRIST, J., Medical Sociology
SIES, H., Physiological Chemistry
STAHL, W. J., Physiological Chemistry
STEIGER, H.-J., Neurology
STEINGRÜBER, H.-J., Medical Psychology
STRAUER, B.-E., Internal Medicine
STÜTTGEN, U., Dentistry
SUNDMACHER, R., Ophthalmology
TARNOW, J., Anaesthesiology
THÄMER, V., Physiology
TRESS, W., Psychiatry
WENDEL, U., Paediatrics
ZILLES, K., Anatomy

Faculty of Law (Universitätsstr. 1, Gebäude 24.91 U1 R65, 40225 Düsseldorf; tel. (211) 81-11414; fax (211) 81-11431; e-mail dekanat .jura@uni-duesseldorf.de; internet www.jura .uni-duesseldorf.de):

ALTENHAIN, K., Criminal Law
BUSCHE, J., Civil Law
DIETLEIN, J., Public Law
FEUERBORN, A., Civil Law, Industrial Law and International Civil Law
FRISTER, H., Criminal Law and Law of Criminal Procedure
HEY, J., Entrepreneurial Tax Law
JANSEN, N., German and International Private Law
LOOSSCHELDERS, D., Civil Law and International Law
LORZ, R. A., German and International Public Law
MICHAEL, L., Public Law
MORFOCK, M., Public Law, Sociology of Law and Economic Law
NOACK, U., Civil Law and Commercial Law
OLZEN, D., Civil Law and Law of Civil Procedure
POHLMAN, P., Civil Law and International Commercial Law
SCHLEHOFER, H., Criminal Law and Law of Criminal Procedure

ATTACHED INSTITUTES

Deutsches Diabetes-Forschungsinstitut an der Heinrich-Heine-Universität Düsseldorf: Auf'm Hennekamp 65, 40225 Düsseldorf; Dir Prof. Dr D. MÜLLER-WIELAND.

Institut für Umweltmedizinische Forschung an der Heinrich-Heine-Universität Düsseldorf: see under Research Institutes.

Neurologisches Therapiezentrum (NTC) an der Heinrich-Heine-Universität Düsseldorf: Hohensandweg 37, 40591 Düsseldorf; Dir Prof. Dr V. HÖMBERG.

Arbeitsgemeinschaft Elektrochemischer Forschungsinstitutionen AGEF e.V.: Universitatsstr. 1, 40225 Düsseldorf; Chair. Prof. Dr J. W. SCHULTZE.

Eichendorff-Institut - Literaturwissenschaftliches Institut der Stiftung Haus Oberschlesien: 6-Hösel, Bahnhofstr. 71, 40883 Ratingen; Dir. Prof. Dr B. WITTE.

Institut für Medizin, Forschungszentrum Jülich GmbH: 52428 Jülich; Dir Prof. Dr K. ZILLES.

Institut für Biotechnologie, Forschungszentrum Jülich GmbH: 52428 Jülich; Dir Prof. Dr H. SAHM.

Institut für Chemie und Dynamik der Geosphäre: 52428 Jülich; Dir Prof. Dr U. SCHURR.

Deutsches Krankenhausinstitut: Tersteegenstr. 3, 40474 Düsseldorf; Dir Dipl.-oec. UDO MÜLLER.

Technische Akademie Wuppertal e.V.: Postfach 100409, 42004 Wuppertal; Man. Dir Dipl. oec. ERICH GIESE.

Institut für Internationale Kommunikation: Hildebrandtstr. 4, 40215 Düsseldorf; Man. Dir Dr M. JUNG.

Institut für die Kultur und Geschichte der Deutschen im ostlichen Europa: Dir Prof. Dr DETLEF BRANDES.

Ostasien-Institut: Dir Prof. Dr MICHIKO MAE.

Düsseldorfer Institut für Dienstleistungs-Management: Dir Prof. Dr W. HAMEL.

Institut für Biologische Informationsverarbeitung, Forschungszentrum Jülich GmbH: Dir Prof. Dr G. BÜLDT.

Institut 'Moderne im Rheinland': Dir Prof. Dr CEPL-KAUFMANN.

KATHOLISCHE UNIVERSITÄT EICHSTÄTT-INGOLSTADT

Ostenstrasse 26–28, 85072 Eichstätt

Telephone: (8421) 93-0
Fax: (8421) 931796
E-mail: info@ku-eichstaett.de
Internet: www.ku-eichstaett.de

Founded 1972, reviving a foundation of 1564
Academic year: April to February

President: Prof. Dr RUPRECHT WIMMER
Vice-President: Prof. Dr HELMUT FISCHER
Chief Administrative Officer: Dr GOTTFRIED FRHR. VON DER HEYDTE
Librarian: Dr ANGELIKA REICH

Library of 1,600,000 vols
Number of teachers: 460
Number of students: 4,400

Publications: *Agora* (2 a year), *Eichstätter Beiträge* (2 a year), *Eichstätter Studien* (3 a year), *Eichstätter Materialen* (2 a year)

DEANS

Faculty of Economic Sciences: Prof. Dr JOHANNES SCHNEIDER
Faculty of History and Social Sciences: Prof. Dr KARSTEN RUPPERT
Faculty of Languages and Literature: Prof. Dr GERHARD ZIMMER
Faculty of Mathematics and Geography: Prof. Dr HANS-PETER BLATT
Faculty of Philosophy and Education: Prof. Dr PETER BRÜNGER
Faculty of Religious Education: Prof. Dr UTO MEIER
Faculty of Social Studies: Prof. Dr ULRICH BARTOSCH
Faculty of Theology: Prof. Dr ALOIS SCHIFFERLE

PROFESSORS

Faculty of Economic Sciences (Auf den Schanz 49, 85049 Eichstätt; tel. (841) 937-1801; fax (841) 937-1950; e-mail elisabeth .batz@ku-eichstaett.de; internet www .ku-eichstaett.de/Fakultaeten/WWF):

BURGER, A., General Business Management
BÜSCHKEN, J., Business Administration and Marketing
DJANANI, C., General Business Management
FISCHER, H., Economics
FISCHER, T. M., General Business Management Controlling
FUCHS, M., Law for Economists
GENOSKO, J., Economic and Social Policy
KUHN, H., Business Administration, Production and Operations Management
KÜSTERS, U., Statistics
KUTSCHKER, M., General Business Management, International Management
LUTTERMANN, C., Law for Economists
RINGLSTETTER, M., General Business Management
SCHNEIDER, J., Economics
STAUSS, B., Business Administration and Services Management
WILDE, K., General Business Management and Economic Information Technology
WILKENS, M., General Business Management, Financing

Faculty of History and Social Sciences (Universitätsallee 1, 85072 Eichstätt; tel. (8421) 931286; fax (8421) 931798; e-mail gertraud .reinwald@ku-eichstaett.de; internet www .ku-eichstaett.de/Fakultaeten/GGF):

DETJEN, J., Political Science
DICKERHOF, H., Medieval History
GRECA, R., Sociology
KÖNIG, H.-J., Latin American History
LAMNEK, S., Sociology
LUKS, L., Contemporary Eastern European History
MALITZ, J., Ancient History
MÜLLER, R. A., Early Modern History
RUPPERT, K., Modern and Contemporary History
SCHREIBER, W., Theory and Teaching of History
SCHUBERT, K., Political Science
SCHWINN, T., Sociology
TREIBER, A., Folklore
ZSCHALER, F., History of Economics and Social Development

Faculty of Languages and Literature (Universitätsallee 1, 85072 Eichstätt; tel. (8421) 931517; fax (8421) 931797; e-mail monika .bittl@ku-eichstaett.de; internet www .ku-eichstaett.de/Fakultaeten/SLF):

BAMMESBERGER, A., English Linguistics
DICKE, G., German Literature
GSELL, O., Romance Linguistics
HÖMBERG, W., Journalism
KLÖDEN, H., Romance Linguistics
KRAFFT, P., Classical Philology
MARTIN, F.-P., Teaching of French Language
MUELLER, K., German as a Foreign Language
NATE, R., English Literature
NEUMANN, M., Modern German Literature
PITTROF, T., New German Literature
RENK, H. E., Teaching of German Language and Literature
RONNEBERGER-SIBOLD, E., Historic German Linguistics
SCHNACKERTZ, H.-J., American Literature
TONNEMACHER, J., Journalism
TSCHIEDEL, H.-J., Classical Philology
WEHLE, W., Romance Literature
WEIGAND, R. U., Medieval German Literature
ZIMMER, G., Classical Archaeology

Faculty of Mathematics and Geography (Ostenstr. 28, 85072 Eichstätt; tel. (8421) 931456; fax (8421) 931789; e-mail claudia .banzer@ku-eichstaett.de; internet www .ku-eichstaett.de/Fakultaeten/MGF):

BECHT, M., Physical Geography
BISCHOFF, W., Mathematics
BLATT, H.-P., Mathematics
DESEL, J., Informatics
DIEHL, S., Informatics
FELIX, R., Mathematics
FISCHER, H., Mathematics
HEMMER, I., Teaching of Geography
HOPFINGER, H., Geography
KUTSCH, H., Physical Geography
PECHLANER, H., Tourism
RESSEL, P., Mathematics
RICKER, W., Mathematics
ROHLFS, J., Mathematics
SOMMER, M., Mathematics
STEINBACH, J., Geography

Faculty of Philosophy and Education (Ostenstr. 26, 85072 Eichstätt; tel. (8421) 931298; fax (8421) 931799; e-mail dekanat .ppf@ku-eichstaett.de; internet www .ku-eichstaett.de/Fakultaeten/PPF):

BRÜNGER, P., Music Education
FELL, M., Adult Education
FETZ, R., Philosophy
GEISER, G., Pedagogics of Work
GRABOWSKI, F., Psychology
HABISCH, A., Central Institute for Marriage and Family in Society
HELLBRÜCK, J., Psychology
JENDROWIAK, H.-W., General Pedagogics
KALS, E., Psychology
KERKHOFF, G., Psychology
KÖCK, M., Pedagogics of Work
KONRAD, F.-M., Historical and Comparative Pedagogy
KÖPPEL, G., Art
LÄMMERMANN, G., Protestant Theology
LOVEN, C., Musicology
LUTTER, K., Sports
SCHMIDT, H.-L., Social Pedagogics
SCHULTHEIS, K., Elementary Education
SCHÖNIG, W., Pedagogics of School
THOMAS, F., Psychology
ZIMMERMANN, M., Art History

Faculty of Religious Education (vocational courses) (Pater-Philipp-Jeningen-Platz 6, 85072 Eichstätt; tel. (8421) 931275; fax (8421) 931784; e-mail dekanat.rpf@ ku-eichstaett.de; internet www.ku-eichstaett .de/Fakultaeten/RPF):

EHAM, M., Music and Voice Training
KURTEN, P., Dogmatics
MEIER, U., Religious Education
OBERRÖDER, W., Theory and Practice of Church Work
SCHUSTER, B., Psychology
SILL, B., Moral Theology and Social Ethics
STAUCHIGL, B., Pedagogics
TAGLIACARNE, P., Old Testament
TRAUTMANN, M., New Testament
WILLERS, U., Fundamental Theology and Philosophy

Faculty of Social Studies (vocational courses) (Ostenstr. 26, 85072 Eichstätt; tel. (8421) 931246; fax (8421) 931773; e-mail dekanat .fsw@ku-eichstaett.de; internet www .ku-eichstaett.de/Fakultaeten/SWF):

BARTOSCH, U., Pedagogics
BECK, C., Social Work
ERATH, P., Social Work
GÖPPNER, H.-J., Psychology
KLUG, W., Social Work
OXENKNECHT-WITZSCH, R., Law
SCHIEREN, S., Political Science

Faculty of Theology (P.-Philipp-Jeningen-Platz 6, 8507 Eichstätt; tel. (8421) 931437; fax (8421) 931779; e-mail karin.lepschy@ ku-eichstaett.de; internet www.ku-eichstaett .de/Fakultaeten/THF):

BÄRSCH, F., Liturgy
BÖTTIGHEIMER, C., Fundamental Theology
FISCHER, N., Philosophy and Basic Questions of Theology
GERWING, M., Dogmatics
GROSS, E., Religious Teaching and Teaching of Catholic Religion
HOFMANN, J., Old Church History and Patrology
MAIER, K., Middle and New Church History
MAYER, B., New Testament
MÖDE, E., Homiletics
MÜLLER, S. E., Moral Theology
SCHIFFERLE, A., Pastoral Theology
WEIß, A., Canon Law/History of Church Law
ZAPFF, B., Old Testament

ATTACHED INSTITUTE

Interdisziplinäres Zentrum für Gesundheitswissenschaften (IZG): Dir (vacant).

Zentralinstitut für Ehe und Familie in der Gesellschaft: Dirs Prof. Dr BERNHARD SUTOR, Prof. Dr HEINZ OTTO LUTHE.

Zentralinstitut für Lateinamerika-Studien: Man. Dir Dr KARL-DIETER HOFFMANN; Dirs Prof. Dr HAN-JOACHIM KÖNIG, Prof. Dr KARL KOHUT.

Zentralinstitut für Mittel- und Osteuropastudien: Dir Prof. Dr NIKOLAUS LOBKOWICZ.

FRIEDRICH-ALEXANDER-UNIVERSITÄT ERLANGEN-NÜRNBERG

Postfach 35 20, 91023 Erlangen
Telephone: (9131) 85-0
Fax: (9131) 8522131
E-mail: pressestelle@zuv.uni-erlangen.de
Internet: www.uni-erlangen.de

Founded 1743; merged with Universität Altdorf 1809

Rector: Prof. Dr KARL-DIETER GRÜSKE
Pro-Rectors: Prof. JOHANNA HABERER, Prof. Dr HARALD MEERKAMM, Prof. Dr HANS-PETER STEINRÜCK
Chancellor: THOMAS A. H. SCHÖCK
Librarian: Dr HANS-OTTO KEUNECKE

Number of teachers: 1,775
Number of students: 25,768

Publications: *Erlanger Bausteine zur fränkischen Heimatforschung, Erlanger Forschungen, Geologische Blätter für Nordost-Bayern und angrenzende Gebiete, Jahresbericht, Jahresbibliographie und Forschungsbericht, Jahrbuch für fränkische Landesforschung, Unikurier, Unikurier aktuell*

DEANS

Faculty of Economic and Social Sciences: Prof. Dr INGO KLEIN
Faculty of Education: Prof. Dr CLAUDIA KUGELMANN
Faculty of Law: Prof. Dr HANS-DIETER SPENGLER
Faculty of Medicine: Prof. Dr BERNHARD FLECKENSTEIN
Faculty of Natural Sciences I: Mathematics and Physics: Prof. Dr FRANK DUZAAR
Faculty of Natural Sciences II: Biology and Chemistry: Prof. Dr NORBERT SAUER
Faculty of Natural Sciences III: Geosciences: Prof. Dr WERNER BUGGISCH
Faculty of Philosophy I: History and Social Sciences: Prof. Dr ROLAND STURM
Faculty of Philosophy II: Languages and Literatures: Prof. Dr MECHTHILD HABERMANN
Faculty of Technology: Prof. Dr ALFRED LEIPERTZ
Faculty of Theology: Prof. Dr ODA WISCHMEYER

PROFESSORS

Faculty of Biology and Chemistry:

ELDIK, R. VAN, Inorganic and Analytical Chemistry
FEY, G., Genetics
GLADYSZ, J. A., Organic Chemistry
GMEINER, P., Pharmaceutical Chemistry
HÄDER, D.-P., Botany
HELVERSEN, O. VON, Zoology
HESS, Theoretical Chemistry
HILLEN, W., Microbiology
HIRSCH, A., Organic Chemistry
KREIS, W., Pharmaceutical Biology
LEE, G., Pharmaceutical Technology
SAUER, N., Botany
SCHNEIDER, S., Physical Chemistry
SCHWEIZER, E., Biochemistry
SELLMANN, D., Inorganic and General Chemistry
STEINRÜCK, H.-P., Physical Chemistry
WASSERTHAL, R., Zoology

Faculty of Economic and Social Sciences:

AMBERG, M., Business Administration (Information Systems III)
BACHER, Sociology
BERNECKER, W. L., Modern and Contemporary History (Latin America, Southern Europe)
BODENDORF, F., Administration (Information Systems)
BUTTLER, G., Statistics and Empirical Economic Research
DILLER, H., Marketing
FELDENKIRCHEN, W., Economic and Business History
GERKE, W., Banking, Finance and Stock Exchange
GRÜSKE, K.-D., Economics and Public Finance
HARBRECHT, W., International Economics
HERRMANN, H., Private Law
HOLTBRÜGGE, D., International Management
HUNGENBERG, Business Management
KLAUS, P., Logistics
KLEIN, I., Statistics and Econometrics
KREUTZ, H., Sociology and Social Anthropology
LACHMANN, W., Economic Policy and Development Economics
MÄNNEL, W., Business Management
MERTENS, P., Business Administration (Information Systems I)

MOSER, Psychology (Economic and Social Psychology)
PEEMÖLLER, V. H., Business Economics and Auditing
PEYKE, Business and Social Geography
REISS, W., German and International Tax Law
SCHACHTSCHNEIDER, K. A., Public Law
SCHEFFLER, W., Business Taxation
SCHNABEL, Labour Market and Regional Policy
SCHÖFFSKI, O., Business Management
SCHULZ, W., Communication Studies and Political Science
VOIGT, Industrial Management and Technology Management

Faculty of Education:
DANN, H.-D., Psychology
EINSIEDLER, W., Primary-School Teaching
ERDMANN, E., History
FREDERKING, V., Teaching of German Language and Literature
HELBIG, P., Primary-School Teaching
LÄHNEMANN, J., Religious Education (Lutheran)
OSWALD, W. D., Psychology
RÜTTEN, A., Sports Science
SACHER, W., School Education
SCHEINPFLUG, A., Educational Theory
SCHMIDT, W., Art
SCHRETTENBRUNNER, H., Geography
SCHROFNER, E., Theology
SPANHEL, D., Education
WALTER, G., English
WETH, Mathematics

Faculty of Geosciences:
BUGGISCH, W., Geology
GÖBBELS, Mineralogy
KOPP, H., Geography
KREUTZMANN, H., Geography
TOBSCHALL, H.-J., Applied Geology
TRETER, U., Geography

Faculty of Languages and Literatures:
ACKERMANN, P. D., Japanese
BREINIG, H., American Studies
FELDMANN, D., English Philology
FREIBURG, R., English Philology
HAUSMANN, F. J., Romance Philology
HERBST, TH., English Philology
HEYDENREICH, T., Romance Philology
HUDDE, H., Romance Philology
JASTROW, O., Semitic Philology
KOSTER, S., Classical Philology
KUGLER, H., German Philology
LACKNER, M., Sinology
LANG, J., Romance Philology
LEHMANN, J., Modern German Literature and Comparative Science of Literature
MUNSKE, H. H., Germanic and German Linguistics
OETTINGER, N., Comparative Indo-Germanic Philology
SCHOENMAKERS, H., Theatre and Media Studies
STEINKE, K., Slavic Philology
VERWEYEN, TH., Modern German Literature

Faculty of Law:
BARTLSPERGER, R., Public Law
BLOMEYER, W., Civil Law, Commercial and Business Law, Labour Law, International Private Law and Comparative Law
ERB, Criminal Law and Criminal Procedure
GREGER, R., Civil Law, Civil Procedure and Non-Contentious Jurisdiction
GRUNDMANN, German and European Private Law
HILLGRUBER, Public Law, International Private Law and Legal Philosophy
HRUSCHKA, J., Criminal Law, Criminal Procedure and Legal Philosophy
ROHE, M., Civil Law
SCHMIDT-PREUSS, M., Public Law
SIEMS, H., History of German and Bavarian Law and Civil Law
SPENGLER, Civil Law, Roman Law and History of Ancient Law
STRENG, F., Criminal Law and Criminology
VEELKEN, W., Civil Law, Commercial and Business Law, Copyright Law and Industrial Property Rights, International Private Law and Comparative Law
VIEWEG, K., Civil Law, Law and Data Processing, Personal Data Protection Law

Faculty of Mathematics and Physics:
ANTON, G., Experimental Physics
BARTH, W., Mathematics
DÖHLER, G., Semiconductor Physics
DUZAAR, Mathematics
FAUSTER, TH., Solid State Physics
GEYER, W.-D., Mathematics
GREVEN, A., Mathematical Stochastics
HÜLLER, A., Theoretical Physics
KNABNER, P., Applied Mathematics
KNAUF, Mathematics
LENZ, F., Theoretical Physics
LEUCHS, G., Optics
LEY, L., Experimental Physics
MAGERL, A., Crystallography
MÜLLER, P., Experimental Physics
PANKRATOV, O., Theoretical Solid State Physics
RITH, K., Physics
SCHULZ, M., Applied Physics
STRAMBACH, K., Mathematics
TÖPFFER, CH., Theoretical Physics

Faculty of Medicine:
BAUTZ, W. A., Diagnostic Radiology
BECKER, C.-M., Biochemistry
BECKMANN, M., Gynaecological Medicine
BEHRENS, J., Experimental Medicine
BETZ, P., Forensic Medicine
BRUNE, K., Pharmacology and Toxicology
DANIEL, W. F., Internal Medicine
DEXLER, Labour and Social Medicine
ESCHENHAGEN, Clinical Pharmacology and Clinical Toxicology
FAHLBUSCH, R., Neurosurgery
FLECKENSTEIN, B., Virology
FORST, Orthopaedics
GEFELLER, Biometry and Epidemiology
HAHN, E. G., Internal Medicine
HANDWERKER, H. O., Physiology and Experimental Physiopathology
HIRSCHFELDER, U., Orthodontics
HOHENBERGER, W., Surgery
IRO, Otorhinolaryngology
KALDEN, J. R., Internal Medicine
KALENDER, W., Radiology
KESSLER, M., Physiology and Cardiology
KIRCHNER, T., Pathology and Anatomy
KORNHUBER, Psychiatry
KUWERT, Clinical Nuclear Medicine
LÜTJEN-DRECOLL, E., Anatomy
MARK, K. VON DER, Experimental Medicine
NAUMANN, G. O. H., Optics
NEUHUBER, W. L., Anatomy
NEUKAM, F. W., Maxillofacial Surgery
NEUNDÖRFER, B., Neurology
PETSCHELT, A., Restorative Dentistry and Periodontology
PLATT, D., Gerontology
RASCHER, W., Paediatrics
RÖLLINGHOFF, M., Clinical Microbiology and Immunology
SAUER, R., Radiotherapy
SCHROTT, K.-M., Urology
SCHULER, G., Dermatology
SCHÜTTLER, J., Anaesthesiology
SIEBER, G., Internal Medicine (Gerontology)
WEGNER, Biochemistry and Pathobiochemistry
WEYAND, Heart Surgery
WICHMANN, Orthodontics
WIESMANN, Human Genetics
WITTERN-STERZEL, R., History of Medicine

Faculty of Philosophy, History and Social Sciences:
ABELE-BREHM, A., Social Psychology
ALTRICHTER, H., East European History
FORSCHNER, M., Philosophy
GEBHARDT, J., Political Science
HAUG, A., Science of Music
HERBERS, Medieval History
JASPER, W., Political Science
KRANZ, P., Classical Archaeology
KULENKAMPFF, J., Philosophy
KURER, O., Economics
LIEBAU, E., Education
LÖSEL, F., Psychology
MÖSENEDER, K., History of Art
NEUHAUS, H., Modern History
OLBRICH, E., Modern History
SCHMIDT, G., Sociology
SCHÖLLGEN, G., Modern History
SRUBAR, I., Sociology
STURM, R., Political Science
STÜRMER, M., Medieval and Modern History
SÜNKEL, W., Education
THIEL, CHR., Philosophy
URBAN, R., Early History
WERBIK, H., Psychology
WÜST, Bavarian and Franconian Local History

Faculty of Technology:
ALBACH, Electromagnetic Fields
DAL CIN, M., Communication Networks
DURST, F., Fluid Mechanics
EHRENSTEIN, G., Raw Materials
EMIG, G., Technical Chemistry
FELDMANN, K., Production Engineering
GEIGER, M., Manufacturing Engineering
GERHÄUSER, Information Technology, Communication Technology
GLAUERT, W., Electrical Engineering
GREIL, P., Raw Materials
GREINER, P., Data Processing
HEROLD, G., Electrical Engineering
HERZOG, U., Communication Networks
HOFMANN, F., Operating Systems
HUBER, J., Communications Technology
KAUP, A., Multimedia Communications and Signal Processing
KOCH, W., Mobile Communications
KUHN, G., Technical Engineering
LEEB, K., Automatic Theory and Formal Languages
LEIPERTZ, A., Technical Chemistry
LERCH, R., Sensors
MEERKAMM, H., Technical Construction
MEYER-WEGENER, Database Systems
MOLERUS, O., Mechanical Engineering
MUGHRABI, H., Materials Science, General Material Properties
MÜNSTEDT, H., Raw Materials
NEESSE, TH., Recycling
NIEMANN, H., Pattern Recognition
PIEPENBREIER, Electrical Drive and Control
ROPPENECKER, G., Automatic Control
RÜDE, Computer Science
RYSSEL, Technical Electronics
SAGLIETTI, Software Engineering
SCHLÜCKER, Process Technology and Machinery
SCHMIDT, High-Frequency Technology
SCHMUKI, P., Corrosion and Surface Engineering
SCHNEIDER, H.-J., Programming Languages
SINGER, R. F., Materials Science, Metals Technology
STEINER, R., Technical Chemistry
STOYAN, H., Artificial Intelligence
STRUNK, H., Materials Science
WECKENMANN, A., Manufacturing Engineering
WINNACKER, A., Materials Science

Faculty of Theology:
- BRANDT, H., Ecumenical Theology, Science of Missions and Religion
- BRENNECKE, H.-C., Early Church History
- FELMY, CH., Theology of the Christian East
- HAMM, B., Historical Theology
- HERON, A., Reformist Theology
- MERK, O., New Testament
- NICOL, M., Pastoral Theology
- SCHMIDT, G., Teaching of Religion
- SCHMIDT, L., Old Testament
- SCHMITT, H.-C., Old Testament Theology
- SPARN, W., Systematic Theology
- ULRICH, J., Systematic Theology
- WISCHMEYER, New Testament

JOHANN WOLFGANG GOETHE-UNIVERSITÄT FRANKFURT

Senckenberganlage 31, Postfach 111932, 60054 Frankfurt am Main

Telephone: (69) 798-0
Fax: (69) 798-28383
E-mail: presse@uni-frankfurt.de
Internet: www.uni-frankfurt.de

Founded 1914

Academic year: October to September (2 semesters)

President: Prof. Dr R. STEINBERG
Vice-Presidents: JÜRGEN BEREITER-HAHN, ANDREAS GOLD
Chancellor: HANS GEORG MOCKEL
Librarian: B. DUGALL

Number of teachers: 2,600
Number of students: 35,000

Publications: *Forschungsbericht* (annually), *Forschung Frankfurt* (4 a year), *Uni-Report* (6 or 7 a year)

DEANS

- Department of Biochemistry, Chemistry and Pharmaceutical Sciences: Prof. Dr HARALD SCHWALBE
- Department of Biological Sciences: Prof. Dr RÜDIGER EWITTIG
- Department of Catholic Theology: Prof. Dr BERND TROCHOLEPCZY
- Department of Computing and Mathematics: Prof. Dr DETLEF KRÖMKER
- Department of Economics: Prof. Dr WOLFGANG KÖNIG
- Department of Education: Prof. Dr ANDREAS GRUSCHKA
- Department of Geosciences and Geography: Prof. Dr HEINRICH THIEMEYER
- Department of Law: Prof. Dr REGINA OGOREK
- Department of Linguistic and Cultural Studies: Prof. Dr RAINER VOßEN
- Department of Medicine: Prof. Dr JOSEF M. PFEILSCHIFTER
- Department of Modern Languages: Prof. Dr V. BOHN
- Department of Philosophy and History: Prof. Dr HARTMUT LEPPIN
- Department of Physics: Prof. Dr WOLF AßMUS
- Department of Protestant Theology: Prof. Dr STEFAN ALKIER
- Department of Psychology and Sport: Prof. Dr HELFRIED MOOSBRUGGER
- Department of Social Sciences: Prof. Dr FRANK NONNENMACHER

PROFESSORS

Department of Biology and Computer Science (Feldbergstr. 42, 60323 Frankfurt am Main; tel. (69) 798-23956):
- BEREITER-HAHN, J., Cell Research
- BRÄNDLE, K., Zoology
- BRENDEL, M., Biology for Doctors
- BRÜGGEMANN, W., Botany
- DROBNIK, O., Architecture and Business Systems
- ENTIAN, K.-D., Microbiology
- FEIERABEND, F., Botany
- FLEISSNER, G., Zoology
- GEIHS, K., Practical Informatics
- GNATZY, W., Zoology
- HAGERUP, T., Theoretical Informatics
- KAHL, G., Botany
- KEMP, R., Applied Informatics
- KOENIGER, N., Apiculture
- KROEGER, A., Microbiology
- KRÖMKER, D., Graphical Data Processing
- KUNZ, W., Drafting Methods
- LANGE-BERTALOT, H., Botany
- MASCHWITZ, U., Zoology
- NOVER, L., Botany
- OSIEWACZ, H., Botany
- PONS, F., Microbiology
- PRINZINGER, R., Zoology
- PROTSCH VON ZIETEN, R., Anthropology
- SANDMANN, G., Botany
- SCHMIDT-SCHAUSS, M., Artificial Intelligence
- SCHNITGER, G., Theoretical Informatics
- STARZINSKI-POWITZ, A., Human Genetics
- STEIGER, H., Microbiology
- STREIT, B., Zoology
- TROMMER, G., Biology Teaching
- WALDSCHMIDT, K., Applied Informatics
- WILTSCHKO, W., Zoology
- WITTIG, R., Botany
- WOTSCHKE, D., Computer Languages
- ZICARI, R., Databases
- ZIMMERMANN, H., Zoology
- ZIZKA, G., Botany

Department of Catholic Theology (Grüneburgplatz 1, 60323 Frankfurt am Main; tel. (69) 798-33344):
- DENINGER-POLZER, G., Catholic Theology
- HAINZ, J., Exegesis of the New Testament
- HOFFMANN, J., Moral Theology, Social Ethics
- KESSLER, H., Systematic Theology
- RASKE, M., Practical Theology
- SCHREIJÄCK, T., Catholic Theology
- WIEDENHOFER, S., Systematic Theology

Department of Chemical and Pharmaceutical Sciences (Biozentrum, Marie-Curie-Str. 9, 60439 Frankfurt am Main; tel. (69) 798-29545; fax (69) 798-29546):
- AUNER, N., Inorganic Chemistry
- BADER, H.-J., Chemistry Teaching
- BAMBERG, E., Biophysical Chemistry
- BRUTSCHY, B., Physical Chemistry
- DINGERMANN, TH., Pharmaceutical Biology
- DRESSMAN, J. B., Pharmaceutical Technology
- EGERT, E., Organic Chemistry
- ENGELS, J., Organic Chemistry
- GÖBEL, M., Organic Chemistry
- KARAS, M., Analytical Chemistry
- KOLBESEN, B., Inorganic Chemistry
- KREUTER, J., Pharmaceutical Technology
- LAMBRECHT, G., Pharmacology for Natural Scientists
- LUDWIG, B., Biochemistry
- MARSCHALEK, R., Pharmaceutical Biology
- MOSANDL, A., Food Chemistry
- MÜLLER, W. E., Pharmacology and Toxicology
- PRISNER, TH. F., Physical Chemistry
- REHM, D., Physical and Organic Chemistry
- RÜTERJANS, H., Physical Biochemistry
- SCHUBERT-ZSILAVECZ, M., Pharmaceutical Chemistry
- STARK, H., Pharmaceutical Chemistry
- STEINHILBER, D., Pharmaceutical Chemistry
- STOCK, G., Theoretical Chemistry
- WACHTVEITL, J., Physical Chemistry
- WAGNER, M., Inorganic Chemistry

Department of Economics (Mertonstr. 17–25, 60054 Frankfurt am Main; tel. (69) 798-22305; fax (69) 798-22678):
- BARTELS, H. G., Business Administration, Operational Research
- BAUER, T., Economic Systems and Transition
- BINDER, M., Macroeconomics
- BLONSKI, M., Microeconomics
- BÖCKING, H.-J., Corporate Governance
- EWERT, R., Controlling and Auditing
- FITZENBERGER, B., Labour Economics
- GEBHARDT, G., Economic Management
- GOMBER, P., e-Finance
- HALIASSOS, M., Macroeconomics and Financial Markets
- HASSLER, U., Statistics
- HOLTEN, R., Business Information Systems
- HOMMEL, M., Audit and Invoicing
- HORLEBEIN, M., Economic Pedogogics
- HUJER, R., Statistics and Econometrics
- ISERMANN, H., Business Administration
- KAAS, K. P., Industrial Economics
- KLAPPER, D., Marketing
- KLUMP, R., Business Development
- KÖNIG, W., Economic Management
- KRAHNEN, J. P., Financial Management
- KRÜGER, D., Macroeconomy
- LAUX, H., Theory of Organization
- MATHES, H. D., Production Planning
- MAURER, R., Investment
- MELLWIG, W., Industrial Economics
- NATTER, M., Trade
- NAUTZ, D., Empirical Macroeconomy
- RANNENBERG, K., Business Computing
- ROMMELFANGER, H., Mathematics for Economists
- SCHEFOLD, B., Political Economics
- SCHLAG, CH., Financial Economics
- SCHMIDT, R., Economic Management
- SKIERA, B., Electronic Commerce
- VELTHUIS, L., Organisation and Management
- WAHRENBURG, M., Business Administration (Banking)
- WALZ, U., Industry Economics
- WEICHENRIEDER, A., Financial Economics
- WIELAND, V., Money Theory and Policy

Department of Education (Senckenberganlage 15, 60054 Frankfurt am Main; tel. (69) 798-22392):
- BRAKEMEIER-LISOP, I., Economic Pedagogics
- BRUMLIK, M., Pedagogics
- CREMER-SCHÄFER, H., Pedagogics and Social Pedagogics
- DEPPE-WOLFINGER, H., Special Education
- DUDEK, P., Pedagogics
- FAUST-SIEHL, G., Primary Education
- GRUSCHKA, A., Teacher Training
- HESS, H., Social Pedagogics
- HOFMANN-MÜLLER, C. H., Pedagogics
- JACOBS, K., Special and Remedial Education
- KADE, J., Theory and Practice of Adult Education
- KALLERT, H., Social Pedagogics
- KAMINSKI, W., Pedagogics
- KATZENBACH, D., Pedagogics
- MARKERT, W., Economic Pedagogics
- MEIER, R., Primary Teacher Training
- NITTEL, D., Social Pedagogics and Adult Education
- NYSSEN, F., Teacher Training
- OVERBECK, A., Special Education
- RADTKE, F.-O., Pedagogics
- RANG, B., History and Pedagogics of Women's Studies
- SCHLÖMERKEMPER, J., Pedagogics
- SCHOLZ, G., Primary Education
- ZANDER, H., Social Pedagogics
- ZENZ, G., Social Pedagogics

Department of Geosciences and Geography (Bockenheimer Landstr. 133, 60325 Frankfurt am Main; tel. (69) 798-22691; fax (69) 798-28416; e-mail dekanat-geowiss@em.uni-frankfurt.de):
- ALBRECHT, V., Teaching of Geography
- ANDRES, W., Physical Geography
- BATHELT, H., Economic Geography

BREY, G., Mineralogy
BRINKMANN, W. L. F., Hydrology
HASSE, J., Teaching of Geography
HERBERT, F., Theoretical Meteorology
HUESSNER, H., Geology and Palaeontology
JUNGE, A., Geophysics
KLEINSCHMIDT, G., Geology
KOWALCZYK, G., Regional Geology
MÜLLER, G., Mathematical Geophysics
OSCHMANN, W., Palaeontology
PÜTTMANN, W., Environmental Analysis
RUNGE, J., Physical Geography
SCHAMP, E., Economic Geography
SCHICKHOFF, I., Human Geography
SCHMELING, H., Solid Earth Physics
SCHMIDT, U., Atmospheric Physics
SCHÖNWIESE, C., Meteorological Environmental Research
SCHROEDER, R., Palaeontology
STEIN, N., Physical Geography
STEININGER, F. F., Palaeontology and Historical Geology
THARUN, E., Cultural Geography
THIEMAYER, H., Hydrology
WOLF, K., Cultural Geography

Department of Law (tel. (69) 798-22201; e-mail dekanat.fb01@jur.uni-frankfurt.de):

ALBRECHT, P., Criminology and Criminal Law
BAUMS, TH., Business Law (Banking and Media)
CAHN, A., Law and Finance
CORDES, A., European History of Law
EBSEN, I., Constitutional, Administrative and Social Law
FABRICIUS, D., Criminal Law, Criminology and Psychology of Law
FRANKENBERG, G., Public Law
GILLES, P., Legal Procedure, Civil and Comparative Law
GÜNTHER, K., Theory of Law, Penal Law and Law of Criminal Procedure
HAAR, BRIGITTE, Civil Law
HASSEMER, W., Theory of Law, Social and Criminal Law
HERMES, G., Public Law
HOFMANN, R., Civil Law
KADELBACH, S., Public Law, European Law
KARGL, W., Theory of Law, Philosophy of Law and Criminal Law
KOHL, H., Civil Law
NEUMANN, U., Social, Criminal, and Criminal Adjective Law and Philosophy of Law
OGOREK, R., Roman Law, Civil Law
OSTERLOH, L., Public Law, Tax Law
PRITTWITZ, C., Criminal Law
REHBINDER, E., Business, Environmental and Comparative Law
RÜCKERT, J., History of Law
SACKSOFSKY, U., Public Law and Comparative Law
SIEKMANN, H., Money and Bank Law
SIRKS, B., History of Law and Civil Law
STOLLEIS, M., Public Law, History of Law
TEUBNER, G., Civic Rights, Commercial Law
VESTING, T., Public Law, Media Law
WANDT, M., German and International Civil Law, Commercial and Insurance Law
WEISS, M., Labour Law and Civic Rights
WELLENHOFER, MARINA, Civil and Process Law
WIELAND, J., Public Law, Financial Law and Tax Law
ZEKOLL, J., Civil Law

Department of Linguistic and Cultural Studies (Bockenheimer Landstr. 133, 60325 Frankfurt am Main; tel. (69) 798-22915; fax (69) 798-28474):

BASTIAN, H. G., Teaching of Music
BÜCHSEL, M., History of European Art
DAIBER, Oriental Studies
ERDAL, M., Turkish Studies
FASSLER, M., European Ethnology
FISCHER, J., Art Teaching
FREIDHOF, G., Slavonic Studies
GIPPERT, J., Comparative Linguistics
HERDING, K., Art History
LANGER, G., Slavonic Studies
MEYER, J.-W., Archaeology
NEU, T., Art Teaching
NEUMEISTER, C., Classical Philology
NOTHOFER, B., Southeast Asian Studies
NOVA, A., Art History
NOWAK, A., Musicology
RAECK, W., Classical Archaeology
RICHARD, B., Art Teaching
SCHLÜTER, M., Jewish Studies
SCHMITZ, TH., Greek Philology
SIEVERT, A., Art Teaching
VOSSEN, R., African Languages
WELZ, G., European Ethnology

Department of Mathematics (Robert-Mayer-Str. 6–8, 60325 Frankfurt am Main; tel. (69) 798-28920; e-mail dekanat@math.uni-frankfurt.de):

BAUMEISTER, J. B., Optimum and Convex Functions
BEHR, H., Pure Mathematics
BIERI, R., Pure Mathematics
BLIEDTNER, J., Pure Mathematics
CONSTANTINESCU, F., Mathematics
DINGES, H., Probability Theory and Statistics
FÜHRER, L., Mathematics Teaching
GROOTE, H. DE, Applied Mathematics
KERSTING, G., Stochastics
KLOEDEN, P. E., Applied Mathematics
KRUMMHEUER, G., Mathematics Teaching
LUCKHARDT, H., Fundamental Mathematics
METZLER, W., Mathematics
MÜLLER, K. H., Applied Mathematics
REICHERT-HAHN, M., Mathematics
SCHNORR, C., Applied Mathematics
SCHWARZ, W., Mathematics
SIEVEKING, M., Applied Mathematics
WAKOLBINGER, A., Probability Theory
WEIDMANN, J., Mathematics
WOLFART, J., Mathematics

Department of Medicine (Theodor-Stern-Kai 7, 60596 Frankfurt am Main; tel. (69) 6301-6010; fax (69) 6301-6301; e-mail kersken-nuelens@em.uni-frankfurt.de):

AUBURGER, G., Applied Neurology
BITTER, K., Maxillo-facial Surgery
BÖHLES, H. J., Paediatrics
BÖTTCHER, H. D., Radiation Therapy
BRAAK, H., Anatomy
BRADE, V., Hygiene, Microbiology
BRANDT, U., Biochemistry
BRATZKE, H., Forensic Medicine
BRETTEL, H.-F., Forensic Medicine
BUSSE, R., Physiology
CASPARY, W., Internal Medicine and Gastroenterology
CHANDRA, P., Therapeutic Biochemistry
DELLER, T., Anatomy
DEPPE, H.-U., Medical Sociology
DOERR, H. W., Medical Virology
DUDZIAK, R., Anaesthesiology
ELSNER, G., Industrial Medicine
ENCKE, A., General and Abdominal Surgery
FELLBAUM, CH., Pathology and Pathological Anatomy
FIEGUTH, H.-B., Thoracic Surgery
FÖRSTER, H., Applied Biochemistry
GALL, V., Child Audiology
GEIGER, H., Internal Medicine
GEISSLINGER, G., Clinical Pharmacology
GIERE, W., Documentation and Data Processing
GRONER, B., Molecular Infection and Tumour Biology
GROSS, W., Physiological Chemistry
GRÜNWALD, F., Nuclear Medicine
GSTÖTTNER, W., Ear, Nose and Throat Surgery
HANSMANN, M.-L., Pathology
HEIDEMANN, D., Dental and Maxillo-facial Medicine
HELLER, K., Surgery
HOELZER, D., Haematology
HOFMANN, D., Child Health
HOFSTETTER, R., Child Cardiology
HOHMANN, W., Materials in Dentistry
JAGOW, G. VON, Psychological Chemistry
JONAS, D., Urology
JORK, K., General Medicine
KAUERT, G., Forensic Toxicology
KAUFMANN, M., Gynaecology
KAUFMANN, R., Dermatology and Venereology
KERSCHBAUMER, F., Orthopaedics and Orthopaedic Surgery
KLINGEBIEL, T., Child Health
KLINKE, R., Physiology
KOCH, F.-H., Ophthalmology
KORF, H.-W., Anatomy
KUHL, H., Experimental Endocrinology
LANGENBECK, U., Human Genetics
LAUER, H.-CHR., Dentistry
LEUSCHNER, U., Gastroenterology
LOEWENICH, V. VON, Child Health
MAURER, K., Psychiatry
MELCHNER VON DYDIOWA, H., Clinical Molecular Biology
MOELLER, M., Medical Psychology
MORITZ, A., Thoracic, Heart and Vessel Surgery
MÜLLER-ESTERL, W., Biological Chemistry
MÜLSCH, A., Physiology
NENTWIG, G.-H., Dental and Maxillo-facial Medicine
NÜRNBERGER, F., Anatomy, Neurobiology
OHRLOFF, CH., Ophthalmology and Experimental Ophthalmology
OVERBECK, G., Psychosomatics
PFEILSCHIFTER, J. M., Pharmacology and Toxicology
PFLUG, B., Psychiatry
POUSTKA, F., Child and Adolescent Psychiatry
RÄTZKE, P., Dental and Maxillo-facial Medicine
SCHMIDT, H., Paediatric Radiology
SCHMITZ-RIXEN, TH., Vascular Surgery
SCHOPF, P., Maxillo-facial Surgery
SCHUBERT, R., Hygiene
SEIFERT, V., Neurosurgery
SIEFERT, H., History of Medicine
SIGUSCH, V., Sexology
STEIN, J., Gastroenterology and Clinical Nutrition
STEINMETZ, H., Neurology
STÜRZEBECHER, E., Medical Acoustics
USADEL, K.-H., Internal Medicine
VOGL, TH., Radiological Diagnosis
WAGNER, TH., Internal Medicine and Allergistics
WINCKLER, J., Anatomy
ZANELLA, F., Neuroradiology
ZEIHER, A. M., Internal Medicine
ZICHNER, L., Orthopaedics

Department of Modern Languages (Grüneburgplatz 1, 60323 Frankfurt am Main; tel. (69) 798-32742; fax (69) 798-32743):

BOHN, V., Modern German Philology
BROGGINI, G., German Philology
BUSCHENDORF, C., American Studies
ERFURT, J., Romance Philology
EWERS, H., German Philology and Literature (Children's Literature)
FREY, W., German
GARSCHA, K., Romance Philology
GREWENDORF, G., German Linguistics
HAMACHER, W., Modern German Philology
HANSEN, O., American Studies
HELLINGER, M., English Studies
HERRMANN, W., Teaching of German Language and Literature

KELLER, U., English
KLEIN, H. G., Romance Philology
KÜHNEL, W., English and American
LAUERBACH, G., English Studies
LEHMANN, H.-T., Theatre Studies
LEUNINGER, H., German Linguistics
LINDNER, B., German Language and Literature Teaching
LOBSIEN, E., English
METZNER, E., German
MITTENZWEI, I., Modern German
OPFERMANN, S., American Studies
OSSNER, J., Language Science of Modern German
QUETZ, J., English Teaching
RAITZ, W., History of German Literature
REICHERT, K., English/American Language
ROSEBROCK, C., Teaching of Literary Appreciation
RÜTTEN, R., French Language and Literature
SCHARLAU, B., Romance Philology
SCHEIBLE, H., German Language and Literature
SCHLOSSER, H. D., German
SCHLÜPMANN, H., Film Science
SCHNEIDER, G., Romance Philology
SCHRADER, H., Teaching of French
SEITZ, D., German
SOLMECKE, G., Teaching of English Language
STEGMANN, T., Romance Languages and Literature
WEISE, W.-D., English Teaching
WIETHÖLTER, W., Modern German Literature
WOLFZETTEL, F., Romance Philology
ZIMMERMANN, TH., Semantics

Department of Philosophy and History (Grüneburgplatz 1, 60323 Frankfurt am Main; tel. (69) 798-32758):

BREUNIG, P., Archaeology
CLAUSS, M., Ancient History
DETEL, W., Philosophy
ESSLER, W. K., Philosophy, Logic and Educational Theory
FEEST, CHR., Ethnology
FRIED, J., Ancient History
GALL, L., Medieval and Modern History
GREFE, E.-H., Teaching of History
HENNING, J., Prehistory
HONNETH, A., Social Philosophy
KAENEL, H. M. VON, Greek and Roman History
KOHL, K.-H., Ethnology
KULENKAMPFF, A., Philosophy
LENTZ, C., Ethnology
LÜNING, J., Prehistory
LUTZ-BACHMANN, M., Medieval Philosophy
MERKER, B., Philosophy
MUHLACK, U., General History
MÜLLER, H., Medieval Philosophy
PLUMPE, W., Economic and Social History
RECKER, M.-L., Recent History
SCHORN-SCHÜTTE, L., The Renaissance

Department of Physics (Gräfstr. 39, 60486 Frankfurt am Main; tel. (69) 798-23313; fax (69) 798-28309):

ASSMUS, W., Experimental Physics
BECKER, R., Applied Physics
DREIZLER, R., Theoretical Physics
ELZE, T., Nuclear Physics
GÖRNITZ, T., Physics Teaching
GREINER, W., Theoretical Physics
HAUG, H., Theoretical Physics
HENNING, W., Experimental Nuclear Physics
JELITTO, R., Theoretical Physics
KEGEL, W., Theoretical Physics
KING, D. A., History of Natural Sciences
KOPIETZ, P., Theoretical Solid State Physics
LACROIX, A., Applied Physics
LANG, M., Experimental Physics
LYNEN, U., Nuclear Physics
MÄNTELE, W., Biophysics
MARUHN, J., Theoretical Physics
MESTER, R., Applied Physics
MOHLER, E., Applied Physics
RATZINGER, U., Applied Physics
RISCHKE, D.-H., Theoretical Heavy Ion Physics
ROSKOS, H., Experimental Physics
SALTZER, W., History of Science
SCHMIDT-BÖCKING, H., Experimental Atomic Physics
SCHUBERT, D., Physics for Doctors
SIEMSEN, F., Physics Teaching
STOCK, R., Experimental Nuclear Physics
STÖCKER, H., Theoretical Physics
STRÖBELE, H., Experimental Nuclear Physics

Department of Protestant Theology (Grüneburgplatz 1, 60323 Frankfurt am Main; tel. (69) 798-33344; fax (69) 798-24992; e-mail stenger@em.uni-frankfurt.de):

DEUSER, H., Protestant Theology
FAILING, W.-E., Protestant Theology
HEIMBROCK, H. G., Protestant Theology
WEBER, E., Protestant Theology

Department of Psychology and Sport (Kettenhofweg 128, 60054 Frankfurt am Main; tel. (69) 798-23267; fax (69) 798-24956):

BALLREICH, A., Training Science
BANZER, W., Prevention and Rehabilitation
BAUER, W., General Psychology
DEGENHARDT-EWERT, A., Diagnostic Psychology
ECKENSBERGER, L. H., Psychology
EMRICH, E., Sport Science
GIESEN, H., Educational Psychology
GOLD, A., Pedagogical Psychology
HAASE, H., Psychology and Sociology of Sport
HODAPP, V., Diagnostic Psychology
KNOPF, M., Psychology
LANGFELDT, H.-P., Pedagogical Psychology
LAUTERBACH, W., Clinical Psychology
MOOSBRUGGER, H., Psychological Methodology, Statistics
PREISER, S., Educational Psychology
PROHL, R., Sports
ROHDE-DACHSER, CH., Psychoanalysis
SARRIS, V., Psychology
SCHMIDTBLEICHER, D., Training Science
SCHWANENBERG, E., Social Psychology
SIRETEANU, R., Physiological Psychology
ZAPF, D., Psychology

Department of Social Sciences (Robert-Mayer-Str. 5, 60054 Frankfurt am Main; tel. (69) 798-22521):

ALLERBECK, K., Sociology
ALLERT, T., Sociology and Social Psychology
APITZSCH, U., Sociology
BOSSE, H., Theory of Socialization
BROCK, L., International Politics
CLEMENZ, M., Sociology of Education
ESSER, J., Study of Politics, Sociology
GERHARD, U., Sociology
GLATZER, W., Social Structures
GRESS, F., Political Science
HELLMANN, G., Foreign Policy
HIRSCH, J., Political Science
HOFMANN, G., Methods of Social Research, Statistics
HONDRICH, K. O., Sociology
KAHSNITZ, D., Polytechnic and Technical Instruction Course
KELLNER, H.-F., Sociology
KRELL, G., Political Science
MANS, D., Methods of Social Research
MAUS, I., History of Political Ideas
MÜLLER, H., Political Science
NEUMANN-BRAUN, K., Sociology
NONNENMACHER, F., Teaching of Social Sciences
OEVERMANN, U., Sociology, Social Psychology
PROKOP, D., Mass Communications Research
PUHLE, H.-J., Political Science
RODENSTEIN, M., Sociology
ROPOHL, G., Polytechnic and Technical Instruction Course
ROTTLEUTHNER-LUTTER, M., Methodology
SCHMID, A., Polytechnic and Technical Instruction Course
SCHUMM, W., Sociology
SIEGEL, T., Sociology of Industrialized Societies
STEINERT, H., Sociology
TATUR, M., Political Science and Political Sociology

EUROPA-UNIVERSITÄT VIADRINA (Viadrina European University)

Grosse Scharrnstr. 59, 15230 Frankfurt an der Oder
Telephone: (335) 5534-0
Fax: (335) 5534-305
E-mail: study@euv-frankfurt-o.de
Internet: www.euv-ffo.de

Founded 1991
Languages of instruction: German, English
Academic year: October to July

President: Prof. Dr GESINE SCHWAN
Chancellor: PETER STRAHL
Registrar: BEATRIX ECKERT
International Office: PETRA WEBER
Librarian: Dr HANS-GERD HAPPEL

Number of teachers: 190
Number of students: 5,300

DEANS

Faculty of Law: Prof. Dr UWE SCHEFFLER
Faculty of Economics: Prof. Dr WOLFGANG PETERS
Faculty of Cultural and Social Studies: Prof. Dr KARL SCHÖGEL

ATTACHED RESEARCH INSTITUTES

Heinrich von Kleist Institute for Literature and Politics.

Frankfurt Institute for Transformation Studies.

Interdisciplinary Ethics Centre

ATTACHED COLLEGE

Collegium Polonicum: (situated in Slubice in Poland, and managed jointly by the Europa-Universität Viadrina and the Adam Mickiewicz University in Poznań).

TECHNISCHE UNIVERSITÄT BERGAKADEMIE FREIBERG

Akademiestr. 6, 09599 Freiberg
Telephone: (3731) 39-0
Fax: (3731) 22195
E-mail: rektorat@zuv.tu-freiberg.de
Internet: www.tu-freiberg.de

Founded 1765
State control
Academic year: October to August

Rector: Prof. Dr-Ing. GEORG UNLAND
Pro-Rectors: Prof. Dr-Ing. CARSTEN DREBENSTEDT, Prof. Dr WOLFGANG VOIGT
Chancellor: Dr GERLINDE DIETZE
Librarian: KARIN MITTENZWEI

Number of teachers: 357
Number of students: 4,700

Publications: *Fakultät Mathematik und Informatik Preprints*, *Freiberger Forschungshefte*, *Wissenschaftliche Mitteilungen des Instituts für Geologie*

DEANS

Faculty of Chemistry and Physics: Prof. Dr rer. nat. MICHAEL SCHLÖMANN

Faculty of Economics and Business Administration: Prof. Dr BRUNO SCHÖNFELDER
Faculty of Geosciences, Geotechnology and Mining: Prof. Dr-Ing. habil. ANTON SROKA
Faculty of Materials Science and Technology: Prof. Dr-Ing. habil. HORST BIERMANN
Faculty of Mathematics and Computer Science: Prof. Dr rer. nat. habil. WOLFGANG MÖNCH
Faculty of Mechanical, Process and Energy Engineering: Prof. Dr-Ing. habil. GEORG HÄRTEL
Interdisciplinary Ecological Centre: Prof. Dr JÖRG MATSCHULLAT

ALBERT-LUDWIGS-UNIVERSITÄT FREIBURG

Fahnenbergplatz, 79085 Freiburg im Breisgau
Telephone: (761) 2030
Fax: (761) 203-4369
Internet: www.uni-freiburg.de

Founded 1457
Academic year: October to July

Rector: Prof. Dr Dr WOLFGANG JÄGER
Pro-Rectors: Prof. Dr GERHARD SCHNEIDER, Prof. Dr KARL-REINHARD VOLZ, Prof. Dr MATHIAS LANGER
Director of Administration: WOLF-ECKHARD WORMSER
Librarian: BÄRBEL SCHUBEL

Number of teachers: 2,400
Number of students: 21,000

DEANS

Faculty of Theology: Prof. Dr HELMUT HOPING
Faculty of Law: Prof. Dr ANDREAS VOSSKHULE
Faculty of Business and Behavioural Science: Prof. Dr HANS SPADA
Faculty of Medicine: Prof. Dr JOSEF ZENTNER
Faculty of Philology: Prof. Dr E. CHEAURÉ
Faculty of Arts: Prof. Dr HERMANN SCHWENGEL
Faculty of Mathematics and Physics: Prof. Dr JOSEF HONERKAMP
Faculty of Chemistry, Pharmacy and Geosciences: Prof. Dr HARALD HILLEBRECHT
Faculty of Biology: Prof. Dr GEORG FUCHS
Faculty of Forestry and Enivronmental Sciences: Prof. Dr ERNST E. HILDEBRAND
Faculty of Applied Sciences: Prof. Dr JAN G. KORVINK

PROFESSORS

Faculty of Theology:

ALBUS, M., Pedagogics and Catechism
ENDERS, M., Philosophy
FRANK, S., Old Church History
GLATZEL, N., Christian Society
HOPING, H., Dogmatics and Liturgical History
IRSIGLER, H., Old Testament
NOTHELLE-WILDFEUER, U., Patoral Theology
OBERLINNER, L., New Testament Literature
POMPEY, H., Caritas Science and Social Work
RAFFELT, A., Dogmatics
SCHOCKENHOFF, E., Moral Theology
SMOLINSKY, H., New Church History
TZSCHEETZSCH, W., Pedagogics and Catechism
UHDE, B., History
VERWEYEN, H. J., Fundamental Theology
WALTER, P., Dogmatics
WARLAND, R., Christian Archaeology and Art History
WINDISCH, H., Pastoral Theology
ZAPP, H., Church Law

Faculty of Law:

BLAUROCK, U., Economic Law
BLOY, R., Penal Law
ESER, A., Penal Law
FRISCH, W., Penal Law
HAGER, G., International Civil Law
HAEDICKE, M., Civil Law
HOHLOCH, G., International Civil Law
HOLLERBACH, A., History of Law, Church Law, Philosophy of Law
KÖBL, U., Social Insurance Law
LEIPOLD, D., Civil, Labour and Procedural Law
LIEBS, D., History of Modern Law
LÖWISCH, M., Civil, Labour, Social Insurance and Commercial Law
MERKT, H., International Civil Law
MURSWIEK, D., State Law
NEHLSEN-VON STRYCK, K., History of Law
PERRON, W., Penal Law
SCHOCH, F., Public Law
SCHWARZE, J., European and International Law
STÜRNER, R., Civil Law
TIEDEMANN, K., Criminal Law and Procedure
WAHL, R., Administrative Law
WÜRTENBERGER, T., State Law
VOßKUHLE, A., History of Law, Philosophy of Law

Faculty of Economics and Behavioural Sciences:

BLÜMLE, G., Mathematical Economics
FUCHS, R., Sport Science
GEHRIG, T., Economic Development
GIEß-STÜBER, P., Sport Science
GOLLHOFER, A., Sport Science
FRANCKE, H. H., Financial Economics
HAUSER, S., Imperial Economics
HILKE, W., Commercial Economics
KESSLER, W., Business Economics
KNIEPS, G., Political Economy
LANDMANN, O., Economic Theory
RAFFELHÜSCHEN, Financial Economics
REHKUGLER, H., Commercial Economics
SCHAUENBERG, B., Management Economics
SCHOBER, F., Computer Science
SCHULTZ, G., Socio-political Economics
STRUBE, G., Cognition Science
TSCHEULIN, D., Health Service Economics
VANBERG, V., Political Economics

Faculty of Medicine:

AKTORIES, K., Pharmacology and Toxicology
BEHRENDS, J., Physiology
BESSLER, W., Immunology
BEYERSDORF, F., Cardiovascular Surgery
BIRNESSER, H., Sports Traumatology
BLUM, H., Gastroenterology
BODE, C., Cardiology
BOGDAN, CH., Microbiology
BORNER, C., Stem Cell Research
BRAND-SABERI, B., Anatomy and Cell Biology
BRANDIS, M., Paediatrics
BRANDSCH, R., Biochemistry
CHRIST, B., Anatomy
DASCHNER, F., Environmental Medicine
DECKER, K., Biochemistry
DICKHUT, H.-H., Rehabilitation and Sports Medicine
FAKLER, Physiology
FROMMHOLD, H., Radiology
FROTSCHER, M., Anatomy
FUNK, J., Eye Hospital
GEIGER, K., Anaesthesiology
GITSCH, G., Gynaecology
GOEPPERT, S., Medical Psychology
GUTTMAN, J., Anaesthesiology
HASSE, J., Surgery
HELLWIG, E., Dentistry
HOFFMAN, H.-D., Anatomy
HOPT, U., General and Visceral Surgery
HUANG, R., Anatomy
JACKISCH, R., Pharmacology and Toxicology
JONAS, Physiology
JONAS, J., Dentistry
KECECIOGLU, D., Paediatric Cardiology
KIST, M., Microbiology
KLAR, R., Medicine Informatics
KORINTHENBERG, R., Neurology and Muscular Diseases
KURZ, H., Anatomy
LANGER, M., Radiology
LASZIG, R., Otorhinolaryngology
LEVEN, K.-H., History of Medicine
MERTELSMANN, R., Internal Medicine
MEYER, D. K., Pharmacology and Toxicology
MOSER, E., Radiology
MÜLLER-QUERNHEIM, J., Pneumology
NIERNEYER, C., Paediatric Haemotology and Oncology
NIKKHAH, G., Neurosurgery
OSTERTAG, C., Neurosurgery
PAHL, H., Anaesthesiology
PANNEN, B., Anaesthesiology
PETER, H. H., Rheumatology
PETERS, C., Molecular Medicine
PFANNER, N., Biochemistry
PIRCHER, H., Immunology
POLLAK, S., Forensic Medicine
REICHELT, A., Orthopaedics
ROSPERT, S., Biochemistry
SCHEMPP, W., Cytogenetics
SCHMELZEISEN, R., Oral and Maxillofacial Surgery
SCHÖPF, E., Dermatology
SCHUMACHER, M., Medical Statistics
SIEBERT, F., Biophysics
STARK, B., Plastic and Hand Surgery
STARKE, K., Pharmacology and Toxicology
STRUB, J., Dentistry
SÜDKAMP, N. P., Traumatology
SZABO, B., Pharmacology and Toxicology
TRÖHLER, U., History of Medicine
TROPSCHUG, M., Biochemistry
TROSCHKE, J. VON, Medical Sociology
VOLK, B., Neuropathology
VOOS, W., Biochemistry
WALZ, G., Nephrology
WERNER, M., Pathology
WETTERAUER, U., Urology
WOLF, U., Human Genetics and Anthropology
ZENTNER, J. F., General Neurosurgery

Faculty of Philology:

ADAMS, J., American Literature
ANZ, H., Scandinavian Studies
ARNHAMMER, A., German Philology
AUER, P., German Philology
BANNERT, R., Scandinavian Studies
BERG, W. B., Literature
BLANK, W., German Philology
BÖNING, T., German Philology
CHEURÉ, E., Slavonics
DANGEL-PELLOQUIN, E., German Philology
DITTMANN, J., German Philology
DREWS, P., Slavonics
FLUDERNIK, M., English Philology
GÜNTHER, H.-C.
HAHN, U., German Philology
HALFORD, B., Oral Language
KILIAN, E., Literature
MAIR, C., Caribbean Language and Literature
HAUSMANN, R., Romance Philology
HERRMANN, H.-P., German Philology
HESS, R., Romance Philology
HOCHBRUCK, W., Literature
JURT, J., Literature
KAISER, G., German Philology
KÄSTNER, H.-J., German Philology
KNOOP, U., German Philology
KOCHENDÖRFER, G., German Philology
KOHL, N., English Literature
KORTE, B., Literature
KORTMANN, B., English Philology
KÜHNE, U., German Philology
KUNZE, K., German Philology
LEFÈVRE, E., Classical Philology
LÖNKER, F., German Philology
MATTHEWS, R., Linguistics

MAUSER, W., German Philology
MICHEL, W., German Philology
MÜRB, F., German Philology
PIETZCKER, C., German Philology
PILCH, H., English Philology
PÖRKSEN, U., German Philology
PÜTZ, M., English Philology
RENNER, R., German Philology
SASSE, G., German Philology
SCHÄFER, E., Latin Philology
SCHMIDT, J., German Philology
SCHOLZ, R., German Philology
SCHWAN, W., German Philology
SIEGERT, R., German Philology
RAIBLE, W., Romance Philology
RIX, H., Indogermanic Languages
THOMAS, C., German Philology
TICHY, E., Indogermanic Languages
TRISTRAM, H., German Philology
WEIHER, E., Slavonics
ZIMMERMAN, B., German Philology
ZUTT, H., German Philology

Faculty of Philosophy:

ASCHE, R., Modern History
BERGER, C., Music
BRÜGGEMEIER, F.-J., Economic and Social History
DEGELE, N., Sociology
ESSBACH, W., Sociology
FIGAL, G., Philosophy
GEHRKE, H.-J., Ancient History
GREINER, P., Sinology
HINÜBER, O., Indology
JÄGER, W., Political Science
JANHSEN, A., History of Art
KÜSTER, K., Music
KUNTZ, A., Ethnology
LAUT, J.-P., Islamic History
MARTIN, J., Ancient History
MATTER, M., Ethnology
MERTENS, D., Medieval History
MEZGER, W., Ethnology
MORDEK, H., Medieval History
NEUTATZ, D., Modern and East European History
NUBER, H. U., Roman Provincial Archaeology
PALETSCHEK, S., Modern History
PRATER, A., History of Art
REBSTOCK, U., Islamic History
RIESCHER, G., Political History
RÜLAND, J., Political History
SCHLEHE, J., Ethnology
SCHLINK, W., History of Art
SCHMIDT, G., Medieval Latin Philology
SCHNITZLER, G., Modern German Literature and Music
SCHWENGEL, H., Sociology
SEITZ, S., Ethnology
SENGER, H., Sinology
STEIBLE, H., Oriental Philology
STEUER, H., Prehistory
STRAHM, C., Prehistory
STROCKA, V., Classical Archaeology
TRÖHLER, U., History of Medicine
WARLAND, R., Christian Archaeology and Byzantine Art
WINDLER, C., Modern History
WINTERLING, A., Ancient History
ZOTZ, T., Medieval History

Faculty of Mathematics and Physics:

BAMBERGER, A., Experimental Physics
BANGERT, V., Mathematics
VAN DER BIJ, J., Theoretical Physics
BLUMEN, A., Theoretical Physics
BRENN, R., Experimental Physics
BRIGGS, J. ST., Theoretical Physics
DZIUK, G., Applied Mathematics
EBBINGHAUS, H.-D., Mathematical Logic
EBERLEIN, E., Stochastics
FLUM, J., Mathematical Logic
GRABERT, H., Theoretical Physics
GROHE, M., Logic
HABERLAND, H., Experimental Physics
HEINZEL, T., Physics
HELM, H., Experimental Physics
HERMES, H., Logic
HERTEN, G., Physics
HONERKAMP, J., Theoretical Physics
JAKOBS, K., Physics
KLAR, H., Physics
KÖNIGSMANN, K., Physics
KRÖNER, D., Applied Mathematics
KUWERT, E., Analysis
LANDGRAF, U., Physics
LUDWIG, J., Physics
POHLMEYER, K., Theoretical Physics
RÖMER, H., Theoretical Physics
RÖPKE, H., Experimental Physics
RUZICKA, M., Applied Mathematics
SCHMIDT, V., Physics
SCHMITT, H., Experimental Physics
SCHNEIDER, R., Mathematics
SIEBERT, B., Geometry
SOERGEL, W., Algebra
SPILKER, J., Actuarial Mathematics
STROBL, G., Experimental Physics
RÜSCHENDORF, L., Stochastics
WAGNER, F., Logic
WEIDEMÜLLER, M., Physics
WITTING, H., Applied Mathematics
WOLKE, D., Mathematics
ZIEGLER, M., Mathematical Logic

Faculty of Chemistry, Pharmacology and Geosciences:

BANNWARTH, W., Organic Chemistry
BECHTHOLD, A., Pharmaceutical Biology
BEHRMANN, J., Geology
BREIT, B., Organic Chemistry
BRÜCKNER, R., Organic Chemistry
BUCHER, K., Mineralogy
EBERBACH, W., Biochemistry
FINKELMANN, H., Molecular Chemistry
FRIEDRICH, K., Organic Chemistry
GLAWION, R., Geography
GOSSMANN, H., Geography
GRAPES, R., Geosciences
GRONSKI, W., Macromolecular Chemistry
HENK, A., Geology
HILLEBRECHT, H., Inorganic Chemistry
JANIAK, CH., Inorganic Chemistry
KELLER, J., Mineralogy
KRAMER, V., Crystallography
LEIBUNDGUT, CH., Hydrology
MÄCKEL, R., Geography
MAYER, H., Meteorology
MERFORT, I., Pharmaceutical Biology
MÜHLHAUPT, R., Macromolecular Chemistry
OTTO, H. H., Pharmaceutical Technology
PLATTNER, D., Organic Chemistry
PRINZBACH, H., Organic Chemistry
RÖHR, C., Inorganic Chemistry
RÜCHARDT, C., Organic Chemistry
SCHWESINGER, R., Organic Chemistry
SCHULZ, G. E., Biochemistry
SEITZ, S., Ethnology
STADELBAUER, J., Geography
TIPPER, J. C., Geology
VAHRENKAMP, H., Inorganic Chemistry
WIMMENAUER, W., Geosciences

Faculty of Biology:

AERTSEN, A., Neurobiology
BAUER, G., Evolutionary Biology
BAUMEISTER, R., Neurogenetics
BECK, C., Biology
BEYER, P., Cell Biology
BOGENRIEDER, A., Geobotany
DEIL, U., Geobotany
DRIEVER, W., Neurobiology
FISCHBACH, K. F., Biology
FUCHS, G., Microbiology
FUKSHANSKY, L., Botany
GÜNTHER, K., Neurobiology
HAEHNEL, W., Biochemistry
HARTMANN, R., Neurobiology
HERTEL, R., Biology
KLEINIG, H., Cell Biology
MÜLLER, J., Chemical Ecology
NEUBÜSER, A., Neurobiology
NEUHAUS, G., Cell Biology
OELZE, J., Microbiology
PESCHKE, K., Zoology
RESKI, R., Biotechnology
RETH, M., Molecular Immunology
ROSSEL, S., Neurobiology
SCHÄFER, E., Botany
SCHRÖDER, J., Biochemistry
VOGT, K., Neurobiology
WAGNER, E., Botany
WECKESSER, J., Microbiology
WELLMANN, E., Botany

Faculty of Forestry and Environmental Sciences:

ABETZ, P., Forest Growth
BAUHAUS, J., Silviculture
BECKER, G., Forest Utilization and Work Science
BECKER, M., Forest Policy
BOPPRÉ, M., Forest Zoology
EISFELD, D., Forest Zoology
ESSMANN, H., Environmental Policy
FINK, S., Forest Botany
HILDEBRAND, E. E., Soil Sciences and Forest Nutrition
JAEGER, L., Meteorology
KOCH, B., Land Information Systems
KONOLD, W., Land Use Planning
KRINGS, T., Cultural Geography
LEWARK, S., Forest Utilization and Work Science
MAYER, H., Meteorology
MEIDINGER, E., Forest Management
MITSCHERLICH, G., Forest Growth
OESTEN, G., Forest Management
PELZ, D. R., Biometrics
REIF, A., Silviculture
RENNENBERG, H., Tree Science
ROEDER, A., Forest Management
SCHMIDT, U., Environmental Policy
SCHRÖDER, E.-J., Cultural Geography
SPIECKER, H., Forest Production
VOLZ, K., Forest Policy

Faculty of Applied Sciences:

ALBERS, S., Parallel and Distributed Computing
BASIN, D., Informatics
BECKER, B., Informatics
BERGARD, W., Autonomous Intelligent Systems
BURKHARDT, H., Informatics
HAUSSELT, J., Microsystems Technology
KORVINK, J. G., Microsystems Technology
KUNTZ, Information Technology
LAUSEN, G., Informatics
LEUE, S., Computer Networks
MANOLI, Information Technology
MENZ, W., Microsystems Technology
NEBEL, B., Informatics
OTTMANN, TH., Informatics
PAUL, Information Technology
RAEDT, L. DE, Machine Learning
RÜHE, Information Technology
SCHOLL, C., Operating Systems
SCHMIDT-THIEME, L., Computer-Based New Media
SCHNEIDER, G., Communication Systems
THIEMANN, P., Programming Languages
URBAN, G. A., Microsystems Technology
WILDE, Information Technology
WOIAS, Information Technology
ZAPPE, Information Technology
ZENGERLE, Information Technology

JUSTUS-LIEBIG-UNIVERSITÄT GIEßEN

Ludwigstr. 23, 35390 Gießen
Telephone: (641) 99-0
Fax: (641) 99-12259
Internet: www.uni-giessen.de

Founded 1607
State control

Academic year: October to September (two terms)
President: Prof. Dr STEFAN HORMUTH
Vice-Presidents: Prof. Dr JÜRGEN JANEK, Prof. Dr JOACHIM STIENSMEIER-PELSTER
Chief Administrative Officer: Dr MICHAEL BREITBACH
Librarian: Dr PETER REUTER
Number of teachers: 380
Number of students: 22,000
Publication: *Spiegel der Forschung* (annually)

DEANS

Department of Agrarian Sciences, Nutritional Sciences, Environmental Management: Prof. W. KÖHLER
Department of Biology, Chemistry and Geosciences: Prof. JÜRGEN MAYER
Department of Economics: Prof. Dr WOLFGANG SCHERF
Department of History and Cultural Studies: Prof. Dr HELMUT KRASSER
Department of Human Medicine: Prof. HANS MICHAEL PIPER
Department of Language, Literature, Culture: Prof. Dr HARTMUT STENZEL
Department of Law: Prof. Dr GABRIELE WOLFSLAST
Department of Mathematics and Information Studies, Physics, Geography: Prof. VOLKER METAG
Department of Psychology and Sport: Prof. Dr JOACHIM STIENSMEIER-PELSTER
Department of Social and Cultural Studies: Prof. Dr KLAUS FRITZSCHE
Department of Veterinary Medicine: Prof. MANFRED REINMACHER

PROFESSORS

Department of Agricultural and Nutritional Sciences, Home Economics and Environmental Management (Bismarckstr. 24, 35390 Gießen; tel. (641) 99-37001; fax (641) 99-37009):

BAUER, S., Project and Regional Planning
BECKER-BRANDENBURG, K., Nutritional Biochemistry
BOLAND, H., Agricultural Extension and Communication
BRÄUNIG, D., Management of Services for Persons
BRÜCKNER, H.-O., Food Science
DZAPO, V., Genetics, Breeding and Husbandry of Pigs and Small Animals
ERHARDT, G., Animal Breeding and Genetics
EVERS, A., Comparative Health and Social Policy
FELIX-HENNINGSEN, P., Soil Science and Soil Conservation
FREDE, H.-G., Resources Management
FRIEDT, W., Plant Breeding
GÄTH, S., Waste Management and Environmental Research
HERRMANN, R., Agricultural and Food Market Analysis
HOFFMANN, I., Nutritional Ecology
HONERMEIER, B., Crop Science
HOY, S., Farm Animal Housing and Biology
HUMMEL, H. E., Biological and Biotechnical Plant Protection
KÄMPFER, P., Recycling Microbiology
KOGEL, K.-H., Molecular Plant Pathology
KÖHLER, W., Biometry and Population Genetics
KRAWINKEL, M., Human Nutrition, International Nutrition
KÜHL, R. W., Food Economics and Marketing Management
KUHLMANN, F., Farm Management
KUNZ, C., Human Nutrition, Evaluation of Food
LEITHOLD, G., Organic Farming
LEONHÄUSER, I.-U., Nutrition Education and Consumer Behaviour
MEIER, U., Economics of Private Households and Family Sciences
MÜHLING, K.-H., Biochemical Aspects of Plant Nutrition
NEUHÄUSER-BERTHOLD, M., Human Nutrition
NUPPENAU, E. A., Agricultural and Environmental Policy
OPITZ VON BOBERFELD, W., Grassland Management and Forage Growing
OTTE, A., Landscape Ecology and Landscape Planning
PALLAUF, J., Animal Nutrition
SCHLICH, E., Home Engineering
SCHMITZ, P. M., Agricultural and Development Economics and Policy Analysis
SCHNELL, S., General and Soil Microbiology
SCHNIEDER, B., Housing and Human Ecology
SCHUBERT, S., Plant Nutrition
SEUFERT, H., Agricultural Engineering
VILCINSKAS, A., Applied Entomology

Department of Biology, Chemistry and Geosciences (Heinrich-Buff-Ring 58, 35392 Gießen; tel. (641) 99-35001; fax (641) 99-35009):

ASKANI, R., Organic Chemistry
VAN BEL, A. J. E., Organic Botany
BINDEREIF, A., Biochemistry
CLAUß, W., Animal Physiology
DORRESTEIJN, A. W. CH., Zoology
EHRENHOFER-MURRAY, A. E., Cosmetics
EMMERMANN, R., Mineralogy
ESSER, G., Plant Ecology
FORCHHAMMER, K., Microbiology
FRANKE, W., Geology
FRÖBA, M., Inorganic Chemistry
GEBELEIN, H., Chemistry Teaching
HAACK, U., Mineralogy
HUGHES, J., Plant Physiology
IPAKTSCHI, J., Organic Chemistry
JÄGER, H.-J., Experimental Plant Ecology
JANEK, J., Physical Chemistry
KLEE, R., Biology Teaching
KLUG, G., Microbiology
KUNTER, M., Anthropology
KUNZE, C., Botany
LAKES-HARLAN, R., Sensory Physiology
MARTIN, M., Immunology
MAYER, J., Teaching of Biology
OVER, H., Physical Chemistry
PINGOUD, A., Biochemistry
RENKAWITZ, R., Genetics
SCHINDLER, S., Inorganic Chemistry
SCHREINER, P., Organic Chemistry
SCHULTE, E., Zoology
SPENGLER, B., Analytical Chemistry
TRENCZEK, M., Zoology
VOLAND, E., Philosophy
WAGNER, G., Botany
WIEKE, T., Zoology and Biodiversity
WOLTERS, V., Animal Ecology

Department of Economics (Licher Str. 74, 35394 Gießen; tel. (641) 99-22001; fax (641) 99-22009; e-mail dekanat@wirtschaft.uni-giessen.de):

ABERLE, G., General Economics, Price Theory, Industrial Organization and Competition Policy, Transport Economics
ALEXANDER, V., General Economics, Money, Credit and Currency
BESSLER, W., General Business Administration, Finance and Banking
ESCH, F.-R., General Business Administration, Marketing
GLAUM, M., Business Administration, International Management, Accounting and Auditing
HEMMER, H.-R., General Economics, Development Economics
KABST, R., General Business Administraion, Human Resource Management
KRÜGER, W., General Business Management, Organization, Leadership
MORLOCK, M., General Business Management, Risk Management and Insurance
MÜLLER, H., General Economics, Economics for Subsidiary Students, Environmental Economics
MECKL, H., General Economics, International Economics
RINNE, H., Statistics and Econometrics
SCHERF, W., General Economics, Public Finance
SCHWICKERT, A., General Business Administration, Computer Science in Business
SPENGEL, C., General Business Administration, Company Taxation
WEIßENBERGER, B., Business Administration, Management of Industrial Corporations, Controlling

Department of History and Cultural Studies (Otto-Behaghel-Str. 10, Haus G, 35394 Gießen; tel. (641) 99-28000; fax (641) 99-28009; e-mail dekanat@fb04.uni-giessen.de):

BÄUMER, F.-J., Religious Education Studies and Teaching of Religion
BAUMGARTNER, M., History of Art
CARL, H., Medieval and Modern History
EISEN, U., Bible Studies, Old Testament and New Testament
GOSEPATH, S., Practical Philosophy
GRÄB-SCHMIDT, E., Systematic Theology
HARTMANN, A., Islamic Studies
HAUSER, L., Systematic Theology
KIRCHNER, M., Turcology
KRASSER, H., Classical Philology
KURZ, W., Religion Lessons
LENGER, F., Medieval and Modern History
LEXUTT, A., History of the Church
MARTINI, W., Classical Archaeology
OSWALT, V., Teaching of History
VON MÖLLENDORFF, P., Greek Philology
OSWALT, V., History Teaching
PROSTMEIER, F., Bible Studies, New Testament
QUANDT, S., History Teaching
REINELE, C., German Regional History
REULECKE, J., Modern History
RÖSENER, W., Medieval and Modern History
SPEITKAMP, W., Modern History
SPICKERNAGEL, E., History of Art
TAMMEN, S., History of Art

Department of Human Medicine (Rudolf-Buchheim-Str. 6, 35392 Gießen; tel. (641)-99-48001; fax (641) 99-48009):

ALZEN, G., Paediatric Radiology
BAUER, R., Nuclear Medicine
BAUMGART-VOGT, E., Anatomy and Cellular Biology
BECK, E., Molecular Biology
BECKMANN, D., Medical Psychology
BEIN, G., Clinical Immunology and Transfusion Medicine
BÖKER, D.-K., Neurosurgery
BOHLE, R., Pathology
BRETZEL, R., Internal Medicine
CHAKRABORTY, T., Medical Microbiology
DREYER, F., Pharmacology and Toxicology
EIKMANN, T., Hygiene
ENGELHART-CABILLIC, R., Radiology
FERGER, D., Dentistry
FLEISCHER, G., Auditory Research
FRIEDRICH, R., Molecular Genetics and Virology
GALLHOFER, B., Psychiatry
GERLICH, W., Medical Virology
GEYER, R., Biochemistry
GIELER, U., Psychosomatics and Psychotherapy
GLANZ, H., Otorhinolaryngology
GRIMMINGER, F., Internal Medicine, Pneumology
HEMPELMANN, G., Anaesthesiology and Operative Intensive Medicine

HOWALDT, H.-P., Surgery of the Mouth, Jaws and Face
KAPS, M., Neurology
KATZ, N., Clinical Chemistry
KAUFMANN, H., Ophthalmology
KIESSLING, J., Audiology
KLIMEK, J., Dentistry
KOCKAPAN, C., Endodontics
KRAWINKEL, M., Paediatrics, Nutritional Science
KREUDER, J., Paediatrics
KUMMER, W., Anatomy and Cellular Biology
LINDEMANN, H., Paediatrics
LOHMEYER, J., Internal Medicine
MEINHARDT, A., Anatomy and Cellular Biology
MERSCH-SUNDERMANN, V., Indoor-air Toxicology and Environmental Toxicology
MEYLE, J., Paradontology
MIDDENDORFF, R., Anatomy and Cellular Biology
MÜLLER, U., Human Genetics
NEUBAUER, B., Paediatrics
PADBERG, W., Visceral, Thoracic and Transplantation Surgery
PANCHERZ, H. J., Dental Orthopaedics
PIPER, H. M., Physiology
PRALLE, H., Internal Medicine
PREISSNER, K., Biochemistry
RAU, W. S., Radiological Diagnostics
REIMER, C., Clinical Psychosomatics and Psychotherapy
REITER, A., Paediatric Haematology and Oncology
ROELCKE, V., History of Medicine
SAUER, H., Physiology
SCHACHENMAYR, W., Neuropathology
SCHÄFFER, R., Cytopathology
SCHILL, W.-B., Dermatology and Andrology
SCHLÜTER, K.-D., Physiology
SCHNETTLER, R., Accident Surgery
SCHRANZ, D., Paediatric Cardiology
SCHULZ, A., Pathology
SEEGER, W., Internal Medicine, Pneumology
SKRANDIES, W., Physiology
STÜRZ, H., Orthopaedics
TILLMANNS, H., Internal Medicine, Cardiology
TINNEBERG, H.-R., Gynaecology
TRAUPE, H., Neuroradiology
VOGT, P., Cardiology, Vascular Surgery
WEIDNER, W., Urology
WEILER, G., Forensic Medicine
WETZEL, W.-E., Paediatric Dentistry
WÖSTMANN, B., Gerodontology and Clinical Aspects of Dental Materials

Department of Language, Literature and Culture (Otto-Behaghel-Str. 10, Haus G, 35394 Gießen; tel. (641) 99-31001; fax (641) 99-31009):

BERSCHIN, H., Romance Linguistics
BORGMEIER, R., Modern English and American Literature
EHLER, S., Teaching of German Language and Literature
EHRISMANN, O., German Language, Historical Linguistics
FEIEKE, H., German Linguistics and Teaching of German Language
FINTER, H., Applied Theatre Studies
FLOECK, W., Spanish Literature
FRITZ, G., German Philology
GANSEL, C., Teaching of German Language and Literature
GAST, W., Teaching of German Language and Literature
GOEBBELS, H., Applied Theatre Studies
GRAF, A., Slavonic Literatures
HORSTMANN, U., Modern English and American Literature
KURZ, G., History of Modern German Literature
LEGUTKE, M., Teaching of English Language
LEIBFRIED, E., General Literature and History of Literature
LOBIN, H., Applied Linguistics and Computer Linguistics
MEISSNER, F.-J., Teaching of Romance Languages and Literature
MUKHERJEE, J., English Language
NÜNNING, A., English and American Literature and Cultural Studies
OESTERLE, G., Modern German Literature
PRINZ, M., Teaching of Romance Languages and Literature
RAMGE, H., German Linguistics
RIEGER, D., Romance Literature
RÖSLER, D., German as a Foreign Language
SEEL, M., Philosophy
STENZEL, H., Romance Literature and Cultural Studies
WINGENDER, M., Slavonic Linguistics
WINKELMANN, O., Romance Linguistics

Department of Law (Licher Str. 72, 35394 Gießen; tel. (641) 99-21000; fax (641) 99-21109; e-mail dekanat@fb01.uni-giessen.de):

BEHNICKE, C., Civil Law, Commercial Law, Comparative Law, International Civil Law
BRITZ, G., Public Law, European Law
BRYDE, B.-O., Public Law
EKKENGA, J., Civil Law, Commercial Law
GIESEN, R., Civil Law, Labour and Social Law
GROPP, W., Criminal Law, Criminal Procedural Law
GROSS, T., Public Law, Administrative Science
HAMMEN, H., Civil Law, Commercial Law
HECKER, B., Criminal Law, Criminal Procedural Law
KREUZER, A., Criminology, Juvenile Criminal Law
LANGE, K., Public Law, Administration Teaching
LIPP, M., German Legal History and Civil Law
MARAUHN, T., Public Law, International Public Law, European Law
SCHAPP, J., Civil Law and Philosophy of Law
WALKER, W.-D., Civil Law, Labour Law, Civil Procedural Law
WOLFSLAST, G., Criminal Law, Criminal Procedural Law

Department of Mathematics and Information Studies, Physics, Geography (Heinrich-Buff-Ring 16, 35392 Gießen; tel. (641) 99-33000; fax (641) 99-33009):

BARTSCH, T., Analysis
BAUMANN, B., Mathematics, Algebra
BEUTELSPACHER, A., Mathematics, Geometry
BUHMANN, M., Numerical Mathematics
BUNDE, A., Theoretical Physics
CASSING, W., Theoretical Physics
DÜREN, M., Experimental Physics
FELIX-HENNINGSEN, P., Soil Science, Land Conservation
FENSKE, C., Mathematics
FRANKE, M., Teaching of Mathematics
GIESE, E., Economic Geography
HÄUSLER, E. K., Stochastics
HAVERSATH, J. B., Teaching of Geography
HERMANN, G., Experimental Physics
KANITSCHEIDER, B., Philosophy of Natural Sciences
KING, L., Geography
KOHL, C.-D., Applied Physics
KÜHN, W., Experimental Physics
METAG, V., Experimental Physics
METSCH, K., Mathematics Geometry
MEYER, B., Experimental Physics
MOSEL, U., Theoretical Physics
MÜLLER, A., Experimental Physics
OVERBECK, L., Mathematics
PROFKE, L., Didactics of Mathematics
SALZBORN, E., Nuclear Physics
SAUER, T., Numerical Mathematics
SCHEID, W., Theoretical Physics
SCHLETTWEIN, D., Applied Physics
SCHOLZ, U., Geography
SCHWARZ, G., Teaching of Physics
SEIFERT, V., Geography
STUTE, W., Mathematical Statistics
TIMMESFELD, F. G., Mathematics, Algebra
WALTHER, H.-O., Mathematics, Analysis
WERLE, O., Didactics of Geography

Department of Psychology and Sport (Otto-Behaghel-Str. 10, Haus F1, 35394 Gießen; tel. (641) 99-26000; fax (641) 99-26009; e-mail dekanat@fb06.uni-giessen.de):

BORG, I., Applied Psychological Methods
BRUNNSTEIN, J., Educational Psychology
ENNEMOSER, M., Special Educational Psychology
FRESE, M., Work and Organizational Psychology
GEGENFURTNER, K., General and Experimental Psychology
GLOWALLA, U., Educational Psychology
HALDER-SINN, P., Psychological Diagnosis
HENNIG, J., Differential Psychology
MUNZERT, J., Sports Psychology
NEUMANN, H., Sport and Training
PROBST, H., Special Educational Psychology
SPORER, S., Social Psychology
SCHUSTER, C., Psychological Methodology
SCHWARZER, G., Developmental Psychology
SCHWIER, J., Sport and Teaching of Sport
STIENSMEIER-PELSTER, J., Educational Psychology

Department of Social and Cultural Studies (Karl-Glöckner-Str. 21, Haus E/B, 35394 Gießen; tel. (641) 99-23001; fax (641) 99-23009; e-mail dekan@fb03.uni-giessen.de; internet www.uni-giessen.de/fb03):

BIRCKENBACH-WELLMANN, H.-M., Political Science, European Studies
BULLERJAHN, C., Political Science, European Studies
CLAUS-BACHMANN, M., Music
DUBIEL, H., Sociology
DUNCKER, L., Educational Science
EBERS, A., Comparative Health and Social Policy
ECARIUS, J., Educational Science
FORNECK, H., Educational Science
FRITZSCHE, K., Political Science
GRONEMEYER, R., Sociology
HOFMANN, C., Educational Science
HOLLAND-CUNZ, B., Political Science, Gender Studies
KREBS, D., Empirical Research in Social Sciences
LEGGEWIE, C., Political Science
LIPPITZ, W., Philosophy of Education, Comparative Studies of Education
MOSER, V., Educational Science
NECKEL, S., Sociology
NITSCHE, P., Music
PHLEPS, T., Music
REIMANN, B., Sociology
RICHTER-REICHENBACH, K.-S., Teaching of Art
SANDER, W., Teaching of Social Sciences
SCHMIDT, P., Empirical Social Research
SCHWANDER, M., Educational Science
SEIDELMANN, R., Political Science, International Relations
SPICKERNAGEL, E., History of Art
STACHOWIAK, F., Educational Science
STANICZEK, J., Art Practice
STÖPPLER, R., Educational Science
WILLEMS, H., Microsociology and Qualitative Methods
WISSINGER, J., Educational Science

Department of Veterinary Medicine (Frankfurter Str. 74, 35392 Gießen; tel. (641) 99-38001; fax (641) 99-38009; e-mail dekanat@vetmed.uni-giessen.de):

BALJER, G., Infectious Diseases and Hygiene
BAUERFEIND, R., Control of Epidemics
BERGMANN, M., Veterinary Anatomy, Histology and Embryology
BOSTEDT, H., Physiology and Pathology of Reproduction
BÜLTE, M., Veterinary Nutrition
CLAUß, W., Animal Physiology
DIENER, M., Veterinary Physiology
DOLL, K., Diseases of Ruminants
EISGRUBER, H., Hygiene of Food of Animal Origin and Consumer Protection
ERHARDT, G., Animal Breeding and Genetics of Domestic Animals
GERSTBERGER, R., Veterinary Physiology
HOFFMANN, B., Physiology and Pathology of Reproduction
KALETA, E., Diseases and Hygiene of Poultry
KÖLLE, S., Veterinary Anatomy, Histology and Embryology
KRAMER, M., Small Animal Surgery
KRESSIN, M., Veterinary Anatomy, Histology and Embryology
LEISER, R., Veterinary Anatomy, Histology and Embryology
LITZKE, L.-F., Equine Surgery
MORITZ, A., Internal Medicine
NEIGER, R., Small Animal Internal Medicine
PETZINGER, E. D., Pharmacology and Toxicology
REINACHER, M., Pathology
REINER, G., Department of Swine Diseases (Internal Medicine and Surgery)
RÜMENAPF, T., Clinical Virology
THIEL, H.-J., Virology
USLEBER, E., Milk Science
WENGLER, G., Virology and Cellular Biology
WÜRBEL, H., Animal Welfare and Ethology
ZAHNER, H., Parasitology

GEORG-AUGUST-UNIVERSITÄT GÖTTINGEN

37073 Göttingen
Telephone: (551) 390
Fax: (551) 399612
E-mail: pressestelle@uni-goettingen.de
Internet: www.uni-goettingen.de

Founded 1737
Academic year: October to July
President: Prof. Dr KURT VON FIGURA
Vice-Presidents: Prof. Dr REINER KREE, Prof. Dr DORIS LEMMERMÖHLE, Prof. Dr JOACHIM MÜNCH
Librarian: Prof. Dr ELMAR MITTLER
Number of teachers: 800
Number of students: 23,000
Publications: *Georgia-Augusta* (2 a year), *Jahresforschungsbericht* (every 2 years), *Spektrum* (4 a year)

DEANS

Faculty of Agriculture: Prof. Dr RAINER MARGGRAF
Faculty of Biology: Prof. Dr THOMAS RAMMSAYER
Faculty of Chemistry: Prof. Dr ULF DIEDERICHSEN
Faculty of Earth Sciences: Prof. Dr WERNER KREISEL
Faculty of Economics: Prof. Dr LOTHAR SCHRUFF
Faculty of Forestry: Prof. Dr REINER FINKELDEY
Faculty of Law: Prof. Dr VOLKER LIPP
Faculty of Mathematics: Prof. Dr INA \KERSTEN
Faculty of Medicine: Prof. Dr CORNELIUS FRÖMMEL
Faculty of Philosophy: Prof. Dr EBERHARD WINKLER
Faculty of Physics: Prof. Dr RAINER G. ULBRICH
Faculty of Social Sciences: Prof. Dr MARGRET KRAUL
Faculty of Theology: Prof. Dr HERMANN SPIEKERMANN

ERNST-MORITZ-ARNDT-UNIVERSITÄT GREIFSWALD

Baderstr. 1, 17487 Greifswald
Telephone: (3834) 86-1150
Fax: (3834) 86-1151
E-mail: rektor@uni-greifswald.de
Internet: www.uni-greifswald.de

Founded 1456
Academic year: October to September
Chancellor: Dr THOMAS BEHRENS
Rector: Prof. Dr rer.nat. RAINER WESTERMANN
Pro-Rectors: Prof. Dr CLAUS DIETER CLASSEN, Prof. Dr med. OTTO-ANDREAS FESTGE
Librarian: Dr PETER WOLFF
Number of teachers: 235
Number of students: 8,200
Publications: *Greifswalder Universitätsreden* (irregular), *Wissenschaftliche Beiträge* (irregular)

DEANS

Faculty of Law and Economics: Prof. Dr rer. pol. ROLAND ROLLBERG
Faculty of Mathematics and Natural Sciences: Prof. Dr rer. nat. KLAUS FESSER
Faculty of Medicine: Prof. Dr rer. nat. HEYO K. KROEMER
Faculty of Philosophy: Prof. Dr soz. wiss. MANFRED BORNEWASSER
Faculty of Theology: Prof. Dr theol. CHRISTFRIED BÖTTRICH

MARTIN LUTHER-UNIVERSITÄT HALLE-WITTENBERG

Universitätsplatz 10, 06099 Halle (Saale)
Telephone: (345) 552-0
Fax: (345) 552-7077
E-mail: rektor@uni-halle.de
Internet: www.uni-halle.de

Founded 1502 (Wittenberg), 1694 (Halle), 1817 (Halle-Wittenberg)
Academic year: October to September
Rector: Prof. Dr WILFRIED GRECKSCH
Number of teachers: 340
Number of students: 18,500
Publication: *Scientia halensis* (4 a year).

UNIVERSITÄT HAMBURG

Edmund-Siemers-Allee 1, 20146 Hamburg
Telephone: (40) 42838-0
Fax: (40) 42838-2449
E-mail: presse@rrz.uni-hamburg.de
Internet: www.uni-hamburg.de

Founded 1919
State control
Academic year: October to July
President: Dr Dr h.c. JÜRGEN LUTHJE
Vice-Presidents: Prof. Dr HOLGER FISCHER, Prof. Dr KARL-WERNER HANSMANN
Chief Administrative Officer: MANFRED NETTEKOVEN
Director for International Affairs: Dr JOCHEN HELLMANN
State and University Librarian: Prof. Dr PETER RAU
Number of teachers: 3,172
Number of students: 40,996

DEANS

Department of Biology: Prof. Dr ARNO FRÜHWALD
Department of Chemistry: Prof. Dr JOACHIM THIEM
Department of Computer Science: Prof. Dr H. SIEGFRIED STIEHL
Department of Cultural History and Science: Prof. Dr BRUNO REUDENBACH
Department of Earth Sciences: Prof. Dr HELMUT SCHLEICHER
Department of Economic Sciences: Prof. Dr LOTHAR STREITFERDT
Department of Education: Prof. Dr KARL-DIETER SCHUCK
Department of History and Philosophy: Prof. Dr JÜRGEN SARNOWSKY
Department of Language, Literature and Media Studies: Prof. Dr KNUT HICKETHIER
Department of Law: Prof. Dr KARL-HEINZ LADEUR
Department of Mathematics: Prof. Dr ALEXANDER KREUZER
Department of Medicine: Prof. Dr CHRISTOPH WAGENER
Department of Oriental Studies and Asia–Africa Institute: Prof. Dr RAINER CARLE
Department of Physics: Prof. Dr GÜNTER HUBER
Department of Physical Education: Prof. Dr K. MICHAEL BRAUMANN
Department of Protestant Theology: Prof. Dr STEFAN TIMM
Department of Psychology: Prof. Dr BERNHARD DAHME
Department of Social Sciences: Prof. Dr MICHAEL GREVEN

PROFESSORS

Department of Biology (Allende-Platz 2, 20146 Hamburg; tel. (40) 42838-0; fax (40) 42838-7025):

ABRAHAM, R., Entomology
ADAM, G., Phytopathology
BAUCH, J., Timber Biology
BEUSMANN, V., Biotechnics, Society and Environment
BOCK, E., General Microbiology
BÖTTGER, M., General Botany
BRANDT, A., Zoology
BRETTING, H., Zoology
BUCHHOLZ, F.
CHOPRA, V., Anthropology
DREYLING, G., Applied Botany
ECKSTEIN, D., Timber Biology
FLEISCHER, A., Work Science
FORTNAGEL, P., Botany
FRÜHWALD, A., Mechanical Processing of Timber
GANZHORN, J., Zoology
GEWECKE, M., Zoology, Animal Physiology
GIERE, O., Zoology
GRIMM, R., Zoology
HAHN, H., Zoology, Ecology
HARTMANN, H., Systematic Botany
HEINZ, E., Botany
HEUVELDOP, J., International Forest Management
KAUSCH, H., Hydrobiology
JÜRGENS, N., Biological Systems, Plant Evolution
KIES, L., General Botany
KRISTEN, U., General Botany
LIEBEREI, R., Phytopathology
LÖRZ, H., Applied Plant Molecular Biology
MANTAU, U., Economics of Forestry
MERGENHAGEN, D., Cell Biology
MÜHLBACH, H.-P., Molecular Genetics
PARZEFALL, J., Zoology
PATT, R., Chemical Timber Technology
PRATJE, E., General Botany
REISE, K., Heligoland Biological Institute
RENWRANTZ, L., Zoology

RESSEL, J., Wood Physics
RODEWALD, A., Anthropology and Human Genetics
SCHÄFER, W., Biology
SCHURIG, V.
STAHL-BISKUP, E., Pharmaceutical Biology
TEMMING, A., Fisheries Sciences
WEBER, A., General Botany
WIENAND, U., General Botany
WIESE, K., Neurophysiology
WILKENS, H., Zoology
ZEISKE, E., Zoology

Department of Chemistry (Martin-Luther-King-Platz 6, 20146 Hamburg; tel. (40) 42838-0; fax (40) 42838-2893):

BASLER, W. D.
BEIER, U., Home Economics
BENNDORF, C., Physical Chemistry
BISPING, B., Food Microbiology and Hygiene
BREDEHORST, R., Biochemistry
DEPPERT, W., Molecular Biochemistry
DUCHSTEIN, H.-J., Pharmaceutical Chemistry
FÖRSTER, S., Physical and Macromolecular Chemistry
FRANCKE, W., Organic Chemistry
GEFFKEN, D., Pharmaceutical Chemistry
HECK, J., Inorganic Chemistry
HEISIG, P., Pharmaceutical Biology, Microbiology
KAMINSKY, W., Inorganic Chemistry
KERSCHER, M., Personal Hygiene
KÖNIG, W., Organic Chemistry
KRAMOLOWSKY, R., Inorganic Chemistry
KRICHELDORF, H., Applied Chemistry
KULICKE, W., Technical Chemistry
LECHERT, H., Physical Chemistry
MARGARETHA, P., Organic Chemistry
MEIER, C., Organic Chemistry
MEYER, B., Organic Chemistry
MIELCK, J., Pharmaceutical Technology
MORITZ, H.-U., Technical and Macromolecular Chemistry
MÜHLHAUSER, I., Health
REHDER, D., Inorganic Chemistry
STAHL-BISKUP, E., Pharmaceutical Biology
STEINHART, J., Food Chemistry
THIEM, J., Organic Chemistry
THORN, E., Technical and Macromolecular Chemistry
WELLER, H., Electrochemistry

Department of Computer Sciences (Vogt-Kölln-Straße 30, 22527 Hamburg; tel. (40) 42883-0; fax (40) 42838-2206):

BRUNNSTEIN, K., Computer Applications
DRESCHLER-FISCHER, L., Cognitive Systems
FLOYD, C., Software Technics
FREKSA, C.
HABEL, C., Information and Documentation
HAHN, W. VON, Natural Language Systems
HEIDE, K. VON DER, Technical Basics of Computer Science
JANTZEN, M., Computer Theory
KAISER, K., Computer Applications
KUDLEK, M., Computer Theory
LAMERSDORF, W., Technical Basics of Computer Science
MENZEL, W.
MERTSCHING, B.
MÖLLER, D.
NEUMANN, B., Cognitive Systems
OBERQUELLE, H., Computer Theory
PAGE, B., Computer Applications
ROLF, A., Computer Theory
SCHEFE, P., Computer Applications
STIEHL, H.-S., Cognitive Systems
VALK, R., Computer Theory
WOLFINGER, B., Computer Organization
ZÜLLIGHOVEN, H.

Department of Cultural History and Cultural Science (Rothenbaumchaussee 67/69, 20148 Hamburg; tel. (40) 42838-4051; fax (40) 42838-6530):

ALTENMÜLLER, H., Egyptology
DÖMLING, W., Music
FEHR, B., Classical Archaeology
GREEVE, B., Music
HENGAUTNER, T., Folklore
HIPP, H., History of Art
KEMP, W., Art History
KOKOT, W., Ethnology
KURTH, D., Egyptology
LANG, H., Ethnology
LEHMANN, A., German Archaeology and Folklore
MISCHUNG, B., Ethnology
NIELSEN, I., Classical Archaeology
PETERSEN, P., Musicology
REUDENBACH, B., Art History
RÖSING, H., Systematic Music
ROLLE, R., Prehistory of Europe
SCHNEIDER, A., Systematic Music
SMAILUS, O., Ancient American Languages and Culture
WAGNER, M., Art History
WARNKE, M., History of Art

Department of Earth Sciences (Bundesstraße 55, 20146 Hamburg; tel. (40) 42838-5230; fax (40) 42838-5270):

BACKHAUS, J., Oceanography
BANDEL, K., Palaeontology and Historic Geology
BETZLER, C., Geology
BISMAYER, U., Mineralogy, Crystallography
BRÜMMER, B., Meteorology
DAHM, T.
FRAEDRICH, K, Meteorology
GAJEWSKI, D., Geophysics
GRASSL, H., Meteorology
GRIMMEL, E., Geography
GUSE, W., Mineralogy
HILLMER, G., Geology and Palaeontology
JASCHKE, D., Geography
LAFRENZ, J., Geography
LEUPOLT, B., Geography
MAKRIS, J., Geophysics
MEINCKE, J., Regional Oceanography
MICHAELIS, W., Organic Geochemistry
MIEHLICH, G., Soil Science
NAGEL, F. N., Geography
OSSENBRÜGGE, J., Geography
POHL, D., Mineralogy
RASCHKE, E., Meteorology
REUTHER, C.-D., Geology
ROSSMANITH, E., Mineralogy
SCHATZMANN, M., Meteorology
SCHLEICHER, H., Mineralogy, Petrography
SCHWARZ, R., Geography
SPAETH, CH., Geology and Palaeontology
SPIELMANN, H.-O., Geography
SÜNDERMANN, J., Oceanography
TARKIAN, M., Mineralogy
THANNHEISER, D., Geography
TIETZ, G. F., Sedimentary Petrography
TOL, R. S., Sustaining the Environment
VINX, R., Mineralogy
WONG, H. K., Geology
ZAHEL, W., Oceanography

Department of Economic Sciences (Von-Melle-Park 5, 20146 Hamburg; tel. (40) 42838-0; fax (40) 42838-6322):

ADAMS, M., Economic Law
ALTROGGE, G., Business Administration
ARNOLD, B., National Economy
CZERANOWSKY, G., Business Administration
ENGELHARDT, G., National Economy
FREIDANK, C.-C., Business Administration, Auditing Taxation
FUNKE, M., National Economy
GROTHERR, S., Business Administration
HANSEN, K., Business Administration
HANSMANN, K.-W., Business Administration
HASENKAMP, G., National Economy
HAUTAU, H., National Economy
HESBERG, D.
HOFMANN, H., National Economy
HOLLER, M., National Economy
HUMMELTENBERG, W., Business Administration
KRAUSE-JUNG, G., International Finance
KÜPPER, W., Business Administration
LAYER, M., Business Administration
LORENZEN, G., National Economy
LUCKE, B., National Economy
MAENNIG, W., National Economy
NELL, M., Insurance
OEHSEN, J. H. VON, Finance
PFÄHLER, W., National Economy
PRESSMAR, D., Business Administration
REITSPERGER, W. D., Business Administration
RIETER, H., National Economy
RINGLE, G., Business Administration
SATTLER, H., Business Administration
SCHÄFER, H.-B., National Economy
SCHEER, C., Finance
SCHLITTGEN, R., National Economy, Statistics
SCHMIDT, H., Business Administration
SEELBACH, H., Business Administration
STAHLECKER, H.-P., National Economy, Statistics
STOBER, R., Economic Law
STRAUBHAAR, T.
STREITFERDT, L., Business Administration
TIMMERMANN, V., National Economy
TOL, R. (Endowed Chair, Sustaining the Environment)
WEGSCHEIDER, K., National Economy, Statistics

Department of Education (Von-Melle-Park 8, 20146 Hamburg; tel. (40) 42838-0; fax (40) 42838-2112):

AUFENANGER, S.
BASTIAN, J.
BECK, I.
BOLLMANN, H.
VON BORRIES, B.
BOS, W.
BRAND, W.
BRUSCH, W.
BÜRGER, W.
BUTH, M.
CLAUßEN, B.
COMBE, A.
DECKE-CORNILL, H.
DEGENHART, S.
DEHN, M.
DUISMANN, G.
EHNI, H. W.
FAULSTICH, P.
FAULSTICH-WIELAND, H.
FIEDLER, U.
FILIPP, K.
GEBHARD, U.
GOGOLIN, I.
GRAMMES, T.
GRENZ, D.
GUDJONS, H.
GÜNTHER, K.-R.
HARTER-MEYER, R.
HARTMANN, W.
HEMMER, K.
HOFSÄSS, T.
JUNG, H. W.
KAISER, G.
KAISER, H.-J.
KIPP, M.
KLEIN, P.
KOKEMOHR, R.
KOLLER, H.-C.
KRAUTHAUSEN, G.
KRETSCHMER, J.
KÜNNE, W.
LECKE, B.

LEGLER, W.
LOHMANN, I.
MARTENS, E.
MAYER, C.
MEYER, H.
MEYER, M.
MIELKE, R.
MITCHELL, G.
NEUMANN, U.
NEVERS, P.
NOLTE, M.
OPASCHOWSKI, H.
PAZZINI, K.-J.
PETERSEN, J.
RAUER, W.
RENZELBERG, G.
RICHTER, H.
ROTHWEILER, M.
SCARBATH, H.
SCHÄFER, H.-P.
SCHENK, B.
SCHERLER, K.
SCHREIER, H.
SCHUCK, K. D.
SEYD, W.
SPRETH, G.
STRUCK, P.
STRUVE, K.
STÜTZ, G.
TENFELDE, W.
TRAMM, T.
VOLLMER, T.
WAGNER, A.
WALLRABENSTEIN, W.
WARZECHA, B.
WEICHERT, W.
WEISSE, W.
WELLING, A.
WILLENBERG, H.
WIMMER, K.-M.
WOCKEN, H.
WUDTKE, H.
ZIMPEL, A.

Department of History and Philosophy (Rothenbaumchaussee 67/69, 20148 Hamburg; tel. (40) 42838-4049; fax (40) 42838-6333):

ANGERMANN, N., Medieval and Modern History
BARTUSCHAT, W., Philosophy
CLEMENS, G., Modern European History (Western European Integration)
DEININGER, J., Ancient History
DIEDERICH, W., Philosophy
DINGEL, J., Classical Philology
EIDENEIER, H., Byzantine and Modern Greek Philology
FINZSCH, N., Modern and North American History
FREDE, D., Philosophy
GÄHDE, U., Philosophy
GALL, D., Classical Philology
GOETZ, H.-W., Medieval and Modern History
GOLCZEWSKI, F., Eastern European History
HALFMANN, H., Ancient History
HARLFINGER, D., Classical Philology
HERGEMÖLLER, B.-U., Medieval History
HERZIG, A., Modern History
KÜNNE, W., Philosophy
MEJCHER, H., Modern History
MOLTHAGEN, J., Ancient History
PIETSCHMANN, H., Modern History
RECKI, B., Philosophy
SARNOWSKY, V., Medieval History
STEINVORTH, U., Philosophy
VOGEL, B., Modern History

Department of Language, Literature and Media Studies (Rothenbaumchaussee 67/69, 20148 Hamburg; tel. (40) 42838-0; fax (40) 42838-5977):

BERG, T., English Linguistics
BLESSIN, S., German Literature, German as a Foreign Language
BÖRNER, W., Linguistics
BRAUNMÜLLER, K., Germanic Philology
BRINKER, K., German Linguistics
BUNGARTEN, T., German Linguistics
CORTHALS, J., Comparative Language Studies
DAMMANN, G., German Literature
DIEWALD, G., German Linguistics
EDMONDSON, W., Language Instruction Research
FISCHER, L., German Literature
FISCHER, R., German Sign Language
FREYTAG, H., German Philology
FREYTAG, W., German Literature
FRIEDL, B., American Studies
GREINER, N., English Literature
GUTJAHR, O., Modern German Literature
GUTKNECHT, C., English Language
HABEL, C., Language Processing
HAHN, W. VON, Natural Language Systems
HARTENSTEIN, K., Russian
HASEBRINK, E., Empirical Communications Science
HELIMEKI, E., Finno-Ugrian Philology
HENKEL, N., German Philology
HENNIG, J., German Linguistics
HICKETHIER, K., German Literature
HILL, P., Slavonic Philology
HODEL, R., Slavonic Philology
HOTTENROTH, P.-M., French and Italian Linguistics
HOUSE, J., Language Instruction Research
HÜHN, P., English Philology
IBANEZ, R., Hispanic Linguistics
KÖSTER, U., German Literature
LATOUR, B., German as a Foreign Language
LEHMANN, V., Language Instruction Research
LLEO, C., Hispanic Linguistics
MEIER, J., German Linguistics
MEISEL, J. M., Romance Philology
MEYER, W., Romance Philology
MEYER-ALTHOFF, M.
MEYER-MINNEMANN, K., Romance Philology
MÜLLER, H.-H., German Literature
NEUMANN, M., Romance Philology
PANTHER, K.-U., English Linguistics
PÉTURSSON, M., General Applied Phonetics
PRESCH, G., German Linguistics
PRILLWITZ, S., German Linguistics
REHBEIN, J., German Linguistics, German as a Foreign Language
REICHARDT, D., Romance Philology
REINITZER, H., German Literature
RODENBURG, H.-P., American Studies
SAGER, S., German Linguistics
SCHLUMBOHM, D., Romance Philology
SCHMID, W., Slavonic Literature
SCHMIDT, J., English Philology
SCHMIDT-KNÄBEL, S., German Linguistics
SCHÖBERL, J., German Literature
SCHÖNERT, J., German Literature
SCHÖPP, J. K., American Studies
SCHULLER, M., German Literature
SCHULMEISTER, R., Higher School Didactics
SCHULTZE, B., English Philology
SEGEBERG, H., German Literature
SETTEKORN, W., French
TERNES, E., Phonetics
TRAPP, F., Modern German Literature
VINKEN, B., Romance Philology
VOIGT, B., Spanish
WERGIN, U., Modern German Literature
WINTER, H.-G., German Literature
WITTSCHIER, H. W., Romance Philology

Department of Law (Rothenbaumchaussee 41, 20148 Hamburg; tel. (40) 42838-0; fax (40) 42838-6352):

BEHRENS, P., Civil, Commercial and International Private Law
BORK, R., Civil, Commercial, Economic and International Private Law
BRUHA, T., Public, European and International Law
BULL, H. P., Constitutional and Administrative Law
FELIX, D., Public and Social Law
FEZER, G., Criminal Law
FROTSCHER, G., International Financial and Taxation Law
GIEHRING, H., Criminal Law
HAAG, F., Sociology
HANSEN, U., Criminal Law
HILF, M., Public, European and International Law
HIRTE, H., Public, Commercial and Business Law
HOFFMANN-RIEM, W., Public, Administrative, Revenue and Tax, and Economic Law
JACHMANN, M., Public, Financial and Taxation Law
JOOST, D., Civil and Labour Law
KARPEN, U., Public Law
KELLER, R., Criminal Law
KOCH, H.-J., Public Law, Philosophy of Law
KÖHLER, M., Criminal Law, Philosophy of Law
KRIECHBAUM, M., Roman Law
LADEUR, K.-H., Public Law
LAGONI, R., Public, Maritime, International and Constitutional Law
LUCHTERHANDT, O., Public and Eastern Law
LÜDICKE, J., International Financial and Taxation Law
MAGNUS, U., Civil Law
MANKOWSKI, P., Civil, Comparative and International Private and Procedural Law
MARTENS, K. P., Civil, Labour and Commercial Law
MERKEL, R., Criminal Law, Philosophy of Law
MORITZ, K., Civil and Labour Law, Sociology of Law
OETER, S., Public, International and European Law
OTT, C., Sociology of Law, Civil, Commercial and Company, and Economic Law
PASCHKE, M., Civil, Commercial and Economic Law
PFARR, H., Civil and Labour Law
RAMSAUER, U., Public Law
RANDZIO, R., Civil Law
RITTSTIEG, H., Public Law
SCHÄFER, H.-B., National Economy
SCHEERER, S., Criminology
SCHWABE, J., Public Law
SESSAR, K., Criminology and Juvenile Criminal Law
SONNEN, B.-R., Criminal Law
STOBER, R., Economic Law
STRUCK, G., Civil Law
VILLMOW, B., Criminology
WALZ, R., Commercial, Economic, Civil and Tax Law
WERBER, M., Civil and Insurance Law

Department of Mathematics (Bundesstraße 55, 20146 Hamburg; tel. (40) 42838-4106; fax (40) 42838-4927):

ANDREAE, T.
BANDELT, H.-J.
BÄR, C.
BERNDT, R.
BRÜCKNER, H.
DADUNA, H.
DIESTEL, R.
ECKHARDT, U.
GEIGER, C.
HASS, R.
HOFMANN, W. D.
HÜBNER, G.
HÜNEMÖRDER, C.
KRÄMER, H.
KREMER, E.
KREUZER, A.
LAUTERBACH,

MICHALICEK, J.
MÜLLER, H.
NEUHAUS, G.
OBERLE, H. J.
ORTLIEB, C.
REICH, K.
RIEMENSCHNEIDER, O.
SCHRÖDER, E.
SEIER, W.
STRADE, H.
STRUCKMEIER, J.
TAUBERT, K.
WERNER, B.
WOLFSCHMIDT, G.

Department of Medicine (Universitätsklinikum Hamburg-Eppendorf, Martinistr. 52, 20246 Hamburg; tel. (40) 42803-0; fax (40) 42803-6752):

ADAM, G., X-ray Diagnosis
AGARWAL, D., Human Genetics
ALBERTI, W., Radiotherapy
BAISCH, H., Biophysics
BAUR, X., Industrial Medicine
BECK, H., Anaesthesiology
BEIL, F. U., Internal Medicine
BEISIEGEL, U., Biochemistry
BENTELE, K., Paediatrics
BERGER, J., Mathematics and Computer Applications of Medicine
BERGER, M., Child Psychology
BERNER, W., Psychiatry
BÖGER, R., Clinical Pharmacology
BOHUSLAVIZKI, H., Nuclear Medicine
BRAENDLE, L.-W., Gynaecology and Obstetrics
BRAULKE, T., Pathophysiology and Molecular Biological Genetic Health
BRAUMANN, K.-M., Internal-Physiological Sports Medicine
BROMM, B., Physiology
BULLINGER, M., Medical Psychology
BURDELSKI, M., Paediatrics
BUSSCHE, H. VAN DEN, Didactics
CLAUSEN, M., Nuclear Medicine
DALLEK, M., Surgery, Accident Surgery
DAVIDOFF, M., Anatomy
DELLING, G., General Pathology and Pathological Anatomy
DENEKE, F.-W., Psychosomatic Medicine
DÖRING, V., Surgery
DRIESCH, P., Dermatology and Venereology
EHMKE, H., Physiology
EIERMANN, T., Transfusion Medicine
ENGELMANN, K., Ophthalmology
FEUCHT, H.-H., Medical Microbiology and Immunology
FIEDLER, W., Internal Medicine
FLEISCHER, B., Immunology, Virology
GAL, A., Medical Genetics
GÖTZE, P., Psychiatry
GRETEN, H., Internal Medicine
HALATA, Z., Anatomy
HAND, I., Psychiatry
HEGEWISCHE-BECKER, S., Internal Medicine
HELLWEGE, H., Paediatrics
HELMCHEN, U., Pathology
HESS, M., Otorhinolaryngology
HÖHNE, K.-H., Information and Data Processing in Medicine
HÖLTJE, W.-J., Maxillary Surgery
HORSTMANN, R., Internal Medicine
HOSSFELD, D., Internal Medicine
HÜBENER, K.-H., Radiology
HULAND, H., Urology
HUNEKE, A., Gynaecology and Obstetrics
IZBICKI, J., Surgery
JÄNICKE, F. K.-H., Gynaecology and Obstetrics
JANKE-SCHAUB, G., Paediatrics
JENTSCH, T., Cell Biology
JÜDE, H. D., Dental Medicine
JUNG, H., Biophysics and Radiobiology
KAHL-NIEKE, B., Orthodontics
KAULFERS, P.-M., Medical Microbiology
KAUPEN-HAAS, H., Medical Sociology
KOCH, U., Otorhinolaryngology
KOCH-GROMUS, U., Medical Psychology
KOHLSCHÜTTER, A., Paediatrics
KOLLEK, R., Biotechnology
KORTH, M., Pharmacology
KRAUSZ, M., Psychiatry
KREYMANN, K. G., Internal Medicine
KRUPPA, J., Physiological Chemistry
KRUSE, H.-P., Internal Medicine
KÜHNL, P., Transfusions, Immuno-Haematology
LAMBRECHT, W., Surgery
LAUFS, R., Medical Microbiology and Immunology
LEICHTWEISS, H.-P., Physiology
LEUWER, R., Otorhinolaryngology
LOCKEMANN, U., Legal Medicine
LÖNING, T., General Pathology, Pathological Anatomy
MACK, D., Medical Microbiology, Infection Epidemiology and Hospital Hygiene
MANGOLD, U., Anatomy
MARQUARDT, H., General Toxicology
MAYR, G. W., Physiological Chemistry
MEINERTZ, T., Cardiology
MESTER, J., Nuclear Medicine
MOLL, I., Dermatology, Venereology
MÜHLHAUSER, I., Health
MÜLLER, D., Neurosurgery
MÜLLER-WIEFEL, D. E., Internal Medicine
MUNZEL, T., Internal Medicine
NABER, D., Psychiatry
NEUBER, K., Dermatology and Venereology
NEUMAIER, M., Clinical Chemistry
NOLDUS, J., Neurology
PANTEL, K., Molecular Genetics in Gynaecological Ontomology
PAUS, R., Dermatology and Venereology
PFEIFFER, E., Hygiene
PFEIFFER, G., Neurology
PFORTE, A., Internal Medicine
PLATZER, U., Dentistry
PONGS, O., Neurology
PÜSCHEL, U., Forensic Medicine
RICHARD, G., Ophthalmology
RICHTER, D., Physiological Chemistry
RICHTER, R., Medical Psychology, Psychosomatics
RIEDESSER, P., Paediatric Psychology
ROGIERS, X., Surgery
ROTHER, U., Radiological Diagnostics on Dental Medicine
RUDAT, T., Radiotherapy
RUEGER, J. M., Accident Surgery
RUMBERGER, E., Physiology
RUTHER, K., Ophthalmology
RUTHER, W., Orthopaedics
SCHÄFER, H., General Pathology and Pathological Anatomy
SCHALLER, C., Neurobiology
SCHIFFNER, U., Dental Medicine
SCHMALE, H., Biochemistry
SCHMELZLE, R., Dental Medicine
SCHMIDT, G., Sexology
SCHMOLDT, A., Forensic Medicine
SCHACHNER CAMARTIN, M., Neurobiology
SCHNEPPENHEIM, R., Paediatric Haematology and Oncology
SCHOLZ, H., Pharmacology and Toxicology
SCHRÖDER, H. J., Physiology
SCHULTE AM ESCH, J., Anaesthesiology
SCHULTE-MARKWORT, M., Child and Youth Psychiatry
SCHULZE, C., Anatomy
SCHULZE, W., Anatomy
SCHUMACHER, U., Anatomy
SCHWARZ, J., Physiology
SCHWORM, H. D., Ophthalmology
SEITZ, H.-J., Physiological Chemistry
SOEHENDRA, N., Surgery
STAHL, R., Internal Medicine
STANDL, T., Anaesthesiology
STAVROU, D., Neuropathology
STEINER, P., Radiology
STRÄTLING, W., Physiological Chemistry
TANNICH, E., Molecular Parasitology
THAISS, F., Internal Medicine
TROJAN, A., Social Medicine
ULLRICH, K. H. O., Paediatrics
UßMULLER, J., Otorhinolaryngology
VONDERLAGE, M., Physiology
WAGENER, C., Clinical Chemistry
WEIL, J., Paediatric Cardiology
WEILLER, C., Neurology
WESTENDORF, J., Toxicology, Pharmacology
WIEDEMANN, K. B., Biological Psychiatry
WIELAND, T., Pharmacology
WILL, H. K., Microbiology
WILLIG, R. P., Paediatrics
WINDLER, E., Internal Medicine
WINTERPACHT, A., Human Genetics
ZANDER, A., Bone Marrow Transplantation
ZEUMER, H., Neuroradiology
ZYWIETE, F., Biophysics, Radiobiology

Department of Oriental Studies and Asia–Africa Institute (Rothenbaumchaussee 67/69, 20148 Hamburg; tel. (40) 42838-4054; fax (40) 42838-6530; e-mail aai@uni-hamburg.de):

CARLE, R., Indonesian and South Seas Languages
CONRAD, L., Islamic Sciences
EBERSTEIN, B., Sinology
EMMERICK, R., Iranian Studies
FRIEDRICH, M., Sinology
GERHARDT, L., African Languages and Cultures
JACKSON, D., Tibetology
KAPPERT, P., Turkish Studies
ORANSKAIA, T., Indic Studies
POHL, M., Japanese Politics
REH, M., African Languages and Cultures
ROTTER, G., Islamic Studies
SASSE, W., Chinese
SCHMITHAUSEN, L., Indology
SCHNEIDER, R., Japanese
STUMPFELDT, H., Sinology
TERWIEL, B., Thai Language and Culture
UHLIG, S., African Languages and Cultures
WEZLER, A., Indology

Department of Physical Education (Mollerstraße 10, 20148 Hanburg; tel. (40) 42838-2474; fax (40) 42838-5666):

BRAUMANN, K.-M.
EICHLER, G.
FUNKE-WIENEKE, J.
LANGE-AMELSBERG, J.
NIEDLICH, H.-D.
STRIPP, K.
TIEDEMANN, C.
TIWALD, H.
WEINBERG, P.

Department of Physics (Dammtorstraße 12, 2. stock, 20354 Hamburg; tel. (40) 42838-4056; fax (40) 42838-6233):

BARTELS, J., Theoretical Physics
BLOBEL, V., Experimental Physics
BÜSSER, F.-W., Experimental Physics
FAY, D., Theoretical Physics
FREDENHAGEN, K., Theoretical Physics
GERAMB, H. V. VON, Theoretical Physics
HANSEN, W., Experimental Physics
HEINZELMANN, G., Experimental Physics
HEITMANN, D., Applied Physics
HEMMERICH, A., Experimental Physics
HEUER, R.-D., Elementary Particle Physics
HEYSZENAU, H., Theoretical Physics
HUBER, G., Experimental Physics
JOHNSON, R., Experimental Physics
KLANNER, R., Experimental Physics
KÖTZLER, J., Applied Physics
KRAMER, B., Theoretical Physics
MACK, G., Theoretical Physics
MERKT, U., Experimental Physics
NAROSKA, B., Experimental Physics
NEUHAUSER, W., Experimental Physics
OEPEN, H. P., Experimental Physics
PFANNKUCHE, D., Theoretical Physics
REIMERS, D., Astronomy
SCHARNBERG, K., Theoretical Physics

SCHMIDT-PARZEFALL, W., Experimental Physics
SCHMITT, J., Astronomy
SCHMÜSER, P., Experimental Physics
SCOBEL, W., Experimental Physics
SENGSTOCK, K., Experimantal Physics
SONNTAG, B., Experimental Physics
SPITZER, H., Fundamental Physics
WAGNER, A., Elementary Particle Physics
WENDKER, H., Astronomy
WICK, K., Experimental Physics
WIESENDANGER, R., Experimental Physics
WURTH, W., Experimental Physics
ZIMMERER, G., Experimental Physics

Department of Protestant Theology (Sedanstr. 19, 20146 Hamburg; tel. (40) 42838-0; fax (40) 42838-4013):

AHRENS, T., Missions
DIERKEN, J., Systematic Theology
GRÜNBERG, W., Practical Theology
GUTMANN, H.-M., Practical Theology
KOCH, T., Systematic Theology
LINDNER, W. V., Practical Theology
LOHR, W., Church and Dogmatic History
MAGER, I., Church History and Dogma
MOXTER, M., Systematic Theology
SCHRAMM, T., New Testament
SCHRÖTER, J., New Testament
SCHUMANN, O., Religious and Missionary Science
SELLIN, G., New Testament
STEIGER, J. A., Church and Dogmatic History
TIMM, S., Old Testament
WILLI-PLEIN, I., Old Testament

Department of Psychology (Von-Melle-Park 5, 20146 Hamburg; tel. (40) 42838-5460; fax (40) 42838-5492):

BAMBERG, E.
BERBALK, H.
BURISCH, M.
BUSE, L.
DAHME, B.
ECKERT, J.
HEINZE, B.
LANGER, I.
OETTINGEN, G
ORTH, B.
PAWLIK, K.
PROBST, P.
RHENIUS, D.
SCHMIDTCHEN, S.
SCHULZ VON THUN, F.
SCHWAB, R.
TONNIES, S.
VAGT, G.
WITT, H.
WITTE, E.

Department of Social Sciences (Allende-Platz 1, 20146 Hamburg; tel. (40) 42838-0; fax (40) 42838-4506):

EICHNER, K., Sociology
GOERTZ, H.-J., Social and Economic History
GREVEN, M., Political Science
HEINEMANN, K., Sociology
JAKOBEIT, C., Political Science
KAUPEN-HAAS, H.
KLEINSTEUBER, H. J., Political Science
LANDFRIED, C., Political Science
LÜDE, R. VON, Sociology
MILLER, M., Sociology
NEVERLA, I., Journalism, Communications
PIEPER, M., Sociology
RASCHKE, P., Political Science
RENN, H., Sociology
RUNDE, P., Sociology
SCHEERER, S., Criminology
SEßAR, K., Criminology
TETZLAFF, R., Political Science
TROITZSCH, U., Social Sciences
VILLMOW, B., Criminology
WEISCHENBERG, S., Communications Science, Journalism

UNIVERSITY INSTITUTES

Office for Continuing Education.

Interdisciplinary Centre for University Didactics.

Computer Centre.

Institute for Theatre, Musical Theatre and Film.

International Tax Institute.

Biotechnology, Society, Environment.

Audio-Visual Centre.

Centre for Oceanography and Climate Research.

Museum of Geology and Palaeontology.

Museum of Zoology.

Museum of Mineralogy.

ASSOCIATED INSTITUTES

Mission Academy.

Institute for Integration Research.

Hans Bredow Institute for Radio and Television.

Institute for Peace Research and Security Policy.

Heinrich Pette Institute for Experimental Virology and Immunology.

Institute for Hormone and Reproduction Research.

HELMUT SCHMIDT UNIVERSITÄT—UNIVERSITÄT DER BUNDESWEHR HAMBURG
(University of the Federal Armed Forces, Hamburg)

Postfach 700822, 22008 Hamburg
Physical location: Holstenhofweg, 22043 Hamburg
Telephone: (40) 6541-0
Fax: (40) 6541-2869
Internet: www.hsu.hh.de

Founded 1972
State control
Languages of instruction: German, English
Academic year: October to September
Chancellor: ECKHARD REDLICH
President: Dr-Ing. HANS-CHRISTOPH ZEIDLER
Vice-President: Prof. Dr WOLF SCHÄFER
Librarian: Dr JOHANNES MARBACH

Library of 750,000 vols
Number of teachers: 103
Number of students: 1,950

Publications: *Uniforum* (annually), *Uniforschung* (annually)

DEANS

Faculty of Economics and Management: Prof. Dr JÖRN KRUSE
Faculty of Educational Science: Prof. Dr THOMAS HOPPE
Faculty of Electrical Engineering: Prof. Dr-Ing. HOLGER GÖBEL
Faculty of Mechanical Engineering: Prof. Dr JENS WULFSBERG

TECHNISCHE UNIVERSITÄT HAMBURG-HARBURG

21071 Hamburg
Telephone: (40) 42878-0
Fax: (40) 42878-2040
E-mail: pressestelle@tu-harburg.de
Internet: www.tu-harburg.de

Founded 1978
Academic year: October to September

President: Prof. Dr EDWIN KREUZER
Vice-President: Prof. Dr ULRICH KILLAT
Chancellor: KLAUS-JOACHIM SCHEUNERT
Librarian: INKEN FELDSIEN-SUDHAUS

Library: *c.* 2,500 vols
Number of teachers: 101
Number of students: 3,800

DEANS

Chemical and Process Engineering: Prof. Dr MÄRKL
Civil Engineering: Prof. Dr WICHMANN
Electrical Engineering: Prof. Dr SINGER
General Engineering Sciences: Prof. Dr BAUHOFER
Mechanical Engineering: Prof. Dr ACKERMANN

MEDIZINISCHE HOCHSCHULE HANNOVER

Carl-Neuberg-Str. 1, 30625 Hannover
Telephone: (511) 532-0
Fax: (511) 532-5550
E-mail: pressestelle@mh-hannover.de
Internet: www.mh-hannover.de

Founded 1965

Pres.: Prof. Dr DIETER BITTER-SUERMANN
Vice-Pres.: HOLGER BAUMANN, Dr ANDREAS TECKLENBURG, HOLGER BAUMANN
Librarian: Dr ANNAMARIE FELSCH-KLOTZ

Library of 280,000 vols
Number of teachers: 614
Number of students: 3,197

DEANS

Biology: Prof. Dr G. GROS
Dentistry: Prof. Dr H. TSCHERNITSCHEK
Medicine: Prof. Dr HERMANN HALLER

PROFESSORS

Professors

Anatomy:

GROTE, C., Neuroanatomy
GRUBE, D., Microscopic Anatomy
PABST, R., Functional and Applied Anatomy
UNGEWICKELL, E., Anatomy

Biochemistry:

GAESTEL, M., Physiological Chemistry
GERARDY-SCHAHN, R., Cellular Chemistry
LENZEN, S., Biochemistry
MANSTEIN, D., Biophysical Chemistry

Laboratory Medicine:

BLASCZYK, R., Transfusion Medicine
FÖRSTER, R., Immunology
GOSSLER, A., Molecular Biology
HEDRICH, H.-J., Animal Research
SCHULZ, T., Laboratory Medicine
SUERBAUM, S., Microbiology and Hospital Hygiene

Medical Technologies:

HECKER, H., Biometry
MATTHIES, H., Medical Computing

Pathology, Genetics and Forensic Medicine:

KREIPE, H.-H., Pathology
SCHLEGELBERGER, B., Pathology, Genetics and Forensic Medicine
SCHMIDTKE, J., Human Genetics
TRÖGER, H.-D., Medical Law

Pharmacology and Toxicology:

JUST, I., Toxicology
RESCH, K., Pharmacology
STICHTENOTH, O., Clinical Pharmacology
WRBITZKY, R., Occupational Medicine

Physiology:

GROS, G., Vegetative Physiology
BRENNER, B., Molecular and Cell Physiology
FAHLKE, C., Neurophysiology
MAASEEN, N., Sports Physiology/Sports Medicine

Public Health Care:

GEYER, S., Medical Sociology
HUMMERS-PRADIER, E., General Medicine
LANGE, K., Medical Psychology

LOHFF, B., History, Ethics and Philosophy of Medicine
SCHWARTZ, F. W., Epidemiology, Social Medicine and Health Systems Research

UNIVERSITÄT HANNOVER

Welfengarten 1, 30167 Hannover
Telephone: (511) 762-0
Fax: (511) 762-3456
E-mail: info@pressestelle.uni-hannover.de
Internet: www.uni-hannover.de

Founded 1831

President: Prof. Dr ERICH BARKE
Vice-Presidents: Prof. Dr KLAUS HULEK, Prof. Dr SABINE E. KUNST, GÜNTER SCHOLZ
Library Director: U. ROSEMANN
Number of teachers: 1,272
Number of students: 31,880

DEANS

Department of Architecture and Landscape: Prof. E. ECKERLE
Department of Civil Engineering: Prof. T. SIEFER
Department of Economics: Prof. S. HOMBURG
Department of Electrical Engineering and Information Technology: Prof. P. PIRSCH
Department of Law: Prof. V. EPPING
Department of Mechanical Engineering: Prof. F. W. BACH
Department of Mathematics and Physics: Prof. O. LECHTENFELDL
Department of Natural Sciences: Prof. W. FISCHER
Department of Philosophy: Prof. F. JOHANNSENS

PROFESSORS

Department of Architecture and Landscape (Schlosswender Str. 1, 30159 Hannover; tel. (511) 762-4276; fax (511) 762-2115; e-mail hobert@dek-arch.uni-hannover.de):

BARTH, H. G., Regional Planning
BRAUM, M., Town Planning
BUCHERT, M., History of Art and Construction
DWORSKY, A., Rural Design
ECKERLE, E., Fine Arts
EHRMANN, W., Work Methods and Processing of Wood and Artificial Materials
FÜRST, D., Regional Planning
FRIEDRICH, J., Design and Building Construction
FURCHE, A., Structural Design and Research
GABRIEL, I., Construction and Design
GANZERT, J., History of Art and Construction
GENENGER, H.-G., Architecture
GERKEN, H., Planning Technology
HAAREN, CHR. V., Conservation
HACKER, E., Conservation
KAPPELER, D., Painting and Graphic Arts
KAUP, P., Construction and Design
KENNEDY, M., Resource-saving in Building
LÉON, H., Building Typology and Design Section
LÖSKEN, G., Open Space Planning and Garden Architecture
LITTMAN, K., Work Methods and Processing of Wood and Artificial Materials
OPPERMANN, B., Open Space Planning
PARAVICINI, U., Theory of Architecture
POHL, W.-H., Building Materials Technology
REICH, M., Plant Ecology
SCHMID-KIRSCH, A., Drawing and Computer-Assisted Design
SCHOMERS, M., Design
SCHULTE, K., Industrial Design
SEGGERN, H. VON, Open Space Planning
SLAWIK, H., Construction and Design
TESSIN, W., Planning-related Sociology
TROJAN, K., Town Planning
TURKALI, Z., Construction and Design
WÖBSE, H. H., Landscape Aesthetics and Design
WEILACHER, U., Landscape Architecture
WOLSCHKE-BULMAHN, J., Open Space Planning and Garden Architecture
ZIBELL, B., Theory of Architecture

Department of Civil Engineering (Callinstr. 34, Hannover; tel. (511) 762-2447; fax (511) 762-4783; e-mail dekanat@fb-bauing.uni-hannover.de; internet www.fb-bauing.uni-hannover.de):

ACHMUS, M., Foundations, Dams
BILLIB, M., Hydrology
BLÜMEL, W., Foundations, Dams
DAMRATH, R., Applied Informatics
DOEDENS, H., Water Supply
FRIEDRICH, B., Traffic Economics, Highway System, Town Planning
GRÜNBERG, J., Concrete Construction
HOFFMANN, B., Hydrology
HOTHAN, J., Traffic Economics, Highway Systems, Town Planning
IWAN, G., Construction Management
KONECNY, G., Photogrammetry and Engineering Surveying
KUNST, S., Water Supply
LECHER, K., Hydrology
LIERSE, J., Building Construction
LOHAUS, L., Building Materials Science
MARKOFSKY, M., Flow Mechanics
MULL, R., Hydrology
MÜLLER, U., Graduate Centre for Environmentally Relevant Fluxes in Water and Soil
MÜLLER-KIRCHENBAUER, H., Foundations, Dams
NACKENHORST, U., Mechanics and Computational Mechanics
PELZER, H., General Surveying
ROKAHR, R., Statics and Geomechanics
ROSEMEIER, G., Flow Mechanics
ROSENWINKEL, K.-H., Water Supply
ROTHERT, H., Statics
SCHAUMANN, P., Steel Construction
SCHELLING, W., Building Technology
SEEBER, G., Geodesy
SESTER, M., Cartography
SIEFERT, T., Railways and Roads
SIEKER, F., Hydrology
VERWORN, H.-R., Hydrology
WRIGGERS, P., Mechanics and Computational Mechanics
ZIELKE, W., Flow Mechanics
ZIMMERMANN, C., Hydroengineering

Department of Economics and Business Administration (Königsworther Platz 1, 30167 Hannover; tel. (511) 762-5350; fax (511) 762-5665; e-mail heer@mbox.vul.uni-hannover.de; internet www.wiwi.uni-hannover.de):

BREITNER, M. H., Computer Science
FÖRSTER, G., Business Taxation
GEIGANT, F., Money, Credit, Currency
GERLACH, K., Political Economy and Labour Economics
HANSEN, U., Marketing
HASLINGER, F., Economics
HEINEMANN, H.-J., International Economic Relations
HOFMANN, CH., Controlling
HOMBURG, S., Public Economics
HÜBL, L., Economic Policy
HÜBLER, O., Econometrics
JÖHNK, M.-D., Econometrics and Statistics
KIRSCH, H.-J., Economics
LÖFFLER, A., Economics
MENKHOFF, L., Money, Credit, Currency
MEYER, W., Economic Policy
MÜLLER, U., Economic Systems, Anti-Trust Policy and Stabilization
RIDDER, H.-G., Personnel Management
SCHMIDT, U., Economics
SCHULENBURG, J.-M. GRAF VON DER, Insurance
SCHWARZE, J., Computer Science
STEINLE, C., Management Economics
WAIBEL, H., Horticultural Economics
WIEDMANN, K.-P., Marketing

Department of Electrical Engineering (Appelstr. 9A, 30167 Hannover; tel. (511) 762-19645; fax (511) 762-19646; e-mail fbbuero@et.uni-hannover.de; internet www.et.uni-hannover.de):

BARKE, E., Microelectronic Systems
EUL, H., High Frequency Technology
GARBE, H., Basic Electrical Engineering
GERTH, W., Control Technology
GOCKENBACH, E., High Voltage
GRABINSKI, H., Theoretical Electrical Engineering
GRAUL, J., Semiconductor Technology and Materials of Electrical Engineering
HAASE, H., Electrical Engineering
HOFMANN, K., Semiconductor Technology and Materials of Electrical Engineering
JOBMANN, K., General Communications Technology
KUCHENBECKER, H.-P., General Communications Technology
LIEDTKE, C.-E., Theoretical Communications Technology
MARQUARDT, J., High Frequency Technology
MATHIS, W., Theoretical Electrical Engineering
MUCHA, J., Theoretical Electrical Engineering
MÜLLER-SCHLOER, C., Computing Sciences
MUSMANN, H.-G., Theoretical Communications Technology
NACKE, B., Electrical Process Technology
NEJDL, W., Knowledge-based Systems
NESTLER, J., Power Electronics
OSTEN, J., Technology and Materials of Electrical Engineering
OSWALD, B. R., Electricity Supply
PIRSCH, P., Microelectronical Engineering
PONICK, B., Electrical Machines and Drives
SEINSCH, H. O., Electrical Machines and Drives
STÖLTING, H.-D., Electrical Machines and Drives
WAGNER, B., Electrical Systems and Teaching of Electrical Engineering

Department of Law (Königsworther Platz 1, 30167 Hannover; tel. (511) 762-8104; fax (511) 762-8107; e-mail dekanat@jura.rw.uni-hannover.de; internet www.jura.uni-hannover.de):

ABELTSHAUSER, T., Civil Law
BUCK, P., Civil Law
BUTZER, H., Public Law
CALLIESS, R.-P., Criminal Law
DORNDORF, E., Civil Law
EPPING, V., Public Law
FABER, H., Public Law
FENGE, H., Civil Law
FOLZ, H.-E., Public Law
FORGÓ, N., Civil Law
FRANK, J., Economics
HESSE, H. A., Teaching of Law, Sociology of Law
KILIAN, W., Civil Law
KÜHNE, J.-D., Public Law
MAGOULAS, G., Economics
MASSING, O., Politics
MEDER, S., Civil Law, History of Law
MEIER, B.-D., Criminal Law
NAHAMOWITZ, P., Theory of Organization and Planning
NOCKE, M., Teaching of Law
OPPERMANN, B., Civil Law
PFEIFFER, C., Criminology
RÜPING, H., Criminal Law
SALJE, P., Civil Law
SCHNEIDER, H.-P., Public Law
SCHWARZE, R., Civil Law

SCHWERDTFEGER, G., Public Law
TREIBER, H., Theory of Organization and Planning
WAECHTER, K., Public Law
WALTHER, M., Teaching of Law and Philosophy
WENDELING-SCHRÖDER, U., Civil Law
WOLF, CH., Civil Law
ZIELINSKI, D., Criminal Law

Department of Mechanical Engineering (Im Moore 11B, 30167 Hannover; tel. (511) 762-2779; fax (511) 762-2763; e-mail dekan@maschinenbau.uni-hannover.de; internet www.maschinenbau.uni-hannover.de):

BACH, F.-W., Materials
BESDO, D., Mechanics
BRAUNE, R., Mechanisms and Machine Elements
DEKENA, B., Production Engineering and Machine Tools
DOEGE, E., Metal Forming and Machines
GATZEN, H.-H., Microtechnology
GERTH, W., Machine Dynamics
GIETZELT, M., Steam and Fuel Engineering
HAFERKAMP, H. D., Materials
HALLENSLEBEN, M. L., Macromolecular Chemistry
HEIMANN, B., Machine Dynamics
KABELAC, S., Thermodynamics
LOUIS, H., Material Testing
MEIER, G. E. A., Fluid Mechanics
MERKER, G. P., Internal Combustion Engine
MEWES, D., Chemical Engineering
NYHUIS, P., Factory Building and Logistics
OVERMEYER, L., Conveying Technology and Mining Machinery
POLL, G., Construction Science
POPP, K., Mechanics
RAUTENBERG, M., Radial Compressors
REDEKER, G., Factory Building
REHFELDT, D., Welding Technology
REITHMEIER, E., Measurement and Control Technology
RIESS, W., Turbo Machinery
ROSEMANN, H., Construction Science
SCHULZE, L., Department Planning, Control of Warehouse and Transport Systems
SCHWERES, M., Labour Science, Ergonomics
SENME, J., Turbo Machinery
STEGEMANN, D., Nuclear Technology
VOSS, G., Railway Machines
WIENDAHL, H.-P., Plant Engineering and Production Control

Department of Mathematics and Physics (tel. (511) 762-4466; fax (511) 762-5819; e-mail dekanat@math.uni-hannover.de):

BÄUERLE, N., Mathematical Stochastics
BARINGHAUS, L., Mathematical Stochastics
BARKE, E., Microelectronic Systems
BESSENRODT, CH., Mathematics
BOTHMER, H.-CH. V., Mathematics
BREHM, B., Atomic Processes
DANZMANN, K., Experimental Physics
DEMMIG, F., Plasma Physics
DRAGON, N., Theoretical Physics
EBELING, W., Mathematics
ERNÉ, M., Mathematics
ERTMER, W., Experimental Physics
ESCHER, J., Applied Mathematics
ETLING, D., Theoretical Meteorology
EVERTS, H.-U., Theoretical Physics
FORSTER, P., Applied Mathematics
GRÜBEL, R., Probability Theory and Statistics
GROSS, G., Meteorology
GROSSER, J., Atomic Processes
HAUF, T., Meteorology
HAUG, R., Experimental Physics
HEINE, J., Applied Mathematics
HENZLER, M., Experimental Physics
HOTJE, H., Mathematics
HULEK, K., Mathematics
KOCK, M., Plasma Physics
LECHTENFELD, O., Theoretical Physics
LEWENSTEIN, M., Theoretical Physics
LIPECK, U., Computer Science
MÜHLBACH, G., Approximation Theory and Numerical Analysis
MÜLLER, D., Computer Science
MIKESKA, H. J., Theoretical Physics
NEJDL, W., Computer Science
OESTREICH, M., Experimental Physics
PARCHMANN, R., Computer Science
PFNÜR, H., Experimental Physics
PIRSCH, P., Microelectronic Systems
PRALLE, H., Head of Regional Computer Centre, Lower Saxony
REINEKE, J., Mathematics
SAUER, P. U., Theoretical Physics
SCHMIDT-WESTPHAL, U., Mathematics
SCHNOEGE, K. J., Applied Mathematics
SCHULZ, E., Plasma Physics
SCHULZ, H., Theoretical Physics
SECKMEYER, G., Meteorology
STARKE, G., Applied Mathematics
STEFFENS, K., Mathematics
STEPHAN, E., Applied Mathematics
SZCZERBICKA, H., Systems Engineering
TIEMANN, E., Experimental Physics
VOLLMER, H., Computer Science
WAGNER, B., Systems Engineering
WELLEGEHAUSEN, B., Applied Physics
WOLTER, F.-E., Applied Systems
ZAWISCHA, D., Theoretical Physics

Department of Natural Sciences (Schneiderberg 50, 30167 Hannover; tel. (511) 762-3318; fax (511) 762-5874; internet www.unics.uni-hannover.de/geo/index.html):

ANDERS, A., Biophysics
ARNOLD, A., Human Geography
AULING, G., Microbiology
BÖTTCHER, J., Soil Science
BECKER, J. A., Physical Chemistry
BEHRENS, P., Inorganic Chemistry
BELLGARDT, K.-H., Technical Chemistry
BERGER, R. G., Applied Chemistry
BINNEWIES, M., Inorganic Chemistry
BLANCKENBURG, F. VON, Mineralogy
BRAKHAGE, A., Microbiology
BUCHHOLZ, H. J., Human Geography
BUHL, J.-CH., Mineralogy
BUTENSCHÖN, H., Organic Chemistry
CARO, J., Physical Chemistry
DUDDECK, H., Organic Chemistry
FENDRIK, I., Biophysics
FISCHER, R., Palaeontology
FISCHER, W. R., Soil Science
HÖRMANN, D., Gardening Management
HÜPPE, J., Palaeoecology
HAHN, A., Domestic Technology
HALLENSLEBEN, M. L., Macromolecular Chemistry
HAU, B., Phytopathology
HEITJANS, P., Physical Chemistry
HESSE, D., Technical Chemistry
HITZMANN, B., Technical Chemistry
HOFFMANN, H. M. R., Organic Chemistry
HOLTZ, F., Mineralogy
HORST, W., Plant Nutrition
HOTHORN, L., Biology Informatics
HUCHZERMEYER, B., Botany
IMBIHL, R., Physical Chemistry
JACOBSEN, H.-J., Molecular Biology
JUG, K., Theoretical Chemistry
KIRSHNING, A., Organic Chemistry
KLOPPSTECH, K., Botany
KOLB, A., Biophysics
KRETZMER, G., Technical Chemistry
KUHLMANN, H., Plant Nutrition
KUHNT, G., Physical Geography
KUSTER, H., Palaeoecology
LIEFNER, I., Economic Geography
MAISS, E., Phytopathology
MARTEN, I., Biophysics
MEYER, H. H., Organic Chemistry
MOSIMANN, T., Physical Geography
NAUMANN, I., Domestic Technology
NIEMEYER, R., Botany
PLOEG, R. VAN DER, Soil Science
POTT, R., Botany
RATH, T., Horticulture
ROTZOLL, G., Technical Chemistry
SCHÄTZL, L., Economic Geography
SCHÖNHERR, J., Fruit Science
SCHÜLKE, I., Geology
SCHÜNGERL, K., Technical Chemistry
SCHENK, E.-W., Gardening Management and Accountancy
SCHENK, M., Plant Nutrition
SCHEPER, T., Technical Chemistry
SCHERER, G., Crop Physiology
SCHMIDT, A., Botany
SCHMIDT, E., Horticultural Economics
SCHMITZ, U. K., Applied Genetics
SEREK, M., Gardening Management and Accountancy
SPETHMANN, W., Nursery Gardening
STÜTZEL, Vegetable Science
TANTAU, H.-J., Horticultural Engineering
TATLIOGLU, T., Applied Genetics
URLAND, W., Inorganic Chemistry
VOGT, C., Inorganic Chemistry
WÜNSCH, G., Inorganic Chemistry
WAIBEL, H., Horticultural Economics
WATKINSON, B. M., Food Science
WINSEMANN, J., Geology
WINTERFELDT, E., Organic Chemistry
ZIMMER, K., Ornamental Plants

Department of Philosophy (Königsworther Platz 1, 30167 Hannover; tel. (511) 762-4556; fax (511) 762-8243; e-mail dekanat@fbls.uni-hannover.de; internet www.fbls.uni-hannover.de):

ACHINGER, G., Sociology
AHLERS, I., Human Geography
ANTES, P., Study of Religions
ASCHOFF, H.-G., Modern History and Ecclesiastical History
AVERKORN, R., Medieval History
BÖNSCH, M., School Pedagogy
BARMEYER-HARTLIEB, H., Modern History
BAUSENHART, G., Roman Catholic Religious Education
BAYER, K., German
BECKER-SCHMIDT, R., Psychology
BERG, D., Medieval History
BEUTLER, K., Education
BEZZEL, CH., German Language
BICKES, H., German Language
BILLMANN-MAHECHA, H., Psychology
BINDEL, W.-R., Special Education
BIRKNER, G., English Philology
BLANKE, B., Political Science
BLELL, G., Teaching of English
BLEY, H., Modern History
BOLSCHO, D., Pedagogy
BRÜGGEMANN, H., Modern German Literature
BRODTMANN, D., Sports
BROKMEIER, P., Political Science
BUCKMILLER, M., Political Science
BULTHAUP, P., Philosophy
CALLIES, H., Ancient History
CLAUSSEN, D., Sociology
DAIBER, K.-F., Study of Religions
DIEWALD, G., Modern German Literature
DISCHNER-VOGEL, G., Modern German Literature
DITTRICH, J.-H., Technology of Clothing and Textiles
DORDEL, H. J., Sports
DUDEN, B., Sociology
EBINGHAUS, H., Physics
EGGERT, D., Psychology
EGGS, E., Romance Philology and Language
EHRHARDT, J., Education
EHRHARDT, M. L., German
FÜLLBERG-STOLLBERG, O., Modern History
FELDMANN, K., Sociology
FISCHER, H., German Literature
FRACKMANN, M., Social Education

FRANZKE, R., Social Education
GÖRTZ, H.-J., Roman Catholic Religious Education
GHOLAMASAD, D., Sociology
GIPSER, D., Special Education
GLAGE, L., English Literature
GLITHO, S., Modern German Literature
HÖLKER, K., Romance Philology and Literature
HAENSCH, D., Political Science
HASEMANN, K., Mathematics
HAUPTMEYER, C.-H., Early Medieval History
HEINEMANN, M., Education
HERWIG, J., Music
HIEBER, L., Sociology
HOECKER, B., Political Science
HOEGES, D., Romance Philology and Literature
HORSTER, D., Education
ILIEN, A., Education
JANSSEN, B., School Pedagogy
JETTER, K., Therapy
JOHANNSEN, F., Evangelical Religious Education
JUNGK, D., Vocational Education
KÖPCKE, K. M., German
KÜHNE, A., Psychology
KENTLER, H., Social Education
KIESELBACH, T., Psychology
KNAPP, G.-A., Psychology
KOETHEN, E., Art and Visual Media, Teaching of Art and Visual Media
KORFF, F.-W., Philosophy
KREUTZER, L., Modern German Literature
KRIWET, I., Education of Mentally Handicapped People
KROVOZA, A., Psychology
KRUIP, G., Roman Catholic Religious Education
KUNTZ, K. M., Education
KUPETZ, R., Teaching of English, Applied Linguistics
LAGA, G., Sociology
LEMKE, C., Political Science
LENK, E., German Literature
LOHRER-PAPE, Arts
LUDWIG, O., German Language
MÜHLHAUSEN, K., Education
MÜLLER, R.-W., Political Science
MANZ, W., Vocational Education
MAYER, R., English Literature
MENSCHING, G., Philosophy
MESCHKAT, K., Sociology
MICKLER, O., Sociology
NARR, R., School Pedagogy
NAUMANN, H., German
NAUMANN, G., Home Technology
NEGT, O., Sociology
NOLL, A.-H., Social Studies
NOLTE, H.-H., Medieval History
NOORMANN, J., Teaching of Evangelical Relations
OELSCHLÄGER, H., Educational Planning and Reform
PAEFGEN, E., German
PEIFFER, L., Sports
PERELS, J., Political Science
PETERS, J., Modern German Literature
RÜTTERS, K., Vocational Education
RAUFUSS, D., Education
RECTOR, M., Modern German Literature
REHKÄMPER, K., Modern German Literature
REISER, H., Special Education
REUMANN, R.-D., Technology of Clothing and Textiles
RIEDEL, M., Modern History
RIEMEN, F., Music
RIES, W., Philosophy
ROHLOFF, H., English Philosophy
RUNTE, A., Modern German Literature
RUST, H., Sociology
SALDERN, A. VON, Modern History
SANDERS, H., Romance Philology and Literature
SAUER, W., German Language
SCHÄFER, G., Political Science
SCHÖNBERGER, F., Special Education
SCHAEFFNER, L., Adult Education
SCHLOBINSKI, P., German Language
SCHMAUDERER, E., Food Science
SCHMID, H.-D., History and History Teaching
SCHMIDT, M., Adult Education
SCHMITZ, K., Education
SCHREIBER, G., Technology of Clothing and Textile
SCHUCHARDT, E., Education
SCHULZE, R., English Language and Linguistics
SCHWARZ, B., Medieval History
SIEBERT, H., Adult Education
STIMPFLE, A., Roman Catholic Religious Education
SWIENTEK, CH., Special Education
TIEDEMANN, J., Psychology
TILCH, H., Social Education
TREBELS, A. H., Sports
TROCHOLEPCZY, B., Roman Catholic Religious Education
URBAN, A., Psychology
VASSEN, F., Modern German Literature
VESTER, M., Political Science
WACKER, A., Psychology
WAGNER-HASEL, B., Ancient History
WATKINSON, B. M., Food Science
WEBER, H., English Philology
WELLENDORF, F., Psychology
WELZER, H., Psychology
WENZEL, F., Scientific and Technical Russian
WERNER, W., Roman Catholic Religious Education
WERNING, R., Education of Mentally Handicapped People
WILHARM, I., History and History Teaching
WILKEN, E., Special Education
WIPPERMANN, H., Mathematics
WÜNDERICH, V., Sociology
WÜNDERICH, V., Latin American History
ZIEHE, T., Education

TIERÄRZTLICHE HOCHSCHULE HANNOVER
(Hanover School of Veterinary Medicine)

Postfach 711180, 30545 Hanover
Bünteweg 2, 30559 Hanover
Telephone: (511) 953-6
Fax: (511) 953-8050
E-mail: presse@tiho-hannover.de
Internet: www.tiho-hannover.de

Founded 1778 as Königliche Rossarzneischule, attained university status 1887
State control
Academic year: October to September

Pres.: Dr GERHARD GREIF
Vice-Pres.: Dr BURKHARD MEINECKE, Dr ANDREA TIPOLD

Number of teachers: 122
Number of students: 2,160

Publications: *TiHo-Anzeiger* (8 a year), *TiHo Forschung fürs Leben* (annually)

HEADS

Department of Analytical Chemistry and Endocrinology: Prof. Dr H.-O. HOPPEN
Department of Biometry, Epidemiology and Data Processing: Prof. Dr L. KREIENBROCK
Department of Fish Pathology and Fish Farming: Prof. Dr WOLFGANG KÖRTING
Department of General Radiology and Medical Physics: Prof. Dr HERMANN SEIFERT
Department of History of Veterinary Medicine and Domestic Animals: Prof. Dr JOHANN SCHÄFFER
Department of Immunology: Prof. Dr WOLFGANG LEIBOLD
Institute of Anatomy: Prof. Dr H. WAIBL
Institute for Animal Behaviour and Protection: Prof. Dr HANSJOACHIM HACKBARTH
Institute of Animal Breeding and Genetics: Prof. Dr OTTMAR DISTL
Institute for Animal Ecology and Cell Biology: Prof. Dr BERND SCHIERWATER
Institute for Animal Hygiene and Protection: Prof. Dr JÖRG HARTUNG
Institute for Animal Nutrition: Prof. Dr J. KAMPHUES
Institute of Epidemics: Prof. Dr THOMAS BLAHA
Institute for Food Quality and Safety: Prof. Dr G. KLEIN
Institute for Microbiology: Prof. Dr JOERCH MERKEL
Institute for Parasitology: Prof. Dr THOMAS SCHNEIDER
Institute for Pathology: Prof. Dr WOLFGANG BAUMGÄRTNER
Institute for Physiology: Prof. Dr GERHARD BREVES
Institute for Physiological Chemistry: Prof. Dr HASSAN Y. NAIM
Institute for Reproductive Medicine: Prof. Dr EDDA TÖPFER-PETERSEN
Institute for Virology: Prof. Dr VOLKER MOENNIG
Institute for Wildlife Research: Prof. Dr KLAUS POHLMEYER
Institute for Zoology: Prof. Dr ELKE ZIMMERMANN
Centre for Food Toxicology: Prof. Dr HEINZ NAU
Clinic for Cattle: Prof. Dr HEINRICH BOLLWEIN
Clinic for Horses: Prof. Dr KARSTEN FEIGE
Clinic for Pigs, Small Ruminants, Forensic Medicine and Ambulatory Service: Prof. Dr K.-H. WALDMANN
Clinic for Poultry: Prof. Dr U. NEUMANN
Clinic for Small Domestic Animals: Prof. Dr INGO NOLTE

RUPRECHT-KARLS-UNIVERSITÄT HEIDELBERG

Postfach 105760, 69047 Heidelberg
Telephone: (6221) 540
Fax: (6221) 542618
E-mail: gb@zuv.uni-heidelberg.de
Internet: www.uni-heidelberg.de

Founded 1386
Academic year: October to September

Rector: Prof. Dr PETER HOMMELHOFF
Pro-Rectors: Prof. Dr ANGELOS CHANIOTIS, Prof. Dr PETER COMBA, Prof. Dr SILKE LEOPOLD, Prof. Dr JOCHEN TRÖGER
Chancellor: Dr MARINA FROST
Librarian: Dr VEIT PROBST

Number of teachers: 2,522
Number of students: 27,000

Publications: *Ruperto Carola* (3 a year), *Pressemitteilungen Personalia* (monthly), *Heidelberger Jahrbücher*, *Alumni Revue* (2 a year)

DEANS

Faculty of Behavioural and Cultural Studies: Prof. Dr KLAUS ROTH
Faculty of Biology: Prof. Dr MICHAEL BRUNNER
Faculty of Chemistry and Earth Sciences: Prof. Dr BERNHARD EITEL
Faculty of Clinical Medicine (Mannheim): Prof. Dr KLAUS VAN ACKERN
Faculty of Economics and Social Studies: Prof. Dr WOLFGANG SCHLUCHTER
Faculty of Law: Prof. Dr THOMAS PFEIFFER
Faculty of Mathematics and Computer Sciences: Prof. Dr KAY WINGBERG
Faculty of Medicine (Heidelberg): Prof. Dr CLAUS R. BARTRAM

Faculty of Modern Languages: Prof. Dr EDGAR RADTKE
Faculty of Philosophy and History: Prof. Dr STEFAN WEINFURTER
Faculty of Physics and Astronomy: Prof. Dr JOHANNA STACHEL
Faculty of Theology: Prof. Dr HELMUT SCHWIER

PROFESSORS (INSTITUTE DIRECTORS)

Faculty of Theology (Hauptstr. 231, 1 OG, 69117 Heidelberg; tel. (6221) 543334):

HOFMEISTER, H., Philosophy of Religion
MÖLLER, C., Practical Theology
SCHMIDT, H., Practical Theology

Faculty of Law (Friedrich-Ebert-Anlage 6–10, 69117 Heidelberg; tel. (6221) 547631; fax (6221) 547654):

BALAUS, C., Historical Law
DÖLLING, D., Criminal Law
KIRCHHOF, P., Fiscal and Tax Law
MÜLLER-GRAFF, P.-C., German and European Company and Business Law
PFEIFFER, T., Foreign and International Private and Business Law

Faculty of Medicine (Heidelberg) (Im Neuenheimer Feld 346, 69120 Heidelberg; tel. (6221) 562700; fax (6221) 565404):

BARTRAM, C. R., Human Genetics
BÜCHLER, M., Surgery
DRAGUHN, A., Physiology and Pathophysiology
ECKART, W. U., History of Medicine
ENK, A., Dermatology
GERNER, H.-J., Orthopaedics
HACKE, W., Neurology
HERZOG, W., Psychosomatic Medicine
HOFFMANN, G. F., Paediatrics
KAUFFMANN, G. W., Radiology
KIRSCH, J., Medical Cell Biology
KRIZ, W., Anatomy
HERZOG, W., Internal Medicine
HURT, E., Biochemistry
KRAÜSSLIAN, H.-G., Hygiene
MARTIN, E., Anaesthesiology
MATTERN, R., Forensic Medicine
MEUER, S., Immunology
MÜHLING, J., Dentistry
MUNDT, C., Psychiatry
OFFERMANNS, S., Pharmacology
PLINKERT, P., Oto-Rhino-Laryngology
SCHIRMACHER, P., Pathology
SOHN, C., Gynaecology
TRIEBIG, G., Social and Industrial Medicine
UNSICKER, K., Neuroanatomy
UNTERBERG, A., Neurosurgery
VIKTOR, N., Medical Biometrics and Computer Science in Medicine
VÖLCKER, H. E., Ophthalmology

Faculty of Clinical Medicine (Mannheim) (Theodor-Kutzer-Ufer, 68167 Mannheim; tel. (621) 3832527; fax (621) 3833802; e-mail beate.schmidt@dekan.ma.uni-heidelberg.de):

VAN ACKERN, K., Anaesthesiology
ALKEN, P., Urology
BLEYL, U., General Pathology and Pathological Anatomy
BORGGREFE, M., Internal Medicine
DÜBER, CH., Radiology
GLADISCH, R., Internal Medicine
GOERDT, S., Dermatology and Venereal Diseases
HEHLMANN, R., Internal Medicine (III)
HENN, F., Social Psychiatry
HENNERICI, M., Neurology
HOF, H., Medical Microbiology and Hygiene
HÖRMANN, K., Ear, Nose and Throat
JONAS, J., Ophthalmology
LEMMER, B., Pharmacology and Toxicology
MELCHERT, F., Obstetrics and Gynaecology
NEUMAIER, M., Clinical Chemistry
NÜTZENADEL, W., Paediatrics
OBERTACKE, U., Casualty Surgery
POST, S., Surgery
SCHADENDORF, D., Clinical Co-operation Unit (Skin Cancer)
SCHMIEDEK, P., Neurological Surgery
SINGER, M. V., Internal Medicine
WAAG, K.-L., Children's Surgery
WEHLING, M., Clinical Pharmacology
VAN DER WOUDE, F., Internal Medicine

Faculty of Philosophy (Hauptstr. 120, 69117 Heidelberg; tel. (6221) 542329; fax (6221) 543635; e-mail phil-hist@uni-heidelberg.de):

AHN, G., Comparative Religion
ARNOLD, W., Semitics
HOLSCHER, T., Ancient, Medieval and Modern History
JÖRDENS, A., Papyrology
KOMMERLING, A., Philosophy
LEDDEROSE, L., History of the Arts
LEOPOLD, S., Musicology
LÖWE, H.-D., History of Eastern Europe
MAUL, S., Sinology
MARAN, J., Egyptology
MOST, G. W., Classics
SAURMA, L., History of Art
SCHAMONI, W., Japanese Studies
SCHMIDT, M. G., Political Science
WAGNER, R., Sinology

Faculty of Modern Languages (Hauptstr. 120, 69117 Heidelberg; tel. (6221) 542891; fax (6221) 543625):

BERSCHIN, W., Latin Philology of the Middle Ages
GVOZDANOVIĆ, J., Slavic Philology
HELLWIG, P., Computer Linguistics
KNOPP, F. P., German Philology
KORNELIUS, J., Translating and Interpreting
NÜNNING, V., English Philology
VON STUTTERHEIM, C, German Studies
WANNER, B., Language Laboratory
WEIAND, CH., Romance Philology

Faculty of Economics and Social Sciences (Grabengasse 14, 2 OG, 69117 Heidelberg; tel. (6221) 542915; fax (6221) 542959; e-mail gudrun.schnecke@mail.awi.uni-heidelberg.de):

KOGELSCHATZ, H., Comparative Economic and Social Statistics
REQUATE, T., Interdisciplinary Institute for Environmental Economics
ROSE, M., Political Economics
SCHREMMER, E., History of Sociology and Economics

Faculty of Behavioural and Cultural Sciences (Hauptstr. 120, 69117 Heidelberg; tel. (6221) 542894; fax (6221) 543650; e-mail dekanat.soverwi@urz.uni-heidelberg.de):

FUNKE, J., Psychology
HEIM, R., Sport
KRUSE, A., Gerontology
LENHART, V., Education
SCHLUCHTER, W., Sociology
WASSMANN, J., Ethnology

Faculty of Mathematics and Computer Sciences (Im Neuenheimer Feld 288, 69120 Heidelberg; tel. (6221) 545758; fax (6221) 548312; e-mail dekanat@mathi.uni-heidelberg.de):

AMBOS-SPIES, K., Computer Science
TOMI, F., Mathematics

Faculty of Chemistry and Earth Sciences (Im Neuenheimer Feld 234, 69120 Heidelberg; tel. (6221) 544844; fax (6221) 544589; e-mail edith.weich@urz.uni-heidelberg.de):

ALTHERR, R., Mineralogy and Petrography
BECHSTÄDT, R., Geology and Geochronology
EITEL, B., Geography
GADE, L. H., Inorganic Chemistry
HELMCHEN, G., Organic Chemistry
SHOTYK, W., Environmental Geochemistry
WOLFRUM, J., Physical Chemistry

Faculty of Biosciences (Im Neuenheimer Feld 346, 69120 Heidelberg; tel. (6221) 546036; fax (6221) 545475; e-mail dekanat.pharmazie@urz.uni-heidelberg.de):

BADING, H., Neurobiology
BAUTZ, E., Molecular Genetics
FRICKER, G., Pharmaceutical Technology
HOLSTEIN, T., Zoology
JÄSCHKE, A., Pharmaceutical Chemistry
LEINS, P., Botany
RAUSCH, T., Botany
ROBINSON, D. G., Cell Biology
SCHALLER, H., Microbiology
WINK, M., Pharmaceutical Biology

Faculty of Physics and Astronomy (Albert-Ueberle-Str. 11, 69120 Heidelberg; tel. (6221) 549298; fax (6221) 549347; e-mail dekanat@physik.uni-heidelberg.de):

BILLE, J., Physics
HUNKLINGER, S., Applied Physics
MEIER, K., High-Energy Physics
ROTH, K., Atmospheric Physics
STACHEL, J., Physics
TSCHARNUTER, W., Theoretical Astrophysics
WETTERICH, C., Theoretical Physics

ATTACHED INSTITUTES

Biochemie-Zentrum Heidelberg (Centre for Biochemistry): Im Neuenheimer Feld 328, 69120 Heidelberg; Dir Prof. Dr F. WIELAND.

Heidelberg Center for American Studies (HCA): Schillerstr. 4-8, 69115 Heidelberg; Dir PD Dr PHILIPP GASSERT.

Interdisziplinäres Zentrum für Neurowissenschaften (Interdisciplinary Centre for Neuroscience): Im Neuenheimer Feld 307, 69120 Heidelberg; Dir Prof. Dr K. UNSICKER.

Interdisziplinäres Zentrum für Wissenschaftliches Rechnen (Interdisciplinary Centre for Scientific Computing): Im Neuenheimer Feld 368, 69120 Heidelberg; Dir Prof. Dr J. WARNATZ.

Südasien-Institut (South Asia Institute): Im Neuenheimer Feld 330, 69120 Heidelberg; Dir Prof. Dr A. MICHAELS.

Zentrum für Molekulare Biologie Heidelberg (Centre for Molecular Biology): Im Neuenheimer Feld 282, 69120 Heidelberg; Dir Prof. Dr K. BEYREUTHER.

UNIVERSITÄT HILDESHEIM

Marienburger Platz 22, 31141 Hildesheim
Telephone: (5121) 883102
Fax: (5121) 883104
E-mail: presse@uni-hildesheim.de
Internet: www.uni-hildesheim.de

Founded 1978
State control
Academic year: October to September

President: Prof. Dr WOLFGANG-UWE FRIEDRICH
Vice-President: Prof. Dr KLAUS AMBROSI, Dr MARGITTA RUDOLPH, Dr BARBARA WEINMANN, Prof. Dr CHRISTA WORMSER-HACKER
Librarian (vacant)

Number of teachers: 157
Number of students: 3,997

Publication: *Uni Hildesheim. Das Magazin* (2 a year)

DEANS

Faculty I (Education and Sociology): Prof. Dr MARTINA SCHREINER
Faculty II (Cultural Education): Prof. Dr WOLFGANG SCHNEIDER
Faculty III (Information and Communication): Prof. Dr HORST KIERDORF

PROFESSORS

Faculty I (Education and Sociology) (tel. (5121) 883-401; fax (5121) 883-402):

BORSCHE, T., Philosophy
BRÄNDLE, W., Protestant Theology
CLOER, E., General Pedagogy
EBERLE, H.-J., Social Pedagogy
FRIEDRICH, W., Political Science
HELFRICH-HÖLTER, W., Psychology
HOPF, CH., Sociology
JAUMANN-GRAUMANN, O., Education
KECK, R., Education
KÖHNLEIN, W., General Science
KUNERT, H., General Education Studies
MEIER-HILBERT, G., Geography
MÜLLER, B., Social Pedagogy
NICKEL, U., Sport
OVERESCH, M., History
SCHREINER, M., Protestant Theology
SIEBERG, H., Sociology
STRANG, H., Social Education Studies
WALLRAVEN, K., Sociology
WERNER, W., Catholic Theology
WOLFF, ST., Social Education Studies

Faculty II (Cultural Education) (tel. (5121) 883-601; fax (5121) 883-602):

BERG, J., Media Education
FRÜHSORGE, G., Fine Arts
GIFFHORN, H., Media Education
GORNIK, H., German Literature and Linguistics
GROMES, H., Theatre
GÜNZEL, R., Fine Arts and Visual Communication
HÜGEL, H.-O., Popular Culture
KURZENBERGER, H.-J., Theatre
LÖFFLER, W., Music and Aural Communication
MENZEL, W., German Language and Linguistics
NOLTE, J., Fine Arts and Visual Communication
SCHNEIDER, W., Cultural Politics
TESKE, U., Fine Arts
VIETTA, J., Literature
WEBER, R., Music and Aural Communication

Faculty III (Information and Communication) (tel. (5121) 883-801; fax (5121) 883-802):

AMBROSI, K., Computer Science
ARNTZ, R., Romance Languages and Linguistics
BENTZ, H.-J., Mathematics
BENEKE, J., English, Linguistics and Intercultural Communication
DIRKS, U., English Studies
FLECHSIG, E., Chemistry
FRANZBECKER, W., Technical Studies
HAUENSCHILD, CH., Computational Linguistics
KAHLE, D., Mathematics
KIERDORF, H., Biology
KOLB, G., General Economics
KREUTZKAMP, TH., Mathematics
SABBAN, A., Romance Languages and Linguistics
SCHWARZER, E., Physics
STURM, H., Biology
WEGNER, N., Technology
WOMSER-HACKER, CH., Information Science

ATTACHED INSTITUTES

Institute of General Educational Theory: Dir Prof. Dr ERNST CLOER.

Institute of Applied Educational Science and General Teaching Methodology: Dir Prof. Dr RUDOLF KECK.

Institute of Primary Education Studies: Dir Prof. Dr WALTER KÖHNLEIN.

Institute of Philosophy: Dir Dr TILMAN BORSCHE.

Institute of Psychology: Dir Prof. Dr HEDE HELFRICH-HÖLTER.

Institute of Social Service Management Studies: Dir Prof. Dr HERWARD SIEBERG.

Institute of Protestant Theology: Dir Prof. Dr MARTIN SHREINER.

Institute of Geography and History: Dir Dr GERHARD MEIER-HILBERT.

Institute of Catholic Theology: Dir Prof. Dr WOLFGANG WERNER.

Institute of Social Service Management Studies: Dir Prof. Dr BURKHARD MÜLLER.

Institute of Sport Science and Sport Education: Dir Prof. Dr ULRICH NICKEL.

Institute of Art and Aesthetics: Dir Prof. Dr JOSEF NOLTE.

Institute of German Language and Literature: Dir Prof. Dr WOLFGANG MENZEL.

Institute of Media and Theatre: Dir Dr HARTWIN GROMES.

Institute of Audiovisual Media: Dir Dr WALTER THISSEN.

Institute of Music: Dir Prof. Dr WOLFGANG LÖFFLER.

Institute of Applied Linguistics: Dir Prof. Dr CHRISTA HAUENSCHILD.

Institute of Work, Business and Technology: Dir Dr WALTER FRANZBECKER.

Institute of Mathematics and Applied Computer Science: Dir Prof. Dr THEO KREUTZKAMP.

Institute for the Theory of Business Management: Dir Prof. Dr KLAUS AMBROSI.

Institute of Physics and Computer Science in Technology: Dir Prof. Dr EBERHARD SCHWARZER.

Institute of Biology and Chemistry: Dir Prof. Dr HORST KIERDORF.

Institute of Cultural Policy: Dir Prof. Dr WOLFGANG SCHNEIDER.

UNIVERSITÄT HOHENHEIM

70593 Stuttgart
Telephone: (711) 459-0
Fax: (711) 459-3960
E-mail: post@uni-hohenheim.de
Internet: www.uni-hohenheim.de

Founded 1818
Academic year: October to September

Rector: Prof. Dr H.-P. LIEBIG
Pro-Rectors: Prof. Dr A. FANGMEIER, Prof. Dr U. MACKENSTEDT, Prof. Dr E. TROSSMANN
Administrative Director: A. FUNK
University Librarian: K.-W. HORSTMANN

Number of teachers: 780
Number of students: 5,500

DEANS

Faculty of Agricultural Sciences: Prof. Dr S. DABBERT
Faculty of Economics and Social Sciences: Prof. Dr M. AHLHEIM
Faculty of Natural Sciences: Prof. Dr K. BOSCH

PROFESSORS

Faculty of Natural Sciences:

BECKER-BENDER, G., Physics
BEIFUSS, U., Bio-organic Chemistry
BIESALSKI, H. K., Biochemistry and Nutrition
BLUM, M., Zoology
BODE, C., Nutrition
BOSCH, K., Mathematics
BREER, H., Zoophysiology
CARLE, R., Food Technology
DEHNHARDT, W., Informatics
DUFNER, J., Mathematics
EHRENSTEIN, W., Applied Physiology
FISCHER, A., Food Technology
FISCHER, L., Biotechnology
GRAEVE, L., Biochemistry and Nutrition
HAMMES, W., Food Technology
HANKE, W., Zoophysiology
HINRICHS, J., Food Technology
ISENGARD, H.-D., Food Analysis
JETTER, K., Applied Mathematics
KOTTKE, V., Food Process Technology
KUHN, A., Microbiology
KUHN, E., Plant Physiology
KÜPPERS, M., Botany
KÜPPERS, M., Botany
MACKENSTEDT, U., Zoology
MENZEL, P., Chemistry and Ecology
PFITZNER, A., Virology
PREISS, A., Genetics
RASSOW, J., Microbiology
RÖSNER, H., Zoology
SCHALLER, J., Animal Ecology
SCHWACK, W., Food Chemistry
SPRING, O., Botany
STRADSEIT, H., Bio-inorganic Chemistry
VETTER, A., Food Technology
WULFMEYER, V., Physics and Meteorology

Faculty of Agricultural Sciences:

AMSELGRUBER, W., Anatomy and Physiology of Domestic Animals
BECKER, K., Animal Nutrition in Tropical and Subtropical Areas
BECKER, T., Rural Markets and Rural Marketing
BESSEI, W., Animal Breeding
BLAICH, R., Viticulture
BÖCKER, R., Landscape Ecology
BÖHM, R., Veterinary Hygiene
BUCHENAUER, H., Plant Protection
CLAUPEIN, W., Plant Production
CLAUS, R., Stockbreeding
DABBERT, S., Production Theory in Agriculture
DOLUSCHITZ, R., Farm Management
DOPPLER, W., Farm Management in Tropical and Subtropical Areas
DROCHNER, W., Animal Nutrition
FANGMEIER, A., Plant Ecology and Ecotoxicology
GEIGER, H. H., Genetics
GELDERMANN, H., Stockbreeding
GROSSKOPF, W., Agricultural Politics
HAUSSMANN, A., Stockbreeding
HEIDHUES, F., Agricultural Economics in Tropical and Subtropical Areas
HOFFMANN, V., Agricultural Communication
HURLE, K., Plant Protection
JUNGBLUTH, T., Agricultural Technology
KANDELER, E., Soil Biology
KLEISINGER, S., Agricultural Technology
KÖLLER, K., Agricultural Technology in Developing Countries
KORFF, H.-R., Socioeconomics in the Tropics and Subtropics
KROMKA, F., Agricultural Sociology
KRUSE, M., Seed Technology
KUTZBACH, H.-D., Agricultural Technology
LIEBIG, H.-P., Vegetable Cropping
MELCHINGER, A., Genetics and Plant Breeding
MOSENTHIN, R., Animal Nutrition
MÜHLBAUER, W., Agricultural Technology in Tropical and Subtropical Areas
OPPEN, M. VON, Agricultural Economics in Developing Countries
PIEPHO, H.-P., Bioinformatics
RÖMHELD, V., Plant Nutrition
SAUERBORN, J., Ecology of Tropical and Subtropical Areas
SCHULTZE-KRAFT, R., Biodiversity and Land Rehabilitation in Tropical and Subtropical Areas
STAHR, K., Soil Sciences
STÖSSER, R., Applied Botany
STRECK, T., Biogeophysics
VALLE ZÁRATE, A., Stockbreeding in Tropical and Subtropical Areas
WEBER, G., Special Plant Breeding

WIRÉN, N. VON, Plant Nutrition
ZEBITZ, C., Plant Protection
ZEDDIES, J., Agricultural Economics
Faculty of Economics and Social Sciences:
AHLHEIM, M., Environmental Economics
BACKES-HAASE, A., Vocational Training
BAREIS, P., Taxation and Management
BELKE, A., International Economics
BUSS, E., Sociology
CAESAR, R., Financing
DITTMAN, A., Law
ESCHER-WEINGART, C, Law
GERYBADZE, A., International Management
HABENICHT, W., Industrial Economics
HACHMEISTER, B., Accounting and Finance
HAGEMANN, H., Economic Theory
HERDZINA, K., Economics
JUNGKUNZ, D., Vocational Teaching
KIRN, C., Informatics
KUHNLE, H., Business Administration
MACHARZINA, K., Management and Organizational Research
MAST, C., Journalism
MELL, U., Theology and Didactics
MÜHLENKAMP, H., Economics of Social Sciences
MÜLLER, C., Entrepreneurship
PFETSCH, B., Communication Policy
SCHENK, M., Communication and Social Research
SCHRAMM, M, Theology and Didactics
SCHULER, H., Psychology
SCHULZ, W., Environmental Management
SCHWALBE, U., Industrial Economics
SEEL, B., Household Management
SPAHN, P., Economics
STREB, D., Social and Economic History
TROSSMANN, E., Controlling
VOETH, M., Marketing
WAGENHALS, G., Statistics and Econometry

TECHNISCHE UNIVERSITÄT ILMENAU

Postfach 100565, 98684 Ilmenau
Premises at: Max-Planck-Ring 14, 98693 Ilmenau
Telephone: (3677) 69-0
Fax: (3677) 69-1701
E-mail: webmaster@tu-ilmenau.de
Internet: www.tu-ilmenau.de

Founded 1953 as Hochschule für Elektrotechnik; present name and status 1992
State control
Academic year: October to September

Rector: Prof. Dr rer. nat. habil. PETER SCHARF
Vice-Rector (Science): Prof. Dr-Ing KLAUS AUGSBURG
Vice-Rector (Teaching): Prof. Dr-Ing. JÜRGEN PETZOLDT
Chancellor: Dr BERNHARD HAUPT
Librarian: GERHARD VOGT

Number of teachers: 625
Number of students: 7,100

Publications: *"Information / Dokumentation"* (proceedings, every 2 years), *Tagungsberichte des Internationalen Kolloquiums* (annually), *Wissenschaftliches Magazin*

DEANS

Faculty of Business Economics: Prof. Dr rer. pol. habil. DIRK STELZER
Faculty of Computer Science and Automation: Prof. Dr-Ing. habil. ANDREAS MITSCHELE-THIEL
Faculty of Electrical Engineering and Information Technology: Prof. Dr-Ing. habil. HEINZ-ULRICH SEIDEL
Faculty of Mathematics and Natural Sciences: Prof. Dr rer. nat. habil. JOCHEN HARANT
Faculty of Mechanical Engineering: Prof. Dr-Ing. habil. PETER KURTZ

FRIEDRICH-SCHILLER-UNIVERSITÄT JENA

Fürstengraben 1, 07743 Jena
Telephone: (3641) 9300
Fax: (3641) 931682
E-mail: aaa@uni-jena.de
Internet: www.uni-jena.de

Founded 1558
Languages of instruction: German, English
Academic year: October to September

Rector: Prof. Dr KARL-ULRICH MEYN
Pro-Rectors: Prof. Dr ROLF STEYER, Prof. Dr CHRISTIAN RÜSSEL
Registrar: Dr KLAUS KÜBEL
Librarian: Dr SABINE WEFERS

Number of teachers: 1,974
Number of students: 19,500

Publications: *Jenaer Reden und Schriften, Mitteilungen der Thüringer Universitäts- und Landesbibliothek, Uni-Journal Jena, Forschungsmagazin*

DEANS

Faculty of Theology: Prof. Dr JÜRGEN VAN OORSCHOT
Faculty of Law: Prof. Dr MICHAEL BRENNER
Faculty of Medicine: Prof. Dr HEINRICH SAUER
Faculty of Philosophy: Prof. Dr WALTER AMELING
Faculty of Economics: Prof. Dr JOHANNES RUHLAND
Faculty of Mathematics and Computer Science: Prof. Dr WERNER ERHARD
Faculty of Chemistry and Geosciences: Prof. Dr DIETER KLEMM
Faculty of Biology and Pharmaceutics: Prof. Dr GABRIELE DIEKERT
Faculty of Physics and Astronomy: Prof. Dr PAUL SEIDEL
Faculty of Social and Behavioural Sciences: Prof. Dr HOLGER GABRIEL

TECHNISCHE UNIVERSITÄT KAISERSLAUTERN

Gottlieb-Daimler-Str., 67663 Kaiserslautern
Telephone: (631) 205-0
Fax: (631) 205-3200
E-mail: auslandsamt@uni-kl.de
Internet: www.uni-kl.de

Founded 1970 as Universität Trier Kaiserslautern, separated 1975
State control
Academic year: October to September

President: Prof. Dr H. J. SCHMIDT
Vice-Presidents: Prof. Dr H.-D. FESER, Prof. Dr W. FREEDEN
Administrative Officer: STEFAN LORENZ
Librarian: Dipl.-Ing. ROLF WERNER WILDERMUTH

Number of teachers: 583
Number of students: 8,600

DEANS

Faculty of Architecture, Regional Planning and Civil Engineering: Prof. Dr jur. WILLY SPANNOWSKY
Faculty of Biology: Prof. Dr rer. nat. REGINE HAKENBECK
Faculty of Chemistry: Prof. Dr-Ing. STEFAN ERNST
Faculty of Computer Science: Prof. Dr MICHAEL RICHTER
Faculty of Electrical Engineering: Prof. Dr-Ing. NORBERT WEHN
Faculty of Mathematics: Prof. Dr JÜRGEN FRANKE
Faculty of Mechanical Engineering: Prof. Dr-Ing. DIETMAR EIFLER
Faculty of Physics: Prof. Dr BURKHARD HILLEBRANDS
Faculty of Social and Economic Sciences: Prof. Dr Dr JÜRGEN ENSTHALER

PROFESSORS

Faculty of Architecture, Regional Planning and Civil Engineering:
BAYER, D., Digital and Methodical Modelling
BECKMANN, R., Ecological Planning and Environmental Compatibilty
BÖHM, W., Theory of Buildings and Design
CASTORPH, M., Component-orientated Planning Processes
DENNHARDT, H., Regional Planning
FILIBECK, R., Construction Management
GÖPFERT, N., Statics of Rising Structures
GOTZ, M., Urban Construction and Planning
HEINRICH, B., Building Physics and Equipment
HOFRICHTER, H., Architecture, History of Town Planning
KAHLFED, P., Industrial Construction III and Design
KLEINE-KRANEBURG, H., Industrial Construction II and Design
KLOPF, H., Load-bearing Structure Design
KOEHLER, G., Civil Engineering
MECHTCHERINE, V., Construction Material Technology
MEDINA-WARMBURG, H., Construction History
MERX, L., Representation and Composition
MEYERSPEER, B., Industrial Construction I and Design
NADLER, M., Building Development
SCHMITT, T. G., Water Management in Residential Areas
SCHNELL, J., Concrete and Building Construction
SEITZ, E., Room Design
SPANNOWSKY, W., Public Law
SPELLENBERG, A., Urban Sociology
STEITZBACH, G., Urban Planning
STREICH, B., Computer-assisted Design and Construction
TOBIAS, K., Ecological Planning and Environmental Compatibility
TOPP, H. H., Traffic Management
TROEGER-WEIß, A., Regional Development and Planning
TRUMPKE, K., Surveying
VRETTOS, C., Soil Mechanics and Foundation Engineering
WASSERMANN, K., Civil Engineering
WITTEK, U., Civil Engineering
WÜST, H.-S., Landscaping

Faculty of Biology:
ANKER, T., Biotechnology
BRÜNE, A., Cell Biology
BÜDEL, D., Systematic Botany
CULLUM, J. A., Genetics
DEITMER, J. W., Zoology
FRIAUF, A., Animal Physiology
HAHN, A., Phytopathology
HAKENBECK, R., Microbiology
LAKATOS, A., Ecology
LEITZ, A., Animal Development
NEUHAUS, A., Physiology of Plants
SCHMIDT, H., Physiological Ecology
ZANKL, H., Human Biology and Genetics

Faculty of Chemistry:
EISENBRAND, G., Food Chemistry and Toxicology
ERNST, S., Technical Chemistry
HARTMANN, M., Chemical Technology
HARTUNG, J., Organic Chemistry
HIMBERT, G., Organic Chemistry
KIETZTMANN, T., Biochemistry
KREITER, C., Inorganic Chemistry
KRÜGER, H. J., Inorganic Chemistry
KUBALL, H.-G., Physical Chemistry
KUBIK, S., Organic Chemistry

MARKO, D., Food Chemistry and Toxicology
MEMMER, R., Physical and Theoretical Chemistry
MEYER, W., Physical and Theoretical Chemistry
NIEDER-SCHATTEBURG, A., Physical and Theoretical
REGITZ, M., Organic Chemistry
SCHERER, O. J., Inorganic Chemistry
SCHRENK, D., Food Chemistry and Toxicology
SITZMANN, H., Inorganic Chemistry
THIEL, W., Inorganic Chemistry
TROMMER, W., Organic Chemistry, Biochemistry

Faculty of Computer Science:
BERNS, K., Robotic Systems
BREUEL, T., Pattern Recognition
DENGEL, A., Knowledge-based Systems
DEßLOCK, S., Heterogenous Informations System
EBERT, A., Visualization
GOTZHEIN, R., Networked Systems
HAGEN, H., Graphic Data Processing, Computer Geometry
HÄRDNER, T., Data Management Systems
HEINRICH, S., Numeral Algorithms in Computer Science
LIGGESMEYER, P., Software Engineering Dependability
MADLENER, K., Principles of Computer Science
MAYER, O., Principles of Programming and Computer Languages
MER, P., Shared Algorithms
MÜLLER, P., Integrated Communication Systems
NEHMER, J., Software Technology
POETZSCH-HEFFTER, A., Software Technology
RAUSCH, A., Software Technology
ROMBACH, D., Software Engineering
SCHMITT, J., Shared Systems (DISCO)
SCHNEIDER, K., Reactive Systems
SCHÜRMANN, B., Modelling of Embedded Systems
UMLAUF, G., Algorithms
WIEHAGEN, R., Algorithmic Learning (Theory)

Faculty of Electrical Engineering:
BAIER, P. W., Radio Frequency Communication
BEISTER, J., Circuits
FREY, A., Agent-based Automation
HAUCK, A., Power Electronics (Teaching)
HUTH, H., Mechatronics and Electrical Drives
KOENIG, A., Integrated Sensor Systems
KUNZ, A., Electronic Design Automation
LITZ, L., Automatic Control
LIU, A., Control Systems
POTCHINKOV, M., Digital Signal Processing
TIELERT, R., Principles of Microelectronics
TUTTAS, A., Power Systems-Transmission and Power Plants (Teaching)
URBANSKY, R., Public Telecommunications Engineering
WEHN, N., Microelectronics
WEISS, P., High-voltage Engineering, Principles of Electrical Engineering
ZENGERLE, R., Theory of Electrical and Electronic Engineering, Optical Communications

Faculty of Mathematics:
BECKER, H., Mathematics
BRAKHAGE, H., Applied Mathematics
DEMPWOLFF, U., Mathematics
FRANKE, J., Stochastics
FREEDEN, W., Mathematics
GREUEL, G.-M., Topology
HAMACHER, H., Econometrics
LÜNEBURG, H., Mathematics
NEUNZERT, H., Mathematics
PFISTER, G., Computer Algebra
PRÄTZEL-WOLTERS, D., Mathematics
RADBRUCH, K., Mathematics, Teaching of Mathematics
SCHOCK, E., Applied Mathematics
SCHWEIGERT, D., Mathematics
TRAUTMANN, G., Pure Mathematics
V. WEIZÄCKER, H., Analysis

Faculty of Mechanical Engineering:
AURICH, J. C., Institute of Manufacturing Engineering and Production Management
BART, H.-J., Chemical Engineering
EIFLER, D., Materials Science
EIGNER, M., Product Development
FLIERL, R., Workgroup for Combustion Engines
HABERLAND, R., Precision Engineering
HELLMANN, D., Fluid Mechanics
MAURER, G., Thermodynamics
RENZ, R., Recyclability in Product Design and Disassembly
RIPPERGER, S., Institute for Particle Technology
SAUER, B., Machine Components
SCHINDLER, C., Institute of Design Engineering
ZÜLKE, D., Production Automation

Faculty of Physics:
AESCHLIMANN, M., Experimental Physics
BEIGANG, R., Experimental Physics
BERGMANN, K., Experimental Physics
DILL, R., Experimental Physics
EGGERT, S., Theoretical Physics
FLEISCHHAUER, M., Theoretical Physics
FOUCKHARDT, H., Experimental Physics
HILLEBRANDS, B., Experimental Physics
HOTOP, H., Experimental Physics
HÜBNER, W., Theoretical Physics
JODL, H.-G., Teaching of Physics, Experimental Physics
KORSCH, J., Theoretical Physics
KRÜGER, H., Theoretical Physics
KUPSCH, J., Theoretical Physics
OESTERSCHULZE, E., Experimental Physics
SCHMORANZER, H., Experimental and Applied Physics
SCHNEIDER, H. C., Theoretical Physics
SCHÜNEMANN, V., Experimental Physics
URBASSEK, H. M., Applied Physics
ZIEGELER, C., Technical Physics

Faculty of Social and Economic Sciences:
ARNOLD, R., Education
BLIEMEL, F., Marketing
CORSTEN, H., Production Management
DUTKE, S., Psychology
ENSTHALER, J., Civil and Economic Law
FESER, H.-D., Economics and Economic Policy I
GESMANN-NUISSL, D., Business Law
VON HAUFF, M., Economics and Economic Policy
HÖLSCHER, R., Finance and Investment
JAINTER, T., Sports
LINGNAU, HV., Management Accounting and Management Control Systems
NEUSER, W., Philosophy
PÄTZOLD, H., Education
RITTBERGER, B., Politics
WENDT, O., Information Systems and Operations Research
WILZEWSKI, J., Politics
ZINK, K. J., Business Management

AFFILIATED INSTITUTES

Deutsches Forschungszentrum für Künstliche Intelligenz GmbH (DFKI) (Research Centre for Artificial Intelligence): Erwin-Schrödinger-Str. (Gebäude 57), Postfach 2080, 67663 Kaiserslautern; Dir (vacant).

Institut für Verbundwerkstoffe GmbH (IVW) (Institute for Composite Materials): Erwin-Schrödinger-Str., 67663 Kaiserslautern; Dir Prof. Dr-Ing. MANFRED NEITZEL.

Institut für Oberflächen- und Schichtanalytik GmbH (Institute for Surface and Coating Analysis): Erwin-Schrödinger-Str. (Gebäude 56), 67663 Kaiserslautern; Dir Prof. Dr rer. nat. HANS OECHSNER.

UNIVERSITÄT KARLSRUHE

Kaiserstr. 12, 76128 Karlsruhe
Telephone: (7210 608-0
Fax: (721) 6084290
E-mail: post@uni-karlsruhe.de
Internet: www.uni-karlsruhe.de

Founded 1825

first technical institute in Germany and the first to acquire university status
State control
Academic year: October to September

Rector: Prof. Dr HORST HIPPLER
Pro-Rectors: Prof. Dr NORBERT HENZE, Prof. Dr VOLKER KREBS, Prof. Dr DORIS WEDLICH
Chief Administrative Officer: Dr DIETER ERTMANN
Librarian: Dipl.-Ing. CHRISTOPH-HUBERT SCHÜTTE

Number of teachers: 700
Number of students: 17,600

Publication: *Fridericiana* (2 a year)

DEANS

Faculty of Mathematics: Prof. Dr ANDREAS KIRSCH
Faculty of Physics: Prof. Dr THOMAS MÜLLER
Faculty of Chemistry and Biosciences: Prof. Dr MANFRED KAPPES
Faculty of Civil, Geo- and Environmental Sciences: Prof. Dr FRANZ NESTMANN
Faculty of Humanities and Social Sciences: Prof. Dr phil. UWE JAPP
Faculty of Architecture: Prof. Dr MATTHIAS PFEIFER
Faculty of Mechanical Engineering: Prof. Dr MARTIN GABI
Faculty of Chemical and Process Engineering: Prof. Dr BETTINA KRAUSHAAR-CZARNETZKI
Faculty of Electrical Engineering and Information Technology: Prof. Dr-Ing. GERT F. TROMMER
Faculty of Computer Science: Prof. Dr M. ZITTERBART
Faculty of Business Engineering and Economics: Prof. Dr WOLFRIED STUCKY

PROFESSORS

Faculty of Architecture:
BAVA, H.
CRAIG, S.
FIERZ, P.
JANSON, A.
KOHLER, N.
KOSSATZ, G.
KRAMM, R.
LEDERER, A.
MEIRER, K.
NÄGELI, W.
NEPPL, M.
PFEIFFER, M.
RASCH, J.
RICHTER, P.
SCHNEIDER, N.
SCHULZE, U.
VOGELEY, J.
WAGNER, A.
WALL, A.

Faculty of Chemical and Process Engineering:
BOCKHORN, H.
BRAUN, A.
BUGGISCH, N.
FRIMMEL, F. H.

KASPER, G.
KIND, M.
KOLB, T.
KRAUSHAAR-CZERNETSKI, B.
MARTIN, H.
NIRSCHL, H.
OELLRICH, L.
POSTEN, C.
REIMERT, R.
SCHABER, K.
SCHAUB, G.
SCHUCHMANN, H.
SYLDATK, C.
ZARZALIS, N.

Faculty of Chemistry and Biosciences:

AHLRICHS, R.
BOCKHORN, H.
BRÄSE, S.
DEUTSCHMANN, O.
FELDMANN, C.
FENSKE, D.
FREYLAND, W.
HIPPLER, H.
HÖGER, S.
KAPPES, M.
KLOPPER, W.
METZLER, M.
NICK, P.
OLZMANN, M.
PAULSEN, R.
PODLECH, J.
POWELL, A.
PUCHTA, H.
RICHERT, C.
RIEDER, N.
SCHNÖCKEL, H.
TARASCHEWSKI, H.
ULRICH, A.
WEDLICH, D.
WEISENSEEL, M.
ZÖLLER, M.
ZUMFT, W.

Faculty of Civil Engineering:

BÄHR, H.-P.
BLAß, H. J.
BURGER, D.
CZURDA, K.
EISBACHER, G.
GEHBAUER, F.
GUDEHUS, G.
HAHN, H. H.
HECK, B.
JIRKA, G.
KILCHENMANN, A.
LENNERTS, K.
MEURER, M.
MÜLLER, H.
NESTMANN, F.
NÜESCH, R.
PRINZ, D.
PUTHLI, R.
RODI, W.
ROOS, R.
SAAL, H.
SCHMITT, G.
SCHOLL, B.
SCHWEIZERHOF, K.
STEMPNIEWSKI, L.
STINNESBECK, W.
STOSCH, H.-G.
STÜBEN, D.
VIELSACK, P.
VOGT, J.
WAGNER, W.
WINTER, J.
ZUMKELLER, D.

Faculty of Electrical Engineering and Information Technology:

BECKER, J.
BOLZ, A.
BRAUN, M.
DÖSSEL, O.
DOSTERT, K.
IVERS-TIFFÉE, E.
JONDRAL, F.
KIENCKE, U.
KREBS, V.
KROSCHEL, K.
LEIBFRIED, T.
LEMMER, U.
LEUTHOLD, J.

Faculty of Humanities and Social Sciences:

BÖHN, A.
BÖS, K.
GLEITSMANN-TOPP, R.-J.
JAPP, U.
LIPSMEIER, A.
REKUS, J.
SCHÄFERS, B.
SCHMALZRIEDT, S.
SCHNEIDER, N.
SCHULZE, U.
SCHÜTT, H.-P.
STEINBACH, P.
STEINER, H.
THUM, B.

Faculty of Mathematics:

ALEFELD, G.
AUMANN, G.
DÖRFLER, W.
HENZE, N.
HERRLICH, F.
HEUVELINE, V.
KAUCHER, E.
KIRSCH, A.
LAST, G.
LEMMERT, R.
LEUZINGER, E.
PLUM, M.
VON RENTELN, M.
RIEDER, A.
SCHERER, R.
SCHMIDT, C.-G.
SCHNEIDER, G.
VOLKMANN, P.
WEIL, W.
WEIS, L.
WIENERS, N.

Faculty of Mechanical Engineering:

ALBERS, A.
ARNOLD, D.
BAUER, H.-J.
BRETTHAUER, G.
CACCUCI, D.
FLEISCHER, J.
FURMANS, K.
GABI, M.
GUMBSCH, P.
HOFFMANN, M. J.
KRAFT, O.
LÖHE, D.
MAAS, U.
OERTEL, H.
OVTCHAROVA, J.
SAILE, V.
SCHMIDT, J.
SCHNACK, E.
SEEMANN, W.
SPICHER, U.
STILLER, C.
WANNER, A.
WAUER, J.
WITTIG, S.
ZÜLCH, G.
ZUM GAHR, K.-H.

Faculty of Physics:

ADRIAN, G.
VON BALTZ, R.
BEHENG, K. D.
BLÜMER, H.
DE BOER, W.
DORMANN, E.
DREXLIN, G.
FEINDT, M.
FISCHER, H.
GEMMEKE, H.
GERTHSEN, D.
HUBRAL, P.
JONES, S.
KALT, H.
KLINGSHIRN, C.
KÜHN, J.
VON LÖHNEYSEN, H.
MIRLIN, A.
MÜLLER, TH.
SCHIMMEL, T.
SCHÖN, G.
WEGENER, M.
WEIß, G.
WENZEL, F.
WÖLFLE, P.
ZEITNITZ, B.

ATTACHED RESEARCH INSTITUTES

German-French Institute for Automation and Robotics: Dir T. LEIBFRIED.

Inter-Faculty Institute for Entrepreneurship: Dir G. WERNER.

Institute for Applied Computer Science: Dir W. STUCKY.

German-French Institute for Environmental Research: Dir O. RENTZ.

Centre for Visually-Impaired Students: Dir R. VOLLMAR.

Research Centre for Functional Nanostructures: Dir M. WEGENER.

Centre for Disaster Management and Risk Reduction Technology: Dir L. STEMPNIEWSKI.

Centre for Elementary Particles and Physics of Astro-Particles: Dir T. MÜLLER.

Computing Centre: Dir W. JULING.

Environmental Research Centre: Dir R. REIMERT.

Centre for Applied Cultural Sciences and Studium Generale: Dir C. ROBERTSON VON TROTHA.

UNIVERSITÄT KASSEL

Präsidialverwaltung, Mönchebergstr. 19, 34109 Kassel
Telephone: (561) 804-0
Fax: (561) 804-2330
E-mail: poststelle@uni-kassel.de
Internet: www.uni-kassel.de

Founded 1971
State control
Language of instruction: German
Academic year: October to July

President: Prof. Dr ROLF-DIETER POSTLEP
Vice-Presidents: Prof. Dr ALEXANDER ROSSNAGEL, Prof. Dr EKKEHART FRIELING
Chancellor: Dr HANS GÄDEKE
Librarian: Dr AXEL HALLE

Library of 1,731,868 books, 10,207 periodicals
Number of teachers: 301
Number of students: 17,076

Publications: *Publik* (9 a year), *Bericht des Präsidiums* (annually)

DEANS

Agriculture, International Rural Development and Environmental Protection: Prof. Dr JÜRGEN HESS
Architecture, Urban Planning, Landscape Planning: Prof. Dr Ing. HELMUT HOLZAPFEL
Business and Economics, Psychology: Prof. Dr REINHARD HÜNERBERG
Civil Engineering: Prof. Dr-Ing. EKKEHARD FEHLING
Education, Humanities and Music: Univ. Prof. Dr ILSE MÜLLNER
Electrical Engineering, Computer Science: Prof. Dr-Ing. JÜRGEN SCHMID
Languages and Literature: Prof. Dr PETER SEIBERT
Mathematics and Computer Science: Prof. Dr BERND WOLLRING

Mechanical Engineering: Prof. Dr-Ing. GUNTER KNOLL
Physics, Biology and Chemistry: Prof. Dr HOLGER WÖHRMANN
Social Work: Prof. Dr WOLFRAM FISCHER
Social Sciences, Geography, Sports Science: Prof. Dr CHRISTOPH SCHERER
School of Art: Prof. Dr KARIN STEMPEL

ATTACHED RESEARCH INSTITUTES

Centre for Environmental Systems Research (CESR): internet www.usf.uni-kassel.de/cesr; Dir Prof. Dr JOSEPH ALCAMO.

Centre for Nanostructure Science and Technology (CINSaT): internet www.cinsat.uni-kassel.de/startseite.php; Dir Prof. Dr FRANK TRÄGER.

International Centre for Higher Education Research (INCHER-Kassel): internet www.uni-kassel.de/incher; Dir Prof. Dr BARBARA KEHM.

East-West Science Centre: Dir (vacant).

CHRISTIAN-ALBRECHTS UNIVERSITÄT ZU KIEL

24098 Kiel
Telephone: (431) 88000
Fax: (431) 880-2072
E-mail: mail@uni-kiel.de
Internet: www.uni-kiel.de

Founded 1665
State control
Academic year: October to July (two terms)

Rector: Prof. Dr JÖRN ECKERT
Vice-Rectors: Prof. Dr THOMAS BAUER, Prof. Dr GERHARD FOUQUET
Chancellor: Dr OLIVER HERRMANN
Librarian: Dr ELSE M. WISCHERMANN

Number of teachers: 600
Number of students: 20,000

Publications: *Christiana Albertina* (2 a year), *Jahresbericht* (annually), *Unizeit* (7 a year)

DEANS

Faculty of Agricultural and Nutritional Sciences: Prof. Dr SIEGFRIED WOLFFRAM
Faculty of Economics and Social Sciences: Prof. Dr ANDREAS DREXL
Faculty of Engineering: Prof. Dr PETER SEEGEBRECHT
Faculty of Law: Prof. Dr jur. JOACHIM JICKELI
Faculty of Mathematics and Natural Sciences: Prof. Dr JÜRGEN GROTEMEYER
Faculty of Medicine: Prof. Dr MICHAEL ILLERT
Faculty of Philosophy: Prof. Dr SIEGFRIED OESCHLE
Faculty of Theology: Prof. Dr theol. ULRICH HÜBNER

PROFESSORS

Faculty of Agricultural and Nutritional Science (Hermann-Rodewald-Str. 4, 24098 Kiel; tel. (431) 880-2591; fax (431) 880-7334; e-mail dekanat@agrar.uni-kiel.de; internet www.agrar.uni-kiel.de):

ABDULAI, A., Food Economics and Food Policy
BRUHN, M., Agricultural Marketing
FOHRER, N., Hydrology and Water Resources Management
HENNING, C., Agricultural Policy
HORN, R., Soil Science
JUNG, C., Plant Breeding and Genetics
KAGE, H., Crop Science
KALM, E., Animal Breeding and Genetics
KRIETER, J., Animal Husbandry, Quality of Products
LATACZ-LOHMANN, U., Farm Management and Production Economics
LOY, J.-P., Agricultural Market Theory
MÜLLER, M. J., Internal Medicine, Human Nutrition
MÜLLER, R. A. E., Agricultural Economics, Information, Innovation
RIMBACH, G., Food Science
ROOSEN, J., Health Economics
ROWECK, H., Landscape Ecology
SATTELMACHER, B., Plant Nutrition
SCHALLENBERGER, E., Animal Husbandry, Hygienics
SCHWARZ, K., Food Technology
SUSENBETH, A., Animal Nutrition
TAUBE, F., Grass and Forage Science, Organic Farming
VERREET, J.-A., Phytopathology, Plant Diseases
WOLFFRAM, S., Animal Nutrition and Nutritional Physiology
WYSS, U., Phytopathology, Biotechnology

Faculty of Economics and Social Sciences (Wilhelm-Seelig-Platz 1, 24098 Kiel; tel. (431) 880-2140; fax (431) 880-1691; e-mail dekanat@bwl.uni-kiel.de; internet www.bwl.uni-kiel.de):

ALBERS, S., Innovation, New Media and Marketing
BRÖCKER, J., Regional Science
DREXL, A., Production Management and Logistics
FRIEDL, B., Controlling
HERWARTZ, H., Econometrics
KLAPPER, D., Marketing
KRAUSE, J., Politics
KRUBER, K.-P., Political and Economic Education
LIESENFELD, R., Statistics and Empirical Economics
LUX, T., Monetary Economics and International Financial Markets
NIPPEL, P., Financial Management
RAFF, H., Industrial Economics
REQUATE, T., Economics of Innovation, Competition and Institutions
SEIDL, C., Public Finance and Choice Theory
SNOWER, D., Economics
VEIT, K.-R., Accounting
WALTER, A., Entrepreneurship and Innovation Management
WOHLTMANN, H.-W., Macroeconomics
WOLF, J., Organization

Faculty of Engineering (Kaiserstr. 2, 24143 Kiel; tel. (431) 880-6001; fax (431) 880-6003; e-mail dekanat@tf.uni-kiel.de; internet www.tf.uni-kiel.de):

BERGHAMMER, R., Computer-Aided Program Development
BROCKS, W., Material Mechanics
DIRKS, H., Electromagnetic Field Theory
FAUPEL, F., Multicomponent Materials
FÖLL, H., General Materials Science
FUCHS, F. W., Power Electronics and Electrical Devices
HACKBUSCH, W., Practical Mathematics
HANUS, M., Programming Languages and Compiler Construction
HANXLEDEN, R. VON, Real-time and Embedded Systems
HEUBERGER, A., Semiconductor Technology
HEUTE, U., Circuits and System Theory
HÖHER, P., Information and Coding Theory Laboratory
JÄGER, W., Centre for Microanalysis
JANSEN, K., Theory of Parallelism
KLINKENBUSCH, I., Computational Electromagnetics Group
KNÖCHEL, R., Microwave Group
KOCH, R., Multimedia Information Processing
LUTTENBERGER, N., Communication Systems
RÖCK, H., Automation and Control Engineering
ROEVER, W. P. DE, Software Technology
ROSENKRANZ, W., Communications
SCHIMMLER, M., Computer Engineering
SCHNEIDER, R., Scientific Computing
SEEGEBRECHT, P., Semiconductor Electronics
SOMMER, G., Cognitive Systems
SRIVASTAV, A., Discrete Optimization
THALHEIM, B., Information Systems Engineering
WEPPNER, W., Sensors and Solid State Ionics
WILKE, T., Theoretical Computer Science

Faculty of Law (Leibnizstr. 4, 24098 Kiel; tel. (431) 880-2125; fax (431) 880-1689; e-mail dekanat@law.uni-kiel.de; internet www.uni-kiel.de/fakultas/jura):

ALEXY, R., Public Law and Legal Philosophy
ECKERT, J., History of German and European Law, Civil Law, Commercial Law
EINSELE, D., Civil Law, Commercial Law, Private International Law, Comparative Law
FISCHER, M., Civil, Commercial and Economic Tax Law
FROMMEL, M., Criminology and Criminal Law
HOYER, A., Penal Law and Procedure
IGL, G., Public Law, Social Law
JICKELI, J., Civil Law, Commercial Law
KRACK, R., Penal Law and Procedure
MEYER-PRITZL, R., Civil Law, Roman Law, History of Law in Modern Times, Comparative Law
MUTIUS, A. VON, Public Law and Administration
REUTER, D., Civil, Commercial and Economic Law
SCHACK, H., International Civil Law, Private and Civil Trial Law, Copyright Law
SCHMIDT-JORTZIG, E., Public Law
SMID, S., Civil Law and Procedure
TRUNK, A., Civil and Civil Trial Law, International Private Law and Comparative Law
ZIMMERMANN, A., German and Foreign Public, International, and European Law, and General Theory of the State

Faculty of Mathematics and Natural Sciences (Christian-Albrechts-Platz 4, 24098 Kiel; tel. (431) 880-2128; fax (431) 880-2320; e-mail dekanat@mnf.uni-kiel.de; internet www.uni-kiel.de/fakultas/mathnat):

ALBAN, S., Pharmaceutical Biology
BÄHR, J., Geography
BAUER, T., Ecology
BAYRHUBER, H., Teaching Methods of Biology
BENDER, H., Mathematics
BENSCH, W., Inorganic Chemistry
BERGWEILER, W., Mathematics
BERNDT, R., Solid-State Physics
BETTEN, D., Mathematics
BILGER, W., Ecology
BISCHOF, K., Marine Biology
BLASCHEK, W., Pharmaceutical Biology
BODENDIEK, R., Mathematics
BÖNING, C., Theoretical Oceanography
BONITZ, M., Theoretical Physics
BORK, H.-R., Ecology System Research
BOSCH, T., General Zoology
BRENDELBERGER, H., Zoology and Limnology
CEMIČ, L., Mineralogy and Petrology
CLEMENT, B., Pharmaceutical Chemistry
COLIJN, F., Coastal Ecology
CORVES, C., Geography
DAHMKE, A., Applied Geology
DEMUTH, R., Teaching of Chemistry
DEPMEIER, W., Mineralogy and Crystallography
DEVEY, C., Geology
DIERSSEN, K., Botany
DOMMENGET, D., Meteorology
DULLO, W. C., Palaeo-Oceanography
DUTTMANN, R., Geography

EISENHAUER, A., Marine Ecogeology
EULER, M., Teaching of Physics
FRANK, M., Geology
GÖTZE, H.-J., Geophysics
GROOTES, P., Experimental Physics, Isotope Research
GROTEMEYER, J., Physical Chemistry
HACKNEY, R., Geophysics
HAMMANN, M., Teaching Methods of Biology
HANEL, R., Fishery Biology
HÄNSEL, W., Pharmaceutical Chemistry
HARTKE, B., Theoretical Chemistry
HARTL, G. B., Zoology
HASSENPFLUG, W., Geography
HEBER, J., Mathematics
HELBIG, V., Physics
HERGES, R., Organic Chemistry
HERZIG, P., Marine Science
HOERNLE, K., Vulcanology, Magmatic Petrology
HOPPE, H. G., Microbiology
IMHOFF, J., Marine Microbiology
IRLE, A., Probability Theory and Mathematical Statistics
KEMPKEN, F., Botany
KIPP, L., Experimental Physics
VON KLITZING, R., Physical Chemistry
KÖNIG, H., Mathematics
KOESTER, D., Astronomy and Astrophysics, Theoretical Physics
KÖRTZINGER, A., Organic Marine Chemistry
KRUPINSKA, K., Cell Biology
KUHNT, W., Geology and Palaeontology
KUNZE, T., Pharmaceutical Chemistry
LATIF, M., Meterology
LEIPPE, M., Zoology
LINDHORST, T., Organic Chemistry
LOCHTE, K., Plankton
LÜNING, U., Organic Chemistry
MACKE, A., Meteorology
MÄDER, H., Physical Chemistry
MAGNUSSEN, O. M., Experimental Physics
MAYERLE, R., Applied Coastal Geology
MIKELSKIS-SEIFERT, S., Teaching Methods of Physics
MÜLLER, B., Pharmaceutical Technology
MÜLLER, D., Mathematics
MÜLLER, M., Physics
NELLE, O. A., Ecology
NERDEL, C., Teaching Methods of Chemistry
NEWIG, J., Geography
PEHLKE, E., Theoretical Physics
PIEL, A., Experimental Physics
PRECHTL, H., Teaching Methods of Biology
RABBEL, W., Geophysics
REISE, K., Biological Oceanography
RESTON, T. J., Marine Geophysics
REVILLA DIEZ, J., Economy of Geography
RIEBESELL, U., Marine Biology
ROEDER, T., Zoology
RÖSLER, U., Stochastics
ROHR, G. VON, Geography
RUPRECHT, E., Meteorology
SAUTER, M., Botany
SCHÄFER, P., Geology
SCHANZE, S., Teaching Methods of Chemistry
SCHENK, V., Petrology and Mineralogy
SCHMIDT, R., Mathematics
SCHMITZ-STREIT, R. A., Microbiology
SCHNACK, D., Ichthyology
SCHNEIDER, R., Geology
SCHÖNHEIT, P., Microbiology
SCHREMPP, B., Theoretical Physics
SCHULZ-FRIEDRICH, R., Botany
SCHUSTER, H. G., Theoretical Physics
SEND, U., Physical Oceanography
SOMMER, U., Sea-Floor Ecology
SPENGLER, U., Teaching Methods of Mathematics
SPINAS, O., Logic
SPINDLER, M., Polar Ecology
STATTEGGER, K., Geology and Palaeontology
STELLMACHER, B., Mathematics
STERR, H., Physical Geography
STOCK, N., Inorganic Chemistry
STOFFERS, P., Geology
SUESS, E., Marine Environmental Geology
TEMPS, F., Physical Chemistry
TUCZEK, F., Inorganic Chemistry
UHLARZ, H., Botany
VISBECK, M., Physical Oceanography
WAHL, M., Marine Biology and Zoology
WALLACE, D., Marine Chemistry
WALTHER, G., Teaching of Mathematics
WILLEBRAND, J., Oceanography
WIMMER-SCHWEINGRUBER, R., Experimental Physics

Faculty of Medicine (Christian-Albrechts-Platz 4, 24098 Kiel; tel. (431) 880-2126; fax (431) 880-2129; e-mail dekanat@med.uni-kiel.de; internet www.uni-kiel.de/fak/med/med.html):

ALBERS, H.-K., Dentistry
ALDENHOFF, J., Psychiatry, Psychotherapy
ALZHEIMER, C., Psychology
AMBROSCH, P., Oto-rhino-laryngology
BARON, R., Neurology
BLEICH, M., Physiology
CREMER, J., Surgery
DEUSCHL, G., Neurology and Neurophysiology
FICKENSCHER, H., Medical Microbiology
FISCHER-BRANDIES, H., Dentistry
FÖLSCH, U. R., Internal Medicine
GERBER, W.-D., Clinical Psychology
GIESELER, F., Internal Medicine
GLÜER, C., Medicinal Physics
GROTE, W., Human Genetics
HASSENPFLUG, J., Orthopaedics
HELLER, M., Radiological Diagnosis
HENZE, E., Nuclear Medicine
HERDEGEN, T., Physiology, Molecular Pharmacology
ILLERT, M., Physiology
JANSEN, O., Neuroradiology
JONAT, W., Gynaecology and Obstetrics
JÜNEMANN, K.-P., Urology
JUST, U., Biochemistry
KAATSCH, H.-J., Legal Medicine
KABELITZ, D., Medical Microbiology and Immunology
KALTHOFF, H., Immunology and Cell Biochemistry
KERN, M., Dentistry
KIMMIG, B. N., Clinical Radiology
KLÖPPEL, G., Pathology and Pathological Anatomy
KNEBA, M., Internal Medicine
KOVACS, G., Clinical Radiology
KRAMER, H.-H., Child Medicine, Child Cardiology
KRAWCZAK, M., Human Genetics
KREMER, B., Surgery
KUNZENDORF, U., Internal Medicine, Nephrology
LUCIUS, R., Anatomy
LÜLLMANN-RAUCH, R., Anatomy
MASER, E., Toxicology
MEHDORN, H., Neurosurgery
METTLER, L., Gynaecology
OEHMICHEN, M., Legal Medicine
PARWARESCH, R., Haematopathology
PLAGMANN, H.-CH., Dentistry
PROKSCH, E., Dermatology and Venereology
ROIDER, J., Opthalmology
ROSE-JOHN, S., Biochemistry
SAFTIG, P., Biochemistry
SCHÖCKLMANN, H., Nephrology, Internal Medicine
SCHOLZ, J., Anaesthesiology
SCHRAPPE, M., Paediatrics
SCHREIBER, S., Internal Medicine and Gastroenterology
SCHRÖDER, J. M., Experimental Dermatology
SCHÜNKE, M., Anatomy
SCHÜTZE, G., Child Psychiatry
SCHWARTZ, T., Dermatology
SIEVERS, J., Anatomy
SIMON, R., Cardiology
STEPHANI, U., Paediatrics, Neuropaediatrics
STICK, C., Physiology
TONNER, P., Anaesthesiology
WEILER, N., Anaesthesiology
WILTFANG, J., Dental Surgery

Faculty of Philosophy (Christian-Albrechts-Platz 4, 24098 Kiel; tel. (431) 880-3055; fax (431) 880-7301; e-mail dekan@philfak.uni-kiel.de; internet www.uni-kiel.de/fakultas/philosophie):

BILLER, K.-H., Pedagogics
BLIESENER, T., Medieval and Modern History
BRINKHAUS, H., Indology
BRINKMANN, W., Pedagogics
CARNAP-BORNHEIM, C. VON, Prehistory and Early History
CONZELMANN, A., Sports Psychology
CORNELISSEN, C., Modern and Contemporary History
DORMEIER, H., Medieval and Modern History
ENGEL, A., Slavic Philology
FERSTL, R., Clinical Psychology
FLEISCHMANN, B., English Philology
FOUQUET, G., Economic and Social History
GÓMEZ-MONTERO, J., Romance Philology
GÖTTSCH-ELTEN, S., Folklore
GROSS, K., English Philology
HAAS, R., English Language and Literature
HAMEYER, U., Pedagogics
HANISCH, M., Teaching of History
HARRINGTON, J., Phonetics
HELDMANN, K., Classical Philology
HOEKSTRA, J., Friesian Philology
HOINKES, U., Romance Philology
HORATSCHEK, A. M., English Philology
JAWORSKI, R., East European History
JOBST, C., Art History
JONGEBLOED, H. C., Pedagogics
KÄPPEL, L., Classical Philology
KAPP, V., Romance Philology
KERSTING, W., Philosophy
KLEIN, D., Old German Literature
KÖHNKEN, G., Diagnostic and Differential Psychology
KONERSMANN, R., Teaching of Philosophy
KONRADT, U., Industrial, Marketing and Organizational Psychology
KROPE, P., Pedagogics
KUDER, U., Art History
KÜHNE, U., Ancient History, Medieval Linguistics
LINCK, G., Sinology
MAROLD, E., Old Norse Philology
MAUSFELD, R., Psychology
MEIER, A., History of Modern German Literature
MEYER, M., English Philology
MIETHLING, W.-D., Sports Pedagogics
MÖLLER, J., Psychology
MOERKE, O., Early Modern and Modern History
MOSEL, U., Linguistics
MÜLLER, J., Prehistory and Early History
MÜLLER, W.-U., Prehistory and Early History
NÜBLER, N., Slavic Philology
OECHSLE, S., Music
PALLASCH, W., Pedagogics
PETERSEN, J., Pedagogics
PISTOR-HATAM, A., Oriental Philology
POHL, K-H., Teaching of History
PRAHL, H.-W., Pedagogics
PRENZEL, M., Pedagogics
RADICKE, J., Classical Philology

REBAS, H., Northern History
RIIS, T., History of Schleswig-Holstein
RÜHLING, L., Modern Scandinavian Literature
SCHMALTZ, B., Classical Archaeology
SCHMIDT, A., Folklore
SIELERT, U., Pedagogics
SIMON, B., Psychology
SOMMER, M., Philosophy
SPONHEUER, B., Music
STEINDORFF, L., East European History
THUN, H., Romance Philology
TUCHOLSKI-DÄKE, B-C., Art
ULRICH, W., German Philology, Teaching of German Language
WEISS, P., Ancient History
WEISSER, B., Sports Medicine
WIESEHÖFER, J., Ancient History
WÜNSCH, M., History of Modern German Literature
WULFF, H. J., Theatre and Film Studies

Faculty of Theology (Leibnitzstr. 4, 24118 Kiel; tel. (431) 880-2124; fax (431) 880-1735; e-mail dekanattheo@email.uni-kiel.de; internet www.uni-kiel.de/fak/theol):

BARTELMUS, R., Old Testament Studies, Biblical and Middle Eastern Languages
VON BENDEMANN, R., New Testament Studies
BOBERT, S., Practical Theology
HÜBNER, U., Old Testament Studies and Biblical Archaeology
MECKENSTOCK, G., Systematic Theology
PREUL, R., Practical Theology
ROSENAU, H., Systematic Theology
SÄNGER, D., New Testament Studies
SCHILLING, J., Church History

ATTACHED INSTITUTES

Institut für Sicherheitspolitik an der Universität Kiel (ISUK) (Institute for Security Policy at Kiel University): Olshausenstr. 40, 24098 Kiel; Dir Prof. Dr J. KRAUSE.

Institut für Weltwirtschaft an der Universität Kiel (Institute for World Economics at Kiel University): Düsternbrooker Weg 120, 24105 Kiel; Pres. Prof. D. SNOWER.

Leibniz-Institut für Meereswissenschaften (IFM-GEOMAR) (Leibniz Institute of Marine Sciences): Wischhofstr. 1–3, 24148 Kiel; Dir Prof. Dr P. HERZIG.

Leibniz-Institut für die Pädagogik der Naturwissenschaften an der Universität Kiel (Leibniz Institute for Science Education): Olshausenstr. 62, 24098 Kiel; Dir Prof. Dr M. PRENZEL.

Lorenz-von-Stein-Institut für Verwaltungswissenschaften an der Universität Kiel (Lorenz von Stein Institute for Management Sciences at Kiel University): Olshausenstr. 40, 24098 Kiel; Dir Prof. Dr JOACHIM JICKELI.

Schleswig-Holsteinisches Institut für Friedenswissenschaften (Schleswig Holstein Institute for Peace Studies): Kaiserstr. 2, 24143 Kiel; Dir Prof. Dr K. POTTHOFF.

WISSENSCHAFTLICHE HOCHSCHULE FÜR UNTERNEHMENSFÜHRUNG, OTTO-BEISHEIM-HOCHSCHULE (Otto Beisheim Graduate School of Management)

Burgplatz 2, 56179 Vallendar
Telephone: (261) 6509-0
Fax: (261) 6509-509
E-mail: info@whu.edu
Internet: www.whu.edu

Founded 1984
Private control
Languages of instruction: German, English
Academic year: September to August

Rector: Prof. Dr PETER J. JOST
Vice-Rectors: Prof. Dr HOLGER ERNST, Prof. Dr MICHAEL FREUKEL, Prof. Dr JÜRGEN WEBER, Prof. Dr PETER WITT, Prof. Dr JÜRGEN WEBER
Librarian: HANNELORE PÖTHIG

Library of 35,000 vols
Number of teachers: 72
Number of students: 460

PROFESSORS

BROCKHOFF, K., Corporate Policy
ERNST, H., Technology and Innovation Management
FASSNACHT, M., Marketing
FISCHER, T., Business Information Science and Information Management
FRENKEL, M., Macroeconomics and International Economics
FÜLBIER, R. U., Accounting
HOLGL, M., Human Resources Management
HUCHZERMEIER, A., Production Management
HUTZSCHENREUTER, T., Corporate Strategy and Electronic Media Management
JOST, P.-J., Organization Theory
KAUFMANN, L., International Management
KORN, O., Corporate Finance
RUDOLF, M., Finance
WEBER, J., Controlling and Telecommunications
WEIGAND, J., Microeconomics and Industrial Organization
WITT, P., Entrepreneurship and Management of Start-Ups

DEUTSCHE SPORTHOCHSCHULE KÖLN

Carl-Diem-Weg 6, 50933 Cologne
Telephone: (221) 4982-1
Fax: (221) 4982-8330
Internet: www.dshs-koeln.de

Founded 1920 in Berlin, reopened in Cologne 1947
State control
Academic year: October to March, April to September

Rector: Prof. Dr WALTER TOKARSKI
Chancellor: Dr JOHANNES HORST
Librarian: Dr HEIKE SCHIFFER

Number of teachers: 230
Number of students: 6,672

DEANS

Faculty of Applied Sports Sciences: Prof. Dr CLAUS BUHREN
Faculty of Medicine and Natural Sciences: Prof. Dr DIETER EßFELD
Faculty of Philosophy and Social Sciences: Prof. ILSE HARTMANN-TEWS

UNIVERSITÄT ZU KÖLN

Albertus-Magnus-Platz, 50923 Köln
Telephone: (221) 470-0
Fax: (221) 4705151
E-mail: aaa@verw.uni-koeln.de
Internet: www.uni-koeln.de

Founded 1388
Academic year: October to July

Rector Magnificus: Prof. Dr AXEL FREIMUTH
First Vice-Rector: Prof. Dr THOMAS KRIEG
Chancellor: Dr jur. JOHANNES NEYSES
Librarian: Prof. Dr W. SCHMITZ

Number of teachers: 2,132
Number of students: 49,000

DEANS

Faculty of Economics, Business Administration and Social Sciences: Prof. Dr NORBERT HERZIG
Faculty of Education: Prof. Dr KLAUS KÜNZEL
Faculty of Law: Prof. Dr MICHAEL WALTER
Faculty of Mathematics and Natural Sciences: Prof. Dr ULRICH RADTKE
Faculty of Medicine: Prof. Dr med. EDGAR SCHÖMIG
Faculty of Philosophy: Prof. Dr HANS-PETER ULLMANN
Faculty of Special Education: Prof. Dr GERHARD LAUTH

PROFESSORS

Faculty of Economics, Business Administration and Social Sciences (tel. (221) 470-5607; fax (221) 470-5179; e-mail dekanat@wiso.uni-koeln.de; internet www.wiso.uni-koeln.de):

ANDEREGG, R. G., Political Economy
BAUM, H., Economics
BEUERMANN, G., Business Administration
DELFMANN, W., Business Administration
DERIGS, U., Information Systems, Operations Research
DONGES, J., Economics
EEKHOFF, J., Economics
EISENFÜHR, F., Business Administration
FELDERER, B., Economics
FELDSIEPER, M., Economics
FISCHER, L., Business Psychology
FRESE, E., Business Administration
FRIEDRICHS, J., Sociology
FUNK, P., Economics
GLÄSSER, E., Economic Geography
HARTMANN-WENDELS, T., Business Administration
HERZIG, N., Business Administration, Taxation
JÄGER, T., Political Science
JAGODZINSKI, W., Sociology
KEMPF, A., Business Administration, Finance
KITTERER, W., Economics
KÖHLER, R., Marketing
KOPPELMANN, U., Business Administration
KUHNER, C., Business Administration
LEIDHOLD, W., Political Science
LINDNER-BRAUN, C., Sociology
LÖBBECKE, C., Electronic Commerce
MELLIS, W., Business Informatics
MEULEMANN, H., Sociology
MOSLER, K., Statistics, Econometrics
MÜLLER-HAGEDORN, L., Business Administration
PIERENKEMPER, T., Economic History
RETTIG, R., Economics
RÖSNER, H. J., Social Politics
SCHELLHAASS, H. M., Economics
SCHMID, F., Statistics
SCHRADIN, H. R., Business Administration, Insurance
SCHULZ-NIESWANDT, F., Social Policy
SEIBT, D., Information Science, Business Administration
STERNBERG, R., Economic Geography
TEMPELMEIER, H., Business Administration
WAGNER, M., Sociology
WEIZSÄCKER, C. C. VON, Economics
WESSELS, W., Political Science
WIED-NEBBELING, S., Economics
WISWEDE, G., Business Psychology
ZERCHE, J., Social Policy

Faculty of Law (tel. (221) 470-2218; fax (221) 470-5106; e-mail jura-dekanat@uni-koeln.de; internet www.dekanat.de):

BAUR, J. F., Civil Law, Commercial Law, European Law
BÖCKSTIEGEL, K.-H., International and Constitutional Law, German and International Commercial Law
DAUNER-LIEB, B., Civil Law, Commercial Law, Industrial Law
DEPENHEUER, O., Public Law, Philosophy of Law
GRUNEWALD, B., Civil Law, Commercial Law
HENSSLER, M., Civil Law, Commercial Law, Industrial Law

HOBE, S., Public Law, International Law, European Law
HÖFLING, W., Constitutional Law, Administrative Law, Financial Law
HORN, N., Civil Law, German and International Commercial and Banking Law, Philosophy of Law
HÜBNER, U., Insurance Law, Civil Law, Commercial Law, Foreign and International Private Law
LANG, J., Tax Law, Public Law
MANSEL, H.-P., Civil Law, International Private Law, Comparative Law
MITTENZWEI, I., Civil Law, Civil Process Law, Philosophy of Law
MUCKEL, S., Public Law, Canon Law
NESTLER, C., Criminal Law, Criminal Case Law
PRÜTTING, H., Civil Law, Industrial Law
SCHIEDERMAIR, H., Public Law, International Law, Philosophy of Law
SCHMITT-KAMMLER, A., Constitutional and Administrative Law
SEIER, J., Criminal Law, Criminal Case Law
TETTINGER, P. J., Constitutional and Administrative Law
WALTER, M., Criminology, Criminal Law
WALTHER, S., Criminal Law, Criminal Procedural Law, Comparative Law
WEIGEND, T., Criminal Law, Criminal Procedural Law, Comparative Criminal Law, Criminology

Faculty of Medicine (tel. (221) 478-0; fax (221) 478-4097; e-mail med-dekanat@medizin.uni-koeln.de; internet www.medizin.uni-koeln.de):

ABKEN, H., Onco-genetics, Cell Biology
ADDICKS, K., Anatomy
BALDAMUS, C., Internal Medicine
BAUMANN, M. A., Dentistry
BERGDOLT, K., History of Medicine, Medical Ethics
BERTHOLD, F., Paediatrics
BÖRNER, U., Anaesthesiology
BRUNKWALL, J. S., Surgery
BUZELLO, W., Anaesthesiology
DECKERT-SCHLÜTER, M., Neuropathology
DIEHL, V., Internal Medicine
DIENES, H. P., Pathology and Pathological Anatomy
DÖPFNER, M., Psychopathology
ENGELMANN, U., Urology
ERDMANN, E., Internal Medicine
FRICKE, U., Pharmacology and Toxicology
FUHR, U., Pharmacology
GOESER, T., Internal Medicine
HACKENBROCH, M. H., Orthopaedics
HAUPT, G., Urology
HEISS, W.-D., Neurology and Psychiatry
HERHOLZ, K., Neurology
HERZIG, S., Pharmacology and Toxicology
HESCHELER, J., Physiology
HÖLSCHER, A. H., Surgery
HÖPP, H.-W., Internal Medicine
KERSCHBAUM, T., Dentistry
KLAUS, W., Pharmacology and Toxicology
KLOSTERKÖTTER, J., Psychiatry
KLUG, N., Neurosurgery
KOEBKE, J., Anatomy
KÖHLE, K., Psychosomatic Medicine and Psychotherapy
KONEN, W., Ophthalmology
KRIEG, T., Dermatology and Venereology
KRIEGLSTEIN, G. K., Ophthalmology
KRÖNKE, M., Hygiene and Microbiology
KRONE, W., Internal Medicine
LACKNER, K., Clinical Radiology
LAUTERBACH, K. W., Health Economics
LECHLER, E., Internal Medicine
LEHMACHER, W., Medical Statistics, Informatics and Epidemiology
LEHMANN, K., Anaesthesiology
LEHMKUHL, G., Child and Adolescent Psychiatry
MAHRLE, G., Dermatology
MALLMANN, P., Gynaecology and Obstetrics
MICHALK, D., Paediatrics
MÖSGES, R., Medical Informatics
MÜLLER, R.-P., Radiology
MÜLLER-WIELAND, D., Internal Medicine
NEISS, W. F., Anatomy
NIEDERMEIER, W., Dental Prosthetics
NOACK, M. J., Dentistry
NOEGEL, A. A., Biochemistry
PAULSSON, M., Biochemistry
PFAFF, H., Medical Sociology
PFEIFFER, P., Dentistry
PFISTER, H., Virology
PFITZER, G., Physiology
PIEKARSKI, C., Industrial Medicine
REHM, K. E., Surgery and Accident Surgery
ROTH, B., Paediatrics
RÜSSMANN, W., Ophthalmology
SCHEFFNER, M., Biochemistry
SCHICHA, H., Nuclear Medicine
SCHIRMACHER, P., Pathology
SCHRÖDER, H., Anatomy
STENNERT, E., Otorhinolaryngology
STURM, V., Neurosurgery
THIELE, J., Pathology
TROIDL, H., Surgery
TSCHUSCHKE, V., Medical Psychology
DE VIVIE, E. R., Thorax- and Cardio-Surgery
WIELCKENS, K., Clinical Chemistry
WIESNER, R. J., Physiology
ZÖLLER, J. E., Dental Surgery

Faculty of Philosophy (tel. (221) 470-2212; fax (221) 470-5133; e-mail Dekan.PhilFak@uni-koeln.de; internet www.uni-koeln.de/phil-fak):

AERTSEN, J., Philosophy
ALEXANDER, M., Modern History
ALLEMANN-GHIONDA, C., Intercultural Education
ANTOR, H., English Philology
ARMBRUSTER, C., Romance Philology
AX, W., Classical Philology
BALD, W.-D., Applied Linguistics
BEHREND-ENGELHARDT, H., African Studies
BENTE, G. M., Psychology
BERRESSEM, H., American Studies
BIEG, L., Modern Chinese Literature
BLAMBERGER, G., Modern German Literature
BLATTMANN, M., Medieval History
BLUMENTHAL, P., Romance Philology
BLUMRÖDER, C. VON, Musicology
BOLLIG, M., Cultural Anthropology
BOS, G., Jewish Studies
BOSCHUNG, D., Classical Archaeology
BOSINSKI, G., Prehistory and Early History
BRENNER, P. J., Modern German Literature
BUCK, E., Theatre, Film and Television Studies
CASIMIR, M., Cultural Anthropology
CLAESGES, U., Philosophy
DÄMMER, H.-W., Prehistory and Early History
DANN, O., Modern History
DIEM, W., Islamic Studies
DIMMENDAAL, G. J., African Studies
DRUX, R., Modern German Literature
DÜLFFER, J., Modern History
DÜSING, K., Philosophy
ECK, W., Ancient History
EHMCKE, F., Japanese Studies
ELEY, L., Philosophy
ENGELS, O., Medieval and Modern History
ERICKSON, J., Applied Linguistics
FISCHER, G., Psychology
FISCHER, T., Classical Archaeology
FRISCH, P., Classical Philology
FROST, U., Education
GARCÍA-RAMÓN, J. L., Linguistics
GAUS, J., History of Art
GEYER, P., Romance Philology
GÖRLACH, M., English Philology
GRAEVENITZ, A. VON, Art History
GREIVE, A., Romance Philology
GROEBEN, N., Psychology
GRONEWALD, M., Classical Philology
GÜNTHER, R., Musicology
HEINE, B., African Studies
HESBERG, H. VON, Classical Archaeology
HEUSER, R., Chinese Law
HÖHN, H.-J., Catholic Theology
HOLKESKAMP, K.-J., Early History
HUSSY, W., Psychology
ISENMANN, E., Medieval History
JÄRVENTAUSTA, M., Finnish Studies
JENAL, G., Medieval History
KABLITZ, A., Romance Philology
KAEHLER, K., Philosophy
KÄMPER, D., Musicology
KAPP, D. B., Indology and Tamil Studies
KINDERMANN, U., Medieval Latin
KLEINSCHMIDT, E., Modern German Literature
KREUTZER, G., Nordic Philology
KUNISCH, J., Medieval and Modern History
KWASMAN, T., Jewish Studies
LEBEK, W. D., Classical Philology
LENERZ, J., German Philology
LIEBRAND, C., Modern German Literature and Gender Studies
MANUWALD, B., Classical Philology
MERTENS, G., Education
NEUHAUS, V., Modern German and Comparative Literature
NEUMEIER, B., English Philology
NITSCH, W., Romance Philology
NUSSBAUM, N., Art History and Urban Conservation
OBST, U., Slavonic Philology
OST, H., Art History
PAPE, W., Modern German Philology
PETERS, U., Medieval German Literature
PLÖGER, W., Education
POTTHAST, B., Latin American History
PRIMUS, B., German Linguistics
ROLSHOVEN, J., Philological and Linguistic Computing
RÜPPELL, H., Education
SALBER, W., Psychology
SASSE, H.-J., Comparative Linguistics
SCHARPING, T., Sinology
SCHMIDT, C., East European History
SCHMIDT-DENTER, U., Psychology
SCHNEIDER, I., Theatre, Film and Television Studies
SCHNEIDER, W., Education
SCHUMACHER, R., Musicology
SEIFERT, U., Musicology
STEPHAN, E., Psychology
STRUVE, T., Medieval History
TAUCHMANN, K., Ethnology
THALLER, M., Informatics in Historical and Cultural Studies
THISSEN, H. J., Egyptology
ULLMANN, H.-P., Modern History
WEIHER, E. VON, Ancient Oriental Philology
WIENBRUCH, U., Philosophy
ZAHRNT, M., Early History
ZELINSKY, B., Slavonic Philology
ZEUSKE, M., Iberian and Latin American History
ZICK, G., Art History
ZIEGELER, H. J., Medieval German Literature
ZIMMERMANN, A., Prehistory and Early History

Faculty of Mathematics and Natural Sciences (tel. (221) 470-5643; fax (221) 470-5108; e-mail math-nat-fakultaet@uni-koeln.de; internet www.uni-koeln.de/math-nat-fak):

ARMBRUST, M., Mathematics
ARNDT, H., Zoology
BACHEM, A., Applied Mathematics and Informatics
BELOW, R., Micropalaeontology and Palaeoecology
BERKESSEL, A., Organic Chemistry

BERKING, S., Zoology
BESLER, H., Geography
BOHATÝ, L., Crystallography
BOTHE, H., Botany
BRUNOTTE, E., Geography
BUNDSCHUH, P., Mathematics
BÜSCHGES, A., Zoology
CAMPOS-ORTEGA, J. A., Developmental Physiology
COENEN, H. H., Nuclear Chemistry
DEITERS, U., Physical Chemistry
DOHMEN, J., Genetics
DOST, M., Physics
ECKART, A., Experimental Physics
EILENBERGER, G., Theoretical Physics
ERMER, O., Organic Chemistry
FAIGLE, U., Applied Mathematics
FLÜGGE, U.-I., Botany
FREIMUTH, A., Experimental Solid State Physics
GOMPPER, G., Theoretical Physics
GRIESBECK, A. G., Organic Chemistry
HAUSEN, K., Zoology
HEHL, F. W., Theoretical Physics
HENKE, W., Mathematics
HERBIG, H.-G., Palaeontology and Historical Geography
HOHLNEICHER, G., Physical Chemistry
HOWARD, J. C., Genetics
HÜLSKAMP, M., Botany
ILGENFRITZ, G., Physical Chemistry
JOLIE, J., Experimental Physics
JÜNGER, M., Informatics
KAUPP, U. B., Biophysical Chemistry
KAWOHL, B., Mathematics
KEMPER, B., Genetics and Genetic Engineering
KERSCHGENS, M., Meteorology
KLEIN, H. W., Biochemistry
KORSCHING, S., Genetics
KRAAS, F., Anthropogeography
KRAMER, R., Biochemistry
KRUMSIEK, K., Geology
KÜPPER, T., Mathematics
LAMOTKE, K., Mathematics
LANGE, H., Mathematics
LANGER, T., Genetics
LEPTIN, M., Genetics
LESCH, M., Mathematics
LEYTHAEUSER, D., Geology
MELKONIAN, M., Botany
MEYER, G., Inorganic Chemistry
MICKLITZ, H., Experimental Physics
MÜHLBERG, M., Crystallography
MÜLLER-HARTMANN, E., Theoretical Physics
NATTERMANN, T., Theoretical Physics
NAUMANN, D., Inorganic and Analytical Chemistry
NEUBAUER, F. M., Geophysics and Meteorology
NEUMANN, M., Applied Mathematics
NEUWIRTH, W., Physics
NIMTZ, G., Physics
NIPPER, J., Geography
PAETZ GEN. SCHIECK, H., Physics
PALME, H., Mineralogy
PLICKERT, G., Zoology
POHLEY, H.-J., Developmental Biology
RADTKE, U., Geography
RAJEWSKY, K., Molecular Genetics
RAMMENSEE, W., Mineralogy
RAPOPORT, M., Mathematics
RECKZIEGEL, H., Mathematics
RICKEN, W., Geology
ROTH, S., Developmental Biology
RUSCHEWITZ, U., Inorganic Chemistry
SCHIEDER, R., Experimental Physics
SCHIERENBERG, E., Zoology
SCHLICHTER, D., Zoology
SCHMALZ, H.-G., Organic Chemistry
SCHMITZ, K., Botany
SCHNEIDER-POETSCH, HJ., Botany
SCHNETZ, K., Genetics
SCHOMBURG, D., Biochemistry
SCHRADER, R., Informatics
SEIDEL, E., Geochemistry
SEYDEL, R., Mathematics
SOYEZ, D., Anthropogeography
SPECKENMEYER, E., Informatics
SPETH, P., Geophysics and Meteorology
STAUFFER, D., Theoretical Physics
STERNER, R., Biochemistry
STREY, R., Physical Chemistry
STRÖHER, H., Experimental Nuclear Physics
STUTZKI, J., Physics
TAUTZ, D., Genetics
TEZKAN, B., Geophysics
THORBERGSSON, G., Mathematics
TIEKE, B., Physical Chemistry
TOPP, W., Zoology
TROTTENBERG, U., Applied Mathematics
WALKOWIAK, W., Zoology
WEISSENBÖCK, G., Botany
WERR, W., Developmental Biology
WESEMANN, L., Inorganic Chemistry
ZIRNBAUER, M., Theoretical Physics
ZITTARTZ, J., Theoretical Physics

Faculty of Education (tel. (221) 470-5777; fax (221) 470-5073; e-mail dekanat@ew.uni-koeln.de; internet www.uni-koeln.de/ew-fak):

ADOLPHI, K., Biology
ANACKER, U., General Education
AUERNHEIMER, G., Intercultural Education
BANNWARTH, H., Biology
BARTELS, G., Geography
BECKER-MROTZEK, M., German
BOMBEK, M., Textile Design
BREULL, W.-R., Biology and Human Biology
BROSSEDER, J., Catholic Theology
BUKOW, W.-D., Sociology
BURSCHEID, H. J., Mathematics
BUTTERWEGGE, C., Political Science
DONNERSTAG, J., English
GLÜCK, G., General Education and School Education
GRÜNEWALD, B., Philosophy
GÜNTHER, HARTMUT, German Language and Literature
GÜNTHER, HENNING, General Education and School Education
HAIDER-HASEBRINK, H., Psychology
HURRELMANN, B., German Language and Literature
KLEIN, K., Biology
KOCH-PRIEWE, B., General Education and School Education
KOENEN, K., Protestant Theology
KÜNZEL, K., Adult Education
LAMM, H., Psychology
LLARYORA, R., Sociology
MESSELKEN, H., German Language and Literature
MINSEL, W.-R., Psychology
OTT, T., Music
RECH, P., Art
REICH, K., General Education
REINERS, C., Chemistry
SCHÄFER, G., General Education
SCHMIDT, S., Mathematics
SCHNEIDER, R., Music
SCHÖN, E., German Language and Literature
SCHOLTEN, C., Roman Catholic Theology
SCHRÖDER, J., History
SEIBEL, H. D., Sociology
STOCK, A., Theology
STRUVE, H., Mathematics
THIEMANN, F., General Education
THIEME, G., Geography
TIMM, U., Biology
TÖNNIS, G., Art
VOLKENBORN, A., Mathematics
WEGENER-SPÖHRING, G., General Education
WEISER, W., Mathematics
WICHARD, W., Biology
WICKERT, J., Psychology
WIEGERSHAUSEN, H.-W., Art
WILKENDING, G., German Language and Literature
ZILLESSEN, D., Protestant Theology

Faculty of Special Education (tel. (221) 470-4640; fax (221) 470-5953; internet www.uni-koeln.de/hp-fak):

BUCHKREMER, H., General Therapy and Social Education
CONINX, F., Education of the Deaf and Hard of Hearing
DREHER, W., Education of the Mentally Handicapped
FENGLER, J., Psychology
FISCHER, K., Physical Education
FORNEFELD, B., Education of the Mentally Retarded
KIRFEL, B., Sociology of the Handicapped
LAUTH, G., Psychology and Psychotherapy
LIST, G., Psychology
MASENDORF, F., Special Education and Rehabilitation of the Educationally Subnormal
OSKAMP, U., Education of the Physically Handicapped
PIEL, W., Music Therapy
SCHLEIFFER, R., Psychiatry and Psychotherapy
SEIFERT, R., Education of the Physically Handicapped
TSCHERNER, K. W. H., Teaching of the Educationally Subnormal
WEINWURM-KRAUSE, E.-M., Psychology and Psychiatry
WICHELHAUS, B., Art Therapy
WILLAND, H., Special Education and Rehabilitation of the Educationally Subnormal
WISOTZKI, K. H., Education of the Deaf and Hard of Hearing
WÖRNER, G., Arts and Crafts

UNIVERSITÄT KONSTANZ

78457 Konstanz
Telephone: (7531) 88-0
Fax: (7531) 88-3688
Internet: www.uni-konstanz.de

Founded 1966
Academic year: October to September

Rector: Prof. Dr GERHART VON GRAEVENITZ
Pro-Rectors: Prof. Dr BRIGITTE ROCKSTROH, Prof. Dr BERNHARD SCHINK, Prof. Dr ASTRID STADLER
Registrar: JENS APITZ
Librarian: Dr jur. K. FRANKEN

Number of teachers: 171
Number of students: 9,363

Publications: *Uni-info*, *Studienführer*

DEANS

Faculty of Sciences: Prof. Dr THOMAS ELBERT
Faculty of Law, Economics and Politics: Prof. Dr FRIEDRICH BREYER
Faculty of Humanities: Prof. Dr ALMUT TODOROW

PROFESSORS

Faculty of Humanities

Department of History and Sociology:

GIESEN, B., Sociology
GOTTER, U., Sociology
HINZ, T., Sociology
KNORR, C., Sociology
OSTERHAMMEL, J., History
PATSCHOVSKY, A., History
PIETROW-ENKER, B., History
REICHHARDT, S., History
RICHTER, M., History
RIEHLE, H., Sports Science
SCHLÖGL, K., History
SOEFFNER, H., Sociology
SÜRENHAGEN, D., History
WISCHERMANN, C., History

WUNDER, B., History
WOLL, A., Sports Science

Department of Linguistics:

BAYER, J.
BREU, W.
BUTT, M.
CORRELL, CH.
EGLI, U.
KAISER, G.
LAHIRI, A.
PLANK, F.

Department of Literature:

ASSMANN, A.
BAUDY, G.
FEICHTINGER, B.
GRAEVENITZ, G. VON
JOAN I TOUS, P.
KOSCHORKE, A.
KÜMMEL, A.
KUHN, B.
MERGENTHAL, S.
MURASOV, J.
NISCHIK, R.
PAECH, J.
SCHNYDER, H.
SMIRNOV, I.
THÜRLEMANN, F.
TODOROW, A.

Department of Philosophy:

SEEBASS, G.
SPOHN, W.
STEMMER, P.
WOLTERS, G.

Faculty of Law, Economics and Politics

Department of Economics:

BREYER, F.
DEISSINGER, TH.
FABEL, O.
FRANKE, G.
GENSER, B.
GRIEBEN, W.-H.
HEILER, S.
JACKWERTH, J.
KAAS, L.
POHLMEIER, W.
RAMSER, H.-J.
SANDER, H.
SCHWEINBERGER, A.
STURM, J.-E.
SÜDEKUM, J.
URSPRUNG, H.
WITTMANN, F.

School of Law:

BOECKEN, W.
EISELE, J.
FEZER, K.-H.
FRANZEN, M.
GLÖCKNER, J.
HAILBRONNER, K.
HAUSMANN, R.
HEINZ, W.
IBLER, M.
RENGIER, R.
RÖHL, H.-C.
STADLER, A.
STRÄTZ, H.
WILMS, H.

Department of Politics and Management:

BOERNER, S.
KELLER, B.
KLIMECKI, R.
KNILL, CH.
SCHNEIDER, G.
SCHNEIDER, V.
SCHNELL, R.
SEIBEL, W.
SIMON, K.
VATTER, A.

Faculty of Sciences

Department of Biology:

ADAMSKA, J.
APELL, H.-J.
BOOS, W.
BÜRKLE, A.
COOK, A.
DIEDRICHS, K.
DIETRICH, D.
ECKMANN, R.
GALIZIA, G.
GHISLA, S.
GROETRUP, M.
HASTUNG, T.
HOFER, H.-W.
KRONECK, P.
KROTH, P.
KÜPPER, H.
KUTSCH, W.
MALCHOW, D.
MENDGEN, K.
MEYER, A.
PEETERS, F.
PLATTNER, H.
ROTHHAUPT, K. O.
SCHINK, B.
SCHEFFNER, M.
STÜRMER, C.
WELTE, W.
WENDEL, A.

Department of Chemistry:

DALTROZZO, E.
EXNOR, T.
FISCHER, H.
GROTH, U.
KROKE, E.
MARX, A.
MECKING, S.
MÜLLER, H.
MÜLLER, G.
PRZYBYLSKI, M.
STEINER, U.
WEYRICH, W.
WITTMANN, V.

Department of Computer and Information Science:

BERTHOLD, M.
BRANDES, U.
DEUSSEN, O.
KEIM, D.
KUHLEN, R.
LEUE, S.
REITERER, H.
SAUPE, D.
SCHOLL, M. H.
WALDVOGEL, H.

Department of Mathematics and Statistics:

BARTHEL, G.
BAUR, W.
BERAN, J.
DENK, R.
DREHER, H.
HOFFMANN, D.
JUNK, M.
KOHLMANN, M.
PRESTEL, A.
RACKE, R.
SCHEIDERER, C.
WATZLAWEK, W.

Department of Physics:

AUDRETSCH, J.
DEKORSY, T.
DIETERICH, W.
FUCHS, M.
GANTEFÖR, G.
LEIDERER, P.
LEITENSDORFER, A.
MARET, G.
NIELABA, P.
RÜDIGER, U.
SCHATZ, G.
SCHEER, E.

Department of Psychology:

ELBERT, TH.
GOLLWITZER, P.
HÜBNER, R.
KIßLER, J.
MCCREA, S.
NEUNER, F.
ROCKSTROH, B.
SCHUPP, H.
SONNENTAG, S.
STECK, P.
TROMMSDORF, G.
WALTER, H.

UNIVERSITÄT LEIPZIG

Postfach 100920, 04009 Leipzig
Located at: Ritterstr. 26, 04109 Leipzig
Telephone: (341) 97108
Fax: (341) 9730099
Internet: www.uni-leipzig.de

Founded 1409
State control
Academic year: October to September (two semesters)

Rector: Prof. Dr FRANZ HÄUSER
Vice-Rector (Education): Prof. Dr CHARLOTTE SCHUBERT
Vice-Rector (Research and Promotion of Young Scientists): Prof. Dr MARTIN SCHLEGEL
Vice-Rector (University Development): Prof. Dr PETER WIEDEMANN
Chancellor: PETER GUTJAHR-LÖSER
Librarian: Dr CHARLOTTE BAUER
Number of students: 31,000

DEANS

Faculty of Biosciences, Pharmacy and Psychology: Prof. Dr KURT EGER
Faculty of Chemistry and Mineralogy: Prof. Dr HARALD MORGNER
Faculty of Economics and Management: Prof. Dr ROLF HASSE
Faculty of Education: Prof. Dr HARALD MARX
Faculty of History, Art and Oriental Studies: Prof. Dr HELMET LOOS
Faculty of Law: Prof. Dr MARTIN OLDIGES
Faculty of Mathematics and Computer Science: Prof. Dr GERHARD HEYER
Faculty of Medicine: Prof. Dr WIELAND KIESS
Faculty of Philology: Prof. Dr ERWIN TSCHIRMER
Faculty of Physics and Earth Science: Prof. Dr GERD TETZLAFF
Faculty of Social Sciences and Philosophy: Prof. Dr WOLFGANG FACH
Faculty of Sports Science: Prof. Dr JÜRGEN KRUG
Faculty of Theology: Prof. Dr WOLFGANG RATZMANN
Faculty of Veterinary Medicine: Prof. Dr GOTTHOLD GÄBEL

PROFESSORS

Faculty of Biosciences, Pharmacy and Psychology (Brüderstr. 35, 04103 Leipzig; tel. (341) 9736700; fax (341) 9736749; e-mail dekanat.bio@uni-leipzig.de):

BECK-SICKINGER, A. G., Biochemistry
BUSOT, F., Terrestrial Ecology
COLLANI, G. VON, Cognitive Social Psychology
EGER, K., Pharmaceutical Chemistry
HARMS, H., Environmental Microbiology
HAUSCHILDT, S., Immunobiology
HOFMANN, H.-J., Biophysical Chemistry
JESCHENIAK, D., Cognitive Psychology
MOHR, G., Industrial and Organizational Psychology
MORAWETZ, W., Special Botany
MÖRL, M., Biochemistry and Molecular Biology
MÜLLER, M., Experimental Psychology and Cognitive Neuroscience
NIEBER, K., Pharmacology
PETERMANN, H., Psychology of Personality and Psychological Intervention
POEGGEL, G., Human Biology
RAUWALD, J.-W., Pharmaceutical Biology

REISSER, W., General and Applied Botany
ROBITZKI, A., Molecular Biological-Biochemical Processing Technology
RÜBSAMEN, R., Neurobiology
SASS, H., Genetics
SCHILDBERGER, K.-M., General Zoology and Animal Behaviour Physiology
SCHLEGEL, M., Molecular Evolution and Systematics of Animals
SCHRÖDER, H., Clinical Psychology
SCHRÖGER, E., Cognitive Psychology and Biological Psychology
WILHELM, CHR., Plant Physiology
WITRUK, E., Educational Rehabilitation Psychology

Faculty of Chemistry and Mineralogy (Johannisallee 29, 04103 Leipzig; tel. (341) 9736000; fax (341) 9736099; e-mail dekanat@chemie.uni-leipzig.de; internet www.uni-leipzig.de/chemie):

BENTE, K., Mineralogy, Crystallography
BERGER, ST., Analytical Chemistry
BREDE, O., Physical Chemistry
GIANNIS, A., Organic Chemistry
HEY-HAWKINS, E., Inorganic Chemistry
HOFFMANN, R., Bioanalytics
KRAUTSCHEID, H., Inorganic Chemistry
MORGNER, H., Physical Chemistry
PAPP, H., Technological Chemistry
REINHOLD, J., Theoretical Chemistry
SCHNEIDER, C., Organic Chemistry
STRÄTER, N., Structural Analysis of Biopolymers

Faculty of Economics and Management (Marschnerstr. 31, 04109 Leipzig; tel. (341) 9733500; fax (341) 9733509; e-mail dekanat@wifa.uni-leipzig.de; internet www.uni-leipzig.de/wifa):

BRUHNKE, K.-H., Industrial Engineering and Structural Engineering: Technical and Infrastructural Management
DIEDRICH, R., Business Management: Controlling and Management Accounting
EISENECKER, U., Manager Information Systems: Software Development, Business and Administration
FRANCZYK, B., Manager Information Systems: Information Management
FÖHR, S., Business Management: Personnel Management
GRAW, K.-U., Industrial Engineering and Structural Engineering: Laying of Foundations/Hydraulic Engineering
HASSE, R., Economics: Economic Policy
HEILEMANN, U., Empirical Economics and Econometrics
HOLLÄNDER, R., Environmental Management in Small and Medium Enterprises
KALISKE, M., Industrial Engineering and Structural Engineering: Statics and Dynamics of Structures
LANG, S., Economics, Statistics
LENK, T., Economics: Public Finance Theory
LÖBLER, H., Business Management: Marketing
PAHL, B., Industrial Engineering and Structural Engineering: Drafting/Construction Design
PARASKEWOPOULOS, S., Economics: Macroeconomics
PELZL, W., Business Management: Real Estate Management
POSSELT, T., Business Management: Service Management
RAUTENBERG, H.-G., Business Management: Management Accounting and Corporate Taxation
RINGEL, J., Urban Management
SCHMIDT, H., Business Management: Accounting and Auditing
SCHUHMACHER, F., Business Management: Corporate Finance
SINGER, H. J., Business Management: Banking
TUE, V., Industrial Engineering and Structural Engineering: Solid Construction/Building Material Technology
VOLLMER, U., Economics and Currency
WAGNER, F., Business Management: Insurance Company Management
WIESE, H., Economics: Microeconomics
WANZEK, T., Industrial Engineering and Structural Engineering: Steel-Girder Construction

Faculty of Education (Karl-Heine-Str. 22B, 04229 Leipzig; tel. (341) 9731400; fax (341) 9731499; e-mail dekanat.fakerz@uni-leipzig.de; internet www.uni-leipzig.de/~erzwiss):

DOBSLAFF, O., Special Education, Language and Speech Pathology
HOFSÄSS, T., Special Education, Learning Disabilities
HOPPE-GRAFF, S., Educational Psychology
HÖRNER, W., Comparative Education
KLAUSER, F., Economics, Business Education and Management Training
KNOLL, J., Adult Education
MARX, H., Psychology in School and Instruction
MELZER, M., School Education
MUTZECK, W., Behaviour Problems and Therapy in Special Education
SCHULZ, D., School Education
TOEPELL, M., Teaching Primary School Mathematics
VON WOLFFERSDORFF-EHLERT, C., Social Education
WOLLERSHEIM, H. W., General Education

Faculty of History, Art and Oriental Studies (Burgstr. 21, 04109 Leipzig; tel. (341) 9737000; fax (341) 9737049; e-mail dekgko@rz.uni-leipzig.de; internet www.uni-leipzig.de/fak/gesch.htm):

BAUMBACH, G., Drama
BAXMANN, J., Drama (Dance)
BÜNZ, E., History of Saxony
CAIN, H.-U., Classical Archaeology
DENZEL, M. A., Social and Economic History
DINER, D., Jewish History and Culture
EBERHARD, W., East and Middle European History
EBERT, H.-G., Islamic Law
FEURICH, H.-J., Teaching of Music
FISCHER-ELFERT, H.-W., Egyptology
FRANCO, E., Indology
VON FRANZ, R., Modern Sinology
GERTEL, J., Economy and Social Geography of the Middle East
GIRSHAUSEN, TH., Drama
VON HEHL, U., Modern History
HEEG, G., Drama
HEYDEMANN, G., Modern History
HÖPKEN, W., East and South-east European History
JONES, A., African History
KAPPEL, R., African Politics and Economy
KLOTZ, S., Systematic Musical Science
LANGE, B., History of Art
LOOS, H., Historical Music Science
MAREK, M., History of Art
MORITZ, R., Classical Sinology
PREISSLER, H., History of Middle Eastern Religions
RICHTER, S., Japanology
RIECKHOFF-HESSE, S., Prehistory and Early History
RIEKENBERG, M., Comparative History and Ibero-American History
RUDERSDORF, M., History of the Early Modern Era
SCHUBERT, CH., Classical History
SCHULZ, E., Arabic Linguistic and Translation Science
SCHULZ, F., Teaching of Art
SEIWERT, H., General and Comparative Religion
SÖRENSEN, P. K., Central Asian Studies
STRECK, B., Ethnology
STRECK, M., Ancient Near East
TOPFSTEDT, TH., History of Art
WOLFF, E., African Studies
ZÖLLNER, F., History of Art

Faculty of Law (Burgstr. 27, 04109 Leipzig; tel. (341) 9735100; fax (341) 9735299; e-mail simue@rz.uni-leipzig.de; internet www.uni-leipzig.de/~jura):

BECKER-EBERHARD, E., Civil Law and Civil Action Law
BERGER, CHR., Civil and Civil Trial Law, Copyright
BOEMKE, B., Civil and Industrial Law, Social Legislation
DEGENHART, C., Commercial, Environmental and Planning Law
DOLEZALEK, G., Civil Law
DRYGALA, T., Civil Law, Commercial, Social and Business Law
ENDERS, CHR., Public Law
GOERLICH, H., Public, Constitutional and Administrative Law
HÄUSER, F., Civil, Industrial and Banking Law
KAHLO, M., Criminal and Criminal Trial Law, Legal Philosophy
KERN, B.-R., Civil and Medical Law, History of Law
KLESCZEWSKI, D., Criminal Trial Law and European Criminal Law
KÖCK, W., Environmental Law
OLDIGES, M., Public Law
RAUSCHER, TH., Private International Law, Comparative and Civil Law
SCHUMANN, H., Criminal and Commercial Law
STADIE, M.-H., Tax Law and Public Law
WELTER, R., Civil Law, German and International Economic Law

Faculty of Mathematics and Computer Science (Augustusplatz 10–11, 04109 Leipzig; tel. (341) 9732100; fax (341) 9732199; e-mail matinf@mathematik.uni-leipzig.de; internet www.uni-leipzig.de/matinf):

BEYER, K., Applied Mathematics
BORNELEIT, P., Teaching of Mathematics
BREWKA, G., Intelligent Systems
FREY, R., Discrete Mathematics
FRITZSCHE, B., Probability Theory
GIRLICH, H.-J., Stochastics
GRUHN, V., Applied Telematics
GÜNTHER, M., Partial Differential Equations
HERRE, H., Formal Concepts of Computer Science
HERZOG, B., Principles of Mathematics, Logic, Theory of Numbers
HEYER, G., Natural Language Processing
HUBER-KLAWITTER, A., Theoretical Mathematics
IRMSCHER, K., Computer Networks and Split Systems
KEBSCHULL, U., Technical Information Technology
KIRSTEIN, B., Mathematical Statistics
KUNKEL, P., Numerical Mathematics and Scientific Computing
KÜRSTEN, K.-D., Operator Algebra
LUCKHAUS, ST., Mathematical Optimization
MIERSEMANN, E., Calculus of Variations
RADEMACHER, H.-B., Differential Geometry
RAHM, E., Databases
SCHMÜDGEN, K., Functional Analysis
SCHUMANN, R., Analysis
SCHWARZ, M., Mathematics in Science
STADLER, P., Bioinformatics
STÜCKRAD, J., Algebra
WOLLENBERG, M., Mathematical Physics

Faculty of Medicine (Liebigstr. 27, 04103 Leipzig; tel. (341) 9715930; fax (341) 9715939; e-mail teichh@medizin.uni-leipzig.de):

ADAM, H., Anaesthesiology and Intensive Therapy
ALEXANDER, H., Obstetrics and Gynaecology
ALLGAIER, C., Pharmacology and Toxicology
ANGERMEYER, M., Psychiatry
ARENDT, T., Neuroanatomy
ARNOLD, K., Medical Physics and Biophysics
ASMUSSEN, G., Physiology
BADER, A., Cell Biology
BAERWALD, C., Internal Medicine, Rheumatology
BAIER, D., Obstetrics and Gynaecology
BLATZ, R., Medical Microbiology
BÖHME, H.-J., Biochemistry
BRÄHLER, E., Medical Psychology
BÜHRDEL, P., Paediatrics
VON CRAMON, Y., Cognitive Neurology
DANNHAUER, K.-H., Orthodontics
DECKERT, F., Diagnostic Radiology
DIETZ, A., Oto-rhino-laryngology
DONATH, E., Medical Physics and Biophysics
EICHFELD, U., Thorax Surgery
EILERS, J., Physiology
EMMRICH, P., Pathology
ENGELE, J., Anatomy, Embryology
ENGELMANN, L., Internal Medicine, Intensive Medicine
ESCHRICH, K., Biochemistry
ETTRICH, C., Child and Adolescent Psychiatry, Psychotherapy
FROSTER, U., Genetics
GEBHARDT, R., Biochemistry
GERTZ, H.-J., Psychiatry
GEYER, M., Psychosomatic Medicine and Psychotherapy
GLANDER, H.-J., Andrology
GRÄFE, H.-G., Paediatric Surgery
GRÜNDER, W., Medical Physics and Biophysics
GUMMERT, J. F., Cardiac Surgery
HÄNTZSCHEL, H., Internal Medicine, Rheumatology
HAUSS, J. P., Abdominal, Transplantation and Vascular Surgery
HEMPRICH, A., Maxillofacial Surgery
HENGSTLER, J., Molecular Toxicology
HERBARTH, O., Environmental Medicine
HIRSCH, W., Diagnostic Radiology
HÖCKEL, M., Obstetrics and Gynaecology
HORN, F., Molecular Immunology
HUMMELSHEIM, H., Neurology
ILLES, P., Pharmacology and Toxicology
JAKSTAT, H., Dental Prosthetics and Materials
JANOUSÈK, J., Paediatric Cardiology
JASSOY, C., Molecular Virology
JENTSCH, H., Parodontology
JOSTEN, CH., Traumatology
KAHN, TH., Diagnostic Radiology
KÄSTNER, I., History of Medicine
KELLER, E., Paediatrics
KIESS, W., Paediatrics
KLEEMANN, W. J., Forensic Medicine
KLÖTZER, B., Surgery
KÖNIG, F., Anaesthesiology and Intensive Therapy
KÖNIG, H.-H., Health Economy
KÖRHOLZ, D., Paediatrics, Haematology and Oncology
KORTMANN, R.-D., Radiotherapy
KOSTELKA, M., Paediatrics, Cardiac Surgery
LIEBERT, U. G., Virology
LÖFFLER, M., Medical Informatics, Statistics and Epidemiology
MEIXENSBERGER, J., Neurosurgery
MERKENSCHLAGER, A., Paediatrics
MERTE, K., Restorative Dentistry
METZNER, G., Clinical Immunology, Allergology
MOHR, F.-W., Cardiac Surgery
MÖSSNER, J., Internal Medicine, Gastroenterology
MOTHES, TH., Clinical Chemistry
NIEDERWIESER, D., Internal Medicine, Haematology
NÖRENBERG, W., Pharmacology and Toxicology
OLTHOFF, D., Anaesthesiology and Intensive Therapy
PASCHKE, R., Internal Medicine, Endocrinology
PFÄFFLE, R., Paediatrics, Endocrinology, Gastroenterology
PFEIFFER, D., Internal Medicine, Cardiology
PLÖTTNER, G., Psychosomatic Medicine and Psychotherapy
PREISS, R., Clinical Pharmacology
REIBER, TH., Dental Prosthetics and Materials
REICHENBACH, A., Neurophysiology
RICHTER, V., Clinical Chemistry, Metabolic Disorders
RIEDEL-HELLER, S., Public Health
RIHA, O., History of Medicine
RODLOFF, A., Medical Microbiology
SABRI, O., Nuclear Medicine
VON SALIS-SOGLIO, G., Orthopaedics
SANDHOLZER, H., Internal Medicine
SCHELLENBERGER, W., Biochemistry
SCHMIDT, F., Diagnostic Radiology
SCHOBER, R., Neuropathology
SCHÖNEBERG, T., Biochemistry, Molecular Endocrinology
SCHREINICKE, G., Industrial Medicine
SCHUBERT, ST., Internal Medicine
SCHULER, G., Internal Medicine, Cardiology
SCHUSTER, V., Paediatrics
SCHWARZ, J., Neurology
SCHWARZ, R., Social Medicine
SCHWOKOWSKI, CH., Surgical Oncology
SEIBEL, P., Molecular Cell Therapy
SIMON, J.-C., Dermatology
SPANEL-BOROWSKI, K., Anatomy
STICHERLING, M., Dermatology
STUMWOLL, M., Internal Medicine, Gastroenterology, Hepatology
TANNAPFEL, A., Pathology
THIERY, J., Laboratory Medicine
TILLMANN, H.-L., Internal Medicine, Gastroenterology and Hepatology
TREIDE, A., Child Dentistry
WAGNER, A., Neurology
WIEDEMANN, P., Ophthalmology
WILD, H. A., Paediatric Orthopaedics
WINTER, A., Medical Informatics
WIRTZ, H., Internal Medicine, Pulmology
WITTEKIND, C., Pathology, Immunopathology
ZIMMER, H.-G., Physiology

Faculty of Philology (Beethovenstr.15, 04107 Leipzig; tel. (341) 9737300; fax (341) 9737349; e-mail dekphilo@uni-leipzig.de; internet www.uni-leipzig.de/~philol):

BARZ, I., Contemporary German Linguistics and Lexicology
BAUMANN, K., Applied Linguistics/LSP Communication (English, Russian, German)
BICKEL, B., Linguistic Typology and Diversity
DEUFERT, M., Classical Philology and Latin Literature
EILERT, H., Modern German Literature
FELTEN, U., French and Italian Literature
FIX, U., Contemporary German Linguistics
GÄRTNER, E., Romance Linguistics
GOTTZMANN, C., Old German Literature
HARRESS, B., Slavic Literature and Cultural History
HINRICHS, U., Southern Slavic Linguistics and Translation Science
HOFFMANN-MAXIS, A., General and Comparative Literature and Literary Theory
KEIL, H., North American Cultural History
KOENEN, A., American Literature
LÖRSCHER, W., English Linguistics
MEIER, B., Teaching of German
MÜLLER, G., General Linguistics
NASSEN, U., Children's Literature and Juvenile Literature
ÖHLSCHLÄGER, G., German Linguistics
PECHMANN, TH., Psycholinguistics
POLLNER, C., English Linguistics
RITZER, M., Modern German Literature
RYTEL-KUC, D., West Slavic Linguistics
SCHENKEL, E., English Literature
SCHMITT, A. P., Linguistics and Translation Studies (English)
SCHWARZ, W., Literature and Cultural History of the Western Slavs
SCHWEND, J., Cultural Studies (Great Britain)
SIER, K., Classical Philology and Greek Literature
STOCKINGER, L., Modern German Literature
DE TORO, A., Romance Literature
TSCHIRNER, E., German as a Foreign Language
UDOLPH, J., Onomastic Science
WERNER, E., Sorbian Studies
WIESE, I., Contemporary German Linguistics
WOTJAK, B., German as a Foreign Language, Lexicology of Contemporary German Linguistics
WOTJAK, G., Romance Linguistics and Translation Science (Spanish and French)
ZYBATOW, G., Slavic Linguistics

Faculty of Physics and Earth Science (Linnéstr. 5, 04103 Leipzig; tel. (341) 9732400; fax (341) 9732499; e-mail dekan@physik.uni-leipzig.de):

BUTZ, T., Experimental Physics
EHRMANN, W., Geology
ESQUINAZI, P. D., Experimental Physics
FREUDE, D., Chemical Physics
GLÄSSER, W., Geology, Hydrogeology
GRILL, W., Experimental Physics
GRUNDMANN, M., Experimental Physics
HEINRICH, J., Physical Geography and Landscape-based Environmental Research
HEINTZENBERG, J., Atmospheric Physics
HERRMANN, H., Chemistry of the Atmosphere
IHLE, D., Theoretical Physics
JACOBI, CHR., Meteorology
JACOBS, F., Geophysics
JANKE, W., Theoretical Physics
KÄRGER, J., Experimental Physics
KÄS, J., Experimental Physics
KIRSTEIN, W., Geography and Geoinformatics
KORN, M., Theoretical Geophysics
KREMER, F., Experimental Physics
KROY, K.-D., Theoretical Physics
LENTZ, S., Regional Geography
LÖSCHE, M., Experimental Physics
MELLES, M., Geology
METZ, W., Theoretical Meteorology
OEHME, W., Teaching of Physics
RAUSCHENBACH, B., Applied Physics
RENNER, E., Modelling of Atmospheric Processes
RUDOLPH, G., Theoretical Physics
SALMHOFER, M., Theoretical Physics
SIBOLD, K., Theoretical Physics
TETZLAFF, G., Meteorology
WEILAND, U., Urban Ecology
WIESSNER, R., Anthropogeography, Economic Geography and the Labour Market

Faculty of Social Sciences and Philosophy (Burgstr. 21, 04109 Leipzig; tel. (341) 9735600; fax (341) 9735699; e-mail foerster@rz.uni-leipzig.de):

BARTELBORTH, TH., Philosophy of Science
BENTELE, G., Public Relations
ELSENHANS, H., Political Science and International Politics
FACH, W., Political Theory
FENNER, C., Comparative Politics
FLAM, H., Sociology
FRÜH, W., Empirical Communications and Media Research
GIESEN, K.-G., International Politics
GOTTWALD, S., Logic
HALLER, M., Journalism and Media Science
HUBER, M., International Politics
KALTER, F., Sociology
KÖHNKE, K., Theory and Philosophy of Culture
KUTSCH, A., Historical and Systematic Communication Studies
LÜBBE, W., Philosophy
MACHILL, M., Journalism and Media Science
MEGGLE, G., Philosophy
MEUSCHEL, S., Political Systems
MÜHLER, K., Sociology
SCHORB, B., Teaching of Media Studies, Further Education
SIEGRIST, H., Comparative History of Modern Europe
STEINMETZ, R., Media and Media Culture
STEKELER-WEITHOFER, P., Philosophy
STIEHLER, H.-J., Empirical Communications and Media Research
VOBRUBA, G., Sociology
VOSS, T., Sociology

Faculty of Sports Science (Jahnallee 59, 04109 Leipzig; tel. (341) 9731600; fax (341) 9731699; e-mail spodekan@rz.uni-leipzig.de; internet www.uni-leipzig.de/~sportfak):

ALFERMANN, D., Psychology of Sport
BUSSE, M., Sports Medicine
INNENMOSER, J., Sports Therapy, Sport for Handicapped People
KRUG, J., General Movement and Training Science

Faculty of Theology (Otto-Schill-Str. 2, 04109 Leipzig; tel. (341) 9735400; fax (341) 9735499; e-mail dekanat@theologie.uni-leipzig.de; internet www.uni-leipzig.de/~theolweb):

BERLEJUNG, A., Old Testament
FITSCHEN, K., Church History
HANISCH, H., Religious Education
HERZER, J., New Testament
LUX, R., Old Testament
PETZOLDT, M., Systematic Theology
PETZOLDT, M., Principles of Theology, Hermeneutics
RATZMANN, W., Practical Theology
SCHNEIDER, G., Systematic Theology
SCHRÖTER, J., New Testament
WARTENBERG, G., Church History
WOHLRAB-SAHR, M., Religious and Church Sociology

Faculty of Veterinary Medicine (An den Tierkliniken 19, 04103 Leipzig; tel. (341) 9738000; fax (341) 9738099; e-mail dekanat@vetmed.uni-leipzig.de):

ALBER, G., Immunology
BLESSING, M., Molecular Pathogenesis
BRAUN, R., Milk Hygiene
DAUGSCHIES, A., Parasitology
EDINGER, J., Orthopedics
EINSPANIER, A., Endocrinology
FEHLHABER, K., Food Hygiene and Consumer Protection
FERGUSON, J., Large-Animal Surgery
FUHRMANN, H., Physiological Chemistry
GÄBEL, G., Physiology
GREVEL, V., Small-Animal Surgery
KRAUTWALD-JUNGHANNS, M.-E., Bird Diseases
KRÜGER, M., Bacteriology and Mycology
LÜCKER, E., Meat Hygiene
MÜLLER, H., Virology
OECHTERING, G., Small-Animal Medicine
SALOMON, F.-V., Anatomy
SCHOON, H.-A., Histopathology and Clinical Pathology
SCHUSSER, G., Large-Animal Medicine
SEEGER, J., Histology and Embryology
SOBIRAJ, A., Obstetrics and Gynaecology
TRUYEN, U., Epidemiology
UNGEMACH, F. R., Pharmacology and Pharmacy

Institute of German Literature (Wächterstr. 34, 04107 Leipzig; tel. (341) 9730300; fax (341) 9730319; e-mail kahl@uni-leipzig.de; internet www.uni-leipzig.de/dll):

HASLINGER, J., Literary Aesthetics
TREICHEL, H.-U., German Literature

MEDIZINISCHE UNIVERSITÄT ZU LÜBECK

Ratzeburger Allee 160, 23538 Lübeck
Telephone: (451) 500-0
Fax: (451) 500-3016
E-mail: presse@uni-luebeck.de
Internet: www.mu-luebeck.de

Founded 1964

Rector: Prof. Dr med. PETER DOMINIAK
Pro-Rectors: Prof. Dr med. THOMAS MARTINETZ, Prof. Dr rer. nat. PETER SCHMUCKER
Chancellor: ASTRID KÜTHER

Number of teachers: 232
Number of students: 2,400

Publications: *Focus MUL* (4 a year), *Forschungsbericht*

DEANS

Faculty of Medicine: Prof. Dr med. WOLFGANG JELKMANN
Faculty of Science and Technology: Prof. Dr rer. nat. ENNO HARTMANN

DIRECTORS

Directors of Institutes

Medicine:

Anaesthesiology: Prof. Dr PETER SCHMUCKER
Anatomy: Prof. Dr JÜRGEN WESTERMANN
Biometry and Statistics: Prof. Dr ANDREAS ZIEGLER
Cardiology: Prof. Dr HANS-HINRICH SIEVERS
Clinical Chemistry: Prof. Dr MICHAEL SEYFARTH
Child Psychology: Prof. Dr ULRICH KNÖLKER
Clinical Rheumatology: Prof. Dr WOLFGANG L. GROSS
Dermatology: Prof. Dr DETLEF ZILLIKENS
Ear, Nose and Throat: Prof. Dr BARBARA WOLLENBERG
Experimental and Clinical Pharmacology and Toxicology: Prof. Dr PETER DOMINIAK
Gynaecology and Childbirth: Prof. Dr KLAUS DIEDRICH
Human Genetics: Prof. Dr GABRIELE GILLESSEN-KAESBACH
Immunology and Transfusion Medicine: Prof. Dr HOLGER KIRCHNER
Jaw and Facial Surgery: Prof. Dr Dr PETER SIEG
Medical Clinic: Prof. Dr WERNER SOLBACH
Medical Clinic I: Prof. Dr HORST LORENZ FEHM
Medical Clinic II: Prof. Dr HERIBERT SCHUNKERT
Medial Clinic III: Prof. Dr PETER ZABEL
Medical Psychology: Prof. Dr Dr FRITZ SCHMIELAU
Molecular Medicine: Prof. Dr GEORG SCZAKIEL
Neuroendocrinology: Prof. Dr JAN BORN
Neurology: Prof. Dr FRITZ HOHAGEN
Neuroradiology: Prof. Dr DIRK PETERSEN
Neurosurgery: Prof. Dr VOLKER TRONNIER
Occupational Medicine: Prof. Dr Dr RICHARD KESSEL
Ophthalmology: Prof. Dr HORST LAQUA
Orthopaedics: Dr MARTIN RUSSLIES
Paediatrics: Prof. Dr EGBERT HERTING
Paediatric Surgery: Prof. Dr LUCAS WESSEL
Pathology: Prof. Dr ALFRED CHRISTIAN FELLER
Physiology: Prof. Dr WOLFGANG JELKMANN
Plastic Surgery: Prof. Dr PETER MAILÄNDER
Psychosomatic Illnesses: Prof. Dr DETLEV-O. NUTZINGER
Radiology and Nuclear Medicine: Prof. Dr THOMAS HELMBERGER
Radiotherapy: Prof. Dr JÜRGEN DUNST
Research Centre Borstel: Prof. Dr Dr SILVIA BULFONE-PAUS
Social Medicine: Prof. Dr Dr HANS-HEINRICH RASPE
Surgery: Prof. Dr HANS-PETER BRUCH
Urology: Prof. Dr DIETER JOCHAM

Science and Technology:

Biochemistry: Prof. Dr ROLF HILGENFELD
Biology: Prof. Dr ENNO HARTMANN
Biomedical Optics: Prof. Dr REGINALD BIRNGRUBER
Chemistry: Prof. Dr THOMAS PETERS
Information Systems: Prof. Dr VOLKER LINNEMANN
International School of New Media: Prof. Dr JOACHIM HASEBROOK
Mathematics: Prof. Dr JÜRGEN PRESTIN
Medical Computing: Prof. Dr SIEGFRIED J. PÖPPL
Molecular Biology: Prof. Dr PETER KARL MÜLLER
Multimedia and Interactive Systems: Prof. Dr MICHAEL HERCZEG
Neuro- and Bioinformatics: Prof. Dr THOMAS MARTINETZ
Physics: Prof. Dr ALFRED X. TRAUTWEIN
Robotics and Cognitive Systems: Prof. Dr ACHIM SCHWEIKARD
Software and Programme Languages: Prof. Dr WALTER DOSCH
Technical Informatics: Prof. Dr ERIK MAEHLE
Telematics: Prof. Dr STEFAN FISCHER
Theoretical Computing: Prof. Dr RÜDIGER K. REISCHUK

PROFESSORS

Faculty of Medicine:

ARNOLD, H., Neurosurgery
BRUCH, H.-P., Surgery
DIEDRICH, K., Gynaecology and Obstetrics
DOMARUS, H., Maxillary and Facial Surgery
DOMINIAK, P., Pharmacology, Toxicology and Clinical Pharmacology
FEHM, H. L., Internal Medicine
FELLER, A. C., Pathology
GROSS, W. L., Rheumatology
HALSBAND, H., Paediatric Surgery
HOHAGEN, F., Psychiatry
JELKMANN, W., Physiology
JOCHAM, D., Urology
KATUS, H. A., Internal Medicine
KESSEL, R., Industrial Medicine
KIRCHNER, H., Immunology and Transfusional Medicine
KNÖLKER, U., Child and Adolescent Psychiatry
KÖMPF, D., Neurology
KRUSE, K., Paediatrics
LAQUA, H., Ophthalmology
LÖHR, J., Orthopaedics
OEHMICHEN, M., Forensic Medicine
RASPE, H.-H., Social Medicine
RICHTER, E., Radiotherapy and Nuclear Medicine
SCHMIELAU, F., Medical Psychology
SCHMUCKER, P., Anaesthesiology
SCHWINGER, E., Human Genetics
SCZAKIEL, G., Molecular Medicine

SEYFARTH, M., Clinical Chemistry
SIEVERS, H. H., Cardiac Surgery
SOLBACH, W., Medical Microbiology and Hygiene
WEERDA, H., Otolaryngology
WEISS, H.-D., Radiology
WESTERMANN, J., Anatomy
WOLFF, H. H., Dermatology and Venereology

Faculty of Science and Technology:

AACH, T., Signal Processing and Process Control
DOSCH, W., Software Engineering
DÜMBGEN, L., Mathematics
ENGELHARDT, D., History of Medicine and Science
FISCHER, B., Mathematics
HARTMANN, E., Biology
HERCZEG, M., Multimedia and Interactive Systems
HOGREFE, D., Telematics
KONECNY, E., Medical Technology
LINNEMANN, V., Practical Informatics
MAEHLE, E., Computer Engineering
MARTINETZ, TH., Neuro- and Bioinformatics
MÜLLER, K.-P., Medical Molecular Biology
PETERS, TH., Chemistry
PÖPPL, S., Medical Informatics and Statistics
PRESTIN, J., Mathematics
REISCHUK, K. R., Theoretical Computer Science
RIETSCHEL, E.-TH., Immunochemistry and Biochemical Microbiology
ROELCKE, V., History of Medicine and Science
SCHÄFER, G., Biochemistry
TRAUTWEIN, A., Physics
VOSWINCKEL, P., History of Medicine and Science
ZEUGMANN, TH., Theoretical Computer Science

UNIVERSITÄT LÜNEBURG

Scharnhorststr. 1, 21335 Lüneburg
Telephone: (4131) 677-0
Fax: (4131) 677-1099
E-mail: info-portal@uni-lueneburg.de
Internet: www.uni-lueneburg.de

Founded 1946
State control
President: Dr SASCHA SPOUN
Vice-Presidents (vacant): Prof. Dr HEINRICH DEGENHART, HOLM KELLER, Prof. Dr FERDINAND MÜLLER-ROMMEL, Prof. Dr SABINE REMDISCH, Prof. Dr FERDINAND SCHALTEGGER
Librarian: TORSTEN AHRENS

Library of 350,000 vols
Number of teachers: 169
Number of students: 7,300

Publication: *Forschungsberichte* (every 3 years)

DEANS

Faculty of Economic, Behavioural and Legal Sciences: Prof. Dr EGBERT KAHLE
Faculty of Educational, Cultural and Social Sciences: Prof. Dr HERBERT-ERNST COLLA
Faculty of Environmental Sciences and Information Technology: Prof. Dr RALF HADELER

PROFESSORS

Faculty of Economics, Behavioural and Legal Sciences (tel. (4131) 78-2001; fax (4131) 78-2009; e-mail woelk@uni-lueneburg.de; internet www.uni-lueneburg.de/fakultaet_2/):

BAXMANN, U., Business Administration
BEHRENDS, T., Small-business Economics
BURKHART, G., Sociology
DONNER, H., Law
DÖRING, U., Business Administration
FISCHER, A., Business Education
GRUNWALD, W., Psychology
GSCHWENDTER, H., Economics
HEILMANN, J., Law
KAHLE, E., Business Administration
KREILKAMP, E., Business Administration, Travel and Tourism
MARTIN, A., Business Administration
MERZ, J., Research on Professions
MÜLLER-ROMMEL, F., Political Sciences
OTT, J., Economics
REESE, J., Business Administration and Business-Related Computer Sciences
RUNKEL, G., Sociology
SCHALTEGGER, ST., Environmental Management
SCHULTE, R., Business Administration
SIMON, J., Law
THAYSEN, U., Political Sciences
WAGNER, J., Economics
WEISENFELD-SCHENK, U., Business Administration
ZÜNDORF, L., Sociology

Faculty of Educational, Cultural and Social Sciences (tel. (4131) 78-1601; fax (4131) 78-1608; e-mail pilzecker@uni-lueneburg.de; internet www.uni-lueneburg.de/fakultaet_1/):

CLASSEN-BAUER, I., Comparative Educational Sciences
COLLA-MÜLLER, H. E., Social Work and Therapy
CZERWENKA, K., Teacher Education
GARBE, C., German Language and Literature
HÖFFKEN, P., Protestant Theology
KARSTEN, M.-E., Social Administration and Management
LENZ-JOHANNS, M., Aesthetic Education
NEUMANN, F.-D., General Education
PAULUS, P., Psychology
PLEWIG, H.-J., Deviant Behaviour
RINGSHAUSEN, G., Protestant Theology
SALDERN, M. VON, Teacher Training
SCHUMACHER, L., Psychology
SIELAND, B., Psychology
STIMMER, F., Social Work and Therapy
STOLTENBERG, U., Social Studies and Science
STÜCKRATH, F., German Language and Literature
TITZE, H., General Education
UHLE, R., General Education
WEINHOLD, S., German Language
WOLFF, J., Judicature and Criminal Law relating to Juvenile Delinquency
ZIEGENSPECK, J., Psychology

Faculty of Environmental Sciences and Information Technology (tel. (4131) 677-2801; fax (4131) 677-2803; e-mail dembeck@uni-lueneburg.de; internet www.uni-lueneburg.de/fakultaet3/):

AßMANN, TH., Biology
BRANDT, E., Environmental Law
COENEN-STASS, D., Ecology
HÄRDTLE, W., Ecology
HOFMEISTER, S., Environmental Planning
LÖRCHER, K.-W., Ecology
MERZYN, G., Physics
MICHELSEN, G., Ecology
RUCK, W., Chemistry
SARETZKI, TH., Environmental Politics
STEFFENSKY, M., Chemistry

ATTACHED INSTITUTES

Institute of Applied Media Research: Dir Prof. Dr WERNER FAULSTICH.

Institute of Business Administration: Dir Prof. Dr EGBERT KAHLE.

Institute of Cultural Theory: Dir Prof. Dr GÜNTER BURKART.

Institute of Ecology and Environmental Chemistry: Dirs Prof. Dr WERNER HÄRDTLE, Prof. Dr-Ing WOLFGANG RUCK.

Institute of Economics: Dir MAIK HEINEMANN.

Institute of Electronic Business Management: Dir Prof. Dr-Ing. MATHIAS GROß.

Institute of English Language and Teaching: Dir Prof. Dr ANITA FETZER.

Institute of Environmental Communication: Dir Prof. Dr GERD MICHELSEN.

Institute of Environmental Strategy: Dir Prof. Dr THOMAS SCHOMERUS.

Institute of Evaluation and Quality Control: Dir Prof. Dr SABINE REMDISCH.

Institute of Experimental Business Psychology: Dir Prof. Dr RAINER HÖGER.

Institute of German Language, Literature and Teaching: Dir Prof. Dr ST STEIN.

Institute of Independent Professions: Dir Prof. Dr JOACHIM MERZ.

Institute of Integrative Studies: Dir Prof. Dr UTE STOLTENBERG.

Institute of Jurisprudence: Dir Prof. Dr JÜRGEN HEILMANN.

Institute of Leisure, Play and Movement Studies: Dir Prof. Dr KARLHEINZ WÖHLER.

Institute of Pedagogics: Dir Dr THOMAS LEHMANN.

Institute of Psychology: Dir Prof. Dr BERNHARD SIELAND.

Institute of School and High School Research: Dir Prof. Dr KURT CZERWENKA.

Institute of Small and Medium-sized Businesses: Dir Prof. Dr ALBERT MARTIN.

Institute of Social Education: Dir Prof. Dr MARIA-ELEONORA KARSTEN.

Institute of Social Sciences: Dir Prof. Dr GÜNTER BURKART.

Institute of Theology and Religious Education: Dir Prof. Dr GERHARD RINGSHAUSEN.

OTTO-VON-GUERICKE-UNIVERSITÄT MAGDEBURG

Universitätsplatz 2, 39106 Magdeburg
Telephone: (391) 67-01
Fax: (391) 11156
E-mail: akaa@uni-magdeburg.de
Internet: www.uni-magdeburg.de

Founded 1953, present status 1993
State control
Academic year: October to September (two semesters)
Chancellor: WOLFGANG LEHNECKE
Rector: Prof. Dr KLAUS ERICH POLLMANN
Vice-Rector (Planning and Development): Prof. Dr HELMUT WEIß
Vice-Rector (Research): Prof. Dr VOLKER HOELT
Vice-Rector (Study): Prof. Dr VOLKER LINNEWEBER
Librarian: Dr-Ing. EKKEHARD OEHMIG

Library of 1,080,000 vols
Number of teachers: 1,326
Number of students: 11,249

Publications: *Forschungsbericht* (annually), *Wissenschaftsjournal* (2 a year), *Unireport* (monthly)

DEANS

Faculty of Computer Science: Prof. Dr THOMAS STROTHOTTE
Faculty of Economics and Management: Prof. Dr JOACHIM WEIMANN
Faculty of Electrical and Information Engineering: Prof. Dr ZBIGNIEW STYCZYNSKI
Faculty of Humanities, Social Sciences and Education: Prof. Dr BERND-PETER LANGE

Faculty of Mathematics: Prof. Dr GERALD WARNECKE
Faculty of Medicine: Prof. Dr ALBERT ROESSNER
Faculty of Mechanical Engineering: Prof. Dr KARL-HEINRICH GROTE
Faculty of Natural Sciences: Prof. Dr RAINER CLOS
Faculty of Process and Systems Engineering: Prof. Dr ANDREAS SEIDEL-MORGENSTERN

PROFESSORS

Faculty of Computer Sciences (Universitätsplatz 2, Building 29, 39106 Magdeburg; tel. (391) 67-18853):
ARNDT, H.-K., Applied Informatics
DASSOW, J., Theoretical Informatics
DITTMANN, J., Technical and Business Information Systems
DUMKE, R., Software Engineering
HORTEN, G., Simulation and Graphics
HUELLERMEIER, E., Technical Computer Science
KAISER, J., Information Systems
KRUSE, R., Neural and Fuzzy Systems
NETT, E., Distributed Systems
PREIM, B., Computer Graphics
RAUTENSTRACH, C., Business Information Systems
ROESNER, D., Knowledge and Language Engineering
SCHIRRA, S., Algorithmics
SPILIPOULOU, M., Business Informatics
STROTHOTTE, T., Computer Graphics and Interactive Systems
TOENNIS, K.-D., Computer Graphics

Faculty of Economics and Management (Universitätsplatz 2, Building 22, 39106 Magdeburg; tel. (391) 67-18585):
BURGARD, U., Law and Economics
CHWOLKA, A., Accounting
ERICHSON, B., Marketing
GISCHER, H., Money Credit
INDERFURTH, K., Logistics
KIESEWETTER, D., Fiscal Theory
LUHMER, A., Controlling
LUSK, E., Business Administration
PAQUE, K.-H., International Business
RAITH, M., Entrepreneurship
REICHLING, P., Finance and Banking
SCHOEB, R., Economics, Finance
SCHWODIAUER, G., Economics, Business Theory
SPENGLER, T., Company Management
VOGT, B., Empirical Economics Research
WAESCHER, G., Management Science
WEIMANN, J., Political Economy
WOLFF, B., International Management

Faculty of Electrical and Information Engineering (Universitätsplatz 2, Building 09, 39106 Magdeburg; tel. (391) 67-18635):
BURTE, E. P., Technology of Semiconductors
KIENLE, A., Automation Engineering
KLEINE, U., Electronics
KORN, U., Control Engineering
LINDEMANN, A., Power Electronics
MICHAELIS, B., Technical Computer Science
NITSCH, J., Theory of Electrical Engineering
OMAR, A. S., Microwave and Communications Engineering
PALIS, F., Power Electronics
RAISCH, J., System Theory
SCHMIDT, B., Measurement Technology and Microsystems
STYCZYNSKI, Z. A., Electrical Power Networks and Renewable Energy Resources
WENDEMUTH, A., Cognitive Systems
WOLLENBERG, G., Theoretical and General Electrical Engineering

Faculty of Humanities, Social Sciences and Education (Zschokkestr. 32, Building 40, 39104 Magdeburg; tel. (391) 67-16541):
ADAM, W., Modern German Literature
BADER, R., Vocational Education
BAUDISCH, W., Special Education and Professional Rehabilitation
BELENTSCHIKOW, R., Slavic Studies
BERGIEN, A., English Linguistics
BLASER, P., Administrative Sciences
BREIT, G., Politics
BRUCHHAEUSER, H.-P., Administrative Management and New Media
BURKHARDT, A., German Language
DITTRICH, E., Macrosociology
DREHER, M., Ancient History
FORNDRAN, E., International Relations and Theory of Politics
FRITSCHE, K.-P., Comparative Political Systems
FROMME, J., Media Education and Adult Education
FUHRER, U., Developmental and Educational Psychology
GIRMES, R., General Didactics and Theory of Education
GOLZ, R., Historical and Comparative Educational Studies
JENEWEIN, K., Didactic Technical Subject Areas
KERSTEN, H., English and American Studies
KOEHLER, J., Music Education
KNOLLE, N., Music Education
LABOUVIE, E., Contemporary History and Gender Research
LANGE, B. P., English Literary and Cultural Studies
LINNEWEBER, V., Social Psychology
LOHMANN, G., Practical Philosophy
MAEKELAE, T., Music Science
MAROTZKI, W., General Education
MUENTE, T. F., Psychology
PAUEN, M., Philosophy
PETERS, S., Work-based Education
POLLMANN, K. E., Modern History and History of Science
RENZSCH, W., Political System and Sociology of the Federal Republic of Germany
ROS, A., Theoretical Philosophy
SCHILLING, M., Older German Literature and Linguistics
SCHUETZE, F., Microsociology
SPRINGER, M., Medieval History
SUEß, H., Chemical Engineering

Faculty of Mathematics (Universitätsplatz 2, Building 03, 39106 Magdeburg; tel. (391) 67-18322):
CHRISTOPH, G., Mathematical Stochastics
DECKELNICK, K., Analysis
GAFFKE, N., Mathematical Stochastics
GRUNAU, H.-C., Analysis
HENK, M., Geometry
JUHNKE, F., Mathematical Optimization
POTT, A., Discrete Mathematics
SCHWABE, R., Mathematical Stochastics
TOBISKA, L., Numerical Analysis
WARNECKE, G., Numerical Mathematics
WEISMANTEL, R., Mathematical Optimization
WILLEMS, W., Mathematics

Faculty of Mechanical Engineering (Universitätsplatz 2, 39106 Magdeburg; tel. (391) 67-18519):
BAETGE, J., Experimental Motive Power Engineering
BERTRAM, A., Strength of Materials
DETERS, L., Machine Elements and Tribology
FLOß, D., Work Design
GABBERT, U., Numerical Mathematics
GATZKY, T., Industry Design
GROTE, K. H., Product Development and Engineering Design
HEILMAYER, M., Materials Engineering
HEROLD, H., Joining Engineering
KARPUSCHEWSKI, B., Metal Cutting and Removal Technology
KASPER, R., Mechatronics
KUEHNLE, H., Factory Operation and Manufacturing Systems
MOLITOR, M., Manufacturing Measurement Technology and Quality Management
POPPY, W., Construction Machinery
REGENER, D., Materials Engineering and Materials Testing
SINAPIUS, M., Adapt Lightweight Construction
STRACKELJAN, J., Technical Dynamics
TSCHOEKE, H., Measurement Technology and Reciprocating Machines
VAJNA, S., Computer Applications in Mechanical Engineering
ZIEMS, D., Logistics

Faculty of Medicine (Leipzigerstr. 44, 39120 Magdeburg; tel. (391) 67-15750):
ALLHOFF, E. P., Urology
BEHRENS-BAUMANN, W., Ophthalmology
BERNARDING, J., Biometry and Medical Informatics
BOGERTS, B., Psychiatry
BOHNENSACK, R., Biochemistry
COSTA, S.-D., Women's Clinic
DÖHRING, W., Radiology
DUEZEL, E., Neurology
FIRSCHING, R., Neurosurgery
FRANKE, A., Haematology and Oncology
FREIGANG, B., Otorhinolaryngology
GADEMANN, G., Radiotherapy
GERLACH, K.-L., Oral and Maxillofacial Surgery
GOLLNICK, H., Dermatology and Venereology
HACHENBERG, T., Anaesthesiology and Intensive Care
HEINZE, H.-J., Neurology
HOELLT, V., Pharmacology and Toxicology
HOFFMANN, W., Molecular Biology and Medical Chemistry
HUTH, C., Cardiothoracic Surgery
JORCH, G., Paediatrics and Neonatology
KLEIN, H., Cardiology, Angiology and Pneumology
KOENIG, W., Medical Microbiology
KRAUSE, D., Medical Law
LEVERKUS, C.-M., Dermatology and Venerology
LIPPERT, H., General Surgery
LULEY, C., Clinical Chemistry
MALFERTHEINER, P., Gastroenterology and Hepatology
MITTLER, U., Paediatric Haematology and Oncology
NAUMANN, M., Experimental Internal Medicine
NEUMANN, H.-W., Orthopaedic Surgery
PAPE, H.-C., Physiology
ROBRA, B.-P., Social Medicine and Health Economics
RÖSSNER, A., Pathology
ROTHKÖTTER, H.-J., Anatomy
SABEL, B., Medical Psychology
SCHLUTER, D., Medical Microbiology
SCHRAVEN, B., Immunology
SKALEJ, M., Diagnostic Radiology
ULLRICH, O., Immunology Institute
WALLESCH, C.-W., Neurology
WEISE, W., Gynaecology
WIEACKER, P., Medical Genetics
WOLF, G., Neurobiological Medicine

Faculty of Natural Sciences (Universitätsplatz 2, Building 16, 39106 Magdeburg; tel. (391) 67-18678):
BRAUN, A. K., Biology and Zoology
BRAUN, J., Cognitive Biology
CHRISTEN, J., Experimental Physics
CLOS, R., Experimental Physics
HERMANN, CH., Biology Psychology
MIßLER, S., Biophysics
MUELLER, S., Biophysics
MUENTE, T. F., Psychology
RICHTER, J., Theoretical Physics

STANNARIUS, R., Experimental Physics and Non-linear Phenomena

Faculty of Process and Systems Engineering (Universitätsplatz 2, Building 10, 39106 Magdeburg; tel. (391) 67-11190):

EDELMANN, F., Inorganic Chemistry
HAUPTMANNS, U., Plant Safety
MOERL, L., Chemical Apparatus Construction
REICHL, U., Biochemical Engineering
SCHINZER, D., Organic Chemistry
SCHMIDT, J., Thermodynamics
SEIDEL-MORGENSTEIN, A., Chemical Reaction Engineering
SPECHT, E., Technical Thermodynamics and Combustion
SUNDMACHER, K., Process System Engineering
THÉVENIN, D., Fluid Dynamics
TOMAS, J., Mechanical Process Engineering
TSOTSAS, E., Thermal Process Engineering
WEIß, H., Chemical Engineering

JOHANNES GUTENBERG-UNIVERSITÄT MAINZ

55099 Mainz
Saarstr. 21, 55128 Mainz
Telephone: (6131) 39-0
Fax: (6131) 39-29-19
Internet: www.uni-mainz.de

Founded 1477; closed 1816; reopened 1946

President: Prof. Dr JÖRG MICHAELIS
Chancellor: GOETZ SCHOLZ
Vice-President (Academic Studies and Teaching): Prof. Dr JÜRGEN OLDENSTEIN
Vice-President (Research): Prof. Dr JOHANNES PREUSS
Librarian: Dr A. ANDERHUB

Library: see Libraries and Archives
Number of teachers: 2,800
Number of students: 34,600

Publications: *Forschungsbericht*, *Forschungsmagazin*

DEANS

Faculty of Applied Languages: KARL-HEINZ STOLL
Faculty of Catholic Theology: Prof. Dr LEONHARD HELL
Faculty of Biology: Prof. Dr HARALD PAULSEN
Faculty of Chemistry, Pharmacy and Earth Sciences: Prof. Dr PETER LANGGUTH
Faculty of Evangelical Theology: Prof. Dr FRIEDRICH-WILHELM HORN
Faculty of History and Cultural Studies: Prof. JAN KUSBER
Faculty of Law and Economics: Dr ROLAND EULER
Faculty of Medicine: Prof. Dr med. Dr rer. nat. R. URBAN
Faculty of Philosophy and Pedagogics: Prof. Dr STEPHAN BÜRMAFÜSSEL NN
Faculty of Physics, Mathematics and Computing: Prof. Dr DIETRICH VON HARRACH
Music College and Academy of Art: Prof. Dr phil. JÜRGEN BLUME

PROFESSORS

Faculty of Catholic and Evangelical Theology (01) (Forum 6, 55099 Mainz; tel. (6131) 39-22215; fax (6131) 39-23501; e-mail kath-dekanat@uni-mainz.de; internet www.theologie.uni-mainz.de):

BAUMEISTER, T.
DIETZ, W.
DINGEL, I.
FECHTNER, K.
FRANZ, A.
HELL, L.
HORN, F. W.
LANDMESSER, C.
LEHNARDT, A.
MEIER, J.
REISER, M.
REITER, J.
RIEDEL-SPANGENBERGER, I.
SIEVERNICH, M.
SIMON, W.
SLENCZKA, N
WEYER-MENKHOFF, S.
WIßMANN, H.
ZWICKEL, W.

Faculty of Social Sciences, Media and Sport (02) (Colonel-Kleinmann-Weg 2, 55128 Mainz; tel. (6131) 39-22247; fax (6131) 39-23347; e-mail fritsche@mail.uni-mainz.de):

AUFENANGER, S.
AUGUSTIN, D.
BÜRMANN, J.
DITTGEN, H.
DORMANN, C.
DRUWE, U.
FALTER, J. W.
GARZ, D.
GROB, N.
HAMBURGER, F.
HECHT, H.
HEINEMANN, E.
HILLER, W.
HRADIL, S.
HUFNAGEL, E.
JUNG, K.
KEPPLINGER, H. M.
KOEBNER, T.
KOLBE, F.-U.
KROHNE, H. W.
KUNCZIK, M.
KUNZ, V.
MEINHARDT, G.
MESSING, M.
MÜLLER, N.
NIENSTEDT, H.-W.
OCHSMANN, R.
PREISENDÖRFER, P.
RENNER, K.N.
RICKER, R.
ROLLER, E.
SCHELLE, C.
SCHNEIDER, N. F.
SCHWEPPE, C.
SEIFFGE-KRENKE, I.
VON FELDEN, H.
WILKE, J.
WOLFF, V.
ZIMMERLING, R.

Faculty of Law and Economics (03) (Jakob-Welder-Weg 9, 55128 Mainz; tel. (6131) 39-22225; fax (6131) 39-23529; e-mail dekanat-fb03@uni-mainz.de; internet www.uni-mainz.de/fachbereiche/1754.php):

BECK, K.
BELLMANN, K.
BOCK, M.
BREUER, K.
BRONNER, R.
DÖRR, D.
DREHER, M.
ERB, V.
EULER, R.
FINK, U.
FRIEDL, G.
GOERKE, L.
GRÖSCHLER, P.
GURLIT, E.
HAAS, U.
HABERSACK, M.
HAIN, K.-E.
HEIL, O. P.
HENTSCHEL, V.
HEPTING, R.
HERGENRÖDER, C. W.
HETTINGER, M
HUBER, F
HUBER, P
HUFEN, F
KAISER, D
KOLMAR, M
KUBE, H.
LEISEN, D.
MÜLBERT, P. O.
OECHSLER, J.
PEFFEKOVEN, R.
RAMMERT, S.
ROTH, A.
RUTHIG, J.
SAUERNHEIMER, K
SCHULZE, P. M.
TRAUTMANN, S.
VOLKMANN, U.
WEDER, B.
ZOPFS, J.

Faculty of Medicine (04) (Obere Zahlbacher Straße 63, 55131 Mainz; tel. (6131) 39-33180; internet dekanat.medizin.uni-mainz.de):

BARTENSTEIN, P.
BEHL, C.
BEHNEKE, N.
BEUTEL, M. E.
BHAKDI, S.
BIRKLEIN, F.
BLETTNER, M.
BORK, K.
BRISENO, B.
BROCKERHOFF, P.
BUHL, R.
D'HOEDT, B.
DICK, B.
DIETERICH, M.
DÜBER, C.
DUSCHNER, H.
FISCHER, T.
FÖRSTERMANN, U.
GALLE, P. R.
HAAF, T.
HEINE, J.
HEINEMANN, M.
HEINRICHS, W.
HIEMKE, C.
HOMMEL, G.
HUBER, C.
JAGE, J.
JANSEN, B.
JUNGINGER, T.
KAINA, B.
KEMPSKI, O.
KIRKPATRICK, C. J.
KLEINERT, H.
KNOP, J.
KÖLBL, H.
KONERDING, M. A.
KRAFT, J.
KÜMMEL, W. F.
LACKNER, K. J.
LETZEL, S.
LEUBE, R.
LOOS, M.
LÜDDENS, H.
LUHMANN, H.
LUTZ, B.
MAEURER, M.
MANN, W.
MICHAELIS, J.
MÜLLER, W. E.G.
MÜLLER-KLIESER, W.
MÜNTEFERING, H.
MÜNZEL, T.
MUSHOLT, T.
NEURATH, M.
NIX, W.
OESCH, F.
OTTO, G.
PAUL, N. W.
PERNECZKY, A.
PFEIFFER, N.
PIETRZIK, C.
PLACHTER, B.
POHLENZ, J.
POLLOW, K.
POMMERENING, K.
REDDEHASE, M. J.
REITTER, B.
RESKE-KUNZ, A. B.
ROMMENS, P. M.

SAHIN, U.
SCHELLER, H.
SCHIER, F.
SCHILD, H.
SCHMIDBERGER, H.
SCHMITT, H. J.
SCHRECKENBERGER, M.
SCHREIBER, W.
SCHULTE, E.
SCHUMACHER, R.
SOMMER, C.
STOETER, P.
STOFFT, E.
STOPFKUCHEN, H.
STREECK, R. E.
THEOBALD, M.
THÜROFF, J. W.
TREEDE, R.-D.
VAUPEL, P.
VON BAUMGARTEN, R.
WAGNER, W.
WAGNER, W.
WEBER, M. M.
WEHRBEIN, H.
WEILEMANN, L. S.
WERNER, C.
WILLERSHAUSEN, B.
WOJNOWSKI, L.
WÖLFEL, T.
ZABEL, B.
ZANDER, R.
ZEPP, F.
ZÖLLNER, E. J.

Faculty of Philosophy and Pedagogics (05) (Jakob-Welder-Weg 18, 55128 Mainz; tel. (6131) 39-20005; fax (6131) 39-20085; e-mail fsb05@uni-mainz.de):

BISANG, W.
BOESCHOTEN, H.
BRENDEL, E..
BREUER, U.
DREYER, M.
ECKEL, W.
EICHLER, K.-D.
ERLEBACH, P.
FISCHER, E.
FÜSSEL, S.
GEISLER, E.
GIRKE, W.
GÖBLER, F.
GRÄTZEL, S.
HORNUNG, A.
KREUDER, F.
KROPP, M.
LAMPING, D.
LEY, K.
MARTIN, A.
MEIBAUER, J.
MEISIG, K.
METZINGER, T.
MÜLLER-WOOD, A.
NÜBLING, D.
PORRA, V.
REITZ, B.
SARHIMAA, A.
SCHEIDING, O.
SCHULTZE, B.
SEELBACH, D.
SIMON, M.
SOLBACH, A.
SPIES, B.
STAIB, B.
STÖRMER-CAYSA, U.
VEITH, W. H.
VON HOFF, D.
WEHR, B.

Faculty of Applied Linguistic and Cultural Studies (06) (An der Hochschule 2, 76711 Germersheim; tel. (7274) 508-0; fax (7274) 508-35429; e-mail dekan06@uni-mainz.de; internet www.fask.uni-mainz.de):

VON BARDELEBEN, R.
FORSTNER, M.
GIPPER, A.
HUBER, D.
KELLETAT, A.
KLENGEL, S.
KLENGEL, S.
KUPFER, P.
LOENHOFF, J.
MENZEL, B.
MÜLLER, K. P.
PERL, M.
PERL, M.
SCHREIBER, M.
STOLL, K.-H.
WORBS, E.

Faculty of History and Cultural Studies (07) (Jakob-Welder-Weg 18, 55128 Mainz; tel. (6131) 39-23346; fax (6131) 39-24619):

ALTHOFF, J.
BEER, A.
BIERSCHENK, T.
BLÜMER, WI.
BRAUN, E. A.
FELTEN, F. J.
GAUDZINSKI-WINDHEUSER, S.
KASTENHOLZ, R.
KIßENER, M.
KREIKENBOM, D.
KUSBER, J.
LENTZ, C.
MATHEUS, M.
MÜLLER, M.
OY-MARRA, E.
PARE, C. F. E.
PESCHLOW, U.
PRECHEL, D.
PRINZING, G.
RÖDDER, A.
SCHUMACHER, L.
VERHOEVEN-VAN ELSBERGEN, U.
WALDE, C.
WIESEND, R.

Faculty of Physics, Mathematics and Computing (08) (Staudingerweg 9, 55128 Mainz; tel. (6131) 39-22267; fax (6131) 39-22994; e-mail info@phmi.uni-mainz.de; internet www.phmi.uni-mainz.de):

ADRIAN, H.
ARENDS, H.-J.
BACH, V.
BINDER, K.
BLOCH, I.
BORRMANN, S.
BROCKMANN, R.
DE JONG, T.
DOLL, T.
ELMERS, H.-J.
GÖTTLER, H.
GRAMSCH, B.
HANKE-BOURGEOIS, M.
HEIL, W.
HÖPFNER, R.
HUBER, G.
JAENICKE, R.
JÜNGEL, A.
KLEINKNECHT, K.
KLENKE, A.
KÖPKE, L.
LEHN, M.
MÜLLER-STACH, S.
OSTRICK, M.
PALBERG, T.
PAPADOPOULOS, N.
PERL, J.
POCHODZALLA, J.
REUTER, M.
ROWE, D. E.
SANDER, H.-G.
SCHILCHER, K.
SCHILLING, R.
SCHLEINKOFER, G.
SCHÖMER, E.
SCHÖNHENSE, G.
SCHUH, H.-J.
TAPPROGGE, S
VAN DONGEN, P. . J.
VAN STRATEN, D.
VON HARRACH, D.
WALZ, J.
WERNLI, H.
WIRTH, V.
WITTIG, H.
ZUO, K.

Faculty of Chemistry, Pharmacy and Earth Sciences (09) (Becherweg 14, 55128 Mainz; tel. (6131) 39-22273; fax (6131) 39-23521; e-mail dekan19@uni-mainz.de; internet www.uni-mainz.de/FB/Chemie/fbhome):

BANHART, F.
BASCHÉ, T.
DANNHARDT, G..
DOMRÖS, M.
EPE, B.
ESCHER, A.
FAHRENHOLZ, F.
FELSER, C.
FOLEY, S. F.
FREY, H.
GAUß, J.
GRUNERT, J.
HOFFMANN, T.
JANSHOFF, A.
KERSTEN, M.
KLINKHAMMER, K.
KLINKHAMMER, K.
KOCH-BRANDT, C.
KRATZ, J. V.
KRÖNER, A.
KUNZ, H.
LANGGUTH, P.
LÖWE, H.
MEIER, H.
MEYER, G.
NUBBEMEYER, U.
NUBBEMEYER, U.
PASSCHIER, C. W.
PINDUR, U.
PREUß, J.
RATTER, B. M. W.
REGENAUER-LIEB, K.
REICH, T.
RENTSCHLER, E.
RÖSCH, F.
SCHENK, D.
SCHMIDT, M.
SIROCKO, F.
STÖCKIGT, J.
TREMEL, W.
WILCKE, W.
WILKEN, R.
WITULSKI, B.
ZENTEL, R.

Faculty of Biology (10) (Gresemundweg 2, 55128 Mainz; tel. (6131) 39-22548; fax (6131) 39-23500; internet www.uni-mainz.de/FB/Biologie/biologie.html):

ALT, K. W.
BÖHNING-GAESE, K.
CLAßEN-BOCKHOFF, R.
DECKER, H.
EISENBEIS, G.
HANKELN, T.
HENKE, W.
KADEREIT, J. W.
KAMP, G.
KÖNIG, H.
MARKL, J.
MARTENS, J.
NEUMEYER, C.
PAULSEN, H.
PFLUGFELDER, G.
ROTHE, G.
SCHMIDT, E. R.
SEITZ, A.
STÖCKER, W.
TECHNAU, G.
TROTTER, J.
UNDEN, G.
WEGENER, G.
WERNICKE, W.
WOLFRUM, U.
ZISCHLER, H.

Music College and Academy of Art (11) (Binger Str. 26, 55122 Mainz; tel. (6131) 39-35538; fax (6131) 39-30146; e-mail wenkel@mail.uni-mainz.de; internet www.musik.uni-mainz.de):

BERNING, A., Academy of Art
BLUME, J., Theory of Music
DAUS, J., College of Music
DELNON, G., Stage Theory
DEUTSCH, N., Oboe
DEWALD, T., Singing
DOBNER, M., Double Bass
DREYER, L., Music Theory
EDER, C., Singing
FRANK, B., Piano
GAVRIC, D., Chamber Music
GERMER, K., Piano
GMEINDER, J., Clarinet
GNANN, G., Church Music
HAHN, G., Academy of Art
HELLMANN, U., Academy of Art
KAISER, H.-J., Church Music
KIEFER, P., Modern Music
KIESSLING, D., Academy of Art
KNOCHE-WENDEL, E., Academy of Art
MARX, K., Chamber Music
REICHERT, M., Modern Music
SHIH, A., Violin
SPACEK, V., Academy of Art
STRIEGEL, L., Music Theory
VETRE, O., Piano
VIRNICH, W., Academy of Art
VOGELGESANG, K., Academy of Art
WALLFISCH, R., Violoncello
ZARBOCK, H., Piano
ZIMMERMANN, J., Academy of Art

ATTACHED INSTITUTES

Forschungsinstitut für Wirtschaftspolitik (Institute for Economic Research): Universität, Jakob-Welder-Weg 4, 55099 Mainz; Dirs Prof. Dr HARTWIG BARTLING, Prof. Dr HELMUT DIEDERICH, Prof. Dr WALTER HAMM, Prof. Dr WERNER ZOHLNHÖFER.

Forschungsinstitut Lesen und Medien (Institute for Media Research): Fischtorplatz 23, 55116 Mainz; Dir Prof. Dr STEPHAN FÜSSEL.

Institut für Europäische Geschichte (Institute for European History): see under Research Institutes.

Institut für Geschichtliche Landeskunde (Institute for Historical Regional Studies of Rhineland-Palatinate): Universität, Johann-Friedrich-von-Pfeiffer-Weg 3, 55099 Mainz; Dirs Prof. Dr A. HAVERKAMP, Prof. Dr W. KLEIBER, Prof. Dr M. MATHEUS.

Institut für Internationales Recht des Spar-, Giro- und Kreditwesens (Institute for International Law of Banking): Universität, Saarstrasse 21, Haus Recht und Wirtschaft, 55122 Mainz; Dirs Prof. Dr W. HADDING, Prof. Dr U. H. SCHNEIDER.

Institut für Mikrotechnik GmbH (Institute for Microtechnology): Postfach 421364, 55071 Mainz;premises at: Carl-Zeiss-Str. 18–20, 55129 Mainz; Dir Prof. Dr W. EHRFELD.

Tumorzentrum Rheinland-Pfalz e.V. (Tumour Centre Rhineland-Palatinate): Am Pulverturm 13, 55101 Mainz; Dir Prof. Dr C. HUBER.

UNIVERSITÄT MANNHEIM

Schloss, 68131 Mannheim
Telephone: (621) 181-0
Fax: (621) 181-1050
E-mail: rektorat@verwaltung.uni-mannheim.de
Internet: www.uni-mannheim.de
Founded 1907 as Städtische Handelshochschule, attached to Heidelberg University 1933, reopened as Wirtschaftshochschule 1946, University status 1967
Languages of instruction: German, English
Academic year: April to February
Rector: Prof. Dr HANS-WOLFGANG ARNDT
Pro-Rectors: Prof. Dr KAI BRODERSEN, Prof. Dr MILA MAJSTER-CEDERBAUM, Prof. Dr WALTER OECHSLER
Chancellor: Dr. SUSANN-ANNETTE STORM
Librarian: Dipl.-Phys. CHRISTIAN BENZ
Number of teachers: 113
Number of students: 11,500

DEANS

Faculty of Business Administration: (vacant)
Faculty of Law: Prof. Dr KONRAD STAHL
Faculty of Mathematics and Information Sciences: Prof. Dr MATTHIAS KRAUSE
Faculty of Philosophy: Prof. Dr THOMAS KLINKERT
Faculty of Social Sciences: Prof. Dr JOSEF BRÜDERL.

ATTACHED INSTITUTES

Institut für Binnenschiffahrtsrecht: Dir Prof. Dr EIBE RIEDEL.

Institut für Deutsches, Europäisches und Internationales Medizinrecht, Gesundheitsrecht und Bioethik der Universitäten Heidelberg und Mannheim: Dir Prof. Dr JOCHEN TAUPITZ.

Institut für Empirische Wirtschaftsforschung: Dir Prof. Dr MARTIN SCHADER.

Institut für Kommunikations- und Medienforschung/Sprachlabor: Dir (vacant) Dipl.-Hdl. WILFRIED KLEIN.

Institut für Landeskunde und Regionalforschung: Dir Prof. Dr PIRMIN SPIESS.

Institut für Mittelstandsforschung: Dir Prof. Dr PETER MILLING.

Institut für Sport: Dir FRIEDRICH HENNINGER.

Institut für Versicherungswissenschaft: Dir Prof. Dr EGON LORENZ.

Institut für Volkswirtschaftslehre und Statistik: Dir Prof. Dr AXEL BÖRSCH-SUPAN.

Otto-Selz-Institut für Psychologie und Erziehungswissenschaft: Dir Prof. Dr WERNER W. WITTMANN.

Mannheimer Zentrum für Europäische Sozialforschung: Dir Prof. Dr JAN VAN DETH.

Rechenzentrum: Dir Dr. HANS GÜNTHER KRUSE.

PHILIPPS-UNIVERSITÄT MARBURG

Biegenstr. 10-12, 35032 Marburg
Telephone: (6421) 2820
Fax: (6421) 2822500
E-mail: grassman@verwaltung.uni-marburg.de
Internet: www.uni-marburg.de
Founded 1527
State control
Academic year: October to July (two terms)
President: Prof. Dr VOLKER NIENHAUS
Vice-President: Prof. Dr GERHARD HELDMAIER
Vice-President: Dr HERBERT CLAAS
Chancellor: Dr FRIEDHELM NONNE
Librarian: Dr DIRK BARTH
Library: see Libraries and Archives
Number of teachers: 650
Number of students: 17,900
Publication: *Journal* (2 a year)

PROFESSORS

Department of Law (Universitätsstr. 6, 35032 Marburg; tel. (6421) 2823101; fax (6421) 2823181; e-mail dekanat01@mailer.uni-marburg.de):

BACKHAUS, R., Roman and Civil Law
BÖHM, M., Public Law
BUCHHOLZ, ST., German Legal History and Civil Law
DETTERBECK, S., Public Law
FREUND, G., Criminal and Procedural Law, Philosophy of Law
FROTSCHER, W., Public Law
GORNIG, G.-H., Public Law
GOUNALAKIS, G., Civil and Comparative Law
HORN, H.-D., Public Law
LANGENBÜCHER, K., Civil Law
LANGER, W., Criminal and Procedural Law
MENKHAUS, H., Japanese Law
MUMMENHOFF, W., Civil and Labour Law
RADTKE, H., Criminal Law, Procedural Law
RÖSSNER, D., Criminal Law, Procedural Law
RUPPRECHT, H.-A., Papyrology
SCHANZE, E., Civil Law
VOIT, W., Civil Law
WERTENBRUCH, J., Civil Law

Department of Economics (Universitätsstr. 25, 35032 Marburg; tel. (6421) 2821722; fax (6421) 2824858; e-mail dekanat@wiwi.uni-marburg.de):

ALPAR, P., Economics, Computer Science
FEHL, U., Economic Theory
FELD, L., Financial Science
FLEISCHER, K., Statistics
GERUM, E., Commerce
GÖPFERT, I., Commerce, Logistics
HASENKAMP, U., Business Management and Economic Information Studies
KERBER, W., Political Economy
KIRK, M., Development Policy, Agricultural Economics and Co-operative Science
KRAG, J., Commerce
LINGENFELDER, M., Marketing
PRIEWASSER, E., Banking
RÖPKE, J., Economic Theory
SCHIMENZ, B., Business Economics
SCHÜLLER, A., Economic Theory
STORZ, C., Japanese Economics
WEHRHEIM, M., Commerce

Department of Social Science and Philosophy (Wilhelm-Röpke-Str. 6B, 35032 Marburg; tel. (6421) 2824726; fax (6421) 2825467; e-mail ciok@mailer.uni-marburg.de):

BERG-SCHLOSSER, D., Political Science
BIELING, H.-J., Political Science
BORIS, H.-D., Sociology
BRANN, K., European Ethnology
BREDOW, W. VON, Political Science
DEPPE, F., Political Science
FÜLBERTH-SPERLING, G., Political Science
FUNDER, M., Sociology
GUTMANN, M., Philosophy
JANICH, P., Philosophy
KÄSLER, D., Sociology
KISSLER, L., Sociology
KURZ-SCHERF, I., Political Science
LÜDTKE, H., Sociology
MERKEL, I., Ethnology
MÜNZEL, M., Ethnology
NOETZEL, T., Political Science
PYE, M., General Religious Science
RUPP, H.-K., Political Science
SCHILLER, TH., Political Science
ZIMMERMANN, H.-P., European Ethnology

Department of Psychology (Gutenbergstr. 18, 35032 Marburg; tel. (6421) 2823674; fax (6421) 2826949; e-mail dekanpsy@mailer.uni-marburg.de):

LACHNIT, H., General Psychology
LIEBHART, E., Educational Psychology
LOHAUS, A., Developmental Psychology
RIEF, W., Clinical Psychology
RÖHRLE, B., Clinical Psychology
RÖSLER, F., Cognitive Psychology, Neuroscience
ROST, D., Educational Psychology

SCHEIBLECHNER, H., Psychological Methodology
SCHMIDT-ATZERT, L., Psychological Diagnostics
SCHULZE, H.-H., Psychological Methodology
SCHWARTING, R., General and Physiological Psychology
SOMMER, G., Clinical Psychology
STELZL, I., Psychological Methodology and Diagnostics
STEMMLER, G., Psychological Diagnostics
WAGNER, U., Social Psychology

Department of Theology (Alte Universität, Lahntor 3, 35032 Marburg; tel. (6421) 2822441; fax (6421) 2828968; e-mail dekan05@mailer.uni-marburg.de):

AVEMARIE, F., New Testament
BARTH, H.-M., Systematic Theology
BIENERT, W., Church History
DABROCK, P., Social Ethics
DRESSLER, B., Practical Theology
ELSAS, C., Religious History
JEREMIAS, J., Old Testament
KAISER, J.-C., Church History
KESSLER, R., Old Testament
KOCH, G., Christian Archaeology
KORSCH, D., Systematic Theology
MARTIN, G. M., Practical Theology
NETHÖFEL, W., Social Ethics
PINGGERA, K., Church History
SCHNEIDER, H., Church History
SCHWEBEL, H., Religious Communication
STANDHARTINGER, A., New Testament
WAGNER-RAU, H., Practical Theology

Department of History and Cultural Sciences (Wilhelm-Röpke-Str. 6C, 35032 Marburg; tel. (6421) 2824518; fax (6421) 2826948; e-mail dekan06@mailer.uni-marburg.de):

BÖHME, H. W., Prehistory
BORSCHEID, P., Social and Economic History
CONZE, E., Modern History
DREXHAGE, H.-J., Ancient History
ERRINGTON, R. M., Ancient History
FRONING, H., Classical Archaeology
HARDACH, G., Social and Economic History
KAMPMANN, C., Modern History
KRIEGER, W., Modern History
LAUTER, H., Classical Archaeology
MEYER, A., Medieval History
MÜLLER-KARPE, A., Prehistory
PAUER, E., Japanese Studies
PLAGGENBORG, S., East European History
POSTEL, V., Medieval History
ÜBELHÖR, M., Sinology
WINTERHAGER, W. E., Modern History

Department of German Studies and Art (Wilhelm-Röpke-Str. 6A, 35032 Marburg; tel. (6421) 2824542; fax (6421) 2827056; e-mail dekan09@mailer.uni-marburg.de):

ALBERT, R., German Language
ANZ, TH., Modern German Literature
BERTELSMEIER-KIERST, C., German Philology
DEDNER, B., Modern German Literature
DOHM, B., Modern German Literature
HEINZLE, J., German Philology
HELLER, H.-B., Modern German Literature
HENZE-DÖHRING, G., Music
HERKLOTZ, I., History of Art
HERRGEN, J., German Linguistics
HEUSINGER, L., Informatics in History of Art
KRAUSE, K., History of Art
KREMERS, E., Graphics and Painting
KÜNZEL, H., Phonetics
MIX, Y.-G., Modern German Literature
OSINSKI, J., Modern German Literature
PRÜMM, K., Media Teaching
SCHLESEWSKY, M., Neurolinguistics
SCHMIDT, J., Dialect and Linguistics
SCHÜTTE, W., History of Art
WIESE, R., German Linguistics

Department of Foreign Languages and Philology (Wilhelm-Röpke-Str. 6D, 35032 Marburg; tel. (6421) 2824764; fax (6421) 2824715; e-mail kissling@mailer.uni-marburg.de):

BISCHOFF, V., American Literature
HAHN, M., Indology
HANDKE, J., English Linguistics
HOFER, H., Romance Philology
IBLER, R., Slavic Philology
KÖNSGEN, E., Latin Philology of the Middle and Modern Ages
KUESTER, M., English Studies
LEONHARDT, J., Classic Philology
POPPE, E., General Language and Celtology
RIEKEN, E., Comparative Language
SCHALLER, H., Slavic Philology
SCHMITT, A., Classic Philology
SOMMERFELD, W., Ancient Oriental Studies
STILLERS, R., Romance Philology
UHLIG, C., English and American Philology
WENINGER, S., Semitistics
ZIMMERMANN, R., English Linguistics
ZOLLNA, J., Romance Philology

Department of Mathematics (Hans-Meerwein-Str., 35032 Marburg; tel. (6421) 2825463; fax (6421) 2825466; e-mail dekan@mathematik.uni-marburg.de):

BAUER, T., Geometrical Algebra
DAHLKE, S., Numerics
FREISLEBEN, B., Practical Informatics
GROMES, W., Analysis
GUMM, H.-P., Theoretical Informatics
HESSE, W., Software Engineering
HÜLLERMEIER, E., Informatics
KNÖLLER, F. W., Topology and Geometry
LOOGEN, R., Functional Programmes
MAMMITZSCH, V., Probability Theory and Mathematical Statistics
PORTENIER, C., Analysis
SCHLICKEWEI, H. P., Algebra
SCHUMACHER, G., Topology and Geometry
SCHWENTICK, T., Theoretical Informatics
SEEGER, B., Databases
SOMMER, M., Practical Informatics
ULTSCH, A., Neuroinformatics
UPMEIER, H., Analysis
WELKER, V., Combinatorics

Department of Physics (Renthof 6, 35032 Marburg; tel. (6421) 2821314; fax (6421) 2821309; e-mail dekanat@physik.uni-marburg.de):

BREMMER, F., Applied Physics
ECKHARDT, B., Theoretical Physics
ECKHORN, R., Applied Physics
GEBHARD, F., Theoretical Physics
HEIMBRODT, W., Experimental Physics
HÖFER, U., Experimental Physics
JAKOB, P., Experimental Physics
KIRA, M., Theoretical Physics
KOCH, S., Theoretical Physics
LENZ, P., Theoretical Physics
NEUMANN, H., Theoretical Physics
PÜHLHOFER, F., Experimental Physics
RIES, H., Experimental Physics
RÜHLE, W., Experimental Physics
STÖCKMANN, H.-J., Experimental Physics
THOMAS, P., Theoretical Physics
WEISER, G., Experimental Physics

Department of Chemistry (Hans-Meerwin-Str., 35032 Marburg; tel. (6421) 2825543; fax (6421) 2828917; e-mail dekanat@chemie.uni-marburg.de):

BRÖRING, M., Inorganic Chemistry
ELSCHENBROICH, CHR., Inorganic Chemistry
ENSINGER, W., Analytical and Nuclear Chemistry
ESSEN, L.-O., Biochemistry
FRENKING, G., Chemistry-Related Computer Studies
GERMANO, G., Physical Chemistry
GREINER, A., Macromolecular Chemistry
HAMPP, N., Physical Chemistry
HARBRECHT, B., Inorganic Chemistry
HILT, G., Organic Chemistry
KOERT, W., Organic Chemistry
MARAHIEL, M., Biochemistry
MÜLLER, U., Inorganic Chemistry
SCHRADER, T., Organic Chemistry
SEUBERT, A., Analytical Chemistry
STUDER, A., Organic Chemistry
SUNDERMEYER, J., Metal-organic Chemistry
UHL, W., Inorganic Chemistry
WEITZEL, K.-M., Physical Chemistry
WENDORFF, J., Physical Chemistry

Department of Pharmacy (Wilhelm-Roser-Str. 2, 35032 Marburg; tel. (6421) 2825890; fax (6421) 2825815; e-mail dekanat.pharmazie@mailer.uni-marburg.de):

FRIEDRICH, C., History of Pharmacy
HANEFELD, W., Pharmaceutical Chemistry
HARTMANN, R., Pharmaceutical Chemistry
KEUSGEN, M., Pharmaceutical Chemistry
KISSEL, T., Pharmaceutical Technology and Biopharmacy
KLEBE, G., Pharmaceutical Chemistry
KRIEGLSTEIN, J., Pharmacology and Toxicology
KUSCHINSKY, K., Pharmacology and Toxicology
LINK, A., Pharmaceutical Chemistry
MATERN, U., Pharmaceutical Biology
MATUSCH, R., Pharmaceutical Chemistry
PETERSEN, M., Pharmaceutical Biology

Department of Biology (Karl-von-Frisch-Str., 35032 Marburg; tel. (6421) 2822047; fax (6421) 2822057; e-mail pega@mailer.uni-marburg.de):

BATSCHAUER, A., Plant Physiology, Photobiology
BÖLKER, M., Genetics
BRANDL, R., Animal Ecology
BREMER, E., Microbiology
BUCKEL, W., Microbiology
GALLAND, P., Plant Physiology, Photobiology
HASSEL, M., Morphology
HELDMAIER, G., Zoology
HOMBERG, U., Animal Physiology
KAHMANN, R., Genetics
KIRCHNER, C., Zoology
KLEIN, A., Molecular Genetics
KOST, G., Botany, Mycology
LINGELBACH, U., Zoology, Parasitology
MAIER, U., Cell Biology and Botany
MATTHIES, D., Plant Ecology
PLACHTER, H., Nature Conservancy Studies
RENKAWITZ-POHL, R., Molecular Genetics
THAUER, R., Microbiology
WEBER, H. C., Botany
ZIEGENHAGEN, B., Nature Conservancy Biology

Department of Geosciences (Hans-Meerwein-Str., 35032 Marburg; tel. (6421) 2823000; fax (6421) 2828919; e-mail napieral@mailer.uni-marburg.de):

BUCK, P., Crystallography
HOFFER, E., Petrology
PRINZ-GRIMM, P., Historical and Regional Geology
SCHMIDT-EFFING, R., Geology
VOGLER, ST., Structural Geology

Department of Geography (Deutschhausstr. 10, 35032 Marburg; tel. (6421) 2825916; fax (6421) 2828950; e-mail jansen@mailer.uni-marburg.de):

BARTHELT, H., Cultural Geography
BENDIX, J., Climatic Geography and Geoecology
BRÜCKNER, H., Morphology and Geoecology
MIEHE, G., Geography of Asia and East Africa
OPP, CH., Physical Geography
PAAL, M., Cultural Geography
PLETSCH, A., Cultural Geography and Geography of North America
STRAMBACH, S., Cultural Geography

Department of Medicine (Baldingerstr., 35032 Marburg; tel. (6421) 2866201; fax (6421) 2861548; e-mail dekanat@post.med.uni-marburg.de):

ARNOLD, R., Internal Medicine
AUMÜLLER, G., Anatomy
AUSTERMANN, K.-H., Maxillo-Facial Surgery
BACK, T., Neurology
BASLER, H.-D., Psychology
BAUER, W., Molecular Biology
BAUM, E., General Medicine
BEHR, T., Nuclear Medicine
BERGER, R., Otorhinolaryngology
BERTALANFFY, H., Neurosurgery
BESEDOVSKY, H., Physiology
BIEN, S., Neurosurgery
CETIN, Y., Anatomy
CZUBAYKO, F., Pharmacology
DAUT, J., Physiology
DIBBETS, J., Dentistry
DONNER-BANZHOFF, N., General Medicine
EILERS, M., Molecular Biology
ENGENHART-CABILLIC, R., Radiotherapy
FEHRENBACH, H.-G., Pneumology
FLORES DE JACOBY, L., Paradontology
GARTEN, W., Virology
GÖKE, R., Internal Medicine
GOTZEN, L., Surgery
GRISS, P., Orthopaedics
GRZESCHIK, K.-H., Human Genetics
GUDERMANN, T., Pharmacology and Toxicology
HAPPLE, R., Dermatology
HASILIK, A., Physiological Chemistry
HEBEBRAND, J., Child Psychiatry
HEEG, K., Microbiology
HOFMANN, R., Urology
JONES, D., Orthopaedics
KANN, P., Internal Medicine
KLENK, H.-D., Virology
KLINGMÜLLER, V., Nuclear Diagnosis
KLOSE, K., Radiology
KRAUSE, W., Andrology
KRETSCHMER, V., Transfusion Medicine
KRIEG, J. C., Psychology
KROLL, P., Ophthalmology
KUHN, K., Medical Informatics
LANG, R. E., Experimental Nuclear Medicine
LILL, R., Cytobiology
LISS, B., Physiology
LOHOFF, M., Microbiology
LOTZMANN, K.-U., Dentistry
MAIER, R., Neonatology
MAISCH, B., Cardiology
MAX, M., Anaesthesiology and Intensive Therapy
MOLL, R., Pathology
MOOSDORF, R., Cardiac Surgery
MÜLLER, R., Molecular Biology
MUELLER, U., Medical Sociology
NEUBAUER, A., Internal Medicine
OERTEL, W., Neurology
PIEPER, K., Dentistry for Children
RADSAK, K., General Medicine
REMSCHMIDT, H., Child Psychology
RENZ, H., Interdisciplinary Medical Centre
RÖPER, J., Physiology
ROSENOW, F., Neurology
ROTHMUND, M., Surgery
RUPP, H., Cardiology
SCHÄFER, H., Medical Biometry
SCHMIDT, S., Obstetrics
SCHWARZ, R., Parasitology
SEITZ, J., Anatomy
SEYBERTH, H. W., Child Medicine, Clinical and Theoretical Pharmacology
SOMMER, N., Neurology (Neuroimmunology)
STACHNISS, V., Dentistry
STEINIGER, B., Anatomy
STREMPEL, J., Ophthalmology
VOGELMEIER, C., Pneumology
VOIGT, K.-H., Physiology
WAGNER, H.-J., Radiology
WAGNER, W., Obstetrics
WEIHE, E., Anatomy
WERNER, J., Otolaryngology, Head and Neck Surgery
WULF, H., Anaesthesiology and Intensive Therapy

Department of Education (Wilhelm-Röpke-Str. 6B, 35032 Marburg; tel. (6421) 2824770; fax (6421) 2828946; e-mail dekan21@mailer.uni-marburg.de):

ACKERMANN, H., General Teaching
BECKER, P., Sociology of Sports
BÜCHNER, P., Sociology of Education
HAFENEGER, B., Extracurricular Education
KÖNIGS, F., General Teaching, Applied Linguistics
KUCKARTZ, U., Education
LAGING, R., Sports Science
LERSCH, R., School Education
NUISSL VON REIN, E., Adult Education
PROKOP, U., Socialization Theory
ROHR, E., Education
ROHRMANN, E., Education
SCHNOOR, H., Pedagogics
SEEWALD, J., Educational Kinesiology
SEITTER, W., Education
SOMMER, H.-M., Sports Medicine

LUDWIG-MAXIMILIANS-UNIVERSITÄT MÜNCHEN

Geschwister-Scholl-Platz 1, 80539 Munich
Telephone: (89) 2180-0
Fax: (89) 2180-2322
Internet: www.lmu.de

Founded 1472
Academic year: October to July

Rector: Prof. Dr rer.pol. BERND HUBER
Pro-Rectors: Prof. Dr med. Dr h.c. REINHARD PUTZ, Prof. Dr paed. FRIEDERIKE KLIPPEL, Dr phil. WERNER SCHUBÖ, Prof. Dr rer. nat. JOCHEN FELDMANN
Chief Administrative Officer: THOMAS MAY
Director of Library: Dr GÜNTER HEISCHMANN

Number of teachers: 4,500
Number of students: 46,800

Publications: *Vorlesungsverzeichnis* (2 a year), *LMU at a glance* (2 a year), *Veranstaltungskalender* (11 a year), *MUM* (4 a year), *'Einsichten'* (annually)

DEANS

Faculty of Ancient Cultures: Prof. Dr HANS VAN ESS
Faculty of Biology: Prof. Dr UTE HARMS
Faculty of Business Administration: Prof. Dr MANFRED SCHWAIGER
Faculty of Catholic Theology: Prof. Dr STEPHAN LEIMGRUBER
Faculty of Chemistry and Pharmacy: Prof. Dr FRANZ BRACHER
Faculty of Economics: Prof. Dr GERHARD ILLING
Faculty of Evangelical Theology: Prof. Dr KLAUS KOSCHORKE
Faculty of Geosciences: Prof. Dr DONALD BRUCE DINGWELL
Faculty of History and Art: Prof. Dr WINFRIED SCHULZE
Faculty of Language and Literature: Prof. Dr ULRICH SCHWEIER
Faculty of Law: Prof. Dr MORIS LEHNER
Faculty of Mathematics: Prof. Dr HEINZ SIEDENTOP
Faculty of Medicine: Prof. Dr DIETRICH REINHARDT
Faculty of Philosophy, Philosophy of Science and Religious Science: Prof. Dr Dr THOMAS BUCHHEIM
Faculty of Physics: Prof. Dr ALEX SCHENZLE
Faculty of Psychology and Pedagogics: Prof. Dr RUDOLF TIPPELT
Faculty of Social Sciences: Prof. Dr HANS-BERND BROSIUS
Faculty of Veterinary Science: Prof. Dr ANDREAS STOLLE

TECHNISCHE UNIVERSITÄT MÜNCHEN

Arcisstr. 21, 80333 Munich
Telephone: (89) 289-01
Fax: (89) 289-22000
E-mail: praesident@tu-muenchen.de
Internet: www.tu-muenchen.de

Founded 1868
State control
Academic year: October to September

President: Prof. Dr Dr h.c. mult. WOLFGANG A. HERRMANN
Vice-Presidents: Prof. Dr rer. nat. Dr-Ing. habil. ARNDT BODE, Dr phil. HANNEMOR KEIDEL, Prof. Dr rer. nat. ERNST RANK, Prof. Dr-Ing. habil. RUDOLF SCHILLING
Chancellor: Dr jur. LUDWIG KRONTHALER
Librarian: Dr REINER KALLENBORN

Number of teachers: 3,357
Number of students: 20,462

Publication: *Jahrbuch* (annually)

DEANS

Faculty of Architecture: Prof. Dr THOMAS HERZOG
Faculty of Chemistry: Prof. Dr JOHANNES A. BUCHNER
Faculty of Civil Engineering and Geodesy: Prof. Dr REINER RUMMEL
Faculty of Economics: Prof. Dr Dr h.c. RALF REICHWALD
Faculty of Electrical Engineering and Information Technology: Univ.-Prof. Dr Ing. JÖRG EBERSPÄCHER
Faculty of Informatics: Prof. Dr rer. nat. JOHANN SCHLICHTER
Faculty of Life Science: Prof. Dr BERTOLD HOCK
Faculty of Mathematics: Prof. Dr rer. nat. MARTIN BROKATE
Faculty of Mechanical Engineering: Prof. Dr HARTMUT HOFFMANN
Faculty of Medicine: Prof. Dr med. MARKUS SCHWAIGER
Faculty of Physics: Prof. Dr ALFRED LAUBEREAU
Faculty of Sports Science: Prof. Dr Dr h.c. JOSEF HACKFORTH

PROFESSORS

Faculty of Architecture (tel. (89) 289-22351; fax (89) 289-28442; e-mail marga.cervinka@lrz.tu-muenchen.de; internet www.arch.tu-muenchen.de):

BARTHEL, R., Structural Engineering
BOCK, T., Building Implementation and Information Technology
COTELO LÓPEZ, V., Design and the Conservation of Historical Buildings
DEUBZER, H., Design, Spatial Art and Lighting Design
EBNER, P., Housing and Housing Economics
EMMERLING, E., Restoration, Art Technology and Conservation
FINK, D., Integrated Construction
HAUSLADEN, G., Indoor Climate and Mechanical Services
HERZOG, T., Building Technology
HORDEN, R., Architecture and Product Development
HUGUES, T., Building Construction and Materials
HUSE, N., History of Art
KIESSLER, U., Integrated Buildings
KOENIGS, W., History of Building and Building Research

KRAU, I., Town Planning and Urban Development
LATZ, P., Landscape Architecture and Planning
MUSSO, F., Design, Building Construction and Materials Science
OSTERTAG, D., House Technology
REICHENBACH-KLINKE, M., Planning and Construction in Rural Areas
STRACKE, F., Urban Development and Regional Planning
THIERSTEIN, A., Territorial and Spatial Development
WIENANDS, R., Principles of Design and Representation
WITTENBORN, R., Visual Design
WOLFRUM, S., Urban and Regional Planning
ZBINDEN, U., Building Construction and Design Methodology

Faculty of Chemistry (Lichtenbergstr. 4, 85748 Garching; tel. (89) 289-3001; fax (89) 289-4386; e-mail dekanat@ch.tum.de; internet www.chemie.tu-muenchen.de):

BACH, T., Organic Chemistry I
BACHER, A., Organic Chemistry and Biochemistry
BONDYBEY, V. E., Physical Chemistry
BUCHNER, J., Biotechnology
DOMCKE, W., Theoretical Chemistry
FÄSSLER, T., Inorganic Chemistry
HEIZ, U., Physical Chemistry I
HERRMANN, W., Inorganic Chemistry
HINRICHSEN, O., Chemical Technology I
KESSLER, H., Organic Chemistry II
KETTRUP, A., Ecological Chemistry and Environmental Analytics
LANGOSCH, D., Bipolymer Chemistry
LERCHER, J., Chemical Technology II
LIMBERG, C., Inorganic Chemistry
NEUMEIER, D., Clinical Chemistry and Pathobiochemistry
NIEßNER, R., Hydrogeology, Hydrochemistry and Environmental Analytical Chemistry
NITSCH, W., Chemical Engineering
NUYKEN, O., Macromolecular Substances
PLANK, J., Construction Chemistry
SCHIEBERLE, P., Food Chemistry
SCHIEMANN, O., Physical Chemistry II
SCHMIDBAUR, H., Inorganic and Analytical Chemistry
SKERRA, A., Biological Chemistry
TÜRLER, A., Radiochemistry
VEPREK, S., Chemistry of Inorganic Materials

Faculty of Civil Engineering and Geodesy (tel. (89) 289-22400; fax (89) 289-23841; e-mail dekanat@bv.tum.de; internet www.bv.tum.de):

ALBRECHT, G., Steel-girder Construction
BLETZINGER, K., Structural Analysis
BÖSCH, H.-J., Tunnel Construction, Building Management
BUSCH, F., Traffic Engineering and Control
EBNER, H., Photogrammetry
FAULSTICH, M., Water Quality Control and Waste Management
GRUNDMANN, H., Building Mechanics
HAUSER, G., Building Physics
KIRCHHOFF, P., Transport and Town Planning
LEYKAUF, G., Road, Railway and Airfield Construction
MAGEL, H., Ground Preparation and Land Development
MENG, L., Cartography
MÜLLER, G., Building Mechanics
RANK, E., Building Informatics
RUMMEL, R., Astronomical and Physical Geodesy
SCHIESS, R., Building Materials and Materials Testing
SCHIESSL, P., Building Materials and Materials Testing
SCHIKORA, K., Analysis of Civil Engineering Structures
SCHUNCK, E., Building Construction
SPAUN, G., Geology
STROBL, TH., Hydraulic and Water Resources Engineering
THURO, K., Geology
VALENTIN, F., Hydraulics and Hydrography
VOGT, N., Foundations, Soil Mechanics and Rock Mechanics
WILDERER, P., Water Quality and Waste Management
WINTER, S., Building Construction
WUNDERLICH, T., Geodesy
ZILCH, K., Concrete Structures
ZIMMERMANN, J., Building Process Management

Faculty of Economics and Social Sciences (tel. (89) 289-25066; fax (89) 289-25070; e-mail dekanat@wi.tum.de; internet www.wi.tu-muenchen.de):

ACHLEITNER, A., KfW Entrepreneurial Finance
ANN, C., Corporate Law and Intellectual Property
BÄUMLER, G., Physical Education (Psychology)
BELZ, F., Brewing and Food Industry
BLÜMELHUBER, C., Maketing and Distribution
BÜSSING, A., Psychology
ENNEKING, U., Agribusiness and Food Industry
GRANDE, E., Political Science
GROSSER, M., Science of Movement and Training
HACKER, W., Psychology
HEINRITZ, G., Geography
HEISSENHUBER, A., Agricultural Economics and Farm Management
HENKEL, J., Technology and Innovation Management
HOFMANN, W., Political Science
HOLZHEU, F., Economics
KARG, G., Consumer Economics
KASERER, C., Financial Management and Capital Markets
KOLISCH, R., Technical Services and Operational Management
LEIST, K.-H., Physical Education Teaching
LÜCK, W., Business Management, Accounting, Auditing and Consulting
MOOG, M., Forest Management
REICHWALD, R., Information, Organization and Management
SALHOFER, K., Environmental Economics and Agricultural Policy
SCHELTEN, A., Pedagogics
STEINMÜLLER, H., Social Policy and Insurance
SUDA, M., Forest Policy and Forest History
TRINCZEK, R., Sociology
WEINDLMAIER, J., Dairy and Food Industry Management
VON WEIZSÄCKER, R. FRHR., Economics
WENGENROTH, U., History of Engineering
WILDEMANN, H., Management, Logistics and Production
WITT, D., Service Management
ZACHMANN, K., History of Technology

Faculty of Electrical Engineering and Information Technology (tel. (89) 289-28378; fax (89) 289-22559; e-mail dekanat@ei.tum.de; internet www.e-technik.tu-muenchen.de):

AMANN, M., Semiconductor Technology
ANTREICH, K., Computer-aided Design
BIRKHOFER, A., Reactor Dynamics and Reactor Safety
BOECK, W., High Voltage Engineering and Power Plants
BUSS, M., Automatic Control Engineering
DIEPOLD, K., Data Processing
EBERSPÄCHER, J., Communication Networks
FÄRBER, G., Real-time Computer Systems
GÜNTHER, C., Communication and Navigation
HAGENAUER, J., Communications Engineering
HEKERSDORF, A., Integrated Systems
KINDERSBERGER, J., High Voltage Engineering and Electric Power Transmission
KOCH, A., Measurement Systems and Sensor Technology
LANG, M., Man–Machine Communication
LUGLI, P., Nanoelectronics
NOSSEK, J., Circuit Theory and Signal Processing
RIGOLL, G., Man–Machine Communication
RUGE, I., Integrated Circuits
RUSSER, P., High Frequency Engineering
SCHLICHTMANN, U., Electronic Design Automation
SCHMIDT, G., Control Engineering
SCHMITT-LANDSIEDEL, D., Technical Electronics
SCHRÖDER, D., Electrical Drives
SWOBODA, J., Data Processing
WACHUTKA, G., Physics of Electrotechnology
WAGNER, U., Energy Economy and Application Technology
WOLF, B., Medical Electronics

Faculty of Informatics (Boltzmannstr 3, 85748 Garching; tel. (89) 289-17590; fax (89) 289-17591; e-mail gemkow@in.tum.de; internet www.informatik.tu-muenchen.de):

BAYER, R., Computer Science
BICHLER, M., Internet-based Information Systems
BODE, A., Computer Organization, Parallel Computer Architecture
BRAUER, W., Theoretical Computer Science and Foundations of Artificial Intelligence
BROY, M., Software and Systems Engineering
BRÜGGE, B., Applied Software Engineering
BUNGARTZ, H.-J., Computer Science in Engineering, Numerical Programming
EICKEL, J., Computer Science
FELDMANN, A., Network Architecture
GRUST, T., Database Systems
HEGERING, H.-G., Technical Informatics – Computer Networks
HUBWIESER, P., Didactics of Informatics
JESSEN, E., Computer Science
KNOLL, A., Robotics and Embedded Systems
KRAMER, S., Bioinformatics
KRCMAR, H., Information Systems
MATTHES, F., Software Engineering for Business Applications
MAYR, E. W., Efficient Algorithms
NAVAB, N., Computer-aided Medical Procedures
RADIG, B., Image Understanding and Knowledge-based Systems
SCHLICHTER, J., Applied Informatics/Collaborative Systems
SEIDL, H., Formal Languages, Compiler Construction, Software Construction
SPIES, P., System Architecture
WESTERMANN, R., Computer Graphics and Visualization
ZENGER, C., Computer Science

Faculty of Life Science (Alte Akademie 8, 85354 Freising; tel. (8161) 71-3258; fax (8161) 71-3900; e-mail dekanat@wzw.tum.de; internet www.wzw.tu-muenchen.de):

AUERNHAMMER, H., Agricultural Engineering
BACK, W., Brewing Technology I
BAUER, J., Animal Hygiene
DANIEL, H., Physiology of Nutrition
DELGADO, A., Fluid Mechanics and Process Automation
ENGEL, K.-H., Food and Nutrition

FAULSTICH, M., Technology of Biogenic Products
FORKMANN, G., Floriculture
FRIEDRICH, J., Physics
FRIES, H.-R., Animal Breeding
GIERL, A., Genetics
GRILL, E., Botany
HABE, W., Landscape Ecology
HAUNER, H., Nutritional Medicine
HOCK, B., Cell Biology
HRABÉ DE ANGELIS, M., Experimental Genetics
KETTRUP, A., Ecological Chemistry and Environmental Analytics
KÖGEL-KNABNER, I., Soil Science
KULOZIK, U., Food Process Engineering
LANGOSCH, D., Biopolymer Chemistry
LANGOWSKI, H.-C., Brewery Installations and Food Packaging Technology
LATZ, P., Landscape Architecture and Planning
MANLEY, G. A., Zoology
MATYSSEK, R., Ecophysiology of Plants
MENZEL, A., Ecoclimatology
MEWES, H.-W., Genome-orientated Bioinformatics
MEYER, H., Physiology
MEYER-PITTROFF, R., Energy and Environmental Technologies of the Food Industry
MOOG, M., Forestry
MOSANDL, R., Silviculture and Forest Planning
PARLAR, H., Chemical-Technical Analysis and Chemical Food Technology
PFADENHAUER, J., Vegetation Ecology
PRETZSCH, H., Forest Yield Science
QUEDNAU, H.-D., Work Science and Applied Computer Science
RECHKEMMER, G., Biofunctionality of Food
ROTHENBURGER, W., Horticultural Economics
SCHEMANN, M., Human Biology
SCHLEIFER, K.-H., Microbiology
SCHMIDHALTER, U., Plant Nutrition
SCHNITZLER, W. H., Vegetable Science
SCHNYDER, H., Grassland
SCHÖN, J., Land Engineering
SCHOPF, R., Animal Ecology
SKERRA, A., Biological Chemistry
SOMMER, K., Machinery and Apparatus
SUDA, M., Politics and History of Forestry
VALENTIEN, C., Landscape Architecture and Design
VOGEL, R., Industrial Microbiology
WARKOTSCH, W., Forest Industry and Applied Computer Science
WEGENER, G., Wood Science and Wood Engineering
WEISSER, H., Brewery Construction and Food Packaging Technology
WENZEL, G., Plant Cultivation
WOLF, P. F. J., Phytopathology
WOLFRAM, G., Human Nutrition
WURST, W., Developmental Genetics
ZANDER, J., Land Use Planning and Nature Conservation

Faculty of Mathematics (Boltzmannstr. 3, 85747 Garching; tel. (89) 289-16806; fax (89) 289-17584; e-mail dekanat@ma.tum.de; internet www.ma.tum.de):

BORNEMANN, F., Scientific Computing
BROKATE, M., Mathematical Modelling
BULIRSCH, R., Numerical Analysis
FRIESEKE, G., Global Analysis
GRITZMANN, P., Combinatorial Geometry
HOFFMAN, K.-H., Mathematical Modelling
KEMPER, G., Algorhythmic Algebra
KLÜPPELBERG, C., Statistics
LASSER, R., Biomathematics
LOSS, M., Global Analysis
RENTROP, P., Numerical Analysis
RICHTER-GEBERT, J., Geometry and Visualization
RITTER, K., Optimization
SCHEURLE, J., Dynamic Systems
SPOHN, H., Mathematical Physics
ZAGST, R., Mathematical Finance

Faculty of Mechanical Engineering (Boltzmannstr. 15, 85748 Garching; tel. (89) 289-5020; fax (89) 289-5024; e-mail wagner@mw.tum.de; internet www.mw.tu-muenchen.de):

ADAMS, N., Aerodynamics
BAIER, H., Lightweight Structures
BENDER, K., Information Technology
BUBB, H., Ergonomics and Human Factors
GREGORY, J. K., Materials
GÜNTHER, A., Material Flow and Logistics
GÜNTHNER, W., Production Technology
HEIN, D., Thermal Power Plants
HEINZL, J., Precision Mechanics and Microengineering
HEISSING, B., Automotive Engineering
HOFFMANN, H., Metal Forming and Casting
HÖHN, -R., Machine Elements
KAU, H. P., Flight Propulsion
LASCHKA, B., Fluid Mechanics
LINDEMANN, U., Product Development
LOHMANN, B., Automatic Control
PEUKERT, W., Solid Fuel Process Engineering
PEUKERT, W., Chemical Process Engineering
REINHART, G., Assembly Systems and Factories
RENIUS, K. T., Agricultural Machinery
SACHS, G., Flight Mechanics and Control
SATTELMAYER, T., Thermodynamics
SCHILLING, R., Fluid Mechanics
SCHMITT, D., Aeronautical Engineering
STICHLMAIR, J., Process Engineering
STROHMEIER, K., Apparatus and Plant Construction
ULBRICH, H., Applied Mechanics
WACHTMEISTER, G., Internal Combustion Engines
WALL, W., Computional Mechanics
WALTER, U., Astronautics
WERNER, E., Materials Science and Mechanics
WEUSTER-BOTZ, D., Biochemical Engineering
WINTERMANTEL, E., Medical Engineering
ZÄH, M., Machine Tools and Industrial Management

Faculty of Medicine (Ismaninger Str. 48, 81675 Munich; tel. (89) 4140-2121; fax (89) 4140-4870; e-mail huebener@nt1.chir.med.tu-muenchen.de; internet www.med.tu-muenchen.de):

ARNOLD, W., Otorhinolaryngology
BURDACH, S., Paediatrics
CLASSEN, M., Internal Medicine
CONRAD, B., Neurology
EISENMENGER, W., Forensic Medicine
EMMRICH, P., Paediatrics
ERFLE, V., Virology
FÖRSTL, H., Psychiatry and Psychotherapy
GÄNSBACHER, B., Experimental Oncology and Therapy Research
GÖTTLICHER, M., Clinic for Industrial and Environmental Medicine
GRADINGER, R., Orthopaedics and Sport Orthopaedics
GREIM, H., Toxicology and Environmental Hygiene
HALLE, M., Preventive and Rehabilitative Sports Medicine
HARTUNG, R., Urology
HAUNER, H., Nutritional Medicine
HESS, J., Paediatric Cardiology
HÖFLER, H., General Pathology and Pathological Anatomy
HOFMANN, F., Molecular Medicine
HOFMANN, F., Pharmacology and Toxicology
HORCH, H.-H., Dentistry
JESCHKE, D., Preventive and Rehabilitative Sports Medicine
KIECHLE, M., Gynaecology
KOCHS, E. F., Anaesthesiology
KUHN, K. A., Medical Statistics and Epidemiology
LANGE, R., Cardiac Surgery
LANZL, I. M., Ophthalmology
MEITINGER, T., Genetics
MERTZ, M., Ophthalmology
MOLLS, M., Radiotherapy and Radiological Oncology
NEISS, A., Medical Statistics and Epidemiology
NEUMEIER, D., Clinical Chemistry and Pathobiochemistry
NOWAK, D., Clinic for Industrial and Environmental Medicine
PESCHEL, C., Internal Medicine III
RING, J., Dermatology and Allergology
RUMMENY, E. J., X-Ray Diagnostics
SCHMID, R., Internal Medicine II
SCHÖMIG, A.-W., Internal Medicine I
SCHWAIGER, M., Nuclear Medicine
SIEWERT, J.-R., Surgery
SPEICHER, M., Genetics
TRAPPE, A. E., Neurosurgery
VON RAD, M., Clinical Psychology and Psychotherapy
WAGNER, H., Clinical Microbiology, Immunology and Hygiene
WILMANNS, J. C., Medical History and Ethics

Faculty of Physics (James Franck Str., 85748 Garching; tel. (89) 289-12492; fax (89) 289-14474; e-mail dekanat@physik.tu-muenchen.de; internet www.physik.tu-muenchen.de):

ABSTREITER, G., Experimental Semiconductor Physics I
BÖNI, P., Experimental Physics
BURAS, A. J., Theoretical Physics IV
DIETRICH, K., Theoretical Physics I
VON FEILITZSCH, F., Experimental Physics and Astro-Particle Physics
FEULNER, P., Physics
FISCHER, S., Theoretical Physics II
FRIEDRICH, H., Theoretical Physics
FRIEDRICH, J., Physics
FRIEDRICH, J., Physics
GROSS, R., Technical Physics
GROß, A., Theoretical Physics
VAN HEMMEN, J. L., Theoretical Physics
KINDER, H., Experimental Physics
KLEBER, M., Theoretical Physics
KOCH, F., Physics
KRÜCKEN, R., Physics
LAUBEREAU, A., Experimental Physics
LINDNER, M., Theoretical Particle and Astro-Particle Physics
NETZ, R., Theoretical Physics II
PARAK, F. G., Physics and Biophysics
PAUL, S., Physics I
PAUL, S., Physics I
PETRY, W., Experimental Physics
RIEF, M., Physics
RING, P., Theoretical Physics
STIMMING, U., Physics
STUTZMANN, M., Experimental Semiconductor Physics II
VOGL, P., Theoretical Physics III
WEISE, W., Theoretical Physics
ZWERGER, W., Theoretical Physics V

Faculty of Sports Science (Connollystr. 32, 80809 Munich; tel. (89) 289-24601; fax (89) 289-24636; e-mail dekanat.sport@sp.tum.de; internet www.sport.tu-muenchen.de):

HACKFORTH, J., Sport, Media and Communication
KELLER, J. A., Sport Psychology
LEIST, K.-H., Sport Pedagogy
MICHNA, H., Sport and Health Promotion
TUSKER, F., Human Movement Science and Training

ATTACHED INSTITUTES

Central Institute Carl von Linde Academy: Dir Prof. Dr PETER GRITZMANN.

Central Institute for Nutrition and Food Research: Dir Prof. Dr SIEGFRIED SCHERER.

Central Institute for Education: Dir Dr KARL GLÖGGLER.

Central Institute for Medical Engineering: Dir Prof. Dr med. ERICH WINTERMANTEL.

Central Institute for the History of Technology: Dir Prof. Dr ULRICH WENGENROTH.

Central Institute for Regional Planning and Environmental Research: Dir Prof. Dr HANSJÖRG LANG.

Central Institute for Sports Sciences: Dir Prof. Dr GÜNTHER BÄUMBER.

Heinz Maier-Leibnitz Research Neutron Source (FRM-II): Dir Prof. Dr KLAUS SCHRECKENBACH.

Media Centre: Dir Prof. Dr rer.nat. Dr-Ing. habil. ARNDT BODE.

Walter Schottky Institute for Basic Research in Semiconductor Electronics: Dir Prof. Dr GERHARD ABSTREITER.

Weihenstephan Bavarian State Brewery: Dir Prof. Dr HEINZ MIEDANER.

Weihenstephan Centre for Nutrition, Land Management and Environmental Studies: Dir Prof. Prof. Dr BERTOLD HOCK.

Weihenstephan Testing and Experimental Institute for Dairy Science: Dir Prof. Dr HEINRICH KARG.

UKRAINISCHE FREIE UNIVERSITÄT

Pienzenauerstr. 15, 81679 Munich

Telephone: (89) 99-738830
Fax: (89) 99-738850
E-mail: ufu@extern.lrz-muenchen.de
Internet: www.ukrainische-freie-universitaet.mhn.de

Founded 1921
Private, State-approved
Languages of instruction: Ukrainian, English, German
Academic year: October to August (including Summer Courses July–August)

Rector: Prof. Dr LEONID RUDNYTZKY
Chancellor: Prof. Dr NICOLAS SZAFOWAL
Librarian: MIROSLAW FICAK

Number of teachers: 56
Number of students: 196

Publications: *Naukovi Zapysky UVU* (annually), *Naukovi Zbirnyky UVU*, *Specimina dialectorum ucrainorum*, *Studien zu deutsch-ukrainischen Beziehungen*

DEANS

Faculty of Law and Economics: Prof. Dr IVAN MYHUL
Faculty of Philosophy: Prof. Dr LEONID RUDNYTZKY
Faculty of Ukrainian Studies: Prof. Dr ANATOLIJ POHRIBNYJ
Pedagogical Institute: Prof. Dr A. KUSILEWSKA-TKACZ
Research Institute for German–Ukrainian Relations: Prof. Dr REINHARD HEYDENREUTER

PROFESSORS

Faculty of Law and Economics (tel. (89) 99-73-88-42):

FUTEY, B., Constitutional Law
ISAJIW, V., Sociology
KOSTYCKY, M., Ukrainian Public Law
MYHUL, I., Political Sciences
NAGY, L., Geography
PYNZENYK, V., Political Economy
SUBTELNY, O., History of Political Ideas
ZLUPKO, S., History of Economic Theories

Faculty of Philosophy (Arts):

ANDRIEWSKY, O., Ukranian History
DACKO, I., Theology
GUDZIAK, B., Church History and History of Philosophy
JERABEK, B., Education
KIPA, A., Comparative Literature
KULCHYCKY, J., European History
KYSILEWSKA-TKACH, A., Education
LABUNKA, M., Ukranian History
MAKSYMTSCHUK, W., Comparative Literature
PIETSCH, R., Philosophy
RUDNYTZKY, L., Comparative Literature
STEPOWYK, D., Ukranian Cultural History
SYSYN, F., History of Eastern Europe
ŽLEPKO, D., History of Eastern Europe
ŽUK, R., History of Architecture

Faculty of Ukrainian Studies:

HROMJAK,, R., Ukrainian Language and Literature
KOPTILOV, V., Ukrainian Language and Literature
KOZAK, S., Slavonic Literature
MUŠINKA, M., Ukranian Ethnology
POHRIBNYJ, A., Ukrainian Language and Literature
PRYSJAZNIJ, M., Journalism
SALYHA, T., History of Ukrainian Literature

UNIVERSITÄT DER BUNDESWEHR MÜNCHEN

Werner-Heisenberg-Weg 39, 85579 Neubiberg

Telephone: (89) 6004-0
Fax: (89) 60042009
E-mail: info@unibw.de
Internet: www.unibw.de

Founded 1973
Academic year: October to September (3 semesters)

President: Prof. Dr MERITH NIEHUSS
Vice-Presidents: Prof. Dr UWE M. BORGHOFF, Prof. Dr THOMAS WÜSTRICH
Chancellor (vacant)
Registrar: INGO FRITZ
Librarian: Dr HANS-JOACHIM GENGE

Library of 773,000 vols
Number of teachers: 200
Number of students: 2,700

Publications: *Forschungsbericht*, *'Der Hochschulkurier'* (3 a year)

DEANS

Faculty of Aviation and Space, Aerospace Engineering: Prof. Dr-Ing. K.-J. SCHWENZFEGER
Faculty of Civil Engineering, Surveying and Geodesy: Prof. Dr-Ing. D. KRAUS
Faculty of Computer and Information Sciences: Prof. Dr rer. nat. S. BRAUN
Faculty of Economics and Organizational Sciences: Prof. Dr rer. pol. P. FRIEDRICH
Faculty of Education: Prof. Dr A. KAISER
Faculty of Electrical Engineering: Prof. Dr-Ing. K. HOFFMANN
Faculty of Social Sciences: Prof. Dr Z. VOIGT
Polytechnical College of Business Administration: Prof. Dr jur. W. ROTTMANN
Polytechnical College of Civil and Electrical Engineering: Prof. Dr-Ing. G. STICHLER
Polytechnical College of Mechanical Engineering: Prof. Dipl.-Ing. J. HERRMANN

WESTFÄLISCHE WILHELMS-UNIVERSITÄT MÜNSTER

Schlossplatz 2, 48149 Münster

Telephone: (251) 830
Fax: (251) 8332090
E-mail: verwaltung@uni-muenster.de
Internet: www.uni-muenster.de

Founded 1780; became Academy in 1818; University status again in 1902
State control
Academic year: October to July (two terms)

Rector: Prof. Dr JÜRGEN SCHMIDT
Pro-Rectors: Prof. Dr Dr WOLFGANG BERDEL, Prof. Dr ULRICH MÜLLER-FUNK, Prof. Dr ULRICH PFISTER, Prof. Dr HARALD ZÜCHNER
Chancellor: Dr BETTINA BÖHM
Librarian: Dr BEATE TRÖGER

Number of teachers: 1,217
Number of students: 40,000

Publications: *Forschungsjournal* (2 a year), *Jahresbericht der Gesellschaft zur Förderung der WWU* (annually)

DEANS

Faculty of Biology: Prof. Dr CHRISTIAN KLÄMBT
Faculty of Catholic Theology: Prof. Dr REINHARD HOEPS
Faculty of Chemistry and Pharmacy: Prof. Dr BERNHARD WÜNSCH
Faculty of Earth Sciences: Prof. Dr HANS KERP
Faculty of Economic Sciences: Prof. Dr THERESIA THEURL
Faculty of Education and Social Sciences: Prof. Dr HANSJÖRG SCHEERER
Faculty of History/Philosophy: Prof. Dr MAGDALENE SÖLDNER
Faculty of Languages: Prof. Dr JÜRGEN HEIN
Faculty of Law: Prof. Dr REINER SCHULZE
Faculty of Mathematics and Computing: Prof. Dr KLAUS H. HINRICHS
Faculty of Medicine: Prof. Dr HERIBERT JÜRGENS
Faculty of Physics: Prof. Dr GERNOT MÜNSTER
Faculty of Protestant Theology: Prof. Dr HANS-RICHARD REUTER
Faculty of Psychology and Sports Science: Prof. Dr BERND STRAUß
Music School: Prof. Dr REINBERT EVERS

ATTACHED INSTITUTES

Musikhochschule der Universität Münster: Dir Prof REINBERT EVERS.

Münster Research Institute for Insurance: Dir Prof. Dr H. KOLLHOSSER.

Research Centre for European Civil Law: Dir Prof. Dr R. SCHULZE.

Central Institute for Development Planning: Dirs Prof. Dr HANS D. JARASS, Prof. Dr Dr Dr W. KRAWIETZ, Prof. Dr U. VAN SUNTUM.

Freiher vom Stein Institute: internet www.uni-muenster.de/Jura.fsi; Dir Dr DÖRTE DIEMERT.

Institute for Commercial Management: Dir Prof. Dr D. AHLERT.

Hornheide Clinic for Tumours, Tuberculosis and Facial and Skin Restoration: Medical Dir Dr V. SCHWIPPER.

Leibniz Institute for Arteriosclerosis Research: internet www.lifa.uni-muenster.de; Dir Prof. Dr G. ASSMANN (acting).

Nephrological Institute: Dir Prof. Dr K.-H. RAHN.

Academy for Manipulative Medicine: internet www.manuellemedizin.de; Dir Dr M. SCHILGEN.

Institute for Psychology and Psychotherapy: Dir AGNES LASSAK.

Institute for Comparative Local History: Dirs Prof. Dr PETER JOHANEK, Prof. Dr JOSEF SUDBROCK.

Institute for Research into the Early Middle Ages: Dir Prof. Dr G. ALTHOFF.

Institute for Chemical and Biological Transmission: Head Prof. Dr K. CAMMANN.

Institute for Informatics in Agriculture: Dir Prof. Dr U. STREIT.

Institute for Applied Informatics: Dirs Prof. Dr H. L. GROB, Dr W. HELD, Prof. Dr W.-M. LIPPE.

CARL V. OSSIETZKY UNIVERSITÄT OLDENBURG

Postfach 2503, 26111 Oldenburg
Located at: Ammerländer Heerstr. 114–118, 26129 Oldenburg
Telephone: (441) 798-0
Fax: (441) 7983000
E-mail: webmaster@uni-oldenburg.de
Internet: www.uni-oldenburg.de
Founded 1974
Academic year: October to September (two terms)
President: Prof. Dr UWE SCHNEIDEWIND
Vice-Presidents: Prof. Dr RETO WEILER, Prof. Dr KAREN ELLWANGER, GERLINE WALTER
Librarian: HANS-JOACHIM WÄTJEN
Number of teachers: 212 professors
Number of students: 12,091
Publications: *Einblicke* (research at the University, 2 a year), *Monoculus* (biology, 2 a year), *Data Work* (computer sciences, 3 a year)

DEANS

Faculty 1 (School of Education): Prof. Dr BARBARA MOSCHNER
Faculty 2 (School of Computer Science, Business Administration, Economics and Law): Prof. Dr HANS-JÜRGEN APPELRATH
Faculty 3 (Linguistics and Cultural Studies): Prof. Dr RALF GRÜTTERMEIER
Faculty 4 (Humanities and Social Sciences): Prof. Dr JÜRGEN HEUMANN
Faculty 5 (Mathematics and Natural Sciences): Prof. Dr JÜRGEN RULLKÖTTER

PROFESSORS

Faculty 1 (School of Education) (Ammerländer Heerstr. 114–118, 26129 Oldenburg; tel. (441) 798-2002; fax (441) 798-2924; e-mail dekanat.fk1@uni-oldenburg.de; internet www.uni-oldenburg.de/fk1):

Department of Education

(Head of Department: Prof. Dr KLAUS WINTER (acting))

HANFT, A., Adult Education and Continuing Vocational Education
KAISER, A., Elementary Science, Elementary Social Studies
KIPER, H., Theory and Practice in Secondary Education
MEYER, H., General Education, School Teaching
MOSCHNER, B., Teaching and Learning Research
NITSCH, W., Theory of Knowledge
SCHMIDTKE, H.-P., Intercultural Education

Department of Special Needs Education)

(Head of Department: Prof. Dr MANFRED WITTROCK)

ORTMANN, M., Education for the Physically Handicapped
SCHULZE, G. C., Special Education Needs
WITTROCK, M., Education for People with Disturbed Behaviour

Faculty 2 (School of Computer Science, Business Administration, Economics and Law) (Ammerländer Heerstr. 114–118, 26129 Oldenburg,; tel. (441) 798-4140; fax (441) 798-4199; internet www.uni-oldenburg.de/fk2):

Business Administration and Education:

BREISIG, T., Organization and Human Resources
LACHNIT, L., Financial and Management Accounting
MOHE, Business Consultancy
MÜLLER, M., Production and Environmental Management
PFRIEM, R., General and Environmental Management
RAABE, T., Marketing
REBMANN, K., Vocational and Business Education
SIEBENHÜNER, Ecological Economics

Computer Science:

APPELRATH, H.-J., Information Systems and Databases
BEST, E., Parallel Systems
DAMM, W., Safety Critical Embedded Systems
FATIKOW, S., Microrobotics, Control Engineering
FRÄNZLE, M., Hybrid Systems
HABEL, A., Formal Languages
HASSELBRING, W., Software Engineering
HEIN, A., Automation and Measurement Engineering
JENSCH, P., Image Processing and Process Control
KOWALK, W., Computer Networks and Telecommunications
MÖBUS, C., Learning Environments and Knowledge-based Systems
NEBEL, W., Embedded Hardware/Software Systems Design
OLDEROG, E.-R., Correct System Design
SONNENSCHEIN, M., Environmental Informatics
STIEGE, G., Graphs and Networks
THEEL, O., System Software and Distributed Systems

Economics:

EBERT, U., Public Finance
LITZ, H.-P., Economic Statistics
SCHEELE, Economic Policy
SCHÜLER, K. W., Econometrics
TRAUTWEIN, H. M., International Economics
WELSCH, H., Economic Theory

Law:

BLANKE, T., Labour Law
FRANK, G., Public Economic Law
SCHIEK, D., European Economic Law
TAEGER, J., Private Law, Business and Economic Law, Legal Informatics

Teaching of Economics and of Technology:

HENSELER, K., Teaching of Technology
KAMINSKI, H., Teaching of Economics
LEWALD, A., Home Economics
REICH, G., Teaching of Technology

Faculty 3 (Linguistics and Cultural Studies) (Ammerländer Heerstr. 114–118, 26129 Oldenburg,; tel. (441) 798-2347; fax (441) 798-2115; e-mail fk3@uni-oldenburg.de; internet www.uni-oldenburg.de/fk3):

Dutch Studies:

GRÜTTEMEIER, R., Dutch Literature

English Studies:

GELUYKENS, R., Pragmatics, Discourse Analysis, Social Variation
HAMANN, C., Acquisition of First and Second Languages, Bilingualism, Formal Syntax and Semantics
KOEHRING, K., American Literature and Culture

Fine Arts and Visual Communication:

HOFFMANN, D., History of Fine Arts
SPRINGER, P., Theory and History of Art
THIELE, J., Fine Arts and Visual Communication
WENK, S., History of Art, Gender Studies

German Studies:

BRANDES, H., Literature
DOERING, S., Literature
EICHLER, W., Didactics and Linguistics
GLOY, J., Linguistics
KYORA, S., Literature
MEVES, U., Medieval German Literature and Language
STÖLTING, W., German as a Second or Foreign Language

Music:

DINESCU, V., Applied Composition
HOFFMANN, F., Music Education
SCHLEUNING, P., History of Music, Music Teaching
STROH, W. M., Theory of Music and Music Pedagogics

Slavonic Studies:

GRÜBEL, R., Slavonic Literature
HENTSCHEL, G., Linguistics and Slavonic Languages

Visual and Material Culture:

ELLWANGER, K., History of Culture
MÖRSCH, C., Teaching of Material Culture

Faculty 4 (Humanities and Social Sciences) (Ammerländer Heerstr. 114–118, 26129 Oldenburg,; tel. (441) 798-2634; fax (441) 798-2624; e-mail dekanat.fk4@uni-oldenburg.de; internet www.uni-oldenburg.de/fk4):

Geography:

HAGEN, D., Cartography and Physical Geography

History:

BUDDE, G., 19th- and 20th-century German and European History
ETZEMÜLLER, T., Contemporary History
FREIST, D., Early Modern History
GÜNTHER-ARNDT, H., Teaching of History
HAHN, H.-H., Modern and East European History (esp. History of Poland)
HOLBACH, R., Medieval History
REEKEN, D. VON, Teaching of History
SCHEER, T., Ancient History

Philosophy:

GERHARD, M., Philosophy of Nature and of Science, Continental Philosophy
KREUZER, J., Philosophy and History of Philosophy
MÖBUSS, S., Philosophy and Jewish Philosophy
PUSTER, E., Epistemology, Philosophy of Language, Ethics
RUSCHIG, U., Philosophy
SCHULZ, R., Philosophy and History of Science
SUKALE, M., Philosophy and Philosophy of Science

Psychology:

BELSCHNER, W., Psychology
COLONIUS, H., Psychological Methods
HELLMAN, A., Psychological Methods
HÖGE, H., Environmental Psychology and Empirical Aesthetics
LAUCKEN, U., Social Psychology
MEES, U., General Psychology
NACHREINER, F., Applied Psychology
SCHICK, A., Psychological Acoustics and Environmental Psychology
SZAGUN, D., Developmental Psychology
VIEBAHN, P., Educational Psychology
WALCHER, K.-P., Psychology of Personality, Environmental Psychology

Social Sciences:

FLAAKE, K., Women's Studies
GRUNENBERG, A., Political Theory and Political Culture
KRAIKER, G., Social and Political Theory
LOEBER, H.-D., Sociology of Labour and Education
MÜLLER-DOOHM, S., Sociology of the Mass Media
NASSMACHER, K.-H., Comparative Politics
WEISMANN, A., Sociology, Methods of Social Research

Sports Science:

ALKEMEYER, T., Sociology and Philosophy of Sport
LIPPENS, V., Motor Control and Learning
SCHIERZ, M., Sports Science
SCHMÜCKER, B., Sports Science and Sports Medicine

Theology:

GOLKA, F., Jewish Studies, Old Testament
HEUMANN, J., Religious Education
LINK-WIECZOREK, U., Systematic Theology and Religious Education
WEISS, W., New Testament

Faculty 5 (Mathematics and Science) (Ammerländer Heerstr. 114–118, 26129 Oldenburg; tel. (441) 798-3442; fax (441) 798-5601; e-mail fk5@uni-oldenburg.de; internet www.uni-oldenburg.de/fk5):

Biology, Earth and Environmental Sciences:

BRUMSACK, H.-J., Geomicrobiochemistry
CYPIONKA, H., Palaeomicrobiology
EBER, W., Botany, Morphology
GIANI, L., Soil Sciences
HAESELER, V., Terrestrial Ecology
HAGEN, D., Cartography and Physical Geography
HOESSLE, C., Biology, School Teaching
JANIESCH, P., Botany, Physiological Ecology
KLEYER, M., Landscape Ecology
KLUMP, G. M., Zoophysiology
KOCH, K.-W., Biochemistry
KRETZBERG, J.
KUMMERER, K., Regional Planning and Development
RICHTER-LANDSBERG, C., Molecular Neurobiology, Neurochemistry
RINKWITZ, S., Neurogenetics
SCHMINKE, H. K., Zoology, Zoosystematics and Morphology
SIMON, U., Biology of Geological Processes
STABENAU, H., Plant Physiology
VARESCHI, E., Aquatic Ecology
WACKERNAGEL, W., Genetics
WEILER, R., Zoology, Neurobiology
WINDELBERG, J., Infrastructure and Environmental Planning

Chemistry:

AL-SHAMERY, K., Physical Chemistry
BECKHAUS, R., Inorganic Chemistry
GMEHLING, J., Industrial Chemistry
KLEINER, T., Physical Chemistry
KÖLL, P., Organic Chemistry
MARTENS, J., Organic Chemistry
METZGER, J. O., Organic Chemistry
POWCHMANN, J., Chemistry, Theory and Practice of School Teaching
RÖSSNER, F., Industrial Chemistry
WICKLEDER, M., Inorganic Chemistry
WITTSTOCK, G., Physical Chemistry

Mathematics:

DEFANT, A., Mathematics, Functional Analysis
HERZBERGER, J., Applied Mathematics, Instrumental Mathematics
KNAUER, U., Mathematics, Algebraic Methods
LEISSNER, W., Mathematics, Geometry
MÜLLER, CH., Mathematics, Stochastics
PFLUG, P., Mathematics, Complex Variables
PIEPER-SEIER, I., Mathematics, Algebra
QUEBBEMANN, H.-G., Mathematics, Number Theory
SCHMALE, W., Mathematics, Dynamic Systems
SCHMIEDER, G., Mathematics, Complex Analysis
SPÄTH, H., Applied Mathematics
VETTER, U., Mathematics, Commutative Algebra

Physics:

BAUER, G. H., Experimental Physics
ENGEL, A., Theoretical Physics
HINSCH, K., Experimental Physics
HOLTHAUS, M., Theoretical Physics
KOLLMEIER, B., Applied Physics
KOLNY, J., Applied Physics
KUNZ-DROLSHAGEN, J., Theoretical Physics, Field Theory
MAIER, K. H., Experimental Physics
MELLERT, V., Applied Physics
MERTINS, A., Applied Physics
PARISI, J., Experimental Physics
PEINKE, J., Experimental Physics
RIESS, F., Teaching of Physics
VERHEY, J., Applied Physics

UNIVERSITÄT OSNABRÜCK

Neuer Graben/Schloss, 49069 Osnabrück
Telephone: (541) 969-0
Fax: (541) 969-4570
E-mail: aaa@uni-osnabrueck.de
Internet: www.uni-osnabrueck.de

Founded 1973
Languages of instruction: German, English
Academic year: October to September

President: Prof. Dr CLAUS R. ROLLINGER
Vice-President: Prof. Dr PETER HERTEL
Vice-President (vacant)
Registrar: Dr UWE SIELEMAN
Librarian: FELICITAS HUNDHAUSEN

Number of teachers: 500
Number of students: 10,500

Publication: *Forschungsbericht* (every 2 years)

HEADS OF DEPARTMENTS

Law: Prof. Dr JÖRN IPSEN
Economics and Business: Prof. Dr MICHAEL WOSNITZER
Social Sciences: Prof. Dr ROLAND CZADA
Education and Culture Sciences: Prof. Dr BEATE EGO
Languages and Literature Sciences: Prof. Dr TRUDER MEISENBURG
Human Sciences: Prof. Dr JULIUS KUHL
Mathematics, Computer Sciences: Prof. Dr ELMER COHORS-FRESENBORG
Physics: Prof. Dr SIEGMAR KAPPHAN
Biology and Chemistry: Prof. Dr JÜRGEN HEINISCH
Culture and Geosciences: Prof. Dr RAINER HAGL

UNIVERSITÄT-GESAMTHOCHSCHULE PADERBORN

Warburger Str. 100, 33098 Paderborn
Telephone: (5251) 600
Fax: (5251) 602519
E-mail: pressestelle@zv.uni-paderborn.de
Internet: www.uni-paderborn.de

Founded 1972
State control
Language of instruction: German
Academic year: October to July

Rector: Prof. Dr NIKOLAUS RISCH
Chancellor: Dr JÜRGEN PLATO
Librarian: Dr DIETMAR HAUBFLEISCH

Library of 1,300,000 vols, 1,900 periodicals
Number of teachers: 950
Number of students: 14,700

Publications: *Forschungsforum* (annually), *Paderborner Universitätsreden* (irregular), *Paderborner Universitätszeitung* (4 a year)

DEANS

Faculty of Business Studies: Prof. Dr PETER SLOANE
Faculty of Cultural Studies: Prof. Dr FRANZ GÖTTMANN
Faculty of Electrical Engineering, Computing and Mathematics: Prof. Dr KLAUS MEERKÖTTER
Faculty of Mechanical Engineering: Prof. Dr JÜRGEN GAUSEMEIER
Faculty of Natural Sciences: Prof. Dr HANS-JOACHIM WARNECKE

PROFESSORS

Department of Agriculture:

BORGMANN, F.-W., Crop Cultivation
BRELOH, B., Stockbreeding, Statistics
FREITAG, M., Anatomy and Physiology, Animal Nutrition
HENSCHE, H.-U., Agricultural Economics
LÜTKE ENTRUP, N., Agriculture
PAUL, V., Crop Cultivation and Protection
SCHÄFERKORDT, H., Agriculture
SCHLAGBAUER, A., Biology
SCHÜTTERT, R., Agriculture
VOLK, L., Agriculture
WECKE, W., Agriculture

Department of Automation Engineering:

BAREISS, M., Automation Engineering
BEATER, P., Automation Engineering
ELIAS, H.-J., Economics
FORSTER, J., Automation Engineering
MEIER, F., Automation Engineering
PETUELLI, G., Machine Tools
RICHTER, W., Automation Engineering
SAADAT, M., Mechanical Engineering
SCHMIDT, W., Automation Engineering
SCHULZ-BEENKEN, A. S., Mechanical Engineering
SCHÜRMANN, E., Automation Engineering
SPÖRER, R., Automation Engineering
STEMMER, F., Mechanical Engineering, Automation Engineering
STÖWER-GROTE, R., Automation Engineering
STUMPE, M., Automation Engineering

Department of Chemistry and Chemical Engineering:

BECKER, H. J., Chemistry
BROECKER, H.-C., Chemistry
FELS, G., Chemistry
GOLDSCHMIDT, A., Chemistry
GROTE, M., Chemistry
HAUPT, H.-J., Chemistry
HUBER, C., Chemistry
KITZEROW, H.-S., Chemistry
KROHN, K., Chemistry
LENDERMANN, B., Chemistry and Chemical Engineering
MARSMANN, H., Chemistry and Chemical Engineering
MASUCH, Biology
POLLMANN, P., Chemistry and Chemical Engineering
REININGER, G., Chemistry and Chemical Engineering
RISCH, N., Chemistry
SCHUBERT, V., Chemistry
WARNECKE, H. J., Chemistry

Department of Data Engineering:

BECHTLOFF, J., Mechanical Engineering
GRONAU, P., Business Administration
HIPP, K. J., Data Engineering
KLEIN, H. W., Mechanical Engineering
KNOBLOCH, T., Data Engineering
OEVENSCHEIDT, W. F., Production Engineering
RIEDEL, U., Mechanical Engineering
SCHÖNFELDER, T., Data Engineering
SCHUSTER, C., Mechanical Engineering
STOLP, W., Mechanical Engineering
STURMATH, R., Data Engineering
TILLNER, W., Mechanical Engineering
WILLMS, J., Data Engineering

Department of Economics:

BARTON, D. M., Private, Commercial and Media Law
BÖHLER, W., English and Economics
DANGELMEIER, W., Economics
DIETL, H., Organization and International Management

DIETRICH, G., Private and Commercial Law
DOBIAS, P., Political Economy
FISCHER, J., Business Administration
GILROY, B. M., International Economics
GOLLERS, R., Economics
GRIES, T., Economics
HARFF, P., Statistics
KAISER, F.-J., Economics
KRAFT, M., Statistics
KRIMPHOVE, D., Commercial Law
LIEPMANN, P., Economics
NASTANSKY, L., Computer Science
NISSEN, H.-P., General Political Economy
PULLIG, K.-K., Business Administration
RAHMANN, B., Political Economy
REISS, W., Political Economy
RESE, M., Economics
ROSENBERG, O., Business Administration
ROSENTHAL, K., Business Administration
SCHILLER, B., Economics
SCHMIDT, K.-H., Business Administration
SKALA, H.-J., Statistics
SUHL, L., Business Administration
WEBER, W., Business Administration
WERNER, T., Business Administration.

Department of Education, Psychology and Physical Education:

ENGFER, A., Psychology
HAGEMANN, W., Education
HAMMEL, W., Education
KLEIN, M.-L., Physical Education
KNIEVEL, H., Education
KOCH, J.-J., Psychology
KÖNIG, E., Education
LIESEN, H., Sports Medicine
SCHNEIDER, P., Education
WEBER, A., Education
WEISS, M., Sports Medicine
WETTLER, M., Psychology
ZIELKE, G., Education

Department of Electrical Engineering:

ALDEJOHANN, A., Information Technology
BARSCHDORFF, D., Electrical Engineering
BELLI, F., Information Technology
CAMBEIS, L., Electrical Engineering
DÖRRSCHEIDT, F., Electrical Engineering
GAUSCH, F., Electrical Engineering
GROTSTOLLEN, H., Electrical Engineering
HARTMANN, G., Electrical Engineering
HORSTICK, G. J., Electrical Engineering
MEERKÖTTER, K., Electrical Engineering
MROZYNSKI, G., Electrical Engineering
NOÉ, R., Electrical Engineering
RENTZSCH-HOLM, I., Electrical Engineering
RÜCKERT, U., Electrical Engineering
TEICH, J., Data Engineering
VOSS, J., Electrical Engineering
WICHERT, H. W., Electrical Engineering

Department of Electrical Power Engineering:

BECKER, W., Electrical Power Engineering
BITZER, B., Electrical Power Engineering
GIESE, K.-G., Electrical Power Engineering
GRAUEL, A., Electrical Power Engineering
KRYBUS, W., Electrical Power Engineering
MEPPELINK, J., Electrical Power Engineering
MÜLLER, K.-H., Electrical Power Engineering
SACHS, G., Electrical Power Engineering
SCHWARZ, U., Electrical Power Engineering
THIEMANN, P., Electrical Power Engineering
WEIMAR, R.-J., Electrical Power Engineering

Department of Environmental Protection Technology:

BIELENBERG, K., Environmental Protection Technology
BITTER, W., Environmental Protection Technology
BRAND, G., Environmental Protection Technology
FETTIG, J., Environmental Protection Technology
GRUPPE, M., Environmental Protection Technology
HENNE, K.-H., Environmental Protection Technology
LOHR, H., Mathematics, Data Processing
MASSMEYER, K., Environmental Protection Technology
MIETHE, M., Environmental Protection Technology
MEON, G., Environmental Protection Technology
MÜLLER, L., Geology, Geotechnology
RAMKE, H.-G., Environmental Protection Technology
RATHKE, K., Environmental Protection Technology
SIETZ, M., Chemistry

Department of Fine Arts, Music and Design:

ALLROGGEN, G., Music
BAUER, G., Art and Works of Art
BEDER, J., Textile Design
BILLMAYER, F., Art, Teaching of Art
FISCHER, W., Music
KAEMPF-JANSEN, H., Art
KEIL, W., Music
KÖHLER, M., Vocational Education
LAUBENTHAL, A., Music
REESE-HEIM, D., Textile Design

Department of Landscape Architecture and Ecological Planning:

BÖTTCHER, H., Land Maintenance
GERKEN, B., Land Maintenance
HARFST, W., Land Maintenance
RÖHR, W.-D., Land Maintenance
SCHITTEK, N., Land Maintenance
SCHMIDT, U., Land Maintenance
SCHULTE, A., Ecology and Climatology
SEYFANG, V., Land Maintenance
WOLF, A., Land Maintenance

Department of Languages and Literature:

ALLKEMPER, A., German Literature
APEL, F., German Literature
ARENS, A., Romance Philology
BREMER, E., German
BREUER, R., English
DURZAK, M., German
ECKER, G., General Literary Research
ECKHARDT, J., German
ELKE, N., German
FELDBUSCH, E., German
FREESE, P., American Studies
FREUND, W., German
GREIF, S., Literature
GRUBITZSCH, H., Literature
HARTIG, M., Language
LANGENBACHER-LIEBGOTT, J., Romance Philology
MICHELS, G., Language and Literature
PASIERBSKY, F., German
PIENEMANN, M., English Language, Teaching English Language
PORSCHE, M., American Studies
ROHDENBURG, English
SCHLESIER, R., Anthropology
SCHÖWERLING, R., English
STEINECKE, H., Modern German Literature
STEINHOFF, H.-H., German
THOMAS, J., Romance Philology
WINKLER, H., Media
ZONS, R. A., Literature

Department of Mathematics and Computer Science:

BENDER, P., Mathematics
BIERSTEDT, K.-D., Mathematics
BÖTTCHER, S., Mathematics
BRUNS, M., Mathematics
DEIMLING, K., Mathematics
DELLNITZ, M., Mathematics
DIETZ, H.-M., Mathematics, Computer Science
DOMIK, B., Computer Science
ENGELS, G., Computer Science
ERNST, B., Mathematics
FUCHSSTEINER, B., Mathematics
GATHEN, J. V. Z., Mathematics
HANSEN, S., Mathematics
HAUENSCHILD, W., Computer Science
HEISS, H.-U., Computer Science
INDLEKOFER, K.-H., Mathematics
KASTENS, U., Practical Computer Science
KEIL-SLAWIK, R., Computer Science
KIYEK, K.-H., Mathematics
KLEINE BÜNING, H., Computer Science
KÖCKLER, N., Mathematics
KÜSPERT, H.-J., Computer Science
LENZING, H., Mathematics
LUSKY, W., Mathematics
MANGENHEIM, J. S., Computer Science
MEYER AUF DER HEIDE, F., Computer Science
MONIEN, B., Computer Science
RAMMIG, F. J., Computer Science
RINKENS, H.-D., Mathematics
SCHÄFER, W., Computer Science
SOHR, H., Mathematics
SPIEGEL, H., Mathematics
SZWILLUS, G., Computer Science

Department of Mechanical Engineering:

GAUSEMEIER, J., Mechanical Engineering
GORENFLO, D., Thermodynamics and Heat Transfer
HAHN, O., Mechanical Engineering
HERRMANN, K., Mechanical Engineering
JORDEN, W., Mechanical Engineering
KOCH, R., Design
LIMPER, A., Mechanical Engineering
LÜCKEN, J., Mechanical Engineering
MAIER, H.-J., Mechanical Engineering
MEIERFRANKENFELD, B., Mechanical Engineering
PAHL, M. H., Mechanical Engineering
POTENTE, H., Mechanical Engineering
RICHARD, H. A., Mechanical Engineering
VOLLERSTEN, F., Mechanical Engineering
WALLASCHEK, J., Mechanical Engineering
ZELDER, U., Mechanical Engineering

Department of Philosophy, History, Geography, Religious and Social Sciences:

BARTELS, A., Philosophy
BARTH, H.-K., Geography
BRIESE, V., Political Science
BUBLITZ, H., Sociology
EICHER, P., Catholic Theology
FLACH, D., History
FRANKEMÖLLE, H., Catholic Theology
FUCHS, G., Geography
GÖTTMANN, H.-M., Protestant Theology
HOFFMANN, M., Physical Geography
JARNUT, J., History
KAGERMEIER, A., Anthropology and Geoinformatics
KLENKE, D., History, Teaching of History
KUHLMANN, H., Evangelical Theology
LEUTZSCH, M., Evangelical Theology
LINK, S., History
METTE, N., Catholic Theology
PIEPMEIER, R., Philosophy
SCHUPP, F., Philosophy
SPRENGER, R., History, Teaching of History
STEINECKE, A., Geography for Economics and Tourism
SZMULA, V., Political Science

Department of Physics:

ANTHONY, K.-H., Physics
AS, D.-J., Applied Physics
FRAUENHEIM, T., Theoretical Physics
HESEKER, H., Home Economics
HOLZAPFEL, W. B., Experimental Physics
LESSNER, G., Theoretical Physics
LISCCHKA, K., Experimental Physics
MEYER ZUR CAPELLEN, F., Physics
MIMKES, J., Experimental Physics
OSTEN, W. VON DER, Experimental Physics
OVERHOF, H., Theoretical Physics
REINHOLD, P., Teaching of Physics
SCHNEIDER, L., Home Economics
SCHWERMANN, W., Physics
SOHLER, W., Applied Physics

SPAETH, J.-M., Experimental Physics
WORTMANN, G., High Pressure Physics, Solid-State Physics
ZIEGLER, H., Applied Physics

Department of Telecommunications:

BREIDE, S., Telecommunications
HAFNER, S., Telecommunications
HAHN, Data Engineering
HUFNAGEL, F., Telecommunications
JÄGER, H.-G., Telecommunications
JANSSEN, W., Telecommunications
KACZMARCZYK, N., Telecommunications
KEUTER, W., Telecommunications
KLASEN, H., Telecommunications
KRAUSE, K., Telecommunications
LÜDERS, C.-F., Physics and Data Engineering
MÖLLER, G., Telecommunications
NERZ, K.-P., Telecommunications
OPIELKA, D., Telecommunications
RIES, S., Telecommunications
SCHULZE, H., Telecommunications
SCHWARZ, K.-D., Telecommunications
SCHWEPPE, E.-G., Telecommunications
STEHLING, T., Software Engineering
WÜNSCHE, C., Telecommunications

UNIVERSITÄT PASSAU

Innstr. 41, 94032 Passau
Telephone: (851) 509-0
Fax: (851) 509-1005
E-mail: auslandsamt@uni-passau.de
Internet: www.uni-passau.de

Founded 1972
State control
Language of instruction: German
Academic year: October to July

Rector: Prof. Dr W. SCHWEITZER
Pro-Rector: Prof. Dr CHRISTIAN LENGAUER
Pro-Rector: Prof. Dr KLAUS DIRSCHERL
Administrative Officer: LUDWIG BLOCH
Librarian: Dr STEFFEN WAWRA

Library of 1,650,000 vols
Number of teachers: 101
Number of students: 8,299

DEANS

Faculty of Business Sciences: Prof. Dr HANS ZIEGLER
Faculty of Law: Prof. Dr BERNARD HAFFKE
Faculty of Mathematics and Computer Sciences: Prof. Dr BURKHARD FREITAG
Faculty of Philosophy: Prof. Dr ERNST STRUCK
Faculty of Theology: Prof. Dr ANTON LANDERSDORFER

PROFESSORS

Faculty of Business Sciences (94030 Passau; tel. (851) 509-2400; fax (851) 509-2402; e-mail dekanat@wiwi.uni-passau.de; internet www.wiwi.uni-passau.de):

BÜHNER, R., Management, Organization and Personnel
HAASE, K. D., Management and Tax Studies
KLEINHENZ, G., Economic Policy
KLEINSCHMIDT, P., Economics-Related Computer Studies
LAMBSDORFF, J. G., Economic Theory
LEHNER, F., Business Computing
LÜDEKE, R., Economics and Finance
MOOSMÜLLER, G., Statistics
PFLÜGNER, M., Economics (Foreign Trade and Payments)
SCHILDBACH, TH., Management, Investment and Accounts
SCHWEITZER, W., Statistics
STEINER, J., Finance and Banking
WILHELM, J., Management
ZIEGLER, H., Business Management and Economic Production

Faculty of Law (94030 Passau; tel. (851) 509-2201; fax (851) 509-2207; e-mail franz.wenninger@uni-passau.de; internet www.jura.uni-passau.de):

ALTMEPPEN, H., Civil Law, Commercial Law I
BETHGE, H., State and Administrative Law
BEULKE, W., Penal Law
BRAUN, J., Civil Law, Civil Procedural Law and Philosophy of Law
FINCKE, M., Penal Law
HAFFKE, B., Criminal Law, Criminal Procedural Law, Philosophy and Sociology of Law
HAU, W., Common Law, International Private Law, Company Law
HECKMANN, D., Public Law
MANTHE, U., Civil Law and Roman Law
SCHURIG, K., Civil, International and Comparative Law
SCHWEITZER, M., State, Administrative, International and European Law
SEEWALD, O., State and Administrative Law
SEIF, U., Civil Law, History of European and German Law, International Private Law
SÖHN, H., State and Administrative Law
STOFFELS, M., Common Law, Labour Law, Commercial Law, Company Law
WILHELM, J., Civil and Commercial Law

Faculty of Mathematics and Computer Studies (94030 Passau; tel. (851) 509-3001; fax (851) 509-3002; e-mail dekanat@fmi.uni-passau.de; internet www.fmi.uni-passau.de):

BRANDENBURG, F.-J., Theoretical Computer Studies
DE MEER, H., Informatics
DENZLER, J., Informatics
DONNER, K., Mathematics
FREITAG, B., Computer Science
GRAF, S., Mathematics
GRASS, W., Computer Science
LEHA, G., Mathematics
LENGAUER, CH., Computer Science and Programming
RITTER, G., Mathematics
SCHMIDT, B., Informatics
SCHWARTZ, N., Mathematics
SNELTING, G., Informatics
WEISPFENNING, V., Mathematics

Faculty of Philosophy (94030 Passau; tel. (851) 509-2601; fax (851) 509-2603; e-mail Bachsleitner@uni-passau.de; internet www.phil.uni-passau.de):

ANHUF, P., Physical Geography
BACH, M., Sociology
BAUER, L., Mathematics Teaching
BECKER, W., Modern History
BENDER, H., Archaeology of the Roman Provinces
BERNERT, W., Teaching of Social Policy
DIRSCHERL, K., Romance Literature
EMONS, R., English Language
ERKENS, R., Medieval History
FELIX, S., General and Applied Linguistics
FRENZ, T., Medieval History and Historical Auxiliary Sciences
GELLNER, W., Politics
HANSEN, K., American Studies
HARNISCH, R., German Language
HEESCH, M., Systematic Theology
HEITZER, H., History Teaching
HIERING, P., Biology Teaching
HINZ, M., Romance Literature
JARFE, G., English Language and Literature
KAMM, J., English Literature and Culture
KORFF, R., Psychology of Development
KRAH, H., Modern German Literature
LENZ, B., British Studies
LÜTTERFELDS, W., Philosophy
MARTSCHINKE, S., Primary School Teaching Methods
MIEDL, O., Aesthetic Education
MOGEL, H., Psychology
MÜLLER, K., Teaching German Language and Literature
NOLTE, T., Old German Literature
OBERREUTER, H., Politics
POLLAK, G., Educational Theory
SCHRÖTER, S., South-East Asian Studies
SCHÜSSLER, G., History of Art and Christian Archaeology
SEIBERT, N., Education
STAMPFL, I., Music
STRUCK, E., Human Geography
TITZMANN, M., History of Modern German Literature and General Literature
WALTER, K.-P., Romance Literary and Regional Studies, with emphasis on France
WOLDAN, A., East Central European Studies
WOLFF, H., Ancient History
WÜNSCH, T., Medieval History
ZEHNPFENNIG, B., Political Theory and History of Ideas

Faculty of Theology (94030 Passau; tel. (851) 509-2001; fax (851) 509-2003; internet www.ktf.uni-passau.de):

BAUMGARTNER, I., Christian Social Studies and Pastoral Theology
FONK, P., Moral Theology
LANDERSDORFER, A., Church History
LISKE, M.-T., Philosophy
MENDL, J., Religious Education and Teaching Methods
SCHWANKL, O., New Testament Exegesis
SCHWIENHORST-SCHÖNBERGER, L., Old Testament Exegesis and Hebrew
STINGLHAMMER, H., Dogmatics
ZECHMEISTER-MACHHART, Basic Theology

ATTACHED INSTITUTES

Bavarian Centre of Research for Knowledge-Based Systems: Dir Prof. Dr KLAUS DONNER.

Centre for European Law (CEP): Dir Prof. Dr M. SCHWEITZER.

Centre for Market-orientated Tourism Research: Dir Dr GÜNTHER HRIBECK.

Centre for Teacher Training and Didactics: Dir Prof. Dr NORBERT SEIBERT.

European Centre for Documentation: Dir Prof. Dr MICHAEL SCHWEITZER.

Institute for Agricultural Law: Dirs Prof. Dr OTFRIED SEEWALD, Prof. Dr MARKUS STOFFELS.

Institute for Applied Ethics in Economy, Training and Further Education: Dir Prof. Dr PETER FONK.

Institute for Financial Planning (IFP): Dirs Prof. Dr JÜRGEN STEINER, Prof. Dr BERNHARD KROMSCHRÖDER.

Institute for the History of Modern Psychology: Dir Prof. Dr WERNER TRAXEL.

Institute for Information Systems and Software Technology (IFIS): Dir Prof. Dr BURKHARD FREITAG.

Institute for Intercultural Communication at the University of Passau: Dir Prof. Dr KLAUS DIRSCHERL.

Institute for International and Foreign Law: Dir Prof. Dr KLAUS SCHURIG (acting).

Institute for Research into East Bavarian History: Dir Prof. Dr EGON BOSHOF.

UNIVERSITÄT POTSDAM

Postfach 601553, 14415 Potsdam
Am Neuen Palais 10, 14469 Potsdam
Telephone: (331) 977-0
Fax: (331) 977-972163

E-mail: presse@rz.uni-potsdam.de
Internet: www.uni-potsdam.de
Founded 1991
Languages of instruction: German, English
Academic year: October to September
Rector: Prof. Dr WOLFGANG LOSCHELDER
Vice-Rector (Teaching and Study): Prof. Dr GERDA HASSLER
Vice-Rector (Research and Scientific Development): Prof. Dr FRIEDER SCHELLER
Vice-Rector (Planning and Finance): Prof. Dr JÜRGEN RODE
Vice-Rector (Scientific and Technology Transfer and Innovation): Prof. Dr HARALD FUHR
Number of teachers: 226 professors, 923 other academic staff
Number of students: 17,200

DEANS

Faculty of Arts: Prof. Dr BERNHARD KROENER
Faculty of Economic and Social Sciences: Prof. Dr DETLEV HUMMEL
Faculty of Human Sciences: Prof. Dr RIA DE BLESER
Faculty of Law: Prof. Dr HEIDRUN POHL-ZAHN
Faculty of Mathematics and Natural Sciences: Prof. Dr ROBERT SECKLER

UNIVERSITÄT REGENSBURG

Universitätsstr. 31, 93053 Regensburg
Telephone: (941) 943-01
Fax: (941) 943-2305
E-mail: rudolf.dietze@verwaltung.uni-regensburg.de
Internet: www.uni-regensburg.de
Founded 1962
Academic year: October to September
Rector: Prof. Dr ALF ZIMMER
Pro-Rectors: Prof. Dr ARMIN KURTZ, Prof. Dr JÜRGEN SCHMUDE
Administrative Officer: CHRISTIAN BLOMEYER
Librarian: Dr F. GEISSELMANN
Number of teachers: 1,339
Number of students: 17,624
Publication: *Research Report* (online at www.uni-regensburg.de/Universitaet/Forschungsbericht)

DIRECTORS OF DEPARTMENTS

Biology and Pre-clinical Medical Studies: Prof. Dr Dr H. R. KALBITZER
Business Management, Economics and Management Information Systems: Prof. Dr J. MÜLLER
Catholic Theology: Prof. Dr K. BAUMGARTNER
Chemistry and Pharmacy: Prof. Dr A. GÖPFERICH
History, Social Sciences and Geography: Prof. Dr. P. SCHMID
Language and Literature: Prof. Dr U. HEBEL
Law: Prof. Dr H. E. MÜLLER
Mathematics: Prof. Dr G. KINGS
Medicine: Prof. Dr M. NERLICH
Philosophy, Sport and Arts: Prof. Dr M. BRÖKING-BERTFELD
Physics: Prof. Dr W. WEGSCHEIDER
Psychology and Pedagogy: Prof. Dr M. HAMMERL

PROFESSORS

Department of Biology and Pre-clinical Medical Studies (tel. (941) 943-3110; fax (941) 943-4341; internet www.biologie.uni-regensburg.de):

BAUMANN, R., Physiology
BRUNNER, E., Biophysics
FÖRSTER, C., Zoology
HAUSKA, G., Botany
HEINZE, J., Zoology
KALBITZER, H. R., Biophysics
KRAMER, B., Zoology
KUNZELMANN, B., Physiology
KURTZ, A., Physiology
MINUTH, W., Anatomy, Cell Biology
NEUMANN, I., Animal Physiology
OBERPRIELER, C., Botany
OERTEL, W., Genetics
POSCHLOD, P., Botany
SCHMÄDEL, D. VON, Medical Sociology
SCHMITT, R., Genetics
SCHNEUWLY, S., Developmental Biology
SPEIERER, G. W., Medical Psychology
STERNER, R., Biology
STROM, E., Zoology
SUMPER, M., Biochemistry
TAMM, E., Anatomy
TANNER, W., Botany
THOMM, M., Microbiology
TSCHOCHNER, H., Biochemistry
WARTH, R., Physiology
WIRTH, R., Microbiology
WROBEL, K.-H., Morphology and Anatomy

Department of Business Management, Economics and Management Information Systems (tel. (941) 943-2392; fax (941) 943-4752; internet www.wiwi.uni-regensburg.de):

ARNOLD, L., Economics, Economic Theory
BARTMANN, D., Business Informatics
BUCHHOLZ, W., Public Finance and Environmental Economics
DOWLING, M., Management of Technology and Innovation
DRUKARCZYK, J., Finance
DRUMM, H. J., Human Resources Management
FEDERRATH, H., Business
GÖMMEL, R., History of Economics
HALLER, A., Financial Accounting and Auditing
HAMERLE, A., Statistics
HEUBES, J., Political Economy
HRUSCHKA, H., Marketing
JERGER, J., International Economy
LEE, G., Real Estate Economics
LORY, P., Mathematics and Information Science
MEYER-SCHARENBERG, D., German Tax System
MÖLLER, J., Political Economy
OTTO, A., Controlling and Logistics
PERNUL, G., Business Informatics
RÖDER, K., Financial Services
SCHÄFERS, W., Real Estate Management
TSCHERNIG, R., Econometry
WIEGARD, W., Political Economy

Department of Catholic Theology (tel. (941) 943-3746; fax (941) 943-4944; internet www.uni-regensburg.de/Fakultaeten/Theologie):

BAUMGARTNER, K., Practical Theology
DEMEL, S., Canon Law
DIRSCHERL, E., Dogmatics
DOHMEN, C., Exegesis and Hermeneutics of the Old Testament
HAUSBERGER, K., Church History
HILGER, G., Religious Education
KNOLL, A., Fundamental Theology
LAUX, B., Theological Anthropology
LEINSLE, U., Philosophical–Theological Propaedeutic
MERKT, A., Old Church History and Patrology
RITT, H. P., New Testament
SCHLÖGEL, H., Moral Theology

Department of Chemistry and Pharmacy (tel. (941) 943-2556; fax (941) 943-4275; internet www.chemie.uni-regensburg.de):

BUSCHAUER, A., Pharmaceutical Chemistry II
DICK, B., Physical Chemistry
ELZ, S., Pharmaceutical Chemistry
GÖPFERICH, A., Pharmaceutical Technology
HEILMANN, J., Pharmaceutical Biology
KOHLER, H.-H., Physical Chemistry
KÖNIG, B., Organic Chemistry
KORBER, N., Inorganic Chemistry
KRIENKE, H., Theoretical Chemistry
KUNZ, W., Physical Chemistry
MERZ, A., Organic Chemistry
PFITZNER, A., Inorganic Chemistry
REISER, O., Organic Chemistry
SCHEER, M., Anorganic Chemistry
SCHMEER, J., Physical Chemistry
SCHÜTZ, A., Theoretical Chemistry
SEIFERT, R., Pharmacology and Toxicology
STEINEM, C., Biosensors
WOLFBEIS, O., Analytical Chemistry

Department of History, Social Sciences and Geography (tel. (941) 943-3587; fax (941) 943-3993; internet www.uni-regensburg.de/Fakultaeten/phil_Fak_III):

BAUER, F., History
BEILNER, H., Didactics of History
BIERLING, S., Political Science, International Politics
BREUER, T., Cultural Geography
EHRIG, F. R., Geography
GOETZE, D., Sociology
HEINE, K., Geography
HERB, K., Political Philosophy and History of Ideas
HERZ, P., Ancient History
HETTLAGE, R., Sociology
KÖHLE, K., Didactics of Social Studies
KORTÜM, H.-H., Medieval History
LUTTENBERGER, A. P., Early Modern History
MA'CKÓV, D., Political Science (Middle and Eastern Europe)
OBERSTE, J., Medieval History
RINSCHEDE, J., Didactics of Geography
SCHAUER, P., Pre- and Early History
SCHMID, P., History of Bavaria
SCHMUDE, J., Economic and Social Geography
SEBALDT, M., Political Science (Western Europe)
VÖLKEL, J., Soil Science

Department of Language and Literature (tel. (941) 943-3592; fax (941) 943-1811; e-mail fachbereich.sl@sprachlit.uni-regensburg.de; internet www.uni-regensburg.de/Fakultaeten/phil_Fak_IV):

BECK, J.-W., Classical Philology (Latin)
BERGER, D. A., English Philology
DAIBER, J., German Philology
DOTZLER, B., Media Science
DRASCEK, D., Study of Civilization
EMIG, R., English Literature
FEISTNER, E., German Literature of the Middle Ages
FISCHER, R., English Linguistics
FRANZ, K., Teaching of German Language and Literature
GELHARD, D., Comparative Literature
GEISENHANSLÜKE, A., Modern German Literature
GREULE, A., German Linguistics
HAMMWÖHNER, R., Linguistic Computer Science
HANSEN, B., Slavic Linguistics
HEBEL, U., American Studies
KLINGENSCHMITT, G., Indo-Germanic Philology
KOSCHMAL, W., Slavic Literatures
MECKE, J., French Literature, Film Studies
NEKULA, M., Bohemian Studies, Western Slavic Philology
NEUMANN-HOLZSCHUH, J., French and Spanish Linguistics
RECHENAUER, G., Classical Philology (Greek)
REGENER, U., German Philology
SCHNEIDER, E. W., English Linguistics
SCHULZ, M., German Linguistics
SELIG, M., Romance Linguistics
THURMAIR, M., German as a Foreign Language, German Linguistics
TIEFENBACH, H., German Linguistics
WETZEL, H., French and Italian Literature
WOLFF, C., Media Informatics

Department of Law (tel. (941) 943-2267; fax (941) 943-2013; internet www.uni-regensburg.de/Fakultaeten/Jura):

ARNOLD, R., Public Law, Foreign Public Law, Comparative Law
BECKER, H.-J., Civil Law, History of European Law and Canon Law
ECKHOFF, R., Public Law, Law of Public Finance and Taxation
FRITSCHE, J., Civil Law, Commercial and Economic Law
GOTTWALD, P., Civil Law, Law Procedure and International Private Law
GRIGOLEIT, H. C., Civil Law, Commercial Law, Company Law, European Private Law
HOFER, S., Civil Law, History of German and European Private Law
KINGREEN, T., Public Law, Social Law, Health Law
MANSSEN, G., Public Law, German and European Administrative Law
MÜLLER, H.E., Criminal Law, Juvenile Criminal Law
PAWLIK, H., Criminal Law, Philosophy of Law
ROTH, H., Civil Law, German, European and International Procedural Law
SPICKHOFF, A., Civil Law, International Private Law, Comparative Law
STEINER, U., Public Law, German and Bavarian State and Administration Law
UERPMANN, R., Public Law, International Law
ZIMMERMAN, R., Civil Law, Roman Law and Historical Comparative Law

Department of Mathematics (tel. (941) 943-2024; fax (941) 943-4923; internet www.uni-regensburg.de/Fakultaeten/nat_Fak_I/):

BINGENER, J.
FINSTER ZIRKER, F.
GARCKE, H.
GOETTE, W.
VOM HOFE, R..
HACKENBROCH, W.
JÄNICH, K.
JANNSEN, U.
KINGS, G.
KNEBUSCH, M.
KNORR, K.
KÜNNEMANN, K.
SCHMIDT, A.

Department of Medicine (Franz-Josef-Strauß Allee 11, 93053 Regensburg; tel. (941) 944-6082; fax (941) 944-6079; internet www.uni-regensburg.de/Fakultaeten/Medizin):

ANDREESEN, R., Internal Medicine I
BIRNBAUM, D., Heart, Thorax and Cardiovascular Surgery
BOGDAHN, U., Neurology
BOßERHOFF, U., Molecular Pathology
BRAWANSKI, A., Neurosurgery
EILLES, CHR., Nuclear Medicine (Radiotherapy)
FEUERBACH, S., Radiology
FÜRAT, A., Colproctology
GABEL, V.-P., Ophthalmology
GEISSLER, E., Experimental Surgery
GRIFKA, J., Orthopaedics
HACKI, T., Otorhinolaryngology, Head and Neck Surgery
HAJAK, G., Psychiatry
HANDEL, G., Prosthodontics
HARTMANN, A., Pathology
HENGSTENBERG, C., Internal Medicine
HOBBHAHN, J., Anaesthesiology
HOFSTÄDTER, F., Pathology
HOHENLEUTNER, U., Dermatology
HOLMER, S., Internal Medicine
JILG, W., Medical Microbiology and Hygiene
KLEIN, H. E., Psychiatry
KÖLBL, O., Radiotherapy
KRÄMER, E., Internal Medicine II
LANDTHALER, M., Dermatology
LEHN, N., Medical Microbiology and Hygiene
LOEW, T., Psychosomatic Medicine and Psychotherapy
LORENZ, B., Ophthalmology
MACK, M., Internal Medicine and Nephrology
MACKENSEN, A., Haematology, Oncology
MALIK, E., Gynaecology
MÄNNEL, D., Tumour Immunology (Pathology)
MULTHOFF, G., Oncology
MÜßIG, D., Orthodontics
NERLICH, M., General Surgery
ORTMANN, O., Gynaecology
OSTERHEIDER, M., Forensic Psychiatry
PFEIFER, M., Internal Medicine II
PISO, P., Surgery
REICHERT, T., Surgery
RIEGGER, G., Internal Medicine II
ROGLER, J., Internal Medicine
RUHL, S., Parodontology
SALZBERGER, B., Internal Medicine
SCHLITT, H. J., Surgery
SCHMALZ, G., Operative Dentistry and Periodontology
SCHMID, F. X., Heart, Thorax and Cardiovascular Surgery
SCHMITZ, G., Clinical Chemistry and Laboratory Medicine
SCHÖLMENICH, J., Internal Medicine I
SEELBACH-GÖBEL, D., Gynaecology and Obstetrics
SEGERER, H., Neonatology
STRAUB, R., Internal Medicine I
STRUTZ, J., Otorhinolaryngology, Head and Neck Surgery
TAEGER, K., Anaesthesiology
VOGT, T., Dermatology
WAGNER, R., Molecular Microbiology
WEBER, B., Human Genetics
WIELAND, F., Urology
WINKLER, J., Neurology
WOERTGEN, C., Neurosurgery
WOLF, H., Medical Microbiology and Hygiene

Department of Philosophy, Sport and Arts (tel. (941) 943-1811; fax (941) 943-3993; e-mail philosophie.sport.kunst@verwaltung.uni-regensburg.de; internet www.uni-regensburg.de/Fakultaeten/phil_Fak_I/):

BRÖKING-BORTFELDT, M., Protestant Theology, Didactics of Religious Education
DITTSCHEID, H.-CHR., Art History
HILEY, D., Music
HOFMANN, B., Music Education
HORN, W., Music
LEBER, H., Art Education
MEINEL, CHR., History of Science
REUSSER, C., Archaeology
ROTT, H., Philosophy
SCHÖLLER, W., Art History
SCHÖNBERGER, R., Philosophy
STEINFATH, H., Philosophy
TRAEGER, J., History of Art
WESENBERG, B., Archaeology
ZINK, J., History of Art

Department of Physics (tel. (941) 943-3967; fax (941) 943-2021; internet www.physik.uni-regensburg.de):

BACK, C., Magnetism, Magneto-Electronics
BAYREUTHER, G., Magnetism, Magnetic Materials, Spintronics
BRACK, M., Finite Fermion Systems
BRAUN, V., Quantum Field Theory and Quantum Chromodynamics
GÖRITZ, D., Polymers
GRIFONI, M., Quantum Transport and Dissipation
LANGFELLNER, H., High-Technology Superconductors
MAIER, M., Optics, Spectroscopy, Laser Physics
MAYER, A., Phonons, Surfaces
MORGENSTERN, I., Superconductivity, Optimization of Industrial Processes
PENZKOFER, A., Femtosecond Spectroscopy of Organic Materials
RENK, K. F., Non-linear Transport, Terahertz Spectroscopy of Semiconductors
RICHTER, K., Complex Quantum Systems
RÖSSLER, U., Semiconductors and Nanostructures
SCHÄFER, A., Quantum Chromodynamics and Hadron Physics
SCHOEPE, W., Suprafluidity, Ultra-low Temperature Physics
SCHÜLLER, C., Optical Spectroscopy on Semiconductor Quantum Structures
STRUNK, D., Mesoscopic Systems
WEISS, D., Semiconducting and Ferromagnetic Nanostructures
WEGSCHEIDER, W., Epitaxy and Characterization of Multi-player Semiconductors
WETTIG, T., Lattice Quantum Chromodynamics, Spintronics, Quantum Chromodynamics in Chips
ZWECK, J., Electron Microscopy

Department of Psychology and Pedagogy (tel. (941) 943-3587; fax (941) 943-3993; internet www.uni-regensburg.de/Fakultaeten/phil_Fak_II):

BÄUML, K.-H., Psychology
FÖLLING-ALBERS, M., Didactics of the Elementary School
GREENLEE, M. W., Psychology
GRUBER, H., Pedagogy
HAMMERL, M., Psychology
LANGE, K., Psychology
LUKESCH, H., Psychology
MULDER, R., Pedagogy
RICHTER, S., Didactics of the Elementary School
THOMAS, A., Psychology
WILD, K. P., Pedagogy
ZIMMER, A., Psychology

UNIVERSITÄT ROSTOCK

Universitätspl. 1, 18051 Rostock
Telephone: (381) 4980
Fax: (381) 4981015
E-mail: kanzler@uni-rostock.de
Internet: www.uni-rostock.de

Founded 1419
State control
Academic year: October to September

Rector: Prof. Dr JÜRGEN WENDEL
Vice-Rectors: Prof. Dr DETLEF CZYBULKA, Prof. Dr KARL HANTZSCHMANN, Prof. Dr GERD RÖPKE
Chancellor: JOACHIM WITTERN
Library Director: Dr JÜRGEN HEEG

Library: see Libraries and Archives
Number of teachers: 332
Number of students: 9,757

Publications: *Archiv der Freunde der Naturgeschichte in Mecklenburg*, *Erziehungswissenschaftliche Beiträge*, *Forschungsbericht der Universität Rostock*, *Pädagogisches Handeln*, *Rostocker Agrar- und Umweltwissenschaftliche Beiträge*, *Rostocker Arbeitspapiere zu Rechnungswesen und Controlling*, *Rostocker Arbeitspapiere zu Wirtschaftsentwicklung und Human Resource Development*, *Rostocker Beiträge zur Deutschen und Europäischen Geschichte*, *Rostocker Beiträge zur Regional- und Strukturforschung*, *Rostocker Beiträge zur Sprachwissenschaft*, *Rostocker Beitrage zur Verkehrswissenschaft und Logistik*, *Rostocker Forum Theologie*, *Rostocker Informatik-Berichte*, *Rostocker Informationen zu Politik und Verwaltung*, *Rostocker Materialen für Landschaftsplanung und Raumentwicklung*, *Rostocker Mathema-*

tisches Kolloquium, Rostocker Medizinische Beiträge, Rostocker Meeresbiologische Beiträge, Rostocker Philosophische Manuskripte, Rostocker Schriften zur Bank und Finanzmarktforschung, Rostocker Schriften zum Bankrecht, Rostocker Studien zur Kulturwissenschaft, Schiffbauforschung, Thunen-Reihe Angewandter Volkswirtschftstheorie, and various faculty publs

DEANS

Faculty of Agricultural and Environmental Science: Prof. Dr WOLFGANG RIEDEL
Faculty of Economics and Social Sciences: Prof. Dr JAKOB RÖSEL
Faculty of Information Technology and Electroscience: Prof. Dr URSULA VAN RIENEN
Faculty of Law: Prof. Dr RALPH WEBER
Faculty of Mathematics and Natural Sciences: Prof. Dr UDO KRAGL
Faculty of Mechanical Engineering and Shipping Technology: Prof. Dr ALFRED LEDER
Faculty of Medicine: Prof. Dr GABRIELE NÖLDGE-SCHOMBURG
Faculty of Philosophy: Prof. Dr WERNER MÜLLER
Faculty of Theology: Prof. Dr HERMANN MICHAEL NIEMANN

UNIVERSITÄT DES SAARLANDES

Postfach 151150, 66041 Saarbrücken
Telephone: (681) 3020
Fax: (681) 302-3900
E-mail: praesident@univw.uni-saarland.de
Internet: www.uni-saarland.de
Founded 1948
Academic year: October to July
President: Prof. Dr MARGRET WINTERMANTEL
Vice-Presidents: Prof. Dr ROLF W. HARTMANN, Prof. Dr MATHIAS HERMANN, Prof. Dr PATRICIA OSTER-STIERLE
Librarian: Prof. Dr BERND HAGENAU
Number of teachers: 1,090
Number of students: 15,500
Publications: *Annales Universitatis Saraviensis* (4 a year), *Campus* (irregular), *Forschungsbericht* (annually), *Jahresbibliographie* (annually), *Vorlesungsverzeichnis* (2 a year)

DEANS

Faculty of Law and Business Studies: Prof. Dr RUDOLF WENDT
Faculty of Medicine: Prof. Dr MATHIAS MONTENARH
Faculty of Natural Sciences and Technology I: Prof. Dr THORSTEN HERFET
Faculty of Natural Sciences and Technology II: Prof. Dr ANDREAS SCHÜTZE
Faculty of Natural Sciences and Technology III: Prof. Dr KASPAR HEGETSCHWEILER
Faculty of Philosophy I: Prof. Dr MICHAEL HÜTTENHOFF
Faculty of Philosophy II: Prof. Dr ULRIKE DEMSKE
Faculty of Philosophy III: Prof. Dr RAINER KRAUSE

PROFESSORS

Faculty of Law and Business (tel. (681) 302-2003; fax (681) 302-4213; e-mail dekanat@rewi.uni-sb.de; internet www.rewi.uni-sb.de):

ALBERT, M., Economics
AUTEXIER, C., French Public Law
BECKMANN, R., Civil, Commercial, Economic and Labour Law
BIEG, H., Business Economics
CHIUSI, T., Civil Law, Roman Law
FRIEDMANN, R., Statistics
GLASER, H., Business Economics
GRÖPPEL-KLEIN, A., Business Economics
GRÖPL, C., State and Management Law
HERBERGER, M., Civil Law, Theory of Law, Computer Applications in Jurisprudence
JUNG, H., Penal and Procedural Law, Criminal Law, Law of Criminal Procedure, Criminology and Comparative Criminal Jurisprudence
KORIATH, H., Criminal Law, Criminal Procedural Law, Philosophy of Law, Sociology of Law
KUßMAUL, H., Business Economics
KÜTING, K., Business Economics
LOOS, P., Business Economics
MARTINEK, M., Civil, Commercial and Economic Law, International Private Law and Comparative Jurisprudence
MATUSCHE-BECKMANN, A., Civil, Commercial and Economic Law and Labour Law
MENG, W., Public Law, International Law, European Community Law
MOMSEN, C., Penal and Procedural Law
NICKEL, S., Business Economics
PIERZIOCH, C., Economics
RANIERI, F., European Civil Law
RÜSSMANN, H., Civil and Procedural Law, Philosophy of Law
SCHMIDT, G., Business Economics
SCHMIDTCHEN, D., Economics
SCHOLZ, C., Business Economics
STEIN, T., European Law, European Public Law, International Law
STROHMEIER, S., Business Economics
WADLE, E., History of German Law, Civil Law
WASCHBUSCH, G., Business Economics
WENDT, R., Constitutional and Administrative Law, Revenue and Tax Law
WETH, S., German and European Procedural and Industrial Law
WITZ, C., French Public Law
ZENTES, J., Business Economics

Faculty of Medicine (Medizinische Fakultät, Universitätskliniken des Saarlandes, 66421 Homburg; tel. (6841) 16-24737; fax (6841) 16-26003; e-mail mfdekan@med-rz.uni-sb.de):

ABDUL-KHALIQ, H., Paediatrics
BOCK, R., Anatomy
BOHLE, R., Pathology
BÖHM, M., Internal Medicine
BRUNS, D., Physiology
BUCHTER, A., Occupational Medicine
CAVALIÉ, A., Pharmacology and Toxicology
FALKAI, P., Psychaitry and Psychotherapy
FASSBENDER, K., Psychaitry and Psychotherapy
FEIDEN, W., Neuropathology
FLOCKERZI, V., Pharmacology and Toxicology
FREICHEL, M., Pharmacology and Toxicology
FUHR, G., Medical Technology
GORTNER, L., Paediatrics
GRAF, N., Paediatrics
HANNIG, M., Oral and Maxillofacial Medicine
HERRMANN, E., Mathematical Modelling in Molecular Medicine
HERRMANN, M., Microbiology
HERRMANN, W., Clinical Chemistry
HOTH, M., Physiology
HÜTTERMANN, J., Biophysics
KIENECKER, E.-W., Anatomy
KINDERMANN, W., Sports Medicine
KIRSCH, C.-M., Nuclear Medicine
KÖHLER, H., Internal Medicine
KOHN, D., Orthopaedics
LARSEN, R., Anaesthesiology
LIPP, P., Molecular Cell Biology
LISSON, J., Oral and Maxillofacial Medicine
LÖBRICH, M., Biophysics and Physical Basis of Medicine
MAURER, H. H., Pharmacology and Toxicology
MEESE, E., Human Genetics and Molecular Biology
MENGER, M., Institute for Clinical and Experimental Surgery
MESTRES-VENTURA, P., Anatomy
MEYERHANS, A., Virology
MONTENARH, M., Medical Biochemistry
MÜLLER-LANTZSCH, N., Virology
PFREUNDSCHUH, M., Internal Medicine
POHLEMANN, T., Casualty Surgery
POSPIECH, P., Oral and Maxillofacial Medicine
REITH, W., Diagnostic Radiology
RETTIG, J., Physiology
RÖSLER, M., Psychiatry, Neurology
RÜBE, CH., Radiotherapy
SCHÄFERS, H.-J., Surgery
SCHEIDIG, A., Structural Biology
SCHILLING, M., Surgery
SCHMIDT, W., Gynaecology and Obstetrics
SCHMITZ, F., Neuroanatomy
SCHULZ, I., Physiology
SEITZ, B., Occular Medicine
SPITZER, W. C., Maxillofacial Surgery
STAHL, H., Medical Biochemistry
STEUDEL, W.-I., Neurosurgery
STÖCKLE, M., Urology
SYBRECHT, G. W., Internal Medicine
THIEL, G., Medical Biochemistry
TILGEN, W., Dermatology and Venereology
VON GONTARD, A., Child Psychiatry
WALLDORF, U., Developmental Biology
WANKE, K., Neurology, Psychiatry
WILSKE, J., Forensic Medicine
ZEUZEM, S., Internal Medicine
ZIMMERMANN, R., Physiological Chemistry

Faculty of Natural Science and Technology I: Mathematics and Computer Science (tel. (681) 302-5070; fax (681) 302-5068; e-mail sekr.fakultaet@mx.uni-saarland.de; internet www.uni-saarland.de/fak6):

ALBRECHT, E., Mathematics
BACKES, M., Computer Science
BLÄSER, M., Computer Science
BROSAMLER, G.-A., Mathematics
DECKER, W., Mathematics
ESCHMEIER, J., Mathematics
FUCHS, M., Mathematics
GEKELER, E.-U., Mathematics
HERFET, T., Computer Science
HERMANNS, H., Computer Science
HISCHER, H., Teaching of Mathematics
JOHN, V., Mathematics
KOCH, C., Computer Science
KOHLER, M., Mathematics
LENHOFF, H., Bioinformatics
LOUIS, A. K., Mathematics
PAUL, W., Information Science
RJASANOW, S., Mathematics
SCHEIDIG, H., Informatics
SCHREYER, F.-O., Mathematics
SCHULZE-PILLOT, R., Mathematics
SEIDEL, R., Theoretical Informatics
SIEKMANN, J., Informatics
SLUSALLEK, P., Informatics
SMOLKA, G., Information Science
WAHLSTER, W., Informatics
WEICKERT, J., Mathematics
ZELLER, A., Software Engineering

Faculty of Natural Science and Technology II: Physics and Electrical Engineering (tel. (681) 302-4943; fax (681) 302-4973; e-mail dekan.fak7@mx.uni-saarland.de; internet www.uni-saarland.de/fak7):

BIRRINGER, R., Physical Engineering
BECHER, C., Physical Engineering
DYCZIJ-EDLINGER, R., Electrical Theory
HARTMANN, U., Experimental Physics
JAKOBS, K., Experimental Physics
JANOCHA, H., Process Automation
KLAKOW, D., SpeechProcessing
KLIEM, H., Electrical Engineering Physics
KNORR, K., Physical Engineering
KÖNIG, K., Microsensor Technology
KRÜGER, J.K., Experimental Physics
KUGI, A., Systems Theory and Control Engineering

LÜCKE, M., Theoretical Physics
MÖLLER, M., Electronics and Circuits
NICOLAY, T., High Frequency Engineering
PELSTER, R. (acting), Experimental Physics
RIEGER, H., Theoretical Physics
SANTEN, L., Theoretical Physics
SCHÜTZE, A., Measurement
SEIDEL, H., Micromechanics
WAGNER, C., Experimental Physics
WICHERT, T., Physical Engineering
XU, CHIHAO, Microelectronics

Faculty of Natural Science and Technology III: Chemistry, Pharmacy, Materials Science (tel. (681) 302-2400; fax (681) 302-3421; e-mail dekan.fak8@mx.uni-saarland.de; internet www.uni-saarland.de/fak8):

BAUER, P., Botany
BECK, H. P., Inorganic and Analytical Chemistry, Radiochemistry
BERNHARDT, I., Biophysics
BERNHARDT, R., Biochemistry
BLEY, H., Production Engineering
BUSCH, R., Metallic Materials
CLASEN, R., Materials Science
DIEBELS, S., Applied Mechanics
GIFFHORN, F., Microbiology
HARTMANN, R. W., Pharmaceutical Chemistry
HEGETSCHWEILER, K., Inorganic Chemistry
HEINZLE, E., Technical Bioengineering
HELMS, V., Computational Biology
HUBER, C., Analytical Chemistry
JAUCH, J., Organic Chemistry
KAZMAIER, U., Organic Chemistry
KIEMER, A.K., Pharmaceutical Biology
KRÖNING, M., Non-destructive Materials Testing
LEHR, C.-M., Pharmaceutical Technology
MAIER, W., Technical Chemistry
MÜCKLICH, F., Work Materials
MÜLLER, R., Pharmaceutical Biotechnology
MÜLLER, U., Zoology and Physiology
POSSART, W., Polymers and Surfaces
SCHMIDT, H., New Materials
SCHMITT, M., Microbiology
SPRINGBORG, M., Physical Chemistry
VEHOFF, H., Materials Science, Methodology
VEITH, M., Inorganic Chemistry
WALTER, J., Genetics
WEBER, C., Construction Engineering
WENZ, G., Macromolecular Chemistry

Faculty of Philosophy I: History and Cultural Sciences (tel. (681) 302-2300; fax (681) 302-4234; e-mail u.weisgerber@pfdek.uni-sb.de):

BEHRINGER, W., Early Times
BRANDOLINI, A., Art Education
DE JONG, R., Art Education
DETZLER, B., Art Education
GIRARDET, K. M., Ancient History
GOERTZ, S., Practical Theology and Social Ethics
GRABAS, M., Economic and Social History
GÜTHLEIN, K., History of Art
HAUSIG, D., Art Education
HECKMANN, H., Philosophy
HINSCH, W., Philosophy
HÜTTENHOFF, M., Protestant Theology
HUDEMANN, R., Modern and Contemporary History
HULLMANN, H., Art Education
KASTEN, B., Medieval History
KRAUS, W., New Testament
KUBISCH, C., Art Education
LICHTENSTERN, C., History of Art
MAKSIMOVIC, I., Art Education
NESTLER, W., Art Education
NORTMANN, U., Philosophy
OHLIG, K.-H., Theology
POPP, H., Art Education
REINSBERG, C., Classical Archaeology
RIEMER, P., Classical Philology
ROMPZA, S., Art Education
ROSENBACH, U., Art Education
SACHSSE, R., Art Education
SCHERZBERG, L., Systematic Theology
SCHMITT, R., Comparative Indo-Germanic Languages
SCHRÖDER, B., Religious Education
SCHNEIDER, H., Medieval History
WALICZKY, M., Art Education
WINZEN, A., Art Education
ZIMMERMANN, C., Cultural History and Media History

Faculty of Philosophy II: Language, Literature and Cultural Studies (tel. (681) 302-3360; fax (681) 302-4535; e-mail g.braun@pfdek.uni-sb.de):

ALBERT, M., Romance Philology
BARRY, W. J., Phonetics, Phonology
BÉHAR, P., German for Francophones
BEM, J., Romance Philology
CROCKER, M., Psycholinguistics
DEMSKE, U., German Linguistics
ENGEL, M., German Language and Literature
GERZYMISCH-ARBOGAST, H., English Translation
GHOSH-SCHELLHORN, M., English Philology
GIL ARROYO, A., Translation Studies, Romance Languages
GÖTZE, L., German as a Foreign Language
HALLER, J., Mechanical Transmission
HAUBRICHS, W., Medieval German Literature
KLEINERT, S., Romance Philology
LOHMEIER, A.-M., Modern German Philology and Literature
LÜSEBRINK, H.-J., Romance Civilization, Intercultural Communication
MARTENS, K., English Philology, American Literature
MARTI, R., Slavonic Philology
NORRICK, N., English Philology, Linguistics
OSTER-STIERLE, P., French Literature
PINKAL, M., Computer Languages
SAUDER, G., Modern German Philology and Literature
SCHMELING, M., General and Comparative Literature
SCHWEICKARD, W., Romance Philology
SPRAUL, H., Russian
STEINER, E., English Linguistics and Translation
USZKOREIT, H., Computer Linguistics

Faculty of Philosophy III: Empirical Humanities (tel. (681) 302-3700; fax (681) 302-2953; e-mail s.mersdorf@pfdek.uni-sb.de; internet www.uni-saarland.de/fak5):

ASCHERSLEBEN, G., Developmental Psychology
BRÜCHER, W., Geography
BRÜNKEN, R., Education Science
EMRICH, E., Kinesiology and Exercise Science
HERZMANN, P., Education Science
KERKOFF, G., Clinical Neuropsychology
KRAUSE, R., Psychology
KUBINIOK, J., Physical Geography
LÖFFLER, E. W., Physical Geography
MAXEINER, J., Education
SPINATH, F., Differential Psychology and Diagnostics
STARK, R., Personal Development and Education
STOCKMANN, R., Sociology
WASSMUND, H., Political Science
WENTURA, D., General Psychology and Methodology
WINTERHOFF-SPURK, P., Psychology
WINTERMANTEL, M., Social Psychology
WYDRA, G., Sports Education
ZIMMERMANN, H. H., Information Science

ATTACHED INSTITUTES

Institut für Konsum- und Verhaltensforschung (Consumer and Behavioural Research Institute): Dir Prof. Dr PETER WEINBERG.

Institut für Handel und Internationales Marketing (Institute of Commerce and International Marketing): Dir Prof. Dr JOACHIM ZENTES.

Institut für Wirtschaftsinformatik (Institute for Information Systems): Dir Prof. Dr Dr h.c. AUGUST-WILHELM SCHEER.

Institut für Wirtschaftsprufung (Institute of Accountancy): Dir Prof. Dr KARLHEINZ KÜTING.

Institut der Gesellschaft zur Förderung der Angewandten Informationsforschung e.V. an der Universität des Saarlandes: Dirs Prof. Dr JOHANN HALLER, Prof. Dr HARALD ZIMMERMANN.

Fraunhofer-Institut für Zerstörungsfreie Prüfverfahren (Fraunhofer Institute of Non-Destructive Testing): Dir Prof. Dr MICHAEL KRÖNING.

Fraunhofer-Institut für Biomedizinische Technik (Fraunhofer Institute of Biomedical Engineering): Dir Prof. Dr G. R. FUHR.

Institut für Neue Materialen gem. GmbH (Institute for New Materials): Dir Prof. Dr HELMUT SCHMIDT.

Deutsches Forschungszentrum für Künstliche Intelligenz GmbH (German Research Centre for Artificial Intelligence): Dir and CEO Prof. Dr Dr h.c. WOLFGANG WAHLSTER.

Max-Planck-Institut für Informatik (Max-Planck-Institute for Informatics): Dir Prof. Dr HARALD GANZINGER.

Internationales Begegnungs- und Forschungszentrum für Informatik gem. GmbH (International Research Centre for Informatics): Dir Prof. Dr REINHARD WILHELM.

Institut für Landeskunde im Saarland (Institute for Regional Studies in Saarland): Dir Prof. Dr HEINZ QUASTEN.

Gesellschaft für umweltkompatible Prozesstechnik mbH (Society for Environmentally Friendly Process Engineering): Dir Prof. Dr HORST CHMIEL.

Institut für Präventivmedizin an der Universität des Saarlandes (Institute for Preventive Medicine).

comprises:

Institut für Präventive Kardiologie (Institute for Preventive Cardiology): Dir Prof. Dr HERMANN-JOSEF SCHIEFFER.

Institut für Medizinische Genetik (Institute for Medical Genetics): Dir Prof. Dr KLAUS ZANG.

Institut für Präventive Pneumonologie (Institute for Preventive Pneumonology): Dir Prof. Dr GERHARD SYBRECHT.

Zentrum zur Prävention, Erforschung und Dokumentation von Muskel- und Hirnkreislaufkrankheiten (Centre for Prevention, Research and Documentation of Circulatory Disorders of Muscles and the Brain): Dir Prof. Dr A. HAASS (acting).

Präventivmedizinisches Zentrum für arbeitsbedingte Erkrankungen (Preventive Medical Centre for Occupational Diseases): Dir Prof. Dr AXEL BUCHTER.

Institut für Präventive Sportmedizin (Institute for Preventive Sports Medicine): Dir Prof. Dr WILFRIED KINDERMANN.

Institut für Prävention in der Pädiatrie (Institute for Preventive Medicine in Paediatrics): Dir Prof. Dr CARL FRIEDRICH SITZMANN.

Institut für Präventive Zahnheilkunde (Institute of Preventive Dentistry): Dir (vacant).

Institut für Präventive Augenheilkunde (Institute of Preventive Ophthalmology): Dir Prof. Dr KLAUS RUPRECHT.

UNIVERSITÄT SIEGEN

Am Herrengarten 3, 57068 Siegen
Telephone: (271) 740-0
Fax: (271) 740-4899
E-mail: buero@rektorat.uni-siegen.de
Internet: www.uni-siegen.de

Founded 1972
State control
Academic year: October to July (2 semesters)

Rector: Prof. Dr THEODORA HANTOS
Vice-Rectors: Prof. Dr SIGRID SCHUBERT, Prof. Dr GERALD ADLBRECHT, Prof. Dr GERO HOCH, Prof. MICHAEL LENHART
Chancellor: Dr JOHANN PETER SCHÄFER
Librarian: WERNER REINHARDT

Library of 1,150,000 vols
Number of teachers: 600
Number of students: 12,200

Publications: Research Report, *Reihe Siegen*, *Siegener Hochschulzeitung*, *Siegener Pädagogische Studien*, *MuK—Massenmedien und Kommunikation*, *SPIEL* (2 a year), *Diagonal*, *Siegen: Sozial* (2 a year), *Navigationen*, *Reihe Medienwissenschaften*, *LiLi—Zeitschrift für Literaturwissenschaft und Linguistik*

DEANS

Department of Sociology, Philosophy, Theology, History and Geography: Prof. Dr THOMAS KLATETZKI
Department of Education Science, Psychology and Physical Education: Prof. Dr SABINE HERING
Department of Languages, Literature and Media Sciences: Prof. Dr INGO PLAG
Department of Art and Music Education: Prof. Dr ANGELA ZIESCHE
School of Economic Disciplines: Prof. Dr PETER KREBS
Department of Mathematics: Prof. Dr RAINER SCHARK
Department of Physics: Prof. Dr CLAUS GRUPEN
Department of Chemistry, Biology: Prof. Dr BERND WENCLAWIAK
Department of Architecture and Town Planning: Prof. Dr-Ing. BERND BORGHOFF
Department of Civil Engineering: Prof. Dr RICHARD HERRMANN
Department of Mechanical Engineering: Prof. Dr-Ing. HANS-JÜRGEN CHRIST
Department of Electrical Engineering: Prof. Dr RAINER LOHE
Department of Electrical Engineering and Computer Science: Prof. Dr RAINER BRÜCK

DEUTSCHE HOCHSCHULE FÜR VERWALTUNGSWISSENSCHAFTEN SPEYER

Freiherr-vom-Stein-Str. 2, 67346 Speyer
Telephone: (6232) 654-0
Fax: (6232) 654-208
E-mail: dhv@dhv-speyer.de
Internet: www.dhv-speyer.de

Founded 1947
State control
Languages of instruction: German, English
Academic year: May to January

Rector: Prof. Dr RUDOLF FISCH
Vice-Rector: Prof. Dr KARL-PETER SOMMERMEYER
Administrative Officer: CHRISTIANE MÜLLER
Librarian: Prof. Dr STEFAN FISCH

Library of 270,000 vols
Number of teachers: 90 (incl. 72 part-time)
Number of students: 500

A postgraduate institution offering courses in administrative sciences for senior civil service managers

PROFESSORS

BOHNE, E., Public Administration
FÄRBER, G., Public Finance and Economics
FISCH, R., Empirical Social Sciences
FISCH, S., Modern History
HILL, H., Public Administration, Public Law
JANSEN, D., Sociology of Organizations
KNORR, A., International Economics
KÖNIG, T., Political Science
MAGIERA, S., Public Law, European Law and Public International Law
MERTEN, D., Public Law, Social Law
MÜHLENKEMP, H., Public Finance
PITSCHAS, R., Public Administration, Development Policy and Public Law
REINERMANN, H., Public Administration, Information Technology
SIEDENTOPF, H., Public Administration, Public Law
SOMMERMANN, K.-P., Public Law, Constitutional Law, Comparative Law
WIRTZ, B., Information and Communication Management
ZIEKOW, J., Public Law and Administrative Law

ATTACHED INSTITUTE

Forschungsinstitut für Öffentliche Verwaltung (Research Institute for Public Administration): Dir Prof. Dr JAN ZIEKOW.

UNIVERSITÄT STUTTGART

Postfach 106037, 70049 Stuttgart
Telephone: (711) 121-0
Fax: (711) 121-3500
Internet: www.uni-stuttgart.de

Founded 1829 as Gewerbeschule; University status 1967
Academic year: October to September

Rector: Prof. Dr-Ing. DIETER FRITSCH
Vice-Rectors: Prof. Dr-Ing. KARL-HEINZ WEHKING (Research and Marketing), Prof. Dr phil. CHRISTOPH HUBIG (Structure and Controlling), Prof. Dr-Ing. PETER GÖHNER (Academic)
Chancellor: J. SCHWARZE
Chief Librarian: W. STEPHAN

Library: see Libraries
Number of teachers: 2,600
Number of students: 18,500

Publications: *Stuttgarter Uni-Kurier* (3–4 a year), *News* (newsletter, on-line), *Science* (newsletter, on-line), *Wechselwirkungen-Aus Lehre und Forschung der Universität Stuttgart* (annually), *Forschung-Entwicklung-Beratung* (in German and English, annually)

PROFESSORS

Architecture and City Planning (Universitätsbereich Stadtmitte, Keplerstr. 11, 70714 Stuttgart; tel. (711) 121-3223; fax (711) 121-2788; e-mail dekanat@f01.uni-stuttgart.de; internet www.architektur.uni-stuttgart.de):

ADAM, J., Design and Construction
BEHLING, S., Building Construction and Design
BOTT, H., City Planning and Urban Design
CHERET, P., Building Construction and Design
DE BRUYN, G., Theory of Architecture and Design
EISENBIEGLER, G., Structures and Constructional Design
ERTEL, H., Building Materials, Building Physics, Mechanical Equipment
HARLANDER, T., Housing and Design
HERRMANN, D., Building Materials, Building Physics, Mechanical Equipment
HÜBNER, P., Building Constructions and Design
JESSEN, J., City and Regional Planning
JOCHER, T., Housing and Design
KAULE, G., Landscape Planning and Ecology
KIMPEL, D., History of Architecture
KNIPPERS, J., Structures and Constructional Design
KNOLL, W., Drawing, Drafting and Modelling
MORO, J. L., Planning and Construction of High-rise Buildings
PESCH, F., City Planning and Urban Design
PODREKA, B., Interior Design and Architectural Design
RIBBECK, E., Planning and Building Development
SCHÖNWANDT, W., Foundations of Planning
SCHÜRMANN, P., Building Materials, Building Physics, Mechanical Equipment
SOBEK, W., Lightweight Structures and Conceptual Design
TRAUB, H., Drawing, Drafting and Modelling
ULLMANN, F., Interior Design and Architectural Design

Civil Engineering and Surveying (Universitätsbereich Vaihingen, Pfaffenwaldring 7, 2.OG, Stuttgart; tel. (711) 685-6234; e-mail dekanat@fak2.uni-stuttgart.de; internet www.uni-stuttgart.de/bauingenieur):

BÁRDOSSY, A., Water Management
BERNER, F., Construction Industry
EHLERS, W., Engineering Mechanics
ELIGEHAUSEN, R., Materials Science in Structural Engineering
ENGESSER, K.-H., Biological Cleaning of Used Air
FRIEDRICH, M., Transport Planning and Traffic Control
GERTIS, K., Building Physics
HELMIG, R., Hydromechanics and Hydrosystems Modelling
KRANERT, M., Sanitary Engineering, Waste Water and Solid Waste Management
KUHLMANN, U., Design and Construction
MARTIN, U., Railway and Transportation Engineering
METZGER, J., Hydrochemistry and Hydrobiology, Sanitary Engineering, Waste Water and Solid Waste Management
MIEHE, C., Engineering Mechanics
MÖHLENBRINK, W., Applied Geodesy
MORO, J. L., Planning and Construction of High-rise Buildings
NOVÁK, B., Large-scale Construction
PINNEKAMP, J., Waste Water Engineering
RAMM, E., Structural Engineering
REINHARDT, H.-W., Materials Science in Structural Engineering
RESSEL, W., Road and Transport Planning and Engineering
ROTT, U., Water Quality Management, Sanitary Engineering
SEDLBAUER, K., Constructional Physics
SOBEK, W., Interdisciplinary Research, Architecture and Civil Engineering
TREUNER, P., Regional Development Planning
VERMEER, P. A., Geotechnology
WIEPRECHT, S., Water Engineering

Chemistry (Universitätsbereich Vaihingen, Pfaffenwaldring 55, 7.OG, Stuttgart; tel. (711) 685-4584; e-mail dekanat@f03.uni-stuttgart.de; internet www.uni-stuttgart.de/chemie):

ALDINGER, F., Non-Metallic Inorganic Materials
ARZT, E., Metallurgy
BECKER, G., Inorganic Chemistry
BERTAGNOLLI, H., Physical Chemistry
CHRISTOFFERS, J., Organic Chemistry

EISENBACH, C., Chemical Engineering
GIESSELMANN, F., Physical Chemistry
GUDAT, D., Inorganic Chemistry
HASHMI, S., Organic Chemistry
JÄGER, V., Organic Chemistry
KAIM, W., Inorganic Chemistry
LASCHAT, S., Organic Chemistry
MITTELMEIJER, E., Metallurgy
RODUNER, E., Physical Chemistry
SCHLEID, T., Inorganic Chemistry
SCHMID, R., Technical Biochemistry
WEITKAMP, J., Chemical Engineering
WERNER, H.-J., Theoretical Chemistry
WOLF, D., Biochemistry
ZABEL, F., Physical Chemistry

Biological and Geo-Sciences (Universitätsbereich Vaihingen, Herdweg 51, 70174 Stuttgart; tel. (711) 121-1334; fax (711) 2237978; e-mail dekanat@g04.uni-stuttgart.de; internet www.uni-stuttgart.de/geowissenschaft):

BLÜMEL, W. D., Geography
GAEBE, W., Cultural Geography
GHOSH, R., Bioenergetics
GOERTZ, H. D., Zoology
HEYER, A., Botany
JESKE, H., Molecular Biology and Virology of Plants
KELLER, P., Mineralogy and Crystal Chemistry
MASSONNE, H.-J., Mineralogy and Crystal Chemistry
MATTES, R., Industrial Genetics
MUTTI, M., Geology and Palaeontology
NUßBERGER, S., Biophysics
PFIZENMAIER, K., Cell Biology and Immunology
SCHEURICH, P., Molecular Immunology
SCHNEIDER, G., Geophysics
SEUFERT, W., Industrial Genetics
SEYFRIED, H., Geology and Palaeontology
SPRENGER, G., Microbiology
WIELANDT, E., Geophysics
WOLF, D. H., Biochemistry
WOLLNIK, F., Animal Physiology

Computer Science, Electrical Engineering and Information Technology (Universitätsbereich Vaihingen, Pfaffenwaldring 47, Zi. 4.116, Stuttgart; tel. (711) 685-7234; fax (711) 685-7236; e-mail dekanat@f-iei.uni-stuttgart.de; internet www.f-iei.uni-stuttgart.de):

BERROTH, M., Communications Engineering
BUNGARTZ, H.-J., Simulation of Large Systems
CLAUS, V., Formal Concepts of Computer Science
DIEKERT, V., Theoretical Computer Science
EGGENBERGER, O., Operating Systems
ERTL, T., Dialogue Systems
ESPARZA, J., Secure and Reliable Software Systems
FRÜHAUF, N., Display Technology
GÖHNER, P., Control Engineering and Process Automation
KASPER, E., Semiconductor Engineering
KÜHN, P. J., Communications Switching and Data Techniques
LAGALLY, K., Operating Systems
LANDSTORFER, F., Radio Frequency Technology
LEHMANN, E., Export Systems
LEVI, P., Computer Vision
LUDEWIG, J., Software Engineering
MITSCHANG, B., User Software
PLÖDEREDER, E., Programming Languages
ROLLER, D., Computer Science Fundamentals
ROTH-STIELOW, J., Power Electronics and Control Engineering
ROTHERMEL, K., Distributed Systems
RUCKER, W., Theory of Electrical Engineering
SCHÄFER, Energy Conversion
SPEIDEL, J., Telecommunications
TENBOHLEN, S., High-Voltage Technology
WERNER, J. H., Physical Electronics
WUNDERLICH, H.-J., Computer Architecture
YANG, B., Network and Systems Theory

Aerospace Engineering and Geodetic Science (Universitätsbereich Vaihingen, Pfaffenwaldring 27, Zi.02, Stuttgart; tel. (711) 685-2400; fax (711) 685-3617; e-mail dekanat@f06.uni-stuttgart.de; internet www.f06.uni-stuttgart.de):

AUWETER-KURTZ, M., Space Transportation Technology
DRECHSLER, K., Aircraft Construction
FRITSCH, D., Photogrammetry and Land Surveying
GRAFAREND, E. W., Geodetic Science
KELLER, W., Physical Geodetic Science
KLEUSBERG, A., Navigation
KRÄMER, E., Aerodynamics
KRÖPLIN, B.-H., Statics and Dynamics of Aerospace Structures
KÜHN, M., Aerodynamics
MÖHLENBRINK, W., Aviation Telemetry
MUNZ, C.-D., Air and Gas Dynamics
REICHEL, R., Aviation Systems
RÖSER, H.-P., Space Systems
STAUDACHER, S., Turbojet Engines
VOIT-NITSCHMANN, R., Aircraft Construction
VON WOLFERSDORF, J., Aerospace Thermodynamics
WAGNER, S., Air and Gas Dynamics
WEIGAND, B., Aerospace Thermodynamics
WELL, K. H., Guidance and Control of Aerospace Vehicles
WOLF, D., Theory and Modelling of Geodetic Systems

Mechanical Engineering (Universitätsbereich Vaihingen, Pfaffenwaldring 9, 5.OG, 70569 Stuttgart; tel. (711) 685-6470; fax (711) 685-6492; e-mail dekanat@f07.uni-stuttgart.de; internet www.f07.uni-stuttgart.de):

ALLGÖWER, F., Systems Theory in Engineering
BARGENDE, M., Combustion Engines
BERTSCHE, B., Machine Elements (Gear Design, Cab Sealing Technology)
BINZ, H., Machine and Gearing Design
BRUNNER, H., Interface Chemistry
BULLINGER, H.-J., Industrial Science and Technology Management
BUSSE, G., Non-destructive Testing
CASEY, M., Thermal Turbo-Engines
EBERHARD, P., Mechanics
EIGENBERGER, G., Chemical Process Engineering
EYERER, P., Polymer Testing and Polymer Science
FRIEDRICH, H., Vehicle Concepts
FRITZ, H. G., Polymer Processing
GADOW, R., Manufacturing Technologies of Ceramic Compounds and Composites
GAUL, L., Mechanics
GILLES, E. D., System Dynamics and Control Systems
GÖDE, E., Fluid Machines and Hydraulic Pumps
GRAF, T., Network Engineering
HAASE, H., Technical Thermodynamics
HEIN, K. R. G., Process Engineering and Steam Boiler Technology
HEISEL, U., Machine Tools
KISTNER, A., Engineering Mechanics
KLEMM, P., Control Engineering
KÜCK, H., Time Measuring, Precision Engineering and Microengineering
LAURIEN, E., Nuclear Engineering
LOHNERT, G., Nuclear Engineering and Energy Systems
MAIER, T., Technical Design
MERTEN, C., Chemical Engineering
MÜLLER-STEINHAGEN, H., Thermodynamics and Heat Engineering
NAGEL, J., Biomedical Technology
OSTEN, W., Technical Optics
PIESCHE, M., Mechanical Production Engineering
PLANCK, H., Textile Technology and Process Engineering
PRITSCHOW, G., Control Technology of Machine Tools and Production Systems
REUSS, H.-C., Automobile Mechatronics
REUSS, M., Biochemical Engineering
ROOS, E., Materials Testing, Materials Science and Strength of Materials
SANDMAIER, H., Time Measuring, Precision Engineering and Microengineering
SCHINKÖTHE, W., Design and Production in Precision Engineering
SCHMAUDER, S., Process Development
SCHMIDT, M., Heating and Air-conditioning Engineering
SEIFERT, H., Thermal Waste Utilization
SIEGERT, K., Metal Forming
SPATH, D., Technology Management
VOSS, A., Energy Economics
WEHKING, K.-H., Conveyer and Transmission Technology, Gear Technology
WEHLAN, H., Process Control Engineering
WESTKÄMPER, E., Industrial Production and Plant
WIEDEMANN, J., Motor Vehicle Engineering
ZEITZ, M., System Dynamics Control

Mathematics and Physics (Universitätsbereich Vaihingen, Pfaffenwaldring 57, 70550 Stuttgart; tel. (711) 685-2400; fax (711) 685-3617; e-mail dekanat@f08.uni-stuttgart.de; internet www.uni-stuttgart.de/mathephysik):

BECHINGER, C., Experimental Physics
BLIND, G., Mathematics
BRÜDERN, J., Mathematics
DENNINGER, G., Physics
DIETRICH, S., Theoretical Physics
DIPPER, R., Mathematics
DOSCH, H., Experimental Physics
DRESSEL, M., Experimental Physics
GEKELER, E., Mathematics
HÄHL, H., Mathematics
HERRMANN, H., Theoretical Physics
HESSE, C., Mathematics
HÖLLIG, K., Mathematics
KÜHNEL, W., Mathematics
LUNK, A., Plasma Research
MAHLER, G., Theoretical Physics
MICHLER, P., Experimental Physics
MIELKE, A., Mathematics
MURAMATSU, A., Theoretical Physics
PFAU, T., Institute of Physics
PÖSCHEL, J., Mathematics
SANTOS, L., Theoretical Physics
SCHWEITZER, D., Experimental Physics
SEIFERT, U., Theoretical Physics
STRAUSS, W., Mathematics
TREBIN, H.-R., Theoretical and Applied Physics
WALK, H., Mathematics
WEIDL, T., Mathematics
WEISS, U., Theoretical Physics
WOHLMUTH, B., Mathematics
WRACHTRUP, J., Experimental Physics
WUNNER, G., Theoretical Physics

Philosophy and History (Universitätsbereich Stadtmitte, Keplerstr. 17, KII, 3.OG, 70174 Stuttgart; tel. (711) 121-3089; fax (711) 121-2803; e-mail dekanat@f09.uni-stuttgart.de; internet www.f09.uni-stuttgart.de):

ALEXIADOU, M., Linguistics and English
BAHLKE, J., Early Modern History
BARK, J., Modern German Literature
CZERWINSKI, P., German Philology
DOGIL, G., Computational Linguistics
GÖBEL, W., American Studies and Modern English Literature
VON HEUSINGER, K., Linguistics and German
HUBIG, C., Theory of Science and Technical Philosophy

KAMP, H., Formal Logic and Philosophy of Language
KRÜGER, R., Roman Studies
MAAG, G., Italian Studies
OLSHAUSEN, E., Ancient History
PAFEL, J., Linguistics and German
PYTA, W., Modern History
QUARTHAL, F., Regional History of Baden-Württemberg
REICHERT, F., History
ROHRER, CH., Computational Linguistics
SEEBER, H. U., Modern English Literature
STEIN, A., Linguistics/Roman Studies
STEINER, R., History of Arts
STÜRNER, W., History
THOMÉ, H., Modern German Literature
WYSS, B., History of Arts

Social Sciences and Economics (Universitätsbereich Stadtmitte, Keplerstr. 17, KII, 10 OG, 70174 Stuttgart; tel. (711) 121-3046; fax (711) 121-2807; e-mail dekanat@wiso.uni-stuttgart.de; internet www.uni-stuttgart.de/wiso):

ACKERMANN, K.-F., Economics
ALT, W., Sports
ARNOLD, U., Economics
BRINKHOFF, K.-P., Sports
ENGLMANN, F., Economics
FRANKE, S. F., Economic Policy and Public Law
FROMM, M., Educational Theory
FUCHS, D., Political Science
GABRIEL, O. W., Political Science
HERZWURM, G., Economics
HORVÁTH, P., Economics
KEMPER, H.-G., Economics
MAJER, H., Economics
NICKOLAUS, R., Vocational and Economic Education
REISS, M., Economics
RENN, O., Sociology of Environment and Technology
SCHÄFER, H., Economics
SCHLICHT, W., Sports
URBAN, D., Sociology
WOECKENER, B., Economics
ZAHN, E., Economics

ATTACHED INSTITUTES

Computer Centre, University of Stuttgart: Dir Prof. Dr ROLAND RÜHLE.

Language Centre: Dir Prof. Dr Dr phil. habil VOLKER SAFTIEN.

Centre for Infrastructural Planning: Dirs Prof. Dr rer. pol. F. C. ENGLMANN, Prof. Dr agr. GISELHER KAULE, Prof. Dr-Ing. W. MÖHLENBRINK.

Computer Applications: Dirs Prof. Dr phil. G. SCHRÖDER, Prof. Dr-Ing. R. RÜHLE.

Centre for Civilization Studies and Cultural Theory: Dirs Prof. Dr phil. G. MAAG, Prof. Dr DIETER FUCHS, Prof. Dr phil. HANS ULRICH SEEBER, Prof. Dr-Ing. HELLMUT BOTT.

Sports Science Institute: Dir Prof. Dr WOLFGANG SCHLICHT.

UNIVERSITÄT TRIER

Universitätsring 15, 54286 Trier
Telephone: (0651) 201-0
Fax: (0651) 201-4299
E-mail: presse@uni-trier.de
Internet: www.uni-trier.de

Founded 1473, reopened 1970
Academic year: October to September

President: Prof. Dr PETER SCHWENKMEZGER
Vice-Presidents: Prof. Dr MICHAEL JÄCKEL, Prof. Dr WOLFGANG KLOOß
Chancellor: Dr KLAUS HEMBACH (acting)
Librarian: Dr HILDEGARD MÜLLER

Number of teachers: 462 full-time
Number of students: 11,046

Publications: *Jahresbericht* (annually), *Trierer Beiträge* (annually), *UNI-Journal* (4 a year)

DEANS

Faculty I: Pedagogy, Philosophy and Psychology: Prof. Dr BERND DÖRFLINGER
Faculty II: Language and Literature: Prof. Dr FRANZISKA SCHÖßLER
Faculty III: History, Political Sciences, Classical Archaeology, Egyptology, Art History, Papyrology: Prof. Dr HELGA SCHNABEL-SCHÜLE
Faculty IV: Management Economics, Sociology, Political Economy, Applied Mathematics, Computer Science and Ethnology: Prof. Dr DIETER SADOWSKI
Faculty V: Law: Prof. Dr MICHAEL REINHARDT
Faculty VI: Geography and Geosciences: Prof. Dr REINHARD HOFFMANN
Faculty VII: Theology: Rector REINHOLD BOHLEN

PROFESSORS

Faculty I: Pedagogy, Philosophy and Psychology (Fachbereich I, 54286 Trier; tel. (651) 2012015; fax (651) 2013942; e-mail kohrg@uni-trier.de; internet www.psychologie.uni-trier.de/fbi):

ANTON, F., Psychobiology
BECKER, P., Psychology
BRANDTSTÄDTER, J., Psychology
CONNY, A., Psychology
DÖRFLINGER, B., Philosophy
FILIPP, S.-H., Psychology
HELLHAMMER, D., Psychology
HOMFELDT, H.-C., Pedagogy
HONIG, M. S., Pedagogy
KRAMPEN, G., Psychology
MEYER, J., Psychobiology
MULLER, C., Psychobiology
MÜLLER-FOHRBRODT, G., Pedagogy
PRECKEL, F., Psychology
RUSTEMEYER, D., Pedagogy
SCHÄCHINGER, H., Psychobiology
SCHELLER, R., Psychology
SCHWENKMEZGER, P., Psychology
WALTHER, E., Psychology
WENDER, K. F., Psychology

Faculty II: Language and Literature (Fachbereich II, 54286 Trier; tel. (651) 2012210; fax (651) 2013901; e-mail dienhart@uni-trier.de; internet www.uni-trier.de/uni/fb2/dekanat):

ALTHAUS, H. P., German Linguistics, Yiddish Language
BENDER, K.-H., Romance Literature
BREUER, H., English Literature
BUCHER, H.-J., Media Studies
CHIAO, W., Sinology
EIGLER, U., Classical Philology
GÄRTNER, K., German Philology
GELHAUS, H., German Linguistics
GÖSSMANN, H., Japanese Studies
HASLER, J., English and American Literature
HÖLZ, K., Romance Literature
HURM, G., English Literature
KLOOSS, W., English Philology
KÖHLER, H., Romance Literature
KÖHLER, R., Linguistic Data Processing
KÖSTER, J.-P., Applied Linguistics, Phonetics
KRAMER, J., Romance Philology
KREMER, D., Romance Philology
KRÖNER, H. O., Classical Philology
KÜHLWEIN, W., English Philology
KÜHN, P., German as a Foreign Language
LOIPERDINGER, M., Media Studies
LIANG, Y., Sinology
MOULIN, C., Old German Philology
NEUBERG, S., Yiddish Studies
NIEDEREHE, H.-J., Romance Philology
PIKULIK, L., Modern German Literature
PLATZ, N., English Literature
POHL, K. H., Chinese Studies
POHL, K. H., Sinology
REINHARDT, H., Modern German Literature
RESSEL, G., Slavistics
RIEGER, B., Linguistic Data Processing, Computer Languages
RÖLL, W., German Philology, Yiddish Language
SCHOLZ-CIONCA, S., Japanese Studies
SCHÖßLER, F., New German Literature
STAHL, H., Slavic Literature
STRAUSS, J., English Philology
STUBBS, M., English Linguistics
THORAU, H.-E., Portuguese Philology
TIMM, E., Yiddish Language
UERLINGS, H., Modern German Literature
WIMMER, R., German Linguistics
WÖHRLE, G., Classical Philology
ZIRKER, H., English Literature

Faculty III: History, Political Science, Classical Archaeology, Egyptology, Art History, Papyrology (Fachbereich III, 54286 Trier; tel. (651) 2012144; fax (651) 2013936; e-mail merz@uni-trier.de; internet www.uni-trier.de/uni/fb3/dekanat/fb3.html):

ANTON, H. H., Medieval History
CLEMENS, L., History
DORN, F., History
EBELING, D., History
FRANZ, G., History
GERHARDT, C., History
GESTRICH, A., Modern History
HAVERKAMP, A., Medieval History
HEINEN, H., Ancient History
HERRMAN-OTTO, E., Ancient History
HOLTMANN, W., History
IRSIGLER, F., Cultural History
KETTENHOFEN, E., History
KÖNIG, I., History
KRAMER, B., Papyrology
MOLT, P., Political Science
RAPHAEL, L., Modern and Recent History
SCHMID, W., History
SCHNABEL-SCHÜLE, H., Modern History
TACKE, A., Art History
VEEN, H. J., Political Science
VOLTMER, E., History
VLEEMING, S. P., Egyptology
WEBER, W., History
WIELING, H., History
WÖHRLE, G., Greek Philology

Faculty IV: Management Economics, Sociology, Political Economy, Applied Mathematics, Computer Science and Ethnology (Fachbereich IV, 54286 Trier; tel. (651) 2012640; fax (651) 2013927; e-mail dekanfb4@uni-trier.de; internet www.uni-trier.de/uni/fb4/dekanat/index.htm):

AMBROSI, C. M., Political Economy
ANTWEILER, C., Ethnology
BAUM, D., Computer Science
BERGMANN, R., Computer Science
BRAUN, H., Sociology
CZAP, H., Computer Science
DICKERTMANN, D., Political Economy
DIEHL, S., Computer Science
ECKERT, R., Sociology
EL-SHAGI, E. S., Political Economy
FILC, W., Political Economy
FEHR, H. J., Accounting
FERNAU, H., Computer Science
GAWRONSKI, W., Mathematics
HAHN, A., Sociology
HAMM, B., Sociology
HARDES, H.-D., Political Economy
HECHELTJEN, P., Political Economy
JÄCKEL, M., Sociology
KLÄS, F., Accounting
KNAPPE, E., Political Economy
LEHMANN, M., Management Economics
LIEBIG, S., Sociology
MILDE, H., Management Economics
MÜNNICH, R., Economics
NÄHER, S., Computer Science

OFFERMANN-CLAS, CH., European Community
RÜCKLE, D., Management Economics
SACHS, E., Mathematics
SADOWSKI, D., Management Economics
SPEHL, H., Political Economy
STURM, P., Computer Science
SCHERTLER, W., Strategic Management
SCHMIDT, A., Economics
SWOBODA, B., Management Economics
WÄCHTER, H., Management Economics
WALTER, B., Computer Science
WEIBER, R., Management Economics

Faculty V: Law (Fachbereich V – Rechtswissenschaft, 54286 Trier; tel. (651) 2012524; fax (651) 2013911; e-mail dekanatfb5@uni-trier.de; internet www.uni-trier.de/uni/fb5/fachbereich/dekanat.htm):

AXER, P., Public Law
BACHMANN, G., Civil Law, Commercial Law
BIRK, R., Private Law, Labour Law, Conflict of Laws
BURMESTER, G., National and International Finance and Tax Law
DORN, F., Private Law, Legal History, Comparative Law
ECKHARDT, D., Civil Law
HENDLER, R., Constitutional and Administrative Law
HOFFMANN, B. VON, Private Law, Conflict of Laws, Comparative Law
JÄGER, C., Criminal Law
KREY, V., Criminal Law, Criminal Procedure, Legal Methods
KÜHNE, H.-H., Criminal Law, Criminology, Criminal Procedure
RAAB, T., Public Law, Commercial Law, Labour Law
REIFF, P., Private Law, Commercial Law, Corporation Law, Insurance Law
REINHARDT, M., Constitutional and Administrative Law
ROBBERS, G., Public Law, Ecclesiastical Law, Philosophy of Law
RÜFNER, T., Public Law, German and International Civil Law
SCHRÖDER, M., Public, International and EC Law

Faculty VI: Geography and Geosciences (Fachbereich VI, 54286 Trier; tel. (651) 2014530; fax (651) 2013939; e-mail dekanatfb6@uni-trier.de; internet dekanatfb6.uni-trier.de):

ALEXANDER, J., Physical Geography
BECKER, CHR., Applied Geography and Geography of Tourism
BLÖMEKE, B., Ecotoxicology
BOLLMANN, J., Cartography
CALTEUX, G., Geography of Tourism
DIESTER-HAAß, L., Biogeography
EBERLE, I., Economic and Social Geography
FISCHER, K., Inorganic and Analytical Chemistry
HEINEMANN, G., Climatology
HILL, J., Remote Sensing
HOFFMANN, R., Geography and its Teaching
MONHEIM, H., Applied Geography, Urban and Regional Planning and Development
RIES, J. B., Physical Geography
SAILER, U., Cultural and Regional Geography
SYMADER, W., Hydrology
THOMAS, F., Geobotany
VOGEL, H., Communal Science
WAGNER, J.-F., Geology

Faculty VII: Theology (Universitätsring 19, 54296 Trier; tel. (651) 2013520; fax (651) 2013951; e-mail theofak@uni-trier.de; internet www.uni-trier.de/uni/theo):

BOHLEN, Biblical Studies
BRANDSCHEIDT, Old Testament
ECKERT, New Testament
EULER, Fundamental Theology
FIEDROWICZ, Medieval Church History and Christian Archaeology
GÖBEL, Moral Philosophy
HEINZ, Liturgical Studies
KRÄMER, Church Law
KRIEGER, Philosophy I
OCKENFELS, Medieval Church History
SCHNEIDER, Church History
SCHÜßLER, Philosophy II
THEIS, Religious Instruction
VODERHOLZER, Dogma and History of Dogma
WAHL, Pastoral Theology

EBERHARD-KARLS-UNIVERSITÄT TÜBINGEN

Wilhelmstr. 7, 72074 Tübingen
Telephone: (7071) 29-0
Fax: (7071) 29-5990
E-mail: registratur@verwaltung.uni-tuebingen.de
Internet: www.uni-tuebingen.de

Founded 1477
Academic year: October to July

President: Prof Dr EBERHARD SCHAICH
Chief Administrative Officer: Dr ANDREAS ROTHFUSS
Librarian: Dr ULRICH SCHAPKA

Number of teachers: 1,650
Number of students: 24,000

Publications: *Tuebinger Universitätsnachrichten* (6 a year), *Attempto! Forum der Universität Tübingen* (2 a year), *Rechenschaftsbericht des Rektors* (annually)

PROFESSORS

Department of Biology (Auf der Morgenstelle 28, 72076 Tübingen; tel. (7071) 29-76853; fax (7071) 295134; e-mail dek-bi@uni-tuebingen.de; internet www.mikrobio.uni-tuebingen.de):

BRAUN, V., Microbiology
ENGELS, E.-M., Development Physiology
GÖTZ, F., Microbiological Genetics
HAMPP, R., Botany
HARTER, K., Plant Physiology
JÜRGENS, G., Development Genetics
MAIER, W., Zoology
MALLOT, H., Cognitive Neurosciences
MICHIELS, N., Evolution Ecology of Animals
NORDHEIM, A., Molecular Biology
OBERWINKLER, F., Botany
SCHNITZLER, H.-U., Zoophysiology
SCHÖFFL, F., Genetics
WOHLLEBEN, W., Microbiology, Biotechnology

Department of Catholic Theology (Liebermeisterstr. 18, 72076 Tübingen; tel. (7071) 29-72544; fax (7071) 29-5407; e-mail u02-info@uni-tuebingen.de; internet www.uni-tuebingen.de/kath-theologie):

BIESINGER, A., Educational Religion
ECKERT, M., Fundamental Theology
FREYER, T., Dogmatic Theology
FUCHS, O., Practical Theology
GROSS, W., Old Testament
HILBERATH, B. J., Systematics
HOLZEM, A., Medieval and Modern Church History
MIETH, D., Moral Theology and Social Sciences
PUZA, R., Church Law
SEELIGER, H.-R., Ancient Church History, Patrology, Christian Archaeology
THEOBALD, M., New Testament

Department of Chemistry and Pharmacy (Auf der Morgenstelle 8, 72076 Tübingen; tel. (7071) 29-72920; fax (7071) 29-5198; e-mail dekanat-chem-pharm@uni-tuebingen.de; internet www.uni-tuebingen.de/Chemie):

HAMPRECHT, B., Biochemistry
HEIDE, L., Pharmacology
LAUFER, S., Pharmacology
MAIER, M., Organic Chemistry
MEIXNER, A., Physical Chemistry
NÜRNBERGER, T., Organic Biochemistry
OBERHAMMER, H., Physical Chemistry
RUTH, P., Pharmacology
STRÄHLE, J., Inorganic Chemistry
STEHLE, T., Biochemistry
WESEMANN, L., Inorganic Chemistry
ZIEGLER, T., Organic Chemistry

Department of Cultural Sciences (Hölderlinstr. 19, 72074 Tübingen; tel. (7071) 29-76858; fax (7071) 551567; e-mail a11-info@uni-tuebingen.de; internet www.uni-tuebingen.de/kultur-dekanat/index.html):

ANTONI, K., Japanology
BUTZENBERGER, K., Indology, Comparative Religion
EGGERT, M., Pre- and Ancient History
GERÖ, ST., Oriental Christian Philology and Culture
HOFMANN, H., Classical Philology
KLEIN, P., Art History
LEITZ, C., Egyptology
LEONHARDT, J., Latin Philology
PERNICKA, E., Archaeometry, Archaeometallurgy
RICHTER-BERNBURG, L., Oriental Studies
SCHAEFER, T., Classical Archaeology
SCHMID, M. H., Music
SCHUBERT, G., Sinology
STELLRECHT, I., Ethnography
SZLEZÁK, TH., Greek Philology
VOGEL, H.-U., Sinology
VOLK, K., Oriental History

Department of Economics (Nauklerstr. 47, 72074 Tübingen; tel. (7071) 29-72563; fax (7071) 29-5179; e-mail w04.dekanat@uni-tuebingen.de; internet www.uni-tuebingen.de/uni/w04):

BATEN, J., Economic History
BERNDT, R., Commerce
BUCH, C.-M., Economics
CANSIER, D., Economics
GRAMMIG, J., Economics and Statistics
HECKER, R., Commerce
HOFMANN, C., Commerce
JAHNKE, B., Commerce
KOHLER, W., Economics
NEUS, W., Commerce
PULL, K., Commerce
SCHAICH, E., Economics and Statistics
SCHÖBEL, R., Commerce
STADLER, M., Economics
STARBATTY, J., Economics
WAGNER, F. W., Commerce

Department of Geosciences (Sigwartstr. 17, 72076 Tübingen; tel. (7071) 29-76861; fax (7071) 550744; e-mail e16-info@uni-tuebingen.de; internet www.uni-tuebingen.de/geo):

CONARD, N., Palaeohistory and Protohistory
EBERLE, D., Geography
FÖRSTER, H., Geography
FRISCH, W., Geology
HADERLEIN, S., Environmental Mineralogy
KUCERA, M., Micropalaeontology
MOSBRUGGER, V., Palaeontology
SATIR, M., Geological Chemistry

Department of Information Science and Computer Science (Sand 13, 72076 Tübingen; tel. (7071) 29-77046; fax (7071) 29-5919; e-mail dekanat@informatik.uni-tuebingen.de; internet www.informatik.uni-tuebingen.de):

CARLE, G., Computer Science
DIEHL, M., Psychology
HAUCK, P., Computer Science
HAUTZINGER, M., Psychology
HESSE, F., Psychology
HUSON, D., Computer Science

KLAEREN, H., Computer Science
KOHLBACHER, O., Computer Science
LANGE, K.-J., Computer Science
ROSENSTIEL, W., Computer Science
SCHWAN, S., Psychology
STAPF, K.-H., Psychology
STRASSER, W., Computer Science
ULRICH, R., Psychology
ZELL, A., Computer Science

Department of Law (tel. (7071) 29-72545; fax (7071) 29-5178; e-mail dekanat@jura.uni-tuebingen.de; internet www.jura.uni-tuebingen.de):

ASSMANN, H.-D., Civil Law, Trade and Commercial Law
GÜNTHER, H.-L., Penal Law
HAFT, F., Penal Law and Procedural Law
KÄSTNER, K.-H., Civil Law, State Church Law
KERNER, H.-J., Criminology
KIRCHHOF, F., Public Law
KÜHL, K., Penal Law and Procedural Law
MAROTZKE, W., Civil Law and Procedural Law
MÖSCHEL, W., Civil, Trade and Commercial Law
NETTESHEIM, M., Public Law, European Law, Civil Law
PICKER, E., Civil Law, Labour and Trade Law
REICHOLD, H., Public Law, Trade and Commercial Law, Labour Law
REMMERT, B., Public Law, European Law and Constitution History
RONELLENFITSCH, M., Public Law
SCHIEMANN, G., Civil Law
SCHRÖDER, J., Penal and Private Law, History of German Law
VITZTHUM, W. GRAF, Public Law
VOGEL, J., Penal Law, Procedural Law
WEBER, U., Penal Law, Procedural Law
WESTERMANN, H. P., Civil, Trade and Commercial Law

Department of Mathematics and Physics (Auf der Morgenstelle 4, 72076 Tübingen; tel. (7071) 29-72567; fax (7071) 29-5400; e-mail dekanat.physik@uni-tuebingen.de; internet www.physik.uni-tuebingen.de/dekanat):

BATYREV, V., Algebra
FÄSSLER, A., Theoretical Physics
HERING, C., Geometry
JOCHUM, J., Experimental Physics
KAUP, W., Complex Analysis
KERN, D., Basic Physical Computer Science
KLEY, W., Computational Physics
LUBICH, C., Numerical Analysis
PLIES, E., Applied Physics
REINHARDT, H., Theoretical Physics
RUDER, H., Theoretical Astrophysics
SANTANGELO, A., Astronomy, Astrophysics
SCHÄTZLE, R., Analysis
SCHOPOHL, N., Theoretical Physics
SCHREIBER, F., Biophysical Structures
TEUFEL, S., Mathematical Methods in Natural Sciences
WERNER, K., Astronomy and Astrophysics
YSERENTANT, H., Numerical Analysis
ZERNER, M., Stochastics
ZIMMERMANN, C., Experimental Physics

Department of Medicine (Geissweg 5, 72076 Tübingen; tel. (7071) 29-72566; fax (7071) 29-5188; e-mail judith.jovanovic@med.uni-tuebingen.de; internet www.medizin.uni-tuebingen.de/pages/med_fakultaet/index.html):

AUTENRIETH, I. B., Medical Microbiology
BAMBERG, M., Radiography
BARES, R., Nuclear Medicine
BARTZ-SCHMIDT, K.-U., Ophthalmology
BECKER, H. D., Surgery
BIRBAUMER, N., Psychology
BUCHKREMER, G., Psychiatry
BÜLTMANN, B., Pathology
CLAUSSEN, C., Radiography
DICHGANS, H., Neurology
DIETZ, K., Medical Biometrics
DREWS, U., Anatomy
FUCHS, J., Child Surgery
GAWAZ, M., Internal Medicine
GOSSER, T., Neurology
GÖZ, G., Dentistry
GREGOR, M., Internal Medicine
HÄRING, H.-U., Internal Medicine
HOFBECK, M., Paediatrics
JAHN, G., Medical Virology
JUCKER, M., Neurology
KANDOLF, R., Molecular Pathology
KANZ, L., Internal Medicine
KLOSINSKI, G., Child and Youth Psychiatry
KNOBLOCH, J., Tropical Medicine
KÖNIGSRAINER, A., Surgery
KRÄGELOH-MANN, J., Paediatrics
LANG, F., Physiology
LÖST, C., Dentistry
MEYERMANN, R., Neuropathology
NIESS, A., Sports Medicine
OSSWALD, H., Pharmacology
POETS, C. F., Paediatrics
RAMMENSEE, H.-G., Immunology
REINERT, S., Maxillofacial Surgery
RIESS, O., Clinical Genetics
RÖCKEN, M., Dermatology
SCHALLER, H.-E., Plastic, Hand and Burns Surgery
SCHWEIZER, P., Child Surgery
SELBMANN, H.-K., Medical Statistics and Data Processing
STENZL, A., Urology
TATAGIBA, M., Neurosurgery
THIER, H. P., Neurology
UNERTL, K., Anaesthesiology
VOIGT, K., Neuroradiology
WAGNER, H.-J., Anatomy
WALLWIENER, D., Gynaecology
WEBER, H., Dentistry
WEHNER, H.-D., Forensic Medicine
WEISE, K., Traumatology
WIESING, U., Medical Ethics
WULKER, N., Orthopaedics
ZENNER, H.-P., Oto-rhino-laryngology
ZIEMER, G., Thoracic and Cardiovascular Surgery
ZIPFEL, S., Psychosomatic Medicine, Psychotherapy
ZRENNER, E., Ophthalmology

Department of Modern Languages (Wilhelmstr. 50, 72074 Tübingen; tel. (7071) 29-72952; fax (7071) 29-4253; e-mail dek-nphil@uni-tuebingen.de; internet www.uni-tuebingen.de/Neuphil-Dekanat/index.htm):

BAUER, M., English Philology
BERGER, T., Slavonic Philology
BRAUNGART, G., German Philology
ENGLER, B., English Philology
FICHTE, J., English Philology
HINRICHS, E., Computing Science of Linguistics
HOTZ-DAVIES, I., English Philology
HUBER, CH., Medieval German Literature
KEMPER, H.-G., German Philology
KILCHER, A., German Philology
KLUGE, R.-D., Slavonic Philology
KOBATEK, J., Romance Philology
KOCH, P., German Philology
KOHN, K., English Philology
MATZAT, W., Romance Philology
MOOG-GRÜNEWALD, M., Romance Philology
REINFANDT, C., English Philology
REIS, M., German Philology
RIDDER, K., Medieval German Literature
SCHAHADAT, S., Slavonic Philology
STECHOW, A. VON, Theoretical Linguistics
UEDING, G., Rhetorics
WERTHEIMER, J., German Philology

Department of Philosophy and History (Philosophy Section, Bursagasse 1, 72070 Tübingen; tel. (7071) 29-76852; fax (7071) 29-5295; e-mail dekanat@philosophie.uni-tuebingen.de; internet www.uni-tuebingen.de/philosophie/index.htmHistory Section, Sigwartstr. 17, 72076 Tübingen; tel. (7071) 29-72568; fax (7071) 29-252897; e-mail stefan.zaunder@uni-tuebingen.de; internet www.uni-tuebingen.de/dekanat-geschichte/index.htm):

BEYRAU, D., East European History
DOERING-MANTEUFFEL, A., Modern and Contemporary History
FRANK, M., Philosophy
HARTMANN, W., Medieval and Modern History
HEIDELBERGER, M., Philosophy
HÖFFE, O., Philosophy
KOCH, A. F., Philosophy
KOLB, F., Ancient History
LANGEWIESCHE, D., Medieval and Modern History
LORENZ, S., Medieval and Modern History
SCHINDLING, A., Medieval and Modern History

Department of Protestant Theology (Liebermeisterstr. 12, 72076 Tübingen; tel. (7071) 29-72538; fax (7071) 29-3318; e-mail ev.theologie@uni-tuebingen.de; internet www.uni-tuebingen.de/ev-theologie):

BAYER, O., Systematic Theology
BLUM, E., Old Testament
DRECOLL, V., Church History
DREHSEN, V., Practical Theology
ECKSTEIN, H.-J., New Testament
HENNIG, G., Practical Theology
HERMS, E., Systematic Theology
HOFIUS, O., New Testament
JANOWSKI, B., Old Testament
KÖPF, U., Church History
LICHTENBERGER, H., New Testament and Ancient Jewish Culture
SCHWEITZER, F., Practical Theology
SCHWÖBEL, C., Systematic Theology

Department of Social and Behavioural Sciences and Pedagogics (Wächterstr. 67, 72074 Tübingen; tel. (7071) 29-76857; fax (7071) 29-5115; e-mail s08info@uni-tuebingen.de; internet www.uni-tuebingen.de/FakSozVer):

BOECKH, A., Political Studies
DEUTSCHMANN, CH., Sociology
DIGEL, H., Theory of Physical Education
GILDEMEISTER, R., Sociology
HORN, K.-P., Pedagogics
HRBEK, R., Political Studies
HUBER, G., Pedagogics
JOHLER, R., Cultural Studies
MÜLLER, S., Social Pedagogics
RITTBERGER, V., Political Studies
SCHRADER, J., Pedagogics
THIEL, A., Theory of Physical Education
TREPTOW, R., Pedagogics
WANK, V., Theory of Physical Education

ATTACHED INSTITUTES

Goethe-Wörterbuch: Frischlinstr. 7, 72074 Tübingen; Dir of Commission Prof. Dr W. KÜHLMANN.

Institut für Wissensmedien (Media Institute): Konrad-Adenauer-Str. 40, 72072 Tübingen; Dir Prof. Dr FRIEDRICH W. HESSE.

UNIVERSITÄT ULM

89069 Ulm
Telephone: (731) 502-01
Fax: (731) 502-2038
E-mail: post@uni-ulm.de
Internet: www.uni-ulm.de

Founded 1967 as Medizinische-Naturwissenschaftliche Hochschule, University charter 1967
State control
Language of instruction: German
Academic year: October to September

Rector: Prof. Dr KARL JOACHIM EBELING
Pro-Rectors: Prof. Dr GUIDO ADLER, Prof. Dr PETER DÜRRE, Prof. Dr WERNER KRATZ
Chancellor: DIETER KAUFMANN
Chief Librarian: SIEGFRIED FRANKE

Number of teachers: 480
Number of students: 5,000

Publication: *Uni Ulm Intern* (8 a year)

DEANS

Faculty of Engineering: Prof. Dr HANS-JÖRG PFLEIDERER
Faculty of Information Science: Prof. Dr H. PARTSCH
Faculty of Mathematics and Mathematical Economics: Prof. Dr ULRICH STADTMÜLLER
Faculty of Medicine: Prof. Dr KLAUS-MICHAEL DEBATIN
Faculty of Natural Sciences: Prof. Dr KLAUS-DIETER SPINDLER

ATTACHED INSTITUTES

Central Institute for Biomedical Engineering: Dir Prof. Dr HANS WOLFF.

Forschungsinstitut fur Anwendungsorientierte Wissensverarbeitung (Research Institute for Applied Knowledge Processing): Dir Prof. Dr Dr FRANZ JOSEF RADERMACHER.

Institut für Lasertechnologien in der Medizin (Institute for Laser Technologies in Medicine): Dir Prof. Dr RUDOLF STEINER.

Institut für Diabetestechnologie GmbH (Institute for Diabetes Technology): Dir Prof. Dr CORNELIA HAUG.

Institut für Dynamische Materialprüfung (Institute for Dynamic Materials Testing): Chair. Prof. Dr HANS-JÖRG FECHT.

Institute for Finance and Actuary Sciences: Dir Prof. Dr JOCHEN RUß, Prof. Dr ANDREAS SEYBOTH.

Institut für Medienforschung und Medienentwicklung (Institute for Media Research and Development): Man. Dirs Prof. G. HÖRMANN, Prof. Dr W. E. REINKE.

Institute for Orthopaedic Research and Biomechanics: Dir Prof. Dr HEIKO REICHEL.

Interdisciplinary Centre for Medical Research: Dir Prof. Dr FRANK LEHMANN-HORN.

Research Institute for Rehabilitation Medicine: Dir Prof. Dr Dr ECKHART JACOBI.

Zentrum für Sonnenenergie- und Wasserstofforschung (Centre for Solar Energy and Hydrogen Technology): internet www.zsw-bw.de; Dir Dr THOMAS SCHOTT.

BAUHAUS-UNIVERSITÄT WEIMAR

Geschwister-Scholl-Str. 8, 99421 Weimar
Telephone: (3643) 58-0
Fax: (3643) 58-1120
E-mail: rektor@uni-weimar.de
Internet: www.uni-weimar.de

Founded 1860
Academic year: October to June

Chancellor: Dr-Ing. HEIKO SCHULTZ
Rector: Prof. Dr GERD ZIMMERMANN
Vice-Rectors: Prof. Dr KARL BEUCKE, Prof. LORENZ ENGELL, Prof. Dr WOLFGANG SATTLER
Librarian: Dr FRANK SIMON-RITZ

Number of teachers: 83
Number of students: 5,000

Publications: *Der Bogen* (9 a year), *Philosophische Diskurse* (annually), *Schriften der Bauhaus-Universität* (2 a year), *Thesis* (6 a year), *VERSO-Architekturtheorie* (annually)

DEANS

Faculty of Architecture: Prof. BERND RUDOLF
Faculty of Arts: Prof. HERMANN STAMM
Faculty of Construction Engineering: Prof. Dr-Ing. JOCHEN STARK
Faculty of Media: Prof. Dr MATTHIAS MAIER

PROFESSORS

Faculty of Architecture (tel. (3643) 583113; fax (3643) 583114; e-mail lars-christian .uhlig@archit.uni-weimar.de; internet www .uni-weimar.de/cms/?297):

BARZ-MALFATTI, H, Design and Settlement Planning I
BÜTTNER-HYMAN, H, Principles of Design
CHRIST, W, Design and Town Planning I
DONATH, D., Information Technology in the Architectural Planning Process
GLEITER, J H., Design and Architectural Theory
GLÜCKLICH, D., Principles of Ecological Construction
GRASHORN, B., Design and Building Construction
GUMPP, R., Design and Structural Engineering
HASSENPFLUG, D., Sociology and Social History of Towns
KÄSTNER, A., Technology of Building Design
KIEßL, K., Building Ecology and Air-conditioning
KLEIN, B., Design and Town Planning II
KOPPÁNDY, J., Landscape Architecture
LOUDON, M., Design and Industrial Buildings
Care of Historic Monuments: (vacant)
NENTWIG, B., Building Industry and Building Management
RIEß, H., Design and Building Construction I
RUDOLF, B., Theory of Building Construction
RUTH, J., Structural Engineering
SCHIRMBECK, E., Design and Interior Design
SCHMITZ, K.-H., Design and Building Construction II
SCHULZ, M., Construction Technology
STAMM-TESKE, W., Design and House-Building
WELCH GUERRA, M., Space Research, Development and Land Planning

Faculty of Arts (tel. (3643) 583206; fax (3643) 583230; e-mail christa.billing@gestaltung .uni-weimar.de; internet www.uni-weimar .de/gestaltung):

BABTIST, G., Product Design
BACHHUBER, L., Free Art
BARTELS, H., Product Design
BOCK, W., Art Science
FRÖHLICH, E., Free Art
GRONERT, S., Art Science
HINTERBERGER, N. W., Free Art
HOLZWARTH, W., Visual Communication
NEMITZ, B., Free Art
PREIß, A., Art Science
RUTHERFORD, J., Visual Communication
SATTLER, W., Product Design
SCHAWELKA, K., Art Science
STAMM, H., Visual Communication
WEBER, O., Art Science
WENTSCHER, H., Visual Communication

Faculty of Construction (tel. (3643) 584415; fax (3643) 584413; e-mail elke.lindner@ bauing.uni-weimar.de; internet www .uni-weimar.de/bauing):

ALFEN, Construction Management
BARGSTÄDT, Construction Site Management
BECKMANN, Waste Management
BERGMANN, Experimental Analysis of Materials and Structures
BEUCKE, Informatics in Construction
BIDLINGMAIER, Waste Management
BRANNOLTE, General Building Materials
BUCHER, Construction Engineering
FREUNDT, Applied Mathematics
GÜRLEBECK, Applied Mathematics
HACK, Preparation of Materials and Recycling
HÜBLER, Information Processing
KAPS, Chemistry for Building
KÖNKE, Building Statistics
KORNADT, Physics of Building
KRANAWETTREISER, Electrical Engineering
LONDONG, Urban Water Management
MÜLLER, Preparation of Materials and Recycling
RAUE, Solid Buildings I
RAUTENSTRAUCH, Wood and Stone Construction
RUTH, Solid Buildings II
SCHANZ, Soil Mechanics
SCHWARZ, Surveying
SCHWARZ, Earthquake Centre
STARK, General Building Materials
TRABERT, Construction Engineering Planning
WERNER, Steel Construction
WITT, Foundation Engineering

Faculty of Media (tel. (3643) 583703; fax (3643) 583701; e-mail medien@uni-weimar .de; internet www.uni-weimar.de/medien):

ENGELL, L., Media Philosophy
FRÖHLICH, B., Virtual Reality Systems
GEELHAAR, J., Interface Design
GROSS, T., Computer Supported Cooperative Work
HENNIG-THURAU, T., Marketing and Media
KISSEL, W., Media Events
LEEKER, M., History and Theory of Artificial Worlds
MAIER, M. (acting), Media Management
MINARD, R., Electronic Sound Production
SIEGERT, B., History and Theory of Cultural Technologies
STEIN, B., Content Management and Web Technology
WÜTHRICH, C., Graphical Data Processing

HOCHSCHULE WISMAR

Philipp-Müller-Str., Postfach 1210, 23952 Wismar
Telephone: (3841) 753-0
Fax: (3841) 753-383
E-mail: postmaster@hs-wismar.de
Internet: www.hs-wismar.de

Founded 1908 as Ingenieurhochschule Wismar, renamed 1939, 1969, 1988; present name 1992
State control
Academic year: September to August

Rector: Prof. Dr rer. nat. NORBERT GRÜNWALD
Pro-Rectors: Prof. Dr-Ing. MANFRED AHN, Prof. Dr MARION WIENECKE, Prof. Dr oec. ERHARD ALDE
Librarian: UTE KINDLER

Number of teachers: 155
Number of students: 4,300

HEADS OF DEPARTMENTS

Architecture: Prof. Dipl.-Ing. JOACHIM JOEDICKE
Civil Engineering: Prof. Dr-Ing. WOLF-RAINER BUSCH
Commerce: Prof. Dr phil. KNUT REESE
Design/Interior Architecture: Prof. Dipl.-Gebrauchsgrafikerin HANKA POLKEHN
Electrical Engineering and Computer Science: Prof. Dr-Ing. ERNST JONAS
Mechanical Engineering/Process and Environmental Engineering: Prof. Dr-Ing. PETER HEINZE
Maritime Studies: Prof. Dr-Ing. MICHAEL RACHOW

UNIVERSITÄT WITTEN/HERDECKE (Witten/Herdecke University)

Alfred-Herrhausen-Str. 50, 58448 Witten
Telephone: (2302) 926-0
Fax: (2302) 926-407
E-mail: public@uni-wh.de
Internet: www.uni-wh.de
Founded 1982
Private control
Languages of instruction: German, English
Academic year: October to July
President: Prof. Dr WOLFGANG GLATTHAAR
Librarian: IRIS KOCH
Library of 150,000 books, 500 periodicals
Number of teachers: 295
Number of students: 1,327

DEANS

Faculty of Dental Medicine: Prof. Dr PETER GÄNGLER
Faculty of Economics and Business Administration: Prof. Dr BERND FRICK
Faculty of Fundamental Studies: Prof. Dr. MATTHIAS KETTNER
Faculty of Medicine: Prof. Dr MATTHIAS SCHRAPPE
Faculty of Natural Sciences: Prof. Dr WOLFGANG WINTERMEYER

BERGISCHE UNIVERSITÄT WUPPERTAL

Gaussstr. 20, 42097 Wuppertal
Telephone: (202) 439-1
Fax: (202) 439-2901
Internet: www.uni-wuppertal.de
Founded 1972
State control
Language of instruction: German
Academic year: October to September
Rector: Prof. Dr rer. pol. VOLKER RONGE
Co-Rector (Academic): Prof. Dr phil. ANNEGRET MAACK
Co-Rector (Science and Research): Prof. Dr WOLFGANG SPIEGEL
Co-Rector (Planning and Finance): Prof. Dr HEINZ-REINER TREICHEL
Chancellor: Dr HANS-JOACHIM VON BUCHKA
Librarian: UWE STADLER
Number of teachers: 298
Number of students: 13,500

DEANS

Faculty of Architecture, Design and Art: Prof. Dr FRANK WERNER
Faculty of Civil, Mechanical and Safety Engineering: Prof. Dr DIETRICH HOEBORN
Faculty of Economics and Social Sciences: Prof. Dr LAMBERT T. KOCH
Faculty of Educational Science: Prof. Dr ANDREAS SCHAARSCHUCH
Faculty of Electrical, Information and Media Engineering: Prof. Dr BERND TIBKEN
Faculty of Humanities: Prof. Dr HANS-JOACHIM LIETZMANN
Faculty of Mathematics and Natural Sciences: Prof. Dr REINT EUJEN

ATTACHED INSTITUTES

Institute for Applied Computer Science: Dir Prof. Dr ANDREAS FROMMER.

Institute for Robotics: Dir Prof. Dr PETER C. MÜLLER.

Institute for European Economic Research: Dir Prof. Dr GERHARD ARMINGER.

Institute for Materials Science: Dir Prof. Dr RONALD FRAHM.

Institute for Environmental Design: Dir Prof. Dr FRANK WERNER.

Institute for Educational Research and Teacher Training: Dir Prof. Dr JÜRGEN BAURMANN.

Institute for Economic and Technological Development: Dir Prof. Dr GEROLD BEHRENS.

Institute for Civil Engineering, Waste Processing and Water Supply: Dir Prof. Dr BERNHARD WALZ.

Institute for Construction Engineering: Dir Prof. Dr GERHARD HANSWILLE.

BAYERISCHE JULIUS-MAXIMILIANS-UNIVERSITÄT WÜRZBURG

Sanderring 2, 97070 Würzburg
Telephone: (931) 310
Fax: (931) 312600
E-mail: universitaet@zv.uni-wuerzburg.de
Internet: www.uni-wuerzburg.de
Founded 1582
State control
Academic year: October to September
President: Prof. Dr rer. nat. A. HAASE
Vice-Presidents: Prof. Dr phil. W. SCHNEIDER, Prof. Dr phil. U. SINN, Dr rer. nat. H. MOLL, Dr rer. nat. G. KAISER
Chancellor: B. FORSTER
Chief Librarian: Dr phil. KARL SÜDEKUM
Library of 3,000,000 vols
Number of teachers: 900
Number of students: 18,000
Publications: *Personal- und Vorlesungsverzeichnis* (2 a year), *Jahresbericht*, *Blick* (2 a year), *Würzburg Heute* (2 a year)

DEANS

Faculty of Biology: Prof. Dr ULRICH SCHEER
Faculty of Catholic Theology: Prof. Dr STEPHAN ERNST
Faculty of Chemistry and Pharmacy: Prof. Dr INGFRIED ZIMMERMANN
Faculty of Economics: Prof. Dr HANSRUDI LENZ
Faculty of Geosciences: Prof. Dr BARBARA HAHN
Faculty of Law: Prof. Dr KLAUS LAUBENTHAL
Faculty of Mathematics and Computer Science: Prof. Dr HANS-GEORG WEIGAND
Faculty of Medicine: Prof. Dr GEORG ERTL
Faculty of Philosophy I (Antiquity, Cultural Studies): Prof. Dr HEINRICH HETTRICH
Faculty of Philosophy II (Philology, History, History of Art): Prof. Dr WOLFGANG RIEDEL
Faculty of Philosophy III (Philosophy, Education, Social Sciences): Prof. Dr PAUL PAULI
Faculty of Physics and Astronomy: Prof. Dr GUSTAV GERBER

PROFESSORS

Faculty of Biology (Am Hubland, Biozentrum, 97074 Würzburg; tel. (931) 8884209; fax (931) 8887123; e-mail f-biologie@biozentrum.uni-wuerzburg.de):

DANDEKAR, TH., Bioinformatics
GOEBEL, W., Microbiology
HEDRICH, R., Botany
HEISENBERG, M., Genetics
LINSENMAIR, K. E., Zoology
MÜLLER, M., Pharmaceutical Biology
RIEDERER, M., Botany
SCHEER, U., Zoology
ZIMMERMANN, U., Biotechnology

Faculty of Catholic Theology (Sanderring 2, 97070 Würzburg; tel. (931) 312252; fax (931) 312673; e-mail thde001@mail.uni-wuerzburg.de):

DROESSER, G., Christian Sociology
DÜNZL, F., Church History
ERNST, S., Moral Theology
GARHAMMER, E., Pastoral Theology
HALLERMANN, H., Theological Law
HEININGER, B., New Testament Exegesis
KLINGER, E., Basic Theology and Comparative Religion
MEUFFELS, O., Dogmatics
SEIDL, TH., Old Testament Exegesis and Biblical Oriental Languages
SIMONIS, W., Dogmatics and History of Dogma
WEISS, W., History of the Frankish Church
ZIEBERTZ, H.-G., Religious Instruction

Faculty of Chemistry and Pharmacy (Am Hubland, 97074 Würzburg; tel. (931) 8885364; fax (931) 8884607; e-mail hopf.dekanat@mail.uni-wuerzburg.de):

BRAUNSCHWEIG, H., Inorganic Chemistry
BRINGMANN, G., Organic Chemistry
FISCHER, U., Biochemistry
HOLZGRABE, U., Pharmaceutical Chemistry
KIEFER, W., Physical Chemistry
MÜLLER, G., Silicate Chemistry
RÜHL, E., Physical Chemistry
SCHREIER, P., Food Chemistry
TACKE, R., Inorganic Chemistry
WÜRTHNER, F., Organic Chemistry
ZIMMERMANN, I., Pharmaceutical Technology

Faculty of Economics (Sanderring 2, 97070 Würzburg; tel. (931) 312901; fax (931) 312101; e-mail f-wifak@wifak.uni-wuerzburg.de):

BERTHOLD, N., Political Economy
BOFINGER, P., Political Economy
BOGASCHEWSKY, R., Industrial Management
FEHR, J., Economics
FREERICKS, W., Business Management Taxation
KUKUK, M., Econometrics
LENZ, H., Accounting and Consultancy
MEYER, M., Marketing
SCHULZ, N., Political Economy
THOME, R., Economics and Computer Science
WÄLDE, K., Political Economy
WENGER, E., Banking

Faculty of Geosciences (Pleicherwall 1, 97070 Würzburg; tel. (931) 312561; fax (931) 312376; e-mail f-geowiss@mail.uni-wuerzburg.de):

BAUMHAUER, R., Geography
BÖHN, D., Geography Teaching
DECH, ST., Geography
FRIMMEL, H., Mineralogy
FÜRSICH, F. T., Palaeontology
HAHN, B., Economic Geography
LÖFFLER, G., Cultural and Economic Geography
LORENZ, V., Geology

Faculty of Law (Domerschulstr. 16, 97070 Würzburg; tel. (931) 312389; fax (931) 312477; e-mail dekanat@jura.uni-wuerzburg.de):

DREIER, H., Philosophy of Law, Political and Administrative Law
HARKE, J., Civil Law, Roman Law and Historical Comparative Law
HILGENDORF, E., Criminal Law, Criminal Procedural Law
KIENINGER, E.-M., German and European Civil Law, International Civil Law
LAUBENTHAL, K., Criminology and Penal Law
PACHE, E., State Law, International Law, International Economic Law, Economic Administrative Law
REMIEN, O., Civil Law and European Economic Law
SCHERER, I., Civil Law
SCHEUING, D. H., German and Foreign Public Law, Civil and European Law
SCHULZE-FIELITZ, H., Public Law, Environmental Law and Administrative Science
SCHWARZ, G. CH., Civil, Procedural and Comparative Law
SOSNITZA, O., Civil Law
SUERBAUM, J., Public and Administrative Law

TIEDTKE, K., Law of Finance and Economics
WEBER, C., Civil Law and Labour Law
WEITZEL, J., Civil Law, History of European Law and Procedural Law
WOLLENSCHLÄGER, M., Public Law
ZIESCHANG, F., Criminal Law, Criminal Procedural Law

Faculty of Mathematics and Computer Science (Am Hubland, 97074 Würzburg; tel. (931) 8885021; fax (931) 8884614; e-mail dekan@mathematik.uni-wuerzburg.de):

ALBERT, J., Computer Science
DOBROWOLSKI, M., Applied Mathematics
FALK, M., Mathematical Statistics
GRUNDHÖFER, TH., Mathematics
HELMKE, U., Mathematics
KANZOW, CH., Applied Mathematics
KOLLA, R., Computer Science
MÜLLER, P., Mathematics and Algebra
NOLTEMEIER, H., Computer Science
PUPPE, F., Computer Science
RUSCHEWEYH, S., Mathematics
SCHILLING, K., Technical Computer Science
TRAN-GIA, P., Computer Science
WAGNER, K. W., Computer Science
WEIGAND, H.-G., Teaching of Mathematics

Faculty of Medicine (Josef-Schneider-Str.2, Klinikum (Haus D7), 97080 Würzburg; tel. (931) 20153855; fax (931) 20153860; e-mail f-medizin@mail.uni-wuerzburg.de):

BECKMANN, H., Psychiatry
BRÖCKER, E.-B., Dermatology, Venerology and Allergology
DIETL, J., Obstetrics and Gynaecology
DRENCKHAHN, D., Anatomy
EINSELE, H., Internal Medicine
ELERT, O., Thoracic and Cardiovascular Surgery
ERTL, G., Internal Medicine
EULERT, J., Orthopaedics
FLENTJE, M., Radiology
FROSCH, M., Hygiene and Microbiology
GREHN, F., Ophthalmology
HACKER, J., Molecular Biology of Infections
HAGEN, R., Molecular Biology of Infections
HAHN, D., Radiodiagnostics
HELMS, J., Oto-rhino-laryngology
HÖHN, H., Human Genetics
HÜNIG, T., Virology
KARSCHIN, A., Neurophysiology
KLAIBER, B., Dentistry
KOEPSELL, H., Anatomy
KUHN, M., Physiology
LOHSE, M., Pharmacologyy
LUTZ, W., Toxicology
MÜLLER-HERMELINK, H. K., Pathology
PATZELT, D., Forensic and Social Medicine
RAPP, U., Medical Radiology
REINERS, CH., Medical Radiology
RETHWILM, A., Virology
REUTHER, J., Dentistry, Maxillo-facial Surgery
RICHTER, E.-J., Dental and Facial Medicine
RIEDMILLER, H., Urology
ROEWER, N., Anaesthesiology
ROOSEN, K., Neurosurgery
SCHARTL, M., Physiological Chemistry
SEBALD, W., Physiological Chemistry
SENDTNER, M., Clinical Neurobiology
SPEER, C., Paediatrics
STELLZIG-EISENHAUER, A., Dental and Facial Orthopaedics
STOLBERG, M., History of Medicine
THIEDE, A., Surgery
THULL, R., Experimental Dentistry
TOYKA, K. V., Neurology
WALTER, U., Clinical Biochemistry and Pathobiochemistry
WARNKE, A., Child Psychiatry

Faculty of Philosophy I (Residenzplatz 2, 97070 Würzburg; tel. (931) 312879; fax (931) 8887050; e-mail f-philfak1@mail.uni-wuerzburg.de):

BRÜCKNER, H., Indology
BRUSNIAK, F., Music Education, Teaching of Music
ERLER, M., Classical Philology
HANNICK, CH., Slavic Philology
HETTRICH, H., Comparative Linguistics
KONRAD, U., Musicology
KUHN, D., Oriental Philology
SCHIER, W., Prehistoric Archaeology
SCHOLZ, U. W., Classical Philology
SCHÖNBEIN, M., Japanology
SINN, U., Classical Archaeology
WILHELM, G., Oriental Philology

Faculty of Philosophy II (Am Hubland, 97074 Würzburg; tel. (931) 8885221; fax (931) 8884601; e-mail f-philfak2@mail.uni-wuerzburg.de):

ACHILLES, J., American Studies
ALT, P.-A., History of Modern German Literature
ALTGELD, W., Modern and Contemporary History
BRUNNER, H., German Philology
BURGSCHMIDT, E., English Linguistics
DAXELMÜLLER, C., European Ethnology
DIETZ, K., Early History
FLACHENECKER, H., Frankish History
FUCHS, F., Medieval History
KOHL, ST. M., English Literature and British Cultural Studies
KUMMER, S., History of Art
NEUGEBAUER, W., Modern History
PENZKOFER, G., Romance Philology
PFOTENHAUER, H., History of Modern German Literature
PÖTTERS, W., Romance Philology
WOLF, N. R., German Linguistics

Faculty of Philosophy III (Wittelsbacherplatz 1, 97074 Würzburg; tel. (931) 8884879; fax (931) 8884880; e-mail f-philfak3@mail.uni-wuerzburg.de):

GÖTZ, M., Elementary Teaching and Education
HANSEN, D., Special Education
HOFFMANN, J., Psychology
HUIZING, K., Protestant Religion
KAPUSTIN, P., Physical Education
LELGEMANN, R., Special Education
LEMBECK, K.-H., Philosophy
MERTENS, K., Practical Philosophy
MÜLLER, W., Education
PAULI, P., Psychology
RUPP, H., Protestant Religion and Religious Education
SCHNEIDER, W., Psychology
STRACK, F., Psychology
VERNOOIJ, M. A., Special Education

Faculty of Physics and Astronomy (Am Hubland, 97074 Würzburg; tel. (931) 8885720; fax (931) 8885508; e-mail f-physik@physik.uni-wuerzburg.de):

CLAESSEN, R., Experimental Physics
DYAKONOV, V., Experimental Physics, Energy Research
FORCHEL, A., Semiconductor Technology and Physics
GERBER, G., Experimental Physics
HANKE, W., Theoretical Physics
HEUER, D., Physics Teaching
JAKOB, P., Biophysics
KINZEL, W., Computational Physics
MANNHEIM, K., Astronomy
MOLENKAMP, L., Experimental Physics
RÜCKL, R., Theoretical Physics
UMBACH, E., Experimental Physics

Colleges

GENERAL

Schiller International University – Germany: Bergstr. 106, 69121 Heidelberg; tel. (6221) 4581-0; fax (6221) 402703; e-mail campus@siu-heidelberg.de; internet www.siu-heidelberg.de; f. 1964 as independent international university; language of instruction: English (all campuses); campuses in France, Germany, Spain, Switzerland, UK and USA (for which see respective chapters); depts of commercial art, computer studies, engineering management, international business, international tourism and hospitality management, international relations and diplomacy, literature, para-legal studies, pre-medicine; degrees at Florida (USA) campus conferred under charter granted by State of Florida; degrees at all other campuses conferred under charter granted by State of Delaware (USA); library: 91,000 vols (total for all campuses); 25 teachers (Heidelberg campus only); 1,519 students (total for all campuses, of which 210 at Heidelberg campus); Pres. Dr WALTER W. LEIBRECHT; Vice-President for Academic Affairs C. F. EBERHART.

Wissenschaftskolleg zu Berlin (Institute for Advanced Study): Wallotstr. 19, 14193 Berlin; tel. (30) 89001-0; fax (30) 89001-300; e-mail wiko@wiko-berlin.de; internet www.wiko-berlin.de; f. 1980; private institution for international and interdisciplinary postdoctoral research; 40 Fellows; library mainly reference collection; Rector Prof. Dr DIETER GRIMM; Sec. Dr JOACHIM NETTELBECK; Librarian Dr GESINE BOTTOMLEY.

ART, ARCHITECTURE

Akademie der Bildenden Künste (Academy of Fine Arts): Akademiestr. 2, 80799 Munich; tel. (89) 3852-0; fax (89) 3852-203; e-mail sekretariat@adbk.mhn.de; internet www.adbk.mhn.de; f. 1770 (Charter conferred 1808 and 1953); languages of instruction: German, English; 35 professors; 630 students; library: 110,000 vols, 100 current periodicals; Rector Prof. NIKOLAUS GERHART; Chancellor BIANCA MARZOCCA; Librarians CHARLOTTE DIEHL, INGE SICKLINGER-SEUß.

Akademie der Bildenden Künste in Nürnberg: Bingstr. 60, 90480 Nuremberg; tel. (911) 94040; fax (911) 9404150; e-mail info@adbk-nuernberg.de; internet www.adbk-nuernberg.de; f. 1662; 27 teachers; 350 students; library: 22,000 vols; President Prof. OTTMAR HÖRL; Vice-Presidents Prof. PETER ANGERMANN, Prof. CLAUS BURY, Prof. PETER ANGERMANN; Chancellor AXEL KLON; Librarian MARTINA KEMMSIES.

Bauhaus Kolleg: see entry for Bauhaus Dessau Foundation.

Deutsche Film- und Fernsehakademie Berlin GmbH (German Film and Television Academy): Potsdamer Straße. 2, 10785 Berlin; tel. (30) 257590; fax (30) 25759161; e-mail info@dffb.de; internet www.dffb.de; f. 1966; 40 teachers; 110 students; library: 80,000 vols; Dir Prof. REINHARD HAUFF.

Hochschule für Bildende Künste Braunschweig: Johannes-Selenka-Platz 1, 38118 Brunswick; tel. (531) 391-9122; fax (531) 391-9292; e-mail hbk@hbk-bs.de; internet www.hbk-bs.de; f. 1963; depts of art (painting, graphics, sculpture, film, video, performing arts and photography), design (industrial and graphic), art teaching, art history; institute for media and film studies, institute for art history and visual research; languages of instruction: German, English; library: 26,000 vols; 1,200 students; President BARBARA STRAKA; publs *Schriftenreihe* (3–5 a year), *Vorlesungsverzeichnis/Studienführer* (2 a year).

Hochschule für Bildende Künste Dresden: 01288 Dresden; premises at: Güntzstr. 34, 01307 Dresden; tel. (351) 49267-0; fax

(351) 4952023; e-mail info@serv1.hfbk-dresden.de; internet www.hfbk-dresden.de; f. 1764; stage and theatre design, costume design, painting, sculpture, graphics, restoration, art therapy; languages of instruction: German, English; 31 teachers; 566 students; Rector Prof. CHRISTIAN SERY; Chancellor HANS-JÜRGEN SCHÖNEMANN; Librarians KARIN HUß, CHRISTINE POSSEGGA.

Hochschule für Bildende Künste Hamburg: Lerchenfeld 2, 22081 Hamburg; tel. (428) 989205; fax (428) 989206; e-mail presse@hfbk.hamburg.de; internet www.hfbk-hamburg.de; depts of art, architecture, industrial design, visual communication, education and technology; Pres. MARTIN KÖTTERING; Chancellor HORST-VOLKERT THIEL; Librarian ELISABETH WILKER.

Hochschule für Film und Fernsehen 'Konrad Wolf' Potsdam-Babelsberg (Academy of Film and Television): Marlene-Dietrich-Allee 11, 14482 Potsdam; tel. (331) 6202-0; fax (331) 6202-549; e-mail info@hff-potsdam.de; internet www.hff-potsdam.de; f. 1954; 100 teachers; 500 students; library: 82,000 vols, 16,000 video titles, 170 film magazines, 1.6m. newspaper cuttings, 2,800 HFF (student) films; President Prof. Dr sc. DIETER WIEDEMANN; publ. *BFF (Beiträge zur Film- und Fernsehwissenschaft)* (irregular).

Hochschule für Grafik und Buchkunst Leipzig (Leipzig State Academy of Graphic Arts and Book Design): Wächterstr. 11, 04107 Leipzig; tel. (341) 2135-0; fax (341) 2135-166; e-mail hgb@hgb-leipzig.de; internet www.hgb-leipzig.de; f. 1764; painting, graphic arts, book art, graphic design, photography, media art; 48 teachers; 350 students; library: 40,000 vols, 100 current periodicals; Rector Prof. JOACHIM BROHM; Chancellor MARIA-CORNELIA ZIESCH; Librarian CLAUDIA-MARIA DARMER.

Hochschule für Künste Bremen: Am Speicher XI 8, 28217 Bremen; tel. (421) 9595-100; fax (421) 9595-2000; e-mail studsek@hfk-bremen.de; internet www.hfk-bremen.de; f. 1988; library: 40,000 vols; 90 teachers; 723 students (623 undergraduate, 100 postgraduate); Rector Prof. Dr PETER RAUTMANN; Chancellor MARKUS WORTMANN; Librarians VERONIKA GREUEL, SIEGFRIED STANGE.

Kunstakademie Düsseldorf, Hochschule für Bildende Künste (Academy of Fine Art, Düsseldorf): Eiskellerstr. 1, 40213 Düsseldorf; tel. (211) 1396-0; fax (211) 1396-225; e-mail postmaster@kunstakademie-duesseldorf.de; internet www.kunstakademie-duesseldorf.de; f. 1773; 50 teachers; 700 students; library: 110,000 vols; Rector Prof. Dr MARKUS LÜPERTZ; Rector Prof. Dr PETER MICHAEL LYNEN; Librarian HELMUT KLEINENBROICH.

Kunsthochschule Berlin-Weissensee, Hochschule für Gestaltung: Bühringstr. 20, 13086 Berlin; tel. (30) 47705-0; fax (30) 47705-290; e-mail rektor@kh-berlin.de; internet www.kh-berlin.de; f. 1946; fine arts, industrial design, ceramics, fashion design, textile design, communication design, architecture, stage design, sculpture; 550 students; 39 teachers; library: 20,000 vols; Rector Prof. GERHARD STREHL.

Staatliche Akademie der Bildenden Künste: Postfach 6267, 76042 Karlsruhe; Reinhold-Frank-Str. 67, 76133 Karlsruhe; tel. (721) 9265210; fax (721) 9265213; e-mail mail@kunstakademie-karlsruhe.de; internet www.kunstakademie-karlsruhe.de; f. 1854; library: 30,000 vols; Rektor Prof. ERWIN GROSS; Chancellor RÜDIGER WEIS; Librarian RENATE WINKLER-WILDE.

Staatliche Akademie der Bildenden Künste: Am Weissenhof 1, 70191 Stuttgart; tel. (711) 28440-0; fax (711) 28440-225; e-mail info@abk-stuttgart.de; internet www.abk-stuttgart.de; f. 1761; art, graphics, sculpture, architecture, design, conservation, ceramics, textiles and industrial design; Rector Dr LUDGER HUENHKEUS; Pro-Rectors Prof. PETER LITZLBAUER, Prof. ANDREAS OPIOLKA.

Staatliche Hochschule für Bildende Künste–Städelschule: Dürerstr. 10, 60596 Frankfurt; tel. (69) 605008-0; fax (69) 605008-52; e-mail rektor@staedelschule.de; internet www.staedelschule.de; f. 1817; art, architecture, film, sculpture, painting, drawing, architecture (conceptual design); 9 profs; 150 students; library: 16,000 vols; Rector Prof. Dr DANIEL BIRNBAUM; Exec. Dir JÜRGEN GRUMANN; Librarian HEIKE BELZER.

ECONOMICS, POLITICAL AND SOCIAL SCIENCES, PUBLIC ADMINISTRATION

European Business School: Schloss Reichartshausen, 65375 Oestrich-Winkel; tel. (6723) 69-0; fax (6723) 69-133; e-mail info@ebs.de; internet www.ebs.de; f. 1971; private, state-recognized diploma courses; 22 teachers; 835 students; library: 22,000 vols, 150 current periodicals; Pres. Prof. Dr HANS TIETMEYER; Rector Prof. ULRICH HOMMEL; Chancellor Dr PETER ADLER; Librarian SILVA SCHELLHAS.

Hochschule für Politik München: Ludwigstr. 8, 80539 Munich; tel. (89) 285018; fax (89) 283705; e-mail hfp-muenchen@hfp.mhn.de; internet www.hfp.mhn.de; f. 1950; 150 teachers; 950 students; library: 35,000 vols; Rector Prof. Dr P. C. MAYER-TASCH; publs *Zeitschrift für Politik* (quarterly), *Junge Wissenschaft* (irregular), *Schriftenreihe* (irregular).

HWP – Hamburger Universität für Wirtschaft und Politik: Von-Melle-Park 9, 20146 Hamburg; tel. (40) 42838-2180; fax (40) 42838-4150; e-mail HildC@hwp-hamburg.de; internet www.hwp-hamburg.de; f. 1948; undergraduate degree courses in business and management, law, economics, sociology; postgraduate degree courses in socio-economics, international business administration, European studies; languages of instruction: German, English; 80 teachers; 2,600 students; Pres. Dr DOROTHEE BITTSCHEIDT; Registrar DIETMAR PLUM.

Stuttgart Institute of Management and Technology: Filderhauptstr. 142, 70599 Stuttgart; tel. (711) 451001-0; fax (711) 451001-45; e-mail info@uni-simt.de; internet www.uni-simt.de; f. 1998; 68 teachers (8 full-time, 60 part-time); 150 students; MBA in International Management, Finance and Investment, Management Information Systems, Technology and Innovation Management; International Executive MBA; part-time programs; Man. Dir Dr BERNHARD SEITZ.

LANGUAGES

Akademie für Fremdsprachen (Academy of Foreign Languages): Postfach 150104, 10663 Berlin; Nürnberger Str. 38, 10777 Berlin; tel. (30) 884302-0; fax 884302-23; e-mail post@akafremd.de; internet www.akafremd.de; f. 1971; translators' and interpreters' courses in German, English, French, Spanish, Italian, Russian, and courses in German as a foreign language; 1,600 students; Sec. NORBERT ZÄNKER.

MEDICINE

Medizinische Akademie Erfurt: Nordhäuser Str. 74, PSF 595, 99089 Erfurt; tel. 790; fax 23697; f. 1954; 121 teachers; 750 students; library: 140,000 vols; Rector Prof. Dr Dr h.c. mult. W. KÜNZEL; Pro-Rector Prof. Dr G. ENDERT; Medical Dir Prof. Dr W. KRAFFT; Librarian Dr B. ADLUNG.

MUSIC AND DRAMA

Hochschule für Musik Saar: Bismarckstr. 1, 66111 Saarbrücken; tel. (681) 96731-0; fax (681) 96731-30; e-mail t.wolter@hfm.saarland.de; internet www.hfm.saarland; f. 1947; 110 teachers; 350 students; library: 82,000 vols; Rector Prof. THOMAS DUIS; Man. Dir ALFONS SIMON; Librarian ILSE HAHN.

Hochschule für Musik: Schwarzwaldstr. 141, 79095 Freiburg im Breisgau; tel. (761) 319150; fax (761) 3191542; e-mail info@mh-freiburg.de; internet www.mh-freiburg.de; f. 1946; 160 teachers; 540 students; Rector MANFRED KLIMANSKI.

Hochschule für Musik 'Hanns Eisler': Charlottenstr. 55, 10117 Berlin; tel. (30) 90269-700; fax (30) 90269-701; e-mail rektorat@hfm.in-berlin.de; internet www.hfm-berlin.de; f. 1950; departments of voice, music, stage and theatre direction; strings, harp and guitar; brass, woodwind, percussion and conducting; and piano, accordion and composition/harmony; 433 teachers (113 full-time, 320 part-time); 702 students; Dir Prof. CHRISTHARD GÖSSLING.

Hochschule für Musik Detmold: Neustadt 22, 32756 Detmold; tel. (5231) 975-5; fax (5231) 975-972; internet www.hfm-detmold.de; f. 1946; 120 teachers; 580 students; library of 157,800 items; Rector Prof. MARTIN CHRISTIAN VOGEL.

Hochschule für Musik 'Carl Maria von Weber' Dresden: Wettiner Platz 13, Postfach 120039, 01001 Dresden; tel. (351) 4923600; fax (351) 4923657; e-mail rektorat@hfmdd.smwk.sachsen.de; internet www.hfmdd.de; f. 1856; library: 50,000 vols, 7,000 records and CDs, contains Heinrich-Schütz archive; 80 teachers; 631 students; attached institute for musicology (in co-operation with the Heinrich-Schütz Archive), institute for music medicine, studio for voice research, studio for electronic music; Rector Prof. Dr STEFAN GIES; Pro-Rectors Prof. HEIDRUN RICHTER, Prof. GÜNTER SOMMER; publs *Schriftenreihe der Hochschule für Musik* (irregular), *Jahrbuch* (annually).

Hochschule für Musik Köln: Dagobertstr. 38, 50668 Cologne; tel. (221) 912818-0; fax (221) 131204; internet www.mhs-koeln.de; f. 1925; centres in Cologne, Aachen and Wuppertal; instrumental music and musicology; 330 teachers; 1,800 students; library: 136,000 vols, 8,600 records, 400 films; Rector Prof. JOSEF PROTSCHKA; Chancellor URSULA WIRTZ-KNAPSTEIN; publ. *Journal* (2 a year).

Hochschule für Musik und Theater 'Felix Mendelssohn Bartholdy' Leipzig: PSF 100809, 04008 Leipzig; located at:Grassistr. 8 , 04107 Leipzig; tel. (341) 214455; fax (341) 2144503; e-mail rektor@hmt-leipzig.de; internet www.hmt-leipzig.de; f. 1843; library: 163,000 vols; 850 students; Rector Prof. KONRAD KÖRNER.

Hochschule für Musik Nürnberg-Augsburg: Veilhofstr. 34, 90489 Nuremberg; tel. (911) 2318443; fax (911) 2317697; e-mail hfm-rektorat@stadt.nuernberg.de; internet www.hfm-n-a.de; f. 1873 as Leopold Mozart Konservatorium; present name 1999; international college of higher education; concerts, productions, International Leopold Mozart Competition for Young Violinists,

Studio for Old and New Music; 98 teachers; 200 students; library: 12,500 vols in Nuremberg and Augsburg libraries; Rector SIEGFRIED JERUSALEM; Chancellor HANS-WERNER ITTMANN.

Hochschule für Musik 'Franz Liszt' Weimar: Platz der Demokratie 2/3, 99423 Weimar; tel. (3643) 555-0; fax (3643) 555-117; f. 1872; 840 students; 132 teachers; library: 65,000 vols and 45,000 tapes; Rector Prof. ROLF-DIETER ARENS; Pro-Rectors Prof. ANNE-KATHRIN LINDIG, Prof. GERO SCHMIDT-OBERLÄNDER; instruction in: keyboard, string and wind instruments, accordion, guitar, jazz/pop instruments and vocal, composition, conducting, singing and music teaching, church music and musicology.

Hochschule für Musik: Hofstallstr. 6–8, 97070 Würzburg; tel. (931) 321870; fax (931) 321872800; e-mail hochschule@hfm-wuerzburg.de; internet www.hfm-wuerzburg.de; f. 1804; 220 teachers; 650 students; library: 14,200 vols, 45,400 music scores, 47 current periodicals; Rector Prof. SILKE-THORA MATTHIES; Chancellor Dr EVA STUMPF-WIRTHS; Librarian BARBARA KONRAD.

Hochschule für Musik und Darstellende Kunst: Eschersheimer Landstrasse 29–39, 60322 Frankfurt am Main; tel. (69) 154007-0; fax (69) 154007-108; internet www.hfmdk-frankfurt.de; 60 teachers; 850 students; f. 1878 as Konservatorium, Hochschule since 1938; Rector Prof. THOMAS RIETSCHEL.

Hochschule für Musik und Theater Hannover: Emmichpl. 1, 30175 Hanover; tel. (511) 31001; fax (511) 3100200; e-mail pressestelle@hmt-hannover.de; internet www.hmt-hannover.de; f. 1961; 280 teachers; 1,100 students; library: 203,000 vols; Pres. Prof. Dr KLAUS-ERNST BEHNE.

Hochschule für Musik und Theater: Harvestehuder Weg 12, 20148 Hamburg; tel. (40) 428482586; fax (40) 428482666; internet www.hfmt-hamburg.de; f. 1950; 250 teachers; 750 students; library: 20,000 vols; Pres. Prof. ELMAR LAMPSON; Chancellor BERNHARD LANGE; Librarians SILKE BROSE, MELANIE KINTZEL.

Hochschule für Musik und Theater München: Arcisstr. 12, 80333 Munich; tel. (89) 289-03; fax (89) 28927419; e-mail verwaltung@musikhochschule-muenchen.de; internet www.musikhochschule-muenchen.de; f. 1846; 300 teachers; 900 students; Pres. Prof. Dr SIEGFRIED MAUSER.

Internationales Musikinstitut Darmstadt (IMD): Nieder-Ramstäder Str. 190, 64285 Darmstadt; tel. (6151) 132416; fax (6151) 132405; e-mail imd@darmstadt.de; internet www.imd.darmstadt.de; f. 1946; international holiday courses on contemporary music (composition, interpretation); international music lending library (works since beginning of 20th c.) of 35,000 scores, 5,000 vols, 4,000 tapes, 1,500 records; Dir SOLF SCHAEFER.

Musikhochschule Lübeck: Gr. Petersgrube 17-29, 23552 Lübeck; tel. (451) 1505-0; fax (451) 1505-300; e-mail info@mh-luebeck.de; internet www.mh-luebeck.de; f. 1933; musical training on all instruments, opera singing and performing, training of music teachers, sacred music (Protestant and Catholic), preparatory training of professional musicians and music teachers; library: 110,000 vols; 130 teachers; 500 students; Rector Prof. INGE-SUSANN RÖMHILD; Admin DETLEF BAUDISCH; Librarian TORSTEN SENKBEIL.

Richard-Strauss-Konservatorium: Kellerstr. 6, 81667 Munich; tel. (89) 48098-4415; fax (89) 48098-4417; e-mail sekretariat@rsk.musin.de; internet www.rsk.musin.de; f. 1962; courses in vocal and instrumental studies, conducting, composition, jazz; 120 teachers; 500 students; library: 20,000 vols; Dir MARTIN MARIA KRÜGER; Librarian TOM HOPFINGER.

Robert-Schumann-Hochschule Düsseldorf: Fischerstr. 110, 40476 Düsseldorf; tel. (211) 49180; fax (211) 4911618; e-mail rsh@rsh-duesseldorf.de; internet www.rsh-duesseldorf.de; f. 1935; languages of instruction: German, English; library: 120,000 vols; 191 teachers; 830 students; Rector Prof. RAIMUND WIPPERMANN; Pro-Rector Prof. BARBARA SZCZEPANSKA; Chancellor BARBARA SZCZEPANSKA.

Staatliche Hochschule für Musik Karlsruhe: Postfach 6040, 76040 Karlsruhe; Am Schloss Gottesaue 7, 76131 Karlsruhe; tel. (721) 662950; fax (721) 662966; internet www.hfm-karlsruhe.de; f. 1884; library: 115,000 vols; 150 teachers; 550 students; Rector Prof. WOLFGANG MEYER; Chancellor WOLFRAM SCHERER; Librarian HANNELORE BERNT.

Staatliche Hochschule für Musik und Darstellende Kunst: Urbanstr. 25, 70182 Stuttgart; tel. (711) 2124631; fax (711) 2124632; e-mail rektor@mh-stuttgart.de; internet www.mh-stuttgart.de; f. 1857; 200 teachers; 770 students; library: 10,000 vols; Rector Prof. Dr WERNER HEINRICHS; Chancellor ALBRECHT LANG.

Staatliche Hochschule für Musik und Darstellende Kunst Heidelberg-Mannheim: N7, 18, 68161 Mannheim; fax (621) 2922072; e-mail rektorat@muho-mannheim.de; internet www.muho-mannheim.de; f. 1899; 200 teachers; 550 students; Rector Prof. R. MEISTER; Man. Dir THILO FISCHER; Librarian KATHRIN WINTER.

PHILOSOPHY, THEOLOGY

Augustana Hochschule: Waldstr. 11, 91564 Neuendettelsau; tel. (9874) 509-0; fax (9874) 509-555; e-mail hochschule@augustana.de; internet www.augustana.de; f. 1947; five depts of theology and one dept of theology; 30 teachers; 200 students; Rector Prof. Dr HELMUT UTZSCHNEIDER; Librarian ARMIN STEPHAN.

Hochschule für Philosophie: Kaulbachstr. 31A, 80539 Munich; tel. (89) 23862300; fax (89) 23862302; e-mail admin@hfph.mwn.de; internet www.hfph.mwn.de; f. 1925; library: 199,000 vols; 20 teachers; 500 students; Rector Prof. Dr MICHAEL BORDT; Chancellor Dr IGNAZ FISCHER-KERLI; Librarian J. OSWALD; publ. *Theologie und Philosophie* (4 a year).

Kirchliche Hochschule Bethel: Postfach 130140, 33544 Bielefeld; premises at: Remterweg 45, 33617 Bielefeld; tel. (521) 144-3948; fax (521) 1443961; e-mail rektorat.kihobethel@uni-bielefeld.de; internet www.kiho-bethel.de; f. 1905; languages of instruction: German, English; library: 125,000 vols; 23 teachers; 200 students; Rector Prof. Dr FRANÇOIS VOUGA; publ. *Jahrbuch—Wort und Dienst* (every 2 years).

Kirchliche Hochschule Wuppertal: Missionstr. 9B, 42285 Wuppertal; tel. (202) 2820-100; fax (202) 2820-101; e-mail rektorat-kiho@uni-wuppertal.de; internet www.kiho.uni-wuppertal.de; f. 1935; Protestant; library: 100,000 vols; 15 teachers; 200 students; Rector Prof. Dr DIETER VIEWEGER.

Lutherische Theologische Hochschule Oberursel:; e-mail verwaltung@lthh-oberursel.de Altkönigstrasse 150, 61440 Oberursel im Taunus; tel. (6171) 9127-0; fax (6171) 9127-70; e-mail lthh@lthh-oberursel.de; internet www.lthh-oberursel.de; f. 1947; library: 35,000 vols; 8 teachers; 30 students; publ. *Lutherische Theologie und Kirche* (4 a year).

Philosophisch-Theologische Hochschule Sankt Georgen: Offenbacher Landstr. 224, 60599 Frankfurt am Main; tel. (69) 60610; fax (69) 6061307; e-mail rektorat@st-georgen.uni-frankfurt.de; internet www.st-georgen.uni-frankfurt.de; f. 1926 (since 1950 combined with Jesuit Theological Faculty, f. 1863); languages of instruction: German, English; library: 390,000 vols; 23 teachers; 460 students; Rector Prof. Dr HELMUT ENGEL; Librarian MARCUS STARK; publs *Theologie und Philosophie* (4 a year), *Frankfurter Theologische Studien* (2–3 a year), *Sankt Georgener Hochschulschriften* (annually).

Theologische Fakultät Fulda (Staatlich anerkannte Wissenschaftliche Hochschule): Eduard-Schick-Platz 2, 36037 Fulda; tel. (661) 87220; fax (661) 87224; e-mail rektorat@thf-fulda.de; internet www.thf-fulda.de; f. 748; languages of instruction: German, English; 20 teachers; 40 students; Rector Prof. Dr theol. Dr phil. BERND WILLMES; publs *Fuldaer Studien*, *Fuldaer Hochschulschriften*.

Theologische Fakultät Paderborn: Kamp 6, 33098 Paderborn; tel. (5251) 1216; fax (5251) 121700; e-mail Theol-Fakultaet-Paderborn@t-online.de; internet www.theofak-pb.de; f. 1615; 26 teachers; 351 students; Rector Prof. Dr GÜNTHER WILHELM; Pro-Rector Prof. Dr MICHAEL KUNZLER; Librarian Prof. Dr KARL HENGST; publ. *Theologie und Glaube* (quarterly).

Theologische Fakultät Trier: Universitätsring 19, 54296 Trier; tel. (651) 201-3520; fax (651) 201-3951; e-mail theofak@uni-trier.de; internet www.uni-trier.de/uni/theo; f. 1950; library: 400,000 vols; 20 ordinary professors; 315 students; Chancellor Dr REINHARD MARX (Bishop of Trie); Rector Prof. Dr REINHOLD BOHLEN; publ. *Trierer Theologische Zeitschrift* (quarterly).

Attached institutes:

Institut für Cusanusforschung, Trier.

Emil Frank Institut, Wittlich.

TECHNOLOGY

Burg Giebichenstein Hochschule für Kunst und Design Halle: 06108 Halle, Neuwerk 7; tel. (345) 7751-50; fax (345) 7751-569; e-mail rektorat@burg-halle.de; internet www.burg-halle.de; f. 1915; language of instruction: German; library: 64,000 vols of various media, 170 journals; 90 teachers; 980 students; Rector Prof. ULRICH KLIEBER; Dean, School of Design Prof. AXEL MÜLLER-SCHÖLL; Dean, School of Fine Arts Prof. THOMAS RUG.

Attached Research Institutes:

Institut Computer Art & Design: tel. (345) 7751-900; fax (345) 7751-907; e-mail ca&d@burg-halle.de; internet cad.burg-halle.de; Dir LEONORE PUNK.

Institut idea (Interior Design, Environment and Architecture): tel. (345) 7751-868; fax (345) 7751-868; e-mail idea@burg-halle.de; internet www.burg-halle.de/~idea.

Institut für Software Consulting und Entwicklung: tel. (345) 7751-701; fax (345) 7751-719; e-mail isce@burg-halle.de; internet www.burg-halle.de/~isce; Dir Prof. JOSEF WALCH.

Hochschule Anhalt (FH): Bernburger Str. 52–57, 06366 Köthen; tel. (3496) 671000; fax (3496) 671099; internet www.hs-anhalt.de; f.

1891, present status 1992; Köthen: mechanical engineering (plant construction), chemical and environmental engineering, biotechnology and food processing, computer science, electrical engineering; Bernburg: business economics, agriculture, landscape architecture and planning, food and health management; Dessau: architecture, civil engineering, surveying, design; President Prof. Dr DIETER ORZESSEK; Vice-Pres Prof. Dr CAROLA GRIEHL, Prof. Dr RUDOLF LÜCKMANN, Prof. Dr NORBERT OTTO.

Hochschule Mittweida (FH)–University of Applied Sciences: Postfach 1457, 09644 Mittweida; tel. (3727) 580; fax (3727) 581379; e-mail info@htwm.de; internet www.htwm.de; f. 1867; electrical engineering, electronics, microelectronics, mechanical engineering, mathematics, physics, economic sciences, social sciences, media technology, media management, microsystems engineering, precision engineering, steel and metal construction, building engineering, physical engineering, environmental engineering, computer sciences; library: 140,000 vols; 298 teachers; 4,824 students; Rector Prof. Dr-Ing. habil. Dr h. c. WERNER TOTZAUER.

Hochschule für Technik, Wirtschaft und Kultur Leipzig (Leipzig University of Applied Sciences): Postfach 301166, 04251 Leipzig; premises at: 04277 Leipzig, Karl-Liebknecht-Str. 132; tel. (341) 3076-0; fax (341) 3076-6456; e-mail studinf@k.htwk-leipzig.de; internet www.htwk-leipzig.de; f. 1992; architecture, civil engineering, electrical engineering, mechanical engineering, printing technology, multimedia technology, publishing, computer science, business mathematics, business administration, social work, library and information science, museology, book trade/publishing, engineering with management (electrical engineering, energy engineering, mechanical engineering, civil engineering), international management; library: 320,000 vols; 180 teachers; 6,000 students; Rector Prof. Dr-Ing. MANFRED NIETNER.

Hochschule Zittau/Görlitz (FH): Postfach 1454, 02754 Zittau; located at:Theodor-Koerner-Allee 16, 02763 Zittau; tel. (3583) 611401; fax (3583) 611402; e-mail info@hs-zigr.de; internet www.hs-zigr.de; f. 1992; architecture, civil engineering, business management, chemistry, electrical engineering, process engineering, power and environmental engineering, real estate and housing management, computer science, mechanical engineering, ecology and environmental protection, mechatronics, tourism, translating English and Czech, social work, social education, special needs education, communications psychology, business mathematics, marketing, electrical and electronic engineering, business studies, industrial engineering; library: 179,254 vols; 121 teachers; 3,800 students; Rector Prof. Dr-Ing. RAINER HAMPEL; Chancellor Dr-Ing. P. REINHOLD.

Westsächsische Hochschule Zwickau (FH): Dr-Friedrichs-Ring 2A, 08056 Zwickau; tel. (375) 536-0; fax (375) 536-1127; e-mail rektorat@fh-zwickau.de; internet www.fh-zwickau.de; f. 1992; Schools of Mechanical and Automotive Engineering, Electrical Engineering, Physical and Computer Sciences, Applied Economics, Applied Arts, Textile and Leather Production Engineering, Architecture, Health and Healthcare Management, Languages; languages of instruction: German, English; library: 198,000 vols; 191 teachers; 4,700 students; Rector Prof. Dr-Ing. habil. KARL-FRIEDRICH FISCHER; publs *Hochschulführer* (annually), *Hochschulforschungsbericht* (annually).

GHANA

The Higher Education System

In 1957 the former British dependencies of Togoland and Gold Coast declared the independent state of Ghana, which subsequently became a republic in 1960. The first institution of higher education, Achimota College, was founded in 1924, and the first university-level institution, University College of the Gold Coast, was founded in 1948 in conjunction with the University of London (United Kingdon), and achieved full university status in 1961; it is now known as University of Ghana, and is based in the capital, Accra. Some 82,346 students were enrolled in higher education in 1996/97, with 23,126 students attending the country's five universities.

Higher education is administered by the Ministry of Education, Science and Sports. The National Council for Tertiary Education is the body that advises the Government on higher education policy. The National Accreditation Board (NAB) classifies institutions of higher education as universities, university colleges, polytechnics, colleges, schools, institutes, academies, or tutorial colleges. The NAB is responsible for accrediting private and public institutions of higher education, approving programmes of study, ensuring quality assurance, and determining degree equivalency. Institutions of higher education usually have two-tier systems of governance, consisting of a Council, which oversees administrative issues such as finance and personnel, and either a Senate or Academic Board, which deals with academic issues. The Chancellor is the head of the University.

Admission to university is based on suitable scores in either six subjects at SSSCE (Senior Secondary School Certificate Examinations) level or three subjects at A-level. The main undergraduate degree is the three- to four-year Bachelors, though both University of Ghana and Kwame Nkrumah University of Science and Technology offer two-year Diploma programmes. The Bachelors degree is based on the US-style 'credit' and semester schema, and students are required to accrue a specified number of credits in major and minor subjects in order to graduate. Only the five state-controlled universities offer postgraduate degrees, which include one- to two-year Masters and Postgraduate Diploma programmes and Doctorate programmes lasting a minimum of three years.

The National Co-ordinating Committee for Technical and Vocational Education and Training is the Government body responsible for technical and vocational education. The leading institutions for technical and vocational education are the polytechnics, which were elevated to higher education-level status in 1993. They offer four main qualifications: Vocational Craft Certificate, Advanced Craft Certificate, Diploma, and Higher National Diploma.

Learned Societies

GENERAL

Centre for National Culture: POB 2738, Accra; tel. (21) 664099; f. 1958; to promote and develop the arts and preserve traditional arts; includes a research section; a regional museum is planned; Chair. Nii Ayitey Agbofu II; Dir M. K. Amoatey; publ. *DAWURO*.

Ghana Academy of Arts and Sciences: POB M.32, Accra; tel. (21) 772002; fax (21) 772032; e-mail gaas@ug.edu.gh; internet www.gaas-gh.org; f. 1959; sections of Arts (Chair. Prof. Kwame Gyekye), Sciences (Chair. Prof. Ivan Addae Mensah); 90 Fellows; Pres. Dr S. K. B. Asante; Hon. Sec. Prof. Kwesi Yankah; publ. *Proceedings* (annual).

UNESCO Office Accra: POB CT4949, Accra; located at: 32 Nortei Ababio St, Airport, Residential, Accra; tel. (21) 765497; fax (21) 765498; e-mail accra@unesco.org; designated Cluster Office for Benin, Côte d'Ivoire, Ghana, Nigeria and Togo; Dir Bruno Lefevre.

ARCHITECTURE AND TOWN PLANNING

Ghana Institute of Architects: POB M.272, Accra; fax (21) 229464; e-mail giarch@internet.com.gh; internet www.internet.com.gh/gia; f. 1962; 300 mems; Pres. Kenneth Ampratwum; Hon. Sec. Joseph E. Hayford; publs *Bulletin* (monthly), *Ghana Architect*, *PATO*.

BIBLIOGRAPHY, LIBRARY SCIENCE AND MUSEOLOGY

Ghana Library Association: POB 4105, Accra; tel. (21) 763523; f. 1962; Pres. Helena Asamoah-Hassan; Sec. Angelina Lily Armah; publs *Ghana Library Journal* (annually), *Ghana Library Newsletter*.

ECONOMICS, LAW AND POLITICS

Economic Society of Ghana: c/o Department of Economics, University of Ghana, POB 57, Legon, Accra; f. 1957; 500 mems; publs *Economic Bulletin of Ghana*, *Social and Economic Affairs* (quarterly).

Ghana Bar Association: POB 4150, Accra; tel. and fax (21) 226748; 2,500 mems; Nat. Pres. Paul Adu-Gyamfi; Nat. Sec. Benson Nutsukpui.

EDUCATION

West African Examinations Council: Headquarters Office, POB GP 125, Accra; tel. (21) 237784; fax (21) 222905; e-mail waechqrs@africaonline.com.gh; internet www.waecheadquartersgh.org; f. 1952 by the four West African Commonwealth countries; nat. offices in Lagos, Nigeria; Accra, Ghana; Freetown, Sierra Leone; Banjul, The Gambia; Monrovia, Liberia; conducts the West African Senior School Certificate Examination (WASSCE) for The Gambia, Sierra Leone and Nigeria, Senior Secondary School Certificate Examination (SSSCE) for Ghana, Basic Education Certificate Examination (GABECE) for The Gambia and 9th and 12th grade examinations for Liberia; also selection examinations for entry into secondary schools and similar institutions and the Public Services; entrance and final examinations for teacher training colleges, commercial and technical examinations at the request of the various Ministries of Education; holds examinations on behalf of the United Kingdom examining authorities and the Educational Testing Service, Princeton, NJ, USA; 5 mem. countries; Chair. Prof. Jerome S. Djangmah; Registrar Matthew P. Ndure; publ. *Research Report* (abstracts and findings of research projects conducted by the Council).

HISTORY, GEOGRAPHY AND ARCHAEOLOGY

Ghana Geographical Association: University of Ghana; f. 1955; Pres. Prof. E. V. T. Engmann; Hon. Sec. Dr L. J. Gyamfi-Fenteng; publ. *Bulletin* (annually).

Historical Society of Ghana: POB 12, Legon; f. 1952; formerly Gold Coast and Togoland Historical Soc.; *c*. 600 mems; Pres. T. A. Osae; Sec. R. Addo-Fening; publ. *Transactions* (annually).

LANGUAGE AND LITERATURE

Alliance Française: Liberation Link, Airport Residential Area, POB CT 4904, Accra; tel. (21) 760278; fax (21) 760279; e-mail info@alliancefrancaiseghana.org; internet www.alliancefrancaiseghana.org; offers courses and exams in French language and culture and promotes cultural exchange with France; attached teaching centres in Cape Coast, Kumasi, Takoradi and Tema.

British Council: Liberia Rd, POB GP 771 Accra; tel. (21) 683068; fax (21) 683062; e-mail infoaccra@gh.britishcouncil.org; internet www.britishcouncil.org/ghana; f. 1943; conducts British examinations, supports personal and professional development through physical and electronic resources; projects include school and higher education partnership, leadership training, and Africa 2007; attached centre in Kumasi; library of 4,000 vols, more than 50 periodicals; 1,500 videos and DVDs, electronic resources; Dir Moses Anibaba.

Ghana Association of Writers: POB 4414, Accra; tel. (21) 776586; f. 1957; aims at bringing together all the writers of the country, to protect and champion the interests of Ghanaian writers, to encourage contact with foreign writers, and to foster the development of Ghanaian literature; literary evenings, annual congress, etc.; Pres. Atukwei Okai; Gen. Sec. J. E. Allotey-Pappoe;

publs *Angla* (anthology, annually), *Takra* (monthly newsletter).

Goethe-Institut: 30 Kakramadu Rd, Cantonments, Accra; tel. (21) 776764; fax (21) 779770; e-mail administration@accra.goethe.org; internet www.goethe.de/af/acc/deindex.htm; offers courses and exams in German language and culture and promotes cultural exchange with Germany; library of 4,000 vols; Dir ELEONORE SYLLA.

MEDICINE

Pharmaceutical Society of Ghana: POB 2133, Accra; tel. (21) 228341; fax (21) 239583; e-mail psgh@ighmail.com; f. 1935; aims to advance chemistry and pharmacy and maintain standards of the profession; 8 regional brs; library of 250 vols; 1,200 mems; Pres. JOHN ARTHUR; Hon. Gen. Sec. FRANCIS ABOAGYE-NYAME; publ. *The Ghana Pharmaceutical Journal* (4 a year).

NATURAL SCIENCES

General

Ghana Science Association: POB 7, Legon; tel. (21) 500253; f. 1959; Nat. Pres. Dr P. A. KURANCHIE; Nat. Sec. I. J. KWAME ABOH; publ. *The Ghana Journal of Science*.

West African Science Association: c/o Botany Dept, POB 7, University of Ghana, Legon; f. 1953; mems: Ghana, Nigeria, Sierra Leone, Côte d'Ivoire, Senegal, Togo, Niger, Benin; observers: Burkina Faso, Liberia; Pres. Prof. ANDRÉ DOVI KUEVI; Sec. Dr J. K. B. A. ATA; publ. *Journal* (annually).

RELIGION, SOCIOLOGY AND ANTHROPOLOGY

Ghana Sociological Association: c/o Dept of Sociology, University of Ghana, Legon; f. 1961; financial aid from the universities and the Academy of Arts and Sciences; academic activities, conferences, etc.; 215 mems; Pres. Prof. J. M. ASSIMENG; Sec. E. H. MENDS; publ. *Ghana Journal of Sociology*.

TECHNOLOGY

Ghana Institution of Engineers: POB 7042, Accra-North; tel. (21) 772005; e-mail ghie@ncs.com.gh; f. 1968; 1,000 mems; Pres. Ing. K. OFORI-KURAGO; Exec. Sec. Ing. LAURI LAWSON; publ. *The Ghana Engineer* (quarterly).

Research Institutes

GENERAL

Council for Scientific and Industrial Research (CSIR): POB M.32, Accra; tel. (21) 777651; fax (21) 777655; e-mail csir@ghana.com; internet www.csir.org.gh; f. 1958; functions include advice to the Government, encouragement of scientific and industrial research relevant to national development and commercialization of research results; co-ordination of research in all its aspects in Ghana, and collation, publication and dissemination of research results; library: Institute for Scientific and Technological Information: see Libraries and Archives; Dir-Gen. Prof. E. OWUSU-BENNOAH; Sec. E. ODARTEI-LARYEA; publs *Annual Report*, *CSIR Handbook*, *Ghana Journal of Agricultural Science*, *Ghana Journal of Science*.

Attached research institutes:

Animal Research Institute: POB AH20, Achimota; tel. (21) 401846; fax (21) 511588; e-mail ari@africaonline.com.gh; f. 1957; Dir Dr K. G. ANING.

Building and Road Research Institute: Univ. POB 40, Kumasi; tel. (51) 60064; fax (51) 60080; f. 1952; library of 8,000 vols; Dir K. AMOA-MENSAH.

Crops Research Institute: POB 3785, Kumasi; tel. (51) 60389; fax (51) 60396; e-mail cri@africaonline.com.gh; Dir Rev. Dr J. N. ASAFU-AGYEI.

Food Research Institute: POB M.20, Accra; tel. (21) 761209; fax (21) 777647; e-mail fri@ghana.com; f. 1964; food processing, preservation, storage, analysis, marketing; Dir Dr W. A. PLAHAR; publ. *Bulletin*.

Forestry Research Institute of Ghana: POB 63, KNUST, Kumasi; tel. (51) 60123; fax (51) 60121; e-mail director@forig.org; Dir Dr J. R. COBBINAH; publ. *Ghana Journal of Forestry* (every 2 years).

Oil Palm Research Institute: POB 74, Kade; tel. (803) 610257; fax (803) 610235; f. 1964; Dir Dr T. E. O. ASAMOAH.

Plant Genetic Resources Centre: POB 7, Bunso; tel. (81) 24124; fax (81) 24124; Dir Dr S. O. BENNETT-LARTEY.

Savanna Agricultural Research Institute: POB 52, Tamale; tel. (71) 22411; fax (71) 23483; e-mail sari@africaonline.com.gh; Dir Dr A. B. SALIFU.

Science and Technology Policy Research Institute: POB CT 519, Cantonments, Accra; tel. (21) 773856; fax (21) 773068; e-mail stepri@africaonline.com.gh; Dir Dr J. O. GOGO.

Soil Research Institute: PMB, Academy PO, Kwadaso, Kumasi; tel. (51) 50353; fax (51) 50308; e-mail soils@africaonline.com.gh; f. 1951; Dir Dr R. D. ASIAMAH.

Water Research Institute: POB AH.38, Achimota; tel. (21) 775357; fax (21) 777170; e-mail wri@ghana.com; Dir Dr C. A. BINEY.

AGRICULTURE, FISHERIES AND VETERINARY SCIENCE

Cocoa Research Institute of Ghana: POB 8, New Tafo-Akim; tel. (27) 609900; fax (27) 609901; e-mail crig@crig.org; f. 1938; research on cocoa, cola, coffee, shea nut and cashew; 3 substations; 3 cocoa plantations for research and development of cocoa by-products; library of 15,000 vols, 8,100 pamphlets, 200 journals; Exec. Dir Dr M. R. APPIAH; publs *Annual Report*, *Newsletter*, *Technical Bulletin*.

MEDICINE

Health Laboratory Services: Ministry of Health, POB 300, Accra; f. 1920; laboratory services, public health reference laboratory, reference haematology laboratory, training of laboratory technicians; research on public health microbiology, abnormal haemoglobins and allied subjects; library of 8,000 vols combined with that of the Ghana Medical School; Head E. C. MARBELL.

NATURAL SCIENCES

Physical Sciences

Geological Survey of Ghana: POB M.80, Accra; tel. (21) 228093; fax (21) 228063; e-mail ghgeosur@ghana.com; f. 1913; geological mapping and geophysical surveying of the country, research and evaluation of mineral resources; library of 30,216 vols; Dir CHARLES EDWARD ODURO; publ. *Annual Report*.

Ghana Meteorological Services Department: POB 87, Legon; f. 1937; serves civil and military aviation, agriculture, forestry, engineering and medical research; 409 mems; Dir S. E. TANDOH; publs numerous regular and irregular reports.

Libraries and Archives

Accra

Accra Central Library: Thorpe Rd, POB 2362, Accra; tel. (21) 665083; f. 1950; central reference library; central lending library; central children's library; mobile library unit; union catalogues; Regional Librarian SUSANNAH MINYILA.

George Padmore Research Library on African Affairs: POB 2970, Accra; tel. (21) 223526; fax (21) 247768; e-mail padmoreresib@yahoo.co.uk; internet www.ghana.com.gh/padmore; f. 1961; collection, processing and dissemination of recorded literature related to history, culture, anthropology, economics, law and public administration of all Africa; incl. Ghana National Collection; 52,651 vols, 80 periodicals; Librarian OMARI MENSAH TENKORANG; publs *Ghana National Bibliography* (6 a year and annually), *special subject bibliographies* (irregular).

Ghana Library Board: POB 663, Accra; tel. (21) 662795; f. 1950; comprises Accra Central Library, regional libraries at Kumasi, Sekondi, Ho, Tamale, Bolgatanga, Cape Coast, Koforidua, Sunyani, Research Library on African Affairs (*q.v.*); 37 branch libraries, mobile libraries, children's libraries; research library 35,029 vols, adults' libraries 1,167,653 vols, children's libraries; 1,383,712 vols; Dir of Library Services DAVID CORNELIUS.

Institute for Scientific and Technological Information (INSTI): POB M.32, Accra; tel. (21) 778808; fax (21) 777655; e-mail insti@ghana.com; internet www.csir.org.gh; f. 1964; attached to Council for Scientific and Industrial Research; 21,873 vols, 60 current periodicals; publishes Union List of Scientific and Technological Journals in Ghana and Union List of Agricultural Serials in Ghana; Dir CLEMENT ENTSUA-MENSAH; publs *Gains News* (4 a year), *Ghana Journal of Agricultural Science* (2 a year), *Ghana Journal of Science* (2 a year), *Ghana Science Abstracts* (annually), *Ghastinet Newsletter* (4 a year).

Public Records and Archives Administration Department: POB 3056, Accra; e-mail praad@4u.com.gh; internet www.praad.gov.gh; f. 1946 as National Archives of Ghana (legal recognition 1955); preserves Ghana's historical records; regional offices in Kumasi, Cape Coast, Sekondi, Tamale, Sunyani, Koforidua and Ho; 128 staff; Dir C. A. AZANGWEO; publs *Brochure*, *Class Lists of the Holdings of PRAAD*.

Kumasi

Ashanti Regional Library: Bantama Rd, POB 824, Kumasi; tel. (51) 2784; f. 1954; lending, reference and extension services for adults, students and schoolchildren; 20,000 vols, incl. local collection on Ghana of 450 vols; Librarian KOFI S. ANTIRI.

Kwame Nkrumah University of Science and Technology Library: University PO, Kumasi; tel. (51) 60133; fax (51) 60358; e-mail library@knust.edu.gh; internet www.knust.edu.gh; f. 1951; 202,810 vols, 340 periodicals, 9,000 e-journals; Librarian H. R. ASAMOAH-HASSAN.

Legon

University of Ghana Library (Balme Library): POB 24, Legon; tel. (21) 512407; fax (21) 502701; e-mail balme@ug.edu.gh; f. 1948; 367,896 vols; comprises Arabic, United Nations, World Bank, Africana, Braille, Volta Basin Research Project collections and Students' Reference libraries; Librarian Prof. A. A. ALEMNA; publ. *Library Bulletin*.

Sekondi

Western Regional Library: Old Axim Rd, POB 174, Sekondi; tel. (31) 46816; f. 1955; 41,480 vols; Librarian S. Y. KWANSA.

Museums and Art Galleries

Accra

Ghana National Museum: Barnes Rd, POB 3343, Accra; tel. (21) 221633; f. 1957; controlled by the Ghana Museums and Monuments Board; archaeological and ethnological finds from all over Ghana and West Africa; modern works by Ghanaian artists; the preservation and conservation of ancient forts and castles and traditional buildings; the achievement of man in Africa; Dir I. N. DEBRAH (acting).

Museum of Science and Technology: POB 3343, Accra; tel. (21) 223963; fax (21) 234843; e-mail gmmb_acc@africaonline.com.gh; f. 1965; a temporary exhibition hall with an open-air cinema is used for the display of working models, charts, films and other exhibits on science and technology; collection of exhibits for permanent galleries has begun; temporary exhibitions are taken to the regions, films shown to colleges and schools and regional and national Science Fairs are organized; Principal Curator K. A. ADDISON.

Cape Coast

Cape Coast Castle Museum: POB 281, Cape Coast; tel. (42) 32701; fax (42) 30264; e-mail ghct@ghana.com; f. 1971; cultural history of Ghana's Central region; Senior Curator ALBERT WUDDAH-MARTEY.

Universities

KWAME NKRUMAH UNIVERSITY OF SCIENCE AND TECHNOLOGY

University PO, KumasiTelephone: (51) 60351
Fax: (51) 60137
E-mail: ustlib@ust.gn.apc.org
Internet: www.knust.edu.gh

Founded 1951 as College of Technology, University status 1961
Language of instruction: English
State control
Academic year: October to June (2 semesters)

Chancellor (vacant)
Vice-Chancellor: Prof. JOHN SEFA KWADWO AYIM
Pro-Vice-Chancellor: Prof. E. Y. SAFO
Registrar: SOPHIA QUASHIE-SAM
Librarian: HELENA ASAMOAH-HASSAN

Number of teachers: 487
Number of students: 11,633

Publication: *Journal of the University of Science and Technology*

DEANS

Faculty of Agriculture: Prof. D. B. OKAI
Faculty of Environmental and Development Studies: Prof. K. K. ADARKWA
Faculty of Pharmacy: Prof. A. K. ABAITEY
Faculty of Science: (vacant)
Faculty of Social Sciences: Prof. A. A. SACKEY
Board of Postgraduate Studies: Prof. ANTHONY A. ADIMADO
College of Art: Dr K. EDUSEI
School of Engineering: Prof. K. A. ANDAM
School of Medical Science: Prof. E. TSIRI AGBENYEGA

DIRECTORS

Bureau of Integrated Rural Development: (vacant)
Centre for Cultural Studies: VESTA ADU-GYAMFI
Distance Education: P. ADOLINAMA
Institute of Land Management and Development: Prof. S. O. ASIAMA
Institute of Mining and Mineral Engineering: Dr E. K. ASIAM
Institute of Renewable Natural Resources: Dr FRIMPONG-MENSAH
Institute of Technical Education: P. ADOLINAMA
Technology Consultancy Centre: PETER DONKOR
Western University College, Tarkwa: Prof. MIREKU-GYIMAH (Provost)

PROFESSORS

ANDAM, K. A., Civil Engineering
BROBBY, G. W., Ear, Eye, Nose and Throat Surgery
KASANGA, K., Land Economy
OSEI, S. A., Animal Science
OWUSU-SARPONG, A. K., Languages
SARPONG, K., Pharmacy
TUAH, A. K., Animal Science

UNIVERSITY OF CAPE COAST

University PO, Cape Coast
Telephone: (42) 32480
Fax: (42) 32485
E-mail: vcucc@yahoo.com
Internet: www.ucc.edu.gh

Founded 1962
Language of instruction: English
State control
Academic year: August to June (2 semesters)

Chancellor: Dr SAM ESSON JONAH
Pro-Chancellor: Dr CHARLES MENSA
Vice-Chancellor: Prof. E. A. OBENG
Pro-Vice-Chancellor: Prof. K. YANKSON
Registrar: S. KOFI OHENE
Librarian: ALFRED K. MARTEY

Number of teachers: 300
Number of students: 11,637

Publications: *ASEMKA* (Faculty of Arts, 2 a year), *Journal of Educational Management* (IEPA, 2 a year), *Journal of the Institute of Education* (IEPA, 2 a year), *Journal of Social Sciences* (Faculty of Social Sciences, 2 a year), *Oguaa Educator* (Faculty of Education, 2 a year), *Primary Teacher* (Dept of Primary Education, 2 a year)

DEANS

Faculty of Arts: Prof. D. D. KUUPOLE
Faculty of Education: Dr J. A. OPARE (acting)
Faculty of Science: Prof. V. P. Y. GADZEKPO
Faculty of Social Sciences: Prof. K. AWUSABO-ASARE
School of Agriculture: Prof. P. K. TURKSON
Graduate Studies: Prof. JANE NAANA OPOKU AGYEMANG

HEADS OF DEPARTMENTS

Faculty of Arts (tel. (42) 34073):

- Classics and Philosophy: J. A. AKAAH-ENNIN (acting)
- English: Prof. NAANA J. OPOKU-AGYEMANG
- French: Dr D. D. KUUPOLE (acting)
- Ghanaian Languages: EDOH TORGAH (acting)
- History: H. K. O. ASAMOAH (acting)
- Music: Prof. N. N. KOFIE
- Religious Studies: Rev. Dr. B. A. NTREH (acting)

Faculty of Education (tel. (42) 34810; fax (42) 35545):

- Arts and Social Sciences Education: E. T. AMUNAH-SEKYI (acting)
- Educational Foundations: Dr J. A. OPARE (acting)
- Health, Physical Education and Recreation: Dr S. L. LAMPTEY (acting)
- Primary Education: C. B. DUEDU (acting)
- Science Education: R. QUARCOO-NELSON (acting)
- Vocational and Technical Education: Dr H. F. AKPLU (acting)

Faculty of Science (tel. (42) 36932; fax (42) 32095):

- Botany: Dr E. C. QUAYE (acting)
- Chemistry: Prof. V. P. Y. GADZEKPO
- Computer Centre: D. OBUOBI (acting)
- Laboratory Technology: Prof. JOHN BLAY, JR
- Laser and Fibre-Optic Centre: Dr P. K. BUAH-BASSUAH
- Mathematics and Statistics: Dr B. K. GORDOR (acting)
- Optometry: Prof. HARUNA YAKUBU
- Physics: Prof. S. YEBOAH-MENSAH
- Zoology: Prof. KOBINA YANKSON

Faculty of Social Sciences (tel. (42) 34072; fax (42) 34072; e-mail csucc@ncs.com.gh):

- African and General Studies: Dr J. V. MENSAH (acting)
- Business Studies: EDWARD MARFO-YIADOM (acting)
- Economics: Dr VIJAY BHASIN (acting)
- Geography and Tourism: Prof. K. AWUSABO-ASARE
- Sociology: Dr MANSAH PRAH

School of Agriculture (tel. (42) 32709; fax (42) 33793; e-mail ieucc@africaonline.com.gh):

- Department of Agricultural Economics and Extension: Dr J. A. KWARTENG (acting)
- Department of Agricultural Engineering: D. L. LAMPTEY (acting)
- Department of Animal Science: Prof. P. K. TURKSON
- Department of Crop Science: Dr A. A. ADDOQUAYE (acting)
- Department of Soil Science: Prof. B. A. OSEI (acting)

School of Biological Sciences:

- Entomology and Wildlife, and Human Biology: Prof. KOBINA YANKSON
- Environmental Science and Biochemistry: Prof. E. C. QUAYE
- Fisheries and Aquaria Sciences: Prof. KOBINA YANKSON
- Molecular Biotechnology: Prof. E. C. QUAYE

DIRECTORS

Centre for Development Studies: Dr S. B. KENDIE (acting)
Centre for Research on Improving the Quality of Primary Education in Ghana: J. M. DZINYELA
Institute of Education: Dr A. K. AKYEMPONG (acting)
Institute for Educational Planning and Administration: Dr A. L. DARE (acting)

UNIVERSITY COLLEGE OF EDUCATION

POB 25, Winneba
Telephone: (432) 22269
Fax: (432) 22268
E-mail: ucew@ug.gn.apc.org

Founded 1992 by merger of 7 colleges
State Control

Vice-Chancellor: JOPHUS ANAMUAH-MENSAH

Library of 65,011 , 567 periodicals
Number of teachers: 205
Number of students: 2,600

Publications: *Ghana Educational Media and Technology Association Journal*, *Journal of Special Education*

DEANS

Applied Arts and Technology: J. K. N. SACKEY
General Culture and Social Studies: S. M. QUARTEY
Languages: L. KORANTENG
Science: H. A. BROWN-ACQUAYE
Specialized and Professional Studies in Education: J. K. ABOAGYE

ATTACHED RESEARCH INSTITUTES

Centre for Basic Education: Co-ordinator R. ESHUN.

Centre for Educational Policy Studies.

Centre for Educational Resources: Co-ordinator R. K. BINEY.

Centre for School and Community Science and Technology Studies.

Institute of Educational Development and Extension: Dir S. K. E. MENSAH.

UNIVERSITY FOR DEVELOPMENT STUDIES

POB 1350, Tamale
Telephone: (71) 22078
Fax: (71) 22369

Founded 1992
State control
Academic year: September to July (three semesters)

Vice-Chancellor: Prof. JOHN B. K. KABURISE (acting)
Pro-Vice-Chancellor: Rev. Prof. SAA DITTOH
Registrar: F. O. AKUFFO
Librarian: I. K. ANTWI

Library of 21,342 vols
Number of teachers: 122
Number of students: 3,991

Publications: *Academic Calendar* (every 5 years), *Faculties and Departments at a Glance* (every 2 years), *Strategic Plan* (every 5 years)

DEANS

Faculty of Agriculture: Dr THOMAS BAYORBOR
Faculty of Applied Sciences: Dr W. M. KPIKPI
Faculty of Integrated Development Studies: Dr DANIEL BAGAH
School of Medicine and Health Sciences: Dr ROWLAND OTCHEWEMAH (acting)
Postgraduate Centre: Dr DAVID MILLAR

UNIVERSITY OF GHANA

POB 25, Legon, Accra
Telephone: (21) 501967
Fax: (21) 502701
E-mail: pad@ug.gn.ape.org
Internet: www.ug.edu.gh

Founded 1948 as University College of Ghana; University status 1961
Language of instruction: English
Academic year: September to June
State control

Vice-Chancellor: Prof. CLIFFORD N. B. TAGOE (acting)
Pro-Vice-Chancellor: Prof. KWESI YANKAH (acting)
Director of Finance: J. E. MINLAH
Registrar: A. T. KONU
Librarian: Prof. A. ALEMNA

Number of teachers: 766
Number of students: 27,414

Publications: *Annual Report*, *Basic Statistics*, *Campus Update*, *Newsfile*, *Universitas*

DEANS

Faculty of Arts: Prof. KWESI YANKAH
Faculty of Law: Prof. NII ASHIE KOTEY
Faculty of Science: Prof. GEORGE ODAMTTEN
Faculty of Social Studies: Prof. ATU AYEE
College of Agriculture: ANNA BARNES
School of Administration: Prof. J. K. A. POKU (acting)
Business School: Prof. KOFI NTI
Dental School: Dr N. O. NARTEY (acting)
Medical School: Prof. R. B. BIRITWUM (acting)
Graduate Studies: Prof. JACOB SONGSORE
International Educational Programmes: Prof. S. SEFA-DEDEH

PROFESSORS

ADDAE, S. K., Physiology
ADDAE-MENSAH, I., Chemistry
ADDO, S. T., Geography and Resource Development
ADU-GYAMFI, Y., Anaesthesia
AHENKORAH, Y., Crop Science
AKYEAMPONG, D. A., Mathematics
ALEMNA, A. A., Information Studies
AMOAH, A. G. B., Medicine and Therapeutics
AMUZU, J. K. A., Physics
ANTESON, R. K., Microbiology
ANYIDOHO, K., English
APT, N. A., Sociology
ARCHAMPONG, E. Q., Surgery
ARDAYFIO-SCHANDORF, E., Geography and Resource Development
ASENSO-OKYERE, K., Institute of Statistical, Social and Economic Research
ASHITEY, G. A., Community Health
ASSIMENG, J. M., Sociology
ASSOKU, R. K. G., Animal Science
AYERTEY, J. N., Crop Science
AYETTEY, A. S., Anatomy
AYETTEY, E., Institute of Statistical, Social and Economic Research
AYISI, N. K., Noguchi Institute for Medical Research
BADOE, E. A., Surgery
BAETA, R. D., Physics
BENNEH, G., Geography and Resource Development
BOADI, L. A., Linguistics
BRITWUM, K., French
CLERK, G. C., Botany
COKER, W. Z., Zoology
DANSO, S. K. A., Soil Science
DOKU, E. V., Crop Science
FYNN, J. K., History
GYASI, E. A., Geography and Resource Development
KROPP DAKUBU, M. E., Sociolinguistics
MINGLE, J. A. A., Microbiology
NEEQUAYE, J. E., Child Health
NKRUMAH, F. K., Paediatrics
NUKUNYA, G. K., Sociology
ODURO, K. A., Anaesthesia
OFORI-AMANKWAH, E. H., Law
OFORI-SARPONG, E., Law
OFOSU-AMAAH, S., School of Public Health
OLIVER-COMMEY, J. O., Child Health
OWUSU, S. K., Medicine and Therapeutics
SEFA-DEDEH, S., Nutrition and Food Science
TAGOE, C. N. B., Anatomy
TETTEH, G. K., Physics
YANKAH, K., Linguistics
YANKSON, P. W. K., Geography and Resource Development
YEBOAH, E. D., Surgery

ATTACHED INSTITUTES

Institute of Adult Education: POB 31, Legon, Accra; Dir R. A. AGGOR.

Institute of African Studies: POB 73, Legon, Accra; Dir Prof. T. MANUH (acting).

Institute of Statistical, Social and Economic Research: POB 74, Legon, Accra; Dir Prof. E. ARYEETEY.

Legon Centre for International Affairs: Legon, Accra; Dir Prof. K. KUMADO (acting).

Noguchi Memorial Institute for Medical Research: POB 25, Legon, Accra; f. 1979; international centre for basic and applied research; Dir Prof. D. OFORI-ADJEI; Provost Rev. Prof. A. S. AYETTEY (acting).

Regional Institute for Population Studies: POB 96, Legon, Accra; f. 1972 with UN aid; Dir Dr S. O. KWANKYE (acting).

Regional Training Centre for Archivists: POB 60, Legon, Accra; Head C. O. KISIEDU.

School of Communication Studies: POB 53, Legon, Accra; Dir Prof. K. ANSU-KYEREMEH.

School of Performing Arts: POB 19, Legon, Accra; Dir Prof. M. OWUSU.

School of Public Health: POB 13, Legon, Accra; Dir Dr I. QUAKYI (acting).

United Nations University Institute for Natural Resources in Africa: Private Mail Bag, Kotoka International Airport, Accra; Dir Dr UZO MOKWUNYE.

Volta Basin Research Project: Legon, Accra; Chair. Prof. S. G. K. ADIKU.

AGRICULTURAL RESEARCH STATIONS

Agricultural Research Station, Accra: POB 38, Legon, Accra; Officer-in-Charge Dr E. A. CANACOO.

Agricultural Research Station, Kade: POB 43, Kade; Officer-in-Charge Dr J. K. OSEI.

Agricultural Research Station, Kpong: POB 9, Kpong; Officer-in-Charge Dr E. O. DARKWA.

Colleges

Accra Polytechnic: POB GP 561, Accra; tel. (21) 662263; fax (21) 664797; f. 1949; technical and vocational education with practical research programmes in manufacturing, commerce, science and technology; from technician to higher national diploma level; library: 15,800 vols; 340 teachers; 6,400 students; Principal Prof. RALPH K. ASABERE.

Accra Technical Training Centre: POB M.177, Accra; f. 1966; attached to Ministry of Education; to train tradesmen for industry and civil service; number of students: 350; library: 10,500 vols; Principal T. K. ADZEI.

Ghana Institute of Management and Public Administration: Greenhill, POB 50, Achimota; tel. (21) 405805; fax (21) 405805; f. 1961; research, consultancy, human resource development, strategic studies and policy analysis and postgraduate studies, diploma, certificate and master's degree programmes; 30 teachers; library: 50,000 vols; Dir-Gen. Dr STEPHEN ADEI; publs *Greenhill Case Studies Book*, *Administrators' Digest*, *Greenhill Journal of Administration* (2 a year), *GIMPA News* (4 a year), *Ghana Economic Outlook* (2 a year).

Ho Polytechnic: POB 217, Ho, Volta Region; tel. (91) 26456; fax (91) 28398; e-mail gafeti@africaonline.com.gh; f. 1968; training of middle-level management personnel and technicians to HND standard; library: 13,000 vols; 100 teachers; 2,500 students; Principal Dr G. M. AFETI; Registrar F. K. DZINEKU.

Koforidua Technical Institute: POB 323, Koforidua; f. 1960; 9 teachers; 206 students; library: 2,000 vols; Principal P. C. NOI.

Kpandu Technical Institute: Technical Division, POB 76, Kpandu, Volta Region; tel. Kpandu 22; f. 1956; 70 teachers; 689 students; library: 4,000 vols; Principal J. Y. VODZI.

National Film and Television Institute (NAFTI): PMB, GPO, Accra; tel. (21) 777610; fax (21) 774522; e-mail nafti@ghana.com; f. 1978 by Government decree; 4-year Bachelor of Fine Arts degree courses in film and television production with special emphasis on the production of educational programmes, and feature, informative, animation, documentary and industrial films; mem. of CILECT, Int. Assn. of Film and Television Schools; receives financial help from public funds and technical assistance from NGOs and Unesco; 2-year diploma courses in film and television production; exchange programmes; 68 students; library: specialized library of 51,000 vols; Dir MARTIN LOH; publ. *NAFTI Concept*.

Sunyani Polytechnic: POB 206, Sunyani; tel. (61) 23278; fax (61) 24921; e-mail spolytec@ghana.com.gh; f. 1967 as Technical Institute; present name and status 1997; technical and business education, electrical and electronic engineering, hotel, catering and institutional management, secretaryship and management studies; accredited by International Professional Managers Association (IPMA—UK) and Charted Institute of Marketing (UK); library: 11,020 vols; 180 teachers; 4,528 students; Principal Dr KWASI NSIAH-GYABAA; Sec. S. A. OBOUR.

Takoradi Polytechnic: POB 256, Takoradi; tel. (31) 22918; fax (31) 25256; f. 1955; 130 teachers; 4,500 students; library: 10,250 vols, 48 periodicals; Principal Dr SAMUEL OBENG APORI; Sec. KOFI MANUKURE-HENAKU.

West Africa Computer Science Institute: POB 1643, Mamprobi, Accra; tel. (21) 229927; fax (21) 229575; e-mail wacsi@internetghana.com; f. 1988; independent college providing training in computers, accounting and related fields; 10 teachers; 300 students; Pres. AIKINS BRIGHT KUMI; Principal LAWRENCE NYARKO.

GREECE

The Higher Education System

The country's first universities were established shortly after Greece secured its independence from Ottoman Turkish rule in 1830. Ethniko Metsovio Polytechneio (National Technical University of Athens) was founded in 1836 and both Anotati Scholi Kalon Technon (Athens School of Fine Art) and Ethnikon Kai Kapodistriakon Panepistimion Athinon (National and Capodistrian University of Athens) were founded in 1837. Institutions of higher education are separated into two categories, Anotera Ekpedeftika Idrimata (AEI) and Technologika Ekpedeftika Idrimata (TEI). AEIs are university-level institutions, which encompass universities, polytechneia (technical universities), and the Athens School of Fine Art. TEIs are technological higher education institutions, which were officially upgraded to university status in 2001 but are still regarded as distinct from AEIs. There are 19 AEIs in Greece. Overall responsibility for higher education lies with the Ministry of National Education and Religious Affairs, and the Constitution stipulates that only public institutions may provide higher education. AEIs and TEIs are autonomous institutions.

Admission to higher education is on the basis of the Apolyterio, the leading secondary school certificate, and Vevaiosi Provasis, a certificate of access to higher education which is calculated according to scores in the Apolyterio. Although Greece is a signatory to the Bologna Process it has yet to implement the required reforms; however, the traditional degree system does consist of three stages. In both AEIs and TEIs the main degree is the Ptychio, which is a four-year programme of study in most subjects, but in some subjects last five years (engineering, agriculture, veterinary studies, dentistry and architecture) and in medicine lasts six years. To take postgraduate degrees students holding the Ptychio must undergo a selection process or sit examinations. The first postgraduate degree is the Metaptychiakon Spoudon, which lasts two years and is broadly equivalent to the Masters. Finally, the Didaktor is a doctoral-level degree awarded following a period of research and submission of a thesis.

The establishment of private institutions of higher education is forbidden by Greek law and qualifications offered by private institutions are not regarded as equivalent to qualifications from public institutions. However, private institutions may operate as laboratories of liberal science, purely with a view to providing education related to the arts and professional studies.

Technical and vocational education is overseen by different government bodies, notably the Ministry of National Education and Religious Affairs, the Organization of Vocational Education and the Ministry of Labour, Employment and Manpower Organization. The Organization of Vocational Education runs Institutes of Vocational Training, which offer courses of study leading to the award of diplomas. The Employment and Manpower Organization has a National Council for vocational training which oversees apprenticeships and on-the-job training.

Learned Societies

GENERAL

Akadimia Athinon (Academy of Athens): Odos Panepistimiou 28, 10679 Athens; tel. 210-3601163; fax 210-3634806; e-mail info@academyofathens.gr; internet www.academyofathens.gr; f. 1926; sections of Literature and Fine Arts (Pres. K. Svolopoulos), Moral and Political Sciences (Pres. I. Zizioulas) and Positive Sciences (Pres. K. Kribas); 223 mems (50 ordinary, 25 foreign, 144 corresp., 4 hon.); attached research institutes: see Research Institutes; library: see Libraries and Archives; Pres. Konstantinos Stefanis; Sec.-Gen. Nikolaos Matsaniotis; publ. *Praktika* (Proceedings, annually).

BIBLIOGRAPHY, LIBRARY SCIENCE AND MUSEOLOGY

Enosi Ellinon Vivliothikonomon kai Epistimon Pliroforisis (EEBEP) (Greek Association of Librarians and Information Scientists): Themistocleus 73, 106 83 Athens; tel. 210-3302128; fax 210-3302128; e-mail info@eeb.gr; internet eeb.gr; f. 1968; 500 mems; Pres. George Yannakopoulos; Gen. Sec. Maria Marinopoulou; publ. magazine.

EDUCATION

Hellenic Association of University Women: 44a Voulis St, 105 57 Athens; tel. 210-3234268; Pres. Irene Dilari; Sec.-Gen. Flora Kamari.

Syllogos pros Diadosin ton Hellenikon Grammaton (Society for the Promotion of Greek Education): Odos Pindarou 15 (136), Athens; f. 1869; 9 mems; Pres. Philip Dragoumis; Sec.-Gen. Alexandratos Panayiotis.

FINE AND PERFORMING ARTS

Enosis Hellinon Mousourgon (Union of Greek Composers): Deinokratous 35, 106 76 Athens; tel. and fax 210-7256607; e-mail gcu@otenet.gr; internet www.gcu.org.gr; f. 1931; 200 mems; Pres. Theodore Antoniou; Sec.-Gen. Iossif Papadatos.

Epimelitirion Ikastikon Technon Ellados (Chamber of Fine Arts): 14 Koletti St, 106 81 Athens; tel. 210-3301206; fax 210-3301408; e-mail chafartg@otenet.gr; f. 1945; promotion of the fine arts, support for artists, organizes exhibitions in Greece and abroad, organizes conferences, etc.; 3,100 mems; library of 2,000 vols; Pres. Michalis Papadakis.

HISTORY, GEOGRAPHY AND ARCHAEOLOGY

Archaeologiki Hetairia (Archaeological Society): Odos Panepistimiou 22, 106 72 Athens; tel. 210-3609689; fax 210-3644996; e-mail archetai@otenet.gr; internet www.archetai.gr; f. 1837; 401 mems; library of 118,500 vols; Pres. Epaminondas Spiliotopoulos; Sec.-Gen. Basil Petrakos; publs *O Mentor* (quarterly), *Archaeologiki Ephimeris* (annually), *Praktika* (annually), *Ergon* (annually).

Hellenic Geographical Society: 11 Voucourestiou St, 106 71 Athens; tel. 210-3631112; f. 1919; 148 mems; Pres. Dimitrios Dimitriadis; Gen. Sec. George Ivantchos; publ. *Bulletin*.

Historical and Ethnological Society of Greece: Old Parliament, Stadiou St, 105 61 Athens; tel. 210-3237617; fax 210-3213786; e-mail info@nhmuseum.gr; internet www.culture.gr; f. 1882; Pres. Constantinos Tsamados; Sec.-Gen. Ioannis C. Mazarakis-Aenian.

LANGUAGE AND LITERATURE

Etairia Ellinon Logotechnon (Society of Greek Men of Letters): 8 Gennadiou St and Acadimias, 106 78 Athens; tel. 210-3634559; f. 1934; 700 mems; Pres. Paul Nathanail; Sec. E. Anagnostaki-Tzavara.

Etairia Ellinon Theatricon Syngrapheon (Greek Playwrights' Society): Asklipiou St 33, 10 680 Athens; tel. 210-3232472; e-mail eeths@otenet.gr; internet www.eeths.gr; f. 1908; 120 mems; Pres. Giorgos Lazaridis; Sec. Giorgos Christofilakis.

British Council: 17 Kolonaki Sq., 106 73 Athens; tel. 210-3692333; fax 210-3614658; e-mail customerservices@britishcouncil.gr; internet www.britishcouncil.org/greece; teaching centre; offers courses and exams in English language and British culture and promotes cultural exchange with the UK; attached office in Thessaloniki; f. 1939; Dir Desmond Lauder.

Goethe-Institut: Omirou 14–16, POB 30383, 100 33 Athens; tel. 210-3661000; fax 210-3643518; e-mail info@athen.goethe.org; internet www.goethe.de/om/ath/deindex.htm; offers courses and exams in German language and culture and promotes cultural exchange with Germany; attached centre in Thessaloniki; library of 15,000 vols; Dir and Regional Head of Operations Horst Deinwallner.

Instituto Cervantes: Skoufá 31, 106 73 Athens; tel. 210-3634117; fax 210-3647233; e-mail cenate@cervantes.es; internet atenas.cervantes.es; offers courses and exams in Spanish language and culture and promotes cultural exchange with Spain and Spanish-speaking Latin and Central America; library of 11,000 vols; Dir NATIVIDAD GÁLVEZ GARCÍA.

NATURAL SCIENCES

Mathematical Sciences

Elliniki Mathimatiki Eteria (Greek Mathematical Society): Odos Panepistimiou 34, 106 79 Athens; tel. 210-3616532; fax 210-3641025; e-mail info@hms.gr; internet www.hms.gr; f. 1918; 15,000 mems; library of 2,000 vols; seminars, lectures, summer schools, educational policy; Pres. Prof. NIC ALEXANDRIS; Gen. Sec. JOHN TYRLIS; publs *Astrolavos* (Informatics Review, 2 a year), *Deltion* (Bulletin, annually), *Euclides* (4 a year), *Mathimatiki Epitheorissi* (Review, 2 a year).

Physical Sciences

Enosis Ellinon Chimikon (Association of Greek Chemists): 27 Odos Kanningos, 106 82 Athens; tel. 210-3621524; e-mail info@eex.gr; internet www.eex.gr; official advisor to the state on matters relating to chemistry; promotes the chemical science in industry, education and research; protects the benefits and the professional rights of chemist; f. 1924; 14,000 mems; library of 5,000 vols, 100 periodicals; Pres. P. HAMAKIOTIS; Gen. Sec. D. PSOMAS; publs *ChemBioChem*, *Chemistry, A European Journal*, *ChemPhysChem*, *European Journal of Inorganic Chemistry*, *European Journal of Organic Chemistry*.

TECHNOLOGY

Elliniki Epitropi Atomikis Energhias (Greek Atomic Energy Commission): POB 60092, 153 10 Aghia Paraskevi, Athens; tel. 210-6506748; fax 210-6533939; internet www.eeae.gr; independent service, supervised by the General Secretariat of Research and Technology (GSRT), under the Ministry of Development; responsible for nuclear power and technology issues and for the protection of the population, workers and environment from the ionization and artificially produced non-ionizing radiation; f. 1954; Pres. Prof. LEONIDAS CAMARINOPOULOS.

Research Institutes

GENERAL

Ethnikon Idryma Erevnon (National Hellenic Research Foundation): 48 Vassileos Constantinou Ave, 116 35 Athens; tel. 210-7273500; fax 210-7246618; internet www.eie.gr; f. 1958; carries out basic and applied research in its own institutes (humanities, natural sciences); library of 2,000 periodicals; Euronet facilities; specialized libraries attached to the humanities institutes; Nat. Documentation Centre: see Libraries and Archives; Dir Prof. DIMITRIOS A. KYRIAKIDIS.

Attached research institutes:

Institute of Biological Research and Biotechnology: 48 Vassileos Constantinou Ave, 116 35 Athens; tel. 210-7273759; fax 210-7273758; e-mail kolisis@eie.gr; internet www.eie.gr/nhrf/institutes/ibrb/index-en.html; Dir Prof. FRAGISKOS KOLISIS (acting).

Institute for Byzantine Research: 48 Vassileos Constantinou Ave, 116 35 Athens; tel. 210-7273619; fax 210-7273629; e-mail tkolias@eie.gr; internet www.eie.gr/nhrf/institutes/ibr/index-en.html; f. 1959; uses archival, literary and archaeological sources for Byzantine cultural history and daily life in the Greek Middle Ages, the relations of Byzantium with the peoples of the Balkans, the East Mediterranean and the West, and the historical geography and historical demography of the Greek world; organizes int. symposia and academic meetings; library of 33,500 vols, microfilm colln of archive material; Dir Prof. TAXIARCHIS KOLIAS; publs *Symmeikta* (annual), *Byzantium Today*.

Institute of Greek and Roman Antiquity: 48 Vassileos Constantinou Ave, 116 35 Athens; tel. 210-7273675; fax 210-7234145; e-mail mhatzkop@eie.gr; internet www.eie.gr/nhrf/institutes/igra/index-en.html; f. 1979; Dir MILTIADES HATZOPOULOS.

Institute for Neohellenic Research: 48 Vassileos Constantinou Ave, 116 35 Athens; tel. 210-7273556; fax 210-7246212; e-mail kne@eie.gr; internet www.eie.gr/nhrf/institutes/inr/index-en.html; f. 1960; Dir Prof. PASCHALIS M. KITROMILIDES; publs *Historical Review* (annual), *Tetradia Ergasias* (annual).

Institute of Organic and Pharmaceutical Chemistry: 48 Vassileos Constantinou Ave, 116 35 Athens; tel. 210-7273868; fax 210-7273831; e-mail ngo@eie.gr; internet www.eie.gr/nhrf/institutes/iopc/index-en.html; f. 1979; research in the fields of organic and organometallic chemistry, pharmaceutical chemistry, structural biology and chemistry, computational chemistry and molecular analysis; carries out the rational design, synthesis, and evaluation of molecules against major diseases with an emphasis on type 2 diabetes, cancer, inflammation and neurodegeneration; Sec. MARIA KALATZI.

Institute of Theoretical and Physical Chemistry: 48 Vassileos Constantinou Ave, 116 35 Athens; tel. 210-7273792; fax 210-7273794; e-mail eikam@eie.gr; internet www.eie.gr/nhrf/institutes/tpci/index-en.html; Dir EFSTRATIOS KAMITSOS.

AGRICULTURE, FISHERIES AND VETERINARY SCIENCE

Benakio Phytopathologiko Institouto (Benaki Phytopathological Institute): 8 Odos Delta, 145 61 Kiphissia, Athens; tel. 210-2128002; fax 210-8077506; e-mail admin1@bpi.gr; internet www.bpi.gr; f. 1930; phytopathology, entomology, agricultural zoology, pesticides; 21 laboratories; museum of zoological and entomological specimens, including 22,000 species, and culture collns; library of 11,000 vols, 30,000 pamphlets, 1,400 current periodicals; Dir Dr A. S. ALIVIZATOS; publ. *Annals* (English edition; irreg.).

Hellenic Centre for Marine Research: POB 712, 190 13 Anavissos, Attica; tel. 229-1076466; fax 229-1076323; internet www.hcmr.gr; f. 1965 as National Centre for Marine Research (NCMR); merged with Institute of Marine Biology of Crete (IMBC) 2003; marine and freshwater fisheries and biology, marine geology and geophysics; operates research vessels, and a hydrobiological research station (with aquarium and museum) on Rhodes; library of 3,000 vols, 541 periodicals; Dir and Pres. Prof. GEORGIOS CHRONIS; publ. *Mediterranean Marine Science* (2 a year).

Attached research institutes:

Institute of Aquaculture: Limani Irakleiou, POB 2214, Heraklion; tel. 2810-346860; fax 2810-241882; Dir Dr PASCAL DIVANACH.

Institute of Inland Waters: POB 712, 190 13 Anavyssos; tel. 22910-76458; fax 22910-76323; Dir Dr ARISTIDIS DIAPOULIS.

Institute of Marine Biological Resources: Agios Kosmas, 166 10 Athens; tel. 210-9821354; fax 210-9811713; Dir Dr K. PAPACONSTANTINOU.

Institute of Marine Biology/Genetics: Gournes Pediados, POB 2214, Heraklion; tel. 2810-337806; fax 2810-337822; Dir Dr A. MAGOULAS.

Institute of Oceanography: POB 17, 190 13 Attica; tel. 22910-76452; fax 22910-76347; Dir Dr EVANGELOS PAPATHANASSIOU.

ECONOMICS, LAW AND POLITICS

Centre of International and European Economic Law: POB 14, 55102 Kalamaria, Thessaloniki; tel. 231-0486900; fax 231-0476366; e-mail kdeod@cieel.gr; internet www.cieel.gr; f. 1977; national documentation and research centre, specializing in European Community law, protection of human rights in Europe, international economic law; European Documentation Centre by decision of the EEC; library of 55,000 vols, 192 periodicals; Dir Prof. ATHANASSIOS KAISSIS; Sec. Prof. PAROULA NASKOU-PERRAKI; publs *Hellenic Review of European Law* (4 a year in Greek, annually in English), *Public Procurement and State Aid Law Review* (3 a year).

Centre of Planning and Economic Research: Amerikis 11, 106 72 Athens; tel. 210-3676300; fax 210-3611136; e-mail kepe@kepe.gr; internet www.kepe.gr; f. 1961; scientific study of the economic problems of Greece, the promotion of economic research, and co-operation with other Greek research institutes; library of 29,425 vols, 700 periodical titles, 315 series of statistical bulletins; Chair. and Scientific Dir. Prof. KYPRIANOS P. PRODROMIDIS; publ. *Economic Perspectives* (3 a year).

Hellenic Centre for European Studies (EKEM): 4 Xenofontos St, 106 80 Athens; tel. 210-3215549; fax 210-3215096; e-mail ekem@ekem.gr; internet www.ekem.gr; f. 1988; non-profit-making independent org. under supervision of the Ministry of Foreign Affairs; advises the govt, academic bodies and private companies on matters of European policy and integration; organizes conferences and seminars; library: maintains Depository Library of the European Community, with 7,000 vols; Pres. of Admin. Council and Dir Assoc. Prof. KOSTAS IFANTIS.

Hellenic Institute of International and Foreign Law: 73 Solonos St, 106 79 Athens; tel. 210-3615646; fax 210-3619777; e-mail hiifl@ath.forthnet.gr; internet www.mfa.gr; f. 1939; library of 40,000 vols; Dir Prof. KONSTANTINOS KERAMEUS; publ. *Revue hellénique de droit international* (in English and French, 2 a year).

Institute of International Public Law and International Relations: Vass. Herakliou St, 546 25 Thessaloniki; tel. 2310-552295; fax 2310-566953; e-mail ipilir@otenet.gr; internet web.auth.gr/institute-iplir; f. 1966; research, documentation and education centre; courses run June-September; library: library and World Bank and UN depository library; Dir Prof. KALLIOPI K. KOUFA; publ. *Thesaurus Acroasium* (annually).

Kentron Ereunes Historias Hellenikou Dikaiou (Centre for Research in the History of Greek Law): Anagnostopoulou 14, 106 73 Athens; tel. 210-3664607; fax 210-3664628; e-mail keied@academyofathens.gr; internet www.academyofathens.gr; f. 1929; attached to Acad. of Athens; collects, studies and publishes legal material of Byzantine and post-Byzantine times; Pres. G. MITSOPOULOS; Dir E. KARABELIAS; publ. *Epetiris* (annually).

FINE AND PERFORMING ARTS

Kentro Erevnas Byzantinis kai Metabyzantinis Technis (Research Centre for Byzantine and Post-Byzantine Art): Odos Anagnostopoulou 14, 106 73 Athens; tel. 210-3664613; fax 210-3664652; e-mail kevmt@academyofathens.gr; internet academyofathens.gr; f. 1994; attached to Acad. of Athens; research on Byzantine wall-paintings in Greece; 5 mems; library of 3,000 vols; Pres. PANAYOTIS L. VOCOTOPOULOS; Dir IOANNA BITHA (acting).

HISTORY, GEOGRAPHY AND ARCHAEOLOGY

Centre for Asia Minor Studies: Kydathineon 11, 105 58 Athens; tel. 210-3239225; fax 210-3229758; e-mail kms@otenet.gr; internet users.otenet.gr/~kms; f. 1930; independent, private, non-profit organization; research into history and civilization of Greek communities in Asia Minor before 1922; library of 15,000 vols, 501 MSS; oral history archive of 150,000 MS pages; photographic archive of *c.* 5,000 photographs; folk music archive of 1,000 records, 700 tapes; special collections: Karamanli books, and Greek books, newspapers and periodicals printed in Turkey, maps, manuscripts; Pres. Prof. M. B. SAKELLARIOU; Dir Dr S. TH. ANESTIDIS (acting); publ. *Deltio K. M. S.* (annually).

Foundation of the Hellenic World: 38 Poulopoulou St, 118 51 Athens; tel. 212-2543800; fax 212-2543838; e-mail webmaster@fhw.gr; internet www.fhw.gr/fhw/en; f. 1993; uses the latest information and computer technology in pursuit of research, awareness and understanding of Hellenic history and culture; Cultural Centre: Hellenic Cosmos located at 254 Pireos St, 177 78 Athens; Pres. LAZAROS D. EFRAIMOGLOU; Man. Dir DIMITRIS EFRAIMOGLOU.

Kentron Erevnis Ellinikis Philosophias (Centre for Research in Greek Philosophy): Anagnostopoulou 14, 106 73 Athens; tel. 210-3664605; fax 210-3615937; e-mail keef@academyofathens.gr; internet www.academyofathens.gr; f. 1966; attached to Acad. of Athens; Pres. C. DESPOTOPOULOS (acting); Dir M. PROTOPAPA-MARNELI (acting); publ. *Philosophia* (annually).

Institute for Balkan Studies: Meg. Alexandrou Ave 31a, 546 41 Thessaloniki; tel. 231-0832143; fax 231-0831429; e-mail imxa_iss@yahoo.gr; internet www.imxa.gr; f. 1953; research centre concerned with the historical, literary, political, economic and social development of the Balkan peoples since early times; library of 30,000 vols, 260 periodicals; Dir Prof. Dr YANNIS MOURELOS; Chair. Prof. BASIL KONDIS; publs *Balkan Studies* (2 a year), *Valkanika Symmeikta* (annually).

International Centre for Classical Research (of the Hellenic Society for Humanistic Studies): 47 Alopekis St, Athens 140; study of and research into ancient Greek culture, scientific research and promotion of popular education through conferences and publications; f. 1959; 700 mems; library of 20,000 vols; Pres. Prof. ARISTOXENOS D. SKIADAS; Sec.-Gen. GEORGE BABINIOTIS; publs *Antiquity and Contemporary Problems*, *Studies and Research*.

Kentron Erevnis Archaiotitos (Research Centre for Antiquity): Odos Anagnostopoulou 14, 106 73 Athens; tel. 210-3664612; fax 210-3602448; e-mail kea@academyofathens.gr; internet www.academyofathens.gr; f. 1977; attached to Acad. of Athens; Supervisor S. IAKOVIDIS; Dir M. PIPILI.

Kentron Erevnis Messeonikou kai Neou Ellinismou (Centre for Research into Medieval and Modern Hellenism): Anagnostopoulou 14, 106 73 Athens; tel. 210-3664610; fax 210-3664637; e-mail kemne@academyofathens.gr; internet www.academyofathens.gr; f. 1930; attached to Acad. of Athens; 7 mems; library of 25,000 vols; Dir K. LAPPAS; publ. *Messeonika kai Nea Ellinika* (annually).

Kentron Erevnis Neoterou Ellinismou (Research Centre for the History of Modern Hellenism): Anagnostopoulou St 14, 106 73 Athens; tel. 210-3664601; fax 210-3664661; e-mail keine@academyofathens.gr; internet www.academyofathens.gr; f. 1957; attached to Acad. of Athens; Greek history since 1821; library of 12,100 vols, 12,000 microfilms; Pres. MICHAEL SAKELLARIOU (acting); Dir KALLIA KALLIATAKI (acting).

LANGUAGE AND LITERATURE

Kentron Ereunes Hellenikes kai Latinikes Grammateias (Centre for the Research of Greek and Latin Literature): Anagnostopoulou 14, 106 73 Athens; tel. and fax 210-3664630; e-mail keelg@academyofathens.gr; internet www.academyofathens.gr; f. 1955; attached to Acad. of Athens; Pres. NIKOLAOS KONOMIS; Supervisor ATHANASIOS KAMBYLIS; Librarian ELENI MASTROGEORGIOU.

Research Centre for Modern Greek Dialectics: Syngrou Ave 129 and Dipla St 1, 117 45 Athens; tel. 210-9344806; fax 210-9316350; e-mail ksilneg@academyofathens.gr; internet www.academyofathens.gr/ksil/homengl.htm; f. 1914; attached to Acad. of Athens; Pres. MICHAEL SAKELLARIOU; Dir Dr GIAKOUMAKI ELEUTHERIA; publ. *Lexicographikon Deltion (Bulletin lexicographique)* (annually).

Research Centre for Scientific Terms and Neologisms: Solonos St 84, 106 80 Athens; tel. 210-3664732; e-mail geon@academyofathens.gr; internet www.academyofathens.gr; f. 2003; attached to Acad. of Athens; Pres. N. KONOMIS; Dir TITOS P. JOCHALAS; publ. *Bulletin of Scientific Terminology and Neologisms*.

MEDICINE

Institut Pasteur Hellénique: 127 Vassilissis Sofias Ave, 115 21 Athens; tel. 210-6478800; fax 210-6423498; internet www.pasteur.gr; f. 1919; study and research of bacteriology, biochemistry, biotechnology, immunology, microbiology, molecular biology, molecular virology, parasitology, virology; library of 3,500 vols and 155 periodicals; Dir A. F. MENTIS.

NATURAL SCIENCES

Physical Sciences

Institouton Geologikon kai Metalleutikon Ereunon (Institute of Geology and Mineral Exploration): 70 Messoghion St, 115 27 Athens; tel. 210-7771438; fax 210-7752211; e-mail dirgen@igme.gr; internet www.igme.gr; f. 1952; operates under the Ministry of Development; consultant to the Government on geoscientific matters and on mine legislation; carries out the geological study of Greece; surveys and evaluates all mineral raw materials, except hydrocarbons, and groundwater resources; 819 mems; library of 9,500 vols, 500 periodicals, 4,000 maps and 6,000 reports; Dir-Gen. ANDREAS N. GEORGAKOPOULOS; publs *Geological and Geophysical Research*, *Special Research*.

Kentron Erevnis Phissikistis Atmospheras kai Climatologias (Research Centre for Atmospheric Physics and Climatology): Odos Panepistimiou 28, Athens; tel. and fax 210-8832048; e-mail phatmcli@otenet.gr; internet www.academyofathens.gr; f. 1977; attached to Acad. of Athens; Pres. C. ALEXOPOULOS; Dir CHR. REPAPIS.

National Observatory of Athens: POB 20048, 118 10 Athens; tel. 210-3490101; fax 210-3490140; internet www.noa.gr/indexen.html; f. 1842; library: library contains 60,000 vols; Pres. of the Administration Board Prof. D. P. LALAS; Dir, Institute of Astronomy and Astrophysics Prof. CHRISTOS GOUDIS; Dir, Institute for Astroparticle Physics Prof. LEONIDAS RESVANIS; Dir, Institute for Environmental Research and Sustainable Development Dr PETRAKIS MICHAEL; Dir, Institute of Geodynamics Dr G. STAVRAKAKIS (acting); Dir, Institute for Space Applications and Remote Sensing Dr I. A. DAGLIS; publs *Annals of the National Observatory of Athens*, *Memoirs, Series I—Astronomy*, *Series II—Meteorology*, bulletins of the Astronomical, Meteorological, Ionospheric and Geodynamics Institutes.

Research Centre of Pure and Applied Mathematics (RCPAM): Odos Panepistimiou 28, Athens; tel. 210-3664717; fax 210-3664718; e-mail nikartem@academyofathens.gr; internet www.academyofathens.gr; f. 1992; attached to Acad. of Athens; Pres. G. KONTOPOULOS; Supervisor N. K. ARTEMIADIS.

PHILOSOPHY AND PSYCHOLOGY

Kentron Erevnis Ellinikis Philosophias (Research Centre for Greek Philosophy): Anagnostopoulou St 14, 106 73 Athens; tel. 210-3664606; e-mail keef@acadmyofathens.gr; internet www.academyofathens.gr; f. 1970; attached to Acad. of Athens; Pres. C. DESPOTOPOULOS; Dir M. PROTOPAPA-MARNELI; publ. *Philosophia*.

RELIGION, SOCIOLOGY AND ANTHROPOLOGY

Athens Center of Ekistics: 24 Strat. Syndesmou St, 106 73 Athens; tel. 210-3623216; fax 210-3629337; e-mail ekistics@otenet.gr; internet www.ekistics.org; f. 1963; research, education, collaboration and documentation in the development of human settlements; secretariat of World Society for Ekistics; library of 1,000 vols, 100 periodical titles (historic colln of 20,000 vols largely transferred in 2003 to School of Architecture, National Technical Univ. of Athens *q. v.*); Dir PANAYOTIS C. PSOMOPOULOS; publ. *Ekistics* (6 a year).

Hellenic Folklore Research Centre of the Academy of Athens (Research Centre for Hellenic Folklore): 3 Ipitou St, 105 57 Athens; tel. 210-3318042; fax 210-3313418; e-mail keel@academyofathens.gr; internet www.academyofathens.gr; f. 1918; folklore, anthropology, ethnology (ethnography), folk music, social, spiritual life, archives of folk material, MSS, tape, video tape, cassette movie, photos, slides; library of 14,500 vols, 4,816, MSS, 28,000 songs, 17,000 folktales and stories, 200,000 proverbs, customs, etc.; Dir Dr AIK. POLYMEROU-KAMILAKIS; publ. *Yearbook*.

Kentron Erevnis Ellinikis Kinonias (Research Centre for Greek Society): 84 Solonos St, 106 80 Athens; tel. 210-3664725; fax 210-3664726; e-mail keek@academyofathens.gr; internet www.academyofathens.gr; f. 1978; attached to Acad. of Athens; research into Greek Society, especially the historical development of the Greek family and the social and economic consequences of migration in Greece; library of 4,000 vols; Dir Prof. M.-G. LILY STYLIANOUDI; publs *Elliniki Koinonia* (Yearbook of the Centre), *Epeteiris tou KEEK*.

National Centre of Social Research (EKKE): 14–18 Messogeion Ave, 115 27 Athens; tel. 210-7491600; fax 210-7489127; e-mail president@ekke.gr; internet www.ekke.gr; f. 1960; operates under the Ministry of Research and Technology; aims to promote the development of the social sciences in Greece, to organize and conduct social research and to act as a link between Greek and foreign social scientists, to promote international co-operation in this field; Dirs THOMAS MALOUTAS, IOANNIS SAKELLIS; publ. *Epitheorissis Koinonikon Erevnon* (Greek Review of Social Research, quarterly).

Patriarchal Institute for Patristic Studies: 64 Eptapyrgiou St, Moni Vlatadon, 546 34 Thessaloniki; tel. and fax 231-0203620; f. 1968; research centre with depts of patrology, palaeography, history of Byzantine art, history of worship and ecclesiastical history; library of 15,000 vols, 300 periodicals, 115 codex MSS, 450 rare books, 10,000 MSS on microfilm, colour slides of illuminated MSS; Dir Prof. JOHN FOUNTOULIS; publ. *Kleronomia* (2 a year).

TECHNOLOGY

'Demokritos' National Centre for Scientific Research: POB 60228, 153 10 Aghia Paraskevi, Athens; tel. 210-6503285; fax 210-6522965; e-mail info@lib.demokritos.gr; internet www.demokritos.gr; f. 1961; study and research by eight institutes: nuclear physics, materials science, microelectronics, biology, nuclear technology and radiation protection, informatics and telecommunications, physical chemistry, radioisotopes and radiodiagnostic products; 659 mems; library of 20,000 vols, 300,000 technical reports, 1,500 periodicals; Dir Prof. EMMANUEL G. FLORATOS; Librarian NORIA CHRISTOPHORIDOU; publ. *DEMO Reports*.

Libraries and Archives

Athens

Academy of Athens Library: Anagnostopolou 14, 106 73 Athens; tel. 210-3664607; fax 210-3364628; e-mail keied@academyofathens.gr; internet www.academyofathens.gr; f. 1926; collects and publishes Greek historical legal documents, including those of the Byzantine and post-Byzantine periods; 5 brs; 500,000 vols; Dir Dr E. KARABELIAS; publ. *Epiteris tou Kentrou Historias Ellenikou Dikaiou*.

Athens University of Economics and Business Library: 76 Patission St, 104 34 Athens; tel. 210-8203355; fax 210-8221456; e-mail library@aueb.gr; internet www.lib.aueb.gr; f. 1928; 75,000 vols, 700 periodicals, 7,000 working papers; three documentation centres: European Documentation Center (EDC) f. 1992, Depository Library of OECD f. 1997, and Depository Library of WTO f. 2004; Dirs Prof. E. J. YANNAKOUDIS, GEORGIA THEOPHANOPOULOU.

Eugenides Foundation Library: Syngrou Ave 387, Paleon Phaleron, 175 64 Athens; tel. 210-9411181; fax 210-9417372; e-mail library@eugenfound.edu.gr; internet www.eugenfound.edu.gr; f. 1966; 23,500 vols, 441 periodicals (science and technology); Librarian HARA BRINDESI.

Gennadius Library: Odos Souidias 61, 106 76 Athens; tel. 210-7210536; fax 210-7237767; e-mail secretarygenn@ascsa.edu.gr; internet www.ascsa.edu.gr/gennadius/g_index.htm; f. 1926; rare book and research library attached to American School of Classical Studies; 115,000 vols; spec. colln on Greece, the Near East, the Balkans and travel accounts; first editions of classics; maps; literary and other archives; Dir Dr MARIA GEORGOPOULOU; Librarian SOPHIE PAPAGEORGIOU; publs *Exhibition Catalogues*, *Gennadeion Monographs*, *The New Griffon* (annually).

Greek Chamber of Deputies Library: Parliament Bldg, 100 21 Athens; tel. 210-3235030; fax 210-3236072; e-mail abadjis@artemis.parl.ariadne-t.gr; f. 1844, damaged by fire 1859, rebuilt 1875; 1,500,000 vols; Dir IRENE CON. ELIOPOULOU.

Music Library of Greece 'Lilian Voudouri': Vasilissis Sofias and Kokkali, 115 21 Athens; tel. 210-7282775; fax 210-7259196; e-mail library@megaron.gr; internet www.mmb.org.gr; f. 1994; holds the Greek Music Archives; 92,000 vols, 66 periodicals, 12,700 recordings, microforms and MSS; Dir STEPHANIA MERAKOU.

National Library of Greece: Odos Panepistimiou 32, 106 79 Athens; tel. 210-3382601; fax 210-3382502; e-mail gzachos@nlg.gr; internet www.nlg.gr; f. 1828; 2,500,000 vols; collection of MSS; serves as the national bibliographical centre and as the national centre for ISBN and ISSN; Gen. Dir Dr GEORGE K. ZACHOS.

National Technical University of Athens Library: Odos Polytechniou 9, Zografou Campus, 157 73 Athens; tel. 210-7722229; fax 210-7721565; e-mail library@central.ntua.gr; internet www.lib.ntua.gr; f. 1836; 80,000 vols; Librarian MARIA KALAMBALIKI.

Nordic Library at Athens: Kavalotti 7, 117 42 Athens; tel. 210-9249210; fax 210-9216487; internet www.norlib.gr; 40,000 vols, 450 periodicals; Greek archaeology and ancient Greek religion and history; jt venture by archaeological institutes of Denmark, Finland, Norway and Sweden; Head Librarian CHRISTINA TSAMPAZI-REID.

Technical Chamber of Greece–Documentation and Information Unit: Odos Lekka 23–25, 105 62 Athens; tel. 210-3245180; fax 210-3237525; e-mail tee_lib@tee.gr; internet library.tee.gr; f. 1926; 55,000 vols, 1,400 periodicals, TCG publications; Head of Unit KATERINA TORAKI.

Canea

Technical University of Crete Library: 731 00 Canea; tel. 821-037273; fax 821-037576; e-mail amlet@library.tuc.gr; internet www.library.tuc.gr; f. 1985; 47,000 vols, 630 current periodicals, maps and dissertations; scientific fields of the institute, arts and history; Library Dir MARIA NTAOUNTAKI.

Chios

Koraes Central Public Historical Library of Chios: 2 Korai St, 821 00 Chios; tel. 22710-44246; fax 22710-28251; e-mail bibkor@aegean.gr; internet vivl-chiou.chi.sch.gr; f. 1792; colln of rare and unique Homeric edns; 200,000 vols; Dir ANASTASIOS SARRIS.

Patras

University of Patras Library and Information Service: 265 00 Patras; tel. 61-997290; internet www.upatras.gr/services/library/library.php?lang=en; 90,000 vols, 2,400 journals; biology, medicine, theatre, mathematics, computer science, economics, literature, applied sciences, education and general reference.

Piraeus

University of Piraeus Library: 80 Dimitriou and Kalaoli Sts, 185 34 Piraeus; internet www.lib.unipi.gr; economics, business admin., industrial management, finance, and maritime studies; 45,000 vols, 350 periodicals.

Rethymnon

University of Crete Library: Gallos Campus, Knossou Ave, 731 00 Rethymnon; tel. 831-77810; fax 831-77850; e-mail webauthor@lib.uoc.gr; internet www.lib.uoc.gr/english; f. 1978; 3 brs at Heraklion; Dir ELENI DIAMANTAKI.

Thessaloniki

Aristotelian University of Thessaloniki Library: 541 24 Thessaloniki; tel. 231-995378; fax 231-995364; e-mail libraryweb@lib.auth.gr; internet www.lib.auth.gr; f. 1927; 181,500 vols, 122,950 journals, 7,055 dissertations; rare books from 18th and 19th c.; Librarians X. AGOROGIANNI, S. ALEXANDRIDOU, EL. KOSEOGLOU.

University of Macedonia, Economic and Social Sciences Library: 156 Egnatia St, 540 06 Thessaloniki; tel. 2310-891752; fax 2310-857794; e-mail maclib@uom.gr; internet www.lib.uom.gr.

Tripolis

Pan Library ('Circle of the Friends of Progress'): Odos Giorgios 43, Tripolis, Arcadia; vols on all subjects.

Veria

Veria Central Public Library: 8 Ellis St, 591 00 Veria; tel. 2331-24494; fax 2331-24600; e-mail vivlver@libver.gr; internet www.libver.gr; f. 1952; 90,000 vols; Central Library for the Prefecture of Imathia.

Volos

Library of the Three Hierarchs: Demetriados-Ogl, 382 21 Volos; tel. and fax 24210-25641; f. 1907; 23,000 vols; literature, religion, history, philosophy, physical sciences; Asst Dir ACHILLES K. GLAVATOS.

University of Thessaly Central Library: Argonafton and Fillelinon Sts, 382 21 Volos; tel. 421-74604; fax 421-74609; internet www.lib.uth.gr; other brs: Veterinary Science in Karditsa; Medicine in Larisa; Physical Education and Sport in Trikala; Humanities, Technological Sciences and Kitsos Makris Folklore Centre in Volos.

Museums and Art Galleries

Athens

Acropolis Museum: Office: Makriyani 2–4, 117 42 Athens; tel. 210-3236665; fax 210-9239023; e-mail aepka@culture.gr; internet www.culture.gr; f. 1874; contains the sculptures discovered on the Acropolis; illustrates the origins of Attic art, pedimental compositions, archaic horsemen, Korai, sculptures of the Parthenon, Temple of Niké, Erechtheion; Dir Dr ALKESTIS CHOREMI.

Benaki Museum: Odos Koumbari 1, 106 74 Athens; tel. 210-3671000; fax 210-3671063; e-mail benaki@benaki.gr; internet www.benaki.gr; f. 1930; Greek art from Neolithic to late Roman period; Byzantine and post-Byzantine; Greek folk art and costumes; historic memorabilia from the War of Independence in 1821 to 1936; 18th–19th c. paintings, engravings and drawings; works of art by N. Hadjikyriakos-Ghikas; Coptic and Islamic art; textiles and embroidery from Far East and Western Europe; neolithic to modern Chinese porcelain; children's toys and games from antiquity to the mid-20th c.; historical and photographic archives (Documentation Centre for Neo-Hellenic Architecture); library of 50,000 vols, 500 MSS; Dir Prof. Dr ANGELOS DELIVORRIAS.

Byzantine and Christian Museum: 22 Vasilissis Sophias Ave, 106 75 Athens; tel. 210-7211027; fax 210-7231883; e-mail protocol@bma.culture.gr; internet www.culture.gr; f. 1914; more than 25,000 objects since 3rd c. AD, incl. sculptures, icons and other works of art; wall paintings, ceramics, textiles, MSS, drawings, anthibola, engravings, incunabula and copies of wall paintings and mosaics of the Byzantine and post-Byzantine eras; Dir Dr DIMITRIOS KONSTANTIOS.

National Archaeological Museum: 1 Tositsa St, 106 82 Athens; tel. 210-8217724; fax 210-8213573; e-mail eam@culture.gr; internet www.culture.gr; f. 1889; original Greek sculptures and Roman copies of Greek originals; sculptures of the Archaic, Classical, Hellenistic and Roman periods; Neolithic objects from Thessaly; Bronze Age relics from the mainland and the Aegean Islands; Mycenaean treasures; frescoes and pottery from Thera; rich collns of Greek vases and terracottas; collns of jewels and bronzes; Egyptian antiquities; Dir Dr NIKOLAOS KALTSAS; Head of Bronzes Colln Dr ROZA PROSKYNITOPOULOU; Head of Prehistoric, Egyptian and Anatolian Antiquities Colln Dr ELENI PAPAZOGLOU; Head of Sculpture Colln Dr ELENI KOURINOU; Head of Vases and Minor Art Colln ELISAVET STASINOPOULOU.

National Art Gallery and Alexander Soutzos Museum: 50 Vassileos Konstantinou Ave, 115 28 Athens; tel. 210-7211010; fax 210-7224889; internet www.nationalgallery.gr; f. 1900; Greek paintings since 17th c., sculptures and prints; European paintings since 14th c., including El Greco, Caravaggio, Jordaens, Poussin, Tiepolo, Delacroix, Mondrian, Picasso; engravings; drawings; library of 8,000 vols; Dir Prof. MARINA LAMBRAKI-PLAKA.

National Historical Museum of Greece: Old Parliament, Stadiou St, 105 61 Athens; tel. 210-3237617; fax 210-3213786; e-mail nhmuseum@tee.gr; internet www.fhw.gr/projects/vouli; f. 1882; chronicles the history of Modern Greece from the 16th to the 20th century; ethnographic colln of traditional regional costumes, jewellery, embroidery and textiles; Dir IOANNIS K. MAZARAKIS-AINIAN.

National Museum of Contemporary Art (EMST): 14 Amvr. Frantzi St, 117 43 Athens; tel. 210-9242111; fax 210-9245200; e-mail protocol@emst.gr; internet www.emst.gr; f. 2000; paintings, installations, photography, video, new media, architecture and industrial design; Dir ANNA KAFETSI.

Stoa of Attalos: 10 555 Athens; tel. 210-3210185; f. as a museum in 1956; the design of the original building (constructed the 2nd c. BC) was exactly reproduced in the reconstruction carried out 1953–56 by the American School of Classical Studies; collections include all material found in the excavations of the Athenian Agora, illustrating 5,000 years of Athenian history; Dir P. KALLIGAS.

Zoological Museum of the University of Athens: Panepistimiopolis, 157 84 Athens; tel. 210-7274609; fax 210-7274619; e-mail zoolmuse@biol.uoa.gr; internet www.uoa.gr/biology/zoology/welcome.htm; f. 1858; permanent and temporary exhibitions on Greek and world fauna: birds, mammals, shells, insects etc.; research in ecology and zoogeography; Dir Prof. M. MORIATOU-APOSTOLOPOULOU.

Canea

Archaeological Museum of Canea: 731 31 Canea; tel. 2821-90334; fax 2821-94487; internet www.culture.gr; f. 1963; housed in the katholikon of the Venetian monastery of St Francis; pre-historic and Minoan artefacts; Dir MARIA VLAZAKI.

Maritime Museum of Crete: Akti Koundourioti , 731 36 Canea; tel. 2821-91875; fax 2821-74484; e-mail mar-museum-crete@cha.forthnet.gr; internet www.greece-museums.com/museum/109; f. 1973; Dir K. MANIOUDAKIS.

Corfu

Archaeological Museum: Armeni Vraila 1, 491 00 Corfu; tel. 2661-30680; fax 2661-43452; internet www.greece-museums.com/museum/116; f. 1967; Bronze statues from Archaic to Roman era; funeral offerings from the Archaic, Classical and Hellenistic eras; findings from Prehistoric era and 7th and 6th c. BC; Menecrates lion, clay pottery, terracotta statuettes from shrines of Corfu; Gorgon-Medusa pediment from the great temple of Artemis, constructed in 585 BC.

Museum of Asian Art: St Michael and St George Palace, 491 00 Corfu; tel. 26610-30443; fax 26610-20193; internet www.greece-museums.com/museum/35; f. 1927; Greek-Buddhistic colln of sculptures from Gadara, Pakistan, dating from the 1st–5th c. AD.

Corinth

Archaeological Museum in Corinth: Corinth 200 10; tel. and fax 210-741031207; f. 1932; items from the Geometric to Hellenistic periods, Roman and Byzantine eras, from excavations at the Asklepieion of Corinth; sculptures and inscriptions; Dir ALEXANDROS MANTIS.

Delphi

Archaeological Museum: 330 54 Delphi; tel. 2265-082313; fax 2265-082966; e-mail protocol@iepka.culture.gr; internet www.culture.gr; f. 1903; finds from the Delphic excavations; library of 5,200 vols; Dir ROZINE KOLONIA.

Heraklion

Archaeological Museum: 2 Xanthoudidou St, 712 02 Heraklion, Crete; tel. 281-0224630; fax 281-0332610; e-mail protocol@amh.culture.gr; f. 1904; contains rich collection of Minoan art (pottery, sealstones, frescoes, jewellery); traces the development of Cretan art up to the Roman period; Dir RETHEMIOTAKI PANAGIOTA.

Nafplion

Komboloi Museum: 25 Staikopoulou St, 211 00 Nafplion; tel. 2752-21618; e-mail arisevag@otenet.gr; internet www.komboloi.gr; f. 1987; 400 komboloi (prayer beads) findings from the period 1750–1950; komboloi belonging to Buddhists, Catholics, Hindus, Muslims and Orthodox Monks.

Peloponnesian Folklore Foundation: Vas. Alexandrou 1, 211 00 Nafplion; tel. 2752-028379; fax 2752-027960; e-mail pff@otenet.gr; internet www.pli.gr; f. 1974; research, presentation, study and preservation of the material culture of Greece (costume, music and dance); br. in Stathmos; library of 9,389 vols; Pres. IOANNA PAPANTONIOU; Curator KANELLOS KANELLOPOULOS; publs *Endymatologica*, *Ethnographica*.

Olympia

Archaeological Museum: 270 65 Olympia; tel. and fax 2624-022529; e-mail protocol@zepka.culture.gr; internet www.culture.gr; f. 1970; Greek geometric and archaic bronzes; two pediments from Temple of Zeus, Hermes of Praxiteles, Victory of Paionios; finds from Sanctuary of Olympia and Pheidias' workshop; Roman sculpture; Dir GEORGIA CHATZI-SPILIOPOULOU.

Attached Museums:

Museum of the History of Excavations in Ancient Olympia: Olympia; tel. and fax 2624-022529; e-mail protocol@zepka.culture.gr; f. 2004; presentation of the history of the 19th c. German excavation and archaeological activity in Ancient Olympia; Dir GEORGIA CHATZI-SPILIOPOULOU.

Museum of the History of the Olympic Games: Olympia; tel. and fax 2624-022529; e-mail protocol@zepka.culture.gr; f. 1888; 463 objects (statues, inscriptions, vases, bronzes, etc.) detailing the history of the Olympic Games from the Mycenean to the Roman periods; Dir GEORGIA CHATZI-SPILIOPOULOU.

Paiania

Vorres Museum of Greek Art: 1 Parodos Diad. Konstantinou, 190 02 Paiania, Attica; tel. 210-6642520; fax 210-6645775; e-mail vores@otenet.gr; internet www.sitemaker.gr/vorres; f. 1983; covers 4,000 years of Greek history; two sections: folk art and architecture (a group of traditional buildings containing artefacts, furniture, etc.) and a museum of contemporary Greek art; Dir IAN VORRES; publ. *Catalogue*.

Rethymnon

Archaeological Museum: 741 00 Rethymnon; tel. 2831-54668; internet www.ellada.net/crete-info/museums/rethymno.php; f. 1991; artefacts from the late Neolithic period, early to late Minoan periods, Geometric and Archaic periods and Hellenistic and Roman periods.

Historical and Folk Art Museum: 30 M. Vernardou St, 741 00 Rethymnon; tel. 2831-23398; fax 2831-23667; internet www.ellada.net/crete-info/museums/rethymno.php; f. 1998; 5,000 items of folk art; history of textiles; Pres. FALY G. VOYATZAKIS.

Rhodes

Archaeological Museum: Medieval City, 85 100 Rhodes; tel. 2241-031048; f. Hospital of the Knights built 1440–89; sculpture, vases and other objects from Rhodes, Ialysos, Kamiros and other sites, from Mycenean to late Roman times, funerary stelae and weapons dating from Middle Ages; library of 27,400 vols.

Rhodes Jewish Museum: Dossiadou St, Rhodes; tel. 31047-54779; fax 31047-58144; e-mail info@rhodesjewishmuseum.org; internet www.rhodesjewishmuseum.org; housed in fmr women's prayer rooms at 16th c. Kahal Shalom synagogue; attached to Rhodes Jewish Historical Foundation; Pres. BELLA RESTIS.

Thessaloniki

Archaeological Museum of Thessaloniki: 6 Manolis Andronikos St, 54621 Thessaloniki; tel. 2310-830538; fax 2310-861306; e-mail amth@culture.gr; internet www.amth.gr; f. 1912; exhibitions on prehistoric Macedonia, the birth of Macedonian cities, Macedonia from the 7th century BC to Late Antiquity, and Thessaloniki; educational activities for children and adults; archaeological and historical lectures; library of 7,000 vols; Asst Dir Dr IGNATIADOU DESPOINA; publs *Archeologiko Ergo ste Makedonia kai Thrace* (annual journal), *Thessaloniki Philippou Vassilissan*.

Macedonian Museum of Contemporary Art of Thessaloniki: 154 Egnatia St, 546 36 Thessaloniki; tel. 2310-240002; fax 2310-281567; e-mail mmcart@mmca.org.gr;

internet www.macedonian-heritage.gr/museums; f. 1979; 2,000 works by Greek and foreign artists; library of 2,500 vols; Dir ANTONIS KOURTIS.

Sports Museum: 18 Aristotelous St, 546 23 Thessaloniki; tel. 2310-224551; fax 2310-241300; e-mail info@olympicsportmuseum.org; internet www.sportmuseum.gr; f. 1998; history of athletics.

State Museum of Contemporary Art at Thessaloniki: Kolokotroni 21, Moni Lazariston, 564 30 Thessaloniki; tel. 2310-589140; fax 2310-600123; e-mail info@greekstatemuseum.com; internet www.greekstatemuseum.com/contact_en; f. 1997; Costakis colln of 1,275 works of Russian avant-garde art; also houses Museum of Photography and Centre of Contemporary Art; Dir MILTIADES PAPANIKOLAOU.

Technical Museum at Thessaloniki: 2nd Road, Bldg 47, Industrial Zone of Thessaloniki, 570 22 Thessaloniki; tel. 2310-799773; fax 2310-796816; e-mail info@tmth.edu.gr; internet www.tmth.edu.gr; f. 1978; objects and multimedia information grouped by theme: Ancient Greek Technology, Spinning and Textile Making, Printing, Electricity, Telecommunications, New Telecommunications Technologies, Electronic Computers, Radio and Television, Amateur Radio, Navigational Instruments, Oil, Rubber, Automobiles, the Railway, Aviation, Air Traffic Control Tower Telecommunications, Human Beings in Space, Meteorology, Instruments for Physics Experiments, Photography, Holograms, Audiovisual Media, Traditional Technology, Medical Apparatus and Instruments; Dir CHRIS G. PAPADAKIS.

Thessaloniki Museum of Photography: Warehouse A, Port of Thessaloniki, 541 10 Thessaloniki; tel. 2310-566716; fax 2310-566717; e-mail mariako@thmphoto.gr; internet www.thmphoto.gr; f. 1997; historical and contemporary Greek and international photography; library of 17,000 vols; Curator I. HERCULES.

Universities

ANOTATI SCHOLI KALON TECHNON (Athens School of Fine Art)

Odos Patission 42, 106 82 Athens
Telephone: 210-3816930
Fax: 210-3816926
E-mail: info@asfa.gr
Internet: www.asfa.gr

Founded 1837

Rector: YANNIS PAPADAKIS

Library of 29,000 vols
Number of teachers: 38
Number of students: 783

DIRECTORS OF SECTIONS

Painting: Prof. CHR. BOTSOGLOU
Printmaking: Prof. G. MILIOS
Sculpture: Prof. G. LAPPAS
Theoretical Studies: Prof. M. LAMBRAKI

Brs in Delphi, Hydra, Mykonos, Rhodes, Lesbos and Rethymnon.

ARISTOTELEIO PANEPISTIMIO THESSALONIKIS (Aristotle University of Thessaloniki)

University Campus, 541 24 Thessaloniki
Telephone: 2310-996000
Internet: www.auth.gr

Founded 1925
State Univ., with autonomous function
Language of instruction: Greek
Academic year: September to August

Rector: Prof. ANASTASIOS MANTHOS
Vice-Rector for Academic Affairs and Personnel: Prof. ATHANASIA TSATSAKOU
Vice-Rector and Head of the Special Account of Research Funds: Prof. STAVROS PANNAS
Vice-Rector for Finance and Devt: Assoc. Prof. ANDREAS GIANNAKOUDAKIS
Head of Int/ Relations: HELEN KOTSAKI
Librarian: Prof. CHRISTOS BABATZIMOPOULOS

Library: see Libraries and Archives
Number of teachers: 2,287
Number of students: 92,509

Publications: *Panepistimioupoli* (quarterly), catalogue, scientific annals and faculty periodicals

DEANS

Faculty of Agriculture: NIKOLAOS MISOPOLINOS (Chair.)
Faculty of Dentistry: Prof. ATHANASIOS ATHANASIOU (Chair.)
Faculty of Education: Prof. SOFRONIOS CHATZISAVIDIS
Faculty of Engineering: Prof. NIKOLAOS MOUSIOPOULOS
Faculty of Fine Arts: Prof. G. KATSAGELOS
Faculty of Forestry and the Natural Environment: Prof. ANASTASIOS NASTIS (Chair.)
Faculty of Law, Economics and Political Sciences: Prof. GIANNOULA KARYMBALI-TSIPTSIOU
Faculty of Medicine: Prof. IOANNIS BONDIS (Chair.)
Faculty of Philosophy: Prof. PHOEVUS GIKOPOULOS
Faculty of Science: Prof. IOANNIS PAPADOGIANNIS
Faculty of Theology: Prof. IOANNIS KOGOULIS
Faculty of Veterinary Medicine: Prof. DIMITRIOS RAPTOPOULOS (Chair.)

CHAIRMEN OF SCHOOLS

Faculty of Education (tel. 2310-995062; fax 2310-995061):
- School of Early Childhood Education: Prof. GIORGIOS TSIAKALOS
- School of Primary Education: Prof. DEMETRIOS GERMANOS

Faculty of Engineering (tel. 2310-995601; fax 2310-995611):
- School of Architecture: Prof. NIKOLAOS KALOGIROU
- School of Chemical Engineering: Prof. VASSILIOS PAPAGEORGIOU
- School of Civil Engineering: Prof. DIMOSTHENIS ANGELLIDIS
- School of Electrical and Computer Engineering: Prof. NIKOLAOS MARGARIS
- School of Mathematics, Physics and Computational Sciences: Prof. GERASIMOS KOUROUKLIS
- School of Mechanical Engineering: Prof. NIKOLAOS MOUSIOPOULOS
- School of Rural and Survey Engineering: Prof. PETROS PATIAS
- School of Urban Regional Planning and Development (Veroia): Prof. NIKOLAOS RODOLAKIS

Faculty of Fine Arts (tel. 231-995071; fax 231-995073):
- School of Drama: Prof. NIKIFOROS PAPANDREOU
- School of Film Studies: Prof. APOSTOLOS-FOKION VETTAS
- School of Musical Studies: Prof. DIMITRIOS GIANNOU
- School of Visual and Applied Arts: Prof. GEORGIOS GOLFINOS

Faculty of Law, Economics and Political Sciences (tel. 2310-996539; fax 2310-996526):
- School of Economics: C. PAPADOPOULOS
- School of Law: K. HATZIKONSTANTINOU

Faculty of Philosophy (tel. 2310-995173; fax 2310-997152):
- School of English Language and Literature: Prof. ANGELIKI ATHANASIADOU
- School of French Language and Literature: Prof. A. NENOPOULOU-DROSOU
- School of German Language and Literature: Prof. IOANNA EKONOMOU-AGORASTOU
- School of History and Archaeology: Prof. THEOHARIS PAZARAS
- School of Italian Language and Literature: Prof. ANTONIOS TSOMPANOGLOU
- School of Philology: Prof. ANTONIOS REGAKOS
- School of Philosophy and Education: Prof. NIKOLAOS TERZIS
- School of Psychology: Prof. G. KIOSEOGLOU

Faculty of Sciences (tel. 2310-998020; fax 2310-998022):
- School of Biology: Prof. Z. SKOURAS
- School of Chemistry: Assoc. Prof. ANDREAS GIANNAKOUDAKIS
- School of Geology: Prof. GEORGIOS CHRISTOFIDIS
- School of Informatics: A. POMBORTZIS
- School of Mathematics: Prof. POLYCHRONIS MOISIADES
- School of Physics: Prof. STERGIOS LOGOTHETIDIS

Faculty of Theology:
- School of Ecclesiastical and Social Theology: Prof. GEORGIOS THEODOROUDIS
- School of Theology: Prof. MILTIADES KONSTANTINOU

Independent Schools:
- School of Journalism and Mass Media Studies: Prof. THEODOROS KORRES
- School of Pharmacy: Prof. ASTERIOS TSIFTSOGLOU
- School of Physical Education and Athletics in Serres: Prof. C. KAMPITSIS
- School of Physical Education and Athletics in Thessaloniki: Prof. ASTERIOS DELIGIANNIS

DIMOKRITEIO PANEPISTIMIO THRAKIS ('Demokritos' University of Thrace)

Administration Building, University Campus, 691 00 Komotini
Telephone: 2531-039000
Fax: 2531-039081
E-mail: intrela@duth.gr
Internet: www.duth.gr

Founded 1973
State control
Language of instruction: Greek
Academic year: September to August

Rector: A. KARABINIS
Vice-Rectors: K. SIMOPOULOS, ATH. KARABINIS, G. HADJICONSTANTINOU
Administrative Officer: E. TSITSOPOULOS

Library of 236,656 vols, 4,060 periodicals
Number of teachers: 495
Number of students: 18,627

DEANS

Faculty of Engineering: I. DIAMANTIS
Faculty of Law: K. KALAVROS
Faculty of Medicine: D. HATSERAS
Faculty of the Science of Physical Education and Sport: G. MAVROMMATIS
Department of Agricultural Development: G. VASSILIOU
Department of Architectural Engineering: C. ATHANASSOPOULOS
Department of Civil Engineering: ATH. KARABINIS
Faculty of Educational Sciences: TH. VOUGIOUKLIS

Department of Electrical Engineering and Computer Engineering: D. PAPADOPOULOS
Department of Environmental Engineering: VASS. TSICHRINTZIS
Department of Forestry and Management of the Environment and Natural Resources: K. SIDERIS
Department of Greek Literature: A. CHARALAMBAKIS
Department of History and Ethnology: D. SAMSARIS
Department of International Economic Relations and Development: G. HADJICONSTANTINOU
Department of Languages, Literature and Culture of the Black Sea Countries: I. SCHINAS
Department of Molecular Biology and Genetics: G. BOURIKAS
Department of Pre-School Education Sciences: L. BEZE
Department of Production and Management Engineering: ATH. KARABINAS
Department of Social Administration: K. REMELIS
Pedagogical Department of Primary Education: E. TARATORI

PROFESSORS

Faculty of Law (University Campus, New Law School, 691 00 Komotini; tel. 2531-039890; fax 2531-039897):
ALIPRANDIS, N., Labour Law
CHARALAMBAKIS, A., Penal Law
KALAVROS, K., Civil Procedural Law
KONSTANDINIDIS, A., Penal Procedural Law
MANIOTIS, D., Civil Procedural Law
PARARAS, P., Constitutional Law
PITSAKIS, K., History of Law
POULIS, G., Ecclesiastical Law
REMELIS, K., Administrative Law
SCHINAS, J., Commercial Law

Faculty of Medicine (Ioakim Kavyri 6, 681 00 Alexandroupoli; tel. 25510-30921; fax 25510-30922):
BOUGIOUKAS, Cardiac Surgery
BOURIKAS, G., Pathology
BOUROS, D., Pneumonology
CHATSERAS, D., Cardiology
CHOURDAKIS, K., Toxicology, Forensic Medicine
DIMITRIOU, TH., Anatomy
KARTALIS, G., Pathology
KOUSKOUKIS, K., Dermatology, Venereal Diseases
KTENIDOU-KARTALI, S., Microbiology
MALTEZOS, E., Pathology
MANOLAS, K., Surgery
MAROULIS, G., Obstetrics and Gynaecology
MINOPOULOS, G., Surgery
PAPADOPOULOS, E., Urology
PRASSOPOULOS, P., Radiology
SIMOPOULOS, K., Surgery
SIVRIDIS, E., Pathology
VARGEMEZIS, V., Nephrology

Faculty of the Science of Physical Education and Sport (7 km on National Rd, Komotini–Xanthi, 691 00 Komotini; tel. 2531-039621; fax 2531-039623; e-mail tefaa@phyed.duth.gr):
CHARACHOUSOU-KABITSI, Y., Mass Sports
GODOLIAS, G., Sports Medicine
KABITSIS, CH., Classical Athletics
KIOUMOURTZOGLOU, E., Basketball Coaching
LAIOS, ATH., Basketball Coaching
LAPARIDIS, K., Nutrition in Sports
MANDIS, K., Tennis
MAVROMATIS, G., Statistics
SERBEZIS, V., Teaching of Greek Folk Dancing
TAXILDARIS, K., Basketball
TOKMAKIDIS, S., Exercise Physiology

Department of Agricultural Development (Pantazidou 193, 682 00 Orestiada; tel. 2552-041161; fax 2552-041191; e-mail ezelidou@ores.duth.gr):
ABAS, Z., General and Special Animal Husbandry
BEZIRTZOGLOU, E., Microbiology, Microbe Ecology
GALANOPOULOS, K., Agricultural Economy
KOTOULA-SYKA, EL., Pests, Pesticides, Pest Control
KOUTROUMANIDIS, TH., Applied Economic Statistics
KOUTROUMBAS, SP., General and Special Agriculture
SPARTALIS, ST., Algebra
TOKATLIDIS, I., Genetics and Plant Improvement
VASSILIOU, G., Agricultural Pharmacology and Ecotoxicology

Department of Architectural Engineering (Vasilissis Sofias 1, 671 00 Xanthi; tel. 2541-079350; fax 2541-079349; e-mail info@arch.duth.gr):
AMERICANOU, E., Architectural Design
BARKAS, N., Building Construction and Architectural Acoustics
EXARCHOPOULOS, P.-L., Architectural Design and Compositions
KOKKORIS, P., Architectural Design
KOLOKOTRONIS, I., History of Art, European and American Art of the 20th Century
LIANOS, N., Architectural Design
MANTZOU, P., Architectural Design, Building Compositions
MICHAELIDIS, A., Architectural and Construction Sculpture
PATRIKIOS, G., Architectural Design, Spatial Organization and Microenvironment
POLYCHRONOPOULOS, D., Urban Planning
POTAMIANOS, I., History of Architecture
PREPIS, ALK., History of Art
THEONI, X., Architectural Design and Compositions, Creation of Building Units for Professional and Private Use
THOMAS, N., Architectural and Construction Drawing
TSIOUKAS, VASS., Topography

Department of Civil Engineering (Vasilissis Sofias 1, 671 00 Xanthi; tel. 2541-079031; fax 2541-020275; e-mail info@civil.duth.gr):
ATHANASSOPOULOS, CHR., Building Construction
GALOUSSIS, EV., Steel Construction
GDOUTOS, EM., Technical Engineering and Applied Mechanics
KARABINIS, ATH., Reinforced Concrete Structures
KARAGIANNIS, CH., Construction of Reinforced Concrete
KARALIS, TH., Soil Mechanics: Foundations
KOTSOVINOS, N., Hydraulics
LABRINOS, P., Higher Mathematics
LIOLIOS, AST., Higher Mathematics
MATSOUKIS, P.-F., Maritime Engineering
PANAGIOTAKOPOULOS, D., Construction Project Management
PANTAZOPOULOU, ST., Construction of Reinforced Concrete
PAPADOPOULOS, V., General Topology
SIDERIS, K., Building Materials
STEPHANIS, VAS., Transport Engineering, Survey Engineering

Department of Electrical Engineering (Vasilissis Sofias 1, 671 00 Xanthi; tel. 2541-079035; fax 2541-079037; e-mail info@ee.duth.gr):
BEKAKOS, M., Computers, Hardware
CHAMZAS, CHR., Signal and Image Processing, Coding, MM Communication Systems, Networks
GEORGOULAS, N., Microelectronic and Optoelectronic Materials and Elements
PAPADOPOULOS, D., Electric Engines
PAPAMARKOS, N., Electric Cicuits, Digital Filters, Digital Image Processing
SARRIS, EM., Electromagnetic Theory
SPARIS, P., Special Mechanical Engineering
THANAILAKIS, A., Electrical and Electronic Materials Technology
TSALIDIS, PH., Computer Science
TSANGAS, N., Nuclear Engineering and Technology

Department of Environmental Engineering (University Campus of Xanthi, Kimmeria, 671 00 Xanthi; tel. 2541-079101; fax 2541-079108; e-mail mlekidou@lib.duth.gr):
AIVAZIDIS, AL., Environmental Technology
OUZOUNIS, K., Environmental Chemistry
RAPSOMANIKIS, SP., Air Pollution, Atmospheric Pollutant Control Technology
TSICHRINTZIS, V., Ecological Engineering Technology
VOUDRIAS, E., Solid Waste Management

Department of Forestry and Management of the Environment and Natural Resources (Pantazidou 193, 682 00 Orestiada; tel. 2552-041171; fax 2552-041192; e-mail impatzio@ores.duth.gr):
AVRAMIDIS, ST., Wood Science
ILIADIS, LAZ., Forestry Informatics
KARANIKOLA, P., Forest Wood Entomology
MANOLAS, EV., Sociology and Environmental Science, Forest Education
MILIOS, IL., Silviculture
PAPAGEORGIOU, AT., Forest Genetics
TSACHALIDIS, E., Game Ecology and Management

Department of Greek Literature (University Campus, 691 00 Komotini; tel. 25310-39900; fax 25310-39901):
IOANNIDOU, CH., Ancient Greek Literature
KAMBAKI-VOUGIOUKLI, P., Applied Linguistics
KONTOGIANNI, VASS., Modern Greek Literature
MANAKIDOU, H., Ancient Greek Literature
MANOS, AND., Ancient Greek Philosophy
PANTELIDIS, N., General Linguistics
TSOURIS, K., Byzantine History and Archaeology
TZIATZI-PAPAGIANNI, M., Byzantine Literature

Department of History and Ethnology (Panaghi Tsaldari 1, 691 00 Komotini; tel. 25310-39462; fax 25310-39462):
CHATZOPOULOS, K., History of Modern Hellenism
GALLIS, K., Prehistoric Archaeology
PAPAZOGLOU, G., History (based on sources such as Codices)
SAMSARIS, D., Roman History
XIROTYRIS, N., Physical Anthropology

Department of International Economic Relations and Development (University Campus, 691 00 Komotini; tel. 2531-039826; fax 2531-039830; e-mail ekostant@ierd.duth.gr; internet www.ierd.duth.gr):
CHATZIKONSTANTINOU, G., Economic Theory
CHIONIS, DION., International (Direct) Investments and Multinationals
KONSTANDINIDIS, E., International Economic Law, International and European Business Law
MOURMOURIS, I., Transportation Economics and Management

Department of Languages, Literature and Culture of the Black Sea Countries (Pan. Tsaldari 1, 691 00 Komotini; tel. 2531-039413; fax 2531-039421; e-mail ddiamant@kom.duth.gr):
FALANGAS, A., History and Civilization of the Western and Northern Black Sea Area
KEKRIDIS, E., Contemporary and Recent Culture of the Black Sea Peoples
THOMADAKI, EV., Theoretical Linguistics

Department of Molecular Biology and Genetics (Dimitras 19, Old Hospital, 681 00 Alexandroupoli; tel. and fax 25510-30610; e-mail secr@mbg.duth.gr):

CHLICHLIA, AIK., Immunobiology
GRIGORIOU, M., Molecular Biology
KOFFA, M., Cell Biology
PHYLAKTAKIDOU, K., Chemistry
SANDALTZOPOULOS, RAF., Molecular Biology

Department of Pre-School Education Sciences (Nea Chili, 681 00 Alexandroupoli; tel. 25510-39623; fax 25510-39624; e-mail secr@psed.duth.gr; internet www.psed.duth.gr):

BEZE, L., Psychology and Sociology of Education
GOGOU-KRITIKOU, L., Sociology of Education
METAXAKI-KOSIONIDOU, CHR., Informatics Applications in Pre-School Education
PETROGIANNIS, KON., Development Psychology

Department of Production and Management Engineering (University Campus of Xanthi, Kimmeria, 671 00 Xanthi; tel. 2541-079345; fax 2541-079361; e-mail secr@pme.duth.gr):

ANAGNOSTOPOULOS, K., Business Economics and Management with Engineering
CHATZOGLOU, P., Information Systems in Administration
SIMINTIRAS, A., Marketing
TOURASSIS, VASS., Industrial Production

Department of Social Administration (Pan. Tsaldari 1, 691 00 Komitini; tel. 25310-39409; fax 25310-39442; e-mail dgogou@kom.duth.gr):

CHATZOPOULOS, VASS., EU Law and Policies
KALLINIKAKI-MANGRIOTI, TH., Social Work
KANDYLAKI, AG., Social Work and Local Development in Multicultural Societies
KATROUNGALOS, G., Public Law
PAPASTYLIANOU, A., Social Psychology
PAPATHEODOROU, CH., Social Policy
PETMEZIDOU-TSOULOUVI, M., Social Policy
VENIERIS, D., Social Policy
VIDALI, SOF., Criminology, Anti-crime Policy

Pedagogical Department of Primary Education (Nea Chili, 681 00 Alexandroupoli; tel. 25510-30024; fax 25510-39630; e-mail tsesmel@eled.duth.gr):

DAVAZOGLOU, ANG., Education of Children with Special Needs
KARAKATSANIS, P., Educational Philosophy
KEKKERIS, G., Informatics, Multimedia in Aesthetics Education
KEVREKIDIS, TH., Biology and Ecology
MICHAS, P., Teaching of Natural Sciences
PAPAGEORGIOU, G., Teaching of Chemistry, Environmental Chemistry
PETROPOULOS, I., Ancient Greek Literature
ROKKA, ANG., Earth Sciences, Geology, Geography
SAKONIDIS, CHAR., Teaching of Mathematics
TARATORI, EL., Teaching Methodology
VOUGIOUKLIS, TH., Mathematics

ELLINIKO ANOIKTO PANEPISTIMIO (Hellenic Open University)

16 Sahtouri–Ag. Andreou St, 262 22 Patra
Telephone: 2610-362564
Fax: 2610-361420
E-mail: info@eap.gr
Internet: www.eap.gr

Founded 1992 as a distance-learning university, offering undergraduate and postgraduate courses to adults
State control

President: ALEXIOS LYKOURGHIOTIS
Secretary-General: CHARALAMPOS RODOPOULOS

Number of teachers: 703
Number of students: 12,706 (8,251 undergraduate, 4,455 postgraduate)

DEANS

Faculty of Applied Arts: DIMITRIOS ZEVGOLIS
Faculty of Humanities: LILA LEONTIDOU
Faculty of Sciences and Technology: SPIROS TZAMARIAS
Faculty of Social Sciences: (vacant)

ETHNIKON KAI KAPODISTRIAKON PANEPISTIMION ATHINON (National and Capodistrian University of Athens)

Odos Panepistimiou 30, 106 79 Athens
Telephone: 210-3614301
Fax: 210-3602145
Internet: www.uoa.gr

Founded 1837
State control
Language of instruction: Greek
Academic year: September to June

Rector: Prof. GEORGE DEMETRIUS BABINIOTIS
Vice-Rectors: Prof. CH. KITTAS (Academic Affairs and Personnel), Prof. M. DERMITZAKIS (Financial Planning and Development), Prof. D. ASIMAKOPOULOS (Strategic Planning Works and Student Affairs)

Number of teachers: 1,709
Number of students: 45,000

DEANS

Faculty of Arts: IOANNIS PARASKEVOPOULOS
Faculty of Health Sciences: KONSTANTINOS DIMOPOULOS
Faculty of Law, Economic and Political Sciences: CHRISTOS ROZAKIS
Faculty of Sciences: NIKOLAOS SIMEONIDIS
Faculty of Theology: CONSTANTINE SCOUTERIS

HEADS OF DEPARTMENTS

Faculty of Arts:

English Language and Literature: B. RAIZIS
French Language and Literature: D. PANTELODEMOS
German Language and Literature: W. BENNING
Greek Language and Literature: G. BABINIOTIS
History and Archaeology: E. MIKROYIANNAKIS
Philosophy, Psychology and Education: I. MARKANTONIS

Faculty of Health Sciences:

Dentistry: Z. MANTZAVINOS
Hospital Care: K. KYRIAKOU
Medicine: K. DIMOPOULOS
Pharmacology: NICOS HOULIS

Faculty of Law, Economics and Political Sciences:

Business and Finance: NIKOLAOS MILONAS
Economic History and the Philisophy of the Social Sciences: KOSTAS KOSTIS
International Economics and Development: KOSTIS VAITSIOS
Mathematics and Informatics: JOHN DEMETRIOU
Political Economy: YANNIS STOURNARAS
Quantitative Methods: DEMETRIS MOSCHOS

Faculty of Sciences:

Biology: E. FRANGOULIS
Chemistry: N. HATZICHRISTIDIS
Communication and Mass Media Studies: G. LAVVAS
Computer Sciences: G. PHILOKYPROU
Geosciences: S. SKOUNAKIS
Mathematics: E. KOUNIAS
Music: The Rector: PETROS A. GAMTOS
Physical Education and Athletics: V. KLEISSOURAS
Physics: P. LASKARIDIS
Teacher Training for Pre-school Education: I. PAPACOSTAS
Teacher Training for Primary Education: TH. EXARHAKOS
Theatre Studies: The Rector: PETROS A. GAMTOS

Faculty of Theology:

Pastoral Studies: ILIAS VOULGARAKIS
Theology: CHRISTOS VOULGAKIS

ETHNIKO METSOVIO POLYTECHNEIO (National Technical University of Athens)

Polytechnioupoli, Zografou, 157 80 Athens
Telephone: 210-7722017
Fax: 210-7722028
Internet: www.ntua.gr

Founded 1836
State control
Language of instruction: Greek
Academic year: September to August

Rector: Prof. ANDREAS ANDREOPOULOS
Vice-Rectors: P. KOTTIS, E. DRIS
Chief Administrative Officer: E. RELAKI
Librarian: M. KALABALIKI

Library: see Libraries and Archives
Number of teachers: 700
Number of students: 1,000

Publications: *Pyrphoros* (every 2 weeks), *Scientific Papers, Scientific Year Book*

HEADS OF DEPARTMENTS

Architecture: Prof. IOANNIS POLYZOS
Chemical Engineering: Prof. S. SIMOPOULOS
Civil Engineering: Prof. K. MOUTSOURIS
Electrical and Computing Engineering: Prof. NIKOLAUS THEODOROU
Applied Mathematics and Physics: Prof. E. GALANIS
Mechanical Engineering: Prof. S. SIMOPOULOS
Mining and Metallurgical Engineering: Prof. P. NEOU-SYNGOUNA
Naval Architecture and Marine Engineering: Prof. G. ATHANASSOULIS
Rural Engineering and Surveying: Prof. A. GEORGOPOULOS

DIRECTORS OF SECTIONS

Applied Mathematics and Physics:

Humanities, Social Science and Law: V. NIKOLAIDOU
Mathematics: K. KYRIAKIS
Physics: P. PISSIS

Architecture:

Architectural Design: AMILIOS KORONAIOS
Design and Technology: ALEKSANDRA MONEMVASITOU
Design, Visual Studies and Communication: IOANNIS TSOUDEROS
Urban and Regional Planning: IOANNIS TERZOGLOU

Chemical Engineering:

Chemical Sciences: A. HARALAMBOUS
Process Analysis and Plant Design: A. BOUDOUVIS
Material Science and Engineering: F. ROUBANI-KALANZOPOULOU
Synthesis and Development of Industrial Processes: A. VLYSSIDIS

Civil Engineering:

Engineering Construction and Management: A. ANAGNOSTOPOULOS
Geotechnical Engineering: (vacant)
Structural Engineering: J. ERMOPOULOS
Transportation Planning and Engineering: J. FRANTSESKAKIS
Water Resources, Hydraulic and Maritime Engineering: A. ADREADAKIS

Electrical and Computing Engineering:
Computer Science: G. STASINOPOULOS
Electrical Power: J. STATHOPOULOS
Electroscience: N. OUZOUNOGLOU

Mechanical Engineering:
Fluid Mechanics Engineering: G. BERGELES
Industrial Management and Operational Research: G. FOKAS-KOSMETATOS
Manufacturing Technology: A. MAMALIS
Mechanical Construction and Automatic Control: P. MAKRIS
Nuclear Engineering: D. LEONIDOU
Thermal Engineering: K. RAKOPOULOS

Mining and Metallurgical Engineering:
Geological Sciences: Prof. Dr E. MPOSKOS
Metallurgy and Materials Technology: Assoc. Prof. K. TSAKALAKIS
Mining Engineering: Prof. ALEXANDROS I. SOFIANOS

PROFESSORS

AFRATI, F., Electrical and Computer Engineering
ANAGNOSTOU, M., Electrical and Computer Engineering
ANASTASSOPOULOU, I., Materials Science and Engineering
ANDREOPOULOS, A., Synthesis and Development of Industrial Processing
ANDROUTSOPOULOS, G., Process Analysis and Plant Design
ANTONOPOULOS, K., Mechanical Engineering
ASSIMAKOPOULO, D., Process Analysis and Plant Design
ASSIMAKOPOULOS, V., Electrical and Computer Engineering
ATHANASOULIS, G., Naval Architecture and Marine Engineering
AVARITSIOTIS, J., Electrical and Computer Engineering
BAFA, G., Process Analysis and Plant Design
BATIS, G., Materials Science and Engineering
BOUDOUVIS, A., Process Analysis and Plant Design
BOURKAS, P., Electrical and Computer Engineering
CAPROS, P., Electrical and Computer Engineering
CAPSALIS, C., Electrical and Computer Engineering
CARAYANNIS, G., Electrical and Computer Engineering
CHRYSSOULAKIS, J., Materials Science and Engineering
CONSTANTINOU, F., Electrical and Computer Engineering
COTTIS, P., Electrical and Computer Engineering
DERVOS, K., Electrical and Computer Engineering
DIALINAS, E., Electrical and Computer Engineering
FRANGOPOULOS, CH., Naval Architecture and Marine Engineering
FRANGOS, P., Electrical and Computer Engineering
FTICOS, CHR., Synthesis and Development of Industrial Processing
GLYTSIS, E., Electrical and Computer Engineering
HATZIARGYRIOU, N., Electrical and Computer Engineering
HIZANIDIS, K., Electrical and Computer Engineering
KAKATSIOS, X., Mechanical Engineering
KAKLIS, P., Naval Architecture and Marine Engineering
KANELLOPOULOS, J., Electrical and Computer Engineering
KASELOURI-RIGOPOULOU, V., Chemical Sciences
KAYAFAS, E., Electrical and Computer Engineering
KOLISIS, FR., Synthesis and Development of Industrial Processing
KOLLIAS, S., Electrical and Computer Engineering
KOUKIOS, E., Synthesis and Development of Industrial Processing
KOULOUMBI, N., Materials Science and Engineering
KOUMANTAKIS, I., Geological Sciences
KOUSSIOURIS, T., Electrical and Computer Engineering
KOUTSOURIS, D., Electrical and Computer Engineering
KRIKELIS, N., Mechanical Engineering
KYRTATOS, N., Naval Architecture and Marine Engineering
LIVADITI, K., Geological Sciences
LOIS, E., Synthesis and Development of Industrial Processing
LOIZIDOU-MALAMIS, M., Chemical Sciences
LOUKAKIS, TH., Naval Architecture and Marine Engineering
MACHIAS, A., Electrical and Computer Engineering
MAGLARIS, V., Electrical and Computer Engineering
MAMALIS, A., Mechanical Engineering
MANIAS, S., Electrical and Computer Engineering
MARAGOS, P., Electrical and Computer Engineering
MARATOS, N., Electrical and Computer Engineering
MARINOS-KOURI, D., Process Analysis and Plant Design
MARKATO, N., Process Analysis and Plant Design
MARKOPOULOU-IGGLESI, O., Chemical Sciences
MAROULI, Z., Process Analysis and Plant Design
MATHIOUDAKIS, K., Mechanical Engineering
MAVRAKOS, S., Naval Architecture and Marine Engineering
MITROU, N., Electrical and Computer Engineering
MOROPOULOU, A., Materials Science and Engineering
MPERGELES, G., Mechanical Engineering
MPOSKOS, E., Geological Sciences
NEOU-SYNGOUNA, P., Metallurgy and Materials Technology
OCHSENKUEHN-PETROPOULOU, M., Chemical Sciences
PANAGIOTOU, G.N., Mining Engineering
PANAGOPOULOS, K.J., Mining Engineering
PANAGOPOULOS, C., Metallurgy and Materials Technology
PAPADIMITRIOU, G., Metallurgy and Materials Technology
PAPAILIOU, K., Mechanical Engineering
PAPAKONSTANTINOU, G., Electrical and Computer Engineering
PAPANIKOLAOU, A., Naval Architecture and Marine Engineering
PAPANTONIS, D., Mechanical Engineering
PAPASPYRIDES, C.D., Synthesis and Development of Industrial Processing
PAPAVASILOPOULOS, G., Electrical and Computer Engineering
PAPAYANNAKI, L., Process Analysis and Plant Design
PAPAYANNAKOS, N., Process Analysis and Plant Design
PAPAZOGLOU, V., Naval Architecture and Marine Engineering
PARASKEVOPOULOS, P., Electrical and Computer Engineering
PASPALIARIS, I., Metallurgy and Materials Technology
PEKMESTZI, K., Electrical and Computer Engineering
PHILIPPOPOULOS, K., Process Analysis and Plant Design
PROTONOTARIOS, E., Electrical and Computer Engineering
PSARAFTIS, CH., Naval Architecture and Marine Engineering
RAKOPOULOS, K., Mechanical Engineering
ROGDAKIS, E., Mechanical Engineering
ROUBANI-KALANZOPOULOU, F., Materials Science and Engineering
ROUMELIOTIS, J., Electrical and Computer Engineering
SAMOUILIDIS, E., Electrical and Computer Engineering
SELLIS, T., Electrical and Computer Engineering
SFANTSIKOPOULOS, M., Mechanical Engineering
SIMITZIS, J., Materials Science and Engineering
SIMOPOULOS, S., Mechanical Engineering
SKORDALAKIS, E., Electrical and Computer Engineering
SPENTZAS, K., Mechanical Engineering
SPYRELLIS, N., Chemical Sciences
STAFYLOPATIS, A.G., Electrical and Computer Engineering
STAMATAKI, S., Mining Engineering
STASSINOPOULOS, G., Electrical and Computer Engineering
STATHOPULOS, I.A., Electrical and Computer Engineering
STOURNAS, S., Synthesis and Development of Industrial Processing
SYKAS, E., Electrical and Computer Engineering
TATSIOPOULOS, I., Mechanical Engineering
THEODOROU, N., Electrical and Computer Engineering
THEODOROU, TH., Materials Science and Engineering
THEOLOGOU, M., Electrical and Computer Engineering
TRIANTAFYLLOU, G., Naval Architecture and Marine Engineering
TSALAMENGAS, J., Electrical and Computer Engineering
TSANAKAS, P., Electrical and Computer Engineering
TSANGARIS, S., Mechanical Engineering
TSANGARIS, G., Materials Science and Engineering
TSEZOS, M., Metallurgy and Materials Technology
TSIMAS, S., Chemical Sciences
TZABIRAS, G., Naval Architecture and Marine Engineering
TZAFESTAS, S., Electrical and Computer Engineering
UZUNOGLOU, N., Electrical and Computer Engineering
VASSILIOU, Y., Electrical and Computer Engineering
VASSILIOU, P., Materials Science and Engineering
VGENOPOULOS, A., Geological Sciences
VLYSSIDIS, A., Synthesis and Development of Industrial Processing
VOMVORIDIS, J., Electrical and Computer Engineering
VOURNAS, C., Electrical and Computer Engineering
XANTHAKIS, J., Electrical and Computer Engineering
YOVA, D., Electrical and Computer Engineering
ZACHOS, S., Electrical and Computer Engineering
ZEVGOLIS, E.N., Metallurgy and Materials Technology

GEOPONIKO PANEPISTIMIO ATHINON
(Athens Agricultural University)

Iera Odos 75, 118 55 Athens
Telephone: 210-5294802
Fax: 210-3460885
E-mail: r@aua.gr

Internet: www.aua.gr
Founded 1920
Rector: Prof. ANDREAS KARAMANOS
Sec.-Gen.: CON. TSAKOUMAKIS
Number of teachers: 177
Number of students: 3,500
Faculties of Agricultural Biotechnology; Animal Science; Crop Science; Food Science and Technology; Natural Resources Management and Agricultural Engineering; Rural Economics and Development; Science.

DIRECTORS

Laboratory of Agribusiness Management: PATSIS PANAGIOTIS
Laboratory of Agricultural Engineering: NICK SIGRIMIS
Laboratory of Agricultural Extension, Agricultural Systems and Rural Sociology: KASIMIS CHARALAMBOS
Laboratory of Agricultural Hydraulics: PETROS G. KERKIDES
Laboratory of Agricultural Zoology and Entomology: NIKOLAOS G. EMMANUEL
Laboratory of Agronomy: ANDREAS KARAMANOS
Laboratory of Anatomy and Physiology of Farm Animals: IOANNIS MENEGATOS
Laboratory of Animal Breeding and Husbandry: ROGDAKIS EMMANUEL
Laboratory of Animal Nutrition: GEORGE ZERVAS
Laboratory of Applied Hydrobiology: SOFRONIOS E. PAPOUTSOGLOU
Laboratory of Botany: GEORGE SARLIS
Laboratory of Dairy Research: IOANNIS KANDARAKIS
Laboratory of Ecology and Environmental Sciences: GERASIMOS ARAPIS
Laboratory of Electron Microscopy: KONSTANTINOS FASSEAS
Laboratory of Enzyme Technology: Y. CLONIS
Laboratory of Floriculture and Landscape Architecture: JOANNIS CHRONOPOULOS
Laboratory of Food Chemistry: M. KOMAITIS
Laboratory of Food Process Engineering, Treatment and Preservation of Agricultural Products: P. RODIS
Laboratory of Food Quality Control and Hygiene: P. ATHANASOPOULOS
Laboratory of General and Agricultural Meteorology: AIKATERINI CHRONOPOULOU-SERELI
Laboratory of General and Agricultural Microbiology: GEORGE AGGELIS
Laboratory of General Chemistry: MOSCHOS POLISSIOU
Laboratory of Genetics: MICHAEL LOUKAS
Laboratory of Informatics: ALEXANDROS SIDERIDIS
Laboratory of Mathematics and Theoretical Mechanics: TAKIS SAKKALIS
Laboratory of Microbiology and Biotechnology of Foods: G. I. NYCHAS
Laboratory of Mineralogy and Geology: GEORGE MIGIROS
Laboratory of Molecular Biology: POLYDEUKIS HATZOPOULOS
Laboratory of Pesticide Science: BASIL ZIOGAS
Laboratory of Physics: ATHANASIOS HOUNTAS
Laboratory of Plant Breeding and Biometry: PANTOUSES J. KALTSIKES
Laboratory of Plant Physiology and Morphology: IOANNIS DROSSOPOULOS
Laboratory of Political Economy and European Integration: MARTINOS NIKOLAOS
Laboratory of Pomology: CONSTANTINE A. PONTIKIS
Laboratory of Rural Economic Development: SOPHIA EFSTRATOGLOU
Laboratory of Rural Policy and Cooperatives: DAMIANOS DIMITRIS
Laboratory of Sericulture and Apiculture: PASCHALIS HARIZANIS
Laboratory of Soil Science and Agricultural Chemistry: KOLLIAS VASSILIKI
Laboratory of Vegetable Crops: CHRISTOS M. OLYMPIOS
Laboratory of Viticulture: MANOLIS N. STAVRAKAKIS

HAROKOPIO PANEPISTIMION
(Harokopio University)

70 El. Venizelou St, 17671 Athens
Telephone: 210-9549100
Fax: 210-9577050
E-mail: haruniv@hua.gr
Internet: www.hua.gr
Founded 1990
State control
Rector: ANDREAS KIRIAKOUSIS
Vice-Rector (Academic Affairs and Staff): KATERINA MARIDAKI-KASSOTAKI
Vice-Rector (Economic Planning and Development): SMARAGDI ANTONOPOULOU
Library of 8,000 vols, 200 journals
Number of teachers: 65430

HEADS OF DEPARTMENTS

Department of Dietetics and Nutritional Science: NIKOLAOS ANDRIKOPOULOS
Department of Geography: KONSTANTINOS HATZIMICHALIS
Department of Home Economics and Ecology: GREGORIOS PAGKAKIS

IKONOMIKON PANEPISTIMION ATHINON
(Athens University of Economics and Business)

Odos Patission 76, 104 34 Athens
Telephone: 210-8203250
Fax: 210-8228419postgraduate studies at: 47 Evelpidon Str. 113 62 Athens
Telephone: 210-8203640
Fax: 210-8228655
Internet: www.aueb.gr
Founded 1920
Rector: Prof. ANDREAS KINTIS
Sec.-Gen.: S. BENOS
Librarian: G. THEOFANOPOULOU
Library of 100,000 vols, 1,000 periodicals: See Libraries and Archives
Number of teachers: 118
Number of students: 11,800
Faculties of Business Administration, Computer Science, Economics, International and European Economic Studies, Management Science and Marketing and Statistics.

IONIO PANEPISTIMIO
(Ionian University)

Rizospaston Voulefton 7, 491 00 Corfu
Telephone: 2661-044878
Fax: 2661-022549
E-mail: int_rel@ionio.gr
Internet: www.ionio.gr
Founded 1984
State control
Academic year: October to July
Rector: DIMITRIOS TSOUGARAKIS
Vice-Rectors: CHARALAMBOS XANTHOUDAKIS (Academic Management and Human Resources), VASILIOS CHRISIKOPOULOS (Financial Management)
Departments of Archives and Library Science, Audio and Visual Arts, Computer Science, Foreign Languages, History, Music Studies and Translation and Interpreting.

PANEPISTIMION AEGAEOU
(University of the Aegean)

University Hill, Admin. Building 2, 811 00 Mytilene
Telephone: 2251-036000
Fax: 2251-036009
Internet: www.aegean.gr
Founded 1984
Rector: Prof. SOKRATIS K. KATSIKAS
Librarian: ELLI VLACHOU
Library of 86,674 vols
Number of teachers: 422
Number of students: 11,828 (7,599 undergraduate, 4,229 postgraduate)
Departments: Chios campus: Business Administration, Shipping, Transport and Trade; Mytilene campus: Environmental Studies, Social Anthropology, Geography, Marine Sciences, Sociology; Rhodes campus: Primary Education, Secondary Education, Mediterranean Studies; Samos campus: Mathematics, Information and Communication Systems.

PANEPISTIMION IOANNINON
(University of Ioannina)

University Campus, 451 10 Ioannina
Telephone: 2651-097446
Fax: 2651-097200
E-mail: intlrel@cc.uoi.gr
Internet: www.uoi.gr
Founded 1964 as a dept of the Aristotle University of Thessaloniki; established as an independent university 1970
State control
Language of instruction: Greek
Academic year: September to June
Rector: Prof. GEORGIOS DIMOU
Vice-Rectors: Prof. NIKI J. AGNANTIS, Prof. IOANNIS GEROTHANASIS, Prof. CHRISTOS MASSALAS
Registrar: L.-N. PAPALOUKAS
Librarian: GEORGIOS ZACHOS (acting)
Library of 310,000 vols
Number of teachers: 500
Number of students: 13,000
Publications: *Eperitis 'Dodoni I'* (History and Archaeology, annually), *Eperitis 'Dodoni II'* (Philology, annually), *Eperitis 'Dodoni III'* (Philosophy, Education and Psychology, annually)

DEANS

School of Educational Sciences: Prof. A. PAPAIOANNOU
School of Medicine: Prof. EPAMINONDAS TSIANOS
School of Natural Resources in Agrinio: Prof. GEORGE LEONTARIS (acting)
School of Natural Sciences: Prof. GEORGIOS KARAKOSTAS
School of Philosophy: Prof. ERATOSTHENIS KAPSOMENOS
School of Science and Technology: (vacant)

PROFESSORS

School of Educational Sciences (tel. 2651-097454; fax 2651-097020):

DIMOU, G., Pedagogics and Psychology of Learning Disabilities
KAPSALIS, G.
KANAVAKIS, M., Pedagogics
KARAFYLIS, G., Society Philosophy
KARPOZILOU, M.
KONSTANTINOU, C., School Pedagogics
STAVROU, L., Psychology of Pre-School Education
TZOULIS, CH., Modern Greek Literature
ZAHARIS, D., Evolutionary Psychology in Education

School of Medicine (tel. 2651-097201; fax 2651-097019):

AGNADI-GIRA, N. J., Pathological Anatomy
ANDRONIKOU, S., Neo-Natology
ASIMAKOPOULOS, C., Oto-Rhino-Laryngology
BERIS, A., Orthopaedics
BOURANTAS, C., Pathology, Haematology
DROSOS, A., Pathology-Rheumatology
EFRAIMIDIS, S., Radiology
EVANGELOU, A., Physiology
FOTSIS, TH., Biological Chemistry
GEORGATOS, S., Biology
GEROULANOS, ST., History of Medicine
GLAROS, D., Medical Physics
HATZIS, I., Dermatology
IOANNIDIS, I., Hygiene
KALEF-EZRA, J., Medical Physics
KANAVAROS, P., Anatomy-Histology
KAPPAS, A., Surgery
KIRITSIS, A., Neurology
KONSTANTOPOULOS, S., Pathology and Pneumonology
LOLIS, D., Obstetrics and Gynaecology
MALAMOU-MITSI, V., Pathology
MARSELOS, M.-A., Medical Pharmacology
MAVREAS, V., Psychiatry
PAPADOPOULOS, G., Anaesthiology
PARASKEVAIDIS, C., Organic Peptide Chemistry
PAVLIDIS, N., Oncology
PSILAS, C., Ophthalmology
SEFERIADIS, C., Biological Chemistry
SIAMOPOULOS, K., Pathology and Nephrology
SIAMOPOULOU-MAVRIDOU, A., Paediatrics
SKEVAS, A., Oto-rhino-laryngology
SOFIKITIS, N., Urology
SOUCACOS, P., Orthopaedics
TSIANOS, E., Oncology
TZAFLIDOU, M., Medical Physics
XENAKIS, T., Orthopaedics

School of Natural Resources in Agrinio:

FOTOPOULOS, CH., Administration of Agricultural Enterprises
MATTHOPOULOS, D., Administration of Environment and Natural Resources

School of Natural Sciences and Computer Science (tel. 2651-097190; fax 2651-097005):

AKRIVIS, G., Computer Science
ALBANIS, T., Environmental Protection
ALISSANDRAKIS, C., Physics of the Sun and Space
ASSIMAKOPOULOS, P., Nuclear Physics and Radio Ecology
BAIKOUSIS, CH., Differential Geometry
BATAKIS, N., Physics
BOLIS, TH., Combinatorial Group Theory
BOLOVINOS, AG., Atomic and Molecular Physics
DOUGIAS, S., Mathematical Analysis
DRAINAS, C., Chemistry
EVMIRIDIS, N., Inorganic Chemistry
EVANGELOU, SP., Physics, Theory of Condensed Matter
FERENTINOS, K., Statistics
FILOS, C., Mathematical Analysis
GALATSANOS, N., Computer Science
GEROTHANASIS, I., Organic Chemistry
GRAMMATIKOPOULOS, M., Differential Equations
HADJILIADIS, N., Inorganic and General Chemistry
HASANIS, T., Differential Geometry
KAMARATOS, E., Physical Chemistry
KAMBANOS, T., Inorganic Chemistry
KARAKOSTAS, G., Mathematical Analysis and Applications
KATSARAS, A., Functional Analysis
KATSOULIS, V., Meteorology and Climatology
KONDOMINAS, M., Chemistry
KOSMAS, M., Chemistry
KOSTARAKIS, P., Physics
KOUFOGIORGOS, TH., Differential Geometry
KOVALA-DEMERTZI, D., Inorganic Chemistry
LAGARIS, I., Computer Science
LEONDARIS, G., Physics, Elemental Multiplets
LOUKAS, S., Statistics
MANESIS, E., Physics, High Energy Theory
MARMARIDIS, N., Algebra
MASSALAS, CH., Continuum Physics and Mechanics
PANTIS, G., Theory of Nuclear Physics
PHILOS, C., Differential Equations
POMONIS, F., Industrial Chemistry
SAKARELLO DAITSO, M., Biochemistry
SAKARELLOS, C., Organic Peptide Chemistry
SDOUKOS, A., Industrial Chemistry
SFIKAS, Y. G., Differential Equations
STAVROULAKIS, I., Differential Equations
TAMVAKIS, K., Elementary Particle Theory and Cosmology
TRIANTIS, F., High-Energy Physics and Related Technological Applications
TSAMATOS, P., Mathematical Analysis
TSANGARIS, J., Inorganic and General Chemistry
VAGIONAKIS, C., Physics
VERGADOS, J., Theoretical Physics

School of Philosophy (tel. 2651-097176):

APOSTOLOPOULOU, G., History, Interpretation and Practice of Philosophy
ATHANASIOU, L., Language Teaching and Evaluation
CHADJIDAKI-BAHARA, T., Byzantine Archaeology
GOTOVOS, A., Pedagogics
HADJIDAKI-BACHARA, T., Byzantine Archaeology
KAPSOMENOS, E., Modern Greek Literature and Literary Theory
KARPOZILOS, A.-D., Medieval Greek Literature
KATSOURIS, A., Ancient Greek Philology
KONDORINI, B., History and Archaeology
KONSTANDINIDIS, C., Ancient and Medieval Greek Literature
KORDOSIS, M., Ancient and Medieval Greek Literature
MARAGOU, E., Classical Archaeology
MAVROMATIS, J., Byzantine Philology and Post-Byzantine Philology
MAVROYIORGOS, Y., Pedagogic Educational Policy
NOUTSOS, CH., History of Education
NOUTSOS, P., Philosophy
PALIOURAS, A., Byzantine Archaeology
PAPACONSTANDINOU, P., Pedagogics
PAPADIMITRIOU, E., Philosophy
PAPADOPOULOS, A., Prehistoric Archaeology
PAPAGEORGIOU, G., Modern History
PAPAPOSTOLOU, J., Classical Archaeology
PERISSINAKIS, J., Ancient Greek Literature
PLOUMIDIS, G., Venetian History and Historical Geography
RAIOS, D., Ancient Greek and Latin Philology
SIOROKAS, G., Modern European History
STASINOS, D., Psychology
SYNODINOU, A., Ancient Greek Philology
TRIANTI, A., Archaeology
TSANGALAS, K., Folklore

School of Science and Technology:

CHARALAMBOPOULOS, A., Material Science
DRAINAS, C., Chemistry
KAXIRAS, E., Materials Science
MASSALAS, CH., Continuum Physics and Mechanics
PSARROPOULOU, A., Animal Physiology

Independent Department of Economics:

PALYVOS, TH., Economics

PANEPISTIMIO KRITIS
(University of Crete)

741 00 Rethymnon, Crete

Telephone: 2831-077900
Fax: 2831-077909
E-mail: rectsecr@cc.uoc.gr
Internet: www.uoc.gr

Founded 1973
State control
Language of instruction: Greek
Academic year: September to June

Rector: Prof. CHRISTOS NIKOLAOU
Vice-Rectors: Prof. MICHAEL DAMANAKIS, Prof. AGELOS KRANIDIS
Director of International and Public Relations: Dr STELLA PAPADAKI-TZEDAKI
Librarian: MICHALIS TZEKAKIS

Library of 145,000 vols
Number of teachers: 580
Number of students: 10,628

Publications: *Ariadne* (faculty of letters), *Mandatoforos* (Modern Greek studies), *Triton* (newsletter)

HEADS OF DEPARTMENTS

Biology: I. PAPAMATHEAKIS
Chemistry: NIKOS MIHALOPOULOS
Computer Science: PANAGIOTIS TSAKALIDES
Economics: EMMANUEL PETRAKIS
History and Archaeology: CHRISTOS LOUKOS
Materials Science and Technology: GEORGIOS FYTAS
Mathematics: JANNIS ANTONIADIS
Philology: NIKOLAIDIS ANASTASIOS
Philosophy and Social Studies: GIANNIS KUGIUMUTZAKIS
Physics: PAPANICOLAOU NIKOS
Political Sciences: DIMITRIS KOTROYIANNOS
Psychology: GALANIS GIORGOS

AFFILIATED INSTITUTION

Foundation for Research and Technology–Hellas: POB 1385, 711 10 Heraklion; tel. 281-391500; fax 281-391555; e-mail central@admin.forth.gr; internet www.forth.grf. 1983; 254 research and teaching staff; 374 graduate students; Chair. Prof. E. N. ECONOMOU.

Constituent institutes:

Institute of Applied and Computational Mathematics: internet www.iacm.forth.gr; Dir Prof. VASSILIOS DOUGALIS.

Institute of Chemical Engineering and High Temperature Chemical Processes: internet www.iceht.forth.gr; Dir Prof. A. C. PAYATAKES.

Institute of Chemical Process Engineering Research Institute: internet www.cperi.forth.gr; Dir Prof. C. KIPARISSIDES.

Institute of Computer Science: internet www.ics.forth.gr; Dir Prof. CONSTANTINE STEPHANIDIS.

Institute of Electronic Structure and Lasers: internet www.iesl.forth.gr; Dir Prof. C. FOTAKIS.

Institute of Mediterranean Studies: internet www.ims.forth.gr; Dir Prof. A. KALPAXIS.

Institute of Molecular Biology and Biotechnology: internet www.imbb.forth.gr; Dir Prof. G. THIREOS.

PANEPISTIMION MAKEDONIAS
(University of Macedonia)

Egnatia 156, POB 1591, 540 06 Thessaloniki

Telephone: 231-0844825
Fax: 231-0844536
E-mail: grad@uom.gr

Internet: www.uom.gr
Founded 1957 as Graduate Industrial School of Thessaloniki
State control
Rector: Prof. KONSTANTINOS VELENZAS
Vice-Rectors: Prof. CONSTANTINOS MARGARITIS, Prof. CONSTANTINOS VELENTZAS
Secretary-General: TSOMOU-FISTA EVAGGELIA
Librarian: ANNA FRANKOU

Number of teachers: 108
Number of students: 8,000

HEADS OF DEPARTMENTS OF UNDERGRADUATE STUDIES

Department of Accounting and Finance: Prof. DIMITRIOS PAPADOPOULOS
Department of Applied Informatics: Prof. ANASTASIOS KATOS (acting)
Department of Balkan, Slavic and Oriental Studies: Prof. KOSTANTINOS VELENTZAS
Department of Business Administration: Prof. GEORGE PIPEROPOULOS
Department of Economics: Prof. DIMITRIOS IOANNIDIS
Department of Educational and Social Policy: Prof. LAZAROS TRIARHOU
Department of International and European, Economic and Political Studies: Prof. MAGDALINI PSAROU
Department of Music Science and Art: Prof. HANS-UWE PAPAMATTHEOU MATSCHKE
Department of Marketing and Operations Management: Prof. ILIAS KOUSKOUVELIS
Department of Technology Management: (vacant)

HEADS OF INTERDEPARTMENTAL POSTGRADUATE STUDIES

Master in Applied Informatics: (vacant)
Master in Business Administration: Prof. DIMITRIOS PAPADOPOULOS
Master in Economics: Assoc. Prof. AGGELIKI NIKOLAOU
Master in Information Systems: Prof. GEORGE HARAMIS

PROFESSORS

ALYGIZAKIS, ANTONIOS, Music Science and Art
BARALEXIS, SPYROS, Accounting and Finance
CHARALAMPOUS, DIMITRIOS, Educational and Social Studies
GEORGANTA, ZOE, Applied Informatics
IOANNIDIS, DIMITRIOS, Economics
KAPSALIS, ACHILEAS, Educational and Social Studies
KARAGIANNI, STELLA, Economics
KARFAKIS, COSTAS, Economics
KATOS, ANASTASIOS, Applied Informatics
KATRANIDIS, STELIOS, Economics
KONSTANTOPOULOU, CHRYSSOULA, Applied Informatics
KOUSKOUVELIS, ILIAS, International, European, Economic and Political Studies
LABRIANIDIS, LOIS, Economics
LAZARIDIS, JOHN, Accounting and Finance
LAZOS, BAIOS, Business Administration
MARGARITIS, KONSTANTINOS, Applied Informatics
MOURMOURAS, IOANNIS, Economics
NOULAS, ATHANASIOS, Accounting and Finance
PALIVOS, THEODORE, Economics
PAPADIMITRIOU, JOHN, Applied Informatics
PAPADOPOULOS, DIMITRIOS, Accounting and Finance
PAPAMATTHEOU MATSCHKE, HANS-UWE, Music Science and Art
PAPARRIZOS, KONSTANTINOS, Applied Informatics
PAULIDIS, GEOGRIOS, Educational and Social Studies
PEKOS, GEORGE, Applied Informatics
PIPEROPOULOS, GEORGE, Business Administration
SKALIDIS, ELEFTHERIOS, Accounting and Finance
TARABANIS, KONSTANTINOS, Business Administration
THEMELI, CHRISANTHI, Accounting and Finance
THEODOSIOU, IOANNIS, Economics
TRIARHOU, LAZAROS, Educational and Social Studies
TSIOTRAS, GEORGE, Business Administration
TSOPELA, VINIA, Music Science and Art
VELENTZAS, KONSTANTINOS, Economics
XIARHOS, STAVROS, Economics
XIROTIRI-KOUFIDOU, STELLA, Business Administration
XOURIS, DIMITRIOS, Business Administration

PANEPISTIMION PATRON
(University of Patras)

University Campus, 265 04 Patras
Telephone: 261-0997608
Fax: 261-0991771
E-mail: rectorate@upatras.gr
Internet: www.upatras.gr

Founded 1964
State control
Language of instruction: Greek
Academic year: September to August

Rector: Prof. CHRISTOS HADJITHEODOROU
Vice-Rector (Academic Affairs and Personnel): Prof. PANAGIOTIS GOUMAS
Vice-Rector (Financial Planning and Development): Prof. IOANNA DAOULI
Vice-Rector (Research and Educational Affairs): Prof. GEORGE STAVROPOULOS
Administrative Officer: SPILIOS PAPATHANASSOPOULOS

Number of teachers: 712
Number of students: 26,000

Publication: *University Bulletin* (annually)

DEANS

School of Engineering: Prof. ALEXANDROS DEMETRACOPOULOS
School of Health Sciences: Prof. IOANNIS VARAKIS
School of Humanities and Social Sciences: Prof. IOANNIS DELLIS
School of Natural Sciences: Prof. NICHOLAS DEMOPOULOS

PROFESSORS

School of Economics and Management Sciences

Department of Business Administration:

PAVLIDES, G.
PECHLIVANIDIS, P.
SAKKAS, D.
VERNARDAKIS, N.
ZAHARATOS, G.

Department of Economics:

DAOULI-DEMOUSI, I.
DEMOUSSIS, M.
SYPSAS, P.

School of Engineering

Department of Architecture:

KATZOURAKIS, D.
KSANTHOPOULOS, K.
POLYDORIDES, N.

Department of Chemical Engineering:

DASSIOS, G.
KOUTSOUKOS, P.
KRAVARIS, K.
LADAS, S.
LYBERATOS, G.
NIKOLOPOULOS, P.
PANDIS, S.
PAPATHEODOROU, G.
PAVLOU, S.
PAYATAKES, A.
RAPAKOULIAS, D.
TSAHALIS, D.
TSAMOPOULOS, J.
VAYENAS, C.
VERYKIOS, X.

Department of Civil Engineering:

ANAGNOSTOPOULOS, S.
ATHANASOPOULOS, G.
ATMATZIDIS, D.
BESKOS, D.
CHRYSIKOPOULOS, K.
DEMETRACOPOULOS, A.
FARDIS, M.
HADJITHEODOROU, C.
KALERIS, V.
MAKRIS, N.
PAPAGEORGIOU, A.
THEODORAKOPOULOS, D.

Department of Computer Engineering and Informatics:

ALEXIOU, G.
CHRISTODOULAKIS, D.
GALLOPOULOS, E.
KAKLAMANIS, CH.
KIROUSSIS, E.
KOSMADAKIS, S.
LIKOTHANASSIS, S.
NIKOLOS, D.
PAPATHEODOROU, TH.
SPIRAKIS, P.
TRIANTAPHILLOU, P.
TSAKALIDIS, A.
VARVARIGOS, E.

Department of Electrical and Computer Engineering:

AVOURIS, N.
BITSORIS, G.
FAKOTAKIS, N.
GIANNAKOPOULOS, G.
GOUTIS, C.
GROUMPOS, P.
HOUSSOS, E.
KOUBIAS, S.
KOUFOPAVLOU, O.
KOUSSOULAS, N.
MAKIOS, V.
PAPADOPOULOS, G.
PIMENIDIS, T.
SAFACAS, A.
SERPANOS, D.
SPYROU, N.
STOURAITIS, A.
TSANAKAS, D.
VOVOS, N.

Department of Engineering Science:

HATZIKONSTANTINOU, P.
IOAKIMIDIS, N.
KOUTROUVELIS, I.
LIANOS, P.
MARKELLOS, V.
PERDIOS, E.
POLITIS, C.
VELGAKIS, M.

Department of Mechanical Engineering and Aeronautics:

ASPRAGATHOS, N.
CHRYSSOLOURIS, G.
FASSOISS, S.
KALLINTERIS, I.
KERMANIDIS, TH.
KOSTOPOULOS, V.
MISSIRLIS, I.
PAIPETIS, S.
PANTELAKIS, S.
PAPAIOANNOU, S.
PAPANICOLAOU, G.
PAPANIKAS, D.
SISSOURAS, A.

School of Health Sciences

Faculty of Medicine:

ALEXOPOULOS, D.
ANASTASIOU, E.
ANDONOPOULOS, A.

ATHANASIADOU-GIKA, A.
BARBALIAS, G.
BASSIARIS, H.
BERATI, S.
BEZERIANOS, A.
BONIKOS, D.
DIMITRACOPOULOS, G.
DIMOPOULOS, J.
DOUGENIS, D.
DRAINAS, D.
FLORDELLIS, CH.
GARTAGANIS, S.
GOGOS, C.
GOUMAS, P.
KALFARENTZOS, F.
KALPAKSIS, D.
KARAVIAS, D.
KOLIOPOULOS, I.-M.
KOSTOPOULOS, G.
KOUVELAS, E.
LAMBIRIS, E.
MANTAGOS, S.
NIKIFORIDIS, G.
PALLIKARAKIS, N.
PANAGIOTAKIS, G.
PAPAPETROPOULOU, M.
PAPAVASILIOU, A.
TSAMBAOS, D.
TZORAKOELETHERAKIS, E.
TZINGOUNIS, V.
VAGENAKIS, A.
VARAKIS, J.
VLACHOJANNIS, J.
ZOUMBOS, N.

Department of Pharmacy:

CORDOPATIS, P.
TZARTOS, S.

School of Natural Sciences

Department of Biology:

ALAHIOTIS, ST.
DEMOPOULOS, N.
DIMITRIADIS, G.
GEORGIADIS, TH.
ILIOPOULOU, I.
KAMARI, G.
MANETAS, I.
MARMARAS, V.
PSARAS, G.
TZANOUDAKIS, D.
YANNOPOULOS, G.
ZACHAROPOULOU, A.
ZAGRIS, N.

Department of Chemistry:

BARLOS, K.
CHRISTOPOULOS, TH.
GLAVAS, S.
IOANNOU, P.
KALLITSIS, I.
KARAISKAKIS, G.
KARAMANOS, N.
KLOURAS, N.
KOUTINAS, A.
LYCOURGHIOTIS, A.
MAROULIS, G.
MATSOUKAS, J.
MIKROYIANNIDIS, J.
PAPAIOANNOU, D.
PERLEPES, S.
POULOS, C.
STAVROPOULOS, G.
TSEGENIDIS, TH.

Department of Geology:

CONTOPOULOS, N.
DOUTSOS, TH.
FERENTINOS, G.
FRYDAS, D.
HATZIPANAGIOTOU, K.
KALLERGIS, G.
KATAGAS, C.
KOTOPOULI, C.
KOUKIS, G.
PAPAMARINOPOULOS, S.
TSAILA-MONOPOLI, S.
TSELENTIS, G.
TSOLIS-KATAGAS, P.
VARNAVAS, S.

Department of Materials Science:

GALIOTIS, C.
PHOTINOS, D.

Department of Mathematics:

BOTSARIS, CH.
BOUNTIS, A.
COTSIOLIS, A.
DROSSOS, C.
ILIADIS, S.
IORDANIDIS, K.
KAFOUSSIAS, N.
KOUROUKLIS, S.
METAKIDES, G.
PAPANTONIOU, V.
PHILIPPOU, A.
PINTELAS, P.
PNEVMATIKOS, S.
SIAFARIKAS, P.
STABAKIS, J.
TSOUBELIS, D.
TZANNES, V.
VRAHATIS, M.
ZAGOURAS, CH.

Department of Physics:

BAKAS, I.
GEORGES, A.
GEROGIANNIS, V.
GOUDIS, CHR.
HARITANTIS, I.
KARAHAILOS, G.
KATSIARIS, G.
MANTAS, G.
MYTILINEOU, E.
PIZANIAS, M.
TOPRAKTSIOGLOU, CH.
YIANOULIS, P.
ZDETSIS, A.

School of Social Sciences and Humanities

Department of Philology:

MARKOS, A.
PANAGOPOULOS, A.
RALLI, A.

Department of Philosophy:

PATELI, I.
TEREZIS, CH.

Department of Pre-School Education:

PATINIOTIS, N.
POLYCHRONOPOULOS, P.
RAVANIS, K.
XIROMERITI, A.

Department of Primary Education:

ALEXOPOULOS, A.
BOUZAKIS, J.
DELLIS, I.
GEORGOGIANNIS, P.
KRIVAS, S.
LAMPROPOULOU, V.
PORPODAS, C.
VERGIDIS, D.

Department of Theatre Studies:

STEFANOPOULOS, TH.
XAAS, D.

PANEPISTIMIO PELOPONNESOU
(University of the Peloponnese)

28 Erithrou Stayrou and Kariotaki Sts, 221 00 Tripolis

Telephone: and fax 2710-230006
E-mail: info@uop.gr
Internet: www.uop.gr

Founded 2002
State control

Chairman, Board of Trustees: CONSTANTIN DIMOPOULOS
Vice-Chairman, Board of Trustees: IOANNIS PARASKEVOPOULOS

HEADS OF DEPARTMENTS

Computer Science and Technology: (vacant)
Social and Education Policy: Prof. DIONYSSIS KLADIS
Telecommunications Science and Technology: Prof. ANDREAS MARAS

PROFESSORS

Department of Social and Education Policy (Damaskinou and Kolokotroni Sts, 201 00 Korinth; tel. 27410-74991; fax 27410-74993; e-mail sep-secr@uop.gr):

KLADIS, D., Education Policy
KOULAIDIS, V., Design of Educational Programmes
KOULOURI, C., History of Modern Greek Education and Society

Department of Telecommunications Science and Technology (End of Karaiskaki St, 221 00 Tripolis; tel. 2710-372163; fax 2710-372160; e-mail ntalagan@uop.gr):

BOUCOUVALAS, A. C.
MARAS, A.

PANEPISTIMION PIREOS
(University of Piraeus)

80 Karaoli and Dimitriou St, 185 34 Piraeus
Telephone: 210-4142000
Fax: 210-4142328
E-mail: publ@unipi.gr
Internet: www.unipi.gr

Founded 1938, university status since 1958

Rector: T. GAMALETSOS
Secretary: A. GOTSIS

Library of 27,000 vols, 200 periodicals
Number of teachers: 90
Number of students: 11,400

Publication: *Spoudai* (quarterly)

Departments of Business Administration, Economics, Statistics and Insurance Science, Financial Management and Banking, Industrial Management, Informatics, Maritime Studies, Teachers Education and Technology.

PANEPISTIMIO THESALIAS
(University of Thessaly)

Argonafton and Filellinon, 382 21 Volos
Telephone: 2421-074000
E-mail: webmaster@uth.gr
Internet: www.uth.gr

Founded 1984
State control

Rector: Prof. CONSTANTINOS BAGIATIS
Vice-Rectors: Prof. CONSTANTINOS GOURGOULIANIS, Prof. NAPOLEON MITSIS

Library of 80,000 books, 828 journals

14 departments in four schools (Agricultural Sciences, Engineering, Health Sciences and Humanities), and two independent departments (Economic Studies and Physical Education and Sport).

PANTEION PANEPESTIMION IKONOMIKON KAI POLITCON EPISTIMON
('Panteios' University of Social and Political Sciences)

Leoforos A. Syngrou 136, 176 71 Athens
Telephone: 210-9220100
Fax: 210-9223690
E-mail: rector@panteion.gr
Internet: www.panteion.gr

Founded 1930

Rector: D. CONSTAS
Gen. Sec.: M. VARELLA
Number of students: 7,500.

POLYTECHNION KRITIS
(Technical University of Crete)

Agiou Markou St, 731 32 Chania
Telephone: 2821-037047
Fax: 2821-028418
E-mail: intoffice@isc.tuc.gr
Internet: www.tuc.gr

Founded 1977, first student intake 1984
State control
Academic year: September to June

Rector: Prof. JOAKIM GRISPOLAKIS
Vice-Rectors: Prof. MICHALIS PATERAKIS (Academic Affairs and Personnel), Prof. NIKOS BAROTSIS (Planning and Development)
Librarian: MARIA NTAOUNTAKI

Library of 30,000 vols
Number of teachers: 212 (incl. 91 full professors)
Number of students: 2,500

HEADS OF DEPARTMENTS

Electronic and Computer Engineering: Prof. MICHAEL PATERAKIS
Environmental Engineering: Prof. VASSILIS GEKAS (acting)
Mineral Resources Engineering: Prof. NIKOLAOS VAROTSIS
Production Engineering and Management: Prof. EVAN DIAMADOPOULOS
Sciences: Assoc. Prof. ELENA PAPADOPOULOU

DIRECTORS OF LABORATORIES

Air, Water and Solid Wastes Management: ALEXANDER P. ECONOMOPOULOS
Analytical and Environmental Chemistry: NIKOLAOS KALLITHRAKAS-KONTOS
Applied Geology: ZACHARIAS G. AGIOUTANTIS
Applied Geophysics: ANTONIS VAFIDIS
Applied Mathematics and Computers: YIANNIS SARIDAKIS
Applied Mechanics: CONSTAS P. PROVIDAKIS
Applied Mineralogy: GEORGE KOSTAKIS
Applied Socio-economic Research: GEORGE LIODAKIS
Atmospheric Aerosol: MIHALIS LAZARIDIS
Automation: MICHALIS ZERVAKIS
Biochemical Engineering and Environmental Biootechnology: NIKOS KALOGERAKIS
Ceramics and Glass Technology: ATHINA TSETSEKOU
Chemical Processes and Wastewater Treatment: DIONYSIOS MANTZAVINOS
Computer-Aided Design and Robotics: NIKOLAOS BILALIS
Computer-Aided Manufacturing: YIANNIS PHILLIS
Data Analysis and Forecasting: CHRISTOS SKIADAS
Decision Support Systems: ATHANASIOS MIGDALAS
Digital Image and Signal Processing: MICHALIS ZERVAKIS
Distributed Multimedia Information Systems and Applications: STAVROS CHRISTODOULAKIS
Drilling Technology and Applied Fluid Mechanics: VASSILIOS KELESSIDIS
Dynamic Systems and Simulation: MARKOS PAPAGEORGIOU
Ecology and Biodiversity: NIKOS KALOGERAKIS
Electric Circuits and Renewable Energy Sources: KOSTAS KALAITZAKIS
Electrical Circuits and Electronics: PAVLOS S. GEORGILAKIS
Electronics: KOSTAS KALAITZAKIS
Environmental Engineering and Management: EVAN DIAMADOPOULOS
Financial Engineering: CONSTANTIN ZOPOUNIDIS
General Geology: EMMANOUEL MANUTSOGLU
Geodesy and Geomatics Enigineering: STELIOS MERTIKAS
Geo-environmental Engineering: GEORGE KARATZAS
Geostatistics: DIONISSIOS T. HRISTOPOULOS
Hydrogeochemical Engineering and Soil Remediation: NIKOLAOS NIKOLAIDIS
Information and Computer Networks: VASSILIS DIGALAKIS
Intelligent Systems: EMMANOUEL KOUMBARAKIS
Inorganic and Organic Geochemistry and Organic Petrography: VASSILIS PERDIKATSIS
Intelligent Systems and Robotics: NIKOS C. TSOURVELOUDIS
Management Systems: VASSILIS MOUSTAKIS
Materials Structure and Laser Physics: STAVROS MOUSTAIZIS
Microprocessor and Hardware: APOSTOLOS DOLLAS
Mine Design: GEORGE EXADAKTYLOS
Mineral Processing: ELIAS STAMBOLIADIS
Minerals Quality Control – Health and Safety: MICHAEL GALETAKIS
Mining and Metallurgical Waste Management: KOSTAS KOMNITSAS
Petrology and Economic Geology: THEODOROS MARKOPOULOS
Physical Chemistry and Chemical Processes: IOANNIS V. YENTEKAKIS
PVT and Core Analysis: NIKOS VAROTSIS
Robotics: ANASTASIOS POULIEZOS
Rock Mechanics: ZACHARIAS G. AGIOUTANTIS
Safety of Work and Cognitive Ergonomics: TOM KONTOGIANNIS
Software Systems and Network Application: EMMANOUEL KOUMBARAKIS
Solid Fuels Benification and Technology: DESPINA VAMVOUKA
Telecommunications: NIKOS SIDIROPOULOS
Toxic and Hazardous Waste Management: EVANGELOS GIDARAKOS
Transport Phenomena and Applied Thermodynamics: VASSILIS GEKAS
Water Resources Management and Coastal Engineering: IOANNIS K. TSANIS

PROFESSORS

AGIOUTANIS, Z.
ALEVIZOS, G.
AVDELAS, G.
BALAS, K.
BILALIS, N.
CHRISTIDIS, G.
CHRISTODOULAKIS, S.
CHRISTODOULOU, M.
CHRISTOPOULOS, D.
DARRAS, T.
DELLIS, A.
DIAMADOPOULOS, E.
DIGALAKIS, V.
DOLLAS, A.
DOUMPOS, M.
ECONOMOPOULOS, A.
ELLINAS, D.
EXADAKTYLOS, G.
FOSCOLOS, A.
FRAGOMIHELAKIS, M.
GALETAKIS, M.
GEKAS, V.
GEORGILAKIS, P.
GIDARAKOS, E.
GRIGOROUDIS, E.
GRYSPOLAKIS, J.
KALAITZAKIS, K.
KALLITHRAKAS, K. N.
KALOGERAKIS, N.
KANDYLAKIS, D.
KARAKASSIS, I.
KARATZAS, G.
KATSANOS, A.
KAVOURIDIS, K.
KELESIDIS, V.
KOMNITSAS, K.
KONTOGIANNIS, T.
KOSMATOPOULOS, E.
KOSTAKIS, G.
KOUBARAKIS, E.
KOUIKOGLOU, V.
LAZARIDIS, M.
LIODAKIS, G.
MANOUTSOGLOU, E.
MANTZAVINOS, D.
MARIA, E.
MARKOPOULOS, T.
MATHIOUDAKIS, M.
MATSATSINIS, N.
MERTIKAS, S.
MIGDALAS, A.
MONOPOLIS, D.
MOUSTAIZIS, S.
MOUSTAKIS, V.
NIKOLAIDIS, N.
NIKOLOS, I.
PANTINAKIS, A.
PAPADOPOULOU, E.
PAPAGEORGIOU, M.
PASADAKIS, N.
PATELIS, D.
PATERAKIS, M.
PERDIKATSIS, V.
PETRAKIS, E.
PETRAKIS, M.
PHILLIS, Y.
PNEVMATIKATOS, D.
POTAMIANOS, A.
POULIEZOS, A.
PROVIDAKIS, K.
SAMELIS, A.
SAMOLADAS, V.
SARIDAKIS, Y.
SIDIROPOULOS, N.
SINOLAKIS, K.
SKIADAS, C.
STAMPOLIADIS, E.
STAVRAKAKIS, G.
STAVROULAKIS, P.
SYNOLAKIS, C.
TRAFALIS, T.
TSANIS, I.
TSETSEKOU, A.
TSOMPANAKIS, I.
TSOURVELOUDIS, N.
VAFIDIS, A.
VAMVOUKA, D.
VAROTSIS, N.
YENTEKAKIS, Y.
ZERVAKIS, M.
ZOPOUNIDIS, K.

ATTACHED INSTITUTES

Institute of Telecommunications Systems: e-mail tsi@tsinet.gr; internet www.tsinet.gr; Dir Prof. MICHALIS PATERAKIS.

Colleges

ARCHAEOLOGY, GREEK STUDIES

American School of Classical Studies at Athens: Odos Souidias 54, 106 76 Athens; tel. 210-7236313; fax 210-7250584; e-mail ascsa@ascsa.edu.gr; internet www.ascsa.edu.gr; f. 1881; research institute and postgraduate school for students of classical and post-classical literature, history and archaeology; controlled by a committee representing 160 American and Canadian universities; library: Gennadius and Blegen libraries with 195,000 vols; 13 teachers; 60 students; Dir STEPHEN V. TRACY; publ. *Hesperia* (4 a year).

British School at Athens: Odos Souedias 52, 106 76 Athens; tel. 210-7210974; fax 210-7236560 *London office*: Senate House, Malet St, London, WC1E 7HU, United Kingdom; tel. (20) 7862-8732; fax (20) 7862-8733; e-mail admin@bsa.ac.uk; internet www.bsa.gla.ac.uk; f. 1886; archaeology and Hellenic studies; Fitch Laboratory for research and analysis; library: over 60,000 vols (ancient, medieval and post-medieval Greek studies and archaeology of all periods) including the Finlay Library (Greek travel and modern Greek studies); Chair. Prof. Lord COLIN RENFREW; Dir Dr A. J. M. WHITLEY; London Sec. HELEN FIELDS.

Deutsches Archäologisches Institut, Abteilung Athen (German Archaeological Institute in Athens): Odos Fidiou 1, 106 78 Athens; tel. 210-3307400; fax 210-3814762; e-mail sekretariat@athen.dainst.org; internet www.dainst.de; f. 1874; library: 66,000 vols; Dirs Prof. Dr WOLF-DIETRICH NIEMEIER, Dr REINHARD SENFF; publs *Athenische Mitteilungen* (annually), *Beihefte*.

Ecole Française d'Athènes (French Archaeological School): Odos Didotou 6, 106 80 Athens; tel. 210-3679900; fax 210-3632101; e-mail efa@efa.gr; internet www.efa.gr; f. 1846; 15 mems and architects; library: 80,000 vols; Dir D. MULLIEZ; Sec.-Gen. M. BRUNET; publs *Bulletin de correspondance hellénique* (annually), *Bulletin des études grecques modernes et contemporaines* (annually).

Italian School of Archaeology at Athens (Scuola Archeologica Italiana di Atene): 14 Parthenonos, 117 42 Athens; tel. 210-9239163; fax 210-9220908; e-mail segretario@scuoladiatene.it; internet www.scuoladiatene.it; f. 1909; post-graduate studies in archaeology, epigraphy and antiquities, ancient architecture; research and excavations in Greece; library: 48,300 vols; Dir Prof. EMANUELE A. GRECO; Library Dir Dr STEFANO GARBIN; publs *Annuario della Scuola Archeologica di Atene e delle Missioni Italiane in Oriente* (annually), *Monografie della Scuola Archeologica di Atene e delle Missoni Italiane in Oriente* (irregular), *Notiziario* (2 a year), *Tripodes* (irregular).

Svenska Institutet i Athen (Swedish Institute at Athens): 9 Mitseon St, 117 42 Athens; tel. 210-9232102; fax 210-9220925; e-mail swedinst@sia.gr; internet www.sia.gr; f. 1948; research into Greek antiquity and archaeology, and cultural exchange between Sweden and Greece; 270 mems; library: 40,000 vols (housed at the Nordic Library, Kavalotti 7, 117 42 Athens); 2 teachers; 15 students; Dir ANNE-LOUISE SCHALLIN; Librarian JENNY WALLENSTEN; publ. *Skrifter utgivna av Svenska Institutet i Athen* (Acta Instituti Atheniensis Regni Sueciae and *Opuscula Atheniensia*).

ARTS, DRAMA, MUSIC

American College of Greece: 6 Gravias St, Aghia Paraskevi, 153 42 Athens; tel. 210-6009800; fax 210-6009811; e-mail acg@acg.edu; internet www.acg.edu; f. 1875; comprises Deree College (BA courses in dance, economics, English, history, history of art, music, philosophy, psychology, sociology, BSc course in business administration, MBA), Junior College (associate degrees in arts and sciences) and Pierce College (high school); library: 150,000 vols; 250 teachers (incl. Junior College division); 5,000 students (incl. Junior College division); Pres. JOHN S. BAILEY; publ. *Library Series*.

Dramatiki Scholi (Drama School): National Theatre, Odos Menandrou 65, Athens; internet www.n-t.gr; f. 1924; open to actors who desire to improve their art and to young people who desire to take up the stage as a career; the staff comprises the director, 11 professors, and 2 teachers.

Kratiko Odeio Thessaloniki (State Conservatory of Music): Leondos Sofou Str. 16, 546 25 Thessaloniki; tel. 231-0510551; fax 231-0522158; e-mail odiokrat@otenet.gr; internet www.odiokrat.gr; f. 1914; instrumental, vocal and theoretical studies; 60 teachers; 630 students; library: 17,000 vols, scores, records, slides, compact discs, video cassettes, including collection in Braille; exhibition of musical instruments; Chair. Prof. P. I. RENTZEPERIS..

Attached conservatory:

Odeion Athenon (Odeon of Athens): Odos Rigillis and Vassileos Georgiou 17–19, Athens; f. 1871; comprises a music section, a drama section, a section for military music, and a section for Byzantine Church music; 53 professors, 40 teachers and 1,200 students; Dir A. GAROUFALIS.

Odeion Ethnikon (National Conservatory): 8 Maizonos and 18 Mayer Sts, Athens 104 38; tel. 210-5233175; fax 210-5245291; e-mail ethnodio@otenet.gr; f. 1926; sections for music and opera; 200 teachers; 5,000 students; Dirs HARA KALOMIRI, PERIKLIS KOUKOS; publ. *Deltio* (annually).

GRENADA

The Higher Education System

Before 1968 higher education in Grenada was limited to the provision of sponsorship for study abroad. In that year Grenada acquired the Extra-Mural Department of the University of the West Indies (UWI) and the Grenada Teacher Training College was founded, its 2-year programme being monitored and certified by the UWI. In 1974 the Government established a number of other colleges relevant to the country's social and economic needs. During 1979–83 the new People's Revolutionary Government enhanced existing teacher training programmes and increased scholarships offered for university and technical education abroad. The Institute of Higher Education in Grenada, which approximated the idea of a university, was also established during this period. In 1988 the restored, post-colonial Government amalgamated a number of institutions, including the Grenada Teachers College and the Institute of Higher Education in Grenada, to form the Grenada National College, which was renamed the T.A. Marryshow Community College (TAMCC) in 1996. In the same year the UWI and St George's University expanded their activities.

The Government is responsible for higher education, although both St George's University and the UWI enjoy a greater degree of autonomy than does the TAMCC. The TAMCC is required by law to report directly to the Ministry of Education, primarily for financial purposes and for powers of jurisdiction. Higher education is governed by the Grenada Education Act, and the St George's University (School of Medicine) Act, 1976. The Ministry of Education is the main source of funding for the TAMCC. It also provides some support for the UWI, although this is largely funded through the collective contributions of the Caribbean countries to the UWI as a whole. St George's University is funded mainly by student fees.

Learned Society

HISTORY, GEOGRAPHY AND ARCHAEOLOGY

Grenada National Trust: Grenada National Museum, Young St, St George's; tel. 440-3725; f. 1967 to preserve evidence of the history and growth of the island, and to support the Grenada National Museum; 240 mems; Pres. GORDON DE LA MOTHE; Sec. KAY SIMON; publ. *Quarterly Newsletter*.

Libraries and Archives

St George's

Founder's Library, St George's University: POB 7, St George's; tel. 444-1573; fax 444-2884; e-mail library@sgu.edu; internet www.sgu.edu; f. 1979; 13,000 vols, 350 periodicals; Dir. JOHN MCGUIRK.

Grenada Public Library: Carenage, St George's; tel. 440-2506; fax 440-6650; e-mail gls@caribsurf.com; f. 1853; 60,000 vols; special West Indian and National Archives of Grenada collections; reference, research and lecture facilities; links its activities with other educational agencies; attached to Ministry of Education; Dir S. LILLIAN SYLVESTER; Librarian DEON DAVID.

Museum

St George's

Grenada National Museum: Young St, St George's; tel. 440-3725; fax 440-9292; f. 1976; history, technology, fauna and flora; Dir. JEANNE FISHER; Curator HUGH THOMAS; publs *Art 'y' Facts* (2 a year), *Newsletter*, *Relics*.

Universities and Colleges

ST GEORGE'S UNIVERSITY

University Centre, POB 7, St George's

Telephone: 444-4175
Fax: 444-4823
E-mail: sguinfo@sgu.edu
Internet: www.sgu.edu

Founded 1977
Language of instruction: English
Academic year: August to June

Chancellor: CHARLES R. MODICA
Registrar: MARGARET LAMBERT
Librarian: JOHN MCGUIRK

Library: see Libraries and Archives
Number of teachers: 776 (76 full-time, 700 part-time)
Number of students: 2,000

DEANS

Arts and Sciences: T. HOLLIS
Basic Sciences: A. PENSICK
Clinical Studies: STEPHEN WEITZMAN
Veterinary Medicine: R. SIS

CHAIRMEN OF DEPARTMENTS

Anatomical Sciences: Dr ROBERT JORDAN
Behavioural Sciences: Prof. DAVID BROWN
Biochemistry: Dr R. HANSFORD
Business: Dr L. BLYTH
English: Dr A. MACDONALD-SMYTHE
Histology: Dr A. PAPARO
Life Sciences: Dr C. MORRALL
Medicine: Prof. S. WEITZMAN
Nutrition: Prof. KEITH TAYLOR
Obstetrics and Gynaecology: Prof. P. BEAUGARD
Paediatrics: Prof T. POTTER
Pathology and Microbiology: Prof. S. BHUSNURMATH
Pharmacology: Dr H. BAER
Physiology: Dr R. HOUSE
Psychiatry: Dr ELIOT SOREL
Public Health: Dr O. AMULERU-MARSHALL
Surgery: Prof. G. LUTCHMAN
Veterinary–Clinical: Dr J. HUMBERG
Veterinary–Para-Clinical: Dr R. N. SHARMA
Veterinary–Pre-Clinical: Dr W. KUGLER

T .A. Marryshow Community College (TAMCC): Tanteen, St George's; tel. 440-1389; fax 440-3079; e-mail tamcc@caribsurf.com; internet www.tamcc.edu.gd; f. 1988 by a merger of The Grenada Teachers College, The Grenada Technical and Vocational Institute, The Institute for Further Education, The National Institute of Handicraft, The Mirabeau Agricultural Training School, The Domestic Arts Institute, The Continuing Education Programme and The School of Pharmacy; present name and status 1996; offers full and part-time programmes leading to Bachelors and Associate Degrees, Certificates and Diplomas; Principal Dr JEFFERY BRITTON (acting); Registrar C. NIGEL GRAVESANDE; Dean of Arts, Sciences and Professional Studies Dr DUNBAR STEELE; Dean of Applied Arts and Technology DESMOND LA TOUCHE.

University of the West Indies School of Continuing Studies: Marryshow House, H. A. Blaize St, POB 439, St George's; tel. 440-2451; fax 440-4985; e-mail rtscsuwi@caribsurf.com; internet www.uwichill.edu.bb/bnccde/grenada/index.htm; f. 1956; first-year university courses, general courses; library and resource collection of 10,000 vols; folk theatre, telecommunications distance teaching centre; 27 teachers; 150 students; Resident Tutor BEVERLEY A. STEELE.

GUATEMALA

The Higher Education System

Under Spanish colonial rule, Guatemala was part of the Viceroyalty of New Spain. Independence was obtained from Spain in 1821, from Mexico in 1824 and from the Federation of Central American States in 1838. The oldest university is Universidad de San Carlos de Guatemala, which was founded by King Carlos II of Spain in 1676.

The main requirement for admission to university is the Bachiller or Bachillerato, the secondary school qualification. The Licenciado is the undergraduate degree and is awarded after four years, though some subjects (such as medicine) require longer periods of study. In professional fields of study a professional title is awarded. Following the Licenciado the first postgraduate degree is the Maestría, which is awarded after two years of study. However, the Doctorado can also be awarded following two years of study after the Licenciado, although some doctoral programmes require a Maestría.

Technical and vocational education is offered by the universities and specialized post-secondary institutions. The Instituto Técnico de Capitación y Productividad provides apprenticeships and courses. The main vocational qualification is the Diplomado, awarded after two-and-a-half to three years of study.

Learned Societies

GENERAL

Academia de Ciencias Médicas, Físicas y Naturales de Guatemala (Academy of Medical, Physical and Natural Sciences): 13 Calle 1–25, Zona 1, Apdo Postal 569, 01001 Guatemala City; tel. 2238-1251; fax 2232-7291; e-mail manuelgonzalez@yahoo.com; f. 1945; 80 mems; library: *c.* 4,000 vols; Pres. MANUEL GONZÁLEZ AVILA; Sec. Dr CARLOS ROLZ ASTURIAS; publs *Annals* (irregular), *research summaries*.

FINE AND PERFORMING ARTS

Sociedad Pro-Arte Musical (Musical Society): 12 Calle 2–09, Zona 3, Apdo 980, Guatemala City; f. 1945; 200 mems; Pres. LULÚ C. DE HERRARTE; Exec. Sec. DORA G. DE MENDIZÁBAL.

HISTORY, GEOGRAPHY AND ARCHAEOLOGY

Academia de Geografía e Historia de Guatemala (Geographical and Historical Academy of Guatemala): 3 Avda 8–35, Zona 1, Guatemala City; tel. 2253-5141; fax 2232-3544; e-mail acgeohis@concyt.gob.gt; f. 1923; 45 mems; library of 30,000 vols; Pres. GUILLERMO DÍAZ ROMEU; Sec. BARBARA KNOKE DE ARATHOON; publs *Anales* (annually), *Biblioteca Goathemala*, *Viajeros*.

LANGUAGE AND LITERATURE

Academia Guatemalteca de la Lengua (Guatemala Academy of Letters): 12 Calle 6–40, Zona 9, Officina 403–404, Edificio Plazuela, Guatemala City; tel. 2332-2824; fax 2332-2824; e-mail aglesp@correo.terra.com.gt; f. 1887; corresp. of the Real Academia Española (Madrid); library of 5,000 vols; Dir MARIO ANTONIO SANDOVAL SAMAYOA; Sec.-Gen. FRANCISCO MORALES SANTOS.

Alliance Française: 13 Avda 16–30, Zona 10 Nueva Guatemala de la Asunción, Apdo Postal 2013, 01001 Guatemala City; tel. 2366-1287; fax 2368-1891; e-mail alianzafr@intelnet.net.gt; offers courses and exams in French language and culture and promotes cultural exchange with France; attached teaching offices in La Antigua and Quetzaltenango.

NATURAL SCIENCES

Biological Sciences

Asociación Guatemalteca de Historia Natural: Jardín Botánico, Universidad de San Carlos, Mariscal Cruz 1–56, Zona 10, Guatemala City; f. 1960; 86 mems; Pres. Dr MARIO DARY RIVERA.

TECHNOLOGY

Colegio de Ingenieros de Guatemala: 7A Avda 39-60, Zona 8, 01008 Guatemala City; tel. 2471-7544; fax 2472-4224; e-mail juntadirectiva@cig.org.gt; internet www.cig.org.gt; f. 1947; 1,965 mems; Pres. Ing. CARLOS GERARDO BRAN GUZMÁN; publ. *Revista Ingeniería* (4 a year).

Research Institutes

ECONOMICS, LAW AND POLITICS

Centro de Investigaciones Económicas Nacionales (Centre for National Economic Studies): 12 Calle 1-25, Zona 10, Edif. Géminis 10, Torre Norte, Nivel 17, Oficina 1702, Guatemala City; tel. 2335-3415; fax 2335-3416; e-mail cien@cien.org.gt; internet www.cien.org.at; f. 1982; study of economic and social problems; Dir JORGE LAVARREDA; publ. *Carta Económica* (monthly).

Instituto Nacional de Estadística (National Statistical Institute): 8a. Calle 9-55, Zona 1, Guatemala City; tel. 2232-3188; fax 2232-4790; e-mail ventas@ine.gob.gt; internet www.ine.gob.gt; f. 1879 as Sección de Estadística; present name 1985; compiles and publishes national statistics; Dir SIEGFRIDO LEE LEIVA; publs *Censo Nacional Agropecuario* (national agricultural census, online), *Censo Nacional de Población y de Habitación* (national population and dwellings census, online), *Indice de Precios al Consumidor* (retail price index; online, monthly).

HISTORY, GEOGRAPHY AND ARCHAEOLOGY

Instituto de Antropología e Historia: 12 Avda 11-11, Zona 1, 01001 Guatemala City; tel. and fax 2232-5956; e-mail guatepazidaeh@yahoo.com; f. 1946; research on Middle-American history, Mayan archaeology, ethnology, philology, and Spanish Colonial history; supervises archaeological sites, monuments and museums; library of 12,000 vols; Dir-Gen. Arq. ARTURO PAZ; publs *Revista Anual de Antropología e Historia de Guatemala* (annually), *books and special publs*.

Instituto Geográfico Nacional 'Ing. Alfredo Obiols Gómez': Avda Las Américas 5-76, Zona 13, Guatemala City; tel. 2332-2611; fax 2331-3548; e-mail ign@ign.gob.gt; internet www.ign.gob.gt; f. 1945; Dir Ing. FERNANDO AMILCAR BOITON VELÁSQUEZ.

MEDICINE

Instituto de Nutrición de Centro América y Panamá (INCAP) (Institute of Nutrition of Central America and Panama): Calzada Roosevelt 6-25, Zona 11, Apdo Postal 1188-01901 Guatemala City; tel. 2472-3762; fax 2473-6529; internet www.incap.org.gt; f. 1949; member countries: Belize, Costa Rica, El Salvador, Guatemala, Honduras, Nicaragua, Panama; administered by Pan American Health Bureau Organization (PAHO)/World Health Organization (WHO); Food and Nutrition Security Program considers food systems, nutrition education and communication, and health and nutrition with an emphasis on mother and child; Master programme and short training courses; well documented library publs scientific articles in Spanish and English, information bulletins, periodic compilations of scientific publications for member governments, annual reports, monographs, various other documents; Dir Dr HERNÁN DELGADO.

NATURAL SCIENCES

Biological Sciences

Centro de Estudios Conservacionistas: Avda La Reforma 0–63, Zona 10, Guatemala City; tel. 2331-0904; fax 2334-7664; e-mail direccioncecon@yahoo.com; internet www.usac.edu.gt/cecon/INDEX%20CECON.htm; f. 1981; management and administration of protected areas; investigation and studies of biodiversity and sustainable management of natural resources; management of nat. botanical garden and nat. biodiversity database; 142 mems; Exec. Dir JORGE ALBERTO RUIZ ORDOÑEZ.

Physical Sciences

Instituto Nacional de Sismología, Vulcanología, Meteorología e Hidrología (National Institute of Seismology, Vulcanology, Meteorology and Hydrology): 7A Avda 14-57, Zona 13, Guatemala City; tel. 2331-5944; fax 2331-5005; e-mail direccion@insivumeh.gob.gt; internet www.insivumeh

.gob.gt; f. 1976; Dir EDDY HARDIE SÁNCHEZ; publs *Boletín Meteorológico Diario* (electronic, daily weather forecast), *Pronóstico de 1 a 3 Dias* (electronic, four-day forecast), *Tiempo Presente* (electronic, current forecast), *Boletín Estacional* (electronic, quarterly forecast), *Boletín Mensual* (electronic, monthly forecast), *Pronóstico de Fin de Semana* (electronic, weekend forecast), *Normales Climáticas* (electronic, climate statistics), *Boletín Sismológico* (electronic, monthly catalogue of earthquakes), *Boletín Sismológico Especial* (electronic, catalogue of significant earthquakes), *Boletín Vulcanológico Diario* (electronic, catalogue of current eruptions), *Boletín Vulcanológico Especial* (electronic, catalogue of significant eruptions), *Boletín de Tsunamis* (electronic, catalogue of tsunamis), *Boletín Anual Hidrológico* (electronic, hydrology, annually), *Mareas Oceánicas* (electronic, monthly tidal forecast).

TECHNOLOGY

Dirección General de Energía Nuclear: 24 Calle 21-12, Zona 12, Apdo postal 1421, Guatemala City; tel. 2477-0746; fax 2476-2007; f. 1978; work concerns peaceful application of nuclear energy in medicine, industry, agriculture, etc.; 50 mems; library of 1,200 vols; Dir Ing. RAÚL EDUARDO PINEDA GONZÁLEZ.

Instituto Centroamericano de Investigación y Tecnología Industrial (ICAITI) (Central American Research Institute for Industry): Apdo Postal 1552-01901, Guatemala City; located at: Avda La Reforma 4–47, Zona 10, Guatemala City; tel. 2331-0631; fax 2331-7470; e-mail general@icaiti.org.gt; internet www.icaiti.org.gt; f. 1956; research on marketing, development of new industries and manufacturing techniques, establishment of Central American standards, information services to industry, and professional advice; library of 36,000 vols; Dir Lic. LUIS FIDEL CIFUENTES ECHEVERRIA (acting).

Libraries and Archives

Guatemala City

Archivo General de Centro América (National Archives): 4 Avda 7–16, Zona 1, Guatemala City; tel. 2232-3037; f. 1846; comprises two sections: La Colonia, archive with 8,427 files of 99,157 documents relating to Guatemala, Chiapas, El Salvador, Honduras, Nicaragua and Costa Rica; library contains ancient and modern historical volumes; periodicals pertaining to the colonial epoch and the period of independence; microfilm and photocopying service for researchers; Dir ARTURO VALDÉS OLIVA; publ. *Boletín*.

Biblioteca Central de la Universidad de San Carlos de Guatemala: Ciudad Universitaria, Zona 12, Guatemala City; tel. 2476-7217; fax 2476-9652; e-mail biblioteca@usac.edu.gt; internet http://biblioteca.usac.edu.gt; f. 1965; economics, humanities and multidisciplinary collections; thesis collection; newspaper and magazine collection; Guatemalan collection, Carlos Mérida collection; 82,881 vols, 756 periodical titles; Dir Licda OFELIA AGUILAR (acting).

Biblioteca del Organismo Judicial: 21 Calle 7-70, Zona 1, Guatemala City; tel. 2248-7000; e-mail biblioteca@oj.gob.gt; f. 1881; 10,000 vols; Dir DORA CRISTINA GODOY LÓPEZ; publs *Informador Bibliotecario* (electronic, weekly), *Informador Bibliotecario Mensual* (electronic, monthly).

Biblioteca del Banco de Guatemala: 7a Avda 22–01, Zona 1, Apdo 365, Guatemala City; tel. 2429-6000; internet www.banguat.gob.gt/biblio; f. 1955; 38,000 vols; Librarian JULIO C. MARISCAL.

Biblioteca del Congreso Nacional: 9 Avda 9–42, Guatemala City; f. 1823; 7,000 vols; Dir CARLOS H. GODOY Z..

Biblioteca Nacional de Guatemala: 5A Avda 7–26, Zona 1, Guatemala City; tel. 2232-2443; fax 2253-9071; e-mail biblioguatemala@intelnett.com; internet www.biblionet.edu.gt; f. 1879; 350,000 vols; Dir Lic. VICTOR CASTILLO LÓPEZ.

Quezaltenango

Biblioteca Pública de Quezaltenango: a/c Casa Cultura Occidente 7a, Calle 11–35, Zona 1, Quezaltenango; reopened 1958; 25,000 vols; Dir JULIO CÉSAR ALVAREZ.

Museums and Art Galleries

Chichicastenango

Museo Regional de Chichicastenango: 5a Avda 4-47, Zona 1, Chichicastenango; f. 1950; articles of the Maya-Quiché culture; Dir RAÚL PÉREZ MALDONADO.

Guatemala City

Museo Nacional de Arqueología y Etnología de Guatemala (Archaeological and Ethnographical Museum): Edif. No. 5, La Aurora, Zona 13, Guatemala City; tel. 2472-0489; fax 2472-0489; f. 1948; collection of some 3,000 archaeological pieces, mainly Mayan art, and 1,000 ethnological exhibits, all from Guatemala; Dir Licda DORA GUERRA DE GONZÁLEZ; publ. *Revista* (2 a year).

Museo Nacional de Arte Moderno: Edif. No. 6, Finca La Aurora, Zona 13, Guatemala City; tel. 2472-0467; fax 2471-1422; f. 1975; paintings, sculpture, engravings, drawings, etc.; Dir J. OSCAR BARRIENTOS.

Museo Nacional de Historia (National Museum of History): 9 Calle 9–70, Zona 1, Guatemala City; tel. and fax 2253-6149; f. 1975; 19th- and 20th-century paintings, sculpture, documents, furniture and tools, all from Guatemala; Dir ITALO MORALES HIDALGO.

Museo Nacional de Historia Natural 'Jorge A. Ibarra': 6A Calle 7–30, Zona 13, Apdo 987, Guatemala City; tel. and fax 2472-0468; fax 2472-0468; f. 1950; collection of geological, botanical and zoological specimens; library of 2,600 vols; Dir and Founder JORGE A. IBARRA.

Universities

UNIVERSIDAD DE SAN CARLOS DE GUATEMALA

Ciudad Universitaria, Zona 12, 01012 Guatemala City
Telephone: 2443-9672
Fax: 2476-7221
E-mail: webmaster@usac.edu.gt
Internet: www.usac.edu.gt

Founded 1676 by King Carlos II, established in its present form 1927, autonomous status 1944
Private control
Language of instruction: Spanish
Academic year: January to November

Rector: Dr M. V. LUIS ALFONSO LEAL MONTERROSO
Secretary-General: Dr CARLOS ENRIQUE MAZARIEGOS MORALES
Director-General of Administration: Lic. CARLOS SIERRA ROMERO
Director-General of Planning: Lic. JOSÉ H. CALDERÓN DÍAZ
Director-General of Research: Dr RODOLFO ESPINOZA SMITH
Director-General of Teaching: Lic. JUAN ALBERTO MARTINEZ
Director-General of University Development: Arq. BYRON RABÉ
Registrar: Ing. ROLANDO GRAJEDA
Librarian: Licda MERCEDES DE BEECK

Library: see Libraries
Number of teachers: 2,600
Number of students: 114,000

Publications: *Revista de la Universidad de San Carlos de Guatemala* (4 a year), *Universidad* (monthly), *USAC al Día* (every 2 weeks)

DEANS

Faculty of Agronomy: Dr ARIEL ABDERRAMAN ORTIZ
Faculty of Architecture: Arq. CARLOS VALLADARES
Faculty of Chemistry and Pharmacy: Lic. GERARDO ARROYO
Faculty of Dentistry: Dr CARLOS ALVARADO CEREZO
Faculty of Economics: Lic. EDUARDO VELASQUEZ
Faculty of Engineering: Ing. SYDNEY SAMUELS
Faculty of Humanities: Lic. MARIO CALDERON
Faculty of Law and Social Sciences: Lic. BONERGE MEJÍA ORELLANA
Faculty of Medicine: Dr CARLOS ALVARADO DUMAS
Faculty of Veterinary Medicine: Dr MARIO LLERENA

DIRECTORS

School of Communications Science: Lic. GUSTAVO ADOLFO BRACAMONTE CERÓN
School of History: Lic. GABRIEL MORALES
School of Political Science: Lic. FERNANDO MOLINA
School of Psychology: Lic. RIQUELMI GASPARICO
School of Social Work: Lic. RUDY RAMÍREZ
School of Teacher-Training: Ing. FRANCISCO ROSALES CEREZO

UNIVERSIDAD DEL VALLE DE GUATEMALA

Apdo Postal No. 82, 01901 Guatemala City
located at: 18 Avda 11-95, Zona 15, Vista Hermosa III, Guatemala City
Telephone: 2364-0336
Fax: 2364-0212
E-mail: info@uvg.edu.gt
Internet: www.uvg.edu.gt

Founded 1966
Language of instruction: Spanish
Private control
Academic year: February to November

Rector: Lic. ROBERTO MORENO GODOY
Vice-Rector and Director of Studies: MSc. MARÍA LUISA DURANDO DE BOEHM
Registrar: Lda. VICTORIA EUGENIA ROSALES
Librarian: Dra MARÍA EMILIA LÓPEZ

Library of 68,000 vols, 130 current periodicals
Number of teachers: 250
Number of students: 2,000

DEANS

Faculty of Education: MA. JACQUELINE GARCÍA DE DE LEÓN
Faculty of Engineering: Ing. CARLOS PAREDES
Faculty of Science and Humanities: MSc. EDUARDO ÁLVAREZ MASSIS

Faculty of Social Sciences: MA. MARÍA DEL PILAR DE RODRÍGUEZ
Research Institute: Ing. CARLOS ROLZ
University College: MSc. EDUARDO ÁLVAREZ MASSIS

UNIVERSIDAD FRANCISCO MARROQUIN

6 Calle Final, Zona 10, Guatemala City
Telephone: 2338-7700
Fax: 2334-6896
E-mail: info@ufm.edu.gt
Internet: www.ufm.edu.gt

Founded 1971
Language of instruction: Spanish
Private control
Academic year: January to November

Rector: Ing. GIANCARLO IBÁRGÜEN D.
Secretary-General: Lic. RICARDO CASTILLO
Librarian: Dr JULIO H. COLE

Library of 75,000 vols
Number of teachers: 450
Number of students: 7,379

Publications: *Laissez-Faire* (2 a year), *Revista de la Facultad de Derecho* (2 a year)

DEANS

School of Architecture: Arq. ERNESTO PORRAS
School of Dentistry: Dr RAMIRO ALFARO
School of Economics: Dr WENCESLAO GIMÉNEZ
School of Law: Dr MILTON ARGUETA
School of Medicine: Dr RODOLFO HERRERA-LLERANDI
Graduate School of Economics and Business Administration: Dr JUAN CARLOS CACHANOSKY

UNIVERSIDAD GALILEO

Calle Dr Eduardo Suger Cofiño (7a Avda Final), Zona 10, 01010 Guatemala City
Telephone: 2423-8000
Fax: 2362-2731
Internet: www.galileo.edu

Founded 2000
Private control

Rector: Dr JOSÉ EDUARDO SUGER COFIÑO
Vice-Rector: Dr JOSÉ CYRANO RUIZ CABARRÚS
Vice-Rector (Academic): Lic. MYRA ROLDAN DE RAMÍREZ
Secretary-General: Lic. JORGE FRANCISCO RETOLAZA

DEANS

Faculty of Education: Dr BERNARDO RENÉ MORALES FIGUEROA
Faculty of Science, Technology and Industry: Ing. JORGE IVÁN ECHEVERRÍA PERMOUT
Faculty of Systems Engineering: Ing. JOSÉ EDUARDO SUGER CASTILLO

DIRECTORS

Institute of Open Education: Ing. STEPHANY OROZCO
School of Graduate Studies: Ing. CARLOS ARNADI-KLEE
School of Professional Development and Training: Lic. LUIS MANUEL ALVAREZ ALVAREZ

UNIVERSIDAD MARIANO GÁLVEZ DE GUATEMALA

Apdo Postal 1811, Guatemala City
Telephone: 2288-7592
Internet: www.umg.edu.gt

Founded 1966
Language of instruction: Spanish
Private control
Academic year: February to November

Rector: Lic. ALVARO R. TORRES MOSS
Vice-Rectors: Lic. HUGO C. MORALES Y MORALES, Dr ALFREDO SAN JOSÉ
Secretary: Licda RUBY SANTIZO DE HERNÁNDEZ
Registrar: Lic. JOSÉ CLODOVEO TORRES MOSS
Librarian: GLORIA MARINA ARROYO

Library of 9,000 vols
Number of teachers: 400
Number of students: 10,000

Publication: *Boletín Mensual* (monthly)

DIRECTORS

School of Architecture: Arq. VÍCTOR HUGO HERNÁNDEZ ORDÓÑEZ
School of Business Administration: Lic. CARLOS F. CÁRDENAS C.
School of Civil Engineering: Ing. HANS JOAQUÍN LOTTMANN
Schools of Economics, Public Auditing and Accounting: Lic. OSCAR EUGENIO DUBÓN PALMA
School of Education: Lic. VÍCTOR EGIDIO AGREDA GODÍNEZ
School of Humanities: Lic. VÍCTOR EGIDIO AGREDA GODÍNEZ
School of Information Systems: Ing. JORGE A. ARIAS TOBAR
School of Law: Lic. RODERIGO SEGURA TRUJILLO
School of Languages: Dr NEVILLE STILES
School of Linguistics: Dr DAVID OLTROGGE
School of Nursing: Licda DELIA LUCILA CHANG CHANG
School of Odontology: Dr ROLANDO DÍAZ LOZZA
School of Theology: Lic. ADALBERTO SANTIZO ROMÁN

UNIVERSIDAD RAFAEL LANDÍVAR

Vista Hermosa III, Zona 16, Apdo Postal 39 'C', Guatemala City
Telephone: 2369-2751
Fax: 2369-2756
E-mail: info@url.edu.gt
Internet: www.url.edu.gt

Founded 1961
Language of instruction: Spanish
Private control
Academic year: January to November

Rector: GONZALO DE VILLA
General Vice-Rector: GUILLERMINA HERRERA
Vice-Rectors: RENÉ POITEVIN (Academic), Arq. CARLOS HAUESLER (Administrative)
General Secretary: LUIS QUAN
Librarian: REGINA ROMERO DE LA VEGA

Number of teachers: 1,008
Number of students: 20,000

Publications: *Estudios Sociales* (quarterly), *Cultura de Guatemala* (3 a year), *Vida Universitaria* (monthly), *Boletín de Lingüística* (6 a year), *Aprapalabra*, *Revista de Literatura*

DEANS

Faculty of Agriculture and Environmental Sciences: Ing. JAIME CARRERA
Faculty of Architecture: Arq. SERGIO TULIO CASTANEDA
Faculty of Economic Sciences: JOSÉ ALEJANDRO AREVADO
Faculty of Engineering: EDWIN ESCOBAR
Faculty of Health Sciences: MIGUEL GARCÉS
Faculty of Humanities: MA. EUGENIA SANDOVAL
Faculty of Political and Social Sciences: RENZO ROSAL
Faculty of Theology: DENIS LEDER

ATTACHED INSTITUTES

Institute of Agriculture, Natural Resources and the Environment: Dir Ing. JUVENTINO GÁLVEZ.

Institute of Dance: Dir Dr SABRINA CASTILLO.

Institute of Economic and Social Research: Dir TOMAS ROSADA.

Institute of Linguistics: Dir Dr LUCIA VERDUGO.

Institute of Musicology: Dir Dr DIETER LEHNHOFF.

Institute of Psychology: Dir Dr FIDELIO SWANA.

Institute of Science and Technology: Dir LYS CIFUENTES.

Schools of Art and Music

Conservatorio Nacional de Música (National Academy of Music): 3a Avda 4-61, Zona 1, 01001 Guatemala City; f. 1875; 40 teachers; 900 students; Dir LUIS A. LIMA Y LIMA.

Escuela Nacional de Artes Plásticas 'Rafael Rodríguez Padilla': 6 Avda 22-00, Zona 1, Guatemala City; f. 1920; library: 2,500 vols; Dir ZIPACNÁ DE LEÓN; publ. *Revista de la Escuela Nacional de Artes Plásticas 'Rafael Rodríguez Padilla'*.

GUINEA

The Higher Education System

Guinea (formerly French Guinea) was part of French West Africa until it gained its independence in 1958, and the education system is still based on the French system. There are two state-controlled universities, Université Gamal Abdel Nasser de Conakry (founded in 1962) and Université Julius Nyéréré de Kankan (founded in 1963, current name and status since 1987). Additional institutions of higher education include professional institutes and schools attached to the universities. The Ministry of Higher Education and Scientific Research is the main controlling body, through the aegis of the Department for Scientific and Technical Research and the Department for Higher Education, but higher education institutions enjoy significant autonomy. Higher education is wholly financed by the Government (except for private institutions).

Students must hold the secondary school qualification, Baccalauréat Deuxième Partie, and sit a competitive entrance examination in order to be admitted to university. There are two undergraduate degrees: the Diplôme d'Etudes Universitaires Générales, which is awarded after two years, and the Licence, which is awarded after four years. Undergraduates may also receive a professional diploma (Diplôme), depending on the subject. After the Licence, the Maîtrise or the Diplôme d'Etudes Supérieures are the first postgraduate qualifications, both awarded after one year of study. Finally, the third stage of university-level qualifications is the Doctorat, which is a research-based, two year course leading to submission of a thesis.

Learned Society

LANGUAGE AND LITERATURE

PEN Centre de Guinée: BP 107, Labé; tel. 30-44-14-75; f. 1989; 32 mems; library of 92 vols; Sec. ZEINAB KOUMANTHIO DIALLO; publ. *Pour Mémoire*.

Research Institutes

GENERAL

Direction Nationale de la Recherche Scientifique et Technique: Conakry, BP 561; f. 1958; 60 mems; 2 libraries; Dir Dr FODE SOUMAH; publ. *Bulletin*.

AGRICULTURE, FISHERIES AND VETERINARY SCIENCE

Centre de Recherche Agronomique de Foulaya: BP 156, Kindia; tel. 30-61-01-48; e-mail iragdq@irag.org.gn; f. 1946; Dir Dr MAHMOUD CAMARA.

Institut de Recherche Agronomique de Guinée: Blvd du Commerce, BP 1523, Conakry; tel. 30-21-19-57; e-mail iragdg@biasy.net.gn.

Institut de Recherche en Animalculture Pastoria: BP 146, Kindia; tel. 30-61-08-11; f. 1923; fmr *Institut Pasteur*, nationalized 1965; research on infectious animal diseases; production of various vaccines; 18 staff; library of 362 vols; Dir Dr ALHASSANE DIALLO.

Libraries and Archives

Conakry

Archives Nationales: BP 1005, Conakry; tel. 30-44-42-97; f. 1960; Dir ALMANY STELL CONTE.

Bibliothèque Nationale: BP 561, Conakry; tel. 30-46-10-10; f. 1958; 40,000 vols, also spec. colln on slavery (c. 500 books, pamphlets and MSS); 225 current periodicals; courses in librarianship; Dir LANSANA SYLLA.

Museum

Conakry

Musée National: BP 139, Conakry; tel. 30-45-10-66; f. 1960; Dir SORY KABA.

Universities

UNIVERSITÉ GAMAL ABDEL NASSER DE CONAKRY

BP 1147, Conakry
Telephone: 30-46-46-89
Fax: 30-46-48-08
E-mail: uganc@mirinet.net.gn

Founded 1962
State control

Rector: OUSMANE SYLLA
Vice-Rector (Academic): JEAN-MARIE TOURÉ
Vice-Rector (Research): Dr M. KODJOUGOU DIALLO
Sec.-Gen: GALEMA GUILAVOGUI
Dir of Library: MANSA KANTÉ

Library of 4,000 vols
Number of teachers: 824
Number of students: 5,000

Publications: *Guinée Médicale*, *Horizons*

DEANS

Faculty of Arts and Humanities: GOUDOUSSY DIALLO
Faculty of Law, Economics and Management: HAWA FOFANA
Faculty of Medicine and Pharmacy: (vacant)
Faculty of Science: Dr DJELIMANDJAN CONDÉ
Polytechnic Institute: Prof. NANAMOUDOU MAGASSOUBA (Director-General)

ATTACHED CENTRES

Computer Centre: Dir Dr BINKO MADY TOURÉ.

Environment Study and Research Centre: Dir Prof. AHMED TIDIANE BOIRO.

UNIVERSITÉ JULIUS NYÉRÉRÉ DE KANKAN

Ministère de l'Enseignement Supérieur et de la Recherche Scientifique, Kankan

Telephone: 30-71-20-93

Founded 1963; univ. status 1987
State control
Academic year: October to June

Rector: Dr SEYDOUBA CAMARA
Vice-Rector (Academic): Dr MAWIATOU BAH
Vice-Rector (Research): Dr SIDAFA CAMARA
Sec.-Gen.: DOMINIQUE KOLY
Dir of Financial and Administrative Affairs: ELHADJ ALPHA OUSMANE DIALLO
Dir of International Relations and Co-operation: MARTIN KOIVOGUI
Dir of Univ. Publs: ELHADJ NAMANDIAN DOUMBOUYA
Library Dir: JOSEPH KOKOLY DRAMOU

Library of 12,160 vols
Number of teachers: 95
Number of students: 3,012

Publication: *Revue Scientifique de l'Université de Kankan* (2 a year)

DEANS

Faculty of Natural Sciences: Dr BAKARY KAMANO
Faculty of Social Sciences: Dr AMADOU BAÏLO BARRY
Ecole Supérieure des Sciences de l'Information: SIBA BILIVOGUI

Colleges

Ecole Nationale des Arts et Métiers: POB 240, Conakry; tel. 30-46-25-62; fax 30-46-25-62; f. 1962; industrial automation, electro-mechanical engineering, electronics, refrigeration and air-conditioning, diesel mechanics, industrial maintenance; Dir MAHMOUDOU BARRY.

Ecole Nationale de la Santé: Conakry; tel. 30-29-52-49; fax 30-46-50-09; Dir BARRY YAYA.

Ecole Supérieure d'Administration: Conakry; f. 1964.

Institut Supérieur Agronomique et Vétérinaire 'Valéry Giscard d'Estaing' de Faranah: BP 131, Faranah; tel. 30-81-02-15; fax 30-81-08-18; e-mail isav1@mirinet.net.gn; f. 1978; library: 3,629 vols, 207 periodicals; 110 teachers; 2,515 students; faculties of agriculture, agricultural engineering, stockbreeding and veterinary medicine, waters and forestry, rural economics, common-core syllabus; Dir-Gen. Dr YAZORA SOROPOGUI.

GUINEA BISSAU

The Higher Education System

Guinea-Bissau was formerly Portuguese Guinea (Guiné), during which time education as a whole was geared to serve a narrow élite, consisting mainly of the colonial rulers' children. The country gained its independence in 1974 following a military coup in Portugal. The first institution of higher education, a school of law, was established in 1979, followed by centres for medicine, education, nursing and sports. In 1999 a Government decree placed all these institutions under the authority of the Ministry of National and Higher Education (formerly Ministry of Education), with a view to establishing a university at the National Institute for Research. In 2003 the Universidade Amílcar Cabral, Guinea-Bissau's first university, was founded. In the same year a private university also opened.

Technical and vocational education is available at two institutions, the Centre of Administrative Training and the Centre of Experimental Training.

Research Institutes

GENERAL

Centro de Estudos da Guiné-Bissau (Study Centre of Guinea-Bissau): CP 37, Bissau; f. 1945.

Instituto Nacional de Estudos e Pesquisa (INEP) (National Institute of Studies and Research): CP 112, Bairro Cobornel, Bissau; located at: Complexo Escolar 14 de Novembro, Bissau; tel. 251867; fax 251125; f. 1987, damaged during conflict between government forces and rebels in 1999, restoration, with the support of international scholars, began in 2000; library of 40,000 vols; includes archives and museum; also holds periodicals, photographs, plays, press cuttings; fees for using facility and for exhibitions.

Libraries and Archives

Bissau

Biblioteca Nacional da Guiné-Bissau (National Library of Guinea-Bissau): Praça do Impéro, CP 37, Bissau; f. 1970.

Museums and Galleries

Bissau

Museu da Guiné-Bissau (Museum of Guinea Bissau): Praca do Império, CP 37, Bissau; f. 1945; library of 14,000 vols; collns of economics, ethnography, history, natural science.

Museu Etnografico Nacional (National Ethnographical Museum): Complexo Escolar 14 de Novembro, CP 338, Bissau; tel. 215600; fax 204400; photographic archive depicting former colln of African masks and statues (largely destroyed during military conflict in 1998).

University and Colleges

UNIVERSIDADE AMÍLCAR CABRAL

Endereço Bairro da Ajuda, 2a fase, CP 659, Bissau

Telephone: 255970

Fax: 202244

E-mail: geral@uac.com

Founded 2003

State control

Rector: Prof. Dr TCHERNO DJALÓ

Faculties of Agricultural and Veterinary Science, Economics, Letters and Communications, Science, Technology; school of Physical Education and Sport.

Faculdade de Direito da Guiné-Bissau: Complexo escolar 14 de Novembro, CP 595, Bissau Codex; tel. 252770; fax 204304; e-mail geral@fdbissau.com; internet www.fdbissau.com; f. 1990; Dir FODÉ ADULAI MANÉ.

Instituto Nacional para o Desenvolvimento da Educação (INDE): Rua Dr Herman Gmeiner, Bairro 7, 2a Fase, CP 132 Bissau; tel. 204534; fax 202054; e-mail indebissau@hotmail.com; Pres. ALFREDO GOMES; Dir-Gen. AUGUSTO PEREIRA.

GUYANA

The Higher Education System

Guyana, formerly British Guiana, a colony of the United Kingdom, achieved independence in 1966. The Free Education Act of 1976 guaranteed the right to free education at all levels from pre-school to higher education. The Ministry of Education is the supreme body for higher education. The state-controlled University of Guyana (founded in 1963) is the only university, but higher education is also available at professional schools, technical institutes and colleges.

The Caribbean Examinations Council Secondary Education Certificate is the standard requirement for admission to higher education, though GCE O-levels and A-levels are also accepted. The main degrees are the undergraduate Bachelors, which is awarded after fours years of study, and the postgraduate Masters, which is awarded after one further year of study. There are also undergraduate and graduate Diploma programmes in mainly professional fields of study. Masters programmes are not offered in all subjects.

The University of Guyana has an Institute of Distance and Continuing Education, which runs extramural courses; the Adult Education Association offers similar programmes. Post-secondary vocational and technical qualifications include Craft Certificate, Technician Certificate and Technician Diploma.

Learned Societies

BIBLIOGRAPHY, LIBRARY SCIENCE AND MUSEOLOGY

Guyana Library Association: c/o National Library, 76–77 Main St, POB 10240, Georgetown; tel. 226-2690; fax 227-4052; f. 1968; 35 personal mems, 13 institutional mems; Pres. IVOR RODRIGUES; Sec. GWYNETH GEORGE; publ. *Bulletin*.

ECONOMICS, LAW AND POLITICS

Guyana Institute of International Affairs: POB 101176, Georgetown; tel. 227-7768; fax 227-7768; f. 1965; 100 mems; library of 5,000 vols; Pres. DONALD A. B. TROTMAN; publs *Annual Journal of International Affairs*, occasional papers.

EDUCATION

Adult Education Association of Guyana: 88 Carmichael St, POB 101111, Georgetown; tel. 225-0758; fax 227-2273; e-mail aea@guyana.net.gy; f. 1957; 1,000 mems; non-governmental org. which aims to provide opportunities for Guyanese to improve their skills, raise the level of awareness of their culture, acquire a critical understanding of major contemporary issues; programmes: academic, technical, scientific, creative art, commercial and professional development; Pres. LUNSFORD BOWEN; Exec. Dir PATRICIA DAVID.

LANGUAGE AND LITERATURE

Alliance Française: The Hive, 27/28 Queen St, Kitty, Georgetown; offers courses and exams in French language and culture and promotes cultural exchange with France.

Research Institutes

AGRICULTURE, FISHERIES AND VETERINARY SCIENCE

Inter-American Institute for Co-operation on Agriculture (IICA)–Co-operation Agency in Guyana: Lot 18, Brickdam, Stabroek, POB 10-1089, Georgetown; tel. 226-8347; fax 225-8358; e-mail iica@networksgy.com; internet www.iica.int; f. 1974; Guyana branch of the specialized agency of the OAS for the agricultural sector; promotes food safety and the prosperity of the rural sector in the Americas; library of 1,550 vols, 25 periodicals; Rep. CROMWELL CONSTANTINE CRAWFORD; publs *Agriview* (4 a year), *Caribbean News* (4 a year), *COMUNIICA* (4 a year), *Tropical Fruits Newsletter* (4 a year).

MEDICINE

Pan-American Health Organization, Guyana Office: Lot 8, Brickdam, Stabroek, POB 10969, Georgetown; tel. 225-3000; fax 226-6654; e-mail e-mail@guy.paho.org; internet www.guy.paho.org; f. 1902; maternal and child health, environmental health, health services development, human resource development, communicable diseases, management programmes for national development; library of 3,500 vols; Rep. Dr BERNADETTE THEODORE-GANDI.

Libraries and Archives

Georgetown

Bank of Guyana Library: POB 1003, Georgetown; tel. 226-3261; fax 227-2965; e-mail boglib@guyana.net.gy; internet www.bankofguyana.org.gy; f. 1966; provides support for the information needs of the staff; 15,000 vols, 150 periodicals; special collections: staff publs, conference papers, IMF documents, World Bank publs; Librarian BEVERLY BAKER.

Documentation Centre, Caribbean Community Secretariat: 3rd Fl., Bank of Guyana Bldg, POB 10827, Georgetown; tel. 226-9281; fax 226-7816; e-mail carisec2@caricom.org; internet www.caricom.org; f. 1980; 24,635 books and pamphlets, 14,169 official documents, 5,039 microfiches, 91 microfilms, 12 reel tapes, 111 cassettes, 99 CD-ROMs; collections (documents): CARICOM, UN, UN agencies; Senior Project Officer MAUREEN C. NEWTON.

Guyana Medical Science Library: Georgetown Hospital Compound, Georgetown; f. 1966; attached to the Ministry of Health; provides medical information to doctors, nurses, and health personnel; 9,914 vols, 300 journals, 1,000 pamphlets; Librarian Mrs JENNIFER WILSON; publs *Bulletin* (quarterly), *Annual Report*.

National Library: 76–77 Church and Main St, POB 10240, Georgetown; tel. 226-2699; fax 226-4053; e-mail natlib@sdnp.org.gy; internet www.natlib.gov.gy; f. 1909; combines the functions of a National Library and Public Library; legal depository for material printed in Guyana; 197,355 vols; special collections: Caribbeana, library science, A. J. Seymour, Unesco deposit; Chief Librarian GWYNETH BROWMAN (acting); publ. *Guyanese National Bibliography* (quarterly).

University of Guyana Library: POB 101110, Georgetown; fax 225-4885; internet fss.uog.edu.gy/university_library.htm; f. 1963; 200,000 vols, 3,000 periodicals; special collections: UN deposit collection, Caribbean Research Library, Law Collection; Librarian YVONNE LANCASTER; publs *Additions in the Humanities* (all every 2 months), *Additions in Science and Technology*, *Caribbean Additions*.

Museums and Art Galleries

Georgetown

Guyana Museum: Company Path, North St, Georgetown; f. 1853 by the Royal Agricultural and Commercial Society; subjects covered include Industry, Art, History, Anthropology, Zoology; Curator CLAYTON RODNEY; publ. *Journal* (annually).

Incorporates:

Guyana Zoo: Company Path, North St, Georgetown; specializes in the display, care and management of South American fauna; Dir GEORGE E. BURNHAM.

University

UNIVERSITY OF GUYANA

POB 101110, Turkeyen, Greater Georgetown
Telephone: 222-4184
Fax: 222-3596
E-mail: pro@uog.edu.gy
Internet: www.uog.edu.gy

Founded 1963
State control
Language of instruction: English
Academic year: two terms, beginning September and January

Chancellor: Dr BERTRAND RAMCHARRAN
Pro-Chancellor: Dr PREM MISIR
Vice-Chancellor: Dr JAMES ROSE
Deputy Vice-Chancellor: AL CREIGHTON
Registrar: Dr DAVID CHANDERBALLI
Librarian: YVONNE LANCASTER

Library: See Libraries and Archives
Number of teachers: 235

Number of students: 5,151

Publications: *Focus on UG* (monthly newsletter), *University of Guyana Bulletin* (annually)

DEANS

Faculty of Agriculture and Forestry: Dr PATSY FRANCIS
Faculty of Health Sciences: Dr EMANUEL CUMMINGS
Faculty of Natural Sciences: Dr PHILLIP DA SILVA
Faculty of Social Sciences: Dr MARK KIRTON
Faculty of Technology: Dr WILLIAM WILSON
School of Education and Humanities: TOTA MANGAR

PROFESSORS

BISHOP, A., Law
BRITTON, P., Law
JAMES, R., Law
LALITHAKUMARI, J., Agriculture
LONCKE, J., French
MCGOWAN, W., History
MASSIAH, K., Law
PERSICO, A., Spanish
ROGERS, D., Creative Arts
THOMAS, C. Y., Economics and Business Administration
VERMA, V. N., Chemistry
WESTMASS, R., Architecture

ATTACHED INSTITUTES

Institute of Development Studies: Dir Prof. C. Y. THOMAS.

Institute of Distance and Continuing Education: Dir SAMUEL SMALL.

Colleges

American International School of Medicine: Oceanview Campus, POB 101728, Georgetown; e-mail info@aism.edu; internet www.aism.edu; tel. 222-3437; fax 225-1646; f. 1997; library: 2,500 vols; 30 teachers; 50 students; Pres. COLIN A. WILKINSON.

Critchlow Labour College: Woolford Ave, Non Pareil Park, Georgetown; tel. 226-2481; f. 1970; library: 2,000 vols; 40 teachers; 600 students; industrial and social studies; Principal T. ANSON SANCHO.

E. R. Burrowes School of Art: 96 Carmichael St, Georgetown; tel. 226-3649; f. 1975; 4-year diploma course; library: 750 vols; 13 teachers; 52 students; Administrator AGNES JONES.

Government Technical Institute: Woolford Ave, Georgetown; tel. 226-2468; f. 1951; library: 3,500 vols; 37 teachers; 2,000 students; Principal LENNOX B. WILLIAMS.

Guyana Industrial Training Centre: Woolford Ave and Albert St, Non Pareil Park, Georgetown; tel. 226-6196; f. 1966; library: 1,600 vols; 6 teachers; 120 full-time, 90 part-time students; Dir SYDNEY R. WALTERS.

Guyana School of Agriculture Corporation: Mon Repos, East Coast Demerara; tel. and fax 220-2297; e-mail gsa@sdnp.org.gy; internet www.sdnp.org.gy/minagro/; f. 1963; library: 7,000 vols; Principal LYNETTE P. CUNHA.

Kuru-Kuru Co-operative College: 128 D'Urban St, D'Urban Backlands, Lodge, Georgetown; tel. 225-8433; e-mail kurukuruguy@netscape.net; f. 1973; library: 5,800 vols; 26 teachers; 270 students; Principal AVRIL BACCHUS (acting); Librarian LINDA CALDER

COURSE CO-ORDINATORS

Accounting: VIBART DUNCAN
Agriculture: TREVOR CALLENDER (acting)
Co-operative Studies: JAMES N. FRASER
Economics: MICHAEL BOBB-SEMPLE
English: ASHLEY B. WOOLFORD
Extra-Mural Studies: DERECK BOSTON
Management and Commercial Law: LLOYD STUART
Statistics: EMANUEL GILKES

Linden Technical Institute: Lot 1, New Rd, Constabulary Compound, Mackenzie, Linden; tel. 444-3333; fax 444-6719; internet www.sdnp.org.gy/geap/lti/; f. 1958; Guyana Technical Education Examination courses in electrical installation, welding, mechanical fitting, metal machining, instrumentation, motor vehicle work, internal combustion engines, carpentry and joinery, driver training; 10 instructors; 86 full-time students; Principal ISAAC LAMAZON (acting).

New Amsterdam Technical Institute: POB 50, Garrison Rd, Fort Ordnance, New Amsterdam, Berbice; tel. 333-2702; f. 1971; Guyana Technical Education Examination in electrical trades, radio and electronic servicing, agricultural mechanics, automotive engineering, wood trades, fitting, welding, masonry, plumbing; secretarial and business studies; Ordinary Technician diploma, Mechanical Engineering Technician course, Agricultural Engineering Technician course; Architectural and Building Construction Technician course; library: 2,186 vols; 32 teachers; 1,000 students; Principal RONALD L. SIMON.

HAITI

The Higher Education System

Haiti (formerly Saint-Domingue) was under French sovereignty until 1804, when it gained its independence, but later came under US supervision from 1915 until 1934. The traditional education system has strong French influences, though some private institutions follow the American system. French and Creole are the official languages of instruction. The Ministry of Education and Professional Training has responsibility for education. There are three universities, the state-controlled Université d'État d'Haiti (founded in 1920) and the private Université Quisqueya (founded in 1988) and Université Roi Henri Christophe (founded in 1980). Other higher education institutions include professional schools and institutes.

The main secondary school qualification, the Baccalauréat, is the leading requirement for admission to higher education. Undergraduates study for three to four years for the Diplôme d'Etudes Supérieures, Certificat d'Etudes Supérieures or a professional title. The first postgraduate degree is the Maîtrise, received after one year of study following the undergraduate degree. The second postgraduate degree is the Doctorat, but is only available in the fields of ethnology and development sciences.

Learned Societies

GENERAL

UNESCO Office Port-au-Prince: 19, Delmas 60, Musseau par Bourdon, Petion Ville, Port-au-Prince; tel. 511-0460; fax 511-0468; e-mail unescohaiti@hainet.net; Dir JORGE ESPINAL.

BIBLIOGRAPHY, LIBRARY SCIENCE AND MUSEOLOGY

Le Bibliophile: Cap Haïtien; f. 1923 to promote knowledge and readership of world literature; 28 mems; Pres. SILVIO FASCHI; Sec. LOUIS TOUSSAINT; publs *La Citadelle* (weekly), *Stella* (monthly).

LANGUAGE AND LITERATURE

Alliance Française: 99, Rue Lamartinière, BP 131, Port-au-Prince; tel. 244-0016; fax 244-0017; e-mail dgalliancefr_haiti@yahoo.fr; offers courses and exams in French language and culture and promotes cultural exchange with France; attached offices in Cap-Haïtien, Gonaives, Jacmel, Jeremies, Les Cayes, Port-de-Paix.

NATURAL SCIENCES

General

Conseil National des Recherches Scientifiques (National Council for Scientific Research): Département de la Santé Publique et de la Population, Port-au-Prince; f. 1963; to co-ordinate scientific development and research, particularly in the field of public health; Pres. Prof. VICTOR NOËL; Sec. M. DOUYON.

Research Institute

RELIGION, SOCIOLOGY AND ANTHROPOLOGY

Bureau National d'Ethnologie: Angle rue St Honoré and ave Magloire Ambroise, Place des Héros de l'Indépendance, BP 915, Port-au-Prince; tel. 222-5232; f. 1941; departments: African and Haitian ethnography, pre-Columbian archaeology; Dir Dr MAX PAUL; publ. *Bulletin* (2 a year).

Libraries and Archives

Port-au-Prince

Archives Nationales d'Haiti: Angle rues Geffrard et Borgella, BP 1299, Port-au-Prince; tel. 222-8566; fax 222-6280; e-mail admin@anhhaiti.org; internet www.anhhaiti.org; f. 1860; Dir-Gen. JEAN WILFRID BERTRAND.

Bibliothèque Haitienne des F. I. C.: Saint-Louis de Gonzague, 180 Rue du Centre, BP 1758, Port-au-Prince; tel. 223-2148; f. 1920; 13,000 vols; Haitian literature, newspapers since the 19th century; Dir ERNEST EVEN.

Bibliothèque Nationale d'Haiti: 193 rue du Centre, Port-au-Prince; tel. 222-0236; fax 223-8773; f. 1940; 23,000 vols, 419 periodicals; 12 brs; Dir FRANÇOISE BEAULIEU THYBULLE.

Museums and Art Galleries

Port-au-Prince

Centre d'Art: 58 rue Roy, Port-au-Prince; tel. 222-2018; f. 1944; Dir FRANCINE MURAT; arranges representative exhibitions of Haitian art in the Americas and Western Europe.

Musée du Panthéon National Haitien: Place des Héros de l'Indépendance, Champ de Mars, Port-au-Prince; tel. 222-3167; fax 221-8838; e-mail mupanah@yahoo.fr; f. 1983; historical artefacts, arts and crafts; Dir-Gen. MARIE-LUCIE VENDRYES.

Universities

UNIVERSITÉ D'ÉTAT D'HAITI

1 rue de Houx, BP 2279, Port-au-Prince

Telephone: 244-2942
Fax: 244-2910

Founded 1920
State control
Language of instruction: French
Academic year: October to July

Rector: PIERRE PAQUIOT
Vice-Rector (Academic): MICHEL HECTOR
Vice-Rector (Administrative): MARIE CARMEL AUSTIN
Secretary-General: LESLIE DUCHATELLIER
Librarian (vacant)

Library of 7,000 vols
Number of teachers: 664
Number of students: 10,446

DEANS AND CO-ORDINATORS

Faculty of Agronomy and Veterinary Medicine: JEAN VERNET HENRY
Faculty of Applied Linguistics: PIERRE VERNET
Faculty of Ethnology: JEAN YVES BLOT, PATRICIA MICHEL FOUCAULT
Faculty of Humanities: JEAN RENOL ELIE
Faculty of Law and Economics: JUSTIN CASTEL
Faculty of Medicine and Pharmacy: Dr MARIO ALVAREZ
Faculty of Odontology: Dr ALIX CHATEIGNE
Faculty of Science: GUICHARD BEAULIEU (Academic: CHRISTIAN ROUSSEAU (Administrative)
Ecole Normale Supérieure: BERARD CENATUS, ROGER PETIT-FRÈRE
Institut d'Etudes et de Recherches Africaines d'Haiti: ERNST BERNADIN
Institut National d'Administration de Gestion et des Hautes Etudes Internationales (INAGHEI): EDDY CARRÉ

UNIVERSITÉ QUISQUEYA

Angle rue Chareron et boulevard Harry Truman, BP 796, Port-au-Prince

Telephone: 222-9103
Fax: 221-4211
E-mail: recteur@uniq.edu
Internet: www.uniq.edu

Founded 1988
Private control
Language of instruction: French
Academic year: September to July

Rector: PAUL SAINT-HILAIRE
Vice-Rectors: EDGARD PRÉVILON (Academic), LIONEL RICHARD (Administration)
General Secretary: MARIE GISÈLE PIERRE
Librarian: CARLO DUPUY

Library of 22,000 vols
Number of teachers: 256
Number of students: 2,036

Publication: *Revue Juridique de l'UniQ* (quarterly)

DEANS

Faculty of Agriculture and the Environment: EDGARD JEANNITON
Faculty of Economics and Management: NARCISSE FIÈVRE
Faculty of Education: ROLAND MATHIEU
Faculty of Health Sciences: KYSS JEAN-MARY
Faculty of Law: MIRLANDE MANIGAT

Faculty of Science and Engineering: GÉRARD-LUC JEAN-BAPTISTE

ATTACHED INSTITUTE

Institute of Research, Training and Counselling in Management of Co-operatives and Small Enterprises: Dir JOEL JEAN-PIERRE.

UNIVERSITÉ ROI HENRI CHRISTOPHE

BP 98, Rues 17-18, H-1, Cap-Haïtien
Telephone: 262-1316
Fax: 262-0802
Founded 1980
Private control

Rector: JOSEPH YVON
Administrator: EDGARD BERNARDIN
Librarian: MARIE-MERCIE PREDESTIN
Number of students: 100

DEANS

Faculty of Agriculture: BRUNEL GARÇON
Faculty of Engineering: (vacant)
Faculty of Medicine: Dr GUY DUGUÉ

Colleges

Ecole Nationale des Arts et Métiers: 266 rue Monseigneur Guilloux, Port-au-Prince; tel. 222-9686; f. 1983; Dirs EMERANTE DE PRADINES MORSE, ROBERT BAU DUY.

Ecole de Technologie Médicale: Rue Oswald Durand, Port-au-Prince; Dir PAULETTE A. CHAMPAGNE.

Institut International d'Etudes Universitaires: c/o Fondation Haitienne de Développement, 106 ave Christophe, Port-au-Prince; Dir Y. ARMAND.

HONDURAS

The Higher Education System

The oldest institution of higher education is the Universidad Nacional Autónoma de Honduras, which was founded in 1847. There are two further universities and a college with a number of attached centres. The Ministry of Public Education is responsible for the provision of higher education. In 2003 75,643 students were enrolled in university-level education.

The secondary school qualification Bachillerato (Académico) is the main requirement for admission to higher education. The primary undergraduate degrees are the Licenciado or professional title, awarded after four years of study, and the Bachillerato Universitario, a technological qualification also awarded after four years. Following the Licenciado, the first postgraduate degree is the Maestría, awarded after two to three years of study. The Bachillerato Universitario does not always guarantee admission to postgraduate studies.

Higher technical and vocational education is offered by professional colleges and schools. The leading qualification is the Técnico or Técnico Universitario, which requires one-and-a-half years of study.

Learned Societies

GENERAL

Academia Hondureña (Honduran Academy): Apdo 4003, Tegucigalpa; located at: Avda Tiburcio Carías Andino 811, Col. Alameda, Tegucigalpa; tel. and fax 232-1322; e-mail ahlengua@hotmail.com; f. 1949; corresp. of the Real Academia Española (Madrid); 28 mems; Dir Óscar Acosta; Sec. María Elba Nieto Segovia; publ. *Boletín*.

ARCHITECTURE AND TOWN PLANNING

Colegio de Arquitectos de Honduras (College of Honduran Architects): Apdo 1974, Tegucigalpa; tel. 235-8828; fax 235-7965; e-mail cah1@e-cah.org; internet www.e-cah.org; f. 1979; 727 mems; library; publ. *Arquitectura y Contexto* (4 a year).

BIBLIOGRAPHY, LIBRARY SCIENCE AND MUSEOLOGY

Asociación de Bibliotecarios y Archivistas de Honduras: 11a Calle, 1a y 2a Avdas No. 105, Comayagüela, DC, Tegucigalpa; f. 1951; 53 mems; library of 3,000 vols; Pres. Francisca de Escoto Espinoza; Sec.-Gen. Juan Angel Ayes R.; publ. *Catálogo de Préstamo* (monthly).

HISTORY, GEOGRAPHY AND ARCHAEOLOGY

Academia Hondureña de Geografía e Historia: Apdo 619, Tegucigalpa; f. 1968; 21 mems; library of 1,535 vols; Pres. Dr Ramón E. Cruz; Sec. Pm Fernando Ferrari Bustillo; publ. *Revista*.

LANGUAGE AND LITERATURE

Alliance Française: Col. Lomas Del Guijarro, Apdo Postal 3445, Tegucigalpa; tel. 239-6164; fax 239-6163; e-mail tegucigalpa@tegus-alfrancaise.net; offers courses and exams in French language and culture and promotes cultural exchange with France; attached teaching offices in La Ceiba, San Pedro Sula, Tegucigalpa and Tela.

Research Institutes

GENERAL

Instituto Hondureño de Cultura Interamericana (IHCI): Apdo 201, Tegucigalpa; located at: 2da. Avda entre 5 y 6, Calle No. 520, Comayagüela; tel. 220-1393; fax 238-0064; e-mail rosario@ihci.sdnhon.org.hn; f. 1939; courses in English, bilingual secretarial studies; art gallery; library of 8,000 vols (English and Spanish); Dir Rosario Elena Córdova.

AGRICULTURE, FISHERIES AND VETERINARY SCIENCE

Instituto Hondureño del Café (Honduran Coffee Institute): Apdo Postal 3147, Tegucigalpa; located at: Col. Las Minitas, Edif. El Faro Contiguo a Embajada de Guatemala, Tegucigalpa; tel. 232-2544; fax 232-2768; e-mail ihcafe@cafesdehonduras.com; internet www.cafedehonduras.hn/IHCAFE2005/ihcafe/quienessomos.html; f. 1970; CEO Juan José Osorto.

Instituto Nacional Agrario (National Agrarian Institute): Col. Alameda, Calle Principal, 4a. Avda entre 10 y 11 Calle, # 1009 Tegucigalpa; tel. 232-4893; fax 239-7398; Dir Erasmo Portillo.

HISTORY, GEOGRAPHY AND ARCHAEOLOGY

Instituto Geográfico Nacional (IGN) (National Geographic Institute): Apdo Postal 3177, Tegucigalpa; Barrio La Bolsa, Tegucigalpa, DC; tel. 225-2759; fax 225-2753; e-mail apsanchezs-rsc@unete.com; f. 1946; delineates natural and mineral resources, their evaluation and their exploitation; 130 staff; library of 8,000 vols; Dir-Gen. Ing. Angel Porfirio Sanchez Sanchez; publs *Boletín de la Dirección General de Cartografía*, *Boletín de la Dirección General de Cartografía del Ministerio de Obras Públicas, Transporte y Viviencia*, *Boletín del Instituto Geográfico Nacional*.

Instituto Hondureño de Antropología e Historia: Apdo 1518, Villa Roy, Barrio Buenos Aires, Tegucigalpa; tel. 222-3470; fax 222-2552; e-mail ihah2003@yahoo.com; internet www.ihah.hn; f. 1952; library of 12,000 vols; research and conservation of cultural property, archaeology, history, ethnography, linguistics, museology; Dir Margarita Durón de Gálvez; publ. *Yaxkin* (annually).

Libraries and Archives

Tegucigalpa

Archivo Nacional de Honduras: Avda Cristóbal Colón, Calle Salvador Mendieta 1117, Tegucigalpa; tel. 222-8338; fax 236-9532; internet www.secad.gob.hn/archi.htm; f. 1880; 700 linear m of documents; 2,700 vols and 100 periodicals; Dir Carlos Wilfredo Maldonado.

Biblioteca Nacional de Honduras: Apdo Postal 4563, Tegucigalpa; located at: Ave Cristobal Colón, Calle 'Salvador Mendieta', POB 1117, Tegucigalpa; tel. 228-0241; fax 222-8577; e-mail binah@sdnhon.org.hn; internet www.binah.gob.hn; f. 1880; 70,000 vols; co-ordinates national and international exchange; shares legal deposit with other centres; Dir Hector Roberto Luna; publ. *Anuario Bibliográfico*.

Biblioteca 'Wilson Popenoe': Escuela Agrícola Panamericana, Apdo 93, Tegucigalpa; tel. 776-6140; fax 776-6113; e-mail hgallo@zamorano.edu; internet www.zamorano.edu/biblioteca; f. 1946; tropical agriculture; 19,000 vols, 950 periodicals, 1,200 DVDs; Librarian Hugo Alberto Gallo M.; publ. *Ceiba* (2 a year).

Sistema Bibliotecario Universidad Nacional Autónoma de Honduras: Edif. de Biblioteca, 3er piso, Carretera a Suyapa, Ciudad Universitaria, Tegucigalpa; tel. 232-2204; fax 232-2204; internet www.biblio.unah.hn; f. 1847; 200,000 vols; Librarian Orfylia Pinel; publ. *Boletín del Sistema Bibliotecario* (quarterly).

Museums and Art Galleries

Comayagua

Museo Arqueológico de Comayagua: Frente a Plaza San Francisco, Ciudad de Comayagua; tel. 772-03-86; f. 1946; archaeological collection from the Comayagua Valley; some contemporary items; Dir Salvador Turcios.

Copán

Museo Regional de Arqueología Maya: Ciudad de Copán; f. 1939; objects relate exclusively to Maya culture; Dir Prof. Osmin Rivera.

Cortés

Museo Nacional de Historia Colonial: Puerto de Omoa, Cortés; f. 1959 in former prison; colonial and historical items; Curator Ramón Zúñiga Andrade.

Universities

UNIVERSIDAD NACIONAL AUTÓNOMA DE HONDURAS

POB 3560, Tegucigalpa, DC

Telephone: 235-3361
Fax: 235-3361
Internet: www.unah.hn

Founded 1847
Autonomous control
Language of instruction: Spanish
Academic year: February to December

Rector: GUILLERMO PÉREZ-CADALSO ARIAS
Vice-Rector: OCTAVIO SÁNCHEZ MIDENCE
Administrative-Secretary: RAÚL FLORES
General Secretary: AFREDO HAWIT
Librarian: ORFYLIA PINEL

Library: see Libraries and Archives
Number of teachers: 3,486
Number of students: 56,077

Publications: *Catálogo de Estudios*, *Memoria Anual*, *Presencia Universitaria*, *Revista de la Universidad*, *and various faculty publs*

DEANS

Faculty of Law and Social Sciences: JESÚS MARTINEZ
Faculty of Economics, Business Administration and Accountancy: GABRIEL ORDOÑEZ
Faculty of Medicine and Nursing: GUSTAVO VALLEJO
Faculty of Chemistry and Pharmacy: GODOFREDO CRUZ
Faculty of Dentistry: RAÚL SANTOS
Faculty of Engineering: ADOLFO RACHEL QUAN

DIRECTORS

Atlantic Coast University Centre (La Ceiba): Ing. JORGE SOTO MONICO
General Studies Centre: RAQUEL ANGULO
Regional Studies Centre: MARTÍN CASTRO
University Centre of the North (San Pedro Sula): DARIO E. TURCOS

UNIVERSIDAD PEDAGÓGICA NACIONAL 'FRANCISCO MORAZÁN'

POB 3394, Calle El Dorado, Blvd Miraflores, Tegucigalpa

Telephone: 239-8037
E-mail: webmaster@upnfm.edu.hn
Internet: www.upnfm.edu.hn

Founded 1957 as Escuela Superior del Profesorado, in co-operation with UNESCO; current name and status since 1989
State control
Academic year: February to November (two semesters)

Rector: RAMÓN ULISES SALGADO
Vice-Rector (Academic): LEA AZUCENA CRUZ
Vice-Rector (Administration): DAVID ORLANDO MARÍN
Vice-Rector (University Centre for Distance Learning): MARCIO BULNES
Secretary-General: GUSTAVO ZELAYA
Librarian: ADÁN BRITO

Library of 35,000 vols
Number of teachers: 520
Number of students: 9,000

Publications: *Codice* (monthly), *Revista Paradigma* (quarterly)

Faculties of Humanities, Science and Technology.

UNIVERSIDAD TECNOLÓGICA DE HONDURAS

Carretera a Armenta, Frente a Rio Blanco, San Pedro Sula

Telephone: 551-2236
Fax: 551-6108
E-mail: mirna.rivera@uth.hn
Internet: www.uth.hn

Founded 1986 as Instituto Superior Tecnológico; current name and status since 1996
State control

President: Lic. ROGER D. VALLADARES
Rector: RICARDO ANTILLÓN
Vice-Rector: Ing. FERNANDO FERRERA
Academic Director: Lic. CELESTINO PADILLA
Number of students: 4,100

DIRECTORS

El Progreso Campus: Ing. ROBERTO CÁCERES
La Ceiba Campus: Lic. LUIS RIETTI
Puerto Cortés Campus: Dr MOHAM MERZKANI

HEADS OF DEPARTMENTS

Business Management: Lic. JAVIER MEJÍA
Computer Engineering: Ing. ANGEL IRÍAS
Electronic Engineering: Ing. JULIO ARRARIBA
Industrial Production Engineering: Ing. JUAN JOSÉ AGUIRRE
Industrial Relations: Lic. LUIS CARACCIOLI
Law: Lic. REYNA MATAMALA
Marketing: Lic. WU
Mathematics: Lic. ALBERTO FAJARDO
Tourism: Lic. CARLOS FLORES

College

Zamorano, Escuela Agrícola Panamericana: Apdo 93, Tegucigalpa; tel. 776-6140; fax 776-6240; e-mail gerencia_mercadeo@zamorano.edu; internet www.zamorano.edu; f. 1942; private, non-profit pan-American instn of higher education; offers 4-year undergraduate degree, with programmes in Agricultural Science and Production, Agroindustry, Agribusiness, and Socioeconomic Development and Environment; 70 teachers; 800 students; library: 14,000 vols, 500 periodicals; Rector Dr KENNETH L. HOADLEY; publ. *CEIBA* (3 a year).

Attached centres:

Centre for Agribusiness.
Centre for Agricultural Policy.
Centre for Apiculture.
Centre for Biological Control.
Centre for Evaluation and Management of Pesticides.
Centre for Food Technology.
Centre for Geographic Information Systems.
Centre for Meat Science.
Centre for Milk Processing.
Centre for Natural Resources Economics.
Centre for Rural Development.
International Seed and Grain Science Centre.
W. K. Kellogg Training Centre.

HUNGARY

The Higher Education System

Higher education in Hungary dates back to the 14th century, with the establishment in 1367 of Pécsi Tudományegyetem (University of Pécs). Other long-established universities include Debreceni Egyetem (University of Debrecen; founded in 1538), Debreceni Református Hittudományi Egyetem (University of Reformed Theology of Debrecen; founded in 1538) and Evangélikus Hittudományi Egyetem (Evangelical–Lutheran Theological University; founded in 1557). In 1999–2000 the system of higher education underwent a major reorganization, as a result of which from 1 January 2000 there were 30 state-run universities and colleges, 26 church universities and colleges and six colleges run by foundations. In 2005 a new Act on Higher Education legislated the creation of a new system of university degrees (see below), and introduced financial and managerial reforms. In 2005/06 an estimated 231,482 students were enrolled in 71 institutions of higher education.

The Ministry of Education and Culture is responsible for establishing and recognizing institutions of higher education, which must gain accreditation from the Hungarian Accreditation Committee and Higher Education and Academic Council. The Act on Higher Education (2005) established an Economic Council to take responsibility for all decisions regarding the financing and management of the higher education sector. Universities and colleges are autonomous institutions and set their own curricula and courses.

Since 2004 admission to higher education has been based purely on results in the Erettsegi or Matura, the main secondary school qualifications. (Previously, admission had been based on a combination of the Erettsegi/Matura and competitive entrance examination.) In September 2006 a Bachelors-Masters-Doctorate degree system was introduced, based on the principles of the Bologna Process. The new courses are based on a 'credit semester' system, with students accruing a specified number of credits each semester in order to graduate. The main undergraduate degree is the Bachelors, which lasts six to eight semesters (three to four years) for which students must accumulate 180–240 credits. Following the Bachelors, the Masters is the first postgraduate degree, lasting two to four semesters (one to two years) during which students must accrue 60–120 credits (teacher training lasts five semesters or two-and-a-half years and requires 150 credits). In total, combined Bachelors and Masters studies must not last less than 10 or more than 12 semesters. Finally, the Doctoral degree (PhD) is a six-semester programme (three years) requiring 180 credits.

Technical and vocational education has been integrated into the mainstream education system and the old system of apprenticeships has been phased out. Courses are offered by post-secondary vocational schools and last two years. Students are awarded the Technikusi Oklevel qualification and the title of Technikus (Technician).

Learned Societies

GENERAL

Magyar Tudományos Akadémia (Hungarian Academy of Sciences): 1051 Budapest, Roosevelt tér 9; tel. (1) 411-6100; e-mail priroda@office.mta.hu; internet www.mta.hu; f. 1825; sections of 1. Linguistic and Literary Sciences (Chair. Miklós Maróth,), 2. Philosophy and Historical Sciences (Chair. Miklós Szabó), 3. Mathematical Sciences (Chair. Domokos Szász), 4. Agricultural Sciences (Chair. Péter Horn), 5. Medical Sciences (Chair. László Romics), 6. Technical Sciences (Chair. József Gyulai), 7. Chemical Sciences (Chair. Kálmán Medzihradszky), 8. Biological Sciences (Chair. Sándor Damjanovich), 9. Economics and Law (Chair. Ádám Török), 10. Earth Sciences (Chair. József Ádám), 11. Physical Sciences (Chair. Zalán Horváth); 707 mems (203 hon., 250 ordinary, 92 corresp., 162 external); attached research institutes: see Research Institutes; library: see Libraries and Archives; Pres. E. Sylvester Vizi; Gen. Sec. Attila Meskó; publs *Acta Agronomica, Acta Alimentaria, Acta Antiqua, Acta Archaeologica, Acta Biologica, Acta Botanica, Acta Chirurgica, Acta Ethnographica, Acta Geodaetica et Geophysica, Acta Historiae Artium, Acta Historica, Acta Juridica, Acta Linguistica, Acta Mathematica, Acta Medica, Acta Microbiologica et Immunologica, Acta Oeconomica, Acta Orientalia, Acta Physica, Acta Physiologica, Acta Phytopathologica, Acta Technica, Acta Veterinaria, Acta Zoologica, Analysis Mathematica, Studia Musicologica, Studia Scientiarium Mathematicarum Hungarica, Studia Slavica*, Bulletins of the Sections of the Academy, in five series.

Müszaki és Természettudományi Egyesületek Szövetsége (Federation of Technical and Scientific Societies): 1055 Budapest, Kossuth L. tér 6–8; tel. (1) 353-2808; fax (1) 353-0317; e-mail mtesz@mtesz.hu; internet www.mtesz.hu; f. 1948; 42 mem. socs; Pres. Dr Gábor Széles; Sec.-Gen. (vacant) Ágota Kósz.

Széchenyi Irodalmi és Művészeti Akadémia (Széchenyi Academy of Letters and Arts): 1051 Budapest, Roosevelt tér 9; tel. (1) 331-4117; fax (1) 331-4117; e-mail szima@ella.hu; internet www.mta.hu; f. 1825 as section of Hungarian Acad. of Sciences, ind. 1992; sections of Letters, of Fine Arts, of Theatre and Film, of Music; 70 mems; Pres. Miklós Jancsó; Exec. Pres. László Lator; Exec. Sec. Anikó Kovács.

AGRICULTURE, FISHERIES AND VETERINARY SCIENCE

Magyar Agrártudományi Egyesület (Hungarian Society of Agricultural Sciences): 1055 Budapest, Kossuth Lajos tér 6–8; tel. (1) 353-1950; fax (1) 353-0651; f. 1951; 8,500 mems; 17 affiliated socs; Sec.-Gen Dr Károly Neszmélyi; Pres. Dr Károly Tamás; publ. *Magyar Mezőgazdaság* (Hungarian Agriculture, monthly).

Magyar Élelmezésipari Tudományos Egyesület (MÉTE) (Hungarian Scientific Society for Food Industry): 1027 Budapest, Fő u. 68; tel. (1) 214-6691; fax (1) 214-6692; e-mail mail.mete@mtesz.hu; internet www.mete.mtesz.hu; f. 1949; poultry breeding and processing, viticulture, sugar industry, confectionery, grain processing, meat industry, cold storage, canning, paprika, tobacco, oil, soap, cosmetics, brewery, bakery, distillery; 3,800 mems; Pres. Dr Peter Biacs; Exec. Dir Dr László Cserháti; publs *A Hús* (Meat, 4 a year), *Ásványvíz-Üdítőital-Gyümölcslé* (Mineral Water-Softdrink-Juice, 4 a year), *Cukoripar* (Sugar Industry, 4 a year), *Édesipar* (Confectionery Industry, 4 a year), *Élelmezési Ipar* (Food Industry, monthly), *Hűtőipar* (Frozen Food Industry, 4 a year), *Konzervújság* (Canning News, 4 a year), *Molnárok Lapja* (Millers' Journal, 6 a year), *Olaj, Szappan, Kozmetika* (Oil, Soap, Cosmetics, 6 a year), *Sütőipar* (Baking Industry, 4 a year), *Szeszipar* (Distilling Industry, 4 a year), *Tejgazdaság* (Dairy Industry, 2 a year).

Országos Erdészeti Egyesület (Hungarian Forestry Association): 1027 Budapest, Fő utca 68; tel. (1) 201-6293; fax (1) 201-7737; e-mail oee@mtesz.hu; internet quercus.emk.nyme.hu/oee; f. 1866; forestry, forest industries, environment protection; 5,000 mems; library of 20,000 vols; Pres. József Káldy; Sec.-Gen. Gábor Barátossy; publ. *Erdészeti Lapok* (Forestry Bulletin).

ARCHITECTURE AND TOWN PLANNING

Építéstudományi Egyesület (Scientific Society for Building): 1027 Budapest, Fő u. 68; tel. and fax (1) 201-8416; e-mail info@eptud.hu; internet www.eptud.mtesz.hu; f. 1949; 3,500 mems; Pres. Dr Celesztin Meszléry; Sec.-Gen. Pál Seenger; publs *Magyar Építőipar* (Hungarian Building Industry), *Magyar Épületgépészet* (Hungarian Sanitary and Installation Engineering).

BIBLIOGRAPHY, LIBRARY SCIENCE AND MUSEOLOGY

Magyar Könyvtárosok Egyesülete (Association of Hungarian Librarians): 1054 Budapest, Hold u. 6; tel. (1) 311-8634; fax (1) 311-8634; e-mail mke@oszk.hu; internet www

.mke.oszk.hu; f. 1935; 2,200 mems; Pres. KLÁRA BAKOS; Sec.-Gen. ANIKÓ NAGY.

Magyar Levéltárosok Egyesülete (Association of Hungarian Archivists): 1014 Budapest, Hess András tér 5; tel. and fax (1) 411-6737; e-mail ek_titkarsag@ludens.elte.hu; internet www.leveltaros.hu; f. 1986; 850 mems; Pres. LÁSZLÓ SZÖGI; Sec. EDIT TAKÁCS.

EDUCATION

Magyar Művelődési Intézet (Hungarian Institute of Culture): 1011 Budapest, Corvin tér 8; tel. (1) 355-6561; fax (1) 201-5764; e-mail mmi@mmi.hu; internet www.mmhir.hu; f. 1951; analyses the social impact of cultural values, the changes in the content and organization of community education and the activities of cultural communities; organizes training for professionals in community education; centre for life-long education, folk art, minority cultures, amateur artistic and leisure pursuits, community development, arts and crafts; 80 mems; library of 60,000 vols; special collection on past and present Hungarian folk high schools; Dir ANDRÁS FÖLDIÁK; publ. *SZIN* (6 a year).

FINE AND PERFORMING ARTS

Liszt Ferenc Társaság (Franz Liszt Society): 1064 Budapest, Vörösmarty u. 35; tel. and fax (1) 342-1573; e-mail lisztferenctarsasag@lft.axelero.hu; internet www.lisztsociety.hu; f. 1893; to promote the work of the composer Franz Liszt (1811–86), and to further the interest of audiences in live music; concerts, competitions, annual Liszt Record Grand Prix; establishment of Liszt memorials; 400 mems; Pres. ISTVÁN LANTOS; Gen. Sec. Dr CSABA KIRÁLY.

Magyar Zenei Tanács (Hungarian Music Council): BMC Hungarian Music Information Center, Lónyay u. 54, 1093 Budapest; tel. (1) 476-1097; fax (1) 210-6908; internet www.bmc.hu; f. 1996 to replace Magyar Zeneművészek Szövetsége; library of 7,400 vols, 13,600 scores, 1,700 CDs, 5,600 records, 800 tapes with 1,400 Hungarian compositions; Dir ADRIENNE MANKOVITS; Exec. Sec. ÁGNES PÁLDY; Head of the Music Information Centre ESZTER VIDA; publs *Polifónia* (irregular), *Magyar Zene* (Hungarian Music, 4 a year).

Magyar Zeneművészeti Társaság (Hungarian Music Society): 1025 Budapest, Pusztaszeri ut. 30; tel. (1) 325-7313; fax (1) 325-7313; f. 1987; 60 mems; aims to foster cultivation of Hungarian music, to promote the interests of musical artists, to educate young people's musical taste, to preserve Hungarian music past and present and to perform foreign contemporary music in Hungary; Pres. JÁNOS DEVICH.

Országos Magyar Cecilia Társulat (National Hungarian Cecilia Society): 1119 Budapest, Fehérvári út 82; f. 1897; 2,800 mems; aims to foster cultivation of Catholic music; Ecclesiastical Chair. GY. SZAKOS.

Országos Színháztörténeti Múzeum és Intézet (Hungarian Theatre Museum and Institute): 1013 Budapest, Krisztina-krt. 57; tel. (1) 375-1184; fax (1) 375-1184; e-mail oszmi@ella.hu; internet www.oszmi.hu; f. 1952; to research into theatre history and theory, information on Hungarian drama and theatre for abroad and on world drama and theatre for Hungarian professionals; controls the theatrical memorial places, and the Bajor Gizi Actors' Museum; 40 mems; Dir. Dr PETER P. MÜLLER; publs *Világszínház* (world theatre, 6 a year), *Szinháztudományi szemle* (theatre studies, annually), *Évkönyv* (yearbook).

HISTORY, GEOGRAPHY AND ARCHAEOLOGY

Magyar Földmérési, Térképészeti és Távérzékelési Társaság (Hungarian Society for Surveying, Mapping and Remote Sensing): 1027 Budapest, Fő utca 68; tel. (1) 201-8642; fax (1) 156-1215; f. 1956; 1,000 mems; Pres. ÁKOS DETREKŐI; Sec.-Gen. FERENC BARTOS; publ. *Geodézia és Kartográfia* (Geodesy and Cartography).

Magyar Földrajzi Társaság (Hungarian Geographical Society): c/o Prof. Dr Ádám Kertész, 1118 Budapest, Budaörsi útja 43–45; tel. (1) 309-2686; fax (1) 309-2686; e-mail kertesza@helka.iif.hu; f. 1872; 1,300 mems; library of 32,000 vols, 800 periodicals, 5,000 maps; Pres. SANDOR MAROSI; Gen. Sec. ANTAL NEMERKÉNYI; publ. *Földrajzi Közlemények* (with English summaries, 4 a year).

Magyar Irodalomtörténeti Társaság (Society of Hungarian Literary History): 1052 Budapest, Piarista köz 1; tel. (1) 337-7819; f. 1912; Pres. SÁNDOR IVÁN KOVÁCS; Gen. Sec. MIHÁLY PRAZNOVSZKY; publ. *Irodalomtörténet* (Literary History, quarterly).

Magyar Régészeti és Művészettörténeti Társulat (Hungarian Society of Archaeology and History of Fine Arts): 1088 Budapest, Múzeum-krt. 14–16; tel. (1) 338-2662; e-mail wollak@hnm.hu; f. 1878; 600 mems; Pres. Dr JENŐ FITZ; Gen. Sec. Dr TIBOR KOVÁCS; Sec. KATALIN WOLLÁK; publs *Archaeológiai Értesítő* (annually), *Henszlmann Lapok* (irregular), *Művészettörténeti Értesítő* (annually).

Magyar Történelmi Társulat (Hungarian Historical Society): 1014 Budapest, Uri u. 53; tel. (1) 375-9011; f. 1867; Pres. DOMOKOS KOSÁRY; Gen. Sec. IGNÁC ROMSICS; publ. *Századok* (every 2 months).

LANGUAGE AND LITERATURE

Alliance Française: 6722 Szeged, Petofi Sandor SGT. 36, POB 1240; tel. and fax (62) 420-427; e-mail szeged@af.org.hu; internet www.af.org.hu; offers courses and exams in French language and culture and promotes cultural exchange with France; attached offices in Debrecen, Gyor, Miskolc and Pécs; Dir SÜMEGI ISTVÁN.

British Council: 1068 Budapest, Benczúr u. 26; tel. (1) 478-4700; fax (1) 342-5728; e-mail information@britishcouncil.hu; internet www.britishcouncil.hu; teaching centre; offers courses and exams in English language and British culture and promotes cultural exchange with the UK; Dir JIM MCGRATH; Teaching Centre and Examinations Man. JOHN PARE.

Goethe-Institut: 1061 Budapest, Andrássy út 24; tel. (1) 374-4070; fax (1) 374-4080; e-mail info@budapest.goethe.org; internet www.goethe.de/ms/bud/deindex.htm; offers courses and exams in German language and culture and promotes cultural exchange with Germany; library of 13,000 vols; Dir Dr BRIGITTE KAISER-DERENTHAL.

Hungarian PEN Centre: 1053 Budapest, Károlyi Mihály u. 16; e-mail hungary@penclub.t-online.hu; f. 1926; 325 mems; Pres. GÁBOR GÖRGEY.

Instituto Cervantes: 1064 Budapest, Vörösmarty ut. 32; tel. (1) 354-3670; fax (1) 302-2954; e-mail cenbud@cervantes.es; internet budapest.cervantes.es; offers courses and exams in Spanish language and culture and promotes cultural exchange with Spain and Spanish-speaking Latin and Central America; Dir JOSEP MARIA DE SAGARRA ÁNGEL.

Magyar Írószövetség (Union of Hungarian Writers): 1062 Budapest, Bajza u. 18; tel. (1) 322-8840; fax (1) 321-3419; f. 1945; 1,100 mems; Pres. MÁRTON KALÁSZ.

Magyar Nyelvtudományi Társaság (Hungarian Linguistic Society): 1052 Budapest, Piarista köz 1; tel. (1) 137-6819; f. 1904; 660 mems; Pres. LORÁND BENKŐ; Gen. Sec. JENŐ KISS; Sec. ANDRÁS ZOLTÁN; publ. *Magyar Nyelv* (quarterly).

Magyar Ujságirók Országos Szövetsége (National Federation of Hungarian Journalists): 1062 Budapest, Andrássy ut. 101; tel. (1) 322-1699; fax (1) 322-1881; 6,800 mems; Pres. ANDRÁS KERESZTY; Gen. Sec. GÁBOR BENCSIK.

MEDICINE

Magyar Gyógyszerészeti Társaság (Hungarian Pharmaceutical Society): 1085 Budapest, Gyulai Pál u. 16; tel. (1) 266-9395; fax (1) 483-1465; e-mail titkarsag@mgyt.hu; internet www.mgyt.hu; f. 1924; 1,200 mems; Pres. Dr Z. VINCZE; Gen. Sec. Dr J. LIPTÁK; publs *Acta Pharmaceutica Hungarica*, *Gyógyszerészet*.

Magyar Orvostársaságok és Egyesületek Szövetsége (MOTESZ) (Association of Hungarian Medical Societies): POB 145, 1443 Budapest; located at: 1051 Budapest, Nádor u. 36; tel. (1) 311-6687; fax (1) 383-7918; e-mail szalma@motesz.hu; internet www.motesz.hu; f. 1966; 30,000 mems, 115 mem. socs; Pres. Prof. Dr PÉTER SÓTONYI; Dir-Gen. Dr BÉLA SZALMA; publ. *MOTESZ Magazine* (8 a year).

NATURAL SCIENCES

General

Tudományos Ismeretterjesztő Társulat (Society for the Dissemination of Scientific Knowledge): 1088 Budapest, Bródy Sándor u. 16; tel. (1) 338-2496; fax (1) 338-3320; e-mail eszter@fok.hu; internet www.tit.online.hu; f. 1841; library of 20,000 vols; 17,000 mems; Gen. Dir ESZTER PIRÓTH (acting); publs *Elet és Tudomány* (Life and Science, weekly), *Természet Világa* (World of Nature, monthly), *Valóság* (Reality, monthly).

Biological Sciences

Magyar Biofizikai Társaság (Hungarian Biophysical Society): 1027 Budapest, Fő utca 68; tel. (1) 202-1216; f. 1961; medical physics, ultrasound, radiation biophysics, photo-biophysics; 450 mems; Pres. Dr LAJOS KESZTHELYI; Sec.-Gen. Dr SÁNDOR GYÖRGYI; publ. *Magyar Biofizikai Társaság Értesítője* (every 3 years).

Magyar Biokémiai Egyesület (Hungarian Biochemical Society): 1518 Budapest, POB 7; premises at: 1113 Budapest, Karolina u. 29; tel. (1) 166-5856; fax (1) 166-5856; f. 1949; Pres. Dr PETER FRIEDRICH; Sec.-Gen. Dr PETER CSERMELY; publ. *Biokémia*.

Magyar Biológiai Társaság (Hungarian Biological Society): 1061 Budapest, Fő u. 68; tel. (1) 201-6484; f. 1952; 1,500 mems; Pres. Dr TAMÁS PÓCS; Sec.-Gen. Dr ERNŐ BÁCSY; publs *Állattani Közlemények*, *Antropológiai Közlemények*, *Botanikai Közlemények*, *Természetvédelmi Közlemények* (all annually).

Magyar Biomassza Társaság (Hungarian Biomass Association): 2103 Gödöllő, Páter Károly u. 1; tel. (28) 410-200; e-mail barotfi.kott.mgk@mgk.gau.hu; f. 1991; Pres. Dr ISTVÁN BARÓTFI (acting).

Magyar Rovartani Társaság (Hungarian Entomological Society): 1088 Budapest, Baross u. 13; tel. (1) 267-7100; fax (1) 267-3462; internet www.magyarrovartanitarsasag.hu; f. 1910; 380 mems; Pres. Dr Z. MÉSZÁROS; Sec. D. RÉDEI; publ. *Folia Entomologica Hungarica / Rovartani Közlemények* (annually).

Mathematical Sciences

Bolyai János Matematikai Társulat (János Bolyai Mathematical Society): 1027 Budapest, Fő u. 68; tel. (1) 225-8410; fax (1) 201-6974; e-mail bjmt@renyi.hu; internet www.bolyai.hu; f. 1891; 2,000 mems; Pres. GYULA KATONA; Gen. Sec. ANDR'AS RECSKI; publs *Abacus* (8 a year), *Alkalmazott Matematikai Lapok* (Gazette for Applied Mathematics, 4 a year), *Combinatorica* (combinatorics and the theory of computing, 4 a year), *Középiskolai Matematikai Lapok* (Mathematical Gazette for Secondary Schools, 9 a year), *Matematikai Lapok* (Mathematical Gazette, 4 a year), *Periodica Mathematica Hungarica* (4 a year).

Physical Sciences

Eötvös Loránd Fizikai Társulat (Roland Eötvös Physical Society): 1027 Budapest, Fő u. 68; tel. (1) 201-8682; fax (1) 201-8682; e-mail mail.elft@mtesz.hu; internet www.kfki.hu/~elfthp; f. 1891; physics and astronomy; 1,800 mems; Pres. JUDIT NÉMETH; Gen. Sec. GÁBOR SZABÓ; publ. *Fizikai Szemle* (Physics Review, monthly).

Hungarian Association for Geo-Information (HUNAGI): 1123 Budapest, Alkotás u. 25; located at: Rm 441, Department of Lands and Mapping, Ministry of Agriculture and Rural Development, 1860 Budapest, Kossuth tér 11; tel. (1) 301-4052; fax (1) 301-4691; e-mail remeteyfg@posta.fvm.hu; internet www.fomi.hu/hunagi; f. 1994; non-profit, interdisciplinary umbrella association promoting and supporting the development and use of geo-information and its associated technologies; 66 governmental and non-governmental mem. orgs; Pres. and Chair. ZSOLT SIKOLYA; Sec.-Gen. Dr GÁBOR REMETEY-FÜLÖPP; publs *Geodézia és Kartográfia*, *Geomatika*.

Magyar Asztronautikai Társaság (Hungarian Astronautical Society): 1027 Budapest, Fő u. 68; tel. (1) 201-8443; f. 1956; 450 mems; Pres. Dr IVÁN ALMÁR; Gen. Sec. ANDRÁS VARGA.

Magyar Geofizikusok Egyesülete (Association of Hungarian Geophysicists): 1027 Budapest, Fő u. 68 I/113; tel. and fax (1) 201-9815; e-mail geophysic@mtesz.hu; internet www.elgi.hu/mge; f. 1954; 650 mems; Pres. Dr FERENC ÁBELE; Sec. ANDRÁS PÁLYI; publ. *Magyar Geofizika* (Hungarian Geophysics, 4 a year).

Magyar Hidrológiai Társaság (Hungarian Hydrological Society): POB 433, 1371 Budapest; tel. (1) 201-7655; fax (1) 202-7244; e-mail mail.mht@mtesz.hu; internet www.mtesz.hu/tagegyesuletek/mht; f. 1917; 5,000 mems; Pres. Dr ÖDÖN STAROSOLSZKY; Sec.-Gen. ZOLTÁN SZÖLLŐSI; publs *Hidrológiai Közlöny* (Hydrological Journal, every 2 months), *Hidrológiai Tájékoztató* (Circular on Hydrology, annually).

Magyar Karszt- és Barlangkutató Társulat (Hungarian Speleological Society): 1025 Budapest, Pusztaszeri út.35; tel. (1) 346-0494; fax (1) 346-0495; e-mail mkbt@mail.matav.hu; f. 1910; 1,000 mems; library of 5,000 vols; Pres. Dr LÁSZLÓ KORPÁS; Sec.-Gen. PÉTER BÖRCSÖK; publ. *Karszt és Barlang* (with summaries in English, annually).

Magyar Kémikusok Egyesülete (Hungarian Chemical Society): 1027 Budapest, Fő u. 68; tel. (1) 201-6883; fax (1) 201-8056; e-mail mail.mke@mtesz.hu; internet www.mtesz.hu; f. 1907; 6,000 mems; Pres. Dr ALAJOS KÁLMÁN; Sec.-Gen. Dr GYULA KÖRTVÉLYESSY; publs *Középiskolai Kémiai Lapok* (Secondary School Chemical Papers, 5 a year), *Magyar Kémiai Folyóirat* (Hungarian Journal of Chemistry, monthly), *Magyar Kémikusok Lapja* (Hungarian Chemical Journal, monthly).

Magyar Meteorológiai Társaság (Hungarian Meteorological Society): 1371 Budapest, Fő u. 68, POB 433; tel. (1) 201-7525; fax (1) 202-1216; e-mail mmt@mtesz.hu; f. 1925; 360 mems; Pres. Dr PÁL AMBRÓZY; Gen. Sec. Dr GYÖRGY GYURÓ.

Magyarhoni Földtani Társulat (Hungarian Geological Society): 1027 Budapest, Fő utca 68; tel. and fax (1) 201-9129; e-mail mail.mft@mtesz.hu; internet www.foldtan.hu; f. 1848; 900 mems; Pres. Dr KÁROLY BREZSNYÁNSZKY; Sec.-Gen. Dr SZOBÓ CSOBA; publ. *Földtani Közlöny* (Bulletin, quarterly).

Optikai, Akusztikai és Filmtechnikai Tudományos Egyesület (Scientific Society for Optics, Acoustics, Motion Pictures and Theatre Technology): 1027 Budapest, Fő u. 68; tel. (1) 202-0452; f. 1933; 1,800 mems; Pres. Dr OLIVER PETRIK; Sec.-Gen. LÁSZLÓ FŰSZFÁS; publs *Elektrónikai Technológia-Mikrotechnika* (Electronic Technology-Microtechnics, monthly), *Kép és Hangtechnika* (Picture and Audio Techniques, every 2 months), *Szinháztechnikai Fórum* (Forum of the Technical Theatre, quarterly).

PHILOSOPHY AND PSYCHOLOGY

Magyar Filozófiai Társaság (Hungarian Philosophical Association): 1364 Budapest, Pf. 107; tel. and fax (1) 266-4195; f. 1987; 400 mems; Pres. KRISTÓF NYÍRI; Gen. Sec. ISTVÁN M. BODNÁR; publ. *MFT-Hírek* (Newsletter, 4 a year).

Magyar Pszichológiai Társaság (Hungarian Psychological Association): 1132 Budapest, Victor Hugo 18–22; tel. (1) 350-0555; fax (1) 350-0555; e-mail mpt@mtapi.hu; f. 1928; 1,293 mems; Pres. MAGDA RITOÓK; Scientific Sec. KATALIN VARGA; publ. *Magyar Pszichológiai Szemle* (Hungarian Psychological Review).

RELIGION, SOCIOLOGY AND ANTHROPOLOGY

Magyar Néprajzi Társaság (Hungarian Ethnographical Society): 1055 Budapest, Kossuth Lajos tér 12; tel. (1) 332-6340; fax (1) 269-1272; e-mail mnt@post.hem.hu; f. 1889; 1,340 mems; Pres. LÁSZLÓ KÓSA; Sec.-Gen. IMRE GRÁFIK; publs *Ethnographia* (quarterly), *Néprajzi Hírek* (Newsletter).

Magyar Szociológiai Társaság (Hungarian Sociological Association): 1014 Budapest, Országház u. 30; tel. (1) 224-6747; fax (1) 224-6745; e-mail mszt@mtapti.hu; f. 1978; 682 mems; Pres. ILDIKÓ HRUBOS; Sec. TIMEA TIBORI; publs *Szociológiai Szemle* (4 a year), *Review of Sociology* (2 a year).

TECHNOLOGY

Bőr-, Cipő-, és Bőrfeldolgozóipari Tudományos Egyesület (Scientific Society of the Leather, Shoe and Allied Industries): 1372 Budapest, Pf. 433; premises at 1027 Budapest, Fő u. 68; tel. (1) 202-0182; f. 1930; Pres. Dr TAMÁS KARNITSCHER; publ. *Bőr és Cipőtechnika* (Leather and Shoe News, monthly).

Energiagazdálkodási Tudományos Egyesület (Scientific Society of Energetics): 1055 Budapest, Kossuth Lajos tér 6–8; tel. (1) 153-2751; fax (1) 153-3894; f. 1949; 4,300 mems; Pres. Dr TAMÁS ZETTNER; Vice-Pres. GYŐZŐ WIEGAND; publ. *Energiagazdálkodás (Energy Economics) (monthly)*.

Faipari Tudományos Egyesület (Scientific Society of the Timber Industry): 1027 Budapest, Fő utca 68; tel. (1) 201-9929; f. 1950; 1,800 mems; Pres. Dr SÁNDOR MOLNÁR; Sec.-Gen. DEZSŐ LELE; publ. *Faipar* (Timber Industry).

Gépipari Tudományos Egyesület (GTE) (Scientific Society of Mechanical Engineers): 1371 Budapest, Fő u. 68, POB 433; tel. (1) 202-0582; fax (1) 202-0252; e-mail mail.gte@mtesz.hu; internet www.mtesz.hu/gtagegy/gte; f. 1949; sciences of mechanical engineering, dissemination of technical culture, assisting the technical and economic development of Hungary; 4,800 mems; library of 1,500 vols; Pres. Prof. Dr JÁNOS TAKÁCS; Sec.-Gen. Dr TAMÁS BÁNKY; publs *Gép* (Machine, monthly), *Járművek* (Vehicles, monthly), *Gépgyártás* (Production Engineering, monthly), *Műanyag és Gumi* (Plastics and Rubber, monthly), *Gépipar* (Machinery, monthly).

Hiradástechnikai Tudományos Egyesület (Scientific Society for Telecommunication): 1372 Budapest, Pf. 451, Kossuth Lajos tér 6–8; tel. (1) 353-1027; fax (1) 353-0451; e-mail hiradastechnika@mtesz.hu; f. 1949; organization of conferences, discussions, seminars, technical exhibitions, postgraduate courses, study trips, expert advice for official organs and enterprises, recommendations for official organs, public discussion and criticism of technical, economic, scientific and educational matters, engineering activities; 2,500 mems; Pres. Prof. Dr LÁSZLÓ PAP; Sec.-Gen. Dr GÁBOR HUSZTY; publs *Híradástechnika* (Telecommunication, monthly), *Hírlevél* (Newsletter, monthly).

Közlekedéstudományi Egyesület (Scientific Association for Transport): 1055 Budapest, Kossuth Lajos tér 6–8; tel. (1) 153-2005; fax (1) 153-2005; e-mail info.kte@mtesz.hu; internet www.mtesz.hu/kte; f. 1949; 6,723 mems; Pres. Dr SÁNDOR GYURKOVICS; Sec.-Gen. Dr ANDRÁS KATONA; publs *Közlekedéstudományi Szemle* (Communications Review), *Közúti és Mélyépitési Szemle* (Civil Engineering Review), *Városi Közlekedés* (Urban Transport).

Magyar Elektrotechnikai Egyesület (Hungarian Electrotechnical Association): 1055 Budapest, Kossuth Lajos tér 6–8; tel. (1) 153-0117; fax (1) 153-4069; f. 1900; 6,500 mems; Pres. Dr ISTVÁN KRÓMER; Dir PÉTER LERNYEI; publ. *Electrotechnika* (Electrical Engineering, monthly).

Magyar Iparjogvédelmi és Szerzői Jogi Egyesület (Hungarian Association for the Protection of Industrial Property and Copyright): 1055 Budapest V, Kossuth Lajos tér 6–8; tel. (1) 353-1661; fax (1) 353-1780; e-mail 2.mie@mtesz.hu; f. 1962; 2,250 mems; Pres. Dr BÉLA KENDE; Sec.-Gen. GEORGE MAROSI; publ. *MIE Közleményei* (report).

Méréstechnikai és Automatizálási Tudományos Egyesület (Scientific Society for Measurement and Automation): 1055 Budapest V, Kossuth tér 6–8; tel. (1) 153-1406; f. 1952; 3,000 mems; Pres. Prof. Dr ISTVÁN MARTOS; Gen. Sec. Dr JÓZSEF HAJAS; publ. *Mérés és Automatika* (Measurement and Automation).

Neumann János Számitógéptudományi Társaság (John v. Neumann Computer Society): 1054 Budapest, Báthori u. 16; tel. (1) 132-9349; fax (1) 131-8140; f. 1968; to promote the study, development and application of computer sciences; 5,500 mems; library of 3,000 vols; Pres. DEZSŐ SIMA; Man. Dir ISTVÁN ALFOLDI.

Országos Magyar Bányászati és Kohászati Egyesület (Hungarian Mining and Metallurgical Society): 1027 Budapest, Fő utca 68; tel. (1) 201-7337; fax (1) 201-7337; e-mail ombke@mtesz.hu; internet www.ombkenet.hu; f. 1892; 4,000 mems; library of 1,500 vols; Pres. Dr LAJOS TOLNAY; Gen. Sec. ÁRPÁD KOVACSICS; publs *Bányászat* (Mining, 6 a year), *Kohászat* (Metallurgy, 6 a year), *Kőolaj és Földgáz* (Oil and Gas, monthly).

Papír- és Nyomdaipari Műszaki Egyesület (Technical Association of the Paper and Printing Industry): 1371 Budapest, Pf. 433; located at: 1027 Budapest, Fő u. 68; tel. (1) 457-0633; fax (1) 202-0256; e-mail mail.pnyme@mtesz.hu; internet www.pnyme.hu; f. 1948; 1,800 individual mems, 130 corporate mems; Pres. Dr ZOLTAN SZIKLA; Sec.-Gen. ENDRE FÁBIAN; publs *Magyar Grafika* (Hungarian Printers and Graphic Designers), *Papíripar* (Paper Industry).

Szervezési és Vezetési Tudományos Társaság (Society for Organization and Management Science): 1027 Budapest, Fő u. 68; tel. (1) 202-1456; fax (1) 202-0856; f. 1970; 5,000 mems; Pres. Dr FERENC TRETHON; Sec.-Gen. Dr JÁNOS PAKUCS; publ. *Ipar-Gazdaság* (Industrial Economy, monthly).

Szilikátipari Tudományos Egyesület (Scientific Society of the Silicate Industry): 1027 Budapest, Fő utca 68; tel. (1) 201-9360; f. 1949; 2,300 mems; library: *c.* 2,500 vols; Pres. JENŐ VIG; Sec.-Gen. Dr MÁRTA FODOR; publ. *Építőanyag* (Building Materials).

Textilipari Műszaki és Tudományos Egyesület (Hungarian Society of Textile Technology and Science): 1027 Budapest, Fő utca 68; tel. (1) 201-8782; fax (1) 224-1454; e-mail info.tmte@mtesz.hu; internet www.tmte.hu; f. 1948; 1,300 mems; Pres. Dr FERENC CSÁSZI; Gen. Sec. Dr KATALIN MÁTHÉ; publs *Magyar Textiltechnika* (Hungarian Textile Engineering), *Textiltisztitás* (Textile Cleaning).

Research Institutes

AGRICULTURE, FISHERIES AND VETERINARY SCIENCE

Állattenyésztési és Takarmányozási Kutatóintézet (Research Institute for Animal Breeding and Nutrition): 2053 Herceghalom; tel. (23) 319-082; fax (23) 319-082; research into large animal breeding, nutrition, reproductive biology, genetics, nutrition biology and microbiology; library of 4,800 vols; Dir Prof. Dr LÁSZLÓ FÉSÜS; publ. *Állattenyésztés és Takarmányozás* (Animal Breeding and Nutrition, 6 a year, with English summaries).

Gabonatermesztési Kutató Kht. (Cereal Research Non-Profit Co.): 6701 Szeged, POB 391; tel. (62) 435-235; fax (62) 434-163; e-mail mtki@mtki.hu; internet www.mtki.hu; f. 1924; research into the cultivation of wheat, barley, oats, maize, triticale, sunflower, oilflax, oil-rape, red clover, onion, garlic, soya, sorghum, Sudangrass, millet; breeding, sowing, seed trading, dietetic foods; library of 12,000 vols; Dir Dr J. MATUZ; publ. *Cereal Research Communications* (quarterly).

Magyar Tejgazdasági Kisérleti Intézet (Hungarian Dairy Research Institute): 9200 Mosonmagyaróvár, Lucsony u. 24; tel. (96) 215-711; fax (96) 215-789; e-mail mtki@mtki.hu; internet www.mtki.hu; f. 1903; brs in Budapest and Pécs; scientific research of raw materials, technology, engineering, chemistry, microbiology, economics; library of 5,700 vols; Dir Dr ANDRÁS UNGER.

Magyar Tudományos Akadémia Állatorvos-tudományi Kutatóintézete (Veterinary Medical Research Institute, Hungarian Academy of Sciences): 1143 Budapest, Hungária krt. 21; tel. (1) 252-2455; fax (1) 252-1069; e-mail harrach@vmri.hu; internet www.vmri.hu; f. 1949; research in infectious and parasitic diseases of domestic and wild animals (virology, bacteriology, fish parasitology); library of 6,600 vols; Dir Dr BALÁZS HARRACH (acting); publ. *Acta Veterinaria Hungarica* (4 a year).

Magyar Tudományos Akadémia Mezőgazdasági Kutatóintézete (Agricultural Research Institute of the Hungarian Academy of Sciences): 2462 Martonvásár; tel. (22) 569-500; fax (22) 460-213; e-mail bedoz@buza.mgki.hu; internet www.mgki.hu; f. 1949; research in plant genetics, plant physiology, plant breeding and plant cultivation of maize and wheat; library of 16,000 vols; Dir ZOLTÁN BEDŐ; publ. *Martonvásár* (2 a year).

Magyar Tudományos Akadémia Növényvédelmi Kutatóintézete (Plant Protection Institute, Hungarian Academy of Sciences): 1525 Budapest II, Herman Ottó út. 15, Box 102; tel. (1) 155-8722; f. 1880, reorganized 1950; research on plant diseases, insect pests, pesticide chemistry and plant biochemistry, biotechnology, virology; 100 mems; library of 20,000 vols; Dir Dr T. KŐMÍVES.

Magyar Tudományos Akadémia Talajtani és Agrokémiai Kutató Intézete (Research Institute for Soil Science and Agricultural Chemistry of the Hungarian Academy of Sciences): 1022 Budapest, Herman Ottó u. 15; tel. and fax (1) 356-4682; e-mail rissac@rissac.hu; internet www.taki.iif.hu; f. 1949; research in soil physics, chemistry, geography and cartography, reclamation of salt-affected and sandy soils, irrigation, conservation, fertilization, soil mineralogy, soil microbiology, soil ecology, recultivation; library of 27,000 vols; Dir Prof. Dr T. NÉMETH; publ. *Agrokémia és Talajtan* (Agrochemistry and Soil Science, 2 a year).

Országos Állategészségügyi Intézet (Central Veterinary Institute): 1149 Budapest, Tábornok u. 2; tel. (1) 252-8444; fax (1) 252-5177; e-mail web@oai.hu; internet sgicenter.oai.hu/oai; f. 1928; diagnostic examinations and research work on the infectious, parasitic and metabolic diseases of animals, also veterinary toxicology and diseases of wild animals; 95 mems; library of 5,966 vols; Dir L. TEKES.

Országos Mezőgazdasági Minősitő Intézet (National Institute for Agricultural Quality Control): 1024 Budapest, Keleti Károly u. 24; tel. (1) 336-9100; fax (1) 336-9099; e-mail neszmelyik@ommi.hu; internet www.ommi.hu; f. 1988 by amalgamation of four orgs; 606 mems; library of 20,000 vols; Dir-Gen. Dr KÁROLY NESZMÉLYI; publs National List of Varieties, Descriptive List of Varieties, List of approved grape and fruit varieties, selections and foreign varieties permitted for propagation (annually), *Yearbook* of cattle, pig, sheep, horse, water fowl, fish breeding and beekeeping.

Szőlészeti és Borászati Kutató Intézet (Research Institute for Viticulture and Oenology): 6000 Kecskemét-Miklóstelep, Úrihegy 5/A, POB 25; tel. (76) 494-888; fax (76) 494-924; e-mail titkarsag@szbkik.hu; f. 1898; viticulture, oenology, economy; library of 7,200 vols; Dir Dr ERNŐ PÉTER BOTOS; publ. *Bor és Piac* (monthly).

Vízgazdálkodási Tudományos Kutató Rt. (VITUKI) (Water Resources Research Centre plc): 1095 Budapest, Kvassay Jenő út. 1; tel. (1) 215-6140; fax (1) 216-1514; e-mail vitukirt@vituki.hu; internet www.vituki.hu; f. 1952; basic, applied and development research associated with hydrological data collection, processing, storage, information; hydrology of ground-, karstic water, regional soil moisture control; hydromechanics of hydraulic structures; pollution and quality control of water; hydrological and hydraulic problems in agricultural water management (drainage, irrigation); international postgraduate course on hydrology; library of 13,000 vols; Dir-Gen. Dr PÉTER BAKONYI; publs *Hydrological Yearbook of Hungary* (annually), *VITUKI Proceedings* (annually).

ECONOMICS, LAW AND POLITICS

Magyar Tudományos Akadémia Jogtudományi Intézete (Institute for Legal Studies of the Hungarian Academy of Sciences): 1014 Budapest, Országház u. 30; tel. (1) 355-7384; fax (1) 375-7858; e-mail lamm@jog.mta.hu; f. 1949; departments of legal theory, international law, constitutional and administrative law, civil law, criminal law, comparative law, human rights; library of 52,000 vols; Dir Prof. Dr VANDA LAMM; publs *Állam- és Jogtudomány* (2 a year), *Acta Juridica Hungarica* (2 a year).

Magyar Tudományos Akadémia Közgazdaságtudományi Kutatóközpont (Institute of Economics of the Hungarian Academy of Sciences): Budaörsi út 45, 1112 Budapest; tel. (1) 309-2651; fax (1) 319-3151; e-mail titkarsag@econ.core.hu; internet www.econ.core.hu; f. 1954; research in macroeconomics and economic policy, labour economics and human resources, public and institutional economics, microeconomics and sectoral economics, international economics, mathematical economics, history of economic thought, agricultural economics, economics of technological change; library of 50,000 vols, 130 periodicals; Dir Prof. JENŐ KOLTAY; publs *Budapesti Munkagazdaságtani Füzetek* (Budapest Working Papers on the Labour Market, in English and Hungarian, 9 or 10 a year), *Műhelytanulmányok* (Discussion Papers, in English and Hungarian, 9 or 10 a year), *Munkatudományi Kutatások* (Labour Research Volumes, annually), *Munkaerőpiaci tükör* (Labour Market Yearbook, with chapters in English).

Magyar Tudományos Akadémia Politikai Tudományok Intézete (Institute for Political Science of the Hungarian Academy of Sciences): 1014 Budapest, Országház u. 30; tel. (1) 224-6724; fax (1) 224-6727; e-mail ipshas@mtapti.hu; internet www.mtapti.hu; f. 1991; study of political systems, party politics, nat. and local government, political culture, elections, problems of integration with the EU, migration, security policy and NATO; library of 43,000 vols; Research Dir Dr IMRE KOVÁCH; publs *Hungarian Political Science Review* (4 a year), *European Studies, City Societies, Local Authority and Local Policy, Scientia Humana—Politology, Integration Studies, Central European Political Science Review* (in English, 4 a year).

Magyar Tudományos Akadémia Világgazdasági Kutató Intézete (Institute for World Economics of the Hungarian Academy of Sciences): 1014 Budapest, Országház u. 30; tel. (1) 224-6760; fax (1) 224-6761; e-mail vki@vki3.vki.hu; internet www.vki.hu; f. 1965; research in world economics; library of 102,000 vols; Dir Prof. ANDRÁS INOTAI; publs *Kihívások* (Challenges, irregular), *Mühelytanulmányok* (Workshop Studies, irregular), *Trends in World Economy, Working Papers* (all irregular, in English).

Teleki László Intézet (László Teleki Institute): 1125 Budapest, Szilágyi Erzsébet fasor 22/C; tel. (1) 391-5700; fax (1) 391-5746; e-mail mki@tla.hu; f. 1972; prepares analytical material and information for foreign policy institutions; research on theoretical issues of international relations; organizes round-table conferences, seminars, lectures; reference library; Dir Prof. GYÖRGY GRANASZTÓI; publs *Külügyi Szemec* (foreign policy; in Hungarian 4 a year, in English 2 a year), *Reyio* (minorities, society, politics; in Hungarian 4 a year, in English annually).

EDUCATION

Felsóoktatási Kutatóintézet (Hungarian Institute for Higher Educational Research): located at: 1145 Budapest, Ajtósi Dürer sor 19–21; tel. and fax (1) 220-8056; e-mail oktataskutato@ella.hu; internet www.hier.iif.hu; f. 1981; applied social research and postgraduate training in school education, higher education and vocational education; library of 23,000 vols; Dir Dr ILONA LISKO; publs *Educatio* (review, 4 a year), *Kutatás Közben* (Research Papers, 6 a year).

FINE AND PERFORMING ARTS

Magyar Tudományos Akadémia Művészettörténeti Kutatóintézet (Research Institute for Art History of the Hungarian Academy of Sciences): 1014 Budapest, Uri-utca 49; tel. (1) 224-6700; fax (1) 375-0493; f. 1969; research on Hungarian art since 10th c.; library of 29,700 vols; Dir LÁSZLO BEKE; publ. *Ars Hungarica* (2 a year).

Magyar Tudományos Akadémia Zenetudományi Intézete (Institute for Musicology of the Hungarian Academy of Sciences): 1014 Budapest, Táncsics M. u. 7; tel. (1) 214-6770; fax (1) 375-9282; e-mail info@zti.hu; internet www.zti.hu; f. 1961; incorporates the Bartók Archives, the Dohnányi Archives, the Museum of History of Music, and depts of Folk Music, Folk Dances, History of Hungarian Music, History of Early Music; library of 150,000 vols; 100,000 recorded melodies; Dir TIBOR TALLIÁN; publ. *Studia Musicologica* (quarterly).

HISTORY, GEOGRAPHY AND ARCHAEOLOGY

Magyar Tudományos Akadémia Földrajztudományi Kutatóintézete (Geographical Research Institute, Hungarian Academy of Sciences): 1112 Budapest, Budaőrsi út 43–45; tel. and fax (1) 309-2686; e-mail schweitf@sparc.core.hu; internet www.mtafki.hu; f. 1950, reorg. 1952; research in physical and human geography; library of 70,129 vols; Dir FERENC SCHWEITZER; publs *Földrajzi Értesítő* (quarterly), *Földrajzi Tanulmányok*, *Studies in Geography in Hungary*, *Geographical Abstracts from Hungary*.

Magyar Tudományos Akadémia Régészeti Intézete (Archaeological Institute of the Hungarian Academy of Sciences): 1250 Budapest, Úri u. 49; tel. (1) 356-4567; fax (1) 224-6719; e-mail konyvtar@archeo.mta.hu; internet www.archeo.mta.hu; f. 1958; research in archaeology and associated sciences; 58 mems; library of 69,900 vols; Dir Prof. CSANÁD BÁLINT; publs *Magyarország Régészeti Topográfiája* (Archaeological Topography of Hungary), *Antaeus* (yearbook in German and English), *Varia Archaeologica Hungarica* (in foreign languages, irreg.).

Magyar Tudományos Akadémia Regionális Kutatások Központja (Research Centre for Regional Studies of the Hungarian Academy of Sciences): 7621 Pécs, Papnövelde u. 22; tel. (72) 523-800; fax (72) 523-803; e-mail postmaster@rkk.hu; internet www.rkk.hu; f. 1943; research into regional planning, geography, economics, government, sociology, ethnography, and history; 60 mems; library of 40,000 vols; Dir-Gen. Prof. GYULA HORVÁTH; publs *Tér és Társadalom* (quarterly), *Alföldi Tanulmányok* (irregular).

Magyar Tudományos Akadémia Történettudományi Intézete (Institute of Historical Science of the Hungarian Academy of Sciences): 1014 Budapest, Uri u. 53; tel. (1) 224-6755; fax (1) 224-6756; e-mail apok@tti.hu; internet www.tti.hu; f. 1949; five depts of Hungarian history and comparative European history, one dept of documentation and bibliography, historiography; library of 100,000 vols; Dir Prof. FERENC GLATZ; publs *Történelmi Szemle* (quarterly), annual bibliography of historical works published in Hungary.

LANGUAGE AND LITERATURE

Magyar Tudományos Akadémia Irodalomtudományi Intézete (Institute of Literary Studies of the Hungarian Academy of Sciences): 1118 Budapest, Ménesi u. 11–13; tel. (1) 385-8790; fax (1) 185-3876; internet www.iti.mta.hu; f. 1956; research in Hungarian and world literature; library of 170,000 vols; Dir Prof. LÁSZLÓ SZÖRÉNYI; publs *Irodalomtörténeti Közlemények* (6 a year), *Helikon* (4 a year), *Literatura* (4 a year), *Irodalomtörténeti Füzetek* (studies, irregular), *Neohelicon* (2 a year).

Magyar Tudományos Akadémia Nyelvtudományi Intézete (Research Institute of Linguistics of the Hungarian Academy of Sciences): 1399 Budapest, POB 701/518; located at: 1068 Budapest, Benczúr u. 33; tel. (1) 351-0413; fax (1) 322-9297; e-mail kiefer@nytud.hu; internet www.nytud.hu; f. 1949; research in theoretical linguistics, phonetics, neuro- and sociolinguistics, historical linguistics, lexicography, corpus linguistics; library of 40,000 vols; Dir Dr ISTVÁN KENESEI; publs *Magyar Fonetikai Füzetek* (Hungarian Papers in Phonetics, 2 a year), *Műhelymunkák a nyelvészet és társtudományai köréből* (Working Papers on Linguistics and Related Sciences, irregular), *Nyelvtudományi Közlemények* (Linguistic Publications, 2 a year).

MEDICINE

Magyar Tudományos Akadémia Kísérleti Orvostudományi Kutatóintézete (Institute of Experimental Medicine of the Hungarian Academy of Sciences): 1083 Budapest, Szigony u. 43; tel. (1) 210-9400; fax (1) 210-9423; e-mail info@koki.hu; internet www.koki.hu; f. 1952; conducts basic biomedical research, primarily in the field of neuroscience, incl. studies on neurotransmission, learning and memory, behaviour, ischaemic and epileptic brain damage, and the central and peripheral control of hormone secretion; library of 18,500 vols; Dir Prof. Dr TAMAS F. FREUND.

Mozgássérültek Pető András Nevelőképző és Nevelőintézete (András Pető Institute for Conductive Education of the Motor Disabled, and Conductors' College): 1125 Budapest, Kutvölgyi u. 6; tel. (1) 224-1500; fax (1) 355-6649; e-mail info@peto.hu; internet www.peto.hu; f. 1945; conductive education for 300 children with motor disability and for 1,200 children and adults with damage to the central nervous system; training of conductor-teachers; postgraduate training for professionals holding a teacher's diploma; Gen. Dir Dr h.c. ILDIKÓ KOZMA; publ. *Conductive Education Occasional Papers* (2 a year).

Országos Epidemiológiai Központ (National Center for Epidemiology): 1097 Budapest, Gyáli út. 2–6; tel. and fax (1) 476-1369; e-mail konyvtar@oek.antsz.hu; internet www.antsz.hu/oek; f. 1927; research in epidemiology, microbiology, virology, bacteriology, parasitology, mycology, vaccines; library of 30,000 vols; Dir-Gen. Dr MÁRTA MELLES; publs *EPINFO* (weekly), *Évi Működés* (Annual Report).

Országos Epidemiológiai Központ, Mikrobiológiai Kutatócsoport (Microbiological Research Group of the National Centre for Epidemiology): 1529 Budapest, Pihenő u. 1; tel. (1) 394-5044; fax (1) 394-5409; e-mail mini@microbi.hu; f. 1963; research into oncogenic viruses, virus tumours, HIV/AIDS, interferon, mycobacteria and mycobacteriophages, DNA methylation; library of 2,000 vols; Dir Dr JÁNOS MINÁROVITS.

Országos 'Fréderic Joliot-Curie' Sugárbiológiai és Sugáregészségügyi Kutató Intézet (National Research Institute for Radiobiology and Radiohygiene): 1775 Budapest, POB 101; tel. (1) 482-2001; fax (1) 482-2003; e-mail radbiol@hp.osski.hu; f. 1957; under Min. of Health; radiohygiene, including protection of workers from radiation; radiobiology research on effects of external ionizing radiation and incorporated radioisotopes; radiation and radioisotope applications including preservation of biological tissue, preparation of radiopharmaceuticals for in vitro and in vivo uses in nuclear medicine; teaching within the Semmelweis Medical School, Budapest; library of 7,000 vols; Dir Prof. Dr G. J. KÖTELES.

Országos Haematológiai és Immunológiai Intézet (National Institute of Haematology and Immunology): 1113 Budapest, Daróczi út. 24; tel. (1) 372-4300; fax (1) 372-4352; internet www.c3.hu/~haemat; f. 1948; research and clinical activities in haematology and immunology, including bone-marrow transplantation; library: *c.* 10,000 vols, 91 periodicals; Dir Prof. Dr GY. PETRÁNYI; publs *Haematologia* (int. 4 a yearin English), *Transzfúzió* (4 a year, in Hungarian).

Országos Onkológiai Intézet (National Institute of Oncology): 1122 Budapest, Ráth György u. 7/9; tel. (1) 224-8600; fax (1) 224-8620; f. 1952; experimental and clinical activities; library of 15,973 vols, 164 periodicals, service for reprints of all publs available; Dir Dr M. KASLER; publ. *Magyar Onkológia* (quarterly).

NATURAL SCIENCES

Biological Sciences

Magyar Tudományos Akadémia Balatoni Limnológiai Kutatóintézete (Balaton Limnological Research Institute of the Hungarian Academy of Sciences): 8237 Tihany, POB 35; tel. (87) 448-244; fax (87) 448-006; e-mail intezet@tres.blki.hu; internet www.blki.hu; f. 1927; research particularly in hydrobiology, and experimental zoology; library of 16,000 vols; Dir Dr SÁNDOR HERODEK; publ. collected reprints, progress report.

Magyar Tudományos Akadémia Ökológiai és Botanikai Kutatóintézete (Ecological and Botanical Research Institute of the Hungarian Academy of Sciences): 2163 Vácrátót; tel. (28) 360-122; fax (28) 360-110; e-mail obki@botanika.hu; internet www.botanika.hu; f. 1952; theoretical and experimental research; vegetation mapping; structure and dynamics of vegetation; ecological basis of nature conservation; hydrobiology of River Danube; library of 8,700 vols; Dir Dr GABOR VIDA.

Magyar Tudományos Akadémia Szegedi Biológiai Központja (Biological Research Centre of the Hungarian Academy of Sciences): 6701 Szeged, Temesvári krt. 62, POB 521; tel. (62) 599-600; fax (62) 432-576; internet www.brc.hu; f. 1971; library of 30,000 vols; Dir-Gen. DÉNES DUDITS.

Attached institutes:

Biofizikai Intézet (Institute of Biophyscs): c/o Magyar Tudományos Akadémia Szegedi Biológiai Központja, 6701 Szeged, Temesvári krt. 62, POB 521; tel. (62) 433-465; f. 1971; Dir PÁL ORMOS.

Biokémiai Intézet (Institute of Biochemistry): c/o Magyar Tudományos Akadémia Szegedi Biológiai Központja, 6701 Szeged,

Temesvári krt. 62, POB 521; tel. (62) 433-506; f. 1971; Dir LÁSZLÓ VÍGH.

Enzimológiai Intézet (Institute of Enzymology): 1113 Budapest, Karolina u. 29; tel. (1) 466-5856; fax (1) 466-5465; f. 1957; Dir PÉTER FRIEDRICH.

Genetikai Intézet (Institute of Genetics): c/o Magyar Tudományos Akadémia Szegedi Biológiai Központja, 6701 Szeged, Temesvári krt. 62, POB 521; tel. (62) 432-232; fax (62) 433-503; f. 1971; Dir ISTVÁN RASKÓ.

Növénybiológiai Intézet (Institute of Plant Biology): c/o Magyar Tudományos Akadémia Szegedi Biológiai Központja, 6701 Szeged, Temesvári krt. 62, POB 521; tel. (62) 433-434; fax (62) 433-434; f. 1970; Dir DÉNES DUDITS.

Természetvédelmi Hivatal, Madártani Intézet (Authority for Nature Conservation, Institute for Ornithology): 1121 Budapest, Költő u. 21; tel. (1) 391-1759; e-mail buki@mail.kvvm.hu; internet www.termeszetvedelem.hu; f. 1893; library of 8,000 vols, 1,000 periodicals; Dir JÓZSEF BÜKI; publ. *Aquila* (annual).

Mathematical Sciences

Magyar Tudományos Akadémia Rényi Alfréd Matematikai Kutatóintézet (Alfréd Rényi Institute of Mathematics, Hungarian Academy of Sciences): 1364 Budapest, POB 127; located at: 1053 Budapest, Reáltanoda u. 13–15; tel. (1) 483-8300; fax (1) 483-8333; e-mail math@renyi.hu; internet www.renyi.hu; f. 1950; research in fields of pure and applied mathematics; 80 mems; library of 60,000 vols; Dir G. O. H. KATONA; publ. *Studia Scientiarum Mathematicarum Hungarica*.

Physical Sciences

Magyar Állami Eötvös Loránd Geofizikai Intézet (Eötvös Loránd Geophysical Institute of Hungary): 1145 Budapest, Columbus u. 17–23; tel. (1) 252-4999; fax (1) 363-7256; e-mail elgi@elgi.hu; internet www.elgi.hu; f. 1907; geophysical exploration for hydrocarbons, coal, bauxite, water, ores; engineering geophysics; geophysical research, gravity, magnetics, lithosphere, ionosphere; library of 30,000 vols; Dir Dr TAMÁS FANCSIK; publ. *Geophysical Transactions* (quarterly).

Attached institute:

Geophysical Observatory: 8237 Tihany; tel. (87) 448-501; fax (87) 538-001; e-mail csontos@elgi.hu; f. 1954; Head LÁSZLÓ HEGYMEGI.

Magyar Tudományos Akadémia Atommagkutató Intézete (Institute of Nuclear Research of the Hungarian Academy of Sciences): 4026 Debrecen, Bem tér 18/c; tel. (52) 509-200; fax (52) 416-181; e-mail rgl@atomki.hu; internet www.atomki.hu; f. 1954; nuclear physics, atomic physics, particle physics, materials science and analysis, earth and cosmic sciences, environmental research, biological and medical research, devt of methods and instruments; 200 mems; library of 55,000 vols; Dir Dr REZSŐ G. LOVAS.

Magyar Tudományos Akadémia Csillagászati Kutatóintézete (Konkoly Observatory of the Hungarian Academy of Sciences): 1121 Budapest, Konkoly Thege Miklós u. 13–17; tel. (1) 175-4122; fax (1) 275-4668; f. 1899; 52 staff; library of 32,000 vols; Mountain Station: Piszkéstető, Galyatető (f. 1962), with Schmidt telescope, Cassegrain-reflector and 100 cm Ritchey-Chretien telescope; Dir BÉLA SZEIDL; publs *Information Bulletin on Variable Stars of Commission 27 of the IAU*, *Mitteilungen der Sternwarte der Ungarischen Akademie der Wissenschaften* (Communications from the Konkoly Observatory of the Hungarian Academy of Sciences).

Magyar Tudományos Akadémia Csillagászati Kutatóintézetének Napfizikai Obszervatóriuma (Heliophysical Observatory of the Hungarian Academy of Sciences): 4010 Debrecen, Egyetem tér 1, POB 30; tel. (52) 311-015; e-mail obs@fenyi.sci.klte.hu; f. 1958; studies of solar activity: sunspots, solar flares, prominences; library of 10,000 vols, 20 periodicals, 5,500 sunspot drawings (1872–1919), 100,000 full-disc solar photographs; Dir B. KÁLMÁN; publ. *Publications*.

Magyar Tudományos Akadémia Geodéziai és Geofizikai Kutató Intézete (Geodetical and Geophysical Research Institute of the Hungarian Academy of Sciences): 9400 Sopron, Csatkai E. u. 6–8; tel. (99) 508-340; fax (99) 508-355; internet www.ggki.hu; f. 1955 as two separate laboratories, merged as one institute 1972; research in advanced problems of geodesy and geophysics including seismology; library of 34,000 vols; Dir Prof J. ZAVOTI; publs *Rapport Microséismique de Hongrie* (annually), *Geophysical Observatory Reports* (annually), *Publications in Geomatics* (annually).

Magyar Tudományos Akadémia, Kémiai Kutatóközpont (Chemical Research Centre of the Hungarian Academy of Sciences): 1025 Budapest, Pusztaszeri u. 59/67; tel. (1) 325-7900; fax (1) 325-7554; e-mail palg@chemres.hu; internet www.chemres.hu; f. 1954; fundamental research in organic, medicinal, biomolecular and bio-organic chemistry, surface reactions and heterogeneous catalysis, nanochemistry, kinetics and mechanism of chemical reactions, theoretical chemistry, electrochemistry and corrosion, polymer chemistry and polymer physics, environmental and analytical chemistry, materials chemistry and molecular structure, spectroscopy and diffraction, nuclear and isotope chemistry, photochemistry; library of 60,000 vols; Dir-Gen. Prof. Dr GÁBOR PÁLINKÁS.

Magyar Tudományos Akadémia Kémiai Kutatóközpont Izotóp- és Felületkémiai Intézet (Institute of Isotope and Surface Chemistry Chemical Research Centre of the Hungarian Academy of Sciences): 1525 Budapest, POB 77; located at: 1121 Budapest, Konkoly Thege M. u. 29–33; tel. (1) 392-2222; fax (1) 392-2533; e-mail wojn@alpha0.iki.kfki.hu; internet www.iki.kfki.hu; f. 1959; research in the fields of catalysis, surface chemistry, adsorption, radiation chemistry, photochemistry, molecular spectroscopy, nuclear spectroscopy, nuclear safety, radioactive tracer technique; library of 14,000 vols; Dir Dr LÁSZLÓ WOJNÁROVITS.

Magyar Tudományos Akadémia, KFKI Anyagtudományi Kutató Intézet (Research Institute for Materials Science of the Hungarian Academy of Sciences): 1525 Budapest, POB 49; located at: 1121 Budapest, Konkoly Thege u. 29–33; tel. (1) 395-9253; fax (1) 395-9284; e-mail gyulai@ra.atki.kfki.hu; f. 1992; library: shares library of 120,000 vols; Dir Prof. JOZSEF GYULAI.

Magyar Tudományos Akadémia, KFKI Atomenergia Kutató Intézet (KFKI Atomic Energy Research Institute of the Hungarian Academy of Sciences): 1525 Budapest, Konkoly Thege M. u. 29–33, POB 49; tel. (1) 169-6762; fax (1) 155-2530; f. 1992; library: shares library of 120,000 vols; Dir JÁNOS GADÓ.

Magyar Tudományos Akadémia, KFKI Mérés- és Számítástechnikai Kutató Intézet (KFKI Research Institute for Measurement and Computing Techniques of the Hungarian Academy of Sciences): 1525 Budapest, Konkoly Thege M. u. 29–33, POB 49; tel. and fax (1) 169-5532; f. 1992; Dir FERENC VAJDA.

Magyar Tudományos Akadémia Műszaki Kémiai Kutató Intézet (Research Institute for Chemical Engineering of the Hungarian Academy of Sciences): 8200 Veszprém, Egyetem u. 2; tel. (88) 425-206; fax (88) 424-424; f. 1960; fundamental and applied research in traditional chemical engineering, bioengineering and systems engineering; library of 8,500 vols; Dir Dr JÁNOS GYENIS; publ. *Hungarian Journal of Industrial Chemistry*.

Uránia Csillagvizsgáló (Urania Public Observatory): 1016 Budapest, Sánc u. 3B; tel. (1) 186-9233; fax (1) 267-1391; f. 1947; centre of the Hungarian amateur astronomy movement; 8-inch Heyde refractor, 6-inch Zeiss reflector; library of 1,700 vols; Dir OTTO ZOMBORI; publ. *Uránia Füzetek* (Urania Letters, annually).

PHILOSOPHY AND PSYCHOLOGY

Magyar Tudományos Akadémia Filozófiai Kutatóintézete (Research Institute for Philosophy of the Hungarian Academy of Sciences): 1398 Budapest 62, POB 594; tel. and fax (1) 312-0243; e-mail office@phil-inst.hu; internet www.phil-inst.hu; f. 1957 for research into problems of epistemology, philosophy of science, social philosophy, methodological problems of social sciences, philosophy of religion, political philosophy, history of philosophical thought; library: institute library of 26,000 vols; Dir Prof. Dr KRISTÓF NYÍRI.

Magyar Tudományos Akadémia Pszichológiai Kutatóintézet (Institute for Psychology of the Hungarian Academy of Sciences): 1394 Budapest, POB 398; tel. (1) 239-6726; fax (1) 239-6727; e-mail czigler@cogpsyphy.hu; internet www.mtapi.hu; f. 1902; basic research on cognitive psychophysiology and neuropsychology, developmental psychology, social psychology and personality, research on educational psychology, psychology of decision-making, cross-cultural psychology; library of 20,000 vols; Dir Dr ISTVÁN CZIGLER; publ. *Pszichológia* (quarterly).

RELIGION, SOCIOLOGY AND ANTHROPOLOGY

Magyar Tudományos Akadémia Néprajzi Kutatóintézete (Institute of Ethnology of the Hungarian Academy of Sciences): 1250 Budapest, POB 29; tel. (1) 375-9011; fax (1) 375-9764; e-mail etnologia@etnologia.mta.hu; internet www.etnologia.mta.hu; f. 1967; research in ethnology of the Hungarian people, general anthropology, folklore and traditions, study of gypsies; library of 68,000 vols; Dir MIHÁLY HOPPÁL; publs *Népi Kultura—Népi Társadalom*, *Magyar Néprajz*, *Folklór Archivum*, *Documentatio Ethnographica*, *Életmód és Tradició*, *Folklór és Tradició*, *Néprajzi tanulmányok*, *Etnolore*.

Magyar Tudományos Akadémia Szociológiai Kutatóintézet (Institute of Sociology of the Hungarian Academy of Sciences): 1014 Budapest, Uri u. 49; tel. (1) 224-6740; fax (1) 224-6741; e-mail h8756tam@ella.hu; internet www.socio.mta.hu; f. 1963; East and Central European comparative research, environmental research, modernization of the economic and technological systems, social justice, sociology of health, sociology of organization and work, sociology of values, systems of management, sociology of women, the family and the elderly; library of 8,000 vols; Dir PÁL TAMÁS; publs *Társadalomkutatás* (Research in the Social Sciences, 4 a year), *INFO – Társadalomtudomány* (INFO – Social Science, 4 a year).

TECHNOLOGY

Magyar Tudományos Akadémia Számítástechnikai és Automatizálási Kutató Intézete (Computer and Automation Research Institute of the Hungarian Academy of Sciences): 1518 Budapest, POB 63; tel. (1) 279-6000; fax (1) 466-7503; e-mail pr@sztaki.hu; internet www.sztaki.hu; f. 1964; conducts research in intelligent computing, control and information systems, new computation structures, and computer applications for engineering, production and administration systems; library of 45,600 vols; Dir Dr PÉTER INZELT; publs *Report* (annually), *Transactions* (irregular).

Szilikátipari Központi Kutató és Tervező Intézet (Central Research and Design Institute for the Silicate Industry): 1034 Budapest, Bécsi út 122–124; tel. (1) 250-1311; fax (1) 168-7626; f. 1953; research and technological design in the silicate sciences and building materials industry; library of 25,000 vols, 7,000 periodicals; Dir CSABA ÁRPÁD RÉTI; publs *Transactions* (irregular, in English, German, French, Russian), *Tudományos Közlemények* (irregular, summaries in English, German, French, Russian).

Villamosenergiaipari Kutató Intézet (Institute for Electric Power Research): 1251 Budapest, POB 80; located at: 1016 Budapest, Gellérthegy u. 17; tel. (1) 457-8273; fax (1) 457-8274; e-mail i.kromer@veiki.hu; internet www.veiki.hu; f. 1949; research and development on safety assessment of nuclear power plants, combustion technology and environmental management, mechanical and power engineering technology, equipment of the electricity networks, high voltage and high power laboratory testing, systems of control engineering and telemechanics; library: technical library of 25,000 vols; Gen. Man. Dr ISTVÁN KRÓMER; publ. *VEIKI Publications* (Hungarian, with abstracts in English, annually).

Libraries and Archives

Budapest

Budapest Főváros Levéltára (Budapest City Archives): 1052 Budapest, Városház u. 9/11; tel. (1) 317-7306; fax (1) 318-3319; e-mail bfl@bparchiv.hu; internet www.bparchiv.hu; f. 1901; 23,000 metres of bookshelves; Dir Dr LÁSZLÓ A. VARGA; publ. *Budapesti Negyed* (quarterly).

Budapesti Corvinus Egyetem Központi Könyvtár (Central Library of Corvinus University of Budapest): 1093 Budapest, Zsil u. 2; tel. (1) 482-7602; fax (1) 482-7500; e-mail konyvtar@uni-corvinus.hu; internet www.lib.uni-corvinus.hu; f. 1850; economic sciences, world economy, management sciences, public administration, business and finance, sociology, political science, social sciences, environment protection, agriculture; 506,988 527,561 vols; Dir-Gen. Dr GABRIELLA ALFÖLDI.

Budapesti Corvinus Egyetem Entz Ferenc Könyvtár és Levéltár (Corvinus University of Budapest, Entz Ferenc Library and Archives): 1118 Budapest, Villányi út. 29–43; tel. (1) 482-6300; fax (1) 482-6334; internet helix.uni-corvinus.hu; f. 1860; horticulture, floriculture, nursery, medicinal plants, fruitgrowing, landscape and garden architecture, urban planning, environmental protection; food industry, canning technology, food fermentation, processing of animal products, processing of cereals and industrial plants, oenology, brewing; 320,000 vols, 365 current periodicals; Dir Dr ÉVA ZALAI-KOVÁCS; publ. *'Lippay János' Tudományos Ülésszak Előadásai* (every 2 years).

Budapesti Műszaki és Gazdaságtudományi Egyetem Országos Műszaki Információs Központ és Könyvtár (BME OMIKK) (Budapest University of Technology and Economics National Technical Information Centre and Library): 1502 Budapest, POB 91; located at: 1111 Budapest XI, Muegyetem rkp. 3; tel. (1) 463-2441; fax (1) 463-2440; e-mail pvasarhelyi@omikk.bme.hu; internet www.omikk.bme.hu; f. 1848; 2,084,352 vols, 340,000 periodicals; Dir-Gen. ILONA FONYO; publ. *Tudományos és Műszaki Tajekoztatas* (Scientific and Technical Information, monthly).

Eötvös Loránd Tudományegyetem Állam- és Jogtudományi Kar Könyvtára (Faculty of Law Library of Eötvös Loránd University): 1053 Budapest, Egyetem tér 1–3; tel. (1) 266-3005; fax (1) 266-4091; e-mail kjager@ludens.elte.hu; f. 1903; 42,000 vols, 8,000 periodicals, 21,000 MSS, 3,720 sundry; Dir JÄGERNÉ FÜRSTNER KRISZTINA; publs *Acta Facultatis Politico-Juridicae, Annales Univ Sci. Budapestinensis Sect. Juridica.*

Eötvös Loránd TudományegyetemEgyetemi Könyvtára (Loránd Eötvös University Library): Ferenciek tere 6, 1053 Budapest; tel. (1) 411-6777; fax (1) 411-6737; e-mail ek_titkarsag@ludens.elte.hu; internet www.library.elte.hu; f. 1635; Central Library of the University and national scientific library for philosophy, psychology, medieval history and history of Christianity; 1,500,000 vols, 1,339 periodicals, 60,000 MSS, 191 codices, 1,100 incunabula, 2,600 old Hungarian printed works (to 1711), 9,600 old and rare books; Dir-Gen. Dr LÁSZLÓ SZÖGI; publ. Egyetemi Könyvtár Évkönyve (University Library Annals, irregular).

Fővárosi Szabó Ervin Könyvtár (Metropolitan Ervin Szabó Library): VIII Szabó Ervin tér 1, Pf. 487, 1371 Budapest; tel. (1) 411-5000; fax (1) 411-5002; e-mail titkar@fszek.hu; internet www.fszek.hu; f. 1904; sociology, humanities, literature, history of Budapest; 3,593,055 vols (1,568,436 vols in central library); 78 brs; Dir PÉTER FODOR; publs *Databases* (CD-ROM), *Yearbook*.

Hadtörténeti Könyvtár és Térképtár (Library of Military History and Cartographic Collection): 1014 Budapest, Kapisztrán tér 2; tel. (1) 325-1672; fax (1) 212-0286; e-mail konyvtar@mail.militaria.hu; e-mail terkeptar@mail.militaria.hu; internet www.hm-him.hu; f. 1920; 190,000 vols, 500,000 maps; Dir LÁSZLÓ VESZPRÉMY; publs *Bibliography* (annually), *Hadtörténelmi Közlemények* (Review of Military History, quarterly).

Iparművészeti Múzeum Könyvtára (Library of the Museum of Applied Arts): 1091 Budapest, Üllői út. 33–37; tel. (1) 456-5177; fax (1) 217-5838; e-mail konyvtar@imm.hu; internet www.imm.hu; f. 1874; scientific research library for the decorative arts; 60,000 vols, 20,000 periodicals; Dir ESTHER TISZAVÁRI; publ. *Ars Decorativa* (annually).

Központi Statisztikai Hivatal Könyvtár és Levéltár (Library and Archive of the Central Statistical Office): 1024 Budapest, Pf. 10, II, Keleti Károly u. 5; tel. (1) 345-6105; fax (1) 345-6112; e-mail kodosz@ksh.hu; internet lib.ksh.hu; f. 1867; 760,000 books, periodicals, maps and electronic documents; national and research library of statistics and demography; Dir-Gen. Dr ERZSEBET NEMES; publs *Magyarország Történeti Helységnévtára* (Historical Gazetteer of Hungary), *Szakbibliográfiák* (Special Bibliographies).

Liszt Ferenc Zeneművészeti Egyetem Könyvtára (Library of the Ferenc Liszt Academy of Music): 1391 Budapest, Liszt Ferenc tér 8, POB 206; tel. (1) 322-0699; e-mail karpati@lib.liszt.hu; internet www.liszt.hu; f. 1875; 350,000 musical scores plus 80,000 vols and periodicals, 20,000 records; research library for music history; Dir JÁNOS KÁRPÁTI.

Magyar Irók Könyvtára (Library of Hungarian Writers' Union): 1062 Budapest, Bajza u. 18; tel. (1) 122-8840; f. 1950; maintained by the Hungarian Writers Federation; collection of belles-lettres, history of literature, linguistics and allied sciences by Hungarian and foreign authors, translated and/or in original languages; 87,100 vols, 48 foreign and 104 Hungarian periodicals; Dir LÁSZLÓ MEZŐVÁRI.

Magyar Nemzeti Galéria Könyvtára (Library of the Hungarian National Gallery): 1250 Budapest, Budavári Palota, Pf. 31; tel. (1) 375-7533; fax (1) 212-7356; f. 1957; books on art from all over the world, specializing in Hungarian sculpture, wood-carvings, panel paintings, Baroque art, art since 12th c.; 80,000 vols, 27,000 catalogues, 8,800 periodicals, 15,000 slides; Dir Mrs ZSUZSA BERÉNYI; publ. *A Magyar Nemzeti Galéria Évkönyve* (Annals).

Magyar Nemzeti Múzeum Régészeti Könyvtára (Archaeological Library of the Hungarian National Museum): 1088 Budapest, Múzeum-körút 14–16; tel. (1) 113-4400; f. 1952; 104,000 vols of Hungarian and foreign archaeology, numismatics and history; Dir Dr ENDRE TÓTH; publs *Folia Archaeologica, Folia Historica, Inventaria Praehistorica Hungariae.*

Magyar Országos Levéltár (National Archives of Hungary): 1014 Budapest, Bécsikapu tér 4; tel. (1) 225-2800; fax (1) 225-2817; e-mail info@mol.gov.hu; internet www.mol.gov.hu; f. 1756; 70,500 m of shelving; records from the 12th century to 1989; Gen. Dir Dr LAJOS GECSÉNYI; publs *Levéltári Közlemények* (journal), *Levéltári Szemle* (journal).

Magyar Tudományos Akadémia Földrajztudományi Kutató Intézet Könyvtára (Library of the Geographical Research Institute of the Hungarian Academy of Sciences): 1388 Budapest, POB 64; located at: 1112 Budapest, Budaörsi út 45; tel. (1) 319-3119; fax (1) 309-2690; e-mail magyar@sparc.core.hu; internet www.mtafki.hu; f. 1952; 70,580 vols, 17,905 maps, 8,128 MSS, 8,088 periodicals; Librarians ÁRPÁD MAGYAR, GABRIELLA PETZ; publs *Elmélet-módszer-gyakorlat* (Theory-Methods-Practice), *Földrajzi Értesítő, Studies in Geography in Hungary.*

Magyar Tudományos Akadémia Könyvtára (Library of the Hungarian Academy of Sciences): 1245 Budapest V, POB 1002, Arany János u. 1; tel. (1) 411-6100; fax (1) 331-6954; e-mail mtak@vax.mtak.hu; internet www.mtak.hu; f. 1826; 1,129,643 vols, 348,265 periodicals, 710,546 MSS, 32,386 microfilms, 396 electronic documents, 59 audiovisual titles; collection includes oriental manuscripts, old prints and incunabula; depository library for Academy's dissertations; Academy's archives; Dir-Gen. Prof. GABOR NARAY-SZABO.

Politikatörténeti Intézet Könyvtára (Library of the Institute of Political History): 1054 Budapest, Alkotmány u. 2; tel. (1) 301-2024; e-mail konyvtar@phistory.hu; internet www.polhist.hu; f. 1948; 175,000 vols; Chief Librarian ÉVA TÓTH.

Nemzeti Kulturális Örökség Minisztériuma, Levéltári Osztály (Archives Department of the Ministry of Cultural Heritage): 1077 Budapest,Wesselényi u. 20–22; tel. (1) 413-2812; fax (1) 413-2813;

internet www.kultura.hu/nkom/nkom/; f. 1950; functions as supervising board of all archives in Hungary; Head RADOJKA GORJÁNÁC.

Országgyűlési Könyvtár (Library of the Hungarian Parliament): 1357 Budapest, Pf. 4, Kossuth Lajos-tér 1–3; tel. (1) 441-4686; fax (1) 441-4853; e-mail ambrusj@ogyk.hu; internet www.ogyk.hu; f. 1870; 820,000 vols; parliamentary papers (Hungarian and foreign), contemporary history, administrative and legal sciences, politics; UN depository library, EU depository library; Librarian JÁNOS AMBRUS; publs *INFO-Társadalomtudomány* (4 a year), *Pressdok* (review on floppy disk and CD-ROM of Hungarian newspapers and periodicals), *Hundok* (review on floppy disk and CD-ROM of foreign newspapers and weekly periodicals dealing with Hungarian issues).

Országos Egészségügyi Információs Intézet és Könyvtár (National Institute and Library for Health Information – MEDINFO): 1444 Budapest, Szentkirályi u. 21, POB 278; tel. (1) 338-4133; fax (1) 266-9710; e-mail medinfo@medinfo.hu; internet www .medinfo.hu; f. 1949; centre for medical libraries, training, promotion of interlibrary co-operation; Hungarian and foreign medical bibliographies and reviews compiled; 102,000 vols; Dir-Gen. Dr GYULA KINCSES; publs *Magyar Orvosi Bibliográfia* (Hungarian Medical Bibliography, 6 a year, English edition 2 a year), *Nővér* (Nurse, 4 a year), *Országtanulmányok* (Country Profiles).

Országos Idegennyelvü Könyvtár (National Library of Foreign Literature): 1056 Budapest, Molnár u. 11; tel. (1) 318-3688; fax (1) 318-0147; e-mail h9126oik@ella .hu; internet www.oik.hu; f. 1956; formerly the Gorky State Library; specializing in foreign literature, the theory of literature, linguistics, musicology, music scores and records, literature concerning national minorities; 331,000 vols; Dir JENŐ JUHÁSZ; publs *Ethnic Minority Bibliography* (annually), *New Books for Nationalities* (irregular).

Országos Mezőgazdasági Könyvtár és Dokumentációs Központ (National Agricultural Library and Documentation Centre): 1253 Budapest, POB 15; tel. (1) 489-4900; fax (1) 489-4939; e-mail omgkref@omgk.hu; internet www.omgk.hu; f. 1951; 279,421 vols, 510 periodicals; Gen. Dir GABRIELLA LÜKŐ-ÖRSI; publs *Az Európai Unió Agrárgazdasága* (monthly), *Agrárkönyvtári Hírvilág* (quarterly), *Magyar Mezőgazdasági Bibliográfia* (on disk, quarterly).

Országos Pedagógiai Könyvtár és Múzeum (National Educational Library and Museum): 1363 Budapest, POB 49; located at: 1055 Budapest, Honvéd u. 19; tel. (1) 312-6862; fax (1) 312-6862; e-mail Balogh.Mihaly@opkm.hu; internet www .opkm.hu; f. 1877, reorganized 1958; methodological library for education; pedagogical museum; 550,000 vols; Dir Dr MIHÁLY BALOGH; publs *Külföldi Pedagógiai Információ* (International Educational Information, on CD-ROM), *Magyar Pedagógiai Irodalom* (Hungarian Educational Literature, on CD-ROM), *Könyv és Nevelés* (Books and Education, 4 a year).

Országos Rabbiképző – Zsidó Egyetem Könyvtára (Library of the Jewish Theological Seminary – University of Jewish Studies): 1428 Budapest, POB 21; located at: 1085 Budapest, Bérkocsis u. 2; tel. (1) 267-5415 ext. 103; fax (1) 318-7049 ext. 150; e-mail konyvtar@or-zse.hu; internet www .rabbi.hu; f. 1877; 100,000 vols; Dir BERTA BIRÓ BÉRI.

Országos Széchényi Könyvtár (National Széchényi Library): 1827 Budapest, Budavári Palota F-épület; tel. (1) 224-3700; fax (1) 202-0804; internet www.oszk.hu; f. 1802; 2,634,000 books and periodicals, 4,750,000 manuscripts, maps, prints, microfilms, etc.; Dir-Gen. ISTVÁN MONOK; publs include *Magyar Nemzeti Bibliográfia, Könyvek bibliográfiája* (Hungarian National Bibliography, Monographs, every 2 weeks , *Magyar Nemzeti Bibliográfia. Időszaki kiadványok repertóriuma* (Hungarian National Bibliography, Repertory of Periodicals, monthly) , *Magyar Nemzeti Bibliográfia, Időszaki kiadványok bibliográfiája* (Hungarian National Bibliography, Periodicals, annually), *Magyar Nemzeti Bibliográfia* (Hungarian National Bibliography, Books and Periodicals CD-ROM, 2 a year); *Hungarika Információ*(Hungarica Information, 3 current indexes, 1 cumulative index a year), *Mikrofilmek cimjegyzéke* (lists of microfilms, irregular), *Az Országos Széchényi Könyvtár Füzetei* (Studies of the National Széchényi Library, irregular), *Magyarországi egyházi könyvtárak kéziratkatalógusai* (Catalogues of the Manuscript Collections in Hungarian Church Libraries, irregular), *Libri de Libris* (irregular), National Collection (irregular), *Margarithe Bibliothecae Nalis Hungariae* (irregular), *A Kárpát-medence koraújkori könyvtáraj* (Libraries of the Early Modern Age in the Carpathian Basin, irregular).

Affiliated libraries:

Könyvtártudományi és Módszertani Központ (Centre for Library and Information Science): 1827 Budapest, Budavári Palota F-épület; tel. (1) 224-3788; f. 1959; research and development, promotion of inter-library co-operation, literature propaganda, public relations, training and library documentation services; library science; 107,000 vols; Dir ERZSÉBET GYŐRI (acting); publs *Könyvtári Figyelő* (Library Review), *A Magyar Könyvtári Szakirodalom Bibliográfiája* (Bibliography of Hungarian Library Literature), *Hungarian Library and Information Science Abstracts* (in English), *Uj Könyvek* (New Books), *Uj Periodikumok* (New Periodicals), *MANCI* (database of library science periodical articles with quarterly updates on floppy disk).

Reguly Antal Historic Library: 8420 Zirc, Rákóczi-tér 1; tel. and fax (88) 593-800; f. 1720; 68,618 vols; Librarian KATALIN URBÁN.

Pázmány Péter Katolikus Egyetem, Hittudományi Kar Könyvtára (Library of the Péter Pázmány Catholic University's Faculty of Theology): 1053 Budapest, Veres Pálné u. 24; tel. (1) 318-1643; fax (1) 484-3054; e-mail ppke_htk@ella.hu; internet www.htk.ppke .hu; f. 1635; history, theology and linguistics; 63,500 vols (books from *c.* 1880, older material kept in the Library of the University); also houses the Collection of the Brothers of St Paul (f. 1775; 12,000 vols; incunabula and MSS from the 15th and 16th centuries), and the Library of the Central Catholic Seminary (Központi Papnevelő Intézet Könyvtára) (f. 1805; 17,300 vols); Dir Dr HUBA RÓZSA.

Semmelweis Egyetem Egészségügyi Főiskolai Kar Könyvtár (Semmelweis University College of Health Care Library): POB 229, 1088 Budapest; Vas u. 17, 1088 Budapest; tel. (1) 486-5955; fax (1) 486-5951; e-mail library@se-efk.hu; internet efk.sote .hu; f. 1975; 54,000 vols; Chief Librarian IMOLA JEHODA.

Semmelweis Egyetem Központi Könyvtára (Central Library of Semmelweis University): 1085 Budapest, Üllői út 26; tel. (1) 317-0948; fax (1) 317-1048; e-mail lvasas@lib .sote.hu; internet www.lib.sote.hu; f. 1828; 537,127 vols; Dir Dr LÍVIA VASAS.

Semmelweis Egyetem Testnevelési és Sporttudományi Kar Könyvtára (Library of the Faculty of Physical Education and Sport Sciences, Semmelweis University): 1123 Budapest, Alkotás u. 44; tel. (1) 487-9200 ext. 12-34; fax (1) 356-6337; e-mail linda@mail.hupe.hu; internet www.hupe.hu; f. 1925; collection covers physical education, sport, human kinesiology, management, mental health, recreation and allied domains, also literature by Hungarian and foreign authors; 98,500 vols, 77 domestic and 4 foreign trade papers; Dir FERENC KRASOVEC.

Szent István Egyetem Állatorvos-tudományi Könyvtár (Veterinary Science Library, Szent István University): 1400 Budapest, Pf. 2; located at: 1078 Budapest, István u. 2; tel. (1) 478-4226; fax (1) 478-4227; e-mail library.univet@aotk.szie.hu; internet konyvtar.univet.hu; f. 1787; 90,000 vols, 178 current periodicals; spec. collns: ancient veterinary literature, historical archives; museum of veterinary history; distance education for veterinary surgeons; Dir JUDIT SZABÓ SZÁVAY; publs *Bibliography of Hungarian Veterinary Literature*, *NOCTUA – Sive Nova ex Bibliotheca Veterinaria* (newsletter, quarterly).

Debrecen

Debreceni Egyetem Egyetemi és Nemzeti Könyvtár (University of Debrecen University and National Library): 4010 Debrecen, Egyetem tér 1, Pf. 39; tel. (52) 410-443; fax (52) 410-443; e-mail marta@lib .unideb.hu; internet www.lib.unideb.hu; f. 1912; 2,178,050 vols and periodicals, 2,618,085 MSS, prints, microfilms, etc.; Dir-Gen. Dr MÁRTA VIRÁGOS; publ. *Könyv és Könyvtár* (annually).

Debreceni Egyetem Orvos- és Egészségtudományi Centrum Kenézy Könyvtár (Life Sciences Library of the Medical and Health Sciences Centre of the University of Debrecen): 4012 Debrecen, Nagyerdei körut 98; tel. (52) 413-847; fax (52) 413-847; e-mail kenezy@lib.unideb.hu; internet www.clib .dote.hu; f. 1947; 170,000 vols; Librarian Dr MÁRTA VIRÁGOS; publ. *Annual Report*.

Tiszántúli Református Egyházkerületi és Kollégiumi Nagykönyvtár (Library of the Reformed College and of the Transtibiscan Church District): 4044 Debrecen, Kálvint tér 16, POB 201; tel. (52) 414-744; fax (52) 414-1919; e-mail theca.silver@drk.hu; f. 1538; 570,000 vols; Dir Dr GÁBORJÁNI SZABÓ BOTOND.

Esztergom

Főszékesegyházi Könyvtár (Library of Esztergom Cathedral): 2500 Esztergom, Pázmány Péter u. 2; tel. (33) 510-130; e-mail bibliotheca@invitel.hu; internet www.ehf.hu/ ~bibliotheca; f. 11th c.; 250,000 items; incl. Fugger, Batthyany and Mayer collns; Dir BÉLA CZÉKLI.

Gödöllő

Szent István Egyetem Gödöllői Tudományos Könyvtár (St Stephen's University Gödöllő Campus Library): 2103 Gödöllő, Páter Károly u. 1; tel. (28) 522-004; fax (28) 410-804; e-mail tibor@gikk.gau.hu; f. 1945; 370,000 vols, 535 current periodicals; Dir Dr TIBOR KOLTAY; publ. *Bibliográfia* (every 2 or 3 years).

Keszthely

Veszprémi Egyetem Georgikon Mezőgazdaságtudományi Kar, Keszthely Központi Könyvtár és Levéltár (Georgikon Faculty of Agriculture, University of Veszprém, Keszthely Central Library and Archives): 8360 Keszthely, Deák F. u. 16, POB 66; tel. (83) 312-330; fax (83) 315-105; e-mail lib@georgikon.hu; f. 1797, reorganized 1954; 150,000 vols; Dir CSILLA PÓR; publ. *Georgikon for Agriculture* (2 a year).

Miskolc

Miskolci Egyetem Könyvtár, Levéltár, Múzeum (Library, Archives and Museum of the University of Miskolc): 3515 Miskolc-Egyetemváros; tel. (46) 565-324; fax (46) 563-489; e-mail konzsamb@gold.uni-miskolc.hu; internet www.lib.uni-miskolc.hu; f. 1735; 612,000 vols, 113,000 periodicals; Dir-Gen. Dr LÁSZLÓ ZSÁMBOKI.

Pannonhalma

Főapátsági Könyvtár Pannonhalma (Benedictine Abbey Library): 9090 Pannonhalma, Vár 1; tel. (96) 570-142; fax (96) 470-011; e-mail fokonyvtar@osb.hu; internet www.osb.hu; f. 1802; collection of early records, MSS, codices, source material for the Hungarian language; 350,000 vols; Dir P. MIKSA BÁNHEGYI.

Pécs

Pécsi Tudományegyetem Könyvtára (Library of the University of Pécs): 7601 Pécs, Pf. 227; premises at: 7621 Pécs, Szepesy I. u. 1–3; tel. (72) 501-600; fax (72) 325-552; e-mail webmaster@lib.pte.hu; internet www.lib.pte.hu; f. 1774; 1,165,000 vols; Gen. Dir. Dr ÁGNES FISCHER-DÁRDAI.

Pécsi Tudományegyetem Orvostudományi és Egészségtudományi Centrum Könyvtára (Medical Centre Library, Pécs University): 7643 Pécs, Szigeti út 12; tel. (72) 536-000; fax (72) 536-293; e-mail konkozi@aok.pte.hu; internet www.aok.pte.hu; f. 1926; collection covers medicine, health sciences, chemistry, physics and biology; 472,413 vols; Dir TÜNDE GRACZA.

Sárospatak

Sárospataki Református Kollégium Tudományos Gyűjteményei Nagykönyvtára (Library of the Scientific Collection of the Reformed College of Sárospatak): 3950 Sárospatak, Rákóczy u. 1; tel. (47) 311-057; f. 1531; 394,000 vols; Dir MICHAEL SZENTIMREI.

Sopron

Nyugat-Magyarországi Egyetem Központi Könyvtára (Central Library of the University of West Hungary): 9400 Sopron, Bajcsy-Zsilinszky u. 4; tel. (99) 518-223; fax (99) 518-287; e-mail library@nyme.hu; internet ilex.efe.hu; f. 1735; 315,639 vols; Dir SÁNDOR SARKADY.

Szeged

Somogyi-könyvtár (Somogyi Library): 6720 Szeged, Dóm tér 1–4; tel. (62) 425-525; fax (62) 426-521; e-mail library@sk-szeged.hu; internet www.sk-szeged.hu; f. 1881; 914,000 vols; Dir ERZSÉBET SZŐKEFALVI-NAGY; publs *Szegedi Műhely* (Workshop of Szeged), *Csongrád Megyei Könyvtáros* (Librarian of Csongrád County).

Szegedi Tudományegyetem Egyetemi Könyvtár (Main Library of the University of Szeged): 6722 Szeged, Ady tér 13; tel. (62) 546-665; fax (62) 546-665; e-mail mader@bibl.u-szeged.hu; internet www.bibl.u-szeged.hu; f. 1921; 1,500,000 vols; Dir Dr BÉLA MADER; publs *Acta Bibliothecaria, Dissertationes ex Bibliotheca Universitatis de Attila József nominatae*.

Szegedi Tudományegyetem Orvostudományi Könyvtára (Library of the former Albert Szent-Györgyi Medical University): 6701 Szeged, Tisza Lajos krt 109; tel. (62) 455-587; fax (62) 455-068; f. 1926; 200,000 vols, 800 current journals; Dir Dr JANOS MARTON.

Veszprém

Veszprémi Egyetem Központi Könyvtára (Library of the University of Veszprém): 8200 Veszprém, Egyetem u. 10; tel. (88) 425-074; fax (88) 425-074; e-mail hazitibo@almos.vein.hu; internet www.vein.hu/library/ve; f. 1949; 196,548 vols; Dir Dr MÁRTA EGYHÁZY; publs *Hungarian Journal of Industrial Chemistry* (4 a year), *Studia Germanica Universitatis Vesprimensis* (4 a year).

Museums and Art Galleries

Badacsony

Egry József Emlékmúzeum (József Egry Memorial Museum): 8261 Badacsony, Egry Sétány 12; tel. (87) 431-044; f. 1973; art gallery of works by Lake Balaton landscape painter Egry.

Baja

Türr István Múzeum: 6501 Baja, Deák Ferenc u. 1, POB 55; tel. (79) 324-173; fax (79) 324-173; f. 1937; archaeological and ethnographic collections, modern Hungarian painters, local history; library of 10,000 vols; Dir ZSUZSA MERK; publs *Türr István Múzeum Kiadványai, Bajai Dolgozatok*.

Balassagyarmat

Palóc Múzeum: 2660 Balassagyarmat, Palóc liget 1; tel. (35) 300-168; fax (35) 300-168; f. 1891; ethnography, local folk art and shepherds' art; collections of Nógrád costumes, embroidery, folk religion and folk instruments; library of 12,000 vols; Dir GABOR LIMBACHER.

Békéscsaba

Munkácsy Mihály Múzeum: 5600 Békéscsaba, Széchenyi u. 9; tel. and fax (66) 323-377; e-mail mmm@bmmi.hu; internet www.munkacsy.hu; f. 1899; archaeological, historical and regional ethnographic collections, modern Hungarian paintings, ornithology, natural science; paintings and legacies of the painter Mihály Munkácsy (1844–1900); library of 19,000 vols; Dir Dr IMRE SZATMÁRI.

Budapest

Bartók Béla Emlékház (Béla Bartók Memorial House): 1025 Budapest, Csalán út. 29; tel. (1) 394-2100; fax (1) 394-4472; f. 1981; organizes musical programmes and concerts; Man. ZSUZSA NYUJTÓ.

Budapesti Történeti Múzeum (Budapest History Museum): 1014 Budapest, Szent György tér 2; tel. (1) 487-8801; fax (1) 487-8872; e-mail btm@mail.btm.hu; internet www.btm.hu; f. 1887; medieval antiquities, medieval royal castle, Gothic statues; library of 45,700 vols; Dir-Gen. Dr SÁNDOR BODÓ; publs *Budapest Régiségei* (Antiquities of Budapest), *Monumenta Historica Budapestinensia* (irreg.), *Tanulmányok Budapest Múltjából* (Studies on the History of Budapest).

Attached museums:

Aquincum Múzeum: 1033 Budapest, Záhony u. 3; 1033 Budapest, Szentendrei út 139; tel. (1) 430-1081; fax (1) 430-1083; e-mail h7442tot@iif.hu; internet www.aquincum.hu; f. 1894; prehistory and Roman history of Budapest; Dir Dr PAULA ZSIDI; publ. *Aquincumi Füzetek* (excavations and rescue work at the Aquincum Museum).

Fővárosi Képtár (Municipal Picture Gallery): 1037 Budapest, Kiscelli út 108; tel. (1) 388-8560; fax (1) 368-7917; e-mail fovarosikeptar@mail.btm.hu; internet www.btmfk.iif.hu; fine arts since the 19th century; Dir PÉTER FITZ.

Kiscelli Múzeum: 1037 Budapest, Kiscelli u. 108; tel. (1) 388-8560; fax (1) 368-7917; e-mail h13293fit@ella.hu; internet www.btm.hu/kiscell/kiscell.htm; f. 1899; history of Budapest since 1686; Dir Dr PÉTER FARBAKY.

Budavári Mátyás-templom Egyházművészeti Gyüjteménye (Matthias Church of Buda Castle Ecclesiastical Art Collection): 1014 Budapest, Szentháromság tér 2; tel. (1) 489-0717; fax (1) 488-7717; e-mail turizmus@matyas-templom.hu; internet www.matyas-templom.hu; f. 1964; permanent collection of Roman Catholic religious objects in the gallery of Matthias Church; Dir MÁTÉFFY BALÁZS.

HM HIM Hadtörténeti Múzeum és Könyvtár (Military History Museum and Library): located at: Tóth Árpád sétány 40, 1014 Budapest; POB 7, 1250 Budapest; tel. and fax (1) 356-1575; e-mail him.muzeum@hm-him.hu; internet www.hm-him.hu; f. 1918; Hungarian and Hungarian-related militaria incl. arms, medals, flags, uniforms, art, books, documents, photographs, posters, prints, mapsetc.; 39 mems; library of 300,025 vols; Dir Colonel Dr JÓZSEF LUGOSI; publ. *A Hadtörténeti Múzeum Értesítője / Acta Musei Militaris in Hungaria* (Yearbook of the Hungarian Military Museum, with summaries in English and German, annually).

Holocaust Memorial Centre: 1094 Budapest, Páva u. 39; tel. (1) 455-3333; fax (1) 455-3399; e-mail info@hdke.hu; internet www.hdke.org; f. 2004; Dir JUDIT MARTINKOVITS.

Iparművészeti Múzeum (Museum of Applied Arts): 1091 Budapest, Üllői út 33–37; tel. (1) 456-5100; fax (1) 217-5838; internet www.imm.hu; f. 1872; European and Hungarian decorative arts; library: see Libraries; Gen. Dir Dr KÁROLY SIMON; publs catalogues, *Ars Decorativa* (annually).

Component museums:

Hopp Ferenc Kelet-Ázsiai Művészeti Múzeum (Ferenc Hopp Museum of Eastern Asiatic Arts): 1062 Budapest, Andrássy u. 103; tel. (1) 322-8476; fax (1) 217-5838; f. 1919; collections of Asiatic arts, exhibition of Japanese miniature carvings; library of 25,000 vols; Chief Curator Dr ZSUZSANNA RENNER.

Nagytétényi Kastélymúzeum (Castle Museum of Nagytétény): 1225 Budapest, Kastélypark u. 9–11; tel. (1) 207-0005; fax (1) 207-4680; internet www.nagytetenyi.hu; f. 1948; European furniture of the 15th–19th c.; Manager ELUIRA KIRÁLY.

Ráth György Múzeum: 1068 Budapest, Városligeti-fasor 12; tel. (1) 342-3916; f. 1906; exhibition of Oriental art and Chinese ceramics; Chief Curator Dr ZSUZSANNA RENNER.

Közlekedési Múzeum (Transport Museum): 1146 Budapest, Városligeti krt 11; tel. (1) 343-0565; fax (1) 344-0322; e-mail km@ella.hu; internet www.km.iif.hu; f. 1896; models of railway locomotives and rolling stock, old vehicles, railway, nautical, aeronautic, road and urban transport collections, road- and bridge-building, etc.; four branch museums including aviation and railway exhibitions with open-air displays; library of 100,000 vols; Dir Dr ANDRÁS KATONA; publs yearbooks, scientific reviews (*c.* every 2 years).

Liszt Ferenc Emlékmúzeum és Kutatóközpont (Ferenc Liszt Memorial Museum and Research Centre): 1064 Budapest VI, Vörösmarty utca 35; tel. (1) 342-7320; fax (1) 413-1526; e-mail eckhardt@lib.liszt.hu; internet www.lisztmuseum.hu; f. 1986; reconstruction of the composer Franz Liszt's (1811–1886) residence in the bldg of the Old Acad. of Music, with his instruments, furniture, library and other memorabilia; permanent and temporary exhibitions; colln of Liszt's music MSS, letters and other documentation, in collaboration with the Research Library for Music History; Dir MÁRIA ECKHARDT.

Magyar Bélyegmúzeum (Stamp Museum): 1400 Budapest, Pf. 86, 1074 Hársfa u. 47; tel. (1) 341-5526; fax (1) 342-3757; e-mail belyegmuzeum@axelero.hu; f. 1930; collections of 12 million Hungarian and foreign stamps; philatelic history; exhibitions locally and abroad; library of 5,000 vols; Dir ROSALIE SOLYMOSI; publ. *Yearbook*.

Magyar Építészeti Múzeum (Hungarian Museum of Architecture): 1036 Budapest, Mókus u. 20; tel. (1) 388-6170; fax (1) 367-2686; f. 1968; architecture and history of architecture; library of 7,000 vols; Dir KÁROLY BUGAR-MÉSZÁROS; publ. *Pavilon* (annually).

Magyar Kereskedelmi és Vendéglátóipari Múzeum (Hungarian Museum of Trade and Tourism): 1051 Budapest, Szent István tér 15; tel. (1) 212-1245; fax (1) 269-5428; e-mail mkvm@iif.hu; internet www.mkvm.hu; catering trade colln f. 1966, covers the subjects of sales and services, particularly in tourism, hotels and hostelry, cuisine, coffee houses, confectionery, shop fittings; commerce colln f. 1970, contains shop fittings, samples, storage pots, packing material, measuring instruments and coins; the 2 depts also contain documents, photos, posters; Dir IMPRE KISS.

Magyar Mezőgazdasági Múzeum (Museum of Hungarian Agriculture): 1146 Budapest, Városliget Vajdahunyadvár; tel. (1) 363-1117; fax (1) 364-0076; e-mail museum@mmgm.hu; internet www.mmgm.hu; f. 1896; library of 55,000 vols; collection, preservation and presentation of objects and documents related to the history of agriculture and agroindustries in Hungary; conferences; provincial brs; Dir-Gen. Dr GYÖRGY FEHÉR; publs *Agrártörténeti Szemle* (Agricultural History Review, 4 a year), *Bibliographia Historiae Rerum Rusticarum Internationalis* (International Bibliography of Agrarian History, every 2 years), *Magyar Mezőgazdasági Múzeum Közleményei* (Proceedings, every 2 years).

Magyar Nemzeti Galéria (Hungarian National Gallery): 1250 Budapest, Budavári Palota, Pf. 31; tel. (1) 375-7533; fax (1) 375-8898; e-mail mng@mng.hu; internet www.mng.hu; f. 1957; collections include Hungarian art since 11th c,; paintings, sculptures, drawings, engravings, medals; library of 76,000 vols; Dir Dr LÓRÁND BERECZKY; publ. *A Magyar Nemzeti Galéria Évkönyve* (Annals).

Magyar Nemzeti Múzeum (Hungarian National Museum): 1088 Budapest, Múzeum krt 14–16; tel. (1) 338-2122; fax (1) 317-7806; e-mail info@hnm.hu; internet www.hnm.hu; f. 1802; history, archaeology, numismatics; library of 240,000 vols; Dir-Gen. Dr TIBOR KOVÁCS; publs *Folia Archaeologica* (annually), *Folia Historica* (annually), *Régészeti Füzetek* (Fasciculi Archaeologici), *Communicationes Archaeologicae Hungariae* (annually), *Múzeumi Műtárgyvédelem* (Protection of Museum Art Objects, annually), *A magyar múzeumok kiadványainak bibliográfiája* (Bibliography of the Hungarian Museum's publications), *Bibliotheca Humanitatis Historica*, *Inventaria Praehistorica Hungariae*.

Magyar Sportmúzeum (Hungarian Museum of Sport): 1146 Budapest, Dózsa György u. 3; tel. (1) 252-1696; fax (1) 469-5012; e-mail lajos.szabo@axeleron.hu; internet www.sportmuzeum.hu; f. 1963; documents and photos of history of sport in Hungary and abroad; 7,000 books, 35,000 plaques and medals, 4,000 trophies, etc., 500,000 photos, films; Dir Dr LAJOS SZABÓ.

Magyar Természettudományi Múzeum (Hungarian Natural History Museum): 1088 Budapest, Baross u. 13; tel. (1) 267-7101; fax (1) 317-1669; e-mail mtmiroda@zoo.zoo.nhmus.hu; internet www.nhmus.hu; f. 1802; depts of Mineralogy and petrography, Geology and palaeontology, Botany, Zoology, Anthropology; library of 250,000 vols; Chief Dir Dr ISTVÁN MATSKÁSI; publs *Annales Historico-Naturales Musei Nationalis Hungarici* (annual), *Folia Entomologica Hungarica* (annual), *Studia Botanica* (annual), *Fragmenta Palaeontologica Hungarica* (annual).

Magyar Zsidó Múzeum és Levéltár (Hungarian Jewish Museum and Archives): 1075 Budapest, Dohány u. 2; tel. (1) 343-6756; fax (1) 343-6756; e-mail bpjewmus@visio.c3.hu; internet www.c3.hu/~bpjewmus; f. 1916; Jewish pieces of archaeology and art history, religious objects; Dir ROBERT B. TURÁN.

Műcsarnok (Palace of Art): 1406 Budapest, POB 35; tel. (1) 460-7000; fax (1) 363-7205; e-mail info@mucsarnok.hu; internet www.mucsarnok.hu; f. 1896; temporary exhibitions of Hungarian and foreign contemporary art; library of 15,000 vols; Dir Dr JULIA FABÉNYI.

Néprajzi Múzeum (Museum of Ethnography): 1055 Budapest, Kossuth Lajos tér 12; tel. (1) 473-2410; fax (1) 473-2411; e-mail info@neprajz.hu; internet www.neprajz.hu; f. 1872; collections and research activities cover peasant and tribal folk cultures; library of 169,000 vols; Ethnographic Archive with 28,000 MSS and 318,000 photographs, 252 films; Folk Music Archive with 62,000 entries; Gen. Dir Dr ZOLTÁN FEJŐS; publs *Néprajzi Értesítő* (Yearbook), *Hungarian Folklore Bibliography* (annually), *Fontes Musei Ethnographiae*, *Tabula* (2 a year), *MaDok-füzetek*.

Öntödei Múzeum (Foundry Museum): 1027 Budapest, Bem József u. 20; tel. (1) 202-5011; f. 1969; attached to the Hungarian Museum of Science and Technology; used by Ábrahám Ganz and others until 1964; original foundry equipment; history of technological development of foundry trade, old mouldings; library of 1,483 vols; Curator KATALIN LENGYEL-KISS.

OMM Elektrotechnikai Múzeuma (Museum of Electrical Engineering): 1075 Budapest, Kazinczy utca 21; tel. and fax (1) 342-5750; e-mail emuzeum@qwertynet.hu; f. 1970; historic colln of electrical engineering; library of 10,000 vols; Dir Dr SÁNDOR JESZENSZKY.

Országos Műszaki Múzeum (National Museum for Science and Technology): 1502 Budapest, POB 311; located at: 1117 Budapest, Kaposvár-utca 13/15; tel. (1) 204-4095; fax (1) 204-4088; e-mail omm@nadir.hmst.hu; internet www.omm.hu; f. 1954 (collection), 1973 (museum); collection covers inventions and prototypes with reference to natural science and technology, historic exhibits from the early days of industry and its development to the present; library of 20,000 vols; Dir Dr ERZSEBET SZENTPETERI; publ. *Technikatörténeti Szemle* (Review of History of Technology).

Petőfi Irodalmi Múzeum és Kortárs Irodalmi Központ (Petőfi Museum of Hungarian Literature and Centre for Contemporary Literature): 1053 Budapest, Károlyi M. u. 16; tel. (1) 317-3611; fax (1) 317-1722; e-mail muzeuminf@pim.hu; internet www.pim.hu; f. 1954; literature since 19th c.; library of 400,000 vols; archive of 950,000 MSS, 30,000 photographs, 4,900 sound recordings; art collection of 20,000 items; Dir Dr RITA RATZKY.

Postamúzeum (Postal Museum): 1061 Budapest, Andrássy út. 3; tel. (1) 268-1997; fax (1) 268-1958; f. 1955; permanent exhibition of the history of post and telecommunications; library of 11,000 vols; Dir Mrs IRÉN KOVÁCS; publ. *Postai és Távközlési Múzeumi Alapítvany Évkönyve* (annually).

Semmelweis Orvostörténeti Múzeum, Könyvtár és Levéltár (Semmelweis Medical Historical Museum, Library and Archives): 1013 Budapest, Apród. u. 1–3 (Museum and Archives); 1023 Budapest, Török u. 12 (Library); tel. (1) 201-1577 (Museum and Archives), (1) 212-5421 (Library); fax (1) 375-3936; e-mail semmelweis@museum.hu; internet www.semmelweis.museum.hu; f. 1951 (Library), 1965 (Museum), 1972 (Archives); administers 12 attached medical museums; library of 112,000 vols, 20,000 periodicals; Gen. Dir Dr KÁROLY KAPRONCZAY; Man. Dir (vacant); publ. *Orvostörténeti Közlemények / Communicationes de Historia Artis Medicinae* (2 a year).

Szépművészeti Múzeum (Museum of Fine Arts): 1146 Budapest, Dózsa György út 41; tel. (1) 363-7336; fax (1) 469-7114; e-mail titkarsag@szepmuveszeti.hu; internet www.szepmuveszeti.hu; f. 1896, opened 1906; collections and galleries include: Egyptian and Greco-Roman antiquities, foreign paintings, sculptures, drawings and engravings; library of 150,000 vols; Dir Dr LÀSZLÓ BAÁN; publ. *Bulletin du Musée Hongrois des Beaux-Arts*.

Attached museum:

Vasarely Múzeum: 1033 Budapest, Szentlélek tér 1; tel. (1) 388-7551; fax (1) 250-1540; e-mail vasarely.budapest@museum.hr; internet www.muzeum.hu/budapest/vasarely; Dir LILLA SZABÓ.

Textil és Textilruházati Ipartörténeti Múzeum (Museum of the Textile and Clothing Industry): 1036 Budapest III, Lajos u. 138; tel. (1) 430-1387; fax (1) 367-5910; e-mail vajk.eva@axelero.hu; internet www.museum.hu/budapest/textilmuzeum; f. 1972; exhibits from Hungary and Central Europe; library of 3,690 vols; Dir ÉVA VAJK; publ. *Évkönyv* (Year Book).

Tűzoltó Múzeum (Fire Brigade Museum): 1105 Budapest, Martinovics tér 12; tel. (1) 261-3586; f. 1955; includes old fire-fighting equipment, pumps and hoses; universal and Hungarian history of fire protection, its means and organization; library of 15,000 vols; Curator GYULA CSICSMANN.

Zenetörténeti Múzeum (Museum of History of Music): 1014 Budapest, Táncsics M. u. 7; tel. (1) 214-6770; fax (1) 375-9282; e-mail info@zti.hu; f. 1969; colln of instruments, MSS, personal objects used by great musicians; Curator ANNA BARANYI.

Cegléd

Kossuth Lajos Múzeum: 2700 Cegléd, Muzeum u. 5; tel. (53) 310-637; fax (53) 310-637; f. 1917; relics of Lajos Kossuth; ethnography, archaeology, arts, numismatics; library of 14,000 vols; Dir GYULA KOCSIS; publ. *Ceglédi Füzetek* (annually).

Debrecen

Déri Múzeum: 4001 Debrecen, Déri tér 1, Pf. 61; tel. (52) 417-577; fax (52) 417-560; e-mail derimuzeum@freemail.hu; internet www.derimuz.hu; f. 1902; archaeological, ethnographic, fine and applied art, natural history, literary and local history collections and exhibitions; library of 50,000 vols, photographic archive of 100,500 negatives and slides; Dir Dr IBOLYA SZATHMÁRI; publs *A Déri Múzeum Évkönyve* (Yearbook), *Múzeumi Kurir* (Review).

Dunaújváros

Intercisa Múzeum: 2400 Dunaújváros, Városháza tér 4; tel. (25) 408-970; fax (25) 411-315; e-mail intercisamuz@freemail.hu; f. 1951; prehistoric, Roman and medieval colIns; regional history, archaeology and ethnography; library of 5,204 vols; Curator Dr LENDVAI MÁRTA MATUSSNÉ.

Eger

Dobó István Vármúzeum: 3301 Eger, Vár 1; tel. (36) 312-744; fax (36) 312-450; e-mail varmuzeum@div.iif.hu; f. 1872; originally archiepiscopal picture gallery and museum; enlarged by Fort Eger excavation material 1949; local remains of archaeology, ethnography, history of literature and of arts; relics of the Turkish occupation; library of 30,000 vols; Dir Dr TIVADAR PETERCSÁK; publs *Agria* (Yearbook), *Studia Agriensia*.

Esztergom

Balassa Bálint Múzeum: 2500 Esztergom, Mindszenty tér 3; tel. (33) 312-185; f. 1894; history, archaeology, numismatics, applied arts; library of 12,000 vols; Curator Dr ISTVÁN HORVÁTH.

Keresztény Múzeum (Christian Museum): 2501 Esztergom, Mindszenty tér 2; tel. (33) 413-880; fax (33) 413-880; e-mail keresztenymuzeum@vnet.hu; internet www.christianmuseum.hu; f. 1875; Hungarian, Italian, Dutch, Austrian and German late medieval and Renaissance paintings and sculpture; colIns of baroque and modern art, decorative arts, prints and drawings; library of 11,000 vols; Dir PÁL CSÉFALVAY.

Magyar Környezetvédelmi és Vízügyi Múzeum (Hungarian Environmental and Water Management Museum): 2500 Esztergom, Kölcsey u. 2; tel. (33) 500-250; fax (33) 500-251; e-mail info@mail.dunamuzeum.org.hu; internet www.dunamuzeum.org.hu; f. 1973; history of water management; library of 9,700 vols; Curator IMRE KAJÁN; publ. *Vizgazdálkodás* (Water Management).

Vármúzeum: 2500 Esztergom, Szent István tér 1; tel. (33) 415-986; fax (33) 500-095; e-mail varmegom@invitel.hu; internet www.mnmvarmuzeuma.hu; f. 1967; excavated and reconstructed royal palace from the times of the Hungarian House of the Árpáds; municipal history of Esztergom as royal seat in the Middle Ages; Curator BÉLA HORVÁTH.

Fertőd

Kastélymúzeum: 9431 Fertőd, Bartók Béla u. 2; tel. (99) 370-971; fax (99) 370-120; f. 1959; historic castle of Esterházy family; local documents, furnishings, applied art, memorabilia of composer Haydn; Dir JOLÁN BAK.

Gyöngyös

Mátra Múzeum (Museum Historico-Naturale Matraense): 3200 Gyöngyös, Kossuth u. 40; tel. (37) 311-447; fax (37) 311-447; e-mail matramuz@enternet.hu; internet www.matramuzeum.hu; f. 1957; natural history: palaeontology, zoology and botany of Hungary and Europe; history of hunting; library of 12,000 vols; Curator Dr LEVENTE FÜKÖH; publs *Folia Historico-naturalia Musei Matraensis* (annually), *Malacological Newsletter* (annually).

Győr

Xántus János Múzeum: 9022 Győr, Széchenyi tér 5; tel. (96) 310-588; fax (96) 310-731; e-mail xantus@gymsmuzeum.hu; f. 1854; archaeological collection containing relics of the ancient town of Arrabona (now Győr); history, art, anthropology, Roman lapidarium; picture gallery; library of 38,000 vols; Dir Dr ESZTER SZŐNYI; publ. *Arrabona* (annually).

Gyula

Erkel Ferenc Múzeum (Ferenc Erkel Museum): 5700 Gyula, Kossuth u. 17; tel. (66) 361-236; e-mail erkelmuzeum@bhn.hu; f. 1868; archaeology, art, local history, musicological and ethnographic collections; library of 9,052 vols; Curator Dr PÉTER HAVASSY.

Hajdúböszörmény

Hajdúsági Múzeum: 4220 Hajdúböszörmény, Kossuth L. u. 1; tel. (52) 371-038; fax (52) 371-038; f. 1924; sections: archaeology, ethnography, history and fine arts; library of 15,000 vols; Curator Dr MIKLÓS NYAKAS; publs *Évkönyv* (in Hungarian and German, every 2 years), *Közlemények* (in Hungarian, German, English and Russian, annually).

Herend

Porcelán Múzeum: 8440 Herend, Kossuth-u. 140; tel. (88) 261-159; fax (88) 261-801; e-mail porcelan@c3.hu; f. 1964; exhibits from the famous china factory, est. 1826; library of 4,500 vols; Dir MAGDOLNA SIMON.

Hódmezővásárhely

Tornyai János Múzeum: 6801 Hódmezővásárhely, Szántó Kovács János-u. 16–18; tel. (62) 344-424; f. 1905; archaeological, ethnographic and folk-art collections, Tornyai paintings and Medgyessy sculptures; pottery and farm-museum; library of 5,500 vols; Curator IMRE NAGY.

Jászberény

Jász Múzeum: 5100 Jászberény, Táncsics-u. 5; tel. and fax (57) 502-610; e-mail jaszmuzeum@mail.datanet.hu; f. 1873; collections from the late Stone, Copper, Bronze and Iron Ages; ethnography, local history; library; library of 6,593 vols; Curator JÁNOS TÓTH.

Kalocsa

Viski Károly Múzeum: 6300 Kalocsa, Szent István Király u. 25, POB 82; tel. (78) 462-351; fax (78) 462-351; f. 1932; regional museum, folk art; library of 9,000 vols; Dir IMRE ROMSICS.

Kaposvár

Somogy Megyei Múzeumok Igazgatósága: 7400 Kaposvár, Fő utca 10; tel. (82) 314-011; e-mail smmi@smmi.hu; internet www.smmi.hu; f. 1909; archaeological and ethnographic collections, contemporary history, fine arts, natural history; library of 13,000 vols; Dir Dr ISTVÁN S. KIRÁLY; publs *Múzeumi Tájékoztató, Somogyi Múzeumok Füzetei, Somogyi Múzeumok Közleményei*.

Karcag

Győrffy István Nagykun Múzeum: 5300 Karcag, Kálvin u. 4; tel. (59) 312-087; f. 1906; regional museum, ethnography; library of 8,000 vols; Curator Dr MIKLÓS NAGY MOLNÁR.

Kecskemét

Katona József Múzeum: 6000 Kecskemét, Bethlen Gábor krt. 1; tel. (76) 481-350; fax (76) 481-122; e-mail katona.kecskemet@museum.hu; f. 1894; archaeological, ethnographical, historical and fine art collections; library of 16,600 vols; Dir Dr JÁNOS BÁRTH; publ. *Cumania* (annually).

Kecskeméti Képtár és Tóth Menyhért Emlékmúzeum: 6000 Kecskemét, Pf. 165, Cifrapalota, Rákóczi u. 1; tel. (76) 480-776; f. 1983; Hungarian paintings since 19th c., particularly by Menyhért Tóth; Dir SIMON MAGDOLNA.

Magyar Naiv Művészek Múzeuma (Museum of Hungarian Naive Art): 6000 Kecskemét, Gáspár A. u. 11; tel. (76) 324-767; f. 1976; exhibitions of works of Hungarian primitive painters and sculptors; Dir Dr PÁL BÁNSZKY; publ. *Magyar Naiv Művészek Múzeuma*.

Szórakaténusz Játékmúzeum (Toy Museum): 6000 Kecskemet, Gáspár A. u. 11; tel. (76) 481-469; fax (76) 481-469; e-mail bacsmuz@matav.hu; f. 1981; library of 3,000 vols; Dir Dr JOZSEF VÍZI KRISTON; publ. *Studies of the History of Play*.

Keszthely

Balatoni Múzeum: 8360 Keszthely, Múzeum-u. 2; tel. (83) 312-351; fax (83) 312-351; e-mail balatonimuz@georgikon.hu; internet www.zmmi.hu; f. 1898; prehistoric and historic collections relating to Lake Balaton; library of 29,000 vols; Director Dr BÁLINT HAVASI.

Helikon Kastélymúzeum: 8360 Keszthely, Kastély u. 1; tel. (83) 312-190; fax (83) 315-039; e-mail khelikon@freemail.hu; f. 1974; 18th c. castle of Festetics family; Helikon Library; Coach Museum; library of 94,000 vols; Dir Dr LÁSZLÓ CZOMA.

Kiskunfélegyháza

Kiskun Múzeum: 6100 Kiskunfélegyháza, Dr Holló L. u. 9; tel. (76) 461-468; fax (76) 462-542; f. 1902; ethnography; library of 20,000 vols; Curator Dr ERZSÉBET MOLNÁR.

Kiskunhalas

Thorma János Múzeum: 6400 Kiskunhalas, Köztársaság-u. 2; tel. (77) 422-864; fax (77) 422-864; f. 1874; ethnography, archaeology and history; library of 7,000 vols; Curator AURÉL SZAKÁL.

Kőszeg

Városi Múzeum (Municipal Museum): 9730 Kőszeg, Jurisics tér 6; tel. and fax (94) 360-156; e-mail museum.koszeg@axelerod.hu; f. 1932; collection of castle and town history; library of 9,300 vols; Dir Prof. Dr KORNÉL BAKAY.

Mátészalka

Szatmári Múzeum: 4700 Mátészalka, Kossuth-ut. 5; tel. and fax (44) 502-646; e-mail szatmari.mateszalka@museum.hu; internet www.museum.hu/mateszalka/szatmari; f. 1972; local history and ethnographic collections; Dir Dr LÁSZLÓ CSERVENYÁK.

Miskolc

Herman Ottó Múzeum: 3529 Miskolc, Görgey Artúr ut. 28; tel. (46) 560-172; fax (46) 555-397; e-mail hermuz@axelero.hu; internet www.hermuz.hu; f. 1899; collections of archaeology, regional ethnography, fine arts and applied arts, natural science, minerals of Hungary, local history, literary history, history of photography; library of 44,000 vols; Dir Dr LÁSZLÓ VERES; publs *A Herman Ottó Múzeum Évkönyve* (Yearbook), *Officina Musei, A Miskolci Herman Ottó Múzeum Közleményei* (Communications), *Néprajzi Kiadványok* (Ethnographical Studies), *Documentatio Borsodiensis, Natura Borsodiensis*.

Központi Kohászati Múzeum (Central Foundry Museum): 3517 Miskolc-Felsőhámor, Palota-u. 22; tel. (46) 379-375; f. 1949; science and technology; archaeological foundry of the 9th–10th c.; 18th-c. foundry; Curator LÁSZLÓ PORKOLÁB.

Mohács

Kamizsai Dorottya Múzeum: 7700 Mohács, Városház u. 1; tel. (69) 311-536; f. 1923; ethnography of the Serbs, Croats and Slavs; library of 2,300 vols; Curator JAKAB FERKOV.

Mosonmagyaróvár

Hansági Múzeum: 9200 Mosonmagyaróvár, Szent István u. 1; tel. (96) 213-834; fax (96) 212-094; f. 1882; regional museum; archaeology, ethnography, lapidarium, local history, paintings by János Szale, Gyurkovits colln; library of 7,216 vols; Dir KÁROLY SZENTKUTI.

Nagycenk

Széchenyi István Emlékmúzeum (Széchenyi Memorial Museum): 9485 Nagycenk, Kiscenki-utca 3; tel. (99) 360-023; fax (99) 360-260; f. 1973; history of the Széchenyi family and life (iconography, bibliography) of 19th-century statesman Count István Széchenyi; library of 5,000 vols; Curator Dr ATTILA KÖRNYEI.

Nagykanizsa

Thury György Múzeum: 8801 Nagykanizsa, Fő tér 5; tel. (93) 314-596; fax (93) 317-233; f. 1919; archaeological and ethnographical collections, local history displays, numismatics; library of 5,000 vols; Curator Dr LÁSZLÓ HORVÁTH.

Nagykőrös

Arany János Múzeum: 2751 Nagykőrös, Ceglédi-u. 19; tel. (53) 350-810; fax (53) 350-770; e-mail ajmpmi@freemail.hu; f. 1928; regional museum; archaeology, ethnography, local history, literary documents of poet J. Arany; library of 20,019 vols; Dir Dr LÁSZLÓ NOVÁK; publs *Acta Musei*, *Archivum Musei*.

Nyirbátor

Báthory István Múzeum: 4300 Nyirbátor, Károlyi-u. 15; tel. and fax (42) 281-760; e-mail batormuz@axelero.hu; f. 1955; archaeology, local history and art; library of 2,900 vols; Curator PILIPKÓ ERZSÉBET.

Nyiregyháza

Jósa András Múzeum: 4400 Nyíregyháza, Benczúr tér 21, Pf. 57; tel. (42) 315-722; fax (42) 315-722; e-mail jam@jam.nyirbone.hu; internet jam.nyirbone.hu; f. 1868; collections of archaeology, ethnography and local history; fine and applied arts, numismatics; library of 20,000 vols; Dir Dr PÉTER NÉMETH; publ. *A nyíregyházi Jósa András Múzeum Évkönyve* (annually).

Pannonhalma

Pannonhalmi Főapátság Gyűjteménye (Abbey of Pannonhalma Collection): 9090 Pannonhalma, Vár 1; tel. (96) 570-142; fax (96) 470-011; f. 1802; paintings, sculptures, applied arts in an ancient Benedictine Abbey.

Pápa

Gróf Esterházy Károly Kastély- és Tájmúzeum (Count Charles Esterházy Castle and Regional Museum): 8501 Pápa, Fő tér 1, Pf. 208, Várkastély; tel. (89) 313-584; f. 1960; ethnographical, archaeological and industrial collections from the town and environment; library of 10,000 vols; Dir Dr PÉTER LÁSZLÓ; publ. *Acta Musei Papensis* (annually).

Pécs

Csontváry Múzeum: 7621 Pécs, Janus Pannonius-u. 11; tel. (72) 310-544; fax (72) 315-694; e-mail jpm@jpm.hu; f. 1973; art gallery comprising selected works by the expressionist painter Tivadar Csontváry Kosztka; Man. GÁBOR TILLAI.

Janus Pannonius Múzeum: 7621 Pécs, Káptalan u. 5; tel. (72) 310-172; fax (72) 315-694; e-mail jpm@jpm.hu; f. 1904; natural sciences, archaeology, ethnography, modern Hungarian art, local history; library of 25,000 vols; Dir ZOLTÁN HUSZÁR; publs *Évkönyv* (Yearbook), *Dunántuli Dolgozatok* (Trans-Danubian Studies).

Modern Magyar Képtár I (Modern Hungarian Gallery I, 1900–1950): 7621 Pécs, Káptalan u. 4; tel. (72) 324-822; f. 1957; paintings by Mednyánszky, Gulácsy, Rippl Rónai, Czóbel, Uitz, Kassák, Egry.

Modern Magyar Képtár II (Modern Hungarian Gallery II, 1950–): 7621 Pécs, Szabadság u. 2; tel. (72) 324-822; f. 1957; paintings by Barcsay, Bizse, Korniss, Lantos, Orosz.

Vasarely Múzeum: 7621 Pécs, Káptalan-u. 3; tel. (72) 324-822; fax (72) 315-694; e-mail jpm@jpm.hu; f. 1976; art gallery comprising works by Hungarian-born French artist Victor Vasarely; Man. GÁBOR TILLAI.

Rudabánya

Alapítvány Érc- és Ásványbányászati Múzeum (Museum of Mining of Metals and Minerals): 3733 Rudabánya, Petőfi u. 24; f. 1956; history of the industry, exhibitions; Curator BÉLA SZUROMI.

Salgótarján

Nógrádi Történeti Múzeum (Nógrád Historical Museum): 3100 Salgótarján, Múzeum tér 2, Pf. 3; tel. (32) 314-169; fax (32) 512-335; e-mail nogradimuzeum@nogradi-muzeumok.hu; internet www.museum.hu; f. 1959; social history since 19th c., history of art, literary history, numismatics, industrial history, esp. mining; library of 16,000 vols; Dir Dr ANNA KOVÁCS; publ. *Yearbook of the Museums of Nógrád County*.

Sárospatak

Rákóczi Múzeum: 3950 Sárospatak, Szent Erzsébet u. 19; tel. (47) 311-083; fax (47) 511-135; e-mail spatak@rakoczimuseum.axelero.net; internet www.spatak.hu; f. 1950; housed in the Castle of Sárospatak; historical, ethnographic, archaeological and applied art collections; library of 18,000 vols; Curator Dr DANKÓ KATALIN JÓSVAINÉ.

Sárvár

Nádasdy Ferenc Múzeum: 9600 Sárvár, Vár-u. 1; f. 1951; late Renaissance and Baroque Hungarian milieu reconstructed in state rooms of 16th-century castle; library of 3,900 vols; Dir ISTVÁN SÖPTEI.

Sopron

Központi Bányászati Múzeum (Central Mining Museum): 9400 Sopron, Templom u. 2; tel. (99) 312-667; fax (99) 338-902; f. 1957; science and technology; history of mining in the Carpathian basin since prehistoric age; Dir ERZSÉBET BIRCHER.

Soproni Múzeum: 9400 Sopron, Fő tér 8; tel. (99) 311-327; fax (99) 311-347; e-mail smuzeum@mail.c3.hu; f. 1867; archaeology, folk art, pharmacy, medieval synagogue, local Baroque art and Storno Collections; library of 29,000 vols; Dir Dr ATTILA KÖRNYEI.

Szarvas

Tessedik Sámuel Múzeum: 5540 Szarvas, Vajda P. u. 1; tel. (66) 216-608; f. 1951; archaeology, ethnography and local history collections; Dir Dr JÓZSEF PALOV.

Szécsény

Kubinyi Ferenc Múzeum: 3170 Szécsény, Ady Endre-u. 7; f. 1973; archaeology and local history; library of 8,400 vols; Curator Dr KATALIN SIMÁN.

Szeged

Móra Ferenc Múzeum: 6701 Szeged, POB 474; located at: 6720 Szeged, Roosevelt tér 1–3; tel. (62) 549-040; fax (62) 549-061; e-mail info@mfm.u-szeged.hu; internet www.mfm.u-szeged.hu; f. 1883; archaeological, ethnographic and biological collections, history of arts and regional collections; library of 50,000 vols; special collections include: Sándor Bálint bequest of 5,500 vols on archaic religions and beliefs, old books of prayers and liturgies, Győző Csongor Bequest of 5,500 vols on local history; Dir Dr GABRIELLA VÖRÖS; publs *Studia Archaeologica* (annually), *Studia Ethnographica* (annually), *Studia Historica* (annually), *Studia Naturalia* (annually), *Studia Historiae Literarum et Artium* (annually), *Monographia Archaeologica* (irregular).

Székesfehérvár

Szent István Király Múzeum: 8002 Székesfehérvár, Fő u. 6, P4. 78; tel. (22) 315-583; fax (22) 311-734; e-mail fmmuz@mail.iif.hu; f. 1873; prehistoric, Roman and medieval collections, anthropological collection, regional ethnography, art gallery, musical collection, numismatic collection, stones of the Basilica of King St Stephen; library of 80,000 vols; Dir GYULA FÜLÖP; publs *Bulletin*, *Alba Regia* (Scientific Almanac).

Szekszárd

Wosinsky Mór Megyei Múzeum: 7101 Szekszárd, Szent István tér 26; tel. (74) 316-222; fax (74) 316-222; e-mail wmmm@terrasoft.hu; f. 1896; collections of folk art, archaeology, history, fine arts and applied arts; library of 11,300 vols; Dir Dr ATTILA GAÁL; publ. *Yearbook*.

Szentendre

Ferenczy Múzeum: 2001 Szentendre, Fő tér 6, pf. 49; tel. (26) 310-244; fax (26) 310-790; e-mail pmmikozmuvelodes@freemail.hu; internet www.pmmi.hu; f. 1951; paintings, drawings, sculptures and Gobelin tapestries; centre for 30 museums in Pest County; library of 24,000 vols, 210 periodicals; Dir Dr LÁSZLÓ SIMON; publ. *Studia Comitatensia* (yearbook of papers published by the Museums of Pest County).

Szabadtéri Néprajzi Múzeum (Hungarian Open Air Museum): 2001 Szentendre, POB 63, Sztaravodai u.; tel. (26) 502-500; fax (26) 502-502; e-mail sznm@sznm.hu; internet www.skanzen.hu; f. 1967; vernacular architecture and furniture; library of 11,000 vols; archive of 90,000 photographs, 13,000 ethnographical, historical, architectural documents, films, maps, drawings, etc.; Dir Dr MIKLÓS CSERI; publs *Téka* (4 a year), *Ház és Ember* (yearbook).

Szentes

Koszta József Múzeum: 6600 Szentes, Szechenyi Liget 1; tel. (63) 313-352; fax (63) 313-352; e-mail muzeum@szentesinfo.hu; f. 1894; archaeological and ethnographical collection and paintings by Koszta; Dir JÁNOS SZABÓ.

Szigetvár

Zrínyi Miklós Vármúzeum: 7900 Szigetvár, Vár-u. 1; f. 1917; local history collection, relating particularly to the period of Turkish occupation (16th–17th c.).

Szolnok

Damjanich János Múzeum: 5001 Szolnok, Kossuth tér 4, Pf. 128; tel. (56) 421-602; fax (56) 341-204; e-mail muzeum@djm.hu; internet www.djm.hu; f. 1933; archaeology, ethnography, palaeontology, fine arts, applied art and local history collections; library of 50,000 vols; Dir Dr RÓBERT KERTÉSZ; publ. *Tisicum* (annually).

Szombathely

Savaria Múzeum: 9701 Szombathely, Kisfaludy Sándor u. 9; tel. (94) 312-554; fax (94) 313-736; e-mail savmuz@c3.hu; f. 1872; natural history, archaeology, local cultural history, ethnography; library of 32,000 vols; Dir Dr SÁNDOR HORVÁTH; publs *Savaria* (Journal, annually), *Praenorica – Folia Historico-Naturalia* (irregular).

Tác

Gorsium Szabadtéri Múzeum (Gorsium Open-Air Museum): 8121 Tác, Fövenypuszta Ady E. u. 56; tel. (22) 362-443; e-mail lak5706@mail.iif.hu; f. 1963; excavations of a Roman city, the ruins showing original shape.; Dir Prof. Dr JENŐ FITZ.

Tata

Kuny Domokos Megyei Múzeum: 2892 Tata, Néppark, Kiskastély, POB 224; tel. (34) 487-888; fax (34) 487-888; e-mail kunyd@freemail.hu; f. 1954; history, archaeology, ethnology, art, palaeobotany; library of 27,000 vols; Dir Dr ANDREA SZILVIA HOLLÓ.

Vác

Tragor Ignác Múzeum: 2600 Vác, Zrínyi u. 41A; tel. (27) 500-750; fax (27) 500-758; e-mail muzeum@dunaweb.hu; internet www.muzeum.vac.hu; f. 1895; archaeology, ethnography, local history and fine arts exhibits; library of 10,565 vols, 4,760 periodicals and newsletters; Dir KŐVÁRI KLÁRA; publ. *Váci Könyvek* (Bulletin).

Várpalota

Magyar Vegyészeti Múzeum (Hungarian Chemical Museum): 8100 Várpalota, Szabadság tér 1; tel. (88) 575-670; fax (88) 471-702; e-mail vegymuz@vegyeszetimuzeum.hu; internet www.vegyeszetimuzeum.hu; f. 1963; history of the chemical industry; library of 18,618 vols; Dir ISTVÁN PRÓDER.

Vértesszőllős

Magyar Nemzeti Múzeum Vértesszőllősi Bemutatóhelye: 2837 Vértesszőllős; tel. (1) 327-7744; e-mail hnm@hnm.hu; internet www.hnm.hu; f. 1975; permanent open-air exhibition; dwelling-place and remains of early man; part of Archaeology Dept of Nat. Museum; Curator Dr VIOLA DOBOSI.

Veszprém

Laczkó Dezső Múzeum: 8201 Veszprém, Erzsébet sétány 1; tel. (88) 564-310; fax (88) 426-081; e-mail titkar@vmmuzeum.hu; internet www.c3.hu/~vmmuzeum; f. 1903; ethnographic, archaeological, historical, fine and industrial arts, history of literature, numismatic exhibits from Veszprém County; library of 36,000 vols; Dir Dr ZSUZSA FODOR; publs *Veszprém Megyei Múzeumok Közleményei*, *Publicationes Museorum Comitatus Vesprimiensis* (Communications of the Museums of Veszprém County).

Visegrád

Mátyás Király Múzeum (King Matthias Museum): 2025 Visegrád, Fő u. 23–25; tel. (26) 398-026; fax (26) 398-252; f. 1933; managed by Magyar Nemzeti Múzeum of Budapest; 13th-century upper and lower castle with Roman and medieval archaeological remains; partially restored 15th-century royal palace; library of 10,000 vols; Dir MÁTYÁS SZŐKE.

Zalaegerszeg

Göcseji Falumúzeum (Village Museum of Göcsej): 8900 Zalaegerszeg, Falumúzeum u. 1; tel. (92) 703-295; e-mail muzeum@zmmi.hu; internet www.zmmi.hu; f. 1968; open-air ethnographical collection; Dir Dr LÁSZLÓ VÁNDOR.

Göcseji Múzeum: 8900 Zalaegerszeg, Batthyányi u. 2, POB 176; tel. (92) 314-537; fax (92) 511-972; e-mail muzeum@zmmi.hu; internet www.zmmi.hu; f. 1950; collections of regional history, archaeology, ethnography, paintings and sculpture; exhibition of sculptures by Zs. Kisfaludi-Strobl; exhibition on the history of County Zala; library of 20,658 vols; Dir Dr LÁSZLÓ VÁNDOR; publ. *Zalai Múzeum* (annually).

Magyar Olajipari Múzeum (Oil Industry Museum): 8900 Zalaegerszeg, Wlassics Gy. u. 13; tel. (92) 313-632; fax (92) 311-081; f. 1969; exhibitions of the history of the professional and technical development of the oil industry; equipment, documents, photos, etc.; library of 9,000 vols; Curator JÁNOS TÓTH.

Zirc

Bakonyi Természettudományi Múzeum (Bakony Mountains Natural History Museum): 8420 Zirc, Rákóczi tér 1, POB 36; tel. (88) 575-300; fax (88) 575-301; e-mail btmz@bakonymuseum.hu; internet www.bakonymuseum.hu; f. 1972; natural history exhibits from Bakony Mountains, minerals from the Carpathian Basin; library of 6,000 vols; Curator ÁGOTA KASPER; publs *A Bakony természettudományi kutatásának eredményei* (Results of Research into the Natural History of Bakony), *Folia Musei Historico-naturalis Bakonyiensis* (A Bakonyi Természettudományi Múzeum Közleményei).

State Universities

BUDAPESTI CORVINUS EGYETEM (Corvinus University of Budapest)

1093 Budapest IX, Fővám tér 8
Telephone: (1) 482-5000
E-mail: intoffice@bkae.hu
Internet: www.uni-corvinus.hu

Founded 1920 as Budapesti Közgazdaságtudományi és Államigazgatási Egyetem
State control
Languages of instruction: Hungarian, English
Languages of instruction: French, German
Academic year: September to June

Rector: Prof. Dr TAMÁS MÉSZÁROS
Vice-Rectors: Dr MIKLÓS IMRE, Prof. Dr ZSOLT HARNOS, Prof. Dr ILDIKÓ HRUBOS
Librarians: Dr H. HUSZÁR, Dr Á. OROSZ, Dr E. ZALAI-KOVÁCS

Number of teachers: 971
Number of students: 17,243

Publications: *Társadalom és Gazdaság* (Society and Economy, in Hungarian, 2 a year; in English, 3 a year), *Applied Ecology and Environmental Research* (2 a year)

DEANS

Faculty of Business Administration: S. KEREKES
Faculty of Economics: L. TRAUTMANN
Faculty of Food Science: CS. BALLA
Faculty of Horticultural Science: M. G. TÓTH
Faculty of Landscape Architecture: I. JÁMBOR
Faculty of Public Administration: A. TAMÁS
Faculty of Social Sciences: Z. SZÁNTÓ

PROFESSORS

ÁGH, A., Politics
ANGYAL, Á, Management and Organization
BALATON, K., Management and Organization
BALÁZS, P., European Studies
BÁNFI, T., Finance
BARICZ, R., Accountancy
BÉKÁSSY-MOLNÁR, E., Food Engineering
BEKKER, ZS., Economic Theory
BERNÁTH, J., Herb and Aroma Products
BENCZÚR, E., Floriculture and Dendrology
BERÁCS, J., Marketing
BLAHO, A., World Economics
BOD, P. Á., Economic Policy
BÚZA, J., Economic History
CHIKÁN, A., Logistics
CSÁKI, CS., Agriculture
CSEMEZ, A., Landscape Planning and Development
CSER, L., Computer Science
CSIMA, P., Landscape Protection
S. CSIZMADIA, Philosophy
D. DEÁK, Economic Law
DOBÁK, M., Management and Organization
FARAGÓ, T., Economic History
FEKETE, A., Physics Control
FODOR, P., Applied Chemistry
FORGÓ, F., Operations Research
GÁBOR, R. I., Human Resources
GÁL, P., World Economics
GALASI, P., Human Resources
GÁLIK, M., Media Economics
GEDEON, P., Comparative Economics
HAJDU, I., Food Economy
HÁMORI, B., Comparative Economics
HARNOS, Z., Mathematics and Informatics
HOÓS, J., Public Administration
HORÁNYI, Ö., Communication
HROTKÓ, K., Pomology
HRUBOS, I., Sociology
JÁMBOR, I., Landscape Technology and Garden Techniques
JENEI, GY., Public Administration
KÁLLAY, H., Oenology
KEREKES, S., Environmental Management
KERÉKGYÁRTÓ, GY., Statistics
KISS, J. L., International Relations
KONCZ, K., Human Resources
KOSÁRY, J., Applied Chemistry
KŐVÁRI, GY., Human Resources
KUCZI, T., Sociology
LADÁNYI, J., Sociology
LÁNG, Z., Technology
LENGYEL, GY., Sociology
LIGETI, S., Finance
LŐRINC ISTVÁNFFY, H., European Studies
MAGYAR, M., Language Centre
MAGYARI-BECK, I., Psychology and Pedagogy
MARÁZ, A., Microbiology
MELLÁR, T., Economic Policy
MÉSZÁROS, L., Entomology
MÉSZÁROS, T., Strategy and Project Management
MÓCZÁR, J., Mathematics
MOKSONY, F., Sociology
NOVÁKY, E., Futurology
PALÁNKAI, T., World Economics
PAPP, J., Pomology
QUITTNER, P., Information Systems
RADICS, L., Ecology and Sustainable Economic Systems
RÁCZ, A., Constitutional Law
RIMÓCZI, I., Botanics
ROSTOVÁNYI, ZS., International Relations
SCHMIDT, G., Floriculture and Dendrology
SURÁNYI, S., World Economics
SZABÓ, K., Comparative Economics
SZAKÁCS, S., Economic History
SZÁZ, J., Finance
TALLOS, P., Mathematics
TARI, E., Management and Organization
TEMESI, J., Operations Research
TÖRÖK, G., Business Law

TÓTH, T., Marketing
TÓTH, G. M., Pomology
VATAI, G., Food Engineering
VELICH, I., Genetics
VERMES, L., Soil Science and Water Management
VITA, L., Statistics
ZALAI, E., Econometrics
ZÁMBORINÉ, N. E., Medicinal and Aromatic Plants
ZELKÓ, L., Finance
ZSOLNAI, L., Business Ethics

ATTACHED INSTITUTES

Institute for Postgraduate Studies in Economics: 1093 Budapest, Lónyay u. 12; tel. (1) 216-4441; fax (1) 216-2809; Dir PÉTER P. GÁSPÁR.

International Studies Centre (ISC): 1093 Budapest, Fővám tér 8; tel. (1) 482-5443; fax (1) 482-5449; 351 students; Dir JÓZSEF BERÁCS.

BUDAPESTI MŰSZAKI ÉS GAZDASÁGTUDOMÁNYI EGYETEM (Budapest University of Technology and Economics)

1111 Budapest, Műegyetem rkp. 3
Telephone: (1) 463-1111
Fax: (1) 463-2220
E-mail: rektor@mail.bme.hu
Internet: www.bme.hu

Founded 1782 as Institutum Geometricum Hydrotechnicum and reorganized as Hungarian Palatine Joseph Technical University in 1871. Építőipari és Közlekedési Műszaki Egyetem (Technical University of Building and Transport Engineering) was incorporated with the university in 1967. Present name 2000
State control
Languages of instruction: Hungarian, English
Languages of instruction: German, French, Russian
Academic year: September to June
Rector: Prof. Dr KÁROLY MOLNÁR
Vice-Rectors: Prof. Dr JÁNOS KÖVESI, Dr GYULA SALLAI, Dr MIKLÓS ZRÍNYI
Librarian: ISTVÁNNÉ FONYÓ
Number of teachers: 1,190
Number of students: 22,567
Publications: *A Budapesti Műszaki Egyetem Évkönyve* (annually), *Periodica Politechnica*, *Research News*

DEANS

Faculty of Architecture: DLA ANTAL LÁZÁR
Faculty of Chemical Engineering: Prof. Dr GYÖRGY POKOL
Faculty of Civil Engineering: Prof. Dr GYÖRGY FARKAS
Faculty of Economic and Social Sciences: Prof. Dr JÓZSEF VERESS
Faculty of Electrical Engineering and Informatics: Prof. Dr PÉTER ARATÓ
Faculty of Mechanical Engineering: Prof. Dr ANTAL PENNINGER
Faculty of Natural Sciences: Prof. Dr TAMÁS KESZTHELYI
Faculty of Transportation Engineering: Prof. Dr ÉVA KÖVES-GILICZE

PROFESSORS

Faculty of Architecture (tel. (1) 463-3521; fax (1) 463-3520; e-mail DekaniHivatal@eszk.bme.hu; internet www.bme.hu/en/organization/faculties/architecture/index.html):

BALOGH, B., Design
BITÓ, J., Housing Design
CSÁGOLY, F., Design of Public Buildings
DOMOKOS, G., Structural Mechanics
ISTVÁNFI, GY., History of Architecture
KASZÁS, K., Design of Public Buildings
KLAFSZKY, E., Building Management and Organization
LÁZÁR, A., Industrial and Agricultural Architecture
MAJOROS, A., Sanitary Engineering
MEGGYESI, T., Urban Studies
NAGY, L., Sanitary Engineering
PETRÓ, B., Building Constructions
TÖRÖK, F., Design of Public Buildings
VÖRÖS, F., Building Construction
ZÖLD, A., Sanitary Engineering

Faculty of Chemical Engineering (tel. (1) 463-3571; fax (1) 463-3570; e-mail dekan@ch.bme.hu; internet www.bme.hu/en/organization/faculties/chemical/index.html):

BITTER, I., Organic Chemical Technology
BORSA, J., Plastics and Rubber Industries
FAIGL, F., Organic Chemical Technology
FEKETE, J., General and Analytical Chemistry
FONYÓ, ZS., Chemical Unit Operations
GÁL, S., General and Analytical Chemistry
GROFCSIK, A., Physical Chemistry
HARGITTAI, I., General and Analytical Chemistry
HENCSEI, P., Inorganic Chemistry
HORVAI, GY., Chemical Informatics
KALAUS, GY., Organic Chemistry
KEGLEVICH, GY., Organic Chemical Technology
KEMÉNY, S., Chemical Unit Operations
KUBINYI, M., Physical Chemistry
MIHÁLTZ, P., Chemical Unit Operations
NOVÁK, B., Agricultural Chemical Technology
NOVÁK, L., Organic Chemistry
NYITRAI, J., Organic Chemistry
NYULÁSZI, L., Inorganic Chemistry
ÖRSI, F., Biochemistry and Food Technology
POKOL, GY., General and Analytical Chemistry
PUKÁNSZKY, B., Plastics and Rubber Industries
RÉFFY, J., Inorganic Chemistry
SALGÓ, A., Biochemistry and Food Technology
SEVELLA, B., Agricultural Chemical Technology
SZÉCHY, G., Chemical Technology
SZEPESVÁRI TOTH, K., General and Analytical Chemistry
TŐKE, L., Organic Chemical Technology
TUNGLER, A., Chemical Technology
VESZPRÉMI, T., Inorganic Chemistry
ZRINYI, M., Physical Chemistry

Faculty of Civil Engineering (tel. (1) 463-3531; fax (1) 463-3530; e-mail tolo@vpszk.bme.hu; internet www.bme.hu/en/organization/faculties/civil/index.html):

ADAM, J., Geodesy and Surveying
BALÁZS, GY., Building Materials and Engineering Geology
BOJTÁR, I., Structural Mechanics
DETREKŐI, Á., Photogrammetry and Geoinformatics
FARKAS, GY., Reinforced Concrete Structures
FARKAS, J., Geotechnics
FÍ, I., Road and Railway Engineering
GÁLOS, M., Building Materials and Engineering Geology
GÁSPÁR, ZS., Structural Mechanics
HEGEDŰS, I., Reinforced Concrete Structures
IJJAS, I., Hydraulic and Water Resources Engineering
IVÁNYI, M., Steel Structures
KISS PAPP, L., Geodesy and Surveying
KURUTZ KOVÁCS, M., Structural Mechanics
MEGYERI, J., Road and Railway Engineering
PATONAI, D., Building Construction
SÁRKÖZY, F., Geodesy and Surveying
SOMLYODY, L., Sanitary and Environmental Engineering
SZALAY, K., Reinforced Concrete Structures
SZÉLL, M., Building Construction
TARNAI, T., Structural Mechanics

Faculty of Economic and Social Sciences (tel. (1) 463-3591; fax (1) 463-3590; e-mail gtk-dekani@gtdh.bme.hu; internet www.bme.hu/en/organization/faculties/fess/index.html):

ANTALOVITS, M., Ergonomics and Psychology
BÁNDI, GY., Environmental Economics and Law
BENEDEK, A., Technical Education
BISZTERSZKY, E., Technical Education
DINYA, L., Industrial Management and Business Economics
FARKAS, J., Sociology
FEHÉR, M., Philosophy and History of Science
HORÁNYI, Ö., Sociology
HRONSZKY, I., Innovation Studies and History of Technology
KERÉKGYÁRTÓ, GY., Economics
KÖVESI, J., Industrial Business and Management
MARGITAY, T., Philosophy and History of Science
PLÉH, CS., Information Management
SÁRKÖZY, T., Law and Business Organization
S. NAGY, K., Sociology
SZLÁVIK, J., Environmental Economics and Technical Law
TÖRÖK, Á., Industrial Business and Management
VERESS, J., Economic and Business Policy
VINCZE, P., Physical Education

Faculty of Electrical Engineering and Informatics (1111 Budapest, Egry F. u. 18; tel. (1) 463-3581; fax (1) 463-3580; ; fax vikdhvez@vik-dh.vdk.bme.hu; internet www.bme.hu/en/organization/faculties/electrical/index.html):

ARATÓ, P., Process Control
BENYÓ, Z., Process Control
BERTA, I., High-Voltage Engineering
FRIGYES, I., Microwave Telecommunications
GORDOS, G., Telecommunications and Telematics
GYŐRFI, L., Mathematics
HALÁSZ, S., Electrical Machines
ILLYEFALVI-VITÉZ, ZS., Electronic Technology
KEVICZKY, L., Automation
KÓCZY, T. L., Telecommunications and Telematics
KOLLÁR, I., Measurement and Instrument Engineering
LANTOS, B., Process Control
LEVENDOVSZKY, J., Telecommunications
MOJZES, I., Electronic Technology
PAPP, L., Telecommunications
PÉCELI, G., Measurement and Instrument Engineering
RECSKI, A., Mathematics
RÓNYAI, L., Mathematics
ROSKA, T., Measurement and Instrument Engineering
SALLAI, GY., Telecommunications and Telematics
SCHMIDT, I., Electrical Machines
SELÉNYI, E., Measurement and Instrument Engineering
SZABÓ, CS., Telecommunications
SZÉKELY, V., Electronic Devices
SZIRMAY-KALOS, L., Process Control
TARNAY, K., Electronic Devices
VAJDA, I., Telecommunications
VAJK, I., Automation
VARJU, GY., Electric Power Plants and Networks

VESZELY, GY., Automation
ZOMBORY, L., Microwave Telecommunications

Faculty of Mechanical Engineering (tel. (1) 463-3541; fax (1) 463-3540; e-mail gepeszd@mail.bme.hu; internet www.bme.hu/en/organization/faculties/mechanical/index.html):

ARTINGER, I., Mechanical Technology
BÉDA, GY., Technical Mechanics
BÜKI, G., Energetics
CZVIKOVSZKY, T., Polymer Engineering and Textile Technology
GARBAI, L., Sanitary Engineering
GINSZTLER, J., Electrical Materials Technology
HALÁSZ, G., Hydraulic Machines
HALMAI, A., Precision Mechanics – Optics
HORVÁTH, M., Machine Production
JÓRI, J. I., Agricultural Machine Design
KOVÁCS, L., Hydraulic Machines
KOZMA, M., Machine Elements
LAJOS, T., Fluid Mechanics
MEGGYES, A., Heat Engines
MOLNÁR, K., Process Engineering
PARTI, M., Fluid Mechanics
PENNINGER, A., Heat Engines
REMÉNYI, K., Energetics
STÉPÁN, G., Technical Mechanics
VÁRADI, K., Agricultural Machine Design
VARGA, L., Machine Elements
ZIAJA, GY., Mechanical Technology

Faculty of Natural Sciences (tel. (1) 463-3561; fax (1) 463-3560; e-mail ttk-dekani@ttdh.bme.hu; internet www.bme.hu/en/organization/faculties/natural/index.html):

CSISZÁR, I., Stochastics
CSOM, GY., Nuclear Technology
DEÁK, P., Atomic Physics
FRITZ, J., Differential Equations
GYULAI, J., Experimental Physics
JÁNOSSY, A., Experimental Physics
KERTÉSZ, J., Physics
MIHÁLY, GY., Quantum Theory
MOLNÁR, E., Geometry
NAGY, B., Analysis
NOSZTICZIUS, Z., Chemical Physics
PETZ, D., Analysis
RICHTER, P., Atomic Physics
RÓNYAI, L., Algebra
SCHMIDT, T., Algebra
SZÁSZ, D., Stochastics
SZATMÁRY, Z., Nuclear Technology
TÓTH, B., Stochastics
VERHÁS, J., Chemical Physics
VIROSZTEK, A., Quantum Theory
ZAWADOWSKI, A., Physics

Faculty of Transportation Engineering (1111 Budapest, Bertalan L. u. 2; tel. (1) 463-3551; fax (1) 463-3550; e-mail felv@kma.bme.hu; internet www.bme.hu/en/organization/faculties/transportation/index.html):

BOKOR, J., Transport Automatics
ELEÖD, A., Machine Elements
KÖVES GILICZE, É., Transport Operation
KULCSÁR, B., Building and Materials-Handling Machines
MÁRIALIGETI, J., Machine Elements
PALKOVICS, L., Motor Vehicles
ROHÁCS, J., Aircraft and Ships
TAKÁCS, J., Machine Production Technology
TÁNCZOS, LNÉ., Transport Economics
TARNAI, G., Transport Automatics
VÁRLAKI, P., Motor Vehicles
ZOBORY, I., Railway Vehicles

Centre for Distance and Adult Learning (1111 Budapest, Egry J. u. 1; tel. (1) 463-3866; fax (1) 463-2561; e-mail info@bme-tk.bme.hu; internet www.bme-tk.bme.hu):

SZŰCS, A.

Centre of Information Studies (1111 Budapest, Műegyetem rkp. 7–9; tel. (1) 463-2421; fax (1) 463-2420; e-mail eiszk@mail.bme.hu; internet www.eik.bme.hu):

HELYBÉLI, Z.

Institute for Continuing Engineering Education (1111 Budapest, Műegyetem rkp. 9; tel. (1) 463-2471; fax (1) 463-2470; e-mail info@mti.bme.hu; internet www.mti.bme.hu):

GINSZTLER, J.

International Education Centre (1111 Budapest, Bertalan L. u. 2; tel. (1) 463-2461; fax (1) 463-2460; e-mail admission@tanok.bme.hu; internet www.tanok.bme.hu/home.ssi):

CSOPAKI, GY.

CENTRAL EUROPEAN UNIVERSITY

1051 Budapest, Nádor u. 9(1) 327-3000
Fax: (1) 327-3005
E-mail: main@ceu.hu
Internet: www.ceu.hu

Founded 1991
Private control
Language of instruction: English
Academic year: September to June

Postgraduate courses only

President and Rector: Prof. YEHUDA ELKANA
Academic Pro-Rector: Prof. LÁSZLÓ MÁTYÁS
Executive Vice-President: Dr ISTVÁN TEPLÁN

Library of 150,000 books, 1,500 periodicals
Number of teachers: 100
Number of students: 900

HEADS OF DEPARTMENTS AND PROGRAMMES

Economics: Prof. JACEK ROSTOWKI
Environmental Sciences and Policy: Prof. RUBEN MNATSAKANIAN
Gender and Culture: Prof. ALLAINE CERWONKA
History: Prof. LÁSZLÓ KONTLER
International Relations and European Studies: Prof. JULIUS HORVATH
Legal Studies: Prof. STEFAN MESSMANN
Mathematics: Prof. GHEORGE MOROSANU
Medieval Studies: Prof. JÓZSEF LASZLOVSZKY
Nationalism Studies: Prof. MÁRIA KOVÁCS
Philosophy: Prof. FERENC HUORANSZKI
Political Science: Prof. GÁBOR TÓKA
Sociology and Social Anthropology: Prof. AYSE CAGLAR
CEU Graduate School of Business: Dr FERENC PÁRTOS
Master of Public Policies Programmes: Prof. DIANE L. STONE

DEBRECENI EGYETEM
(University of Debrecen)

4010 Debrecen, Egyetem tér 1, POB 37
Telephone: (52) 512-900
Fax: (52) 310-007
E-mail: rector@admin.unideb.hu
Internet: www.unideb.hu

Founded 1538; became Kossuth Lajos Tudományegyetem (Lajos Kossuth University) 1912; present name 2000 upon integration with Debreceni Agrártudományi Egyetem (Debrecen University of Agricultural Sciences), Debreceni Orvostudományi Egyetem (University Medical School of Debrecen) and Wargha István Pedagógiai Főiskola (István Wargha College of Education)

State control
Languages of instruction: Hungarian, English
Academic year: September to June

Rector: Prof. Dr LÁSZLÓ IMRE
Vice-Rector (Academic Affairs): Dr LÁSZLÓ KOVÁCS
Vice-Rector (Educational Affairs): Dr JÁNOS NAGY
Vice-Rector (General Affairs): Dr KÁLMÁN GYŐRY
Vice-Rector (International Relations and University Advancement): Dr ZOLTÁN ABÁDI-NAGY
Vice-Rector (Strategic Affairs): Dr LÁSZLÓ FÉSÜS
Vice-Rector (Teacher Education): Dr JÓZSEF SZABÓ
Director for Policy of Social Affairs and Quality Management: Dr ÉVA BAKOSI
Senior Adviser to the Rector: Dr SÁNDOR NAGY
Registrar: ZSUZSA BORBÉLY
Director of Finance: ÁGNES HARSÁNYI
Director of Human Resources Management: Dr GYÖRGY NÁDAS
Director of the University and National Library: Dr MÁRTA VIRÁGOS

Library: Libraries with a total of 5,300,000 vols
Number of teachers: 1,638
Number of students: 25,888

Publications: *Acta Andragogiae* (annually), *Acta Classica* (annually), *Acta Debrecina* (annually), *Acta geographica ac geologica et meteorologica Debrecina* (annually), *Acta Neerlandica* (annually), *Acta pericemonologica rerum ambientum Debrecina* (irregular), *Acta Physica et Chimica* (annually), *A Debreceni Egyetem évkönyve* (annually), *A Debreceni Egyetem Magyar Nyelvtudományi Intézetének kiadványai* (annually), *Agrártudományi közlemények* (irregular), *Annual Report* (annually), *Collectio iuridica Universitatis Debreceniensis* (irregular), *Competitio* (4 a year), *Debreceni szemle* (4 a year), *Ethnica* (irregular), *English Programme Bulletin Dentistry* (annually), *English Programme Bulletin Faculty of Medicine* (annually), *Ethnographica Folcloristica Carpatica* (annually), *Folia Uralica Debreceniensia* (annually), *Gond* (4 a year), *Hungarian Journal of English and American Studies* (2 a year), *Italianistica Debreceniensis* (annually), *Journal of Agricultural Sciences* (irregular), *Kitaibelia* (2 a year), *Könyv és Könyvtár* (annually), *Magyar Nyelvjárások* (annually), *Módszerek és eljárások* (annually), *Ókortudományi Értesítő* (annually), *Poszbizánci Közlemények* (every 2 years), *Publ. Mathematicae* (2 a year), *Sprachteorie und Germanistiche Linguistik* (2 a year), *Studia Litteraria* (annually), *Studia Romanica* (linguistics, annually), *Studies in Linguistics* (annually), *Teaching Mathematics and Computer Science* (2 a year), *Történeti Tanulmányok* (irregular)

DEANS

Faculty of Agriculture: Dr P. PEPÓ
Faculty of Agronomics and Rural Development: Dr A. NÁBRÁDI
Faculty of Arts and Humanities: Dr E. BARTHA
Faculty of Dentistry: Dr ILDIKÓ MÁRTON
Faculty of Economics and Business Administration: Dr L. MURAKÖZY
Faculty of General Medicine: Dr A. BERTA
Faculty of Law: Dr BÉLA SZABÓ
Faculty of Pharmacy: Dr ÁRPÁD TÓSAKI
Faculty of Science: Dr GYÖRGY BORBÉLY

DIRECTORS

Hajdúböszörményi College Faculty of Education: Dr GY. VARGA (Dir-Gen.)
College Faculty of Engineering: Dr A. KŐSZEGHY (Dir-Gen.)
Faculty of Health College: Dr MIKLÓS OROSZ-TÓTH
Centre of Agricultural Sciences: Dr I. ERTSEY
Conservatory of Debrecen: M. DUFFEK
Experimental Farm and Regional Research Institute: GY. SZABÓ

Institute of Information Technology: Dr A. PETHŐ
Institute of Public Health: Dr R. ÁDÁNY
Medical and Health Science Centre: Dr L. FÉSÜS
Research and Experiment Institute: Dr T. KONCZ
Research Institute of Karcag: Dr L. BLASKÓ
Research Institute of Nyíregyháza: Dr S. TŐGYI

PROFESSORS

Faculty of Agriculture (4032 Debrecen, Böszörményi út 138; tel. (52) 414-329; fax (52) 347-596; e-mail pepopeter@fs2.date.hu):

BODÓ, I., Animal Husbandry, Breeding and Nutrition
CSIZMAZIA, Z., Agricultural Engineering
GUNDEL, J., Animal Husbandry, Breeding and Nutrition
GYŐRI, Z., Food Processing and Quality Control
HÓDOSSI, S., Horticulture
KÁTAI, J., Soil Science and Microbiology
LOCH, J., Agricultural Chemistry
MIHÓK, S., Animal Husbandry, Breeding and Nutrition
NAGY, J., Land Cultivation
PEPÓ, PÁL, Genetics and Plant Breeding
PEPÓ, PÉTER, Crop Production and Applied Ecology
PETHŐ, M., Agricultural Botany and Plant Physiology
RUZSÁNYI, L., Crop Production and Applied Ecology
SINÓROS SZABÓ, B., Land Cultivation
SZARUKÁN, I., Crop Production and Applied Ecology
THYLL, SZ., Water and Environmental Management

Faculty of Agroeconomics and Rural Development (4032 Debrecen, Böszörményi út 138; tel. (52) 414-329; fax (52) 347-596; e-mail csapone@helios.date.hu):

BÁNSZKI, T., Rural Development
BORSOS, J., Farm Business Management
ERTSEY, I., Economic Analysis and Statistics
KOZMA, A., Accounting and Finance
LAKATOS, D., Agricultural and General Economics
LAZÁNYI, J., Rural Development
NÁBRÁDI, A., Farm Business Management
NAGY, G., Rural Development
NAGY, T., Labour Science
NEMESSÁLYI, ZS., Farm Business Management
PALOTÁS, G., Nature Conservation, Zoology and Game Management
PFAU, E., Farm Business Management
SZABÓ, G., Agricultural and General Economics

Faculty of Arts and Humanities (tel. (52) 512-900 ext. 2701; fax (52) 412-336; e-mail nemesne@tigris.klte.hu):

ABÁDI-NAGY, Z., North American Studies
BARTA, J., Medieval and Early Modern World History
BARTHA, E., Ethnography
BITSKEY, I., Old Hungarian Literature
CZIGLER, I., General Psychology
GORILOVICS, T., French Language and Literature
GÖRÖMBEI, A., Modern Hungarian Language
GUNST, P., Modern and Contemporary World History
HALÁSZ, K., French Language and Literature
HAVAS, L., Classical Philology
HUNYADI, L., Applied Linguistics
IMRE, L., 19th-century Hungarian Literature
KERESZTES, L., Finno-Ugrian Linguistics
KERTÉSZ, A., German Linguistics
KLEIN, S., Psychology
KOZMA, T., Education
LŐKÖS, I., Comparative Literature
MOLNÁR, D. I., Polish Language and Literature
NÉMETH, GY., Ancient History
NOVÁK RÓZSA, E., History of Philosophy
NYIRKOS, I., Hungarian Linguistics
OROSZ, I., Medieval and Early Modern World History
POZSGAY, I., Political Science
SOLYMOSI, L., History
SZABÓ, L., Ethnography
TAXNER, E., Old Hungarian Literature
VAJDA, M., Philosophy
VIRÁGOS, ZS., North American Studies

Faculty of Dentistry (4012 Debrecen, Nagyerdei krt. 98; tel. (52) 417-571; fax (52) 419-807; e-mail angyal@fogaszat.dote.hu):

MÁRTON, I., Conservatory Dentistry
MÓDIS, L., Dental Anatomy

Faculty of Economics and Business Administration (4028 Debrecen, Kassai út 26; tel. (52) 416-580; fax (52) 419-728; e-mail mura@tigris.klte.hu):

CSABA, L., Economics
FÜLÖP, GY., Management and Marketing
HÁMORI, B., Economics
POLÓNYI, I., Management and Marketing
PRUGBERGER, T., Business Law
SZABÓ, K., Economics

Faculty of Law (4028 Debrecen, Kassai út 26; tel. (52) 512-900 ext. 7101; fax (52) 512-900 ext. 7105; e-mail jogszabe@gold.uni-miskolc.hu):

DÉNES, I. Z., Social Sciences
SZABADFALVI, J., Philosophy and Sociology of Law
SZABÓ, B., History of Law

Faculty of Medicine (4032 Debrecen, Nagyerdei krt. 94; tel. (52) 455-865; fax (52) 410-006; e-mail mfux@jaguar.dote.hu):

ANTAL, M., Anatomy, Histology and Embryology
BAKÓ, GY., Internal Medicine
BALÁZS, GY., Surgery
BALLA, GY., Neonatology
BARABÁS, GY., Human Genetics
BERECZKI, D., Neurology
BERTA, A., Ophthalmology
BÍRÓ, V., Traumatology and Hand Surgery
BODA, Z., Internal Medicine
BORSOS, A., Obstetrics and Gynaecology
BURIS, L., Forensic Medicine
CSÉCSEI, GY., Neurosurgery
CSIBA, L., Neurology
DAMJANOVICH, S., Biophysics and Cell Biology
DEGRELL, I., Psychiatry
DOMBRÁDI, V., Medical Chemistry
ÉDES, I., Cardiology
FACHET, J., Immunology
FÉSÜS, L., Biochemistry and Molecular Biology
FURKA, I., Operative Techniques and Surgical Research
GÁSPÁR, R., Biophysics and Cell Biology
GERGELY, L., Medical Microbiology
GERGELY, P., Medical Chemistry
GOMBA, SZ., Pathology
HEGEDŰS, K., Neurology
HERNÁDI, Z., Obstetrics and Gynaecology
HORKAY, I., Dermatology and Venereology
HUNYADI, J., Dermatology and Venereology
ILYÉS, J., Family Medicine
KAKUK, GY., Internal Medicine
KOVÁCS, L., Physiology
LUKÁCS, G., Surgery
MARÓDI, L., Paediatrics
MATESZ, K., Anatomy, Histology and Embryology
MECHLER, F., Neurology
MOLNÁR, P., Behavioural Sciences
MOLNÁR, P., Pathology
MUSZBEK, L., Clinical Biochemistry and Molecular Pathology
NÁNÁSI, P., Physiology
NEMES, Z., Pathology
OLÁH, É., Paediatrics
PARAGH, GY., Internal Medicine
PÉTER, M., Radiology
PÉTERFFY, Á., Cardiac Surgery
RAJNAVÖLGYI, S., Immunology
SÁPY, P., Surgery
SIPKA, S., Internal Medicine
SZABÓ, G., Biophysics and Cell Biology
SZEGEDI, GY., Internal Medicine
SZEPESI, K., Orthopaedics
SZIKLAI, I., Otolaryngology
SZILVÁSSY, Z., Pharmacology
SZÖLLŐSI, J., Biophysics and Cell Biology
SZŰCS, G., Physiology
TÓTH, CS., Urology
TÓTH, F., Microbiology
TÓTH, Z., Obstetrics and Gynaecology
TRÓN, L., Positron Emission Tomography Centre
UDVARDY, M., Internal Medicine
URAY, E., Anaesthesiology and Intensive Care
VARGA, S., Central Service Laboratory
WÓRUM, F., Internal Medicine
ZEHER, M., Internal Medicine
ZS. NAGY, I., Gerontology

Faculty of Pharmacy (fax (52) 416-490; e-mail tosaki@king.pharmacol.dote.hu):

KOVÁCS, P., Pharmacology
TÓSAKI, Á., Pharmacological Effects

Faculty of Science (tel. (52) 512-900 ext. 2358; fax (52) 310-936; e-mail labalogh@kltesrv.klte.hu):

ANTUS, S., Organic Chemistry
BÁNFALVI, G., Comparative Anatomy and Physiology
BAZSA, GY., Physical Chemistry
BEKE, D., Solid State Physics
BÓDI, B., Mathematics and Informatics
BORBÉLY, GY., Botany
BRINDZA, B., Mathematics and Informatics
BRÜCHNER, E., Inorganic and Analytical Chemistry
DARÓCZY, Z., Mathematics and Informatics
DÉVAI, GY., Ecology
DÖMÖSI, P., Mathematics and Informatics
FARKAS, E., Inorganic and Analytical Chemistry
GYŐRY, K., Mathematics and Informatics
JOÓ, F., Physical Chemistry
KERÉNYI, A., Applied Landscape Geography
KISS, Á. Z., Physics
KÓNYA, J., Isotope Applications
LIPTÁK, A., Biochemistry
LOSONCZI, L., Mathematics and Informatics
MAJOR, P., Mathematics and Informatics
NAGY, Á., Theoretical Physics
PÁLES, ZS., Mathematics and Informatics
PÁLINKÁS, J., Experimental Physics
PAP, GY., Mathematics and Informatics
PETHŐ, A., Mathematics and Informatics
RUZSA, I., Mathematics and Informatics
SAILER, K., Theoretical Physics
SIPICZKI, M., Genetics and Molecular Biology
SÓVÁGÓ, I., Inorganic and Analytical Chemistry
STOYAN, G., Mathematics and Informatics
SÜLI-ZAKAR, I., Social Geography and Regional Development
SZABÓ, J., Physical Geography
SZÉKELYHIDI, L., Mathematics and Informatics
SZILÁGYI, L., Organic Chemistry
SZŐŐR, GY., Mineralogy and Geology
TÓTHMERÉSZ, B., Ecology
TRÓCSÁNYI, Z., Experimental Physics
VARGA, V., Zoology

VARGA, Z., Evolutionary Zoology and Human Biology
ZSUGA, M., Applied Chemistry

Conservatory (4032 Debrecen, Egyetem tér 2; tel. (52) 411-226; fax (52) 411-226; e-mail adamk@dragon.klte.hu):

ÁDÁM, K., Stringed Instruments
KAMMERER, A., Brass and Percussion
KEDVES, T., Stringed Instruments
KISS, V. P., Stringed Instruments
KÖKÉNYESSY, M., Stringed Instruments
MATÚZ, I., Woodwind
SZESZTAY, ZS., Music Theory, Choir Conducting

Hajdúböszörményi College Faculty of Education (4220 Hajdúböszörmény, Désány I u. 1–9; tel. (52) 229-433; fax (52) 229-559; e-mail TIT8003@helka.iif.hu):

BAKOSI, É., Children's Education
FRÁTER, K., Children's Education
KÖVÉR, I., Children's Education
VARGA, GY., Social Studies

College Faculty of Engineering (4028 Debrecen, Ótemető u. 2/4; tel. (52) 415-155; fax (52) 417-979; e-mail kati@infosrv.tech.klte.hu):

BÁRSONY, I., Mechanical and Maintenance Engineering
EGRI, I., General and Management Training
HOMMONNAI, GY., Engineering
HORVÁTH, R., Chemical Engineering
IBRAHIM, M., General and Management Training
KŐSZEGHI, A., Settlement Engineering
KULCSÁR, A., Construction Industry
NAGY, G., General Machinery
POKRÁDI, L., General Machinery
TIBA, ZS., General Machinery

Faculty of Health College (4400 Nyíregyháza, Sóstói út 2; tel. (42) 404-403; fax (42) 408-656; e-mail sztunde@creative.doteefk.hu):

CSELÉNYI, I., Applied Public Health Sociology
GÓTH, L., Labour Analysis and Clinical Diagnostics
KALAPOS, I., Preventive Medicine for District Nurses
LUKÁCSKÓ, ZS., Social Work
OROSZ TÓTH, M., Preventive Medicine for District Nurses

Farm and Regional Research Institute (4032 Debrecen, Böszörményi út 138; tel. (52) 347-888; fax (52) 413-385; e-mail csapone@helios.date.hu):

GONDA, I., Horticulture

Institute of Information Technology:

GISPERT, S.
MAJOR, P.
PAP, G.
PETHŐ, A.

School of Public Health (4028 Debrecen, Kassai út 26; tel. (52) 460-194; fax (52) 460-195; e-mail bardos@jaguar.dote.hu):

ÁDÁNY, R., Hygiene and Epidemiology

ATTACHED INSTITUTES

Ferenc Kölcsey Calvinist Teachers' Training College: Dir-Gen. Dr PÉTER CSORBA.

Nuclear Research Institute of the Hungarian: see entry under Research Institutes.

University of Reformed Theology: see separate entry under Other Colleges.

EÖTVÖS LORÁND TUDOMÁNYEGYETEM
(Loránd Eötvös University)

1056 Budapest, Egyetem tér 1–3, POB 109
Telephone: (1) 411-6500
Fax: (1) 411-6712
Internet: www.elte.hu
Founded 1635
State control
Academic year: September to June (two terms)

Rector: Dr ISTVÁN KLINGHAMMER
Pro-Rector: Dr LAJOS IZSÁK
Pro-Rector (Education and Scientific Affairs): Dr FERENC HUDECZ
Pro-Rector (International Affairs): Dr LÁSZLÓ BOROS
Secretary-General: Dr GYÖRGY RÁK
Head Librarian: Dr LÁSZLÓ SZÖGI

Library: see Libraries and Archives
Number of teachers: 1,820
Number of students: 32,486

Publications: *Acta Facultatis Politico-iuridicae Universitatis Scientiarum Budapestinensis*, *Annales* (geological, juridical and geological series, annually)

DEANS

Faculty of Arts: Dr KÁROLY MANHERZ
Faculty of Elementary and Nursery Teacher's Training: Dr ISTVÁN HORTOBÁGYI
Faculty of Informatics: Dr LÁSZLÓ KOZMA
Faculty of Law and Political Science: Dr BARNA MEZEY
Faculty of Pedagogy and Psychology: Dr GYÖRGY HUNYADY
Faculty of Science: Dr FERENC LÁNG
Faculty of Social Sciences: Dr TAMÁS RUDAS
Faculty of Special Education: Dr GYÖRGY KÖNCZEI

PROFESSORS

Faculty of Arts (1088 Budapest, Múzeum körút 4/a):

ADAMIK, T., Latin Language and Literature
BALÁZS, G., Linguistics
BALOGH, A., Modern World History
BANCZEROWSKI, J., Polish Language and Literature
BÁRDOSI, V., Romance Studies
BENCE, GY., Ethics and Social Philosophy
BERTÉNYI, I., Medieval and Early Modern Hungarian History
BÍRÓ, F., 18th- and 19th-Century Hungarian Literature
DÁVID, G., Oriental Studies
DOMOKOS, P., Finno-Ugric Linguistics
ERDÉLYI, Á., Philosophy
FODOR, S., Semitic Philology and Arabic Studies
GAÁL, E., Egyptology
GÉHER, I., English
GERGELY, A., History
GERGELY, J., Modern and Contemporary Hungarian History
GERŐ, A., Economic and Social History
GIAMPAOLO, S., Romance Studies
GLATZ, F., Historical Auxiliary Sciences
GYIVICSÁN, A., Slavonic Studies
GÓSY, M., Linguistics
GRANASZTÓI, G., Romance Studies
HESSKY, P., German Linguistics
HORVÁTH, I., Old Hungarian Literature
JEREMIÁS, E., Oriental Studies
KARDOS, J., History
KARA, GY., Central Asian Studies
KARDOS, J., Historical Auxiliary Sciences
KELEMEN, J., Ethics and Social Philosophy
KÉLÉNYI, G., History of Art
KENYERES, Z., Modern Hungarian Literature
KESZLER, B., Contemporary Hungarian Linguistics
KISS, J., Hungarian Historical Linguistics and Dialectology
KLAUDY, K., Linguistics
KNIPF, E., German
KOMORÓCZY, G., Assyriology and Hebrew Studies
KÓSA, L., Cultural History
KOVÁCS, A., Slavonic Studies
KOVÁCS, S. I., Old Hungarian Literature
KÖVECSES, Z., English
KRAUSZ, T., History
KULCSÁR SZABÓ, E., Comparative Literature
LUDASSY, M., Ethics and Social Philosophy
LUFT, U., Egyptology
MANHERZ, K., Germanic Linguistics
MAROSI, E., Art History
MASÁT, A., Scandinavian Languages and Literature.
MEDGYES, P., English Teacher Training
MISKOLCZY, A., Romance Studies
NÉMETH, G., History
NYOMÁRKAY, I., Slavic Philology
OROSZ, M., German
PALÁDI-KOVÁCS, A., Ethnography
PALOTÁS, E., East European History
PASSUTH, K., Art History
PÉTER, M., Eastern Slavonic and Baltic Philology
PROKOPP, M., History of Art
PUSKÁS, I., History
RACZKY, P., Archaeology
RADNÓTI, S., Aesthetics
ROMSICS, I., Modern and Contemporary Hungarian History
RÓNAY, L., Modern Hungarian Literature
SIPOS, L., Literary History
SOLYMOSI, L., History
STEIGER, K., Philosophy
SZABICS, I., French Language and Literature
SZABÓ, K., Medieval World History
SZABÓ, M., Classical Archaeology
SZÁVAI, J., Comparative and World Literature
SZEGEDY-MASZÁK, M., Comparative Literature
SZÉKELY, G., History
SZVÁK, G., History
TOLCSVAI, N. G., Linguistics
TÓTH, B., Romance Studies
TVERDOTA, G., Literary History
VARGA, L., English
VARGYAI, GY., Historical Auxiliary Sciences
VÁSÁRI, I., Turkish Studies
VOIGT, V., Folklore
VÖRÖS, I., French Language and Literature

Faculty of Law (1053 Budapest, Egyetem tér 1–3):

BIHARI, M., Political Science
BÖHM, A., Political Science
BURJÁN, L., International Law
ERDEI, Á., Criminal Procedural Law
FICZERE, L., Public Administration Law
FÖLDESI, T., Philosophy
FÖLDI, A., Roman Law
GÖNCZÖL, K., Criminology
HAMZA, G., Roman Law
HARMATHY, A., Civil Law
HORVÁTH, P., Universal Legal and Political History
KARÁCSONY, A., Philosophy
KÖRÖSNYI, A., Political Science
KUKORELLI, I., Constitutional Law
LENKOVITS, B., Civil Law
LÉVAY, M., Criminology
LÓRINCZ, L., Public Administration Law
MEZEI, B., Universal Legal and Political History
PACSOLAY, P., Political Science
PÁNDI, G., Public Administration Law
POKOL, B., Political Science
SÁJO, A., Civil Law
SÁRI, J., Constitutional Law
SCHLETT, I., Political Science
STUMPF, I., Political Science
SZABÓ, MÁRTON, Political Science
SZABÓ, MÁTÉ, Political Science
SZILÁGYI, P., Theory of Law
TAMÁS, A., Theory of Law
VALKI, L., International Law

VÉKÁS, L., Civil Law

Faculty of Science (1088 Budapest, Rákoczi út 5):

BERCZIK, Á., Systematic Zoology and Ecology
BODZSÁR, É., Biology
BÖDDI, B., Biology
CSÁNYI, V., Behaviour Genetics
CSIKOR, F., Theoretical Physics
DEMETROVICS, J., Information Systems
DÉTÁRI, L., Biology
DÓZSA-FARKAS, K., Biology
ERDEI, A., Immunology
FARSANG, GY., Inorganic and Analytical Chemistry
FODOR, Z., Theoretical Physics
FRANK, A., Operational Research
GALÁCZ, A., Palaeontology
GERE, G., Biology
GESZTI, T., Physics of Complex Systems
GRÁF, L., Biochemistry
GYENIS, G., Biology
GYURJÁN, I., Plant Anatomy
HEGYI, G., Biology
HORVÁTH, Z., Theoretical Physics
KISS, Á., Atomic Physics
KISS, E., Mathematics
KOMJÁTH, P., Computer Science
KONDOR, I., Physics of Complex Systems
KOVÁCS, J., Biology
KÜRTI, J., Physics
LACZKOVICH, M., Analysis
LÁNG, F., Biology
LENDVAI, J., General Physics
LOVÁSZ, L., Computer Science
NAGY, D. L., Atomic Physics
ORMOS, P., Physics
OROSZ, L., Biology
PÁLFY, P., Algebra and Number Theory
PALLA, L., Theoretical Physics
PATKÓS, A., Atomic Physics
PODANI, J., Biology
POLONYI, J., Atomic Physics
SÁRMAY, G., Immunology
SASS, M., General Zoology
SZABÓ, K., Physical Chemistry
SZALAY, S., Atomic Physics
SZATHMÁRI, E., Plant Taxonomy and Ecology
SZIGETI, Z., Biology
TÉL, T., Theoretical Physics
TICHY, G., Solid State Physics
UNGÁR, T., General Physics
VESZTERGOMBI, G., Physics
VICSEK, T., Biological Physics
VINCZE, I., Physics
ZÁVODSZKÝ, P., Biological Physics

Institute and Postgraduate Centre for Sociology and Social Policy (1088 Budapest, Pollack Mihály tér 10):

ANGELUSZ, R., Sociology
CSEPELI, GY., Social Psychology
FERGE, ZS., Social Policy
HUSZÁR, T., Historical Sociology
NÉMEDI, D., Social Theory
PATAKI, F., Social Psychology
SOMLAI, P., Social Theory

Teacher-Training Faculty (1075 Budapest, Kazinczy u. 23–27):

CS. VARGA, I., Hungarian Language and Literature
DEMETER, J., Hungarian Language and Literature
DRUZSIN, F., Hungarian Language and Literature
DUKKON, Á., Hungarian Language and Literature
ESTÓK, J., History
FRIED, I., Italian Language and Literature
GAIZER, F., Chemistry
GÖDÉNY, E., Hungarian Language and Literature
GRÉTSY, L., Hungarian Linguistics
HAJDU, P., Social Theory
HEGYVÁRI, N., Mathematics
HELTAI, P., English
HORVÁTH, G., Geography
JÁSZÓ, A., Hungarian Linguistics
MADARÁSZ, I., Hungarian Linguistics
MILKOVITS, I., Biology
NÉMETH, A., Educational Science
SALAMON, K., History
SAPSZON, F., Music
SIPOSNÉ-JÁGER, K., Biology
UZONYI, P., German
ZÁVODSKY, G., History
ZIRKULI, P., French Language and Literature

ATTACHED INSTITUTE

Biological Research Station.

Botanical Garden: Dir Dr ISTVÁN ISÉPI.

Centre for Foreign Languages.

Centre Universitaire d'Etudes Françaises: Dir Dr JUDIT KARAFIÁTH.

European Educational Centre: Dir Dr LÁSZLÓ BOROS.

Gothard Astrophysical Observatory.

Postgraduate Institute of Law and Political Science: 1053 Budapest, Egyetem tér 1–3; Dir Dr REZSŐ HÁRSFALVI.

KAPOSVÁRI EGYETEM (University of Kaposvár)

7401 Kaposvár, Guba Sándor u. 40
Telephone: (82) 412-613
Fax: (82) 320-175
Internet: www.u-kaposvar.hu

Founded 2000 from Faculty of Animal Husbandry of Pannon Agrártudományi Egyetem (Pannon University of Agricultural Sciences) and Csokonai Vitéz Mihály Teacher-Training College
State control
Language of instruction: Hungarian
Academic year: September to June

Rector: Prof. PÉTER HORN

Number of teachers: 150
Number of students: 2,643

Publication: *Acta Agraria Kaposváriensis* (4 a year)

DEANS

Faculty of Animal Science: Prof. JENŐ PAÁL
Csokonai Vitéz Mihály College Faculty of Teacher-Training: SÁNDOR LEITNER

PROFESSORS

Faculty of Animal Science:

BABINSZKY, L., Animal Nutrition
BOGENFÜRST, F., Poultry Breeding
CSAPÓ, J., Biochemistry
DÉR, F., Plant Production
GYENIS, J., Process Engineering
HECKER, W., Academy of Equitation
HORN, P., Pig Production
HORVÁTH, GY., Social Sciences
KOVÁCS, M., Physiology and Animal Hygiene
PAÁL, J., Mathematics and Computer Science
REPA, I., Digital Imaging, Radiology
SARUDI, J., Chemistry and Biochemistry
STEFLER, J., Cattle Production
SZAKÁLY, S., Food Science
SZÉLES, GY., Farm Economics
SZENDRŐ, ZS., Animal Breeding
TAKÁTSY, T., Agricultural Engineering

LISZT FERENC ZENEMŰVÉSZETI EGYETEM (Ferenc Liszt Academy of Music (State University))

1391 Budapest, POB 206, Liszt Ferenc tér 8
Telephone: (1) 462-4600
Fax: (1) 462-4648
Internet: www.liszt.hu

Founded 1875
State control
Academic year: September to June

Rector: Dr ANDRÁS BATTA
Vice-Rector: Prof. LÁSZLO TIHANYI
Librarian: Dr. J. KÁRPÁTI

Library of 187,000 vols
Number of teachers: 158
Number of students: 767

HEADS OF DEPARTMENTS

Chamber Music: M. GULYÁS
Church Music: J. SZENDREY
Composition: Z. JENEY
Foreign Language Faculty: Á. SIMON
Keyboard Instruments and Harp: Prof. I. LANTOS
Musicology: Prof. T. TALLIÁN
Music Theory: Dr K. KOMLÓS
Secondary School Singing Teachers and Choir Conductors: É. KOLLÁR
Singing and Opera: É. ANDOR
Stringed Instruments: A. KISS
Wind Instruments and Percussion: Prof. G. HŐHNA

ATTACHED INSTITUTES

Bartók Béla Zeneművészeti Szakközépiskola és Gimnázium (Béla Bartók Conservatory of Music and Secondary School): 1065 Budapest, Nagymező u.1; Dir T. SZABÓ.

Budapesti Tanárképző Intézet (Teacher Training Institute in Budapest): 1052 Budapest, Semmelweiss u. 12; Dir Prof. LEHEL BOTH.

MAGYAR IPARMŰVÉSZETI EGYETEM (Hungarian University of Craft and Design)

1121 Budapest, Zugligeti út 11–25
Telephone: (1) 392-1180
Fax: (1) 392-1188
E-mail: rektori@mie.mie.hu
Internet: www.mif.hu

Founded 1880, present status 1985
State control
Academic year: September to June

Rector: Prof. JUDIT DROPPA
Vice-Rectors: Prof. GÁBOR KOPEK, Prof. PÉTER REIMHOLZ
General Secretary: Dr SÁNDOR BANKÓ
Librarian: KLÁRA LÉVAI

Library of 42,000 vols
Number of teachers: 98
Number of students: 570

Publications: *Kék Ég* (4 a year), *Diploma* (annually)

DIRECTORS OF INSTITUTES AND HEADS OF DEPARTMENTS

Institute of Foundation Studies: Prof. JÓZSEF SCHERER
Institute of Humanities: Prof. GYULA ERNYEY
Institute for Manager Training: Prof. Dr ÁGNES KAPITÁNY
Department of Architecture: Prof. GÁBOR TURÁNYI
Department of Education: Prof. EMIL GAUL
Department of Product Design: Prof. STEFAN LENGYEL
Department of Silicate Design: Prof. ÉVA KÁDASI
Department of Textile Design: Prof. CSABA POLGÁR
Department of Visual Communication: Prof. GYULA MOLNÁR

MAGYAR KÉPZŐMŰVÉSZETI FŐISKOLA (University of Fine Arts)

1062 Budapest, Andrássy út 69–71
Telephone: (1) 342-1738
Fax: (1) 342-1563
E-mail: rektor@mke.hu
Internet: www.mke.hu

Founded 1871

Rector: JÁNOS WELSCH
Vice-Rector: KÁLMÁN MOLNÁR
International Affairs: RITA ROMÁN
Librarian: KATALIN BLASKÓ

Library of 47,500 vols
Number of teachers: 134
Number of students: 552

PROFESSORS

FARKAS, Á., Sculpture
KOCSIS, I., Graphic Art
MENRÁTH, P., Restoration
MOLNÁR, K., Applied Graphic Art
NAGY, G., Painting
PETERNÁK, M., Multimedia Studies
SZABADI, J., Art History
SZÉKELY, L., Stage and Costume Design
TÖLG-MOLNÁR, Z., Painting

MAGYAR TÁNCMŰVÉSZETI FŐISKOLA (Hungarian Dance Academy)

1372 Budapest, POB 439
Telephone: (1) 273-3434
Fax: (1) 273-3433
E-mail: info@mtf.hu
Internet: www.mtf.hu

Founded 1950
Academic year: September to June

Director: IMRE DÓZSA

Library of 19,000 vols
Number of teachers: 109
Number of students: 930.

MISKOLCI EGYETEM (University of Miskolc)

3515 Miskolc-Egyetemváros
Telephone: (46) 565-111
Fax: (46) 565-014
E-mail: stbes@uni-miskolc.hu
Internet: www.uni-miskolc.hu

Founded 1735 in Selmecbánya, Academy status 1770; moved 1919 to Sopron; reorganized 1949 in Miskolc
State control
Languages of instruction: Hungarian, Englishfor foreign students
Academic year: September to June

Rector: Prof. LAJOS BESENYEI
Vice-Rector (Educational Affairs): Prof. GYÖRGY BÍRÓ
Vice-Rector (General Affairs): Prof. GYULA PATKÓ
Vice-Rector (International Relations): Prof. ALADÁR NAGY
Vice-Rector (Scientific Affairs): Prof. MIHÁLY DOBRÓKA
Secretary-General: VIKTOR KOVÁCS
Librarian: Dr L. ZSÁMBOKI

Number of teachers: 920
Number of students: 13,571

Publications: *Évkönyv* (yearbook), *Miskolci Egyetem Közleményei* (papers in Hungarian, irregular), *Publications of the University of Miskolc* (papers in German, English and Russian, irregular)

DEANS

Faculty of Arts: Dr J. BESSENYEI
Faculty of Earth Sciences Engineering: Dr J. BŐHM
Faculty of Economics: Dr I. SZINTAY
Faculty of Law: Dr M. SZABÓ
Faculty of Materials Science and Engineering: Dr GY. KAPTAY
Faculty of Mechanical Engineering: Dr A. DÖBRÖCZÖNI

HEADS OF DEPARTMENT AND PROFESSORS

Faculty of Arts (tel. (46) 565-211; fax (46) 563-459; e-mail boleborb@uni-miskolc.hu; internet www.bolcsweb.hu):

ANDRIK-HELL, J., Philosophy
BAÁN, I., Medieval and Early Modern Hungarian History and Associated Sciences of History
BESSENYEI, J., Medieval and Early Modern Hungarian History and Associated Sciences of History
CZÖVEK, I., World History
DOMÁNSZKY, G., Comparative Literature and Cultural History
FERENCZI, L., Literature of the Enlightenment, Romanticism and Regional History
FORRAI, G., History of Philosophy
FÜLÖP, ZS., English Literature
FURMAN-PANKUCSI, M., Sociology
GYAPAY, L., Literature of the Enlightenment, Romanticism and Regional History
GYULAI, É, Cultural History and Museology
HELTAI, J., Old Hungarian Literature
HORVÁTH, E., World History
ILLÉS-KOVÁCS, M., Hungarian Linguistics
KABDEBÓ, L., Contemporary Hungarian Literature
KLAUDY, K., Applied Linguistics
KOTICS, J., Cultural and Visual Anthropology
MOLNÁR, I., German Literature
Ö. KOVÁCS, J., Modern Hungarian History
PETHŐ, S., Classical Philology and Religion
PETNEKI, Á., Central European Literature and Culture
RINGER, Á., Prehistory and Antiquity
SALÁNKI, A., German Linguistics
SIMIG-FENYŐ, S., Applied Linguistics
SIMON, J., Political Science
SZIGETI, J., Central European Literature and Culture
SZILI-JUHÁSZ, E., Contemporary Hungarian Literature
VÁRADI, T., English Linguistics

Faculty of Earth Sciences Engineering (tel. (46) 565-051; fax (46) 563-465; e-mail rekbdhiv@uni-miskolc.hu; internet www.uni-miskolc.hu/~mfk):

BOBOK, E., Natural Gas Engineering
BŐHM, J., Environmental Management
BUÓCZ, Z., Mining and Geotechnology
CSETE, J., Natural Gas Engineering
CSŐKE, B., Process Engineering
DOBRÓKA, M., Geophysics
FÖLDESSY, J., Geology and Mineral Resources
GYULAI, Á., Geophysics
HAHN, GY., Human Geography
HAVASI, I., Geodesy and Mine Surveying
HEVESI, A., Geography and Environmental Sciences
KOCSIS, K., Human Geography
KOVÁCS, F., Mining and Geotechnology
LAKATOS, I., Mining Chemistry
PÁPAY, I., Petroleum Engineering
SOMOSVÁRI, ZS., Mining and Geotechnology
SZABÓ, I., Hydrogeology and Engineering Geology
SZAKÁLL, S., Mineralogy
TAKÁCS, G., Petroleum Engineering
TIHANYI, L., Natural Gas Engineering
VŐNEKI, GY., Equipment for Geotechnology

Faculty of Economics (tel. (46) 565-190; fax (46) 563-471; e-mail gazddek@uni-miskolc.hu; internet www.gtk.uni-miskolc.hu):

BESENYEI, L., Business Statistics and Forecasting
BOZSIK, S., Finance
CZABÁN, J., Business Economics
DANKÓ, L., International Marketing
FEKETE, I., Human Resources
ILLÉS, M., Business Economics
KOCZISZKY, GY., Regional Economics
NAGY, A., Economic Theory
PÁL, T., Accounting
PELCZ-GÁLL, I., Entrepreneurship
PISKÓTI, I., Marketing Strategy and Communication
SZAKÁLY, D., Innovation and Technology Management
SZINTAY, I., Management
SZILÁGYI, D., World Economy and Comparative Economics
VERES-SOMOSI, M., Organizational Behaviour

Faculty of Law (tel. (46) 565-170; fax (46) 367-933; e-mail rekrat@uni-miskolc.hu; internet www.uni-miskolc.hu/law):

BIRÓ, GY., Civil Law
BRAGYOVA, A., Constitutional Law
CSÁK, CS., Labour Law and Agricultural Law
FARKAS, Á., Criminal Procedural Law and Law Enforcement
FEHÉR, L., Criminal Law and Criminology
GÖRGÉNYI, I., Criminal Law and Criminology
KALAS, T., Administrative Law
KOVÁCS, P., International Law
LÉVAY, M., Criminal Law and Criminology
LÉVAY-FAZEKAS, J., European and International Private Law
MISKOLCZI BODNÁR, P., Commercial Law
PÁSZTOR-ERDŐS, É., Financial Law
PÉTER, O., Roman Law
PETROVICH-WOPERA, ZS., Civil Procedural Law
PRUGBERGER, T., Labour Law and Agricultural Law
STIPTA, I., Legal History
SZABADFALVI, J., Legal Theory and Legal Sociology
SZABÓ, B., Roman Law
SZABÓ, M., Legal Theory and Legal Sociology
TORMA, A., Administrative Law

Faculty of Materials Science and Engineering Science (tel. (46) 565-090; fax (46) 565-408; e-mail rekkdzbm@uni-miskolc.hu; internet www.akk.uni-miskolc.hu):

BÁRÁNY, S., Chemistry
BÁRCZY, P., Polymer Engineering
GÖMZE, A. L., Ceramics and Silicate Engineering
KAPROS, T., Energy Utilization
KAPTAY, GY., Chemistry
KÁROLY, GY., Metallurgical and Foundry Engineering
KOVÁCS, K., Quality Assurance
KOVÁCS, K., Chemistry
PALOTÁS, A. B., Combustion Technology and Thermal Energy
ROÓSZ, A., Physical Metallurgy

Faculty of Mechanical Engineering (tel. (46) 565-131; fax (46) 563-453; e-mail gkdh3@uni-miskolc.hu; internet gepesz.uni-miskolc.hu):

ÁDÁM, T., Automation
AJTONYI, I., Automation
BALLA, K., Mathematical Analysis
CSELÉNYI, J., Materials Handling and Logistics
CSER, L., Information Engineering
DÖBRÖCZÖNI, Á., Machine Elements
DUDÁS, I., Production Engineering
FEGYVERNEKI, S., Applied Mathematics

GALÁNTAI, A., Applied Mathematics
ILLÉS, B., Materials Handling and Logistics
JÁRMAI, K., Materials Handling and Logistics
JUHÁSZ, I., Descriptive Geometry
KACSUK, P., Automation
KOVÁCS, E., Electrotechnology and Electronics
KUNDRÁK, J., Production Engineering
LUKÁCS, J., Mechanical Technology
ORTUTAY, M., Chemical Machinery
PÁCZELT, I., Mechanics
PARIPÁS, B., Physics
PATKÓ, GY., Machine Tools
RONTÓ, M., Mathematical Analysis
SZABÓ, SZ., Heat and Fluid Engineering
SZEIDL, GY., Mechanics
SZIGETI, J., Mathematical Analysis
TISZA, M., Mechanical Technology
TÓTH, L., Mechanical Technology
TÓTH, T., Information Engineering
VADÁSZ, D., Information Technology

ASSOCIATE INSTITUTES

Bela Bartók Music Institute: 3530 Miskolc, Bartók tér 1; Dir Dr SÁNDOR KOVÁCS.

Comenius Teachers' Training College: 3950 Sárospatak, Eötvös u. 7; Dir LÁSZLÓ HEGEDÜS.

Faculty of Health Care Studies: 3508 Miskolc, Mész u. 1; Dir Dr MÁRTA PEJA.

Research Institute of Applied Chemistry: 3515 Miskolc, Pf. 2; Dir Dr ISTVÁN LAKATOS.

NYUGAT-MAGYARORSZÁGI EGYETEM (University of West Hungary)

9400 Sopron, Bajcsy-Zs. u. 4
Telephone: (99) 518-100
Fax: (99) 311-103
E-mail: rectoro@nyme.hu
Internet: www.nyme.hu

Founded 2000 upon merger of Soproni Egyetem (University of Sopron, f. 1762 as Academy of Mining and Forestry), Mosonmagyaróvár Faculty of Agriculture (f. 1818) of Pannon Agrártudományi Egyetem (Pannon University of Agricultural Sciences), Apáczai Csere János Teacher Training College (f. 1778), and Benedek Elek College of Education (f. 1959)
State control
Language of instruction: Hungarian
Academic year: September to June

Rector: Prof. Dr SÁNDOR FARAGÓ
Pro-Rectors: Prof. Dr KÁROLY MÉSZÁROS, Prof. Dr RESZŐ SCHMIDT, Prof. Dr PÉTER TAKÁTS
Economic Director: LÁSZLÓ HERCZEG
Administrative Officer: Dr MÁRIA MERÉNYI
Librarian: Dr SÁNDOR SARKADY, Jr

Library of 380,000 vols
Number of teachers: 618
Number of students: 12,570

Publications: *Acta Agronomica Ovariensis* (in German and English, 2 a year), *Acta Facultatis Forestalis* (in German and English), *Acta Facultatis Ligniensis* (in German and English), *Apáczai Csere János Tanítóképző Főiskolai Kar Tanulmánykötet* (in Hungarian, annually), *Benedek Elek Pedagógiai Főiskolai Kar Tudomány napja* (in Hungarian, annually), *Erdészeti Tallózó* (in Hungarian, monthly), *Faipar* (Wood Science, in Hungarian with English summary, 5 a year), *Magyar Apróvad Közlemények* (Hungarian Small Game Bulletin, in Hungarian and English, 1 or 2 a year), *Magyar Vízivad Közlemények* (Hungarian Waterfowl Publication, in Hungarian and English, 1 or 2 a year), *Tilia* (in Hungarian, 1 or 2 a year)

DEANS AND DIRECTORS

Faculty of Agricultural Sciences: Dr VINCE ÖRDÖG
Faculty of Economic Sciences: Prof. Dr ERZSÉBET GIDAI
Faculty of Forestry: Prof. Dr KÁROLY MÉSZÁROS
Faculty of Wood Sciences: Prof. Dr SÁNDOR MOLNÁR
Benedek Elek College of Education: Dr ERZSÉBET ALPÁRNÉ SZÁLA
College of Geoinformatics: Dr BÉLA MÁRKUS
Apáczai Csere János Teacher-Training College: Dr SÁNDOR CSEH

DIRECTORS OF INSTITUTES

Faculty of Agricultural and Food Sciences (9200 Mosonmagyaróvár, Vár 2; tel. (96) 566-637; fax (96) 566-620; e-mail ordogvin@mtk.nyme.hu; internet www.mtk.nyme.hu):

Institute of Agricultural Economics and Social Sciences:
Agricultural Economics and Marketing: Dr TAMÁS SÁNTHA
Social Sciences: Prof. Dr ISTVÁN SZABÓ

Institute of Agricultural, Food and Environmental Engineering:
Biological and Environmental Engineering: Prof. Dr KÁROLY KACZ
Food Process Engineering and Environmental Techniques: Prof. Dr MIKLÓS NEMÉNYI

Institute of Animal Breeding Husbandry:
Cattle- and Sheep-breeding: Dr ERNŐ BÁDER
General Animal Husbandry: Dr LÁSZLÓ GULYÁS
Poultry- and Pig-breeding: Prof. Dr KATALIN GAÁL

Institute of Biological and Environmental Sciences:
Animal Health: Prof. Dr BORISZ EGRI
Botany: Prof. Dr ÁKOS MÁTHÉ
Soil Science and Water Management: Prof. Dr MIHÁLY SZŰCS
Zoology: Prof. Dr PÁL BENEDEK

Institute of Crop Sciences:
Crop Production: Prof. Dr KÁROLY POCSAI
Genetics and Plant Breeding: Dr JÓZSEF KISS
Plant Physiology and Plant Biotechnology: Prof. Dr VINCE ÖRDÖG
Soil Management: Prof. Dr RESZŐ SCHMIDT

Institute of Farm Business Management:
Farm Management: Prof. Dr LAJOS SALAMON
Accountancy and Financial Management: Prof. Dr BARNABÁS REKE
Statistics and Economic Information Management: Dr RÓZSA CSATAI

Institute of Food Sciences:
Food Technology and Microbiology: Prof. Dr JENŐ SZIGETI
Food Quality Assurance: Dr ZSOLT AJTONY
Dairying Science: Dr LÁSZLÓ VARGA

Institute of Management and Labour Sciences:
Labour Organization and Production Techniques: Dr JÓZSEF ORBÁN
Management and Organizational Development: Dr LEONA MORVAY

Departments not within an Institute:
Animal Nutrition: B. KISS, Dr GERTRÚD KELEMEN
Animal Physiology and Biotechnology: Dr ELEMÉR GERGÁCZ
Chemistry: Prof. Dr PÁL SZAKÁL
EU Educational Centre: Prof. Dr FRIGYES NAGY
Foreign Languages: JÓZSEF OLÁH
Horticulture: Dr JÓZSEF IVÁNCSICS
Mathematics and Physics: Dr OTTÓ DÓKA
Physical Training: MIHÁLY MÉSZÁROS
Plant Protection: Prof. Dr PÉTER REISINGER

Faculty of Economic Sciences (9400 Sopron, Ady E. u. 5; tel. (99) 518-257; fax (99) 518-257; e-mail ecoman@ktk.nyme.hu; internet ktk.nyme.hu):

Institute of Applied Economics:
Business Economics: Dr FERENC TÓTH
Business Studies: Dr CHAUDHURI SUJIT
Sectoral Economics: Dr LAJOS JUHÁSZ

Institute of Applied Mathematics and Statistics:
Applied Mathematics: Dr JÓZSEF ZÁVOTI
Statistics: Dr LASZLÓ SZALAY

Institute of Business Informatics:
Applied Business Informatics: (vacant): Dr ISTVÁN SZŰTS
Theoretical Business Informatics: Dr ATTILA KOVÁCS

Institute of Economics:
Economic Policy and Collective Management: Dr EMESE ÉGETŐ
Economics: Prof. Dr ERZSÉBET GIDAI
International and Comparative Economics: Dr ATTILA FÁBIÁN

Institute of Finance and Accounting:
Accounting: Dr LÁSZLÓ NYIKOS
Finance: Dr CSABA LENTNER

Institute of Management:
Management: Dr JÁNOS HERCZEG
Marketing: Dr ESZTER PATAKI SZABÓNÉ
Service Organization and Tourism: Dr MÁTYÁS FEKETE

Institute of Social Economics and Law:
Human Resource Economics: Dr GYULA LAKATOS
Law: Dr ATTILANÉ TÓTH
Social Economics: Dr ATTILANÉ TÓTH

Institute of Social Geography and World Economics:
Foreign Economics and European Integration: Dr EMESE FAYNÉ PÉTER
Social Geography: Prof. Dr JUDIT BALÁZS
World Economics: Prof. Dr JUDIT BALÁZS

Departments not within an Institute:
Centre for European Studies: Dr EMESE FÁYNÉ PÉTER
Regional Economy Research Institute: Prof. Dr ERZSÉBET GIDAI

Faculty of Forestry (9400 Sopron, Ady E. u. 5; tel. (99) 518-207; fax (99) 329-808; e-mail fdoffice@emk.nyme.hu):

Institute of Botany Forest Site:
Botany: Prof. Dr DÉNES BARTHA
Forest Site: Dr GÁBOR KOVÁCS

Institute of Environmental Sciences:
Ecology and Genetics: Prof. Dr CSABA MÁTYÁS
Environmental Biology: Dr ERNŐ FÜHRER
Environmental and Nature Protection: Dr JÓZSEF PÁJER
Landscape and Regional Planning: Dr ÉVA KONKOLYNÉ GYÚRÓ

Institute of Forest Resource Management:
Forestry Management: Dr GÁBOR VEPERDI
Forestry Policy and Economics: Prof. Dr KÁROLY MÉSZÁROS
Practical Training Centre: Dr GÁBOR HALÁSZ

Institute of Forestry and Environmental Engineering:
Energetics: Prof. Dr BÉLA MAROSVÖLGYI
Forestry Mechanics: Prof. Dr BÉLA HORVÁTH
Forest Utilization: Prof. Dr JÁNOS RUMPF

Institute of Geomatics and Civil Engineering:

Forest Development and Water Management: Prof. Dr MIKLÓS KOSZTKA
Geodesy and Remote Sensing: Prof. Dr LÁSZLÓ BÁCSATYAI

Departments not within an Institute:

Foreign Language Centre: IMRE KRISCH
Silviculture: Prof. Dr JÓZSEF KOLOSZÁR

Faculty of Wood Sciences (9400 Sopron, Ady E. u. 5; tel. (99) 518-101; fax (99) 518-259; e-mail fadek@fmk.nyme.hu; internet www.nyme.hu):

Institute of Applied Arts: GYÖRGY MÉSZÁROS
Institute of Applied Mechanics and Structures: Dr JÓZSEF SZALAI
Institute of Informatics: Dr LÁSZLÓ JEREB
Institute of Physics: Dr GYÖRGY PAPP
Institute of Product Development and Technology: Dr ZSOLT KOVÁCS
Institute of Wood and Paper Technology: Prof. Dr ANDRÁS WINKLER
Institute of Wood Sciences: Dr SÁNDOR MOLNÁR
Institute of Woodworking Machinery: Dr MIKLÓS LANG
Teacher Training Institute: Dr ISTVÁN LÜKŐ

HEADS OF DEPARTMENTS

Benedek Elek College of Education (9400 Sopron, Ferenczi J. u. 5; tel. (99) 512-821; fax (99) 332-390; e-mail szala@bepf.hu):

Hungarian Language and Literature: Dr ILDIKÓ GÖDÉNÉ TÖRÖK
Minority and Foreign Languages: PÉTER TÁRNOK
Music: ÁRPÁD DÁRDAI
Pedagogy: Dr TAMÁS SIMON
Physical Education: Dr EMŐKE BUCSY
Psychology: Dr FERENC BLÜMEL
Social Pedagogy: Dr BÉLA TELEKI
Social Sciences: Dr ERZSÉBET ALPÁRNÉ SZÁLA
Visual Communication: GÁBOR KOVÁCS-GOMBOS

College of Geoinformatics (8000 Székesfehérvár, Pirosalma u. 1–3; tel. (22) 516-522; fax (22) 516-560; e-mail geo@geo.info.hu; internet www.geo.info.hu):

Foreign Languages: JÁNOS JANURIK
Geodesy: Dr SZABOLCS CSEPREGI
Geoinformation Science: Prof. Dr BÉLA MÁRKUS
Geoinformation Technology: Dr SZABOLCS MIHÁLY
Law: Dr MIHÁLY KURUCZ
Natural and Social Sciences: Prof. Dr JÓZSEF ZÁVOTI
Photogrammetry and Remote Sensing: Dr PÉTER ENGLER
Surveying and Land Management: Dr LÁSZLÓ VINCZE
Foreign Language Centre: JÁNOS JANURIK

Apáczai Csere János Teacher-Training College (9022 Győr, Liszt Ferenc u. 42; tel. (96) 516-732; fax (96) 329-934; e-mail apaczai@atif.hu; internet www.atif.hu):

Education: Dr MÁRIA KOVÁTSNÉ NÉMETH
Foreign Languages and Literature: ILDIKÓ LŐRINCZ
Hungarian Literature and Linguistics: Dr ZOLTÁN ZSÁVOLYA
Mathematics and Natural Sciences: Dr GÉZA CSÓKA
Music: ISTVÁN BEYER
Physical Training: Dr MIKLÓS BÁNHIDI
Social Education: Dr IRÉN FEHÉR
Sociology and Cultural Management: Dr ZOLTÁN GÁL
Tourism: Dr LÁSZLÓ CSIZMADIA
Visual Training: KÁROLY BORBÉLY

PÉCSI TUDOMÁNYEGYETEM
(University of Pécs)

7633 Pécs, Szántó K. J. u. 1/b
Telephone: (72) 510-509
Fax: (72) 251-527
E-mail: int@iro.pte.hu
Internet: www.pte.hu

Founded 1367, re-founded 1923 as Janus Pannonius Tudományegyetem (Janus Pannonius University); present name 2000 upon integration with Pécsi Orvostudományi Egyetem (Pécs University Medical School) and Illyés Gyula Pedagógiai Főiskola (Gyula Illyés College of Education)
State control
Academic year: September to May (two terms)
Rector: Prof. LÁSZLÓ LÉNÁRD
Senior Vice-Rector: Dr JÓZSEF VÖRÖS
Vice-Rectors: MÁTYÁS HÜBNER (Development and Investment), Prof. ANTAL BÓKAY (Education), Dr BÉLA SIPOS (Informatics and Grant Applications), Prof. LÁSZLÓ IMRE KOMLÓSI (Research and External Relations)
Chief Administrative Officer: FERENCNÉ NAGY
Chief Librarian: Dr Fischerné Dr ÁGNES DÁRDAI
Number of teachers: 2,000
Number of students: 36,000
Publications: *Pécsi Orvostudományi Egyetem Évkönyve* (annually), *Specimina Fennica* (irregular), *Specimina Geographica* (irregular), *Specimina Nova Dissertationum ex Institutio Historico* (irregular), *Specimina Sibirica* (irregular), *Studia Iuridica Auctoritatae Universitatis Pécs Publicata* (4 a year), *Studia Oeconomica Auctoritatae Universitatis Pécs Publicata* (4 a year), *Studia Paedagogica Auctoritate Universitatis Pécs Publicata* (irregular), *Studia Philosophica et Sociologica Auctoritatae Universitatis Pécs Publicata* (4 a year), *Szép Literatúrai Ajándék* (4 a year), *Tudományos Dialóg* (6 a year), *Univ Pécs* (every 2 weeks)

DEANS

Faculty of Adult Education and Human Resources Development: Dr DÉNES KOLTAI
Faculty of Business and Education: Dr GÁBOR RAPPAI
Gyula Illyés Faculty of Education: Dr GYÖRGY FUSZ
Mihály Pollack Faculty of Engineering: Dr JÓZSEF MECSI
Faculty of Health Sciences: Dr GÁBOR KOVÁCS L.
Faculty of Humanities: Dr RÓBERT SOMOS
Faculty of Law: Dr ERZSÉBET SZALAYNÉ-SÁNDOR
Faculty of Music and Visual Arts: Dr COLIN FOSTER
Faculty of Sciences: Dr RÓBERT GÁBRIEL
School of Medicine: Dr BALÁZS SÜMEGI

PROFESSORS

Faculty of Business and Economics (7622 Pécs, Rákóczi u. 80; tel. (72) 211-433; fax (72) 501-553; internet www.ktk.pte.hu):

BARAKONYI, K., Strategic Management
BÉLYÁCZ, I., Corporate Finance and Accounting
BUDAY-SÁNTHA, A., Agricultural, Environmental and Regional Economics
DOBAY, P., Business Informatics
FARKAS, F., Management
KOMLÓSI, S., Decision-making
LÁSZLÓ, GY., Corporate Finance and Accounting
OROSZI, S., Economics
REKETTYE, G., Marketing
SIPOS, B., Strategic Management
TAKÁCS, B., Marketing
TÖRŐCSIK, M., Marketing
TÓTH, T., Economic History
VARGA, J., Decision-making
VÖRÖS, J., Decision-making

Gyula Illyés Faculty of Education (7100 Szekszárd, Rákóczi u. 1; tel. (74) 528-300; fax (74) 528-301; e-mail szaboe@igyfk.pte.hu; internet www.igyfk.pte.hu):

ANDRÁSSY, GY., Philosophy
BAJNER, M., Foreign Languages
BORBÉLY, S., Hungarian Language and Literature
BÚS, I., Education
FUSZ, GY., Visual Education
HORVÁTH, B., Hungarian Language and Literature
KURUCZ, R., Education and Psychology
NAGY, J. T., Philosophy of Law
TOLNAI, GY., Social Policy
TOTHNÉ LITOVKINA, A., Foreign Languages
VÁRADY, Z., History of Science

Mihály Pollack Faculty of Engineering (7624 Pécs, Boszorkany út 2; tel. (72) 211-968; fax (72) 214-682; internet www.pmmf.pte.hu):

ARADI, L., Public Utilities, Geodesy and Environmental Protection
ÁSVÁNYI, J., Automation
BACHMAN, Z., Design and Architecture
BÁRSONY, J., Statics and Supporting Structures
BUDAY, L., Education
CSÉBFALVI, GY., Statics and Supporting Structures
FÜLÖP, L., Building Structures
HÜBNER, M., Urban Development
JÓZSA, L., Electric Networks
KISS, E., Education
KISTELEGDI, I., Building Structures
KLINCSIK, M., Mathematics
LENKEI, P., Statics and Supporting Structures
ORBAN, F., Mechanical Engineering
ORBÁN, J., Materials, Geotechnics and Transport Engineering
TÓTH, Z., Urban Development
VAJDA, J., Building Construction
VARGA, L., Education
VÍG MIKLÓSNE, L. A., Mathematics

Faculty of Health Sciences (7624 Pécs, Rét u. 4):

BÓDIS, J., Obstetrics and Gynaecology
BUDA, J., Public Health
CHOLNOKY, P., Paediatrics
CSERE, T., Radiology
FARKAS, M., Nuclear Medicine
FIGLER, M., Gastroenterology
GYÓDI, GY., Paediatrics
HARTMANN, G., Physiology
HORVÁTH, B., Obstetrics and Gynaecology
ILLEI, GY., Obstetrics and Gynaecology
JEGES, S., Biostatistics
KELEMEN, J., Chemistry
KISS, T., Biology
KOMÁROMY, L., Biology
KOPA, J., Neurosurgery
KOVÁCS, L. G., Neuroendocrinology
KRÁNITZ, J., Orthopaedics
LAKY, R., Traumatology
ROZSOS, I., Surgery
SULYOK, E., Paediatrics
TAHIN, T., Medical Sociology
TÁRNOK, F., Gastroenterology

Faculty of Humanities (7624 Pécs, Ifjúság útja 6; tel. (72) 503-600; fax (72) 501-558; internet www.btk.pte.hu):

ANDRÁSFALVY, B., Ethnography
BÓKAY, A., Literature and Culture of the English-Speaking People
BOROS, J., History of Philosophy
ERŐS, F., Psychology
FISHER, F., Modern History
FONT, M., Medieval and Early Modern History

FORRAY, R. K., Linguistics
HETESI, I., Classical Literary History and Comparative Literature
KÁLMÁN, C. GY., Modern Literary History and Theory of Literature
KARSAI, GY., Classical Philology
KASSAI, I., Linguistics
KÉZDI, B., Personality, Development and Clinical Psychology
KISBÁN, E., Ethnography
KOMLÓSI, L., English Linguistics
KUPA, L., Sociology and Social Policy
LÁSZLÓ, J., Psychology
NAGY, E., Sociology and Social Policy
NAGY, I., Classical Literary History and Comparative Literature
ORMOS, M., Modern History
PÓCS, E., Ethnography
ROHONYI, Z., Classical Literary History and Comparative Literature
SZÉPE, GY., Linguistics
TASSONI, L., Italian Studies
THOMKA, B., Modern Literary History and Theory of Literature
VARGYAS, P., Ancient History and Archaeology
VISY, ZS., Ancient History and Archaeology
WEISS, J., History of Philosophy
WILD, K., German Linguistics

Faculty of Law (7622 Pécs, 48-as tér 1; tel. (72) 211-433; fax (72) 215-148; internet www.law.pte.hu):

ANDRÁSSY, GY., Political Science and Social Theory
BRUHÁCS, J., International and European Law
KAJTÁR, I., History of Law and Roman Law
KECSKÉS, L., Civil Law
KENGYEL, M., Civil Procedural Law and Sociology of Law
KISS, GY., Labour Law and Social Welfare Law
KISS, L., Administrative Law
KORINEK, L., Criminal Law
TÓTH, M., Criminal Law
TREMMEL, F., Criminal Procedural Law
VISEGRÁDY, A., Philosophy of Law and State

Faculty of Medicine (7624 Pécs, Szigeti út 12; tel. (72) 536-200; fax (72) 536-104; internet www.aok.pte.hu):

ÁNGYÁN, L., Physiology
BAJNÓCZKY, I., Forensic Medicine
BARTHÓ, L., Pharmacology
BARTHÓNÉ SZEKERES, J., Medical Microbiology and Immunology
BELÁGYI, J., Central Research Laboratory
BELLYEI, Á., Orthopaedics
BOGÁR, L., Anaesthesiology and Intensive Therapy
CZIRJÁK, L., Internal Medicine
CZOPF, J., Neurology
DÓCZI, T., Neurosurgery
EMBER, I., Public Health
EMŐDY, L., Microbiology
ERTL, T., Obstetrics and Gynaecology
FEKETE, M., Paediatrics
FISCHER, E., Pharmacology
GALLYAS, F., Neurosurgery
GÖTZ, F., Urology
GREGUS, Z., Pharmacology
HIDEG, K., Central Research Laboratory
HORVÁTH, L., Radiology
HORVÁTH ÖRS, P., Surgery
KAJTÁR, P., Paediatrics
KARÁTSON, A., Internal Medicine
KELÉNYI, G., Pathology
KELLERMAYER, M., Clinical Biochemistry
KETT, K., Surgery
KILÁR, F., Central Research Laboratory
KOLLÁR, L., Surgery
KOSZTOLÁNYI, GY., Paediatrics
KOVÁCS, B., Ophthalmology
KOVÁCS, S., Pathophysiology
KRÁNICZ, J., Orthopaedics
KROMMER, K., Obstetrics and Gynaecology
LÁZÁR, GY., Anatomy
LÉNÁRD, L., Physiology
LUDÁNY, A., Clinical Chemistry
MÉHES, K., Paediatrics
MEZŐNÉ FARKAS, B., Dermatology
MOLNÁR, D., Paediatrics
MÓZSIK, GY., Internal Medicine
NAGY, L., Family Medicine
NÉMETH, P., Immunology and Biotechnology
NYÁRÁDY, J., Traumatology
PAJOR, L., Pathology
PAPP, L., Cardiology
PÁR, L., Internal Medicine
PINTÉR, A., Paediatrics
PYTEL, J., Otorhinolaryngology
SÁNDOR, A., Biochemistry
SCHNEIDER, I., Dermatology
SÉTÁLÓ, GY., Anatomy
SOLTÉSZ, GY., Paediatrics
SOMOGYI, B., Biophysics
SÜMEGI, B., Biochemistry
SZABÓ, GY., Oral Medicine
SZABÓ, I., Behavioural Science
SZABÓ, I., Obstetrics and Gynaecology
SZEBERÉNYI, J., Biology
SZÉKELY, M., Pathophysiology
SZELÉNYI, Z., Pathophysiology
SZOLCSÁNYI, J., Pharmacology
TEKERES, M., Intensive Therapy and Anaesthesia
TÉNYI, J., Public Health
THAN, G., Obstetrics and Gynaecology
TÓTH, GY., Chemistry
TRIXLER, M., Psychiatry and Medical Psychology
VERECZKEI, L., Behavioural Science
VÉRTES, M., Physiology

Faculty of Sciences (7624 Pécs, Ifjúság útja 6; tel. (72) 503-600; fax (72) 501-527; e-mail hatvani@ttk.pte.hu; internet www.ttk.pte.hu):

AGÁRDI, P., Cultural Studies
BERGOU, J., Theoretical Physics
BORHIDI, A., Botany
CSOKNYA, M., Zoology and Neurobiology
ERDŐSI, F., Institute of Geography
FISCHER, E., Zoology and Neurobiology
HÁMORI, J., Zoology and Neurobiology
KLEIN, S., Human Resource Development
KOLLÁR, L., Inorganic Chemistry and Technology
KORPA, CS., Theoretical Physics
KŐSZEGFALVI, GY., Institute of Geography
KOZMA, L., Adult Education
LOVÁSZ, GY., Institute of Geography
MAJER, J., General and Applied Ecology
NAGY, G., General Physics and Chemistry
PESTI, M., General and Environmental Microbiology
SZABÓ, L., Botany
SZEIDL, L., Mathematics
TOMCSÁNYI, T., Genetics and Molecular Biology
TÓTH, J., Institute of Geography
UHRIN, B., Mathematics
VUICS, T., Institute of Geography

Faculty of Visual Arts and Music (7624 Pécs, Damjanics u. 30; tel. and fax (72) 501-540; e-mail mail@art.pte.hu; internet www.art.pte.hu):

BENCSIK, I., Sculpture
JOBBÁGY, V., Music
KESERÜ, I., Painting
KIRCS, L., Music
PINCZEHELYI, S., Painting
RÉTFALVI, S., Sculpture
TILLAI, A., Music
VIDOVSZKY, L., Theory of Art

SEMMELWEIS EGYETEM
(Semmelweis University)

1085 Budapest VIII, Üllői u. 26
Telephone: (1) 459-1500
Fax: (1) 317-2220
E-mail: rekhiv@rekhiv.sote.hu
Internet: www.sote.hu

Founded 1769 as Medical Faculty of the University of Nagyszombat; independent 1951 as Semmelweis Orvostudományi Egyetem (Semmelweis University of Medicine); present name 2000 upon integration with Haynal Imre Egészségtudományi (Imre Haynal University of Health Sciences) and Magyar Testnevelési Egyetem (Hungarian University of Physical Education)
State control
Languages of instruction: Hungarian, English, German
Academic year: September to June

Rector: Prof. Dr T. TULASSAY
Vice-Rectors: Prof. Dr V. ÁDÁM, Prof. Dr M. KOLLAI, Prof. Dr P. FEJÉRDY
General Secretary (vacant)

Library of 261,624 vols
Number of teachers: 1,133
Number of students: 9,473

Publication: *Pathology Oncology Research* (4 a year)

DEANS

Faculty of Dentistry: Dr I. GERA
Faculty of Medicine: Dr I. KARÁDI
Faculty of Pharmacy: Dr B. NOSZÁL
Faculty of Physical Education and Sport Sciences: Dr M. NYERGES
College of Health Care: Dr J. MÉSZÁROS (Dir-Gen.)
School of Doctoral Studies: Dr Á. SZÉL (Pres.)

PROFESSORS

Faculty of Dentistry (tel. (1) 266-0453; fax (1) 266-1967; e-mail gera@szajseb.sote.hu):

BARABAS, J., Oral, Dental and Maxillofacial Surgery
BOROS, I., Oral Biology
DIVINYI, T., Oral, Dental and Maxillofacial Surgery
FÁBIÁN, T., Prosthodontics
FAZEKAS, A., Preservation Dentistry
FEJÉRDY, P., Prosthetic Dentistry
GERA, I., Periodontics
KAÁN, M., Prosthodontics
SIMON, GY., Oral Biology
SZABÓ, GY., Oral and Maxillofacial Surgery
VARGA, G., Oral Biology
ZELLES, T., Oral Biology

Faculty of Medicine (tel. (1) 317-9057; fax (1) 266-0441; e-mail vegan@rekhiv.sote.hu):

ACSÁDY, GY., Cardiovascular Surgery
ÁDÁM, E., Medical Microbiology
ÁDÁM, V., Medical Biochemistry
ALFÖLDY, F., Transplantation and Surgery
ANTMANN, I., Medical Microbiology
BANAI, J., Surgery
BIRKÁS, J., Military and Disaster Medicine
BITTER, J., Psychiatry and Psychotherapy
BODÓ, M., Oncopathology and Cytodiagnostics
BODOR, E., Cardiovascular Surgery
BÖHM, Á., Cardiology
BÖSZÖRMÉNYI NAGY, GY., Pulmonology
CSÁSZÁR, A., Obstetrics and Gynaecology
CSERMELY, P., Medical Chemistry, Molecular Biology and Pathobiochemistry
CSILLAG, A., Anatomy, Histology and Embryology
DARVAS, K. I., Surgery
DE CHÂTEL, R., Internal Medicine
DEMETER, J., Internal Medicine
DOSZPOD, J., Obstetrics and Gynaecology
DZSINICH, CS., Cardiovascular Surgery

EGYED, J., Obstetrics and Gynaecology
ENGLONER, L., Internal Medicine
ENYEDI, P., Physiology
FALLER, J., Surgery
FALUS, A., Biology
FARAGÓ, A., Medical Chemistry, Molecular Biology and Pathobiochemistry
FARSANG, G., Internal Medicine
FEHÉR, E., Anatomy, Histology and Embryology
FEKETE, B., Immunology
FEKETE, GY., Paediatrics
FERENCZ, A., Laboratory Medicine, Dermatology and Venereology
FIDY, J., Biophysics and Radiology
FLAUTNER, L., Surgery
FÜREDI, J., Psychiatry, Addiction and Paediatric Psychiatry
FÜRST, ZS., Pharmacology
FÜST, GY., Internal Medicine
GÉHER, P., Pneumatology and Physiotherapy
GERENDAI, I., Human Morphology and Developmental Biology
GERGELY, P., Dermatology and Venereology
GERŐ, L., Internal Medicine
GÖMÖR, B., Rheumatology and Physiotherapy
GÓTH, M., Obstetrics and Gynaecology
GYIRES, K., Pharmacology and Pharmacotherapy
HALÁSZ, P., Vascular Neurology
HORVÁTH, A., Dermatology and Venereology
HUNYADY, L., Physiology
JÁRAY, J., Transplantation and Surgery
JENEY, A., Pathology and Experimental Cancer Research
KÁDÁR, A., Pathology
KALABAY, L., Family Medicine
KÁLMÁNCHEY, R., Paediatrics
KARÁDI, I., Internal Medicine
KÁRPÁTI, S., Dermatology and Venereology
KÁSLER, M., Oncotherapy
KECSKEMÉTI, V., Pharmacology and Pharmacotherapy
KELEMEN, Z., Urology
KOLLER, Á., Pathophysiology
KELTAI, M., Cardiology
KEMPLER, P., Internal Medicine
KENÉZ, J., Neuroradiology
KERÉNYI, T., Pathology
KERPEL-FRONIUS, S., Pharmacology and Pharmacotherapy
KISS, J., Surgery
KOLLAI, M., Physiology and Experimental Laboratory for Clinical Research
KOPP, M., Behavioural Sciences
KOPPER, L., Pathology and Experimental Cancer Research
KÖTELES, GY., Occupational and Environmental Health
KÖVES, K., Human Morphology and Developmental Biology
KUPCSULIK, P., Surgery
LIGETI, L., Physiology
LOSONCZY, GY., Pulmonology
LOZSÁDI, K., Cardiology
MACHAY, T., Paediatrics
MACHOVICH, R., Medical Biochemistry
MADÁCSY, L., Paediatrics
MAGYAR, P., Pulmonology
MAKÓ, E., Radiology
MANDL, J., Medical Chemistry, Molecular Biology and Pathobiochemistry
MATOLCSY, A., Pathology and Experimental Cancer Research
MONOS, E., Human Physiology
MORAVA, E., Public Health
MORVAI, V., Internal Medicine
MÓZES, T., Traumatology
NAGY, GY., Human Morphology and Developmental Biology
NAGY, Z., Cardiovascular Surgery
NEMES, A., Cardiovascular Surgery
NÉMETH, GY., Radiotherapy, Oncoradiology
NÉMETH, J., Ophthalmology
NYÁRY, I., Neurosurgery
OLÁH, I., Human Morphology and Developmental Biology
ONDREJKA, P., Surgery
PAJOR, A., Obstetrics and Gynaecology
PÁLÓCZI, K., Immunology
PAPP, GY., Andrology
PAPP, J., Internal Medicine
PAPP, Z., Obstetrics and Gynaecology
PAULIN, F., Obstetrics and Gynaeology
PERNER, F., Transplantology and Surgery
PÉNZES, I., Anaesthesiology and Intensive Therapy
POÓR, GY., Rheumatology and Physiology
PRÉDA, I., Cardiology
RÁCZ, K., Internal Medicine
RAJNA, P., Psychiatry and Psychotherapy
REGÖLY-MÉREI, J., Surgery
RÉPÁSSY, G., Otorhinolaryngology, Head and Neck Surgery
RÉTHELYI, M., Anatomy, Histology and Embryology
REUSZ, GY., Paediatrics
ROMICS, I., Urology
ROMICS, L., Internal Medicine
RONTÓ, GY., Biophysics and Radiation Biology
ROSIVALL, L., Pathophysiology
ROZGONYI, F., Microbiology
SALACZ, GY., Ophthalmology
SÁNDOR, P., Human Physiology
SÁRVÁRY, A., Traumatology
SCHAFF, ZS., Pathology
SELMECI, L., Cardiovascular Surgery
SIKLÓSI, GY., Obstetrics and Gynaecology
SIMON, T., Public Health
SÓLYOM, J., Paediatrics
SÓTONYI, P., Forensic Medicine
SPÄT, A., Physiology
SRÉTER, L., Internal Medicine
STAUB, M., Medical Chemistry, Molecular Biology and Pathobiochemistry
SÜVEGES, I., Ophthalmology
SZALAY, F., Internal Medicine
SZÁNTÓ, I., Surgery
SZÉKÁCS, B., Geriatrics
SZÉL, Á., Human Morphology and Developmental Biology
SZENDE, B., Pathology and Experimental Cancer Research
SZENDRŐI, M., Orthopaedics
SZIGETVÁRI, I., Obstetrics and Gynaecology
SZIRMAI, I., Neurology
SZOLLÁR, L., Pathophysiology
TAMÁS, GY., Internal Medicine
TIHANYI, T., Surgery
TIMÁR, J., Pathology and Experimental Cancer Research
TIMÁR, L., Paediatrics, Infectious Diseases
TÓTH, M., Medical Chemistry, Molecular Biology and Pathobiochemistry
TRINGER, L., Psychiatry and Psychotherapy
TULASSAY, T., Paediatrics
TULASSAY, ZS., Internal Medicine
UNGVÁRY, GY., Public Health
VASTAG, E., Pulmonology
VEREBÉLY, T., Paediatrics
VIZI, E., Pharmacology and Pharmacotherapy
WENGER, T., Human Morphology and Developmental Biology

Faculty of Pharmacy (tel. (1) 266-0449; fax (1) 317-5340; e-mail nosbel@hogyes.sote.hu):
BORVENDÉG, J., Medical Regulation
KLEBOVICH, J., Pharmaceutics
LEMBERKOVICS, É., Pharmacognosy
LIPTÁK, J., Medical Regulation
MARTON, S., Pharmaceutics
MÁTYUS, P., Organic Chemistry
NOSZÁL, B., Pharmaceutical Chemistry
PAÁL, T., Medical Regulation
SZŐKE, É., Pharmacognosy
TAKÁCSNÉ NOVÁK, K., Pharmaceutical Chemistry
TEKES, K., Pharmacodynamics
TÖRÖK, T., Pharmacodynamics
VINCZE, Z., University Pharmacy, Pharmacy Administration

Faculty of Physical Education and Sport Sciences (1123 Budapest, Alkotás u. 44; tel. (1) 487-9214; fax (1) 356-6337; e-mail nyerges@mail.hupe.hu):
FÖLDESY, T., Social Sciences
FRENKL, R., Health Sciences and Sports Medicine
GOMBOCZ, J., Theory and Teaching of Physical Education
ISTVÁNFI, CS., Theory and Teaching of Physical Education
KERTÉSZ, I., Social Sciences
MÉSZÁROS, J., Health Sciences and Sports Medicine
MOHÁCSI, J., Health Sciences and Sports Medicine
NYAKAS, CS., Health Sciences and Sports Medicine
PAVLIK, G., Health Sciences and Sports Medicine
RADÁK, ZS., Sport Sciences Research
RIGLER, E., Sport Games
SIPOS, K., Psychology
TAKÁCS, F., Social Sciences
TIHANYI, J., Biomechanics
TOMCSÁYI, T., Mental Health

College of Health Care (1088 Budapest, Vas u. 17; tel. (1) 369-1241; fax (1) 369-1241; e-mail meszarosj@seefk.hu):
CZINNER, A., Paediatrics
SZABOLCS, J., Dietetics

ATTACHED INSTITUTE

Health Services Management Training Centre: Dir Dr M. SZÓCSKA.

SZÉCHENYI ISTVÁN EGYETEM
(Széchenyi István University)

9026 Győr, Egyetem tér 1
Telephone: (96) 503-400
Fax: (96) 329-263
E-mail: sze@sze.hu
Internet: www.sze.hu

Founded 1968 as Széchenyi István Főiskola; present name and status 2002
State control
Academic year: September to June

Rector: Prof. Dr IMRE CZINEGE
Vice-Rector (Education): Prof. Dr GYULA SZALAY
Vice-Rector (Institutional Development): Prof. Dr ATTILA KOPPÁNY
Vice-Rector (Research Relations): Prof. Dr PÉTER SCHARLE
Secretary-General: Prof. Dr BÉLA ÍRÓ
Library Director: JULIANNA MÁRKUS

Library of 240,000 vols, 1,000 periodicals
Number of teachers: 300
Number of students: 10,600 (6,800 undergraduate, 1,200 postgraduate, 2,600 distant learning)
Publication: *Hungarian Electronic Journal of Sciences* (online)

DEANS

Faculty of Law and Economics: Prof. Dr JÁNOS RECHNITZER
Faculty of Technical Sciences: Prof. Dr LÁSZLÓ KÓCZY
Institute of Health and Community Studies: Prof. Dr SÁNDOR GARDÓ
Institute of Music: Prof. JÓZSEF GÁBOR

SZEGEDI TUDOMÁNYEGYETEM
(University of Szeged)

6720 Szeged, Dugonics tér 13
Telephone: (62) 544-001
Fax: (62) 546-371
E-mail: rekthiv@rekt.u-szeged.hu
Internet: www.u-szeged.hu

Founded 1872, refounded 1921; become József Attila Tudományegyetem (Attila József University) 1962; present name 2000 upon merger with Szent-Györgyi Albert Orvostudományi Egyetem (Albert Szent-Györgyi University of Medicine) and other instns

State control
Academic year: September to June

Rector: Prof. Dr GÁBOR SZABÓ
Vice-Rectors: Prof. Dr IMRE DÉKÁNY (Scientific and Foreign Affairs), Prof. Dr BÉLA RÁCZ (Strategic Affairs), Dr ATTILA BADÓ (Student Affairs and Public Relations), Dr BÉLA PUKÁNSZKY (Education), Prof. Dr JÁNOS LONOVICS (General Affairs)
Librarian: Dr BÉLA MADER

Library: see Libraries and Archives
Number of teachers: 2,279
Number of students: 31,478

Publications: *Acta Biologica Szegediensis, Acta Climatologica, Acta Cybernetcia, Acta Scientarum Mathematicarum*

DEANS

Faculty of Arts: Prof. Dr TIBOR ALMÁSI
Faculty of Law: Prof. Dr IMRE SZABÓ
Faculty of Economics and Business Administrations: Dr BEÁTA FARKAS
Faculty of Medicine: Prof. Dr GYÖRGY BENEDEK
Faculty of Pharmacy: Prof. Dr GYÖRGY ISTVÁN FALKAY
Faculty of Science: Prof. Dr JÁNOS CSIRIK
College Faculty of Agriculture: Prof. Dr IMRE MUCSI
College Faculty of Food Engineering: Prof. Dr JÓZSEF FENYVESSY
College Faculty of Health Sciences: Dr MAGDOLNA POGÁNY
College Faculty of Music: Prof. Dr FERENC KEREK
College Faculty of 'Juhász Gyula' Teachers' Training College: Prof. Dr GÁBOR GALAMBOS

PROFESSORS

Faculty of Arts (6722 Szeged, Egyetem u. 2; tel. (62) 544-166; fax (62) 425-843; e-mail kelemen@arts.u-szeged.hu; internet www.arts.u-szeged.hu):

ANDERLE, Á., Hispanic Studies
BAKRÓ-NAGY, M., Finno-Ugrian Linguistics
BALÁZS, M., Early Hungarian Literature
BASSOLA, P., German Linguistics
BERNÁTH, Á., German Literature
BERTA, A., Altaic Studies
CSAPÓ, B., Education
CSEJTEI, D., Philosophy
CSÚRI, K., Austrian Culture and Literature
JUHÁSZ, A., Ethnography
KARSAI, L., Modern World History and Mediterranean Studies
KENESEI, I., English and American Studies
KONTRA, M., English Language Teacher Education and Applied Linguistics
MAKK, F., Auxiliary Sciences of History
NAGY, L., Modern World History and Mediterranean Studies
OLAJOS, T., Auxiliary Sciences of History
PÁL, J., Italian Language and Literature
PÁLFY, M., French Language and Literature
SAJTI, E., Modern World History and Mediterranean Studies
SZABÓ, J., Hungarian Linguistics
SZAJBÉLY, M., Classic Hungarian Literature
SZIGETI, L., Modern Hungarian Literature
SZÖRÉNYI, L., Comparative Literature
WOJTILLA, GY., Ancient History

Faculty of Economics and Business Administration (6722 Szeged, Honvéd tér 6; tel. (62) 544-485; fax (62) 544-499; e-mail bfarkas@eco.u-szeged.hu; internet www.eco.u-szeged.hu):

BOTOS, K., Finance
BENET, I., World Economics and European Economic Integration
DINYA, L., Marketing and Management
GARAI, L., Economic Psychology
LENGYEL, I., Economics and Economic Development

Faculty of Law (6722 Szeged, Tisza L. krt. 54; tel. (62) 544-206; fax (62) 544-204; e-mail ajtk.dekani@juris.u-szeged.hu; internet www.juris.u-szeged.hu):

BALOGH, E., Legal History
BESENYEI, L., Civil Law and Civil Procedure
BLAZOVICH, L., Legal History
BODNÁR, L., International Law
CZÚCZ, O., Social and Labour Law
HERCZEG, J., Statistics and Demography
JAKAB, É., Roman Law
KATONA, T., Statistics and Demography
MARTONYI, J., International Private Law
NAGY, F., Criminal Law and Criminal Procedure
PACZOLAY, P., Political Sciences
POKOL, B., Philosophy and Sociology of Law
RUSZOLY, J., Legal History
STIPTA, I., Legal History
TRÓCSÁNYI, L., Constitutional Law

Faculty of Medicine (6720 Szeged, Dóm tér 12; tel. (62) 545-015; fax (62) 426-529; e-mail aokdh@medea.szote.u-szeged.hu; internet www.szote.u-szeged.hu):

BALOGH, Á., Clinical Surgery
BARI, F., Physiology
BÁLINT, G., Psychiatry
BÁRTFAI, G., Tocology and Gynaecology
BENEDEK, GY., Physiology
BODOSI, M., Neurological Surgery
BORBÉLYI, Z., Internal Medicine and Cardiology
BOROS, M., Experimental Surgery
CSANÁDY, M., Internal Medicine
CZÍGNER, J., Otolaryngology
DOBOZY, A., Dermatology
DUDA, E., Medical Microbiology
DUX, L., Biochemistry
ENGELHARDT, J., Neurology
FARKAS, G., Surgery
FAZEKAS, A., Prosthetic Dentistry
FORSTER, T., Internal Medicine and Cardiology
FRÁTER, L., Radiology
FÜZESI, K., Paediatrics
GELLEN, J., Tocology and Immunology
HAJNAL, M., Early Hungarian Literature
HANTOS, F., Family Medicine
HORVÁTH, A. R., Clinical Chemistry
HŐGYE, M., Internal Medicine and Cardiology
HUSZ, S., Dermatology and Allergology
IVÁNYI, B., Pathology
JANKA, Z., Neurology and Psychiatry
JANCSÓ, G., Physiology
JÁRDÁNHÁZY, T., Neurology
JÓRI, J., Oto-Rhino-Laryngology and Head and Neck Surgery
JULESZ, J., Endocrinology
KEMÉNY, L., Dermatology and Allergology
KOLOZSVÁRI, L., Ophthalmology
KOVÁCS, A., Oral Surgery
KÓSA, F., Forensic Medicine
KRASZKÓ, P., Pulmonology
LÁZÁR, G, Surgery
LEPRÁN, I., Pharmacology and Pharmacotherapy
LONOVICS, J., Internal Medicine
MÁNDI, Y., Medical Microbiology and Immunology
MÉRAY, J., Anaesthesiology
MÉSZÁROS, T., Orthopaedics
MIHÁLY, A., Anatomy, Histology and Embryology
MIKÓ, T., Pathology
NAGY, E., Clinical Microbiology
NAGYMAJTÉNYI, L., Public Health
PAJOR, L., Urology
PALKÓ, A., Radiology
PAPP, G., Paediatrics
PAPP, J. G., Pharmacology
PÁL, A., Tocology and Gynaecology
PÁVICS, L., Nuclear Medicine
PENKE, B., Medical Chemistry
PETRI, A., Surgery
POKORNY, G., Rheumatology
PRÁGAI, B., Medical Microbiology and Immunology
PUSZTAI, R., Medical Microbiology and Immunology
RESCH, B., Tocology and Gynaecology
SIMONKA, J. A., Traumatology
SONKODI, I., Oral Medicine
SONKODI, S., Nephrology, Dialysis
SZABAD, J., Medical Biology
SZABÓ, G., Pathophysiology
SZABÓ, J., Medical Genetics
SZÖLLŐSSY, J., Tocology and Gynaecology
TAKÁCS, T., Internal Medicine
TELEGDY, G., Pathophysiology
THURZÓ, L., Oncotherapy
TÓTH, K., Orthopaedics
TÚRI, S., Paediatrics
VARGA, G., Internal Medicine and Cardiology
VARGA, T., Forensic Medicine
VÁRKONYI, Á., Paediatrics
VARRÓ, T., Pharmacology and Pharacotherapy
VÉCSEI, L., Neurology
VÉGH, Á., Pharmacology and Pharmacotherapy
VIMLÁTA, L., Anaesthiology
WITTMANN, T., Internal Medicine

Faculty of Pharmacy (6720 Szeged, Zrinyi u. 9; tel. (62) 545-022; fax (62) 541-906; e-mail gytkdh@medea.szote.u-szeged.hu; internet www.szote.u-szeged.hu):

DOMBI, G., Pharmaceutical Analysis
ERŐS, I., Pharmaceutical Technology
FALKAY, GY., Pharmacodynamics
FÜLÖP, F., Pharmaceutical Chemistry
HÓDI, K., Pharmaceutical Technology
HOHMANN, J., Pharmacognosy
MÁTHÉ, I., Pharmacognosy
PÁAL, T., Drug Regulatory Affairs
RÉVÉSZ, P., Pharmaceutical Technology
STÁJER, G., Pharmaceutical Chemistry

Faculty of Science (6720 Szeged, Aradi vértanúk tere 1; tel. (62) 544-681; fax (62) 426-221; e-mail annuse@sci.u-szeged.hu; internet www.sci.u-szeged.hu):

BECSEI, J., Economic Geography
BOR, ZS., Optics and Quantum Electronics
BOROS, I., Genetic and Molecular Biology
CSIRIK, J., Computer Science
CSÖRGŐ, S., Applied Analysis
CZÉDLI, G., Algebra and Number Theory
DÉKÁNY, I., Colloid Chemistry
ERDEI, L., Plant Physiology
ERDŐHELYI, A., Solid State Chemistry and Radiochemistry
ÉSIK, Z., Principles of Computer Science
FEHÉR, L., Theoretical Physics
FÜLÖP, Z., Foundations of Computer Science
GALLÉ, L., Ecology
GÉCSEG, F., Computer Science
GULYA, K., Zoology and Cell Biology
HANNUS, I., Applied and Environmental Chemistry
HATVANI, L., Analysis

HETÉNYI, M., Mineralogy, Geochemistry and Petrography
IGLÓI, F., Theoretical Physics
KÉRCHY, L., Analysis
KEVEI, F., Climatology and Landscape Ecology
KIRICSI, I., Applied Chemistry
KISS, T., Inorganic Chemistry
KOVÁCS, K., Biotechnology
KRÁMLI, A., Applications of Analysis
KRISZTIN, T., Applied Numerical Mathematics
LEHOCZKI, E., Botany
LEINDLER, L., Analysis
MARÓTI, P., Biophysics
MARÓY, P., Genetic and Molecular Biology
MÉSZÁROS, R., Economic Geography
MEZŐSI, G., Physical Geography
MOLNÁR, Á., Organic Chemistry
MÓRICZ, F., Applications of Analysis
NAGY, L., Inorganic and Analytical Chemistry1
NAGYPÁL, I., Physical Chemistry
NEMCSÓK, J., Biochemistry
NOTHEISZ, F., Organic Chemistry
NOVÁK, M., Physical Chemistry
RÁCZ, B., Optics and Quantum Electronics
SIMÁNYI, N., Geometry
SZABÓ, G., Optics and Quantum Electronics
SZATMÁRI, S., Experimental Physics
SZENDREI, Á., Algebra and Number Theory
SZENDREI, M., Algebra and Number Theory
SZENTE, M., Comparative Physiology
TOLDI, J., Comparative Physiology
TOTIK, V., Set Theory and Mathematical Logic
VISY, C., Physical Chemistry

College Faculty of Agriculture (6800 Hódmezővásárhely, Andrássy ut. 15; tel. (62) 241-779; fax (62) 241-779; e-mail mucsi@mfk.u-szeged.hu; internet www.mfk.u-szeged.hu):

MUCSI, I., Animal Husbandry
PÉTER, J., Nutrition

College Faculty of Food Engineering (6724 Szeged, Mars tér 7; tel. (62) 546-003; fax (62) 546-003; e-mail fotit@szef.u-szeged.hu; internet www.szef.u-szeged.hu):

FENYVESSY, J., Food Technology
KOVÁCS, E. T., Food Science
SZABÓ, G., Unit Operation and Environmental Techniques
TANÁCS, L., Food Science

College Faculty of Health Sciences (6726 Szeged, Temesvári krt. 31; tel. (62) 545-024; fax (62) 545-515; e-mail poma@efk.u-szeged.hu; internet www.efk.u-szeged.hu):

BÁRÁNY, F., Social Work and Social Policy

College Faculty of Music (6722 Szeged, Tisza L. krt. 79–81; tel. (62) 544-600; fax (62) 544-066; e-mail zfk@muzik.u-szeged.hu; internet www.muzik.u-szeged.hu):

HUSZÁR, L., Music Theory
KEREK, F., Piano
SZECSŐDI, F., Strings
TEMESI, M., Voice

College Faculty of 'Juhász Gyula' Teacher Traing College (6722 Szeged, Boldogasszony sgt. 6; tel. (62) 546-050; fax (62) 420-953; e-mail galambos@jgytf.u-szeged.hu; internet www.jgytf.u-szeged.hu):

BÉKÉSI, I., Hungarian Language
GALAMBOS, G., Computer Science
GALGÓCZI, L., Hungarian Language
NAGY, J., Hungarian Language
NÁNAI, L., Physics
SERES, L., Chemistry

SZENT ISTVÁN EGYETEM
(St Stephen's University)

2103 Gödöllő, Páter Károly u. 1
Telephone: (28) 410-971
Fax: (28) 410-804
E-mail: rector@gau.hu
Internet: www.gau.hu

Founded 1945; as Gödöllői Agrártudományi Egyetem (Gödöllő University of Agricultural Sciences), merged with Állatorvostudomanyi Egyetem (University of Veterinary Science) (Budapest), Kertészeti és Élelmiszeripari Egyetem (University of Horticulture and Food Technology) (Budapest), Jászberényi Tanítóképző Főiskola (Jászberény Teacher-Training College) and Ybl Miklós Műszaki Főiskola (Miklós Ybl Polytechnic) in 2000, adopting present name
State control
Languages of instruction: Hungarian, English
Languages of instruction: Russian, French
Academic year: September to May
Rector: Dr PÉTER SZENDRŐ
Number of teachers: 1,079
Number of students: 23,704

DEANS

Faculty of Agricultural Engineering: Dr ATTILA VAS
Faculty of Agricultural Sciences: Dr GYÖRGY HELTAI
Faculty of Economic and Social Sciences: Dr JÓZSEF MOLNÁR
Faculty of the Food Industry: Prof. Dr ANDRÁS FEKETE
Faculty of Horticulture: Dr JENŐ BERNÁTH
Faculty of Landscape Architecture: Dr ILONA BALOGH ORMOS
Faculty of Veterinary Science: Prof. Dr L. SOLTI
College Faculty of Jászberény: (vacant)
Ybl Miklos Technical College Faculty: Prof. Dr GEORGE SAMSONDI KISS
Institute of Scientific Training: Dr PÉTER SZENDRŐ

DIRECTORS

College Faculty of Agricultural Economics, Gyöngygös: Dr SÁNDOR MAGDA

PROFESSORS FROM THE FORMER GÖDÖLLŐ UNIVERSITY OF AGRICULTURAL SCIENCES

Faculty of Agricultural Engineering:

BARÓTFY, I., Environmental Engineering
GY. BEER, Agricultural Engineering
FARKAS, I., Physics
GYÜRK, I., Mechanics
JESZENSZKY, Z., Agricultural Engineering
KÓSA, A., Mathematics
SEMBERY, P., Food Engineering
SZENDRŐ, P., Agricultural Mechanization
ZS. SZÜLE, Agricultural Mechanization
VAS, A., Agricultural Engineering

Faculty of Agricultural Sciences:

BEDŐ, S., Animal Breeding
GY. FÜLEKY, Soil Science
GY. HELTAI, Chemistry
HESZKY, L., Plant Genetics
HORNOK, L., Microbiology
HORVÁTH, L., Animal Genetics
KISS, J., Plant Protection
MÁTÉ, A., Crop Production
MÉZES, M., Animal Feeding
OROSZ, L., Biotechnology
PÉCZELY, P., Animal Breeding
PEKLI, J., Tropical Agriculture
SAJGÓ, M., Biochemistry
GY. SZALAI, Water Management
SZEMÁN, L., Grassland Management
TUBA, Z., Botany and Plant Physiology

Faculty of Economic and Social Sciences:

BARKÓ, E., Education
BIRÓ, S., Economic Law
HAJÓS, L., Labour Science
KISS, K., Statistics
KULCSÁR, L., Rural Sociology
RATHMANN, J., Philosophy
CS. SZÉKELY, Agricultural Economics
TÓTH, P., Accounting and Finance
VÖLGYESY, P., Psychology

PROFESSORS FROM THE FORMER UNIVERSITY OF VETERINARY SCIENCE

ÉLIÁS, B., Zoology
FEKETE, S., Animal Nutrition
FODOR, L., Microbiology
FRENYÓ, V. L., Immunology and Biochemistry
GAÁL, T., Internal Medicine
HAJÓS, F., Anatomy and Histology
HUSZENICZA, GY., Obstetrics and Reproduction
LACZAY, P., Pharmacology
RAFAI, P., Animal Hygiene
RUDAS, P., Physiology and Biochemistry
RUSVAI, M., Microbiology
SCHEIBER, P., Chemistry
SEMJÉN, G., Pharmacology
SOLTI, L., Obstetrics and Reproduction
SZENCI, O., Obstetrics and Reproduction
VARGA, I., Parasitology
VARGA, J., Microbiology
VETÉSI, F., Pathology
VETTER, J., Botany
VÖRÖS, K., Internal Medicine
ZÖLDÁG, L., Animal Husbandry

PROFESSORS FROM THE FORMER UNIVERSITY OF HORTICULTURE AND FOOD TECHNOLOGY

BALÁZS, S., Vegetable Production
BALOGH, S., Food Industry Economics
BÉKÁSSY-MOLNÁR, E., Food Technology
BERNÁTH, J., Medicinal Plants
BOROSS, L., Chemistry and Biochemistry
CSEMEZ, A., Landscape Architecture
CSEPREGI, P., Viticulture
DALÁNYI, L., Landscape Architecture
DEÁK, T., Microbiology
DIMÉNY, I., Agricultural Economics
DINYA, L., Economics and Marketing
EPERJESI, I., Oenology
ERDÉLYI, E., Food Technology
FARKAS, J., Food Preservation
FEKETE, A., Food Physics
FODOR, P., Chemistry and Biochemistry
GLITS, M., Plant Pathology
ZS. HARNOS, Mathematics
HORVÁTH, G., Plant Physiology
HOSCHKE, A., Brewing and Distillation
JÁMBOR, I., Landscape Architecture
KISS, I., Food Preservation
KOSÁRY, J., Chemistry and Biochemistry
KÖRMENDY, I., Food Preservation
LÁNG, Z., Technical Department
MÉSZÁROS, Z., Entomology
MŐCSÉNYI, M., Landscape Architecture
PAIS, I., Chemistry
PAPP, J., Fruit Growing
RIMÓCZI, I., Botany
SÁRAI, T., Food Technology
SÁRKŐZY, P., Agricultural Economics
SASS, P., Fruit Growing
SCHMIDT, G., Floriculture and Dendrology
SZABÓ, S. A., Food Chemistry
VARSÁNYI, I., Food Preservation
VELICH, I., Plant Genetics and Selection
VERMES, L., Agrometeorology and Water Management

ATTACHED INSTITUTES

Academy of Trading and Enterprise: Dir Dr B. HAUK.

Agricultural Research Institute: Dir Dr A. FEHÉR.

Environmental and Landscape Management Institute: Dir Dr J. ANGYÁN.

Farm Machinery Historical Museum: Dir GY. PÁLFY.

Institute of Management and Business Training: Dir Dr F. NEMES.

Research Institute of Veterinary Science: Dir Dr J. SEREGI.

SZINHÁZ- ÉS FILMMŰVÉSZETI FŐISKOLA
(University of Drama and Film)

1088 Budapest, Vas u. 2C

Telephone: (1) 318-8111
Fax: (1) 338-4749
Internet: www.filmacademy.hu

Founded 1865

Rector: GÁBOR SZÉKELY
Vice-Rectors: LÁSZLÓ BABARCZY, ÁDÁM HORVÁTH
Secretary-General: L. TISZEKER
Number of teachers: 97
Number of students: 269

HEADS OF DEPARTMENTS

Drama: PÉTER HUSZTI
Film: JÁNOS ZSOMBOLYAI

VESZPRÉMI EGYETEM
(University of Veszprém)

8200 Veszprém, Egyetem u. 10, POB 158

Telephone: (88) 422-022
Fax: (88) 423-866
E-mail: rekti@almos.vein.hu
Internet: www.vein.hu

Founded 1949; absorbed Georgikon Faculty of Agriculture of the former Pannon Agrártudományi Egyetem (Pannon University of Agricultural Sciences) 2000
State controlled
Languages of instruction: Hungarian, English
Academic year: September to June

Rector: Prof. ZOLTÁN GAÁL
Pro-Rectors: Prof. FERENC HUSVÉTH, Prof. JÁNOS KRISTÓF, Prof. FERENC OLTI, Prof. ÁKOS RÉDEY
Librarian: Dr M. EGYHÁZY

Library: see Libraries
Number of teachers: 435
Number of students: 6,794 (6,313 full-time, 481 part-time)

Publication: *Hungarian Journal of Industrial Chemistry* (4 a year)

DEANS

Georgikon Faculty of Agriculture: Prof. KÁROLY DUBLECZ
Faculty of Economics: Prof. ZOLTÁN KOVÁCS
Faculty of Engineering: Prof. GÉZA HORVÁTH
Faculty of Information Technology: Prof. FERENC FRIEDLER
Faculty of Teacher Training: Prof. CSABA FÖLDES

PROFESSORS

ALMÁDI, L., Botany
ANDA, A., Water Management
BAKOS, J., Organic Chemistry
BÁRDOS, J., English Language
BENCZE, L., Organic Chemistry
BÉRES, I., Botany
BUDAI, L., English Language
BUZÁS, GY., Economics
FISCHL, G., Plant Pathology
FÖLDES, CS., German Language
FRIEDLER, F., Systems Engineering in Computer Science
GAÁL, Z., Management and Economy
GÁBORJÁNYI, R., Plant Pathology
GYŐRI, I., Mathematics
HANGOS, K., Systems Engineering in Computer Science
HLAVAY, J., Analytical Chemistry
HORVÁTH, A., Inorganic Chemistry
HORVÁTH, GY., Pedagogy and Psychology
HORVÁTH, J., Plant Pathology
HORVÁTH, O., Inorganic Chemistry
HUSVÉTH, F., Zoology
KANYÁR, B., Radiochemistry
KARDOS, Z., Social Sciences
KARDOS, Z., Economics
KISMÁNYOKI, T., Agronomy
KOCSONDI, J., Management and Economy
KOVÁCS, Z., Management and Economy
KOZMANN, GY., Informatics
KRISTÓF, J., Analytical Chemistry
LENGYEL, ZS., Applied Linguistics
LISZI, J., Physical Chemistry
LÖRINCZ, A., International Economics
MAJOR, I., Economics
MARTON, GY., Chemical Process Engineering
MÉSZÁROS, E., Environmental Sciences
MIHALOVICS, Á., French Language
MIHÁLYI, P., Economics
MINK, J., Analytical Chemistry
NAGY, I., Theatre Studies
PADISÁK, F., Limnology
PALKOVICS, M., Agricultural Economics
PAPP, S., Inorganic Chemistry
PUPOS, T., Economics
RÉDEY, Á., Chemical Technology, Environmental Engineering
SOMOGYI, S., Management and Economics
SPEIER, G., Organic Chemistry
SUGÁR, L., Zoology
SZABÓ, F., Animal Husbandry
SZABÓ, F., Hungarian Linguistics
SZABÓ, I., Botany
SZABÓ T, A., Biology
SZIRDNYI, T., Image Processing and Neurocomputing
SZILÁGYI, I., Social Sciences
SZOLGAY, P., Display Optics, Colour Image Sensing
TÖRÖK, A., Economics
TUZA, ZS., Mathematics
UNGVÁRY, F., Organic Chemistry
VARGA, K., Radiochemistry
VÁRNAGY, L., Agricultural Hygiene
VERESS, G., Informatics and Control
VINCZE, L., Inorganic Chemistry
VINCZE, L., Animal Nutrition
ZSOLNAY, F., Pedagogy

Theological Universities

DEBRECENI REFORMÁTUS HITTUDOMÁNYI EGYETEM
(University of Reformed Theology of Debrecen)

4044 Debrecen, Kálvin tér 16

Telephone: (52) 414-744
Fax: (52) 516-822
E-mail: info@drhe.drk.hu
Internet: www.drhe.drk.hu

Founded 1538

Rector: KÁROLY FEKETE

Library of 600,000 vols
Number of teachers: 36
Number of students: 306.

EVANGÉLIKUS HITTUDOMÁNYI EGYETEM
(Evangelical-Lutheran Theological University)

1141 Budapest, Rózsavölgyi köz 3

Telephone: (1) 383-4537
Fax: (1) 363-7454
E-mail: teologia@lutheran.hu
Internet: teol.lutheran.hu

Founded 1557

Rector: Dr LAJOS SZABÓ

Library of 55,000 vols, 119 periodicals
Number of teachers: 20
Number of students: 200

Departments of Church History, Church Music, New Testament Theology, Old Testament Theology, Practical Theology, Religious and Social Studies and Systematic Theology.

KÁROLI GÁSPÁR REFORMÁTUS EGYETEM
(Gáspár Károli University of the Reformed Church in Hungary)

1092 Budapest, Ráday u. 28

Telephone: (1) 217-2403
Fax: (1) 217-2403
E-mail: dekani.hivvez.htk@kre.hu
Internet: www.kre.hu

Founded 1855

Rector: EZTHER KOVÁCS

Library of 150,000 vols
Number of teachers: 19
Number of students: 190

DEANS

Faculty of Divinity: Prof. Dr DÁVID NÉMETH
Faculty of Humanities
Dr ERNŐ RAFFAY

ORSZÁGOS RABBIKÉPZŐ–ZSIDÓ EGYETEM
(Jewish Theological Seminary–University of Jewish Studies)

1084 Budapest, Bérkocsis u. 2

Telephone: and fax (1) 317-2396
E-mail: vzs@or-zse.hu
Internet: www.or-zse.hu

Founded 1877

Rector: Rabbi Dr Y. A. SCHÖNER

Library of 110,000 vols
Number of teachers: 87
Number of students: 264

Faculty of Rabbinical Studies; College Faculty/Paedagogium.

PÁZMÁNY PÉTER KATOLIKUS EGYETEM
(Péter Pázmány Catholic University)

1088 Budapest, Szentkirályi u. 28–30

Telephone: (1) 429-7211
Fax: (1) 318-0507
E-mail: rector@ppke.hu
Internet: www.ppke.hu

Founded 1635
Academic year: September to June

Rector: Rev. Dr GYÖRGY FODOR
Vice-Rector (vacant): Rev. Dr MIHÁLY KRÁNITZ
Financial Director: MIKLÓS RÓKA
Technical Director: PÉTER BOROSS-TÓBY
Chief Counsellor (vacant)
Co-ordinator of Education and Science: GÉZA BITTSÁNSZKY
Chief of International Relations: Dr ANDRÁS SZABÓ

Library of 400,000 vols
Number of teachers: 650
Number of students: 8,500

Publications: *Folia Canonica* (review of Eastern and Western Canon Law in five languages, annually), *Folia Theologica* (in five languages, annually), *Kánonjog* (Canon Law, in Hungarian, 2 a year), *Teológia* (in Hungarian, 4 a year), *VERBUM Analecta Neolatina* (in several European languages, 2 a year)

DEANS

Faculty of Humanities: Prof. IDA FRÖHLICH
Faculty of Information Technology: Prof. TAMÁS ROSKA
Faculty of Law and Political Science: Prof. GYULA BÁNDI
Faculty of Theology: Rev. Prof. ZOLTÁN ROKAY

Other Colleges

GENERAL

Collegium Budapest: 1014 Budapest, Szentháromság u. 2; tel. (1) 224-8300; fax (1) 224-8310; e-mail colbud@colbud.hu; internet www.zeus.colbud.hu; f. 1991; centre for interdisciplinary advanced and postdoctoral research and international scholarly exchange between East and West; library: 7,500 vols; 30 to 50 fellows; Rector GÁBOR KLANICZAY; Sec. FRED GIROD.

BUSINESS AND COMMERCE

Budapesti Gazdasági Főiskola Kereskedelmi, Vendéglátóipari és Idegenforgalmi Főiskolai Kar (College of Commerce, Catering and Tourism of Budapest Business School): 1054 Budapest, Alkotmány u. 9–11; tel. (1) 374-6207; fax (1) 302-2956; internet www.kvif.bgf.hu; f. 1969; library: 100,000 vols; 151 teachers; 6,500 students; Dir Dr KATALIN MEDVE.

Külkereskedelmi Főiskola Kar, Budapesti Gazdasági Főiskola (College for Management and Business Studies, Budapest Business School): 1165 Budapest, Diósy Lajos u. 22–24; tel. (1) 467-7800; fax (1) 407-1556; internet www.kkf.hu; f. 1971; 172 teachers; 3,331 students; library: 65,000 vols, 413 periodicals; Gen. Dir Dr ENDRE MARINOVICH.

Pénzügyi és Számviteli Főiskola (College of Finance and Accountancy): 1149 Budapest, Buzogány u. 10; tel. (1) 383-4799; fax (1) 383-4799; internet www.pszfb.hu; f. 1962; 172 teachers; 3,500 students; library: 125,000 vols; Dir Dr JÓZSEF ROÓZ.

TECHNOLOGY

Budapesti Műszaki Főiskola (Budapest Tech (Polytechnical Institution)): 1034 Budapest, Doberdó u. 6; tel. (1) 250-0333; fax (1) 453-4149; e-mail rektor@bmf.hu; internet www.bmf.hu; f. 2000 as a result of the merger of Könnyüipari Műszaki Főiskola (College of Technology for Light Industry) (Budapest), Bánki Donát Gépipari Műszaki Főiskola (Donát Bánki Polytechnic) (Budapest), Kandó Kálmán Műszaki Főiskola (Kálmán Kandó College of Engineering) (Budapest) and other instns; 417 teachers; 12,500 students; Rector Dr IMRE RUDAS.

Dunaújvárosi Főiskola (Dunaújváros Polytechnic): 2400 Dunaújváros Táncsics M. u. 1/A; tel. (25) 410-848; fax (25) 412-620; f. 1969; 111 teachers; 3,513 students; Dir-Gen. Dr ENDRE KISS.

Gépipari és Automatizálási Műszaki Főiskola (College of Mechanical Engineering and Automation): 6001 Kecskemét, Izsáki u. 10, Pf. 91; tel. (76) 481-291; fax (76) 481-304; e-mail gamf@gandalf.gamf.hu; f. 1964; training of production engineers in tool designing, product design, informatics, machine production, plastics production, plastics processing and cybernetics; 80 teachers; 1,300 students; library: 65,000 vols; Dir Dr A. SZABÓ; publ. *GAMF Közlemények*.

ICELAND

The Higher Education System

The Icelandic higher education system dates back to the foundation the University of Iceland in 1911. The University of Iceland remains the principal institution of higher learning in Iceland, but since the 1970s new institutions of higher education have emerged with a more specialized focus, providing greater diversity at that level. In 2007 there were nine higher education institutions in Iceland.

Legislation on higher education institutions (the Universities Act, No. 136/1997) enacted in 1997 establishes the general framework for the activities of these institutions. In this Act, the term 'háskóli' is used to refer both to traditional universities and institutions which do not carry out research. Separate legislation for each public higher education institution, and the charters of privately run universities, define their engagement in research, internal organization, etc. Iceland is a signatory of the Bologna Declaration and all legislative reforms and regulations are handled by a national Bologna follow-up group based in the Ministry of Education and Culture. A two-cycle degree system which conforms to the Bologna regulations is well established for most courses with the exception of medical-related subjects.

Public and private higher education institutions receive individual appropriations from the state budget. The administration of each public university is entrusted to the Senate, the rector, faculty meetings, faculty councils and deans, if the university is divided into faculties. The Senate issues final rulings in the affairs of the university and its institutions, formulates their overall policy and furthers their development. The Senate is the supreme decision-making body in each institution unless otherwise provided for explicitly in the relevant act. The state draws up performance-related contracts with all higher education institutions, defining how the institution intends to achieve its objectives and what the Government's financial contribution shall be.

Entry to undergraduate courses is based on the Stúdentspróf (matriculation examination). Many institutions have restricted admission based on the average mark obtained or marks in subjects that are deemed relevant. Mature students are not always required to hold the Stúdentspróf if they have specific work experience. Courses are assessed in terms of credits. Short courses resulting in a certificate or diploma are available in a limited number of subjects. The Baccalaureatus (Bachelors degree), usually in arts, science or education, is three to four years in length (a minimum of 90 credits). The University of Iceland awards the Kandidatspróf (Candidatus degree), which is offered in professional subject areas (law, medicine, engineering, etc.) and is four to six years in length. A number of institutions provide one- to two-year programmes following the Baccalaureatus leading to postgraduate certificates in various subjects. The University of Iceland awards the Meistarapróf (Masters degree) after a two-year course for holders of the Baccalaureatus. In some cases a first-class Baccalaureatus is required. The Magister Paedagogiae degree in education is only offered in Icelandic studies. All courses require completion of a major thesis or research project. The Iceland University of Education offers a two-year Master of Education course. There are two types of Doktorspróf (Doctorate degree) available either at the University of Iceland or the Iceland University of Education. The Doctor Philosophiae is three or four years in length and follows the Meistarapróf. The Doctor Scientiarum and the Doctor Medicinae degree courses are based on the Kandidatspróf or the Meistarapróf degrees. In exceptional circumstances, a holder of a good Baccalaureatus may be allowed to undertake a Doctorate degree; however, studies would have to last for four years. The course is completely research-based.

Specialized vocational schools, known as Sérskóli, offer courses for specialized employment. Since the 1990s many Sérskóli have been upgraded to the higher education level. Students are required to take 25 unit-credits in general academic subjects to complement their technical training. Apprentices completing their studies take the Sveinspróf (Journeyman's examination). Students may progress to become a Meistarabréf (Master Craftsman) after a period of work experience and advanced study. Alternatively, students may progress to university after a specified period of additional studies. The Meistarabréf gives the right to train apprentices, operate a business or manage an enterprise.

Icelandic students have a long tradition of studying abroad for their higher education. About 16% of Icelandic students in higher education study abroad, most of them in post-graduate studies.

Learned Societies

AGRICULTURE, FISHERIES AND VETERINARY SCIENCE

Bændasamtök Íslands (Farmers' Association of Iceland): Baendahöllinni við Hagatorg, POB 7080, 127 Reykjavík; tel. 563-0300; fax 562-3058; e-mail vefstjori@bondi.is; internet www.bondi.is; f. 1995; 4,000 farmer mems in 15 district assocs and 13 sector orgs; library of 10,000 vols; Chair. ARI TEITSSON; Dir Dr SIGURGEIR THORGEIRSSON; publs *Bændablaðið* (Farmers' News, every 2 weeks), *Freyr* (monthly).

BIBLIOGRAPHY, LIBRARY SCIENCE AND MUSEOLOGY

Information–The Icelandic Library and Information Science Association: Lágmúla 7, 108 Reykjavík; tel. 553-7290; fax 588-9239; e-mail upplysing@bokis.is; internet www.bokis.is; f. 1960; 500 mems; Pres. ÞÓRDÍS T. ÞÓRARINSDÓTTIR; Sec. INGIBJÓRG BALDURSDÓTTIR; publs *Bókasafnið* (annually), *Fregnir* (3 a year), *A Leið til Upplýsingar* (History of Icelandic Library Associations, with summary in English).

FINE AND PERFORMING ARTS

Bandalag Íslenzkra Listamanna (Union of Icelandic Artists): Laugavegur 24, POB 637, 101 Reykjavík; tel. 822-3699; e-mail bil@mmedia.is; internet www.bil.is; f. 1928; Pres. ÞORVALDUR ÞORSTEINSSON; 1,712 mems.

Constituent organizations:

Arkítektafélag Íslands (Icelandic Architects' Association): Engjateigi 9, 105 Reykjavík; tel. 551-1465; fax 562-0465; e-mail ai@ai.is; internet www.ai.is; 226 mems; Chair. ÞÓRARINN ÞÓRARINSSON.

Félag Íslenzkra Leikara (Icelandic Actors' Association): Lindargötu 6, 101 Reykjavík; tel. 552-6040; fax 562-7706; e-mail fil@fil.is; internet www.fil.is; Chair. RANDVER THORLAKSSON; 310 mems.

Félag Íslenzkra Listdansara (Association of Icelandic Dance Artists): POB 8654, 128 Reykjavík; e-mail olof.i@li.is; 55 mems; Chair. ÓLÖF INGÓLFSDÓTTIR.

Félag Íslenzkra Myndlistarmanna (Association of Icelandic Visual Artists): Klapparstíg 25–27, 101 Reykjavík; e-mail sim@simnet.is; Chair. PJETUR STEFÁNSSON; 263 mems.

Félag Íslenzkra Tónlistarmanna (Icelandic Musicians' Association): Lindargötu 46, 101 Reykjavík; fax 562-6455; e-mail fiston@centrum.is; Chair. MARGRÉT BÓASDÓTTIR; 92 mems.

Félag Kvikmyndagerdarmanna (Icelandic Film Makers' Association): POB 5162, 128 Reykjavík; internet www.filmmakers.is; f. 1966; 156 mems; Chair. BJORN BJÖRNSSON.

Félag Leikstjóra á Íslandi (Icelandic Association of Stage Directors): Lindargötu 6, 101 Reykjavík; tel. 562-6656; 68 mems; Chair. PETER EINARSSON.

Rithöfundasamband Íslands (Icelandic Writers' Association): Dyngjuvegi 8, 104 Reykjavík; tel. 568-3190; fax 568-3192;

e-mail rsi@rsi.is; internet www.rsi.is; f. 1974; 365 mems; Chair. PETUR GUNNARSSON.

Samband Íslenzkra Myndlistarmanna (Icelandic Visual Artists' Association): Hafnarstræti 16, POB 1115, 121 Reykjavík; tel. 551-1346; fax 562-6656; e-mail sim@simnet.is; internet www.sim.is; 355 mems; Chair. SOLVEIG EGGERTSDÓTTIR.

Samtök Kvikmundaleikstjóra (Guild of Icelandic Film Directors): Sudurgata 14, 101 Reykjavík; 50 mems; Chair. FRIDRIK THOR FRIDRIKSSON.

Tónskáldafélag Íslands (Icelandic Composers' Society): Laufásvegi 40, 101 Reykjavík; tel. 552-4972; 50 mems; Chair. JOHN SPEIGHT.

Tónlistarfélagið (Music Society): Bjarmaland 19, 108 Reykjavík; f. 1930; operates a College of Music; affiliated societies in major towns; Chair. BALDVIN TRYGGVASON; Man. RUT MAGNÚSSON; Headmaster of College HALLDÓR HARALDSSON.

HISTORY, GEOGRAPHY AND ARCHAEOLOGY

Íslenzka fornleifafélag (Icelandic Archaeological Society): POB 177, 121 Reykjavík; f. 1879; Pres. THÓR MAGNÚSSON; 600 mems; Sec. GUDMUNDUR ÓLAFSSON; publ. *Árbók* (Year Book).

Sögufélagið (Icelandic Historical Society): Fischerssundi 3, 101 Reykjavík, POB 1078, R 121; tel. 14620; f. 1902; 1,600 mems; Pres. HEIMIR THORLEIFSSON; Sec. SVEINBJÖRN RAFNSSON; publs *Ný saga* (annually), *Saga* (annually).

LANGUAGE AND LITERATURE

Hið Íslenzka bókmenntafélag (Icelandic Literary Society): Skeifan 3b, POB 8935, 128 Reykjavík; e-mail hib@islandia.is; internet www.hib.is; f. 1816; research work and publishing; 2,000 mems; Pres. SIGURDUR LÍNDAL; Sec. REYNIR AXELSSON; publ. *Skírnir* (2 a year).

NATURAL SCIENCES

General

Vísindafélag Íslendinga (Icelandic Academy of Sciences and Letters): Bárugötu 3, 101 Reykjavík; f. 1918; 159 mems; Pres. SIGURDUR STEINTHORSSON; publs *Ráðstefnurit* (irregular), *Rit*.

Biological Sciences

Íslenzka náttúrufrædifélag (Icelandic Natural History Society): Hlemmi 3, POB 5320, 125 Reykjavík; tel. 590-0500; fax 590-0595; e-mail ni@ni.is; internet www.ni.is; f. 1889; 1,600 mems; library of 9,000 vols, 600 periodicals; Pres. JÓN OTTÓSSON; publ. *Náttúrufrædingurinn* (quarterly journal of natural history).

Physical Sciences

Jöklarannsóknafélag Íslands (Iceland Glaciological Society): POB 5128, 125 Reykjavík; fax 552-1347; internet www.jorfi.is; f. 1950; 550 mems; Pres. MAGNÚS T. GUDMUNDSSON; Sec. STEINUNN JAKOBSDÓTTIR; publ. *Jökull* (annually).

TECHNOLOGY

Verkfrædingafélag Íslands (Association of Chartered Engineers in Iceland): Engjateigi 9, Reykjavík 105; tel. 568-8511; fax 568-9703; f. 1912; 1,100 mems; Pres. STEINAR FRIDGEIRSSON; Sec. LOGI KRISTJÁNSSON; publs *Árbók Verkfrædingafélags Íslands* (annually), *Verktækni* (newsletter, 10 a year).

Research Institutes

ECONOMICS, LAW AND POLITICS

Hagstofa Íslands (Statistics Iceland): Borgartun 21A, 150 Reykjavík; tel. 528-1000; fax 528-1098; e-mail information@statice.is; internet www.statice.is; f. 1914; Dir-Gen. HALLGRÍMUR SNORRASON; publs *Hagtíðindi* (Statistics Monthly), *Hagskýrslur Íslands* (Statistics of Iceland), *Landshagir* (Statistical Yearbook of Iceland).

MEDICINE

Rannsóknastofa Háskólans (University Institute of Pathology): Barónsstígur, POB 1465, 121 Reykjavík; tel. 543-8351; f. 1917; 52 mems; Dir Prof. JOHANNES BJORNSSON.

Tilraunastöð Háskóla Íslands i meinafræði að Keldum (Institute for Experimental Pathology, University of Iceland): við Vesturlandsveg, 112 Reykjavík; tel. 585-5100; fax 567-3979; e-mail bo@hi.is; internet www.keldur.hi.is; f. 1948; affiliated to University of Iceland; library of 4,000 vols; Dir SIGURDUR INGRARSSON; publ. *Icelandic Agricultural Sciences* (1–2 a year).

NATURAL SCIENCES

General

Rannsóknarrád Íslands (Icelandic Research Council): Laugavegur 13, 101 Reykjavík; tel. 515-5800; fax 552-9814; internet www.rannis.is; f. 1994 to advise the Government and Parliament on all aspects of science, technology and innovation, and to promote international co-operation in science and technology; a government institution subordinate to the Ministry of Culture and Education; Dir Dr HANS KRISTJÁN GUÐMUNDSSON.

Attached research institutes:

Hafrannsóknastofnunin (Marine Research Institute): Skulagata 4, 121 Reykjavík; tel. 575-2000; fax 575-2001; e-mail hafro@hafro.is; internet www.hafro.is; research into marine biological and oceanographic sciences; special divisions for pelagic fish, demersal fish, flat-fish, technology and fishing gear, hydrography, phytoplankton, zooplankton and benthos; Government institution subordinate to the Ministry of Fisheries; Chair. FRIÐRIK BALDURSSON; Dir JÓHANN SIGURJÓNSSON.

Idntæknistofnun Íslands (Technological Institute of Iceland): c/o Rannsóknarrád Íslands, Laugavegur 13, 101 Reykjavík; research and service institution for industry; research on raw materials, machinery and end products to improve quality and competitiveness of Icelandic industrial production; special divisions for training and information, industrial development, technical services and for research; Government institution subordinate to the Ministry of Industry; Chair. MAGNÚS FRIÐGEIRSSON; Dir HALLGRÍMUR JÓNASSON.

Rannsóknastofnun byggingaidnadarins (Building Research Institute): c/o Rannsóknarrád Íslands, Laugavegur 13, 101 Reykjavík; f. 1965; scientific research and services for the construction and building industries; Government institution subordinate to the Ministry of Industry; Chair MAGNUS FRIÐGEIRSSON; Dir HÁKON ÓLAFSSON.

Rannsóknastofnun fiskidnadarins (Icelandic Fisheries Laboratories): Skulagata 4, 101 Reykjavík; tel. 530-8600; fax 530-8601; e-mail info@rf.is; internet www.rfisk.is; research and services for the fish industry, quality control, etc.; divisions for chemistry, bacteriology and technology; Government institution subordinate to the Ministry of Fisheries; Chair. FRIÐRIK FRIÐRIKSSON.

Rannsóknastofnun landbúnadarins (Agricultural Research Institute): c/o Rannsóknarrád Íslands, Laugavegur 13, 101 Reykjavík; internet www.rala.is; government-financed research and experimental development in agriculture; special divisions for animal-breeding, ecology and cultivation and farming technology; Government institution subordinate to the Ministry of Agriculture; Chair. PÉTUR HELGASON; Dir THORSTEINN TÓMASSON.

Surtseyjarfélagið (Surtsey Research Society): POB 352, 121 Reykjavík; e-mail surtsey@ni.is; f. 1965; to promote and co-ordinate scientific work in geo- and biological sciences on the island of Surtsey; 104 mems; Chair. STEINGRIMUR HERMANNSSON; Sec. SVEINN JAKOBSSON; publ. *Surtsey Research*.

Biological Sciences

Náttúrufrædistofnun Íslands (Icelandic Institute of Natural History): POB 5320, 125 Reykjavík; tel. 590-0500; fax 590-0595; e-mail ni@nattfs.is; f. 1889 by Hið Íslenzka Náttúrufrædifélag (The Icelandic Natural History Society) and maintained by this Society until 1946; taken over by the State 1947; library of 8,000 vols, 500 periodicals; Dir-Gen. JÓN G. OTTÓSSON; Dir AEVAR PETERSEN (Reykjavík); Dir KRISTINN J. ALBERTSSON; publs *Bliki* (irregular), *Fjölrit Náttúrufræðistofnunar* (irregular), *Acta Botanica Islandica* (2 a year).

Physical Sciences

Vedurstofa Íslands (Icelandic Meteorological Office): Bústadavegur 9, 150 Reykjavík; tel. 522-6000; fax 522-6001; e-mail office@vedur.is; internet www.vedur.is; f. 1920; weather forecasts, climatology, aerology, sea ice, seismology, avalanches and landslides; library of 10,000 vols; Dir MAGNÚS JÓNSSON; publs *Vedráttan* (monthly), *Greinargerd* (Report, irreg.).

Libraries and Archives

Reykjavík

Borgarbókasafn Reykjavíkur (City Library of Reykjavík): Grófarhús, Tryggvagötu 15, 101 Reykjavík; tel. 563-1750; fax 563-1705; e-mail borgarbokasafn@borgarbokasafn.is; internet www.borgarbokasafn.is; f. 1923; 500,000 vols; Dir ANNA TORFADOTTIR.

Landsbókasafn Íslands-Háskólabókasafn (National and University Library of Iceland): Arngrímsgötu 3, 107 Reykjavík; tel. 525-5600; fax 525-5615; e-mail lbs@bok.hi.is; internet www.bok.hi.is; f. 1994 by amalgamation of the National Library of Iceland (f. 1818) and the University Library (f. 1940); 870,000 books, 16,000 MSS; Dir Dr SIGRÚN KLARA HANNESDÓTTIR.

Thjódskjalasafn Íslands (National Archives of Iceland): Laugavegur 162, Reykjavík; tel. 590-3300; fax 590-3301; e-mail upplysingar@skjalasafn.is; internet www.archives.is; f. 1882; collection of historical documents since 12th c.; Dir ÓLAFUR ÁSGEIRSSON.

Museums and Art Galleries

Gardabær

Thjóðminjasafn (National Museum): Lynghàls 7, 210 Garðabær; tel. 530-2200; fax

530-2201; e-mail natmus@natmus.is; internet www.natmus.is; f. 1863; the main collection is of Icelandic antiquities; collection of folk art and ethnology; Dir MARGRÉT HALLGRÍMSDÓTTIR (State Antiquary); publs *Árbók hins islenzka fornleifafélags*, *Asa G. Wright Memorial Lectures*, *Rit Hins islenska fornleifafélags og Thjódminjasafns Islands*.

Reykjavík

Listasafn Einars Jónssonar (National Einar Jónsson Museum): Eiriksgata, POB 1051, 121 Reykjavík; tel. 551-3797; fax 562-3909; e-mail skulptur@skulptur.is; internet www.skulptur.is; sculpture and paintings by Einar Jónsson (1874–1954); Dir JULIANA GOTTSKALKSDOTTIR; publ. catalogue.

Þjóðminjasafn Íslands (National Museum of Iceland): Suðurgötu 41, 101 Reykjavík; tel. 530-2200; fax 530-2201; e-mail natmus@natmus.is; internet www.natmus.is; f. 1863; 2,000 objects, dating from the Settlement Age to the present; 1,000 photographs since beginning of 20th c.; Dir (vacant).

Universities

HÁSKÓLINN Á AKUREYRI
(University of Akureyri)

Nordurslod, 600 Akureyri
Telephone: 463-0900
Fax: 463-0999
E-mail: international@unak.is
Internet: www.unak.is
Founded 1987
Languages of instruction: Icelandic, English
Academic year: August to June
Rector: THORSTEINN GUNNARSSON
Number of teachers: 70
Number of students: 1,500
Faculties: education, health sciences, information technology, management, natural resource sciences, social sciences and law..

ATTACHED RESEARCH INSTITUTES

Research Institute: Þingvallastræti 23, 600 Akureyri; tel. 463-0570; fax 463-0998; e-mail rha@unak.is; Dir GRÉTAR THOR EYTHORSSON.

HÁSKÓLI ÍSLANDS
(University of Iceland)

Suðurgata, 101 Reykjavík
Telephone: 525-4000
Fax: 552-1331
E-mail: hi@hi.is
Internet: www.hi.is
Founded 1911
State control
Academic year: September to June
Rector: Prof. KRISTÍN INGÓLFSDÓTTIR
Vice-Rector: Prof. EIRÍKUR TÓMASSON
Director (Academic Affairs): THÓRDUR KRISTINSSON
Director (Finances): GUNNLAUGUR H. JÓNSSON
Director (International Relations): KARITAS KVARAN
Director (Operations and Construction): GUÐMUNDUR R. JÓNSSON
Director (Research): HALLDÓR JÓNSSON
Library: see Libraries and Archives
Number of teachers: 2,300 (430 tenured, 1,800 non-tenured)
Number of students: 9,000
Publications: *Árbók Háskóla Íslands* (annually), *Ritaskrá Háskóla Íslands* (annually)

DEANS

Faculty of Economics and Business Administration: Assoc. Prof. GYLFI MAGNÚSSON
Faculty of Engineering: Prof. SIGURÐUR BRYNJÓLFSSON
Faculty of Humanities: Assoc. Prof. ODDNÝ G. SVERRISDÓTTIR
Faculty of Law: Prof. EIRÍKUR TÓMASSON
Faculty of Medicine: Prof. STEFÁN B. SIGURÐSSON
Faculty of Natural Sciences: Prof. THORSTEINN VILHJÁLMSSON
Faculty of Nursing: Prof. ERLA KOLBRÚN SVAVARSDÓTTIR
Faculty of Odontology: Assoc. Prof. EINAR RAGNARSSON
Faculty of Pharmacy: Prof. ÞORSTEINN LOFTSSON
Faculty of Science: Assoc. Prof. HÖRÐUR FILIPPUSSON
Faculty of Social Sciences: Prof. ÓLAFUR HARÐARSON
Faculty of Theology: Prof. EINAR SIGURBJÖRNSSON

ATTACHED RESEARCH INSTITUTES

Árni Magnússon Institute in Iceland.
Centre for International Studies.
Centre for Research in the Humanities.
Centre for Women's and Gender Studies.
Dental Institute.
Engineering Research Institute.
Ethical Research Institute.
Fisheries Research Institute.
Icelandic Language Institute.
Institute of Anthropology.
Institute of Biology.
Institute of Business Research.
Institute of Economic Studies.
Institute of Experimental Pathology.
Institute of History.
Institute of Lexicography (Ordabók).
Institute of Linguistics.
Institute of Literary Research.
Institute of Nursing Research.
Institute of Philosophy.
Institute of Theology.
Law Institute.
Nordic Volcanological Institute.
Science Institute.
Sigurdur Nordal Institute: medieval and modern Icelandic culture.

HÁSKÓLINN Í REYKJAVIK
(University of Reykjavik)

Ofanleiti 2, 103 Reykjavik
Telephone: 510-6200
Fax: 510-6201
E-mail: ru@ru.is
Internet: www.ru.is
Founded 1998
Academic year: August to June
Rector: Dr GUÐFINNA S. BJARNADOTTIR
Dir: HANNA KATRÍN FRIÐRIKSSON
Head Librarian: GUÐRÚN TRYGGVADÓTTIR

DEANS

School of Business: AGNAR HANSSON
School of Computer Science: GÍSLI HJÁLMTÝSSON
School of Law: THÓRÐUR S. GUNNARSSON

KENNARHÁSKÓLI ÍSLANDS
(Iceland University of Education)

Stakkahlíð, 105 Reykjavik
Telephone: 563-3800
Fax: 563-3833
E-mail: khi@khi.is
Internet: www.khi.is
Founded 1908, as Teachers' College of Iceland, present name and status 1997
Academic year: August to July
Rector: Dr ÓLAFUR PROPPÉ
Number of teachers: 170
Number of students: 1,800
Departments of undergraduate and postgraduate studies.

LANDBUNAÐARHÁSKÓLI ÍSLANDS
(Agricultural University of Iceland)

Hvanneyri, 311 Borgarnes
Telephone: 433-5000
Fax: 433-5001
E-mail: lbhi@lbhi.is
Internet: www.hvanneyri.is
Founded 1889
Rector: Dr ÁGÚST SIGURÐSSON,
Library of 18,650 vols
Number of teachers: 28
Number of students: 246
Publication: *Fjölrit Bændaskólans* (annually).

LISTAHÁSKÓLI ÍSLANDS
(Iceland Academy of Arts)

Skipholt 1, Reykjavík
Telephone: 552-4000
Fax: 562-3629
E-mail: lhi@lhi.is
Internet: www.lhi.is
Founded 1998, following merger of Reykjavik College of Music, Icelandic College of Arts and Crafts, and Icelandic Drama School
State control
Rector: HJALMAR H. RAGNARSSON
Director of Academic Affairs: SIGRUN KR. MAGNUSDOTTIR
International Relations Co-ordinator and Student Counsellor: HANNA BACHMAN
Library Director: LÍSA VALDIMARSDÓTTIR
Departments: architecture, drama, graphic design, music, product design, visual art.

TÆKNISKÓLI ÍSLANDS
(Icelandic College of Engineering and Technology)

Höfðabakka 9, 110 Reykjavík
Telephone: 577-1400
Fax: 577-1401
E-mail: icet@ti.is
Internet: vefur.ti.is
Founded 1964
Languages of instruction: Icelandic, English
Academic year: August to May
Rector: GUDBRANDUR STEINTHORSSON
Library of 9,000 vols
Number of teachers: 115 (45 full-time, 70 part-time)
Number of students: 700.

VIÐSKIPTAHÁSKÓLINN Á BIFRÖST
(Bifröst School of Business)

311 Borgarnes
Telephone: 433-3000
Fax: 433-3001
E-mail: bifrost@bifrost.is
Internet: www.bifrost.is
Founded 1918
Private, non-profit
Languages of instruction: Icelandic, English
Academic year: September to August
Library of 7,000 vols
Rector: RUNÓLFUR ÁGÚSTSSON
Vice-Rector: MAGNÚS ÁRNI MAGNÚSSON

Librarian: ANDREA JÓHANNSDÓTTIR
International Coordinators: KRISTÍN ÓLAFSDÓTTIR, Dr IAN WATSON
Number of teachers: 30
Number of students: 700 (500 undergraduate, 120 graduate, 80 preparatory)

DEANS

Faculty of Business: BERNHARD ÞÓR BERNHARDSSON
Faculty of Law: BRYNDÍS HLÖÐVERSDÓTTIR
Faculty of Social Sciences and Economics: MAGNÚS ÁRNI MAGNÚSSON

PROFESSORS

BJARNASON, A., Business
EYÞÓRSSON, G., Social Sciences and Economics
JÓNSSON, I., Social Sciences and Economics
MÓSESDÓTTIR, L., Business
ÓLAFSSON, J., Social Sciences and Economics
ÞORGEIRSDÓTTIR, H., Law

College

Búnadarskólinn á Hólum i Hjaltadal (Agricultural School): Hólum i Hjaltadal, 551 Sauðárkrókur; tel. 453-6300; fax 453-6301; e-mail holaskoli@holar.is; f. 1882; library: 6,000 vols; 4 professors; 50 students; depts of aquaculture and rural tourism; International Center for Icelandic Horses; Dir HAUKUR JØRUNDARSON.

INDIA

The Higher Education System

The modern higher education system was established while India was under British rule. Among the oldest institutions are Presidency College (founded in 1817), Deccan College Post-graduate and Research Institute (founded in 1821) and Sanskrit College (founded in 1824). In 1857 major universities were founded at Mumbai (formerly Bombay), Madras and Kolkata (formerly Calcutta). The main representative body of Indian universities, the Association of Indian Universities, was founded in 1925 and re-established as a statutory body in 1947, when India gained its independence. In 1953 the University Grants Commission was created to act between the Government and States as the co-ordinating body on higher education. In the same year a National Council for Higher Education in Rural Areas was established. India had a total of 277 universities and institutions with university status in 2003, and some 13,150 university and affiliated colleges in 2001/02. University enrolment was 9.2m. in 2002/03.

Universities are autonomous institutions, mostly funded by the States' governments, except for the 'central' universities, which are funded by the central Government. Universities are classified as either 'unitary' or 'affiliating'. Unitary universities conduct all undergraduate and postgraduate teaching, while in affiliating universities the teaching of undergraduates is conducted by affiliated colleges. There are also two other types of universities, 'deemed' and 'institutions of national importance'. Deemed universities are single-discipline institutions which have been granted university status by the University Grants Commission, and the institutions of national importance are funded directly by the Government but are distinct from central universities. The States account for 90% of university funding, with the rest coming from central Government. Student fees account for a small percentage of universities' income. The National Assessment and Accreditation Council (founded 1994) is the national body responsible for accreditation and quality assurance.

Universities have broadly the same administrative structure. The Vice-Chancellor is both the administrative and the academic head of the university. The Senate or Court, Syndicate and Executive Council or Board of Management are the primary administrative bodies, responsible for institutional budgets and management. The Academic Council oversees all academic aspects of the institution, including teaching and research. Faculties are the most important academic divisions, and are headed by Deans. Boards of Study determine programmes of study.

Admission to higher education is on the basis of one of the different Higher Secondary School Certificates. Standard undergraduate Bachelors degrees last three years, although some programmes in professional fields of study last four years (engineering, dentistry and pharmacy) or five years (architecture). The Bachelor of Laws is either a five-year first degree or a two- to three-year second degree. The first postgraduate degree is the Masters. Admission to the Masters may vary depending on the institution; a Bachelors is the most common requirement, but institutions may also set an entrance examination, while applicants for Masters programmes in the fields of architecture, engineering, pharmacy and technology must sit the Graduate Aptitude Test in Engineering. Masters programmes are two to three years in length. Following the Masters there is a pre-doctoral programme called the Master of Philosophy (MPhil), a one-and-a-half year course. Finally, the Doctorate (PhD) is awarded three years after the Masters and at least two years after the MPhil. The PhD consists of a thesis based on original research.

Technical and vocational education is overseen by several different bodies: the Central Apprenticeship Council, the National Council for Training in Vocational Trades, the National Council for Educational Research and Training, the Joint Council for Vocationalisation of Education and the All India Council for Technical Education. The Joint Council for Vocationalisation of Education was founded in 1990 and is the body tasked with implementing and maintaining the national standard of vocational education. Universities, polytechnics and colleges offer one- to four-year Diploma courses in most subjects.

Regulatory and Representative Bodies

GOVERNMENT

Bureau of University and Higher Education, Minorities Education, Book Promotion and Copyrights, Ministry of Human Resources Development: Shastri Bhavan, New Delhi 110 001; tel. (11) 23382298; fax (11) 23070036; e-mail skumar@nic.in; internet education.nic.in; Minister of Human Resource Devt ARJUN SINGH; Jt Sec., Bureau of Univ. and Higher Education SUNIL KUMAR.

Ministry of Culture: Room 334, 'C' Wing, Shastri Bhavan, New Delhi 110 001; tel. (11) 23381198; fax (11) 23382907; e-mail js .culture@nic.in; internet indiaculture.nic.in; Minister AMBIKA SONI.

Ministry of Human Resource Development: Shastri Bhavan, New Delhi 110 001; tel. (11) 23782698; fax (11) 23382365; internet education.nic.in; Minister ARJUN SINGH.

ACCREDITATION

National Assessment and Accreditation Council: POB 1075, Nagarbhavi, Bangalore, Karnataka; tel. (80) 23210261; fax (80) 23210270; e-mail vsprasad@naacindia.org; internet www.naacindia.org; Dir Prof. V. S. PRASAD.

FUNDING

University Grants Commission: Bahadur Shah Zafar Marg, New Delhi 110002; tel. (11) 23319628; f. 1953 to promote and co-ordinate univ. education; to determine and maintain the standards of teaching, examination and research in univs; may allocate grants to univs and colleges for these purposes; library of 41,850 vols; receives 50 journals; Chair. Prof. A. S. DESAI; Sec. Dr G. D. SHARMA; publs *University Development in India* (annual statistical review), *Journal of Higher Education*, *Bulletin of Higher Education*.

NATIONAL BODIES

All India Council for Technical Education: I.G. Sports Complex, I.P. Estate, New Delhi 110 002; tel. (11) 23392506; fax (11) 23392554; e-mail admin@aicte.ernet.in; internet www.aicte.ernet.in; Chair. of Council Prof. DAMODAR ACHARYA.

Association of Indian Universities: AIU House, 16 Kotla Marg, New Delhi 110002; tel. (11) 23236105; fax (11) 23232131; e-mail aiu@del2.vsnl.net.in; internet www.aiuweb .org; f. 1925; facilitates exchange of information between univs, organizes meetings, conferences of vice-chancellors, inter-univ. youth festivals and sports events, researches into contemporary problems and issues relating to higher education and overseas degree equivalence, liaises with foreign univs; 256 mem. univs; library of 30,000 vols, 130 periodicals; Pres. Prof. S. VENKATESWARAN; Sec.-Gen. Prof. K. B. POWAR; publs *Universities Handbook* (every 2 years), *Handbook of Medical Education*, *Handbook of Distance Education*, *Handbook of Engineering Education*, *Handbook of Management Education*, *Handbook of Computer Education*, *Handbook of Library and Information Science*, *Scholarships for Study Abroad and at Home* (all annual), *Equivalence of Foreign Degrees* (irreg.).

Indian Adult Education Association: 17B Indraprastha Estate, New Delhi 110002; tel. (11) 23319282; fax (11) 23355306; f. 1939; recognized by nat. govt; training, research, publs and field programmes; 1,500 mems; library of 12,000 vols; Pres. B. S. GARG; Sec. K. C. CHOUDHARY; publs *Indian Journal of Adult Education* (quarterly), *Proudh Shiksha* (Hindi monthly), *IAEA Newsletter* (monthly), *Jago Aur Jagao* (Hindi monthly).

National Council of Educational Research and Training: Sri Aurobindo Marg, New Delhi 110016; tel. (11) 26560620; fax (11) 26868419; e-mail directorncert@vsnl.com; internet www.ncert.nic.in; f. 1961 with the aim of improving school education; academic adviser to the Min. of Human Resource Devt; co-ordinates research and devt in all branches of education; organizes pre- and in-service training; publishes school textbooks, instructional material for teachers and educational surveys; 8 major constituent units: Nat. Institute of Education and Central Institute of Educational Technology in New Delhi, Central Institute of Vocational Education in Bhopal and 5 regional Institutes of Education at Ajmer, Bhopal, Bhubaneswar, Mysore and Shillong; Pres. The Union Min. of Human Resource Devt; Dir Prof. KRISHNA KUMAR; publs *Indian Education*, *Journal of Value Education*, *School Science*, *Primary Teacher*.

Learned Societies

GENERAL

India International Centre: 40 Max Mueller Marg, New Delhi 110003; tel. (11) 24619431; f. 1958; international cultural organization for promotion of amity and understanding between the different communities in the world; programme of lectures, discussions, film evenings, etc.; mems: 3,746 individuals, 256 corporate (including 35 univs); library of 31,000 vols, also houses the India Collection of 3,500 rare documents on British India and the Himalayan Club Library of 900 vols; Pres. Dr KAPILA VATSYAYAN; Dir N. N. VOHRA; Sec. N. H. RAMACHANDRAN; publs *IIC Quarterly*, *IIC Diary* (every 2 months).

Indian Council for Cultural Relations: Azad Bhawan, Indraprastha Estate, New Delhi 110002; tel. (11) 23318303; fax (11) 23712639; f. 1950 to establish and strengthen cultural relations between India and other countries; branch offices in Mumbai, Calcutta, Madras, Bangalore, Chandigarh, Lucknow, Trivandrum and Hyderabad; cultural centres in Georgetown (Guyana), Paramaribo (Suriname), Moscow (Russia), Port Louis (Mauritius), Jakarta (Indonesia), Berlin (Germany), Cairo (Egypt), Tashkent (Uzbekistan), Almaty (Kazakhstan) and London (United Kingdom); activities include exchange visits between scholars, artists and men of eminence in the field of art and culture; exchange of exhibitions; international conferences and seminars, lectures by renowned scholars including Azad Memorial Lectures; establishment of chairs and centres of Indian studies abroad and welfare of overseas students in India; administration of Jawaharlal Nehru Award for International Understanding; prestation of books and Indian art objects to universities, libraries and museums in other countries; library: over 75,000 vols on India and other countries; Pres. VASANT SATHE; Dir-Gen. SHIV SHANKER MUKHERJEE; publs interpretations of Indian art and culture and translations of Indian works into foreign languages, *Indian Horizons*, *African Quarterly* (in English, quarterly), *Thaqafat-ul-Hind* (in Arabic, quarterly), *Papeles de la India* (in Spanish, quarterly), *Rencontre avec l'Inde* (in French, quarterly), *Gagananchal* (Hindi, quarterly).

Indian Institute of World Culture: POB 402, 6 Shri B.P. Wadia Rd, Basavangudi, Bangalore 560004; tel. (80) 26678581; e-mail iiwc@vsnl.net; f. 1945; Mumbai Office: Theosophy Hall, 40 New Marine Lines, Mumbai 400020; 3,100 mems; library of 45,000 vols, 400 periodicals; objects: to provide opportunities for cultural and intellectual development, to promote exchange of thought between India and other countries and to raise the consideration of national and world problems to the plane of moral and spiritual values and to foster a sense of universal brotherhood; Pres. Justice M. N. VENKATACHALIAH; Hon. Sec. L. CHANDRASHEKAR; publs *Annual Report*, *Bulletin* (monthly), *Transactions*.

Jammu and Kashmir Academy of Art, Culture and Languages: Srinagar, Kashmir 190001; tel. (191) 2542640 (Jammu); tel. (8649) 232379 (Srinagar); fax (191) 2542640 (Jammu); fax (8649) 232379 (Srinagar); f. 1958; to promote arts, culture and languages of the State; library of 20,000 vols, 650 rare MSS, 250 laminated photographs, 90 opera and folk song recordings; collections of gramophone records, cassettes, paintings, jewellery, calligraphy, costumes, contemporary paintings and sculpture; Pres. Gen. K. V. KRISHNA RAO; Sec. B. THAKUR; publs *Sheeraza* (monthly in Urdu, every 2 months in Kashmiri, Dogri, Punjabi and Hindi, quarterly in Ladakhi, Pahari, Gojri and annually in English and Balti), *Hamara Adab* (annual anthology in Urdu, Kashmiri, Gojri, Pahari, Dogri, Punjabi, Hindi, Ladakhi), *Akademi* (Newsletter), *Encyclopaedia Kashmirana*.

AGRICULTURE, FISHERIES AND VETERINARY SCIENCE

Agri-Horticultural Society of India: Alipore Rd, Kolkata 700027; tel. (33) 24791713; f. 1820; 1,300 mems; library of 400 vols; Pres. S. G. KHAITAN; Sec. Dr S. K. BASU; publ. *Horticultural Journal* (quarterly).

Agri-Horticultural Society of Madras: Cathedral PO, Chennai 600086; f. 1835; 3,410 mems; Patron HE The GOVERNOR OF TAMIL NADU; Chair. R. SADASIVAM; Hon. Sec. Prof. J. RAMCHANDRAN.

Crop Improvement Society of India: Dept of Plant Breeding, Punjab Agricultural University, Ludhiana 141004; tel. (161) 2401960; f. 1974; aims to disseminate knowledge on crop improvement through lectures, symposia, publications, to arrange excursions and explorations, and to co-operate with national and international organizations; 200 mems; Pres. Dr G. S. SIDHU; Sec. Dr G. S. CHAHAL; publ. *Crop Improvement* (2 a year).

Indian Dairy Association: IDA House, Sector IV, R. K. Puram, New Delhi 110022; 3,000 mems; library of 700 vols; 100 periodicals; Pres A. BANERJEE; publs *Indian Journal of Dairy Science* (6 a year), *Indian Dairyman* (monthly).

Indian Society of Agricultural Economics: 46–48 Esplanade Mansions, 3rd Fl., Mahatma Gandhi Rd, Fort, Mumbai 400001; tel. (22) 22842542; fax (22) 22838790; e-mail isae@bom7.vsnl.net.in; internet www.isaeindia.org; f. 1939; promotes the study of social and economic problems of agriculture and rural areas, and technical competence for teaching and research in agricultural economics and allied subjects; 1,700 mems and subscribers; library of 20,928 vols; Pres. Dr S. S. JOHL; Hon. Jt Sec. Dr C. L. DADHICH; publs *The Indian Journal of Agricultural Economics* (quarterly), books, reports, papers.

Indian Society of Soil Science: Division of Soil Science and Agricultural Chemistry, Indian Agricultural Research Institute, New Delhi 110012; tel. (11) 5850991; fax (11) 5755529; e-mail isss@vsnl.com; internet www.indiansocietyofsoilscience.org; f. 1934; aims to cultivate and promote soil science and its allied disciplines and to disseminate knowledge of soil science and its applications; co-operation with Int. Soc. of Soil Science and similar organizations; 2,350 mems; Pres. Dr P. K. CHHONKAR; Sec. Dr G. NARAYANASAMY; publs *Journal* (quarterly), *Bulletin* (occasional).

ARCHITECTURE AND TOWN PLANNING

Indian Institute of Architects: 5th Fl., Prospect Chambers Annexe, Dr D. N. Rd, Mumbai 400001; tel. (22) 22046972; fax (22) 22832516; e-mail iia@vsnl.com; internet www.iia-india.org; f. 1929; aims: to promote aesthetic, scientific and practical efficiency of the architectural profession; to sponsor architectural education; to set qualifying standards for the profession; to provide a forum for discussing related subjects; mems: 10,233, incl. 1,191 Fellows, 28 Hon. Fellows, 8,624 Assocs, 95 Licentiates, 1,850 students, 65 retired; library of 3,000 vols; Pres. GURUNATH DALVI; Hon. Secs PARESH KAPADIA, DIVYA KUSH; publs *Journal* (monthly), *News Letter* (monthly).

BIBLIOGRAPHY, LIBRARY SCIENCE AND MUSEOLOGY

Indian Association of Special Libraries and Information Centres (IASLIC): P. 291, CIT Scheme No. 6M, Kankurgachi, Kolkata 700054; tel. (33) 3349651; e-mail iaslic@vsnl.net; internet www.iaslic.org; f. 1955 to promote study and research into special librarianship and information science; to conduct short-term training courses on the subject, hold conferences and co-ordinate activities among special libraries and special interest groups; publishes seminar and conference papers and books on information and library science; translation and reprographic services; 2,200 mems; library of 2,600 vols, 50 current periodicals; Hon. Pres. Prof. Dr S. B. GHOSH; Hon. Gen. Sec. D. K. NAG; publs *Annual Report*, *Conference Proceedings*, *IASLIC Bulletin* (4 a year), *IASLIC Newsletter* (monthly), *Indian Library Science Abstracts (ILSA)* (annually), *Seminar Proceedings*.

Indian Library Association: A/40-41, Flat 201, Ansal Bldgs, Dr Mukherjee Nagar, Delhi 110009; tel. and fax (22) 27651743; e-mail info@ilaindia.org; internet www.ilaindia.org; f. 1933; 4,000 mems; library of 600 vols; Pres. Prof. C. R. KARISIDDAPPA; Sec. D. V. SINGH; publs *ILA Bulletin* (quarterly), *Newsletter* (monthly).

Museums Association of India: c/o State Museum, Lucknow 226001; f. 1944; professional discussions, seminars, conferences, exhibitions, etc.; 700 individual and institutional mems; Pres. Dr S. D. TRIVEDI; Sec. Dr S. K. SRIVASTAVA; publ. *Journal of Indian Museums*.

National Book Trust, India: A-5, Green Park, New Delhi 110016; tel. (11) 26568052; fax (11) 26851795; e-mail nbtindia@ndb.vsnl.net.in; internet www.nbtindia.org.in; f. 1957; an autonomous body set up by the Government; activities include publishing moderately-priced books for general readers in 12 Indian languages and English, giving assistance to authors, illustrators and publishers for producing books for children, neo-literates and the higher education sector, organizing book fairs, exhibitions, seminars and workshops, and promoting Indian books abroad; Chair. Prof. BIPAN CHANDRA; Dir NUZHAT HASSAN.

ECONOMICS, LAW AND POLITICS

Bar Association of India: Chamber 93, Supreme Court Bldg, New Delhi 110001; publ. *The Indian Advocate* (quarterly).

Indian Council of World Affairs: Sapru House, Barakhamba Rd, New Delhi 110001; f. 1943; non-governmental institution for the study of Indian and international questions; 2,625 mems; library of 124,122 vols, 523 periodicals, and all UN publs; Pres. HARCHARAN SINGH JOSH; Hon. Sec.-Gen. S. C. PARASHER; publs *India Quarterly*, *Foreign Affairs* (monthly).

Indian Economic Association: Delhi School of Economics, Delhi 110009; f. 1918; Pres. Prof. V. M. DANDEKAR; Hon. Sec. Prof. K. A. NAQVI; publ. *Indian Economic Journal*.

Indian Law Institute: Opp. Supreme Court, Bhagwandas Rd, New Delhi 110001; tel. (11) 23386321; fax (11) 23782140; e-mail ili@nde.vsnl.met.in; internet www.ilidelhi.org; f. 1956 to promote advanced studies and research in law and reform of administration of law and justice; 2,600 mems; library of 70,000 vols; Pres. CHIEF JUSTICE OF INDIA; Registrar DALIP KUMAR; publs *Journal* (4 a year), *Annual Survey*, *Newsletter* (4 a year).

Institute of Chartered Accountants of India: Indraprastha Marg, New Delhi 110002; tel. (11) 23312055; fax (11) 23721334; f. 1949; 62,000 mems; library of 40,000 vols; Pres. N. P. SARDA; Sec. A. K. MAJUMDAR; publ. *The Chartered Accountant* (monthly).

EDUCATION

All India Association for Educational Research: N1/55 IRC Village, Bhubaneswar 751015; tel. (674) 2550611; e-mail indianeducationalresearch@gmail.com; internet www.geocities.com/aiaer15; f. 1987; 1,682 mems; Pres. Prof. B. K. PASSI; Gen. Sec. Dr SUNIL B. MOHANTY; publ. *Journal* (4 a year).

Hyderabad Educational Conference: 19 Bachelors' Quarters, Jawaharlal Nehru Rd, Hyderabad, Deccan; f. 1913; to promote academic research, assist needy students and further education in Andhra Pradesh; library: over 9,500 vols; Pres. SYED MASOOD ALI; Sec. GHOUSE MOHIUDDIN; publs *Proceedings of Public Sessions* (in Urdu), *Educational Annual* (in Urdu), *Ruh-e-tarraqui* (in Urdu).

J. N. Petit Institute: 312 Dr Dadabhoy Naoroji Rd, Fort, Mumbai 400001; tel. (22) 22048463; f. 1856; organizes lectures and makes accessible literary, scientific and philosophic works; 4,210 mems; library: see Libraries and Archives; Pres. Sir DINSHAW M. PETIT; Jt Hon. Secs K. P. DRIVER, N. M. PATEL.

National Bal Bhavan: Kotla Rd, New Delhi 110002; f. 1958; an autonomous institution set up by the Ministry of Human Resource Development; provides planned environment and creative activities based on Arts and Science to children between the ages of 5 and 16; provides leadership and guidance to teachers towards fostering a creative approach in teaching of art and science, organizes orientation courses for teachers and parents, runs a repertory theatre for children, the National Children's Museum and a national training resource centre; library: children's library of 43,347 vols and a reference library of 11,584 vols; Chair. SAROJ DUBEY; Sec. MADHU PANT.

FINE AND PERFORMING ARTS

All-India Fine Arts and Crafts Society: Old Mill Rd (Rafi Marg), New Delhi 110001; tel. (11) 23711315; f. 1928; holds art exhibitions including the All India Annual Art Exhibition, exhibitions of Indian art abroad and exhibitions of arts and crafts from foreign countries in India, talks and film shows on art; 600 mems; library of 5,000 vols; Pres. Prof. JAGMOHAN CHOPRA; Sec. S. S. BHAGAT; publs *Roopa Lekha* (annually), *Arts News* (monthly).

Art Society of India: Sandhurst House, 524 S.V.P. Rd, Mumbai 400004; f. 1918; 650 mems; library of 2,000 vols; Pres. P. DAHANUKAR; Hon. Sec. B. R. KULKARNI.

India International Photographic Council: 21 Bharti Artists Colony, Vikas Marg, New Delhi 110092; tel. (11) 22248766; fax (11) 22254608; e-mail fotoarte-1@hotmail.com; f. 1983; promotes art and science of photography; 4,000 mems; publ. *Indian Photography and Cinematography* (monthly).

Indian Society of Oriental Art (Calcutta): 15 Park St, Kolkata 700016; f. 1907; 320 mems; to promote and research all aspects of ancient and contemporary Indian and Oriental art; library of 3,500 vols; Sec. Smt. INDIRA NAG CHAUDHURI; publ. *Journal* (annually).

Mumbai Art Society: Jehangir Art Gallery, Mumbai 400023; tel. (22) 22044058; f. 1888; Pres. K. K. HEBBAR; Hon. Sec. G. S. ADIVREKAR; 450 Life mems; 150 ord. mems; 200 student mems; holds All India Annual Art Exhibition; publs *Art Journal*, illustrated catalogues of exhibitions.

National Academy of Art/Lalit Kala Akademi: Rabindra Bhavan, New Delhi 110001; tel. (11) 23387241; fax (11) 23782485; e-mail lka@bol.net.in; f. 1954; autonomous, government-financed; sponsors national and international exhibitions, such as the National Exhibition of Art (annually) and Triennale-India; arranges seminars, lectures, films, etc.; Sec. Dr SUDHANAR SHARMA; publs Lalit Kala Contemporary (4 a year), *Lalit Kala Ancient* (2 a year), *Samkaleen Kala* (in Hindi, 4 a year).

National Academy of Music, Dance and Drama/Sangeet Natak Akademi: Rabindra Bhavan, Feroze Shah Rd, New Delhi 110001; tel. (11) 23381833; fax (11) 23385715; e-mail sangeetnatak@bol.net.in; internet www.sangeetnatak.org; f. 1953 for the preservation and development of the performing arts of India; documents the performing arts through films, tapes and photographs; maintains a museum of musical instruments, costumes, masks and puppets; offers financial assistance to music, dance and theatre institutions; administers the Jawaharlal Nehru Manipur Dance Academy, Imphal, Kathak Kendra, Delhi, and Rabindra Rangashala, Delhi; conducts festivals, seminars; gives awards and fellowships for outstanding work; 66 mems; library of 22,000 vols and audio-visual library of tapes and discs; Chair. Dr BHUPEN HAZARIKA; Sec. JAYANT KASTUAR; publ. *Sangeet Natak* (4 a year).

South India Society of Painters: No. 13, 111 Trust Cross, Chennai 600028.

HISTORY, GEOGRAPHY AND ARCHAEOLOGY

Bharata Itihasa Samshodhaka Mandala: 1321 Sadashiva Peth, Pune, 411030; tel. (20) 24472581; e-mail bismpune@redifmail.com; f. 1910 for collecting, conserving and publishing historical materials; collection of 3,500 coins; 33,000 Persian, Sanskrit and Marathi MSS; 1,600,000 documents, about 1,200 old Indian paintings; 1,000 copperplates, sculptures and other antiquarian objects, museum of paintings; 675 mems; library of 40,000 vols; Pres. (vacant); Chair. Dr S. GOKHALE; Sec. Dr S. M. BHAVE; publs *Journal* (quarterly), *Sviya Granthamala Series*, *Puraskrita Granthamala*.

Geographical Society of India: c/o Dept of Geography, University of Calcutta, 35 Ballygunge Circular Rd, Kolkata 700019; tel. (33) 24753681; f. 1933; 750 mems; library of 14,200 vols, 5,709 journals; geographical lectures, seminars, excursions and exhibitions; encouragement of geographical research and training; Pres. S. P. DASGUPTA; Sec. DURGADAS SAHA; publ. *Geographical Review of India* (quarterly).

LANGUAGE AND LITERATURE

Alliance Française: 2 Aurangzeb Rd, New Delhi 110011; tel. (11) 23014682; fax (11) 23014364; e-mail dgaf@afindia.org; internet www.afindia.org; offers courses and exams in French language and culture and promotes cultural exchange with France; attached teaching centres in Ahmedabad, Bangalore, Bhopal, Chandigarh, Chennai, Coimbatore, Hyderabad, Indore, Jaipur, Karikal, Kochi, Kolkata, Madurai, Mahe, Mumbai, Panjim, Pondichery, Pune, Rajkot, Secunderabad and Trivandrum.

British Council: British High Commission, 17 Kasturba Gandhi Marg, New Delhi 110001; tel. (11) 23711401; fax (11) 23710717; e-mail delhi.enquiry@in.britishcouncil.org; internet www.britishcouncil.org/india; teaching centre; offers courses and exams in English language and British culture and promotes cultural exchange with the UK; attached offices in Chennai, Kolkata and Mumbai; library of 30,000 vols; Dir EDMUND MARSDEN.

Central Hindi Directorate: Department of Education, Ministry of Human Resource Development, West Block 7, R. K. Puram, New Delhi 110022; f. 1960; preparation and publication of bilingual and trilingual dictionaries of Indian and foreign languages; teaching of Hindi by correspondence courses to Indians and foreigners; extension courses; *c.* 300 mems; library of 83,100 vols; Dir Dr G. P. VIMAL; publs *Bhasha* (quarterly), *Varshiki* (annually), *UNESCO DOOT* (monthly).

Linguistic Society of India: c/o Deccan College, Pune 411006; tel. (20) 26692113; fax (20) 26690104; e-mail info@linguisticsociety.8m.com; internet www.linguisticsocietyofindia.org; f. 1928; 700 mems; library of 6,000 vols; Pres. Dr PREM SINGH; Sec. Dr S. R. SHARMA; publ. *Indian Linguistics* (annually).

Madras Literary Society: College Rd, Chennai 600006; tel. (44) 28279666; f. 1812; Pres. M. GOPALAKRISHNAN; Hon. Sec. U. RAMESH RAO.

Max Müller Bhavan (Goethe-Institut): 3 Kasturba Gandhi Marg, New Delhi 110001; tel. (11) 23329506; fax (11) 23722573; e-mail info.mmb@delhi.goethe.org; internet www.goethe.de/newdelhi; the six branches of the Goethe Institut in India are named after the German Indologist, Max Müller (1823–1900); offers courses and exams in German language and culture and promotes cultural exchange with Germany; attached centres in Bangalore, Chennai, Mumbai and Pune; Dir and Commissioner of South Asia Region Dr STEFAN DREYER.

Mythic Society: 2 Nrupathunga Rd, Bangalore 560002; tel. (80) 22215034; f. 1909 to promote the study of mythology, archaeology, indology and Karnataka history; 400 mems;

library of 24,000 vols, incl. special collections of Mysore history; Pres. Dr SURYANATH U. KAMATH; Sec. Dr M. K. L. N. SASTRY; publ. *Journal* (quarterly).

PEN All-India Centre: Theosophy Hall, 40 New Marine Lines, Mumbai 400020; tel. (22) 22032175; e-mail arsirkar@gems.vsnl.net.in; f. 1933; Founder SOPHIA WADIA; Pres. ANNADA SHANKAR RAY; Sec.-Treas. RANJIT HOSKOTE (acting); publ. *The Indian PEN* (4 a year).

Sahitya Akademi/National Academy of Letters: Rabindra Bhavan, 35 Ferozeshah Rd, New Delhi 110001; tel. (11) 23387064; fax (11) 23382428; e-mail secy@ndb.vsnl.net.in; internet www.sahitya-akademi.org; f. 1954 for the devt of Indian literature, the co-ordination of literary activities in the Indian languages and research in Indian languages and literature; publ. of literary works; promotion of cultural exchanges with other countries; awards annual prizes for original works and translations; organizes seminars, symposia and workshops on literary subjects; General Council consists of 8 eminent persons in the field of letters elected in their personal capacity, nominees of the Central and State Govts, 20 reps of the univs and one rep. of each of the 22 languages of India recognized by the Akademi, and 1 rep. each of the Lalit Kala Akademi, the Sangeet Natak Akademi, the Indian Council for Cultural Relations, the Raja Rammohun Roy Library Foundation and the Indian Publishers' Asscns; library of 125,000 vols; Pres. Prof. GOPI CHAND NARANG; Sec. A. KRISHNA MURTHY; publs *Indian Literature* (in English, 6 a year), *Sanskrita Pratibha* (in Sanskrit, 2 a year), *Samakaleena Bharatiya Sahitya* (in Hindi, 6 a year).

Samskrita Academy: Mata Mandir Gali, Jhandewala, New Delhi 110055; tel. (11) 23517689; e-mail samskrit@satyam.net.in; f. 1927; promotion and propagation of Sanskrit language, publication of studies and expositions of Sanskrit works, organization of oratorical and recitation competitions, regular lectures and seminars in Sanskrit and Tamil on well-known Sanskrit poets and philosophers by eminent scholars, occasional production of Sanskrit drama; 200 mems; publ. *Sambhashana Sandeshah* (monthly).

Tamil Nadu Tamil Development and Research Council: Fort St George, Chennai 600009; f. 1959; development of Tamil in all its aspects, especially as a modern language; library of 27,000 vols, 320 MSS, 85 periodicals; 16 teachers; 50 students; Chair. CHIEF MINISTER; Vice-Chair. MINISTER FOR EDUCATION; Sec. DIRECTOR OF TAMIL DEVELOPMENT; publ. *Tamil Nadu Tamil Bibliography*.

MEDICINE

All-India Ophthalmological Society: c/o Prof. Rajvardhan Azad, Dr R. P. Centre for Ophthalmic Sciences, All-India Institute of Medical Sciences, Ansari Nagar, New Delhi 110029; tel. (11) 26593187; fax (11) 26852919; e-mail rajvardhanazad@hotmail.com; internet www.aios.org; f. 1930; cultivation and promotion of the study and practice of ophthalmic sciences with a view to render service to the community and to promote social contacts among ophthalmologists; 7,394 mems; Pres. Dr B. SHUKLA; Gen. Sec. Prof. RAJVARDHAN AZAD; publ. *Indian Journal of Ophthalmology* (quarterly).

Association of Medical Physicists of India: c/o Radiological Physics Division, Bhabha Atomic Research Centre, Mumbai 400085; tel. (22) 25563060 ext. 2201; fax (22) 25560750; e-mail mpssrphd@magnum.bareti.ernet.in; f. 1976; 680 mems representing medical physicists, radiation oncologists and others interested in this field; organizes annual conference, workshops, lectures, awards, research grants, travel fellowships within India; Pres. Dr A. V. LAKSHAMAN; Sec. K. N. GOVINDA RAJAN; publ. *Journal of Medical Physics* (quarterly).

Association of Surgeons of India: 21 Swamy Sivananda Salai, Chepauk, Chennai 600005; tel. (44) 25383459; fax (44) 25367095; e-mail asi@md5.vsnl.net.in; internet www.asiindia.org; f. 1938; 12,006 mems; library: c. 12,000 vols; Pres. Dr C. PALANIVELU; Hon. Sec. Dr A. RATHNASWAMI; publ. *Indian Journal of Surgery* (every 2 months).

Federation of Obstetric & Gynaecological Societies of India: 6th Floor, New Bldg, Cama & Albless Hospital, Mahapalika Marg, Mumbai 400001; tel. (22) 2672044; fax (22) 2676405; e-mail fogsi@bom7.vsnl.net.in; internet www.fogsi.org; f. 1950; organizes annual congress for the exchange of views in the various aspects of the subject; organizes workshops on family planning, etc.; medical education programme; holds periodic international seminars; 18,500 mems; Pres. Dr SADHANA K. DESAI; Hon. Sec.-Gen. Dr SHYAM V. DESAI; publ. *Journal of Obstetrics & Gynaecology of India* (6 a year).

Helminthological Society of India: Dept of Parasitology, UP College of Veterinary Science and Animal Husbandry, Mathura; Pres. Prof. S. N. SINGH; Treas.-Sec. Prof. B. P. PANDE; publ. *Indian Journal of Helminthology* (2 a year).

Indian Association of Parasitologists: 110 Chittaranjan Ave, Kolkata 700012; Pres. Dr H. N. RAY; Sec. Dr A. B. CHAUDHURY.

Indian Cancer Society: 74 Jerbai Wadia Rd, Parel, Mumbai 400012, and Eucharistic Bldg, 5 Convent St, Mumbai 400039; tel. (22) 22047642; f. 1951; charitable trust subsisting on donations; objects: to support cancer research, to aid sufferers from cancer, to improve facilities for diagnosis, treatment and rehabilitation, to educate the public and the profession and to organize national conferences; diagnostic, treatment and research centre in South Mumbai (Lady Ratan Tata Medical and Research Centre); Hon. Founder Sec. and Man. Trustee Dr D. J. JUSSAWALLA; publ. *Indian Journal of Cancer* (quarterly).

Indian Medical Association: I.M.A. House, Indraprastha Marg, New Delhi 110002; tel. (22) 23319009; fax (22) 23316270; e-mail inmedici@ndb.vsnl.net.in; internet www.ima1928.com; f. 1928; 125,000 mems; Pres. Dr V. C. PATEL; Hon. Gen. Sec. Dr PREM AGGARWAL; publs *Journal* (monthly), *Your Health* (monthly), *I.M.A. News* (monthly), *Apka Swasthya* (monthly), *Family Medicine India* (4 a year).

Indian Pharmaceutical Association: Kalina, Santacruz (East), Mumbai 400098; tel. (22) 26671072; fax (22) 26670744; e-mail ipacentre@mtnl.net.in; internet www.indianpharma.org; f. 1939; 10,000 mems; Pres. P. D. SHETH; Hon. Gen. Sec. Dr M. K. RAINA; publs *Indian Journal of Pharmaceutical Sciences* (6 a year), *Pharma Times* (monthly).

Indian Public Health Association: 110 Chittaranjan Ave, Kolkata 700073; tel. (33) 22413831; e-mail jiten-ksingh@yahoo.com; internet www.ipha.net; f. 1957; promotion of public health and allied sciences; 22 state and local brs; holds Annual Convention, meetings, conferences, etc.; organizes training programme on various areas of interest of public health; 3,890 mems; Pres. Dr ASHOK KUMAR; Gen. Sec. Prof. Dr SANDIP K. RAY; publ. *Indian Journal of Public Health* (quarterly).

Indian Society for Medical Statistics: c/o Institute for Research in Medical Statistics (ICMR), Mayor Ramanathan Rd, Chetput, Chennai 600031; tel. (44) 28265308; fax (44) 28264963; e-mail icmrtrc@ren.nic.in; f. 1983 to contribute to the development of medical statistics and strengthen the application of statistics in medicine, health and related disciplines; organizes annual conferences, refresher courses, symposia; 480 mems; Pres. Prof. P. P. TALWAR; Gen Sec. Dr M. KACHIRAYAN; publs *ISMS Bulletin*, proceedings of annual meetings, monographs.

Indian Society of Anaesthetists: c/o Dept of Anaesthesiology, K.E.M. Hospital, Parel, Mumbai 400012; f. 1947; 4,000 mems; Pres. Dr K. P. RAMCHANDRAN; Hon. Sec. Dr D. DAS GUPTA; publ. *Indian Journal of Anaesthesia* (every 2 months).

Medical Council of India: Aiwan-e-Galib Marg, Kotla Rd, New Delhi 110002; tel. (11) 23235178; fax (11) 23236604; e-mail mci@del13.vsnl.net.in; internet www.mciindia.org; f. 1933, maintenance of uniform standards of medical education, reciprocity in mutual recognition of medical qualifications with other countries, maintenance of Indian Medical Register; Pres. Dr P. C. KESAVANKUTTY NAYAR (acting); Sec. Dr A. R. N. SETALVAD; publs *Indian Medical Register*, *MCI Bulletin of Information*, *Report of the Programme on Continuing Medical Education*.

Mumbai Medical Union: Blavatsky Lodge Bldg, Chowpatty, Mumbai 400007; f. 1883; 250 mems; Pres. Dr U. N. BASTODKAR; Sec. Dr Smt. M. K. THACKER.

National Academy of Medical Sciences: Ansari Nagar, Ring Rd, New Delhi 110029; tel. (11) 26561418; fax (11) 26857592; e-mail nams@bol.net.in; f. 1961; 2,039 mems (700 fellows, 1,339 ordinary mems); Pres. Dr HARI GAUTAM; Sec. Dr P. K. KHOSLA.

Pharmacy Council of India: 2nd Floor, Combined Councils' Building, Temple Lane, Kotla Rd, POB 7020, New Delhi 110002; f. 1949 to set and maintain educational standards for qualification and registration in pharmacy and to co-ordinate the practice thereof; Pres. Prof. J. S. QADRY; Asst Sec. ARCHNA MUGDAL.

NATURAL SCIENCES

General

Indian Academy of Sciences: CV Raman Ave, POB 8005, Sadashivanagar, Bangalore 560080; tel. (80) 23614592; fax (80) 23616094; e-mail madhavan@ias.ernet.in; internet www.ias.ac.in; f. 1934; promotes the cause of science in its pure and applied forms; activities incl. publication of scientific journals and special volumes, organizing meetings of the Fellowship and discussions on important topics, recognizing scientific talent, improvement of science education and supporting issues of concern to the scientific community; 925 full individual mems (877 fellows, 48 hon. fellows), 27 assoc. mems; library of 1,000 vols; Pres. Prof. T. V. RAMAKRISHNAN; Secs Prof. S. CHANDRASEKARAN, Prof. A. K. SOOD; Exec. Sec. G. MADHAVAN; publs *Bulletin of Materials Science* (6 a year), *Current Science* (every 2 weeks), *Journal of Astrophysics and Astronomy* (4 a year), *Journal of Biosciences* (4 a year), *Journal of Earth System Science* (6 a year), *Journal of Genetics* (4 a year), *Patrika* (newsletter), *Pramana* (journal of physics, monthly), *Proceedings Chemical Sciences* (6 a year), *Proceedings Mathematical Sciences* (4 a year), *Resonance: Journal of Science Education* (monthly), *Sadhana* (engineering sciences, 6 a year), *Year Book*.

Indian National Science Academy (formerly National Institute of Sciences of India): Bahadur Shah Zafar Marg, New Delhi 110002; tel. (11) 23231038; fax (11) 23235648; e-mail insa@giasdlol.vsnl.in; f. 1935 to promote scientific knowledge, co-ordination between scientific bodies, and safeguard the interests of scientists in India; adhering organization of ICSU; 676 Fellows, 104 Foreign Fellows; library of 21,000 vols; Pres. Dr S. VARADARAJAN; Secs Prof. N. APPAJI RAO, Prof. P. T. MANOHARAN; publs *Proceedings, Monographs, Bulletin, Progress of Science in India, Indian Journal of History of Science, Year Book, Indian Journal of Pure and Applied Mathematics, Biographical Memoirs.*

Indian Science Congress Association: 14 Dr Biresh Guha St, Kolkata 700017; tel. and fax (33) 22402551; e-mail isca.assocn@gems.vsnl.net.in; f. 1914 to advance and promote science in India; holds annual congress; 12,001 mems; library of 8,000 vols, 60 periodicals; Pres. Dr R. S. PARODA; Secs Prof. A. B. BANERJEE, Prof. UMA KANT; publs *Proceedings* (annually, in 4 parts), *Everyman's Science* (4 a year).

National Academy of Sciences: 5 Lajpatrai Rd, Allahabad 211002, Uttar Pradesh; f. 1930 for the cultivation and promotion of science in all its branches; 2,580 mems excluding 732 fellows, 48 honorary fellows and 23 foreign fellows; Pres. Prof. U. S. SRIVASTAVA; Secs Dr O. M. PRASAD, Dr SANDEEP K. BASU; Foreign Sec. Prof. ALOK K. GUPTA; publs *Proceedings* in two sections— *Section A: Physical Sciences, Section B: Biological Sciences* (quarterly), *National Academy of Sciences Letters* (monthly), *Annual Number* (annually).

Biological Sciences

Academy of Zoology: Church Rd 2/95, Civil Lines, Agra 282002; f. 1954; 1,500 mems; library of 91,000 vols, exchange service with other zoological institutions; international organization and forum for the advancement of zoology; Pres. and Sec. Dr D. P. S. BHATI; publ. *The Annals of Zoology*.

Association of Microbiologists of India: c/o Div. of Microbiology, Indian Agricultural Research Institute, New Delhi 110012; tel. (11) 25847649; e-mail ijm@iari.res.in; internet www.iari.res.in/divisions/microbiology/; f. 1938; 1,500 mems; library of 3,000 vols; Pres. Dr B. D. KAUSHIK; publ. *Indian Journal of Microbiology* (quarterly).

Bombay Natural History Society: Hornbill House, Shahid Bhagat Singh Rd, Mumbai 400023; tel. (22) 22821811; fax (22) 22837615; e-mail bnhs@bom4.vsnl.net.in; internet www.bnhs.org; f. 1883; studies natural history, ecology and conservation in the Indian sub-continent; research programmes in field zoology; 5,000 mems; library of 17,000 vols; Pres. B. G. DESHMUKH; Hon. Sec. J. C. DANIEL; Dir A. R. RAHMANI; publs *Journal, Hornbill*.

Indian Association of Biological Sciences: Life Science Centre, Calcutta University, Kolkata 700019; tel. (33) 224753681; f. 1968; 400 mems; Sec. and Editor Prof. T. M. DAS; publ. *Indian Biologist* (2 a year).

Indian Biophysical Society: Saha Institute of Nuclear Physics, 1/AF, Bidhannagar, Kolkata 700064; tel. (33) 25565611; internet www.saha.ac.in/cmb/www/biop.html; f. 1965; *c.* 200 mems; Pres. Prof. DIPAK DASGUPTA; publ. *Proceedings* (annually).

Indian Botanical Society: Dept of Botany, University of Madras, Chepauk, Chennai 600005; Pres. K. S. THIND; Sec. Prof. K. S. BHARGAVA; publ. *Journal*.

Indian Phytopathological Society: Division of Plant Pathology, Indian Agricultural Research Institute, New Delhi 110012; tel. (11) 25781474; fax (11) 25766420; e-mail dharam-vir@hotmail.com; internet www.ipsdis.com; f. 1947; 1,600 mems; virology, bacteriology, mycology, nematology and plant pathology; holds seminars, symposia, etc.; Pres. Dr C. MANOHARACHARY; Sec. Dr D. K. AGARWAL; publs *Indian Phytopathology* (4 a year), *IPS* (4 a year).

Indian Society of Genetics and Plant Breeding: Indian Agricultural Research Institute, Genetics Division, New Delhi 110012; f. 1941; plant breeding and genetic research; 1,400 mems; Pres. Prof. V. L. CHOPRA; Sec. Dr R. B. MEHRA; publ. *Journal*.

Marine Biological Association of India: Cochin, Kerala (South India); f. 1958; Pres. Dr E. G. SILAS; Vice-Pres. Dr R. R. PRASAD, Dr R. NATARAJAN; publs *Journal* (2 a year), *Memoirs* (irregular), Proceedings of symposia (irregular).

Society of Biological Chemists, India: Indian Institute of Science, Bangalore 560012; f. 1930; 1,600 mems; Pres. Dr P. M. BHARGAVA; publs *Biochemical Reviews* (annually), *Proceedings and Abstracts* (annually), *News Letter* (quarterly).

Zoological Survey of India: 34 Chittaran Ave, Kolkata 700012; e-mail zsi@envfor.delhi.nic.in; f. 1916; exploration and survey of fauna in India; taxonomic studies; status survey of endangered species; publication of results through departmental journals; maintenance and development of national zoological collections; maintenance of museums at headquarters and regional stations; environmental impact studies produced on behalf of Min. of Environment and Forests; library of 37,100 vols, 875 periodicals; publ. *Journal of Indian Zoology* (annually).

Mathematical Sciences

Allahabad Mathematical Society: 10 C. S. P. Singh Marg, Allahabad 211001; tel. (532) 2623553; fax (532) 2623221; e-mail pramila8@sancharnet.in; internet www.amsallahabad.org; f. 1958; to further the cause of advanced study and research in various branches of mathematics, including theoretical physics and mathematical statistics; 270 mems; library of 5,000 vols; Pres. Prof. PRAMILA SRIVASTAVA; Sec. Dr MONA KHARE; publs *Indian Journal of Mathematics* (3 a year), *Bulletin* (annually).

Bharata Ganita Parisad: Dept of Mathematics and Astronomy, University, Lucknow 226007; tel. (522) 2740019; f. 1950; mathematics; 185 mems; library of 16,000 vols; Pres. Prof. J. B. SHUKLA; Gen. Sec. Prof. A. NIGAM; publ. *Ganita* (2 a year).

Calcutta Mathematical Society: Asutosh Bhavan, AE-374, Sector I, Saltlake City, Kolkata 700064; tel. (33) 23378882; fax (33) 23376290; e-mail cms@cal2.vsnl.net.in; f. 1908; lectures, seminars, symposia, workshops in mathematical sciences; research projects sponsored by various funding agencies; 1,182 mems; library of 22,500 vols; Pres. Prof. Dr K. RAMACHANDRA; Sec. Prof. Dr MAHIMARANJAN ADHIKARI; publs *Bulletin* (6 a year), *Journal* (2 a year), *News Bulletin* (monthly), *Review Bulletin* (2 a year).

Indian Mathematical Society: Department of Mathematics, Maitreyi College, Bapu Dham Complex, Chanakyapuri, New Delhi 110021; tel. (11) 25264358; fax (11) 25264358; e-mail drsparya@vsnl.net; f. 1907; 1,000 mems; library of 4,000 vols; Pres. Prof. M. A. PATHAN; Admin. Sec. Prof. M. K. SINGAL; publs *Journal, Mathematics Student* (4 a year).

Physical Sciences

Astronomical Society of India: Dept of Astronomy, Osmania University, Hyderabad 500007; tel. (80) 23340122; fax (80) 23340492; e-mail pati@iiap.ernet.in; f. 1973; 750 mems; Pres. Prof. G. SRINIVASAN; Sec. Dr ASHOK PATI; publs *Bulletin* (4 a year), *Memoirs* (irregular).

Electrochemical Society of India: Indian Institute of Science Campus, Bangalore 560012; tel. (80) 23340977; fax (80) 23341683; e-mail mahesh@cedt.iisc.ernet.in; f. 1964 to promote the science and technology of electrochemistry, electro-deposition and plating, corrosion including high-temperature oxidation, electrometallurgy and metal finishing, semi-conductors and electronics, batteries, solid electrolytes, solid state electrochemistry, and protection of metals and materials against environmental attack; 670 mems; library of 4,000 vols; Pres. M. RAVINDRANATH; Sec. Dr G. ANANDA RAO; publ. *Journal* (quarterly).

Indian Association for the Cultivation of Science: 2–3 Raja S. C. Mallick Rd, IACS Campus, Jadavpur, Kolkata 700032; tel. (33) 24734971; fax (33) 24732805; e-mail director@mahendra.iacs.res.in; internet www.iacs.res.in; f. 1876 to promote fundamental research in the developing areas of basic sciences; 703 mems (625 life, 50 ordinary, 10 assoc., 18 hon.); Pres. Prof. A. P. MITRA; Dir Prof. D. MUKHERJEE; publ. *Indian Journal of Physics* (monthly).

Indian Chemical Society: University Science College Bldgs, 92 Acharya Prafulla Chandra Rd, Kolkata 700009; tel. (33) 23503478; f. 1924; 2,000 mems; library of 10,500 vols; Pres. Dr JAI P. MITTAL; Hon. Sec. Prof. P. L. MAJUMDER; publ. *Journal* (monthly).

Optical Society of India: Dept. of Applied Optics and Photonics, Applied Physics Bldg, Calcutta Univ., 92 Acharya Prafulla Chandra Rd, Kolkata 700009; tel. (33) 23522411; e-mail osi_india@rediffmail.com; internet www.osiindia.org; f. 1965 to promote and diffuse the knowledge of optics in all its branches, pure and applied; organizes seminars, workshops and conferences; 678 mems; library of 400 vols; Pres. J. A. R. KRISHNA MOORTY; Gen. Sec. Prof. L. N. HAZRA; publ. *Journal of Optics* (quarterly).

RELIGION, SOCIOLOGY AND ANTHROPOLOGY

Anthropological Society of Mumbai: 209 Dr Dadabhai Naoroji Rd, Fort, Mumbai 400001; f. 1886; Pres. Dr. J. F. BULSARA; Hon. Sec. SAPUR F. DESAI.

Asiatic Society: 1 Park St, Kolkata 700016; internet www.asiaticsocietycal.com; f. 1784; to study humanities and sciences in India; 1,292 mems; 64 research Fellows; library of 149,000 vols; 47,000 MSS in 26 languages, 80,000 journals, 24,000 old coins, 75 oil paintings; research on Indology and Oriental studies; Pres. Prof. BISWANATH BANERJI; Sec. Prof. DILIP COOMER GHOSE; publ. *Journal* (quarterly).

Asiatic Society of Mumbai: Town Hall, Mumbai 400023; tel. (22) 22660956; f. 1804 to investigate and encourage sciences, arts and literature in relation to Asia and India in particular; established Dr P. V. Kane Research Institute for Oriental Studies; 2,811 mems; library of 235,000 vols, 2,357 MSS, 10,443 old coins; Pres. Dr D. R. SARDESAI; Hon. Sec. VIMAL SHAH; publs *Journal*, monographs, reports.

Indian Anthropological Association: Department of Anthropology, University of Delhi, Delhi 110007; tel. (11) 27667329;

e-mail iaadelhi@rediffmail.com; internet www.indiananthropology.org; f. 1964; 400 mems; Pres. Prof. Dr S. M. PATNAIK; publs *Indian Anthropologist* (2 a year), *News Bulletin* (annually), *Directory of Anthropologists in India* (every 4–5 years).

Indian Society for Afro-Asian Studies: 297 Sarswati Kunj, I.P. Ext., New Delhi 110092; tel. (11) 22722801; fax (11) 22725024; e-mail isaas@giasdl01.vsnl.net.in; f. 1980; aims at analysing political, economic, social and cultural situation of Afro-Asian countries; 621 mems; Pres. LALIT BHASIN; Sec. Dr DHARAMPAL; publ. *ISAAS Newsletter* (annually).

Theosophical Society: International Headquarters, Adyar, Chennai 600020; tel. (44) 24912474; e-mail theossoc@satyam.net.in; internet www.ts.adyar.org; f. 1875 in New York; 32,000 mems throughout the world; library of 152,000 vols and 18,000 palm-leaf and paper MSS; aims: to form a nucleus of the Universal Brotherhood of Humanity without distinction of race, creed, sex, caste or colour, to encourage the study of comparative religion, philosophy and science, and to investigate unexplained laws of nature and the powers latent in man; Pres. RADHA BURNIER; Sec. MARY ANDERSON; publs *The Theosophist* (monthly), *Adyar Library Bulletin* (annually), *Adyar Newsletter* (4 a year).

TECHNOLOGY

Aeronautical Society of India: 13B, Indraprastha Estate, New Delhi 110002; tel. (11) 23370516; fax (11) 23370768; e-mail aerosoc@bol.net.in; internet www.aesi.org; f. 1948 for the promotion and diffusion of knowledge of aeronautical sciences and aircraft engineering, and for the advancement of the aeronautical profession; 6,500 mems; library of 4,000 vols; Pres. N. R. MOHANTY; Hon. Sec. B. K. JOSHI; Admin. Sec. Group Capt. H. C. BHATIA; publs *Journal* (4 a year), *Avia* (newsletter, monthly).

Geological, Mining and Metallurgical Society of India: c/o Geology Dept, University of Calcutta, 35 B.C. Rd, Kolkata 700019; tel. (33) 24753681; f. 1924; 315 mems; Pres. Prof. A. K. BANERJI; Joint Secs Dr B. K. SAMANTA, Dr A. SENGUPTA; publs *Journal* (quarterly), *Bulletin*.

India Society of Engineers: 12-B Netaji Subhas Rd, Kolkata 700001; f. 1934; library of 20,000 vols; 8,000 mems; Pres. A. C. SINHA; Gen. Sec. D. B. CHOWDHURY; publ. *Science and Engineering* (monthly in English).

Indian Association of Geohydrologists: c/o Geological Survey of India, 4 Chowringhee Lane, Kolkata 700016; f. 1964; 440 mems; Pres. V. SUBRAMANYAM; Hon. Sec. A. K. ROY; publ. *Indian Geohydrology*.

Indian Ceramic Society: c/o Central Glass and Ceramic Research Institute, Kolkata 700032; tel. and fax (33) 24138878; e-mail incers@cal2.vsnl.net.in; f. 1928; 2,000 mems; Pres. Prof. F. D. G. NANAM; Sec. S. CHAKRABARTI; publ. *Transactions* (quarterly).

Indian Institute of Metals: Metal House, Plot 13/4, Block AQ, Sector V, Salt Lake, Kolkata 700091; tel. (33) 23675004; fax (33) 23675335; e-mail iiomcal@dataone.in; internet www.iim-india.net; f. 1947; 8,650 mems; Pres. B. MUTHURAMAN; Sec. Gen. J. C. MARWAH; publs *Transactions* (6 a year), *IIM Metal News* (6 a year).

Indian National Academy of Engineering: 117 Visiting Faculty, Nalanda House, IIT Campus, Hauz Khas, New Delhi 110016; tel. (11) 26968475; fax (11) 26968635; e-mail inae@nda.vsnl.net.in; f. 1987 to promote the general advancement of engineering and technology and related sciences and disciplines; awards Professorship, Fellowship and Scholarship; 299 Fellows; Pres. Prof. P. V. INDIRESAN; Exec. Sec. Maj.-Gen. J. C. AHLUWALIA.

Indian Society of Mechanical Engineers (ISME): c/o Dept of Mechanical Engineering, Indian Institute of Technology, New Delhi 110016; tel. (11) 26311259; fax (11) 26311261; f. 1975; 480 mems; Pres. Prof. G. S. SEKHON; Sec. Dr S. G. DESHMUKH; publs *Journal of Engineering Production* (quarterly), *Journal of Thermal Engineering* (quarterly), *Journal of Engineering Design* (quarterly).

Institution of Electronics and Telecommunication Engineers (IETE): 2 Institutional Area, Lodi Rd, New Delhi 110003; tel. (11) 24631810; f. 1953 to promote the advancement of electronics and telecommunications engineering and related fields; 40,000 mems; Pres. Prof. R. K. ARORA; Sec. Maj.-Gen. K. B. JHALDIYAL; publs *IETE Journal of Research* (6 a year), *IETE Technical Review* (6 a year), *IETE Journal of Education* (4 a year).

Institution of Engineers (India): 8 Gokhale Rd, Kolkata 700020; tel. (33) 22238311; fax (33) 22238345; e-mail sdg@ieindia.org; internet www.ieindia.org; f. 1920; inc. by Royal Charter 1935; non-formal eng. education; 94 centres; 60 libraries; over 500,000 mems; Pres. D. K. GOWDA; Sec. and Dir-Gen. Cdr (retd) ARVIND K. POOTHIA; publs *Technorama* (2 a year), *Journal* (monthly), *IEI News* (monthly), *Inter-Disciplinary* (2 a year).

Mineralogical Society of India: Manasa Gangotri, Mysore 6; f. 1959; objects: to advance knowledge of crystallography, mineralogy, petrology, etc. by means of research and the holding of conferences, meetings and discussions; 400 mems; library of 1,500 vols; Pres. Dr VISWANATHIAH; Sec. Dr P. N. SATISH; publ. *The Indian Mineralogist*.

Systems Society of India: c/o The Associate Director (R and D), Vikram Sarabhai Space Centre, Thiruvananthapuram 695022; tel. (471) 2565576; fax (471) 2564092; e-mail bn_suresh@vssc.org; internet www.sysi.org; f. 1982; nat. professional org.; systems science and engineering; 500 mems; Pres. Dr S. C. GUPTA; Sec. Dr B. N. SURESH; publ. *Paritantra* (journal, 2 a year).

Research Institutes

GENERAL

Council of Scientific and Industrial Research: Rafi Marg, New Delhi; tel. (11) 23711251; fax (11) 23714788; e-mail csirhq@sirnetd.ernet.in; internet www.csir.res.in; f. 1942; the nat. research laboratories described below have been established under the Council, which is itself responsible to the Min. of Science and Technology (Govt of India); library: library of 20,000 vols; Indian Nat. Scientific Documentation Centre: see Libraries and Archives; Pres. THE PRIME MINISTER; Dir-Gen. Dr R. A. MASHELKAR; Joint Sec. (Admin.) AJAY KUMAR; publ. *Technical Manpower Bulletin* (monthly).

Attached research institutes:

Central Building Research Institute: Roorkee 247667, Uttar Pradesh; tel. (1332) 272243; fax (1332) 272272; e-mail general@cscbri.ren.nic.in; f. 1947; research and devt in all aspects of building science and technology; work divided into 5 areas: shelter planning, new materials, structural and foundation eng., disaster mitigation and process devt; library of 44,778 vols; Dir Dr R. NARAYANA IYENGAR; publs *CBRI Newsletter* (in English, quarterly), *Bhavanika* (in Hindi, quarterly).

Central Drug Research Institute: Chattar Manzil Palace, PB 173, Lucknow; tel. (522) 2223286; fax (522) 2223405; e-mail cdrilk@sirnetd.ernet.in; f. 1951; biochemical, molecular biological, pharmacological, chemical, microbiological, endocrinological, biophysical, parasitological and medical research; library of 21,300 vols; Dir Dr C. M. GUPTA; publs *Industry Highlights* (quarterly), *Ocean Drugs Alert* (quarterly).

Central Electrochemical Research Institute: Karaikudi 630006, Tamil Nadu; tel. (4565) 222065; fax (4565) 222088; e-mail cecrik@cscecri.ren.nic.in; f. 1953; electrochemical and allied research; library of 31,755 vols; Dir Dr M. RAGHVAN; publs *Bulletin of Electro-chemistry*, *Battery Newsletter*.

Central Electronics Engineering Research Institute: Pilani, Rajasthan; tel. (1596) 242111; fax (1596) 242294; e-mail root@ceeri.ernet.in; f. 1953; design and construction of electronic equipment, components and test equipment; Dir Dr S. AHMAD; publ. *CEERI News* (quarterly).

Central Food Technological Research Institute: Cheluvamba Mansion, Food Technology PO, Mysore 570013; tel. (821) 2517760; fax (821) 2516308; e-mail director@nicfos.ernet.in; internet www.mylibnet.org.in/cftri/cftri.htm; f. 1950; library of 36,300 vols; Dir Dr V. PRAKASH; publs *Food Technology Abstracts* (monthly), *Food Digest* (quarterly), *Food Patents* (quarterly), *CFTRI Newsletter* (6 a year), *Library Bulletin* (quarterly), *Performance Report* (annual).

Central Fuel Research Institute: PO Fuel Research Institute, Jealgora, Dhanbad 828108, Bihar; tel. (326) 2460141; fax (326) 2469350; e-mail director@cscfri.ren.nic.in; f. 1945; research on technological and industrial aspects of coal; library of 10,129 vols, 35,000 periodicals; Dir Dr KALYAN SEN; publ. *Fuel Science and Technology* (quarterly).

Central Glass and Ceramic Research Institute: 196 Raja S.C. Mullick Rd, Jadavpur, Kolkata 700032; tel. (33) 24735829; fax (33) 24730957; e-mail cscgcri@giascl.l.vsnl.net.in; f. 1950; fundamental and applied research on special kinds of glass, ceramics, sol-gel, refractories, ceramic coatings, composites and allied areas; library of 25,000 vols; Dir Dr H. S. MAITY.

Central Institute of Medicinal and Aromatic Plants: PO CIMAP, Lucknow 226015; tel. (522) 2359623; fax (522) 2342666; e-mail roor@cimap.sirnetd.ernet.in; f. 1959; co-ordination of activities in the devt of cultivation and use of medicinal and aromatic plants on organized basis; library of 2,688 vols; Dir Dr SUSHIL KUMAR; publs *Farm Bulletin* (irreg.), *Journal of Medicinal and Aromatic Plant Sciences* (quarterly), *CIMAP Newsletter* (quarterly), *Yatharth* (quarterly).

Central Leather Research Institute: Adyar, Chennai 600020; tel. (44) 24910846; fax (44) 24912150; e-mail clrim@giasmd01.vsnl.net.in; internet www.clri.org; f. 1948; library of 17,225 vols; Dir Dr T. RAMASAMI; publ. *Leather Science Abstract Services* (monthly).

Central Mechanical Engineering Research Institute: Mahatma Gandhi Ave, Durgapur 713209, West Bengal; tel. (343) 2546749; fax (343) 2546745; e-mail root@cscmeri.ren.nic.in; internet www

.cmeri.com; f. 1958; library of 60,000 vols; Dir Shri HARDYAL SINGH; publ. *Mechanical Engineering Bulletin* (quarterly).

Central Mining Research Institute: Barwa Rd, Dhanbad, 826001 Bihar; tel. (326) 2203043; fax (326) 2205028; e-mail director@csemri.ren.nic.in; f. 1956; research on safety, health and efficiency in mining; library of 26,382 vols; Dir Dr T. N. SINGH; publ. *Newsletter* (quarterly).

Central Road Research Institute: PO CRRI, Delhi-Mathura Rd, New Delhi 110020; tel. (11) 26848917; fax (11) 26845943; e-mail director@cscrri.ren.nic.in; f. 1952; research and devt in highway eng., traffic and transportation, transport environment and safety, bridge eng., pavement design; library of 90,000 vols; Dir Dr A. K. GUPTA; publs *CRRI Road Abstracts* (quarterly), *Highway Documentation* (monthly), *Roadsearch Bulletin* (2 a year), *CRRI WIN Bulletin* (quarterly).

Central Salt and Marine Chemicals Research Institute: Waghawadi Rd, Bhavnagar 364002, Gujarat; tel. (278) 2569496; fax (278) 2566970; e-mail general@csmcri.ren.nic.in; f. 1954; preparation of salt, magnesium compounds, bromine and bromides, cultivation and use of marine algae, desalination of water by solar stills, electrodialysis and reverse osmosis, waste water treatment using membrane processes; library of 48,000 vols; Dir Dr P. K. GHOSH; publ. *Newsletter* (fortnightly).

Central Scientific Instruments Organization: Sector 30-C, Chandigarh 160020; tel. (172) 2657190; fax (172) 2657267; e-mail root@cscsia.ren.nic.in; internet www.nio.org/csir/csio.htm; f. 1959; research, design, devt, repair and maintenance of scientific and industrial instruments; technical training and diploma courses in instrument technology; library of 38,700 vols, 180 periodicals; Dir Dr R. P. BAJPAI (acting); publ. *Communications in Instrumentation* (quarterly).

Centre for Biochemicals Technology: Mall Rd, Delhi Univ. Campus, Delhi 110007; tel. (11) 27257298; fax (11) 27257471; e-mail central@cbt.res.in; internet www.cbt.res.in; f. 1966; uses the results obtained in basic biological research to provide commercially viable technologies for health care; Dir SAMIR K. BRAHAMCHARI.

Centre for Cellular and Molecular Biology: Hyderabad; tel. (40) 27173487; fax (40) 27171195; e-mail lalji@ccmb.ap.nic.in; internet www.ccmbindia.org; f. 1977; research in frontier areas and multi-disciplinary areas of modern biology with a view to aiding devt of biochemical and biotechnological technology in India by providing centralized facilities and training; Dir Dr LALJI SINGH; publ. *CCMB Highlights*.

Indian Institute of Chemical Biology: 4 Raja S.C. Mullick Rd, Jadavpur, Kolkata 700032; tel. (33) 24735197; fax (33) 24735197; e-mail iichbio@giascl01.vsnl.net.in; f. 1956; solution of medical problems through fundamental and applied research in the basic biological sciences, with emphasis on projects bearing directly on the country's current biological and medical needs; library of 30,000 vols; Dir Dr D. K. GANGULY (acting).

Indian Institute of Chemical Technology: Hyderabad 500007; tel. (40) 27173874; fax (40) 27173387; e-mail root@csiict.ren.nic.in; f. 1944; agrochemicals, drugs and pharmaceuticals, inorganic chemicals and materials, organic coatings and polymers, design engineering of chemical plant, oils and fats, biotechnology; library of 40,000 vols, 500 periodicals; Dir Dr K. V. RAGHVAN; publ. *Bulletin* (quarterly).

Indian Institute of Petroleum: Dehradun 248005; tel. (135) 2624508; fax (135) 2671986; e-mail iipddn@de12.vsnl.net.in; f. 1960; research and devt in the field of petroleum, natural gas, and petrochemicals and use of petroleum products; trains technical personnel; assists Bureau of Indian Standards in framing standards for petroleum products; library of 15,000 vols, 14,000 periodicals; the institute is a Patents Inspection Centre of the Indian Patents Office and is open to the public for studying patent specifications; Dir S. SINGHAL (acting); publs *R & D Newsletter* (quarterly), *Vikalp* (quarterly).

Industrial Toxicology Research Centre: Mahatma Gandhi Marg, Lucknow 226001, Uttar Pradesh; tel. (522) 2221856; fax (522) 2228227; e-mail intox@itrc.sirnetd.ernet.in; f. 1965; studies the effects of industrial pollution; library of 25,200 vols; Dir Dr P. K. SETH.

Institute of Himalayan Bioresources Technology, Palampur: Dist. Kangra, 176061 Himachal Pradesh; tel. (1894) 230411; fax (1894) 230433; e-mail director@csihbt.ren.nic.in; f. 1983; biodiversity conservation, tea husbandry and manufacture, agro-technology, processing and postharvest technologies for floriculture, aromatic and herbal plants; Dir Dr P. S. AHUJA.

Institute of Microbial Technology: Sector 39A, Chandigarh 160036; tel. (172) 2690785; fax (172) 2690585; e-mail root@imtech.ernet.in; internet www.imtech.ernet.in; f. 1983; research and devt in genetic eng. and microbiology, protein eng., immunology and fermentation technology; library of 15,809 vols; Dir Dr AMIT GHOSH.

National Aerospace Laboratories: PB 1779, Kodihalli, Bangalore 560017; tel. (80) 25270584; fax (80) 25260862; e-mail viman@csnal.ren.in; internet www.cmmacs.ernet.in/nal; f. 1959; research and devt in aircraft design, testing and operation, and support for nat. aerospace programmes; library of 110,000 vols; Dir Dr T. S. PRALAHAD.

National Botanical Research Institute: Rana Pratap Marg, Lucknow 226001; tel. and fax (522) 2282881; e-mail manager@nbri.sirnetd.ernet.in; f. 1953; research into economic botany and collection, introduction, propagation and improvement of ornamental and economic plants; 520 mems; library of 53,414 vols; Dir Dr P. PUSHPANGADAN; publs *NBRI Newsletter* (quarterly), *Applied Botany Abstracts* (quarterly).

National Chemical Laboratory: Pune 336151; tel. (22) 25893303; fax (22) 25893355; e-mail prs@ems.ncl.res.in; f. 1950; advanced materials, biotechnology, catalysis, organic chemical technology and polymers; library of 75,000 vols; Dir Dr PAUL RATNASAMY; publ. *NCL Bulletin* (quarterly).

National Environmental Engineering Research Institute: Nehru Marg, Nagpur 440020, Maharashtra; tel. (712) 2249885; fax (712) 2249900; e-mail director@neeri.res.in; internet www.neeri.res.in; f. 1958; research and devt in environmental monitoring, environmental biotechnology, solid and hazardous waste management, environmental systems design, modelling and optimization, air and water pollution control, sewage and industrial wastewater treatment, instrumentation and environmental impact studies; library: more than 44,700 vols, journals, reports, conference proceedings, CDs and audiovisual films; 200 int. and nat. peer-reviewed current periodicals; online access to 3,000 scientific and technical journals; Dir Dr SUKUMAR DEVOTTA (acting); publs *Paryavaran Patrika* (2 a year), *Journal of Environmental Science and Engineering* (quarterly).

National Geophysical Research Institute: Uppal Rd, Hyderabad 500007; tel. (40) 27170141; fax (40) 27171564; e-mail postmast@csngri.ren.nic.in; internet www.ngri.com; f. 1961; basic and applied research into mineral exploration and investigation of the earth's interior through seismic, geomagnetic, electric, geochemical and paleogeophysical studies; library of 19,173 vols, 13,895 bound vols of journals, 120 subscribed journals; Dir Dr HARSH K. GUPTA.

National Institute of Oceanography: Miramar, Panaje, 403004 Goa; tel. (8251) 221322; fax (8251) 223340; e-mail ocean@csnio.ren.nic.in; internet www.nio.org; f. 1966; investigates physical, chemical, geological and biological oceanography, also functions as the Nat. Oceanographic Data Centre; research on marine geophysics and instrumentation; maintenance of data pertaining to the Indian Ocean at Planning and Data Div.; library of 24,000 vols; Dir Dr E. DESA.

National Institute of Science, Technology and Development Studies: Hillside Rd, New Delhi 110012; tel. (11) 25743227; fax (11) 25754640; e-mail postmast@csnistad.ren.nic.in; f. 1981; research on technological and social change, and resource planning and use for regional devt; library of 15,000 vols, 250 periodicals; Dir Dr S. PRUTHI (acting); publs *Report* (every 2 years), *CLOSS* (quarterly).

National Metallurgical Laboratory: Jamshedpur 831007, Singhbhum District, Bihar; tel. (657) 2431131; fax (657) 2426527; e-mail nml@csnml.ren.nic.in; f. 1950; ore dressing, production, physical and chemical metallurgy; library of 43,875 vols; Dir Prof. P. R. RAO; publs *Technical Journal* (quarterly), *News Bulletin* (quarterly).

National Physical Laboratory: Hillside Rd, New Delhi 110012; tel. (11) 25741440; fax (11) 25752678; f. 1947; fundamental and applied research in physics; maintenance of standards; testing and calibration of equipment; library of 109,000 vols; Dir Prof. A. K. RAYCHAUDHARY; publs *Sameeksha* (quarterly), *Ionospheric Data* (quarterly).

Regional Research Laboratory: Bhubaneshwar 4, Orissa; tel. (674) 2581126; fax (674) 2586126; f. 1964; research in problems relating to the industry and raw materials of the region; Dir Prof. H. S. RAY; publ. *RRL Bulletin* (quarterly).

Regional Research Laboratory: Canal Rd, Jammu-Tawi 180001, Jammu and Kashmir; tel. (191) 2546368; fax (191) 2548607; e-mail rrlj@nde.vsnl.net.in; f. 1957; drug and medicinal plants; introduction of exotic plants, particularly from temperate zones; plant chemistry, extraction and processing of drugs; library of 16,522 vols; Dir Prof. S. S. HANDA.

Regional Research Laboratory: Jorhat, 785006 Assam; tel. (376) 2320353; fax (376) 2321158; e-mail director@csrrljt.ren.nic.in; f. 1961; research into coal, petroleum, pulp and paper, natural product chemistry, cement, drugs and pharmaceuticals, synthetic organic chemistry, essential oils and medicinal plants, general and earthquake eng., biochemistry, material science, building materials, soil eng., testing and analysis; library of 15,750 vols; Dir Dr J. S. SANDHU; publ. *RRL News* (6 a year).

Regional Research Laboratory: Library Bldg, Hoshangabad Rd, Univ. of Bhopal, Habibganj Naka, Bhopal 462026; tel. (755) 2587105; fax (755) 2587042; e-mail root@rrlbpl.onp.nic.in; f. 1981; research and devt on minerals and materials with particular focus on aluminium; Dir Prof. T. C. RAO.

Regional Research Laboratory: Industrial Estate, Trivandrum; tel. (471) 2490324; fax (471) 2491712; e-mail root@csrrltd.ren.nic.in; f. 1976 to develop technologies for the optimal use of regional resources, to help industry in the region through research, devt and technology transfer; Dir Dr G. V. NAIR.

Structural Engineering Research Centre: Chennai 600113; tel. (44) 22352139; fax (44) 22350508; e-mail sercm@sirnetm.ernet.in; design and testing of skeletal steel structures, fatigue and fracture of industrial structures and components, computer-aided design of structures and software devt, structural dynamics and experimental mechanics, construction engineering, concrete composites and special concretes, wind engineering and cyclone disaster mitigation; library of 7,300 vols, 146 periodicals; Dir Dr T. V. S. R. APPA RAO; publ. *Journal of Structural Engineering* (quarterly).

Structural Engineering Research Centre: Central Govt Enclave, Kamla Nehru Nagar, Ghaziabad 201002, Uttar Pradesh; tel. (575) 2721874; fax (575) 2721882; e-mail root@cssercg.ren.nic.in; f. 1965; research into various aspects of structural eng., incl. problems connected with bridges and long-span structures and high-rise bldgs, natural disaster mitigations and materials science; library of 8,500 vols; Dir V. K. GHANEKAR; publ. *Journal* (quarterly).

AGRICULTURE, FISHERIES AND VETERINARY SCIENCE

Agro-Economic Research Centre: Visva-Bharati University, Santiniketan, West Bengal; tel. (3463) 252751; fax (3463) 252672; e-mail aere@vbharat.ernet.in; f. 1954; conducts research in agricultural economics; library of 6,000 vols; Dir KAZI M. B. RAHIM.

Central Arid Zone Research Institute: Jodhpur 342003; tel. (291) 2740584; fax (291) 2740706; e-mail pratap@cazri.raj.nic.in; internet cazri.raj.nic.in; f. 1959; seven divisions: Resource Survey and Monitoring, Resource Management, Arable Cropping System, Perennial Cropping System, Animal Sciences and Rodent Control, Energy Management, Engineering and Product Processing; Outreach programme; Regional Research Stations in Pali, Bikaner, Jaisalmer, Bhuj; library of 19,000 books, 164 current journals, 1,990 reprints; Dir Dr PRATAP NARAIN; publs *Annals of Arid Zone* (4 a year), *Annual Progress Report*, *DEN News* (4 a year).

Central Inland Capture Fisheries Research Institute: Barrackpore 700120, West Bengal; tel. (33) 25921190; fax (33) 25920388; e-mail director@cifri.wb.nic.in; internet www.icar.org.in/cicfri.html; f. 1947; research into: ecology of rivers, reservoirs, flood plain wetlands, estuaries and lakes; fisheries management of selected rivers, reservoirs, ox-bow lakes and estuaries; pen culture of carp and prawns; biology of fish and prawns; water pollution studies, conservation and environmental modelling; fish diseases and their control; also conducts information and training programmes; library of 9,000 vols and 90 journals; Dir Dr V. V. SUGUNAN; publs *Newsletter* (4 a year), *Indian Fisheries Abstracts* (2 a year), *Annual Report*.

Central Rice Research Institute: Cuttack, 753006 Orissa; tel. 21887; f. 1946; research on basic and applied aspects of all disciplines of rice culture; 530 mems; library of 12,000 vols, 200 periodicals; Dir Dr H. K. PANDE; publs *Annual Report*, *Oryza* (quarterly), *Rice Research News* (quarterly).

Central Tobacco Research Institute: Rajahmundry 533105, Andhra Pradesh; tel. (883) 2449871; fax (883) 2448341; e-mail ctri@sify.com; internet www.ctriindia.com; f. 1947; library of 22,000 vols, 159 periodicals; under the Indian Council of Agric. Research (Ministry of Agriculture and Rural Reconstruction, Govt of India); applied and fundamental research on all types of tobacco grown in India; regional stations at Guntur, Vedasandur, Pusa, Hunsur, Dinhata, Jeelugumilli and Kandukur; 250 mems; Dir Dr KAPIL DEO SINGH; publs *Newsletter* (4 a year), *Annual Report*.

Indian Agricultural Statistics Research Institute: Library Ave, Pusa, New Delhi 110012; tel. (11) 25847121; fax (11) 25841564; e-mail director@iasri.res.in; internet www.iasri.res.in; f. 1959; part of ICAR (see below); research in experimental designs, sample surveys, biometric techniques, forecasting techniques, econometrics and computer applications; conducts postgraduate courses and in-service training in agricultural statistics and computer application; provides advisory service to agricultural scientists; provides consultancy service in data processing; develops computer software and information systems; library of 25,106 vols, 6,721 journals, 53 online journals, 8,009 reports, 835 theses; Dir Dr S. D. SHARMA; publ. *Agricultural Research Data Book* (annually).

Indian Council of Agricultural Research (ICAR): Krishi Bhavan, Dr Rajendra Prasad Rd, New Delhi 110001; tel. (11) 23382629; e-mail mrai.icar@nic.in; internet www.icar.org.in; f. 1929 to promote agricultural and animal husbandry research in conjunction with State Governments, Central and State Research Institutions, etc.; attached to Min. of Agriculture; provides consultancy and information on agriculture, horticulture, resource management, animal sciences, agricultural engineering, fisheries, agricultural extension, agricultural education, home science and agricultural communication; coordinates agricultural research and development programmes and develops links at nat. and intl level with related organisations to enhance the quality of life of the farming community; research centres; human resource development in the field of agricultural sciences; oversees numerous agricultural universities nationally; establishes Krishi Vigyan Kendras (farm training centres) responsible for training, research and demonstration of the latest agricultural technology; Pres. SHARAD PAWAR; Dir-Gen. Dr MANGALA RAI; publs *Indian Journal of Agricultural Sciences*, *Indian Journal of Animal Sciences*, *Indian Farming*, *Kheti* (all monthly), *Indian Horticulture*, *Phal-Phool*, *Krishi Chayanika* (all quarterly).

Indian Council of Forestry Research and Education: New Forest, Dehradun 248006; tel. (135) 2759382; fax (135) 2758614; e-mail dg@icfre.org; internet www.icfre.org; f. 1906; library of 160,000 vols, 600 periodicals; Dir-Gen. R. P. S. KATWAL; publs *Indian Forest Records*, *ICFRE Newsletter*, *Annual Report*, *ENVIS Forestry Bulletin*.

Indian Plywood Industries Research and Training Institute: Post Bag 2273, Tumkur Rd, Bangalore 560022; tel. (80) 28394341; fax (80) 28396361; e-mail cnpandey@vsnl.net; f. 1962; research on saw-milling, plywood manufacturing techniques, preservative treatment of wood and wood-based panels, devt of synthetic and natural adhesives; testing of panel products; training in mechanical wood processing technology; specialized short-term courses; library of 8,500 vols; Dir Dr C. N. PANDEY.

Indian Veterinary Research Institute: Izatnagar 243122, Uttar Pradesh; tel. (581) 2301375; fax (581) 2302179; e-mail dirivri@ivri.up.nic.in; internet www.ivri.nic.in; f. 1889; Deemed University status 1983; campuses at Bangalore, Bhopal, Kolkata, Mukteswar, Palampur and Srinagar; research divisions of Animal Biochemistry, Animal Biotechnology, Animal Genetics and Breeding, Animal Nutrition, Animal Physiology, Avian Diseases, Biostatistics, Livestock Products Technology, Livestock Production and Management, Poultry Science, Veterinary Bacteriology, Veterinary Epidemiology, Veterinary Extension Education, Veterinary Gynaecology and Obstetrics, Veterinary Immunology, Veterinary Medicine, Veterinary Parasitology, Veterinary Pathology, Veterinary Pharmacology, Veterinary Public Health, Veterinary Surgery and Veterinary Virology; library: library of 207,000 vols, 300 periodicals; Dir Dr M. P. YADAV; publs *Annual Report*, *Annual Scientific Report*.

National Dairy Research Institute: Karnal, Haryana 132001; tel. (184) 2252800; fax (184) 2250042; e-mail bnm@ndri.hry.nic.in; internet karnal.nic.in/res_ndri.asp; f. 1923; training, research and extension; regional stations at Bangalore and Kalyani; library of 75,000 vols and 22,000 periodicals; Dir Dr NAGENDRA SHARMA; Registrar Cptn MEHER SINGH; publs *Annual Report*, *Dairy Samachar* (quarterly).

National Sugar Institute: Kalyanpur, Kanpur 208017, Uttar Pradesh; tel. (512) 2250541; fax (512) 2250247; f. 1936 to undertake research, teaching and consultancy activities in all aspects of sugar technology; library of 7,368 vols; Dir RAM KUMAR; publs *Sharkara*, *N.S.I. News*.

Rubber Research Institute of India: Kottayam 686009, Kerala; tel. (481) 2353311; fax (481) 2353327; e-mail rrii@vsnl.com; internet www.rubberboard.com; f. 1955 to promote the development of the industry; scientific, technological and economic research in improved methods of planting, cultivation, processing and consumption of natural rubber; library of 50,000 vols; Chair. S. M. DESALPHINE; Rubber Production Commr Dr A. K. KRISHNAKUMAR; Dir of Research Dr N. M. MATHEW; publs *Indian Journal of Natural Rubber Research* (2 a year), *Rubber* (in Malayalam, monthly), *Indian Rubber Statistics* (annually), *Rubber Growers' Companion* (annually), *Rubber Statistical News* (monthly), *Annual Report*.

Vasantdada Sugar Institute: Manjari (Bk.), 412307 Tal. Haveli, Dist. Pune, Maharashtra; tel. (20) 26902151; fax (20) 26902244; e-mail vsilib@vsnl.com; internet www.vsisugar.com; f. 1975; library of 18,000 vols; Dir-Gen. SHIVAJIRAO DESHMUKH; publ. *Bulletin* (quarterly).

BIBLIOGRAPHY, LIBRARY SCIENCE AND MUSEOLOGY

Documentation Research and Training Centre (Indian Statistical Institute): 8th

Mile, Mysore Rd, R. V. College Post, Bangalore 560059; tel. (80) 28483002; fax (80) 28484265; e-mail drtc@isibang.ac.in; f. 1962; conducts research in the fields of library science, documentation and information science; trains documentalists; provides an advisory service to industry, academic and research institutions; library of 20,000 vols; Head Prof. I. K. RAVICHANDRA RAO; publ. *DRTC Annual Seminar*.

ECONOMICS, LAW AND POLITICS

Indian Institute of Public Administration: Indraprastha Estate, Ring Rd East, New Delhi 110002; tel. (11) 23702400; fax (11) 23702440; e-mail diriipa@bol.net.in; f. 1954 to promote the study of public administration; research, training, consultancy; library of 192,000 vols, 400 periodicals; Dir Dr P. L. SANJEEV REDDY; Registrar S. N. SURI; publs *The Indian Journal of Public Administration* (4 a year), *Documentation in Public Administration* (4 a year), *Nagarlok* (4 a year), *Newsletter* (monthly).

Institute for Defence Studies and Analyses: Sapru House Annexe, Barakhamba Rd, New Delhi 110001; tel. (11) 23314951; fax (11) 23321851; f. 1965; research on national security, undertakes study on methods of warfare, strategy, disarmament and international relations; library of 45,000 vols, and 1,500 maps; Pres. DINESH SINGH; Dir J. SINGH; publs *Strategic Digest* (monthly), *Strategic Analysis* (monthly), *News Reviews* (monthly).

Institute for Social and Economic Change: Nagarabhavi PO, Bangalore 560072; tel. (80) 23387010; fax (80) 23387008; f. 1972; social and economic development in India; library of 81,000 vols, 300 periodicals; Pres. THE GOV. OF KARNATAKA; Dir Dr M. G. RAO; publ. *Journal of Social and Economic Development* (2 a year).

Madras Institute of Development Studies: 79 Second Main Rd, Gandhinagar, Adyar, Chennai 600020; tel. (44) 24412589; fax (44) 24910872; e-mail ssmids@ren.nic.in; f. 1970; aims to contribute to the economic and social development of Tamil Nadu State and India; undertakes studies and research in micro-development problems; aims at upgrading economic research in the South Indian universities through research methodology courses and studies; fosters inter-university co-operation of southern states and promotes inter-disciplinary research; recognized by Univ. of Madras for PhD courses; library of 43,500 vols; Chair Prof. C. T. KURIEN; Dir Dr V. K. NATRAJ; publ. *Review of Development and Change* (2 a year).

National Council of Applied Economic Research: Parisila Bhavan, 11 Indraprastha Estate, New Delhi 110002; tel. (11) 23379861; fax (11) 23370164; e-mail infor@ncaer.org; internet www.ncaer.org; f. 1956; autonomous research organization to study economic problems for government, international organizations and private business; library of 73,400 vols, 400 periodicals, microfiche collection of census of India 1872–1951, CD databases; Dir-Gen. SUMAN BERY; publs *Margin* (4 a year), *Artha Suchi* (4 a year), *Macro Track* (4 a year).

National Productivity Council: 5–6 Institutional Area, Lodi Rd, New Delhi 110003; tel. (11) 24690331; fax (11) 24615002; e-mail npc@ren02.nic.in; internet www.npcindia.org; f. 1958 by the Government of India to help increase productivity in every sector of the national economy; 12 regional directorates (Kanpur, Chandigarh, Kolkata, Madras, Bangalore, Guwahati, Mumbai, Ahmedabad, Delhi, Bhopal, Hyderabad, Patna); library of 30,000 vols, 80 journals; Dir-Gen. K. SRINIVASANY; publs *Productivity* (quarterly), *Productivity News* (monthly), *Utpadakta* (Hindi, monthly).

Socio-Economic Research Institute: C-19 & C-39 College Street Market, Kolkata 700007; tel. (33) 22410775; economics and economic history, sociology and social history, demography focusing on the historical demography of India; Dir Prof. DURGAPRASAD BHATTACHARYA.

EDUCATION

Indian Institute of Advanced Study: Rashtrapati Nivas, Shimla 171005; tel. (177) 2230006; fax (177) 2231389; f. 1965 to undertake post-doctoral research, especially in the humanities and social sciences; also functions as Inter-University Centre for Humanities and Social Sciences on behalf of the University Grants Commission of India; library of 145,000 vols and 340 periodicals; Dir (vacant); Chair. Prof. B. C. MUNGEKAR; publ. two journals.

Indian Psychometric and Educational Research Association: Dept of Education, Patna Training College Campus, Patna 800004; f. 1969 to promote and develop the study of, and undertake research into, psychology, education, statistics, etc.; 330 mems; library of 3,700 vols; Pres. Dr A. K. P. SINHA; Gen. Sec. Dr R. P. SINGH; publ. *Indian Journal of Psychometry and Education*.

FINE AND PERFORMING ARTS

National Institute of Design: Paldi, Ahmedabad 380007; tel. 79692; f. 1961; established by the Government of India as a research, training and service organization in industrial and communication design; Diploma in Design after 2–3 years' training (graduate) or 5 years' training (undergraduate) in Industrial Design or Communication Design; library of 23,000 vols, 130 current periodicals, 75,000 slides, 2,044 tapes and records, 1,545 other audio-visual aids and 600 well-designed objects for reference; Exec. Dir VIKAS SATWALEKAR.

National Research Laboratory for Conservation of Cultural Property: Sector E-3, Aliganj Scheme, Lucknow 226020; tel. and fax (522) 2372378; e-mail nrlclko@lw1.vsnl.net.in; f. 1976 by the Ministry of Human Resource Development, Dept of Culture; conducts research into conservation techniques of objects of art and provides technical assistance to museums and related institutions; training in conservation for Asian countries sponsored by UNESCO; regional laboratory at Mysore; library: *c.* 12,000 vols, 130 periodical subscriptions; Dir TEJ SINGH.

HISTORY, GEOGRAPHY AND ARCHAEOLOGY

Archaeological Survey of India: Government of India, New Delhi 110011; f. 1902; excavating, preservation, surveying and maintenance of archaeological sites; advanced archaeological training; library of 80,000 vols containing rare material; Dir-Gen. Dr M. S. NAGARAJA RAO; publs *Memoirs*, *Indian Archaeology—A Review*.

Bihar Research Society: Museum Bldgs, Patna 800001, Bihar; f. 1915; 180 mems; library of 31,000 vols; Pres. Dr J. C. JHA; Sec M. S. PANDEY; publ. *Journal*.

Indian Council of Historical Research: 35 Ferozeshah Rd, New Delhi 110001; gives grants for doctoral theses, research projects, historical journals, and for bibliographical and documentation works; organizes and supports seminars, workshops and conferences for promotion of historical research; Dir Dr T. R. SAREEN; publ. *The Indian Historical Review*.

Jayaswal, K. P., Research Institute: Patna 800001; f. 1904 to promote historical research; library of 31,650 vols; Dir Dr JATA SHANKAR JHA.

Kamarupa Anusandhana Samiti (Assam Research Society): Gauhati, Assam; f. 1912; historical and archaeological research; 250 mems; Pres. Dr BISWANARAYAN SHASTRI; Joint Sec. ATULANANDA GOSWAMI; publ. *Journal of Assam Research Society* (annually).

Karnatak Historical Research Society: Diwan Bahadur Rodda Rd, Dharwad 1, Karnataka; f. 1914; to promote historical research in the Karnatak; to popularize the study of history and culture by lectures, slides, exhibitions, celebrations of historical events, excursions etc.; sections for research in language, culture and Vedic literature, socio-economic problems; 100 mems; library of 3,000 vols; Pres. RAJA S. G. ACHARYA; Chair. Dr P. R. PANCHAMUKHI; Secs A. R. PANCHAMUKHI, G. G. NADGIR; publs *Karnatak Historical Review* (2 a year in English and Kannada), and research publications.

National Atlas and Thematic Mapping Organisation: C.G.O. Complex, DF Block, Salt Lake, Kolkata 700064; e-mail natmo@vsnl.net; internet www.natmo.gov.in; fax (33) 23346460; f. 1956; engaged in cartographical research and preparation of national atlas of India; library of 19,000 vols, 78,000 maps, 350 atlases; Dir PRITHVISH NAG; publs *Agricultural Resources Atlas of India* (in English), *Atlas of Forest Resources* (in English), *Atlas of Water Resources*, *Irrigation Atlas of India* (in English), *National Atlas of India* (English and Hindi editions), *Tourist Atlas of India* (in English), other maps and monographs.

Survey of India: Map Record and Issue Office, Hathibarkala, Dehradun 248001, Uttar Pradesh; f. 1767; engaged in topographical, geographical and geodetic preparation of large scale development project maps; acts as adviser to the Government of India on all survey matters.

LANGUAGE AND LITERATURE

Abul Kalam Azad Oriental Research Institute: Public Gardens, Hyderabad 500004, Andhra Pradesh; f. 1959; research in history, philosophy, culture, Islamic Studies and languages; Pres. MAHMOOD BIN MUHAMMAD; Hon. Sec. and Dir M. K. ALI KHAN.

Academy of Sanskrit Research: Melkote 571431, Mandya Dist., Karnataka State; tel. (8236) 258741; e-mail asrmel@vsnl.com; internet www.geocities.com/athens/ithaca/2455; f. 1978; affiliated to Mysore University and Kannada University, Hampi; affiliated to Rashtriya Sanskrit Sansthan, New Delhi, for undergraduate, postgraduate and doctoral courses; research and study of Vedas, Agamas and comparative philosophy, with primary focus on Visistadvaita; library of 25,000 vols, 10,500 palm leaf and paper manuscripts; Pres. M. A. S. RAJAN; Dir M. A. LAKSHMITHATHACHAR; publs *Tattva Dipah* (2 a year), *Newsletter* (4 a year).

All-India Oriental Conference: Bhandarkar Oriental Research Institute, Deccan Gymkhana, Pune 411004; tel. (20) 25656932; e-mail bori@ip.eth.net; f. 1919; 1,500 mems; mem. International Union for Oriental and Asian Studies; academic sessions every two years; Sec. Dr SAROJA BHATE; publ. Proceedings of Sessions (every 2 years).

Anjuman-i-Islam Urdu Research Institute: 92 Dr Dadabhoy Nowroji Rd, Mumbai 400001; tel. (22) 22620177; fax (22)

22621610; f. 1947; research in Urdu; PhD in Arabic, Persian, Urdu and Islamic Studies; library of 20,200 vols; Chair. SAMI KHATIB; Dir SHAMIM TARIQ; publ. *Nawa-e-Adab* (4 a year).

Bhandarkar Oriental Research Institute: Pune 411004; tel. (20) 25656932; fax (20) 25661362; e-mail bori1@vsnl.net; f. 1917; Sanskrit, Indological and Oriental studies; library of 99,700 vols, 28,000 MSS; Hon. Sec. Prof. SAROJA BHATE; publ. *Annals* (annually).

Cama, K. R., Oriental Institute: 136 Mumbai Samachar Marg, Fort, Mumbai 400023; tel. (22) 22843893; fax (22) 22876593; e-mail krcamaoi@vsnl.com; f. 1916; 320 mems; library of 25,671 vols, 2,000 MSS, 182 journals; Pres. MUNCHERJI N. M. CAMA; Jt Hon. Secs H. N. MODI, Dr N. B. MODY; publ. *Journal* (annual).

Deccan College Postgraduate and Research Institute: Deccan College Rd, Yeravada, Pune 411006; tel. (20) 26692113; fax (20) 26692104; e-mail dakshina@pn2.vsnl.net.in; f. 1939; postgraduate research in linguistics, archaeology, history and Vedic Sanskrit; library of 136,000 books and periodicals, 12,000 MSS; Joint Dirs Dr V. D. GOGTE, Dr K. PADDAYYA; publ. *Annual Bulletin*.

Ganganatha Jha Kendriya Sanskrit Vidyapeetha (Central Sanskrit Research Institute): Azad Park, Allahabad 211002, Uttar Pradesh; f. 1943; research into Sanskrit and other Indological subjects; library of 60,000 vols, 50,000 MSS; Principal Dr G. C. TRIPATHI; publs *Quarterly Research Journal*, catalogues, bibliographies, Sanskrit texts and studies.

Gujarat Research Society: Dr Madhuri Shah Campus, Ramkrishna Mission Marg, Khar (West), Mumbai 400052; tel. (22) 26462691; fax (22) 26047398; f. 1936 to organize and co-ordinate research in social and cultural activities; teacher-training; library of 10,000 vols; Pres. K. P. HAZARAT; publ. *Journal* (quarterly).

International Academy of Indian Culture: J 22 Hauz Khas Enclave, New Delhi 110016; tel. (22) 26515800; f. 1935 to study India's artistic, literary and historic relations with other Asian countries; library of 200,000 vols, 40,000 MSS; Pres. Dr LOKESH CHANDRA; publ. *Satapitaka Series*.

Kuppuswami Sastri Research Institute: 84 Thiru V. Kalayanasundaranar Rd, Mylapore, Chennai 600004; f. 1944; govt-sponsored and affiliated to University of Madras; promotion of Oriental learning especially Indology; lectures, seminars and workshops; 400 mems; library of 30,000 vols (including palm-leaf manuscripts); Dir Dr S. S. JANAKI; publs *Journal of Oriental Research*, and numerous research publs.

Mumbai Marathi Granth Sangrahalaya: Dadar, Mumbai 400014; f. 1898; research in Marathi language and literature; library of 185,020 vols; Pres. S. K. PATIL.

Nava Nalanda Mahavihara (Nalanda Institute of Buddhist Studies and Pali): PO Nalanda, Bihar 803111; tel. and fax (6112) 274820; f. 1951; administered by Dept of Culture, Ministry of Human Resources Development; studies and research in Pali, Buddhism, philosophy, ancient Indian and Asian studies; diploma in languages: Chinese, Japanese, Tibetan, Hindi, Sanskrit and Pali; library of 36,000 vols; Dir Prof. Dr DIPAK KUMAR BARUA; publs *Pali Tipitaki, Atthakatha*.

Oriental Institute of Indian Languages: Univ. of Mysore, Kautilya Circle, Mysore 570005, Karnataka; tel. (821) 2423136; e-mail orimys5@yahoo.co.in; f. to promote inter-regional and inter-continental understanding through the study of languages; Dir Dr H. P. DEVAKI.

Oriental Research Institute: Mysore, 570005; tel. 23136; library of 28,300 vols and 50 periodicals; collection of 60,000 ancient MSS; Dir K. RAJAGOPALACHAR.

Sri Venkateswara University Oriental Research Institute: Tirupati, Andhra Pradesh 517502; tel. (877) 2249666; fax (877) 2224111; e-mail orientalresearchinstitute@yahoo.co.in; f. 1939; given by T. T. DEVASTHANAMS to the University in 1956; research in language and literature, philosophy and religion, art and archaeology, ancient Indian history and culture; library of 30,000 vols, 16,948 palm-leaf and paper MSS; Dir Dr V. VENKATARAMANA REDDY; publ. *SVU Oriental Journal*.

Vishveshvaranand Vedic Research Institute: Sadhu Ashram, Hoshiarpur 146021; tel. (1882) 223582; e-mail vvrinstitute@yahoo.co.in; f. 1903; 3,230 mems; academic and cultural studies on Indian literatures and religion; Pres. Prof. G. P. CHOPRA; Dir Prof. I. D. UNIYAL; publs *Vishva Jyoti* (cultural, Hindi monthly), *Vishva Samskritam* (cultural research, Sanskrit, 4 a year), *Research Bulletin* (annually, in English).

Attached institute:

Vishveshvaranand Vishva Bandhu Institute of Sanskrit and Indological Studies: Sadhu Ashram, Hoshiarpur 146021; tel. (1882) 221002; f. 1965; postgraduate teaching, research and study in Indology; Prak-Shastri and Shastri MA classes in Sanskrit; 12 fellows; library of 76,500 vols, 3,000 ancient MSS; Chair. G. D. BHARADWAJ; publs *Acharya Vishva Bandhu Memorial Lecture Series* (annually), *Panjab University Indological Series*, *Vishveshvaranand Indological Journal* (research, English and Sanskrit, 2 a year).

MEDICINE

Advanced Centre for Treatment, Research and Education in Cancer (ACTREC): Tata Memorial Centre, Sector 22, Kharghar, Navi Mumbai 410208; tel. (22) 27405000; fax (22) 27412894; e-mail mail@actrec.res.in; f. 1952 as Cancer Research Centre; library: 5,481 books, 9,642 bound vols of journals, 51 current periodicals; Dir Dr R. SARIN; publ. *Scientific Report* (annually).

B. M. Institute of Mental Health: Ashram Rd, near Nehru Bridge, Ahmedabad 380009, Gujarat; tel. (79) 26578256; fax (79) 26578259; e-mail bminstitute_ahm@yahoo.com.in; f. 1951; comprehensive mental health services, teaching, and research; psychiatric clinic for the emotionally disturbed; clinic for children with learning difficulties; occupational therapy and rehabilitation services; speech clinic; postgraduate training in psychodiagnostics and counselling; offers diploma in working with the developmentally handicapped; library of 6,484 vols; Dir Dr S. R. APTE; publ. *Mental Health Review* (annual).

Central Jalma Institute for Leprosy: POB 101, Taj Ganj, Agra 282001, Uttar Pradesh; tel. (562) 2331756; fax (562) 2331755; e-mail jalma@zyberway.com; f. 1966; part of Indian Council of Medical Research; treatment, research and training on leprosy, tuberculosis and HIV/AIDS; library of 2,496 books, 40 journals; Dir Dr V. M. KATOCH; publ. *Quarterly Bulletin*.

Central Leprosy Teaching and Research Institute: POB 24, Thirumani, Chingalpattu, Tamil Nadu 603001; tel. (4114) 226274; fax (4114) 226064; e-mail lepoltri@md3.vsnl.net.in; internet education.vsal.com/cltri; f. 1955; a WHO regional training centre; library of 11,000 vols, 44 periodicals; Dir Dr P. K. OOMMEN; publs *News Bulletin* (4 a year), *Annual Report*.

Central Research Institute: Kasauli, Himachal Pradesh; f. 1905; medical research, graduate and postgraduate training, manufacture of biological products; Institute of the Govt of India; library of 30,000 vols; Dir Dr J. SOKHEY; publ. *Annual Scientific Report*.

Haffkine Institute for Training, Research and Testing: Acharya Donde Marg, Parel, Mumbai 400012; tel. (22) 24160847; fax (22) 24150826; f. 1897; principal centre of research in communicable diseases, biomedical and allied sciences in India; library of 40,000 vols; Depts: Bacteriology, Biochemistry, Chemotherapy, Clinical Pathology, Immunology, Pharmacology and Phytochemistry, Radiation Biology Unit, Testing Unit, Zoonosis, Human Pharmacology and Virology, each with its staff of scientists; Dir Dr V. L. YEMUL; publ. *Annual Report*.

Indian Brain Research Association: Dept of Biochemistry, University of Calcutta, 35 Ballygunge Circular Rd, Kolkata 700019; f. 1964; 300 mems; library of 2,000 vols; Pres. and Ed. Sec. Prof. J. J. GHOSH; publ. *Brain News* (2 a year).

Indian Council of Medical Research: V. Ramalingaswami Bhawan, Ansari Nagar, New Delhi 110029; tel. (11) 26588204; fax (11) 26589258; e-mail icmrhqds@sansad.nic.in; internet www.icmr.nic.in; f. 1911; promotes, co-ordinates and funds medical research; maintains the National Institute of Nutrition (Hyderabad), National Institute of Virology (Pune), Tuberculosis Research Centre (Chennai), National Institute of Cholera and Enteric Diseases (Kolkata), Institute of Pathology (New Delhi), National Institute of Occupational Health (Ahmedabad), Institute of Immunohaematology (Mumbai), National Institute for Research in Reproductive Health (Mumbai), Entero Virus Research Centre (Mumbai), Vector Control Research Centre (Pondicherry), Central Jalma Institute for Leprosy (Agra), Malaria Research Centre (Delhi), Institute for Research in Medical Statistics (New Delhi), National Institute of Epidemiology (Chennai), Institute of Cytology and Preventive Oncology (New Delhi), Rajendra Memorial Research Institute of Medical Sciences (Patna), National AIDS Research Institute (Pune), National Centre for Laboratory Animal Sciences (Hyderabad), Food and Drug Toxicology Research Centre (both Hyderabad), Centre for Research in Medical Entomology (Madurai), ICMR Genetic Research Centre (Mumbai), and six Regional Medical Research Centres (Bhubaneswar, Dibrugarh, Jabalpur, Jodhpur, Port Blair, Belgaum); library of 20,000 vols; Dir-Gen. N. K. GANGULY; publs *Indian Journal of Medical Research* (monthly, with supplements), *ICMR Bulletin* (monthly), *Indian Journal of Malariology* (4 a year), *ICMR Patrika* (in Hindi, monthly), Annual Reports of the Council.

Institute of Child Health: 11 Dr Biresh Guha St, Kolkata 700017; f. 1953; affiliated to College for Child Health, University of Calcutta; Dir Dr SISIR KUMAR BOSE; departments of Clinical Paediatrics, Paediatric Surgery, Biochemistry, Radiology, Pathology, Preventive Paediatrics, Physiotherapy, Psychiatry, Dermatology, Ophthalmology and Oto-rhino-laryngology.

King Institute of Preventive Medicine: Guindy, Chennai 600032; f. 1899; postgraduate training in microbiology; library of 20,137 vols; Dir Dr K. V. MURTHY; publ. *Annual Report*.

National Institute of Communicable Diseases: 22 Sham Nath Marg, Delhi 110054; tel. (11) 23966065; fax (11) 23922677; e-mail dirnicd@bol.net.in; internet www.nicd.org; f. 1963; formerly Malaria Institute of India, f. 1909; research and training centre in field of communicable and vector-borne diseases; brs at Alwar (Rajasthan), Coonoor (Tamil Nadu) and Jagdalpur (Madhya Pradesh) (all for research and training in epidemiology), Calicut (Kerala), Rajahmundry (Andhra Pradesh) and Varanasi (Uttar Pradesh) (all for research and training on helminthology), Patna (medical entomology and vector control), Bangalore (zoonosis); library of 34,430 vols, 265 maps; Dir Dr SHIV LAL; publs *CD Alert* (monthly), *Health News Clipping* (monthly).

Attached institute:

National Anti-Malaria Eradication Programme: 22 Sham Nath Marg, Delhi 110054; tel. (11) 22918576; fax (11) 22518329; f. 1958; co-ordination, technical guidance, planning, monitoring and evaluation of a nation-wide malaria control and eradication programme; library of 4,000 vols; Dir Dr SHIV LAL; publ. *Malaria Watch* (4 a year).

National Institute of Nutrition: Indian Council of Medical Research, Jamai-Osmania, Hyderabad 500007, Andhra Pradesh; tel. (40) 27008921; fax (40) 27019074; e-mail nin@ap.nic.in; internet ninindia.org; f. 1918; principal research and training centre for South and South-East Asia; includes centres for Food and Drug Toxicology Research, National Centre for Laboratory Animal Sciences and National Nutrition Monitoring Bureau; library of 15,000 vols, 27,000 periodicals, 10,000 reports; Dir Dr B. SIVAKUMAR; Library and Information Officer DEVIDAS MAHINDRAKAR; publs *Annual Report*, *NCLAS Newsletter* (2 a year), *NIN Library Newsletter* (6 a year), *Nutrition* (4 a year), *Nutrition News* (6 a year).

National Tuberculosis Institute: Govt of India, 'Avalon', 8 Bellary Rd, Bangalore 560003; tel. (80) 23362431; fax (80) 23440952; e-mail ntiindia@blr.vsnl.net.in; internet ntiindia.kar.nic.in; f. 1959; 240 mems; research in epidemiology, applied tuberculosis bacteriology, sociological aspects and systems research with regard to tuberculosis control; training and control programme; information centre on tuberculosis; digital library of institute papers published in periodicals and publications; Dir Dr PRAHLAD KUMAR; publs *Bulletin* (2 a year), *Annual Report*.

Pasteur Institute and Medical Research Institute: Shillong, Assam; f. 1915; library of 7,311 vols; Dir N. G. BANERJEE.

Pasteur Institute of India: Coonoor 643103 (Nilgiris), Tamil Nadu; tel. (423) 31250; fax (423) 31655; e-mail piicnr@md4.vsnl.net.in; f. 1907; work on virus diseases incl. polio and rabies, development of vaccines; a WHO international reference centre for quality control and production of rabies vaccines; a WHO National Polio Surveillance Project; library of 20,000 vols; Dir Dr L. N. RHAO BHAU.

Vallabhbhai Patel Chest Institute: POB 2101, University of Delhi, Delhi 110007; tel. (11) 27666180; fax (11) 27667420; e-mail vpci@delnet.ren.nic.in; internet www.vpci.org.in; f. 1949; attached to Univ. of Delhi; postgraduate teaching and research in respiratory diseases and allied biomedical sciences; library of 25,000 vols; Dir Prof. V. K. VIJAYAN; publ. *Indian Journal of Chest Diseases and Allied Sciences* (quarterly).

Vector Control Research Centre: Medical Complex, Indira Nagar, Pondicherry 605006; tel. (413) 2272396; fax (413) 2272041; e-mail vcrc@vsnl.com; internet www.pon.nic.in/fil-free/vcrc/da5.html; f. 1975; develops epidemiological surveillance tools and strategies for the prevention and control of vector-borne diseases, including malaria, filariasis and dengue fever; research and postgraduate training; attached to Indian Council of Medical Research; affiliated with Central Univ., Pondicherry; library of 10,000 vols; Dir P. K. DAS; publ. *Annual Report*.

NATURAL SCIENCES

General

Bose Institute: 93/1 Acharya Prafulla Chandra Rd, Kolkata 700009; tel. (33) 23342403; fax (33) 23506790; e-mail dbt@boseinst.ernet.in; internet dst.gov.in/autoinst/bose_institute.htm; f. 1917 to advance the science and diffusion of knowledge; research undertaken by depts of Physics, Chemistry, Botany, Microbiology, Biochemistry and Biophysics; experimental stations at Falta, Shamnagar, Madhyamgram and Darjeeling; library of 24,883 vols; Co-ordinator Dr PINAKPANI CHAKRABARTI; publs *Transactions*, *Annual Report*, *News Letter*.

Indian Association for the Cultivation of Science (IACS): Jadavpur, Kolkata 700032; tel. (33) 24734971; fax (33) 24732805; e-mail root@mahendra.iacs.res.in; f. 1876; research in theoretical physics, spectroscopy, material science, solid state physics, physical chemistry, biological chemistry, energy research unit, polymer science unit, organic and inorganic chemistry; 1,600 mems; library of 63,205 vols; Pres. Prof. A. K. SHARMA; Dir Prof. D. CHAKRABORTY; publs *Indian Journal of Physics*, *Bulletin of the IACS*.

Raman Research Institute: C. V. Raman Ave, Sadashivanagar, Bangalore 560080; tel. (80) 23610122; fax (80) 23610492; e-mail root@rri.res.in; internet www.rri.res.in; f. 1948; liquid crystals, astrophysics, radio astronomy, theoretical physics and quantum optics; library of 23,920 books, 34,523 bound periodicals, 170 journal subscriptions (of which 100 online); Dir Prof. RAVI SUBRAHMANAYAN.

UNESCO Office New Delhi and Asia-Pacific Regional Bureau for Communication and Information: B-5/29 Safdarjung Enclave, New Delhi 110029; tel. (11) 26713000; fax (11) 26713001; e-mail newdelhi@unesco.org; internet unescodelhi.nic.in; f. 1948; designated Cluster Office for Bangladesh, Bhutan, India, Maldives, Nepal and Sri Lanka, working in co-operation with national and regional organizations; activities in all areas of UNESCO competence: special focus on education for all, science and technology for development, science for progress and the environment, environment and natural resources management, culture and communicators of information; library: documentation centre of 30,000 UNESCO documents, reports, etc.; special collections: science and technology, education, social sciences, culture and communication; films library, posters, CD-ROMs, CDs; Dir Prof. M. TAWFIK; publs *UNESCO New Delhi Newsletter* (4 a year), *Annual Report*.

Biological Sciences

Birbal Sahni Institute of Palaeobotany: 53 University Rd, Lucknow 226007; tel. (522) 2324291; fax (522) 2381948; e-mail registrar@bsip.res.in; internet www.bsip-india.org; f. 1946; scientific research on the fundamental and applied aspects of fossil plants and their bearing on the origins of life; evolutionary linkages; biostratigraphy; fossil fuel exploration; phytogeography and biodiagenesis; repository of fossil plants; library of 5,000 vols, 10,000 current periodicals, 35,000 reprints and 300 microfilms, etc.; Dir Prof. ANSHU K. SINHA; publ. *The Palaeobotanist* (3 a year).

Botanical Survey of India: P/8 Brabourne Rd, Kolkata 700001; tel. (33) 22424922; fax (33) 22429330; f. 1890; botanical surveys and research; Headquarters: Central National Herbarium and Indian Botanic Garden at Howrah; Industrial Section, Indian Museum at Calcutta; regional circles at Allahabad, Pune, Coimbatore, Jodhpur, Port Blair, Shillong, Dehra Dun, Itanagar and Gangtok; library of more than 250,000 vols; 491 scientific staff; Dir Dr B. D. SHARMA; publs *Bulletin* (quarterly), *Reports* (annually), *Indian Floras*, etc.

Indian Association of Systematic Zoologists: c/o Zoological Survey of India, 34 Chittaranjan Ave, Kolkata 700012; f. 1947; Pres. Dr A. P. KAPUR.

Institute of Plant Industry: Indore, Madhya Pradesh; f. 1924; research in cotton genetics, and in crop improvement of cotton and rotation crops; Dir RAI BAHADUR R. L. SETHI.

Tropical Botanic Garden and Research Institute: Pacha-Palode, Trivandrum 695562, Kerala; tel. (472) 2869246,; fax (472) 2869646; e-mail gmnair@satyam.net.in; f. 1979; to establish a botanical garden, an arboretum, a medicinal plant garden and laboratories for botanical, horticultural, plant biotechnical ethnomedicinal, ethnopharmacological and phytochemical research; conservation of rare and endangered tropical plant species; promotion of research and development studies of plants of medicinal and economic importance; library of 5,000 vols, 65 journals; herbarium of 17,800 mounted specimens and 30,000 duplicates of vascular plants; museum; Dir Prof. Dr G. M. NAIR; publs *Annual Report*, *Index Seminum*, *Information Brochures*, *Quarterly Newsletter*.

Zoological Survey of India: M Block, New Alipur, Kolkata 700053; f. 1916; activities include maintenance of National Zoological Collections, conduct of faunistic surveys and research on systematic zoology, wildlife, environmental conservation, etc; regional stations at Berhampur, Canning, Chennai, Dehradun, Digha, Hyderabad, Itanagar, Jabalpur, Jodhpur, Kozhikode, Patna, Port Blair, Pune, Shillong, Solan; library of 60,000 vols, 800 periodicals; Dir Dr ASISH K. GHOSH; publs *Records* (quarterly), *Memoirs*, *Annual Reports*, *Fauna of India*, *Occasional Papers*, *Handbooks*, *State Fauna Series*, *Bibliography of Indian Zoology*, *and a series of monographs*.

Mathematical Sciences

Institute of Mathematical Sciences: CIT Campus, Taramani, Chennai 600113; tel. (44) 22541856; fax (44) 22541586; e-mail postmaster@imsc.ernet.in; internet www.imsc.ernet.in; f. 1962; research in pure and applied mathematics, theoretical physics and theoretical computer science; library of 44,996 vols, 260 periodicals; Dir Prof. R. BALASUBRAMANIAN; publ. *I.M.Sc. Reports*.

Physical Sciences

Alipore Observatory and Meteorological Office: Kolkata; f. 1877; publ. *The India Meteorological Department*.

Astronomical Observatory: Presidency College, Kolkata; f. 1898; Dir Dr P. CHOUDHURY.

Astronomical Observatory of St Xavier's College: 30 Park St, Kolkata 700016; f. 1875; Dir Rev. F. GOREUX.

Bhabha Atomic Research Centre: Trombay, Mumbai 400085, Maharashtra; tel. (22) 25505050; fax (22) 25505151; e-mail director@barc.gov.in; internet www.barc.gov.in; f. 1957; national centre for research in and development of atomic energy for non-military purposes; facilities include: three research reactors; Van de Graaff accelerator; laboratories at Srinagar, Gulmarg, and Gauribidanur; isotope production unit; central workshops; pilot plants for production of heavy water, zirconium, titanium; uranium metal plant; food irradiation and processing laboratory; reactor engineering laboratory and test facilities; library of 200,000 vols, 1,200 technical journals, 450,000 technical reports; Dir Dr SRIKUMAR BANERJEE; publs *Newsletter* (monthly), *Technical Reports*.

Central Seismological Observatory: Shillong; headquarters at New Delhi.

Geodetic and Research Branch, Survey of India: POB 77, Dehradun 248001; f. 1800; geodetic and allied geophysical activities, including development and research of instrumentation; library of 55,000 vols; Dir Dr M. G. ARUR; publs reports, and technical publications.

Geological Survey of India: 27 J. L. Nehru Rd, Kolkata 700016; tel. (33) 22496941; fax (33) 22496956; e-mail gsi_chq@vsnl.com; internet www.gsi.gov.in; f. 1851; devoted to surveying and mapping, mineral exploration, specialized investigations, other exploration, research and development, information dissemination, human resource development and project modernization and replacement; library of 5,003,500 vols; Dir-Gen. K. N. MATHUR; publs *Memoirs of the Geological Survey of India* (irregular), *Records of the Geological Survey of India. Part I–VIII* (annually), *Bulletin, Series A, B, C* (irregular), *Palaeontologica Indica* (irregular), *Special Publications* (irregular), *Miscellaneous Publications* (irregular), *Catalogue Series* (irregular), *Manual Series* (irregular), *Indian Minerals* (4 a year).

India Meteorological Department: Lodi Rd, New Delhi 110003; tel. (11) 24619415; fax (11) 24669216; e-mail rrkelkar@imd.ernet.in; f. 1875; six regional offices at New Delhi, Mumbai, Kolkata, Madras, Nagpur and Guwahati; 11 meteorological centres at Thiruvananthapuram, Bangalore, Hyderabad, Bhubaneshwar, Lucknow, Jaipur, Srinagar, Ahmedabad, Patna, Chandigarh and Bhopal; 10 cyclone detection radars; Positional Astronomy Centre at Kolkata; provides weather service; scientific activities cover research in all branches of meteorology, including agricultural and hydrometeorology, radio-meteorology, satellite and environmental meteorology, atmospheric electricity, seismology; New Delhi is Regional Telecommunication Hub and Regional Meteorological Centre under WMO World Weather Watch; Regional Specialised Meteorological Centre for Tropical Cyclones; also Regional Area Forecast Centre under ICAO; Dir-Gen. Dr R. R. KELKAR (acting); publs *Indian Astronomical Ephemeries* (annually), *Mausam* (quarterly), *Indian Weather Review*, *Regional/State Daily Weather Reports*, occasional Memoirs, Monographs and Reviews.

Indian Bureau of Mines: 'Indira Bhavan', Civil Lines, Nagpur 440001; tel. (712) 2524500; fax (712) 2533041; e-mail ibmnag@mah.nic.in; f. 1948; Government dept responsible for the conservation and development of mineral resources and protection of mining environment; aid in mine and mineral development, technical consultancy in mining and mineral processing, collection and dissemination of mineral statistics and information, preparation of feasibility reports of mining projects, including benefication plants, and preparation of environmental management plans; conducts market surveys on minerals and mineral commodities; regional offices at Ajmer, Bangalore, Bhubaneswar, Chennai, Dehradun, Goa, Hyderabad, Jabalpur, Kolkata, Ranchi, Udaipur; mineral processing laboratory and pilot plant at Nagpur; library of 50,000 vols, 10,000 periodicals; Controller-Gen. A. N. BOSE; publs *Indian Minerals Yearbook*, *Monthly Statistics of Mineral Production*, *Mineral Industry at a Glance* (annually).

Indian Institute of Astrophysics: Bangalore 560034; tel. (80) 25530672; fax (80) 25534043; f. 1786 as private observatory in Madras; study of solar physics, stellar physics, solar system objects, theoretical astrophysics incl. ionosphere, cosmology, solar-terrestrial relationship and instrumentation; library: more than 18,000 vols and access to 140 online journals; field stations at Kavalur, Kodaikanal, Hanle and Gauribidanur, and a research unit at Hosakote; Dir Prof. S. S. HASAN; publs *Newsletter*, *Reprints*.

Indian Institute of Geomagnetism: Dr Nanabhai Moos Marg, Colaba, Mumbai 400005; tel. (22) 22150293; fax (22) 22189568; e-mail root@iig.iigm.res.in; f. 1971; observatories in Alibag, Jaipur, Nagpur, Ujjain, Gulmarg, Shillong, Pondicherry, Silchar, Tirunelveli, Vishakapatnam; World Data Centre WDC-C2 for geomagnetism; operates geomagnetic observatory over Antarctica; library of 15,000 vols (books, bound periodicals and magnetic data); Dir Prof. G. S. LAKHINA; publs *Newsletter* (2 a year), *Indian Magnetic Data* (annually), *Annual Report*.

Indian Space Research Organization (ISRO): Antariksh Bhavan, New BEL Rd, Bangalore 560094; tel. (80) 23416356; fax (80) 23412253; e-mail kitta@isro.ernet.in; internet www.isro.org; f. 1972; development of satellites, launch vehicles and ground stations for satellite-based communications, resources survey and meteorological services; operates Vikram Sarabhai Space Centre, Space Applications Centre at Ahmedabad, ISRO Satellite Centre at Bangalore, SHAR Centre at Sriharikota Island, Liquid Propulsion System Unit at Trivandrum and Bangalore, Development & Educational Communications Unit at Ahmedabad, ISRO Telemetry Tracking and Command Network at Bangalore, ISRO Inertial Systems Unit, Trivandrum, INSAT Master Control Facility, Hassan; the Nat. Remote Sensing Agency at Hyderabad, the Physical Research Laboratory at Ahmedabad and the Nat. Mesosphere-Stratosphere-Troposphere Radar Facility at Gadanki are grant-in-aid instns; Chair. G. MADHAVAN NAIR; Scientific Sec. K. R. SRIDHAR MURTHY; publs *Space India* (4 a year), *Journal of Spacecraft Technology* (2 a year).

Indira Gandhi Centre for Atomic Research: Department of Atomic Energy, Kalpakkam 603102, Tamil Nadu; tel. (4114) 280267; fax (4114) 280060; e-mail dir@igcar.ernet.in; internet www.igcar.ernet.in; f. 1969; attached to Dept of Atomic Energy, Govt of India; research in Fast Reactor technology and related disciplines; library of 63,400 vols, 820 journals, 200,000 research reports; Dir Dr RAJ BALDEV; publs *IGC Newsletter* (4 a year), *IGC Annual Report*.

Institute for Plasma Research: Bhat, Gandhinagar 382428; tel. (79) 23969001; fax (79) 23969017; e-mail postmaster@plasma.ernet.in; internet www.plasma.ernet.in; f. 1986; research in plasma physics; library of 19,174 vols, 10,323 technical reports, 1,330 reprints, 110 periodicals; Dir P. K. KAW; publs *Annual Report*, *Plasma Processing Update* (4 a year).

Inter-University Centre for Astronomy and Astrophysics: Post Bag 4, Ganeshkhind, Pune University Campus, Pune 411 007; tel. (20) 25604100; fax (20) 25604699; e-mail root@iucaa.ernet.in; internet www.iucaa.ernet.in; f. 1988; fundamental research and training in all aspects of astronomy and astrophysics; MSc and PhD, refresher courses, research workshops, etc.; Dir Prof. NARESH K. DADHICH; publs *Khagol* (quarterly), *Annual Report*, *Lecture Notes*.

Mining, Geological and Metallurgical Institute of India: GN-38/4, Sector V, Salt Lake, Kolkata 700091; tel. (33) 23573482; fax (33) 22204653; e-mail csrpcil@cal2.vsnl.net.in; f. 1906; 2,500 mems from 16 brs; library of 3,500 vols; Pres. U. KUMAR; Hon. Sec. DEBASISH SARKAR; publs *Transactions* (2 a year), *Newsletter* (6 a year).

National Institute of Rock Mechanics: Champion Reefs P.O., Kolar Gold Fields 563117, Karnataka; tel. (8153) 261169; fax (8153) 260937; e-mail nirm@giasbg01.vsnl.net.in; f. 1989; library of 1,400 vols; Dir Dr N. M. RAJU; publs *Bulletin* (3 a year), *Annual Report*.

Nizamiah and Japal-Rangapur Observatories and Centre of Advanced Study in Astronomy: Osmania University, Hyderabad 500007; tel. (40) 27017306; e-mail pies@ouastr.ernet.in; f. 1908, transferred to control of Osmania Univ. 1919; library of 15,000 vols, 4,000 periodicals; Dir Prof. P. V. SUBRAHMANYAM; publ. *Astronomical*.

Physical Research Laboratory: Ahmedabad, Gujarat 380009; tel. (79) 26302129; fax (79) 26301502; e-mail info@prl.res.in; internet www.prl.res.in; f. 1947; atomic and molecular physics, nuclear and particle physics, laser physics and quantum optics, gravitational physics, non-linear dynamics and quantum chaos, optical and infrared astronomy, solar physics, astrophysics, atmospheric sciences and planetary aeronomy, oceanography and climate studies, solar system and geochronology, planetary science and exploration; library of 50,000 vols, 2,500 scientific reports and 1,200 maps; Dir Prof. G. S. AGARWAL.

Saha Institute of Nuclear Physics: 1/AF, Bidhannagar, Kolkata 700064; tel. (33) 23375345; fax (33) 23374637; e-mail library@saha.ac.in; internet www.saha.ac.in; f. 1951; conducts advanced research and teaching in nuclear science (radioactive ion beams; high energy physics, quark gluon plasma); research in physics (atomic physics, condensed matter physics, high energy physics, microelectronics, nuclear physics, plasmic physics, surface and general mathematical physics) and biophysical sciences (cell biology genetic toxicology, macromolecular crystallography; membrane biophysics, molecular genetics, nuclear and radiochemistry, photochemistry, radiation chemistry and biology, structural biology and biomolecular spectroscopy, ultrastructural research); library of 31,952 books, 45,056 journals, 21,076 reports, 515 CD-ROMs; Dir Prof. BIKASH SINHA.

PHILOSOPHY AND PSYCHOLOGY

Pratap Centre of Philosophy: Dept of Philosophy, University of Poona, Amalner, District Jalgaon, Maharashtra 425401; f. 1916 as Indian Inst. of Philosophy, taken over by Univ. and renamed 1972; comparative study of Indian and European philosophy; 12 mems; library of 6,000 vols; 3 fellowships awarded yearly for research; Dir Dr A. P. DEOGAONKAR; publs *The Philosophical Quarterly* (quarterly), *Tatvadnyan Mandir* (in Marathi).

Yoga Institute: Santa Cruz, Prabhat Colony, Mumbai 400055; tel. (22) 26122185; e-mail yoga@vsnl.net; internet www.yogainstitute.org; f. 1918 to promote self-education, physical, mental, moral and psychic, aided by the science of Yoga; to conduct academic and scientific research in Yoga culture and technique; runs teacher training Inst. of Yoga and a Psychosomatic Clinic based on Yoga; library of 4,500 vols; Dir HANSA SAVADEVA; publs *Yoga Studies*, *Cyclopaedia Yoga*, *Yoga and Total Health* (monthly).

RELIGION, SOCIOLOGY AND ANTHROPOLOGY

Anjuman-i-Islam Islamic Research Association: 92 Dadabhoy Nowroji Rd, Mumbai 400001; library of 5,000 vols; Pres. Dr M. ISHAQUE JAMKHANAWALA; Dir Prof. N. S. GOREKAR; publ. 12 vols of research work on Islamic studies.

Anthropological Survey of India: 27 Jawaharlal Nehru Rd, Kolkata 700016; tel. (33) 22498731; fax (33) 22497696; f. 1945; research in cultural and physical anthropology, human ecology, linguistics, psychology, folklore, biochemistry and radiology; library of 40,935 vols; Dir Dr R. K. BHATTACHARYA; publ. *Journal* (quarterly).

Applied Interdisciplinary Development Research Institute, Youth Entrepreneurship Development Organisation (YEDO): 20 Thiruvenkadapuram Main Rd, Choolaimedu, Chennai 600094; tel. (44) 23745579; fax (44) 23741564; e-mail peteraidri@hotmail.com; f. 1985; interdisciplinary development education, training, research, consultancy, information dissemination in fields of sustainable agricultural development, youth empowerment, empowerment of street children, women's empowerment, indigenous knowledge and local resources development, environmental education, and entrepreneurship development; Exec. Dir Dr A. PETER.

Ethnographic and Folk Culture Society: C-24, K Rd, Mahanagar Extn, Lucknow 226006; tel. and fax (522) 2372362; e-mail efcs@sancharnet.in; internet www.efcsindia.com; f. 1945; research into anthropological sciences; museum of Folk Life and Culture; library; Pres. B. D. SANWAL; Hon. Gen. Sec. Dr NADEEM HASNAIN; publs *The Eastern Anthropologist* (4 a year), *Indian Journal of Physical Anthropology and Human Genetics* (2 a year), *Manav* (in Hindi, 2 a year).

Giri, V. V., Labour Institute: POB 68, Sector 24, Noida 201301, Uttar Pradesh; tel. (120) 4535171; fax (120) 4532974; e-mail vvgnli@vsnl.com; internet www.vvgnli.org; f. 1964; research, training and consultancy; library of 50,000 vols; Dir UDAY KUMAR VARMA; publs *Award Digest* (4 a year), *Labour and Development* (2 a year), *Shram Jagat* (6 a year), *Shram Vidhan* (6 a year).

Indian Council of Social Science Research: JNU Institutional Area, Aruna Asaf Ali Marg, New Delhi 110067; tel. (11) 26176771; fax (11) 26179836; e-mail icssr@ren.nic.in; internet www.icssr.org; regional centres in Mumbai, Kolkata, Chandigarh, Delhi, Hyderabad, and Shillong; f. 1969; sponsors and co-ordinates research in social science, provides financial assistance for research programmes, awards fellowships and grants; sponsors conferences, seminars, training programmes and publications; provides partial support to 28 social science research institutes; collaborates with international bodies in research programmes; National Social Science Documentation Centre (NASSDOC: see Libraries); Data Archives; library of 35,000 books, 150,000 periodicals; Chair. Dr V. R. PANCHAMUKHI; Member-Sec. BHASKAR CHATTERJEE; publs *Indian Social Science Review*, *ICSSR Journal of Abstracts and Reviews: Sociology and Social Anthropology* (2 a year), *ICSSR Journal of Abstracts and Reviews: Economics* (2 a year), *ICSSR Journal of Abstracts and Reviews: Geography* (2 a year), *ICSSR Journal of Abstracts and Reviews: Political Science* (2 a year), *Indian Psychological Abstracts and Reviews* (2 a year), *Newsletter* (4 a year).

Institute of Applied Manpower Research: Plot 25, Sector A-7, Institutional Area, Narela, Delhi 110040; tel. (11) 27783468; fax (11) 27783467; e-mail iamr@del2.vsnl.net.in; internet www.iamrindia.org; f. 1962; autonomous body under Planning Commission; studies and disseminates information on the nature, characteristics and utilization of human resources in India; develops methodologies for forecasting demand and supply; compiles information on technical manpower; organizes seminars, conferences, study courses and training programmes in techniques of manpower planning at nat. and int. levels and provides consultancy services; conducts degree and diploma courses in Human Resource Planning and Development for int. participants, in collaboration with Commonwealth Secretariat, London; library of 25,000 vols, 150 journals; Pres. Hon. SH. MONTEK SINGH AHLUWALIA; Dir Prof. H. RAMACHANDRAN; publs *Manpower Journal* (4 a year), *Manpower Documentation* (12 a year), *Manpower Profile India* (annually), *Technical Manpower Bulletin* (4 a year), *Technical Manpower Profile* (every 5 years).

Institute of Economic Growth: University Enclave, Delhi 110007; tel. (11) 27257260; fax (11) 27257101; e-mail system@ieg.ernet.in; internet ieg.nic.in; f. 1958; an autonomous body recognized by the University of Delhi as a national-level multidisciplinary centre for advanced research and training, including Ph.D. supervision in the fields of economic and social development; specialized library and documentation service; Dir Prof. PRAVIN VISARIA; publs *Contributions to Indian Sociology: New Series* (2 a year), *Studies in Asian Social Development* (irregular), *Studies in Economic Development and Planning*.

Namgyal Institute of Tibetology/fmrly Sikkim Research Institute of Tibetology: Gangtok, Sikkim; tel. and fax (3592) 281525; e-mail nitsikkim@yahoo.co.in; internet www.tibetology.net; f. 1958; research centre for study of Mahayana (Northern Buddhism); museum of icons and art objects; library: library of Tibetan literature (canonical of all sects and secular) in MSS and xylographs; Dir TASHI DENSAPA; publ. *Bulletin of Tibetology* (2 a year).

National Institute of Rural Development: Rajendranagar, Hyderabad 500030; tel. (40) 24015001; fax (40) 24015277; e-mail karaju@nird.ap.nic.in; internet www.nird.org; f. 1958; autonomous servicing and consultancy agency for central and state governments; training for government and non-government officials; a Centre on Rural Documentation (CORD) provides computerized library services; development research into all facets of rural life; offers consultancy service to national and international organizations; aims to repackage govt and other literature on rural development for wider dissemination; library of 95,000 vols; Dir-Gen. R. C. CHOWDHURY; publs *CORD Index* (monthly), *Journal of Rural Development* (quarterly), *Newsletter*, *CORD Abstracts* (every 2 months), *CORD Alerts* (every 2 weeks), *Research Highlights* (annually), *Handbook of Rural Development Statistics* (annually), *Annual Report*, *Recommendations of Seminars and Workshops* (annually).

Rural Development Organization: Lamsang Bazar, PO Lamsang, Manipur; tel. (85) 310961; f. 1975; research, socio-economic development programme for the rural poor, skill training programme; Library and Documentation Centre, AIDS Prevention and Control Programme, Community Health Centre, Micro-credit scheme, rural bank, all set up with govt aid; library of 10,000 vols; Gen. Sec. W. BRAJABIDHU SINGH; publ. *Loyalam* (monthly).

Sinha, A. N., Institute of Social Studies: Patna 800001, Bihar; tel. (612) 2221395; fax (612) 2226226; e-mail ansiss@sancharnet.in; internet www.ansiss.bihar4all.com; f. 1958 to undertake teaching and research in the social sciences, especially economics, sociology, social psychology and political science; library of 58,206 vols; Dir NAVIN VERMA; Sec. JITENDRA PANDEY; publ. *Journal of Social and Economic Studies* (4 a year).

Sri Aurobindo Centre: Adhchini, Junction of Sri Aurobindo Marg and Qutab Hotel Rd, New Delhi 110017; multi-disciplinary research and training in the integral study of Man; research in comparative religions, Indian cultural values; lectures, seminars, study groups, summer programmes; homeopathic dispensary; research facilities; library; Chair. DHARMA VIRA; Hon. Sec. K. M. AGARWALA.

TECHNOLOGY

Ahmedabad Textile Industry's Research Association: PO Ambavadi Vistar, Ahmedabad 380015; tel. (79) 26307921; fax (79) 26302874; e-mail atiraad1@sancharnet.in; internet www.atira-tex-rnd.org; f. 1949; textile consultation, training and research, information and testing services; library of 41,000 vols; Dir Dr M. M. GHARIA; publs *ACT (ATIRA Communications on Textiles)* (4 a year), *UPDATIRA-ATIRA Newsletter* (6 a year), *TEXINCON* (4 a year).

Automotive Research Association of India: POB 832, Vetal Hill, Pune 411004; tel. (20) 25437180; fax (20) 25434190; e-mail arai@vsnl.com; internet www.araiindia.com; f. 1966; research institution of the Automotive Industry with the Ministry of Industry; provides facilities for research and development; product design; evaluation of equipment and standardization; certification for the Indian automotive and component industry; compilation and dissemination of technical information to the automotive and engineering industry; testing laboratories; library of 10,000 vols, 60 periodicals; Dir B. BHANOT; publs *Automotive Abstracts* (monthly), *ARAI Newsletter* (quarterly), *Automotive Abstracts*.

Bengal Ceramic Institute: Kolkata 10; f. 1941.

Bengal Textile Institute: Serampore; f. 1904.

Berhampore Textile Institute: Berhampore; f. 1925.

Birla Research Institute for Applied Sciences: Birlagram 456331, Nagda, Madhya Pradesh; f. 1965; registered society to help national industrial growth; research in pulp, paper, cellulose fibre and pollution abatement; Pres. D. P. Mandelia; Dir-Gen. S. K. Roy Moulik; publs *Annual Report*, *Bulletin* (quarterly).

Bombay Textile Research Association: Lal Bahadur Shastri Marg, Ghatkopar (West), Mumbai 400 086; tel. (22) 25003651; fax (22) 25000459; e-mail btra@vsnl.com; internet www.btraindia.com; f. 1954; research on process and product devts with emphasis on cleaner processing technologies; textile testing services; technical consultancy services in textile manufacturing; certification and training services; recognized for postgraduate studies by Univ. of Mumbai; 100 institutional mems; library of 20,200 vols; Dir Dr Ashok N. Desai; publs *BTRA Scan* (quarterly), *BTRA Bulletin* (monthly).

Bureau of Indian Standards (BIS): 9 Bahadur Shah Zafar Marg, New Delhi 110002; tel. (11) 23230131; fax (11) 23234062; e-mail bis@vsnl.com; internet www.del.vsnl.net.in/bis.org; f. 1947; library of 740,000 standards and technical publications and 416 periodicals; Dir-Gen. Sh. K. M. Sahni; Dir (Library Services) A. Sinha; publs *Current Published Information on Standardization*, *Standards Worldover – Monthly Additions to Library*, *Standards India*.

Central Institute for Research on Cotton Technology: Adenwala Rd, Matunga, Mumbai 400019; tel. (22) 24127273; f. 1924; part of Indian Council of Agricultural Research; library of 11,800 vols; Dir Dr K. R. Krishna Iyer.

Central Water and Power Research Station: PO Khadakwasla Research Station, Pune 411024; tel. (20) 24380511; fax (20) 24381004; e-mail wapis@mah.nic.in; internet www.cwprs.gov.in; f. 1916; basic and applied research in hydraulic engineering and allied subjects; activities in fields of hydrology and water resources analysis, river engineering, reservoir and appurtenant structures, coastal and offshore engineering, ship hydrodynamics, hydraulic machinery, foundations and structures, mathematical modelling, instrumentation and control, applied earth sciences; library of 70,000 vols, 200 periodicals; Dir V. M. Bendre; publs *Annual Report*, *Jalashakti* (Newsletter, 4 a year).

Indian Lac Research Institute: Namkum, Ranchi 834010; tel. (651) 2260117; fax (651) 2260202; e-mail lac@ilri.bih.nic.in; f. 1924; library of 40,128 vols; Dir Dr K. K. Kumar; publs *Annual Report*, *Newsletter* (4 a year).

Indian Rubber Manufacturers Research Association: Plot No. B–88, Rd U–2, Wagle Industrial Estate, Thane 400604, Maharashtra; f. 1959; research and development relating to rubber and allied industries; 45 staff; Dir Dr W. Millns.

Institute of Hydraulics and Hydrology: Poondi 602023, (Via) Trivellore, Chingleput District, Tamil Nadu; f. 1945; library of 8,000 vols and 5,870 journals; Dir K. Subramaniam; publ. *Annual Report*.

Irrigation and Power Research Station: Amritsar; conducts research in fields of irrigation and hydraulic engineering; Dir J. Nath.

National Council for Cement and Building Materials: 34 Km-Stone, Delhi-Mathura Rd, Ballabgarh 121004, Haryana; tel. (129) 2242051; fax (129) 2242100; e-mail nccbm@giasdl01.vsnl.net.in; internet www.ncbindia.com; f. 1966; provides intensive and planned research and development support to the cement, concrete and allied industries in the fields of new materials, technology development and transfer, continuing education and industrial services; library of 44,700 vols, 151 periodicals; Dir-Gen. S. Raina; publs *NCB Current Contents* (documentation list, every 2 months), *Research Reports*, *Annual Report*, *Cement Standards of the World*, *Newsletter* (4 a year).

National Institute of Hydrology: Jalvigyan Bhawan, Roorkee, Uttar Pradesh 247667; tel. (1332) 272106; fax (1332) 272123; e-mail sharmakd@nih.ernet.in; f. 1978; under Min. of Water Resources; research in all aspects of water resources; library of 7,000 vols, 3,000 technical reports, 87 periodicals, etc.; Dir Dr K. D. Sharma; publs *Jal Vigyan Sameeksha*, *Research Reports*.

Pulp and Paper Research Institute: Jaykaypur 765017, Orissa; tel. (6856) 222050; fax (6856) 222238; e-mail jkpaper@jkpm.jkmail.com; f. 1974; research in pulp and paper technology, forestry, environment and pigment; library of 6,188 vols, periodicals, etc.; Deputy Dir A. K. Biswal; publs *Abstract Index of Periodicals* (6 a year), *PAPRI Information Bulletin* (6 a year).

Research Designs and Standards Organization: Ministry of Railways, Government of India, Manak Nagar, Lucknow 226011; tel. (522) 2451200; fax (522) 2458500; f. 1957; conducts studies on the design and standardization of all railway infrastructure and equipment and tests and trials of new railway stock and other assets, and research into the economic and effective maintenance of operating practices; library of 154,000 vols, 130 periodicals; Dir-Gen. Hari Mohan; publs *Annual Report*, *RDSO Highlights*, *Indian Railway Technical Bulletin* (4 a year), Research Reports, Technical Papers, etc.

Synthetic and Art Silk Mills' Research Association: Sasmira, Sasmira Marg, Worli, Mumbai 400030; tel. (22) 24935351; fax (22) 24930225; f. 1950; research and devt in man-made textiles; technical education (postgraduate and diploma courses) in the field of man-made fibres, textile technology, textile chemistry, knitting technology and marketing and management of man-made textiles; library of 26,000 vols; Dir M. K. Bardhan; publ. *Man Made Textiles in India*.

Libraries and Archives

Ahmedabad

British Council Library: Bhakaka Bhavan, Law Garden Rd, Ellisbridge, Ahmedabad 380006; tel. (79) 26464693; fax (79) 26469493; e-mail bl.ahmedabad@in.britishcouncil.org; f. 1979; 24,000 vols; English Language Devt Colln; Head Librarian Satish Deshpande.

Gujarat Vidyapith Granthalaya: Ahmedabad 380014; tel. (79) 27541148; fax (79) 27542547; e-mail gvpahd@ad1.vsnl.net.in; f. 1920; University, State Central and Public Library combined; 474,000 vols; depository collection; Librarian Navalsinh Vaghela.

Sheth Maheklal Jethabhai Pustakalaya (Free Public Library): Ellis Bridge, Ahmedabad, Gujarat State; f. 1933; 25,012 mems; 178,317 vols; UNESCO programmes for children's libraries; Librarian M. M. Patel.

Allahabad

Allahabad Public Library: Rajkeeya Public Library, Alfred Park, Allahabad 211002; f. 1864; 72,601 vols; Librarian Dr K. K. Saxena.

Bangalore

Bangalore State Central Library: Cubbon Park, Bangalore 1, Karnataka; f. 1914; 140,000 vols; State Librarian and Head of Public Libraries N. D. Bageri.

British Council Library: Prestige Takt, 23 Kasturba Rd Cross, Bangalore 560001; tel. (80) 22213485; fax (80) 22240767; e-mail bl.bangalore@in.britishcouncil.org; 28,000 vols; Man. I. H. Jahagirdhar.

Karnataka Government Secretariat Library: Room No. 28, Ground Floor, Vidhana Soudha, Bangalore 560001; tel. (80) 22257686; fax (80) 22200620; e-mail bngvslib@kar.nic.in; internet vslib.kar.nic.in; f. *c*.1919; 117,846 vols, 15 newspapers, 90 periodicals; Chief Librarian Daniel Baretto.

Baroda

Central Library: Baroda 390006, Gujarat; f. 1910; 280,000 vols; State Librarian Bakulesh Bhuta; publ. *Granth Deep* (quarterly).

Bhopal

British Council Library: Guru Teg Bahadur Complex, Roshanpura Naka, Bhopal 462003; tel. (755) 2553767; fax (755) 2765211; e-mail bl.bhopal@in.britishcouncil.org; 15,000 vols; Librarian Bipin Kumar.

Chandigarh

British Library: SCO 36-38, Sector 8C, Madhya Marg, Chandigarh 160008; tel. (172) 2546540; fax (172) 2547540; e-mail bl.chandigarh@in.britishcouncil.org; 8,000 vols; Man. Sushant Banerjee.

Chennai

Adyar Library and Research Centre: Adyar, Chennai 600020; tel. (44) 24913528; e-mail adyarlibrary@vsnl.net; f. 1886; research in Indology; 200,000 vols, 18,000 MSS; specializes in religion, philosophy, civilization; Dir Dr S. Sankaranarayanan; Librarian Prof. C. A. Shinde (acting); publ. *Brahmavidya* (annual).

Connemara (State Central) Public Library: Pantheon Rd, Egmore, Chennai 600008; tel. (44) 28193751; f. 1896; deposit library from 1954 for all Indian publications; information centre for UN and allied agencies and for Asian Development Bank; 556,003 vols; Librarian N. Avudaiappan; publ. *Tamil Nadu State Bibliography* (in Tamil, monthly and cumulated annually).

Indian Institute of Technology Central Library: Chennai 600036; tel. (44) 22571365; fax (44) 22350509; e-mail lib@iitm.ernet.in; internet www.iitm.ac.in; f. 1959; includes collection of technical and scientific books (German and English); partial archive of scientific films; 264,097 vols, 700 current periodicals, 400 films, 1,600 microfilms and microfiches; user education programmes; Chief Librarian Dr Harish Chandra; publ. *New Additions to the Library*.

Madras Literary Society Library: Chennai 600006; f. 1812; 105,000 vols; Man. P. N. Balasundaram; Hon. Sec. S. V. B. Row.

Tamil Nadu Government Oriental Manuscripts Library: University Bldg, Chepauk, Chennai 600005; tel. (44) 25365130; f. 1869; acquisition, preservation and publication of rare and important collection of MSS in Sanskrit, Islamic and South Indian languages; 25,373 vols, 72,314 MSS; Curator Dr S. Soundarapandian; publ. *Bulletin*.

Delhi

Central Archaeological Library: Annexe bldg of National Archives of India, Janpath, New Delhi 110001; tel. (11) 23387475; fax (11) 23385883; e-mail asi@dell3.vsnl.net.in; f.

1902; attached to Archaeological Survey of India; 102,180 vols, 5,776 maps, 85 current periodicals; Dir-Gen. C. BABU RAJEEV.

Central Secretariat Library: Department of Culture, Govt of India, G Wing, Shastri Bhavan, New Delhi 110001; tel. (11) 23389684; fax (11) 23384846; e-mail csl@delnet.ren.nic.in; f. 1890; lending, reference, reprographic divisions, background material on selected topics and biographies; 810,000 vols, 730 periodicals; special collections: area study, Indian official documents, foreign official documents, Hindi and Indian regional languages publs; Dir KALPANA DASGUPTA.

Delhi Public Library: H-Block, nr Main Market, Sarojini Nagar, Delhi 110023; tel. (11) 24101261; fax (11) 24673220; e-mail dpl1@vsnl.net; f. 1951 in association with UNESCO; established as a model for public library development in south-east Asia; central library, 3 br. libraries, braille section, 4 mobile libraries and 59 sub-br. and community libraries; 1,557,000 vols in English, Hindi, Urdu, Punjabi, Bengali, Sindhi and other Indian languages and in Braille; Dir Dr BANWARI LAL.

Indian Council of World Affairs Library: Sapru House, Barakhamba Rd, New Delhi 110001; tel. (11) 23317246; fax (11) 23310638; f. 1950; 128,000 vols, 376 periodicals, 2,458,000 press clippings; research collections on social sciences with special reference to international relations, international law and international economics; Press library; maps, microfilms and microfiches; United Nations and EU documents; Librarian MAN SINGH DEORA (acting).

Indira Gandhi National Centre for the Arts: Central Vista Mess, Janpath, New Delhi 110001; tel. (11) 23384901; fax (11) 23381139; e-mail ignca@de12.vsnl.in; internet www.nic.in/ignca; f. 1987; resource centre with reference material relating to Indian arts and culture; Academic Dir Dr KAPILA VATSYAYAN.

National Archives of India: Janpath, New Delhi 110001; tel. (11) 23383436; fax (11) 23384127; f. 1891; valuable collections of public records, maps, private papers and microfilm covering 35km of shelf space; 200,000 vols; Dir-Gen. S. SARKAR; publs *Indian Archives* (2 a year), *Annual Report*, *Bulletin of Research Theses and Dissertations* (every 2 years).

National Institute of Science Communication and Information Resources: Dr K. S. Krishnan Marg, New Delhi 110012; tel. (11) 25746024; fax (11) 25787062; e-mail vkg@niscair.res.in; internet www.niscair.res.in; f. 2002; attached to Council of Scientific and Industrial Research; national science library; disseminates scientific and technological information to the scientific community and the general public; provides networking services and network-based online services; bibliographical information retrieval from national and international online and CD-ROM databases; 178,000 vols; Dir V. K. GUPTA; publs *Journal of Scientific and Industrial Research* (monthly), *Indian Journal of Experimental Biology* (monthly), *Indian Journal of Biochemistry and Biophysics* (6 a year), *Indian Journal of Biotechnology* (4 a year), *Indian Journal of Marine Sciences* (4 a year), *Indian Journal of Traditional Knowledge* (4 a year), *Journal of Intellectual Property Rights* (6 a year), *Natural Product Radiance* (6 a year), *Bharatiya Vaigyanic evam Audyogic Anusandhan Patrika* (2 a year), *Indian Journal of Chemistry, Sec A* (monthly), *Indian Journal of Chemistry, Sec B* (monthly), *Indian Journal of Chemical Technology* (6 a year), *Indian Journal of Engineering and Materials Sciences* (6 a year), *Indian Journal of Pure and Applied Physics* (monthly), *Indian Journal of Radio and Space Physics* (6 a year), *Indian Journal of Fibre and Textile Research* (4 a year), *Annals of Library and Information Studies* (4 a year), *Medicinal and Aromatic Plants Abstracts* (6 a year), *Indian Science Abstracts* (every 2 weeks).

National Social Science Documentation Centre: 35 Ferozshah Rd, New Delhi 110001; tel. (11) 23074393; fax (11) 23383091; internet www.icssr.org; f. 1970; division of Indian Council of Social Science Research (ICSSR); provides information and documentation service for social scientists, policymakers and others working in the academic and govt sectors, business and industry; provides library and reference services, document delivery and reprographic services, consultancy service, select bibliography service, training courses; library of 850 current periodicals, 150,000 serial vols, 28,000 monographs including Ph.D. theses, research project reports and reference books, conference papers, working papers; Dir Dr P. R. GOSWAMI; publs *Annotated Index of Indian Social Science Journals* (2 a year), *Bibliographic Reprints* (irregular), *Conference Alert* (quarterly).

Nehru Memorial Museum and Library: Teen Murti House, New Delhi 110011; tel. (11) 23015333; fax (11) 23793296; e-mail nmml@vsnl.net; internet www.nehrumemorial.org; f. 1964; archival collections on modern Indian history with emphasis on Indian nationalism; research centre for interdisciplinary studies in modern Indian history and society; large collection of newspapers, microfilms, private papers, institutional records, photographs and oral history recordings; 226,603 vols; Dir K. JAYAKUMAR.

Dharamsala

Library of Tibetan Works and Archives: Gangchen Kyishong, Dharamsala 176215; tel. (1892) 222467; fax (1892) 223723; e-mail ltwa@ndf.vsnl.net.in; f. 1971; 80,000 vols; 10,000 photographs, 25,000 hours of audio/video tape, 1,200 icons and artefacts; Dir Ven. ACHOK RINPOCHE; publ. *The Tibet Journal* (4 a year).

Hyderabad

British Council Library: 5-9-22 Sarovar Centre, Secretariat Rd, Hyderabad 500063; tel. (40) 23483333; fax (40) 23483100; e-mail bl.hyderabad@in.britishcouncil.org; internet www.britishcouncilonline.org; 25,000 vols, 1,000 DVDs; information on higher education in the UnitedKingdom; Librarian SUDHAKAR GOUD.

State Central Library: Afzalgunj, Hyderabad 500012, Andhra Pradesh; tel. (40) 24615621; fax (40) 24600107; f. 1891; 347,000 vols; Librarian T. V. VEDAMRUTHAM.

Kolkata

Centre for Asian Documentation: K-15, CIT Bldgs, Christopher Rd, POB 11215, Kolkata 700014; provides reference services; Dir S. CHAUDHURI; publs *Index Indo-Asiasticus* (quarterly), *Index Internationalis Indicus* (every 3 years), *Index Asia Series in Humanities* (irregular), *Indian Science index* (every 2 years), *Indian Biography* (annually).

National Library: Belvedere, Kolkata 700027; tel. (33) 24791381; fax (33) 24791462; f. 1903 by the amalgamation of the Calcutta Public Library and the Imperial Library; depository and research library; 2,186,500 vols, 84,952 maps, 3,127 MSS; 4,145 microfilms, 94,500 microfiches, 17,650 periodicals; ind. Central Reference Library, at the same address, compiles *Indian National Bibliography*, but does not hold a book colln; Dir HARJIT SINGH; publs *India's National Library—Systematization and Modernization*, *The National Library and Public Libraries in India*, *Conservation of Library Materials*, *Rabindra Grantha Suchi* (vol 1 part 1), *Bibliographical Control in India*, *Indological Studies and South Asia Bibliography*, *General Collection Author and Subject Catalogues*, *Bibliographies*, *Reports*, *Newsletter* (quarterly), etc.

Lucknow

Acharya Narendra Dev Pustakalaya: 10 Ashoka Marg, Lucknow; f. 1959; public library, with special emphasis on social sciences; 79,636 vols; 150 periodicals; Librarian T. N. MISRA.

Ludhiana

Panjab University Extension Library: Civil Lines, Ludhiana, Punjab; tel. (161) 2449558; f. 1960; serves educational institutions within a radius of 60 km; 138,000 vols; Librarian Dr K. C. AHUJA (acting).

Mumbai

Petit, J. N., Institute Library: 312 Dr Dadabhoy Naoroji Rd, Fort, Mumbai 400001; tel. (22) 22048463; f. 1856 as 'Fort Improvement Library'; 160,000 vols; Admin. J. R. MODY.

Patna

Bihar Secretariat Library: Patna 800015; f. 1885; 106,300 vols; Chief Librarian P. N. SINHA DOSHI.

Khuda Bakhsh Oriental Public Library: Ashok Rajpath, Patna 800004, Bihar; tel. (612) 2300209; e-mail pat_khopl@dataone.in; internet www.kblibrary.nic.in; f. 1891; autonomous instn under Min. of Culture and declared as an instn of nat. importance; awards fellowships for Ph.D. and D.Litt. students; designated as a Manuscript Resource Centre (MRC) and Manuscript Conservation Centre (MCC) by the Nat. Mission for Manuscripts, Govt of India; Dir Dr AHMAD IMTIAZ; contains more than 21,000 MSS in Arabic, Persian, Urdu, Pushto, Pali, Turkish, Hindi and Sanskrit, 247,032 vols, 39,419 bound periodicals, 2,222 audio and video cassettes, Mughal, Iranian, Central Asian and Rajput paintings; publ. *Journal* (quarterly).

Shrimati Radhika Sinha Institute and Sachchidananda Sinha Library (State Central Library, Bihar): G.P.O., Patna 800001; tel. (612) 2221674; f. 1924; 157,089 vols, 523 periodicals; Librarian Dr R. S. P. SINGH.

Rajahmundry

Gowthami Regional Library: Rajahmundry 533104, Andhra Pradesh; tel. (883) 2476908; f. 1898; management transferred to Andhra Pradesh Government in 1979; research library of 58,643 vols, 428 palm leaf MSS; special collection of rare 19th-century periodicals in English and Telugu, rare collection of old Telugu books; Librarian VENNA POLI REDDY.

Thiruvananthapuram

British Library, Thiruvananthapuram: YMCA Bldg, Thiruvananthapuram 695001, Kerala; tel. (471) 2330716; fax (471) 2330717; e-mail bl.trivandrum@in.britishcouncil.org; internet www.britishcouncil.org.in; f. 1964; lending of books, journals, DVDs and CDs; online information service; reference service; information and counselling on education in the United Kingdom; travel information; administration of British examinations; children's library; 23,000 vols, 1,000 DVDs, 600 CDs; Librarian SUBRAMONI KRISHNASWAMI.

Trivandrum

Trivandrum Public Library (State Central Library): Trivandrum, Kerala State; tel. (471) 2322895; f. 1829; 263,056 vols; Librarian SARAMMA GEORGE.

Museums and Art Galleries

Ahmedabad

Calico Museum of Textiles: Sarabhai Foundation, Shahibag, Ahmedabad 380004; tel. (79) 22868172; fax (79) 22865759; e-mail sarafound@icenet.net; internet www.calicomuseum.com; f. 1948; colln of 17th- and 18th-century Indian textiles and costumes, and reconstructed carved wooden façades from the 17th–19th centuries; Sec. D. S. MEHTA.

Ajmer

Rajputana Museum: Ajmer 305001, Rajasthan; f. 1908; archaeology; rare sculptures, architectural carvings, old coins, epigraphs, Rajput paintings, arms and armour of Rajasthan; Curator R. D. SHARMA.

Banares

Bharat Kala Bhavan: Banaras Hindu University, Varanasi 221005; tel. (542) 2316337; f. 1920; attached to univ. 1950; art objects, miniature paintings, sculpture, textiles, archaeology, seals; library: *c.* 14,000 vols and periodicals, 26,511 MSS; Dir Prof. R. C. SHARMA; publs *Chhavi*, catalogues, etc.

Bangalore

Government Museum: Kasturba Rd, Bangalore 560001, Karnataka; f. 1866; art, archaeology, industrial art and natural history; library of 2,000 vols; Curator (vacant); publ. *Annual Report*.

Visvesvaraya Industrial and Technological Museum: Kasturba Rd, PMB 5216, Bangalore 560001, Karnataka; tel. (80) 22864563; fax (80) 22864114; e-mail vitm@vsnl.com; internet www.vismuseum.org; f. 1962; aims to encourage interest in science and technology, and to explain the application of technology in industry and human welfare; library of 10,230 vols, also audio-visual materials; Dir K. V. BHATTA.

Baroda

Baroda Museum and Picture Gallery: Baroda 390005, Gujarat; f. museum 1894 and picture gallery 1920; Indian archaeology; prehistoric and historic; Indian art: ancient, medieval and modern; numismatic collections; modern Indian paintings; industrial art; Asiatic and Egyptian collections; Greek, Roman, European civilizations and art; European paintings; ethnology, zoology, geology, economic botany; library of 19,000 vols; Dir S. K. BHOWMIK; Curators R. K. MAKWANA (Art and Archaeology), G. M. PATHAK (Natural History); publ. *Bulletin*.

Bhubaneswar

Orissa State Museum: Bhubaneswar 751006, Orissa; f. 1932; archaeology, epigraphy, numismatics, armoury, arts and crafts, anthropology, palmleaf MSS, natural history; library of 22,000 vols, 2,000 periodicals; Dir Dr H. C. DAS; publ. *Orissa Historical Research Journal*.

Bikaner

Government Museum: Bikaner 334001, Rajasthan; tel. (151) 2528894; f. 1937; collection of terracottas, sculptures, bronzes, coins, inscriptions, Rajasthani paintings, documents, arms and costumes, specimens of folk-culture; Superintendent P. C. BHARGAVA.

Bodh Gaya

Archaeological Museum: Bodh Gaya, Bihar State; stone and bronze sculpture, etc.; Curator S. SINGH.

Chennai

Fort Museum: Fort St George, Chennai 600009; tel. (44) 25361117; f. 1948; exhibits belong mainly to the days of the East India Co.; Dir Dr D. JITHENDRADAS.

Government Museum and National Art Gallery: Pantheon Rd, Egmore, Chennai 600008; tel. (44) 28193238; fax (44) 28193035; e-mail govtmuse@md4.vsnl.net.in; internet www.chennaimuseum.org; f. 1851; archaeology, ancient and modern Indian art, South Indian bronzes, Buddhist sculptures, numismatics, philately, anthropology, botany, zoology, geology, chemical conservation education, contemporary art, design and display; Dir THIRU M. A. SIDDIQUE; publs *Madras Museum Bulletins*, *Newsletter* (2 a year).

Delhi

Archaeological Museum Red Fort Delhi: Mumtaz Mahal, Red Fort; f. 1909; library of 420 vols; historical collections of the Mughal period; old arms, seals and signets, letters, MSS, coins, miniatures, Mughal dresses and relics of India's War of Independence; Curator S. K. SHARMA.

Crafts Museum: Pragati Maidan, Bhairon Rd, New Delhi 110001; tel. (11) 23371641; fax (11) 23371515; f. 1952; Indian traditional crafts and tribal arts; library of 11,000 vols; Dir Dr JYOTINDRA JAIN.

National Gallery of Modern Art: Jaipur House, India Gate, Sher Shah Rd, New Delhi 110003; tel. (11) 23382835; f. 1954; contemporary art (paintings, sculpture, drawings, graphics, architecture, industrial design, photography, prints and minor arts); Dir Dr ANIS FAROOQI.

National Gandhi Museum and Library: Rajghat, New Delhi 110002; tel. (11) 23310168; fax (11) 23311793; e-mail gandhimk@nda.vsnl.net.in; internet www.gandhimuseum.org; f. 1953 by the Gandhi Memorial Museum Society to collect and display Gandhi's records and mementos and to promote the study of his life and work; library of 45,000 vols, 50,000 documents, 91 periodicals; 130 films and recordings; 9,000 photographs; large picture gallery; Chair. B. R. NANDA; Dir Dr Y. P. ANAND.

National Museum of India: Janpath, New Delhi 110011; tel. (11) 23018159; fax (11) 23019821; f. 1949; Departments of Art, Archaeology, Anthropology, Modelling, Presentation, Preservation, Publication, Library and Photography; Indian prehistoric tools, protohistoric remains from Harappa, Mohenjodaro, etc., representative collections of sculptures, terracottas, stuccos and bronzes from 2nd century BC to 18th century AD; illustrated MSS and miniatures; Stein Collection of Central Asian murals and other antiquities; decorative arts; textiles, coins and illuminated epigraphical charts; armour; copper-plate etchings; woodwork; library of 43,400 vols; Dir-Gen. Dr R. C. SHARMA; publs *Bulletin* (annually), special publs on art and archaeology.

National Museum of Natural History: FICCI Museum Bldg, Barakhamba Rd, New Delhi 110001; tel. and fax (11) 23314932; e-mail sksaraswat@yahoo.co.uk; f. 1978; exhibits on natural history, ecology, environment, conservation; educational programmes for children and other groups, school loan service, mobile museum for rural extension service; controls regional museums of natural history in Mysore, Bhopal and Bhubneshwar; library of 25,000 vols; Dir S. K. SARASWAT.

National Rail Museum: Chanakyapuri, New Delhi 110021; tel. (11) 26881816; fax (11) 26880804; e-mail rajesh_agrawal@vsnl.com; internet www.railmuseum.org; f. 1977; library of 5,000 vols; Dir RAJESH AGRAWAL; publ. *Newsletter* (monthly).

Rabindra Bhavan Art Gallery: 35 Ferozeshah Rd, New Delhi; tel. (11) 23387241; fax (11) 23782485; e-mail lka@bol.net.in; f. 1955; permanent gallery of the Lalit Kala Akademi (National Academy of Art), and venue of the National Exhibition of Art and Triennale-India (international art); Chair. Dr SARAYU V. DOSHI; publs *Lalit Kala Ancient* (2 a year), *Lalit Kala Contemporary* (4 a year), *Samkaleen Kala* (in Hindi, 4 a year).

Shankar's International Dolls Museum: Nehru House, 4 Bahadur Shah Zafar Marg, New Delhi 110002; tel. (11) 23316970; fax (11) 23721090; e-mail cbtnd@vsnl.com; internet www.childrensbooktrust.com; f. 1965; 6,000 exhibits from all over the world; Curator SHANTA SRINIVASAN.

Gauhati

Assam State Museum: Gauhati 781001, Assam; f. 1940; indological and archaeological studies; library of 5,850 vols; Dir Dr R. D. CHOUDHURY; publ. *Bulletin* (annually).

Guntur

Archaeological Museum: Nagarjunakonda, Guntur, Andhra Pradesh; f. 1966; prehistoric and historical antiquities, mainly sculptures, Buddhist and Hindu; Curator K. VEERABHADRA RAO.

Hyderabad

Andhra Pradesh State Museum: Hyderabad 500034; f. 1930; sculpture, epigraphy, arms and weapons, Bidriware, bronze objects, miniatures and paintings, MSS, numismatics, European paintings (prints), decorative and modern arts, textiles; excavations at Yeleswaram Pochampal, Peddabankur; Dir Dr V. V. KRISHNA SASTRY; publ. various on numismatics.

Salarjung Museum: Hyderabad 500002, Andhra Pradesh; tel. (40) 24523211; fax (40) 24572558; e-mail salarjung@hotmail.com; internet www.salarjungmuseum.com; f. 1951; paintings, textiles, porcelain, jade, carpets, MSS, antiques, ivory, glass, silver- and bronze-ware; children's section; library of 60,000 vols incl. Persian, Arabic and Urdu MSS; Dir Dr A. K. V. S. REDDY; publs *Research Journal* (every 2 years), Guide Book and Manuscript Catalogue.

Imphal

Manipur State Museum: Polo-ground, Imphal, Manipur; general collection.

Jaipur

Maharaja Sawai Man Singh II Museum: City Palace, Jaipur 302002, Rajasthan; tel. (141) 2615681; fax (141) 2603880; e-mail citypalace@pinkline.net; internet www.royalfamilyjaipur.com; f. 1959; textiles and costumes, armoury, Mughal and Rajasthani miniature paintings, Persian and Mughal carpets, transport accessories, regalia, historical documents, maps and plans, manuscript library of 10,000 Sanskrit, Persian, Hindi and Rajasthani MSS; Dir B. M. S. PARMAR.

Kolkata

Asutosh Museum of Indian Art: Centenary Building, University of Calcutta, Kolkata

700073; f. 1937; library: over 2,000 vols and periodicals; Curator NIRANJAN GOSWAMI; publ. catalogues.

Birla Industrial and Technological Museum: 19A Gurusaday Rd, Kolkata 700019; tel. (33) 22477241; fax (33) 22476102; e-mail bitm@cal2.vsnl.net.in; internet www.bitmcal.org; f. 1959; administered by the National Council of Science Museums; portrays the history and development of science and technology; eight satellite centres and eight mobile science exhibition buses in rural areas; educational programmes for students and teachers and the general public; library of 14,000 vols incl. periodicals; film and CD library; archives; special collections on history and development of science and technology, arts, painting, museology etc.; Dir Dr JAYANTA STHANAPATI; publ. *Popscience* (2 a year).

Indian Museum: 27 Jawaharlal Nehru Rd, Kolkata 700016; tel. (33) 22861679; fax (33) 22861696; f. 1814; collections of archaeology, art, coins, anthropology, geology, botany, zoology; library; herbarium; library of 45,000 vols; Dir-in-Charge Prof. Dr CHITTARANJAN PANDA; Librarian Dr PATRA CHITTARANJAN; publs *Bulletin* (annually), monographs, etc.

Victoria Memorial Hall: 1 Queens Way, Kolkata 700071; tel. and fax (33) 22231889; fax (33) 22235142; e-mail victomen@cal2.vsnl.net.in; internet www.victoriamemorial-cal.org; f. 1906; museum of medieval Indian history and culture, and British Indian history of the late 18th and early 19th c.; wide collection of oil-paintings and water colours by European artists of 18th and 19th c.; sketches, miniatures, engravings, photographs, sculptures, maps, MSS, furniture, stamps, coins, medals, textiles, arms and armour; library: almost 13,030 vols; Sec. and Curator Prof. C. PANDA.

Lucknow

Uttar Pradesh State Museum: Banarasibagh, Lucknow, Uttar Pradesh; tel. and fax (522) 2273146; f. 1863; collections of sculptures, terracottas, copper plates, numismatics, paintings, manuscripts, textiles and natural history specimens; library of 15,000 vols; Dir S. D. TRIVEDI; publ. *Bulletin* (2 a year).

Mathura

Government Museum: Dampier Nagar, Mathura 281001, Uttar Pradesh; f. 1874; 40,000 items, dominated by sculptures, terracottas of Mathura School to Kushana and Gupta period; coins, paintings, etc.; library: reference library of 20,000 vols.

Mumbai

Chhatrapati Shivaji Maharaj Vastu Sangrahalay: 159–161 Mahatma Gandhi Rd, Fort, Mumbai 400023; tel. (22) 22844484; fax (22) 22045430; e-mail powm@vsal.com; f. 1905; fmrly Prince of Wales Museum of Western India; sections: Art, Painting, Archaeology, Natural History; library of 25,000 vols; Dir Dr K. DESAI; publs *Bulletin*, catalogues.

Dr Bhau Daji Lad Museum: 91A Dr B. Ambedkar Rd, Byculla, Mumbai 400027; tel. (22) 23757943; f. 1855; reference library on Indian and foreign art, archaeology, ethnology, geology, history, numismatics and museology; exhibits of agriculture and village life, armoury, cottage industries, ethnology, fine arts, crafts, fossils, Indian coins, minerals, miscellaneous collection, Old Mumbai, collection; Curator M. GANDHI; publs catalogues, etc.

Nagpur

Central Museum: Civil Lines, Nagpur 440001, Maharashtra; tel. (712) 2546314; e-mail curator@centralmuseumnagpur.com; internet www.centralmuseumnagpur.com; f. 1863; objects relating to archaeology, art, tribal art and culture, natural history, sculpture, weapons and metal objects; Curator Y. KATHANE.

Nalanda

Archaeological Museum: Nalanda, Bihar State; f. 1958; collections of antiquities, specializing in Buddhist sculptures; Curator S. K. SHARMA.

Patna

Patna Museum: Patna-Gaya Rd, Buddha Marg, Patna 800001, Bihar; tel. (612) 2235731; f. 1917; archaeology, bronzes, ethnology, geology, arms and armour, natural history, art, coins, plaster casts, Tibetan paintings; Dr Rajendra Prasad's colln (first Pres. of India); Buddha Relic casket; publishes research on art, archaeology and ethnology; seminars and lectures; Dir J. P. AGRARWAL; Curator K. K. SHARMA.

Rajahmundry

Sri Rallabandi Subbarao Government Museum (formerly the Andhra Historical Research Society): Godavari Bund Rd, Rajahmundry, East Godavari District, Andhra Pradesh 533101; f. 1967; art, archaeology, epigraphy, history and numismatics; collection of coins, sculpture, pottery, terra cotta, palm-leaf MSS, inscriptions, etc.; Dir Dr V. V. KRISHNA SASTRY; publ. *Journal of the AHRS*.

Santiniketan

Rabindra-Bhavana (Tagore Museum and Archives): Visva-Bharati, PO Santiniketan 731235; tel. (3463) 252773; fax (3463) 252672; f. 1942; collection of MSS, letters, books, newspaper clippings, gramophone records, photographs, cine-film, paintings by Tagore and tape recordings of his voice; library of 41,000 vols; inside the Uttarayana Campus where the poet spent the last days of his life; publ. *Rabindra-Viksa* (2 a year).

Sarnath

Sarnath Museum: District Varanasi Pin 221007, Uttar Pradesh; archaeological site museum; f. 1904; Buddhist and Hindu collection from 3rd century BC to 12th century AD; Superintending Archaeologist Dr B. BANDYOPADHYAY.

Srinagar

Sri Pratap Singh Museum: Lalmandi, Srinagar 190008-72078, Jammu and Kashmir; tel. (8649) 232374; f. 1898; general collection of Jammu and Kashmir; library of 1,300 vols about cultural subjects; Curator M. S. ZAHID.

Trichur

Kerala State Museums, Zoos, Art Galleries and Government Gardens: include: (1) State Museum and Zoo, Trichur, f. 1885; (2) Govt Museums and Zoological and Botanical Gardens, Trivandrum, f. 1857; natural history collections, Indian arts and crafts; (3) Art Gallery and Krishna-Menon Museum, Calicut; f. 1976; (4) Govt Botanical Garden, Olavanna; f. 1991.

Trivandrum

Sri Chitra Art Gallery, Gallery of Asian Paintings: Trivandrum 695001, Kerala; f. 1935; sections: Pure Indian Art, Rajput, Mughal and Persian, Tanjore, Tibetan, Chinese, Japanese, Balinese, Indo-European (water and oil), etchings and woodcuts; Modern Indian Contemporary Art and Murals; library of 736 vols; Dir K. RAJENDRA BABU; publ. *Administration Report*.

Universities

There are three types of university in India: Affiliating and Teaching (most teaching done in colleges affiliated to the university, but some teaching, mostly postgraduate, undertaken by the university); Unitary (all teaching done on one campus); Central (universities established by Acts of Parliament). It is not possible, for reasons of space, to give details of affiliated colleges.

ACHARYA N. G. RANGA AGRICULTURAL UNIVERSITY

Hyderabad 500030, Andhra Pradesh

Telephone: (40) 24015011

Fax: (40) 24015031

E-mail: root@apau.ren.nic.in

Internet: www.angrau.net

Founded 1964

Languages of instruction: English, Telugu

Academic year: July to June

Chancellor: HE THE GOVERNOR OF ANDHRA PRADESH

Vice-Chancellor: S. P. SINGH

Registrar: Dr S. RAGHU VARDHAN REDDY

Librarian: Dr G. SAIPRASAD

Library of 200,000 vols

Number of teachers: 1,786

Number of students: 3,853

Publication: *ANGRAU Journal of Research* (4 a year)

DEANS

Faculty of Agriculture and Forestry: Dr S. RAGHUVARDHAN REDDY (acting)

Faculty of Home Science: Dr VIJAYA KHADER

Faculty of Veterinary and Animal Science: Dr M. V. SUBBA RAO

Faculty of Postgraduate Studies: Dr M. V. SUBBA RAO (acting)

CONSTITUENT COLLEGES

Agricultural College: Aswaraopet; Principal Dr B. GOPAL SINGH.

Agricultural College: Bapatla; Principal Dr G. LAKSHMI KANTHA REDDY.

Agricultural College: Naira; Principal Dr M. R. NAIDU.

Agricultural College: Rajendranagar; Principal Dr G. BHEEMAIAH.

Agricultural College: Mahanandi; Principal Dr K. SRINIVASA REDDY (acting).

Agricultural Polytechnic: Anakapalle; Principal Dr K. SUBRAMANYAM.

Agricultural Polytechnic: Jagtial; Principal Dr B. BHASKAR REDDY (acting).

Agricultural Polytechnic: Maruteru; Principal Dr P. RAGHAVA REDDY.

Agricultural Polytechnic: Palem; Principal Dr N. VENKAT REDDY.

Animal Husbandry Polytechnic: Palamaner; Principal Dr S. T. VEEROJI RAO.

College of Agricultural Engineering: Bapatla; Principal Dr C. R. SUKUMARAN (acting).

College of Fishery Science: Muthukur; Principal Dr K. GOPALA RAO.

College of Home Science: Bapatla; Principal Dr PREMA RAMACHANDRAN.

College of Home Science: Hyderabad; Principal Dr V. VIMALA.

College of Veterinary Science: Gannavaram; Principal Dr K. KRISHNA REDDY.

College of Veterinary Science: Rajendranagar; Principal Dr G. NARASIMHA RAO.

College of Veterinary Science: Tirupathi; Principal Dr A. SESHAGIRI RAO.

S. V. Agricultural College: Tirupati; Principal Dr K. CHANDRASEKHARA RAO.

UNIVERSITY OF AGRICULTURAL SCIENCES

G. K. V. K., Bangalore 560065, Karnataka
Telephone: (80) 23330153
Fax: (80) 23330277
Internet: uasbng.kar.nic.in
Founded 1964
Residential
Languages of instruction: English, Kannada
State control
Academic year: September to August (two terms)
Chancellor: HE THE GOVERNOR OF KARNATAKA
Pro-Chancellor: THE MINISTER OF AGRICULTURE, KARNATAKA
Vice-Chancellor: Dr S. BISLAIAH
Dean: Dr M. C. DEVAIAH
Registrar: Dr. K. M. JAYARAMAIAH
Administrative Officer: B. GANGADHAR
Librarian: K. T. SOMASHEKHAR
Library: Libraries of 168,000 vols
Number of teachers: 1,082
Number of students: 2,214
Publications: *Annual Report*, *Calendar*, *Current Research* (monthly), *Dairy* (monthly), *Extension Series*, *Krishi Vijana* (4 a year, in Kannada), *Miscellaneous Series* (irregular), *Mysore Journal of Agricultural Sciences* (4 a year), *Research Series*, *Technical Series*

PROFESSORS

ABDUL RAHMAN, S., Parasitology
ANANTHANARAYANA, R., Chemistry and Soils
ANILKUMAR, T. B., Plant Pathology
ASHOK, T. H., Horticulture
AVADHANI, K. K., Genetics and Plant Breeding
BHAT, G. S., Dairy Chemistry
CHALLAIAH, Agricultural Extension
CHANDRAKANTH, M. G., Agricultural Economics
CHANDRAMOULI, K. N., Anatomy
CHANDRAPPA, H. M., Plant Breeding
CHANDRASHEKAR GUPTA, T. R., Fishery Oceanography
CHANNAPPA, T. C., Agricultural Engineering
CHENGAPPA, P. G., Agricultural Marketing
CHIKKADEVAIAH, Seed Processing Engineering
CHOWDEGOWDA, M., Agricultural Engineering
DAS, T. K., Animal Nutrition
DEVEGOWDA, G., Poultry
ESHWARAPPA, G., Agricultural Extension
FAROOQ MOHAMMED, Veterinary Physiology
FAROOQI, A. A., Medicinal and Aromatic Plants
GANGADHAR, K. S., Gynaecology and Obstetrics
GEETHA RAMACHANDRA, Biochemistry
GIRIJA, P. R., Psychology
GOPALA GOWDA, H. S., Agricultural Microbiology
GOPALAKRISHNA HEBBAR, Agricultural Economics
GOPALAKRISHNA RAO, Agricultural Extension
GOVINDAIAH, M. G., Animal Genetics and Breeding
GOVINDAN, R., Entomology
GOWDA, H., Pharmacology
GUNDURAO, D. S., Mathematics
GURUMURTHY, Statistics
GURURAJ HUNSIGI, Agronomy
HEGDE, S. V., Microbiology
HONNEGOWDA, Pharmacology
HUDDAR, A. G., Horticulture
JAGADISH, A., Entomology
JAGADISH KUMAR, Pharmacology
JAGANNATH, M. S., Parasitology
JANARDHANA, K. V., Crop Physiology
JAVAREGOWDA, S., Agricultural Engineering
JAYADEVAPPA, S. M., Surgery
JAYARAMAIAH, M., Sericulture
JOSEPH BHAGYARAJ, D., Agricultural Microbiology
JOSHI SHAMASUNDAR, Botany
KAILAS, M. M., Dairy Production
KARUNASAGAR, I., Fishery Microbiology
KATTEPPA, Y., Agricultural Extension
KESHAVAMURTHY, K. V., Plant Pathology
KESHAVANATH, P., Aquaculture
KHAN, M. M., Horticulture
KRISHNA, K. S., Agricultural Extension
KRISHNAPPA, A. M., Soil Science
KRISHNAPRASAD, Agricultural Entomology
KRISHNAPRASAD, P. R., Pathology
KRISHNEGOWDA, K. T., Agronomy
KULAKARNI, R. S., Agricultural Botany
KUMARASWAMY, A. S., Water Management and Plant Breeding
LAKKUNDI, N. H., Agricultural Entomology
LOKANATH, G. R., Poultry for Meat
MALLIK, B., Acarology
MALLIKARJUNAIAH, R. R., Microbiology
MANJUNATH, A., Plant Breeding
MELANTA, R., Horticulture
MOHAN JOSEPH, Fishery Biology
MUNI LAL DUBEY, B., Gynaecology and Obstetrics
MUNIYAPPA, V., Plant Pathology
MUNIYAPPA, T. V., Agricultural Extension
MUSHTARI BEGUM, J., Home Science
NAGARAJA SETTY, M. V., Plant Breeding
NAGARAJU, Animal Sciences
NANJEGOWDA, D., Nematology
NARASIMHAMURTHY, S., Mathematics
NARAYANA, K., Pharmacology
NARAYANA GOWDA, K., Agricultural Extension
NARAYANAGOWDA, J. V., Horticulture
NARENDRANATH, R., Physiology
PANCHAKSHARAIAH, S., Agronomy
PARAMASHIVAIAH, B. M., Animal Science
PARAMESWAR, N. S., Plant Breeding
PARASHIVAMURTHY, A. S., Soil Science
PARVATHAMMA, S., Mathematics
PARVATHAPPA, H. C., Soil Science and Agricultural Chemistry
PRABHAKAR HEGDE, B., Dairy Production
PRABHAKAR SETTY, T. K., Agronomy
PRABHUSWAMY, H. P., Agricultural Entomology
PRASAD, T. G., Crop Physiology
PRATAP KUMAR, K. S., Poultry Science
PUTTASWAMY, Entomology
RAGHAVAN, R., Veterinary Microbiology
RAJ, J., Microbiology
RAJAGOPAL, D., Apiculture
RAMACHANDRAPRASAD, T. V., Agronomy
RAMANJANEYULU, G., Dairy Technology
RAMAPRASANNA, K. P., Seed Technology
RANGANATHAIAH, K. G., Plant Pathology
RAVI, P. C., Agricultural Marketing
SAMIULLA, R., Horticulture
SATHYAN, B. A., Plant Breeding
SATHYANARAYANA RAO, G. P., Agricultural Extension
SESHADRI, V. S., Agricultural Extension
SHAKUNTALA SRIDHARA, Zoology
SHANBHOGUE, S. L., Fishery Biology
SHANKAR, P. A., Dairy Microbiology
SHANKAREGOWDA, B. T., Plant Sciences
SHANTHA JOSEPH, Fishery Economics
SHANTHA R. HIREMATH, Plant Breeding
SHANTHAMALLAIAH, N. R., Crop Production
SHARIEF, R. A., Plant Science
SHESHAPPA, D. S., Fishery Engineering
SHIVAPPA SHETTY, K., Microbiology
SHIVARAJ, B., Agronomy
SHIVASHANKAR, K., Agronomy
SHIVANNA, H., Plant Breeding and Genetics
SIDDARAMAIAH, A. L., Plant Pathology
SIDDARAMAIAH, B. S., Agricultural Extension
SIDDARAMAPPA, R., Soil Science
SIDDARAMEGOWDA, T. K., Biotechnology
SINGLACHAR, M. A., Agronomy
SOMASHEKARAPPA, G., Agricultural Extension
SRIHARI, K., Zoology
SRINIVASA GOWDA, M. V., Economics
SRINIVASA GOWDA, R. N., Poultry Pathology
SRIKAR, L. N., Biochemistry
SUSHEELA DEVI, L., Soil Science and Agricultural Chemistry
SURYA PRAKASH, S., Agricultural Economics
THIMME GOWDA, S., Agronomy
UDAYAKUMAR, M., Crop Physiology
UPADHYA, A. S., Veterinary Microbiology
UTTAIAH, B. C., Horticulture
VAIDEHI, M. P., Home Science
VAJRANABAIAH, S. N., Crop Physiology
VASUDEVAPPA, Inland Fisheries
VEERABHADRAIAH, V., Agricultural Extension
VENKATASUBBAIAH, K., Botany
VENKATESH REDDY, T., Post-Harvest Technology
VENUGOPAL, Agricultural Extension
VENUGOPAL, N., Agricultural Meteorology
VIDYACHANDRA, B., Plant Breeding
VIJAYASARATHI, S. K., Veterinary Microbiology
VIRAKTHAMATH, C. A., Agricultural Entomology
VISHWANATH, D. P., Soil Science
VISWANATH, S., Virology
VISWANATHA, S. R., Plant Breeding
VISWANATHA REDDY, V. N., Gynaecology and Obstetrics
VISWANATHA SASTRY, K. M., Veterinary Medicine
YADAHALLI, Y. H., Agronomy

CONSTITUENT COLLEGES

College of Agriculture: G. K. V .K., Bangalore; f. 1946; Dir Dr M. B. CHANNEGOWDA.

College of Agriculture: Hassan; f. 1996; Dir Dr M. B. CANNEGOWDA.

College of Agriculture: Mandiya; f. 1991; Dir S. KUMARASWAMY.

College of Agriculture: Shimoga; f. 1990; Dir Dr K. SHIVAPPA SHETTY.

College of Basic Sciences and Humanities: Bangalore; f. 1967; Dir Dr R. V. RAMA MOHAN.

College of Fisheries, Mangalore: f. 1970; Dir Dr S. L. SHANBHOGUE.

College of Forestry: Ponnampet; f. 1995; Dir Dr N. SWAMY RAO.

College of Horticulture: Mudigere; f. 1991; Dir Dr N. VIJAYAKUMAR.

College of Post-Graduate Education: G.K.V.K., Bangalore; f. 1967; Dir Dr J. V. VENKATARAM.

College of Sericulture: Chinthamani; f. 1995; Dir Dr D. K. NAGESHCHANDRA.

Dairy Science College: Hebbal, Bangalore; f. 1979; Dir Dr P. A. SHANKAR.

Veterinary College: Hebbal, Bangalore; f. 1957; Dir Dr S. ABDUL REHMAN.

ALAGAPPA UNIVERSITY

Alagappa Nagar, Karaikudi 630003, Tamil Nadu
Telephone: (4565) 235205
E-mail: kkd_alagappa@sancharnet.in
Internet: www.aluniv.org
Founded 1985
Chancellor: HE THE GOVERNOR OF TAMIL NADU
Vice-Chancellor: Dr A. RAMASAMY
Registrar: Dr R. DHANASEKARAN

Number of teachers: 101
Number of students: 1,545

HEADS OF DEPARTMENTS

Commerce: Dr M. A. ARULANADAM
Computer Applications: Dr S. SAKTHIVEL
Corporate Secretaryship: Dr R. NEELAMEGAM
Education: Dr S. MOHAN
Industrial Chemistry: Dr T. VASUDEVAN
Physical Education: Dr A. M. MOORTHY
Mathematics: Dr K. C. RAO
Physics: Dr R. SABESAN
Tamil: Dr A. VISVANATHAN
Women's Studies: Dr S. GOKILAVANI
Alagappa Institute of Management: Dr A. R. UMAMAHESWAR
Crystal Research Centre: Dr R. DHANASEKARAN

PRINCIPALS

College of Education: Karaikudi 630003; T. N. SHAMALA.

College of Physical Education: Karaikudi 630004; Dr E. K. CHINNAMA REDDY.

ALIGARH MUSLIM UNIVERSITY

Aligarh, Uttar Pradesh 202002
Telephone: (571) 2700220
Fax: (571) 2700528
E-mail: amupro@sancharnet.in
Internet: www.amu.nic.in

Founded as Anglo-Mohamedan Oriental College, 1875; raised to university status, 1920

Central university
Language of instruction: English
Indian govt control
Academic year: July to May

Chancellor: SYEDNA BURHANUDDIN
Vice-Chancellor: MOHAMMAD HAMID ANSARI
Registrar: S. M. AFZAL
Librarian: Prof. NOORUL HASAN KHAN

Library of 965,000 vols; MSS in Arabic, Persian, Urdu and Hindi
Number of teachers: 1,191
Number of students: 16,211

Publications: *Gazette* (monthly), *Tehzibul Akhlaq* (monthly)

DEANS

Faculty of Agriculture: Prof. P. K. SRIVASTAVA
Faculty of Arts: Prof. JAFAR RAZA ZAIDI
Faculty of Commerce: Prof. MAHFOOZ-UR-REHMAN
Faculty of Engineering and Technology: Prof. FARID GHANI
Faculty of Law: Prof. QAISER HAYAT
Faculty of Life Sciences: Prof. JAMEEL AHMAD
Faculty of Management Studies and Research: Prof. KALEEM MOHD KHAN
Faculty of Medicine: Prof. KAMLESH TIWARI
Faculty of Science: Prof. SIRAJUR REHMAN
Faculty of Social Sciences: Prof. MANSURA HAIDER
Faculty of Theology: Prof. ABDUL ALEEM
Faculty of Unani Medicine: Prof. AFZAL AHMAD KHAN

ATTACHED RESEARCH INSTITUTES

Centre of West-Asian Studies: Dir Prof. TAYYABA HUSAIN.

Institute of Agriculture: Dir GHULAM MOHAMMAD KHAN.

Institute of Biotechnology: Dir Prof. SALEEMUDDIN.

Institute of Ophthalmology: Dir Prof. LEOLA AHUJA.

Institute of Petroleum Studies: Chair. Prof. HAMID ALI.

UNIVERSITY OF ALLAHABAD

Allahabad 211002, Uttar Pradesh
Telephone: (532) 2461089
Fax: (532) 2545021
E-mail: gkm@allduniv.edu
Internet: www.allduniv.edu

Founded 1887

Unitary
Languages of instruction: English, Hindi
Academic year: July to April

Chancellor: HE THE GOVERNOR OF UTTAR PRADESH
Vice-Chancellor: Prof. G. K. MEHTA
Registrar: Dr KAILASH NATH PANDEY
Librarian: Dr A. P. GAKHAR

Library of 710,000 vols
Number of students: 37,694

DEANS

Faculty of Arts: Prof. U. N. AGARWALA
Faculty of Commerce: Prof. ALKA AGARWAL
Faculty of Law: Prof. R. K. SINHA
Faculty of Medicine: Prof. KESHAV KUMAR
Faculty of Science: Prof. A. K. GUPTA

UNIVERSITY COLLEGES

J. K. Institute of Applied Physics and Technology: Allahabad; Head Prof. M. S. BISHT.

Kali Prasad University College: Allahabad; Principal Dr RAJ SHEKHAR.

Madan Mohan Malaviya University College: Allahabad; Principal Dr M. P. SINGH.

William Holland University College: Allahabad; Principal Dr E. S. K. GHOSH.

CONSTITUENT COLLEGE

Motilal Nehru Medical College: Allahabad; f. 1961; Principal Prof. KESHAV KUMAR.

There are 11 associated colleges

AMRAVATI UNIVERSITY

Amravati, Maharashtra 444602
Telephone: (721) 2662373
Fax: (721) 2662135
E-mail: amtunivc@amtuni.com
Internet: www.amtuni.com

Founded 1983

Teaching and Affiliating
Languages of instruction: English, Marathi, Hindi
Academic year: July to April

Chancellor: HE THE GOVERNOR OF MAHARASHTRA
Vice-Chancellor: Dr SUDHIR N. PATIL
Registrar: Dr P. S. NARKHEDE
Librarian: S. P. POTDAR

Library of 59,387 vols
Number of students: 108,217

Faculties of Arts, Commerce, Education, Engineering and Technology, Home Science, Law, Science and Social Sciences

There are 248 affiliated colleges.

ANDHRA UNIVERSITY

Visakhapatnam 530003, Andhra Pradesh
Telephone: (891) 2754871
Fax: (891) 2755324
E-mail: aureg@kadli.nio.org

Founded 1926

Affiliating
Languages of instruction: English, Telugu
Academic year: July to March

Chancellor: HE THE GOVERNOR OF ANDHRA PRADESH
Vice-Chancellor: Prof. Y. C. SIMHADRI
Registrar: Prof. M. S. PRASADA RAO
Librarian: Prof. P. V. KRISHNA RAO

Library of 431,800 vols
Number of teachers: 883
Number of students: 100,000

Publications: *Annual Report*, *Handbook*

The faculties are in the process of reorganization.

CONSTITUENT COLLEGES

Erskine College of Natural Sciences: Waltair; f. 1941; Principal Prof. V. LAKSHMINARAYANA.

J. V .D. College of Science and Technology: Waltair; f. 1932; Principal Prof. G. GORRAREDDY.

University College of Arts and Commerce: Waltair; f. 1931; Principal Prof. G. SUBRAHMANYAM.

University College of Engineering: Waltair; f. 1955; Principal Prof. V. RADHAKRISHNA MURTHY.

University College of Law: Waltair; f. 1934; Principal Prof. C. RAMA RAO.

University College of Science and Technology: Waltair; Principal Prof. V. RADHA KRISHNAMURTHY.

There are 160 affiliated colleges. The University also runs postgraduate courses at Kakinada and Srikakulam.

ANNA UNIVERSITY

Sardar Patel Rd, Guindy, Chennai 600025
Telephone: (44) 22351723
Fax: (44) 22350397
E-mail: vc@annauniv.edu
Internet: www.annauniv.edu

Founded 1978 as Perarignar Anna University of Technology, name changed 1982
Autonomous control
Language of instruction: English
Academic year: July to May

Vice-Chancellor: Dr ADINARAYANA KALANIDHI
Registrar: Dr S. GANAPATHY
Director of University Library: Dr LALITHA JAYARAMAN

Library of 161,405 vols
Number of teachers: 672
Number of students: 6,633

Publications: *Annual Report*, *News Bulletin*

DEANS

Architecture and Planning: Dr A. N. SACHITHANANDAN
Civil Engineering: Dr A. R. SANTHAKUMAR
Electrical Engineering: Dr S. R. PARANJOTHI
Engineering (Madras Institute of Technology): Dr S. RANGANATHAN
Mechanical Engineering: Dr G. RAMAIYAN
Science and Humanities: Dr PONNAMMAL NATARAJAN
Technology: Dr V. MOHAN

HEADS OF DEPARTMENTS

Aeronautical Engineering: Dr K. JAYARAMAN
Architecture and Planning: Prof. SURESH KUPPUSAMY
Chemical Engineering: Dr M. RAJENDRAN
Chemistry: Dr V. MURUGESAN
Civil Engineering: Dr S. THAYUMANAVAN
Computer Science and Engineering: Dr K. M. MEHATA
Electrical and Electronics Engineering: Dr M. A. PANNEERSELVAM
Electronics and Communication Engineering: Dr G. RAVINDRAN
Electronics Engineering: Dr S. KALIYUGAVARADHAN
Geology and Geophysics: Dr C. MOHANA DOSS
Humanities and Social Sciences: Prof. V. CHELLAMMAL
Instrumentation Engineering: Dr P. KANAGASABAPATHY

Leather Technology: Dr T. Ramasami
Management Studies: R. B. Kumar
Mathematics: Dr A. Vijayakumar
Mechanical Engineering: Dr K. Jeyachandran
Mining Engineering: Dr K. V. Shankar
Physics: Dr T. S. Subbaraman
Printing Technology: Dr K. Sankaranarayanan
Production Technology: Dr G. S. Kandasami
Rubber Technology: Dr K. Balasubramanian
Textile Technology: Dr M. Mathusoothanan
Institute of Remote Sensing: Dr A. R. Santhakumar
Audio-Visual Research Centre: Dr D. Viswanathan
Centre for Biotechnology: Dr P. Kaliraj
Centre for Environmental Studies: Dr S. Thayumanavan
Centre for New and Renewable Sources of Energy: Dr S. Renganarayanan
Centre for Water Resources: Dr M. Karmegam
Crystal Growth Centre: Dr P. Ramasamy
Ramanujan Computer Centre: Dr V. Sankaranarayanan

ANNAMALAI UNIVERSITY

Annamalai Nagar Post, Tamil Nadu 608002
Telephone: (4144) 238259
Fax: (4144) 238080
E-mail: au_regr@yahoo.co.in
Internet: www.annamalaiuniversity.ac.in

Founded 1929
Languages of instruction: Tamil, English
Academic year: July to June

Chancellor: Thiru Surjit Singh Barnala
Pro-Chancellor: Dr M. A. M. Ramaswamy
Vice-Chancellor: Dr L. B. Venkatrangan
Registrar: Dr M. Rathinasabapathi
Librarian: Dr M. Suriya

Library of 473,225 vols
Number of teachers: 2,000
Number of students: 18,567

Publication: *Annamalai University Research Journal*

DEANS

Faculty of Agriculture: Dr G. Kuppusamy
Faculty of Arts: Dr A. Subbian
Faculty of Dentistry: Dr C. R. Ramachandran
Faculty of Education: Dr K. Vaithianathan
Faculty of Engineering and Technology: Prof. B. Palaniappan
Faculty of Fine Arts: Prof. O. S. Thiagarajan
Faculty of Indian Languages: Dr S. Natanasabapathy
Faculty of Medicine: Dr M. Ramanathan
Faculty of Science: Dr L. S. Ranganathan

ARUNACHAL UNIVERSITY

Rono Hills, Itanagar 791112
Telephone: (3781) 247252
Fax: (3781) 247317

Founded 1984
State control
Language of instruction: English

Chancellor: Mata Prasad
Vice-Chancellor: Dr K. K. Dwivedi
Registrar: Joram Begi
Librarian (vacant)

Number of teachers: 46
Number of students: 385

Publications: *Newsletter* (annually), *Research Journal* (annually)

DEANS

Faculty of Social Sciences: Prof. S. Dutta

HEADS OF DEPARTMENTS

Commerce: Dr Ranjit Tamuli
Economics: Dr A. Mitra
Education: Prof. J. C. Soni
English: Dr B. N. Singh
Geography: Dr R. S. Yadav
History: Prof. S. Dutta
Political Science: Prof. A. C. Talukdar
Tribal Studies: Prof. Tamo Mibang

ASSAM AGRICULTURAL UNIVERSITY

Jorhat 785013, Assam
Telephone: (376) 2320989

Founded 1969

Teaching, research and extension at undergraduate and postgraduate levels in agriculture (Jorhat campus and Biswanath Chariali), home science (Jorhat campus), animal husbandry and veterinary science (Khanapara campus and Azad, North Lakhimpur) and fisheries (Raha)
Language of instruction: English
Autonomous control

Chancellor: HE The Governor of Assam
Vice-Chancellor: Prof. A. N. Mukhopadhyay
Registrar: Dr M. N. Chetia
Librarian: Mahendra Nath Borah

Library of 90,000 vols (main campus)
Number of teachers: 530
Number of students: 2,500

Publications: *Ghare-Pathare* (Assamese, monthly), *Journal of Research*, *Krishibikshan* (Assamese, quarterly), *Newsletter* (English, every 2 weeks), *Package of Practices for Kharif Crops* (English, 2 a year), *Package of Practices for Rabi Crops* (English, 2 a year)

DEANS

Faculty of Agriculture: Dr D. N. Dutta
Faculty of Home Science: Dr Labonya Majumder
Faculty of Veterinary Science: Dr A. R. Gogoi

HEADS OF DEPARTMENTS

Faculty of Agriculture:
- Agricultural Economics and Farm Management: R. N. Sarma
- Agricultural Engineering: Dr P. K. Dutta
- Agricultural Statistics: Dr B. K. Bhattacharyya
- Agronomy: Dr S. R. Baroova
- Animal Production and Management: Dr H. Gogoi
- Botany and Plant Pathology: Dr A. C. Thakur
- Crop Physiology and Agricultural Botany: Dr S. C. Dey
- Extension Education: Dr R. C. Sarma (acting)
- Genetics and Plant Breeding: Dr P. K. Duara (acting)
- Horticulture: Dr A. Sadeque
- Language: Dr M. N. Choudhury
- Nematology: Dr P. N. Phukan
- Physics and Meteorology: Dr K. K. Nath (acting)
- Tea Husbandry and Technology: A. K. Neog
- Zoology and Entomology: Dr J. N. Khound

Faculty of Home Science:
- Child Development and Family Relations: Dr M. Phukon
- Clothing and Textiles: Dr Amiya Gogoi
- Extension Education: Dr S. Siddiqui
- Food and Nutrition: Dr B. Baroova
- Home Management: Dr M. Pathak

Faculty of Veterinary Science:
- Anatomy: Dr C. C. Bordoloi
- Animal Breeding and Genetics: Dr D. Das
- Animal Production and Management: Dr N. N. Bora
- Extension Education: Dr K. Sahariah
- Gynaecology: Dr B. N. Borgohain
- Medicine: Dr C. C. Kalita
- Microbiology: Dr G. P. Patgiri (acting)
- Nutrition: Dr P. C. Das
- Parasitology: Dr B. C. Lahkar
- Pathology: Dr A. Mukit
- Pharmacology: Dr H. N. Khanikar
- Physiology: Dr B. N. Chakravartty
- Poultry Science: Dr K. K. Dutta
- Surgery: Dr S. C. Pathak

ASSAM UNIVERSITY

Silchar, Assam 788011
Telephone: (3842) 270801
Fax: (3842) 270802
E-mail: auves@sancharnet.in
Internet: www.assamuniversity.nic.in

Founded 1994

Central university
Academic year: July to June

Chancellor: Dr R. A. Mushlekar
Vice-Chancellor: Prof. S. C. Saha
Registrar: S. Sengupta
Librarian: V. D. Shrivastava

Library of 60,562 vols, 317 periodicals
Number of teachers: 140
Number of students: 1,446

Publications: *Journal*, *Proceedings*

DEANS

School of Environmental Sciences: Prof. B. K. Dutta
School of Humanities: Dr N. B. Biswas
School of Information Sciences: Prof. D. Chakrabarty
School of Languages: Prof. T. Bhattacharjee
School of Life Sciences: Prof. B. K. Dutta
School of Management Studies: Dr A. Mazaindar
School of Physical Sciences: Prof. M. R. Islam
School of Social Sciences: Prof. K. Sengupta

HEADS OF DEPARTMENTS

School of Environmental Science:
- Ecology and Environmental Science: Dr A. K. Das

School of Humanities:
- Education: Dr N. B. Biswas
- Fine Arts: Prof. B. Mate
- Philosophy: Dr Gautam Biswas

School of Information Science:
- Mass Communication: Dr G. P. Pandey

School of Languages:
- Arabic: Dr A. M. Bhuiya
- Bengali: Dr Rama Bhattacharjee
- English: Dr D. Purkayastha
- Hindi: Dr Biswanath Prasad
- Linguistics: (vacant)
- Manipuri: Dr Saratchandrea Singh
- Sanskrit: Dr H. P. Chakraborty

School of Life Sciences:
- Life Science: Dr D. Kar

School of Management Studies:
- Business Administration: Dr R. K. Raul
- Commerce: Dr N. B. Dey

School of Physical Science:
- Chemistry: Dr N. V. S. Rao
- Computer Science: Dr B. Prikayasthan
- Mathematics: Dr T. Sum
- Physics: Dr A. K. Sen

School of Social Sciences:
- Economics: Dr N. Roy
- History: Dr R. K. Vey
- Political Science: Dr D. Bhattacharjee
- Social Work: Dr A. Sarkar
- Sociology: Dr G. Ram

There are 50 affiliated colleges

AVADH UNIVERSITY

PB 17, Faizabad, Uttar Pradesh 224001
Telephone: (527) 2814230
Founded 1975
Teaching and Affiliating
Languages of instruction: English, Hindi
Academic year: July to June
Chancellor: HE The Governor of Uttar Pradesh
Vice-Chancellor: Prof. K. P. Nautiyal
Registrar: A. N. Seth
Librarian: S. K. Singh
Number of teachers: 19 (university), 2,006 (affiliated colleges)
Number of students: 45,220 (university and affiliated colleges)

DEANS

Arts: Prof. V. K. Pandey
Commerce: Dr S. M. Verma
Education: Dr S. P. Singh
Law: Dr K. N. Pandey
Science: Prof. L. K. Singh

There are 33 affiliated colleges.

AWADHESH PRATAP SINGH UNIVERSITY

Rewa 486003, Madhya Pradesh
Telephone: (7662) 230050
Fax: (7662) 242175
Founded 1968
Affiliating, Teaching and Research
Languages of instruction: Hindi, English
Academic year: July to June
Chancellor: HE The Governor of Madhya Pradesh
Vice-Chancellor: Prof. A. D. N. Bajpai
Registrar: Dr R. S. Pandey
Librarian: G. K. Singh
Library of 31,000 vols
Number of teachers: 841 (42 at university, 799 at affiliated colleges)
Number of students: 47,254 (incl. affiliated colleges)
Publication: *Vindhya Bharati* (quarterly)

DEANS

Faculty of Arts: R. R. Mathur
Faculty of Ayurveda: Dr R. V. Sohgunra
Faculty of Commerce: Prof. I. P. Tripathi
Faculty of Education: Dr Rashami Shukla
Faculty of Home Science: Dr A. K. Shrivastava
Faculty of Law: R. R. Mathur
Faculty of Life Science: Dr R. N. Shukla
Faculty of Medicine: Dr M. K. Rathore
Faculty of Prachya Sanskrit: Dr Bhashkaracharya Tripathi
Faculty of Science: Dr S. K. Nigam
Faculty of Social Science: Dr A. K. Shrivastava

There are 62 affiliated colleges

BABA FARID UNIVERSITY OF HEALTH SCIENCES

Kotakapura Rd, Faridkot 151203, Punjab
Telephone: (1639) 256232
Fax: (1639) 256234
E-mail: generalinfo@babafariduniv.com
Internet: www.babafariduniv.com
Founded 1998
Affiliating
Chancellor: HE The Governor of Punjab
Vice-Chancellor: Dr J. S. Gural
Registrar: Dr A. S. Sekhon
Number of students: 8,326

There are 48 affiliated colleges.

BABASAHEB BHIMRAO AMBEDKAR UNIVERSITY

Vidya Vihar, Rai Bareilly Rd, Lucknow 226025
Telephone: (522) 2440826
Fax: (522) 2440821
E-mail: info@bbauindia.org
Internet: www.bbauindia.org
Founded 1989
Central university
Academic year: July to June
Vice-Chancellor: Prof. Gummadi Nancharaiah
Registrar: Prof. N. K. Shastri
Librarian: A. K. Katna

DEANS

School for Amdebkar Studies: Prof. S. K. Bhatnagar
School for Biosciences and Biotechnology: Prof. M. Yunus
School for Environmental Sciences: Prof. M. Yunus
School for Information Science and Technology: Prof. M. Yunus
School for Legal Studies: Prof. S. K. Bhatnagar

DEPARTMENTAL CO-ORDINATORS

Applied Animal Science: Dr Kamal Jaiswal
Applied Plant Science: Dr R. B. Ram
Computer Science: Dr Vipin Saxena
Economics: Dr N. M. P. Verma
Environmental Science: Prof. M. Yunus
History: Dr L. K. Kenadi
Human Rights: Prof. S. K. Bhatnagar
Library and Information Science: Dr K. L. Mahawar

BANARAS HINDU UNIVERSITY

Varanasi 221005, Uttar Pradesh
Telephone: (542) 2316558
Fax: (542) 2317074
E-mail: bhu@banaras.ernet.in
Internet: www.bhu.ac.in
Founded 1915
State control
Central university (residential and teaching)
Languages of instruction: Hindi, English
Academic year: July to April (three terms)
Visitor: President of the Republic of India
Vice-Chancellor: Prof. P. Ramachandra Rao
Registrar: Prof. P. C. Upadhyay
Librarian: Prof. O. N. Srivastava
Library of 916,821 vols
Number of teachers: 1,085
Number of students: 16,105
Publications: *BHU Journal*, *Prajna*

DEANS

Faculty of Agriculture: Prof. A. K. Richania
Faculty of Ayurveda: Prof. R. H. Singh
Faculty of Commerce: Prof. M. N. A. Ansari
Faculty of Education: Prof. Asha Pandey
Faculty of Engineering and Technology: Prof. B. N. Roy
Faculty of Management Studies: Prof. R. M. Srivastava
Faculty of Medicine: Prof. Gajendra Singh
Faculty of Performing Arts: Dr Krishna Chakravorty
Faculty of Sanskrit Vidya Dharm Vigyan: Prof. N. R. Srinivasan
Faculty of Science: Prof. S. N. Lal
Faculty of Social Sciences: Prof. A. P. Singh
Faculty of Visual Arts: Dr R. N. Mishra

HEADS OF DEPARTMENTS

Faculty of Agriculture:

Agronomy: Prof. H. C. Sharma
Agricultural Economics: Dr C. Sen
Animal Husbandry and Dairying: Prof. R. K. Yadava
Entomology and Agricultural Zoology: Prof. J. Singh
Extension Education: Prof. V. K. Dubey
Farm Engineering: Prof. S. R. Singh
Genetics and Plant Breeding: Prof. Bhupendra Rai
Horticulture: Prof. C. B. S. Rajput
Mycology and Plant Pathology: Prof. D. C. Pant
Plant Physiology: Prof. B. Bose
Soil Science and Agricultural Chemistry: Prof. R. C. Tiwari

Faculty of Arts:

Ancient Indian History, Culture, Archaeology: Prof. P. Singh
Arabic: Dr N. Faruqui
Bengali: Dr K. B. Chakravorty
English: Prof. A. K. Toipathi
Foreign Languages: Dr A. Jha
French Studies: Dr H. N. Das
German Studies: Dr Indu Bhave
Linguistics: Dr R. B. Mishra
Hindi: Prof. Srinivas Pandey
History of Art: Dr D. B. Pandey
Indian Languages: Ghanshyam Nepal
Journalism and Mass Communication: Dr B. R. Gupta
Library and Information Science: Dr H. N. Prasad
Marathi: Dr S. P. Bhriguwar
Pali and Buddhist Studies: Dr H. S. Shukla
Persian: Dr S. Akhtar
Philosophy and Religion: Prof. R. R. Pandey
Physical Education: Dr D. K. Dureha
Sanskrit: Prof. S. N. Mishra
Telugu: Dr G. Trivikramaiah
Urdu: Dr Qamar Jahan

Faculty of Ayurveda:

Ayurveda Samhita: Prof. J. Ogha
Basic Principles: Prof. I. P. Singh
Dravya Guna: Dr S. D. Dubey
Kaya Chikitsa: Dr B. N. Upadhyaya
Medicinal Chemistry: Dr Mahendra Sahai
Prasuti Tantra: Dr R. D. Sharma
Rasa Shastra: Dr C. B. Jha
Shalya Shalakya: Dr M. Sahu

Faculty of Engineering and Technology:

Applied Chemistry: Prof. D. C. Rupainwar
Applied Mathematics: Prof. K. N. Bhowmik
Applied Physics: Prof. S. P. Ojha
Chemical Engineering: Prof. P. Mishra
Civil Engineering: Prof. V. P. Mishra
Ceramic Engineering: Prof. S. P. Singh
Computer Engineering: Dr A. K. Tripalhi
Electrical Engineering: Prof. T. Srinivason
Electronics Engineering: Prof. S. K. Srivastava
Mechanical Engineering: Prof. J. N. Dubey
Metallurgical Engineering: Prof. V. Singh
Mining Engineering: Prof. R. Nath
Pharmaceutics: Prof. S. K. Patnaik

Faculty of Medicine:

Anatomy: Prof. M. Singh
Anaesthesiology: Prof. A. Lal
Biochemistry: Prof. R. Shankar
Biophysics: Prof. A. K. Bhattacharya
Cardiology: Dr P. R. Gupta
Cardiothoracic Surgery: Prof. T. K. Lahiri
Dentistry: Prof. B. P. Singh
Dermatology and Venereology: Prof. S. S. Pandey
Endocrinology: Prof. J. K. Agrawal
Forensic Medicine: Prof. C. B. Tripathi
Gastroenterology: Prof. A. K. Jain
Medicine: Prof. K. K. Tripathi
Microbiology: Prof. A. K. Gulati
Nephrology: Prof. R. G. Singh
Neurology: Prof. Surendra Mishra
Neurosurgery: Prof. S. Mohanti

Obstetrics and Gynaecology: Prof. L. K. Pandey
Ophthalmology: Prof. R. P. S. Bhatiya
Otorhinolaryngology: Dr R. K. Jain
Orthopaedics: Dr S. K. Saraf
Paediatric Surgery: Prof. S. Chooramami Gopal
Physiology: Prof. R. K. Sharma
Pharmacology: Prof. S. B. Acharya
Pathology: Prof. P. K. Shukla
Plastic Surgery: Prof. F. M. Tripathi
Preventive and Social Medicine: Prof. J. Tadon
Psychiatry: Prof. Indra Sharma
Paediatrics: Prof. P. N. Singla
Radiology: Prof. A. K. Agrawal
Surgery: Prof. H. S. Shupla
Radiotherapy and Radiation Medicine: Dr A. K. Asthana
Tuberculosis and Chest Diseases: Dr S. C. Matah
Urology: Dr P. B. Singh

Faculty of Oriental Learning and Theology:
Bauddha and Jain Darshan: Prof. S. S. Shashtri
Dharmagam: Dr K. Jha
Dharmashastra and Mimamsa: Dr N. R. Srinivasan
Jyotish: Dr R. C. Pandey
Sahitya: Dr C. M. Dwivedi
Vaidic Darshan: Prof. K. K. Sharma
Veda: V. Mishra
Vyakaran: Prof. B. Shastri

Faculty of Performing Arts:
Instrumental Music: Prof. R. P. Shashtri
Musicology: Prof. C. R. Jyotishi
Vocal Music: Prof. C. R. Jyolishi

Faculty of Science:
Biochemistry: Dr S. Rathour
Biotechnology: Prof. B. D. Singh
Botany: Prof. K. P. Singh
Chemistry: Prof. R. Balaji Rao
Computer Science: Prof. S. K. Basu
Geography: Dr S. B. Singh
Geology: Prof. B. K. Chatterjee
Geophysics: Prof. B. R. D. Gupta
Home Science: Prof. P. Srivastava
Mathematics: Prof. R. S. Pathak
Physics: Prof. A. N. Mantri
Statistics: Dr K. N. S. Yadava
Zoology: Prof. A. K. Mittal

Faculty of Social Sciences:
Economics: Prof. P. K. Bhargava
History: Dr Aruna Sinha
Political Science: Prof. A. S. Upadhyaya
Psychology: Prof. C. B. Durivedi
Sociology: Prof. A. L. Srivastava

Faculty of Visual Arts:
Painting: Dr R. N. Mishra
Plastic Arts: Dr P. C. Vinod
Applied Arts: S. Dasgupta

CONSTITUENT COLLEGE

Mahila Maha Vidyalaya: Varanasi; f. 1929; Principal Prof. K. R. Ranganayakalu.

ATTACHED INSTITUTES

Institute of Agricultural Sciences: Dir Prof. A. N. Maurya.

Institute of Medical Sciences: Dir Prof. V. P. Singh.

Institute of Technology: Dir Prof. P. M. Prasad.

There are four affiliated colleges

BANASTHALI VIDYAPITH

PO Banasthali Vidyapith, Rajasthan 304022
Telephone: (1438) 228324
Fax: (1438) 228365
E-mail: adityashastri@yahoo.com
Internet: www.banasthali.org

Founded 1935; university status 1983
Autonomous control
Academic year: July to April
Languages of instruction: Hindi, English

President: Prof. Diwakar Shastri
Vice-President: Kamla Shastri
Director: Prof. Aditya Shastri
Secretary: Prof. Chitra Purohit

Library of 215,000 vols, 660 periodicals
Number of teachers: 260
Number of students: 3,237

DEANS

Faculty of Education: Prof. T. K. S. Lakshmi
Faculty of Fine Arts: Dr B. S. Sharma
Faculty of Home Science: Dr Indu Bansal
Faculty of Humanities: Prof. Kunjbala Goel
Faculty of Management: Prof. Siddharth Shastri
Faculty of Science: Prof. Vinay Sharma
Faculty of Social Sciences: Prof. Siddharth Shastri
AIM and ACT: Prof. Rekha Govil

BANGALORE UNIVERSITY

Jnana Bharathi, Bangalore 560056, Karnataka
Telephone: (80) 23214001
Fax: (80) 23219295
E-mail: bnguni@kar.nic.in
Internet: www.bangaloreuniversity.net

Founded 1964
Affiliating
Languages of instruction: Kannada, English
Academic year: June to March

Chancellor: HE The Governor of Karnataka
Vice-Chancellor: Dr M. S. Thimmappa
Registrar: Arvind G. Risbud
Librarian: Dr Anjanappa

Library of 315,000 vols
Number of teachers: 456
Number of students: 419,132

Publications: *Bash Bharathi* (2 a year), *Janapriya Vignana* (monthly), *Sadhane* (Kannada, quarterly), *Vignana Bharathi*, *Vidya Bharathi*

DEANS

Faculty of Arts: Dr Siddalingaiah
Faculty of Commerce: Dr K. Eresi
Faculty of Communication: Dr Leela Rao
Faculty of Education: Dr M. S. Talwar
Faculty of Engineering and Technology: Dr K. Ranga
Faculty of Law: Prof. K. M. Hanumantharayappa
Faculty of Science: Dr D. S. Chandrashekariah

HEADS OF DEPARTMENTS

Architecture: K. V. Guruprasad
Botany: Dr B. H. M. Nijalingappa
Chemistry: Dr N. M. Nanje Gowda
Civil Engineering: Dr K. Ranga
Commerce: Dr P. N. Reddy
Communication: Dr Leela Rao
Drama, Dance and Music: Rajalakshmi Tirunarayanan
Economics: S. N. Nanje Gowda
Education: M. S. Talawar
Electrical Engineering: Prof. K. Mallikarjun Chetty
Electronics and Computer Engineering: Prof. H. N. Shivashankar
English: Dr Vimala Rao
Geography: Dr B. Eshwarappa
Geology: K. G. Gubbaiah
Hindi: Dr T. G. Prabha Shankar
History: Dr Shadakshariah
Kannada: Dr K. Marulasiddappa
Law: Prof. V. B. Coutinho
Library Science: Dr A. Y. Asundi
Mathematics: Dr H. T. Rathod
Mechanical Engineering: Dr V. K. Basalalli
Philosophy: Dr Srinivasa Rao
Physical Education: L. R. Vydyanathan
Physics: Dr C. Raghavendra Rao
Political Science: R. L. M. Patil
Psychology: Dr Indira Jai Prakash
Sanskrit: Dr M. Shivakumaraswamy
Sericulture: S. R. Ananthanarayana
Social Work: Dr L. S. Gandhi Doss
Sociology: Dr Srinivasa Rao
Statistics: Dr K. Harischandra
Telugu: Dr G. S. Mohan
Urdu: Dr M. Nooruddin
Zoology: Dr S. Ravichandra Reddy
Centre for Rural Development Studies: K. Rangaswamy

UNIVERSITY COLLEGES

University College of Physical Education: Bangalore; Principal Dr M. S. Talwar.

University Law College: Bangalore; Principal Dr K. M. Hanumantharayappa.

University Visvesvaraya College of Engineering: Bangalore.

There are 450 affiliated colleges

BARKATULLAH VISHWAVIDYALAYA

Bhopal 462026, MP
Telephone: (755) 2547151

Founded 1970 as Bhopal University, name changed 1989
Teaching and Affiliating
Languages of instruction: English, Hindi

Chancellor: HE The Governor of Madhya Pradesh
Vice-Chancellor: Prof. H. V. Tiwary
Registrar: Dr N. S. Verma
Librarian: R. K. Mishra

Library of 52,700 vols
Number of teachers: 1,100
Number of students: 40,000 (incl. affiliated colleges)

DEANS

Faculty of Arts: Dr Arifa Simmin
Faculty of Commerce: Dr D. P. Sharma
Faculty of Education: P. K. Khanna
Faculty of Engineering: Dr C. S. Bhatnagar
Faculty of Home Science: Dr Madhu Mishra
Faculty of Law: H. L. Jain
Faculty of Medicine: Dr N. R. Bhandari
Faculty of Science: (vacant)
Faculty of Social Science: Dr I. S. Chauhan
Faculty of Life Science: Dr Santosh Kumar
Faculty of Technical Education: Prof. G. S. Chandaran

There are 43 affiliated colleges

BERHAMPUR UNIVERSITY

Berhampur 760007, Orissa
Telephone: (3482) 200615
Fax: (3482) 202322
Internet: bamu.nic.in

Founded 1967
Teaching and Affiliating
State control
Language of instruction: English
Academic year: June to May

Chancellor: HE The Governor of Orissa
Vice-Chancellor: Dr Aditya Prasad Padhy
Registrar: R. N. Mishra
Librarian: B. Panda

Library of 73,000 vols
Number of teachers: 168
Number of students: 31,550

Publication: *Research Journal* (annually)

PROFESSORS

Acharya, S., Oriya
Baral, J. K., Political Science

DAS, D., Oriya
DAS, G. N., Linguistics
DAS, H. H., Political Science
DAS, N. C., Physics
KHAN, P. A., Botany
MAJHI, J., Electronics
MISHRA, S. K., English
MISRA, B. N., Botany
MISRA, D.
MISRA, P. M., Marine Science
MOHANTY, S. P., Physics
MOHAPATRA, N. C., Physics
PADHISHARMA, R., Economics
PANDA, C. S., Chemistry
PANDA, G. P., Law
PANDA, G. S., Business Administration
PANDA, J., Commerce
PANDA, P., Economics
PANIGRAHY, G. P., Chemistry
PARHI, N., Mathematics
PATI, S. C., Chemistry
PATNAIK, B. K., Zoology
PATRA, G. C., Industrial Relations and Labour Welfare
PRASAD, R., Zoology
RAO, E. R., English
RATH, D., Mathematics
SAHU, P. K., Commerce
SAMAL, J. K., History
VERMA, G. P., Zoology

There are 48 affiliated colleges

BHARATHIAR UNIVERSITY

Coimbatore, Tamil Nadu 641046

Telephone: (422) 2422222
Fax: (422) 2422387
E-mail: regr@bharathiaruni.org
Internet: www.bharathiaruni.org

Founded 1982

Teaching and Affiliating
Academic year: July to April

Chancellor: HE THE GOVERNOR OF TAMIL NADU
Vice-Chancellor: Prof. S. SIVASUBRAMANIAN
Registrar: Dr C. SUBRAMANIAM
Librarian: Dr S. SELVASEKARAPANDIAN

Library of 86,572 vols

DEANS

Arts: Dr C. SHUNMUGOM
Commerce: Dr M. MANICKAM
Education: Dr R. ANANTHASAYANAM
Science: Dr S. NATARAJAN
Social Sciences: Dr S. NARAYANAN

HEADS OF DEPARTMENTS

Botany: Dr K. UDAIYAN
Computer Science: Dr K. CHELLAPPAN (acting)
Chemistry: Dr K. NATARAJAN
Economics: Dr S. PERUMALSAMY
Environmental Sciences: Dr V. GOPAL
Linguistics: Dr C. SHANMUGOM (acting)
Mathematics: Dr M. R. RAGHAVACHAR
Physical Education: K. R. MUTHUSAMY
Physics: Dr SA. K. NARAYANDASS
Psychology: Dr S. NARAYANAN
Sociology: Dr M. LAKSHMANASINGH
Statistics: Dr V. SOUNDARARAJAN
Tamil: Dr P. BALASUBRAMANIAM
Zoology: Dr R. MANAVALALARAMANUJAM (acting)
School of Management and Entrepreneur Development: Dr P. MUTHUSAMY

There are 85 affiliated colleges and 19 affiliated research institutes

BHARATHIDASAN UNIVERSITY

Palkalaiperur, Tiruchirappalli, Tamil Nadu 620024

Telephone: (431) 2407092
Fax: (431) 2407045
E-mail: office@bdu.ernet.in
Internet: www.bdu.ernet.in

Founded 1982

Affiliating
Languages of instruction: English, Tamil
State control
Academic year: June to April

Chancellor: HE THE GOVERNOR OF TAMIL NADU
Vice-Chancellor: Dr MUTHIAH MARIAPPAN
Registrar: Dr V. RAJAGOPALAN (acting)
Librarian: P. SEETHARAMAN (acting)

Library of 68,000 vols
Number of teachers: 2,779
Number of students: 99,802

Publications: *Annual Report*, *BARD News Letter*, *Information Bulletin*

DEANS

Arts: Dr K. PARTHASARATHY
Indian and Other Languages: Dr A. NOEL JOSEPH SEETHARAMAN
Science: Dr M. LAKSHMANAN

HEADS OF DEPARTMENTS

Animal Sciences: Dr M. R. CHANDRAN
Biotechnology: Dr M. VIVEKANANDAN
Chemistry: Dr M. KRISHNA PILLAY
Earth Sciences: Dr S. M. RAMASWAMY
Economics: Dr C. THANGAMUTHU
Educational Technology: Dr S. PURUSHOTHAMAN
English: Dr A. JOSEPH
Mathematics: Dr N. RAMANUJAM
Microbiology: Dr G. SUBRAMANIAN
Physical Education: Dr P. MARIAYYAH
Physics: Dr M. LAKSHMANAN
Plant Science: Dr K. V. KRISHNAMURTHY
Social Work: Dr S. PALANISAMY
Sociology: Dr R. SHANKAR
Tamil: Dr M. RAMALINGAM
Adult, Continuing Education and Extension: Dr K. PARTHASARATHY
Centre for History: Dr N. RAJENDRAN

There are 108 affiliated colleges

ATTACHED INSTITUTES

Bharathidasan Institute of Engineering and Technology: Tiruchirappalli 620023; Co-ordinator Dr N. RAMANUJAM.

Bharathidasan Institute of Management: Tiruchirappalli 620014; Dir Prof. N. JAYASANKARAN.

BHAVNAGAR UNIVERSITY

Gaurishanker Lake Rd, University Campus, Bhavnagar 364002, Gujarat

Telephone: (278) 2430002
Fax: (278) 2426706
E-mail: naresh_ved@rediffmail.com
Internet: www.bhavuni.edu

Founded 1978

Teaching and Affiliating
State control
Language of instruction: Gujarati
Academic year: June to March (two terms)

Chancellor: HE THE GOVERNOR OF GUJARAT
Vice-Chancellor: Dr NARESH VED
Registrar: BHARATSINH J. PARMAR
Librarian: NIMESH D. OZA

Library of 98,600 vols
Number of teachers: 400
Number of students: 20,959

DEANS

Faculty of Arts: Dr P. V. MEHTA
Faculty of Commerce: Dr B. K. OZA
Faculty of Education: Dr C. K. BHOGAYATA
Faculty of Engineering: Prof. M. R. PATEL
Faculty of Law: J. A. PANDYA
Faculty of Management: Dr A. KUMAR
Faculty of Medicine: Dr D. R. JALA
Faculty of Rural Studies: ARUN DAVE
Faculty of Science: Dr G. M. AKOLIA

There are 28 affiliated colleges

ATTACHED INSTITUTES

B. V. Patel Pharmaceutical Education and Research: Ahmedabad.

Central Salt and Marine Chemicals Research Institute: see under Research Institutes.

Dholakia School of Music: Sihor.

K. K. Jani Institute of Medical Laboratory Technology, Amargadh: Dir Dr R. M. Thakkar.

K. L. Institute for Deaf and Dumb: Vidyanagar.

BHUPENDRA NARAYAN MANDAL UNIVERSITY

Madhepura 852113, Bihar

Founded 1992
State control

Vice-Chancellor: Dr JAI K. PRASAD YADAV
Registrar: Prof. B. P. MANDAL.

BIDHAN CHANDRA KRISHI VISWAVIDYALAYA

PO Krishi Viswavidyalaya, Mohanpur 741252, Nadia, West Bengal

Telephone: (33) 25879772
Fax: (3473) 222275
E-mail: vcbckv@vsnl.net.in

Founded 1974

Residential
Academic year: July to June

Chancellor: HE THE GOVERNOR OF WEST BENGAL
Vice-Chancellor: Prof. DEBABRATA DAS GUPTA
Registrar: ASOK BANERJEE (acting)
Asst Librarian: DIPIKA NEOGI

Library of 101,535 vols
Number of students: 466

DEANS

Faculty of Agricultural Engineering: Prof. D. K. DUTTA
Faculty of Agriculture: Prof. M. M. ADHIKARY
Faculty of Horticulture: Prof. T. P. MUKHOPADHYAY

BIJU PATNAIK UNIVERSITY OF TECHNOLOGY

Rourkela 769004, Orissa

Telephone: (661) 2501349
Fax: (661) 2501345
Internet: www.bput.org

Founded 2002

Chancellor: HE THE GOVERNOR OF ORISSA
Vice-Chancellor: Dr DAMODAR ACHARYA

Courses in architecture, business administration, computer application, engineering, pharmacy and technology.

BIRLA INSTITUTE OF TECHNOLOGY

Mesra, Ranchi

Telephone: (651) 2301565
Fax: (651) 2300615
Internet: www.bitmesra.edu

Founded 1955, university status 1986

Vice-Chancellor: Dr B. KANTA RAO
Registrar: Prof. G. SAHAY (acting)
Librarian: Dr U. N. SINGH

Library of 60,000 vols
Number of teachers: 149

Number of students: 1,650

HEADS OF DEPARTMENTS

Applied Chemistry: Dr J. PAUL
Applied Mechanics: Prof N. R. RAO
Applied Physics: Dr J. RAM
Civil Engineering: Prof. B. S. RAJEEVALOCHANAM
Computer Science: Dr P. K. MAHANTI
Electrical and Electronic Engineering: Prof. S. H. KEKRE
Electronics and Communication Engineering: Prof. S. C. GOEL
Management: Prof. A. PRASAD
Mathematics: B. B. MISHRA
Mechanical Engineering: Prof. K. M. SIRBHAYA
Pharmaceutical Sciences: Dr A. K. SHARMA
Polymer Engineering: Dr M. MUKHERJEE
Production Engineering: Dr S. KUMAR
Space Engineering and Rocketry: Dr N. L. MUNJAL

ATTACHED INSTITUTE

Technology Centre, Lalpur: Dir Dr B. B. MISHRA.

BIRLA INSTITUTE OF TECHNOLOGY AND SCIENCE

Pilani, Rajasthan 333031
Telephone: (1596) 242192
Fax: (1596) 244183
E-mail: mmsanand@bits-pilani.ac.in
Internet: www.bits-pilani.ac.in

Founded 1964
Language of instruction: English
Academic year: July to May (two semesters)

Chairman: Dr K. K. BIRLA
Vice-Chancellor: Prof. S. VENKATESWARAN
Deputy Director (Academic): Prof. L. K. MAHESHWARI
Deputy Director (Administration): Prof. K. E. RAMAN
Deputy Director (Off-Campus Programmes): Prof. V. S. RAO
Registrar: Prof. M. M. S. ANAND
Librarian: ISHWARA BHAT M.

Library of 218,972 vols
Number of teachers: 489
Number of students: 15,964; includes both on campus (6,339 students) and off campus (9,625 students)

Publication: *Bulletin*

DEANS

Academic Registration and Counselling Division: Prof. R.K. MITTAL
Distance Learning Programmes Division: Prof. B.R. NATARAJAN
Educational Development Division and Faculty Division III: Prof. RANENDRA N. SAHA
Educational Hardware Division: Prof. RAJIV GUPTA
Educational Services Division: Prof. K.E. RAMAN
Faculty Division II: Prof. G. RAGHURAMA
Instruction Division and Faculty Division I: Prof. ASHOKE KUMAR SARKAR
Practice School Division: Prof. V. S. RAO
Research and Consultancy Division: Prof. RAVI PRAKASH
Students Welfare Division: Prof. G. SUNDAR

GROUP LEADERS

Biological Sciences: Assoc. Prof. SANJAY KUMAR VERMA
Chemical Engineering: Prof. B. V. BABU
Chemistry: Prof. S. C. SIVASUBRAMANIAN
Civil Engineering: Assoc. Prof. K RAJU
Computer Science and Information Systems: Assoc. Prof. S. BALUSUBRAMANIAM
Economics and Finance: Prof. ARYA KUMAR
Electrical and Electronics Engineering: Prof. S. BALASUBRAMANIAN
Electronics and Instrumentation: Prof. SUREKHA BHANOT
Engineering Technology: Prof. KODALI RAMBABU
Humanities: Prof. NIRUPAMA PRAKASH
Languages: Assoc. Prof. MEENAKSHI RAMAN
Management: Prof A.K. BHATT
Mathematics: Prof. RAM AVTAR
Mechanical Engineering: Prof. KODALI RAMBABU
Pharmacy: Assoc. Prof. R MAHESH
Physics: Prof. R.R. MISHRA

BIRSA AGRICULTURAL UNIVERSITY

Kanke, Ranchi 834006, Jharkhand
Telephone: (651) 2450500
Fax: (651) 2450850
E-mail: bau@bitsmart.com

Founded 1981
Languages of instruction: English, Hindi
Academic year: July to June

Chancellor: HE THE GOVERNOR OF JHARKHAND
Vice-Chancellor: Dr S. N. PANDEY
Registrar: Dr K. P. SINGH
Librarian (vacant)

Library of 70,000 vols
Number of teachers: 200
Number of students: 700

Publications: *BAU* (2 a year), *Journal of Research*

DEANS

Faculty of Agriculture: Dr A. K. SARKAR
Faculty of Forestry: Dr O. N. PANDEY
Faculty of Veterinary Science and Animal Husbandry: Dr A. K. SINHA

CHAIRMEN OF DEPARTMENTS

Faculty of Agriculture (Kanke, Ranchi 834006, Jharkhand; tel. (651) 2450626):
- Agricultural Economics: Dr R. P. SINGH
- Agricultural Engineering: (vacant)
- Agricultural Extension: (vacant)
- Agricultural Physics: (vacant)
- Agronomy: Dr R. A. RAFEY
- Entomology: (vacant)
- Horticulture: (vacant)
- Plant Breeding and Genetics: (vacant)
- Plant Pathology: (vacant)
- Soil Science and Agricultural Chemistry: Dr A. K. SARKAR

Faculty of Veterinary Science and Animal Husbandry:
- Anatomy: (vacant)
- Animal Breeding and Genetics: (vacant)
- Animal Production: (vacant)
- Gynaecology: Dr A. K. SINHA
- Medicine: (vacant)
- Microbiology: (vacant)
- Nutrition: (vacant)
- Parasitology: Dr K. D. PRASAD
- Pathology: (vacant)
- Pharmacology: (vacant)
- Physiology: (vacant)
- Surgery: (vacant)
- Veterinary Biochemistry: Dr R. L. PRASAD
- Veterinary Public Health: (vacant)

BUNDELKHAND UNIVERSITY

Jhansi, Uttar Pradesh 284003
Telephone: (517) 2320497; (517) 2320761
E-mail: info@bundelkhanduniv.org
Internet: www.bundelkhanduniv.org

Founded 1975
Affiliating

Vice-Chancellor: Dr SATYAVATI PANDEY RAHGIR
Registrar: Dr RADHEY SHYAM BANSAL
Librarian: Dr S. C. SROTIA

Library of 10,000 vols
Number of teachers: 434
Number of students: 38,000

DEANS

Faculty of Agriculture: Dr G. N. LODHI
Faculty of Arts: Dr V. S. SHUKLA
Faculty of Commerce: Dr N. S. SRIVASTAVA
Faculty of Education: Dr TAQDIR SINGH
Faculty of Law: M. P. DIXIT
Faculty of Medicine: Dr R. N. SRIVASTAVA
Faculty of Science: Dr R. K. DIXIT

There are 20 affiliated colleges

UNIVERSITY OF BURDWAN

Burdwan 713104, West Bengal
Telephone: (342) 2533913
Fax: (342) 2530452
E-mail: vcbu@satyam.net.in
Internet: www.bur.univ.ac.in

Founded 1960
Teaching and Affiliating
Languages of instruction: English, Bengali
Academic year: June to May

Chancellor: HE THE GOVERNOR OF WEST BENGAL
Vice-Chancellor: Prof. AMIT KUMAR MALLIK
Registrar: Dr S. M. DAN
Finance Officer: T. N. SARKAR
Director (Correspondence Courses): Dr H. BHATTACHARYYA
Librarian: SAMIR KUMAR DE (acting)

Library of 210,481 vols
Number of teachers: 205
Number of students: 3,293

Publications: *Bengali Journal*, *English Journal*, *History Journal*, *Journal of Mass Communication*, *Law Review*, *Philosophy Journal*, *Political Science Journal*, *Sanskrit Journal*, *Science Journal*, *Socio-Political Journal*, *University Annual Report*

PROFESSORS

BAGCHI, S., Chemistry
BAGCHI, S. B., Statistics
BANDOPADHYAY, D. N., English
BANDYOPADHYAY, M. K., Sanskrit
BANDYOPADHYAY, T. C., Zoology
BANERJEE, A. K., Economics
BANERJEE, C., Mathematics
BANERJEE, G., Mathematics
BANERJEE, K., Geography
BANERJEE, M., Chemistry
BASU, D. K., Philosophy
BASU, P. S., Botany
BASU, S., Bengali
BASU, S., Chemistry
BHATTACHARYYA, A., Philosophy
BHATTACHARYYA, A. K., Physics
BHATTACHARYYA, A. K., USIC
BHATTACHARYYA, A., Sanskrit
BHATTACHARYYA, G. N., Sanskrit
BHATTACHARAYYA, K., Chemistry
BHATTACHARAYYA, K., Mathematics
BHATTACHARAYYA, P. K., Botany
BHATTACHARYYA, R. P., Sanskrit
BISWAS, S. C., Library and Information Science
BISWAS, S. K., Commerce
CHAKRABARTI, T., Sanskrit
CHAKRABORTY, B., Bengali
CHAKRABORTY, C. S., Zoology
CHAKRABORTY, K., Bengali
CHAKRABORTY, N. D., Mathematics
CHAKRABORTY, P., Economics
CHAKRABORTY, P., Zoology
CHAKRABORTY, P. C., English
CHAKRABORTY, P. K., Economics
CHAKRABORTY, S., Bengali
CHAKRABORTY, S., Zoology
CHAKRABORTY, S. K., Mathematics
CHATTERJEE, K. K., English

Chatterjee, S. K., Institute of Science Education
Chattopadhyay, A., Statistics
Chattopadhyay, K. C., Mathematics
Chattopadhyay, N. C., Botany
Chattopadhyay, R. R., Bengali
Chaudhury, M. K., Bengali
Chaudhury, P. K., Zoology
Das, A. K., Chemistry
Das, P., Commerce
Das, T. K., Physics
Dasgupta, S. S., Physics
De, A. K., Bengali
De, G. S., Chemistry
De, N. K., Geography
Dutta, D. M., Business Administration
Ghosh, B., Sociology
Gupta, K., Botany
Gupta, L. N., Bengali
Hoque, A., Philosophy
Hui, A. K., English
Khan, G. C., Philosophy
Kundu, R. K., English
Kushari, D. P., Botany
Maharatna, A., Economics
Majumdar, G., Zoology
Mallik, A. K., Commerce
Mallik, P., Physics
Mallik, U. K., Commerce
Mitra, A., Sociology
Mitra, C., Geography
Mondal, K. K., Mathematics
Mondal, P. K., Philosophy
Mukherjee, A., Botany
Mukherjee, B., Sanskrit
Mukherjee, R. N., Mathematics
Mukhopadhyay, A. K., Botany
Mukhopadhyay, A. K., Chemistry
Mukhopadhyay, A. K., Political Science
Mukhopadhyay, R. N., Botany
Mukhopadhyay, S., Computer Science
Nandi, A. P., Zoology
Nandi, B., Botany
Pramanik, N. C., Political Science
Prasad, N., Geography
Ray, A. B., Political Science
Ray, M. K., English
Ruy, A., History
Roy, D., Business Administration
Roy, R. K., Physics
Roy, S., Zoology
Roy, S. K., Physics
Roy, S. K., Political Science
Roy Choudhury, S. K., Mathematics
Samad, A., Mathematics
Samanta, B. C., Physics
Samanta, L. K., Physics
Sarkar, A. K., Zoology
Sarkar, B. C., Physics
Sarkhel, J., Commerce
Sarma, P., Botany
Sengupta, S. K., Business Administration
Siddhanta, U. K., Instrumentation Centre
Singh, S. S., Law
Sinha, B. C., Hindi
Thakur, S., Chemistry

There are 101 affiliated colleges

ATTACHED INSTITUTES

Binoy Krishna Choudhury Rural Technology Centre: Dir Dr S. Chattopadhyay.

Institute of Science Education: Golapbag, Burdwan; Head Dr S. Chattopadhyay.

University Institute of Technology: Principal Dr M. N. Gupta.

UNIVERSITY OF CALCUTTA

Senate House, 87/1, College St, Kolkata, West Bengal 700 073
Telephone: (33) 22410071
Fax: (33) 22413222
E-mail: univlibrarian@caluniv.ac.in
Internet: www.caluniv.ac.in

Founded 1857
Teaching and Affiliating
Language of instruction: English
Academic year: July to June

Chancellor: Viren J. Shah
Vice-Chancellor: Prof. Asis Kumar Banerjee
Pro-Vice-Chancellors: Prof. Suranjan (Academic Affairs), Prof. Tapan Kumar Mukherjee (Business Affairs and Finance)
Registrar: Prof. Ujjwal Basu
Librarian: Dr Soumitra Sarkar

Library of 795,000 vols
Number of teachers: 667
Number of students: 300,000

Publications: *Calcutta Review* (4 a year), *UNICAL* (4 a year)

DEANS

Faculty of Agriculture and Veterinary Science: Prof. Mrinal Kanti Majumdar
Faculty of Arts: Prof. Rakhahari Chatterjee
Faculty of Commerce and Business Management: Prof. Ranajit Chakraborty
Faculty of Education, Journalism and Library Information Science: Prof. Arjun Dasgupta
Faculty of Engineering and Technology: Prof. Pranab Kumar Daspoddar
Faculty of Fine Arts, Music and Home Science: Prof. Diptis Sengupta
Faculty of Law: Prof. Imtiaz Gulam Ahmed
Faculty of Medicine, Nursing, Homeopathy, Ayurveda and Dental Science: Dr Manoj Kumar Bhattacharyya
Faculty of Science: Prof. Pradip Narayan Ghosh

PROFESSORS

University College of Agriculture (5 Ballygunge Circular Rd, Kolkata 700 019):

Basu, R. N.
Bhattacharyya, B.
Ghosh, K.
Gupta, S. K.
Majumdar, B. C.
Majumdar, M. K.
Sadhu, M. K.

University College of Arts (1 Reformatory St, Kolkata 700 027; tel. 2241-0071; fax (33) 2241-3222):

Acharya, S. N., Sanskrit
Alquadri, S. M. S., Ancient Indian History and Culture
Bandyopadhyay, A., History
Bandyopadhyay, B. N., Sociology
Bandyopadhyay, S., Ancient Indian History and Culture
Banerjee, A. K., Economics
Banerjee, H., History
Banerjee, H. K., Economics
Banerjee, M., Philosophy
Banerjee, S., Economics
Banerjee, S., English
Basu, R., Sanskrit
Bhattacharya, A., Ancient Indian History and Culture
Bhattacharya, A., Philosophy
Bhattacharya, B., Pali
Bhattacharya, K., Linguistics
Bhattacharyya, S. K., Sociology
Bhaumik, A. C., Museology
Burke, I. K., Ancient Indian History and Culture
Chakrabarti, B., Library and Information Science
Chakrabarti, D., English
Chakrabarti, R., Ancient Indian History and Culture
Chakrabarti, R., Philosophy
Chakrabarti, S., English
Chatterjee, R., Islamic History and Culture
Chatterjee, R., Political Science
Chattopadhyay, S.
Chaturvedi, J., Hindi
Chaudhuri, A., Economics
Chaudhuri, B., South and South-East Asian Studies
Choudhuri, S., Islamic History and Culture
Das, S., History
Dasgupta, A., Library and Information Science
Dasgupta, A., Economics
De, B. B., Ancient
Dutta, P. K., Political Science
Dutta Gupta, S., Political Science
Ganguly, M. K., Sanskrit
Ganguly, S. S., Bengali
Ghosh, D., Sanskrit
Ghosh, J., Bengali Language and Literature
Ghosh, P., South and South-East Asian Studies
Goswami, K. R., Philosophy
Gupta, C., Archaeology
Gupta, D., Philosophy
Khan, M., Bengali Language and Literature
Mahapatra, R., Tamil
Maitra, J., Ancient Indian History and Culture
Majumdar, M., Bengali Language and Literature
Mallik, A., Economics
Mukherjee, B., Political Science
Mukherjee, B. K., Bengali Language and Literature
Mukherjee, S. K., Museology
Mukhopadhyay, B. K., Bengali Language and Literature
Mukhopadhyay, S. K., Political Science
Nath, M. K., Linguistics
Pandey, C., Hindi
Paramanik, S. K., Sociology
Ray, A., Islamic History and Culture
Ray, J. K., History
Roy, A. K., South and South-East Asian Studies
Roy, D. K., Museology
Roy, S., English
Sanyal, J., English
Sanyal, K., Economics
Sen, K., Philosophy
Sen, P. K., Philosophy
Sen, R., Philosophy
Sen, S. K., Linguistics
Sengupta, S., Sanskrit
Sharma, A., Hindi
Shaw, S., Hindi
Sikdar, S. N., Economics
Taqi, Y. R., Urdi
Vasudevan, H. S., History

University College of Commerce (87/1 College St, Kolkata 700 073; tel. (33) 2241-0071; fax (33) 2241-3222):

Banerjee, B.
Banerjee, S.
Sinha, G. C.

University College of Law (51/1 Hazra Rd, Kolkata 700 019; tel. (33) 2475-5801):

Ahmed, I. G.

University College of Management (1 Reformatory St, Kolkata 700 027; tel. (33) 2479-1645):

Chakrabarti, R.
Dhar, S., Business Management
Khasnabis, R., Business Management

University College of Science (35 Ballygunge Circular Rd, Kolkata 700 019
92 Acharya Prafulla Chandra Rd, Kolkata 700 009):

Acharya, S. K., Pure Mathematics
Adhikary, M. R., Pure Mathematics
Bagchi, B., Applied Mathematics
Bandhyopadhyay, M. K., Geography
Banerjee, A., Chemistry

BANERJEE, A. B., Biochemistry
BANERJEE, D., Physics
BANERJEE, J., Chemistry
BANERJEE, M., Botany
BANERJEE, S. B., Zoology
BASU, A., Statistics
BASU, S. R., Geography
BHATTACHARYYA, A., Zoology
BHATTACHARYYA, A., Marine Science
BHATTACHARYYA, A. K., Biochemistry
BHATTACHARYYA, C., Geology
BHATTACHARYYA, D. K., Pure Mathematics
BHATTACHARYYA, M., Anthropology
BHATTACHARYYA, P. K., Physics
CHAKRABARTI, B. C., Pure Mathematics
CHAKRABARTI, C. G., Applied Mathematics
CHATTERJEE, A., Botany
CHATTERJEE, N. B., Zoology
CHATTERJEE, P. K., Psychology
CHATTERJEE, S. P., Physiology
CHATTOPADHYAY, D., Biochemistry
CHOUDHURI, P. K., Applied Mathematics
CHOWDHURY, U., Biophysics
CHOWDHURY, B., Anthropology
DAS, J., Pure Mathematics
DAS, J. N., Applied Mathematics
DAS, K. C., Physics
DAS, K. P., Applied Mathematics
DAS, T. K., Physics
DASCHOWDHURY, A. B., Anthropology
DASGUPTA, C. K., Biophysics
DASGUPTA, U., Biophysics
DATTA GUPTA, A. K., Zoology
DE, S. S., Applied Mathematics
GANGULY, S., Pure Mathematics
GHATAK, K. P., Electronics Science
GHOSH, C. K., Biochemistry
GHOSH, P. N., Physics
GHOSH, S., Botany
LAHIRI, P., Zoology
MAITY, B. R., Zoology
MALLICK, R., Botany
MANNA, B., Zoology
MONDAL, A., Biochemistry
MUKHERJEE, D., Geology
MUKHERJEE, M., Biochemistry
MUKHERJEE, P., Botany
MUKHERJEE, S., Botany
MUKHERJEE, S., Geology
MUKHOPADHYAY, A. S., Zoology
MUKHOPADHYAY, S. C., Geography
NANDA, D. K., Zoology
PAL, S. G., Zoology
PAN, N. R., Physics
PRAMANIK, A. K., Applied Mathematics
PURAKAYASTHA, R., Botany
RAY, S., Botany
ROY, R., Anthropology
ROYCHAUDHURY, P., Applied Mathematics
ROYCHOUDHURY, D., Electronics Science
ROYCHOWDHURY, A., Physics
ROYCHOWDHURY, P., Physics
ROYCHOWDHURY, R., Botany
SAHA, G. B., Psychology
SAHA, P. K., Geography
SAMAJPATI, N., Botany
SAMANTA, B. K., Geology
SANYAL, A. B., Biophysics
SARKAR, S. K., Physics
SEN, R. N., Applied Mathematics
SEN, S., Botany
SENGUPTA, A., Geology
SENGUPTA, D., Biochemistry
SIRCAR, P. K., Botany
THAKUR, A. R., Biophysics

University College of Technology:

BANDHYOPADHYAY, S., Computer Science
BANIK, A. K., Chemical Engineering
BASU, A. K., Chemical Technology
BASU, D. K., Applied Physics
BASU, P. K., Radiophysics and Electronics
BHATTACHARJEE, A. K., Computer Science
BHATTACHARYYA, D. K., Chemical Technology
BHATTACHARYYA, S., Chemical Engineering
BHATTACHARYYA, T. K., Chemical Technology
CHAKRABORTY, A. K., Applied Physics
CHAKRABORTY, A. N., Radiophysics and Electronics
CHATTERJEE, N. K., Chemical Technology
CHATTOPADHYAY, D., Radiophysics and Electronics
DAS, V., Polymer Science and Technology
DASGUPTA, A. K., Radiophysics and Electronics
DAS PODDAR, P. K., Chemical Technology
DATTA, A. K., Applied Physics
DATTA, A. N., Radiophysics and Electronics
DATTA, B. K., Chemical Engineering
GHOSH, P., Polymer Science and Technology
GUPTA, S. N., Polymer Science and Technology
LAHIRI, C. R., Chemical Technology
MAJUMDER, R. N., Chemical Technology
MITRA, N. K., Chemical Technology
MITRA, T. K., Applied Physics
MUKHOPADHYAY, A. K., Applied Physics
NATH, N. G., Radiophysics and Electronics
PARIA, B. B., Chemical Engineering
PARIA, H., Radiophysics and Electronics
PURKAIT, N. N., Radiophysics and Electronics
RAKSHIT, P. C., Radiophysics and Electronics
ROY, P., Chemical Engineering
ROY, S. K., Radiophysics and Electronics
SAHA, P. K., Radiophysics and Electronics
SEN, A. K., Radiophysics and Electronics
SENGUPTA, P. K., Polymer Science and Technology

UNIVERSITY COLLEGES

University Colleges of Agriculture: Kolkata; Sec. M. K. SENGUPTA.

University Colleges of Arts: Kolkata; f. 1954; Sec. Dr D. P. DE.

University Colleges of Commerce, Social Welfare and Business Management: Kolkata; f. 1954; Sec. Dr D. P. DE.

University Colleges of Education, Journalism and Library Science: Sec. Dr A. K. CHAKRABORTI.

University Colleges of Fine Arts, Music and Home Science: Sec. (vacant).

University Colleges of Law: Kolkata; f. 1909; Sec. M. K. NAG.

University Colleges of Medicine: Kolkata; f. 1957; Sec. Dr D. BAGCHI.

University Colleges of Science: Kolkata; f. 1954; Sec. M. K. SENGUPTA.

University Colleges of Technology: Kolkata; f. 1954; Sec. M. K. SENGUPTA.

CONSTITUENT COLLEGES

All India Institute of Hygiene and Public Health: Dir Dr B. N. GHOSH; see under Colleges.

Institute of Post-Graduate Medical Education and Research: 244 Acharyya J. C. Bose Rd, Kolkata 700 020; Dir Prof. D. SEN.

Presidency College: 86/1 College St, Kolkata; f. 1817; Principal (vacant).

Sanskrit College: Bankim Chatterjee St, Kolkata; f. 1824; Principal B. P. BHATTACHARYYA.

School of Tropical Medicine: Kolkata; Dir Dr B. D. CHATTERJEE.

There are also 37 professional colleges and 207 affiliated colleges

UNIVERSITY OF CALICUT

PO Calicut University, Malappuram 673635, Kerala
Telephone: (494) 2401144
Fax: (494) 2400269
E-mail: reg@unical.ac.in
Internet: www.unical.ac.in

Founded 1968

Teaching and Affiliating
State control
Languages of instruction: English, Malayaam
Academic year: June to March

Chancellor: HE THE GOVERNOR OF KERALA
Vice-Chancellor: Prof. SYED IQBAL HASNAIN
Pro-Vice Chancellor: Prof. M. SALIM
Registrar: Dr P. P. MOHAMED
Librarian: Dr ROSAMMA JOSEPH

Library of 90,900 vols
Number of teachers: 166 (University Depts), 5,920 (Affiliated Colleges)
Number of students: 275,000 (University Depts and Affiliated Colleges)

Publications: *Calicut University Research Journal* (2 a year), *Development Review* (2 a year), *University News* (quarterly)

DEANS

Faculty of Ayurveda: Dr P. K. WARRIER
Faculty of Commerce and Management Studies: Dr E. P. SAINUL ABIDEEN
Faculty of Dentistry: Dr M. HARINDRANATH
Faculty of Education: Dr K. P. MANOJ
Faculty of Engineering: Dr M. P. CHANDRA SEKHARAN
Faculty of Fine Arts: Dr VAYALA VASUDEVAN PILLAI
Faculty of Health Science: T. SANKARAN NAIR
Faculty of Homeopathy: Dr M. P. PRAKASAN
Faculty of Humanities: Dr D. P. NAIR
Faculty of Journalism: Dr SYED AMJAD AMAMED
Faculty of Languages and Literature: Dr IQBAL AHAMMAD
Faculty of Law: Prof. K. V. NARAYANIKUTTY
Faculty of Medicine: Dr R. VELAYUDHAN NAIR
Faculty of Science: Dr P. RAMESAN

HEADS OF DEPARTMENTS

Applied Zoology: Dr U. V. K. MOHAMED
Arabic: Dr E. K. AHAMEDKUTTY
Biotechnology: Dr M. V. JOSEPH
Botany: Dr N. NEELAKANTAN
Chemistry: Dr M. P. KANNAN
Commerce and Management Studies: Dr E. P. SAINUL ABIDEEN
Drama and Fine Arts: Dr VAYALA VASUDEVAN PILLAI
Economics: Dr D. PRABHAKARAN NAIR
Education: Dr P. KELU
English: Dr N. RAMACHANDRAN NAIR
Hindi: Dr G. GOPINATHAN
History: Dr S. M. MOHAMMED KOYA
Journalism: Dr C. D. CHAKKAPPAN
Library Science: M. BAVAKUTTY
Life Science: Dr V. K. SASIDHARAN
Malayalam: Dr M. M. PURUSHOTHAMAN NAIR
Mathematics: Dr V. KRISHNA KUMAR
Philosophy: Dr K. KANTHAMANI
Physical Education: S. MURALICHKARAN (Assistant Director in charge)
Physics: Dr K. NEELAKANDAN
Psychology: Dr ANITHA RAVINDRAN
Russian: Dr S. NIRMALA
Sanskrit: Dr N. V. P. UNNITHIRI
Statistics: Dr M. MANOHARAN
School of Distance Education: K. KUNHIKRISHNAN (Dir)
Academic Staff College: Dr T. K. NARAYANAN (Dir)
Adult Education and Extension Services: Dr K. KARUNAKARAN (Co-ordinator in Charge)

There are 146 affiliated colleges

CENTRAL AGRICULTURAL UNIVERSITY

Iroisemba, Imphal 795004, Manipur
Telephone: (385) 2415933
Fax: (385) 2415196
E-mail: snpuri04@yahoo.co.in

Founded 1993

Central university

Academic year: August to July (two semesters)

Chancellor: V. L. Chopra
Vice-Chancellor: Dr S. N. Puri
Registrar: Dr M. Premjit Singh

Library of 18,527 vols, 241 periodicals
Number of teachers: 103
Number of students: 437

DEANS

College of Agriculture: Prof. N. I. Singh
College of Fisheries: Dr M. L. Bhowmik
College of Home Science: Dr R. S. Raghuvanshi
College of Horticulture and Forestry: Prof. D. S. Rathore
College of Veterinary Science and Animal Husbandry: Dr H. C. Kalita

PROFESSORS

Bhattacharya, D., Soil Science and Agricultural Chemistry
Laishram, J. M., Plant Breeding and Genetics
Meitei, W. I., Horticulture
Nandeesha, M. C., Aquaculture
Raghuvanshi, R. S., Food and Nutrition
Rathore, D. S., Pomology
Singh, M. D., Animal Husbandry and Dairying
Singh, M. P., Agricultural Entomology
Singh, M. R. K., Plant Breeding and Genetics
Singh, N. I., Plant Pathology
Singh, N. R., Agricultural Economics
Singh, R. K. K., Soil Science and Agricultural Chemistry
Singh, Y. J., Agricultural Engineering

CHANDRA SHEKHAR AZAD UNIVERSITY OF AGRICULTURE AND TECHNOLOGY

Nawabganj, Kanpur 208002, Uttar Pradesh
Telephone: (512) 2294557
Fax: (512) 2210408
E-mail: csauknp@hotmail.com
Internet: www.csauk.org

Founded 1975
State control
Languages of instruction: Hindi, English
Academic year: July to June

Chancellor: HE The Governor of Uttar Pradesh
Vice-Chancellor: Dr P. K. Singh
Registrar: Dr R. S. Bisen
Librarian: Dr R. P. Singh

Library of 100,000 vols
Number of teachers: 318
Number of students: 1,187

DEANS

Faculty of Agriculture: Dr K. D. Upadhyay
Faculty of Home Science: Dr Rachel George
Faculty of Technology: Dr M. R. Verma

CHAUDHARY CHARAN SINGH HARYANA AGRICULTURAL UNIVERSITY

Hissar 125004, Haryana
Telephone: (1662) 237720
Fax: (1662) 234613

Founded 1970
State control
Languages of instruction: English, Hindi
Academic year: July to June

Chancellor: HE The Governor of Haryana
Vice-Chancellor: Sh. M. K. Miglani
Registrar: Dr M. S. Kuhad
Librarian: Sh. Prem Singh

Library of 287,130 vols
Number of teachers: 1,066
Number of students: 3,462

Publications: *HAU Journal of Research* (4 a year), *Thesis Abstracts* (4 a year), *Haryana Kheti* (monthly)

DEANS

College of Agricultural Engineering and Technology: Dr Pratap Singh
College of Agriculture: Dr Satyavir
College of Animal Sciences: Dr K. L. Raheja (Officiating)
College of Basic Sciences and Humanities: Dr R. C. Sihag
College of Home Science: Dr Savita Singal
College of Veterinary Science: Dr A. P. Singh
Postgraduate Studies: Dr R. K. Malik
Sports College: Dr K. S. Solanki

CHAUDARY CHARAN SINGH UNIVERSITY

Meerut 250005, Uttar Pradesh

Founded 1966 as Meerut University

Affiliating and Teaching
Languages of instruction: Hindi, English

Chancellor: HE The Governor of Uttar Pradesh
Vice-Chancellor: Dr B. B. L. Saxena
Registrar: Dr V. B. Bansal

Library of 102,064 vols
Number of students: 125,365

DEANS

Faculty of Agriculture: Dr P. K. Gupta
Faculty of Arts: Dr S. S. Sharma
Faculty of Commerce: Dr K. N. Nagar
Faculty of Education: Dr K. G. Sharma
Faculty of Law: O. P. Garg
Faculty of Medicine: Dr J. S. Mathur
Faculty of Science: Dr D. Banerjee

There are one constituent college and 61 affiliated colleges

CHAUDHARY DEVI LAL UNIVERSITY

Barnala Rd, Sirsa 125055, Haryana
Internet: www.cdluonline.net

Founded 2003

Teaching and Affiliating
Language of instruction: English
Academic year: July to May (three terms)

Departments of Biotechnology, Environmental Studies, Information Technology and Computer Education and Management Studies.

CHAUDHARY SARWAN KUMAR HIMACHAL PRADESH KRISHI VISHVAVIDYALAYA

Palampur 176062, Dist. Kangra, Himachal Pradesh

Telephone: (1894) 230511
Fax: (1894) 230565
E-mail: vc@hillagrc.ernet.org
Internet: www.hillagric.ernet.org

Founded 1978; fmrly Faculty of Agriculture of Himachal Pradesh University
State control
Language of instruction: English
Academic year: July to June

Chancellor: HE The Governor of Himachal Pradesh
Vice-Chancellor: Dr Manoranjan Kalia (acting)
Comptroller: M. C. Jublani (acting)
Registrar: Sanjeev Pathania
Librarian: Dr H. B. Singh (acting)

Library: library of 41,383 vols, 26,028 bound periodicals, 2,995 theses, 799 other items
Number of teachers: 363
Number of students: 805

Publications: *Annual Report*, *CSKHPKV Newsletter* (4 a year), *Himachal Journal of Agricultural Research* (2 a year), *Parvatiya Khetibari* (4 a year)

DEANS

College of Agriculture (Palampur): Dr P. C. Katoch (acting)
College of Basic Sciences: Dr S. K. Sharma
College of Home Science: Dr Manoranjan Kalia
College of Veterinary and Animal Sciences: Dr R. C. Katoch
Postgraduate Studies: Dr B. Prasad (acting)

ATTACHED REGIONAL RESEARCH STATIONS

Regional Research Centre, Bajaura: Bajaura, Dist. Kullu 175125, Himachal Pradesh; tel. (1905) 287235; fax (1905) 287235; Assoc. Dir B. S. Deor.

Regional Research Centre, Dhaulakuan: Dhaulakuan, Dist. Sirmour 173001, Himachal Pradesh; tel. (1794) 257421; fax (1794) 257421; Assoc. Dir H. L. Thakur.

Regional Research Centre, Kukumseri: Kukumseri, Dist. Lahoul and Spiti, Himachal Pradesh; tel. (1909) 222210; Assoc. Dir Vijay Singh Thakur.

CHHATRAPATI SHAHUJI MAHARAJ UNIVERSITY, KANPUR

Kalyanpur, Kanpur 208024, Uttar Pradesh
Telephone: (512) 2250301
Internet: www.kanpuruniversity.org

Founded 1966 as Kanpur University; present name 1997

Affiliating
State control
Languages of instruction: English, Hindi
Academic year: July to June

Chancellor: HE The Governor of Uttar Pradesh
Vice-Chancellor: Prof. Sarvagya S. Katiyar
Registrar: Dr R. S. Bansal
Librarian: Dr S. D. Misra

Library of 47,000 vols
Number of students: 220,000

DEANS

Faculty of Advanced Studies in Commerce, Business and Industrial Management: Dr A. P. Gupta
Faculty of Advanced Studies in Life Sciences: Dr L. C. Misra
Faculty of Advanced Studies in Social Sciences: Dr S. S. Awasthi
Faculty of Agriculture: Dr D. P. Sharma
Faculty of Arts: Dr M. M. Saxena
Faculty of Ayurvedic and Unani Medicine: Dr K. K. Thakral
Faculty of Commerce: Dr A. Narain
Faculty of Education: Dr K. M. Rai Saxena
Faculty of Engineering and Technology: Dr A. K. Vashistha
Faculty of Law: Sri Ramesh Charan
Faculty of Medicine: Dr R. K. Srivastava
Faculty of Science: Dr R. K. Nigam

COCHIN UNIVERSITY OF SCIENCE AND TECHNOLOGY

Cochin University PO, Cochin 682022, Kerala
Telephone: (484) 2577595
Fax: (484) 2575396

E-mail: register@cusat.ac.in
Internet: www.cusat.ac.in

Founded 1971
State control
Language of instruction: English
Academic year: July to April

Chancellor: HE THE GOVERNOR OF KERALA
Pro-Chancellor: THE MINISTER FOR EDUCATION, KERALA
Vice-Chancellor: Dr N. UNNIKRISHNAN
Registrar: Dr K. V. KUNHIKRISHNAN
Librarian: Dr M. D. BABY

Library of 82,000 vols, 200 periodicals
Number of teachers: 197
Number of students: 2,100

Publications: *Law Review*, *Marine Sciences Bulletin*, *Indian Manager*, *Management Information Service*, *Anuseelam*, *Cochin University News*, *Tejus* (univ. newsletter), *Statistical Methods*

DEANS

Faculty of Engineering: Dr BABU T. JOSE
Faculty of Environmental Studies: Dr A. MOHANDAS
Faculty of Humanities: Dr SHAMIM ALIYAR
Faculty of Law: Dr K. N. CHANDRASEKHARA PILLAI
Faculty of Marine Science: Dr R. DAMODARAN
Faculty of Medical Science: Dr C. K. SASIDHARAN
Faculty of Science: Dr K. P. RAJAPPAN NAIR
Faculty of Social Sciences: Dr D. RAJASENAN
Faculty of Technology: Dr K. G. BALAKRISHNAN

PROFESSORS

ALIYAR, S., Hindi
ARAVINDAKSHNAN, A., Hindi
BABU, T. J., Civil Engineering
BABU SUNDAR, S., Computer Application
BALACHAND, A. N., Physical Oceanography
BALAKRISHNAN, K. G., Electronics
CHACKO, J., Chemical Oceanography
CHANDRASEKHARAN, M., Biotechnology
CHANDRASEKHARAN, N. S., Legal Studies
CHANDRASEKHARAN PILLAI, K. N., Legal Studies
DAMODARAN, K. T., Marine Sciences
DAMODARAN, R., Marine Sciences
EASWARI, M., Hindi
FRANCIS, C. A., Management Studies
GEORGE, K. E., Polymer Science and Rubber Technology
GEORGE, K. K., Management Studies
GEORGE VARGHESE, K., Management Studies
GIRIJAVALLABHAN, C. P., Physics
GOPALAKRISHNA KURUP, P., Marine Sciences
HRIDAYANATHAN, C., Industrial Fisheries
JACOB, P. K., Computer Science
JATHAVEDAN, M., Mathematics
JOSEPH, R., Polymer Science and Rubber Technology
KORAKANDY, R., Industrial Fisheries
KRISHNAMURTHY, A., Mathematical Sciences
KRISHNANKUTTY, P., Ship Technology
KURIAKOSE, A. P., Polymer Science and Rubber Technology
KURIAKOSE, V. L., Physics
MADHUROADANA KENUP, B., Industrial Fisheries
MARY JOSEPH, T., Management Studies
MATHAI, E., Physics
MATHEW, K. T., Electronics
MATHEW, S., Industrial Fisheries
MATHEWS ABRAHAM, B., Civil Engineering
MOHAMMED YUSSUF, K., Applied Chemistry
MOHAN KUMAR, K., Atmospheric Science
MOHANAN, N., Hindi
MOHANAN, P., Electronics
MOHANDAS, A., Environmental Studies
MURALEEDHARAN NAIR, K. R., Statistics
MURUGESAN REDDIAR, K., German
NANDAKUMARAN, V. M., Photonics
NARAYANAN NAMPOOTHIRI, V. P., Photonics
PAVITHRAN, K. B., Management Studies
PHILIP, B., Marine Biology, Microbiology and Biochemistry
PHILIP, J., Instrumentation
PILLAI, P. R. S., Electronics
POULOSE JACOB, K., Computer Science
RADHAKRISHNAN, P., Photonics
RAJAN, C. K., Atmospheric Science
RAJAPPAN NAIR, K. P., Physics
RAJASENAN, D., Applied Economics
RAMACHANDRAN, A., Industrial Fisheries
RAMACHANDRAN NAIR, V. K., Statistics
RAVINDRA-NATHA MENON, N. R., Marine Sciences
RAM MOHAN, H. S., Marine Sciences
SABIR, M., Physics
SADASIVAN NAIR, G., Legal Studies
SAJAN, K., Marine Sciences
SALIH, M., Marine Biology, Microbiology and Biochemistry
SASIDHARAN, R., Hindi
SEBASTIAN, K. L., Applied Chemistry
SERALATHAN, P., Marine Geology and Geophysics
SHANMUGHAN, M., Hindi
SIVASANKARA PILLAI, V. N., Environmental Studies
SOMASEKHARAN NAIR, E. M., Ship Technology
SUDARSHANAN PILLAI, P., Management Studies
SUGUNAN, S., Applied Chemistry
SUKUMARAN NAIR, H. K., Applied Economics
SUKUMARAN NAIR, M. K., Applied Chemistry
SUNEETHA BAI, L., Hindi
THRIVIKRAMAN, T., Mathematical Sciences
UNNIKRISHNAN NAIR, N., Statistics
VALLABHAN, G., Photonics
VASUDEVAN, K., Electronics
VIJAYAKUMAR, K. P., Physics
WILSON, P. R., Management Studies
YUSUFF, M., Applied Chemistry

DAYALBAGH EDUCATIONAL INSTITUTE

Dayalbagh, Agra, Uttar Pradesh 282005
Telephone: (562) 2281545
Fax: (562) 2281226
E-mail: dei@sancharnet.in

Founded 1981
Academic year: July to June

President: Justice G. D. SAHGAL
Director: Prof. P. S. SATSANGI
Registrar: Dr P. K. SINHA

Library of 101,213 books
Number of teachers: 180
Number of students: 2,302

Publication: *Journal of Science and Engineering Research* (annually)

DEANS

Arts: Prof. CHANDAR KANTA
Commerce: Dr PRAMOD KUMAR
Education: Prof. SAHEB DAYAL
Engineering: Prof. S. B. RAO
Science: Prof. SATYA PRAKASH
Social Sciences: Dr POORNIMA JAIN

ATTACHED INSTITUTES

DEI Prem Vidyalaya Girls' Intermediate College: Principal M. DAS.

DEI Technical College: Principal P. P. DUA.

DEEN DAYAL UPADHYAY GORAKHPUR UNIVERSITY

Gorakhpur, Uttar Pradesh 273009
Telephone: (551) 2330767
Fax: (551) 2340459

Founded 1957 as Gorakhpur University; present name 1997
Teaching and Affiliating
Languages of instruction: Hindi, English
Academic year: July to April (two terms)

Chancellor: HE THE GOVERNOR OF UTTAR PRADESH
Vice-Chancellor: Prof. R. RAMAN PANDE
Registrar: MAHESH CHANDAR
Librarian: J. L. UPADHYAY

Library of 387,100 vols, 800 periodicals
Number of teachers: 300
Number of students: 115,000, including students of the colleges

DEANS

Faculty of Agriculture: Prof. V. S. SHUKLA
Faculty of Arts: Prof. A. K. MITTAL
Faculty of Commerce: Prof. I. A. ANSARI
Faculty of Education: Prof. R. D. SINGH
Faculty of Engineering and Technology: Prin.: Dr SATAYA SHEEL
Faculty of Law: Prof. O. P. TIWARI
Faculty of Medicine: Dr R. B. VERMA
Faculty of Science: Prof. K. PANDEY

There are four professional colleges and 82 affiliated colleges

UNIVERSITY OF DELHI

Delhi 110007
Telephone: (11) 27667725
Fax: (11) 27666350
E-mail: vcdu@vsnl.com
Internet: www.du.ac.in

Founded 1922
Central university
Languages of instruction: English, Hindi
Academic year: July to April (three terms)

Chancellor: VICE-PRESIDENT OF INDIA
Pro-Chancellor: CHIEF JUSTICE OF INDIA
Vice-Chancellor: Prof. DEEPAK NAYYAR
Registrar: Dr ATINDRA SEN
Librarian: M. L. SAINI

Library of 1,387,000 vols
Number of professors: 270
Number of students: 309,203

DEANS

Faculty of Applied Sciences and Humanities: Prof. RASHMI AGGARWAL
Faculty of Arts: Prof. K. SHAILIE
Faculty of Ayurvedic and Unani Medicine: Hkm M. A. LARI
Faculty of Education: Prof. SHYAM B. MENON
Faculty of Interdisciplinary and Applied Sciences: Prof. SHEELA SRIVASTAVA
Faculty of Law: Prof. PARMANAND SINGH
Faculty of Management: Prof. O. P. CHOPRA
Faculty of Mathematics: Prof. V. P. SRIVASTAVA
Faculty of Medical Sciences: Prof. B. K. JAIN
Faculty of Music and Fine Arts: Prof. SUNITA DHAR
Faculty of Planning and Administrative Reforms: Prof. V. S. VARMA
Faculty of Science: Prof. S. P. TEWARI
Faculty of Social Sciences: Prof. T. K. V. SUBRAMANIAM
Faculty of Technology: Prof. G. S. BRAR

CONSTITUENT COLLEGES

Atma Ram Sanatan Dharam College: New Delhi; f. 1959.

Bharati Mahila College: New Delhi; f. 1971.

Daulat Ram College: Delhi 7; f. 1960.

Gargi College: New Delhi; f. 1967.

Guru Gobind Singh College of Commerce: Delhi; f. 1984.

Gyan Devi Salwan College: New Delhi; f. 1970.

Hamdard College of Pharmacy: New Delhi; f. 1972.

Hamdard Tibbi College: Delhi; f. 1977.

Hans Raj College: Delhi; f. 1948.
Hindu College: Delhi; f. 1922.
Indraprastha College for Women: Delhi; f. 1925.
Institute of Home Economics: Delhi; f. 1969.
Janki Devi Mahavidyalaya: New Delhi; f. 1959.
Jesus and Mary College: New Delhi; f. 1968.
Kalindi College: New Delhi; f. 1967.
Kamla Nehru College: New Delhi; f. 1964.
Lady Irwin College: New Delhi; f. 1950.
Lady Shri Ram College for Women: New Delhi; f. 1956.
Lakshmibai College: Delhi; f. 1965.
Maitreyi College: New Delhi; f. 1967.
Mata Sundri College: New Delhi; f. 1967.
Moti Lal Nehru College: New Delhi; f. 1964.
P.G.D.A.V. College: New Delhi; f. 1957.
Rajdhani College: New Delhi; f. 1964.
Ramjas College: Delhi; f. 1917.
Satyawati Co-educational College: Delhi; f. 1972.
Shaheed Bhagat Singh College: New Delhi; f. 1967.
Shivaji College: New Delhi; f. 1961.
Shri Aurobindo College: New Delhi; f. 1972.
Shri Guru Teg Bahadur Khalsa College: Delhi; f. 1951.
Shri Ram College of Commerce: Delhi; f. 1926.
Shyam Lal College: Delhi; f. 1964.
Shyama Prasad Mukherjee College: New Delhi; f. 1969.
Sri Venkateswara College: New Delhi; f. 1961.
St Stephen's College: Delhi; f. 1922.
Swami Shardhanand College: Delhi; f. 1967.
Vivekanand Mahila College: Delhi; f. 1970.
Zakir Hussain College: Delhi; f. 1948.

UNIVERSITY MAINTAINED COLLEGES

Deshbandhu College: Kalkaji, New Delhi; f. 1952.
Dyal Singh College: New Delhi; f. 1959.
Kirori Mal College: Delhi; f. 1954.
Miranda House for Women: Delhi; f. 1948.
School of Correspondence Courses and Continuing Education: Delhi; f. 1962.
University College of Medical Sciences: Delhi; f. 1971.
Vallabhbhai Patel Chest Institute: see under Research Institutes.
College of Vocational Studies: New Delhi; f. 1972.

GOVERNMENT MAINTAINED COLLEGES

Ayurvedic and Unani Tabbia College: New Delhi; f. 1974.
College of Art: New Delhi; f. 1972.
College of Nursing: New Delhi; f. 1946.
College of Pharmacy: New Delhi; f. 1971.
Delhi College of Engineering: Kashmeri Gate, Delhi 6; f. 1959.
Delhi Institute of Technology: Delhi; f. 1983.
Lady Hardinge Medical College: New Delhi; f. 1949.
Maulana Azad Medical College: New Delhi; f. 1958.

DEV SANSKRITI VISHWAVIDYALAYA

Gayatrikunj, Shantikunj, Hardwar 249411, Uttaranchal
Telephone: (1334) 261367
Fax: (1334) 260723
E-mail: administrator@dsvv.org
Internet: www.dsvv.org

Founded 2002
Academic year: July to May

Chancellor: Dr PRANAV PANDYA
Vice-Chancellor: Dr S. P. MISHRA
Registrar: GOURISHANKAR SHARMA

Library of 25,000 vols
Number of teachers: 15
Number of students: 136

HEADS OF DEPARTMENTS

Foreign Languages: B. P. UPADHYAY
Holistic Health Management: Dr VANDANA SRIVASTAVA
Indian Culture: Dr PRAVEEN JOSHI
Psychology: Prof. O. P. MISHRA
Theology: DURGESH DIWEDI
Yogic Science: SURESH BARNWAL

Faculties of Education, Health, Sadhana and Self-Employment

DEVI AHILYA VISHWAVIDYALAYA

Nalanda Parishar, Indore 452001, Madhya Pradesh
Telephone: (731) 2527532
Internet: www.dauniv.ac.in

Founded 1964 as University of Indore
Teaching and Affiliating
Languages of instruction: Hindi, English
Private control
Academic year: July to May (three terms)

Chancellor: HE THE GOVERNOR OF MADHYA PRADESH
Vice-Chancellor: Prof. A. A. ABBASSI
Registrar: Dr S. K. BEGDE
Librarian: Dr G. H. S. NAIDU (deputy)

Library of 117,210 vols
Number of teachers: 1,251
Number of students: 35,394

DEANS

Faculty of Arts: Dr C. DEOTALE
Faculty of Ayurved: Dr P. P. AGRAWAL
Faculty of Commerce: Dr D. D. MUNDRA
Faculty of Dentistry: Dr H. C. NEEMA
Faculty of Education: Dr S. VAIDYA
Faculty of Electronics: Dr RAJKAMAL
Faculty of Engineering: (vacant)
Faculty of Engineering Sciences: (vacant)
Faculty of Life and Home Sciences: Dr R. BHARADWAJ
Faculty of Management Studies: Dr R. D. PATHAK
Faculty of Medicine: Dr K. BHAGAWAT
Faculty of Pharmacy: Dr S. C. CHATURVEDI
Faculty of Physical Education: (vacant)
Faculty of Science: Dr K. K. PANDEY
Faculty of Social Sciences and Law: Dr B. Y. LALITHAMA

There are 65 affiliated colleges

DIBRUGARH UNIVERSITY

Dibrugarh 786004, Assam
Telephone: (373) 2370231
Fax: (373) 2370323
E-mail: registrar@dibru.ernet.in
Internet: www.dibru.ernet.in

Founded 1965
Affiliating and teaching
State control
Languages of instruction: Assamese, English
Academic year: January to December

Chancellor: HE THE GOVERNOR OF ASSAM
Vice-Chancellor: Dr K. PATHAK
Registrar: Dr K. K. DEKA
Librarian (vacant)

Library of 159,271 vols
Number of teachers: 181 (University depts)
Number of students: 58,850 (including affiliated colleges)

Publications: *The North Eastern Research Bulletin*, *Padartha Vigyan Patrika* (physics, in Assamese, annually), *Dibrugarh University Journal of English Studies*, *Assam Economic Journal*, *Anthropology Bulletin*, *Assam Statistical Review*, *Life Sciences Bulletin*, *Mathematical Forum*, *Dibrugarh University Journal of Education*, *Journal of Historical Research*, *Pharmray*

HEADS OF DEPARTMENTS

Anthropology: Dr S. SENGUPTA
Applied Geology: Dr D. MAJUNDAR
Assamese: Dr A. KONWAR
Chemistry: Dr P. K. GOGOI
Commerce: Dr A. SAHA
Economics: Dr J. K. GOGOI
Education: Dr D. BARA TALUKDAR
English: Dr B. K. DANTA
History: Dr A. HUSSAIN
Life Sciences: Dr M. ISLAM
Mathematics: Dr B. R. SARMA
Petroleum Technology: Dr M. DAS
Pharmaceutical Sciences: Dr S. DAS
Physics: Dr N. C. SHARMA
Political Science: Dr A. U. YASIN
Sociology: Dr B. N. BARTNAKUR
Statistics: Dr B. GOGOI

There are 121 affiliated colleges

DR B. R. AMBEDKAR OPEN UNIVERSITY

Prof. G. Ram Reddy Marg, Rd 46, Jubilee Hills, Hyderabad 500033, Andhra Pradesh
Telephone: (40) 23544830
Fax: (40) 23544830
E-mail: info@braou.ac.in
Internet: www.braou.ac.in

Founded 1982
Academic year: July to June

Chancellor: HE THE GOVERNOR OF ANDHRA PRADESH
Vice-Chancellor: Prof. G. V. SUBRAHMANYAM
Registrar: P. KRISHNA RAO

Library of 29,912 vols
Number of teachers: 63
Number of students: 63,575

DEANS

Faculty of Arts: Prof. R. VASUNANDAN
Faculty of Commerce: Prof. Y. S. KIRANMAYI
Faculty of Science: Prof. M. RAMACHANDRAIAH
Faculty of Social Sciences: Prof. A. VIDYAVATHI

PROFESSORS

CHANDRASEKHARA RAO, V., Library Science
DAMAYANTHI DEVI, I., Zoology
GNANAPRASUNA, K., Physics
HAYAT, S., Urdu
JADHAO, Y., Hindi
KIRANMAYI, Y. S., Business Management
KOTESWARA RAO, K., Commerce
KUPPUSWAMY RAO, K., Mathematics
NETHI, G., Zoology
PRASAD, V. S., Public Administration
PUSHPA RAMAKRISHNA, C., English
RAJASHEKAR REDDY, S. V., Geology
RAMACHANDRAIAH, G., Chemistry
RAMACHANDRAIAH, M., Botany
RAMAIAH, P., Economics
SRINIVASACHARYULU, G., Evaluation
SUNDARA RAO, B., Economics
UMAPATHI VARMA, Y. V., Educational Technology
VASUNADAN, R., Telugu

VENKAIAH, V., Business Management
VIDYAVATHI, A., Sociology

There are 140 Study Centres located in the state of Andhra Pradesh

DR BABASAHEB AMBEDKAR MARATHWADA UNIVERSITY

Aurangabad 431004, Maharashtra
Telephone: (240)2400491
Fax: (240) 2400431
E-mail: registrar@bamuniversity.org
Internet: www.bamuniversity.org

Founded 1958
Teaching and Affiliating
Languages of instruction: English, Marathi
Academic year: June to April (two terms)

Chancellor: HE THE GOVERNOR OF MAHARASHTRA
Vice-Chancellor: K. P. SONAWANE
Registrar: Dr G. G. SURASE
Librarian: Dr SNEHLATA M. MOHAL

Library of 304,473 vols(incl. affiliated colleges):
Number of teachers: 3,275
Number of students: 130,534

Publications: *Annual Report*, *University Journal*, *University Handbook*, *Rabindranath Tagore Lecture Series*

DEANS

Arts: N. Z. WAGH
Ayurveda: D. V. KULKARNI
Commerce: K. G. LAGHANE
Education: M. P. SURWASE
Engineering: S. D. DESHMUKH
Homeopathy: Dr S. M. DESARADA
Management Studies: Dr SYED ABDUL MANNAN
Medicine: Dr R. M. AMBULGEKAR
Physical Education: V. B. PATHRIKAR
Science: Dr A. D. MOHEKAR
Social Science: D. V. PAWAR

There are 146 affiliated colleges

DR BABASAHEB AMBEDKAR OPEN UNIVERSITY

Govt Bungalow 9, Nr Dafnala, Shahibaug, Ahmedabad 380003, Gujarat
Telephone: (79) 22869690
Fax: (79) 22869691
E-mail: baou@sancharnet.in

Founded 1994
State control
Academic year: August to July

Chancellor: HE THE GOVERNOR OF GUJARAT
Vice-Chancellor: Dr AMRAPALI M. MERCHANT
Registrar: S. H. BAROT

Faculties of Arts and Humanities, Management, Science and Social Sciences

There are 69 study centres.

DR BABASAHEB AMBEDKAR TECHNOLOGICAL UNIVERSITY

Tal Mangaon, District Raigad, Lonere 402103, Maharashtra
Telephone: (2140) 275101

Founded 1989

Chancellor: HE THE GOVERNOR OF MAHARASHTRA
Vice-Chancellor: Dr S. D. AWALE
Registrar: Dr VIJAY BABU

Departments of Chemical Engineering, Chemistry, Computer Engineering, Electrical Engineering, Electronics and Telecommunications Engineering, English, Mathematics, Mechanical Engineering, Petrochemical Engineering and Physics.

DR BALASAHEB SAWANT KONKAN KRISHI VIDYAPEETH

Ratnagiri, Dapoli 415712, Maharashtra
Telephone: (2358) 282411
Fax: (2358) 282074
E-mail: root@kkv.ren.nic.in

Founded 1972
State control
Academic year: July to May
Language of instruction: English

Chancellor: HE THE GOVERNOR OF MAHARASHTRA
Vice-Chancellor: Dr S. S. MAGAR
Registrar: R. N. KULKARNI
Librarian: S. M. RODGE

Library of 40,000 vols

Publication: *Newsletter*

DEANS

Faculty of Agricultural Engineering: Dr A. G. PAWAR
Faculty of Agriculture: Dr V. B. MEHTA
Faculty of Fisheries: Dr P. C. RAJE

DR BHIM RAO AMBEDKAR UNIVERSITY

Senate House, Paliwal Park, Agra 282004, Uttar Pradesh
Telephone: (562) 2152373
Fax: (562) 2152118
E-mail: uccibs@sancharnet.in
Internet: www.brauagra.ac.in

Founded 1927 as Agra University; present name 1995
Affiliating and Teaching
Languages of instruction: English, Hindi
Academic year: July to May (one term)

Chancellor: HE THE GOVERNOR OF UTTAR PRADESH
Vice-Chancellor: Dr G. C. SAXENA
Registrar: Dr B. L. ARYA
Hon. Librarian: Dr SUNDER LAL

Library of 169,027 vols
Number of students: 123,000

DEANS

Faculty of Agriculture: Dr J. P. VERMA
Faculty of Commerce: Dr K. K. BANSAL
Faculty of Education: Dr CHANDER HANS PATHAK
Faculty of Fine Arts: Dr S. BHARGAVE
Faculty of Homeopathic Medicine: Dr MOTI LAL SHUKLA
Faculty of Home Science: Dr H. KUMAR
Faculty of Law: Dr V. K. KAUSHIK
Faculty of Medicine: Dr U. C. MISRA
Faculty of Science: Dr JAI SHANKER

CONSTITUENT INSTITUTES

Dau Dayal Institute of Vocational Education: Agra.

Deen Dayal Upadhyay Institute of Rural Development: Agra.

Institute of Basic Sciences: Agra.

Institute of Home Science: Agra; library: library of 10,218 vols; 10 teachers; Dir Dr H. KUMAR (acting).

Institute of Social Sciences: Agra; library: library of 18,000 vols; 14 teachers; Dir Dr S. V. PANDEY.

K.M. Institute of Hindi Studies and Linguistics: Agra; library: library of 39,000 vols; Dir Dr JAI SINGH NEERAD.

Lalit Kala Sansthan (Institute of Fine Arts): Agra.

School of Life Sciences: Agra.

Seth Padam Chandjain Institute of Commerce, Business Management and Economics: Agra; Dir Dr M. R. BANSAL (acting).

There are 65 affiliated colleges

DR HARI SINGH GOUR UNIVERSITY

Gour Nagar, University Campus, Sagar, Madhya Pradesh 470003
Telephone: (7582) 222574
Fax: (7582) 223236
E-mail: sagaruniversity@hotmail.com

Founded 1946
Teaching, Affiliating and Residential
Languages of instruction: Hindi, English
Academic year: July to April (two terms)

Chancellor: HE THE GOVERNOR OF MADHYA PRADESH
Vice-Chancellor: Prof. SANTOSH KUMAR
Registrar: Dr S. K. BEGDE
Librarian: MUKESH KUMAR SAHU (acting)

Library of 309,625 vols
Number of teachers: 213
Number of students: 17,545

Publication: *Madhya Bharti—Research Journal* (annually, Hindi and English)

DEANS

Faculty of Arts: Prof. G. DWIVEDI
Faculty of Commerce: Prof. A. K. GANGELE
Faculty of Education: Prof. V. D. JHA
Faculty of Engineering: Prof. P. P. RODDAY
Faculty of Law: Prof. H. N. GIRI
Faculty of Life Sciences: Prof. S. SAHAI
Faculty of Science: Prof S. C. GARG
Faculty of Social Sciences: Prof. V. D. JHA
Faculty of Technology: Prof. S. P. VYAS

There are 70 affiliated colleges

DR PANJABRAO DESHMUKH AGRICULTURE UNIVERSITY

Krishi Nagar, Akola 444104, Maharashtra
Telephone: (724) 2258200
Fax: (724) 2258219
E-mail: root@pdkv.mah.nic.in

Founded 1969
State control
Languages of instruction: English, Marathi
Academic year: July to June

Chancellor: HE THE GOVERNOR OF MAHARASHTRA
Pro-Chancellor: THE MINISTER FOR AGRICULTURE, MAHARASHTRA
Vice-Chancellor: Dr S. A. NIMBALKAR
Registrar: RAM CHIMURKAR

Library of 140,500 vols
Number of teachers: 650
Number of students: 3,650

Publications: *PKV Research Journal* (2 a year), *Post Graduate Institute Research Journal* (annually), *Krishi Patrika* (Marathi, monthly), *PKV Newsletter* (monthly)

DEANS

Faculty of Agricultural Engineering: Dr D. S. KHARCHE
Faculty of Agriculture: Dr V. D. PATIL

CONSTITUENT COLLEGES

College of Agricultural Engineering: Akola; f. 1970; Assoc. Dean Dr D. S. KHARCHE.

College of Agriculture: Akola; f. 1950; Assoc. Dean V. D. PATIL.

College of Agriculture: Nagpur; f. 1906; Assoc. Dean Dr C. S. CHOUDHARI.

College of Forestry: Akola; f. 2001; Assoc. Dean Dr J. S. ZOPE.

College of Horticulture: Akola; f. 2001; Assoc. Dean Dr V. K. MAHORKAR.

Postgraduate Institute: Akola; f. 1970; Assoc. Dean Dr R. B. SOMANI.

There are two affiliated colleges and 19 research stations

DR YASHWANT SINGH PARMAR UNIVERSITY OF HORTICULTURE AND FORESTRY

Nauni (Solan) 173 230, HP

Telephone: (1792) 252219
Fax: (1792) 252242
E-mail: vc@yspuhf.hp.nic.in
Internet: www.ysparmaruniversity.org

Founded 1985
State control
Academic year: August to July

Chancellor: V. S. KOKJE
Vice-Chancellor: Dr S. S. NEGI
Registrar: PADAM SINGH CHAUHAN
Librarian: Dr S. D. SHARMA

Library of 55,000 vols
Number of teachers: 258
Number of students: 542

DEANS

College of Forestry: Dr V. K. MISHRA
College of Horticulture: Dr J. M. SINGH CHAUHAN

PROFESSORS

AGNIHOTRI, A. K., Directorate of Research
AGNIHOTRI, R. P., Regional Horticultural Research Station, Jachh
AMIT NATH, Entomology and Apiculture
ANAND, S. A., Pomology
BADAYALA, S. D., Regional Horticulture and Forestry Research Station, Bhota
BHARDWAJ, L. N., Mycology and Plant Pathology
BHARDWAJ, N. R., Seed Technology and Production Centre
BHARDWAJ, S. D., Silviculture and Agroforestry
BHARDWAJ, S. P., Regional Horticulture Research Station, Mashobra
BHARDWAJ, S. S., Mycology and Plant Pathology
BHARDWAJ, S. V., Biotechnology
CHAUHAN, K. C., Tree Improvement and Genetic Resources
CHAUHAN, N. S., Forest Products
CHAUHAN, PREM SAGAR, Regional Horticultural Research Station, Mashobra
FARMAHAN, H. L., Pomology
GARG, R. C., Directorate of Extension Education
GAUTAM, D. R., Pomology
GULERIA, S. P. S., Regional Horticulture Research Station
GUPTA, P. R., Entomology and Apiculture
JANDAIK, C. L., Mycology and Plant Pathology
JULKA, N. K., Pomology
KANBID, B. R., Social Sciences
KAKKAR, K. L., Regional Horticultural Research Station, Mashobra
KARKARA, V. K., Regional Research Station, Dhaulakuan
KASHYAP, A. S., Horticulture Research Station, Kandaghat
KASHYAP, S. D., Directorate of Research
KAUSHAL, P., Regional Centre (NAEB)
KHAN, M. L., Entomology and Apiculture
KHOKHAR, U. U., Pomology
KHURANA, D. K., Tree Improvement and Genetic Resources
KOHLI, U. K., Vegetable Crops
KORLA, B. N., Vegetable Crops
MAHAJAN, S., Computer and Information Centre
NARANG, M. L., Entomology and Apiculture
NAYITAL, R. K., Silviculture and Agroforestry
REHALIA, A. S., Pomology
SEHGAL, R. N., Tree Improvement and Genetic Resources
SHARMA, A. K., Basic Sciences
SHARMA, D. R., Biotechnology
SHARMA, I. P., Directorate of Research
SHARMA, J. P., Regional Horticultural Research Station, Bajaura
SHARMA, J. R., Regional Horticultural Research Station, Mashobra
SHARMA, R. K., Seed Technology and Production Centre
SHARMA, R. C., Mycology and Plant Pathology
SHARMA, S. D., Fruit Breeding and Genetic Resources
SHARMA, S. K., Vegetable Crops
SHARMA, SUDESH KUMAR, Mycology and Plant Pathology
SHARMA, Y. D., Floriculture and Landscaping
SHARMA, Y. P., Directorate of Extension Education
SHIRKOT, C. K., Basic Sciences
SINGH, N. B., Forest Products
SINGH, R. P., Pomology
SOOD, G., Regional Horticultural Research Station, Jachh
SOOD, S. K., Directorate of Extension Education
THAKUR, G. C., Directorate of Extension Education
THAKUR, M. C., Vegetable Crops
VERMA, A. K., Entomology and Apiculture
VERMA, T. D., Entomology and Apiculture

DRAVIDIAN UNIVERSITY

Chitoor District, Kuppam 517425, Andhra Pradesh

Telephone: (8570) 278220
Fax: (8570) 278230

Founded 1997

Teaching, Residential and Affiliating
Academic year: July to June

Chancellor: HE THE GOVERNOR OF ANDHRA PRADESH
Vice-Chancellor: Prof. R. SRI HARI
Registrar: Dr S. DAMODARA NAIDU

Library of 25,000 vols
Number of students: 165.

FAKIR MOHAN UNIVERSITY

Vyasa Vihar, Balasore 756019, Orissa

Telephone: (6782) 254480
Fax: (6782) 254881

Founded 1999
Academic year: July to May

Chancellor: HE THE GOVERNOR OF ORISSA
Vice-Chancellor: Prof. SUKADEV NANDA
Registrar: Dr HEMANT KUMAR PARIJA

Library of 2,143 vols
Number of students: 23,542

There are 61 affiliated colleges.

GANDHIGRAM RURAL INSTITUTE

Gandhigram 624302, Dindigul District, Tamil Nadu

Telephone: (451) 2452371
Fax: (451) 2454466
E-mail: gricc@rsnl.com
Internet: www.ruraluniv.org

Founded 1956, university status 1976
Central Government control
Language of instruction: English
Academic year: July to June

Chancellor: Sri BHAIRON SINGH SHEKHAWAT
Vice-Chancellor: Dr G. PANKAJAM
Registrar: Dr P. KANNIAPPAN
Controller of Examinations: Dr M. SUNDARAVADIVELU
Finance Officer: Sri N. KARUNAKARAN
Deputy Registrar (Academic): Dr A. P. A. JUSILA KIRUBAVATHY
Deputy Registrar (Development): Sri B. ARUNACHALAM
Librarian: N. ARUMUGAM (Deputy Librarian)

Library of 100,673 vols, 320 periodicals
Number of teachers: 118
Number of students: 2,057

Publications: *Annual Report*, *GRI News* (monthly), *Journal of Extension and Research* (2 a year)

DEANS

Agriculture and Animal Husbandry: Dr T. RENGANATHAN
English and Foreign Languages: Dr M. R. KUBENDRAN
Rural Development: Dr A. SURIAKANTHI
Rural Health and Sanitation: Dr S. PONNURAJ
Rural Oriented Sciences: Dr R. BALASUBRAMANIAN
Rural Social Sciences: Dr G. PALANITHURAI
Tamil, Indian Languages and Rural Arts: Dr G. PANKAJAM (acting)

HEADS OF DEPARTMENTS

Adult and Continuing Education and Extension Education: Dr A. SURIAKANTHI
Agriculture and Animal Husbandry: Dr T. T. RENGANATHAN
Applied Research: Dr M. A. SUDHIR
Biology: Dr C. THILAGAVATHI DANIEL
Chemistry: Dr N. S. NAGIARAJAN
Computer Science and Applications: Dr K. SOMASUNDARAM
Co-operation: Dr B. SUBBURAJ
Economics: Dr P. SUMANGIALA
English: Dr M. R. KUBENDRAN
Futurology: Dr K. THANGIAVEL
Gandhian Thought and Peace Science: Dr S. WILLIAM BASKARAN (acting)
Home Science: Dr N. KAMALAMMA
Mathematics: Dr K. THANGIAVEL
Physical Education: (vacant)
Physics: Dr R. BALASUBRAMANIAN
Political Science and Development Administration: Dr G. PALANITHURAI
Rural Development: Dr A. SURIAKANTHI
Rural Health and Sanitation: Dr S. PONNURAJ
Rural Industries and Management: Dr N. THILLAINAYAGIAM
Rural Technology Centre: Dr R. UDAYAKUMAR (Dir)
Sociology: Dr S. GIURUSAMY
Tamil: Dr M. KURUVAMMAL

GAUHATI UNIVERSITY

Gauhati 781014, Assam

Telephone: (361) 2570415
Fax: (361) 2570133
E-mail: mcsarma@rediffmail.com
Internet: www.gu.nic.in

Founded 1948

Teaching, Residential and Affiliating
Language of instruction: English
Academic year: July to May (three terms)

Chancellor: HE THE GOVERNOR OF ASSAM
Vice-Chancellor: Dr G. N. TALUKDAR
Registrar: Dr MADHAB C. SARMA
Librarian: B. C. GOSWAMI

Library of 517,000 vols
Number of teachers: 281
Number of students: 118,213

DEANS

Faculty of Arts: Prof. M. BORA
Faculty of Commerce: Prof. G. C. DEKA
Faculty of Engineering: Prof. D. BHATTACHARJEE
Faculty of Law: Prof. N. SANAJAOBA
Faculty of Medicine: Dr P. D. BORA
Faculty of Science: Prof. M. M. DAS

HEADS OF DEPARTMENTS

Anthropology: Dr B. K. MEDHI
Arabic: Dr R. K. CHAUDHARY

Assamese: Dr L. Saikia Bora
Bengali: U. R. Bhattacharjee
Biotechnology: Dr A. K. Handique
Botany: Dr S. P. Borah
Chemistry: Dr K. G. Bhattacharyya
Commerce: Dr G. C. Deka
Communication and Journalism: Dr K. K. Barman
Computer Science: Dr A. K. Mahanta
Economics: Dr R. D. Baruah
Education: Dr S. Das
Electronics Science: P. Datta
English: R. K. Dev Goswami
English Language Teaching: A. Tamuli
Environmental Science: Dr D. C. Goswami
Folklore: Dr K. K. Bhattacharjee
Foreign Languages: Dr G. Jha
Geography: Dr M. M. Das
Geology: Dr A. D. Patgiri
Hindi: Dr B. N. Roychoudhury
History: Dr R. Bezbarua
Law: Dr N. S. Singh
Library and Information Science: Dr N. Lakhar
Linguistics: Dr J. P. Tamuley
Management of Business Administration: Prof. M. Kakati
Mathematics: Prof. T. K. Duta
Modern Indian Languages: Dr U. Deka
Persian: Dr R. Ahmed (acting)
Philosophy: Dr S. Sarma
Physics: Dr M. Devi
Political Science: Prof. M. Hussain
Psychology: Dr Indrani Phukan
Sanskrit: Prof. M. Borah
Statistics: Dr D. C. Nath
University Science of Instrumentation Centre: Dr G. Dutta Mujumdar
Zoology: Prof. A. Dutta

CONSTITUENT COLLEGE

University Law College: Gauhati; Principal Dr B. K. Chakraborty.

ATTACHED RESEARCH INSTITUTES

Population Research Centre: Hon. Dir Dr D. C. Nath.

Women's Studies Research Centre: Dir Dr Archana Sarma (acting).

There are 194 affiliated colleges

GOA UNIVERSITY

Sub Post Office Goa University, Taleigao Plateau, 403203, Goa
Telephone: (832) 2451375
Fax: (832) 2451184
E-mail: vc@unigoa.ernet.in
Internet: www.goacom.com/unigoa

Founded 1985
Academic year: June to April

Vice-Chancellor: Prof. P. S. Zacharias
Registrar: Prof. Jayant S. Budkuley
Librarian: P. V. Konnur

Library of 120,000 vols
Number of students: 7,080

DEANS

Faculty of Engineering and Architecture: Dr A. R. Naik
Faculty of Languages and Literature: Dr A. K. Joshi
Faculty of Life Science and Environment: Prof. D. J. Bhat
Faculty of Management Studies: Prof. A. Sreekumar
Faculty of Medicine: Prof. V. G. Dhume
Faculty of Natural Science: Prof. P. R. Sarode
Faculty of Social Sciences: Prof. A. V. Afonso

GOVIND BALLABH PANT UNIVERSITY OF AGRICULTURE AND TECHNOLOGY

Udham Singh Nagar, Pantnagar 263145 Uttar Pradesh
Telephone: (5944) 233640
Fax: (5944) 233473
E-mail: vc@gbpuat.ernet.in
Internet: www.gbpuatindia.org

Founded 1960
Languages of instruction: English, Hindi
State control
Academic year: July to June (two terms)

Chancellor: HE The Governor of Uttar Pradesh
Vice-Chancellor: Dr P. L. Gautam
Registrar: Dr D. C. Thapliyal
Librarian: Dr S. P. Jain

Library of 349,356 vols
Number of teachers: 783
Number of students: 3,166

Publications: *Indian Farmers Digest* (monthly), *Kisan BHARTI* (monthly), *Pantnagar Journal of Research* (2 a year)

DEANS

Faculty of Agribusiness Management: Dr V. P. S. Arora
Faculty of Agriculture: Dr R. V. Singh
Faculty of Basic Sciences and Humanities: Dr B. N. Johan
Faculty of Fisheries: Dr A. P. Sharma
Faculty of Forestry: Dr M. C. Nautiyal
Faculty of Home Science: Dr Rachel George
Faculty of Postgraduate Studies: Dr D. K. Gupta
Faculty of Technology: Dr K. N. Shukla
Faculty of Veterinary and Animal Sciences: Dr Amresh Kumar

There are 10 constituent colleges and 70 teaching departments

GUJARAT AGRICULTURAL UNIVERSITY

Sardar Krushinagar 385506, District Banaskantha
Telephone: (2748) 278222
Fax: (2748) 278261
E-mail: vc@gauskn.guj.nic.in
Internet: gau.guj.nic.in

Founded 1972
Academic year: July to March

Chancellor: Sundarsingh Bhandari
Vice-Chancellor: Dr M. H. Mehta
Registrar: Dr H. N. Kher

Library of 22,490 vols
Number of teachers: 1,336
Number of students: 2,181

Publications: *G. A. U. News* (4 a year), *G. A. U. Research Journal* (2 a year)

DEANS

Faculty of Agricultural Engineering and Technology: Dr S. C. B. Siripurapu
Faculty of Agriculture: Dr S. R. S. Dange (acting)
Faculty of Dairy Science: Dr R. S. Sharma
Faculty of Fisheries Science: Dr A. Y. Desai (acting)
Faculty of Forestry and Horticulture: Dr B. M. Patel (acting)
Faculty of Home Science: Dr M. M. Patel (acting)
Faculty of Veterinary Science: Dr M. B. Pande (acting)
Post-Graduate Research: Dr R. P. S. Ahlawat

CONSTITUENT COLLEGES

Aspee College of Home Science: Sardar Krushinagar; Prin. Dr M. M. Patel (acting).

Aspee College of Horticulture and Forestry: Navsari; Prin. Dr B. M. Patel (acting).

B. A. College of Agriculture: Anand; Prin. Dr D. J. Patel.

College of Agricultural Engineering and Technology: Junagadh; Prin. Dr S. C. B. Siripurapu.

College of Agriculture, Junagadh: Prin. Dr D. D. Malavia.

College of Agriculture, Sardar Krushinagar: Prin. Dr S. R. S. Dange (acting).

College of Fisheries Science: Veraval; Prin. Dr A. Y. Desai (acting).

College of Veterinary Science and Animal Husbandry, Anand: Prin. Dr M. B. Pande (acting).

College of Veterinary Science and Animal Husbandry, Sardar Krushinagar: Prin. Dr M. C. Desai.

Mansukhlal Chhaganlal College of Dairy Science: Anand; Prin. Dr R. S. Sharma.

N. M. College of Agriculture: Navsari; Prin. Dr H. N. Vyas.

GUJARAT AYURVED UNIVERSITY

Chanakya Bhavan, Jamnagar, Gujarat 361008
Telephone: (288) 2676854
Fax: (288) 2555966
E-mail: info@ayurveduniversity.com
Internet: www.ayurveduniversity.com

Founded 1967
Affiliating and teaching
Languages of instruction: Gujarati, Hindi
Languages of instruction: English, Sanskrit
Academic year: June to April (two terms)

Chancellor: HE The Governor of Gujarat
Vice-Chancellor: Dr P. N. V. Kurup
Registrar: Rajendrasinh M. Jhala (acting)
Director of Pharmacy: Dr G. L. Atata (acting)
Dean of Faculty: Prof. Gurdipsingh (acting)
Librarian: S. M. Jani

Library of 28,950 vols
Number of teachers: 219
Number of students: 2,071

Publications: *Ayu* (research at the University, monthly), *Traditional Medicine International* (4 a year), *News Letter* (monthly).

GUJARAT UNIVERSITY

Navrangpura, Ahmedabad 380009, Gujarat
Telephone: (79) 26301341
Fax: (79) 26302654
Internet: www.gujaratuniversity.org.in

Founded 1949
Teaching and Affiliating
Languages of instruction: Gujarati, Hindi, English
Academic year: June to April (two terms)

Chancellor: HE The Governor of Gujarat
Vice-Chancellor: Prof. A. U. Patel
Pro-Vice-Chancellor: Prof. Chaitanya Khambholja
Registrar: M. P. Jadia
Librarian: Ramanbhai L. Patel

Library: Libraries of 334,110 vols
Number of teachers: 3,075
Number of students: 153,379

DEANS

Faculty of Arts: Prof. K. B. Desai
Faculty of Commerce: Principal: K. K. Shah
Faculty of Engineering and Technology: Prof. H. V. Trivedi
Faculty of Law: Principal: R. S. Desai
Faculty of Medicine: Dr H. P. Bhalodiya

Faculty of Science: Principal: R. G. BHATT

There are 224 affiliated colleges and 14 recognized institutions (some listed under Research Institutes)

GUJARAT VIDYAPITH

Ashram Rd, Ahmedabad 380014, Gujarat
Telephone: (79) 27541148
Fax: (79) 27542547
E-mail: gvpahd@vsnl.com
Internet: www.gujaratvidyapith.org

Founded 1920, university status 1963
Languages of instruction: Gujarati, Hindi
Academic year: June to April

Chancellor: RAVINDRABHAI VARMA
Vice-Chancellor: Dr ARUNKUMAR DAVE
Registrar: Dr RAJENDRA KHIMANI (acting)
Librarian: NAVALSINH VAGHELA

Library of 515,854 vols
Number of teachers: 102
Number of students: 1,410

Publication: *Vidyapith* (3 a year)

DEANS

Education: Dr ILA NAIK
Social Sciences: Dr USHA UPADHYAY

PROFESSORS

DUBE, M., Hindi
NAIK, I., Education
PATEL, M., Education
UPADHYAY, U., Gujurati
VORA, S., Gandhian Thought and Peace Research

GULBARGA UNIVERSITY

Gulbarga 585106, Karnataka
Telephone: (8472) 445446
Fax: (8472) 445927
E-mail: reggug@rediffmail.com
Internet: www.gulbargauniversity.kar.nic.in

Founded 1980
State (Govt of Karnataka) control
Languages of instruction: English, Kannada
Academic year: June to March

Chancellor: Sri KURSHEED ALAM KHAN
Vice-Chancellor: Prof. V. B. COUTINHO
Registrar: Sri KANWARPAL
Librarian: Dr R. B. GADDAGIMATH

Library of 180,980 vols
Number of students: 18,314

DEANS

Faculty of Arts: Dr D. B. NAIK
Faculty of Commerce: Dr RAJNALKAR LAXMAN
Faculty of Education: Prof. SYEDA AKTHAR
Faculty of Engineering and Technology: Dr C. R. ACHARAYALU
Faculty of Law: Dr J. S. PATIL
Faculty of Medicine: Dr S. RAMBHIMAIAH
Faculty of Science and Technology: Dr Y. F. NEELGUND
Faculty of Social Science: Dr M. S. KALLUR

There are 160 affiliated colleges, 35 university departments and postgraduate centres in Bellary, Bidar, Raichur and Sandur

GURU GHASIDAS UNIVERSITY

Bilaspur 495009, Chhattisgarh
Telephone: (7752) 260283
Fax: (7752) 260352
Internet: gguniversity.nic.in

Founded 1983

Vice-Chancellor: Prof. J. L. GUPTA
Registrar: SONMONI BORAH
Librarian: Prof. J. S. DANGI

HEADS OF DEPARTMENTS

Adult Education: Dr RANU SHUKLA
Anthropology: Prof. B. M. MUKHERJEE
Biotechnology: Dr RAGINI GOTHALWAL
Commerce: Prof. L. M. MALVIYA
Computer Science: Dr A. K. SAXENA
Economics: Prof. ANILLA GUPTA
English: ANURAG CHOUHAN
Forestry and Environmental Science: Dr RASHMI AGRAWAL
Hindi: Dr HEMLATA MAHESHWAR
History: Dr P. K. SHUKLA
Information Technology: Dr ANURAG SHRIVASTAVA
Journalism: Dr GOPA BAGCHI
Library Science: Dr BRAJESH TIWARI
Management: Prof. HARISH KUMAR
Mathematics: Prof. S. P. SINGH
Pharmaceutical Science: Prof. J. S. DANGI
Physical Education: SHARADA KASHYAP
Physics and Electronics: Dr P. K. BAJPAI
Political Science: Dr ANUPAMA SAXENA
Rural Technology: Dr M. S. K. KHOKHAR
Social Work: Dr S. V. S. CHAUHAN

ATTACHED INSTITUTES

Chhattisgarh Institute of Medical Sciences: tel. (7752) 254300; fax (7752) 501684; f. 2001; Dean Prof. ANIL SARANGI

PROFESSORS

BADGAIYA, Y. D.
BEHARA, P. K., Biochemistry
CHHABRA, B., Anaesthesia
DHURIYA, A., Anatomy
HAJARI, S. K., Anatomy
JAINA, R. S., Orthopaedics
KAR, C. R., Surgery
MITRA, J. P., Microbiology
PANDA, B. K., Surgery
PATIL, S. K. B., Biochemistry
PATLE, D. R., Surgery
RATH, S. K., Obstetrics and Gynaecology
SARANGI, A., Dean
SHARMA, D. K., Physiology
SINGH, P. C., Venerology and Dermatology
SINGH, P. D., Pharmacology

Institute of Technology: Dir Prof. S. N. SAHA.

GURU GOBIND SINGH INDRAPRASTHA UNIVERSITY

Kashmere Gate, Delhi 110006Telephone: (11) 23869313
Fax: (11) 23865941
E-mail: mail@ipu.edu
Internet: ipu.ac.in

Founded 1998
Teaching and Affiliating
Academic year: August to July

Chancellor: VIJAI KAPOOR
Vice-Chancellor: Prof. K. K. AGGARWAL
Registrar: Prof. NALIN KUMAR SHASTREE
Librarian: A. K. KATNA

Library of 15,690

DEANS

School of Architecture and Planning: Prof. M. B. SAXENA
School of Basic and Applied Sciences: Prof. SAROJ AGGARWAL
School of Biotechnology: Prof. P. C. SHARMA
School of Chemical Technology: Prof. D. V. GUPTA
School of Information Technology: Prof. YOGESH SINGH
School of Law and Legal Studies: Prof. NOMITA AGGARWAL
School of Management Studies: Prof. AJAY PANDIT

GURU JAMBESHWAR UNIVERSITY

Delhi Rd, Hisar 125001, Haryana
Telephone: (1662) 263101
Fax: (1662) 276240
E-mail: gju_tech@yahoo.com
Internet: www.gju.ernet.in

Founded 1995

Chancellor: HE THE GOVERNOR OF HARYANA
Vice-Chancellor: VISHNU BHAGWAN
Registrar: D. K. KASNIA
Librarian: Prof. M. S. TURAN

Library of 34,563 vols, 178 periodicals

DEANS

Faculty of Engineering and Technology: Prof. J. K. SHARMA
Faculty of Information Technology and Computer Science: Prof. M. S. TURAN
Faculty of Management Studies: Prof. M. S. TURAN
Faculty of Media Studies: Prof. B. K. KUTHIALA
Faculty of Non-Conventional Sources of Energy and Environment Science: Prof. C. P. KAUSHIK
Faculty of Pharmaceutical Sciences: Prof. A. S. DHAKE
Faculty of Religious Studies: Prof. B. K. KUTHIALA
Faculty of Science and Technology: Prof. J. K. SHARMA

HEADS OF DEPARTMENTS

Advertising Management: Prof. B. K. KUTHIALA
Applied Chemistry: Prof. J. K. SHARMA
Applied Mathematics: Dr KULDEEP BANSAL
Applied Physics: Prof. NAVAL KISHORE
Applied Psychology: Prof. M. S. TURAN
Biotechnology: Dr ASHOK CHAUDHARY
Business Economics: Prof. M. S. TURAN
Business Management: Prof. M. S. TURAN
Communication Management and Technology: Dr MANOJ DAYAL
Computer Science and Engineering: Dr DHARMINDER KUMAR
Environment Science and Engineering: Prof. C. P. KAUSHIK
Food Processing and Technology: Dr B. S. KHATKAR
Institute of Engineering and Technology: Prof. J. K. SHARMA (Dir)
Pharmaceutical Sciences: Prof. A. S. DHAKE
Printing Technology: Prof. J. K. SHARMA

GURU NANAK DEV UNIVERSITY

Amritsar 143005, Punjab
Telephone: (183) 2258802
Fax: (183) 2258820
Internet: www.gnduonline.org

Founded 1969
Affiliating and Teaching; campuses at Gurdaspur, Jalandhar, Ladhewali and Punjab
Autonomous, partly funded by state government
Languages of instruction: English, Hindi, Punjabi
Academic year: July to June

Chancellor: HE THE GOVERNOR OF PUNJAB
Vice-Chancellor: Dr SURENDER PAL SINGH
Registrar: Dr R. S. BAWA

Library of 390,036 vols
Number of teachers: 2,991 (including external staff)
Number of students: 98,850 (including external students)

Publications: *Amritsar Law Journal* (annually), *Annual Report*, *Calendar* (annually), *Guru Nanak Journal of Sociology* (2 a year), *Indian Journal of Quantitative Economics* (2 a year), *Journal of Management Studies* (annually), *Journal of Regional History* (annually), *Journal of Sikh Studies* (English, 2 a year), *Journal of Sports Traumatology and Allied Sports*

Science (annually), *Khoj Darpan* (Punjabi, 2 a year), *Personality Study and Group Behaviour* (annually), *Perspectives on Guru Granth Sahib* (annually), *Pradhikrit* (Hindi, annually), *PSE Economic Analyst* (English, 2 a year), *Punjab Journal of English Studies* (annually), *Punjab Journal of Politics* (2 a year), *University Samachar* (quarterly)

HEADS OF TEACHING FACULTIES

Faculty of Agriculture and Forestry: Dr. S. S. JOHL
Faculty of Applied Sciences: Prof. M. P. S. ISHER
Faculty of Arts and Social Sciences: Prof. R. S. SANDHU
Faculty of Economics and Business: Dr PARAMJIT KAUR DHINDSA
Faculty of Education: Dr JEEVAN JYOTI
Faculty of Engineering and Technology: Dr HARDEEP SINGH
Faculty of Humanities and Religious Studies: Dr JASWINDER KAUR DHILLON
Faculty of Languages: Dr H. S. BEDI
Faculty of Law: KULDEEP SINGH
Faculty of Life Sciences: Prof. S. K. GARG
Faculty of Music and Fine Arts: Dr BHAGWANT KAUR
Faculty of Physical Education: Dr KANWALJIT SINGH
Faculty of Physical Planning and Architecture: Dr S. S. BEHL
Faculty of Sciences: Dr R. K. BEDI
Faculty of Sport Medicine and Physiotherapy: Dr JASPAL SINGH

HEADS OF DEPARTMENTS

Applied Chemical Sciences and Technology: Dr HARKAMALJIT SINGH
Applied Chemistry: Dr M. P. MAHAJAN
Applied Physics: Dr S. S. SEKHON
Architecture: Prof. PARAMJIT SINGH
Biotechnology: Dr PRABHJEET SINGH
Botanical and Environment Sciences: Dr RENU KUMARI
Business and Commerce: Dr AMARJIT SINGH SIDHU
Chemistry: Dr RAKESH KUMAR MAHAJAN
Computer Science and Engineering Science: Dr HARDIP SINGH
Electronics Technology: Prof. DERICK ANGLES
English: Dr GURUPDESH SINGH
Food Science and Technology: Dr DALBIR SINGH SOGI
Foreign Languages: Dr P. S. SHARMA
Guru Nanak Studies: Dr BALWANT SINGH DILLON
Guru Ram Dass Postgraduate School of Planning: Prof. B. R. BATRA
Hindi: Dr SUDHA RANI
History: Dr RADHA RANI
Human Genetics and Human Biology: Dr A. S. BHANWAR
Laws: Dr MOHINDER DEEP SINGH
Library and Information Science: Dr AMRIT PAL
Mathematics: Dr OM PARKASH
Microbiology: Dr BHUPINDER SINGH CHADDA
Molecular Biology and Biochemistry: Dr JATINDER SINGH
Music: Dr BHAGWANT KAUR
Pali, Sanskrit and Prakrit: Dr RENU BALA
Pharmaceutical Sciences: Dr GAJENDRA SINGH
Physical Education: Dr SUKHDEV SINGH
Physics: Dr KULWANT SINGH
Political Science: Dr JAGROOP SINGH
Psychology: Dr SUNITA GUPTA
Punjab School of Economics: Dr PARAMJEET KAUR DHINDSA
School of Punjabi Studies: Dr MAJIT PAL KAUR
Sociology: Dr MANMOHAN SINGH GILL
Sports Medicine and Physiotherapy: Dr JASPAL SINGH
Urdu and Persian: Dr BARKAT ALI
Zoology: Dr PUSHPINDER KAUR

There are 107 affiliated colleges

UNIVERSITY OF HEALTH SCIENCES, ANDHRA PRADESH

Vijayawada 520008, Andhra Pradesh
Telephone: (866) 2451206
Fax: (866) 2450463

Founded 1986

Residential and Teaching
Language of instruction: English
State control
Academic year: June to June

Chancellor: HE THE GOVERNOR OF ANDHRA PRADESH
Vice-Chancellor: Prof. GURNURKAR SHAM SUNDER
Registrar: Dr S. NARASIMHA REDDY
Librarian: K. SRINIVASA RAO

Library: Library in process of formation
Number of teachers: 3,000
Number of students: 9,000 undergraduate, 3,000 postgraduate

Publications: *UHS News* (quarterly), *University Information and Employment*

Faculties of Dental Sciences, Indian Systems of Medicine, Medical Laboratory Technology, Modern Medicine, Nursing, Nutrition and Physiotherapy

There are 103 affiliated colleges.

HEMCHANDRACHARYA NORTH GUJARAT UNIVERSITY

University Rd, POB 21, Patan 384265, Gujarat
Telephone: (2766) 230427
Fax: (2766) 231917
E-mail: vc@ngu.ac.in
Internet: www.ngu.ac.in

Founded 1986
State control
Language of instruction: Gujarati
Academic year: June to April

Chancellor: HE THE GOVERNOR OF GUJARAT
Vice-Chancellor: Dr M. M. PATEL
Registrar: B. N. SHAH
Librarian: M. K. PRAJAPATI

Library of 42,000 vols
Number of teachers: 1,829
Number of students: 85,665

Publications: *Udichya* (every 2 weeks), *Anart* (annually)

DEANS

Faculty of Arts: Dr P. J. PATEL
Faculty of Commerce: Prin.: N. N. SHAH
Faculty of Education: Dr J. H. PANCHOLI
Faculty of Engineering: H. R. DARE
Faculty of Homeopathy: Prin.: JAGNNATHAN
Faculty of Law: Prin.: P. N. THAKAR
Faculty of Management Studies: Dr B. A. PRAJAPATI
Faculty of Pharmacy: Prin.: MADHABHAI M. PATEL
Faculty of Rural Studies: SARTENBHAI DESAI
Faculty of Science: Dr M. I. PATEL

There are 132 affiliated colleges

HEMVATI NANDAN BAHUGUNA GARHWAL UNIVERSITY

Srinagar (Garhwal) 246174, Uttaranchal
Telephone: (1368) 252167
Fax: (1368) 252174
E-mail: root@hnbgugrw.ren.nic.in
Internet: www.hnbgu.in

Founded 1973, fmrly Garhwal University, renamed 1989
Teaching and Affiliating
State control
Languages of instruction: Hindi, English
Academic year: July to May

Chancellor: HE THE GOVERNOR OF UTTAR PRADESH
Vice-Chancellor: Dr N. NATARAJAN (acting)
Registrar: C. S. MEHTA
Hon. Librarian: Prof. B. S. SEMWAL

Library of 280,000 vols
Number of teachers: 280
Number of students: 100,000 (incl. colleges)

DEANS

Faculty of Agriculture: Prof. N. D. TODARIYA
Faculty of Arts: Prof. B. M. KHANDURI
Faculty of Ayurveda: Dr PUJA BARDWAJ
Faculty of Commerce: Prof. ALOK SAKLANI
Faculty of Education: Prof. K. B. BUDHORI
Faculty of Engineering: Dr M. L. DEWAL
Faculty of Law: Dr S. K. MITTAL
Faculty of Medicine: Dr A. N. MEHROTRA
Faculty of Non-Formal Education: Prof. A. MISRA
Faculty of Science: Prof. R. D. GAUR

There are three constituent colleges and 49 affiliated colleges

HIDAYATULLAH NATIONAL LAW UNIVERSITY

Raipur 492001, Chhattisgarh
Telephone: (771) 5080114
Fax: (771) 5080118
E-mail: registrar@hnluraipur.com
Internet: www.hnluraipur.com

Founded 2003

Vice-Chancellor: Prof. JOSE P. VERGHESE
Director, Bilaspur Centre: T. V. RAMAKRISHNAN

Schools: Constitutional Governance; Administration of Criminal Justice; International Legal Studies; Human Sciences; Science, Technology and Sustainable Development; Continuing and Clinical Legal Education; regional centre in Bilaspur.

HIMACHAL PRADESH UNIVERSITY

Summer Hill, Shimla 171005, Himachal Pradesh
Telephone: (177) 2830890
Fax: (177) 2830775
E-mail: webhpu@hp.nic.in
Internet: hpuniv.nic.in

Founded 1970

Affiliating and Teaching
State control
Languages of instruction: English, Hindi
Academic year: July to May

Chancellor: HE THE GOVERNOR OF HIMACHAL PRADESH
Vice-Chancellor: Prof. L. R. VERMA
Registrar: ASHOK SHARMA
Librarian: R. C. DATTA

Library of 188,402 vols
Number of teachers: 258
Number of students: 3,678

DEANS

Faculty of Ayurveda: Dr J. P. S. OBEROI
Faculty of Commerce and Management Studies: Prof. MUNEET KUMAR
Faculty of Dental Sciences: Prof. S. C. SHARMA
Faculty of Education: Prof. BUDH PRAKASH
Faculty of Engineering and Technology: Prin.: R. E. C. HAMIRPUR
Faculty of Languages: Prof. KISHAN KUMAR
Faculty of Life Sciences: Prof. L. R. VERMA
Faculty of Medical Sciences: Dr R. C. SHARMA
Faculty of Performing and Visual Arts: Prof. C. L. VERMA

Faculty of Physical Science: Prof. R. C. SHARMA
Faculty of Social Sciences: Prof. D. K. MALHOTRA

There are 59 affiliated colleges and institutions

UNIVERSITY OF HYDERABAD

Central University PO, Hyderabad 500046, Andhra Pradesh
Telephone: (40) 23010500
Fax: (40) 23010145
E-mail: yakkala@uohyd.ernet.in
Internet: www.uohyd.ernet.in

Founded 1974

Central university
State control
Language of instruction: English
Academic year: July to April

Chief Rector: HE THE GOVERNOR OF ANDHRA PRADESH
Chancellor: Justice P. N. BHAGWATI
Vice-Chancellor: Dr KOTA HARINARAYANA
Registrar: Dr Y. NARASIMHULU
Librarian: E. RAMA REDDY

Library of 257,000 vols
Number of teachers: 200
Number of students: 2,000

Publications: *Newsletter* (2 a year), *Annual Report*

DEANS

School of Chemistry: Prof. E. D. JEMMIS
School of Humanities: Prof. PROBAL DASGUPTA
School of Life Sciences: Prof. T. SURYANARAYANA
School of Management Studies: Prof. A. A. WAQIF
School of Mathematics and Computer and Information Sciences: Prof. R. TANDON
School of Performing Arts, Fine Arts and Communication: Prof. E. HARIBABU
School of Physics: Prof. S. N. KAUL
School of Social Sciences: Prof. D. NARASIMHA REDDY

INDIRA GANDHI KRISHI VISHWA VIDYALAYA

Krishak Nagar, Raipur 492006, Madhya Pradesh
Telephone: (771) 2443166
Fax: (771) 2442131
Internet: www.geocities.com/igkvin

Chancellor: HE THE GOVERNOR OF CHHATTISGARH
Vice-Chancellor: Dr C. R. HAZRA.

INDIRA GANDHI NATIONAL OPEN UNIVERSITY

Maidan Garhi, New Delhi 110068
Telephone: (11) 26862707
Fax: (11) 26862312
Internet: www.ignou.ac.in

Founded 1985

Central university
Autonomous control
Languages of instruction: English, Hindi
Academic year: January to December

Vice-Chancellor: Prof. H. P. DIKSHIT
Pro-Vice-Chancellor: Prof. S. C. GARG
Registrar: Prof. S. P. NARANG
Librarian: Dr SIBHA BRATA GHOSH

Library: Central library of 80,000 vols, 500 periodicals
Number of teachers: 255
Number of students: 594,227

Publications: *Indian Journal of Open Learning* (2 a year), *Newsletter* (3 a year)

DIRECTORS

School of Communication: Prof. MADHULIKA KAUSHIK
School of Computer and Information Science: Prof. MANOHAR LAL
School of Continuing Education: Prof. G. THOMAS
School of Education: Prof. S. V. S. CHAUDHARY
School of Health Sciences: Dr A. K. AGARWAL
School of Humanities: Prof. P. N. PANDIT
School of Management Studies: Prof. B. B. KHANNA
School of Sciences: Prof. S. S. HASAN
School of Social Sciences: Prof. KAPIL KUMAR

INDIRA KALA SANGIT UNIVERSITY

Khairagarh 491881, Chhattisgarh
Telephone: (7820) 234232
Fax: (7820) 234108
E-mail: umusart@sancharnet.in
Internet: www.mp.nic.in/kghuniv

Founded 1956

Teaching and Affiliating
Languages of instruction: Hindi, English
Academic year: July to April (two terms)

Chancellor: HE THE GOVERNOR OF CHHATTISGARH
Vice-Chancellor: Prof. INDRANI CHAKRAVARTI
Registrar: PHANI BHUSHAN TRIVEDI
Deputy Librarian: RAMESH PATEL

Library of 44,000 vols, 41 periodicals, 90 MSS
Number of teachers: 586
Number of students: 9,680

Publications: *Shiv Mangalam*, *Bharat Bhashyam*, *Bhatkhande Smriti Granth*, *Kala Saurabh*, *Sangit Suryodaya*, *Meri Dakshin Bharat*, *Ki Sangit Yatra*

DEANS

Faculty of Arts: Prof. R. K. SHRIVASTAVA
Faculty of Dance: Prof. MANDAVI SINGH
Faculty of Folk Music and Arts: Prof. S. MOHAMMED
Faculty of Music: Prof. R. K. SONI
Faculty of Visual Arts: Prof. S. K. SHRIVASTAVA

There are 46 affiliated colleges

JADAVPUR UNIVERSITY

PO Jadavpur University, Kolkata 700032
Telephone: (33) 24735339
Fax: (33) 24137121
E-mail: anb@jufs.ernet.in
Internet: www.jadavpur.edu

Founded 1955

Residential and Teaching
Language of instruction: English
Academic year: July to June (two terms)

Chancellor: HE THE GOVERNOR OF WEST BENGAL
Vice-Chancellor: Prof. Dr A. N. BASU
Registrar: R. BANDYOPADHYAY
Chief Librarian (vacant)

Library of 482,000 vols, including periodicals
Number of teachers: 661
Number of students: 7,990

Publications: *Essays and Studies* (2 a year), *Journal of International Relations* (annually), *Journal of Philosophy* (2 a year), *Journal of Comparative Literature* (annually), *Journal of History* (annually), *Journal of the Department of Bengali* (annually)

DEANS

Faculty of Engineering and Technology: Prof. Dr S. KR. SANYAL
Faculty of Science: Dr DIPAK CHANDRA GHOSH
Faculty of Arts: Prof. Dr A. KR. BANERJEE

HEADS OF DEPARTMENTS

Architecture: Prof. S. MUKHERJEE
Bengali: Prof. PINAKESH CHANDRA SARKAR
Chemical Engineering: Prof. TAPAS DUTTA
Chemistry: Prof. SUBHAS CHANDRA BERA
Civil Engineering: Prof. SAKTI RANJAN BHATTACHARYA
Comparative Literature: SIBAJI BANDYOPADHYAY
Construction Technology: Prof. SUBHAJIT SARASWATI
Computer Science and Engineering: Prof. BIJAN BEHARI BHOWMIK
Economics: Dr SUSMITA RAKSHIT
English: MALABIKA SARKAR
Electrical Engineering: Prof. SHYAMAL GOSWAMI
Electronics and Telecommunications Engineering: Prof. RABINDRA NATH NANDI
Film Studies: SANJAY MUKHERJEE
Food Technology and Biochemical Engineering: UTPAL RAY CHAUDHURI
Geological Sciences: Prof. Dr SUDIPTA SENGUPTA
History: Dr KUNAL CHATTOPADHYAY
International Relations: Prof. Dr S. GHOSH
Instrumentation Engineering: R. BANDYOPADHYAY
Library and Information Science: Prof. A. CHATTERJEE
Life Science and Biotechnology: Prof. SUKUMAR CHATTOPADHYAY
Mathematics: Prof. ARUN KUMAR GHOSH
Mechanical Engineering: Prof. SAMIR KUMAR SAHA
Metallurgical Engineering: Prof. BIMAL CHAUDHURI
Philosophy: SREELEKHA DUTT
Physical Education: P. DEBNATH
Physics: Prof. Dr DHIRANJAN RAY
Power Plant Engineering: AMITAVA DUTT
Production Engineering: BALENDRA NATH LAHIRI
Pharmaceutical Technology: Prof. Dr CHANDANA SENGUPTA
Printing Engineering: ARUN KUMAR PAL
Sanskrit: ABHIJIT GHOSH

CO-ORDINATORS OF INTERDISCIPLINARY COURSES

Bioengineering and Science (M.Tech.): Prof. S. PAL
Electronics (M.Sc.): Prof. D. P. BHATTACHARYA
Energy Science and Engineering (M.Tech.): Prof. S. BASU
Environmental Sciences (M.Phil.): Dr U. K. DEY

There are two affiliated colleges

JAGADGURU RAMBHADRACHARYA HANDICAPPED UNIVERSITY

Chitrakoot Dham, Lucknow, Uttar Pradesh
Internet: www.jrhu.com

Founded 2001

Registrar: Dr AVANISH C. MISHTRA.

JAI NARAIN VYAS UNIVERSITY, JODHPUR

Jodhpur 342001, Rajasthan
Telephone: (291) 2649733
Fax: (291) 2649733
E-mail: vcjnvu@sancharnet.in

Founded 1962

Languages of instruction: English, Hindi
Academic year: July to April

Chancellor: HE THE GOVERNOR OF RAJASTHAN
Vice-Chancellor: Dr NASEEM BHATIA
Registrar: M. L. BHATT
Librarian: Dr R. K. DAVE

Library of 277,229 vols
Number of teachers: 336
Number of students: 24,063

Publications: *Jai Narain Vas University Gazette and News Bulletin*, *The Beacons* (Engineering), *Annals of Economics*, *The University Times* (Students' Union), *International Journal of Finance and Economic Studies* (annually), *Journal of Accounting and Control* (annually)

DEANS

Faculty of Arts, Social Sciences and Education: Dr U. R. NAHAR
Faculty of Commerce: Dr S. J. LALWANI
Faculty of Engineering: Prof. V. P. GUPTA
Faculty of Law: Dr M. K. VYAS
Faculty of Science: Dr B. S. PALIWAL

DIRECTORS

Institute of Evening Studies: Dr P. S. BHATI
K. Nehru College for Women: Dr ANAND MATHUR

PROFESSORS

BANERJI, K. K., Chemistry
BHANDARI, S., Mining Engineering
DHARIWAL, S. R., Physics
GUPTA, V. P., Civil Engineering
LALWANI, S. J., Commerce
MALI, S. L., Electrical Engineering
OHRI, M. L., Civil Engineering
SETRIA, M. R., Structural Engineering
SHARMA, D., Civil Engineering
SHARMA, U. S., Civil Engineering
SHEKHANAT, K. S., Rajasthani
SHRIVASTAVA, R. S., Sociology
SURANA, D. M., Mining Engineering
SURANA, P., Sociology
SURANA, S. L., Electrical Engineering
TIWARI, R. P., Mechanical Engineering

There are eight affiliated colleges

JAI PRAKASH VISHWAVIDYALAYA

Chapra 841301, Bihar.

JAMIA MILLIA ISLAMIA

Jamia Nagar, New Delhi 110025
Telephone: (11) 26981717
Fax: (11) 26840229
E-mail: vc@jmi.ernet.in
Internet: jmi.nic.in

Founded 1920

Central university

Autonomous control (government financed)
Languages of instruction: Urdu, Hindi, English
Academic year: July to July
Chancellor: FAKHRUDDIN T. KHORAKIWALA
Vice-Chancellor: Prof. MUSHIRUL HASAN
Registrar: Prof. Z. H. KHAN
Librarian: Dr GAYAS MAKHDUMI

Library of 336,857 vols, 379 periodicals, 3,000 MSS
Number of teachers: 612
Number of students: 12,851

Publications: *Islam Aur Asr-i-Jadeed* (quarterly, Urdu), *Islam and the Modern Age* (quarterly, English), *Jamia Monthly* (in Urdu)

DEANS

Faculty of Education: Prof. MOHAMMED MIYAN
Faculty of Engineering and Technology: Prof. N. U. KHAN
Faculty of Humanities and Languages: Prof. AKHTARUL WASEY
Faculty of Law: Prof. TAHIR HASAN KHAN
Faculty of Natural Sciences: Prof. IQBAL AHMAD
Faculty of Social Sciences: Prof. NAUSHAD ALI AZAD

HEADS OF DEPARTMENTS

Faculty of Education (tel. (11) 26823108):
- Fine Arts: Prof. MOHAMMED MIYAN
- Foundations of Education: Prof. ILYAS HUSAIN
- Teacher Training and Non-Formal Education: Prof. M. AKHTAR SIDDIQUI

Faculty of Engineering and Technology (tel. (11) 26981717):
- Civil Engineering: Prof. N. U. KHAN
- Electrical Engineering: Prof. IBRAHEEM
- Electronics: Prof. D. R. BHASKAR
- Mechanical Engineering: Prof. R. A. KHAN
- University Polytechnic: Principal: IQBAL AZAM

Faculty of Humanities and Languages (tel. (11) 26983578):
- Arabic: Prof. Z. A. FARROQUI
- English: Prof. SHYAMALA A. NARYAN
- Hindi: Prof. S. A. WAJAHAT
- History and Culture: Prof. SUNITA ZAIDA
- Islamic Studies: Prof. I. H. A. FAROOQI
- Persian: Dr QAMAR GHAFFAR
- Urdu: Prof. Q. O. R. HASHMI

Faculty of Natural Sciences (tel. (11) 26985177):
- Bio-Sciences: Prof. S. AKHTAR HUSAIN
- Chemistry: Prof. MAZHARUL HAQ
- Geography: Prof. M. ISHTIYAQ
- Mathematics: Prof. SHARFUDDIN AHMED
- Physics: Prof. MOHAMMED ZAHID

Faculty of Social Sciences (tel. (11) 28985178):
- Adult and Continuing Education: Prof. S. K. BHATI
- Commerce: Dr ALTAB AHMED KHAN
- Economics: Prof. KHAN. MASOOD AHMED
- Political Science: Prof. M. MUJTABA KHAN
- Psychology: Prof. M. GHALIB HUSAIN
- Social Work: Prof. HAJRA KUMAR
- Sociology: Dr SHEENA JAIN

ATTACHED INSTITUTES

Academic Staff College: Dir Prof. M. AKHTAR SIDDIQUI.

Academy of Third World Studies: Dir Prof. MUSHIRUL HASAN.

Coaching/Career Planning: Dir H. Z. ZAID.

Dr Zakir Husain Institute of Islamic Studies: Dir Prof. AKHTARUL WASEY.

Mass Communication Research Centre: Dir IFTIKHAR AHMED.

State Resource Centre: Dir NISHAT FAROOQI.

UNIVERSITY OF JAMMU

Baba Sahib Ambedkar Rd, Jammu (Tawi) 180006, Jammu and Kashmir
Telephone: (191) 2435248
Fax: (191) 2450014
E-mail: nodalpoint@jammuuniversity.in
Internet: www.jammuuniversity.in

Founded 1969

Affiliating and Teaching
Languages of instruction: English, Hindi
Languages of instruction: Urdu, Sanskrit
Languages of instruction: Dogri, Punjabi
Academic year: July to March

Chancellor: HE THE GOVERNOR OF JAMMU AND KASHMIR
Vice-Chancellor: Prof. AMITABH MATTOO
Registrar: Prof. O. S. SUDAN
Librarian: Prof. VERINDER GUPTA (acting)

Library of 340,810 vols, 282 periodicals
Number of teachers: 259
Number of students: 33,453

Publications: *University News Bulletin*, *Social Science Journal*, *Distance Education Journal*

DEANS

Faculty of Arts: Prof. POSH CHARAK
Faculty of Ayurveda: Dr C. R. GUPTA
Faculty of Behavioural Sciences: Prof. J. R. PANDA
Faculty of Commerce: Prof. DESH BANDHU
Faculty of Engineering Technology: Dr R. N. SHARMA
Faculty of Law: Prof. LALITA PARIHAR
Faculty of Life Sciences: Prof. M. K. JYOTI
Faculty of Management Studies: Prof. M. R. RANA
Faculty of Medicine: Dr ANIL GOSWAMY
Faculty of Music and Fine Arts: SAVITA BAKSHI
Faculty of Oriental Learning: Prof. VEENA GUPTA
Faculty of Science: Prof. I. B. SHARMA
Faculty of Social Sciences: Prof. HARI OM

PROFESSORS

AIMA, A., Management Studies
ANAND, V. K., Botany
BADYAL, S. K., Physics and Electronics
BANDHU, D., Distance Education
BHAT, B. L., Economics
CHARAK, P., English
CHOUDHARY, R., Political Science
DHAR, B. L., Geology
DHOTRA, J. R., Management Studies
DUTTA, S. P., Environmental Science
GANAI, N. A., Law
GOHIL, R. N., Botany
GUPTA, N., Hindi
GUPTA, R., Chemistry
GUPTA, R., Economics
GUPTA, S. C., Zoology
GUPTA, S. P., Commerce
GUPTA, V., Dogri
GUPTA, V. K., Physics and Electronics
HAMAL, I. A., Botany
JYOTI, M. K., Zoology
KALSOTRA, B. L., Chemistry
KAHN, S. R., Psychology
KAUR, K., Political Science
KESAR, A., Dogri Studies
KHOSA, S. K., Physics and Electronics
KOMAL, B. S., Mathematics
KOUL, G. L., Computer Science
KUMAR, R., Hindi
LANGER, A., Botany
MAGOTRA, L. K., Physics and Electronics
MAGOTRA, V. P., Law
MALHAN, I. V., Library Science
MANDOKA, R., English
MASOODI, G. S., Law
MOHD, J., History
OM, H., History
PANDA, J. R., Sociology
PARIHAR, L., Law
PRASAD, G. V. R., Geology
RANA, M. R., Management Studies
RAZDAN, K. B., English
SEHGAL, B. P. S., Law
SHARMA, I. B., Chemistry
SHARMA, K., Management Studies
SHARMA, N. R., Education
SHARMA, O. P., Economics
SHARMA, R. D., Commerce
SHARMA, R. L., Chemistry
SHARMA, S. K., Law
SIDDIQUI, K. H., Urdu
SINGH, A. P., Mathematics
SINGH, G., Computer Science
SINGH, G., Geography
SINGH, S., Law
SUDAN, C. S., Geology
SUMBLI, K., Education
SURI, S. P., Education
TIWARI, R. J., Statistics
VERMA, L., Education
WADAN, D. S., Punjabi

WAKHLU, A. K., Botany
WANGOO, C. L., Mathematics

There are 44 constituent colleges and 17 affiliated colleges

JAWAHARLAL NEHRU AGRICULTURAL UNIVERSITY

PB 80, Krishnagar, Jabalpur 482004, MP
Telephone: (761) 343771
Fax: (761) 343606
E-mail: psingh@jnaump.nic.in

Founded 1964
Languages of instruction: Hindi, English
Academic year: July to June

Chancellor: HE THE GOVERNOR OF MADHYA PRADESH
Vice-Chancellor: Dr P. SINGH
Registrar: Sri A. B. L. BHAGOLIWAL
Assistant Librarian: J. S. BHATTA

Library of 202,000 vols, including periodicals
Number of students: 2,282

Publications: *JNKVV News* (quarterly), *JNKVV Research Journal* (quarterly)

DEANS

Faculty of Agricultural Engineering: Dr M. C. SHRIVASTAVA
Faculty of Agriculture: Dr A. S. TIWARI
Faculty of Veterinary Science and Animal Husbandry: Dr K. S. JOHAR

DIRECTORS

Extension: Dr B. L. MISHRA
Farms: Dr R. K. GUPTA
Instruction: Dr A. S. TIWARI
Instrumentation: Dr S. N. MURTHY
Research: Dr R. K. GUPTA

HEADS OF DEPARTMENTS

Faculty of Agricultural Engineering:

Farm Machinery and Power: (vacant)
Post-Harvest Process and Food Engineering: Dr C. K. TECKCHANDANI
Soil and Water Engineering: Dr M. C. SHRIVASTAVA

Faculty of Agriculture:

Agricultural Economics: Dr A. K. CHENDHARY
Agronomy: Dr K. L. TIWARI
Entomology: Dr S. M. VAISAMPAYAN
Extension: Dr B. D. RAI
Food Science: Y. K. SHARMA
Plant Breeding and Genetics: C. B. SINGH
Plant Pathology: Dr N. D. SHARMA
Pomology and Fruit Preservation: Dr G. S. RATTUSE
Soil Science and Agrochemistry: Dr M. K. MEMA
Vegetable Crops and Floriculture: Dr R. P. PANDY

Faculty of Veterinary Science and Animal Husbandry:

Anatomy: Dr G. P. TIWARI
Animal Breeding: Dr H. K. B. PAREKH
Animal Nutrition: (vacant)
Animal Production: Dr V. P. SINGH
Biochemistry: Dr H. S. KUSHWALS
Medicine: K. N. P. RAO
Parasitology: Dr V. K. SHAHANSHRISUDHE
Poultry Science: (vacant)
Veterinary Pathology: (vacant)

Basic Science:

Mathematics and Statistics: Dr M. L. CHANDAK
Physics: V. K. GUPTA

CONSTITUENT COLLEGES

College of Agricultural Engineering, Jabalpur: Dean Dr M. C. SHRIVASTAVA.

College of Agriculture, Gwalior: Dean Dr J. S. RAGHU.

College of Agriculture, Indore: Dean Dr R. M. SARAN.

College of Agriculture, Jabalpur: Dean Dr C. B. SINGH.

College of Agriculture, Khandwa: Dean Dr K. C. MANDLAI.

College of Agriculture, Rewa: Dean Dr R. A. KHAN.

College of Agriculture, Sehore: Dean Dr V. S. TOMAR.

College of Veterinary Science and Animal Husbandry, Jabalpur: Dean Dr H. K. B. PAREKH.

College of Veterinary Science and Animal Husbandry, Mhow: Dean Dr G. P. TIWARI.

JAWAHARLAL NEHRU TECHNOLOGICAL UNIVERSITY

Kukatpally, Hyderabad 500072, Andhra Pradesh
Telephone: (40) 23158661
Fax: (40) 23156184
E-mail: info@jntu.ac.in
Internet: www.jntu.ac.in

Founded 1972
State control
Academic year: July to April

Chancellor: HE THE GOVERNOR OF ANDHRA PRADESH
Vice-Chancellor: Prof. Y. VENKATARAMI REDDY
Registrar: Dr P. RAM REDDY
Librarian: B. SATYANARAYANA

Library of 162,620 books, 48,500 bound periodicals, 555 periodicals
Number of teachers: 457
Number of students: 34,000 (incl. affiliated colleges)

DIRECTORS

School of Continuing and Distance Education: Dr I. V. RAMANA
School of Information Technology: Dr L. V. A. R. SHARMA
School of Planning and Architecture: Dr M. V. RAMASEHU
Institute of Postgraduate Studies and Research: Dr I. V. RAMANA
Oil Technology and Research Institute: Dr K. N. JAYAVEERA
Bureau of Industrial Consultancy, Research and Development: Dr B. L. P. SWAMY

PROFESSORS

School of Continuing and Distance Education:

APPLANAIDU, P.
SATYANARAYANA MURTY, N.

School of Planning and Architecture:

DHARMARAJ, P. J., Architecture
PADMAVATHI, P., Architecture
RAMA SESHU, M. V., Architecture

Institute of Postgraduate Studies and Research:

PEDDY, D. V., Water Resources
ANJANEYULU, Y., Chemistry
LAKSHMI NARAYANA, P., Hydraulics
MURALIKRISHNA, I. V., Remote Sensing
NARASIMHA MURTHY, D., Mathematics
PRATAP REDDY, S., Industrial Engineering
SRINIVAS BHATT, M., Management Science
SAMBASIVA RAO, I., Placement and Training
VENKATA SESHAIAH, P., Energy

College of Engineering, Anantapur:

ANJANEYULU, K. S. R., Electrical and Electronics Engineering
BHASKAR DESAI, V., Civil Engineering
GOVINDARAJULU, K., Mechanical Engineering
KAMESWARA RAO, P., Physics
KRISHNAMACHARYULU, J., Chemistry
NARASAIAH CHETTY, K., Mechanical Engineering
PANDU RANGADU, V., Mechanical Engineering
PRASAD, E. V., Computer Science
RAJAGOPAL, K., Mechanical Engineering
SANKARAIAH, C., Mathematics
SATYA PRASAD, K., Electronics and Communication Engineering
SHANKAR, V., Electrical and Electronics Engineering
SOUNDERRAJAN, K., Electronics and Communication Engineering
SRINIVASULU, N., Electrical and Electronics Engineering
SUBBRAYUDU, M., Electronics and Communication Engineering
SUBRAHMANYAM, R., Physics
SUDARSHAN RAO, H., Civil Engineering
SWAMY, A. V. N., Chemical Engineering
UMAMAHESWARA GOUD, B., Mechanical Engineering

College of Engineering, Hyderabad:

ACHYUTA RAO, T., Physics
ASTHANA, A. K., Civil Engineering
BABU, V., Computer Science
BELLUBI, B. S., Physics
CHANDRA SEKHAR, M., Physics
CHENNAKESAVULU, N., Civil Engineering
DUBEY, P. K., Chemistry
JAYARAM KUMAR, S. V., Electrical and Electronics Engineering
KHALEELULLAH, M., Chemistry
KISHEN KUMAR REDDY, T., Mechanical Engineering
KOTAIAH, R., Metallurgy
KRISHNA GANDHI, B., Mathematics
KUMAR, A. C. S., Mechanical Engineering
KUMAR, S. P., Physics
LALKISHORE, K., Electronics and Communication Engineering
NAIDU, A., Chemistry
NARASIMHULU, Y., Mathematics
PARADESI RAO, C. D. V., Electronics and Communication Engineering
PRASADA RAO, A., Civil Engineering
RADHA KRISHNA, T., Physics
RAMA KRISHNA RAO, A., Humanities
RAMA KRISHNA RAO, G., Mathematics
RAMAIAH, M. G., Mathematics
RAMANA RAO, N. V., Civil Engineering
SAGAR, G., Computer Science
SAIBABA REDDY, E., Civil Engineering
SESHAGIRIRAO, M. V., Civil Engineering
SOMASEKHARA, P. V. D., Electronics and Communication Engineering
SRIHARI RAO, V., Mathematics
TAGORE, G. N., Mechanical Engineering
TULASI RAM DAS, G., Electrical and Electronics Engineering
VISWANADHAM, M., Civil Engineering

College of Engineering, Kakinada:

ANANDA MOHAN, D., Mechanical Engineering
ANANDA MOHAN, K., Electronics and Communication Engineering
CHALAMAIAH, N., Computer Science
GANDHI, N. S. V. V. S. J., Civil Engineering
GUPTA, L. S., Mechanical Engineering
HARINARAYANA RAO, B., Electrical and Electronics Engineering
KAMARAJU, V., Electrical and Electronics Engineering
KRISHNA MOHAN, P. G., Electronics and Communication Engineering
KRISHNAVENAMMA, M., Humanities
MURALI MOHANA RAO, D., Chemistry
PENCHALAIAH, C., Mechanical Engineering
RAJAGOPALA RAO, A., Civil Engineering
RAMANA, B. V., Mathematics
SARVARAYUDU, G. P. R., Electronics and Communication Engineering

SARVESH, S., Electrical and Electronics Engineering
TULASI RAM, S. S., Electrical and Electronics Engineering
VENU GOPAL REDDY, A., Computer Science
YESURATNAM, G., Civil Engineering

College of Fine Arts:

DASARATHA REDDY, K., Applied Arts
MANDHAN DUTT, M. S., Painting
PRAKASH, N., Photography
SADANAND, P., Applied Arts
SHARMA, A. C., Applied Arts

JAWAHARLAL NEHRU UNIVERSITY

New Mehrauli Rd, New Delhi 110067
Telephone: (11) 26167557
Fax: (11) 26198234
E-mail: webmaster@mail.jnu.ac.in
Internet: www.jnu.ac.in

Founded 1969

Central university
Academic year: July to May

Chancellor: Prof. KARAN SINGH
Vice-Chancellor: Prof. G. K. CHADHA
Registrar: RAMESH KUMAR (acting)
Librarian: S. K. KHULLAR (acting)

Library of 484,702 vols, 700 periodicals
Number of teachers: 371
Number of students: 3,843

Publications: *International Studies* (4 a year), *Studies in History* (2 a year), *Hispanic Horizon* (2 a year), *Journal of School of Languages* (2 a year), *JNU News* (6 a year)

DEANS

School of Arts and Aesthetics: Prof. JYOTINDRA JAIN
School of Computer and Systems Sciences: Prof. KARMESHU
School of Environmental Sciences: Prof. KASTURI DATTA
School of International Studies: Prof. R. R. SHARMA
School of Language, Literature and Culture Studies: Prof. H. C. PANDE
School of Life Sciences: Prof. ALOK BHATTACHARYA
School of Physical Sciences: Prof. A. K. RASTOGI
School of Social Sciences: Prof. M. K. PALAT
Centre for Biotechnology: Prof. B. BHATNAGAR
Centre for Sanskrit Studies: Assoc. Prof. S. P. KUMAR
Centre for the Study of Law and Governance: Prof. N. G. JAYAL

HEADS OF CENTRES

School of International Studies:

Centre for American and West European Studies: Prof. C. S. RAJ
Centre for East Asian Studies: Prof. R. R. KRISHNAN
Centre for International Politics, Organization and Disarmament: Dr K. D. BAJPAI
Centre for Russian, Central Asian and East European Studies: Prof. N. M. JOSHI
Centre for South, Central South-East Asian and South-West Pacific Studies: Prof. I. N. MUKHERJI
Centre for Studies in Diplomacy, International Law and Economics: Prof. S. K. DAS
Centre for West Asian and African Studies: Dr G. C. PANT

School of Language, Literature and Culture Studies:

Centre for Arabic and African Studies: Prof. M. A. ISLAHI
Centre for Chinese and South-East Asian Languages: Dr P. MUKHERJI
Centre of French and Francophone Studies: Prof. C. SIVAM
Centre of German Studies: Prof. REKHA VAIDYARAJAN
Centre for Indian Languages: Prof. MANAGER PANDEY
Centre for Japanese and North-East Asian Languages: Prof. RAJENDER TOMAR
Centre of Linguistics and English: Prof. H. C. NARANG
Centre for Persian and Central Asian Studies: Prof. M. ALAM
Centre of Russian Studies: Prof. A. K. BASU
Centre of Spanish Studies: Prof. S. P. GANGULY

School of Social Sciences:

Centre for Economic Studies and Planning: Prof. PRABHAT PATNAIK
Zakir Husain Centre for Educational Studies: Prof. KARUNA CHANANA
Centre for Historical Studies: Prof. M. K. PALAT
Centre of Philosophy: Prof. P. B. MEHTA
Centre for Political Studies: Prof. BELVEER ARORA
Centre of Social Medicine and Community Health: Dr MOHAN RAO
Centre for Studies in Science Policy: Prof. ANJAN MUKHERJEE (acting)
Centre for the Study of Regional Development: Prof. SUDESH NANGIA
Centre for the Study of Social Systems: Prof. DIPANKAR GUPTA

JAYPEE UNIVERSITY OF INFORMATION TECHNOLOGY

Waknaghat, PO Dumehar Bani, District Solan, Kandaghat 173215, Himachal Pradesh
Telephone: (1792) 239242
Fax: (1792) 245362
Internet: www.jiit.ac.in/juit

Founded 1992
Academic year: July to June

Chancellor: SHRI JAIPRAKASH GAUR JI
Vice-Chancellor: Dr YAJULU MEDURY
Director: Dr NAVEEN PRAKASH
Dean: Dr R. M. VASAN
Registrar: Brig. BALBIR SINGH

Library of 13,000 cols, 26 periodicals
Number of teachers: 68
Number of students: 832

Departments of Bioinformatics, Civil Infrastructure Engineering, Computer Science and Engineering, Electronics and Communication Engineering, Humanities, Mathematics, Communications, Management Studies and Physics

PROFESSORS

BHOOSAN, S. V., Electronics and Communication Engineering
KATYAL, S. C., Electronics and Communication Engineering
PRAKASH, N., Computer Science and Information Technology
SINGH, H., Mathematics

JIWAJI UNIVERSITY

Vidya Vihar, Gwalior 474002, Madhya Pradesh
Telephone: (751) 2341896
Fax: (751) 2341450

Founded 1964

Teaching and Affiliating
Languages of instruction: Hindi, English
Academic year: July to June

Chancellor: HE THE GOVERNOR OF MADHYA PRADESH
Vice-Chancellor: Dr R. R. DASS
Registrar: S. S. DIKSHIT
Librarian (vacant)

Library of 57,000 vols
Number of students: 47,358

Publications: *Humanities*, *Science* (2 a year)

DEANS

Faculty of Arts: Dr H. C. GUPTA
Faculty of Ayurved: Dr B. M. GUPTA
Faculty of Commerce: Dr D. C. SHARMA
Faculty of Education: Dr D. S. SHUKLA
Faculty of Engineering: Dr R. N. SAPRE
Faculty of Home Science: Dr Smh VEENA SHIRASTAM
Faculty of Law: S. P. SHARMA
Faculty of Medicine: Dr Smh S. OPOHAYA
Faculty of Physical Education: (vacant)
Faculty of Science: (vacant)
Faculty of Social Sciences: Dr P. L. SABLOOK

There are 71 affiliated colleges

KACHCHH UNIVERSITY

Kachchh 370001, Gujarat

Founded 2003.

KAKATIYA UNIVERSITY

Vidyaranyapuri, Warangal 506009
Telephone: (8712) 277687
Fax: (8712) 278935
E-mail: kakatiya@ap.nic.in
Internet: www.kuwarangal.com

Founded 1976

Teaching and Affiliating
Languages of instruction: English, Telugu, Urdu

Chancellor: HE THE GOVERNOR OF ANDHRA PRADESH
Vice-Chancellor: Prof. CHANDRAKANT KOKATE
Registrars: Prof. G. SREENIVAS REDDY, M. UPENDER RAO
Librarian: K. RAMANAIAH (Deputy Librarian)

Library of 104,000 vols
Number of students: 72,000

Publications: *Kakatiya Journal of English Studies and Vimarshini*, *Syllabus*, *University Act*

DEANS

Faculty of Arts: Prof. P. SHIV KUMAR
Faculty of Commerce: Prof. O. GHANSHYAMDAS
Faculty of Education: Prof. G. RAMESH
Faculty of Engineering and Technology: Prof. K. KISHAN RAO
Faculty of Law: Justice S. V. MARUTHI
Faculty of Pharmaceutical Sciences: Prof. C. K. KOKATE
Faculty of Science: Prof. D. V. KRISHNA REDDY
Faculty of Social Sciences: Prof. G. SREENIVAS REDDY

KALYANI UNIVERSITY

Kalyani 741235, Nadia, West Bengal
Telephone: (33) 25828220
Fax: (33) 25828282
E-mail: klyunivrgs@yahoo.co.in

Founded 1960

Teaching and Research
Language of instruction: English
Academic year: June to May

Chancellor: HE THE GOVERNOR OF WEST BENGAL
Vice-Chancellor: Prof. NITYANANDA SAHA
Registrar: UTPAL BATTACHARYYA
Librarian (vacant)

Library of 128,790 vols
Number of teachers: 210

Number of students: 4,000

DEANS

Faculty of Arts and Commerce: Prof. P. K. BHATTACHARYYA
Faculty of Education: Prof. A. K. BANERJEE
Faculty of Science: Prof. ASIT GUHA

PROFESSORS

Bengali (tel. (33) 25828220 ext. 233):
BANERJEE, R.
CHOUDHURI, D.
GHATAK, K.
GHATAK, K. S.
SHAW, R.
Biophysics and Biochemistry (tel. (33) 25828750):
BHATTACHARYYA, D. K.
ROY, P. K.
Botany (tel. (33) 25825750 ext. 317):
BHATTACHARYYA, S.
BISWAS, A. K.
CHAUDHURI, S.
GHOSH, P. D.
SEN, T.
Chemistry (tel. (33) 25828220 ext. 305):
DEY, K.
GUHA, A.
LAHIRI, S. C.
MAJUMDER, K. C.
MAJUMDER, M. N.
MUKHERJEE, J.
SARKAR, A. R.
Commerce (tel. (33) 25828750):
BHATTACHARYYA, P. K.
KONAR, D. N.
MAJHI, M. M.
Ecology:
SANTRA, S. C.
Economics (tel. (33) 25828750):
DUTTA, M.
GHOSH, B.
BHATTACHARYYA, R. N.
PAL, D. P.
Education (tel. (33) 25828750):
BASU, M. K.
English (tel. (33) 25828750):
BHATTACHARYYA, D. P.
CHAKRABORTY, B.
DAS, N.
DEB, P. K.
Folklore:
CHAKRABORTY, B. K.
History:
CHAKRABORTY, B. K.
Mathematics (tel. (33) 25828750):
BASU, M.
CHAKRABORTY, H.
DAS, A. G.
DEY, U. C.
KONAR, A.
MUKHERJEE, S.
SANYAL, D. C.
SENGUPTA, P. R.
Physical Education (tel. (33) 25820184 ext. 232):
BANERJEE, A. K.
BHOWMICK, S.
GHOSH, S. R.
Physics (tel. (33) 25820184):
BHATTACHARYYA, A. B.
BISWAS, S.
CHAUDHURI, S.
DASGUPTA, P.
DEB, S. K.
ROY, A. C.
ROY, S.
RUDRA, P.
Political Science:
MUKHOPADHYAY, A.
Sociology:
DASGUPTA, H.
DASGUPTA, S. K.
MANNA, S.
Statistics:
DAS, P.
MITRA, T. K.
PANDA, R. N.
Zoology (tel. (33) 25828750):
BHATTACHARYYA, D. K.
CHAKRABORTY, S.
CHAKRABORTY, S.
DEY, N. C.
HALDER, D. P.
JANA, B. B.
KHUDA BAX, A. R.
KONAR, S. K.
KUNDU, S.
MANNA, C. K.
MUKHERJEE, D. K.
SAHU, C. R.

KAMESHWARA SINGH DARBHANGA SANSKRIT UNIVERSITY

Darbhanga, Bihar 846004
Telephone: (6272) 222178; (6272) 222217
Founded 1961
Teaching and Affiliating
Autonomous control
Languages of instruction: Sanskrit, Hindi
Academic year: July to June
Chancellor: HE THE GOVERNOR OF BIHAR
Vice-Chancellor: Dr MUNISHWAR JHA
Registrar: KANHALYA JEE CHOUBEY
Librarian: J. MAHTO
Library of 100,000 vols, 15,000 periodicals, 10,000 MSS
Number of students: 515,000
Publication: *Vishwa Maneesha* (quarterly)

DEANS

Faculty of Darshan: R. S. JHA
Faculty of Jyotish: R. C. JHA
Faculty of Puran: (vacant)
Faculty of Samaj Shstra: K. MISHRA
Faculty of Veda: S. MISHRA
Faculty of Vyakaran: V. MISHRA

There are 38 constituent colleges and 37 affiliated colleges

KANNADA UNIVERSITY HAMPI

Vidyaranya, Hospet (Taluk) 583276, Karnataka
Telephone: (839) 2441337
Fax: (839) 2441334
E-mail: mail@kavihampi.org
Internet: www.kavihampi.org
Founded 1991
Unitary and Residential
Vice-Chancellor: Dr H. J. LAKKAPPA GOWDA
Registrar: Dr K. V. NARAYANA
Publications: *Kannada Adhyayana,* (Kannada Studies), *Mahila Adhyayana* (Women Studies), *Janapada Karnataka* (Folklore of Karnataka), *Budakattu Karnataka* (Tribal Karnataka), *Namma Kannada* (Kannada Linguistics), *Journal of Karnataka Studies* (in English)
Faculties of Languages, Fine Arts, Sciences and Social Sciences

DEANS

Fine Arts: Prof. H. N. DORAI
Language: Prof. A. V. NAVADA
Social Sciences: Dr H. C. KARIGOWDA

HEADS OF DEPARTMENTS

Development Studies: Dr M. CHANDRA POJJARY
Dravidian Culture Studies: Prof. MALLEPURAM G. VENKATESH
Epigraphy: Dr DEVARAKONDA REDDY
Folklore Studies: Dr MANJUNATH BEVINAKATTI
History: Dr T. P. VIJAY
Kannada Language Studies: Prof. D. PANDURANGA BABU
Kannada Literature Studies: Dr RAHAMAT TARIKERE
Music and Dance: Prof. HANUMANNA NAIK DORE
Translation Studies: Prof. B. K. KARIGOWDA
Women Studies: Dr H. S. SREEMATHI

KANNUR UNIVERSITY

PO Kalliasseri, Kannur 670562, Kerala
Telephone: (497) 2705330
Fax: (497) 2705380
Internet: www.kannuruniversity.ac.in
Founded 1996
Vice-Chancellor: Prof. P. K. RAJAN
Pro Vice-Chancellor: Prof. M. O. KOSHY
Registrar: Dr K. H. SUNRAMANIAN
Library of 10,300 vols, 123 periodicals

DEANS

Faculty of Ayurveda: Dr C. R. SASIDHARAN PILLAI
Faculty of Commerce and Management: Prof. P. SUDARSHANAN PILLAI
Faculty of Communication: Prof. C. D. CHAKKAPPAN
Faculty of Education: Prof. P. M. JALEEL
Faculty of Engineering: Dr M. K. RADHAKRISHNAN
Faculty of Humanities: Prof. D. PRABHAKARAN NAIR
Faculty of Languages and Literature: Prof. M. DASAN
Faculty of Law: Dr M. C. PRAMODAN
Faculty of Modern Medicine: Dr S. HARIHARAN
Faculty of Science: Prof. M. P. KANNAN
Faculty of Social Science: Prof. M. INDUKUMARI

There are 43 affiliated colleges

KARNATAKA STATE OPEN UNIVERSITY

Manasagangotri, Mysore 570006, Karnataka
Telephone: (821) 2514848
Fax: (821) 250084612
Internet: www.ksoumysore.com
Founded 1969 as Institute of Correspondence Course and Continuing Education; present name and status 1996
Academic year: August to June
Vice-Chancellor: Prof. K. SUDHA RAO
Registrar: V. RAMANNA
Dean (Academic): Prof. CHAMBI PURANIK
Dean (Study Centres): Dr K. T. SHIVANNA
Regional Directors: D. SHIVANNA (Davanagere): Dr K. G. SURESH (Bangalore): Dr KAMBLE ASHOK (Gulbarga): G. V. CHANDRA SHEKAR (Dharwad): Prof. HOOVAJAH GOWDA (Shimoga)
Library of 80,000 vols
Number of teachers: 60
Number of students: 30,000

CHAIRS OF DEPARTMENTS

Commerce and Management: Prof. K. G. RAMAKRISHAN
Economics: SATHYA PREMA
Education: M. K. SACHIDANANDA
English: Y. ALIJAZ AHMED
Hindi: B. G. CHANDRALEKHA
History: Dr G. RAMANATHAN

Kannada: D. T. BASAVARAJ
Management: Dr JAGADEESH
Political Science and Public Administration: S. M. SEETHAMMA
Sanskrit: Dr N. RADHAKRISHNA BHAT
Sociology: N. DODDASIDIAH
Tamil: M. TAMILMARAN
Telugu: Dr A. RAMANATHAM NAIDU
Urdu: BALQUEES BANU

KARNATAKA STATE WOMEN UNIVERSITY

Station Rd, Nr Dr B. R. Ambedkar Circle, Bijapur 586101, Karnataka
Telephone: (8352) 240023
E-mail: ku_bij@mail.kar.nic.in
Internet: womenuniversity.kar.nic.in

Founded 2003

Vice-Chancellor: Prof. SYEDA AKHTAR

Library of 15,000 vols, 240 periodicals

Departments of Economics, Education, English, Kannada, Sociology and Women's Studies

There are 41 affiliated colleges.

KARNATAK UNIVERSITY

Dharwad, Karnataka 580003
Telephone: (836) 2747121
Fax: (836) 2747884
E-mail: vckud@ren.nic.in

Founded 1949

Teaching and Affiliating
Language of instruction: English
Academic year: June to April

Chancellor: HE THE GOVERNOR OF KARNATAKA
Vice-Chancellor: Prof. M. KHAJAPEER
Registrar: S. C. KALASAD
Deputy Librarian: C. G. MESTRI

Library of 350,000 vols

Number of postgraduate teachers: 310
Number of college teachers: 5,556
Number of students: 3,779 (postgraduate)
Number of students in affiliated and constituent colleges: 100,562

Publications: *Bharati Vidyarthi* (4 a year), *Humanities, Journal of the Karnataka University—Science, Social Sciences; Karnataka Bharati* (4 a year)

DEANS

Faculty of Arts: Dr V. B. RAJUR
Faculty of Business Management: Dr M. S. SUBHAS
Faculty of Commerce: Dr S. S. HUGAR
Faculty of Education: Dr SASHIKALA DESHPANDE
Faculty of Law: Dr C. RAJASHEKHAR
Faculty of Science and Technology: Dr S. K. SAIDAPUR
Faculty of Social Sciences: Dr S. RAJASHEKHARA

CHAIRMEN OF POSTGRADUATE DEPARTMENTS

Faculty of Arts:
English: Dr G. A. GIRADDIYAVAR
Foreign Languages: Dr M. S. MULLA
Hindi: Dr T. R. BHAT
Janapad: Dr S. G. IMRAPUR
Marathi: Dr B. D. GIAKWAD
Music, Dance and Painting: Dr S. G. IMRAPUR
Sanskrit: Dr M. B. PARADDI
Institute of Kannada Studies: Dr B. R. HIREMATH

Faculty of Business Management:
Business Management: M. S. SUBHAS

Faculty of Commerce:
Commerce: Dr S. S. HUGAR

Faculty of Education:
Education: Dr SHASHIKALA DESHPANDE
Physical Education: (vacant)

Faculty of Law:
Law: Dr S. S. VISHWESHWARAIAH

Faculty of Science and Technology:
Biochemistry: Dr S. R. HINCHIGERI
Botany: Dr S. C. HIREMATH
Chemistry: Prof. A. H. H. SIDDHALINGAIAH
Geography: Dr S. G. KADARAMANDALGI
Geology: Dr S. G. TENGINKAI
Marine Biology, Karwar: Dr B. NEELAKANTHAN
Mathematics: Dr P. S. NEERALAGI
Physics: Dr T. S. MUDHOLE
Sericulture: Dr C. J. SAVANURMATH
Statistics: Dr S. H. KUNCHUR
Zoology: Dr R. D. KANAMADI

Faculty of Social Sciences:
Ancient Indian History and Epigraphy: Dr LEELASHANTAKUMARI
Anthropology: Dr P. B. GAI
Criminology: A. S. INAMDAR
Economics: Dr R. V. DADIBHAVI
Gandhian Studies: Dr V. S. HEGDE
History and Archaeology: Dr M. T. KAMBLE
Library and Information Science: Prof. B. V. RAJASHEKHAR
Mass Communication and Journalism: Dr A. S. BALASUBRAMANYA
Philosophy: Dr B. P. SHIDDASHRAM
Political Science: Dr S. Y. GUBBANNAVAR
Psychology: Dr P. S. HALYAL
Social Work: Dr N. A. GANIHAR
Sociology: Dr K. M. GOUDAR
Yoga Studies: Dr LEELASHANTAKUMARI

CONSTITUENT COLLEGES

Karnatak Arts College: Dharwad; f. 1917; Prin. Dr VEENA SHANTESHWAR.

Karnatak Science College: Dharwad; f. 1919; Prin. Dr B. G. NADAKATTI.

University College of Education: f. 1962; Prin. Dr R. T. JANTALI.

University College of Law: f. 1962; Prin. C. S. PATIL.

University College of Music and Fine Arts: f. 1975; Prin. H. A. KHAN.

There are 246 affiliated colleges

UNIVERSITY OF KASHMIR

Hazratbal, Srinagar 190006, Jammu and Kashmir
Telephone: (194) 2523345
Fax: (194) 2421357
E-mail: info@kashmiruniversity.net
Internet: www.kashmiruniversity.net

Founded 1948
Academic year: March to December

Teaching and Affiliating

Vice-Chancellor: Prof. JALEES AHMAD KHAN TAREEN
Registrar: Prof. ABDUL MAJEED MATTOO
Dean of Academic Affairs: Prof. A. S. BHAT
Dean of Student Welfare: Prof. S. M. AFZAL QADRI
Librarian: REYAZ RUFAI

Library of 400,000 vols
Number of teachers: 280
Number of students: 2,900

DEANS

Faculty of Arts: Prof. M. S. NIYAZMAND
Faculty of Commerce and Management Studies: Prof. AIJAZ RASOOL MATTOO
Faculty of Education: Prof. NAZIR AHMAD NADEEM
Faculty of Engineering: Prof. A. M. WANI
Faculty of Law: Prof. S. M. AFZAL QADRI
Faculty of Medicine: Prof. G. R. MIR
Faculty of Music and Fine Arts: Prof. M. S. SHOUQ
Faculty of Oriental Learning: Prof. M. SHAFI SHOUQ
Faculty of Science: Prof. JALESS AHMAD KHAN TAREEN
Faculty of Social Science: Prof. A. M. MATTOO

PROFESSORS

ABDUL AZIZ, Mathematics
ALVI, W. A., Library and Information Science
AZURDAH, M. Z., Urdu
BABA, N. A., Political Science
BHAT, A. S., Law
BHAT, G. M., Economics
BHAT, M. I., Geology
BHAT, R. C., Zoology
CHANNA, A., Zoology
CHESTI, M. Z., Zoology
DABLA, B. A., Sociology
DHAR, R. L., Zoology
DHAR, T. N., English
DOST, M., Economics
FAROOQ, A., Physics
JAMWAL, K. S., Physics
JAVAID, A. Q., Urdu
KANT, T. A.
KAW, M. A., Central Asian Studies
KHAN, A. H., Distance Education
KHAN, A. M., Central Asian Studies
KHAN, A. R., Zoology
KHAN, B. A., Economics
KHAN, M. I., History
KURSHID, A., Management Studies
LONE, M. S., Kashmiri
MALIK, G. M., Education
MALIK, G. R., English
MALIK, N. A., Urdu
MASOODI, M. M., Persian
MATTOO, A. M., Central Asian Studies
MATTOO, A. R., Management Studies
MIR, A. A., Law
MIR, G. Q., Law
MIR, M., Law
MIR, M. A., Law
MUNSHI, A. H., Botany
MUZAMER, A. M., Urdu
NADEEM, N. A., Education
NIAZMAND, M. S., Persian
NISAR, A., Economics
PEER, M. A., Computer Science
PUNJABI, R., Distance Education
QUADRI, S. M. A., Law
QURESHI, A. W., Economics
QURESHI, M. A., Chemistry
RAFIQUI, A. Q., History
RAIS, A., Geography
RATHER, A. R., Education
SAPRU, B. L., Botany
SHAH, A. M., Environmental Services
SHAH, A. M., Management Studies
SHAH, G. M., Zoology
SHAH, N. A., Electronics
SIKANDAR, F., Botany
SOFI, M. A., Mathematics
SYED, F. A., Commerce
TAK, A. H., English
TANTRAY, G. N., Centre of Adult Continuing Education and Extension
WAFAI, B. A., Botany
WANI, M. A., History

There are 39 constituent, 22 affiliated and seven oriental institutions

KAVILKULGURU KALIDAS SANSKRIT VISHWAVIDYALAYA

Baghele Bhavan, Mouda Rd, Sheetalwadi, District Nagpur, Ramtek 441106, Maharashtra
Telephone: (7114) 255546
Fax: (7114) 255549
E-mail: admin@sanskrituni.com
Internet: www.sanskrituni.org

Founded 1997

Academic year: July to May
Chancellor: HE The Governor of Maharashtra
Vice-Chancellor: Dr Pankaj Chande
Registrar: Dr H. H. Dave
Dean of Faculty: Dr N. J. Puri
Librarian: R. M. Deshpande

Number of teachers: 22
Number of students: 1,148

Undergraduate and postgraduate courses in Sanskrit

There are 40 affiliated colleges.

UNIVERSITY OF KERALA

Thiruvananthapuram 695034, Kerala
Telephone: (471) 2306634
Fax: (471) 2307158
E-mail: keralauniversity@vsnl.com
Internet: www.keralauniversity.edu

Founded 1937

Teaching and Affiliating
Language of instruction: English
Academic year: June to May

Chancellor: HE The Governor of Kerala
Pro-Chancellor: The Minister for Education, Government of Kerala
Vice-Chancellor: Dr B. Ekbal
Pro-Vice-Chancellor: Dr S. Kevin
Registrar: Dr D. Jayadeva Das
Librarian: N. Parameswaran

Library of 280,804 vols
Number of teachers: 5,799
Number of students: 123,310

DEANS

Faculty of Applied Sciences: Dr V. Nanda Mohan
Faculty of Arts: Dr M. Thangadurai
Faculty of Ayurveda: Dr K. Sankaran
Faculty of Commerce: Dr R. Gangadharan Nair
Faculty of Dentistry: Dr Sobha Kuriakose
Faculty of Education: Dr K. R. Sivadasan
Faculty of Engineering and Technology: K. Balachandra Sarma
Faculty of Fine Arts: K. Sumana Devi
Faculty of Homoeopathic Medicine: Dr M. Abdul Lethif
Faculty of Law: Dr N. K. Jayakumar
Faculty of Management Studies: Dr M. Sivaraman
Faculty of Medicine: Dr Joy Philip
Faculty of Oriental Studies: Dr T. Devarajan
Faculty of Physical Education: Dr S. S. Hasrani
Faculty of Science: Dr P. R. Sudhakaran
Faculty of Social Sciences: Dr M. Indukumari

HEADS OF DEPARTMENTS

Aquatic Biology and Fisheries: Dr R. Kaleysa Raj
Biochemistry: Dr P. R. Sudhakaran
Biotechnology: Dr V. Thankamani
Botany: Dr B. Vijayavalli
Chemistry: Dr P. Indrasenan
Commerce: Dr K. Sarngadharan
Computer Science: Dr M. R. Kaimal
Demography: Dr P. Sadasivan Nair
Economics: Dr K. Ramachandran Nair
Education: Dr Vasantha Ramkumar
English: Dr K. Radha
Environmental Science: Dr V. Sobha
Futures Studies: Dr V. Nanda Mohan
Geology: Dr P. K. Rajendran Nair
German: Dr S. Santhakumari
Hindi: Dr N. Ravindranath
History: Dr K. K. Kusuman
Islamic Studies and Culture: Dr K. T. Muhammed Ali
Journalism: Dr M. Thangadorai
Law: Dr N. K. Jayakumar
Library and Information Science: Dr G. Devarajan
Linguistics: Dr V. R. Prabodhachandran Nair
Malayalam: Dr M. R. Gopinatha Pillai
Management Studies: Dr M. K. Ramachandran Nair
Mathematics: Dr M. I. Jinnah
Opto-Electronics: Dr V. Unnikrishnan Nayar
Oriental Research Institute: Dr K. Vijayan
Philosophy: Dr K. Saratchandran
Physics: Dr S. Devanarayanan
Politics: Dr M. Bhaskaran Nair
Psychology: Dr B. Dharmangadan
Russian: Dr R. Gopi
Sanskrit: Dr T. Devarajan
Sociology: Dr M. Indukumari
Statistics: Dr T. S. Krishnan Moothathu
Tamil: Prof. Dr C. Subramonia Pillai
Zoology: Dr Oommen V. Oommen

There are 91 affiliated colleges

KERALA AGRICULTURAL UNIVERSITY

Vellanikkara 680654, Trichur, Kerala
Telephone: (487) 2370432
Fax: (487) 2370019
E-mail: kauhqr@hub.nic.in

Founded 1972
Language of instruction: English
Academic year: June to March

Chancellor: HE The Governor of Kerala
Vice-Chancellor: Dr K. V. Peter
Registrar: O. P. Kaler
Librarian: M. C. Lalitha (acting)

Library of 115,000 vols
Number of teachers: 823
Number of students: 2,445

Publications: *Journal of Tropical Agriculture* (2 a year), *Journal of Veterinary and Animal Science* (2 a year)

DEANS

Faculty of Agricultural Engineering: Dr K. John Thomas
Faculty of Agriculture: Dr A. N. Ramadevi
Faculty of Fisheries: Dr D. D. Namboodiri
Faculty of Veterinary and Animal Sciences: Dr E. Nanu

CONSTITUENT COLLEGES

College of Agriculture, Nilesaher: Nilesaher; Dean Dr M. Abdul Salam (acting).

College of Agriculture, Trivandrum: Vellayani, Trivandrum; (formerly affiliated to University of Kerala); Dean Dr A. N. Remadevi.

College of Co-operative Banking and Management: Mannuthy, Trichur; f. 1981; Dean Dr M. Mohandas.

College of Dairy Science and Technology: Mannuthy, Trichur; f. 1994; Dean Dr V. Prasad.

College of Fisheries: Panangad; f. 1979; Dean Dr Damodaran Namboodiri (acting).

College of Forestry: Vellanikkara, Trichur; Dean Dr Luckins C. Babu.

College of Horticulture: Vellanikkara, Trichur; f. 1972; Dean Dr G. S. L. H. V. Prasada Rao (acting).

College of Veterinary and Animal Sciences, Trichur: Mannuthy, Trichur; (formerly affiliated to University of Calicut); Dean Dr E. Nanu (acting).

College of Veterinary and Animal Science, Wayanad: Pookot, Wayanad; f. 1999; Dean Dr P. P. Balakrishnan.

Kelappaji College of Agricultural Engineering and Technology: Tavanur, Malappuram; Dean Dr K. John Thomas.

KUMAUN UNIVERSITY

Nainital 263001, Uttar Pradesh
Telephone: (5942) 235068; (5942) 235576
E-mail: vc@kumuni.ren.nic.in

Founded 1973

Teaching and Affiliating
Languages of instruction: Hindi, English
Academic year: July to June (two terms)

Chancellor: HE The Governor of Uttar Pradesh
Vice-Chancellor: Prof. R. C. Pant
Registrar: S. C. Joshi
Librarian: Prof. C. C. Pant

Library of 90,000 vols
Number of teachers: 485
Number of students: 29,000

DEANS

Faculty of Arts: Prof. O. P. Singh
Faculty of Commerce: Prof. N. S. Rana
Faculty of Education: Prof. S. Durgapal
Faculty of Law: Prof. P. C. Joshi
Faculty of Science: Prof. G. C. Joshi

PROFESSORS

Faculty of Arts:
- Bisht, H. S., Geography
- Bisht, L. S., Economics
- Bisht, L. S., Hindi
- Dube, M. P., Political Science
- Gupta, R. K., Hindi
- Pande, G. C., Economics
- Pandey, D. C., Economics
- Pathak, S., History
- Pokharia, D. S., Hindi
- Rawat, A. S., History
- Ruwali, K. D., Hindi
- Sah, N. K., Economics
- Sahai, V., History
- Singh, O. P., Geography
- Tripathi, D. R., Sanskrit

Faculty of Commerce:
- Bisht, N. S., Business Administration
- Rana, N. S., Commerce
- Tiwari, J. C., Commerce

Faculty of Education:
- Durgapal, S.
- Joshi, J. K.
- Juyal, P. D.
- Shukla, S. C.

Faculty of Science:
- Bhatt, S. D., Zoology
- Bisht, C. S., Mathematics
- Bisht, G., Chemistry
- Bisht, M., Zoology
- Chandra, M., Chemistry
- Chandra, S., Botany
- Dhami, H. S., Mathematics
- Joshi, G. C., Botany
- Joshi, L., Chemistry
- Kaushal, B. R., Zoology
- Khami, K. S., Chemistry
- Khetwal, K. S., Chemistry
- Kumar, S., Geology
- Kumar, S., Zoology
- Lohani, A. B., Mathematics
- Mathela, C. S., Chemistry
- Mathpal, K. N., Chemistry
- Mehrotra, R. M., Chemistry
- Mehta, S. P. S., Chemistry
- Melkani, K. B., Chemistry
- Mishra, V. N., Chemistry
- Pandey, K., Physics
- Pandey, K. N., Botany
- Pandey, S. B., Mathematics
- Pangeti, Y. P. S., Botany
- Pant, C. C., Geology
- Pant, D. N., Mathematics
- Pant, M. C., Physics
- Pant, R. P., Mathematics
- Pant, T. C., Physics
- Shah, L., Zoology

Singh, R. P., Forestry
Singh, S. P., Botany
Varma, K. R., Botany

There are two constituent colleges and 29 affiliated colleges

KURUKSHETRA UNIVERSITY

Kurukshetra 136119, Haryana
Telephone: (1744) 238039
Fax: (1744) 238277
E-mail: kulib@kuk.ernet.in
Internet: kuk.ernet.in

Founded 1956

Teaching and Affiliating
State control
Languages of instruction: English, Hindi
Academic year: July to June

Chancellor: HE The Governor of Haryana
Vice-Chancellor: Dr A. K. Chawla
Registrar: Dr J. S. Kadian
Librarian: R. D. Mehla

Library of 288,312 vols, 660 periodicals
Number of teachers: 390
Number of students: 5,584

Publications: *Annual Report* (in English and Hindi), *Research Journal for Arts and Humanities* (in English and Hindi), *Sambhawana* (in Hindi), *Kurukshetra Law Journal* (in English), *Journal of Haryana Studies* (in English), *Jeevanti* (in Hindi), *Kuru Jyoti* (in English, Sanskrit and Hindi), *Praci Jyoti* (in English), *Kalanidhi* (magazine, in Hindi)

DEANS

Faculty of Arts and Languages: Dr Lal Chand Gupta
Faculty of Ayurvedic Medicine: Dr S. S. Saini (acting)
Faculty of Commerce and Management: Dr D. S. Bhardwaj
Faculty of Education: Dr N. S. Mavi
Faculty of Engineering and Technology: Dr Krishan Gopal
Faculty of Indic Studies: Dr Amar Singh
Faculty of Law: Dr Devinder K. Raheja
Faculty of Medicine and Dentistry: Dr S. K. Khindsia
Faculty of Science: Dr Hari Singh
Faculty of Social Sciences: Dr Amir Singh

PROFESSORS

Faculty of Arts and Languages (tel. (1744) 234374):
Gupta, L. C., Hindi
Kaang, A. S., Punjabi
Sharma, S. D., English

Faculty of Commerce and Management:
Bansal, M. L., Commerce
Bhardwaj, D. S., Tourism
Dwivedi, R. S., Management
Gupta, S. L., Management
Hooda, R. P., Commerce
Jain, M. K., Management
Mittal, R. K., Commerce
Sharma, V. D., Management

Faculty of Education:
Malhotra, S. P.
Mavi, N. S.
Yadav, D. S.

Faculty of Indic Studies (tel. (1744) 238347):
Kushwaha, S. K., Fine Arts
Saxena, Madu Bala, Music
Sharma, Indu Bala, ISIS
Singh, A., Sanskrit

Faculty of Law:
Aggarwal, V. K.
Kumari, D.
Varandani, G.

Faculty of Science (tel. (1744) 239235):
Aneja, K. R., Microbiology
Arya, S. P., Chemistry
Asthana, V. K., Geography
Chaturvedi, D. K., Physics
Chopra, G., Zoology
George, P. J., Electronics Science
Gupta, S. C., Chemistry
Kakkar, L. R., Chemistry
Lunkad, S. K., Geology
Matta, N. K., Botany
Mehta, J. R., Chemistry
Mittal, I. C., Zoology
Mukherjee, D., Botany
Nand, Lal, Earth Sciences
Rohtash, C., Zoology
Sharda Kumari, Statistics
Sharda Rani, Botany
Sharma, N. D., Physics
Sharma, V. K., Geography
Singh, H., Biochemistry
Suri, P. K., Computer Science
Trehan, K., Botany
Vinod Kumar, Mathematics

Faculty of Social Sciences:
Kundu, T. R., Economics
Khurana, G., History
Sharma, P. D., Political Science
Sharma, R. K., History
Singh, H., Public Administration
Sunita Pathania, History
Tanwar, R., History
Tuteja, K. L., History
Upadhyaya, R. K., Social Work
Vashist, B. K., Economics

There are 122 affiliated colleges and three maintained colleges

KUVEMPU UNIVERSITY

Shankaraghatta, Shimoga District, Karnataka 577451
Telephone: (8282) 656222
Fax: (8282) 656255
E-mail: root@shikuv.kar.nic.in
Internet: www.kuvempuuniversity.org

Founded 1987
Academic year: August to April

Chancellor: T. N. Chaturvedi
Vice-Chancellor: Prof. Chidananda Gowda
Registrar: Praveen Chandra
Librarian: Dr K. C. Ramakrishne Gowda

Library of 55,500 vols
Number of teachers: 93
Number of students: 950 (postgraduate)

DEANS

Faculty of Arts: Prof. T. N. Shankaranarayana
Faculty of Commerce: Prof. B. Bakkappa
Faculty of Education: Prof. P. Basavakumaraiah
Faculty of Engineering: Prof. G. P. Prabhukumara
Faculty of Law: Prof. T. Satyamurthy
Faculty of Science: Prof. C. S. Bagewadi

There are 119 affiliated colleges

LALIT NARAYAN MITHILA UNIVERSITY

Kameshwarnagar, POB 13, Darbhanga 846004, Bihar
Telephone: (6272) 222428; (6272) 222598

Founded 1972

Teaching and Affiliating
Languages of instruction: Hindi, English
Academic year: June to May

Chancellor: HE The Governor of Bihar
Vice-Chancellor: Dr Janardan Kumar
Registrar: B. L. Das
Librarian: K. K. Kamal

Library of 168,854 vols
Number of teachers: 1,251
Number of students: 110,355

DEANS

Faculty of Arts: Prof. R. N. Thakur
Faculty of Commerce: Dr Gopal Lal
Faculty of Education: (vacant)
Faculty of Law: Prof. D. K. Jha
Faculty of Medicine: Dr S. N. Singh
Faculty of Science: Prof. S. Pandey

PROFESSORS

Jha, B. N., Mathematics
Jha, S. M., Maithili
Lall, G., Commerce
Pandey, S., Zoology
Pathak, R. K., Hindi
Prasad, A. B., Botany
Rahman, M., Urdu
Roy, B. K., History
Thakur, B., Economics
Thakur, R. N., Political Science
Thakur, Y., Chemistry

UNIVERSITY OF LUCKNOW

Badshah Bagh, Lucknow 226007, Uttar Pradesh
Fax: (522) 2330065

Founded 1921

Residential and Teaching
Languages of instruction: English, Hindi
Academic year: July to April

Chancellor: HE The Governor of Uttar Pradesh
Vice-Chancellor: Prof. D. P. Singh
Pro Vice-Chancellor: Prof. H. N. Verma
Registrar: R. S. Ram
Librarian: Prof. P. C. Misra

Library of 510,000 vols
Number of teachers: 661
Number of students: 48,625

DEANS

Faculty of Architecture: Nehru Lal
Faculty of Arts: Prof. S. N. Misra
Faculty of Ayurveda: Dr B. N. Singh
Faculty of Commerce: Dr S. B. Singh
Faculty of Dental Sciences: Prof. D. N. Kapoor
Faculty of Education: R. J. Singh
Faculty of Engineering Technology: Prof. G. N. Pandey
Faculty of Fine Arts: J. K. Agarwal
Faculty of Law: K. C. Srivastava
Faculty of Medicine: P. K. Mishra
Faculty of Science: Prof. V. K. Srivastava

HEADS OF DEPARTMENTS

Anaesthesiology: Dr B. K. Singh
Anatomy: Dr D. R. Singh
Ancient Indian History and Archaeology: Dr S. N. Misra
Anthropology: Dr B. R. K. Shukla
Applied Economics: Dr R. Sharma
Applied Sciences: Dr S. K. Srivastava
Arabic: Dr U. Farahi
Architecture: N. Lal
Biochemistry: Dr R. K. Singh
Botany: Dr N. K. Mehrotra
Business Administration: Dr B. L. Bajpai
Cardiology: Dr V. K. Puri
Civil Engineering: A. K. Shukla
Commerce: Dr S. B. Singh
Commercial Art: P. C. Little
Computer Science: Dr S. K. Bajpai
Chemistry: Dr A. Khare
Dravya Gun: Dr R. A. Gupta
Economics: Dr A. K. Sengupta
Education: Dr R. J. Singh
Electrical Engineering: Smt. B. Dwivedi
Electronics: Dr N. Malaviya
English and Modern European Languages: Dr M. S. Kushwah

Fine Arts: J. K. AGARWAL
Forensic Medicine: Dr B. SINGH
Geology: Dr I. B. SINGH
Hindi: Dr S. P. DIKSHIT
Kaya Chikitsa: Dr C. C. PATHAK
Law: Sri K. C. SRIVASTAVA
Library Science: Dr N. R. SATYANARAYANA
Linguistics: Dr V. P. JAIN
Mathematics and Astronomy: Dr S. DUTTA
Maulik Siddhant and Sanhita: Dr S. SRIVASTAVA
Mechanical Engineering: Dr R. C. GUPTA
Medicine: Dr A. R. SIRCAR
Medieval and Modern Indian History: Dr N. K. ZUTSHI
Microbiology: Dr U. C. CHATURVEDI
Neurology: Dr DEVIKA NAG
Obstetrics and Gynaecology: Dr CHANDRAWATI
Ophthalmology: Dr V. B. PRATAP
Orthopaedic Surgery: Dr U. K. JAIN
Otorhinolaryngology: Dr S. C. MISRA
Paediatrics: Dr P. K. MISHRA
Pathology: Dr PRAMOD NATH
Persian: Dr ASIFA ZAMANI
Pharmacology and Therapeutics: Dr R. C. SAXENA
Philosophy: Dr R. R. VERMA
Physics: Dr L. M. BALI
Physiology: Dr S. SINGH
Plastic Surgery: Dr RAMESH CHANDRA
Political Science: Dr S. M. SAYEED
Prasuti Stri Avam Balrog: Dr D. N. MISHRA
Psychiatry: Dr A. K. AGARWAL
Psychology: Dr NEELIMA MISRA
Public Administration: Dr C. P. BARTHWAL
Radio Diagnosis: Dr V. K. TANDON
Radiotherapy: Dr H. R. MALI
Ras Shastra: Dr K. K. SRIVASTAVA
Sanskrit and Prakrit Languages: Dr NAVJEERAN RASTOGI
Sculpture: R. N. MAHAPATRA
Shalya Shalakya: Dr PRAMOD KUMAR
Sharir: Dr J. R. YADAV
Social and Preventive Medicine: Dr R. CHANDRA
Social Work: Dr SURENDRA SINGH
Sociology: Dr A. AWASTHI
Statistics: Dr V. K. SRIVASTAVA
Surgery: Dr K. N. SINHA
Tuberculosis: Dr P. K. MUKERJI
Urdu: Dr S. SULAIMAN HUSAIN
Western History: Dr R. N. MEHRA
Zoology: Dr VINOD GUPTA

CONSTITUENT COLLEGES

College of Arts and Crafts: Lucknow; Prin. J. K. AGARWAL.

Government College of Architecture: Lucknow; Prin. Prof. N. LAL.

Institute of Engineering and Technology: Lucknow; Dir Prof. G. N. PANDEY.

King George's Medical College: Lucknow; f. 1911; 4-year postgraduate medical courses have been established; Prin. Dr P. K. MISHRA.

State College of Ayurveda: Lucknow; f. 1954; Prin. Prof. B. N. SINGH.

There are 20 associated colleges

MADHYA PRADESH BHOJ (OPEN) UNIVERSITY

Red Cross Bhavan, Shivaji Nagar, Bhopal 462016, Madhya Pradesh
Telephone: (755) 2576555
Fax: (755) 2550606
Internet: www.bhojvirtualuniversity.com

Founded 1992
Academic year: July to June

Vice-Chancellor: Prof. R. K. SINGH
Registrar: Prof. C. K. JAIN
Librarian: J. P. SONI

Library of 7,000 vols

DIRECTORS OF REGIONAL CENTRES

Bhopal: Dr PRAVEEN JAIN
Bilaspur: Dr S. L. KOKA
Gwalior: Dr U. P. VERMA
Indore: Dr ANIL DIXIT
Jabalpur: Dr K. K. TIWARI
Jagdalpur: Dr ALI
Raipur: Dr S. K. SINGH
Rewa: Dr K. S. TIWARI
Ujjain: Dr D. K. SHARMA

HEADS OF DEPARTMENTS

Basic Sciences: Dr PRAVEEN JAIN
General Education: Prof. J. S. GREWAL
Health Sciences: Dr PRAVEEN JAIN
History, Archaeology and Tourism: Dr SUSMITA PANDE
Information Technology: Dr JYOTSNA DIKSHIT
Management: (vacant)
Special Education: Prof. G. GURU

PROFESSORS

DHAKAD, S. K.
DUBEY, S. K.
GARDE, V. D.
GOEL, R. M.
GREWAL, J. S.
MISRA, R. D.
SAXENA, M. C.
SESHADRI, C. S.
TOMAR, S. K.

ATTACHED RESEARCH INSTITUTES

National Institute of Education and Research for the Empowerment of Differently-Abled Persons.

UNIVERSITY OF MADRAS

Chepauk, Triplicane PO, Chennai 600005, Tamil Nadu
Telephone: (44) 25368778
Fax: (44) 25366693
E-mail: vc@unom.ac.in

Founded 1857

Teaching and Affiliating
Languages of instruction: English, Tamil
Academic year: July to April

Chancellor: HE THE GOVERNOR OF TAMIL NADU
Vice-Chancellor: Prof. S. P. THYAGARAJAN
Registrar: Dr N. MANI
Librarian: Dr R. VENGAN (acting)

Library of 506,295 vols
Number of students: 107,518

Publications: *Annals of Oriental Research*, *University Bulletin* (monthly), *University Calendar*, *University Journals*

FACULTY PRESIDENTS

Faculty of Arts: Dr R. THANDAVAN
Faculty of Fine Arts: Dr N. RAMANATHAN
Faculty of Indian and Other Languages: Dr V. JAYADEVAN
Faculty of Law: Dr N. BALU
Faculty of Science: Dr D. LALITHA KUMARI
Faculty of Teaching: Dr D. RAJA GANESAN

There are 276 affiliated colleges

MADURAI-KAMARAJ UNIVERSITY

Palkalai Nagar, Madurai 625021, Tamil Nadu
Telephone: (452) 2458471
Fax: (452) 2458449
E-mail: registrarmku@rediffmail.com
Internet: www.mkuniversity.org

Founded 1966

Teaching and Affiliating
Languages of instruction: English, Tamil
Academic year: June to April

Chancellor: HE THE GOVERNOR OF TAMIL NADU
Vice-Chancellor: Prof. P. K. PONNUSWAMY
Registrar: Dr V. ALAGAPPAN
Librarian: A. SRIMURUGAN

Library of 251,000 vols
Number of teachers: 377 (excluding affiliated colleges)
Number of students: 133,100 (including affiliated colleges)

Publication: *Journal of Biology Education* (quarterly)

There are 109 affiliated colleges.

MAGADH UNIVERSITY

Bodh-Gaya 824234, Bihar
Telephone: (631) 2200490
Fax: (631) 2222717

Founded 1962

Teaching and Affiliating
Languages of instruction: English, Hindi
Academic year: June to May

Chancellor: HE THE GOVERNOR OF BIHAR
Vice-Chancellor: Justice SURESH C. MOOKHERJI
Pro-Vice-Chancellor: Dr B. N. SINGH
Registrar: Dr B. N. PANDEY
Librarian (vacant)

Library of 220,000 vols
Number of teachers: 5,000
Number of students: 170,500

Publications: *Annual Report*, *Handbook*

DEANS

Faculty of Business Management: (vacant)
Faculty of Commerce: Dr N. C. AGRAWAL
Faculty of Humanities: Dr C. N. MISHRA
Faculty of Medicine: Dr M. P. SINGH
Faculty of Science: Prof. G. P. SINGH
Faculty of Social Science: Dr K. B. SINGH

PROFESSORS

AGRAWAL, N. C., Commerce
AGRAWAL, B. N., Political Science
AMBASHTHA, A. V., Commerce
GUPTA, L. N., Commerce
JHA, B. K., Political Science
LAL, B. K., Philosophy
MISHRA, C. N., Sanskrit
NATH, B., Philosophy
PRASAD, B. K., Philosophy
PRASAD, B. N., Mathematics
PRASAD, N., English
ROY, L. M., Economics
ROY, P., Hindi
SAHAI, S., Ancient Indian and Asian Studies
SHRIVASTAVA, J. P., Chemistry
SINGH, A. N., Physics
SINGH, B. K., Psychology
SINGH, B. P., Political Science
SINGH, G. P., Physics
SINGH, H. G., Economics
SINGH, J. P., English
SINGH, R. C. P., Ancient Indian and Asian Studies
SINGH, S., Mathematics
SINGH, S. B., Zoology
SINHA, D. P., Zoology
SINHA, H. P., Philosophy
SINHA, N. C. P., Psychology
SINHA, S. P., Economics
SINHA, V. N., Philosophy
THAKUR, U., Ancient Indian and Asian Studies
TIWARY, P., Mathematics
VERMA, B. B., Commerce
VISHESHWARAM, S., Mathematics

ATTACHED INSTITUTES

Mishra, L. N., Institute of Economic Development and Social Change: Hon. Dir Dr CHAKERDHAR SINGH.

Nava Nalanda Mehavihar: Nalanda; postgraduate teaching in Pali and research in

Pali literature with special reference to Buddhism; Dir Dr U. THAKUR.

Rajendra Memorial Research Institute of Medical Science: postgraduate research in conjunction with the Faculty of Medicine; Dir Dr LALA SURAYNANDAN PRASAD.

Sri D. K. Jain Orient Research Institute: Arrah; postgraduate research in Prakrit, Jain philosophy and religion; Hon. Dir Dr RAJA RAM JAIN.

There are 50 constituent colleges and 60 affiliated colleges

MAHARAJA SAYAJIRAO UNIVERSITY OF BARODA

Vadodara 390002, Gujarat
Telephone: (265) 2514778
Fax: (265) 2514778
Internet: www.msub.edu

Founded 1949

Residential and Teaching
Language of instruction: English
Academic year: June to April (two terms)

Vice-Chancellor: Dr ANIL S. KANE
Pro-Vice-Chancellor: Prof. DIPAK KUMAR
Registrar: D. P. CHHAYA
Librarian: Prof. M. K. R. NAIDU

Library of 404,043 vols
Number of teachers: 1,230
Number of students: 32,609

Publications: *Handbook*, *Annual Report*, *Journal of Oriental Institute*, *Journal of Education and Psychology*, *Journal of Animal Morphology and Physiology*, *Swadhyaya*, *Pavo*, *Journal of Technology and Engineering* (annually)

DEANS

Faculty of Arts: Prof. D. H. MOHITE
Faculty of Commerce: Prof. B. S. PATEL
Faculty of Education and Psychology: Prof. S. M. YOSHI
Faculty of Fine Arts: Prof. P. D. DHUHAL
Faculty of Home Science: Dr ANUPAMA SHAH
Faculty of Journalism and Communication: Dr H. N. DESAI
Faculty of Law: Prof. L. J. PAREKH
Faculty of Management Studies: Prof. M. M. DADI
Faculty of Medicine: Dr KAMAL J. PATHAK
Faculty of Performing Arts: Prof. D. K. BHONSALE
Faculty of Science: Prof. L. J. PAREKH
Faculty of Social Work: Prof. S. B. SAXENA
Faculty of Technology and Engineering: Prof. H. V. BHAVNANI

PROFESSORS

Faculty of Arts:

JUNEJA, O. P., English
KAR, P., English
MEHTA, S. Y., Gujarati
MOHITE, D. H., Political Science
PANDYA, N. M., Economics
PANTHAM, T., Political Science
PAREKH, V. S., Archaeology
PATEL, K. H., Environmental Archaeology
PATEL, P. J., Sociology
REDE, L. A., Economics
Mrs SHAH, M. N., Economics
SIDDIQI, M. H., Persian
SONAWANE, V. H., Archaeology

Faculty of Commerce:

BHATT, A. S., Commerce and Business Administration
MOHITE, M. D., Co-operation
PANCHOLI, P. R., Business Economics
PATEL, B. S., Commerce and Business Administration
SANDHE, A. G., Commerce and Business Administration
SHAH, K. R., Economics
SINGH, S. K., Business Economics
SYAN, J. K., Banking and Business Finance
VYAS, I. P., Commerce and Business Administration

Faculty of Education and Psychology:

GOEL, D., Education
JOSHI, S. M., Educational Administration
YADAV, M. S., Education

Faculty of Fine Arts:

PANCHAL, R. R., Sculpture
PATEL, V. S., Graphic Arts

Faculty of Home Science:

BALKRISHNAIH, B., Clothing and Textiles
MANI, U. V., Foods and Nutrition
SARASWATI, T. S., Human Development and Family Studies
SHAH, A., Home Science Extension and Communication

Faculty of Law:

PARIKH, S. N., Law
RATHOD, J. C., Law

Faculty of Management Studies:

DADI, M. M., Management
DHOLAKIA, M. N., Management
JOSHI, K. M., Management
MAHESHWARI, G. C., Management

Faculty of Medicine:

BHOTI, S. J., Ophthalmology
BONDRE, K. V., Anatomy
BUCH, V. P., Radiology
CHANDWANI, S., Physiology
CHAUHAN, L. M., Obstetrics and Gynaecology
DESAI, M. R., Obstetrics and Gynaecology
GHOSH, S., Biochemistry
HATHI, G., Physiology
HEMAVATI, K. G., Pharmacology
JHALA, D. R., Paediatrics
JOSHI, G. D., Preventative and Social Medicine
KARELIA, L. S., Pathology
MAZUMDAR, U., Dentistry
MEHTA, J. P., Surgery
MEHTA, N. C., Medicine
PATHAK, K., Medicine
PATRA, B. S., Surgery
PATRA, S. B., Pathology
RAWAL, H. H., Anaesthesia
SAINATH, M., Ophthalmology
SANGHVI, N. G., Medicine
SAXENA, S. B., Microbiology
SHAH, A. U., Preventative and Social Medicine
SHAH, D. N., Preventative and Social Medicine
SHAK, K. D., Surgery
SHARMA, S. N., Plastic Surgery
SHETH, R. T., Ophthalmology
SHUKLA, G. N., Surgery
TIWARI, R. S., Ear, Nose and Throat
VAISHNAVI, A. J., Orthopaedics
VANKAR, G. K., Psychiatry
VOHRA, P. A., Radiology
VYAS, D. C., Anatomy

Faculty of Performing Arts:

BHONSLE, D. K., Vocal Music
SHAH, P., Dance

Faculty of Science:

AMBADKAR, P. M., Zoology
BHATTACHARYA, P. K., Chemistry
CHATTOO, B., Microbiology
CHHATPAR, H. S., Microbiology
DESAI, N. D., Geology
DESAI, S. J., Geology
DEVI, S. G., Chemistry
GOYAL, O. P., Mathematics
KATYARE, S. S., Biochemistry
MEHTA, T., Biochemistry
PADH, H., Biochemistry
PAREKH, L. J., Biochemistry
PATEL, H. C., Statistics
PATEL, M. P., Geology
PATEL, N. V., Mathematics
PILO, B., Zoology
RAKSHIT, A. K., Chemistry
RAMCHANDRAN, A. V., Zoology
RANGASWAMY, V. C., Geography
RAO, K. K., Microbiology
SHAH, A. C., Chemistry
SHREEHARI, M., Statistics
SOMAYAJULU, D. R. S., Physics
TELANG, S. D., Biochemistry

Faculty of Social Work:

ANJARIA, V. N., Social Work
NAVALE, A. S., Social Work
SAXENA, S. B., Social Work

Faculty of Technology and Engineering:

AGRAWAL, S. K., Metallurgical Engineering
AGRAWAL, S. R., Applied Mathematics
BALARAMAN, R., Pharmacy
BANGLORE, V. A., Textile Engineering
BASA, D. K., Metallurgical Engineering
BHAGIA, R. M., Applied Mechanics
BHATT, G. D., Mechanical Engineering
BHATT, R. D., Civil Engineering
BHAVNANI, H. V., Civil Engineering
BHAVSAR, N., Electrical Engineering
BIYANI, K. R., Applied Mechanics
CHUDASAMA, U. V., Applied Chemistry
DE, D. K., Textile Engineering
DESAI, P. B., Mechanical Engineering
DESHPANDE, S. V., Architecture
DIVEKAR, M. H., Chemical Engineering
ETHIRAJULU, K., Chemical Engineering
GADGEEL, V. I., Metallurgical Engineering
GOROOR, S. P., Water Management
GUHA, S., Textile Chemistry
GUPTE, S. G., Electrical Engineering
JOSHI, S. M., Electrical Engineering
JOSHI, T. R., Applied Physics
KANITKAR, S. A., Electrical Engineering
KAPADIA, V. H., Textile Engineering
LOIWAL, A. S., Mechanical Engineering
MISHRA, A. N. R., Pharmacy
MISHRA, S. H., Pharmacy
MODI, P. M., Water Management
MOINUDDIN, S., Chemical Engineering
MORTHY, R. S. R., Pharmacy
NANAVATI, J. I., Mechanical Engineering
PAI, K. B., Metallurgical Engineering
PAREKH, B. S., Computer Science
PARMAR, N. B., Civil Engineering
PATEL, A. A., Mechanical Engineering
PATEL, B. A., Electrical Engineering
PATEL, H. J., Computer Science
PATEL, N. M., Applied Mechanics
PATHAK, V. D., Applied Mathematics
PATODI, S. C., Applied Mechanics
POTBHARE, V. N., Applied Physics
PRAJAPATI, J. J., Civil Engineering
PURANIK, S. A., Chemical Engineering
PUTHANPURAYIL, P., Mechanical Engineering
RAJPUT, H. G., Training and Placement
SAVANI, A. K., Civil Engineering
SHAH, A. N., Civil Engineering
SHAH, D. L., Applied Mechanics
SHAH, S. G., Electrical Engineering
SHROFF, A. V., Applied Mechanics
SUKLA, H. J., Mechanical Engineering
SUBRAMANYAM, N., Chemical Engineering
SUNDAR MORTI, N. S., Metallurgical Engineering
SUTARIA, P. N., Civil Engineering
THAKUR, S. A., Electrical Engineering
TRIVEDI, A. I., Electrical Engineering
VASDEV, S., Chemical Engineering
VORA, R. A., Applied Chemistry
VYAS, J. K., Applied Mechanics
YADAV, R., Pharmacy

Centre for Continuing and Adult Education and Community Services:

PARALIKAR, K. R.

Oriental Institute:

NANAVATI, R. I.
WADEKAR, M. L.

CONSTITUENT COLLEGES

Baroda Sanskrit Mahavidyalaya: Vadodara; f. 1915; Principal U. H. SHUKLA.

Manibhai Kashibai Amin Arts and Science College and College of Commerce: Padra; f. 1965; Principal Dr W. V. AHIRE.

Polytechnic: Vadodara; f. 1957; Principal A. G. TELPANDE.

ATTACHED CENTRE

Women's Studies Research Centre: Dir Prof. AMITA VERMA.

MAHARANA PRATAP UNIVERSITY OF AGRICULTURE AND TECHNOLOGY

Udaipur 313001, Rajasthan
Telephone: (294) 2471101
Fax: (294) 2470682
E-mail: vc@mpuat.ac.in
Internet: www.mpuat.ac.in
Founded 1999
Chancellor: HE THE GOVERNOR OF RAJASTHAN
Vice-Chancellor: Dr S. L. MEHTA
Registrar: VEENITA BOHRA
Librarian: ASHU SATHI

DEANS

Rajasthan College of Agriculture: Dr G. S. SHARMA
College of Dairy and Food Science Technology: Dr N. S. RATHORE
College of Fisheries: Dr G. S. SHARMA
College of Home Science: Dr PUSHPA GUPTA
College of Horticulture and Fisheries (Jhalawar): Dr SHAAFAT MOHAMMED
College of Technology and Engineering: Dr A. N. MATHUR

HEADS OF DEPARTMENTS

Rajasthan College of Agriculture:
- Agricultural Chemistry and Soil Science: Dr B. N. SWAMI
- Agricultural Economics: Dr K. P. SHARMA
- Agronomy: Dr H. S. DUNGARWAL
- Animal Production: Dr L. S. JAIN
- Basic Science: (vacant)
- Biochemistry: Dr G. C. NANAWATI
- Extension Education: Dr V. P. SHARMA
- Horticulture: Dr A. K. AHLAWAT
- Limnology and Fisheries: Dr L. L. SHARMA
- Nematology: Dr A. U. SIDDIQUI
- Plant Breeding and Genetics: Prof. V. N. JOSHI
- Plant Pathology: Dr H. N. GAUR
- Plant Physiology: Dr K. B. SHUKLA
- Statistics and Mathematics: Dr P. K. DASHORA

College of Dairy and Food Science Technology:
- Dairy and Food Chemistry: Dr A. K. SANKHLA
- Dairy and Food Engineering: Dr L. K. MURDIA
- Dairy and Food Microbiology: Dr P. SUBRAMANIUM
- Food Technology: S. H. QURESHI

College of Engineering and Technology:
- Basic Sciences: Dr SUDHA MATHUR
- Civil Engineering: B. S. SINGHVI
- Computer Science and Engineering: P. M. JAT
- Electrical Engineering: R. R. JOSHI
- Farm Machinery and Power Engineering: Dr Y. C. BHATT
- Mechanical Engineering: Dr B. P. NANDWANA
- Mining Engineering: S. S. RATHORE
- Processing and Food Engineering: Dr A. N. MATHUR
- Renewable Energy Sources: Dr N. S. RATHORE
- Soil and Water Conservation Engineering: Dr RAJVIR SINGH

College of Home Science:
- Child Development: Dr C. DAVE
- Family Resource Management: Dr RITU SINGHVI
- Foods and Nutrition: Dr MAYA CHOUDHARY
- Home Science Extension and Communication Management: Dr ASHA SINGHAL
- Textiles and Apparel Designing: Dr MEENU SRIVASTAVA (acting)

ATTACHED RESEARCH INSTITUTE

Land and Water Management Research Institute: Dir Dr RAJVEER SINGH.

MAHARASHTRA ANIMAL AND FISHERY SCIENCES UNIVERSITY

Seminary Hills, Nagpur 440006, Maharashtra
Telephone: (712) 2511259
Fax: (712) 2510883
E-mail: adnvc@sancharnet.in
Internet: www.mafsu.com
Founded 2000
Chancellor: HE THE GOVERNOR OF MAHARASHTRA
Vice-Chancellor: Dr A. T. SHERIKAR
Registrar: Dr DEEPAK G. MHAISEKAR
Colleges of Animal, Fishery and Veterinary Science (Parbhani), Veterinary and Animal Sciences (Latur), Veterinary Science (Mumbai) and Veterinary Science (Nagpur).

MAHARASHTRA UNIVERSITY OF HEALTH SCIENCES

Anandvalli, Gangapur Rd, Nashik 422013, Maharashtra
Telephone: (253) 2340271
Fax: (253) 2344343
E-mail: registrar@muhsnashik.com
Internet: www.muhsnashik.com
Founded 1998
Academic year: June to May
Chancellor: HE THE GOVERNOR OF MAHARASHTRA
Vice-Chancellor: Dr RAVINDRA BAPAT
Registrar: Dr P. M. DURGAWALE
Faculties of Allied Health Sciences, Ayurveda, Dentistry, Homeopathy and Medicine
There are 210 affiliated colleges.

MAHARISHI MAHESH YOGI VEDIC VISHWAVIDYALAYA

871 Napier Town, Jabalpur 482001, Madhya Pradesh
Telephone: (7625) 220285
E-mail: vcmmyvv@rediffmail.com
Internet: www.maharishi-india.org
Founded 1995
Vice-Chancellor: Prof. BHUVNESH SHARMA
Registrar: PYARE L. KADALBAJU.

MAHARSHI DAYANAND SARASWATI UNIVERSITY

Ajmer
Founded 1987 as Ajmer University; present name *c.* 1992
Vice-Chancellor: Prof. R. B. UPADHYAYA
Registrar: Dr J. P. GUPTA

PROFESSORS

BHARDWAJ, T. N., Botany
DUBE, S. N., Mathematics
JOSHI, R. P., Political Science
VASHISHTHA, V. K., History

MAHARSHI DAYANAND UNIVERSITY, ROHTAK

Rohtak 124001, Haryana
Telephone: (1262) 294133
Fax: (1262) 294133
E-mail: md_university@yahoomail.com
Internet: www.mduonline.org
Founded 1976
Affiliating
Languages of instruction: English, Hindi
Academic year: June to May
Chancellor: HE THE GOVERNOR OF HARYANA
Vice-Chancellor: Maj.-Gen. BHIM S. SUHAG (Retd)
Registrar: Dr AJAY K. RAJAN
Librarian: Dr RAJBIR SINGH
Library of 235,155 vols, 400 periodicals
Number of teachers: 385
Number of students: 95,000
Publications: *Sahityanushilan*, *MDU* (quarterly)

DEANS

Faculty of Ayurvedic and Unani System of Medicine: Dr B. N. SINGH
Faculty of Commerce: Dr S. N. MITTAL
Faculty of Dental Sciences: Prof. S. C. ANAND
Faculty of Education: Dr S. B. DAHIYA
Faculty of Engineering and Technology: Dr ASHOK KUMAR
Faculty of Humanities: Dr R. N. MISHRA
Faculty of Law: Dr C. P. SHEORAN
Faculty of Life Sciences: Dr RAVI PARKASH
Faculty of Management Studies: Dr S. K. BEDI
Faculty of Medical Sciences: Maj. Gen. VIRENDRA SINGH
Faculty of Physical Sciences: Dr NATHI SINGH
Faculty of Social Sciences: Dr SURINDER KUMAR
There are 130 affiliated colleges and two maintained colleges

MAHATAMA GANDHI ANTARRASHTRIYA HINDI VISHWAVIDYALAYA

POB 16, Panchtila, Umari Village, Arvi Rd, Wardha 442001, Maharashtra
Telephone: (7152) 230901
Fax: (7152) 230903
E-mail: hindiunv@nda.vsnl.net.in
Internet: www.hindivishwa.org
Founded 1997
Central university
Academic year: July to May
Vice-Chancellor: Prof. G. GOPINATHAN
Registrar: Dr R. K. TIWARI
Publications: *Bahuvachan* (in Hindi, quarterly), *Hindi: Language, Discourse, Writing* (in English, quarterly).

MAHATMA GANDHI CHITRAKOOT GRAMODAYA UNIVERSITY

District Satna, Chitrakoot 485331, Madhya Pradesh
Telephone: (7670) 265413
Fax: (7670) 265411
E-mail: mgcgv@rediffmail.com
Internet: www.ruraluniversity-chitrakoot.org
Founded 1991
Academic year: July to June
Vice-Chancellor: Prof. T. KARUNAKARAN
Registrar: B. K. UPADHYAY
Library of 25,000 vols
Faculties of Agriculture and Animal Science, Ayurveda and Yogic Science, Education, Humanities and Social Science, Rural Reconstruction, Science and Technology.

MAHATMA GANDHI KASHI VIDYAPEETH

Varanasi 221002, Uttar Pradesh
Telephone: (542) 2222689
Fax: (542) 2221168
Chancellor: HE The Governor of Uttar Pradesh
Vice-Chancellor: Ram J. Singh
Registrar: Babu R. Kanaujia.

MAHATMA GANDHI UNIVERSITY

Priyadarshini Hills PO, Kottayam 686560, Kerala
Telephone: (481) 2731050
Fax: (481) 2731009
E-mail: mgu@md2.vsnl.net.in
Internet: www.mguniversity.edu
Founded 1983 as Gandhiji University
State control
Language of instruction: English
Academic year: June to March
Chancellor: HE The Governor of Kerala
Vice-Chancellor: Dr Cyriac Thomas
Pro-Vice-Chancellor: Dr N. Ravindranath
Registrar: Prof. Jose James
Librarian: K. J. Jayamal
Number of teachers: 5,000
Number of students: 125,000
Publications: *Annual Report*, *Newsletter*

HEADS OF DEPARTMENTS

Bio-Sciences: Dr Shankar Shashidhar
Behavioural Science: Prof. Razeena Padmam
Chemical Sciences: Prof. V. N. Rajasekharan Pillai
Computer Science: Dr K. N. Ramachandran Nair
Gandhian Thought and Development Studies: Prof. Mahajan P. Mani
International Relations and Politics: Dr A. K. Ramakrishnan
Indian Legal Thought: Prof. K. Vikraman Nair
Printing and Publishing: O. V. Usha
Pure and Applied Physics: Dr C. S. Menon
Social Sciences: Prof. P. M. Rajan Gurukkal
School of Communication and Information Science: Madavan Balkrishna Pillai
School of Distance Education: Prof. Baby Thomas
School of Environmental Studies: Dr A. P. Thomas
School of Letters: Prof. R. Narendra Prasad
School of Life Sciences: Dr K. C. John
School of Management and Business Studies: Dr K. Sreeranganathan
School of Medical Education: Dr George Paul
School of Pedagogical Science: Prof. P. M. Jaleel
School of Sports Science and Physical Education: Dr Jose James
School of Technology and Applied Sciences: Dr K. A. Jose
Adult Continuing Education and Extension: C. Thomas Abraham
There are 155 affiliated colleges

MAHATMA PHULE KRISHI VIDYAPEETH

Rahuri 413722, Ahmednagar District, Maharashtra
Founded 1968
Academic year: July to May
Chancellor: HE The Governor of Maharashtra
Pro-Chancellor: The Minister for Agriculture
Vice-Chancellor: Dr S. N. Puri
Registrar: Babasaheb R. Pardhe
Librarian: A. G. Karande
Library of 93,195 vols
Number of students: 2,200
Publications: *Journal of Maharashtra Agricultural University* (in English, 3 a year), *Shi Suga* (in Marathi, 3 a year)

DEANS

Faculty of Agricultural Engineering: Dr H. G. More
Faculty of Agriculture: Dr S. S. Kadam

CONSTITUENT COLLEGES

Agricultural College: Dhulia; f. 1960; Assoc. Dean Dr T. A. More.

Agricultural College: Kolhapur; f. 1963; Assoc. Dean Dr S. H. Shinde.

Agricultural College: Pune; f. 1906; Assoc. Dean Dr D. L. Sale.

College of Agricultural Engineering: Rahuri; f. 1969; Assoc. Dean Prof. G. B. Bangal.

Postgraduate Agricultural Institute: Rahuri; f. 1972; Assoc. Dean Dr V. M. Pawar.

MAKHANLAL CHATURVEDI RASHTRIYA PATRAKARITA VISHWAVIDYALAYA

POB RSN/560, Trilochan Singh Nagar, Shahpura, Bhopal 462039, Madhya Pradesh
Telephone: (755) 2725307
Fax: (755) 2561970
E-mail: query@mcu.ac.in
Internet: www.mcu.ac.in
Founded 1990
Academic year: August to July
Director-General: Sharad C. Behar
Registrar: Joshi Sachchidanand
Librarian: G. N. Vyas
Library of 15,000 vols
Publication: *Vidura* (in Hindi and English)
Departments of Broadcast Journalism, Communication and Public Relations, Computer Applications and Journalism, Library and Information Science.

MANGALORE UNIVERSITY

Mangalagangotri 574199, Karnataka
Telephone: (824) 2287276
Fax: (824) 2287367
E-mail: info@mangaloreuniversity.ac.in
Internet: www.mangaloreuniversity.ac.in
Founded 1980
Languages of instruction: English, Kannada
Academic year: June to April
Chancellor: HE The Governor of Karnataka
Vice-Chancellor: Prof. B. Hanumaiah
Registrar: K. Sundar Naik
Librarian: Dr M. K. Bhandi
Library of 150,428 vols
Number of teachers: 2,849
Number of students: 1,303 (university), 41,579 (affiliated colleges)
Publications: *Mangalore University Library* (4 a year), *Newsletter* (4 a year)

DEANS

Faculty of Arts: Prof. B. A. Vivek Rai
Faculty of Commerce: Prof. P. Pakkeerappa
Faculty of Education: Prof. K. R. Rangaraju
Faculty of Law: M. M. Nadig
Faculty of Science and Technology: K. M. Kaveriappa

CHAIRMEN OF DEPARTMENTS

Applied Botany: Prof. K. M. Kaveriappa
Applied Zoology: Dr K. K. Vijayalaxmi
Biosciences: Prof. M. Jayarama Hegde
Chemistry: Prof. Thimme Gowda
Commerce: Dr A. Raghurama
Computer Science: Dr Doreswamy
Economics: Prof. G. V. Joshi
English: Dr R. Shashidhar
History: Prof. B. Surendra Rao
Kannada: Prof. B. A. Viveka Rai
Library and Information Science: Dr A. K. Baradol
Marine Geology: Prof. K. R. Subramanya
Mass Communication and Journalism: Prof. K. V. Nagaraj
Materials Science: Prof. Jayagopal Uchil
Mathematics: Dr Sampath Kumar
MBA Studies: Dr T. Mallikarjunappa
Physical Education: S. Nagalingappa
Physics: Prof. K. Siddappa
Political Science: Prof. Valerian Rodrigues
Sociology: Prof. Jogan Shankar
Statistics: Dr K. K. Acharya
There are 108 affiliated colleges

MANIPUR UNIVERSITY

Canchipur, Imphal 795003, Manipur
Telephone: (385) 2435276
Fax: (385) 2435145
E-mail: vcmu@sancharnet.in
Founded 1980
Teaching and Affiliating
State control
Language of instruction: English
Academic year: July to June
Chancellor: HE The Governor of Manipur
Vice-Chancellor: Prof. N. Bijoy Singh
Registrar: Dr R. K. Ranjan Singh
Librarian: Ch. Radheshyam Singh
Library of 99,916 vols
Number of teachers: 157 (postgraduate depts only)
Number of students: 1,666 (postgraduate depts only)
Publications: *Manipur University Bulletin* (4 a year), *Manipur University Magazine* (annually), *Manipur University Annual Report*

DEANS

Humanities: Prof. H. Behari Singh
Science: Prof. C. Amuba Singh
Social Sciences: Prof. K. Bimola Devi
There are 71 affiliated colleges

MANONMANIAM SUNDARANAR UNIVERSITY

Abishekapatti, Tirunelveli 627012, Tamil Nadu
Telephone: (462) 2333741
Fax: (462) 2334363
E-mail: tvl_regismsu@sancharnet.in
Internet: www.msuniversitytvl.net
Founded 1990
Teaching and Affiliating
Chancellor: HE The Governor of Tamil Nadu
Vice-Chancellor: Dr K. Chockalingam
Registrar: Dr P. Nagarajan
Finance Officer: S. Ramakrishnan
Librarian: P. Alangarababu

HEADS OF DEPARTMENTS

Chemistry: Prof. M. Sivasankaran Nair (acting)
Communication: Prof. P. Govindraju
Computer Science and Engineering: Prof. V. Sadasivam
Criminology and Criminal Justice: Dr P. Madhava Soma Sundaram
English: Prof. S. Ravindranathan
Environmental Science: Prof. N. Sukumaran
History: Prof. K. Sadasivan
Information Technology and Engineering: Dr N. Krishnan

Library and Information Science: P. ALANGARABABU
Management Studies: Dr B. RAJASEKARAN
Marine Science and Technology: Dr M. PETER MARIAN
Mathematics: Prof. T. TAMIZH CHELVAM
Physics: Prof. N. ARUNACHALAM
Sociology: Prof. G. KARUNANITHI
Sports and Physical Education: Dr D. SHUNMUGANATHAN
Statistics: Prof. V. S. SAMPATH KUMAR
Tamil: Prof. T. PARAMASIVAN

There are 61 affiliated colleges

MARATHWADA AGRICULTURAL UNIVERSITY

Parbhani 431402, Maharashtra
Telephone: (2452) 223801
Fax: (2452) 223582
E-mail: vcmau@rediffmail.com

Founded 1972
State control
Language of instruction: English
Academic year: June to May

Chancellor: HE THE GOVERNOR OF MAHARASHTRA
Vice-Chancellor: Dr V. M. PAWAR
Registrar: Dr B. N. CHAVAN
Librarian: B. T. MUNDHE

Library of 70,000 vols
Number of teachers: 282
Number of students: 2,017

Publications: *News Letter* (English and Marathi, monthly), *Research Bulletin* (English, monthly), *Sheti Bhati* (Marathi, monthly)

PROFESSORS

Faculty of Agricultural Technology:
KULKARNI, D. N., Food Science and Cereal Technology
WANKHEDE, D. B., Biochemistry

Faculty of Agriculture:
CHAVAN, B. N., Agronomy
DHAVAN, A. S., Agricultural Chemistry and Soil Science
GORE, K. P., Agricultural Engineering
JANDHALE, S. G., Agricultural Extension
KULKARNI, U. G., Plant Physiology
NADRE, K. R., Agricultural Extension
NARWADKAR, P. R., Horticulture
PAWAR, N. D., Agricultural Economics and Statistics
SHELKE, D. K., Agronomy
SONTAKKE, M. B., Horticulture

Faculty of Home Science:
MURALI, D., Home Management
PATANAM, V., Child Development and Family Relations
ROHINDEVI, P., Food and Nutrition

CONSTITUENT COLLEGES

College of Agricultural Engineering: Parbhani; Principal Dr G. R. MORE.

College of Agricultural Technology: Parbhani; Principal Dr D. B. WANKHEDE.

College of Agriculture, Ambajogai: Ambajogai; Principal Dr B. K. DHANORKAR.

College of Agriculture, Badnapur: Badnapur; Principal Dr H. N. PATIL.

College of Agriculture, Latur: Latur; Principal Dr K. K. ZOTE.

College of Agriculture, Osmanabad: Osmanabad; Principal Dr V. G. REDDY.

College of Agriculture, Parbhani: Parbhani; Principal Dr M. V. DHOBALE.

College of Home Science: Parbhani; Principal Prof. D. MURALI.

College of Horticulture: Parbhani; Principal Dr B. A. KADAM.

There are 16 affiliated research stations

MAULANA AZAD NATIONAL URDU UNIVERSITY

Gochibowli, Hyderabad 500032, Andhra Pradesh
Telephone: (40) 23006601
Fax: (40) 23006603
E-mail: manuu@indiainfo.com
Internet: www.manuu.ac.in

Founded 1998
Central university
State control

Vice-Chancellor: Prof. A. M. PATHAN
Registar: B. NARAYANA
Librarian: Dr ABBAS KHAN A. A.

Library of 9,040 vols, 47 periodicals
Number of students: 22,000

There are three regional centres (Delhi, Patna, Bangalore) and 70 study centres.

MAULANA MAZHARUL HAQUE ARABIC AND PERSIAN UNIVERSITY

Sandal Nagar, Mahendru, Patna 800006.

MIZORAM UNIVERSITY

Aizwal 796012, Mizoram
Telephone: (389) 2342348
Fax: (389) 2340313
E-mail: mzuuni@hotmail.com

Founded 2001
Central university
Academic year: August to July

Vice-Chancellor: Prof. A. K. SHARMA
Registrar: P. C. LAWMKUNGA
Asst Librarian: R. K. NVURTINKHUMA

Library of 18,000 vols

Faculties of Applied Science, Arts, Commerce, Education, Law and Science

There are 31 affiliated colleges.

MOHAN LAL SUKHADIA UNIVERSITY

Pratap Nagar, Udaipur 313001, Rajasthan
Telephone: (294) 2471035
Fax: (294) 2471150
E-mail: sgk@mlsu.org
Internet: www.mlsu.org

Founded 1962 as Rajasthan Agricultural University, present name 1982
Teaching and Affiliating
Autonomous control
Languages of instruction: English, Hindi
Academic year: July to June

Chancellor: HE THE GOVERNOR OF RAJASTHAN
Vice-Chancellor: Prof. A. K. SINGH
Registrar: MOHAN LAL SHARMA
Librarian: Prof. K. K. SUD

Library of 287,000 vols
Number of teachers: 264
Number of students: 47,209

Publications: *Information Bulletin* (annually), *Annual Report*

DEANS

Faculty of Commerce: Prof. I. V. TRIVEDI
Faculty of Education: Dr M. P. SHARMA
Faculty of Humanities: Prof. S. R. VYAS
Faculty of Law: Dr R. L. BHATT
Faculty of Postgraduate Studies: Prof. H. R. S. TYAGI
Faculty of Science: Prof. B. L. CHOUDHARY
Faculty of Social Sciences: Prof. C. N. MATHUR

PROFESSORS

Faculty of Commerce:
JAIN, P. K., MBA
RAO, N. S., Accountancy and Statistics
SODANI, K. C., Business Administration
TRIVEDI, I. V., Banking and Business Economics

Faculty of Humanities and Social Sciences:
CHATURVEDI, A., Political Science
JOSHI, C. P., Psychology
JOSHI, H., Geography
KOHLI, A., Economics
MATHUR, C. N., Psychology
VYAS, R. N., Geography
VYAS, S. R., Philosophy

Faculty of Science:
AERY, N. C., Botany
AMETA, S. C., Chemistry
BHATNAGAR, M., Zoology
BHATT, D. K., Zoology
CHOUDHARY, B. L., Botany
GYANI, K. C., Geology
KALRA, M. L., Physics
KAPOOR, K., Botany
KATARIA, P., Geology
RAMAWAT, K. G., Botany
RANAWAT, P. S., Geology
SHARMA, M. S., Zoology
SHARMA, S. S., Physics
SUD, K. K., Physics
TYAGI, H. R. S., Zoology

There are 45 affiliated colleges

CONSTITUENT COLLEGES

College of Commerce and Management Studies: Udaipur; Dean Prof. I. V. TRIVEDI.

College of Law: Udaipur; Assoc. Dean Dr R. L. BHATT.

College of Science: Udaipur; Dean Prof. B. L. CHOUDHARY.

College of Social Sciences and Humanities: Udaipur; Dean Prof. C. N. MATHUR.

MOTHER TERESA WOMEN'S UNIVERSITY

Kodaikanal 624102, Tamil Nadu
Telephone: (4542) 241122
Fax: (4542) 241122
E-mail: mtwuni@md2.vsnl.net.in

Founded 1984
State control
Languages of instruction: English, Tamil
Academic year: June to May

Chancellor: HE THE GOVERNOR OF TAMIL NADU
Vice-Chancellor: Dr ANANDHAVALLI MAHADEVAN
Registrar: S. NAGALAKSHMI
Assistant Librarians: K. P. PADMAVATHY, P. SEMBIANMADEVI

Library of 47,000 vols
Number of teachers: 34
Number of students: 1,000

Courses in economics, education, English, family life management, historical studies, sociology, Tamil, computer science, music, women's studies, guidance and counselling, population studies, business economics, history and tourism, entrepreneurship and industrial training, health and family welfare

PROFESSORS

ANEES, A., Economics
ARAVANAN, T., Tamil
SUBBAMMAL, K., Education
SURYAKUMARI, A., Historical Studies and Tourism

UNIVERSITY OF MUMBAI

University Rd, Fort, Mumbai 400032, Maharashtra
Telephone: (22) 22656789
Fax: (22) 22652832

E-mail: vc@fort.mu.ac.in
Internet: www.mu.ac.in
Founded 1857 as University of Bombay; present name 1996
Teaching and Affiliating
Language of instruction: English
Academic year: June to April (two terms)
Chancellor: HE THE GOVERNOR OF MAHARASHTRA
Vice-Chancellor: Dr VIJAY KHOLE
Pro Vice-Chancellor: Dr ARUN D. SAWANT
Registrar: L. R. MANE
Librarian: Prof. VIJAYA RAJHAMA
Library of 837,978 vols
Number of students: 262,350
Publications: *Journal of the University of Bombay*, *Prakrit and Pali*, *Sanskrit*, *University of Bombay Studies*, *University Economics Series*, *University Series in Monetary and International Economics*, *University Sociology Series*

DEANS

Faculty of Arts: Dr A. M. PETHE
Faculty of Commerce: Principal: MALLIKARJUN G. SHIRAHATTI
Faculty of Fine Arts: Prof. N. D. VICHARE
Faculty of Law: Dr P. C. WARKE
Faculty of Science: Dr JAYANT P. DIGHE
Faculty of Technology: Dr P. V. PARAMESWARAN

PROFESSORS

Faculty of Arts:
ABHEDI, R. S. A., Urdu
ANNAKUTY, V. K., German Literature and Russian
BANDIVADEKAR, C. M., Comparative Literature
BHARADWAJ, M. A., Econometrics
BHARUCHA, N., Post-Colonial Literature
BHAT NAYAK, V., Mathematics
BHONGLE, N., 20th-Century Indian Literature in English
BOKIT, S. V., Industrial Policy and Development Banking
BHOWMIK, S. K., Sociology
CHAWATHE, P. D., Graphs Theory
CORREA, R., Economics
DALVI, A. M. I., Urdu
DESHPANDE, J. V., Mathematics
DOSSAL, M., History
GIRI, R. D., Mathematics
GUHA, S. B., Geography
GUMMADI, N., General Economics
JADHAV, A. S., Geography
JANWA, H. L., Algebra
JOGDAND, P. G., Sociology
JOSHI, S. A., Philosophy
JOSHI, S. M., Statistical Inference
KAMATH, P. M., American Studies
KHOKLE, V. S., Socio-linguistics
KUMARESAN, S., Mathematics
LIMAYE, N. B., Mathematics
LUKMANI, V. M., English
MODY, N. B., Civics and Politics
MOHANTY, S. P., Social Demography
MOMIN, A. R., Cultural Anthropology
MUNGEKAR, B. I., Economics
NABAR, S. P., Statistics
NABAR, V., Indo-English Literature
NACHANE, D. N., Quantitative Economics
NADKARNI, M. G., Mathematics
NEMADE, B. V., Comparative Literature
PETHE, A. M., Economics
PHADKE, V. S., Geography
RAJHANSA, V. P., Reference Service
RAO, M. J. M., General Economics
SABNIS, R. S., Monetary and Industrial Economics
SANDESARA, J. C., Industrial Economics
SANE, S. S., Mathematics
SAWANT, S. D., Agricultural Economics
SEETA PRABHU, K., Economics
SEN, M., Experimental Psychology
SIRDESHPANDE, M. R., French
SRIRAMAN, S., Transport Economics
TIKEKAR, A. C., Library Science
TIWARI, R., Hindi
VAIDYA, S. S., Marathi
VANAJA, N., Algebra
VASANT KARNIK, A., Economics
VASANTKUMAR, T., Kannada Literature
VYAS, V. S., Music

Faculty of Commerce:
ANAGOL, M., Banking
GHOSH, P. K., Personnel Management
IYER, V. R., Management
MANERIKAR, V. V., Research Methodology
MURTHY, G. N., Finance and Accounts
SANTANAM, H., Operational Research

Faculty of Law:
KHODIE, N., Mercantile Law
RAO, M., Law
WARKE, P. C., Law

Faculty of Science:
BAGADE, U. S., Life Sciences
FULEKAR, M. H., Life Sciences
GAJBHIYE, N. S., Physics
GOGAVALE, S. V., Experimental Electronic and Plasma Physics
HOSANGADI, B. D., Organic Chemistry
JOSHI, V. N., Computer Science
KULKARNI, A. R., Plant Sciences
NARAYANAN, P., Life Sciences
NARSALE, A. M., Physics
PATEL, S. B., Experimental Nuclear Physics
PRATAP, R., Electronics
RANGWALA, A. A., Theoretical Physics
SHETHNA, Y. I., Life Sciences
SIVAKAMI, S., Life Sciences
VASANTHAKUMAR, T., Kannada

Faculty of Technology:
AKAMANCHI, K. G., Pharmaceutical Chemistry
ATHAWALE, V. D., Chemistry
BHAT, N. V., Physics
CHANDALIA, S. B., Chemical Engineering
DIXIT, S. G., Physics
JOSHI, J. B., Chemical Engineering
KALE, D. D., Polymer Technology
KULKARNI, P. R., Food Science and Technology
KULKARNI, V. M., Medicinal Chemistry
LOKHANDE, H. T., Fibre Science
MALSHE, V. C., Paint Technology
MASHRAQUI, S. H., Chemistry
MHASKAR, R. D., Chemical Engineering
NYAYADHISH, V. B., Mathematics
PAI, J. S., Biochemical Engineering
PANGARKAR, V. G., Chemical Engineering
RAJADYAKSHA, R. A., Physical Chemistry
RAO, H. M., Engineering
SESHADRI, S., Dyestuffs Technology
SHARMA, M. M., Chemical Engineering
SHENAY, V. A., Textile Chemistry
SUBRAMANIAN, V. V. R., Oil Technology
TELI, M. D., Fibre Science
TIWARI, K. K., Chemical Engineering
TUNGARE, S. A., Architecture
VENKATESEN, T. K., Oil Chemistry
VARADARAJAN, T. S., Applied Physics
YADAV, G. D., Chemical Engineering

There are 315 constituent colleges and 79 recognized postgraduate institutions (mostly listed under Research Institutes)

UNIVERSITY OF MYSORE

POB 407, Mysore 570005, Karnataka
Telephone: (821) 2438666
Fax: (821) 2421263
Internet: www.universityofmysore.com
Founded 1916
Teaching and Affiliating
Languages of instruction: English, Kannada
Academic year: June to March (two terms)
Chancellor: HE THE GOVERNOR OF KARNATAKA
Vice-Chancellor: Prof. S. N. HEGDE
Registrar: Prof. V. G. TALWAR
Registrar (Evaluation): Prof. K. N. UDAYA KUMAR
Librarian: Prof. H. R. ACHYUTHA RAO
Library of 750,000 vols (incl. undergraduate library)
Number of students: 74,555 (62,966 undergraduate, 11,589 postgraduate)

DEANS

Faculty of Arts: Prof. C. P. SIDDHASHRAMA
Faculty of Commerce: Prof. B. R. ANANTHAN
Faculty of Education: Prof. A. S. RAGHAVA KUMARI
Faculty of Engineering: Prof. CHENNA VENKATESH
Faculty of Law: Dr H. K. NAGARAJA
Faculty of Medicine: Dr KAMALA
Faculty of Science and Technology: Prof. Y. SRINIVASA REDDY

UNIVERSITY COLLEGES

College of Fine Arts for Women.

Maharaja's College.

University College of Physical Education.

University Evening College.

Yuvaraja's College.

There are 122 affiliated colleges, 2 evening colleges and 2 postgraduate centres

NAGALAND UNIVERSITY

Lumami, Kohima 797001, Nagaland
Telephone: (370) 2290488
Fax: (370) 2290246
E-mail: nagalanduniversity@yahoo.co.in
Founded 1994
Central university
State control
Language of instruction: English
Academic year: September to August
Chief Rector: HE THE GOVERNOR OF NAGALAND
Chancellor (vacant): Prof. YOGINDER K. ALAGH
Vice-Chancellor: Prof. G. D. SHARMA
Registrar: Dr KUHOI K. ZHIMOMI
Library of 30,000 vols, 87 periodicals
Number of teachers: 112
Number of students: 19,151 (18,349 undergraduate, 802 postgraduate)

DEANS

School of Agricultural Sciences and Rural Development: Prof. D. N. UPADHYA
School of Humanities and Education: Prof. S. K. GUPTA
School of Sciences: Prof. R. P. KACHHARA
School of Social Sciences: Dr A. L. AO
There are 42 affiliated colleges

NAGARJUNA UNIVERSITY

Nagarjuna Nagar 522510, Andhra Pradesh
Telephone: (863) 2293378
Founded 1976
Language of instruction: English
Academic year: July to April
Chancellor: HE THE GOVERNOR OF ANDHRA PRADESH
Vice-Chancellor: Prof. CHITTURI V. RAGHAVULU
Principal: Prof. V. L. NARASIMHAM
Registrar: Prof. LAM PRAKASA
Librarian: J. RAMA RAO
Library of 86,000 vols
Number of teachers: 148
Number of students: 1,700

DEANS

Faculty of Commerce: Prof. D. DAKSHINA MURTHY
Faculty of Education: Dr M. SHYAM SUNDAR
Faculty of Engineering: Prof. V. V. SUBBA RAO
Faculty of Humanities: Prof. B. R. SUBRAHMANYAM
Faculty of Law: Prof. D. VIJAYANARAYANA REDDY
Faculty of Natural Sciences: Prof. P. NARASIMHAM
Faculty of Physical Sciences: Prof. V. L. NARASIMHAM
Faculty of Social Sciences: (vacant)

PROFESSORS

Faculty of Commerce:
- BRAHMANANDAM, G. N., Commerce
- DAKSHINA MURTHY, D., Commerce
- GANJU, M. K., Commerce
- HANUMANTHA RAO, K., Commerce
- NARASIMHAM, V. V. L., Commerce
- PRASAD, G., Commerce
- UMAMAHESWARA RAO, T., Commerce
- VIYYANNA RAO, K., Commerce

Faculty of Engineering:
- THRIMURTY, P., Computer Science and Engineering

Faculty of Humanities:
- BALAGANGADHARA RAO, Y., Telugu and Languages
- KRUPACHARY, G., Telugu and Languages
- KUMARASWAMY, Y., Ancient History and Archaeology
- NIRMALA, T., Telugu and Oriental Languages
- PUNNA RAO, A., Telugu and Oriental Languages
- RAMA SASTRY, N. A., Telugu and Languages
- RAMALAKSHMI, P., Ancient History and Archaeology
- BHASKARA MURTHY, D., Ancient History and Archaeology
- SARASWATHI, R., English
- SUBRAHMANYAM, B. R., Ancient History and Archaeology

Faculty of Law:
- HARAGOPAL REDDY, Y. R.
- RANGAIAH, N., Law
- VIJAYANARAYANA REDDY, D.

Faculty of Natural Sciences:
- BALAPARAMESWARA RAO, M., Aquaculture
- DURGA PRASAD, M. K., Zoology
- GOPALAKRISHNA REDDY, T., Zoology
- LAKSHMI, N., Botany
- MALLAIAH, K. V., Botany
- NARASIMHA RAO, P., Botany
- NIRAMALA MARY, T., Botany
- RAMAMOHANA RAO, P., Botany
- RAMAMURTHY NAIDU, K., Botany
- RANGA RAO, V., Geology
- SANTHA KUMARI, D., Botany
- SHARMA, S. V., Zoology

Faculty of Physical Sciences:
- ANJANEYULU, Y., Chemistry
- GOPALA KRISHNA MURTHY, P. V., Physics
- HARANADH, C., Physics
- KOTESWARA RAO, G., Mathematics
- NARASIMHAM, V. L., Statistics
- NARAYANA MURTHY, P., Physics
- PRAKASA RAO, L., Mathematics
- PRAKASA RAO, N. S., Chemistry
- RAMA BADRA SARMA, I., Mathematics
- RAMAKOTAIAH, D., Mathematics
- RANGACHARYULU, H., Physics
- SATYANANDAM, G., Physics
- SATYANARAYANA, P. V. V., Chemistry
- SHYAM SUNDAR, B., Chemistry
- SIVA RAMA SARMA, B., Chemistry
- VENKATACHARYULU, P., Physics
- VENKATESWARA REDDY, Y., Mathematics

Faculty of Social Sciences:
- ASHEERVADH, N., Political Science
- BAPUJI, M., Political Science
- BHAVANI, V., Political Science
- NARAYANA RAO, C., Political Science
- RAGHAVULU, C. V., Political Science and Public Administration
- RAJA BABU, K., Economics
- RAJU, C. S. N., Economics
- SUDHAKARA RAO, N., Economics

There are 174 affiliated colleges

UNIVERSITY OF NAGPUR

Rabindranath Tagore Marg, Nagpur 440001, Maharashtra
Telephone: (712) 2523045
Internet: www.nagpur-university.com

Founded 1923

Teaching and Affiliating

Languages of instruction: English, Hindi, Marathi

Academic year: June to March (two terms)

Chancellor: HE THE GOVERNOR OF MAHARASHTRA
Vice-Chancellor: M. T. GABHE
Registrar: P. B. MISTRI
Librarian: Dr P. S. G. KUMAR

Library of 319,000 vols, including 14,313 MSS
Number of teachers: 4,074
Number of students: 95,664

DEANS

Faculty of Arts: A. K. DEY
Faculty of Ayurvedic Medicine: S. SHARMA
Faculty of Commerce: N. H. KHATRI
Faculty of Education: R. S. DAGAR
Faculty of Engineering and Technology: H. THAKARE
Faculty of Home Science: Dr A. G. MOHARIL
Faculty of Law: SUNDARAM
Faculty of Medicine: Dr W. B. TAYADE
Faculty of Science: Dr T. M. KARDE
Faculty of Social Sciences: V. H. GHORPADE

CHAIRMEN OF BOARDS OF STUDIES

Faculty of Arts (including Fine Arts):
- Arabic: Dr A. MAJID
- English: K. SATYANARAYANA
- Fine Arts: A. S. MOREY
- Hindi: H. CHAURASIA
- Linguistics: Dr R. P. SAXENA
- Marathi: Prof. S. W. SWAN
- Music: S. S. PALDHIKAR
- Other Foreign Languages: P. R. DEO
- Other Indian Languages: Dr R. N. ROY
- Pali and Prakrit: Prof. M. S. WAGHMARE
- Persian: Q. JOHAN
- Sanskrit: Dr M. GULAB
- Urdu: Dr ARSHAD JAMAL

Faculty of Ayurvedic Medicine:
- Clinical: Dr G. N. TIWARI
- Paraclinical: H. B. DESHPANDE
- Preclinical: J. T. CHOTAI
- Pharmaceutical Surgery: M. M. JUMALE

Faculty of Commerce:
- Accounts and Statistics: Prof. T. D. LODHI
- Business Administration and Business Management: Prof. V. M. CHOPDE
- Business Economics: B. A. MEGDE
- Commerce: V. S. AINCHWAR
- Languages: D. JOG

Faculty of Education:
- Education: Dr P. B. GUPTA
- Physical Education and Recreation: R. S. DAGAR

Faculty of Engineering and Technology:
- Applied Science and Humanities: V. S. GOGULWAR
- Architecture: Prof. A. L. CHHATRE
- Chemical Engineering: Dr R. L. SONULIKAR
- Chemical Technology: Dr J. D. DHAKE
- Civil Engineering: R. S. BAIS
- Electrical Engineering: Dr N. T. KHOBRAGADE
- Electronics Engineering: J. B. HELONDE
- Fire Engineering: (vacant)
- Mechanical Engineering: Prof. I. K. CHOPDE
- Metallurgical Engineering: Dr S. U. PATHAK
- Mining Engineering: L. L. MUTHREJA
- Production Engineering: Prof. V. M. KRIPLANI

Faculty of Home Science:
- Dr P. AKHANI

Faculty of Law:
- V. R. MANOHAR

Faculty of Medicine:
- Dentistry (Clinical): Dr P. V. HAZARE
- Dentistry (Preclinical): V. K. HAZARE
- Clinical Medicine: (vacant)
- Clinical Medicine II: Dr N. D. WASUDEV
- Homoeopathy: Dr V. P. MISHRA
- Modern Medicine (OT and PT): Dr G. J. RAMTEKE
- Paraclinical Medicine: Dr B. D. PARANJAPE
- Preclinical Medicine: Dr V. M. SATHE
- Pharmaceutical Sciences: Dr K. P. BHUSARI
- Surgery: Dr R. NARANG

Faculty of Science:
- Biochemistry: Dr S. CHARI
- Botany: Dr K. M. MAKDE
- Chemistry: Dr V. G. DESHMUKH
- Electronics: Dr A. A. SAKALE
- Geology: Dr N. K. MOHOBEY
- Languages: K. M. THOMAS
- Mathematics: Dr T. M. KARDE
- Microbiology: A. V. GOMASE
- Physics: S. R. BAJAJ
- Statistics: C. P. CHOLKAR
- Zoology: Dr P. G. PURANIK

Faculty of Social Sciences:
- Ancient Indian History, Culture and Archaeology: Dr C. S. GUPTA
- Economics: M. K. GURPUDE
- Geography: V. H. GHORPADE
- Gandhian Thought: B. M. MANDEOKAR
- History: Dr Y. N. GUJAR
- Home Economics: P. DHOBLE
- Library and Information Science: Dr P. S. G. KUMAR
- Mass Communication: (vacant)
- Philosophy: Dr B. Y. DESHPANDE
- Political Science: Dr B. L. BHOLE
- Psychology: Dr A. V. KULKARNI
- Public Administration: Dr P. L. JOSHI
- Rural Services: R. B. GHATE
- Social Work: A. W. DHAGE
- Sociology: M. B. BUTE

CONSTITUENT COLLEGES

Laxminarayan Institute of Technology: Nagpur; f. 1942; 50 teachers; 510 students; Dir Dr G. D. NAGESHWAR.

University College of Education: Nagpur; f. 1945; 16 teachers; 320 students; Principal C. K. NAGOSE.

University College of Law: Nagpur; f. 1925; 10 teachers; 2,571 students; Principal V. D. THAKARE.

There are 218 affiliated colleges

NALANDA OPEN UNIVERSITY

Patna 800001, Bihar
Telephone: (612) 2201013
Fax: (612) 2201001
E-mail: nalopuni@bih.nic.in
Internet: www.nalandaopenuniversity.info

Founded 1987

Academic year: June to May

Chancellor: HE THE GOVERNOR OF BIHAR

Pro-Vice-Chancellor: Prof. USHA SINGH
Vice-Chancellor: VIJAY SHANKAR DUBEY
Registrar: Dr S. P. SINHA

Library of 10,000 vols

There are study centres in Ara, Bhagalpur, Patna, Ranchi and Saharsa.

NARENDRA DEVA UNIVERSITY OF AGRICULTURE & TECHNOLOGY

Narendranagar, Kumarganj, Faizabad 224229, Uttar Pradesh
Telephone: (5270) 262035
Fax: (5270) 262097
E-mail: nduat@up.nic.in
Internet: UPgov.up.nic.in/nduat

Founded 1974
State control
Languages of instruction: Hindi, English
Chancellor: HE THE GOVERNOR OF UTTAR PRADESH
Vice-Chancellor: Prof. B. B. SINGH
Registrar: Prof. B. V. S. SISODIA

Library of 42,000 vols
Number of teachers: 67
Number of students: 432

Publication: *NDUAT News Bulletin*

DEANS

Faculty of Agricultural Engineering and Technology: Prof. E. RAM KISHORE
Faculty of Agriculture: Dr D. S. YADAV
Faculty of Home Science: Dr A. C. VERMA
Faculty of Veterinary Science: Dr D. N. VERMA

NATIONAL ACADEMY OF LEGAL STUDIES AND RESEARCH UNIVERSITY

Justice City, Shameerpet, Rangareddy District, Hyderabad 500014, Andhra Pradesh
Telephone: (8418) 245159
Fax: (8418) 245161
E-mail: director@nalsarlawuniv.org
Internet: www.nalsarlawuniv.org

Founded 1998
Academic year: July to June
Dir: Prof. RANBIR SINGH
Registrar: Prof. A. LAKSHMINATH

Library of 14,300 vols

Publication: *NALSAR Law Review* (2 a year).

NATIONAL LAW INSTITUTE UNIVERSITY

Bhopal Bhadbhada Rd, Barkheri Kalan, POB 369, Bhopal 462003, Madhya Pradesh
Telephone: (755) 2646905
Fax: (755) 2696965
E-mail: nliu@sancharnet.in
Internet: www.nliu.org

Founded 1998

Director: Prof. M. C. SHARMA
Registrar: ANIL THAKRE.

NATIONAL LAW UNIVERSITY

NH-65, Nagaur Rd, Mandore, Jodhpur 342004, Rajasthan
Telephone: (291) 2577530
Fax: (291) 2577540
E-mail: nlu-jod@raj.nic.in
Internet: www.nlujodhpur.nic.in

Founded 1999

Chancellor: ANIL DEV SINGH (Chief Justice of Rajasthan)
Vice-Chancellor: Prof. N. L. MITRA
Registrar: RATAN LAHOTI
Librarian: DEEPA AWASTHI

Library of 3,500 vols

DEANS

Faculty of Law: Prof. Y. K. TIWARI
Faculty of Management: Prof. H. K. BEDI
Faculty of Policy Science: Prof. RAMLAL SHARMA
Faculty of Science: Prof. AKSHYA M. BHANDARI

PROFESSORS

BANERJEE, D., Crystallography
BANERJI, K. K., Chemistry
BEDI, H. K., Management Studies
BHANDARI, A. M., Organic Chemistry
DAGA, U. R., Financial Management, Accounting and Quantitative Technology
KALLA, N. R., Life Science
SHARMA, R., Macroeconomics, Monetary Economics and Econometrics
TIWARI, Y. K., Family Law and Labour Law
VIBHUTE, K. I., Criminal Law, Criminology and Legal Research Methodology

ATTACHED RESEARCH INSTITUTES

Center for Criminal Law Studies: Dir Prof. K. I. VIBHUTE.

Center for Forensic Science: Dir Prof. P. CHANDRA SEKHARAN.

Center for Human Rights Education and Research: Dir SESHAIAH SHASTHRI VEDANTAM.

Center for Insurance Studies and Research: Dir K. N. BHANDARI.

Center for Studies in Agriculture and Law: Dir SANJAY K. PANDEY.

Center for Studies in Banking and Finance: Dir MADHAV M. MEHTA.

Center for WTO Studies: Dir SANJAY PANDEY.

NETAJI SUBHAS OPEN UNIVERSITY

1 Woodburn Park, Kolkata 700020, West Bengal
Telephone: (33) 22835157
Fax: (33) 22871082
E-mail: admin@wbnsou.com
Internet: www.wbnsou.com

Founded 1997
Language of instruction: Bengali
Chancellor: HE THE GOVERNOR OF WEST BENGAL
Vice-Chancellor: Prof. SURABHI BANERJEE
Registrar: DIPAK ROY
Director (Study Centres): Prof. PRADIP BHRAMA
Director (Humanities): Prof. SWAPAN BANERJEE
Director (Science): Prof. ASOK CHOUDHURI
Number of students: 30,000

Undergraduate and postgraduate degree programmes in accountancy, Bengali, botany, chemistry, commerce, computer science, economics, education, English, environmental science, geography, history, management, mathematics, physics, political science, public administration, sociology and zoology

There are 90 study centres.

NIRMA UNIVERSITY OF SCIENCE AND TECHNOLOGY

Sarkhej Gandhinagar Highway, Village Chharodi, Ahmedabad 382481, Gujarat
Telephone: (2717) 241911
Fax: (2717) 241917
Internet: www.nirmauniversity.ac.in

Founded 1994; present name and status 2003
Privately controlled by Nirma Education and Research Foundation
Vice-Chancellor: Dr N. V. VASANI.

CONSTITUENT INSTITUTES

Institute of Diploma Studies

Sarkhej Gandhinagar Highway, Village Chharodi, Ahmedabad 382481, Gujarat
Telephone: (2717) 241911
Fax: (2717) 241917
E-mail: registrar@nids.edu
Internet: www.nids.edu

Founded 1997
Principal: Prof. G. N. GANDHI
Registrar: D. P. CHHAYA

Library of 3,173 vols, 42 periodicals

HEADS OF DEPARTMENTS

Chemical Engineering: (vacant)
Computer Engineering: Prof. B. B. KADAM
Electronics and Communication Engineering: Prof. B. B. KADAM
General Department: Dr A. S. PATEL
Information Technology: Prof. B. B. KADAM
Mechanical Engineering: Prof. R. R. MANSURI
Plastic Engineering: Prof. G. K. LALCHANDANI

Institute of Management

Sarkhej Gandhinagar Highway, Village Chharodi, Ahmedabad 382481, Gujarat
Telephone: (2717) 241900
Fax: (2717) 241916
E-mail: director@nim.ac.in
Internet: www.nim.ac.in

Founded 1996

Director: Dr ANUP K. SINGH
Deputy Registrar: G. RAMACHANDRAN NAIR
Dean: Dr G. S. GUPTA
Librarian: Prof. H. ANIL KUMAR

PROFESSORS

BAHL, S.
BHATTACHARYA, A.
CHUGAN, P. K.
DHANAK, D.
GUPTA, G. S.
GUPTA, P.
MAHAKUD, J.
MALLIKARJUN, M.
MUNCHERJI, N.
NATH, V.V.
PETHE, S.
SAHU, C.
SAHU, S.
SAXENA, S.
TRIVEDI, H.
YADAV, P. K.

Institute of Pharmacy

Sarkhej Gandhinagar Highway, Village Chharodi, Ahmedabad 382481, Gujarat
Telephone: (2717) 241900
Fax: (2717) 241916
Internet: www.nids.edu/pharmacy

Founded 2004

Director: Dr Y. K. AGRAWAL.

Institute of Technology

Sarkhej Gandhinagar Highway, Village Chharodi, Ahmedabad 382481, Gujarat
Telephone: (2717) 241911
Fax: (2717) 241917
Internet: www.nit.edu

Founded 1995

Director: Dr H. V. TRIVEDI

Library of 22,000 vols

HEADS OF DEPARTMENTS

Chemical Engineering: Dr A. K. BHARADWAJ
Civil Engineering: Prof. G. N. PATEL
Electrical, Electronics and Communication: Dr M. D. DESAI
Information Technology and Computer Engineering: Prof. D. J. PATEL

Mathematics and Humanities: Dr K. R. KACHOT
Mechanical Engineering: Prof. A. B. PATEL

UNIVERSITY OF NORTH BENGAL

PO North Bengal University, Raja Rammohunpur 734430, Darjeeling District, West Bengal
Telephone: (353) 2582099
Fax: (353) 2581212
E-mail: regnbu@sancharnet.in
Internet: www.nbu.ac.in

Founded 1962
Teaching and Affiliating
Academic year: July to June
Chancellor: HE THE GOVERNOR OF WEST BENGAL
Vice-Chancellor: Prof. P. K. SAHA
Registrar: Dr T. K. CHATTERJEE
Deputy Librarian: Dr SOUMITRA SARKAR
Library of 151,126 vols
Number of teachers: 154
Number of students: 61,528
Publications: *North Bengal University Review (Humanities and Social Sciences)* (2 a year), *North Bengal University Review (Science and Technology)* (2 a year)

DEANS

Faculty of Arts, Commerce and Law: Prof. P. K. SENGUPTA
Faculty of Medicine: Prof. R. K. DEB
Faculty of Science: Prof. D. K. HAZRA

PROFESSORS

Arts, Commerce and Law:
BHADRA, R. K., Sociology
BHATTA, A., Bengali
BHATTACHARJEE, C., Philosophy
CHAKRABORTY, B. B., Philosophy
CHAKRABORTY, U., English
GHOSH, R., Philosophy
MONDAL, SK. R., Centre for Himalayan Studies
MUKHOPADHYAY, C., Economics
MUKHOPADHYAY, R. S., Sociology
ROY MOULIK, S. K., English
SAHU, R., Centre for Himalayan Studies
SENGUPTA, P. K., Political Science
SENGUPTA, P. R., Commerce
UPADHYAY, B. K., Nepali

Science:
BOSE, M. K., Mathematics
DAS, A. P., Botany
DASGUPTA, D., Physics
HAZRA, D. K., Chemistry
KARANJAI, S. B., Mathematics
MANNA, N. R., Computer Science and Applications
MUKHOPADHYAY, A., Zoology
NANDI, K. K., Mathematics
ROY, A., Chemistry
ROY, P. S., Chemistry
SAHA, S. K., Chemistry
SARKAR, P. K., Botany

There are three university colleges and 55 affiliated colleges

NORTH-EASTERN HILL UNIVERSITY

PO NEHU Campus, Shillong 793002
Telephone: (364) 2250705
Fax: (364) 2250076
Internet: www.nehu.ac.in

Founded 1973
Central university
Language of instruction: English
Academic year: July to June
Chancellor: Dr K. R. NARAYANAN
Vice-Chancellor: Prof. BARRISTER PAKEM
Pro-Vice Chancellors: Prof. LALTHANTLUANGA, Prof. K. S. LYNGDOH, Prof. M. S. SANGMA
Registrar: P. S. RYNJAH
Librarian: Dr LALIT P. PATHAK
Library of 187,000 vols
Number of teachers: 271
Number of students: 23,709
Publications: *NEHU Journal of Social Sciences and Humanities* (quarterly), *NEHU News* (monthly)

DEANS

School of Economics, Management and Information Science: Prof. S. K. MISHRA
School of Human and Environmental Sciences: Prof. A. C. MOHAPATRA
School of Humanities and Education: (vacant)
School of Life Sciences: Prof. A. RAGHUVERMAN
School of Physical Sciences: Prof. S. N. BHATT
School of Social Sciences: Prof. J. P. SINGH

There are 54 affiliated colleges

NORTH MAHARASHTRA UNIVERSITY

PB No. 80, Jalgaon 425002, Maharashtra
Telephone: (257) 2252187
Fax: (257) 2252183
E-mail: info@nmu.ac.in
Internet: www.nmu.ac.in

Founded 1990
State control
Academic year: July to April
Vice-Chancellor: Prof. R. S. MALI
Registrar: Dr R. H. GUPTA
Library of 11,000 vols
Number of teachers: 3,174
Number of students: 47,974

DEANS

Faculty of Arts: GHANSHYAM MOHARIR
Faculty of Ayurveda: Prof. T. N. PATIL
Faculty of Commerce and Management: Dr SHAMKANT G. DESHPANDE
Faculty of Education: Prof. R. K. MAHAJAN
Faculty of Engineering: Prin.: P. D. PATIL
Faculty of Law: Prin.: PRAVINCHANDRA JANGALE
Faculty of Medicine and Pharmacy: Dr BHAIDAS PATIL
Faculty of Mental, Moral and Social Sciences: Prin.: P. D. DEORE
Faculty of Science: Dr D. A. PATIL

There are 143 affiliated colleges

NORTH ORISSA UNIVERSITY

Baripada 757003, Orissa
Telephone: (6792) 255127
Fax: (6792) 255127

Founded 1998
State control
Academic year: June to May
Chancellor: HE THE GOVERNOR OF ORISSA
Vice-Chancellor: Dr BIRANCHINARAYAN N. PUHAN
Registrar: Dr HARIPRASAD P. PANDA
Librarian: S. K. TANTI
Library of 2,647 vols
Number of students: 10,320

Faculties of Arts, Commerce, Computer Applications, Education, Engineering, Law, Medicine, Science and Tribal Studies

There are 79 affiliated colleges.

ORISSA UNIVERSITY OF AGRICULTURE AND TECHNOLOGY

Bhubaneswar 751003, District Khurda, Orissa
Telephone: (674) 2402677
Fax: (674) 2407780
E-mail: vc@ouat.ac.in
Internet: www.ouat.ac.in

Founded 1962
Teaching and Research
State control
Language of instruction: English
Academic year: July to July
Chancellor: HE THE GOVERNOR OF ORISSA
Vice-Chancellor: SAHADEVA SAHOO
Registrar: BIJOY KUMAR PARIDA
Library of 175,000 vols
Number of teachers: 294
Number of students: 3,046

DEANS

College of Agricultural Engineering and Technology: Dr S. N. SWAIN
College of Agriculture (Bhubaneswar): Dr B. SENAPATI
College of Agriculture (Chiplima): Dr M. M. PANDA
College of Basic Science and Humanities: Dr J. C. MUDULI
College of Engineering and Technology: Dr B. S. PATRO
College of Fisheries: Dr R. K. RATH
College of Home Science: Prin.: P. DAS
College of Veterinary Science and Animal Husbandry: Dr SARAT CHANDRA MISHRA

OSMANIA UNIVERSITY

Hyderabad 500007, Andhra Pradesh
Telephone: (40) 27098043
Internet: www.osmania.ac.in

Founded 1918
Teaching, Residential and Affiliating
Languages of instruction: English, Hindi
Languages of instruction: Telugu, Urdu, Marathi
Academic year: June to April (two terms)
Chancellor: HE THE GOVERNOR OF ANDHRA PRADESH
Vice-Chancellor: Prof. D. C. REDDY
Registrar: Prof. PANNALAL
Librarian: URMILA VEMI REDDY
Library of 422,000 vols
Number of students: 78,212
Publications: *Journal of Osmania University, List of Recognized Examinations of Other Universities, Osmania Journal of English Studies, Research Bulletin of Department of Psychology, Syllabuses, University Act, University Diary, University Hand Book*

DEANS

Faculty of Arts: Prof. C. RAMA RAO
Faculty of Ayurvedha and Unani: Dr K. G. K. SASTRY
Faculty of Commerce: Prof. P. SUBRAHMANYAM
Faculty of Education: Prof. V. EASHWAR REDDY
Faculty of Engineering: Prof. D. C. REDDY
Faculty of Law: Justice BHASKAR RAO
Faculty of Medicine: Dr P. S. RAO
Faculty of Science: Prof. P. RAMCHANDER RAO
Faculty of Social Sciences: Prof. N. Y. REDDY
Faculty of Technology: Prof. P. SADASHIVA RAO

HEADS OF DEPARTMENTS

Faculty of Arts:
Ancient Indian History, Culture & Archaeology: Dr S. DHARESWARI
Arabic: Prof. SULTAN MOHIUDDIN
English: Prof. M. SIVARAMA KRISHNA
French: Dr PRAMILA VENKAT RAO
German: Dr D. SATYANARAYANA
Hindi: Dr T. MOHAN SINGH
Islamic Studies: Dr SULEMAN SIDDIQUI
Journalism: ABDUR RAHIM

Kannada: Dr K. G. NARAYAN PRASAD
Linguistics: Dr A. K. SHARMA
Marathi: Dr KAVITA KATKE
Persian: Dr SYEDA BASHEERUNNISA BEGUM
Philosophy: Prof. P. SITARAM REDDY
Russian: MADHAV MARURKAR
Sanskrit: Prof. K. KAMALA
Tamil: G. PRABALAMBAL
Telugu: Prof. V. SITA KALYANI
Theatre Arts: Dr PRADEEP KUMAR
Urdu: Prof. S. YOUSUF SHARIFUDDIN

Faculty of Commerce:
Business Management: Prof. A. V. SATYANARAYAN RAO
Commerce: Prof. S. RAMA MURTHY

Faculty of Education:
Education: Prof. R. KRISHNA RAO

Faculty of Engineering:
Civil Engineering: Prof. D. SHANTA RAM
Computer Science Engineering: Prof. K. V. CHALAPATTI RAO
Electrical Engineering: Prof. P. ETHIRAJULU
Electronics and Communication Engineering: Prof. SADASIV SHARMA
Mechanical Engineering: Prof. M. KOMARAIAH
Mining Engineering: Prof. VEERENDER SINGH

Faculty of Law:
Law: Prof. P. SHESHADRI

Faculty of Science:
Astronomy: Prof. B. LOKANADHAM
Biochemistry: Dr. G. VENKATESWALU
Botany: Prof. M. NUSRATH
Chemistry: Prof. P. K. SAI PRAKASH
Genetics: Prof. T. POPI REDDY
Geology: Prof. M. VENKATESHWARA RAO
Geophysics: Prof. J. B. RAMAPRASADA RAO
Mathematics: Prof. V. SHIVA RAMA PRASAD
Microbiology: Prof. G. SEENAYYA
Physics: Prof. K. RAMA REDDY
Statistics: Dr Y. SIVARAMA KRISHNA
Zoology: Prof. T. SATYANARAYAN SINGH

Faculty of Social Sciences:
Economics: Prof. H. VENKATESWARA RAO
Geography: Prof. RAM MOHAN RAO
History: Prof. P. JHANSI LAXMI
Library Science: N. LAXMAN RAO
Political Science: Prof. S. D. JATKAR
Psychology: Prof. N. YADAGIRI REDDY
Public Administration: Prof. M. A. ALEEM
Sociology: Prof. J. V. RAGHVENDER RAO

Faculty of Technology:
Chemical Engineering and Technology: Prof. M. BHAGWANTH RAO

UNIVERSITY COLLEGES

University College of Arts: Hyderabad; f. 1918; Principal Prof. K. SUBHASHCHANDRA REDDY.

University College of Commerce and Business Management: Hyderabad; f. 1975; Principal Prof. B. GOVERDHAN REDDY.

University College of Education: Hyderabad; f. 1928; Principal Prof. R. KRISHNA RAO.

University College of Engineering: Hyderabad; f. 1929; Principal Prof. P. S. R. MURTHY.

University College of Law: Hyderabad; f. 1960; Principal V. KRISHNAMA CHARY.

University College of Science: Hyderabad; f. 1918; Principal Prof. M. GOVIND RAM REDDY.

University College of Technology: Hyderabad 7; f. 1969; Principal M. BHAGAWANTHA RAO.

University College for Women: Hyderabad; f. 1924; Principal Prof. V. R. LALITHA.

CONSTITUENT COLLEGES

Kothagudem School of Mines: Kothagudem 507101; f. 1976; Principal Prof. G. S. N. RAJU.

Nizam College: Hyderabad; f. 1887; Principal Prof. G. GOPALA KRISHNA.

Postgraduate Centre, Biknoor: f. 1976; Head Prof. Dr D. MALLESHWAR.

Postgraduate Centre, Godavari Khani: f. 1976; Head Prof. M. LAKSHRIPATHI RAO (acting).

Postgraduate Centre, Kothagudem: f. 1976; Head Prof. A. A. MOIZ (acting).

Postgraduate Centre, Mahaboobnagar: f. 1987; Head Prof. C. R. ANAND RAO.

Postgraduate Centre, Mirzapur: f. 1980; Head Dr K. S. K. RAO PATNAIK.

Postgraduate Centre, Nalgonda: f. 1987; Head Prof. D. O. REDDY.

Postgraduate College of Law, Hyderabad: f. 1954; Principal G. MANCHAR RAO.

Postgraduate College of Science: Saifabad, Hyderabad; f. 1951; Principal Prof. K. SHANKARAIAH.

Postgraduate College, Secunderabad: f. 1947; Principal Prof. N. UMAPATHY.

Satavahana P. G. Centre: Karimnagar; f. 1976; Head Prof. V. SURENDER.

There are 120 affiliated colleges and 16 Oriental colleges

PANDIT RAVISHANKAR SHUKLA UNIVERSITY, RAIPUR

Raipur 492010, Chhattisgarh
Telephone: (771) 2533957
Fax: (771) 2534283

Founded 1964

Teaching and Affiliating
Languages of instruction: Hindi, English
Private control
Academic year: July to June (two terms)

Chancellor: HE THE GOVERNOR OF CHHATTISGARH
Vice-Chancellor: Dr B. P. CHANDRA
Registrar: A. MINJ
Librarian: M. I. AHMED

Library of 160,000 vols
Number of students: 28,496

DEANS

Faculty of Arts: Dr CHITTARANJAN KAR
Faculty of Ayurved: Dr D. K. KATARIA
Faculty of Commerce: AMIR CHAND JAIN
Faculty of Education: Dr B. K. MEHTA
Faculty of Engineering: Dr H. KUMAR
Faculty of Home Science: Dr V. RAJ
Faculty of Law: Dr A. A. KHAN
Faculty of Management: Dr R. P. DAS
Faculty of Science: Dr G. L. MUNDHRA
Faculty of Social Sciences: Dr M. A. KHAN
Faculty of Technology: Dr SHAILENDRA SARAF

There are 132 affiliated colleges

PANJAB UNIVERSITY

Sector 14, Chandigarh 160014
Telephone: (172) 2541022
Fax: (172) 2534299
E-mail: regr@pu.ac.in
Internet: www.pu.ac.in

Founded 1947

Teaching and Affiliating
Languages of instruction: English, Punjabi
Languages of instruction: Urdu, Hindi
Academic year: July to April

Chancellor: THE VICE-PRESIDENT OF INDIA
Vice-Chancellor: Prof. K. N. PATHAK
Registrar: Prof. PARAMJIT SINGH
Librarian: A. R. SETHI

Library: Libraries of 590,000 vols
Number of teachers: 746
Number of students: 20,554

Publications: *Research Bulletin* (Arts), *Parakh*, *Parishodh*, *Social Sciences Research Journal*, *P. U. News*, *P. U. Research Journal* (science)

DEANS

Faculty of Arts: Dr MADAN MOHAN PURI
Faculty of Business Management and Commerce: Prof. S. P. SINGH
Faculty of Design and Fine Arts: JOGINDER SINGH
Faculty of Education: NIRMAL KAUR
Faculty of Engineering and Technology: Prof. D. K. VOHRA
Faculty of Languages: Dr ANIRUDH JOSHI
Faculty of Law: GOPAL KRISHAN CHATRATH
Faculty of Medical Sciences: Dr K. S. CHUGH
Faculty of Pharmaceutical Sciences: Prof. V. K. KAPOOR
Faculty of Science: (vacant)

There are 115 affiliated colleges

PATNA UNIVERSITY

Patna 800005, Bihar State
Telephone: (612) 2670531; (612) 2670852

Founded 1917

Residential and Teaching
Languages of instruction: Hindi, English
Academic year: June to May (three terms)

Chancellor: HE THE GOVERNOR OF BIHAR
Vice-Chancellor: Dr K. K. JHA
Registrar: Dr VIBHASH KUMAR YADAV
Librarian: Dr U. M. THAKUR

Library of 300,000 vols
Number of teachers: 895
Number of students: 11,000

Publications: *Patna University News Bulletin* (monthly), *University of Patna Journal*

DEANS

Faculty of Commerce: Dr JYOTI SHEKHAR
Faculty of Education: G. K. PRAJAPATI
Faculty of Engineering: Dr P. K. SINHA
Faculty of Fine Arts: Dr N. K. P. SINGH
Faculty of Humanities: Dr R. R. SAHAY
Faculty of Law: Dr L. L. B. SHARAN
Faculty of Medicine: Dr B. K. SINGH
Faculty of Science: Dr S. N. GUHA
Faculty of Social Science: Dr SAVITRI SHARMA

PROFESSORS

ADHIKARI, S., Geography
AHMAD, S. U., Sociology
AKHTAR, M. M., Physics
ALAM, M. S., Persian
ALAM, P. A., Urdu
ARSHAD, E. A., Urdu
ARYA, R. S., Philosophy
ASHOK, S. M., English
AZAD, A., Urdu
AZAD, R., Chemistry
BANERJEE, N. N., Botany
BANERJEE, S., Political Science
BEGAM, S., Urdu
BHAKTA, C., Chemistry
BHATT, P., Zoology
BLAKTA, S., Mathematics
CHOUDHARY, A. K., Physics
CHOUDHARY, M. N., Hindi
CHOUDHARY, N. K., Economics
CHOUDHARY, R., Philosophy
CHOUDHARY, R. B., Sanskrit
CHOUDHARY, S., Political Science
DAS, R. N., Mathematics
DUBEY, G. R., Education
DUBEY, S., Psychology
DUBEY, V. S., Geology
DUTTA, P., History
DUTTA, S. A., English
GHOSH, A. K., Chemistry

GHOSH, P., History
GUHA, S. N., Physics
GUPTA, A. D., Sociology
GUPTA, A. K., Botany
GUPTA, F., Sanskrit
HASANARAN, S. J., Mechanical Engineering
JAISWAL, R., Mathematics
JHA, B., Maithili
JHA, H., Sociology
JHA, I., Education
JHA, K., Psychology
JHA, N. N., Physics
JHA, R., Ancient Indian History and Archaeology
JHA, R., English
JHA, S. M., Mathematics
JHA, U., Chemistry
KALIM, Z., English
KARAN, V., Maithili
KATHURIA, S., Botany
KHAN, S. A., Statistics
KUMAR, A., English
KUMAR, A., Sanskrit
KUMAR, B., Chemistry
KUMAR, B., Statistics
KUMAR, B. S., History
KUMAR, N., Mechanical Engineering
KUMAR, R. V., History
KUMAR, S., Civil Engineering
KUMAR, S., Sociology
KUMARI, A., Statistics
KUMARI, R., Sociology
KUMARI, S., Hindi
LAL, S., Chemistry
MAHTO, K., Geography
MAHTO, R. U., Commerce
MALTIYAR, K. K., Geography
MATHUR, K. N. L., Physics
MIRZA, K., Political Science
MISHRA, A., Statistics
MISHRA, B. K., Geology
MISHRA, H., English
MISHRA, J. S., History
MISHRA, N. M., Physics
MISHRA, R. G., Sanskrit
MISHRA, R. N., Statistics
MISHRA, R. S., Statistics
MISHRA, U., Commerce
MITRA, K. A., Physics
MOHAN, M., Zoology
MUKHERJEE, D., Physics
MUKHERJEE, I., Botany
MURARI, R., Economics
NATH, A., Zoology
NILIMA, N., Hindi
OJHA, G. P., Political Science
PADAMDEO, S. R., Botany
PANDEY, B. N., Commerce
PANDEY, M. K., Sanskrit
PANDEY, N. M., English
PANDEY, N. N., Physics
PASWAN, B., Hindi
PASWAN, K. N., Geography
PODAR, P. K., History
PRAJAPATI, G. K., Education
PRAKASH, D., Chemistry
PRASAD, A., Chemistry
PRASAD, A., Statistics
PRASAD, B., Mathematics
PRASAD, D., Mathematics
PRASAD, D., Sociology
PRASAD, K., Geology
PRASAD, K., History
PRASAD, R. K., Chemistry
PRASAD, R. P., Chemistry
PRASAD, R. D., Hindi
PRASAD, R. N., Philosophy
PRASAD, S. A. K., Mathematics
PRASAD, S. L., Geography
QUADRI, E. A., Civil Engineering
RAJGARHIA, C., Mathematics
RANI, P., Zoology
ROHATAGI, A. K., Geology
ROY, D. N., Bengali
ROY, R., English
ROY, R. B. R., Hindi
ROY, S., Chemistry
ROY, V. R., Psychology
RUDRA, S., Economics
SAHAY, R. R., Philosophy
SHARDENDU, Hindi
SHARMA, B., Mathematics
SHARMA, D. K., Mathematics
SHARMA, D. K., Physics
SHARMA, J. P., Education
SHARMA, M. D., Bengali
SHARMA, N. K., Hindi
SHARMA, P. L., History
SHARMA, R. N., Sociology
SHARMA, S., Psychology
SHARMA, S. N., Botany
SHARMA, S. N., Physics
SHARMA, S. N., Political Science
SHAW, G., Home Science
SHEKHAR, J., Commerce
SHREE, V., Philosophy
SHUKLA, H., Political Science
SHUKLA, K. N., Zoology
SHUKLA, P., Psychology
SHUKLA, R., Geology
SIDDIQUI, F. K., Arabic
SIDDIQUI, M. G., Persian
SIDDIQUI, M. O., Botany
SINGH, A., Economics
SINGH, A. K., Ancient Indian History and Archaeology
SINGH, A. K., History
SINGH, A. K., Psychology
SINGH, A. K. S., Hindi
SINGH, A. N., History
SINGH, B. P., Economics
SINGH, C., Commerce
SINGH, D. P., Hindi
SINGH, G., Hindi
SINGH, J., Physics
SINGH, J. M. P., Hindi
SINGH, J. P., Sociology
SINGH, K. N., Mechanical Engineering
SINGH, K. P., English
SINGH, K. S. P., Civil Engineering
SINGH, L. K. P., Geography
SINGH, N. K., Geology
SINGH, N. K. P., History
SINGH, N. N. P., History
SINGH, P., Philosophy
SINGH, P. D., Chemistry
SINGH, R. B. P., Geography
SINGH, R. P., Chemistry
SINGH, S., Botany
SINGH, S., Home Science
SINGH, S. C., History
SINGH, S. D. N., Sociology
SINGH, S. K., Mechanical Engineering
SINGH, S. K., Statistics
SINGH, S. K. P., Economics
SINGH, S. K. P., History
SINGH, S. N., Chemistry
SINGH, S. N., Economics
SINGH, S. P. Y., Hindi
SINGH, S. S., Ancient Indian History and Archaeology
SINHA, A. K., Civil Engineering
SINHA, A. K., Statistics
SINHA, A. K., Statistics
SINHA, A. P., Economics
SINHA, B. K., Mathematics
SINHA, G., Psychology
SINHA, H. B. P., Mathematics
SINHA, K., Economics
SINHA, K. S., Mathematics
SINHA, L., Political Science
SINHA, M., Psychology
SINHA, M., Sanskrit
SINHA, M. N., Geology
SINHA, M. P., Zoology
SINHA, M. R., English
SINHA, N., Geology
SINHA, P., Psychology
SINHA, P. K., Mathematics
SINHA, P. K., Mechanical Engineering
SINHA, R. C., Philosophy
SINHA, R. J., Chemistry
SINHA, R. K., Zoology
SINHA, R. M. P., Physics
SINHA, S., English
SINHA, S., Philosophy
SINHA, S. K., Civil Engineering
SINHA, S. S., Education
SINHA, V., Psychology
SINHA, V. N. P., Geography
SINHA, U. K., Botany
SINHA, V. K., Zoology
SIRKAR, J., Economics
SRINIVASAN, P., Physics
SRIVASTAVA, S. K., Zoology
SRIVASTAVA, U. K., Civil Engineering
SUKLA, B., Sociology
TAHAN, K., Persian
THAKUR, B. K., Geology
THAKUR, J., Physics
THAKUR, S. J., English
THAKUR, V. K., History
TIWARI, B., Hindi
TIWARY, N. P., Philosophy
TIWARY, P. N., History
TRIPATHY, A. N., Sanskrit
TULSIYAN, S. S., Economics
VARMA, M., Philosophy
VERMA, C., Zoology
VERMA, J., Psychology
VERMA, M., Economics
VERMA, P. C., Economics
VERMA, R. K., Mathematics
VERMA, S. P., Physics
VERMA, U., Geography
YADAV, A., Physics
YADAV, A. K. P., Physics
YASIN, S., Zoology

CONSTITUENT COLLEGES

Arts and Crafts College: Patna 800001; f. 1938; 5 teachers; 150 students; Principal P. S. NATHSINHA.

Bihar College of Engineering: Mahendru, Patna; f. 1924; 4-year course; 46 teachers; 450 students; Principal Dr A. K. SINHA.

Bihar National College: Bankipur, Patna 4; f. 1917; 84 teachers; 1,263 students; Principal Dr MADAN PRASAD SINHA.

Directorate of Distance Education: Dir Dr R. R. SAHAY.

Institute of Psychological Research and Service: Dir Dr PRABHA SHUKLA.

Institute of Public Administration: Dir Dr G. P. OJHA.

Magadh Mahila College: Patna; f. 1946; 30 teachers; 918 students; Principal Dr MANJU RANI SINHA.

Patna College: PO Bankipur, Patna, Bihar; f. 1863; the oldest college in the province, and the parent institution of three other colleges; 48 teachers; 2,363 students; Principal Dr S. S. TULSYAN.

Patna Law College: PO Mahendru, Patna, Bihar; f. 1906; 20 teachers; 868 students; Principal Prof. L. L. B. SHARAN.

Patna Medical College: Bankipur, Patna; f. 1925; under administrative control of the Govt of Bihar; 60 teachers; 900 students; Principal Dr M. SINGH.

Patna Training College: Patna; f. 1908; 10 teachers; 126 students; Principal Dr INDIRA SINHA.

Patna Women's College: Patna; f. 1940; 44 teachers; 2,309 students; Principal Sister Dr DORIS D'SOUZA.

Science College: Bankipur, Patna; f. 1927; 56 teachers; 1,002 students; Principal Dr JAGANNATH THAKUR.

Vanijya Mahavidyalaya: Patna 4; f. 1953; 12 teachers; 704 students; Principal Dr UMESH MISHRA.

Women's Training College: Patna; f. 1951; 11 teachers; 244 students; Principal Dr SAROJ BALA SINHA.

PERIYAR UNIVERSITY

Government College of Engineering Campus, Salem 636011, Tamil Nadu
Founded 1997
State control
Academic year: July to June
Languages of instruction: English, Tamil
Chancellor: HE THE GOVERNOR OF TAMIL NADU
Vice-Chancellor: Dr R. SETHUPATHI RAMALINGAM
Registrar: Dr G. BALASUBRAMANIAN
Library of 13,000 vols
Faculties of Arts, Commerce, Education, Engineering, Languages and Science
There are 51 affiliated colleges.

UNIVERSITY OF PETROLEUM AND ENERGY STUDIES

Petroleum House, Vasant Vihar Enclave, Dehradun 284006, Uttaranchal
Telephone: (135) 2764370
E-mail: info@upesindia.org
Internet: www.upesindia.org
Founded 2003
Regional centre in Delhi
Chancellor: Dr S. J. CHOPRA
Pro-Chancellor: Prof. U. K. DIKSHIT
Vice-Chancellor: Dr PARAG DIWAN
Registrar: SANDEEP MEHTA
Number of teachers: 20

DEANS
College of Engineering Studies: Dr B. P. PANDEY
College of Legal Studies: (vacant)
College of Management and Economic Studies: Dr MOHAMMED WASHID

PONDICHERRY UNIVERSITY

R. Venkataraman Nagar, Kalapet, Pondicherry 605014
Telephone: (413) 2655991
Fax: (413) 2655211
Internet: www.pondiuni.org
Founded 1985
Central university
State control
Languages of instruction: English, French
Languages of instruction: Tamil, Hindi
Languages of instruction: Malayalam, Telegu, Sanskrit
Academic year: July to June
Chancellor: HE THE VICE-PRESIDENT OF INDIA
Vice-Chancellor: Dr A. K. BHATNAGAR
Chief Rector: HE THE LT-GOVERNOR OF PONDICHERRY
Registra: Dr J. SAMPATH (acting)
Librarian: P. RAMANATHAN
Number of teachers: 140
Number of students: 1,217 (University), 15,909 (affiliated colleges and institutes)
Publications: *Annual Report*, *Handbook*, *Quarterly Newsletter*

DEANS
Sri Aurobindo School of Eastern and Western Thought: Dr V. C. THOMAS
Salim Ali School of Ecology and Environmental Sciences: (vacant)
School of International Studies: Dr NALINI KANT JHA
School of Management: Dr K. RAMACHANDRAN
Ramanujam School of Mathematics and Computer Science: Dr S. KUPPUSWAMI
Sri Sankaradass Swami School of Performing Arts: (vacant)
Subramania Bharathi School of Tamil Language and Literature: Dr A. ARIVUNAMBI

HEADS OF DEPARTMENTS
Anthropology: Dr T. SUBRAMANYAM NAIDU
Biological Sciences: Prof. E. VIJAYAN
Biotechnology: Dr S. JAYACHANDRAN
Chemistry: Dr H. S. P. RAO
Commerce: Dr K. CHANDRASEKHARA RAO
Computer Science: Dr R. SUBRAMANIAN
Earth Sciences: Dr S. BALAKRISHNAN
Economics: Dr K. SHAM BHAT
English: Dr P. BALASWAMY
French: Prof. R. KICHENAMOURTY
Hindi: Dr V. VIZIALAKSHMI
History: Dr I. S. VISWANATH
Mathematics: Dr S. RAMASWAMY
Physical Education: Dr N. GOVINDARAJULU
Physics: Dr S. MOHAN
Political Science: Dr N. K. JHA
Sanskrit: Dr E. DHARANEEDHARAN
Sociology: Dr S. GUNASEKARAN

ATTACHED INSTITUTES
Bioinformatics Centre: Dir Dr P. P. MATHUR.
Centre for Adult and Continuing Education: Dir Dr R. PRABHAKARA RAYA.
Centre for Entrepreneurship Training and Development.
Centre for Futures Studies: Dir T. SUBRAMANYAM.
Centre for Human Rights: Dir Dr T. S. N. SASTRY.
Centre for Nehru Studies: Dir Dr B. KRISHNAMURTHY.
Centre for Ocean and Island Studies: Dir Dr P. M. MOHAN.
Centre for Pollution Control and Energy Technology: Dir Dr S. A. ABBASI.
Centre for Tourism Studies: Dir Dr G. ANJANEYA SWAMY.
Centre for Women's Studies: Dir Dr V. T. USHA.
Centre for Yoga Studies: Dir Dr D. SAKTHIGNANAVEL.

POTTI SREERAMULU TELUGU UNIVERSITY

Public Gardens, Nampally, Hyderabad 500004, Andhra Pradesh.

UNIVERSITY OF PUNE

Ganeshkhind, Pune 411007, Maharashtra
Telephone: 56061
Internet: www.unipune.ernet.in
Founded 1949
Teaching and Affiliating
Languages of instruction: English (optional), Marathi
Academic year: June to March (two terms)
Chancellor: HE THE GOVERNOR OF MAHARASHTRA
Vice-Chancellor: Dr ARUN NIGAVEKAR
Registrar: V. S. POL
Librarian: Dr S. G. MAHAJAN
Library of 272,000 vols
Number of students: 96,000 (including affiliated colleges)

DEANS
Faculty of Arts: Prof. SUDHAKER PANDEY
Faculty of Ayurvedic Medicine: P. H. KULKARNI
Faculty of Commerce: Dr J. R. GODHA
Faculty of Education: Prof. S. V. KHER
Faculty of Engineering: Prof. H. M. GANESHRAO
Faculty of Law: VIJAYRAO MOHITE
Faculty of Medicine: Dr M. J. JOSHI
Faculty of Mental, Moral and Social Science: Dr D. B. KERUR
Faculty of Science: Dr S. C. GUPTE

HEADS OF DEPARTMENTS
Anthropology: Prof. B. V. BHANU
Archaeology: Dr V. N. MISRA
Botany: Dr S. B. DAVID
Chemistry: Dr N. S. NARASIMHAN
Defence Studies: Maj. GANTAM SEN
English: Dr SUDHAKAR PANDEY
Experimental Psychology: Dr M. N. PALSANE
Geology: (vacant)
Geography: Dr K. R. DIKSHIT
Hindi: Dr A. P. DIKSHIT
History: Dr A. R. KULKARNI
Journalism: P. N. PARANJPE
Law: Dr S. K. AGRAWALA
Linguistics: Dr P. BHASKARRIO
Marathi: Dr M. S. KANADE
Mathematics: Dr S. S. ABHYANKAR
Modern European Languages: Prof. S. R. SALKAR
Philosophy: Dr M. P. MARATHE
Physics: Dr A. S. NIGVEKAR
Politics: Dr N. R. INAMDAR
Sanskrit and Prakkrit Languages: Dr S. D. JOSHI
Sociology: (vacant)
Statistics: Dr S. R. ADKE
Zoology: Dr S. MODAK

CONSTITUENT COLLEGES
Adarsha College of Education: Erandawana, Karve Rd, Pune 4; f. 1970.
Adhyapak Mahavidyalaya College of Education: Aranyeshwar, Pune 9; f. 1970.
Armed Forces Medical College: Pune 1; f. 1948.
Arts and Commerce College: Hadapsar, Pune 28; f. 1971.
Ashtang Ayurved Mahavidyalaya: Pune 30.
Bharati Vidyapeeth Pune College of Pharmacy: Pune 4.
Bharati Vidyapeeth New Law College: Pune 4.
Chandrasekhar Agashe College of Physical Education: Pune 9.
B.J. Medical College: Pune 1; f. 1946.
Brihan Maharashtra College of Commerce: Pune 4; f. 1943.
College of Architecture: Pune 30.
College of Engineering: Pune 4; f. 1854.
Fergusson College: Pune 4; f. 1885.
Jain College of Arts and Commerce: Chinchwad, Pune 19; f. 1971.
Law College: Pune 4; f. 1924.
M.E. Society's Abasaheb Garware College of Commerce: Pune 4; f. 1967.
M.E. Society's Abasaheb Garware College of Arts and Sciences: Pune 4; f. 1945.
Modern College of Arts, Science and Commerce: Shivajinagar, Pune 5.
Ness Wadia College of Commerce: Pune 1; f. 1969.
Nowrosjee Wadia College: 19 Bund Rd, Pune 1; f. 1932.
Pune College of Arts, Science and Commerce: Compound of Anglo-Urdu High School, Shankarsheth Rd, Pune 1; f. 1970.
St Mira's College for Girls: Pune 1; f. 1962.
Shahu Mandir Mahavidyalaya: Pune 9; f. 1960.
Sir Parashurambhau College: Pune 30; f. 1916.
St Vincent College: 2004 St Vincent St, Pune 1; f. 1970.

Symbiosis Institute of Management: Senapati Bapat Marg, Pune 411004.

Tilak College of Education: Pune 30; f. 1941.

Tilak Ayurveda Mahavidyalaya: 583/2 Rasta Peth, Pune 11; f. 1933.

Yeshwantrao Mohite Arts, Science and Commerce College: Pune 4.

There are 117 affiliated colleges

PUNJAB AGRICULTURAL UNIVERSITY

Ludhiana 141004, Punjab

Telephone: (161) 2401960
Fax: (161) 2400955
E-mail: registrar@pau.edu
Internet: www.pau.edu

Founded 1962

Teaching, Research and Extension
Autonomous control
Languages of instruction: English, Punjabi
Academic year: August to July (two terms)

Chancellor: HE THE GOVERNOR OF PUNJAB
Vice-Chancellor: Dr K. S. AULAKH
Director of Extension Education: Dr S. S. GILL
Director of Research: Dr G. S. NANDA
Dean of Postgraduate Studies: Dr DARSHAN SINGH
Registrar: Dr V. K. SHARMA
Librarian: Dr S. S. GILL

Library of 336,496 vols
Number of teachers: 1,182
Number of students: 2,067

Publications: *Changi Kheti* (in Punjabi, monthly), *Journal of Research* (in English, quarterly), *Package of Practices for Crops of the Punjab* (2 a year), *Progressive Farming* (in English, monthly), *Punjab Agricultural Handbook* (annually)

DEANS

College of Agricultural Engineering: Dr S. K. SONDHI
College of Agriculture: Dr M. S. TIWANA
College of Basic Science and Humanities: Dr A. P. S. MANN
College of Home Science: Dr M. K. DHILLON
College of Veterinary Science: Dr M. S. OBEROI

HEADS OF DEPARTMENTS

College of Agricultural Engineering (tel. and fax (161) 2402456):
- Civil Engineering: Dr N. K. KHULLAR
- Computer Science and Electrical Engineering: Prof. DINESH GROVER
- Farm Power and Machinery: Dr S. S. AHUJA
- Mechanical Engineering: Dr PAWAN KUMAR GUPTA
- Processing and Agricultural Structures: Dr B. S. GHUMAN
- Soil and Water Engineering: Dr H. S. GULATI
- School of Energy Structures for Agriculture: Dr PAWAN KUMAR GUPTA

College of Agriculture (tel. and fax (161) 2403006):
- Agronomy and Agrometrology: Dr LAL SINGH BRAR
- Entomology: Dr G. S. DEOL
- Extension Education: Dr RANBIR RANDHAWA
- Floriculture and Landscaping: Dr RAMESH KUMAR SADAWARTI
- Food Science and Technology: Dr G. S. PADDA
- Forestry and Natural Resources: Dr S. S. GILL
- Horticulture: Dr YOG RAJ CHANANA
- Plant Breeding, Genetics and Biotechnology: Dr N. S. MALHI
- Plant Pathology: Dr GURDIP SINGH
- Seeds: Dr J. S. SAMRA (Dir)
- Soils: Dr G. S. CHAHAL
- Vegetable Crops: Dr A. S. SIDHU

College of Basic Sciences and Humanities (tel. and fax (161) 2403533; e-mail apsmann@pau.edu):
- Biochemistry and Chemistry: Dr B. S. SEKHON
- Botany: Dr NEELAM SETIA
- Business Management: Dr S. K. SINGLA
- Economics: Dr A. S. JOSHI
- Mathematics, Statistics and Physics: Dr JOGINDER SINGH
- Microbiology: Dr P. K. KHANNA
- Zoology and Fisheries: Dr H. S. SEHGAL

College of Home Science (tel. (161) 2403179; fax (161) 2403179; e-mail deanhsc@pau.edu):
- Clothing and Textiles: Dr SURINDERPAL SIDHU
- Family Resources Management: Dr RUPA BAKSHI
- Food and Nutrition: Dr S. VERMA
- Human Development and Sociology: Dr A. K. GUPTA

College of Veterinary Science (tel. and fax (161) 2400822; e-mail msoberoi@glide.net.in):
- Animal Breeding and Genetics (including Biostatistics): Dr O. S. PARMAR
- Animal Nutrition: Dr BALDEV KRISHAN
- Animal Reproduction, Gynaecology and Obstetrics: Dr G. S. DHALIWAL
- Livestock Production and Management: Dr M. C. HANDA
- Livestock Products Technology: Dr JHARI SAHOO
- Veterinary Anatomy and Histology: Dr K. S. ROY
- Veterinary Biochemistry: Dr K. C. CHAUDHRY
- Veterinary Clinical Medicine, Ethics and Jurisprudence: Dr P. S. DHALIWAL
- Veterinary Clinical Services: Dr SUKHEEP SINGH SIDHU
- Veterinary Epidemiology and Preventative Medicine: Dr KULBIR SINGH SANDHU
- Veterinary Medicine and Animal Husbandry Extension: Dr S. P. S. SANGHA
- Veterinary Microbiology: Dr S. K. JAND
- Veterinary Parasitology: Dr PARAYAG DUTT JUGAL
- Veterinary Pathology: Dr R. S. BRAR
- Veterinary Pharmacology and Toxicology: Dr HARPAL SINGH SANDHU
- Veterinary Physiology: Dr RAJVIR SINGH
- Veterinary Public Health: Dr J. K. SHARMA
- Veterinary Surgery and Radiology: Dr SIMRAT SAGAR SINGH

PUNJAB TECHNICAL UNIVERSITY

REC Post Office, Jalandhar 144001, Punjab

Telephone: (181) 2297046
Fax: (181) 2290079
E-mail: info@punjabtechnicaluniversity.com
Internet: www.punjabtechnicaluniversity.com

Founded 1997

Chancellor: HE THE GOVERNOR OF PUNJAB
Vice-Chancellor: Dr S. K. SALWAN
Registrar: Dr M. S. GREWAL

Courses in engineering, natural sciences and technology

There are 35 affiliated colleges.

PUNJABI UNIVERSITY

Patiala 147002, Punjab

Telephone: (175) 2237455
Fax: (175) 2237305
E-mail: regpup@pbi.ernet.in
Internet: www.universitypunjabi.org

Founded 1962

Languages of instruction: Punjabi, English
State control
Academic year: July to May (three terms)

Chancellor: HE THE GOVERNOR OF PUNJAB
Vice-Chancellor: SWARAN SINGH BOPARAI
Registrar: Prof. PARM BAKHSHISH SINGH
Librarian: Dr DEVINDER KAUR

Library of 312,192 vols
Number of students: 53,399

Publications: *Journal of Religious Studies* (quarterly), *Punjabi University Bulletin*

DEANS

Faculty of Arts and Culture: Prof. ANIL NARULA
Faculty of Education and Information Science: Prof. MEENAKSHI SHARMA
Faculty of Languages: Prof. RANJIT KAUR
Faculty of Life Sciences: Prof. MANJIT SINGH
Faculty of Physical Sciences: Prof. G. L. GARG
Faculty of Professional Courses: Prof. U. C. SINGH
Faculty of Social Science: Prof. NIRMAL SINGH AZAD

There are 71 affiliated colleges

RABINDRA BHARATI UNIVERSITY

56A Barrackpore Trunk Rd, Kolkata 700050

Telephone: (33) 25568019
Fax: (33) 25568079

Founded 1962

Languages of instruction: Bengali, English
State control
Academic year: June to May (three terms)

Chancellor: HE THE GOVERNOR OF WEST BENGAL
Vice-Chancellor: Dr SUBHANKAR CHAKRABORTY
Registrar: O. S. ADHIKARI
Librarian: B. B. DAS

Library of 83,500 vols
Number of teachers: 165
Number of students: 6,759

Publications: *Rabindra Bharati Journal* (English, annually), *Rabindra Bharati University Patrika* (Bengali, annually), *R.. B. U. Newsletter*, departmental journals (annually: Bengali, Sanskrit, English, Education, Economics, Library and Information Science, Vedic Studies, Study and Research on Tagore, Rabindra Sangeet)

Departments of Bengali, English, Sanskrit, Philosophy, History, Economics, Political Science, Dance, Drama, Vocal Music, Instrumental Music, Rabindra Sangeet, Painting, Graphics, Applied Art, Sculpture, History of Art, Education and Library and Information science.

UNIVERSITY OF RAJASTHAN

Gandhi Nagar, Jaipur 302004, Rajasthan

Telephone: (141) 2706813
Fax: (141) 2709582
E-mail: vicechancellor@uniraj.ernet.in
Internet: www.uniraj.ernet.in

Founded 1947

Teaching and Affiliating
Independent control
Languages of instruction: English, Hindi
Academic year: July to May (two terms)

Chancellor: HE THE GOVERNOR OF RAJASTHAN
Vice-Chancellor: Prof. K. L. SHARMA
Registrar: B. L. GUPTA
Librarian: Dr ASHWANI KUMAR

Library of 371,500 vols, 65,000 bound periodicals
Number of teachers: 575

Number of students: 175,000

DEANS

Faculty of Arts: Prof. SANTOSH GUPTA
Faculty of Ayurveda: (vacant): Prof. KRISHAN SHARMA
Faculty of Commerce: Dr N. S. RATHORE
Faculty of Engineering and Technology: Prof. N. C. BHANDARI
Faculty of Fine Arts, Music and Drama: Prof. MAYA RANI TAK
Faculty of Homeopathy: Prof. J. D. DARYANI
Faculty of Law: Prof. N. C. JAIN
Faculty of Management Studies: Dr ANJALI R. SAXENA
Faculty of Medicine and Pharmacy: Dr ANAND K. SINGHAL
Faculty of Science: Prof. H. S. SHARMA
Faculty of Social Sciences: Prof. MADHUKAR SHYAM CHATURVEDI

There are 206 affiliated colleges

UNIVERSITY COLLEGES

Commerce College: Jaipur; f. 1956.
Evening Law College: Jaipur.
Law College: Jaipur.
Maharaja's College: Jaipur; f. 1944.
Maharani's College: Jaipur; f. 1944.
Rajasthan College: Jaipur; f. 1956.

RAJASTHAN AGRICULTURAL UNIVERSITY, BIKANER

Bikaner 334002, Rajasthan
Telephone: (151) 2250025
Fax: (151) 2250336
Founded 1988
Vice-Chancellor: Prof. PARMATMA SINGH
Registrar: M. L. NEHRA
Librarian: CHETAN RAJPUROHIT
Library: Central Library of 10,000 vols
Number of teachers: 425
Number of students: 2,250

DEANS

Faculty of Agriculture (Bikaner): Dr B. L. POONIA
Faculty of Agriculture (Jobner): Dr P. JOSHI
Faculty of Home Science: Dr MADHU GOYAL
Faculty of Veterinary and Animal Science: A. K. GAHLOT
Institute of Agri-business Management: Prof. A. K. DAHAMA (Dir)

There are four affiliated colleges

RAJASTHAN AYURVEDA UNIVERSITY

Jodhpur, Rajasthan
Telephone: (21) 22722070
Fax: (21) 22722070
Founded 2003
Academic year: July to June
Vice-Chancellor: Prof. R. H. SINGH
Controller of Examinations: Prof. S. N. SONI
Number of teachers: 15
Number of students: 65.

RAJASTHAN SANSKRIT UNIVERSITY

Dungri, Rajasthan Textbook Board Bldg, Jaipur 302004, Rajasthan
Telephone: (141) 2704068
Fax: (141) 2711050
Founded 2001
Academic year: July to May
Chancellor: HE THE GOVERNOR OF RAJASTHAN
Vice-Chancellor: Prof. SATYA DEVA MISRA
Registrar: B. D. GUPTA.

RAJENDRA AGRICULTURAL UNIVERSITY

Pusa, Samastipur 848125, Bihar
Telephone: (6274) 274226
E-mail: rau@bih.nic.in
Founded 1970
Languages of instruction: Hindi, English
Academic year: July to June (two terms)
Chancellor: HE THE GOVERNOR OF BIHAR
Vice-Chancellor: Dr K. S. CHAUHAN
Registrar: Dr R. P. ROY SHARMA
Librarian: Dr B. N. VERMA
Library of 42,000 vols and 2,000 MSS
Number of teachers: 400
Number of students: 1,200
Publications: *Adhunik Kisan* (monthly), *Research Journal* (quarterly)

DEANS

Faculty of Agricultural Engineering: Dr A. P. MISHRA
Faculty of Agriculture: Dr P. N. JHA
Faculty of Basic Science: Dr A. K. SRIVASTAVA
Faculty of Home Science: Dr A. P. MISHRA
Faculty of Veterinary Science: Dr R. R. P. SINHA
Postgraduate Faculty: Dr T. P. SINGH

PROFESSORS

Faculty of Agricultural Engineering:
KUMAR, A., Soil Conservation
RAM, R. B., Farm Machinery

Faculty of Agriculture:
CHOUDHARY, L. B., Plant Breeding
MISHRA, S. S., Agronomy
OJHA, K. L., Plant Pathology
PRASAD, B., Soil Science
SAKAL, R., Soil Science
SHARMA, R. P. ROY, Agronomy
SINGH, B. K., Agronomy
SINGH, R. K., Seed Technology
THAKUR, R., Plant Breeding
YAZDANI, S. S., Entomology and Agricultural Zoology

Faculty of Veterinary Science:
MANI MOHAN, Animal Breeding and Genetics
PRASAD, C. B., Veterinary Microbiology
SINGH, M. K., Veterinary Pharmacology
SINHA, R. R. P., Animal Nutrition
SRIVASTAVA, P. S., Veterinary Parasitology

There are eight constituent colleges

RAJIV GANDHI PROUDYOGIKI VISHWAVIDYALAYA

Airport Bypass, Gandhi Nagar, Bhopal 462036, Madhya Pradesh.

RAJIV GANDHI UNIVERSITY OF HEALTH SCIENCES, KARNATAKA

Bangalore 560041, Karnataka
Telephone: (80) 26637058
Fax: (80) 26658569
E-mail: vc@rguhs.ac.in
Internet: www.rguhs.ac.in
Founded 1996
Vice-Chancellor: Dr R. CHANDRASHEKHARA
Registrar: K. M. SRINIVASA GOWDA
Librarian: Dr R. RAMA RAJ URS

Courses in anaesthesia, Ayurveda, cardiology, dentistry, homeopathy, hospital management, medical laboratory technology, medicine, naturopathy and yogic sciences, nursing, perfusion technology, pharmacy, physiotherapy, psycho-social rehabilitation, radiography, renal dialysis technology, respiratory technology, surgery, Unani medicine.

RANCHI UNIVERSITY

Ranchi 834008, Bihar
Telephone: (651) 2206062; (651) 2301077
Founded 1960
Teaching and Affiliating
Chancellor: HE THE GOVERNOR OF BIHAR
Vice-Chancellor: Dr L. S. SINGH
Registrar: M. ORAON
Library of 70,100 vols
Number of teachers: c. 2,000
Number of students: 67,500
Publications: *The University Journal*, *Journal of Social Research*, *The Geographical Outlook*, *Journal of Historical Research*, *Research Journal of Philosophy*, *Political Scientist*, *Journal of Agricultural Science*

DEANS

Faculty of Commerce: Dr V. L. SRIVASTAVA
Faculty of Education: Dr N. DATKEOLYAR
Faculty of Engineering: Prin.: Dr S. N. SINHA
Faculty of Humanities: Dr A. P. SINGH
Faculty of Law: B. K. PRASAD
Faculty of Medicine: N. L. DAS
Faculty of Science: Dr G. JHA
Faculty of Social Sciences: Dr S. M. PATHAK

There are 53 constituent colleges and 34 affiliated colleges

RANI DURGAVATI UNIVERSITY

Saraswati Vihar, Jabalpur 482001, Madhya Pradesh
Telephone: (761) 2600567
Fax: (761) 2603752
E-mail: rdvvcc@sancharnet.in
Internet: www.rdunijbpin.org
Founded 1957 as Jabalpur University, name changed 1983
Teaching and Affiliating
Languages of instruction: Hindi, English
Academic year: July to April (four terms)
Chancellor: HE THE GOVERNOR OF MADHYA PRADESH
Vice-Chancellor: Justice GULAB GUPTA
Registrar: Dr S. M. PATEL
Librarian: Y. L. CHOPRA
Library of 183,000 vols
Number of teachers: 1,053
Number of students: 95,000

DEANS

Faculty of Arts: Dr CHHAYA RAI
Faculty of Ayurveda: Dr G. S. KALCHURI
Faculty of Commerce: Dr K. B. AGARWAL
Faculty of Education: RAJENDRA TIWARI
Faculty of Engineering: Dr M. CHOUBEY
Faculty of Home Science: S. BATALIA
Faculty of Law: Dr M. A. QURESHI
Faculty of Life Science: Dr K. VERMA
Faculty of Management: Prof. P. K. JOSHI
Faculty of Mathematical Science: Prof. S. D. TRIPATHI
Faculty of Medicine: Dr A. KAUR
Faculty of Science: Dr K. K. MISHRA
Faculty of Social Sciences: Dr C. S. S. THAKUR

There are 116 affiliated colleges

ROHILKHAND UNIVERSITY

Bareilly, Uttar Pradesh 243001
Telephone: (581) 2458475
Fax: (581) 2453627
Founded 1975
State control
Languages of instruction: Hindi, English
Academic year: July to June
Chancellor: HE THE GOVERNOR OF UTTAR PRADESH
Vice-Chancellor: Dr MURLIDHAR TIWARY
Registrar: S. M. SRIVASTAVA

Number of teachers: 1,062
Number of students: 65,000

DEANS

Faculty of Agriculture: Dr S. K. Rajput
Faculty of Arts: Dr U. P. Arora
Faculty of Commerce: Dr P. K. Yadav

There are 32 affiliated colleges

UNIVERSITY OF ROORKEE

Roorkee, UP 247667
Telephone: (1332) 272349
E-mail: regis@rurkiu.ernet.in
Internet: www.uor.org
Founded in 1847 as Thomason College; inaugurated as a university 1949
Residential and Teaching; specializes in all branches of engineering
Language of instruction: English
Academic year: July to May (two terms)
Chancellor: HE The Governor of Uttar Pradesh
Vice-Chancellor: Dr N. C. Nigam
Registrar: G. G. Chhabra
Librarian: Yogendra Singh
Library of 260,000 vols
Number of teachers: 400
Number of students: 2,860.

SAMBALPUR UNIVERSITY

PO Jyoti Vihar, Burla, Sambalpur 768019, Orissa
Telephone: (663) 2430157
Fax: (663) 2430158
E-mail: info@sambalpuruniversity.net
Internet: ww.sambalpuruniversity.net
Founded 1967
Teaching and Affiliating
Language of instruction: English
Academic year: June to May
Chancellor: The Governor of Orissa
Vice-Chancellor: Prof. Madhav Chandra Dash
Registrar: Gangadhar Mahanand
Librarian: Dr B. P. Mohapatra
Library: Library of 105,000 books, 15,000 vols of periodicals
Number of teachers: 1,653
Number of students: 36,225
Publications: *Journal* (Science, annually), *Journal of Humanities* (annually), *Saptarshi* (monthly)

DEANS

Faculty of Arts: Prof. S. Nanda
Faculty of Commerce: Prof. D. P. Nayak
Faculty of Education: (vacant)
Faculty of Engineering: Dr R. K. Mishra
Faculty of Law: Prof. G. K. Rath
Faculty of Medicine: Prof. A. K. Sarangi
Faculty of Science: Dr M. K. Behera

There are 183 affiliated colleges and three constituent colleges

SAMPURNANAND SANSKRIT UNIVERSITY

Varanasi 221002, Uttar Pradesh
Telephone: (542) 2204089; (542) 2206617
Founded 1958
Teaching and Affiliating
Chancellor: The Governor of Uttar Pradesh
Vice-Chancellor: Dr Mandan Mishra
Registrar: Ram Prasad Ambast
Librarian: V. N. Misra
Library of 262,000 vols
Number of students: 35,000

There are two affiliated colleges on-campus, and 1,998 off-campus.

SARDAR PATEL UNIVERSITY

Vallabh Vidyanagar, Kaira 388120, Gujarat
Telephone: (2692) 236475
Fax: (2692) 236546
Internet: www.spuvvn.edu
Founded 1955
Teaching and Affiliating
Languages of instruction: Hindi, English, Gujarati
Academic year: June to April (two terms)
Chancellor: HE The Governor of Gujarat
Vice-Chancellor: Dr P. J. Patel
Registrar: Dr B. Natraj
Librarian: Dr S. M. Charan
Number of teachers: 1,050, including 241 postgraduate
Number of students: 21,629, including 3,606 postgraduate
Publications: *Journal of Education and Psychology*, *Arth-Vikas* (Economics Journal), *Pragna* (Journal of Engineering and Technology), *Prasna* (Journal of Social Sciences), *Mimansa* (Journal of English Literature), *Sheel Shrutam*

DEANS

Faculty of Arts: Prof. D. S. Mishra
Faculty of Business Studies: Dr V. G. Patel
Faculty of Education: Principal: N. R. Patel
Faculty of Engineering and Technology: Principal: F. S. Umrigar
Faculty of Home Science: Dr Rema Subhash
Faculty of Homoeopathy: Dr P. C. Dave
Faculty of Law: P. M. Patel
Faculty of Management: Principal: N. M. Zaveri
Faculty of Medicine: Dr S. H. Shrivastav
Faculty of Pharmaceutical Science: Prof. B. G. Patel
Faculty of Science: Dr L. M. Manocha

There are 39 affiliated colleges and one constituent college

SARDAR VALLABH BHAI PATEL UNIVERSITY OF AGRICULTURE AND TECHNOLOGY

Modipuram, Meerut 250110, Uttar Pradesh
Telephone: (121) 2571941
Fax: (121) 2571941
Founded 2000
Chancellor: HE The Governor of Uttar Pradesh
Vice-Chancellor: Dr B. Ram
Registrar: Dr H. S. Verma.

SAURASHTRA UNIVERSITY

University Campus, University Rd, Rajkot 360005, Gujarat
Telephone: (281) 2578501
Fax: (281) 2577633
Internet: www.saurashtrauniversity.edu
Founded 1967
Teaching and Affiliating
State control
Languages of instruction: Gujarati, Hindi, English
Academic year: June to March/April (two terms)
Chancellor: HE The Governor of Gujarat State
Vice-Chancellor: Prof. H. M. Joshi
Pro-Vice-Chancellor: K. T. Trivedi
Registrar: V. H. Joshi
Librarian (vacant)
Library of 136,000 vols
Number of teachers: 2,266 (inc. affiliated colleges)
Number of students: 63,548 (inc. affiliated colleges)
Publications: *Annual Budget*, *Annual Report*, *Samachar Patrika*, *Syllabus*, *Vol*

DEANS

Faculty of Arts: Prin.: D. M. Acharya
Faculty of Commerce: Prin.: C. D. Patel
Faculty of Education: Prin.: D. A. Uchat
Faculty of Home Science: Prof. Vasuben Trivedi
Faculty of Law: Prof. D. G. Modi
Faculty of Medicine: Dr H. M. Mangal
Faculty of Rural Studies: P. S. Gajera
Faculty of Science: Prof. U. V. Manavar
Faculty of Technology and Engineering: Prin.: D. B. Desai

HEADS OF DEPARTMENTS

Biosciences: Dr S. M. Pandya
Chemistry: Dr A. R. Parikh
Commerce: Dr N. M. Khandelwal
Economics: Dr K. K. Khakhkhar
Education: Dr D. A. Uchat
Electronics: Dr H. N. Pandya
English: Dr Avdhesh Singh
Gujarati: Dr B. S. Jani
Hindi: Dr S. P. Sharma
History: Dr A. M. Kikani
Home Science: (vacant)
Law: Dr N. K. Indrayan
Library and Information Science: (vacant)
Mathematics: (vacant)
Physics: Prof. R. G. Kulkarni
Psychology: Dr D. J. Bhatt
Sanskrit: Dr M. V. Joshi
Sociology: H. V. Rao
Statistics: Dr D. K. Ghosh
Computer Centre: Dr V. R. Rathod
A. D. Sheth Department of Journalism: Dr Y. A. Dalal
Post-Graduate Centre in Business Management: Dr D. G. Naik
Postgraduate Centre in Computer Science and Application: Dr N. N. Jani

There are 108 affiliated colleges

SHER-E-KASHMIR UNIVERSITY OF AGRICULTURAL SCIENCES AND TECHNOLOGY JAMMU

Railway Rd, Jammu 180012, Jammu and Kashmir
Telephone: (191) 2473417
Fax: (191) 2473883
Internet: www.skuastjammu.org
Founded 1999
State control
Academic year: July to June
Chancellor: HE The Governor of Jammu and Kashmir
Vice-Chancellor: Dr Nagendra Sharma
Registrar: Dr H. N. Khajuria
Librarian: S. C. Uppal
Library of 11,412 vols, 125 current periodicals

DEANS

Faculty of Agriculture: Dr R. K. Sharma (Assoc. Dean)
Faculty of Veterinary Sciences and Animal Husbandry: Dr A. K. Srivastava

SHER-E-KASHMIR UNIVERSITY OF AGRICULTURAL SCIENCES AND TECHNOLOGY OF KASHMIR

Shalimar Campus, Srinagar 191121, Jammu and Kashmir
Telephone: (194) 2462160
Fax: (194) 2462160
E-mail: skuast.aris@yahoo.com

Founded 1982
State control
Academic year: August to July
Chancellor: HE THE GOVERNOR OF JAMMU AND KASHMIR
Vice-Chancellor: Dr ANWAR ALAM
Registrar: Dr M. A. GORA
Faculties of Agriculture, Postgraduate Studies, Veterinary Sciences and Animal Husbandry.

SHIVAJI UNIVERSITY

Vidyanagar, Kolhapur 416004, Maharashtra
Telephone: (231) 2690571
Fax: (231) 2691533
E-mail: info@shivajiuniversity.com
Internet: www.unishivaji.ac.in
Founded 1962
Teaching and Affiliating
Languages of instruction: English, Marathi
Academic year: June to April (two terms)
Chancellor: HE THE GOVERNOR OF MAHARASHTRA
Vice-Chancellor: Dr M. M. SALUNKHE
Registrar: Dr S. N. DESAI
Librarian: SUMITRA JADHAV (acting)
Library of 250,000 vols, 6,300 MSS
Number of teachers: 7,075
Number of students: 149,427
Publication: *University Journal* (Humanities and Social Sciences sections)

DEANS
Faculty of Arts: Dr A. G. JOSHI
Faculty of Ayurvedic and Homeopathic Medicine: Dr S. S. SUNGARE
Faculty of Commerce: Dr K. V. BACHUTE
Faculty of Education: P. R. SHINDE
Faculty of Engineering and Technology: T. D. SAYAD
Faculty of Law: Prin.: H. G. KULKARNI
Faculty of Medicine: Dr V. M. YEMUL
Faculty of Science: Dr R. S. ADSUL
Faculty of Social Sciences: Dr V. B. JUGALE
There are 266 affiliated colleges and recognized institutes

SHREEMATI NATHIBAI DAMODAR THACKERSEY WOMEN'S UNIVERSITY

1 Nathibai Thackersey Rd, Mumbai 400020, Maharashtra
Telephone: (22) 22031879
Fax: (22) 22018226
E-mail: admin@sndt.org
Internet: sndt.org
Founded 1916
Teaching and Affiliating
State control
Languages of instruction: English, Gujarati
Languages of instruction: Marathi, Hindi
Academic year: June to March (two terms)
Chancellor: HE THE GOVERNOR OF MAHARASHTRA
Vice-Chancellor: Prof. RUPA B. SHAH
Registrar: Prof. P. V. DABLI
Librarian: Prof. HARSHA PAREKH
Library of 335,000 vols
Number of teachers: 744 full-time
Number of teachers: 238 part-time
Number of students: 50,000

DEANS
Faculty of Arts: Dr VILAS KHOLE
Faculty of Commerce: MUKUL SHAH
Faculty of Education: Prof. HEMALATA PARASNIS
Faculty of Fine Arts: NITIN MULEY
Faculty of Home Sciences: Prof. RAVIKALA KAMATH
Faculty of Library Science: Dr BHARATI SEN
Faculty of Nursing: ALKA KALAMBI
Faculty of Social Science: Dr B. B. PRADHAN

CONSTITUENT COLLEGES
Shreemati Nathibai Damodar Thackersey College of Arts, and Shreemati Champaben Bhogilal College of Commerce and Economics for Women: 1 Nathibai Thackersey Rd, Mumbai 400020; f. 1931; Principal ARUN N. KAMBLE.
Shreemati Nathibai Damodar Thackersey College of Arts and Commerce for Women: Karve Rd, Maharshi Karve Vidyavihar, Pune 411038; f. 1916; Principal Dr ASHWINI DHONGDE.
Premcoonverbai Vithaldas Damodar Thackersey College of Education for Women: Nathibai Thackersey Rd, Mumbai 400020; f. 1959; Principal Dr A. G. BHALWANKAR.
Shreemati Nathibai Damodar Thackersey College of Education for Women: Karve Rd, Maharshi Karve Vidyarihar, Pune 411038; f. 1964; Principal Dr C. K. NAGOSHE.
Shreemati Nathibai Damodar Thackersey College of Home Science: Karve Rd, Maharshi Karve Vidyarihar, Pune 411038; f. 1968; Principal I. P. AWASTHEE.
Sir Vithaldas Thackersey College of Home Science: Sir Vithaldas Vidyavihar, Juhu Rd, Mumbai 400049; f. 1959; Principal Dr SHALINI INAMDAR (acting).
Shree Hansraj Pragji Thackersey College of Library Science: 1 Nathibai Thackersey Rd, Mumbai 400020; f. 1961; Principal Prof. HARSHA PAREKH.
Leelabai Thackersey College of Nursing: Nathibai Thackersey Rd, Mumbai 400020; f. 1952; Principal JOY KUTTY.
C. U. Shah College of Pharmacy: Sir Vithaldas Vidyavihar Juhu Rd, Mumbai 400049; f. 1980; Principal Dr S. Y. GABHE.
Premlila Vithaldas Polytechnic: Sir V. Vidyavihar Juhu Rd, Mumbai 400049; f. 1976; Principal RADHA SINHA.
Centre of Education: PVDT College of Education, 1 Nathibai Thackersey Rd, Mumbai 400020; Co-ordinator Dr S. S. JOGIEKAV.
Department of Postgraduate Studies and Research: 1 Nathibai Thackersey Rd, Mumbai 400020; f. 1983; Dir Dr S. K. G. SUNDARAM.
Department of Postgraduate Studies and Research in Home Science: Sir Vithaldas Vidyavihar Juhu Rd, Mumbai 400049; Dir Dr RAVIKALA KAMATH.
There are 44 affiliated colleges

SHRI JAGANNATH SANSKRIT VISHWAVIDYALAYA

Srivihar, Puri 752003, Orissa
E-mail: sjsv@ori.nic.in
Internet: sjsv.nic.in
Founded 1981
Library of 23,000 vols
Departments of Dharmashastra, Nyaya, Sahitya, Sarvadarshan, Veda, Vedanta and Vyakarana
Publication: *Jagannath Jyotih* (irregular).

SHRI MATA VAISHNO DEVI UNIVERSITY

Gandhinagar 180004, Jammu and Kashmir
Telephone: (191) 2439404
Fax: (191) 2439566
E-mail: vcsmvdu@sancharnet.in
Internet: www.smvdu.org
Founded 1999
Residential and Teaching
Chancellor: HE THE GOVERNOR OF JAMMU AND KASHMIR
Vice-Chancellor: Prof. B. B. CHATTOO
Registrar: Dr C. M. SETH.

SIDHU KANHU UNIVERSITY

Santal Parganas, Dumka 814101, Jharkhand.

SIKKIM MANIPAL UNIVERSITY OF HEALTH, MEDICAL AND TECHNOLOGICAL SCIENCES

Fifth Mile, Tadong, Gangtok 737102, Sikkim
Telephone: (3592) 231938
Fax: (3592) 231147
E-mail: smu@dte.vsnl.net.in
Internet: www.smuhmts.edu
Founded 1995
Academic year: August to July
Chancellor: HE THE GOVERNOR OF SIKKIM
Pro-Chancellor: Dr RAMDAS PAI
Vice-Chancellor: L. C. AMARNATHAN
Registrar: S. D. DHAKAL.

CONSTITUENT INSTITUTIONS
Sikkim Manipal Institute of Medical Science: Dean Dr D. M. VASUDEVAN.
Sikkim Manipal Institute of Technology: Dean Dr S. MADHAVKUMAR.

SOUTH GUJARAT UNIVERSITY

PB 49, Surat 395007, Gujarat
Telephone: (261) 2227141
Fax: (261) 2227312
E-mail: sgsurat@guj.nic.in
Founded 1967
Teaching and Affiliating
State control
Language of instruction: Gujarati
Academic year: June to March (two terms)
Chancellor: HE The Governor of Gujarat KAILASHPATIJI MISHRA
Vice-Chancellor: P. K. SHARDA
Registrar: Dr V. D. NAIK (acting)
Librarian: E. R. J. CHRISTIE (acting)
Library of 150,000 vols
Number of teachers: 102 (University), 1,666 (colleges)
Number of students: 88,323
Publication: *University Journal*

DEANS
Faculty of Arts: Prin. GHANSHYAM PRASAD SANADHYA
Faculty of Commerce: J. B. SHAH
Faculty of Education: Dr S. G. SHAH
Faculty of Engineering and Technology: (vacant)
Faculty of Law: Prin. V. B. DESAI
Faculty of Medicine: (vacant)
Faculty of Rural Studies: (vacant)
Faculty of Science: Dr P. K. HIRADHAR
There are 140 affiliated colleges

SREE SANKARACHARYA UNIVERSITY OF SANSKRIT

Sree Sankarapuram, Ernakulam, Kalady 683574, Kerala
Telephone: (484) 2463380
Fax: (484) 2463480
E-mail: ssus@vsnl.com
Internet: www.ssus.ac.in
Founded 1994
Academic year: June to April
Chancellor: HE THE GOVERNOR OF KERALA
Vice-Chancellor: Dr K. N. PANIKKAR
Registrar: Dr V. K. ABDUL JALEEL
Principal and Dean of Studies: Dr N. K. SANKARAN

Library of 40,000 vols, 125 periodicals, 200 MSS

Faculties of Arts, Education, Sanskrit Studies and Social Sciences

Regional Centres in Ettumanoor, Kalady, Koyilandy, Payyannur, Thrissur, Thuravoor and Tirur.

SRI KRISHNADEVARAYA UNIVERSITY

Sri Venkateswarapuram PO, Anantapur 515003, Andhra Pradesh

Telephone: (8554) 255244

Internet: www.skuhyd.com

Founded 1967, university status 1981

Postgraduate Teaching and Research

Language of instruction: English

Academic year: December to October

Chancellor: HE THE GOVERNOR OF ANDHRA PRADESH

Vice-Chancellor: Prof. Y. SARASWATHY RAO

Principal (University College): Prof. D. V. KRISHNA

Registrar: B. LAKSHMIPATHY

Librarian: Dr P. KAMAIAK

Library of 63,000 vols, *c.* 500 periodicals

Number of teachers: 154

Number of students: 1,500

DEANS

Faculty of Arts: Prof. V. T. NAIDU

Faculty of Commerce: Prof. T. SUBBI REDDY

Faculty of Law: Prof. T. P. SUDARSHANA RAO

Faculty of Science: Prof. R. SEETHARMASWAMY

PROFESSORS

ANKI REDDY, K. C., Mathematics
BASHA MOHIDEEN, M., Zoology
BRAHMAJI RAO, S., Chemistry
ENOCK, K., Telugu
GHOUSE, M., Law
GOPAL, B. R., History
KAMESWARA RAO, A.
KANTHA RAO, M. L., Economics
KOTESWARA RAO, T., Telugu
KRISHNA, D. V., Mathematics
MANOHARA MURTHY, N., Physics
NAIDU, V. T., Rural Development
NARAYANA, N., Economics
PRAKASHA RAO, C. G., Botany
RAGHUNATHA SARMA, S., Telugu
RAJGOPAL, E.
RAMA MURTHY, V., Physics
RAMAKRISHNA RAO, A., English
RAMAKRISHNA RAO, P., Biochemistry
RAMAKRISHNA RAO, T. V., Physics
RAMAVATHARAM, S. I., Law
SEETHARAMASWAMY, R., Mathematics
SHARMA, D. P., Commerce
SUBBA RAO, C., English
SUBBARAMAIAH, S., Economics
SUBBI REDDY, T., Commerce
SUBRAHMANYAM, S. V., Physics
SUDARSHAN RAO, T. P., Law
SWAMINATHAN, E., Geography
TIRUPATHI NAIDU, V., Rural Development
VENKATA REDDY, C., Economics
VENKATA REDDY, D., Chemistry
VENKATA REDDY, K., English
VENKATA REDDY, K., Rural Development
VENKATASIVA MURTHY, K. N., Mathematics

SRI PADMAVATHI MAHILA VISVAVIDYALAYAM

Tirupati 517502, Andhra Pradesh

Telephone: (877) 2248417

Fax: (877) 2248417

E-mail: vcspmvv@yahoo.com

Founded 1983

Academic year: July to June

Chancellor: HE THE GOVERNOR OF ANDHRA PRADESH

Vice-Chancellor: Prof. R. MADHAVI

Registrar: Prof. P. MURALI MOHAN (acting)

Deputy Librarian: Dr D. RAJESWARI

Library of 46,000 books, 8,000 vols of periodicals

Number of students: 1,032

Faculties of Education, Humanities, Law, Science and Management.

SRI SATHYA SAI INSTITUTE OF HIGHER LEARNING

Prasanthi Nilayam, Anantapur District, Andhra Pradesh 515134

Telephone: (8555) 287239

Fax: (8555) 287390

Internet: www.srisathyasai.org.in/pages/instts/secschl.htm

Founded 1981

Private control

Language of instruction: English

Academic year: June to March (two terms)

Chancellor: BHAGWAN SATHYA SAI BABA

Vice-Chancellor: S. V. GIRI

Registrar: Prof. A. V. LAKSHMINARASIMHAM

Librarian: Dr K. TATA RAO (Deputy Librarian)

Library: Libraries (3 campuses) with 150,000 vols

Number of teachers: 115

Number of students: 1,100

Publications: *Journal of Applied Mathematics and Stochastic Analysis* (4 a year), *Bulletin of Pure and Applied Sciences* (4 a year), *International Journal of Modern Physics* (4 a year), *Third Concept: An International Journal of Ideas* (6 a year)

DEANS

Business Management and Finance: Prof. U. S. RAO

Commerce: Prof. U. S. RAO

Science: Prof. K. SRINIVASAN

HEADS OF DEPARTMENTS

Bioscience: Prof. P. V. BHIRAVAMURTHY

Business Management, Finance and Accounting: Prof. U. S. RAO

Chemistry: Dr C. JANARDHANA (Dir)

Commerce: Prof. U. S. RAO

Education: Dr M. KAPANI (Dir)

Home Science: Dr R. KAPOOR (Dir)

Mathematics and Computer Science: Prof. C. J. M. RAO

Physics: Prof. K. SRINIVASAN

Telugu Language and Literature: Dr. PADMAVATHAMMA (Dir)

SRI VENKATESWARA UNIVERSITY

Tirupati 517502, District Chittoor, Andhra Pradesh 2166

Telephone: (877) 2249611

Founded 1954 as Residential and Teaching; Affiliating since 1956

Languages of instruction: English, Telugu

Academic year: June to April (two terms)

Chancellor: HE THE GOVERNOR OF ANDHRA PRADESH

Vice-Chancellor: Prof. RALLAPALLI RAMAMURTHI

Registrar: K. JAYADEVA REDDY (acting)

Librarian: Dr M. R. CHANDRAN

Library: Libraries of 278,974 vols

Number of teachers: 498

Number of students: 3,259

Publications: *Annual Report*, *College Magazine*, *Research Bulletin*, *SV University Central Journal*, *SV University News*

DEANS

Faculty of Arts: Prof. G. NAGESWARA RAO

Faculty of Commerce: Prof. M. CHANDRASEKHAR

Faculty of Education: Prof. A. VENKATARAMI REDDY

Faculty of Engineering: Prof. T. RANGASWAMY

Faculty of Law: Prof. P. KOTESWARA RAO

Faculty of Medicine: (vacant)

Faculty of Oriental Learning: (vacant)

Faculty of Science: (vacant)

Faculty of Teaching: (vacant)

School of Biological and Earth Sciences: Prof. M. V. NAYUDU

School of Humanities and Extension: Prof. V. ANJANEYA SARMA

School of Mathematical and Physical Sciences: Prof. M. S. R. NAIDU

School of Social and Behavioural Sciences: Prof. V. RAMI REDDY

HEADS OF DEPARTMENTS

School of Biological and Earth Sciences:

- Biochemistry: Dr K. THYAGARAJU
- Botany: Prof. P. M. SWAMY
- Geography: Dr. P. NARAYANAMMA
- Geology: Prof. K. R. REDDY
- Home Science: B. DEVAKI
- Virology: Prof. M. V. NAYUDU
- Zoology: (vacant)

School of Humanities and Extension Studies:

- Adult Education: Dr M. C. REDDEPPA REDDY
- Education: Dr B. RAMACHANDRA REDDY
- English: Prof. G. NAGESWARA RAO
- Hindi: Dr T. RAJESWARANDA SARMA
- Indian Culture: Prof. S. S. RAMACHANDRA MURTHY
- Linguistics: Prof. P. C. NARASIMHA REDDY
- Philosophy: Dr K. MUNIRATHNAM CHETTY
- Population Studies: Prof. K. MAHADEVAN
- Sanskrit: Dr K. PRATAP
- Tamil: Dr R. MANUVEL
- Telugu Studies: Prof. K. SARVOTNAMA RAO
- Urdu, Arabic and Persian: Dr K. BASHEER AHMED

School of Mathematical and Physical Sciences:

- Chemistry: Prof. Y. KRISHNA REDDY
- Mathematics: Dr L. NAGAMUNI REDDY
- Physics: Dr B. JAGANNADHA REDDY
- Statistics: Dr P. BALASIDDAMUNI

School of Social and Behavioural Sciences:

- Business Management: Prof. B. V. V. N. MURTHY
- Commerce: Dr B. BHAGAVAN REDDY
- Econometrics: Prof. L. KANNAIAH NAIDU
- Economics: Dr Y. JAYASIMHULU NAIDU
- History: Sri A. R. RAMACHANDRA REDDY
- Indo-China: Prof. A. LAKSHMANNA CHETTY
- Law: Prof. P. KOTESWARA RAO
- Library Science: Prof. N. GURUSWAMY NAIDU
- Physical Anthropology and Prehistoric Archaeology: Prof. V. RAMI REDDY
- Political Science and Public Administration: Prof. K. V. NARAYANA RAO
- Psychology: Dr B. NAGARATHNAMMA
- Social Anthropology: Prof. A. MUNIRATHNAM REDDY
- Sociology: Dr M. HANUMANTHA RAO

College of Engineering:

- Chemical Engineering: Prof. D. CHENGAL RAJU
- Chemistry: Prof. S. JAYARAMA REDDY
- Civil Engineering: Prof. K. SRINIVASA RAO
- Computer Applications: Dr M. MUNIRATHNAM NAIDU
- Electrical and Electronics Engineering: Prof. B. SUBRAMANYAM
- Mathematics and Humanities: Dr M. SUNDARA MURTHY

Mechanical Engineering: Dr G. GURUNADHAN
Physics: Dr M. KRISHNAIAH

There are also three university postgraduate centres, three oriental colleges, two engineering colleges, three training colleges, six law colleges, four physical education colleges, one music college, one inst. of research in yoga and allied sciences, and 55 affiliated degree colleges

SWAMI RAMANAND TEERTH MARATHWADA UNIVERSITY

Vishnupuri, Nanded 431606, Maharashtra
Telephone: (2462) 229243
Fax: (2462) 229245
E-mail: srtmun@vsnl.com
Internet: www.srtmun.org

Founded 1994

Teaching and Affiliating
Academic year: June to April
Chancellor: HE THE GOVERNOR OF MAHARASHTRA
Vice-Chancellor: Dr SHESHRAO SURYAWANSHI
Registrar: Dr S. M. SONAWANE
Librarian: Dr S. P. SATARKAR

Library of 25,000 vols

Publication: *New Vision*

HEADS OF DEPARTMENTS

School of Chemical Sciences: Prof. B. P. BANDGAR
School of Commerce and Management Sciences: Prof. J. V. JOSHI
School of Earth Sciences: Prof. D. B. YEDEKAR
School of Languages and Literature: Prof. ANAND PATIL
School of Life Sciences: Prof. S. MOHAN KARUPPAYIL
School of Mathematics, Statistics and Computational Sciences: S. D. KHAMITKAR
School of Physical Sciences: Prof. SURESH CHANDRA
School of Social Sciences: Prof. B. C. BARIK

There are 182 affiliated colleges

TAMIL UNIVERSITY

Administrative Bldg, Trichy Rd, Thanjavur 613005, Tamil Nadu
Telephone: (4362) 227040
Fax: (4362) 227040

Founded 1981

Languages of instruction: Tamil, English
Academic year: July to April
Chancellor: HE THE GOVERNOR OF TAMIL NADU
Vice-Chancellor: Dr E. SUNDARAMOORTHI
Registrar: R. JEYAKUMAR
Library Director: Dr B. SUNDARESAN

Number of teachers: 74
Number of students: 265

Publications: *News Bulletin*, *Seithi Malar* (monthly)

DEANS

Faculty of Arts: Dr S. RAJUKALIDOSS
Faculty of Developing Tamil: Dr AROMA GLORY SAM
Faculty of Languages: Dr T. SEENISAMY
Faculty of Manuscript Studies: T. K. PARAMAVISA
Faculty of Science: Dr S. PREMA

ATTACHED INSTITUTES

Centre for Underwater Archaeology: New Campus, Trichy Rd, Thanjavur, Tamil Nadu 613005; Dir (vacant).

School of Philosophy: New Campus, Trichy Rd, Thanjavur 613005; research in philosophy; Dir Dr G. BASKARAN.

Tribal Research Institute: Tamil University, Thanjavur, Tamil Nadu 613005; Dir Dr V. CHIDAMBARANATHANPILLAI.

TAMIL NADU AGRICULTURAL UNIVERSITY

Coimbatore 641003, Tamil Nadu
Telephone: (422) 2431222
Fax: (422) 2431672
E-mail: registrar@tnau.ac.in
Internet: www.tnau.ac.in

Founded 1971
State control
Language of instruction: English
Academic year: July to June (two semesters)
Chancellor: HE THE GOVERNOR OF TAMIL NADU
Pro-Chancellor: THE MINISTER OF AGRICULTURE, GOVERNMENT OF TAMIL NADU
Vice-Chancellor: Dr C. RAMASAMY
Registrar: Dr S. D. SUNDAR SINGH
Deputy Librarian: K. PERUMALSAMY

Library of 161,146 vols
Number of teachers: 955
Number of students: 2,791

Publications: *TNAU News Letter* (in English, monthly), *Valarum Velanmai* (in Tamil, monthly), *Madras Agricultural Journal* (in English, monthly), *South Indian Horticulture* (in English, 4 a year), *Journal of External Education* (in English, 4 a year), *Alumni Newsletter* (in English, 4 a year), *Education Newsletter* (in English, 4 a year), *Journal of Agriculture Resource Management* (in English, 2 a year), *Annual Report* (in English and Tamil)

DEANS

Agricultural College and Research Institute, Coimbatore: Dr R. KRISHNASAMY
Agricultural College and Research Institute, Killikulam: Dr T. M. THIAGARAJAN
Agricultural College and Research Institute, Madurai: Dr N. KEMPUCHETTY
Agricultural Engineering College and Research Institute, Coimbatore: Dr R. MANIAN
Agricultural Engineering College and Research Institute, Kumulur: Dr C. T. DEVADAS
Anbil Dharmalingham Agricultural College and Research Institute, Tiruchirappalli: Dr S. ANTHONI RAJ
Forest College and Research Institute, Mettupalayam: Prof. K. S. NEELAKANDAN
Home Science College and Research Institute, Madurai: Dr K. SHEELA
Horticultural College and Research Institute, Coimbatore: Dr E. VADIVEL
Horticultural College and Research Institute, Periyakulam: Dr S. ANBU
School of Post Graduate Studies, Coimbatore: Dr S. KOMBAIRAJU

DIRECTORS

Centre for Agriculture and Rural Development Studies: Dr N. RAVEENDRAN
Centre for Plant Breeding and Genetics: Dr T. S. RAVEENDRAN
Centre for Plant Molecular Biology: Dr K. RAMASAMY
Centre for Plant Protection Studies: Dr T. MARIMUTHU
Extension Education: Dr G. DORAISWAMY
Open and Distance Learning: Dr V. ALAGESAN
Planning and Mentoring: Dr D. VEERARAGAVATHATHAM
Research: Dr S. RAMANATHAN
Soil and Crop Management Studies: Dr V. MURUGAPPAN
Student Welfare: Dr V. THANDAPANI
Tamil Nadu Rice Research Institute, Aduthurai: Dr B. CHANDRASEKARAN
Water Technology Centre: Dr K. PALANISAMI
Controller of Admissions: Dr B. SANTHANAKRISHNAN

HEADS OF DEPARTMENTS

Coimbatore Campus:

Agricultural Economics: Dr M. CHANDRASEKARAN
Agricultural Entomology: Dr S. PALANISAMY
Agricultural Extension and Rural Development Studies: Dr P. ATHIMUTHU
Agricultural Meteorology: Dr R. JAGANNATHAN
Agricultural Microbiology: Dr T. NATARAJAN
Agricultural and Rural Management: Dr N. AJJAN
Agronomy: Dr O. S. KANDASAMY
Animal Husbandry: Dr R. BALAGOPAL
Biochemistry: Dr R. BALASARASWATHI
Bio-Energy: Dr G. CHINNACHETTY
Central Farm Unit, SCMS: Dr K. VAIRAVAN
Cotton: Dr A. RAMALINGAM
Crop Physiology: Dr U. BANGARUSAMY
Environmental Sciences: Dr P. SINGARAM
Farm Machinery: Dr K. KATHIRVAL
Floriculture and Landscaping: Dr M. JAWAHARLAL
Food and Agricultural Process Engineering: Dr L. NARAYANAN
Forage Crops: Dr G. VIJAYKUMAR
Fruit Crops: Dr T. N. BALAMOHAN
Krishi Vigyan Kendra: Dr M. MANOHARAN
Millets: Dr B. SELVI
Nematology: Dr E. I. JONATHAN
Oilseeds: Dr P. VINDHYAVARMAN
Physical Science and Information Technology: Dr C. R. RANGANATHAN
Plant Pathology: Dr M. RAMIAH
Plant Molecular Biology and Biotechnology: Dr P. BALASUBRAMANIAN
Post-Harvest Technology Centre: Dr K. THANGAVEL
Pulses: Dr S. RAJARATHINAM
Rice: Dr K. MOHANASUNDARAM
Seed Science and Technology: Dr A. S. PONNUSWAMY
Sericulture: Dr N. CHANDRAMOHAN
Soil and Agricultural Chemistry: Dr M. GOVINDASAMY
Soil and Water Conservation: Dr M. V. RANGASAMY
Spice and Plantation Crops: Dr G. BALAKRISHNAMOORTHY
Vegetable Crops: Dr S. NATARAJAN
Zonal Research Centre: Dr D. ANANTHAKRISHNAN

Killikulam Campus:

Agricultural Economics: Dr M. CHINNADURAI
Agricultural Engineering: Dr V. J. F. KUMAR
Agricultural Entomology: Dr P. MANIDURAI MANOHARAN DAVID
Agricultural Extension: Dr S. SOMASUNDRAM
Agricultural Microbiology: Dr R. SRIDHAR
Agronomy: Dr A. MUTHUSANKARANARAYANAN
Horticulture: Dr P. PARAMAGURU
Plant Breeding: Dr S. CHIDAMBARAM
Plant Pathology: Dr E. ERAIVAN ARUTKANI AIYANATHAN
Soil Science: Dr V. SUBRAMANIAN

Kumulur Campus:

Agricultural Processing and Basic Sciences: Dr K. ALUGUSUNDARAM
Agricultural Sciences: Dr R. MARIMUTHU
Farm Machinery and Bio-energy: Dr V. MURUGESAN
Soil, Water Conservation and Agricultural Structures: Dr S. SANTHANA BOSE

Madurai Campus:

Agricultural Economics: Dr D. DAVID RAJASEKAR
Agricultural Engineering: Dr S. KAMARAJ
Agricultural Entomology: Dr R. RAJENDRAN

Agricultural Extension and Rural Development Studies: Dr V. SEKAR
Agricultural Microbiology: Dr J. PRABHAKARAN
Agronomy: Dr B. GURURAJAN
Animal Husbandry: Dr B. GURURANJAN
Apparel Design and Fashion Technique: Dr P. VENNILA
Family Resource Management: Dr M. R. PREMALATHA
Food Science and Nutrition: Dr D. MALATHI
Horticulture: Dr S. KUMAR
Human Development: Dr S. PARVATHI
Home Science and Extension: Dr A. ANDAL
Physical Science: Dr N. ARUNACHALAM
Plant Breeding and Genetics: Dr P. VIVEKANANDAN
Plant Pathology: Dr R. BASKARAN
Soils and Environment: Dr A. SARAVANAN

Mettupalayam Campus:

Agroforestry: Dr M. AYYASAMY
Forest Biology: Dr M. GANESHKUMAR
Forest Soils: Dr A. K. MANI
Silviculture: Dr K. K. SURESH
Tree Breeding: Dr M. PARAMATHMA

Periyakulam Campus:

Agronomy and SS&AC: Dr K. R. LATHA
Horticultural Botany: Dr A. BALAN
Olericulture: Dr D. SARALADEVI
Plant Protection: Dr R. SUNDARAM
Pomology: Dr M. SELVARAJAN

Tiruchirappalli Campus:

Crop Protection: Dr G. ARJUNAN
Plant Breeding and Genetics: Dr S. BALASUBRAMANIAN
Social Sciences and Languages: Dr G. RANGANATHAN

AFFILIATED COLLEGES

Adhiparasakthi Agricultural College, Kalavai: Dean Dr K. VANANGAMUDI.

Pandit Jawaharlal Nehru College of Agriculture and Research Institute, Karaikal: Dean Dr P. SUNDARAVADIVELU.

There are 30 research stations and 12 Krishi Vigyan Kendra (basic skills institutions)

TAMIL NADU DR AMBEDKAR LAW UNIVERSITY

5 Greenways Rd, Chennai 600028, Tamil Nadu

Telephone: (44) 24641212
Fax: (44) 24957414
E-mail: alu@tndalu.org
Internet: www.tndalu.org

Founded 1997

Chancellor: HE THE GOVERNOR OF TAMIL NADU
Vice-Chancellor: S. S. P. DARWESH
Registrar: Prof. C. ROBIN
Number of students: 7,300

Publications: *Newsletter* (quarterly), *Law Journal* (annually)

There are 5 affiliated colleges.

TAMIL NADU DR M. G. R. MEDICAL UNIVERSITY

69 Anna Salai, Guindy, Chennai 600032, Tamil Nadu

Telephone: (44) 22353574
Fax: (44) 22353698
E-mail: tnmmu@hotmail.com
Internet: www.tnmmu.ac.in

Founded 1987

Chancellor: HE THE GOVERNOR OF TAMIL NADU
Vice-Chancellor: Prof. C. V. BHIRMANANDHAM

HEADS OF FACULTIES

Faculty of Ayurveda: Prof. VIJAYA SESHADHRI
Faculty of Basic Medical Sciences: Prof. A. NALINI
Faculty of Biomedical Sciences: Prof. N. M. SAMUEL
Faculty of Community Health, Social Sciences and History of Medicine: Dr JAYAPRAKASH MULLIYAL
Faculty of Dentistry: Dr E. MUNIRATHINAM
Faculty of Homeopathy: Dr V. C. VAIDYALINGAM
Faculty of Medicine and Medical Specialities: Prof. C. V. BHIRMANANDHAM
Faculty of Nursing: Ms SEETHALAXMI
Faculty of Obstetrics and Gynaecology and Related Specialities: Prof. SHANTHA SAMBANDAN
Faculty of Paediatrics and Paediatric Specialities: Prof. C. S. R. SARKUNAM
Faculty of Pharmacy: Dr T. K. RAVI
Faculty of Siddha: Prof. G. GANAPATHY
Faculty of Surgery and Surgical Specialities: Prof. SRIKUMARI DAMODARAN
Faculty of Unani: Dr SHAIK SHAHUL HAMEED

PROFESSORS

Faculty of Ayurveda:

SESHADHRI, V.

Faculty of Basic Medical Sciences:

BANUMATHY, S. P., Anatomy
MANICKAVASAGAM, S.
NALINI, A., Pharmacology
RAJESWARI, C., Microbiology
SHERIFF, Biochemistry
VADIVELU, Forensic Medicine

Faculty of Biomedical Sciences:

SAMUEL, N. M.

Faculty of Community Health, Social Sciences and History of Medicine:

PRITHVI, A.

Faculty of Dentistry:

JAGANNATHAN, J., Conservative Dentistry
SWAMINATHAN, T. N., Prosthodontics

Faculty of Medicine and Medical Specialities:

BHIRMANANDHAM, C. V., Cardiology
JAGANNATHAN, K., Thoracic Medicine
JAYANTHI, Gastroenterology
PALANIAPPAN, V., Psychiatry
PANCHAPAKESA RAJENDRAN, C., Rheumatology
RAJAN, S. K., General Medicine
RAVIKANNAN, Medical Oncology
SENTHAMIL SELVI, G., Dermatology
USMAN, N., Venerology

Faculty of Nursing:

SAHU, G.

Faculty of Obstetrics and Gynaecology and Related Specialities:

ANUSUYA, P., Obstetrics and Gynaecology
MATHAI, M., Obstetrics and Gynaecology
RAMACHANDRAN, M., Obstetrics and Gynaecology
SAMBANDAN, S., Obstetrics and Gynaecology
SOUNDARAM, K., Obstetrics and Gynaecology
TAMILMANI, D., Obstetrics and Gynaecology

Faculty of Paediatrics and Paediatric Specialities:

CHANDRASEKARAN, K., Paediatrics
CHERIAN, T., Paediatrics
SARKUNAM, C. S. R., Paediatrics
TAMILARASU, P. T., Paediatrics
TAMILVANAN, S., Paediatrics

Faculty of Pharmacy:

PRAKASH, M. S.
RAJENDRAN, A.
RAO, G. S.
SRIDHARAN, A.

Faculty of Siddha:

GANAPATHY, G.
IQBAL, P. I.
PATRAYAN, A.
RAJESWARI, A.
SAKUNTHALA, P. R.

Faculty of Surgery and Surgical Specialities:

CHANDRASEKARAN, M., Surgical Endocrinology
DAMODARAN, S., Surgical Gastroenterology
JESUDASON, B., Surgery
PUSHPARAJ, K., Neurosurgery
RATHINAM, T., Ears, Nose and Throat

TAMIL NADU VETERINARY AND ANIMAL SCIENCES UNIVERSITY

Madhavaram Milk Colony, Chennai 600051, Tamil Nadu

Telephone: (44) 25551586
Fax: (44) 25551575
E-mail: tanuvas@vsnl.com
Internet: www.tanuvas.com

Founded 1989
State control
Academic year: July to June

Chancellor: HE THE GOVERNOR OF TAMIL NADU
Vice-Chancellor: Dr N. BALARAMAN
Registrar: Dr V. THIAGARAJAN

Number of teachers: 466
Number of students: 1,457

Publications: *Cheiron* (every 2 months), *Tanuvas Newsletter* (monthly), *Kalnadai Kathir* (every 2 months), *Cheidhi Madal* (monthly).

CONSTITUENT INSTITUTIONS

Centre for Animal Health Studies: Madhavaram Milk Colony, Chennai 600051, Tamil Nadu; Dir Dr A. KOTEESWARAN.

Centre for Animal Production Studies: Madhavaram Milk Colony, Chennai 600051, Tamil Nadu; Dir Dr K. GAJENDRAN.

Fisheries College and Research Institute: Thoothukudi 628008, Tamil Nadu; Dir Dr R. SANTHANAM.

Institute of Animal Nutrition: LRS Campus, Kattankolathur PO, Kattupakkam 603203, Tamil Nadu; Dir Dr T. SIVAKUMAR.

Institute of Food and Dairy Technology: Koduvalli, Chennai 600052, Tamil Nadu; Dir Dr ROBINSON J. J. ABRAHAM.

Madras Veterinary College: Chennai 600007, Tamil Nadu; Departments of Animal Genetics and Breeding, Animal Nutrition, Animal Reproduction, Bioinformatics, Dairy Science, Livestock Production and Management, Meat Science and Technology, Obstetrics and Gynaecology, Poultry Science, Veterinary Anatomy and Histology, Veterinary and Animal Husbandry Extension and Entrepreneurship, Veterinary Clinical Medicine, Ethics and Jurisprudence, Veterinary Microbiology, Veterinary Parasitology, Veterinary Pathology, Veterinary Pharmacology and Toxicology, Veterinary Physiology and Biochemistry, Veterinary Preventive Medicine and Epidemiology and Veterinary Surgery and Radiology; library of 60,363 vols; Dean Dr P. THANGARAJU.

Veterinary College and Research Institute: Namakkal 637001, Tamil Nadu; Dir Dr N. KANDASAMY.

TEZPUR UNIVERSITY

Napaam, Tezpur 784028, Assam

Telephone: (3712) 267004
Fax: (3712) 267006
E-mail: administration@tezu.ernet.in
Internet: www.tezu.ernet.in

Founded 1994
Academic year: July to June

Central university
Vice-Chancellor: Prof. P. C. DEKA
Registrar: Prof. M. AHORN
Library of 25,000 vols
Number of teachers: 100
Number of students: 700

DEANS

School of Energy, Environment and Natural Resources: Prof. D. KONWER
School of Humanities and Social Sciences: Prof. M. M. SARWA
School of Management Sciences: Prof. S. S. KHANKA
School of Science and Technology: Prof. S. K. DOLUI

HEADS OF DEPARTMENTS

School of Energy, Environment and Natural Resources (tel. (3712) 267007; fax (3712) 267006):
- Energy: Prof. P. K. BORDOLOI
- Environmental Sciences: Prof. K. K. BARVA

School of Humanities and Social Sciences:
- Cultural Studies: Dr S. K. DUTTA
- English and Foreign Languages: Prof. M. M. SARWA
- Mass Communication and Journalism: P. AMBARASAN

School of Management Sciences:
- Business Administration: Prof. S. S. KHANKA

School of Science and Technology:
- Chemical Sciences: Prof. N. S. ISLAM
- Computer Science and Information Technology: Prof. D. K. SAIKIA
- Electronics: Prof. B. D. PHUKAN
- Mathematical Sciences: Prof. A. K. BORKAKATI
- Molecular Biology and Biotechnology: Prof. B. K. KONWAR
- Physics: Dr A. KUMAR

THAPAR INSTITUTE OF ENGINEERING AND TECHNOLOGY

Patiala 147001
Telephone: (175) 2393021
Fax: (175) 2214498
Internet: www.tiet.ac.in
Founded 1956
President: L. M. THAPAR
Director: Dr M. P. KAPOOR
Registrar: Prof. A. JUNEJA
Librarian: Dr JANAK RAJ
Library of 38,000 vols
Number of teachers: 102
Number of students: 1,340

HEADS OF DEPARTMENTS

Chemical Engineering: Dr P. K. BAJPAI
Civil Engineering: Dr V. S. BATRA
Computer Science and Engineering: Dr G. K. SHARMA
Electrical and Electronics Engineering: Dr P. S. BIMBHRA
Mechanical and Industrial Engineering: Dr T. P. SINGH

HEADS OF SCHOOL

School of Basic and Applied Sciences: Dr K. K. RAINA
School of Biotechnology: Dr V. RAMAMURTHY
School of Management Studies: Dr D. S. BAWA

THIRUVALLUVAR UNIVERSITY

Vellore, Tamil Nadu
Vice-Chancellor: A. SUSHEELA THIRUMARAN
Registrar: Dr S. MAHALINGAM.

TILKA MANJHI BHAGALPUR UNIVERSITY

Bhagalpur 812007, Bihar
Telephone: (641) 2620100
Fax: (641) 2620353
E-mail: mustafams@yahoo.com
Internet: www.tmbu.org
Founded 1960 as Bhagalpur University; present name 1993
Teaching and Affiliating
Academic year: June to May
Chancellor: HE THE GOVERNOR OF BIHAR
Vice-Chancellor: Dr RAM ASHAY YADAV
Registrar: Dr M. G. MUSTAFA
Deputy Librarian: Dr ANIRUDHA PRASAD
Library of 120,000 vols
Number of teachers: 2,038
Number of students: 43,500

DEANS

Faculty of Commerce: Dr R. K. SINHA
Faculty of Education: HARENDRA P. SINGH
Faculty of Engineering: Dr C. R. PRATAP
Faculty of Humanities: Dr G. N. JHA
Faculty of Medicine: Dr ANIL KUMAR VERMA
Faculty of Science: Dr J. OJHA
Faculty of Social Science: Dr R. D. SHARMA

There are 29 constituent colleges and 24 affiliated colleges

TRIPURA UNIVERSITY

PO Suryamaninagar, Tripura West 799130, Tripura
Telephone: (381) 2374801
Fax: (381) 2374801
E-mail: tridm@dte.vsnl.net.in
Founded 1987
State control
Languages of instruction: English, Bengali
Academic year: June to May
Chancellor: HE THE GOVERNOR OF TRIPURA
Vice-Chancellor: Prof. D. K. BASU
Registrar: S. DEB
Librarian (vacant)
Library of 45,000 vols
Number of teachers: 63
Number of students: 19,000 (incl. affiliated colleges)
Publication: *News Letter* (quarterly)

PROFESSORS

AGGARWAL, B. K., Life Science
BHOWMIK, R. N., Mathematics
CHAUDHURIU, M., Bengali
CHAUDHURY, D. K., History
DEBNATH, P., Commerce
DEY, A., Mathematics
DEY, B. K., Physics
DEY, S. N., Sanskrit
DINDA, B., Chemistry
GHOSH, D., Life Science
HALDAR, P. K., Commerce
ROY, A. D., Life Science
SAHA, A., Economics
SRIVASTAVA, R. C., Life Science

There are 21 affiliated colleges

UTKAL UNIVERSITY

PO Vani Vihar, Bhubaneswar 751004, Orissa
Telephone: (674) 2581850
Fax: (674) 2581850
Internet: www.utkaluniversity.org
Founded 1943
Teaching and Affiliating
State control
Languages of instruction: English, Oriya
Academic year: July to June
Chancellor: HE THE GOVERNOR OF ORISSA
Vice-Chancellor: Prof. G. K. DAS
Registrar: Dr A. K. PAUL (acting)
Librarian: Dr NILAKANTHA SARANGI (acting)
Library of 233,000 vols, 256 periodicals
Number of teachers: 8,521
Number of students: 200,000

DEANS

Faculty of Arts: Prof. K. M. PATRA
Faculty of Commerce: Dr GUNANIDHI SAHOO
Faculty of Education: M. DAS
Faculty of Engineering: Dr NILAKANTHA PATTANAIK
Faculty of Law: INDRAJIT RAY
Faculty of Medicine: Dr R. N. DASH
Faculty of Science: Dr P. K. JESTHI

CONSTITUENT COLLEGES

Madhusudan Law College: Cuttack; f. 1949; Prin. Dr D. P. KAR.

University Law College: Vani Vihar, Bhubaneswar 751004; f. 1975; Prin. Dr P. K. PADHI.

There are 362 affiliated colleges

UTKAL UNIVERSITY OF CULTURE

POB 4, Bhubaneswar 751001, Orissa
Telephone: (674) 2530213
Fax: (674) 2535486
E-mail: mailbox@utkaluniversityculture.com
Internet: utkaluniversityculture.com
Founded 1999
Teaching and Affiliating
Academic year: July to June
Chancellor: HE THE GOVERNOR OF ORISSA
Vice-Chancellor: NARENDRA KUMAR MISHRA
Registrar: Dr SUBHENDU MUND
Library of 3,000 vols
Publication: *Sanskruti* (Bulletin)
Schools of Architecture and Archaeology, Language and Literature, Visual Arts, Performing Arts, Culture Studies, Occupational Studies and Orissan Studies
There are 13 affiliated colleges.

UTTAR PRADESH RAJARSHI TANDON OPEN UNIVERSITY

17 Maharshi Dayanand Marg, Thornhill Rd, Allahabad 211001, Uttar Pradesh
Telephone: (532) 2621839
Fax: (532) 2624368
E-mail: contact@uprtou.org
Internet: www.uprtou.org
Founded 1998
Chancellor: HE THE GOVERNOR OF UTTAR PRADESH
Vice-Chancellor: Prof. D. P. SINGH
Registrar: A. K. SINGH
Schools of Computer and Information Technology, Health Sciences, Journalism and Mass Communication, Management, Social Sciences, Humanities and Languages and Tourism and Hotel Management.

UTTAR PRADESH TECHNICAL UNIVERSITY

IET Campus, Sitapur Rd, Lucknow 226021, Uttar Pradesh
Telephone: (522) 2732193
Fax: (522) 2732185
E-mail: dameleak@rediffmail.com
Internet: www.uptu.org
Founded 2000
Chancellor: HE THE GOVERNOR OF UTTAR PRADESH
Pro-Chancellor: Prof. A. K. KHARE
Vice-Chancellor: Prof. D. S. CHAUHAN
Registrar: A. K. DAMELE

Finance Officer: SHEO HORI SINGH YADAV
Number of students: 90,000
There are 190 affiliated colleges.

V. B. S. PURVANCHAL UNIVERSITY

Devkali Jasopur, Saraykhaja, Jaunpur 222001, Uttar Pradesh
Telephone: (5452) 252244
Fax: (5452) 252222
Internet: www.purvanchaluniversity.org
Founded 1987
Residential and Affiliating
Vice-Chancellor: Prof. NARESH CHAND GAUTAM
Registrar: RAM S. RAM
Faculties of Agriculture, Applied Social Sciences, Arts, Commerce, Education, Engineering and Technology, Law, Management Studies and Science
There are more than 300 affiliated colleges.

VARDHAMAN MAHAVEER OPEN UNIVERSITY

Rawatbatha Rd, Akhelgarh, Kota 324010, Rajasthan
Telephone: (744) 2470971
Fax: (744) 2470451
E-mail: admin@koukota.com
Internet: www.vmoukota.org
Founded 1987
Chancellor: HE THE GOVERNOR OF RAJASTHAN
Vice-Chancellor: Dr R. V. VYAS
Registrar: B. L. KOTHARI
Library of 85,000 vols
Departments of Commerce, Computer Science, Economics, Education, History, Indian Tradition and Culture, Law, Library and Information Science, Management and Political Science
There are six regional centres and 32 study centres.

VEER KUNWAR SINGH UNIVERSITY

Arrah 802301, Bihar
Telephone: (6182) 223559
Fax: (6182) 223559
Founded 1992
Academic year: June to May
Chancellor: HE THE GOVERNOR OF BIHAR
Vice-Chancellor: Dr I. C. KUMAR
Registrar: Dr QAMAR AHSAN
Librarian: Dr J. P. SINGH

DEANS

Faculty of Commerce: Dr D. K. TIWARI
Faculty of Humanities: Dr R. P. RAI
Faculty of Science: Dr R. P. PANDEY
Faculty of Social Science: Dr GANDHIJEE RAI
There are 17 constituent colleges and 45 affiliated colleges

VIDYASAGAR UNIVERSITY

PO Vidyasagar University, West Midnapore 721102, West Bengal
Telephone: (32) 22275297
Fax: (32) 22275329
E-mail: registrar@vidyasagar.ac.in
Internet: www.vidyasagar.ac.in
Founded 1981
State control
Languages of instruction: English, Bengali
Academic year: July to June
Chancellor: HE THE GOVERNOR OF WEST BENGAL
Vice-Chancellor: Prof. SWAPAN KUMAR PRAMANICK
Registrar: Dr HIMANSU GHOSH
Librarian: AMIYA SARKAR (acting)
Library of 70,000 vols
Number of teachers: 105
Number of students: 36,500 (incl. affiliated colleges)
Publications: *Journal of Physical Sciences* (annually), *Journal of Philosophy and the Life World* (annually), *Journal of Commerce* (annually), *Journal of Biological Sciences* (annually), *Politics and Society* (annually), *Journal of Library and Information Science* (annually)

DEANS

Faculty of Arts and Commerce: Prof. P. K. MISRA
Faculty of Science: Prof. R. N. JANA
There are 39 affiliated colleges

PROFESSORS

BANERJEE, T. K., Political Science with Rural Administration
BATTACHARYA, T., Zoology
KHAN, L. A., Bengali
MAHAPATRA, P. K., Physics
MAITI, M., Applied Mathematics
MISRA, P. K., Philosophy and Life-World
MUKHOPADHAYA, S., Computer Science and Electronics
PATI, B. R., Microbiology
RANJAN DE, B., Chemistry and Chemical Technology
SAHA, S. C., Electronics

VIKRAM UNIVERSITY

University Rd, Ujjain 456010, Madhya Pradesh
Telephone: (734) 2552072
Fax: (734) 2552076
Founded 1957
Teaching and Affiliating
Languages of instruction: Hindi, English
Academic year: July to June
Chancellor: HE THE GOVERNOR OF MADHYA PRADESH
Vice-Chancellor: Dr R. K. S. CHAUHAN
Registrar: Dr S. K. BEGDE
Librarian (vacant)
Library of 140,000 vols
Number of students: 31,472

DEANS

Faculty of Arts: Dr K. N. JOSHI
Faculty of Ayurveda: Dr S. L. SHARMA
Faculty of Commerce: Prof. T. L. JAIN
Faculty of Education: Dr R. R. MISHRA
Faculty of Engineering: Dr M. G. SHARMA
Faculty of Law: Dr K. N. JOSHI
Faculty of Life Science: Dr O. P. MALL
Faculty of Science: Dr S. N. GUPTA
Faculty of Social Sciences: (vacant)
There are 55 affiliated colleges

VINOBA BHAVE UNIVERSITY

POB 31, Hazaribag 825301, Jharkhand
Telephone: (6546) 264279
Fax: (6546) 264279
E-mail: root@vbharat.ernet.in
Founded 1992
State control
Academic year: July to May
Chancellor: HE THE GOVERNOR OF JHARKHAND
Vice-Chancellor: Dr BAHURA EKKA
Registrar: PHOOLAN PRASAD VERMA
Librarian-in-charge: Dr PARMANAND MAHTO

DEANS

Faculty of Commerce: Dr B. N. SINGH
Faculty of Engineering: Dr S. SINGH
Faculty of Humanities: Dr Y. PRASAD
Faculty of Medicine: Dr RENU BALA
Faculty of Science: Dr K. P. KARNAL
Faculty of Social Sciences: Dr ENAYATULLAH
There are 19 constituent colleges and 40 affiliated colleges

VISVA-BHARATI

PO Santiniketan, Birbhum 731235, West Bengal
Telephone: (3463) 252751
Fax: (3463) 252672
E-mail: root@vbharat.ernet.in
Internet: www.visva-bharati.ac.in
Founded 1951
Central university
Central Government control
Languages of instruction: English, Bengali
Academic year: July to April (three terms)
Rector: HE THE GOVERNOR OF WEST BENGAL
Chancellor: A. B. BAJPAL
Vice-Chancellor: Dr SUJIT K. BASU
Registrar: SUNIL KUMAR SARKAR
Librarian: Prof. P. JASH (acting)
Library of 750,000 vols
Number of teachers: 516
Number of students: 6,357
Publications: *Visva-Bharati Patrika* (4 a year), *Visva-Bharati News*, *Journal of Philosophy*

HEADS OF DEPARTMENTS

Agricultural Extension, Agricultural Economics and Agricultural Statistics: Dr SARTHAK CHOUDHURI
Ancient Indian History, Culture and Archaeology: Prof. GANAPATHY SUBBIAH
Arabic, Persian, Urdu and Islamic Studies: Prof. HAFIZ MOHAMMED TAHIR ALI
ASEPAN: Prof. DULAL CHANDRA GHOSH
Bengali: Prof. RAMBAHAL TIWARI
Biotechnology: Prof. AJIT KUMAR ADITYA
Botany: Prof. SUSIL KUMAR PAL
Centre for Rural Studies: Prof. ONKAR PRASAD
Chemistry: Prof. UDAY SANKAR ROY
Chinese Language and Culture: Dr JAYEETA GANGULY
Classical Music: Prof. MOHAN SING KHANGURA
Computer and System Science: Dr BALARAM BHATTACHARYA
Cottage Industry Training: Prof. RAJ KUMAR KONAR
Crop Improvement, Horticulture and Argricultural Botany: Dr DEBOTOSH SANYAL
Design: SHIBAPRASAD KAR CHOUDHURY
Economics and Politics: Prof. SIBRANJAN MISHRA
Education: Prof. HIMADRI RANJAN BHATTACHARYA
English and Other Modern European Languages: Dr NIRANJAN MOHANTY
Environmental Studies: Prof. SUDHENDU MONDA
Geography: Prof. ARABINDA BISWAS
Graphic Art: Dr NIRMALENDU DAS
Hindi: Dr RAMESWAR PRASAD
History: Sen Dr SUCHIBRATA
History of Art: Prof. JANAK JHANKAR NARZARY
Indo-Tibetan Studies: Dr NARENDRA KUMAR DASH
Japanese Studies: Dr PADMARUCHI MUKHERJEE
Journalism and Mass Communication: DWIJADAS BANERJEE
Mathematics: Prof. DULAL KUMAR PAL
Oriya: Prof. NILADRI BHUSAN
Painting: Prof. NANDADULAL MUKHERJEE
Philosophy and Comparative Religion: Dr SABUJKALI MITRA
Physical Education: MAONIMOY MITRA
Physics: Prof. PRABIR KUMAR GHOSH

Plant Protection: Dr NAKUL CHANDRA MONDAL
Rabindra Music and Dance: Prof. GORA SARBADHIKARY
Sanskrit, Pali and Prakrit: Prof. DIPAK BHATTACHRYA
Sculpture: Prof. SUSHENDRA KUMAR GHOSH
Social Work: Prof. MANJU MOHAN MUKHERJEE
Zoology: Prof. ARUN KUMAR ROY

There are eight constituent colleges

VISVESWARAIAH TECHNOLOGICAL UNIVERSITY

Santhibastawad Rd, Machhe, Belgaum 590014, Karnataka
Telephone: (831) 2405468
E-mail: info@vtu.ac.in
Internet: www.vtu.ac.in

Founded 1998
Teaching and Affiliating
Academic year: September to June

Chancellor: HE THE GOVERNOR OF KARNATAKA
Pro-Chancellor: THE MINISTER FOR HIGHER EDUCATION, KARNATAKA
Vice-Chancellor: Dr K. BALAVEERA REDDY
Registrar: Prof. M. S. SHIVAKUMAR

Courses in chemical engineering, civil engineering, computer science, electrical engineering, electronics engineering, industrial production engineering, mechanical engineering and textile engineering

There are 97 affiliated colleges and regional centres in Bangalore, Belgaum, Gulbarga and Mysore.

WEST BENGAL UNIVERSITY OF ANIMAL AND FISHERY SCIENCES

68 Kshudiram Bose Sarani, Kolkata 700037, West Bengal
Telephone: (33) 25565021
Fax: (33) 25571986
E-mail: wbuafs@wb.nic.in

Founded 1995
State control
Academic year: July to June

Chancellor: HE THE GOVERNOR OF WEST BENGAL
Vice-Chancellor: Dr SATYA S. GHOSH
Registrar: Dr D. N. JANA
Librarian-in-charge: Dr RANAJIT KUMAR GHOSH

Library of 22,000 vols

Faculties of Dairy Technology, Fishery Sciences and Veterinary and Animal Sciences.

WEST BENGAL UNIVERSITY OF TECHNOLOGY

West Bengal State Archives Bldg, 43 Shakespeare Sarani, Kolkata 700017, West Bengal
Telephone: (33) 23217578
Fax: (33) 23217578
E-mail: vcwbut@sify.in
Internet: www.wbut.net

Founded 2001
State control
Academic year: January to December

Chancellor: HE THE GOVERNOR OF WEST BENGAL
Vice-Chancellor: Prof. A. R. THAKUR
Registrar: Dr S. K. BANDYOPADHYAY

Courses in architecture, biotechnology, business administration, ceramics and glass technology, chemical engineering, civil engineering, computer engineering, computer science, cooking and catering, electrical engineering, electronic engineering, hotel management, information technology, leather technology, marine engineering, mechanical engineering, optometry, power engineering, production engineering, telecommunications engineering, textile technology and town planning

There are 73 affiliated colleges.

YASHWANTRAO CHAVAN MAHARASHTRA OPEN UNIVERSITY

Nashik 422222, Maharashtra
Telephone: (253) 2231714
Fax: (253) 2231716
E-mail: registrar@ycmou.com
Internet: www.ycmou.com

Founded 1999
State control
Languages of instruction: English, Hindi, Marathi
Academic year: July to June

Chancellor: HE THE GOVERNOR OF MAHARASHTRA
Vice-Chancellor: RAJAN MADHAORAO WELUKAR
Registrar: Dr NANASAHEB R. KAPADNIS

Library of 25,000 vols
Number of teachers: 4,300
Number of students: 400,000

Publications: *Wamvad* (monthly), *Dnyangangotri* (quarterly), *Mukta Vidya* (every 6 months)

DIRECTORS

School of Agricultural Science: Prof. SURYA GUNJAL
School of Commerce and Management: Prof. PANDIT PALANDE
School of Computer Science: Prof. RAMCHANDRA TIWARI
School of Continuing Education: Prof. RAJENDRA VADNERE
School of Education: Dr A. N. JOSHI
School of Health Sciences: Dr SHYAM ASHTEKAR
School of Humanities and Social Sciences: Dr RAMESH WARKHEDE
School of Science and Technology: MANOJ KILLEDAR

There are eight regional centres and 2,500 recognized study centres

Institutes of National Importance

Institutes of National Importance are established, or so designated, through Acts of Parliament and are thereby granted degree-awarding powers.

ALL-INDIA INSTITUTE OF MEDICAL SCIENCES

Ansari Nagar, New Delhi 110029
Telephone: (11) 26588500
Fax: (11) 26588663
E-mail: webmastr@aiims.ac.in
Internet: www.aiims.ac.in

Founded 1956

Director: Prof. P. VENUGOPAL
Registrar: V. P. GUPTA
Librarian: Dr R. P. KUMAR

Library of 115,000 vols, 570 periodicals
Number of teachers: 475 faculty staff
Number of students: c. 1,000students

Publications: *AIIMS News* (bulletin, quarterly), *The National Medical Journal of India* (6 a year)

PROFESSORS

Anaesthesiology:
ARORA, M. K.
BATRA, R. K.
CHANDERLEKHA
DUREJA, G. P.
JAYALAKSHMI, T. S.
PAWAR, D. K.
SAXENA, R.

Anatomy:
AJMANI, M. L.
KUCHERIA, K.
KUMAR, R.
MEHRA, R. D.
SABHERWAL, U.
WADHWA, S.

Biochemistry:
RAO, D. N.
SINGH, N.
SINHA, S.

Biomedical Engineering:
ANAND, S.
RAY, A. R.
SINGH, H.
TANDON, S. N.

Biophysics:
MISHRA, R. K.
RAO, G. S.
SINGH, T. P.

Biostatistics:
SUNDARAM, K. R.

Biotechnology:
PRASAD, H. K.
SHARMA, Y. D.
TYAGI, J. S.

Cardiology:
BAHL, V. K.
KOTHARI, S. S.
REDDY, K. S.
SAXENA, A.

Centre of Community Medicine:
KAPOOR, S. K.
PANDAV, C. S.
REDDAIAH, V. P.

Dental Surgery:
PARKASH, H.
SHAH, N.

Dermatology and Venereology:
KHANNA, N.
SHARMA, V. K.
VERMA, K. K.

Endocrinology and Metabolism:
AMMINI, A. C.

Forensic Medicine:
DOGRA, T. D.

Gastroenterology and Human Nutrition:
ACHARYA, S. K.
JOSHI, Y. K.
KAPIL, U.

Gastrointestinal Surgery:
CHATTOPADHYAY, T. K.

Haematology:
CHOUDHRY, V. P.
KUMAR, R.
SAXENA, R.

Transplant Immunology and Immunogenetics:
MEHRA, N. K.

Hospital Administration:
CHAUBEY, P. C.
SHARMA, R. K.

Laboratory Medicine:
JAILKHANI, B. L.
MUKHOPADHYAY, A. K.

Medicine:
GULERIA, R.

KUMAR, A.
MISRA, A.
SHARMA, S. K.
SOOD, R.

Microbiology:
BANERJEE, U.
BROOR, S.
SAMANTARAY, J. C.
SETH, P.

Nephrology:
DASH, S. C.
TIWARI, S. C.

Nuclear Medicine:
BANDOPADHYAYA, G. P.
MALHOTRA, A.
PANT, G. S.

Nuclear Magnetic Resonance Imaging:
JAGANNATHAN, N. R.

Obstetrics and Gynaecology:
KRIPLANI, A.
KUMAR, S.
MITTAL, S.

Orthopaedics:
BHAN, S.
JAYASWAL, A.
KOTWAL, P. P.
RASTOGI, S.

Otorhinolaryngology:
BAHADUR, S.
DEKA, R. C.
SHARMA, S. C.

Paediatric Surgery:
GUPTA, D. K.
MITRA, D. K.

Paediatrics:
ARORA, N. K.
ARYA, L. S.
BHAN, M. K.
KALRA, V.
PAUL, V. K.

Pathology:
CHOPRA, P.
DAWAR, S.
KAPILA, K.
PANDA, S. K.
SARKAR, C.
SINGH, M. K.
VERMA, K.
VIJAYARAGHAVAN, M.

Pharmacology:
GROVER, J. K.
GUPTA, Y. K.

Physiology:
BIJLANI, R. L.
KUMAR, V. M.
SENGUPTA, J.

Psychiatry and Deaddiction Centre:
KHANDELWAL, S. K.
MEHTA, M.
RAY, R.
TRIPATHI, B. M.

Radio Diagnosis:
GUPTA, A. K.
MUKHOPADHYAY, S.
VASHIST, S.

Reproductive Biology:
KUMAR, A.
SARKAR, N. N.

Physical Medicine and Rehabilitation:
SINGH, U.

Surgical Disciplines:
KUMAR, A.
MEHTA, S. N.
MISRA, M. C.
SRIVASTAVA, A.

Urology:
GUPTA, N. P.
HERNAL, A. K.

AFFILIATED COLLEGE

College of Nursing: Principal M. VATSA.

DAKSHINA BHARAT HINDI PRACHAR SABHA

POB 1419, Thyagaraya Nagar, Chennai 600017, Tamil Nadu
Telephone: (44) 24341824
Fax: (44) 24388420
Internet: www.tnuniv.ac.in/dbhps

Founded 1918; present name and status 1964
Academic year: July to June
Language of instruction: Hindi

Chancellor: Dr B. D. JATTI
Vice-Chancellor: M. MAHADEV
Pro-Chancellor: V. A. SHARMA
Registrar: R. F. NEERLAKATTI
Registrar: Dr P. H. SETHUMADHAVA RAO

Library of 100,000 vols (within National Hindi Research Library)

There are 20 affiliated colleges.

INDIAN INSTITUTE OF TECHNOLOGY, BOMBAY

Powai, Mumbai 400076, Maharashtra
Telephone: (22) 25722545
Fax: (22) 25723480
E-mail: director@iitb.ac.in
Internet: www.iitb.ac.in

Founded 1958
Language of instruction: English
Academic year: July to April
Residential

Dir: Prof. ASHOK MISRA
Registrar: Dr TARUNADIRYA SAHAY
Librarian: Dr DAULAT JOTHWANI

Library of 388,174 vols, 1,400 periodicals
Number of teachers: 409
Number of students: 5,270

depts of Aerospace eng., Chemical eng., Chemistry, Civil eng., Computer science and eng., Earth sciences, Electrical eng., Humanities and social sciences, Mathematics, Mechanical eng., Metallurgical eng. and materials science, Physics.

ATTACHED RESEARCH CENTRES

Advanced Centre for Research in Electronics: Head Prof. A. N. CHANDORKAR.

Centre for Aerospace Systems Design and Engineering: tel. (22) 25722545 ext. 7113; Head Prof. P. M. MUJUMDAR.

Centre for Environmental Science and Engineering: Head Prof. S. R. ASOLEKAR.

Centre for Formal Design and Verification of Software: tel. (22) 25722545 ext. 8700; Head Prof. G. SIVAKUMAR.

Centre for Research in Nanotechnology and Science: Head Prof. RAMGOPAL RAO.

Centre for Studies in Resources Engineering: tel. (22) 25722545 ext. 7660; Head Prof. D. CHANDRASEKHARAM.

Centre for Technology Alternatives in Rural Areas: tel. (22) 25722545 ext. 7522; Head Prof. A. W. DATE.

Computer Centre: Head Prof. ANURAG MEHRA.

Industrial Design Centre: Head Prof. RAVI POOVAIAH.

Sophisticated Analytical Instrumentation Facility: tel. (22) 25722545 ext. 7690; Head Prof. A. R. KULKARNI..

ATTACHED SCHOOLS

School of Biosciences and Bioengineering: Head Prof. K. K. RAO.

Kanwal Rekhi School of Information Technology: Head Prof. BERNARD L. MENEZES.

Shailesh J. Mehta School of Management: Head Prof. KARUNA JAIN.

INDIAN INSTITUTE OF TECHNOLOGY, DELHI

Hauz Khas, New Delhi 110016Telephone: (11) 26582222
Fax: (11) 26582277
E-mail: malhotraas@hotmail.com
Internet: www.iitd.ac.in

Founded 1961; present status 1963
Academic year: July to May

Director: Prof. R. S. SIROHI
Registrar: SINGH MALHOTRA

Library of 307,832 vols
Number of teachers: 484
Number of students: 4,854

HEADS OF DEPARTMENTS

Applied Mechanics: Prof. K. S. SHISHODIA
Biochemical Engineering and Biotechnology: Prof. S. MISHRA
Chemical Engineering: Prof. A. K. GUPTA
Chemistry: Prof. H. M. CHAWLA
Civil Engineering: Prof. K. G. SHARMA
Computer Science and Engineering: Prof. M. BALAKRISHNAN
Electrical Engineering: Prof. M. GOPAL
Humanities and Social Sciences: Prof. V. UPADHYAY
Management Studies: Prof. R. BAISYA
Mathematics: Prof. J. B. SRIVASTAVA
Mechanical Engineering: Prof. K. GUPTA
Physics: Prof. L. K. MALHOTRA
Textile Technology: Prof. V. K. KOTHARI

HEADS OF RESEARCH CENTRES

Centre for Applied Research in Engineering: Prof. S. K. KOUL
Centre for Atmospheric Sciences: Prof. G. JAYARAMAN
Centre for Biomedical Engineering: Prof. H. SINGH
Centre for Energy Studies: Prof. C. AVINASH
Centre for Polymer Science and Engineering: Prof. V. CHOUDHARY
Centre for Rural Development and Technology: Prof. SANTOSH
Computer Services Centre: Prof. B. P. PAL
Educational Technology Services Centre: Dr V. KUMAR
Industrial Tribology, Machine Dynamics and Maintenance Engineering Centre: Prof. V. P. AGRAWAL
Instrument Design and Development Centre: Prof. A. L. AYAL

INDIAN INSTITUTE OF TECHNOLOGY, GUWAHATI

North Guwahati, Guwahati 781039, Assam
Telephone: (361) 2583000
Fax: (363) 2690762
E-mail: webmaster@iitg.ernet.in
Internet: www.iitg.ernet.in

Founded 1994

Director: Prof. GAUTAM BARUA
Registrar: Dr M. C. BORGOHAIN

HEADS OF DEPARTMENTS

Biotechnology: Asst Prof. R. SWAMINATHAN
Chemical Engineering: Prof. D. S. DE
Chemistry: Prof. J. B. BARUAH
Civil Engineering: Assoc. Prof. S. TALUKDAR
Computer Science and Engineering: Prof. SUKUMAR NANDI
Design: Prof. K. RAMCHANDRAN
Electronics and Communication Engineering: Prof. A. K. GOGOI

Humanities and Social Sciences: Assoc. Prof. S. Borbora
Mechanical Engineering: Assoc. Prof. P. S. Robi
Mathematics: Assoc. Prof. D. C. Dalal
Physics: Assoc. Prof. A. Srinivasan

PROFESSORS

Barua, G., Computer Science and Engineering
Baruah, J. B., Chemistry
Bora, P. K., Electronics and Communication Engineering
Chattopadhyay, A., Chemistry
Chaudhuri, M. K., Chemistry
De, D. S., Chemical Engineering
Gogoi, A. K., Electronics and Communication Engineering
Khan, A. T., Chemistry
Mahanta, A., Electronics and Communication Engineering
Mishra, S. C., Mechanical Engineering
Nandi, S., Computer Science and Engineering
Ramchandran, K., Design
Sahasrabudhe, A. D., Mechanical Engineering
Yammiyavar, P. G., Design

INDIAN INSTITUTE OF TECHNOLOGY, KANPUR

IIT PO, Kanpur 208016, Uttar Pradesh
Telephone: (512) 2590151
Founded 1960
State control
Language of instruction: English
Director: Prof. R. C. Malhotra
Registrar: V. Narasimhan
Librarian: Dr Bhooshan Lal
Library of 390,000 vols and 900 periodicals
Number of teachers: 319
Number of students: 2,061
Publications: *Courses of Study* (annually), *Research, Design and Development Capabilities* (annually), *Research Reports*.

INDIAN INSTITUTE OF TECHNOLOGY, KHARAGPUR

PO Kharagpur Technology, Kharagpur 721302, West Bengal
Telephone: (3222) 255221
Fax: (3222) 255303
E-mail: director@iitkgp.ernet.in
Internet: www.iitkgp.ernet.in
Founded 1950
Academic year: July to April
Director: Dr Shishir K. Dube
Registrar: Dr D. Gunasekaran
Chair, Central Library: Prof. P. K. J. Mahapatra
Library of 362,852 vols, 1,130 periodicals
Number of teachers: 431
Number of students: 3,604
Publication: *Newsletter* (3 a year)

HEADS OF DEPARTMENTS

Aerospace Engineering: Prof. A. K. Ghosh
Agricultural and Food Engineering: Prof. S. Kar
Architecture and Regional Planning: Prof. Mridula Banerji
Chemical Engineering: Prof. A. K. Biswas
Chemistry: Prof. Jayasree Ghosh
Civil Engineering: Prof. M. Bandyopadhyay
Computer Science and Engineering: Prof. A. K. Majumdar
Electrical Engineering: Prof. T. K. Basu
Electronics and Electrical Communication Engineering: Prof. R. Garg
Geology and Geophysics: Prof. A. Chakraborty
Humanities and Social Sciences: Prof. B. P. Sandilya
Industrial Engineering and Management: Prof. P. K. J. Mahapatra
Mathematics: Prof. J. C. Mishra
Mechanical Engineering: Prof. P. K. Nag
Metallurgical and Materials Engineering: Prof. M. Charaborty
Mining Engineering: Prof. B. S. Sastry
Ocean Engineering and Naval Architecture: Prof. S. K. Satsangi
Physics and Meteorology: Prof. H. N. Acharya

HEADS OF CENTRES

Biotechnology Centre: Prof. S. C. Kundu
Cryogenics Engineering Centre: Prof. V. R. Kalvey
Materials Science Centre: Prof. D. Bhattacharya
Rubber Technology Centre: Prof. G. B. Nando
Rural Development Centre: Prof. S. C. Mahapatra

HEADS OF SCHOOLS

Advanced School of Medical Science and Technology: (vacant)
G. S. Sanyal School of Telecommunication: Assoc. Prof. S. Chakraborty
School of Information Technology: Assoc. Prof. A. Gupta
Vinod Gupta School of Management: Prof. D. Acharya

INDIAN INSTITUTE OF TECHNOLOGY, MADRAS

IIT PO, Chennai 600036, Tamil Nadu
Telephone: (44) 22578100
Fax: (44) 22570509
E-mail: registrar@iitm.ac.in
Internet: www.iitm.ac.in
Founded 1959
State control
Language of instruction: English
Academic year: July to April
Director: Prof. M. S. Ananth
Registrar: Dr Usha Titus
Librarian: Dr H. Chandra
Library: see Libraries and Archives
Number of teachers: 334
Number of students: 4,031
Publications: *Annual Report*, *I. I. T. Madras News* (4 a year), *Journal of Mathematical and Physical Science* (6 a year), *Research Consultancy, Expertise and Facilities* (annually)

HEADS OF DEPARTMENTS

Aerospace Engineering: Prof. S. Santhakumar
Applied Mechanics: Prof. J. Raamachandran
Chemical Engineering: Prof. M. Chidambaram
Chemistry: Prof. B. Viswanathan
Civil Engineering: Prof. M. S. Mathews
Computer Science and Engineering: Prof. S. Raman
Electrical Engineering: Prof. C. Venkatasešhaiah
Humanities and Social Sciences: Prof. T. T. Narendran
Mathematics: Prof. A. Avudainayagam
Mechanical Engineering: Prof. V. Ganesan
Metallurgical Engineering: Prof. K. Prasada Rao
Ocean Engineering: Prof. K. Muthukrishnaiah
Physics: Prof. V. R. K. Murthy

ATTACHED RESEARCH CENTRES

Central Electronic Centre: Head Dr M. Kumaravel.

Centre for Continuing Education: Head Prof. K. Krishnaiah.

Composite and Technology Centre: Head Dr S. K. Malhotra.

Materials Science and Research Centre: Head Prof. B. Viswanathan.

Sophisticated Analytical Instrumentation Centre: Head Prof. S. Sankararaman.

INDIAN INSTITUTE OF TECHNOLOGY, ROORKEE

Roorkee 247667, Uttaranchal
Telephone: (1332) 272349
Fax: (1332) 273560
E-mail: img@iitr.ernet.in
Internet: www.iitr.ernet.in
Founded 1847
Director: Dr Prem Vrat
Regitrar: A. K. Srivastava
Departments of Alternate Hydro Energy, Architecture, Biotechnology, Chemical Engineering, Chemistry, Civil Engineering, Earth Sciences, Earthquake Engineering, Electrical Engineering, Electronic and Computer Engineering, Humanities, Hydrology, Management Studies, Mathematics, Mechanical and Industrial Engineering, Metallurgical Engineering, Paper Technology Engineering, Physics and Water Resources.

INDIAN STATISTICAL INSTITUTE

203 Barrackpore Trunk Rd, Kolkata 700108, West Bengal
Telephone: (33) 25778085
Fax: (33) 25776680
E-mail: dean@isical.ac.in
Internet: www.isical.ac.in
Founded 1931
State control
Academic year: July to June
ISI regional centres located in Bangalore, Chennai, Coimbatore, Hyderabad, Mumbai, New Delhi, Pune and Vadodara
Dir: Prof. K. B. Sinha
Dean of Studies: Prof. G. M. Saha
Chief Librarian: Prof. D. Dasgupta (acting)
Library of 215,000 vols
Publications: *Sankhya: The Indian Journal of Statistics*, *Technical Reports*, *Memoranda*

HEADS OF DIVISIONS

Applied Statistics: Prof. A. Dewanji
Biological Sciences: Prof. M. Ghose
Computer Science and Communication Science: Prof. B. B. Bhattacharyya
Physical and Earth Science: Prof. Dilip Saha
Social Sciences: Prof. Atis Dasgupta
Theoretical Statistics and Mathematics: Prof. S. C. Bagchi

PROFESSORS

Bagchi, B.
Bagchi, D. K.
Bagchi, S.
Bagchi, S. C.
Bandyopadhay, S.
Bhat, B. V. R.
Bhatia, R.
Bhatt, A. G.
Bhattacharya, B.
Bhattacharya, B. B.
Bhattacharya, S.
Bhattacharya, S.
Bhimasankaram, P.
Bose, A.
Bose, M.
Chakravarty, S. R.
Chanda, B.
Chanda, S.

CHANDRA, T. K.
CHATTOPADHYAY, M.
CHAUDHURI, P.
CHOWDHURI, B. B.
COONDOO, D.
DANDAPAT, B. S.
DAS, A.
DAS, J.
DAS, N.
DAS, S.
DAS, S. P.
DASGUPTA, A. K.
DASGUPTA, D.
DASGUPTA, R.
DELAMPADY, M.
DEWANJI, A.
DEY, A.
DUTTA GUPTA, J.
GHOSE, M.
GOSWAMI, A.
GUPTA, M. R.
GUPTA, R.
JEGANATHAN, P.
KARANDIKAR, R. L.
KUNDU, M. K.
MAITI, P.
MAJUMDER, A.
MAJUMDER, H. P.
MAJUMDER, P. K.
MAJUMDER, P. P.
MAZUMDER, B. S.
MITRA, S.
MONDAL, B. N.
MUKHERJEA, K. K.
MURTHY, C. A.
MUTHURAMALINGAM, P. L.
NARAYANA, N. S. S.
PAL, N. R.
PARUI, S. K.
PAUL, M.
RAHA, A. B.
RAJEEV, B.
RAMACHANDRAN, V. K.
RAMAMURTHY, K.
RAMASUBRAMANIAM, S.
RAMASWAMY, B.
RAO, A. R.
RAO, I. K.
RAO, S. B.
RAO, T. J.
RAO, T. S. S. R. K.
RAY, K. S.
REDDY, B. M.
ROY, B. K.
ROY, P.
ROY, R.
ROY, S.
ROY CHOWDHURY, P.
SAHA, D.
SAHA, G. M.
SAMANTA, T.
SARBADHIKARI, H.
SARKAR, A.
SARKAR, N.
SASTRY, N. S. N.
SEN, A.
SENGUPTA, A.
SENGUPTA, D.
SENGUPTA, D.
SIKDAR, K.
SINHA, B. P.
SINHA, K. B.
SITARAM, A.
SRIVASTAVA, S. M.
SWAMINATHAN, M.
THANGAVALU, S.
TRIPATHI, T. P.
VIJAYAN, K. S.

NATIONAL INSTITUTE OF PHARMACEUTICAL EDUCATION AND RESEARCH

Sector 67, SAS Nagar, Mohali 160062, Punjab
Telephone: (172) 2214682
Fax: (172) 2214692
E-mail: director@niper.nic.in
Internet: www.niper.nic.in

Founded 1991

Academic year: July to June

Director: Prof. P. R. RAO
Dean: Dr K. K. BHUTANI

Library of 3,139 vols, 103 periodicals

Publication: *Current Research & Information on Pharmaceutical Sciences (CRIPS)* (quarterly)

HEADS OF DEPARTMENTS

Biotechnology: Prof. C. S. DEY
Medicinal Chemistry: Prof. A. K. CHAKRABORTI
Natural Products: Prof. K. K. BHUTANI
Pharmaceutical Analysis: Prof. S. SINGH
Pharmaceutical Management: Asst Prof. P. GARG
Pharmaceutical Technology: Prof. U. C. BANERJEE
Pharmaceutics: Prof. R. PANCHAGNULA
Pharmacology and Toxicology: Prof. P. R. RAO
Pharmacy Practice: Assoc. Prof. P. TIWARI

POSTGRADUATE INSTITUTE OF MEDICAL EDUCATION AND RESEARCH

Sector 12, Chandigarh 160012
Telephone: (172) 2747585
Fax: (172) 2744401
E-mail: pgimer@chd.nic.in
Internet: www.pgimer.nic.in

Founded 1962

Academic year: January to December or July to June

Director: Prof. K. K. TALWAR
Deputy Director (Administration): Prof. SARLA GOPALAN
Registrar: D. R. YADAVA
Dean: Prof. SUDHA SURI

Library of 85,000 vols, 577 periodicals

Publications: *Bulletin* (quarterly), *Drugs Bulletin* (quarterly), *Annual Report*, *Bulletin of Pediatric Gastroentrology Hepatology and Nutrition* (quarterly)

HEADS OF DEPARTMENTS

Anaesthesia: Prof. PROMILA CHARI
Anatomy: Prof. MADHUR GUPTA
Biochemistry: Prof. G. K. KHULLER
Biophysics: Prof. K. L. KHANDUJA
Blood Transfusion: Dr NEELAM MARWAHA
Cardiology: Prof. K. K. TALWAR
Cardiovascular and Thoracic Surgery: Prof. R. S. DHALIWAL
Community Medicine: Prof. RAJESH KUMAR
Cytology and Gynaecological Pathology: Prof. ARVIND RAJWANSHI
Dermatology, Venereology and Leprosy: Prof. BHUSHAN KUMAR
Endocrinology: Prof. SUBHASH VERMA
Experimental Medicine and Biotechnology: Prof. S. MAJUMDAR
Forensic Medicine: Prof. DALBIR SINGH
Gastroenterology: Prof. B. NAGI
General Surgery: Prof. J. D. WIG
Haematology: Prof. GURJEEWAN GREWAL
Hepatology: Prof. Y. K. CHAWLA
Histopathology: Prof. KUSUM JOSHI
Hospital Administration: Dr A. K. GUPTA
Immunopathology: Dr RAKESH KUMAR VASISHTA
Internal Medicine: Prof. SUBHASH VERMA
Medical Microbiology: Prof. MEERA SHARMA
Nephrology: Prof. V. SAKHUJA
Neurology: Prof. S. PRABHAKAR
Neurosurgery: Prof. V. K. KHOSLA
Nuclear Medicine: Prof. S. K. JINDAL
Obstetrics and Gynaecology: Prof. SARALA GOPALAN
Ophthalmology: Prof. AMOD GUPTA
Oral Health Sciences: Prof. H. S. CHAWLA
Orthopaedics: Prof. O. N. NAGI
Otolaryngology: Prof. S. B. S. MANN
Paediatrics: Prof. ANIL NARANG
Paediatric Surgery: Prof. K. L. N. RAO
Parasitology: Prof. NANCY MALLA
Pharmacology: Prof. PROMILA PANDHI
Plastic Surgery: Prof. R. K. SHARMA
Psychiatry: Prof. SAVITA MALHOTRA
Pulmonary Medicine: Prof. S. K. JINDAL
Radio Diagnosis and Imaging: Prof. SUDHA SURI
Radiotherapy: Prof. S. C. SHARMA
Urology: Prof. A. K. MANDAL
Virology: Dr R. K. RATHO

PROFESSORS

Department of Anaesthesia:
BATRA, Y. K.
CHARI, P.
GROVER, V. K.
MALHOTRA, S. K.
WIG, J.

Department of Anatomy:
GUPTA, M.

Department of Biochemistry:
GILL, K. D.
KHULLAR, G. K.
KOHLI, K. K.

Department of Biophysics:
KHANDUJA, K. L.

Department of Cardiovascular and Thoracic Surgery:
DHALIWAL, R. S.

Department of Cardiology:
TALWAR, K. K.

Department of Community Medicine:
KUMAR, R.

Department of Cytology and Gynaecological Pathology:
RAJWANSHI, A.

Department of Dermatology, Venereology and Leprosy:
KANWAR, A. J.
KUMAR, B.

Department of Experimental Medicine and Biotechnology:
MAJUMDAR, S.

Department of Gastroenterology:
BHASIN, D. K.
NAGI, B.
SINGH, K.

Department of General Surgery:
MINZ, M.
SINGH, R.
WIG, J. D.

Department of Haematology:
DASH, S.
GAREWAL, G.

Department of Hepatology:
CHAWLA, Y. K.

Department of Histopathology:
JOSHI, K.

Department of Hospital Administration:
GUPTA, A. K.

Department of Internal Medicine:
BAMBERY, P.
SINGH, S.
VARMA, S. C.

Department of Medical Microbiology:
SHARMA, M.

Department of Nephrology:
SAKHUJA, V.

Department of Neurology:
PRABHAKAR, S. K.
Department of Neurosurgery:
KHOSLA, V. K. K.
MATHURIYA, S. N.
Department of Obstetrics and Gynaecology:
GOPALAN, S.
GUPTA, I.
MALHOTRA, S.
Department of Ophthalmology:
GUPTA, A.
RAM, J.
Department of Oral Health Sciences:
CHAWLA, H. S.
UTREJA, A. K.
Department of Orthopaedics:
GILL, S. S.
NAGI, O. N.
RAI, J.
Department of Otolaryngology:
MANN, S. B. S.
Department of Paediatric Surgery:
RAO, K. L. N.
Department of Paediatrics:
MARWAHA, R. K.
NARANG, A.
SINGHI, P. D.
SINGHI, S.
Department of Parasitology:
MALLA, N.
Department of Pharmacology:
GARG, S. K.
PANDHI, P.
Department of Psychiatry:
KULHARA, P.
MALHOTRA, S.
Department of Pulmonary Medicine:
BEHERA, D.
JINDAL, S. K.
Department of Radio Diagnosis and Imaging:
SURI, S.
Department of Radiotherapy:
PATEL, F.
SHARMA, S. C.

SREE CHITRA TIRUNAL INSTITUTE FOR MEDICAL SCIENCES AND TECHNOLOGY

Thiruvananthapuram 695011, Kerala
Telephone: (471) 2443152
Fax: (471) 2446433
E-mail: sct@sctimst.ker.nic.in
Internet: sctimst.ker.nic.in
Founded 1973; present status 1980
Academic year: January to December
President: Dr R. CHIDAMBARAM
Director: Dr K. MOHANDAS
Registrar: Dr A. V. GEORGE

HEADS OF DIVISIONS
Anaesthesiology: Dr R. C. RATHOD
Artificial Internal Organs: Dr G. S. BHUVANESHWAR
Biochemistry: Dr K. SUBRAMONIA IYER
Biomaterials Technology: Dr R. SIVAKUMAR
Biosurface Technology: Dr C. P. SHARMA
Blood Transfusion: Dr JAISY MATHAI
Cardiology: Dr K. G. BALAKRISHNAN
Cardiovascular Thoracic Surgery: Dr M. P. MOHANSINGH
Cellular and Molecular Cardiology: Dr C. C. KARTHA
Clinical Engineering: K. VIJHYAKUMAR
Engineering Services: NEELAKANTAN NAIR
Microbiology: Dr J. SHANMUGHAM
Neurology: Dr K. RADHAKRISHNAN
Neurosurgery: Dr D. ROUT
Pathology: Dr V. V. RADHAKRISHNAN
Pathophysiology: Dr MOHANTY MIRA
Polymer Chemistry: Dr A. JAYAKRISHNAN
Radiology: Dr A. K. GUPTA
Toxicology: Dr K. RATHINAM
Vivarium: A. VIJAYANLAL

Deemed Universities

Deemed Universities (also known as Deemed-to-be Universities) are institutions that have been conferred the status of a university by virtue of their long tradition of teaching, or specialization and excellence in a particular field of study.

Allahabad Agricultural Institute: Allahabad 211007, Uttar Pradesh; tel. (532) 2684281; fax (532) 2684394; e-mail registrar@aaidu.org; internet www.aaidu.org; f. 1910; Deemed University status 2000; faculties of Agriculture, Business Studies, Engineering and Technology, Health and Medical Sciences, Humanities, Social Sciences, Arts and Culture, Science, Theology, Veterinary Science and Animal Husbandry; library: library of 40,000 vols; Chancellor Dr MANI JACOB; Vice-Chancellor Prof. RAJENDRA B. LAL; Registrar Prof. SARVJEET HERBERT.

Amrita Vishwa Vidyapeetham: Ettimadai PO, Coimbatore 641105, Tamil Nadu; tel. (422) 2656422; fax (422) 2656274; e-mail webmaster@amrita.edu; internet www.amrita.edu; Deemed University status 2003; constituent institutions: Amrita Institute of Technology and Science, Amrita Institute of Management, Amrita Institute of Medical Sciences (Kochi, Kerala); research institute: Centre of Excellence in Computational Engineering and Networking; Vice-Chancellor Dr P. VENKAT RANGAN.

Avinashilingam Institute for Home Science and Higher Education for Women: Mettupalayam Rd, Coimbatore 641043, Tamil Nadu; tel. (422) 2440241; fax (422) 2438786; e-mail webmaster@avinuty.ac.in; internet www.avinashilingam.edu; f. 1957; Deemed University status 1988; faculties of Business Administration, Education, Engineering, Community Education and Entrepreneurship Development, Home Science, Humanities, Science; library: library of 130,000 vols; 4,436 students; Vice-Chancellor Dr M. CHANDRAMANI; Registrar Dr SAROJA PRABHAKARAN.

Ayal Bihari Vajpayee Indian Institute of Information Technology and Management: Gwalior, Madhya Pradesh; tel. (751) 2460315; fax (751) 2460313; internet www.iiitm.ac.in; f. 2001; departments of computer science, electronics, finance, human resources, information technology, marketing and networking; Dir Prof. D. P. AGRAWAL.

Banasthali Vidyapith: Banasthali 304022, Rajasthan; tel. (1438) 228348; fax (1438) 228365; e-mail director@banasthali.ac.in; internet www.banasthali.ac.in; f. 1935; Deemed University status 1983; faculties of Education, Fine Arts, Home Science, Humanities, Management, Science and Social Sciences; library: library of 180,757 vols, 530 periodicals; 210 teachers; 4,182 students; Dir Prof. ADITYA SHASTRI; Librarian Dr S. D. VYAS.

Bengal Engineering College: PO Botanic Garden, Howrah 711103, West Bengal; tel. (33) 26684561; fax (33) 26604564; e-mail vc@becs.ac.in; internet www.becs.ac.in; f. 1856; departments of applied mechanics and drawing, architecture and town and regional planning, chemistry, civil engineering, computer science and technology, electrical engineering, electronics and telecommunication, humanities, mathematics, mechanics, metallurgical engineering, mining, engineering and geology and physics; Dir AMALJYOTI SENGUPTA; Registrar PRADIP RAY.

Bharath Institute of Higher Education and Research: 29 Tilak St, Chennai 600017, Tamil Nadu; tel. (44) 28341865; fax (44) 28348776; internet bharathuniv.com; f. 1984; Deemed University status 2003; constituent institutions: Bharath Institute of Science and Technology, Sree Balaji Dental College and Hospital; library: 40,000 vols, 80 periodicals; Vice-Chancellor Dr S. RENGANATHAN; Registrar Dr K. P. THOOYAMANI.

Bharati Vidyapeeth: Lal Bahadur Shastri Marg, Pune 411030, Maharashtra; tel. (20) 24331317; fax (20) 24339121; e-mail bharati@vsnl.com; internet www.bharatividyapeeth.edu; f. 1996; composed of 17 constituent institutions: Medical College, Dental College and Hospital, College of Ayurved, Homoeopathic Medical College, College of Nursing, Yashwantrao Mohite College of Arts, Science and Commerce, New Law College, Yashwantrao Chavan Institute of Social Science Studies and Research, Social Science Centre, Research and Development Centre in Pharmaceutical Sciences and Applied Chemistry, Institute of Environment Education and Research, Pune College of Pharmacy, Institute of Management and Entrepreneurship Development, College of Engineering, College of Physical Education, Rajiv Gandhi Institute of Biotechnology and Information Technology, Interactive Research School for Health Affairs; library: total colln of 99,125 vols; 8,386 students; Vice-Chancellor Prof. S. F. PATIL; Registrar B. R. ARBAD.

Bhatkhande Music Institute: 1 Kaiserbagh, Lucknow 226001, Uttar Pradesh; tel. (522) 2210318; fax (522) 2222926; f. Deemed University status 2000; faculties of dance, instrumental music, musicology and training and vocal music; Vice-Chancellor PURNIMA PANDE; Registrar B. SINHA.

Bihar Yoga Bharati (Bihar Yoga University): Ganga Darshan Fort, Munger 811201, Bihar; tel. (6344) 222430; fax (6344) 220169; e-mail byb@yogavision.net; internet www.biharyogabharati.net; f. 1994; Deemed University status 2000; temporarily closed for restructuring from 2005; Vice-Chancellor SWAMI SHANKARANANDA SARASWATI.

Birla Institute of Technology, Ranchi: Mesra 835215, Ranchi; tel. (651) 275868; fax (651) 535401; e-mail birlatech@bitsmart.com; internet www.bitmesra.edu; f. 1955, Deemed University status 1986; extension centres in Allahabad, Bhimtal, Kolkata, Hyderabad, Jaipur and Noida; international centre in Bahrain (Iran); library: 60,000 vols; 149 teachers; 1,650 students; Vice-Chancellor Prof. S. K. MUKHERJEE; Registrar Dr K. V. KRISHNAMURTHY (acting).

Birla Institute of Technology and Science: Vidhya Vihar Campus, Pilani 333031, Rajasthan; tel. (1596) 245073; fax (1596) 244183; e-mail mmsanand@bits-pilani.ac.in; internet www.bits-pilani.ac.in; f. 1964; campuses in Goa and Dubai (United Arab Emirates); library: 208,319 vols; 300 teachers; 11,070 students; Vice-Chancellor Prof. S. VENKATESWARAN; Registrar Prof. M. M. S. ANAND; Librarian M. A. BHATT; publ. *Bulletin*.

Central Institute of English and Foreign Languages: Hyderabad, Andhra Pradesh 500007; tel. (40) 27098131; fax (40) 27098402; e-mail ciefors@ciefl.ac.in; internet www.ciefl.ac.in; f. 1958; Deemed University status 1973; academic year June to May; postgraduate and research degrees, diplomas, certificates; correspondence course; library: 125,282 vols; 98 teachers; 2,276 students; Vice-Chancellor Prof. KOTA HARINARAYANA; Registrar Dr G. VENKATESHWER RAO.

Central Institute of Fisheries Education: Seven Bungalows, University Rd, Anderi, Mumbai 400061, Maharashtra; tel. (22) 26361446; fax (22) 26361573; e-mail root@cife.bom.nic.in; internet www.cife.bom.nic.in; f. 1961; Deemed University status 1989; library: 27,326 vols; Dir Dr S. C. MUKHERJEE; Registrar SURESH KUMAR.

Central Institute of Higher Tibetan Studies: Sarnath, Varanasi 221007, Uttar Pradesh; tel. (542) 2585148; fax (542) 2585150; e-mail cihts@hotmail.com; internet www.cihts.ac.in; f. 1977; Deemed University status 1988; Dir NGAWANG SAMTEN; Registrar R. D. AGARWAL.

Dayalbagh Educational Institute: Dayalbagh, Agra 282005, Uttar Pradesh; tel. (562) 2121545; fax (562) 2121226; e-mail dei@nde.vsnl.net.in; f. 1981; faculties of Arts, Commerce, Education, Engineering, Science and Social Sciences; library: 101,213 books; 180 teachers; 2,493 students; Dir Prof. SANT SARAN BHOJWANI; Registrar Prof. N. SATYANARAYANA MURTHY; publ. *Journal of Science and Engineering Research* (annually).

Deccan College Postgraduate and Research Institute: Yeravada, Pune 411006, Maharashtra; tel. (20) 26693794; fax (20) 26692104; e-mail deccan.college@gems.vsnl.net.in; internet www.deccancollegepune.org; f. 1821; Deemed University status 1990; postgraduate courses in ancient history, archaeology, linguistics and Sanskrit; library: 128,764 books, 31,647 vols of bound periodicals; 127 students; Dir Dr K. PADDAYYA.

Dharmsinh Desai Institute of Technology: POB 35, College Rd, Nadiad 387001, Gujarat; tel. (268) 2520502; fax (268) 2520501; e-mail vc@ddit.ac.in; internet www.ddit.ac.in; f. 1968; Deemed University status 2000; undergraduate and postgraduate courses in engineering and computer applications; library: 26,400 vols; Pres. Dr N. D. DESAI; Vice-Chancellor Dr H. M. DESAI.

Dr B. R. Ambedkar National Institute of Technology: Jalandhar 144004, Punjab; tel. (181) 2690301; fax (181) 2690320; e-mail admin@nitj.ac.in; internet www.nitj.ac.in; f. 1987; Deemed University status 2002; departments of applied chemistry, applied mathematics, applied physics, chemical and biological engineering, civil engineering, computer science, electronics and communication engineering, humanities, industrial engineering, instrumentation and control engineering, leather technology engineering, management, mechanical engineering and textile technology engineering; Dir Prof. PRAMOD S. MEHTA.

Dr D. Y. Patil Vidyapeeth: Pimpri, Pune 411018, Maharashtra.

Dr M. G. R. Educational and Research Institute: E. V. R. Periyar Salai (NH4 Highway), Maduravoyal, Chennai 600095, Tamil Nadu; tel. (44) 23782176; fax (44) 23783165; internet www.drmgrec.ac.in; f. 1988; Deemed University status 2003; faculties of engineering and technology, humanities and sciences, medicine and dental sciences; library: 50,000 vols, 302 periodicals; Vice-Chancellor Prof. R. M. VASAGAM; Registrar J. P. RAJAPANDIAN.

Forest Research Institute: Kaulagarh Rd, Dehradun 248195, Uttaranchal; tel. (135) 2751826; fax (135) 2756865; e-mail arorasd@icfre.org; f. 1906; Deemed University status 1991; MSc degree courses in Wood Science and Technology, Forestry, Environment Management; also offers postgraduate diploma courses and doctorate degree courses; library: 159,286 vols; 82 students; Dir Dr P. P. BHOJVAID; Registrar S. D. ARORA.

Gandhigram Rural Institute: Dindigul District, Gandhigram 624302, Tamil Nadu; tel. (451) 2452371; fax (451) 2453071; e-mail gricc@vsnl.com; internet www.ruraluniv.org; f. 1956, Deemed University status 1976; Faculties of Agriculture and Animal Husbandry, English and Foreign Languages, Rural Development, Rural Health and Sanitation, Rural Oriented Sciences, Rural Social Sciences; library: 93,422 vols, 320 periodicals; 118 teachers; 2,024 students; Vice-Chancellor Dr G. PANKAJAM; Registrar Dr P. KANNIAPPAN; publs *GRI News* (monthly), *Annual Report*, *Journal of Extension and Research* (2 a year).

Gokhale Institute of Politics and Economics: 846 Shivajinagar, Pune 411004, Maharashtra; tel. (20) 25650287; fax (20) 25652579; e-mail gokhaleinstitute@gipe.ernet.ingipe; internet www.gipe.ernet.in; f. 1930; Deemed University status 1993; postgraduate courses in politics and economics; library: 261,537 vols, 440 periodicals; Dir Prof. V. S. CHITRE; Registrar Dr N. BENJAMIN; publ. *Artha Vijanana* (in English, quarterly).

Gujarat Vidyapith: Ashram Rd, Ahmedabad 380014, Gujarat; tel. (79) 27541148; fax (79) 27542547; e-mail gvpahd@vsnl.com; internet www.gujaratvidyapith.org; f. 1920, university status 1963; library: 515,854 vols; 102 teachers; 1,410 students; Chancellor RAVINDRABHAI VARMA; Vice-Chancellor Dr ARUNKUMAR DAVE; Registrar Dr RAJENDRA KHIMANI (acting); Librarian NAVALSINH VAGHELA; publ. *Vidyapith* (3 a year).

Gurukul Kangri Vishwavidyalaya: PO Gurukul Kangri, Hardwar 249404, Uttar Pradesh; tel. (1334) 246811; fax (1334) 246366; e-mail swantantrak56@yahoo.com; f. 1900; Deemed University status 1962; library: 133,667 vols; 103 teachers; 1,558 students; Vice-Chancellor Prof. SWATANTRA KUMAR; Registrar Prof. MAHAVIR AGARWAL; Librarian Dr J. P. VIDYALANKAR; publs *Gurukula Patrika* (monthly), *Prahlad* (4 a year), *Arya Bhatt* (4 a year), *Vedic Path* (4 a year).

Indian Agricultural Research Institute: Pusa Campus, New Delhi 110012; tel. (11) 25847438; fax (11) 25846420; e-mail pakhale@iari.res.in; internet www.iari.res.in; f. 1905; Deemed University status 1958; postgraduate courses in all major branches of agriculture; Schools of Basic Sciences, Crop Improvements, Crop Protection, Resource Management and Social Sciences; library: 600,000 vols; 360 teachers; 600 students; Dir Prof. S. NAGARAJAN; Registrar P. C. JACOB; Dean Dr R. C. GAUTAUM; Librarian N. S. PAKHALE; publs *Current Events* (monthly, online), *IARI News* (quarterly), *Annual Report*.

Indian Institute of Foreign Trade: Bhawan, B-21, Qutab Institutional Area, New Delhi 110016; tel. (11) 26965124; fax (11) 26853956; e-mail iift@iift.ac.in; internet www.iift.edu; f. 1963; attached research centres: Centre for International Trade in Technology, Centre for World Trade Organization Studies; library: 84,000 vols and 800 periodicals; Dir PRABIR SENGUPTA; publs *Focus WTO*, *Foreign Trade Review*, *Technology Exports*, *Compendium*.

Indian Institute of Information Technology, Allahabad: Nehru Science Centre, Kamla Nehru Rd, Allahabad 211011, Uttar Pradesh; tel. (532) 2461374; fax (532) 2608469; e-mail contact@iiita.ac.in; internet www.iiita.ac.in; f. 1999; Deemed University status 2000; undergraduate and postgraduate courses in information technology; Dir Dr M. D. TIWARI.

Indian Institute of Science: Bangalore, Karnataka 560012; tel. (80) 22932001; fax (80) 23600085; e-mail regr@admin.iisc.ernet.in; internet www.iisc.ernet.in; f. 1909; library: 468,000 vols; 434 teachers; 1,794 students; Dir Prof. GOVERDHAN MEHTA; Registrar Dr UDAY BALAKRISHNAN; Librarian Dr S. VENKADESAN; publ. *Journal*

DEANS

Faculty of Engineering: Prof. Y. V. VENKATESH
Faculty of Science: Prof. RENUKA RAVINDRAN

CHAIRMEN OF DIVISIONS

Biological Sciences: Prof. P. BALARAM
Chemical Sciences: Prof. S. CHANDRASEKARAN
Electrical Sciences: Prof. H. P. KHINCHA
Information Sciences: Prof. N. BALAKRISHNAN
Mechanical Sciences: Prof. M. L. MUNJAL
Physical and Mathematical Sciences: Prof. A. K. SOOD

CHAIRMEN OF DEPARTMENTS, CENTRES AND UNITS

Biological Sciences (tel. (80) 22932809; fax (80) 223600416; e-mail dcbio@admin.iisc.ernet.in):

- Biochemistry: Prof. K. MUNIYAPPA
- Central Animal Facility: Prof. R. NAYAK
- Centre for Ecological Sciences: Prof. R. GADAGKAR
- Microbiology and Cell Biology: Prof. R. NAYAK
- Molecular Biophysics Unit: Prof. A. SUROLIA
- Molecular Reproduction, Development and Genetics: Prof. V. NANJUNDIAH

Chemical Sciences (tel. (80) 22932810; fax (80) 223600416; e-mail dcche@admin.iisc.ernet.in):

- Inorganic and Physical Chemistry: Prof. A. R. CHAKRAVARTY
- Materials Research Centre: Prof. K. CHATTOPADHYAY
- Organic Chemistry: Prof. A. SRIKRISHNA
- Solid State and Structural Chemistry: Prof. T. N. GURU ROW
- Sophisticated Instruments Facility: Prof. K. V. RAMANATHAN

Electrical Sciences (tel. (80) 22932808; fax (80) 223600416; e-mail dcele@admin.iisc.ernet.in):

- Centre for Electronic Design Technology: Prof. H. S. JAMADAGNI
- Computer Science and Automation: Prof. Y. N. SRIKANT
- Electrical Communication Engineering: Prof. ANURAG KUMAR
- Electrical Engineering: Prof. V. RAMANARAYANAN
- High Voltage Engineering: Prof. G. R. NAGABHUSHANA

Information Sciences (tel. (80) 22932808; fax (80) 223600416):

- Management Studies: Prof. N. J. RAO
- National Centre for Science Information: Prof. A. G. MENON
- Supercomputer Education and Research Centre: Prof. S. M. RAO
- Bioinformatics Centre: Prof. S. RAMAKUMAR
- Digital Information Services Centre: Prof. G. RANGARAJAN

Mechanical Sciences (tel. (80) 22932953; fax (80) 223600416; e-mail demec@admin.iisc.ernet.in):

- Aerospace Engineering: Prof. B. N. RAGHUNANDAN
- Centre for Atmospheric and Oceanic Sciences: Prof. J. SRINIVASAN
- Centre for Product Design and Manufacturing: Dr B. GURUMOORTHY

Centre for Sustainable Technologies: Prof. N. H. RAVINDRANATH
Chemical Engineering: Prof. J. M. MODAK
Civil Engineering: Prof. B. K. RAGHU PRASAD
Mechanical Engineering: Prof. S. K. BISWAS
Metallurgy: Prof. K. A. NATARAJAN
IISc-ISRO Space Technology Cell: Prof. M. SEETHARAMA BHAT
Joint Advanced Technology Programme: Prof. P. J. PAUL

Physical and Mathematical Sciences (tel. (80) 22932807; fax (80) 223600416; e-mail dcphy@admin.iisc.ernet.in):

Centre for Cryogenic Technology: Dr SUBHASH JACOB
Centre for Condensed Matter Theory: Prof. CHANDAN DASGUPTA
Instrumentation: Prof. R. M. VASU
Astronomy and Astrophysics: A. R. CHOUDHURI (Co-ordinator)
Mathematics: Prof. G. RANGARAJAN
Physics: Prof. H. L. BHAT

Departments outside Divisions:

Centre for Continuing Education: Prof. T. S. MRITHYUNJAYA
Centre for Scientific and Industrial Consultancy: Dr P. P. IYER
Hindi Cell: Prof. R. GADAGKAR
Centre for Sponsored Schemes and Projects: Prof. C. E. VENIMADHAVAN

Indian School of Mines: Dhanbad 826004, Jharkhand; tel. (326) 2205403; fax (326) 2203042; e-mail director@perl.ism.ac.in; internet www.ism.ac.in; f. 1926; residential; language of instruction: English; academic year July to June; bachelor degree courses, postgraduate courses in engineering and management, postgraduate research; library: 74,550 books, 550 journals, 3,000 online journals; 105 teachers; 1,035 students; Dir Prof. B. B. BHATTACHARYA; Registrar Col S. M. MEHTA; Librarian Dr PARTHA DE (acting)

HEADS OF DEPARTMENTS

Applied Geology: Prof. T. MAJUMDAR
Applied Geophysics: Prof. B. B. BHATTACHARYA
Applied Chemistry: Dr D. D. PATHAK
Applied Mathematics: Prof. B. K. RAJHANS
Applied Physics: Prof. P. S. GUPTA
Computer Science and Engineering: Prof. A. CHATTOPADHYAY
Electronics and Instrumentation: B. S. R. SASTRY
Engineering and Mining Machinery: Prof. M. K. SHARMA
Fuel and Mineral Engineering: Prof. R. VENUGOPAL
Humanities and Social Sciences: Prof. R. K. SINGH
Management Studies: Prof. K. MUKHERJEE
Mining Engineering: Prof. S. B. SRIVASTAVA
Petroleum Engineering: Prof. S. LAIK
Continuing Education: Prof. P. K. BANIK

HEADS OF CENTRES

Centre of Longwall Mine Mechanization: Prof. S. N. MUKHERJEE
Centre of Mine Environment: Prof. G. SINGH
Computer Centre: S. MITRA

Indian Veterinary Research Institute: Izatnagar 243122, Uttar Pradesh; tel. (581) 2301375; fax (581) 2302179; e-mail dirivri@ivri.up.nic.in; internet www.ivri.nic.in; f. 1889; Deemed University status 1983; campuses at Bangalore, Bhopal, Kolkata, Mukteswar, Palampur and Srinagar; research divisions of Animal Biochemistry, Animal Biotechnology, Animal Genetics and Breeding, Animal Nutrition, Animal Physiology, Avian Diseases, Biostatistics, Livestock Products Technology, Livestock Production and Management, Poultry Science, Veterinary Bacteriology, Veterinary Epidemiology, Veterinary Extension Education, Veterinary Gynaecology and Obstetrics, Veterinary Immunology, Veterinary Medicine, Veterinary Parasitology, Veterinary Pathology, Veterinary Pharmacology, Veterinary Public Health, Veterinary Surgery and Veterinary Virology; library: library of 207,000 vols, 300 periodicals; Dir Dr M. P. YADAV; publs *Annual Report*, *Annual Scientific Report*.

Indira Gandhi Institute of Development Research: Gen. A.K.Vaidya Marg, Goregaon (E), Mumbai 400065, Maharashtra; tel. (22) 28400919; fax (22) 28402752; e-mail rrk@igidr.ac.in; internet www.igidr.ac.in; f. 1987; Deemed University status 1995; postgraduate courses in economics and development studies; library: library of 50,000 vols, 500 periodicals; 36 teachers; Dir Dr ROKKAM RADHAKRISHNA; Registrar T. V. SUBRAMANIAN; Librarian G. K. MANJUNATH.

Institute of Advanced Studies in Education: Gandhi Vidya Mandir, Sardarshahr 331401, Rajasthan; tel. (1564) 220025; fax (1564) 220057; e-mail gandhivmandir@yahoo.com; internet www.gandhividyamandir.org; f. 1950; Deemed University status 2002; faculties of Education, Information Technology, Management and Medicine; library: library of 95,000 vols; Dir MILAP DUGAR; Registrar R. S. SUROLIA.

Institute of Armament Technology: Girinagar, Pune 411025, Maharashtra; fax (20) 24389411; f. 1952; Deemed University status 1999; Dir Prof. G. S. MANI.

International Institute for Population Sciences: Govandi Station Rd, Deonar, Mumbai 400088, Maharashtra; tel. (22) 25563254; fax (22) 25563257; e-mail diriips@vsnl.com; internet www.iipsindia.org; f. 1956; Deemed University status 1985; 30 teachers; 120 students; library: 70,000 books, 11,500 bound periodicals; Dir Prof. T. K. ROY; publ. *Newsletter*

HEADS OF DEPARTMENTS

Development Studies: Dr HAZISH SRIVASTAVA
Fertility Studies: Dr F. RAM
Mathematical Demography and Statistics: Dr G. RAMA RAO
Migration and Urban Studies: Dr K. GUPTA
Population Policies and Development Programme: Dr BALRAM PASWAN
Public Health and Mortality Studies: Dr S. LAHIRI

International Institute of Information Technology: Gachibowli, Hyderabad 500019, Andhra Pradesh; tel. (40) 23001967; fax (40) 23001413; e-mail query@iiit.net; internet www.iiit.net; f. 1998; undergraduate and postgraduate courses in various disciplines of information technology; research centres in data engineering, visual information technology, visual embedded systems technology, communications, technology consultancy, open software, bioinformatics, building science, earthquake engineering, education; library: library of 6,000 vols; Dir Prof. RAJEEV SANGAL; Librarian Dr P. KRISHNA REDDY.

Jain Vishva Bharati Institute: Dist. Nagaur, Ladnun 341306, Rajasthan; tel. (1581) 222110; fax (1581) 222116; e-mail registrar@rjvbi.org; internet www.jvbi.org; f. 1970; Deemed University status 1991; Schools of Jainology and Oriental Studies, Non-Violence and Social Sciences; library: library of 46,260 books, 116 periodicals, 6,000 MSS; Vice-Chancellor SUDHAMAHI REGHUNATHAN; Registrar Dr JAGAT RAM BHATTACHARYYA; Librarian H. C. R. SIDDAPPA.

Jamia Hamdard: Hamdard Nagar, New Delhi 110062; tel. (11) 26059677; fax (11) 26059663; e-mail inquiry@jamiahamdard.edu; internet www.jamiahamdard.edu; f. 1963; Deemed University status 1989; faculties of Allied Health Sciences, Islamic Studies and Social Science, Management Studies and Information Technology, Medicine, Nursing, Pharmacy and Science; library: 141,021 books, 124 periodicals, 5,000 MSS; 2,100 students; Vice-Chancellor SIRAJ HUSSAIN; Registrar Dr S. H. HASAN; Librarian Dr M. A. PRODHANI.

Janardan Rai Nagar Rajasthan Vidyapeeth: Pratap Nagar, Udaipur 313001, Rajasthan; tel. (294) 2492441; fax (294) 2492440; e-mail icervu@sancharnet.com; internet www.rajasthanvidyapeeth.com; f. 1937; Deemed University status 1987; faculties of Arts, Commerce, Education, Management, Medicine and Social Work; 12 constituent institutions; library: 244,000 books, 140 periodicals; 5,300 students; Vice-Chancellor Prof. L. BHATT; Registrar Dr M. TRIVEDI; Librarian K. L. VAISHNAV.

Jawaharlal Nehru Centre for Advanced Scientific Research: Jakkur, Bangalore 560064, Karnataka; tel. (80) 22082769; fax (80) 22082766; internet www.jncasr.ac.in; f. 1989; Deemed University status 2002; library: 10,000 vols, 71 periodicals; 31 teachers; Pres. M. R. S. RAO; publs *Chemistry and Physics of Materials*, *Engineering Mechanics*, *Evolutionary and Organismal Biology*, *Geodynamics*, *Molecular Biology and Genetics*, *Theoretical Science*.

Kalinga Institute of Industrial Technology: Bhubaneshwar 751024, Orissa; tel. (674) 2741998; e-mail info@kiit.org; internet www.kiit.org; f. Deemed University status 2004; constituent institutions: IBAT School of Management, KITS School of Technology, Kalinga Polytechnic; Vice-Chancellor Prof. MRITTUNJAY BHATTACHARYYA; publ. *KIIT Review* (quarterly).

Karunya Institute of Technology and Sciences: Karunya Nagar, Coimbatore 641114, Tamil Nadu; e-mail kaint@vsnl.com; internet www.karunya.edu; tel. (42) 22615618; fax (42) 22615615; f. 1986; Deemed University status 1999; 275 teachers; 3,300 students; faculties of civil engineering, computer application, computer science and engineering, electrical and electronics engineering, electronic and instrumentation engineering, electronics and communication engineering, information technology, management studies, mechanical engineering, production engineering, science and humanities and software engineering; Chancellor Dr D. G. S. DHINAKARAN.

Lakshmibai National Institute of Physical Education: Mela Rd, Shakti Nagar, Gwalior 474002, Madhya Pradesh; tel. (751) 2500902; fax (751) 2340553; e-mail info@lnipe.edu; internet www.lnipe.edu; f. 1957; Deemed University status 1995; library: 31,000 vols; Dir Prof. K. K. VERMA; Registrar Dr SANJAY P. TIWARI.

Malaviya National Institute of Technology: Jaipur 302017, Rajasthan; tel. (141) 2702955; fax (141) 2702107; e-mail director@mnit.ac.in; internet www.mnit.ac.in; f. 1963; Deemed University status 2002; departments of Architecture, Chemical Engineering, Chemistry, Civil Engineering, Computer Engineering, Electrical Engineering, Electronics and Communication Engineering, Humanities, Mathematics, Mechanical Engineering, Metallurgical Engineering, Physics and Structural Engineering; library: library of 135,000 vols; 150 teachers; 1,700 students; Dir ASHOK K. JAIN; Registrar S. K. POKHARNA; Librarian DEEP SINGH.

Manipal Academy of Higher Education: University Building, Madhav Nagar, Manipal 576119, Karnataka; tel. (8252) 271300; fax (8252) 270062; e-mail office.mahe@manipal.edu; internet www.manipal.edu; f. 1953; Deemed University status 1993; privately-controlled network of 50 institutions run by the Manipal Group, incl. Kasturba Medical College, Melaka Manipal Medical College, Manipal College of Dental Sciences, Manipal College Of Nursing, Manipal College of Pharmaceutical Sciences, Manipal Institute of Technology, International Center for Applied Sciences, Manipal Center of Information Sciences, Welcomgroup Graduate School of Hotel Administration, TA Pai Management Institute, Manipal Institute of Management, Manipal Institute of Communication, Kasturba Medical College, Manipal College of Dental Sciences; library: library of 50,000 vols, 600 periodicals; Chancellor Dr RAMDAS M. PAI; Vice-Chancellor Dr H. S. BALLAL; Registrar Dr S. GURUMADHVA RAO.

Maulana Azad National Institute of Technology: Bhopal 462007, Madhya Pradesh; tel. (751) 2670900; fax (751) 2670562; internet www.manit.nic.in; f. 1960; Deemed University status 2002; undergraduate and postgraduate courses in architecture, civil engineering, computer science, electrical, electronics and communication engineering, information technology and mechanical engineering; library: 96,000 vols; Dir Prof. P. K. CHANDE; Registrar AJIT NARAYAN; Librarian V. K. MATHUR.

Meenakshi Academy of Higher Education and Research: Virugambakkam, Tamil Nadu.

Mody Institute of Technology and Science: Dist. Sikar, Lakshmangarh 332311, Rajasthan; tel. (1573) 225001; fax (1573) 225041; e-mail contact@mitsuniversity.info; internet www.mitsuniversity.info; f. 1998; Deemed University status 2004; faculties of Engineering and Technology, and Management Studies; library: library of 23,362 vols; 74 teachers; 1,250 students; Pro-Vice-Chancellor Dr MAHIPAL JAIN.

Narsee Monjee Institute of Management Studies: JVPD Scheme, Vile Parle (W), Mumbai 400056, Maharashtra; tel. (22) 26130858; fax (22) 26114512; e-mail enquiry@nmims.edu; internet www.nmims.edu; f. 1981; Deemed University status 2003; library: 31,000 books, 210 periodicals; Vice-Chancellor Dr N. M. KONDAP; Registrar Dr SUNIL KARVE; publ. *NMIMS Management Review*.

National Brain Research Centre: Nr NSG Campus, Manesar 122050, Haryana; tel. (124) 2338922; fax (124) 2338910; e-mail info@nbrc.ac.in; internet www.nbrc.ac.in; f. 2003; main research areas: molecular and cellular neuroscience, systems neuroscience, theoretical neuroscience; Dir Prof. VIJAYALAKSHMI RAVINDRANATH.

National Dairy Research Institute: Karnal, Haryana 132001; tel. (184) 2252800; fax (184) 2250042; e-mail bnm@ndri.hry.nic.in; internet karnal.nic.in/res_ndri.asp; f. 1923; training, research and extension; regional stations at Bangalore and Kalyani; library: 75,000 vols and 22,000 periodicals; Dir Dr NAGENDRA SHARMA; Registrar Cptn MEHER SINGH; publs *Annual Report*, *Dairy Samachar* (quarterly).

National Institute of Mental Health and Neurosciences: POB 2900, Hosur Rd, Bangalore 560029, Karnataka; tel. (80) 26564140; fax (80) 26562121; e-mail registrar@nimhans.kar.nic.in; internet www.nimhans.kar.nic.in; f. 1974; Deemed University status 1994; library: library of 75,000 vols, 315 periodicals; Dir Prof. D. NAGARAJA; Registrar M. E. SHIVALINGA MURTHY; Librarian-in-charge Dr H. S. SIDDAMALLAIAH.

National Institute of Technology, Calicut: Calicut 673601, Kerala; tel. (495) 2286101; fax (495) 2287250; e-mail pvr@nitc.ac.in; internet www.nitc.ac.in; f. 1961; Deemed University status 2002; library: 100,000 vols; Dir Dr S. S. GOKHALE; Registrar T. G. RADHAKRISHNA PAI.

National Institute of Technology, Durgapur: Mahatma Gandhi Ave, Durgapur 713209, West Bengal; tel. (343) 2546397; fax (343) 2547375; e-mail director@nitdgp.ac.in; internet www.nitdgp.ac.in; f. 1960; Deemed University status 2002; library: 22,000 vols, 150 periodicals; 162 teachers; 1,800 students; Dir Dr A. C. GANGULI.

National Institute of Technology, Hamirpur: Hamirpur 177005, Himachal Pradesh; internet recham.ernet.in; f. 1986; Deemed University status 2002; 68 teachers; 900 students; Dir Dr S. K. BHOWMIK.

National Institute of Technology, Jamshedpur: Jamshedpur 831014, Jharkhand.

National Institute of Technology, Karnataka: Surathkal, Dakshina Kannada, Srinivasnagar 575025, Karnataka; tel. (824) 2475984; fax (824) 2476090; e-mail registrar@nitk.ac.in; internet www.nitk.ac.in; f. 1960; Deemed University status 2002; library: 100,000 vols; 195 teachers; Dir Prof. S. SRINIVASA MURTHY; Registrar Dr A. H. SEQUEIRA; Librarian M. K. MOHANDAS.

National Institute of Technology, Kurukshetra: Kurukshetra 136119, Haryana; tel. (1744) 238491; fax (1744) 238050; e-mail nit_kkr@rediffmail.com; internet www.nitkkr.net; f. 1963; Deemed University status 2002; departments of Chemistry, Civil Engineering, Computer Engineering, Electrical Engineering, Electronics and Communication Engineering, Humanities, Mathematics, Mechanical Engineering and Physics; library: library of 50,000 vols; Dir Dr S. N. MAHENDRA; Registrar R. P. S. LOHCHAB; Librarian KRISHAN GOPAL.

National Institute of Technology, Rourkela: Rourkela 769008, Orissa; tel. (661) 2477001; fax (661) 2471169; e-mail info@nitrkl.ac.in; internet www.nitrkl.ac.in; f. 1955; Deemed University status 2002; departments of Applied Mathematics, Ceramic Engineering, Chemical Engineering, Chemistry, Civil Engineering, Computer Science and Engineering, Electrical Engineering, Electronics and Instrumentation Engineering, Humanities, Mechanical Engineering, Metallurgical and Materials Engineering, Mining Engineering and Physics; library: library of 150,000 vols; Dir Prof. SUNIL K. SARANGI; Registrar J. P. PADHY; Librarian-in-charge Prof. K. N. SINGH.

National Institute of Technology, Silchar: Silchar 788010, Assam; tel. (3842) 233179; fax (3842) 233797; e-mail contactus@nits.ac.in; internet www.nits.ac.in; f. 1967; library: library of 45,000 books and 150 periodicals; 880 students; Dir Prof. GAUTAM BARUA; Registrar Dr FAZAL A. TALUKDAR.

National Institute of Technology, Srinagar: Srinagar 190006, Jammu and Kashmir.

National Institute of Technology, Tiruchirapalli: Tanjore Rd, Tiruchirappalli 620015, Tamil Nadu; tel. (431) 2501801; fax (431) 2500133; e-mail director@nitt.edu; internet www.nitt.edu; f. 1964; Deemed University status 2003; departments of Architecture, Chemical Engineering, Chemistry, Civil Engineering, Computer Applications, Computer Science and Engineering, Electrical and Electronics Engineering, Electronics and Communication Engineering, English, Humanities, Instrumentation and Control Engineering, Management Studies, Mathematics, Mechanical Engineering, Metallurgical Engineering, Physics and Production Engineering; Center for Energy and Environmental Science and Technology; library: 100,000 books, 15,943 bound periodicals, 200 current periodicals, 4,500 online journals; Dir Dr P. SUBRAMANIAN.

National Institute of Technology, Warangal: Warangal 506004, Andhra Pradesh; tel. (870) 2459191; fax (870) 2459547; e-mail director@nitw.ernet.in; internet www.recw.ernet.in; f. 1959; 200 teachers; 3,000 students; Dir Prof. D. K. TRIPARTHY; Registrar Prof. G. R. K. ACHARYA.

National Law School of India University: Nagarbhavi, PB 7201, Bangalore 560072, Karnataka; tel. (80) 23211303; fax (80) 23217858; e-mail registrar@nls.ac.in; internet www.nls.ac.in; f. 1987; library: 18,000 books, 15,000 bound periodicals; 30 teachers; 400 students; Dir Dr A. JAYAGOVIND; Registrar Prof. V. S. MALLAR; publs *National Law School Journal* (annually), *March of the Law* (annually), *Law and Medicine* (annually), *Gender Justice Reporter* (annually).

National Museum Institute of History of Art, Conservation and Museology: Janpath, New Delhi 110011; tel. (11) 23011901; fax (11) 23011901; e-mail nminstitute1@vsnl.net; internet www.nationalmuseumindia.org/nmi; f. 1983; Deemed University status 1989; postgraduate courses in history of art, conservation and restoration of works of arts and museology; library: 2,500 books, 60,000 slides; Vice-Chancellor Dr R. D. CHOUDHARY; Registrar Dr B. VENUGOPAL.

Padmashree Dr D. Y. Patil Vidyapeeth: Vidyanagar Sector 7, Nerul, Navi Mumbai 400706, Maharashtra; tel. (22) 27715000; fax (22) 27714598; e-mail info@dypatil.edu; internet www.dypatil.ac.in; f. 2002; constituent colleges: Padmashree Dr D. Y. Patil Medical College and Padmashree Dr D. Y. Patil Dental College and Hospital; Vice-Chancellor D. K. GHOSH; Registrar Prof. B. G. BHANDARKAR.

Punjab Engineering College: Sector 12, Chandigarh; e-mail admissions@pec.ac.in; internet www.pec.ac.in; f. 1947; library: library of 106,000 vols; Dir Dr BALJEET S. KAPOOR.

Rashtriya Sanskrit Sansthana: Janakpuri, New Delhi 110016; internet www.sanskrit.nic.in; f. 1970; campuses in Allahabad, Bhopal, Jaipur, Jammu, Lucknow, Mumbai, Puri, Sringeri and Trichur; library: total library colln of 213,581 vols, 51133 MSS; Vice-Chancellor Prof. V. KUTUMBA SASTRY; publ. *Sanskrit Vimarsh* (annually).

Rashtriya Sanskrit Vidyapeetha: Tirupati 517507, Andhra Pradesh; tel. (8574) 227937; fax (8574) 227937; e-mail rsvp@nettlix.com; internet www.sansknet.org; f. 1961; library: 60,000 vols and 5,000 MSS; Vice-Chancellor Prof. D. PRAHLADA CHAR; Registrar CH. SAMBAIAH.

S. R. M. Institute of Science and Technology: Chennai 600033, Tamil Nadu; tel. (4114) 252270; fax (4114) 253903; e-mail srmec@giasmd01.vsnl.net.in; Vice-Chancellor P. SATHYANARAYANAN.

Sardar Vallabhbhai National Institute of Technology: Ichhchha Nath, Surat 395007, Gujarat; tel. (261) 2223371; fax (261) 2228394; e-mail director@svnit.ac.in; internet www.svnit.ac.in; f. 1961; library: 100,000 vols; Dir Dr A. K. DAVE.

Sathyabama Institute of Science and Technology: Jeppiaar Nagar, Old Mamallapuram Rd, IT High Way, Chennai 600119,

Tamil Nadu; tel. (44) 24501644; fax (44) 24502344; e-mail directors@sathyabamauniv.ac.in; internet www.sathyabamauniv.ac.in; f. 1987; Deemed University status 2001; departments of Architecture, Bioinformatics, Biomedical Engineering, Biotechnology, Chemical Engineering, Civil Engineering, Computer Application, Computer Science and Engineering, Electrical and Electronics Engineering, Electronics and Communication Engineering, Electronics and Control Engineering, Electronics and Instrumentation Engineering, Electronics and Telecommunication Engineering, Information Technology, Management Sciences, Mechanical Engineering, Production Engineering, Science and Visual Communication; library: 50,000 books, 290 periodicals; Vice-Chancellor Prof. V. S. R. K. Mouly; Registrar Prof. R. Rangarajan.

School of Planning and Architecture: 4 Block B, Indraprastha Estate, New Delhi 110002; tel. (11) 23702382; fax (11) 23702383; e-mail regspa@indiatimes.com; internet www.indiawatch.org/SPA; f. 1955; library: 70,875 vols; 62 teachers; 694 students; Dir-in-Charge Prof. J. H. Ansari; Dean of Studies Prof. T. M. Vinod Kumar; Registrar D. R. Bains

HEADS OF DEPARTMENTS

Architectural Conservation: Prof. Nalini M. Thakur
Architecture: Prof. Arvind Krishan
Building Engineering and Management: Dr V. Thiruvengadam
Environmental Planning: Prof. Shovam K. Saha
Housing: Prof. Subir Shah
Industrial Design: Prof. I. M. Chisti
Landscape Architecture: Prof. Dr Surendra Suneja
Physical Planning: Prof. S. D. Joardar
Regional Planning: Prof. H. B. Singh
Transport Planning: A. K. Sharma
Urban Design: Prof. K. T. Ravindran
Urban Planning: Prof. Kavas Kapadia.

Attached centres:

Centre for Advanced Studies in Architecture: 4 Block B, Indraprastha Estate, New Delhi 110002; tel. (11) 23702391; fax (11) 23702381; Dir-in-Charge J. H. Ansari; 19 teachers; 354 students.

Centres for Analysis and Systems Studies: 4 Block B, Indraprastha Estate, New Delhi 110002; tel. (11) 23702378; fax (11) 23702383; e-mail regspa@indiatimes.com; internet www.indiawatch.org/SPA; Dir Prof. K. Chander.

Centre for Conservation Studies: 4 Block B, Indraprastha Estate, New Delhi 110002; tel. (11) 23702387; fax (11) 23702383; Dir Prof. Nalini Thaken; 3 teachers; 18 students.

Centre for Environmental Studies: 4 Block B, Indraprastha Estate, New Delhi 110002; tel. (11) 23702389; fax (11) 23702383; Dir Prof. Shovan K. Saha; 3 teachers; 24 students.

Centre for Geographic Information Systems: Dir Dr S. Gupta.

Centre for Housing Studies: 4 Block B, Indraprastha Estate, New Delhi 110002; tel. (11) 23702388; fax (11) 23702383; Dir Prof. Subir Saha; 3 teachers; 30 students.

Centre for Remote Sensing: Dir Prof. Dr Mahavir.

Centre for Rural Development: 4 Block B, Indraprastha Estate, New Delhi 110002; tel. (11) 23702389; fax (11) 23702383; Dir Prof. H. B. Singh; 2 teachers; 21 students.

Centre for Transport Studies: 4 Block B, Indraprastha Estate, New Delhi 110002; tel. (11) 2370239; fax (11) 23702383; Dir Prof. A. K. Sharma; 5 teachers; 31 students.

Centre for Urban Studies: 4 Block B, Indraprastha Estate, New Delhi 110002; tel. (11) 23702378; fax (11) 23702383; Dir Prof. Kavas Kapadia; 6 teachers; 43 students.

Shanmugha Arts, Science, Technology and Research Academy: Shanmugha Campus, Tirumalaisamaduram, Thanjavur 613402, Tamil Nadu; tel. (4362) 264101; fax (4362) 264120; e-mail registrar@sastra.edu; internet www.sastra.edu; f. 1984; Deemed University status 2001; schools of Chemical Engineering and Biotechnology, Civil Engineering, Computing, Electrical and Electronics Engineering, Humanities and Sciences, Management and Mechanical Engineering; Vice-Chancellor Prof. R. Sethuraman; Registrar Prof. R. Kandaswamy; publ. *Newsletter* (annually).

Shri Lal Bahadur Shastri Rashtriya Sanskrit Vidyapeetha: New Mehrauli Rd, Katwaria Sarai, New Delhi 110016; tel. (11) 26564003; fax (11) 26520255; e-mail vidyapeetha@vsnl.net; f. 1962; Deemed University status 1987; library: 65,000 vols; Vice-Chancellor Prof. Vachaspati Upadhyaya; Registrar B. K. Mohapatra.

Sri Chandrasekharenda Saraswathi Viswa Mahavidyalaya: Sri Jayendra Saraswathi St, Enathur 631561, Tamil Nadu; tel. (4112) 264301; fax (4112) 264285; e-mail kanchiuniv@yahoo.co.in; internet www.kanchiuniv.ac.in; f. 1993; library: library of 200,000 vols; Vice-Chancellor N. Jayasankaran.

Sri Ramachandra Medical College and Research Institute: Sri Ramachandra Medical Center, 1 Ramachandra Nagar, Porur, Chennai 600116, Tamil Nadu; tel. (44) 24768403; fax (44) 24767008; e-mail srmc@giasmd01.vsnl.net.in; internet www.srmc.edu; f. 1985; Deemed University status 1994; departments of Anaesthesiology, Cardiac Care, Chest and Tuberculosis, Dermatology, Emergency, Trauma and Critical Care, Endocrinology, Ears, Nose and Throat, General Medicine, General Surgery, Medical Gastroenterology, Nephrology, Neurology, Neurosurgery, Obstetrics and Gynaecology, Ophthalmology, Orthopaedics, Paediatric Medicine, Paediatric Surgery, Paediatric Urology, Plastic and Reconstructive Surgery, Radiology and Imaging Sciences, Psychiatry, Surgical Gastroenterology and Urology; Vice-Chancellor S. Thanikachalam; Registrar Radha Venkatachalam.

Sri Sathya Sai Institute of Higher Learning: Prasanthi Nilayam, Anantapur District, Andhra Pradesh 515134; tel. (8555) 287239; fax (8555) 287390; internet www.srisathyasai.org.in/pages/instts/secschl.htm; f. 1981; library: library of 150,000 vols; 115 teachers; 1,100 students; Vice-Chancellor S. V. Giri; publs *Journal of Applied Mathematics and Stochastic Analysis* (4 a year), *Bulletin of Pure and Applied Sciences* (4 a year), *International Journal of Modern Physics* (4 a year), *Third Concept: An International Journal of Ideas* (6 a year).

Swami Vivekananda Yog Anusandhana Samsthana: Bangalore 560018, Karnatake.

Symbiosis International Education Centre: Senapati Bapat Rd, Pune 411004, Maharashtra; tel. (20) 25673520; e-mail siec@vsnl.net; internet siec.ac.in; f. 1979; Deemed University status 2002; constituent institutes: Symbiosis Society's Law College, Symbiosis Institute of Business Management, Symbiosis Institute of Computer Studies and Research; 217 teachers (43 full-time, 7 part-time, 167 visiting); 6,116 students; Vice-Chancellor Lt-Gen. Dr M. A. Tutakne; Registrar V. S. Pol.

Tata Institute of Fundamental Research: Homi Bhabha Rd, Mumbai 400005, Maharashtra; tel. (22) 22804545; fax (22) 22804610; e-mail webmaster@tifr.res.in; internet www.tifr.res.in; f. 1945; Deemed University status 2003; attached research centres: National Centre for Biological Sciences (Bangalore), National Centre for Radio Astrophysics (Pune), Homi Bhabha Centre for Science Education (Mumbai); attached field stations: TIFR Centre Maths (Bangalore), Balloon Facility (Hyderabad), High Energy Gamma Ray Observatory (Panchmarhi), TIFR Gravitation Laboratory (Gauribidanur), Radio Astronomy Centre (Ooty); Dir Prof. Sabyasachi Bhattacharya.

Tata Institute of Social Sciences: POB 8313, Deonar, Mumbai 400088, Maharashtra; tel. (22) 25563289; fax (22) 25562912; e-mail swaraj@tiss.edu; internet www.tiss.edu; f. 1936; Deemed University status 1964; postgraduate courses and professional training in social work and personnel management and industrial relations; health and hospital administration; research; library: 105,000 vols; 106 students; Dir Prof. S. Parasuraman; Registrar Dr S. K. Bandyopadhyay; Librarian Dr M. Koganuramath; publ. *The Indian Journal of Social Work*.

TERI School of Advanced Studies: Darbari Seth Block, Habitat Place, Lodi Rd, New Delhi 110003; tel. (11) 24682100; fax (11) 24682144; e-mail registrar@teri.res.in; internet www.terischool.ac.in; f. 1998; Deemed University status 1999; Dir Dr Vibha Dhawan; Registrar Rajiv Seth.

Thapar Institute of Engineering and Technology: Patiala 147004, Punjab; tel. (175) 2393021; fax (175) 2364498; e-mail info@mail.tiet.ac.in; internet www.tiet.ac.in; f. 1956; Deemed University status 1985; schools of Chemistry and Biotechnology, Management and Social Sciences, Mathematics and Computer Applications, Physics and Material Science; library: 55,000 vols; 102 teachers; 1,340 students; Dir Dr S. C. Saxena; Registrar Brig. Paramjit Singh.

Tilak Maharashtra Vidyapeeth: Vidyapeeth Bhavan, Gultekdi, Pune 411037; tel. (20) 4265665; fax (20) 4266068; e-mail timavee@pn2.vsnl.net.in; internet www.tilakvidyapeeth.org; f. 1921; faculties of Arts and Fine Arts, Ayurveda and Moral and Social Sciences; library: 77,674 vols; 35 teachers; 5,508 students; Vice-Chancellor Prof. Hira B. Adyanthaya; Registrar R. K. Dhavalikar.

Vinayaka Mission's Research Foundation: NH-47 Sankari Main Rd, Ariyanoor, Salem 636308, Tamil Nadu; tel. (427) 2477316; fax (427) 2477903; e-mail enquiry@vinayakamission.com; internet www.vinayakamission.com; f. 2001; constituent institutions: Aarupadai Veedu Institute of Technology, Annapoorana College of Nursing, College of Pharmacy, College of Physiotherapy, Homoeopathic Medical College, Kirupanananda Variyar Enginnering College, Kirupananda Variyar Medical College, Sankarachariyar Dental College; Chancellor Dr A. Shanmugasundaram; Vice-Chancellor J. S. Sathish Kumar; Registrar Prof. V. R. Rajendran.

Visvesvaraya National Institute of Technology: South Ambazari Rd, Nagpur 440011, Maharashtra; tel. (712) 2226240; fax (712) 2223230; e-mail registrar@vnitnagpur.ac.in; internet www.vnitnagpur.ac.in; f. 1960; Deemed University status 2002; departments of Applied Chemistry,

Applied Mechanics, Applied Physics, Architecture, Civil Engineering, Electrical Engineering, Electronics and Computer Science, Humanities, Mathematics, Mechanical Engineering, Metallurgical Engineering and Mining Engineering; library: 75,000 vols, 166 periodicals; Dir Dr C. S. MOGHE; Registrar B. M. GANVEER.

Colleges

BUSINESS

Administrative Staff College of India: Bella Vista, Raj Bhavan Rd, Hyderabad 500082; tel. (40) 23310952; fax (40) 23312954; e-mail webmaster@asci.org.in; internet www.asci.org.in; f. 1956; conducts post-experience management development programmes for officials in government, executives and managers in industry and non-government organisations; undertakes research and consultancy assignments for nat. and intl organizations; library: 74,000 vols, 500 periodicals, online databases; Principal S. K. RAO; Librarian N. G. SATISH; publ. *ASCI Journal of Management* (2 a year).

Indian Institute of Management, Ahmedabad: Vastrapur, Ahmedabad 380015; tel. (79) 26307241; fax (79) 26306896; e-mail director@iimahd.ernet.in; internet www.iimahd.ernet.in; f. 1962; 2-year postgraduate, 4-year doctoral programme in management; general and functional management programmes for practising managers, and special programmes for government officials, university teachers and sectors such as agriculture, public systems; undertakes project research and consulting in the field of management; 80 faculty members; 400 postgraduate programme students; 50 PhD level students; library: 148,600 vols; Dir JAHAR SAHA; publs *Vikalpa* (4 a year), *Alumnus* (3 a year).

Indian Institute of Management, Bangalore: Bannerghatta Rd, Bangalore 560076; tel. (80) 26582450; fax (80) 26584050; f. 1973; postgraduate programmes; 80 teachers; 425 students; Dir Prof. M. RAMMOHAN; publs *IIMB Management Review* (2 a year), *IIMB Campus News* (6 a year), *IIBM Alumni* (6 a year).

Indian Institute of Management, Kolkata: Joka, Diamond Harbour Rd, POB 16757, PO Alipore, Kolkata 700027; tel. (33) 24678310; fax (33) 24678307; e-mail director@iimcal.ac.in; f. 1961 to promote improvement in management through education, research and consultancy; two-year MBA course in Computer-Aided Management, three-year part-time MBA in business management; doctoral and extension courses; centres for studies in human values, development and environment policy, rural development and environment management; executive development; faculty development through research and consulting services; library: Dr B. C. Roy Memorial library of 125,000 vols; 77 teachers; 669 students; Dir Dr AMITAVA BOSE; publs *Decision*, *Journal on Human Values* (2 a year).

Indian Institute of Management, Indore: Pigdamber, Rau, Indore 453331, Madhya Pradesh; tel. (731) 2399101; fax (731) 2399115; e-mail webman@iimidr.ac.in; internet www.iimidr.ac.in; f. 1997; library: 15,000 vols and 425 periodicals; 27 teachers; Dir Dr S. P. PARASHAR.

Indian Institute of Management, Kozhikode: Calicut R. E. C. PO, Kozhikode 673601, Kerala; tel. (495) 2803001; fax (495) 2803010; e-mail osd@iimk.ren.nic.in; internet www.iimk.org; f. 1996; library: 7,000 books, 1,120 periodicals; Dir Dr AMARLAL H. KALRO.

Indian Institute of Management, Lucknow: Prabandh Nagar, Off Sitapur Rd, Lucknow 226013; tel. (522) 2734101; fax (522) 2734025; e-mail dsingh@iiml.ac.in; internet www.iiml.ac.in; f. 1984; 2-year postgraduate programme in agri-business management, exec. development programmes; undertakes research and consulting projects in the field of management; main areas: agriculture, health, education, rural development, state public enterprises, corporate management, information technology and systems, entrepreneurship, corporate communication and media relations, leadership and human values; centre for entrepreneur development and new venture management, agricultural management centre; library: library of 60,000 documents; 66 teachers; 480 postgraduate students; Dir Dr DEVI SINGH; publs *Newsletter* (every 2 weeks), *Annual Report*, *Innovision* (annually), *L'Essence* (annually), *Metamorphosis* (2 a year), *MUDRA* (annually).

EDUCATION

National Institute of Educational Planning and Administration: 17-B Sri Aurobindo Marg, New Delhi 110016; tel. (11) 26863562; fax (11) 26853041; f. 1962; diploma courses for education personnel of developing countries and district education officers; other in-service training courses; research in various aspects of educational planning and management; consultancy service for developing countries, State govts and other organizations; collaboration with UNESCO and other foreign agencies; library: 45,963 vols, 350 current journals; Dir Prof. KULDEEP MATHUR; publs *Journal of Educational Planning and Administration* (quarterly), *Pariprakshya* (in Hindi).

LANGUAGES

Central Institute of Indian Languages: Ministry of Human Resource Development, Department of Education, Government of India, Manasagangotri, Mysore 570006; tel. (821) 2515820; fax (821) 2515032; internet www.ciil.org; f. 1969; assisting and co-ordinating the development of Indian languages; preparation of grammars and dictionaries of tribal and border languages; inter-disciplinary research; preparation of materials for teaching and learning; 290 academic and technical staff; 7 Regional Language Centres in Mysore (languages: Kannada, Telugu, Malayalam, Tamil), Bhubaneswar (languages: Assamese, Bengali, Oriya), Pune (languages: Marathi, Gujarati, Sindhi), Patiala (languages: Urdu, Punjabi, Kashmiri), Solan (Urdu), Lucknow (Urdu) and Guwahati (north-eastern languages); library: 65,000 vols and 400 periodicals in 75 Indian and 30 foreign languages; Dir Dr I. S. BORKAR; publ. *New Language Planning Newsletter* (quarterly).

LAW

Indian Academy of International Law and Diplomacy: 9 Bhagwan Dass Rd, New Delhi 110001; tel. (11) 23384458; fax (11) 23383783; e-mail rpanand@giasdl01.vsnl.net.in; internet www.isil-aca.org/indian-academy.htm; f. 1964; part of the Indian Society of International Law; includes a research institute and library; offers courses in international law and diplomacy, human rights, international humanitarian and refugee laws, international trade and business law, law of air transport and aviation liability, international law and law of international institutions; library: 25,000 vols; Pres. RAM NIWAS MIRDHA; publ. *Indian Journal of International Law* (4 a year).

MEDICINE

All India Institute of Hygiene and Public Health: 110 Chittaranjan Ave, Kolkata 700073; f. 1932; constituent college of University of Calcutta; administered by Directorate-General of Health Services and Ministry of Health and Family Welfare; facilities for postgraduate work and medical research; depts of Behavioural Sciences, Biochemistry and Nutrition, Epidemiology and Health Education, Maternal and Child Health, Microbiology, Occupational Health, Public Health Administration, Public Health Nursing, Sanitary Engineering, Social and Preventive Medicine; Statistics and Demography, Veterinary Public Health, Rural Health and Training Centre, Urban Health and Training Centre; offers diploma, certificate, and orientation courses; academic year July to June; 112 teachers (incl. 14 professors); 300 students; library: 85,000 vols, 250 current periodicals; Dir Prof. K. J. NATH; publs *Annual Report*, *Prospectus*.

National Institute of Health and Family Welfare (NIHFW): New Mehrauli Rd, Munirka, New Delhi 110067; tel. (11) 26165959; fax (11) 26101623; e-mail info@nihfw.org; internet www.nihfw.org; f. 1977; in-service training, MD course in community health administration, biomedical research, research and consultancy; regional centre for health management; documentation and reprographic services; library: specialized library of 41,000 vols and 308 periodicals; Dir Dr N. K. SETHI; publs *Newsletter* (quarterly, in English), *NIHFW Journal* (quarterly), and Technical Report series.

TECHNOLOGY

See Institutes of National Importance for details of Indian Institutes of Technology.

Institute of Radiophysics and Electronics, University of Calcutta: 92 Acharya Prafulla Chandra Rd, Kolkata 700009; tel. (33) 23509115; fax (33) 23515828; e-mail hod@inraphel.ernet.in; internet www.irpel.org; f. 1949; houses postgraduate teaching and research dept of Univ. of Calcutta, Faculty of Technology; 3-year post-B.Sc. integrated course leading to BTech. degree, and two-year post-BTech./BE course leading to MTech. degrees in radiophysics and electronics and in information technology; conducts training programmes; research facilities in ionosphere, radio wave propagation, radio astronomy, solid state and microwave electronics, millimetre wave technology, solid state devices, plasma and quantum electronics, optoelectronics, control systems and micro-computers, communication theory and systems, microelectronics and VLSI technology; maintains ionosphere field station at Haringhata and radio astronomy field station at Kalyani; recognized as a Centre of Advanced Study by the University Grants Commission; 36 teachers; 240 students; library: 18,000 vols, 5000 journal issues; Head Prof. P. K. BASU; publ. *Yearbook*.

National Institute of Fashion Technology: Hauz Khas, Near Gulmohar Park, New Delhi 110016; tel. (11) 26965080; fax (11) 26851198; e-mail webmaster@niftindia.com; internet www.niftindia.com; f. 1986; undergraduate and postgraduate diploma courses relevant to the textiles and clothing industries; library of 17,000 books and documents; campuses in New Delhi, Mumbai, Kolkata, Gandhinagar, Hyderabad and Chennai; Dir-

Gen. GAURI KUMAR; publ. *Fashion and Beyond* (quarterly).

Schools of Art and Music

Academy of Architecture: Plot No. 278, Shankar Ghanekar Marg, next to Tyresoles Co., Prabhadevi, Mumbai 400025, Maharashtra; f. 1955; five-year Govt Diploma courses in architecture; library: 5,600 vols and 2,000 slides; Principal P. P. AMBERKAR.

Bharatiya Vidya Bhavan: Kulapati Munshi Rd, Mumbai 400007, Maharashtra; tel. (22) 3634462; f. 1938; aims to revitalize ancient Indian values to suit modern needs; postgraduate courses in Indology; colleges of arts, science, commerce and engineering; runs schools, Academy of Foreign Languages, College of Sanskrit; dept of Ancient Insights and Modern Discoveries; Ayurveda Research Centre; Institute of Communication and Management; Institute of Management and Research; schools of music, dancing, dramatic art; library: 76,688 vols and 1,404 MSS; 31,450 mems; Pres. C. SUBRAMANIAM; Hon. Dir Prof. J. H. DAVE; Dir-Gen. and Exec. Sec. S. RAMAKRISHNAN; publs *Bharatiya Vidya* (quarterly), *Samvid* (Sanskrit, quarterly), *Bhavan's Journal* (every 2 weeks), *Navaneet* (Hindi, monthly), *Navaneet-Samarpan* (Gujarati, monthly), 11 vols of the *History and Culture of the Indian People*, and various series.

Kalakshetra Foundation: Tiruvanmiyur, Chennai 600041, Tamil Nadu; tel. (44) 24911836; fax (44) 24914359; f. 1936; centre for education in classical music, dancing, theatrical art, painting and handicrafts; maintains a weaving-centre for the production of silk and cotton costumes in traditional design and a Kalamkari Unit for dyeing and hand-block printing with vegetable dyes; Dr U. V. Swaminatha Aiyar library noted for classical MSS and literature in Tamil; Dir S. RAJARAM; Sec R. V. RAMANI.

Music Academy: 306 T.T.K. Rd, Royapettah, Chennai 600014, Tamil Nadu; tel. (44) 28275619; f. 1927; research and study of Indian music; directs the Teachers' College of Music; library: 5,300 vols; Pres. T. T. VASU; Secs T. S. PARTHASARATHY, M. RAMADURAI, M. S. VENKATARAMAN, N. RAMJI; publs *Journal*, and books.

National School of Drama: Bahawalpur House, Bhagwandas Rd, New Delhi 110001; tel. (11) 23389402; fax (11) 23384288; e-mail nsdr@bol.net.in; internet schoolofdrama.india.com; f. 1959; three-year diploma course for a maximum of 20 students in each class, short-term theatre training workshops; Theatre-in-Education Company working with and performing for children; library: 28,000 vols, 2,500 slides, records, etc.; 16 teachers; 60 students; Dir Prof. RAM GOPAL BAJAJ; Registrar A. N. ROY; publs *N.S.D. Newsletter* (4 a year), *Theatre India* (in English, 2 a year), *Rang Prasang* (in Hindi, 2 a year).

Sri Varalakshmi Academies of Fine Arts: Ramavilas, Kashipathy Agarahar, Chamaraja Double Rd, Mysore 4; f. 1945; educational and cultural research institution; gives advanced courses of study in Karnataka music; library: 5,000 vols; Prin. Vidwan C. V. SRIVATSA; Head Research Dept Prof. R. SATHYANARAYANA.

INDONESIA

The Higher Education System

The oldest institution of higher education is the Institut Teknologi Bandung (Bandung Institute of Technology), which was founded in 1920 when Indonesia was part of the Dutch East Indies. In 1949 Indonesia gained independence from the Netherlands. The Portuguese colony of Timor-Leste (formerly East Timor) was annexed in 1975 and administered as a province of Indonesia until 1999, when it was transferred to a UN transitional administration before achieving sovereign independence in 2002. Higher education consists of different types of institutions, which include public and private universities (universitas), higher colleges (sekolah tinggi), teacher training institutes (institut keguruan dan ilmu pendidikan), Islamic universities (universitas Islam), Christian universities (universitas Kristen), academies (akademi) and polytechnics (politeknik). Universities (including the three technical institutes) offer a full range of undergraduate and postgraduate degrees; teacher training institutes and Islamic universities have degree-awarding powers; academies are specialized institutions of higher education related to a particular profession; and polytechnics are technical and vocational institutions offering diploma-level education. In 2004/05 there were 2,516 institutions of higher education, with a total enrolment of 2.8m. The Directorate General of Higher Education is the Government body responsible for overall control of higher education, but the Directorate of Islamic Higher Education is responsible for the Islamic universities.

Admission to public universities is on the basis of the Entrance Examination to State Universities (Ujian Masuk Perguruan Tinggi Negeri), while admission to polytechnics requires the applicant to complete secondary education and sit and entrance examination (Ujian Masuk Politeknik). The Entrance Examination to State Universities is divided into two streams, social sciences and natural sciences. Institutions may also make an offer of admission based on Interest and Ability Tracing (Penelusuran Minat dan Kemampuan), a system for monitoring secondary school students.

Indonesia operates a US-style 'credit semester' system for awarding undergraduate and postgraduate degrees, divided into three stages (sarjana). The first stage is the undergraduate degree (Sarjana Satu), which lasts a minimum of eight semesters (four years) and requires 144–160 credits. Degrees in professional fields, such as medicine, dentistry, veterinary science and engineering, may last for an additional one to three years. The second stage (and first postgraduate degree) is the Magister, a course of study requiring 36–50 credits and lasting at least four semesters (two years). The third and last stage is the Doktor, also lasting at least four semesters (two years) and requiring a further 40–60 credits.

Post-secondary technical and vocational education is offered by polytechnics and academies. Students are awarded one of four diplomas (D1–D4) depending on length of course (one to four years) or area of specialization. The diploma D4 is regarded as equivalent to the Sarjana Satu. There are also two 'specialist' vocational qualifications, Ijazah Spesialis (SP1), awarded after two years and requiring 26–50 credits, and Ijazah Spesialis (SP2), awarded after 40–50 credits have been accrued following SP1.

The National Accreditation Board for Higher Education (Badan Akreditasi Nasional Perguruan Tinggi) was founded in 1994 as part of the Directorate General of Higher Education and is the body responsible for accrediting both public and private institutions of higher education. Courses are ranked on a scale A–D, with A being 'very good' and D 'unsatisfactory'. C is the minimum requirement for accreditation.

Learned Societies

GENERAL

Jajasan Kerja-Sama Kebudajaan (Foundation for Cultural Co-operation): Jl. Gajah Mada 13, Bandung; to promote co-operation and mutual understanding between the countries of Western Europe and Indonesia; Rep. for Indonesia A. KOOLHAAS.

BIBLIOGRAPHY, LIBRARY SCIENCE AND MUSEOLOGY

Indonesian Library Association: Jl. Imam Bonjol 1, POB 3624, Jakarta 10002; tel. 34-25-29; f. 1954; Pres. M. H. PRAKOSO; Sec.-Gen. SOEMARNO.

EDUCATION

UNESCO Office Jakarta and Regional Science Bureau for Asia and the Pacific: Jl. Galuh (II) No. 5, Kebayoran Baru, POB 1273/JKT, Jakarta 12110; tel. (21) 7399818; fax (21) 72796489; e-mail jakarta@unesco.org; internet www.unesco.or.id; represents Brunei, Indonesia, Malaysia, Philippines, and Timor-Leste; Dir QUNLI HAN.

LANGUAGE AND LITERATURE

Alliance Française: Jalan Purnawarman 32, Bandung 40117; tel. (22) 4212417; fax (22) 4207877; e-mail ccfbdg@rad.net.id; offers courses and exams in French language and culture and promotes cultural exchange with France; attached teaching centres in Balikpapan, Bogor, Denpassar Jati, Padang, Makassar, Manado, Medan, Semarang and Yogyakarta.

British Council: S. Widjojo Centre, Jalan Jenderal Sudirman Kav 71, Jakarta 12190; tel. (21) 2524115; fax (21) 2524129; e-mail information@britishcouncil.or.id; internet www.britishcouncil.org/indonesia; teaching centre; offers courses and exams in English language and British culture and promotes cultural exchange with the UK; attached office in Surabaya; library of 18,000 vols; Dir Dr PATRICK BRAZIER; Man., English Language Services SIMON COLLEDGE.

Goethe-Institut: Jl. Sam Ratulangi 9–15, Jakarta 10350; tel. (21) 23550208; fax (21) 23550021; e-mail info@jakarta.goethe.org; internet www.goethe.de/jakarta; f. 1961; offers courses and exams in German language and culture and promotes cultural exchange with Germany; attached centre in Bandung; library of 8,500 vols, 1,600 audiovisual items, 40 periodicals; Dir Dr PETER J. BUMKE.

MEDICINE

Ikatan Dokter Indonesia (Indonesian Medical Association): Jl. Dr Sam Ratulangi 29, Jakarta; tel. (21) 3150679; fax (21) 3900473; e-mail yapenidi@mail.idi.or.id; f. 1950; 45,131 mems; Chair. Prof. Dr Dr M. AHMAD DSOSOSONGITO; Sec.-Gen. Dr FACHMI IDRIS; publs *Majalah Kedokteran Indonesia* (monthly), *BIDI* (26 a year).

NATURAL SCIENCES

Physical Sciences

Astronomical Association of Indonesia: Jakarta Planetarium, Cikini Raya 73, Jakarta; f. 1920; to promote the advancement of astronomical science; Chair. Prof. Dr BAMBANG HIDAYAT; Sec. Drs S. DARSA; Treas. Dr WINARDI SUTANTYO.

TECHNOLOGY

Persatuan Insinyur Indonesia (Indonesian Institute of Engineers): 39 Jl. Halimun, Jakarta 12980; tel. (21) 835-2180; fax (21) 837-00663; e-mail info@pii.or.id; internet www.pii.or.id; 27,000 mems; Pres. ABURIZAL BAKRIE; Sec.-Gen. I. SUCIPTO UMAR.

Research Institutes

GENERAL

Lembaga Ilmu Pengetahuan Indonesia (Indonesian Institute of Sciences): Jl. Jendral Gatot Subroto no. 10, Jakarta 12710; tel. (21) 5251542; fax (21) 5207226; e-mail kepala@lipi.go.id; internet www.lipi.go.id; f. 1967; government agency to promote the development of science and technology, to serve as the national centre for regional and international scientific co-operation, to organize national research centres; library of 150,000 titles; Head Prof. Dr UMAR ANGGARA JENIE; publs *Journal of Tropical Ethnobiology* (2 a year), *Jurnal Ekonomi dan Pembangunan* (2 a year), *Jurnal Elektronika dan Pembangunan* (every 2 months), *Jurnal Masyarakat dan Budaya* (2 a year), *Korosi: Majalah Ilmu dan Teknologi* (2 a year), *Limnotek* (2 a year), *Majalah Widyariset* (monthly), *Masyarakat Indonesia: Majalah Ilmu-ilmu Sosial Indonesia* (2 a year), *Oseanologi dan Limnologi di Indonesia* (every 2 months), *Reinwardtia: A Journal on Taxonomic Botany, Plant Sociology and Ecology* (irregular), *Riset Geologi dan Pertambangan*, *Telaah: Berkala Ilmu Pengetahuan dan Teknologi* (2 a year), *Treubia: Journal on Zoology of the Indo-Australian Archipelago* (irregular), *Warta Biotek* (quarterly), *Warta Oseanografi* (quarterly), *Berita Iptek* (quarterly), *Jurnal Penduduk dan Pembangunan* (2 a year), *Prosea Newsletter* (quarterly), *Berita Biologi* (quarterly), *IPT Technical Journal* (quarterly), *Jurnal Kimia Terapan Indonesia* (3 a year), *Warta Kimia Analitik* (2 a year), *Jurnal Teknologi Informasi* (3 a year), *Warta KIM* (monthly).

AGRICULTURE, FISHERIES AND VETERINARY SCIENCE

Badan Penelitian dan Pengembangan Kehutanan (Agency for Forestry Research and Development): Gedung Manggala Wanabakti Lt. 11, Jl. Gatot Subroto, POB 51/JKWB, Jakarta 10270; e-mail wwardojo@yahoo.com; internet www.dephut.go.id; f. 1983; 114 research scientists; library of 25,000 vols; Dir Gen. WAHJUDI WARDOJO; Inspector Gen. SUHARIYANTO; Sec. Gen. ROEN M. PURNAMA; publs *Journal of Forestry Research*, *Jurnal Analisis Kebijakan Kehutanan* (Journal of Forestry Policy Analysis), *Buletin Penelitian Hutan* (Forest Research Bulletin), *Jurnal Penelitian Hasil Hutan* (Forest Products Research Journal), *Pengumuman, Penelitian Hasil Hutan* (Communication, Forest Products Research), *Jurnal Penelitian Hutan Tanaman* (Journal of Plantation Forest Research), *Jurnal Penelitian Hutan & Konservasi* (Journal of Forest and Nature Conservation Research), *Jurnal Penelitian Sosial Ekonomi & Kebijakan Kehutanan* (Journal of Social, Economic and Forestry Policy Research), *Buletin Teknologi Perbenihan* (Bulletin of Seed Technology), *Info Hutan* (Forest Information), *Info Hasil Hutan* (Forest Products Information), *Info Sosial Ekonomi Kehutanan* (Social Economy of Forestry Information), *Warta Benih & Informasi Teknis* (News of Seed and Technical Information), *Warta Penelitian dan Pengembangan Kehutanan* (Forestry Research and Development News).

Balai Besar Industri Agro (Centre for Agro-Based Industry): Jl. Ir H. Juanda 11, Bogor 16122; tel. (251) 324068; fax (251) 323339; e-mail irdabi@indo.net.id; internet www.bbia.go.id; f. 1909; attached to Min. of Industry and Trade; provides services for agriculture-based industry through training, consultancy, chemical and microbiological testing, research and development, certification, environmental management, and calibration; Dir YANG YANG SETIAWAN; publ. *Warta IHP* (Journal of agro-based industry, 2 a year).

Balai Penelitian Veteriner (Research Institute for Veterinary Science, Agency of Agricultural Research and Development, Ministry of Agriculture): Jl. R.E. Martadinata 30, POB 151, Bogor 16114; tel. (251) 331048; fax (251) 336425; e-mail balivet@indo.net.id; f. 1908; depts of bacteriology, pathology and epidemiology, toxicology, parasitology, mycology, virology, balitvet culture collection; library of 12,270 vols, 1,136 periodicals; Dir Dr SJAMSUL BAHRI; publs *Annual Report*, *Newsletter* (2 a year).

Pusat Penelitian dan Pengembangan Hortikultura (Indonesian Centre for Horticulture Research and Development (ICHORD)): Jl. Ragunan 19, Pasarminggu, Jakarta 12520; tel. (21) 7890990; fax (21) 7805135; e-mail yamto@indo.net.id; research and development of horticultural crops; Dir Dr SUYAMTO; publ. *Jurnal Hortikultura* (4 a year).

Attached institutes:

Balai Penelitian Tanaman Hias (Indonesian Ornamental Crops Research Institute (IOCRI)): Jl. Raya Ciherang Segunung, Pacet-Cianjur 43253, Kotak Pos 8 SdL; tel. (263) 512607; fax (263) 514138; e-mail segunung@indoway.net; Dir Dr KUSUMAH EFFENDIE.

Balai Penelitian Tanaman Sayur (Indonesian Vegetable Research Institute (IVEGRI)): Jl. Tangkuban Perahu 517, Lembang; tel. (22) 2786245; fax (22) 2786416; e-mail ivegri@balitsa.or.id; Dir Dr UDIN S. NUGRAHA.

Balai Penelitian Tanaman Buah (Indonesian Fruit Research Institute (IFRURI)): Jl. Raya Aripan Km 8, Kotak Pos No 5, Solok 27301, Sumatera Barat; tel. (755) 20137; fax (755) 20592; e-mail rif@padang.wasantara.net.id; Dir Dr I. DJATNIKA.

Pusat Penelitian dan Pengembangan Peternakan (Central Research Institute for Animal Sciences): Jln. Raya Pajajaran, Bogor, West Java; tel. 322185; fax 328382; e-mail criansci@indo.net.id; f. 1950; research into farm animals and animal parasites and diseases; library of 14,000 vols, 1,199 periodicals; Dir Dr KUSUMA DIWYANTO; publs *Ilmu Peternakan dan Veteriner* (4 a year), *Wartazoa* (2 a year), *Proceedings of the National Seminar* (annually).

Pusat Penelitian dan Pengembangan Tanaman Pangan (Central Research Institute for Food Crops): Jl. Merdeka 147, Bogor 16111; tel. (251) 334089; fax (251) 312755; f. 1961; food crops research and development; library of 3,000 vols; Dir Dr ACHMAD M. FAGI; publ. *Contributions of CRIFC* (4–6 a year).

Attached institutes:

Balai Penelitian Tanaman Pangan Lahan Rawa (Research Institute for Food Crops on Swampy Areas): Jl. Kebun Karet, Lok Tabat, Kotak Pos 31, Banjarbaru 70712, Kalimantan Selatan; tel. (511) 4772534; fax (511) 4773034; Dir ACHMADI; publ. *Pemberitaan Penelitian* (2–4 a year, in Indonesian and English).

Balai Penelitian Bioteknologi Tanaman Pangan (Research Institute for Biotechnology of Food Crops): Jl. Tentara Pelajar 3A, Bogor 1611; tel. (251) 337975; fax (251) 338820; Dir Dr DJOKO S. DAMARDJATI; publs *Penelitian Pertanian* (Agricultural Research, 3–4 a year, in Indonesian and English), *Buletin Penelitian* (Research Bulletin, 2–4 a year).

Balai Penelitian Tanaman Kacangkacangan dan Umbi-umbian Malang (Research Institute for Legumes and Root Crops): Jl. Raya Kendal Payak, Kotak Pos 66, Malang 65101, Jawa Timur; tel. (341) 81468; fax (341) 318148; Dir Dr SUYAMTO; publ. *Penelitian Palawija* (Palawija Research, 2 a year, in Indonesian, and abstract in English).

Balai Penelitian Tanaman Jagung dan Serealia Lain (Research Institute for Maize and Other Cereals): Jl. Ratulangi, Kotak Pos 173, Maros 90511, Ujung Pandang, Sulawesi Selatan Telp; tel. (411) 371016; fax (411) 318148; Dir Dr MARSUM DAHLAN; publ. *Agrikam: Buletin Penelitian Pertanian* (Agricultural Research Bulletin, 2–4 a year, with English summary).

Balai Penelitian Tanaman Padi (Research Institute for Rice): Jl. Raya 9, Sukamandi – Tromol Pos 11, Cikampek Subang 41255, Jawa Barat; tel. (264) 520157; fax (264) 520158; Dir Dr ANDI HASANUDDIN; publ. *Media Sukamandi* (Research at Sukamandi, 2–4 a year, with English summary).

Pusat Penelitian Kelapa Sawit (Indonesian Oil Palm Research Institute): POB 104, Medan; f. 1916; to promote agricultural improvement on the member estates; 500 mems; library of 11,000 vols, 20,000 periodicals; Dir Dr H. ADLIN U. LUBIS; publs *Bulletin* (quarterly, in Indonesian with English summaries), *Berita* (in Indonesian), *Annual Report* (in Indonesian), *Oil Palm Statistics* (in Indonesian), *Rainfall Records* (in Indonesian).

Pusat Penelitian Perkebunan Gula Indonesia (Indonesian Sugar Research Institute): Jl. Pahlawan 25, Pasuruan 67126; tel. (343) 421086; fax (343) 421178; e-mail isri@telkom.net; f. 1887; library of 15,000 vols; 150 staff; Dir Dr MIRZAWAN PDN; publs *Majalah Penelitian Gula* (Sugar Journal, quarterly), *Berita* (Communications), *Laporan Tahunan* (Annual Report), *Bulletin* (2 a year).

Pusat Penelitian Tanah dan Agroklimat (Soil and Agricultural Climate Research Centre): Jl. Ir. H. Juanda 98, Bogor 16123; f. 1905; library of 4,000 vols; Dir Dr SYARIFUDDIN KARAMA.

Balai Penelitian Bioteknologi Perkebunan Indonesia (Indonesian Biotechnology Research Institute for Estate Crops): Jl. Taman Kencana 1, POB 179/Bgr 16001, Bogor 16151; tel. (251) 324048; fax (251) 328516; e-mail briec@indo.net.id; internet www.ipard.com; f. 1933; supportive research in plant molecular biology and immunology, microbes and bioprocessing; library of 13,493 vols, 1,597 periodicals, 3,109 reprints, 70 theses; Head of Unit Dr Ir. DARMONO TANIWIRYONO; publ. *Menara Perkebunan* (in English and Indonesian, 2 a year).

ARCHITECTURE AND TOWN PLANNING

Research Institute for Human Settlements and United Nations Regional Centre for Research on Human Settlements: Jl. Panyawungan, Cileunyi, Wetan, Kab. Bandung 40393; tel. (22) 798393; fax (22) 798392; f. 1953; research on housing, building etc.; library of 29,000 vols; Dir SUTIKUI UTORO; publs *Masalah Bangunan* (quarterly, in English), *Jurnal Penelitian Pemutiman* (4 a year, in Bahasa Indonesian), *Buku Petunjuk Pedesaan* (in Bahasa Indonesian).

ECONOMICS, LAW AND POLITICS

Badan Pusat Statistik (BPS Statistics Indonesia): Jl. Dr Sutomo 6-8, Jakarta 10710; tel. (21) 3841195; fax (21) 3857046; e-mail bpshq@bps.go.id; internet www.bps.go.id; f. 1920; library of 60,000 vols, 1,100 periodicals; Dir Dr SOEDARTI SURBAKTI.

Centre for Strategic and International Studies: Jl. Tanah Abang IIIkav 23-27, Jakarta 10610; tel. (21) 3865532; fax (21) 3847517; e-mail csis@csis.or.id; internet www.csis.or.id; f. 1971; library of 50,000 vols; policy-oriented studies in international and national affairs in collaboration with industry, commerce, and the political, legal and journalistic communities; Executive Dir Dr HADI SOESTASTRO; publs *The Indonesian Quarterly (English)*, *Analisis CSIS* (4 a year).

Indonesian Institute of World Affairs: c/o University of Indonesia, Jakarta; Chair. Prof. SUPOMO; Sec. Mr SUDJATMOKO.

Lembaga Administrasi Negara (Institute of Public Administration): Jl. Veteran 10, Jakarta 10110; tel. (21) 3868208 ext. 09; fax (21) 3848792; e-mail kr050546@rad.net.id; internet www.lan.go.id; f. 1958; library of 50,262 vols; Chair. Dr NASRI EFFENDI; publ. *Manajemen Pembangunan*.

Lembaga Pers dan Pendapat Umum (Press and Public Opinion Institute, Ministry of Information): Pegangsaan Timur 19B, Jakarta; f. 1953; audience research of press, film and radio; library: *c.* 4,500 vols; Dir Dr MARBANGUN.

HISTORY, GEOGRAPHY AND ARCHAEOLOGY

Dinas Intelijen Medan & Geografi Jawatan Topografi TNI-AD (Geographical Institute): Jl. Dr Wahidin 1/11, Jakarta; Dir Capt. AMARUL AMRI.

Direktorat Perlindungan dan Pembinaan Peninggalan Sejarah dan Purbakala (Directorate for the Protection and Development of the Historical and Archaeological Heritage): Jl. Cilacap 4, POB 2533, Jakarta; Dir UKA TJANDRASASMITA.

Pusat Penelitian Arkeologi (Research Centre of Archaeology): Jl. Raya Condet Pejaten 4, Pasar Minggu, Jakarta 12510; tel. (21) 7988131; fax (21) 7988187; e-mail arkenas@bit.net.id; brs in Yogyakarta, Denpasar, Palembang, Bandung, Banjarmasin, Makassar, Manado, Ambon and Jayapura; library of 15,000 vols; Dir Dr HARIS SUKENDAR; publs *Bulletin*, *reports*, *monographs*, *Aspects*, *Amerta*, *Kalpataru*.

LANGUAGE AND LITERATURE

Pusat Bahasa. Departemen Pendidikan Nasional (Language Centre of the Ministry of National Education): POB 6259, Jl. Daksinapati Barat IV, Rawamangun, Jakarta 13220; tel. (21) 4706678; fax (21) 4750407; e-mail masterfbs@bahasa-sastra.web.id; f. 1975; language planning policies, research in linguistics and vernaculars, compiling of dictionaries, co-ordinating and supervising language development and cultivation, applied research in language education; library of 80,000 vols; Dir DENDY SUGONO; publs *Bahasa dan Sastra* (6 a year), *Lembar Komunikasi* (6 a year), *Informasi Pustaka Kebahasaan* (4 a year).

MEDICINE

Badan Pengawas Obat dan Makanan (National Agency of Drug and Food Control): Jl. Percetakan Negara 23, Jakarta 10560; tel. (21) 4245331; fax (21) 4244947; e-mail informasi@pom.go.id; internet www.pom.go.id; f. 2000; legislation, regulation and standardization of drug and food industries; licensing and certification of pharmaceutical industry; evaluation of products; sampling and laboratory testing of products; inspection of production and distribution facilities; investigation and law enforcement; auditing of product advertisement and promotion; research on drug and food policy implementation; public communication, information and education; Head Drs H. M. SAMPURNO; Sec. Dra MAWARWATI DJAMALUDDIN.

Central Institute for Leprosy Research: Jl. Kimia 17, Jakarta; f. 1935; Institute includes a clinic and laboratory; Dir MOH. ARIF.

Laboratorium Kesehatan Daerah (Pathological Laboratory, Ministry of Health): Jl. Laboratorium 5, Medan; f. 1906; investigation and control of contagious and endemic diseases in Sumatra; library: *c.* 3,000 vols; Dir Dr ISKAK KOIMAN.

Laboratorium Kesehatan Pusat Lembaga Eijkman (Eijkman Institute): Library, Clinical Pathology Dept, Medical Faculty of the University of Indonesia, Ciptomangunkusumo Hospital, Jl. Diponegoro 69–71, Jakarta 10010; tel. 332265; fax 3147713; f. 1888; bacteriological-serological department, chemical department and virus division; Head Dr HENDRO JOEWONO; publs Reports, Papers.

Lembaga Malaria (Malaria Institute, Ministry of Health): Jl. Percetakan Negara 29, Jakarta; tel. (21) 417608; fax (21) 4207807; f. 1920; Dir Dr P. R. ARBANI.

Perusahaan Negara Bio-Farma (Pasteur Institute): Jl. Pasteur 9, POB 47, Bandung; Dir M. S. NASUTION.

Pusat Penelitian dan Pengembangan Pelayanan dan Technologi Kesehatan (Health Services and Technology Research and Development Centre): Jl. Indrapura 17, Surabaya 60176; tel. (31) 3528748; fax (31) 3528749; e-mail suwandimakmur@lithang.depkes.go.id; internet www.litbang.depkes.go.id Jl. Percetakan Negara 23A, Jakarta 10560; tel. (21) 4243314; fax (21) 4211013; f. 1975; library of 13,604 vols, 751 journals; Dir Dr H. SUWANDI MAKMUR; publs *Bulletin of Health System Research* (2 a year), *Warta JIP* (4 a year).

Unit Diponegoro (Nutrition Institute): c/o Nutrition Centre, Seameo Tropmed–U.I., Campus University of Indonesia, Salemba 4, Jakarta; f. 1937; Dir Dradjat D. PRAWIRANEGARA.

NATURAL SCIENCES

General

Institut de Recherche pour le Développement (IRD): Wisma Anugraha, Jalan Taman Kemang 32B, Jakarta 12730; tel. (21) 71792114; fax (21) 71792179; e-mail ird-indo@rad.net.id; internet www.ird.fr; f. 1944; (see main entry under France); geography, agroforestry, anthropology, aquaculture, agronomy, fishery, archaeology, ethnoecology; Dir Dr PATRICE LEVANG.

Biological Sciences

Pusat Penelitian dan Pengembangan Biologi (Research and Development Centre for Biology): Jl. Raya Juanda 18, POB 110, Bogor 16122; f. 1817; 156 mems; library of 14,995 vols, 4,393 bound periodicals, *c.* 600 current periodicals, 24,587 reprints, 4,377 unpubl. reports, 7,155 newspaper clippings, 2,463 maps; Dir Dr SOETIKNO WIRJOATMODJO; publs *Berita Biologi*, *Reinwardtia*, *Treubia* (all irregular), *Laporan Tahunan*, *Laporan Teknik* (annually), *Laporan Kemajuan* (quarterly), *Warta Biologi* (every 2 months), *pamphlets*.

Attached institutes:

Balai Penelitian dan Pengembangan Botani (Research and Development Institute for Botany): Jl. Raya Juanda 22, Bogor; f. 1884; Head Dr JOHANIS PALAR MOGEA.

Balai Penelitian dan Pengembangan Mikrobiologi (Research and Development Institute for Microbiology): c/o Kebun Raya Indonesia; f. 1884; Head Dr SUBADRI ABDULKADIR.

Balai Penelitian dan Pengembangan Zoologi (Research and Development Institute for Zoology): Jl. Raya Juanda 3, Bogor; Head Drs MOHAMAD AMIR.

UPT Balai Pengembangan Kebun Raya (Bogor Botanical Gardens):; f. 1817; Head Dr SUHIRMAN; publs *Buletin Kebun Raya* (quarterly), *Index Seminum* (annually), *Alphabetical List of Plant Species*, *Warta Kebun Raya* (irregular), *pamphlets*.

Physical Sciences

Badan Meteorologi dan Geofisik (Meteorological and Geophysical Agency): Jl. Aarif Rahman Hakim 3, Jakarta; Dir Drs C. SOETRISNO.

Dinas Geodesi, Jawatan Topografi TNI-AD (Geodetic Section, Army Topographic Service): Jl. Bangka 1, Bandung; f. 1855; library: *c.* 2,000 vols, 2,500 periodicals; Dir Ir. MOH TAWIL.

National Atomic Energy Agency: Jl. Kuningan Barat, Mampang Prapatan, POB 4390, Jakarta 12043; tel. 5204246; fax 511110; Dir-Gen. Ir. DJALI AHIMSA.

Observatorium Bosscha (Bosscha Observatory): Lembang, Java; tel. Lembang 1; f. 1925; since 1951 the observatory has been part of the Dept of Astronomy, Bandung Institute of Technology, Bandung; Dir Dr BAMBANG HIDAYAT; publs *Annals* (irregular), *Contributions* (irregular), *Annual Report*.

Pusat Penelitian dan Pengembangan Geologi (Geological Research and Development Centre): Jl. Diponegoro 57, Bandung 40122; tel. (22) 7272601; fax (22) 7202669; e-mail grdc@melsa.net.id; internet www.grdc.dpe.go.id; f. 1979; geological and geophysical research and systematic mapping; library: see Libraries; geological research and systematic museum; Dir BAMBANE DWIYANTO; publs *Publikasi Teknik* (Technical Papers: Geophysics, Palaeontology Series), *Publikasi Khusus* (Special Publications), *Buletin*, *Laporan Tahunan* (Annual Reports), *Geosurvey Newsletter*, *Journal of Geology and Mineral Resources*, *Peta Geologi*, *Geofisika dan Tematik*.

Pusat Penelitian Oseanografi (Research Centre for Oceanography): Jl. Pasir Putih 1, Ancol Timur, POB 4801/JKTF, Jakarta 11048; tel. 683850; fax 681948; e-mail p30.lipi@jakarta.wasantara.net.id; internet www.oseanologi.lipi.go.id; f. 1905; library of 2,000 vols, 250 periodical titles; Dir Dr Ir KURNAN SUMADHIHARYA; publs *Marine Research in Indonesia* (irregular), *Oseanologi di Indonesia* (irregular), *Oseana* (quarterly).

TECHNOLOGY

Akademi Teknologi Kulit (Academy of Leather Technology): Jl. Diponegoro 101, Yogyakarta; Dir P. SUKARBOWO.

Balai Besar Penelitian dan Pengembangan Industri Barang Kulit, Karet dan Plastik (BBKKP) (Centre for Leather, Rubber and Plastic (CLRP)): Jl. Sokonandi 9, Yogyakarta 55166; tel. (274) 563939; fax (274) 563655; e-mail bbkkp@jogjamedianet.com; internet bbkkp.go.id; f. 1927; library of 4,000 vols; Dir Ir. SARDJONO.

Balai Fotogrametri (Institute of Photogrammetry, Ministry of Defence): Jl. Gunung Sahar 90, Jakarta; f. 1937; research on problems relative to photogrammetry, aerotriangulization, topographical maps, etc.; library of *c.* 1,500 books and periodicals; Head Maj. R. E. BEAUPAIN.

Balai Penelitian Batik & Kerajinan (Batik and Handicraft Research Institute): Jl. Kusumanegara 2, Yogyakarta; f. 1951; research, testing, and training courses; 108 mems; library of 1,792 vols; Dir SOEPARMAN S. TEKS.

Dinas Hidro-Oseanografi (Naval Hydro-Oceanographic Office): Jalan Pantai KutaV1, Jakarta 14430; f. 1947; hydrographical survey of Indonesia; staff of 700; Dir Col. P. L. KATOPPO; publs Tide Tables, etc.

Direktorat Metrologi (Directorate of Metrology): Jl. Pasteur 27, Bandung 40171;

tel. (22) 4203597; fax (22) 4207035; e-mail ditmet@bdg.Centrin.net.id; f. 1923; Dir of Metrology AMIR SAHARUDDIN SJABRIAL.

Institut Teknologi Tekstil (Institute of Textile Technology): Jl. Jond. A. Yani 318, Bandung; f. 1922; Dir Maj. JON SEORJOSEOJARSO.

Jajasan Dana Normalisasi Indonesia (Indonesian Standards Institution): Jl. Braga 38, (Atas) Bandung; f. 1920; Chair. Prof. Ir. R. SOEMONO; Sec. GANDI.

Lembaga Research dan Pengujian Materiil Angkatan Darat (Military Laboratory for Research and Testing Material, Ministry of Defence): Jl. Ternate 6–8, Bandung; f. 1865; library of 1,500 vols; Dir Brig.-Gen. N. A. KUSOMO.

Pusat Penelitian dan Pengembangan Sumber Daga Air (Research Institute for Water Resources): Jl. Ir. H. Juanda 193, POB 841, Bandung 40135; tel. (22) 2504053; fax (22) 2500163; e-mail pusair@bdg.centrin.net.id; internet www.pusair.domainvalet.com; f. 1966; attached to Agency for Research and Development, Ministry of Settlement and Regional Infrastructure; survey, investigation and research in the field of water resources development; experimental stations for hydrology, water resources, the environment, hydraulic structures and geotechnics, irrigation, swamps and coastal regions, rivers, and sabo; library of 6,000 vols, 3,000 reports, 9,000 periodicals; Dir Ir. DYAH RAHAYU PANGESTI; publs *Jurnal Penelitian dan Pengembangan Pengairan* (2 a year), *Bulletin Pusair* (2 a year), *Technical and Research Report* (annually).

Libraries and Archives

Bandung

Perpustakaan Pusat Institut Teknologi Bandung (Central Library, Bandung Institute of Technology): Jl. Ganesya 10, Bandung 40132; tel. (22) 2500089; fax (22) 2500089; e-mail library@itb.ac.id; internet www.lib.itb.ac.id; f. 1920; science, technology, fine arts and business; 227,000 vols, 791 current periodicals, 40,000 bound vols; rare books, pamphlets and reports on Indonesia, colln on fine arts; Dir Dr YANNES MARTINUS PASARIBU; publ. *ITB Proceedings*.

Perpustakaan Pusat Penelitian dan Pengembangan Geologi (Library of Geological Research and Development Centre): Jl. Diponegoro 57, Bandung 40122; tel. (22) 703205; fax (22) 702669; e-mail grdc@melsa.net.id; 11,000 vols, 904 periodicals, 4,609 maps, 11,021 reports, 9,034 reprints, 400 microfiches; Chief Librarian RINI H. MARINO.

Pusat Perpustakaan Angkatan Darat (Central Military Library): Jl. Kalimantan 6, Bandung; 36,000 vols in Central Library, and about 20,000 vols in departmental, territorial and college and office libraries; Dir Brig.-Gen. SOESATYO.

Bogor

Pusat Perpustakaan Pertanian dan Komunikasi Penelitian (Centre for Agricultural Library and Research Communication): Jl. Ir. Haji Juanda 20, Bogor 16122; tel. (251) 321746; fax (251) 326561; f. 1842; 400,000 vols; Dir Dr PRABOWO TJITROPRANOTO; publs *Bibliography* (irregular), *Indek Biologi Pertanian Indonesia* (6 a year), *Abstrak Hasil Penelitian Pertanian* (2 a year), *Indonesian Agricultural Bibliography* (annually), *Daftar Tambahan Koleksi* (quarterly), *Indonesian Journal of Crop Science* (2 a year), *Indonesian Agricultural Research and Development Journal* (quarterly), *Journal Penelitian dan Pengembangan Pertanian* (quarterly), *Warta Penelitian dan Pengembangan Pertanian* (6 a year).

UPT Perpustakaan Institut Pertanian Bogor (Bogor Agricultural University Library): Kampus Darmaga, POB 199, Bogor 16001; tel. (251) 621073; fax (251) 623166; e-mail uptperpus@ipb.ac.id; f. 1963; 159,000 vols, 3,500 periodicals; Chief Officer Ir ABDUL RAHMAN SALEH; publs *Forum Pasca Sarjana*, *Indonesian Journal of Tropical Agriculture*.

Jakarta

Arsip Nasional Republik Indonesia (National Archives): Jl. Ampera Raya, Cilandak Timur, Jakarta 12560; tel. (21) 7805851; fax (21) 7805812; e-mail anrinet@indosat.net.id; f. 1892; preservation of documents as a national heritage and national account of the planning, execution and performance of the national life; to provide records for government and public activities; supervises the management of current operational records and the collection, storage, preservation, safe-keeping and use of historical archives; *c.* 25 km archives; 8,437 vols of books and other publications, 48,000 films, 10,000 video recordings, 4,000 oral history recordings, 1,600,000 photographs; Dir Dr NOERHADI MAGETSARI; publs *Penerbitan Sumber Sejarah* (irregular), *Penerbitan Sumber Sejarah Lisan* (irregular), *Lembaran Berita Sejarah Lisan Arsip Nasional RI* (irregular), *Berita Arsip Nasional RI* (2 a year).

Central Documentation and Library of the Ministry of Information: Medan Merdeka Barat 9, Jakarta; f. 1945; specializes in mass communication, social and political subjects, and supplies regional branch offices; press-cutting service from Indonesian newspapers since 1950; temporarily acting as Exchange Centre for government publications and official documents; 10,000 vols; Head Drs P. DALIMUNTHE; Librarian Mrs SAMPOERNO.

Library of Political and Social History: Medan Merdeka Seletan 11, Jakarta; f. 1952; 65,000 vols; includes the National Bibliographic Centre (Kantor Bibliografi Nasional) deposit library; Librarian Drs SOEKARMAN; publs *Berita Bulanan* (Monthly Bulletin), *Regional Bibliography of Social Sciences, Publications—Indonesia, Checklist of Serials in the Libraries of Indonesia*.

Perpustakaan Bagian Pathologi Klinik R. S. Dr Tjipto Mangunkusumo (Dr Tjipto Mangunkusumo Hospital Library): Jl. Diponegoro 69, Jakarta; 3,000 vols; medicine, public health; Dir Prof. Dr JEANNE LATU.

Perpustakaan Dewan Perwakilan Rakyat Republik Indonesia (Library of Indonesian Parliament): Jl. Jenderal Gatot Subroto, Jakarta 10270; tel. 5715220; fax 584804; f. 1946; 200,000 vols; Librarian Mrs ROEMNINGSIH.

Perpustakaan Nasional (National Library of Indonesia): Jl. Salemba Raya 28, POB 3624, Jakarta 10002; tel. 3101411; f. 1980 by a merger of four libraries; depository library of Indonesia; *c.* 750,000 vols; special collections: Indonesian newspapers since 1810, Indonesian periodicals since 1779, Indonesian maps since 17th century, Indonesian dissertations, Indonesian monographs since 17th century; Dir Ms MASTINI HARDJO PRAKOSO; publs *Bibliografi Nasional Indonesia* (quarterly), *Indexs artikel suratkabar* (Press Index, quarterly), *subject bibliographies, catalogues*, etc.

Pusat Dokumentasi dan Informasi Ilmiah – Lembaga Ilmu Pengetahuan Indonesia (PDII-LIPI) (Centre for Scientific Documentation and Information of the Indonesian Institute of Sciences): Jl. Jendral Gatot Subroto 10, POB 4298, Jakarta 12042; tel. (21) 5733465; fax (21) 5733467; e-mail admin@pdii.lipi.go.id; internet www.pdii.lipi.go.id; f. 1965; 58,552 books, 4,783 periodicals, 14,022 theses and dissertations, 75,000 microforms, 40,000 research reports, 11,679 patents; Head Dra JUSNI DJATIN; publs *Baca* (Read, 3 a year), *Directory of Special Libraries and Information Sources in Indonesia* (irregular), *Index of Indonesian Learned Periodicals, Abstract of Research and Survey Reports* (irregular), *Index to Papers Submitted to Seminars* (irregular), *Daftar Terbitan Berkala Indonesia yang Telah Mempunyai ISSN* (Indonesian Serials with ISSN, irregular), *Union Catalog of Serials* (irregular), *FOKUS* (issues covering 17 subjects, every 2 months).

UPT Perpustakaan dan Dokumentasi, Biro Pusat Statistik (Library and Statistical Documentation, Central Bureau of Statistics): POB 1003, Jl. Dr Sutomo 8, Jakarta; tel. (21) 3810291; fax (21) 3857046; 60,000 vols; Librarian DAME MUNTHE.

Ujung Pandang

Hasanuddin University Library: Kampus UNHAS Tamalanrea, Jl. Perintis Kemerdekaan km 10, Ujung Pandang 90245; tel. (411) 512026; fax (411) 510088; f. 1956; open to public; 122,000 vols, 3,821 periodicals, 23,421 dissertations and theses; Head Dra ROSDIANI RACHIM; publs *Warta Perpustakan*, *Iaporan Tahunan*, *Info Pustaka*.

Perpustakaan Umum Makassar (Makassar Public Library): Jl. Madukelleng 3, POB 16, Ujungpandang 90112; f. 1969; organizes lending library services in brs throughout South Sulawesi Province; film and music programmes; foreign language courses; children's library services; exhibitions and talks; 42,000 vols; Dir (vacant).

Yogyakarta

Perpustakaan Islam (Islamic Library): C/o Ministry of Religious Affairs, Jl. Lapangan Banteng Barat 3–4, Jakarta Pusat; located at: Jl. P. Mangkubumi 38, Yogyakarta; f. 1942; under the Ministry of Religious Affairs; 70,000 vols; MSS and periodicals; Dir Drs H. ASYHURI DAHLAN; Librarian MOH. AMIEN MANSOER.

Perpustakaan Jajasan Hatta (Hatta Foundation Library): Malioboro 85, Yogyakarta; 43,000 vols; Librarian R. SOEDJATMIKO.

Perpustakaan Wilayah (Regional Library): Malioboro 175, Yogyakarta; f. 1949; 120,000 vols; Librarian ST. KOSTKA SOEGENG.

Museums and Art Galleries

Denpasar

Museum Bali: Jl. Letnan Kolonel Wisnu 1, Denpasar, Bali; f. 1932; exhibits of Bali culture; library of 1,970 vols, 1,605 magazines, 1,023 transcriptions of lontars (palm leaves); Dir Drs PUTU BUDIASTRA; publs *Majalah Saraswati, Karya Widia tak berkala, reports*, etc.

Jakarta

Museum Nasional (National Museum): Jl. Merdeka Barat 12, Jakarta Pusat; tel. 360796; f. 1778, formerly Museum Pusat; library of 360,000 vols (now part of National Library); departments of ceramics, ethnography, pre-history, classical archaeology, anthropology, manuscripts and education; Dir Drs BAMBANG SUMADIO; publs subject catalogues.

State Universities

UNIVERSITAS AIRLANGGA

Jl. Mulorejo, Kampus C, Surabaya 60115
Telephone: (31) 5914042
Fax: (31) 5981841
E-mail: bapsi@unair.ac.id
Internet: www.unair.ac.id

Founded 1954
Language of instruction: Indonesian
Academic year: September to August

Rector: Prof. Dr Dr PURUHITO
Vice-Rector for Academic Affairs: Prof. Dr H. FASICH
Vice-Rector for General Administration: Drs EDY JUWONO SLAMET
Vice-Rector for Student Affairs: Drs SUKO HARDONO
Chief, Bureau for General Academic Administration and Student Affairs: Dr ZAINAL ARIFIN
Chief, Bureau for General Administration: Dra Hj. SUNARTI
Chief, Bureau for Planning Administration and Information Systems: ROSMELYANI
Librarian: RR. RATNANINGSIH

Number of teachers: 1,434
Number of students: 20,719

Publications: *Majalah Kedokteran Tropis Indonesia* (4 a year), *Majalah Kedokteran Surabaya* (4 a year), *Majalah Kedokteran Gigi* (4 a year), *Yuridika* (4 a year), *Majalah Masyarakat Kebudayaan Politik* (4 a year), *Folia Medika Indonesiana* (4 a year), *Majalah Kesehatan Masyarakat* (4 a year), *Surabaya Journal of Surgery* (4 a year), *Buletin Toraks Kardiovaskular Indonesia* (4 a year)

DEANS

Faculty of Dentistry: Prof. Dr Drg. MOHAMAD RUBIANTO
Faculty of Economics: Drs KARJADI MINTAROEM
Faculty of Law: H. MACHSOEN ALI
Faculty of Letters: Prof. HERU SUPRIYADI
Faculty of Mathematics and Natural Sciences: Drs H. ABDUL LATIEF BURHAN
Faculty of Medicine: Prof. Dr Dr H. M. S. WIYADI
Faculty of Pharmacy: Prof. Dr NOOR CHOLIES ZAINI
Faculty of Psychology: Prof. Dr H. M. ZAINUDIN
Faculty of Public Health: Dr Dr TJIPTO SUWANDI
Faculty of Social and Political Sciences: Dr Drs HOTMAN SIAHAAN
Faculty of Veterinary Medicine: Dr Drh. ISMUDIONO
Postgraduate Programmes: Prof. Dr Dr H. MUHAMMAD AMIN

ATTACHED INSTITUTES

Research Institute for Public Services: Dir Prof. Dr H. SARMANU.

Tropical Disease Centre: Dir Prof. Dr YOES PRIJATNA DACHLAN.

UNIVERSITAS ANDALAS

Kampus Limau Manis, Padang, 25163 West Sumatra
Telephone: (751) 71389
Fax: (751) 71085
E-mail: rektorat@unand.ac.id
Internet: unand.ac.id

Founded 1956
Language of instruction: Indonesian
Academic year: September to June

Rector: MARLIS RAHMAN
Vice-Rector for Academic Affairs: AMIRMUSLIM MALIK
Vice-Rector for Administration and Finance: DJASWIR ZEIN
Vice-Rector for Student Affairs: FIRMAN HASAN
Head Librarian: MARAMIS

Number of teachers: 1,396
Number of students: 13,009

Publications: *Jurnal Penelitian Andalas*, *Warta Pengabdian Andalas*, *Jurnal Pembangunan dan Perubahan Sosial Budaya*, *Jurnal Ekonomi Manajemen*, *Jurnal Peternakan dan Lingkungan*, *Jurnal Matematika dan Ilmu Pengetahuan Alam*, *Jurnal Teknologi Pertanian* (Journal of Agricultural Technology), *Potetika*, *Teknika*, *Justisia*, *Andalas Medical Journal*, *Jurnal Antropologi*, *Lingua: Jurnal Bahasa dan Sastra*

DEANS

Faculty of Law and Social Science: AZHAR RAUF
Faculty of Medicine: RUSDAN DJAMIL
Faculty of Mathematics and Natural Sciences: HAZLI NURDIN
Faculty of Agriculture: BUJANG RUSMAN
Faculty of Animal Husbandry: AZINAR KAMARUDDIN
Faculty of Economics: SJAFRIZAL
Faculty of Arts: SYAFRUDDIN SULAIMAN
Faculty of Engineering: DAHNIL ZAINUDDIN
Faculty of Political and Social Sciences: DAHRUL DAHLAN
Polytechnic of Engineering: ALIZAR HASAN
Polytechnic of Agriculture: MASRUL JALAL

ATTACHED INSTITUTES

Research Centre: Dir DAYAR ARBAIN.

Social Research Centre: Dir MUSLIAR KASIM.

Institute for Regional Economic Research: Dir FIRMAN TAN.

Institute for Management: Dir YOHANES KHATIB.

Institute for Demography: Dir SYAHRUDDIN.

Sumatra Nature Study: Dir ANAS SALSABILA.

Environmental Study: Dir ARDINIS ARBAIN.

Women's Studies: Dir SYARIDAL DAHLAN.

Irrigation Study: Dir SJOFJAN ASNAWI.

Forestry Study: Dir ANWAR KASIM.

Environmental Law Study: Dir ARDINIS ARBAIN.

Centre for Manpower Research: Dir AZHAR MAKMUR.

Centre for Human Resources Research: Dir ROSDIWATI.

INSTITUT TEKNOLOGI BANDUNG (Bandung Institute of Technology)

Jl. Tamansari 64, Bandung 40132
Telephone: (22) 2503147
Fax: (22) 431792
E-mail: webmaster@itb.ac.id
Internet: www.itb.ac.id

Founded 1920, present form 1959 as a merger of the faculties of mathematics, natural sciences and engineering of the University of Indonesia
State control
Language of instruction: Indonesian
Academic year: August to July

Rector: Prof. Dr Ir LILIK HENDRAJAYA
Vice-Rector for Academic Affairs: Dr Ir. ADANG SURAHMAN
Vice-Rector for General Administration: Prof. Dr Ir DJOKO SANTOSO
Vice-Rector for Development, Planning, Administration and Information Systems: Dr Ir RIZAL ZAINUDDIN TAMIN
Librarian: Dr Ir ROBERT MANURUNG

Number of teachers: 1,263
Number of students: 15,031

Publications: *Journal of Mathematics and Science* (2 a year), *Maalah Ilmiah Himpunan Matematika Indonesia* (2 a year), *Kontribusi Fisika* (4 a year), *Akta Farmasetika Indonesia* (12 a year), *Jurnal Teknologi Mineral* (3 a year), *Buletin Geologi* (3 a year), *Majalah Mesin* (3 a year), *Majalah Ilmiah Teknik Electro* (3 a year), *Jurnal Teknik dan Manajemen Industri* (3 a year), *Jurnal Teknik Sipil* (4 a year), *Geodesi dan Surveying* (2 a year), *Jurnal Atap* (annually), *Jurnal Teknik Lingkungan* (2 a year), *Journal Pusat Pengembangan Perencanaan Wilayah Kota* (annually)

DEANS

Faculty of Mathematics and Natural Sciences: Dr Ing. CYNTHIA LINAYA RADIMAN
Faculty of Civil Engineering and Planning: Prof. Dr Ir TOMMY FIRMAN
Faculty of Industrial Technology: Prof. Dr Ir DJOKO SUJARTO
Faculty of Mineral Technology: Prof. Dr Ir MADE EMMY RELAWAT
Faculty of Fine Arts and Design: Drs SETIAWAN SABANA
School of Business and Management: Prof. Dr SURNA TJAHJA DJAJADININGRAT
Graduate Program: Prof. Dr Ir. SOELARSO (Dir)

PROFESSORS

ACHMAD, S. A., Chemistry
AGOES, G., Pharmacy
ALGAMAR, K., Environmental Engineering
ANSJAR, M., Mathematics
ARIFIN, A., Mathematics
ARISMUNANDAR, W., Mechanical Engineering
ASIKIN, S., Geology
BAGIASNA, K., Mechanical Engineering
BARMAWI, M., Physics
SJAFRUDDIN, A., Civil Engineering
BINTORO, S. B., City Planning
BRODJONEGRO, S. S., Mechanical Engineering
BROTOSISWOJO, B. S., Physics
CHATIB, B., Environmental Engineering
SUDRADJAT, I., Architecture
DHANUTIRTO, H., Pharmacy
DIRAN, O., Mechanical Engineering
DJAJADININGRAT, A. H., Environmental Engineering
DJAJADININGRAT, S. T., Industrial Engineering
DJAJAPUTRA, A. A., Civil Engineering
DJAJASUGITA, F. A., Electrical Engineering
DJALARI, Y. A., Design
DJAUHARI, M. A., Mathematics
DJOJODIHARDJO, H., Mechanical Engineering
FIRMAN, K., Pharmacy
FIRMAN, T., City Planning
GANI, A. Z., Industrial Engineering
GDE RAKA, I. D., Industrial Engineering
HANDOJO, A., Engineering Physics
HARAHAP, F., Mechanical Engineering
HARJOSUPARTO, S., Chemical Engineering
HARLANDJA, B., Civil Engineering
HAROEN, Y., Electrical Engineering
HARSOKOESOEMO, D., Mechanical Engineering
HENDRADJAYA, L., Physics
HIDAYAT, B., Astronomy
JENJIE, S. D., Mechanical Engineering
KAHAR, J., Geodesy
KAMIL, S., Mechanical Engineering
KANA, J. C., Petroleum Engineering
KARSA, K., Electrical Engineering
KOESOEMADINATA, R. P., Geology
KUSBIANTORO, City Planning

LIANG, O. B., Chemistry
LIONG, T. H., Physics
MANGUNWIJAYA, A., Mining Engineering
MARDIHARTANTO, F. X., Industrial Engineering
MARDISEWOJO, P., Petroleum Engineering
MARTODJOJO, S., Geology
MARTOJO, W., Mining Engineering
MERATI, I. G. W., Civil Engineering
MIRA, S., Geodesy
NABANAN, S. M., Mathematics
ON, T. M., Physics
PADMAWINATA, K., Pharmacy
PIROUS, A. D., Design
PRINGGOPRAWIRO, H., Geology
PRINGGOPRAWIRO, M., Physics
PRODJOSOEMARTO, P., Mining Engineering
PULUNGGONO, A., Geology
RAHAYU, S. I., Chemistry
RAIS, J., Geodesy
RELAWATYI, S. E., Geology
RIDWAN, A. S., Civil Engineering
SAMADIKUN, S., Electrical Engineering
SAMPURNO, Geology
SANTOSO, D., Geophysics
SAPIIE, S., Electrical Engineering
SASMOJO, S., Chemical Engineering
SASTRAMIHARDJA, I., Chemical Engineering
SASTRODIHARDJO, S., Biology
SATIADARMA, K., Pharmacy
SEMBIRING, R. K., Mathematics
SILABAN, P., Physics
SIRAIT, K. T., Electrical Engineering
SIREGAR, C., Pharmacy
SIREGAR, H. P. S., Petroleum Engineering
SISWOSUWARNO, M., Mechanical Engineering
SJUIB, F., Pharmacy
SLAMET, J. S., Environmental Engineering
SOEDIRO, I., Pharmacy
SOEDJITO, B. B., City Planning
SOEGIJANTO, R. M., Engineering Physics
SOEGIJOKO, S., Electrical Engineering
SOELARSO, Mechanical Engineering
SOEMARTO, S., Environmental Engineering
SOEMINTAPOERA, K., Electrical Engineering
SOEMODINOTO, W., Mining Engineering
SOENARKO, B., Engineering Physics
SOEPANGKAT, H. P., Physics
SOERIA-ATMADJA, R., Geology
SOERIAATMADJA, R. E., Biology
SUDARWATI, S., Biology
SUDIRMAN, I., Industrial Engineering
SUHARTO, D., Mechanical Engineering
SUHUD, R., Civil Engineering
SUJARTO, D., City Planning
SUKARMADIJAYA, H., Environmental Engineering
SULE, D., Mining Engineering
SUMAWIGANDA, S., Civil Engineering
SURAATMADJA, D., Civil Engineering
SURDIA, N. M., Chemistry
SURDIA, T., Metallurgical Engineering
SUTJIATMO, B., Mechanical Engineering
SUWONO, A., Mechanical Engineering
TABRANI, P., Design
TAROEPRATJEKA, H., Industrial Engineering
TJAHJATI, S. B., City Planning
TOHA, I. S., Industrial Engineering
TUAH, H., Civil Engineering
UMAR, F., Mining Engineering
WANGSADINATA, W., Civil Engineering
WARDIMAN, A., Engineering Physics
WIDAGDO, Design
WIDODO, R. J., Electrical Engineering
WIRASONJAYA, S., Architecture
WIRJOMARTONO, S. H., Mechanical Engineering
WIRJOSUMARTO, H., Mechanical Engineering
WISJNUPRAPTO, Environmental Engineering
WAWOROENTOE, W. J., City Planning
ZAINUDDIN, I. M., Design
ZEN, M. T., Geology

UNIVERSITAS BENGKULU

Jl. Raya Kandang Limun, Bengkulu
Telephone: (736) 32105
Internet: himita.freehomepage.com
Founded 1982
Rector: Dr Ir SOEKOTJO
Chief Administrative Officer: SYAIFUL AKHMAD
Librarian: Mrs ROSDIANAH ASSAUDI
Library of 20,600 vols
Number of teachers: 444
Number of students: 3,320

DEANS

Faculty of Agriculture: TOEKIDJO MARTOREJO
Faculty of Economics: ILYAS YAKUB
Faculty of Social Sciences: HASNUL BASRI
Faculty of Law: HIDJAZIE K.
Faculty of Education: AZNAM YATIM

INSTITUT PERTANIAN BOGOR
(Bogor Agricultural University)

Jl. Lingkar Akademik, Kampus IPB Darmaga, Bogor
Telephone: (251) 622642
Fax: (251) 622708
Internet: www.ipb.ac.id
Founded 1963
State control
Languages of instruction: Indonesian, and English for foreign visiting professors
Academic year: September to June (two semesters)
Rector: Prof. Dr H.R.M. AMAN WIRAKARTAKUSUMAH
Vice-Rector (Academic Affairs): Prof. Dr A. A. MATTJIK
Vice-Rector (Administration): Ir DARWIN KADARISMAN
Vice-Rector (Student Affairs): Prof. Dr SUPIANDI SABIHAM
Vice-Rector (Co-operative Affairs): Dr DARNAS DANA
Registrar: Dr SETYO PERTIWI
Administrator: Ir UDIN M. WAHJUDIN
Librarian: Ir ABDUL R. SALEH
Number of teachers: 1,327
Number of students: 19,440
Publications: *Indonesian Journal of Tropical Agriculture, Jurnal Ilmu Pertanian Indonesian, Forum Pasca Sarjana, Media Peternakan, Media Veteriner, Communication Agriculture, Buletin Hama dan Penyakit Tumbuhan, Gema Penelitian, Buletin Ilmu Tanah, Media Konservasi, Teknologi, Jurnal Primatologi, Feed and Nutrition Journal*

DEANS

Faculty of Agriculture: Prof. Dr M. CHOSIN
Faculty of Veterinary Medicine: Dr F. H. PASARIBU
Faculty of Animal Science: Prof. Dr H. SOEDARMADI
Faculty of Forestry: Prof. Dr YUSUF SUDOHADI
Faculty of Fisheries and Marine Science: Dr E. HARIS
Faculty of Agricultural Technology: Prof. Dr M. BAMBANG PRAMUDYA NOORACHMAT
Faculty of Mathematics and Natural Sciences: Dr SISWADI
Faculty of Economics and Management: Prof. Dr BUNASOR SANIM

ATTACHED INSTITUTES AND CENTRES

Research Institute: Chair. Dr AUNUDIN.

Constituent centres:

Environmental Studies Centre.
Engineering Applications in Tropical Agriculture Research Centre.
Tropical Biology Studies Centre.
Tropical Biodiversity Studies Centre.
Primates Studies Centre.
Food and Nutrition Policy Studies Centre.
Women's Studies Centre.
Development Studies Centre.
Tropical Fruits Studies Centre.
Marine Commodities Studies Centre.
Coastal and Marine Resources Studies Centre.
Traditional Food Studies Centre.

Postgraduate School: Dir Prof. Dr SJAFRIDA MANUWOTO.

Institute for Community Service: Dir Prof. Dr RIZAL SYARIEF.

Institute for Information Resources: Dir Dr KHAIRIL ANWAR NOTODIPUTRO.

Institute for the Assessment and Development of Education: Dir Dr SUDARMAN YAHYA.

Centre for Food and Nutrition: Dir Dr ADIL BASUKI AHZA.

Centre for Life Sciences: Dir Prof. Dr DODI NANDIKA.

Centre for Biotechnology: Dir Dr A. MACHMUD THOHARI.

UNIVERSITAS BRAWIJAYA

Jl. Veteran, Malang, Jawa Timur 65145
Telephone: (341) 575777
Fax: (341) 565420
E-mail: rektorat@brawijaya.ac.id
Internet: www.brawijaya.ac.id
Founded 1963
State control
Language of instruction: Indonesian
Academic year: September to August
Rector: Prof. Dr Ir BAMBANG GOERITNO
Vice-Rectors: Prof. Dr Ir YOGI SUGITO, Prof. Dr MUNIR, Drs TJAHJANULIN DOMAI, Prof. Dr UMAR NIMRAN
Head of General Administration Bureau: GOERID HARDJITO
Head of Planning and Information System Bureau: Dra Hj. SITI ROMLAH
Head of Student and Academic Administration Bureau: Dra Haja SITI ROMLAH
Librarian: Dra WELMIN SUNYI ARININGSIH
Number of teachers: 1,271
Number of students: 28,105
Publications: *Administrator* (monthly), *Agrivita* (monthly), *Agrotek* (4 a year), *Aqua* (4 a year), *Arena Hukum* (monthly), *Buletin* (monthly), *Canopy* (monthly), *Dian* (monthly), *Diagnostika* (annually), *Febra* (monthly), *Habitat* (3 a year), *Indicus* (monthly), *Indikator* (monthly), *Jurnal* (2 a year), *Jurnal Administrasi Bisnis* (2 a year), *Jurnal Administrasi Negara* (2 a year), *Jurnal Ilmu Peternakan* (2 a year), *Jurnal Penelitian Ilmu – Ilmu Hayati* (2 a year), *Jurnal Penelitian Ilmu – Ilmu Sosial* (2 a year), *Jurnal Penelitian Ilmu–Ilmu Teknik* (2 a year), *Jurnal Teknik* (3 a year), *Jurnal Teknologi Pertanian* (2 a year), *Lintasan Ekonomi* (2 a year), *Mafaterna* (2 a year), *Majalah Kedokteran Universitas Brawijaya* (3 a year), *Manifest* (2 a year), *Media Karya Ilmiah* (2 a year), *Mimbar Universitas Brawijaya* (6 a year), *Mitra Akademika* (2 a year), *Natural Jurnal* (2 a year), *Prasetya* (48 a year), *Solid* (2 a year), *Techno* (2 a year), *Wartamina* (6 a year)

DEANS

Faculty of Administrative Sciences: Dr SUHADAK
Faculty of Agricultural Technology: Prof. Dr Ir. SIMON BAMBANG WIDJANARKO
Faculty of Agriculture: Prof. Dr Ir. SYEKHFANI

Faculty of Animal Husbandry: Prof. Dr Ir. IFAR SUBAGIYO
Faculty of Economics: Prof. Dr BAMBANG SUBROTO
Faculty of Engineering: Ir. IMAM ZAKY
Faculty of Fishery: Ir. SUKOSO
Faculty of Law: WARKUM SUMITRO
Faculty of Medicine: Dr HARIJANTO
Faculty of Natural Science and Mathematics: Ir. ADAM WIRYAWAN
Polytechnic: Ir. BUDI TJAHJONO
Postgraduate Studies Programme: Prof. Dr Dr DJANGGAN SARGOWO

PROFESSORS

ACHMAD, H., Medicine
ACHMADY, Z. A., Administration
ACHMANU, Animal Husbandry
ALHABSJI, T., Administration
ALI, M. M., Medicine
ARIFFIN, Aeroclimatology
ASHARI, M. S., Agriculture
ASTUTI, M. S., Law
BAISOENI, H., Mathematics
CHUZAEMI, S., Animal Husbandry
FADJAR, A. M., Law
FANANI, Z., Animal Husbandry
FAUZI, A., Administration
GINTING, E., Animal Husbandry
GURITNO, B., Agriculture
HADIASTONO, T., Agriculture
HAIRIAH, K., Agriculture
HAKIM, L., Animal Husbandry
HANDAYANTO, E., Agriculture
HARIJONO, Agricultural Technology
HARSONO, O. S. H., Economics
HIDAYAT, A., Medicine
HIDAYAT, M., Medicine
ICHSAN, M., Administration
IDRUS, M. S., Economics
ISLAMY, M. I., Administration
ISMANI, Administration
KALIM, H., Medicine
KIPTIYAH, S. M., Economics
KOENTJOKO, Animal Husbandry
KUMALANINGSIH, S., Agricultural Technology
LOEKITO, R. M., Medicine
LUTH, T., Law
MARTAWIJAYA, S., Economic Development
MIMBAR, S. M., Agriculture
MISMAIL, B., Electrical Engineering
MOELJADI, H., Economics
MOENANDIR, J., Agriculture
MUNIR, M., Agriculture
MUNIR, M., Law
MUSTADJAB, M. M., Agriculture
NIMRAN, U., Administration
NUGROHO, W. H., Mathematics
PURNOMO, H., Animal Husbandry
RASYID, Y., Agriculture
RUBAI, M., Law
SALEH, M., Economics
SARGOWO, D., Medicine
SASTRAHIDAYAT, I. R., Agriculture
SEMAOEN, M. I., Agriculture
SITOMPUL, S. M., Agriculture
SJAMSUDDIN, S., Administration
SODIKI, A., Law
SOEBAKTININGSIH, Medicine
SOEBARINOTO, Animal Husbandry
SOEHONO, L. A., Mathematics
SOEKARTAWI, Agriculture
SOEMARNO, Agriculture
SOEPARMAN, S., Engineering
SOEPRAPTO, R., Administration
SOETANTO, H., Animal Husbandry
SOEWARTO, S., Medicine
SUBROTO, B., Accounting
SUGIJANTO, Agriculture
SUHARDJONO, Research Methodology
SUDARMA, M. S., Accounting
SUGITO, Y., Agriculture
SUHARTO, B., Agricultural Technology
SUKESI, K., Agriculture
SULISTYOWATI, L., Agriculture
SUMITRO, S. B., Agricultural Technology
SUNUHARYO, B. S., Administration
SUPRIYANTO, E., Fisheries
SUSANTO, M. H., Economics
SUSANTO, T., Agricultural Technology
SYAFRADJI, M. S., Economics
SYAMSIDI, S. R. C., Agriculture
SYAMSULBAHRI, Agriculture
SYEKHFANI, Agriculture
THANTAWI, Economics
TRIADJI, B., Economics
TRISUNUWATI, P., Epidemiology
TROENA, E. A., Economics
UTOMO, W. H., Agriculture
WAHAB, S. A., Administration
WARDANA, N. G., Engineering
WARDIYATI, T., Agriculture
WIDJANARKO, S. B., Agricultural Technology
WIDODO, M. A., Medicine
ZAIN, D., Economics

UNIVERSITAS CENDERAWASIH

Jl. Kamp Wolker, Kampus UNCEN Waena, Jayapura, Papua 99358
Telephone: (967) 572108
Fax: (967) 572102
E-mail: uncen@uncen.ac.id
Internet: www.uncen.ac.id

Founded 1962
Language of instruction: Indonesian
Academic year: September to July

Rector: Ir FRANS A. WOSPAKRIK
Vice-Rectors: Drs ISAAK AJOMI, Drs DAAN DIMARA, Ir ROBERT LALENOH
General Administration Officer: Ir H. SUMANTO
Academic and Student Administration Officer: Drs M. HATTU
Librarian: Drs A. C. SUNGKANA HADI

Library of 56,000 vols
Number of teachers: 519
Number of students: 6,789

Publications: *Bulletin of Irian Jaya Development*, *Tifa Agro*

Faculties of law, social and political sciences, education and teacher training, economics, mathematics, natural sciences, agriculture, civil engineering.

UNIVERSITAS DIPONEGORO

Jl. Prof. Sudarto, Tembalang, Semarang 1269, Central Java
Telephone: (24) 7460012
Fax: (24) 7460013
E-mail: prlundip@indosat.net.id
Internet: www.undip.ac.id

Founded 1956
Academic year: September to August

Rector: Prof. Ir. EKO BUDIHARDJ
Vice-Rector (Academic Affairs): Prof. Dr S. P. HADI
Vice-Rector (Administration and Finance): Prof. Dr Ir. Y. S. DARMANTO
Vice-Rector (Development and Co-operation): Dr Dr SUSILO WIBOWO
Vice-Rector (Student Affairs): Dr Ir. BAMBANG TRIONO BASUKI
Head of Administration and Academic Bureau: Drs PRIYO SANTOSO
Head of General Administration Bureau: Dra KUSRINI
Head of Planning Administration and Information Systems Bureau: Dra ISMARTINI
Head of Student Administration Bureau: Dra PRANTIKASIH
University Librarian: Dra ARI WIDJAYANTI

Library of 191,224 vols
Number of teachers: 1,618
Number of students: 38,522

Publications: *Manunggal*, *UNDIP Newsletter*, *Forum*, *Berita Penelitian*, *Teknis*, *Media*, *Info*, *Media Ekonomi & Bisnis*, *Masalah-Masalah Hukum*, *Masalah Teknik*, *Buletin Fekom*, *Berita UNDIP*, *Transient*, *Opini*, *Gema Teknologi*, *Bhakti*, *Cakrawala*, *Prasasti*, *Pulsa*, *Publica*, *Mahaprika*, *Nuansa*, *Konsolidasi*, *Kinetika*, *Gallery*, *Respect*, *Zigma*, *Gema*, *Majalah*, *Ilmiah Politeknik*, *Gema Keadilan*, *Edent*, *Majalah Kedokteran*, *Bulletin Fakultas Peternakan & Perikanan*, *Lembaran Imu Sastra*, *Hayam Wuruk*, *Warta Perpustakaan*, *Bulletin Dharma Wanita*

DEANS

Faculty of Animal Husbandry: Dr Ir. BAMBANG SRIGANDONO
Faculty of Economics: Dr H. M. CHABACHIB
Faculty of Engineering: Prof. Ir. EKO WAHYUNI
Faculty of Fisheries and Marine Science: Prof. Dr Ir. YOHANES HUTALIRAT
Faculty of Law: ACHMAD BUSRO
Faculty of Letters: Prof. Dr RAHAYU PRIHATMI
Faculty of Mathematics and Natural Sciences: Dr Drs WALIYU SETIA RUDI
Faculty of Medicine: Prof. Dr KABULRACHMAN
Faculty of Public Health: Dr LUDFI SANTOSO
Faculty of Social and Political Sciences: Drs WARSITO

DIRECTORS

Community Service Institute: Drs SUWARSO
Education Development Institute: Drs YUSMILARSO
Research Institute: Prof. Dr dr I. RIWANTO

PROFESSORS

ANGGORO, S., Aquatic Biology
ATMOMARSONO, U., Animal Science
BUDIHARDJO, E., Architecture
BUDI PRAYITNO, S., Aquaculture
DARMANTO, Y. S., Fisheries Resources
DARMONO, S., Nutrition
DJOKO MOELJANTO, S., Internal Medicine
DJULIATI SUROYO, A. M., Social and Economic History
FAIK HEYDER, A., Surgery
FATIMA MUIS, S., Nutrition
GHOZALI, I., Methodology
HADIHARDAJA, J., Steel Construction
HADISAPUTRO, S., Public Health
HARRY KISTANO, N., Letters
HARTONO, B., Neurology
HARTONO, S. R., Commercial Law
HUTABARAT, S., Oceanography
HUTABARAT, Y., Aquatic Culture
KABULRACHMAN, Dermatovenerology
KARYANA, S., Traditional Javanese Culture
KELIB, A., Islamic Law
KRISTIANTI, L., Paediatrics
MANGUNWIHARDJO, S., Financial Management
MIYASTO, Economics
MULADI, H., Criminal Law
MUSTAFID, Mathematics
NAWAWI ARIEF, B., Criminal Law
NASUTION, I., Pharmacology and Theraputics
NOTOATMOJO, H., Paediatrics
PARSUDI ABDULROCHIM, I., Internal Medicine
P. HADI, S., Environmental Studies
PRAMONO, N., Obstetrics and Gynaecology
PRAPTOHARDJO, U., Gynaecology and Obstetrics
PRIHATMI, M. S. R., Literature
RACHMATULLAH, P., Physiology
RAHAYU PRIHATMI, S., Literature
REDJEKI, H. S., Law
RIWANTO, Surgery
SARJADI, H., Anatomy, Pathology
SATOTO, Nutrition
SERIKAT PUTRAJAYA, N., Criminal Law
SOEBOWO, Anatomy, Pathology
SOEDARSONO, Animal Production
SOEDJARWO, Indonesian Literature
SOEDJATI, Linguistics
SOEJOENOES, A., Obstetrics and Gynaecology
SOEMANTRI, A., Paediatrics, Haematology

SOENARTO, S., Internal Medicine
SOETOMO, I., Linguistics
SOETOMO, S., Planology
S. TRASTOTENOJO, M., Paediatrics
SUDARYONO, Linguistics
SUDIGBIA, Paediatrics
SUGANGGA, Proscriptive Law
SULTANA, A., Histology
SUNARTI, D., Animal Production
SUNARJO, S., Anaesthiology
SUPRIHARYONO, A., Fishery
SUSANTO, I. S., Criminal Law
SUTRISNO, I., Animal Husbandry
SURYANTO, B., Agribusiness Management
SYA'RANI, L., Fishery
WARELLA, Y., Sociology and Politics
WARASIH, E., Law and Society
WIBOWO, S., Andrology
WILARDJO, S., Ophthalmology

ATTACHED INSTITUTES

Citizenship and Ethical Course Unit: Chair. JOKO WASISTO.

Computer Center and Data Processing: Chair. Drs DJALAL ER RIYANTO.

English Service Unit: Chair. Drs SUNARWOTO.

Entrepreneurship Unit: Chair. Drs WAHYU HIDAYAT.

UNIVERSITAS GADJAH MADA

Bulaksumur, Yogyakarta 55281

Telephone: (274) 562011
Fax: (274) 565223
E-mail: rektor@ugm.ac.id
Internet: www.ugm.ac.id

Founded 1949
Language of instruction: Indonesian
Academic year: September to June

Rector: Prof. Dr SOFIAN EFFENDI
Vice-Rector for Education and Quality Control: Prof. Dr Ir. SUDJARWADI
Vice-Rector for Research and Community Services: Prof. Dr Dra. RETNO SUNARMININGSIH
Vice-Rector for Administration and Human Resources: Dr GOEDONO
Vice-Rector for Students and Alumni: Prof. Dr Ir. ZAENAL BACHARUDDIN
Vice-Rector for Co-operation and Business Development: Prof. Dr AGUS DWIYANTO

Number of teachers: 2,277
Number of students: 45,787

Publications: *Biologi* (biology, 2 a year), *Majalah Farmasi Indonesia* (pharmacy, 4 a year), *Indonesian Journal of Geography* (2 a year), *Majalah Geografi Indonesia* (geography, 2 a year), *Berkala Ilmu Kedokteran* (medicine, 4 a year), *Berita Kedokteran Masyarakat* (medicine, 4 a year), *Buletin Kehutanan* (forestry, 4 a year), *Berkala Ilmiah MIPA* (mathematics and natural sciences, 2 a year), *Jurnal Fisika Indonesia* (mathematics and natural sciences, 4 a year), *Buletin Peternakan* (animal husbandry, 4 a year), *Humaniora* (humanities, 4 a year), *Media Teknik* (engineering, 4 a year), *Forum Teknik* (engineering, 3 a year), *Agritech* (agricultural technology, 4 a year), *Perlindungan Tanaman Indonesia* (agricultural technology, 2 a year), *Indonesian Food and Nutrition Progress* (2 a year), *Warta Pengabdian* (community service, 3 a year), *Manusia dan Lingkungan* (environmental studies, 3 a year)

DEANS

Faculty of Agriculture: Dr Ir. SUSAMTO SOMOWIYARJO
Faculty of Agricultural Technology: Prof. Dr Ir. KAPTI RAYAHU KUSWANTO
Faculty of Animal Science: Prof. Dr Ir. ZAENAL BACHRUDDIN
Faculty of Biology: Prof. Dr SUKARTI MOELJOPAWIRO
Faculty of Cultural Sciences: Prof. Dr TIMBUL HARYONO
Faculty of Dentistry: Dr Drg. SUDIBYO
Faculty of Economics: Prof. Dr ZAKI BARIDWAN
Faculty of Engineering: Dr Ir. INDARTO
Faculty of Forestry: Dr Ir. SOFYAN PARTIDJO WARSITO
Faculty of Geography: Prof. Dr SUDARMADJI
Faculty of Law: Dr MOHAMMAD BURHANTSANI
Faculty of Mathematics and Natural Sciences: Prof. Dr Drs. SUBANAR
Faculty of Medicine: Prof. Dr HARDYANTO
Faculty of Pharmacy: Prof. Dr IBNU GHOLIB GANJAR
Faculty of Philosophy: Prof. Dr R. SOEJADI
Faculty of Psychology: Drs SAIFUDIN AZWAR
Faculty of Social and Political Sciences: Prof. Dr SUNYOTO USMAN
Faculty of Veterinary Medicine: Prof. Drh. R. WASITO
Graduate Programmes: Prof. Dr MULYADI (Dir)

ATTACHED RESEARCH INSTITUTES

Research Institute: Chairman Dr Ir ABDUL ROZAQ.

Agroindustrial Study Centre: Head Prof. Dr SOEMANTRI.

Asia Pacific Study Centre: Head Prof. Dr DIBYO PRABOWO.

Biological Control Study Centre: Head Prof. Dr Ir SEBASTIAN MARGINO.

Biotechnology Study Centre: Head Prof. Dr ABDUL SALAM MUDZAKIR S.

Clinical Pharmacology and Drugs Study Centre: Head Dr Dra SURYAWATI.

Cultural Study Centre: Head Dr FARUK.

Diasaster Study Centre: Head Prof. Dr H. SUTIKNO.

Economics and Public Policy Study Centre: Head Dr CATUR SUGYIANTO.

Energy Study Centre: Head Dr Ir YUDI UTOMO IMARDJOKO.

Environmental Study Centre: Head Dr Ir. BAKTI SETIAWAN.

Food and Nutrition Study Centre: Head Prof. Dr Ir TRANGGONO.

German Study Centre: Head Dr Ing. Ir. ACHMAD MUNAWAR.

Higher Education Planning and Study Centre: Head Dr Ir SAHID SUSANTO.

Japanese Study Centre: Head Dr Ir ERNI MARTANI.

Korean Study Centre: Head Prof. Dr DJOKO SURYO.

Land Resources Study Centre: Head Dr Ir AZWAR MAAS.

Marine Resources and Technology Study Centre: Head Prof. Dr Ir KAMISO HANDOYO NITIMULYO.

Pancasila Study Centre: Head Dr DAMARDJATI SUPADJAR.

Population and Policy Study Centre: Head Dr AGUS DWIYANTO.

Regional Planning and Development Study Centre: Dir Ir GUNUNG RADJIMAN.

Security and Peace Study Centre: Head Drs SAMSU RIZAL PANGGABEAN.

Social and South-East Asia Study Centre: Head Dr BAMBANG PURWANTO.

Technical Sciences Study Centre: Head Prof. Dr NUR YUWONO.

Tourism Study Centre: Head Drs HENDRIE ADJIE KUSWORO.

Traditional Medicine Study Centre: Head Dr SUDARSONO.

Transportation and Logistics Study Centre: Head Dr Ir HERU SUTOMO.

Villages and Regional Study Centre: Head Dr Ir MOCHAMAD MAKSUM.

Womens' Study Centre: Head Prof. Dr Ir MARY ASTUTI.

UNIVERSITAS HALUOLEO

Kampus Bumi Tridharma Anduonohu, Kendari, Sulawesi Tenggara 93232

Telephone: (401) 25104
Fax: (401) 22006

Founded 1981
Academic year: September to June

Rector: Prof. Dr Ir. H. SOLEH SOLAHUDDIN
Vice-Rectors: Drs SULEMAN, Drs H. AHMAD BAKKARENG, Drs LA ODE MUH. ARSYAD TENO, Drs H. ALIBAS YUSUF
Librarian: Drs L. HAISU

Library of 43,342 vols
Number of teachers: 452
Number of students: 9,029

Publications: *Journal Haluoleo* (quarterly), *Agri Plus* (6 a year), *Gema Pendidikan* (6 a year), *Sosial Politik* (6 a year), *Majalah Ekonomi* (6 a year)

DEANS

Faculty of Education: Drs H. MUHAMMAD GAZALI
Faculty of Economics: HASAN AEDY
Faculty of Social and Political Sciences: Drs H. M. NUR RAKHMAN
Faculty of Agriculture: Ir. H. MAHMUD HAMUNDU

ATTACHED INSTITUTES

Institute of Social Research: Dir Prof. H. USMAN D. MASIKI.

Institute of Community Service: Dir Prof. Dr H. ABDURRAUF TARIMANA.

Centre for Ecological Studies: Dir Ir. ABDUL MANAN.

Centre for Population Studies: Dir Drs ABD AZIS RASAKE.

Centre for Women's Studies: Dra Ny. Hj. SAARTJE DJARUDJU ROMPAS.

Centre for Computer Science and Information Systems: Dir Ir. GATOT ILHAMTO.

Small Earth Station and Electronic Classroom for Distance Learning: Dir Drs H. AHMAD BAKKARENG.

Centre for Rural Areas Development: Dir MUH. IDRUS MUFTI.

Open University: Dir Drs SULEMAN.

Centre for Dry Land Area: Dir Dr Ir. Y. B. PASOLON.

Centre for Education and Humanities: Dir Drs GUSARMIN SOFYAN.

Centre for Economics and Social Research: Dir ABD. AZIS ABD. MUTHALIB.

UNIVERSITAS HASANUDDIN

Jl. Perintis Kemerdekaan, Kampus Unhas Tamalanrea, Makassar 90245

Telephone: (411) 584002
Fax: (411) 585188
E-mail: cio@unhas.ac.id
Internet: www.unhas.ac.id

Founded 1959
Academic year: September to February

Rector: Prof. Dr Ir. RADI A. GANY
Deputy Rectors: Prof. Dr DJABIR HAMZAH (Academic Affairs), Prof. Dr Ir. H. A. SYAMSUL ARIFIN P. (Administrative and Financial Affairs), Prof. Dr Ir. AMBO ALA

(Student and Alumni Affairs), Prof. Dr Ir. A. MAPPADJANTJI AMIEN (Co-operative and Development Affairs)
Registrar: Dra RATNA ARDJO
Librarian: Dr SYARIFUDDIN ATTJE (acting)

Number of teachers: 1,684
Number of students: 20,816

Publications: *Identitas UNHAS* (monthly), *Interaski/LPPM* (3 a year), *Jupiter/Perpustakaan* (2 a year)

DEANS

Faculty of Agriculture and Forestry: Prof. Dr Ir. SYAWAL
Faculty of Animal Husbandry: Prof. Dr Ir. H. BASIT WELLO
Faculty of Dentistry: Dr M. AMIN KANSI
Faculty of Economics: Dr H. FATTAH KADIR
Faculty of Engineering: Dr Ir. SALEH PALLU
Faculty of Law: ABDUL RAZAK
Faculty of Letters: Dr. H. M. DARWIS
Faculty of Marine Sciences and Fisheries: Ir. HAMZAH SUNUSI
Faculty of Mathematics and Natural Sciences: Prof. Dr ALFIAN NOOR
Faculty of Medicine: Prof. Dr Dr IDRUS A. PATURUSI
Faculty of Public Health: Prof. Dr Dr RAZAK THAHA
Faculty of Social and Political Sciences: Prof. Dr HAFIED CANGARA

DIRECTORS

Central Workshop: Dr Ir. DUMA HASAN
Language Centre: Dr ETTY BAZERGAN
Postgraduate Studies Programme: Prof. Dr Ir. H. M. NATSIR NESSA
UNHAS Information Centre: Dr Ir. MUH. IVAN AZIS

UNIVERSITAS INDONESIA

Jl. Salemba Raya 4, Jakarta Pusat
Telephone: (21) 31930355
Fax: (21) 31930343
E-mail: pusadmui@makara.cso.ui.ac.id
Internet: www.ui.ac.id

Founded 1950
Language of instruction: Indonesian
Academic year: August to June (two semesters)

Rector: Prof. Dr USMAN CHATIB WARSA
Vice-Rector for Academic Affairs: Prof. Dr Ir. SUTANTO SOEHODHO
Vice-Rector for Co-operation and Facilities: EDI TOET HENDRATNO
Vice-Rector for Development: Prof. MARTANI HUSEINI
Vice-Rector for General Administration: DARMINTO
Vice-Rector for Student Affairs: Drs ARIE SETIABUDI SOESILO
University Secretary: Dr WIDIJANTO S. NUGROHO
Librarian: LUKI WIDJAJANTI

Number of teachers: 2,050
Number of students: 36,142

Publications: *Makara* (Technology edition) (every 4 months), *Makara* (Science edition) (every 4 months), *Makara* (Social Sciences edition) (every 4 months), *Makara* (Health Sciences edition) (every 4 months), and various faculty bulletins

DEANS

Faculty of Computer Sciences: Dr T. BASARUDIN
Faculty of Dental Medicine: Dr SRI ANGKY SOEKANTO
Faculty of Economics: Dr BAMBANG P. S. BRODJONEGORO
Faculty of Humanities: Prof. Dr IDA SUNDARI HUSEN
Faculty of Law: Prof. HIKMAHANTO JUWANA
Faculty of Mathematics and Natural Sciences: Drs ADI BASUKRIADI
Faculty of Medicine: Dr MENALDI RASMIN
Faculty of Nursing Sciences: Prof. Dra ELLY NURRACHMAH
Faculty of Psychology: Dra DHARMAYATI B. UTOYO LUBIS
Faculty of Public Health: Prof. Dr HASBULLAH THABRANY
Faculty of Social and Political Sciences: Dr GUMILAR R. SOMANTRI
Faculty of Technology: Dr Ir RENALDY DALIMI
Programme of Postgraduate Studies: Dr PURNAWAN JUNADI

ATTACHED RESEARCH INSTITUTES

APEC Study Centre: Dir Prof. Dr LEPI TANADJAJA TARMIDI.

Centre for American Studies: Dir SUZIE SUDARMAN.

Centre for Australian Studies: Dir Dr RENI WINATA.

Centre for European Studies: Dir Prof. Dr NYAJU JENNI M. T. HARDJATNO.

Centre for Family Welfare: Dir Dr ANHARI ACHADI (acting).

Centre for Health Research: Dir Dr SABARINAH B. PRASETYO.

Centre for Japanese Studies: Dirs Dr BACHTIAR ALAM.

Centre for Middle Eastern and Islamic Studies: Dir ACHMAD RAMZY TADJOEDIN.

Centre for Research Development: Dir Prof. Dr A. DAHANA (acting).

Centre for Research in Science and Technology: Dir Prof. Dr A. DAHANA (acting).

Centre for Research in Society and Culture: Dir Dr SUPRATIKNO RAHARJO (acting).

Centre for Studies of the Environment and Human Resources: Dir Dr SUYUD WARNO UTOMO.

Directorate for Research and Community Services: Dir Prof. Dr A. DAHANA.

SEAMEO-TROPMED Regional Centre for Community Nutrition: Dir Dr WIDJAJA LUKITO.

AFFILIATED COLLEGES AND INSTITUTES

Lembaga Demografi (Institute of Demography): Kampus UI-Depok; Dir Dr Sri HARIJATI HATMADJI.

Lembaga Konsultasi Hukum dan Bantuan Hukum (Legal Consultation and Legal Aid Department): Kampus UI-Depok; Dir RETNO MURNIATI.

Lembaga Management (Institute of Management): Jl. Salemba 4, Jakarta; Dir Dr Ir. RUSLAN PRIJADI.

Lembaga Penyelidikan Ekonomi dan Masyarakat (Institute for Economic and Social Research): Jl. Salemba 4, Jakarta; Dir Dr MOHAMAD IKHSAN.

Lembaga Psikologi Terapan (Institute of Applied Psychology): Jl. Salemba 4, Jakarta; Dir Dra INDARWAHYANTI GRAITO.

Lembaga Teknologi (Institute of Technology): Jl. Salemba 4, Jakarta; Dir Ir YUSUF LATIEF.

Pusat Dokumentasi Hukum (Legal Documentation Centre): Jl. Cirebon 5, Jakarta; Dir AGUS SUPRIYANTO.

UNIVERSITAS JAMBI

Kampus Universita Jambi, Jl. Raya Jambi, Muara Bulian, Km 15 Mendalo, Jambi, 36361
Telephone: (741) 583377
Fax: (741) 583111
E-mail: unja@unja.ac.id
Internet: www.unja.ac.id

Founded 1963
Language of instruction: Indonesian
Academic year: September to August

Rector: H. KEMAS ARSYAD SOMAD
Vice-Rector (Academic Affairs): Drs H. ARDINAL
Vice-Rector (Administration): Dr Ir. SA'AD MURDY
Vice-Rector (Student Affairs): Drs AFFAN MALIK
Registrar: H. N. ZAWAWI
Librarian: Drs AZHAR WAHAB

Library of 99,000 vols
Number of teachers: 600
Number of students: 13,000

Publication: *Berita UNJA* (monthly)

DEANS

Faculty of Agriculture: Dr Ir. ZILKIFLI
Faculty of Animal Husbandry: Ir. SYAFRIL HADI
Faculty of Economics: Dr AFRIZAL
Faculty of Education: Drs AMIN SAIB
Faculty of Law: Dr ANSORULLAH

UNIVERSITAS JEMBER

Jl. Kalimantan III/24, Jember, East Java, 6812
Telephone: (331) 330224
Fax: (331) 339029
Internet: www.unej.ac.id

Founded 1964
State controlIndonesian, English, French
Academic year: July to June

Rector: Prof. Dr H. KABUL SANTOSO
Vice-Rector (Academic Affairs): Dr Ir. IDHA HARIYANTO
Vice-Rector (Administration and Finance): Prof. Drs KADIMAN
Vice-Rector (Student Affairs): PURNOMO
Registrar: Drs MADE PEDUNGAN SARDHA
Director of Agricultural Polytechnic: Ir. H. SUHARJO WIDODO
Director of University Research Institute: Drs LIAKIP
Librarian: Drs MAHFUD A.

Library of 117,441 vols
Number of teachers: 783
Number of students: 12,933

Publications: *Gema Universitas*, *Argopuro*, *Dian Wanita*

DEANS

Faculty of Law: SAMSI KUSAIRI
Faculty of Social and Political Sciences: Prof. Drs H. BARIMAN
Faculty of Agriculture: Ir. Hj. SITI HARTANTI
Faculty of Economics: Drs H. SUKUSNI
Faculty of Teacher Training & Educational Sciences: Drs SUKARDJO
Faculty of Letters: Drs SUDJADI
Faculty of Agricultural Technology: Ir. WAGITO
Faculty of Dentistry: Drg. BOB SOEBIJANTORO

HEADS OF DEPARTMENTS

Faculty of Law:
- Criminal Law: MULTAZAM MUNTOHA
- Civil Law: SUGIYONO
- Basic Law: HARDIMAN
- Constitutional Law: TOTOK SUDARYANTO

Faculty of Social and Political Science:
- International Relations: Drs SYUKRON SYAH
- Administration: Drs AGUS BUDIHARJO
- Social Welfare: Drs HUSNI ABDUL GANI

Faculty of Agriculture:
- Soil Science: Dr Ir. SUTIKTO
- Social Economics: Ir. SIGIT SUSANTO

Agronomy: Dr Ir. M. SETIO PURWOKO
Plant Protection: Ir. SUTJIPTO

Faculty of Teacher Training & Educational Sciences:
General Education: Drs SOEDARMO
Social Science Education: Drs SUMARNO
Mathematics and Physics Education: Drs SOETARTO
Language and Art: Drs HARI SATRIYONO

Faculty of Letters:
Indonesian Literature: Drs KUSMADI
English Literature: Dr SUPARMIN
Indonesian History: Drs SUDIRO

Faculty of Economics:
Economics and Development: Dra AMINAH
Management: Drs ABDUL HALIM

Faculty of Agricultural Technology:
Agricultural Technology: Ir. SETYO HARRI
Agricultural Product Technology: Ir. SUSIYOHADI

MIPA Study Programme:
Mathematics: Drs MOH HASAN
Physics: Drs SUJITO
Chemistry: Drs ZULFIKAR
Biology: Dr W. HIDAYAT TEGUH

UNIVERSITAS JENDERAL SOEDIRMAN

Kampus UNSOED Grendeng, POB 115, Purwokerto 53122, Central Java
Telephone: (281) 635292
Fax: (281) 631802
E-mail: rektor@unsoed.ac.id
Internet: www.unsoed.ac.id

Founded 1963
Language of instruction: Indonesian
Academic year: September to August (two semesters)

Rector: Prof. RUBIJANTO MISMAN
Vice-Rector (Academic Affairs): Dr SUDJARWO
Vice-Rector (Administration Affairs): Prof. Dr H. KAMIO
Vice-Rector (Student Affairs): KOMARI
Chief Registrar: Ir. BAMBANG PURNOMO
Librarian: Drs CHAMDI

Number of teachers: 750
Number of students: 13,000

Publications: *Majalah Ilmiah Unsoed* (biological scientific journal, quarterly), *Journal of Rural Development* (quarterly)

DEANS

Faculty of Agriculture: Ir. SUMIRAT BRONTO WALUYO
Faculty of Biology: Prof. Dr Haji TRIANI HARDIYATI
Faculty of Animal Husbandry: Prof. Dr Ir. SWANDIARINI
Faculty of Economics: Drs GATOT SUPRIHANTO
Faculty of Law: ABDUL AZIS NASIHUDIN
Faculty of Social Sciences and Politics: Drs SUHARI

UNIVERSITAS LAMBUNG MANGKURAT

Kampus UNLAM, Jl. Brigjen H. Hasan Basry, POB 279, Banjarmasin 70123, South Kalimantan
Telephone: (511) 54177
Fax: (511) 54177
E-mail: bjm.unlam@bjm.mega.net.id

Founded 1958 as private university, state control 1960
Language of instruction: Indonesian
Academic year: September to August

Rector: Prof. H. ALFIAN NOOR
Vice-Rector (Administrative Affairs): Ir. Hj. MAHYAR DIANA
Vice-Rector (Student Affairs): Ir. H. MULYADI YUSUF
Vice-Rector (Academic Affairs): Dr Ir. ATHAILLAH MURSYID
Head of Academic Administration, Student Affairs, Planning and Information Systems: Drs H. M. SYACHRIAR ACHMAD
Head of General Administration, Financial and Employee Affairs: Dra Hj. SUNDUSIAH
Librarian: H. MARCONY KHALID

Number of teachers: 830
Number of students: 10,734

Publications: *Kalimantan Scientiae* (2 a year), *Orientasi* (4 a year), *Vidya Karya* (2 a year), *Kalimantan Agriculture* (4 a year)

DEANS

Faculty of Teaching Training and Education: Drs RUSTAM EFFENDI
Faculty of Law: RIDUAN SYACHRANI
Faculty of Economics: Drs H. YUSRIANSYAH AZIS
Faculty of Social and Political Sciences: Drs H. BURHAN ACHMAD
Faculty of Agriculture: Ir. H. M. RASMADI
Faculty of Forestry: Dr Ir. H. M. RUSLAN
Faculty of Fisheries: Ir. SAALUDDIN HUSIN
Faculty of Engineering: Ir. H. ZAIN HERNADY ARIFIN
Faculty of Medicine: Dr H. HASNI HASAN BASRI

UNIVERSITAS LAMPUNG

Kampus UNILA, Gedong Meneng, Kedaton, Bandar Lampung
Telephone: 52673
Internet: www.unila.ac.id

Founded 1965
State control
Languages of instruction: Indonesian, English
Academic year: August to June (two terms)

Rector: Prof. Dr MUHAJIR UTOMO
Vice-Rector (Academic Affairs): Dr BAMBANG SUMITRO
Vice-Rector I: Prof. Dr TIRZA HANUM
Vice-Rector II: Drs SOFIE AKRABI
Vice-Rector III: Drs M. THOHA JAYASAMPURNA
Vice-Rector IV: Prof. Dr SUTOPO GHANI NUGROHO
Administration Bureau: NURDIN IBRAHIM
Library Director: DIANA AMISANI

Number of teachers: 969
Number of students: 23,934

Publications: *Buletin Penelitian*, *Warta Pengabdian pada Masyarakat*

DEANS

Faculty of Law: Prof. Dr SANUSI HUSIN
Faculty of Economics: TOTO GUNARTO
Faculty of Education and Teacher Training: Prof. Drs H. M. YASUN
Faculty of Social and Political Sciences: Prof. Dr BAMBANG SUMITRO
Faculty of Technology: ANSHORI DJAUSAL
Faculty of Mathematics: Prof. Dr SUGENG P. HARIANTO

DIRECTORS

Bureau of Legal Consultation and Aid: M. PULUNG
Centre of Public Services: Drs KANTAN ABDULLAH
Research Centre: Dr FADDEL DJAUHAR
Institute of Environmental Studies: Ir. SUGENG HARIJANTO
Institute of Demography: MUCHSIN BADAR
Institute of Management: SUDANAR
Institute of Languages: Dra ROSITA S. PANJAITAN

UNIVERSITAS MATARAM

Jl. Majapahit 62, Mataram 83125, Nusa Tenggara Barat
Telephone: (370) 633007
Fax: (370) 636041
E-mail: rektorat@unram.org
Internet: www.unram.ac.id

Founded 1962
Academic year: September to August

Rector: Dr MANSUR MA'SHUM
Vice Rectors: Dr ARIFUDDIN SAHIDU (Academic Affairs), Drs HASBULLAH (Administrative Affairs), MUHAMMAD DARWIN (Student Affairs), ROSIADY SAYUTI (External Co-operation)
Registrar: MUHIBAH NASRUDDIN
Administrative Officer: FATHULLAH NATSIR
Librarian: LALU BUDIMAN

Library of 73,156 vols
Number of teachers: 851
Number of students: 11,541

Publications: *Agroteksos* (4 a year), *Research Journal* (3 a year), *Komunitas* (2 a year)

DEANS

Faculty of Economics: SUKARDAN
Faculty of Agriculture: Dr PARMAN
Faculty of Law: ZAINAL ASIKIN
Faculty of Animal Science: M. S. MUHZIE
Faculty of Education and Teaching: Dr SYAHDAN
Faculty of Engineering: Prof. HADI SUTRISNO
Faculty of Medicine: Prof. MULYANTO

ATTACHED INSTITUTES

Research Institute: Dir Dr CHAIRUSSYUHUR.

Community Service Institute: Dir UMAR AR.

Centre for Agribusiness Studies: Dir Dr M. ICHSAN.

Centre for Environmental Studies: Dir MUCHTAR DJOBENG.

Centre for Language and Cultural Studies: Dir Dr HUSNI MUADZ.

Centre for Law and Human Resources Development Studies: Dir I. WAYAN GDE WANGE.

Centre for Natural Resources Development Studies: Dir MEIDIWARMAN.

Centre for Population Studies: Dir M. RAMLI.

Centre for Rural Development Studies: Dir Dr ROSIADY H. SAYUTI.

Centre for Small and Medium Enterprises Studies: Dir EDDY ACHMAD.

Centre for Women's Role Studies: Dir HANARTANI.

UNIVERSITAS MULAWARMAN

Kampus Gunung. Kelua, Samarinda, East Kalimantan 75119
Telephone: (541) 741118
Fax: (541) 732870
E-mail: rektorat@unmul.ac.id
Internet: www.unmul.ac.id

Founded 1962
Academic year: September to August

Rector: Prof. RACHMAD HERNADI
Vice-Rector, Academic Affairs: Prof. Dr ARIFFIEN BRATAWINATA
Vice Rector, Administration and Finance: MAKMUN ALI BADRUN
Vice Rector, Student Affairs: Prof. Drs H. ARIFIN LEO
Vice Rector, Development and Cooperation: Prof. Dr H.BANDI SUPRATONO
Head of General Administration and Finance Bureau: H. IRIANTO
Library Director: DRS SURIANSYAH

Number of teachers: 540
Number of students: 4,603
Publication: *Frontir* (2 a year)

DEANS

Faculty of Economics: Prof. H. A. WARIS
Faculty of Social and Political Sciences: SAROSA HAMONG PRANOTO
Faculty of Agriculture: JUREMI GANI
Faculty of Forestry: Prof. Dr WAWAN KUSTIAWAN
Faculty of Education and Teacher Training: Drs EDDY SUBANDRIJO
Faculty of Fisheries and Marine Science: Dr AHMAD SYAFEI SIDIK

UNIVERSITAS NUSA CENDANA

Jl. Adisucipto, Penfui, Kupang 85001 Nusa Tenggara Timur
Telephone: (380) 881180
Fax: (380) 881180
E-mail: puskom@kupang.wasantara.net.id

Founded 1962
State control
Languages of instruction: Indonesian, English
Academic year: July to June

Rector: Prof. Dr A. BENU
Vice-Rector (Academic Affairs): Drs I. GUSTI BAGUS ARJANA
Vice-Rector (Administration Affairs): Drs ANSGAR DJAHIMO
Vice-Rector (Student Affairs): Drs ELIAS KOPONG
Chief Administrative Officer (Finance and Facilities): Drs KAREL TAHITOE
Chief Administrative Officer (Academic, Students and Information System): Drs JOHN FRANS
Librarian: Dra JANSE ENGGELINA MALELAK

Number of teachers: 813
Number of students: 5,207
Publications: *Sinergia*, *Warta Undana* (monthly), *Liguminesa Journal* (quarterly), *Nusa Cendana Journal* (quarterly), *Media Eksakta Journal* (quarterly)

DEANS

Faculty of Agriculture: Ir DOPPY ROY NENDISA
Faculty of Animal Husbandry: Drs ERNA HARTATI
Faculty of Engineering: Drs DANIEL ADUTE
Faculty of Law: Dr MIKAEL DJAWA
Faculty of Public Health: Drs J. I. MANAFE
Faculty of Science and Mathematics: Drs M. J. PELLA
Faculty of Social and Political Sciences: Prof. Dr JENY EOH
Faculty of Teacher Training and Education: Drs LUKAS BILI BORA

UNIVERSITAS PADJADJARAN

Jl. Dipati Ukur 35, Bandung 40184, Java
Telephone: (22) 2503271
Fax: (22) 2501977
E-mail: rektor@unpad.ac.id
Internet: www.unpad.ac.id

Founded 1957
State control
Languages of instruction: Indonesian, English
Academic year: August to July (two semesters)

Rector: Prof. Dr H. A. HIMENDRA WARGAHADIBRATA
Vice-Rector for Academic Affairs: Prof. Dr H. PONPON S. IDJRADINATA
Vice-Rector for Administration: M. WAHYUDIN ZARKASYI
Vice-Rector for Co-operation: Prof. Dr H. USMAN HARDI
Vice-Rector for Planning, Information Systems and Supervision: Prof. T. SUGANDA
Vice-Rector for Student Affairs: SYARIF A. BARMAWI
Librarian: Prof. Dr I. NURPILIHAN

Library of 178,441 vols
Number of teachers: 1,868
Number of students: 40,482
Publications: *Agrikulture* (Agriculture, 3 a year), *Bionatura* (Sciences, 3 a year), *Jurnal Ekonomi* (Economics, 2 a year), *Jurnal Kedokteran Bandung* (Medicine, 3 a year), *Jurnal Keperawatan* (Nursing, 2 a year), *Puslitbangkum* (Law, 2 a year), *Sosiohumaniora* (Social Sciences, 3 a year)

DEANS

Faculty of Agriculture: Prof. Dr SADELI NATASASMITA
Faculty of Animal Husbandry: Prof. Dr NASIPAN USRI
Faculty of Communication Science: Drs SOLEH SOEMIRAT
Faculty of Dentistry: Dr SETIAWAN NATASAMITA
Faculty of Economics: Prof. Dr H. SURIPTO SAMID
Faculty of Law: Prof. Dr MAN SUPARMAN SASTRAWIDJAJA
Faculty of Letters: Prof. Dr H. EDI SUHARDI EKADJATI
Faculty of Mathematics and Natural Sciences: Prof. Dr SUPRIATNA
Faculty of Medicine: Dr FIRMAN FUAD WIRAKUSUMAH
Faculty of Social and Political Science: Drs TACHJAN
Faculty of Psychology: Dr H. SURYANA SUMANTRI

ATTACHED INSTITUTES

Public Service Institute: Dir Prof. Dr KUSNAKA ADIMIHARDJA.

Research Institute: Dir Prof. Dr JOHAN MASJHUR.

UNIVERSITAS PALANGKARAYA

Jl. Yos Sudarso, Kotak Pos 2, Palangka Raya, Kalimantan Tengah 73112
Telephone: (536) 26878
Fax: (536) 21722
E-mail: info@universitaspalangkaraya.ac.id
Internet: www.universitaspalangkaraya.ac.id

Founded 1963
Language of instruction: Indonesian
Academic year: July to June

Rector: Drs NAPA J. AWAT
Vice-Rector I: Drs HERIYANTO M. GARANG
Vice-Rector II: Drs DADANG LORIDA
Vice-Rector III: H. M. DAMIRI
Vice-Rector IV: Prof. Dr H. AHMADI ISA
Academic and Students' Administrative Officer: Drs LEUNHARD BAN YEN
Librarian: Dra ISTIRAHAYU

Number of teachers: 501
Number of students: 5,265
Publications: *Suara Tunjung Nyaho* (monthly), *Garantung* (monthly), *Optimal* (monthly), *Wahana* (monthly)

DEANS

Faculty of Economics: Drs EFENDY D. TIMBANG
Faculty of Education and Teacher Training: Drs HENRY SINGARASA
Faculty of Agriculture: Ir. SINTO R. NOEHAN

HEADS OF DEPARTMENTS

Faculty of Economics:
- Public Economics: Drs SUFRIDSON
- Management: Drs Y. KALVIN ANGGEN
- General Subjects: Drs BERLIE A. LABIH

Faculty of Education and Teacher Training:
- Education Science: Dra DALIKAH
- Educational Technology and Curriculum: Drs SARLES
- Non-formal Education: Drs HANNES M. B. HAMUN
- Educational Administration: Drs SITJAI MANDAGIE
- Guidance and Counselling: Drs SUNARYO
- Civics: Drs EDDY
- English: Drs SURYA TAIB
- Indonesian: Drs MARIYEDIE
- Mathematics: Drs WALTER PUNDING
- Accountancy: Drs TIMBUL
- Business: Drs DEHEN ERANG
- Social Science: Drs ARNIANSYAH
- Art and Language: Drs RUS ANDIANTO
- Mathematic Natural Science: Dra UMINASTUTI
- Biology: Dra YULA MIRANDA
- Co-operation: Drs MIDDAY
- Physics: Drs KOMANG GDE SWASTIKA
- Chemistry: Drs ABDUL MUM'IN

Faculty of Agriculture:
- Agriculture (Social Economics): Ir. NYELONG I. SIMON
- Agriculture (Agronomy): (vacant)
- Forestry: Ir. BAMBANG WALDY
- Civil Engineering: Ir. MOH. AMIN
- Fishery: Ir. PETRUS SENAS

UNIVERSITAS RIAU

Kampus Bina Widya Km 12.5, Simpang Baru, Pekanbaru 28293, Sumatra
Telephone: (761) 63266
Fax: (761) 63279
E-mail: rektor@unri.ac.id
Internet: www.unri.ac.id

Founded 1962
Academic year: September to July

Rector: Prof. Dr MUCHTAR AHMAD
Vice-Rector (Academic Affairs): Prof. Dr DADANG ISKANDAR
Vice-Rector (Administration): Drs AMIR HASAN
Vice-Rector (Student Affairs): Ir ARIFIEN MANSYOER
Vice-Rector (Planning and Co-operation): Ir SUWARDI LOCKMAN
Registrar: Prof. Dr DADANG ISKANDAR
Librarian: Ir PUTU SEDANA

Number of teachers: 919
Number of students: 14,223
Publications: *Terubuk* (Fisheries Bulletin, 4 a year), *Jurnal Penelitian* (General Scientific Research, 4 a year), *Dawat* (Journal of Malay Language and Culture, 4 a year), *Jurnal Ilmu Sosial dan Politik* (Social and Political Sciences, 4 a year), *Jurnal Ekonomi* (Economics, 4 a year), *Jurnal Agritek* (Agricultural Technology, 2 a year), *Jurnal Perikanan dan Ilmu Kelautan* (Fisheries and Marine Science, 2 a year), *Jurnal Natur Indonesia* (2 a year)

DEANS

Faculty of Politics and Social Science: Drs ALFIAN
Faculty of Economics: Drs MUCHTAR MARISO
Faculty of Natural Sciences and Mathematics: Dra CHAINULFIFAH
Faculty of Fisheries: Dr Ir FELIATRA
Faculty of Teacher Training and Education: Drs M. ZEIN MAADAP
Faculty of Agriculture: Dr ASLIM RASYAD
Faculty of Engineering: Drs RAHMAD

PROFESSORS

ADAM, D., Government and Law
AHMAD, M., Marine Sciences and Fisheries
DAHRIL, T., Planktonology and Water Quality

DIAH, M., Education
HASAN, K., Education
IMRAN, A., Islamology
ISKANDAR, D., Physics
KASMY, M. F., Physics
KASRY, A., Aquatic Resources Management
MAHMUD, S., Education
MARZUKI, S., History Education
RAB, T., Enzymology
RAHMAN, M., Mathematics
RASYAD, A., Agriculture
SAAD, M., Rural Sociology
SAMAD, R., Education
SUWARDI, History
UMAR, S. M., Education
USMAN, F., Agriculture

UNIVERSITAS SAM RATULANGI

Kampus UNSRAT Bahu, Manado, North Sulawesi 95115
Telephone: 63786
Internet: www.unsrat.ac.id

Founded 1961
State control
Language of instruction: Indonesian
Academic year: starts September

Rector: Prof. Dr J. PARUNTU
Vice-Rector for Academic Affairs: Prof. B. H. MONINGKA
Vice-Rector for Administration and Finance: Prof. Dr JOHN HEIN GONI
Vice-Rector for Student and Alumni Affairs: MARTHEN RONDO
Vice-Rector for Secretariat and Co-operation: Dr B. TULUNG
Vice-Rector for Planning: Dr R. TENDA
Vice-Rector for Inspection: Prof. JAHYA BIN SMITH
Head of Bureau for Academic and Student Administration: H. J. MEWENGKANG
Head of Central Library: D. SILANGEN
Number of teachers: 1,496
Number of students: 12,526
Publication: *Palakat-Inovasi*

DEANS

Faculty of Letters: Drs ROBERT TANDI
Faculty of Mathematics and Natural Science: Dr S. RONDONUWU
Faculty of Law: Prof. ADOLF DAPU
Faculty of Social Sciences and Politics: Drs J. J. LONTAAN
Faculty of Economics: Prof. NY. I. NAJOEN
Faculty of Agriculture: Dr Ir. D. T. SEMBEL
Faculty of Animal Husbandry: Prof. Dr D. A. KALIGIS
Faculty of Fisheries and Maritime Sciences: Prof. Dr S. BERHIMPON
Faculty of Medicine: Dr J. W SIAGIAN
Faculty of Engineering: R. J. M. MANDAGI

PROFESSORS

ALAMSJAH, Soil Physics
BUDIARSO, Technology
DUNDU, B., Microbiology
JAN, H., Statistics
KAKAUHE, R. P. L., Management Accounting
KAPOJOS-MONGULA, I. C. R., Civil Law
KARINDA, D. S., English and Dutch
KASINEM-S., Commercial Law
KORAH, M. W., Marketing Management Science
MANDANG, J. H. A., Ahli Mata
MUNIR, M., Paediatrics
MUSA, A., Modern Indonesian History
MUSA KARIM, Indonesian Literature
PALAR, W. T., Agrarian Studies
PALENEWEN, J. L., Ecology
PANDA, H. O., Surgery
PUNUH-GO, S., Civil Law
ROGI, M., Economic Development
SALEH, M., Indonesian Government System
SINOLUNGAN, J. M., Medical Psychology
SOEPENO, Customary Law
SUPIT, J. T., Sociology
TANGKUDUNG, R. S., Civil Administration
TIMBOELENG, K. W., Physics and Research Methodology
TUSACH, N. A., Civil Law
WANTASEN, D., Soil Physics
WAWOROENTOE, S. A., Physics
WAWOROENTOE, W. J., Urban and Regional Planning
WILAR, A. F., Veterinary Science
WOKAS, F. H. M., Plant Protection
WOWOR, G. E., Gynaecology
WUMU, J., History of Economics

UNIVERSITAS SEBELAS MARET

Jl. Ir. Sutami 36A, Surakarta 57126
Telephone: (271) 646994
Fax: (271) 642282
Internet: www.uns.ac.id

Founded 1976
State control
Language of instruction: Indonesian
Academic year: August to July

Rector: Dr Dr MOHAMMED SYAMSULHADI
Vice-Rector (Academic Affairs): Dr RAVIK KARSIDI
Vice-Rector (Administration Affairs): Dr Ir. SHOLAHUDDIN
Vice-Rector (Student Affairs): Drs TOTOK SARSITO
Librarian: Drs HARMAWAN
Library of 140,612 vols
Number of teachers: 1,418
Number of students: 19,732
Publications: *Widya Bhawana*, *Varia Budaya* (Journal of Cultural Studies), *Buletin UNS* (monthly)

DEANS

Teacher-Training and Education: Drs TRISNO MARTONO
Letters and Arts: Dr D. MARYONO
Social and Political Science: Drs DWI TIYANTO
Law: Dr ADI SULISTYO
Economics: Dra SALAMAH WAHYUNI
Medicine: Dr Dr A. A. SUBIYANTO
Agriculture: Prof. Dr Ir. SUNTORO
Engineering: Ir. SUMARYOTO
Mathematics and Natural Sciences: Drs MARSUSI
Postgraduate Programme: Prof. Drs HARIS MUDJIMAN

UNIVERSITAS SRIWIJAYA

Jl. Jaksa Agung R. Suprapto, Palembang, South Sumatra
Telephone: 26004, 26388, 23155
Internet: www.unsri.ac.id

Founded 1960
State control
Language of instruction: Indonesian
Academic year: July to June

Rector: Prof. Dr ZAINAL RIDHO DJAFAR
Vice-Rector I: Dr RUJITO AGUS SUWIGNYO
Vice-Rector II: KIAGUS ABDUL RACHMAN ACHMAD
Vice-Rector III: H. FUAD RUSYDI SUWARDI
Vice-Rector IV: Dr ABDUL HAMID RASYID
Administration Bureau: Drs HERMAN MURSAL
Librarian: Dra CHUZAIMAH DIEM

Number of teachers: 540 full-time

Number of teachers: 617 part-time
Number of students: 8,427

Publications: *Majalah Universitas Sriwijaya* (3 a year), and faculty bulletins

DEANS

Faculty of Economics: BADIA PERIZADE
Faculty of Law: SOFYAN HASAN
Faculty of Engineering: Dr HASAN BASRI
Faculty of Dentistry: Prof. Dr ARSUAD
Faculty of Agriculture: ZULJATI SYAHRUL
Faculty of Teacher Training: Prof. Dr DJAHIR BASIR
Faculty of Education: Dr ZULKIFLI DAHLAN (acting)

PROFESSORS

HALIM, A., Linguistics
HARDJOWIJONO, G., Paediatrics
MUKTI, H. D., Advanced Management
MUSLIMIN, A., Administrative Law
SOELAIMAN, M., Adat Law

ATTACHED INSTITUTES

Institute of Research: Chair. Ir. BUCHORI RAHMAN.

Institute of Community Service: Chair. Drs DJAKFAR MUROD.

University Planning and Development Board: Chair. Dr A. BAGHOWI BACHAR.

UNIVERSITAS SUMATERA UTARA
(University of North Sumatra)

Jl. Dr. T. Mansur No. 9, Kampus USU, Medan
Telephone: (61) 8216575
Fax: (61) 8219411
E-mail: usu@karet.usu.ac.id
Internet: www.usu.ac.id

Founded 1952
State control
Languages of instruction: Indonesian, English
Academic year: August to July

Rector: Prof. CHAIRUDDIN P. LUBIS
Vice-Rector (Academic Affairs): Prof. Dr SUMONO
Vice-Rector (Administrative Affairs): Dr SUBHILHAR
Vice-Rector (Student Affairs): Dr LINDA MAAS
Vice-Rector (Planning, Co-operation and Foreign Affairs): Prof. Dr SUKARIA SINULINGGA
Vice-Rector (Asset Management): Ir. ISMAN NURIADI
Head of Library and Information System: Drs. A. RIDWAN SIREGAR
Library of 500,000 vols
Number of teachers: 1,750
Number of students: 28,000

DEANS

Faculty of Medicine: Dr T. BAHRI ANWAR
Faculty of Dentistry: Prof. ISMET D. NASUTION
Faculty of Agriculture: Dr ZULKIFLI NASUTION
Faculty of Engineering: Dr NAWAWY LOEBIS
Faculty of Mathematics and Sciences: Prof. EDDY MARLIANTO
Faculty of Economics: Drs JHON T. RITONGA
Faculty of Law: Prof. Dr RUNTUNG
Faculty of Letters: Prof. BAHREN UMAR SIREGAR
Faculty of Political and Social Science: Drs M. ARIF NASUTION
Faculty of Public Health: (vacant)
School of Postgraduate Studies: Dr T. CHAIRUN NISA

ATTACHED INSTITUTES

Institution of Research: Dir Prof. Dr HSR PARLINDUNGAN SINAGA.

Institution of Community Service: Dir Dr DARWIN DALIMUNTHE.

ICT Center: Dir Prof. SUTOMO KASIMAN.

UNIVERSITAS SYIAH KUALA

Jl. Darussalam, Kopelma Darussalam Banda Aceh 23111
Telephone: (651) 7410250
E-mail: rektor@unsyiah.ac.id
Internet: www.unsyiah.ac.id

Founded 1961
State control
Language of instruction: Indonesian
Academic year: August to June

Rector: PAPA DIES NATALIS
Vice-Rector for Academic Affairs: Dr ABDI A. WAHAB
Vice-Rector for Administrative Affairs: Dr DARNI M. DAUD
Vice-Rector for Co-operation Affairs: Drs SAIFUDDIN ISHAK
Vice-Rector for Financial Affairs: Drs ALFIAN IBRAHIM
Vice-Rector for Student Affairs: Drs AZHAR PUTEH
Chief Academic Administrative Officer: Drs BACHTIAR EFENDI
Chief Administrative Officer: Drs MUSTAFA USMAN
Librarian: Drs SANUSI

Number of teachers: 1,278
Number of students: 16,715

Publications: *Agripet* (2 a year), *Agrista*, *Ekobis*, *Jurnal Kedokteran Syiah Kuala*, *Jurnal Teknik Sipil* (3 a year), *Kanun Fakultas Hukum*, *Managemen dan Bisnis*, *Medica Veterinaria*, *Mekanikal Komputasi & Numerical*, *Mon Mata* (4 a year), *Natural*, *Rekayasa Elektrika*, *Rekayasa Kimia & Lingkungan*, *Teknorama*, *Telaah dan Riset*, *Wacana Pendidikan* (4 a year), *Warta Unsyiah*

DEANS

Faculty of Agriculture: Ir. ISMAYANI
Faculty of Economics: Prof. Dr SAID MUHAMMAD
Faculty of Engineering: Prof. Dr Ir. HUSAINI
Faculty of Law: MAWARDI ISMAIL
Faculty of Mathematical and Natural Sciences: Dr MUSTANIR
Faculty of Medicine: Dr SYAHRUL
Faculty of Teacher Training and Education: Dr M. YUSUF AZIZ
Faculty of Veterinary Science: Dr MAHDI ABRAR

UNIVERSITAS TADULAKO

Kampus Bumi Tadulako Tondo, Palu 94118, Sulawesi
Telephone: (451) 422611
Fax: (451) 422844
E-mail: webmaster@untad.ac.id
Internet: www.untad.ac.id

Founded 1981

Rector: Drs MOHAMMAD RASYID
Vice-Rectors: T. A. M. TILAAR, ARIFUDDIN BIDIN, SAHABUDDIN MUSTAPA, Dr MAIN LABASO
Head of General Administration Bureau: RAFIGA PONULELE
Librarian: Drs MUH. ASRI HENTE

Library of 30,042 vols
Number of teachers: 660
Number of students: 6,500

DEANS

Faculty of Teacher Training: Drs H. TJATJO THAHA
Faculty of Social and Political Sciences: Drs ZAINUDDIN BOLONG
Faculty of Law: ISMAIL KASIM
Faculty of Economics: ARSYAD MAARDANIN
Faculty of Agricultural Sciences: Ir. MASRIL BUSTAMI
Diploma Programme for Technical Sciences: Ir. GALIB ISHAK

UNIVERSITAS TANJUNGPURA

Jl. A. Yani Pontianak, Kalbar, Pontianak 78124
Telephone: (561) 734439
Fax: (561) 743946
E-mail: untan@untan.ac.id
Internet: www.untan.ac.id

Founded 1959
Language of instruction: Indonesian
Academic year: begins September

Rector: Prof. HJ. ASNIAR ISMAIL
First Vice-Chancellor: Prof. Dr HENDRO S. SUDAGUNG
Registrar: RADJALI HADIMASPUTRA
Head of General Administration Bureau: MAYARANA RANITA
Librarian: SUTARMIN

Number of teachers: 734
Number of students: 9,305

DEANS

Faculty of Law: Prof. ANWAR SALEH
Faculty of Social and Political Sciences: Prof. Dr Sy. IBRAHIM ALKADRIE
Faculty of Engineering: Ir. Hj. PONY SEDYANINGSIH
Faculty of Economics: ASNIAR SUBAGYO
Faculty of Agriculture: Prof. Ir. ALAMSYAH
Faculty of Teaching and Education: Prof. Drs JAWADI HASID

HEADS OF DEPARTMENTS

Civil Law: Ny. WIWI WIDARSIH KARSUM
Criminal Law: SAMPUR DONGAN SIMAMORA
State Law: MASLEH M. YAMAN
State Administration Science: Drs BACHTIAR
Sociology: Dra ROHANI YAHYA
Civil Engineering: Ir. HERRY SANTOSO
Electrical Engineering: Ir. DASRIL
Management: EVI ASMAYADI
Economics and Developmental Study: ZAINAL SYAMSU
Forestry: Dr HERUYONO HADISUPARTO
Agriculture: Ir. SURYADI ALIMIN
Language and Arts Teaching: Drs SUKAMTO
Educational Science: Dra H. SUTIAH ANY ADWAN
Social Studies Teaching: Drs BACHTIAR A. WAHAB

UNIVERSITAS TERBUKA
(Indonesian Open Learning University)

Jl. Cabe Raya, Pondok Cabe, Ciputat Tangerang 15418, POB 6666, Jakarta 15418
Telephone: (21) 7490941
Fax: (21) 7490147
E-mail: info@p2m.ut.ac.id
Internet: www.ut.ac.id

Founded 1984
State control
Language of instruction: Bahasa Indonesia

President: Prof. Dr ATWI SUPARMAN
Registrar: Drs MUCHSINSIN
Librarian: Drs EFFENDI WAHYONO

Library of 30,000 vols
Number of teachers: 766
Number of students: 225,203

Publications: *Journal of Indonesian Studies* (2 a year), *Komunika* (4 a year), *Suara Terbuka* (monthly), *Journal of Education* (2 a year), *Indonesian Journal of Open and Distance Learning* (2 a year), *Journal of Mathematics, Science and Technology* (2 a year)

DEANS

Faculty of Economics: NADIA SRI DAMAYANTI
Faculty of Education: Dr PAULINA PANNEN
Faculty of Mathematics and Natural Science: Dr Ir DJOKOSETYANTO
Faculty of Social and Political Science: Drs ZAINUL ITTIHAD AMIN

INSTITUT SENI INDONESIA YOGYAKARTA
(Indonesia Institute of the Arts Yogyakarta)

Jl. Parangtritis Km 6.5, POB 1210, Yogyakarta 55188
Telephone: (274) 373659
Fax: (274) 371233
E-mail: arts@isi.ac.id
Internet: www.isi.ac.id

Founded 1984; university status
Language of instruction: Indonesian
Academic year: September to June

Rector: Prof.Dr I. MADE BANDEM
Vice-Rectors: Prof. Dr AM. HERMIN KUSMAYATI (Academic Affairs), I. WAYAN DANA (Administrative Affairs), Drs A. B. DWIANTORO (Student Affairs)
Registrar: Dra KUSMINIASTUTI
Librarian: Dra HERLIN NOVIAR SUBARYANTI

Library of 21,000 vols
Number of teachers: 298
Number of students: 2,644

Publication: *SENI, Journal for the Arts* (4 a year)

DEANS

Faculty of Performing Arts: Dr TRIYONO BRAMANTYO PAMUJO SANTOSO
Faculty of Fine Arts: Drs SUKARMAN
Faculty of Art of Recorded Media: Dr SOEDRANJO SOEDJONO

HEADS OF DEPARTMENTS

Faculty of Performing Arts (tel. and fax (274) 379133):
- Dance: Dra SUPRIYANTI
- Traditional Music: Drs SUBUH
- Western Music: Drs BUDI SANTOSA
- Drama: CHATRUL ANWAR
- Ethnomusicology: Drs BUDI RAHARJO
- Puppetry: Drs JOKO SUSENO

Faculty of Fine Arts:
- Fine Art: Drs ANDANE SUPRIHADI
- Crafts: Drs PURWIJO
- Design: Drs M. UMARHADI

INSTITUT TEKNOLOGI SEPULUH NOPEMBER
(Technology Institute of Sepuluh Nopember)

POB 900/SB, Surabaya 60008, East Java
Located at: Kampus ITS, Sukolilo, Surabaya 60111, East Java
Telephone: and fax (31) 5939632
E-mail: bpsi@its.ac.id
Internet: www.its.ac.id

Founded 1960
State control
Language of instruction: Indonesian
Academic year: September to June

Rector: Dr Ir. MUHAMMAD NUH
Vice-Rector for Academic Affairs: Prof. Ir. NOOR ENDAH B. MOCTAR
Vice-Rector for Administration: Ir. R. SYARIF WIDJAYA
Vice-Rector for Student Affairs: Dr Ir. ACHMAD JAZIDIE
Head of the Academic Administration and Student Affairs Bureau: Drs HARRY SANTOSO
Head of the General Administration and Finance Bureau: NURIJATI HAMID
Head of the Administration Planning and Information System Bureau: Ir. ARIE KISMANTO
Librarian: Drs ACHMAD

Library of 45,994 vols
Number of teachers: 1,043
Number of students: 17,384

Publications: *Berita ITS*, *Iptek*, *various faculty bulletins*

DEANS

Faculty of Civil Engineering and Planning: Prof. Dr Ir. PRIYO SUPROBO
Faculty of Mathematics and Sciences: Prof. Dr SUASMORO
Faculty of Industrial Technology: Dr Ir. TRIYOGI YUWONO
Faculty of Ocean Engineering: Ir. ASJHAR IMRON
Faculty of Information Technology: Prof. Ir. ARIEF DJUNAIDI

DIRECTORS

Research and Public Service Institute: Prof. Ir. I. NYOMAN SUTANTRA
Polytechnic of Ship Building: Ir. SUWARNO TAHID
Polytechnic of Electronics: Dr Ir. TITON DUTONO

PROFESSORS

ALTWAY, A., Chemical Engineering
ANWAR, N., Civil Engineering
BAKTIR, A., Chemical Engineering
DJANALI, S., Informatics Engineering
DJUNAIDY, A., Information System Engineering
ERSAM, T., Chemical Engineering
HADI, W., Environmental Engineering
KOESTALAM, P., Civil Engineering
LINUWIH, S., Statistics
MOCHTAR, I. B., Civil Engineering
MOCHTAR, N. E., Civil Engineering
NUH, M., Electrical Engineering
NURSUHUD, D., Mechanical Engineering
PENANGSANG, H. O., Electrical Engineering
PRATIKTO, W. A., Ocean Engineering
PURNOMO, M. H., Electrical Engineering
PURWONO, R., Structural Engineering
PUTU RAKA, I. G., Civil Engineering
RACHIMOELLAH, M., Chemistry
RAMELAN, R., Mechanical Engineering
RENANTO, Chemical Engineering
SANTOSA, M., Architecture
SANTOSO, H. R., Architecture
SARNO, R., Informatics Engineering
SILAS, J., Architecture
SOEBAGIO, Electrical Engineering
SOEGIONO, Ocean Engineering
SUASMORO, H., Physics
SUKARDJONO, S., Electrical Engineering
SUPROBO, P., Civil Engineering
SUTANTRA, N., Mechanical Engineering
SUTRISNO, H., Electrical Engineering
SUWARNO, J., Chemical Engineering
SUWARNO, N., Chemical Engineering
TJANDRASA, H., Informatics Engineering
WAHYUDI, H., Civil Engineering

UNIVERSITAS UDAYANA

Universitas Udayana, Kampus Bukit Jimbaran, Badung 80361, Bali
Telephone: (361) 704625
Fax: (361) 701907
E-mail: info@unud.ac.id
Internet: www.unud.ac.id

Founded 1962
State control
Language of instruction: Indonesian

Rector: Prof. Dr WAYAN WIA
Deputy Rector for Academic Affairs: Prof. Dr I. KETUT NEHEN
Deputy Rector for Administrative Affairs: Prof. Dr IDA BAGUS TJITARSA
Deputy Rector for Student Affairs: Prof. Dr Ir. I. GEDE SUYATNA
Librarian: Drs I. GUSTI NYOMAN TIRTAYASA

Number of teachers: 1,702
Number of students: 10,853

Publications: *Majalah Ilmiah Universitas Udayana* (4 a year), *Majalah Kedokteran Unud* (4 a year), *Berita Udayana* (monthly)

DEANS

Faculty of Letters (Arts): Drs A. A. BAGUS WIRAWAN
Faculty of Medicine: Prof. Dr I. KETUT SUATA
Faculty of Animal Husbandry: Prof. I. MADE MASTIKA
Faculty of Law: Prof. Dr DEWA GEDE ATMAJA
Faculty of Engineering: Ir. MADE DANA
Faculty of Economics: Dr KOMANG GEDE BENDESA
Faculty of Agriculture: Dr Ir. NYOMAN SUTJIPTA
Faculty of Sciences: Ir. I. DPP. SASTRAWAN
Faculty of Veterinary Science: Dr Drh. NYOMAN SADRA DHARMAWAN

PROFESSORS

ADIPUTRA, N., Occupational Health
ARDANA, G. G., History
ARDIKA, W., Archaeology
ARGA, Agricultural Economics
ARHYA, N., Biochemistry
ARKA, B., Veterinary Science
ARYANTA, W. R., Food Microbiology
ASTININGSIH, K., Poultry Production
ASTITI, T I. P., Custom Law
ATMAJA, D. G., Law
BAGUS, G. N., Social Anthropology
BAGUS, G. N., Indonesian Language
BAKTA, M., Internal Medicine
BAWA, W., Indonesian Language
BHINAWA, N., Animal Production
BUDHA, K., Surgery
BUNGAYA, G., Management
DJAGRA, I. B., Animal Production
KALAM, A. A. R., Arts and Design
LANA, K., Animal Nutrition
LANANG, O., Genetics
MANIK, G., Animal Husbandry
MANUABA, I. B. A., Human Physiology
MARDANI, N. K., Biology (Environmental Studies)
MASTIKA, M., Animal Nutrition
MATRAM, R. B., Veterinary Physiology
NALA, G. N., Human Physiology
NEHEN, K., Economic Development
NETRA SUBADIYASA, N., Soil Science
NITIS, M., Animal Nutrition
OKA, I. B., Pharmacology
PANGKAHILA, J. A., Sexology
PUTHERA, G. A. G., Human Histology
PUTRA, D. K. H., Animal Physiology
RATA, I. B., Archaeology
RIKA, K., Forage Science
SAIDI, H. S., Islamology
SIRTA, N., Custom Law
SOEWIGIONO, S., Gastroenterology
SUARNA, I. M., Forage Science
SUATA, I. K., Microbiology
SUDHARTA, T. R., Sanskrit Language
SUDJATHA, W., Food and Technology
SUKARDI, E., Human Anatomy
SUKARDIKA, K., Microbiology
SURAATMAJA, S., Paediatrics
SURYADHI, N. T., Public Health
SUTAWAN, N., Social and Agricultural Economics
SUTER, K., Food Technology
SUTHA, G. K., Law
SUTJIPTA, N., Social and Agricultural Economics
SUWETA, G. P., Veterinary Science
SUYATNA, G., Social Economics
TJITARSA, I. B., Public Health
WIDNYANA, M., Law
WINAYA, P. D., Soil Fertility
WIRAWAN, D. N., Public Health
WITA, W., Cardiology

CHAIRMEN OF STUDY PROGRAMMES

Veterinary Science: Drh I. GUSTI MADE GEDE
Tourism: Drs MADE SUKARSA
Fine Arts and Design: Drs NYOMAN SUKAYA
Agricultural Technology: Prof. I. WAYAN REDI ARYANTA

Private Universities

UNIVERSITAS 17 AGUSTUS 1945, SURABAYA
(17th of August 1945 University)

Telephone: (31) 5931800
Fax: (31) 5927817
E-mail: humus@untag-sby.ac.id
Internet: www.untag-sby.ac.id

Founded 1958
Language of instruction: Indonesian
Academic year: September to August

Faculties of Social and Political Sciences, Law, Economics, Psychology, Letters, Agricultural Science.

UNIVERSITAS HKBP NOMMENSEN

Jl. Sutomo 4A, POB 1133, Medan
Telephone: (61) 4522922
Fax: (61) 4571426
E-mail: nomensen@idola.net.id

Founded 1954
Private control: Batak Christian Protestant Church (HKBP)
Language of instruction: Indonesian
Academic year: September to July

Rector: Ir B. RICSON SIMARMATA
Vice-Rector (Academic Affairs): Drs RAFLES D. TAMPUBOLON
Vice-Rector (Financial Affairs): Drs PANTAS SILABAN
Vice-Rector (Student Affairs): Ir HOTMAN MANURUNG
Director of Community Service: Ir B. T. SIMANJORANG
Director of Research: Dr Ir JONGKER TAMPUBOLON

Number of teachers: 310
Number of students: 7,549

Publication: *VISI* (scientific magazine)

DEANS

Faculty of Economics: Drs ADANAN SILABAN
Faculty of Public and Business Administration: Drs MONANG SITORUS
Faculty of Engineering: Ir SINDAK HUTAURUK
Faculty of Law: TULUS SIAMBATON
Faculty of Animal Husbandry: Ir HERLINA SARAGI
Faculty of Agriculture: Ir P. PARLIN LUMBANRAJA
Faculty of Education: Dr TAGOR PANGARIBUAN
Faculty of Arts: Drs BEN M. PASARIBU

UNIVERSITAS IBN KHALDUN

Jl. Pemuda, Kav. 97, POB 1224, Rawamangun, Jakarta, Timur 13220
Telephone: (21) 4702564
Fax: (21) 4702564

Founded 1956
Languages of instruction: Indonesian, English, Arabic

Rector: Prof. Drs H. AMURA
Vice-Rectors: Drs TWK. ABBAS ABDULLAH, MUHSIN SOLEMAN, Drs H.M. ZIDNI NURI
Registrar: Drs M. UMAR BAAY
Librarian: Drs H. AIDIL FITRI M. HATTA

Number of teachers: 115
Number of students: 3,000

Publication: *Media UIC*

DEANS

Faculty of Communication: Drs HAMID SUCHAS
Faculty of Social and Political Science: (vacant)
Faculty of Law: ZULFATLI
Faculty of Economics: Ir. DJADID ASSEGAF
Faculty of Theology: ABD. KHALIK NUR ALI
Faculty of Agriculture: Ir. WASIS GUNADI
Institute of Islamic Mass Communication: Drs H. MOH. ALI
Institute of Social Research: Ir. RUSLI DJOHAN

UNIVERSITAS IBN KHALDUN BOGOR

Jl. K. H. Sholeh Iskandar Km. 2, POB 172, Bogor 16162
Telephone: (251) 356884
Fax: (251) 356884
E-mail: rector@mail.uika-bogor.ac.id
Internet: www.uika-bogor.ac.id

Founded 1961
Private control
Language of instruction: Indonesian
Chancellor: Prof. Dr Ir H. AFFENDI ANWAR
Rector: Dr Ir SUNSUN SAEFULHAKIM
Head of Academic Administration: Dra HERAWATI
Head of General Administration: Hj TITING SUHARTI
Librarian: Dra TATI TARSITI

Number of teachers: 300
Number of students: 4,293

Publication: *Islamic Journal of Technology, Institutional and Humanity Development* (2 a year)

DEANS

Faculty of Education: Drs YUSUF SHOBIRI
Faculty of Economics: H. AHMAD MUBAROK
Faculty of Law: BARLY
Faculty of Islamic Studies: Drs H. E. BAHRUDDIN
Faculty of Engineering: Dr Ir PRAWOTO
Graduate School of Islamic Studies: Dr K. H. DIDIN HAFIDHUDDIN

UNIVERSITAS ISLAM INDONESIA (Islamic University of Indonesia)

Gedung Rektorat, Jl. Kaliurang Km 14.5, Yogyakarta 55584, Java
Telephone: (274) 898444
Fax: (274) 898459
E-mail: rektorat@uii.ac.id
Internet: www.uii.ac.id

Founded 1945
An independent and private Islamic university
Language of instruction: Indonesian
Academic year: July to June

Rector: Dr LUTHFI HASAN
Vice-Rector (Academic Affairs): Dr S. F. MARBUN
Vice-Rector (Administrative and Financial Affairs): Dr H. MUQODIM
Vice-Rector (Student Affairs): Ir. H. BACHNAS
Vice-Rector (Collaborative Affairs): Dr A. AKHYAR ADNAN
Chief Administrative Officer: Drs H. SYAFARUDDIN ALWI
Librarian: Dra MURYANTI

Library of 73,000 vols
Number of teachers: 365
Number of students: 18,375

Publication: *UII News* (monthly)

DEANS

Faculty of Economics: Drs SUWARSONO
Faculty of Law: Dr JAWAHIR THONTOWI
Faculty of Civil Engineering and Planning: Prof. Dr IR. WIDODO
Faculty of Islamic Science: Drs H. MUDHOFAR AKHWAN
Faculty of Industrial Technology: Ir. H. BACHRUN SUTRISNO
Faculty of Psychology: Dr SUKARTI
Faculty of Mathematics and Science: JAKA NUGRAHA
Faculty of Medical Science: Prof. Dr Dr RUSDI LAMSUDDIN

HEADS OF DEPARTMENTS

Centre for Research: Dr Ir. RUZADI
Centre for Computerization and Statistics: Drs DEKAR URUMSAH
Centre for Public Service: Drs H. AMIR MUALIM
Centre for Islamic Guidance and Development: Drs H. AUNUR ROCHMAN FAQIH
Centre for Foreign Language: WIDYASARI LISTYOWULAN

PROFESSORS

AHMAD ANTONO, Concrete Structures
ASYMUNI, H., Islamic Court
ATMADJA, M. K., International Law
BAHARUDDIN LOPA, Criminal Law
BERNADIB, S. I., Methods of Educational Evaluation, Educational Philosophy
CHOTIB, H. A., Ushl al-Fiqh
DAHLAN, H. Z., Principles of Islamic Law
FATKHURRAHMAN, History of Islam and Islamic Law
HADITONO, S. R., Individual Psychology
HARDJOSO, R., Irrigation
HASAN POERBOHADIWIDJAJA, Environmental Planning
KOESNOE, H. M., Private Procedural Law
KUSNADI HARDJOSUMANTRI, Environment Law
MOCHTAR YAHYA, H., General Philosophy
MUH ZEIN, Method and Evaluation of Islamic Education
MULADI, Politics of Law
PARLINDUNGAN, A. P., Agrarian Law
PARTADIREDJA, H. A., Indonesian Economy
PRAGNYONO, R., Fluid Mechanics
PURNOMO, B., Criminal Law
RIYANTO, B., Development Economy
SATJIPTO RAHARDJO, Sociology of Law
SITI RAHAYU, Psychology
SOEDIKNO MERTOKOESOEMO, Civil Law, Jurisprudence
SOEDIRDJO, Educational Counselling, Curriculum Advancement
SOEKANTO, Business Policy
SOELISTYO, International Economy
SOEPARNO, Analytical Geometry
SRI SUMANTRI, Constitutional Law
SUNARDJO, R., Irrigation Technology
SUYUTI, H. Z., Statistics
SYACHRAN BASAH, Administrative Law
SYAFTI MA'ARIF, A., Islamic Cultural History
TUGIMAN, N., Indonesian Language
UMAR, H. M., Modern Islamic Ideology
UMAR ASSASUDDIN, English
WARSITO, Polymer Chemistry
YUSUF, H. H., Hadiths I, II, III

UNIVERSITAS ISLAM INDONESIA CIREBON (Islamic University of Indonesia in Cirebon)

Jl. Kapten Samadikun 31, Cirebon
President: SA'DILLAH FATHONI
Secretary: M. Z. ABIDIEN

DEANS

Faculty of Law: S. PRAWIRO
Faculty of Economics: Drs ROSYADI
Faculty of Theology: H. MAS'OED

UNIVERSITAS ISLAM JAKARTA

Jl. Balai Takyat, Utan Kayu, Jakarta 13120
Telephone: (21) 8566451
Fax: (21) 8504818
E-mail: informasi@uid.ac.id
Internet: www.uid.ac.id

Founded 1951
President: Prof. Dr SOEMEDI
Rector: SOEDJONO HARDJOSOEDIRO
Registrar: RASJIDI OESMAN
Librarian: ZAINAL ABIDIN

Number of teachers: 34
Number of students: 309

DEANS

Faculty of Law and Social Sciences: Drs H. NAZARUDIN
Faculty of Economics: TAHER IBRAHIM
Faculty of Education: H. M. NUR ASJIK

UNIVERSITAS ISLAM NUSANTARA

Jl. Soekarno-Hatta 530, POB 1579, Bandung 40286
Telephone: (22) 7509655
E-mail: humus@uninus.ac.id
Internet: www.uninus.ac.id

Founded 1959 as Universitas Nahdlatul Ulama; present name 1976
Academic year: September to August

Chancellor: Mayjen H. ACHMAD RUSTANDI
Rector: Dr H. DEDI MULYASANA
Deputy Rectors: Drs SUHENDRA YUSUF, WAHDI SUARDI, H. RUBI ROBANA
Registrar: Drs RUSLI
Librarian: Drs UNDANG SUDAR SANA

Number of teachers: 402
Number of students: 6,574

Publications: *Suara UNINUS* (4 a year), *Literat* (4 a year)

DEANS

Faculty of Law: Drs ENJANG SURACHMAN
Faculty of Economics: Drs KUSMANA
Faculty of Education and Literature: Dr DIDIN WAHIDIN
Faculty of Engineering: Ir. AGUS EDY PRANOTO
Faculty of Agriculture: Ir. RUBI ROBANA
Faculty of Communication Sciences: Drs H. S. INSAR MARTADIKUSUMAH
Faculty of Islamology: Drs HANAFI

PROFESSORS

Faculty of Law:
BASYAH, S., Public Administration Law
RASYIDI, L., Family Law
SANUSI, H. A., Law, Public Administration and Education

Faculty of Economics:
SURACHMAN, H., Management Economics

Faculty of Education and Literature:
EFFENDY, E. R., Mathematics
EMUH, Arabic
FAISAL, Y. A., Indonesian Literature
RUSYANA, Y., Indonesian Literature
SLAMET, H. A., Indonesian Language
SOEHARTO, B., Non-Formal Education
SYAMSUDDIN, Curriculum Development and Methodology

Faculty of Engineering:
HANDALI, D., Mathematics
SUMARNO, Mathematics

Faculty of Agriculture:
AISYAH, H., Pedology
SADELI, H.

Faculty of Communication Sciences:
HUSEIN, S. I., Communications Sciences

Faculty of Islamology:
DJATNIKA, H. R., Islamology
HELMY, H., Islamology
SALIMUDDIN, Islamology

UNIVERSITAS ISLAM RIAU
(Islamic University of Riau)

Jl. Kaharuddin Nasution 113, Perhentian, Marpoyan, Pekanbaru 28284, Riau

Telephone: (761) 674834
Fax: (761) 674834
Internet: www.unri.ac.id

Founded 1962
Academic year: July to June

Rector: Prof. Dr MUCHTAR AHMAD
Vice-Rector I: Prof. Dr DADANG ISKANDAR
Vice-Rector II: AMIR HASAN
Vice-Rector III: ARIFFIEN MANSYOER
Vice-Rector IV: Drs SUARDI LOEKMAN
Librarian: FIRDAUS

Library of 5,150 vols
Number of teachers: 660 (160 full-time, 500 part-time)
Number of students: 7,391

Publications: *Dinamika Pertanian* (4 a year), *Alam* (4 a year), *Presfektif* (2 a year), *Saintis* (2 a year), *Siasat* (2 a year)

DEANS

Faculty of Islamic Theology: ALI NUR
Faculty of Law: ARIFIN BOER
Faculty of Engineering: ALI MUSNAL
Faculty of Agriculture: Ir. T. ISKANDAR JOHAN
Faculty of Economics: Drs SHAHDANUR
Faculty of Political and Sociological Sciences: ZAINI ALI
Faculty of Education: Drs NAZIRUN

HEADS OF DEPARTMENTS

Faculty of Islamic Theology (tel. (761) 674669):
- Islamic Aqidah and Philosophy: ALINOUR SAG

Faculty of Law (tel. (761) 72127):
- Civil Law: SUNIMAR MARBUN
- Criminal Law: Dr YULIDA ARYANTI
- State Law: Dr H. SYAFRINALDI

Faculty of Engineering (tel. (761) 674717):
- Civil Engineering: Ir. ARHAN WANIM
- Petroleum Engineering: Ir. RINALDI IMRAN
- Mechanical Engineering: Ir. N. PERANGIN ANGIN

Faculty of Agriculture (tel. (761) 674681):
- Agronomy: Ir. T. ISKANDAR JOHAN
- Aquaculture: Dr AGUSNIMAR
- Agricultural Economics: Ir. ASRUL

Faculty of Economics (tel. (761) 674681):
- Management: SUYADI
- Economic Development Study: ELLYAN SASTRANINGSIH
- Accounting: YUSRAWATY

Faculty of Social Sciences and Politics (tel. (761) 674635):
- Government Sciences: Dra MONALISA
- Public and Business Administration: Drs TARMISI

Faculty of Education (tel. (761) 674775):
- Indonesian Teaching: Drs NAZIRUN
- English Teaching: Dra SYOFIANIS
- Biology Teaching: Dra SURYANTI
- Mathematics and Physics Teaching: Dra Hj. HANIFAH BOER

ATTACHED INSTITUTES

Centre for Rural Development Studies: Perhentian Marpoyan, Pekenbaru, Riau; Dir Ir. T. ISKANDAR JOHAN.

Management Development Centre: c/o Faculty of Economics, Perhentian Marpoyan, Pekanbaru, Riau; Dir Dr DETRI KARYA.

Centre for South-East Asian Studies (ASEAN): Dir (vacant).

Legal Aid Institution: Dir SH. RAMLI ZEIN.

Institute for Social Services: Dir AZAM AWANG.

Institute for Research: Jl. Perhentian Marpoyan, Pekanbaru, Riau; Dir Dr YULIDA ARYANTI.

Institute for Public Services: Dir T. ROSMAWATY.

UNIVERSITAS ISLAM SUMATERA UTARA
(Islamic University of North Sumatra)

Campus Munawarah, Teladan, Medan 20217, Sumatra

Telephone: (61) 716790
Fax: (61) 716790
Internet: www.uisu.ac.id

Founded 1952
Private control
Language of instruction: Indonesian
Academic year: July to June

Chancellor: Brig.-Gen. (retd) H. A. MANAF LUBIS
Rector: Drs H. M. YAMIN LUBIS
Registrar: Drs ABDUL HAKIM SIREGAR
Librarian: Drs SUDIAR SUDARGO

Number of teachers: 808
Number of students: 10,000

Publications: *Al Jamiah-UISU* (3 a year), *Buletin Fakultas Pertanian* (quarterly), *Buletin Fakultas Hukum* (6 a year)

DEANS

Faculty of Law: AMRIZAL PULUNGAN
Faculty of Islamic Law: Drs SAID ALHINDUAN
Faculty of Economics: Drs AHMAD GHAZALI
Faculty of Education and Teaching: Drs H. ADLIN AHMAD
Faculty of English: Drs MISRAN SUDIONO
Faculty of Islamic Education: H. MAHMUD AZIZ SIREGAR
Faculty of Islamic Communication: Drs MUSTAFA KAMIL
Faculty of Political Science: Drs DANAN JAYA
Faculty of Agriculture: Ir. MEIZAL
Faculty of Medicine: Prof. Dr H. HABIBAH HANUM NASUTION
Faculty of Engineering: Ir. H. M. ICHWAN NASUTION

UNIVERSITAS JAYABAYA

Jl. Pulomas Selatan kav 23, Jakarta Timur 13210

Telephone: (21) 4705466
Fax: (21) 4705482
E-mail: info@jayabaya.ac.id
Internet: www.jayabaya.ac.id

Founded 1958

Chancellor: Dr H. MOESLIM TAHER
Rector: Drs RIDWAN LUBIS
Rector II: H. A. RIYADI
Vice-Rector III: Drs MANSYUR

Number of teachers: 782
Number of students: 15,000

DEANS

Faculty of Law: Prof. Dr H. YUDHA BHAKTI
Faculty of Economics: Prof. Dr HJ. MIRRIAM
Faculty of Political and Social Sciences: H. AMIR SANTOSO
Faculty of Communication Science: DARMA SETIAWAN
Faculty of Technology: DARMA SETIAWAN
Faculty of Law and Management: H. INDARTONO RIVAI

ATTACHED RESEARCH INSTITUTES

Research and Development Institute: Dir Drs M. O. TAMBUNAN.

Business Research and Development: Dir CHALID ISMAIL.

Law Research and Legal Aid Bureau: Dir Mrs IDA.

Business Administration Aid Bureau: Dir Drs SUTRISNO.

UNIVERSITAS KATOLIK INDONESIA ATMA JAYA

Jl Jemdral Sudirman 51, Jakarta 12930

Telephone: (21) 5703306
Fax: (21) 5708811
E-mail: rek@atmajaya.ac.id
Internet: www.atmajaya.ac.id

Founded 1960
Languages of instruction: Indonesian, English
Academic year: July to June

Chairman of Board: Drs R. DJOKOPRANOTO
Rector: Prof. Dr BERNADETTE N. SETIADI
Vice-Rectors: IR. ST. NUGROHO KRISTONO, Dr MARCELLINUS MARCELLINO, Drs. PETRUS PIUS SALAMIN, Dr LILIANA SUGIHARTO
Librarian: Dr DIAO AI LIEN

Library of 70,260 vols
Number of teachers: 1,071
Number of students: 13,452

Publications: *Atma nan Jaya* (science, 3 a year), *Respons* (social ethics, 2 a year), *Jurnal Ekonomi dan Bisnis* (economics and business, 2 a year), *Jurnal Administrasi dan Bisnis* (administration and business, 4 a year), *Metris* (science and technology, 4 a year), *Majalah Kedokteran* (medical science, 3 a year), *Gloria Juris* (law and human rights, 2 a year)

DEANS

Faculty of Business Administration: Dr POL A. Y. AGUNG NUGROHO
Faculty of Economics: Drs SOFIAN SUGIOKO
Faculty of Engineering: Dr M. M. LANNY W. PANDJAITAN
Faculty of Law: ANTONIUS P. S. WIBOWO
Faculty of Medicine: Dr SATYA JOEWANA
Faculty of Psychology: Dr ENGELINA TANZIL BONANG
Faculty of Teacher Training and Education: Dr LAURA F. N. SUDARNOTO
Faculty of Technobiology: Prof. Dr ANTONIUS SUWANTO
Graduate School: Dr ALOISIUS AGUS NUGROHO

ATTACHED CENTRES

Centre for the Development of Ethics: Dir Dr MIKHAEL DUA (acting).

Centre for Health Research: Dir Prof. Dr Dr CHARLES SURJADI.

Centre for Language and Culture: Dir Prof. Dr BAMBANG KASWANTI PURWO.

Centre for Language Teaching: Dir Dra KATHARINA ENDRIATE SUKAMTO.

Centre for the Promotion of Professional Skills: Dir ALEXIUS BAMBANG SUNGKOWO.

Centre for Societal Development: Dir Dr LAMTIUR H. TAMPUBOLON.

Centre for Societal Empowerment: Dir VERONICA H. S. TENIZAR.

Community Service Institute: Chair. Ir PETRUS TAHIR URSAM.

Research Institute: Chair. Dr IRWANTO.

UNIVERSITAS KATOLIK PARAHYANGAN
(Parahyangan Catholic University)

Ciumbuleit 94, Bandung 40141

Telephone: (22) 2032655
Fax: (22) 2031110
E-mail: humas@home.unpar.ac.id
Internet: www.unpar.ac.id

Founded 1955
Private control
Language of instruction: Indonesian

Academic year: August to June
Chairman, Board of Trustees: Prof. Dr B. S. Kusbiantoro
Rector: Dr Pius Suratman Kartasasmita
Vice-Rector for Academic and Student Affairs: Dr Aloysius Rusli
Vice-Rector for Organization and Personnel: Dr Miryam L Wijaya
Vice-Rector for Financial Affairs: Drs Arthur Purboyo
Librarian: Dra Melina L. Tardia
Number of teachers: 1,321 (334 full-time, 687 part-time)
Number of students: 9,781
Publications: *Research Journal* (2 a year), *Bina Ekonomi* (4 a year), *Pro Justitia* (4 a year), *Potensia* (4 a year), *Jurnal Administrasi Publik* (2 a year), *Jurnal PACIS* (2 a year), *Melintas* (4 a year), *Integral* (4 a year), *Rekasaya* (4 a year), *Profil* (4 a year)

DEANS

Faculty of Economics: Dra Catharina Tan Lin Soei
Faculty of Law: R. Ismadi S, Bekti
Faculty of Social and Political Sciences: Drs. Denny Marcelinus Tri Aryadi
Faculty of Engineering: Dr Ir. R. W. Triweko
Faculty of Philosophy: Dr Ir. F. X. Rudiyanto Subagio
Faculty of Industrial Technology: Dr Budi Husodo Bisowarno
Faculty of Mathematics and Natural Sciences: Dra Rosa de Lima
Graduate School: Prof. Dr Ir. Paulus Pramanto Rahardjo

PROFESSORS

Brotosiswojo, B. S., Computer Physics
Dirjosisworo, S., Law
Djajaputera, A., Civil Engineering
Nimpoeno, J. S., Psychology
Rahardjo, P. P., Geotechnology
Sjafruddin, A., Law
Sidharta, B. A., Law
Siregar, S., Architecture
Soelarnosidji, D., Geotechnology in Civil Engineering
Suharto, Ign., Chemical Engineering
Sundjaja, R. S., Management
Surjoatmono, B., Civil Engineering
Winardi, Economics

ATTACHED INSTITUTE

Research Institute: Dir Dr Mauro P. Rahardjo.
Community Service Institute: Dir Drs P. C. Suroso.

UNIVERSITAS KRISNADWIPAJANA

Jl. Raya Jati Waringin, Pondok Gede, Jakarta 13077
Telephone: (21) 8462229
Fax: (21) 8462461
E-mail: humas@unkris.ac.id
Internet: www.unkris.ac.id
Founded 1952
Language of instruction: Indonesian
Academic year: February to December
Rector: Dr T. Gayus Lumbuun
Vice-Rector I: H. Syamsu Djalal
Vice-Rector III: H. Dahlan Mansur
Vice-Rector IV: Drs. Hermawan Pramulo
Director of Postgraduate Programmes: Prof. Dr Rusli Ramli
Secretary: Wayan Sugiyana
Librarian: Dr Daspan
Number of teachers: 128
Number of students: 2,000

DEANS

Faculty of Law: Dr Lodewijk Gultom
Faculty of Economics: Drs. Muhadi Riyanto
Faculty of Science Administration: Drs. Jack R. Sidabutar
Faculty of Technology: Rusjdi Hadjerat

UNIVERSITAS KRISTEN INDONESIA
(Christian University of Indonesia)

Jl. Mayjen Sutoyo, Cawang, Jakarta 13630
Telephone: (21) 8092425
Internet: www.uki.ac.id
Founded 1953
Rector: Prof. Dr K. Tunggul Sirait
Vice-Rector for Academic Affairs: Dr A. S. L. Rampen
Vice-Rector for Administration Planning and Development: E. Gunawan
Vice-Rector for Student Affairs: A. Siregar
Number of teachers: 739
Number of students: 8,000
Publications: *UKI Bulletin*, *Logos*, *Jurnal Ekonomi*, *Honeste Vivere*, *Dialektika*, *Dinamika Pendidikan*, *Emas*

DEANS

Faculty of Education: Togap Linanjuntak
Faculty of English Language and Literature: Dr L. S. Bangun
Faculty of Economics: Drs A. Zabua
Faculty of Law: Dr Bernard Hutabarak
Faculty of Medicine: Dr S. M. L. Toruan
Faculty of Technology: Dr A. Soebagio
Faculty of Social and Political Science: Prof. Dr Payung Bangun

ATTACHED INSTITUTES

Department of Languages.
Department of Legal Aid.
Department of Educational Research.
Computer Centre.
Educational Technology Centre.
Centre for Guidance and Counselling.
Community Development Centre.
Institute of Management.

UNIVERSITAS KRISTEN MARANATHA
(Maranatha Christian University)

Jl. Prof. Suria Sumantri 65, Bandung 40164
Telephone: (22) 2012186
Fax: (22) 2015154
E-mail: humas@maranatha.edu
Internet: www.marantha.edu
Founded 1965
Language of instruction: Indonesian
Academic year: September to August
Rector: Dr Bambang S. P. Abednedo
Number of teachers: 850
Number of students: 7,000
Publications: *Majalah Ilmiah Maranatha* (Maranatha Scientific Magazine, 4 a year), *Media Komunikasi Maranatha* (Maranatha Communication Media, 3 a year), *Journal Kedoktoran* (Medicine Journal, annually)

DEANS

Faculty of Medicine: Sulaiman Sastrawinata
Faculty of Psychology: Sawitri Supardi
Faculty of Engineering: Ibrahim Surya
Faculty of Literature: Jusak Supardjan
Faculty of Economics: R. Sanusi

HEADS OF DEPARTMENTS

Civil Engineering: Noek Sulandari
Electrical Engineering: Aan Darmawan
Industrial Engineering: Imam Istiyanto
English: Trisnowati Tanto
Japanese: Endah S. Satari
Management: Tedy Wahyusaputra
Accounting: Soddin Mangunsong
Non-degree Program for English: (vacant)

UNIVERSITAS KRISTEN SATYA WACANA
(Satya Wacana Christian University)

Jl. Diponegoro 52–60, Salatiga 50711, Central Java
Telephone: (298) 321212
Fax: (298) 321433
E-mail: pr4@uksw.edu
Internet: www.uksw.edu
Founded 1956
Languages of instruction: Indonesian, English(for special programmes only)
Academic year: August to July
Rector: Prof.Dr John Titaley
Deputy Rector for Academic Affairs: Dr Ir Danny Manongga
Deputy Rector for Finance and Administration: Prapto Yuwono
Deputy Rector for Student Affairs: Entri Sulistari Gundo
Deputy Rector for External Affairs: Raema Andreyana
Registrar: Sudi Winarno
Librarian: Drs Djasmani
Number of teachers: 306 (full-time)
Number of students: 9,325
Publications: *Citra Wacana* (4 a year), *Kritis* (3 a year), *Annual Report* (annually), *Dian Ekonomi* (2 a year)

DEANS

Faculty of Law: J. Danny Zacharias
Faculty of Economics: Prof. Hendrawan Supratikno
Faculty of Biology: Drs Agna Sulis Krave
Faculty of Agriculture: Ir Suprihati
Faculty of Technology: Ir Budihardja Murtianta
Faculty of Science and Mathematics: Dr Agus Kristijanto
Faculty of Theology: Drs. Daniel Nuhamara
Faculty of Education and Teacher Training: Drs. Augus Herman Naiola
Faculty of Social and Political Sciences: Dr Kutut Suwondo
Faculty of Languages and Letters: Drs Urip Sutiyono
Faculty of Psychology: Dra Hari Sutjiningsih
Faculty of Pedagogy: Dr Lobby Lukmono
Faculty of Performing Arts: Drs Agastya Rama Listya
Postgraduate Programmes: Prof. Daniel daud Kameo
Professional Programmes: Lina Sinatra

UNIVERSITAS MUHAMMADIJAH

Jl. K. H. Ahmad Dahlan, Cirendeu Ciputat, Jakarta 15419
Telephone: (21) 7401894
Fax: (21) 7430756
Internet: www.umj.ac.id
Rector: Agus Sunarto
Faculties of Social and Political Sciences, Law, Economics, Technology, Agriculture, Religion, Medicine.

UNIVERSITAS MUHAMMADIYAH MALANG
(Muhammadiyah University of Malang)

Jl. Raya Tlogomas 246, Malang 65144, East Java
Telephone: (341) 464318
Fax: (341) 460782
E-mail: webmaster@unix.umm.ac.id
Internet: www.umm.ac.id
Founded 1966
Languages of instruction: Indonesian, English
Academic year: September to June
Rector: Drs H. Muhadjir Effendy

Vice-Rector for Academic Affairs: Ir H. MUH. HAMZAH
Vice-Rector for Financial Affairs: Drs H. WAKIDI
Vice-Rector for Student Affairs: Ir H. ALI SAIFULLAH
Chief of Public Administration: Drs H. FAUZAN
Chief of Academic Administration: Ir DAMAT
Librarian: WAHJOE DWI PRIJONO

Number of teachers: 816
Number of students: 20,274

Publications: *Bestari Journal* (4 a year), *Bestari Tabloid* (monthly)

DEANS

Faculty of Agriculture: Ir MISBAH RUHIYAT
Faculty of Economics: Drs WAHYU HIDAYAT RIYANTO
Faculty of Engineering: Ir SUNARTO
Faculty of Islamic Education: Drs MOH. NURHAKIM
Faculty of Law: MOKH. HAJIH
Faculty of Psychology: Drs LATIPUN
Faculty of Social and Political Science: Dra VINA SALVIANA
Faculty for Teacher Training and Education: Drs AHSANUL IN'AM
Faculty of Animal Husbandry: Ir ABDUL MALIK
Faculty of Medicine: Ir H. MUH. HAMZAH (acting)

UNIVERSITAS NASIONAL

Jl. Sawo Manila, Pasar Minggu, Jakarta 12520
Telephone: (21) 7806700
Fax: (21) 7802719
E-mail: info@unas.ac.id
Internet: www.unas.ac.id

Founded 1949
Academic year: September to August

Rector: Prof. Drs UMAR BASALIM
Vice-Rectors: Ir. NGADINO SURIP (Academic Affairs), EL AMRY BERMAWI PUTERA (Financial and General Administrative Affairs), Drs EKO SUGIYANTO (Student and Alumni Affairs), Drs UMAR SAID (University Relations)
Chief Administrative Officer: Ir. SJAHROEL SJARIF
University Librarian: AMRAN BANUREA

Number of teachers: 550
Number of students: 6,523

Publication: *Ilmu Dan Budaya* (monthly)

DEANS

Faculty of Agriculture: Ir. TRI WALUYO
Faculty of Biology: Dr KHOE SUSANTO KUSUMAHADI
Faculty of Economics: MOCH. ROEM ALIM
Faculty of Law: T. YUZAD FIDDIAN
Faculty of Letters: Drs FALDY RASYIDIE
Faculty of Social and Political Science: Drs HASTO ATMOJO SUROYO
Faculty of Technology and Science: Ir. IDRIS KUSUMA

UNIVERSITAS PAKUAN

Jl. Pakuan, POB 452, Bogor
Telephone: (251) 312206
Internet: www.unpak.ac.id

Founded 1961

Chancellor: Dr H. MASHUDI
Rector: ACHMAD SUBROTO
Secretary: R. H. NATANEGARA

Number of teachers: 60
Number of students: 350

DEANS

Faculty of Law: BINTATAR SINAGA
Faculty of Economics: Drs USMAN ZAKARIA
Faculty of Technology: DJAUHARI NOOR
Faculty of Mathematics and Natural Science: IR. SOEDARSONO

UNIVERSITAS PANCASILA

Srengseng Sawah, Jagakarsa, Pasar Minggu, Jakarta Selatan 12640
Telephone: (21) 7270086
Fax: (21) 7271868
E-mail: upancas@cbn.net.id
Internet: www.univpancasila.ac.id

Founded 1966
Language of instruction: Indonesian
Academic year: September to August

Chairman: Dr Ir. SISWONO YUDOHUSODO
Rector: EDIE TOET HENDRATNO
Vice-Rectors: Prof. Ir. ANTONIUS ANTON (Academic Affairs and Finance and Administration), H. ALWI ASSEGAF (Student Affairs), Drs ANANG FADILLAH RIVAI
Registrar: Dr SAPTADI WIDJAYA SETIABUDI
Librarian: WAKIM

Library of 30,906 vols
Number of teachers: 860
Number of students: 12,017

Publications: *Media Humas*, *Buletin Farmasi*, *Suara Ekonomi*, *Retorika*, *Jurnal Teknik*

DEANS

Faculty of Pharmacy: Drs I. WAYAN REDJA
Faculty of Economy: Dra DEWI TRIRAHAYU
Faculty of Law: INDAH HARLINA
Faculty of Engineering: Prof. Ir. ANTONIUS ANTON

PETRA CHRISTIAN UNIVERSITY

Jl. Siwalankerto 121-131, Surabaya 60236, East Java
Telephone: (31) 8439040
Fax: (31) 8436418
E-mail: info@peter.petra.ac.id
Internet: www.petra.ac.id

Founded 1961
Private control
Languages of instruction: Indonesian, English
Academic year: August to June

Rector: PAULUS NUGRAHA
Vice-Rector for Academic Affairs: F. JONES SYARANAMUAL
Vice-Rector for Finance and Administration: J. HERYANTO
Vice-Rector for Student Affairs: HERRY SAPTONO WARPINDYASMORO
Vice-Rector for Co-operation and Institutional Development: PAUL NUGRAHA (acting)
Registrar: WIDIARTI SUPRAPTO
Librarian: HENNY LINGGAWATI

Library: 104,138 books, 6,916 audiovisual items
Number of teachers: 758 (incl. 227 full-time)
Number of students: 10,161

Publications: *Architecture Dimension* (2 a year), *Civil Engineering Dimension* (2 a year), *Mechanical Engineering Journal* (2 a year), *Informatic Journal* (2 a year), *Industrial Engineering Journal* (2 a year), *Electrical Journal* (2 a year), *Nirmana* (visual communication design, 2 a year), *Accounting and Finance Journal* (2 a year), *Management and Entrepreneur Journal* (2 a year), *K@TA* (language and literature, 2 a year)

DEANS

Faculty of Letters: Drs BINTORO
Faculty of Civil Engineering and Planning: Ir PAULUS H. SOEHARGO
Faculty of Industrial Technology: Ir OEGIK SUGIHARDJO
Faculty of Economics: Drs DEVIE
Faculty of Art and Design: Ir LUKITO KARTONO
Faculty of Communication Studies: Ir JONES SYARANAMUAL (acting)

HEADS OF DEPARTMENTS

English: Drs RIBUT BASUKI
Chinese: Drs STEFANUS SUPRAJITNO
Civil Engineering: Ir RUSLAN DJAJADI
Architecture: TIMOTICIN KWANDA
Mechanical Engineering: Ir JONI DEWANTO
Industrial Engineering: Ir JULIANINGSIH
Electrical Engineering: Ir EMMY HOSEA
Informatics Engineering: Ir DJONI H. SETIABUDI
Management: PETER REMY YOSY PASLA
Accounting: SETYARINI SANTOSA
Hotel Management: Dra DEWI ASTUTI
Tourism and Leisure Management: WIDJOJO SUPRAPTO
International Business Management: RICKY
Accounting: SETYARINI SENTOSA
Interior Design: STEPHANUS P. HONGGOWIDJAJA
Visual Design Communications: ANDRIAN DEKTISA HAGIJANTO
Communications Studies: Drs RONNY H. MUSTAMU
Architecture and Interior Communication Program: HERU DWI WALUYANTO
Postgraduate Program in Civil Engineering: Ir RATNA SETIAWARDANI ALIFEN

ATTACHED INSTITUTES

Language Education Centre: Dir VYRNA SANTOSO.

Continuing Education Centre: Dir Ir IMA MULJATI GINSAR.

Computing Centre: Dir Ir THERESIA LESTIOWATI.

Research Center: Dir Ir KRISWANTO WIDIAWAN.

UNIVERSITAS TRISAKTI

Jl. Kyai Tapa, Grogol, Jakarta 11440
Telephone: (21) 5663232
Fax: (21) 5673001
E-mail: info@trisakti.ac.id
Internet: www.trisakti.ac.id

Founded 1965
Language of instruction: Indonesian
Academic year: September to August

Rector: Prof. Dr THOBY MUTIS
Vice-Rectors: ASRI NUGRAHANTI ADJIDARMO (Academic Affairs), Drs H. YUSWAR Z. BASRI (Personnel, Administration and Finance), I. KOMANG SUKA'ARSANA (Student Affairs), Ir. N. SUTAN ASSIN (Co-operation and Human Resources)
Secretariat: H. SOFAN
Head of Library: FARIDA SALIM

Number of teachers: 2,406 (991 full-time, 1415 part-time)
Number of students: 31,626

Publication: *Warta Usakti* (monthly)

DEANS

Faculty of Dentistry: Drg. BAMBANG S. TRENGGONO
Faculty of Medicine: Dr YULIUS E. SURYAWIDJAJA
Faculty of Law: H. ADI ANDOJO SUTJIPTO
Faculty of Economics: Dr CHAIRUMAN ARMIA
Faculty of Civil Engineering and Planning: Ir. SOERJATMO WREKSOATMODJO
Faculty of Industrial Technology: Prof. Dr Ing. H. FARAZ UMAR
Faculty of Landscape Architecture and Environmental Technology: Prof. Dr Ir. SOEPANGAT SOEMARTO

Faculty of Mineral Technology: Ir. ASRI NUGRAHANTI IRDJIANTO
Faculty of Art and Design: Dra J. PAMUDJI SUPTANDAR
Postgraduate Programme: Prof. Dr THOBY MUTIS

HEADS OF DEPARTMENTS

Faculty of Law:
Civil Law: HASNI
Criminal Law: ERIYANTOU WAHID
International Law (Public): G. P. H. HARYO MATARAM
Faculty of Economics:
Management: Dra Hj. NIDJAT IBRAHIM
Accountancy: Drs BAMBANG SUDARYONO
Economics and Developmental Studies: Dra TIKTIK S. PRATOMO
Faculty of Civil Engineering and Planning:
Civil Engineering: Dr Ir. BUDI WIBAWA
Architectural Engineering: Ir. DJOKO SANTOSO
Faculty of Industrial Technology:
Electrical Engineering: Ir. MAULA SUKMAWIDJAJA
Mechanical Engineering: Ir. TRIYONO
Industrial Engineering: Ir. DOCKY SARASWATI
Computer Engineering: Ir. DJASLI DJAMARUS
Faculty of Landscape Architecture and Environmental Technology:
Landscape Architecture: Ir. RUSTAM HAKIM
Environmental Technology: Ir. WIDYO ASTONO
Planning Engineering: Ir. AIDAD A. GAFAR
Faculty of Mineral Technology:
Petroleum Engineering: Ir. SITI NURAINI SIBUEA
Geological Engineering: Ir. HIDARTAN
Mining Engineering: Ir. ATMOSO SOEHOED
Faculty of Art and Design:
Art: Drs UDANARTO
Design: Dra TETTY SEKARYATI

ATTACHED INSTITUTES

Research Institute: Dir Dr Ir. DADAN UMAR DAIHANI.

Institute for Community Service: Dir Ir. ADHY R. THAHIR.

ATTACHED COLLEGES AND ACADEMIES

Academy of Tourism: Dir MARYAM MIHARDJO.

College of Economics: Dir HANDOKO KARYANTORO.

College of Transport Management: Dir H. SJAHRIR SOELAIMAN.

Academy of Insurance: Dir Drs SAFRI AYAT.

Academy of Graphical Engineering: Dir Drs FAREL SITANGGANG.

UNIVERSITAS VETERAN REPUBLIK INDONESIA

Jl. G. Bawakaraeng 72, Ujung Pandang

Faculties of history, law and education.

Schools of Art and Music

Akademi Seni Karawitan Indonesia Padang Panjang (Academy for Traditional Music and Dance): Jl. Puti Bungsu 35, Padang Panjang, Sumatera Barat; tel. (752) 82077; fax (752) 82803; f. 1966; Diploma courses in ballet, dance, music and music performance; library: 6,196 vols; 62 teachers; 428 students; Dir Prof. MARDJANI MARTAMIN; Registrar BAHRUL PADEK; Librarian Drs ANNAS HAMIR

HEADS OF DEPARTMENTS

Traditional Music: Drs DJARUDDIN AMAR
Traditional Dance: NIRWANA MURNI
School Music: DIRWAN WAKIDI

Akademi Seni Tari Indonesia: Jl. Buahbatu 212, Bandung, Jawa Barat; tel. (22) 421532; f. 1970; degree courses in traditional music and dance; library: *c.* 5,113 vols; c. 74 teachers; c. 342 students; Dir Drs MA'MUR DANASASMITA; Librarian R. OETJE ROEKMIATI

HEADS OF DEPARTMENTS

Dance: IYUS RUSLIANA
Traditional Music: TATANG SURYANA
Theatre: YOYO C. DURACHMAN

INSTITUT SENI INDONESIA (Indonesia Institute of the Arts)

Jalan Parangtritis Km 6.5, Sewon, Yogyakarta
Telephone: (274) 379133
Fax: (274) 371233
E-mail: arts@isi.ac.id
Internet: www.isi.ac.id

Rector: Prof. Dr I. MADE BANDEM
Rector I: Dr HERMIN KUSMAYATI
Rector II: WAYAN DANA
Rector III: Drs. A. B. DWIANTORO.

Sekolah Tinggi Seni Indonesia Surakarta (Ex ASKI Surakarta) (Indonesia College of the Arts): Kampus STSI, Surakarta, Jl. ki Hajar Dewantara 19, Kentingan, Jebres, Surakarta Jawa Tengah 57126; tel. (271) 647658; fax (271) 646175; e-mail direct@stsi-ska.ac.id; internet www.stsi-ska.ac.id; f. 1964; diploma and master's degree courses, postgraduate programme; library: 36,588 vols; 203 teachers; 852 students; Dir Prof. Dr SOETARNO; Vice Dirs Drs SOEGENG TOEKIO M. SUMANTO, SUTARNO HARYONO; Librarian SULISTYOWATI

HEADS OF DEPARTMENTS

Music: I WAYAN SADRA
Puppetry: SUYANTO
Dance: HADI SUBAGYO
Fine Arts: Drs GUNTUR

IRAN

The Higher Education System

The first modern institution of higher education was the Dar al-Fanun, a technical institute founded in 1851. In 1928 two more technical institutes were founded, now known as Iran University of Science and Technology and K. N. Toosi University of Technology. In 1934 Dar al-Fanun was incorporated into the newly-established University of Tehran, the first multi-disciplinary institution of higher education. Universities were closed following the Islamic revolution in 1979 but gradually reopened from 1983. Public universities and colleges are administered by the Ministry of Science, Research and Technology, and medical universities (which are classified separately) are controlled by the Ministry of Health and Medical Education. In 1980 an 'open' university, Islamic Azad University, was founded, which now has 80 centres in cities and towns. It is not funded by central government, it administers its own entrance examination and charges tuition fees. Payame Noor University was founded in 1987 and offers correspondence courses and continuing adult education. There are 37 universities, and in 2004/05 1,018,980 students were enrolled at public institutions of higher education, in addition to the 1,098,491 students enrolled at the Islamic Azad University. Other higher education institutions include general and professional colleges, technological institutes and vocational establishments.

To enter higher education students must gain the Pre-University Certificate and sit and the National Entrance Examination. (Islamic Azad University administers its own entrance examination—Kunkur). Iranian higher education is based on a 'credit semester' system; one credit is gained following 17 hours of taught classes, 34 hours of laboratory work or 51 hours of practical ('workshop') experience. The first undergraduate qualification is the Associate degree, awarded after four semesters (two years) and requiring 67–72 credits. Colleges of Further Education offer an equivalent degree known as Kardani. The Bachelors is the second (and main) undergraduate degree, lasting eight semesters (four years) and requiring 130–35 credits. First degrees offering professional titles are available in pharmacy, medicine, dentistry and veterinary science; these last 11 semesters (six years). A student with the Bachelors may progress to postgraduate education, which consists of the Masters (Karshenasi-Arshad or Fogh-Licence) and Doctorate. The Masters is a course lasting four semesters (two years) and requiring 28–32 credits (of which the thesis accounts for four to 10 units). The final university degree is the Doctorate, which consists of two stages: firstly, the student must complete 12–30 credits of classroom-based learning; secondly, a period of original research leading to submission of a thesis is required. The course lasts a total of four to five years.

University courses must be accredited by either the Ministry of Science, Research and Technology Directorate of Development or the Ministry of Health and Medical Education.

Learned Societies

GENERAL

UNESCO Office Tehran: Bahman Bldg, Sa'ad Abad Palace Complex, Tehran 14168; tel. (21) 2740141; fax (21) 2740144; e-mail a.salih@unesco.org; designated Cluster Office for Afghanistan, Iran, Pakistan and Turkmenistan; Dir ABDIN MOHAMED ALI SALIH.

ECONOMICS, LAW AND POLITICS

Iran Management Association: POB 15855-359, Tehran; located at: Karimkhan Blvd 1/53 corner of Asjodi St, Tehran; tel. (21) 8827878; fax (21) 8835278; e-mail info@iranmanagement.org; internet www.iranmanagement.org; f. 1960 to promote sound management principles and techniques for the improvement of management in Iran, and to create understanding and co-operation among managers in Iran and other countries; 200 individual and 200 institutional mems; library of 8,000 vols; Sec.-Gen. PARVIZ BAYAT; publs *Management Magazine* (in Persian, with summary in English, monthly), *Modiriat* (Management, 6 a year).

HISTORY, GEOGRAPHY AND ARCHAEOLOGY

Ancient Iran Cultural Society: Jomhorie Eslamie Ave, Shahrokh St, Tehran; f. 1961; Man. Dir A. QUORESHI.

British Institute of Persian Studies: c/o The British Acad., 10 Carlton House Terrace, London, SW1Y 5AH, United Kingdom; tel. (20) 7969-5203; fax (20) 7969-5401; e-mail bips@britac.ac.uk *in Tehran:* POB 11365-844, Khiaban-e Dr Ali Shariati, Qolhak, Tehran; tel. (21) 2601937; fax (21) 2604901; e-mail bips@parsonline.net; internet www.britac.ac.uk/institutes/bips; f. 1961; cultural institute, with special emphasis on history, archaeology and all aspects of Iranian studies; 400 mems; library of 10,000 books and MSS; Hon. Sec. Prof. ROBIN CONINGHAM; Sec. ELAHE YAZDI; publ. *Iran* (annual).

LANGUAGE AND LITERATURE

British Council: Qolhak, Khiabane Dr. Shariati, 200 m below Sadr Expressway opp. Bonbaste Elahieh, Tehran 19396 13661; tel. (21) 2001222; fax (21) 2007604; e-mail enquiries@britishcouncil.org.ir; internet www.britishcouncil.org/iran; offers courses and exams in English language and British culture and promotes cultural exchange with the UK; Dir MICHAEL WILSON.

MEDICINE

Iranian Society of Microbiology: Department of Microbiology and Immunology, Faculty of Medicine, University of Tehran; f. 1940; 185 mems; Gen. Sec. G. H. NAZARI.

NATURAL SCIENCES

Mathematical Sciences

Iranian Mathematical Society: POB 13145-418, Tehran; tel. (21) 880-8855; fax (21) 880-7775; e-mail iranmath@rose.ipm.ac.ir; f. 1971; 2,750 mems; Secs. R. ZAARE-NAHANDI, A. ALIMADAD; publs *Bulletin* (2 a year), *Farhang va Andishaye Riyazi* (2 a year), *Khabarnameh* (newsletter, 4 a year).

Research Institutes

GENERAL

Institute for Humanities and Cultural Studies (IHCS): 64 St, Seyyed Jamal-eddin Ave, Tehran 14374; tel. (21) 8048037; fax (21) 8036317; f. 1981; research faculties: literature, history, history and philosophy of science, religious studies, linguistics, social sciences, cultural studies; languages of instruction: Arabic, English; library of 120,000 vols; Dir Prof. MEHDI GOLSHANI; publs *The Farhang* (quarterly), *Journal of Humanities* (quarterly), *Afaq al-Hizarah al-Islamiyyah* (2 a year), *Science and Religion Bulletin* (2 a year).

AGRICULTURE, FISHERIES AND VETERINARY SCIENCE

Animal Science Research Institute: POB 31585-1483, Karaj, Tehran; tel. (261) 430010; fax (261) 413258; e-mail ahri@abdnet.com; f. 1933; research on cattle, water buffalo, sheep, goats, poultry and honey-bees; library of 6,425 books, 176 periodicals; Gen. Dir. Dr MOHAMMAD ALI KAMALI; publ. *Animal Husbandry Research Institute*.

Plant Pests and Diseases Research Institute: POB 19395, Evin/Tabnak St Tehran 1454; tel. (21) 2403012; fax (21) 2403691; e-mail a-abdullahi@areeo.or.ir; internet www.irib.com/PPDRI; f. 1943; research on pests and diseases of agricultural crops; botany, entomology, biological control, pesticides and agricultural zoology; library of 55,000 vols (English and Farsi), 480 periodicals (English and Farsi); Dir Dr G. A. ABDOLLAHI; publs *Applied Entomology and Phytopathology* (annually, in Farsi and English), *Rostaniha – Botanical Journal of Iran* (annually, in Farsi and English), *Iranian Journal of Plant*

Pathology (annually, in Farsi and English), *Journal of the Entomological Society of Iran* (annually, in Farsi and English).

Razi Vaccine and Serum Research Institute: POB 11365-1558, Karaj, Hesarak; tel. (261) 4570038; fax (261) 4552194; e-mail admin@rvsri.com; internet www.rvsri.com; f. 1930; epizootological and ecological studies of animal diseases and human and animal biology; research and preparation of all veterinary vaccines, some human vaccines and therapeutic sera; postgraduate courses in virology and microbiology; languages of instruction: Persian, English; library of 13,000 books, 800 periodicals; Gen. Dir Dr MOHAMMAD ALI AKHAVIZADEGAN; publs *Archives of the Razi Institute* (in English, annually), *Annual Report* (in Persian).

Seed and Plant Improvement Institute (SPII): POB 4119, Mardabad Ave, Karaj 31585; tel. (261) 2228558; fax (261) 229405; e-mail spii.int@abdnet.com; Dir-Gen. Dr E. MADJIDI.

ECONOMICS, LAW AND POLITICS

Institute for Political and International Studies (IPIS): Shahid Bahonar Ave, Shahid Aghaee St, POB 19395/1793, Tehran; tel. (21) 2802671; fax (21) 2802649; e-mail ipis@dre-mfa.gov.ir; internet www.dre-mfa.gov.ir; f. 1983; acts as a research and information centre on international relations, law, economics and Islamic studies, with emphasis on the Middle East, the Persian Gulf and Central Asia; holds conferences and seminars on contemporary international issues; library of 80,000 vols; Pres. SEYED SADEGH KHARRAZI; Dir-Gen. Dr SEYED M. K. SAJJADPOUR; publs *Foreign Policy Quarterly* (in Farsi), *Iranian Journal of International Affairs Quarterly* (in English), *Central Asia and Caucasus Review Quarterly* (in Farsi), *Amyu Darya* (in English and Russian), *Islam and International Relations* (in Farsi), *Journal of Alalaghat Aliranieh* (in Arabic).

Institute for Trade Studies and Research: 240 North Kargar St, POB 14185-671, Tehran 14187; tel. (21) 6425118; fax (21) 6938374; e-mail scient-relations@irtp.com; internet itsr.irtp.com; f. 1980; library of 70,000 vols; Dir Dr A. R. EFTEKHARI.

HISTORY, GEOGRAPHY AND ARCHAEOLOGY

Institut Français de Recherche en Iran: Ave Shahid Nazari, 52 rue Adib, POB 15815-3495, Tehran 94371; tel. (21) 640-11-92; fax (21) 6405501; e-mail ifri@ifriran.org; internet www.ifriran.org; f. 1897, present name 1983; research into Iranian civilization, contact between French and Iranian scholars; library of 42,000 vols; Dir CHRISTOPHE BALAIJ; publs *Abstracta Iranica* (annually), *Cahiers de la DAFI, Bibliothéque Iranienne*.

National Cartographic Centre: POB 13185-1684, Azadi Sq., Meraj Ave, Tehran; tel. (21) 600-0031; fax (21) 600-1971; f. 1953; library of 4,000 vols, 2,500 reports; Dir Dr M. MADAD; publ. *Naghshebardari* (Journal of Surveying, 4 a year).

MEDICINE

Institut Pasteur: 69 Pasteur Ave, Tehran; tel. (21) 6469871; fax (21) 6465132; e-mail office@institute.pasteur.ac.ir; internet www.pasteur.ac.ir; f. 1921; vaccines, research in microbiology, biochemistry, biopharmaceuticals, biotechnology and human genetics, molecular biology, parasitology and mycology, physiology and pharmacology; teaching and postgraduate training; Dir-Gen. Dr M. TAGHIKHANI; publ. *Iranian Biomedical Journal*.

RELIGION, SOCIOLOGY AND ANTHROPOLOGY

Anthropological Research Institute: Azadi Ave, Zanjan Int., POB 13445-719, Tehran; tel. (21) 6016367; fax (21) 6018628; f. 1937; attached to Iranian Cultural Heritage Organization; Dir MOHAMMAD MIRSHOKRAEE.

Islamic Research Foundation, Astan Quds Razavi: POB 91735-366, Mashhad; tel. (511) 2232501; fax (511) 2230005; e-mail info@islamic-rf.org; internet www.islamic-rf.org; f. 1984; research into Islamic subjects: the Qu'ran, the Hadith, jurisprudence, scholastic theology, Islamic text editing, translating Islamic books, study of Islamic arts, production of Islamic CDs; national and international seminars; 180 mems; library of 62,000 vols; Man. Dir Prof. ALI AKBAR ELAHI KHORASANI; publ. *Mehkat* (quarterly).

TECHNOLOGY

Electric Power Research Centre: POB 15745–448, Shahrak Ghods, Pounak Bakhtari Blvd, Tehran; tel. (21) 8079401; fax (21) 8094774; e-mail eprc@dci.iran.com; f. 1983; attached to Min. of Energy; library of 12,000 vols, 151 periodicals; Pres. S. M. TABATABAEE; publ. *Journal of Electrical Science and Technology* (quarterly).

Libraries and Archives

Isfahan

Municipal Library: Shahied Nikbakht St, POB 81638, Isfahan; tel. (31) 621200; fax (31) 621100; f. 1991; 60,000 vols.

University of Isfahan Library: Isfahan; 112,150 vols, half in Persian and Arabic, the remainder in European languages; Persian MSS and incunabula; Dir Dr HOSSEIN HARSIJ.

Mashhad

Ferdowsi University of Mashhad Central Library and Documentation Centre: POB 331-91735, Mashhad; tel. (511) 8789263; fax (511) 8796822; e-mail cent-lib@ferdowsi.um.ac.ir; internet c-library.um.ac.ir; 280,000 vols; Dir-Gen. Prof. Dr M. PARIROKH.

Organizations of Libraries, Museums and Documents Center of Astan-e Quds-e Razavi: POB 91735-177, Mashhad; tel. (511) 2216555; fax (511) 2220845; e-mail info@aqlibrary.org; internet www.aqlibrary.org; f. 15th c.; general library and assistance for researchers, 33 br. libraries, document centre, museums; 2,000,000 vols, 65,000 MSS and 6,000,000 other documents; 78,200 vols of foreign books (in 64 languages); Gen. Dir Dr ALI MUHAMMAD BARADRAN RAFIEI.

Tabriz

Tabriz Public Library (*Ketabkhaneh Melli Tabriz*): Tabriz; 12,816 vols; Dir MAJID FARHANG.

Tarbiat Library: Daneshsara Sq., Tabriz; tel. (41) 5222190; f. 1921; 29,750 vols; Dir HOSSEIN ASADI.

University of Tabriz Central Library and Documentation Centre: Tabriz; tel. (411) 3344705; fax (411) 3355993; e-mail a-assadzadeh@tabrizu.ac.ir; internet www.tabrizu.ac.ir/libraries; f. 1967; 95,871 vols, 6,231 microfiches, 4,300 maps, 6,231 microfilms, 1,643 periodicals, 647 tapes; Librarian A. ASSADZADEH.

Tehran

Central Library and Documentation Centre of Shahid Beheshti University: Evin, Tehran 19834; tel. (21) 293155; f. 1960; 315,529 vols, 3,190 periodicals; Librarian Dr ZAHRA GOOYA; publs *Tazebaye Ketabkhaneh, Sourat Ketabhaye Fehrest Shodeh*.

Central Library and Documentation Centre of Tehran University: Enghelab Ave, Tehran; f. 1949, re-housed 1970; Central Library of 850,000 vols, faculty libraries of 950,000 vols; Librarian Dr A. A. ENAYATI.

Centre for Socio-Economic Documentation and Publications: Baharestan Sq., Tehran 11365; tel. 3271; fax 301135; f. 1962, reorganized 1982; attached to Planning and Budget Organization; branches in 6 divisions: technical services, information services and network affairs, libraries (Central Library, Archive for Development Maps and Projects and 25 regional libraries), editing, graphics and production, distribution; libraries: 49,000 vols, 576 periodicals, 1,627 titles microforms, 16,000 titles development projects, 18,000 maps and plans, databases of selected articles; Dir MEHDI PAZOUKI; publs *Plan and Budget* (6 a year), *Periodical Index to Socio-Economic Articles* (quarterly), *List of Acquisitions* (monthly), *Informatics Newsletter* (monthly), subject bibliographies and catalogues, technical reports.

Institute for Political and International Studies Library and Documentation Centre: POB 19395-1793, Tajrish, Tehran; tel. (21) 2571010; internet www.dre-mfa.gov.ir; f. 1983; attached to the Foreign Ministry; special library and assistance for researchers; 20,000 vols on Islamic science, history, politics, economics, law, geography, diplomacy, military studies; 400 periodicals; Dir-Gen. Dr S. M. K. SAJJADPOUR; publs *New Books Review* (monthly), *Siyasat-e-Khare* (Journal of Foreign Policy, 4 a year), *Iranian Journal of International Affairs* (4 a year), *Asiyaje Miyaneh va Ghofghaaz* (4 a year), *Amu Darya* (4 a year), *Views and Analysis Bulletin* (monthly), *Al-Alaaghaat* (4 a year), *Newsletter* (monthly), *African Studies Journal* (2 a year).

Iran University of Medical Sciences and Health Services Central Library and Documentation Centre: POB 14155-6439, Tehran; tel. (21) 8058644; fax (21) 8054360; e-mail centrlib@iums.ac.ir; f. 1975; 37,000 books, 524 current periodicals, 11,000 theses, 3,000 audiovisual titles; Dir SUSSAN ERTEJAEI.

Iran Bastan Museum Library: Khiaban-e Imam Khomeini, Khiaban-e Sium-e Tir, Tehran 11365; f. 1964; 17,000 vols; Dir M. R. RIYAZI KESHE.

Iran National Archives Organization: Anahita Alley, Africa St, Tehran 19176; tel. (21) 8787335; fax (21) 8788950; internet www.archives.org.ir; f. 1970; Dir MOHAMMAD KAZEM MOUSAVI BOJNOURDI.

Iranian Cultural Heritage Organization Documentation Centre: POB 13445-1594, Tehran; tel. and fax (21) 6003126; e-mail ichodoc@hotmail.com; internet www.ichodoc.ir; f. 1994; 36,000 vols, 237 periodicals, 15,667 research reports, 2,030 films; 22,180 maps, 70,000 photographs, 155,560 slides, 125,000 negatives, 122 video cassettes, 204 audio cassettes, 771 CDs, 923 posters, 4,000 microfiches; Dir FARIBA FARZAM.

Iranian Information and Documentation Centre (IRANDOC): POB 13185/1371, Tehran; tel. (21) 6462548; fax (21) 6462254; e-mail info@irandoc.ac.ir; internet www.irandoc.ac.ir; f. 1968; work in the fields of basic sciences, agriculture, medical sciences, humanities and technology; advises and assists in the establishment of specialized information centres and acts as the national reference centre; part of the Ministry of Culture and Higher Education; 24,000 vols, 210 current periodicals, 70,000 student dissertations; Dir H. GHARIBI; publs *Directory of Scientific Meetings held in Iran* (quarterly), *Current Research in Iranian Universities and Research Centres* (quarterly), *Iranian Dissertation Abstracts* (quarterly), *Abstracts of Scientific/Technical Papers* (quarterly), *Iranian Government Reports* (quarterly), *Dissertation Abstracts of Iranian Graduates Abroad* (quarterly), *Iranian Scholars and Experts* (annually), *Ettela s Resani* (Technical Bulletin, quarterly).

Library of the Bank Markazi Jomhouri Islami Iran (Central Bank of the Islamic Republic of Iran): Pegah St, Mirdamad Blvd, POB 11365/8531, Tehran; tel. (21) 29953263; fax (21) 29953290; e-mail lib@cbi.ir; internet www.cbi.ir; f. 1960; 110,000 books and reports; Dir MAHROKH LOTFI.

Malek Library: Melale Mottahed Ave, Janb e Vezarat Omour Kharege, Tehran; tel. (21) 5204920; fax (21) 6717364; e-mail khoddari@yahoo.com; f. 1937; 50,000 vols covering the sciences, 19,000 titles, 6,400 MSS; attached to the Malek Museum; Dir-Gen. (Malek Museum and Malek Library) IZAT ALLAH DEHGHAN; Dir (Malek Library) Dr SHEIKH HASSAN PAHLAVAN HUSSEIN.

National Library and Archives of Iran: National Library Blvd, Haqani Expressway (West–East), POB 15875-3693, Tehran 1537614111; tel. (21) 8644000; fax (21) 8644082; e-mail nlai@nlai.ir; internet www.nlai.ir; f. 1937; 684,465 books (510,479 in Farsi and Arabic, 173,986 in other languages), 1,000,000 periodicals, 172,000 MSS documents and patchworks, 14,729 Arabic and Farsi MSS, 67,280 pamphlets and sheets, 9, 848 lithographic prints, 320,093 non-book items; maintains library higher education centre for library science; Dir KAZEM MOOSAVI BOJNOURDI; publ. *Iranian National Bibliography* (online and CD-ROM, annually).

Parliament Library (1): Ketabkhane-ye Majles-e Shora-ye Eslami 1, Baharestan Sq., POB 11365-866, Tehran; tel. (21) 33126092; fax (21) 33130919; e-mail frelations@majlislib.com; internet www.majlislib.com; f. 1912; 272,000 books, 28,000 bound vols of 5,000 Persian, Arabic and Latin periodicals, 24,000 manuscripts vols, 12,000,000 national and historical documents, 10,000 photographs, 460 magnetic tapes, 90 old maps, 17,500 manuscripts on microfilm, 3,000 CDs of manuscripts, 27 vols of theses and dissertations, 12,000 government reports, 300 microfilms and 250 CDs of old Iranian periodicals; UN depository; museum (see Museums and Art Galleries); Dir SEYYED MOHAMMAD ALI AHMADI ABHARI; publs *Name-ye Baharestan* (2 a year), *Payam-e Baharestan* (12 a year).

Attached library:

Parliament Library (2): Ketabkhaneh Majles-e Shora-ye Eslami 2, Emam Khomeini Ave, Tehran 13174; tel. (21) 6135335; fax (21) 3130919; f. 1959; special collection on Iranian, Islamic and Oriental studies: 49,554 printed books, 5,166 bound vols of 395 Persian, Arabic and Latin periodicals; Dir SEYYED MOHAMMAD ALI AHMADI ABHARI.

Museums and Art Galleries

Isfahan

Armenian Museum of All Saviour's Cathedral: POB 81735-115, Julfa, Isfahan; tel. (311) 6243471; fax (311) 6270999; e-mail sourbv@yahoo.com; internet www.newjulfa.org; f. 1930, rehoused 1971 with additions; under the supervision of the Diocesan Council of the Armenians in Isfahan; 750 ancient MSS, 570 paintings, miniatures and antique church vestments, tomb portraits; library of 25,000 vols.

Chehel Sotun Museum: Isfahan; Dir KARIM NIKZAD.

Mashhad

Astan-i-Quds Razavi Museums: Sahn-e-Imam Khomeini, Mashhad 91735; tel. (511) 2224570; fax (511) 2220845; e-mail info@aqlibrary.org; internet www.aqlibrary.org; f. 1945; depts: Weapons Museum, Koran Museum, Stamp Museum, Astronomical Instruments and Clocks Museum, Natural Objects and Shells Museum, Crystal and Porcelain Museum, Coins and Medals Museum, Carpet Museum, Museum of Holy Qur'an and Precious Objects presented by His Eminence Ayatollah Khamenei, History of Mashhad Museum and Paintings Museum; Dir SYED MOHAMMAD BEHROOZ.

Qom

Qom Museum: Eram St, Qom; tel. 7741491; f. 1936; under the supervision of the Archaeological Service; Dir B. YOSEFZADEH.

Shiraz

Pars Museum: Shiraz; f. 1938; exhibits include manuscripts, earthenware, ancient coins; Dir MOHAMMED HOSSEIN ESTAKHR; Curator HASRAT ZADEH SORUDE.

Tehran

Golestan Palace Museum: Maidan Panzdah Khordad, POB 11365-9595, Tehran 11149; tel. (21) 3113335; fax (21) 3111811; e-mail info@golestanpalace.org; internet golestanpalace.org; f. 1894; Dir PARVIN SADR SEGHT-OL-ESLAMI.

Iran Bastan Museum: Khiaban-e Imam Khomeini, Khiaban-e Sium-e Tir, Tehran 11364; tel. 672061; f. 1946; archaeological and cultural research; conservation, repair and exhibition of cultural material; four departments; library of 15,924 vols; Dir J. GOLSHAN; publ. *Catalogue*.

Malek Museum: Melale Mottahed Ave, Tehran; tel. (21) 66726613; fax (21) 66717364; e-mail khoddari@yahoo.com; internet www.aqmlm.ir; f. 1937; various objects of historical interest: coins, paintings, metalwork and woodwork, royal decrees, carpets, philatelic colln; library: Library: see Libraries and Archives; Man. and Curator SAID KHODDARI NAINI.

Mardom Shenassi Museum (Ethnological Museum): Maidan Panzdah Khordad, POB 11365-9595, Tehran 11149; tel. (21) 3110653; fax (21) 3111811; f. 1888; Dir ALIREZA ANISI.

Parliament Museum: Muze-ye Majles-e Shora-ye Eslami, POB 11365–866, Baharestan Square, Tehran; tel. and fax (21) 3130919; e-mail frelations@majlislib.com; internet www.majlislib.com; f. 1999; 294 old Iranian paintings, 714 artistic and traditional handicrafts and gifts presented to the speakers of the Islamic Consultative Assembly by foreign dignitaries, 150 rolls of old carpets, 70 chairs and tables and a small collection of antiques; Dir SEYYED MOHAMMAD ALI AHMADI ABHARI.

Tehran Museum of Contemporary Art: Karegar Ave, Laleh Park, Tehran; tel. and fax (21) 8951664; e-mail info@ir-tmca.com; internet www.ir-tmca.com; f. 1977; library of 20,000 vols in formation; Dir ALE REZA SAMI AZAR.

Universities

AHWAZ JONDISHAPOUR UNIVERSITY OF MEDICAL SCIENCES

Golestan-bol, University City Central Building, Ahwaz 61357-15794
Telephone: (611) 3367543
Fax: (611) 3330794
E-mail: info@ajums.ac.ir
Internet: www.ajums.ac.ir

Founded 1988; previously part of Shahid Chamran University
Academic year: September to June

President: Dr HAYAT MOMBEINI
Registrar: Dr M. E. MOTLAQ
Librarian: B. DASHTBOZORGI

Number of teachers: 408
Number of students: 5,276

Publications: *Jondishapour Journal of Pharmaceutical Sciences* (2 a year), *Scientific Medical Journal* (quarterly)

DEANS

College of Dentistry: Dr M. SHOKRI
College of Health: M. LATIFI
College of Nursing: Z. ABBASPOUR
College of Pharmacology: Dr A. HEMATI
College of Physiotherapy: Dr M. J. SHATERZADEH
Medical College: Dr M. FEGHHI
Paramedicine College: Dr M. KARANDISH

PROFESSORS

ASHNAGHAR, A.
BEHROOZ, M.
KALANTARI, H.
MAKVANDI, M.
MARAGHI, S.
MOGHADAM, A. Z.
PEDRAM, M.
ZANDIAN, K.

AL-ZAHRA UNIVERSITY

Vanak, Tehran 19934
Telephone: (21) 8058940
Fax: (21) 8035187
E-mail: office@alzahra.ac.ir
Internet: www.alzahra.ac.ir

Founded 1965, name changed 1981
State control
Language of instruction: Farsi
Academic year: September to June

Chancellor: Dr ZAHRA RAHNAVARD
Vice-Chancellor (Academic Affairs): Dr MAHNAZ AKHAUAN TAFTI
Vice-Chancellor (Administration and Finance): Dr MAHDI PEDRAM
Vice-Chancellor (Research): Dr FAEZEH FARZANEH
Vice-Chancellor (Student Affairs): ZAHRA VAHID MANESH
Director of International Relations: Dr MOHAMMAD MEHDI FEIZABADI
Librarian: Dr QODSI ZIARANI MOHAMMADI

Library of 55,000 vols
Number of teachers: 550
Number of students: 7,932

Publications: *Journal of Art 'Jelveye Honar'*, *Journal of Humanities*, *Journal of Science*

DEANS

Faculty of Engineering: Dr JAFAR BAGHERI NEJAD
Faculty of Fine and Applied Arts: Dr ABULQASEM DADVAR
Faculty of Literature, Foreign Languages and History: Dr AZAM SAZVAR
Faculty of Physical Education and Sports Science: Dr PARVANEH NAZAR ALI
Faculty of Psychology and Education: Dr SUSAN SAIF
Faculty of Sciences: Dr NILOOFAR DOLATSHAHI

Faculty of Social Sciences and Economics: Dr SUSAN BASTANI
Faculty of Theology: Dr FATEMEH ALAIE RAHMANI

HEADS OF DEPARTMENTS

Faculty of Engineering (Vanak, Tehran; tel. (21) 8041469; fax (21) 8041469; e-mail jbagheri@alzahra.ac.ir):
- Computer Engineering: Dr BEHROOZ GHOLIZADEH
- Industrial Engineering: Dr REZA SAMIZADEH
- Information Technology Management: Dr FARIBORZ MOOSAVI MADANI

Faculty of Fine and Applied Arts (Vanak, Tehran; tel. (21) 8035801; fax (21) 8041341; e-mail mazaheri@alzahra.ac.ir):
- Art Research: Dr ABOLGHASEM DADVAR
- Graphic Design: EFFAT AFZAL TOOSI
- Handicrafts: PARVIZ HASSELI
- Industrial Design: BEHZAD SOLEIMANI
- Painting: Dr PARISA SHAD GHAZVINI
- Textile and Fashion Design: SEDIGHEH PAKBIN

Faculty of Literature, Foreign Languages and History (Vanak, Tehran; tel. (21) 8048038; fax (21) 8048038):
- Arabic: Dr ENSIEH KHAZALI
- English: PARIVASH BEHGAM
- French: SEDIGHEH MIRZA EBRAHIM TEHRANI
- History: Dr ALI MOHAMMAD VALAVI
- Linguistics: Dr FARIDEH HAGHBIN
- Persian: Dr MAHIN PANAHI

Faculty of Physical Education and Sports Science (Vanak, Tehran; tel. (21) 8041468; fax (21) 8041468; e-mail nazarali@alzahra.ac.ir):
- Physical Education and Fitness: AMENEH RAZAVI
- Physical Education of the Handicapped: Dr MASUMEH SHOJAIE
- Teaching Physical Education and Fitness: Dr NAHID ATGHIA

Faculty of Psychology and Education (Vanak, Tehran; tel. (21) 8049937; fax (21) 8041464; e-mail susan-seif@alzahra.ac.ir):
- Consultation: Dr SIMIN HOSSEINIAN
- Educational Management: Dr PARVIN SAMADI
- Educational Psychology: Dr FERESHTEH NAZERZADEH KERMANI
- Library Science: Dr MANSOOREH BAGHERI
- Psychology: Dr ZOHREH KHOSRAVI

Faculty of Sciences (Vanak, Tehran; tel. (21) 8047861; fax (21) 8047861; e-mail ndolat@alzahra.ac.ir):
- Biology: Dr SHAYESTEH SEPEHR
- Chemistry: Dr RAHIM HEKMAT SHOAR
- Mathematics: Dr YADOLLAH URDUKHANI
- Physics: Dr AHMAD SHARIATI

Faculty of Social Sciences and Economics (Vanak, Tehran; tel. (21) 8047862; fax (21) 8047862; e-mail latif@alzahra.ac.ir):
- Accountancy: Dr HUSSEIN ALAVI TABARI
- Economics: Dr JAVAD POUR MOQIN
- Family Studies: Dr SUSAN BASTANI
- Management: Dr MIR AHMAD AMIR SHAHI
- Social Sciences: Dr MANSOOREH AZAM AZADEH

Faculty of Theology (Vanak, Tehran; tel. (21) 8041469; fax (21) 8048038):
- History of Islamic Civilization: Dr ZAHRA ALHUIE NAZARI
- Philosophy: Dr NARGESS NAZAR NEJAD
- Qoran Studies: SHAHIN GHAHRAMAN IZADI
- Religions and Mysticism: Dr HAJAT-ALLAH JAVANI
- Religious Jurisprudence: MUSLIM HUSSEINI ADYANI

ATTACHED RESEARCH CENTRE

Women's Research Centre: tel. (21) 8049809; fax (21) 8049809; e-mail golkhoo@alzahra.ac.ir; Dir Dr SHEKOOFEH GOLKHOO.

ALLAMEH TABATABA'I UNIVERSITY

POB 15815/3487, TehranTelephone: (21) 8901521
Fax: (21) 8902536

Founded 1984 following merger of the University Complex for Literature and Humanities and the University Centre for Public and Business Administration
State control
Languages of instruction: English, Persian
Academic year: September to June

Chancellor: Prof. Dr NAJAF-GHOLI HABIBI
Vice-Chancellors: Prof. Dr HOSSEIN RAHMANSERESHT (Research and International Relations), Prof. Dr AHMAD TAMIMDARI (Academic Affairs), Prof. Dr JAFAR BABAJANI (Administration and Finance), Prof. Dr HOSSEIN SALIMI (Student Affairs)
Registrar: Ms SEPEHRI
Chief Librarian: Dr ZAHRA SEIFKASHANI

Number of teachers: 361 (full-time)
Number of students: 12,177

Publication: Each faculty publishes its own journal

DEANS

Accounting and Management: Asst Prof. Dr ABULFAZL KAZZAI
Economics: Prof. Dr HAMID SHORAKA
Education and Psychology: MORTEZA AMINFAR
Law and Politics: Asst Prof. Dr GHOLAM-ALI CHEGENIZADE
Persian Literature and Foreign Languages: Prof. Dr SAEED VAEZ
Social Sciences: Asst Prof. Dr MAHAMMAD ZAHEDIASL

ATTACHED RESEARCH INSTITUTES

International Centre for Insurance Education and Research (ICIER): Dean Asst Prof. Dr MOHAMMAD-GHOLI YOSEFI.

Center for Studies on Iranian Economy (CSIE): Dean Asst Prof. Dr SAEED MOSHIRI.

AMIRKABIR UNIVERSITY OF TECHNOLOGY

424 Hafez Ave, Tehran 15875-4413
Telephone: (21) 64540-1
Fax: (21) 641-3969
E-mail: intoff1@aut.ac.ir
Internet: www.aut.ac.ir

Founded 1958 as Tehran Polytechnic
State control
Academic year: September to June

President: Dr A. FAHIMIFAR
Vice-President (Research): Dr M. KABGANIAN
Director of International Affairs: Dr M. M. AGHDAM
Librarian: Dr MOGHANI

Number of teachers: 420
Number of students: 8,000

Publication: *Amirkabir Journal of Science and Technology* (quarterly)

HEADS OF DEPARTMENTS

Aerospace Engineering: Dr H. HOSSEINI
Chemical Engineering: Prof. B. DABIR
Civil Engineering: Dr A. SOROUSH
Computer and Information Technology: Dr AKBARI
Electrical Engineering: Dr R. MOEINI
Industrial Engineering: Dr M. MOATTAR HOSSEINI
Mathematics: Dr M. DEHGHAN
Mechanical Engineering: Dr B. AREZOO
Medical Engineering: Dr F. TOHIDKHAH
Mining and Metallurgical Engineering: Dr RAMAZI
Physics: Dr S. NOUR AZAR
Polymer Engineering: Dr GHAFFARIAN
Marine Engineering: Dr M. FADAVI
Textile Engineering: Dr M. LATIFI

ATTACHED INSTITUTES

Research Centre: Electrical and Electronics: Dir Dr A. H. AFSHAR.

Research Centre: Energy: Dir Prof. B. DABIR.

Research Centre: Food Industry: Dir Dr F. VAHHAB ZADEH.

Research Centre: Industrial Engineering and Productivity: Dir Dr S. ISFAHANI.

Research Centre: New Technologies: Dir Dr A. ABDULLAH.

Research Centre: Textile Industry and Synthetic Fibre: Dir Dr M. R. BABAEI.

UNIVERSITY OF ART

POB 14155-6434, Tehran
Located at: 42 First St, Parvin Etesami St, Dr Fatemi Ave, Tehran 14146
Telephone: (21) 8954606
Fax: (21) 8954609
E-mail: art-university@art.ac.ir
Internet: www.art.ac.ir

Founded 1980 through amalgamation of the Conservatory of Music, College of Decorative Arts, College of Dramatic Arts, College of National Music and Farabi University; present name 1991
State control
Language of instruction: Farsi
Academic year: October to July

President: Dr MOHAMMAD REZA HAFEZI
Vice-President for Administration and Finance: SEYED ABUTORAB AHMADPANAH
Vice-President for Instruction: Dr MOHAMMAD TAGHI ASHOURI
Vice-President for Research: PARVIN PARTOVI
Vice-President for Student Affairs: SEYED JAVAD SALIMI

Library of 50,000 vols
Number of teachers: 252 (82 full-time, 170 part-time)
Number of students: 2,200

Publications: *Honarnameh* (4 a year), *Dastavard* (4 a year)

DEANS

Visual and Applied Arts: Mr ESKANDARI
Cinema and Theatre: Mr BANI-ARDALAN
Music: Mr LOTFI
Architecture and Urban Planning: Dr VAHID GHOMASHCHI
Applied Arts and Graduate Studies: Mr HOSSEINI

BU-ALI SINA UNIVERSITY

Shariati Ave, University Square, Hamadan 65174
Telephone: (811) 8273952
Fax: (811) 8272046
Internet: www.basu.ac.ir

Founded 1973
State control
Academic year: September to June

President: Dr M. GHOLAMI
Vice-Presidents: Dr G. R. KHANLARI (Education), Dr S. J. SABOUNCHI (Research), Dr A. KAREGAR BIDEH (Administration and Finance), Dr M. SHARIFIAN (Student Affairs), M. R. TAHMASEBI (Development)
Librarian: Dr M. S. GHAEMIZADEH

Number of teachers: 272
Number of students: 7,450

Publications: *Bulletin*, *Agricultural Research* (2 a year)

DEANS

Faculty of Agriculture: Dr M. J. SOLEIMANI
Faculty of Engineering: Dr M. NILI
Faculty of Letters and Humanities: Dr F. MIRZAII
Faculty of Science: Prof. H. ILUKHANI
Faculty of Teacher Training (Malayer): Dr M. JALALI
Faculty of the Veterinary College: Dr H. SHOKRIAN

HEADS OF DEPARTMENTS

Faculty of Agriculture:
Agricultural Education and Extension: M. OTRASHI
Agricultural Machinery: D. MANSOURI-RAD
Animal Science: Dr A. SAKI
Crop Production and Plant Breeding Engineering: Dr H. HOJJAT
Horticulture: M. FARID
Irrigation Engineering: Dr S. MAAROUFI
Plant Protection Engineering: Dr M. J. SOLEIMANI
Soil Science Engineering: Dr R. HOSSAINPOUR
Veterinary Science: Dr N. MIRAZI

Faculty of Engineering:
Architecture: G. R. TALISCHI
Civil Engineering: Dr M. NILLI
Computer Engineering: Dr M. H. DEZFULIN
Electrical Engineering: H. MUSAVI
Industrial Engineering: Dr F. JULALI
Mechanical Engineering: Dr F. FERESHTAE SANIEE

Faculty of Letters and Humanities:
Arabic Literature: H. FATEHI
Economics: Dr M. NAZARI
Educational Science: M. R. ARDALAN
Foreign Languages: Dr M. NAGHZGUYEH-KOHAN
Law: H. NAAEMAH
Library Science: A. ZAREIE
Persian Literature: Dr E. SHAFAGH
Physical Education: Dr F. NAZEM
Social Science: K. FARZADSEEAR

Faculty of Science:
Biology: Dr M. ATRI
Chemistry: Dr D. NEAMATOLLAHI
Geology: Dr F. ALIANI
Mathematics: E. NASIR-ALISLAM
Physics: Dr NASIR-ALISLAM

Faculty of Teacher Training:
Mathematics: B. HAYATI
Training Technology: M. ASGARY

FERDOWSI UNIVERSITY OF MASHHAD

Azadi Square, Ferdowsi University Campus, Mashhad 91774-48974
Telephone: (511) 8797363
Fax: (511) 8763637
E-mail: intr@um.ac.ir
Internet: www.um.ac.ir

Founded 1949
State control
Language of instruction: Farsi
Academic year: September to June (two semesters)

Chancellor: Prof. ALI REZA ASHOURI
Vice-Chancellor for Academic Affairs: Dr. MAHDI. KHAJAVI
Registrar: Dr MAHMOOD REZAI ROKENABAD
Director of the International Office: Dr MOHAMMAD TAGHI HAMED MOUSAVIAN
Librarian: Dr BEHROOZ MAHRAM

Library of 13,000 vols
Number of teachers: 700
Number of students: 17,000

Publications: *Agricultural Science and Technology* (4 a year), *Iranian Food Science and Technology Research Journal* (4 a year), *Iranian Journal of Field Crop Research* (4 a year), *Journal of the School of Economics and Business Administration* (4 a year), *Journal of the School of Engineering* (4 a year), *Journal of the School of Literature* (4 a year), *Journal of the School of Sciences* (4 a year), *Journal of Theology and Islamic Studies* (4 a year)

DEANS

Faculty of Administration and Economics: Dr M. LOTFALIPOOR
Faculty of Agriculture: Dr REZA VALIZADEH
Faculty of Education and Psychology: Dr BAKHTIYAR SHABANI
Faculty of Engineering: Dr HOSSAIN NOEEI BAGHBAN
Faculty of Letters and Humanities: Dr A. MOHAMMAD ZADEH REZAI
Faculty of Mathematical Sciences: Dr H. R. TAREGHIAN
Faculty of Physical Education: R. HASHEMI JAVAHERI
Faculty of Sciences: Dr REZA EIZADI
Faculty of Theology: Dr H. HAERI
Faculty of Veterinary Science: Dr A. NAGHIBI
Shirvan School of Agriculture: Dr MAHMOOD SHOOR
Nishabour School of Fine Arts: Dr HADI MANSOORI MGHADAM

HEADS OF DEPARTMENTS

Accounting: Dr MAHMOOD NASIR ZADEH
Agricultural Economics: Dr NASSER SHAHNOOSH
Agronomy: Dr MEHDI NASSRI MAHALATI
Animal Disease Prevention: Dr MERDAD MEHRI
Animal Sciences: Dr ALI REZA MOUSAVI HERAVI
Arabic Language and Literature: Dr HOSSEIN SAEADI
Biology: Dr MOGHIMI
Biotechnology: Dr FARAJ SHAHRIYARI
Chemical Engineering: Dr MOHAMMAD ALI FANAI
Chemistry: Dr MOHAMMAD REZA HOSSAIN DOKHT
Civil Engineering: Dr MAHMMOD FGHFOOR MAGHRABE
Computer Engineering: Dr POORREZA
Crop Production Technology: MOHAMMAD KHEIRKHAH
Economics: Dr SHASDIN HOSHMAND
Education: Dr HOSSEIN JAFARI SANI
Electrical Engineering: Dr NASSER PARIZ
English Language and Literature: Dr BEHZAD GHONSOOLI
Food Hygiene: Dr ABDOLAH JAMSHIDI
Geography: Dr KHAKPOOR
Geology: Dr AHMAD MAZAHERI
Graphics: FARZANEH FAROHKFAR
Herbal plants: MOHAMMAD KHEIRKHAH
History and Islamic Civilization: Dr MEHDI JALALI
Islamic Philosophy: FAYAZ SABERY
Jurisprudence: Dr MOHAMMAD TAGHI DORRAFSHAN
Koranic Studies: Dr HASSAN TAGHI ZADEH
Law: Dr HOSSEIN HOSSEINI
Librarianship: Dr MOHAMMAD REZA DAVARPANAH
Linguistics: Dr NADER GAHANGRI
Management: Dr NAZEMI
Material Engineering: Dr MOJTABA ZEBARJAD
Mathematics: Dr FATEMEH HELEN GHANE OSTAD GHASEMI
Mechanical Engineering: Dr. MEHRAN KADKHODAYAN
Painting: ALI SEIDANI
Persian Language and Literature: Dr MOHAMMAD ALI GHOLAMI NEJAD
Physical Education: Dr AKBAR MAREFATI
Physics: Dr MOHSSEN SARBISHEI
Plant Pathology: Dr ESMAT MAHDIKHANI
Poltical Science: Dr MORTEZA MANSHADI
Religion and Comparative Mysticism: Dr MANSOOR MOTEMDI
Sculpture: ARDESHIR BOOROJANI
Social Sciences: Dr ALI HAERIZADEH
Soil Sciences: Dr AHMAD MAZAHERI
Statistics: Dr NASSER REZA ARGHAMI
Water Conservation: MOHAMMAD KHEIRKHAH

PROFESSORS

AFSHARNEJAD, Z., Mathematics
ASHOURI, A., Physics
BAGHERI, A., Agronomy
HAERIAN, A., Material Engineering
TOOTOONIYAN, F., Mathematics

UNIVERSITY OF GILAN

POB 1841, Mellat Street, Rasht
Telephone: (131) 3221999
Fax: (131) 3227022
E-mail: khazar@cd.gu.ac.ir
Internet: www.gu.ac.ir

Founded 1977
State control
Language of instruction: Farsi
Academic year: September to June (two semesters)

Chancellor: Dr DAWOUD AHMADI DASTJERDI
Vice Chancellor (Finance and Administration): ESMAEIL MAGHSODI
Vice-Chancellor (Academic Affairs): Dr REZA FOTOUHI GHAZVINI
Vice-Chancellor (Research Affairs): Dr ABOLFAZL DARVIZEH
Vice-Chancellor (Student Affairs): Dr MALEK-MOHAMMAD RANJBAR
Office of Public Relations: Dr HASSAN TAJIK
Office of International and Scientific Relations: Dr MASOUD VAHABI MOGHADDAM
Librarian: Dr REYHANEH SARIRI

Number of teachers: 308
Number of students: 6,705

Publication: *Mahnameh* (12 a year, in Farsi)

DEANS

Faculty of Agriculture: Dr AHAD SAHRAGARD
Faculty of Engineering: Dr HOSSEIN HAFTHCHENARI
Faculty of Fine Arts and Architecture: HAMZEH GHOLAM-ALI-ZADEH
Faculty of Fishery and Aquatic Animals: Dr MSOUD SATTARI
Faculty of Humanities: Dr MOHAMMAD KAZEM YOUSEFPOUR
Faculty of Natural Resources: Dr ZYAEDDIN MIRHOSSEINI
Faculty of Physical Education: Dr ARSALAN DAMIRCHI
Faculty of Sciences: Dr ESMAEIL ANSARI

HEADS OF DEPARTMENTS

Animal Biotechnology: ABOLGHASEM AWHADI
Animal Husbandry: Dr MEHRADAD MOHAMMADI
Arabic Literature: Dr AKBAR SHAHRAKI-KALHOR
Architecture: HAMZEH GHOLAMALI-ZADEH
Biology: Dr NADER SHABANIPOUR
Chemistry: Dr ALI GHANAD-ZADEH
Civil Engineering: Dr ABDOLHAMID MEHRDAD
Electronics: HAMID ZABET KHOSUSI
Entomology: Dr JALA JALALI-SANDI
Environmental Sciences: Dr NOURADIN AZIMI
Fisheries: AKBAR NASROLLAH-ZADEH
Forestry: Dr KAMBEEZ TAHERI
Horticulture: Dr ABDOLLAH HATAM-ZADEH
Irrigation: Dr MASOUD PARSI-NEZHAD
Islamic Sciences: MOHAMMAD HASSAN-ZAHEDI
Law: AKBAR EIMAANPOOR
Management: Dr MOHAMMAD NOWEPASAND
Mathematics: Dr SHAHAB-AL-DEINE EBRAHIMI

Mechanics: Dr NADR NARIMAN-ZADEH
Pedology and Plant Protection: Dr MASOUD ESFAHANI
Persian Language and Literature: SORAYA MOSLEHI
Physical Education: Dr RAHIM RAMAZANI-NEZHAD
Physics: Dr M. ROWZATI
Plant Production Biotechnology: AHMAD ARDABBEL
Psychology: Dr FATEME KARIMI
Sociology: Dr FAROGH KHARABI
Soil Science: Dr MOHAMMAD-REZA HAGHPARAST
Textile Engineering: Dr AKBAR KHODAPARAST-HAGHI

IRAN UNIVERSITY OF MEDICAL SCIENCES AND HEALTH SERVICES

Crossroads of Shahid Hemmat and Shahid Chamran Expressways, POB 15875-6171, Tehran 144961-4535
Telephone: (21) 88052234
Fax: (21) 88052235
E-mail: ofintrel@iums.ac.ir
Internet: www.iums.ac.ir

Founded 1974 as Iran Medical Centre
State control
Language of instruction: Persian
Academic year: September to June

Chancellor: Dr M. FATHI
Vice-Chancellors: Dr N. LATIFI (Academic Affairs), Dr M. BEYGLAR (Admin. and Financial Affairs), Dr S. A. RAZAVI AFZAL (Food and Pharmaceutical Affairs), Dr M. NASEH (Health Affairs), Dr A. KHOSRAVI (Research), Dr S. A. GOOSHEHGIR (Student and Cultural Affairs)
Registrar: Dr M. AFKARI
Head of Central Library: S. ERTEJAEI

Library of 43,000 vols, 3,936 journals, 14.010 theses, 161 research projects
Number of teachers: 725
Number of students: 5,564

Publications: *Annals of Iranian Medicine* (quarterly), *Five Star Doctor* (quarterly), *Iran Journal of Nursing* (quarterly), *Iranian Journal of Pharmacology and Therapeutics* (quarterly, online), *Journal of Iran University of Medical Sciences* (quarterly), *Journal of Medical Laboratory Sciences* (quarterly), *Journal of Medical Management* (quarterly), *Journal of Students* (monthly), *Journal of Thought and Behavior* (quarterly), *Medical Education* (quarterly), *Rehabilitation Letter* (quarterly), *Rehabilitation Message* (quarterly), *University Bulletin* (monthly)

DEANS

School of Allied Medical Sciences: Dr M. J. GHARAVI
School of Management and Medical Information: Dr M. MALEKI
School of Medicine: Dr S. J. HAJ MIR ESMAEILI
School of Nursing and Midwifery: Dr F. HAGHDOOST OSKOUEI
School of Public Health: Dr M. H. TAGHDISI
School of Rehabilitation Sciences: Dr E. EBRAHIMI TAKAMJANI

IRAN UNIVERSITY OF SCIENCE AND TECHNOLOGY

Narmak, Tehran 16844
Telephone: (21) 7451120
Fax: (21) 7451143
E-mail: interiust@iust.ac.ir
Internet: www.iust.ac.ir

Founded 1928
State control
Language of instruction: Farsi
Academic year: September to June

Chancellor: Dr SEYED TAGHI SALEHI
Vice-Chancellors: Dr SEYED HOSSEIN SEYDEN (Administration and Finance), Dr MOHAMMAD REZA ABOUTALEBI (Education), Dr MAHDI BIDABADI (Research), Dr SEYED MOHAMMAD-ALI BOUTORABI (Students)
Director of the Office of International and Scientific Co-operation: Dr. FARHAD GOLESTANI FARD
Head of Graduate Studies: Dr MOHSEN KALANTAR
Registrar: Dr MAHDI NAVIDBAKHSH
Librarian: Dr N. MOZAYANI

Library of 120,000 vols
Number of teachers: 714 (361 full-time, 353 part-time)
Number of students: 8,350

Publications: *International Journal of Civil Engineering* (quarterly, in English), *International Journal of Electrical Engineering* (quarterly, in English), *International Journal of Engineering* (quarterly, in Persian and English), *International Journal of Materials Science and Engineering* (quarterly, in English)

DEANS

School of Architecture and Urban Design: Dr E. SHIEH
College of Automotive Engineering: Dr M. H. SHOJAEE FARD
College of Chemical Engineering: Dr N. KASIRI BIDHENDI
College of Chemistry: Dr S. M. MILANI HOSSEINI
College of Civil Engineering: Dr H. BAZIAR
College of Computer Engineering: Dr M. SHARIFI
College of Electrical Engineering: Dr S. A. A. BEHESHTI SHIRAZI
College of Industrial Engineering: Dr M. S. JABAL-AMELI
College of Mathematics: Dr R. FARNOUSH
College of Mechanical Engineering: Dr A. H. DAVAIE MARKAZI
College of Materials Science and Metallurgical Engineering: Dr M. SHAIKHSHAB BAFGHI
College of Physics: Dr B. GHAFFARY
School of Railway Engineering: Dr S. MOHAMMADZADEH
Arak College of Technology: Dr M. HOSSEINNEJAD
Behshahr College of Technology: Dr M. ALAEEYAN

PROFESSORS

AFSHAR, A., Civil Engineering
ARIANEJAD, M. B., Industrial Engineering
AFSHAR, A., Civil Engineering
BAZIAR, M. H., Civil Engineering
BEHBAHANI, H., Civil Engineering
BOUTORABI, M. A., Materials Science and Metallurgical Engineering
ESRAFILIAN, E., Mathematics
FALLAHI MOGHIMI, M., Foreign Languages
FARMAN, H., Physics
GOLESTANI FARD, F., Materials Science and Metallurgical Engineering
HABIBNEJAD KORAYEM, M., Mechanical Engineering
HAJ KARIM KHARAZI, Y., Materials Science and Metallurgical Engineering
HOJAT KASHANI, F., Electrical Engineering
JASBI, J. A., Industrial Engineering
KASPARI MARGHOSIAN, V., Metallurgy and Materials Engineering
KAVEH, A., Civil Engineering
MAJIDI ZULBANIN, H., Physics
MALEKNEJAD, K., Mathematics
MIRDAMADI, SH., Materials Science and Metallurgical Engineering
ORAIZI ISFAHANI, H., Electrical Engineering
ROEENTAN LAHIJI, GH., Electrical Engineering
SANAEE, E., Civil Engineering
SHAYANFAR, H. A., Electrical Engineering
SHIDFAR, A., Mathematics
SHOJAEEFARD, M. H., Mechanical Engineering
SHOULAIE, A., Electrical Engineering
SLOEIMANI, M. R., Electrical Engineering
TAEB, A., Chemical Engineering

ATTACHED RESEARCH INSTITUTES

Aluminium Research Center: tel. (21) 7724059; fax (21) 7724050; Dir Dr M. T. SALEHI.

Architecture Research Center: tel. (21) 77491243; fax (21) 77491243; Dir Eng. M. A. KHANMOHAMMADI.

Automobile Research Center: tel. (21) 77491224; fax (21) 77491224; Dir Dr M. H. SHOJAEEFARD.

Cement Research Center: tel. (21) 77240475; fax (21) 77240397; Dir Dr M. KHANZADI.

Electronic Research Center: tel. (21) 77240487; fax (21) 77240487; Dir Dr A. JALALI.

Green Research Center: tel. (21) 77491223; fax (21) 77491242; e-mail Jadid@iust.ac.ir; Dir Dr S. JADID.

Information and Communication Technology Research Center: 17 Shahid Hosseinali Ave, Farjam St, Tehran; tel. (21) 7749778; fax (21) 77899955; e-mail incubator@iust.ac.ir; internet www.inc.iust.ac.ir; Dir (vacant).

Information Technology Research Center: tel. (21) 77240391; fax (21) 77240469; e-mail akbari@iust.ac.ir; Dir Dr A. RAHMANI.

Iran Composites Institute: tel. (21) 73912858; fax (21) 77491206; e-mail shokrieh@iust.ac.ir; internet www.irancomposits.org; Dir Dr M. M. SHOKRIEH.

Refractories Research Center: tel. (21) 7724050; fax (21) 7724050; e-mail rmrc@iust.ac.ir; Dir Dr F. GOLESTANI FARD.

UNIVERSITY OF ISFAHAN

Isfahan, Darvazeh Shiraz 81746-73441Telephone: (311) 7932001
Fax: (311) 6687396
E-mail: administrator@ui.ac.ir
Internet: www.ui.ac.ir

Founded 1950
State control
Language of instruction: Persian
Academic year: September to June

Chancellor: Dr HOOSHANG TALEBI
Vice-Chancellor for Finance and Administration: Dr NEMATOLAH AKBARI
Vice-Chancellor for Research Affairs: Dr MOHAMMAD ALI SHAHZAMANIAN
Vice-Chancellor for Student Affairs: Dr MOHAMMAD REZA IRAVANI
Vice-Chancellor for Academic Affairs: Dr IRAJ NAHVI
Office of International and Scientific Relations: Dr SEYED KOMAIL TAYYEBI
Librarian: Dr HAMID REZA FALLAH

Number of teachers: 570
Number of students: 13,950

Publications: *Payame Daneshgah* (Message of the University, monthly), *Islamic Revolution Research Journal* (quarterly), *Research Journal of the Faculty of Letters and Humanities* (quarterly, in Persian and English), *Research Bulletin* (humanities, 2 a year, in Persian and English), *Research Bulletin* (pure science, 2 a year, in Persian and English), *Journal of Administrative Sciences and Economics* (quarterly), *Journal of the Faculty of Educational Sciences* (quarterly), *Journal of the Theology Department* (quarterly)

DEANS

Faculty of Administrative Sciences and Economics: Dr KARIM AZARBAIJANI
Faculty of Educational Sciences and Psychology: Dr MOHAMMAD JAVAD LIAGHATDAR
Faculty of Engineering and Technology: Dr SEYED MOHSEN MOOSAVI
Faculty of Foreign Languages: Dr HOSSEIN VAHID DASTJERDI
Faculty of Letters and Humanities: Dr MORTAZA MAJIHOSSEINI
Faculty of Mathematics and Computer Studies, Khansar: Dr MEHDI MESBAH
Faculty of Physical Education: Dr VAHID ZOLAKTAF
Faculty of Pure Sciences: Dr MOHAMMAD HASSAN HABIBI
Faculty of Technology: Dr AHMAD BARAANI

HEADS OF DEPARTMENTS

Faculty of Administrative Sciences and Economics (tel. (311) 7932622; fax (311) 6683116; e-mail aseadmin@ui.ac.ir; internet www.ltr.ui.ac.ir):

Accountancy: Dr MIR SHAMS SHAHSHAHANI
Economics: Dr HOOSHANG SHAJARI
Management: Dr MEHDI JAMSHIDIAN
Political Science: Dr SAYED JAVAD IMAM JOMEH ZADEH
Law: Dr MAHMOUD JALALI KARVEH

Faculty of Educational Sciences and Psychology (tel. (311) 7932500; fax (311) 6683107; e-mail eduadmin@edus.ui.ac.ir; internet www.edu.ui.ac.ir):

Education: Dr SEYED ALI SIADAT
Library Science: Dr ASHRAF SADAT MIRSHAHZADE
Psychology: Dr HAMID TAHER NESHATDOST
Counselling and Guidance: Dr MOHAMMAD REZA ABEDI

Faculty of Engineering (tel. (311) 7932685; fax (311) 6682887; e-mail engadmin@ui.ac.ir; internet www.eng.ui.ac.ir):

Computing: Dr ABBAS VAFAEI
Surveying: VAHHAB NAFISI
Chemical Engineering: Dr FOAD AGHAMIRI
Technology: Dr KAMAL JAMSHIDI
Biomedical Engineering: Dr AMIN KHODABAKHSHIAN
Electrical Engineering: Dr BEHZAD MIRZAEIAN

Faculty of Foreign Languages (tel. (311) 7932101; fax (311) 6687391; e-mail fgnadmin@fgn.ui.ac.ir; internet www.fgn.ui.ac.ir):

Arabic: Dr M. KHAGHANI
Armenian and German Languages: Dr JAHANGIR ERSHAD
English: Dr A. AFGHARI
French: Dr SUSAN BEIZAVI

Faculty of Letters and Humanities (tel. (311) 6680070; fax (311) 7933151; e-mail ltradmin@ui.ac.ir; internet www.ltr.ui.ac.ir):

Geography: Dr HAMIDREZA WARESI
History: Dr ALI AKBAR KAJBAF
Persian Literature: Dr MOHAMMAD REZA NASR-ESFAHANI
Philosophy: Dr MOHAMMAD ALI EJEII
Social Sciences: Dr FEREIDOON VAHIDA
Theology and Islamic Studies: Dr MOHAMMAD REZA HAJ-ESMAEILI

Faculty of Mathematics and Computer Studies in Khansar (POB 87915-116, Namaz Blvd, Khansar 87931; tel. (371) 2220691; fax (371) 2220692; e-mail ashofteh@sci.ui.ac.ir; internet sci.ui.ac.ir/stat):

Applied Mathematics: AFSHIN ASHOFTEH

Faculty of Physical Education (tel. (311) 7932572; fax (311) 6687572; e-mail Varzesh83@yahoo.com; internet www.ui.ac.ir/uiitems/fclts/phy):

Physical Education: Dr VAHID ZOLAKTAF

Faculty of Pure Sciences (tel. (311) 7932400; fax (311) 6680066; e-mail sciadmin@ui.ac.ir; internet www.sci.ui.ac.ir):

Biology: Dr JAMAL MOSHTAGHIAN
Chemistry: Dr HAMID REZA MEMARIAN
Geology: Dr M. KHALILI
Mathematics: Dr SAEED AZAM
Physics: Dr MOHAMMAD TAGHI FALLAHI
Statistics: Dr M. BAHRAMI

ISFAHAN UNIVERSITY OF MEDICAL SCIENCES

Hezar-Jerib Avenue, Isfahan
Telephone: (311) 7923077
Fax: (311) 6687898
E-mail: international@mui.ac.ir
Internet: www.mui.ac.ir

Founded 1950
State control
Language of instruction: Persian
Academic year: September to June

Chancellor: Dr ABBAS REZAIE
Vice-Chancellor for Finance and Administration: Dr M. B. TAVAKOLI
Vice-Chancellor for Student Affairs: Dr M. JALALI
Vice-Chancellor for Academic Affairs: Dr B. SHAMS
Vice-Chancellor for Research Affairs: Dr M. NEMATBAKHSH
Registrar: M. MARDANI
Head of Libraries: H. RASTEGARI

Number of teachers: 595
Number of students: 6,105

Publications: *Journal of Research at the Isfahan Medical School* (4 a year), *Journal of Nursing and Midwifery* (4 a year), *Iranian Journal of Medical Education*, *Journal of Research in Medical Sciences* (quarterly)

DEANS

Faculty of Medicine: Dr H. TABAN
Faculty of Dentistry: Dr A. KHADEMI
Faculty of Pharmacy: Dr JAFARIAN DEHKORDI
Faculty of Health: Dr MOHAMMAD ZADEH
Faculty of Nursing and Midwifery: Dr H. ABEDI
Faculty of Rehabilitation Sciences: Dr F. BAHMANI
Faculty of Management and Information Services: Dr M. YARMOHAMMADIAN

HEADS OF DEPARTMENTS

Faculty of Medicine (tel. (311) 7922435; fax (311) 6688597; internet med.mui.ac.ir):

Anaesthesiology: Dr K. MONTAZERI
Anatomy: E. ESFANDIARI
Applied Pathology: Dr P. RAJABI
Community-Oriented Medicine: Dr A. R. ZAMANI
Dermatology: Dr A. ASSILIAN
ENT: Dr N. BERJIS
Genetics: Dr R. SALEHI
Gynaecology and Obstetrics: Dr ARAM
Infectious Diseases: Dr I. KARIMI
Internal Medicine: Dr SANEIE
Medical Physics: Dr A. MEHRI
Microbiology: Dr TAMIZIFAR
Mycology and Parasitology: Dr HEJAZI
Neurology: Dr ZIAEI
Neurosurgery: Dr H. MOIN
Ophthalmology: Dr H. RAZMJOO
Orthopaedics: Dr A. EBRAHIMZADEH
Paediatrics: Dr M. SABRI
Physiology: Dr ROSTAMI
Psychiatry: Dr G. ASADOLLAHI
Radiology: Dr FOROOZMEHR
Radiotherapy: Dr H. EMAMI
Surgery: Dr M. SAFAIE
Urology: Dr MOHAMMADI
Virology and Immunology: Dr POURAZAR

Faculty of Pharmacy:

Biochemistry: Dr H. OROOJI
Medicinal Chemistry and Toxicology: Dr G. KHODARAHMI
Pharmaceutics: Dr A. MOSTAFAVI
Pharmacognosy: Dr A. GHANADI
Pharmacology: Dr T. GHAFGHAZI

Faculty of Dentistry (tel. (311) 7922821; fax (311) 6687080; internet dnt.mui.ac.ir):

Dental Diseases Diagnosis: Dr H. KHADEMI
Dental Pathology: Dr P. DEYHIMI
Dental Surgery: Dr GH. FIROOZEIE
Endodontics: Dr M. BARATI
Orthodontics: Dr M. ABDOLLAHI
Paediatric Dentistry: Dr S. MORTAZAVI
Periodontics: Dr M. TAVAKOLI
Permanent and Temporary Prosthesis: Dr M. SABOOHI
Prosthetics: Dr R. MOSHARRAF
Radiology: Dr M. SHEIKHI
Restoration: Dr V. MORTAZAVI

Faculty of Nursing and Midwifery (tel. (311) 7922928; fax (311) 6247080; internet nm.mui.ac.ir):

Health: K. TAVAKOL
Medical Surgical Nursing: Mr DARYABEIGI
Midwifery: Mrs BAHADORAN
Paediatrics: Mrs GOLCHIN
Psychiatric Nursing: Mr YAZDANI
Nursing Technology: N. A. ASEMANRAFAT

Faculty of Rehabilitation Sciences (tel. (311) 7922024; fax (311) 6687270; internet rehab.mui.ac.ir):

Basic Sciences: S. M. MIRBOD
Physiotherapy: J. MOSTAMAND
Speech Therapy: N. BAHARLOOIE
Technical Orthopaedics: T. TAHMASEBI

AFFILIATED CENTRE

Amin Research Centre, Seddigheh Tahereh Research and Treatment Hospital: Dir Dr M. NEMAT BAKHSH.

ISFAHAN UNIVERSITY OF TECHNOLOGY

Isfahan 84154
Telephone: (31) 891-2505
Fax: (31) 8913112
E-mail: isco@cc.iut.ac.ir
Internet: www.iut.ac.ir

Founded 1977
State control
Language of instruction: Persian
Academic year: September to July

President: Dr ALI AHOONMANESH
Vice-President for Academic Affairs: Dr MOJTABA AZHARI
Vice-President for Research: Dr EBRAHIM SHIRANI
Vice-President for Student Affairs: Dr ALI AKBAR ALEM RAJABI
Vice-President for Finance and Administration: Dr MOHAMMAD HASSAN ABBASI
Registrar: Dr SOROUSH ALIMORADI
Library Director: Dr MOSTAFA KARIMIAN EGHBAL

Library of 88,000 vols, 2,500 periodicals
Number of teachers: 440
Number of students: 8,978

Publications: *Esteghlal* (Journal of Engineering, 2 a year), *Journal of Agricultural Engineering and Natural Resources*, *Peyke Ryazy*, *Iranian Journal of Physics Research*

DEANS

Faculty of Mathematics: Dr H. R. ZOHOURI-ZANGENAH
Faculty of Physics: Dr H. AKBARZADEH
Faculty of Electrical and Computer Engineering: Dr M. A. MONTAZERI
Faculty of Civil Engineering: Dr M. M. SAADATPOUR
Faculty of Mechanical Engineering: Dr A. SABONCHI
Faculty of Materials Engineering: Dr M. A. GOLOZAR
Faculty of Industrial Engineering: Dr GH. A. RAISSI ARDALI
Faculty of Agriculture: Dr R. EBADI
Faculty of Mining Engineering: Dr J. TAJADOD
Faculty of Textile Technology: Dr S. H. AMIRSHAHI
Faculty of Chemical Engineering: Dr GH. ETEMAD
Faculty of Chemistry: Dr S. H. GHAZIASKAR
Faculty of Natural Resources: Dr A. JALALIAN

PROFESSORS

AKBARZADEH, H., Physics
AMINI, S. M., Computational Physics
AMINZADEH, A., Chemistry
BASSIR, H., Mining Engineering
HAGHANY, A., Pure Mathematics
HAJRASOOLIHA, SH., Soil Science
KALBASI, M., Soil Science
MALLAKPOUR, S. E., Chemistry
MOLKI, M., Mechanical Engineering
MOUSAVI, S. F., Agriculture
PARSAFAR, GH., Chemistry
PARSIAN, A., Statistics
REZAEI, A., Plant Breeding, Cytogenetics
ROSTAMI, A. A., Mechanical Engineering
SAADATPOUR, M. M., Civil Engineering
TAHANI, V., Electronic Engineering

ISLAMIC AZAD UNIVERSITY

POB 19585/466, 9th Nayestan, Pasdaran Ave, Tehran
Telephone: (21) 2565149
Fax: (21) 2547787
E-mail: iau@dpimail.net
Internet: www.azad.ac.ir

Founded 1982
Academic year: September to September

President: Dr A. JASSBI
Vice-President (Research): Dr F. LARIJANI
Vice-President (Academic Affairs): Dr H. SADEGHISHOJA
Vice-President (Student Affairs): Dr J. AZIZIAN
Vice-President (Medical Affairs): Dr H. YAHYAVI
Vice-President (Financial and Administrative Affairs): M. ZAHABION
Vice-President (Construction and Development): A. SHAHRAKI
Vice-President (Co-ordination Affairs): M. S. KALHOR
Vice-President (Cultural Affairs): M. PIRAYANDEH
Vice-President (International Affairs): M. S. A. AMIRI
Vice-President (Parliamentary Affairs): Dr F. FARMAND
Vice-President (Non-Profit Schools): M. MIRSHAMSI
Librarian: P. MAHASTI SHOTORBANI

Library of 4,875,000 vols
Number of teachers: 25,310
Number of students: 850,000

Publications: *Mobin* (4 a year), *Amol Campus* (4 a year), *Arak Campus* (4 a year), *Babol Campus* (4 a year), *Rahavard* (4 a year), *Selselat - Al-Zahab* (4 a year), *Geographic Space* (4 a year), *Daneshnameh* (4 a year), *Journal of Agricultural Sciences* (4 a year), *Journal of Sciences* (4 a year), *Economics and Management* (4 a year), *Journal of Medical Sciences* (4 a year), *Tazeha* (4 a year), *Zakaria Razi* (4 a year), *Sedaye Didar* (4 a year), *Karname-Y-Pazhooheshi* (research report, 4 a year), *Pazhoheshnameh I* (4 a year), *Scientific Research Quarterly* (4 a year), *Scientific Research Periodical* (4 a year), *Bassirat* (Vision, 4 a year), *Yeganeh* (4 a year), *Sokhane Ashna* (4 a year), *Ensan Va Andishe* (Man and Thought, 4 a year), *Chemistry Newsletter* (4 a year), *Pooyesh* (4 a year), *Rah-avar* (4 a year), *Scientific-Cultural Letter of Research* (4 a year), *Scientific Research Journal* (4 a year), *Nedaye Golestan* (4 a year), *Peyke Dime* (4 a year), *Namaye Pazhoohosh* (4 a year), *Jelvegahe-dopayam* (4 a year), *Armane-e-Pazhouhesh*, *Danesh va Pezhouhesh* (4 a year), *Pazhuhesh – DINI* (4 a year), *Omran* (4 a year), *Nourolelm* (4 a year), *Tolu-e-Andishe* (4 a year), *Nedaye-Daneshgah* (4 a year), *Pouya* (4 a year), *Rouyesh* (4 a year), *Koushk* (4 a year)

Colleges of Agricultural Engineering, Arts, Civil Engineering, Humanities, Medicine and Basic Sciences. Each of the University's 145 branches, which are located throughout Iran, offers a selection of the courses run by the University.

K. N. TOOSI UNIVERSITY OF TECHNOLOGY

POB 15875-4416, 322 Mirdamad Ave West, 19697-64499 Tehran
Telephone: (21) 8881003
Fax: (21) 8882997
E-mail: oisc@kntu.ac.ir
Internet: www.kntu.ac.ir

Founded 1928; present name 1987
State control
Languages of instruction: Farsi, English
Academic year: September to June

President: Dr ALI KHAKI-SEDIGH
Vice-Chancellors: Dr K. MOHAMED-POOR (Education), Dr M. JAFARIAN (Research), Dr M. BAZARGAN (Student Affairs), Dr M. MOOSAVI-NAINIAN (Administration and Finance)
Librarian: Dr F. VAFAIE

Library of 28,900 vols
Number of teachers: 230
Number of students: 4,400

Publications: *Abangan Magazine* (4 a year), *Olum-o-Mohandesi'ye Nasir* (2 a year)

DEANS

Faculty of Civil Engineering (Vali-asr St, after Vanak Sq., Tehran):
Dean: Dr M. R. ABDI

Faculty of Electrical Engineering (Stariati St, Seyyed-Khandan Bridge, POB 16315-1355 Tehran):
Dean: Dr M. AHMADIAN

Faculty of Geodesy and Geomatics Engineering (Vali-asr St, After Vanak Sq., Tehran):
Dean: Dr M. J. VALADAN ZOOJ

Faculty of Industrial Engineering (Dabestan St, Resalat St, Seyyed-Khandan Bridge, POB 16315-989 Tehran):
Dean: Dr A. ASL HADDAD

Faculty of Mechanical Engineering (East Vafadar St, Tehranpars' 4th Sq., POB 16765-3381 Tehran):
Dean: Dr M. R. KHALILI

Faculty of Science (Shahid Mojtabaei St, Seyyed-Khandan Bridge, Tehran):
Dean: Dr A. JABBARI

KERMANSHAH UNIVERSITY OF MEDICAL SCIENCES

Building No. 2, POB 67147-1688, Bolvar-e-shahid Dr Beheshti, Kermanshah
Telephone: (831) 59795
Fax: (831) 50013
E-mail: contacts@kums.ac.ir
Internet: kums.ac.ir

Founded 1986; previously part of Razi University
State control
Academic year: September to July

Chancellor: Dr MOHAMMAD REZA SAEEDI
Vice-Chancellor for Financial and Administrative Affairs: Dr ALI SOROOSH
Vice-Chancellor for Educational and Research Affairs: Dr FEIZOLLAH MANSOURI
Librarian: FAYZOLLAH FROUYBI

Library of 36,000 vols
Number of teachers: 183
Number of students: 1,883

DEANS

Faculty of Health: Dr ALI ALMASI
Faculty of Medicine: Dr JALAL SHAKERI
Faculty of Nursing and Midwifery: Dr MOJDEH ASAREHZADEGAN
Night Faculty of Nursing and Midwifery: SAYED GALAL KAZEMI

MASHHAD UNIVERSITY OF MEDICAL SCIENCES

Daneshghah St, POB 91735-588, Mashhad
Telephone: (511) 8413005
Fax: (511) 8413006
E-mail: med-lib2@mums.ac.ir
Internet: www.mums.ac.ir

Founded 1945
Academic year: October to July

Chancellor: Dr A. BAHRAMI
Vice-Chancellor (Education): Dr M. H. BAHREINI-TOOSI
Vice-Chancellor (Research): Dr B. S. FAZLI BAZAZ
Vice-Chancellor (Financial and Administrative Affairs): Dr R. GHARAVIAN
Vice-Chancellor (Student and Cultural Affairs): Dr M. R. DARABI MAHBOUB
Vice-Chancellor (Health): Dr M. J. PARIZADEH
Vice-Chancellor (Remedy): Dr A. AFSHARI SALEH
Librarians: P. MODIRAMANI, Z. JANGI

Library of 100,000 vols
Number of teachers: 554
Number of students: 5,688

Publications: *Iranian Journal of Basic Medical Sciences* (quarterly), *Journal* (quarterly), *Iranian Journal of Oto-rhino-laryngology* (quarterly)

DEANS

Faculty of Dentistry: Dr A. A. HOSSEINI
Faculty of Medicine: Dr M. MAHMOUDI
Faculty of Nursing: Dr A. DANESH
Faculty of Paramedical and Health Sciences: Dr J. MOVAFFAQ
Faculty of Pharmacy: Dr H. HOSSEINZADEH

MAZANDARAN UNIVERSITY

POB 416, Babolsar
Telephone: (11252) 32095
Fax: (11252) 33702
E-mail: um@umz.ac.ir
Internet: www.umz.ac.ir

Founded 1975 as Reza Shah Kabir University, name changed 1980
State control
Language of instruction: Farsi
Academic year: September to June

Chancellor: Dr SEYED KHALAGH MIRNIA

Vice-Chancellors: Dr KOUROSH NOZARI (Administration and Finance), Dr ALI KARIMI (Education), Dr KOUROSH SEDIGHI (Research), Dr ALI REZA KHESALI (Student Affairs)
Registrar: Dr ALI BAGHERI KHALILI
Librarian: Dr REZA NOORZAD
Number of teachers: 320
Number of students: 11,280

DEANS

Faculty of Art: Dr F. MAHMOUDI
Faculty of Agricultural Sciences: Dr H. SADEGHI
Faculty of Basic Sciences: Dr A. RAOUF
Faculty of Engineering: Dr J. WASEGHI
Faculty of Humanities and Social Sciences: Dr S. MIRDAR
Faculty of Natural Resources: Dr J. OLADI

PAYAME NOOR UNIVERSITY

POB 19395-4697, Lashkarak Rd, Tehran 19569
Telephone: (21) 22442042
Fax: (21) 22441511
E-mail: int@pnu.ac.ir
Internet: www.pnu.ac.ir
Founded 1987
State control
Languages of instruction: Farsi, English
Academic year: September to July (two terms)
Pres.: Prof. ALIREZA ALI-AHMADI
Vice-Pres. for Academic Affairs and Assessment: Dr ASGHAR ABOLHASSANI
Vice-Pres. for Admin. and Finance: Dr MOHAMMAD TAGHI AMINI
Vice-Pres. for Information Technology: Dr DAVOOD KARIMZADEGAN MOGHADDAM (acting)
Vice-Pres. for Planning and Devt: Dr GHOLAMREZA KATEB
Vice-Pres. for Research: Dr ABOLFAZL FARAHANI
Vice-Pres. for Student Affairs and Culture: Dr ABBAS NAZIFI
Dir of the Int. Office: Prof. MOHAMMAD HASSAN BIJAN-ZADEH
Librarian: Dr MANOOCHEHR JAFARIGOHAR
Library of 1,400,000 vols (total for all centres)
Number of teachers: 7,600 (600 full-time, 7,000 part-time)
Number of students: 641,654
Publications: *Newsletter* (monthly), *Peyke Noor Journal* (6 a year), *Journal of Basic Sciences* (quarterly), *Journal of Humanities* (quarterly)
Distance education; 272 study centres and units in Iran; depts of Accountancy, Agricultural economics eng., Agricultural machinery and mechanization eng., Agricultural sciences eng., Animal husbandry, Arabic literature, Art, Biology, Business admin., Chemistry, Computer sciences, Economics, Education, Electronic commerce, English language and linguistics, Environmental health, Ethics and mysticism, Geography, Geology, Hardware eng., History, Industrial eng., Information technology management, Islamic civilization, history and culture, Islamic studies, Jurisprudence and basics of Islamic laws, Koranic sciences and tradition, Management of rural devt eng., Mathematics, Natural resources and environmental eng., Persian language and literature, Philosophy and speech, Physical education, Physics, Professional health, Product management eng., Project management eng., Psychology, Public admin., Public health, Social sciences, Software eng., Statistics, Water and soil eng.

DEANS

Faculty of Agricultural Sciences: Dr GHOLAMREZA BAKHSHI KHANIKI
Faculty of Basic Sciences: Dr PARVIZ PARVARESH
Faculty of Eng.: Dr SEYED SEPEHR GHAZI NOORI
Faculty of Health and Basic Medical Sciences: Dr MOHAMMAD ALI EBRAHIMI
Faculty of Humanities: Dr BAHMAN ZANDI
Faculty of Information Technology: Dr AHMAD FARAAHI
Faculty of Theology and Islamic Sciences: Dr NASER MOHAMMADI

PETROLEUM UNIVERSITY OF TECHNOLOGY

569 Hafez Ave, Tehran 15996-45313
Telephone: (21) 8804272
Fax: (21) 8807687
E-mail: info@put.ac.ir
Internet: www.put.ac.ir
Founded 1939 as Abadan Institute of Technology
State control, under Ministry of Petroleum
Languages of instruction: English, Farsi
Academic year: September to June
Chancellor: Dr D. H. PANJESHAHI
Vice-Chancellor (Academic): Dr M.R. SHISHESAZ
Vice-Chancellor (Finance and Administration): A. ALIMORADY
Vice-Chancellor (Research Affairs): Dr B. ROUZBEHANI
Vice-Chancellor (Research and Postgraduate Studies): Dr A. EMAMZADEH
Vice-Chancellor (Student Affairs): Dr N. NABHANI
Registrar: Dr M. FARZAM
Number of teachers: 100
Number of students: 1,500
Publication: *P. U. T. Monthly News*

DEANS

Faculty of Accounting and Finance (Tehran): Dr A. EMAMZADEH
Faculty of Chemical and Petrochemical Engineering (Abadan): Dr T. JADIDI
Faculty of Petroleum Engineering (Ahwaz): Dr K. SALAHSHOOR

ATTACHED INSTITUTES

Mahmood-Abad Institute for Marine Sciences: POB 161, Mahmood-Abad; Dir H. RAZAEE.

RAZI UNIVERSITY

Kermanshah Azadi Square, Kermanshah
Telephone: 28050
Fax: 26183
Internet: www.razi.ac.ir
Founded 1974
State control
Academic year: January to September
Chancellor: Dr M. MEHDI KHODAEI
Vice-Chancellor: Dr M. MOTALEBI
Administrative Officer: Mr GHAHRAMANI
Librarian: Dr GHASEMPOR
Number of teachers: 175
Number of students: 3,550

DEANS

College of Agriculture: Mr A. POPZAN
College of Engineering: Dr G. SHIESI
College of Letters: Mr V. SABZIANPOOR
College of Science: Dr M. ELAHI
College of Veterinary Sciences: Dr A. CHALEHCHALEH

SEMNAN UNIVERSITY OF MEDICAL SCIENCES

POB 35195-163, Molavi Blvd, Semnan
Telephone: (231) 3320112
Fax: (231) 3327316
E-mail: med_Semnan@sem-ums.ac.ir
Internet: www.sem-ums.ac.ir
Founded 1988 as Semnan College of Medical Sciences; present name and status 1990
Academic year: September to June (two semesters)
Works in collaboration with seven hospitals in the Semnan province
Chancellor: Dr ALI RASHIDI-POUR
Vice-Chancellor (Academic and Research Affairs): Dr VAHID SEMNANI
Vice-Chancellor (Financial and Administrative Affairs): Dr BEHPOUR YOUSEFI
Vice-Chancellor (Treatment): Dr MOHAMMAD BAGHER SABERI ZAFARGHANDI
Vice-Chancellor (Health Affairs): Dr JAFAR JANDAGHI
Vice-Chancellor (Student Affairs): Dr MOHAMMAD AMOUZADEH KHALILI
Vice-Chancellor (Drugs and Food): Dr SIAMAK YAGHMAIAN
Head Librarian: Dr GHOLAMREZA IRAJIAN
Library of 41,863 vols, 125 current periodicals, 417 theses
Number of teachers: 119
Number of students: 1,420
Publications: *Koomesh Medical Journal* (in Persian4 a year), *Avay-e-Elm* (medical research in Persian, 2 or 3 a year), *Health communicators, focus on Health* (in Persian, 2 a year), *Health magazine* (in Persian, 2 a year)

DEANS

Faculty of Health: MOHAMMAD BAGHER DELKHOSH
Faculty of Medicine: Dr MOHAMMAD E. AMINBEIDOKHTI
Faculty of Nursing and Paramedical Sciences: SAEED HAJIAGHAJANI
Faculty of Rehabilitation: Dr AMIR H. BAKHTIARI

SHAHED UNIVERSITY

115 North Kargar Ave, POB 15875-5794, Tehran
Telephone: (21) 6413734
Fax: (21) 6419568
Founded 1989
State control
Academic year: September to June
Chancellor: Dr MAHMOOD NOORISAFA
Vice-Chancellors: Dr SOGHRAT FAGHIHZADEH (Research), Dr SEIYED KAZEM FOROOTAN (Academic Affairs), Dr KAMRAR SAGHAFI (Student Affairs), Dr MOSTAFA KIAIE (Administrative and Financial Affairs, and Development), Dr ALI AZAM KHOSRARI (Cultural Affairs)
Librarian: ABFOLREZA NOROOZI CHACOLI
Library of 150,000 vols
Number of teachers: 215
Number of students: 3,000
Publication: *Daneshvar* (4 a year)

DEANS

Faculty of Agriculture: Dr MASOOD ISFAHANI
Faculty of Art: ALI ASGAR SHIRAZI
Faculty of Basic Sciences: Dr IRAJ RASOOLI
Faculty of Dentistry: Dr SEIYED SHOJAEDDIN SHAYEGH
Faculty of Engineering: Dr JALAL NAZARZADEH
Faculty of Humanities and Literature: Dr MOHAMMAD REZA IMAM
Faculty of Medical Sciences: Dr SEIYED SAEID SEIYED MORTAZ

SHAHID BAHONAR UNIVERSITY OF KERMAN

POB 76169-133, Kerman
Telephone: (341) 237001
Fax: (341) 235391
Internet: www.uk.ac.ir

Founded 1974, teaching commenced 1975
State control
Languages of instruction: Farsi, English
Academic year: September to June

Chancellor: Dr ALI MOSTAFAVI
Registrar: Dr M. A. VALI
Librarian: M. SHAFIIE

Number of teachers: 550
Number of students: 14,680

Faculties: engineering, sciences, mathematics and computer sciences, arts, economics, literature and human sciences, agriculture, physical education and sports science, veterinary science; other faculties at: Jiroft (agriculture), Sirjan (applied sciences), Zarand (industry and mining), Bam (higher education).

SHAHID BEHESHTI UNIVERSITY

Evin, 19834 Tehran
Telephone: (21) 29901
Fax: (21) 22403003
E-mail: int-re@cc.sbu.ac.ir
Internet: www.sbu.ac.ir

Founded 1960 as National University of Iran; present name 1983
State control
Language of instruction: Farsi
Academic year: September to June

President (and with responsibility for Complementary Education): Dr HADI NADIMI
Vice-President for Academic Affairs: Dr SEYED ABOLGHASSEM FATEMI
Vice-President for Administrative and Financial Affairs: Dr AKBAR ZARGAR
Vice-President for Research: Dr ZAHRA SABBAGHIAN
Vice-President for Student Services: Dr MOHAMAD ROSHAN
Registrar: Dr MASOOD SHARIFI

Library: see Libraries and Archives
Number of teachers: 453
Number of students: 13,576

Publications: *Earth Sciences*, *Journal of Administrative Sciences*, *Journal of Economics*, *Journal of Law Research*, *Pazhoohesh Nameh* (literature and humanities), *Soffeh* (architecture)

DEANS

Faculty of Architecture: Dr ALI GHAFFARI
Faculty of Computer and Electrical Engineering: Dr JAVAD ESMAILI
Faculty of Earth Sciences: Dr SEYED HASSAN SADOUGH
Faculty of Economics and Political Sciences: Dr MOHAMMAD NASER SHERAFAT
Faculty of Education and Psychology: MOHAMMAD HASSAN PARDAKHTCHI
Faculty of Law: Dr GOODARZ EFTEKHAR JAHROMI
Faculty of Literature and Humanities: Dr FRAMARZ RAFIPOUR
Faculty of Management and Accounting: Dr MOHAMMAD ESMAEIL FADAEI NEJAD
Faculty of Mathematical Sciences: Dr MOHAMMAD ZOKAEI
Faculty of Nuclear Engineering: Dr ABDOL HAMID MINOOCHEHR
Faculty of Physical Education and Sports Sciences: Dr MOHAMMAD ALI ASLANKHANI
Faculty of Sciences: Dr AHMAD SHABANI

SHAHID BEHESHTI UNIVERSITY OF MEDICAL SCIENCES AND HEALTH SERVICES

Shahid Chamran Highway, Evin, POB 4139-19395, Tehran

Telephone: (21) 2401022
Fax: (21) 2400052
E-mail: icrd@sbmu.ac.ir
Internet: www.sbmu.ac.ir

Founded 1961 as Melli University; present name 1986
State control
Language of instruction: Farsi
Academic year: September to June

Chancellor: Dr HABIBOLLA PEYRAVI
Vice-Chancellor (Academic Affairs): Dr D. YADEGARI
Vice-Chancellor (Administration and Finance): Dr R. ABOUFAZELI
Vice-Chancellor (Curative and Pharmaceutical Affairs): Dr S. S. RAZAVI
Vice-Chancellor (Health): Dr A. RAMEZANKHANI
Vice-Chancellor (Research): Dr M. JORJANI
Vice-Chancellor (Student and Cultural Affairs): Dr M. HOSSEINI KHAMENE
Director of International Relations and Congress Management: Dr F. OKHOVATIAN
Librarian: A. MOHADES RAAD

Library of 5,458 vols, 3,000 current journals, 60 e-books
Number of teachers: 1,039
Number of students: 5,961

Publications: *Bina* (Journal of Ophthalmology, 4 a year), *Iranian Journal of Infectious Disease and Tropical Medicine* (4 a year), *Pejouhandeh* (4 a year), *Research in Medical Subjects* (in Farsi, 4 a year), *Tanaffos* (Respiration, 4 a year), *Journal of Medical Education* (4 a year), *Journal of Dentistry* (4 a year), *Iranian Journal of Urology* (4 a year), *Iranian Journal of Plastic and Reconstructive Surgery* (4 a year), *Journal of the Pharmaceutical Research Centre* (4 a year), *International Journal of Endocrinology and Metabolism* (4 a year), *Digestive Disease Digest* (monthly)

DEANS

Faculty of Allied Medicine: Dr S. H. MOGHADAM-NIA
Faculty of Dentistry
Faculty of Medicine: Dr M. MARDANI
Faculty of Nutrition and Food Industrial Sciences: Dr N. KALANTARI
School of Nursing and Midwifery: Dr M. YAZDJERDI
Faculty of Pharmacy: Dr M. MOSADEGH
School of Public Health: Dr H. KHATAMI
Faculty of Rehabilitation: Dr M. GHASSEMY BOROMAND

ATTACHED INSTITUTES

Institute of Nutrition and Food Industrial Sciences: Dir Dr N. KALANTARI.

WHO Collaborating Centre for Educational Development of Medical and Health Personnel: Dir Dr SH. YAZDANI.

Endocrinology Research Centre: Dir Dr F. AZIZI.

Neuroscience Research Centre: Dir Dr F. MOTAMEDI.

Research Centre for Gastroenterology and Liver Transplantation: Dir Dr M.R. ZALI.

National Research Institute of Tuberculosis and Lung Disease: Dir Dr A. A. VELAYATI.

Dentistry Research Centre: Dir Dr M.R. SAFFAVI.

Centre for Eye Research: Dir Dr M.A. JAVADI.

Skin Research Centre: Dir Dr P. TOOSI.

Urology and Nephrology Research Centre: Dir Dr A. BASSIRI.

Cell and Molecular Biology Research Centre: Dir Dr A. HOSSEINI.

Traditional Medicine and Medicinal Plants Research Centre: Dir Dr M. MOSADEGH.

Pharmaceutical Sciences Research Centre: Dir Dr H. R. MOGHIMI.

Cardiovascular Research Centre: Dir Dr M. R. MOTAMEDI.

SHAHID CHAMRAN UNIVERSITY

Ahvaz, Khuzestan
Telephone: (611) 3330022
Fax: (611) 3332040
E-mail: webmaster@cua.ac.ir
Internet: www.cua.ac.ir

Founded 1955 as Jundi Shapur University, present name 1983
State control
Language of instruction: Farsi
Academic year: September to June

Chancellor: Dr MASOUD SAFAEE MOGHADAM
Vice-Chancellor (Academic Affairs): Dr ROAYAEE
Vice-Chancellor (Research): Dr B. NAJJARIAN
Vice-Chancellor (Student Affairs): Mr HOSEIN-ZADEH
Vice-Chancellor (Administration and Finance): Dr GHOMESHI
Director of International Affairs: Mr SADROSSADAT
Registrar: HAJIPOUR
Librarian: Dr A. FARAJPAHLOU

Number of teachers: 503
Number of students: 13,000

Publications: *Scientific Journal of Agriculture* (in Farsi, 4 a year), *University Journal of Science* (in Farsi, annually), *Journal of Education and Psychology* (in Farsi, 4 a year), *Journal of Engineering* (in Farsi, annually), *Journal of Veterinary Medicine* (in Farsi, annually), *Journal of Literature and Islamic Studies* (in Farsi, annually)

DEANS

Faculty of Agriculture: Dr MAHMOODIAN-SHOOSHTARI
Faculty of Science: Dr CHINEPARDAZ
Faculty of Economic and Social Science: Dr AHANGARI
Faculty of Engineering: Dr KOUSARIAN
Faculty of Veterinary Science: Dr KHAJEH
Faculty of Education and Psychology: Dr MEHRABIZADEH
Faculty of Literature and Humanities: Dr ALAM
Faculty of Theology and Islamic Studies: Dr GANJI
Faculty of Physical Education: Dr ALIJANI
Education and Research Centre in Ramin: Dr BIGDELI
Junior College of Engineering: SHAYESTEH MEHR
Faculty of Marine Science and Oceanography: Dr SAVARI

SHAHID SADOUGHI UNIVERSITY OF MEDICAL SCIENCES

2 - Bouali Ave, POB 89195-734, Yazd
Telephone: (351) 82470171
Fax: (351) 8245446
E-mail: info@ssu.ac.ir
Internet: www.ssu.ac.ir

Founded 1983
State control
Language of instruction: Farsi

Academic year: September to June
Chancellor: Dr AHMAD HAERIAN
Vice-Chancellor (Research Affairs): Dr S. M. YASSINI
Vice-Chancellor (Academic Affairs): Dr MR. MANSORIAN
Vice-Chancellor (Student Services): Dr HOSSEINI
Vice-Chancellor (Administrative and Financial Affairs): Dr MH. EHRAMPOUSH
Vice-Chancellor (Health): Dr M. KARIMI
Director of International Affairs: Dr SM. KALANTAR
Registrar: A. M. ALI HEIDARI

Library of 40,000 vols, 278 journals
Number of teachers: 236
Number of students: 1,800

DEANS

Faculty of Dentistry: Dr TALEBI
Faculty of Medicine: Dr RAFIEAN
Nursing and Midwifery: Dr SEYED HASSANI
Faculty of Paramedicine: Dr KHALILI
Faculty of Public Health: Dr EHRAMPOUSH

ATTACHED RESEARCH INSTITUTES

Diabetes Research Centre: Dir Dr AFKHAMI.

Heart Research Centre: Dir Dr RAFIEI.

Research and Clinical Centre for Infertility: Dir Dr A. AFLATONIAN.

SHAHREKORD UNIVERSITY OF MEDICAL SCIENCES

Kashany Ave, POB 88184, Shahrekord
Telephone: (381) 34590
Fax: (381) 34588

Founded in 1986
State control
Language of instruction: Persian

President: Dr M. HASHEMZADEH
Vice-Chancellor for Education and Research: Dr M. R. SAMIEY NASAB
Vice-Chancellor for Curative, Drug and Food Affairs: Dr E. NOORIAN
Vice-Chancellor for Student and Cultural Affairs: Dr H. DAVOODPOUR
Vice-Chancellor for Administrative and Financial Affairs: F. SHARAFATI
Librarian: Dr A. AMINI

Library of 33,000 vols
Number of teachers: 130
Number of students: 1,357

DEANS

Faculty of Medicine: Dr M. ROGHANY
Faculty of Nursing and Midwifery: M. RAHIMY
Broujen Faculty of Nursing: SH BANAEYAN

SHARIF UNIVERSITY OF TECHNOLOGY

POB 11365-8639, Tehran
Telephone: (21) 66005419
Fax: (21) 66012983
E-mail: scientia@sharif.edu
Internet: www.sharif.edu

Founded 1965 as Aryamehr University, present name 1979
State control
Languages of instruction: Farsi, English
Academic year: September to May

Library of 168,000 vols

President: Prof. SAEED SOHRABPOUR
Vice-President of Education: Prof. ALI MEGHDARI
Vice-President of Research: Dr MOHAMMAD KERMANSHAH
Vice-President of Student Affairs: Dr BIJAN VOSOOGHI VAHDAT
Vice-President of Administration and Finance: Prof. SEYED ALI AKBAR EKRAMI
Chairman, Office of International and Scientific Co-operation (OISC): Prof. ABOLHASSAN VAFAI
Dean of Graduate School: Prof. NADER TABATABAEE
Librarian: Prof. HAMID MEHDIGHOLI

Number of teachers: 850
Number of students: 8,000, including 2000 M.S. and 400 Ph.D. students

Publications: *Research Proceedings* (in Farsi, annually), *Scientia Iranica* (4 a year, in English), *Sharif* (scientific and research, 4 a year, in Farsi), *Sharif News* (in Farsi, monthly)

CHAIRMEN OF DEPARTMENTS

Aerospace Engineering: Dr MOHAMMAD FARSHCHI
Chemical Engineering: Dr CYRUS GHOTBI
Chemistry: Prof. FEREIDOON MOATTAR
Civil Engineering: Dr FAYAZ RAHIMZADEH ROFUEI
Computer Engineering: Dr SAEED BAGHERI SHOURAKI
Electrical Engineering: Dr SEYED MOHAMMAD HOSSEIN ALAVI
Industrial Engineering: M. H. CHAMRAN
Materials Science and Engineering: Prof. SEYED MORTEZA SEYED REIHANI
Mathematical Sciences: Prof. EBADOLLAH MAHMOUDIAN
Mechanical Engineering: Dr ALI ASGAR MOZAFARI
Physics: Prof. HESAM-E-DDIN ARFAEI
Graduate School of Management and Economics: Prof. MANOOCHEHR NAJMI

HEADS OF DEPARTMENTS

Mechanical Engineering: Dr. FARZAM FARAHMAND
Philosophy of Science: Dr. MAHDI GOLSHANI
Graduate School of Management and Economics: Dr. MANOUCHEHR NAJMI

ATTACHED RESEARCH CENTRES

Advanced Information and Communication Technology Centre: Dir Dr HAMID REZA RABIEE.

Advanced Manufacturing Research Centre (AMRC): Dir MOJTABA TAHMOURES.

Biochemical and Bio-environmental Research Centre: Azadi St, Tehran; tel. (21) 66005417; fax (21) 66022893; e-mail bioinfo@sharif.edu; internet http://sina.sharif.edu/~bioinfo; Dir Dr ALI AKBAR SEIF KORDI.

Centre of Excellence in Design, Robotics and Automation: Dir Prof. A. MEGHDARI.

Earthquake Engineering Research Centre: Dir Prof. M. T. KAZEMI.

Electronics Research Centre: Dir Prof. MAHMOUD TABIANI.

Green Card Project Research Centre: Dir Dr ALI REZA TAVAKOLI.

Institute for Transportation Studies and Research: Dir Dr HOSSEIN POURZAHEDI.

Philosophy of Science: Dir Prof. MEHDI GOLSHANI.

Sharif Energy Research Institute: Dir Dr YADDOLLAH SABOUHI.

Water Energy Research Centre: Dir Dr AYOOB TORKIAN.

SHIRAZ UNIVERSITY

Jam-e-Jam Ave, Shiraz 71946-84636
Telephone: (71) 6286416
Fax: (71) 6286419
Internet: www.shirazu.ac.ir

Founded 1946 as Pahlavi University, present name 1979
State control
Languages of instruction: Farsi, English
Academic year: October to July (two semesters)

Chancellor: Dr MAJID ERSHAD
Vice-Chancellor (Academic Affairs): Dr KHOSROW J'FARPOOR SETAYESH
Vice-Chancellor (Administrative and Financial Affairs): Dr MOHAMMAD HOSSEIN SETAYESH
Vice-Chancellor (Development Affairs): Dr GHOLAMREZA RAKHSHANDERO
Vice-Chancellor (Research): Dr HABIB SHARIF
Vice-Chancellor (Student Affairs): Dr MORTEZA AKHOND
Librarian: Dr ZAHIR HAYATI

Number of teachers: 573
Number of students: 12,446

Publications: *Iran Agricultural Research Journal of Social Sciences and Humanities, Iranian Journal of Science and Technology*

DEANS

College of Agriculture: Dr ALIASGHAR GHAEMI
College of Education: Dr MOHAMMAD KHAYYER
College of Engineering: Dr SIROOS JAVADPOUR
College of Law: Dr M. HADI SADEGHI
College of Literature and Human Sciences: Dr ABDULMAHDI RIAZI
College of Science: Dr NOZAR SAMANI
College of Veterinary Medicine: Dr MOHAMMAD MOAZZENI
Junior Agricultural College, Darab: Dr MOHAMMAD GHOLAMI
Teacher Training College, Kazeroon: Dr REZA POOLADI

UNIVERSITY OF SISTAN AND BALUCHISTAN

POB 98135-987, Zahedan
Telephone: (541) 2445981
Fax: (541) 2446771
Internet: www.usb.ac.ir

Founded 1974
State control
Language of instruction: Farsi
Academic year: September to July (two semesters)

Chancellor: Dr A. AKBARI
Vice-Chancellor for Academic Affairs: M. H. SANGTARASH
Vice-Chancellor for Administration and Finance: Dr AMIN REZA KAMALYAN
Vice-Chancellor for Research: Dr RAHBAR RAHIMI
Vice-Chancellor for Student Affairs: Dr A. A. MORYDI FARIMANI
Registrar: Dr ABDOLLAH WASIGH ABBASI
Director of Central Library: Dr RAHMATOLLAH LASHKARIPOUR

Number of teachers: 300
Number of students: 12,000

Publications: *Journal of Humanities* (in Farsi, 4 a year), *Journal of Engineering and Science* (in Farsi, 2 a year), *Iranian Journal of Fuzzy System* (2 a year), *Geography & Development* (in Farsi, 2 a year), *Divine and Law* (in Farsi, 2 a year), *Applied Engineering* (in Farsi, 2 a year), *Persian Language and Literature* (in Farsi, 2 a year), *History and Archaeology* (in Farsi, 2 a year), *Train Science and Psychology* (in Farsi, 2 a year)

DEANS

Engineering College: Dr S. FARAHAT
Science College: Dr A. A. MIRZAIE
College of Humanities (Zahedan): Dr A. A. AHANGAR
Fine Arts College: Dr M. MEHRAN

College of Humanities (Iranshar): Eng. AZARAG

PROFESSORS

AKBARI, A., Agricultural Economics
ATASHI, H., Chemical Engineering
AZIMI, P., Mathematics
ESHGI, H., Chemistry
KHOSHNOODI, M., Chemical Engineering
LASHKARIPOUR, G. R., Geology
MANSORI-TORSHIZI, H. M., Chemistry
NOORA, A. A., Mathematics
RAHIMI, R., Chemical Engineering
REZVANI, A. R., Chemistry
SARDASHTI, A. R., Chemistry
SHARIATI, H., Mathematics
TORMANZAHI, A., Agriculture
VALIZADEH, J., Agriculture
YAZDANI, B.-O., Humanities

TABRIZ UNIVERSITY OF MEDICAL SCIENCES

Golgasht Ave, Tabriz
Telephone: (411) 3346147
Fax: (411) 3342761
E-mail: jodati@tbzmed.ac.ir
Internet: www.tbzmed..ac.ir

Founded 1985, fmrly part of University of Tabriz
State control
Languages of instruction: Farsi, English
Academic year: October to July

Chancellor: Dr A. R. JODATI
Vice-Chancellor for Education: Dr J. HANAEE
Vice-Chancellor for Food and Medicines: Dr A. GARJANI
Vice-Chancellor for Research: Dr RASHIDI
Vice-Chancellor for Administration and Finance: Dr A. JAVAD ZADEH
Vice-Chancellor for Treatment: Dr M. KHOSHBATEN
Vice-Chancellor for Health Services: Dr A. R. NIKNIAZ
Vice-Chancellor for Student Affairs: Dr A. A. TAHER AGDAM
Registrar: Dr M. VARSCHOCHI
Librarian: Mrs MASOOMI

Number of teachers: 500
Number of students: 4,664

Publications: *Medical Journal*, *Journal of Basic Science in Medicine*, *Research Journal*, *Pharmaceutical Science*, *Journal of Nursing and Obstetrics*

DEANS

Faculty of Dentistry: Dr J. YAZDANI
Faculty of Medical Rehabilitation Science: Dr R. KHANDAGI
Faculty of Medicine: Dr M. BARZEGAR
Faculty of Nursing and Obstetrics: Dr Z. MAYABI
Faculty of Paramedical Sciences: Dr A. RAFI
Faculty of Pharmacy: Dr M. H. ZARRINTAN
Faculty of Public Health and Nutrition: Dr M. R. SIYAHI

UNIVERSITY OF TABRIZ

Tabriz 51666-14766
Telephone: (411) 3355994
Fax: (411) 3344272
E-mail: administer@tabrizu.ac.ir
Internet: www.tabrizu.ac.ir

Founded 1946, formerly University of Azarabadegan
State control
Language of instruction: Farsi
Academic year: September to June (two semesters)

Chancellor: Prof. M. R. POURMOHAMMADIE
Vice-Chancellor (Academic): Dr M. H. SADEGHI
Vice-Chancellor for Research Affairs: Dr H. NAMAZIE
Vice-Chancellor for Student Affairs: Dr Y. NOZHOOR
Vice-Chancellor for Finance and Administrative Affairs: Dr H. KATEBI
Vice-Chancellor for Postgraduate Affairs: Prof. M. MOGHADDAM-VAHED
Registrar: Dr M. H. REZAEI MOGHADDAM
Director of International Academic Collaboration: Dr M. RAHIMPOUR
Librarian: Dr M. T. ALAVIE

Library: see Libraries & Archives
Number of teachers: 492
Number of students: 11,500

Publications: *Pazhoohesh* (Record of University Research Activities, 2 a year), *Journal of Agricultural Sciences* (4 a year), *Journal of the Faculty of Engineering* (4 a year), *Journal of the Faculty of Humanities and Social Sciences* (4 a year)

DEANS

Faculty of Agriculture: Dr A. BABAEI-AHARI
Faculty of Agriculture (Maragheh Campus): M. R. AZAM-PARSA
Faculty of Chemistry: Dr H. ASHASIE
Faculty of Education and Psychology: Dr D. HOSSEINI-NASAB
Faculty of Engineering: Dr A. AGHA GOLZADEH
Faculty of Humanities and Social Sciences: Dr M. BEHESHTIE
Faculty of Mathematics: Dr A. A. MEHRVARZ
Faculty of Natural Sciences: Dr Y. SATTARZADEH
Faculty of Persian Literature and Foreign Languages: Dr A. ASSADOLLAHI TAJARRAG
Faculty of Physics: Dr D. JASSOR

PROFESSORS

Faculty of Agriculture (tel. (411) 3341316; fax (411) 3345332; e-mail agri-dean@tabrizu.ac.ir):

MASSIHA, S., Horticulture
MOGHADDAM-VAHED, M., Plant Breeding
PEYGHAMIE, E., Plant Pathology
RAHIMZADEH KHOEI, F., Agronomy
VALIZADEH, M., Genetics and Breeding

Faculty of Chemistry (tel. (411) 3355998; fax (411) 3340191; e-mail chemfac@tabrizu.ac.ir):

BLOURCHIAN, S. M., Organosilicon Chemistry
DJOZAN, DJ., Analytical Chemistry
ENTEZAMI, A. A., Polymer Chemistry
GOLABI, S. M., Electroanalytical Chemistry
MANZOORI, J., Analytical Chemistry, Spectroscopy
POURNAGHI AZAR, M. H., Electroanalytical Chemistry
SOROURADDIN ABADI, M. H., Analytical Chemistry
ZAFARANI-MOATTAR, M. T., Physical Chemistry

Faculty of Education and Psychology (tel. (411) 3341133; fax (411) 3356009):

HOSSEINI-NASAB, D., Training Psychology

Faculty of Engineering (tel. (411) 3356022; fax (411) 3346287; e-mail joeng@tabrizu.ac.ir):

BEHRAVESH, A., Structural Engineering
DILMAGHANI, S., Civil Engineering
HASANZADEH, Y., Heat and Fluid Transfer Engineering
HOSSEINI, S. H., Power Electronics
KEYANVASH, A., Metallurgy
KHANMOHAMMADI, S., Automatic Engineering
KHOSHRAVAN-AZAR, M.E., Heat Transfer Engineering
PIROUZ-PANAH, V., Internal Combustion Engines

Faculty of Humanities and Social Sciences (tel. (411) 3344286; fax (411) 3356013):

BANIFATEMEH, H., Social Sciences
ESFAHANIYAN, D., History
HARIRI-AKBARI, M., Political Sociology
RAJAEI ASL, A. H., Physical Geography

Faculty of Mathematics (tel. (411) 3356032; fax (411) 3344015):

MEHRVARZ, A.A., Algebra
N-DEHGAN, Y., Mathematical Analysis
SHAHABI, M. A., Mathematics
TOOMANIAN, A., Differential Geometry

Faculty of Natural Sciences (tel. (411) 3356027; fax (411) 3341244):

HOSSEINPOUR FEIZI, M.A., Radiobiology

Faculty of Persian Literature and Foreign Languages (tel. (411) 3341150; fax (411) 3356017):

BAGHERI, M., Culture and Ancient Languages
EJLALI, A. P., Persian Language and Literature
IRANDOOST, R., French Language and Literature
LOTFIPOUR SAEDI, K., Applied Linguistics
NAVALI, M., Philosophy
SARKARATI, B., Ancient Iranian Languages

Faculty of Physics (tel. (411) 3356030; fax (411) 3341244):

BIDADI, H., Solid-state Physics
JAFARIZADEH, M.A., Physics of Elementary Particles
KALAFI, M., Solid-state Physics
MOHAMMAD-ZADEH JASSUR, D., Atomic Physics
SOBHANIAN, S., Atomic Physics, Plasma
TAJALLI SAIFI, H., Atomic Physics, Lasers

ATTACHED COLLEGES

College of Engineering (Bonab Campus): Dir M.R.A. PARSA.

College of Engineering (Marand Campus): Dir S. HOSSEINI.

College of Veterinary Medicine: Dir Dr H. KARIMIE.

ATTACHED RESEARCH CENTRES

Centre for Applied Physics and Astrophysical Research: Dir Prof. H. TAJALLI.

Centre for Geographical Research: Dir Dr M. ZAHERIE.

Research Institute of Basic Sciences: Dir Prof. S. SOBHANIAN.

Khajeh Nassir-Alddin Toussi Observatory: Dir A. AJABSHIRIZADEH.

TARBIAT MODARRES UNIVERSITY

Intersection of Chamran and Ale-Ahmad Highways, POB 14155-4838, Tehran
Telephone: (21) 8011001
Fax: (21) 8006544
E-mail: intl@modares.ac.ir
Internet: www.modares.ac.ir

Founded 1982
Academic year: September to June

President: Dr SAEED SEMNANIAN
Vice-President for Research: Dr M. F. MOUSAVI
Vice-President for Academic Affairs: Dr M. T. AHMADY
Vice-President for Student Affairs: Dr A. MALEKI MOGHADDAM
Vice-President for Administrative and Financial Affairs: Dr H. BAHRAMI
Librarian: Dr GHOLAM ALI MONTAZER

Library of 80,000 vols, 2,552 periodicals
Number of teachers: 393
Number of students: 3,595

DEANS

Faculty of Humanities: Dr S. AYEENEVAND
Faculty of Basic Sciences: Dr H. NADERIMANESH
Faculty of Engineering: Dr SHOJAOSSADATI
Faculty of Agriculture: Dr T. TAVAKOLI
Faculty of Arts: Dr M. R. POORJAAFAR
Faculty of Basic Medical Sciences: Dr M. RASAEE
Faculty of Natural Resources and Marine Sciences: Dr SAHARI

TEHRAN UNIVERSITY OF MEDICAL SCIENCES AND HEALTH SERVICES

23 Dameshgh Ave, Vali-e-Asr St, Tehran 14155-14167
Telephone: (21) 8896692
Fax: (21) 8898532
E-mail: iro@sina.tums.ac.ir
Internet: www.tums.ac.ir

Founded 1935 following devolution of medical schools from the University of Tehran and merger with other Tehran-based medical institutions

Chancellor: MOHAMMAD REZA ZAFARGHANDI

Number of teachers: 1,300
Number of students: 13,000

Publications: *Daru* (quarterly), *Acta Medica* (quarterly), *Journal of Dentistry* (quarterly)

Schools of medicine, pharmacy, dentistry, public health, rehabilitation, nursing and midwifery

Research centres: science and technology in medicine, rheumatology, auditory, digestive diseases, skin diseases and leprosy, trauma, haematology and oncology, cardiovascular diseases, endocrinology and metabolism, reproductive health, urology, immunology, asthma and allergies, ethics and medical history, cancer, addiction, bank of transplantation products of Iran; 11 Educational and Health Research Centres in 10 provinces, 15 teaching hospitals; 40 br libraries and one digital library with access to more than 5,000 full text medical journals.

UNIVERSITY OF TEHRAN

Enghelab Ave, Tehran 14174
Telephone: (21) 61112500
Fax: (21) 6409348
E-mail: international@ut.ac.ir
Internet: www.ut.ac.ir

Founded 1934
Language of instruction: Farsi
Academic year: September to July (two semesters)

President: Prof. REZA FARAJI DANA
Vice-Presidents: Dr HOSSEIN HOSSEINI (Academic Affairs), Dr GHANDI (Administration and Finance), Dr SALEHI (Head of e-Learning Centre), Dr MAGHARI (Planning), Dr RAHIMIAN (Research), Dr KHODAYARI (Student Affairs)
Director-General: Dr M. FAEZIPOUR
University Librarian: Dr ALI AKBAR ENAYATI

Library: see Libraries and Archives
Number of teachers: 1,500
Number of students: 32,000

DEANS

Faculty of Agriculture: Dr ALI REZA TALAEI
Faculty of Economics: Dr HOSSEIN ABBASINEJAD
Faculty of Education: Dr KAMAL DORRANI
Faculty of Engineering: Dr MAHMOOD NILI AHMADABADI
Faculty of Environmental Studies: Dr HOSSAIN BAHRINI
Faculty of Fine Arts: Dr M. MEHDI AZIZI
Faculty of Foreign Languages: Dr NADER HAGHANI
Faculty of Geography: Dr GHADIRI
Faculty of Law and Political Science: Dr HASSAN ALI DOROODIAN
Faculty of Literature and Humanities: Dr SHIKHOLSLAMI
Faculty of Management and Business Administration: Dr ALI TASLIMI
Faculty of Natural Resources: Dr MOHAMMAD JAFARI
Faculty of Physical Education: Dr BAGHEZADEH
Faculty of Science: Dr HASSAN EBRAHIMZADEH
Faculty of Social Science: Dr AZAD ARMAKI
Faculty of Theology and Islamic Studies: Dr ALI ALIABADI
Faculty of Veterinary Medicine: Dr S. MEHDI GHAMSARI

DIRECTORS

Institute of Biophysics and Chemistry: Dr OZRA RABANI
Institute of Comparative Law: Dr SAFAEI
Institute of Dehghoda Encyclopaedias: Dr S. JAFAR SHAHEIDI
Institute of Desert Regions and Arid Zones: Dr ZEHTABIAN
Institute of Geography: Dr FARHOODI
Institute of Geophysics: Dr JAVAHERIAN
Institute of Psychology: Dr MOHAMMAD ALI KARDAN
Centre for International Studies: Dr MOSAFA
Aboureihan Educational Complex: Dr MAHMOOD REZA BEHBAHANI
Ghom Higher Educational Complex: Dr MOHSEN RAHAMI

URMIA UNIVERSITY

POB 165, Urmia 57153
Telephone: (441) 3445409
Fax: (441) 3443442
E-mail: chancellor@urmia.ac.ir
Internet: www.urmia.ac.ir

Founded 1965
Academic year: September to July

Chancellor: Dr GOUDARZ SADEGHI-HASHJIN
Vice-Chancellor (Personnel and Finance): GHOLAMREZA MANSOORFAR
Vice-Chancellor (Education): Dr ESMAIL AYAN
Vice-Chancellor (Research): Dr MOHAMMAD MEHDI BARADARANI
Vice-Chancellor (Student Affairs): Dr MAHMOOD RAZAZADEH
Vice-Chancellor (Development): Dr ESFANDYAR MARDANI
Registrar: Dr ALIREZA MOZAFFARI
Librarians: Dr FARHAD FARROKHI ARDEBILI, MOHAMMADREZA FARHADPOOR

Library of 58,000 vols
Number of teachers: 284
Number of students: 8,431

Publications: *Neda* (monthly), *Pajooheshgaran* (quarterly)

DEANS

Agriculture: Dr ASGHAR KHOSROWSHAHI
Engineering: Dr IRAJ MIRZAEE
Literature and Humanities: Dr ABDOLLAH TOLOEE-AZAR
Science: Dr SAMAD ZAREAE
Veterinary Medicine: Dr HOSEIN TAJIK

YAZD UNIVERSITY

POB 89195-741, Yazd
Telephone: (351) 7250220
Fax: (351) 7250110
E-mail: Interoff@yazduni.ac.ir
Internet: www.yazduni.ac.ir

Founded 1988
State control
Languages of instruction: Farsi, English
Academic year: September to June

Chancellor: Dr MOHAMMAD ALI VAHDAT ZAD
Vice-Chancellor (Finance and Administration): Dr GHAZANFAR MIRJALILI
Vice-Chancellor (Research): Dr ABBASS BEHJAT
Vice-Chancellor (Development and Construction): Dr AHMAD SADEGHIYE
Vice-Chancellor (Student Affairs): Dr MOHAMMAD ALI AMROLLAHI
Vice-Chancellor (Registrar): Dr ALI AKBAR DEHGHAN
Librarian: Dr BAGHIYAN

Number of teachers: 306
Number of students: 7,485

Publications: *Bulletin*, *Kavoshnameh* (humanities research, 2 a year)

DEANS

School of Art and Architecture: Dr M. NOGHSAN-MOHAMMADI
School of Basic Sciences: Dr SAYED MANSOUR VAEZPOUR
School of Engineering: Dr MAHMOOD KHODADAD
School of Humanities: Dr KERAMATLAH ZIYARI
Faculty of Natural Resources and Desert Studies: Dr MOHAMMAD HUSSEIN MOBIN

HEADS OF DEPARTMENTS

School of Art and Architecture (tel. (351) 6223700; fax (351) 6223700; e-mail art-arch@yazduni.ac.ir):

- Architecture: Dr SAYED MOHAMMAD H. AYATLLAHI (acting)
- Painting: BAHRAM AHMADI (acting)
- Urban Planning: H. NOOR MOHAMMADZADE (acting)

School of Basic Sciences (tel. and fax (351) 8246467; e-mail science@yazduni.ac.ir):

- Chemistry: Dr HAMID REZA ZARE
- Mathematics: Dr FARID MALEK
- Physics: Dr ABODFAZL MIRYALILI

School of Engineering (tel. and fax (351) 8247100; e-mail engineering@yazduni.ac.ir):

- Civil Engineering: Dr NADER ABDOLI YAZDI
- Computer Engineering: Dr F. ADIBNIA
- Electronic Engineering: Dr REZA SAADAT
- Industrial Engineering: Dr HASSAN HOSSEINI NASAB
- Materials Engineering: Dr MEHDI KALANTAR
- Mechanical Engineering: Dr MANSOOR RAFIEIAN
- Mining Engineering: Dr AMIR HUSSEIN KOOHSARI
- Textile Engineering: Dr ALI A. ALAMDAR

School of Humanities (tel. and fax (351) 8240310; e-mail humanities@yazduni.ac.ir):

- Accounting: JAMAL BARZEGARI
- Arabic Literature and Language: NAZERI
- Business Management: Dr FARID
- Economy: Dr SAYED NEZAMODIN MAKIYAN
- Education: Dr SAYED KAZEM ALAVI LANGROUDI
- English Language: Dr ANITA LASHKARIAN
- Geography: Dr GHOLAM ALI MAZAFARI
- History: Dr MOHAMMDA ALI RANJBAR
- Industrial Management: Dr ABBAS QAZAEI
- Islamic Sciences: Dr H. ABOOEE
- Library and Information Sciences: MIS MAKIZADEH
- Persian Literature and Language: Dr MEHDI MALEKSABET
- Physical Education: HOSSEIN AKBARZADE
- Political Sciences: Dr ABEDI
- Principles of Islamic Law: Dr MOSSAVIZADEH
- Social Science and Anthropology: Dr SAEEDI MADANI
- Theology: Dr FALLAH

Faculty of Natural Resources and Desert Studies (tel. (351) 8247320; fax (351) 8247329; e-mail DDRI@yazduni.ac.ir):

Natural Resources Engineering–Environment: JALIL SARHANGZADE

Natural Resources Engineering–Range and Watershed Management: Dr JANGJOO

ATTACHED COLLEGE

Ardakan College of Natural Resources and Desert Studies: tel. (351) 8247320; fax (351) 7226767; e-mail DDRI@yazduni.ac.ir; Head AHMAD FATTAHI.

Colleges

There are *c.* 50 colleges of higher education in Iran, and *c.* 40 technological institutes, of which the following are a selection only.

Iran Banking Institute: 207 Pasdaran Ave, POB 19395/4814, Tehran; tel. (21) 2848000; fax (21) 2842618; f. 1963; four-year BA degree courses in banking, accounting and computer scince, and MA degree courses in banking, accounting and law; 2,139 students; Chancellor Dr MEHDI EMRANI.

Military Academy: Sepah Ave, Tehran; depts of military history, military science and tactics, international relations and treaties, general engineering science, physics and electronics, military armaments, nuclear warfare.

College of Surveying: POB 1844, Azadi Sq., Tehran; f. 1965; national training centre for surveyors; 80 students; affiliated to National Cartographic Centre; Dir Dr H. NAHAVANDCHI.

IRAQ

The Higher Education System

The University of Baghdad (founded 1957) is the oldest university in Iraq. As a result of increasing petroleum revenues in the 1970s the higher education sector expanded significantly, and in addition to the universities a large number of technical institutes were established. However, during the 1980s and 1990s higher education was affected by economic privations caused by war with Iran (1980–88) and sanctions imposed by the international community following Iraq's invasion of Kuwait in 1990 and defeat by a US-led coalition in 1991. In March–April 2003 another US-led coalition invaded Iraq, captured Baghdad and toppled the Baathist regime of Saddam Hussein. Since 2003 higher education has been subject to reform, including the establishment of new universities; however, many academics have been killed, moved abroad or taken permanent leave of absence, student numbers have fallen and in some areas Islamist groups have imposed segregated classes or forced female students to adopt Islamic forms of dress. The Ministry of Higher Education and Scientific Research oversees the administration of the 20 public universities and other colleges and technical institutes. In 2002/03 there were approximately 240,000 undergraduates attending 65 institutions of higher education.

Students must complete secondary education to be admitted to public universities. Each year the Ministry of Higher Education and Scientific Research determines entry requirements, which vary from programme to programme. The main undergraduate degree is the Bachelors, which lasts four years, although longer periods of study are required for pharmacy, architecture, dentistry, veterinary medicine (all five years) and medicine (six years). The first postgraduate degree is the Masters, lasting two to three years and incorporating both taught and research elements. The final university degree is the Doctor of Philosophy, which also includes both taught and research elements, with students required to pass examinations based on classroom-based work before proceeding to the research element.

Technical and vocational education is dominated by technical colleges and institutes, most of which were founded during the 1970s. The Commission for Technical education is the government body responsible for administering these institutions and technical degrees and diplomas. The Technician Diploma is a two-year course offered by technical institutes, of which there were 37 in 2004. (Some technical institutes are directly affiliated to Government ministries, depending on the area of specialization.) Holders of the Technician Diploma can gain direct entry to the second year of the four-year Bachelor of Technology programme, offered by technical colleges. The majority of these courses are in the fields of engineering and medicine. Following the Bachelor of Technology, technical colleges offer a two-year Higher Diploma of Technology, mainly in engineering disciplines. The Master of Technology is similar to the Higher Diploma of Technology, but contains a greater element of research.

During the US-led military campaign to oust the regime of Saddam Hussain in early 2003, and in the subsequent period of social unrest, damage and looting were reported at a number of Iraq's public institutions.

Learned Societies

EDUCATION

Arab Literacy and Adult Education Organization (ARLO): POB 3217, 113 Abu Nawas St, Baghdad; tel. 7186246; f. 1966 by ALECSO to promote co-operation in all aspects of literacy and adult education between the Arab states; all Arab states are mems; library of 14,700 vols; Dir HASHIM ABU ZEID EL SAFI (acting); publ. *The Education of the Masses* (2 a year).

FINE AND PERFORMING ARTS

Iraqi Artists' Society: Damascus St, Baghdad; f. 1956; exhibitions and occasional publs; Pres. NOORI AL RAWI; Sec. AMER ALUBIDI.

LANGUAGE AND LITERATURE

British Council: 10 Spring Gardens, London, SW1A 2BN, United Kingdom; tel. (161) 957-7755; fax (161) 957-7762; e-mail britishcouncil.iraq@fco.gov.uk; internet www .britishcouncil.org/iraq; f. 1940; offers courses and exams in English language and promotes cultural exchange with the United Kingdom; based in London until further notice; Chief Exec. MARTIN DAVIDSON.

Iraqi Academy: Waziriya, Baghdad; tel. (1) 4224202; fax (1) 4222066; e-mail iraqacademy@yahoo.com; internet www .iraqacademy.org; f. 1947 with the aims of maintaining the Arabic language and heritage, supporting research in Arabic and Muslim history, the history of Iraq and Arabic language and heritage, maintaining Kurdish and Assyrian languages; 37 mems; Pres. Prof. Dr AHMED MATLOUB (acting); publ. *Majallat Al Mejmah Al Ilmi* (literary, quarterly).

MEDICINE

United Iraqi Medical Society: Maari St, Al Mansoor, Baghdad; f. 1920; Dir Dr AHMED AL-HEETY.

NATURAL SCIENCES

General

Federation of Arab Scientific Research Councils: POB 13027, Baghdad; tel. (1) 8881709; fax (1) 8867511; f. 1976; aims to strengthen collaboration among scientific research councils, institutions, centres and universities in all Arab states; to adopt the Arabic language in scientific research and technology and to encourage the use of Arabic in scientific research and promote the Arabization of scientific terminology; to plan joint research projects among Arab states, especially those related to Arab development plans; 15 mem. states; library of 800 vols, 600 periodicals, 1,100,000 patent documents from USA, EPO, WIPO; Sec.-Gen. Prof. Dr TAHA T. AL-NAIMI; publs *Journal of Computer Research*, *Federation News*.

Research Institutes

GENERAL

Scientific Research Council: POB 2441, Jadiriya, Baghdad; f. 1963; Pres. Dr NAJIH M. KHALIL.

Attached research centres:

Agriculture and Water Resources Research Centre: Fudhailiyah; Dir Dr SAMIR A. AL-SHAKER.

Biological Research Centre: Jadiriya; Dir Dr AZWAR N. KHALAF.

Building Research Centre: Jadiriya; Dir Dr M. AL-IZZI.

Electronics and Computer Research Centre: Jadiriya; Dir Dr M. N. BEKIR.

Genetic Engineering and Biotechnology Research Centre: Jadiriya; Dir Dr FARUQ YASS AL-ANI.

Petroleum Research Centre: Jadiriya; Dir Dr A. H. A. K. MOHAMMED.

Psychological and Educational Research Centre: Jadiriya; Dir Dr GHASSAN H. SALIM.

Scientific Affairs Office: Jadiriya; Dir Dr RADHWAM K. A. HALIM.

Scientific Documentation Centre: Jadiriya; library: see under Libraries.

Solar Energy Research Centre: Jadiriya; Dir N. I. AL-HAMDANY.

Space Research Centre: Jadiriya; Dir Dr ALI AL-MASHAT.

AGRICULTURE, FISHERIES AND VETERINARY SCIENCE

Agriculture and Water Resources Research Centre: POB 2416, Karada Al-Sharkiya, Baghdad; tel. 7512080; f. 1980 to carry out research to improve and develop water and agricultural resources; 75 researchers; library of 6,000 vols, 450 periodicals; Dir-Gen. Dr SAMIR A. H. AL-SHAKIR;

publ. *Journal of Agriculture and Water Resources Research*.

EDUCATION

Centre for Educational and Psychological Research: University of Baghdad, 9 Waziriya, Baghdad; f. 1966; educational and psychological research studies to make education an effective power for the acceleration of economic and social development; library: *c.* 6,000 vols; Dir Dr MOHAMMED ALI KHALAF; publ. *Journal of Educational Psychological Research* (2 a year).

HISTORY, GEOGRAPHY AND ARCHAEOLOGY

British School of Archaeology in Iraq: 10 Carlton House Terrace, London, SW1Y 5AH, United Kingdom; tel. (20) 7969-5274; fax (20) 7969-5401; e-mail bsai@britac.ac.uk; internet www.britac.ac.uk/institutes/iraq; f. 1932; promotes, supports and undertakes research in Iraq and neighbouring countries; covers the subjects of archaeology, history, anthropology, geography, language and other related domains from earliest times to the present; grants are available for research; 750 mems; library: the library is currently housed by the British Embassy in Baghdad, the number of volumes is unknown; Pres. RACHEL MAXWELL-HYSLOP; Chair. Prof. ROGER MATTHEWS; Sec. JOAN PORTER MACIVER; publ. *Iraq* (annual).

TECHNOLOGY

Department of Scientific and Industrial Research: Directorate-General of Industry, Baghdad; f. 1935; staff 42; Dir-Gen. of Industry SHEETH NA'AMANN; publs *Technical Bulletin*, *Annual Report*.

Nuclear Research Centre: Tuwaitha, Baghdad; f. 1967; fmr main establishment of Iraq Atomic Energy Commission, now under control of International Atomic Energy Agency; administrative responsibility assumed by the Iraq Ministry of Science and Technology.

Libraries and Archives

Arbil

University of Salahaddin Central Library: Arbil; tel. 23102; f. 1968; 263,705 vols, 530 current periodicals; Dir Dr ABDULL S. ABBAS.

Baghdad

Al-Awqaf Central Library (Ministry of Endowments and Religious Affairs Central Library): POB 14146, Baghdad; f. 1928; library building looted and burnt down April 2003; library staff were able to preserve approx. 5,250 of the total collection of 7,000 MSS; Contact HASAN FREIH; publ. *Al-Rissala-Al-Islamiya*.

Al-Mustansiriya University Library: POB 14022, Waziriya, Baghdad; f. 1963; 311,800 vols, 30,000 vols of periodicals, 330 rolls of film, 280 current periodicals; also 11 college libraries with 33,000 vols, 850 periodicals; part of the collection was looted 2003; Dir FAISAL ANWAN AL-TAEE.

Arab Gulf States Information and Documentation Center: POB 5063, Baghdad; tel. 5433914; f. 1981; affiliated to the Board of Ministers of Information of the Arab Gulf States; aims to gather information from many sources, and to systematize, analyse and exchange it; supports the basic structure of existing information services; seven mem. states; provides a consultancy service; databases, microfilms; specialized library of 8,000 vols; Dir-Gen. HAYFA A. JAJAWI.

Educational Documentation Library: Ministry of Education, Educational Campus, Baghdad; tel. 8860000-2178; f. 1921; 37,000 vols, 73 periodicals; Librarian Dr KADHIM G. AL-KHAZRAJI.

Ibn Hayyan Information House: Iraqi Atomic Energy Commission, POB 765, Tuwaitha, Baghdad; up-to-date references, reports, pamphlets, microcards, magazines and film reels; Dir ISAM ATTA AJAJ.

Iraqi Academy Library: Waziriya, Baghdad; f. 1947; 60,000 vols, 32 original MSS, 1,600 copied MSS, 1,500 microfilms; Librarian SABAH NOAH.

Iraqi Museum Library: Salhiya Quarter, Baghdad West; tel. 8840876; f. 1934; archaeology, history of civilization, art, architecture, cultural heritage; evacuation of collection undertaken before the US-led military intervention 2003, currently in storage; 229,000 vols, 34,000 MSS; Dir ZAINAT AL-SAMAKRI; publ. *Al-Maskukat*.

National Archives of Iraq: POB 594, Baghdad; f. 1964; attached to the Ministry of Culture and Information; building looted and burnt down April 2003; collection subsequently subject to flooding and is currently frozen to prevent deterioration.

National Library: POB 594, Baghdad; tel. 4164190; f. 1961; building looted and burnt down April 2003; approx. 500,000 vols destroyed in fire; some holdings were subsequently subject to flooding and are currently frozen to prevent deterioration; legal deposit centre and national bibliographic centre; Dir-Gen. SAAD ESKANDER.

Scientific Documentation Centre: Abu Nuas Rd, POB 2441, Baghdad; tel. 7760023; f. 1972; scientific information services to researchers at the institutes/centres of the Scientific Research Council (*q.v.*), and to others working in Iraqi laboratories, including UNDP experts; seven libraries are being developed, each attached to a research centre of the Council, including the Central Science Library; in-service training for students of Library Science and Documentation and librarians; 20 staff mems; Dir Dr FAIK ABDUL S. RAZZAQ.

University of Baghdad Central Library: POB 47303, Jadiriya, Baghdad; f. 1960; looted and significant parts of library collection destroyed April 2003; major reconstruction underway; govt and UN depository library; acts as Exchange and governmental Bibliographical Centre; publ. *Current Contents of Iraqi Universities' Journals* (2 a year).

Basrah

University of Basrah Central Library: Basrah; f. 1964; 200,000 vols, 700 MSS, 1,400 current periodicals; Librarian Dr TARIK AL-MANASSIR; publ. catalogue (irregular).

Mosul

University of Mosul Central Library: Mosul; tel. 810162; fax 814765; f. 1967; looted April 2003, although its collections were left intact; 24 br. libraries; 140,000 vols, 3,500 periodicals, depository of UN and Iraqi govt publications; Dir MAHMUD JIRJIS; publs *Adab Al-Rafidarn* (irregular), *Research Work of University Faculty Members* (annually), *Catalogue* (annually), *Mesopotamia Journal of Agriculture*, *Journal of Rafidain Development*, *Annals of the College of Medicine-Mosul*, *Al-Rafidain Engineering*, *Iraqi Journal of Veterinary Sciences*, *Journal of Education and Science* (all irregular).

Museums and Art Galleries

Arbil

Arbil Museum: Arbil; objects from Iraqi history up to Arabic-Islamic period.

Babylon

Babylon Museum: Babylon; f. 1949; contains models, pictures, and paintings of the remains at Babylon; the museum is situated amongst the ruins.

Baghdad

Abbasid Palace Museum: Baghdad; a restored palace dating back to the late Caliphs of the Abbasid dynasty (13th c. AD); an exhibition of Arab antiquities and scale models of important Islamic monumental buildings in Iraq. Opened as a Museum in 1935.

Baghdad Museum: Sahat Al-Risafi, Baghdad; tel. 4165317; f. 1970; museum of folklore and costumes, natural history; photographic exhibition on history of Baghdad; Memorial Exhibition, containing the royal relics of King Faisal I; picture gallery; Dir (vacant).

Iraq Military Museum: A'dhamiya, Baghdad; f. 1974 combining Arms Museum (f. 1940) and Museum of War (f. 1966); contains old Arabian weapons, Othmanic firearms and contemporary Iraqi weapons.

Iraq National Museum: Salhiya quarter, Baghdad West; f. 1923; looted April 2003 resulting in theft or destruction of approx. 15,000 items; closed indefinitely; collection includes antiquities dating from the early Stone Age to the beginning of 18th c. AD, including large collection of Islamic objects; Al-Sarraf gallery contains Islamic coins; library: see Libraries; Dir Dr NAWALA AL-MUTAWALLI; publs *Sumer* (annually), *Al-Maskukat* (2 a year).

Iraq Natural History Research Centre and Museum: Bab Al-Muadham, Baghdad; f. 1946; attached to the University of Baghdad; includes sections on zoology, botany and geology; research work in Natural History; exhibitions of animals, plants, rocks and minerals pertaining to Iraq; organizes cultural, educational and scientific training programmes; library of 31,000 vols, 850 periodicals; Dir H.-A. ALI; publ. publs scientific papers in English (with Arabic summaries) dealing with the natural history of Iraq and neighbouring countries in the series *Iraq Natural History Research Centre Publications*, *Bulletin of the Iraq Natural History Research Centre* and *Annual Report*..

National Museum of Modern Art: Al-Nafoura Square, Bal Al-Sharqi, Baghdad; f. 1962; Supervisor AMER AL-UBAIDI.

Basrah

Natural History Museum of the University of Basrah: Corniche St, POB 432, Basrah; tel. 213494; f. 1971; study of flora and fauna of the marshes of South Iraq and the Arabian Gulf; sections on mammals, birds, reptiles and amphibia, and fishes; scientific collections in all sections accessible to specialists and exhibits open to public; Dir Dr KHALAF AL-ROBAAE; publ. *Bulletin*.

Mosul

Mosul Museum: Dawassa, Mosul; f. 1951; collections of Assyrian antiquities of the 9th–8th c. BC found at Nimrud, objects uncovered in the ruins of Hatra dating back to the 2nd c. BC–2nd c. AD, agricultural tools and pottery vessels from 5000–4000 BC, photographs of excavated buildings at Tepe Gawra, maps of the Assyrian Empire, Nimrud and Hatra;

Prehistoric and Islamic exhibits; assists in discovery and maintenance of several archaeological sites; library: *c.* 2,000 vols; Dir HAZIM A. AL HAMEED.

Nasiriya

Nasiriya Museum: Nasiriya; Sumerian and other archaeological objects found in Ur, Al-Abeed and Aridu.; Dir ABDUL AMIR HAMDANI.

Samarra

Samarra Museum: Samarra; f. 1936; it is housed in one of the old city gates, and contains objects excavated in the ruins of ancient Samarra; also historic maps, writings, pictures.

Universities

UNIVERSITY OF AL-ANBAR

Ramadi, Al-Anbar governorateTelephone: (1) 8864814
Fax: (1) 8178849
E-mail: anb.unv@uruklink.net

Founded 1987
State control

President: ABDUL HADI RAJEB HABEEB (acting)
Vice-President (Administration and Scientific): ABDUL MAJEED ABOUL HAMEED ALI AL-ANNI (acting)

Number of teachers: 464.

AL-MUSTANSIRIYA UNIVERSITY

POB 14022, Waziriya, Baghdad
Telephone: (1) 4168501
Fax: (1) 4165521
E-mail: mustuni@uruklink.net

Founded 1963
State control
Languages of instruction: Arabic, English
Academic year: September to June

President: Dr TAHER KH. AL-BAKAA (acting)
Vice-President (Administration): TAKI A. AL-MOUSAWI (acting)
Vice-President (Scientific): Dr MOHAMMED Y. AL-ANI (acting)
Librarian: FAISAL ALWAN AL-TAEE

Library: see Libraries
Number of teachers: 1,555
Number of students: 23,748

Publications: *Al-Mustansiriya Journal of Science, Al-Mustansiriya Literary Review, Journal of Administration and Economics, Journal of the College of Education, Journal of the College of Teachers, Journal of Dialah Education, Journal of Engineering and Pollution, Journal of the Founding Leader for National and Socialist Studies, Journal of Medical Research, Journal of Middle Eastern Studies*

DEANS

College of Administration and Economics: Prof. Dr JAMAL D. SALMAN
College of Arts: Dr SAMI M. AL-ANI
College of Engineering: Dr ADIL IBRAHIM AL-HADITHI
College of Medicine: Dr SABAH AL-OBEIDI
College of Science: Asst Prof. RA'AD K. AL-MUSLIH
First College of Education: Dr SABAH MAHMOOD-MUHAMMAD
Second College of Education: Asst Prof. Dr SAAD MOHAMMAD AL-MASHHADANI
First College of Teachers: Asst Prof. Dr ABDUL MUNAF SHUKIR AL-NADAWI
Second College of Teachers: Asst Prof. Dr JASSIM MOHAMMAD AL-NADAWI

ATTACHED INSTITUTES

Centre for Middle East Studies: Dir Asst Prof. Dr KHALIL AL-AZZAWA.

Environment Research Centre: Dir Asst Prof. Dr MUTHANNA KHALIS AL-DOORI.

Institute for National and Socialist Studies: Dir Dr AZMI S. AL-SALIHI.

National Diabetes Centre: Dir Asst Prof. Dr MAJEED ABDUL AMIR SAEED.

Polymer Units Centre: Dir Prof. Dr SALAH MOHSIN ALEIWI.

AL-NAHRAIN UNIVERSITY

POB 64074, Jadiriyah, Baghdad
Fax: (1) 7787810
E-mail: saduni@uruklink.net

Founded 1993 as Saddam University; present name 2003

President: MAHMOOD H. HAMMASH (acting)
Vice-President (Administration): FAYEK J. AL-AZZAWI
Librarian: ZAINAB H. RASHID

Library of 65,963 vols
Number of teachers: 285
Number of students: 1,180

DEANS

College of Engineering: Dr MAZIN A. KADHIM
College of Law: Dr BASIM M. SALEH
College of Medicine: Dr MAHMOOD H. HAMASH
College of Political Sciences: Dr MAZIN I. AL-RAMADANI
College of Science: Dr FALAH A. ATTAWI

HEADS OF DEPARTMENTS

Bacteriology: Dr TARIQ I. AL-JUBOORI
Chemical Engineering: Dr TALIB B. KASHMOOLA
Chemistry: Dr AMIR A. TOBIA
Chemistry and Biochemistry: Dr KANAN M. JAMEEL
Civil Engineering: Dr HANI M. FAHMI
Community Medicine: Dr AMJAD D. NIAZI
Computer Sciences: Dr MOHAMED A. SHALLAL
Electronics: Dr FAWZI M. MUNIR AL-NAAMA
Human Anatomy: Dr MAHMOOD H. HAMASH
Mathematics and Computer Applications: (vacant)
Mechanics: Dr MUAYID D. HANNA
Medicine: KHALID A. MOHAMMED
Obstetrics and Gynaecology: Dr QAIS A. KOBAA
Paediatrics: Dr NAJIM ALDIN AL-ROZNAMAJI
Pathology: Dr RAJI H. MOHAMMED
Pharmacology: Dr FAROUQ HASSAN AL-JAWAD
Physics: Dr SHAKIR J. SHAKIR
Physiology: Dr NABEEL A. ANTEWAN
Surgery: Dr USAMA N. RAFAAT

UNIVERSITY OF AL-QADISIYA

POB 88, Diwaniya, Al-Qadisiya governorate
Telephone: (36) 628066
Fax: 8164160
E-mail: unv.qadisia@uruklink.net

Founded 1988
State control

President: Dr MOHAMMAD H. AL-JABIRI (acting)
Vice-President (Administration): D. HIKMAT (acting)

Library of 2,000 vols
Number of teachers: 407.

UNIVERSITY OF AL-TA'AMEEM

Baghdad Rd, Kirkuk, Al-Ta'ameem governorate
Telephone: 418531
E-mail: fqislam@uruklink.net

Founded 2003
State control

President: KAMAK OTHMAN OMEAR (acting)
Vice-President (Administration): ABRAHIM ATEA SALIH (acting)
Vice-President (Scientific): NAJAT QADIR OMEAR (acting)

Number of teachers: 60.

UNIVERSITY OF BABYLON

POB 4, Hilla, Babylon governorate
Telephone: (30) 249551

Founded 1991
State control

President: JAFER ABD AMEER AL-GASSEN (acting)
Vice-President (Administration): HAMDIA ABBAS (acting)
Vice-President (Scientific): ABD-AMEER AL-GANEMI (acting)

Number of teachers: 450.

UNIVERSITY OF BAGHDAD

POB 17635, Jadiriya, Baghdad
Telephone: 7787819
Fax: 7763592

Founded 1957
State control
Languages of instruction: Arabic, English
Academic year: September to June

President: MOSA JAWAD AZIZ AL-MOSAWE
Vice-Presidents: Dr NIHAD M. ABDUL RAHMAN AL-RAWI (acting) (Administration), Dr HATAN JABAR ATTIYA (Scientific)
Registrar: TUMADHR ABDULLAH
Librarians: AMIR ABID MAJBOUR, YUSRA R. ZAHAWI

Library: see Libraries. Each institute and college has its own library of Arabic and foreign books
Number of teachers: 3,675
Number of students: 85,000

Publications: *Bulletin of the College of Arts* (quarterly), *Current Awareness* (quarterly), *Ibn Al-Haitham Journal for Pure and Applied Sciences* (every 6 months), *Iraqi Journal of Pharmaceutical Sciences* (quarterly), *Iraqi Journal of Science* (quarterly), *Iraqi Journal of Veterinary Medicine* (every 6 months), *Iraqi Natural History Museum Bulletin* (annually), *Journal of Agricultural Sciences* (every 6 months), *Journal of the College of Administration and Economics* (quarterly), *Journal of the College of Dentistry* (irregular), *Journal of the College of Education for Women* (every 6 months), *Journal of the College of Languages* (annually), *Journal of the College of Sharia* (every 6 months), *Journal of Engineering* (irregular), *Journal of the Faculty of Medicine* (quarterly), *Journal of Legal Sciences* (quarterly), *Journal of Political Science* (quarterly), *Journal of Sports Education* (irregular), *Statistical Bulletin* (annually), *The Academic* (quarterly), *The Professor* (quarterly)

COLLEGE DEANS

Administration and Economics: Dr ADIL H. SALIH
Agriculture: Dr BAQIR ABID KHALAF
Arts: Dr NOURI HAMMOUDI AL-QAYSI
Dentistry: Dr ISAM ABDUL AZIZ ALI
Education (Ibn Al-Haitham): Dr FAROUK ABDUL SALAM AWNI
Education (Ibn Rushd): Dr MALIK IBRAHIM SALIH
Education for Women: Dr FADHIL AL-SAQI
Engineering: Dr LAITH ISMAIL
Fine Arts: Dr ABDUL MURSIL AL-ZAYDI

Islamic Sciences: Dr ABDUL MUNIM AHMED SALIH
Languages: Dr ADNAN AL-JUBOURI
Law: Dr MUHAMMED AL-DOURI
Medicine: Dr FAKHRI M. AL-HADITHI
Nursing: BADIA AL-DAGHSTANI
Pharmacy: Dr WALEED R. A. SULAIMAN
Political Science: Dr SHAFIK AL-SAMARRAIE
Science: Dr FAROUK AL-ANI
Sports Education: Dr ALI TURKI
Veterinary Medicine: Dr KHALIL IBRAHIM ALTAYIF

AFFILIATED CENTRES

Astronomical Research Unit (attached to the College of Science): Dir Dr HAMEED MIJWIL AL-NIAIMI.

Centre for International Studies (attached to the College of Political Science): Dir Dr ABDUL GHAFOUR KARIM ALI.

Centre for Palestinian Studies (attached to the College of Political Science): Dir Dr KHLDOUN NAJI MAROUF.

Centre for the Revival of Arab Scientific Heritage: Dir NABILA ABDUL MUNIM.

Centre for Urban and Regional Planning (Post-graduate studies): Dir Dr WADHAH SAID YAHYA.

Educational and Psychological Research Centre (attached to the College of Education, Ibn Rushd): Dir MAHDI AL-SAMARRAE.

UNIVERSITY OF BASRAH

POB 49, Basrah
Telephone: (1) 8868520
Fax: (1) 8862998
E-mail: basrahyni@uruklink.net

Founded 1964
State control
Languages of instruction: Arabic, English
Academic year: September to June

President: DAWOOD SULEIMAN
Vice-President (vacant)
Librarian: Dr AMER ABID MUHSIN AL-SAAD

Number of teachers: 1,033
Number of students: 19,781

Publications: *Arab Gulf Journal*, *Basrah Journal of Agricultural Sciences*, *Basrah Journal of Sciences*, *Basrah Journal of Surgery*, *Economic Studies*, *Gulf Economics Journal*, *Iraqi Journal of Polymers*, *Journal of Arts*, *Journal of Basrah Research*, *Journal of Physical Education*, *Marina Mesopotamica*, *Medical Journal of Basrah University*

DEANS

Faculty of Administration and Economics: Dr JALIL S. THAMAD
Faculty of Agriculture: Dr NAZAR A. SHUKRI
Faculty of Arts: Dr RAAD ZAHRAW AL-MUSAWI
Faculty of Education: Dr GALIB BAKIR M. GALIB
Faculty of Education (at Theequar): Dr MAHDI ORYBY HUSSAIN AL-DAKHIL
Faculty of Engineering: Dr ABDULAMIR S. RESAN
Faculty of Fine Arts: MUAYAD ABDULSAMAD
Faculty of Law: Prof. Dr ABDULMAHDI SALEEM AL-MUDHAFFAR
Faculty of Medicine: Prof. Dr ALIM ABDULHAMID YACOUB
Faculty of Physical Education: Dr SALAH ATTYA KADHUM
Faculty of Science: Prof. Dr GOURGIS ABIDAL ADAM
Faculty of Teaching-Training: Dr HAMEED HASSAN TAHIR
Faculty of Veterinary Science: Dr ABDULMUTTALIB Y. YOUSIF

DIRECTORS

Centre for Arab Gulf Studies: Dr OWDA SULTAN
Centre for Marine Sciences: Dr ABDULRAZAK MAHMOOD
Computer Centre: Dr WALEED A. J. MOHAMMAD ALI
Medical Centre: Dr ABDULKHALIQ Z. BNAYAN

UNIVERSITY OF DIYALA

Baqubah, Diyala governorate
Telephone: (5) 8866108
Fax: (5) 8853610
E-mail: diyala_university@yahoo.com

Founded 1999
State control

President: HUSHAM ATA SHEHATHA (acting)
Vice-President: ALA'A SHAKIR MAHMOUD (acting)

Number of teachers: 271.

UNIVERSITY OF DOHUK

Dohuk
Telephone: 7222292
E-mail: unidohuk@aol.com

Founded 1992
State control

President: ASMAT M. KHALID (acting)
Vice-President (Administration): SALIM H. HADJI (acting)
Vice-President (Scientific): AMAD M. SALEM (acting)

Library of 11,770 vols
Number of teachers: 277

Colleges: Administration and Economics; Agriculture; Arts; Engineering; Islamic Legislation and Islamic Studies; Law and Politics; Medicine; Science; Veterinary Medicine.

ISLAMIC UNIVERSITY

Adhmai, Habiet Khatoun, Baghdad
Telephone: (1) 4253574
E-mail: fqislam@uruklink.net

Founded 1989
State control

President: ABD AL-STIAR HAMED AL-DABAG (acting)
Vice-President (Scientific): ABRAHEEM AB SAEEL (acting)

Library of 11,000 vols
Number of teachers: 66.

UNIVERSITY OF KARBALA

Al-Dhbbat district, Karbala, Karbala governorate
Telephone: (32) 321364

Founded 2003
State control

President: A. H. ALWAN (acting)

Number of teachers: 222.

UNIVERSITY OF KUFA

Kufa, Al-Najaf governorate
Telephone: (33) 346034
E-mail: kufa@uruklink.net

Founded 1987
State control

President: HASSAN ISAA AL-HAKEEM (acting)
Vice-President (Administration): NOORIE AL-HAKKNIE (acting)
Vice-President (Scientific): MAJID KADHUM HUSSAIN (acting)

Number of teachers: 410.

UNIVERSITY OF MOSUL

Al-Majmoa al-Thaqafia, Mosul
Telephone: (60) 810733
Fax: (60) 815066
E-mail: unmocha@yahoo.com

Founded 1967 as a separate university; formerly part of the University of Baghdad
State control
Languages of instruction: Arabic, English
Academic year: September to June (two terms)

President: OBAY S. AL-DEWACHI (acting)
Vice-President (Administration): Dr BURHAN MAHMOOD AHMAD AL-ALI (acting)
Vice-President (Scientific Affairs): Dr NAZAR MAJEED QIBI (acting)
Librarian: Dr NASSER ABDUL RAAZAQ MULLA JASSIM

Number of teachers: 2,548
Number of students: 22,526

Publications: *Adab Al-Rafidian* (quarterly), *Al-Rafidian Engineering Sciences* (quarterly), *Al-Rafidain Dental Journal* (quarterly), *Al-Rafidain Journal of Computer Science* (quarterly), *Al-Rafidain Journal of Earth Science* (quarterly), *Al-Rafidain Journal of Law* (quarterly), *Al-Rafidain Journal of Science* (quarterly), *Al-Rafidain Journal of Statistical Science* (quarterly), *Al-Rafidain Sports Science Journal* (quarterly), *Annals of The Medical College* (quarterly), *College of Basic Education Research Journal* (quarterly), *Iraq Journal of Agricultural Science* (quarterly), *Iraqi Journal of Pharmacy* (quarterly), *Iraqi Journal of Veterinary Medicine* (quarterly), *Journal of Education and Science* (quarterly), *Regional Studies* (quarterly), *Studies Mosulia* (quarterly), *Tanmiat al-Rafidain* (quarterly)

DEANS

College of Administration: Dr FAWAZ GARALLA AL-DOLUMY
College of Agriculture: Dr MOWAFAK TAYEB AL-LAYLA
College of Arts: MUHAMMAD-BASIL AL-AZZAWI
College of Basic Education: Dr FADHIL KHALHL IBRAHIM
College of Dentistry: Dr ABDUL HAQ ADUL MAGEED SULIMAN
College of Education: Dr ABDL WAHID DH. TAHA
College of Electronics Engineering: Dr BAYEZ K. AL-SULAIFANIE
College of Engineering: Dr MOHAMMAD TAYEB AL-LAYLA
College of Fine Arts: Dr ADEL SAEED AL-SAFAR
College of Islamic Sciences: Dr DURIAD ABDUL QAADER NURI
College of Law: Dr GAFAR MOHAMMAD GAWAD AL-FADHLI
College of Medicine: Dr MUZHIM AL-KHYATT
College of Medicine (Nineveh): Dr NAZAR MAJEED QIBI
College of Mathematics and Computer Science: Dr THAFER RAMATHAN MUTTAR
College of Nursing: Dr SUBHE HUSEIN AL-GUBORE
College of Pharmacy: Dr SABAH G. AL-DABBAGH
College of Physical Education: Dr YASSIN TAHA MOHAMMAD ALI
College of Political Science: Dr TALAL YOUNIS AL-GALILI
College of Science: Dr IHSAN A. MUSTAFA AL-ABDULLAH
College of Veterinary Medicine: Dr FOUAD KASIM MOHAMMAD

ATTACHED INSTITUTES

Centre for Dams and Water Resources: Dir SALIM QASIM AL-NAQUIB.

Centre for the Development of Teaching Methods: Dir QUSAY TAWFEQ GHAZAL.
Computer Centre: Dir Dr HYTAM ABD AL-WAHAB.
Environmental Research Centre: Dir Dr TARIQ AHMAD MAHMOUD.
Mosul Studies Centre: Dir THANOON Y. AL-TAEE.
Regional Studies Centre: Dir GHANIM MOHAMMED AL-HAFOU.
Remote Sensing Centre: Dir Dr MOHAMMED Y. AL-ALAAF.

UNIVERSITY OF SALAHADDIN

Arbil
Telephone: (566) 21422
E-mail: salahhaw@web-sat.com
Internet: www.salun.org
Founded 1968 in Sulaimaniya as University of Sulaimaniya; relocated in Arbil and acquired present name 1981
State control
Languages of instruction: Kurdish, Arabic, English
Academic year: September to June (two terms)
President: Dr MOHAMMAD S. MOHAMMAD
Vice-President for Scientific Affairs: Dr AHMAD ANWAR AMIN DEZAYE
Library: see Libraries
Number of teachers: 800
Number of students: 10,965 (10,597 undergraduate, 368 postgraduate)
Publications: *University News* (monthly, Arabic), *Statistical Abstract* (annually), *Zanco* (scientific journal, Arabic and English)

DEANS
College of Administration and Economics: Asst Prof. Dr DLER ISMAIL HAQI
College of Agriculture: Asst Prof. Dr FARHAD HASSAN AZEEZ
College of Arts: Prof. Dr AZAD MUHAMMAD AMEEN NAQISHBANDI
College of Dentistry: Dr DASHTI BAIZ DZAYI
College of Education: Prof. Dr KAREEM SALIH ABDUL
College of Engineering: Dr FARAYDOON HADI MAROUF
College of Law: NAJDAT SABRI AQRAWI
College of Medicine: Asst Prof. Dr HAMA NAJIM JAFF
College of Nursing: Dr FARHAD JALEEL KHAYAT
College of Pharmacy: Dr TAFUR JALAL KHLEL
College of Physical Education: IIDREES MUHAMMAD TAHIR
College of Political Science: Dr AHMED MUSTAFA SULAIMAN
College of Science: Asst Prof. ROSTEM KAREEM SAED
College of Teacher Training: Asst Prof. Dr AZAD JALAL SHAREEF

UNIVERSITY OF SULAIMANIYA

2/3/205 Kani-Askan, Sulaimaniya
Telephone: 2127453
E-mail: info@univsul.com
Founded 1968
State control
Languages of instruction: Arabic, English, Kurdish
President: KAMAL KHOSHNAW (acting)
Vice-President (Administration): SHAWNM ABDUL QADIR (acting)
Vice-President (Scientific Affairs and Postgraduate Research): NAZAR M. MUHAMMAD AMIN (acting)
Library of 24,689 vols
Number of teachers: 489
Number of students: 8,000
Colleges of Agriculture, Science, Law, Physical Education, Languages, Engineering, Fine Arts, Education, Medicine, Veterinary Medicine, Administration and Economics, Nursing, Humanities, Dentistry and Commerce.

UNIVERSITY OF TECHNOLOGY

Al-Sinah St, Baghdad
Telephone: (1) 7746532
Fax: (1) 7199446
E-mail: shekhly@uruklink.net
Founded 1975; formerly the College of Engineering Technology of the University of Baghdad
State control
Languages of instruction: Arabic, English
Academic year: October to July
President: Dr WAIL NOORALDEN AL-RIFAIE (acting)
Vice-President (Administration and Scientific): KRIKOR SIROB (acting)
Registrar: Dr ABDU AL-HUSAIN SAKHI
Librarian: AYAD J. SHAMIS ELDEN
Library of 25,000 vols
Number of teachers: 961 (668 full-time, 293 part-time)
Number of students: 7,752

PROFESSORS
AL-HADEETHI, A., Structural Engineering
AL-HAIDARY, J. T., Production Engineering and Metallurgy
AL-MUTALIB IBRAHIM, A., Applied Sciences
AL-SAMAAUI, A., Structural Engineering
AL-SAMRAAI, J. M. A., Electrical Engineering
AL-TOORNAJI, M., Production Engineering and Metallurgy
HAMMUDI, W. KH., Applied Sciences
KHAIRI, W., Computer and Control Engineering
KHORSEED, N., Structural Engineering
MAJEED, J., Mechanical Engineering
TAWFICK, H., Mechanical Engineering

UNIVERSITY OF THI-QAR

Nasiriya, Thi-Qar governorate
Founded 2002
State control
President: RIYAD SHANTAH JABER (acting)
Vice-President (Administration): ADHEEM DRAFISH (acting)
Vice-President (Scientific): M. K. KASSIM (acting)
Number of teachers: 155.

UNIVERSITY OF TIKRIT

POB 42, Salah al-Din, Tikrit
Fax: (21) 825386
E-mail: tikrituniversity@hotmail.com
Founded 1987
State control
Languages of instruction: Arabic, English
Academic year: September to June
President: Prof. Dr MAHER S. AL-JUBORI (acting)
Librarian: SABAH S. KHALEFE
Number of teachers: 701
Number of students: 6,824
Publications: *Iraqi Journal of Educational and Psychological Sciences and Sociology, Surra Min Raa Journal, Tikrit Journal of Agricultural Sciences, Tikrit Journal of Economic Sciences* (all quarterly), *Tikrit Journal of Engineering Sciences, Tikrit Journal of Humanities, Tikrit Journal of Pharmaceutical Sciences, Tikrit Journal of Pure Sciences, Tikrit Medical Journal*

DEANS
College of Administration and Economics: Asst Prof. Dr SABAH F. MAHMOOD
College of Agriculture: Prof. Dr ABDULLAH AHMED AL-SAMARRAIE
College of Dentistry: Prof. Dr ADNAN H. MOHAMMED
College of Education: Asst Prof. Dr ALI SALIH HUSSEIN
College of Education (Samarra): Asst Prof. Dr MUHAMMAD IBRAHIM HUSSEIN
College of Education for Women: Asst Prof. Dr JAID Z. MUKHLIF
College of Engineering: Asst Prof. Dr HAYDAR SAAD YASEEN AL-JUBAIR
College of Law: Asst Prof. Dr DHAMIN HUSSEIN
College of Medicine: Asst Prof. Dr ABID AHMAD SALMAN
College of Pharmacy: Prof. Dr ALI ISMAIL UBEID
College of Science: Asst Prof. Dr SUBHI ATIA MAHMOOD

PROFESSORS
ABDOON, H. F., Islamic Jurisprudence
ABDULLAH, A. A.-M., Veterinary Science
ALAAH, M. M., Microbiology
AL-AZIZ, M. A., Veterinary Science
AL-BAYDHANI, I. S., Modern History
AL-HUSSEIN, S. A., Biology
ALI, A. A.-G. M., Medicine
ALI, K. I., Politics
ALI, N. H., Physical Education
AL-OMER, A. K., Arabic Language
AL-JUBURI, A. H. M., Arabic Language
AL-JUBURI, M. S. A., Arabic Language
AL-JUMAILI, S. H. A., Arabic Language
AL-KUTUBI, S. H., Mathematics
AL-NAJAFEE, H. M., Civil Engineering
ALRAHMAN, Y. A. A., Medicine
AL-SAMARRAIE, A. A.-K. M., Physical Education
AL-SAMARRAIE, A. A.-M. H., Chemistry
AL-SHIQARCHI, S. T., Chemistry
AL-TAAI, A. A. H., Arabic Language
AUBED, A. I., Pharmacology and Toxicology
AZIZ, A. A., Chemistry
DAWOOD, A. S., Plant Protection
DAWOOD, I. S., Biology
DEKRAAN, S. B., Chemistry
GHANIM, Y. M.-A., Medicine
HAMAD, G. Q., Arabic Language
HANTOSH, F. G., Chemistry
HUSEIN, M. H., Civil Engineering
KAMEL, A. A.-M., Modern History
KAMEL, F. M., Food Technologies
LATEEF, R. A., Crops
MAHMOUD, S. A., Chemistry
MOHAMMED, A. H., Dentistry
MOHAMMED, A. H., Economics
MOHAMMED, M. M., Medicine
MUKHIF, J. Z., Arabic Language
MUSA, M. M., Veterinary Science
RASEED, A. A-M., Economics
SAIED, J. M., Animal Production
SHIHAB, A. F., Biology
WADY, A. A.-R. A., History

UNIVERSITY OF WASSIT

Kut, Wassit governorate
Telephone: 313861
Founded 2003
State control
President: Dr MAHMOUD HAYAWEI HAMMASH
Number of teachers: 109.

Colleges

Al-Imam Al-A'dham College: Karkh, Baghdad; f. 1967, affiliated to Baghdad

University 1978; degree course in Islamic studies; 34 teachers; 516 students; Dean Dr SUBHI MOHAMMAD JAMIL AL-KHAYYAT; publ. *Journal* (annually).

Foundation for Technical Institutes: Baghdad; f. 1972; attached to the Ministry of Higher Education; groups all the institutes of technology; Pres. H. M. S. ABDUL WAHAB.

Incorporated institutes:

Institute of Administration: Rissafa, Baghdad; f. 1964; Dean A. S. AL-MASHAT.

Institute of Administration, Karkh (Baghdad): f. 1976; Dean T. SHAKER.

Institute of Applied Arts: Baghdad; f. 1969; Dean A. NOOR-EDDIN.

Institute of Technology: Baghdad; f. 1969; Dean N. S. MUSTAFA.

Technical Institute, Basrah: f. 1973; UNDP/Unesco project; technology and administration; 1,660 students; Dean H. I. MOHAMMED.

Technical Institute, Hilla: f. 1976; technology and administration; Dean S. B. DERWISH.

Technical Institute, Kirkuk: f. 1976; technology and administration; Dean M. ABDUL RAHMAN.

Technical Institute, Mosul: f. 1976; technology and administration; Dean M. S. SAFFO.

Technical Institute, Missan: f. 1979; technology and administration.

Technical Institute, Najaf: f. 1978; technology and administration; Dean M. A. JASSIM.

Technical Institute, Ramadi: f. 1977; technology and administration; Dean J. M. AMIN.

Technical Institute, Sulaimaniya: f. 1973; medical technology and administration; Dean R. M. ABDULLAH.

Technical Institute of Agriculture: Abu-Ghraib, Baghdad; f. 1964; Dean S. A. HASSAN.

Technical Institute of Agriculture, Arbil: Aski-Kalak, Arbil; f. 1976; Dean M. S. ABBASS.

Technical Institute of Agriculture, Kumait: Kumait, Missan; f. 1976; Dean H. L. SADIK.

Technical Institute of Agriculture, Mussaib-Babylon: Mussaib-Babylon; f. 1979.

Technical Institute of Agriculture, Shatra-Thi Qar: Shatra-Thi Qar; f. 1979.

Technical Institute of Medicine: Baghdad; f. 1964; Dean A. S. AL-MASHAT.

IRELAND

The Higher Education System

Higher education in Ireland dates from the foundation of the University of Dublin Trinity College in 1592; the next oldest institutions are the Royal College of Physicians of Ireland (founded 1654) and the National University of Ireland, Maynooth (formerly St Patrick's College, founded 1795). Until 1920 the 32 counties of Ireland were part of the United Kingdom; however, in that year Ireland was partitioned: the six north-eastern counties remained part of the United Kingdom, and the 26 southern counties sought independence. In 1922 the southern counties achieved dominion status, under the British Crown, as the Irish Free State. Ireland achieved full sovereignty within the Commonwealth in 1937 and the Republic of Ireland was declared in 1949. There are four universities, as well as other institutions of higher education including colleges, institutes of technology, schools of art and music and professional establishments. Under the Universities Act (1997) and the Qualifications Act (1999), Ireland participates in the Bologna Process. In 2003/04 77,491 full-time students were enrolled at universities and Higher Education Authority Institutions and 53,586 students were enrolled at technology colleges.

Admission to higher education is administered by the Central Applications Office. In accordance with the Bologna Process the university awards system consists of Bachelors, Masters and Doctorate degrees. The Bachelors is the main undergraduate degree and lasts for three to four years. However, degrees in some disciplines, such as dentistry, veterinary medicine, architecture (all five years) and medicine (six years), may last longer. Following the Bachelors a student may take the Masters, the first postgraduate degree. The Masters is a one- to two-year programme of study, and may be either a taught or a research degree. The second postgraduate degree (and final university-level award) is the Doctor of Philosophy, which is a research-based course lasting two to five years. In addition to the universities, higher education is offered by other types of institution, including Institutes of Technology and so-called 'Designated' Institutions. Awards from these establishments are assured by the Higher Education and Training Awards Council (founded 2001).

Technical and vocational education is offered by colleges, the Dublin Institute of Technology and Industrial Training Authority centres. The Higher Education and Training Awards Council oversees all continuing and adult education and administers a wide range of certificated courses. The most prominent vocational award is the National Vocational Certificate (Levels 1–3).

Regulatory and Representative Bodies

GOVERNMENT

Department of Arts, Sport and Tourism: 23 Kildare St, Dublin 2; tel. (1) 6313800; fax (1) 6611201; e-mail webmaster@dast.gov.ie; internet www.dast.gov.ie; Minister SÉAMUS BRENNAN.

Department of Education and Science: Marlborough St, Dublin 1; tel. (1) 8896400; fax (1) 8892367; e-mail info@education.gov.ie; internet www.education.ie; Minister MARY HANAFIN.

ACCREDITATION

ENIC/NARIC Ireland: Nat. Qualifications Authority of Ireland, 5th Floor, Jarvis House, Jarvis St, Dublin 1; tel. (1) 8871500; fax (1) 8871595; e-mail info@qualificationsrecognition.ie; internet www.qualificationsrecognition.ie; Co-ordinator, Qualifications Recognition CARMEL KELLY.

Higher Education and Training Awards Council: 26–27 Denzille La., Dublin 2; tel. (1) 6314567; fax (1) 6314577; e-mail info@hetac.ie; internet www.hetac.ie; f. 2001 under the Qualifications (Education and Training) Act 1999; develops higher education outside the univ. system in the Republic of Ireland; approves and recognizes courses; grants and confers nat. awards (degrees, diplomas, certificates); co-ordinates courses within and between institutions; successor to the Nat. Council for Educational Awards (NCEA—f. 1972); may delegate authority to make awards to recognized institutions under the Qualifications (Education and Training) Act 1999; 15 ; Chief Exec. S. PÚIRSÉIL; publ. *Policy Documents* (also available online).

National Qualifications Authority of Ireland: 5th Floor, Jervis House, Jervis St, Dublin 1; tel. (1) 8871500; fax (1) 8871595; e-mail info@nqai.ie; internet www.nqai.ie; f. 2001; objects: the establishment and maintenance of a framework of qualifications for the devt, recognition and award of qualifications based on standards of knowledge, skill or competence to be acquired by learners; the establishment and promotion of the maintenance and improvement of the standards of awards of the further and higher education and training sector, other than in the existing univs; the promotion and facilitation of access, transfer and progression throughout the span of education and training provision; the Authority is not an awarding body; Chair. PAUL HARAN; Chief Exec. SEÁN O FOGHLÚ.

FUNDING

Higher Education Authority: Brooklawn House, Crampton Ave, Shelbourne Rd, Dublin 4; tel. (1) 2317100; fax (1) 2317172; e-mail info@hea.ie; internet www.hea.ie; the statutory planning and devt body for higher education and research in Ireland; has wide advisory powers throughout the whole of the third-level education sector; is also the funding authority for the univs and a number of designated higher education instns; Chair. MICHAEL KELLY; Deputy Chief Exec. MARY KERR.

NATIONAL BODIES

Central Applications Office: Tower House, Eglinton St, Galway; tel. (91) 509800; fax (91) 562344; internet www.cao.ie; f. 1976; processes applications for first year undergraduate courses offered by the higher-education instns in the Republic of Ireland; CEO IVOR GLEESON.

Irish Universities Association (IUA): 48 Merrion Sq., Dublin 2; tel. (1) 6764948; fax (1) 6622815; e-mail info@iua.ie; internet www.iua.ie; the rep. body of the heads of the 7 Irish univs; seeks to advance univ. education and research through the formulation and pursuit of collective policies and actions on behalf of the Irish univs thereby contributing to Ireland's social, cultural and economic well-being; Pres. Dr JOHN HEGARTY; Chief Exec. NED COSTELLO; publ. *IUA Review* (irreg.).

Further Education and Training Awards Council: East Point Plaza, East Point Business Park, Dublin 3; tel. (1) 8659500; fax (1) 8650067; e-mail information@fetac.ie; internet www.fetac.ie; f. 1999; makes quality-assured awards in accordance with nat. standards within the nat. framework, creating opportunities for all learners in further education and training to have their achievements recognized and providing access to systematic progression pathways; Chief Exec. STAN MCHUGH.

Learned Societies

GENERAL

Royal Dublin Society: Ballsbridge, Dublin 4; tel. (1) 6680866; fax (1) 6604014; e-mail info@rds.ie; internet www.rds.ie; f. 1731 for the advancement of agriculture, industry, science and the arts; 6,000 mems; library: library: see Libraries and Archives; Pres. Dr AUSTIN MESCAIL; Chief Exec. MICHAEL DUFFY; Registrar EILEEN BYRNE; publ. *Minerva* (3 a year).

Royal Irish Academy: Academy House, 19 Dawson St, Dublin 2; tel. (1) 6762570; fax (1) 6762346; e-mail info@ria.ie; internet www.ria.ie; f. 1785; academy for the sciences and humanities in the Republic of Ireland; promotes excellence in scholarship, recognizes achievements in learning and undertakes research projects; advises on and contributes to public debate and public policy formation in science, technology and culture; maintains a library and is the largest Irish publisher of scholarly and scientific journals, books and monographs; 447 mems (387 ordinary, 60 hon.); library of 35,000 vols, 31,000 pamphlets, 1,800 sets of current periodicals, 2,500 MSS; Pres. JAMES A. SLEVIN; Sec. HOWARD B. CLARKE; Exec. Sec. PATRICK BUCKLEY; publs *Biology and Environment Proceedings* (3 a year), *Ériu* (annual), *Irish Journal of Earth Sciences* (annual), *Irish Studies in International Affairs* (annual), *Mathematical Proceedings* (2 a year), *Proceedings Section C* (Archaeology, Celtic Studies, History, Linguistics, Literature, 5 a year).

AGRICULTURE, FISHERIES AND VETERINARY SCIENCE

Royal Horticultural Society of Ireland: Cabinteely House, The Park, Cabinteely, , Dublin 18; tel. and fax (1) 2353912; e-mail info@rhsi.ie; internet www.rhsi.ie; f. 1816; 1,100 mems; Pres. MARIA PRENDIVILLE; Sec. ROISIN MARKHAM; publ. *Newsletter* (monthly).

Society of Irish Foresters: Enterprise Centre, Ballintogher, Co. Sligo; tel. (71) 9164434; fax (71) 9134904; e-mail sif@eircom.net; internet www.societyofirishforesters.ie; f. 1942 to advance and spread the knowledge of forestry in all its aspects, to promote professional standards in forestry and the regulation of the forestry profession in Ireland; annual study tour, field days, annual symposium, lectures; continuous professional development programme; 650 mems; Pres. MICHAEL BULFIN; Sec. CLODAGH DUFFY; publs *Irish Forester* (4 a year), *Irish Forestry* (2 a year).

Veterinary Council: 53 Lansdowne Rd, Ballsbridge, Dublin 4; tel. (1) 6684402; fax (1) 6604373; e-mail info@vci.ie; internet www.vci.ie; f. 1931; 2,370 registered mems; Registrar V. BEATTY.

ARCHITECTURE AND TOWN PLANNING

Architectural Association of Ireland: 8 Merrion Sq., Dublin 2; tel. (1) 6761703; internet www.irish-architecture.com/aai; f. 1896 to promote the practice and study of architecture, and to foster co-operation among architects; 450 mems; Pres. MAXIM LAROUSSI; Hon. Sec. KEVIN DONOVAN; publ. *Building Material* (monthly).

Royal Institute of the Architects of Ireland: 8 Merrion Sq., Dublin 2; tel. (1) 6761703; fax (1) 6610948; e-mail info@riai.ie; internet www.riai.ie; f. 1839; 2,600 mems; Pres. JAMES PIKE; publs *Architecture Ireland* (monthly), *Irish Architectural Review* (annually), *RIAI Year Book* (annually).

Society of Chartered Surveyors: 5 Wilton Place, Dublin 2; tel. (1) 6765500; fax (1) 6761412; e-mail info@scs.ie; internet www.scs.ie; constituent body of the Royal Institution of Chartered Surveyors; Chief Exec. A. P. SMITH; Exec. Officer LOUISE RYAN.

BIBLIOGRAPHY, LIBRARY SCIENCE AND MUSEOLOGY

Library Association of Ireland (Cumann Leabharlann na hÉireann): 53 Upper Mount St, Dublin 2; tel. (21) 4546499; e-mail president@libraryassociation.ie; internet www.libraryassociation.ie; f. 1928, incorporated 1952; 650 mems; Pres. RUTH FLANAGAN; Hon. Sec. MICHAEL PLAICE; publs *An Leabharlann/The Irish Library* (quarterly), *Directory of Libraries and Information Services in Ireland* (jointly with Northern Ireland Branch of the Library Association, online only).

ECONOMICS, LAW AND POLITICS

Institute of Chartered Accountants in Ireland: Offices and Library: 83 Pembroke Rd, Ballsbridge, Dublin 4; Belfast Office: 11 Donegall Sq. South, Belfast, BT1 5JE, UK; tel. (1) 6680400; fax (1) 6680842; e-mail ca@icai.ie; internet www.icai.ie; inc. by Royal Charter 1888; 10,000 mems; library of 20,000 vols; Pres. JOHN P. GREELY; Chief. Exec. PAT COSTELLO; publ. *Accountancy Ireland* (6 a year).

King's Inns, Honorable Society of: Henrietta St, Dublin 1; tel. (1) 8744840; fax (1) 8726048; e-mail info@kingsinns.ie; internet www.kingsinns.ie; f. 1542; provides training course to enable students to be admitted to the degree of barrister-at-law; 4,000 mems; library of 98,900 vols; Under-Treas. CAMILLA MCALEESE; Dir of Education MARCELLA HIGGINS; Dean of School of Law SARAH MACDONALD; Librarian JONATHAN ARMSTRONG; publ. *Irish Student Law Review* (annually).

Law Society of Ireland: Blackhall Place, Dublin 7; tel. (1) 6724800; fax (1) 6724801; e-mail general@lawsociety.ie; internet www.lawsociety.ie; f. 1852; 7,000 mems; library of 14,000 vols; Dir-Gen. KEN MURPHY; Librarian MARGARET BYRNE; publs *Law Directory* (annually), *Gazette* (monthly).

Statistical and Social Inquiry Society of Ireland: c/o Robert Watt, Indecon House, 25 Wellington Quay, Dublin 2; tel. (1) 6600311; e-mail info@ssisi.ie; internet www.ssisi.ie; f. 1847 to promote the study of social and economic developments; *c.* 500 mems; Pres. Prof. A. PUNCH; Hon. Secs T. N. CAVEN, P. WALSH, S. F. WHELAN; publ. *Journal* (annually).

EDUCATION

Church Education Society: c/o Church of Ireland House, Church Ave, Rathmines, Dublin 6; tel. (1) 4978422; fax (1) 4978821; e-mail ces@ireland.anglican.org; f. 1839; Asst Sec. and Treas. JENNIFER BYRNE; publ. *Annual Report*.

FINE AND PERFORMING ARTS

Aosdána: 70 Merrion Sq., Dublin 2; tel. (1) 6180200; fax (1) 6761302; e-mail aosdana@artscouncil.ie; internet www.artscouncil.ie/aosdana; f. 1981; attached to the Arts Council; an affiliation of artists engaged in literature, music and visual arts; membership limited to 250 mems; Registrar PAUL JOHNSON.

Arts Council: 70 Merrion Square, Dublin 2; tel. (1) 6180200; fax (1) 6761302; e-mail info@artscouncil.ie; internet www.artscouncil.ie; f. 1951; the statutory body appointed by the Minister for Arts, Culture and Gaeltacht to promote and assist the arts; in addition to organizing and promoting exhibitions and other activities itself, the Council gives grant-aid to many organizations including the theatre, opera, arts centres, arts festivals, exhibitions and publishers; also awards bursaries and scholarships to individual artists; Chair. OLIVE BRAIDEN.

Music Association of Ireland Ltd: Waltons School of Music, 69 South Great Georges St, Dublin 2; tel. (1) 4785368; fax (1) 4754426; e-mail music.association@eircom.net; f. 1948; organises schools recital and workshop scheme, composer workshops, and Irish auditions for the European Union Youth Orchestra; Chair. RODNEY SENIOR; publs *Annual Report*, *Music Events Diary*, *Policy Statement of Music Education*.

Royal Hibernian Academy: 15 Ely Place, Dublin 2; tel. (1) 6612558; fax (1) 6610762; e-mail rhagallery@eircom.net; internet www.royalhibernianacademy.com; f. 1823; painting, sculpture, installation and mixed media; 87 mems (47 hon., 30 acads, 10 assoc.); Pres. A. GIBNEY; Sec. JAMES HANLEY.

HISTORY, GEOGRAPHY AND ARCHAEOLOGY

Cork Historical and Archaeological Society: c/o Hon. Treasurer, Lackenroe, Glenmore Cross, Glanmire, Cork; tel. (21) 541076; internet www.ucc.ie/chas; f. 1891; 400 mems; Pres. Dr ELIZABETH TWOHIG; Hon. Sec. MARY LANTRY; publ. *Journal* (annually).

Folklore of Ireland Society: c/o UCD Delargy Centre for Irish Folklore and the Nat. Folklore Colln, School of Irish, Celtic Studies, Irish Folklore and Linguistics, Newman Bldg, Belfield, Dublin 4; tel. (1) 7168216; fax (1) 7161144; e-mail eolas@bealoideas.ie; internet www.bealoideas.ie; f. 1926; 650 mems; Pres. ANRAÍ Ó BRAONÁIN; Sec. EMER NÍ NÍ CHEALLAIGH; publ. *Béaloideas* (annual).

Geographical Society of Ireland: c/o GSI Treasurer, Dept of Geography, St Patrick's College, Drumcondra, Dublin 9; internet www.geographical-society-ireland.org; f. 1934; seeks to provide information and promote discussion about a wide range of topics of geographical interest, within Ireland and abroad; organizes lectures and seminars, field trips; 200 mems; Pres. Prof. JIM HOURIHANE; Treas. Dr RUTH MCMANUS; publs *Geonews* (2 a year), *Irish Geography* (2 a year).

Military History Society of Ireland: University College Dublin, Newman House, 86 St Stephen's Green, Dublin 2; tel. (1) 2985617; fax (1) 7067211; e-mail padraick1@eircom.net; internet www.mhsirl.com; f. 1949; 1,000 mems; Hon. Secs Dr PATRICK MCCARTHY (Correspondence), Col PATRICK G. KIRBY (Membership); publ. *The Irish Sword* (2 a year).

Old Dublin Society: 44 Warrenhouse Rd, Baldoyle, Dublin 13; f. 1934; promotes study of history and antiquities of Dublin; 325 mems; library of 1,300 vols; Pres. Rev. DUDLEY A. LEVISTONE-COONEY; Sec. DAMIEN ROBINSON; publ. *Dublin Historical Record* (2 a year).

Royal Society of Antiquaries of Ireland: 63 Merrion Sq., Dublin 2; tel. (1) 6761749; e-mail rsai@rsai.ie; internet www.rsai.ie; f. 1849; 1,100 mems; library of 13,000 vols; Pres. AIDEEN IRELAND; Hon. Gen. Secs. CHARLES DOHERTY, Dr LINDA DORAN; publ. *Journal* (annual).

LANGUAGE AND LITERATURE

Alliance Française: 1 Kildare St, Dublin 2; tel. (1) 6761732; fax (1) 6764077; e-mail info@alliance-francaise.ie; internet www.alliance-francaise.ie; offers courses in general French, French conversation, specialized French, French for primary schools; also offers diploma courses and corporate courses; promotes French culture; attached offices in Cork, Kilkenny, Limerick, Waterford and Wexford; Dir JEAN-MICHEL GARCIA.

British Council: Newmount House, 22/24 Lower Mount St, Dublin 2; tel. (1) 6764088; fax (1) 6766945; e-mail tom.farrell@ie.britishcouncil.org; internet www.britishcouncil.org/ireland; offers courses and exams in English language and British culture and promotes cultural exchange with the UK; Dir TONY REILLY.

Conradh na Gaeilge (Gaelic League): 6 Sráid Fhearchair, Dublin 2; tel. (1) 4757401; fax (1) 4757844; e-mail eolas@cnag.ie; internet www.cnag.ie; f. 1893; 250 brs; Pres. TOMÁS MAC RUAIRÍ; Gen. Sec. SEÁN MAC MATHÚNA; publs *An tUltach* (monthlies), *Feasta*.

Goethe-Institut: 37 Merrion Sq., Dublin 2; tel. (1) 6611155; fax (1) 6611358; e-mail info@dublin.goethe.org; internet www.goethe.de/dublin; offers courses and examinations in German language and culture and promotes cultural exchange with Germany; library of 12,000 vols; Dir ROLF STEHLE.

Instituto Cervantes: 58 Northumberland Rd, Ballsbridge, Dublin 4; tel. (1) 6682936; fax (1) 6688416; e-mail cendub@cervantes.es; internet dublin.cervantes.es; offers courses and exams in Spanish language and culture and promotes cultural exchange with Spain and Spanish-speaking Latin and Central America; library: library of 11,000 vols; Dir AURORA SOTELO MORILLO.

Irish PEN: 'Tully', Ballinteer Rd, Dublin 12; e-mail irishpen@ireland.com; internet www.irishpen.com; f. 1921; 62 mems; Chair. MARITA CONLON MCKENNA; Sec. and Treas. NESTA TUOMEY.

Irish Texts Society: c/o Royal Bank of Scotland, 49 Charing Cross Rd, London, SW1A 2DX, UK; e-mail hon.sec@irishtextssociety.org; internet www.irishtextssociety.org; f. 1898 to advance public education by promoting the study of Irish literature, and to publish texts in the Irish language, with translations, notes, etc.; 640 mems; Pres. Prof. PÁDRAIG Ó RIAIN; Hon. Sec. SEÁN HUTTON; publs *Main Series: 58 vols of Irish-language texts with English translation, Subsidiary Series: 15 vols.*

MEDICINE

Dental Council: 57 Merrion Sq., Dublin 2; tel. (1) 6762226; fax (1) 6762069; e-mail info@dentalcouncil.ie; internet www.dentalcouncil.ie; f. 1928 as the Dental Board, superseded by the Dental Council in 1985; registers dentists and controls standards of education and conduct among dentists in Ireland; Pres. DANIEL I. KEANE; Chief Officer and Registrar THOMAS FARREN.

Irish Medical Organisation: IMO House, 10 Fitzwilliam Place, Dublin 2; tel. (1) 6767273; fax (1) 6612758; e-mail imo@imo.ie; internet www.imo.ie; f. 1936; 6,000 mems; CEO GEORGE MCNEICE; publ. *Irish Medical Journal* (10 a year).

Medical Council: Lynn House, Portobello Court, Lower Rathmines Rd, Dublin 6; tel. (1) 4983100; fax (1) 4983102; e-mail nfo@mcirl.ie; internet www.medicalcouncil.ie; f. 1978; 17,000 mems; Pres. Dr JOHN HILLERY.

Pharmaceutical Society of Ireland: 18 Shrewsbury Rd, Dublin 4; tel. (1) 2184000; fax (1) 2837678; e-mail info@pharmaceuticalsociety.ie; internet www.pharmaceuticalsociety.ie; f. 1875; Pres. RONAN QUIRKE; Registrar and Sec. Dr AMBROSE MCLOUGHLIN; publ. *Calendar* (annually).

Royal Academy of Medicine in Ireland: International House, 2nd Fl., 20–22 Lower Hatch St, Dublin 2; tel. (1) 6616677; fax (1) 6762920; e-mail secretary@rami.ie; f. 1882; 1,500 fellows; Pres. Prof. DAVID J. BOUCHIER-HAYES; Gen. Sec. and Treas. ARNOLD D. K. HILL; publ. *Irish Journal of Medical Science* (quarterly).

NATURAL SCIENCES

Biological Sciences

Dublin University Biological Association: Trinity College, Dublin; f. 1874; 400 mems; Pres. Prof. IAN TEMPERLEY; Hon. Sec. EMER LOUGHREY.

Dublin Zoo: Phoenix Park, Dublin 8; tel. (1) 4748900; fax (1) 6771660; e-mail info@dublinzoo.ie; internet www.dublinzoo.ie; f. 1830; 9,000 mems; Pres. MICHAEL MACNULTY; Hon. Sec. DOROTHY KILROY; Dir LEO OOSTERWEGHEL.

Physical Sciences

Institute of Chemistry of Ireland: PO Box 9322, Cardiff Lane, Dublin 2; e-mail info@instituteofchemistry.org; internet www.chemistryireland.org; f. 1950; 850 mems; Pres. Dr P. E. CHILDS; Hon. Sec. J. P. RYAN; publ. *Irish Chemical News* (2 a year).

Irish Astronomical Society: POB 2547, Dublin 14; tel. (1) 2981268; e-mail ias1937@hotmail.com; internet www.irishastrosoc.org; f. 1937; 150 mems; library: video and book libraries; Pres. BRIAN KEANE; Sec. ANGELA O'CONNELL; publs *Orbit* (6 a year), *Sky High* (annually).

Irish Branch of the Institute of Physics: c/o Department of Experimental Physics, University College Dublin, Belfield, Dublin, 4; tel. (1) 7162216; fax (1) 2837275; e-mail alison.hackett@iop.org; internet ireland.iop.org; f. 1964; learned society and professional body for the advancement of physics and physics education on the island of Ireland; 1,700 mems; Chair. Dr MARTIN LAMB; Sec. Dr EMMA SOKELL.

PHILOSOPHY AND PSYCHOLOGY

Psychological Society of Ireland: CX House, 2A Corn Exchange Pl., Poolbeg St, Dublin 2; tel. (1) 4749160; fax (1) 4749161; e-mail pres@psihq.ie; internet www.psihq.ie; f. 1970 to advance psychological knowledge and research in Ireland, to ensure maintenance of high standards of professional training and practice, to seek the devt of psychological services; 2,000 mems; Pres. Dr MITCHEL FLEMING; Hon. Sec. IAN STEWART; publs *The Irish Journal of Psychology*, *The Irish Psychologist*.

Theosophical Society in Ireland: 31 Pembroke Rd, Dublin 4; tel. (1) 6602517; e-mail theosophy@eircom.net; f. 1919; Pres. Rep. N. CLANCY; Sec. F. O'KELLY DE GALLAGH; publ. *Bulletin* (monthly).

University Philosophical Society: Graduate Memorial Building, Trinity College, Dublin 2; tel. (85) 1419072; fax (1) 6778996; e-mail president@tcdphil.com; internet www.tcdphil.com; f. 1684, re-founded 1854; 'Major Society' for composition, reading and discussion of papers on literary, political, philosophical and scientific subjects; regular guest speakers; 7,500 mems; Pres. DAIRE HICKEY; Sec. EDWARD GAFFNEY; publs *Laws*, *Philander* (annually).

TECHNOLOGY

Biomedical Engineering Association of Ireland: c/o Dept of Medical Physics and Clinical Engineering, Adelaide and Meath Hospital, Tallaght, Dublin 24; tel. (1) 4145888; internet www.beai.org; f. 1992; Chair. PATRICK PENTONY; Sec. SCOTT BARKLEY.

Institution of Civil Engineers (Republic of Ireland Division): 8 Ardglas Dundrum, Dublin, 16; tel. (1) 4114260; f. 1818; *c.* 550 mems; Chair. DON N. MCENTEE; publs *Municipal Engineer* (quarterly), *New Civil Engineer* (weekly).

Institution of Electrical Engineers Ireland Branch: ESB National Grid, Lower Fitzwilliam St, Dublin 2; tel. (1) 7026071; internet local.iee.org/ireland; Chair. KEVIN O'RIORDAN; Hon. Sec. DAVID HEALY.

Institution of Engineers of Ireland: 22 Clyde Rd, Ballsbridge, Dublin 4; tel. (1) 6684341; fax (1) 6685508; e-mail info@engineersireland.ie; internet www.iei.ie; f. 1835; promotes knowledge and advancement of the engineering profession, conducts examinations and confers the designations 'Chartered Engineer', 'Associate Engineer' and 'Engineering Technician'; 21,000 mems; Dir-Gen. KEVIN KERNAN; publs *Academic Reviews*, *Annual Report*, *Engineers Journal*, *Ezine* (electronic), *Papers*, *Transactions*.

Research Institutes

GENERAL

Science Policy Research Centre: Faculty of Commerce, Univ. College Dublin, Belfield, Dublin 4; tel. (1) 7068263; fax (1) 7061132; f. 1969 to carry out research and to undertake commissioned studies in areas related to technology and innovation policy; small private library; Dir Prof. DENIS J. COGAN.

AGRICULTURE, FISHERIES AND VETERINARY SCIENCE

Teagasc (Agriculture and Food Development Authority): Oak Park, Carlow, Dublin 4; tel. (59) 9170200; fax (59) 9182097; e-mail publications@hq.teagasc.ie; internet www.teagasc.ie; f. 1988; national body providing advisory, research, education and training services to the agriculture and food industry; activities are integrated and managed through six divisions; Dir JIM FLANAGAN; publ. *Irish Journal of Agricultural and Food Research* (2 a year).

Divisions:

Kildalton College of Agriculture: Piltown, Co. Kilkenny; tel. (51) 643105; fax (51) 643797; e-mail mgalvin@kildalton.teagasc.ie; national crops division and headquarters for advisory and training services in Teagasc South; Dir MICHAEL GALVIN.

Kinsealy Research Centre: Malahide Rd, Dublin, 17; tel. (1) 8460644; fax (1) 8460524; e-mail bfarrell@grange.teagasc.ie; national beef division; headquarters for advisory and training services in Teagasc North; Dir DONAL CAREY.

Moorepark Research and Development Division (Teagasc): Fermoy, Co. Cork; tel. (25) 42222; fax (25) 42340; national centre for research in dairying and pig production; Head of Dairy Husbandry Dr PATRICK DILLON; Head of Pig Husbandry BRENDAN LYNCH.

National Dairy Products Research Centre: Moorepark, Fermoy, Co. Cork; tel. (25) 42222; fax (25) 42340; e-mail ldonnelly@moorepark.teagasc.ie; national centre providing research, development and consultancy services; Dir Dr PATRICK DILLON.

National Food Centre: Dunsinea, Castleknock, Dublin 15; tel. (1) 8059500; fax (1) 8059550; e-mail v.tarrant@nfc.teagasc.ie; centre providing research, development and consultancy services for all aspects of food production (except dairy products), food safety and nutrition, and market studies; Dir Dr DECLAN TROY.

Rural Development Division (Teagasc): Athenry, Co. Galway; tel. (91) 845845; fax (91) 845847; e-mail pseery@athenry.teagasc.ie; national centre for rural development; Dir PETER SEERY.

BIBLIOGRAPHY, LIBRARY SCIENCE AND MUSEOLOGY

Irish Manuscripts Commission: 45 Merrion Sq., Dublin 2; tel. (1) 6761610; fax (1) 6623832; e-mail admin@irishmanuscripts.ie; internet www.irishmanuscripts.ie; f. 1928; 19 mems; Chair. JAMES MCGUIRE; Research Officer Dr MICHAEL J. HAREN; 170 published vols of historical interest; publ. *Analecta Hibernica* (irreg.).

ECONOMICS, LAW AND POLITICS

Economic and Social Research Institute: 4 Burlington Rd, Dublin 4; tel. (1) 6671525; fax (1) 6686231; e-mail admin@esri.ie; internet www.esri.ie; f. 1960; 130 individual mems, 400 corporate mems; library of 40,000 vols; Dir Prof. BRENDAN J. WHELAN; publs *Economic and Social Review* (4 a year), *Medium Term Review* (every 2 years), *Quarterly Economic Commentary*.

HISTORY, GEOGRAPHY AND ARCHAEOLOGY

Office of the Chief Herald/incorporating State Heraldic Museum: 2 Kildare St, Dublin; tel. (1) 6030311; fax (1) 6621062; e-mail herald@nli.ie; internet www.nli.ie; f. 1552; granting, confirming and registering of armorial bearings; 1,000 MSS since the 16th century, 100,000 archive items since 1800; Keeper FERGUS GILLESPIE.

LANGUAGE AND LITERATURE

Institiúid Teangeolaíochta Éireann/Linguistics Institute of Ireland: 31 Fitzwilliam Place, Dublin 2; tel. (1) 6765489; fax (1) 6610004; e-mail ite@ite.ie; internet www.ite.ie; f. 1972; research in applied linguistics with special reference to the Irish language and teaching and learning of languages generally; 30 mems; library of 10,000 books, 151 periodicals; Chair. CLÍONA DE BHALDRAITHE MARSH; Dir EOGHAN MAC AOGÁIN; publs *Teangeolas* (2 a year), *Annual Report*, *Language, Culture and Curriculum* (3 a year).

MEDICINE

Health Research Board: 73 Lower Baggot St, Dublin 2; tel. (1) 6761176; fax (1) 6611856; e-mail hrb@hrb.ie; internet www.hrb.ie; f. 1987; Chief Exec. Dr RUTH BARRINGTON.

NATURAL SCIENCES

Physical Sciences

Dunsink Observatory: School of Cosmic Physics, Castleknock, Dublin 15; tel. (1) 8387911; fax (1) 8387090; e-mail astro@dunsink.dias.ie; internet www.dunsink.dias.ie; f. 1785; part of Dublin Institute for Advanced Studies; library of 5,000 vols, 75 periodicals; Dir Prof. EVERT MEURS; Sec. CAROL WOODS.

Libraries and Archives

Cork

Cork City Libraries: 57–61 Grand Parade, Cork; tel. (21) 4924900; fax (21) 4275684; e-mail libraries@corkcity.ie; internet www.corkcity.ie; 75,000 vols, of which 30,000 contained in the Reference Library and 45,000 in the Lending Library and Children's Department; Music Library contains 20,000 records, CDs and tapes; City Librarian LIAM RONAYNE.

Cork County Library: Model Business Park, Model Farm Rd, Cork; tel. (21) 4546499; fax (21) 4343254; e-mail corkcountylibrary@corkcoco.ie; internet www.corkcoco.ie; 1,080,000 vols, 90 periodicals; 28 brs, 5 mobile libraries; Librarian RUTH FLANAGAN.

Cork Institute of Technology Bishopstown Library: Bishopstown Campus, Cork; tel. (21) 4326501; internet library.cit.ie; brs at Crawford College of Art and Design, Cork School of Music and National Maritime College of Ireland; Librarian DERRY DELANEY.

University College Cork Library: The Boole Library, University College Cork, College Rd, Cork; tel. (21) 4902794; fax (21) 4273428; e-mail library@ucc.ie; internet booleweb.ucc.ie; f. 1849; 500,000 vols, including Irish Manuscript collection (microfilm), Senft (philosophy), Torna (Irish), Cooke (travel), John E. Cummings Memorial Collection (humour), Langlands Collection (Africa); Postgraduate Research Library currently under construction; EU documentation centre; Irish copyright privilege; Librarian JOHN FITZGERALD.

Dublin

Central Catholic Library: 74 Merrion Sq., Dublin 2; tel. (1) 6761264; fax (1) 6787618; e-mail catholicresearch@eircom.net; internet www.catholiclibrary.ie; f. 1922; controlled by the Central Catholic Library Association; open to the public; lending and reference depts containing material on every aspect of Catholicism, on other Christian denominations and other religions, Irish history and culture, philosophy; audio and video cassettes; 130,000 vols, incl. large journal collection, special collection of 2,000 vols on Christian art, Ireland Collection; Librarian TERESA WHITINGTON.

Chester Beatty Library: The Clock Tower Building, Dublin Castle, Dublin 2; tel. (1) 4070750; fax (1) 4070760; e-mail info@cbl.ie; internet www.cbl.ie; f. 1953; donated to the Irish nation by Sir Alfred Chester Beatty in 1968; contains one of the world's leading collections of Islamic and Far Eastern art, and important Western and Biblical MSS and miniatures; incunabula and other printed books; Dir Dr MICHAEL RYAN.

Dublin City Public Libraries and Archive: 138-144 Pearse St, Dublin 2; tel. (1) 6744800; fax (1) 6744879; e-mail dublin.city.libs@iol.ie; internet www.dublincity.ie/living_in_the_city/libraries; f. 1884; 2,400,000 vols; special collections include early Dublin printing and fine binding, incunabula, political pamphlets and cartoons, Dublin periodicals and 18th-century plays, Abbey Theatre material, Swift and Yeats material; extensive local history collection in books, newspapers and pictures; representative holdings of modern Dublin presses; special music library; language learning centre; City Librarian DEIRDRE ELLIS-KING.

Irish Theatre Archive: c/o Dublin City Library and Archive, 138–144 Pearse St, Dublin 2; tel. (1) 6744800; fax (1) 6744881; e-mail cityarchives@dublincity.ie; internet www.dublincity.ie; f. 1981 to collect and preserve Ireland's theatre heritage; large collection of material: programmes, posters, play-scripts, prompt-books, etc.; organizes lecture series, exhibitions; Archivist MARY CLARK.

Law Library of Ireland: Four Courts, Dublin 7; tel. (1) 8720622; fax (1) 8720455; internet www.lawlibrary.ie; controlled by the Council of the Bar of Ireland; open to mems of the Irish Bar only; 100,000 vols; Chair., Library Cttee PAUL MCGARRY.

Library Council: 53–54 Upper Mount St, Dublin 2; tel. (1) 6761167; fax (1) 6766721; e-mail info@librarycouncil.ie; internet www.librarycouncil.ie; f. 1947 by Public Libraries Act; advises local authorities and the Min. for the Environment, Heritage and Local Govt on the devt of public library services; provides an information service on libraries and librarianship; operates the inter-library lending system for Ireland, and provides the Secretariat for the Cttee on Library Co-operation in Ireland; Dir NORMA MCDERMOTT; publ. *Irish Library News*.

Marsh's Library: St Patrick's Close, Dublin 8; tel. and fax (1) 4543511; e-mail keeper@marshlibrary.ie; internet www.marshlibrary.ie; f. 1701; 25,000 vols and 300 MSS; Keeper MURIEL MCCARTHY.

National Archives of Ireland: Bishop St, Dublin 8; tel. (1) 4072300; fax (1) 4072333; e-mail mail@nationalarchives.ie; internet www.nationalarchives.ie; f. 1988 (merger of Public Record Office, f. 1867, and State Paper Office, f. 1702), under the Nat. Archives Act, to preserve and make accessible the records of Depts of State, courts, other public service orgs and private donors; 50,000 linear metres of archives; Dir Dr DAVID CRAIG.

National Library of Ireland: Kildare St, Dublin 2; tel. (1) 6030200; fax (1) 6766690; e-mail info@nli.ie; internet www.nli.ie; f. 1877; more than 1,000,000 vols including Irish printing colln, pamphlets, periodicals, newspapers, 70,000 MSS, including 1,200 Gaelic MSS, 300,000 photographic negatives, 90,000 prints and drawings, ephemera and music; Dir AONGUS Ó HAONGHUSA; Keeper of Printed and Visual Collections COLETTE O'FLAHERTY.

Oireachtas Library: Leinster House, Dublin 2; tel. (1) 6183412; fax (1) 6184109; internet www.irlgov.ie/oireachtas; selective works of parliamentary interest, the nucleus of which was the Chief Secretary's Office, Dublin Castle; Librarian MAURA CORCORAN.

Representative Church Body Library: Braemor Park, Churchtown, Dublin 14; tel. (1) 4923979; fax (1) 4924770; e-mail library@ireland.anglican.org; internet www.ireland.anglican.org; f. 1932; theological library controlled by the Representative Body of the Church of Ireland; 40,000 vols, mainly theology, history, ethics and education; Church of Ireland archives; MSS collection, mainly ecclesiastical; Librarian and Archivist Dr RAYMOND REFAUSSÉ.

Royal College of Surgeons in Ireland Library (The Mercer Library): Mercer St Lower, Dublin 2; tel. (1) 4022407; fax (1) 4022457; e-mail library@rcsi.ie; internet www.rcsi.ie/library; f. 1784; 75,000 vols; special collections: archives of RCSI and Dublin hospitals, 20,000 rare books, medical pamphlets from 17th c.; Librarian BEATRICE M. DORAN.

Royal Dublin Society Library: Ballsbridge, Dublin 4; tel. (1) 6680866; fax (1) 6604014; f. 1731; 100,000 vols, including more than 4,000 relating to Ireland, many of them old and rare; 6,000 works and pamphlets on all branches of agricultural science up to 1920, including 1,500 works of equestrian interest; reference collection of more than 2,000 vols, including the 'Thoms Street' directory on Dublin, since the 1840s; the scientific and private correspondence of Professor George Francis Fitzgerald (1851–1901, physicist at Trinity College, Dublin, who first suggested a method of producing radio waves) of which there are more than 1,000 letters; the papers of Dr Horace H. Poole, Richard M. Barrington and John Edmund Carew; the records of the Radium Institute and the Maymes Ansell Archive of Equestrian Photographs; Librarian MARY KELLEHER.

Trinity College Library: College St, Dublin 2; tel. (1) 6081665; fax (1) 6083774; internet www.tcd.ie/library; f. 1592; University and British/Irish legal deposit library; 4,500,000 printed books, 6,000 MSS, incl. the Book of Kells and other medieval manuscripts, collections of 17th and 18th c. French printed materials, caricatures and an extensive colln of music scores and maps; visitor centre; 4,500,000 vols; Librarian and College Archivist ROBIN ADAMS; publ. *Long Room* (annually).

University College Dublin Library: Belfield, Dublin 4; tel. (1) 7167067; fax (1) 2837667; e-mail library@ucd.ie; internet www.ucd.ie/library; f. 1908; 1,200,000 vols, 8,000 periodicals; special collections include pre-1850 imprints, Baron Palles (Law) Library of 2,500 vols, Zimmer (Celtic) Library of 2,000 vols, C. P. Curran (Irish literature), John McCormack (music), Colm Ó Lochlainn (Irish printing), F. J. O'Kelley (Irish printing) and John L Sweeney (Literature) collections; manuscripts collection; literary archives and papers include those of Sean O'Riordain, Patrick Kavanagh, Mary Lavin, Maeve Binchy and Frank McGuinness; Librarian SEAN PHILLIPS.

Galway

Galway City Library: St Augustine St, Galway; tel. (91) 561666; fax (91) 565039; e-mail info@galwaylibrary.ie; internet www.galwaylibrary.ie; Librarian PAT MCMAHON.

Galway County Libraries: Island House, Cathedral Square, Galway; tel. (91) 562471; fax (91) 565039; e-mail info@galwaylibrary.ie; internet www.galwaylibrary.ie; f. 1927; 350,000 vols; County Librarian PATRICK MCMAHON; publ. *Annual Report*.

National University of Ireland, Galway, James Hardiman Library: National University of Ireland, Galway; tel. (91) 524411; fax (91) 522394; e-mail library@nuigalway.ie; internet www.library.nuigalway.ie; f. 1849; 257,000 vols; extensive collection of books in Irish published since 1890; EEC Documentation Centre; enjoys Irish copyright privilege; Librarian MARIE REDDAN.

Limerick

Limerick City Library: City Hall, Merchants Quay, Limerick; tel. (61) 314668; fax (61) 415266; e-mail citylib@limerickcity.ie; internet www.limerickcorp.ie/services/library; Librarian DOLORES DOYLE.

Limerick County Library: 58 O'Connell St, Limerick; tel. (61) 496526; fax (61) 318570; e-mail libinfo@limerickcoco.ie; internet www.lcc.ie/library; 5 brs and 19 part-time brs; Librarian DAMIEN BRADY.

Maynooth

John Paul II Library, National University of Ireland, Maynooth: Maynooth, Co. Kildare; tel. (1) 7083884; fax (1) 6286008; e-mail library.information@nuim.ie; internet www.library.nuim.ie; f. 1795; 442,500 vols; Librarian AGNES NELIGAN.

Waterford

Waterford City Council Central Library: Lady Lane, Waterford; tel. (51) 849975; e-mail library@waterfordcity.ie; internet www.waterfordcity.ie/library; 3 brs; audio listening and language learning facilities; Librarian JANE CANTWELL.

Waterford County Library Headquarters: Lismore, Co. Waterford; tel. (58) 21370; e-mail libraryhq@waterfordcoco.ie; internet www.waterfordcountylibrary.ie; 8 brs; County Librarian DONALD BRADY.

Museums and Art Galleries

Cork

Cork Public Museum: Fitzgerald Park, Cork; tel. (21) 4270679; fax (21) 4270931; e-mail museum@corkcity.ie; f. 1910; sections devoted to Irish history and archaeology, also municipal, social and economic history, Cork glass, silver and lace; items of special interest include the Cork helmet horns, the Garryduff gold bird, the Roche silver collar, civic maces, municipal oar, freedom boxes and Grace Cup of Cork Corporation; Curator STELLA CHERRY.

Dublin

Civic Museum: 58 South William St, Dublin; tel. (1) 6794260; f. 1953; attached to Dublin Public Libraries; original exhibits of antiquarian and historical interest pertaining to Dublin; subjects in the permanent colln incl. streets and buildings of Dublin, traders, industry, transport, political history, maps; Curator THOMAS P. O'CONNOR.

Dublin City Gallery, The Hugh Lane: Charlemont House, Parnell Sq. North, Dublin 1; tel. (1) 2225550; fax (1) 8722182; e-mail info.hughlane@dublincity.ie; internet www.hughlane.ie; f. 1908; works of Irish, English and European schools of painting, and pictures from the Sir Hugh Lane colln; sculptures; Dir BARBARA DAWSON.

Dublin Writers Museum: 18 Parnell Sq., Dublin 1; tel. (1) 8722077; fax (1) 8722231; e-mail writers@dublintourism.ie; internet www.writersmuseum.com; f. 1991; history of Irish literature; library; Operations Man. MARIA O'CALLAGHAN.

Irish Museum of Modern Art: Royal Hospital, Military Rd, Kilmainham, Dublin 8; tel. (1) 6129900; fax (1) 6129999; e-mail info@modernart.ie; internet www.modernart.ie; f. 1991; works by Irish and non-Irish artists since beginning of 20th c.; Dir PHILOMENA BYRNE (acting).

James Joyce Museum: Martello Tower, Sandycove, Co. Dublin; tel. and fax (1) 2809265; e-mail joycetower@dublintourism.ie; internet www.visitdublin.com; f. 1962; papers and personal effects of the writer (1882–1941) and critical works about him; library of 550 vols; Curator ROBERT NICHOLSON.

National Botanic Gardens Glasnevin: Glasnevin, Dublin 9; tel. (1) 8377596; fax (1) 8360080; e-mail botanicgardens@opw.ie; internet www.botanicgardens.ie; f. 1795; includes Irish National Herbarium; visitor centre combines a lecture hall, restaurant and display area with exhibits relating to the history and purpose of the gardens; library of 40,000 vols, including colln of illustrated botanical works; Dir DONAL SYNNOTT; publ. *Glasra–Contributions from the National Botanic Gardens, Glasnevin* (annually).

National Gallery of Ireland: Merrion Sq. West, Dublin 2; tel. (1) 6615133; fax (1) 6615372; e-mail info@ngi.ie; internet www.nationalgallery.ie; f. 1854; nat., historical and portrait galleries; continental European, British and Irish masters since 1250; 2,500 oil paintings, 300 sculptures, 5,200 drawings and watercolours, 3,000 prints; Dir RAYMOND KEAVENEY.

National Museum of Ireland: Kildare St, Dublin 7; tel. (1) 6777444; fax (1) 6777450; e-mail marketing@museum.ie; internet www.museum.ie; f. est.1877 by the Science and Arts Museums Act; incl. (1) Irish Antiquities Div. (Keeper EAMONN P. KELLY); (2) Art and Industrial Div. (Keeper MICHAEL KENNY); (3) Irish Folklife Div. (Keeper TONY CANDON); (4) Natural History Div., which incl. zoological and geological sections (Keeper NIGEL MONAGHAN); Dir Dr PATRICK F. WALLACE.

Royal College of Surgeons in Ireland Museum: St Stephen's Green, Dublin 2; f. 1820; Asst Curator Prof. DOROTHY BENSON.

Strokestown

Strokestown Park House Garden and Famine Museum: Strokestown Park, Strokestown, Co. Roscommon; tel. (78) 9633013; fax (78) 9633712; e-mail info@strokestownpark.ie; internet www.strokestownpark.ie/museum.html; f. 1994; collns related to the history of the Great Irish Famine of the 1840s; Man. JOHN O'DRISCOLL.

Universities

DUBLIN CITY UNIVERSITY

Dublin 9
Telephone: (1) 7005000
Fax: (1) 8360830
E-mail: registry@dcu.ie
Internet: www.dcu.ie

Founded 1980 as National Institute for Higher Education, Dublin; University status 1989
State control
Academic year: September to May

President: Prof. FERDINAND VON PRONDZYNSKI
Vice-President for Learning Innovation: MARIA SLOWEY
Vice-President for Research: DERMOT DIAMOND
Registrar: KEVIN GRIFFIN
Secretary: MARTIN CONRY
Librarian: PAUL SHEEHAN

Number of teachers: 264
Number of students: 10,000

Publications: *Annual Report*, *NewsLink* (3 a year)

DEANS

Faculty of Engineering and Computing: Prof. CHARLES MCCORKELL
Faculty of Humanities and Social Sciences: Prof. EITHNE GUILFOYLE
Faculty of Science and Health: Prof. MALCOLM SMYTH
Joint Faculty of Education: PÁID MAGEE
Joint Faculty of Humanities: Prof. MICHAEL CRONIN
Dublin City University Business School: Prof. BERNARD PIERCE
Oscail–National Distance Education Centre: Dr RONNIE SAUNDERS

HEADS OF SCHOOLS

Faculty of Engineering and Computing:
- Computing: Prof. MICHAEL RYAN
- Electronic Engineering: Prof. MICHAEL MCCORKELL
- Mechanical and Manufacturing Engineering: Prof. SALEEM HASHMI

Faculty of Humanities and Social Sciences:
- Applied Language and Intercultural Studies: Prof. JENNY WILLIAMS
- Communications: BRIAN TRENCH
- Education Studies: Dr GERARD MCNAMARA
- Fiontar (Business Studies, taught in Gaelic): Dr CAOILFHIONN NIC PHÁIDÍN
- Law and Government: Prof. ROBERT ELGIE

Faculty of Science and Health:
- Biotechnology: Prof. IAN W. MARISON
- Chemical Sciences: Prof. HAN VOS
- Health and Human Performance: Dr NIALL MOYNA
- Mathematical Sciences: Prof. JOHN CARROLL
- Nursing: Prof. ANNE SCOTT
- Physical Sciences: Prof. JOHN COSTELLO

RESEARCH CENTRES

Centre for International Studies: Co-Dirs Dr JOHN DOYLE, Dr PEADAR KIRBY.

Centre for Digital Video Processing: Dir Prof. ALAN F. SMEATON.

Centre for Modelling with Differential Equations: Dir Prof. EUGENE O'RIORDAN.

Centre for Technology, Society and Media (STeM): Dir PASCHAL PRESTON.

Centre for Research in Management Learning and Development: Dir Prof. BERNARD PIERCE.

Centre for Software Engineering: Dir Prof. MICHAEL O'DUFFY.

Centre for Translation and Textual Studies: Dir Prof. MICHAEL CRONIN.

International Centre for Neurotherapeutics: Dir Prof. Dr J. OLIVER DOLLY.

Materials Processing Research Centre: Dir Dr LISA LOONEY.

National Centre for Plasma Science and Technology: Dir Prof. MILES TURNER.

National Centre for Sensor Research: Dir Prof. MALCOLM SMYTH.

National Centre for Software Engineering: Dir R. COCHRAN.

National Centre for Technology in Education: Dir JEROME MORRISSEY.

National Institute for Cellular Biotechnology: Dir Prof. MARTIN CLYNES.

National Institute for Language Technology: Dir Prof. JOSEF VAN GENABITH.

Optronics Ireland: Dir Prof. M. HENRY.

PEI Technologies (Power Electronics): Dir J. DOWLING.

Research Institute for Networks and Communications Engineering: Dir Prof. PATRICK MCNALLY.

Sensor Technology Instrumentation and Process Analysis Centre: Dir Prof. D. DIAMOND.

TELTEC (Communications): Dir Dr T. CURRAN.

Vascular Health Research Centre: Dir Prof. PAUL A. CAHILL.

ATTACHED INSTITUTE

National Distance Education Centre: Dublin 9; a faculty of the universityf. 1982; the executive arm of the Nat. Distance Education Ccl; Dir Dr DENIS BANCROFT.

ATTACHED COLLEGES

Mater Dei Institute of Education: Clonliffe Ave, Dublin 3; tel. (1) 8376027; fax (1) 8370776; e-mail info@materdei.dcu.ie; internet www.materdei.ief. 1966; College of the University since 1999; courses in Irish Studies and Theology; 50 teachers; 545 students; library of 160,000 vols; Pres. Rev. Dr MICHAEL DRUMM; Registrar Rev. Dr EOIN G. CASSIDY; publ. *Religion, Education and the Arts* (annually).

St Patrick's College: Drumcondra, Dublin 9; tel. (1) 8842000; fax (1) 8376197; e-mail presidents.office@spd.dcu.ie; internet www .spd.dcu.ief. 1875; College of the University since 1993; academic depts participate in the Joint Faculties of Education and Humanities; 58 teachers; 2,000 students; library of 100,000 vols; Pres. Dr PÁURIC TRAVERS; Registrar Dr LIAM MAC MATHÚNA; publ. *Studia Hibernica* (annually), *The Irish Journal of Education* (2 a year).

UNIVERSITY OF DUBLIN TRINITY COLLEGE

Dublin 2
Telephone: (1) 6772941
Fax: (1) 6772694
Internet: www.tcd.ie
Founded 1592

Academic year: September to July
Chancellor: M. T. W. ROBINSON
Pro-Chancellors: Sir A. J. F. O'REILLY, S. J. G. DENHAM, E. SAGARRA, P. J. MOLLOY
Provost: J. HEGARTY
Vice-Provost: J. B. GRIMSON
Registrar: D. J. DICKSON
Secretary to the College: M. GLEESON
Librarian: D. R. H. ADAMS

Library: see Libraries and Archives
Number of teachers: 741
Number of students: 15,428 (including postgraduate)

Publication: *Hermathena*

DEANS

Faculty of Arts (Humanities): H. V. SMITH
Faculty of Arts (Letters): E. NÍ CHUILLEANÁIN
Faculty of Business, Economic and Social Studies: C. KEARNEY
Faculty of Engineering and Systems Sciences: J. B. FOLEY
Faculty of Health Sciences: D. B. SHANLEY
Faculty of Science: M. J. CARROLL
Graduate Studies: P. J. PRENDERGAST

PROFESSORS

Faculty of Arts (Humanities):

BIGGAR, N. J., Theology
BINCHY, W., Law
FITZPATRICK, D. P. B., Modern History
GREEN, S. M., Childhood Research
HORNE, J. N., Modern European History
MAYES, A. D. H., Hebrew
O'HALPIN, E. J., Contemporary Irish History
OHLMEYER, J. H., Modern History
RICE, J. V., Education (Research)
ROBERTSON, I. H., Psychology
STALLEY, R. A., History of Art

Faculty of Arts (Letters):

BROWN, T. P. MCC., Anglo-Irish Literature
DILLON, J. M., Greek
GRATTON, J., French
GRENE, N., English Literature
KENNEDY, D., Drama and Theatre Studies
MCGOWAN, N. M., German
NELIS, D. P., Latin
SCATTERGOOD, V. J., Medieval and Renaissance Literature (English)
SCOTT, D. H. T., French (Textual and Visual Studies)

Faculty of Business, Economic and Social Studies:

GILLIGAN, R. H., Social Work and Social Policy
HILL, R. J., Comparative Government (Political Science)
HOLTON, R., Sociology
KEARNEY, C., International Business
LANE, P. R., International Macroeconomics
MATTHEWS, A. H., European Agricultural Policy (Economics)
MURRAY, J. A., Business Studies
NORMAND, C. E. M., Health Policy and Management
O'ROURKE, K. H., Economics
WICKHAM, J. J. R., European Labour Market Studies

Faculty of Engineering and Systems Sciences:

BOLAND, F. M., Electronic and Electrical Engineering
FITZPATRICK, J. A., Mechanical Engineering
GRIMSON, J. B., Computer Science
HASLETT, J., Statistics
VIJ, J. K., Electronic Materials

Faculty of Health Sciences:

BEGLEY, C. M., Nursing and Midwifery
BELL, C., Physiology
CASSIDY, L., Clinical Ophthalmology
CLAFFEY, N. M., Periodontology
CLARKSON, J., Public Dental Health
COAKLEY, D., Medical Gerontology
CONLON, K. C. P., Surgery
FEELY, J., Pharmacology and Therapeutics
FITZGERALD, M., Child and Adolescent Psychiatry
GEARY, M. P. P., Clinical Obstetrics and Gynaecology
GILL, A. M., Psychiatry
HOEY, H. M. C. V., Paediatrics
HOLLYWOOD, D. P., Clinical Oncology
KELLEHER, D. P. A., Medicine
KENNY, R. A. M., Geriatric Medicine
LAWLOR, B., Old Age Psychiatry
LEE, R. T., Orthodontics
MCCANN, S. R., Haematology
MCKEON, P., Clinical Psychiatry
MALONE, J. F., Medical Physics
NORMAND, C. E. M., Health Policy and Management
NUNN, J., Special Care Dentistry
O'CONNELL, B., Restorative Dentistry
O'DOWD, T. C., General Practice
O'LEARY, J. J., Pathology
O'MORAIN, C. A., Medicine
REYNOLDS, J. V., Surgery
ROGERS, T. R. F., Clinical Microbiology
SCOTT, J. M., Experimental Nutrition
SHANLEY, D. B., Oral Health
SMITH, O. P., Haematology
STASSEN, L. F., Oral and Maxillo-facial Surgery
TIMON, C. V. I., Clinical Otolaryngology

Faculty of Science:

BOLAND, J., Chemistry (Research)
BLAU, W. J., Physics of Advanced Materials
COEY, J. M. D., Experimental Physics
CONSTANTIN, A., Mathematics
CORISH, J., Physical Chemistry
CORRIGAN, O. I., Pharmaceutics
CUNNINGHAM, E. P., Animal Genetics
DORMAN, C. J., Microbiology
DRURY, L., Astronomy
FOSTER, T. J., Molecular Microbiology
HUMPHRIES, P., Medical Molecular Genetics
JARVIS, S. P., Physics (Research)
JONES, M. B., Botany
MCCONNELL, D. J., Genetics
MARTIN, S. J., Medical Genetics
MILLS, K. H. G., Experimental Immunology
PETHICA, J. B., Physics (Research)
RAMASWAMI, M., Neuroscience
ROGERS, T. R. F., Clinical Microbiology
SCOTT, J. M., Experimental Nutrition
SENGE, M., Organic Chemistry
SHATASHVILI, S., Natural Philosophy (Mathematics)
TAYLOR, D., Geography
TIPTON, K. F., Biochemistry
WEAIRE, D. L., Physics

HEADS OF DEPARTMENTS

(Non-Professorial)

Faculty of Arts (Humanities):

Education: A. M. E. O'MOORE
History of Art: P. D. MCEVANSONEYA
Law: H. DELANY
Medieval History: C. E. MEEK
Music: W. M. TAYLOR
Philosophy: J. LEVINE
Psychology: R. M. J. BYRNE

Faculty of Arts (Letters):

Centre for Language and Communication Studies: D. G. LITTLE
Deaf Studies: L. LEESON
Drama: B. R. SINGLETON
English: S. J. MATTERSON
Hispanic Studies: C. B. COSGROVE
Irish: P. D. J. MCMANUS
Italian: R. BERTONI
Russian: S. SMYTH

Faculty of Business, Economic and Social Studies:
- Business Studies: G. McHugh
- Economics: A. H. Matthews
- Political Science: M. A. Marsh

Faculty of Engineering and Systems Sciences:
- Civil, Structural and Environmental Engineering: R. P. West
- Computer Science: D. M. Abrahamson
- Electronic and Electrical Engineering: R. A. Moore
- Mechanical and Manufacturing Engineering: A. A. Torrance
- Statistics: T. E. Mullins

Faculty of Health Sciences:
- Anatomy: P. Glacken
- Clinical Speech and Language Studies: M. M. Smith
- Obstetrics and Gynaecology: B. L. Sheppard
- Occupational Therapy: D. M. Connolly
- Physiotherapy: J. Hussey (acting)
- Radiation Therapy: M. A. Coffey

Faculty of Science:
- Biochemistry: L. J. A. O' Neill
- Botany: J. A. N. Parnell
- Genetics: T. A. Kavanagh
- Geology: J. R. Graham
- Microliology: C. J. Smyth
- Pharmacy: I. L. I. Hook
- Zoology: C. V. Holland

RECOGNIZED COLLEGES

Church of Ireland College of Education: 96 Upper Rathmines Rd, Dublin 6; tel. (1) 4970033; 3-year course leading to BEd pass degree; Principal Sydney Blain.

Coláiste Mhuire, Marino: Griffith Ave, Dublin 9; tel. (1) 8057700; 3-year course leading to BEd pass degree; Principal (vacant).

Froebel College of Education: Sion Hill, Blackrock, Co. Dublin; tel. (1) 2888520; 3-year course leading to BEd pass degree; Principal Sr Darina Hosey.

Irish School of Ecumenics (Trinity College Dublin): Bea House, Milltown Park, Dublin 6; tel. (1) 2601144; Dir J. D.'A. May.

St Catherine's College of Education for Home Economics: Sion Hill, Blackrock, Co. Dublin; tel. (1) 2884989; f. 1929; 4-year course leading to BEd (Home Econ.) honours degree; Pres. Madeleine Mulrennan.

NATIONAL UNIVERSITY OF IRELAND

49 Merrion Sq., Dublin 2
Telephone: (1) 4392424
Fax: (1) 4392466
E-mail: registrar@nui.ie
Internet: www.nui.ie
Founded 1908

Chancellor: Dr Garret FitzGerald
Vice-Chancellor: Prof. John G. Hughes
Registrar: Dr Attracta Halpin

Publications: *Calendar* (annually), *Éigse: A Journal of Irish Studies* (irregular).

CONSTITUENT COLLEGES

University College Cork

Western Rd, Cork
Telephone: (21) 4903000
Fax: (21) 4273428
E-mail: registrar@ucc.ie
Internet: www.ucc.ie

Founded 1845 as Queen's College, Cork; changed to above in 1908
Academic year: October to September

President: Prof. G. T. Wrixon
Vice-Presidents: Prof. Aine Hyland, Prof. Paul Giller (Academic Affairs, and Registrar), Michael F. Kelleher (Finance and Administration, and Secretary and Bursar), Michael O'Sullivan (Planning, Communications and Development), Prof. J. Kevin Collins (Research, Policy and Support)
Librarian: John A. Fitzgerald

Number of teachers: 2,280 (539 full-time, 1,741 part-time)
Number of students: 15,556 full-time (12,622 undergraduate, 2,923 postgraduate)

Publication: *Chimera* (annually)

DEANS

Faculty of Arts and Celtic Studies: Prof. David H. Cox
Faculty of Commerce: Prof. Denis I. F. Lucey
Faculty of Engineering: Dr Richard Kavanagh (acting)
Faculty of Food Science and Technology: Prof. Yrjo H. Roos
Faculty of Law: Prof. Caroline Fennell
Faculty of Medicine and Health: Prof. Michael Murphy
Faculty of Science: Prof. Patrick Fitzpatrick

PROFESSORS

(Some professors also have responsibilities in other faculties)

Faculties of Arts and Celtic Studies (tel. (21) 4902773; fax (21) 4903364; e-mail ArtsFaculty@arts.ucc.ie):
- Clarke, D., Philosophy
- Cox, D. H., Music
- Howard, M. P., German
- Hyland, A., Education
- Kearney, C. J., Modern English
- Keogh, D. F., Modern History (European Integration Studies)
- Lee, J. J., Modern History
- MacKenzie, D., Hispanic Studies
- Ó Carragáin, E., Old and Middle English
- Ó Coileáin, S., Modern Irish Language
- O'Corrain, D., History
- O'Donovan, P. T., French
- Ó Riain, P. S., Early Irish Language and Literature
- Powell, F. W., Applied Social Studies
- Saccone, E., Italian
- Scakolczai, A. I., Sociology
- Smyth, W. J., Geography
- Taylor, M., Applied Psychology
- Woodman, P. C., Archaeology

Faculty of Commerce (tel. (21) 4902136; fax (21) 4903251; e-mail commerce@ucc.ie):
- Cahill, E. P., Accounting and Finance
- Collins, N., Government
- Fanning, C. M., Economics
- Green, S., Management and Marketing
- Murphy, C. M., Business Information Systems

Faculty of Engineering (tel. (21) 4903081; fax (21) 4276648; e-mail engfac@ucc.ie):
- Campbell, J.
- Crean, G.
- Kennedy, P.
- Kiely, G.
- Murphy, P.
- O'Kane, J. P. J., Civil Engineering
- Oliveira, F. A., Process Engineering

Faculty of Food Science and Technology (tel. (21) 4902007; fax (21) 4276389; e-mail fcoyne@foodscience.ucc.ie):
- Cashman, K. D., Food Science and Technology
- Condon, J. J., Microbiology
- Daly, C., Food Technology
- Lucey, D. I. F., Food Economics
- Morrissey, P. A., Nutrition
- Morris, E. R., Food Chemistry
- Ross, Y. H., Food Science and Technology

Faculty of Law (Aras Na Laois, Cork; tel. (21) 4903249; fax (21) 4903413; e-mail lawfac@ucc.ie):
- Carroll, B. A., Law
- Morgan, D. G., Law

Faculty of Medicine and Health (3 Elderwood, College Rd, Cork; tel. (21) 4902455; fax (21) 4270339; e-mail Medfac@ucc.ie):
- Bradley, C. P., General
- Daly, R. J., Psychiatry
- Fraher, J. P., Anatomy
- Hall, W. J., Physiology
- Higgins, J. R., Obstetrics and Gynaecology
- Kearney, P. J., Paediatrics
- McCarthy, G., Nursing Studies
- McConnell, R. J., Restorative Dentistry
- Murphy, M. B., Clinical Pharmacology
- O'Mullane, D. M., Preventive and Paediatric Dentistry
- Parfrey, N., Pathology
- Perry, I. J., Epidemiology and Public Health
- Quigley, E. M., Medicine
- Redmond, H. P., Surgery
- Shanahan, F. L. J., Medicine
- Shorten, N., Surgery
- Sleeman, D., Dental Surgery

Faculty of Science (tel. (21) 4902299; fax (21) 4270380; e-mail sciencefaculty@ucc.ie):
- Bowen, J. A., Software Engineering
- Brück, P. M., Geology
- Cassells, A. C., Plant Science
- Condon, J. J., Microbiology
- Cotter, T. G., Biochemistry
- Davenport, J., Zoology and Animal Ecology
- Guilbault, G. G., Analytical Chemistry
- Jennings, W. B., Organic Chemistry
- McInerney, J. G., Physics
- Moran, M. A., Applied Statistics
- Mortell, M. P., Applied Mathematics
- O'Reilly, E., Physics
- O'Sullivan, F., Statistics
- Pawltan, Y., Statistics
- Sodeau, J., Physical Chemistry
- Spalding, T. R., Inorganic Chemistry
- Sreenan, C. J., Computer Science

University College Dublin

Belfield, Dublin 4
Telephone: (1) 7167777
Fax: (1) 2694409
E-mail: info@ucd.ie
Internet: www.ucd.ie
Languages of instruction: English, Irish
Founded 1908
Academic year: September to May

President: Dr Hugh Brady
Registrar, Deputy President and Vice-President: Dr Philip Nolan
Vice-President for Innovation and Corporate Partnerships: Prof. Catherine Godson
Vice-President for International Affairs: Prof. William Hall
Vice-President for Research: Prof. Desmond Fitzgerald
Vice-President for Staff and Administrative Systems: Mr Eamon Drea
Vice-President for Students: Prof. Mary Clayton
Vice-President for University Relations: Dr Padraic Conway
Librarian: Sean Phillips

Library: see Libraries and Archives
Number of teachers: 2,531 (837 full-time 1,694 part-time)
Number of students: 18,357

Publications: *Irish University Review* (2 a year), *President's Report*

DEANS

Arts and Celtic Studies, Principal of College: Prof. Mary E. Daly

Business and Law, Principal of College: Mr PAUL HARAN
Engineering, Mathematical and Physical Sciences, Principal of College: Prof. NICK QUIRKE
Human Sciences, Principal of College: Prof. BRIGID LAFFAN
Life Sciences, Principal of College: Prof. BRIAN M. MCKENNA

HEADS OF DEPARTMENTS

School of Agriculture, Food Science and Veterinary Medicine: Prof. MAURICE BOLAND
School of Applied Social Science: Dr VALERIE RICHARDSON
School of Archaeology: Dr MUIRIS O'SUILLEABHÁIN
School of Architecture, Landscape and Civil Engineering: Dr MARK G. RICHARDSON
School of Art History and Cultural Policy: Dr PAULA MURPHY
School of Biology and Environmental Science: Prof. THOMAS BOLGER
School of Biomolecular and Biomedical Science: Dr PAUL MOYNAGH
School of Chemical and Bioprocess Engineering: Prof. DON MACELROY
School of Chemistry and Chemical Biology: Prof. MICHAEL MCGLINCHEY
School of Business: Prof. TOM BEGLEY
School of Classics: Dr MICHAEL LLOYD
School of Computer Science and Informatics: Prof BARRY SMYTH
School of Economics: Prof. RODNEY THOM
School of Education and Lifelong Learning: Prof. SHEELAGH DRUDY
School of Electrical, Electronic and Mechanical Engineering: Dr DAVID P. FITZPATRICK
School of English and Drama: Prof. ANDREW CARPENTER
School of Geological Sciences: Prof. PATRICK SHANNON
School of Geography, Planning and Environmental Policy: Dr JOE BRADY
School of History and Archives: Dr MICHAEL LAFFAN
School of Information and Library Studies: Prof. MARY BURKE
School of Irish, Celtic Studies, Irish Folklore and Linguistics: Prof. SÉAMAS Ó'CATHÁIN
School of Languages, Literatures and Film: Ms CLÍONA DE BHALDRAITHE MARSH
School of Law: Prof. PAUL O'CONNOR
School of Mathematical Sciences: Prof. ADRIAN OTTEWILL
School of Medicine and Medical Science: Prof. WILLIAM POWDERLY
School of Music: Dr WOLFGANG MARX
School of Nursing, Midwifery and Health Systems: Dr MARIE CARNEY
School of Philosophy: Dr GERARD CASEY
School of Physics: Prof. GERRY O'SULLIVAN
School of Physiotherapy and Performance Science: Dr CATHERINE BLAKE
School of Politics and International Relations: Prof. ATTRACTA INGRAM
School of Psychology: Dr BARBARA DOOLEY
School of Public Health and Population Science: Prof. CECILY KELLEHER
School of Social Justice: Dr SARA CANTILLON
School of Sociology: Dr KIERAN ALLEN

PROFESSORS

(Many professors are members of more than one faculty; entry here is shown under one faculty only)

College of Arts and Celtic Studies (Newman Building, Belfield, Dublin 4; tel. (1) 7168101; e-mail artsceltic@ucd.ie):

BARNES, J. C., Italian
BARTLETT, T., Modern Irish History
BREATNACH, P. A., Classical Irish
CALDICOTT, C. E. J., French
CLAYTON, M., Old and Middle English
CRUICKSHANK, D. W., Spanish
FANNING, J. R., Modern History
KIBERD, D., Anglo-Irish Literature and Drama
MCCARTHY, M. J., History of Art
MAYS, J. C. C., Modern English and American Literature
MEIKLE, J. L., American Studies
NÍ CATHÁIN, M. P., Early (incl. Medieval) Irish Language and Literature
Ó CATHÁIN, S., Irish Folklore
RAFTERY, B., Celtic Archaeology
RIDLEY, H. M., German
SMITH, A., Classics
WATSON, S., Modern Irish Language and Literature
WHITE, H., Music

College of Business and Law (Carysfort Ave, Blackrock,, Dublin 4; tel. (1) 7168852; fax (1) 7168954):

BOURKE, P., Banking and Finance
BRADLEY, M. F., International Marketing
BRENNAN, N., Management
CASEY, J. P., Law
DEEGAN, A., Management Information Systems
HOURIHAN, A. P., Management of Financial Institutions
KELLY, W. A., Business Administration
LAMBKIN, M. V., Marketing
O'BRIEN, F. J., Accountancy
OSBOROUGH, W. N., Jurisprudence and Legal History
ROCHE, W. K., Industrial Relations and Human Resources
WALSH, E., Accounting

College of Engineering, Mathematical and Physical Sciences (UCD Engineering and Materials Science Centre, Belfield, Dublin 4; tel. (1) 7161864; fax (1) 7161155; e-mail engscience@ucd.ie):

BOLAND, P.
BRAZIL, T.
BYRNE, G., Mechanical Engineering
DINEEN, S.
GARDINER, S. J.
GRUNEWALD, M.
IVANKOVIC, A.
KEALY, L., Architecture
LYNCH, P.
MACELROY, J. M. D.
O'BRIEN, E. J., Civil Engineering
OTTEWILL, A.
SHANNON, P. M.
SMYTH, B.

College of Human Sciences (Newman Building (Room G210), Belfield, Dublin 4; tel. (1) 7168619; fax (1) 7168355; e-mail mary .buckley@ucd.ie):

BENSON, C., Psychology
BOLAND, P. J., Statistics
BURKE, M., Library and Information Studies
BUTTIMER, A., Geography
DINEEN, S., Mathematics
DRUDY, S., Education
GARVIN, T. C., Politics
LAFFAN, B., European Politics
LAFFEY, T. J., Mathematics
MENNELL, S., Sociology
MORAN, D., Philosophy
NEARY, J. P., Political Economy
OUHALLA, J., Linguistics
WALSH, B. M., National Economics of Ireland and Applied Economics

College of Life Sciences (Belfield, Dublin 4; tel. (1) 7162684; fax (1) 7162685; e-mail life-sciences@ucd.ie):

BAIRD, A., Veterinary Physiology and Biochemistry
BANNIGAN, J. G., Anatomy
BELLENGER, C. R., Veterinary Surgery
BOLAND, M. P., Animal Husbandry
BRADY, H. R., Medicine and Therapeutics
BRESNIHAN, B., Rheumatology
BURY, G., General Practice
CARRINGTON, S., Veterinary Anatomy
CASEY, P. R., Clinical Psychiatry
COLLINS, J. D., Farm Animal Clinical Studies
CURRY, J., Agricultural Zoology
CUSACK, D. A., Legal Medicine
DAWSON, K. A., Physical Chemistry
DERVAN, P. A., Pathology
DRUMM, B., Paediatrics
DUKE, E., Zoology
ENGEL, P. C., Biochemistry
ENNIS, J. T., Radiology
FITZGERALD, M. X., Medicine
FITZPATRICK, C., Child and Adolescent Psychiatry
FITZPATRICK, J. M., Surgery
GARDINER, J. J., Forestry
GREEN, A., Medical Genetics.
HALL, W. W., Medical Microbiology
HEGARTY, A. F., Organic Chemistry
HENNERTY, M. J., Horticulture
JONES, B. R., Small Animal Clinical Studies
KEANE, M., Computer Science
KENNEDY, M. J., Geology
MACERLEAN, D. P., Radiology
MCKENNA, B., Food Science
MCKENNA, T. J., Investigative Endocrinology
MCNICHOLAS, F., Child and Adolescent Psychiatry
MORIARTY, D. C., Anaesthesiology
O'BRIEN, C., Ophthalmology
O'CALLAGHAN, E., Mental Health Research
O'HERLIHY, C., Obstetrics and Gynaecology
O'HIGGINS, N. J., Surgery
POWELL, D., Investigative Endocrinology
QUINN, P. J., Veterinary Microbiology and Parasitology
ROCHE, J. F., Animal Husbandry and Production
RYAN, M. P., Pharmacology
SHEAHAN, B., Veterinary Pathology
STEER, M., Botany
TREACY, M. M., Nursing
WALSH, E., Crop Science

ATTACHED SCHOOL

Michael Smurfit Graduate School of Business: Dean Dr DAMIEN MCLOUGHLIN.

National University of Ireland, Galway

Galway
Telephone: (91) 524411
Fax: (91) 525700
Internet: www.nuigalway.ie

Founded 1845 as Queen's College, Galway; became University College, Galway in 1908; present name 1997
Languages of instruction: English, Irish
Academic year: September to June

President: Dr I. Ó MUIRCHEARTAIGH
Deputy President: Prof. J. BROWNE
Vice-Presidents: Prof. G. HURLEY MARY O'RIORDAN, Prof. J. J. WARD
Secretary for Academic Affairs: Dr S. MAC MATHÚNA
Bursar: Dr MARY DOOLEY

Library: see Libraries and Archives
Number of teachers: 550
Number of students: 15,000

DEANS

Faculty of Arts: Prof. J. MARSHALL
Faculty of Celtic Studies: Dr M. NÍ DHONNCHADHA
Faculty of Commerce: Prof. R. GREEN
Faculty of Engineering: Prof. P. O'DONOGHUE
Faculty of Law: G. QUINN
Faculty of Medicine: Dr P. A. CARNEY
Faculty of Science: Dr P. MORGAN

PROFESSORS

Faculties of Arts and Celtic Studies:

BARRY, K., English
BRADLEY, D., Spanish
CANNY, N. P., History
CURTIN, C. A., Political Science and Sociology
ERSKINE, A. W., Classics
JAMES, J., Psychology
MAC CRAITH, M., Modern Irish
NÍ DHONNCHADHA, M., Old and Middle Irish and Celtic Philology
O'BRIEN, C., Italian
Ó GORMAILE, P., French
RICHARDSON, W., German
SCHMIDT-HANISSA, H., German
STROHMAYER, U., Geography
WADDELL, J., Archaeology
WORNER, M. H., Philosophy

Faculty of Commerce:

COLLINS, J. F., Accountancy and Finance
CUDDY, M. P., Economics
GREEN, R. H., Management
WARD, J. J., Marketing

Faculty of Engineering:

CUNNANE, C., Hydrology
LYONS, G. J., Information Technology
MCNAMARA, J. F., Mechanical Engineering
O'DONOGHUE, P. E., Civil Engineering
WILCOX, D., Electronic Engineering

Faculty of Law:

O'MALLEY, W. A., Business Law
QUINN, G., Law
SCHABAS, W., Human Rights Law

Faculty of Medicine:

CALLAGY, G., Pathology
CORMICAN, M., Bacteriology
DOCKERY, P., Anatomy
KERIN, M., Surgery
LOFTUS, B. G., Paediatrics
MCCARTHY, P. A., Radiology
MCDONAGH, C., Psychiatry
MORRISON, J., Obstetrics and Gynaecology
MURPHY, A., General Practice
O'BRIEN, T., Medicine

Faculty of Science:

BUTLER, R., Chemistry
COLLERAN, E., Microbiology
GUIRY, M. D. R., Botany
HINDE, J. P., Statistics
HURLEY, T. C., Mathematics
KANE, M. T., Physiology
LOWNES, N., Biochemistry
RICHARDSON, W., Spanish
RYAN, P. A., Geology
SMITH, T. J., Biomedical Engineering and Science
WALTON, P. W., Applied Physics

National University of Ireland, Maynooth

Maynooth, Co. Kildare
Telephone: (1) 7086000
E-mail: admissions@nuim.ie
Internet: www.nuim.ie

Founded 1795 as St Patrick's College, Maynooth, which divided in 1997 into National University of Ireland, Maynooth, and a continuing St Patrick's College, Maynooth
State control
Languages of instruction: Irish, English
Academic year: September to June

President: Prof. JOHN G. HUGHES
Vice-President (Planning and Governance): Dr F. J. MULLIGAN
Registrar: DAVID REDMOND
Librarian: AGNES NELIGAN

Library: see Libraries and Archives
Number of teachers: 200
Number of students: 5,500

Publications: *Archivium Hibernicum* (annually), *Irisleabhar Mhá Nuad* (annually), *Maynooth University Record* (annually), *Social Studies* (4 a year)

DEANS

Faculty of Arts: Dr PETER DENMAN
Faculty of Celtic Studies: Dr TADHG Ó DÚSHLÁINE
Faculty of Engineering: Prof. JOHN RINGWOOD
Faculty of Philosophy: Rev. Prof. JAMES MCEVOY
Faculty of Science: Dr R. O'NEILL.

RECOGNIZED COLLEGES OF THE UNIVERSITY

Institute of Public Administration: 57–61 Lansdowne Rd, Ballsbridge, Dublin 4; tel. (1) 2403600; fax (1) 6689135; e-mail information@ipa.ie; internet www.ipa.ie; 1,500 individual mems, corporate mems; library of 40,000 vols, 300 periodicals; 1,400 students; Dir-Gen. JOHN CULLEN; publ. *Administration* (quarterly), *Administration Yearbook & Diary* (annually), *Personnel & Industrial Relations Directory* (every two years).

Milltown Institute of Theology and Philosophy: Milltown Park, Ranelagh, Dublin 6; tel. (1) 2698388; fax (1) 2692528; e-mail info@milltown-institute.ie; internet www .milltown-institute.ie; Pres. Dr BRIAN GROGAN.

National College of Art and Design: 100 Thomas St, Dublin 8; tel. (1) 6364200; fax (1) 6364207; e-mail fios@ncad.ie; internet www .ncad.ief. 1746; faculties of design, education, fine art and history of art and design and complementary studies; 75 ; 750 students; Dir COLM Ó BRIAIN

HEADS OF FACULTIES

Design: Prof. ANGELA WOODS
Education: Prof. GARY GRANVILLE
Fine Art: Prof. BRIAN MAGUIRE
History of Art and Design and Complementary Studies: Prof. JOHN TURPIN

Royal College of Surgeons in Ireland: 123 St Stephens Green, Dublin 2; tel. (1) 4022100; e-mail info@rcsi.ie; internet www .rcsi.ief. 1784; faculties of dentistry, nursing, radiology, sports and exercise medicine; college of anaesthetists; 125 teachers; 900 students; Chief Exec. and Registrar MICHAEL HORGAN; publ. *Journal* (quarterly)

DEANS OF POSTGRADUATE FACULTIES

Faculty of Dentistry: SEAN SHERIDAN
Faculty of Nursing: Prof. SEAMUS COWMAN (Head)
Faculty of Radiologists: Dr ÉAMANN BREATNACH
Faculty of Sports Science and Exercise Medicine: Dr MICHAEL G. MOLLOY
College of Anaesthetists: Prof. HOWARD FEE (Pres.)

PROFESSORS

BOUCHIER-HAYES, D., Surgery
CAHILL, K. M., Tropical Medicine
COLLINS, P. B., Biochemistry
COLLUM, L., Ophthalmology
CUNNINGHAM, A., Anaesthesia
DINAN, T., Psychiatry
DOHERTY, J., Physiology
GILL, D. G., Paediatrics
GRAHAM, I., Epidemiology and Preventive Medicine
HARBISON, J., Forensic Medicine and Toxicology
HARRISON, R., Obstetrics and Gynaecology
HUMPHRIES, H., Microbiology
LEADER, M., Pathology
LYONS, J. B., History of Medicine
MCELVANEY, N., Medicine
MCGEE, H., Psychology
MONKHOUSE, S., Anatomy
NOLAN, K., Chemistry
O'BOYLE, C., Psychology
SHANNON, W., General Practice
WADDINGTON, J., Clinical Neuroscience
WALSH, M., Otolaryngology

St Angela's College of Education: Lough Gill, Sligo; tel. (71) 9143580; fax (71) 9144585; e-mail mcapilitan@stacs.edu.ie; internet college.stangelas.ie; undergraduate courses in education, home economics and nursing; Pres. Dr ANNE TAHENY.

Shannon College of Hotel Management: Shannon International Airport, Shannon, Co. Limerick; tel. (61) 712210; fax (61) 475160; internet www.shannoncollege.com; Dir PHILLIP SMYTH.

UNIVERSITY OF LIMERICK

Limerick
Telephone: (61) 202700
Fax: (61) 330316
Internet: www.ul.ie

Founded 1972 as National Institute for Higher Education, Limerick; University status 1989
State control
Language of instruction: English
Academic year: September to May

President and Vice-Chancellor: Prof. ROGER G. H. DOWNER
Vice-President (Academic) and Registrar: Prof. DON BARRY
Vice-President (Administration) and Secretary: JOHN O'CONNOR
Vice-President (External Affairs): Prof. NOEL WHELAN
Vice-President (Research): Prof. VINCENT CUNNANE
Director, Human Resources: ANNA DOUGHAN

Library of 330,000 vols
Number of teachers: 554
Number of students: 10,500

Publications: *Degree Programmes* (undergraduate brochure, annually), *President's Report* (annually), *Prospectus: postgraduate* (every 2 years), *Prospectus: undergraduate* (annually)

DEANS

College of Education: Dr JOHN O'BRIEN (acting)
College of Engineering: Prof. HUW LEWIS
College of Humanities: Prof. PAT O'CONNOR
College of Informatics and Electronics: Prof. CYRIL BURKLEY
College of Science: Prof. DAVID O'BEIRNE
Kemmy Business School: Prof. DONAL DINEEN
Graduate Studies: Prof. NICHOLAS REES
Teaching and Learning: Dr SARAH MOORE

HEADS OF DEPARTMENTS

College of Education (tel. (61) 202252; fax (61) 331673; e-mail brigeteclancy@ul.ie; internet www.ul.ie/education):

Education and Professional Studies: TOM GEARY
Primary-Level Education: JAMES DEEGAN

College of Engineering (tel. (61) 202421; fax (61) 202567; e-mail huw.lewis@ul.ie; internet www.ul.ie/~engineer):

Manufacturing and Operations Engineering: Prof. PAT PHELAN
Materials Science and Technology: Prof. CONLETH HUSSEY
Mechanical and Aeronautical Engineering: Prof. MICHAEL MCCARTHY

College of Humanities (tel. (61) 202329; fax (61) 202602; e-mail pat.oconnor@ul.ie; internet www.humanities.ul.ie):

Arts: Dr JOHN HAYES

History: Dr Bernadette Whelan
Languages and Cultural Studies: Martin Chappell
Law: Prof. Paul McCutcheon
Politics and Public Administration: Dr Neil Robinson
Sociology: Brian Keary

College of Informatics and Electronics (tel. (61) 202784; fax (61) 202561; internet www.ul.ie/~informat):

Computer Science and Information Systems: Prof. Tony Cahill
Electronic and Computer Engineering: Dr Elfred Lewis
Mathematics and Statistics: Dr Alan Hegarty

College of Science (tel. (61) 202845; fax (61) 202602; internet www.ul.ie/~science):

Chemical and Environmental Science: Prof. Richard Moles
Life Sciences: Prof. Sean Arkins
Nursing and Midwifery: Bernie Quillinan
Occupational Therapy: Dr Elizabeth McKay
Physical Education and Sports Science: Dr Alan Donnelly
Physics: Dr George McClelland
Physiotherapy: Dr Ann Taylor
Speech and Language Therapy: Prof. Sue Franklin

Kemmy Business School (tel. (61) 202116; fax (61) 336559; e-mail lynn.odoherty@ul.ie; internet www.ul.ie/business):

Accounting and Finance: Philip O'Regan
Economics: Prof. Bernadette Andreosso-O'Callaghan
Management and Marketing: Dr Fergal McGrath
Personnel and Employment Relations: Joseph Wallace

ATTACHED INSTITUTES

Advanced Manufacturing Technology: attached to College of Informatics and Electronics; Dir Prof. Eamonn Murphy, Prof. Khalil Arshak.

Advanced Manufacturing Technology (AMT) Ireland: attached to College of Engineering; Dir Dr Mark Whelan.

Automation Research Centre: attached to College of Engineering; Dir Hassan Kaghazchi.

Biomedical Environmental Sensor Technology (BEST): attached to College of Science; Dir Dr Vincent Casey.

CAMET Centre for Advance of Mathematical Education in Technology: attached to College of Informatics and Electronics; Dir Prof. John O'Donoghue.

Centre for Applied Language Studies: attached to College of Humanities; Dir Prof. Angela Chambers.

Centre for Biomedical Electronics: attached to College of Informatics and Electronics; Dir Dr Gerard Lyons.

Centre for Computational Musicology and Computer Music: attached to College of Informatics and Electronics; Dir Dr Donnacha O'Maidin.

Centre for Criminal Justice: attached to College of Humanities; Dir Prof. Dermot Walsh.

Centre for Entrepreneurial Studies: attached to Kemmy Business School; Dir Prof. Patricia Fleming.

Centre for European Studies: attached to College of Humanities; Dir Prof. Eddie Moxon Browne.

Centre for Historical Research: attached to College of Humanities; Dir Prof. Anthony McElligott, Dr Deirdre McMahon.

Centre for Industrial and Applied Mathematics: attached to College of Informatics and Electronics; Dir Prof. Frank Hodnett.

Centre for Information and Knowledge Management: attached to Kemmy Business School; Dir Dr Fergal McGrath.

Centre for Irish-German Studies: attached to College of Humanities; Dir Dr Joachim Fischer, Dr Gisela Holfter.

Centre for Peace and Development Studies: attached to College of Humanities; Dir Dr Neil Robinson (acting).

Centre for Project Management: attached to Kemmy Business School; Dir Terence O'Donnell.

Centre for Research in Industrial Biochemistry: attached to College of Science; Dir Prof. Tony Pembroke.

Centre for Sports Research: attached to College of Science; Dir Prof. Philip Jakeman.

Circuits and System Research Centre (CSRC): attached to College of Informatics and Electronics; Dirs Prof. Phil Burton, Prof. Oliver McCarthy.

Composites Research Centre: attached to College of Engineering; Dirs Prof. Michael McCarthy, Dr Trevor Young.

Computational Intelligence Group: attached to College of Informatics and Electronics; Dir Dr Malachy Eaton, Dr John Kinsella.

Control and Instrumentational Systems Group: attached to College of Informatics and Electronics; Dir Dan Toal.

Curriculum Development Unit: attached to Faculty of Education; Dir Dr David O'Grady.

Curriculum Development, Evaluation and Policy Research Unit: attached to Faculty of Education; Dir Dr Jim Gleeson.

Data Communication Security Laboratory: attached to College of Informatics and Electronics; Dir Prof. Tom Coffey.

Educational Media Research Centre: attached to College of Informatics and Electronics; Dir Tim Hall.

Education Practice Research Unit: attached to Faculty of Education; Dir Prof. Diarmuid Leonard.

Employment Relations Research Unit: attached to Kemmy Business School; Dir Prof. Paddy Gunnigle.

Environmental Research Centre: attached to College of Science; Dir Prof. Richard Moles.

Euro-Asia Research Centre: attached to Kemmy Business School; Dir Prof. Bernadette Andreosso.

Food Science Research Centre: attached to College of Science; Dir Prof. David O'Beirne.

Graduate Centre of Business: attached to Kemmy Business School; Dir Dr Michael Morley.

Growth and Development Research Centre: attached to College of Science; Dir Dr Alan Donnelly.

Human Resource Management Research Group: attached to Kemmy Business School; Dir Prof. Patrick Flood.

Interaction Design Centre: attached to College of Informatics and Electronics; Dir Prof. Liam Bannon.

International Equine Institute: attached to College of Science; Dir Prof. Sean Arkins, Frank McGourty.

Irish Natural Resources Research Centre: attached to College of Humanities and College of Science; Dir Prof. Richard Moles.

Irish World Music Centre: attached to College of Humanities; Dir Prof. Michael O'Sulleabhain.

John Holland Research Centre: attached to College of Engineering; Dir Dr Patrick Frawley, Dr Andrew Niven.

Lightwave Technology Research Centre: attached to College of Engineering; Dir Prof. Con Hussey.

Localisation Research Centre: attached to College of Informatics and Electronics; Dir Reinhard Schaler.

Magnetic Research Laboratory Group: attached to College of Science; Dir Dr I. A. Rahman.

Marketing Centre for Small Business: attached to Kemmy Business School; Dir Mark O'Connell.

Materials Ireland Research Centre: attached to College of Engineering; Dirs Prof. Stuart Hampshire, Deidre O'Reilly.

Materials and Surface Science Research Institute: attached to College of Engineering; Dir Dr Edmond Magner.

Microelectronics and Semiconductor Research Group: attached to College of Informatics and Electronics; Dir Prof. Khalil Arshak.

National Centre for Environmental Education: attached to Faculty of Education; Dir Dr Roland Tormey.

National Centre for Quality Management and Statistical Analysis: attached to Kemmy Business School and College of Informatics and Electronics; Dir Prof. Eamonn Murphy.

National Centre for Tourism Policy Studies: attached to Kemmy Business School; Dir Jim Deegan.

Optical Fibre Communications and Sensors Group: attached to College of Informatics and Electronics; Dirs Dr Michael Connolly, Dr Elfed Lewis.

Power Electronics Ireland and Analog Design (PEI) Technologies: attached to College of Informatics and Electronics; Dirs Prof. Phil Burton, Alan Dunne.

Ralahine Centre for Utopian Studies: attached to College of Humanities; Dir Prof. Tom Moylan.

Schools Information Centre on the Irish Chemical Industry: attached to College of Science; Dir Dr Peter Childs.

Stoke Research Institute (Fluid Dynamics): attached to College of Engineering; Dirs Prof. Mark Davies, Tara Dalton.

Sustainable Agriculture Research Centre: attached to College of Science; Dir Dr George Mullen.

Telecommunication Research Centre: attached to College of Informatics and Electronics; Dir Dr Martin O'Droma.

University-Level Institutions

DUBLIN INSTITUTE FOR ADVANCED STUDIES

10 Burlington Rd, Dublin 4
Telephone: (1) 6140100
Fax: (1) 6680561
E-mail: registrarsoffice@admin.dias.ie
Internet: www.dias.ie
Founded 1940

Chairman of Council: Prof. D. M. X. DONNELLY
Registrar: CECIL KEAVENEY.

CONSTITUENT SCHOOLS

School of Celtic Studies: Chair. Prof. B. Ó MADAGÁIN

SENIOR PROFESSORS

BREATNACH, L.
KELLY, F.
Ó MURCHÚ, M.

School of Cosmic Physics: Chair. Prof. G. WRIXON

SENIOR PROFESSORS

DRURY, L. O'C.
JONES, A. G.
MEURS, E. J. A.

School of Theoretical Physics: Chair. Sir M. ATIYAH

SENIOR PROFESSORS

DORLAS, T. C.
NAHM, W.
O'CONNOR, D.

ROYAL COLLEGE OF PHYSICIANS OF IRELAND

2nd Fl., International House, 20–22 Lower Hatch St, Dublin 2
Telephone: (1) 6616677
Fax: (1) 6762920
E-mail: info@rcpi.ie
Internet: www.rcpi.ie

Founded 1654

President: Prof. T. J. MCKENNA
Registrar: Prof. N. G. MCELVANEY
Secretary: J. W. BAILEY

Faculties of obstetrics and gynaecology, paediatrics, public health medicine, occupational medicine, pathology; awards a Fellowship, a Membership, and a Diploma in Obstetrics and Women's Health.

Institutes of Technology

Athlone Institute of Technology: Dublin Rd, Athlone, Co. Westmeath; tel. (902) 24400; fax (902) 24417; internet www.ait.ie; f. 1970; two-year Nat. Certificate courses, three- and one-year Nat. Diploma courses, four-year degree/professional courses, one-year post-Diploma degree courses, graduate Diploma courses, master's degree courses, postgraduate research; library: 50,000 vols; 300 teachers; 4,000 students; Dir Prof. CIARÁN Ó CATHÁIN; Registrar Dr JOSEPH RYAN

HEADS OF SCHOOLS

Business Studies: J. CUSACK
Engineering: A. HANLEY
Humanities and Hospitality Studies: Dr M. FITZGIBBON
Science: Dr P. TOMKINS

Cork Institute of Technology: Rossa Ave, Cork; tel. (21) 326100; fax (21) 545343; f. 1912; library: 65,000 vols, 550 periodicals; 1,050 teachers; 12,200 students; Dir P. KELLEHER; Registrar B. GOGGIN

HEADS OF DEPARTMENTS

Applied Physics and Instrumentation: Dr E. M. CASHELL
Biological Sciences: Dr J. O'MULLANE
Building and Civil Engineering: L. F. HODNETT
Business Studies: T. J. RIGNEY
Chemical and Process Engineering: J. T. O'SHEA
Chemistry: Dr J. O. WOOD
Electrical and Electronics Engineering: L. J. M. POLAND
Mathematics and Computing: Dr B. J. BRENDAN MURPHY
Mechanical and Manufacturing Engineering: D. A. FITZPATRICK
Nautical Studies: D. C. BURKE
Printing, Graphics and Editorial Studies: D. POWER
Social and General Studies: D. A. COURTNEY
Tourism and Catering Studies: J. KILLILEA
Transport and Automobile Engineering: D. DEMPSEY
Continuing Adult Education: P. MAHONY.

Attached centres:

Centre for Advanced Manufacturing and Management Systems: Dir M. COTTERELL.
Centre for Clean Technology: Dir D. CUNNINGHAM.
Centre for Educational Opportunities: Dir M. BERMINGHAM.
Centre for Innovation in Education: Dir R. P. COUGHLAN.
Centre for Nautical Enterprise: Dir G. TRANT.
Centre for Surface and Interface Analysis: Dirs E. M. CASHELL, L. MCDONNELL.

Constituent schools:

Cork School of Music: Union Quay, Cork; tel. (21) 270076; fax (21) 276595; f. 1878; Principal G. SPRATT.
Crawford College of Art and Design: Sharman Crawford St, Cork; tel. (21) 966343; fax (21) 962767; f. 1884; Principal GEOFFREY STEINER-SCOTT.

Dublin Institute of Technology: Fitzwilliam House, 30 Upper Pembroke St, Dublin 2; tel. (1) 4023000; fax (1) 4023399; internet www.dit.ie; f. 1978 by bringing together six established colleges; formally established 1993; academic year September to June; 1,500 (incl. part-time); 25,000 (incl. part-time); President Prof. B. NORTON; Director of Academic Affairs Dr F. MCMAHON; Director of Finance R. WILLS; Director of Human Resources D. CAGNEY; Director of Research and Enterprise Dr D. GLYNN; Registrar Dr T. DUFF

DIRECTORS OF FACULTIES

Faculty of Applied Arts: Dr E. HAZELKORN
Faculty of the Built Environment: Prof. J. RATCLIFFE
Faculty of Business: P. O'SULLIVAN
Faculty of Engineering: Dr M. MURPHY
Faculty of Science: Dr M. HUSSEY
Faculty of Tourism and Food: Dr M. MULVEY

HEADS OF SCHOOLS

Faculty of Applied Arts (Rathmines Rd, Dublin 6):
School of Art, Design and Printing: J. O'CONNER
School of Conservatory of Music and Drama: B. GRANT
School of Languages: H. CONWAY
School of Media: Dr B. O'NEILL
School of Social Sciences and Legal Studies: Dr N. HAYES

Faculty of the Built Environment (Bolton St, Dublin 2):
School of Architecture: J. HORAN
School of Construction: P. MURRAY
School of Environmental Planning and Management: H. VAN DER KAMP
School of Real Estate and Construction Economics: T. DUNNE

Faculty of Business (Aungier St, Dublin 2):
School of Accounting and Finance: Dr T. BARRETT
School of Management: R. BURNS
School of Marketing: K. UI GHALLACHOIR
School of Retail and Services Management: J. JAMESON
Graduate Business School: Dr J. URQUHART

Faculty of Engineering (Bolton St, Dublin 1):
School of Civil and Building Services Engineering: J. TURNER
School of Manufacturing Engineering: J. LAWLOR
School of Control Systems and Electrical Engineering: Dr E. COYLE
School of Electronic and Communication Engineering: Dr G. FARRELL
School of Mechanical and Transport Engineering: Dr J. MCGOVERN

Faculty of Science (Kevin St, Dublin 8):
School of Biological Sciences: B. A. RYAN
School of Chemistry: Dr N. RUSSELL
School of Computing: Dr B. O'SHEA
School of Mathematical Sciences: Dr J. M. GOLDEN
School of Physics: Dr V. TOAL

Faculty of Tourism and Food (Cathal Brugha St, Dublin 1):
School of Culinary Arts and Food Technology: Dr J. HEGARTY
School of Food Science and Environmental Health: Dr S. CASSIDY (acting)
School of Tourism and Hospitality Management: Dr J. RUDDY (acting)

Dun Laoghaire Institute of Art, Design and Technology: Carraiglea Park, Kill Ave, Dun Laoghaire, Co. Dublin; tel. 2144600; fax 2144700; certificate, diploma and degree programmes; Dir ROISIN HOGAN; Registrar JIM DEVINE.

Dundalk Institute of Technology: Dundalk; tel. (42) 34785; fax (42) 33505; f. 1970; certificate, diploma and degree courses; library: 30,000 vols; Dir SEAN MCDONAGH; Registrar S. MCMANUS

HEADS OF SCHOOLS

Business Studies: PETER FULLER
Engineering: JOHN CONNOLLY
Science: Dr SIMON O'BRIEN

Galway-Mayo Institute of Technology: Dublin Rd, Galway; tel. (91) 753161; fax (91) 751107; internet www.gmit.ie; f. 1972; degree, diploma and certificate courses; library: 95,000 vols; 300 teachers; 9,000 students (5,000 full-time, 4,000 part-time); Dir MARION COY; Registrar BERNARD O'HARA; Librarian ANN JOYCE WALSH

HEADS OF SCHOOLS

Art, Design and Humanities: JOHN TUNNEY
Business Studies: LARRY ELWOOD
Engineering: GERARD MACMICHAEL
Hotel and Catering: STUART JAUNCEY
Science: DES FOLEY

HEADS OF CENTRES

Castlebar Campus: KATIE SWEENEY
Letterfrack Campus: MICHAEL HANNON

Institute of Technology Blanchardstown: Blanchardstown Road North, Dublin 15; tel. (1) 8851000; fax (1) 8851001; e-mail college.support@itb.ie; internet www.itb.ie; f. 1999; bachelor's and master's degrees; national certificates, national and graduate diplomas; 67 teachers; 1,060 students (626 full-time, 356 part-time, 78 apprentices); Dir Dr MARY MEANEY; publ. *Journal* (2 a year)

HEADS OF SCHOOLS

School of Business and Humanities: DES MOORE
School of Informatics and Engineering: LARRY MCNUTT

Institute of Technology Carlow: Kilkenny Rd, Carlow; tel. (59) 9170400; fax (59)

9170500; e-mail info@itcarlow.ie; internet www.itcarlow.ie; f. 1970; higher certificate, ordinary degree, honours degree and postgraduate courses; library: 25,000 vols; 200 teachers; 4,000 students; Dir Dr RUAIDHRÍ NEAVYN; Registrar BRIAN L. BENNETT

HEADS OF DEPARTMENTS

Applied Biology and Chemistry: Dr DAVID RYAN
Business and Management Studies: COLM KELLY
Computing, Physics and Mathematics: MIKE BAKER
Electronic Engineering: BRENDAN LAFFAN
Humanities and Applied Languages: MARTIN MEAGHER
Mechanical, Civil and Construction Engineering: JOHN DOYLE

Institute of Technology Sligo: Ballinode, Sligo; tel. (71) 9155222; fax (71) 9144096; internet www.itsligo.ie; f. 1970; national certificate and diploma courses; degree courses; professional courses; library: 23,000 vols; 180 teachers; 3,385 full-time students; 732 part-time students; 250 apprentices; Dir Dr RICHARD THORN

HEADS OF SCHOOLS

Business and Humanities: T. YOUNG
Engineering: B. MCCORMACK
Science: J. P. TIMPSON
Development: D. MCCONVILLE

Institute of Technology Tallaght: Tallaght, Dublin 24; tel. (1) 4042000; fax (1) 4042700; e-mail info@it-tallaght.ie; internet www.it-tallaght.ie; f. 1992; higher Certificates, ordinary bachelor degrees and honours bachelor degrees; Dir Dr TIM CREEDON; Registrar JOHN VICKERY

HEADS OF DEPARTMENTS

School of Business and Humanities: Dr DAMIEN ROCHE
School of Engineering: PAT MCLAUGHLIN
School of Science: Dr MIKE AHERN

Institute of Technology Tralee: Clash, Tralee, Co. Kerry; tel. (66) 7145600; fax (66) 7125711; e-mail info@ittralee.ie; internet www.ittralee.ie; f. 1977; full-time Nat. Certificate courses, Nat. Diploma courses, bachelor's and master's degrees and doctorates, part-time degree courses; library: 30,000 vols; 200 teachers; 4,000 students; Dir MICHAEL CARMODY; Administration Officer DICK CARMODY

HEADS OF SCHOOL

Business Studies: BRIAN O'CONNOR
Engineering: KEVIN LYNCH
Science: SEAMUS O'SHEA

Letterkenny Institute of Technology: Port Rd, Letterkenny, Co. Donegal; tel. (74) 64100; fax (74) 64111; courses at certificate, diploma and degree levels in engineering, science, design and business studies; library: 30,000 vols; 170 teachers; 1,300 students; Dir PAUL HANNIGAN; Registrar DANIEL BRENNAN

HEADS OF SCHOOLS

Business Studies: S. Ó CNÁIMHSÍ
Science: W. J. W. HINES
Engineering: C. Ó SOMACHÁIN

Limerick Institute of Technology: Moylish Park, Limerick; tel. (61) 208209; fax (61) 208209; e-mail information@lit.ie; internet www.lit.ie; f. 1852; 500 teachers; 6,000 students; Dir V. N. MCCARTHY; Registrar T. TWOMEY (acting)

HEADS OF SCHOOLS AND DEPARTMENTS

School of Art and Design: R. RUTH
School of Business: H. CHADDA (acting)
School of the Built Environment: J. HEALY (acting)
Department of Humanities: T. MANGAN
Department of Information Technology: I. KAVANAGH (acting)
Department of Electrical and Electronic Engineering: B. CALLAN
Department of Mechanical and Automobile Engineering: P. RYAN
Department of Science: F. BARRY (acting)

Tipperary Institute: Nenagh Rd, Thurles, Co. Tipperary; tel. (504) 28000; fax (504) 28001; e-mail info@tippinst.ie; internet www.tippinst.ie; f. 1998; bachelor degrees and higher certificates; library: 17,479 vols, 330 periodicals; 600 students; Chief Exec. PÁDRAIG CULBERT

HEADS OF DEPARTMENT

Department of Business: MOYA BREEN
Department of Information and Communications Technology: JAMES GREENSLADE
Department of Sustainable Rural Development: CIARAN LYNCH

Waterford Institute of Technology: Cork Rd, Waterford; tel. (51) 302000; fax (51) 378292; e-mail enquiries@wit.ie; internet www.wit.ie; f. 1969; degree courses, doctorates, Diplomas, Certificates; library: 90,000 vols, 400 periodicals; 200 full-time teachers; 10,000 students (6,000 full-time 4,000 part-time); Dir Prof. KIERAN R. BYRNE; Registrar P. DOWNEY

HEADS OF SCHOOLS

Accountancy and Business: Dr TOM O'TOOLE
Engineering: D. MORAN
Science and Information Technology: Dr E. MARTIN
Humanities: Dr J. P. ENNIS

Other Institutions of Higher Education

National College of Ireland: Sandford Rd, Ranelagh, Dublin 6; tel. (1) 4060504; fax (1) 44972200; e-mail info@ncirl.ie; internet www.ncirl.ie; f. 1951; 30 teachers; 4,000 students; Ph.D., master's degree, diploma and certificate courses, full-time and part-time; also short courses; specialist areas: human resource management, personnel management, industrial relations, trade union studies, accountancy, business management, languages and European studies, computing, information technology law, management of change, leadership, community-based learning; Pres. Prof. JOYCE O'CONNOR.

St Patrick's College: Maynooth, Co. Kildare; tel. (1) 6285222; fax (1) 6289063; f. 1795; comprises National Seminary and Pontifical University; Bachelor's, Master's and Doctoral degrees, and Diplomas and Licentiates; library: 65,000 vols; 24 teachers; 392 students; Pres. Mgr DERMOT FARRELL.

Schools of Art and Music

National College of Art and Design: see under National University of Ireland–Recognized Colleges of the University.

ROYAL IRISH ACADEMY OF MUSIC

36 Westland Row, Dublin 2
Telephone: (1) 6764412
Fax: (1) 6622798
E-mail: info@riam.iol.ie

Founded 1848, incorporated 1889
Director: JOHN O'CONOR
Secretary: DOROTHY SHIEL
Registrar: TONY MADIGAN
Number of teachers: 75
Number of students: 1,000.

ISRAEL

The Higher Education System

The earliest institutions of higher education were founded when Palestine was a province of the Ottoman Turkish Empire, and tended to be religious, technical or arts schools. The oldest specialist institution is the Etz Hayim, General Talmud, Torah and Grand Teshivah (founded 1847), and the oldest university-level institution is Technion—Israel Institute of Technology (founded 1912; inaugurated 1924). Following the First World War (1914–18) Palestine became a League of Nations mandate under British administration and increased Jewish immigration led to the expansion of the higher education sector: the Hebrew University of Jerusalem was founded in 1918 and inaugurated in 1925. The Arab and Jewish communities began to develop parallel forms of communal government, including separate education systems. In May 1948 the United Kingdom terminated its Palestinian mandate, and an independent Jewish State of Israel was declared. Several university-level institutions were established shortly after, including the Weizmann Institute of Science (founded 1949), Bar-Ilan University (founded 1953; inaugurated 1955) and Tel-Aviv University (founded 1953; inaugurated 1956). In addition to the eight universities, other institutions of higher education include colleges and higher institutes. The Council for Higher Education Law (1958) established the Council for Higher Education to oversee Israeli higher education, including accreditation of institutions and quality assurance. There is a three stage process of accreditation. First, the institution is allowed to advertise programmes of study, invite applications from students and start teaching courses; however, the institution is not allowed to award degrees or other qualifications. Secondly, an institution is permitted to be opened and maintained as a provisional institution of higher education but without accreditation and without awarding the relevant qualifications. Thirdly, and finally, the institution is accredited as an institution of higher education and authorized to award degrees.

The school leavers' certificate or bagrut (matriculation) is the main criteria for admission to higher education. Applicants may also be required to undergo psychometric testing and attend a personal interview, depending on the institution. The Bachelors degree is the standard university-level undergraduate qualification, and the course usually lasts three years. However, some disciplines require longer periods of study, such as nursing (four years) and medicine (six years). Bachelors degrees from non-university institutions, usually Colleges and Higher Institutes, tend to be awarded in conjunction with a professional title or indicate the area of specialization. The first postgraduate-level degree is the Masters, a one- to two-year programme of study that may or may not include a thesis component. A Masters with a thesis component (Type A) allows admission to doctoral studies; a Masters without a thesis (Type B) does not. The second (and highest) postgraduate qualification is the Doctorate (most commonly a PhD) and lasts two years.

Technical and vocational education at the post-secondary level is offered by technical colleges and non-university institutions of higher education. The first qualification at this level is the Technai (Qualified Technician), which lasts one year. The other main qualification is the Handassai (Practical Engineer), which is divided into two tracks, Type A and Type B. Handassai (Type A) is a one-year programme of study, and Handassai (Type B) lasts two years. Admission to Technai and Handassai courses requires bagrut or completion of 12 years of education.

Learned Societies

GENERAL

Israel Academy of Sciences and Humanities: POB 4040, 91 040 Jerusalem; tel. (2) 5676222; fax (2) 5666059; e-mail academy@academy.ac.il; internet www.academy.ac.il; f. 1959; sections of Humanities (Chair. YOHANAN FRIEDMANN), Sciences (Chair. RAPHAEL MECHOULAM); 80 mems; Pres. Prof. MENAHEM YAARI; Vice-Pres. RUTH ARNON; Exec. Dir MEIR ZADOK.

BIBLIOGRAPHY, LIBRARY SCIENCE AND MUSEOLOGY

Israel Librarians' Association: POB 303, 61 002 Tel Aviv; f. 1952; general organization of librarians, archivists and information specialists; promotes the interests and advances the professional standards of librarians; professional and examining body; 850 mems; Chair. BENJAMIN SCHACHTER; Sec. NAAMA RAVID; publs *Yad-La-Kore* (Libraries and Archives Magazine), *Meida La Sefran*.

Israel Society of Libraries and Information Centers (ASMI): POB 28273, 97 Yaffo St (Klal House, Room 707), 91281 Jerusalem; tel. (2) 6249421; fax (2) 6249421; e-mail asmi@asmi.org.il; internet www.asmi.org.il; f. 1966 to promote the utilization of recorded knowledge by disseminating information in the fields of science, technology and the humanities, and to facilitate written and oral communication; 900 mems; Chair. SHOSHANA LANGERMAN; publs *Igeret* (6 a year), *Information and Librarianship* (2 a year).

Israeli Center for Libraries: POB 3251, 51103 Benei Berak; tel. (3) 6180151; fax (3) 5798048; e-mail icl@icl.org.il; internet www.icl.org.il; f. 1965; provides centralized processing and other services for libraries; organizes non-academic librarianship courses; Chair. JACOB AGMON; Dir ORLY ONN; publs *Yad Lakore* (annually), *Basifriyot* (monthly).

Museums Association of Israel: POB 71117, 91710 Jerusalem; tel. (2) 6708811; fax (2) 5631833; f. 1964 to foster public interest in museums and cooperation among association members; affiliated to International Council of Museums (ICOM); 55 mems; Dir Dr MARTIN WEYL.

ECONOMICS, LAW AND POLITICS

International Association of Jewish Lawyers and Jurists: 10 Daniel Frish St, 64 731 Tel-Aviv; tel. (3) 6910673; fax (3) 6953855; e-mail iajli@goldmail.net.il; internet www.intjewishlawyers.org; f. 1969 to contribute towards establishing international order based on law and the promotion of human rights; examines legal problems related to Jewish communities; holds international congresses and seminars; 10 centres (in Israel and abroad); affiliated with the World Jewish Congress (WJC); Pres. ALEX HERTMAN; Exec. Dir ARIEL AINBINDER; publ. *Justice* (quarterly).

Israel Bar: 10 Daniel Frish St, Tel-Aviv 64731; tel. (3) 6918691; fax (3) 6918696; e-mail vaadmerkazi@israelbar.org.il; internet www.israelbar.org.il; f. 1961; autonomous statutory body to incorporate and represent lawyers in Israel; 16,000 mems; Pres. Dr SHLOMO COHEN; Gen. Dir ILAH KATZ; Chair., National Council ORNA LIN; publs *Hapraklit* (monthly), *Orech Hadin* (2 a year).

Attached Organizations:

David Rotlevi National Mediation Institute of the Israel Bar: tel. (3) 6092268; fax (3) 6091641; Joint Chair. SHAY SEGAL, MOSHE TCHETCHIK.

Institute for Continuing Legal Studies: 3rd Fl., Hachashmonaim Tower, 100 Hachashmonaim St Tel Aviv 67133; tel. (3) 5616550; fax (3) 5616551; e-mail machon@israelbar.org.il; Jt Chairs Dr YORAM DANZIGER, Prof. AHARON NAMDAR.

International Association of Jewish Lawyers and Jurists Secretariat: tel. (3) 6910673; fax (3) 6953855; e-mail iajlj@goldmail.net.il; internet www.intjewishlawyers.org; Man. ARIEL AINBINDER.

Israel Political Science Association: c/o Dept of Political Studies, Bar-Ilan University, 52 900 Ramat Gan; tel. (3) 5318578; fax (3) 9234511; e-mail wilzis@ashur.cc.biu.ac.il; 100 mems; Chair. Prof. SAM LEHMAN-WILZIG; publ. *Research Newsletter*.

EDUCATION

Council for Higher Education: POB 4037, 91 040 Jerusalem; tel. (2) 5679911; fax (2) 5679955; e-mail info@che.org.il; internet www.che.org.il; f. 1958; recommends to the government the granting of licences to higher education institutes, accreditation, and authorizes awarding of degrees; 25 mems; Chair. THE MINISTER OF EDUCATION AND CULTURE; Dir-Gen. SHOSH BERLINSKY; Sec. NAFTALI WEITMAN; publ. *Report* (in Hebrew).

FINE AND PERFORMING ARTS

ACUM Ltd. (Society of Authors, Composers and Music Publishers in Israel): ACUM House, 9 Tuval St, POB 1704, Ramat Gan 52117; tel. (3) 6113400; fax (3) 6122629; e-mail acum@acum.org.il; f. 1936; copyright; promotion of music and literature; 3,500 mems; Dir-Gen. YORIK BEN-DAVID; publ. *ACUM News* (4 a year).

Israel Music Institute: 55 Menachem Begin Rd., POB 51197, 12 Ben Josef St, 52474 Ramat Gan; tel. (3) 6729747; fax (3) 5612826; e-mail musicinst@bezeqint.net; internet www.imi.org.il; f. 1961; publishes and promotes Israeli music and musicological works throughout the world; produces CDs; Israel Music Information Centre; Central Library of Israeli Music; mem. of the Int. Asscn of Music Information Centres and Int. Fed. of Serious Music Publishers; library: 2,500 scores, 2,000 audio recordings; Chair. DANIELA RABINOWITZ; Dir PAUL LANDAU; publ. *IMI News* (3 a year).

Israel Painters and Sculptors Association: 9 Alharizi St, Tel-Aviv 64244; tel. (3) 5246685; fax (3) 5226433; e-mail artassoc@netvision.net.il; f. 1934 to advance plastic arts in Israel and protect artists' interests; affiliated to the International Association of Art; organizes group exhibitions and symposia; provides assistance to immigrant artists; maintains a gallery for members' exhibitions; graphic arts workshop and materials supply store; 3 branches; 2,000 mems; Chair. RACHEL SHAVIT.

HISTORY, GEOGRAPHY AND ARCHAEOLOGY

Historical Society of Israel: POB 4179, 91041 Jerusalem; tel. (2) 5650444; fax (2) 6712388; e-mail shazar@shazar.org.il; internet www.shazar.org.il; f. 1926 to promote the study of general and Jewish history; 1,000 mems; library: Library of Jewish History, Judaica, 7,000 vols; Chair. Prof. MICHAEL HEYD; Sec.-Gen. ZVI YEKUTIEL; publs *Historia* (general history, in Hebrew, with summary in English, 2 a year), *Zion* (Jewish history, in Hebrew with summary in English, 4 a year).

Israel Antiquities Authority: POB 586, 91004 Jerusalem; tel. (2) 6204622; fax (2) 6289066; internet www.antiquities.org.il; f. 1948; govt authority; engages in archaeological excavations and surveys, inspection and preservation of antiquities and ancient sites, scientific publications; custodianship of all antiquities; Dir of Antiquities S. DORFMAN; Sec. H. MENAHEM; publs *Archaeological Survey of Israel* (irregular), *Atiqot* (irregular), *Excavations and Surveys in Israel* (2 a year).

Israel Geographical Association: c/o Dept of Geography, Bar-Ilan University, 52900 Ramat-Gan; f. 1961; 650 mems; Pres. Prof. AMIRAM GONEN; Sec. Dr GABI LIPSHITZ; publ. *Ofakim*.

Israel Prehistoric Society: POB 1502, Jerusalem; f. 1958; 100 mems; includes the 'M. Stekelis' Museum of Prehistory; Chair A. GOPHER; Sec. N. GOREN; publ. *Mitekufat Haeven* (annually).

Jerusalemer Institut der Görres-Gesellschaft (Jerusalem Institute of the Görres Society): Notre Dame of Jerusalem Center, POB 4595, Jerusalem; tel. (2) 6271170; f. 1908; fmrly Orientalisches Institut der Görres-Gesellschaft; art, history, archaeology, biblical studies, Christian iconography; library, photo archive, computerized index of Christian monuments in the Holy Land; Exec. Dir GUSTAV KÜHNEL.

LANGUAGE AND LITERATURE

Academy of the Hebrew Language: Givat Ram Campus, 91904 Jerusalem; tel. (2) 6493555; fax (2) 5617065; e-mail acad2u@vms.huji.ac.il; internet hebrew-academy.huji.ac.il; f. 1953; studies the vocabulary, structure and history of the Hebrew language and is the official authority for its devt; is compiling a historical dictionary of the Hebrew language; library: library specializing in Hebrew and Semitic languages; 44 mems (29 full, 15 advisory); Pres. Prof. M. BAR-ASHER; Chief Scientific Sec. R. GADISH; publs *Leshonenu* (quarterly), *Leshonenu La'am* (quarterly), *Zikhronot*.

Association of Religious Writers: POB 7440, Jerusalem; tel. (2) 5660478; fax (2) 5660478; f. 1963; Chair. Dr ZAHAVA BEN-DOV; publ. *Mabua*.

British Council: Crystal House, 12 Hahilazon St, Ramat Gan 52136, Tel Aviv; tel. (3) 6113600; fax (3) 6113640; e-mail bcta@britishcouncil.org.il; internet www.britishcouncil.org.il; teaching centre; offers courses and exams in English language and British culture and promotes cultural exchange with the UK; attached offices in Nazareth and West Jerusalem; Dir KEVIN LEWIS; Dir of Studies, Israel PETA SAREMBOCK.

Goethe-Institut: 15 Sokolov St, 92144 Jerusalem; tel. (2) 5610627; fax (2) 5618431; e-mail goetheje@actcom.co.il; internet www.goethe.de/om/jer/deindex.htm; offers courses and exams in German language and culture and promotes cultural exchange with Germany; attached centre in Tel Aviv; Dir DR FRIEDRICH DAHLHAUS.

Hebrew Writers Association in Israel: POB 7111, Tel-Aviv; tel. (3) 6953256; fax (3) 6919681; f. 1921; 400 mems; publ. *Moznayim* (monthly).

Instituto Cervantes: Shulamit 7, Tel Aviv 64371; tel. (3) 5279992; fax (3) 5299558; e-mail centel@cervantes.es; internet telaviv.cervantes.es; offers courses and exams in Spanish language and culture and promotes cultural exchange with Spain and Spanish-speaking Latin and Central America; library: library of 14,000 vols; Dir JUAN CARLOS VIDAL GARCÍA.

Palestinian PEN Centre: Wadi al-Juz, Al-Khaldi St 4, Jerusalem; tel. (2) 6262970; fax (2) 6264620; e-mail palpenc@palnet.com; Pres. HANAN AWWAD.

MEDICINE

Israel Gerontological Society: POB 2371, 55000 Kiryat Ono; tel. (3) 5357161; fax (3) 6359399; e-mail igs@netvision.net.il; f. 1956; 600 mems; Chair. Prof. JACOB LOMRANZ; Vice-Chair. Dr YITSHAL BERNER; publ. *Gerontology* (4 a year).

Israel Medical Association: POB 3604, 52136 Ramat Gan; located at: 35 Jabotinsky St, 2 Twin Towers, Level 11, 52136 Ramat Gan; tel. (3) 6100444; fax (3) 5751616; internet www.ima.org.il; f. 1912; Pres. Dr YORAM BLACHAR; publs *Harefuah* (every 2 weeks in Hebrew, abstracts in English), *Zman Harefuah* (in Hebrew, monthly), *Israel Medical Association Journal* (monthly).

Israel Society of Internal Medicine: Division of Medicine, Sapir Medical Centre, Meir Hospital, Kfar Sava 44281; tel. (9) 7472591; fax (9) 7472671; e-mail mlahav@post.tau.ac.il; f. 1958; four regional centres; a division of the Israel Medical Association (IMA), and affiliated to the International Society of Internal Medicine (ISIM); organizes scientific meetings and congresses; participates in the planning of postgraduate education in internal medicine and improving conditions of internal medicine practitioners; 750 mems; Chair. Prof. MORDECHAI RAVID; Sec. Dr MEIR LAHAV.

Society for Medicine and Law in Israel: POB 6451, Haifa 31063; tel. (4) 8375219; fax (4) 8381587; e-mail acarmi@research.haifa.ac.il; f. 1972; 3 branches; affiliated to the World Association for Medical Law (WAML); examines and recommends amendments to medical laws; organizes international conferences; 2,300 mems; Pres. A. CARMI; publ. *Refuah U Mishpat* (Medicine & Law, in Hebrew, 4 a year).

NATURAL SCIENCES

General

Association for the Advancement of Science in Israel: c/o Prof. M. Jammer, Dept of Physics, Bar-Ilan University, 52100 Ramat-Gan; tel. (3) 5318433; fax (3) 5353298; f. 1953; 5,200 mems; Pres. Prof. M. JAMMER; publ. *Proceedings of Congress of Scientific Societies*.

Biological Sciences

Botanical Society of Israel: c/o Dept of Biology, Technion-Israel Institute of Technology, Haifa 32000; tel. (4) 8294211; fax (4) 8225153; f. 1936; aims to promote the advancement of the fundamental and applied branches of botanical science; conducts research, organizes lectures and field work; over 300 mems; Pres. Prof. SHIMON GEPSTEIN; Sec. Prof. PETER NEWMANN.

Entomological Society of Israel: POB 6, 50 250 Bet-Dagan; tel. (3) 9683729; fax (3) 9604428; e-mail vtada@volcani.agri.gov.il; internet entymology.org.il; f. 1965 to promote, improve and disseminate the science of entomology (incl. acarology) in Israel; holds 1 full-day meeting per year; 224 mems; Pres. Prof. ADA RAFAELI; Sec. Dr VICTORIA SOROKER; publ. *Israel Journal of Entomology*.

Israel Society of Biochemistry and Molecular Biology: POB 9095, 52 190 Ramat Efal; tel. (3) 6355038; fax (3) 5351103; e-mail mrgzur@ibm.net; 350 mems; Pres. Prof. A. LEVITZKI.

Society for the Protection of Nature in Israel: 4 Hashfela St, Tel-Aviv 66183; tel. (3) 5375063; fax (3) 5377695; f. 1953 to promote nature conservation and quality of the environment; operates 24 local branches, 26 field-study centres, 7 biological information centres; research centres on birds, mammals, reptiles, insects, plants and caves; maintains close cooperation with the Nature Reserves Authority, the Environmental Protection Service and the Council for Beautiful Israel; organizes international seminars on nature conservation education; 45,000 mems; Chair. YOAV SAGI; Exec. Dir EITAN GEDALIZON; publs *Eretz Magazine* (in English, 6 a year), *Pashosh* (children's in Hebrew, monthly), *Teva Va'aretz* (Nature & Land, in Hebrew, every 2 months).

Zoological Society of Israel: c/o Dept of Zoology, Tel-Aviv University, Ramat Aviv; f. 1940; 300 mems; Chair. B. S. GALIL.

Mathematical Sciences

Israel Mathematical Union: c/o University of Haifa, Dept of Mathematics, 31905 Haifa;

fax (4) 8240024; e-mail imu@math.haifa.ac.il; f. 1953; 210 mems; Pres. Prof. J. ZAKS; Sec. Dr S. ABRAMOVICH.

Physical Sciences

Israel Chemical Society: Dept of Chemistry, Ben-Gurion University of the Negev, POB 653, 84105 Be'ersheva; tel. (7) 6461196; fax (7) 6472943; e-mail ashani@bgumail.bgu.ac.il; internet www.weizmann.ac.il/ICS; a scientific and professional association; holds two conventions each year and organizes lectures and symposia in various parts of Israel; the society represents Israel in the International Union of Pure and Applied Chemistry; Chair. Exec. Council Dr HERBERT BERNSTEIN; Gen. Sec. Dr I. BLANK.

Israel Geological Society: POB 1239, Jerusalem 91000; e-mail gsi@igs.org.il; internet www.igs.org.il; f. 1951; 400 mems; Pres. NAOMI PORAT; Sec. RONIT KESSEL; publ. *Israeli Journal of Earth Sciences*.

Israel Physical Society: c/o Dept of Physics, Bar-Ilan University, 52900 Ramat-Gan; tel. (3) 5318431; fax (3) 5353298; e-mail havlin@ophir.ph.biu.ac.il; f. 1954; 250 mems; Pres. Prof. S. HAVLIN; Sec. Prof. V. HALPERN; publs *IPS Bulletin* (annually), *Annals of the IPS*.

PHILOSOPHY AND PSYCHOLOGY

Israel Psychological Association: 74 Frishman St, POB 65244, 61 652 Tel-Aviv; tel. (3) 5239393; fax (3) 5230763; e-mail psycho@inter.net.il; f. 1958; 2,623 mems; Chair. NIRIT APELOIG-ESHKAR; publ. *Bulletin* (quarterly).

RELIGION, SOCIOLOGY AND ANTHROPOLOGY

Israel Oriental Society: The Hebrew University, Jerusalem; tel. (2) 5883633; e-mail ios49@hotmail.com; f. 1949; aims to promote interest in and knowledge of history, politics, economics, culture and life in the Middle East; arranges lectures and symposia to study all aspects of contemporary Middle Eastern, Asian and African affairs; Chair. NEHEMIA LEVTZION; Sec. NIMROD GOREN; publ. *Hamizrah Hehadash* (The New East, annually).

TECHNOLOGY

Association of Engineers and Architects in Israel: 200 Dizengoff Rd, 63 462 Tel-Aviv, POB 3082; tel. (3) 5224746; fax (3) 5220191; e-mail aeai@netvision.net.il; internet www.engineers.org.il; f. 1922; brs in Tel-Aviv, Jerusalem, Haifa, Beersheba; 20,000 mems; Pres. Prof. Y. NEEMAN; Chair. Eng. E. COHEN-KAGAN; publs *Journal of Engineering and Archaeology* (monthly, in Hebrew with English summaries), *Electrical Engineers* (6 a year), *Chemical Engineering* (6 a year).

Israel Society of Aeronautics and Astronautics: POB 2956, 61028 Tel-Aviv; f. 1951 as Israel Society of Aeronautical Sciences, merged 1968 with Israel Astronautical Society; lectures and conferences to foster the growth of aerospace science; 400 mems; Chair. DOV SA'AR; Sec. RAMI SKLEDMAN; publ. *BIAF-Israel Aviation and Space Magazine* (2 to 4 a year).

Society of Municipal Engineers of Israel: 200 Dizengoff St, Tel-Aviv; f. 1937; 120 mems; Pres. Ing. J. KOEN; Sec. Ing. J. KORNBLUM.

Research Institutes

GENERAL

Samuel Neaman Institute for Advanced Studies in Science and Technology: Technion-Israel Institute of Technology, Technion City, 32000 Haifa; tel. (4) 8237145; fax (4) 8231889; e-mail info@neaman.org.il; internet www.neaman.org.il; f. 1978; independent public policy institute researching national problems in science and technology, education, and economic, health and social development; Dir Prof. N. LIRON; publ. *Bulletin* (annually).

Technion Research and Development Foundation Ltd: Senate House, Technion City, 32000 Haifa; tel. (4) 8231219; fax (4) 8323056; f. 1952; operates Industrial Testing Laboratories (building materials, geodetic research, soils and roads, hydraulics, chemistry, metals, electro-optics, vehicles); administers sponsored research at Technion—Israel Institute of Technology (see under Universities) in aeronautical, agricultural, biomedical, chemical, civil, computer, electrical, food and biotechnology, industrial, management and mechanical engineering; biology, chemistry, mathematics, and physics (sciences); and architecture and town planning, education in technology and science, general studies, medicine; 22 subsidiaries in fields of electronics, energy, agriculture, food and medicine; Man. Dir Prof. ZVI KOHAVI.

AGRICULTURE, FISHERIES AND VETERINARY SCIENCE

Agricultural Research Organization: Volcani Center, POB 6, 50250 Bet-Dagan; tel. (3) 9683111; fax (3) 9665327; e-mail research@volcani.agri.gov.il; internet www.agri.gov.il; f. 1921; fundamental and applied research in agriculture; numerous scientific projects at 7 institutes and 3 experiment stations; part of the Min. of Agriculture; library of 30,000 vols and periodicals; Dir Dr ELI PUTIEVSKY; publs *Israel Agresearch* (Hebrew with English summaries and captions), *Bulletin*.

Attached institutes:

Institute of Agricultural Engineering: c/o Agricultural Research Organization, Volcani Center, POB 6, 50250 Bet-Dagan; tel. (3) 9683303; fax (3) 9604704; internet www.agri.gov.il; Dir Dr BOAZ ZION.

Institute of Animal Science: c/o Agricultural Research Organization, Volcani Center, POB 6, 50250 Bet-Dagan; tel. (8) 9484400; fax (8) 9475075; internet www.agri.gov.il; Dir Dr BRUCKENTAL ISRAEL.

Institute of Field and Garden Crops: c/o Agricultural Research Organization, Volcani Center, POB 6, 50250 Bet-Dagan; tel. (3) 9683482; fax (3) 9669642; e-mail vcfield@volcani.agri.gov.il; internet www.agri.gov.il; Dir Prof. YORAM KAPULNIK.

Institute of Horticulture: c/o Agricultural Research Organization, Volcani Center, POB 6, 50250 Bet-Dagan; tel. (3) 9683405; fax (3) 9669583; internet www.agri.gov.il; Dir Dr ELI TOMER.

Institute of Plant Protection: c/o Agricultural Research Organization, Volcani Center, POB 6, 50250 Bet-Dagan; tel. (3) 9683530; fax (3) 9683543; internet www.agri.gov.il; Dir Dr Y. BEN-YEPHET.

Institute of Soils and Water: c/o Agricultural Research Organization, Volcani Center, POB 6, 50250 Bet-Dagan; tel. (3) 9683272; fax (3) 9604017; internet www.agri.gov.il; Dir Dr Y. COHEN.

Institute for Technology and the Storage of Agricultural Products: c/o Agricultural Research Organization, Volcani Center, POB 6, 50250 Bet-Dagan; tel. (3) 9683588; internet www.agri.gov.il; Dir Dr DOV PRUSKY.

Beth Gordon, A. D. Gordon Agriculture, Nature and Kinnereth Valley Study Institute: Deganya A, 15 120 Emeq Ha-Yarden; tel. (6) 750040; f. 1935; inaugurated 1941; regional and research centre and museum of natural history and agriculture and history of the Kinneret (Lake of Galilee) Region; library of 60,000 vols; Dir S. BEN-NOAM; Curator of Archaeology Z. VINOGRADOV; Curator of Natural History S. LULAV.

ECONOMICS, LAW AND POLITICS

Institute for Counter-Terrorism (ICT): Interdisciplinary Center Herzliya, POB 167, Herzliya 46150; fax (9) 9513073; e-mail info@ict.org.il; internet www.ict.org.il; f. 1996; research into terrorism worldwide; Exec. Dir BOAZ GANOR.

Jerusalem Institute for Israel Studies: 20 Radak St, 92 186 Jerusalem; tel. (2) 5630175; fax (2) 5639814; f. 1981; independent non-profit organization to study policy issues and social, economic and political processes in Jerusalem in order to facilitate and improve public policy-making; and to study and disseminate research and environmental policy issues in Israel; Dir ORA AHIMEIR; Exec. Dir Prof. JAACOV BAR-SIMAN-TOV.

Research Institute of the Yitzhak Rabin Center for Israel Studies: 26 Chaim Levanon St, POB 17538, 61 175 Tel- Aviv; tel. (3) 6436545; fax (3) 6436546; e-mail forum@rabincenter.org.il; internet www.rabincenter.org.il; f. 1997; history, society and culture of the State of Israel; associated Rabin archive, library and museum; Head of Research Institute Prof. ANITA SHAPIRA; Exec. Dir of Research Institute IRIT KEYNAN.

Weitz Center for Development Studies: POB 2355, 76122 Rehovot; tel. (8) 9474111; fax (8) 9475884; f. 1963; research, training and planning activities related to the promotion of rural regional development, tourism and entrepreneurship in Israel and the developing world; library of 50,000 vols, World Bank depository library; Gen. Dir JULIA MARGULIES.

EDUCATION

Henrietta Szold Institute—National Institute for Research in the Behavioural Sciences: 9 Columbia St, Kiryat Menachem, Jerusalem; tel. (2) 6494444; fax (2) 6437698; e-mail szold@szold.org.il; internet www.szold.org.il; f. 1941; non-profit organization undertaking research on psychology, psychometry, sociology and education; information retrieval centre for the social sciences in Israel; database of 40,000 records; Dir Prof. ISAAC FRIEDMAN; publ. *Megamot—Behavioral Sciences Quarterly*.

HISTORY, GEOGRAPHY AND ARCHAEOLOGY

Albright, William Foxwell, Institute of Archaeological Research in Jerusalem: 26 Salah ed-Din St, Jerusalem, POB 19096; tel. (2) 6288956; fax (2) 6264424; e-mail director@albright.org.il; internet www.aiar.org; f. 1900; 2,000 mems; library of 28,000 vols; research projects in Semitic languages, literatures, and history; archaeological surveys and excavations; Pres. J. EDWARD WRIGHT; Dir S. GITIN.

Israel Exploration Society: Avida St 5, POB 7041, 91 070 Jerusalem; tel. (2) 6257991; fax (2) 6247772; e-mail ies@vms.huji.ac.il; internet www.hum.huji.ac.il/ies; f. 1913; aims to engage in excavations and allied research into the history, archaeology and geography of Israel; to publish the results of such research; to educate the public in these matters by means of congresses, general meetings, etc.; 4,000 mems; Chair. of Exec. Cttee Prof. E. STERN; Dir J. AVIRAM; publs *Eretz-Israel* (in Hebrew and English, every 3 years), *Israel Exploration Journal* (in English, 2 a year), *Qadmoniot* (in Hebrew, 2 a year).

Joe Alon Centre for Regional and Folklore Studies: Kibbutz Lahav, 85335 D.N. Negev; tel. (7) 9913322; fax (7) 9919889; internet www.lahavnet.co.il/joalon//; f. 1972; centre for research, study and survey of the Southern Shefelah (the hilly region between Jerusalem and Beersheba); includes an Archaeological Museum, a Museum of Bedouin Culture, a Museum for the New Jewish Settlement in the Negev, the Fehalin Exhibit, housed in a restored dwelling cave complex, at the foot of a major site; awards grants for research in the region; library of 900 vols, 3,500 slides; Exec. Dir UZZI HALAMISH.

Kenyon Institute: POB 19283, Jerusalem 91192; tel. (2) 5828101; fax (2) 5323844; e-mail cbrl@netvision.net.il; internet www.britac.ac.uk/institutes/cbrl/; f. 1920 as British School of Archaeology in Jerusalem; part of the Council for British Research in the Levant (see parent institution in Research Institutes in Jordan); undertakes and promotes study of all aspects of the archaeology, history and culture of the Levant from prehistoric times to the present; hostel and library; library of 10,000 vols; Research Officer Dr ROBERT ALLAN; Research Scholar TIM MOORE.

Leo Baeck Institute Jerusalem: 33 Bustenai St, Jerusalem; tel. (2) 5633790; fax (2) 5669505; e-mail leobaeck@netvision.net.il; internet www.leobaeck.org; f. 1955; research and publication on history and culture of Central European Jewry; library: library and archive of items in German, English and Hebrew; special colln: microfilm archive of Jewish newspapers; publs *Yearbook*, *Juedischer Almanach*.

MEDICINE

Rogoff-Wellcome Medical Research Institute: Beilinson Medical Center, Petah-Tikva; tel. (3) 9376742; f. 1955; Dir Prof. A. NOVOGRODSKY.

NATURAL SCIENCES

Biological Sciences

Israel Institute for Biological Research: POB 19, 74 100 Ness-Ziona; tel. (8) 9381656; fax (8) 9401404; internet www.iibr.gov.il; f. 1952; conducts biomedical research in drug design, synthesis of fine chemicals and development of newly-advanced products and processes in biotechnology; three research divisions: Chemistry, Biology and Environmental Sciences; 320 scientists and supporting staff; library of 50,000 vols and 800 periodicals; Dir A. SHAFFERMAN; publ. *OHOLO Annual International Scientific Conference*.

National Institute for Psychobiology in Israel: Hebrew University, Givat Ram Campus, Jerusalem; f. 1971 with funds from the Charles E. Smith Family Foundation, to create a network of scientists engaged in research in psychobiology, to further co-operative programmes between existing institutions, and to train personnel in the field of psychobiology; administers Charles E. Smith Family Laboratory for Collaborative Research in Psychobiology; operates through the Research and Development Authority of the Hebrew University; Dir Prof. BERNARD LERER; Sec. HADASSAH FINDLEY-SHARON.

Physical Sciences

Earth Sciences Research Administration: 30 Malkhei Israel, 95501 Jerusalem; tel. (2) 5314246; fax (2) 5380688; e-mail mbeyth@gsi.gov.il; f. 1949; defines scientific issues involved in energy, environment and infrastructure; Chief Scientist and Dir Dr MICHAEL BEYTH.

Subordinate institutions:

Geological Survey of Israel: 30 Malkhei Israel St, 95501 Jerusalem; tel. (2) 5314220; fax (2) 5380688; f. 1949; geological mapping, research and exploration of mineral, water and energy resources; environmental geology; mitigation of earthquake hazards; Dir Dr A. BEIN.

Geophysical Institute of Israel: 1 Hamashbir St, POB 2286, 58122 Holon; tel. (3) 5576050; fax (3) 5502925; internet www.gii.co.il; f. 1957; activities devoted chiefly to the exploration of petroleum, water and mineral resources and to engineering studies in Israel and abroad, using geophysical methods; documentation unit; data processing centre; monitoring and mitigation of earthquake hazards; Dir Dr Y. ROTSTEIN.

Israel Oceanographic and Limnological Research: POB 1793, 31000 Haifa; tel. (4) 8515202; fax (4) 8511911; internet www.ocean.org.il; f. 1967; physical, chemical and biological oceanography and limnology; aquaculture; Dir. Dr Y. COHEN.

Israel Meteorological Service: POB 25, 50250 Bet Dagan; tel. (3) 9682121; fax (3) 9682176; f. 1936; provides general service to public and detailed service to various orgs; library; various publications; Dir Z. ALPERSON.

RELIGION, SOCIOLOGY AND ANTHROPOLOGY

Harry Fischel Institute for Research in Talmud and Jewish Law: Bucharim Quarter, 14 David St (Corner Fischel St), POB 5289, 91052 Jerusalem; tel. (2) 5322517; fax (2) 5326448; f. 1932; seminary for Rabbis and Rabbinical Judges; legislation and research publications; codification of Jewish law; Jewish adult education centre; 80 mems; Chancellor Chief Rabbi SHEAR-YASHUV COHEN.

World Jewish Bible Center: POB 7024, Jerusalem; tel. (2) 6255965; f. 1957; aims to disseminate a knowledge of the Bible and of Bible research by publications, lectures and exhibitions; Chair. S. J. KREUTNER; publ. *Beit Mikra* (Hebrew, 4 a year).

Yad Izhak Ben-Zvi: POB 7660, 91076 Jerusalem; tel. (2) 5398888; fax (2) 5638310; e-mail ybz@ybz.org.il; internet www.ybz.org.il; f. 1964 as a non-profit foundation by the Government to commemorate Israel's second President; aims to encourage research into the history of Israel and Jerusalem, to promote the study of Jewish communities in the Middle East, Izhak Ben-Zvi and the Zionist and Labour Movements of Israel; library; library of 65,000 vols; Dir Dr ZVI ZAMERET; publs *Cathedra* (4 a year), *Et-mol* (6 a year), *Pe'amim* (4 a year), *Sefunot* (irregular), *Shalem* (irregular).

Subordinate institutions:

Ben-Zvi Institute for the Study of Jewish Communities in the East: POB 7660, 91076 Jerusalem; tel. (2) 5398844; fax (2) 5612329; e-mail mbz@ybz.org.il; internet www.ybz.org.il; f. 1947; operated jtly with the Hebrew University of Jerusalem; sponsors research into the history and culture of Jewish communities in Muslim countries since the 7th c.; maintains a large collection of MSS, and other historical documents; library; Dir Prof. MENAHEM BEN-SASSON; publs *Pe'amim* (in Hebrew, 4 a year), *Sefunot* (in Hebrew, irregular).

Institute for Research of Eretz Israel: POB 7660, 91076 Jerusalem; tel. (2) 5398822; fax (2) 5398836; e-mail lahav@ybz.org.il; internet www.ybz.org.il; promotes research on the history of Eretz Israel from Biblical times to the mid-20th c., and publishes studies on the history and culture of the Jewish people in Israel from the destruction of the Second Temple to the first years of the State of Israel's existence; research and studies based on the work of scientists at the main universities; Dir Prof. URI BIALER; publs *Cathedra* (in Hebrew, 4 a year), *Shalem* (irregular).

TECHNOLOGY

Israel Atomic Energy Commission: POB 7061, 61 070 Tel-Aviv; premises at: 26 Rehov Chaim Levanon, Ramat Aviv, Tel Aviv; tel. (3) 6462922; fax (3) 6462974; f. 1952; advises the Government on long-term policies and priorities in the advancement of nuclear research and development; supervises the implementation of policies approved by the Government, including the licensing of nuclear power plants; promotion of technological industrial applications; represents Israel in relations with scientific institutions and organizations abroad (Israel is a mem. of IAEA); Chair. The PRIME MINISTER; Dir-Gen. G. FRANK.

Attached research centres:

Soreq Nuclear Research Centre: 81800 Yavne; tel. (8) 9434290; f. 1958; swimming-pool research reactor IRR-1 of 5 MW thermal; Dir. URI HALAVEE.

Negev Nuclear Research Centre: Dimona; natural uranium fuelled and heavy water moderated reactor IRR-2 of 26 MW thermal; Dir MICHA DAPHT.

Office of the Chief Scientist—Industrial Research Administration, Ministry of Industry and Trade: 5 Bank Israel St, POB 3166, Jerusalem 91036; tel. (2) 6662486; fax (2) 6662928; f. 1970; promotes industrial research and development in industry, research institutes and higher education institutes by financing projects; encourages establishment of science-based industrial parks near universities and research institutes; proposes policies to promote innovative industry through legislation, developing physical and technical infrastructure and intergovernmental industrial R&D agreements; Chief Scientist ELI OPER.

Associated institutions:

Institutes for Applied Research, Ben-Gurion University of the Negev: POB 1025, 84110 Be'ersheva; tel. (8) 5778382; f. 1956; engage in applied research in water desalination, membrane and ion-exchange technologies, chemical technologies, irrigation with brackish and seawater, development of salt- and drought-resistant crops and ornamentals, natural products from higher plants and algae, development of mechanical and electromechanical products, utilization of non-conventional energy sources; 120 staff; library of 13,200 vols; Dir Prof. A. SHANI; publ. *Scientific Activities* (2 a year).

Israel Ceramic and Silicate Institute: Technion City, 32 000 Haifa; tel. (4) 8222107; f. 1962; provides the local ceramic industry with technical assistance and with research and development into advanced and new fields in ceramics technology; 12 staff; Dir Dr ADRIAN GOLDSTEIN.

Israel Fiber Institute: POB 8001, Jerusalem; tel. (2) 5707377; fax (2) 5245110; f. 1953; to advance textile, polymer, paper, leather and related industries; applied R&D, testing services, quality control, training courses for engineers and technicians, M.Sc. and Ph.D. courses in conjunction with the Hebrew University; 45 staff; library of 4,000 vols and 30 periodicals; Dir Dr HILDA GUTTMAN.

Israel Institute of Metals: Technion City, 32 000 Haifa; tel. (4) 8294473; f. 1962; serves industry in metallurgy and powder technology, foundry, corrosion and coating technology, vehicle and mechanical engineering; Dir Prof. A. ROSEN.

Israel Institute of Plastics: POB 7293, 31 072 Haifa; tel. (4) 8225174; fax (4) 8225173; f. 1981; R&D and information centre for promoting the plastic industry; Dir Dr S. ABRAHAMI.

Israel Wine Institute: POB 2329, 4 Ha-Raz St, 76 310 Rehovot; tel. (8) 9475693; f. 1957 to improve the country's wines by means of quality control and applied research and promote their export; Dir SHLOMO COHEN.

National Physical Laboratory: Hebrew University, Danziger A Bldg, Givat Ram Campus, 91 904 Jerusalem; tel. (2) 5584475; fax (2) 5520797; attached to Min. of Industry and Trade Dept; f. 1950; basic physical standards, energy saving, ecology, solar energy, applied research with industrial orientation; Dir Dr A. SHENHAR.

Rubber Research Association Ltd: Technion City, 32 000 Haifa; tel. (4) 8222124; fax (4) 8227582; f. 1951; the advancement of the rubber industry in Israel; Dir D. CZIMERMAN.

Standards Institution of Israel: POB 39020, 61390 Tel-Aviv; tel. (3) 5454154; fax (3) 5419683; f. 1923; tests the compliance of commodities with the requirements of standards and specifications; grants standards mark; conducts technological research; publishes the National Standards Specifications and Codes; 550 staff; library of 300,000 standards; Dir-Gen. ELI HADAR; publ. *Mati* (quarterly).

Libraries and Archives

Be'ersheva

Ben Gurion University of the Negev Library: POB 653, 84 105 Be'ersheva; tel. (7) 6461401; fax (7) 6472940; f. 1966; 720,000 vols, 5,000 current periodicals, 1,300 microfilms, 15,000 microfiche; Dir AVNER SHMUELEVITZ.

Haifa

Borochov Library: c/o Haifa Labour Council, POB 5226, Haifa; f. 1921; 40,000 vols, in central library, 60,000 in 24 brs; Chief Librarian EZECHIEL OREN.

Haifa AMLI Library of Music: 23 Arlosoroff St, POB 4811/25, Haifa; tel. and (4) 8644485; f. 1958; lending library including books, scores, records and cassettes; Librarian LEAH MARCUS.

Pevsner Public Library: 54 Pevsner St, POB 5345, Haifa; tel. (4) 8667766; f. 1934; 200,000 vols covering all fields of literature and science, in Hebrew, English and German; 15 brs; Chief Librarian Dr S. BACK.

Technion—Israel Institute of Technology, Library System: Technion City, Haifa 32000; tel. (4) 8292507; fax (4) 8295662; e-mail roitberg@tx.technion.ac.il; internet library.technion.ac.il; f. 1925; science, technology, architecture and medicine; Elyachar (Central) Library, 18 departmental libraries; 1,000,000 vols, 12,000 current periodicals; Dir Dr NURIT ROITBERG.

University of Haifa Library: Mount Carmel, 31905 Haifa; tel. (4) 8240289; fax (4) 8257753; e-mail webmaster@lib.haifa.ac.il; internet www-lib.haifa.ac.il; f. 1963; 1,050,000 vols, 19,500 periodical titles; 8,000 current periodicals; 480,000 microfiches and -films; 27,000 maps; 168,000 slides; 5,600 films (incl. videos); special collections include integrated law collection, rare books, media centre, laboratory for children's librarianship; Dir Prof. BARUCH A. KIPNIS; Admin. Dir. NEHAMA REKEM.

Jerusalem

Archive and Library of Ashkenaz House: Hechal Shlomo, 58 King George St, Jerusalem; tel. (2) 6233225; fax (2) 6233226; e-mail synagog@netvision.net.il; internet www.ashkenazhouse.org; research material related to German Jewry; collects material about Ashkenaz Jewry and documents about 'Kristallnacht' in Germany, November 1938; ongoing compilation of a series of memorial books, documenting the synagogues and Jewish communities destroyed in the 20th century; Dir Prof. em. Dr MEIER SCHWARZ.

Awkaf Supreme Council Library: c/o Supreme Muslim Council, POB 19859, Jerusalem; located at: Haram al-Sharif, Jerusalem; f. 1931; contains Arabic and Islamic MSS.

Bibliothèque de l'Ecole Biblique et Archéologique Française: 6 Nablus Rd, POB 19053, 91 190 Jerusalem; tel. (2) 6264468; fax (2) 6282567; e-mail biblio@ebaf.edu; internet www.ebaf.edu; f. 1890; 140,000 vols; archaeology and epigraphy of the ancient Near East, biblical studies; Librarian Rev. PAWEL TRZOPEK; publs *Cahiers de la Revue Biblique*, *Etudes Bibliques*, *Revue Biblique* (quarterly).

Central Archives for the History of the Jewish People (formerly Jewish Historical General Archives): POB 39077, 91 390 Jerusalem; tel. (2) 6586249; fax (2) 6535426; e-mail archives@vms.huji.ac.il; internet sites.huji.ac.il/archives; f. 1969; Dir HADASSAH ASSOULINE; intended to serve as the central archives of Jewish history; publ. *Newsletter-Ginzei Am Olam*.

Central Zionist Archives: POB 92, Jerusalem; tel. (2) 6204800; fax (2) 6204837; e-mail cza@shani.net; internet www.wzo.org.il/cza/index.htm; f. 1919; 125,000 vols; 8,180 metres of files; 8,430 newspapers; 545,000 pictures; 1,000 private archives and collections; 490 magnetic tapes; 240,000 items of small printed matter; Dir Prof. H. AVNI; Librarian G. BAR-TIKVA.

Gulbenkian Library: Armenian Patriarchate, POB 14106, 91140 Jerusalem; tel. (2) 6282331 ext. 222; f. 1929; donated by the late Calouste Gulbenkian; one of the three great Armenian libraries in the diaspora, the others being the Mekhitarist Fathers' Library in Venice and another in Vienna; public library of 100,000 vols, of which one-third are in Armenian and the rest in foreign languages, primarily English and French; receives more than 360 newspapers, magazines, periodicals (of which more than half are Armenian) from foreign countries; collections of newspapers and magazines since the 1850s; a copy of the first printed Armenian Bible (1666); 3,890 Armenian MSS; Sec. and Librarian Rev. NORAYO KAZAZIAN; publ. *Sion* (official organ of the Armenian Patriarchate, monthly).

Israel Antiquities Authority Archives Branch: POB 586, 91004 Jerusalem; tel. (2) 6204680; fax (2) 6271173; e-mail arieh@israntique.org.il; internet www.israntique.org.il; f. 1948; written, computerized and photographic records, maps and plans; Asst to Head of Archives ARIEH ROCHMAN-HALPERIN.

Israel State Archives: Prime Minister's Office, Kiryat Ben-Gurion, 91 919 Jerusalem; tel. (2) 5680680; fax (2) 6793375; f. 1949; comprises seven sections: Department of Files and Manuscripts, Library Department, Records Management, Supervision Department of Public and Private Archives, Services to the Public, Technical Services Department and Publication of State Papers; holdings include files occupying 30 kilometres of shelving, 150,000 printed items and 25,000 books; administrative records, including foreign relations, are available after 30 years and records on defence after 50 years; State Archivist E. FRIESEL; Dir M. MOSSEK; publs *Israel Government Publications* (bibliography, annually), *Documents on the Foreign Policy of Israel*.

Jerusalem City (Public) Library: POB 1409, Jerusalem; tel. (2) 6256785; fax (2) 6255785; f. 1961; 750,000 vols; 20 brs and 2 Bookmobiles; Dir ABRAHAM VILNER.

Jewish National and University Library: POB 34165, 91 341 Jerusalem; tel. (2) 6584651; fax (2) 6511771; f. 1892; 4,000,000 vols, including those in departmental libraries; 10,000 MSS; 49,000 microfilmed Hebrew MSS; microfilms of Jewish and Israeli newspapers; 200 incunabula (120 Hebrew and 80 in other languages); 15,000 current periodicals; special collections include the Abraham Schwadron Collection of Jewish Autographs and Portraits, the Harry Friedenwald Collection on the History of Medicine, the National Sound Archives and the Jacob Michael Collection of Jewish Music, the Sidney M. Edelstein Collection on the History of Chemistry, the Eran Laor Cartographic Collection, the Archives of Albert Einstein; Dir Prof. SARA JAPHET; publs *Kiryat Sefer* (bibliography, quarterly), *Index of Articles on Jewish Studies* (annually).

Library of the Central Bureau of Statistics: 66 Kanfei Nesharm St, POB 34525, 95464 Jerusalem; tel. (2) 6592666; fax (2) 6521340; internet www.cbs.gov.il; f. 1948; *c.* 40,000 vols; special collection: all publs of (British) Palestine Dept of Statistics (due to be transferred to the Israel State Archives); most publs available for exchange; Librarian MARIAN ROMAN.

Library of the Israel Antiquities Authority: POB 586, 91004 Jerusalem; tel. (2) 6204685; fax (2) 6260684; e-mail brandl@israntique.org.il; internet www.israntique.org.il; f. 1935; collections mainly on the archaeology, ancient history and civilizations of Israel and the ancient Near East; 80,000 vols; Librarian BARUCH BRANDL.

Library of the Knesset: Knesset, 91 950 Jerusalem; tel. (2) 6753333; fax (2) 6662733; e-mail sifri@2netvision.net.il; internet www.knesset.gov.il; f. 1949; principally for members' use; 150,000 vols, including books, bound periodicals and collection of all Israeli Government publications, UN publications and foreign parliamentary papers; Librarian NAOMI KIMHI.

Library of the Studium Biblicum Franciscanum: POB 19424, Monastery of the Flagellation, Via Dolorosa, 91 193 Jerusalem; tel. (2) 6282936; fax (2) 6264519; e-mail sbfnet@netvision.net.il; f. 1924; 48,000 vols chiefly on archaeology, judaeo-christianism, biblical and patristic studies; 20 mems; Librarian D. ROBAERT.

Muriel and Philip Berman National Medical Library–Library Authority, Hebrew University of Jerusalem: POB 12272, 91 120 Jerusalem; tel. (2) 6758795; fax (2) 6757106; e-mail mdlibinfo@savion.huji.ac.il; internet library.md.huji.ac.il; f. 1919; 65,000 book titles, 5,000 electronic journal titles, 200 annual print periodical subscriptions; Dir SHARON LENGA.

Schocken Library: 6 Balfour St, 92 102 Jerusalem; e-mail Library@schocken-jts.org.il; tel. (2) 5636857; f. 1900; 55,000 vols, 200 MSS, 20,000 photostats (Hebrew Liturgy and Poetry); Dir Dr SHMUEL GLICK.

Supreme Court Library: Supreme Court of Israel, Rehov Sha'arei Mishpat, Kiryat Ben Gurion, 91 950 Jerusalem; tel. (2) 6759665; e-mail liba@supreme.court.gov.il; f. 1949; 80,000 vols; Librarian LIBA BORCK.

Kfar Giladi

Kfar Giladi Library: Kfar Giladi, 12 210 Upper Galilee; f. 1934; 35,000 vols, 110 periodicals; Librarian SHULAMIT ROSENTHAL.

Kiryat Shmona

Library of Tel-Hai Academic College: Upper Galilee, 12210, nr Kiryat Shmona; tel. (4) 6900907; fax (4) 6900906; internet www.telhai.ac.il; includes the Calvary Collection, the Ofer Collection, the Kapeliuk Middle East collection, Dvir Collection in Environmental Studies, the Lubin art collection and the Gail Chasin art collection, Littauer Judaic Collection, Silvia Sheim Collection; 80,000 vols, 600 periodicals, 1,200 videotapes, 4,200 e-Journals; Library Dir IRIS CHAI.

Nahariya

Municipal Library in Memory of William and Chia Boorstein: 61 Herzl St, Nahariya; tel. (4) 9879870; f. 1946; under the supervision of the Ministry of Education and Culture, Jerusalem; 70,000 vols; Chief Librarian SHOSHANA GIBLEY.

Ramat-Gan

Bar-Ilan University Library System: POB 90000, 52900 Ramat-Gan; tel. (3) 5318486; fax (3) 5349233; e-mail dolinsm@mail.biu.ac.il; internet www.biu.ac.il/lib; f. 1955; serves faculties of Humanities, Judaica, Law, Social Sciences, Exact Sciences, and Life Sciences; 1,000,000 vols, 4,500 current journals; special collections include the Mordecai Margulies collection of rare 16th and 17th c. Hebrew books and 800 Hebrew Oriental MSS, Berman collection of early Eastern European Hebrew imprints, rare Latin and German books on Jewish studies, Old Testament criticism, material on the Dead Sea Scrolls and the Samaritans; a collection of material on the development of Religious Zionism; collection of Responsa and Jewish studies; Moussaieff colln of 220 Kabbalistic MSS; Librarian MENAHEM MOLINSKY; publs *Hebrew Subject Headings* (online), *Index to Literary Supplements of the Daily Hebrew Press* (online).

'Dvir Bialik' Municipal Central Public Library: Hibat-Zion St 14, Ramat-Gan; f. 1945; 400,000 vols, including special Rabbinic literature and Social Sciences collection; maintains 11 branches; Chief Librarian HADASSAH PELACH.

Rehovot

Hebrew University of Jerusalem, Central Library of Agricultural Science: POB 12, 76 100 Rehovot; tel. (8) 9481270; f. 1960; National Agricultural Library, operated jointly by the Volcani Centre of the Ministry of Agriculture's Agricultural Research Organization and the Hebrew University's Faculty of Agriculture; maintains exchange relations all over the world; 300,000 vols, 3,200 current periodicals and serials, 180,000 documents; regional libraries at Gilath, Dor and N've Ya'ar; Dir N. BARZELY.

Weizmann Archives: POB 26, 76 100 Rehovot; tel. (8) 9343487; fax (8) 9344146; e-mail merav.segal@weizman.ac.il; f. 1950; contains assembled letters, papers, photographs, and other documents relating to political and scientific activities of Dr Chaim Weizmann, first President of Israel; approx. 180,000 items; Dir MERAV SEGAL.

Weizmann Institute of Science Libraries: POB 26, 76 100 Rehovot; tel. (8) 9343583; fax (8) 9344176; e-mail ilana.pollack@weizmann.ac.il; internet www.weizmann.ac.il/wis-library/home.htm; f. 1934 as Ziff Institute Libraries; renamed 1949; Wix Central Library, 3 faculty libraries, 1 departmental library and approx. 50 departmental collections; 260,000 vols, incl. bound periodicals and 1,032 current print periodicals in science and technology, and access to several databases and several thousand electronic journals; Chief Librarian ILANA POLLACK.

Tel-Aviv

Felicja Blumental Music Center and Library: 26 Bialik St, 65241 Tel-Aviv; tel. (3) 5250499; fax (3) 5281032; e-mail irit_s@tzion.tel-aviv.gov.il; f. 1950; 75,920 vols, 64 periodicals, 18,000 records, 3,446 compact discs, 170 video cassettes; Bronislav Huberman archive, Joachim Stutschewsky archive, Shulamith Conservatory (1910), Beit Levi'im (1919), etc.; Dir IRIT SCHÖNHORN.

General Archives of the City of Tel-Aviv-Yafo: City Hall, Kikar Malkhei Israel, 64 162 Tel-Aviv; tel. (3) 6438554; f. 1967; Archivist JUDITH Z. FASTOVSKY.

Sourasky Central Library, Tel-Aviv University: POB 39038, Ramat-Aviv, 69 978 Tel-Aviv; tel. (3) 6408745; fax (3) 6409598; f. 1954; 880,000 vols, 4,800 current periodicals and 96,000 microforms; 7 specialized br. libraries with a further; 788,000 vols; includes the Pevsner Collection of Hebrew Press, the Faitlovitch collection, the Collection of Yiddish Literature and Culture in memory of Benzion and Pearl Margulies, the Wiener Library collection, which concerns the Second World War, especially the Holocaust, and the history of antisemitism, the Herbert Cohen collection of rare books, the Dr Horodisch collection on the history of books and the Jaffe collection of Hebrew poetry; Dir Dr DAN SIMON.

Tel-Aviv Central Public Library 'Shaar Zion': 25 King Saul Blvd, POB 33235, Tel-Aviv; tel. (3) 6910141; fax (3) 6919024; internet www.tel-aviv.gov.il/tarbut/ariela.htm; f. 1891; 900,000 vols (in 23 branches); General Library in 8 languages; special collections: Rambam Library (*q.v.*, Judaica), Ahad ha-Am Library (history and geography of Eretz Israel), Dance Library; Dir ORA NEBENZAHL.

Museums and Art Galleries

Acre

Okashi Art Museum, Acre: Old City of Akko, El- Jazz'ar St; permanent exhibition of works by Avsalom Okashi (1916–1980); temporary exhibitions by Israeli artists.

Be'ersheva

Negev Museum: Derech Ha'atsmaut, POB 5188, 84100 Be'ersheva; tel. (7) 6282057; fax (7) 6277603; f. 1954; exhibits from regional excavations, mainly from the Chalcolithic, Israelite, Roman and Byzantine periods; exhibitions of Israeli contemporary art; Dir GALIA GAVISH.

Haifa

Haifa Museum of Art: 26 Shabbetai Levy St, Haifa; tel. (4) 8523255; fax (4) 8552714; f. 1951; collns of Israeli and world contemporary art, prints, art posters, paintings and sculptures; library of 10,000 vols; Curator Dir NISSIM TAL.

National Maritime Museum: 198 Allenby Rd, POB 44855, 31447 Haifa; tel. (4) 8536622; fax (4) 8539286; e-mail nautic@netvision.net.il; f. 1954; large collection of artefacts and ship models illustrating 5,000 years of navigation and shipbuilding, old maps and engravings, undersea archaeology, a Hellenistic bronze ram, and stamps and ancient coins connected with seafaring and maritime symbols; archaeology and civilizations of ancient peoples; scientific instruments; library: research library of 6,000 vols; Chief Curator AVSHALOM ZEMER; publs *Sefunim*, *Bulletin* (irregular).

Tikotin Museum of Japanese Art: 89 Hanassi Ave, 34642 Haifa; tel. (4) 8383554; fax (4) 8379824; e-mail japanmus@netvision.net.il; internet www.haifa.gov.il; f. 1960; paintings, prints, drawings, textiles, netsuke, lacquer work, ceramics, metalwork, collection of Mingei (folk art); courses for children and adults; library of 3,000 vols; Chief Curator Dr ILANA SINGER.

Jerusalem

Archaeological (Rockefeller) Museum: Rockefeller Bldg, Suleiman Rd, POB 586, Jerusalem 91004; tel. (2) 6282251; fax (2) 6271926; internet www.imj.org.il; f. 1938; formerly Palestine Archaeological Museum; archaeology of Israel from earliest times up until end of Islamic period; largely material found in excavations before 1948; Curator FAWZI IBRAHIM.

Beit Ha'Omanim (Jerusalem Artists' House): 12 Shmuel Hanagid St, Jerusalem; tel. (2) 6253653; fax (2) 6258594; e-mail artists@zahav.net.il; Dir RUTH ZADKA; f. 1965; Israeli and foreign contemporary art exhibitions and permanent gallery of works by Israeli artists.

Bible Lands Museum Jerusalem: POB 4670, 91046 Jerusalem; premises at: 25 Granot St, 93706 Jerusalem; tel. (2) 5611066; fax (2) 5638228; e-mail contact@blmj.org; internet www.blmj.org; f. 1992; ancient Near Eastern history and Biblical archaeology; Dir BATYA BOROWSKI; Curator YEHUDA KAPLAN.

Israel Museum: POB 71117, 91710 Jerusalem; tel. (2) 6708811; fax (2) 6771332; e-mail sb@imj.org.il; internet www.imj.org.il; f. 1965; fine art, Judaica and archaeology from Biblical times to the present; Shrine of the Book housing Dead Sea Scrolls; Billy Rose Sculpture Garden; library of 65,000 vols; Dir JAMES S. SNYDER; publ. *Journal* (annually).

Mayer, L.A., Museum for Islamic Art: POB 4088, 2 Hapalmach St, 92 542 Jerusalem; tel. (2) 5661291; fax (2) 5619802; f. 1974; collection of Islamic art: metalwork, glass, miniatures, ceramics, ivories, jewellery; Sir David Salomons collection of antique clocks and watches; educational activities in Jewish and Arab sectors; library of 14,000 vols, 50 periodicals; photographs and slides; Dir RACHEL HASSON.

Museum of Prehistory, Institute of Archaeology, Hebrew University: Mt Scopus Campus, Jerusalem; tel. (2) 5882099; f. 1955; large collection of objects from prehistoric sites in Israel; library.

Museum of Taxes: POB 3100, 91036 Jerusalem; tel. (2) 6258978; fax (2) 5317553; e-mail misim@mof.gov.il; internet www.mof.gov.il/museum; f. 1964; 5 sections: artefacts from the Land of Canaan and environs, taxes levied specifically on Jews in the Diaspora, general section for tax-related items from all over the world, taxation in Israel, prevention of smuggling and importation of illegal goods and other customs-related issues; Dir MIRA DROR; publ. *Israeli Tax Review* (quarterly).

Museum of the Studium Biblicum Franciscanum: POB 19424, Monastery of the Flagellation, Via Dolorosa, Jerusalem; tel. (2) 6282936; f. 1923; Palestinian archaeology: city coins of Palestine, Roman-Byzantine-Crusader pottery and objects; Curator M. PICCIRILLO; publ. *S. B. F Museum*.

Yad Vashem, Holocaust Martyrs' and Heroes' Remembrance Authority: POB 3477, Mount Herzl, Jerusalem 91034; tel. (2) 6443400; fax (2) 6443443; e-mail general.information@yadvashem.org.il; internet www.yadvashem.org; f. 1953; the Jewish people's national memorial to the Holocaust; museum: permanent exhibition of photographs and documents; Hall of Remembrance; Children's Memorial; Valley of the Communities; Memorial to the Deportees, Hall of Names; Avenue and Garden of the Righteous Among the Nations; art museum; Int. Institute for Holocaust Research is responsible for expanding academic and research activities; Int. School for Holocaust Studies organizes seminars and develops teaching materials; library of 87,000 vols; world's largest repository of archival and documentary information on the Holocaust: 60 million pages of documents, microfilms, testimonies, diaries, artefacts; Chair. AVNER SHALEV.

Kibbutz Hazorea

Wilfrid Israel Museum of Oriental Art and Studies: Kibbutz Hazorea, 30060 Post Hazorea; f. 1947; opened 1951 in memory of the late Wilfrid Israel; a cultural centre for study and art exhibitions incl. modern art and all areas of the plastic arts; houses the Wilfrid Israel collection of Near and Far Eastern art and cultural materials; local archaeological exhibits from neolithic to Byzantine times; art library; Dir EHUD DOR.

Kibbutz Lahav

Museum of Bedouin Culture: Joe Alon Centre, Kibbutz Lahav, 85335 D. N. Negev; tel. (8) 9913322; fax (8) 9919889; e-mail joealon@lhv.org.il; internet www.joealon.org.il; f. 1985; part of the Colonel Joe Alon Centre for Regional and Folklore Studies; exhibition of contemporary arts and crafts, educational lectures and guided tours, photographs, demonstrations of Bedouin life (weaving, cooking, etc.); museum of Jewish settlement in the Negev; art gallery; museum of the Bar-Kokba Rebellion; awards grants for research in Bedouin and regional studies; library of 150 vols, 3,000 slides; Gen. Dir UZI HALMISH.

Kiryat Shmona

Tel Hai Museum: Tel Hai, 12 210 Upper Galilee; reconstruction of a Jewish settlement from the beginning of the 20th c.; documents of Joseph Trumpeldor and his defence of the region in 1920.

Ma'ayan Baruch

Ma'ayan Baruch Prehistory Museum of the Huleh Valley: Ma'ayan Baruch, 12220 Upper Galilee; tel. (4) 6954611; fax (4) 6950724; f. 1952; pre-history of the Huleh Valley from the Palaeolithic (including large colln of Ashulian handaxes) to the Chalcolithic period; locally excavated Bronze Age and Roman-Byzantine objects; colln of stone grain mills and oil presses; the Earliest Dog in the World, buried with a woman from the Natufian period (10,000 BC); plaster skull from Neolithic era (7000 BC); world ethnographic exhibition of tools fashioned by people who still live as in prehistoric times; Dir A. ASSAF.

Nazareth

Terra Sancta Museum: Terra Sancta Monastery, POB 23, 96 100 Nazareth; tel. (4) 6572501; fax (4) 6460203; f. 1920; Byzantine (and later) remains, coins, Roman and Byzantine glass; colln of antiquities from excavations made in the monastery compound; Vicar of Monastery Rev. P. JOSÉ MONTALVERNE DE LANCASTRE.

Safad

Israel Bible Museum: c/o POB 1396, Safed; tel. (4) 6999972; e-mail info@israelbiblemuseum.com; internet www.israelbiblemuseum.com; f. 1984; exhibition of the biblical art of Phillip Ratner; permanent and changing exhibitions including Kabbalah and art for children; Dir AMI SHOSHAN.

Sha'ar Ha-Golan

Museum of Prehistory: Sha'ar Ha-Golan, Jordan Valley; f. 1950; large number of exhibits from the neolithic Yarmukian culture excavated in the region; Dir Y. ROTH.

Tel-Aviv

Ben-Gurion House: 17 Ben-Gurion Blvds, Tel-Aviv 63454; tel. (3) 5221010; fax (3) 5247293; e-mail bghouse@bezegint.net; internet www.ben-gurion-house.org.il; f. 1974; residence of David Ben-Gurion, first Prime Minister of the State of Israel; museum and research and study centre; library of 20,000 vols and periodicals on history of Zionist movement, land and state of Israel, ancient peoples, cultures, religions and philosophies, general and military history; Dir HANNI HERMOLIN.

Beth Hatefutsoth (The Nahum Goldmann Museum of the Jewish Diaspora): POB 39359, 61 392 Tel-Aviv; tel. (3) 6408000; fax (3) 6405727; e-mail bhmuseum@post.tau.ac.il; f. 1978; permanent exhibition tells the story of Jewish survival and life in the Diaspora; temporary exhibitions portray Jewish communities all over the world; seminars and youth educational activities; photographic and film archives; Jewish Genealogy and music centre; Dir RANNY FINZI.

Eretz-Israel Museum: 2 Chaim Levanon St, POB 17068, Ramat Aviv, 61 170 Tel-Aviv; tel. (3) 6415244; fax (3) 6412408; Tel-Aviv region archaeology and history, Jewish ethnography and folklore, ceramics, ancient glass, numismatics, history of Jewish theatre, tools and technology, planetarium; library of 40,000 vols.

Tel-Aviv Museum of Art: 27 Shaul Hamelech Blvd, POB 33288, 61332 Tel-Aviv; also at: Helena Rubinstein Pavilion for Contemporary Art, 6 Tarsat Blvd, Tel-Aviv; tel. (3) 6077000; fax (3) 6958099; e-mail yaffag@tamuseum.com; internet www.tamuseum.com; f. 1932; art collection consisting of works since 16th c.; Israeli art; library: art library of 60,000 vols, periodicals, microfiches; Dir and Chief Curator Prof. MORDECHAI OMER.

Tiberias

Municipal Museum of Antiquities: Lake Front, Tiberias; f. 1953; collection of antiquities from Tiberias and region, mainly of the Roman, Byzantine and Arab periods; Dir ELISHEVA BALLHORN.

Universities

BAR-ILAN UNIVERSITY

52100 Ramat-GanTelephone: (3) 5318111
Fax: (3) 5344622
Internet: www.biu.ac.il

Founded 1953; inaugurated 1955
State control
Language of instruction: Hebrew
Academic year: October to June

Chancellor: Prof. E. RACKMAN
President: Prof. M. KAVEH
Rector: Prof. Y. YESHURUN
Vice-Rector: Prof. Z. MEVARECH
Pro-Rector: Prof. H. LAVEE
Vice-President for Research: Prof. H. BASCH
Director-General: Dr S. LUBEL
Academic Registrar: M. MISHAN
Librarian (vacant)

Library: see Libraries and Archives
Number of teachers: 1,500
Number of students: 28,600

Publications: *Bar-Ilan Annual*, *Philosophia* (4 a year)

DEANS

Faculty of Exact Sciences: Prof. K. HOCHBERG
Faculty of Humanities: Prof. D. SCHWARTZ
Faculty of Jewish Studies: Prof. Y. SCHWARTZ
Faculty of Law: Prof. Y. ZILBERSHATZ
Faculty of Life Sciences: Prof. H. BREITBART
Faculty of Social Sciences: Prof. Y. WOLF

PROFESSORS

Faculty of Exact Sciences (tel. (3) 5318586; fax (3) 5344766; e-mail exacts@mail.biu.ac.il):

AGRONOVSKY, M., Mathematics
AMIR, A., Computer Science
BASCH, H., Chemistry
BERKOWITZ, R., Physics
DEUTSCH, M., Physics
EHRENBERG, B., Physics
EISENBERG, L., Mathematics
FREULIKHER, V., Physics
FREUND, Y., Physics
FRIEDMAN, L., Mathematics
FRIMER, A., Chemistry
GEDANKEN, A., Chemistry
GOLDSCHMIDT, Z., Chemistry
GORDON, A., Chemistry
HALPERN, H., Physics
HAVLIN, S., Physics
HOCHBERG, K., Mathematics
HOZ, S., Chemistry
KANTOR, I., Physics
KAVEH, M., Physics
KAY, K., Chemistry
KESSLER, D., Physics
KRAUSS, S., Computer Science
KRUSHKAL, S., Mathematics
MARGEL, S., Chemistry
MARGOLIS, S., Mathematics
MARZBACH, E., Mathematics
NUDELMAN, A., Chemistry
ORBACH, D., Chemistry
PERSKY, A., Chemistry
RABIN, I., Physics
RAPPAPORT, D., Physics
ROSENBLUH, M., Physics
ROWEN, L., Mathematics
SHAPIRA, B., Physics

SHLIMAK, I., Physics
SHNIDER, S., Mathematics
SUKENIK, H., Chemistry
TEICHER, M., Mathematics
ULMAN, A., Chemistry
YESHURUN, Y., Physics
ZALCMAN, L., Mathematics

Faculty of Humanities (tel. (3) 5318370; fax (3) 5347601; e-mail segalil@mail.biu.ac.il):

ABRAHAMOV, B., Arabic
FINE, J., English
HALAMISH, M., Philosophy
HANDELMAN, S., English
HARVEY, S., Philosophy
HASSINE, J., Comparative Literature
KATZOFF, R., Classical Studies
KOREN, R., French Culture
LANGERMAN, Z., Arabic
PERL, J., English
REICHELBERG, R., Comparative Literature
ROTHSTEIN, S., English
SAGUY, A., Philosophy
SCHWARTZ, D., Philosophy
SPOLSKY, E., English
WIDOKER, D., Philosophy

Faculty of Jewish Studies (tel. (3) 5318233; fax (3) 5351233; e-mail jsfcty@mail.biu.ac.il):

BAR TIKVAH, B., Literature of the Jewish People
BAUMGARTEN, A., Jewish History
COHEN, M., General History
COHEN, T., Literature of the Jewish People
DISHON, Y., Literature of the Jewish People
FEINER, S., Jewish History
GENIZI, H., General History
HAVLIN, S. Z., Talmud and Information Sciences
HAZAN, E., Literature of the Jewish People
KASHER, R., Bible
KLONER, A., Land of Israel Studies
KOGEL, J., Bible
LIPSKER, A., Literature of the Jewish People
MICHMAN, D., Jewish History
MILIKOWSKI, H., Talmud
ORFALI, M., Jewish History
ROSMAN, M., Jewish History
SAFRAI, Z., Land of Israel Studies
SCHWARTZ, J., Land of Israel Studies
SCHWARTZWALD, O., Hebrew Language
SHARVIT, S., Hebrew Language
SOKOLOFF, M., Hebrew and Semitic Languages
SPERBER, D., Talmud
SPIEGEL, Y., Talmud
TABORI, Y., Talmud
TAUBER, E., History of the Middle East
TOAFF, A., Jewish History
VARGON, S., Bible
WEISS, H., Literature of the Jewish People

Faculty of Law (tel. (3) 5318417; fax (3) 5351856; e-mail olmertr@mail.biu.ac.il):

COHEN, Z.
LERNER, S.

Faculty of Life Sciences (tel. (3) 5318721; fax (3) 7369928; e-mail landmar@mail.biu.ac.il):

ACHITUV, Y.
BREITBART, H.
BRODIE, C.
COHEN, Y.
HAAS, E.
KISLEV, M.
MALIK, Z.
MAYEVSKY, A.
SAMPSON, S.
SHAINBERG, A.
SHOHAM, Y.
SREDNI, B.
STEINBERGER, J.
SUSSWEIN, A.

Faculty of Social Sciences (tel. (3) 5318452; fax (3) 5351825; e-mail socials@mail.biu.ac.il):

ADAD, M., Criminology
ALPEROVITCH, G., Economics
BABKOFF, H., Psychology
COHEN, S., Political Science
DON-YEHIEH, E., Political Science
FRIEDMAN, M., Sociology
GAZIEL, H., School of Education
GOLDREICH, Y., Geography
GREILSAMMER, I., Political Studies
HALEVY-SPIRO, M., Social Work
HILLMANN, A., Economics
INBAR, E., Political Science
IRAM, Y., Education
JAFFE, E., Business Administration
KATZ, J., Geography
KLEIN, P., Education
KOSLOWSKY, M., Psychology
KRAWITZ, S., Psychology
LAUTERBACH, B., School of Business Administration
LAVEE, H., Geography
LEVI-SHIFF, R., Psychology
MENIS, J., Education
MEVARECH, Z., Education
MIKULINCER, M., Psychology
NACHSHON, I., Criminology
NITZAN, S., Economics
ORBACH, I., Psychology
RABINOWITZ, J., Social Work
SANDLER, S., Political Science
SHULMAN, S., Psychology
SCHWARZWALD, J., Psychology
SILBER, J., Economics
TAPIERO, C., Economics
TZURIEL, D., School of Education
VAKIL, E., Psychology
WELLER, A., Psychology
WOLF, Y., Criminology
YEHUDA, S., Psychology
YITZCHAKI, H., Social Work
ZIDERMAN, A., Economics
ZISSER, B., Political Science

AFFILIATED SCHOOLS AND INSTITUTES

School of Education: Dir Prof. D. TSURIEL.

School of Social Work: Dir Prof. H. YITZCHAKI.

Institute for the History of Jewish Bible Research: Dir Prof. Y. KOGEL.

Institute for Post-Talmudic Research: Dir Prof. H. MILIKOWSKY.

Kramer Institute of Assyriology: Dir Dr Y. ZAFATI.

S. Daniel Abraham School of Business Administration: Dir Prof. Y. WEISBERG.

B. Kurzweil Institute for the Literature of the People of Israel: Dir Dr S. RAPHAEL.

Institute for Research in the History of Oriental Jewry: Dir Prof. A. TOAFF.

Naftal Centre for the Study of Oral Law and its Dissemination: Dir Prof. D. HANSCKE.

J. M. Kaplan Centre for Legal Research, Praxis and Theory: Dir Prof. Y. STERN.

Finkler Institute for Research of the Holocaust: Dir Prof. D. MICHMAN.

Institute for the Study of Jews in Diaspora: Dir Prof. D. MICHMAN.

Institute for Advanced Torah Studies: Dir Rabbi A. KATZ.

Rena Costa Yiddish Centre: Dir Dr A. LIPSKER.

Institute for Research into Religious Zionism: Dir Prof. YEHUDA FRIEDLANDER.

Institute for Information Retrieval and Computational Linguistics: Dir Prof. Y. CHOUEKA.

Centre for Lexicography: Dir Prof. M. SOKOLOFF.

Menachem Begin Institute for Research in Resistance Movements: Dir Prof. E. TAUBER.

Institute for Contemporary Judaism: Dir Prof. J. BAUMEL.

Rivlin Institute for the History of Israel and its Settlements: Dir Dr Z. AMAR.

Institute for Computerized Data in Jewish Studies: Dir Prof. S. FRIEDMAN.

Institute for the Study of Tiberias: Dir Dr M. HILDESHEIMER.

Kukin Center for Study of the Family (social work): Dir Prof. Y. RABINOWITZ.

Lechter Institute for Literary Research: Dir Prof. M. KRAMER.

Institute for Economic Research: Dir Prof. S. NEUMAN.

William Farber Centre for Alzheimer's Research: Dir Prof. S. YEHUDA.

Dr Joseph H. Lookstein Institute for Jewish Education in the Diaspora: Dir Prof. Y. RICH.

Institute for Social Integration in the Educational System: Dir Prof. H. GAZIEL.

Institute for Sociological Research of Ethnic Groups: Dir Prof. A. LASLO.

Institute for the Research and Advancement of Religious Education: Dir Prof. Y. RICH.

Institute for Research in Jewish Economic History: Dir Prof. Y. ROSENBERG.

Centre for Documentation of Contemporary Jewish Communities: Dir Prof. M. FRIEDMAN.

Shlomo Argov Centre for Israel–Diaspora Relations: Dir Prof. D. YEHIYE.

Midrasha for Women: Dir Rabbi Y. KRAUSS.

Institute for Local Government: Dir Dr S. ROZVITZ.

Center for Retail Management and Marketing: Dir Prof. E. JAFFE.

Abraham Gelbart Research Institute in Mathematical Sciences: Dir Prof. L. ZALZMAN.

Dr Jaime Lusinchi Center for Applied Research in the Life Sciences: Dir Prof. M. ALBECK.

Haddad Centre for Research in Dyslexia and Reading Disorders: Dir Prof. D. TSURIEL.

Centre for the Study of Mountainous Areas in Judea and the Ezion Bloc: Dir Prof. J. KATZ.

The Cancer, AIDS and Immunology Research Institute: Dir Prof. B. SREDNI.

The David J. Azrieli Institute for Research on the Economy of Israel: Dir Dr A. BEREZIS.

The Edward I. and Fannie Baker Center for the Study of Developmental Disorders in Infants and Young Children: Dir Prof. PNINA KLEIN.

The Institute for Research on the European Community: Dir Prof. I. GREILSAMMER.

The Center for International Policy and Communication: Dir Prof. S. LEHMANN.

The Center for Commercial Law: Dir Prof. S. LERNER.

Emmy Noether Mathematics Institute in Algebra, Geometry, Function Theory and Summability: Dir Prof. M. TEICHER.

Center for Strategic Studies: Dir Prof. E. INBAR.

Rehabilitation Center for IDF Head-Injured Disabled Veterans: Dir Prof. S. KRAWITZ.

Rabbi Joseph Carlebach Institute for Studies in Jewish Thought: Dir Dr MIRIAM GILLIS.

Institute for Education and Community Research: Dir Prof. Y. KATZ.

Health Sciences Research Center: Dir Prof. S. R. SAMPSON.

Pearl and Jack Resnick Institute for Advanced Technology: Dir Prof. M. KAVEH.

Jacob Taubes Minerva Centre for Religious Anthropology: Dir Prof. A. BAUMGARTEN.

J. M. Kaplan Program for American Literature: Dir Dr SHARON BARIS.

Sal van Gelden Centre for Teaching and Research of Holocaust Literature: Dir Prof. HANNA YAOZ.

Lewis Family Foundation for International Conferences in the Humanities: Dir Prof. E. SPOLSKY.

Arnold and Anita Lorber Entrepreneurial Award Program: Dir Dr R. ALDOR.

Schnitzer Foundation for Research on the Israeli Economy and Society: Dir Prof. H. BABKOFF.

Program in Journalism and Communications: Dir Dr Y. ORBACH.

Pollack Foundation in Basic and Applied Research in the Natural Sciences.

Samuel M. and Helene K. Soref Young Scientist Endowment Program: Dir Prof. M. KAVEH.

Jerome Schottenstein Cell Scan Centre for the Early Detection of Cancer: Dir Prof. M. DEUTSCH.

Edith Wolfson Instrumentation Research Centre: Dir Dr H. GOTTLIEB.

Fanya Gottesfeld Heller Centre for the Study of Women in Judaism: Dir Prof. T. COHEN.

Ingeborg Rennert Centre for Jerusalem Studies: Dir Prof. Y. SCHWARTZ.

Centre for Basic Jewish Studies: Dir Prof. A. TOAFF.

Gerson and Judith Leiber Jewish Art Exhibition Centre: Dir Prof. D. SPERBER.

Language Policy Research Centre: Dir Dr J. WALTERS.

Bernard W. Marcus Centre for Pharmaceutical and Medicinal Chemistry: Dir Prof. A. NUDELMAN.

Centre for Teaching Science: Dir Prof. Z. MEVARECH.

Minerva Centre for Physics of Mesoscopics: Dir Prof. M. KAVEH.

Minerva Centre for High-Temperature Superconductivity (in collaboration with Tel Aviv University and the Technion): Bar-Ilan Dir Prof. Y. YESHURUN.

Minerva Centre for Fractals: Dir Prof. S. HAVLIN.

Minerva Centre for Neurons: Dir Prof. IDO KANTOR.

Halpern Centre for Research into Jewish Consciousness: Dir Dr A. SHREMER.

Centre for Economic Security and Peace: Dir Prof. B. Z. ZILBERFARB.

Pelleg-Billig Centre for Research into Quality of Family Life: Dir Prof. M. MIKULINCER.

Gonda Goldschmidt Centre for Diagnostic Medicine: Dir Prof. S. HAVLIN.

Centre for Industrial Mathematics: Dir Prof. E. MERZBACH.

Jewish Identity Centre: Dir (vacant).

David and Jemima Jeselsohn Epigraphic Centre of Jewish History: Dir Prof. H. ESHEL.

Dahan Centre for Research of Sephardic Jewry: Dir Prof. E. HAZAN.

Florrie Tanzeri Foundation for Research on Women in Hebrew Literature: Dir Prof. Y. DISHON.

Strochlitz Centre for Advancement of Research on Professional Jewish Education: Dir Prof. S. VARGON.

Centre for Research on Kabbala: Dir Dr A. ELYAKIM.

Rahel Gewirtz Centre for Gender Studies: Dir Prof. T. COHEN.

Raymond Damedian NMR Centre: Dir Prof. E. HAAS.

Aharan Meir Centre for Education in Banking: Dir Prof. B. ZILBERFARB.

Pasternak Institute for the Furthering of Studies and Publication in the Field of Hebrew Language: Dir Prof. M. SOKOLOFF.

Burg Centre for Education, Values, Peace and Tolerance: Dir Prof. Y. IRAM.

Minerva Centre for Microscale and Nanoscale Particles and Films as Tailored Biomaterial Interfaces: Dir Prof. C. SUKENIK.

Centre for Advanced Materials and Nanotechnology: Dir Prof. C. SUKENIK.

Optometry Program: Dir Prof. Y. NITZAN.

Trend for Finance and Banking for Second Degree in Economics and Finance: Dir Dr M. KRAUS.

Naiftal Centre for Research in Oral Law: Dir Prof. D. HANSHKE.

Rapaport Centre for Assimilation and Strengthening the Vitality of Judaism: Dir Prof. Z. ZOHAR.

Ladino Centre in name of Yehoshua and Neima Salti: Dir Dr S. RAPHAEL.

Centre for Study of Commentaries: Dir Prof. A. SAGUY.

Centre for Advancement of Status of Women: Dir Dr RUTH HALPERN KADDARI.

BEN GURION UNIVERSITY OF THE NEGEV

POB 653, 84105 Be'ersheva
Telephone: (8) 6461223
Fax: (8) 6479434
E-mail: acadsec@bgumail.bgu.ac.il
Internet: www.bgu.ac.il

Founded 1965
Languages of instruction: Hebrew, English
Academic year: October to June

President: Prof. AVISHAY BRAVERMAN
Rector: Prof. JIMMY WEINBLATT
Director-General: DAVID BAREKET
Senior Vice-President: Dr ISRAEL GERMAN
Vice-President and Dean for Research and Development: Prof. MORDECHAY HERSKOWITZ
Deputy Rector: Prof. SHRAGA SEGAL
Vice-Rector: Prof. LILY NEUMANN
Academic Secretary: AVRAHAM BAR-ON
Librarian: AVNER SCHMUELEVITZ

Library: see Libraries and Archives
Number of teachers: 1,000
Number of students: 17,000

Publications: *Israel Social Science Research Journal*, *Geography Research Forum*, *Israel Studies*, *Shvut – Studies in Russian and East European Jewish History and Culture*, *MIKAN – Research Journal of Hebrew Literature*, *HAGAR – International Social Science Review*, *JAMA'A – Interdisciplinary Journal for the Study of the Middle East*

DEANS

Engineering Sciences: Prof. YIGAL RONEN
Health Sciences: Prof. RIVKA CARMI
Humanities and Social Sciences: Prof. AVISHAI HENIK
Management: Prof. ARIE REICHEL
Natural Sciences: Prof. ABRAHAM PAROLA

PROFESSORS

Faculty of Engineering Sciences (tel. (8) 6461212; fax (8) 6472936; e-mail offcdean@bgumail.bgu.ac.il; internet www.bgu.ac.il/html/academics.html):

AHARONI, H., Electrical and Computer Engineering
ALFASSI, Z., Nuclear Engineering
APELBLAT, A., Chemical Engineering
ARAZI, B., Electrical and Computer Engineering
BEN-DOR, G., Mechanical Engineering
BEN-YAAKOV, S., Electrical and Computer Engineering
CENSOR, D., Electrical and Computer Engineering
DARIEL, M., Materials Engineering
DINSTEIN, I., Electrical and Computer Engineering
DUBI, A., Nuclear Engineering
EILON, A., Electrical and Computer Engineering
ELIEZER, D., Materials Engineering
ELPERIN, T., Mechanical Engineering
FINGER, N., Industrial Engineering and Management
FUKS, D., Materials Engineering
GALPERIN, A., Nuclear Engineering
GOTTLIEB, M., Chemical Engineering
HAVA, S., Electrical and Computer Engineering
HERSKOWITZ, M., Chemical Engineering
IGRA, O., Mechanical Engineering
JACOB, I., Nuclear Engineering
KAPLAN, B., Electrical and Computer Engineering
KOPEIKA, N., Electrical and Computer Engineering
KOST, J., Chemical Engineering
LADANY, S., Industrial Engineering and Management
LETAN, R., Mechanical Engineering
MENIPAZ, E., Industrial Engineering and Management
MERCHUK, J., Chemical Engineering
MOND, M., Mechanical Engineering
PERL, M., Mechanical Engineering
PLISKIN, J., Industrial Engineering and Management
PLISKIN, N., Industrial Engineering and Management
PORTMAN, V., Mechanical Engineering
RONEN, Y., Nuclear Engineering
ROTMAN, S., Electrical and Computer Engineering
SCHULGASSER, K., Mechanical Engineering
SEGEV, R., Mechanical Engineering
SHACHAM, M., Chemical Engineering
SHANI, G., Nuclear Engineering
SHER, E., Mechanical Engineering
SHINAR, D., Industrial Engineering and Management
SHUVAL, P., Information Systems Engineering
SINUANI-STERN, Z., Industrial Engineering and Management
SLONIM, M., Electrical and Computer Engineering
TALYANKER, M., Materials Engineering
TAMIR, A., Chemical Engineering
VILNAY, O., Construction Engineering

VOLLICH, D., Electrical and Computer Engineering
WISNIAK, J., Chemical Engineering
ZARETSKY, E., Mechanical Engineering

Faculty of Health Sciences (tel. (8) 6477409; fax (8) 6477632; e-mail rtemes@bgumail.bgu.ac.il; internet www.fohs.bgu.ac.il):

ABOUD, M., Microbiology and Immunology
ALKAN, M., Internal Medicine
APPELBAUM, A., Cardiology
APTE, R., Microbiology and Immunology
BASHAN, N., Clinical Biochemistry
BENJAMIN, J., Psychiatry
BUSKILA, D., Internal Medicine
CARMEL, S., Health Sociology
CARMI, R., Clinical Genetics
CLARFIELD, M., Geriatrics
FRASER, D., Epidemiology
GROSSMAN, Y., Physiology
GURMAN, G., Anaesthesiology
HALEVI, S., Dermatology
HALLAK, M., Gynaecology
HELDMAN, E., Physiology
HERZANO, Y., Radiology
ILIA, R., Cardiology
ISAKOV, N., Microbiology and Immunology
KATZ, M., Gynaecology
LEVY, R., Biochemistry
LEVY, Y., Biochemistry
LUNENFELD, E., Gynaecology
MARGULIS, C., Medical Education
MAZOR, M., Gynaecology
MEYERSTEIN, N., Physiology
MORAN, A., Physiology
NAGGAN, L., Epidemiology
NEUMANN, L., Epidemiology
PIURA, B., Gynaecology
PORATH, A., Internal Medicine
POTASHNIK, G., Gynaecology
RAGER, B., Microbiology and Immunology
SCHLESINGER, M., Paediatrics
SCHVARTZMAN, P., Family Medicine
SEGAL, S., Microbiology and Immunology
SHARONI, Y., Clinical Biochemistry
SHANY, SH., Clinical Biochemistry
SCHLAEFFER, F., Internal Medicine
SIKULER, E., Internal Medicine
SOFER, S., Paediatrics
SUKENIK, S., Internal Medicine
TAL, A., Paediatrics
WEINSTEIN, J., Microbiology
WHITE, E., Morphology

Faculty of Humanities and Social Sciences (tel. (8) 6461105; fax (8) 6472945; e-mail henik@bgumail.bgu.ac.il; internet www.bgu.ac.il/html/academics.html):

ALEXANDER, T., Hebrew Literature
BAR-ON, D., Behavioural Sciences
BENZION, U., Economics
BLIDSTEIN, G., Jewish Thought
BORG, A., Hebrew Language
BOWMAN, D., Geography and Environmental Development
BRAVERMAN, A., Economics
BREGMAN, D., Hebrew Literature
CASPI, D., Communication Studies
DANZINGER, L., Economics
DREMAN, S., Behavioural Sciences
EINY, E., Economics
GELMAN, Y., Philosophy
GILAD, I., Bible and Ancient Near-Eastern Studies
GORDON, D., Education
GORDON, H., Education
GORODETSKY, M., Education
GRADUS, Y., Geography and Environmental Development
GRIES, Z., Jewish Thought
GRUBER, I., Bible and Ancient Near-East Studies
HENIK, A., Behavioural Sciences
HOCHMAN, O., Economics
HUROWITZ, V., Bible and Ancient Near-Eastern Studies
ISRALOWITZ, R., Social Work
JUSTMAN, M., Economics
KRAKOVER, S., Geography and Environmental Development
KREISEL, H., Jewish Thought
LARONNE, J., Geography and Environmental Development
LASKER, D., Jewish Thought
LAZIN, F., Behavioural Sciences
LIBERLES, R., History
LURIE, Y., Philosophy
MEIR, A., Geography and Environmental Development
MORRIS, B., Middle East Studies
OREN, E., Bible and Ancient Near-Eastern Studies
PARUSH, A., Philosophy
POZNANSKI, R., Politics and Government
PRIEL, B., Behavioural Sciences
QIMRON, E., Hebrew Language
REGEV, U., Economics
ROSEN, S., Bible and Ancient Near-Eastern Studies
SALMON, Y., History
SHAROT, S., Behavioural Sciences
SHINAR, D., General Studies
SIVAN, D., Hebrew Language
STERN, E., Geography and Environmental Development
TALSHIR, Z., Bible and Ancient Near-East Studies
TOBIN, I., Foreign Languages and Literature
TROEN, I., History
TSAHOR, Z., History
TSOAR, H., Geography and Environmental Development
TZELGOV, Y., Behavioural Sciences
VINNER, S., Science and Technology Education
WEINBLATT, J., Economics

School of Management (tel. (8) 6472250; fax (8) 6472868; e-mail sompr@nihul.bgu.ac.il; internet www.bgu.ac.il/som):

BAR-ELI, M., Business Administration
DRORY, A., Business Administration
GIDRON, B., Business Administration
MALACH-PINES, A., Business Administration
PREISS, K., Business Administration
REICHEL, A., Hotel and Tourism Management

Faculty of Natural Sciences (tel. (8) 6461633; fax (8) 6472954; e-mail mia@math.bgu.ac.il; internet www.bgu.ac.il/html/academics.html):

ABRAHAM, U., Mathematics
ABRAMSKY, Z., Life Sciences
ALPAI, D., Mathematics
ALTSHULER, A., Mathematics
AVISHAI, Y., Physics
BAHAT, D., Geological and Environmental Sciences
BAND, Y., Chemistry
BARAK, Z., Life Sciences
BECKER, J., Chemistry
BELITSKI, H., Mathematics
BEREND, D., Mathematics
BERNSTEIN, J., Chemistry
BITTNER, S., Chemistry
BRUSTEIN, R., Physics
CHIPMAN, D., Life Sciences
COHEN, M., Mathematics
DAVIDSON, A., Physics
EFRIMA, S., Chemistry
EICHLER, D., Physics
EISENBERG, T., Mathematics
FEINTUCH, A., Mathematics
FONF, V., Mathematics
FUHRMANN, P. A., Mathematics
GEDALIN, M., Physics
GERSTEN, A., Physics
GLASER, R., Chemistry
GOLDSHTEIN, V., Mathematics
GOREN, S., Physics
GORODETSKY, G., Physics
GRANOT, Y., Life Sciences
HODORKOVSKY, V., Chemistry
HOROVITZ, B., Physics
HOROWITZ, Y., Physics
KISCH, H., Geological and Environmental Sciences
KOJMAN, M., Mathematics
KOST, D., Chemistry
LIN, M., Mathematics
MEIR, Y., Physics
MIZRAHI, Y., Life Sciences
MOALEM, A., Physics
MORDECHAI, S., Physics
MOREH, R., Physics
OWEN, D., Physics
PAROLA, A., Chemistry
POLAK, M., Chemistry
PRIEL, Z., Chemistry
PROSS, A., Chemistry
RABINOVITSCH, A., Physics
ROSENWAKS, S., Physics
RUBIN, M., Mathematics
SCHARF, B., Chemistry
SEGEV, Y., Mathematics
SHOSHAN-BARMATZ, V., Life Sciences
SHUKER, R., Physics
TKACHENKO, V., Mathematics
ZARITSKY, A., Life Sciences

Blaustein Institute for Desert Research (Sde Boker Campus, 84990 Be'ersheva; tel. (8) 6596700; fax (8) 6596703; e-mail bidr@bgumail.bgu.ac.il; internet www.bgu.ac.il/bidr):

BEN-ASHER, J.
BOUSSIBA, S.
BURDA, G.
DEGAN, A.
ETZION, Y.
FEIMAN, D.
GORDON, J.
GUTTERMAN, Y.
HA COHEN, Z.
HEIMER, Y.
KOTLER, B.
KRESSEL, G.
LUBIN, Y.
MERON, E.
ORON, G.
PINSHOW, B.
RUBINSTEIN, I.
SHACHAK, M.
SOREK, S.
VONSHAK, A.
ZANGWIL, A.
ZARMI, Y.
ZEMEL, A.

Institutes for Applied Research (84990 Be'ersheva; tel. (8) 6461927; fax (8) 6472969; e-mail applied@bgumail.bgu.ac.il; internet www.bgu.ac.il/iar):

ARAD, S., Applied Biosciences
BAR-ZIV, E., Chemistry and Chemical Technology
ZABICKY, J., Chemistry and Chemical Technology

UNIVERSITY OF HAIFA

Mount Carmel, 31905 Haifa
Telephone: (4) 8240111
Fax: (4) 8342104
E-mail: rector@research.haifa.ac.il
Internet: www.haifa.ac.il

Founded 1963
Independent
Language of instruction: Hebrew
Academic year: October to June

Pres.: Prof. AARON BEN-ZE'EV
Rector: Prof. YOSSI BEN-ARTZI
Vice-Rector: Prof. DAVID FARAGGI
Vice-Pres. for Admin.: Prof. BARUCH MARZAN
Vice-Pres. for Public Relations and Resource Devt: ADA SPITZER
Registrar: RUTH RABINOWITZ

Academic Sec.: SHOSHANA LANDMAN
Dean of Graduate Studies: Prof. SOPHIA MENACHE
Dean of Research: Prof. MAJID EL-HAJ
Librarian: Prof. HAYA BAR-ITZHAK

Number of teachers: 1,125
Number of students: 16,000

Publications: *Jewish History* (every 2 years), *Dappim – Research in Literature* (annual, Hebrew, with English abstracts), *Studies in Education* (every 2 years, Hebrew), *Studies in Children's Literature* (annual, Hebrew), *JTD Haifa University Studies in Theatre and Drama* (annual), *Mishpat Umimshal Law and Government in Israel* (every 2 years, Hebrew)

DEANS AND HEADS OF SCHOOLS

Faculty of Education: Prof. OFRA MAYSELLES
Faculty of Humanities: Prof. MENACHEM MOR
Faculty of Law: Prof. ELI SALZBERGER
Faculty of Sciences: Prof. ABRAHAM HAIM
Faculty of Social Science: Prof. SAMMY SAMOOHA
Faculty of Social Welfare and Health Sciences: Prof. PERLA WERNER
School of Political Sciences: Prof. GABRIEL BEN DOR
School of Social Work: Dr AMNON LAZAR
Graduate School of Business: Prof. SHEIZAF RAFAELI

PROFESSORS

Faculty of Education (tel. (4) 8240726; fax (4) 8240911):

ALEXANDER, H., Education
BARAK, A., Education
BEN-PERETZ, M., Education
BREZNITZ, Z., Education
COHEN, A., Education
HERTZ-LAZAROWITZ, R., Education
KATRIEL, T., Education
KLINGMAN, A., Education
LINN, R., Education
NESHER, P., Education
SALOMON, G., Education
SEGINA, R., Education
SCHECHTMAN, Z., Education
SHIMRON, J., Education
YERUSHALMY, M., Education
ZEIDNER, M., Education

Faculty of Humanities (tel. (4) 8240125; fax (4) 8240128):

AVISHUR, Y., Hebrew Language
AZAR, M., Hebrew Language
BARAM, A., Middle Eastern History
BARNAI, J., Land of Israel Studies
BEN-ARTZI, Y., Land of Israel Studies
CHETRIT, J., French
CHISICK, H., History
DAVID, E., General History
DIMANT, D., Jewish History
DOLGOPOLSKY, A., Hebrew Language
ELBAZ, R., French
ELDAR, I., Hebrew Language
EVRON., M., Archaeology
FREEDMAN, W., English
GELBER, Y., Land of Israel Studies
GILBAR, G., Middle-East History
GILEAD, A., Philosophy
GINAT, J., Land of Israel Studies
GOLDSTEIN, Y., Land of Israel Studies
GOODITCH, M., General History
GRABOIS, A., History
HAHLILI, R., Archaeology
HELTZER, M., Bible
HOFFMAN, J., Hebrew Language
KAGAN, Z., Hebrew and Comparative Literature
KANAZI, G., Arabic Language and Literature
KELLNER, M., Jewish History
KOCHAVI, A., History
KUSHNIR, D., Middle East History
LAUFER, M., English
LUZ, E., Jewish Thought
MALUL, M., Biblical Studies
MANSOUR, Y., Hebrew Language
MART, Y., Maritime Civilizations
MENACHE, S., General History
MICHEL, J., French
ODED, B., Jewish History
ORKIN, M., Theatre, English Literature
PECHTER, M., Jewish History
RAPPAPORT, U., Jewish History
REICH, R., Archaeology
ROBIN, R., General History
RONEN, A., Archaeology
ROZEN, M., Jewish History
SANDLER, W., English
SCHATZKER, C., Jewish History
SEGAL, A., Archaeology
SHENHAR, A., Hebrew and Comparative Literature
SHICHOR, Y., Multidisciplinary Studies
SHOHAM, R., Hebrew and Comparative Literature
SMILANSKY, S., Philosophy
SOBEL, M., History
SPANIER, E., Maritime Civilizations
STATMAN, D., Philosophy
STOW, K., Jewish History
TOBI, J., Hebrew and Comparative Literature
WARBURG, G., Middle Eastern History
YARDENI, M., History
YEHOSHUA, A. B., Hebrew and Comparative Literature
ZINGUER, I., French

Faculty of Law (tel. (4) 8240633; fax (4) 8249247):

EDREY, Y., Law
GROSS, E., Law

Faculty of Sciences (tel. (4) 8288076; fax (4) 8288108):

BUTNARIO, D., Mathematics
CARO, Y., Mathematics
CENSOR, Y., Mathematics
DAFNI, A., Biology
GOLAN, J., Mathematics
GORDON, A., Physics
HAIM, A., Biology
KOZENIKOV, A., Mathematics
MORAN, G., Mathematics
NEVO, E., Biology
REISNER, S., Mathematics
RUBINSTEIN, Z., Mathematics
SKOLNICK, A., Biology
SOKER, N., Physics
VAISMAN, I., Mathematics
WASSER, S., Biology
WEIT, I., Mathematics
YITZHAKI, I., Biology
ZACKS, J., Mathematics
ZOLLER, U., Chemistry

Faculty of Social Sciences (tel. (4) 8240331; fax (4) 8246814):

AL-HAJ, M., Sociology
ARAZY, J., Mathematics and Computer Science
ARIAN, A., Political Science
BARAK, A., Psychology
BAR-GAL, Y., Geography
BAR-LEV, S., Statistics
BEIT-HALLAHMI, B., Psychology
BEN-DOR, G., Political Science
BERG, M., Statistics and Business Administration
BERMAN, E., Psychology
BIGER, N., Business Administration
BRAUN, A., Mathematics and Computer Science
BREZNITZ, S., Psychology
CENSOR, Y., Mathematics and Computer Science
DAFNI, A., Biology
EDEN, B., Economics
FARAGGI, D., Statistics
FELZENTAL, D., Political Science
FISHMAN, G., Sociology
GOLAN, J., Mathematics and Computer Science
GOLOMBIC, M., Computer Science
GUIORA, A. Z., Psychology
HARPAZ, Y., Sociology and Business Administration
HAYUTH, Y., Geography
INBAR, M., Geography
ISHAI, Y., Political Science
KATRIEL, T., Communication
KELLERMAN, A., Geography
KEREN, G., Psychology
KIPNIS, B., Geography
KLIOT, N., Geography
KORIAT, A., Psychology
KRAUS, V., Sociology
KUTIEL, H., Geography
LANDAU, G., Computer Science
LANDSBERGER, M., Econ.
LANGBERG, N., Statistics
LIEBERMAN, O., Econ.
MAKOV, E., Land of Israel Studies
MATTRAS, Y., Sociology
MELNIK, A., Econ.
MESHIULAM, I., Business Admin.
MINTZ, A., Political Science
MORAN, G., Mathematics and Computer Science
NAVON, D., Psychology
NEVO, B., Psychology
PERRY, D., Statistics
RAFAELI, S., Business Admin.
RAKOVER, S., Psychology
REISER, B., Statistics
RICHTER-LEVIN, G., Psychology
ROITMAN, M., Mathematics
ROSENFELD, H., Sociology
ROSNER, M., Sociology
ROZENBLATT, M., Business Admin.
RUBIN, S., Psychology
RUBINSTEIN, Z., Mathematics and Computer Science
SAFIR, M., Psychology
SAGI-SCHWARTZ, A., Psychology
SAMUEL, Y., Sociology
SHECHTER, M., Econ.
SHITOVITZ, B., Econ.
SHLIFER, E., Business Admin.
SMOOHA, S., Sociology
SOBEL, Z., Sociology
SOFFER, A., Geography
VAINSHTEIN, A., Mathematics and Computer Science
VAISMAN, I., Mathematics and Computer Science
WATERMAN, S., Geography
WEIMAN, G., Sociology and Communication
WEISS, G., Statistics
WEIT, I., Mathematics and Computer Science
ZAKS, J., Mathematics and Computer Science

Faculty of Social Welfare and Health Sciences (tel. (4) 8249950; fax (4) 8249946):

EISIKOVITS, Z., Social Work
GILBAR, O., Social Work
GUTTMAN, D., Social Work
LEV-WIESEL, R., Social Work
LINN, S., Public Health
LOEWENSTEIN, A., Gerontology
RIMMERMAN, A., Social Work
SHARLIN, S., Social Work
WEISS, T., Occupational Therapy
WERNER, P., Gerontology

ATTACHED RESEARCH INSTITUTES, CENTRES, LABORATORIES

Center for Alternatives in Education.

Center for the Research and Study of Aging.

Center for Information Society Research.

Center for the Interdisciplinary Research of Emotions.

Center for Jewish Education in Israel and the Diaspora.

Center for Multi-Culturalism and Educational Research.

Center for Research and Study of the Family.

Actuarial Research Center.

Center for Research on Peace Education.

Center for the Study of Eretz Israel and its Yishuv of Yad Yitzhak Ben-Zvi and the University of Haifa.

Center for Rehabilitation Research and Human Development.

Center for the Study of Child Development.

Center for the Study of Crime, Law and Society.

Center for the Study of Jewish Culture in Spain and Islamic Lands.

Center for the Study of Pilgrimage, Tourism and Recreation.

Center of Educational Administration and Evaluation.

Center for the Study of Jewish Culture.

Center for the Study of Organizations and Management of Human Resources.

Center for the Research of French Civilization.

Call Center – Computer Language Learning Center.

Golan Research Institute.

Gotteiner Institute for the History of the Bund and the Jewish Labor Movement.

Gottlieb Schumacher Institute for Research of Christian Activities in 19th-Century Palestine.

Haifa Interdisciplinary Center for Advanced Computer Science.

Herzl Institute for Research Studies of Zionism.

Institute for the Study of French History and Culture.

Institute for Research into the Kibbutz and the Cooperative Idea.

Institute of Evolution.

Institute of Information Processing and Decision-Making.

International Centre for Health Law and Ethics.

Jewish–Arab Center (Gustav Heinemann Institute of Middle Eastern Studies).

Leon Recanati Institute for Maritime Studies.

Ian Karten Laboratory for Rehabilitation and Therapy (Nazareth).

Laboratory of Psychopharmacology.

Fear and Avoidance Laboratory.

Laboratory of Animal Learning and Behavior.

Laboratory of Developmental Psychology and Mineral Appetites.

Brain and Behavior Laboratory.

Face Recognition Laboratory.

Social Laboratory.

Attention and Perception Laboratory.

Cognitive Laboratory.

MMPI Laboratory.

Laboratory for the Study and Assessment of Intelligence.

Clinical – Education Laboratory.

Laboratory for the Study of Human Intelligence.

Multimedia Laboratory of the Faculty of Humanities.

Sign Language, Linguistics and Cognition Research Laboratory.

Primary Mathematics Laboratory.

Computer Laboratory.

Laboratory of Computer-Aided Cartography.

Laboratory for Research on Drama, Theatre and Education.

Laboratory for Statistical Counselling.

Laboratory for Geographical Information Systems (GIS) Remote Sensing.

Laboratory for Cross-Cultural Research in Personality and Individual Differences.

Laboratory for Research and Development of Computers for Learning.

Laboratory for Neurocognitive Research.

Laboratory for Learning Disabilities.

Laboratory for Audio-Visual Productions.

Laboratory for Experimental Research in Education.

Laboratory for Learning and Teaching.

Max Wertheimer Minerva Center for Cognitive Processes and Human Performance.

Minerva Center for Youth Studies.

National Security Studies Center.

Natural Resources and Environmental Research Center.

Ray D. Wolfe Center for the Study of Psychological Stress.

Research Unit for the Study of Memory Functioning in the Elderly.

Research Unit for the Cultures of Spain.

Shlomo Zalman Strochlitz Institute of Holocaust Studies.

Wydra Institute of Shipping and Aviation Research.

Zinman Institute of Archaeology.

Caesarea Edmund Benjamin de Rothschild Institute for Interdisciplinary Applications of Computer Science.

Bucerius Center for Contemporary German History and Society.

Brain and Behaviour Center: Dir Prof. GAL RICHTER-LEVIN.

Center for Computational Mathematics and Scientific Computation: Dir Prof. YAIR CENSOR.

Center for the Study of the United States: Dir Prof. MECHAL SOBEL.

Genome Diversity Center: Dir Prof. EDWARD N. TRIFONOV.

AFFILIATED INSTITUTIONS AND REGIONAL COLLEGES

Oranim—School of Education of the Kibbutz Movement: Dir Prof. YAIR CARO.

Zinman College of Physical Education and Sports Sciences at the Wingate Institute.

HEBREW UNIVERSITY OF JERUSALEM

Mount Scopus, 91905 Jerusalem

Telephone: (2) 5882111

Fax: (2) 5322545

Internet: www.huji.ac.il

Founded 1918; inaugurated 1925

Private control, partially supported by the Government

Academic year: October to June

Language of instruction: Hebrew

Chairman, Board of Governors: YIGAL ARNON

President: Prof. MENACHEM MAGIDOR

Rector: Prof. HAIM D. RABINOWITCH

Vice-Presidents: AVINOAM ARMONI, HERVÉ BERCOVIER, MOSHE VIGDOR

Academic Secretary: JOEL ALPERT

Library Director: Prof. YORAM TSAFRIR

Library: see Jewish National and University Library

Number of teachers: 1,095

Number of students: 24,142

Publications: *Research* (in English), *Yahadut Zemanenu* (Studies in Contemporary Jewry, annually, in English and Hebrew editions), *Jews in Eastern Europe* (in English, 3 a year), *Antisemitism* (annotated bibliography, annually, multilingual), *Tarbebiz* (Jewish studies, in Hebrew, annually), *Shnaton* (Biblical and ancient Near Eastern studies, in Hebrew, annually), *Aleph* (historical studies in science and Judaism, in Hebrew, annually), *Jerusalem Studies in Jewish Thought* (in Hebrew, annually), *Jerusalem Studies in Jewish Folklore* (in Hebrew, annually), *Jerusalem Studies in Hebrew Literature* (in Hebrew, annually), *Italia* (research in the history, culture and literature of the Jews in Italy, annually, multilingual), *Hispania Judaica Bulletin* (in English, 1 year)

DEANS AND DIRECTORS

Faculty of Agricultural, Food and Environmental Science: Prof. YITZHAK HADAR

Faculty of Dental Medicine: Prof. JONATHAN MANN

Faculty of Humanities: Prof. STEVEN KAPLAN

Faculty of Law: Prof. EYAL ZAMIR

Faculty of Mathematics and Natural Science: Prof. AVRAHAM GAL

Faculty of Medicine: Prof. DANIEL SHUVAL

Faculty of Social Sciences: Prof. NACHMAN BEN-YEHUDA

Jerusalem School of Business Administration: Prof. JONATHAN KORNBLUTH

School of Education: Prof. ELISHA BABAD

School of Library, Archive and Information Studies: Prof. CATRIEL BEERI

School of Nutritional Sciences: Dr RANA REIFEN

School of Pharmacy: Prof. GERSHON GOLOMB

Paul Baerwald School of Social Work: Prof. HILLEL SCHMID

Centre for Pre-Academic Studies: Prof. RUTH SPERLING

Hebrew University—Hadassah School of Occupational Medicine: Prof. NAOMI KATZ

Hebrew University—Hadassah School of Public Health and Community Medicine: Prof. ELLIOT BEERY

Henrietta Szold-Hebrew University—Hadassah School of Nursing: Dr MIRI ROM

Koret School of Veterinary Medicine: Prof. GADI GLAZER

Rothberg School for Overseas Students: (vacant)

PROFESSORS

Faculty of Agricultural, Food and Environmental Quality Science

(including the School of Nutritional Sciences and the Koret School of Veterinary Medicine)

ADIN, A., Soil and Water Sciences
CAHANER, A., Field Crops, Vegetables and Genetics
CHEN, Y., Soil and Water Sciences
COHEN, E., Entomology
CZOSNEK, H., Molecular Genetics

FEINERMAN, E., Agricultural Economics
FRIEDMAN, A., Animal Sciences
GOLDSCHMIDT, E. E., Horticulture
GUTNICK, J. M., School of Veterinary Medicine
HADAR, Y., Plant Pathology and Microbiology
HELLER, D. A., Animal Sciences
HILLEL, J., Field Crops, Vegetables and Genetics
MADAR, Z., Agricultural Biochemistry
MAHRER, Y., Soil and Water Sciences
MUALEM, Y., Soil and Water Sciences
NAIM, H., Food Science and Nutrition
NATIV, R., Soil and Water Sciences
NOY-MEIR, I., Horticulture
NUSSINOVITCH, A., Food Science and Nutrition
OKON, Y., Plant Pathology and Microbiology
RABINOWITCH, H. D., Field Crops, Vegetables and Genetics
RIOV, J., Horticulture
RUBIN, B., Field Crops, Vegetables and Genetics
SAGUY, I., Agricultural Biochemistry
SELA, I., Virology
TEL-OR, E., Agricultural Economics
TSUR, Y., Agricultural Economics
WALLACH, R., Soil and Water Sciences
WOLFENSON, D., Animal Sciences
YARDEN, O., Plant Pathology and Microbiology
ZAMIR, D., Field Crops, Vegetables and Genetics
ZAMSKI, E., Agricultural Botany

Faculty of Dental Medicine (En Karem Campus, POB 12272, 91120 Jerusalem; tel. 6158595; fax 6439219; e-mail hujident@cc.huji.ac.il; internet dental.huji.ac.il):

(Hebrew University-Hadassah School of Dental Medicine)

BAB, I., Oral Pathology
BIMSTEIN, E., Paediatric Dentistry
CHEVION, M., Biochemistry
DEUTSCH, D., Oral Biology
GARFUNKEL, A., Oral Medicine
GAZIT, D., Oral Pathology
HOROWITZ, M., Physiology
MANN, J., Community Dentistry
SCHWARTZ, Z., Periodontics
SELA, J., Oral Pathology
SELA, M., Maxillofacial Rehabilitation
SELA, M., Oral Biology
SHAPIRA, L., Periodontics
SMITH, P., Anthropology
SOSKOLNE, A., Periodontics
STABHOLZ, A., Endodontics

Faculty of Humanities

(the Joseph and Ceil Mazer Center for the Humanities, including the Institutes of: Jewish Studies; Contemporary Jewry; Asian and African Studies; Archaeology, Philosophy and History; Languages, Literatures and Art; School of Education)

ABITBOL, M., Contemporary Jewry and African Studies
AMISHAI-MAISELS, Z., History of Art
ARAZI, A., Arabic Language and Literature
ASCHHEIM, S., History
ASSIS, Y.-T., Jewish History
BABAD, E., Education
BAR ASHER, M., Hebrew Language
BAR-ELLI, G., Philosophy
BARTAL, I., Jewish History
BAR YAFFE, Y., Spanish and Latin American Studies
BELFER-COHEN, A., Archaeology
BEN-SASSON, M., Jewish History
BEN-SHAMMAI, H., Arabic Language and Literature
BESSERMAN, L., English Literature
BLUM-KULKA, S., Education, Communication
BRODY, R., Talmudic Studies
BUDICK, E., American Studies
BUDICK, S., English Literature
COGAN, M., History of Jewish Studies
COHEN, R., Jewish History
COHEN, S., Education
COTTON, H., History and Classics
DELLA PERGOLA, S., Contemporary Jewry
DINER, D., History
ELBOIM, Y., Hebrew Literature
ELIOR, R., Jewish Thought
ELIZUR, S., Hebrew Literature
ETKES, I., Education and History of the Jewish People
FERRETTI CUOMO, L., Italian Language and Literature
GAFNI, I., Jewish History
GATI, I., Education, Psychology
GERBER, H., Islamic Studies
GOREN-INBAR, N., Archaeology
HACKER, J. R., History of the Jewish People
HALBERTAL, M., Jewish Thought and Philosophy
HARVEY, Z., Jewish Thought
HASAN-ROKEM, G., Literature and Folklore
HEVER, H., Hebrew Literature
HEYD, D., Philosophy
HEYD, M., History
HIRSHBERG, J., Musicology
HOPKINS, S. A., Arabic
IDEL, M., Jewish Thought
KADISH, A., History
KAHANA, M., Talmudic Studies
KAPLAN, S., Comparative Religion and African Studies
KAPLAN, Y., History of the Jewish People
KAREEV, Y., Education
KARK, R., Geography
KARTUN-BLUM, R., Modern Hebrew Literature
KEDAR, B., History
KISTER, M., Jewish Studies
KOHLBERG, E., Arabic Language and Literature
KÜHNEL, B., Art History
KVART, I., Philosophy
LAVSKY, H., Contemporary Jewry and Jewish History
LECKER, M., Arabic
LEVIN, A., Arabic Language and Literature
LEWIN, I., Archaeology and History of the Jewish People
LIEBES, Y., Jewish Thought
MAMAN, A., Hebrew Language
MARGALIT, A., Philosophy
MAZAR, A., Archaeology
MEDDING, P., Contemporary Jewry and Political Science
MENDELS, D., History
OFER, D., Education, Contemporary Jewry
OLSHTAIN, E., Education
PATRICK, J., Archaeology
PITOWSKY, I., History and Philosophy of Science
POZY, C., Philosophy
PRIMORATZ, I., Philosophy
RAPPAPORT-HOVAV, M., English Literature
RAVITZKY, A., Jewish Thought
RICCI, D., American Studies and Political Science
ROJTMAN, B., French Language and Literature
ROSENTHAL, D., Talmudic Studies
SCHULMAN, D., Indian Studies and Comparative Religion
SCHWARTZ, D., History of the Jewish People
SEGAL, D., Russian and Slavic Studies and Comparative Literature
SHARON, M., Islamic Studies
SHESHA-HALEVY, A., General and Egyptian Philology
SHILLONY, B. A., Japanese History
SHINAN, A., Hebrew Literature
SIVAN, E., History
SOLOTOREVSKY, M., Spanish and Latin-American Studies
STEINER, M., Philosophy
STEWART, F., Islamic Studies
STONE, M., Indo-Iranian and Armenian Studies
STROUMSA, G., Comparative Religion
STROUMSA, S., Jewish Thought
SZEINTUCH, Y., Yiddish
TAUBE, M., Linguistics and Slavic Studies
TOCH, M., History
TOKER, L., English Literature
TORREFRANCA, M. A., Musicology
TOV, E., Bible
TZAFRIR, Y., Archaeology
ULLMAN-MARGALIT, E., Education
VAN CREVELD, M., History
WEXLER, P., Education
WISTRICH, R., History, and History of the Jewish People
WOLOSKY, S., English Literature
YAHALOM, Y., Hebrew Literature
YUVAL, I., History of Jewish Studies
ZAKOVITCH, Y., Bible
ZIMMERMANN, M., History

Faculty of Law (tel. (2) 5882528; fax (2) 5823042; internet http://mishpatim.mscc.huji.ac.il):

(including the Harry Sacher Institute for Legislative Research and Comparative Law, the Israel Matz Institute for Research in Jewish Law)

BEN-MENAHEN, H., Jewish Law, Philosophy of Law
GAVISON, R., Philosophy of Law and Public Law
GILEAD, I., Tort Law
GUR-ARYE, M., Criminal Law
HAREL, A., Jurisprudence, Theory of Rights, Economic Analysis of Law
KREMITZER, M., Criminal and Constitutional Law
KRETZMER, D., Public Law
LANDAU, S., Violence, Stress and Crime
LIBSON, G., Islamic Law
LIFSCHITZ, B., Jewish Law
SEBBA, L., Victimology, Penology
SHETREET, S., Public Law and the Judiciary
SHIFMAN, P., Family Law and Succession Law
WEISBURD, D., White Collar Crime, Policing
ZAMIR, E., Contract Law

Faculty of Medicine

(the Hebrew University-Hadassah Medical School, including the School of Pharmacy, School of Social Medicine and Public Health, the Hadassah-Henrietta Szold School of Nursing, the School of Occupational Therapy)

ABRAMSKY, O., Neurology
ARGOV, A., Neurology
BACH, G., Genetics
BAIDER, L., Psycho-oncology
BAR-TANA, J. (acting), Biochemistry
BAR-ZIV, J., Diagnostic Radiology
BARENHOLZ, Y., Biochemistry
BEERI, E., Medicine
BEN-BASSAT, Experimental Surgery
BEN-CHETRIT, E., Medicine
BEN-EZRA, D., Ophthalmology
BEN-NERIAH, Y., Immunology
BEN-SASSON, Z., Immunology
BEN-YEHUDA, D., Haematology
BENITA, S., Pharmacy
BERCOVIER, H., Clinical Microbiology
BERGMAN, H., Physiology
BERGMAN, Y., Experimental Medicine
BIALER, M., Pharmacology
BRANSKY, D., Paediatrics
BRENNER, T., Neurology
BREZIS, M., Medicine
CEDAR, H., Molecular Biology

Chajek-Shaul, T., Medicine
Deutsch, J., Pharmaceutical Chemistry
Domb, A., Pharmacology
Eilat, D., Immunology
Elidan, J., Laryngology
Fibach, E., Experimental Haematology
Freund, H., Surgery
Friedlander, Y., Epidemiology
Friedman, G., Medicine
Friedman, M., Pharmacy
Gabizon Barchilom, A., Oncology
Glaser, B., Endocrinology
Glaser, G., Biochemistry
Godfrey, S., Paediatrics
Goldberg, I., Microbiology
Golomb, G., Pharmacology
Gomori, M. (acting), Radiology
Granot, E., Paediatrics
Gretz, D., Anatomy
Hansky, E., Microbiology
Hershko, Ch., Haematology
Ilan, Y., Medicine
Kaempfer, R., Molecular Virology
Kalcheim, C., Anatomy
Kanner, B. I., Biochemistry
Kark, J., Social Medicine
Kedar, E., Immunology
Keren, A., Cardiology
Keshet, E., Virology
Kotler, M., Pathology
Laufer, N., Obstetrics and Gynaecology
Leitersdorf, E., Medicine
Lerer, B., Psychiatry
Lev-Tov, A., Anatomy and Cell Biology
Levy, M., Medicine
Levy-Shaffer, F., Pharmacology
Lichtenstein, D., Physiology
Manny, J., Surgery
Mayer, M., Clinical Biochemistry
Merin, G., Cardiothoracic Surgery
Meyuchas, O., Biochemistry
Milgrom, Ch., Orthopaedics
Minke, B., Physiology
Mitrani-Rosenbaum, S., Molecular Biology
Naparstek, J., Medicine
Ornoy, A., Anatomy
Panet, A., Virology
Peer, J., Ophthalmology
Penchas, S., Organization and Management of Health Services
Polliak, A., Haematology
Rachmilewitz, D., Medicine
Rahamimoff, R., Physiology
Raz, I., Internal Medicine
Razin, E., Biochemistry
Reches, A., Neurology
Rotem, S., Clinical Microbiology
Rotshenker, S., Anatomy
Shalev, A., Psychiatry
Shapira, Y., Paediatrics
Shlomai, J., Molecular Biology
Shohami, E., Pharmacology
Shouval, D., Medicine
Siegal, T., Neurology and Neuro-Oncology
Silver, J., Nephrology
Slavin, S., Medicine
Sprung, Ch. L., Medicine
Steiner, I., Neurology
Tovito, E., Pharmacology
Tzivoni, D., Medicine
Umansky, F., Neurosurgery
Vaadia, E., Physiology
Vlodavsky, I., Oncology
Weinstein, D., Obstetrics and Gynaecology
Weissman, Ch., Anaesthesiology
Yaari, E., Physiology
Yagel, S., Obstetrics and Gynaecology
Yanai, J., Anatomy and Embryology
Yedgar, S., Biochemistry
Yefenof, E., Immunology

Faculty of Science

(including the Institute of Mathematics; Institute of Computer Science; Racah Institute of Physics; Institute of Chemistry; Alexander Silberman Institute of Life Sciences; Institute of Earth Sciences; Fredy and Nadine Herrmann Graduate School of Applied Science and Technology; Amos de Shalit Science Teaching Centre; Heinz Schteinitz Interuniversity Institute for Marine Biological Research)

Agmon, Chemistry
Agranat, A., Applied Physics
Aizenshtat, Z., Applied Chemistry
Asscher, M., Physical Chemistry
Atlas, D., Biological Chemistry
Avnir, D., Organic Chemistry
Balberg, Y., Experimental Physics
Barak, A., Computer Science
Barkat, Z., Physics
Beckenstein, Y., Theoretical Physics
Beeri, C., Computer Science
Belkin, S., Life Sciences
Ben-Artzi, M., Mathematics
Ben-Or, M., Computer Science
Ben-Shaul, A., Theoretical Chemistry
Ben-Tzvi, N., Science Teaching
Ben-Yosef, N., Applied Physics
Benvenisty, N., Life Sciences
Bercourier, M., Computer Science
Biali, S., Organic Chemistry
Bino, A., Theoretical and Analytical Chemistry
Buch, V., Chemistry
Cabantchik, Y., Biophysics
Camhi, J. M., Cell and Animal Biology
Cohen, A., Atmospheric Sciences
Davidov, D., Experimental Physics
Dekel, A., Theoretical Physics
De-Shalit, E., Mathematics
Devor, M., Zoology
Dolev, D., Computer Science
Dror-Farjoun, E., Mathematics
Elitzur, S., Theoretical Physics
Erez, J., Oceanography
Farkas, H., Mathematics
Feinberg, J., Physics
Felner, I., Experimental Physics
Friedland, L., Theoretical Physics
Friedman, E., Experimental Physics
Gal, A., Theoretical Physics
Garfunkel, Z., Geology
Garti, N., Applied Chemistry
Gerber, R. B., Theoretical Chemistry
Gilon, C., Organic Chemistry
Giveon, A., Physics
Glaberson, W., Experimental Physics
Gruenbaum, Y., Genetics
Grushka, E., Inorganic and Analytical Chemistry
Gutfreund, H., Theoretical Physics
Haas, Y., Physical Chemistry
Harel, E., Plant Sciences
Hart, S., Mathematics
Hirschberg, J., Genetics
Hochstein, S., Neurobiology
Hrushovski, E., Mathematics
Kalai, G., Mathematics
Kaplan, A., Plant Sciences
Kerem, B., Life Sciences
Khain, A., Atmospheric Sciences
Khazdan, D., Mathematics
Kifer, Y., Mathematics
Kosloff, R., Physical Chemistry
Laikhtman, B., Physics
Lehmann, D., Computer Science
Lev, O., Ecology
Levanon, H., Physical Chemistry
Levin, G., Mathematics
Levine, R., Theoretical Chemistry
Levitski, A., Biological Chemistry
Lewis, A., Applied Physics
Linial, N., Computer Science
Livne, R., Mathematics
Loyter, A., Biological Chemistry
Lubotzky, A., Mathematics
Luria, M., Applied and Environmental Science
Luz, B., Plant Sciences
Magdassi, S., Applied Chemistry
Magidor, M., Mathematics
Mandelzweig, V., Theoretical Physics
Mandler, D., Chemistry
Mann, A., Mathematics
Marom, G., Applied Chemistry
Matthews, A., Geology
Meerson, B., Experimental Physics
Mozes, S., Mathematics
Nebenzahl, I., Physics
Nechushtai, R., Plant Sciences
Neyman, A., Mathematics and Economics
Nisan, N., Computer Science
Nowik, I., Experimental Physics
Oren, A., Ecology
Orly, J., Biological Chemistry
Ottolenghi, M., Physical Chemistry
Ovadyahu, Z., Experimental Physics
Padan, E., Microbiological Ecology
Paldor, N., Plant Sciences
Parnas, H., Neurobiology
Paul, M., Experimental Physics
Peleg, S., Computer Science
Piran, Z., Theoretical Physics
Rabinovici, E., Theoretical Physics
Rips, E., Mathematics
Rosenfeld, D., Plant Sciences
Ruhman, S., Chemistry
Sagiv, Y., Computer Science
Sasson, Y., Applied Chemistry
Schuldiner, S., Microbial Ecology
Schwob, J. L., Experimental Physics
Segev, I., Neurobiology
Sever, M., Mathematics
Shaik, S. S., Organic Chemistry
Shalev, A., Mathematics
Shappir, Y., Applied Physics
Shashua, A., Computer Science
Shelah, S., Mathematics
Shmida, A., Botany
Simchen, G., Genetics
Solomon, S., Theoretical Physics
Sompolinsky, H., Physics
Soreq, H., Biological Chemistry
Sperling, R., Genetics
Spira, M., Neurobiology
Tikochinsky, Y., Physics
Tishby, N., Computer Science
Wagschal, J. J., Physics
Weinshall, D., Computer Science
Weiss, B., Mathematics
Werman, M., Computer Science
Willner, I., Organic Chemistry
Yarom, Y., Neurobiology
Zigler, A., Physics

Faculty of Social Sciences

(the Eliezer Kaplan School of Economics and Social Sciences)

Adler, E., International Relations
Bar-Siman-Tov, Y., International Relations
Ben-Ari, E., Sociology, Anthropology
Ben-Shakhar, G., Psychology
Ben-Yehuda, N., Sociology
Bentin, S., Psychology and Education
Bialer, V., International Relations
Bienstock, M., Economics
Bilo, Y., Psychology and Sociology
Bornstein, G., Psychology
Cohen, R., International Relations
Ebstein, R., Psychology
Ezrahi, Y., Political Science
Frost, R., Psychology
Galnoor, I., Political Science
Galor, O., Economics
Gati, I., Psychology and Education
Gilula, Z., Statistics and Social Work
Goldberg, H., Sociology
Hart, S., Economics
Haviv, M., Statistics
Hasson, S., Geography and Urban Studies
Kark, R., Geography
Kella, O., Statistics
Kimmerling, B., Sociology, Anthropology

LAVIH, V., Economics
LIEBES, T., Communication
LIEBLICH, A., Psychology
METZER, J., Economics
NINIO, A., Psychology
OMAN, S., Statistics
PERRY, M., Economics, Rationality Centre
PFEFFERMAN, D., Statistics
POLLAK, M., Statistics
RICCI, D., Political Science
RINOTT, Y., Statistics
RITOV, Y., Statistics
SALOMON, I., Geography and Urban Studies
SCHUL, Y., Psychology
SHAMIR, B., Sociology, Anthropology
SHANON, B., Psychology
SHEFFER, G., Political Science
TEUBAL, M., Economics
VERTZBERGER, Y., International Relations
WOLFSFELD, G., Political Science
YERMIYA, R., Psychology
YITZHAKI, S., Economics

Jerusalem School of Business Administration (tel. (2) 5883235; fax (2) 5881576; internet bschool.huji.ac.il):

BAR-LEV, B., Business Administration
BAR-YOSEF, S., Accounting
GALAI, D., Banking
GOLDMAN, A., Business Administration
KORNBLUTH, J., Business Administration
LANDSKRONER, Y., Business Administration
LEVY, H., Business Administration
MAZURZKY, O., Marketing
VENEZIA, I., Business Administration
ZUCKERMAN, D., Business Administration

School of Library, Archive and Information Studies (Givat Ram POB 1255, Jerusalem, 91904; tel. (2) 6585044; fax (2) 6585707; e-mail secretar@libs.huji.ac.il; internet sites .huji.ac.il/slais):

BEIT-ARIE, M., Palaeography and Codicology

Paul Baerwald School of Social Work (tel. (2) 5881477; fax (2) 5823587; e-mail social-work@savion.huji.ac.il; internet www .sw.huji.ac.il):

AUSLANDER, G.
BAR GAL, D.
BENBEMISHTY, R.
LITWIN, H.

RESEARCH CENTRES AND INSTITUTES

Institute for Advanced Studies, The: Givat Ram, 91904 Jerusalem; tel. (2) 6584735; fax (2) 6523429; internet www.as .huji.ac.il; Dir Prof. ELIEZER RABINOVICH.

Harry S. Truman Research Institute for the Advancement of Peace: tel. (2) 5882300; fax (2) 5828076; internet http:// truman.huji.ac.il; Dir Prof. EYAL BEN-ARI.

Dinur Center for Research in Jewish History: Room 2205, Rabin Building, Mount Scopus, 91905 Jerusalem; tel. (2) 5884894; fax (2) 5883894; e-mail dinurcenter@mscc .huji.ac.il; internet www.dinur.org; Dir Prof. IMMANUEL ETKES.

Center for Research on Dutch Jewry: Rm.1301, Rabin Building, Mount Scopus, 91905 Jerusalem; tel. (2) 5880242; fax (2) 5880241; e-mail dutchjew@cc.huji.ac.il; internet http://dutchjewry.huji.ac.il; Dir Prof. YOSEF KAPLAN.

Center for Research on the History and Culture of Polish Jews: Room 2303, Rabin Building, Mount Scopus, 91905 Jerusalem; tel. (2) 5881769; Dir Prof. ISRAEL BARTAL.

Center for the Study of Jewish Languages and Literature: Room 2106, Rabin Building, Mount Scopus, 91905 Jerusalem; tel. (2) 5880244; fax (2) 5881206; e-mail otirosh@mscc.huji.ac.il; Dir Prof. MOSHE BAR-ASHER.

Folklore Research Center: Room 1306, Rabin Building, Mount Scopus, 91905 Jerusalem; tel. (2) 5881797; Dir Prof. GALIT HASAN-ROKE.

Vidal Sassoon International Center for the Study of Antisemitism: Gastev Building, Mount Scopus, Jerusalem; tel. (2) 5882494; fax (2) 5881002; e-mail sicsa@mscc .huji.ac.il; internet http://sicsa.huji.ac.il; Dir Prof. ROBERT WISTRICH.

Orion Center for the Study of the Dead Sea Scrolls and Associated Literature, The: Room 3102, Rabin Building, Mount Scopus, 91905 Jerusalem; tel. (2) 5881966; fax (2) 5883584; e-mail msdss@mscc.huji.ac .il; internet http://orion.mscc.huji.ac.il; Dir Dr ESTHER CHAZON.

Philip and Muriel Berman Center for Biblical Archaeology: Philosophy Dept., Hebrew University, 91905 Jerusalem; tel. (2) 5882403; fax (2) 5825548; Dir Prof. TRUDE DOTHAN.

S. H. Bergman Center for Philosophical Studies: tel. (2) 5883762; fax (2) 5880148; Dir Dr ELHANAN YAKIRA.

Sidney M. Edelstein Center for the History and Philosophy of Science, Technology and Medicine: Givat Ram, 91905 Jerusalem; tel. (2) 6585652; fax (2) 6586709; e-mail Travis@cc.huji.ac.il; Dir Prof. ITAMAR PITOWSKY.

Richard Koebner Center for German History: tel. (2) 5883766; fax (2) 5816501; e-mail mskoeb@pluto.mscc.huji.ac.il; Dir Prof. MOSCHE ZIMMERMAN.

Center for Literary Studies: tel. (2) 5883925; fax (2) 5880203; e-mail cis@savion .huji.ac.il; Dir Dr JON DAVID WHITMAN.

Franz Rosenzweig Center for the Study of German Culture and Literature: tel. (2) 5881909; fax (2) 5811369; e-mail Rosenzweig@vms.huji.ac.il; Dir Prof. PAUL MENDES FLOHR.

Center for Slavic Languages and Literatures: tel. (2) 5883901; fax (2) 5881245; e-mail romantimenchik@excite.com; Dir Prof. WOLF MOSCOWICH.

Center for Jewish Art: tel. (2) 5882281; fax (2) 5400105; e-mail cja@vms.huji.ac.il; Dir Dr RINA TALGAM.

Robert H. and Clarice Smith Center for Art History: tel. (2) 5883872; fax (2) 5883944; e-mail anat@savion.huji.ac.il; Dir Prof. ZIVA AMISHAI-MAISELS.

Jewish Music Research Center: tel. (2) 6585059; fax (2) 5611156; e-mail jmrc_inf@ savion.huji.ac.il; Dir Prof. EDWIN SEROUSSI.

Paul Desmarais Centre for the Study of French Culture European Forum at the Hebrew University: Faculty of Social Sciences, Mount Scopus, 91905 Jerusalem; tel. (2) 5883286; fax (2) 5881535; e-mail mseuro@mscc.huji.ac.ill; internet www.ef .huji.ac.il; Dir (vacant).

Misgav Yerushalaim Center for the Study of Sephardi and Oriental Jewry: tel. (2) 5815460; fax (2) 5815460; e-mail misgav@h2.hum.huji.ac.il; internet http:// www.hum.huji.ac.il/misgav/index2.htm; Dir Dr MEIR BUZAGLO.

Cherrick Center for the Study of Zionism, the Yishuv and the State of Israel: tel. (2) 5882867; fax (2) 5882986; e-mail cherrick@mscc.huji.ac.il; internet http:// cherrick.huji.ac.il; Dir Dr UZI REBHUN.

Ben-Zvi Institute for the Study of Jewish Communities in the East: POB 7660, Jerusalem; tel. (2) 539884; fax (2) 5612329; e-mail bzi@ybz.org.il; internet www.ybz.org .il; Chair. Prof. HAGGAI BEN-SHAMAI.

Jewish Oral Traditions Research Center: Room 1302, Rabin Building, Mount Scopus, 91905 Jerusalem; tel. (2) 5881828; e-mail dornirit@zahav.net.il; Dir Prof. AHARON MAMAM.

Center for Research on Romanian Jewry: Room 2204, Rabin Building, Mount Scopus, 91905 Jerusalem; tel. (2) 5881672; fax (2) 5881673; e-mail rumjewry@vms.huji .ac.il; Dir Prof. EZRA FLEISCHER.

Center for the Study of Christianity: tel. (2) 5883819; fax (2) 5883819; e-mail centerc@ savion.cc.huji.ac.il; Dir Dr DAVID SATRAN.

Center for Austrian Studies European Forum at the Hebrew University: Faculty of Social Sciences, Mount Scopus, 91905 Jerusalem; tel. (2) 5883286; fax (2) 5881535; e-mail mseuro@mscc.huji.ac.il; internet www .ef.huji.ac.il; Dir (vacant).

National Council of Jewish Women Research Institute for Innovation in Education.

Goldie Rotman Center for Cognitive Science in Education: tel. (2) 5882102; Dir Prof. YAACOV KAREEV.

Leonard Davis Institute for International Relations: tel. (2) 5882312; fax (2) 5825534; e-mail msdavis@mscc,huji.ac.il; internet http://davis.huji.ac.il; Dir Prof. RAYMOND COHEN.

Levi Eshkol Institute for Economic, Social and Political Research: tel. (2) 5883032; fax (2) 5324339; e-mail eshkol@ mscc.huji.ac.il; internet http://eshkol.huji.ac .il; Dir Prof. GAD WOLSFELED.

Levin Center for the Study of Normal Child and Adolescent Development: tel. (2) 5883370; fax (2) 5881159; e-mail levinc@ mscc.huji.ac.il; internet http://psychology .mscc.huji.ac.il; Dir Prof. RUTH BUTLER.

Scheinfeld Center for Human Genetics in the Social Sciences: tel. (2) 536855; fax (2) 536853; e-mail ebstein@mscc.huji.ac.il; Dir Prof. RICHARD EBSTEIN.

Sigmund Freud Center for Study and Research in Psychoanalysis: tel. (2) 5883380; fax (2) 5322132; e-mail msfreud@ pluto.mscc.huji.ac.il; internet http://atar .mscc.huji.ac.il/%7EFreud; Dir Prof. GABY SHEFLER.

Sturman Center for Human Development: Dept. of Psychology, Mount Scopus, Jerusalem; tel. (2) 5883409; fax (2) 5881159; e-mail msmerava@mscc.huji.ac.il; Dir Prof. RAM FROST.

Brian Y. Davidson Center for Agribusiness: Jerusalem School of Business Administration, Jerusalem; tel. (2) 5883224; fax (2) 5883685; e-mail dinam@savion.huji.ac.il; internet bschool.huji.ac.il; Dir Prof. CHEZI OFIR.

Lafer Center for Women and Gender Studies: tel. (2) 5883455; fax (2) 5883364; e-mail mslaferc@mscc.huji.ac.il; internet www.lafer.huji.ac.il; Chair. Dr TAMAR EL-OR.

Shaine Center for Research in the Social Sciences: tel. (2) 5883032; fax (2) 5324339; e-mail msschein@mscc.huji.ac.il; Dir Dr AMALIA OLIVER.

Krueger Center for Finance: The Jerusalem School of Business Administration, Jerusalem; tel. (2) 5883224; fax (2) 5883685; e-mail dinam@savion.huji.ac.il; internet bschool.huji.ac.il; Dir Prof. HAIM LEVY.

K Mart International Retail and Marketing Center: The Jerusalem School of Business Administration, Jerusalem; tel. (2) 5883224; fax (2) 5883685; e-mail dinam@ savion.huji.ac.il; internet bschool.huji.ac.il; Dir Prof. DAVID MAZURSKY.

Gal-Edd Center for Industrial Development: The Jerusalem School of Business Administration, Jerusalem; tel. (2) 5883224; fax (2) 5883685; e-mail dainam@savion.huji.ac.il; internet bschool.huji.ac.il; Dir Dr NIRON HASHAI.

Recanati Center for Research in Business Administration: The Jerusalem School of Business Administration, Jerusalem; tel. (2) 5883224; fax (2) 5883685; e-mail dainam@savion.huji.ac.il; internet bschool.huji.ac.il; Dir Dr YISHAI YAFE.

Mordechai Zagagi Center for Finance and Accounting: The Jerusalem School of Business Administration, Jerusalem; tel. (2) 5883224; fax (2) 5883685; e-mail dinam@savion.huji.ac.il; internet bschool.huji.ac.il; Dir Prof. YORAM LANDSKRONER.

Center for Rationality and Interactive Decision Theory: Givat Ram, Jerusalem; tel. (2) 6584135; fax (2) 6513681; e-mail ratio@math.huji.ac.il; internet www.ratio.huji.ac.il; Dir Prof. MAYA BAR-HILLEL.

Smart Family Foundation Communication Institute: Room 5416, Faculty of Social Sciences, Hebrew University, 91905 Jerusalem; tel. (2) 5883210; fax (2) 5817008; e-mail msmartc@mscc.huji.ac.il; internet http://smart.huji.ac.il; Dir Prof. MENACHEM BLONDHEIM.

Institute for European Studies European Forum at the Hebrew University: Faculty of Social Sciences, Mount Scopus, 91905 Jerusalem; tel. (2) 5883286; fax (2) 5881535; e-mail mseuro@mscc.huji.ac.il; internet www.ef.huji.ac.il; Dir Prof. BIANCA KUEHNEL.

Marjorie Mayrock Center for Russian, Eurasian and East European Research Forum at the Hebrew University: Faculty of Social Sciences, Mount Scopus, 91905 Jerusalem; tel. (2) 5883286; fax (2) 5881535; e-mail mseuro@mscc.huji.ac.il; internet www.ef.huji.ac.il; Dir (vacant).

Israel Matz Institute for Research in Jewish Law: tel. (2) 5882501; fax (2) 5882567; e-mail jewishlaw@savion.cc.huji.ac.il; internet law.mscc.huji.ac.il/law1/newsite/hebrew.html; Dir Prof. GIDEON LIBSON.

Harry and Michael Sacher Institute for Legislative Research and Comparative Law, The: tel. (2) 5882535; fax (2) 5882565; e-mail yaffal@savion.huji.ac.il; internet http://law.mscc.huji.ac.il/law1/sache; Dir Prof. SHIMON SHETREET.

Minerva Center for Human Rights: tel. (2) 5881156; fax (2) 5819371; e-mail mchr@savion.huji.ac.il; internet law.mscc.huji.ac.il/law1/minerva/english/index.htm; Dir Dr MICHAEL KARAYAMI.

Moshe Shilo Center for Marine Biogeochemistry: The Institute of Life Sciences, Givat Ram, Jerusalem; tel. (8) 6374329; fax (8) 6360122; e-mail anton@pob.huji.ac.il; internet www.ivi-eilat.ac.il; Dir Prof. YEHUDA COHEN.

G. W. Leibnitz Minerva Center for Research in Computer Sciences: School of Computer Science and Engineering, Jerusalem; tel. (2) 6586299; fax (2) 6585439; e-mail josko@cs.huji.ac.il; internet www.cs.huji.ac.il; Dir Prof. LEO JOSKOWICZ.

Edmund Landau Minerva Center for Research in Mathematical Analysis and Related Areas: The Institute of Mathematics, Givat Ram, Jerusalem; tel. (2) 6584091; fax (2) 5630702; e-mail mbartzi@math.huji.ac.il; internet www.ma.huji.ac.il; Dir Prof. YURI KIFER.

Fritz Haber Research Center for Molecular Dynamics: The Institute of Chemistry, Givat Ram, Jerusalem; tel. (2) 6585271; fax (2) 5618033; e-mail abs@fh.huji.ac.il; internet www.chemistry.huji.ac.il; Dir Prof. AVINOAM BEN-SHAUL.

Minerva Avron Even-Ari Center of Photosynthesis Research: The Institute of Life Sciences , Givat Ram, Jerusalem; tel. (2) 6585338; fax (2) 6586103; e-mail hirschu@vms.huji.ac.il; internet www.bio.huji.ac.il; Dir Prof. JOSEPH HIRSCHBERG.

Knune Minerva Farkas Center for the Study of Light Induced Processes: The Institute of Chemistry, Givat Ram, Jerusalem; tel. (2) 6585067; fax (2) 5618033; e-mail yehuda@chem.cc.huji.ac.il; internet www.chemistry.huji.ac.il; Dir Prof. SANFORD RUHMAN.

Sudarsky Center for Computational Biology: Givat Ram, Jerusalem; tel. (2) 6585425; fax (2) 6586103; e-mail michall@cc.huji.ac.il; internet www.cbc.huji.ac.il; Dir Prof. MICHAL LINEAL.

Otto Loewi Center for Cellular and Molecular Neurobiology: The Institute of Life Sciences, Givat Ram, Jerusalem; tel. (2) 6583172; fax (2) 6586103; e-mail yarom@vms.huji.ac.il; internet www.bio.huji.ac.il; Dir Prof. YOSEF YARAM.

Wolfson Center for Applied Structural Biology: The Institute of Life Sciences, Givat Ram, Jerusalem; tel. (2) 6586894; fax (2) 6586103; e-mail livnah@cc.huji.ac.il; internet www.bio.huji.ac.il; Dir Prof. ZVI SELINGER.

Lisa Meitner-Minerva Center for Computational Quantum Chemistry: The Institute of Chemistry, Givat Ram, Jerusalem; tel. (2) 6585909; fax (2) 6585345; e-mail sason@yfaat.ch.huji.ac.il; internet www.chemistry.huji.ac.il; Dir Prof. SASSON SHAIK.

National Institute for Psychobiology in Israel: Life Sciences Building, Givat Ram, 91904 Jerusalem; tel. (2) 6584086; fax (2) 5635267; e-mail psychobi@cc.huji.ac.il; internet http://psychobiology.org.il; Dir Prof. BERNARD LERER.

Harry Stern National Center for the Study and Treatment of Alzheimer's Disease and Related Topics: Life Sciences Building, Givat Ram, 91904 Jerusalem; tel. (2) 6584086; fax (2) 5635267; internet http://psychobiology.org.il; Dir Prof. BERNARD LERER.

Center for Geographical Information Systems: tel. (2) 6586345; e-mail bennun@cc.huji.ac.il; internet http://shum.huji.ac.il/~bennun/toc.htm; Dir Prof. RONEN KADMON.

Herbarium of Middle Eastern Flora (Israel National Herbarium): Dir (vacant).

Interdisciplinary Center for Neural Computation: Givat Ram, Jerusalem; tel. (2) 6585984; fax (2) 98/9485; e-mail idan@lobster.ls.huji.ac.il; internet www.icoc.huji.ac.il; Dir Prof. IDAN SEGEV.

Center for the Study of Bone Metabolism: Nephrology Services, Hadassah Hospital, POB 12000, 91120 Jerusalem; tel. (2) 6436778; fax (2) 6421234; e-mail silver@cc.huji.ac.il; internet http://www.hadassah.org.il/atarim/medicine/e1.htm; Dir Prof. JUSTIN SILVER.

Institute for Dental Science: Faculty of Dental Medicine, Hebrew University, POB 12272, 91120 Jerusalem; tel. (2) 6758576; fax (2) 6424144; e-mail jjsela@cc.huji.ac.il; Dir Prof. YONA SELA.

D. Walter Cohen Middle East Center for Dental Education: Faculty of Dental Medicine, Hebrew University, POB 12272, 91120 Jerusalem; tel. (2) 6758596; fax (2) 6439219; e-mail hujident@cc.huji.ac.il; Dir Dr RAFAEL BENOLIEL.

Ronald E. Goldstein DDS Research Center for Dental Materials and Aesthetics in Dentistry: Faculty of Dental Medicine, Hebrew University, POB 12272, 91120 Jerusalem; tel. (2) 6776193; fax (2) 6429683; e-mail nitzan@bichacho.net; Dir Prof. ERVIN WEISS.

Sanford F. Kuvin Center for the Study of Infectious and Tropical Diseases: Hadassah Medical School, Hebrew University, Jerusalem; tel. (2) 6758089; fax (2) 6727425; e-mail josephs@ekmd.huji.ac.il; internet http://kuvin.huji.ac.il; Dir Prof. JOSEPH SHLOMAI.

Lautenberg Center for General and Tumour Immunology: Hadassa Medical School, Hebrew University, POB 12272, Jerusalem; tel. (2) 6758726; fax (2) 6430834; e-mail dkraut@pob.huji.ac.il; internet http://immunology.huji.ac.il; Dir Prof. EITAN YEFENOF.

Hubert H. Humphrey Center for Experimental Medicine and Cancer Research: POB 12272, 12272 Jerusalem; tel. (2) 6758350; fax (2) 6414583; e-mail katzav@md.huji.ac.il; Dir Prof. SHULAMIT KATZAN.

Center for Diabetes Research: Faculty of Medicine, Hebrew University, Jerusalem; tel. (2) 6758798; fax (2) 6758741; e-mail sassolo@cc.huji.ac.il; Chair. Prof. SHLOMO SASSON.

Center for the Study of Pain: internet http://paincenter.huji.ac.il/index.htm; Dir Prof. YAIR SHARAV.

Kühne-Minerva Center for Studies of Visual Transduction: Dept. of Physiology, Faculty of Medicine, Hebrew University, Jerusalem; tel. (2) 6758407; fax (2) 6431736; e-mail minb@md.huji.ac.il; Dir Prof. BARUCH MINKE.

Center for Trauma Research: fax (2) 6417997; e-mail rivkind@hadassah.org.il; Dir Prof. AVI RIVKIND.

Center for Agricultural Economic Research: Hebrew University of Jerusalem, POB 12, Rehovot; tel. (8) 9489230; fax (8) 9466267; e-mail finkelsh@agri.huji.ac.il; internet http://departments.agri.huji.ac.il/economics/econocene.html; Dir Dr ISRAEL FINKELSHTAIN.

Seagram Center for Soil and Water Sciences: Hebrew University of Jerusalem, POB 12, 76100 Rehovot; tel. (8) 9489340; fax (8) 9475181; e-mail soil@agri.huji.ac.il; internet http://departments.agri.huji.ac.il/soils; Dir Prof. YECHEZKEL MAHRER.

Benjamin Triwaks Bee Research Center: Hebrew University of Jerusalem, POB 12, 76100 Rehovot; tel. (8) 9489401; fax (8) 9489842; e-mail shafir@agri.huji.ac.il; internet http://departments.agri.huji.ac.il/entomology/staff_pages/shafir.html; Dir Dr SHARONI SHAFIR.

Leo Picard Groundwater Research Center: Hebrew University of Jerusalem, POB 12, 76100 Rehovot; tel. (8) 9489174; fax (8) 9475181; e-mail mualem@agri.huji.ac.il; Dir Prof. YECHEZKEL MUALEM.

Otto Warburg Minerva Center for Agricultural Biotechnology: Hebrew University of Jerusalem, POB 12, 76100 Rehovot; tel. (8) 9489973; fax (8) 9363882; e-mail ingel@agri.huji.ac.il; internet http://departments.agri.huji.ac.il/biotech; Dir Prof. SHMUEL WOLF.

Herb and Frances Brody Center for Food Sciences: Hebrew University of Jerusalem, POB 12, 76100 Rehovot; tel. (8) 9489292; fax (8) 9462384; e-mail feiner@agri.huji.ac.il; Dir Prof. ELI FEINERMAN.

Center for Agricultural Research in Desert and Semi-Arid Zones: Hebrew

University of Jerusalem, POB 12, 76100 Rehovot; tel. (8) 9489234; fax (8) 9468565; e-mail yonachen@agri.huji.ac.il; internet http://departments.agri.huji.ac.il/economics/econocene.html; Dir Prof. YONA CHEN.

Kennedy Leigh Centre for Horticultural Research: Hebrew University of Jerusalem, POB 12, 76100 Rehovot; tel. (8) 9489251; fax (8) 9489899; e-mail shimony@agri.huji.ac.il; internet http://departments.agri.huji.ac.il/horticulture/kennedy.html; Dir Prof. ALEXANDER. VAINSTEIN.

Center for Integrated Pest Management: Hebrew University of Jerusalem, POB 12, 76100 Rehovot; tel. (8) 9489223; fax (8) 9466768; e-mail coll@agri.huji.ac.il; Dir Dr MOSHE COLL.

Niznick Dental Implant and Research Center: POB 12272, 91120 Jerusalem; tel. (2) 6776170; fax (2) 6776175; e-mail kohavi@cc.huji.ac.il; internet www.hadassah.org.il; Dir Prof. D. KOHAVI.

Asper Center for Entrepreneurship: The Jerusalem School of Business Administration, Jerusalem; tel. (2) 5882994; fax (2) 5883685; e-mail refo@mscc.huji.ac.il; internet bschool.huji.ac.il; Dir Prof. JACOB GOLDENBERG.

Center for Nanoscience and Nanotechnology: Givat Ram, Jerusalem; tel. (2) 6584515; fax (2) 6584148; e-mail banin@chem.ch.huji.ac.il; internet www.nanoscience.huji.ac.il; Dir Prof. URI BANIN.

Zigi and Lisa Daniel Swiss Center: Faculty of Social Sciences, Mount Scopus, 91905 Jerusalem; tel. (2) 5883056; fax (2) 5880004; e-mail crmr@savion.huji.ac.il; internet www.crmr.huji.ac.il; Dir Prof. YAACOV BAR SIMAM TOV.

Gilo Citizenship, Democracy and Civil Education Center: Faculty of Social Sciences, Mount Scopus, 91905 Jerusalem; tel. (2) 5882267; fax (2) 5881532; e-mail gilocenter@mscc.huji.ac.il; internet www.gilocenter.huji.ac.il; Dir Dr DAN AVNON.

Scholion Interdisciplinary Research Center in Jewish Studies: Room 1107, Rabin Building, Mount Scopus, 91905 Jerusalem; tel. (2) 5882430; fax (2) 5881196; e-mail scholion@savion.huji.ac.il; internet http://scholion.huji.ac.il; Dir Prof. ISRAEL J. YUVAL.

Leonid Nevzlin Research Center for Russian and East European Jewry: Room 6003, Rabin Building, Mount Scopus, 91905 Jerusalem; tel. (2) 5881959; fax (2) 5881950; e-mail merkaznev@savion.huji.ac.il; internet www.nevzlin.huji.ac.il; Dir Prof. ISRAEL BARTAL.

Chais Center for Jewish Studies in Russian, The: Room 2113, Rabin Building, Mount Scopus, 91905 Jerusalem; tel. (2) 5881770; fax (2) 5881795; e-mail chais_center@savion.huji.ac.il; Dir Dr ALEXANDER KULILS.

Roland Center for the Research of Neurodegenerative Disease: Faculty of Medicine, Hebrew University, POB 12272, 91120 Jerusalem; tel. (2) 6757388; fax (2) 6439736; e-mail hagaib@md.huji.ac.il; Dir (vacant).

OPEN UNIVERSITY OF ISRAEL

108 Ravutski St, POB 808, Raanana 43107Telephone: (9) 7780778
Fax: (9) 7780642
E-mail: president@openu.ac.il
Internet: www.openu.ac.il

Founded 1974; formerly Everyman's University; present name 1989; a distance-learning institution serving students on a nationwide basis. Academic and general adult education using written material and integrating technology (including online and satellite transmission) in a self-study system supplemented by tutorial instruction. Offers 500 courses in history, philosophy, Judaic studies, literature, language, the arts, education, psychology, economics, management, sociology, democracy, political science, communication, mathematics, computer science and natural sciences
Language of instruction: Hebrew
Academic year: September to June (two semesters) and summer semester

Chancellor: Lord WOOLF
Deputy Chancellor: Lord ROTHSCHILD
Vice-Chancellor: Prof. ABRAHAM GINZBURG
President: Prof. GERSHON BEN-SHAKHAR
Vice-President (Academic Affairs): Prof. ORA LIMOR
Director General: DAVID KLIBANSKI
Dean of Academic Studies: Prof. ITZHAK DOTAN
Dean of Students: Dr HAIM SAADOUN
Director of the Library: HAVA MUSTIGMAN

Library of 75,000 vols, 500 e-books, 92 databases, 20,000 electronic periodicals
Number of teachers: 1,693 (55 senior faculty members, 428 junior faculty members and 1,210 tutors throughout Israel teaching in 100 study centres)
Number of students: 36,315, 2,598 graduate students, 7,000 students in countries of the former USSR.

ATTACHED RESEARCH INSTITUTES

Center for Information Technology in Distance Education: Dir Dr YOAV YAIR.

Chair Research Center for the Integration of Technology in Education: Dir Prof. YORAM ESHET.

Extra-Academic Studies Center: Dir LIPATZ VINITZKY.

School of Technology: Dir ISRAEL ZILBERSTEIN.

TEL-AVIV UNIVERSITY

Ramat-Aviv, 69978 Tel-Aviv
Telephone: (3) 6407777
Fax: (3) 6408601
Internet: www.tau.ac.il

Founded 1953; inaugurated 1956
Private control, partially supported by the Government
Language of instruction: Hebrew
Academic year: October to June (two terms)

President: Prof. I. RABINOWICH
Rector: Prof. D. LEVIATAN
Vice-Rector (vacant)
Vice-President (Foreign Relations): Y. BEN-ZVI
Vice-President (Research and Development): Prof. R. SHALGI
Director-General: Prof. G. LANGHOLTZ
Academic Secretary: H. BEN-SHEFFER
Dean of Students: Prof. T. LOBEL

Library: see Libraries and Archives
Number of teachers: 2,302
Number of students: 26,000

Publications: *Hasifrut* (4 a year), *Iunei Mishpat* (4 a year), *Poetics Today* (4 a year), *Zemanim* (4 a year), *Mideast File* (4 a year), *Middle East Contemporary Survey* (annually), *Jahrbuch des Instituts für Deutsche Geschichte* (annually), *Dinei Israel* (annually), *Israel Yearbook in Human Rights* (annually), *Studies in Zionism* (2 a year), *Mediterranean Historical Review* (2 a year), *Michael* (8 every 18 months), *Shvut* (9 a year), *Studies in Educational Evaluation* (4 a year), *International Perspective on Education and Society* (annually), *Ph.D. Abstracts* (annually), *Theoretical Inquiries in Law* (2 a year), *Israeli Society* (in Hebrew), *Kesher*

DEANS

Yolanda and David Katz Faculty of Arts: Prof. F. ROKEM
Iby and Aladar Fleischman Faculty of Engineering: Prof. T. MILOH
Raymond and Beverly Sackler Faculty of Exact Sciences: Prof. J. LICHTENSTADT
Faculty of Humanities: Prof. S. BIDERMAN
Buchmann Faculty of Law: Prof. A. PORAT
George S. Wise Faculty of Life Sciences: Prof. Y. KLOOG
Faculty of Management (Leon Recanati Graduate School of Business Administration): Prof. S. BENNINGA
Sackler Faculty of Medicine: Prof. D. LICHTENBERG
Faculty of Social Sciences: Prof. I. VINER

HEADS OF SCHOOLS

David Azrieli School of Architecture: Prof. M. MARGALIT
School of Chemistry: Prof. O. CHESHNOVSKY
School of Computer Science: Prof. R. SHAMIR
School of Continuing Medical Education: Prof. M. PHILLIP
Shirley and Leslie Porter School of Cultural Studies: Prof. E. ROZEN
Maurice and Gabriella Goldchlager School of Dental Medicine: Prof. I. KAFFE
Eitan Berglas School of Economics: Prof. I. GILBOA
School of Education: Prof. D. NEVO
School of Electrical Engineering: Prof. E. HEYMAN
Porter School of Environmental Studies: Prof. H. M. YARON
School of Government and Policy: Prof. Y. SHAIN
School of Health Professions: Prof. T. KRULIK
Aranne School of History: Prof. E. TOLEDANO
Chaim Rosenberg School of Jewish Studies: Prof. D. PORAT
School of Mathematical Sciences: Prof. C. FUCHS
School of Mechanical Engineering: Prof. M. FUCHS
School of Medicine: Prof. R. TUR-KASPA
Buchman-Mehta School of Music: Prof. T. LEV
Lowy School of Overseas Students: Prof. D. MENASHIRI
School of Philosophy: Prof. M. FISH
School of Physics and Astronomy: Prof. A. LEVY
School of Public Health: Prof. M. SHAHI
Bob Shapell School of Social Work: Prof. T. RONEN
Executive M. B. A. of Recanati School (in Hebrew): Prof. G. ARIAV

PROFESSORS

AARONSON, J., Mathematics
ABBOUD, S., Biomedical Engineering
ABRAMOWICZ, H., Physics
AHARONOWITZ, Y., Microbiology
AHARONY, A., Physics
AHITUV, N., Management
AKSELROD, S., Physics
ALGOM, D., Psychology
ALON, N., Mathematics
ALONI, R., Botany
ALPERT, P., Geophysics and Planetary Sciences
AMIRAV, A., Chemistry
AMIT, Y., Bible
AMOSSY, R., French Literature
ANDELMAN, D., Physics
ANILY, S., Management
APTER, A., Psychiatry
ARBEL, A., Industrial Engineering
ARBEL, B., History
ARBER, N., Medicine

ARON, S., History
ASHKENAZI, S., Paediatrics
AVERBUCH, A., Computer Sciences
AVRON, A., Computer Sciences
AYALON, A., History of the Middle East and Africa
AZAR, Y., Computer Sciences
AZRIEL, P., Anaesthiology and Intensive Care
BANKS-SILLS, L., Mechanical Engineering
BAR-KOCHVA, B., History of the Jewish People
BAR-MEIR, S., Medicine
BAR-NAVI, E., History
BAR-NUN, A., Planetary Sciences
BAR-TAL, D., Education
BARBASH, G., Preventive Medicine, Social Medicine
BARKAI, R., History
BARNEA, D., Mechanical Engineering
BARZILAY, Z., Paediatrics
BATTLER, A., Cardiology
BE'ERY, Y., Electrical Engineering
BEER, S., Plant Sciences
BELHASSEN, B., Cardiology
BELKIN, A., Theatre Arts
BELKIN, M., Ophthalmology
BEN, E. S., Psychology
BEN-AVRAHAM, Z., Geophysics
BEN-BASSAT, I., Haematology
BEN-DAVID, Y., Anatomy and Anthropology
BEN-JACOB, E., Physics
BEN-RAFAEL, E., Sociology and Anthropology
BEN-RAFAEL, Z., Gynaecology and Obstetrics
BEN-ZVI, A., Political Science
BEN-ZVI, L., Theatre Arts
BENAYAHU, Y., Zoology
BENJAMINI, Y., Statistics
BENNINGA, S., Management
BENVENISTE, Y., Mechanical Engineering
BENVENISTI, E., Law
BERECHMAN, J., Urban Planning
BERGMAN, D., Physics
BERNHEIM, J., Medicine
BERNSTEIN, J., Mathematics
BIDERMAN, S., Philosophy
BIXON, M., Chemistry
BOXMAN, R., Electrical and Electronic Engineering
BRACHA, B., Law
BRAUNER, N., Mechanical Engineering
BREIMAN, A., Plant Sciences
BUCHNER, A., Oral Pathology
CARMELI, S., Physics
CASHER, A., Physics
CHEN, R., Physics
CHESHNOVSKY, O., Chemistry
CHESKIS, S., Chemistry
CHOR, B., Computer Sciences
COHEN, A., Communication
COHEN, G., Molecular Microbiology and Biotechnology
COHEN, J., History of the Jewish People
COHEN, N., Law
CUKIERMAN, A., Economics
DAGAN, H., Law
DASCAL, M., Philosophy
DASCAL, N., Physiology
DAVIDSON, M., Psychiatry
DAYAN, D., Oral Pathology
DAYAN, T., Zoology
DEKEL, E., Economics
DERSHOWITZ, N., Computer Sciences
DEUTCH, M., Law
DINARI, G., Paediatrics
DOR, J., Obstetrics and Gynaecology
DRAZEN, A., Economics
DREYFUS, T., Teaching of Science
DYN, N., Applied Mathematics
ECKSTEIN, Z., Economics
EDEN, D., Management
EINAV, S., Biomedical Engineering
ELAD, D., Biomedical Engineering
ELDAR, M., Cardiology
ENTIN, O., Physics
EPEL, B. L., Botany
ESHEL, I., Statistics
EVEN, U., Chemistry
EVEN-ZOHAR, I., Theory of Literature
FABIAN, I., Cell Biology and Histology
FAINARU, M., Medicine
FARBER, M., Mathematics
FARFEL, Z., Medicine
FEDER, M., Electrical Engineering
FERSHTMAN, CH., Economics
FIAT, A., Computer Sciences
FINKELBERG, M., Classics
FINKELSTEIN, I., Archaeology
FISHELSON, Z., Cell and Development Biology
FISHER, M., Classical Archaeology
FLEUROV, V., Physics
FRANKFURT, L. L., Physics
FREEMAN, A., Biotechnology
FRENK, H., Psychology
FRENKEL, J., Economics
FRENKEL, N., Cell Research and Immunology
FRIEDLAND, N., Psychology
FRIEDMAN, M. A., Talmud
FUCHS, C., Statistics
FUCHS, M., Mechanical Engineering
GADOTH, N., Neurology
GAFTER, U., Medicine
GANS, CH., Law
GANZACH, Y., Management
GAT, A., Political Sciences
GAZIT, A., Human Microbiology
GERCHAK, Y., Industrial Engineering
GERSHONI, I., History of the Middle East
GERSHONI, Y., Cell Research and Immunology
GILBOA, I., Management, Economics
GINSBURG, D., Mathematics
GITIK, M., Mathematics
GLASNER, S., Mathematics
GLAZER, J., Management
GLEZERMAN, M., Obstetrics and Gynaecology
GLUSKIN, E., Mathematics
GOFER, A., Archaeology
GOLANI, I., Zoology
GOLDBERG, I., Chemistry
GOLDBOURT, U., Preventive Medicine, Social Medicine
GOLDHIRSCH, I., Mechanical Engineering
GOLDMAN, B., Genetics
GORODETSKY, G., History
GOVER, A., Electrical and Electronic Engineering
GOZES, I., Clinical Biochemistry
GRAUR, D., Zoology
GREEN, M., Preventive Medicine, Social Medicine
GREENSTEIN, E., Bible
GRODEZINSKY, Y., Psychology
GROSSMAN, E., Medicine
GUREVITZ, M., Plant Sciences
GUTNIK, D., Microbiology
HALKIN, H., Medicine
HALPERN, Z., Medicine
HAMMEL, I., Pathology
HARAN, D., Mathematics
HARATS, D., Medicine
HARDY, A., Electrical and Electronic Engineering
HASSIN, R., Statistics
HATIVA, N., Education
HAZAN, H., Sociology and Anthropology
HEFETZ, A., Zoology
HENIG, M., Management
HENIS, Y., Biochemistry
HERSHKOVITZ, I., Anatomy and Anthropology
HEYMAN, E., Electrical Engineering
HILDESHEIMER, M., Communication Disorders
HIZI, A., Cell Biology
HOCHBERG, Y., Statistics
HOFFMAN, Y., Bible
HOLZMAN, A., Hebrew Literature
HOMBURG, R., Obstetrics and Gynaecology
HORNIK, J., Management
HOROWITZ, A., Geology
HOROWITZ, M., Cell Research and Immunology
HUPPERT, D., Chemistry
ICHILOV, O., Education
ISAAC, B., Classics
ITZCHAK, Y., Diagnostic Radiology
IZRE'EL, S., Semitic Linguistics
JARDEN, M., Mathematics
KAFFE, I., Oral Radiology
KAHANE, Y., Management
KALAY, A., Management
KALDOR, U., Chemistry
KANDEL, SH., Management
KANTOR, Y., Physics
KARLINER, M., Physics
KARNIOL, R., Psychology
KASHMAN, Y., Chemistry
KATZ, D., History
KATZIR, A., Physics
KAUFMAN, G., Biochemistry
KEISARI, Y., Human Microbiology
KENAAN-KEDAR, N., History of Arts
KEREN, G., Cardiology
KIT, E., Mechanical Engineering
KLAFTER, J., Chemistry
KLEIN, A., Mathematics
KLEIN, S., Jewish Philosophy
KLIEMAN, A., Political Science
KLOOG, Y., Biochemistry
KORCZYN, A., Neurology
KORENSTEIN, R., Physiology
KOSLOFF, D., Geophysics
KREITLER, S., Psychology
KRONFELD, I., Geophysics and Planetary Sciences
KUPIEC, M., Microbiology
LAMED, R., Biotechnology
LANDMAN, F., Linguistics
LANGHOLZ, G., Electrical Engineering
LAOR, D., Hebrew Literature
LAOR, N., Psychiatry
LASS, Y., Physiology
LAVI, S., Cell Biology
LEDERMAN, E., Law
LEHRER, E., Statistics
LEIBOWITZ, E., Physics and Astronomy
LEIDERMAN, L., Economics
LESSING, J., Gynaecology and Obstetrics
LEVANON, N., Electrical and Electronic Engineering
LEVIATAN, D., Mathematics
LEVIN, D., Applied Mechanics
LEVIN, E., Physics
LEVIN, Z., Atmospheric Sciences
LEVO, Y., Medicine
LEVY, A., Physics
LEVY, S., Theatre Arts
LEWIN, N., Sociology and Anthropology
LIBERMAN, U. A., Statistics
LICHTENBERG, D., Pharmacology
LICHTENSTADT, J., Physics
LITSYN, S., Electrical Engineering
LIVSHITS, Z., Anatomy and Anthropology
LOBEL, T., Psychology
LOTAN, I., Physiology
LOYA, Y., Zoology
MAIMON, O., Industrial Engineering
MALKIN, I., Ancient History
MANSOUR, Y., Computer Sciences
MAOZ, D., Physics and Astronomy
MAOZ, Z., Political Science
MARGALIT, M., Education
MARGALIT, R., Biochemistry
MATZKIN, H., Surgery
MAUTNER, M., Law
MAZEH, T., Physics
MEDIN, Z., History
MEILIJSON, I., Statistics
MEKORI, Y., Medicine
MELAMED, E., Neurology
MENASHIRI, D., History of the Middle East
MESSER, H., Electrical Engineering
MEVARECH, M., Microbiology
MICHAELSON, D., Biochemistry
MILMAN, V., Mathematics
MILOH, T., Engineering
MIMOUNI, F., Paediatrics
MINTS, R., Physics
MOHR, R., Surgery
MOTRO, M., Cardiology
MULLER, E., Management
NAAMAN, N., History of the Jewish People

NADLER, A., Psychology
NAOR, Z., Biochemistry
NAVON, R., Human Genetics
NELSON, N., Biochemistry
NETZER, H., Physics
NEVO, D., Education
NITZAN, A., Chemistry
NUSSINOV, R., Biochemistry
NUSSINOV, S., Physics
OFEK, I., Human Microbiology
OFER, A., Management
OLEVSKII, A., Mathematics
OPPENHEIMER, A., History of the Jewish People
OR, U. G., Surgery
ORON, U., Zoology
ORON, Y., Pharmacology
OVADIA, M., Zoology
PASSWELL, J., Paediatrics
PAZ, G., Physiology
PELED, E., Chemistry
PHILLIP, M., Paediatrics
PIASETZKY, E., Physics
PICK, E., Immunology
PITARU, S., Oral Biology
PODOLACK, M., Planetary Science
POLAK, F., Bible
POLTEROVICH, L., Mathematics
PORAT, A., Law
PORTUGALI, J., Geography
RABEY, M., Neurology
RABINOVICH, I., History of the Middle East
RABINOWITZ, B., Cardiology
RAK, Y., Anatomy and Anthropology
RAVID, M., Medicine
RAVIV, A., Psychology
RAZ, A., Biochemistry
RAZ, J., East Asian Studies
RAZ, T., Management
RAZI, Z., History
RAZIN, A., Economics
RECHAVI, G., Haematology
REHAVI, M., Pharmacology
REIN, R., History
REPHAELI, Y., Physics
RISHPON, J., Biotechnology
ROKEM, F., Theatre Arts
ROLL, I., Classical Archaeology
RON, E., Microbiology
RON-EL, R., Gynaecology and Obstetrics
RONEN, B., Management
ROSENAU, P., Applied Mathematics
ROSENBAUM, M., Psychology
ROSENBERG, M., Human Microbiology
ROSENMAN, G., Electrical Engineering
ROSSET, SH., Mathematics
ROZEN, S., Chemistry
RUBIN, U., Arabic Language and Literature
RUBIN, Z., History
RUBINSTEIN, A., Economics
RUBINSTEIN, E., Medicine
RUDNICK, Z., Mathematics
RUPIN, E., Computer Science
RUPIN, E., Physiology
RUSCHIN, SH., Electrical Engineering
SABAR, B., Education
SADAN, J., Islamic Culture, Arabic Literature
SADKA, E., Economics
SAFRA, Z., Management
SAMET, D., Management
SAND, SH., History
SARNE, Y., Physiology
SAVION, N., Clinical Biochemistry
SCHMEIDLER, D., Statistics and Economics
SCHWARTZ, M., Physics
SEMYONOV, M., Sociology
SHACHAM-DIAM, Y., Electrical Engineering
SHAI, A., History
SHAKED, U., Electrical and Electronic Engineering
SHALGI, R., Embryology
SHAMIR, M., Political Science
SHAMIR, R., Computer Sciences
SHAMIR, Z., Hebrew Literature
SHANI, M., Health Systems Management
SHAPIRA, A., History of the Jewish People
SHAPIRA, Y., Electrical and Electronic Engineering
SHAPIRO, Y., Physiology
SHARIR, M., Computer Sciences
SHAVIT, Y., History of the Jewish People
SHAVIT, Y., Sociology and Anthropology
SHAVIT, Z., Semiotics and Cultural Research
SHEMER, J., Medicine
SHEMER, L., Mechanical Engineering
SHENKMAN, L., Medicine
SHILOH, Y., Human Genetics
SHOENFELD, Y., Medicine
SHOHAMY, E., Education
SHOHAT, M., Paediatrics
SHUSTIN, E., Mathematics
SIDI, Y., Medicine
SINGER, I., Cultures of the Ancient East
SINGER, S., Electrical Engineering
SIVASHINSKY, G., Applied Mathematics
SKORNICK, Y., Surgery
SKUTELSKY, E., Pathology
SNEH, B., Botany
SNYDERS, I., Electrical Engineering
SODIN, M., Mathematics
SOLOMON, B., Biotechnology
SOLOMON, Z., Social Work
SOUDRY, D., Mathematics
SPIEGLER, I., Management
STAVY, R., Teaching of Science
STEINBERG, B., Electrical Engineering
STERN, N., Medicine
STERNBERG, A., Physics
STERNBERG, M., Theory of Literature
STONE, L., Zoology
STRAUSS, S., Educational Psychology
TAL, H., Periodontology
TAMARKIN, M., History of Africa
TAMIR, A., Statistics
TAMSE, A., Endodontology
TARSI, M., Computer Sciences
TAUMAN, Y., Management
TEBOULLE, M., Operation Research and Statistics
TE'ENI, D., Management
TEICHMAN, M., Psychology
TEICHMAN, Y., Psychology
TERKEL, J., Zoology
TIROSH, D., Teaching of Science
TISHLER, A., Management
TODER, V., Embryology
TOLEDANO, E., History of the Middle East
TOURY, G., Theory of Literature, Comparative Literature
TSAL, Y., Psychology
TSIRELSON, B., Statistics
TUR, M., Electrical and Electronic Engineering
TUR-KASPA, R., Medicine
TURKEL, E., Mathematics
TYANO, S., Psychiatry
URBAKH, M., Chemistry
VERED, Z., Cardiology
VIDNE, B., Surgery
VOLKOV, S., History
WEINER, I., Psychology
WEINSTEIN, E., Electrical and Electronic Engineering
WEISMAN, Y., Paediatrics
WEISS, A., Electrical Engineering
WEISS, Y., Economics
WEIZMAN, A., Psychiatry
WEIZMAN, R., Psychiatry
WIENTROUB, S. H., Orthopaedic Surgery
WOLFSON, H., Computer Sciences
YAKAR, J., Archaeology
YANKIELOWICZ, S., Physics
YAROSLAVSKY, L., Electrical Engineering
YASSIF, E., Hebrew Literature
YEHUDAI, A., Computer Sciences
YINON, U., Physiology
YOGEV, A., Sociology of Education
YOM-TOV, Y., Zoology
ZADOK, R., History of the Jewish People and Cultures of the Ancient East
ZAGAGI, N., Classical Studies
ZAHAVI, J., Management
ZAKAY, D., Psychology
ZALTZMAN, N., Law
ZANG, I., Management
ZILCHA, I., Economics
ZISAPEL, N., Biochemistry
ZONNENSCHEIN, J., Physics
ZWICK, U., Computer Sciences

ATTACHED RESEARCH INSTITUTES

Diaspora Research Institute.

Benzion Katz Institute for Research in Hebrew Literature.

Sonia and Marco Nadler Institute of Archaeology.

Dayan Center for Middle Eastern and African Studies.

Cummings Center for Soviet and East European Studies.

Institute for German Studies.

Porter Institute for Poetics and Semiotics.

Jaffee Center for Strategic Studies.

Foerder Institute for Economic Research.

Institute for Social Research.

David Horowitz Research Institute for Developing Countries.

Golda Meir Institute for Labor and Social Research.

Israel Institute of Business Research.

Operations Research Center.

Florence and George S. Wise Observatory.

Cohn Institute for the History and Philosophy of Sciences and Ideas.

Institute for Nature Preservation Research.

Institute for Cereal Crops Improvement.

Center for Nuclear Research, Nahal Soreq.

Center for Research in the Biology of Cancer.

Institute for Petroleum Research and Geophysics: see Research Institutes.

Interdisciplinary Center for Technological Analysis and Forecasting.

Pinchas Sapir International Center for Development.

Eva and Marc Besen Institute for the Study of Contemporary Historical Consciousness.

Marcel and Annie Adams Institute for Business Management Information Systems.

Joseph Kasirer Institute for Research in Accounting.

Institute of Occupational Health.

Djerassi-Elias Institute of Oncology.

Neufeld Cardiac Research Institute.

Institute for Petroleum and Energy.

Raymond and Beverly Sackler Institute of Theoretical Physics.

Vladimir Schreiber Institute of Mathematical Sciences.

Max and Betty Kranzberg Institute for Electronic Devices Research.

Prof. Dr Raphael Taubenschlag Institute of Criminal Law.

Institute for Continuing Legal Studies.

Cegla Institute of Comparative and Private International Law.

Mortimer and Raymond Sackler Institute of Advanced Studies.

Gordon Center for Energy Studies.

Kovens Health Systems Management Center.

Ruth and Albert Abramson Center for Medical Physics.

Institute for Research of the Jewish Press.

Sackler Institute for Economic Studies.

Dead Sea Research Center.

Interdisciplinary Institute of Biotechnology.

Tami Steinmetz Center for Peace Research.

Raymond and Beverly Sackler Institute for Physical Chemistry.

Ela Kodesz Institute for Research on Cancer Development and Prevention.

Herczeg Institute on Aging.

David and Anne Warsaw Center for Entrepreneurial Studies.

Morris E. Curiel Center for International Studies.

Adams Super-Center for Brain Studies.

Ela Kodesz Institute for Cardiac Physical Sciences and Engineering.

Stanly Steyer Institute for Cancer Epidemiology and Research.

Porter Super-Center for Environmental and Ecological Studies.

Raymond and Beverly Sackler Institute of Astronomy.

Wolfson Center for Material Sciences.

Zwitzerland Institute of Developmental Biology.

Shalom and Varda Yoran Institute for Human Genome Research.

Elizabeth and Nicholas Slezak Center for Cardiac Research and Medical Engineering.

Science and Technology Education Center.

Maurice and Gabriela Goldschleger Eye Research Institute.

Sackler Institute of Molecular Medicine.

Minerva Research Center on Cholesterol Gallstones and Lipid Metabolism in the Liver.

Julius F. Cohnheim Center of Cellular and Molecular Phagocyte Research.

Felsenstein Medical Research Center.

Minerva Center for Human Rights.

Erhard Center for Higher Studies and Research in Insurance.

Max Perlman Center for Global Business.

B. I. Cohen Institute for Public Opinion Research.

Deutsch Institute of Computer Sciences.

Reymond and Beverly Sackler Institute of Scientific Computation.

Heinrich Herts Minerva Center for High Temperature Superconductivity.

Hermann Minkowski Center for Geometry.

Chaim Weizmann Institute for Research in the History of Zionism.

Ela Kodesz Institute for Host Defence against Infectious Diseases.

Institute for International Scientific Exchanges in Medical Sciences.

Institute for Latin American History and Culture.

Miriam and George Faktor Entrepreneurial Center.

Peres Institute for Diplomacy and Regional Co-operation.

Raymond and Beverly Sackler Institute for Solid State Physics.

Stephen Roth Institute for Study of Contemporary Anti-Semitism and Racism.

Game Theory Center.

Adler Research Center for Child Welfare and Protection.

Claire and Amedee Maratier Institute for the Study of Blindness and Visual Disorders.

Joan and Jaime Constantiner Institute for Molecular Genetics.

Laura Shwarz-Kipp Institute for Advanced Technology in the Humanities.

Yael Family Institute for Plant Biotechnology.

Andrea and Charles Bronfman Center for Media and the Jewish People.

Levie-Edersheim-Gitter Institute for Functional Brain Imaging.

Institute for Continuous Legal Education.

Saban Institute for the Study of the American Political System.

Marian Gertner Institute for Medical Nanosystems.

Yitzhak and Chaya Weinstein Research Institute for Signal Processing.

TECHNION—ISRAEL INSTITUTE OF TECHNOLOGY

32000 Haifa
Telephone: (4) 8292111
Fax: (4) 8221581
Internet: www.technion.ac.il

Founded 1912; inaugurated 1924
State control
Language of instruction: Hebrew
Academic year: October to July

President: Prof. Yitzhak Apeloig
Senior Vice-President: Prof. Aviv Rosen
Deputy Senior Vice-President: Prof. David Degani
Deputy Senior Vice-President and Co-ordinator of International Academic Relations and Student Exchange: Prof. David Degani
Vice-President for Academic Affairs: Prof. Moshe Moshe
Vice-President for Administration and Finance: Prof. Michael Rubinivitch
Vice-President for Research: Prof. Moshe Eizenberg
Vice-President for Resource Development and External Relations: Prof. Peretz Lavie
Dean of Graduate School: Prof. Alfred Bruckstein
Dean of Undergraduate Studies: Prof. Shmuel Zaks

Library: see Libraries and Archives
Number of teachers: 993
Number of students: 13,291 (9,273 undergraduate, 4,018 postgraduate)

Publications: *Bulletin* (weekly), *Catalogue* (annually), *HaTechnion* (3 a year), *President's Report* (annually), *Research Report* (annually), *Shlomo Kaplansky Memorial Series* (incorporated in *Israel Journal of Technology*), *Technion Focus Newsletter* (in English, 4 a year), *The Joseph Wunsch Lectures* (annually)

DEANS

Faculty of Aerospace Engineering: Prof. D. Givoli
Faculty of Architecture and Town Planning: Prof. A. Churchman
Faculty of Biology: Assoc. Prof. D. Zilbershtine
Faculty of Biotechnology and Food Engineering: Prof. S. Mizrahi
Faculty of Chemical Engineering: Prof. Y. Talmon
Faculty of Chemistry: Prof. E. Keinan
Faculty of Civil and Environmental Engineering: Prof. A. Laufer
Faculty of Computer Science: Prof. A. Itai
Faculty of Electrical Engineering: Prof. M. Sidi
Faculty of Industrial Engineering and Management: Prof. D. Monderer
Faculty of Materials Engineering: Prof. E. Zolotoyabko
Faculty of Mathematics: Prof. R. Pinsky
Faculty of Mechanical Engineering: Prof. Z. Palmor
Faculty of Medicine: Prof. I. Perlman
Faculty of Physics: Prof. E. Ehrenfreund
Department of Biomedical Engineering: Prof. J. Mizrahi (Head)
Department of Education in Technology and Science: Assoc. Prof. M. Moore (Head)
Department of Humanities and Art: Prof. M. Moore

PROFESSORS

Faculty of Aerospace Engineering (tel. (4) 8292308; fax (4) 8231848; e-mail aerdean@aerodyne.technion.ac.il):

Bar-Itzhack, I., Navigation, Guidance and Control
Durban, D., Aerospace Structure
Gany, A., Rocket Propulsion
Givoli, D., Aerospace Structures, Computational Mechanics
Greenberg, B., Combustion Theory
Guelman, M., Space Engineering
Karpel, M., Aeroelasticity, Optimization
Rand, O., Rotary Wings, Aerospace Structures
Rosen, A., Rotary Wings, Aerospace Structure
Tambour, Y., Combustion of Fuel Sprays
Weihs, D., Fluid Mechanics, Bio-Mechanics and Stability Theory
Weller, T., Aerospace Structures, Smart Structures Technology

Faculty of Architecture and Town Planning (tel. (4) 8294001; fax (4) 8294617; e-mail deanarc@tx.technion.ac.il; internet arc.technion.ac.il):

Alterman, R., Land Development
Amir, S., Regional Planning
Burt, M., Ocean Architecture
Carmon, N., Social Policy
Churchman, A., Environmental Psychology
Shaviv, E., Energy and Architecture
Shefer, D., Urban and Regional Economics

Faculty of Biology (tel. (4) 8294211; fax (4) 8225153; e-mail ddafna@tx.technion.ac.il; internet www.biology.technion.ac.il):

Cassel, D., G-Proteins and Membrane Traffic
Schuster, G., Molecular Biology

Department of Biomedical Engineering (tel. (4) 8239431; fax (4) 8294599; internet www.bm.technion.ac.il):

Dinnar, U., Cardiovascular Fluid Dynamics, Minimal Invasive Diagnosis
Lanir, Y., Tissues Mechanics and Structure, Cardiac Mechanics, Coronary Circulation
Mizrahi, J., Orthopaedic and Rehabilitation Biomechanics

Faculty of Biotechnology and Food Engineering (tel. (4) 8293068; fax (4) 8293399; e-mail biotech@tx.technion.ac.il; internet www.technion.ac.il/biotech):

Cogan, U., Food Chemistry

LEVI, B. Z., Mammalian Cell Biotechnology, Transcriptional Regulation, Innate Immunity
MILTZ, J., Packaging Engineering
SHOHAM, Y., Biochemical Engineering, Industrial Microbiology, Applied Enzymology

Faculty of Chemical Engineering (tel. (4) 8292820; fax (4) 8295672; e-mail chemeng@tx.technion.ac.il; internet http://chemeng.technion.ac.il):

COHEN, Y., Polymer Science and Engineering
GRADER, G., Ceramic Materials, Sol-Gel Systems
LEWIN, D. R., Process Design and Control
MARMUR, A., Interfaces and Colloids
NIR, A., Fluid Mechanics, Transport Phenomena
SEMIAT, R., Process Development, Separation Processes, Desalination, Electro-Optical Techniques for Fluid-Flow
SHEINTUCH, M., Chemical Reaction Engineering, Catalysis, Non-linear Dynamics
TALMON, Y., Complex Liquids, Electron Microscopy

Faculty of Chemistry (tel. (4) 8293664; fax (4) 8295703; e-mail chsabine@techunix.technion.ac.il; internet www.technion.ac.il/technion/chemistry):

APELOIG, Y., Organosilicon and Computational Chemistry
BAASOV, T., Bio-organic Chemistry, Enzymology
EISEN, M., Polymer Chemistry, Organometallic Chemistry
GROSS, Z., Catalysis, Inorganic Chemistry, Bioinorganic Chemistry
KAFTORY, M., Chemical Crystallography
KEINAN, E., Biocatalysis, Organic Synthesis, Molecular Computing
KOLODNEY, E., Molecular Beams, Surface Chemistry
MAREK, I., Organic Synthesis
MOISEYEV, N., Quantum Chemistry
SCHLECTER, I., Analytical Chemistry
SPEISER, S., Laser Photophysics

Faculty of Civil and Environmental Engineering (tel. (4) 8231508; fax (4) 8220133; e-mail yta@techunix.technion.ac.il):

BENTUR, A., Cementitious and Composite Building Materials
CEDER, A., Transportation Planning and Operation
DOYTSHER, Y., Mapping and Geo-Information Engineering
EISENBERGER, M., Computational Mechanics-Static, Dynamics, Stability Analysis
FROSTIG, Y., Sandwich Structures, Prestressed Concrete, Retrofitting of Concrete Structures, Tile-Wall Systems
FRYDMAN, S., Geotechnical Engineering
KIRSCH, U., Structural Engineering
LAUFER, A., Project Management
MAMANE, Y., Air Pollution Meteorology, Atmospheric Aerosols
MURAVSKI, G., Soil Structure Interaction
NEUMANN, P. M., Plant Physiology
POLUS, A., Traffic Flow and Congestion Modelling, Safety of Transportation Systems
RUBIN, H., Contaminant Hydrology
SHEINMAN, I., Post-Buckling, Dynamics, Static, Damage, Vibration Induced by People
STIASSNIE, M., Water Waves
UZAN, J., Pavement Engineering
YANKELEVSKY, D., Impact Engineering, Mechanics of Reinforced Concrete, Earthquake Engineering
ZIMMELS, Y., Environmental and Process Engineering

Faculty of Computer Science (tel. (4) 8294313; fax (4) 8294353; e-mail itai@cs.technion.ac.il; internet www.cs.technion.ac.il):

BARAM, Y., Pattern Recognition, Artificial Neural Network
BIHAM, E., Cryptology
BRUCKSTEIN, A., Image Processing
BSHOUTY, N., Computational Learning Theory
FRANCEZ, N., Semantics and Verification, Computational Linguistics
GRUMBERG, O., Formal Verification
ISRAELI, M., Scientific Computing, Numerical Methods, Computational Linguistics
ITAI, A., Analysis of Algorithms and Data Structures, Computational Linguistics
KUSHILEVITZ, E., Complexity and Cryptography
MAKOWSKY, J., Mathematical Logic Computability and Complexity, Combinatorial Algorithms, Database Theory
MORAN, S., Search Methods on the Web
ROTH, R., Coding Theory
SIDI, A., Theoretical Numerical Analysis and Scientific Computing
SHMUELI, O., Databases: Systems and Theory
UNGARISH, M., Modelling and Numerical Simulation of Fluid Flows
ZAKS, S., Distributed Computing and Communication Networks

Faculty of Electrical Engineering (tel. (4) 8294679; fax (4) 8294715; e-mail eedean@ee.technion.ac.il; internet www.ee.technion.ac.il):

CIDON, I., Communication Networks
EISENSTEIN, G., Optoelectronics
FEUER, A., Automatic Control
FINKMAN, E., Quantum Hetrostructure
FISCHER, B., Optoelectronics
LEVIATAN, Y., Electromagnetic Waves
MALAH, D., Digital Signal Processing of Speech and Images
MERHAV, N., Information Theory
ROM, R., Communication Networks
SALZMAN, J., Optoelectronics
SCHIEBER, D., Energy Conversion
SEGALL, A., Computer Networks
SHAMAI, S., Information Theory
SHWARTZ, A., Large Deviations Theory
SIDI, M., Computer Networks
TANNENBAUM, A., Robust Control Theory
ZEEVI, Y., Vision and Image Sciences
ZEITOUNI, Z., Large Deviations Theory
ZIV, J., Statistical Communication, Information Theory

Faculty of Industrial Engineering and Management (tel. (4) 8294444; fax (4) 8295676; e-mail iedean@ie.technion.ac.il; internet http://ie.technion.ac.il):

ADLER, R., Stochastic Processes
BEN-TAL, A., Non-linear Optimization
EREZ, M., Organizational Psychology
DE-HAAN, U., Entrepreneurship
EREV, I., Behavioural Sciences and Experimental Economics
FEIGIN, P., Applied Statistics
GOLANY, B., Industrial Engineering
GOPHER, D., Human Factors
KASPI, H., Probability and Stochastic Processes
MANDELBAUM, A., Operations Research, Stochastic Processes and their Applications
MONDERER, D., Game Theory
NEMIROVSKY, A., Optimization Complexity Theory
NOTEA, A., Non-Destructive Testing
ROTHBLUM, U. G., Operations Research
RUBINSTEIN, R., Stochastic Systems
SHTUB, A., Project Management
TENNENHOLTZ, M., Artificial Intelligence
WEISSMAN, I., Probability and Statistics

Faculty of Materials Engineering (tel. (4) 8294591; fax (4) 8295677; e-mail bzipi@tx.technion.ac.il):

EIZENBERG, M., Electronic Materials
GUTMANAS, E., Processing of High-Performance Material
KOMEM, Y., Electronic Materials
LIFSHITZ, Y., Nanostructured Inorganic Materials
SHECHTMAN, D., Properties and Microstructure of Intermetallic Compounds
SIEGMANN, A., Polymers and Plastic Structuring
ZOLOTOYABKO, E., X-Ray Diffraction

Faculty of Mathematics (tel. (4) 8223071; fax (4) 8324654; e-mail mathsee@tx.technion.ac.il):

AHARONI, R., Combinatorics
AHARONOV, D., Complex Analysis
BENYAMINI, Y., Banach Spaces
BERMAN, A., Matrix Theory
BSHOUTY, D., Complex Analysis, Probability Theory, Mathematical Statistics
CHILLAG, D., Algebra Group Theory
CWIKEL, M., Functional Analysis and Interpolation Space
GOLDBERG, M., Numerical Analysis
GORDON, Y., Functional Analysis
HERSHKOWITZ, D., Matrix Theory
IOFFE, A., General Theory of Sub-differentials
KATCHALSKI, M., Combinatorial Geometry
LERER, L., Linear Algebra, Operator Theory
LIRON, N., Applied Mathematics
LOEWY, R., Linear Algebra
MARCUS, M., Partial Differential Equations, Non-linear Analysis
NEPOMNYASHCHY, A., Fluid Mechanics
PINKUS, A., Approximation Theory
PINSKY, R., Probability and Stochastic Processes, Partial Differential Equations
REICH, S., Non-linear Analysis
RUBINSTEIN, J., Applied Mathematics
SOLEL, B., Operator Theory, Functional Analysis
SONN, J., Algebraic Number Theory
WAJNRYB, B., Algebraic Geometry
ZEITOUNI, O., Probability and Stochastic Processes
ZIEGLER, Z., Theory of Approximation

Faculty of Mechanical Engineering (tel. (4) 8292079; fax (4) 8295710):

ALTUS, E., Micro-Mechanics of Solids
BAR-YOSEPH, P., Finite Element Analysis
BEN-HAIM, Y., Decisions under Uncertainty, Reliability
DEGANI, D., Computational Fluid Dynamics
ELIAS, E., Thermohydraulics, Nuclear Engineering
ETSION, I., Tribology, Lubrication
GROSSMAN, G., Thermodynamics, Heat Pumps, Cooling and Air-Conditioning
GUTMAN, S., Relative Stability of Linear Dynamic Systems
HABER, S., Particulate Systems
PALMOR, Z., Digital Control of Industrial and Mechanical Systems
RUBIN, M., Continuum Mechanics
SHAPIRO, M., Porous Media, Aerosols
SHITZER, A., Bio-Heat Transfer
SHOHAM, M., Robotics and Medical Robotics
SHPITALNI, M., CAD/CAM, Manufacturing
TIROSH, J., Fracture Mechanics
YARIN, A., Rheology, Fluid Mechanics
YARIN, L. P., Two-Phase Flow, Combustion
ZVIRIN, Y., Solar Energy, Internal Combustion Engines

Faculty of Medicine (POB 9649, Bat Galim, Haifa, 31096; tel. (4) 8514722; fax (4) 8517008; e-mail medicine@tx.technion.ac.il; internet www.technion.ac.il/medicine):

AVIRAM, M., Lipid Research Laboratory

BENJAMIN, B., Haematology
BEYAR, R., Invasive Cardiology
CIECHANOVER, A., Intercellular Breakdown of Proteins
ETZIONI, A., Paediatrics and Immunology
FINBERG, J., Neuropharmacology
FINSOD, M., Neurosurgery
FRY, M., Enzymology of DNA Replication
GAVISH, M., Molecular Pharmacology
HASIN, Y., Cardiology
HERSHKO, A., Intracellular Protein Degradation
ITSKOVITZ, J., Human Embryonic Stem Cells
KRAUSZ, M., General Surgery
LAVIE, P., Psychobiology, Sleep Research
LEWIS, B., Cardiology
NEUFELD, G., Angiogenesis
PALTI, Y., Physiology and Biophysics
PERLMAN, I., Vision Neurophysiology
PRATT, H., Behavioural Sciences
ROWE, Y., Haematology
SHALEV, E., Obstetrics and Gynaecology
SKORECKI, K., Nephrology, Molecular Medicine
VOLDAVSKY, I., Vascular and Tumour Biology, Biochemistry
YOUDIM, M., Neuropharmacology

Faculty of Physics (tel. (4) 8293551; fax (4) 8295755; e-mail office@physics.technion.ac.il; internet physics.technion.ac.il):

AKKERMANS, E., Theory of Condensed Matter Physics, Mesoscopic Quantum
AUERBACH, A., Condensed Matter Theory
AVRON, J., Mathematical Physics
BRAUN, E., Biophysics, Non-linear Dynamics of Systems out of Equilibrium
COHEN, E., Spectroscopic Properties of Laser Materials
DADO, S., High-Energy Physics Experimentation
DAR, A., Astroparticle Physics
EHRENFREUND, E., Semi-conducting Quantum Structures and Polymers
EILAM, G., Elementary Particle Physics
FELSTEINER, J., Condensed Matter Physics, Plasma Physics
FISHMAN, S., Quantum Chaos
GERSHONI, D., Semiconducting Quantum Heterostructures
GRONAU, M., Theoretical High Energy Physics
KALISH, R., Ion-Implantation—Hyperfine Interactions
KOREN, G., Superconductivity and Lasers
LIPSON, S., Low Temperature Physics
MANN, A., Theoretical Physics
MOSHE, M., Theoretical High Energy Physics
ORI, A., General Relativity, Black Holes, Gravitational Radiation
POLTURAK, E., High Temperature Superconductors
REGEV, O., Astrophysics
RIESS, I., Solid State Electrochemistry
SHAPIRO, B., Theory of Condensed Matter
SHAVIV, G., Astrophysics
SEGEV, M., Nonlinear Optics
SIVAN, U., Mesoscopic Physics, Bio-Electronics
SOKER, N., Astrophysics Theory

AFFILIATED INSTITUTES

Technion Research and Development Foundation Ltd: see under Research Institutes.

Attached research centres:

Aeronautical Research Center.
Agricultural Engineering Research Center.
Architectural Heritage Research Center.
Center for Architectural Research and Development.
Norman and Helen Asher Space Research Institute.
Center for Biological Research.
Center for Chemical Research.
Center for Research in Energy and Environmental Conservation Engineering.
Center for Research in Environmental and Water Resources Engineering.
Chemical Engineering Research Center.
Electrical Engineering Research Center.
Food Industries Research and Development Center.
Philip M. and Ethel Klutznick Center for Urban and Regional Studies.
Izhak Kidron Microelectronics Research Center.
Materials Engineering Research Center.
Material Mechanics Center.
National Building Research Institute.
Quality and Reliability Research Center.
Research Center for Intelligent Systems.
Research Center for Mapping and Geodesy.
Research and Development Center for Education in Technology and Science and for Vocational Training.
Research Center for Very Large Scale Integrated Systems (VLSI).
Research Center for Work Safety and Human Engineering.
Russell Berrie Nanotechnology Institute.
J. Silver Institute for Bio-Medical Engineering.
Solid State Institute.
Transportation Research Institute.
J. W. Ullman Center for Manufacturing Systems and Robotics.
Stephen and Nancy Grand Water Research Institute: .

Coastal and Marine Engineering Research Institute.

Israel Institute of Metals: see under Research Institutes.

Samuel Neaman Institute for Advanced Studies in Science and Technology: see under Research Institutes.

Rappaport Family Institute for Research in Medical Science.

WEIZMANN INSTITUTE OF SCIENCE

POB 26, 76 100 Rehovot
Telephone: (8) 9342111
Fax: (8) 9344107
Internet: www.weizmann.ac.il

Founded 1949; includes the Daniel Sieff Research Institute (f. 1934).

The Institute is a private non-profit corporation for fundamental and applied research in the natural and exact sciences. The Feinberg Graduate School offers MSc and PhD courses

Chairman (Board of Governors): STUART E. EIZENSTAT
Chairperson (Scientific Council): Prof. YEHIAM PRIAM
President: Prof. ILAN CHET
Vice-President: Prof. SAMUEL SAFRAN
Vice-President (Administration and Finance): GAD KOBER
Vice-President (International Affairs and Public Relations): AMY MATCHEN
Vice-President (Technology Transfer): Prof. HAIM GARTY
Chief Librarian: Mrs I. POLLACK

Library: see Libraries and Archives
Number of teachers: 300
Number of students: 785 postgraduates

Publications: *Annual Report of Scientific Activities*, *Interface*, *Current Research Activities*

DEANS

Faculty of Biochemistry: Prof. B.-Z. SHILO
Faculty of Biology: Prof. B. GEIGER
Faculty of Chemistry: Prof. MORDECHAI SHEVES
Faculty of Mathematical Sciences: Prof. ZVI ARTSTEIN
Faculty of Physics: Prof. YARON SILBERBERG
Feinberg Graduate School: Prof. YOSEF YARDEN

HEADS OF DEPARTMENTS

Faculty of Biochemistry (internet www.weizmann.ac.il/homepage/pages/dbiochem.shtml):

Biological Chemistry: Prof. ZVI LIVNEH
Molecular Genetics: Prof. ADI KIMCHI
Plant Sciences: Prof. GAD GALILI
Biological Services: Prof. CHAIM KAHANA

Faculty of Biology (internet www.weizmann.ac.il/homepages/pages/dbio.shtml):

Molecular Cell Biology: Prof. VARDA ROTTER
Immunology: Prof. Z. ESHHAR
Biological Regulation: Prof. NAVA DEKEL
Neurobiology: Prof. YADIN DUDAI
Veterinary Resources: Dr A. HARMELIN

Faculty of Chemistry (internet www.weizmann.ac.il/homepage/pages/dchem.shtml):

Chemical Physics: Prof. SHIMON VEGA
Environmental Sciences and Energy Research: Prof. DAN YAKIR
Materials and Interfaces: Prof. RESHEF TENNE
Organic Chemistry: Prof. D. MILSTEIN
Structural Biology: Prof. AMNON HOROVITZ
Solar Energy Facilities Unit: M. EPSTEIN
Chemical Research Support: Prof. B. BERKOVICH

Faculty of Mathematics and Computer Science (internet www.weizmann.ac.il/homepages/pages/dmath.shtml):

Computer Science and Applied Mathematics: Prof. TAMAR FLASH
Mathematics: Prof. G. SCHECHTMAN

Faculty of Physics (internet www.weizmann.ac.il/homepage/pages/dphys.shtml):

Condensed Matter Physics: Prof. I. BAR-JOSEPH
Physics of Complex Systems: Prof. G. FALKOVICH
Particle Physics: Prof. I. TSERRUYA
Physics Services: Prof. D. ZAJFMAN

Feinberg Graduate School (internet www.weizmann.ac.il/homepage/pages/dfgs.shtml):

Science Teaching: Prof. ABRAHAM ARCAVI
Young@Science: Dr ZVI PALTIEL

DIRECTORS OF CENTRES

Faculty of Biochemistry:

Dr Joseph Cohn Minerva Center for Biomembrane Research: Prof. ZVI LIVNEH
Mel Dobrin Center for Nutrition: Prof. GAD GALILI
Charles W. and Tillie K. Lubin Center for Plant Biotechnology: Prof. GAD GALILI

Avron-Wilstätter Minerva Center for Research in Photosynthesis: Prof. A. SCHERZ
Harry and Jeanette Weinberg Center for Plant Molecular Genetics Research: Prof. GAD GALILI
Crown Human Genome Center: Prof. DORON LANCET
Leo and Julia Forchheimer Center for Molecular Genetics: Prof. A. KIMCHI
Y. Leon Benoziyo Institute for Molecular Medicine: Prof. BEN-ZION SHILO
M.D. Moross Institute for Cancer Research: Prof. YORAM GRONER
Kekst Family Center for Medical Genetics: Prof. YORAM GRONER
David and Fela Shapell Family Center for Genetic Disorders Research: Prof. YORAM GRONER

Faculty of Biology:

Belle S. and Irving E. Meller Center for Biology of Ageing: Prof. ZELIG ESHHAR
Nella and Leon Benoziyo Center for Neurosciences: Prof. YADIN DUDAI
Murray H. and Meyer Grodetsky Center for Research of Higher Brain Functions: Prof. A. GRINVALD
Carl and Micaela Einhorn-Dominic Institute for Brain Research: Prof. YADIN DUDAI
Norman and Helen Asher Center for for Brain Imaging: Prof. YADIN DUDAI
Wilner Family Center for Vascular Biology: Prof. NAVA DEKEL
Yad Abraham Research Center for Cancer Diagnostics and Therapy: Prof. VARDA ROTTER
Gabrielle Rich Center for Transplantation Biology Research: Prof. YAIR REISNER
Women's Health Research Center: Prof. VARDA ROTTER
Nella and Leon Benoziyo Center for Neurological Diseases: Prof. MENAHEM SEGAL

Faculty of Chemistry:

Center for Energy Research: Prof. JACOB KARNI
Gerhard M. J. Schmidt Minerva Center for Supermolecular Architecture: Prof. R. TENNE
Fritz Haber Center for Physical Chemistry: Prof. SHIMON VEGA
Helen and Milton A. Kimmelman Center for Biomolecular Structure and Assembly: Prof. A. E. YONATH
Joseph and Ceil Mazer Center for Structural Biology: Prof. AMNON HOROVITZ
Sussman Family Center for the Study of Environmental Sciences: Prof. DAN YAKIR
Helen and Martin Kimmel Center for Molecular Design: Prof. DAVID MILSTEIN
Helen and Martin Kimmel Center for Archaeological Sciences: Prof. STEPHEN WEINER
Ilse Katz Institute for Material Sciences and Magnetic Resonance Research: Prof. MORDECHAI SHEVES
Helen and Martin Kimmel Center for Nanoscale Science: Prof. RESHEF TENNE

Faculty of Mathematics and Computer Science:

Arthur and Rochelle Belfer Institute of Mathematics and Computer Science: Prof. ZVI ARTSTEIN
Minerva Center for Formal Verification of Reactive Systems: Prof. A. PNUELI
Ida Cohen Centre for Mathematics: Prof. ZVI ARTSTEIN

Faculty of Physics:

Joseph H. and Belle R. Braun Center for Submicron Research: Prof. M. HEIBLUM
Albert Einstein Minerva Center for Theoretical Physics: Prof. ELI WAXMAN
Nella and Leo Benoziyo Center for High Energy Physics: Prof. G. MIKENBERG
Minerva Center for Non-linear Physics of Complex Systems: Prof. ITAMAR PROCACCIA
Maurice and Gabriela Goldschleger Center for Nanophysics: Prof. ISRAEL BAR-JOSEPH
Center for Experimental Physics: Prof. YARON SILBERBERG

Feinberg Graduate School:

Aharon Katzir-Katchalsky Center: Prof. Y. YARDEN

INSTITUTION-WIDE CENTRES

Dolfi and Lola Ebner Center for Biomedical Research: Dir Prof. SAMUEL SAFRAN.

Clore Center for Biological Physics: Dir Prof. BENNY GEIGER.

Center for New Scientists: Dir Prof. SAMUEL SAFRAN.

Center for Scientific Excellence: Dir Prof. SAMUEL SAFRAN.

J & R Center for Scientific Research: Dir Prof. SAMUEL SAFRAN.

Prospective Center for Systems Biology: Dir Prof. EYTAN DOMANY.

Colleges and Higher Institutes

Academic Center Ruppin: PO Academic Center Ruppin, 40250 Emek Hefer; tel. (9) 8983005; fax (9) 8983021; e-mail rani@ruppin.ac.il; internet www.ruppin.ac.il; f. 1949; three-year degree courses in economics, accounting, business administration and the behavioural sciences; two-year courses in architecture, basic trades, computers, electrical engineering, industrial management, landscape architecture, megatronics, soil and water engineering; short courses in basic economics, accounting and mechanics; School of Engineering: electrical, industrial and computer science; library: 40,000 vols; 350 teachers; 5,000 students; Dir RANI IDAN.

Academic College of Law: 87 Pinchas St, Ramat-Gan 52275; tel. (3) 5745206; fax (3) 5742974; internet www.rg-law.ac.il; depts of Human Rights, Criminal Law and Criminology and Law, Communication and Technology; 1,000 students; Man. Dir NITZA MAZAR; Dean Prof. CLAUDE KLEIN.

Academic College of Tel-Aviv-Yaffo: 4 Antokolsky St, POB 16131, Tel-Aviv 61161; tel. (3) 5211840; fax (3) 5211870; e-mail acty@mta.ac.il; internet www.mta.ac.il; Bachelor of Arts degrees in society and politics, behavioural science, management, computer science.

Bezalel Academy of Arts and Design: Mount Scopus, POB 24046, 91240 Jerusalem; tel. (2) 5893333; fax (2) 5823094; e-mail liv@bezalel.ac.il; internet www.bezalel.ac.il; f. 1906; degree courses in fine arts, design, gold- and silver-smithing, architecture, industrial design, animation, visual communication, jewellery and fashion accessories design, photography, video and computer imaging, ceramics and glass design; library: 35,000 vols; 300 teachers; 1,600 students; Dir Dr RAN SAPOZNIK.

Ecole Biblique et Ecole Archéologique Française: POB 19053, 91190 Jerusalem; tel. (2) 6264468; fax (2) 6282567; e-mail directeur@ebaf.edu; internet ebaf.op.org; f. 1890; research, Biblical and Oriental studies, exploration and excavation in Palestine; 14 professors; library, see Libraries; Dir JEAN-MICHEL POFFET; publs *Revue Biblique* (4 a year), *Etudes Bibliques*, *Cahiers de la Revue Biblique*, *Etudes Annexes*, *Littératures anciennes du Proche Orient*.

Etz Hayim, General Talmud, Torah and Grand Teshivah: POB 300, Jerusalem; f. 1841; 1,400 students; library: 10,000 vols; Pres. Rabbi I. Z. MELTZER.

Hadassah College: 37 Hanevi'im St, POB 1114, Jerusalem 91010; tel. (2) 6291911; fax (2) 6250619; e-mail info@hadassah-col.ac.il; internet www.hadassah-col.ac.il; f. 1970; comprises Hadassah Academic College (depts of Optometry, Communication Disorders, Medical Laboratory Sciences, Computer Sciences), Hadassah College of Technology (depts of Technical Software Engineering, Printing and Computer Graphics, Photography and Digital Media, Cinema and Television Production, Industrial Design, Dental Technology, Hotel Management), Tachlit Center for Lifelong Learning; Pres. Prof. NAVA BEN ZVI.

Hebrew Union College—Jewish Institute of Religion, Jerusalem School: 13 King David St, 94101 Jerusalem; tel. (2) 6203333; fax (2) 6251478; e-mail mzakai@huc.edu; internet www.huc.edu; f. 1963; branch of the same institution in the United States of America; the first year of graduate rabbinic studies, Jewish education, cantorial training and programme in biblical archaeology, including summer excavations; Rabbinic programme for Israel Reform (Progressive); English 'Lehrhaus' study programmes in classical Jewish Literature for general public (Bet Midrash); Skirball Museum of Biblical Archaeology; library: Abramov library of 40,000 vols; microfilm collection from American Jewish Archives; 35 teachers; 150 students; Pres. Dr DAVID ELLENSON; Dean Rabbi MICHAEL MARMUR.

International Institute of Histadrut: Beit Berl, 44905 Kfar Saba; tel. (9) 7612323; fax (9) 7421868; e-mail info@peoples.org.il; internet www.peoples.org.il; f. 1958 to train labour and co-operative movements, professional assocs and women's and youth orgs; candidates nominated by trade unions, co-operatives, universities, international labour organizations, etc.; courses and seminars in fields of labour, social and economic development and co-operative studies in English, French, Spanish, Russian and Arabic; 41,400 graduates from 140 countries; library: 15,000 vols, and monographs and periodicals; 8 teachers; 1,400 students; Dir-Gen. GABRIEL LOUSQUI; Academic Dir ZVI GALOR.

Jerusalem College of Technology: 21 Havaad Haleumi St, POB 16031, 91 160 Jerusalem; tel. (2) 6751111; fax (2) 6422075; e-mail pr@mail.jct.ac.il; internet www.jct.ac.il; f. 1969; 4-year first degree courses; library: 20,000 vols; 106 teachers (66 full-time, 40 part-time); 1,300 students; Pres. Prof. JOSEPH BODENHEIMER; Rector Prof. YAAKOV FRIEDMAN; Librarian ZVI SOBEL

CHAIRMEN OF DEPARTMENTS

Applied Mathematics: Prof. Y. AHARONI
Applied Physics/Electro-Optics: ZVI WEINBERGER
Computer Science: Prof. RAPHAEL YEHAZKEL
Electronics: Dr ARYEH WEISS
Managerial Accounting: Prof. ALAN STOLMAN
Science Teaching: Dr REUVEN FREEMAN
Technology Management and Marketing: Dr GERSHON MILES

Jerusalem Academy of Music and Dance: Givat Ram Campus, Jerusalem 91904; tel. (2) 6759911; fax (2) 6527713; internet www.jmd.ac.il; f. 1947; performing arts, composition, conducting and theory, music education, dance; awards B. Mus., B.Ed.Mus., B. Dance and Artists' Diplomas;

courses leading to B.A.Mus., M.A.Mus. and M.Mus. in co-operation with the Hebrew University; Conservatory and High School (Music and Dance); 190 teachers; 550 students; library: 60,000 vols; collection of musical instruments; electroacoustic laboratory; Head AVNER BIRON.

Jerusalem University College: POB 1276, Mount Zion, 91012 Jerusalem; tel. (2) 6718628; fax (2) 6732717; e-mail paulwright@juc.edu; internet www.juc.edu; f. 1957; Christian study centre at university level; graduate and undergraduate courses in the geography, history, languages, religions and cultures of Israel in the Middle East context; field trips and archaeological excavation programme; 20 teachers; 200 students; Pres. Dr PAUL WRIGHT; publ. *From Mount Zion* (newsletter, 2 a year).

Mosad Harav Kook: POB 642, Jerusalem; tel. (2) 6526231; fax (2) 6526968; f. 1937 to educate and train young men for research in the field of Torah Literature and to infuse the original Hebrew culture in all classes of the people; library: Rav Maimon Library of Judaica; religious Zionist Archives; publs Torah-Science books, including the printing of MSS of previously unpublished *Rishonim* works that are still retained in Genizah form, popular commentary to the entire Bible; incorporates Institute for Chasiduth; Dir Rabbi JOSEPH MOVSHOVITZ.

ORT Braude College: POB 78, 21982 Karmiel; tel. (4) 9901911; fax (4) 9882016; e-mail ykatz@ort.org.il; f. 1988; B.Tech degree programmes in Biotechnology Engineering, Electrical and Electronics Engineering, Mechanical Engineering, Industrial and Management Engineering, and Software Engineering; also Practical Engineering 2-year degree programmes; library: 50,000 vols; 320 teachers; 1,200 undergraduate students; Pres. Dr PINHAS SHWINGER.

Pontifical Biblical Institute: POB 497, 3 Paul-Emile Botta St, Jerusalem; tel. (2) 6252843; fax (2) 6241203; e-mail pbijer@netvision.net.il; f. 1913 as a branch of the Pontifical Biblical Institute of Rome; fosters the study of Biblical geography and archaeology; provides courses for students and graduates of Roman Institute; Prehistorical Museum containing discoveries of Teleilat Ghassul, a chalcolithic site in the Jordan valley, excavated by the Institute; library: 26,000 vols for biblical studies; Dir Rev. TOM FITZPATRICK.

Shenkar College of Engineering and Design: 12 Anne Frank St, 52526 Ramat-Gan; tel. (3) 7521133; fax (3) 7521141; e-mail info@mail.shenkar.ac.il; f. 1970; bachelor degrees and research in industrial management and marketing, computer science, plastics engineering, industrial chemistry, industrial engineering, fashion design, textile and interior design, jewellery design, industrial design; library: 20,000 vols, 250 periodicals; 50 teachers; 2,180 students (680 full-time, 1,500 part-time); Pres. Prof. AMOTZ WEINBERG; Man. Dir BARUCH SAGIV.

Studium Biblicum Franciscanum: POB 19424, Monastery of the Flagellation, 91 193 Jerusalem; tel. (2) 6282936; fax (2) 6264519; e-mail secretary@studiumbiblicum.org; internet www.custodia.org/sbf; f. 1927; centre of archaeological research sponsored by the Franciscan Custody of the Holy Land, biblical and archaeological faculty of the *Pontificium Athenaeum Antonianum*, Rome, for degrees of Bachelor in Theology, Licentiate and Doctorate in Biblical Sciences and Archaeology, and diploma in Oriental Biblical Studies and Archaeology and in Biblical Formation; 15 teachers; 80 students; Dean G. C. BOTTINI; publs *Liber Annuus*, *Collectio Maior*, *Collectio Minor*, *Analecta*, *Museum*.

Tel Hai Academic College: 12 210 Upper Galilee; tel. (4) 6900859; fax (4) 6900919; e-mail telhai@telhai.ac.il; internet www.telhai.ac.il; f. 1957; bachelor degree courses in biotechnology and environmental sciences, nutrition sciences, education, economics and management, social work, computer science, multidisciplinary studies; diploma courses in architecture, construction, electronics and electricity, computers, mechanics and machinery, industrial management, telemedia and communication, drama therapy; Art Institute courses in sculpture, drawing, ceramics, photography and ethnic crafts; 500 teachers; 4,000 students; Pres. Prof. MORDECHAI SHECHTER.

Ulpan Akiva Netanya, International Hebrew Study Centre: POB 6086, 42 160 Netanya; tel. (9) 8352312; fax (9) 8652919; e-mail ulpanakv@netvision.net.il; f. 1951; basic and supplementary courses in Hebrew and Arabic; cultural studies; 45 teachers; Dir EPHRAIM LAPID.

Yeshivat Dvar Yerushalayim (Jerusalem Academy of Jewish Studies): 53 Katzenellenbogen, Har Nof, POB 5454, 91 053 Jerusalem; tel. (2) 6522817; fax (2) 6522827; e-mail dvar@dvar.org.il; internet www.dvar.org.il; f. 1970; runs courses in English, French, Spanish, Russian and Hebrew on the Bible, Hebrew, Talmud, philosophy, ethics and Halacha; 500 mems; library: 5,000 vols; 7 teachers; 70 students; Dean Rabbi B. HOROVITZ; Exec. Dir DOV HOROVITZ; publ. *Jewish Studies Magazine* (annually).

Zinman College of Physical Education and Sport Sciences at the Wingate Institute: 42 902 Netanya; tel. (9) 8639222; fax (9) 8650960; e-mail zinman@wincol.macam.ac.il; f. 1944; four-year B.Ed programme, M.P.E. programme at the college, M.A. programme in conjunction with Haifa Univ.; in-service training; library: 52,000 vols, 180 periodicals; 450 teachers; 950 regular students, 3,000 students on other courses; Rector Prof. Dr MICHAEL SAGIV.

ISRAELI-OCCUPIED TERRITORIES AND PALESTINIAN AUTONOMOUS AREAS

Learned Societies

GENERAL

UNESCO Office Ramallah: POB 2154, Ramallah, West Bank, Palestinian Authority; located at: 17 Ahliyya College St, Ramallah, West Bank, Palestinian Authority; tel. (2) 2959740; fax (2) 2959741; e-mail ramallah@unesco.org; Dir BECHIR LAMINE.

LANGUAGE AND LITERATURE

Alliance Française: Peace Center, POB 1166, Bethlehem; tel. (2) 2766677; e-mail mangerb@p-ol.com; offers courses and exams in French language and culture and promotes cultural exchange with France.

British Council: 31 Nablus Rd, POB 19136, Jerusalem 97200; tel. (2) 6267111; fax (2) 6283021; e-mail british.council@ps.britishcouncil.org; internet www.ps.britishcouncil.org; offers courses and exams in English language and British culture and promotes cultural exchange with the UK; attached offices in Gaza (building destroyed during civil unrest in March 2006), Hebron, Khan Yunis, Nablus and Ramallah; Dir-Gen. KEN CHURCHILL.

Libraries and Archives

Nablus

Nablus Municipality Public Library: Nablus, West Bank, via Israel; tel. (9) 2383356; fax (9) 2374690; e-mail nabm-plib@zaytona.com; f. 1960; 70,000 vols, mainly in Arabic and English; Librarian ALI MUHAMMED WASEF TUQAN.

Ramallah

Public Library: Ramallah, West Bank, via Israel; f. 1962; 3,500 vols; Librarian ADEL UWAIS.

Universities

AL-AQSA UNIVERSITY

POB 144 Gaza, Gaza Strip
Telephone: (8) 2821109
Fax: (8) 2821109
E-mail: alaqsa@alaqsa.edu.ps
Internet: www.alaqsa.edu.ps

Founded 1991
State control

President: ALI ZAYDANE ABU ZAHRI

Faculties of Applied and Natural Sciences, Education and Humanities and Quality Sciences; (Educational Studies Campus destroyed by Israeli military in March 2004).

AL-AZHAR UNIVERSITY

POB 1277, Gaza, Gaza Strip
Telephone: (8) 2824020
Fax: (8) 2823180
E-mail: alazhar@palnet.com
Internet: www.alazhar-gaza.edu

Founded 1991
State control
Languages of instruction: Arabic, English
President: RIYAD EL-KHOUDARY
Number of teachers: 352
Number of students: 10,162
Publication: *Journal*

DEANS

Faculty of Agriculture and Environment: HATEM EL-SHANTY
Faculty of Applied Medical Sciences: RAJAI BARAKA
Faculty of Arts and Humanities: SADEK ABU SULAIMAN
Faculty of Economics and Administrative Sciences: MOEEN RAJAB
Faculty of Education: SALLAH ABU NAHIA
Faculty of Information Technology: NABIL ABU SHABAN
Faculty of Intermediate Studies: HAZIM SAKEEK
Faculty of Law: MUSTAFA AYAD
Faculty of Medicine: SHEHATTA ZOROUP
Faculty of Pharmacy: SULEIMAN AL-JPOUR
Faculty of Science: SHEHATA ZOROUP

ATTACHED CENNTRES

Centre for Continuing Education: Dir MUSTAFA EL-BABA.

Centre for Drug Analysis and Research: Dir NASSER KHUDAIR.

Centre for Food Analysis: Dir ABED AL-RAZEQ SALAMA.

Centre for Information Technology: Dir HAZEM SAKEEK.

Centre for Water Research: Dir YOUSIF ABU MAYLA.

BETHLEHEM UNIVERSITY

POB 9, Bethlehem, West Bank, via Israel
Telephone: (2) 2741241
Fax: (2) 2744440
E-mail: info@bethlehem.edu
Internet: www.bethlehem.edu

Founded 1973
Private control (Roman Catholic)
Languages of instruction: Arabic, English
Academic year: September to June

Chancellor Archbishop: ANTONIO FRANCO
Vice-Chancellor: Br DANIEL CASEY
President: Archbishop FOUD TWAL
Vice-President (Academic): Br FERGUS MCARDLE
Vice-President (Development): Br JACK CURRAN
Vice-President (Finance): SAMI EL YOUSEF
Registrar: MARY JUHA
Librarian: Br DOMINIC SMITH

Library of 70,000 vols
Number of teachers: 184 (132 full-time, 52 part-time)
Number of students: 2,488 (day)
Publications: *University Journal*, *Bethlehem University News*

DEANS

College of Arts: Dr WALID MUSTAFA
College of Business Administration: FADI KATTAN
College of Sciences: Dr ALFRED ABED RABBO

DIRECTORS

College of Arts:
- Department of Arabic: Dr IBRAHIM EL-ALAM
- Department of English: Dr HANNA TUSHYEH
- Department of Humanities: Dr MANUEL HASSASSIAN
- Department of Social Sciences: Dr BERNARD SABELLA

College of Business Administration:
- Faculty of Nursing: DIANNE ABRAHAM
- College of Education: Dr VIOLET FASHEH
- Institute of Hotel Management: A. WALID DAJANI

College of Sciences:
- Department of Chemistry: Dr ALFRED ABED RABBO
- Department of Life Sciences: Dr NAIM IRAQI
- Department of Mathematics: KARIM ABDUL NOUR

BIRZEIT UNIVERSITY

POB 14, Birzeit, West Bank, Palestinian National Authority
Telephone: (2) 2982000 via Palestinian National Authority
Fax: (2) 2810656 via Palestinian National Authority
E-mail: bzu-pr@birzeit.edu
Internet: www.birzeit.eduAlso Birzeit University Liaison Office, POB 950666, Amman, Jordan
Telephone: (6) 5527181
Fax: (6) 5527202

Founded 1924 as school, 1951 college, present status 1975
Private autonomous control
Languages of instruction: Arabic, English
Academic year: September to June (two semesters), summer session July–August

President: Dr NABEEL KASSIS
Vice-President for Academic Affairs: Dr ABDUL LATIF ABU HIJLEH
Vice-President for Administrative and Financial Affairs: Dr CARMELA OMARI
Vice-President for Planning and Development: RAMZI RIHAN
Head Librarian: DIANA SAYEJ NASSER

Library of 126,000 vols, 246 periodicals
Number of teachers: 314 (232 full-time, 82 part-time)
Number of students: 6,655

Publications: *Birzeit University Newsletter* (in English and Arabic), *Birzeit Human Rights Record* (in English)

DEANS

Arts: Dr AHMAD HARB
Commerce and Economics: Dr ADEL ZAGHA
Engineering: Dr FAISAL AWADALLAH
Law and Public Administration: Dr MUDAR KASSIS (acting)
Science: Dr AZIZ SHAWABKEH
Graduate: Dr LISA TARAKI

ATTACHED RESEARCH INSTITUTES

Continuing Education Centre: Dir WALID NANMOUR.

Institute of Community and Public Health: Dir Dr RANA AL-KHATIB.

I. Abu Lughud Institute of International Studies: Dir Dr MAJDI EL-MALKI.

Institute of Law: Dir Dr MUDAR KASSIS.

Institute of Water Studies: Dir Dr ZIAD AL-MIMI.

Institute of Women's Studies: Dir EILEEN KUTTAB.

Media Institute: Dir AREF HIJJAWI (acting).

HEBRON UNIVERSITY

POB 40, Hebron, West Bank, via Israel
Telephone: (2) 2220995
Fax: (2) 2229303
E-mail: info@hebron.edu
Internet: www.hebron.edu

Founded 1971
Independent national university
Languages of instruction: Arabic, English
Academic year: October to June

Chairman of the Board of Trustees: Dr NABEEL JABARI
President: Prof. FAKHRI HASSAN
Vice-President (Academic Affairs): Dr SAMIR ABU ZNEID
Vice-President (Planning and Development): Dr AKRUM TAMIMI
Director (Finance): SAMIA IMAM
Director (Personnel Affairs): IZ JABARI
Director (Public Relations): NAIM DAOUR
Registrar: M. ZIAD JA'BARI
Librarian: NO'AMAN SHAHEEN

Library of 60,000 vols
Number of teachers: 200
Number of students: 5,400

DEANS

Agriculture: AYED GHALEB
Arts: Dr HASAN FLEAFEL
Education: Dr JAMAL ABU MARAK
Finance and Management: Dr RATEB JABARI
Islamic Studies: Dr HAROUN SHARABATI
Nursing: YOUSEF JARADAT
Postgraduate Faculty: Dr RADWAN BARAKAT
Science and Technology: Dr BASSAM MANASRAH

HEADS OF DEPARTMENTS

Animal Husbandry: Dr AYED GHALEB
Arabic: Dr HASSAN FLAFEL
Biology: JAMIL RABBA
Chemistry: Dr FAHED TAKRURI
Education: Dr ALAM DEEN KHATEEB
English: Dr AHMAD ATTAWNEH
Figh: Dr HANI SAID
History: Dr ABED AL-QADER JABARIN
Islamic Law: Dr HAFEZ JAABARI
Mathematics: Dr MOHAMMED ABU EIDEH
Plant Production and Protection: Dr RADWAN BARAKAT

ISLAMIC UNIVERSITY OF GAZA

POB 108, Gaza, via Israel
Telephone: (8) 2860700 via Israel
Fax: (8) 2860800 via Israel
E-mail: public@mail.iugaza.edu
Internet: www.iugaza.edu

Founded 1978
Academic year: September to June

President: Prof. MOHAMMED EID SHUBAIR
Vice-President for Academic Affairs: Dr KAMALAIN SHA'AT
Vice-President for Administrative Affairs: Prof. MOHAMMED SHABAT
Dean of Library: Dr ESMAEL RADWAN
Dean of Planning: Dr RIFAT RUSTOM
Dean of Registration: Dr BASSAM SAQQA

Library of 100,300 vols in central library
Number of students: 16,210 (12,995 undergraduate, 301 postgraduate, 2,659 Community College, 255 Education Diploma)
Publication: *Journal* (2 a year)

DEANS

Faculty of Arts: Dr MAHMOUD A. AMOUDI
Faculty of Commerce: Dr FARIS M. ABOU MUAMMAR
Faculty of Education: Dr MOHAMMAD ASQOUL
Faculty of Engineering: Dr MOHAMED AWAD
Faculty of Islamic Law: Dr AHMED D. SHWIDEH
Faculty of Nursing: ATEF J. ISMAIL

Faculty of Foundations of Religion: Dr SALEM SALAMEH
Faculty of Science: Prof. JASSER SARSOUR
Technical and Applied Sciences Community College: Dr YAHYA R. SARRAJ

PROFESSORS

Faculty of Arts:
ABO ALI, N. KH.
AMOUDI, M. A.
OLWAN, M. SH.
OLWAN, N. S.

Faculty of Commerce:
EDWAN, A. I.

Faculty of Education:
ASQOUL, M.
EL-HELOU, M. W.

Faculty of Engineering:
AWAD, M.
ENSHASSI, A.
KUHAIL, Z. S.

Faculty of Foundations of Religion:
HALABIYA, A. A.
HAMMAD, N. H.

Faculty of Science:
ABDEL-LATIF, M.
ASHOUR, M. M.
EL-ATRASH, M. S.
EL-AZIZ, E. E. A.
EL-NAKHAL, H. A.
HABIL, E.
SARSOUR, M. E.
SHABAT, M. M.
SHUBAIR, M. E.

UNITS AND CENTRES

Business Research Unit: Dir ISMAEL MAHFOUZ.

Community Services and Continuing Education Centre: Dir Dr JAMAL AZEBDA.

Computer Laboratories: Dir HASSAN ALAMOUDY.

Environmental and Rural Research Unit: Dir Dr SAMIR AFIFI.

Journalism Laboratories: Dir FATHI NAJY.

Measurement, Electric, Electronics, Communication and Microwave Laboratories: Dir Eng. JAWDAT ABU TAHA.

Medical Technology Laboratories: Dir Dr ABDELMEN'EM LUBBAD.

Soil Laboratory: Dir Dr SHAFIQ JENDEIA.

AN-NAJAH NATIONAL UNIVERSITY

Omar Ibn Khattab St, POB 7, Nablus, West Bank, Palestinian Authority
Telephone: (9) 2394960 (old campus), (9) 2340200 (new campus)
Fax: (9) 2387982
E-mail: info@najah.edu
Internet: www.najah.edu

Founded 1977
Public control
Academic year: September to June
Languages of instruction: Arabic, English(for science faculties)
Academic year: September to June

Chairman of the Board of Trustees: SALAH AL-MASRI
President: Prof. RAMI HAMDALLAH
Vice-President (Academic Affairs): Prof MAHER AL-NATSHEH
Vice-President (Administrative Affairs): Dr MOHAMMAD HANNOUN (acting)
Public Relations: RAFE DARAGHME
Registrar: Dr JABR ABU JUOKHA
Research Centres Co-ordinator: Dr SULAIMAN KHALIL
Librarian: HANI JABER
Library of 162,000 vols
Number of teachers: 541 (408 full-time, 133 part-time)
Number of students: 11,500 (excluding Community College)
Publications: *An-Najah Journal of Research* (separate series for natural sciences and humanities), *University Yearbook*, *An-Najah Newsletter* (in Arabic and English), *University Student Guidebook*, *An-Najah Academic Catalog* (in Arabic and English), *An-Najah in Brief* (in Arabic and English), *An-Najah "A base of Science and Technology"* (in Arabic and English)

DEANS

Faculty of Agriculture: Dr MA'EN SAMARA (acting)
Faculty of Arts: Prof. MOHAMMAD ABU SAFAT
Faculty of Economics and Administrative Sciences: Dr SA'ED AL KOUNI
Faculty of Educational Sciences: Prof. GHASSAN HILO
Faculty of Engineering: Dr RIYAD ABDUL KARIM
Faculty of Fine Arts: Dr MOHAMMED ATTA
Faculty of Information Technology: Dr RA'ED AL QADI
Faculty of Islamic Law (Shari'a): Dr NASER AL-SHA'ER
Faculty of Law: Dr AHMAD AL-KHALDI
Faculty of Medicine: Dr HUSSNI MAQBOUL (acting)
Faculty of Nursing: ANSAM SAWALHA
Faculty of Optometry: Prof. MAHER NATSHEH
Faculty of Pharmacy: Dr WALEED SWEILEH
Faculty of Science: Dr SAMI JABER
Faculty of Veterinary Medicine: Dr RATEB AREF
Faculty of Graduate Studies: Dr KHALEEL ODEH
Scientific Research: Prof. MOHAMMED JAWD NOURI
Community College: Dr WA'EL ABU SALEH
Hisham Hijawi College of Technology: Dr SMER MAYYALAH

HEADS OF DEPARTMENTS

Faculty of Agriculture:
Animal Husbandry: Dr JAMAL ABU OMAR
Plant Production: Dr HASSAN ABU QA'OUD

Faculty of Arts:
Arabic: Prof. ADEL OSTA
English: Dr ABDALLAH HAMAD
French: Dr BILAL AL-SHAFI
Geography: Dr AHMAD RA'FAT
Sociology: Dr MAHER ABU ZANAT
History: Dr ADNAN MOLHEM
Archaeology: ATEF KHWAIREH
Journalism: Dr SAMAR SHUNNAR

Faculty of Economics and Administrative Sciences:
Economics: Dr BASSEM MAKHOUL
Business Administration: NADER QARIOTI
Political Science: Dr RA'ED NUAIRAT
Accounting: Dr HATEM AL KUKHUN
Finance: Dr HESHAM JABR
Marketing: ABDALLAH SAMARA

Faculty of Education and Psychology:
Elementary Education: Dr GHASSAN HILO
Psychology: Dr ABED ASSAF
Physical Education: Dr SUBHI NEMR
Teaching Methodology: Dr SUZAN ARAFAT

Faculty of Engineering:
Architectural Engineering: Dr EYMAN AMAD
Building Engineering: Dr NAJEH TAMIM
Chemical Engineering: Dr ABDALRAHIM ABUSAFA
Civil Engineering: Dr SHAKER BITAR
Computer Engineering: Dr LU'AI MALHIS
Electronic Engineering: Dr ALLAM MUSSA
Industrial Engineering: Dr AHMAD RAMAHI
Mechanical Engineering: Dr AHMAD RAMAHI

Faculty of Fine Arts:
Music: AHMAD MOUSA
Painting and Design: AHMAD ALHAJ

Faculty of Information Technology:
Computer Science: Dr NEZAR AWARTANI
Management Information Systems: Dr RA'ED AL QADI

Faculty of Islamic Law (Shari'a):
Ussul Al-Deen (Holy Quran and Sayings of the Prophet): Dr KHALED OLWAN
Fiqh wa Tashree (Science of Islamic Law): Dr JAMAL HASHASH

Faculty of Science:
Biology: Dr SAMI YA'EESH
Chemistry: Dr MOHAMMAD NOURI
Mathematics: Dr MOHAMMED NAJIB
Medical Laboratory Sciences: Dr YAHYA FAIDI
Physics: Dr GHASSAN SAFARINI
Statistics: Dr ALI BARAKAT

Faculty of Graduate Studies:
Humanities: Dr AHMAD HAMAD
Natural Sciences: Dr MOHAMMAD ABU JAFAR

ATTACHED RESEARCH INSTITUTES

Academic Programme for the Study of Involuntary Migration: Dir SAMER AQROUQ.

Arabic for Non-Native Speakers' Program: Co-ordinator RAFI' DARAGHMEH.

Center for Chemical and Biological Analysis: Dir Dr NIDAL ZATAR.

Center for Continuing Education: Dir Dr SULAIMAN KHALIL.

Center for Earth Sciences and Seismic Engineering: Dir Dr JALAL AL-DABBIK.

Center for Energy Research: Dir Dr EMAD BRAIK.

Center for Measurement and Evaluation: Dir Dr ALI SHAKIA.

Center for Opinion Polls and Survey Studies: Dir Dr HUSSEIN AHMAD.

Center for Urban and Regional Planning: Dir Dr ALI ABDUL HAMEED.

Community Service Center: Dir SAMI KILANI.

Computer Research Center: Dir NAJEH ABU SAFYYEH.

Construction and Transport Research Center: Dir Dr KHALED AL-SAHILI.

Medical Lab Center: Dir Dr SULAIMAN KHALIL.

UNESCO Chair on Human Rights and Democracy: Dir SAMER AQROUQ.

Water and Environmental Studies Institute: Dir AMMAR JARRAR.

Youth Exchange Program (Zajel): Co-ordinator ALAA YOUSEF.

PALESTINE POLYTECHNIC UNIVERSITY

Hebron, West Bank
Telephone: (2) 2229812
Fax: (2) 2217248
E-mail: info@ppi.edu
Internet: www.ppu.edu

Founded 1978
State control

President: DAWOD AL-ZATARY

Faculties of Applied Sciences, Business and Information Systems and Engineering.

AL-QUDS UNIVERSITY

POB 51000, Jerusalem, via Israel
Telephone: (2) 2274980
Fax: (2) 2277166
Internet: www.alquds.edu
Founded 1979
Private control
Language of instruction: English
Academic year: October to August
President: Dr Sari Nusseibeh
Vice-President: Dr Toufik Shakhashir
Assistant to the President for Academic Affairs: Dr Khaled Kanan
Dean of Research and Academic Studies: Dr Ziad Abdeen
Registrar: Dr Hanna Abdul Nur
Librarian: Randa Kamal
Library of 100,000 vols
Number of teachers: 244
Number of students: 2,800

DEANS

Faculty of Allied Health Professions: Prof. Varseen Shaheen
Faculty of Arts: Prof. Hasan Silwadi
Faculty of Law: Prof. Ali Khashan
Faculty of Medicine: Prof. Na'el Shihabi
Faculty of Jurisprudence: Prof. Hamzeh Theeb
Faculty of Quran and Islamic Studies: Prof. Ismail Nawahdah
Faculty of Science and Technology: Prof. Adnan Rashid

ATTACHED INSTITUTES

Centre for Area Studies: Dir Prof. Musa Budeiri.

Centre for Commerce and Economic Science: Dir Prof. Mahmoud Jafari.

Higher Institute of Islamic Archaeology: Dir Prof. Marwan Abu-Khalaf.

Institute of Modern Media: Dir Daoud Kuttab.

Institute of Phonetics and Language Sciences: Dir Prof. Yousef El-Hallis.

Islamic Research Centre: Dir Prof. Hasan Silwadi.

Language Centre: Dir Prof. Omar Abu-Hommos.

AL-QUDS OPEN UNIVERSITY

POB 51800, Sheikh Jarrah, Musa Feidi St, East Jerusalem
Telephone: (2) 5816239
Fax: (2) 5816734
E-mail: administrative@qou.edu
Internet: www.qou.edu
Founded 1991
State control
President: Dr Younis Amr
Library of 20,800 vols (16,000 in Arabic, 4,800 in English), 80 periodicals
Number of teachers: 911
Number of students: 40,501
Programmes in agriculture, education, management and entrepreneurship, social and family development and technology and applied science; campus in Riyadh, Saudi Arabia, open to Palestinian nationals or people of Palestinian origin.

College

Tulkarm Community College: West Bank, via Israel; f. 1931; library: 30,000 vols; 27 teachers; 400 students; a teacher-training college preparing teachers of agriculture, science, mathematics, computer science, Arabic, Islamic and social studies, English and physical education; Dean Dr M. Z. Ghazaleh.

ITALY

The Higher Education System

Italy's first universities were established during the 10th–13th centuries and are amongst the oldest in Europe; in fact, Università degli Studi di Parma (AD 962) is Europe's oldest university, and other long-established universities include Università di Bologna (founded 1088), Università degli Studi di Modena e Reggio Emilia (founded 1175) and Università degli Studi di Perugia (founded 1200). Several universities date from the 14th–16th centuries. In 2005/06 there were 1.8m. undergraduate students enrolled at 74 institutes of higher education. Italian universities operate on the European Credit Transfer System (ECTS) and Italy also participates in the Bologna Process to establish a European Higher Education Area. The Ministry of Universities and Scientific Research is the government agency responsible for higher education. In addition to universities, there are four other types of State-recognized institutions of higher education: academies of arts education, higher institutes of applied arts, the national school for cinema studies and national institutes or schools for cultural restoration and preservation.

Admission to higher education is primarily based on the higher secondary school certificate (Diploma di Esame di Stato), though institutions may also administer entrance examinations. Since the implementation of the Bologna Process in 1999 the universities have adopted a two-tier Bachelors and Masters degree system. The Bachelors degree (Laurea) is a three-year programme which requires 180 credits. Undergraduates in specialized or professional fields which require longer periods of study, such as medicine (six years), pharmacy, architecture and law (all five years), may carry credits over into the Laurea Specialistica. Alternatively, the Laurea Specialistica may be awarded as a conventional Masters-type degree after one to three years study following the Laurea. Dottorato di Ricerca is the standard doctoral degree programme, and admission is on the basis of the Laurea Specialistica and institutional requirements.

Regulatory and Representative Bodies

GOVERNMENT

Ministry of Universities and Research: Piazzale Kennedy 20, 00144 Rome; tel. 06-58491; e-mail ufficio.stampa@miur.it; internet www.miur.it; Minister FABIO MUSSI.

Ministry of Education: Viale Trastevere 76A, 00153 Rome; tel. 06-58491; fax 06-5803381; e-mail uffstampa@istruzione.it; internet www.istruzione.it; Minister BEPPE FIORONI.

Ministry of Cultural Assets and Activities: Via del Collegio Romano 27, 00186 Rome; tel. 06-67231; fax 06-6798441; e-mail urp@beniculturali.it; internet www.beniculturali.it; Minister FRANCESCO RUTELLI.

ACCREDITATION

Comitato Nazionale per la Valutazione del Sistema Universitario (National Committee for the Evaluation of the University System): P.le Kennedy 20, 00144 Rome; tel. 06-58496401; fax 06-58496480; e-mail valuniv@miur.it; internet www.cnvsu.it; Pres. Prof. LUIGI BIGGERI.

ENIC/NARIC Italy: Information Centre on Academic Mobility and Equivalence, Viale Ventuno Aprile 36, 00162 Rome; tel. 06-86321281; fax 06-86322845; e-mail cimea@fondazionerui.it; internet www.cimea.it; Dir Dr CARLO FINOCCHIETTI.

Istituto Nazionale per la Valutazione del Sistema dell'Istruzione (National Institute for the Assessment of the Educational System): Villa Falconieri, 00044, Frascati; tel. 06-941851; fax 06-94185215; e-mail invalsi@invalsi.it; internet /www.invalsi.it; f. 1974; library of 8,400 vols, 300 current periodicals; research on planning and funding educational systems, permanent and recurrent education, learning processes, educational innovation and in-service training, educational technology; nat. agency for the evaluation of quality in education; Pres. Prof. BENEDETTO VERTECCHI; Dean Dott. SALVATORE CINA.

NATIONAL BODIES

Conferenza dei Rettori delle Università Italiane (Italian University Rectors' Conference): Palazzo Rondanini, Piazza Rondanini 48, 00186 Rome; tel. 06-684411; fax 06-68441399; e-mail segreteriacrui@crui.it; internet www.crui.it; f. 1963; Pres. Prof. GUIDO TROMBETTI; Exec. Dir Dott.ssa EMANUELA STEFANI.

Consiglio Universitario Nazionale (National University Council): Piazza J. F. Kennedy 20, 00144 Rome; tel. 06-97727502; fax 06-97726031; e-mail cun@miur.it; internet www.cun.it; Pres. Prof. ANDREA LENZI; Sec. Dott. ANTONIO VALEO.

Istituto per la Co-operazione Universitaria (Institute for University Co-operation): Viale G. Rossini 26, 00198 Rome; tel. 06-85300722; fax 06-8554646; e-mail info@icu.it; internet www.icu.it; f. 1967; to promote cultural relations between different countries, chiefly through university co-operation, int. meetings and study groups; int. technical co-operation by sending volunteers and experts to developing countries; Pres. Prof. UMBERTO FARRI; Gen. Sec. CARLO DE MARCHI; publs *SIPE—Servizio Stampa Educazione e Sviluppo* (6 a year), *Educazione e Sviluppo* (irreg.).

Fondazione Rui: Viale XXI Aprile 36, 00162 Rome; tel. 06-86321281; fax 06-86322845; e-mail info@fondazionerui.it; internet www.fondazionerui.it; f. 1959; promotes the training of univ. students and researchers; manages int. halls of residence and cultural centres in nine cities; awards scholarships; carries out research in the int. educational field in collaboration with local and nat. authorities, the EU; holds int. conferences on secondary and higher education; library of 3,000 vols; Pres. Dr MARIO ROVERARO; Dir Dr Ing. ALFREDO RAZZANO; publs *Documenti di Lavoro* (quarterly), *Fondazione Rui* (quarterly).

Learned Societies

GENERAL

Accademia delle Scienze dell'Istituto di Bologna (Academy of Sciences of the Bologna Institute): Via Zamboni 31, 40126 Bologna; tel. 051-222596; fax 051-265249; e-mail accademiascienze@libero.it; internet www.unibo.it/Portale/Divulgazione+scientifica/Accademia/default.htm; f. 1711; organizes national and international conventions and conferences; promotes studies of art restoration and art history; 60 mems; 200 corresp. mems; Pres. Prof. ILLIO GALLIGANI; Sec. Prof. RUGGERO BORTOLAMI.

Accademia delle Scienze di Ferrara (Academy of Sciences of Ferrara): Via Romei 3, 44100 Ferrara; tel. 0532-205209; fax 0532-205209; e-mail academia@dns.unife.it; internet web.unife.it/associazioni/accademia_delle_scienze; f. 1823; sections of Medical Sciences, Mathematics, Physics and Natural Sciences, Law, Economics, History and Moral Sciences; 270 mems; library of 12,500 vols; Pres. Prof. Avv. GIOVANNA CAVALLARO; Sec. Avv. VINCENZO CAPUTO; publ. *Atti*.

Accademia delle Scienze di Torino (Academy of Sciences of Turin): Via Maria Vittoria 3, 10123 Turin; tel. 011-5620047; fax 011-532619; e-mail info@accademia.csi.it; internet www.accademiadellescienze.it; f. 1783; sections of Physics, Mathematics and Natural Sciences, Moral Sciences, History and Philology; 310 mems; library: see Libraries and Archives; Pres. Prof. PIETRO ROSSI; publs *Memorie* (edns for physical, mathematical and natural sciences, and for philosophy, law, history and philology, each annually), *Atti* (edns for physical, mathematical and natural sciences, and for the philosophy, law, history and philology, each annually), *Quaderni* (irregular).

Accademia Etrusca (Etruscan Academy): Palazzo Casali, Piazza Signorelli 9, 52044 Cortona; tel. 0575-637248; fax 0575-637248; e-mail accademia_etrusca@libero.it; internet www.accademia-etrusca.org; f. 1727 to promote knowledge of the culture and history of the Cortona area and of Etruscan archaeological discoveries; 80 mems; 50 hon. mems;

80 corresp. mems; Pres. Dott. GUGLIELMO MAETZKE; Vice-Pres. and Sec. Prof. EDOARDO MIRRI; publs *Annuario* (every 2 years), *Note e Documenti*, *Fonti e Testi*.

Accademia Gioenia di Catania: Corso Italia 55, 95129 Catania; e-mail rcristof@unict.it; internet www.unict.it/gioenia; f. 1824; sections of Natural Sciences, Physics, Chemistry and Mathematics, and Applied Sciences; 56 mems, 57 corresp. mems; library of 20,000 vols, 400 periodicals; Pres. Prof. SALVATORE FOTI; Gen. Sec. Prof. RENATO CRISTOFOLINI; publs *Bollettino delle Sedute della Accademia Gioenia di Scienze Naturali in Catania*, *Atti della Accademia Gioenia di Scienze Naturali in Catania*.

Accademia Ligure di Scienze e Lettere (Ligurian Academy of Sciences and Letters): Piazza G. Matteotti 5, 16123 Genoa; tel. 010-565570; fax 010-566080; f. 1798; 180 mems (30 ordinary and 50 corresp. in each class; 20 hon.); library of 60,000 vols; Pres. Prof. E. SALVIDIO; Sec.-Gen. Dr G. P. PELOSO; publs *Atti* (annual), *Studi e Ricerche*.

Accademia Nazionale dei Lincei: Palazzo Corsini, Via della Lungara 10, 00165 Rome; tel. 06-680271; fax 06-6893616; e-mail segreteria@lincei.it; internet www.lincei.it; f. 1603; sections of Physical, Mathematical and Natural Sciences (Academic Secs Prof. GIANCARLO SETTI, Prof. ANNIBALE MOTTANA), Moral, Historical and Philological Sciences (Academic Secs Prof. ALBERTO QUADRIO CURZIO, Prof. ANTONIO GIULIANO); 540 mems (180 nat., 180 corresp., 180 foreign); library: see Libraries and Archives; Pres. Prof. GIOVANNI CONSO; Vice-Pres. Prof. LAMBERTO MAFFEI; Academic Administrators Prof. ANGELO FALZEA; publs *Rendiconti Lincei: Scienze Fisiche e Naturali* (quarterly), *Rendiconti Lincei: Matematica e Applicazioni* (quarterly), *Rendiconti: Classe di Scienze Morali, Storiche e Filologiche* (quarterly), *Memorie Lincee, Classe di Scienze Morali, Storiche e Filologiche* (irreg.), *Memorie Lincee, Matematica e Applicazioni* (irreg.), *Memorie Lincee, Scienze Fisiche e Naturali* (irreg.), *Notizie degli Scavi di Antichità*.

Accademia Nazionale di San Luca (National Academy of San Luca): Piazza dell'Accademia di San Luca 77, 00187 Rome; tel. 06-6798850; fax 06-6789243; e-mail segreteria@accademiasanluca.it; internet www.accademiasanluca.it; f. 14th c.; sections of Painting, of Sculpture, of Architecture; 54 mems; 90 corresp. mems; 30 foreign mems; 47 cultural and hon. mems; library: see Libraries and Archives; Pres. CARLO AYMONINO; Sec.-Gen. GIORGIO CIUCCI.

Accademia Nazionale di Santa Cecilia (National Academy of Santa Cecilia): Auditorium Parco della Musica, l.go Luciano Berio 3, 00196 Rome; tel. 06-80242501; fax 06-80242301; e-mail info@santacecilia.it; internet www.santacecilia.it; f. 1566; promotes symphonic concert music, has own symphony orchestra and chorus, carries out professional music training; 100 mems (70 nat., 30 foreign); Pres. BRUNO CAGLI; publs *Studi Musicali* (2 a year), *E. M. Rivista degli Archivi di Etnomusicologia* (annually).

Accademia Nazionale Virgiliana di Scienze, Lettere e Arti (Virgilian National Academy of Sciences, Literature and Arts): Via dell'Accademia 47, 46100 Mantua; tel. 0376-320314; fax 0376-222774; internet www.accademiavirgiliana.it; f. early 17th c., present name 1981; 90 mems; 20 hon. mems; 60 corresp. mems; library: see Libraries and Archives; Pres. Prof. CLAUDIO GALLICO; Sec. Dott. A. ZANCA; publ. *Atti e Memorie N. S.* (annually).

Accademia Petrarca di Lettere, Arti e Scienze (Petrarch Academy of Literature, Arts and Science): Via dell'Orto 28, 52100 Arezzo; tel. 0575-24700; e-mail info@accademiapetraca.it; internet www.accademiapetrarca.it; f. 1810; 413 mems; library of 15,000 vols; Pres. Prof. GIULIO FIRPO; Sec. Prof. ANTONIO BATINTI; publs *Atti e Memorie* (annually), *Studi Petrarcheschi* (annually).

Accademia Pugliese delle Scienze (Puglia Academy of Sciences): Palazzo dell'Ateneo, Piazza Umberto I, 70121 Bari; tel. and fax 080-5714578; e-mail accademia.pugliese@ateneo.uniba.it; internet www.ateneo.uniba.it/accademiapugliese; f. 1925; divided into two classes: Physical, Medical and Natural Sciences, and Moral Sciences, with 120 ordinary mems, 200 corresp. mems and 20 hon. mems; library of 6,600 vols, 270 periodical titles; Pres. Prof. VITTORIO MARZI; Sec. GIOVANNA PANEBIANCO; publ. *Atti e Relazioni* (annually).

Accademia Roveretana degli Agiati: Piazza Rosmini 5, 38068 Rovereto; tel. 0464-436663; fax 0464-487672; e-mail info@agiati.org; internet www.agiati.org; f. 1750; fosters the development of sciences, literature and art; 330 mems; library of 50,000 vols; Pres. Prof. LIVIO CAFFIERI; publs *Atti* (Series A (human sciences, literature, art), online), *Atti* (Series B (mathematics, physics, natural science), online).

Accademia Tiberina: Via del Vantaggio 22, 00186 Rome; tel. 06-3619305; internet www.pontificiaaccademiatiberina.it; f. 1813; 200 mems and 2,000 assoc., corresp., resident and hon. mems; applied sciences, psychology, arts, hygiene and health, anthropology, Yoga-Vedanta centre; library of 10,000 vols; Pres. Prof. Dott. FERNANDO MARIOTTI; Sec. (vacant).

Accademia Toscana di Scienze e Lettere 'La Colombaria' (La Colombaria Tuscan Academy of Science and Literature): Via S. Egidio 23, 50122 Florence; tel. and fax 055-2396628; internet www.colombaria.it; f. 1735; library of 30,000 vols; Pres. Prof. FRANCESCO ADORNO; Gen. Sec. STEFANO SPILLI; publs *Atti e Memorie* (annually), *Studi* (4–5 a year), *Corpus dei papiri filosofici greci e latini* (irregular).

Istituto Lombardo Accademia di Scienze e Lettere: Via Brera 28, 20121 Milan; tel. 02-864087; fax 02-86461388; e-mail istituto.lombardo@unimi.it; internet www.istitutolombardo.it; f. 1802; Pres. Prof. ALBERTO QUADRIO CURZIO; Vice-Pres. Prof. GIANANTONIO SACCHI LANDRIANI; it is divided into two classes: Mathematics and Natural Sciences (Sec. Prof. FIORENZA DE BERNARDI; 66 mems, 88 corresponding associates, 31 foreign mems); Moral Sciences (Sec. ISABELLA GUALANDRI; 51 mems, 80 corresponding associates, 42 foreign mems); library of 450,000 vols, 330 Italian periodicals, 600 foreign periodicals; publs *Cicli di Conferenze*, *Memorie della Classe di Scienze Matematiche e Naturali*, *Memorie della Classe di Scienze Morali*, *Rendiconti–Classe di Lettere e Scienze Morali*, *Rendiconti–Parte Generale e Atti Ufficiali*, *Rendiconti–Sez.A: Scienze Matematiche e Naturali*, *Rendiconti–Sez.B: Scienze Biologiche e Mediche Chimica e Fisica*, Proceedings of Symposiums.

Istituto Veneto di Scienze, Lettere ed Arti (Venetian Institute of Sciences, Literature and Arts): Campo S. Stefano 2945, 30124 Venice; tel. 041-2407711; fax 041-5210598; e-mail ivsla@istitutoveneto.it; internet www.istitutoveneto.it; f. 1838; functions as academy; also organizes postdoctoral courses; sections of Physical, Mathematical and Natural Sciences (Academic Sec. Prof. GIAN ANTONIO DANIELI), Moral Sciences, Literature and Arts (Academic Sec. Prof. MANLIO PASTORE STOCCHI); 78 mems; 110 corresp. mems; 29 foreign mems; library of 200,600 vols; Pres. Prof. LEOPOLDO MAZZAROLLI; publs *Atti* (Proceedings (moral sciences series), 4 a year), *Atti* (Proceedings (physical sciences series), 4 a year), *Memorie*.

Società di Letture e Conversazioni Scientifiche (Scientific Society): Palazzo Ducale ammezzato ala est, Piazza Matteotti 5, Genoa; tel. and fax 010-565141; e-mail letturescientifiche@libero.it; internet www.letturescientifiche.it; f. 1866; holds conferences and debates on scientific, historical, literary and political topics; library of 15,310 vols; Pres. UMBERTO COSTA.

Società Nazionale di Scienze, Lettere ed Arti (National Society for Sciences, Literature and Art): Via Mezzocannone 8, 80134 Naples; tel. and fax 081-5527549; e-mail socnazsla@virgilio.it; internet www.socnazsla.unina.it; library of 35,000 vols; Pres. Prof. FULVIO TESSITORE; Sec.-Gen. Prof. CARLO SBORDONE.

UNESCO Office in Venice–UNESCO Regional Bureau for Science and Culture in Europe (BRESCE): 4930 Castello–Palazzo Zorzi, 30122 Venice; tel. 041-2601511; fax 041-5289995; e-mail veniceoffice@unesco.org; internet www.unesco.org/venice; f. 1988; science policy, education and research throughout South-eastern Europe; environmental policy in local govt (incl. management of water resources and prevention of natural disasters); development of cultural activities and identifying priorities in South-east Europe, such as protection and promotion of cultural heritage; training programmes for cultural conservation; promotes cultural dialogue and artistic creation, and handicraft as a symbol of cultural diversity; library of 2,000 UNESCO publs; Dir Dr ENGELBERT RUOSS.

AGRICULTURE, FISHERIES AND VETERINARY SCIENCE

Accademia di Agricoltura di Torino (Academy of Agriculture of Turin): Via Andrea Doria 10, 10123 Turin; tel. 011-8127470; fax 011-8127470; e-mail to0323@biblioteche.reteunitaria.piemonte.it; internet http://web.tiscali.it/accagri; f. 1785; 155 mems; library of 26,000 vols, 50 current periodicals; Pres. Dott. Prof. SILVANO SCANNERINI; publs *Annali Dell'Accademia di Agricoltura di Torino* (annually), *Nuovo Calendario Georgico* (annually).

Accademia dei Georgofili (Academy of Georgofili): Logge degli Uffizi, 50122 Florence; tel. 055-212114; fax 055-2302754; e-mail accademia@georgofili.it; internet www.georgofili.it; f. 1753; promotes the application of sciences to agriculture and environmental protection, and the development to rural areas; 522 ; library of 60,000 vols; Pres. Prof. FRANCO SCARAMUZZI; publs *Atti*, *Quaderni*, *Rivista di Storia della Agricoltura*.

Accademia Italiana di Scienze Forestali (Italian Academy of Forestry Science): Piazza Edison 11, 50133 Florence; tel. 055-570348; fax 055-575724; e-mail info@aisf.it; internet www.aisf.it; f. 1951; 327 mems; library of 6,000 vols; Pres. Prof. A. MANCINI; publs *Annali* (annually), *L'Italia Forestale e montana* (every 2 months).

Accademia Nazionale di Agricoltura (National Academy of Agriculture): Via Castiglione 11, 40124 Bologna; tel. 051-268809; fax 051-263736; e-mail segreteria@accademia-agricoltura.it; internet www.accademia-agricoltura.unibo.it; f. 1807; 80 mems and 140 corresponding mems; library of 20,000 vols; Pres. Prof. GIORGIO AMADEI;

Sec. Dott. ANDREA SEGRÉ; publ. *Annali* (4 a year).

Istituto Agronomico per l'Oltremare (Agronomic Institute for Overseas): Via Antonio Cocchi 4, 50131 Florence; tel. 055-50611; fax 055-5061333; e-mail iao@iao.florence.it; internet www.iao.florence.it; f. 1904; 50 mems; library of 127,000 vols, 800 current periodicals; Dir-Gen. Dott. ALICE PERLINI; publ. *Journal of Agriculture and Environment for International Development* (4 a year).

Società Italiana delle Scienze Veterinarie (Italian Society of Veterinary Sciences): Via A. Bianchi 1, 25124 Brescia; tel. 030-223244; fax 030-2420569; e-mail seren@vet.unibo.it; internet www.sisvet.it; f. 1947; 1,700 mems; Pres. Prof. ERALDO SEREN; Gen. Sec. Dott. GIOVANNI SCIMONE; publ. *Atti*.

Società Italiana di Economia Agraria (Italian Agrarian Economics Society): Istituto di Zooeconomia, Coviolo, 42100 Reggio Emilia; tel. 0522-21745; e-mail mario.prestamburgo@econ.univ.trieste.it; internet brezza.iuav.it/~ramirez; f. 1962; 300 mems; Pres. Prof. MARIO PRESTAMBURGO; publ. *Atti* (annually).

ARCHITECTURE AND TOWN PLANNING

Centro Internazionale di Studi di Architettura 'Andrea Palladio' (Andrea Palladio International Centre for the Study of Architecture): Palazzo Barbaran da Porto, contra' Porti 11, CP 835, 36100 Vicenza; tel. 0444-323014; fax 0444-322869; e-mail segreteria@cisapalladio.org; internet www.cisapalladio.org; f. 1959 to make known the work of Andrea Palladio, b. Padua 1508, and to encourage the study of Palladianism and of Venetian architecture of all ages; Pres. AMALIA SARTORI; Dir GUIDO BELTRAMINI; publ. *Annali* (online, annually).

Istituto Nazionale di Architettura (IN-ARCH) (National Architectural Institute): Via Crescenzio 16, 00193 Rome; tel. 06-68802254; fax 06-6868530; e-mail inarch@inarch.it; internet www.inarch.it; f. 1959; organizes meetings, debates and exhibitions; 2,000 mems; Pres. Ing. ADOLFO GUZZINI.

Istituto Nazionale di Urbanistica (INU) (National Institute of Town Planning): Piazza Farnese 44, 00186 Rome; tel. 06-68801190; fax 06-68214773; e-mail segreteria@inu.it; internet www.inu.it; f. 1930; 2,654 mems (960 ordinary, 1,694 assoc.); Pres. Prof. Arch. PAOLO AVARELLO; Sec. MASSIMO GIULIANI; publs *Urbanistica* (3 a year), *Urbanistica Informazioni* (6 a year), *Urbanistica Dossier* (monthly).

Italia Nostra—Associazione Nazionale per la Tutela del Patrimonio Storico, Artistico e Naturale della Nazione (Italia Nostra—National Association for the Preservation of the Historical, Artistic and Natural Heritage of the Nation): Via Nicolò Porpora 22, 00198 Rome 00198; tel. 06-8440631; fax 06-8844634; e-mail info@italianostra.org; internet www.italianostra.org; f. 1955; 20,000 mems, subscribers, delegates; library of 4,500 vols; brs in 206 towns; Pres. ANTONIETTA PASOLINI DALL'ONDA; Sec.-Gen. GAIA PALLOTTINO; publ. *Italia Nostra* (9 a year).

BIBLIOGRAPHY, LIBRARY SCIENCE AND MUSEOLOGY

Associazione Italiana Biblioteche (Italian Library Association): CP 2461, 00185 Rome AD; c/o Biblioteca nazionale centrale, viale Castro Pretorio 105, 00185 Rome; tel. 06-4463532; fax 06-4441139; e-mail aib@aib.it; internet www.aib.it; f. 1930 to support the org. and devt of libraries and a library service in Italy, and to act as a professional representative in all cultural, scientific, technical, legal and legislative spheres; 4,500 mems; library of 8,000 vols, 500 journals; Pres. Prof. MAURO GUERRINI; Sec. MARCELLO SARDELLI; publs *Bollettino AIB* (quarterly), *AIB Notizie* (monthly).

Associazione Nazionale dei Musei Italiani (National Association of Italian Museums): Piazza San Marco 49, 00186 Rome; tel. and fax 06-6791343; Pres. Prof. D. BERNINI; Sec. Dott. L. BARBACINI; publ. *Musei e Gallerie d'Italia*.

Centro Di (International Documentation Centre): Piazza de'Mozzi 1, 50125 Florence; f. 1968; documentation, distribution of books and catalogues in the field of art, architecture, visual communication; library of 8,000 vols; Dir F. MARCHI; publs bulletin of catalogues, indexes.

Istituto Centrale per la Patologia del Libro (Central Institute of Book Pathology): Via Milano 76, 00184 Rome; tel. 06-482911; fax 06-4814968; e-mail ic-pl@beniculturali.it; internet www.patologialibro.beniculturali.it; f. 1938; book restoration and preservation; 77 mems; library of 15,000 vols; Dir ARMIDA BATORI; publ. *Cabnewsletter* (6 a year).

ECONOMICS, LAW AND POLITICS

Accademia Italiana di Economia Aziendale (Academy of Business Economics): Via Cairoli 11, 40121 Bologna; tel. 051-558798; fax 051-6492446; e-mail redazione@accademiaaidea.it; internet www.accademiaaidea.it; f. 1813; divided into 3 classes; 375 national mems; 50 foreign mems; 10 hon. mems; reps from all Italian universities; Pres. Prof. ROBERTO CAFFERATA; Secs Prof. UMBERTO BOCCHINO, Prof. GIORGIO INVERNIZZI.

Cenacolo Triestino: Piazza della Borsa 14, 34121 Trieste; tel. 040-64210; f. 1946; academy of economic and social studies; Pres. BENIAMINO ANTONINI; Sec.-Gen. SPIRIDIONE NICOLAIDI; publ. *Osservatore Economico e Sociale*.

CIRGIS (International Centre for Juridical Research and Scientific Initiatives): Via Manzoni 45, 20121 Milan; tel. 02-6552167; f. 1979 to promote cultural relations between scholars of Italian and foreign law; aims for the realization of exchanges of thought and experience between Italian and foreign jurists, the knowledge of laws and institutions of different countries through meetings, publications etc.; *c*. 400 mems; Pres. Avv. Prof. FRANCESCO OGLIARI; International Sec. Avv. GIUSEPPE AGLIALORO.

Istituto di Diritto Romano e dei Diritti dell'Oriente Mediterraneo (Institute of Roman Law and Laws of the Near East): Facoltà di Giurisprudenza, Piazzale Aldo Moro 5, 00185 Rome; tel. 06-49910608; fax 06-49910241; e-mail marilena.zanatatritto@uniroma1.it; internet http://151.100.28.159; f. 1937; library of 70,000 vols, 80 current periodicals; Dir Prof. ANDREA DI PORTO; Academic Sec. Dott.ssa MARILENA ZANATA TRITTO.

Istituto per il Rinnovamento Economico (IRE): Via Petronio Arbitro 4, 00136 Rome; f. 1924; promotes international economic and monetary reform; Pres. G. DI DOMENICO.

Società Italiana degli Economisti (Italian Economists' Society): Piazzale Martelli, 8, 60121 Ancona; tel. 071-2207111; fax 071-200494; e-mail sie@dea.unian.it; internet www.sie.unian.it; f. 1950; 594 mems; Pres. Prof. GIORGIO LUNGHINI; Gen. Sec. Prof. GIULIANO CONTI; publs *Lettera* (annually), *Bollettino dei Soci*, *Rivista Italiana degli Economisti*.

Società Italiana di Economia, Demografia e Statistica: c/o Dip. di Teoria Economica e Metodi Quantitativi per le Scelte Politiche, Università 'La Sapienza', Piazzale Aldo Moro 5, 00185 Rome; tel. 06-4462991; f. 1938; *c*. 600 mems; Pres. Prof. ORNELLO VITALI; Sec. Gen. Prof. FRANCO VACCINA; publs *Rivista Italiana di Economia, Demografia e Statistica* (quarterly), *Collana di Studi e Monografie* (irregular).

Società Italiana di Filosofia Giuridica e Politica: c/o Ist. di Filosofia del Diritto, Facoltà di Giurisprudenza, Università La Sapienza, 00185 Rome; tel. 06-490489; fax 06-49910951; f. 1936; 200 mems; Pres. GAETANO CARCATERRA; Sec. MAURIZIO BASCIU; publ. *Rivista internazionale di filosofia del diritto* (quarterly).

Società Italiana di Statistica (Italian Statistics Society): Salita de' Crescenzi 26, 00186 Rome; tel. 06-6869845; fax 06-6540742; internet www.ips.it/musis/scheda77.html; f. 1939; 1,000 mems; statistics and demography; Pres. Prof. LUIGI BIGGERI; Gen. Sec. Prof. MAURIZIO VICHI; publs Proceedings of the Scientific Meetings, *SIS-Bollettino* (4 a year), *SIS-Informazioni* (monthly), *Journal of the Italian Statistical Society* (4 a year).

Società Italiana per l'Organizzazione Internazionale (SIOI) (UN Association for Italy): Piazza di S. Marco 51, Palazzetto di Venezia, 00186 Rome; tel. 06-6920781; fax 06-6789102; e-mail sioi@sioi.org; internet www.sioi.org; f. 1944; sections in Florence, Milan, Naples, Turin; library: see Libraries; Pres. UMBERTO LA ROCCA; Sec.-Gen. MARIO ALESSI; publ. *La Comunità Internazionale* (quarterly).

EDUCATION

Associazione Pedagogica Italiana (Italian Educational Association): Via Zamboni 34, 40126 Bologna; tel. 051-2098442; fax 051-228847; e-mail info@aspei.it; internet www.aspei.it; f. 1950; aims to promote the development of schools in general and all other institutions of education, also studies and research in education; 50 brs; 5,000 mems; Pres. SIRA SERENELLA MACCHIETTI; Sec.-Gen. ALDO D'ALFONSO; publ. *Bollettino* (4 a year).

FINE AND PERFORMING ARTS

Academia Española de Bellas Artes en Roma (Spanish Fine Arts Academy in Rome): Piazza San Pietro in Montorio 3 (Gianicolo), 00153 Rome; f. 1873; Dir Prof. FELIPE V. GARIN LLOMBART.

Accademia di Francia (French Academy in Rome): Villa Medici, Viale Trinità dei Monti 1, 00187 Rome; tel. 06-6761291; fax 06-6761278; e-mail standard@villamedici.it; internet www.villamedici.it; f. 1666; organizes exhibitions, concerts, symposia and seminars on artistic and literary topics, and on their history; library of 27,000 vols; Dir RICHARD PEDUZZI; Gen. Sec. ELIZABETH FLEURY; publ. *Newsletter* (monthly).

Accademia Raffaello: Via Cesare Battisti 54, 61029 Urbino; tel. (0722) 329695; e-mail segreteria@accademiaraffaello.it; internet www.accademiaraffaello.it; f. 1869; promotes fine art; 108 mems; library of 16,000 vols; Pres. Dr GAETANO SAVOLDELLI PEDROCCHI.

Consiglio Nazionale per i Beni Culturali e Ambientali (National Council for Culture and the Environment): Ministry of Culture and the Environment, Via del Collegio Romano 27, 00186 Rome; tel. 06-6789529; six committees: environment and architecture (Pres. Prof. ROBERTO DI STEFANO); archaeology (Pres. Prof. ATTILIO STAZIO); history of art (Pres. Prof. FRANCESCO NEGRI

ARNOLDI); archives (Pres. Prof. GIUSEPPE PANSINI); books (Pres. Dott. LETIZIA VERGNANO PECORELLA); cultural institutes (Pres. Prof. AURELIO RIGOLI); Pres. of the Council, Minister for Culture and the Environment; Sec. Dott. MARILISA CORDONE CAMETTI.

Istituto Italiano per la Storia della Musica (Italian Institute for the History of Music): c/o Accademia Nazionale di Santa Cecilia, Via Vittoria 6, 00187 Rome; tel. and fax 06-36000146; fax 06-36000146; e-mail info@iism.it; internet www.iism.it; f. 1938; Pres. Prof. BRUNO CAGLI; publ. *Bollettino*.

Istituto Nazionale di Studi Verdiani (National Institute of Verdi Studies): Strada della Repubblica 56, 43100 Parma; tel. 0521-286044; fax 0521-287949; e-mail direzione@studiverdiani.it; internet www.studiverdiani.it; f. 1960 under the patronage of the International Music Council and the Italian Ministry of Cultural Affairs and Education; to study the life and works of Giuseppe Verdi; library of 15,000 vols, archives of 16,000 documents; Pres. MARIA MERCEDES CARRARA VERDI; Dir PIERLUIGI PETROBELLI; publs *Quaderni*, *Proceedings of Congresses*, *Studi Verdiani* (annually), *Carteggi Verdiani*, *Premio Internazionale Rotary Club di Parma 'Giuseppe Verdi'*.

Istituto Universitario Olandese di Storia dell'Arte (Dutch University Institute for the History of Art): Viale Torricelli 5, 50125 Florence; tel. 055-221612; fax 055-221106; e-mail iuo@iuo.iris.firenze.it; internet www.iuoart.org; f. 1958; library of 50,000 vols; Dir BERT W. MEIJER.

Kunsthistorisches Institut in Florenz–Max-Planck-Institut/Istituto di Storia dell'Arte di Firenze (Institute for the History of Art in Florence): Via Giuseppe Giusti 44, 50121 Florence; tel. 055-249111; fax 055-2491155; internet www.khi.fi.it; f. 1897; 32 mems; library of 270,000 vols, 2,450 periodicals and 560,000 reproductions; spec. collns incl. art in Northern Italy, Italian art since 19th c.; Dir Prof. Dr GERHARD WOLF; publs *Jahresbericht* (every 2 years), *Kleine Schriftenreihe des KHI* (annually), *Mitteilungen* (annually), *Monographienreihe: Italienische Forschungen* (every 2 years).

Società d'Incoraggiamento d'Arti e Mestieri (Society for the Encouragement of Arts and Crafts): Via Santa Marta 18, 20123 Milan; tel. 02-86450125; fax 02-86452542; e-mail segreteria@siam1838.it; internet www.siam1838.it; f. 1838; education in mechanics, electronics, electrotechnics, chemistry, computer studies; library: *c.* 6,000 vols; Pres. BRUNO SORESINA; Gen. Sec. ALBERTO PIANTA.

Società Italiana di Musicologia (Italian Musicological Society): CP 7256, Ag. Roma Nomentano, 00162 Rome; located at: Via dei Greci 18, 00187 Rome; tel. 340-5941462; e-mail segreteria@sidm.it; internet www.sidm.it; f. 1964; 800 mems; Pres. BIANCA MARIA ANTOLINI; publs *Rivista Italiana di Musicologia* (2 a year), *Fonti Musicali Italiane* (annually), *Bollettino* (electronic, 2 a year).

Società Italiana Musica Contemporanea: Piazza Buenos Aires 20, 00198 Rome; tel. 06-868012; Pres. M. PERAGALLO; Sec. M. R. MANN.

HISTORY, GEOGRAPHY AND ARCHAEOLOGY

Accademia Archeologica Italiana: Via Archimede 139, 00197 Rome; tel. 06-8072575; f. 1952; 60 academicians in five classes: archaeology, history, art, literature, science; Pres. Prof. LEO MAGNINO; Sec. Prof. VITALIANO ROCCHIERO; publ. *La Cultura nel Mondo* (quarterly).

Associazione Archeologica Romana (Roman Archaeological Society): Piazza B. Cairoli 117, 00186 Rome; tel. 06-6865647; internet www.associazionearcheologicaromana.it; f. 1902; 400 mems; library of 3,000 vols; Pres. Prof. CLAUDIO STRINATI; Sec. PAOLA MANETTO; publ. *Romana Gens* (quarterly).

Istituto Geografico Militare (Military Geographical Institute): Via C. Battisti 10, 50122 Florence; tel. 055-27321; fax 055-282172; e-mail info@geomil.esercito.difesa.it; internet www.igmi.org; f. 1872; geodetic and topographical surveying; official cartography; library of 120,000 vols, 700 atlases, 19,000 cartographic items; Dir-Gen. Lt-Gen. MICHELE CORRADO; publs *L'Universo* (6 a year), *Bollettino di Geodesia e Scienze Affini* (4 a year).

Istituto Italiano di Numismatica (Italian Numismatics Society): Palazzo Barberini, Via Quattro Fontane 13, 00184 Rome; tel. 06-4743603; fax 06-4743603; e-mail ist.italnumismatica@flashnet.it; internet www.istitutoitalianonumismatica.it; f. 1936; library of 20,000 vols; Pres. Prof. ATTILIO STAZIO; Dir Prof. SARA SORDA; publ. *Annali* (annually).

Istituto Italiano di Paleontologia Umana (Italian Institute of Human Palaeontology): Piazza Mincio 2, 00198 Rome; tel. 06-8557598; internet w3.uniroma1.it/isipu; f. 1913; quaternary environment, geology, palaeontology, palaeoanthropology, archaeology; 250 mems; library of 5,800 vols, 31 periodicals; extensive offprints series; Pres. Prof. AMILCARE BIETTI; Gen. Sec. GIORGIO MANZI; publs *Memorie* (irregular), *Quaternaria* (annually).

Istituto Italiano per la Storia Antica (Italian Institute for Ancient History): Via Milano 76, 00184 Rome; tel. and fax 06-4880597; e-mail storia.antica@virgilio.it; f. 1935; library of 17,000 vols; Pres. Prof. ANDREA GIARDINA; publs *Miscellanea Greca e Romana*, *Dizionario Epigrafico di Antichità Romane*, *Studi pubblicati dall'Istituto Italiano per la Storica Antica*, *Quaderni della Scuola di Storia Antica* (3 a year).

Istituto Nazionale di Archeologia e Storia dell'Arte (National Institute of Archaeology and History of Art): Piazza San Marco 49, 00186 Rome; tel. 06-6780817; fax 06-6798804; e-mail inasa@inasa-roma.it; internet www.inasa-roma.it; f. 1918; library of 500,000 vols; Pres. (vacant); Chief Officer ADRIANO LA REGINA; publ. *Rivista* (annually).

Istituto Nazionale di Studi Etruschi ed Italici (National Institute for Etruscan and Italic Studies): Via della Pergola 65, 50121 Florence; tel. 055-2396846; fax 055-2396846; e-mail studietruschi@interfree.it; f. 1932; 206 mems; library of 14,915 vols; Pres. Prof. GIOVANNANGELO CAMPOREALE; Sec. Prof. LUIGI DONATI; publ. *Studi Etruschi* (annually).

Istituto per la Storia del Risorgimento Italiano (Institute for the History of the Italian Revival): Vittoriano, Piazza Venezia, 00186 Rome; tel. 06-6793598; fax 06-6782572; e-mail ist.risorgimento@tiscalinet.it; internet www.risorgimento.it/risorgimento/home_istituto.htm; f. 1935; 3,400 mems; Pres. Prof. GIUSEPPE TALAMO; Gen. Sec. Prof. SERGIO LA SALVIA; publs *Rassegna Storica del Risorgimento dal 1914* (4 a year), *Biblioteca Scientifica* (3 series).

Istituto Storico Italiano per il Medio Evo (Italian Institute of Medieval History): Piazza dell'Orologio 4, 00186 Rome; tel. 06-68802075; fax 06-68195963; e-mail istituto@isime.it; internet www.isime.it; f. 1883; library of 120,000 vols; Pres. MASSIMO MIGLIO; publs *Bullettino*, *Fonti per la storia dell'Italia medievale*, *Nuovi Studi Storici*, *Repertorium Fontium Historiae Medii Aevi*.

Istituto Storico Italiano per l'Età Moderna e Contemporanea (Italian Historical Institute for the Contemporary and Modern Era): Via Michelangelo Caetani 32, 00186 Rome; tel. 06-68806922; fax 06-6875127; e-mail iststor@libero.it; f. 1934; historical research and publications; Pres. Prof. LUIGI LOTTI; publ. *Annuario*.

Società di Minerva: Piazza Hortis 4, 34123 Trieste; tel. 040-660245; fax 040-660245; internet www.retecivica.trieste.it/minerva/home.htm; f. 1810 for the study of the history, art and culture of Trieste, Istria and Gorizia; 150 mems; Pres. Prof. arch. GINO PAVAN; Sec. Dott.ssa ELENA CLARI; publs *Archeografo Triestino* (annually), *Quaderni di Minerva* (irregular).

Società di Studi Geografici (Society for Geographical Studies): Via San Gallo 10, 50129 Florence; tel. 055-2757956; fax 055-2757956; e-mail info@societastudigeografici.it; internet www.societastudigeografici.it; f. 1895; 600 mems; library of 20,000 vols; Pres. MARIA TINACCI MOSSELLO; Sec. CRISTINA CAPINERI; publ. *Rivista Geografica Italiana* (4 a year).

Società Geografica Italiana: Palazzetto Mattei in Villa Celimontana, Via della Naviocella 12, 00184 Rome; tel. 06-7008279; fax 06-77079518; e-mail segretaria@societageografica.it; internet www.societageografica.it; f. 1867; library: see Libraries and Archives; Pres. Prof. FRANCO SALVATORI; publs *Bollettino* (quarterly), *Ricerche e Studi*, *Memorie*.

Società Napoletana di Storia Patria (Neapolitan Society of Italian History): Piazza Municipio Maschio Angioino, 80133 Naples; tel. 081-5510353; fax 081-2528206; e-mail snsp@unina.it; internet www.storia.unina.it/snsp; f. 1876; library of 300,000 vols, 900 current periodicals; 650 mems; Pres. Prof. GIUSEPPE GALASSO; Vice-Pres. Prof. RAFFAELE AJELLO; publ. *Archivo Storico per le Province Napoletane*.

Società Romana di Storia Patria (Roman Society of Italian History): Piazza della Chiesa Nuova 18, 00186 Rome; tel. 06-68307513; e-mail srsp@libero.it; f. 1876; *c.* 100 mems; Pres. LETIZIA ERMINI PANI; Sec. PASQUALE SMIRAGLIA; publs *Archivio della Società* (annually), *Miscellanea della Società* (irregular), *Codice diplomatico di Roma e della Regione Romana* (irregular).

Società Storica Lombarda (Lombardy Historical Society): Via Morone 1, 20121 Milan; tel. 02-860118; fax 02-72002108; e-mail storica@tiscalinet.it; internet www.societastoricalombarda.it; f. 1873; 450 mems; library of 27,000 vols; Pres. Co. Ing. GAETANO BARBIANO DI BELGIOJOSO; Sec. Dott. LUIGI OROMBELLI; publ. *Archivio Storico Lombardo* (annually).

LANGUAGE AND LITERATURE

Accademia della Crusca: Villa Medicea di Castello, Via di Castello 46, 50141 Florence; tel. 055-454277; fax 055-454279; e-mail segretaria@crusca.fi.it; internet www.accademiadellacrusca.it; f. 1583; library of 140,000 vols; Pres. Prof. FRANCESCO SABATINI; Dir of Philological Studies DOMENICO DE ROBERTIS; Dir of Lexicographical Studies D'ARCO SILVIO AVALLE; Dir of Grammatical Studies GIOVANNI NENCIONI; Sec. SEVERINA PARODI; publs *La Crusca Per Voi* (2 a year), *Studi di Filologia Italiana* (annual), *Studi di Grammatica Italiana* (annual), *Studi di Lessicografia Italiana* (annual).

Alliance Française: Via Montebello 104, 00185 Rome; tel. 06-4474061; fax 06-

4456370; e-mail federation@alliancefr.it; internet www.alliancefr.it; offers courses and exams in French language and culture and promotes cultural exchange with France; attached offices in Aosta, Avellino, Bari, Biella, Bologna, Borgomanero, Catania, Catanzaro, Fermo, Foggia, Forli, Ivrea, L'Aquila, La Spezia, Lecce ,Livorno, Lucques, Messina, Pavia, Piacenza, Sassari, Sulmona, Trieste, Venice, Verona, Viareggio and Ventimiglia; Dir CHARLES DE TINGUY DE LA GIROULIÈRE.

British Council: Via Quattro Fontana 20, 00184 Rome; tel. 06-478141; fax 06-4814296; e-mail studyandcultureuk@britishcouncil.it; internet www.britishcouncil.org/italy; teaching centre; offers courses and exams in English language and British culture and promotes cultural exchange with the UK; attached teaching centres in Bologna, Milan and Naples (Vomero and Chiaia); Dir, Italy PAUL DOCHERTY.

Goethe-Institut: Via Savoia 15, 00198 Rome; tel. 06-8440051; fax 06-8411628; e-mail VL@rom.goethe.org; internet www.goethe.de/it/rom/deindex.htm; offers courses and exams in German language and culture and promotes cultural exchange with Germany; attached centres in Genoa, Milan, Naples and Turin; library of 29,000 vols; Dir MICHAEL KAHN-ACKERMANN.

Instituto Cervantes: Via di Villa Albani 14–16, 00198 Rome; tel. 06-8537361; fax 06-8546232; e-mail cenrom@cervantes.es; internet roma.cervantes.es; offers courses and exams in Spanish language and culture and promotes cultural exchange with Spain and Spanish-speaking Latin and Central America; attached centres in Milan and Naples; library: library of 24,000 vols; Dir LUIS JAVIER RUÍZ SIERRA.

PEN International Centre, Italy: Via Daverio 7, 20122 Milan; tel. 02-5461365; fax 02-5461365; e-mail penclub@tiscalinet.it; internet http://web.tiscalinet.it/pen_club_it; promotes freedom of expression; 250 mems; Pres. FERDINANDO CAMON; Sec.-Gen. VITTORIO SOZZI; publ. *Scritture* (4 a year).

Società Dante Alighieri: Palazzo di Firenze, Piazza Firenze 27, 00186 Rome; tel. 06-6873694; fax 06-6873685; e-mail seg.gen@flashnet.it; internet www.soc-dante-alighieri.it; f. 1889; promotes Italian language and culture throughout the world; Sec.-Gen. Comm. Dott. ALESSANDRO MASI; publ. *Pagine della Dante* (3 a year).

Società Dantesca Italiana (Italian Dante Society): Pallagio dell'Arte della Lana, Via Arte della Lana 1, 50123 Florence; tel. 055-287134; fax 055-211316; e-mail sdi@leonet.it; internet www.dantesca.it; f. 1888; library of 25,000 vols, 1,500 microfilms; Pres. Prof. FRANCESCO MAZZONI; publs *Studi Danteschi, Studi Danteschi–Rivista Annuale, Manoscritti Danteschi e d'Interesse Dantesco, Quaderni del Centro di Studi e Documentazione Dantesca e Medievale, Edizione Nazionale delle Opere di Dante Alighieri*.

Società Filologica Romana: Dipartimento di Studi Romanzi, Sapienza Università di Roma, Facoltà di Scienze Umanistiche, P. le Aldo Moro 5, 00185 Rome; tel. 06-72595105; e-mail beggiato@lettere.uniroma2.it; internet cisadu2.let.uniroma1.it/fil_rom/sfr/frame_visualizzazione.htm; f. 1901; library of 8,000 vols; Pres. FABRIZIO BEGGIATO; Sec. SERGIO MARRONI; publ. *Studi Romanzi*.

Società Italiana degli Autori ed Editori (SIAE) (Italian Authors' and Publishers' Society): Viale della Letteratura 30, 00144 Rome; tel. 06-59901; fax 06-59647050; e-mail urp@siae.it; internet www.siae.it; f. 1882; protects authors' and publishers' rights; 50,000 mems; administers the Museo e Biblioteca Teatrale del Burcardo (35,000 vols); Pres. SILVANO GUARISO (acting); Gen. Dir Prof. GIANNI PROFITA; publs *Il Diritto d'Autore, Lo Spettacolo* (quarterly), *Bollettino SIAE, Teatro in Italia* (annually), *Lo Spettacolo in Italia* (annually).

Società Letteraria di Verona (Verona Literary Society): Piazzetta Scalette Rubiani 1, 37121 Verona; tel. 045-595949; fax 045-595949; e-mail societaletteraria@societaletteraria.it; internet www.societaletteraria.it; f. 1808; promotes appreciation of sciences, literature and art; library of 200,000 vols; Pres. Dott. GIAMBATTISTA RUFFO; publ. *Bollettino* (annually).

MEDICINE

Accademia delle Scienzi Mediche di Palermo: Clinica Chirurgica B, Via Liborio Giuffrè 5, 90127 Palermo; tel. 091-230808; f. 1621; library; Pres. Prof. P. LI VOTI; Sec. Prof. P. BAZAN; publ. *Atti* (annually).

Accademia di Medicina di Torino (Turin Academy of Medicine): Via Po 18, 10123 Turin; tel. and fax 011-8179298; internet www.accademiadimedicina.unito.it; f. 1846; 120 ordinary mems, 30 hon. mems, 29 corresp. mems; library of 11,240 vols; Pres. Prof. GIUSEPPE POLI; Sec.-Gen. Prof. GIOVANNI CARLO ISAIA; publ. *Giornale* (2 a year).

Accademia Medica di Roma: Policlinico Umberto I, 00161 Rome; tel. 06-4957818; f. 1875; 400 mems; Pres. Prof. ANDREA SCIACCA; Sec. Prof. MARIO STEFENINI; publ. *Bolletino ed Atti* (annually).

Associazione Italiana di Dietetica e Nutrizione Clinica (Italian Association for Dietetics and Clinical Nutrition): Via Sallustio Bandini 10, 00191 Rome; tel. and fax 06-36306018; e-mail info@adiitalia.com; internet www.adiitalia.com; f. 1950; education and training; application of research in nutrition; 200 mems; Pres. Prof. MARIA ANTONIA FUSCO; Gen. Sec. Dr GIUSEPPE FATATI; publ. *ADI Magazine* (4 a year).

Associazione Italiana di Medicina Aeronautica e Spaziale (Italian Association for Aeronautical and Space Medicine): Servizio Medicina Gruppo Alitalia, Largo Forlanini, Aeroporto Leonardo da Vinci, 00050 Fiumicino; tel. 06-65632660; e-mail info@aimas.it; internet www.aimas.it; f. 1963; Pres. GIACOMO C. MODUGNO; Gen. Sec. FLAVIO BARETTI; publ. *Bollettino* (irregular).

Associazione Italiana di Radiologia Medica e Medicina Nucleare: III Cattedra di Radiologia, Instituto di Radiologia, Policlinico Umberto I, 00161 Rome; Pres. Prof. CARISSIMO BIAGINI; Sec. Prof. VINCENZO CAVALLO.

Centro di Studi e Ricerche di Medicina Aeronautica e Spaziale dell'Aeronautica Militare: Via Piero Gobetti 2A, 00185 Rome; f. 1951; library of 4,300 vols; Dir Col. GIORGIO MEINERI.

Fondazione Luigi Villa: Via Pace 9, 20122 Milan; tel. 02-5510709; fax 02-54100125; e-mail fondazionevilla@libero.it; f. 1969; research in molecular biology, genetics and haematology; library of 9,500 vols; Pres. Prof. PIER MANNUCCIO MANNUCCI; Sec.-Gen. Dott. OLGA MOSCA.

Società Italiana di Anestesiologia e Rianimazione: Ist. An. Rean. Nuovo Policlinico, Viale Bracci 53, 53100 Siena; tel. 0577-50103; f. 1934; 2,000 mems; Pres. Prof. GUALTIERO BELLUCCI; Sec. Dott. ANDREA DI MASSA; publ. *Minerva Anestesiologica*.

Società Italiana di Cancerologia (Italian Society of Cancerology): Via G. Venezian, 1, 20133 Milan; tel. 02-2666895; fax 02-2664342; e-mail sic@istitutotumori.mi.it; internet www.cancerologia.it; f. 1952; Pres. MARCO A. PIEROTTI; publ. *Tumori*.

Società Italiana di Chirurgia (Italian Society for Surgery): Viale Tiziano, 19, 00196 Rome; tel. 06-3221867; fax 06-3220676; e-mail sic@sichirurgia.org; internet www.sichirurgia.org; f. 1882; Pres. Prof. CLAUDIO CORDIANO; Gen. Sec. Prof. ALDO ROMALDI; publ. *Chirurgia Italiana* (6 a year).

Società Italiana di Farmacologia (Italian Pharmacological Society): Viale Abruzzi 32, 20131 Milan; tel. 02-29520311; fax 02-29520179; e-mail sif.farmacologia@segr.it; internet sif.unito.it; f. 1939; to develop pharmacological studies and their applications; 1,152 mems (1,115 ordinary, 13 hon., 24 assoc.); Pres. Prof. ACHILLE CAPUTI; Exec. Sec. Prof. PIER LUIGI CANONICO; publs *Pharmacological Research* (monthly), *Quaderni della SIF* (quarterly).

Società Italiana di Ginecologia ed Ostetricia (Italian Society for Gynaecology and Obstetrics): Via dei Soldati 25, 00186 Rome; tel. 06-6875119; fax 06-6868142; e-mail federazione@sigo.it; internet www.sigo.it; f. 1892; 5,300 mems; Pres. ANTONIO AMBROSINI; Sec. NICOLA COLACURCI; publs *Atti* (annually), *Italian Journal of Gynaecology and Obstetrics* (4 a year), *SIGO Notizie* (3 a year).

Società Italiana di Medicina Interna (Italian Society for Internal Medicine): Viale dell'Università 25, 00185 Rome; tel. 06-44340373; fax 06-44340474; e-mail simimail@tin.it; internet www.simi.it; f. 1887; 2,355 mems; Pres. Prof. PIER MANNUCCIO MANNUCCI; Sec. Prof. FRANCESCO VIOLI; publs *Journal Annali Italiani di Medicina Interna* (in Italian and English, annual special supplements, 4 a year), *Bollettino* (in Italian, 4 a year).

Società Italiana di Medicina Legale e delle Assicurazioni (Italian Society for Legal Medicine and Assurance): Istituto di Medicina Legale, Via Mangiagalli 37, 20133 Milan; e-mail staff@simlaweb.com; internet www.simlaweb.com; f. 1897; Pres. Prof. ANTONIO FARNETI; publ. *Rivista Italiana di Medicina Legale*.

Società Italiana di Odontostomatologia e Chirurgia Maxillo-Facciale (Italian Society for Odontostomatology and Maxillofacial Surgery): Via Eugubina 42, 06122 Perugia; tel. 075-5729867; fax 075-5737378; e-mail siocmf@tin.it; internet main.netemedia.net/siocmf; f. 1957; 2,000 mems; Pres. Prof. PIERLUIGI SAPELLI; Sec.-Gen. and Treas. Prof. MAURIZIO PROCACCINI; publ. *Minerva Stomatologica* (monthly).

Società Italiana di Ortopedia e Traumatologia (Italian Society for Orthopaedics and Traumatology): Via Nicola Martelli 3, 00197 Rome; tel. 06-80691593; fax 06-80687266; e-mail segreteria@siot.it; internet www.siot.it; f. 1906; 3,100 mems; Pres. Prof. VITTORIO MONTELEONE; Sec. Dott. VINCENZO CASTELLI; publ. *Giornale Italiano di Ortopedia e Traumatologia* (quarterly).

Società Italiana di Reumatologia (Italian Society for Rheumatology): Corso Plebisciti 9, 20129 Milan; tel. 02-7382330; fax 02-7385763; e-mail reumatologia@unipd.it; internet www.reumatologia.it; f. 1950; 915 mems; Pres. STEFANO BOMBARDIERI; Gen. Sec. VITTORIO MODENA; publs *Reumatismo* (4 a year), *Bollettino*.

Società Italiana di Traumatologia della Strada (Italian Society for Road Accident Traumatology): c/o Istituto di Clinica Ortopedica e Traumatologica dell' Universita La Sapienza, Piazzale A. Moro 5, 00185 Rome; tel. 06-49982399; fax 06-4462650; e-mail socitras@socitras.org; internet www.socitras.org; f. 1984; 200 mems; Pres. ANDREA COSTANZO; Sec.-Gen. Dr ROBERTO SAPIA.

Società Medica Chirurgica di Bologna (Society of Medicine and Surgery): Palazzo dell'Archiginnasio, Piazza Galvani 1, 40124 Bologna; tel. and fax 051-231488; e-mail info@medchir.bo.it; internet www.medchir.bo.it; f. 1802; holds scientific meetings; 250 mems; library of 15,000 vols; Pres. Prof. RUGGERO BAZZOCCHI; Sec. Prof. ENNIO MANZINI; Dir of Library Prof. STEFANO ARIETI; publ. *Bullettino delle Scienze Mediche*.

NATURAL SCIENCES

General

Accademia Nazionale delle Scienze, detta dei XL (National Academy of Sciences, known as the Forty): Via L. Spallanzani 7, 00161 Rome; tel. 06-44250465; fax 06-44250871; e-mail segreteria@accademiaxl.it; internet www.accademiaxl.it; f. 1782 as the Italian Society of Sciences; 65 mems (40 Italian, 25 foreign); Pres. Prof. G. T. SCARASCIA MUGNOZZA; Sec. Prof. M. CUMO; publs *Rendiconti: Memorie Scienze Fisiche e Naturali* (annually), *Memorie di Matematica* (annually), *Scritti e Documenti* (irregular), *Annuario* (every 2 years).

Federazione delle Associazioni Scientifiche e Tecniche (Federation of Scientific and Technological Associations): Piazzale R. Morandi 2, 20121 Milan; tel. 02-77790300; fax 02-782485; e-mail fast@fast.mi.it; internet www.fast.mi.it; f. 1897; aims at fostering cultural debate and promotion of the fields of science policy, technological and industrial research and development, with particular reference to: energy and resources, chemistry and materials, electronics and information, biotechnology, technological research and innovation, ecology and environment, training, professionalism and job organization; mems: 40 scientific orgs, 55,000 individuals; Pres. Prof. ADOLFO COLOMBO; Gen. Sec. Dr ALBERTO PIERI.

Società Adriatica di Scienze (Adriatic Society of Sciences): CP 1029, 34100 Trieste; e-mail adriscie@univ.trieste.it; internet www.units.it/~adriscie; f. 1874; 200 mems; library of 27,000 vols; Pres. Prof. FRANCO CUCCHI; Sec. BERNARDINO CRESSERI; publ. *Bollettino* (annual).

Società Italiana di Scienze Naturali (Italian Society of Natural Sciences): Museo Civico di Storia Naturale, Corso Venezia 55, 20121 Milan; tel. 02-795965; fax 02-795965; e-mail info@scienzenaturali.org; internet www.scienzenaturali.org; f. 1857; promotes and carries out scientific research; organizes meetings to present and discuss members' research results; 1,000 mems; library: library of 1,600 periodicals; Pres. CARLO VIOLANI; Sec. MAMI AZUMA; publs *Atti* (2 a year), *Natura* (2 a year), *Memorie*, *Rivista di Ornitologia* (2 a year), *Paleontologia Lombarda*.

Società Italiana per il Progresso delle Scienze (Italian Society for Scientific Progress): Viale dell'Università 11, 00185 Rome; tel. 06-4451628; fax 06-4440515; e-mail sips@sipsinfo.it; internet www.sipsinfo.it; f. 1839; library of 30,000 vols; Pres. Prof. MAURIZIO CUMO; Sec. Prof. ROCCO CAPASSO; publs *Atti Riunioni SIPS* (annually), *Scienza e Tecnica* (monthly).

Società Toscana di Scienze Naturali (Tuscan Society of Natural Sciences): Via S. Maria 53, 56126 Pisa; e-mail info@stsn.it; internet www.stsn.it; f. 1847; 412 mems; library of 75,000 vols, 300 current periodicals; Pres. Prof. S. MERLINO; Gen. Sec. F. RAPETTI; publs *Atti – Memorie serie A (abiologica)* (electronic, annual), *Atti – Memorie serie B (biologica)* (electronic, annual), *Palaeontographia Italica* (annual).

Biological Sciences

Società Botanica Italiana Onlus (Italian Botanical Society Onlus): Via Giorgio La Pira 4, 50121 Florence; tel. 055-2757379; fax 055-2757467; e-mail sbi@unifi.it; internet www.societabotanicaitaliana.it; f. 1888; 1,300 mems; library of 9,000 vols; Pres. Prof. DONATO CHIATANTE; Sec. Prof. GRAZIELLA BERTA; publs *Plant Biosystems* (3 a year), *Informatore Botanico Italiano* (2 a year).

Società Entomologica Italiana (Italian Entomological Society): c/o Museo Civico di Storia Naturale, Via Brigata Liguria 9, 16121 Genoa; internet www.socentomit.it; f. 1869; pure and applied entomology; library (Corso Torino 19/4 sc. A. Genoa); 750 mems; Pres. Prof. A. VIGNA TAGLIANTI; publs *Bollettino* (3 a year), *Memorie* (annual).

Società Italiana di Biochimica Clinica e Biologia Molecolare Clinica (Italian Society of Clinical Biochemistry and Clinical Molecular Biology): Via Libero Temolo 4, 20126 Milan; tel. 02-87390041; fax 02-87390077; e-mail segreteria@sibioc.it; internet www.sibioc.it; f. 1969; 2,500 mems; mem. of Intl Federation of Clinical Chemistry; Pres. Prof. LUCA DEIANA; publ. *Biochimica Clinica* (monthly).

Società Italiana di Biochimica e Biologia Molecolare (Italian Society for Biochemistry and Molecular Biology): Dipartimento di Scienze Biochimiche 'A. Rossi Fanelli', Università di Roma 'La Sapienza', Piazzale Aldo Moro 5, 00185 Rome; tel. 06-4450291; fax 06-4440062; e-mail info@biochimica.it; internet www.biochimica.it; f. 1951; 1,300 mems; Pres. Prof. GIAMPETRO RAMPONI; Sec ANDREA BELLELLI; publ. *Biochimica in Italia*.

Società Italiana di Ecologia (SItE) (Italian Ecological Society): c/o Dipartimento di Scienze Ambientali, Università di Parma, Area Parco delle Scienze 33A, 43100 Parma; fax 0521-905402; e-mail site@dsa.unipr.it; internet www.dsa.unipr.it/site; f. 1976; aims to promote theoretical and applied ecological research, to disseminate knowledge of ecology, encourage the devt of cultural exchange among researchers, and to facilitate nat. and int. co-operation; operates working groups, congresses, etc.; 705 mems; Pres. Prof. PIERLUIGI VIAROLI; Sec.-Gen. ALBERTO BASSET; publs *SITE Atti* (proceedings of congresses and symposia, annual), *Lettera ai Soci* (newsletter, 6 a year).

Società Italiana di Microbiologia (Italian Microbiological Society): c/o Istituto di Microbiologia, Via Androne 81, 95124 Catania; tel. 095-312633; e-mail sim@societasim.org; internet www.societasim.org; f. 1962; promotes the study of microbiology, holds congresses and conventions; Pres. GIUSEPPE NICOLETTI; Sec. and Treas. S. RIPA; publ. *Bollettino* (online, annually).

Physical Sciences

Associazione Geofisica Italiana (Italian Geophysical Association): c/o CNR, V.le dell'Università 11, 00185 Rome; tel. and fax 06-44702989; e-mail info@associazionegeofisica.it; internet www.associazionegeofisica.it; f. 1951; promotes, co-ordinates and disseminates knowledge, studies and research on pure and applied geophysics; 200 mems; library of 1,500 vols; Pres. Prof. Dr H. COLACINO; Sec. Dr M. AVERSA; publ. *Bollettino Geofisico* (quarterly).

Associazione Geotecnica Italiana (Italian Geotechnical Association): Viale dell'Università 11, 00185 Rome; tel. 06-44704349; fax 06-44361035; e-mail agiroma@iol.it; internet www.associazionegeotecnica.it/~agi; f. 1947; independent; aims to encourage, carry out and support geotechnical studies and research in Italy through publications, conferences, scholarships, etc.; 1,100 mems; Pres. Prof. GIOVANNI BARLA; publ. *Rivista Italiana di Geotecnica* (4 a year).

Associazione Italiana Nucleare: Corso Vittorio Emanuele II 244, 00186 Rome; tel. 06-94005401; fax 06-94005314; e-mail info@assonucleare.it; internet www.assonucleare.it; f. 1998 by merger of ANDIN (Associazione Italiana di Ingegneria Nucleare e Sicurezza Impiantistica), FIEN (Forum Italiano dell'Energia Nucleare) and SNI (Società Nucleare Italiana); promotes debate and research into the role of nuclear power, in order to promote the peaceful and safe use of nuclear technology, in the national interest; Chair. Prof. RENATO ANGELO RICCI.

Società Astronomica Italiana (Italian Astronomical Society): Largo E. Fermi 5, 50125 Florence; tel. 055-2752270; fax 055-220039; e-mail sait@arcetri.astro.it; internet www.sait.it; f. 1920; 700 mems; Pres. Prof. SALVATORE SERIO; Sec. Dr FABRIZIO MAZZUCCONI; publs *Memorie* (4 a year), *Giornale di Astronomia* (print and electronic versions, 4 a year).

Società Chimica Italiana (Italian Chemistry Society): Viale Liegi 48/C, 00198 Rome; tel. 06-8549691; fax 06-8548734; e-mail soc.chim.it@agora.stm.it; internet www.sci.uniba.it; f. 1909; 4,800 mems; library of 2,300 vols; Pres. Prof. FRANCESCO DE ANGELIS; publs *Annali di Chimica* (6 a year), *Il Farmaco* (medicinal and pharmaceutical chemistry, in English, monthly), *La Chimica e l'Industria* (monthly), *La Chimica nella Scuola* (6 a year).

Società Geologica Italiana (Italian Geological Society): c/o Dipartimento di Scienze della Terra, Università La Sapienza, Piazzale Aldo Moro 5, 00185 Rome; tel. 06-4959390; fax 06-49914154; e-mail sgi@socgeol.it; internet www.socgeol.it; f. 1881; 2,400 mems; Sec. Dott. ACHILLE ZUCCARI; publs *Bollettino* (4 a year), *Memorie* (irregular), *Rendiconti*.

Società Italiana di Fisica (Italian Physics Society): Via Saragozza 12, 40123 Bologna; tel. 051-331554; fax 051-581340; e-mail sif@sif.it; internet www.sif.it; f. 1897; 1,500 mems; library of 6,500 vols; Pres. Prof. FRANCO BASSANI; publs *European Physical Journal* (owned in conjunction with two other learned socs, monthly), *Il Nuovo Cimento B* (monthly), *Il Nuovo Cimento C* (6 a year), *Europhysics Letters* (2 a month), *Rivista del Nuovo Cimento* (monthly), *Bollettino* (6 a year), *Giornale di Fisica* (4 a year).

PHILOSOPHY AND PSYCHOLOGY

Società Filosofica Italiana (Italian Philosophical Society): c/o Dip. di Studi Filosofici ed Epistemologici, Università di Roma 'La Sapienza', Villa Mirafiori, Via Nomentana 118, 00161 Rome; tel. and fax 06-8604360; e-mail sfi@sfi.it; internet www.sfi.it; f. 1902; independent organization to promote philosophical research on a scientific level, to safeguard the professional status of philosophy lecturers, to encourage contact and collaboration in Italy and internationally between philosophic disciplines; helps set up local centres of study; 1,350 mems; Pres. MAURO DI GIANDOMENICO; Sec. and Treas. Prof.ssa CARLA GUETTI; publ. *Bollettino* (3 a year).

Società Italiana di Psicologia: Via Tagliamento 76, 00198 Rome; tel. and fax 06-8845136; e-mail sipsit@tin.it; f. 1910; carries out activities in conjunction with university institutions for study and research; organizes national congresses every three years; Pres. LEONARDO ANCONA; publ. *Psicologia Italiana*.

RELIGION, SOCIOLOGY AND ANTHROPOLOGY

Fondazione Internazionale Premio E. Balzan – 'Premio': Piazzetta U. Giordano 4, 20122 Milan; tel. 02-76002212; fax 02-76009457; e-mail balzan@balzan.it; internet www.balzan.it; f. 1957; annual prizes for the world-wide promotion of the arts and sciences; Pres. Amb. B. BOTTAI; publ. *Premi Balzan* (annual).

Fondazione Marco Besso (Marco Besso Foundation): Largo di Torre Argentina 11, 00186 Rome; tel. 06-6865611; fax 06-68216313; e-mail segreteriadue@fondazionemarcobesso.it; internet www.fondazionemarcobesso.it; f. 1918; promotes development of Roman cultural world; library: see Libraries and Archives; Pres. GLORIA SONAGLIA LUMBROSO; Dir ANTONIO MARTINI.

Gruppo Interdisciplinare per la Ricerca Sociale (Interdisciplinary Group for Social Research): Facoltà di Scienze Statistiche, Demografiche e Attuariale, Piazzale Aldo Moro 5, 00185 Rome; tel. 06-4453828; f. 1937; Italian section of Int. Institute of Sociology; library of 8,000 vols, 100 current periodicals; Pres. Prof. AMMASSARI.

Società Italiana di Antropologia e Etnologia: Via del Proconsolo 12, 50122 Florence; tel. 055-2396449; fax 055-219438; e-mail musant@unifi.it; f. 1871; 200 mems; library of 5,760 vols, 70 periodicals; Pres. Prof. CLETO CORRAIN; Librarian CATERINA SCARSINI; publ. *Archivio per l'Antropologia e la Etnologia* (annually).

TECHNOLOGY

Associazione Elettrotecnica ed Elettronica Italiana (AEI) (Italian Electrical and Electronics Association): Piazzale Morandi 2, 20121 Milan; tel. 02-77790200; fax 02-798817; e-mail sartori@federaeit.it; internet www.aei.it; f. 1896; Pres. FRANCESCO GAGLIARDI; Gen. Sec. ANDREA BONATI; publs *AEIT—Federazione di Elettrotecnica, Elettronica, Automazione, Informatica e Telecomunicazioni* (monthly), *L'Energia Elettrica* (6 a year), *European Transactions on Telecommunications* (6 a year, in English), *Mondo Digitale* (monthly).

Associazione Idrotecnica Italiana (Italian Water Resources Association): Via Nizza 53, 00198 Rome; tel. 06-8845064; fax 06-8852974; e-mail info@idrotecnicaitaliana.it; internet www.idrotecnicaitaliana.it; f. 1923; study of problems concerning the utilization and management of water resources, and the safeguarding of the environment; 1,500 mems; library of 200 vols; Pres. UGO MAJONE; Gen. Sec. OLIMPIA ARCELLA; publ. *L'Acqua* (6 a year).

Associazione Italiana di Aeronautica e Astronautica (Italian Association of Aeronautical and Space Sciences): Casella Postale 227, 00187 Rome V.R.; tel. and fax 06-88346460; e-mail info@aidaa.it; internet www.aidaa.it; f. 1920; promotes and co-ordinates research in aeronautical and space sciences, co-operates with nat. and int. bodies in this field; 400 mems in 8 sections; Pres. Dr Ing. FAUSTO CERETI; Gen. Sec. Prof. ANTONIO CASTELLANI; publ. *Aerotecnica Missili e Spazio* (quarterly).

Associazione Italiana di Metallurgia (Italian Metallurgical Association): Piazzale R. Morandi 2, 20121 Milan; tel. 02-76021132; fax 02-76020551; e-mail aim@aimnet.it; internet www.aimnet.it; f. 1946; promotes and develops all aspects of science, technology and use of metals and materials closely related to metals; 2,000 mems; Pres. OTTAVIO LECIS; Gen. Sec. (vacant); publ. *La Metallurgia Italiana* (monthly).

Associazione Italiana Nucleare (Italian Nuclear Association): Corso Vittorio Emanuele II 244, 00186 Rome; tel. 06-94005401; fax 06-94005314; Chair. Prof. RENATO ANGELO RICCI; Sec.-Gen. Ing. UGO SPEZIA.

Associazione Termotecnica Italiana (Italian Thermal Engineering Association): Via Pacini 11, 20131 Milan; tel. 02-26626540; fax 02-26626550; e-mail panvini@cti2000.it; internet www.cti2000.it; f. 1947; Pres. Prof. UMBERTO RUGGIERO; Sec.-Gen. GIOVANNI RIVA; publs *La Termotecnica* (10 a year), *Ricerche di Termotecnica* (occasional), *Atti Congressi Nazionali*.

Comitato Elettrotecnico Italiano (CEI) (Italian Electrotechnical Committee): Via Saccardo 9, 20134 Milan; tel. 02-210061; fax 02-21006210; e-mail cei@ceiweb.it; internet www.ceiweb.it; Pres. Ing. ALDO BOLZA.

Comitato Termotecnico Italiano (CTI) (Italian Thermotechnical Committee): Via G. Pacini 11, 20131 Milan; tel. 02-2662651; fax 02-26626550; e-mail cti@cti2000.it; internet www.cti2000.it; f. 1933; Pres. CESARE BOFFA; Gen. Sec. Prof. GIOVANNI RIVA; publ. *La Termotecnica* (10 a year).

Ente Nazionale Italiano di Unificazione (UNI) (Italian National Standards Association): Via Battistotti Sassi 11B, 20133 Milan; tel. 02-700241; fax 02-70106149; e-mail uni@uni.com; internet www.uni.com; f. 1921; Pres. PAOLO SCOLARI; Exec. Vice-Pres. Dr Ing. ENRICO MARTINOTTI; publ. *Unificazione* (quarterly).

Istituto di Studi Nucleari per l'Agricoltura (ISNA) (Institute of Nuclear Studies applied to Agriculture): Via IV Novembre 152, 00187 Rome; tel. 06-6784991; f. 1959; Pres. Avv. Prof. GIUSEPPE GESUALDI; Sec.-Gen. Prof. M. L. SCARSELLI; publs *Agricoltura d'Italia* (monthly), *Il Corriere di Roma*, *Quaderni ISNA*.

Istituto Italiano del Marchio di Qualità (IMQ) (Italian Institute of the Quality Mark): Via Quintiliano 43, 20138 Milan; tel. 02-50731; fax 02-5073271; e-mail mkt@imq.it; internet www.imq.it; f. 1951; tests electrical and gas products to grant the IMQ safety mark; undertakes EU Directives conformity assessment and certifies company quality and management systems as part of the CSQ scheme; Pres. GIORGIO SCANAVACCA; Man. Dir GIANCARLO ZAPPA; publs *Guida agli Acquisti IMQ* (list of products and companies approved by IMQ, 2 a year), *IMQ Notizie* (News, 4 a year).

Istituto Italiano della Saldatura (Italian Welding Institute): Lungobisagno Istria 15A, 16141 Genoa; tel. 010-83411; fax 010-8367780; e-mail iis@iis.it; internet www.iis.it; f. 1948; consultancy training, research, standardization, certification, laboratory tests and diploma courses in welding; 800 mems; library of 15,000 vols; Sec.-Gen. Dott.-Ing. MAURO SCASSO; publ. *Rivista Italiana della Saldatura* (every 2 months).

Research Institutes

GENERAL

Consiglio Nazionale delle Ricerche (CNR) (National Research Council of Italy): Piazzale Aldo Moro 7, 00185 Rome; tel. 06-49931; fax 06-4461954; e-mail urp@urp.cnr.it; internet www.cnr.it; f. 1923; research is carried out by 110 institutes in 5 groups: Basic Sciences; Earth and Environmental Sciences; Human and Social Sciences; Life Sciences; and Technological, Engineering and Information Sciences; 20 Aree di Ricerca provide the institutes with logistical, technical and administrative support: Bari (Pres. Prof. ANGELO VISCONTI), Bologna (Pres. Dott. GIANCARLO SECONI), Cosenza (Pres. Dott. MARINO SORRISO VALVO), Florence (Pres. Prof. PIER LUIGI EMILIANI), Genoa (Pres. Ing. FILIPPO GRASSIA), Milan 1 (Pres. Dott. ALCIDE BERTANI), Milan 2 (Pres. Dott. VALTER ESPOSTI), Milan 3 (Pres. Dott. EMILIO OLZI), Milan 4 (Pres. Prof. ALBERTO ALBERTINI), Naples 1 (Pres. Prof. CATELLO POLITO), Naples 2 (Pres. Prof. MOSÈ ROSSI), Naples 3 (Pres. Dott. GUIDO CIMINO), Padua (Pres. Dott. SERGIO DAOLIO), Palermo (Pres. Dott. PIERLUIGI SAN BIAGIO), Pisa (Pres. Prof. LUIGI DONATO), Potenza (Pres. Prof. VINCENZO CUOMO), Rome 1–Montelibretti (Pres. Dott. SESTO VITICOLI), Rome 2–Tor Vergata (Pres. Dott. PAOLO PERFETTI), Rome 3 (Pres. Prof. PIETRO CALISSANO), Turin (Pres. Prof. MAURIZIO CONTI); Pres. Prof. FABIO PISTELLA; Dir-Gen. Dott. ANGELO GUERRINI; publs *Ricerca e Futuro* (print and electronic versions, quarterly), *Almanacco della Scienza* (electronic, fortnightly), *Notiziario Neutroni e Luce di Sincrotrone* (print and electronic versions, in Italian and English, 2 a year), *CNR Report* (annual).

Basic Sciences:

Istituto per le Applicazioni del Calcolo 'Mauro Picone' (Institute for Applied Mathematics): Viale del Policlinico 137, 00161 Rome; tel. 06-884701; fax 06-4404306; e-mail direttore@iac.cnr.it; internet www.iac.cnr.it; f. 2000; Dir Prof. MICHIEL BERTSCH.

Istituto di Astrofisica Spaziale e Fisica Cosmica (Cosmic Physics and Space Astrophysics Institute): Via del Fosso del Cavaliere 100, 00133 Rome; tel. 06-49934472; fax 06-20660188; e-mail gev@rm.iasf.cnr.it; internet www.rm.iasf.cnr.it; f. 2000; Dir Dott. GABRIELE VILLA.

Istituto di Chimica dei Composti Organo Metallici (Institute of Organometallic Compounds Chemistry): Via Madonna del Piano snc, 50019 Sesto Fiorentino; tel. 055-52251; fax 055-5225203; e-mail claudio.bianchini@iccom.cnr.it; internet www.iccom.cnr.it; f. 2001; Dir Dott. CLAUDIO BIANCHINI.

Istituto di Chimica Inorganica e delle Superfici (Institute of Inorganic and Surface Chemistry): Corso Stati Uniti 4, 35127 Padua; tel. 049-8295940; fax 049-8702911; e-mail zanella@icis.cnr.it; internet www.icis.cnr.it; f. 2000; Dir Dott. PIERINO ZANELLA.

Istituto di Chimica e Tecnologia dei Polimeri (Institute of Polymer Chemistry and Technology): Via Campi Flegrei 34, 80078 Pozzuoli; tel. 081-8675077; fax 081-8675230; e-mail direttore@ictp.cnr.it; internet www.ictp.cnr.it; f. 2001; Dir Prof. COSIMO CARFAGNA.

Istituto di Cibernetica 'Edoardo Caianiello' (Cybernetics Institute): Via Campi Flegrei 34, 80078 Pozzuoli; tel. 081-8675111; fax 081-8675128; e-mail s.termini@cib.na.cnr.it; internet www.cib.na.cnr.it; f. 2001; Dir Prof. SETTIMO TERMINI.

Istituto di Cristallografia (Institute of Crystallography): Via Giovanni Amendola 122/O, 70126 Bari; tel. 080-5929140; fax 080-5929170; e-mail carmelo.giacovazzo@ic.cnr.it; internet www.ic.cnr.it; f. 2001; Dir Prof. CARMELO GIACOVAZZO.

Istituto per l'Energetica e le Interfasi (Institute for Energetics and Interphases): Corso Stati Uniti 4, 35127 Padua; tel. 049-8295850; fax 049-8295853; e-mail s.daolio@

ieni.cnr.it; internet www.ieni.cnr.it; f. 2000; Dir Dott. SERGIO DAOLIO.

Istituto di Fisica Applicata 'Nello Carrara' (Institute of Applied Physics): Via Panciatichi 64, 50127 Florence; tel. 055-42351; fax 055-410893; e-mail p.l.emiliani@ifac.cnr.it; internet www.ifac.cnr.it; f. 2001; Dir Dott. PIER LUIGI EMILIANI.

Istituto di Fisica del Plasma 'Piero Caldirola' (Institute for Plasma Physics): Via Roberto Cozzi 53, 20125 Milan; tel. 02-66173238; fax 02-66173239; e-mail direttore@ifp.cnr.it; internet www.ifp.cnr.it; f. 1974; library of 3,000 vols, 100 periodical titles; Dir Dott. ENZO LAZZARO.

Istituto di Fisica dello Spazio Interplanetario (Institute for Interplanetary Space Physics): Via del Fosso del Cavaliere 100, 00133 Rome; tel. 06-4993460; fax 06-49934383; e-mail angioletta.coradini@ifsi.rm.cnr.it; internet www.ifsi.rm.cnr.it; f. 2001; Dir Dott.ssa ANGIOLETTA CORADINI.

Istituto di Fotonica e Nanotecnologie (Institute for Photonics and Nanotechnologies): Via Cineto Romano 42, 00156 Rome; tel. 06-415221; fax 06-41522220; e-mail evangelisti@ifn.cnr.it; internet www.ifn.cnr.it; f. 2000; study and development of photonics from points of view of radiation-matter interaction and of developing materials, devices and systems; study and development of nanotechnologies for the fabrication of nanoscale-size devices; development of microelectronic and micromechanical devices; Dir Prof. FLORESTANO EVANGELISTI.

Istituto di Matematica Applicata e Tecnologie Informatiche (Institute of Applied Mathematics and Information Technology): Via Ferrata 1, 27100 Pavia; tel. 0382-548211; fax 0382-548300; e-mail direttore@imati.cnr.it; internet www.imati.cnr.it; f. 2000; Dir Prof. FRANCO BREZZI.

Istituto per i Materiali Compositi e Biomedici (Institute for Composite and Biomedical Materials): Piazzale Vincenzo Tecchio 80, 80125 Naples; tel. 081-7682401; fax 081-7682666; e-mail nicolais@unina.it; f. 2001; Dir Prof. LUIGI NICOLAIS.

Istituto dei Materiali per l'Elettronica ed il Magnetismo (Institute of Materials for Electronics and Magnetism): Parco Area delle Scienze 37A, 43100 Fontanini, Parma; tel. 0521-2691; fax 0521-269206; e-mail direttore@imem.cnr.it; internet www.imem.cnr.it; f. 2001; library of 1,300 vols; Dir Dott. LUCIO ZANOTTI.

Istituto di Metodologie Chimiche (Institute for Methodological Chemistry): Via Salaria Km 29.3, CP 10, 00016 Monterotondo Stazione; tel. 06-9062511; fax 06-90672519; e-mail imc@imc.cnr.it; internet www.mlib.rm.cnr.it; f. 2001; Dir Dott. GIANCARLO ANGELINI.

Istituto di Metodologie Inorganiche e dei Plasmi (Institute of Inorganic Methodologies and Plasmas): Via Salaria Km. 29.3, CP 10, 00016 Monterotondo Stazione; tel. 06-90672213; fax 06-90672238; e-mail direttore.imip@imip.cnr.it; internet www.imip.cnr.it; f. 2000; Dir Dott. MARIO CACCIATORE.

Istituto per la Microelettronica e Microsistemi (Institute for Microelectronics and Microsystems): Stradale Primosole 50, 95121 Catania; tel. 095-5968211; fax 095-5968312; e-mail emanuele.rimini@imm.cnr.it; internet www.imm.cnr.it; f. 2000; Dir Prof. EMANUELE RIMINI.

Istituto per i Processi Chimico-Fisici (Institute for Chemical and Physical Processes): Via Giuseppe Moruzzi 1, 56124 Pisa; tel. 050-3152234; fax 050-3152234; e-mail direttore@ipcf.cnr.it; internet www.ipcf.cnr.it; f. 2000; Dir Dott. MASSIMO MARTINELLI.

Istituto di Radioastronomia (Institute of Radioastronomy): Via Piero Gobetti 101, 40129 Bologna; tel. 051-6399385; fax 051-6399431; e-mail gtofani@ira.cnr.it; internet www.ira.cnr.it; f. 2000; Dir Prof. GIANNI TOFANI.

Istituto di Scienze e Tecnologie Molecolari (Institute of Molecular Science and Technologies): Via Camillo Golgi 19, 20133 Milan; tel. 02-70635452; fax 02-50314300; e-mail g.casalone@istm.cnr.it; internet www.istm.cnr.it; f. 2000; Dir Dott. GIANLUIGI CASALONE.

Istituto per la Sintesi Organica e la Fotoreattività (Institute for Organic Syntheses and Photoreactivity): Via Piero Gobetti 101, 40129 Bologna; tel. 051-6399770; fax 051-6399844; e-mail direzione@isof.cnr.it; internet www.isof.cnr.it; f. 2000; Dir Dott. GIANCARLO SECONI.

Istituto dei Sistemi Complessi (Sperimentale) (Institute for Experimental Complex Systems): Via dei Taurini 19, 00185 Rome; tel. 06-49934598; fax 06-49934003; e-mail luciano.pietronero@isc.cnr.it; internet www.isc.cnr.it; f. 2004; Dir Prof. LUCIANO PIETRONERO.

Istituto Sperimentale di Acustica 'Orso Mario Corbino' (Institute of Acoustics): Via del Fosso del Cavaliere 100, 00133 Rome; tel. 06-49934482; fax 06-20660061; e-mail damico@idac.rm.cnr.it; internet www.idac.rm.cnr.it; f. 2001; Dir Prof. ARNALDO D'AMICO.

Istituto di Struttura della Materia (Institute for the Structure of Matter): Via del Fosso del Cavaliere 100, 00133 Rome; tel. 06-49934476; fax 06-49934153; e-mail perfetti@ism.cnr.it; internet www.ism.cnr.it; f. 2000; Dir Dott. PAOLO PERFETTI.

Istituto per lo Studio delle Macromolecole (Institute for Macromolecular Studies): Via Edoardo Bassini 15, 20133 Milan; tel. 02-23699366; fax 02-2362946; e-mail locatelli@ismac.cnr.it; internet www.ismac.cnr.it; f. 2000; Dir Dott. PAOLO LOCATELLI.

Istituto per lo Studio dei Materiali Nanostrutturati (Institute of Nanostructured Materials): Via dei Taurini 19, 00185 Rome; tel. 06-49937741; fax 06-49937760; e-mail s.viticoli@dcas.cnr.it; internet www.ismn.cnr.it; f. 2000; Dir Dott. SESTO VITICOLI.

Istituto per la Tecnologia delle Membrane (Institute for Membrane Technology): Via P. Bucci, 87030 Rende; tel. 0984-402706; fax 0984-402103; e-mail e.drioli@itm.cnr.it; internet www.itm.cnr.it; f. 2001; Dir Prof. ENRICO DRIOLI.

Earth and Environmental Sciences:

Istituto per l'Ambiente Marino Costiero (Institute for the Coastal Marine Environment): Calata Porta di Massa, 80133 Naples; tel. 081-5423811; fax 081-5423888; e-mail dargenio@gms01.geomare.na.cnr.it; f. 2001; Dir Prof. BRUNO D'ARGENIO.

Istituto per la Dinamica dei Processi Ambientali (Institute for the Dynamics of Environmental Processes): Calle Larga Santa Marta 2137, 30123 Venice; tel. 041-2348547; fax 041-2578549; e-mail paolo.cescon@idpa.cnr.it; internet www.idpa.cnr.it; f. 2001; Dir Prof. PAOLO CESCON.

Istituto di Geologia Ambientale e Geoingegneria (Institute of Environmental Geology and Geoengineering): Via Bolognola 7, (Via Salaria Km 11.6), 00138 Rome; tel. 06-88070001; fax 06-8804463; e-mail g.cavarretta@igag.cnr.it; internet www.igag.cnr.it; f. 2001; Dir Dott. GIUSEPPE CAVARRETTA.

Istituto di Geoscienze e Georisorse (Institute of Geosciences and Earth Resources): Via Giuseppe Moruzzi 1, 56124 Pisa; tel. 050-3152384; fax 050-3152323; e-mail direttore@igg.cnr.it; internet www.igg.cnr.it; f. 2001; Dir Prof. PIERO MANETTI.

Istituto sull'Inquinamento Atmosferico (Institute for Atmospheric Pollution): Via Salaria Km 29.3, CP 10, 00016 Monterotondo Stazione; tel. 06-90625349; fax 06-90672660; e-mail allegrini@iia.cnr.it; internet www.iia.cnr.it; f. 2001; Dir Dott. IVO ALLEGRINI.

Istituto di Metodologie per l'Analisi Ambientale (Institute of Methodologies for Environmental Analysis): Contrada S. Loja, C.P. 27, 85050 Tito Scalo; tel. 0971-427262; fax 0971-427222; e-mail cuomo@imaa.cnr.it; internet www.imaa.cnr.it; f. 2001; Dir Prof. VINCENZO CUOMO.

Istituto di Ricerca sulle Acque (Water Research Institute): Via Reno 1, 00198 Rome; tel. 06-8841451; fax 06-8417861; e-mail direzione@irsa.rm.cnr.it; internet www.irsa.rm.cnr.it; f. 2001; Dir Prof. ROBERTO PASSINO.

Istituto di Ricerca per la Protezione Idrogeologica (Research Institute for Geo-hydrological Protection): Via Madonna Alta 126, 06128 Perugia; tel. 075-5014402; fax 075-5014420; e-mail direzione@irpi.cnr.it; internet www.irpi.cnr.it; f. 2001; Dir Prof. LUCIO UBERTINI.

Istituto di Scienze dell'Atmosfera e del Clima (Institute of Atmospheric Sciences and Climate): Via Piero Gobetti 101, 40129 Bologna; tel. 051-6399619; fax 051-6399658; e-mail direzione@isac.cnr.it; internet www.isac.cnr.it; f. 2000; Dir Prof. FRANCO PRODI.

Istituto di Scienze Marine (Institute of Marine Sciences): San Polo 1364, Palazzo Papadopoli, 30125 Venice; tel. 041-5216811; fax 041-2602340; e-mail direttore@ismar.cnr.it; internet www.ismar.cnr.it; f. 2001; Dir Prof. ENRICO BONATTI.

Istituto per lo Studio degli Ecosistemi (Institute of Ecosystem Study): Largo Vittorio Tonolli 50–52, 28922 Pallanza; tel. 0323-518300; fax 0323-518349; e-mail r.debernardi@ise.cnr.it; internet www.ise.cnr.it; f. 2001; Dir Dott. RICCARDO DE BERNARDI.

Human and Social Sciences:

Istituto per i Beni Archeologici e Monumentali (Institute of Archeological Heritage – Monuments and Sites): Prov.le Lecce-Monteroni, 73100 Lecce; tel. 0832-422200; fax 0832-422225; e-mail francesco.dandria@unile.it; internet www.ibam.cnr.it; f. 2001; Dir Prof. FRANCESCO D'ANDRIA.

Istituto per la Conservazione e Valorizzazione dei Beni Culturali (Institute for the Conservation and Promotion of Cultural Heritage): Vai Madonna del Piano, Edificio C, 50019 Sesto Fiorentino; tel. 055-5225484; fax 055-5225403; e-mail matteini@icvbc.cnr.it; internet www.icvbc.cnr.it; f. 2001; Dir Dott. MAURO MATTEINI.

Istituto per il Lessico Intellettuale Europeo e la Storia delle Idee (Institute for the European Intellectual Lexicon and the History of Ideas): Via Nomentana 118,

Villa Mirafiori, 00161 Rome; tel. 06-86320527; fax 06-49917215; e-mail iliesi@iliesi.cnr.it; internet www.iliesi.cnr.it; f. 2001; Dir Prof. TULLIO GREGORY.

Istituto di Linguistica Computazionale (Institute of Computational Linguistics): Via Giuseppe Moruzzi 1, 56124 Pisa; tel. 050-3152870; fax 050-3152839; e-mail direttore@ilc.cnr.it; internet www.ilc.cnr.it; f. 2001; Dir Dott.ssa NICOLETTA ZAMORANI CALZOLARI.

Istituto Opera del Vocabolario Italiano (The Italian Dictionary): Via di Castello 46, 50141 Florence; tel. 055-452841; fax 055-4250678; e-mail beltrami@ovi.cnr.it; internet www.ovi.cnr.it; f. 2001; Dir Prof. PIETRO BELTRAMI.

Istituto di Ricerche sulle Attività Terziarie (Institute for Service Industry Research): Via Michelangelo Schipa 115, 80122 Naples; tel. 081-2470911; fax 081-2470933; e-mail a.morvillo@irat.cnr.it; internet www.irat.cnr.it; f. 2001; Dir Dott. ALFONSO MORVILLO.

Istituto di Ricerca sull'Impresa e lo Sviluppo (Institute of Research on Business Firms and Their Development): Via Real Collegio 30, 10024 Moncalieri; tel. 011-6824911; fax 011-6824966; e-mail s.rolfo@ceris.cnr.it; internet www.ceris.cnr.it; f. 2001; Dir Dott. SECONDO ROLFO.

Istituto di Ricerche sulla Popolazione e le Politiche Sociali (Institute for Research on Population and Social Policies): Via Nizza 128, 00198 Rome; tel. 06-49932805; fax 06-85834506; e-mail e.pugliese@irpps.cnr.it; internet www.irpps.cnr.it; f. 2001; Dir Prof. ENRICO PUGLIESE.

Istituto di Ricerca sui Sistemi Giudiziari (Institute for Research on Judicial Systems): Via Zamboni 26, 40126 Bologna; tel. 051-237044; fax 051-260250; e-mail direttore@irsig.cnr.it; internet www.irsig.cnr.it; f. 2002; Dir Prof. GIUSEPPE DI FEDERICO.

Istituto di Storia dell'Europa Mediterranea (Institute of Mediterranean European History): Via G. B. Tuveri 128, 09129 Cagliari; tel. 070-40367; fax 070-498118; e-mail casula@isem.cnr.it; internet www.isem.cnr.it; f. 2001; Dir Prof. FRANCESCO CESARE CASULA.

Istituto per la Storia del Pensiero Filosofico e Scientifico Moderno (Institute for the History of Philosophical and Scientific Thought in the Modern Age): Via Porta di Massa 1, 80133 Naples; tel. 081-2535580; fax 081-2535515; e-mail enrico.rambaldi@unimi.it; internet www.ispf.cnr.it; f. 2001; Dir Prof. ENRICO ISACCO RAMBALDI FELDMANN.

Istituto di Studi sulle Civiltà dell'Egeo e del Vicino Oriente (Institute for Aegean and Near Eastern Studies): Via Giano della Bella 18, 00162 Rome; tel. 06-4416131; fax 06-44237724; e-mail direzione@icevo.cnr.it; internet www.icevo.cnr.it; f. 2001; Dir Prof. MIROSLAVO SALVINI.

Istituto di Studi sulle Civiltà Italiche e del Mediterraneo Antico (Institute for the Study of the Italic and Ancient Mediterranean Civilizations): Viale di Villa Massimo 29, 00161 Rome; tel. 06-85301934; fax 06-44239379; e-mail etruschi@iaei.rm.cnr.it; internet soi.cnr.it/iscima; f. 2001; Dir Prof. FRANCESCO RONCALLI DI MONTORIO.

Istituto di Studi Giuridici Internazionali (Institute for International Legal Studies): Via dei Taurini 19, 00185 Rome; tel. 06-49937660; fax 06-44340025; e-mail sergio.marchisio@isgi.cnr.it; internet www.isgi.cnr.it; f. 1986, present name 2001; research in international law; the international protection of human rights; international environmental law; library of 2,000 vols; Dir Prof. SERGIO MARCHISIO.

Istituto di Studi sui Sistemi Regionali Federali e sulle Autonomie 'Massimo Severo Giannini' (Institute for Regional and Federal Studies): Via dei Taurini 19, 00185 Rome; tel. 06-49937740; fax 06-490704; e-mail dir.issirfa@issirfa.cnr.it; internet www.issirfa.cnr.it; f. 2001; Dir Prof. ANTONIO D'ATENA.

Istituto di Studi sulle Società del Mediterraneo (Institute of Studies on Mediterranean Societies): Via Pietro Castellino 111, 80131 Naples; tel. 081-6134086; fax 081-5799467; e-mail malanima@issm.cnr.it; internet www.issm.cnr.it; f. 2001; Dir Prof. PAOLO MALANIMA.

Istituto per le Tecnologie Applicate ai Beni Culturali (Institute for Technologies Applied to Cultural Heritage): Via Salaria Km. 29.3, C.P. 10, 00016 Monterotondo Stazione; tel. 06-90625274; fax 06-90672373; e-mail direttore@itabc.cnr.it; internet www.itabc.cnr.it; f. 2001; Dir Dott. SALVATORE GARRAFFO.

Istituto di Teoria e Tecniche dell'Informazione Giuridica (Institute of Legal Information Theory and Technology): Via Panciatichi 56/16, 50127 Florence; tel. 055-43995; fax 055-4221637; e-mail nicola.palazzolo@ittig.cnr.it; internet www.ittig.cnr.it; f. 2001; Dir Prof. NICOLA PALAZZOLO.

Life Sciences:

Istituto di Biochimica delle Proteine (Institute of Protein Biochemistry): Via Guglielmo Marconi 10, 80125 Naples; tel. 081-6132273; fax 081-6132277; e-mail m.rossi@ibp.cnr.it; internet www.ibp.cnr.it; f. 2001; Dir Prof. MOSÈ ROSSI.

Istituto di Biofisica (Institute of Biophysics): Via De Marini 6, Torre di Francia, 16149 Genoa; tel. 010-6475592; fax 010-6475500; e-mail direttore@pi.ibf.cnr.it; internet www.ibf.cnr.it; f. 2001; Dir Dott. FRANCO CONTI.

Istituto di Bioimmagini e Fisiologia Molecolare (Institute of Molecular Bioimaging and Physiology): Via Fratelli Cervi 93, 20090 Segrate; tel. 02-21717514; fax 02-21717558; e-mail ferruccio.fazio@hsr.it; internet www.ibfm.cnr.it; f. 2001; Dir Prof. FERRUCCIO FAZIO.

Istituto di Biologia Agro-ambientale e Forestale (Institute of Agro-environmental and Forest Biology): Via Guglielmo Marconi 2, 05010 Porano; tel. 0763-374911; fax 0763-374980; e-mail giuseppe.scarascia@ibaf.cnr.it; internet www.ibaf.cnr.it; f. 2001; Dir Prof. GIUSEPPE SCARASCIA MUGNOZZA.

Istituto di Biologia e Biotecnologia Agraria (Institute of Agricultural Biology and Biotechnology): Via Edoardo Bassini 15, 20133 Milan; tel. 02-23699403; fax 02-23699411; e-mail direttore@ibba.cnr.it; internet www.ibba.cnr.it; f. 2001; Dir Dott. ALCIDE BERTANI.

Istituto di Biologia Cellulare (Institute of Cell Biology): Via E. Ramarini 32, 00016 Monterotondo Scalo; tel. 06-90091207; fax 06-90091260; e-mail gtocchini@ibc.cnr.it; f. 2001; Dir Prof. GLAUCO TOCCHINI-VALENTINI.

Istituto di Biomedicina e di Immunologia Molecolare 'Alberto Monroy' (Institute of Biomedicine and Molecular Immunology): Via Ugo La Malfa 153, 90146 Palermo; tel. 091-6809134; fax 091-6809122; e-mail bonsignore@ibim.cnr.it; internet www.ibim.cnr.it; f. 2001; Dir Prof. GIOVANNI BONSIGNORE.

Istituto di Biometeorologia (Institute for Biometeorology): Via Giovanni Caproni 8, 50145 Florence; tel. 055-301421; fax 055-308910; e-mail maracchi@ibimet.cnr.it; internet www.ibimet.cnr.it; f. 2000; Dir Prof. GIAMPIERO MARACCHI.

Istituto di Biologia e Patologia Molecolari (Institute of Molecular Biology and Pathology): Piazzale Aldo Moro 5, 00185 Rome; tel. 06-4940543; fax 06-4440062; e-mail emilia.chiancone@uniroma1.it; internet www.ibpm.cnr.it; f. 2001; Dir Prof.ssa EMILIA CHIANCONE.

Istituto di Biomembrane e Bioenergetica (Institute of Biomembrane and Bioenergetics): Via Giovanni Amendola 165/A, 70126 Bari; tel. 080-5443389; fax 080-5443317; e-mail papabchm@cimedoc.uniba.it; f. 2001; Dir Prof. SERGIO PAPA.

Istituto di Biostrutture e Bioimmagini (Institute of Biostructure and Bioimaging): Via Mezzocannone 16, 80134 Naples; tel. 081-2536651; fax 0825-34560; e-mail pedone@chemistry.unina.it; internet www.ibb.cnr.it; f. 2001; Dir Prof. CARLO PEDONE.

Istituto di Chimica Biomolecolare (Institute of Biomolecular Chemistry): Via Campi Flegrei 34, 80078 Pozzuoli; tel. 081-8675024; fax 081-8041770; e-mail gcimino@icmib.na.cnr.it; internet www.icmib.na.cnr.it; f. 2001; Dir Dott. GUIDO CIMINO.

Istituto di Chimica del Riconoscimento Molecolare (Institute of Chemistry of Molecular Recognition): Via Mario Bianco 9, 20131 Milan; tel. 02-28500024; fax 02-28901239; e-mail direttore@icrm.cnr.it; internet www.icrm.cnr.it; f. 2001; Dir Dott. GIACOMO CARREA.

Istituto per l'Endocrinologia e l'Oncologia 'Gaetano Salvatore' (Institute for Experimental Endocrinology and Oncology): Via Sergio Pansini 5, 80131 Naples; tel. 081-7463036; fax 081-7701016; e-mail consigli@ieos.cnr.it; internet ieos.cnr.it; f. 2001; Dir Prof. EDUARDO CONSIGLIO.

Istituto di Fisiologia Clinica (Institute of Clinical Physiology): Via Giuseppe Moruzzi 1, 56124 Pisa; tel. 050-3152216; fax 050-3152166; e-mail ldonato@ifc.cnr.it; internet www.ifc.cnr.it; f. 2001; Dir Prof. LUIGI DONATO.

Istituto di Genetica e Biofisica 'Adriano Buzzati Traverso' (Institute of Genetics and Biophysics): Via Pietro Castellino 111, 80131 Naples; tel. 081-6132401; fax 081-6132706; e-mail polito@igb.cnr.it; internet www.igb.cnr.it; f. 2000; Dir Prof. CATELLO POLITO.

Istituto di Genetica Molecolare (Institute of Molecular Genetics): Via Abbiategrasso 207, 27100 Pavia; tel. 0382-5461; fax 0382-422286; e-mail riva@igbe.pv.cnr.it; internet www.igm.cnr.it; f. 2000; Dir Dott. SILVANO RIVA.

Istituto di Genetica delle Popolazioni (Institute of Population Genetics): Casella Postale, 07040 Santa Maria la Palma; tel. 079-946706; fax 079-946714; e-mail pirastu@igm.ss.cnr.it; f. 2001; Dir Dott. MARIO PIRASTU.

Istituto di Genetica Vegetale (Institute of Plant Genetics): Via Giovanni Amendola 165/A, 70126 Bari; tel. 080-5583400; fax 080-5587566; e-mail direttore.igv@igv.cnr.it; internet www.igv.cnr.it; f. 2001; Dir Prof. LUIGI MONTI.

Istituto di Neurobiologia e Medicina Molecolare (Institute of Neurobiology and Molecular Medicine): Viale Marx 15, 00137

Rome; tel. 06-86090246; fax 06-86090370; e-mail calissano@in.rm.cnr.it; f. 2000; Dir Prof. PIETRO CALISSANO.

Istituto di Neurogenetica e Neurofarmacologia (Institute of Neurogenetics and Neuropharmacology): Via Boccaccio 8, Località Su Planu, 09047 Selargius; tel. 070-540342; fax 070-540722; e-mail c.flore@inn.cnr.it; f. 2001; Dir Prof. ANTONIO CAO.

Istituto di Neuroscienze (Neuroscience Institute): Via Giuseppe Moruzzi 1, 56124 Pisa; tel. 050-3153211; fax 050-3153220; e-mail maffei@in.cnr.it; internet www.in.cnr.it; f. 2001; Dir Prof. LAMBERTO MAFFEI.

Istituto per la Protezione delle Piante (Plant Protection Institute): Via Madonna del Piano (edificio E), 50019 Sesto Fiorentino; tel. 055-5225580; fax 055-5225666; e-mail p.raddi@ipp.cnr.it; internet www.ipp.cnr.it; f. 2001; Dir Dott. PAOLO RADDI.

Istituto di Scienza dell'Alimentazione (Institute of Food Science): Via Roma 52 a/c, 83100 Avellino; tel. 0825-299111; fax 0825-781585; e-mail leone@isa.cnr.it; internet www.isa.cnr.it; f. 2001; Dir Prof. ANTONIO MALORNI.

Istituto di Scienze Neurologiche (Institute of Neurological Sciences): Località Burga, Piano Lago, 87050 Mangone; tel. 0984-98011; fax 0984-969306; e-mail a.quattrone@isn.cnr.it; internet www.isn.cnr.it; f. 2001; Dir Prof. ALDO QUATTRONE.

Istituto di Scienze delle Produzioni Alimentari (Institute of Food Production Sciences): Via Amendola 122/O, 70126 Bari; tel. 080-5929333; fax 080-5929373; e-mail angelo.visconti@ispa.cnr.it; internet www.ispa.cnr.it; f. 2001; Dir Dott. ANGELO VISCONTI.

Istituto di Scienze e Tecnologie della Cognizione (Institute of Cognitive Sciences and Technologies): Viale Carlo Marx 15, 00137 Rome; tel. 06-86090235; fax 06-824737; e-mail c.castelfranchi@istc.cnr.it; internet www.istc.cnr.it; f. 2001; Dir Prof. CRISTIANO CASTELFRANCHI.

Istituto per i Sistemi Agricoli e Forestali del Mediterraneo (Institute for Mediterranean Agriculture and Forest Systems): Via Patacca 85, 80056 Ercolano; tel. 081-7717325; fax 081-7718045; e-mail m.menenti@ispaim.na.cnr.it; internet www.isafom.cnr.it; f. 2001; Dir Prof. MASSIMO MENENTI.

Istituto per il Sistema Produzione Animale in Ambiente Mediterraneo (Institute for Animal Production in the Mediterranean Environment): Via Argine 1085, 80147 Ponticelli; tel. 081-5966006; fax 081-5965291; e-mail lino@iabbam.na.cnr.it; internet www.iabbam.na.cnr.it; f. 2001; Dir Dott. LINO FERRARA.

Istituto di Tecnologie Biomediche (Institute of Biomedical Technologies): Via Fratelli Cervi 93, 20090 Segrate; tel. 02-26422702; fax 02-26422770; e-mail director@itb.cnr.it; internet www.itb.cnr.it; f. 2001; Dir Prof. ALBERTO ALBERTINI.

Istituto per i Trapianti d'Organo e Immunocitologia (Organ Tranplantation and Immunology Institute): Piazzale Collemaggio, 67100 L'Aquila; tel. 0862-27129; fax 0862-410758; e-mail d.adorno@itoi.cnr.it; internet www.itoi.cnr.it; f. 2001; Dir Prof. DOMENICO ADORNO.

Istituto di Virologia Vegetale (Institute of Plant Virology): Strada delle Cacce 73, 10135 Turin; tel. 011-39771; fax 011-343809; e-mail m.conti@ivv.cnr.it; internet www.ivv.cnr.it; f. 2001; Dir Prof. MAURIZIO CONTI.

Technological, Engineering and Information Sciences:

Istituto di Analisi dei Sistemi ed Informatica 'Antonio Ruberti' (Institute for Systems Analysis and Computer Science): Viale Manzoni 30, 00185 Rome; tel. 06-77161; fax 06-7716461; e-mail rinaldi@iasi.cnr.it; internet www.iasi.cnr.it; f. 2001; Dir Dott. GIOVANNI RINALDI.

Istituto di Calcolo e Reti ad Alte Prestazioni (Institute for High-performance Computing and Networking): Via Pietro Bucci, Cubo 41C, 87030 Rende; tel. 0984-831720; fax 0984-839054; e-mail sacca@icar.cnr.it; internet www.icar.cnr.it; f. 2001; Dir Prof. DOMENICO SACCÀ.

Istituto di Elettronica e di Ingegneria dell'Informazione e delle Telecomunicazioni (Institute of Electronics, Computer and Telecommunications Engineering): Corso Duca degli Abruzzi 24, 10129 Turin; tel. 011-5645400; fax 011-5645429; e-mail ajmone@polito.it; internet www.ieiit.cnr.it; f. 2001; Dir Prof. MARCO AJMONE MARSAN.

Istituto Gas Ionizzati (Ionized Gas Institute): Corso Stati Uniti 4, 35127 Padua; tel. 049-829500; fax 049-8700718; e-mail giorgio.rostagni@igi.cnr.it; internet www.igi.cnr.it; f. 2001; Dir Prof. GIORGIO ROSTAGNI.

Istituto di Informatica e Telematica (Institute for Informatics and Telematics): Via Giuseppe Moruzzi 1, 56124 Pisa; tel. 050-3152112; fax 050-3152593; e-mail franco.denoth@iit.cnr.it; internet www.iit.cnr.it; f. 2001; Dir Prof. FRANCO DENOTH.

Istituto di Ingegneria Biomedica (Institute of Biomedical Engineering): Corso Stati Uniti 4, 35127 Padua; tel. 049-829570; fax 049-8295763; e-mail isib.cnr@polimi.it; internet www.isib.cnr.it; f. 2001; Dir Dott. FERDINANDO GRANDORI.

Istituto per le Macchine Agricole e Movimento Terra (Institute for Agricultural and Earth-moving Machines): Via Canal Bianco 28, 44044 Cassana; tel. 0532-735611; fax 0532-735666; e-mail gl.zarotti@imamoter.cnr.it; internet www.imamoter.cnr.it; f. 2001; Dir Ing. GIAN LUCA ZAROTTI.

Istituto di Metrologia 'Gustavo Colonnetti' (Institute of Metrology): Strada delle Cacce 73, 10135 Turin; tel. 011-3977; fax 011-346761; e-mail a.sacconi@imgc.cnr.it; internet www.imgc.cnr.it; f. 2001; Dir Dott. ATTILIO SACCONI.

Istituto Motori (Motors Institute): Via Marconi 8, 80125 Naples; tel. 081-7177111; fax 081-2396097; e-mail a.dilorenzo@im.cnr.it; internet www.im.cnr.it; f. 2001; Dir Dott. ALDO DI LORENZO.

Istituto Nazionale di Ottica Applicata (INOA) (National Institute of Applied Optics): Largo Enrico Fermi 6, 50125 Florence; tel. 055-23081; fax 055-2337755; e-mail direttore@ino.it; internet www.ino.it; f. 1927; quantum, instrumental and physiological optics; library of 7,000 vols; Pres. Prof. FABIO PISTELLA; Gen. Dir. Dr CARLO CASTELLINI.

Istituto di Ricerche sulla Combustione (Institute for Research on Combustion): Piazzale Vincenzo Tecchio 80, 80125 Naples; tel. 081-7682245; fax 081-5936936; e-mail grusso@irc.na.cnr.it; internet www.irc.na.cnr.it; f. 2001; Dir Prof. GENNARO RUSSO.

Istituto per il Rilevamento Elettromagnetico dell'Ambiente (Institute for Electromagnetic Sensing of the Environment): Via Diocleziano 328, 80124 Naples; tel. 081-5707999; fax 081-5705734; e-mail bucci.om@irea.cnr.it; internet www.irea.cnr.it; f. 2001; Dir Prof. OVIDIO MARIO BUCCI.

Istituto di Scienza e Tecnologia dei Materiali Ceramici (Institute of Ceramics Science and Technology): Via Granarolo 64, 48018 Faenza; tel. 0546-699711; fax 0546-699719; e-mail babini@istec.cnr.it; internet www.istec.cnr.it; f. 2001; Dir Dott. GIAN NICOLA BABINI.

Istituto di Tecnologie Avanzate per l'Energia 'Nicola Giordano' (Institute for Advanced Energy Technologies): Via Salita S. Lucia sopra Contesse 5, 98126 Messina; tel. 090-6241; fax 090-624247; e-mail cacciola@itae.cnr.it; internet www.itae.cnr.it; f. 2000; Dir Dott. Ing. GAETANO CACCIOLA.

Istituto per le Tecnologie della Costruzione (Construction Technologies Institute): Via Lombardia 49, 20098 San Giuliano Milanese; tel. 02-98061; fax 02-98280088; e-mail valter.esposti@itc.cnr.it; internet www.itc.cnr.it; f. 2001; Dir Ing. VALTER ESPOSTI.

Istituto per le Tecnologie Didattiche (Institute for Educational Technology): Via De Marini 6, Torre di Francia, 16149 Genoa; tel. 010-64751; fax 010-6475300; e-mail olimpo@itd.cnr.it; internet www.itd.cnr.it; f. 2001; Dir Dott. GIORGIO OLIMPO.

Istituto di Scienza e Tecnologie dell'Informazione 'Alessandro Faedo' (Institute of Information Science and Technology): Via Giuseppe Moruzzi 1, 56124 Pisa; tel. 050-3152878; fax 050-3152811; e-mail direttore@isti.cnr.it; internet www.isti.cnr.it; f. 2000; Dir Prof. PIERO MAESTRINI.

Istituto di Studi sui Sistemi Intelligenti per l'Automazione (Institute of Intelligent Systems for Automation): Via Giovanni Amendola 122/D-I, 70126 Bari; tel. 080-5929420; fax 080-5929460; e-mail distante@ba.issia.cnr.it; internet www.issia.cnr.it; f. 2001; Dir Dott. ARCANGELO DISTANTE.

Istituto di Tecnologie Industriali e Automazione (Institute of Industrial Technologies and Automation): Viale Lombardia 20A, 20131 Milan; tel. 02-23699995; fax 02-23699941; e-mail f.jovane@itia.cnr.it; internet www.itia.cnr.it; f. 2000; Dir Prof. FRANCESCO JOVANE.

Istituto per la Valorizzazione del Legno e delle Specie Arboree (Tree and Timber Institute): Via Madonna del Piano snc, 50019 Sesto Fiorentino; tel. 055-52251; fax 055-5225507; e-mail ario.ceccotti@ivalsa.cnr.it; internet www.ivalsa.cnr.it; f. 2002; Dir Prof. ARIO CECCOTTI.

AGRICULTURE, FISHERIES AND VETERINARY SCIENCE

Istituto Sperimentale per la Cerealicoltura (Experimental Institute for Cereal Crops): Via Cassia 176, 00191 Rome; tel. 06-3295705; fax 06-36306022; e-mail cerealicoltura@cerealicoltura.it; internet www.cerealicoltura.it; f. 1919; cereal crops improvement; cereal genetics; library of 10,000 vols, 318 current periodicals; Dir Dott. NATALE DI FONZO; publs *Journal of Genetics and Breeding* (4 a year), *Maydica* (maize and allied species, 4 a year).

Istituto Sperimentale per la Zoologia Agraria (Experimental Institute of Agricultural Zoology): Via Lanciola 12A, Cascine del Riccio, 50125 Florence; tel. 055-24921; fax 055-209177; e-mail isza@isza.it; internet www.isza.it; f. 1875; library of 55,000 vols; Dir Dott. MARCO VITTORIO COVASSI; publ. *Redia* (annually).

Ufficio Centrale di Ecologia Agraria (Meteorological and Ecological Centre): Via del Caravita 7A, 00186 Rome; tel. 06-695311; fax 06-69531215; e-mail ucea@ucea.it; internet www.ucea.it; f. 1876; controls 100 observatories; 18 mems; Dir Dott. DOMENICO VENTO; publs *Bollettino Agrometeorologico Nazionale* (monthly), *Bollettino Avversità Meteo*, *Osservazioni Meteo Collegio Romano* (electronic, annually), *Indici Agroclimatici: Velocità e direzione del vento*.

ECONOMICS, LAW AND POLITICS

Centro di Ricerche Economiche e Sociali (CERES) (Centre for Economic and Social Research): Via Po 102, 00198 Rome; tel. 06-8541016; fax 06-85355360; e-mail info@ceres-italia.org; internet www.ceres-italia.org; f. 1970 as an autonomous body promoted by a trade union (CISL); aims to improve economic and social conditions of workers; fosters contact and collaboration between national and international centres and institutes interested in problems of economic and social development; Pres. Prof. LUIGI FREY; Sec.-Gen. Prof. RENATA LIVRAGHI; publs *Quaderni di Economia del Lavoro* (3 a year), *Benessere degli Anziani* (monthly).

Fondazione Giangiacomo Feltrinelli: Via Romagnosi 3, 20121 Milan; tel. 02-874175; fax 02-86461855; e-mail segretaria@fondazionefeltrinelli.it; internet www.feltrinelli.it/fondazione/index.htm; f. 1949; history of international socialism, communism and the labour movement; economic and social history; library of 400,000 vols, 20,000 periodicals; Pres. CARLO FELTRINELLI; publ. *Annali*.

Istituto Affari Internazionali (International Affairs Institute): Via Angelo Brunetti 9, 00186 Rome; tel. 06-3224360; fax 06-3224363; e-mail iai@iai.it; internet www.iai.it; f. 1965; library of 17,000 vols; Pres. STEFANO SILVESTRI; Dir GIANNI BONVICINI; publs *The International Spectator* (4 a year, in English), *L'Italia e la Politica Internazionale* (annually), *FP Global* (published in partnership with another company, 6 a year).

Istituto di Studi Europei 'Alcide De Gasperi': Via Poli 29, 00187 Rome; tel. 06-6784262; fax 06-6794101; e-mail kipsc@tin.it; internet www.ise-ies.org; f. 1953; promotes research and organizes meetings on legal, economic, political and social issues in the field of European co-operation and integration, and within a broader pan-European context; the Postgraduate School of European Studies organizes courses of varying duration and specialized seminars; courses are also held on the specialized English and French terminology of European int. orgs; library of 5,000 vols; Pres. Prof. Dott. GIUSEPPE SCHIAVONE; Admin Officer CLAUDIA BATTISTI.

Istituto Italiano di Studi Legislativi (Italian Institute for Legislation Studies): Via del Corso 267, 00186 Rome; tel. 06-6789488; fax 06-69941306; f. 1925 to promote the scientific and technical studies of legislation; Pres. Prof. GIAN PIERO ORSELLO; Gen. Sec. Dssa FRANCA CIPRIGNO; publs *Yearbook of Comparative Law and Legislative Studies*, *L'Italia e l'Europa*.

Istituto Nazionale di Statistica (National Institute of Statistics): Via Cesare Balbo 16, 00184 Rome; tel. 06-46731; fax 06-46733107; e-mail redazioneweb@istat.it; internet www.istat.it; f. 1926; library of 500,000 vols, 2,700 current periodicals; Pres. LUIGI BIGGERI; Dir-Gen. P. GARONNA; publs *Annuario statistico italiano*, *Bollettino mensile di statistica* (monthly).

Istituto per gli Studi di Politica Internazionale (Institute for the Study of International Politics): Palazzo Clerici, Via Clerici 5, 20121 Milan; tel. 02-8633131; fax 02-8692055; e-mail ispi.segreteria@ispionline.it; internet www.ispionline.it; f. 1933; public and private funding; aims to provide information and analysis of the great global issues of today, to identify opportunities for more effective Italian participation in int. affairs, to identify the domestic factors which constrain or enhance Italy's int. role; research in int. politics and economics, strategic problems and the history of foreign relations, European integration, int. economic co-operation, consolidation of peace and security among nations, strengthening of political freedoms and democratic instns; library of 100,000 vols, historical archive, press archive; postgraduate training courses; organizes conferences, lectures, etc.; Pres. BORIS BIANCHERI; Dir PAOLO MAGRI; publs *ISPI Relazioni Internazionali* (electronic, 3 a year), *L'Italia e la Politica Internazionale* (annual).

Istituto per le Relazioni tra l'Italia e i Paesi dell'Africa, America Latina e Medio Oriente (IPALMO) (Institute for relations between Italy and the countries of Africa, Latin America and the Middle East): Via degli Scipioni 147, 00192 Rome; tel. 06-32699701; fax 06-32699750; e-mail ipalmo@ipalmo.com; internet www.ipalmo.com; f. 1971 to promote and develop political, economic and cultural relations between countries in these regions; research and promotion of information at all levels of Italian society; to organize conferences, seminars, etc.; library of 20,000 vols, 500 periodicals; Pres. GIANNI DE MICHELIS; Scientific Dir UMBERTO TRIULZI; publ. *Politica Internazionale* (6 a year).

UNICEF Innocenti Research Centre: Piazza SS. Annunziata 12, 50122 Florence; tel. 055-20330; fax 055-244817; e-mail florence@unicef.org; internet www.unicef-icdc.org; f. 1988; conducts research vital to the work of the United Nations Children's Fund (UNICEF), especially in the field of children's rights; Dir MARTA SANTOS PAIS.

EDUCATION

Istituto per Ricerche ed Attività Educative (Institute for Educational Research and Activity): Riviera di Chiaia 264, 80121 Naples; tel. 081-2457074; e-mail ipe@ipeistituto.it; internet www.ipeistituto.it; f. 1979; aims to give young people access to education, culture and jobs; offers grants, promotes study and research in education; 32 mems; library of 6,500 vols; Pres. Prof. RAFFAELE CALABRÓ; Sec.-Gen. Dott. LORENZO BURDO; publ. *IPEnews* (monthly).

FINE AND PERFORMING ARTS

Istituto Centrale per il Restauro (Central Institute for the Restoration of Works of Art): Piazza S. Francesco di Paola 9, 00184 Rome; tel. 06-488961; fax 06-4815704; e-mail icr@arti.beniculturali.it; internet www.icr.arti.beniculturali.it; f. 1939; research on the influence of environment on cultural property and on prevention of deterioration; studies formulation of rules on theory of conservation and restoration and on techniques to be used; advises institutes of the Min. of Culture, and regional organizations; in-service teaching and refresher courses; carries out restoration of complex works or those of interest in research and teaching; library of 43,000 vols, 800 periodicals; archive of 51,600 negatives, 4,664 X-rays, 31,900 slides on restoration; Dir CATERINA BON VALSASSINA; publs *DIMOS* (series), preprints of International Conferences on non-destructive testing, micro-analytical methods and environment evaluation for study and conservation of works of art (quinquennial), *Bollettino ICR* (2 a year), *News.Icr* (electronic, Italian and English versions, 6 a year).

Istituto Internazionale per la Ricerca Teatrale/International Institute for Theatre Research: Casa di Goldoni, S. Tomà 2794, 30124 Venice; tel. 041-714883; f. 1953 by the International Federation for Theatre Research; library of 30,000 vols; special collections: critical works, Italian and foreign dramatic works, Venetian musical theatre scores, periodicals, editions of the playwright Carlo Goldoni, Maddelena (miscellany), Ortolani miscellany, Vendramin Archive; Pres. MARIA TERESA MURARO; Gen. Sec. Doc. MARIA IDA BIGGI.

Villa I Tatti/Harvard University Center for Italian Renaissance Studies: Via di Vincigliata 26, 50135 Florence; tel. 055-603251; fax 055-603383; e-mail info@itatti.it; internet www.itatti.it; f. 1961 for the post-doctoral study of the Italian Renaissance: history of art, political, economic and social history, history of philosophy and religion, history of literature, music and science; the Villa is the former residence of Bernard Berenson, who left his library and art collection to Harvard; library of 150,000 vols, 500 current periodicals, 300,000 photographs; Dir JOSEPH CONNORS; publs *I Tatti Studies* (every 2 years), *Newsletter* (annually).

HISTORY, GEOGRAPHY AND ARCHAEOLOGY

Academia Belgica (Belgian Academy in Rome): Via Omero 8, 00197 Rome; tel. 06-3201889; fax 06-3208361; e-mail direttore@academiabelgica.it; internet www.academiabelgica.it; f. 1939; research centre and residence; library of 96,000 vols; Dir Prof. WALTER GEERTS; publ. *Bulletin de l'Institut Historique Belge de Rome*.

Accademia di Danimarca (Danish Institute of Science and Art in Rome): Via Omero 18, 00197 Rome; tel. 06-3265931; fax 06-3222717; e-mail accademia@dkinst-rom.org; internet www.dkinst-rom.dk; f. 1956; archaeology, philology, art and architecture, history of art, history of music, literature; library of 25,000 vols; Dir Dr ERIK BACH (acting); Sec. and Librarian Dr MARIA ADELAIDE ZOCCHI; publ. *Analecta Romana Instituti Danici*.

Accademia Tedesca (German Academy in Rome): Villa Massimo, Largo di Villa Massimo 1–2, 00161 Rome; tel. 06-4425931; fax 06-44259355; e-mail villamassimo.roma@katamail.com; Dir Dr JOACHIM BLÜHER.

American Academy in Rome: Via Angelo Masina 5, 00153 Rome; tel. 06-58461; fax 06-5810788; f. 1894; fellowships for independent study and advanced research in fine arts, classical studies, art history, Italian studies and archaeology; library of 135,000 vols; Pres. ADELE CHATFIELD-TAYLOR; Dir CARMELA VIRCILLO FRANKLIN; Librarian CHRISTINA HUEMER; publ. *Memoirs* (annually).

British Institute of Florence: Piazza Strozzi 2, 50123 Florence; tel. 055-26778200; fax 055-26778222; e-mail info@britishinstitute.it; internet www.britishinstitute.it; f. 1917; aims to develop cultural understanding between the UK and Italy through the teaching of their respective languages and cultures; offers a range of Italian language and History of Art courses, and an extensive programme of English language courses for the host population; a number of special programmes are run in conjunction with British and American univs; library of 50,000 vols; 1,700 students; Dir VANESSA HALL-SMITH.

British School at Rome: Via Gramsci 61, 00197 Rome; tel. 06-3264939; fax 06-3221201; e-mail info@bsrome.it; internet www.bsr.ac.uk; f. 1901, inc. by Royal Charter 1912; postgraduate residential centre for higher research in the humanities and for the practice of the fine arts and architecture; 40 residents; library of 60,000 vols, 600 current periodicals; Dir Prof. A. WALLACE-HADRILL; Librarian VALERIE SCOTT; publ. *Papers of the British School at Rome* (annual).

Centro Camuno di Studi Preistorici (Centre for Prehistoric Studies): Via Marconi 7, 25044 Capo di Ponte Valcamonica; tel. 0364-42091; fax 0364-42572; e-mail info@ccsp.it; internet www.ccsp.it; f. 1964; research centre specializing in prehistoric rock art; archaeological research, early religions, anthropology and ethnology; seminars, intl symposia, individual tutoring in prehistoric and tribal art; co-ordinator of World Archives of Rock Art; provides advisers and consultants on conservation, exhibition and evaluation of prehistoric and tribal art; park and museum planning; field research in Europe, Asia and Australia; Valcamonica summer school; library of 38,000 vols, 300,000 photographs; Dir Prof. EMMANUEL ANATI; publs *Archivi*, *BC Notizie:CCSP Newsletter*, *BCSP: The World Journal of Prehistoric and Tribal Art*.

Centro Italiano di Studi sul Basso Medioevo Accademia Tudertina: Via Ciuffelli 31, 06059 Todi; tel. 075-8942521; all aspects of late medieval civilization; Pres. Prof. TULLIO GREGORY; Dir Prof. ENRICO MENESTÒ.

Fondazione Centro Italiano di Studi sull'Alto Medioevo (Central Italian Foundation for Studies on Early Medieval Civilization): Palazzo Ancaiani, Piazza della Libertà 12, 06049 Spoleto; tel. 0743-225630; fax 0743-49902; e-mail cisam@cisam.org; internet www.cisam.org; f. 1951; promotes research, conferences and scientific publications on all aspects of early medieval civilization; library of 3,000 vols; Pres. Prof. ENRICO MENESTÒ; publ. *Studi Medievali III Serie* (4 a year).

Deutsches Archäologisches Institut Rom (German Archaeological Institute Rome): Via Sardegna 79, 00187 Rome; tel. 06-4888141; fax 06-4884973; e-mail sekretariat@rom.dainst.org; internet www.dainst.org; f. 1829; library of 220,000 vols, 1,200 current periodicals; Dirs Prof. Dr HENNER VON HESBERG, Prof. Dr KLAUS S. FREYBERGER; Library Dir Dr THOMAS FRÖHLICH; publs *Römische Mitteilungen*, *Series*, *Sonderschriften des Deutschen Archäologischen Instituts Rom*.

Ecole Française de Rome/Scuola Francese di Roma (French School in Rome): Piazza Farnese 67, 00186 Rome; tel. 06-686011; fax 06-6874834; f. 1873; French school of archaeology and history, specializing in Rome and medieval and modern Italy; library of 180,000 vols, 1,650 periodicals and 32,000 off-prints; Dir MICHEL GRAS; Dirs of Studies JEAN-FRANÇOIS CHAUVARD, MARILYN NICOUD, YANN RIVIÈRE; Librarian YANNICK NEXON; publ. *Mélanges de l'Ecole Française de Rome* (series *Antiquité, Moyen Age, Italie et Méditerranée*).

Escuela Española de Historia y Arqueología, CSIC Roma (Spanish School of History and Archaeology in Rome): Via di Torre Argentina 18-3°, 00186 Rome; tel. 06-6810001; fax 06-68309047; e-mail escuela@csic.it; internet www.csic.it; f. 1910; history of Italian-Spanish interaction; organizes conferences, seminars; research programmes and support for Spanish historians and archaeologists in Italy; 15 mems; library of 20,000 vols; special collections: Monumenta Albornotiana, documents on Spanish music in Italy; Dir Prof. RICARDO OLMOS ROMERA.

Institutum Romanum Finlandiae: Passeggiata del Gianicolo 10, 00165 Rome; tel. 06-68801674; fax 06-68802349; e-mail orma@irfrome.org; internet www.irfrome.org; f. 1954; Classical and Italian studies; library of 17,000 vols; Dir Prof. MIKA KAJAVA; publ. *Acta Instituti Romani Finlandiae*.

Istituto di Norvegia in Roma di Archeologia e Storia dell'Arte (Norwegian Institute of Archaeology and History of Art in Rome): Viale Trenta Aprile 33, 00153 Rome; tel. 06-58391007; fax 06-5880604; e-mail info@roma.uio.no; internet www.hf.uio.no/roma/; f. 1959; library of 23,000 vols; Dir SIRI SANDE; publ. *Acta ad Archaeologiam et Artium Historiam Pertinentia* (annually).

Istituto Ellenico di Studi Bizantini e Postbizantini di Venezia (Hellenic Institute of Byzantine and Post-Byzantine Studies of Venice): Castello 3412, 30122 Venice; tel. 041-5226581; fax 041-5238248; e-mail info@institutoellenico.org; internet www.institutoellenico.org; f. 1951; library of 25,000 vols, and archives containing 200,000 documents of 16th–19th c. relating to the Greek Orthodox community of Venice; Dir CHRYSSA MALTEZOU; Sec. DEMETRA FARASI; publs *Thesaurismata* (annually), Monograph series.

Istituto Italiano di Studi Germanici (Italian Institute for Germanic Studies): Via Calandrelli 25, 00153 Rome; tel. 06-588811; fax 06-5888139; e-mail chiarini@studigermanici.it; internet www.studigermanici.it; f. 1932; library of 80,000 vols; Dir Prof. PAOLO CHIARINI; publs *Studi Germanici* (3 a year), *Wissenschaftliche Reihen: Testi e Materiali*, *Atti*, *Studi e ricerche*, *Poeti e prosatori tedeschi*, *Strumenti*.

Istituto Italiano per gli Studi Storici (Italian Institute for Historical Studies): Via Benedetto Croce 12, 80134 Naples; tel. 081-5512390; fax 081-5514813; e-mail istituto@iiss.it; internet www.iiss.it; f. 1947; studies and teaching in history, philosophy and the humanities; awards 20 student grants annually and offers scholarships to Italian and non-Italian postgraduates; library of 120,000 vols, 400 current periodicals; Pres. Prof. NATALINO IRTI; Dir Prof. GENNARO SASSO; publs *Annali* (annually), *Collana delle monografie* (2 a year), *Carteggi di Benedetto Croce* (2 a year), *Ristampe Anastatiche* (4 a year), *Testi storici filosofici e letterari* (annually), *Inventari* (annually).

Istituto Nazionale di Studi Romani (National Institute of Roman Studies): Piazza dei Cavalieri di Malta 2, 00153 Rome; tel. 06-5743442; fax 06-5743447; e-mail studiromani@studiromani.it; internet www.studiromani.it; f. 1925; promotes the study of Rome from ancient to modern times in all aspects; 120 mems; library of 26,000 vols, 1,500 periodicals; Pres. Prof. MARIO MAZZA; Dir Dott. FERNANDA ROSCETTI; publs *Studi Romani* (quarterly), *Rassegna d'Informazioni* (monthly).

Istituto Nazionale di Studi sul Rinascimento (National Institute of Renaissance Studies): Palazzo Strozzi, 50123 Florence; tel. 055-287728; fax 055-280563; e-mail sbassi@iris.firenze.it; internet www.insr.it; f. 1938; publishes critical texts and results of research; 10-mem. council; library of 45,000 vols, 500 periodicals, special collection 'Machiavelli-Serristori', art photo library of 78,000 items, 700 micro-films; Pres. Prof. MICHELE CILIBERTO; publ. *Rinascimento* (annually).

Istituto Papirologico 'Girolamo Vitelli' (Papyrological Institute): Borgo degli Albizi 12–14, 50122 Florence; tel. 055-2478969; fax 055-2480722; e-mail simona.russo@unifi.it; f. 1908; study of Greek and Latin papyri; library of 20,000 vols; colln of papyri; Scientific Dir Prof. GUIDO BASTIANINI; publs *Comunicazioni*, *Notiziario di Studi e Ricerche in Corso*, *Papiri Greci e Latini della Società Italiana*, *Studi e Testi di Papirologia*.

Istituto Siciliano di Studi Bizantini e Neoellenici 'B. Lavagnini' (Sicilian Institute for Byzantine and Neo-hellenic Studies): Via Noto 34, 90141 Palermo; tel. 6259541; fax 308996; e-mail istbizantino@issbi.org; f. 1952; 120 mems (60 ordinary, 60 corresp.); library of 10,000 vols; Pres. Prof. VINCENZO ROTOLO; Sec.-Gen. Prof. RENATA LAVAGNINI.

Istituto Storico Austriaco a Roma (Austrian Historical Institute in Rome): Viale Bruno Buozzi 113, 00197 Rome; tel. 06-36082601; fax 06-3224296; e-mail iarom@librs6k.vatlib.it; f. 1881; Dir Prof. Dr RICHARD BOESEL; publs *Römische Historische Mitteilungen* (annually), *Publikationen des Historischen Instituts beim ÖKI in Rom* (irregular).

Istituto Storico Germanico (German Historical Institute): Via Aurelia Antica 391, 00165 Rome; tel. 06-6604921; fax 06-6623838; e-mail verwaltung@dhi-roma.it; internet www.dhi-roma.it; f. 1888; medieval and modern history, history of music; library of 205,000 vols, 640 current periodicals; Dir Prof. Dott. MICHAEL MATHEUS; publs *Quellen und Forschungen aus italienischen Archiven und Bibliotheken*, *Bibliothek des Deutschen Historischen Instituts*, *Rapporto Annuale* (online, annually).

Real Colegio de San Clemente de los Españoles (Royal College of Spain): Via del Collegio di Spagna 4, 40123 Bologna; tel. 051-330408; f. 1364 under Will of Cardinal Don Gil de Albornoz; study centre for 20 Spanish postgraduates; library of 25,000 vols; Rector Prof. Dr JOSÉ GUILLERMO GARCÍA VALDECASAS; publ. *Studia Albornotiana* (irregular).

Svenska Institutet i Rom (Swedish Institute in Rome): Via Omero 14, 00197 Rome; tel. 06-3201966; fax 06-3230265; e-mail srisv@vatlib.it; internet www.svenska-institutet-rom.org; f. 1926; library of 58,000 vols; Swedish courses for students of classical archaeology and history of art; fellowships in classical philology, archaeology, architecture, history of art and conservation; excavations at various sites in Italy; Dir Prof. BARBRO SANTILLO FRIZELL; publs *Acta Instituti Romani Regni Sueciae*, *Opuscula Romana*, *Suecoromana*.

Reale Istituto Neerlandese a Roma (Royal Netherlands Institute): Via Omero 10–12, 00197 Rome; tel. 06-3269621; fax 06-3204971; e-mail general@nir-roma.it; internet www.nir-roma.it; f. 1904; classical archaeology, modern history, history of art; residence for scholars from Dutch universities; library of 30,000 vols; Dir Prof. Dr MARJAN SCHWEGMAN; publs *Mededelingen* (annually), *Studien*, *Scripta Minora*, *Scrinium*.

MEDICINE

Istituto di Ricerche Farmacologiche 'Mario Negri' (Institute of Pharmacological Research): Via Eritrea 62, 20157 Milan; tel. 02-390141; fax 02-3546277; e-mail mnegri@marionegri.it; internet www.marionegri.it; f. 1961; non-profit org. for research and education in pharmacology and biomedicine; library of 8,848 scientific publications; Pres. Dott. PAOLO MARTELLI; Dir Prof. SILVIO GARATTINI; publs *Negri News* (monthly), *Research and Practice* (every 2 months).

Istituto Nazionale di Ricerca per gli Alimenti e la Nutrizione (National Institute for Research on Food and Nutrition): Via Ardeatina 546, 00178 Rome; tel. 06-514941; fax 06-51494550; e-mail dgferrari@inran.it; internet inn.ingrm.it; f. 1936 as part of CNR, independent 1958 on budget of Min. of Agricultural Resources, supported by contracts and grants from Min. of Health, CNR and intl bodies; biological research in human nutrition, analyses and surveys on composition and nutritive value of foods; Pres. Prof. FERDINANDO ROMANO; Gen. Dir Dr PATRIZIA FERRARI.

Istituto Nazionale per la Ricerca sul Cancro (National Institute for Cancer Research): Largo Rosanna Benzi 10, 16132 Genoa; tel. 010-56001; fax 010-358032; internet www.istge.it; f. 1978; research in all fields of cancer prevention, diagnosis, cure and rehabilitation; holds conferences, seminars, training courses; library of 1,808 books, 148 periodicals; Chief Exec. Dr MAURIZIO MAURI; Scientific Dir RICCARDO ROSSO; publ. *IST Insieme* (6 a year).

Istituto Sieroterapico Milanese (Milan Serum Institute): Via Darwin 22, 20143 Milan; tel. 02-8397441; f. 1896; research on immunological products and pharmaceuticals; library of 32,487 vols; Dir Prof. S. CANESCHI; publs *Bollettino*, *La Clinica Veterinaria*.

Istituto Superiore di Sanità (Higher Institute of Health): Viale Regina Elena 299, 00161 Rome; tel. 06-49901; fax 06-49387118; e-mail web@iss.it; internet www.iss.it; f. 1934; aims to promote public health through scientific research, surveys, controls and analytical tests in the various fields of health sciences; library of 200,000 vols, 3,500 current periodicals; Pres. Prof. ENRICO GARACI; Dir-Gen. Dr SERGIO LICHERI; publs *Annali dell' Istituto Superiore di Sanità* (4 a year), *Notiziario dell' Istituto Superiore di Sanità* (monthly), *Rapporti ISTISAN* (40 a year), *Strumenti di Riferimento* (irregular), *Istisan Congressi* (5 a year).

NATURAL SCIENCES

General

Istituto per l'Interscambio Scientifico (Institute for Scientific Interchange): Viale Settimo Severo 65, 10133 Turin; tel. 011-6603090; fax 011-6600049; e-mail isi@isi36a.isi.it; internet www.isi.it; f. 1982; promotes basic research in molecular biology, chemistry, computer sciences, economics, mathematics, theoretical physics; Pres. Prof. TULLIO REGGE; Exec. Dir TIZIANA BERTOLETTI.

Biological Sciences

Herbarium Universitatis Florentinae—Sezione Botanica, Museo di Storia Naturale Universitá di Firenze: Via La Pira 4, 50121 Florence; tel. 055-2757462; f. 1842; systematic botany, plant geography; Dir Dr CHIARA NEPI; publ. *Pubblicazioni del Museo Botanico*.

Stazione Zoologica 'Anton Dohrn' di Napoli (Zoological Station of Naples): Villa Comunale, 80121 Naples; tel. 081-5833111; fax 081-7641355; e-mail szadohrn@szn.it; internet www.szn.it; f. 1873; conducts biological research on marine organisms and marine ecosystems; library of 93,000 vols, 180 periodicals, 1,180 electronic resources; Pres. Prof. GIORGIO BERNARDI; Dir Dott. LUCIO CARIELLO; publs *History and Philosophy of Life Sciences*, *Marine Ecology*.

Mathematical Sciences

Istituto Nazionale di Alta Matematica Francesco Severi (National Institute of Higher Mathematics): Piazzale Aldo Moro 5, 00185 Rome; tel. 06-490320; fax 06-4462293; e-mail indam@altamatematica.it; internet www.altamatematica.it; f. 1939; promotes training of researchers in mathematics, conducts research in pure and applied mathematics; Pres. Prof. CORRADO DE CONCINI; publs *Rendiconti di Matematica*, *Symposia Mathematica*.

Physical Sciences

Comitato Glaciologico Italiano (Italian Glaciological Committee): Via Accademia delle Scienze 5, 10123 Turin; tel. 011-3977251; fax 011-6707155; e-mail g.mortara@irpi.to.cnr.it; internet www.disat.unimib.it/comiglacio/comitatoglaciologico.htm; f. 1895; glaciology and alpine climatology; *c.* 50 mems; library of 700 books, 15,000 photographs; Pres. CLAUDIO SMIRAGLIA; Gen. Sec. GIOVANNI MORTARA; publ. *Geografia Fisica e Dinamica quaternaria* (2 a year).

Dipartimento di Ingegneria Nucleare, Centro Studi Nucleari Enrico Fermi (CESNEF) (E. Fermi Centre for Nuclear Studies): Politecnico di Milano, Via Ponzio 34/3, 20133 Milan; tel. 02-23996300; fax 02-23996309; e-mail dipnuc@polimi.it; internet www.cesnef.polimi.it; f. 1957; one of the Departments of the Politecnico di Milano; trains technical personnel in the fields of nuclear energy, physics of materials, and electronics; library of 7,000 vols, 31 current periodicals; Dir Prof. GIUSEPPE CAGLIOTI.

Istituto Gemmologico Italiano (Italian Gemmological Institute): Viale A. Gramsci 228, 20099 Sesto S. Giovanni; tel. 02-2409354; fax 02-2406257; e-mail info@igi.it; internet www.igi.it; f. 1973; courses in gemmology, laboratory analysis, research; 1,500 mems; Pres. GIAN-MARIA BUCCELLATI.

INAF – Osservatorio Astronomico di Trieste (National Institute of Astrophysics – Trieste Astronomical Observatory): Via Tiepolo 11, 34143 Trieste; tel. 040-3199111; fax 040-309418; e-mail segreteria@oats.inaf.it; internet www.ts.astro.it; f. 1753; attached to Istituto Nazionale di Astrofisica; research in astrophysics, astrophysical techniques; library of 23,900 vols, 300 periodicals; Dir Prof. STEFANO CRISTIANI.

Istituto Idrografico della Marina (Naval Institute of Hydrography): Passo dell'Osservatorio 4, 16100 Genoa; tel. 010-24431; fax 010-261400; e-mail iim.sre@marina.difesa.it; internet www.marina.difesa.it/idro/Index.htm; f. 1872; library of 35,000 vols; Library Dir Mrs P. PRESCIUTTINI BELLEZZA.

Istituto Italiano di Speleologia: Dip. Scienze della Terra e Geologico-Ambientali, Via Zamboni 67, 40127 Bologna; tel. 051-2094547; fax 051-2094522; e-mail paolo.forti@unibo.it; f. 1929; exploration and scientific research in natural caves; 5 mems; library of 65,000 vols; Dir Prof. PAOLO FORTI; publ. *Memorie* (irreg.).

Istituto Nazionale di Astrofisica: Viale del Parco Mellini 84, 00136 Rome; tel. 06-355331; fax 06-35533219; e-mail inaf@inaf.it; internet www.inaf.it; promotes, carries out and co-ordinates research in the fields of astronomy, radioastronomy, spatial astrophysics and cosmic physics; has observatories in: Bologna, Cagliari, Catania, Florence, Milan, Naples, Padua, Palermo, Rome, Teramo, Turin and Trieste; finances the Telescopio Nazionale Galileo (*q.v.*) located on La Palma, Canary Islands; has a part ownership in the Large Binocular Telescope at the Mount Graham Int. Observatory (*q.v.*), AZ, USA; Pres. Prof. SERGIO DE JULIO.

Istituto Nazionale di Fisica Nucleare (INFN) (National Institute of Nuclear Physics): Piazza dei Caprettari 70, 00186 Rome; tel. 06-6840031; fax 06-68307924; e-mail presidenza@presid.infn.it; internet www.infn.it; f. 1951; promotes and undertakes research in fundamental nuclear physics; consists of: Central Administration (Frascati), 19 sections, 4 National Laboratories (Frascati, Legnaro, Gran Sasso (L'Aquila), Catania), the National Centre for Informatics and Networking (CNAF Bologna) and 8 groups; the sections are at the Institutes of Physics at the Universities of Turin, Milan, Padua, Genoa, Trieste, Bologna, Pisa, Pavia, Florence, Rome, Rome II, Rome III, Naples, Bari, Catania, Cagliari, Ferrara, Perugia, Lecce; the groups are at the Institutes of Physics at the Universities of Parma, Trento, Udine, Salerno, Messina, L'Aquila, Cosenza, Sanità; Pres. ROBERTO PETRONZIO.

Istituto Nazionale di Geofisica e Vulcanologia (National Institute of Geophysics and Volcanology): Via di Vigna Murata 605, 00143 Rome; tel. 06-518601; fax 06-5041181; e-mail info@ingv.it; internet www.ingv.it; f. 1936; seismology, geomagnetism, aeronomy, environmental geophysics; library of 6,000 vols, 150 current periodicals; Pres. Prof. ENZO BOSCHI; publs *Annali di Geofisica* (6 a year), *Bollettino sismico* (quarterly), *Bollettino macrosismico* (annually), *Annuario geomagnetico*, *Bollettino indici K* (monthly), *Bollettino dei valori istantanei alle ore 0, 2* (3 a year), *Bollettino ionosferico* (monthly), *Tavole di previsione ionosferica* (every 2 weeks).

Istituto Nazionale di Oceanografia e di Geofisico Sperimentale (National Institute for Oceanography and Experimental Geophysics): Borgo Grotta Gigante 42/C, 34010 Sgonico; tel. 040-21401; fax 040-327307; e-mail mailbox@ogs.trieste.it; internet www.ogs.trieste.it; f. 1958; library of 3,000 vols; Pres. Prof. IGINIO MARSON; publ. *Bollettino di Geofisica Teorica e Applicata* (4 a year).

Laboratori Nazionali di Frascati dell' INFN (National Laboratories of INFN, Frascati): Via E. Fermi 40, 00044 Frascati; tel. 06-94031; fax 06-94032582; e-mail dirlnf@lnf.infn.it; internet www.lnf.infn.it; f. 1953; 450 MeV Linear accelerator for electrons and positrons, 1.5 GeV electron positron storage ring; theoretical research group, high energy and nuclear physics research, electronics and radio-frequency laboratory, laboratory of technology and vacuum; library of 20,000 vols; Dir MARIO CALVETTI.

Osservatorio Astronomico di Capodimonte (Astronomical Observatory at Capodimonte): Salita Moiariello 16, 80131 Naples; tel. 081-5575111; fax 081-456710; e-mail capaccioli@na.astro.it; internet www.na.astro.it; f. 1819; uses a 1.6 m mirror telescope for studies and research; library of 24,000 vols; Dir Prof. MASSIMO CAPACCIOLI; publ. *Annuario* (online, annually).

Osservatorio Astronomico di Padova (Padua Astronomical Observatory): Vicolo dell' Osservatorio 5, 35122 Padua; tel. 049-8293411; fax 049-8759840; e-mail oa-padova@pd.astro.it; internet www.pd.astro.it; f. 1767; attached to Istituto Nazionale di Astrofisica; library of 10,000 vols; Dir Prof. MASSIMO CALVANI.

Osservatorio Astronomico di Roma (Rome Astronomical Observatory): Viale del Parco Mellini 84, 00136 Rome; tel. 06-35347056; fax 06-35347802 and at Via Frascati 33, 00040 Monteporzio Catone; tel. 06-9428641; fax 06-9447243; e-mail buonanno@mporzio.astro.it; internet www.mporzio.astro.it; f. 1923; library of 25,000 vols, 51 astronomical and astrophysical periodicals; astronomical museum; attached astronomical station at Campo Imperatore; Dir Prof.

ROBERTO BUONANNO; publs *Solar Phenomena*, *Annual Report*.

Osservatorio Vesuviano (Vesuvius Observatory): Via Diocleziano 328, 80124 Naples; tel. 081-6108483; fax 081-6100811; e-mail info@ov.ingv.it; internet www.ov.ingv.it; f. 1841; chiefly concerned with monitoring the active volcanic areas of Mount Vesuvius, Campi Flegrei Caldera and the island of Ischia; Dir Prof. GIOVANNI MACEDONIO; publs *Open File Report* (online, annually), *Monitoring Report* (online, irregular).

PHILOSOPHY AND PSYCHOLOGY

Centro Superiore di Logica e Scienze Comparate (Centre for Logic and Comparative Science): Via Belmeloro 3, 40126 Bologna; f. 1969; promotes the study of Logic and contributes to research in this field; 1,250 mems; library and archives; Pres. Prof. FRANCO SPISANI.

Istituto di Studi Filosofici 'Enrico Castelli' (Institute of Philosophy): Via Nomentana 118, c/o Facoltà di Filosofia, Università, 00161 Rome; tel. 06-8441491; f. 1939; Dir Prof. M. M. OLIVETTI; publs *Edizione Naz. dei Classici del pensiero italiano*, *Settimana di studi filosofici internazionali* (annually), *Archivio di Filosofia* (quarterly), *Bibliografia filosofica Italiana*, *Edizione Naz. A. Rosmini*, *Edizione Naz. V. Gioberti*, *Studi Filosofici e Religiosi*.

RELIGION, SOCIOLOGY AND ANTHROPOLOGY

Fondazione di Ricerca 'Istituto Carlo Cattaneo' ('Istituto Carlo Cattaneo' Research Foundation): Via Santo Stefano 11, 40125 Bologna; tel. 051-239766; fax 051-262959; e-mail catt@cattaneo.org; internet cattaneo.org; f. 1965; study and research in the field of social science with particular regard to education, electoral behaviour, politics, crime, terrorism, family, immigration and public policy; Pres. Prof. RAIMONDO CATANZARO; Dir Prof. GIANCARLO GASPERONI; Sec. ADRIANA GUELFI; publs *Cattaneo* (irregular), *Misure/Materiali di ricerca dell'Istituto Carlo Cattaneo* (irregular), *Polis-Ricerche e studi su società e politica in Italia* (3 a year), *Italian Politics — A Review* (annually), *Stranieri in Italia* (irregular).

Istituto Italiano di Antropologia (Italian Institute of Anthropology): Università di Roma 'La Sapienza', Dipart. di Biologia Animale e dell'Uomo, P.le Aldo Moro 5, 00185 Rome; tel. 06-49912273; fax 06-49912271; e-mail isita@uniroma1.it; internet www.isita-org.com; f. 1893; promotes the biological, social and cultural study of the evolution of man; organizes scientific meetings; library of 5,000 vols; Pres. Prof. ERNESTO CAPANNA; Sec. Assoc. Prof. GIOVANNI DESTRO-BISOL; publ. *Journal of Anthropological Sciences* (annual).

Istituto Italiano per l'Africa e l'Oriente (IsIAO) (Italian Institute for Africa and the East): Via Ulisse Aldrovandi 16, 00197 Rome; tel. 06-328551; e-mail info@isiao.it; internet www.isiao.it; f. 1995; Pres. Prof. GHERARDO GNOLI; Gen. Dir GIANCARLO GARGARUTI; a library and museum of oriental art are attached to the Institute; publs *East and West* (in English, 4 a year), *Africa* (4 a year), *Cina* (annually), *Il Giappone* (annually), *Yemen* (irregular), *Ming Qing Yanjiu* (annually), *Rome Oriental Series*, *Archaeological reports*, *Reports and Memoirs*, *Restorations*.

Istituto Luigi Sturzo: Via delle Coppelle 35, 00186 Rome; tel. 06-6840421; fax 06-68404244; e-mail segretaria@sturzo.it; internet www.sturzo.it; f. 1951; sociological and historical research; library of 80,000 vols; Pres. Prof. GABRIELE DE ROSA; Sec.-Gen. Dott. FLAVIA NARDELLI; publs *Sociologia* (3 a year), *Civitas* (3 a year).

Istituto per l'Oriente C. A. Nallino: Via Alberto Caroncini 19, 00197 Rome; tel. 06-8084106; fax 06-8079395; e-mail ipocan@ipocan.it; internet www.ipocan.it; f. 1921; research on modern and ancient Near East; library of 35,000 vols, 300 periodicals; Pres. Prof. CLAUDIO LO JACONO; publs *Eurasian Studies* (2 a year), *Oriente Moderno* (3 a year), *Rassegna di Studi Etiopici* (annual).

TECHNOLOGY

Centro Radioelettrico Sperimentale 'Guglielmo Marconi' (Marconi Experimental Radio-electric Centre): Padriciano 99, 34012 Trieste; tel. 040-3755517; fax 040-3755519; internet http://marconi.area.trieste.it; f. 1933; attached to the Istituto Superiore delle Poste e Telecomunicazioni; experimental research on radio waves; Pres. Prof. GIANCARLO CORAZZA.

Centro Sviluppo Materiali SpA: Via di Castel Romano 100, 00128 Rome; tel. 06-5055829; fax 06-5055202; e-mail info@c-s-m.it; internet www.c-s-m.it; f. 1963; reference centre for innovation in materials and in related production, design and application technologies; library of 40,000 vols; Man. Dir Dr R. BRUNO; Gen. Man. Dr A. MASCANZONI.

Ente per le Nuove Tecnologie, l'Energia e l'Ambiente (ENEA) (Agency for New Technology, Energy and the Environment): Lungotevere Thaon di Revel 76, 00196 Rome; tel. 06-36271; fax 06-36272591; e-mail com@sede.enea.it; internet www.enea.it; f. 1960; scientific research and technological development, implementing advanced research programmes and conducting complex projects for Italy's social and economic development; library of 250,000 vols; Pres. Prof. CARLO RUBBIA; Gen. Dir Ing. GIOVANNI LELLI; publs *Energia Ambiente e Innovazione* (6 a year), *Rapporto Energia e Ambiente* (online, annually).

Fondazione Guglielmo Marconi (Guglielmo Marconi Foundation): Via Celestini 1, 40044 Pontecchio Marconi; tel. 051-846121; fax 051-846951; e-mail fgm@fgm.it; internet www.fgm.it; f. 1938; research in telecommunications; library of 3,500 vols; Chair. Prof. GABRIELE FALCIASECCA.

Istituto Elettrotecnico Nazionale 'Galileo Ferraris' (Galileo Ferraris National Electrotechnical Institute): Strada delle Cacce 91, 10135 Turin; tel. 011-39191; fax 011-346384; e-mail info@ien.it; internet www.ien.it; f. 1934; carries out research in metrology and on new materials and devices; tests materials, components and apparatus; contributes to education and training of students; 155 mems; library of 11,000 vols, 1,000 periodicals, CEI standards; Pres. ELIO BAVA; Gen. Dir PAOLO A. MASTROENI; publ. *Scientific Report* (annually).

Istituto Nazionale per Studi ed Esperienze di Architettura Navale (National Institute of Naval Architecture Studies and Experiments): Via Vallerano 139, 00128 Rome; tel. 06-5071580; fax 06-5070619; e-mail secretary@insean.it; internet www.insean.it; f. 1927; library of 3,500 vols; Pres. Adm. GIANO PISI; Dir Ing. PAOLINO MANISCALCO; publ. *Quaderni* (annual).

SORIN Biomedica SpA: Via Borgonuovo 14, 20121 Milan; tel. and fax 02-63321; internet www.sorin.com; f. 1956; applied research in biomedicine; production and development of radiopharmaceuticals and immunodiagnostic kits (using radioactive and enzymatic tracers), pace-makers, artificial cardiac valves (mechanical and biological), oxygenators, dialysers, haemodialysis and haemoperfusion accessories; 2,112 staff; Chair. UMBERTO ROSA; CEO DRAGO CERCHIARI.

Libraries and Archives

Alessandria

Biblioteca Civica: Piazza Vittorio Veneto 1, (ang. Via Machiavelli), 15100 Alessandria; tel. 0131-515911; internet www.comune.alessandria.it/flex/cm/pages/serveblob.php/l/it/idpagina/1315; f. 1806; 180,000 vols, 217 current periodicals; Dir (vacant).

Ancona

Archivio di Stato di Ancona: Via Maggini 80, 60127 Ancona; tel. 071-2802053; fax 071-2800356; e-mail asan@archivi.beniculturali.it; internet archivi.beniculturali.it/ASAN; f. 1941; provincial archives dating from before Italian unification; 8,000 vols, 280 periodicals; Dir Dott.ssa GIOVANNA GIUBBINI; publ. *Archivio di Stato-Ancona* (series, irregular).

Biblioteca Comunale Luciano Benincasa: Via Bernabei 32, Piazza Plebiscito 33, 60121 Ancona; tel. 071-222-5020; fax 071-222-5020; e-mail aiaale@comune.ancona.it; f. 1669; 155,000 vols, 62 incunabula, 124 periodicals, 347 MSS, 3,000 cinquecentine; Dir ALESSANDRO L. AIARDI.

Arezzo

Biblioteca della Città di Arezzo: Palazzo Pretorio, Via dei Pileati 8, 52100 Arezzo; tel. 0575-22849; fax 0575-370419; e-mail direzione@bibliotecaarezzo.it; internet www.bibliotecaarezzo.it; f. 1603; 250,000 vols, pamphlets and miscellanea, 587 MSS and 197 incunabula; Dir Dott. SILVIO SANTINI.

Ascoli Piceno

Biblioteca Comunale 'Giulio Gabrielli': Piazza Arringo 6, 63100 Ascoli Piceno; tel. 0736-298212; fax 0736-298232; internet www.cultura.marche.it/musamarche/arim/11.html; f. 1849; 180,000 vols, 265 incunabula, 900 MSS, 2,000 *cinquecentine*, 340 periodicals; Dir Dott.ssa EMANUELA IMPICCINI.

Avellino

Biblioteca Provinciale Scipione e Giulio Capone: Corso Europa 41, 83100 Avellino; tel. and fax 0825-782382; e-mail info@mediateca.avellino.it; internet avellino.ebiblio.it; f. 1913; 120,000 vols; Dir Dott. MARIO SARRO.

Bari

Archivio di Stato di Bari: Via Demetrio Marin 3, 70125 Bari; tel. 080-5024860; fax 080-5024870; e-mail archivio.stato@teseo.it; internet www.teseo.it/archiviodistato; f. 1835; 6,192 vols, 224 periodicals, 139 MSS; Dir Dr GIUSEPPE DIBENEDETTO.

Bergamo

Biblioteca Civica 'Angelo Mai': Piazza Vecchia 15, 24129 Bergamo; tel. 035-399430; fax 035-240655; e-mail info@bibliotecamai.org; internet www.bibliotecamai.org; f. 1760; 650,000 vols, 9,380 MSS, 37,478 documents, 2,140 incunabula; Dir GIULIO ORAZIO BRAVI.

Bologna

Archivio di Stato di Bologna: Piazza dei Celestini 4, 40123 Bologna; tel. 051-223891; fax 051-220474; e-mail asbo@archivi.beniculturali.it; internet www.archiviodistatobologna.it; f. 1874; 230,000 items; 23,000 vols, 331 periodicals; Dir Dott.ssa MARIA ROSARIA CELLI GIORGINI.

Biblioteca Carducci: Piazza Carducci 5, 40125 Bologna; tel. 051-347592; fax 051-4292820; e-mail casacarducci@comune.bologna.it; internet www.casacarducci.it/htm/info_cont/bibl1.htm; given to the commune of Bologna in 1907 by Marguerite of Savoy, inaugurated in 1921; the library preserves the surroundings of the poet Giosuè Carducci and contains his collected works, as well as many rare editions of other works; 35,000 vols; Dir PIERANGELO BELLETTINI.

Biblioteca Comunale dell'Archiginnasio: Piazza Galvani 1, 40124 Bologna; tel. 051-276811; fax 051-261160; e-mail archiginnasio@comune.bologna.it; internet www.archiginnasio.it; f. 1801; 829,000 vols (incl. 2,500 incunabula, 20,000 16th-century editions), 12,000 MSS, 500,000 letters and documents; Dir Dott. PIERANGELO BELLETTINI; publ. *L'Archiginnasio – Bollettino della Biblioteca Comunale di Bologna* (annually).

Biblioteca del Dipartimento di Scienze Giuridiche 'A. Cicu': Via Zamboni 27–29, 40126 Bologna; tel. 051-2099626; fax 051-2099624; e-mail bibgiur@giuri.unibo.it; internet www.jus.unibo.it; f. 1926; 292,000 vols; Chief Librarian LEONARDA MARTINO.

Biblioteca San Domenico: Piazza San Domenico 13, 40124 Bologna; tel. 051-6400493; fax 051-6400492; e-mail biblsand@iperbole.bologna.it; internet www.comune.bologna.it/iperbole/biblsand; f. 1218; more than 70,000 vols, incunabula and MSS; spec. collns incl. philosophy and theology; Dir P. ANGELO PIAGNO.

Biblioteca Universitaria di Bologna: Via Zamboni 33–35, 40126 Bologna; tel. 051-243420; fax 051-252110; e-mail direzione@bub.unibo.it; internet www.bub.unibo.it; f. 1712; 1,348,688 vols, 309,475 pamphlets, 12,820 MSS, 1,021 incunabula, 76,708 microforms, 11,224 periodicals; Dir Dr BIANCASTELLA ANTONINO; publ. *BUBLife* (3 a year).

Brescia

Biblioteca Queriniana: Via Mazzini 1, 25121 Brescia; tel. 030-2978200; fax 030-2400359; e-mail queriniana@comune.brescia.it; internet queriniana.comune.brescia.it; f. 1747; 500,511 vols; Dir ALDO PIROLA.

Cagliari

Archivio di Stato di Cagliari: Via Gallura 2, 09125 Cagliari; tel. 070-669450; fax 070-653401; e-mail archivio@unica.it; internet www.alizar.it/welcome/archiviostatocagliari; f. 19th c.; 26,556 vols, 2,690 periodicals, 407,000 microfiches; Dir Dott. MARINELLA FERRAI COCCO ORTU.

Biblioteca Universitaria: Via Università 32A, 09124 Cagliari; tel. 070-660017; fax 070-652672; f. 1792; 460,470 vols; 1,033 MSS, 5,469 letters and documents, 241 incunabula, 2,784 magazines; Gabinetto delle Stampe 'Anna Marongiu Pernis' contains 4,541 etchings; Dir Dott. GRAZIELLA SEDDA DELITALA.

Campobasso

Archivio di Stato di Campobasso: Via Orefici 43, 86100 Campobasso; tel. 0874-411488; fax 0874-411525; e-mail ascb@archivi.beniculturali.it; f. 1818; 19,000 vols, 802 periodicals, 29 MSS; Dir Dott.ssa ELENA GLIELMO.

Catania

Archivio di Stato di Catania: Via Vittorio Emanuele 156, 95131 Catania; tel. 095-7159860; fax 095-7150465; e-mail asct@archivi.beniculturali.it; internet archivi.beniculturali.it/ASCT; f. 1854; 161,790 items; 11,700 vols; Dir Dott. ALDO SPARTI.

Biblioteca Regionale Universitaria: Piazza Università 2, 95124 Catania; tel. 095-7366111; fax 095-326862; f. 1755; 400,000 vols, 117 incunabula, 590 MSS; Dir UGO GIOVALE.

Biblioteche Riunite Civica e A. Ursino Recupero: Via Biblioteca 13, 95124 Catania; tel. 090-316883; f. 1931 as municipal library, fmrly a Benedictine monastery library, nationalized in 1867; 210,000 vols, specializing in Sicily and Catania; Dir Prof.ssa MARIA SALMERI.

Cesena

Istituzione Biblioteca Malatestiana: Piazza Bufalini 1, 47023 Cesena; tel. 0547-610892; fax 0547-21237; e-mail malatestiana@sbn.provincia.ra.it; internet www.malatestiana.it/manoscritti/index.htm; f. 1452; 400,000 vols, 286 incunabula, 2,180 MSS; Dir Dr.ssa DANIELA SAVOIA; publ. *Newsletter* (online, irregular).

Como

Biblioteca Comunale: Via Indipendenza 87, 22100 Como; tel. 031-270187; fax 031-240183; e-mail biblioteca@comune.como.it; f. 17th c.; 370,000 vols; Dir RICCARDO TERZOLI.

Cremona

Biblioteca del Seminario Vescovile: Via Milano 5, 26100 Cremona; tel. 03-7220267; fax 03-7229135; e-mail seminario.cr@libero.it; f. 1592; 138,450 vols, 400 MSS, 18 incunabula; Dir Prof. FOGLIA DON ANDREA.

Biblioteca Statale e Libreria Civica: Via Ugolani Dati 4, 26100 Cremona; tel. 0372-495611; fax 0372-495615; f. *c.*1600; 680,000 vols, 2,380 MSS, 18,600 letters and documents, 394 incunabula, 6,000 16th c. editions; Dir Dott. EMILIA BRICCHI PICCIONI; publs *Annali*, *Fonti e Sussidi*, *Mostre*.

Fermo

Biblioteca Comunale: Piazza del Popolo7, 63023 Fermo; tel. 0734-284310; fax 0734-215112; e-mail biblioteca@comune.fermo.net; internet www.fermo.net/ita/egov/biblioteca.html; f. 1688; 332,000 vols, 681 incunabula, 15,000 *cinquecentine*, 3,000 MSS, 110 current periodicals; Dir NATALIA TIZI.

Ferrara

Biblioteca Comunale Ariostea: Via Scienze 17, 44100 Ferrara; tel. 0532-418200; fax 0532-204296; e-mail info.ariostea@comune.fe.it; internet www.artecultura.fe.it/index.phtml; f. 1753; 420,000 vols; Dir Dott. E. SPINELLI.

Florence

Archivio di Stato di Firenze: Viale G. Italia 6, 50122 Florence; tel. 055-263201; fax 055-2341159; internet www.archiviodistato.firenze.it; f. 1852; 604,580 items; 43,000 vols, 350 periodicals; Dir Dott.ssa ROSALIA MANNO TOLU.

Biblioteca degli Uffizi: Loggiato degli Uffizi, 50122 Florence; tel. 055-2388647; fax 055-2388648; e-mail biblioteca@polomuseale.firenze.it; internet www.polomuseale.firenze.it/biblioteche/bib_uffizi.asp; f. 1770; 64,000 vols; Dir Dr CLAUDIO DI BENEDETTO.

Biblioteca del Gabinetto Scientifico Letterario G. P. Vieusseux: Palazzo Strozzi, Piazza Strozzi, 50123 Florence; tel. 055-288342; fax 055-2396743; e-mail biblioteca@vieusseux.fi.it; internet www.vieusseux.fi.it/biblio.html; f. 1819; 600,000 vols; Dir Prof. ENZO SICILIANO; publ. *Antologia Vieusseux* (quarterly).

Attached archive:

Archivio Contemporaneo 'A. Bonsanti': Palazzo Corsini-Suarez, Via Maggio 42, 50125 Florence; tel. 055-290131; fax 055-213188; e-mail archivio@vieusseux.fi.it; internet www.vieusseux.fi.it/archivio.html; f. 1975; 500,000 vols, 85,000 records; Man. GLORIA MANGHETTI.

Biblioteca Marucelliana: Via Cavour 43–47, 50129 Florence; tel. 055-27221; fax 055-294393; e-mail marucelliana@maru.firenze.sbn.it; internet www.maru.firenze.sbn.it; f. 1752; 553,992 vols; 2,574 MSS; 489 incunabula, 3,200 drawings, 53,000 prints, 8,000 16th c. editions, 30,405 letters and documents, 9,322 periodicals; Dir MARIA PRUNAI FALCIANI.

Biblioteca Medicea-Laurenziana: Piazza S. Lorenzo 9, 50123 Florence; tel. 055-210760; fax 055-2302992; e-mail medicea@unifi.it; internet www.bml.firenze.sbn.it; f. 1571; contains the private Medici Library, collections of MSS from the Grand Dukes of Lorena, S. Croce, S. Marco, Badia Fiesolana, cathedral of Florence, and private family collections; 15th and 16th c. first editions; 14,000 MSS of the 5th–19th c.; 2,500 papyri, 80 ostraca, 150,000 vols; Dir Dr FRANCA ARDUINI.

Biblioteca Moreniana: Via dei Ginori 10, 50123 Florence; tel. and fax 055-2760331; e-mail moreniana@provincia.fi.it; internet www.provincia.fi.it/moreniana.htm; f. 1869; 34,000 vols, about 2,000 MSS, specializing in ancient Tuscan history; Dir Dr.ssa SIMONETTA MERENDONI.

Biblioteca Nazionale Centrale: Piazza Cavalleggeri 1, 50122 Florence; tel. 055-249191; fax 055-2342482; e-mail info@bncf.firenze.sbn.it; internet www.bncf.firenze.sbn.it; f. 1747; 5,300,000 vols, pamphlets, 115,000 periodicals, 25,000 MSS, 4,000 incunabula, 29,000 16th c. editions; Dir Dr ANTONIA IDA FONTANA; publ. *Bibliografia nazionale italiana* (monthly, annual accumulations, quarterly CD-ROM).

Biblioteca Pedagogica Nazionale: c/o Biblioteca di Documentazione Pedagogica, Palazzo Gerini, Via M. Buonarroti 10, 50122 Florence; tel. 055-2380364; fax 055-2380330; e-mail biblioteca@indire.it; f. 1941; 80,000 vols, 1,600 periodicals, rare books, drawings, etc.; data banks on education; Pres. Dott.ssa MARIA CRISTINA DOTTORINI; publs *Schedario* (review of children's literature, 3 a year), *Segnalibro* (review of literature for young people, annually).

Biblioteca Riccardiana: Via dei Ginori 10, 50123 Florence; tel. 055-212586; fax 055-211379; e-mail riccardiana@riccardiana.firenze.sbn.it; internet www.riccardiana.firenze.sbn.it; f. 1815; 61,675 vols, 4,415 MSS, 725 incunabula, 3,856 16th c. editions, 192 periodicals; Dir Dott. GIOVANNA LAZZI.

Biblioteca Umanistica dell' Università: Piazza Brunelleschi 3, 50121 Florence; tel. 055-2757811; fax 055-243471; e-mail floriana.tagliabue@unifi.it; internet www.sba.unifi.it/biblio/umanistica; f. 1959; 1,600,000 vols; Dir Dr FLORIANA TAGLIABUE.

Forlì

Biblioteca Comunale 'Aurelio Saffi': Corso della Repubblica 72, 47100 Forlì; tel. 0543-712600; fax 0543-712616; e-mail biblioteca-saffi@comune.forli.fo.it; internet www.provincia.forli-cesena.it/cultura/biblioteche/ita/saffi.htm; 490,000 vols, 250 incunabula, 8,000 16th c. editions, 2,000 MSS, 2,200 periodicals; Dir Dr FRANCO FABBRI.

Genoa

Archivio di Stato di Genova: Piazza S. Maria in Via Lata, 7, 16128 Genoa; tel. 010-5957581; fax 010-5538220; e-mail asge@archivi.beniculturali.it; internet archivi.beniculturali.it/ASGE/asge.htm; f. 1817; *c.*

13,000 vols, 145 periodicals; Dir PAOLA CAROLI.

Biblioteca Durazzo Giustiniani: Via XXV Aprile 12, 16123 Genoa; tel. 010-2476232; fax 010-2474122; f. 1760–1804; 20,000 17th and 18th c. vols, 1,000 *cinquecentine*, 448 incunabula, 300 MSS; Curator Dr SANDRA MACCHIAVELLO.

Biblioteca di Storia dell'Arte: Via ai Quattro Canti di San Francesco, 16121 Genoa; tel. 010-5574957; fax 010-5574970; e-mail biblarte@comune.genova.it; internet www.comune.genova.it/turismo/biblioteche/bibliociv/welcome.htm; f. 1908; 56,000 vols; specialized library relating to Italian and Genoese fine arts (since 11th century); Curator Dr ELISABETTA PAPONE; publ. *Bollettino dei Musei Civici Genovesi*.

Biblioteca Universitaria: Via Balbi 3, 16126 Genoa; tel. 010-254641; fax 010-2546420; e-mail segreteria@bibliotecauniversitaria.ge.it; internet www.bibliotecauniversitaria.ge.it; f. 18th c.; 540,000 vols, 1,037 incunabula, 1,861 MSS; 14,148 letters and documents; Dir Reg. ERNESTO BELLEZZA.

Gorizia

Biblioteca Statale Isontina di Gorizia: Via Mameli 12, 34170 Gorizia; tel. 0481-580210; fax 0481-580260; e-mail isontina@librari.beniculturali.it; internet www.isontina.librari.beniculturali.it; f. 1629; lending and reference library, bibliographical information service; 300,000 vols, 39 incunabula, 690 *cinquecentine*, 873 current periodicals, 443 MSS, 1,181 microfiches; Dir Dott. MARCO MENATO; publ. *Studi Goriziani* (2 a year).

Imola

Biblioteca Comunale: Via Emilia 80, 40026 Imola; tel. 0542-602636; fax 0542-602602; e-mail bim@comune.imola.bo.it; f. 1761; 419,000 vols, 520 current periodicals, 1,692 MSS, 140 incunabula; Dir Dott.ssa GRAZIA-VITTORIA GURRIERI.

L'Aquila

Biblioteca Provinciale 'Salvatore Tommasi': Piazza Palazzo 30, 67100 L'Aquila; tel. 0862-299262; fax 0862-61964; e-mail biblioteca@provincia.laquila.it; internet www.provincia.laquila.it; f. 1848; 250,000 vols, 490 current periodicals, 128 incunabula, 1,011 MSS, 3,200 *cinquecentine* (rare 16th c. editions), 450 videos; Dir Dr PAOLO COLLACCIANI.

Livorno

Biblioteca Comunale 'Labronica' Francesco Domenico Guerrazzi: Via del Forte S. Pietro 15, 57123 Livorno; tel. 0586-219265; fax 0586-219151; e-mail bottinidellolio@comune.livorno.it; internet www.comune.livorno.it/_livo/pages.php?id=127; f. 1816; 380,000 vols incl. 2,000 15th- and 16th-century edns, 850 current periodicals, various MSS and 60,000 letters and documents; Dir Dott. DUCCIO FILIPPI; publ. *Quaderni della Labronica* (quarterly).

Lucca

Biblioteca Statale di Lucca: Via S. Maria Corteorlandini 12, 55100 Lucca; tel. 0583-491271; fax 0583-496770; e-mail bslu@librari.beniculturali.it; internet www.bslu.librari.beniculturali.it; f. 17th century; 449,200 vols, 594 current periodicals, 10,000 cinquecentine, 835 incunabula, 4,321 MSS, 19,462 letters and documents, 2,595 graphic items; musical collection of 68 MSS, 500 scores; Dir Dott.ssa DANILA ANDREONI.

Macerata

Biblioteca Comunale Mozzi-Borgetti: Piazza Vittorio Veneto 2, 62100 Macerata; tel. 0733-256360; fax 0733-256338; e-mail biblioteca@comune.macerata.it; internet www.comune.macerata.it/Entra/Engine/RAServePG.php3/P/2508110417; f. 1773; 350,000 vols, 10,000 MSS, 300 incunabula, 20,000 photographs; Dir Dott.ssa ALESSANDRA SFRAPPINI.

Mantua

Biblioteca Comunale Teresiana: Via Roberto Ardigò 13, 46100 Mantua; tel. 0376-321515; fax 0376-310801; e-mail biblioteca.centrale@comune.mantova.it; internet www.comune.mantova.it/cultura_turismo/sistemaculturale/biblioarchivi/teresiana; f. 1780; 330,000 vols, 1,375 MSS, 1,425 incunabula, 8,500 *cinquecentine*; Dir Dssa IRMA PAGLIARI.

Biblioteca dell' Accademia Nazionale Virgiliana: Via dell'Accademia 47, 46100 Mantua; tel. 0376-320314; fax 0376-222774; e-mail cgallic@tin.it; f. early 17th c.; 30,000 vols; Librarian Prof. MARIO VAINI; publs *Atti e Memorie* (annually), *Nuova Serie* (annually).

Messina

Biblioteca Regionale: Via dei Verdi 71, 98122 Messina; tel. 090-663332; fax 090-771909; e-mail brs.me@regione.sicilia.it; internet www.regione.sicilia.it/beniculturali/dirbenicult/biblioteche/biblioteche.html; f. 1731; 400,000 vols, 461 current periodicals, 1,307 MSS, 423 incunabula, 3,637 *cinquecentine*; Dir Dott.ssa SANDRA CONTI.

Milan

Archivio di Stato di Milano: Via Senato 10, 20121 Milan; tel. 02-7742161; fax 02-774216230; e-mail asmi@cilea.it; internet archivi.beniculturali.it/ASMI/indice.html; f. 1886; 27,096 vols and pamphlets, 18,814 periodicals; Dir Dott. MARIA BARBARA BERTINI.

Archivio Storico Civico e Biblioteca Trivulziana: Castello Sforzesco, 20121 Milan; tel. 02-88463690; fax 02-88463698; e-mail ascb.trivulziana@comune.milano.it; internet www.comune.milano.it; f. 1872 (Archivio Storico Civico), 1935 (Biblioteca Trivulziana); 170,000 vols, 1,500 MSS dating from the 8th c., 2,000 incunabula, and rare editions of works on history and literature; local historical artefacts; Dir Dr IVANOE RIBOLI; publ. *Libri & Documenti* (3 a year).

Biblioteca Ambrosiana: Piazza Pio XI 2, 20123 Milan; e-mail info@ambrosiana.it; internet www.ambrosiana.it; tel. 02-806921; fax 02-80692210; f. 1607; 850,000 vols and rare prints, 35,000 MSS mostly Latin, Greek, and Oriental, 2,100 incunabula, 12,000 parchments, 20,000 prints, 10,000 drawings; Dir Dott. GIANFRANCO RAVASI.

Biblioteca d'Arte: Castello Sforzesco, 20121 Milan; tel. 02-88463751; fax 02-88463819; e-mail info@bibdarte.it; internet www.bibdarte.it; f. 1930; art library and Leonardo da Vinci Collection; 120,000 vols, 1,500 periodicals, 310 current periodicals; Librarian Dott. LIA GANDOLFI.

Biblioteca d'Ateneo dell' Università Cattolica del Sacro Cuore: Largo Gemelli 1, 20123 Milan; tel. 02-72342230; fax 02-72342701; e-mail biblioteca.direzione-mi@unicatt.it; internet www.unicatt.it/library; f. 1921; 1,720,000 vols and pamphlets, 33,760 periodicals, 8,535 electronic journals, 237 online and CD-ROM-based databases; Head of Library Dott.ssa ELLIS SADA.

Biblioteca Centrale di Ingegneria–Leonardo: Piazza Leonardo da Vinci 32, 20133 Milan; tel. 02-23992550; fax 02-23992560; e-mail ingegneria@mail.biblio.polimi.it; internet bci.biblio.polimi.it; 153,400 vols, 350 MSS, 3,780 periodicals, 270 current periodicals; Head of Library SIMONETTA MORELLI.

Biblioteca del Centro Nazionale di Studi Manzoniani: Via Morone 1, 20121 Milan; tel. 02-86460403; fax 02-875618; e-mail manzoni@energy.it; f. 1937; 25,000 vols; Dir Prof. GIANMARCO GASPARI; publs *Annali*, *Bollettino Bibliografico*, *Edizione Nazionale ed Europea delle Opere di Alessandro Manzoni*.

Biblioteca Comunale: Palazzo Sormani, Corso di Porta Vittoria 6, 20122 Milan; tel. 02-88463397; fax 02-88463353; e-mail biblioteca.sormani@comune.milano.it; internet www.comune.milano.it/biblioteche; f. 1886; 644,432 vols, 2,414 current periodicals, 48,909 audio and video items, 483 electronic resources; Dir Dr ANNA MARIA ROSSATO.

Biblioteca del Conservatorio di Musica 'Giuseppe Verdi': Via Conservatorio 12, 20122 Milan; tel. 02-762110219; fax 02-76003097; e-mail biblioteca@consmilano.it; internet www.consmilano.it; f. 1808; 500,000 items; 50,000 MSS, 30,000 books on music, 400 periodicals; Librarian LICIA SIRCH; publ. *Annuario del Conservatorio*.

Biblioteca della Facoltà di Agraria: Università degli Studi di Milano, Via G. Celoria 2, 20133 Milan; tel. 02-50316428; fax 02-50316427; e-mail bib.agraria@unimi.it; internet users.unimi.it/biblioteche/agraria; f. 1871; 51,000 vols; Scientific Dir Prof. A. SCHIRALDI; Librarian Dott. ANGELO BOZZOLA.

Biblioteca delle Facoltà di Giurisprudenza e di Lettere e Filosofia dell' Università: Via Festa del Perdono 7, 20122 Milan; tel. 02-50312273; fax 02-50312598; e-mail alessandra.dallera@unimi.it; internet users.unimi.it/~biblio; f. 1923; 930,000 vols; Dir MARIA ALESSANDRA DALL'ERA.

Biblioteca dell' Istituto Lombardo Accademia di Scienze e Lettere: Via Borgonuovo 25, 20121 Milan; tel. 02-864087; fax 02-86461388; e-mail istituto.lombardo@unimi.it; internet www.istitutolombardo.it/biblioteca.html; f. 1802; 495,000 vols, 2,600 periodicals; Dir Dr ADELE BIANCHI ROBBIATI.

Biblioteca Nazionale Braidense: Via Brera 28, 20121 Milan; tel. 02-86460907; fax 02-72023910; e-mail info@braidense.it; internet www.braidense.it; f. 1770; 965,183 vols, 17,149 periodicals, 26,455 autographs, 2,107 MSS; Dir ROBERTO DI CARLO.

Biblioteca dell' Università Commerciale Luigi Bocconi: Via Gobbi 5, 20136 Milan; tel. 02-58365101; fax 02-58365100; e-mail library.staff@unibocconi.it; internet www.unibocconi.it/biblioteca; f. 1903; borrowing and reference services, user instruction services; European Documentation Centre; 735,064 vols, 2,810 current periodicals, 47,182 theses, 4,335 current electronic periodicals, 44 databases; Head Librarian Dr MARISA SANTARSIERO.

Raccolte Storiche del Comune di Milano, Biblioteca e Archivio: Palazzo De Marchi, Via Borgonuovo 23, 20121 Milan; tel. 02-8693549; fax 02-72001483; e-mail risorgi@energy.it; f. 1884; 250,000 vols, newspapers and pamphlets, 3,825 files of documents since 1750; Dir Dott. ROBERTO GUERRI.

Modena

Biblioteca Estense Universitaria: Palazzo dei Musei, Largo Porta S. Agostino 337, 41100 Modena; tel. 059-222248; fax 059-230195; e-mail biblio.estense@cedoc.mo.it; internet www.cedoc.mo.it/estense; 549,719 vols, 11,066 MS vols, 157,961 loose MSS,

1,662 incunabula, 15,966 *cinquecentine*, 101,545 pamphlets, 4,332 periodicals; Dir Dott. AURELIO AGHEMO.

Naples

Archivio di Stato di Napoli: Piazzetta Grande Archivio 5, 80138 Naples; tel. 081-5638111; e-mail asna@archivi.beniculturali.it; internet http://archivi.beniculturali.it/ASNA; f. 1808; 544,000 items; 25,000 vols; Dir Dott.ssa FELICITA DE NEGRI.

Biblioteca del Conservatorio S. Pietro a Majella: Via S. Pietro a Majella 35, 80138 Naples; tel. (81) 5644427; fax (81) 5644415; e-mail biblioteca@sanpietroamajella.it; f. 1791; 300,000 vols, 18,000 MSS, 10,000 costume designs, 8,000 opera libretti, 10,000 letters, 200 *cinquecentine*; Dir Dr FRANCESCO MELISI.

Biblioteca della Facoltà di Scienze Agrarie dell' Università degli Studi di Napoli Federico II: Via Università 100, 80055 Portici; tel. 081-2539321; e-mail petricci@unina.it; internet www.agraria.unina.it/biblio; f. 1872; 65,000 vols, 3,130 periodicals, 441 current periodicals; Dir OLIMPIA PETRICCIONE.

Biblioteca della Pontificia Facoltà Teologica dell' Italia Meridionale, sezione 'San Tommaso d'Aquino': Viale Colli Aminei 2, 80131 Naples; tel. 081-7413343; fax 081-7437580; e-mail presidenzapftim@libero.it; internet www.teologia.it/pftim; f. 1687; 120,000 vols; 11 incunabula, 600 MSS, 1,000 periodicals, 450 current periodicals; Dir Prof. FRANCESCO RUSSO.

Biblioteca della Società Napoletana di Storia Patria: Piazza Municipio, Maschio Angioino, 80133 Naples; tel. 081-5510353; fax 081-5529238; e-mail bibl.snsp@libero.it; internet www.storia.unina.it/snsp; f. 1875; 300,000 vols, 2,400 MSS, 2,955 periodicals, 900 current periodicals, 1,300 *cinquecentine*, 59 incunabula; Librarian MARIA CONCETTA VILLANI; publ. *Archivio Storico per le Province Napoletane*.

Biblioteca di Castelcapuano: Piazza dei Tribunali, Palazzo di Giustizia, 80138 Naples; tel. 081-269416; f. 1848; 40,000 vols; Dir Dott. ROSSI BUSSOLA RAFFAELLO.

Biblioteca Nazionale 'Vittorio Emanuele III': Palazzo Reale, 80132 Naples; tel. 081-7819111; fax 081-403820; e-mail emanuele@librari.beniculturali.it; internet www.bnnonline.it; f. 1804; 1,800,000 vols, 19,000 MSS, 8,300 periodicals, 4,563 incunabula, 1,792 papyri from Herculaneum; Dir Dott. MAURO GIANCASPRO; publ. *I Quaderni*.

Biblioteca Oratoriana del Monumento Nazionale dei Girolamini: Via Duomo 142, 80138 Naples; tel. and fax 081-294444; e-mail biblioteca@girolamini.it; internet www.girolamini.it/biblioteca.htm; f. 1580; 159,700 vols, 120 incunabula, 5,000 *cinquecentine*, 485 periodicals, 57 current periodicals; Dir P. GIOVANNI FERRARA.

Biblioteca Universitaria di Napoli: Via G. Paladino 39, 80138 Naples; tel. 081-5517025; fax 081-5528275; e-mail buna@librari.beniculturali.it; internet www.bun.unina.it; f. 1816; 1,200,000 vols, 18,000 periodicals, 5,200 *cinquecentine*, 468 incunabula, 144 MSS; open to the public; Dir LUCIANA COZZOLINO.

Novara

Biblioteca Comunale Negroni: Corso Felice Cavallotti 4, 28100 Novara; tel. 0321-623040; fax 0321-628068; f. 1906; 250,000 vols, 3,052 periodicals, 5,540 records, 131 incunabula, 771 microfilms, 420 MSS, maps, etc.; Dir Dr M. CARLA UGLIETTI.

Padua

Biblioteca Antoniana: Piazza del Santo 11, 35123 Padua; tel. and fax 049-8751492; e-mail info@bibliotecaantoniana.191.it; internet www.basilicadelsanto.org/ita/chiostri/biblio.asp; f. 13th century; 85,000 vols, 800 MSS; Dir Prof. SERGIO CATTAZZO.

Biblioteca Civica: Via Orto Botanico 5, 35123 Padua; tel. 049-656375; fax 049-8753207; e-mail biblioteca.civica@comune.padova.it; internet www.padovanet.it/biblioteche; f. 1858; art, Italian literature, history, local history (Padua and Veneto); 500,000 vols, 5,500 MSS, 385 incunabula, 2,000 periodicals; Head Librarian Dr GILDA P. MANTOVANI; publ. *Bollettino del Museo Civico di Padova*.

Biblioteca del Seminario Vescovile: Via Seminario 29, 35122 Padua; tel. 049-9983635; fax 049-8761934; e-mail biblio.seminariopadova@unipd.it; internet www.seminariopadova.it; f. 1671; 300,000 vols, 1,135 MSS, 417 incunabula, 800 periodicals; Dir Prof. RICCARDO BATTOCCHIO.

Biblioteca Universitaria: Via S. Biagio 7, 35121 Padua; tel. 049-8240211; fax 049-8762711; e-mail bupd@librari.beniculturali.it; internet www.cab.unipd.it/bibphp/scheda.php3?CampoID=96; f. 1629; 676,982 vols; 2,708 MSS, 1,280 incunabula, 1,530 music scores, 1,055 maps, 6,471 periodicals, 898 current periodicals, 9,635 *cinquecentine*, 3,000 prints and engravings; Dir Dott. FRANCESCO ALIANO.

Palermo

Archivio di Stato di Palermo: Corso Vittorio Emanuele 31, 90133 Palermo; tel. 091-589693; fax 091-6110594; e-mail aspa@archivi.beniculturali.it; internet archivi.beniculturali.it/ASPA; f. 1814; 386,918 items; 22,000 vols; Dir CLAUDIO TORRISI.

Biblioteca Centrale della Regione Siciliana: Corso Vittorio Emanuele 429–431, 90134 Palermo; tel. 091-7077642; fax 091-7077644; e-mail bcrs@regione.sicilia.it; internet www.regione.sicilia.it/beniculturali/bibliotecacentrale; f. 1782; 580,000 vols; 1,930 MSS and 1,044 incunabula, 5,907 periodicals, 15,000 letters and documents, 5,066 rare books, 4,125 maps, prints and engravings, 47,664 microforms, 3,541 photographs and slides; Dir GAETANO GULLO.

Biblioteca Comunale: Casa Professa, 90134 Palermo; tel. 091-7407570; fax 091-7407584; internet librarsi.comune.palermo.it; f. 1760; 365,000 vols; 1,038 incunabula, 15,000 *cinquecentine*; Dir Dott. FILIPPO GUTTUSO.

Parma

Biblioteca Palatina: Strada alla Pilotta 3, 43100 Parma; tel. 0521-220411; fax 0521-235662; e-mail palatina@unipr.it; internet www.bibpal.unipr.it; f. 1761; 715,000 vols, 6,671 MSS, 556 periodicals, 3,044 incunabula, 52,601 engravings and drawings; musical section: Via del Conservatorio 27; tel. 0521-289429; Dir Dr LEONARDO FARINELLI.

Biblioteca Palatina–Sezione Musicale presso il Conservatorio di Musica 'A. Boito': Strada Conservatorio 27, 43100 Parma; tel. 0521-289429; fax 0521-235662; e-mail sez.musicale@biblcom.unipr.it; f. 1889; 72,449 vols, 16,288 MSS, 30 periodicals; Dir Dr DANIELA MOSCHINI.

Pavia

Biblioteca Civica 'Carlo Bonetta': Piazza Petrarca 2, 27100 Pavia; tel. 0382-21635; fax 0382-33580; e-mail fmilani@comune.pv.it; internet www.comune.pv.it/on-line/index.jsp?instance=1&node=198; f. 1887; Dir Dott. FELICE MILANI.

Biblioteca Universitaria: Strada Nuova 65, 27100 Pavia; tel. 0382-24764; fax 0382-25007; e-mail bupv.infbib@librari.beniculturali.it; internet siba.unipv.it/buniversitaria; f. 1763; 500,000 vols, 1,402 MSS, 689 incunabula, 5,391 periodicals, 718 current periodicals, 7,000 *cinquecentini*, 1,394 microfilms; Librarian Dott.ssa ANNA MARIA CAMPANINI STELLA.

Perugia

Biblioteca Augusta del Comune di Perugia: Palazzo Conestabile della Staffa, Via delle Prome 15, 06122 Perugia; tel. 075-5772500; fax 075-5722231; e-mail augusta@comune.perugia.it; internet www.comune.perugia.it/canale.asp?id=822; f. 1615; 365,000 vols, 3,370 MSS, 1,330 incunabula, 3,660 periodicals, 16,500 *cinquecentine*; Dir Dott. MARIA FOP.

Pesaro

Biblioteca e Musei Oliveriani: Via Mazza 97, 61100 Pesaro; f. 1793; 250,000 vols on general culture and local history; Librarian Prof. Dott. ANTONIO BRANCATI; publ. *Studia Oliveriana* (annually).

Piacenza

Biblioteca Comunale Passerini Landi: Via Carducci 14, 29100 Piacenza; tel. 0523-492401; fax 0523-492400; e-mail biblio.centrale@comune.piacenza.it; internet www.biblioteche.piacenza.it/passerini; f. 1774; 50,000 vols, 1,000 incunabula, 5,000 *cinquecentine*; Dir Dott. CARLO EMANUELE MANFREDI.

Pisa

Biblioteca Universitaria: Via Curtatone e Montanara 15, 56126 Pisa; tel. 050-913411; fax 050-42064; e-mail bupi@librari.beniculturali.it; internet www.pisa.sbn.it; f. 1742; 668,000 vols, 1,389 MSS, 24,087 documents, 161 incunabula, 1,034 current periodicals; Dir Dott.ssa ALESSANDRA PESANTE.

Pistoia

Biblioteca Comunale Forteguerriana: Piazza della Sapienza 5, 51100 Pistoia; tel. 0573-24348; fax 0573-371466; e-mail biblioteca@comune.pistoia.it; internet www.comune.pistoia.it/museibiblioteche/forteguerriana/index.htm; f. 1696; 300,000 vols, 223 current periodicals, 1,000 MSS, 126 incunabula, 3,000 *cinquecentine*, 1,000 CDs; Dir Dr MAURIZIO VIVARELLI.

Portici

Biblioteca del Dipartimento di Entomologia e Zoologia Agraria, Università degli Studi di Napoli Federico II: Via Università 100, 80055 Portici; tel. 081-2539188; fax 081-7755145; e-mail gaeiorio@unina.it; f. 1872; applied entomology and biological control; 100,000 vols; Dir GAETANO IORIO; publ. *Bollettino del Laboratorio di Entomologia Agraria 'Filippo Silvestri'*.

Potenza

Archivio di Stato: Via Nazario Sauro 1, 85100 Potenza; tel. 0971-56144; fax 0971-56223; e-mail aspz@aspz.it; internet aspz.it; f. 1818; 10,000 linear m of records (since 11th c.); administrative and judicial archives since 1687; notarial archives since 1524; archives of religious houses dissolved in the 19th c.; private and feudal archives since 1500; collections of parchments (since 10th c.) and municipal statutes; also archives of ecclesiastical bodies incl. those of the Venosa cathedral chapter (since 11th c.); 17,000 vols, 2,500 periodicals; Dir Prof. Dott. DONATO TAMBLÉ.

Biblioteca Nazionale: Via del Gallitello, 85100 Potenza; tel. 0971-54829; fax 0971-

55071; internet www.bnpz.librari.beniculturali.it; f. 1985; functions as univ. library (Univ. della Basilicata) and regional library; 300,000 vols, 1,681 periodicals; Dir Dott. MAURIZIO RESTIVO.

Ravenna

Istituzione Biblioteca Classense: Via Baccarini 3, 48100 Ravenna; tel. 0544-482112; fax 0544-482104; e-mail informazioni@classense.ra.it; internet www.classense.ra.it; f. 1707–1711; 790,000 vols; Dir Dott. DONATINO DOMINI; publ. *Letture Classensi*.

Reggio Emilia

Biblioteca Panizzi: Via Farini 3, 42100 Reggio Emilia; tel. 0522-456084; fax 0522-456081; e-mail panizzi@comune.re.it; internet panizzi.comune.re.it; f. 1796; 500,000 vols, 10,000 MSS; Dir Dr MAURIZIO FESTANTI.

Rimini

Biblioteca Civica Gambalunga: Via Gambalunga 27, 47900 Rimini; tel. 0541-51105; fax 0541-26167; e-mail gambalunghiana@comune.rimini.it; internet www.comune.rimini.it/cultura/biblioteca/biblioteca_pagina.htm; f. 1619; 220,000 vols (including 7,000 *cinquecentine*), 384 incunabula, 1,350 MSS, 350 current periodicals, 1,960 bound periodicals, 8,000 drawings and engravings, 40,000 photographs; Dir Prof. MARCELLO DI BELLA.

Rome

Archivio Centrale dello Stato: Piazzale degli Archivi 27, 00144 Rome; tel. 06-545481; fax 06-5413620; e-mail acs@archivi.beniculturali.it; internet archivi.beniculturali.it/ACS; f. 1875; 130,000 vols, also periodicals, etc.; political, administrative, cultural and judicial archives of the Kingdom of Italy and Italian Republic; Dir ALDO G. RICCI.

Archivio di Stato di Roma: Corso del Rinascimento 40, 00186 Rome; tel. 06-6819081; fax 06-6864123; e-mail asroma@asrm.archivi.beniculturali.it; internet archivi.beniculturali.it/ASRM/index.html; f. 1871; conservation of archives produced by the central offices of the Papal State from the Middle Ages to 1870, together with documents produced by other agencies in the Rome area; papal provincial treasuries (incl. Avignon and Benevento); archives of religious orders since 14th c. and of brotherhoods, academies, corporate bodies, the University of Rome and notary registers since 13th c.; conservation of govt office records of the Italian State with seat in Rome; School of Archival Science, Latin Palaeography and Diplomatics; 52,000 vols, with three important collections: Statutes, MSS, Decrees; Dir Dott. LUIGI LONDEI.

Biblioteca Angelica: Piazza Sant'Agostino 8, 00186 Rome; tel. 06-6875874; fax 06-6832312; e-mail angelica.polosbn@inroma.roma.it; internet biblioroma.sbn.it/angelica; f. 1605; 200,000 vols, 2,704 MSS, 1,156 incunabula; 15th–18th c. literature; Augustinian, Jansenist, Reformation and Counter-reformation collections; Dir Dssa ARMIDA BATORI.

Biblioteca Archeologia e Storia dell'Arte: Piazza Venezia 3, 00187 Rome; tel. 06-6780982; fax 06-6781167; e-mail archeologica@librari.beniculturali.it; internet www.archeologica.librari.beniculturali.it; f. 1922; 599,000 vols, 3,500 periodicals, 1,489 MSS, 16 incunabula, 20,000 prints, 59,411 microfiches, 740 *cinquecentine*; Dir STEFANIA MURIANNI.

Biblioteca Casanatense: Via S. Ignazio 52, 00186 Rome; tel. 06-6976031; fax 06-69920254; e-mail casanatense@biblioroma.sbn.it; internet www.casanatense.it; f. 1701; 400,000 vols, 6,459 MSS, 2,200 incunabula, 30,000 engravings, 2,000 periodicals, 220 current periodicals; Dir Dr ANGELA A. CAVARRA.

Biblioteca Centrale del Consiglio Nazionale delle Ricerche (Central Library of National Research Council): Piazzale Aldo Moro 7, 00185 Rome; tel. 06-49933221; fax 06-49933834; e-mail biblioce@bice.rm.cnr.it; internet www.bice.rm.cnr.it; f. 1927; 1,000,000 vols, 10,000 periodicals, EU depository library; scientific and technical subjects; Dir Prof. ENZO CASOLINO.

Biblioteca Centrale Giuridica presso il Ministero di Grazia e Giustizia: Palazzo di Giustizia, Piazza Cavour, 00193 Rome; tel. 06-68834900; e-mail bcg@giustizia.it; internet www.giustizia.it/ministero/bcg/webnew.htm; f. 1866; 200,000 vols, 2,300 periodicals, 1,000 current periodicals; Dir Dr ORAZIO FRAZZINI.

Biblioteca Centrale del Ministero dell'Interno: Palazzo del Viminale, Via Agostino Depretis, 00184 Rome; tel. 06-46525703; fax 06-46536689; internet www.interno.it/sezioni/viminale; f. 1872; 110,000 vols; Dir ARTURO LETIZIA.

Biblioteca del Ministero degli Affari Esteri: Piazza della Farnesina 1, 00194 Rome; tel. 06-36913279; e-mail giuseppina.dipietro@esteri.it; internet www.esteri.it/ita/5_47_188.asp; f. 1850; 200,000 vols, 1,500 periodicals, 168 current periodicals; international relations, contemporary history; Dir Dott.ssa MARIA ADELAIDE FRABOTTA.

Biblioteca del Ministero delle Risorse Agricole, Alimentari e Forestali: Via XX Settembre 20, 00187 Rome; tel. 06-4743482; fax 06-4743079; internet biblioteca.dsmc.uniroma1.it/Ricerca/cittanascosta.html; f. 1860; 500,000 vols, 300 current periodicals; Dir Dott.ssa MILVIA SVIBENS.

Biblioteca del Senato 'Giovanni Spadolini': Piazza della Minerva, 38, 00186 Rome; tel. 06-67063717; fax 06-67064338; e-mail bibliotecaminerva@senato.it; internet www.senato.it/biblioteca; f. 1848; 600,000 vols, 3,000 periodicals, 1,100 current periodicals, 209 MSS, 30 incunabula; chiefly works on law, history and politics; medieval statutes; Sr Counsellor Dott. SANDRO BULGARELLI.

Biblioteca dell'Accademia Nazionale dei Lincei e Corsiniana: Via della Lungara 10, 00165 Rome; tel. 06-6861983; fax 06-68027343; e-mail segreteria@lincei.it; internet www.lincei.it/biblioteca/index.php; f. 1754; 552,000 vols on history of arts, sciences and culture, 7,000 periodicals, 4,600 MSS, 2,307 incunabula; oriental section on Arabic and Islamic civilization, with 35,000 books, 350 periodicals, 500 MSS; online catalogue for modern collection; Dir Dott. MARCO GUARDO; Librarian (ancient printed books) Dr EBE ANTETOMASO; Librarian (bibliographical exchanges) Dott.ssa LAURA FORGIONE; Librarian (Oriental Section) Dott.ssa VALENTINA SAGARIA ROSSI; Librarian (Manuscripts) Dott.ssa ENRICA SCHETTINI; Librarian (Periodicals) MARINA TOMEI.

Biblioteca della Camera dei Deputati: Via del Seminario 76, 00186 Rome; tel. 06-67603476; fax 06-6786886; e-mail bib_segreteria@camera.it; f. 1848 in Turin; 1,000,000 vols, 10,000 bound periodicals, 2,500 current periodicals; Dir Dott.ssa E. LAMARO; publ. *Bollettino Nuove Accessioni* (monthly).

Biblioteca della Fondazione Marco Besso: Largo di Torre Argentina 11, 00186 Rome; tel. 06-6865611; fax 06-68216313; e-mail biblioteca@fondazionemarcobesso.it; internet www.fondazionemarcobesso.it/nuovobesso; 60,000 vols and 5,000 pamphlets; special collections: Rome, Dante, Proverbs, Tuscia; Cur. ANNA MARIA AMADIO.

Biblioteca della Società Geografica Italiana: Villa Celimontana, Via della Navicella 12, 00184 Rome; tel. 06-7008279; fax 06-77079518; e-mail biblioteca@societageografica.it; internet www.societageografica.it/archivio/biblioteca/index.htm; f. 1867; 300,000 vols, 2,000 periodicals; Library Counsellor Prof. M. DI ANGELO ANTONIO; publ. *Bollettino*.

Biblioteca della Società Italiana per l'Organizzazione Internazionale (SIOI): Piazza di S. Marco 51, Palazzetto di Venezia, 00186 Rome; tel. 06-6920781; fax 06-6789102; e-mail sioi@sioi.org; f. 1944; 70,000 vols, 800 periodicals, 500,000 UN documents; Librarian Dr SARA CAVELLI.

Biblioteca della Soprintendenza Speciale alla Galleria Nazionale d'Arte Moderna e Contemporanea: Viale delle Belle Arti 131, 00196 Rome; tel. 06-32298246; fax 06-3221579; e-mail biblioteca.gnam@arti.beniculturali.it; internet www.gnam.arti.beniculturali.it/biblioteca.htm; f. 1945; 65,000 vols, 1,500 periodicals, 40,000 miscellaneous items, on art since 19th c.; Dir Prof. LEANDRO VENTURA; Assoc. Dir Dr MARINA GARGIULO; Librarian Dott. DINA MACERA; publ. *Bollettino mensile delle nuove accessioni* (monthly, online).

Biblioteca di Storia Moderna e Contemporanea: Via M. Caetani 32, 00186 Rome; tel. 06-6828171; fax 06-68807662; e-mail informazioni@bsmc.it; internet www.bsmc.it; f. 1917; 450,000 vols, 11,000 MSS, 7,200 bound periodicals, 600 current periodicals, 3,000 microfilms and microfiches; Dir ROSSELLA CAFFO.

Biblioteca Istituto Italo-Latino Americano: Piazza B. Cairoli 3, 00186 Rome; tel. 06-684921; fax 06-6872834; e-mail biblioteca@iila.org; internet www.iila.org; f. 1966; specializes in contemporary Latin-American life; 80,000 vols, 1,000 periodicals, 100 CD-ROMs; services: offsets of any item in library, in-service library loans, information service; audio-visual collection; Librarian Prof. RICCARDO CAMPA; publs annotated bibliographical catalogues, lists of book exhibits.

Biblioteca Lancisiana: Borgo S. Spirito 3, 00193 Rome; tel. 06-68352449; fax 06-68352442; e-mail biblio@aslrme.com; internet www.lancisiana.it; f. 1711; history of medicine, history of science; 18,013 vols, 374 MSS, 60 incunabula, 2,000 *cinquecentine*; Dir Dr SAVERIO MARCO FIORILLA.

Biblioteca Medica Statale: Viale del Policlinico 155, 00161 Rome; tel. 06-490778; fax 06-4457265; e-mail medica@librari.beniculturali.it; internet biblioroma.sbn.it/medica; f. 1925; 130,000 vols, 1,193 periodicals; Dir Dr GIOVANNI ARGANESE; publ. *Bollettino bimestrale nuove accessioni*.

Biblioteca Musicale S. Cecilia: Via dei Greci 18, 00187 Rome; f. 1584; 145,367 MSS and printed works; Dir Dott. DOMENICO CARBONI.

Biblioteca Nazionale Centrale di Roma: Viale Castro Pretorio 105, 00185 Rome; tel. 06-49891; fax 06-4457635; e-mail bncrm@bnc.roma.sbn.it; internet www.bncrm.librari.beniculturali.it; f. 1876; 6,000,000 vols, 84,000 MSS, 1,938 incunabula, 25,000 *cinquecentine*, 20,000 maps, 44,000 periodicals, 10,000 prints and drawings; Dir Dott. OSVALDO AVALLONE.

Biblioteca Storica dei Ministeri delle Finanze e del Tesoro: Via XX Settembre 97, 00187 Rome; tel. 06-47613120; fax 06-4814086; internet www.tesoro.it/web/area_biblioteche/biblioteca_storica.htm; f. 1857; 100,000 vols; Dir Prof. WALTER D'AVANZO.

Biblioteca Universitaria Alessandrina: Piazzale Aldo Moro 5, 00185 Rome; tel. 06-4474021; fax 06-44740222; internet alessandrina.librari.beniculturali.it; f. 1661; 1,000,000 vols, 16,000 bound periodicals, 6,000 current periodicals, 450 MSS, 680 incunabula; Dir MARIA CONCETTA PETROLLO.

Biblioteca Vallicelliana: Piazza della Chiesa Nuova 18, 00186 Rome; tel. 06-68802671; fax 06-6893868; e-mail info@vallicelliana.it; internet www.vallicelliana.it; f. 1581; 150,000 vols, 2,558 MSS, 403 incunabula; also contains library of 'Società Romana di Storia Patria', 50,000 vols; Dir Dr BARBARA TELLINI SANTONI.

Bibliotheca Hertziana—Max-Planck-Institut für Kunstgeschichte: Via Gregoriana 28, 00187 Rome; tel. 06-69993242; fax 06-69993333; e-mail info@biblhertz.it; internet www.biblhertz.it; f. 1913; 260,000 vols on the history of Italian art, 1,130 current periodicals, 2,430 bound periodicals, 740,000 photographs of Italian art; Librarian Dr ANDREAS THIELEMANN; publ. *Römisches Jahrbuch der Bibliotheca Hertziana*.

Cineteca Nazionale: Via Tuscolana 1524, 00173 Rome; tel. 06-72294278; fax 06-7211619; e-mail biblioteca@snc.it; internet www.csc-cinematografia.it/csc/pages/info.php; f. 1935; includes the National Film Archive and the Luigi Chiarini Library; 42,763 vols, 10,976 scenarios, 871 bound periodicals, 170 current periodicals; Gen. Dir GABRIELE TESTI; Library Dir Dott.ssa FIAMMETTA LIONTI; publ. *Bianco e Nero* (3 a year).

Discoteca di Stato e Museo dell'Audiovisivo (National Sound Archive): Via M. Caetani 32, 00186 Rome; tel. 06-68406901; fax 06-6865837; e-mail discoteca@dds.it; internet www.dds.it; f. 1928; collection of recordings of eminent Italians; 220,000 records of classical and light music, jazz; 25,000 records and tapes on anthropology and folklore; collection of sound reproduction equipment; 9,000 vols; Dir Dott. MASSIMO PISTACCHI.

Istituto Centrale per il Catalogo Unico delle Biblioteche Italiane e per le Informazioni Bibliografiche (Central Institute of the Union Catalogue of Italian Libraries and Bibliographical Information): Viale del Castro Pretorio 105, 00185 Rome; tel. 06-4989484; fax 06-4959302; internet www.iccu.sbn.it; f. 1951; Dir Dr MARCO PAOLI.

David Lubin Memorial Library, Food and Agriculture Organization (FAO) of the United Nations: Viale delle Terme di Caracalla, 00100 Rome; tel. 06-57053784; fax 06-57052002; e-mail fao-library-reference@fao.org; internet www.fao.org/library; f. 1946; 1,000,000 vols and more than 8,000 current journals, of which 2,500 electronic; reference and information services, briefings and seminars, and electronic reproduction of FAO documents.; Chief Librarian JANE M. WU.

Rovigo

Pinacoteca dell'Accademia dei Concordi: Piazza V. Emanuele II 14, 45100 Rovigo; tel. 0425-27991; fax 0425-27993; e-mail concordi@concordi.it; internet www.concordi.it; f. 1580; Egyptian and Roman colln; numismatic colln of 2,000 items; colln of paintings from 15th–19th centuries; 250,000 vols.

Sassari

Biblioteca Universitaria: Piazza Università 21, 07100 Sassari; tel. 079-235179; fax 079-235787; internet www.comune.sassari.it/guida/biblioteche/biblioteca_universitaria.htm; f. between 1558 and 1562; 350,000 vols, 1,200 bound periodicals, 1,000 current periodicals, 2,864 MSS, 1,431 microfilms, 71 incunabula, 3,500 *cinquecentine*; Dir Dott.ssa PINA ULERI.

Siena

Biblioteca Comunale degli Intronati: Via della Sapienza 5, 53100 Siena; tel. 0577-280704; fax 0577-44293; e-mail biblio@comune.siena.it; internet www.biblioteca.comune.siena.it; f. 1758; 386,419 vols, 3,679 bound periodicals, 1,091 current periodicals, 5,699 MSS, 1,038 incunabula, 20,000 prints, 5,810 microfiches, 32,500 slides; Dir Dott. DANIELE DANESI.

Teramo

Biblioteca Provinciale 'Melchiorre Delfico': Via Dèlfico 16, 64100 Teramo; tel. 0861-252744; fax 0861-254197; e-mail biblioteca@provincia.teramo.it; internet www.provincia.teramo.it/?area=1066381515305; f. 1816; 260,000 vols, 5,000 bound periodicals, 600 current periodicals, 1,200 *cinquecentine*, 55 incunabula, 15,000 MSS, 100,000 photographs; Dir LUIGI PONZIANI.

Trento

Biblioteca dell' Archivio di Stato di Trento: Via Maccani 161, 38100 Trento; tel. 0461-829008; fax 0461-828981; e-mail astn@archivi.beniculturali.it; internet www.biblio.unive.it/sba/biblioteche/altrebiblioteche.asp; f. 1919; administered by the Ministero per i Beni Culturali e Ambientali; cultural function and to promote historical research; 7,141 vols, 100 periodicals, holds archives of state offices from pre-unification Italy and single documents and archives belonging to or deposited with the State; Dir Dr SALVATORE ORTOLANI.

Biblioteca Comunale: Via Roma 55, 38100 Trento; tel. 0461-275521; fax 0461-275552; e-mail tn.viaroma@biblio.infotn.it; internet www.bibcom.trento.it; f. 1856; 623,569 vols, 536 incunabula and 4,242 16th-c. editions, music section of 18,000 vols; 20,000 MSS, 6,000 periodicals, 10,000 maps; collection of 139,202 vols on history and culture of Trentino-Alto Adige; Austrian Library (6,448 vols); Dir Dr FABRIZIO LEONARDELLI; publs *Studi trentini di scienze storiche*, *BIB – Notiziario della Biblioteca Comunale di Trento* (4 a year), *A TUTTO BIB—Novita per Ragazzi* (4 a year).

Treviso

Biblioteca Comunale: Borgo Cavour 20, 31100 Treviso; tel. 0422-545342; fax 0422-583066; e-mail info@biblioteca.treviso.it; internet www.bibliotecatreviso.it; f. 1770; 450,000 vols, 4,000 MSS, 810 incunabula; Dir Dr EMILIO LIPPI; publ. *Studi Trevisani*.

Trieste

Archivio di Stato di Trieste: Via Lamarmora 17, 34139 Trieste; tel. 040-390020; fax 040-9380033; e-mail asts@archivi.benicultural.it; internet www.newton.it/webif/biblioteca.htm; f. 1926; 41,004 vols, 1,079 periodicals; Dir Dott. GRAZIA TATÒ.

Biblioteca Civica 'A. Hortis': Piazza Attilio Hortis 4, 34123 Trieste; tel. 040-6758200; fax 040-6758199; e-mail bibcivica@comune.trieste.it; internet www.retecivica.trieste.it/triestecultura/biblioteche/bibciv/civicaframe.htm; f. 1793; 400,000 vols, 401 MSS, drawings and maps; Petrarch, Piccolomini, Svevo and Joyce sections and historical archives; Dir Dott. BIANCA CUDERI.

Biblioteca Statale di Trieste: Largo Papa Giovanni XXIII 6, 34123 Trieste; tel. 040-300725; fax 040-301053; e-mail bsts@librari.beniculturali.it; internet www.bsts.librari.beniculturali.it; f. 1956; 196,000 vols; Dir MARCO MENATO.

Narodna in študijska knjižnica v Trstu (Slovene National Study Library): Via S. Francesco 20, 34133 Trieste; tel. 040-635629; fax 040-3484684; e-mail bibslo@spin.it; internet www.nsk-trst.sik.si; f. 1947; 100,000 vols, 500 periodicals.

Turin

Archivio di Stato di Torino: Piazza Castello 209, 10124 Turin; tel. 011-540382; fax 011-546176; e-mail astoto@ipsnet.it; internet www.multix.it/asto; f. 12th century, building 1731; houses documents of the House of Savoy up to 1861, and those of the provincial State administrations of the 19th century; archives: 70 shelf-kms; 50,000 vols, MS collections; Dir Dr ISABELLA MASSABÒ RICCI.

Biblioteca dell' Accademia delle Scienze di Torino: Via Maria Vittoria 3, 10123 Turin; tel. 011-5620047; fax 011-532619; e-mail biblioteca@accademia.csi.it; internet www.accademiadellescienze.it; f. 1783; a conservation library covering most fields of the sciences and humanities; rare books dating from the 15th–19th centuries; colln of books, letters and MSS from the late 18th–19th centuries; 200,000 vols, 500 current periodicals and 3,500 others, 35,000 letters, MSS; online catalogue; Head Librarian Dott.ssa ELENA BORGI; publs *Memorie della Accademia* (annual), *Atti della Accademia* (annual), *Quaderni della Accademia* (annual).

Biblioteche Civiche e Raccolte Storiche: Via Cittadella 5, 10122 Turin; tel. 011-4429812; fax 011-4429830; e-mail biblioteche.civiche@comune.torino.it; internet www.comune.torino.it/cultura/biblioteche; f. 1869; 433,000 vols, 67 incunabula, 2,375 MSS, 1,600 *cinquecentine*, 1,105 rare vols, 4,376 microfilms, 1,257 bound periodicals, 1,243 current periodicals; 12 br. libraries; Dir GISELDA RUSSO.

Biblioteca Matematica dell' Università di Torino: Via Carlo Alberto 10, 10123 Turin; fax 011-534497; f. 1883; 50,000 vols; Dir Prof. L. RODINO.

Biblioteca Nazionale Universitaria: Piazza Carlo Alberto 3, 10123 Turin; tel. 011-8101111; fax 011-8121021; e-mail bnto@librari.beniculturali.it; internet www.bnto.librari.beniculturali.it; f. 1723; 817,657 vols, 171,700 vols of periodicals, 4,500 MSS, 1,603 incunabula, 10,063 *cinquecentine*, 12,440 drawings and prints; Dir Dott. AURELIO AGHEMO.

Biblioteca del Politecnico di Torino: Castello del Valentino, Viale Mattioli 39, 10125 Turin; tel. 011-5646710; fax 011-5646799; e-mail direttore@sb.polito.it; internet www.biblio.polito.it; 15,000 vols; Dir Dott.ssa MARIA VITTORIA SAVIO.

Biblioteca Reale: Piazza Castello 191, 10122 Turin; tel. 011-543855; fax 011-5178259; e-mail to0263@biblioteche.reteunitaria.piemonte.it; f. 1831; 187,614 vols, 4,391 MSS, 1,491 parchments, 3,096 drawings, 1,107 periodicals, 188 incunabula; library of the Savoy family; historical documents on heraldry, military matters, the Sardinian States, the *Risorgimento* and the Piedmont; Dir GIOVANNA GIACOBELLO BERNARD.

Udine

Biblioteca Civica 'Vincenzo Joppi': Piazza Marconi 8, 33100 Udine; tel. 0432-

271583; fax 0432-271580; e-mail bcu@comune.udine.it; internet www.comune.udine.it/biblioteca.htm; f. 1864; 527,647 vols, 11,000 MSS, 124 incunabula; Dir Dott. ROMANO VECCHIET.

Urbino

Biblioteca Universitaria: Via Aurelio Saffi 2, 61029 Urbino; tel. 0722-305212; fax 0722-305286; e-mail bibhum@uniurb.it; internet www.uniurb.it/bib/home.htm; f. 1720; 436,755 vols; Dir Dott. GOFFREDO MARANGONI.

Venice

Biblioteca dell' Accademia Armena di S. Lazzaro dei Padri Mechitaristi: Isola S. Lazzaro, 30126 Venice; tel. 041-5260104; fax 041-5268690; f. 1701; 100,000 vols, 4,000 MSS; Dir Dr SAHAK DJEMDJEMIAN.

Biblioteca del Civico Museo Correr: Piazza S. Marco 52, Procuratie Nuove, 30124 Venice; tel. 041-2405211; fax 041-5200935; e-mail biblioteca.correr@comune.venezia.it; internet www.museiciviciveneziani.it; f. 1830; specializes in history of art and Venetian history; 116,933 vols, 1,022 periodicals, 13,018 MSS, 700 MSS on microfiche; Dir GIANDOMENICO ROMANELLI.

Biblioteca Nazionale Marciana: Piazzetta San Marco 7, 30124 Venice; tel. 041-2407211; fax 041-5238803; e-mail biblioteca@marciana.venezia.sbn.it; internet marciana.venezia.sbn.it; f. 1468; 900,000 vols, 3,731 periodicals, 2,883 incunabula, 24,055 cinquecentine, 13,000 MSS; Dir Dott. MARINO ZORZI.

Fondazione Scientifica Querini-Stampalia: Castello 5252, 30122 Venice; tel. 041-2711411; fax 041-2711445; e-mail biblioteca@querinistampalia.org; internet www.querinistampalia.it/biblioteca/; f. 1869; 300,000 vols, 400 current periodicals; Dir CHIARA RABITTI.

Verona

Biblioteca Civica: Via Cappello 43, 37121 Verona; tel. 045-8079710; fax 045-8009727; e-mail civica@comune.verona.it; internet www.comune.verona.it; f. 1792; 540,000 vols; 1,188 incunabula; 3,477 MSS; Dir Dott. AGOSTINO CONTO.

Vicenza

Biblioteca Civica Bertoliana: Contrà Riale 5, 36100 Vicenza; tel. 0444-578211; fax 0444-578234; e-mail bertoliana@bibliotecabertoliana.it; internet www.bibliotecabertoliana.it; f. 1696; 800,000 vols, 850 incunabula, 3,564 MSS, 615 current periodicals; Librarian GIORGIO LOTTO.

Museums and Art Galleries

Ancona

Museo Archeologico Nazionale delle Marche: Palazzo Ferretti, Via Ferretti 1, 60121 Ancona; tel. 071-202602; fax 071-202134; internet www.archeomarche.it/museoanc.htm; f. 1906; pre-historic and Roman archaeology; large collection from Iron Age Picene and Celtic Cultures; Dir Prof. Dr GIULIANO DE MARINIS.

Aquileia

Museo Archeologico Nazionale: Via Roma 1, 33051 Aquileia; tel. 0431-91016; fax 0431-919537; e-mail archeologico@museoarcheo-aquileia.it; internet www.museoarcheo-aquileia.it; f. 1882; collection of Roman architecture, sculpture, inscriptions, mosaics, etc. from excavations in the town; library of 10,000 vols; Dir Dott.ssa FRANCA MASELLI SCOTTI; publ. *Aquileia Nostra* (annually).

Attached museum:

Museo Paleocristiano: Via Monastero, 33051 Aquileia; tel. 0431-91131; fax 0431-919537; e-mail paleocristiano@museoarcheo-aquileia.it; internet www.museoarcheo-aquileia.it; f. 1961; mosaics and inscriptions from the palaeo-Christian era; Dir Dott.ssa FRANCA MASELLI SCOTTI.

Ardea

Raccolta Manzù: Via Laurentina Km 32.8, 00040 Ardea; tel. 06-9135022; e-mail gnam@arti.beniculturali.it; internet www.gnam.arti.beniculturali.it/manzco.htm; f. 1969; paintings and sculptures by Giacomo Manzù (b. 1908 in Bergamo); part of Nat. Gallery of Modern Art in Rome; Dir LIVIA VELANI.

Arezzo

Museo Archeologico: Via Margaritone 10, 52100 Arezzo; tel. and fax 0575-20882; internet www.mega.it/archeo.toscana/samuar.htm; f. 1832; Etruscan, Greek and Roman antiquities, coralline vases of Augustan period, sarcophagi, mosaics, coins and bronzes; Dir Dott.ssa P. ZAMARCHI.

Museo Statale d'Arte Medievale e Moderna: Palazzo Bruni Ciocchi, Via San Lorentino 8, 52100 Arezzo; tel. 0575-409050; fax 0575-299850; internet brunelleschi.imss.fi.it/ist/luogo/museostataleartemedievalemoderna.html; f. 1957; Italian paintings from 13th–19th c., Majolica ware, glass, ivories, seals and coins; Curator Dott. STEFANO CASCIU.

Assisi

Museo-Tesoro della Basilica di S. Francesco: Piazza S. Francesco 2, 06082 Assisi; tel. 075-819001; fax 075-8190035; e-mail centrodf@tiscali.it; internet www.sanfrancescoassisi.org; f. 1927; historical and artistic collections relating to the Basilica church of St Francis, F. M. Perkins colln of 13th–15th c. European art; Dir Fr PASCHAL M. MAGRO.

Bari

Museo Archeologico: Palazzo dell'Ateneo, Piazza Umberto I, 70121 Bari; tel. 080-5211559; internet www.archeologia.beniculturali.it/pages/atlante/S89.html; f. 1882; library of 2,500 vols; Dir Dott. GIUSEPPE ANDREASSI.

Pinacoteca Provinciale: Via Spalato 19, 70121 Bari; tel. 080-5412421; fax 080-15583401; e-mail pinacotecaprov.bari@tin.it; f. 1928; Apulian, Venetian and Neapolitan paintings and sculpture from 11th–19th c.; paintings from the 'Macchiaioli'; library of 3,000 vols; Dir Dssa CLARA GELAO.

Bergamo

Accademia Carrara di Belle Arti–Museo: Accademia Carrara di Belle Arti, Piazza Giacomo Carrara 82/A, 24121 Bergamo; tel. 035-399640; fax 035-224510; e-mail segr@accademiacarrara.bergamo.it; internet www.accademiacarrara.bergamo.it; f. 1796; colln incl. paintings by Bellini, Raffaello, Pisanello, Mantegna, Botticelli, Beato Angelico, Previtali, Tiepolo, Lotto, Moroni, Baschenis, Galgario; drawings, prints and sculptures since 15th century; Pres. Dott. WILLI ZAVARITT; Curator GIOVANNI VALAGUSSA.

Bologna

Museo Civico Archeologico: Via dell'Archiginnasio 2, 40124 Bologna; tel. 051-2757211; fax 051-266516; e-mail mca@comune.bologna.it; internet www.comune.bologna.it/bologna/museoarcheologico; f. 1881; prehistoric, Egyptian, Greek, Roman, Villanovan, Etruscan and Celtic antiquities; numismatic colln; library of 28,000 vols; Dir Dssa CRISTIANA MORIGI GOVI.

Pinacoteca Nazionale: Via Belle Arti 56, 40126 Bologna; tel. 051-4209411; e-mail spsadbo@arti.beniculturali.it; internet www.pinacotecabologna.it; f. 1808; Bolognese paintings and other Italian schools from 14th–18th centuries; German and Italian engravings; Dir Prof. ANDREA EMILIANI.

Bolzano

Museo Archeologico dell'Alto Adige/Südtiroler Archäologiemuseum (South Tyrol Museum of Archaeology): Via Museo 43, 39100 Bolzano; tel. 0471-320100; fax 0471-320122; e-mail museum@iceman.it; internet www.iceman.it; history and archaeology of the South Tyrol region from the Palaeolithic to the Carolingian period (800 AD); also 'Ötzi', 5,000-year old mummified man discovered in the Schnalstal Glacier in 1991; Dir Dr ANGELIKA FLECKINGER.

Museo Civico di Bolzano: Via Cassa di Risparmio 14, 39100 Bolzano; tel. 0471-974625; fax 0471-980144; e-mail museo.civico@comune.bolzano.it; internet www.comune.bolzano.it; f. 1902; history of art since medieval period; archaeology, numismatics, furniture, liturgical items; library of 27,000 vols, 77 periodicals; Dir Dr STEFAN DEMETZ.

Brescia

Fondazione Brescia Musei: Via Musei 81, 25121 Brescia; tel. 030-2400640; fax 030-2990267; internet www.bresciamusei.com; Dir Dtt.ssa RENATA STRADIOTTI.

Constituent museums and galleries:

Museo delle Armi 'Luigi Marzoli': Via Castello 9, 25121, Brescia; tel. 030-293292; f. 1988; 14th- to 18th-century arms.

Museo del Risorgimento: Via Castello 9, 25121 Brescia; tel. 030-293292; f. 1959; 19th-century historical exhibits.

Pinacoteca Tosio Martinengo: Piazza Moretto 4, 25121 Brescia; tel. 030-3774999; f. 1906; art from the 13th to 18th centuries.

Santa Giulia–Museo della Città: Via dei Musei 81/bis, 25121 Brescia; tel. 030-2977834; f. 1882; art and archaeology and three churches; incl. collection of the former Museo Romano (prehistoric, pre-Roman and Roman artefacts).

Museo Civico di Scienze Naturali: Via Ozanam 4, 25128 Brescia; tel. 030-2978672; fax 030-3701048; e-mail mtonon@comune.brescia.it; f. 1949; botanical, geological, zoological and palaeoethnographical collns; library of 60,000 vols; Dir MARCO TONON; publs *Natura Bresciana*, *Annuario Civica Specola Cidnea*.

Museo Diocesano d'Arte Sacra: Via Gasparo da Salò 13, 25122 Brescia; tel. 030-3751064; fax 030-40233; e-mail musdioc@mus-dioc.bs.it; internet www.mus-dioc.bs.it; f. 1978; Dir IVO PANTEGHINI.

Cagliari

Museo Archeologico Nazionale: Cittadella dei Musei, Piazza Arsenale 1, 09124 Cagliari; tel. 070-662496; f. 1806; Sardinian antiquities (prehistorical, Punic, Roman periods); library of 8,000 vols; Dir Dr VINCENZO SANTONI.

Capua

Museo Provinciale Campano: Via Roma, 81043 Capua; tel. 0823-961402; fax 0823-620035; e-mail info@museocampano.it; internet www.museocampano.it; f. 1870;

library of 57,000 vols, 2,956 MSS; Dir Prof. GIUSEPPE CENTORE.

Chieti

Museo Archeologico Nazionale d'Abruzzo: Via Villa Comunale 3, 66100 Chieti; tel. 0871-331668; fax 0871-330946; e-mail musarc@muvi.org; internet www.muvi.org/musarc; f. 1959; pottery, weapons and ornaments from 9th to 4th-century BC burial sites, sculpture from 6th and 5th-centuries BC; Dir Dott.ssa MARIA RUGGERI.

Cividale

Museo Archeologico Nazionale: Piazza del Duomo 13, 33043 Cividale; tel. 0432-700700; fax 0432-700751; e-mail archeologicocividale@libero.it; f. 1817; prehistoric, Roman and medieval archaeology, jewellery and miniatures; library of 15,000 vols and archives; Dir Dott.ssa AURORA CAGNANA; publ. *Forum Iulii* (annually).

Cosenza

Museo Civico: Piazza XV Marzo, 87100 Cosenza; tel. 0984-813324; f. 1898; history and archaeology; Dir Dr VINCENZO ZUMBINI; publ. *Guide*.

Faenza

Museo Internazionale delle Ceramiche: Via Campidori 2, 48018 Faenza; tel. 0546-697311; fax 0546-27141; e-mail micfaenza@provincia.ra.it; internet www.micfaenza.org; f. 1908; history, art and techniques of ceramics; library of 53,000 vols; Dir (vacant); publ. *Faenza* (6 a year).

Ferrara

Gallerie d'Arte Moderna e Contemporanea: Corso Porta Mare 9, 44100 Ferrara; tel. 0532-243415; e-mail artemoderna@comune.fe.it; Dir Dott. ANDREA BUZZONI.

Constituent galleries:

Museo Michelangelo Antonioni: Corso Ercole i d'Este 17, 44100 Ferrara; tel. 0532-209988; e-mail diamanti@comune.fe.it.

Palazzo dei Diamanti: Corso Ercole I d'Este 21, 44100 Ferrara; tel. 0532-209988; fax 0532-203064; e-mail diamanti@comune.fe.it; incorporates Galleria d'Arte Moderna e Contemporanea, Museo M. Antonioni.

Palazzo Massari: Corso Porta Mare 5–9, 44100 Ferrara; tel. 0532-243415; fax 0532-205035; e-mail artemoderna@comune.fe.it; incorporates Museo d'Arte Moderna e Contemporanea Filippe de Pisis, Museo dell'Ottocento, Museo G. Boldini, Padiglione d'Arte Contemporanea.

Museo Archeologico Nazionale di Spina: Via XX Settembre 124 (Palazzo di Ludovico il Moro), 44100 Ferrara; tel. 0532-66299; f. 1935; Greco-Etruscan vases, statuettes, bronzes and gold ornaments from the graves of Spina; Dir Dr FEDE BERTI.

Florence

Comune di Firenze–Direzione Cultura–Servizio Musei: Via delle Conce 28, 50122 Florence; tel. 055-2625961; fax 055-2625984; internet www.comune.fi.it; Dir Dott.ssa CHIARA SILLA.

Museums and galleries under its control:

Cappella Brancacci: Piazza del Carmine, 50124 Florence; tel. 055-2382195; frescoes in the Church of Santa Maria del Carmine painted by Masolino (1383–1447) and Masaccio (1401–1428), and completed by Filippino Lippi (1457–1504).

Fondazione Romano nel Cenacolo di Santo Spirito: Piazza Santo Spirito 29, 50125 Florence; tel. 055-287043; colln of sculptures given by Salvatore Romano; incl. 2 pieces by Tino di Camaino, and 2 fragments attributed to Donatello.

Galleria Rinaldo Carnielo: Piazza Savonarola 3, 50132 Florence; works by the sculptor Rinaldo Carnielo (1853–1910).

Museo Bardini: Piazza dei Mozzi 1, 50125 Florence; tel. 055-2342427; f. 1925; paintings by Pollaiuolo, Beccafumi, Lucas Cranach, Mirabello Cavalori, Giovanni da S. Giovanni, Cecco Bravo, Guercino, Carlo Dolci, Luca Giordano, Il Volterano; sculptures by Nicola and Giovanni Pisano, Tino di Camaino, Andrea della Robbia, Donatello, Michelozzo; oriental rugs, bronzes, arms, furniture, medals, etc.

Museo Marino Marini: Piazza San Pancrazio, 50123 Florence; tel. 055-219432; fax 055-219432; e-mail marini@fol.it; works by the sculptor Marino Marini (1901–1980).

Museo di Palazzo Vecchio: Quartieri Monumentali, Piazza della Signoria, 50122 Florence; tel. 055-2768325; paintings, furnishings; frescoes by Ghirlandaio, Salviati, Bronzino, Vasari; Michelangelo's 'Victory' statue.

Museo di Santa Maria Novella: Piazza S. Maria Novella, 50123 Florence; tel. 055-282187; museum built in part of a Dominican church; 15th-century frescoes of the Genesis story by Paolo Uccello, Dello Delli; 14th-century frescoes by Andrea di Bonaiuto depicting the Dominican order and the Church Triumphant.

Museo Stibbert: Via F. Stibbert 26, 50134 Florence; tel. 055-486049; fax 055-475721; e-mail info@museostibbert.it; internet www.museostibbert.it/web.it; f. 1908; Etruscan, Roman and medieval arms and armour; European and Oriental arms from 15th–19th centuries; holy objects and vestments; European and Oriental costumes, etc. from 18th–19th centuries; Flemish tapestries from 15th–17th centuries, Italian and foreign paintings and furniture from 14th–19th centuries; library of 3,500 vols; Dir KIRSTEN ASCHENGREEN.

Museo Storico Topografico 'Firenze com' era': Via dell'Oriolo 24, 50122 Florence; tel. 055-2616545; depicts the history of the city.

Raccolta d'Arte Contemporanea 'Alberto della Ragione': Via S.Egidio, 21, 50122 Florence; tel. 055-283078; c. 250 works donated by Alberto della Ragione in 1970; Italian art 1914–60.

Gabinetto Disegni e Stampe degli Uffizi: Via Ninna 5, 50123 Florence; tel. 055-2388671; fax 055-2388624; e-mail gdsu@polomuseale.firenze.it; internet www.polomuseale.firenze.it; Dir MARZIA FAIETTI.

Galleria d'Arte Moderna di Palazzo Pitti: Piazza Pitti 1, 50125 Florence; tel. 055-2388601; fax 055-2654520; e-mail gam@polomuseale.firenze.it; internet www.polomuseale.firenze.it/musei/artemoderna; f. 1914; paintings and sculptures since 19th c.; library of 2,000 vols on the history of art; Dir Dott. CARLO SISI.

Galleria dell' Accademia: Via Ricasoli 60, 50122 Florence; tel. 055-2388609; fax 055-2388609; e-mail galleriaaccademia@sbas.firenze.it; internet www.sbas.firenze.it; f. 1784; contains the most complete collection of Michelangelo's statues in Florence and works of art of 13th- to 19th-century masters, mostly Tuscan; colln of musical instruments from the Medici and Lorena families; Dir Dssa FRANCA FALLETTI.

Galleria Palatina: Palazzo Pitti, Piazza Pitti 1, 50125 Florence; tel. 055-2388614; fax 055-2388613; e-mail galleriapalatina.galleri@tin.it; internet www.polomuseale.firenze.it/musei/palatina; f. 17th c.; contains a fine collection of paintings from 16th–17th c.; library of 2,000 vols on the history of art; Dir SERENA PADOVANI.

Galleria Palatina e Appartamenti Reali: Palazzo Pitti, Piazza Pitti 1, 50125 Florence; tel. 055-2388611; fax 055-2388613; e-mail galleriapalatina.galleri@tin.it; internet www.sbas.firenze.it; f. 18–19th c.; Italian and European masterpieces from the 16th–17th c., incl. works by Raphael, A. del Sarto, Carvaggio, Titian, Rubens and Van Dyck; Dir Dott.ssa SERENA PADOVANI.

Galleria degli Uffizi: Piazzale degli Uffizi, 50122 Florence; tel. 055-2388651; fax 055-2388694; e-mail direzione.uffizi@polomuseale.firenze.it; internet www.polomuseale.firenze.it/uffizi; f. 16th century; Florentine Renaissance paintings and sculpture, and paintings by German, Dutch and Flemish masters; library of 64,000 vols, 470 MSS relating to the Florentine collections, 5 incunabula. 996 bound periodicals, 140 current periodicals; Dir ANTONIO PAOLUCCI.

Istituto e Museo di Storia della Scienza: Piazza dei Giudici 1, 50122 Florence; tel. 055-265311; fax 055-2653130; e-mail imss@imss.fi.it; internet www.imss.fi.it; f. 1927; museum of scientific instruments and institute dedicated to the research, documentation and dissemination of the history of science; library of 100,000 vols; Dir Prof. PAOLO GALLUZZI; publs *Nuncius Annali di Storia della Scienza* (2 a year), *Galilaeana* (annually).

Museo Archeologico Nazionale: Via della Colonna 38, 50121 Florence; tel. 055-23575; fax 055-242213; e-mail sat@comune.firenze.it; internet www.comune.firenze.it/soggetti/sat; f. 1870; Egyptian, Etruscan and Greco-Roman archaeology; Dir Dott. ANGELO BOTTINI.

Museo degli Argenti: Palazzo Pitti, Piazza Pitti 1, 50125 Florence; tel. 055-2388709; fax 055-2388710; e-mail argenti@polomuseale.firenze.it; internet www.polomuseale.firenze.it/musei/argenti; summer state apartments of the Medici Grand Dukes; collections of gold, silver, enamel, *objets d'art*, hardstones, ivory, amber, cameos and jewels, principally from the 15th–18th c.; Dir ORNELLA CASAZZA.

Attached gallery:

Galleria del Costume: Palazzo Pitti, 50125 Florence; tel. and fax 055-2388763; e-mail costume.pitti@virgilio.it; internet www.polomuseale.firenze.it/musei/costume; period costumes, principally since 18th c., shown in the neo-classical Meridiana wing of the palace; Dir Dr CARLO SISI.

Museo della Casa Buonarroti: Via Ghibellina 70, 50122 Florence; tel. 055-241752; fax 055-241698; e-mail fond@casabuonarroti.it; internet www.casabuonarroti.it; f. 1858; works by Michelangelo and others; large collection of drawings by Michelangelo, sculptures, majolica and archaeological items from the Buonarroti family collections; Dir P. RAGIONIERI.

Museo Horne: Fondazione Horne, Via dei Benci, 50122 Florence; tel. 055-244661; furniture and works of art from 14th–16th c.; Pres. Dr UMBERTO BALDINI.

Museo Mediceo: Palazzo Medici-Riccardi, Via Cavour 1, 50129 Florence; tel. 055-2760340; fax 055-2760451; e-mail a.belisario@provincia.fi.it; internet www.palazzo-medici.it; chapel built by Michelozzo and frescoed by Benozzo Gozzoli (1459); gallery with frescoes by Luca Giordano (1680); Dir ALESSANDRO BELISARIO.

Museo Nazionale del Bargello: Via del Proconsolo 4, 50122 Florence; tel. 055-

2388606; fax 055-2388756; e-mail museobargello@libero.it; internet www.sbas.firenze.it/bargello; f. 1859; medieval and modern sculpture and *objets d'art*; Dir BEATRICE PAOLOZZI STROZZI; publs *Lo Specchio del Bargello*, *Mostre del Museo Nazionale del Bargello*, *Inventari Medicei*.

Museo dell' Opera del Duomo: Piazza del Duomo 9, 50122 Florence; tel. 055-2302885; fax 055-2302898; e-mail opera@operaduomo.firenze.it; internet www.operaduomo.firenze.it; f. 1891; Dir PATRIZIO OSTICRESI.

Museo di Palazzo Davanzati (Casa Fiorentina Antica): Via Porta Rossa 13, 50123 Florence; tel. 055-2388610; fax 055-2388699; e-mail segreteria@sbas.firenze.it; internet www.sbas.firenze.it; f. 1956; applied arts, specializing in lace and ceramics; Dir Dssa ROSANNA CATERINA PROTO PISANI.

Museo delle Porcellane: Piazza Pitti, 50125 Florence; tel. 055-2388709; fax 055-2388710; e-mail argenti@polomuseale.firenze.it; internet www.polomuseale.firenze.it/musei/porcellane; collection of European porcelain from *c.* 1720–1850; Dir Dr MARIA MADDALENA MOSCO.

Museo di S. Marco o dell' Angelico: Piazza San Marco 3, 50121 Florence; tel. 055-2388608; fax 055-2388704; e-mail museosanmarco@polomuseale.firenze.it; internet www.polomuseale.firenze.it/musei/sanmarco; f. 1869; contains the largest existing colln of paintings by Fra Angelico; Dir Dtt.ssa MAGNOLIA SCUDIERI.

Forlì

Istituti Culturali ed Artistici: Corso della Repubblica 72, 47100 Forlì; tel. 0543-712600; fax 0543-712616; comprises a picture gallery, collection of prints and engravings, archaeological and ethnographical museums, ceramics, sculpture and local history; Piancastelli collection of paintings, medals and coins; Dir Dr FRANCO FABBRI.

Pinacoteca e Musei Comunali: Corso Repubblica 72, 47100 Forlì; tel. 0543-712606; fax 0543-712616; Dir Dr FRANCO FABBRI.

Genoa

Comune di Genova Direzione Cultura, Sport e Turismo–Settore Musei: Largo Pertini 4, 16121 Genoa; tel. 010-5574700; fax 010-5574701; e-mail museicivici@comune.genova.it; internet www.comune.genova.it/turismo/musei/welcome.htm; f. 1908; library of 40,000 vols; Dir GUIDO GANDINO; publ. *Bollettino dei Musei Civici Genovesi* (quarterly).

Museums and galleries under its control:

Archivio Fotografico del Comune di Genova: Via Garibaldi 18, 16124 Genoa; tel. 010-2476351; fax 010-2475357; e-mail bculturalifoto@comune.genova.it; internet www.comune.genova.it/turismo/musei/archivi/welc_archivi.htm; f. 1910; 200,000 photographs (1860–1946) on Genoese customs and history, 19th-century landscapes, war damage, Genoese art and architecture; photographs of museum collns; Curator ELISABETTA PAPONE.

Archivio Storico del Comune di Genova: Palazzo Ducale, Piazza Matteotti 10, 16123 Genoa; tel. 010-5574808; fax 010-5574823; e-mail archiviostorico@comune.genova.it; internet www.archiviostoricogenova.it; f. 1906; documents since 15th century; coins, weights and measures; Curator RAFFAELLA PONTE.

Castello D'Albertis: Corso Dogali 18, 16136 Genoa; tel. 010-2723820; fax 010-2721456; e-mail castellodalbertis@comune.genova.it; internet www.castellodalbertisgenova.it; f. 1932; Museum housed in a Neo-Gothic castle with archaeological and ethnological collns from Africa, Oceania and the Americas; Curator MARIA CAMILLA DE PALMA.

Civico Museo di Storia e Cultura Contadina Genovese e Ligure: Salita al Garbo 47, 16159 Genoa Rivarolo; tel. 010-7401243; fax 010-5574701; f. 1983; colln of tools and utensils relating to local rural life since 19th century; Curator PATRIZIA GARIBALDI.

Galata Museo del Mare: Calata de Mari 1, Darsena, Porto Antico, 16128 Genoa; fax 010-2345655; e-mail info@galatamuseodelmare.it; internet www.galatamuseodelmare.it; maritime history of the city; exhibits incl. 17th-century galleon, arsenal, docks, ancient atlases and naval instruments.

Galleria di Palazzo Bianco: Via Garibaldi 11, 16124 Genoa; tel. 010-5572193; fax 010-2475357; e-mail museopalazzobianco@comune.genova.it; internet www.museopalazzobianco.it; f. 1889; paintings by Genoese and Flemish masters and other schools (15th–18th centuries); Curator CLARIO DI FABIO.

Galleria di Palazzo Rosso: Via Garibaldi 18, 16124 Genoa; tel. 010-2476351; fax 010-2475357; e-mail museopalazzorosso@comune.genova.it; internet www.museopalazzorosso.it; f. 1874; the fine art colln of a noble Genoese family: paintings and sculpture, frescoes and stuccos, nativity models, ceramics; also a colln of textiles; Curator PIERO BOCCARDO.

Museo di Archeologia Ligure: Villa Durazzo-Pallavicini, Via Pallavicini 11, 16155 Genoa–Pegli; tel. 010-6981048; fax 010-6974040; e-mail archligure@mail.it; f. 1892; Ligurian archaeology of the periods up to the Roman era; colln of Greek and Roman antiquities; Curators PATRIZIA GARIBALDI, GUIDO ROSSI.

Museo d'Arte Contemporanea Villa Croce: Via Jacopo Ruffini 3, 16128 Genoa; tel. 010-585772; fax 010-532482; e-mail museocroce@comune.genova.it; internet www.museovillacroce.it; f. 1985; works by key Italian artists; documentation on artistic research in Genoa and Liguria from the Second World War onwards; sculpture by Genoese and Ligurian artists; specialized library and archive open to the public; Curator GUIDO GIUBBINI.

Museo d'Arte Orientale 'Edoardo Chiossone': Villetta di Negro, Piazzale Mazzini 1, 16122 Genoa; tel. 010-542285; fax 010-580526; e-mail museochiossone@comune.genova.it; internet www.museochiossonegenova.it; f. 1905; Japanese works of art from 11th–19th centuries (about 20,000 pieces), collected in Japan during the Meiji period by Edoardo Chiossone; Curator DONATELLA FAILLA.

Museo Civico di Storia Naturale 'Giacomo Doria': Via Brigata Liguria 9, 16121 Genoa; tel. 010-564567; fax 010-566319; e-mail museodoria@comune.genova.it; internet www.museodoria.it; f. 1867; zoology, botany and geology; library of 78,000 vols; Curator Dr GIULIANO DORIA; publs *Annali* (every 2 years), *Doriana* (irreg.).

Museo 'Giannettino Luxoro': Via Mafalda di Savoia 3, 16167 Genoa–Nervi; tel. 010-322673; fax 010-322396; f. 1945; Flemish and Genoese paintings of the 17th and 18th centuries, furniture, ceramics and pottery in the rooms of an early 20th-century villa; Curator LOREDANA PESSA.

Museo Navale: Villa Doria, Piazza Bonavino 7, 16156 Genoa–Pegli; tel. 010-6969885; fax 010-5574701; f. 1930; models of ships, nautical instruments, navigation maps, prints; Curator PIERANGELO CAMPODONICO.

Museo del Risorgimento e Istituto Mazziniano: Casa di Mazzini, Via Lomellini 11, 16124 Genoa; tel. 010-2465843; fax 010-2541545; e-mail museorisorgimento@comune.genova.it; internet www.istitutomazziniano.it; f. 1934; exhibits illustrating life and work of Mazzini, 19th-century documents and arms, specialized library containing works since 18th century; Curator LEO MORABITO.

Museo di Sant'Agostino: Piazza Sarzano 35r., 16128 Genoa; tel. 010-2511263; fax 010-2464516; e-mail museoagostino@comune.genova.it; internet www.museosantagostino.it; f. 1938; sculpture from 10th–18th centuries, architecture and painting; Curator CLARIO DI FABIO.

Museo del Tesoro della Cattedrale di San Lorenzo: Piazza San Lorenzo, 16123 Genoa; tel. 010-2471831; fax 010-5574701; e-mail info@arti-e-mestieri.it; internet www.museosanlorenzo.it; f. 1892; gold and silver objects; Curator CLARIO DI FABIO.

Padiglione del Mare e della Navigazione: Porto Antico—Magazzini del Cotone, 16126 Genoa; tel. 010-2463678; fax 010-2467746; f. 1996; maritime collection; works of art, models and reproductions; Curator PIERANGELO CAMPODONICO.

Raccolte Frugone in Villa Grimaldi: Villa Grimaldi Fassio, Via Capolungo 9, Nervi, 16167 Genoa; tel. 010-322396; fax 010-3724405; e-mail raccoltefrugone@comune.genova.it; internet www.raccoltefrugone.it; f. 1993; colln of sculpture and paintings by Italian artists since 19th century; Curator MARIA FLORA GIUBILEI.

Galleria Nazionale di Palazzo Spinola: Piazza Pellicceria 1, 16123 Genoa; tel. 010-2705300; fax 010-2705322; e-mail galspinola@libero.it; internet www.palazzospinola.it; f. 1958; Dir Dssa FARIDA SIMONETTI; publ. *Quaderni* (annually).

Soprintendenza per i Beni Archeologici della Liguria: Palazzo Reale, Via Balbi 10, 16126 Genoa; tel. 010-27181; fax 010-2465925; e-mail archeoge@arti.beniculturali.it; internet www.archeoge.arti.beniculturali.it; f. 1939; preservation of monuments and excavations of Liguria (prehistoric, Roman and medieval) and conservation of the ancient city of Luni and prehistoric caves of Balzi Rossi; library of 13,000 vols; Superintendent Dott. GIUSEPPINA SPADEA.

Grosseto

Museo Archeologico e d'Arte della Maremma: Piazza Baccarini 3, 58100 Grosseto; tel. 0564-488750; fax 0564-488753; e-mail maam@gol.grosseto.it; internet www.gol.grosseto.it/maam; f. 1865; archaeological and medieval findings from the Maremma; library of 3,000 vols; Dir Dott.ssa MARIAGRAZIA CELUZZA.

L'Aquila

Museo Nazionale d'Abruzzo: Forte Spagnolo, 67100 L'Aquila; tel. 0862-6331; fax 0862-413096; e-mail mna@muvi.org; internet muvi.org/museonazionaledabruzzo; f. 1949; art from the early Middle Ages to contemporary times; Dir Dott. CALCEDONIO TROPEA.

Lecce

Museo 'Sigismondo Castromediano': Viale Gallipoli 28, 73100 Lecce; tel. 0832-307415; fax 0832-304435; f. 1868; archaeology and art gallery; library of 1,900 vols,

2,500 pamphlets and offprints; Dir ANTONIO CASSIANO.

Lucca

Museo Nazionale di Villa Guinigi: Villa Guinigi, Via della Quarquonia, 55100 Lucca; tel. and fax 0583-496033; e-mail luccamuseinazionali@libero.it; internet www.liberologico.com/sbaaaspi/flash/musei/villa-guinigi; collection of Roman and late Roman sculptures and mosaics; Romanesque, Gothic, Renaissance and Neoclassical sculpture; paintings from 12th–18th c. including Fra Bartolomeo and Vasari; wood inlays, textiles, medieval goldsmiths' art; Dir Dott.ssa MARIA TERESA FILIERI.

Museo e Pinacoteca Nazionale di Palazzo Mansi: Via Galli Tassi 43, 55100 Lucca; tel. 0583-55570; fax 0583-312221; f. 1868; paintings by Titian, Tintoretto, etc., and Tuscan, Venetian, French and Flemish Schools; Dir Dr MARIA TERESA FILIERI.

Mantua

Palazzo Ducale: Piazza Sordello 40, 46100 Mantua; tel. 0376-352100; fax 0376-366274; e-mail info@mantovaducale.it; internet www.mantovaducale.it; incorporates Museo e Galleria di Pittura (13th–18th c. paintings) and Museo Statuario d'Arte Greca e Romana; Dir Dott. FILIPPO TREVISANI.

Matera

Museo Nazionale D. Ridola: Via D. Ridola 24, 75100 Matera; tel. 0835-310058; internet www.archeologia.beniculturali.it/pages/atlante/S201.html; f. 1910; local prehistory; funerary items from 6th–4th c. BC, bronzes; Dir Dott.ssa MARIA LUISA NAVA.

Messina

Museo Regionale: Viale della Libertà 465, 98121 Messina; tel. 090-361292; fax 090-361294; internet www.regione.sicilia.it/beniculturali/dirbenicult/musei/musei2/engarmessina.htm; f. 1922; local art and culture from 12th–18th c.; Dir Dott.ssa CARMELA ANGELA DI STEFANO.

Milan

Civiche Raccolte Archeologiche e Numismatiche, Biblioteca Archeologicae Numuismatica: Castello Sforzesco, Piazza Castello, 20121 Milan; tel. 02-88463737; fax 02-88463800; e-mail biblioteca.casra@comune.milano.it; internet www.comune.milano.it/casra; library of 30,000 vols; f. 1808; prehistoric, Roman, Etruscan, Greek and Egyptian archaeology; coins and medals; library and archives; Dir Dr RINA LA GUARDIA; publ. *Rassegna di Studi* (2 a year).

Galleria d'Arte Moderna: Villa Belgiojoso Bonoparte, Museo Dell'Ottocento, Via Palestro 16, 20121 Milan; tel. and fax 02-77809761; f. 1861; painting and sculpture from Neo-Classical period until late 19th c.: includes the Grassi and Vismara collections and Museo Marino Marini; Dir Dott. MARIA TERESA FIORIO.

Museo d'Arte Antica: Castello Sforzesco, 20121 Milan; tel. 02-88463695; fax 02-88463650; f. 1893; sculpture from the middle ages–16th c., including the *Pietà* of Michelangelo; paintings, including works by Mantegna, Foppa, Lippi, Bellini, Lotto, Tintoretto, Tiepolo, Guardi, etc.; furniture, silver, bronzes, ivories, ceramics, musical instruments, tapestries by Bramantino, Bertarelli stamp collection; library of 41,000 vols; Dirs Dr CLAUDIO SALSI (decorative art), Prof. MARIA TERESA FIORIO (painting and sculpture), Dr CLAUDIO SALSI (decorative art).

Museo Civico di Storia Naturale di Milano: Corso Venezia 55, 20121 Milan; tel. 02-88463280; fax 02-88463281; internet www.comune.milano.it/museostorianaturale; f. 1838; all branches of natural history; depts of Vertebrate Palaeontology, Invertebrate Palaeontology, Mineralogy, Vertebrate Zoology, Invertebrate Zoology, Entomology, Botany; library of 140,000 vols; Dir Dr ENRICO BANFI; publs *Atti della Società Italiana di Scienze Naturali e del Museo Civico di Storia Naturale di Milano* (2 a year), *Memorie della Società Italiana di Scienze Naturali e del Museo Civico di Storia Naturale di Milano* (irregular), *Natura* (2 a year).

Museo Nazionale della Scienza e della Tecnica 'Leonardo da Vinci': Via San Vittore 21, 20123 Milan; tel. 02-485551; fax 02-48010016; e-mail museo@museoscienza.org; internet www.museoscienza.org; f. 1953; scientific and technical activities, displaying relics, models and designs, with particular emphasis on Leonardo's work; library of 32,000 vols, mostly history of science and technology, 150 16th c. vols, large section on Leonardo, including facsimile of every MS; Dir FIORENZO GALLI; publ. *Museoscienza* (2 a year).

Museo Poldi Pezzoli: Via A. Manzoni 12, 20121 Milan; tel. 02-796334; fax 02-45473811; e-mail info@museopoldipezzoli.org; internet www.museopoldipezzoli.it; f. 1881; paintings from 14th to 19th century; armour, tapestries, rugs, jewellery, porcelain, glass, textiles, furniture, clocks and watches, etc.; library of 5,500 vols; Dir Dott. ANNALISA ZANNI.

Pinacoteca Ambrosiana: Piazza Pio XI 2, 20123 Milan; tel. 02-806921; fax 02-80692210; e-mail info@ambrosiana.it; internet www.ambrosiana.it; f. 1618; paintings by Raphael, Botticelli, Titian, Luini, Jan Brueghel, Leonardo da Vinci, Jacobo Bassano, Bramantino, etc.; miniatures, enamels, ceramics and medallions; Dir Dott. GIANFRANCO RAVASI.

Pinacoteca di Brera: Via Brera 28, 20121 Milan; tel. 02-722631; fax 02-72001140; e-mail brera.artimi@arti.beniculturali.it; internet www.brera.beniculturali.it; f. 1809; pictures of all schools, especially Lombard and Venetian; paintings by Mantegna, Bellini, Crivelli, Lotto, Titian, Veronese, Tintoretto, Tiepolo, Foppa, Bergognone, Luini, Piero della Francesca, Bramante, Raphael, Caravaggio, Rembrandt, Van Dyck, Rubens; also 20th c. works, mostly Italian; Dir Dr.ssa MARIA TERESA FIORIO.

Raccolte Storiche del Comune di Milano, Museo del Risorgimento: Palazzo De Marchi, Via Borgonuovo 23, 20121 Milan; tel. 02-88464170; fax 02-88464181; e-mail risorgi@energy.it; internet www.museidelcentro.mi.it; f. 1884; documents, relics, etc., of the period 1796–1870; library of 130,000 vols; Dir Dott. ROBERTO GUERRI.

Modena

Galleria Estense: Palazzo dei Musei, Piazza Sant' Agostino 337, 41100 Modena; tel. 059-4395711; fax 059-230196; e-mail galleria.estense@interbusiness.it; internet www.galleriaestense.it; f. 15th century in Ferrara, transferred to Palazzo Ducale, Modena, 1598, to Palazzo dei Musei 1894; collections include about 2,000 paintings and drawings of 14th–18th c., sculpture, engravings, medals, etc.; library of 15,000 vols; Superintendent MARIA GRAZIA BERNARDINI.

Museo Civico Archeologico Etnologico: Palazzo dei Musei, Viale Vittorio Veneto 5, 41100 Modena; tel. 059-200100; fax 059-200110; e-mail museo.archeologico@comune.modena.it; internet www.comune.modena.it/museoarcheologico; f. 1871; prehistory and ethnology; library of 5,000 vols, 2,700 pamphlets; Curator Dott. ILARIA PULINI; publ. *Quaderni*.

Museo Civico d'Arte: Largo Porta Sant'Agostino 337, 41100 Modena; tel. 059-200100; fax 059-200110; e-mail museo.arte@comune.modena.it; internet www.comune.modena.it/museoarte; f. 1871; paintings, sculpture, decorative arts; library of 7,500 vols, 3,500 pamphlets; Curator Dssa FRANCESCA PICCININI.

Museo Lapidario Estense: Piazza Sant' Agostino 337, 41100 Modena; tel. 059-4395711; fax 059-230196; e-mail galleria.estense@beniculturali.it; internet www.galleriaestense.it; f. 1828; Roman and medieval archaeological collections; Dir Dott. MARIA GRAZIA BERNARDINI.

Naples

Museo Archeologico Nazionale: Piazza Museo 19, 80135 Naples; tel. 081-440166; fax 081-440013; e-mail sanc@interbusiness.it; internet www.marketplace.it/museo.nazionale; f. 18th c.; Greek, Roman, Italian and Egyptian antiquities; Superintendent Dr STEFANO DE CARO.

Museo Civico 'Gaetano Filangieri': Via Duomo 288, 80138 Naples; tel. 081-203211; fax 081-203175; internet www.cib.na.cnr.it/remuna/filang/indice.html; f. 1888; paintings, furniture, archives, photographs, majolica, arms and armour; library of 30,000 vols, and coin collection of Neapolitan history; Dir ANTONIO BUCCINO GRIMALDI.

Museo 'Duca di Martina' alla Floridiana: Via Cimarosa 77, 80127 Naples; tel. and fax 081-5788418; e-mail martina.artina@beniculturali.it; f. 1931; decorative art; exhibits donated by the Duke; spec. colln of oriental art; Dir Dr LUISA AMBROSIO.

Museo e Gallerie Nazionali di Capodimonte: Via Miano 1, 80131 Naples; tel. 081-7499111; fax 081-7445032; e-mail capodimonte.artina@arti.beniculturali.it; f. 1738; paintings from 13th–19th c.; sculpture from 19th c.; contemporary art; collection of arms and armour; medals and bronzes of the Renaissance; porcelain; library of 2,000 vols; Dir Prof. MARCIELLA UTILI.

Museo Nazionale di S. Martino: Largo S. Martino 5, 80129 Naples; tel. 081-5585942; e-mail artina@arti.beniculturali.it; f. 1872; ancient church of S. Martino with 16th–18th c. pictures, 13th–19th c. sculpture, majolica and porcelain, Neapolitan historical records and topographical collection, naval collection, arms and military costumes, opaline glass, section of modern painting, prints and engravings; Dir Dott.ssa ROSSANA MUZII.

Soprintendenza Archeologica di Pompei: Via Villa dei Misteri 2, 80045 Pompei; tel. 081-8575111; fax 081-8613183; e-mail info@pompeiisites.org; internet www.pompeiisites.org; f. 1982; Supt Prof. PIETRO GIOVANNI GUZZO.

Supervised sites:

Antiquarium Nazionale di Boscoreale: Via Settetermini 15, Loc. Villa Regina, 80041 Boscoreale; tel. 081-5368796; fax 081-8613183; e-mail info@pompeiisites.org; internet www.pompeiisites.org; Dir Dssa GRETE STEFANI.

Scavi di Ercolano: Corso Resina, 80056 Ercolano; tel. 081-7324311; fax 081-8613183; e-mail info@pompeiisites.org; internet www.pompeiisites.org; Dir Dssa MARIA PAOLA GUIDOBALDI.

Scavi di Oplontis: Via Sepolcri, 80058 Torre Annunziata; tel. 081-8621755; fax 081-8613183; e-mail info@pompeiisites.org; internet www.pompeiisites.org; Dir Dott. LORENZO FERGOLA.

Scavi di Pompei: Via Villa dei Misteri 2, 80045 Pompei; tel. 081-8575400; fax 081-8613183; e-mail info@pompeiisites.org; internet www.pompeiisites.org; Dir Dott. ANTONIO D'AMBROSIO.

Scavi di Stabia: Via Passeggiata Archeologica, 80053 Castellammare di Stabia; tel. 081-8714541; fax 081-8613183; e-mail info@pompeiisites.org; internet www.pompeiisites.org; Dirs Dssa GIOVANNA BONIFACIO.

Padua

Musei Civici di Padova: Piazza Eremitani 8, 35121 Padua; tel. 049-82045450; fax 049-8204585; e-mail musei@comune.padova.it; internet padovacultura.padovanet.it/musei/archivio/000046.html; f. 1825; Dir DAVIDE BANZATO; publ. *Bollettino del Museo Civico di Padova*.

Constituent institutions:

Museo Archeologico: Piazza Eremitani, 35121 Padua; tel. 049-82045450; fax 049-8204585; e-mail zampierig@comune.padova.it; internet padovacultura.padovanet.it/musei/archivio/000065.html; f. 1825; pre- and early historic and Roman finds; Curator Dott. GIROLAMO ZAMPIERI.

Museo d'Arte Medioevale e Moderna: c/o Musei Civici, Piazza Eremitani 8, 35121 Padua; tel. 049-82045450; fax 049-8204585; e-mail musei@comune.padova.it; internet padovacultura.padovanet.it/musei/archivio/000066.html; f. 1825; paintings, sculptures, bronzes, ceramics; Curator Dtt.ssa FRANCA PELLEGRINI.

Museo Bottacin: Palazzo Zuckermann, Corso Garibaldi 33, 35122 Padua; tel. 049-8766959; fax 049-8774671; internet padovacultura.padovanet.it/musei/archivio/000148.html; f. 1865; Graeco-Roman, Paduan, Venetian, Italian, Napoleonic coins, seals and medals, 19th-century sculptures and paintings; Curator Dott.ssa ROBERTA PARISE.

Cappella degli Scrovegni: Piazza Eremitani 8, 35121 Padua; tel. 049-82045450; fax 049-8204585; e-mail musei@comune.padova.it; internet padovacultura.padovanet.it/musei/archivio/000071.html; f. 1300; Giotto frescoes; Dir DAVIDE BANZATO.

Sala del Palazzo della Ragione 'Il Salone': Via Otto Febbraio, 35122 Padua; tel. 049-8205006; fax 049-8204566; e-mail musei@comune.padova.it; internet padovacultura.padovanet.it/musei/archivio/000082.html; f. 1218; works by Fra Giovanni degli Eremitani, frescoes by Nicolò Miretto and Stefano Da Ferrara; Dir DAVIDE BANZATO.

Palermo

Museo Archeologico Regionale A. Salinas: Via Bara all'Olivella 24, 90133 Palermo; tel. 091-6116805; fax 091-6110740; e-mail a.salinas@tin.it; f. 1866; prehistoric, Egyptian, Greek, Punic, Roman and Etruscan antiquities; library of 25,000 vols and pamphlets; Superintendent Prof. Dott.ssa CARMELA ANGELA DI STEFANO.

Parma

Galleria Nazionale: Piazzale della Pilotta 15, 43100 Parma; tel. 0521-233309; fax 0521-206336; e-mail sbaspr@libero.it; internet www.artipr.arti.beniculturali.it/htm/Galleria.htm; f. 1752, later reconstructed and added to; paintings from 13th–19th c., including works by Correggio, Parmigianino, Cima, El Greco, Piazzetta, Tiepolo, Holbein, Van Dyck, Mor, Nattier, and several painters of the school of Parma; 19th c. paintings by Parmesan painters; library of history of art; library of 15,000 vols; Superintendent LUCIA FORNARI SCHIANCHI.

Museo Archeologico Nazionale: Via della Pilotta 5, 43100 Parma; tel. 0521-233718; fax 0521-386112; e-mail manpr@libero.it; f. 1760; archaeological collection of sculptures and other monuments from Veleia; Prehistoric and Bronze Age collections; Roman monuments from province of Parma; Egyptian, Greek, Etruscan and Roman art documents; Dir Dr MARIA BERNABÒ BREA.

Museo Bodoniano: c/o Biblioteca Palatina, Palazzo della Pilotta 3A, 43100 Parma; tel. 0521-220411; fax 0521-235662; e-mail mubodoni@unipr.it; internet www.mb-museobodoniano.it; f. 1963; dedicated to art of printing: punches, original matrices and moulds (approx. 80,000) from Bodoni's printing works; rare editions, technical manuals, press and tools of 'the prince of printers'; Dir LEONARDO FARINELLI; Curator CATERINA SILVA; publ. *Bollettino* (irreg.).

Pavia

Civici Musei—Castello Visconteo: Piazza Castello, 27100 Pavia; tel. 0382-33853; fax 0382-303028; e-mail museicivici@comune.pv.it; internet www.comune.pv.it; f. 1838; library of 21,000 vols; Dir Dott. DONATA VICINI.

Perugia

Galleria Nazionale dell'Umbria: Palazzo dei Priori, Corso Vannucci 1, 06122 Perugia; tel. 075-57411; fax 075-5720316; e-mail uffinfo@gnu.it; internet www.gallerianazionaleumbria.it; f. 1863; paintings of Umbrian school, 13th–19th c.; also sculptures and jewellery; library of 5,300 vols; Dir Dott.ssa VITTORIA GARIBALDI.

Museo Archeologico Nazionale dell'Umbria: Piazza Giordano Bruno 10, 06121 Perugia; tel. 075-5720345; fax 075-5728200; e-mail archeopg@arti.beniculturali.it; internet www.archeopg.arti.beniculturali.it; f. 1948; prehistoric, Roman, Hellenistic and Etruscan remains; primitive pottery, bone tools, funerary urns, amulets, archaic bronzes, coins; Dir A. E. FERUGLIO.

Pesaro

Musei Civici (Pinacoteca e Museo delle Ceramiche): Piazza Toschi Mosca 29, 61100 Pesaro; tel. 0721-387541; fax 0721-387524; e-mail musei@comune.pesaro.ps.it; internet www.museicivicipesaro.it; f. 1936; art gallery and ceramics and decorative arts museum; Dir Prof. GIAN CARLO BOJANI.

Pisa

Museo Nazionale di S. Matteo: Piazza San Matteo in Soarta, Lungarno Mediceo, 56127 Pisa; tel. 050-541865; fax 050-500099; internet www.humnet.unipi.it/linguistica/corsiit/pisa/museo_nazionale_di_san_matteo.htm; f. 1949; sculptures by the Pisanos and their school; colln of the Pisan school from 12th–14th centuries, and paintings and sculpture of the 15th–17th centuries (works by Simone Martini, Masaccio, Beato Angelico, Benozzo Gozzoli, Ghirlandaio, Donatello, Della Robbia), 10thto 17th-centuries ceramics, colln of coins and medals; Dir Dott.ssa MARIAGIULIA BURRESI.

Portoferraio

Museo Napoleonico di S. Martino: 57037 Portoferraio.

Ravenna

Museo Nazionale di Ravenna: Via Benedetto Fiandrini, 48100 Ravenna; tel. 0544-34424; fax 0544-37391; e-mail sbapravenna@beniculturali.it; f. 1885; State property since 1885; art, numismatics and archaeology; Dir Dott. CETTY MUSCOLINO.

Reggio Calabria

Museo Nazionale: Piazza De Nava 26, 89122 Reggio Calabria; tel. 0965-812255; fax 0965-25164; e-mail archeorc@arti.benicultura.it; internet www.museonazionalerc.it; f. 1958; archaeological objects from Calabria from prehistoric era to Roman times; also *Antiquarium di Locri* (Locri), *Museo Archaeologico* (Vibo Valentia), *Museo Archaeologico* (Crotone), *Museo della Sibaritide* (Sibari); library of 10,000 vols; art gallery; Dir Dott.ssa ELENA LATTANZI; publ. *Klearchos* (annual).

Rome

Galleria Borghese: Piazzale del Museo Borghese, 5, 00197 Rome; tel. 06-8413979; e-mail info.servizimusei@libero.it; internet www.galleriaborghese.it; f. *c*.1616; picture gallery, collections of classical and Baroque sculpture; Dir Dott.ssa ALBA COSTAMAGNA.

Galleria Nazionale d'Arte Antica di Palazzo Barberini: Via Quattro Fontane 13, 00184 Rome; tel. 06-4824184; e-mail info@galleriaborghese.it; internet www.galleriaborghese.it; Italian and European paintings from 12th–18th centuries, Baroque architecture; Dir ANNA LO BIANCO; Corsini colln at Galleria Corsini, Via della Lungara 10; Dir Dott. SIVIGLIANO ALLOISI.

Istituto Nazionale per la Grafica: Calcografia, Via della Stamperia 6, 00187 Rome; tel. 06-699801; fax 06-69921454; internet www.grafica.arti.beniculturali.it; f. 1895; Italian and foreign prints and drawings from since 14th c.; collection of matrices since 16th c.; Dir Dott.ssa SERENITA PAPALDO.

Keats-Shelley House: Piazza di Spagna 26, 00187 Rome; tel. 06-6784235; fax 06-6784167; e-mail info@keats-shelley-house.org; internet www.keats-shelley-house.org; f. 1907; library: reference library of 9,000 vols, access by appointment and dependent upon a letter of recommendation from an academic institution or publisher; Dir's permission required prior to consulting books published before 1900; Dir CATHERINE PAYLING; publ. *Review* (annual).

Musei Capitolini: Piazza del Campidoglio 1, 00186 Rome; tel. 06-67102475; fax 06-6785488; e-mail info.museicapitolini@comune.roma.it; internet www.museicapitolini.org; f. 1471; archaeology, art history; Dir Dott.ssa ANNA MURA SOMMELLA.

Museo Barracco: Corso Vittorio Emanuele 168, 00186 Rome; tel. and fax 06-68806848; e-mail crusuam@comune.roma.it; internet www2.comune.roma.it/museobarracco; f. 1905; evolution of sculpture from Egyptian to Roman styles; Dir Dott.ssa MARESITA NOTA.

Museo della Civiltà Romana: Piazza G. Agnelli 10, 00144 Rome; tel. 06-5926041; fax 06-5926135; internet www2.comune.roma.it/museociviltaromana; f. 1952; history of Rome from its origins; Curator Dott.ssa ANNA MURA SOMMELLA.

Museo di Palazzo Venezia: Via del Plebiscito 118, 00186 Rome; tel. 06-69994319; internet www.museionline.it/ita/cerca/museo.asp?id=2362; f. 1921; medieval and Renaissance decorative art; 16th–17th c. ceramics; furniture, prints, textiles; Dir MARIA LETIZIA CASANOVA UCCELLA.

Museo di Roma: Via di San Pantaleo (Piazza Navona), 00186 Rome; tel. 06-82077304; fax 06-67108303; e-mail museodiroma@comune.roma.it; internet www.museodiroma.comune.roma.it; f. 1930; topographic, cultural, social, historical and artistic development of Rome since medieval times; Dir Dott.ssa MARIA ELISA TITTONI.

Museo Nazionale d'Arte Orientale: Palazzo Brancaccio, Via Merulana 248, 00185 Rome; tel. 06-4874415; fax 06-4870624; e-mail orientale@arti.beniculturali.it; internet www.viavenetoroma.it/it/musei/DettaMusei.asp?id=69; f. 1957; library of 8,000 vols; Dir Dssa DONATELLA MAZZEO.

Museo Nazionale delle Arti e Tradizioni Popolari: Piazza Marconi 8/10, 00144 Rome; tel. 06-5926148; fax 06-5911848; e-mail popolari@arti.beniculturali.it; internet www.popolari.arti.beniculturali.it; f. 1923; library of 30,000 vols; archives of musical, spoken and photo-cinematographic material; Dir Dott.ssa STEFANIA MASSARI.

Museo Nazionale di Castel Sant'Angelo: Lungotevere Castello 50, 00193 Rome; tel. 06-6819111; fax 06-68191196; internet www.galleriaborghese.it/castello/it; f. 1925; ancient armoury; architectural and monumental remains, frescoes, sculptures, pictures and period furniture; library of 11,000 vols, 60 periodicals; Dir Arch. RUGGERO PENTRELLA.

Museo Nazionale di Villa Giulia: Piazzale di Villa Giulia 9, 00196 Rome; tel. 06-3226571; fax 06-3202010; internet www.roma2000.it/zvilagiu.htm; f. 1889; Etruscan and Italian antiquities; Dir Dott.ssa FRANCESCA BOITANI.

Museo Nazionale Preistorico Etnografico 'Luigi Pigorini': Piazzale G. Marconi 14, 00144 Rome; tel. 06-549521; fax 06-54952310; e-mail pigorini@arti.beniculturali.it; internet www.pigorini.arti.beniculturali.it; f. 1875; prehistory and ethnology; library of 63,000 vols, 500 bound periodicals, 500 current periodicals; Superintendent Dr MARIA ANTONIETTA FUGAZZOLA; publ. *Bullettino di Paletnologia Italiana* (annually).

Scavi di Ostia: Viale dei Romagnoli 717, 00119 Ostia Antica, Rome; tel. 06-56358099; fax 06-5651500; e-mail ostia@arti.beniculturali.it; internet www.itnw.roma.it/ostia/scavi; Roman antiquities, monuments, paintings, sculptures, mosaics; Curator Dssa ANNA GALLINA ZEVI.

Soprintendenza Archeologica di Roma: Piazza S. Maria Nova 53, 00186 Rome; tel. 06-6990110; fax 06-6787689; e-mail info@archeorm.arti.beniculturali.it; internet www.archeorm.arti.beniculturali.it/sar2000; Superintendent Prof. ADRIANO LA REGINA.

Attached sites:

Il Colosseo (The Colosseum): Anfiteatro Flavio (Colosseo), Piazza del Colosseo, 00184 Rome; tel. 06-39967700; internet www.archeorm.arti.beniculturali.it/sar2000/colosseo/colosseo.asp; f. 80AD.

Terme di Caracalla: Viale Terme di Caracalla 52, 00153 Rome; tel. 06-39967700; internet www.archeorm.arti.beniculturali.it/sar2000/caracalla/caracalla.asp; f. AD216; remains of large complex of Roman baths.

Terme di Diocleziano (Baths of Diocletian): Via Enrico de Nicola 78, 00185 Rome; tel. 06-39967700; internet www.archeorm.arti.beniculturali.it/sar2000/diocleziano/default.asp; f. 3rd century AD; museum f. 1889; sculpture, sarcophagi, inscriptions, mosaics and frescoes.

Villa dei Quintili: Via Appia Nuova 1092, 00178 Rome; tel. 06-39967700; internet www.archeorm.arti.beniculturali.it/sar2000/villa_quintili/villa_dei_quintili.asp; f. 2nd century AD; extensive villa with rooms for masters and servants, bath quarters.

Museo Nazionale Romano: Piazza dei Cinquecento 79, 00185 Rome; tel. 06-483617; fax 06-4814125; f. 1889; Greek, Hellenistic and Roman sculpture and bronzes, paintings and mosaics, numismatics; archaeological colln; Dir Prof. ADRIANO LA REGINA.

Constituent centres:

Crypta Balbi: Via delle Botteghe Oscure 31, 00186 Rome; tel. 06-39967700; internet www.archeorm.arti.beniculturali.it/sar2000/cripta/cripta.asp; f. 13BC; remains of an arcaded courtyard and theatre; material and tools from a 7th-century workshop.

Domus Aurea (Golden House): Via della Domus Aurea 00184 Rome; tel. 06-39967700; internet www.archeorm.arti.beniculturali.it/sar2000/domus/domus_aurea.asp; remains of Nero's villa built after the great fire of 64AD.

Mausoleo di Cecilia Metella: Viale Appia Antica 161, 00179 Rome; tel. 06-39967700; internet www.archeorm.arti.beniculturali.it/sar2000/cecilia_metella/cecilia_metella.asp; f. 20–30 AD; funeral monument.

Palatino (Palatine Hill): Piazza S. Maria Nova 53, 00186 Rome; tel. 06-39967700; internet www.archeorm.arti.beniculturali.it/sar2000/palatino/palatino.asp; history of Rome from 8th century BC.

Palazzo Altemps: Piazza di Sant'Apollinare 48, 00186 Rome; tel. 06-39967700; internet www.archeorm.arti.beniculturali.it/sar2000/altemps/pal_altemps.asp; f. 1997; Greek and Roman sculpture.

Palazzo Massimo: Largo di Villa Peretti, 1, 00185 Rome; tel. 06-480201; fax 06-48903504; internet www.archeorm.arti.beniculturali.it/sar2000/museo_romano/pal_massimo.asp; f. 1998; statues, mosaic pavement, numismatics, frescoes, bronzes and jewellery from 1st century BC to 4th century AD.

Soprintendenza alla Galleria Nazionale d'Arte Moderna e Contemporanea: Viale delle Belle Arti 131, 00196 Rome; tel. 06-322981; fax 06-3221579; e-mail comunicazione.gnam@arti.beniculturali.it; internet www.gnam.arti.beniculturali.it; Superintendent Dott.ssa SANDRA PINTO.

Attached sites:

Galleria Nazionale d'Arte Moderna: Viale delle Belle Arti 131, 00196 Rome; tel. 06-322981; fax 06-3221579; e-mail comunicazione.gnam@arti.beniculturali.it; internet www.gnam.arti.beniculturali.it/gnamco.htm; f. 1883; art since 19th c.; library of 60,000 vols, 1,500 periodicals; Dir Dott.ssa SANDRA PINTO.

Museo Boncompagni Ludovisi: Via Boncompagni 18, 00187 Rome; tel. 06-42824074; e-mail gnam@arti.beniculturali.it; internet www.gnam.arti.beniculturali.it/boncco.htm; modern decorative arts and fashion; Dir GIANNA PIANTONI.

Museo Hendrik Christian Andersen: Via Pasquale Stanislao Mancini, 20 (Piazzale Flaminio), 00196 Rome; tel. 06-3219089; fax 06-3221579; e-mail edimajo.gnam@arti.beniculturali.it; internet www.gnam.arti.beniculturali.it/andeco.htm; f. 1998; paintings and sculpture by Hendrik Christian Andersen (1872–1940); Dir ELENA DI MAJO.

Museo Mario Praz: Palazzo Primoli, Via Zanardelli 1, 00186 Rome; tel. 06-6861089; fax 06-3221579; e-mail gnam@arti.beniculturali.it; internet www.gnam.arti.beniculturali.it/prazco.htm; f. 1995; furniture, paintings, sculpture, carpets, miniatures and objects made of bronze, crystal, porcelain, silver and marble collected by Mario Praz (1896–1982); Dir PATRIZIA ROSAZZA FERRARIS.

Raccolta Manzù: Via Laurentina Km 32.8, 00040 Ardea; tel. 06-9135022; e-mail gnam@arti.beniculturali.it; internet www.gnam.arti.beniculturali.it/manzco.htm; f. 1981; work by the sculptor Manzù; Dir LIVIA VELANI.

Villa della Farnesina: Via della Lungara 230, 00165 Rome; tel. 06-68027268; fax 06-68027345; e-mail farnesina@lincei.it; internet www.lincei.it/informazioni/villafarnesina; now the property of the Accademia Nazionale dei Lincei; built 1509 by Peruzzi; decorated by Raphael, Peruzzi and others; Curator Geom. RODOLFO DONZELLI.

Rovigo

Museo dell'Accademia dei Concordi: Piazza Vittorio Emanuele 14, 45100 Rovigo; tel. 0425-21654; fax 0425-27993; internet www2.regione.veneto.it/cultura/musei/inglese/pag4176e.htm; Protovillanovian, Egyptian and Roman antiquities; numismatic collection of 4,500 items; Dir ADRIANO MAZZETTI.

Pinacoteca dell'Accademia dei Concordi: Piazza Vittorio Emanuele 14, 45100 Rovigo; tel. 0425-21654; fax 0425-27993; internet www2.regione.veneto.it/cultura/musei/inglese/pag4176e.htm; f. 1833; contains 650 Venetian paintings (15th–18th c.), including work by Seminario Vescovile di Rovigo; Dir ADRIANO MAZZETTI.

Sarsina

Museo Archeologico Nazionale: Via Cesio Sabino 39, 47027 Sarsina; tel. 0547-94641; internet www.comune.sarsina.fo.it/museoarch/museo.htm; f. 1890; exhibition of archaeological remains from the Roman age; Dir Dott.ssa CHIARA GUARNIERI.

Sassari

Museo Nazionale G. A. Sanna: Via Roma 64, 07100 Sassari; tel. 079-272203; fax 079-272505; internet www.archeologia.beniculturali.it/pages/atlante/S156.html; f. 1932; archaeology, medieval and modern art, ethnography; Dir Dott. FRANCESCO NICOSIA.

Siena

Museo Archeologico: Piazza Duomo 2, 53100 Siena; tel. 0577-224811; fax 0577-224829; e-mail infoscala@comune.siena.it; internet www.santamaria.comune.siena.it; antiquities from the local area; Etruscan section; numismatic collection; Dir ENRICO TOTI.

Museo Aurelio Castelli: Via dell'Osservanza 7, 53100 Siena; tel. 0577-332444; internet www.museionline.it/ita/cerca/museo.asp?id=4060; 14th–15th c. sculpture, paintings and drawings from the 15th–18th c.; library of 28,000 vols.

Pinacoteca Nazionale: Palazzo Buonsignori, Via San Pietro 29, 53100 Siena; tel. 0577-286143; fax 0577-270508; internet www.museionline.it/ita/cerca/museo.asp?id=4069; f. 1930; 650 paintings exhibited; Dir Dott.ssa ANNA MARIA GUIDUCCI.

Syracuse

Museo Archeologico Regionale 'Paolo Orsi': Viale Teocrito 66, 96100 Syracuse; tel. 0931-464022; fax 0931-462347; e-mail museo.orsi@tin.it; internet www.regione.sicilia.it/beniculturali/dirbenicult/musei/musei2/orsi.htm; f. 1886; prehistory, statuary and antiques from the excavations of the

Greco-Roman city and from prehistoric and classical sites of Eastern Sicily; Dir Dott. GIUSEPPE VOZA.

Taranto

Museo Archeologico Nazionale: Corso Umberto 141, 74100 Taranto; tel. 099-4532112; fax 099-4594946; e-mail archeologica.taranto@libero.it; internet www.tarantocitta.it/museo.htm; f. 1887; local prehistory and Greco-Roman remains; Dir Dott. GIUSEPPE ANDREASSI.

Tarquinia

Museo Nazionale Tarquiniense: Palazzo Vitelleschi, 01016 Tarquinia; tel. 0766-856036; internet www.tarquinia.net/citta/turismo/museo_nazionale.asp; f. 1924; Etruscan sarcophagi 4th–3rd c. BC, Etruscan and Greek vases, bronzes, ornaments; Etruscan paintings; Dir Dott.ssa MARIA CATALDI.

Trento

Castello del Buonconsiglio–Monumenti e Collezioni Provinciali: Via B. Clesio 5, 38100 Trento; tel. 0461-233770; fax 0461-239497; e-mail castellodelbuonconsiglio@provincia.tn.it; internet www.buonconsiglio.it; f. 1924; ancient, medieval and modern art; Dir Dott. FRANCO MARZATICO.

Trieste

Civici Musei di Storia ed Arte: Via Cattedrale 15, 34121 Trieste; tel. 040-310500; fax 040-300687; e-mail museostoriaarte@comune.trieste.it; internet www.triestecultura.it; Dir Dott. ADRIANO DUGULIN.

Constituent museums and galleries:

Castello di San Giusto e Civico Museo del Castello, Lapidario Tergestino: Piazza Cattedrale 3, 34121 Trieste; tel. 040-309362; fax 040-300687; e-mail museostoriaarte@comune.trieste.it; internet www.triestecultura.it; f. 1936, Lapidario 2001.; Dir Dott. ADRIANO DUGULIN.

Civico Museo d'Arte Orientale: Via S. Sebastiano 1, 34121 Trieste; tel. 040-3220736; fax 040-300687; e-mail museoarteorientale@comune.trieste.it; internet www.triestecultura.it; f. 2001; Dir Dott. ADRIANO DUGULIN.

Civico Museo de Guerra per la Pace 'Diego de Henriquez': Via Revoltella 37, 34139 Trieste; tel. 040-948430; fax 040-944390; e-mail museodehenriquez@comune.trieste.it; internet www.triestecultura.it; f. 1998; Dir Dott. ADRIANO DUGULIN.

Civico Museo della Risiera di S. Sabba – Monumento Nazionale: Ratto della Pileria 43, 34148 Trieste; tel. 040-826202; fax 040-300687; e-mail museostoriaarte@comune.trieste.it; internet www.triestecultura.it; f. 1975; Dir Dott. ADRIANO DUGULIN.

Civico Museo del Risorgimento e Sacrario Oberdan: Via XXIV Maggio 4, 34133 Trieste; tel. 040-361675; fax 040-300687; e-mail museostoriaarte@comune.trieste.it; internet www.triestecultura.it; f. 1934; Dir Dott. ADRIANO DUGULIN.

Civico Museo Sartorio: Largo Papa Giovanni XXIII 1, 34123 Trieste; tel. 040-301479; fax 040-300687; e-mail museostoriaarte@comune.trieste.it; internet www.triestecultura.it; f. 1947; Dir Dott. ADRIANO DUGULIN.

Civico Museo di Storia ed Arte e Orto Lapidario: Via Cattedrale 15, 34121 Trieste; tel. 040-308686; fax 040-300687; e-mail museostoriaarte@comune.trieste.it; internet www.triestecultura.it; f. Orto Lapidario 1843, Civico Museo di Storia 1873.; Dir Dott. ADRIANO DUGULIN.

Civico Museo di Storia Patria—Civico Museo Morpurgo de Nilma: Via Imbriani 5, 34122 Trieste; tel. 040-636969; fax 040-636969; e-mail museostoriaarte@comune.trieste.it; internet www.triestecultura.it; f. Museo Morpurgo 1947, Civico Museo di Storia Patria 1950; Dir Dott. ADRIANO DUGULIN.

Civico Museo Teatrale 'Carlo Schmidl': Via Rossini, 4, 34122 Trieste; tel. 040-366030; fax 040-636969; e-mail museoschmidl@comune.trieste.it; internet www.triestecultura.it; f. 1950; Dir Dott. ADRIANO DUGULIN.

Museo Postale e Telegrafico della Mitteleuropa: Piazza Vittorio Veneto 1, 34132 Trieste; tel. 040-6764264; fax 040-6764570; e-mail museopostaletrieste@posteitaliane.it; internet www.triestecultura.it; f. 1997, in association with Poste Italiane S.p.A.; Dir Dott. ADRIANO DUGULIN.

Turin

Armeria Reale: Piazza Castello 191, 10122 Turin; tel. 011-543889; fax 011-5188063; e-mail armeriareale@artito.arti.beniculturali.it; internet www.artito.arti.beniculturali.it; f. 1837; collection of arms; includes the equestrian armour of Otto Heinrich and works by Pompeo della Chiesa, Etienne Delaune and the engravers of the Munich school, Emanuel Sadeler, Daniel Sadeler and Caspar Spät; Dir FULVIO CERVINI.

Città di Torino–Settore Musei: Via San Francesco da Paola 3, 10123 Turin; tel. 011-4434470; fax 011-4434494; e-mail daniele.jalla@comune.torino.it; internet www.comune.torino.it/musei; Dir DANIELE LUPO JALLÀ.

Attached museums:

Borgo e Rocca Medioevale: Parco del Valentino, Viale Virgilio, 10126 Turin; tel. 011-4431701; fax 011-4431719; e-mail borgo.medioevale@comune.torino.it; internet www.comune.torino.it/musei/civici/bm; Superintendent Dott.ssa ENRICA PAGELLA.

Galleria Civica d'Arte Moderna e Contemporanea: Via Magenta 31, 10128 Turin; tel. 011-5629911; fax 011-4429550; e-mail gam@comune.torino.it; internet www.gamtorino.it; f. 1953; Pres. GIOVANNA INCISA CATTANEO; Dir PIERGIOVANNI CASTAGNOLI.

Museo Civico d'Arte Antica e Palazzo Madama: Piazza Castello, 10122 Turin; tel. 011-4429911; fax 011-4429929; e-mail palazzo.madama@comune.torino.it; internet www.comune.torino.it/palazzomadama/museo.html; f. 1863; Dir ENRICA PAGALLA.

Museo Civico Pietro Micca: Via Guicciardini 7, 10121 Turin; tel. 011-546317; fax 011-5069382; internet www.comune.torino.it/musei; f. 1861; Hon. Curator GUIDO AMORETTI.

Galleria Sabauda: Via Accademia delle Scienze 6, 10123 Turin; tel. 011-547440; fax 011-530501; e-mail galleriasabauda@artito.arti.beniculturali.it; f. 1832; one of principal Flemish and Dutch collections, and early Italian, also Bronzino, Veronese, Tiepolo and Lombard and Piedmontese schools, furniture, sculpture and jewellery; Dir Dott.ssa PAOLA ASTRUA.

Museo di Antichità: Via XX Settembre 88C, 10124 Turin; tel. 011-5211106; fax 011-5213145; e-mail info@museoarcheologico.it; internet www.museoantichita.it; f. 1940; Piedmontese prehistory; Etruscan, Sardinian and Gallo-Roman remains; Greek and Cypriot ceramics; Roman statues; silverware; Dir Dott.ssa LILIANA MERCANDO.

Museo Egizio: Via Accademia delle Scienze 6, 10123 Turin; tel. 011-5617776; fax 011-5623157; e-mail ufficio.segreteria@museoegizio.org; internet www.museoegizio.org; f. 1824; Pharonic, Ptolemaic and Coptic antiquities; entire furnishings of the tomb of architect Kha and his wife from Deir el-Medina, Temple of Ellesija (reconstructed Nubian temple of 18th dynasty) presented by the Egyptian Govt; objects from Droveth colln and Schiaparelli excavations in Egypt; Dir ELENI VASSILIKA.

Udine

Civici Musei e Gallerie di Storia e Arte: Castello, Piazza Libertà, 33100 Udine; tel. 0432-501824; fax 0432-501681; f. 1866; history, art; Dir Dott. GIUSEPPE BERGAMINI.

Urbino

Galleria Nazionale delle Marche—Palazzo Ducale: Piazza Duca Federico 107, 61029 Urbino; tel. 0722-27601; fax 0722-377483; e-mail info.servizimusei@libero.it; internet www.galleriaborghese.it/nuove/einfourbino.html; f. 1912; medieval and Renaissance works of art originating in the town of Urbino and the provinces of Marche; Dir Prof. PAOLO DAL POGGETTO.

Venice

Biennale di Venezia: Ca' Giustinian, San Marco 1364, 30124 Venice; tel. 041-5218711; fax 041-2728329; e-mail infogruppi@labiennale.org; internet www.labiennale.org; f. 1895; an autonomous body; organizes artistic and cultural events throughout the year: visual arts, architecture, cinema, theatre, music, dance; the Biennale owns historical archives of contemporary art; library of 100,000 vols and catalogues, photographs, etc.; Pres. DAVIDE CROFF; Gen. Dir GAETANO GUERCI.

Gallerie dell'Accademia: Campo della Carità, Dorsoduro 1050, 30130 Venice; tel. 041-5222247; fax 041-5212709; e-mail polove@arti.beniculturali.it; internet www.gallerieaccademia.org; f. 1807; Venetian painting 1310–1700; Superintendent Dott.ssa GIOVANNA SCIRÈ NEPI.

Galleria Giorgio Franchetti alla Ca' d'Oro: Cannaregio 3932, 30121 Venice; tel. 041-5238790; fax 041-5222349; e-mail polove.franchetti@arti.beniculturali.it; internet www.artive.arti.beniculturali.it; f. 1927; sculpture, bronzes, medals, coins, tapestries, ceramics, and Venetian, central Italian and Flemish art; Dir Dott.ssa ADRIANA AUGUSTI.

Museo Archeologico: Piazza S. Marco 17, 30122 Venice; tel. 041-5225978; fax 041-5210547; e-mail artive@arti.beniculturali.it; f. 1523, reorganized 1923–26 and again after 1945; Greek and Roman sculpture, gems and coins, mosaics and sculptures from the 5th c. BC–11th AD; library of 3,000 vols; Dir Dott. GIOVANNA NEPI SCIRÈ.

Museo d'Arte Orientale: Santa Croce 2076, 30135 Venice; tel. and fax 041-5241173; e-mail polove.orientale@arti.beniculturali.it; internet www.artive.arti.beniculturali.it/index_x.htm; 17th–19th c. decorative arts from the Far East; Dir Dott.ssa FIORELLA SPADAVECCHIA.

Musei Civici Veneziani: Piazza San Marco 52, 30124 Venice; tel. 041-5225625; fax 041-5200935; e-mail info@turismovenezia.it; internet www.museiciviciveneziani.it; Dir Prof. GIANDOMENICO ROMANELLI.

Constituent institutions:

Ca' Rezzonico: Dorsoduro 3136, 30123 Venice; tel. and fax 041-2410100; e-mail mkt.musei@comune.venezia.it; internet www.museicivicivenezìani.it; f. 1935; 18th-century Venetian art, sculpture, etc.

Casa di Carlo Goldoni: San Polo 2794, 30125 Venice; tel. 041-2759325; fax 041-2440081; e-mail mkt.musei@comune.venezia.it; internet www.museicivicivenezìani.it; house of the comic playwright (1707–93).

Galleria Internazionale d'Arte Moderna di Ca' Pesaro: Santa Croce 2076, 30135 Venice; tel. 041-5240695; fax 041-5241075; e-mail mkt.musei@comune.venezia.it; internet www.museicivicivenezìani.it; f. 1897; works of art since the 19th century.

Museo Correr: Piazza San Marco 52, 30124 Venice; tel. 041-2405211; fax 041-5200935; e-mail mkt.musei@comune.venezia.it; internet www.museicivicivenezìani.it; f. 1830 by Teodoro Correr who bequeathed his collections to the City; Venetian art (13th–16th centuries) and history of the Serenissima, Renaissance coins, ceramics; publ. *Bollettino* (quarterly).

Museo Fortuny: San Marco 3780, 30124 Venice; tel. 041-5200995; fax 041-5223088; e-mail mkt.musei@comune.venezia.it; internet www.museicivicivenezìani.it; closed for restoration.

Museo del Merletto: Piazza Galuppi 187, 30012 Burano; tel. 041-730034; fax 041-735471; e-mail mkt.musei@comune.venezia.it; internet www.museicivicivenezìani.it; f. 1981; examples of lace since 19th century in the former Lace School.

Museo di Storia Naturale: Santa Croce 1730, 30125 Venice; tel. 041-2750206; fax 041-7210000; e-mail mkt.musei@comune.venezia.it; internet www.museicivicivenezìani.it; f. 1923; natural history; entomology, malacology, ornithology, icthyology, African ethnology.

Museo del Vetro: Fondamenta Giustinian 8, 30121 Murano; tel. and fax 041-739586; e-mail mkt.musei@comune.venezia.it; internet www.museicivicivenezìani.it; f. 1861; Venetian glass from middle ages to the present; also colins of Roman glass from 1st century AD, Spanish, Bohemian and English collns; archives and photographic colln; spec. exhibitions and educational projects.

Palazzo Ducale (Doge's Palace): Piazza San Marco 1, 30124 Venice; tel. 041-2715911; fax 041-5285028; e-mail mkt.musei@comune.venezia.it; internet www.museicivicivenezìani.it; f. 1340; doge's apartments, institutional chambers, armoury and prisons.

Palazzo Mocenigo: Santa Croce 1992, 30126 Venice; tel. 041-721798; fax 041-5241614; e-mail mkt.musei@comune.venezia.it; internet www.museicivicivenezìani.it; palace of the noble Venetian family which provided several of the doges; colln of fabrics and costumes; library on history of fashion.

Planetario di Venezia: Ass.Astrofili Veneziani, Casella Postale 36, Venice Lido; tel. 041-731518; e-mail planetario@astrovenezia.net; internet www.astrovenezia.net.

Torre Civica di Mestre: Piazza Erminio Ferretto, 30174 Mestre; tel. 041-2749062; fax 041-2749049; internet www.comune.venezia.it/torre_mestre; f. 13th century.

Torre dell'Orologio (Clock Tower): Piazza San Marco, 30124 Venice; tel. 041-2715911; fax 041-5285028; e-mail mkt.musei@comune.venezia.it; internet www.museicivicivenezìani.it; f. 15th century; closed for restoration.

Museo Civico di Storia Naturale: Fontego dei Turchi, Santa Croce 1730, 30135 Venice; tel. 041-721852; fax 041-5242592; e-mail nat.mus.ve@comune.venezia.it; internet www2.regione.veneto.it/cultura/musei/Scheda.asp?ID=36; f. 1921; marine fauna of the Adriatic, ornithology, entomology, minerals and fossils, plants and algae of the world; library of 30,000 vols, 2,350 periodicals; Dir Dr E. RATTI; publs *Bollettino* (annually), *Quaderni* (irregular).

Museo della Fondazione Querini Stampalia: Palazzo Querini Stampalia, Castello 5252, 30122 Venice; tel. 041-2711411; fax 041-2711445; e-mail querini.stampalia@provincia.venezia.it; internet www.querinistampalia.it; f. 1869; 14th- to 19th-century Italian paintings, 18th- and 19th-century furniture, china; Dir Dr GIORGIO BUSETTO.

Museo Storico Navale: Riva S. Biasio Castello 2148, 30122 Venice; tel. 041-2441399; fax 041-5200276; internet www.marina.difesa.it/venezia; f. 1919; library of 3,000 vols; Dir RUDY GUASTADISEGNI.

Peggy Guggenheim Collection (Solomon R. Guggenheim Foundation, New York): Palazzo Venier dei Leoni, 701 Dorsoduro, 30123 Venice; tel. 041-2405411; fax 041-5206885; e-mail info@guggenheim-venice.it; internet www.guggenheim-venice.it; f. 1980; permanent collection includes masterpieces of cubism, futurism, metaphysical painting, European abstraction, surrealism, and American abstract expressionism; Italian Futurist works on loan from the Gianni Mattioli collection; sculpture garden; Dir PHILIP RYLANDS.

Pinacoteca Manfrediniana: Dorsoduro 1, 30123 Venice; tel. 041-2411018; fax 041-2743998; e-mail seminario@patriarcato.venezia.it; internet www.marcianum.it; f. 1827; paintings and sculpture of the Roman, Gothic, Renaissance, Baroque, Neo-classical periods; library of 80,000 vols; Dir LUCIO CILIA.

Verona

Musei Civici d'Arte di Verona: Corso Castelvecchio 2, 37121 Verona; tel. 045-8062611; fax 045-8010729; e-mail castelvecchio@comune.verona.it; internet www.comune.verona.it; f. 1857; Dir Dott.ssa PAOLA MARINI.

Constituent museums and galleries:

Art Library and Graphic Collections: Corso Castelvecchio 2, 37121 Verona; tel. 045-8005817; fax 045-8010729; e-mail castelvecchio@comune.verona.it; internet www.comune.verona.it; f. 1957; library of 33,000 vols, 14,000 prints and drawings; Dir Dott. GIORGIO MARINI.

Galleria Comunale d'Arte Moderna e Contemporanea: Via Forti 1, 37121 Verona; tel. 045-8001903; fax 045-8003524; Dir Dott. G. ROSSI CORTENOVA.

Museo degli Affreschi e Tomba di Giulietta: Via del Pontiere, 37122 Verona; tel. 045-8000361; e-mail castelvecchio@comune.verona.it; f. 1973; Dir Dr PAOLA MARINI.

Museo Archeologico al Teatro Romano: Regaste Redentore, 37129 Verona; tel. 045-8000360; fax 045-8010587; e-mail castelvecchio@comune.verona.it; Dir Dott.ssa MARGHERITA BOLLA.

Museo di Castelvecchio: Corso Castelvecchio 3, 37121 Verona; tel. 045-8005817; fax 045-8010729; e-mail castelvecchio@comune.verona.it; Dir Dott.ssa PAOLA MARINI.

Museo Lapidario Maffeiano: Piazza Brà, 37121 Verona; tel. 045-590087; f. 1745; Curator Dra MARGHERITA BOLLA.

Vicenza

Musei Civici: Piazza Matteotti, 36100 Vicenza; tel. 0444-4222811; fax 0444-4546619; e-mail assturismo@comune.vicenza.it; internet www.comune.vicenza.it/ente/musei/index.php; Dir Dott.ssa MARIA ELISA AVAGNINA.

Attached museums:

Museo Naturalistico Archeologico: Contrà S. Corona, 36100 Vicenza; tel. 0444-320440; fax 0444-325627; e-mail museo.nat.archeo.vi@libero.it; internet www.comune.vicenza.it/vicenza/musei/scorona.php; f. 1991; fossils, flora and fauna; Paleolithic and local Roman remains; Dir Dott. ANTONIO DAL LAGO.

Museo del Risorgimento e della Resistenza: Villa Guiccioli, Viale X Giugno 115, 36100 Vicenza; tel. 0444-322998; fax 0444-326023; e-mail museorisorgimento@comune.vicenza.it; internet www.comune.vicenza.it/vicenza/musei/risorgimento.php; Dir Dott. MAURO PASSARIN.

Pinacoteca Civica: Palazzo Chiericati, Piazza Matteotti 37–39, 36100 Vicenza; tel. 0444-321348; fax 0444-546619; e-mail museocivico@comune.vicenza.it; internet www.comune.vicenza.it/vicenza/musei/pinacoteca.php; f. 1855; 13th–19th c. paintings and sculpture by artists including Montagna, Veronese, Tintoretto and Tiepolo; manuscripts, drawings, prints and coins; Dir Dott.ssa MARIA ELISA AVAGNINA.

Viterbo

Museo Civico: Piazza Crispi 2, 01100 Viterbo; tel. 0761-348275; fax 0761-348276; e-mail museocivico@comune.viterbo.it; internet www.viterboonline.com/muscivicus.html; f. 1912; archaeology, art history; Dir Dott.ssa ADRIANA EMILIOZZI.

Volterra

Museo Diocesano d'Arte Sacra: Palazzo Vescovile, Via Roma 13, 56048 Volterra; tel. 058-886290; fax 058-886290; e-mail museoartesacravolterra@nemail.it; internet www.diocesivolterra.it; f. 1932; sculpture, paintings, costumes, ornaments; Dir Dott. UMBERTO BAVONI.

Museo Etrusco Guarnacci: Via Don Minzoni 15, 56048 Volterra; tel. 0588-86347; fax 0588-90987; e-mail musei@comune.volterra.pi.it; internet www.comune.volterra.pi.it/english/museiit/metru.html; f. 1761; Roman and Etruscan coins, urns, bronzes, etc.; Dir Dott. GABRIELE CATENI.

State Universities

UNIVERSITÀ DEGLI STUDI DI ANCONA

Piazza Roma 22, 60121 Ancona

Telephone: 071-2201
Fax: 071-2202324
Internet: www.unian.it

Founded 1969
Academic year: November to October

Rector: Prof. MARCO PACETTI
Vice-Rector: Prof. MARIO GOVERNA
Director: Dott. SANDRO FERRI
Librarian: Dssa SILVIA SOTTILI

Library of 26,000 vols
Number of teachers: 430
Number of students: 13,000

DEANS

Faculty of Engineering: Prof. GIOVANNI LATINI
Faculty of Medicine and Surgery: Prof. TULLIO MANZONI
Faculty of Economics: Prof. ENZO PESCIARELLI
Faculty of Agronomy: Prof. EDOARDO BIONDI
Faculty of Sciences: Prof. ETTORE OLMO

UNIVERSITÀ DEGLI STUDI DI BARI

Palazzo Ateneo, 70121 Bari
Telephone: 080-311111
Internet: www.uniba.it
Founded 1924
Rector: Prof. ATTILIO ALTO
Registrar: Dott. M. NATALE
Number of teachers: 700
Number of students: 42,439

DEANS

Faculty of Agriculture: Prof. E. BELLITTI
Faculty of Economics and Commerce: Prof. G. CHIASSINO
Faculty of Pharmacology: Prof. V. TORTORELLA
Faculty of Jurisprudence: Prof. G. PIEPOLI
Faculty of Engineering: Prof. B. MAIONE
Faculty of Letters and Philosophy: Prof. F. TATEO
Faculty of Foreign Languages: Prof. V. MASIELLO
Faculty of Education: Prof. M. DELL'AQUILA
Faculty of Medicine: Prof. V. MITOLO
Faculty of Veterinary Medicine: Prof. G. O. MARCOTRIGIANO
Faculty of Science: Prof. A. COSSU

UNIVERSITÀ DEGLI STUDI DELLA BASILICATA

Via Nazario Sauro 85, 85100 Potenza
Telephone: 0971-474111
Fax: 0971-474102
Internet: www.unibas.it
Founded 1982
Rector: Prof. GIANFRANCO BOARI
Vice-Rector: Prof. PASQUALE PIAZZOLLA
Administrative Director: Dr MARIO ROSARIO CAVALIERE
Librarians: Prof. CARLO MARIA SIMONETTI, Prof. GABOR KORCHMAROS
Library of 85,000 vols
Number of teachers: 307
Number of students: 4,845
Publications: *Basilicata Università*, *Collana 'Atti e Memorie'*, *Collana 'Strutture e Materiali'*, *Quaderni*

DEANS

Faculty of Agriculture: Prof. F. BASSO
Faculty of Engineering: Prof. V. COPERTINO
Faculty of Letters and Philosophy: Prof. A. DE FRANCESCO
Faculty of Sciences: Prof. A. M. TAMBURRO

HEADS OF DEPARTMENTS

Faculty of Sciences:
- Mathematics: Prof. G. M. MASTROIANNI
- Chemistry: Prof. A. S. FRACASSINI

Faculty of Engineering:
- Structures, Geotechnology, Geology applied to Engineering: Prof. M. DOLCE
- Architecture, Planning and Transport Infrastructure: Prof. A. CAPPELLI
- Engineering and Environmental Physics: Prof. B. DE BERNARDINIS

Faculty of Letters and Philosophy:
- Literature and Philology: Prof. E. GIACCHERINI
- History, Linguistics and Anthropology: Prof. C. M. SIMONETTI

Faculty of Agriculture:
- Plant Biology, Protection and Biotechnology: Prof. P. RICCIO
- Animal Production: Prof. MICHELE LANGELLA
- Plant Production: Prof. C. XILOYANNIS
- Forest Economics: Prof. E. BOVE

UNIVERSITÀ DEGLI STUDI DI BERGAMO

Via Salvecchio 19, 24129 Bergamo
Telephone: 035-227111
Fax: 035-243054
Internet: www.unibg.it
Founded 1968
Rector: Prof. PIETRO ENRICO FERRI
Administrative Director: Dott. DOMENICO DANISI
Librarian: Dott. ENNIO FERRANTE
Library of 142,000 vols
Number of teachers: 211
Number of students: 6,317

DEANS

Faculty of Economics: Prof. MARIA IDA BERTOCCHI
Faculty of Foreign Languages and Literature: Prof. ALBERTO CASTOLDI
Faculty of Engineering: Prof. ANTONIO PERDICHIZZI

PROFESSORS

Faculty of Economics:
- AMADUZZI, A., Business Administration
- ARCUCCI, F., International Trade and Finance
- BERTOCCHI, M. I., Financial Mathematics
- BIFFIGNANDI, S., Statistics Applied to Economics
- FENGHI, F., Commercial Law
- FERRI, P. E., Economic Analysis
- GAMBARELLI, G., General Mathematics
- GRAZIOLA, G., Economics of Enterprise
- LEONI, R., Labour Economics
- MASINI, M., Banking
- RENOLDI, A., Value Management
- SACCHETTO, C., Tax Law
- SPEDICATO, E., Operations Research
- TAGI, G., Industrial Operations Management
- TAGLIARINI, F., Commercial Penal Law

Faculty of Foreign Languages and Literature:
- BELLER, M., German Language and Literature
- CASTOLDI, A., French Language and Literature II
- CERUTI, M., Epistemology
- CORONA, M., Anglo-American Languages and Literature
- GOTTI, M., History of the English Language
- LOCATELLI, A., English Language and Literature
- MARZOLA, A., English Language and Literature
- MIRANDOLA, G., French Language and Literature I
- MOLINARI, M. V., Germanic Philology
- MORELLI, G., Spanish Language and Literature
- PAPA, E., Modern and Contemporary History
- VILLA, C., Medieval and Humanist Philology

Faculty of Engineering:
- BUGINI, A., Industrial Management of Quality
- COLOMBI, R., Statistics and Probability
- PERDICHIZZI, A., Energetic Powerplants
- RIVA, R., Theoretical and Applied Mechanics
- SALANTI, A., Economics

UNIVERSITÀ DI BOLOGNA

Via Zamboni 33, 40126 Bologna
Telephone: 051-2099111
Fax: 051-2099372
Internet: www.unibo.it
Founded 1088
Academic year: October to July
Rector: Prof. PIER UGO CALZOLARI
Administrative Director: Dssa INES FABBRO
Library of 1,250,000 vols and 400 video cassettes; additional departmental libraries
Number of teachers: 3,001
Number of students: 101,488

DEANS

Faculty of Agriculture: Prof. DOMENICO REGAZZI
Faculty of Architecture: Prof. GIANNI BRAGHIERI
Faculty of Arts and Philosophy: Prof. GIUSEPPE SASSATELLI
Faculty of Economics: Prof. SANDRO SANDRI
Faculty of Economics, Forli: Prof. GIUSEPPE FARNETI
Faculty of Economics, Rimini: Prof. GUIDO CANDELA
Faculty of Education: Prof. FRANCO FRABBONI
Faculty of Engineering: Prof. FRANCO PERSIANI
Faculty of Engineering II: Prof. GUIDO MASETTI
Faculty of Foreign Languages and Literature: Prof. ALBERTO DESTRO
Faculty of Industrial Chemistry: Prof. FERRUCCIO TRIFIRÒ
Faculty of Jurisprudence: Prof. STEFANO CANESTRARI
Faculty of Mathematics, Physics and Natural Sciences: Prof. LORENZO DONATIELLO
Faculty of Medicine: Prof. MARIA PAOLA LANDINI
Faculty of Pharmacy: Prof. GIORGIO CANTELLI FORTI
Faculty of Political Science: Prof. ANNA STAGNI
Faculty of Political Science, Forli: Prof. GILIBERTO CAPENA
Faculty of Psychology: Prof. GUIDO SARCHIELLI
Faculty of Sport Science: Prof. SALVATORE SQUATRITO
Faculty of Statistics and Demography: Prof. PAOLA MONARI
Faculty of Veterinary Medicine: Prof. STEFANO CINOTTI
School of Modern Languages for Interpreters and Translators: Prof. CHRISTOPHER GUY ASTON

UNIVERSITÀ DEGLI STUDI DI BRESCIA

Piazza Mercato 15, 25121 Brescia
Telephone: 030-29881
Fax: 030-2988329
Internet: www.unibs.it
Founded 1982
Rector: AUGUSTO PRETI
Vice-Rector: PIER LUIGI MAGNANI
Administrative Officer: ANGELO BRESCIANI
Librarians: RICCARDO FAINI (Economics and Law), FRANCESCO GENNA (Engineering), PIER FRANCO SPANO (Medicine and Surgery)
Number of teachers: 355
Number of students: 12,020

DEANS

Faculty of Economics: GIANCARLO PROVASI
Faculty of Engineering: ANDREA TARONI

Faculty of Law: VINCENZO ALLEGRI
Faculty of Medicine and Surgery: LUIGI CAIMI

HEADS OF DEPARTMENTS

Faculty of Economics and Commerce:
- Business Management: ANTONIO PORTERI
- Quantitative Methods: LIVIA DANCELLI
- Economics: FRANCESCO SPINELLI
- Social Studies: GIUSEPPE STALUPPI
- Foreign Languages: CAMILLO MARAZZA

Faculty of Engineering:
- Mechanical Engineering: PIERLUIGI MAGNANI
- Civil Engineering: BALDASSARE BACCHI
- Electronics for Automation: DANIELE MARIOLI
- Materials Chemistry and Physics: EVANDRO LODI RIZZINI

Faculty of Law:
- Law Studies: SALVATORE PROSDOCIMI

Faculty of Medicine and Surgery:
- Experimental and Applied Medicine: GIUSEPPE NARDI
- Mother and Child Unit and Biomedical Technology: PIERGIOVANNI GRIGOLATO
- Medical Sciences: VITTORIO GRASSI
- Biomedical Sciences and Biotechnology: DANIELA COCCHI
- Surgical Sciences: GIOVANNI MARINI
- Surgical Pathology: CARLO ALBERTO QUARANTA

UNIVERSITÀ DI CAGLIARI

Via Università 40, 09124 Cagliari, Sardinia
Telephone: 070-662493
Internet: www.unica.it
Founded 1606 by Pope Paul V
Rector: Prof. DUILIO CASULA
Administrative Director: Dott. E. TOXIRI
Librarian: Dott. GRAZIELLA SEDDA DELITALA
Number of teachers: c. 1,000
Number of students: c. 18,000
Publication: Publications: *Studi economico-giuridici* and publications from each faculty

DEANS

Faculty of Economics and Commerce: Prof. G. USAI
Faculty of Pharmacy: Prof. A. MACCIONI
Faculty of Law: Prof. F. SITZIA
Faculty of Engineering: Prof. CARLO VIVANET
Faculty of Letters and Philosophy: Prof. G. RESTAINO
Faculty of Education: Prof. S. TAGLIAGAMBE
Faculty of Medicine: Prof. A. BALESTRIERI
Faculty of Science: Prof. F. RAGA
Faculty of Political Science: Prof. G. SOTGIU

UNIVERSITÀ DI CALABRIA

Via P. Bucci, 87030 Arcavacata di Rende
Telephone: 0984-4911
Fax: 0984-493616
E-mail: diramm@amministrazione.unical.it
Internet: www.unical.it
Founded 1972
Academic year: November to October
Rector: Prof. GIOVANNI LATORRE
Administrative Officer: Dott. BRUNA ADAMO
Number of teachers: 1,240; 640 full-time, 600 part-time
Number of students: 32,000

DEANS

Faculty of Economics: Prof. GIUSEPPE DE BARTOLO
Faculty of Engineering: Prof. MARIA LAURA LUCHI
Faculty of Letters and Philosophy: Prof. FRANCO CRISPINI
Faculty of Mathematical, Physical and Natural Sciences: Prof. ROBERTO BARTOLINO
Faculty of Pharmacy: Prof. SEBASTIANO ANDÒ
Faculty of Political Sciences: Prof. SILVIO GAMBINO

HEADS OF DEPARTMENTS

Archaeology and Arts: Prof. GIUSEPPE ROMA
Cellular Biology: Prof. GIOVANNA DE BENEDICTIS
Chemical Engineering: Prof. GABRIELE IORIO
Chemistry: Prof. NINO RUSSO
Earth Sciences: Prof. GINO M. CRISCI
Ecology: Prof. MARIA BEATRICE BITONTI
Economics and Statistics: Prof. ANTONIO AQUINO
Education: Prof. GIUSEPPE SPADAFORA
Electronics: Prof. SERGIO GRECO
History: Prof. FILIPPO BURGARELLA
Land Planning: Prof. DEMETRIO C. FESTA
Law: Prof. ENRICO CATERINI
Linguistics: Prof. ROBERTO GUARASCI
Management and Public Administration: Prof. IVAR MASSABO
Mathematics: Prof. ANNAMARIA CANINO
Mechanics: Prof. GAETANO FLORIO
Pharmaceutical Sciences: Prof. FRANCESCO MENICHINI
Pharmacology and Biology: Prof. GIUSEPPE GENCHI
Philology: Prof. NICOLA MEROLA
Philosophy: Prof. DANIELE GAMBARARA
Physics: Prof. PIERLUIGI VELTRI
Sociology: Prof. PIETRO FANTOZZI
Soil Conservation: Prof. FRANCESCO CALOMINO
Structures: Prof. DOMENICO BRUNO

UNIVERSITÀ DI CAMERINO

Via Gentile III Da Varano, 62032 Camerino
Telephone: 0737-4011
Fax: 0737-402085
Internet: www.unicam.it
Founded 1336; University status 1727
Academic year: November to October
Rector: Prof. FULVIO ESPOSITO
Administrative Director: Dr LUIGI TAPANELLI
Number of teachers: 301
Number of students: 10,055
Publications: *Studi geologici camerti*, *Index—International Survey of Roman Law*, *Quaderni Camerti*, *Documents Phytosociologiques*, *Laboratorio di Studi linguistici*, *Medicina legale — Quaderni camerti*

DEANS

Faculty of Architecture: Prof. GIOVANNI GUAZZO
Faculty of Jurisprudence: Prof. GUIDO BISCONTINI
Faculty of Science: Prof. RICARDO PIERGALLINI
Faculty of Pharmacy: Prof. MAURIZIO MASSI
Faculty of Veterinary Medicine: Prof. BENIAMINO TESEI

DIRECTORS

Faculty of Architecture:
- Department of Environmental Planning and Construction: Prof. UMBERTO CAO

Faculty of Jurisprudence:
- Department of Legal and Political Sciences: Prof. GIUSEPPE PALMISANO
- Department of Substantive and Procedural Law: Prof. GIOVANNI ARIETA

Faculty of Pharmacy:
- Department of Biology: Prof. DOMENICO AMICI
- Department of Chemistry: Prof. FRANCESO CLAUDI
- Department of Experimental Medicine: Prof. FRANCO CANTALAMESSA
- Department of Hygiene and Sanitation: Prof. MARIO COCCHIONI

Faculty of Science:
- Department of Botany and Ecology: Prof. CARMELA CORTINI
- Department of Comparative Morphology and Biochemistry: Prof. GIOVANNI MATERAZZI
- Department of Earth Sciences: Prof. ANNA MARIA MANCINELLI
- Department of Mathematics and Computer Science: Prof. RENATO DE LEONE
- Department of Mathematics and Physics: Prof. PAOLO TOMBESI

Faculty of Veterinary Medicine:
- Department of Veterinary Science: Prof. CARLO RENIERI

ATTACHED INSTITUTES

School of Clinical-Chemical Research: Dir Prof. ROSALIA TACCONI.

School of Postgraduate Studies in Civil Law: Dir Prof. ANTONIO FLAMINI.

School of Specialization in Hospital Pharmacy: Dir Prof. IPPOLITO ANTONINI.

UNIVERSITÀ DEGLI STUDI DI CASSINO

Via G. Marconi, 03043 Cassino (Frosinone)
Telephone: 0776-2991
Fax: 0776-310562
Internet: www.unicas.it
Founded 1979
State control
Rector: Prof. FEDERICO ROSSI
Administrative Director: Dott. LUIGI PELUSO CASSESE
Number of teachers: 160
Number of students: 9,500

DEANS

Faculty of Letters and Philosophy: GIANFRANCO RUBINO
Faculty of Economics and Commerce: Prof. MARIA CLAUDIA LUCCHETTI
Faculty of Engineering: Prof. GUIDO CARPINELLI
Faculty of Education: Prof. GIANFRANCO RUBINO

UNIVERSITÀ DEGLI STUDI DI CATANIA

Piazza dell' Università 2, 95124 Catania
Telephone: 095-310355
Fax: 095-325194
Internet: www.unict.it
Founded 1434
Rector: Prof. ENRICO RIZZARELLI
Pro-Rector: Prof. ROMILDA RIZZO
Administrative Director: Dr ETTORE GILOTTA
Number of teachers: 1,517
Number of students: 53,674

DEANS

Faculty of Jurisprudence: Prof. VINCENZO ZAPPALA
Faculty of Political Science: Prof. VINCENZO SCIACCA
Faculty of Economics and Commerce: Prof. EMILIO GIARDINA
Faculty of Literature and Philosophy: Prof. GIUSEPPE GIARRIZZO
Faculty of Medicine: Prof. GIOVANNI RUSSO
Faculty of Mathematics, Physics, Chemistry and Natural Sciences: Prof. RENATO PUCCI
Faculty of Architecture: Prof. UGO CANTONE
Faculty of Pharmacy: Prof. GIUSEPPE RONSISVALLE
Faculty of Agriculture: Prof. GIUSEPPE PERROTTA

Faculty of Engineering: Prof. GIUSEPPE COZZO
Faculty of Education: Prof. ROSARIO SORACI

UNIVERSITÀ DEGLI STUDI DI FERRARA

Via Savonarola 9, 44100 Ferrara
Telephone: 0532-293111
Fax: 0532-248927
E-mail: mgn@dns.unife.it
Internet: www.unife.it
Founded 1391
Academic year: November to October
Rector: Prof. PATRIZIO BIANCHI
Pro-Rector (vacant)
Administrative Director: Dott. ALESSANDRO FABBRI
Number of teachers: 714
Number of students: 17,000
Publications: *Annali dell' Università*, *Annuario*, *Ateneo* (6 a year)

DEANS

Faculty of Law: Prof. GIOVANNI CAZZETTA
Faculty of Letters and Philosophy: Prof. CARLO ALBERTO CAMPI
Faculty of Medicine and Surgery: Prof. ADOLFO SEBASTIANI
Faculty of Mathematical, Physical and Natural Sciences: Prof. REMIGIO ROSSI
Faculty of Pharmacy: Prof. ALESSANDRO BRUNI
Faculty of Engineering: Prof. ROBERTO POMPOLI
Faculty of Architecture: Prof. GRAZIANO TRIPPA
Faculty of Economics: (vacant)

PROFESSORS

Faculty of Law (Corso Ercole I d'Este 37, 44100 Ferrara; tel. 0532-205521; fax 0532-200188; e-mail infogiur@unife.it; internet www.giuri.unife.it):

ADAMI, F. E., Canon and Ecclesiastical Law
BALANDI, G. G., Labour Law
BERNARDI, A., Penal Law
BIN, R., Constitutional Law
BORGHI, P., Agrarian Law
BRUNELLI, G., Institutions of Public Law
BRUZZO, A., Political Economy
CARIELLO, V., Commercial Law
CASAROTTO, G., Agrarian Law
CAZZETTA, G., History of Medieval and Modern Law
CIACCIA, B., Civil Procedure Law
COSTATO, L., Agrarian Law
DE GIORGI, M. V., Private Law
GRIPPO, G., Commercial Law
MANFREDINI, A., Roman Law and Laws of Antiquity
NAPPI, P., Agrarian Law
PASTORE, B., Philosophy of Law
PELLIZZER, F., Administrative Law
PUGIOTTO, A., Constitutional Law
SALERNO, F., International Law
SCARANO USSANI, V., Roman Law and Laws of Antiquity
SOMMA, A., Comparative Private Law
ZAMORANI, P., Roman Law and Laws of Antiquity

Faculty of Letters and Philosophy (Via Savonarola 38, 44100 Ferrara; tel. 0532-293416; fax 0532-202689; internet www.unife.it/facolta/facolta-300035.htm):

BELLATALLA, L., History of School and Educational Institutions
BOLLINI, M., Roman History
CAMPI, C. A., Geography
CHERCHI, P., Italian Literature
FABBRI, P., Musicology and Musical History
FAVA, E., Glottology and Linguistics
FOLLI, A., Contemporary Italian Literature
GALLI, M., German Literature
GENOVESI, G., General and Social Pedagogy
MATARRESE, S., Italian Language
MAZZI, M. S., Medieval History
MAZZOCCHI, G., Spanish Literature
MERCI, P., Romance Philology and Linguistics
NESPOR, M. A., Glottology and Linguistics
PANCERA, C., History of Schools and Educational Institutions
RICCI, G., Modern History
SECHI, S., Contemporary History
TEMPERA, M., English Literature
TROVATO, P., Italian Language
VARESE, R., History of Modern Art
ZANOTTI, A., General Sociology

Faculty of Medicine and Surgery (Via Fossato di Mortara 64/b, 44100 Ferrara; tel. 0532-291545; fax 0532-291546; e-mail preside.medicina@unife.it; internet web.unife.it/facolta/medicina):

AVATO, F. M., Forensic Medicine
AZZENA, G. F., General Surgery
BERGAMINI, C., Clinical Biochemistry and Clinical Molecular Biology
BERTI, G., General Pathology
BOREA, P. A., Pharmacology
BORGNA, C., General and Specialized Paediatrics
CALURA, G., Odontostomatological Diseases
CALZOLARI, E., Medical Genetics
CAPITANI, S., Human Anatomy
CARUSO, A., Histology
CASSAI, E., Microbiology and Clinical Microbiology
CASTOLDI, G. L., Haematology
CAVAZZINI, L., Anatomical Pathology
CIACCIA, A., Diseases of the Respiratory Tract
CONCONI, F., Biochemistry
CROCE, C. M., Medical Oncology
DALLOCCHIO, F. P. F., Biochemistry
DE ROSA, E., Industrial Medicine
DEGLI UBERTI, E., Endocrinology
DEL SENNO, L., Molecular Biology
DI VIRGILIO, F., General Pathology
DONINI, I. G., General Surgery
DURANTE, E., General Surgery
FAVILLA, M., Physiology
FELLIN, R., Internal Medicine
FERRARI, R., Cardiovascular Diseases
GRANIERI, E., Neurology
GRAZI, E., Biochemistry
GREGORIO, P., General and Applied Hygiene
GUALDI, E., Anthropology
LIBONI, A., General Surgery
LONGHINI, C., Internal Medicine
MANNELLA, P., Imaging and Radiotherapy Diagnostics
MARTINI, A., Audiology
MOLINARI, S., Clinical Psychology
MOLLICA, G., Obstetrics and Gynaecology
NENCI, I., Anatomy and Pathological Histology
PASTORE, A., Otolaryngology
PINAMONTI, S., Applied Biology
RAMELLI, E., Psychiatry
REGOLI, D., Pharmacology
SEBASTIANI, A., Eyesight Diseases
SICILIANI, G., Odontostomatological Diseases
SPIDALIERI, G., Physiology
TOGNON, M., Applied Biology
TRAINA, G. C., Ambulatory Diseases
TROTTA, F., Rheumatology
TURINI, D., Urology
VIGI, V., General and Specialized Paediatrics
VIRGILI, A., Skin and Venereal Diseases

Faculty of Mathematical, Physical and Natural Sciences (Via Luigi Borsari 46, 44100 Ferrara; tel. 0532-291347; fax 0532-291348; internet www.unife.it/facolta/facolta-275017.htm):

ABELLI, L., Comparative Anatomy and Cytology
ALBERTI, A., Mineralogy
BARBUJANI, G., Genetics
BECCALUVA, L., Petrology and Petrography
BERNARDI, F., Biochemistry
BIASINI, L., Numerical Analysis
BIGNOZZI, C. A., General and Inorganic Chemistry
BOSELLINI, A., Stratigraphic and Sedimentological Geology
BROGLIO, A., Anthropologyy
CANESCHI, L., Theoretical Physics and Mathematical Models and Methods
CIMIRAGLIA, R., Physical Chemistry
COLTORTI, M., Petrology and Petrography
CORALLINI, A., General Microbiology
DALPIAZ, P., General Physics
DEL CENTINA, A., Geometry
DI CAPUA, E., Experimental Physics
DONDI, F., Analytical Chemistry
DONDONI, A., Organic Chemistry
ELLIA, P., Geometry
FAGIOLI, F., Environmental and Conservation Chemistry
FASULO, M. P., General Botany
FIORENTINI, G., Nuclear and Subnuclear Physics
FOA', A. G., Zoology
GERDOL, R., Environmental and Applied Botany
GILLI, G., Physical Chemistry
LASCU, A., Geometry
MARTINELLI, G., Experimental Physics
MASSARI, U., Mathematical Analysis
MENINI, C., Algebra
NANNI, T., Applied Geology
NIZZOLI, F., Solid-State Physics
PEPE, L., Complementary Mathematics
PERETTO, C., Anthropology
PICCOLINO, M., Physiology
PRODI, F., Earth Physics
ROSSI, R., Ecology
RUGGIERO, V., Numerical Analysis
SACCHI, O., Physiology
SACERDOTI, M., Mineralogy
SALVATORELLI, G., Comparative Anatomy and Cytology
SCANDOLA, F., General and Inorganic Chemistry
SCHIFFRER, G., Theoretical Physics and Mathematical Models and Methods
SIENA, F., Petrology and Petrography
SOLONNIKOV, V., Mathematical Physics
TRAVERSO, O., General and Inorganic Chemistry
TRIPICCIONE, R., Theoretical Physics and Mathematical Models and Methods
ZANGHIRATI, L., Mathematical Analysis

Faculty of Pharmacy (Via Fossato di Mortara 17/19, 44100 Ferrara; tel. 0532-291265; fax 0532-291296; e-mail farmline@unife.it; internet web.unife.it/facolta/farmacia):

BARALDI, P. G., Pharmaceutical Chemistry
BIANCHI, C., Pharmacology
BIONDI, C., Physiology
BRANDOLINI, V., Food Chemistry
BRUNI, A., Pharmocological Biology
GAMBACCINI, M., Applied Physics (Conservation, Environmental, Biological and Medical)
GAMBARI, R, Biochemistry
MANFREDINI, S., Pharmaceutical Chemistry
MANSERVIGI, R., Microbiology and Clinical Microbiology
MENEGATTI, E., Applied Pharmaceutical Technology
POLLINI, G. P., Organic Chemistry
RIZZUTO, R., General Pathology
SALVADORI, S., Pharmaceutical Chemistry
SCATTURIN, A., Applied Pharmaceutical Chemistry
SIMONI, D., Pharmaceutical Chemistry
TANGANELLI, S., Pharmacology
TOMATIS, R., Pharmaceutical Chemistry

TRANIELLO, M. S., Biochemistry

Faculty of Engineering (Via Saragat 1, 44100 Ferrara; tel. 0532-974871; fax 0532-760162; internet www.unife.it/facolta/facolta-300076.htm):

BEGHELLI, S., Automatic Controls
BETTOCCHI, R., Energy and Environmental Systems
DAL CIN, R., Stratigraphic and Sedimentological Geology
DALPIAZ, G., Applied Machine Mechanics
DEL PIERO, G., Construction Theory
FERRETTI, P., Experimental Physics
FRANCHINI, M., Hydraulic and Marine Hydraulic Engineering
FRONTERA, F., Experimental Physics
LAMMA, E., Information Processing Systems
OLIVO, P., Electronics
PADULA, M., Mathematical Physics
PIVA, S., Industrial Technical Physics
POMPOLI, R., Environmental Technical Physics
RUSSO, P., Topography and Cartography
TRALLI, A., Construction Theory
ZUCCHI, F., Chemical Foundations of Technology

Faculty of Architecture (Via Quartieri 8, 44100 Ferrara; tel. 0532-293613; fax 0532-293611; e-mail faf@unife.it; internet architettura.fe.infn.it):

ACOCELLA, A., Architectural Technology
ALESSANDRI, C., Construction Theory
CECCARELLI, P., Urban Planning
DI FEDERICO, I., Industrial Technical Physics
LAUDIERO, F., Construction Methods
MINARDI, B., Urban and Architectonic Composition
TRIPPA, G., Architectural Technology

Faculty of Economics (Vicolo del Gregorio 13–15, 44100 Ferrara; tel. 0532-293000; fax 0532-293012; internet www.economia.unife.it):

BIANCHI, P., Applied Economics
CALAMANTI, A., Economics of Financial Mediators
COCOZZA, F., Economic Law
PINI, P., Political Economy
POLA, G., Finance
SEGALA, F., Mathematical Analysis

UNIVERSITÀ DEGLI STUDI DI FIRENZE

Piazza San Marco 4, 50121 Florence
Telephone: 055-27571
Fax: 055-264194
Internet: www.unifi.it
Founded 1321
Academic year: September to August
Rector: Prof. PAOLO BLASI
Vice-Rector: Prof. GIANCARLO ZAMPI
Registrar: Dott. GAETANO SERAFINO
Librarian: Dott. A. M. TAMMARO
Number of teachers: 2,236
Number of students: 59,847

DEANS

Faculty of Jurisprudence: Prof. PAOLO CARETTI
Faculty of Political Sciences: Prof. CLAUDIO FRANCHINI
Faculty of Economics: Prof. CARLO VALLINI
Faculty of Letters and Philosophy: Prof. PAOLO MARRASSINI
Faculty of Education: Prof. PAOLO OREFICE
Faculty of Medicine and Surgery: Prof. GIOVANNI ORLANDINI
Faculty of Mathematical, Physical and Natural Sciences: Prof. P. MALESANI
Faculty of Pharmacy: Prof. SERGIO PINZAUTI
Faculty of Architecture: Prof. FRANCESCO GURRIERI
Faculty of Agriculture and Forestry: Prof. AUGUSTO MARINELLI
Faculty of Engineering: Prof. ENNIO CARNEVALE

DIRECTORS OF INSTITUTES

Faculty of Agriculture and Forestry:

Forestry Management and Technology: Prof. O. CIANCIO
Forestry Pathology and Zoology: Prof. G. SURICO
Silviculture: Prof. G. BERNETTI

Faculty of Architecture:

Mathematics: Prof. O. ARENA

Faculty of Economics:

Law: Prof. R. ALESSI
Linguistics: Prof. R. E. SCHMIDT
Economic History: Prof. G. MORI

Faculty of Education:

Germanic and Oriental Languages and Literature: Prof. I. HENNEMANN
English and North American Language and Literature: Prof. A. SERPIERI

Faculty of Letters and Philosophy:

Germanic, Slav and Ugro-Finnish Languages and Literatures: Prof. C. CORTI

Faculty of Medicine and Surgery:

Anatomy and Pathological Histology: Prof. G. ZAMPI
Anaesthesiology and Resuscitation: Prof. G. P. NOVELLI
Dermosyphilopathy: Prof. B. GIANNOTTI
General Surgery: Prof. C. CORTESINI
General Surgery and Surgical Therapy I: Prof. M. PACE
General Medicine and Cardiology: Prof. G. G. NERI SERNERI
Internal Medicine: Prof. P. GENTILINI
Internal Medicine and Immunoallergology: Prof. S. ROMAGNANI
General Clinical Medicine and Medical Therapy IV: Prof. M. CAGNONI
Ophthalmology: Prof. G. SALVI
Orthopaedics and Traumatology: Prof. G. STRINGA
Obstetrics and Gynaecology: Prof. G. B. MASSI
Otorhinolaryngology: Prof. O. FINI STORCHI
Gerontology and Geriatrics: Prof. A. D'ALESSANDRO
Labour Medicine: Prof. G. GIULIANO
Microbiology 'Renzo Davoli': Prof. G. GARGANI
Odonto-stomatology: Prof. P. PIERLEONI

Faculty of Mathematical, Physical and Natural Sciences:

Anthropology: Prof. G. ARDITO

Interfaculty:

Geography: Prof. L. ROMBAI
Forensic and Insurance Medicine: Prof. C. FAZZARI
General Pathology: Prof. A. FONNESU

UNIVERSITÀ DEGLI STUDI 'GABRIELE D'ANNUNZIO'

Via dei Vestini, 66013 Chieti Scalo
Telephone: 0871-3551
Fax: 0871-3556007
Internet: www.unich.it
Founded 1965 as a private university; became a state university 1982
State control
Rector: Prof. FRANCO CUCCURULLO
Vice-Rector: Prof. GIUSEPPE PAOLONE
Administrative Director: Dr MARCO NAPOLEONE
Number of students: 19,000

DEANS

Faculty of Foreign Languages and Literature: Prof. FRANCESCO MARRONI
Faculty of Literature and Philosophy: Prof. GAETANO BONETTA
Faculty of Medicine and Surgery: Prof. CARMINE DI ILIO
Faculty of Mathematical, Physical and Natural Sciences: Prof. BRUNO DI SABATINO
Faculty of Commerce: Prof. MARIO GIACCIO
Faculty of Architecture: Prof. TOMMASO SCALESSE
Faculty of Pharmacy: Prof. MICHELE VACCA

UNIVERSITÀ DEGLI STUDI DI GENOVA

Via Balbi 5, 16126 Genoa
Telephone: 010-20991
Fax: 010-2099227
E-mail: webmaster@unige.it
Internet: www.unige.it
Founded 1670
Academic year: November to October
Rector: Prof. S. PONTREMOLI
Vice-Rector (vacant)
Administrative Director: Dott. D. PELLITTERI
Number of teachers: 1,719
Number of students: 40,125
Publications: *Annuario dell'Università di Genova* (sections on research and teaching units, each annually), *Genuense Atenaeum* (6 a year)

DEANS

Faculty of Jurisprudence: Prof. V. PIERGIOVANNI
Faculty of Political Sciences: Prof. A. M. DEL GROSSO
Faculty of Economics and Commerce: Prof. L. CASELLI
Faculty of Letters and Philosophy: Prof. M. G. ANGELI
Faculty of Education: Prof. A. DAL LAGO
Faculty of Medicine and Surgery: Prof. U. MARINARI
Faculty of Mathematics, Physics and Natural Science: Prof. M. GIANNINI
Faculty of Pharmacy: Prof. G. BIGNARDI
Faculty of Engineering: Prof. A. SQUARZONI
Faculty of Architecture: Prof. A. E. CALCAGNO
Faculty of Foreign Languages: Prof. P. CROVETTO

UNIVERSITÀ DELL'INSUBRIA

Via Ravasi 2, 21100 Varese
Telephone: 0332-219780
Fax: 0332-219789
Internet: www3.uninsubria.it
Rector: Prof. RENZO DIONIGI
Vice-Rector: Prof. ALBERTO SDRALEVICH
Administrative Director: Dr MARINO BALZANI

DEANS

Faculty of Medicine and Surgery: Prof. PAOLO CHERUBINO
Faculty of Economics: Prof. ROSSELLA LOCATELLI
Faculty of Sciences in Varese: Prof. ROBERTO VALVASSORI
Faculty of Sciences in Como: Prof. ALDO GAMBA
Faculty of Law: Prof. CLAUDIA STORCHI

UNIVERSITÀ DEGLI STUDI DELL' AQUILA

Piazza Rivera 1, 67100 L'Aquila
Telephone: 0862-4311
Fax: 0862-412948
Internet: www.univaq.it
Founded 1952

Rector: Prof. GIOVANNI SCHIPPA
Administrative Director: Dott. LAURA PAONI

Library of 171,356 vols
Number of teachers: 509
Number of students: 8,260

DEANS

Faculty of Sciences: Prof. ARMANDO REALE
Faculty of Engineering: Prof. LUIGI BIGNARDI
Faculty of Education: Prof. ENRICO MONTANARI
Faculty of Medicine: Prof. FERDINANDO DI ORIO
Faculty of Business Economics: STELIO VALENTINI

UNIVERSITÀ DEGLI STUDI DI LECCE

Viale Gallipoli 49, 73100 Lecce
Telephone: 0832-291111
Fax: 0832-292204
E-mail: rettore@unile.it
Internet: www.unile.it

Founded 1956
Academic year: November to October

Rector: Prof. ORONZO LIMONE
Administrative Director: Dott. ANTONIO SOLOMBRINO
Librarian: Dssa GIOVANNA BASCIA

Library of 500,000 vols
Number of teachers: 673
Number of students: 28,403

Publication: *Unile* (quarterly)

DEANS

Faculty of Arts: Prof. MARCELLO GUAITOLI
Faculty of Economics: Prof. NICOLA DI CAGNO
Faculty of Education: Prof. MARCELLO STRAZZERI
Faculty of Engineering: Prof. DOMENICO LAFORGIA
Faculty of Foreign Languages: Prof. ANTONIO FINO
Faculty of Law: Prof. NICOLA DE LISO
Faculty of Letters and Philosophy: Prof. BRUNO PELLEGRINO
Faculty of Science: Prof. CARLO STORELLI

UNIVERSITÀ DEGLI STUDI DI MACERATA

Piaggia dell'Università 11, 62100 Macerata
Telephone: 0733-2581
Fax: 0733-2582689
E-mail: rel.esterne@unimc.it
Internet: www.unimc.it

Founded 1290

Rector: Prof. ROBERTO SANI
Vice-Rector: Prof. LUIGI LACCHÉ
Head of Administration: Dr ROLANDO GARBUGLIA
Deputy Rectors: Prof. ANTONELLA PAOLINI (Budget and Financial Planning), Prof. ADRIANO BALLARINI (Buildings and Property), Prof. ANDREA SIMOCINI (International Relations), Prof. ENZO CANIZZARO (Library System), Prof. CARLO MENGHI (Organization and Staff), Prof. CRISTIANA MAMMANA (Professional and Corporate Relations), Prof. DIEGO POLI (Public Relations), Prof. MAURO MARCONI (Computing and Multimedia Centre (CAIM)), Prof. PIER GIUSEPPE ROSSI (e-Learning and Integrated Teacher Training Centre (CELFI)), Prof. MARINA CAMBONI (Equal Opportunities Committee), Prof. BARBARA POJAGHI (Orientation Centre), Prof. MARCELLO VERDENELLI (Theatre and Artistic Events), Prof. DANIELLE LÉVY (University Language Centre (CLA)), Prof. LUIGI LACCHÉ (University of Macerata Publications Centre)

Number of teachers: 300
Number of students: 15,000

DEANS

Faculty of Arts and Humanities: Prof. DANIELE MAGGI
Faculty of Communication Sciences: Prof. MAURIZIO CIASCHINI
Faculty of Economics: Prof. MAURO MARCONI
Faculty of Educational Sciences: Prof. MICHELE CORSI
Faculty of Law: Prof. RINO FROLDI
Faculty of Political Sciences: Prof. VITANTONIO GIOIA

DIRECTORS OF INSTITUTES

Faculty of Arts and Humanities:
- Classical Philology: Prof. MARCELLO SALVADORE

Faculty of Law:
- Forensic Medicine and Insurance: Prof. MARIANO CINGOLANI
- Historical Studies: Prof. MARIO SBRICCOLI
- History and Philosophy of Law and Ecclesiastic Law: Prof. CARLO MENGHI
- International and European Union Law: Prof. VINCENZO CANNIZZARO
- Law of Civil Procedure: Prof. ANTONIO CARRATTA
- Law and Criminal Procedure: Prof. GLAUCO GIOSTRA
- Legal Practice: Prof. FRANCO BOLOGNINI
- Roman Law: Prof. SANDRO SERANGELI

DIRECTORS OF DEPARTMENTS

Economic Development Studies: Prof. DIEGO PIACENTINO
Economic and Financial Institutions: Prof. ANTONELLA PAOLINI
Education Sciences and Teacher Training: Prof. GIUSEPPE GALLI
Historical, Documentary, Artistic and Area Studies: Prof. GIUSEPPE AVARUCCI
Literary and Philological Linguistic Research: Prof. DIEGO POLI
Modern Languages and Literatures: Prof. MARINA CAMBONI
Philosophy and Human Sciences: Prof. GIANFRANCO PACI
Private Law, Italian and Comparative Labour Law: Prof. FRANCESCO PROSPERI
Public Law and Political Theory: Prof. GIULIO SALERNO
Studies on Social Change, Legal Institutions and Communication: Prof. ALBERTO FEBBRAJO

ATTACHED RECORDS AND RESEARCH CENTRES

Antoine Barnave Laboratory of Constitutional History: Dir Prof. ROBERTO MARTUCCI.

Attilio Moroni Centre of Studies: Dir Prof. GINESIO MANTUANO.

Centre for Autobiographical Studies: Dir (vacant).

Centre for European Records (C. D. E.): Dir Prof. ENZO CANNIZZARO.

Centre for Legal Computing (C. I. G.): Dir Prof. ENRICO DEL PRATO.

Centre for Records on Contemporary Parties and Political Movements in Le Marche: Dir Prof. ANGELO VENTRONE.

Centre for Records and Research on the History of the School Textbook and Children's Literature: Dir Prof. ROBERTO SANI.

Centre for Records and Research on North African Archaeology: Dir Prof. ANTONINO DI VITA.

Centre for Research into the Psychology of Communication: Dir Prof. ANDRZEJ ZUZCKOWSKI.

Centre for Research into the Psychology of Development and Education: Dir Prof.ssa ANNA ARFELLI.

Centre for Studies on Juvenile Justice: Dir Prof. GLAUCO GIOSTRA.

Centre for Studies and Records of the University of Macerata: Dir Prof. SANDRO SERANGELI.

Fausto Vicarelli Laboratory for the Study of the Relations between Banks and Industry: Dir Prof. ANDREA NIUTTA.

Ghino Valenti Laboratory on Agricultural, Environmental and Alimentary Policies: Dir Prof. FRANCESCO ADORNATO.

Interdepartmental Centre on the Reform of the State of Welfare Policies: Dir Prof.ssa PAOLA OLIVELLI.

Inter-University Centre for Research, Teaching and Teacher Training (C. I. R. DI. FOR.): Dir Prof. MICHELE CORSI.

Laboratory of Computer Records: Dir Prof. STEFANO PIGLIAPOCO.

Laboratory of European Mediterranean and Oriental History: Dir Prof. ANGELO VENTRONE.

Laboratory of Experimental Phonetics (LA. FO. S.): Dir Prof. DIEGO POLI.

UNIVERSITÀ DEGLI STUDI DI MESSINA

Piazza Salvatore Pugliatti 1, 98122 Messina
Telephone: 090-6761
Fax: 1717762
E-mail: prorettore.vicario@unime.it
Internet: www.unime.it

Founded 1548
Academic year: November to June

Rector: Prof. FRANCESCO TOMASELLO
Pro-Rector: Prof. GIOVANNI DUGO
Admin. Dir: Dr VINCENZO FERLUGA

Number of teachers: 1,300
Number of students: 40,000

DEANS

Faculty of Econ.: Prof. L. FERLAZZO NATOLI
Faculty of Education: Prof. A. PENNISI
Faculty of Eng.: Prof. S. GALVAGNO
Faculty of Jurisprudence: Prof. S. BERLINGÒ
Faculty of Literature and Philosophy: Prof. V. FERA
Faculty of Mathematics, Physics and Natural Sciences: Prof. M. GATTUSO
Faculty of Medicine: Prof. E. SCRIBANO
Faculty of Pharmacy: Prof. M. G. VIGORITA
Faculty of Politics: Prof. A. ROMANA
Faculty of Statistical Sciences: Prof. L. LA TONA
Faculty of Veterinary Medicine: Prof. G. GERMANÀ

UNIVERSITÀ DEGLI STUDI DI MILANO

Via Festa del Perdono 7, 20122 Milan
Telephone: 02-503111
Fax: 02-50312627
Internet: www.unimi.it

Founded 1923
Academic year: October to September

Rector: Prof. E. DECLEVA
Vice-Rector: Prof. D. CASATI
Administrative Director: Dott. FILIPPO SORI
Librarian: Dott. GIULIANA GIUSTINO

Number of teachers: 716
Number of students: 63,000

Publication: *Sistema Università* (online at www.sisuni.unimi.it)

DEANS

Faculty of Agriculture: Prof. C. SORLINI
Faculty of Law: Prof. V. FERRARI
Faculty of Letters and Philosophy: Prof. E. FRANZINI
Faculty of Medicine: Prof. G. COGGI

Faculty of Motor Sciences: Prof. G. PIZZINI
Faculty of Pharmacy: Prof. R. PAOLETTI
Faculty of Political Sciences: Prof. M. REGINI
Faculty of Sciences: Prof. M. PIGNANELLI
Faculty of Veterinary Medicine: Prof. G. POLI

PROFESSORS

Faculty of Agriculture (Via Celoria 2, 20133 Milan; tel. 02-50316500; fax 02-50316508; e-mail preside.agraria@unimi.it; internet www.unimi.it/ateneo/facol/agraria.htm):

ANDREONI, V., Agricultural Microbiology
BASSI, D., Fruit Farming
BELLI, G., Plant Pathology
BIANCO, P. A., Plant Pathology
BODRIA, L., Agricultural Mechanics
BONOMI, F., Biochemistry
CASATI, D., Agrofood Economy
CASTELLI, G., Agricultural Mechanics
CASTROVILLI, C. M., Zooculture
COCUCCI, M., Physiology of Farmed Plants
CORTESI, P., Plant Pathology
CROVETTO, G. M., Animal Nutrition and Foodstuffs
DE WRACHIEN, D., Irrigation and Drainage
DESIMONI, E., Analytical Chemistry
DURANTI, M. M., Biochemistry
ECCHER, T., General Arboriculture
ELIAS, G., Environmental Technical Physics
FRISIO, D. G., Rural Economics and Surveying
GALLI, A., Foods Microbiology
GANDOLFI, C., Agricultural and Forest Hydraulics
GARLASCHI, F. M., Vegetable Physiology
GASPARETTO, E., Agricultural Mechanization
GAVAZZI, G., Plant Genetic Improvement
GENEVINI, P., Soil Chemistry
GIURA, R., Agricultural Hydraulics
GREPPI, M., Hydraulic Systems, Forestry
LOCATELLI, D. P., General and Applied Entomology
LOZZIA, G. C., General and Applied Entomology
LUCISANO, M., Food Science and Technology
MAGGIORE, T., Herbaceous Farming
MANACHINI, P., General Microbiology
MANNINO, S., Chemico-Physical and Sensory Analysis of Food
MERLINI, L., Organic Chemistry
MONDELLI, R., Organic Chemistry
PAGANI, S., Enzymology
PELLEGRINO, L. M., Food Science and Technology
PIERGIOVANNI, L., Food Science and Technology
POLELLI, M., Rural Evaluation
POMPEI, C., Food Technology Processes
PORRINI, M., Physiology
PRETOLANI, R., Rural Economics and Surveying
QUARONI, S., Vegetable Pathology
RAGG, E. M., Organic Chemistry
RESMINI, P., Agricultural Industry
ROSSI, M., Food Science and Technology
SACCHI, G. A., Organic Chemistry
SALAMINI, F., Genetics and Biotechnology
SANGIORGI, F., Rural and Forest Construction
SCHIRALDI, A., Physical Chemistry
SCIENZA, A., General Arboriculture and Tree Cultivation
SORLINI, C., Agricultural and Forest Microbiology
SUCCI, G., Special Animal Husbandry
SÜSS, L., Agricultural Entomology
TANO, F., Herbaceous Farming
TATEO, F., Food Science and Technology
TESTOLIN, G., Human Food and Nutrition
TOCCOLINI, A., Rural and Forest Construction
VOLONTERIO, G., Agricultural Industry
ZOCCHI, G., Food Science and Technology

Faculty of Law (Via Festa del Perdono 7, 20122 Milan; tel. 02-50312400; fax 02-50312653; e-mail presidenza.giurisprudenza@unimi.it; internet www.unimi.it/ateneo/facol/giurisp.htm):

ALBISETTI, A., Ecclesiastical Law
AMODIO, E., Procedural Penal Law
ANGIOLINI, V., Constitutional Law
BARIATTI, S., International Law
BENATTI, F., Institutions of Private Law
BOSCHIERO, N., International Law
CANDIAN, A., Comparative Private Law
CANTARELLA, E., Institutions of Roman Law
CARINCI, M. T., Labour Law
CARNEVALI, U., Institutions of Private Law
CASTAGNOLA, A., Civil Procedural Law
CASUSCELLI, G., Ecclesiastical Law
CAVALLONE, B., Civil Procedural Law
CONDINANZI, M., International Law
D'AMICO, M. E., Constitutional Law
DE NOVA, G., Civil Law
DENOZZA, F., Commercial Law
DI RENZO, M. G., History of Italian Law
DOLCINI, E., Penal Law
DOMINIONI, O., Procedural Penal Comparative Law
FERRARI, E., Administrative Law
FERRARI, S., Canon Law
FERRARI, V., Sociology of Law
FLORIDA, G., Comparative Public Law
FRASSI, P. A., Commercial Law
GAFFURI, G., Tributary Law
GALANTINI, M. N., Procedural Penal Law
GAMBARO, A., Comparative Private Law
GITTI, G., Institutions of Private Law
GNOLI, F., Roman Law
GOISIS, G., Political Economy
GRECO, G., Administrative Law
GREZZI, M. L., Philosophy of Law
GUERCI, C. M., Political Economy
JAEGER, P., Commercial Law
JORI, M., Philosophy of Law
LANCELLOTTI, E., Financial Science
LUZZATI, C. R., Philosophy of Law
LUZZATTO, R., International Law
MARINUCCI, G., Penal Law
MASSETTO, G., History of Italian Law
MERLIN, E., Civil Procedural Law
MORELLO, U. M., Private Law
NASCIMBENE, B., European Community Law
PADOA SCHIOPPA, A., History of Italian Law
PALIERO, C., Penal Law
PARISI, F., Institutions of Private Law
PELOSI, A. C., Institutions of Private Law
PERICU, G., Administrative Law
PISANI, M., Procedural Penal Law
POCAR, F., International Law
POLARA, G., Institutions of Roman Law
RICCI, E., Bankruptcy Law
RIMINI, E., Commercial Law
ROSSIGNOLI, B., Economics of Credit Institutions
SACCHI, R., Commercial Law
SALETTI, A., Civil Procedural Law
SANTA MARIA, A., International Law
SPAGNUOLO VIGORITA, L., Labour Law
TENELLA SILLANI, C., Institutions of Private Law
TREVES, T., International Private and Procedural Law
TRIMARCHI, F., Administrative Law
TRIMARCHI, P., Civil Law
VIGANÒ, F., Penal Law
VILLA, G., Institutions of Private Law
VILLATA, R., Administrative Law
VIOLINI, L., Constitutional Law
VITALI, E. G., Ecclesiastical Law
ZANON, N., Constitutional Law

Faculty of Letters and Philosophy (Via Festa del Perdono 7, 20122 Milan; tel. 02-50312701; fax 02-50312543; e-mail elio.franzini@unimi.it; internet www.unimi.it/ateneo/facol/letfil.htm):

ALBINI, G., Medieval History
ANTONIELLI, L., History of Political Institutions
ANZI, A., History of the English Theatre
BARONI, M. F., Paleography
BEJOR, G., Classical Archaeology
BERRA, C., Italian Literature
BIANCHI, E., Geography
BIGALLI, D., History of Philosophy
BIGNAMI, M., English Language and Literature
BOCCALI, G., Sanskrit Language and Literature
BOELLA, L., Moral Philosophy
BOLOGNA, M., Archives, Bibliography and Library Science
BOLOGNA, M. P., Glottology and Linguistics
BONOMI, A., Philosophy of Language
BONOMI, I., Italian Linguistics
BOSISIO, P., Dramatic Arts
BRAMBILLA, E., Modern History
BRIOSCHI, F., History of Literary Criticism
BROGI, G., History of the Russian Language
BRUTI LIBERATI, L., Modern History
CADIOLI, A. V., Contemporary Italian Literature
CAIZZI, F., History of Ancient Philosophy
CANAVERO, A., Modern History
CANZIANI, G., History of Philosophy
CAPRA, C., Modern History
CASALEGNO, P., Philosophy and Theory of Languages
CATTANEO, M. T., Spanish Language and Literature
CAVAJONI, G., Latin Language and Literature
CHIAPPA, M. L., Medieval History
CERCIGNANI, F., German Language and Literature
CHITTOLINI, G., Medieval History
CIANCI, G., English Language and Literature
CICALESE, M. L, Theory and History of Historiography
COLOMBO, M., French
COMBA, R., Medieval History
COMETTA, M., German Philology
CONCA, F., History of the Greek Language
CORDANO, F., Greek History
D'AGOSTINO, A., Romance Philology
DAVERIO, G., Greek History
DE ANGELIS, V, Humanistic Philology
DECLEVA, E., Contemporary History
DE FRANCESCO, A., Modern History
DEGRADA, F., History of Modern and Contemporary Music
DE MARINIS, R. C., Early and Recorded History
DEVECCHI, P., History of Modern Art
DI SALVO, M. G., Slavonic Philology
DOGLIO, M., French Literature
DONATI, C., History of the Ancient Italian States
DONINI, P., History of Ancient Philosophy
FIACCADORI, G., Christian and Medieval Archaeology
FORABOSCHI, D., Roman History
FRANZINI, E., Aesthetics
FUMAGALLI, M. J., History of Medieval Philosophy
GALLAZZI, C., Papyrology
GIACOMELLI, R., Glottology and Linguistics
GIORELLO, G., Philosophy of Science
GORI, G., History of Modern Philosophy
GUALANDRI, I., Latin Literature
IAMARTINO, G., English
LANARO, G. V., History of Philosophy
LEHNUS, L. A., Classical Philology
MARI, M., Italian Literature
MASINI, A., Italian Linguistics
MAZZOCCA, F., Museology, Art Criticism and Restoration Criticism
MENEGHETTI, M. L., Romance Philology
MERLO, G., History of the Medieval Church and Heresy

MERZARIO, R., Economic History
MICHELI, G., History of Science and Technology
MILANINI, C., Italian Literature
MODENESI, M., French Literature
MONTALEONE, C., Moral Philosophy
MONTECCHI, G., Bibliography and Archive and Library Science
MORGANA, S., Italian Language History
NEGRI, A., History of Modern Art
NISSIM, L., French Language and Literature
ORLANDI, G., Medieval Latin Literature
PAGETTI, C., English Language and Literature
PERASSI, E., Hispano-American Languages and Literatures
PETTOELLO, R., History of Philosophy
PEYRONEL, S., Medieval and Early Modern History
PIACENTINI, P., Egyptology and Coptic Civilization
PIRETTO, G. P., Slavic Studies
PIVA, P., History of Medieval Art
PUNZO, M., Modern History
RAMBALDI, E., Moral Philosophy
ROSA, G., Contemporary Italian Literature
RUMI, G., Contemporary History
SAMPIETRO, L., Anglo-American Languages and Literatures
SAPELLI, G., Economic History
SCARAMELLINI, G., Geography
SCARAMUZZA, G., Aesthetics
SCARAMUZZA, M. E., Spanish Literature
SINI, C., Theoretical Philosophy
SPAGGIARI, W., Italian Literature
SPERA, F., Italian Literature
TREVES, A. L., Geography
VALOTA, B., History of Eastern Europe
VISMARA, P., History of Christianity and the Churches
ZANETTO, G., Greek Language and Literature
ZECCHI, S., Aesthetics
ZERBI, M. C., Geography

Faculty of Medicine (Via Festa del Perdono 7, 20122 Milan; tel. 02-50312360; fax 02-50312365; e-mail preside.medicina@unimi.it; internet www.unimi.it/ateneo/facol/medchir.htm):

AGUS, G. B., Vascular Surgery
ALESSI, E., Dermatology
ALLEGRA, L., Diseases of the Respiratory System
ALLEVI, P., Biochemistry
ALTAMURA, A. C., Psychiatry
ALTOMARE, G., Dermatology
ANASTASIA, M., Chemistry and Biochemical Propaedeutics
AUSTONI, E., Urology
AUXILIA, F., Hygiene
BA, G., Psychiatry
BALDISSERA, F. G., Human Physiology
BALSARI, A., General Pathology
BEK PECCOZ, P., Endocrinology
BELLINI, T., Applied Physics (Arts, Environment, Biology and Medicine)
BERTAZZI, P. A., Industrial Medicine
BIANCHI PORRO, G., Gastroenterology
BIGLIOLI, P., Cardiac Surgery
BLASI, F. B., Diseases of the Respiratory System
BOCK, G., History of Medicine
BOLIS, G., Obstetrics and Gynaecology
BORTOLANI, E., General Surgery
BRAGA, P., Pharmacology
BRESOLIN, N., Neurology
BRESSANI DOLDI, S., General Surgery
BRUSATI, R., Maxillo-facial Surgery
BUSACCA, M., Obstetrics and Gynaecology
CABITZA, P., Orthopaedics and Traumatology
CAIRO, G., General Pathology
CAJONE, F., General Pathology
CANTALAMESSA, L., Internal Medicine
CAPETTA, P., Obstetrics and Gynaecology
CAPPELLINI, M. D., Internal Medicine
CAPUTO, R., Dermatology
CARACCIOLO, E., Clinical Psychology
CARRASSI, A., Special Odontostomatological Pathology
CARRUBA, M., Pharmacology
CATTANEO, M. N., Internal Medicine
CAVAGNA, G., Human Physiology
CAVAGNINI, F., Endocrinology
CAVALLARI, P., Physiology
CESARANI, A., Audiology
CESTARO, B. A., Biological Chemistry
CHIESARA, E., Toxicology
CHIGORNO, V. L., Clinical Biochemistry and Molecular Biology
CIANCAGLINI, R., Clinical Gnathology
CICARDI, M., Internal Medicine
CLEMENTI, F., Cellular and Molecular Pharmacology
CLERICI, M. S., General Pathology
COGGI, G., Pathological Anatomy and Histology
COLOMBI, A., Industrial Medicine
COLOMBO, M., Internal Medicine
COMI, P., General Pathology
CONTE, D., Gastroenterology
CORNALBA, G., Imaging and Radiotherapy Diagnostics
CORTELLARO, M., Internal Medicine
CORTI, M., Medical Physics
CROSIGNANI, P., Obstetrics and Gynaecology
CROSTI, C., Dermatology
CUSI, D. M., Nephrology
D'ANGELO, E., Human Physiology
DE FRANCHIS, R., Gastroenterology
DECARLI, A., Medical Statistics
DELLE FAVE, A., General Psychology
DESIDERIO, M. A., General Pathology
DI FIORE, P. P., General Pathology
DI GIULIO, A. M., Pharmacology
DONATELLI, F., Cardiac Surgery
DUBINI, F., Microbiology
FANTINI, F., Rheumatology
FARGION, S. R., Internal Medicine
FARNETI, A., Forensic Medicine
FARRONATO, G., Odontostomatological Diseases
FASSATI, L. R., General Surgery
FEDELE, L., Obstetrics and Gynaecology
FERRARIO, V. F., Human Anatomy
FERRERO, M. E., General Pathology
FIORENTINI, C., Cardiology
FOÀ, V., Industrial Hygiene
FOSCHI, D., General Surgery
GABRIELLI, L., Vascular Surgery
GAINI, S. M., Neurosurgery
GALLI, M., Infectious Diseases
GALLI, M. G., Hygiene
GALLUS, G. V., Medical Statistics and Biometrics
GATTINONI, L., Anaesthesiology and Resuscitation
GELMETTI, C., Dermatology
GHIDONI, R., Biological Chemistry
GIANNI, A., Medical Oncology
GINELLI, E., General Biology
GIOIA, M. A., Human Anatomy
GIOVANNINI, M., Paediatrics
GRANDI, M. A., Forensic Medicine
GROPPETTI, A., Pharmacology
GUAZZI, M., Cardiology
GUIDOBONO CAVALCHIN, F., Pharmacology
IAPICHINO, G., Anaesthesiology
INVERNIZZI, G., Psychiatry
LAMBERTENGHI DELILIERS, G., Internal Medicine
LARIZZA, L., Medical Genetics
LEDDA, M., Histology
LENTI, C., Child Neuropsychiatry
LEONETTI, G., Medical Semiology and Methodology
LODI, F., Forensic Toxicology
LUCIGNANI, G., Imaging and Radiotherapy Diagnostics
MAGRINI, F., Internal Medicine
MALCOVATI, M., Molecular Biology
MALLIANI, A., Internal Medicine
MANNUCCI, P. M., Internal Medicine
MANTOVANI, A., General Pathology
MARIANI, C., Neurology
MARIOTTI, M., Physiology
MARONI, M., Industrial Medicine
MASSIMINI, F., General Psychology
MATTINA, R., Microbiology
MATTURRI, L., Pathological Anatomy and Histology
MELZI D'ERIL, G., Clinical Biochemistry and Molecular Biology
MEOLA, G., Neurology
MERONI, P., Internal Medicine
MEZZETTI, M., Thoracic Surgery
MILANESI, G., Cellular Biology
MILANI, F., Radiotherapy
MOJA, E., General Psychology
MONTORSI, M., General Surgery
MORABITO, A., Medical Statistics
MORACE, G., Microbiology and Clinical Microbiology
MORGANTI, A., Internal Medicine
MORONI, M. E., Infectious Diseases
MÜLLER, E., Pharmacology
NICOLIN, A. N., Pharmacology
ORECCHIA, R., Radiotherapy
ORZALESI, N., Ophthalmology
OTTAVIANI, F., Oto-rhino-laryngology
PAGANI, M., Internal Medicine
PAGANO, A., Hygiene
PARDI, G., Obstetrics and Gynaecology
PELICCI, P. G., General Pathology
PERETTI, G., Orthopaedics and Traumatology
PERRELLA, M., Physical Biochemistry
PODDA, M., Internal Medicine
POLI, M., General Psychology
PONTIROLI, A., Internal Medicine
PRINCIPI, N., Paediatrics
RATIGLIA, R., Ophthalmology
RIVA, E., General and Specialist Paediatrics
ROCCO, F., Urology
RONCALLI, M., Pathological Anatomy
RONCHETTI, F., Chemistry and Biochemical Propaedeutics
RONCHI, E., Forensic Medicine
ROVIARO, G. C., General Surgery
SALVATO, A., Orthognathodontics
SAMBATARO, G., Oto-rhino-laryngology
SANTAMBROGIO, L., Thoracic Surgery
SANTANIELLO, E., Chemistry and Biochemical Propaedeutics
SANTORO, F., Odontostomatology
SCALABRINO, G., General Pathology
SCARONE, S., Psychiatry
SCORZA, R., Clinical Immunology and Allergology
SCORZA, R., General Surgery
SETTEMBRINI, P., Vascular Surgery
SICCARDI, A., General Biology
SMIRNE, S., Neurology
SONNINO, S., Biological Chemistry
SPINNLER, H., Neurology
STEFANI, M., Anatomy and Pathological Histology
STROHMENGER, L., Pedodontics
SURACE, A., Orthopaedics and Traumatology
TAROLO, G. L., Nuclear Medicine
TASCHIERI, A., General Surgery
TEALDI, D. G., Vascular Surgery
TENCHINI, M. L. G., General Biology
TETTAMANTI, G., Human Systematic Biochemistry
TRABUCCHI, E., General Surgery
VAGO, G., Pathological Anatomy
VERGANI, C., Gerontology and Geriatrics
VIALE, G., Pathological Anatomy and Histology
VICENTINI, L., Pharmacology
VILLA, M. L., Immunology
WEINSTEIN, R., Parodontology

ZANETTI, A., Hygiene
ZOCCHI, L., Physiology

Faculty of Motor Sciences (Via Kramer 4A, 20129 Milan; tel. 02-50315151; fax 02-50315152; e-mail scienze.motorie@unimi.it; internet www.unimi.it/ateneo/facol/scmot.htm):

CARANDENTE, F., Internal Medicine
FIORILLI, A., Applied Dietetics
LUZI, L., Physiology
PETRUCCIOLI, M. G., Human Anatomy
PIZZINI, G., Human Anatomy
SFORZA, C., Human Anatomy
VEICSTEINAS, A., Physiology
VENERANDO, B., Biochemistry

Faculty of Pharmacy (Viale Balzaretti 9, 20133 Milan; tel. 02-50318402; fax 02-50318266; e-mail presidenza.farmacia@unimi.it; internet www.unimi.it/ateneo/facol/farmacia.htm):

ABBRACHIO, M. P., Pharmacology
ALBINATI, A., General and Inorganic Chemistry
BARLOCCO, D., Pharmaceutical Chemistry
BECCALLI, E., Organic Chemistry
BERINGHELLI, T., General and Inorganic Chemistry
BERRA, B., Biological Chemistry
BOMBIERI, G., Drug Analysis
CARINI, M., Pharmaceutical Chemistry
CASTANO, P., Human Anatomy
CATAPANO, A. L., Pharmacology
CATTABENI, F., Applied Pharmacology
CATTANEO, E., Pharmacology
CELOTTI, F., General Pathology
CESAROTTI, E., General and Inorganic Chemistry
COLONNA, S., Organic Chemistry
CORSINI, A., Pharmacology
D'ALFONSO, G., General and Inorganic Chemistry
DALLA CROCE, P., Heterocyclic Chemistry
DE AMICI, M., Pharmaceutical Chemistry
DE GIULI MORGHEN, C., General Microbiology
DE MICHELI, C., Pharmaceutical and Toxicological Chemistry
DEL PRA, A., General and Inorganic Chemistry
FERRI, V., Pharmaceutical and Toxicological Chemistry
FOLCO, G., Pharmacology and Pharmacognosy
FRANCESCHINI, G., Pharmacology
GALLI, C., Pharmacological Tests and Measuring
GALLI, C. L., Pharmacology
GAVEZZOTTI, A., Physical Chemistry
GAZZANIGA, A., Applied Pharmaceutical Technology
GELMI, M. L., Organic Chemistry
MAFFEI FACINO, R., Drug Analysis
MAGGI, A. C., Pharmacology
MONTANARI, L., Pharmaceutical Technology, Socioeconomy and Legislation
MOTTA, M., General Physiology
PALLAVICINI, M., Pharmaceutical Chemistry
PIVA, F., Physiology
POCAR, D., Organic Chemistry
RACAGNI, G., Pharmacology and Pharmacognosy
SIRTORI, C., Clinical Pharmacology
SPARATORE, A., Pharmacological Chemistry
STRADI, R., Physical Methods in Organic Chemistry
TARAMELLI, D., General Pathology
TOMÈ, F., Pharmaceutical Biology
TREMOLI, E., Pharmacology
VALOTI, E., Pharmaceutical Chemistry

Faculty of Political Sciences (Via Conservatorio 7, 20122 Milan; tel. 02-50321000; fax 02-50321005; e-mail presidenza.scienze.politiche@unimi.it; internet www.unimi.it/ateneo/facol/scpol.htm):

ALBERICI, A., Economics of Credit Institutions
ANTONIOLI, M., Contemporary History
BARBA NAVARETTI, G., Political Economy
BECCALLI, B. Z., Sociology of Economic and Labour Processes
BERNAREGGI, G. M., Public Economy
BESUSSI, A., Political Philosophy
BILANCIA, P., Institutions of Public Law
BOGNETTI, G., Financial Sciences
BORDOGNA, L., Sociology of Economic and Labour Processes
CAFARI PANICO, R., European Community Law
CALVI, M. V., Spanish Language and Translation
CELLA, G. P., Economic Sociology
CHECCHI, D., Political Economy
CHIARINI, R., History of Political Parties and Political Movements
CHIESI, A. M., General Sociology
CLERICI, R., International Private Law
DE CARLI, P. G., Economics and Law
DE MARCO, E., Institutions of Public Law
DONZELLI, F., Political Economy
ESCOBAR, R., Political Philosophy
FACCHI, A., Philosophy of Law
FERRARA, M., Political Science
FERRARI, A., Contemporary History
FERRARI, P. A., Statistics
FLORIO, M., Financial Science
FRIGO, M., International Law
GALEOTTI, M. D., Political Economy
GANINO, M., Comparative Public Law
GARAVELLO, O., Economic Politics
GARZONE, G. E., English
ICHINO, P., Labour Law
ISENBURG, T., Political and Economic Geography
ITALIA, V., Institutions of Public Law
JULLION, M. C., French Language and Translation
LACAITA, G. C., Contemporary History
LAMBERTI ZANARDI, P., International Law
LAVAGNINO, A., Chinese and South East Asian Languages and Literatures
LEONINI, L., Sociology of Cultural and Communicative Processes
LIVORSI, F., History of Political Doctrine
LUPONE, A. M. G., International Law
MARAFFI, M., General Sociology
MARTELLI, P., Political Science
MARTINELLI, A., Political Science
MAURI, A., Economics of Credit Institutions
MAZZOLENI, F., Sociology of Cultural and Communicative Processes
MISSALE, A., Political Economy
MOIOLI, A., Economic History
MOLTENI, C., Japanese and Korean Languages and Literatures
MOSS, D. M., Demo-etno-anthropology
NICOLINI, G., Statistics
OLLA, M. P., History of International Relations
PEDRAZZI, M., International Law
PILOTTI, L., Economics and Management Studies
REGALIA, I., Sociology of Economic and Labour Processes
REGINI, M., Industrial Relations
REGONINI, G., Political Science
RIMINI, C. P., Institutions of Private Law
RIOSA, A., Contemporary History
RIVOLTA, G. C., Commercial Law
RONFANI, P., Juridical Sociology of Deviance and Social Change
RUFFINI, M. L., Comparative Private Law
SALVATI, M. A., Political Economy
SANTONI, M., Public Economy
SEGATTI, P., Political Phenomena and Sociology
TURSI, A., Labour Law
VENTURINI, G., International Law
VIARENGO, I., International Law
VIVAN, I., English Literature
ZICCARDI, F. E., Comparative Private Law

Faculty of Sciences (Via Saldini 50, 20133 Milan; tel. 02-50316001; fax 02-50316004; e-mail presidenza.scienze@unimi.it; internet www.unimi.it/ateneo/facol/smfn.htm):

ACERBI, E., Physics Experiments
ANNUNZIATA, R., Organic Chemistry
APOLLONI, B., Informatics
ARDIZZONE, S., Physical Chemistry
ARTIOLI, G., Mineralogy
BAMBUSI, D. P., Mathematical Physics
BELLINI, G., Physics Experiments
BELLOBONO, I. R., General and Inorganic Chemistry
BELLONE, E., History of Science and Technology
BERETTA, G. P., Applied Geology
BERTIN, G., Astronomy and Astrophysics
BERTINO, E., Database and Information Systems
BERTOLINI, M., Geometry
BERTONI, A., Theoretical Computer Science
BIRATTARI, C., Physics
BLASI, A., Mineralogy
BOLOGNESI, M., Biochemistry
BONETTI, R., Nuclear and Sub-Nuclear Physics
BONIFACIO, R., Institutions of Theoretical Physics
BORIANI, A., Petrography
BORTIGNON, P. F., Nuclear and Sub-Nuclear Physics
BOTTAZZINI, U., Complementary Mathematics
BRACCO, A., Physics Experiments
BROGLIA, R. A., Theory of Nuclear Structures
BRUSCHI, D., Informatics
CAMPADELLI, P., Informatics
CANDIA, M. D., Zoology
CANUTO, G., Geometry
CAPASSO, V., Mathematical Statistics
CARACCIOLO, S., Theoretical Physics and Mathematical Models and Methods
CASTANO, S., Computer Science
CAVALLINI, G., General Pedagogy
CENINI, S., General and Inorganic Chemistry
CESA BIANCHI, N. A., Informatics
CIANI, G. F., Inorganic Chemistry
CINQUINI, M., Organic Chemistry
COLOMBO, R., Cytology and Histology
COTTA RAMUSINO, P., Theoretical Physics and Mathematical Models and Methods
COZZI, F., Organic Chemistry
DAMIANI, E., Informatics
DANIELI, B., Physical Methods in Organic Chemistry
D'ANTONA, O., Informatics
DE BERNARDI, F., Zoology
DE FALCO, D., Calculus of Probability and Mathematical Statistics
DE MICHELIS, M., Plant Physiology
DEDÒ, M., Geometry
DEGLI ANTONI, G., Applied Computer Science (Programming)
DEHÒ, G., Genetics
DEJANA, E., General Pathology
D'ESTE, G., Algebra
DESTRO, R., Physical and Chemical Laboratory
DI FRANCESCO, D., General Physiology
ERBA, E., Palaeontology and Palaeoecology
FAELLI, A., General Physiology
FERRAGUTI, M., Zoology
FERRARI, R., Statistical Mechanics
FERRARIO, A., Mineral Deposits
FERRUTI, P., Macromolecular Chemistry
FOIANI, M., Molecular Biology
FORNI, L., Physical Chemistry
FORNILI, S. L., Physics
FORTE, S., Theoretical Physics and Mathematical Models and Methods

GADIOLI, E., Nuclear Physics
GAETANI, M., Geology
GALASSI, S., Ecology
GALGANI, L., Pure Mechanics
GALLI, E. A., General Microbiology
GARLASCHELLI, L., General and Inorganic Chemistry
GENNARI, C., Organic Chemical Laboratory
GHILARDI, S., Logic and Philosophy of Science
GIANINETTI, E., Theoretical Chemistry
GIAVINI, E., Comparative Anatomy
GIGLIO, M., Physics Experiments
GORLA, M., Genetics
GOSSO, G., Structural Geology
GRAMACCIOLI, C., Physical Chemistry
GREGNANIN, A., Petrography
HAUS, G., Computer Science
JADOUL, F., Regional Geology
JENNINGS, R., Photobiology
LANDINI, D., Industrial Chemistry
LANTERI, A., Geometry
LANZ, L., Institutions of Theoretical Physics
LICANDRO, E., Physical Chemistry
LONGHI, P., Electrochemistry
LONGO, C., Botany
LORENZI, A., Mathematical Analysis
MAIORANA, S., Organic Chemistry
MANDELLI, L., General Physics
MANITTO, P. M., Chemistry of Natural Organic Substances
MANTOVANI, R., Genetics
MARANESI, P., Electronics
MARTELLA, G., Information Systems
MERONI, E., Experimental Physics
MILANI, P., Material Structure
MILAZZO, M., Physical Methodology in the Arts
MOSCA, A., Clinical Biochemistry and Molecular Biology
MUSSINI, T., Electrochemistry
MUSSIO, P., Informatics
NALDI, G., Numerical Analysis
NICOLA, P. C., Mathematical Economics
NICORA, A., Palaeontology and Palaeoecology
ORSINI, F., Organic Chemistry
PAGANONI, L., Mathematical Analysis
PALLESCHI, M., Institutions of Advanced Geometry
PANERAI, A., Pharmacology
PAULMICHL, M., Physiology
PAVARINO, L. F., Numerical Analysis
PAVERI, F. S., Institutions of Mathematics
PEROTTI, M. E., Cytology and Histology
PESOLE, G., Molecular Biology
PIGHIZZINI, G., Computer Science
PIGNANELLI, M., Institutions of Nuclear and Subnuclear Physics
PIURI, V., Information Processing Systems
PIZZOTTI, M., General and Inorganic Chemistry
PLEVANI, P., Molecular Biology
POLI, S., Petrology and Petrography
POZZOLI, R., Material Structure
PREMOLI SILVA, I., Micropalaeontology
PROVINI, A., Ecology
RAGAINI, V., Chemical Industrial Processes and Systems
RAGUSA, F., Experimental Physics
RAIMONDI, M., Physical Chemistry
REATTO, L., Material Structure
RIGOLI, M., Geometry
ROSSI, G. P., Informatics
ROSSI, M., General and Inorganic Chemistry
RUF, B., Mathematical Analysis
RUSSO, G., Organic Chemistry
SABADINI, R., Terrestrial Physics
SAINO, N., Ecology
SALA, F., Botany
SAMARATI, P., Computer Science
SANNICOLÒ, F., Organic Chemistry
SCARABOTTOLO, N., Computer Science
SCOLASTICO, C., Organic Chemistry
SEGALE, A., Rural Economics and Surveying
SERRA, E., Mathematical Analysis
SIRONI, A., General and Inorganic Chemistry
SIRONI, G., Genetics
SMIRAGLIA, C., Physical Geography and Geomorphology
SOAVE, C., Plant Physiology
SPERANZA, G., Organic Chemistry
STURANI, E. P., Cellular Biochemistry
TANTARDINI, G. F., Physical Chemistry
TINTORI, A., Palaeontology and Palaeoecology
TONELLI, C., Genetics
TRASATTI, S., Electrochemistry
TUCCI, P., History of Physics
UGO, R., General Inorganic Chemistry
VALLE, G., Computer Science
VAN GEEMAN, L., Geometry
VANONI, M. A., Biochemistry
VERDI, C., Institutions of Mathematics
VITELLARO, L., Comparative Anatomy and Cytology
ZAMBELLI, V., Algebra
ZANETTI, G., Biological Chemistry
ZANON, D., Theory of Physics, Mathematical Models and Methods

Faculty of Veterinary Medicine (Via Celoria 10, 20133 Milan; tel. 02-50318002; fax 02-50318004; e-mail presveter@unimi.it; internet www.unimi.it/ateneo/facol/medvet.htm):

ADDIS, F., Clinical Veterinary Surgery
BALDI, A., Animal Nutrition and Foodstuffs
BELLOLI, A. G., Medical Veterinary Semiology
BERETTA, C., Pharmacology, Pharmacodynamics and Veterinary Pharmacy
BONIZZI, L., Veterinary Microbiology and Immunology
BONTEMPO, V., Animal Nutrition and Diet
CAIROLI, F., Clinical Obstetrics and Veterinary Gynaecology
CANTONI, C. A., Animal Food Products Inspection and Control
CARENZI, C., Morpho-Functional Evaluation of Animal Production
CARLI, S., Veterinary Pharmacology and Toxicology
CATTANEO, P., Animal Food Products Inspection and Control
CLEMENT, M. G., Veterinary Physiology
CODAZZA, D. M., Infectious Diseases of Domestic Animals
CORINO, C., Animal Feedstuffs and Nutrition
CREMONESI, F., Veterinary Obstetrics and Gynaecology
CRIMELLA, C., Special Zootechnics
DE GRESTI DI SANLEONARDO, A., Surgical Veterinary Semiology
DELL' ORTO, V., Animal Foodstuffs and Nutrition
DOMENEGHINI, C., Systematic and Comparative Veterinary Anatomy
FERRANDI, B., Systematic and Comparative Veterinary Anatomy
FERRO, E., Clinical Veterinary Medicine
FINAZZI, M., Veterinary Pathological Anatomy
FONDA, D., Surgical Veterinary Semiology
GANDOLFI, F., Anatomy of Domestic Animals
GALLAZI, D., Infectious Diseases of Domestic Animals
GENCHI, C., Parasitic Diseases
GUIDOBONO CAVALCHINI, A., Mechanization of Farming Processes.
GUIDOBONO CAVALCHINI, L., Aviculture
LANFRANCHI, P., Veterinary Parasitology
LAURIA, A., Veterinary, Systematic and Comparative Anatomy
MORTELLARO, C., Veterinary Surgical Pathology
NAVAROTTO, P., Rural and Forest Construction
PAGNACCO, G., Animal Genetic Improvement and General Husbandry
PEZZA, F., Clinical Veterinary Medicine
PIRANI, A., Rural Economics and Surveying
POLI, G., Veterinary Microbiology and Immunology
POMPA, G., Veterinary Toxicology
PONTI, W., Infectious Diseases of Domestic Animals
PORCELLI, F., General and Special Histology and Embryology
POZZA, O., Pathology of Domestic Animals
RONCHI, S., Biochemistry
RUFFO, G., Infectious Diseases, Prophylaxis and Veterinary Inspection
SALA, V., Infectious Diseases of Domestic Animals
SARTORELLI, P., Veterinary General Pathology and Pathological Anatomy
SAVOINI, G., Feedstuffs Technology
SCANZIANI, E., General and Veterinary Anatomical Pathology
SECCHI, C. L., Biochemistry
VALFRÈ, F., Supply, Markets and Rural Industries
VERGA, M., Specialized Zootechnics
ZECCONI, A., Infectious Diseases of Domestic Animals

UNIVERSITÀ DEGLI STUDI DI MILANO-BICOCCA

Piazza dell'Ateneo Nuovo 1, 20126 Milan
Internet: www.unimib.it
Director: Rag. PIERO CASSANI.

UNIVERSITÀ DEGLI STUDI DI MODENA E REGGIO EMILIA

Via Università 4, 41100 Modena
Telephone: 059-2056457
Fax: 059-245156
E-mail: rettore@unimo.it
Internet: www.casa.unimo.it
Founded 1175
Academic year: November to October
Rector: Prof. GIAN CARLO PELLACANI
Administrator: Dssa PAOLA REGGIANI GELMINI
Library of 294,000 vols
Number of teachers: 700
Number of students: 14,564
Publications: *Annuario*, *Notiziario*

DEANS

Faculty of Economics: Prof. A. FERRARI
Faculty of Engineering: Prof. G. S. BAROZZI
Faculty of Jurisprudence: Prof. R. LAMBERTINI
Faculty of Mathematics, Physics and Natural Sciences: Prof. C. JACOBONI
Faculty of Medicine and Surgery: Prof. M. PONZ DE LEON
Faculty of Pharmacy: Prof. F. FORNI

PROFESSORS

Faculty of Agricultural Science and Technology (Via Kennedy 17, 42100 Reggio Emilia; tel. 0522-383232; fax 0522-304217; internet www.rcs.re.it/corsi/agraria.htm):

BIANCHI, U., Genetics
GIUDICI, P., Agroalimentary and Environmental Microbiology
PELLEGRINI, M., Applied Geology
TONGIORGI, P., Zoology

Faculty of Arts and Philosophy (Via Berengario 51, 41100 Modena; tel. 059-2056911; fax 059-2056917):

BONDI, M., English Linguistics
DRUMBL, J., German Linguistics
TOCCI, G., Modern History

Faculty of Economics (Via Berengario 51, 41100 Modena; tel. 059-2056911; fax 059-2056917; e-mail preside.economia@unimo.it; internet www.economia.unimo.it):

BISONI, C., Professional and Banking Procedures
BOSI, P., Finance and Financial Law
BRUSCO, S., Economics and Industrial Policy
BURSI, T., Industrial and Commercial Techniques
FERRARI, A., Stock Exchange Techniques
GINZBURG, A., Economic and Financial Policy
GOLZIO, L. E., Work Study
GRANDORI, A., Personnel Management
LANE, D. A., Statistics
RICCI, G., Financial Mathematics

Faculty of Engineering (Via Campi 213/A, 41100 Modena; tel. 059-2055107; fax 059-366293; e-mail preside.ingegneria@unimo.it; internet www.ing.unimo.itViale Allegri 15, 42100 Reggio Emilia; tel. 0522-406356; fax 0522-496466; e-mail preside.ingre@unimo.it; internet www.ingre.unimo.it):

ALBERIGI, A., Electronics
ANDRISANO, A. O., Industrial Design
BAROZZI, G. S., Technical Physics
BERGAMASCHI, S., Information Elaboration Systems
BISI, O., General Physics
CAMPI, S., Mathematical Analysis
CANALI, C., Applied Electronics
CANNAROZZI, M., Construction Theory
CANTORE, G.
CECCHI, R., Environmental Sanitary Engineering
FANTINI, F., Industrial Electronics
FRANCESCHINI, V., Rational Mechanics
GRASSELLI, L., Geometry
IMMOVILLI, G., Electronic Communications
NANNARONE, S., Physics
PELLACANI, G. C., General and Inorganic Chemistry
PILATI, F., Macromolecular Chemistry
RIMINI, B., Industrial Plant Mechanics
SANDROLINI, S., Hydraulic Machinery
STROZZI, A.
TIBERIO, P., Information Elaboration Systems
ZOBOLI, M.

Faculty of Jurisprudence (tel. 059-2056589; fax 059-417522; e-mail preside .giurisprudenza@unimo.it; internet www .giurisprudenza.unimo.it):

ALESSANDRINI, S., Economic Policy
ANTONINI, A., Navigation Law
BIONE, M., Commercial Law
BONFATTI, S., Banking Law
BORGHESI, D., Law of Civil Procedure
CALANDRA BUONAURA, V., Commercial Law
DONINI, M., Penal Law
GALANTINO, L., Labour Law
GASPARINI CASARI, V., Administrative Law
GIANOLIO, R. C., Administrative Law
GUERZONI, L., Ecclesiastical Law
LAMBERTINI, R., Institutions of Roman Law
LUBERTO, S., Anthropology and Criminology
MARANI, F., General Private Law
PANFORTI, M. D., Comparative Private Law
SILINGARDI, G., Transport Law
VIGNUDELLI, A., Constitutional Law

Faculty of Mathematics, Physics and Natural Sciences (Via Campi 213/A, 41100 Modena; tel. 059-371834; fax 059-270809; e-mail preside.scienze@unimo.it; internet www .scienze.unimo.it):

ACCORSI, C. A., Phytogeography
BERTOLANI, R., Zoology
BERTONI, C. M., Theoretical Physics
BONI, M., Mathematical Analysis
BORTOLANI, V., Solid State Physics
CALANDRA BUONAURA, C., Structure of Materials
CAPEDRI, S., Petrography
CAVICCHIOLI, A., Institutes of Advanced Geometry
CHITI, G., Mathematical Analysis
CREMA, R., Ecology
DEL PRETE, C., Botany
DIECI, G., Micropalaeontology
FANTIN, A. M., Histology and Embryology
FAZZINI, P., Geology
FUNARO, D., Numerical Analysis
GAGLIARDI, C., Geometry II
JACOBONI, C., Atomic Physics
LARATTA, A., Numerical Analysis and Programming
LAZZERETTI, P., Physical Chemistry
LEVONI, S., Foundations of Mathematical Physics
MAGHERINI, P.C., General Physiology
MARINI, M., Comparative Anatomy
MENABUE, L., General and Inorganic Chemistry
MESCHIARI, M., Geometry
MIRONE, P., Physical Chemistry
MOMICCHIOLI, F., Physical Chemistry
OTTAVIANI, E., Comparative Anatomy and Cytology
OTTAVIANI, G., Physics (Preparation of Experiments)
PAGLIAI, A. M., Zoology
PAGNONI, U. M., Organic Chemistry
PALYI, G., Chemical Composition
PANIZZA, M., Physical Geography
PASSAGLIA, E., Mineralogy
PRUDENZIATI, M., Applied Electronics
QUATTROCCHI, P., Advanced Elementary Mathematics
RIVALENTI, G., Metamorphic Petrography
RUSSO, A., Palaeoecology
SANTANGELO, R., Terrestrial Physics
SEGRE, U., Electrochemistry
SERPAGLI, E., Palaeontology
SIGHINOLFI, G., Geochemistry
TADDEI, F., Advanced Organic Chemistry
TORRE, G., Organic Chemistry

Faculty of Medicine and Surgery (Via del Pozzo 71, 41100 Modena; tel. 059-422398; fax 059-374037; e-mail preside.medicina@unimo .it; internet wwww.medicina.unimo.it):

AGGAZZOTTI, G., Hygiene and Dentistry
AGNATI, L. F., Human Physiology
ALBERTAZZI, A., Nephrology
ARTIBANI, W., Urology
BAGGIO, G. G., Pharmacology
BALLI, R., Otorhinolaryngology
BARBOLINI, G., Anatomy, Histology and Pathology
BEDUSCHI, G., Forensic Medicine
BERGOMI, M., Hygiene and Odontology
BERNASCONI, S., Paediatrics
BERTOLINI, A., Pharmacology
BLASI, E., Microbiology
BOBYLEVA, V., General Pathology
BON, L., Human Physiology
BORELLA, P., General and Applied Hygiene
CALANDRA BUONAURA, S., General Pathology
CANÈ, V.
CARULLI, N., Medical Pathology and Clinical Methodology
CAVAZZUTI, G. B., Clinical Paediatrics
CELLI, L., Orthopaedics and Traumatology
CONSOLO, U., Odontostomatological Special Surgery
CORAZZA, R., Human Physiology
CORTESI, N., General Clinical Surgery and Surgical Therapy
CORTI, A., Biological Chemistry
CURCI, P., Psychiatry
DE BERNARDINIS, G., General Surgery
DE FAZIO, F. A., Forensic and Insurance Medicine
DE GAETANI, C., Foundations of Medicine and Histological Pathology
DELLA CASA, L., Infectious Diseases
ESPOSITO, R., Infectious Diseases
FABBRI, L., Respiratory Diseases
FABIO, U., Microbiology
FAGLIONI, P., Clinical Neurology
FERRARI, F., Pharmacology
FERRARI, S., Biological Chemistry
FERRARI, S., Applied Biology
FORABOSCO, A., Histology and Embryology
GALETTI, G., Clinical Otorhinolaryngology
GIANNETTI, A., Clinical Dermatology
GUARALDI, G. P., Clinical Psychiatry
GUERRA, R., Clinical Ophthalmology
JASONNI, V. M., Obstetrics and Gynaecology
LODI, R. G., Thoracic Surgery
MANENTI, F., Gastroenterology
MAROTTI, G., Human Anatomy
MATTIOLI, G., Cardiology
MODENA, M. G., Cardiology
MONTI, M. G., Biological Chemistry
MORUZZI, M. S., Chemical Biology
MUSCATELLO, U., General Pathology
PASETTO, A., Anaesthesiology
PONZ DE LEON, M., Internal Medicine
PORTOLANI, M., Virology
ROMAGNOLI, R., Radiology
SALVIOLI, G., Surgical Pathology
SAVIANO, M., Surgical Pathology
SEIDENARI, S., Allergological Dermatology
SILINGARDI, V., Special Medical Pathology and Clinical Methodology
STELLA, A., Vascular Surgery
STERNIERI, E., Clinical Pharmacology
TOMASI, A., General Physiopathology
TORELLI, G., Haematology
TORELLI, U., General Clinical Medicine and Therapy
TRENTINI, G. P., Anatomy and Pathological History
VENTURA, E., General Clinical Medicine and Therapy
VIVOLI, G., Hygiene
VOLPE, A., Physiopathology of Human Reproduction
ZENEROLI, M. L., Semiotics
ZINI, I., Human Physiology

Faculty of Pharmacy (Via Campi 183, 41100 Modena; tel. 059-2055169; fax 059-373602; e-mail preside.farmacia@unimo.it; internet www.farmacia.unimo.it):

ALBASINI, A., Applied Pharmaceutical Chemistry and Toxicology
BARALDI, M., Pharmacology
BERNABEI, M. T., Pharmaceutical Procedures and Legislation
BRASILI, L., Pharmaceutical and Toxicological Chemistry
CAMERONI, R., Applied Pharmaceutical Chemistry
FORNI, F., Pharmaceutical Procedures and Legislation
GALLI, E., Mineralogy
GAMBERINI, G., Pharmaceutical Chemical Analysis
MELEGARI, M., Pharmaceutical Chemical Analysis II
MONZANI, V. A., Pharmaceutical Chemical Analysis
PECORARI, P., Pharmaceutical Chemical Analysis
PIETRA, P., General Physiology
QUAGLIO, G., Hygiene

UNIVERSITÀ DEGLI STUDI DEL MOLISE

Via Mazzini 8/12, 86100 Campobasso
Telephone: 0874-4041
Fax: 0874-63968
Internet: www.unimol.it

Founded 1982

Rector: Prof. LUCIO D'ALESSANDRO

Administrative Director: Dr GIUSEPPE PATRIZI

DEANS

Faculty of Agriculture: Prof. RAIMONDO CUBADDA
Faculty of Economics and Social Sciences: Profa LUCIANA FRANGIONI
Faculty of Law: Prof. ANTONIO PROCIDA MIRABELLI DI LAURO

UNIVERSITÀ DI NAPOLI 'FEDERICO II'

Corso Umberto I, 80138 Naples
Telephone: 081-5477111
Fax: 081-2537330
E-mail: uffpubrel@ceda.unina.it
Internet: www.unina.it

Founded 1224

Rector: Prof. G. TROMBETTI
Administrative Director: Dott. T. PELOSI

Number of teachers: 1,668
Number of students: 83,975

DEANS

Agriculture: A. SANTINI
Architecture: A. CESARANO
Economics: M. MARRELLI
Pharmacy: E. NOVINELLO
Law: L. LABRUNA
Political Science: T. D'APONTE
Engineering: V. NASO
Literature and Philosophy: A. V. NAZZARO
Mathematics and Natural Sciences: A. DI DONATO
Medicine: A. RUBINO
Sociology: E. PUGLIESE
Veterinary Medicine: F. ROPERTO

UNIVERSITÀ DEGLI STUDI DI NAPOLI 'PARTHENOPE'

Via Ammiraglio Acton 38, 80133 Naples
Telephone: 081-5475111
Fax: 081-5521485
Internet: www.uninav.it

Founded 1920 as Istituto Universitario Navale; present name *c.* 2000

Rector: Prof. GENNARO FERRARA
Administrative Director: Dr FERDINANDO FIENGO

Library of 50,000 vols
Number of teachers: 102
Number of students: 5,689

Publication: *Annali*

Faculties: Economics, Law, Engineering, Motor Sciences, Maritime Sciences.

UNIVERSITÀ DEGLI STUDI DI PADOVA

Via 8 Febbraio 2, 35122 Padua
Telephone: 049-8275111
Fax: 049-8273009
Internet: www.unipd.it

Founded 1222

Rector: Prof. GIOVANNI MARCHESINI
First Pro-Rector: Prof. VINCENZO MILANESI
Pro-Rectors: Prof. ACHILLE PESSINA, Prof. P. N. BISOL, Prof. F. BOMBI, Prof. G. ZACCARIA
Secretary: Dott. D. ARTMANN
Librarian: Prof. P. DEL NEGRO

Number of teachers: 1,382
Number of students: 65,579

Publications: *Annuario*, *Bollettino-Notiziario* (annually), *Guida dello Studente*

DEANS

Faculty of Jurisprudence: Prof. A. BURDESE
Faculty of Political Science: Prof. G. ZACCARIA
Faculty of Statistical Sciences: Prof. L. BERNARDI
Faculty of Letters and Philosophy: Prof. S. COLLODO
Faculty of Education: Prof. M. CHIARANDA
Faculty of Medicine and Surgery: Prof. A. GATTA
Faculty of Psychology: Prof. V. RUBINI
Faculty of Veterinary Medicine: Prof. B. BIOLATTI
Faculty of Mathematics, Physics, and Natural Sciences: Prof. C. PECILE
Faculty of Pharmacy: Prof. F. DALL' ACQUA
Faculty of Engineering: Prof. G. B. GUARISE
Faculty of Agriculture: Prof. U. ZILIOTTO
Faculty of Economics: (vacant)

HEADS OF DEPARTMENTS

Physics: Prof. L. PERUZZO
Biology: Prof. G. CASADORO
Pharmacology: Prof. L. CIMA
Paediatrics: Prof. F. ZACCHELLO
Pharmaceutical Science: Prof. M. NICOLINI
Geography: Prof G. BRUNETTA
Developmental Psychology: Prof. A. MAZZOCCO
Statistical Sciences: Prof. S. RIGATTI LUCCHINI
Linguistics: Prof. M. MELI
Education Science: Prof. F. ANTINORI
Inorganic, Metallorganic and Analytical Chemistry: Prof. M. VIDALI
Organic Chemistry: (vacant)
Physical Chemistry: Prof. R. BOZIO
Sociology: Prof. T. R. MINGIONE
General Psychology: Prof. E. GIUS
International Studies: Prof. E. DEL VECCHIO
History: Prof. A. RIGON
Astronomy: Prof. F. LUCCHIN
History of the Fine Arts and Music: Prof. G. CATTIN
Pure and Applied Mathematics: Prof. G. B. DI MASI
Agrarian Biotechnology: Prof. P. SPETTOLI
Electronics and Information Science: Prof. G. TONDELLO
Anglo-Germanic Languages and Literature: Prof. G. BRUNETTI
Electrical Engineering: Prof. S. LUPI
Mechanical Engineering: Prof. G. SCARINCI
Land and Forest Management: Prof. F. VIOLA
Biological Chemistry: Prof. A. RIGO
Mineralogy and Petrology: Prof. A. DAL NEGRO
Geology, Palaeontology and Geophysics: Prof. D. RIO
Mathematical Methods and Models for the Applied Sciences: Prof. M. PITTERI
New Technology and Management Restructuring: P. BARIANI
Biomedical Sciences: Prof. T. POZZAN
Economics: Prof. F. FAVOTTO
Ancient History: Prof. M. PERI
Zootechnical Sciences: Prof. I. ANDRIGHETTO
Agronomy: Prof. G. MOSCA
Italian Studies: Prof. G. CAPOVILLA
Comparative Law: Prof. N. OLIVETTI RASON
Clinical and Experimental Medicine: Prof. A. TIENGO
Psychology and Neurological Sciences: Prof. G. TESTA
Construction and Transport: Prof. B. SCHREFLER
Philosophy: Prof. E. BERTI
Oncology: Prof. L. CHIECO BIANCHI

There are 50 attached Institutes.

UNIVERSITÀ DEGLI STUDI DI PALERMO

Piazza Marina 61, 90133 Palermo
Telephone: 091-270111
Internet: www.unipa.it

Founded 1777

Rector: Prof. GIUSEPPE SILVESTRI
Administrative Director: CARMELO MAZZÈ

Number of teachers: c. 1,300
Number of students: c. 20,000

Publications: *Annali del Seminario Giuridico*, *Circolo Giuridico L. Sampolo*, *Annali della Facoltà di Economia e Commercio*

DEANS

Agriculture: G. FIERROTTI
Architecture: M. DE SIMONE
Economics: V. FAZIO
Pharmacy: S. GIAMMANCO
Law: S. MAZZAMUTO
Engineering: E. OLIVIERI
Letters and Philosophy: A. BUTTITA
Education: G. A. PUGLISI
Medicine: A. GULLOTTI
Mathematics: F. MAGGIO

UNIVERSITÀ DEGLI STUDI DI PARMA

Via Università 12, 43100 Parma
Telephone: 0521-032111
E-mail: uniparma@unipr.it
Internet: www.unipr.it

Founded 962
Academic year: November to October

Rector: Prof. GINO FERRETTI
Administrative Director: Dott. RODOLFO POLDI

Number of teachers: 1,074
Number of students: 29,853

DEANS

Faculty of Jurisprudence: Prof. G. BONILINI
Faculty of Medicine: Prof. A. NOVARINI
Faculty of Pharmacy: Prof. G. PELIZZI
Faculty of Physical, Mathematical and Natural Sciences: Prof. A. MANGIA
Faculty of Veterinary Medicine: Prof. C. F. FLAMMINI
Faculty of Economics and Commerce: Prof. A. GUENZI
Faculty of Arts: Prof. G. BIONDI
Faculty of Engineering: Prof. A. VILLA
Faculty of Agricultural Science: Prof. R. MARCHELLI
Faculty of Architecture: Prof. G. BASSANELLI

UNIVERSITÀ DEGLI STUDI DI PAVIA

Corso Strada Nuova 65, 27100 Pavia
Telephone: 0382-504217
Fax: 0382-504529
Internet: www.unipv.it

Founded 1361 by Emperor Charles IV
Academic year: November to October

Rector: Prof. ROBERTO SCHMID
Vice-Rector: Prof. PAOLA VITA-FINZI
Administrative Director: Dr GAETANO SERAFINO

Number of teachers: 1,033
Number of students: 22,789

Publications: *Annuario*, *Guida dello Studente* (for each faculty), *Guida dello Studente Straniero* and many faculty publs

DEANS

Faculty of Law: Prof. S. SEMINARA
Faculty of Political Sciences: Prof. S. VECA
Faculty of Economics: Prof. L. RAMPA
Faculty of Arts and Philosophy: Prof. G. FRANCIONI
Faculty of Medicine and Surgery: Prof. C. MELONI
Faculty of Mathematics, Physics and Natural Science: Prof. G. FLOR
Faculty of Pharmacy: Prof. C. CARAMELLA
Faculty of Engineering: Prof. N. CANTONI
Faculty of Musicology: Prof. G. BORIO

HEADS OF DEPARTMENTS AND INSTITUTES

Law (tel. 0382-504315; fax 0382-33573; e-mail giurispv@unipv.it; internet www.unipv.it/giurisprudenza):
- Economics: Prof. A. MAIOCCHI
- Law Studies: Prof. P. V. AIMO
- Law and Penal Procedure: Prof. V. GREVI
- Roman Law and History of Law: Prof. D. MANTOVANI

Political Science (tel. 0382-504427; fax 0382-504672; e-mail emfac09@unipv.it; internet www.unipv.it/wwwscpol/homepage.htm):
- Economics: Prof. F. OSCULATI
- Political and Social Studies: Prof. G. P. CALCHI NOVATI
- Statistics: Prof. P. SCARAMOZZINO
- Legal-Political Studies: Prof. P. G. GRASSO
- Foreign Languages: Prof. R. CARPANINI

Economics (Via S. Felice 5, 27100 Pavia; tel. 0382-506203; fax 0382-22486; e-mail dvelo@eco.unipv.it; internet 3weco.unipv.it/web/_index.htm):
- Business Research: Prof. A. ZUCCHELLA
- Economics, Politics and Quantitative Methods: Prof. G. VAGGI

Arts and Philosophy (tel. 0382-504533; fax 0382-504304; e-mail presidenza-lettere@unipv.it; internet lettere.unipv.it):
- Philosophy: Prof. M. VEGETTI
- Modern Languages: Prof. L. GUERRA
- Antiquities: Prof. E. ROMANO
- History and Geography: Prof. A. ZAMBARBIERI
- Linguistics: Prof. A. GIACALONE
- Medieval and Modern Literature and Arts Science: Prof. L. GARGAN
- Psychology: Prof. T. VECCHI

Medicine and Surgery (P.le Volontari del Sangue, 27100 Pavia; tel. 0382-527147; fax 0382-526390; internet www.unipv.it/facolta/eletac.html):
- Biochemistry: Prof. T. SPEZIALE
- Surgery: Prof. P. DIONIGI
- Internal Medicine: Prof. E. FERRARI
- Occupational and Community Preventive Medicine: Prof. A. CAVALLERI
- Human Pathology: Prof. G. RABBIOSI
- Physiology: Prof. V. TAGLIETTI
- Legal Medicine and Insurance: Prof. G. PIERUCCI
- Institute of General Surgery and Organ Transplant: Prof. M. VIGANO
- Neurological Sciences: Prof. A. MOGLIA
- Clinical, Morphological and Eidological Sciences: Prof. E. ROMERO
- Morphological Sciences: Prof. E. ROMERO
- Applied Health Sciences: Prof. A. MARINONI
- Ematology, Pneumology: Prof. P. SCHWARTZ
- Clinical Surgery: Prof. E. FORNI
- Paediatrics: Prof. G. RONDINI
- Experimental Medicine: Prof. V VANNINI
- Sensorial Sciences: Prof. E. MIRA
- Odontostomatology: Prof. S. BIANCHI
- Infectious Diseases: Prof. L. MINOLI
- Neurology: Prof. V. COSI

Mathematics, Physics and Natural Sciences (Via Ferrata 1, 27100 Pavia; tel. 0382-505771; fax 0382-505775; internet www.unipv.it/webbio/facscie.htm):
- Biochemistry: Prof. P. SPEZIALE
- Animal Biology: Prof. M. FASOLA
- Physical Chemistry: Prof. A. MAGISTRIS
- General Chemistry: Prof. L. FABBRIZZI
- Organic Chemistry: Prof. A. ALBINI
- General Physics: Prof. G. GUIZZETTI
- Nuclear and Theoretical Physics: Prof. D. SCANNICCHIO
- Genetics and Microbiology: Prof. G. RANZANI
- Mathematics: Prof. H. L. BERNARDI
- Earth Sciences: Prof. N. TAZZOLI
- Pharmacology: Prof. S. GOVONI
- Botany: Prof. A. PIROLA
- Physics: Prof. C. B. AZZONI
- Environmental Studies: Prof. F. SARTORI

Pharmacology (Viale Taramelli 12, 27100 Pavia; tel. 0382-5071; fax 0382-529095; e-mail mc@chifar.unipv.it; internet chifar.unipv.it/el_perfacolta.htm):
- Pharmaceutical Chemistry: Prof. L. COLOMBO
- Pharmacology: Prof. S. GOVONI
- Cellular-Molecular Pharmacology and Physiological Sciences: Prof. V. TAGLIETTI

Engineering (Via Ferrata 1, 27100 Pavia; tel. 0382-5051; fax 0382-505922; internet www.unipv.it/webing):
- Electronics: Prof. P. ARCIONI
- Computer Science: Prof. G. DANESE
- Civil Engineering: Prof. A. SPALLA
- Hydraulic and Environmental Engineering: Prof. M. GALLATI
- Structural Mechanics: Prof. F. AURICCHIO
- Electrical Engineering: Prof. E. DALLAGO

Musicology:
- Musicology and Philological Sciences: Prof. M. CARACI VELA

UNIVERSITÀ DEGLI STUDI DI PERUGIA

Piazza dell' Università, 06100 Perugia
Telephone: 075-5851
Fax: 075-5852067
Internet: www.unipg.it

Founded 1200
State control
Academic year: November to October

Rector: Prof. G. CALZONI
Administrative Director: Dott. P. SANTINI
Pro-Rector: Prof. A. TATICCHI
Librarian: Dott. M. PIERONI

Number of teachers: 312
Number of students: 31,746

Publications: *L'Università*, *Rivista di Idrobiologia*, *Rivista di Dermatologia*, *Rivista di Biologia*, *La Salute Umana*

DEANS

Faculty of Jurisprudence: Prof. S. CAPRIOLI
Faculty of Political Science: Prof. M. RAVERAIRA
Faculty of Economic Science: Prof. T. SEOIARI
Faculty of Letters and Philosophy: Prof. A. PIERETTI
Faculty of Education: Prof. E. MIRRI
Faculty of Medicine and Surgery: Prof. R. ROSSI
Faculty of Mathematical, Physical and Natural Sciences: Prof. C. MANTOVANI
Faculty of Pharmacy: Prof. C. M. FIORETTI CECCHERELLI
Faculty of Agrarian Science: Prof. B. ROMANO
Faculty of Veterinary Medicine: Prof. A. GAITI
Faculty of Engineering: Prof. R. SORRENTINO

DIRECTORS OF DEPARTMENTS

Plant Biology: Prof. A. MENGHINI
Chemistry: Prof. F. FRINGUELLI
Physics: Prof. F. SACCHETTI
Hygiene: Prof. A. M. IORIO
Mathematics and Computer Science: Prof. G. COLETTI
Experimental Medicine and Biochemical Science: Prof. R. F. DONATO
Earth Sciences: Prof. L. PASSERI
Linguistic and Philological-literary Science of the Anglo-Germanic Area: Prof. S. RUFINI
Statistical Science: Prof. G. CICCHITELLI
Historical Science: Prof. L. TOSI
Historical Science (Antiquity): Prof. F. RONCALLI DI MONTORIO
Internal Medicine and Endocrinology: Prof. P. BRUNETTI
Surgery: Prof. A. DELOGU
Surgery and Emergency Surgery: Prof. L. MOGGI
Cellular Biology: Prof. A. ORLACCHIO
Clinical and Experimental Medicine: Prof. C. RICCARDI

PROFESSORS

Faculty of Jurisprudence:
- AZZARITI, G., Constitutional Law
- BADIALI, G., International Law
- BARBERINI, G., Ecclesiastical Law
- CAPRIOLI, S., History of Modern Italian Law
- CARDI, E., Procedural Law
- CAVALAGLIO, A., Bankruptcy Law
- CAVALLO, B., Administrative Law
- CINELLI, M., Labour Law
- DALLERA, G. F., Finance and Financial Law
- GAITO, A., Penal Law
- MIGLIORINI, L., Administrative Law
- MORSELLI, E., Penal Law
- PALAZZO, A., Institutions of Private Law
- PALAZZOLO, N., History of Roman Law
- PEPPE, L., Roman Law
- SALVI, C., Civil Law
- SASSANI, M., Civil Procedural Law
- TALAMANCA, A., Canon Law
- TINELLI, G., Tax Law
- VOLPI, M., Constitutional Comparative Law

Faculty of Letters and Philosophy:
- AGOSTINIANI, L., Linguistics
- BONAMENTE, G., Roman History
- CARANCINI, G. L., European Protohistory
- COARELLI, F., Greek and Roman Antiquity
- DI PILLA, F., French Language and Literature
- FALASCHI, G., Italian Literature
- FROVA, C., Medieval History
- GIORDANI, R., Christian Archaeology
- ISOLA, A., Ancient Christian Literature
- MADDOLI, G., Greek History
- MELELLI, A., Geography
- MENESTÒ, E., Medieval Latin Literature
- MORETTI, G., Italian Dialectology
- PICCINATO, S., Anglo-American Literature
- PIERETTI, A., Theoretical Philosophy
- PIZZANI, U., Latin Literature
- PRIVITERA, G. A., Greek Literature
- RONCALLI DI MONTORIO, F., Etruscan Studies and Italic Antiquity
- RUFINI, S., English Language and Literature
- SANTACHIARA, U., Church History
- SCARPELLINI PANCRAZI, P., History of Medieval Art
- SEPPILLI, T., Cultural Anthropology
- SPAGGIARI PERUGI, B., Romance Philology
- TORELLI, M., Archaeology and History of Greek and Roman Art
- TORTI, A., English Language and Literature

Faculty of Political Science:
- BONO, S., History and Institutions of Afro-Asian Countries
- CARINI, C., History of Political Doctrine
- COMPARATO, V. I., Modern History
- CRESPI, F., Sociology
- D'AMOJA, F., History of International Relations
- DI GASPARE, G., Economic Law
- GALLI DELLA LOGGIA, E., History of Political Parties and Movements
- GROHMANN, A., Economic History
- MARCHISIO, S., International Law
- MELOGRANI, P., Contemporary History
- MERLONI, F., Administrative Justice
- RAVERAIRA, M., Institutions of Public Law
- TEODORI, M., American History
- TOSI, L., History of Treaties and International Politics

TRAMONTANA, A., Finance

Faculty of Economics:

BORGIA, R., Institutions of Private Law
BRACALENTE, B., Economics Statistics
CALZONI, G., Political Economy
CAVAZZONI, G., Accountancy
CHIARELLE, R., Institutions of Public Law
CICCHITELLI, G., Statistics
CORALLINI, S., Banking
FORCINA, A., Statistics
GRASSELLI, P. M., Political Economy
MEZZACAPO, V., Banking Legislation
MORICONI, F., Mathematics
PAGLIACCI, G., General Mathematics
PERONI, G., Marketing
RIDOLFI, M., Political Economy
SEDIARI, T., Agrarian Economics and Politics
SEVERINO, P., Commercial Penal Law

Faculty of Medicine and Surgery:

ABBRITTI, G., Industrial Medicine
AMBROSIO, G., Cardiology
ARIENTI, G., Biological Chemistry
BARTOLI, A., General Surgery
BECCHETTI, E., Histology
BINAGLIA, L., Chemistry and Biomedicine
BISTONI, F., Microbiology
BOLIS, G. B., Anatomy and Pathological Histology
BOLLI, G., Metabolic Diseases
BORRI, P. F., Psychiatry
BRUNETTI, P., Internal Medicine
BUCCIARELLI, E., Anatomy and Pathological Histology
CALANDRA, P., Dermatology
CAPRINO, G., Radiology
CASALI, L., Diseases of the Respiratory System
DADDI, G., Surgical Pathology and Clinical Propaedeutics
DELOGU, A., Ophthalmology
D'ERRICO, P., Dental Prosthesis
DONATO, R. F., Neuroanatomy
FABRONI, F., Forensic Medicine
FALORNI, A., Paediatrics
FIORE, C., Physiopathological Optics
FRONGILLO, R. F., Infectious Diseases
FURBETTA, M., Preventive and Social Paediatrics
GALLAI, V., Neurology
GIOVANNINI, E., General Biology
GORACCI, G. F., Biological Chemistry
GRIGNANI, F., Internal Medicine
LATINI, P., Radiotherapy
LAURO, V., Gynaecology and Obstetrics
LIOTTI, F. S., General Biology
LISI, P., Dermatology
MAGNI, F., Human Physiology
MAIRA, G., Neurosurgery
MANNARINO, E., Internal Medicine
MARCONI, P., Immunology
MARTELLI, M. F., Haematology
MASTRANDREA, V., Hygiene
MODOLO, M. A., Hygiene
MOGGI, L., General Surgery
MORELLI, A., Gastroenterology
NEGRI, P. L., Paradontology
NENCI, G. G., Internal Medicine
NORELLI, G. A., Forensic Medicine
PALUMBO, R., Nuclear Medicine
PAULUZZI, S., Infectious Diseases
PECORELLI, F., Orthopaedics and Traumatology
PEDUTO, V. A., Anaesthesia and Resuscitation
PETTOROSSI, V. E., Human Physiology
PORENA, M., Urology
PUXEDDU, A., Internal Medicine
RIBACCHI, R., Anatomy and Pathological Histology
RICCARDI, C., Pharmacology
RINONAPOLI, E., Orthopaedics and Traumatology
ROSI BARBERINI, G., Cellular Biology
ROSSI, R., General Pathology
SALVADORI, P., Physics
SANTEUSANIO, F., Endocrinology
SENIN, U., Geriatrics and Gerontology
STAFFOLANI, N., Oral Surgery
STAGNI, G., Infectious Diseases
TRISTAINO, B., General Surgery
VACCARO, R., Paediatrics
VALORI, C., Internal Medicine
VILLANI, C., Oncological Gynaecology
VIOLA MAGNI, M. P., General Pathology

Faculty of Pharmacy:

CORSANO LEOPIZZI, S., Pharmaceutical and Toxicological Chemistry
COSTANTINO, U., General and Inorganic Chemistry
DAMIANI, P., Food Science Chemistry
FIORETTI CECCHERELLI, M. C., Pharmacology and Pharmacognosy
FLORIDI, A., Biochemistry
FRAVOLINI, A., Pharmaceutical and Toxicological Chemistry
GRANDOLINI, G., Socioeconomic Technology and Pharmaceutical Legislation
MENGHINI, A., Pharmaceutical Botany
PELLICCIARI, R., Pharmaceutical and Toxicological Chemistry
PUCCETTI, P., Pharmacology
ROSSI, C., Applied Pharmaceutical Chemistry
SCASSELLATI, S. G., Hygiene
TESTAFERRI, L., Organic Chemistry
TIECCO, M., Organic Chemistry
VECCHIARELLI, A., Microbiology

Faculty of Agrarian Science:

ABBOZZO, P., Farm Evaluation
BENCIVENGA, M., Systematic Agricultural Botany
BERNARDINI BATTAGLINI, M., Animal Husbandry
BIANCHI, A. A., Herbaceous Cultivation
BIN, F., Biological Techniques
BONCIARELLI, F., Cultivation of Special Herbaceous Plants
BUSINELLI, M., Soil Chemistry
CIRICIOFOLO, E., Biology, Production and Technology of Seeds
COSTANTINI, F., Animal Nutrition and Feeding
COVARELLI, G., Weed Control
DURANTI, E., Physiology of Animals in Stockbreeding
FALCINELLI, M., Genetic Improvement in Cultivated Plants
FANTOZZI, P., Alimentation
FATICHENTI, F., Agrarian and Arboreal Microbiology
GIOVAGNOTTI, C.
LORENZETTI, F., Agrarian Genetics
MANNOCCHI, F., Agrarian Hydraulics
MARTE, M., Plant Pathology
MARTINI, A., Agrarian Microbiology
MARUCCHINI, C., Introductory Agrarian Chemistry
MENNELLA, V. G., Agricultural and Forestry Planning
MONOTTI, M., General Agriculture
MONTEDORO, G., Agricultural Industries
PENNACCHI, F., Agrarian Economics
RAGGI, V., Plant Pathology
ROMANO, B., Morphology and Plant Physiology
ROSSI, A. C., Economics and Agrarian Policy
ROSSI, J., Dairy Food Microbiology
SARTI, D. M., Stockbreeding
SCARPONI, L., Agrarian Biochemistry
SOLINAS, M., Agricultural Entomology
STANDARDI, A., Specialist Fruit Growing
TOMBESI, A., General Fruit Growing
VERONESI, F., Genetic Biotechnology
ZAZZERINI, A., Phytotherapy

Faculty of Veterinary Medicine:

ASDRUBALI, G., Pathology of Birds
AVELLINI, G., Clinical Veterinary Medicine
BATTISTACCI, M., Clinical Veterinary Surgery
BEGHELLI, V., Veterinary Physiology and Ethology
BELLUCCI, M., Veterinary Radiology and Nuclear Medicine
BOITI, C., Veterinary Physiology and Ethology
CASTRUCCI, G., Infectious Diseases and Prophylaxis
CECCARELLI, P., Topographical Veterinary Anatomy
CHIACCHIARINI, P., Obstetrics and Gynaecology
DEBENEDETTI, A., Endocrinology of Domestic Animals
DI ANTONIO, E., Inspection and Control of Foodstuffs of Animal Origin
FRUGANTI, G., Veterinary Medical Pathology
GAITI, A., Biochemistry
GARGIULO BERSIANI, A. M., Histology and General Embryology
LORVIK, S., Anatomy of Domestic Animals
MALVISI, J., Pharmacology and Pharmacodynamics
MANGILI PECCI, V., Laboratory Diagnosis
MANOCCHIO, I., Pathological Anatomy
MORICONI, F., Veterinary Surgical Pathology
OLIVIERI, O., Animal Nutrition
POLIDORI GIROLAMO, A. B., Veterinary Parasitology
RANUCCI, S., Veterinary Medical Semiology and Clinical Methodology
SILVESTRELLI, M., Special Stockbreeding
VALENTE, C., Infectious Diseases
VITELLOZZI, G., Veterinary Pathological Anatomy

Faculty of Mathematical, Physical and Natural Sciences:

ALBERTI, G., Inorganic Chemistry
AMBROSETTI, P. L., Palaeontology
ANTONIELLI, M., Plant Physiology
AQUILANTI, V., General and Inorganic Chemistry
AVERNA, A.
BARSI, F., Theory and Application of Mechanical Calculation
BARTOCCI, U., Geometry
CATALIOTTI, R. S., Physical Chemistry
CIOFI DEGLI ATTI, C., Institutions of Nuclear Physics
CIONINI, P. G., Botany
CIROTTO, C., Cytology and Histology
CLEMENTI, S., Organic Chemistry
COLETTI, G., Institutions of Mathematics
DE TOLLIS, B. A., Institutions of Theoretical Physics
DI GIOVANNI, M. V., Zoology
FAINA, G., Geometry
FAVARO MAZZUCATO, G., Physical Chemistry
FRINGUELLI, F., Organic Chemistry
GAINO, E., Zoology
GIANFRANCHESCHI, G. L., General Physiology
GRANETTI, B., Botany
GUAZZONE, S., Algebra
IORIO, A. M., Virology
LAGANÀ, A., General and Inorganic Chemistry
LARICCIA, P., Physics Laboratory
MAFFEI, P., Astrophysics
MANTOVANI, G., General Physics
MARINO, G., Organic Chemistry
MAZZUCATO, U., Physical Chemistry
MONTANINI MEZZASOMA, I., Biochemistry
MOROZZI, G., Hygiene
MORPURGO, G. P., Genetics
NAPPI, A., General Physics
ONORI, G., Physics
ORLACCHIO, A., Biochemistry
PASCOLINI, R., Comparative Anatomy
PASSERI, L., Sedimentology

PECCERILLO, A., Petrography
PERUZZI, M. I., General Physics
PIALLI, G., Geology
PIOVESANA, O., General and Inorganic Chemistry
PUCCI, P., Mathematical Analysis
RINALDI, R., Mineralogy
SACCHETTI, F., Solid State Physics
SANTUCCI, S., Physics Laboratory
SAVELLI, G., Organic Chemistry
SGAMELLOTTI, A., Inorganic Chemistry
SRIVASTAVA YOGENDRA, N., Quantum Theory
TATICCHI, A., Organic Chemistry
TATICCHI, M. I., Ecology
TULIPANI, S., Computer Science
VERDINI, L., Structure of Matter
VOLPI, G., General and Inorganic Chemistry
ZANAZZI, P. F., Crystallography

Faculty of Education:

BALDINI, M., History of Philosophy
BUCCI, S., General Education
DOTTI, U., Italian Language and Literature
FINZI, C., History of Political Doctrine
FISSI MIGLIORINI, R., Dantesque Philology
FURIOZZI, G. B., History of Umbria
MANCINI, F. F., History of Umbrian Art
MIRRI, E., Philosophy
PERUGI, M., Romance Philology
PETRONI, F., History of Modern and Contemporary Italian Literature
RICCIOLI, G., French Language and Literature
ROSATI, L., Teaching
SANTINI, C., Latin Language and Literature
SETAIOLI, A., Latin Grammar
UGOLINI, R., Contemporary History
ZURLI, L., Latin Philology

Faculty of Engineering:

BALLI, R., Applied Mechanics
BASILI, P., Electromagnetic Fields
BATTISTON, R., Physics
BERNA, L., Urban Technology
BIDINI, G., Machines
BORRI, A., Construction Theory
BRANDI, P., Mathematical Analysis
BURRASCANO, P., Electrotechnology
CANDELORO, D., Mathematical Analysis I
CONTI, P., Industrial Technical Drawing
CORRADINI, C., Technical Hydrology
FELLI, M., Technical Physics
LA CAVA, M., Automatic Controls
LIUTI, G., Chemistry
MAZZOLAI, F. M., Physics
PALMIERI, L., Physics
PARDUCCI, A., Construction Technology
PUCCI, E., Advanced Mechanical Engineering
SOCINO, G., Physics
SOLETTI, A. C., Design
SORRENTINI, R., Electromagnetic Fields
TACCONI, P., Applied Geology
VECCHIOCATTIVI, F., Chemistry

UNIVERSITÀ DEGLI STUDI DI PISA

Lungarno Pacinotti 43, 56126 Pisa

Telephone: 050-920115
Fax: 050-42446
E-mail: rettore@unipi.it
Internet: www.unipi.it

Founded 1343
State control
Academic year: November to October

Rector: Prof. LUCIANO MODICA
Chief Admin. Officer: Dott. GIORGIO COLUCCINI
Librarian: Dott. RENATO TAMBURRINI

Number of teachers: 300
Number of students: 47,000

DEANS

Faculty of Law: Prof. U. SANTARELLI
Faculty of Economics: Prof. R. FERRARIS
Faculty of Political Science: Prof. A. MASSERA
Faculty of Letters and Philosophy: Prof. G. FIORAVANTI
Faculty of Foreign Languages and Literature: Prof. G. DI STEFANO
Faculty of Medicine and Surgery: Prof. M. CAMPA
Faculty of Mathematical, Physical and Natural Sciences: Prof. M. PASQUALI
Faculty of Pharmacy: Prof. A. LUCACCHINI
Faculty of Eng.: Prof. P. CORSINI
Faculty of Agrarian Science: A. ALPI
Faculty of Veterinary Medicine: A. BUONACCORSI

UNIVERSITÀ DEGLI STUDI MEDITERRANEA DI REGGIO CALABRIA

Via Zecca 4, 89125 Reggio Calabria

Telephone: 0965-331701
Fax: 0965-332201
E-mail: rettore@unirc.it
Internet: www.unirc.it

Founded 1982

Rector: Prof. ALESSANDRO BIANCHI
Pro-Rector: Prof. ROSARIO GIUFFRE'

DEANS

Faculty of Agriculture: Prof. R. C. FICHERA
Faculty of Architecture: Prof. M. GIOVANNINI
Faculty of Law: S. CICCARELLO
Faculty of Engineering: C. MORABITO

UNIVERSITÀ DEGLI STUDI DI ROMA 'LA SAPIENZA'

Piazzale Aldo Moro 5, 00185 Rome

Telephone: 06-49911
Fax: 06-49910348
E-mail: rettore@uniroma1.it
Internet: www.uniroma1.it

Founded 1303 by Pope Boniface VIII, with the Papal Bull 'In Supremae praeminentia dignitatis'

Rector: Prof. GIUSEPPE D'ASCENZO
Director: CARLO MUSTO D'AMORE
Librarian: Prof. GIOVANNI CICLOTTI

Number of teachers: 4,312
Number of students: 189,000

DEANS

Faculty of Jurisprudence: Prof. CARLO ANGELICI
Faculty of Political Science: FULCO LANCHESTER
Faculty of Economics and Commerce: Prof. ATTILIO CELANT
Faculty of Statistics, Demography and Actuarial Science: Prof. RENATO GUARINI
Faculty of Letters and Humanities: Prof. GUIDO PESCOSOLIDO
Faculty of Humanities: Prof. PAOLO MATTHIAE
Faculty of Philosophy: Prof. MARCO MARIA OLIVETTI
Faculty of Oriental Studies: Prof. FEDERICO NASINI
Faculty of Medicine I: Prof. L. FRATI
Faculty of Medicine II: Prof. ALDO VECCHIONE
Faculty of Mathematics, Physics and Natural Science: Prof. FRANCESCO BOSSA
Faculty of Pharmacy: Prof. DOMENICO MISITI
Faculty of Engineering: Prof. TULLIO BUCCIARELLI
School of Aerospace Engineering: Prof. U. PONZI
Faculty of Architecture I: Prof. LUCIO VALERIO BARBERA
Faculty of Architecture II: Prof. ROBERTO PALUMBO
Faculty of Sociology: LUCIANO BENADUSI
Faculty of Psychology I: STEFANO PUGLISI ALLEGRA
Faculty of Psychology II: Prof. FRANCESCO AVALLONE
School of Librarianship and Archivists: Prof. ATTILIO DE LUCA
Faculty of Communication Studies: Prof. DOMENICO DE MASI

ATTACHED CENTRE

Interuniversity Research Centre on Developing Countries (CIRPS): internet www.cirps.it; Dir Prof. VINCENZO NASO.

Interdepartmental Research Centre of European and International Studies: internet www.eco.uniroma1.it/europe; Dir Prof. GIUSEPPE BURGIO.

UNIVERSITÀ DEGLI STUDI DI ROMA 'TOR VERGATA'

Via Orazio Raimondo, 00173 Rome

Telephone: 06-72591
Fax: 06-7234368
Internet: www2.uniroma2.it

Founded 1985

Rector: Prof. ALESSANDRO FINAZZI AGRÒ
Administrative Director: Dr ERNESTO NICOLAI

Publications: *L'Osservatorio*, *I Quaderni di Tor Vergata*

DEANS

Faculty of Law: Prof. FILIPPO CHIOMENTI
Faculty of Engineering: Prof. FRANCO MACERI
Faculty of Literature and Philosophy: Prof. FRANCO SALVATORI
Faculty of Medicine and Surgery: Prof. RENATO LAURO
Faculty of Mathematics, Physics and Natural Sciences: Prof. PAOLO LULY
Faculty of Economics: Prof. LUIGI PAGANETTO

HEADS OF DEPARTMENTS

Biology: Prof. F. AUTORI
Surgery: CARLO UMBERTO CASCIANI
Law and Civil Procedure: Prof. G. GALLONI
Public Law: Prof. A. ANZON
Physics: Prof. S. TAZZARI
Civil Engineering: Prof. A. NUZZOLO
Electronic Engineering: Prof. R. LOJACONO
Mechanical Engineering: Prof. F. GORI
Modern Languages: Prof. F. BEGGIATO
Mathematics: Prof. A. PICARDELLO
Internal Medicine: Prof. G. FEDERICI
Experimental Medicine: Prof. C. FAVALLI
Philosophical Research: Profssa M. CRISTIANI
Public Health: Prof. G. SIRACUSA
Chemical Science and Technology: Prof. G. PALLESCHI
History: Profssa V. VON FALKENHAUSEN
History and Theory of Law: Prof. F. CASTRO
Finance and Quantitative Methods: Prof. MARTINO LO CASCIO
Business Studies: Prof. ERICO CAVALIERI
Physical Science and Technology and Energy Sources: Prof. S. MARTELLUCCI
Data Processing, Systems and Production: Prof. A. LA BELLA
Economics and Institutions: Prof. M. BAGELLA
Neuroscience: Profssa M. G. MARCIANI
Biopathology and Diagnosis through Imaging: Prof. L. G. SPAGNOLI

UNIVERSITÀ DEGLI STUDI DI SALERNO

Strada Provinciale, Ponte don Melillo 24, 84084 Fisciano (Salerno)

Telephone: 089-961111
Internet: www.unisa.it

Founded 1970

Rector: GIORGIO DONSÌ

Administrative Director: FRANCO LUCIANI

DEANS

Faculty of Economics and Commerce: Prof. N. POSTIGLIONE
Faculty of Law: Prof. M. PANEBIANCO
Faculty of Letters and Philosophy: Prof. A. TRIMARCO
Faculty of Education: Prof. A. MANGO
Faculty of Science: Prof. G. SODANO
Faculty of Engineering: Prof. R. PASQUINO
Faculty of Political Science: Prof. A. MUSI

UNIVERSITÀ DEGLI STUDI DI SASSARI

Piazza Università 21, 07100 Sassari, Sardinia
Telephone: 079-228811
Fax: 079-228820
Internet: www.uniss.it

Founded 1562
State control
Academic year: November to October

Rector: Prof. ALESSANDRO MAIDA
Administrative Director and Secretary: Dott. GIOVANNINO SIRCANA
Librarian: Dott. ELISABETTA PILIA
Number of teachers: 604
Number of students: 16,319

Publication: *Annuario*

DEANS

Faculty of Law: Prof. GIOVANNI LOBRANO
Faculty of Medicine and Surgery: Prof. GIULIO ROSATI
Faculty of Pharmacy: Prof. RICCARDO CERRI
Faculty of Veterinary Medicine: Prof. ANTONELLO LEONI
Faculty of Agronomy: Prof. GAVINO DEL RIO
Faculty of Mathematics, Physics and Natural Sciences: Prof. BRUNO MASALA
Faculty of Economics and Commerce: Prof. CARLO IBBA
Faculty of Political Science: Prof. VIRGILIO MURA
Faculty of Letters and Philosophy: Prof. GIOVANNI MELONI
Faculty of Languages: Prof. SIMONETTA SANNA

UNIVERSITÀ DEGLI STUDI DI SIENA

Banchi di Sotto 55, 53100 Siena
Telephone: 0577-298000
Fax: 0577-298202
Internet: www.unisi.it

Founded 1240

Rector: Prof. PIERO TOSI
Vice-Rector: Prof. FRANCESCO FRANCIONI

Number of teachers: 514
Number of students: 19,093

Publication: *Annuario Accademico*

DEANS

Faculty of Law: R. MARTINI
Faculty of Medicine and Surgery: L. ANDREASSI
Faculty of Mathematics, Physics and Natural Sciences: R. DALLAI
Faculty of Pharmacy: C. PELLERANO
Faculty of Economics: G. ROLLA
Faculty of Education: F. ABBRI
Faculty of Letters and Philosophy: M. BETTINI
Faculty of Arts and Humanities: T. DETTI
Faculty of Engineering: R. TIBERIO

DIRECTORS

Faculty of Law:
- Institute of Economics and Statistics: Prof. R. CAMAITI
- Institute of Forensic Medicine and Criminology: Prof. I. PIVA
- Institute of Modern History and International Relations: Prof. G. BUCCIANTI
- Institute of Penal Law: Prof. L. MAZZA
- Institute of Private Law: Prof. M. COMPORTI
- Institute of Procedural Law: Prof. P. MOSCARINI
- Institute of Public and International Law: Prof. A. L. RAVÀ BAGNOLI
- Institute of Roman Law: Prof. R. MARTINI

Faculty of Medicine and Surgery:
- Institute of General Histology and Embryology: Prof. R. GERLI
- Institute of Labour Medicine: Prof. E. SARTORELLI
- Institute of General Pathology: Prof. M. COMPORTI
- Institute of Special Medical Pathology: Prof. C. GENNARI
- Institute of Social Paediatrics and Puericulture: Prof. M. DETTORI
- Institute of Rheumatology: Prof. F. R. MARCOLONGO
- Institute of Radiology: Prof. P. STEFANI
- Institute of Pharmacology: Prof. A. TAGLIAMONTE
- Institute of Medical Semiotics and Geriatrics: Prof. S. FORCONI
- Institute of Surgical Sciences: Prof. A. CARLI
- Institute of Human Anatomy: Prof. L. COMPARINI
- Institute of Thoracic and Cardiovascular Surgery and Biomedical Technology: Prof. M. TOSCANO
- Institute of General and Specialist Surgery: Prof. L. LORENZINI
- Institute of General Medicine and Medical Therapy: Prof. T. DI PERRI
- Institute of Clinical Obstetrics and Gynaecology: Prof. N. D'ANTONA
- Institute of Clinical Paediatrics: A. FOIS
- Institute of Anaesthesiology: Prof. G. BELLUCCI
- Institute of Neurological Sciences: G. GUAZZI
- Institute of Orthopaedics and Traumatology: Prof. L. BOCCHI
- Institute of Oto-Rhino-Laryngology: D. PASSALI
- Institute of Infectious Diseases: Prof. A. ROSSOLINI
- Institute of Hygiene: Prof. G. BOSCO
- Institute of Clinical Dermosyphilopathy: Prof. L. ANDREASSI
- Institute of General and Clinical Psychology: Prof. M. A. REDA
- Institute of Psychiatry: Prof. N. BATTISTINI
- Institute of Phthisiology and Respiratory Diseases: Prof. M. VAGLIASINDI
- Institute of Human Physiology: Prof. G. CARLI
- Institute of General Surgery and Surgical Therapy: Prof. S. ARMENIO
- Institute of Pathological Anatomy and Histology: Prof. P. TOSI
- Institute of Biochemistry and Enzymology: Prof. E. MARINELLO

Faculty of Mathematics, Physics and Natural Sciences:
- Institute of Mineralogy and Petrography: Prof. G. SABATINI
- Institute of General Physiology: Prof. A. PACINI BRANDANI
- Institute of General Biology: Prof. B. BACCETTI

Faculty of Pharmacy:
- Institute of General Physiology and Alimentation: Prof. V. BOCCI
- Institute of Organic Chemistry: G. ADEMBRI
- Institute of Pharmacology: G. P. SCARAGLI

Faculty of Economics:
- Institute of Economic Technology: Prof. F. CAPARRELLI

Faculty of Letters and Philosophy:
- Institute of Ancient History: Prof. F. FABBRINI

UNIVERSITÀ DEGLI STUDI DI TERAMO

Viale Crucioli 122, 64100 Teramo
Telephone: 0861-2661
Fax: 0861-245350
E-mail: webmaster@unite.it
Internet: www.unite.it

Founded 1993 upon independence of Teramo campus of Università degli Studi 'Gabriele D'Annunzio'

Rector: Prof. LUCIANO RUSSI
Pro-Rector: Prof. MAURO MATTIOLI
Administrative Director: Dott. FELICE ALEANDRI
Librarian: Dott. FRANCO D'AMBROSIO

Number of teachers: 200
Number of students: 10,000

Publications: *Il Cubo di Tangram* (monthly), *Trimestre* (2 a year)

DEANS

Faculty of Agriculture: Prof. IVO COZZANI
Faculty of Law: Prof. MICHELE AINIS
Faculty of Veterinary Medicine: Prof. PIER AUGUSTO SCAPOLO
Faculty of Political Science: Prof. FRANCESCO ZACCARIA

UNIVERSITÀ DEGLI STUDI DI TORINO

Via Verdi 8, 10124 Turin
Telephone: 011-6702200
Fax: 011-6702218
E-mail: rettore@unito.it
Internet: www.unito.it

Founded 1404
Academic year: October to September

Rector: Prof. EZIO PELIZZETTI
Pro-Rector: Prof. SERGIO RODA
Administrative Director: Dott. PASQUALE MASTRODOMENICO
Number of teachers: 2,050
Number of students: 65,000

DEANS

Agriculture: Prof. BRUNO GIAU
Arts and Philosophy: Prof. LORENZO MASSOBRIO
Economics: Prof. SERGIO CONTI
Education: Profa ANNAMARIA POGGI
Foreign Languages: Prof. LIBORIO TERMINE
Law: Prof. MARIO DOGLIANI
Mathematics, Physics and Natural Sciences: Prof. ENRICO PREDAZZI
Medicine: Prof. GIORGIO PALESTRO
Pharmacy: Prof. CARLO BICCHI
Political Sciences: Prof. FRANCO GARELLI
Psychology: Prof. GIAN PIERO QUAGLINO
Veterinary Medicine: Prof. CARLO GIRARDI

UNIVERSITÀ DEGLI STUDI DI TRENTO

Via Belenzani 12, 38100 Trento
Telephone: 0461-881111
Fax: 0461-881258
E-mail: DirezioneGenerale@amm.unitn.it
Internet: www.unitn.it

Founded 1962
State control (since 1982)
Academic year: October to September

President: Dott. INNOCENZO CIPOLLETTA
Rector: Prof. DAVIDE BASSI

Administrative Director: Dott. MARCO TOMASI
Librarian: Dott. PAOLO BELLINI

Library of 350,000 vols and 12,400 periodicals

Number of teachers: 474
Number of students: 14,183

Publications: *Unitn* (monthly), *Unitrentomagazine* (3 a year)

DEANS

Faculty of Arts and Philosophy: Prof. FABRIZIO CAMBI
Faculty of Cognitive Science: Prof. REMO JOB
Faculty of Economics: Prof. CARLO BORZAGA
Faculty of Engineering: Prof. RICCARDO ZANDONINI
Faculty of Law: Prof. ROBERTO TONIATTI
Faculty of Mathematics, Physics and Natural Sciences: Prof. MARCO ANDREATTA
Faculty of Sociology: Prof. ANTONIO SCAGLIA

HEADS OF DEPARTMENTS

Civil and Environmental Engineering: Prof. ALBERTO BELLIN
Cognitive Sciences and Education: Prof. FRANCO FRACCAROLI
Computer and Management Sciences: Prof. LUCA ERZEGOVESI
Economics: Prof. ROBERTO TAMBORINI
Human and Social Sciences: Prof. GUSTAVO CORNI
Information and Communication Technology: Prof. FAUSTO GIUNCHIGLIA
Legal Sciences: Prof. LUCA NOGLER
Materials Engineering and Industrial Technologies: Prof. ALBERTO MOLINARI
Mathematics: Prof. ALBERTO VALLI
Philological and Historical Sciences: Prof. PAOLO GATTI
Physics: Prof. ANTONIO MIOTELLO
Sociology and Social Research: Prof. MARIO DIANI
Structural Mechanical Engineering: Prof. MAURO DA LIO

UNIVERSITÀ DEGLI STUDI DI TRIESTE

Piazzale Europa 1, 34127 Trieste
Telephone: 040-6767111
Fax: 040-6763093
Internet: www.univ.trieste.it

Founded 1924

Rector: LUCIO DELCARO
Vice-Rector: LIVIO COSSAR
Administrative Director: CHIARA RICCI ZINGONE
Librarian: M. LUISA NESBEDA

Number of teachers: 1,200
Number of students: 24,500

Publication: *Piazzale Europa* (3 a year)

DEANS

Faculty of Economics: L. COSSAR
Faculty of Education: L. LAGO
Faculty of Engineering: L. DELCARO
Faculty of Humanities: S. MONTI
Faculty of Law: F. TOMMASEO
Faculty of Medicine: A. LEGGERI
Faculty of Natural Sciences: L. FONDA
Faculty of Pharmacy: G. STEFANCICH
Faculty of Political Science: D. COCCOPALMERIO
Faculty of Psychology: W. GERBINO
Data Processing Centre: Dr M. GREGORI (Dir)
Modern Languages for Interpreters and Translators: J. M. DODDS

DIRECTORS OF DEPARTMENTS

Anglo-German Literature and Civilization: R. S. CRIVELLI
Applied Chemistry and Materials Engineering: S. MERIANI
Applied Mathematics and Actuarial Sciences: S. HOLZER
Archaeology: S. SCONOCCHIA
Astronomy: F. MARDIROSSIAN
Biochemistry, Biophysics and Macromolecular Chemistry: G. SANDRI
Biology: P. L. NIMIS
Biomedical Sciences: C. MONTI BRAGADIN
Chemical Engineering, the Environment and Raw Materials: P. ALESSI
Chemistry: G. DE ALTI
Civil Engineering: A. AMODEO
Earth Sciences: C. EBBLIN
Economic and Statistical Sciences: R. FINZI
Economics and Business: V. NANUT
Economics and the Commodity Studies of Natural Resources and Production: L. FAVRETTO
Education: C. DESINAN
Electrical and Electronic Engineering: M. POLICASTRO
Energetics: S. TOMMASI
Geological, Environmental and Marine Sciences: A. BRAMBATI
Geography and History: G. BATTELLI
Human Morphology: P. NARDUCCI
Human Sciences: G. GIORIO
Italian Studies, Linguistics, Communication and Performing Arts: G. NEGRELLI
Languages and Literature of the Mediterranean: G. TRISOLINI
Law Sciences: G. SPANGHER
Mathematics: E. MITIDIERI
Medieval and Modern History: G. TODESCHINI
Naval Architecture, Ocean and Environmental Engineering: R. NICOLICH
Pharmaceutical Sciences: L. VIO
Philosophy: E. MATTIOLI
Physics: E. CASTELLI
Physiology and Pathology: P. P. BATTAGLINI
Political Science: C. BONVECCHIO
Psychology: C. SEMENZA
Theoretical Physics: G. GHIRARDI

ATTACHED INSTITUTES

Institute of History of Medieval and Modern Art: Dir R. GIORDANI.

Institute of Law: Dir P. CENDON.

Institute of Physiology: Dir A. BAVA.

Institute of General Pathology: Dir L. PATRIARCA.

Institute of Hygiene: Dir C. CAMPELLO.

Institute of Forensic Medicine: Dir B. M. ALTAMURA.

Institute of Pathological Anatomy: Dir L. DI BONITO.

Institute of Radiology: Dir L. DALLA PALMA.

Institute of General Clinical Medicine: Dir G. GUARNIERI.

Institute of General Surgery: Dir A. LEGGERI.

Institute of Surgical Pathology: Dir A. NEMETH.

Institute of Ophthalmology: Dir G. RAVALICO.

Institute of Orthopaedics: Dir F. MAROTTI.

Institute of Otorhinolaryngology: Dir M. RUSSOLO.

Institute of Venereal Diseases and Dermatology: Dir C. SCARPA.

Institute of Paediatrics: Dir F. PANIZON.

Institute of Obstetrics and Gynaecology: Dir S. GUASCHINO.

Institute of Nervous and Mental Diseases: Dir G. CAZZATO.

Institute of Anaesthesiology and Intensive Care: Dir A. GULLO.

Institute of Dentistry: Dir M. SILLA.

Institute of Psychiatry: Dir E. AGUGLIA.

Institute of Industrial Medicine: Dir F. GOBBATO.

Institute of Urology: Dir E. BELGRANO.

UNIVERSITÀ DEGLI STUDI DELLA TUSCIA

Via. S. Maria in Gradi 4, 01100 Viterbo
Telephone: 0761-357900
Fax: 0761-321771
E-mail: rettore@unitus.it
Internet: www.unitus.it

Founded 1979
State control
Academic year: November to October

Rector: Prof. MARCO MANCINI
Vice-Rector: Prof. STEFANO GREGO
Administrative Director: Dr GIOVANNI CUCULLO

Number of teachers: 320
Number of students: 10,000

DEANS

Faculty of Agriculture: Prof. E. RUGINI
Faculty of Modern Languages and Literature: Prof. G. PLATANIA
Faculty of Mathematics, Physics and Natural Sciences: Prof. V. BUONOCORE
Faculty of Conservation of Cultural Heritage: Prof. M. ANDALORO
Faculty of Economics: Prof. E. PERRONE
Faculty of Political Sciences: Prof. M. FERRARI ZUMBINI

HEADS OF DEPARTMENTS

Agrobiology and Agrochemistry: Prof. G. GIOVANNOZZI SERMANNI
Economics and Appraisal: Prof. L. ANGELI
Forestry-Environment Sciences and Resources: Prof. E. GIORDANO
Plant Protection: Prof. M. OLMI
Environmental Sciences: Prof. S. CANNISTRARO
Crop Production: Prof. B. LO CASCIO
History of Writing and Documents: Prof. P. INNOCENTI

UNIVERSITÀ DEGLI STUDI DI UDINE

Via Palladio 8, 33100 Udine
Telephone: 0432-556111
Fax: 0432-507715
Internet: www.amm.uniud.it

Founded 1978
State control

Rector: Prof. FURIO HONSELL
Pro-Rector: Prof. MARIA AMALIA D'ARONCO
Administrative Director: Dr DANIELE LIVON
Librarian: Dr PIER GIORGIO SCLIPPA

Library of 630,000 vols
Number of teachers: 780
Number of students: 16,800

Publication: *RES* (5 a year)

DEANS

Faculty of Agriculture: Prof. ANGELO VIANELLO
Faculty of Economics: Prof. FLAVIO PRESSACCO
Faculty of Education: Prof. FRANCO FABBRO
Faculty of Engineering: Prof. ANDREA STELLA
Faculty of Law: Prof. MARIA RITA D'ADDEZIO
Faculty of Literature: Prof. CATERINA FURLAN
Faculty of Medicine and Surgery: Prof. FRANCO QUADRIFOGLIO
Faculty of Medicine and Veterinary Medicine: Prof. MARCO GALEOTTI
Faculty of Modern Languages: Prof. VINCENZO ORIOLES
Faculty of Sciences: Prof. CARLO TASSO

DIRECTORS OF DEPARTMENT

Agricultural and Environmental Sciences: Prof. RAFFAELE TESTOLIN
Agricultural and Industrial Biology and Economics: Prof. EDOARDO VELICOGNA
Animal Sciences: Prof. DOMENICO LANARI
Biomedical Science and Biotechnology: Prof. PAOLO VIGLINO
Business Administration and Financial Markets: Prof. PAOLO PECORARI
Central and Eastern European Languages, Civilization and Literatures: Prof. GIORGIO ZIFFER
Chemical Science and Technology: Prof. GINO BONTEMPELLI
Civil Engineering: Prof. GAETANO RUSSO
Clinical and Experimental Medicine: Prof. ALFRED TENORE
Crop Protection Biology: Prof. RUGGERO OSLER
Economic Sciences: Prof. LUCIANO CECCON
Economics, Society and Environment: Prof. FRANCA BATTIGELLI
Electrical and Mechanical Engineering: Prof. PIER LUCA MONTESSORO
Energy and Machinery: Prof. CARLO NONINO
Food Science: Prof. ENRICO MALTINI
Germanic and Romance Languages and Literatures: Prof. SILVANA SERAFIN
Glottology and Classical Philology: Prof. ROBERTO GUSMANI
Historical and Documentary Sciences: Prof. GIORGIO. PETRACCHI
History and the Protection of Cultural Heritage: Prof. ARNALDO MARCONE
Italian Studies: Prof. GIAMPAOLO BORGHELLO
Land Resources and Environment: Prof. ADRIANO ZANFERRARI
Law: Prof. MARINA BROLLO
Mathematics and Computer Science: Prof. VITO. ROBERTO
Medical and Morphological Research: Prof. MAURIZIO MARCHINI
Philosophy: Prof. FEDERICO VERCELLONE
Physics: Prof. MARISA MICHELINI
Statistical Sciences: Prof. LUIGI PACE
Surgical Sciences: Prof. ALFIO FERLITO

UNIVERSITÀ DEGLI STUDI DI URBINO

Via Saffi 2, 61029 Urbino
Telephone: 0722-374203
Fax: 0722-374242
E-mail: rettore@uniurb.it
Internet: www.uniurb.it

Founded 1506
Academic year: November to October

Rector: Prof. Dott. GIOVANNI BOGLIOLO
Vice-Rector: Prof. Dott. MAURO MAGNANI
Administrative Director: Dott. ROBERTO PETRUCCI

Library: see Libraries
Number of teachers: 483
Number of students: 22,088

Publications: *Studi Urbinati—A* (law and economics), *Studi Urbinati—B* (history, philosophy and literature), *Notizie da Palazzo Albani* (art review), *Hermeneutica* (philosophy), *Quaderni di Hermeneutica* (philosophy), *Quaderni Urbinati di Cultura Classica* (philology), *Fonti e Documenti* (history), *Documents de Travail* (semiotics, in 6 series), *Storie Locali* (history), *Quaderni dell'Istituto di Filosofia* (philosophy), *Le Carte* (history)

DEANS

Faculty of Law: LUIGI MARI
Faculty of Economics: GIANCARLO FERRERO
Faculty of Letters and Philosophy: GIORGIO CERBONI BAIARDI
Faculty of Education: NANDO FILOGRASSO
Faculty of Pharmacy: GIORGIO TARZIA
Faculty of Mathematics, Physics and Natural Sciences: PAOLO COLANTONI
Faculty of Foreign Languages: STEFANO PIVATO
Faculty of Sociology: GRAZIELLA MAZZOLI
Faculty of Political Sciences: VITTORIO PARLATO
Faculty of Environmental Sciences: FILIPPO MANGANI
Faculty of Physical Education and Health: VILBERTO STOCCHI

PROFESSORS

(Some staff serve in more than one faculty)

Faculty of Law (Via Matteotti 1, 61029 Urbino; tel. 0722-3031; fax 0722-2955; e-mail presidigiur@giur.uniurb.it; internet www.uniurb.it):

DONDI, A., Civil Procedural Law
FANTAPPIÈ, C., History of Canon Law
FERRONI, L., Institutes of Private Law
GILIBERTI, G., Roman Law
MARI, L., International Law
MOROZZO DELLA ROCCA, P., Civil Law
ROZO ACUNA, E., Comparative Public Law

Faculty of Economics (Via Saffi 42, 61029 Urbino; tel. 0722-305500; fax 0722-305566; e-mail presecon@uniurb.it; internet www.econ.uniurb.it):

ANTONELLI, G., Marketing of Agroindustrial Products
CIAMBOTTI, M., Economic Planning and Auditing
FERRERO, G., Marketing
GARDINI, L., Mathematics for Economic Applications
GIAMPAOLI, A., Banking
MARCHINI, I., Business Economics
PAOLONI, M., General and Applied Accountancy
PENCARELLI, T., Economics and Management
POLIDORI, G., Transport Economics
RINALDI, R., Financial Law
STEFANINI, L., General Mathematics

Faculty of Letters and Philosophy (Piano S. Lucia 6, 61029 Urbino; tel. 0722-320125; fax 0722-320125; e-mail preslet@lettere.uniurb.it):

ARBIZZONI ARTUSI, G., Philosophy of Italian Literature
BERNARDINI, P., Greek Language and Literature
BOLDRINI, S., Latin Language and Literature
CECCHINI, E., Humanist Medieval Latin Literature
CECCHINI, F. M., Contemporary History, History of the Risorgimento
CERBONI BAIARDI, G., Italian Literature
CUBEDDU, I., Theoretical Philosophy
FRANCHI, A., Glottology and Linguistics
GORI, F., History of Christianity and the Church
GUERCIO, M., Archives, Bibliography and Librarianship
ILLUMINATI, A., History of Philosophy
LANCIOTTI, S., Latin Language and Literature
PERINI, G., Museum Organization and Art and Restoration Criticism
PERUSINO, F., Greek Language and Literature
QUESTA, C, Classical Philology
RAFFAELLI, R., Latin Language and Literature
RINALDI TUFI, S., Classical Archaeology
SCODITTI, G., Anthropological Demoethnic Studies
TAROZZI, G., Logic and Philosophy of Science

Faculty of Education (Via Bramante 17, 61029 Urbino; tel. 0722-327628; fax 0722-327628; e-mail lisa@uniurb.it; internet www.uniurb.it/Sciform/home.htm):

BALDACCI, M., General Pedagogy
CUBELLI, R., General Psychology
FILOGRASSO, N., General Pedagogy
LOSURDO, D., History of Philosophy
PERSI, P., Geography
PIRANI, P., Educational Psychology
RIPANTI, G., Theoretical Philosophy
ROSSI, S., Theory and Techniques of Psychological Discourse
SALA, G., Dynamic Psychology

Faculty of Pharmacy (Via Saffi 2, 61029 Urbino; tel. 0722-329881; fax 0722-2737; e-mail farmacia@uniurb.it):

ACCORSI, A., Biological Chemistry
CANTONI, O., Pharmacotherapy
DACHÀ, M., Applied Biochemistry
PIATTI, E., Food Science
TARZIA, G., Pharmaceutical Chemistry and Toxicology
VETRANO, F., Physics

Faculty of Mathematics, Physics and Natural Sciences (Località Crocicchia, 61029 Urbino; tel. 0722-304283; fax 0722-304240; e-mail scienze.mmffnn@uniurb.it):

ATTANASI, O. A., Organic Chemistry
BALSAMO, M., Zoology
BERETTA, E., Mathematical Analysis
COCCIONI, R., Micropalaeontology
COLANTONI, P., Sedimentology
DEL GRANDE, P., Comparative Anatomy
GAZZANELLI, G., Cytochemistry and Histochemistry
GORI, U., Applied Geology
MAGNANI, M., Biological Chemistry
MICHELONI, M., General and Inorganic Chemistry
NINFALI, P., Comparative Biochemistry
PAPA, S., Human Anatomy
PERRONE, V., Stratigraphic Geology

Faculty of Foreign Languages (Piazza Rinascimento 7, 61029 Urbino; tel. 0722-328506; fax 0722-328506; e-mail pres.facolta.lingue@uniurb.it):

BOGLIOLO, G., French Literature
MORISCO, G., Anglo-American Languages and Literatures
MULLINI, R., English Literature
OSSANI, A. T., Italian Literature
PIVATO, S., Contemporary History
SAURIN DE LA IGLESIA, M. R., Spanish Literature
VENTURELLI, A., History of German Culture
ZAGANELLI, G., Romance Philology

Faculty of Sociology (Via Saffi 15, 61029 Urbino; tel. 0722-327343; fax 0722-322343; e-mail presidenza@soc.uniurb.it; internet www.soc.uniurb.it):

ALFIERI, L., Political Philosophy
DEI, M., Sociology of Education
DEL TUTTO, L., General Linguistics
DIAMANTI, I., Political Science
FRANCI, A., Social Statistics
GRASSI, P., Philosophy of Religions
MAGGIONI, G., Sociology of Law
MAZZOLI, G., Communication Sociology
NEGROTTI, M., Methodology in Human Sciences
PIAZZI, G., Sociological Theory
VALLI, B., Mass-Media Sociology

Faculty of Political Sciences (Via Bramante 17, 61029 Urbino; tel. 0722-328557; fax 0722-328656; e-mail sc.politiche@uniurb.it):

DELLA CANANEA, G., Administrative Law
GREGOIRE, R., History of Christianity
GUDERZO, M., History of International Relations
MAZZONI, R., Political Economy
PARLATO, V., Canon Law
TENELLA-SILLANI, C., Institutes of Private Law

Faculty of Environmental Sciences (Località Crocicchia, 61029 Urbino; tel. 0722-304271; fax 0722-305265; e-mail sc.ambientali@uniurb.it; internet www.uniurb.it/SA/index.html):

CECCHETTI, G., Principles of Environmental Protection
CONFORTO, G., Laboratory of General Physics
MAGNANI, F., Environmental Chemistry
WEZEL FORESE, C., Stratigraphy
ZUMINO, M. E., Biogeography

Faculty of Physical Education and Health (Via Oddi 14, 61029 Urbino; tel. 0722-3517278; fax 0722-328829; e-mail presid.smotorie@uniurb.it):

FALCIERI, E., Human Anatomy
STOCCHI, V., Applied Biochemistry

UNIVERSITÀ DEGLI STUDI DI VENEZIA

Dorsoduro 3246, Ca' Foscari, 30123 Venice

Telephone: 041-2578111
Fax: 041-52101112
Internet: www.unive.it

Founded 1868, formerly Istituto Universitario di Economia e Commercio e di Lingue e Letterature Straniere

Academic year: November to October

Rector: Prof. PAOLO COSTA
Pro-Rector: Prof. FRANCESCO GATTI
Administrative Director: Dott. FRANCESCO COSTANZI
Librarian: Sig. ALESSANDRO BERTONI

Number of teachers: 494
Number of students: 17,427

Publications: *Cafoscarinotizie* (quarterly), *Cafoscariappuntamenti* (every 2 months), *Annuario*

DEANS

Faculty of Economics and Commerce: Prof. F. MASON
Faculty of Foreign Languages and Literature: Prof. M. CICERI
Faculty of Letters and Philosophy: Prof. G. LEVI
Faculty of Mathematical, Physical and Natural Sciences: Prof. G. A. MAZZOCCHIN

DIRECTORS OF DEPARTMENTS

Faculty of Economics and Commerce:

Applied Mathematics and Computer Science: Prof. E. CANESTRELLI
Economics: Prof. D. SARTORE
Business Economics and Management: Prof. M. RISPOLI
Statistics: Prof. P. MANTOVAN
Economic History: Prof. U. MEOLI
Law: Prof. M. L. PICCHIO FORLATI

Faculty of Foreign Languages and Literature:

Anglo-Germanic Literature and Civilization: Prof. F. MARUCCI
French Literature: Prof. G. CACCIAVILLANI
Iberian Literature: Prof. E. PITTARELLO
History of Art: Prof. A. BETTAGNO
Indology and Far Eastern Studies: Prof. A. BOSCARO
Linguistics and Language Teaching: Prof. G. CINQUE

Faculty of Letters and Philosophy:

Classical Studies: Prof. A. MARINETTI
History and Criticism of Art: Prof. L. PUPPI
Philosophy and Theory of Science: Prof. M. RUGGENINI
Archaeology and Eastern Studies: Prof. F. G. TRAVERSARI
History: Prof. M. ISNENGHI
Italian Studies and Romance Philology: Prof. F. BRUNI
Eurasian Studies: Prof. R. ZIPOLI

Faculty of Mathematical, Physical and Natural Sciences:

Chemistry: Prof. G. MARANGONI
Environmental Sciences: Prof. P. GHETTI
Physical Chemistry: Prof. S. GHERSETTI

UNIVERSITY CENTRES AND SCHOOLS

Interfaculty Linguistics Centre: Santa Croce 2161, 30125 Venice; tel. 5241642; Dir Prof. G. CINQUE.

Statistical Documentation Centre: Dorsoduro 3246, 30123 Venice; tel. 5298111; Dir Prof. R. VEDALDI.

Computer Centre: Dorsoduro 3861, 30123 Venice; tel. 5229823; Pres. Prof. G. PACINI.

Interuniversity Centre for Venetian Studies: San Marco 2945, Ca' Loredan, 30124 Venice; tel. 5200996; Dir Prof. G. PADOAN.

Administrative Computer Centre: Dorsoduro 2169, Santa Marta, 30123 Venice; Pres. Dott. G. BUSETTO.

Interdepartmental Experimental Centre: Dorsoduro 2137, 30123 Venice; tel. 5298111; Pres. Prof. G. A. MAZZOCCHIN.

UNIVERSITÀ DEGLI STUDI DI VERONA

Via dell'Artigliere 8, 37129 Verona

Telephone: 045-8098111
Fax: 045-8098255
Internet: www.univr.it

Founded 1982

Rector: Prof. MARIO MARIGO
Pro-Rector: Prof. GIUSEPPE BRUNI
Administrative Director: Dott. RENZO PICCOLI

Number of teachers: 258
Number of students: 13,087

DEANS

Faculty of Economics and Commerce: Prof. G. BORELLI
Faculty of Arts and Philosophy: Prof. L. SECCO
Faculty of Medicine and Surgery: Prof. R. CORROCHER
Faculty of Languages and Foreign Literature: Prof. E. MOSELE
Faculty of Mathematics, Physics and Natural Sciences: Prof. E. BURATTINI

POLITECNICO DI MILANO

Piazza Leonardo da Vinci 32, 20133 Milan

Telephone: 02-23991
Fax: 02-23992206
Internet: www.polimi.it

Founded 1863

Academic year: November to October

Rector: Prof. ADRIANO DE MAIO
Vice-Rector: Prof. MARIA CRISTINA TREU
Pro-Rector: Prof. GIAMPIO BRACCHI
Administrative Director: Dott. PIERO ZANELLO
Librarians: Prof. MAURIZIO BORIANI, Prof. ENNIO LAZZARINI, Prof. MARIA GIOVANNA SAMI

Number of teachers: 1,013
Number of students: 42,402

Publication: *Politecnico* (4 a year)

DEANS

Faculty of Architecture (Milano Bovisa): Prof. ANTONIO MONESTIROLI
Faculty of Architecture (Milano Bovisa – Industrial Design): Prof. ALBERTO SEASSARO
Faculty of Architecture (Milano Leonardo): Prof. CESARE STEVAN
Faculty of Engineering: Prof. OSVALDO DE DONATO
Faculty of Engineering (Como): Prof. PIERLUIGI DELLA VIGNA
Faculty of Engineering (Lecco): Prof. MICHELE GASPARETTO
Faculty of Engineering (Milano Bovisa): Prof. LUIGI PUCCINELLI
Faculty of Engineering (Milano Leonardo): Prof. NICOLA SCHIAVONI

HEADS OF DEPARTMENTS

Aerospace Engineering: Prof. MARCO BORRI
Applied Physical Chemistry: Prof. ALBERTO CIGADA
Architectural Projects: Prof. GIANNI OTTOLINI
Chemistry: Prof. FRANCESCO MINISCI
Conservation and History of Architecture: Prof. GIULIANA RICCI
Economics and Production: Prof. EMILIO BARTEZZAGHI
Electrical Engineering: Prof. ARNALDO BRANDOLINI
Electronics and Information Technology: Prof. MAURO SANTOMAURO
Energetics: Prof. GIANCARLO GIAMBELLI
Hydraulic, Environmental and Surveying Engineering: Prof. CARLO MONTI
Industrial Chemistry and Chemical Engineering: Prof. PIO FORZATTI
Industrial Design and Architectural Technology: Prof. ANTONIO SCOCCIMARRO
Mathematics: Prof. SANDRO SALSA
Mechanics: Prof. MARZIO FALCO
Nuclear Engineering: Prof. GIUSEPPE CAGLIOTI
Physics: Prof. RINALDO CUBEDDU
Planning and Building Engineering: Prof. SERGIO CROCE
Regional and Urban Planning: Prof. PIERCARLO PALERMO
Structural Engineering: Prof. VINCENZO PETRINI
Transport and Motion Systems: Prof. GUIDO RUGGIERI

POLITECNICO DI TORINO

Corso Duca degli Abruzzi 24, 10129 Turin

Telephone: 011-5646111
Fax: 011-5646329
Internet: www.polito.it

Founded 1859

Higher Institute of Engineering and Architecture

Academic year: November to October

Vice-Chancellor: Prof. R. ROSCELLI
Rector: Prof. R. ZICH
Administrative Director: Dssa A. M. GAIBISSO
Librarian: Prof. G. GHIONE

Library of 175,000 vols
Number of teachers: 774
Number of students: 23,000

DEANS

Faculty of Architecture (Turin): Prof. V. COMOLI
Faculty of Engineering (Turin): Prof. R. CONTI
Faculty of Engineering (Vercelli): Prof. A. GUGLIOTTA
Faculty of Information Engineering (Turin): Prof. C. NALDI

HEADS OF DEPARTMENTS

Faculty of Engineering:

Computer and Control Engineering: Prof. L. CIMINIERA
Electronics: Prof. F. FERRARIS
Industrial Electrical Engineering: Prof. A. VAGATI
Energetics: Prof. G. BUSSI
Physics: Prof. B. MINETTI
Georesources and Land: Prof. F. DEQUAL

Aeronautical and Space Engineering: Prof. P. M. CALDERALE
Building and Territorial Systems: Prof. L. MORRA
Structural Engineering: Prof. P. MARRO
Mathematics: Prof. G. MONEGATO
Mechanics: Prof. G. BELFORTE
Materials Science and Chemical Engineering: Prof. B. DE BENEDETTI
Hydraulics, Transportation and Civil Infrastructures: Prof. L. BUTERA
Manufacturing Systems and Economics: Prof. S. ROSSETTO

Faculty of Architecture (Viale Mattioli 39, 10125 Turin):
Town and Housing: Prof. M. DALLA COSTA
Architectural Design: Prof. C. OLMO
Technical Science for Settlement Processes: Prof. G. DEMATTEIS
Regional Urban and Environmental Studies and Planning: Prof. A. PEANO

Other Universities, Colleges and Institutes

AMERICAN UNIVERSITY OF ROME

Via Pietro Roselli 4, 00153 Rome
Telephone: 06-58330919
Fax: 06-58330992
E-mail: aurinfo@aur.edu
Internet: www.aur.edu
Office in USA: 1025 Connecticut Ave, NW, Suite 601, Washington, DC 20036, USA
Telephone: (202) 331-8327
Fax: (202) 296-9577
Founded 1969
Academic year: August to July
President: MARGARET MELADY
Provost: ROBERT MARINO
Student Services: JAMES LYNCH
Admissions: MARIA NISDEO
Library of 8,000 vols, ProQuest databases containing 4,336 periodicals
Number of teachers: 60
Number of students: 450
Departments: anthropology, art and art history, biology, business administration, cinema, classics, communications, computer science, drama, economics, English, English as a Foreign Language (EFL), history, Italian, mathematics, music, philosophy, political science, psychology, sociology, Spanish, studio art.

EUROPEAN UNIVERSITY INSTITUTE

Via dei Roccettini 9, 50016 San Domenico di Fiesole (FI),
Telephone: 055-46851
Fax: 055-4685298
E-mail: webmaster@iue.it
Internet: www.iue.it
Founded 1972 by the member states of the European Communities (present-day European Union)
Academic year: September to JuneEU languages
President: YVES MÉNY
Secretary-General: GIANFRANCO VARVESI
Librarian: VEERLE DECKMYN
Library of 500,000 vols
Number of teachers: 50 (full-time)
Number of students: 600 (postgraduate)
Publications: *EUI Working Papers*, *European Journal of International Law*, *European Foreign Policy Bulletin*, *President's Annual Report*, *European Law Journal*, *EUI Review*, *Robert Schuman Centre Newsletter*

HEADS OF DEPARTMENTS
Economics: Prof. M. MOTTA
History: Prof. A. MOLHO
Law: Prof. W. SADURSKI
Political Science: Prof. M. KEATING

ATTACHED INSTITUTIONS
Academy of European Law: Dirs B. DE WITTE, G. DE BÚRCA F. FRANCIONI.
European Forum: Dir H. WALLACE.
Robert Schuman Centre for Advanced Studies: Dir H. WALLACE.

FREIE UNIVERSITÄT BOZEN/LIBERA UNIVERSITÀ DI BOLZANO
(Free University of Bozen/Bolzano)

Via Sernesi 1, 39100 Bolzano
Telephone: 0471-012200
Fax: 0471-012209
E-mail: info@unibz.it
Internet: www.unibz.it
Founded 1997
Provincial state controlGerman, Italian, English
Rector: Prof. Dr JOHANN DRUMBL
President: Dr. FRIEDRICH SCHMIDL
Library of 77,300 books, 1,036 periodicals, 4,250 online journals, 68 databases
Number of teachers: 25
Number of students: 1,965

DEANS
School of Economics: Prof. MAURIZIO MURGIA
Faculty of Education: Prof. GERALD WALLNÖFER
Faculty of Computer Science: Prof. MICHAEL BÖHLEN
Faculty of Design and Art: Prof. KUNO PREY

JOHN CABOT UNIVERSITY

Via della Lungara, 00165 Rome
Telephone: 06-6819121
Fax: 06-832088
Internet: www.johncabot.edu
Office in USA: 101B De Vos Center, 401 W Fulton St, Grand Rapids, MI 49504-6431, USA
Fax: (616) 336-7391
E-mail: usoffice@johncabot.edu
Founded 1972
Independent, four-year institution of liberal arts
President: JAMES CREAGAN
Dean of Academic Affairs: FRANCO PAVONCELLO
Dean of Students and Director of Administration and Enrollment: L. CHRIS CURRY
Registrar: CARMEN SCARPATI
Director of Admissions: FRANCESCA R. GLEASON
Library Supervisor: SUSAN FULLER
Library: Frohring Library: reference material, curriculum-related items, newspapers, 1,000 online journals
Number of teachers: 50

PROFESSORS
CREAGAN, J. F., International Relations
GRAY, L. E., Political Science

UNIVERSITÀ CATTOLICA DEL SACRO CUORE
(Catholic University of the Sacred Heart)

Largo A. Gemelli 1, 20123 Milan
Telephone: 02-72345407
Fax: 02-72343796
Internet: www.unicatt.it
Founded 1920; recognized by the Government 1924
Rector: Prof. L. ORNAGHI
Administrative Officer: Dott. A. CICCHETTI
Librarian: Dott. ELLIS SADA
Number of teachers: 3,292
Number of students: 41,519
Publication: Publications: various, published by individual faculties

DEANS
Faculty of Jurisprudence: Prof. G. PASTORI
Faculty of Political Sciences: Prof. A. QUADRIO CURZIO
Faculty of Economics (Milan): Prof. A. COVA
Faculty of Letters and Philosophy: Prof. G. PICASSO
Faculty of Educational Sciences: Prof. M. LENOCI
Faculty of Agrarian Sciences: Prof. G. PIVA
Faculty of Medicine and Surgery: Prof. P. MARANO
Faculty of Mathematical, Physical and Natural Sciences: Prof. M. DEGIOVANNI
Faculty of Banking, Finance and Insurance Sciences: Prof. B. V. FROSINI
Faculty of Lingustic Sciences and Foreign Literatures: Prof. S. CIGADA
Faculty of Economics (Piacenza): Prof. E. CICIOTTI
Faculty of Psychology: Prof.ssa E. SCABINI
Faculty of Jurisprudence (Piacenza): Prof. G. NEGRI
Faculty of Sociology: Prof. M. COLASANTO

HEADS OF DEPARTMENTS
Private and Public Law of Economics: Prof. M. NAPOLI
Philosophy: Prof. A. GHISALBERTI
Foreign Languages and Literature: Prof. B. CAMBIAGHI
Mathematics and Physics (Niccolò Tartaglia): Prof. A. BALLARIN DENTI
Pedagogy: Prof. C. SCURATI
Psychology: Prof. A. ANTONIETTI
Political Sciences: Prof. G. ANCARANI
Religious Sciences: Prof. L. PIZZOLATO
Sociology: Prof. V. CESAREO
Medieval, Humanistic and Renaissance Studies: Prof. G. ANDENNA
Communications and Visual Sciences: Prof. F. CASETTI
Economic and Business Management Sciences: Prof. A. FUSCONI
Social and Economic Sciences: Prof. E. CICIOTTI
International, Institutional and Development Economics: Prof. C. L. BERETTA
Contemporary History: Prof. A. GIOVAGNOLI
Law Sciences: Prof. R. ASTORRI

HEADS OF HEALTH DEPARTMENTS
Cardiovascular Medicine: Prof. G. POSSATI
Surgical Sciences: Prof. A. PICIOCCHI
Gerontological, Geriatrical and Physiatrical Sciences: Prof. P. CARBONIN
Post-Natal Care: Prof. S. MANCUSO
Health Security, Health Technology and Drug Usage: Prof. P. PREZIOSI
Emergency and Admittance: Prof. R. PROIETTI
Pediatric Sciences, Medical-Surgical Sciences and Developmental Neuroscience: Prof. C. DI ROCCO
Neuroscience: Prof. P. A. TONALI

UNIVERSITÀ COMMERCIALE LUIGI BOCCONI

Via R. Sarfatti 25, 20136 Milan
Telephone: 02-58361
Fax: 02-58362000
Internet: www.uni-bocconi.it
Founded 1902; private control

Academic year: November to October
President: Prof. MARIO MONTI
Rector: Prof. CARLO SECCHI
Vice-President: Prof. LUIGI GUATRI
Chief Exec. and General Manager: Dott. GIOVANNI PAVESE
Librarian: MARISA SANTASIERO

Number of teachers: 971
Number of students: 12,600

Publications: *Giornale degli Economisti e Annali di Economia, Economia delle Fonti di Energia, Finanza Marketing e Produzione, Sviluppo e Organizzazione, Economia e Management, Economia e Politica Industriale, Commercio, Azienda Pubblica*

DEANS

Department of Economics: Prof. ALDO MONTESANO
Department of Business Administration: Prof. PAOLO MOTTURA
SDA Bocconi School of Management: Prof. MAURIZIO DALLOCCHIO (Dir)
CESDIA Centre for Teaching and Learning: Prof. V. CODA (Dir)

DIRECTORS

Department of Economics:
'Ettore Bocconi' Institute of Economics: Prof. R. ARTONI
Institute of Quantitative Methods: Prof. D. M. CIFARELLI
'Angelo Sraffa' Institute of Comparative Law: Prof. P. MARCHETTI
Institute of Economic History: Prof. A. M. ROMANI

Department of Business Administration:
'Giorgio Pivato' Institute of Corporate Economics and Management: Prof. S. PODESTÀ
Institute of Business Administration, Control and Finance: Prof. L. GUATRI
'Gino Zappa' Institute of Strategic Management: Prof. V. CODA
Institute of Business Organization and Information Systems: Prof. V. PERRONE
Institute of Public Administration and Health Care Management: Prof. F. PEZZANI
'Giordano Dell'Amore' Institute of Financial Markets and Institutions: Prof. R. RUOZI

PROFESSORS

AIROLDI, G., Business Administration
ALESSANDRI, A., Commercial Law
AMATORI, F., Economic History
AMIGONI, F., Business Administration
ARTONI, R., Public Finance
BATTIGALLI, P., Economics
BELTRATTI, A., Economics
BERTONI, A., Corporate Finance
BIANCHI, L. A., Company and Business Law
BINI, M., Corporate Finance
BORGONOVI, E., Public Administration
BRUGGER, G., Corporate Finance
BRUNETTI, G., Business Administration
BRUNI, F., International Monetary Theory and Policy
BUSACCA, B., Business Administration and Management
CASTAGNOLA, A., Civil Law
CASTAGNOLI, E., Mathematics
CATTINI, M., Economic History
CIFARELLI, D. M., Statistics
CODA, V., Business Administration
DE PAOLI, L., Business Administration and Management
DEMATTÈ, C., Financial Intermediaries
FABRIZI, P. L., Securities Market
FAVERO, C. A., Monetary Economics
FERRARI, G., Monetary Economics
FILIPPINI, C., Economic Development
FORESTIERI, G., Financial Intermediaries
FRACCHIA, F., Administrative Law
FROVA, A., Corporate Finance
GIAVAZZI, F., Economics
GOLFETTO, F., Business Administration and Management
GRANDORI, A., Corporate Organisation
GUARNERI, A., Comparative Civil Law
INVERNIZZI, G., Business Administration
IUDICA, G., Civil Law
LIEBMAN, S., Labour Law
MALERBA, F., Business Administration
MARCHETTI, P., Industrial Law
MASSARI, M., Capital Budgeting
MONTESANO, A., Economics
MONTI, M., Economics
MOTTURA, P., Financial Intermediaries
MULIERE, P., Statistics
ONIDA, F., International Economics
PACI, S., Management of Insurance Companies and Savings Institutions
PECCATI, L., Mathematics for Economics and Finance
PERRONE, V., Organization Theory
PEZZANI, F., Business Administration
PIVATO, S., Industrial Management
PODESTÀ, S., Commercial Management
PORTA, A., Monetary Theory and Policy
PROVASOLI, A., Cost Accounting and Management Control Systems
ROMANI, A., Economic History
RUOZI, R., Banking
SACERDOTI, G., International Law
SALVEMINI, S., Human Resources Management
SECCHI, C., Economics of the European Communities
SENN, L., Regional Economics
SITZIA, B., Econometrics
TABELLINI, G., Economics
URBANI, G., Political Science
VALDANI, E., Marketing
VALOTTI, G., Business Administration
VERONESE, P., Statistics
VICARI, S., Management of Industrial Companies
VIGANO, A., Cost Accounting and Management Control Systems

ATTACHED RESEARCH INSTITUTES

Centre for Monetary and Financial Economics 'Paolo Baffi': Dir Prof. A. PORTA.

CESPRI Centre for Research on Process Innovation and Internationalization: Dir Prof. F. MALERBA.

ECONPUBBLICA Research Centre on the Public Sector: Dir Prof. R. ARTONI.

ELEUSI Centre for Research on the Analysis and Systematic Use of Information: Dir Prof. D. M. CIFARELLI.

IEFE Economics and Policy on Energy and Environment Institute: Dir Prof. L. DE PAOLI.

ISESAO Institute of Economic and Social Studies of East Asia: Dir Prof. C. FILIPPINI.

ISLA Institute of Latin-American Studies: Dir Prof. C. SECCHI.

POLEIS Research Centre for Comparative Politics: Dir Prof. G. URBANI.

CERGAS Research Centre for Health Care Management: Dir Prof. E. BORGONOVI.

CERMES Centre for Research on Markets and the Industrial Sector: Dir Prof. S. PODESTÀ.

CESAD Business Administration Research Centre: Dir Prof. F. AMIGONI.

CRORA Centre for Research into Business Organization: Dir Prof. A. GRANDORI.

FINDUSTRIA Centre for Finance and Industry Studies: Dirs Prof. G. BRUGGER, Prof. S. PIVATO.

NEWFIN Financial Innovation Research Centre: Dir Prof. P. MOTTURA.

SPACE Centre for Research on Security and Protection against Crimes and Emergencies: Dir Prof. S. PIVATO.

CREA Research Centre for Entrepreneurship 'Furio Cicogna': Dir Prof. A. BERTONI.

CERAP Centre for Research on Insurance and Social Security: Dir Prof. S. PACI.

CERTET Centre for Regional Transport and Tourism Economics: Dir Prof. L. SENN.

CERTI Centre for Research on Business Taxation: Dir Prof. A. PROVASOLI.

I-LAB Centre for Research on the Digital Economy: Dir Prof. E. VALDANI.

IGIER 'Innocenzo Gasparini' Institute for Economic Research: Dir Prof. G. TABELLINI.

UNIVERSITÀ ITALIANA PER STRANIERI

Palazzo Gallenga, 06100 Perugia
Telephone: 075-57461
Fax: 075-62014
Internet: www.unistrapg.it

Founded 1921
Academic year: January to December

Founded for the diffusion abroad of Italian language and culture; courses in Italian language and civilization for foreigners of all nationalities. There are courses in advanced culture on Italian institutions, literature, pedagogy, history of art, the geography of Italy, Italian history, and Italian thought throughout the centuries; also courses in Italian language and culture, divided into three sections: Preparatory, Intermediate, Advanced; there are also in the summer term special courses in Etruscology, History of Art and Modern Italian and a course for teachers of Italian abroad. Lectures and classes are given by professors of Italian universities, leading members of academies, etc.

Rector: Prof. GIORGIO SPITELLA
Pro-Rector: ALBERTO MAZZETTI
Administrator: Dott. CARMELO SAETTA

Library of 70,000 vols
Number of teachers: c. 100
Number of students: c. 7,000 annually

Publication: *Annali dell'Università.*

VENICE INTERNATIONAL UNIVERSITY

Isola di S. Servola, 30100 Venice
Telephone: 041-2719511
Fax: 041-2719510
E-mail: viu@univiu.it
Internet: www.univiu.org

Founded 1997
Academic year: September to May

Pres.: UMBERTO VATTANI
Dean: IGNAZIO MUSU
Sec.-Gen.: ANTONELLA ATTARDO

Staff and students provided by the constituent univs.

RESEARCH AND TRAINING CENTRES

Centre for Studies on Technologies in Distributed Intelligence Systems (TeDIS).

International Centre of Economics and Finance (ICEF).

Thematic Environmental Networks (TEN).

ENI CORPORATE UNIVERSITY – SCUOLA ENRICO MATTEI

Via S. Salvo 1, 20097 San Donato Milanese
Telephone: 02-52057969
Fax: 02-52057908
E-mail: info.scuolamattei@eni.it
Internet: www.enicorporateuniversity.it/scuolamattei/
Founded 1957
Academic year: September to June
Dean: Prof. PIERANGELO CIGNOLI
Library of 15,000 vols
Number of teachers: 50
Number of students: annual intake of 55
Publication: *Quaderni* (3 a year)
Economic and management studies; higher degree in energy and environmental economics.

ISTITUTO REGIONALE DI STUDI E RICERCA SOCIALE

Piazza S. Maria Maggiore 7, 38100 Trento
Telephone: 0461-220110
Fax: 0461-233821
E-mail: dir@irsrs.tn.it
Internet: www.irsrs.tn.it
Founded 1947; until *c.* 1993, Scuola Superiore Regionale di Servizio Sociale
President: Prof. CARLO FAIT
Director: Dott. GIAMPIERO GIRARDI
Library of 15,000 vols
Number of teachers: 350
Number of students: 6,000
Publication: *Annali* (annually).

CONSTITUENT INSTITUTES

Scuola per Educatore Professionale (School for Professional Educators).

Scuola per Operatore Socio-Assistenziale (School for Social Service Workers).

Università della Terza Età e del Tempo Disponibile (Open University): training for social workers, and adult education.

ISTITUTO UNIVERSITARIO DI STUDI EUROPEI
(University Institute of European Studies)

Via Maria Vittoria 26, 10123 Turin
Telephone: 011-8394660
Fax: 011-8394664
E-mail: iuse@iuse.it
Internet: www.iuse.it
Founded 1952
President: Prof. LIONELLO JONA CELESIA
Library of 15,000 vols; 23,000 documents from intl orgs.
Postgraduate courses and research in law and international economics.

ISTITUTO UNIVERSITARIO DI ARCHITETTURA

Tolentini 191, 30135 Venice
Telephone: 041-2571111
Fax: 041-2571760
E-mail: comesta@iuav.it
Internet: web.iuav.it
Founded 1926
State control
Academic year: November to October
Rector: Prof. M. FOLIN
Administrative Director: Dott. PIERPAOLO MINELLI
Librarian: Dssa LAURA CASAGRANDE
Library of 123,000 vols, 2,500 periodicals
Number of teachers: 372
Number of students: 12,000.

ISTITUTO UNIVERSITARIO ORIENTALE

Largo San Giovanni Maggiore 30, 80134 Naples
Telephone: 081-5526948
Fax: 081-5526928
Internet: www.iuo.it
Founded 1732
Rector: Prof. ADRIANO ROSSI
Administrative Director: Dr M. R. CAVALIERE

DEANS

Faculty of Letters and Philosophy: Prof. G. D'ERME
Faculty of Political Science: Prof. P. FRASCANI
Faculty of Foreign Languages and Literatures: Prof. G. DE CESARE
School of Islamic Studies: Prof. L. SERRA

LIBERA UNIVERSITÀ DI LINGUE E COMUNICAZIONE IULM

Via Carb Bo 1, 20143 Milan
Telephone: 02-891411
Fax: 02-89141410
E-mail: iulm.orienta@iulm.it
Internet: www.iulm.it
Founded 1968
Academic year: October to May
Rector: Prof. GIOVANNI A. PUGLISI
Administrative Director: Dott. CIRO FRACCACRETA
Librarian: Dott. GIOVANNI MOSCATI
Library of 122,000 vols
Number of teachers: 350
Number of students: 8,500

DEANS

Faculty of Foreign Languages and Literature: Profa PATRIZIA NEROZZI
Faculty of Communications Science: Prof. CARLO A. RICCIARDI

LIBERA UNIVERSITÀ INTERNAZIONALE DEGLI STUDI SOCIALI GUIDO CARLI IN ROMA
(Independent International University of Social Studies in Rome)

Viale Pola 12, 00198 Rome
Telephone: 06-852251
Fax: 06-85225300
Internet: www.luiss.it
Founded 1945, recognized by the Government 1966
President: Dr LUIGI ABETE
Rector: Prof. MARIO ARCELLI
Registrar: Dott. MARIO TEANE PANUNEI
Library of 118,000 vols and 2,133 periodicals
Number of teachers: 515
Number of students: 4,800

DEANS

Faculty of Law: Prof. M. FOSCHINI
Faculty of Political Science: Prof. G. C. DE MARTIN
Faculty of Economics: Prof. F. FONITANE

LIBERA UNIVERSITÀ MARIA SS. ASSUNTA

Via della Traspontina 21, 00193 Rome
Telephone: 06-684221
Fax: 06-6878357
E-mail: lumsa@lumsa.it
Internet: www.lumsa.it
Founded 1939
Academic year: October to July
President: GIUSEPPE DALLA TORRE DEL TEMPIO DI SANGUINETTO
Registrar: Dott. GIANNINA DI MARCO
Librarian: Dott. GIUSEPPINA D'ALESSANDRO
Library of 100,000 vols
Number of teachers: 350
Number of students: 5,200
Faculties of Law, Letters and Philosophy, and Education
Publications: *I Quaderni della Lumsa* (annually), *Nuovi Studi Politici* (4 a year).

BOLOGNA CENTER OF THE JOHNS HOPKINS UNIVERSITY PAUL H. NITZE SCHOOL OF ADVANCED INTERNATIONAL STUDIES (SAIS)

Via Belmeloro 11, 40126 Bologna
Telephone: 051-2917811
Fax: 051-228505
E-mail: admission@jhubc.it
Internet: www.jhubc.it
Founded 1955
Language of instruction: English
Academic year: September to May
Interdisciplinary graduate programme in int. relationswith an emphasis on int. econ., European studies, int. devt, and the many subfields of int. relations (conflict management, global theory and history, int. law and orgs, int. policy, strategic studies). 1- and 2-year programmes are available, with the possibility of combining a year in Bologna and Washington, DC (USA). A strong language programme is available to enable students to achieve a foreign language proficiency, necessary for any career in int. relations
Dir: Prof. KENNETH KELLER
Dir of Finance and Admin.: BART DRAKULICH
Registrar: HANNELORE ARAGNO
Librarian: GAIL MARTIN
Library of 76,000 vols
Number of teachers: 50
Number of students: 185
Publication: *Bologna Center Journal of International Affairs*.

SCUOLA INTERNAZIONALE SUPERIORE DI STUDI AVANZATI IN TRIESTE

Via Beirut 2–4, 34014 Trieste
Telephone: 040-37871
Fax: 040-3787528
Internet: www.sissa.it
Founded 1978; sponsored by the Italian GovernmentEnglish and Italian
Academic year: November to October
Director: Prof. STEFANO FANTONI
Administrator: GIULIANA ZOTTA VITTUR
Library of 10,000 vols
Number of teachers: 59
Number of students: 205
Higher degrees in physics, mathematics and neuroscience; research; fellowships for students from developing countries.

SCUOLA NORMALE SUPERIORE DI PISA

Piazza dei Cavalieri 7, 56126 Pisa
Telephone: 050-509111
E-mail: direzione@sns.it
Internet: www.sns.it
Founded 1813
State control
Dir: Prof. SALVATORE SETTIS
Chief Admin. Officer: Dott. CLAUDIO CAPECCHI
Librarian: Dott.ssa SANDRA DI MAJO
Library of 500,000 vols
Number of teachers: 36
Number of students: 279

Publications: *Annali* (Arts series, Science series), *Studi e Testi*, *Studi Linguistici e Filologici*, *Quaderni di Matematica*, *Testi umanistici inediti o rari*, *Italia dialettale*.

Schools of Music and Art

MUSIC

Accademia Filarmonica Romana (Rome Philharmonic Academy): Via Flaminia 118, 00196 Rome; tel. 06-3201752; fax 06-3210410; f. 1821; library: 1,500 vols; Pres. ROMAN VLAD.

Accademia Musicale Chigiana: Via di Città 89, 53100 Siena; tel. 0577-22091; fax 0577-288124; e-mail accademia.chigiana@chigiana.it; internet www.chigiana.it; f. 1932; master classes, seminars, lectures, concerts, operas, international research conventions; 26 teachers; 351 students; Artistic Director Maestro ALDO BENNICI.

Conservatorio di Musica 'Santa Cecilia': Via dei Greci 18, 00187 Rome; tel. 06-6784552; Dir Maestro GIORGIO CAMBISSA.

Conservatorio Statale di Musica G. B. Martini: Piazza Rossini 2, 40126 Bologna; tel. 051-221483; f. 1804; Dir (vacant).

Conservatorio di Musica G. Verdi: Via Conservatorio 12, 20122 Milan; tel. 02-76001755; fax 02-76014814; f. 1808; library: see Libraries; Dir MARCELLO ABBADO.

Conservatorio di Musica 'Gioacchino Rossini': Piazza Olivieri 5, 61100 Pesaro; tel. 0721-33670; f. 1882; library: *c.* 25,000 vols; Dir MARIO PERRUCCI.

Conservatorio Statale di Musica 'Giuseppe Verdi': Via Mazzini 11, 10123 Turin; tel. 011-8178458; fax 011-885165; f. 1867; Dir GIORGIO FERRARI.

Conservatorio Nazionale di Musica 'Benedetto Marcello': Palazzo Pisani, San Marco 2809, 30124 Venice; tel. 041-5225604; fax 041-5239268; f. 1877; 90 teachers; 480 students; library: 50,000 vols, 70 periodicals; Dir GIOVANNI UMBERTO BATTEL.

Conservatorio di Musica Niccolò Piccinni: Via Brigata Bari 26, 70124 Bari; tel. 080-347962; f. 1959; library: 11,000 vols; Dir G. ROTA; Sec. Dr V. A. DELLEGRAZIE.

Conservatorio Statale di Musica 'C. Monteverdi': Piazza Domenicani 19, 39100 Bolzano; tel. 0471-978764; f. 1940; library: 10,000 vols; international Busoni Piano Competition held annually; Dir Prof. V. BRUNETTI; Admin. Dir Dott. N. MARCHESONI.

Conservatorio Statale di Musica 'G. Pierluigi da Palestrina': Piazza Porrino 1, 09128 Cagliari; tel. 070-493118; fax 070-487388; internet www.conservatoriocagliari.it; f. 1939; Dir NINO BONAVOLONTÀ.

Conservatorio di Musica 'L. Cherubini': Piazzetta delle Belle Arti 2, 50121 Florence; tel. 055-292180; fax 055-2396785; e-mail conservatoriofirenze@tin.it; internet www.bdp.it/conservatorio-firenze; f. 1861; 107 teachers; 702 students; Dir Maestro GIOVANNI CICCONI; Sec. Dssa M. POLLICINA.

Conservatorio di Musica 'S. Pietro a Majella': Via S. Pietro a Majella 35, 80138 Naples; tel. 081-459255; Dir Dr A. COLLUCCI.

Conservatorio di Musica 'V. Bellini': Via Squarcialupo 45, 90133 Palermo; tel. 091-580921; fax 091-586742; e-mail paconsediwin@hotmail.com; f. 1721; library: 40,000 vols, collection of 18th- and 19th-century MSS; Pres. (vacant); Dir CARMELO CAPUSO; publ. *Quaderni del Conservatorio* (irregular).

Conservatorio di Musica 'A. Boito': Via Conservatorio 27A, 43100 Parma; tel. 0521-381911; fax 0521-200398; e-mail direzione.cons-pr@iol.it; internet www.conservatorio.pr.it; f. 1825; library: 70,000 vols; 140 teachers; 800 students; Dir EMILIO GHEZZI.

Conservatorio di Musica Giuseppe Tartini: Via Carlo Ghega 12, 34132 Trieste; tel. 040-6724911; fax 040-370205; e-mail erasmus@conservatorio.trieste.it; internet www.conservatorio.trieste.it; f. 1903; 93 teachers; 630 students; Dir MASSIMO PAROVEL.

ART

Accademia Albertina di Belle Arti: Via Accademia Albertina 6, 10123 Turin; tel. 011-889020; fax 011-8125688; e-mail albertina@itbox.net; internet www.accademialbertina.torino.it; f. 1652; 70 teachers; 550 students; Pres. Dott. Proc. A. M. MAROCCO; Dir Prof. CARLO GIULIAMO.

Accademia di Belle Arti di Bologna (Academy of Fine Arts of Bologna): Via Belle Arti 54, 40126 Bologna; tel. 051-243064; f. 1710; library: 15,000 vols; Dir Prof. A. BACCILIERI; Librarian Prof. M. V. RICCARDI SCASSELLATI; publ. *Prontuario* (annually).

Accademia di Belle Arti e Liceo Artistico (Academy of Fine Arts): Via Roma 1, 54033 Carrara; tel. 0585-71658; courses in painting, sculpture and scene-painting.

Accademia di Belle Arti di Firenze (Academy of Fine Arts of Florence): Via Ricasoli 66, 50122 Florence; tel. 055-215449; f. 1801; library: 22,000 vols; Pres. Sen. L. BAUSI; Dir Prof. D. VIGGIANO.

Accademia di Belle Arti di Lecce (Academy of Fine Arts of Lecce): Via Libertini 3, 73100 Lecce; Dir Prof. S. SPEDICATO.

Accademia di Belle Arti di Milano (Academy of Fine Arts of Milan): Palazzo di Brera, Via Brera 28, 20121 Milan; tel. 02-869551; fax 02-86403643; e-mail accademia@accademiadibrera.milano.it; internet www.accademiadibrera.milano.it; f. 1776; library: 25,000 vols; 400 ; 3,500 ; Pres. Prof. STEFANO ZECCHI; Dir Prof. FERNANDO DE FILIPPI.

Accademia di Belle Arti di Napoli (Academy of Fine Arts of Naples): Via S. M. Constantinopoli 107A, 80138 Naples; f. 1838; library: 7,000 vols; Dir Prof. C. LORENZETTI.

Accademia di Belle Arti di Palermo (Academy of Fine Arts of Palermo): Via Papireto 20, 90134 Palermo; tel. 091-580876.

Accademia di Belle Arti di Perugia (Academy of Fine Arts of Perugia): Piazza S. Francesco al Prato 5, 06123 Perugia; tel. 075-5730631; fax 075-5730632; f. 1573; 96 Academicians, 143 Hon. Academicians; collections of paintings, engravings, drawings, etc.; library: 13,330 vols; Pres. CLAUDIO SPINELLI; Dir Prof. EDGARDO ABBOZZO.

Accademia di Belle Arti di Ravenna (Academy of Fine Arts of Ravenna): Loggetta Lombardesca, Via di Roma 13, 48100 Ravenna; tel. 0544-482874; fax 0544-213641; f. 1827; library: 10,000 vols; Dir VITTORIO D'AUGUSTA; Sec.-Gen. PATRIZIA POGGI.

Accademia di Belle Arti di Roma (Academy of Fine Arts of Rome): Via Ripetta 222, 00186 Rome; tel. 06-3227025; fax 06-3218007; f. 1873; Dir Prof. ANTONIO PASSA.

Accademia di Belle Arti di Venezia (Academy of Fine Arts of Venice): Campo della Carità 1050, 30123 Venice; tel. 041-5225396; fax 041-5230129; e-mail info@accademiavenezia.edu; internet www.accademiavenezia.edu; f. 1750; 76 teachers; 870 students; Dir Prof. RICCARDO RABAGLIATI.

Istituto Statale d'Arte: Piazza d'Armi 16, CP 105, 07100 Sassari; tel. 079-234466; woodwork, metalwork, weaving, painting, ceramics, graphic art and architecture; Pres. Prof. NICOLÒ MASIA.

Istituto Statale d'Arte per la Ceramica: Corso Baccarini 17, 48018 Faenza; tel. 0546-21091; basic courses in ceramic art and technology; higher courses in stoneware, porcelain, restoration, ceramic building coatings, traditional ceramics, technology of special ceramics.

Istituto Statale d'Arte 'Enrico e Umberto Nordio': Via di Calvola, 34143 Trieste; tel. 040-300660; f. 1955; courses in architecture, interior decorating, design and printing of textiles; library: 5,450 vols; Dir Prof. TEODORO GIUDICE.

Istituto Statale d'Arte: Piazza Duca Federico 1, 61029 Urbino; tel. 0722-329892; fax 0722-4830; e-mail ia.scuolalibro@provincia.ps.it; f. 1865; engraving techniques, cartoon drawing, ceramics, photography, editorial graphics, publicity art; library: 20,000 vols; 110 teachers; 714 students; Pres. Prof. MAURIZIA RAGONESI.

DANCE AND DRAMA

Accademia Nazionale di Arte Drammatica 'Silvio d'Amico': Via Vincenzo Bellini 16, 00198 Rome; tel. 06-8543680; fax 06-8542505; f. 1935; 45 teachers; 100 students; Dir Prof. LUIGI MARIA MUSATI.

Accademia Nazionale di Danza: Largo Arrigo VII 5, Castello dei Cesari (Aventino), 00153 Rome; tel. 06-5743284; fax 06-5780994; f. 1948; Pres. CARLO SCARASCIA MUGNOZZA; Dir LIA CALIZZA.

JAMAICA

The Higher Education System

The University of Technology, Jamaica (formerly Jamaica Institute of Technology) was founded in 1958, while Jamaica was under British colonial administration. In 1962 Jamaica achieved full independence within the Commonwealth, and in the same year the University of the West Indies (founded 1948), which has a campus on the island at Mona, was elevated to university status. In 2003/04 there were 11,600 students enrolled in higher education. The Tertiary Unit of the Ministry of Education and Youth is the Government agency responsible for higher education.

Admission to higher education is on the basis of two or more GCE A-levels. The Bachelors is the standard undergraduate degree and lasts three years, followed by the Masters, the first postgraduate degree. The University of the West Indies offers either a two-year, coursework-based Masters programme or a research-based Masters of Philology (MPhil). The highest university degree is the Doctorate, which lasts for two years after award of the Masters.

Technical and vocational education at the post-secondary level is supervised by the Human Employment and Resource Training Agency and National Council on Technical and Vocational Education and Training. The Human Employment and Resource Training Agency runs several academies and vocational training centres and the National Council on Technical and Vocational Education and Training is the official body responsible for awarding the National Vocational Qualification of Jamaica (Levels 1–4). A three-year Associate of Science degree is offered by the College of Agriculture, Science and Education.

The University Council of Council is responsible for quality assurance and accreditation of higher education institutions.

Learned Societies

GENERAL

Institute of Jamaica: 12–16 East St, Kingston; tel. 922-0620; fax 922-1147; e-mail ioj.jam@mail.infocham.com; internet www.instituteofjamaica.org.jm; f. 1879; comprises the National Library of Jamaica (see Libraries); two Junior Cultural Centres; Natural History Division; Arawak (Indian) Museum; Jamaica Folk Museum; Military Museum; Maritime Museum; the National Gallery of Jamaica; the African-Caribbean Institute/Jamaica Memory Bank; Institute of Jamaica Publications; Exec. Dir. Vivian Crawford (acting); publ. *Jamaica Journal*.

UNESCO Office Kingston: 3rd Fl., The Towers, 25 Dominica Drive, Kingston 5; tel. 929-7087; fax 929-8468; e-mail kingston@unesco.org; internet www.unescocaribbean.org; designated Cluster Office for Antigua and Barbuda, Bahamas, Barbados, Belize, Dominica, Grenada, Guyana, Jamaica, St Christopher and Nevis, St Lucia, St Vincent and the Grenadines, Suriname, Trinidad and Tobago; Dir Helene-Marie Gosselin.

AGRICULTURE, FISHERIES AND VETERINARY SCIENCE

Jamaican Association of Sugar Technologists: c/o Sugar Industry Research Institute, Kendal Rd, Mandeville; tel. 962-2241; fax 962-1288; f. 1937 by the local sugar industry to conduct research and investigate technical problems of the Jamaican sugar industry; 266 mems; uses library of Sugar Industry Research Institute; Pres. Michael G. Hylton; Sec. H. M. Thompson; publ. *JAST Journal* (annually).

ARCHITECTURE AND TOWN PLANNING

Jamaican Institute of Architects: 2A Caledonia Crescent, Kingston 5; POB 251, Kingston 10; tel. 926-8060; fax 920-3589; e-mail jia@cwjamaica.com; internet www.jia.org.jm; f. 1957; 87 mems (71 full, 16 associate); Pres. Louise McLeod; Hon. Sec. William Saunders; publ. *Jamaica Architect* (annually).

BIBLIOGRAPHY, LIBRARY SCIENCE AND MUSEOLOGY

Library and Information Association of Jamaica: POB 125, Kingston 5; tel. and fax 927-1614; e-mail liajapresident@yahoo.com; internet www.liaja.org.jm; f. 1949 as Jamaica Library Association; 215 mems; Pres. P. Kerr; Sec. F. Salmon; publs *JLA News* (2 a year), *LIAJA Annual Report*, *LIAJA Bulletin* (annually), *LIAJA News* (monthly), *LIAJA Newslink* (monthly).

HISTORY, GEOGRAPHY AND ARCHAEOLOGY

Jamaica National Heritage Trust: POB 8934, 79 Duke St, Kingston CSO; tel. 922-1287; fax 967-1703; e-mail jnht@wtjam.net; internet www.jnht.com; f. 1958; protection, preservation, restoration and promotion of Jamaica's material and cultural heritage, particularly through declaration of national monuments and designation of protected national heritage; Chair. Rev. Devon Dick; Exec. Dir Susanne Lyon.

LANGUAGE AND LITERATURE

Alliance Française: 12b, Lilford Ave (off Lady Musgrave Rd), Kingston 10; tel. 978-4622; fax 978-1836; e-mail alliance.francaisekingston@laposte.net; offers courses and exams in French language and culture and promotes cultural exchange with France.

British Council: The British High Commission, 28 Trafalgar Rd, Kingston 10; tel. 929-7090; fax 960-3030; e-mail bcjamaica@britishcouncil.org.jm; internet www.britishcouncil.org/caribbean; offers courses and exams in English language and British culture and promotes cultural exchange with the UK; Man. Nicola Johnson.

MEDICINE

Medical Association of Jamaica: 19A Windsor Ave, Kingston 5; tel. 946-1105; fax 946-1102; e-mail medassnjam@kasnet.com; internet www.medicalassnjamaica.com; f. 1877 as branch of British Medical Association; independent body 1966; for the promotion of medical and allied sciences and of the medical profession; 707 mems; Pres. Dr Alverston Bailey; Hon. Sec. Dr Ann Jackson-Gibson; publs *Journal* (annually), *Newsletter* (quarterly).

TECHNOLOGY

Jamaica Institution of Engineers: 2 Winchester Rd, Kingston 10; tel. 929-6741; fax 929-4655; e-mail jie@anngel.com.jm; internet www.jieng.org; f. 1960, present name 1977; to promote the advancement of the engineering profession and the practice and science of engineering, and to facilitate the exchange of information and ideas on those subjects among the mems and others; Pres. Howard Chin; Hon. Sec. Hermon Edmonson; publ. *JIE Advisor* (monthly).

Research Institutes

AGRICULTURE, FISHERIES AND VETERINARY SCIENCE

Sugar Industry Research Institute: Kendal Rd, Mandeville; tel. 962-2241; fax 962-1288; e-mail sirijam@jamaicasugar.org; internet www.jamaicasugar.org; f. 1973; research into sugar cane cultivation and environmental management; library of 660 vols, 2,500 bound vols of periodicals; Dir of Research Earle Roberts; publs *Annual Report*, *Newsletter* (quarterly).

ECONOMICS, LAW AND POLITICS

Planning Institute of Jamaica: Ministry of Finance and Planning, 10–16 Grenada Way, POB 634, Kingston 5; tel. 906-3636; fax 906-5032; e-mail doccen@mail.colis.com; internet www.pioj.gov.jm; f. 1955; for social and economic development projects, especially sustainable development; 118 mems; Dir-Gen. Dr Wesley Hughes; publs *Economic and Social Survey of Jamaica* (annually), *Economic Update and Outlook* (4 a year), *People Magazine* (4 a year), *The Labour Market Information Newsletter* (4 a year).

MEDICINE

Caribbean Food and Nutrition Institute (CFNI): Jamaica Centre, POB 140, Mona, Kingston 7; tel. 927-1540; fax 927-2657; e-mail e-mail@cfni.paho.org; internet www.cfni.paho.org; f. 1967; conducts research and training courses and provides technical advisory services to 18 govts of the English-speaking Caribbean on matters relating to food and nutrition; library of 4,500 vols; there is a centre in Trinidad; Dir Dr FITZROY HENRY; publs *Cajanus* (4 a year), *Nyam News* (2 a month), *Nutrient-Cost Tables* (4 a year).

Medical Research Council Laboratories: University of the West Indies, Mona, Kingston 7; tel. 927-2471; fax 927-2984; e-mail grserjnt@uwimona.edu.jm; f. 1974; attached to Medical Research Council, London; research into sickle-cell disease; 20 staff; Dir G. R. SERJEANT.

NATURAL SCIENCES

General

Scientific Research Council: POB 350, Kingston 6; tel. 927-1771; fax 927-1990; e-mail adminsrc@toj.com; internet www.src-jamaica.org; f. 1960; undertakes, fosters and co-ordinates scientific research in the island; library of 10,000 vols; Exec. Dir Dr AUDIA BARNETT; publs *Conference Proceedings* (annually), *Jamaican Journal of Science and Technology* (annually).

Libraries and Archives

Kingston

Jamaica Library Service: POB 58, 2 Tom Redcam Drive, Kingston 5; tel. 926-3310; fax 926-2188; e-mail jamlibs@cw-jamaica.com; internet www.jamlib.org.jm; f. 1948; provides an island-wide network of 656 service points, including 13 parish libraries, and 121 branch libraries; oversees 925 school and higher education libraries; total bookstock 2,711,000 vols, 70 periodicals; 1,121,000 vols in primary schools and 428,000 vols in secondary schools; Dir PATRICIA ROBERTS; publ. *Statistical Report of the Jamaica Library Service* (annually).

National Library of Jamaica: 12 East St, POB 823, Kingston; tel. 967-2494; fax 922-5567; e-mail nlj@infochan.com; internet www.nlj.org.jm; f. 1979; 47,000 printed items, 29,600 maps and plans, 4,400 serials, 27,100 photographs, 3,150 MSS, 2,550 items of audiovisual material on Jamaica and the West Indies; Exec. Dir WINSOME HUDSON; publs *Jamaica National Bibliography* (quarterly), *National Library News* (quarterly).

University of the West Indies Library: Mona, Kingston 7; tel. 512-3396; fax 927-1926; e-mail main.library@uwimona.edu.jm; internet www.mona.uwi.edu/library/; f. 1948; 518,981 vols including 6,349 current and 6,495 non-current periodicals in the Main Library and two branch libraries for the Medical (32,896 vols) and Scientific (97,634 vols) Collections; University and Campus Librarian NORMA Y. AMENU-KPODO; (see also Barbados, and Trinidad and Tobago).

Spanish Town

Jamaica Archives: cnr King and Manchester Sts, Spanish Town PO; tel. 984-2581; fax 984-8254; e-mail jarchives@jard.gov.jm; internet www.jard.gov.jm; f. 1659; national archives of Jamaica; special collection of ecclesiastical and private records of historical value; Government Archivist JOHN AARONS.

Museum

Kingston

Institute of Jamaica Museum: see Institute of Jamaica.

Universities

UNIVERSITY OF TECHNOLOGY, JAMAICA

237 Old Hope Rd, Kingston 6

Telephone: 927-1680

Fax: 927-4388

E-mail: regist@utech.edu.jm

Internet: www.utechjamaica.edu.jm

Founded 1958 as Jamaica Institute of Technology; became College of Arts, Science and Technology 1959; present name and status 1995

Academic year: September to May

Chancellor: Sir WILLIAM MORRIS

Pro-Chancellor: Dr BLOSSOM O'MEALLY-NELSON

President: Dr RAE DAVIS

Senior Vice-President (Academic Affairs): GEORGE ROPER

Senior Vice-President (Corporate Services): SANDRA GLASGOW

Senior Vice-President (Planning, Development and Technology): Dr NEVILLE SADDLER

Vice-President (Finance and Business Services): KOFI NKRUMAH-YOUNG

Vice-President (Student Services) and Registrar: DIANNE MITCHELL

Hon. Treasurer: VIVIAN CRAWFORD

University Librarian: HERMINE SALMON

University Orator: Dr VETA LEWIS

Number of teachers: 400

Number of students: 7,000

Serves Antigua and Barbuda, Anguilla, Barbados, Bahamas, Belize, British Virgin Islands, Dominica, Grenada, Guyana, Jamaica, St Lucia, St Vincent, Trinidad and Tobago, and Turks and Caicos Islands

Publication: *Journal*

DEANS

Faculty of the Built Environment: AUDREY THOMAS (acting)

Faculty of Business and Management: GARTH KIDDOE

Faculty of Education and Liberal Studies: Dr GERALDENE HODELIN

Faculty of Engineering and Computing: Dr GOSSETT OLIVER

Faculty of Health and Applied Science: CARROL WHITE

UNIVERSITY OF THE WEST INDIES, MONA CAMPUS

Mona, Kingston 7

Telephone: 927-1661

Fax: 927-2765

E-mail: oadmin@uwimona.edu.jm

Internet: www.mona.uwi.edu

Founded 1948, University 1962

Serves 16 territories: Jamaica, Anguilla, Bahamas, Belize, British Virgin Islands, Cayman Islands; Barbados, Antigua and Barbuda, Dominica, Grenada, Montserrat, St Christopher and Nevis, St Lucia, Turks and Caicos, St Vincent and the Grenadines, Trinidad and Tobago. The faculties of humanities and education, medical sciences and social sciences are located on all three campuses. The faculty of law is in Barbados, agriculture and engineering in Trinidad, and the faculties of pure and applied sciences are in Barbados and Jamaica

Academic year: August to July

Chancellor: Sir GEORGE ALLEYNE

Vice-Chancellor: Prof. NIGEL HARRIS

Principal: Prof. KENNETH HALL

University Registrar: GLORIA BARRETT-SOBERS

Librarian: STEPHNEY FERGUSON

Number of teachers: 400

Number of students: 11,000

Publications: *Arts Review* (2 a year), *Caribbean Journal of Criminology and Social Psychology* (2 a year), *Caribbean Journal of Education*, *Caribbean Law Bulletin* (2 a year), *Caribbean Law Review* (2 a year), *Caribbean Quarterly*, *Journal of Tropical Agriculture* (4 a year), *Social Economics Studies* (4 a year), *West Indian Journal of Engineering* (2 a year), *West Indian Law Journal* (annually), *West Indian Medical Journal* (4 a year)

DEANS AT MONA

Faculty of Humanities and Education: Prof. AGGREY BROWN

Faculty of Medical Sciences: Prof. ARCHIBALD MCDONALD

Faculty of Pure and Applied Sciences: Prof. RONALD YOUNG

Faculty of Social Sciences: MARK FIGUEROA

PROFESSORS

AHMAD, M., Biotechnology
BAILEY, W., Geography and Geology
BAIN, B., Community Health and Psychiatry
BENNETT, F., Pathology
BORNHOP, D., Applied Chemistry
BRANDAY, J., Surgery, Radiology, Anaesthesia and Intensive Care
BROWN, A., Mass Communication
BURTON, E., Medicine
CAMPBELL, C., History
CHEN, A., Physics
CHEVANNES, B., Social Anthropology
CHRISTIE, C., Obstetrics, Gynaecology and Child Health
DASGUPTA, T., Inorganic Chemistry
DENBOW, C., Medicine
DEVONISH, H., Language, Linguistics and Philosophy
DONOVAN, S., Palaeozoology
DURRANT, F., Library and Information Studies
FLETCHER, P., Clinical Surgery
FORRESTER, T., Tropical Medicine
FREEMAN, B., Ecology
HANCHARD, B., Anatomical Pathology
HICKLING, F., Psychiatry
JACKSON, T., Igneous Petrology
JACOBS, H., Chemistry
JONES, E., Public Administration
LENNARD, J., English and American Literature
LEO-RHYNIE, E., Women and Development Studies
LEWIS, R., Political Thought
MILLER, E., Teacher Education
MORGAN, O., Medicine
MOORE, B., History
MORRIS, M., Creative Writing and West Indian Literature
MORRISON, E., Biochemistry
MUNROE, T., Government and Politics
NETTLEFORD, R. N., Continuing Studies
REICHGELT, J., Computer Science
REID, H., Clinical Haemorheology
ROBINSON, E., Geology
SHIRLEY, G., Management Studies
SPENCER, H., Cardiothoracic Surgery
THOMAS-HOPE, E., Environmental Development
UCHE, C., Sociology and Social Work
WALKER, S., Epidemiology
WARNER-LEWIS, M., African Caribbean Language and Orature
WILKS, R., Epidemiology
WINT, A., International Business
YOUNG, R., Physiology

ATTACHED INSTITUTES

Biotechnology Centre: Dir Prof. M. AHMAD.

Caribbean Institute of Media and Communication: Dir Drs M. DE BRUIN.

Centre for Gender and Development Studies: Dir Dr B. BAILEY.

Centre for Environment and Development: Dir Prof. A. BINGER.

Centre for Management Development: Dir Dr J. COMMA.

Centre for Marine Sciences: Dir Dr G. WARNER.

Chronic Disease Research Centre: Dir Prof. H. FRASER.

Institute of Caribbean Studies: Dir J. PEREIRA.

Institute of Education: Dir J. TUCKER.

International Centre for Environment and Nuclear Sciences: Dir Prof. G. C. LALOR.

Philip Sherlock Centre for Creative Arts: Mona, Kingston 7; f. 1967; term-to-term activity in painting, sculpture, dance, theatre, writing, exhibitions, readings, etc.; acting as the home for ICC Week activities; the mounting of a small Caribbean Arts Festival; Sec. CAROLYN ALLEN.

School of Business: Dir Prof. G. SHIRLEY.

School of Continuing Studies: Mona, Kingston 7; Dir Prof. L. CARRINGTON.

Sir Arthur Lewis Institute for Social and Economic Studies: Mona, Kingston 7; tel. (92) 72409; applied research relating to the Caribbean; Dirs Prof. N. DUNCAN (Mona Prof. A. DOWNES (Cave Hill Prof. S. RYAN (St. Augustine.

Trade Union Education Institute: Mona, Kingston 7; Dir of Studies Prof. L. CARRINGTON.

Tropical Medicine Research Institute: Mona, Kingston 7; Dir Prof. TERRENCE FORRESTER.

AFFILIATED INSTITUTIONS

Caribbean Institute for Meteorology and Hydrology: Dir Dr COLIN DEPRADINE.

Mico Teachers' College: Dir Dr CLAUDE PACKER.

St John Vianney and the Uganda Martyrs: Dir Rev. MICHAEL DE VERTEUIL.

St Michael's Seminary: Mona, Kingston 7; awards degrees of the Univ. of the West Indies; Director Sr THERESA LOWE CHING.

United Theological College of the West Indies: Mona, Kingston 7; awards degrees and licentiates of the Univ. of the West Indies; Pres. Dr LEWIN WILLIAMS (acting).

College

College of Agriculture, Science and Education: POB 170, Passley Gardens, Port Antonio, Portland; tel. 993-3246; fax 993-2208; internet www.case.edu.jm; f. 1995 by merger of College of Agriculture and Passley Gardens Teachers College; two-year degree course in all aspects of agriculture; 47 faculty mems; 533 full-time students; 86 part-time; 24 evening; faculties of agriculture, education and science; community college and continuing education programmes; library: 35,000 vols, special collections: UN publs, West Indian works, Jamaica Govt publs; Pres. Dr PAUL IVEY (acting); Registrar PATRICIA WRIGHT-CLARKE.

JAPAN

The Higher Education System

Higher education in Japan consists of four categories of institution: universities (daigaku), junior colleges (tanki-daigaku), vocational colleges and technology colleges (koto-senmongakko) and professional graduate schools (the latter since 2003). Institutions are either publicly or privately administered. In 2004 there were 709 universities and graduate schools, with 2.8m. students, and 571 junior and technical colleges, with 292,452 students. Universities offer the full range of undergraduate and postgraduate degrees, and since incorporation in 2004 have become autonomous from the Ministry of Education, Culture, Sports, Science and Technology with regard to decisions about finance, staffing and self-assessment. Junior colleges specialize in two- or three-year Associate Degrees (Jun-Gakushi), credits from which may be accepted towards completion of the university Bachelors degrees. Technology colleges offer five-year training programmes in specialist fields of engineering and technology and professional graduate schools, first established in 2003, offer two-year programmes of study aimed at bridging the gap between formal education and professional experience. The Ministry of Education, Culture, Sports, Science and Technology is responsible for education at all levels, sets the centrally compiled curriculum guidelines and authorizes textbooks.

Admission to university is a three-stage process, based on completion of secondary education, results in the Unified First Stage Examination, administered by the National Centre for University Entrance, and each institution's entrance examination. Applicants can only take an institution's entrance examination depending upon their results in the Unified First Stage Examination. The Bachelors (Gakushi) is the undergraduate degree, and is awarded on a 'credit' system following four (or up to six, for some subjects) years of study. Students must accrue at least 124 credits in 'major' and 'minor' subjects. The two-year Associate Degree offered by junior colleges requires a minimum of 62 credits and the three-year Associate Degree 93 credits. The first postgraduate degree is the Masters (Shushui), and is only available at university postgraduate schools (daigaku-in). The Masters is mainly a research-based degree, lasting two years and requiring 30 credits. The Doctorate (Hakushi) is the second postgraduate degree and highest university-level qualification. It is an entirely research-based programme of study, culminating with submission of a thesis.

Technical and vocational education qualifications include the Special Training School Advanced Course Certificate (Senshu gakko Senmon-ka shuryo shosho), Special Training School Upper Secondary Certificate (Senshu gakko koto-ka sotsugyuo menjo), Technical Associate Degree or Diploma from a Special Training College (Senmonshi) and Vocational Training Certificate or Diploma (awarded by Vocational Training College of the Ministry of Labour).

Regulatory and Representative Bodies

GOVERNMENT

Ministry of Education, Culture, Sports, Science and Technology: 3-2-2, Kasumigaseki, Chiyoda-ku, Tokyo 100-8959; tel. (3) 5253-4111; fax (3) 3595-2017; internet www.mext.go.jp; Minister BUNMEI IBUKI.

ACCREDITATION

Daigaku Kijun Kyokai (Japan University Accreditation Association): 2-7-13, Ichigaya Sadohara-cho, Sinjuku-ku, Tokyo 162-0842; tel. (3) 5228-2020; fax (3) 5228-2323; internet www.juaa.or.jp; f. 1947; promotes the qualitative improvement of univs in Japan through the voluntary efforts and mutual assistance of mem. univs; Pres. TOYOOMI NAGATA.

NATIONAL BODIES

Chuo Kyoiku Shingikai (Central Council for Education): Min. of Education, Culture, Sports, Science and Technology, 3-2-2, Kasumigaseki, Chiyoda-ku, Tokyo 100-8959; tel. (3) 5253-4111; internet www.mext.go.jp; f. 1952; advises the Minister; carries out research and considers issues relating to the promotion of education, lifelong learning and sports; has 5 working groups concerned with: education systems, lifelong learning, elementary and lower secondary education, univs, and sports and youth; Chair. MASAKAZU YAMAZAKI.

Kokuritsu Daigaku Kyokai (Japan Association of National Universities): 4F, Nat. Centre of Sciences Bldg, 1-2, Hitotsubashi 2-chome, Chiyoda-ku, Tokyo 101-0003; tel. (3) 4212-3506; fax (3) 4212-3509; e-mail info@janu.jp; internet www.janu.jp; Pres. MASUO AIZAWA.

Koritsu Daigaku Kyokai (Japan Association of Municipal and Prefectural Colleges and Universities): Toranomon-Yoshiara Bldg, 9th Floor, 1-6-13 Nishi-Shimbashi, Minato-ku, Tokyo 105-0003; tel. (3) 3501-3336; fax (3) 3501-3337; e-mail jimu@kodaikyo.jp; internet www.kodaikyo.jp; f. 1949; 74 mems; Pres. TAKAO KODAMA.

Nihon Shiritsu Daigak Kyokai (Association of Private Universities of Japan): 4-2-25 Kudan-kita, Chiyoda-ku, Tokyo 102; tel. (3) 3261-7048; fax (3) 3261-0769; f. 1946; 266 mem. univs; Pres. Dr SHIGEYOSHI KITTAKA; Sec. Gen. Dr YUKIYASU HARANO; publ. *Kyoikugakujutsu*.

Learned Societies

GENERAL

Nihon Gakujutsu Kaigi (Science Council of Japan): 22–34 Roppongi 7-chome, Minato-ku, Tokyo 106; tel. (3) 3403-6291; fax (3) 3403-6224; f. 1949; governmental org. co-ordinating Japan's scientific research; divisions of Literature, Philosophy, Pedagogy, Psychology, Sociology and History (Chair. YASUNAO NAKADA), Law and Political Science (Chair. KAZUHISA NAKAYAMA), Economics, Commerce and Business Administration (Chair. TOSHINOSUKE KASHIWAZAKI), Pure Science (Chair. MUNEYUKI DATE), Engineering (Chair. MORIYA UCHIDA), Agriculture (Chair. TEITARO KITAMURA), Medicine, Dentistry and Pharmacology (Chair. KAZUHIKO ATSUMI); 210 mems; library: see Libraries and Archives; Pres. MASAO ITO; Sec.-Gen. YASUHIKO NAGASHIMA.

Nihon Gakujutsu Shinko-kai (Japan Society for the Promotion of Science): 6 Ichibadncho, Chiyoda-ku, Tokyo 102-8471; tel. (3) 3263-1722; fax (3) 3221-2470; internet www.jsps.go.jp; f. 1932; independent admin. institution and funding agency; administers grants-in-aid for scientific research, research fellowships for young scientists, univ./industry co-operation, scientific outreach, etc.; has co-operative agreements with 82 overseas orgs; operates JSPS overseas offices in 10 cities; 99 mems; Pres. MOTOYUKI ONO; publs *Japanese Scientific Monthly*, *JSPS Quarterly*.

Nippon Gakushiin (Japan Academy): 7-32 Ueno Park, Taito-ku, Tokyo 110-0007; tel. (3) 3822-2101; fax (3) 3822-2105; e-mail international@japan-acad.go.jp; internet www.japan-acad.go.jp; f. 1879; 150 mems; Pres. Prof. SABURO NAGAKURA; Sec.-Gen. Prof. MASAMI ITO; Section Chair. (Humanities and Social Sciences) Prof. MASAAKI KUBO; Section Chair. (Pure and Applied Sciences) Prof. TAKASHI SUGIMURA; publs *Proceedings* (2 series, 10 a year), *Nippon Gakushiin Kiyo* (3 a year).

AGRICULTURE, FISHERIES AND VETERINARY SCIENCE

Danchi-Nogaku Kenkyu-Kai (Southern Agricultural Society): Miyazaki University, Faculty of Agriculture, Gakuen Kibanadai Nishi, 1-1, Miyazaki 889-21; f. 1947; 200 mems; Pres. TAIJI ADACHI; publ. *Danchi-Nogaku*.

Engei Gakkai (Japanese Society for Horticultural Science): Business Center for Academic Societies Japan, 16–9 Honkomagome 5-chome, Bunkyo-ku, Tokyo 113; tel. (3) 5814-5801; fax (3) 5814-5820; f. 1923; 2,795 mems; Pres. ICHIRO KAJIURA; Sec. TADASHI BABA; publ. *Journal* (6 a year).

Gyogyo Keizai Gakkai (Fisheries Economic Society): Tokyo-Suisan University, 4-5-7 Kohnan, Minato-ku, Tokyo 108; f. 1953; 220 mems; Pres. RYUZO TAKAYAMA; publ. *Journal* (quarterly).

Nihon Ikushu Gakkai (Japanese Society of Breeding): c/o Faculty of Agriculture, University of Tokyo, Bunkyo-ku, Tokyo 113-8657; tel. (3) 5841-5065; fax (3) 5841-5063; e-mail kishima@abs.agr.hokudai.ac.jp; internet www.nacos.com/jsb/e; f. 1951; 2,300 mems; Pres. ATSUCHI HIRAI; publs *Breeding Science* (4 a year), *Ikushugaku Kenkyu* (4 a year).

Nihon Ju-í Gakkai (Japanese Society of Veterinary Science): Tokyo RS Bldg 8th Fl., 6-26-12 Hongo, Bunkyo-ku, Tokyo 113-0033; tel. (3) 5803-7761; fax (3) 5803-7762; e-mail office@jsvs.or.jp; internet wwwsoc.nii.ac.jp/jsvs; f. 1885; 4,100 mems; Pres. KUNIO DOI; publ. *The Journal of Veterinary Medical Science* (monthly).

Nihon Oyo Toshitsu Kagaku Kai (Japanese Society of Applied Glycoscience): c/o National Food Research Institute, 2-1-2 Kannondai, Tsukuba, Ibaraki 305; tel. (298) 38-7991; fax (298) 38-8005; f. 1952; 1,147 mems; Pres. KEIJI KAINUMA; Sec. TAKAFUMI KASUMI; publ. *Oyo Toshitsu Kagaku* (Journal of Applied Glycoscience, 4 a year).

Nihon Sanshi Gakkai (Japanese Society of Sericultural Science): c/o National Institute of Agrobiological Sciences Tsukuba, Ibaraki 305-8634; tel. (29) 838-6056; fax (29) 838-6056; e-mail jsss@silk.or.jp; internet jsss.ac.affrc.go.jp; f. 1930; 800 mems; Pres. MASAHIKO KOBAYASHI; publs *Journal of Sericultural Science of Japan* (3 a year), *Journal of Insect Biotechnology and Sericology* (3 a year).

Nihon Seibutsu-Kogaku Kai (Society for Biotechnology, Japan): c/o Faculty of Engineering, Osaka Univ., 2-1 Yamadaoka, Suita, Osaka 565-0871; tel. (6) 6876-2731; fax (6) 6879-2034; e-mail sbbj@bio.eng.osaka-u.ac.jp; internet wwwsoc.nii.ac.jp/sfbj; f. 1923; provides training and development opportunities for students and young researchers; 4,500 mems; Pres. Prof. YASUO IGARASHI; publs *Journal of Bioscience and Bioengineering* (monthly, in English), *Seibutsu-kogaku Kaishi* (monthly, in Japanese).

Nihon Shinringakkai (Japanese Forestry Society): c/o Japan Forest Technical Association, Rokubancho 7, Chiyoda-ku, Tokyo; tel. and fax (3) 3261-2766; f. 1914; forestry research; 2,900 mems; Pres. KAZUMI KOBAYASHI; publs *Journal* (every two months), *Shinrin Kagaku* (bulletin, 3 a year).

Nippon Chikusan Gakkai (Japanese Society of Animal Science): 201 Nagatani Corporas, Ikenohata 2-9-4, Taito-ku, Tokyo 110-0008; tel. (3) 3828-8409; fax (3) 3828-7649; e-mail tikusan@blue.ocn.ne.jp; internet wwwsoc.nii.ac.jp/jszs; f. 1924; animal science; 2,706 mems; Pres. HIDEO YANO; publs *Animal Science Journal* (6 a year), *Nihon Chikusan Gakkaihou* (4 a year).

Nippon Dojo-Hiryo Gakkai (Japanese Society of Soil Science and Plant Nutrition): 26-10-202 Hongo, 6 chome, Bunkyo-ku, Tokyo; tel. (3) 3815-2085; fax (3) 3815-6018; e-mail jssspm@wwwsoc.nii.ac.jp; f. 1914; 2,300 mems; Pres. TADAKATU YONEYAMA; publs *Journal* (every 2 months), *Soil Science and Plant Nutrition* (every 2 months).

Nippon Nogei Kagaku Kai (Japan Society for Bioscience, Biotechnology and Agrochemistry): 4–16 Yayoi 2-chome, Bunkyo-ku, Tokyo 113-0032; fax (3) 3815-1920; e-mail shomu-b@jsbba.or.jp; internet www.jsbba.or.jp; f. 1924; 13,751 mems; Pres. KENJI MORI; publs *Bioscience, Biotechnology and Biochemistry* (in English, monthly), *Nippon Nögeikagaku Kaishi* (in Japanese, monthly), *Kagaku To Seibutsu* (in Japanese, monthly).

Nippon Sakumotsu Gakkai (Crop Science Society of Japan): c/o Faculty of Agriculture, University of Tokyo, Hongo, Bunkyo-ku, Tokyo 113-8657; fax (22) 717-8637; e-mail y-goto@bios.tohoku.ac.jp; f. 1927; 1,500 mems; Pres. Dr SHIGEMI AKITA; Sec. YUSEKE GOTO; publs *Japanese Journal of Crop Science* (quarterly), *Plant Production Science* (quarterly).

Nippon Shokubutsu-Byori Gakkai (Phytopathological Society of Japan): Shokubo Bldg, Komagome 1-43-11, Toshima-ku, Tokyo 170; tel. (3) 3943-6021; fax (3) 3943-6021; f. 1916 to promote research on plant diseases; 1,880 regular mems; Pres. S. OUCHI; publ. *Annals* (6 a year).

Nippon Suisan Gakkai (Japanese Society of Fisheries Science): C/o Tokyo University of Fisheries, 4-5-7 Konan, Minato-ku, Tokyo 108-8477; tel. (3) 3471-2165; fax (3) 3471-2054; f. 1932; research in fishing science and technology, mariculture, aquaculture, marine environmental science and related fields; 4,879 mems; library of 69 vols; Pres. Prof. T. WATANABE; publs *Fisheries Science* (in English, 6 a year), *Nippon Suisan Gakkaishi* (6 a year).

Nogyokikai Gakkai (Japanese Society of Agricultural Machinery): C/o BRAIN, 1-40-2 Nisshin-cho, Saitama 331-8537; tel. (48) 652-4119; fax (48) 652-4119; e-mail jsam@iam.brain.go.jp; internet wwwsoc.nii.ac.jp/jsam; f. 1937; 1,500 mems; Pres. TOMOHIKO ICHIKAWA; publ. *Journal of the Japanese Society of Agricultural Machinery* (every 2 months).

ARCHITECTURE AND TOWN PLANNING

Kansai Zosen Kyokai (Kansai Society of Naval Architects): C/o Dept of Naval Architecture & O.E., Osaka University, 2-1 Yamada-oka, Suita, Osaka 565; tel. (6) 879-7593; fax (6) 878-5364; f. 1912; 2,400 mems; Pres. S. FURUTA; publs *Journal* (2 a year), *Bulletin* (quarterly).

Nihon Zoen Gakkai (Japanese Institute of Landscape Architecture): Zoen Kaikan 6th Fl., 1-20-11 Jinnan, Shibuya-ku, Tokyo 150-0041; tel. (3) 5459-0515; fax (3) 5459-0516; e-mail info@landscapearchitecture.or.jp; internet www.landscapearchitecture.or.jp; f. 1924; 1,800 mems; Pres. AKIRA HOMMA; publ. *Journal*.

Nihon Zosen Gakkai (Japan Society of Naval Architects and Ocean Engineers):e-mail info@jasnoe.or.jp; internet www.jasnoe.or.jp; f. 2005 by merger of Society of Naval Architects of Japan, Kansai Society of Naval Architects, Japan, and the West-Japan Society of Naval Architects; publ. *Kanrin*.

Nippon Toshi Keikaku Gakkai (City Planning Institute of Japan): Ichibancho-West Building 6F, Ichibancho 10, Chiyoda-ku, Tokyo 102; f. 1951; 5,322 mems; Pres. KAZUO YODA; publ. *City Planning Review* (every 2 months).

BIBLIOGRAPHY, LIBRARY SCIENCE AND MUSEOLOGY

Gakujutsu Bunken Fukyu-Kai (Association for Science Documents Information): c/o Tokyo Institute of Technology, 2-12-1 O-okayama, Meguro-ku, 152 Tokyo; f. 1933; Pres. SHU KANBARA; publs *Reports on Progress in Polymer Physics in Japan* (English, annually), *Proceedings*, etc.

Information Processing Society of Japan: Shibaura-Maekawa Bldg, 7F, 3-16-20, Shibaura, Minato-ku, Tokyo 108-0023; tel. (3) 5484-3535; fax (3) 5484-3534; e-mail somu@ipsj.or.jp; f. 1960; 30,000 mems; Pres. Dr IWAO TODA; publs *Joho Shori* (monthly), *Transactions* (monthly).

Joho Kagaku Gijutsu Kyokai (Information Science and Technology Association): Sasaki Bldg, 5–7 Koisikawa 2, Bunkyo-ku, Tokyo; f. 1950; 2,020 mems; Pres. T. GONDOH; publ. *Journal* (monthly).

Kagaku-Gijutsu Shinko Kiko (JST) (Japan Science and Technology Agency): 5-3 Yonban-cho, Chiyoda-ku, Tokyo 102-0081; tel. (3) 5214-8401; fax (3) 5214-8400; e-mail www-admin@tokyo.jst.go.jp; internet www.jst.go.jp; f. 1957; preparation of abstracts, on-line and manual search services, translation and photo-duplication service, library service, computer processing; 470 mems; Pres. K. OKIMURA; publs *Current Bibliography on Science and Technology* (Abstracts from about 16,200 journals, 12 series), *Journal of Information Processing and Management*, *JST Thesaurus*, *Current Science and Technology Research in Japan* (in English and Japanese), *JST Holding List of Serials and Proceedings*.

Nihon Hakubutsukan Kyokai (Japanese Association of Museums): Shoyu-Kaikan 3-3-1, Kasumigaseki, Chiyoda-ku, Tokyo 100-8925; tel. (3) 3591-7190; fax (3) 3591-7170; e-mail webmaster@j-muse.or.jp; internet www.j-muse.or.jp; f. 1928; Gen. Man. YOKO NIIZUMA; 1,330 mems; publ. *Museum Studies* (monthly).

Nihon Toshokan Kyokai (Japan Library Association): 1-11-14, Shinkawa, Chuo-ku, Tokyo 104-0033; tel. (3) 3523-0811; fax (3) 3523-0841; e-mail info@jla.or.jp; internet www.jla.or.jp; f. 1892; all aspects of library development; 8,900 mems; library of 10,000 vols; Sec.-Gen. KATSURA YOKOYAMA; publs *Toshokan Zasshi* (monthly), *Gendai no Toshokan* (quarterly), *Nihon no Sankotosho Shikiban* (quarterly), *Nihon no Toshokan* (annually), *Toshokan Nenkan* (annually).

Nippon Toshokan Joho Gakkai (Japan Society of Library and Information Science): c/o Graduate School of Library and Information Science, Univ. of Tsukuba, 1–2 Kasuga, Tsukuba-shi, Ibaraki-ken 305-8550; fax (29) 859-1380; e-mail jslis-info@slis.tsukuba.ac.jp; internet wwwsoc.nii.ac.jp/jslis; f. 1953; 750 mems; Pres. SHUICHI UEDA; Sec. YUKO YOSHIDA; publ. *Journal* (quarterly).

ECONOMICS, LAW AND POLITICS

Ajia Seikei Gakkai (Japan Association for Asian Political and Economic Studies): c/o Prof. S. AMAKO, School of International Politics, Economics and Business, Aoyama Gakuin University, 4-4-25 Shibuya, Shibuya-ku, Tokyo 150; f. 1953; 900 mems; Pres. T. WATANABE; publ. *Aziya Kenkyu* (Asian Studies, quarterly).

Hikaku-ho Gakkai (Japan Society of Comparative Law): c/o Faculty of Law, Tokyo University, Hongo, Bunkyo-ku, Tokyo 113; f. 1950; studies in comparative law; holds conferences; issues publications; 780 mems; Pres. H. TANAKA; publ. *Hikakuhô Kenkyû* (Comparative Law Journal, annually).

Hogaku Kyokai (Jurisprudence Association): Faculty of Law, University of Tokyo, Hongo, Bunkyo-ku, Tokyo; tel. (3) 3812-2111; f. 1884; 600 mems; Pres. TAKESHI SASAKI; publs *Hogaku Kyokai Zasshi*, *Journal*.

Hosei-shi Gakkai (Japan Legal History Association): Tohoku University, Kawauchi, Aoba-ku, Sendai 980-8576; tel. (22) 217-6237; fax (22) 217-6249; f. 1949; 495 mems; Pres. S. KOYAMA; publ. *Legal History Review* (annually).

Hosokai (Lawyers' Association): 1, 1-chome, Kasumigaseki, Chiyoda-ku, Tokyo; f. 1891;

20,000 mems; library of 30,000 vols; Pres. RYOHACHI KUSABA; Dir ISAO IMAI; publ. *Hoso Jiho*.

Keizai-ho Gakkai (Association of Economic Jurisprudence): Hitotsubashi University, Kunitachi, Tokyo 186; f. 1951; 280 mems; publ. *Journal* (annually).

Keizai Riron Gakkai (Japan Society of Political Economy): Faculty of Economics, Rikkyo University, 3 Ikebukuro, Toshima-ku, Tokyo; f. 1959; 865 mems; Pres. H. OOUCHI.

Keizaigaku-shi Gakkai (Japan Society for the History of Economic Thought): Dept of Economics, Tohoku University, Kawauchi, Sendai; tel. (22) 217-6275; fax (22) 217-6231; e-mail mawatari@econ.tohoku.ac.jp; internet society.cpm.ehime-u.ac.jp/shet/shet.html; f. 1949; 810 mems; Pres. SHOHKEN MAWATARI; publs *Annual Bulletin, History of Economic Thought, Society Newsletter*.

Kinyu Gakkai (Financial Science Association): c/o Toyo Keizai, Motoishi 1–4 Nihonbashi, Chuo-ku, Tokyo; f. 1943; 459 mems; Pres. T. TAKAGAKU; publ. *Report* (2 a year).

Kokusaiho Gakkai (Association of International Law): Faculty of Law, University of Tokyo, Hongo, Bunkyo-ku, Tokyo; tel. (3) 3812-2111; f. 1897; 804 mems; Pres. SHIGERU KOZAI; publs *Kokusaiho Gaiko Zasshi, Journal of International Law and Diplomacy*.

Nichibei Hougakukai (Japanese American Society for Legal Studies): c/o Faculty of Law, Univ. of Tokyo, Hongo, Bunkyo-ku, Tokyo 113-0033; f. 1964; to seek and develop mutual understanding of Japanese and American law and legal scholarship, especially through co-operation of members of the legal profession; 900 mems; Dir I. TAKAHASHI; publ. *Amerika Hō* (Law in the USA, 2 a year).

Nihon Keizai Gakkai (Japanese Economics Association): c/o The Institute of Statistical Research, 1-18-16 Shimbashi, Minato-ku, Tokyo 105-0004; tel. (3) 3591-8496; fax (3) 3595-2220; f. 1934; 2,598 mems; Pres. KAZUO NISHIMURA; publ. *Japanese Economic Review* (4 a year).

Nihon Koho Gakkai (Japan Public Law Association): University of Tokyo, Hongo, Bunkyo-ku, Tokyo; f. 1948; 1,200 mems; Pres. K. SATO; publ. *Koho-Kenkyu* (Public Law Review, annually).

Nihon Minji Soshoho Gakkai (Japan Association of Civil Procedure Law): c/o Faculty of Law, Osaka City University, 3-3-138 Sugimoto, Sumiyoshi-ku, Osaka; tel. (6) 6605-2327; fax (6) 6605-2920; f. 1949; 815 mems; Pres. H. MATSUMOTO; publ. *Journal of Civil Procedure* (annually).

Nihon Tokei Gakkai (Japan Statistical Society): c/o The Institute of Statistical Mathematics, 4-6-7 Minami-azabu, Minato-ku, Tokyo 106; f. 1931; 1,312 mems; Pres. KIYOSHI TAKEUSHI; publ. *Journal* (2 a year).

Nihon Zaisei Gakkai (Japanese Association of Fiscal Science): Hitotsubashi University, Kunitachi, Tokyo 186; f. 1940; 195 mems.

Nippon Gyosei Gakkai (Japanese Society for Public Administration): Meiji University, Kanda-surugadai 1-1, Chiyoda-ku, Tokyo; f. 1945; 400 mems; Pres. A. SATO; publ. *Nenpo* (Annals, annually).

Nippon Hoshakai Gakkai (Japan Association of Sociology of Law): University of Tokyo, Hongo, Bunkyo-ku, Tokyo; f. 1947; 805 mems; Pres. N. TOSHITANI; publ. *Sociology of Law* (annually).

Nippon Hotetsu-Gakkai (Japan Association of Legal Philosophy): Faculty of Law, Kyoto University, Yoshida Honmachi, Sakyo-ku, Kyoto 606-01; tel. (75) 753-3204; fax (75) 753-3290; f. 1948; 486 mems; Pres. Prof. SHIGEAKI TANAKA; publ. *The Annals of Legal Philosophy*.

Nippon Keiei Gakkai (Japan Society of Business Administration): Hitotsubashi Univ., 2-1 Naka, Kunitachi, Tokyo 186-8601; tel. (42) 580-8571; internet wwwsoc.nii.ac.jp/jsba; f. 1926; 2,127 mems; Pres. S. KOBAYASHI; publs *Annual Review of Business Administration, Journal of Business Management*.

Nippon Keiho Gakkai (Criminal Law Society of Japan): University of Tokyo, Hongo, Bunkyo-ku, Tokyo; f. 1949; 1,000 mems; Pres. K. SHIBAHARA; publ. *Journal* (quarterly).

Nippon Keizai Seisaku Gakkai (Japan Economic Policy Association): Keio University, Mita, Minato-ku, Tokyo; f. 1940; 862 mems; Pres. T. YAMANAKA; publ. *Annals*.

Nippon Kokusai Seiji Gakkai (Japan Association of International Relations): Hosei University, Fujimi-cho, Chiyoda-ku, Tokyo; f. 1956; 512 mems; Pres. H. KAMIKAWA; publ. *International Relations* (quarterly).

Nippon Rodo-ho Gakkai (Japanese Labour Law Association): University of Tokyo, 7-3-1 Hongo, Bunkyo-ku 113, Tokyo; tel. (3) 3812-2111, extn 3243; fax (3) 3816-7375; f. 1950; 595 mems; Pres. Y. YAMAMOTO; publ. *Journal* (2 a year).

Nippon Seizi Gakkai (Japanese Political Science Association): Faculty of Law, Rikkyo University, 3-34-1, Nishi-Ikebukuro, Toshima-ku, Tokyo 171; 820 mems; Pres. JIRO KAMISHIMA.

Nippon Shiho Gakkai (Japan Association of Private Law): C/o Tokyo Daigako Hogakubu Kenkyushitsu, 7-3-1 Hongo, Bunkyo-ku, Tokyo 113-0033; tel. (3) 5841-3131; fax (3) 5841-3174; f. 1948; 688 mems; Pres. T. SUZUKI; publ. *Journal* (annually).

Nippon Shogyo Gakkai (Japan Society of Commercial Sciences): Meiji University, Surugadai Kanda, Chiyoda-ku, Tokyo; f. 1951; 429 mems; Pres. K. FUKUDA.

Tokyo Daigaku Keizai Gakkai (Society of Economics): Faculty of Economics, University of Tokyo, 7-3-1 Hongo, Bunkyo-ku, Tokyo 113-0033; e-mail journal@e.u-tokyo.ac.jp/fservice/ronshu/index.htm; f. 1922; 200 mems; Pres. NAOHIKO JINNO; publ. *Journal of Economics* (4 a year).

EDUCATION

Asia–Pacific Cultural Centre for UNESCO (ACCU): 6 Fukuromachi, Shinjuku-ku, Tokyo 162-8484; tel. (3) 3269-4435; fax (3) 3269-4510; e-mail general@accu.or.jp; internet www.accu.or.jp; f. 1971; children's books, music, literacy materials development, training programmes, adult learning materials, protection of cultural heritage, photo contest, personnel exchange programmes, and other regional cultural activities; library of 29,000 vols; Pres. KAZUO SUZUKI; Dir-Gen. KOJI NAKANISHI; publs *Activity Report* (annually), *ACCU News* (Japanese, 6 a year), *Asian/Pacific Book Development* (English, quarterly).

Kyoiku Tetsugakkai (Society of Educational Philosophy): Sophia University, Kioi-cho, Chiyoda-ku, Tokyo; f. 1957; 510 mems; Pres. T. OURA; publ. *Studies in the Philosophy of Education*.

Nihon Gakko-hoken Gakkai (Japanese Association of School Health): Dept of Health Education, Faculty of Education, University of Tokyo, Hongo 7-3-1, Bunkyo-ku, Tokyo 113; tel. (3) 3812-2111; f. 1954; 1,500 mems; Pres. ATSUHISA EGUCHI; publ. *Gakko-hoken Kenkyu* (Japanese Journal of School Health, monthly).

Nihon Hikaku Kyoiku Gakkai (Japan Comparative Education Society): c/o Dept of Education, Graduate School of Human Environment Studies, Kyushu University, 6-19-1, Hakozaki, Higashi-ku, Fukuoka City, Fukuoka Prefecture 812-8581; tel. and fax (92) 632-8426; f. 1965; 905 mems; Pres. K. MOCHIDA; Sec.-Gen. H. TAKEKUMA; publs *Comparative Education* (2 a year), *Newsletter* (2 a year).

Nihon Kyoiku Gakkai (Japan Society for the Study of Education): 2-29-3-3F Hongo, Bunkyo-ku, Tokyo 113-0033; tel. (3) 3818-2505; fax (3) 3816-6898; f. 1941; 3,200 mems; Pres. TERUHISA HORIO; publ. *The Japanese Journal of Educational Research* (quarterly).

Nihon Kyoiku-shakai Gakkai (Japan Society of Educational Sociology): Faculty of Education, University of Tokyo, Hongo 7-3-1, Bunkyo-ku, Tokyo 113; tel. (3) 5800-6813; fax (3) 5800-6814; e-mail jses2@wwwsoc.nii.ac.jp; internet wwwsoc.nii.ac.jp/jses2; f. 1949; 1,200 mems; Pres. HIDENORI FUJITA; publ. *Journal of Educational Sociology* (2 a year).

Nihon Kyoiku-shinri Gakkai (Japanese Association of Educational Psychology): Yaguchi Bldg, 5th Fl., Hongo 2-11-7, Bunkyo-ku, Tokyo 113-0033; tel. (3) 3818-1534; fax (3) 3818-1575; internet wwwsoc.nii.ac.jp/jaep; f. 1952; 7,300 mems; Pres. NOBORU SAKANO; publs *Annual Report of Educational Psychology in Japan, Japanese Journal of Educational Psychology* (quarterly).

Nippon Kagaku Kyoiku Gakkai (Japan Society for Science Education): c/o National Institute for Educational Policy Research, 6-5-22 Shimomeguro, Meguro-ku, Tokyo 153-8681; e-mail jimukyoku@jsse.jp; internet www.jsse.jp; f. 1977; science and mathematics education and educational technology; 1,200 mems; Pres. M. OGAWA; publs *Journal* (quarterly), *Letter* (every 2 months), *Proceedings of Annual Meeting*.

Nippon Sugaku Kyoiku Gakkai (Japan Society of Mathematical Education): POB 18, Koishikawa, Tokyo 112-8691; tel. (3) 3946-2267; fax (3) 3946-3736; e-mail jsme@mb.infoweb.ne.jp; internet www.sme.or.jp; f. 1919; 3,334 mems; Pres. Prof. T. SAWADA; publs *Journal* (monthly), *Supplementary issue* (report on mathematical education, 2 a year), *Yearbook* (annually).

Nippon Taiiku Gakkai (Japanese Society of Physical Education): Kishi Memorial Hall (Rm 508), Jinnan 1-1-1, Shibuya-ku, Tokyo 150; tel. (3) 3481-2427; fax (3) 3481-2428; f. 1950; 6,752 mems; Pres. Dr JUJIRO NARITA; publs *Research Journal* (quarterly), *Journal of Health and Physical Education* (monthly).

FINE AND PERFORMING ARTS

Bijutsu-shi Gakkai (Japanese Art History Society): c/o Tokyo National Research Institute of Cultural Properties, 13–27 Ueno Park, Taito-ku, Tokyo 110; f. 1949; 665 mems; publ. *Journal* (quarterly).

Nihon Engeki Gakkai (Japanese Society for Theatre Research): Waseda University, 1-6-1 Nishi-Waseda, Shinjuku-ku, Tokyo; f. 1949; Pres. T. MORI; publ. *Kiyō* (News Bulletin, annually).

Nippon Ongaku Gakkai (Musicological Society of Japan): 3-3-3-201 Iidabashi, Chiyoda-ku, 102-0072 Tokyo; tel. (3) 3288-5616; f. 1952; 1,350 mems; Pres. T. ISOYAMA; publ. *Ongaku Gaku* (Journal, 3 a year).

HISTORY, GEOGRAPHY AND ARCHAEOLOGY

Keizai Chiri Gakkai (Japan Association of Economic Geographers): Institute of Economic Geography, Faculty of Economics, East Bldg, Hitotsubashi University, Naka 2-1, Kunitachi-shi, Tokyo 186; tel. (425) 72-1101, ext 5374; fax (425) 71-1893; f. 1954; 700 mems; Pres. K. TAKEUCHI; publ. *Annals* (quarterly).

Kokushi-Gakkai (Society of Japanese Historical Research): Kokugakuin University, 10–28, Higashi 4-chome, Shibuya-ku, Tokyo; f. 1910; Sec. H. ROMIE TSUBAKI; publ. *Kokushigaku* (Journal of Japanese History).

Nihon Kokogakkai (Archaeological Society of Japan): C/o Tokyo National Museum, Ueno Park, Taito-ku, Tokyo; f. 1895; 2,200 mems; Pres. Dr FUJITA KUNIO; publ. *Kokogaku Zasshi* (4 a year).

Nippon Chiri Gakkai (Association of Japanese Geographers): C/o Building of Japan Academic Societies Center, Yayoi 2-4-16 Bunkyo-ku, Tokyo 113-0032; tel. (3) 3815-1912; fax (3) 3815-1672; e-mail ajgeography@ma4.justnet.ne.jp; internet wwwsoc.nii.ac.jp/ajg; f. 1925; 3,200 mems; Pres. S. YAMAMOTO; publs *Chirigaku Hyoron* (Geographical Review of Japan, monthly, in Japanese), *Geographical Review of Japan, English Edition* (2 a year).

Nippon Kokogaku Kyokai (Japanese Archaeological Association): 5-15-5, Hirai, Edogawa-ku, Tokyo 132-0035; tel. (3) 3618-6608; fax (3) 3618-6625; internet www.soc.nii.ac.jp/jaa2; f. 1948; 4,072 mems; library of 37,790 vols; Pres. TADASHI NISHTANI; publ. *Nihon Kōkogaku* (journal).

Nippon Oriento Gakkai (Society for Near Eastern Studies in Japan): Tokyo-Tenrikyokan 9, 1-chome 9, Kanda Nishiki-cho, Chiyoda-ku, Tokyo 101-0054; tel. (3) 3291-7519; fax (3) 3291-7519; f. 1954; 800 mems; Pres. KOJI KAMIOKA; publs *Oriento* (2 a year in Japanese), *Orient* (annually in European languages).

Nippon Seibutsuchiri Gakkai (Biogeographical Society of Japan): C/o Prof. Dr S. Sakai, 2-26-12 Sendagi, Bunkyo-ku, Tokyo 113; tel. (3) 3828-0445; fax (3) 3828-0445; e-mail QYV04336@nifty.ne.jp; internet wwwsoc.nii.ac.jp/tbsj; f. 1928; 300 mems; Pres. Prof. Dr SEIROKU SAKAI; publs *Bulletin*, *Biogeographica*, *Fauna Japonica*.

Nippon Seiyoshigakukai (Japanese Society of Western History): Dept of Western History, Graduate School of Letters, Osaka Univ., 1–5 Machikaneyama-cho, Toyonaka, Osaka 560-8532; tel. (6) 6850-5105; fax (6) 6850-5105; e-mail seiyousihgaku@mti.biglobe.ne.jp; f. 1948; 880 mems; Pres. Prof. A. EGAWA; publ. *Studies in Western History* (quarterly).

Shigaku-kai (Historical Society of Japan): University of Tokyo, Hongo, Bunkyo-ku, Tokyo 113; f. 1889; *c*. 2,470 mems; Pres. OSAMU NARUSE; publ. *Shigaku-Zasshi* (Historical Journal of Japan).

Tokyo Chigaku Kyokai (Tokyo Geographical Society): 12-2 Nibancho, Chiyoda-ku, Tokyo 102; f. 1879; 810 mems; Pres. ISAMU KOBAYASHI; publ. *Journal of Geography* (6 a year, and one special issue annually).

Toyoshi-Kenkyu-Kai (Society of Oriental Researches): Kyoto University, Sakyo-ku, Kyoto City; tel. (75) 753-2790; f. 1935; 1,400 mems; Pres. I. MIYAZAKI; publ. *Toyoshi-Kenkyu* (Journal of Oriental Researches, quarterly).

LANGUAGE AND LITERATURE

Alliance Française: Imamura Bldg, 9th Fl., 2-2-11 Tenjinbashi, Kita-Ku, Osaka 530-0041; tel. (6) 358-7391; fax (6) 358-7393; e-mail info@calosa.com; internet www.calosa.com; offers courses and exams in French language and culture and promotes cultural exchange with France; attached teaching centres in Nagoya, Sapporo, Sendai and Tokushima; Dir ERIC GALMARD.

British Council: 1–2 Kagurazaka, Shinjuku-ku, Tokyo 162-0825; tel. (3) 3235-8031; fax (3) 3235-8040; e-mail enquiries@britishcouncil.or.jp; internet www.britishcouncil.org/japan; teaching centre; offers courses and exams in English language and British culture and promotes cultural exchange with the UK; attached teaching centres in Kyoto, Nagoya and Osaka; Dir, Japan ALAN CURRY.

Goethe-Institut: Doitsu Bunka Kaikan, 7-5-56 Akasaka, Minato-ku, Tokyo 107-0052; tel. (3) 3584-3201; fax (3) 3586-3069; e-mail info@tokyo.goethe.org; internet www.goethe.de/os/tok/deindex.htm; offers courses and exams in German language and culture and promotes cultural exchange with Germany; attached centres in Kansai, Kyoto and Osaka; library of 20,000 vols, 50 periodicals; Dir and Regional Dir, East Asia DR UWE NITSCHKE.

Japanese Centre of International PEN: 20-3 Kabuto-cho, Nihonbashi, Chuo-ku, Tokyo 103-0026; e-mail secretariat01@japanpen.or.jp; internet www.japanpen.or.jp; f. 1935; Pres. KAZUNARI YOSHIZAWA.

Kokugogakkai (Society for the Study of Japanese Language): Faculty of Letters, University of Tokyo, Hongo, Bunkyo-ku, Tokyo 113; f. 1944; 1,500 mems; Pres. ETSUTARO IWABUCHI; publ. *Studies in the Japanese Language* (quarterly).

Manyo Gakkai (Society for Manyo Studies): Kansai University, Senriyama Suita-shi, Osaka; f. 1951; 810 mems; publ. *The Manyo* (quarterly).

Nihon Dokubungakkai (Japanese Society of German Literature): C/o Ikubundo, Hongo 5-30-21, Bunkyo-ku, Tokyo 113-0033; tel. (3) 3813-5861; fax (3) 3813-5861; e-mail jgg@tokyo.email.ne.jp; internet wwwsoc.nii.ac.jp/jgg; f. 1947; 2,600 mems; Pres. Prof. TERUAKI TAKAHASHI; publs *Doitsu Bungaku / German Literature* (2 a year), *Doitsugo Kyoiku / Deutschunterricht in Japan* (annually).

Nihon Eibungakkai (English Literary Society of Japan): 501 Kenkyusha Bldg, 9 Surugadai 2-chome, Kanda, Chiyoda-ku, Tokyo 101; tel. (3) 3293-7528; fax (3) 3293-7539; f. 1928; 4,000 mems; Pres. YOSHIYUKI FUJIKAWA; publ. *Studies in English Literature* (3 a year).

Nihon Esperanto Gakkai (Japan Esperanto Institute): Waseda-mati 12-3, Sinzyuku-ku, Tokyo 162; tel. (3) 3203-4581; fax (3) 3203-4582; e-mail chb71944@biglobe.ne.jp; f. 1919; 1,435 mems; linguistics; Pres. YAMASAKI SEIKÔ; Sec. ISINO YOSIO; publ. *La Revuo Orienta* (monthly).

Nihon Gengogakkai (Linguistic Society of Japan): Shimotachiuri Ogawa Higashi, Kami Kyoku, Kyoto 602-8048; tel. (75) 415-3661; fax (75) 415-3662; e-mail lsj@nacos.com; internet www.tooyoo.l.u-tokyo.ac.jp/~lsj/jap; f. 1938; 2,050 mems; publ. *Gengo Kenkyu* (Journal, 2 a year).

Nihon Mass Communication Gakkai (Japanese Society for Studies in Journalism and Mass Communication): C/o Institute of Socio-Information and Communication Studies, University of Tokyo, 7-3-1 Hongo, Bunkyo-ku, Tokyo 113-0033; tel. (3) 3812-2111, ext. 5921; f. 1951; 1,300 mems; Pres. I. TAKEUCHI; publ. *Journal of Mass Communication Studies* (2 a year).

Nippon Bungaku Kyokai (Japanese Literature Association): 2-17-10 Minami-otsuka, Toshima-ku, Tokyo; tel. (3) 3941-2740; fax (3) 3941-2740; f. 1946; 1,500 mems; library of 2,000 vols; Pres. KUNIAKI MITANI; publ. *Japanese Literature* (monthly).

Nippon Hikaku Bungakukai (Comparative Literature Society of Japan): Aoyamagakuin University, Shibuya-ku, Tokyo; f. 1948; 400 mems; Pres. K. NAKAJIMA; Gen. Sec. SABURO OTA; publs *Journal* (annually), *Bulletin* (quarterly).

Nippon Onsei Gakkai (Phonetic Society of Japan): Business Centre for Academic Studies, 5-16 Honkomagome, Bunkyo-ku, Tokyo 113-8622; tel. (3) 5814-5825; fax (3) 5814-5810; internet www.psj.gr.jp; f. 1926; study of sound phenomena of human speech; 780 mems; library of 30,000 vols; Pres. MIYOKO SUGITO; publ. *Bulletin* (3 a year).

Nippon Seiyo Koten Gakkai (Classical Society of Japan): Dept of Classics, Faculty of Letters, Kyoto Univ., Kyoto 606-8501; tel. (75) 753-2821; e-mail i54241@sakura.kudpc.kyoto-u.ac.jp; internet www.bun.kyoto-u.ac.jp/classics/CSJ/csj.html; f. 1950; 570 mems; Pres. KATSUTOSHI UCHIYAMA; Sec. TETSUO NAKATSUKASA; publ. *Journal of Classical Studies* (annually).

MEDICINE

Japanese Society for the Study of Pain: C/o Dr K. Mori, Dept of Anaesthesia, Kyoto University Hospital, 54 Kawahara-cho Syogoin, Sakyo-ku, Kyoto 606-01; tel. (75) 751-3433; fax (75) 752-3259; f. 1973; research into pain mechanism and pain management; 698 mems; Sec.-Gen. Prof. K. MORI; publ. *Pain Research* (4 a year).

Nihon Eisei Gakkai (Japanese Society for Hygiene): Dept of Preventive Medicine and Public Health, Keio University School of Medicine, 35 Shinanomachi, Shinjuku-ku, Tokyo 160-8582; tel. (3) 3353-1211; fax (3) 3358-0614; f. 1902; 2,750 mems; Chief Officer Prof. HARUHIKO SAKURAI; publs *Japanese Journal of Hygiene* (in Japanese, 4 a year), *Environmental Health and Preventive Medicine* (in English, 4 a year).

Nihon Hinyokika Gakki: (Japanese Urological Association); Saito Bldg, 5F, 2-17-15 Yushima, Bunkyo-ku, Tokyo 113-0034; f. 1912; 7,200 mems; Pres. Prof. AKIHIKO OKUYAMA; publs *International Journal of Urology* (monthly), *Japanese Journal of Urology* (6 a year).

Nihon Ishi-Kai (Japan Medical Association): Bunkyo-ku, Tokyo 113; f. 1916; 121,514 mems; Pres. Y. KARASAWA; publs *Journal* (in Japanese, monthly), *Japan Medical Association Journal* (in English, 6 a year).

Nihon Junkanki Gakkai (Japanese Circulation Society): Kinki Invention Center, 14 Yoshida Kawahara-cho, Sakyo-ku, Kyoto 606-8305; tel. (75) 751-8643; fax (75) 771-3060; e-mail admin@j-circ.or.jp; internet www.j-circ.or.jp; f. 1935; cardiology; 21,096 mems; Chief Dir AKIRA TAKESHITA; publs *Circulation Journal* (monthly in English; supplement in Japanese, 3 a year), *Journal of Board Certified Members of the Japanese Circulation Society* (in Japanese, 2 a year).

Nihon Kakuigakukai (Japanese Society of Nuclear Medicine): c/o Japan Radioisotope Association, 2-28-45 Honkomagome, Bunkyo-ku, Tokyo 113-0021; tel. (3) 3947-0976; fax (3) 3947-2535; f. 1963; 3,500 mems; Pres. Dr TOMIO INOUE; publs *Annals of Nuclear Medicine* (10 a year), *Japanese Journal of Nuclear Medicine* (4 a year).

Nihon Koku Eisei Gakkai (Japanese Society for Dental Health): c/o Koku Hoken Kyokai 44-2, Komagome 1-chome Toshima-ku, Tokyo 170; f. 1952; 2,000 mems; Pres. Y. SAKAKIBARA; publ. *Journal* (quarterly).

Nihon Koku Geka Gakkai (Japanese Society of Oral and Maxillofacial Surgeons): Seven-Ster Mansion Takanawa (2nd floor), 20-26-202 Takanawa 2-chome, Minato-Ku, Tokyo; tel. (3) 5791-1791; fax (3) 5791-1792; e-mail office@jsoms.org; internet www.jsoms.org; f. 1952; 8,500 mems; Gen. Sec. Dr KAN-ICHI SETO; publ. *Japanese Journal of Oral and Maxillofacial Surgery* (monthly).

Nihon Kokuka Gakkai (Japanese Stomatological Society): Department of Oral Surgery, School of Medicine, University of Tokyo, 7-3-1 Hongo, Bunkyo-ku, Tokyo; tel. (3) 3815-5411; f. 1947; 3,600 mems; Dir ICHIRO YAMASHITA; publ. *Journal* (quarterly).

Nihon Kyosei Shikagakkai (Japan Orthodontic Society): c/o Koku Hoken Kyokai, 1-44-2 Komagome, Toshima-ku, Tokyo 170; tel. (3) 3947-8891; fax (3) 3947-8341; f. 1932; 4,200 mems; Pres. KAZUO YAMAUCHI; Vice-Pres. MASAYAKI SEBATA; publ. *Journal of the Japan Orthodontic Society* (every 2 months).

Nihon Masuika Gakkai (Japan Society of Anaesthesiologists): TY Bldg 6F, 18-11 Hongo 3-chome, Bunkyo-ku, Tokyo 113-0033; tel. (3) 3815-0590; fax (3) 3814-0464; e-mail anesth@gamma.ocu.ne.jp; internet www.anesth.or.jp; f. 1954; 8,677 mems; Pres. K. HANAOKA; Sec. Y. SHIMIDA; publs *Masui* (monthly), *Journal of Anaesthesia* (quarterly).

Nihon Naika Gakkai (Japanese Society of Internal Medicine): Hongo Daiichi Bldg, 34-3, Hongo 3-chome, Bunkyo-ku, Tokyo 113; f. 1903; 73,000 mems; Chief Dir ICHIRO KANAZAWA; publs *Journal* (monthly in Japanese), *Internal Medicine* (monthly, English).

Nihon No-Shinkei Geka Gakkai (Japan Neurosurgical Society): Ishikawa Bldg 4F, 5-25-16 Hongo, Bunkyo-ku, Tokyo; tel. (3) 3812-6226; fax (3) 3812-2090; e-mail jns@ss.iij4u.or.jp; internet jns.umin.ac.jp; f. 1948; 8,088 mems; Chair. TAKASHI YOSHIMOTO; publ. *Neurologia Medico-Chirurgica* (monthly in English).

Nihon Ronen Igakukai (Japan Geriatrics Society): Kyorin Bldg No 702, 4-2-1 Yushima, Bunkyo-ku, Tokyo 113; f. 1959; 4,500 mems; Chair. Prof. H. ORIMO; publ. *Japan Journal of Geriatrics* (every 2 months).

Nihon Seishin Shinkei Gakkai (Japanese Society of Psychiatry and Neurology): Wing Bldg 52, 5-25-18 Hongo, Bunkyo-ku, Tokyo 113-0033; 8,200 mems; Pres. MASAHIRO ASAI; publ. *Seishin Shinkeigaku Zasshi* (Japanese, monthly).

Nihon Shika Hoshasen Gakkai (Japanese Society for Oral and Maxillofacial Radiology): C/o Hitotsubashi Printing Co. Ltd, Gakkai Business Center, 2-4-11 Fukagawa, Koutou-ku, Tokyo 135-0033; tel. (3) 5620-1953; fax (3) 5620-1960; e-mail tsuchimochi@ngt.ndu.ac.jp; f. 1951; 1,200 mems; Sec.-Gen. S. KANDA; publs *Dental Radiology* (quarterly, in Japanese), *Oral Radiology* (in English, every 6 months).

Nihon Shokaki-byo Gakkai (Japanese Society of Gastroenterology): Ginza Orient Bldg, 8F, Ginza 8-9-13, Chuo-ku, Tokyo; tel. (3) 3573-4297; fax (3) 3289-2359; e-mail info@jsge.or.jp; internet www.jsge.or.jp; f. 1898; 25,000 mems; Pres. KENJI FUJIWARA; publs *Nihon Shokaki-byo Gakkai Zasshi* (Japanese, monthly), *Journal of Gastroenterology* (English, monthly).

Nihon Shonika Gakkai (Japan Paediatric Society): 4F Daiichi Magami Bldg, 1-1-5 Koraku, Bunkyo-ku, Tokyo 112-0004; tel. (3) 3818-0091; fax (3) 3816-6036; internet jpeds.or.jp; f. 1896; 16,311 mems; Pres. M. NISHIDA; publs *Pediatrics International* (in English, 6 a year), *Journal of the Japan Paediatric Society* (in Japanese, monthly).

Nihon Syoyakugakkai (Japanese Society of Pharmacognosy): Business Center for Academic Societies, 4–16, Yayoi 2-chome, Bunkyo-ku, Tokyo 113; f. 1946; 1,027 mems; Pres. M. KONOSHIMA; publ. *Japanese Journal of Pharmacognosy* (quarterly).

Nihon Teii Kinou Shinkei Geka Gakkai (Japan Society for Stereotactic and Functional Neurosurgery): c/o Dept of Neurological Surgery, School of Medicine, Nihon University, 30-1 Ohyaguchi Kamimachi, Itabashi-ku, Tokyo 173-8610; tel. (3) 3972-8111, ext. 2481; fax (3) 3554-0425; e-mail teii@med.nihon-u.ac.jp; internet jssfn.umin.ac.jp; f. 1963; 518 mems; Sec.-Gen. Dr C. FUKAYA; publ. *Functional Neurosurgery* (2 a year).

Nihon Yakuri Gakkai (Japanese Pharmacological Society): Yayoi 2-4-16, Bunkyo-ku, Tokyo 113-0032; tel. (3) 3814-4828; fax (3) 3814-4809; e-mail society@pharmacol.or.jp; internet www.pharmacol.or.jp; f. 1927; 6,100 mems; Chair. KEITARO HASHIMOTO; publs *Folia Pharmacologica Japonica* (monthly, in Japanese), *Journal of Pharmacological Sciences* (monthly, in English).

Nippon Bitamin Gakkai (Vitamin Society of Japan): 2nd Floor, Kyodai Kaikan, 15–9 Kawaramachi Yoshida, Sakyo-ku, Kyoto 606-8305; tel. (75) 751-0314; fax (75) 751-2870; e-mail vsojkn@mbox.kyoto-inet.or.jp; internet web.kyoto-inet.or.jp/people/vsojkn; f. 1947; 2,000 mems; Pres. Y. TANI; Chief Sec. TAKESHI MATUMOTO; publs *Journal of Nutritional Science and Vitaminology* (English, 6 a year), *Vitamins* (Japanese, monthly).

Nippon Byorigakkai (Japanese Society of Pathology): New Akamon Bldg 4F, 2-40-9 Hongo, Bunkyo-ku, Tokyo 113-0033; tel. (3) 5684-6886; fax (3) 5684-6936; e-mail jsp@ma.kcom.ne.jp; internet jsp.umin.ac.jp; f. 1911; 4,200 mems; Chair. SHIGEO MORI; publs *Pathology International* (monthly in English), *Proceedings* (Japanese), *Annual of Pathological Autopsy Cases in Japan* (Japanese).

Nippon Gan Gakkai (Japanese Cancer Association): C/o Cancer Institute, Kami-Ikebukuro 1-37-1, Toshima-ku, Tokyo 170-0012; tel. (3) 3918-0111, ext. 4231; fax (3) 3918-5776; f. 1907; 16,976 mems; Pres. Dr TOMOYUKI KITAGAWA; publs *Japanese Journal of Cancer Research* (Gann, monthly), *Gann Monograph on Cancer Research* (irregular).

Nippon Ganka Gakkai (Japanese Ophthalmological Society): 2-4-11-402, Sarugaku-cho, Chiyoda-ku, Tokyo 101; f. 1897; 8,800 mems; Pres. YASUO UEMURA; publ. *Acta Societatis Ophthalmologicae Japonicae* (monthly).

Nippon Geka Gakkai (Japan Surgical Society): Hakuoh Bldg, 2-3-10 Koraku, Bunkyo-ku, Tokyo; f. 1899; 37,405 mems; Pres. K. SUGIMACHI; publ. *Journal* (monthly).

Nippon Hifu-ka Gakkai (Japanese Dermatological Association): Taisei Bldg, 14-10 3-chome, Hongo, Bunkyo-ku, Tokyo; tel. (3) 3811-5099; fax (3) 3812-6790; f. 1901; 8,567 mems; Pres. S. HARADA; publs *Japanese Journal of Dermatology* (Japanese, 14 a year), *Journal of Dermatology* (English, monthly).

Nippon Hoi Gakkai (Medico-Legal Society of Japan): Department of Forensic Medicine, Faculty of Medicine, University of Tokyo, 7-3-1 Hongo, Bunkyo-ku, Tokyo 113; tel. (3) 5800-5416; fax (3) 5800-5416; e-mail legalmed@m.u-tokyo.ac.jp; internet web.sapmed.ac.jp/JSLM; f. 1914; 1,400 mems; Pres. YOSHINAO KATSUMATA; publs *Japanese Journal of Legal Medicine* (2 a year), *Legal Medicine* (4 a year).

Nippon Hoshasen Eikyo Gakkai (Japan Radiation Research Society): National Institute of Radiological Sciences, 9-1 Anagawa-4, Inage-ku, Chiba 263-8555; tel. (43) 251-2111; fax (43) 251-4531; f. 1959; 1,095 mems; Pres. T. OHNISHI; publ. *Journal of Radiation Research* (4 a year).

Nippon Hotetsu Shika Gakkai (Japan Prosthodontic Society): c/o Koku Hoken Kyokai, 1-44-2 Komagome, Toshima-ku, Tokyo; f. 1931; 6,000 mems; Pres. YOSHINORI KOBAYASHI; publ. *Journal* (every 2 months).

Nippon Igaku Hōshasen Gakkai (Japan Radiological Society): Room 301 Akamon Habitation, 5-29-13 Hongo, Bunkyo-ku, Tokyo; tel. (3) 3814-3077; fax (3) 5684-4075; f. 1923; 5,986 mems; Pres. Y. ONOYAMA; publ. *Nippon Acta Radiologica* (monthly).

Nippon Jibi-Inkoka Gakkai (Oto-Rhino-Laryngological Society of Japan, Inc.): 3-23-14-807 Takanawa, Minato-ku, Tokyo; tel. (3) 3443-3085; fax (3) 3443-3037; e-mail office@jibika.or.jp; internet www.jibika.or.jp; f. 1893; 10,500 mems; Pres. TAKUYA UEMURA; publ. *Nippon Jibi-Inkoka Gakkai Kaiho (Tokyo)* (monthly).

Nippon Kaibo Gakkai (Japanese Association of Anatomists): c/o Business Center for Academic Societies Japan, 5-16-9 Honkomagome, Bunkyo-ku, Tokyo 113; f. 1893; 2,700 mems; Pres. Dr SHIGEO UCHINO; publs *Kaibogaku Zasshi*, *Acta Anatomica Nipponica* (every 2 months).

Nippon Kansenshoh Gakkai (Japanese Association for Infectious Diseases): Sankei 8 Bldg 6F, 1-8-7 Ebisu, Shibuya-ku, Tokyo 150; tel. (03) 3473-5095; fax (3) 3442-1196; f. 1926; 5,300 mems; Pres. KAORU SHIMADA; publ. *The Journal* (monthly).

Nippon Kekkaku-byo Gakkai (Japanese Society for Tuberculosis): 1-24, Matsuyama 3-chome, Kiyose-shi, Tokyo 204-8533; tel. 0424-92-2091; fax 0424-91-8315; f. 1923; 3,000 mems; Chair. Dr K. AOKI; publ. *Kekkaku* (monthly).

Nippon Ketsueki Gakkai (Japanese Society of Haematology): C/o Kinki Chiho Invention Center, 14 Kawahara-cho, Yoshida, Sakyo-ku, Kyoto 606-8305; tel. (75) 752-2844; fax (75) 752-2842; e-mail ijh-ind@umin.ac.jp; internet www.jshem.or.jp; f. 1937; 6,066 mems; Pres. MINORU OKUMA; publ. *International Journal of Hematology* (10 a year with 1 supplement).

Nippon Kikan-Shokudo-ka Gakkai (Japan Broncho-Esophagological Society): 5th Floor, Hakuo Bldg, 2-3-10 Koraku, Bunkyo-ku, Tokyo 112-0004; tel. (3) 3818-3030; fax (3) 3815-2810; e-mail kishoku@hi-ho.ne.jp; f. 1949; 3,600 mems; Dir Dr Y. MURAKAMI; publ. *Journal* (every 2 months).

Nippon Kisei-chu Gakkai (Japanese Society of Parasitology): Department of Parasitology, Gunma University School of Medicine, 3-39-22 Showa-machi, Maebashi 371-8511; tel. (27) 220-8024; fax (27) 220-8025; f. 1926; 998 mems; Pres. Prof. M. SUZUKI; Sec. Prof. S. KOJIMA; publ. *Parasitology International* (4 a year).

Nippon Koshu-Eisei Kyokai (Japan Public Health Association): Koei Building, 29–8, Shinjuku 1-chome, Shinjuku-ku, Tokyo; f. 1883; 5,000 mems; Pres. MINORU SEIJO; publs *Japanese Journal of Public Health*, *Public Health Information* (monthly).

Nippon Naibumpigaku-Kai Tobu-bukai (Eastern Branch of Japan Endocrinological Society): c/o Department of Urology, School of Medicine, Gumma University, Maebashi; f. 1954; 1,300 mems; Pres. K. SHIDA; publ. *Endocrinologia Japonica* (every 2 months in English, German, French).

Nippon Rai Gakkai (Japanese Leprosy Association): 4-2-1, Aoba-cho, Higashimurayama-shi, Tokyo 189-0002; tel. (42) 391-

8085; fax (42) 394-9092; e-mail jla-hp-admin@hansen-gakkai.jp; internet www.hansen-gakkai.jp; f. 1927; 355 mems; Pres. NORIHASA ISHII; publ. *Japanese Journal of Leprosy* (every 4 months).

Nippon Saikingakkai (Japanese Society for Bacteriology): C/o Oral Health Association of Japan, 1-44-2 Komagome, Toshima-ku, Tokyo 170; tel. (3) 3947-8891; fax (3) 3947-8341; e-mail gakkai@kokuhiken.or.jp; internet wwwsoc.nii.ac.jp/jsb; f. 1927; 3,400 mems; Pres. Dr HIDEO HAYASHI; publs *Japanese Journal of Bacteriology* (4 a year), *Microbiology and Immunology* (monthly).

Nippon Sanka-Fujinka Gakkai (Japan Society of Obstetrics and Gynaecology): Twin View Ochanomizu Bldg, 2-3-9 Hongo, Bunkyo-ku, Tokyo 113-0033; tel. (3) 5842-5452; fax (3) 5842-5470; e-mail nissanfu@jsog.or.jp; internet www.jsog.or.jp; f. 1949; 15,500 mems; Chair. Prof. YUJI TAKETANI; publ. *Acta Obstetrica et Gynaecologica Japonica* (monthly).

Nippon Seikei Geka Gakkai (Japanese Orthopaedic Association): 2-40-18, Hongo, Bunkyo-ku, Tokyo 113-8418; tel. (3) 3816-3671; fax (3) 3818-2337; e-mail joa@joa.or.jp; internet www.joa.or.jp; f. 1926; 20,742 mems; Pres. Prof. HIROSHI YAMAMOTO; publs *Journal* (12 a year, in Japanese), *Journal of Orthopaedic Science* (6 a year, in English).

Nippon Seiri Gakkai (Physiological Society of Japan): Fuse Bldg, Hongo 3-30-10, Bunkyo-ku, Tokyo 113; f. 1922; 3,700 mems; Pres. M. ITO; publ. *Journal*.

Nippon Shika Hozon Gakkai (Japanese Society of Conservative Dentistry): Tokyo Dental Univ., 1 Misaki-cho Kanda, Chiyoda-ku, Tokyo; f. 1955; 826 mems; Pres. E. SEKINE; publ. *Journal* (2 a year).

Nippon Shika Igakkai (Japanese Association for Dental Science): 4-1-20 Kudan-kita, Chiyoda-ku, Tokyo; tel. (3) 3262-9214; fax (3) 3262-9885; f. 1949; 80,000 mems; 14 mem. socs; Pres. Prof. K. ETO; publs *Journal* (annual, in Japanese), *Dentistry in Japan* (annual).

Nippon Shinkei Gakkai (Japanese Society of Neurology): Ichimaru Building 2-31-21 Yushima, Bunkyo-ku, Tokyo 113-0034; fax (3) 3815-1931; e-mail m-iwata@nij.twmu.ac.jp; internet www.neurology-jp.org/index.html; f. 1960; 6,895 mems; Chair. ICHIRO KANAZAWA; publ. *Clinical Neurology* (monthly).

Nippon Shinkeikagaku Gakkai (Japan Neuroscience Society): Inagaya Building 504, 37-6 Hongo 2-chome, Bunkyo-ku, Tokyo 113-0033; tel. (3) 3813-0272; fax (3) 3813-0272; e-mail jnss@mb.neweb.ne.jp; internet www.jnss.org; f. 1974; 4,000 mems; Pres. K. OBATA; publs *News*, *Neuroscience Research* (monthly).

Nippon Tonyo-byo Gakkai (Japan Diabetes Society): 5-25-18, Hongo, Bunkyo-ku, Tokyo 113-0033; tel. (3) 3815-4364; fax (3) 3815-7985; f. 1958; 15,533 mems; Pres. KOICHI YOKONO; publ. *Journal* (monthly).

Nippon Uirusu Gakkai (Society of Japanese Virologists): Business Centre for Academic Societies, 5-16-9 Honkomagome, Bunkyo-ku, Tokyo 113; f. 1953; 3,000 mems; Pres. Dr HIROSHI YOSHIKURA; publs *Virus* (Japanese text with English summary, 2 a year), *Microbiology and Immunology* (monthly).

Nippon Yakugaku-Kai (Pharmaceutical Society of Japan): 12-15-201, Shibuya 2-chome, Shibuya-ku, Tokyo; tel. (3) 3406-3321; fax (3) 3498-1835; e-mail gigy_win@pharm.or.jp; f. 1880; 21,541 mems; Pres. O. YONEMITSU; Exec. Dir M. OHZEKI; publs *Farumashia* (monthly), *Chemical and Pharmaceutical Bulletin* (monthly), *Japanese Journal of Toxicology and Environmental Health* (6 a year), *Biological and Pharmaceutical Bulletin* (monthly).

Nippon Yuketsu Gakkai (Japan Society of Blood Transfusion): Metropolitan Tokyo Red Cross Blood Centre, 1-31-4 Hiroo, Shibuya-ku, Tokyo; tel. (3) 5485-6020; fax (3) 5466-3111; internet www.yuketsu.gr.jp; f. 1954; 3,000 mems; Pres. TAKEO JUJI; publ. *Japanese Journal of Transfusion Medicine* (6 a year).

NATURAL SCIENCES

General

Nihon Kagakushi Gakkai (History of Science Society of Japan): Shimazu Bldg 202, 2-13-1 Hirakawa-cho, Chiyoda-ku, Tokyo 102-0093; tel. (3) 3239-0545; fax (3) 3239-0545; internet wwwsoc.nii.ac.jp/jshs; f. 1941; 1,000 mems; Pres. SHUNTARO ITOH; publs *Kagakushi Kenkyu* (quarterly), *Historia Scientiarum* (3 a year).

Biological Sciences

Hassei Seibutsu Gakkai (Japanese Society of Developmental Biologists): Biological Institute, Graduate School of Science, Tohoku University, Aramaki-Aza-Aoba, Aoba-ku, Sendai 980-8578; tel. (22) 217-3489; fax (22) 217-3489; e-mail isdb@bcasj.or.jp; internet www.bcasj.or.jp/jsdb; f. 1968; 1,500 mems; Pres. M. TAKEICHI; publ. *Development, Growth and Differentiation* (every 2 months, English).

Nihon Jinrui Iden Gakkai (Japan Society of Human Genetics): Dept of Human Genetics, Tokyo Medical and Dental University, 1-5-45 Yushima, Bunkyo-ku, Tokyo; tel. (3) 3813-6111; f. 1956; 1,046 mems; Pres. E. MATSUNAGA; publ. *Journal* (quarterly).

Nihon Kairui Gakkai (Malacological Society of Japan): National Science Museum, 3-23-1, Hyakunin-cho, Shinjuku-ku, Tokyo 169-0073; tel. (3) 3364-7124; f. 1928; scientific research on molluscs; 900 mems; Pres. T. OKUTANI; publs *Venus* (quarterly), *Chiribotan* (in Japanese with English abstract, quarterly).

Nihon Kontyû Gakkai (Entomological Society of Japan): c/o Dept of Zoology, National Science Museum (Natural History), 3-23-1 Hyakunin-chô, Shinjuku, Tokyo 169; f. 1917; 1,300 mems; Pres. M. SASAKAWA; publ. *Japanese Journal of Entomology* (quarterly).

Nihon Mendel Kyokai (Japan Mendel Society): Editorial and Business Office, Cytologia, c/o Toshin Bldg, Hongo 2-27-2, Bunkyo-ku, Tokyo 113-0033; fax (3) 3814-5352; f. 1929; 1,100 mems; Pres. HIDEO HIROKAWA; publ. *Cytologia* (quarterly).

Nihon Seitai Gakkai (Ecological Society of Japan): 1-8 Nishihanaikecho, Koyama, Kitaku Kyoto 603-8148; tel. and fax (75) 384-0250; e-mail office@mail.esj.ne.jp; internet www.esj.ne.jp/es; f. 1953; research in all aspects of ecology; 3,800 mems; Pres. K. KIKUZAWA; Sec.-Gen. H. KOIZUMI; publs *Japanese Journal of Ecology* (in Japanese, 3 a year), *Ecological Research* (in English, 6 a year), *Japanese Journal of Conservation Ecology* (in Japanese, 2 a year).

Nihon Shokubutsu Bunrui Gakkai (Japanese Society for Plant Systematics): Faculty of Symbiotic Systems Science, Fukushima University, Fukushima 960-1296; e-mail kurosawa@sss.fukushima-u.go.jp; internet wwwsoc.nii.ac.jp/jsps; f. 2001; 900 mems; plant taxonomy and phytogeography; Pres. JIN MURATA; Sec. TAKAHIDAE KUROSAWA; publ. *Acta Phytotaxonomica et Geobotanica* (2 a year).

Nippon Chô Gakkai (Ornithological Society of Japan): C/o Laboratory of Wildlife Ecology, Obihiro University of Agriculture and Veterinary Medicine, Inada, Obihiro 080-8555; tel. (155) 49-5500; fax (155) 49-5504; f. 1912; 1,000 mems; library of 600 vols; Pres. Y. FUJIMAKI; publ. *Japanese Journal of Ornithology* (quarterly).

Nihon Dobutsu Gakkai (Zoological Society of Japan): Toshin Bldg, Hongo 2-27-2, Bunkyo-ku, Tokyo 113-0033; tel. (3) 3814-5461; fax (3) 3814-6216; e-mail zsocj@a1.rimnet.ne.jp; internet www.soc.nii.ac.jp/zsj/index-j.html; f. 1878; 2,610 mems; Pres. MAKOTO ASASHIMA; publ. *Zoological Science* (monthly).

Nippon Eisei-Dobutu Gakkai (Japanese Society of Medical Entomology and Zoology): C/o Dept of Parasitology, School of Medicine, Aichi Medical University, Nagakute, Aichi 480-1195; tel. (561) 62-3311; fax (561) 63-3645; internet wwwmez.med.uoeh-u.ac.jp/~mez; f. 1943; 750 mems; Pres. Prof. YASUO CHINZEI; publ. *Medical Entomology and Zoology* (4 a year).

Nippon Iden Gakkai (Genetics Society of Japan): National Institute of Genetics, 1, 111 Yata, Mishima 411-8540, Shizuoka; f. 1920; 1,500 mems; Pres. M. SEKIGUCHI; publ. *Fukuoka Dental College* (6 a year).

Nippon Kin Gakkai (Mycological Society of Japan): c/o Business Center for Academic Societies Japan, 16-9 Honkomagome 5-chome, Bunkyo-ku, Tokyo 113; tel. (3) 5814-5801; fax (3) 5814-5820; f. 1956; 1,600 mems; Pres. MAKOTO MIYAJI; publs *Mycoscience* (quarterly), *Nippon Kingakukai Kaiho* (quarterly).

Nippon Kumo Gakkai (Arachnological Society of Japan): c/o Biological Laboratory, Otemon Gakuin Univ., 2-1-15, Nishi-Ai, Ibaraki, Osaka 567-8502; tel. (72) 641-9550; fax (72) 643-9432; e-mail kamura@res.otemon.ac.jp; f. 1936; 340 mems; Pres. Dr NOBUO TSURUSAKI; publ. *Acta Arachnologica* (2 a year).

Nippon Oyo-Dobutsu-Konchu Gakkai (Japanese Society of Applied Entomology and Zoology): c/o Japan Plant Protection Association, 43-11, 1-chome, Komagome, Toshima-ku, Tokyo 170; f. 1957; 2,000 mems; Pres. YOSHIO TAMAKI; publs *Applied Entomology and Zoology* (in English, quarterly), *Japanese Journal of Applied Entomology and Zoology* (Japanese with English synopsis, quarterly).

Nippon Rikusui Gakkai (Japanese Society of Limnology): c/o School of Environmental Science, University of Shiga Prefecture, 2500 Hassaka-cho, Hikone, Shiga 522-8533; tel. (749) 28-8307; fax (749) 28-8463; e-mail ban@ses.usp.ac.jp; internet wwwsoc.nii.ac.jp/jslim; f. 1931; 1,288 mems; Pres. Dr NORIO OGURA; Gen. Sec. Dr OSAMU MITAMURA; publs *Japanese Journal of Limnology* (3 a year), *Limnology* (3 a year).

Nippon Seibutsu Kankyo Chosetsu Gakkai (Japanese Society of Environment Control in Biology): Faculty of Horticulture, Chiba University, 684 Matsudo, Chiba 271-8510; tel. (47) 308-8843; fax (47) 308-8843; f. 1963; 1,090 mems; Pres. T. TAKAKURA; publ. *Seibutsu Kankyo Chosetsu* (quarterly).

Nippon Shokubutsu Gakkai (Botanical Society of Japan, The): C/o Toshin Bldg, 2-chome 27-2 Hongo, Bunkyo-ku, Tokyo; tel. (3) 3814-5675; fax (3) 3814-5352; e-mail bsj@bsj.or.jp; internet bsj.or.jp; f. 1882; 2,300 mems; Pres. M. WADA; publ. *Journal of Plant Research* (6 a year).

Nippon Shokubutsu Seiri Gakkai (Japanese Society of Plant Physiologists): Shimotachiuri Ogawa Higashi, Kamikyoku, Kyoto

602-8048; tel. (75) 415-3661; fax (75) 415-3662; e-mail jspp@nacos.com; internet www.nacos.com/jspp; f. 1959; 3,201 mems; Pres. KIYOTAKA OKADA; Sec.-Gen. AKIRA NAGATANI; publ. *Plant and Cell Physiology* (monthly).

Mathematical Sciences

Nihon Sugaku Kai (Mathematical Society of Japan): 34-8, Taito-1-chome, Taito-ku, Tokyo 110-0016; tel. (3) 3835-3483; fax (3) 3835-3485; f. 1877; 5,000 mems; Pres. SADAYOSHI KOJIMA; publs *Journal* (4 a year), *Sugaku* (4 a year), *Sugaku-Tsushin* (bulletin, 4 a year), *Japanese Journal of Mathematics* (2 a year), *MSJ Memoirs* (irregular), *Advanced Studies in Pure Mathematics* (irregular).

Physical Sciences

Butsuri Tansa Gakkai (Society of Exploration Geophysicists of Japan): San-es Bldg, 2-2-18 Nakamagome, Ota-ku, Tokyo; f. 1948; 1,420 mems; Pres. T. KAWAMURA; publ. *Butsuri Tansa* (Geophysical Exploration, every 2 months).

Chigaku Dantai Kenkyu-kai (Association for Geological Collaboration in Japan): Kawai Bldg, 2–24–1, Minami-Ikebukuro, Toshima-ku, Tokyo 171-0022; tel. (3) 3983-3378; fax (3) 3983-7525; e-mail chidanken@tokyo.email.ne.jp; internet wwwsoc.nii.ac.jp/agcj/index.html; f. 1947; study of geology, mineralogy, palaeontology and related earth sciences; 2,500 mems; Pres. YUKIO OHTOMO; Sec. SATORU TAKEGOSHI; publs *Sokuhō* (News, monthly), *Chikyu-Kagaku* (Earth Science, 6 a year), *Senpō* (Monograph, irregular), *Chigaku Kyoiku To Kagaku-undo* (Education of Earth Science, 3 a year).

Chikyu-Denjiki Chikyu-Wakuseiken Gakkai (Society of Geomagnetism and Earth, Planetary and Space Science): c/o Business Centre for Academic Societies, 5-16-9 Honkomagome, Bumkyo-ku, Tokyo 113-8622; tel. (3) 5814-5801; fax (3) 5814-5820; internet www.kurasc.kyoto-u.ac.jp/sgepss; f. 1947; frmly Nippon Chikyu Denki Ziki Gakkai; 695 mems; Pres. Prof. RYOICHI FUJII; publ. *Earth, Planets and Space* (monthly).

Ikomasan Tenmon Kyokai (Ikomasan Astronomical Society): Ikoma-Sanzyo, Ikoma-gun, Nara Ken; f. 1942; 705 mems; Pres. JOE UETA; Sec. H. HAMANE; publ. *Tenmon Kyositu* (Astronomical Class, monthly).

Japan Weather Association: Sunshine 60 Bldg 3-1-1, Higashi-Ikebukuro, Toshima-ku, Tokyo 170; tel. (3) 5958-8161; fax (3) 5958-8162; e-mail webmaster@jwa.go.jp; f. 1950; Pres. NAOSHI MACHIDA; publs *Kisho*, *Daily Weather Maps*, *Journal of Meteorological Research* (monthly), *Geophysical Magazine*, *Oceanographical Magazine* (quarterly).

Kaiyoo Kisho Gakkai (Oceanographical and Meteorological Society): 7-chome, Ikutaku, Kobe; f. 1921; 310 mems; Pres. HAYATO OIDA; publ. *Sea and Sky* (every 2 months).

Kobunshi Gakkai (Society of Polymer Science, Japan): Shintomicho Tokyu Building, 3-10-9 Irifune, Chuo-ku, Tokyo 104-0042; tel. (3) 5540-3771; fax (3) 5540-3737; e-mail kokusai@spsj.or.jp; internet www.spsj.or.jp; f. 1951; 12,598 mems; Pres. TISATO KAJIYAMA; publs *Kobunshi* (monthly), *Kobunshi Ronbunshu* (monthly), *Polymer Journal* (in English, monthly), *Polymer Preprints* (in English, 2 a year).

Nihon Bunseki Kagaku-Kai (Japan Society for Analytical Chemistry): Gotanda Sanhaitsu, 26-2, Nishigotanda 1-chome, Shinagawa-ku, Tokyo 141; f. 1952; 9,108 mems; Pres. M. TANAKA; Sec.-Gen. Dr TADASHI FUJINUKI; publs *Bunseki Kagaku* (monthly), *Bunseki* (monthly), *Analytical Sciences* (every 2 months).

Nihon Ganseki Kobutsu Kosho Gakkai (Japanese Association of Mineralogists, Petrologists and Economic Geologists): c/o Graduate School of Science, Tohoku University, Sendai 980-8578; tel. (22) 224-3852; fax (22) 224-3852; e-mail kyl04223@nifty.ne.jp; internet wwwsoc.nii.ac.jp/jampeg/index_e.html; f. 1929; 750 mems; library of 17,000 vols; Pres. MASAAKI OBATA; publ. *Journal of Mineralogical and Petrological Sciences* (6 a year).

Nihon Nensho Gakkai (Combustion Society of Japan): c/o Department of Mechanical Engineering, Osaka Prefecture University, 1-1 Gakuen-cho, Sakai, Osaka 599-8531; tel. (72) 255-7037; fax (72) 255-7037; e-mail office@combustionsociety.jp; internet combustionsociety.jp; f. 1953; 700 mems; Pres. TOSHIKAZU KADOTA; publ. *Journal* (4 a year).

Nihon Nogyo-Kisho Gakkai (Society of Agricultural Meteorology of Japan): c/o Division of Agrometeorology, National Institute of Agro-Environmental Sciences, Tsukuba, Ibaraki 305; tel. (298) 388217; fax (298) 388211; f. 1942; study of protected cultivation, agricultural meteorology and resources of food production; 1,150 mems; Pres. YOSHINORI SUZUKI; publ. *Nogyo-Kisho* (Journal of Agricultural Meteorology, quarterly).

Nihon Seppyo Gakkai (Japanese Society of Snow and Ice): 3rd Fl., Kagaku-Kaikan, Kanda Surugadai 1-5, Chiyoda-ku, Tokyo 101-0062; tel. (3) 5259-5245; fax (3) 5259-5246; e-mail jimu@seppyo.org; internet www.seppyo.org; f. 1939; 1,050 mems; Pres. Dr SHINJI MAE; publs *Seppyo* (Journal of the Japanese Society of Snow and Ice, 6 a year in Japanese and English), *Bulletin of Glaciological Research* (annually, in English), *occasional papers and bibliography*.

Nippon Bunko Gakkai (Spectroscopical Society of Japan): c/o Industrial Hall, 1-13, Kanda-Awaji-cho, Chiyoda-ku, Tokyo 101; tel. (3) 3253-2747; fax (3) 3253-2740; f. 1951; 1,300 mems; Pres. M. TASUMI; Sec. Y. F. MIZUGAI; publ. *Journal* (every 2 months).

Nippon Butsuri Gakkai (Physical Society of Japan, The): 5th Fl., Eishin-kaihatsu Bldg, 5-34-3 Shimbashi, Minato-ku, Tokyo 105-0004; tel. (3) 3434-2671; fax (3) 3432-0997; e-mail jps-office@jps.or.jp; internet wwwsoc.nii.ac.jp/jps; f. 1946; 18,223 mems; Pres. SUKEKATSU USHIODA; publs *Butsuri* (in Japanese, monthly), *Journal of the Physical Society of Japan* (monthly), *Progress of Theoretical Physics* (monthly), *Physics Education in Universities* (in Japanese, 3 a year).

Nippon Chishitsu Gakkai (Geological Society of Japan): Igeta Bldg, 8-15 Iwamoto-cho 2-chome, Chiyoda-ku, Tokyo 101-0032; tel. (3) 5823-1150; fax (3) 5823-1156; e-mail main@geosociety.jp; internet www.geosociety.jp; f. 1893; stratigraphy, petrology, tectonics, volcanology, etc; 5,000 mems; library of 10,000 vols; Pres. ASAHIKO TAIRA; publ. *Journal* (monthly).

Nippon Dai-Yonki Gakkai (Japan Association for Quaternary Research): 3rd Fl., Rakuyo Bldg, Waseda-Tsurumaki-cho 519, Shinjuku, Tokyo 162-0041; tel. (3) 5291-6231; fax (3) 5291-2176; e-mail daiyonki@shunkosha.com; internet wwwsoc.nii.ac.jp/qr/index.html; f. 1956; 1,800 mems; Sec. of Exec. Cttee SUMIKO KUBO; publ. *Quaternary Research* (5 a year).

Nippon Denshi Kenbikyo Gakkai (Japanese Society of Electron Microscopy): c/o Business Centre for Academic Societies, 4-16 Yayoi 2-chome, Bunkyo-ku, Tokyo 113; f. 1949; 2,690 mems; Pres. KAZUO OGAWA; publ. *Journal* (quarterly).

Nippon Kagakukai (Chemical Society of Japan): 5, 1-chome, Kanda-Surugadai, Chiyoda-ku, Tokyo 101-0062; f. 1878; 39,000 mems; Pres. TADASU TACHI; Exec. Dir ATSUO NAKANISHI; publs *Kagaku to Kogyo*, *Kagaku to Kyoiku*, *Nippon Kagaku Kaishi*, *Chemistry Letters*, *Bulletin of the Chemical Society of Japan* (monthly).

Nippon Kaisui Gakkai (Society of Sea Water Science, Japan): c/o Sea Water Science Research Laboratory, Salt Industry Centre of Japan, 4-13-20, Sakawa, Odawara-shi, Kanagawa; f. 1950; 414 mems; Pres. SHINICHI NAKAO; publ. *Journal*.

Nippon Kaiyo Gakkai (Oceanographic Society of Japan): MACAS, 9th Fl., Palaceside Bldg, 1-1-1 Hitotsubashi, Chiyoda-ku, Tokyo 100-0003; tel. (3) 3211-1412; fax (3) 3211-1413; e-mail jos@mycom.co.jp; internet wwwsoc.nii.ac.jp/kaiyo; f. 1941; 2,379 mems; Pres. SHIRO IMAWAKI; publs *Journal of Oceanography* (6 a year), *Umi no Kenkyu* (Oceanography in Japan, 6 a year).

Nippon Kazan Gakkai (Volcanological Society of Japan): C/o Earthquake Research Institute, University of Tokyo, 1-1-1 Yayoi, Bunkyo-ku, Tokyo 113-0032; tel. (3) 3813-7421; fax (3) 5684-2549; e-mail kazan@eri.u-tokyo.ac.jp; internet hakone.eri.u-tokyo.ac.jp/kazan/jishome/VSJ1.html; f. 1932; 1,200 mems; Pres. TADAHIDE UI; publ. *Bulletin* (6 a year).

Nippon Kessho Gakkai (Crystallographic Society of Japan): Nissei Otuka 3-chome Bldg, 3-11-6 Otuka, Bunkyo-ku, Tokyo 112-0012; tel. (3) 5940-7640; fax (3) 5940-7980; e-mail cr-info@rlz.co.jp; internet wwwsoc.nii.ac.jp/crsj/index.html; f. 1950; 1,000 mems; Pres. KAZUMAZA OHSUMI; Sec-Gen. MASAKI TAKATA; publ. *Journal* (every 2 months).

Nippon Kisho Gakkai (Meteorological Society of Japan): c/o Japan Meteorological Agency, Ote-machi, Chiyoda-ku, Tokyo; f. 1882; 4,300 mems; Pres. T. ASAI; publs *Tenki* (monthly), *Journal* (every 2 months).

Nippon Kokai Gakkai (Japan Institute of Navigation): c/o Tokyo University of Mercantile Marine, 2-1-6 Etchujima, Koto-ku, Tokyo; tel. (3) 3630-3093; fax (3) 3630-3093; f. 1948; 920 mems; Pres. Prof. S. KUWASIMA; publs *Journal* (2 a year), *Navigation* (quarterly).

Nippon Koseibutsu Gakkai (Palaeontological Society of Japan): c/o Business Centre for Academic Societies, 5-16-9 Honkomagome, Bunkyo-ku, Tokyo 113; f. 1935; 1,050 mems; Pres. NORIYUKI IKEYA; publs *Paleontological Research* (4 a year), *Fossils* (2 a year).

Nippon Onkyo Gakkai (Acoustical Society of Japan): Nakaura 5th Bldg, 2-18-20 Sotokanda, Chiyoda-ku, Tokyo 101-0021; fax (3) 5256-1022; e-mail kym05145@nifty.ne.jp; internet wwwsoc.nii.ac.jp/asj; f. 1936; 3,600 mems; Pres. T. SONE; publs *Journal* (monthly), *Reports of Spring and Autumn Meetings* (2 a year).

Nippon Sokuchi Gakkai (Geodetic Society of Japan): Geographical Survey Institute, 1 Kitasato, Tsukuba-shi, Ibaraki 305-0811; internet wwwsoc.nii.ac.jp/geod-soc; f. 1954; studies astronomy, crustal activity, earth tide, geodesy, geomagnetism, gravity, etc; 600 mems; library of 5,000 vols; Pres. JIRO SEGAWA; publ. *Journal* (4 a year).

Nippon Temmon Gakkai (Astronomical Society of Japan): National Astronomical Observatory, Osawa Mitaka, Tokyo; f. 1908; 2,640 mems; Pres. Y. UCHIDA; publs *Publications* (every two months), *The Astronomical Herald* (monthly in Japanese).

Nippon Yukagaku Kai (Japan Oil Chemists' Society): 7th Floor, Yushi Kogyo Kaikan, 13-11, Nihonbashi 3-chome, Chuo-ku, Tokyo 103-0027; tel. (3) 3271-7463; fax (3) 3271-7464; e-mail yukagaku@blue.ocn.ne.jp; internet wwwsoc.nii.ac.jp/jocs; f. 1951; 2,426 mems; Pres. ISAO IKEDA; publ. *Journal of Oleo Science* (monthly).

Sen-i Gakkai (Society of Fibre Science and Technology, Japan): 3-3-9-208 Kamiosaki, Shinagawa-ku, Tokyo 141; f. 1943; *c.* 3,000 mems; Pres. HIROSHI INAGAKI; publ. *Journal* (monthly).

Shokubai Gakkai (Catalysis Society of Japan): Shin-Ikeda-yama Mansions, Room 302, 5-21-13, Higashi-Gotanda, Shinagawa-ku, Tokyo 141; tel. (3) 3444-2126; fax (3) 3444-8794; f. 1958; 2,370 mems; Pres. Y. MOROOKA; publ. *Shokubai* (Catalyst, 8 a year).

Zisin Gakkai (Seismological Society of Japan): 6-26-12 Tokyo RS Building, Hongo, Bunkyo-ku, Tokyo 113-0033; tel. (3) 5803-9570; fax (3) 5803-9577; e-mail zisin@tokyo.email.ne.jp; internet wwwsoc.nii.ac.jp/ssj; f. 1929; 2,400 mems; Chair. MASAKAZU OHTAKE; publs *Zisin* (Journal, 4 a year), *Earth Planets and Space* (monthly), *Newsletter* (6 a year).

PHILOSOPHY AND PSYCHOLOGY

Bigaku-Kai (Japanese Society for Aesthetics): Faculty of Arts and Letters, Seijo University, Seijo 6-1-20, Setagaya-ku, Tokyo 157; f. 1950; 1,500 mems; Pres. KEIJI ASANUMA; publs *Bigaku* (quarterly, in Japanese), *Aesthetics* (every 2 years).

Moralogy Kenkyusho (Institute of Moralogy): 1-1, 2-chome, Hikarigaoka, Kashiwashi, Chiba-ken; tel. (4) 7173-3252; fax (4) 7173-3263; e-mail rc@moralogy.jp; internet rc.moralogy.jp; f. 1926; 267 mems; library of 71,294 vols; Pres. M. HIROIKE; publ. *Studies in Moralogy* (2 a year).

Nihon Oyo Shinri-gakkai (Japan Association of Applied Psychology): Dept of Psychology, College of Humanities and Sciences, Nihon University, 3-25-40 Sakurajosui, Setagaya-ku, Tokyo; tel. (3) 3329-1151; f. 1931; Pres. HARUO YAMAMOTO; Sec. KENSUKE MURAI.

Nihon Rinrigakukai (Japanese Society for Ethics): Department of Ethics, Faculty of Letters, The University of Tokyo, Bunkyo-ku, Tokyo 113; f. 1950; 800 mems; Pres. YÔKICHI YAZIMA; publs *Rinrigakunenpo* (Annals), *Rinrigakukaironshu* (Transactions of annual meeting).

Nippon Dobutsu Shinri Gakkai (Japanese Society for Animal Psychology): Shinkyobashi, 5th Fl., Daiichi-Nagoaka Bldg, 3-9-8 Hachobori, Chuo-ku, Tokyo 104-0032; tel. and fax (3) 3523-3078; e-mail dousin@psy.flet.keio.ac.jp; internet wwwsoc.nii.ac.jp/jsap2; f. 1933; 400 mems; Pres. SHIGERU WATANABE; publ. *The Japanese Journal of Animal Psychology* (2 a year).

Nippon Shakai Shinri Gakkai (Japanese Society of Social Psychology): c/o International Academic Printing Co. Ltd, 4-4-19 Takadanobaba, Shinjuku-ku, Tokyo 169-0075; tel. (3) 5389-6217; fax (3) 3368-2822; e-mail jssp-post@bunken.co.jp; internet wwwsoc.nii.ac.jp/jssp; f. 1950; 1,896 mems; Pres. IKUO DAIBO; publs *Japanese Journal of Social Psychology*, *Bulletin* (3 a year).

Nippon Shinrigakkai (Japanese Psychological Association): 5-23-13-7F, Hongo, Bunkyo-ku, Tokyo 113; tel. (3) 3814-3953; fax (3) 3814-3954; internet wwwsoc.nii.ac.jp/jpa; f. 1927; 7,000 mems; Pres. KEIICHIRO TSUJI; publs *Japanese Journal of Psychology* (every 2 months), *Japanese Psychological Research* (quarterly).

Tetsugaku-kai (Philosophical Society): Faculty of Letters, University of Tokyo, Hongo, Bunkyo-ku, Tokyo 113; f. 1884; 500 mems; Pres. JUICHI KATSURA; publ. *Tetsugaku-zasshi* (annually).

RELIGION, SOCIOLOGY AND ANTHROPOLOGY

Japanese Society of Cultural Anthropology: 2-1-1-813 Mita, Minato-ku, Tokyo 108-0073; tel. (3) 5232-0920; fax (3) 5232-0922; e-mail hoya@t3.rim.or.jp; internet wwwsoc.nii.ac.jp/jse; f. 1934; 2,000 mems; publ. *Bunkajinruigaku* (Japanese Journal of Cultural Anthropology, 4 a year).

Nihon Indogaku Bukkyôgakukai (Japanese Association of Indian and Buddhist Studies): Hongo Bldg 2F, 3-33-5 Bunkyo-ku, Hongo Tokyo 113-0033; e-mail jaibs@l.u~tokyo.ac.jp; f. 1951; 2,350 mems; Pres. KIYOTAKA KIMURA; publ. *Indogaku Bukkyôgaku Kenkyû* (Journal of Indian and Buddhist Studies).

Nihon Shūkyō Gakkai (Japanese Association for Religious Studies): 1-29-7-205 Hongo, Bunkyo-ku, Tokyo 113; tel. (3) 5684-5473; fax (3) 5684-5474; f. 1930; 2,000 mems; Pres. FUJIO IKADO; publ. *Journal of Religious Studies* (4 a year).

Nippon Dokyo Gakkai (Japan Society of Taoistic Research): Kansai University, Faculty of Letters, 3-35 Yamate-cho 3-chome, Suita-shi, Osaka 564-8680; tel. (6) 368-0326; f. 1950; 650 mems; Pres. Y. SAKADE; publ. *Journal of Eastern Religions* (2 a year).

Nippon Jinruigaku Kai (Anthropological Society of Nippon): Business Center for Academic Societies, 5-16-9 Honkomagome, Bunkyo-ku, Tokyo 113-8622; tel. (3) 5814-5801; fax (3) 5814-5820; internet wwwsoc.nii.ac.jp/jinrui; f. 1884; 700 mems; Pres. TASUKU KIMURA; publs *Anthropological Science* (4 a year), *Anthropological Science (Japanese Series)* (2 a year).

Nippon Shakai Gakkai (Japanese Sociological Society): Department of Sociology, Faculty of Letters, The University of Tokyo, 7-3-1 Hongo, Bunkyo-ku, Tokyo 113-0033; tel. (3) 5841-8933; fax (3) 5841-8932; e-mail jss@wwwsoc.nii.ac.jp; internet wwwsoc.nii.ac.jp/jss; f. 1923; 3,600 mems; Pres. TAKASHI HOSOYA; publs *Shakaigaku Hyôron* (quarterly), *International Journal of Japanese Sociology* (annually in English).

Tōhō Gakkai (Institute of Eastern Culture): 4-1, Nishi Kanda 2-chome, Chiyoda-ku, Tokyo 101-0065; tel. (3) 3262-7221; fax (3) 3262-7227; e-mail iec@tohogakkai.com; internet www.tohogakkai.com; f. 1947; Asian studies; 1,600 mems; Chair. TOGAWA YOSHIO; Sec.-Gen. YANASE HIROSHI; publs *Acta Asiatica* (bulletin, 2 a year), *Tōhōgaku* (Eastern Studies, 2 a year), *Transactions of the International Conference of Eastern Studies* (annually).

TECHNOLOGY

Denki Gakkai (Institute of Electrical Engineers of Japan (IEEJ)): Homat Horizon Bldg, 6-2 Goban-cho, Chiyoda-ku, Tokyo 102-0076; tel. (3) 3221-7256; fax (3) 3221-3704; e-mail jimkyoku@iee.or.jp; internet www.iee.or.jp; f. 1888; 26,000 mems; Pres. HISAO OKA; publs *Journal of the IEEJ* (in Japanese, monthly), *IEEJ Transactions on Fundamentals and Materials* (in Japanese and English, monthly), *IEEJ Transactions on Power and Energy* (in Japanese and English, monthly), *IEEJ Transactions on Electronics, Information and Systems* (in Japanese and English, monthly), *IEEJ Transactions on Industry Applications* (in Japanese and English, monthly), *IEEJ Transactions on Sensors and Micromachines* (in Japanese and English, monthly).

Denshi Joho Tsushin Gakkai (Institute of Electronics, Information and Communication Engineers): Kikai-Shinko-Kaikan Bldg, 5-8, Shibakoen 3-chome, Minato-ku, Tokyo 105-0011; tel. (3) 3433-6691; fax (3) 3433-6659; f. 1917; 40,000 mems; Pres. HISASHI KANEKO; publs *Journal*, *Transactions* (9 series, incl. *Original Contributions in English and Abstracts in English from the Transactions*, monthly).

Doboku-Gakkai (Japan Society of Civil Engineers): Yotsuya 1-chome, Shinjuku-ku, Tokyo; tel. (3) 3355-3441; fax (3) 5379-0125; e-mail web@jsce.or.jp; internet www.jsce.or.jp; f. 1914; 40,742 mems; library of 45,000 vols; Pres. MICHIO SUZUKI; Exec. Dir. ITSUJI MIYOSHI; publs *Journal* (monthly), *Coastal Engineering in Japan* (in English, 2 a year), *Transactions* (monthly), *Civil Engineering, JSCE* (annually).

Doshitsu Kogakkai (Japanese Society of Soil Mechanics and Foundation Engineering): Sugayama Bldg 4F, Kanda Awaji-cho 2-23, Chiyoda-ku, Tokyo; tel. (3) 3251-7661; fax (3) 3251-6688; f. 1949; 13,000 mems; Pres. YOSHIAKI YOSHIMI; publs *Soils and Foundations* (quarterly), *Tsuchi to Kiso* (monthly).

Keikinzoku Gakkai (Japan Institute of Light Metals): Tukamoto-Sazan Bldg, 2-15, Ginza 4 chome, Chuo-ku, Tokyo 104-0061; tel. (3) 3538-0232; fax (3) 3538-0226; f. 1951; 2,222 mems; Pres. AKIHIKO KAMIO; publ. *Journal* (monthly in Japanese and synopsis in English).

Keisoku Jidouseigyo Gakkai SICE (Society of Instrument and Control Engineers): 35-28-303, Hongo 1-chome, Bunkyo-ku, Tokyo 113; tel (03) 3814-4121; fax (3) 3814-4699; f. 1962; 9,183 mems; Pres. MAKOTO IBUKA; Sec.-Gen. YASUTAKA SAITO; publs *Journal* (monthly), *Transactions* (monthly).

Kuki-Chowa Eisei Kogakkai (Society of Heating, Air-conditioning and Sanitary Engineers of Japan): 8-1, 1-chome, Kitashinjuku, Shinjuku-ku, Tokyo; f. 1917; 17,000 mems; Pres. M. KAMATA; publs *Journal* (monthly), *Transactions* (monthly).

Nihon Genshiryoku Gakkai (Atomic Energy Society of Japan): Shimbashi 2-3-7, Minato-ku, Tokyo 105-0004; tel. (3) 3508-1261; fax (3) 3581-6128; e-mail atom@aesj.or.jp; internet wwwsoc.nii.ac.jp/aesj; f. 1959; peaceful uses of atomic energy; 7,700 mems; Pres. Dr M. TAKUMA; Sec.-Gen. Y. TARUISHI; publs *Nihon-Genshiryoku-Gakkai Shi* (monthly), *Journal of Nuclear Science and Technology* (monthly), *Transactions of the Atomic Energy Society of Japan* (quarterly).

Nihon Kasai Gakkai (Japanese Association for Fire Science and Engineering): Business Center for Academic Science, 2-chome 4-16 Yayoi, Bunkyo-ku, Tokyo 113; f. 1951; 2,000 mems; Pres. TAKAO WAKAMATU; publs *Bulletin* (2 a year), *Kasai* (Fire, every 2 months).

Nihon Kikai Gakkai (Japan Society of Mechanical Engineers): Shinanomachi-Rengakan 5F, 35 Shinanomachi, Shinjuku-ku, Tokyo 160-0016; tel. (3) 5360-3500; fax (3) 5360-3508; e-mail wwwadmin@jsme.or.jp; internet www.jsme.or.jp; f. 1897; 40,000 mems; Pres. AKIRA NAGASHIMA; publs *Journal* (monthly), *Transactions* (monthly), *JSME International Journal* (in English, monthly).

Nihon Shashin Sokuryo Gakkai (Japan Society of Photogrammetry and Remote Sensing): Daichi Honan Bldg 502, 2-8-17 Minami Ikebukoro, Toshima-ku, Tokyo 171; tel. (3) 3984-7040; fax (3) 3984-7402; internet jsprs.iis.u-tokyo.ac.jp; f. 1962; 1,067 mems; Pres.

K. OTAKE; Sec.-Gen. RYUTARO TATEISHI; publ. *Shashinsokuryo to Rimotosenshingu* (6 a year).

Nippon Kinzoku Gakkai (Japan Institute of Metals): 1-14-32 Ichibancho, Aoba-ku, Sendai 980-8544; tel. (22) 223-3685; fax (22) 223-6312; e-mail secgnl@jim.or.jp; f. 1937; 10,000 mems; Pres. KIYOHITO ISHIDA; publs *Journal* (monthly), *Bulletin* (monthly), *Materials Transactions* (monthly, in English).

Nippon Kogakukai (Japan Federation of Engineering Societies): Nogizaka Bldg, 6-41, Akasaka 9-chome, Minato-ku, Tokyo 107; f. 1879.

Nippon Koku Ūchu Gakkai (Japan Society for Aeronautical and Space Sciences): 18-2 Shinbashi 1-chome, Minato-ku, Tokyo 105; tel. (3) 3501-0463; f. 1934; 4,400 mems; Pres. Prof. KANICHIROU KATO; publs *Journal* (monthly), *Transactions* (quarterly).

Nippon Seramikusu Kyoukai (Ceramic Society of Japan): 22-17, 2-chome, Hyakunin-cho, Shinjuku-ku, Tokyo 169-0073; fax (3) 3362-5714; e-mail information@cersj.org; internet www.ceramic.or.jp; f. 1891; 5,546 mems; Pres. YOSHINORI KOKUBU; publs *Journal*, *Ceramics Japan* (Bulletin).

Nippon Shashin Gakkai (Society of Photographic Science and Technology of Japan): Tokyo Polytechnic Institute, 2-9-5 Hon-cho, Nakano-ku, Tokyo 164; f. 1925; 1,550 mems; Pres. T. WAKABAYASHI; publ. *Journal* (every 2 months).

Nippon Tekko Kyoukai (Iron and Steel Institute of Japan): Niikura Building, 2-Kanda-Tsukasacho 2-chome, Chiyoda-ku, Tokyo 101-0048; tel. (3) 5209-7011; fax (3) 3257-1110; e-mail admin@isij.or.jp; internet www.isij.or.jp; f. 1915; 9,274 mems; Pres. Dr NAOKI OKUMURA; publs *Tetsu-to-Hagané* (Iron and Steel, monthly, Japanese), *ISIJ International* (monthly, English), *Ferrum* (bulletin, monthly, Japanese).

Nippon Tribologi Gakkai (Japanese Society of Tribologists): c/o Kikai Shinko Kaikan No. 407-2, 3-5-8, Shibakoen, Minato-ku, Tokyo 105-0001; tel. (3) 3434-1926; fax (3) 3434-3556; f. 1956; 3,044 mems; Pres. K. KIMURA; publ. *Tribologists* (monthly).

Nogyo-Doboku Gakkai (Japanese Society of Irrigation, Drainage and Reclamation Engineering): Nogyo Doboku-Kaikan, 34-4 Shinbashi 5-chome, Tokyo 105-0004; tel. (3) 3436-3418; fax (3) 3435-8494; e-mail suido@jsidre.or.jp; internet www.jsidre.or.jp; f. 1929; 13,000 mems; Pres. Prof. HASEGAWA TAKASHI; publs *Journal* (monthly), *Transactions* (every 2 months), *Journal of Rural and Environmental Engineering* (2 a year, English).

Seisan Gijutsu Kenkyusho (Institute of Industrial Science): c/o The University of Tokyo, 4-6-1 Komaba, Meguro-ku, Tokyo 153-8505; tel. (3) 5454-6024; fax (3) 5452-6094; e-mail kokusai@iis.u-tokyo.ac.jp; internet www.iis.u-tokyo.ac.jp; f. 1949; Dir-Gen. Prof. S. NISHIO; publs *Seisan-Kenkyu* (monthly), *Annual Report*.

Shigen Sozai Gakkai (Mining and Materials Processing Institute of Japan): Nogizaka Bldg, 9-6-41 Akasaka, Minato-ku, Tokyo 107; tel. (3) 3402-0541; fax (3) 3403-1776; f. 1885; 2,627 mems; Sec.-Gen. YAMAGUCHI TAKASHI; publs *Journal* (monthly), *Metallurgical Review* (2 a year), *MMIJ Proceedings* (2 a year).

Sisutemu Seigyo Jyouhou Gakkai (Institute of Systems, Control and Information Engineers): 14 Yoshidakawaharacho, Sakyo ward, Kyoto City, Kyoto 606; f. 1957; 2,744 mems; Pres. MINORU ABE; publ. *Systems, Control and Information* (monthly).

Yosetsu Gakkai (Japan Welding Society): 1-11 Sakuma-cho, Kanda, Chiyoda-ku, Tokyo; tel. (3) 3253-0488; fax (3) 3253-3059; internet wwwsoc.nii.ac.jp/jws; f. 1925; 5,000 mems; Pres. Dr SHUZO SUSEI; publ. *Journal* (monthly).

Research Institutes

GENERAL

Kokusai Nihon Bunka Kenkyu Center (International Research Center for Japanese Studies): 3–2 Oeyama-cho, Goryo, Nishikyo-ku, Kyoto 610-1192; tel. (75) 335-2222; fax (75) 335-2091; e-mail www-admin@nichibun.ac.jp; internet www.nichibun.ac.jp; f. 1987; attached to the Nat. Institutes for the Humanities (an Inter-Univ. Research Institute Corporation); interdisciplinary and comprehensive research on Japanese studies, and research co-operation; library: approx. 400,000 vols, 5,500 periodicals; Dir-Gen. Dr MOTOKO KATAKURA; publs *Japan Review* (English), *Nihon Kenkyu* (Japanese).

Sogo Kenkyu Kaihatsu Kiko (National Institute for Research Advancement): 34F Yebisu Garden Place Tower, 4-20-3 Ebisu, Shibuya-ku, Tokyo 150-6034; tel. (3) 5448-1700; fax (3) 5448-1743; e-mail www@nira.go.jp; internet www.nira.go.jp; f. 1974 under parliamentary legislation to promote and conduct inter-disciplinary research that focuses on the problems facing modern society and their alleviation; conducts its own research, also commissions and subsidizes research by other bodies; promotes international exchange of research affecting policy-making around the world; research results are made public through lectures, symposia or publication of reports; Chair YOTARO KOBAYASHI; Pres. MOTOSHIGE ITO; Executive Vice-Presidents YOSHIO EZAKI YASUO SAWAI; publs *Almanac of Think Tanks in Japan*, *NIRA Kenkyu Hokokusho*, *NIRA News*, *NIRA Research Output* (in English), *NIRA Review* (in English), *NIRA Seisaku Kenkyu*, *NIRA's World Directory of Think Tanks* (in English).

AGRICULTURE, FISHERIES AND VETERINARY SCIENCE

Forest and Forest Products Research Institute: 1 Matsunosato, Tsukuba Ibaraki 305-8687; tel. (29) 873-3211; fax (29) 874-3720; internet www.ffpri.affrc.go.jp; f. 1878; library of 383,000 vols (incl. Br. Stations); Pres. KAZUO SUZUKI; publ. *Bulletin* (quarterly).

National Agriculture Research Center: 3-1-1 Kannondai, Tsukuba, Ibaraki 305-8666; tel. (29) 838-8481; fax (29) 838-8484; e-mail www@narc.affrc.go.jp; internet naro.narc.affrc.go.jp; f. 1981; 208 mems; library of 151,000 vols, 5,800 periodicals; Dir-Gen. SHIGEO MATSUI; publs *Bulletin* (2 a year), *Miscellaneous* (annually), *Farming System Research* (annually).

National Food Research Institute: 2-1-12 Kannondai, Tsukuba, Ibaraki 305-8642; tel. (29) 838-7971; fax (29) 838-7996; internet www.nfri.affrc.go.jp; f. 1934; food processing, chemistry, technology, storage, engineering, distribution, nutrition; applied microbiology, analysis, radiation, etc.; 121 mems; library of 40,000 vols; Dir Dr S. TANIGUCHI; publs *Report of the National Food Research Institute*, *Food Science and Technology*.

National Institute for Rural Engineering: 2-1-6 Kannondai, Tsukuba-shi, Ibaraki-ken 305-8609; tel. (298) 38-7513; fax (298) 38-7609; internet www.nkk.affrc.go.jp; f. 1988; Research on engineering technologies for agriculture and rural community areas; 115 mems; library of 38,000 vols; Director-General HIROSHI SATO; publs *Bulletin* (monthly), *Technical Report* (irregular).

National Institute of Animal Health: 3-1-5, Kannondai, Tsukuba-shi, Ibaraki 305-0856; tel. (29) 838-7708; fax (29) 838-7907; e-mail ref-niah@ml.affrc.go.jp; internet niah.naro.affrc.go.jp/index.html; f. 1921; veterinary medicine, animal husbandry, biology; 3 br. laboratories; library of 21,422 vols, 2,099 serial titles; Dir-Gen. Dr TOSHIAKI TANIGUCHI; publs *Bulletin* (annually), *Animal Health* (research report, annually).

National Institute of Crop Science: 2-1-18 Kannondai, Tsukuba, Ibaraki 305-8518; tel. (298) 38-7849; fax (298) 38-7488; e-mail www@nics.affrc.go.jp; internet nics.naro.affrc.go.jp; f. 1893; library of 130,000 vols; publ. *Bulletin* (irregular).

National Institute of Fruit Tree Science: 2-1 Fujimoto, Tsukuba, Ibaraki 305-8605; tel. (29) 838-6451; fax (29) 838-6437; e-mail www@fruit.affrc.go.jp; internet fruit.naro.affrc.go.jp; f. 1902; library of 60,000 vols; Dir Dr ICHIRO KAJIURA; publ. *Bulletin* (annually).

National Institute of Livestock and Grassland Science: 2 Ikenodai, Kukizaki, Inashiki Ibaraki 305-0901; tel. (298) 38-8618; fax (298) 38-8573; e-mail www@nilgs-t.affrc.go.jp; internet www.nilgs.naro.affrc.go.jp; f. 1916; library of 51,000 vols; publs *Bulletin* (irregular), *Annual Report*.

National Institute of Sericultural and Entomological Science: 1-2, Ohwashi, Tsukuba, Ibaraki 305-8634; tel. (298) 38-6011; internet www.nises.affrc.go.jp; f. 1988; research on development of new techniques for the promotion of sericulture, and use of functions of other insects and invertebrates; 184 mems; library of 75,000 vols; Dir S. KIMURA; publs *Bulletin* (1–2 a year), *Acta Sericologica et Entomologica* (2 or 3 a year), *Annual Report*, *News* (4 a year).

National Institute of Vegetable and Tea Science: 360 Kusawa, Ano, Age Mie 514–2392; tel. (59) 268-4621; fax (59) 268-1339; e-mail www@vegetea.affrc.go.jp; internet vegetea.naro.affrc.go.jp; f. 1902; publ. *Bulletin* (annually).

Policy Research Institute, Ministry of Agriculture, Forestry and Fisheries: 2-2-1 Nishigahara, Kita-ku, Tokyo; tel. (3) 3910-3946; fax (3) 3940-0232; e-mail www@primaff.affrc.go.jp; internet www.primaff.affrc.go.jp; f. 1946; library of 331,495 vols; Dir T. SHINOHARA; publ. *Journal of Agricultural Policy Research* (in Japanese).

ECONOMICS, LAW AND POLITICS

Chuto Chosakai (Middle East Institute of Japan): Sanko Park Bldg, 5th Fl., 7-3-1 Nishi-Shinjuku-ku, Tokyo 160-0023; tel. (3) 3371-5798; fax (3) 3371-5799; internet www.meij.or.jp; f. 1960; government-aided; exchanges information with other countries; research activities in four areas: political and diplomatic affairs, industry, economy, natural resources; library in process of formation; Chair. KOSAKU INABA; publs *Chuto Kenkyu* (Journal of Middle East Studies, monthly), *Chuto Kitaafurika Nenkan* (Yearbook of the Middle East and North Africa).

Japan Center for International Exchange: 9-17 Minami-Azabu 4-chome, Minato-ku, Tokyo 106; tel. (3) 3446-7781; fax (3) 3443-7580; f. 1971 to promote dialogue between Japan and the rest of the world; international conferences and seminars, overseas programme planning, promotion of policy studies and exchange programmes among philanthropic organizations; Japanese Secretariat of the Trilateral Commission; Pres. TADASHI YAMAMOTO.

Japan Economic Research Institute: 6th Floor, Kowa 32 Bldg, 2-32, Minami-Azabu 5-chome, Minato-ku, Tokyo 106-0047; tel. (3) 3442-9400; fax (3) 3442-9403; internet www.nikkeicho.or.jp; f. 1962; research and study of domestic and foreign economic and business management; library of 8,000 vols; Exec. Dir HIROSHI KIYASU; Sec.-Gen. ITSUROU ARIMITSU; publs *Annual Report*, research reports.

Japan Maritime Development Association: Kaiun Bldg, 6-4, 2-chome, Hirakawa-cho, Chiyoda-ku, Tokyo; tel. (3) 3265-5231; fax (3) 3265-5035.

Kabushikikaisha Mitsubishi Sogo Kenkyusho (Mitsubishi Research Institute, Inc.): 3-6, Otemachi 2-chome, Chiyoda-ku, Tokyo 100-8141; tel. (3) 3270-9211; fax (3) 3279-1308; e-mail webmaster@www.mri.co.jp; internet www.mri.co.jp; f. 1970; aims to meet new social, economic and industrial requirements in an age of advanced information systems and internationalization; research on national and international scale to serve the needs of government agencies and industry in the fields of economic, political, industrial and management affairs, techno-economics, social engineering, technology and data processing; 900 mems; library of 63,000 vols, 1,000 periodicals; Pres. SADAMI TAKAHASHI; publs *Outlook for the Japanese Economy* (2 a year), *MRI Newsletter*, *Journal* (2 a year), *Top Management Service (Membership)* (monthly), *MRI Analysis of Japanese Corporations* (2 a year).

Keidanren (Japan Federation of Economic Organizations): 1-9-4, Otemachi, Chiyoda-ku, Tokyo 100; tel. (3) 3279-1411; f. 1946; an independent body which aims to maintain contact with various economic sectors, to sound out opinions in business circles on economic problems, domestic and international, and to obtain practical solutions to these problems thereby promoting sound development of the national economy; carries out surveys, research studies; gives assistance in the exchange of information, dissemination of materials, etc.; 1,192 mems; library of 100,000 vols; Chair. TOYODA SHOICHIRO; Pres. and Dir-Gen. KOZO UCHIDA.

National Institute of Population and Social Security Research: 1-2-3 Kasumigaseki, Chiyoda-ku, Tokyo 100-0013; tel. (3) 3503-1711; fax (3) 3591-4816; e-mail soumuka@ipss.go.jp; f. 1939; part of Ministry of Health and Welfare; library of 16,000 vols; Dir Dr YUICHI SHIONOYA; publs *The Journal of Population Problems* (quarterly), *Annual Report*, *Field Survey Report* (annually), *Latest Demographic Statistics* (annually).

Nihon Baeki Shinkokai Ajia Keizai Kenkyusho (Institute of Developing Economies): 42 Ichigaya-Hommura-cho, Shinjuku-ku, Tokyo 162-8442; tel. (3) 3353-4231; fax (3) 3226-8475; e-mail info@ide.go.jp; internet www.ide.go.jp; f. 1960; library of 350,000 vols; Chair. NOBORU HATAKEYAMA; Pres. IPPEI YAMAZAWA; publs *Ajia Keizai* (monthly), *The Developing Economies* (in English, 4 a year), *Ajiken World Trend* (monthly).

Nihon Keizai Kenkyu Center (Japan Center for Economic Research): Nikkei Kayaba-cho Bldg, 2-6-1 Nihombashi-kayaba-cho, Chuo-ku, Tokyo 103; tel. (3) 3639-2801; fax (3) 3639-2839; f. 1963; 372 institutional, 280 individual mems; library of 45,813 vols, 920 periodicals; Pres. S. TOSHIDA; publs *Keizai Kenkyu Center Kaiho* (every 2 weeks), *Quarterly Forecast of Japan's Economy*, *Five-year Economic Forecast*, *Long-term Economic Forecast* (annually).

Nikko Research Center Ltd: 8-1 Nihonbashi, Kabuto-cho, Chuo-ku, Tokyo 103-0026; tel. (3) 5644-1600; fax (3) 5644-1698; e-mail nrc@nrc.nikko.co.jp; internet www.nikko-fi.co.jp; f. 1970; provides investment information for Nikko Securities Ltd and its clients; economic research on Japanese economy; business research on Japanese companies; projects research sponsored by governments and corporations; *c.* 200 mems; library of 20,000 vols; Pres. TAKAO FURUMI; Dir-Gen. MASAO YOKOMIZO; publs various monthly reports, *Nikko Monthly Bulletin* (in English), *NRC Chartroom—A Graphic Survey of the Japanese Economy and Securities Market* (monthly, in English).

Nippon Research Center Ltd: Shuwa-Sakurabashi Bldg, 4-5-4 Hatchobori, Chuo-ku, Tokyo 104; f. 1960 by interdisciplinary researchers and business men to meet the needs of industrial and economic circles; marketing and public opinion research, marketing consultancy, public relations, economic forecasting and urban and regional development; 96 staff; library: *c.* 3,000 vols; Chair. MATSUO SUZUKI; Pres. KOHJI NIKI; publ. *Bulletin of Marketing Research* (annually, in Japanese).

Rôdô Kagaku Kenkyusho (Institute for Science of Labour): 2-8-14, Sugao, Miyamae-ku, Kawasaki-shi, Kanagawa-ken 216-8501; e-mail isl.info@isl.or.jp; f. 1921; work stress, human-technology interaction, systems safety, human work environment management, chemical health risk management, occupational epidemiology, employment and working life conditions, local industries and welfare support; Chair. ISAO AMAGI; Dir of Research KAZUTAKA KOGI; publs *Rôdô Kagaku* (Journal of Science of Labour, monthly), *Rôdô no Kagaku* (Digest of Science of Labour, monthly), *Reports and Monographs*.

Seisaku Kagaku Kenkyusho (Institute for Policy Sciences, Japan): Friend Bldg, 2-4-11, Nagata-cho, Chiyoda-ward, Tokyo; tel. (3) 3581-2141; fax (3) 3581-2143; f. 1971; independent institute authorized by the Ministries of Finance and International Trade and Industry; undertakes its own and contractual research in the problems of advanced societies caused by technological innovation, industrialization, urbanization, etc.; research in the fields of regional development, environmental problems, energy and natural resources, economic and social problems, etc.; Chair. and Exec. Dir. SHIGERU WATANABE; publs research reports, *The 21st Century Forum* (quarterly).

EDUCATION

Kokuritsu Kyoiku Seisaku Kenkyujo (National Institute for Educational Policy Research): 6-5-22 Shimomeguro, Meguro-ku, Tokyo 153-8681; tel. (3) 5721-5150; fax (3) 3714-7073; e-mail info@nier.go.jp; internet www.nier.go.jp; f. 1949; conducts basic research on specific issues for use in the planning and formulation of education policy and also pursues a wide range of activities such as providing academic sectors with information about educational studies, conducting research studies in conjunction with schools, pursuing practical research into social education, and conducting joint int. initiatives (incl. research studies) in the education field; library: see Libraries; Dir-Gen. SHIGERU YOSHIDA; publs *Bulletin* (in Japanese, annual; in English, irreg.), *Koho* (in Japanese, 6 a year), *Unesco-NIER Newsletter* (in English, 3 a year), *Kenkyushuroku* (in Japanese, 2 a year).

FINE AND PERFORMING ARTS

Tokyo Bunkazai Kenkyu-jo (Tokyo National Research Institute of Cultural Properties): 13–43 Ueno Park, Taito-ku, Tokyo 110-8713; tel. (3) 3823-2241; fax (3) 3828-2434; internet www.tobunken.go.jp; f. 1930; depts incl. Research Programming, Intangible Cultural Heritage; also Centre for Conservation Science and Restoration Techniques, Japan Centre for Int. Co-operation in Conservation and Div. of General Affairs; library of 110,000 vols; Dir-Gen. SUZUKI NORIO; publs *Bijutsu Kenkyu* (Journal of Art Studies, quarterly), *Nihon Bijutsu Nenkan* (Year Book of Japanese Art), *Hozon Kagaku* (Science for Conservation, annual), *Proceedings of the International Symposium on the Conservation and Restoration of Cultural Property* (annual).

Tōyō Ongaku Gakkai (Society for Research in Asiatic Music): 201 Daini Hachikou House, 5-9-25 Yanaka, Taito-ku, Tokyo 110-0001; tel. (3) 3823-5173; fax (3) 3823-5174; e-mail leno3210@nifty.com; internet wwwsoc.nii.ac.jp/tog; f. 1936; aims to promote research in Japanese and other Asian music and ethnomusicology; 750 mems; Pres. KAZUYUKI TANIMOTO; publ. *Tōyō Ongaku Kenkyū* (annually).

HISTORY, GEOGRAPHY AND ARCHAEOLOGY

Geographical Survey Institute: Kitasato-1, Tsukuba-shi, Ibaraki-ken 305-0811; tel. (29) 864-1111; fax (29) 864-8087; f. 1869; part of Ministry of Construction; library of 32,000 vols; Dir YOSHIHISA HOSHINO; publ. *Bulletin* (irregular).

LANGUAGE AND LITERATURE

Gengo Bunka Kenkyujo (Research Institute for Linguistic Culture): 16-26 Nampeidai-machi, Shibuya-ku, Tokyo; Pres. MORITO NAGANUMA; publ. *Nippongo Kyoiku Kenkyu* (2 a year, Japanese).

Kokubungaku Kenkyu Siryokan (National Institute of Japanese Literature): 16-10 Yutaka-cho 1-chome, Sinagawa-ku, Tokyo 142-8585; tel. (3) 3785-7131; fax (3) 3785-4452; internet www.nijl.ac.jp; f. 1972 by the Ministry of Education, Science and Culture at the recommendation of the Japan Science Council and in response to requests for a centre for the preservation of Japanese classical literature; surveys, collects (largely in microfilm), studies, processes, preserves and provides access to MSS and old printed books relating to Japanese literature before 1868; also undertakes research in this field; provides scholarly community with facilities for consultation and reproduction of materials; historical documents division collects and preserves documents of *kinsei* (1600–1867); library: see Libraries; Dir-Gen. Dr YOICHI MATSUNO; publs *Bulletin* (annually), *NIJL Technical Report* (irregular), *NIJL Report* (2 a year), *Bibliographic Reports* (annually), *Bibliography of Research in Japanese Literature* (annually), *Proceedings of the International Conference on Japanese Literature in Japan* (annually), *Bulletin of the Dept of Historical Documents* (annually).

Kokuritu Kokugo Kenkyuzyo (National Language Research Institute): 3-9-14, Nisigaoka, Kita-ku, Tokyo 115; tel. (3) 3900-3111; fax (3) 3906-3530; f. 1948; library of 105,000 vols; Dir O. MIZUTANI; publs *Annual Report*, *Report*, *Linguistic Atlas of Japan* (6 vols).

MEDICINE

Cancer Institute, Japanese Foundation for Cancer Research: Kami-Ikebukuro, Toshima-ku, Tokyo, 170; tel. (3) 3918-0111; fax (3) 5394-3893; f. 1908; departments of pathology, experimental pathology, cell biology, viral oncology, biochemistry, gene research, physics, cancer chemotherapy, molecular biotherapy and human genome analysis; library of 5,000 vols, 10,000 periodicals; Cancer Institute Hospital and Cancer Chemotherapy Centre attached; Dir TOMOYUKI KITAGAWA; publ. *Japan Journal for Cancer Research* (monthly).

Fujisawa Foundation: Doshomachi 3-4-7, Chuo-ku, Osaka 541; tel. (6) 201-5894; f. 1946; fmrly Foundation for the Promotion of Research on Medicinal Sources; Chair. Dr T. FUJISAWA; publ. *ZAIDANHO* (2 a year).

Institute of Brain and Blood Vessels: 6-23 Ootemachi, Isezaki-city, Gumma; tel. (270) 25-0112; fax (270) 23-5522; f. 1963; clinical and basic research on cerebrovascular disease; 95 mems; Dir Dr TATSURU MIHARA; publ. *Nosotchu No Kenkyu* (Studies on Apoplexy).

Institute of Chemotherapy: 6-1-14 Kohnodai, Ichikawa-city, Chiba; tel. (473) 75-1111; fax (473) 73-4921; f. 1939; Dir Prof. TSUGUO HASEGAWA; publ. *Bulletin of the Institute of Chemotherapy*.

Institute of Public Health: 4-6-1 Shirokanedai, Minato-ku, Tokyo 108-8638; tel. (3) 3441-7111; fax (3) 3446-4314; e-mail webmas@iph.go.jp; internet www.iph.go.jp; f. 1938; part of Ministry of Health and Welfare; postgraduate education and research in public health; library of 68,000 vols, 1,500 periodicals; Dir K. FURUICHI; publ. *Bulletin* (quarterly).

Kekkaku Yobo Kai Kekkaku Kenkyujo (Research Institute of Tuberculosis, Japan Anti-Tuberculosis Association): 1-24 Matsuyama 3-chome, Kiyose-shi, Tokyo 204; tel. (424) 93-5711; fax (424) 92-4600; f. 1939; research on tuberculosis and respiratory diseases; information, surveillance and training centre; health education campaign against tuberculosis; 56 mems; library of 15,000 vols; Dir Dr T. MORI; publs *Information and Review of Tuberculosis and Respiratory Disease Research* (in Japanese, 4 a year), *Red Double-Barred Cross* (in Japanese, 6 a year), *Review of Tuberculosis for Public Health Nurses* (in Japanese, 2 a year).

Kitasato Institute: 9-1 Shirokane 5-chome, Minato-ku, Tokyo 108; tel. (3) 3444-6161; f. 1914; research on the cause, prevention and therapy of various diseases; 1,100 mems; library of 86,000 vols; Dir S. OMURA.

Kohno Clinical Medicine Research Institute: 1-28-15 Kita-Shinagawa, Shinagawa-ku, Tokyo; tel. (3) 474-1351; f. 1951; 62 staff; library of 3,000 vols; Dir M. KOHNO; publs *Archives*, *Bulletin*.

Leprosy Research Centre: 4-2-1, Aoba-cho, Higashi-murayama-city, Tokyo; tel. (423) 91-8211; fax (423) 94-9092; f. 1955; part of Ministry of Health and Welfare; Dir S. YAMAZAKI; publ. *Japanese Journal of Leprosy* (4 a year).

Miyake Medical Institute: 1-3 Tenjin-mae, Takamatsu-city, Kagawa; f. 1949; Dir T. MIYAKE.

National Cancer Centre: 5-1-1 Tsukiji, Chuo-ku, Tokyo 104-0045; tel. (3) 3542-2511; fax (3) 3542-3567; e-mail www-admin@ncc.go.jp; internet www.ncc.go.jp; f. 1962; diagnosis, treatment and research of cancer and allied diseases; Dept of Ministry of Health and Welfare; 800 staff; library of 56,000 vols, 17,000 monographs, 500 periodicals; Pres. TADAO KAKIZOE; Dirs KAZUHIRO NOMURA (Hospital), SETSUO HIROHASHI (Research Institute); publs *Collected Papers of Hospital* (in Japanese and English, annually, distributed free to libraries), *Collected Papers of Research Inst.* (in English, annually, distributed free to libraries), *Tumour Registration of Bone, Lung, Stomach, Blood, Brain, etc.* (in Japanese, distributed free to libraries).

National Institute of Genetics: 1111, Yata, Mishima-city, Shizuoka 411-8540; tel. (55) 981-6707; fax (55) 981-6715; e-mail shomuka@lab.nig.ac.jp; internet www.nig.ac.jp/home.html; f. 1949; part of Ministry of Education, Science, Sports and Culture; library of 20,000 vols; Dir Dr YOSHIKI HOTTA; publ. *Annual Report*.

National Institute of Health and Nutrition: 1-23-1 Toyama, Shinjuku-ku, Tokyo; tel. (3) 3203-5721; fax (3) 3202-3278; f. 1920; part of Ministry of Health and Welfare; library of 30,000 vols; Dir S. KOBAYASHI; publs *Annual Report*, *Japanese Journal of Nutrition* (in Japanese, every 2 months).

National Institute of Health Sciences: 1-18-1 Kamiyoga, Setagaya, Tokyo 158; tel. (3) 3700-1141; fax (3) 3707-6950; f. 1874; research in connection with the regulation of foods, drugs, medical devices, cosmetics and environmental chemicals; Dir MITSURU UCHIYAMA; publ. *Bulletin* (annually).

National Institute of Industrial Health: 21-1, Nagao 6-chome, Tama-ku, Kawasaki-city 214-8585, Kanagawa; tel. (44) 865-6111; fax (44) 865-6116; e-mail info@niih.go.jp; internet www.niih.go.jp; f. 1956; part of Ministry of Labour; library of 26,000 vols; Dir SHUNICHI ARAKI; publ. *Industrial Health* (quarterly).

National Institute of Infectious Diseases: Toyama 1-23-1, Shinjuku-ku, Tokyo 162-8640; tel. (3) 5285-1111; fax (3) 5285-1150; f. 1947; part of Ministry of Health, Labour and Welfare; research on communicable diseases, including an AIDS Research Centre; assay of biological products and antibiotics; library of 30,000 vols; Dir HIROSHI YOSHIKURA; publ. *The Japanese Journal of Infectious Diseases* (6 a year).

National Institute of Mental Health, National Centre of Neurology and Psychiatry: 1-7-3 Kohnodai, Ichikawa, Chiba 272; f. 1952; part of Ministry of Health and Welfare; Dir A. FUJINAWA; publ. *Journal of Mental Health* (annually).

Neuropsychiatric Research Institute: 91 Benten-cho, Shinjuku-ku, Tokyo; tel. (3) 3260-9171; fax (3) 3260-9191; e-mail info@seiwa-hp.com; internet www.seiwa-hp.com; f. 1951; research on sleep disorders, mood disorders; art therapy; Chief Dir Y. HONDA; Exec. Dir T. HIROSE.

Nukada Institute for Medical and Biological Research: 5-18 Inage-cho, Chiba-city, Chiba; f. 1939; Dir Dr H. NUKADA; publ. *Report* (irregular).

Ogata Institute for Medical and Chemical Research: 2-10-14 Higashi-Kanda, Chiyoda-ku, Tokyo 101-0031; tel. (03) 3865-7500; fax (03) 3865-7510; f. 1962; library of 12,000 vols; Pres. MASAHIDE ABE; publ. *Igaku to Seibutsugaku* (Medicine and Biology, monthly).

Tokyo Metropolitan Institute of Medical Science: Honkomagome 3-18-22, Bunkyo-ku, Tokyo 113-8613; tel. (3) 3823-2101; fax (3) 3823-2965; e-mail ui@rinshoken.or.jp; internet www.rinshoken.or.jp; f. 1975; research in aetiology and pathogenesis of intractable diseases and application of molecular and cellular biology to the aetiology of these diseases; library of 30,000 vols; Dir MICHIO UI; publs *Rinshoken News* (in Japanese, monthly), *Annual Report* (in Japanese).

NATURAL SCIENCES

General

Kokuritsu Kyokuchi Kenkyujyo (National Institute of Polar Research): 9-10 Kaga 1-chome, Itabashi-ku, Tokyo 173-8515; tel. (3) 3962-4712; fax (3) 3962-2529; e-mail shomu@nipr.ac.jp; internet www.nipr.ac.jp; f. 1973; attached to Joho Shisutemu Kenkyu Kiko (Research Organization of Information Systems); replaces the former Polar Research Centre of the National Science Museum; government-sponsored; implements programmes of the Japanese Antarctic Research Expeditions (JARE), organizes postgraduate courses in polar subjects, offers research facilities to national and foreign universities and individual researchers; library of 44,200 vols and bound periodicals57 full-time staff; Dir Prof. OKISUGU WATANABE; publs include *Nankyoku Shiryo* (Antarctic Record, 3 a year), *Memoirs of the National Institute of Polar Research* (Special Issue), *JARE Data Reports* (10 a year), *Journal* (annually), *Arctic Data Reports*, *Antarctic Geological Map Series*.

Biological Sciences

Kihara Institute for Biological Research: Yokohoma City University, Maioka-cho 641, Totsuka-ku, Yokohama 244; f. 1942; library of 20,000 vols; Dir M. UMEDA; publs *Seiken Ziho* (annually), *Wheat Information Service* (2 a year).

Mitsubishi Kasei Institute of Life Sciences: 11 Minamiooya, Machida-shi, Tokyo 194-8511; tel. (427) 24-6202; fax (427) 29-1252; e-mail hishi@libra.ls.m-kagaku.co.jp; internet www.m-kagaku.co.jp; f. 1971; research in human and general life science; library of 5,000 vols; Dir of Research Co-ordination FUNIO HISHINUMA; publ. *Annual Report*.

Osaka Bioscience Institute: 6-2-4 Furuedai, Suita-shi, Osaka 565-0874; tel. (6) 6872-4812; fax (6) 6872-4818; e-mail office@obi.or.jp; internet www.obi.or.jp; f. 1987; library of 12,000 vols; Dir Dr HIDESABURO HANAFUSA.

Tokyo Biochemical Research Institute: 41-8 Takada, 3-chome, Toshima-ku, Tokyo; f. 1950; Dir M. OKADA; publ. *Report* (annually).

Mathematical Sciences

Institute of Statistical Mathematics: 4-6-7 Minami Azabu, Minato-ku, Tokyo 106-8569; tel. (3) 5421-8719; fax (3) 5421-8719; internet www.ism.ac.jp; f. 1944; National Inter-University Research Institute; research in statistics; library of 52,000 vols, 2,250 periodicals; Dir Prof. GENSHIRO KITAGAWA; publs *Annals* (4 a year), *Proceedings* (2 a year).

Physical Sciences

Fukada Geological Institute: 2-13-12 Hon-Komagome, Bunkyo-ku, Tokyo 113-0021; tel. (3) 3944-8010; fax (3) 3944-5404; e-mail fgi@fgi.or.jp; internet www.fgi.or.jp; f. 1954; Chair TADASHI SATO; publs *Nenpo* (annually, Japanese or English, both with English abstract), *Fukadaken Library* (10 a year).

Institute of Physical and Chemical Research (RIKEN): 2-1 Hirosawa, Wako-shi, Saitama 351-0198; tel. (48) 462-1111; fax (48) 462-4714; e-mail library@postman.riken.go.jp; internet www.riken.go.jp; f. 1917; studies related to science and technology; 621 mems; library of 100,000 vols; Pres. KOBAYASHI SHUN-ICHI; publs *RIKEN Review* (6 a year), *Annual Report of Research Activities of RIKEN* (annually), *RIKEN Accelerated Progress Report* (annually).

Japan Atomic Energy Research Institute (JAERI): Fukoku-Seimei Bldg, 2-2-2

Uchisaiwai-cho, Chiyoda-ku, Tokyo; f. 1956; library of 36,000 vols; Pres. MASAJI YOSHIKAWA; publs *Nuclear Science Information of Japan* (irregular), *JAERI Reports* (irregular), *JAERI Research* (irregular), *JAERI-Data/Code (irregular)*, *JAERI-Tech* (irregular), *JAERI-Review* (irregular), *JAERI-Conf* (irregular).

Kobayasi Institute of Physical Research: 3-20-41 Higashi-Motomachi, Kokubunji, Tokyo 185-0022; tel. (42) 321-2841; fax (42) 322-4698; e-mail info@kobayasi-riken.or.jp; internet www.kobayasi-riken.or.jp; f. 1940; acoustics (noise and vibration, acoustic material, piezoelectric material); Pres. M. YAMASHITA; Dir K. YAMAMOTO; publ. *Annual Report*.

Meteorological Research Institute: 1-1 Nagamine, Tsukuba, Ibaraki 3050052; tel. (29) 853-8546; fax (29) 853-8545; www.mri-jma.go.jp; f. 1942; 174 mems; meteorology, geophysics, seismology, oceanography, geochemistry; Dir S. KADOWAKI; publ. *Papers in Meteorology and Geophysics* (quarterly).

National Astronomical Observatory, Mizusawa VERA Observatory: 2-12 Hoshigaoka-cho, Oshu-shi Mizusawa, Iwate-ken 023-0861; tel. (197) 22-7111; fax (197) 22-7120; internet www.miz.nao.ac.jp; f. 1899; astronomy, geophysics, geodesy; part of Institute of Natural Sciences; library of 68,400 vols; Prof. H. KOBAYASHI; publ. *National Astronomical Observatory Technical Reports of the Mizusawa Kansoku Centre*.

National Institute for Materials Science: 1-2-1 Sengen, Tsukuba, Ibaraki 305-0047; tel. (29) 859-2000; e-mail info@nims.go.jp; internet www.nims.go.jp; f. 2001; Pres. Prof. TERUO KISHI.

Space Activities Commission: 2-2-1 Kasumigaseki, Chiyoda-ku, Tokyo 100-8966; tel. (3) 3581-5271; fax (3) 3503-2570; f. 1968; contributes to a comprehensive and streamlined execution of government programmes on space development, including organization of administrative agencies, planning of general policies and outlining training programmes for researchers and technicians; Chair. SADAKAZU TANIGAKI; publ. *Monthly Report*.

RELIGION, SOCIOLOGY AND ANTHROPOLOGY

Okura Institute for the Study of Spiritual Culture: 706 Futoo-cho, Kohoku-ku, Yokohama; tel. (45) 542-0050; fax (45) 542-0051; f. 1929; Dir N. SASAI; publ. *Okuravama Ronshu*.

Zinbun Kagaku Kenkyusho: (Institute for Research in Humanities): 1 Ushinomiyacho, Yoshida, Sakyo-ku 606-8501, Kyoto; f. 1939; 54 staff; library: see Libraries; attached to Kyoto University; Pres. YUZO YAMAMOTO; the Institute is divided into three sections, dealing with Japanese, Oriental and Western Culture; publs *Zinbun Gakuho* (annually), *Toho Gakuho* (annually), *Annual Bibliography of Oriental Studies*, *Social Survey Reports* (annually), *Annales Zinbun* (annually), *News Letter Zinbun* (annually).

TECHNOLOGY

Applied Science Research Institute: 49 Tanaka Ohi-cho, Sakyo-ku, Kyoto 606; tel. (75) 701-3164; fax (75) 701-1217; f. 1916; metals engineering, surface modification, heat treatment, chemical engineering; Pres. B. KONDO.

Building Research Institute: 1 Tachihara, Tsukuba-shi, Ibaraki Pref.; tel. (29) 864-2151; fax (29) 864-2989; e-mail bri@kenken.go.jp; internet www.kenken.go.jp; f. 1946; 101 mems; town planning, building economics, building materials, construction techniques, structural engineering, earthquake engineering, fire safety, environmental engineering, building design and use; library of 50,000 vols; Dir-Gen. H. YAMANOUCHI; publ. *BRI Research Papers*.

Civil Engineering Research Institute of Hokkaido/Hokkaido Development Agency: Hiragishi 1-3, Toyohira-ku Sapporo 062-8602; internet www.ceri.go.jp; f. 1937; library of 36,000 vols in library; Pres. TOMONORI SAITO; publs *Monthly Report* (quarterly), *Report* (quarterly), *Annual Report*.

Communications Research Laboratory: 4-2-1 Nukui-Kitamachi, Koganei, Tokyo 184-8795; tel. (42) 327-5392; fax (42) 327-7587; e-mail publicity@crl.go.jp; internet www.crl.go.jp; f. 1952; next-generation information-communication networks, radio, space and optical communication, space weather forecasting, and related fields; library of 160,000 vols; Dir T. IIDA; publs *CRL News* (in Japanese, monthly), *CRL Annual Bulletin* (in Japanese), *Review* (in Japanese, 4 a year), *Journal* (4 a year), *Ionospheric Data in Japan* (monthly).

Engineering Research Institute: Faculty of Engineering, University of Tokyo, 11-16, Yayoi, 2 chome, Bunkyo-ku, Tokyo; f. 1939; 67 staff; library of 6,747 vols; Dir YOICHI GOSHI; publ. *Annual Report*.

Institute for Fermentation, Osaka: 17-85, Juso-honmachi 2-chome, Yodogawaku, Osaka 532; tel. (6) 302-7281; fax (6) 300-6814; f. 1944; preservation and distribution of micro-organisms and animal cells; 23 staff; library of 800 vols; Dir Dr TORU HASEGAWA; publs *List of Cultures*, *IFO Research Communications* (every 2 years).

Institute for Future Technology: Tomiokabashi Bldg, 2-6-11 Fukagawa, Koto-ku, Tokyo; f. 1971; research in the fields of technology forecasting, technology assessment and other socio-economic research in future technologies (electronics, telecommunications, space and energy); library of 15,000 vols; Pres. HIROEI FUJIOKA; Chief Sec. TAKAMITSU KOSHIKAWA; publ. *Kenkyu Seika Gaiyo* (research results, annually, in Japanese).

Institute of Energy Economics, Japan: Inui Bldg, 13-1 Kachidoki 1-chome, Chuo-ku, Tokyo 104-0054; tel. (3) 5547-0211; fax (3) 5547-0223; e-mail otoiawase@tky.ieej.or.jp; internet eneken.ieej.or.jp; f. 1966; co-ordinates information related to energy, its use, supply, conservation and economic aspects; provides material as basis for planning and policy formation by government and private business; int. co-operation on energy projects; 155 mems incl. energy-related industries and research institutions; library of 33,000 vols; Pres. MASAHISA NAITOH; Man. Dirs MASAHARU FUJITOMI, KOKICHI ITO, KENSUKE KANEKIYO, HIDEKI OKAMOTO, TSUTOMU TOICHI; publs *Energy Balance Table* (annually, in Japanese), *Energy Economy* (4 a year, in Japanese), *Energy Statistics* (annually, in Japanese).

Institute of Research and Innovation, Japan: 1-6-8 Yushima, Bunkyo-ku, Tokyo 113; tel. (3) 5689-6356; fax (3) 5689-6350; f. 1959; fmrly Industrial Research Institute, Japan; independent; innovative research and development in technology and socio-technology, including alternative energy sources, nuclear technologies and related innovative problems; 70 research staff; library: *c.* 2,000 vols; Pres. SHO NASU; Dir JIRO MIYAMOTO; publ. *Bulletin* (quarterly, in Japanese).

International Association of Traffic and Safety Sciences: 6-20, 2-chome, Yaesu, Chuo-ku, Tokyo 104-0028; f. 1974; aims to contribute to the realization of a better traffic society through the practical application of research conducted in a variety of fields; research surveys on traffic and its safety; collection and retrieval of information on traffic-related sciences; sponsorship of domestic and international symposia and study meetings; provision of awards; IATSS Forum, human resource devt programme for south-east Asian countries; Exec. Dir HIROSHI ISHIZUKI; publs *IATSS Research* (2 a year, in English), *IATSS Review* (quarterly, in Japanese with English abstracts), *Statistics: Road Accidents in Japan* (annual, in English), *White Paper on Traffic Safety* (annual, in English).

Japan Construction Method and Machinery Research Institute: 3154 Obuchi, Fuji-shi, Shizuoka-ken; tel. (545) 35-0212; fax (545) 35-3719; e-mail nakashima@cmi.or.jp; f. 1964; construction machine testing and associated research; Dir HIDESUKE NAKASHIMA; publ. *Annual Report*.

Kokudo Gijyutsu Seisaku Sougou Kenkyujo (National Institute for Land and Infrastructure Management, Ministry of Land, Infrastructure and Transport): 1 Asahi, Tsukuba-shi, Ibaraki-ken 305-0804; tel. (29) 864-4593; fax (29) 864-4322; e-mail kokusai@nilim.go.jp; internet www.nilim.go.jp; f. 2001; 43 research divisions; 386 staff; research on environment, roads, rivers, urban planning, building, housing, land and construction management, water quality control, coastal and marine environments, ports, harbours, airports, advanced information technology and disaster risk management; library of 193,000 vols; Dir TSUNEYOSHI MOCHIZUKI; publs *Annual Report* (in Japanese and English), *NILIM News Letter* (in English).

National Aerospace Laboratory: 7-44-1 Jindaiji Higashi-machi, Chofu-City, Tokyo 182-8522; tel. (422) 40-3000; fax (422) 40-3121; e-mail wwwadmin@nal.go.jp; internet www.nal.go.jp; f. 1955; part of Science and Technology Agency; library of 157,000 vols; Dir-Gen. S. TODA; publs *Technical Report* (irregular), *Technical Memorandum* (irregular), *Newsletter* (4 a year).

National Institute of Advanced Industrial Science and Technology: Tokyo Headquarters, 1-3-1, Kasumigaseki Chiyoda-ku, Tokyo 100-8921; tel. (3) 5501-0851; fax (3) 5501-0855; e-mail pl-publ@m.aist.go.jp; internet www.aist.go.jp; f. 2001; government-sponsored research institute; Dir Dr HIROYUKI YOSHIKAWA.

National Research Institute for Earth Science and Disaster Prevention (NIED): 3-1 Tennodai, Tsukuba-shi, Ibaraki-ken 305; f. 1963; library of 71,232 vols; Dir SHIGETSUGU UEHARA; publs *Report of NIED* (2 a year), *Major Disaster Field Study* (irregular), *NIED Research Notes* (irregular), *NIED Bulletin* (2 a year), *Strong-motion Earthquake Records in Japan* (annually), *Prompt Report of Strong-motion Earthquake Records* (irregular).

Branches:

Nagaoka Institute of Snow and Ice Studies: 187-16, Maeyama, Suyoshi Omachi, Nagaoka-shi, Niigata-ken 940; study of techniques for the prevention of snow damage.

Shinjyo NIED Branch of Snow and Ice Studies: 1400, Takadan, Toka-machi, Shinjo-shi, Yamagata-ken 996; study of the prevention of disasters caused by snow and ice.

National Research Institute of Brewing: 2-6-30 Takinogawa, Kita-ku, Tokyo; f. 1904; Dir H. MURAKAMI; publ. *Report* (annually).

Noguchi Institute: 1-8-1 Kaga, Itabashi-ku, Tokyo 173-0003; tel. (3) 3961-3255; fax (3) 3964-4071; e-mail noguchik@mb.infoweb.or.jp; f. 1941; research into carbohydrate chemistry, solid-state catalysts for ecoprocess; Pres. ITSUHO AISHIMA; publ. *Annual Report*.

Port and Harbour Research Institute: 3-1-1 Nagase, Yokosuka, Kanagawa 239; fax (468) 42-9265; f. 1962; attached to Ministry of Transport; research on harbour and coastal hydraulic engineering; library of 20,000 vols; Dir S. NODA; publs *Report* (quarterly), *Technical Notes* (quarterly), *Annual Report*.

Railway Technical Research Institute: 2-8-38 Hikari-cho, Kokubunji-shi, Tokyo 185-8540; tel. (425) 73-7258; fax (425) 73-7356; internet www.rtri.or.jp; f. 1907; research in railway engineering and magnetic levitated vehicles; 530 mems; library of 350,000 vols; Chair. YOSHIJI MATSUMOTO; Pres. HIROUMI SOEJIMA; publs *Quarterly Report of RTRI*, *Souken Hokoku* (RTRI Report, in Japanese, monthly), *Railway Research Review* (in Japanese, monthly).

Research Institute for Production Development: 15 Shimo Kamomori Honmachi, Sakyo-ku, Kyoto; f. 1947; Dir A. OKUDA.

Research Institute of Printing Bureau: 6-4-20 Sakawa, Odawara, Kanagawa; tel. (465) 49-4246; f. 1891; Dir H. NONAKA; publ. *Research Bulletin* (2 a year).

Ship Research Institute: 38-1, 6-chome, Shinkawa, Mitaka, Tokyo 181-0004; tel. (422) 41-3015; fax (422) 41-3026; e-mail bunsho@srimot.go.jp; f. 1916; attached to Ministry of Transport; shipbuilding and marine engineering; library of 68,000 vols; Dir NOBUTAKA NANBU; publ. *Papers* (6 a year).

Shobo-kenkyujo (National Research Institute of Fire and Disaster Management): 14-1 Nakahara, 3-chome, Mitaka-city, Tokyo; tel. (422) 44-8331; fax (422) 42-7719; f. 1948; library of 17,500 vols; Dir ASAMICHI KAMEI; publs *Shobo-kenkyujo Hokoku*, *Shoken Syuho* (annually).

Tensor Society: c/o Kawaguchi Institute of Mathematical Sciences, Matsu-ga-oka 2-7-15, Chigasaki 253; fax (467) 86-4713; e-mail tensorsociety@ybb.ne.jp; f. 1937; undertakes original research in the field of Tensor Analysis and its applications; library of 23,000 vols; Pres. Prof. Dr T. KAWAGUCHI; Sec. Prof. Dr H. KAWAGUCHI; publ. *Tensor* (3 a year).

Uchu Kagaku Kenkyusho: (Institute of Space and Astronautical Science): 3-1-1, Yoshinodai, Sagamihara, Kanagawa 229; tel. (427) 51-3911; f. 1981; government-sponsored central institute for organization of scientific space research; facilities in all fields: implements research, development and operation of balloons, sounding rockets, satellites and launch vehicles; 290 mems; library of 60,000 vols; Dir Prof. ATSUHIRO NISHIDA; publs *Uchuken Hokoku* (Japanese, irregular), *ISAS Report* (English, irregular), *ISAS Research Note* (English, irregular).

Libraries and Archives

Akita

Akita Prefectural Library: 2-52 Senshu-meitoku-cho, Akita-shi; tel. (188) 33-5411; f. 1899; 403,162 vols; Librarian N. FUJITA.

Chiba

Chiba Prefectural Central Library: 26 Ichiba-machi, Chiba City; 268,488 vols; Librarian S. TATEISHI.

Hakodate

Hakodate City Library: 23 Aoyagi-cho, Hakodate City; 122,500 vols (including branch library); Librarian I. FUKUDA.

Hiroshima

Hiroshima Prefectural Library: 3-7-47 Senda-machi, Naka-ku, Hiroshima City; tel. (82) 241-4995; fax (82) 241-9799; f. 1951; public library; 399,957 vols; Librarian K. HATAKEYAMA.

Ise

Jingu Bunko: 1711 Kodakushimoto-cho, Ise, Mie Prefecture 516-0016; tel. (596) 222737; fax (596) 225066; internet www.isejingu.or.jp/bunka/bunbody4.htm; 260,000 vols on Shinto; Librarian KUNIO KOBORI.

Kagoshima

Kagoshima Prefectural Library: 1-1 Shiroyama-machi, Kagoshima City; 222,357 vols; Librarian H. KUBOTA.

Kanazawa

Kanazawa City Library: 2-20 Tamagawa-cho, Kanazawa City 920; 510,000 vols; Librarian N. YOSHIMOTO.

Kanazawa Municipal Izumino Library: 22-22, 4-chome Izumino-machi, Kanazawa City 921-8034; tel. (76) 280-2345; fax (76) 280-2342; e-mail m-m@lib.kanazawa.ishikawa.jp; internet www.lib.kanazawa.ishikawa.jp; f. 1995; 360,000 vols; Dir S. KIDO.

Kobe

Kobe City Library: 7-2 Kununoki-cho, Ikuta, Kobe; f. 1911; 240,000 vols; Librarian S. AKAI.

Kobe University Library: Rokkodai-cho, Nada-ku, Kobe; tel. (78) 803-7315; fax (78) 803-7320; e-mail kikaku@lib.kobe-u.ac.jp; internet www.lib.kobe-u.ac.jp; f. 1908; 2,958,000 vols; Dir TAKESHI SASAKI.

Kochi

Kochi Prefectural Library: 3 Marunouchi, Kochi City; 141,927 vols; Librarian N. SHIMESHINO.

Kyoto

Institute for Research in Humanities Library: 1 Ushinomiyacho, Yoshida, Sakyo-ku, Kyoto 606-8501; attached to Kyoto University; 493,000 vols; Dir Prof. YUZO YAMAMOTO.

Kyoto Prefectural Library: Okazaki Park, Kyoto-shi, Kyoto; tel. (75) 771-0069; fax (75) 771-2743; f. 1898; 350,000 vols; Dir MINORU SHIBATA; publs *Toshokan Kyoto* (bulletin, annually), *Jigyou Gaiyou* (annual report).

Kyoto University Library: Yoshida Honmachi, Sakyo-ku, Kyoto 606-8501; tel. (75) 753-2613; fax (75) 753-2629; f. 1899; 6,228,385 vols; central library and 51 libraries of 13 graduate schools and 15 research institutes; Dir YUZO OHNISHI.

Ryukoku University Library: 67 Tsukamoto-cho, Fukakusa, Fushimi-ku, Kyoto 612; tel. (75) 645-7885; fax (75) 641-7955; f. 1639; 1,180,367 vols; Librarian JITSUZO SHIGETA.

Matsuyama

Matsuyama University Library: 4-2 Bunkyo-cho, Matsuyama 790; tel. (89) 925-7111; fax (86) 926-9116; e-mail mu-libs@matsuyama-u.jp; internet www.matsuyama.ac.jp; f. 1923; 540,000 vols; collection of rare books, including first editions of 18th and 19th c. works on political economy; Librarian Prof. K. SHISHIDO.

Nagoya

Nagoya City Tsuruma Central Library: 43 Tsurumai-cho, Tsurumai 1-1-155, Showa-ku, Nagoya City; tel. (52) 741-3131; fax (52) 732-9872; internet www.tsuruma-lib.showa.nagoya.jp; f. 1923; 1,040,400 vols; Librarian Y. WADA.

Nagoya University Library: Furo-cho, Chikusa-ku, Nagoya 464-8601; f. 1939; central library and 9 school and 3 institute libraries; 2,635,000 vols; Dir Dr M. KAINOH.

Naha

Ryukyu Islands Central Library: Central Library Building, Naha, Okinawa; f. 1950; 45,926 vols; central deposit library.

Nara

Nara Prefectural Library: 48 Nobori Oojicho, Nara City 630; f. 1909; 296,000 vols; Librarian KATSUKO TOYODA; publ. *Untei*.

Niigata

Niigata Prefectural Library: 2066 Meike, Niigata City; tel. (25) 284-6001; fax (25) 284-6832; f. 1915; 456,147 vols; Librarian K. SHIBUYA.

Niigata University Library: Ikarashi 2-Nocho, Niigata City 950-21; f. 1949; 1,397,560 vols; Dir S. KOBAYASHI.

Nishinomiya

Kwansei Gakuin University Library: 1-1-155 Uegahara, Nishinomiya, Hyogo 662-8501; tel. (798) 54-6121; fax (798) 54-6448; internet library.kwansei.ac.jp; f. 1889; 1,200,000 vols, nearly 40 per cent in foreign languages; br. libraries for 8 schools, 11 graduate schools, 2 satellite campuses; Dean of University Library Services TAKUTOSHI INOUE; publ. *Tokeidai* (Bulletin).

Okayama

Okayama University Library: 1-1 Naka 3-chome, Tsushima, Okayama City 700-8530; tel. (86) 252-1111; fax (86) 251-7314; internet www.lib.okayama-u.ac.jp; f. 1949; 2 br. libraries; 1,870,000 vols; Dir H. INOUE; publ. *Kai* (Library News, 2 a year).

Osaka

Kansai University Library: 3-3-35 Yamate-cho, Suita-shi, Osaka; tel. (6) 368-1121; fax (6) 330-1464; f. 1914; 1,528,962 vols (including 567,775 foreign), 21,168 periodicals; Librarian K. URANISHI.

Osaka Prefectural Nakanoshima Library: 1-2-10 Nakanoshima, Kita-ku, Osaka; tel. (6) 203-0474; fax (6) 203-4914; f. 1903; 509,000 vols; Head Librarian HARUYUKI YAMAMOTO; publ. *Osaka Furitsu Tosyokan Kiyou* (annually).

Sapporo

Hokkaido University Library: Kita 8 Nishi 5, Kita-ku, Sapporo 060-0808; tel. (11) 716-2111; fax (11) 747-2855; internet www.lib.hokudai.ac.jp/index_e.html; f. 1876; 20 br. libraries; 3,455,005 vols (including 1,693,682 foreign language texts); special collections on Slavic studies and North Eurasian culture studies; Librarian D.Med.Sc. YOSHIRO INOUE; publ. *Yuin* (quarterly).

Sendai

Tohoku University Library: Kawauchi, Aoba-ku, Sendai 980-77; f. 1911; 2,247,000 vols, including Kano Collection (108,000 vols) in Japanese and Chinese, the Tibetan Buddhist Canons (6,652 vols), Wundt Collection (15,800 vols) and several other special collections; Dir S. KOYAMA; publs *Annual Report*, *Bulletin*.

Shizuoka

Shizuoka Prefectural Central Library: 53-1 Yada, Shizuoka City; tel. (54) 262-1242; fax (54) 264-4268; e-mail mailmaster@tosyokan.pref.shizuoka.jp; internet www.tosyokan.pref.shizuoka.jp; f. 1925; 430,000 vols, 7,500 periodicals, 4,000 films and videotapes; Librarian YOSHIHIKO SUZUKI; publs *Aoi* (annually), *Toshokan-Dayori* (6 a year).

Tenri

Tenri Central Library: 1050 Somanouchi, Tenri, Nara 632-8577; tel. (743) 63-9200; fax (743) 63-7728; e-mail info@tcl.gr.jp; internet www.tcl.gr.jp; f. 1930; 2,000,000 vols (including 480,000 in foreign languages); special libraries: Yorozuyo Library on Christian Missions (including Jesuit mission printings in Japan), Kogido Library of Ito Jinsai on Confucian Studies, Wataya Library on Renga and Haikai Works (20,000 items), Africana Collection (6,000 vols); Chief Librarian KEIICHIRO MOROI; publ. *Biblia* (in Japanese, 2 a year).

Tokyo

Chuo University Library: 742 Higashinakano, Hachioji-shi, Tokyo 192-03; f. 1885; 1,365,024 vols (577,826 in foreign languages), 14,561 periodicals; Librarian Prof. NOBUO YASUI.

Hitotsubashi University Library: Naka 2-1, Kunitachi-city, Tokyo 186; tel. (425) 72-1101; f. 1887; 1,518,000 vols (including Kodaira branch); Librarian MASANORI NAKAMURA; houses branch library for Institute of Economic Research; f. 1940; 242,500 vols; Dir Y. KIKOKAWA.

Imperial Household Agency Library: 1-1 Chiyoda, Chiyoda-ku, Tokyo; tel. (3) 3213-1111; fax (3) 3214-2792; f. 1948; 87,946 vols; Librarian Mr MOMOTA.

International Christian University Library: 10-2 Osawa 3-chome, Mitaka-city, Tokyo 181-8585; tel. (422) 33-3301; fax (422) 33-3305; e-mail library@icu.ac.jp; internet www-lib.icu.ac.jp; 525,000 vols (incl. 257,000 foreign), 5,580 periodicals; Dir YUKI NAGANO.

Japan Meteorological Agency, Office of Archives and Library: 1-3-4 Ote-machi, Chiyoda-ku, Tokyo 100-8122; e-mail jma-library@met.kishou.go.jp; f. 1875; 110,000 vols; Chief Librarian TADAHIKO NODA.

Keio University MediaNet—Library and Computer Services: 2-15-45 Mita, Minato-ku, Tokyo 108; Chair. Y. KURASAWA.

Kokugakuin University Library: 4-10-28 Higashi, Shibuya-ku, Tokyo; f. 1882; 1,087,663 vols; Librarian Prof. TOSHIO SAWANOBORI; publ. *Kokugakuin Daigaku Toshokan Kiyo* (Library Journal).

Kokuritsu Kobunshokan (National Archives): 3-2 Kitanomaru Park, Chiyoda-ku, Tokyo 102-0091; tel. (3) 3214-0621; fax (3) 3212-8806; internet www.archives.go.jp; f. 1971; attached to Cabinet office; archives, Cabinet Library of 480,000 vols, and government records of 406,000 vols; Pres. MITSUOKI KIKUCHI; publs *Annual Report*, *Kitanomaru* (annually), *Archives* (3 a year).

Kokuritsu Kyoiku Kenkyusho Kyoiku Toshokan (National Institute for Educational Research Library): 6-5-22 Shimomeguro, Meguro-ku, Tokyo 153-8681; tel. (3) 5721-5096; fax (3) 5721-5164; e-mail library@nier.go.jp; internet www.nier.go.jp/homepage/jouhou/toshokan/index.html; f. 1949; 430,000 vols; publ. *Kyoiku Kenkyu Ronbun Sakuin* (Education Index, annually).

Ministry of Education Library: 3-2-2 Kasumigaseki, Chiyoda-ku, Tokyo 100; 120,000 vols; Librarian TARO SUZUKI.

Ministry of Foreign Affairs Library: 2-2 Kasumigaseki, Chiyoda-ku, Tokyo 100; 90,638 vols and 175 periodicals; Librarian S. UCHIDA.

Ministry of Justice Library: 1-1, 1-chome, Kasumigaseki, Chiyoda-ku, Tokyo 100; f. 1928; 278,000 vols; Chief Librarian FUSAO MURATA.

National Diet Library: 1-10-1 Nagatacho, Chiyoda-ku, Tokyo 100-8924; tel. (3) 3581-2331; fax (3) 3508-2934; e-mail kokusai@ndl.go.jp; internet www.ndl.go.jp; f. 1948; deposit library for Japanese publs and publs of the UN, UNESCO, ILO, WHO, ICAO, WTO, etc.; IFLA PAC centre for Asia, ISSN centre for Japan; is divided into one bureau and six departments: Administrative, Research and Legislative Reference, Acquisitions, Books, Serials, Special Materials and Library Co-operation; consists of the Main Library, Detached Library in the Diet, International Library of Children's Literature, Toyo Bunko (Oriental) Library and 27 branch libraries in the Executive and Judicial agencies of the Government; 7,490,000 books, 167,000 periodicals; Librarian MASAO TOBARI; publs *Japanese National Bibliography* (weekly), *National Diet Library Monthly Bulletin*, *General Index to the Debates* (each Diet Session), *Index to the Japanese Laws and Regulations in Force* (annually), *Reference* (monthly), *Annual Report of the National Diet Library*, *National Diet Library Newsletter* (in English, 6 a year online), *CDN LAO Newsletter* (in English, 3 a year).

National Institute of Japanese Literature Library: 16-10 Yutaka-cho 1-chome, Sinagawa-ku, Tokyo 142-8585; fax (3) 3785-7805; internet www.nijl.ac.jp; f. 1972; 184,225 vols old and current books; microforms of woodcuts, old printed books and MSS; 40,084 reels of microfilm, 57,358 sheets of microfiche, 74,169 vols of paper copy, 7,256 titles of serials; Archives for Japanese Historical Documents: 500,000 items (holdings), 5,808 reels of microfilm, 11,038 vols of paper copy, 5,000 articles of folk materia; Dir Y. OTAKA.

Norin Suisansho Toshokan: (Ministry of Agriculture, Forestry and Fisheries Library): 2-1, Kasumigaseki, 1-chome, Chiyoda-ku, Tokyo 100; f. 1948; 275,000 vols; Librarian TATEKI ARAI; publs *Norin Suisan Tosho Shiryo Geppo* (monthly review of publs on agriculture, forestry and fisheries), *Norin Suisan Bunken Kaidai* (annual annotated bibliography).

Ochanomizu University Library: 1-1 Otsuka 2-chome, Bunkyo-ku, Tokyo 112-8610; tel. (3) 5978-5835; fax (3) 5978-5849; f. 1874, reorganized 1949; 563,000 (including 179,000 foreign) vols; Dir YUJIRO OGUCHI.

Patent Office Library: 3-4-3 Kasumigaseki, Chiyoda-ku, Tokyo 100-8915; internet www.jp.go.jp; 144,502 vols; Librarian T. NAKASHIBA.

Science Council of Japan Library: 22-34, Roppongi 7-chome, Minato-ku, Tokyo 106; tel. (3) 3403-6291; f. 1949; 54,000 vols; Librarian MASATO OKAMOTO.

Seikado Bunko Library: 2-23-1 Okamoto, Setagaya-ku, Tokyo; 200,000 vols of Chinese and Japanese classics.

Sophia (Jôchi) University Library: 7-1 Kioi-cho, Chiyoda-ku, Tokyo 102-8554; tel. (3) 3238-3511; fax (3) 3238-3268; f. 1913; 920,000 vols, 10,500 periodicals; Librarian MIKITO HAYASHI.

Statistical Library, Statistics Bureau, Management and Co-ordination Agency: 19-1, Wakamatsu-cho, Shimjuku-ku, Tokyo 162; tel. (3) 3202-1111; f. 1946; *c.* 400,000 vols; Librarian KENJI OKADA; publs numerous reports, statistical handbooks.

Supreme Court Library: 4-2 Hayabusa-cho, Chiyoda-ku, Tokyo 102-8651; f. 1949; 260,000 vols; Librarian S. OGAWA.

Tokyo Geijutsu Daigaku Toshokan (Tokyo National University of Fine Arts and Music Library): Ueno Park 12–8, Taito-ku, Tokyo 110-8714; tel. (3) 5685-7736; fax (3) 5685-7804; internet www.lib.geidai.ac.jp; f. 1887; over 328,330 vols, 2,216 microfilms, 714 microfiches; also music and audiovisual collections (122,809 scores, 32,520 records, 5,463 CDs, 2,627 video recordings); Dir H. UENO.

Tokyo Metropolitan Central Library: 5-7-13 Minami-Azabu, Minato-ku, Tokyo 106-0047; tel. (3) 3442-8451; fax (3) 3447-8924; f. 1972; research and reference centre, centre of library co-operation in Tokyo; 1,471,000 vols and 10,000 periodicals; Yedo Collection, Kaga Collection (rare books of the Yedo Era), Morohashi Collection (Chinese classics), Sanetoh Collection (Chinese literature) and others; Dir TETSUYA SAITO; publs *Hibiya*, *Library Science Bulletin* (annually), *Annual Report*.

Tokyo University of Foreign Studies Library: 4-51-21 Nishigahara, Kita-ku, Tokyo 114-8580; f. 1899; 697,433 vols (including 442,235 foreign); Dir S. TAKAHASHI.

Tokyo University of Marine Science and Technology Library: Konan 4-5-7, Minato-ku, Tokyo 108-8477; tel. (3) 5463-0444; fax (3) 5463-0445; e-mail to-joho@s.kaiyodai.ac.jp; internet lib.s.kaiyodai.ac.jp; f. 1888; 296,000 vols (including 74,000 foreign); Chief Librarian HIROSHI OKADA; publ. *Journal* (annually).

Toyo Bunko (Oriental Library): Honkomagome 2-28-21, Bunkyo-ku, Tokyo 113-0021; tel. (3) 3942-0121; fax (3) 3942-0258; e-mail webmaster@toyo-bunko.or.jp; internet www.toyo-bunko.or.jp; f. 1924; 898,542 vols; research library specializing in Asian studies; special collections: Morrison collection of Western books on Asia, Iwasaki collection of old and rare Japanese and Chinese books and manuscripts, Kawaguchi collection of Tibetan and Buddhist classics; Dir YOSHINOBU SHIBA; publs *Toyo Gakuho* (4 a year), *Memoirs of the Research Department of the Toyo Bunko* (annually, joint publ. with National Diet Library).

University of Tokyo Library System: Hongo 7-3-1, Bunkyo-ku, Tokyo 113-0033; tel. (3) 5841-2612; fax (3) 5841-2636; e-mail kikaku@lib.u-tokyo.ac.jp; internet www.lib.u-tokyo.ac.jp; f. 1877; 8,120,000 vols, including Nanki collection (96,000 vols) and several other special collections; general library, Komaba library, Kashiwa library and 52 faculty and institute libraries; Dir K. SAIGO; publ. *Bulletin*.

Waseda University Library: 1-6-1 Nishi-waseda, Shinjuku-ku, Tokyo 169-8050; fax (3) 5272-2061; e-mail info@wul.waseda.ac.jp; internet www.wul.waseda.ac.jp/index.html; f. 1882; 4,480,219 vols; Librarian TETSUO KATO; publ. *Bulletin* (annual).

Toyonaka

Osaka University Library: 1-4, Machikaneyama-cho, Toyonaka, Osaka 560-0043; tel. (6) 6850-5045; fax (6) 6850-5052; e-mail service@library.osaka-u.ac.jp; internet www.library.osaka-u.ac.jp; f. 1931; 3,050,000 vols; Main library and 2 branch libraries; Dir MINORU KAWAKITA.

Utsunomiya

Tochigi Prefectural Library: 1-2-23 Hanawada, Utsunomiya, Tochigi 320; tel.

(286) 225111; fax (286) 247855; 196,579 vols; Librarian T. IZUMI.

Yamaguchi

Yamaguchi Prefectural Library: 150-1 Matsue, Ushirogawa, Yamaguchi City; f. 1903; 389,104 vols; Librarian TANAKA HIROSHI; publ. *Toshokan Yamaguchi*.

Yamaguchi University Library: Yoshida, Yamaguchi City 753; f. 1949; 2 br. libraries; 1,552,323 vols, 29,501 periodicals.

Yokohama

Kanagawa Prefectural Library: 9-2 Momijigaoka, Nishi-ku, Yokohama City; f. 1954; 76 mems; 540,875 vols; Librarian M. ANDO; publ. *Kanagawa Bunka* (every 2 months).

Yokohama National University Library: 79–6 Tokiwadai, Hodogaya-ku, Yokohama City 240-8501; tel. (45) 339-3221; fax (45) 339-3229; e-mail ref@lib.ynu.ac.jp; internet www.lib.ynu.ac.jp; f. 1949; 1,200,000 vols; Dir Prof. Y. GONJO.

Museums and Art Galleries

Abashiri

Abashiri Kyodo Hakubutsukan (Abashiri Municipal Museum): Katsuramachi 1-1-3, Abashiri-shi, Hokkaido 093; tel. (152) 43-3090; f. 1936; 600 local products, 25,000 articles of historical, geographical and archaeological interest, and 1,800 ethnological objects; Dir M. TATEWAKI.

Asahikawa

Asahikawa Kyodo Hakubutsukan (Asahikawa Folk Museum): Daisetsu Crystal Hall, Kagura 3-7, Asahi-chi, Hokkaido 070-8003; internet www.htokai.ac.jp/dd/museum/museum.html; f. 1952; cultural objects of Ainu people, many archaeological items.

Atami

MOA Museum of Art: 26-2, Momoyama, Atami 413-85; tel. (557) 84-2511; fax (557) 84-2570; e-mail art-admin@moaart.or.jp; internet www.moaart.or.jp; f. 1957, reorganized 1982 by Mokichi Okada Asscn; Japanese and Oriental fine arts: paintings, ceramics, lacquers, calligraphy and sculptures; library of 25,000 vols; Dir YOJI YOSHIOKA; publs *Digest Catalogue*, *MOA Museum Members Club* (4 a year), *Selected Catalogue* (5 vols).

Gora

Hakone Museum of Art: 1300 Gora, Kanagawa Pref.; tel. (460) 2-2623; fax (460) 2-0124; e-mail art-admin@moaart.or.jp; internet www.moaart.or.jp; f. 1952; private collection of Japanese ceramic works of art belonging to Okada Mokichi; Dir YOJI YOSHIOKA (Director of MOA Foundation).

Hakodate

Hakodate City Museum: Hakodate Park, 17-1 Aoyagi-cho, Hakodate City; f. 1879; oldest local museum in Japan; Dir M. ISHIKAWA.

Hiraizumi

Chuson-ji Sanko-zo (Chuson-ji Temple Sanko Repository): Hiraizumi-machi, Nishi-Iwai-gun; f. 1955 to preserve treasures and possessions of the Fujiwara family who were important in the late period of Heian (801–1185).

Hiroshima

Hiroshima Children's Museum: 5-83, Moto-machi, Naka-ku, Hiroshima City 730; tel. (82) 222-5346; fax (82) 222-7020; internet www.pyonta.city.hiroshima.jp; f. 1980; scientific and cultural programmes; planetarium; exhibits on science, transport, astronomy; Dir HIROSHI OKIMOTO; publs *Kagakukan Dayori* (monthly), *Planetarium* (4 a year), *Report of Activities* (annually).

Ikaruga

Hōryuji (Hōryūji Temple): Aza Hōryūji, Ikaruga-cho, Ikoma-gun, Nara Prefecture; a large number of Buddhist images and paintings; the buildings date from the Asuka, Nara, Heian, Kamakura, Ashikaga, and Tokugawa periods.

Ise

Jingu Chokokan (Jingu Historical Museum): Kuratayama, Ise-city; 1,734 exhibits, including treasures of the Grand Shrine of Ise (Naiku Shrine and Geku Shrine) and many objects of historical interest; library of 1,082 vols, MSS and pictures; Dir and Chief of Cultural Section of the Grand Shrine of Ise YASUJI AKIOKA.

Jingu Nogyokan (Agricultural Museum): Kuratayama, Ise-city; f. 1905; 9,583 exhibits connected with agriculture, forestry, and fishing (including collection of over 40 species of shark); Dir YASUJI AKIOKA.

Itsukushima

Itsukushima Jinja Homotsukan (Treasure Hall of the Itsukushima Shinto Shrine): Miyajima-cho, Saeki-gun; f. 1934; 4,000 exhibits of paintings, calligraphy, sutras, swords, and other ancient weapons; Curator and Chief Priest MOTOYOSHI NOZAKA.

Kamakura

Kamakura Kokuhokan (Kamakura Museum): 2-1-1 Yukinoshita, Kamakura City; tel. (467) 22-0753; fax (467) 23-5953; f. 1928; Japanese art and history in the Middle Ages; 3,521 valuable specimens of Japanese fine arts; 12 mems; library of 6,587 vols; Dir TATSUTO NUKI; publ. *Kokuhokan-zuroku*.

Museum of Modern Art, Kamakura: 2-1-53 Yukinoshita, Kamakura, Kanagawa 248-0005; tel. (467) 22-5000; fax (467) 23-2464; e-mail kinbi.4313@pref.kanagawa.jp; internet www.planet.pref.kanagawa.jp/city/kinbi.htm; f. 1951; modern and contemporary art in Japan and Europe; Dir TADAYASU SAKAI; publ. *Annual Report*.

Kobe

Hakutsuru Bijitsukan (Hakutsuru Fine Art Museum): 6-1-1 Sumiyoshiyamate, Higashinada-ku, Kobe 658; tel. (78) 851-6001; fax (78) 851-6001; f. 1934; 1,300 specimens of fine art, including noted Chinese ceramics, old bronze vases and silver ware, and oriental carpets; library of 10,000 vols; Dir HIDEO KANO.

Kobe City Museum: 24 Kyo-machi, Chuo-ku, Kobe 650-0034; tel. (78) 391-0035; fax (78) 392-7054; internet www.city.kobe.jp/cityoffice/57/museum; f. 1982; theme of museum is the historical view of international cultural intercourse, especially contact between eastern and western cultures; 38,000 items including 21 national treasure items, important collections of Namban and Kohmoh arts, 17th–19th c. maps, also historical and archaeological items; library of 55,000 vols; Sec.-Gen. KAZUO KOBAYASHI; publs *Yearbook*, *Museum Tayori* (newsletter, 3 a year), *Bulletin* (annually).

Kochi

Kochi Kaitokukan (Museum in Kochi Park): 1-2-1 Marunouchi, 780-0850 Kochi City, Kochi Prefecture; tel. (888) 24-5701; fax (888) 24-9931; e-mail 310073@ken.pref.kochi.lg.jp; internet www.pref.kochi.jp/~kochijo; f. 1913; 800 exhibits, including autographs and material of interest in Japanese historical research; Dir YUTAKA KONDO.

Kotohira

Kotohira-gü Hakubutsukan (Museum in the Kotohira Shrine): Kotohira-gü Shrine, Kotohira-machi, Nakatado-gun; 3,011 exhibits; Chair. MITSUSHIGE KOTOOKA; Sec. HAZIME HIRAO KOTOHIRA.

Kumamoto

Kumamoto Museum: 3-2 Furukyōmachi, Kumamoto City 862; tel. (96) 324-3500; fax (96) 351-4257; f. 1952; 10,000 books; 80,000 items of natural scientific interest (sea shells, minerals, rocks etc.) and 30,000 items of historical interest (folklore, archaeology etc.); Chief Officer NOBUO TOMOZOE; publ. *Gazette*.

Kurashiki

Ohara Bijutsukan (Ohara Museum of Art): 1-1-15 Chuo, Kurashiki City; tel. (86) 422-0005; fax (86) 427-3677; e-mail info@ohara.or.jp; internet www.ohara.or.jp; f. 1930; Western paintings since 19th c. and contemporary arts; modern Japanese ceramics and fabrics; modern Japanese oil paintings; Asiatic art; artwork from Ancient Egypt and Medieval Islam; Dir SHUJI TAKASHINA.

Kushiro

Kushiro-shiritsu Hakubutsukan (Kushiro City Museum): Harutori Park 1-7, Shunkodai, Kushiro; tel. (154) 41-5809; fax (154) 42-6000; e-mail ku7011@city.kushiro.hokkaido.jp; internet kcweb.city.kushiro.hokkaido.jp/museum/index.html; f. 1936; 12,130 earthenware articles, natural history museum; Dir KENGO ONOZAKI; publs *Memoirs of the Kushiro City Museum* (annually), *Science Report of the Kushiro City Museum* (4 a year).

Kyoto

Chishakuin (Treasure Hall of the Chishakuin Temple): Higashi-Kawaramachi, Higashiyama-ku, Kyoto; Buddhist equipment and utensils, old documents, paintings, calligraphy, sutras, and books in Japanese and in Chinese.

Daigoji Reihokan (Treasure Hall of the Daigoji Temple): Daigo, Fushimi-ku, Kyoto; f. 1936; contains 1,500 old art objects and 120,000 historical documents relating chiefly to Buddhism.

Jishoji (Ginkakuji) (Silver Temple): Ginkakuji-cho, Sakyo-ku, Kyoto; f. 1482 by Yoshimasa, eighth Shogun of Ashikaga, as twelve separate buildings in the grounds of his villa; only the Ginkaku or Silver Hall, and the Togudo are now left; Curator R. ARIMA.

Kitano Temmangu Homotsuden (Treasure Hall of Kitano-Temmangu shrine): Kitano Bakuro-cho, Kamigyo-ku, Kyoto; shrine dedicated to Michizane Sugawara, statesman and great scholar of Heian period; exhibits of treasure hall include the 'Kitano-Tenjin' history picture scrolls and an ancient copy of the 'Nihon Shoki'.

Korūji Reihōden (Treasure Museum of the Koryuji Temple): Koryuji Temple, Uzumasa, Ukyo-ku, Kyoto; f. 1922; many Buddhist images and pictures, including the two images of 'Miroku Bosatsu'; Curator EIKO KIYOTAKI.

Kyoto Kokuritsu Hakubutsukan (Kyoto National Museum): 527 Chaya-machi, Higashiyama-ku, Kyoto; tel. (75) 541-1151; fax (75) 531-0263; e-mail welcome@kyohaku.go.jp; internet www.kyohaku.go.jp; f. 1897 as Imperial Kyoto Museum; 52,692 books and 188,528 research photographs; 11,513 exhibits, including fine art and applied art exhibits and historical materials of Asia, chiefly of Japan; Dir Dr HISAYASU NAKAGAWA; Chief Curator KENICHI YUYAMA; publs *Gakuso* (annually), *Shaji Chosa Hokoku* (annually).

Kyoto-shi Bijutsukan (Kyoto Municipal Museum of Art): Okazaki Park, Sakyo-ku, Kyoto; tel. (75) 771-4107; fax (75) 761-0444; f. 1933; contemporary fine arts objects (mostly Japanese); Dir MITSUGI UEHIRA; publs *Annual Report*, *Museum Newspaper*.

Myōhōin (Treasure House of the Myōhōin Temple): Myohoin-maegawa-cho, Higashiyama-ku, Kyoto; possessions of Toyotomi-Hideyoshi and many other national treasures.

National Museum of Modern Art, Kyoto: Enshoji-cho, Okazaki, Sakyo-ku, Kyoto; tel. (75) 761-4111; fax (75) 752-0509; e-mail info@momak.go.jp; internet www.momak.go.jp; f. 1963; Japanese-style painting, oil painting, print, modern art, crafts, design, photography, sculpture; Dir TAKEO UCHIYAMA; Chief Curator YASUHIRO SHIMADA; publs *Museum News* (6 a year), *Annual Report*, *Membership* (quarterly).

Ninnaji Reihóden (Treasure Hall of the Ninnaji Temple): Ninnaji Temple, Omuro Daimon-cho, Ukyo-ku, Kyoto.

Rengeoin (Sanjusangendo) (Treasure House of the Rengeoin Temple): Mawari-cho, Higashiyama-ku, Kyoto; 'One Thousand Images' and many other Buddhist images.

Rokuonji (Treasures of the Rokuonji Temple): Kinkakuji-cho, Kita-ku, Kyoto; famed for its garden and gold pavilion.

Shoren-in (Treasure House of the Shōren-in Temple): Sanjōbō-machi, Awadaguchi, Higashiyama-ku, Kyoto; f. 1153; Dir JIKO HIGASHIFUSHIMI; library of 5,000 vols; rare books, writings, paintings, etc.

Taiten Kinen Kyoto Shokubutsuen (Kyoto Prefectural Museum Botanical Garden): Hangi-machi, Shimogamo, Sakyô-ku, Kyoto; 70,000 plants and 5,500 botanical specimens.

Toyokuni Jinja Hómotsuden (Treasure Hall of the Toyokuni Shrine): Shomen Chaya-machi Yamato-Ooji, Higashiyama-ku, Kyoto; treasures and possessions of Toyotomi-Hideyoshi, including paintings, painted screens, swords, etc.

Yogen-In (Treasure Hall of the Yōgen-In Temple): Sanju-sangendō-mae, Yamato-ōji Shichijō Higashi Iru, Higashiyama-ku, Kyoto.

Yūrinkan (Yurinkan Collection): 44 Okazaki-Enshōjichyô, Sakyō-ku, Kyoto; f. 1926; privately owned by the Fujii Foundation; rare antique Chinese fine arts and curios, including bronze and jade ware, porcelain, seals, Buddhist images, pictures, and calligraphy; Dir Z. FUJII.

Matsue

Koizumi-Yakumo Kinenkan (Lafcadio Hearn Memorial Museum): 322 Okudani-machi, Matsue City 690-0872; tel. (852) 21-2147; fax (852) 21-2156; f. 1933; collection of items belonging to Lafcadio Hearn; library of 492 vols (works by and on Hearn); Dir TOSHIO UCHIDA.

Shimane Prefectural Museum: 1 Tono-machi, Matsue City; tel. (852) 22-5750; fax (852) 22-6728; e-mail kodai@pref.shimane.jp; internet www2.pref.shimane.jp/kodai; f. 1959; bronze bells, bronze swords and other ancient heritage; Dir SYO KATSUBE; publs *News of the Institution for Ancient Study* (4 a year), *Studies of Ancient Culture* (annually), *Ancient Culture in Shimane* (annually).

Matsumoto

Matsumoto City Museum: 4-1 Marunouchi, Matsumoto City, Nagano 390-0873; tel. (263) 32-0133; fax (263) 32-8974; e-mail mcmuse@city.matsumoto.nagano.jp; internet www.city.matsumoto.nagano.jp; f. 1906; folklore, history, archaeology, star festival dolls, popular belief tools, fine art, agricultural tools; Dir KENICHI KUMAGAI.

Minobu

Minobusan Homotsukan (Treasury of the Kuonji Temple): Kuonji Temple, Minobu-machi, Minami-Koma-gun; 300 articles, examples of the fine arts, and materials connected with the history of the Nichiren Sect of Buddhism, the biography of Saint Nichiren.

Mount Koya

Kōyasan Reihōkan (Museum of Buddhist Art on Mount Kōya): Kōyasan, Kōya-cho, Ito-gun; f. 1926; 50,000 exhibits, including Buddhist paintings and images, sutras and old documents, some of them registered National Treasures and Important Cultural Properties; a centre of Buddhism in Japan; Dir CHIKYŌ YAMAMOTO.

Nagoya

Nagoya Castle Donjon: 1-1 Hon-maru, Naka-ku, Nagoya; tel. (52) 231-1700; built in 1612 by Ieyasu Tokugawa; destroyed by fire 1945; restored to its original form 1959; exhibition rooms, galleries and observatory; 1,049 paintings of the Kano school on sliding doors and ceilings; armoury and swords.

Nara

Kasugataisha Homotsuden (Treasure Hall of the Kasugataisha Shrine): Kasugataisha Shrine, Kasugano-cho, Nara City; f. 1934; the ancient, curvilinear style of architecture is called 'Kasuga Zukuri' after this shrine; Shrine Master CHIKATADA KASANNOIN.

Museum Yamato Bunkakan: 1-11-6 Gakuen-minami, Nara City; tel. (742) 45-0544; fax (742) 49-2929; internet www.kintetsu.jp/kouhou/yamato/index.html; f. 1960; art objects of East Asia, chiefly Japan, China and Korea; library of 20,000 vols; Dir Prof. AKIRA MIZUTA; publs *Yamato Bunka* (2 a year), *Catalogues of the Museum Collection* (English), *Bi-no-Tayori* (4 a year).

Nara National Museum: 50 Nobori-oji-cho, Nara-shi 630-8213; tel. (742) 22-7771; fax (742) 26-7218; internet www.narahaku.go.jp; f. 1895; Buddhist sculptures, paintings, applied arts, calligraphy, archaeological objects, etc.; also special exhibitions; library of 59,750 vols; Dir KENICHI YUYAMA.

Neiraku Museum: Isuien Park, 74 Suimon-cho, Nara City; tel. (742) 22-2173; fax (742) 25-0781; f. 1939; ancient Chinese bronze mirrors, seals, etc., and Korean potteries; Dir JUNSUKE NAKAMURA.

Todaiji: 406-1 Zōshi-cho, Nara City; tel. (742) 22-5511; fax (742) 22-0808; f. 752; headquarters of Kegonshū Buddhist sect; Daibutsuden: Main Hall of the Todaiji Temple, the largest wooden edifice in the world, the world-famous Great Image of Buddha and 2 Bodhisattvas; attached bldgs are the Hokkedō, Kaidan-in, Nigatsudō, which contain many famous images of Buddha and Bodhisattva; library of 70,000 vols, 10,000 manuscripts; Dir (vacant); publ. *Nanto Bukkyō: Journal of the Nanto Society for Buddhist Studies* (annual).

Yakushiji (Yakushiji Temple): 457 Nishi-no-Kyō-machi, Nara City 630-8563; tel. (742) 33-6001; fax (742) 33-6004; e-mail yksj8@mahoroba.or.jp; internet www.nara-yakushiji.com; f. 697; famous bronze images of the Yakushi Trinity; a pagoda 1,300 years old; Dir Lord Abbot S. MATSUKUBO.

Narita

Naritasan Reikokan Museum (Treasure Hall of the Naritasan-Shinshoji Temple): Narita Park, Narita-City, Chiba Pref.; f. 1947; contains treasures dedicated to the shrine and archaeological pieces from the region, 12,113 MSS and books, sculptures, botanical specimens; Curator SHOSEKI TSURUMI.

Omishima

Oyamazumi Jinja Kokuhokan (Treasure Hall of the Oyamazumi Shrine): Oyamazumi Shrine, Omishima town, Ochigun; f. AD1; 2,000 exhibits, including a large collection of ancient armour, swords, and the oldest mirrors in Japan; library of 20,000 vols; Curator YASUHISA MISHIMA.

Osaka

National Museum of Ethnology: 10-1 Senri Expo Park, Suita, Osaka 565-8511; tel. (6) 6876-2151; fax (6) 6875-0401; internet www.minpaku.ac.jp; f. 1974; 256,436 artefacts from Japan and abroad; conducts anthropological research and promotes general understanding and awareness of peoples, societies and cultures around the world; established as Inter-Univ. Research Institute; library of 587,115 vols, 15,586 journals, 69,325 audiovisual items; Dir-Gen. MAKIO MATSUZONO; publs *Bulletin* (in Japanese, English, French, Spanish, Russian, Chinese and German, quarterly), *Minpaku Anthropology Newsletter* (2 a year, in English), *Minpaku Tsushin* (newsletter, in Japanese), *Senri Ethnological Reports* (irreg.), *Senri Ethnological Studies* (in English and selected other European languages, irreg.).

Osaka Municipal Museum of Art: 1-82 Chausuyama-cho, Tennoji-ku, Osaka 543-0063; tel. (6) 6771-4874; fax (6) 6771-4856; internet www.city.osaka.jp/museum-art; f. 1936; Chinese, Korean and Japanese fine art; library of 11,000 vols; Dir YUTAKA MINO; publ. *Miotsukushi* (Bulletin, 2 a year).

Osaka Museum of Natural History: Nagai Park, Higashisumiyoshi-ku, Osaka 546-0034; tel. (6) 6697-6221; fax (6) 6697-6225; internet www.mus-nh.city.osaka.jp; f. 1952; entomology, zoology, botany, geology and palaeontology; Dir TAKAYOSHI NASU; Head Curator MOTOHARU OKAMOTO; publs *Bulletin*, *Nature Study*, *Occasional Paper* (annually), *Special Publications* (annually).

Tenri

Tenri University Sankokan Museum: 250 Morimedo-cho, Tenri City, Nara Prefecture 632-8540; tel. (743) 63-8414; fax (743) 63-7721; f. 1930; attached to Tenri University; ethnographic and archaeological items from all parts of the world.

Tokyo

Ancient Orient Museum: 1-4 Higashi Ikebukuro 3-chome, Toshima-ku, Tokyo 170; tel. (3) 3989-3494; fax (3) 3590-3266; f. 1978; archaeology and ancient history of Middle and Near East, Egypt, India and Central Asia; library of 9,000 vols; Dir Prof. NAMIO EGAMI; publ. *Bulletin* (annual).

Bridgestone Museum of Art, Ishibashi Foundation: 10-1, Kyobashi 1-chome, Chuo-ku, Tokyo 104-0031; tel. (3) 3563-0241; fax (3) 3561-2130; f. 1952 by Shojiro Ishibashi; private museum of 19th- and 20th-century European paintings and modern Japanese Western-style paintings; Dir NORIO SHIMADA.

Gotoh Museum: 9-25 3-chome Kaminoge, Setagaya-ku, Tokyo; f. 1960; Japanese, Chinese and Korean art; about 2,000 exhibits, incl. the 'Tales of Genji' scroll and the 'Diary of Lady Murasaki' scroll.

Inokashira Onshi Koen Shizen Bunkaen (Natural Science Park in Inokashira Park): 1-17-6 Gotenyama, Musashinoshi, Tokyo; zoo, botanical garden, research room, marine biology room.

Kokuritsu Kagaku Hakubutsukan (National Science Museum): Ueno Park 7-20, Taito-ku, Tokyo 110-8718; tel. (3) 3822-0111; fax (3) 5814-9898; e-mail webmaster@kahaku.go.jp; internet www.kahaku.go.jp; f. 1877; merged with Research Institute for Natural Resources in 1971; exhibits of natural history, physical science and engineering; library of 87,567 vols; Dir HIDEKI HAYASHIDA; publs *Bulletin* (in 5 series), *Memoirs* (annual).

Kotsu Hakubutsukan (Transportation Museum): 25 1-chome, Kanda-Sudacho, Chiyoda-ku, Tokyo; tel. (3) 3251-8481; fax (3) 3251-8489; e-mail gakugei@kouhaku.or.jp; internet www.kouhaku.or.jp; f. 1921; locomotives, electric equipment, motor-cars, aircraft, ships, etc.; Dir TATSUHIKO SUGA.

Meguro Parasitological Museum: 1-1 Shimomeguro, 4-Chome, Meguro-ku, Tokyo 153-0064; tel. (3) 3716-7144; fax (3) 3716-2322; f. 1953; science of parasites; Chief Curator SHUNYA KAMEGAI.

Meiji Jingu Homotsuden (Meiji Shrine Treasure Museum): Yoyogi, Shibuya-ku, Tokyo; f. 1921; 102 treasures and possessions of Emperor Meiji and 74 objects belonging to Empress Shoken; there is also a Memorial Picture Gallery.

Mori Art Museum: 53rd Fl., Mori Tower, Roppongi, Minato-ku, Tokyo; tel. (3) 6406-6100; fax (3) 6406-9351; e-mail info@mori.art.museum; internet www.mori.art.museum/; f. 2003; Dir DAVID ELLIOTT.

Museum of Contemporary Art: Metropolitan Kiba Park, 4-1-1 Miyoshi Koto-ku, Tokyo 135-0022; tel. (3) 5245-4111; Japanese and foreign art since 1945.

National Museum of Modern Art, Tokyo: 3 Kitanomaru Koen, Chiyoda-ku, Tokyo 102-8322; tel. (3) 5777-8600; internet www.momak.go.jp; f. 1952; colln of Japanese-style paintings, oil paintings, prints, sculpture, drawings, watercolours and photographs, and European and American works; incl. Crafts Gallery and Film Centre; Dir TETSUO TSUJIMURA; publs *Gendai no Me* (6 a year, Japanese), *National Film Centre Newsletter* (6 a year, Japanese).

National Museum of Western Art: 7-7 Ueno-koen, Taito-ku, Tokyo 110-0007; tel. (3) 3828-5131; fax (3) 3828-5135; e-mail wwwadmin@nmwa.go.jp; internet www.nmwa.go.jp; f. 1959 (building designed by Le Corbusier); 19th-century European paintings and sculptures collected by the late Kojiro Matsukata and new acquisitions of old masters; Dir KOICHI KABAYAMA.

Nezu Institute of Fine Arts: 6-5-1 Minami-Aoyama, Minato-ku, Tokyo 107-0062; tel. (3) 3400-2536; fax (3) 3400-2436; e-mail nezu@nezu-muse.or.jp; internet www.nezu-muse.or.jp; f. 1940; private colln by Kaichiro Nezu of 7,195 paintings, calligraphy, sculpture, swords, ceramics, lacquer-ware, archaeological exhibits; 187 items designated as nat. treasures; Dir KOICHI NEZU.

Nippon Mingeikan (Japan Folk Crafts Museum): 4-3-33 Komaba, Meguro-ku, Tokyo 153-0041; tel. (3) 3467-4527; fax (3) 3467-4537; internet www.mingeikan.or.jp; f. 1936; Japanese traditional folk craft and craft from around the world; spec. collns from founding mems of Mingei Movement: Soetsu Yanagi, Kanjiro Kawai, Shoji Hamada, Keisuke Serizawa, Bernard Leach, Shiko Munakata, Kenkichi Tomimoto and others; Dir SORI YANAGI; publ. *Mingei* (monthly).

Okura Cultural Foundation Okura Shukokan Museum: 2-10-3, Toranomon, Minato-ku, Tokyo; f. 1917; 1,700 articles of fine arts; library of 36,000 vols Chinese classics; Pres. NOBORU NISHITANI.

Shitamachi Museum: 2–1 Ueno-koen, Taito-ku, Tokyo; tel. (3) 823-7451; f. 1980; re-creation of the old commercial district of Tokyo; incl. typical street, wooden houses, life-size figures, furniture, pictures, books and letters, religious material, domestic utensils, Second World War items, games and musical instruments, cosmetics and accessories, etc.; Dir HIDENOBU HIROSE.

Shodo Hakubutsukan (Calligraphy Museum): 125 Kaminegishi, Daito-ku, Tokyo; f. 1936; colln of the calligrapher, the late F. Nakamura; 1,000 rubbed copies of the stone tablets and 'hōjō', ancient texts of calligraphy (10,000 articles).

Tokyo Daigaku Rigaku Kenkyu-ka Fuzoku Shokubutsuen (Botanical Gardens, Graduate School of Science, University of Tokyo): 7-1, Hakusan 3, Bunkyo-ku, Tokyo 112; tel. (3) 3814-2625; fax (3) 3814-0139; f. 1684, transferred to Univ. 1877; Nikko br.; research in systematic botany and conservation of plants; 6,000 kinds of plants; 2,500 in Nikko; associated with the herbarium TI with approx. 700,000 specimens; library of 20,000 vols; Dir Prof. Dr JIN MURATA.

Tokyo Kokuritsu Hakubutsukan (Tokyo National Museum): 13-9 Ueno Park, Taito-ku, Tokyo 110-8712; tel. (3) 3822-1111; fax (3) 3822-0086; internet www.tnm.jp; f. 1872; largest art museum in Japan; Eastern fine arts, incl. paintings, calligraphy, sculpture, metal work, ceramic art, textiles, lacquerware, archaeological exhibits, etc.; Dir-Gen. HIROSHI NOBAKI; publs *Museum* (monthly), *Tokyo National Museum News* (monthly).

Tokyo-to Bijutsukan (Tokyo Metropolitan Art Museum): Ueno Park 8–36, Taito-ku, Tokyo; tel. (3) 3823-6921; fax (3) 3823-6920; e-mail tobi@tobikan.jp; internet www.tobikan.jp; f. 1926; ancient and modern art exhibition, educational service, art library and gallery for group exhibitions; Dir YOSHITAKE MAMURO; publ. *Bulletin* (annual).

University Art Museum, Tokyo National University of Fine Arts and Music: Ueno Park, Taito-ku, Tokyo 110-8714; tel. (3) 5525-2200; fax (3) 5525-2532; internet www.geidai.ac.jp/museum; paintings, sculptures and applied art of Japan, China and Korea.

Waseda Daigaku Tsubouchi Hakase Kinen Engeki Hakubutsukan (Tsubouchi Memorial Theatre Museum, Waseda University): 1-6-1 Nishi-Waseda, Shinjuku-ku, Tokyo 169-8050; tel. (3) 5286-1829; f. 1928; 92,000 (Japanese), 30,000 (foreign) books on drama, 46,000 wood-block colour prints, 23,000 pictures and 518 costumes, properties, and other items used on the stage; Dir BUNZO TORIGOE; publs *News Bulletin*, *Catalogues*, *Studies in Dramatic Art*.

Yasukuni Jinja: Kudan Kita, 3-1-1, Chiyoda-ku, Tokyo 102-8246; located at: Chiyoda-ku, Tokyo; tel. (3) 3261-8326; fax (3) 3261-0081; internet www.yasukuni.or.jp; f. 1869; nat. shrine dedicated to the war dead; museum displays items from wars fought by Japan since the establishment of the shrine.

Ueno

Iga-ryu Ninja Museum: 117 Ueno-marunouchi, Iga Ueno, Iga City, Mie Prefecture; tel. (595) 23-0311; fax (595) 23-0314; e-mail iga-ueno@mxs.mesh.ne.jp; internet iganinja.jp; history and exhibits on Ninjas, spies who played an important role during periods of civil war in medieval Japan.

Yokohama

Kanagawa Prefectural Kanazawa Bunko Museum: 142 Kanazawa-cho, Kanazawa-ku, Yokohama; tel. (45) 701-9069; fax (45) 788-1060; internet www.planet.pref.kanagawa.jp/city/kanazawa.htm; f. 1972; nat. treasures (figure of Hojo-Sanetoki, etc.); library: library f. 1275; 20,000 old books and 4,149 documents; Curator YOSHIAKI SUZUKI.

National Universities

AICHI PREFECTURAL UNIVERSITY

1522-3 Ibaragabasama, Kumabari, Nagakute-cho, Aichi-gun, Aichi 480-1198

Telephone: (561) 64-1111
E-mail: jim@bur.aichi-pu.ac.jp
Internet: www.aichi-pu.ac.jp

Founded 1947

President: MASAO MORI

Library of 450,000 vols

PROFESSORS

Faculty of Letters:

- KOTANI, S., Department of Japanese Language and Letters
- TOUYAMA, I., Department of English
- YAMADA, M., Department of Japanese History and Culture
- KAWAGUCHI, A., Department of Childhood Education
- SHIMIZU, K., Department of Social Welfare

Faculty of Foreign Studies:

- KICHISE, S., Department of British and American Studies
- HAYAMIZU, Y., Department of French Studies
- SHIGA, I., Department of Spanish and Latin American Studies
- HIOKI, M., Department of German Studies
- KURAHASHI, M., Department of Chinese Studies

Faculty of Information Science and Technology:

- SAKURAI, K., Department of Information Systems
- HANDA, N., Department of Applied Information Science and Technology

UNIVERSITY OF THE AIR

2-11 Wakaba, Mihama-ku, Chiba City 261-8586

Telephone: (43) 276-5111
Fax: (43) 298-4378
Internet: www.u-air.ac.jp

Founded 1981

Chairman: TAKAYOSHI INOUE
President: NORIHITO TAMBO
Vice-Presidents: MAKOTO ASO, MORIAKI WATANABE
Director-General: YUKIO OSAWA
Librarian: HITOSHI ABE

Library of 630,643 vols
Number of teachers: 67 full-time
Number of teachers: 371 part-time
Number of students: 87,169

HEADS OF DEPARTMENTS

Living and Welfare: TOYOKO SAKAI
Human Development and Education: YASUTO MIYAZAWA
Social and Economic Studies: KAHEI ROKUMOTO
Industry and Technology: AKIO AKAGI
Humanities: KAZUHIRO EBUCHI
Natural Sciences: KAZUYUKI AIHARA

ASAHIKAWA MEDICAL COLLEGE

2-1-1-1 Midorigaoka, Asahikawa 078-8510
Telephone: (166) 65-2111
Fax: (166) 66-0025
E-mail: ipc@asahikawa-med.ac.jp
Internet: www.asahikawa-med.ac.jp

Founded 1973
Independent (National University Corporation)
Academic year: April to March

President: SUNAO YACHIKU
Executive Directors: HIYOSHI SHIONO, MUTSUO ISHIKAWA
Executive Secretary-General: SUSUMU OHTA
Library Director: KATSUHIRO OGAWA

Library of 139,000 vols
Number of teachers: 263
Number of students: 953 (845 undergraduate, 108 postgraduate)

Publication: *Asahikawa Medical College* (annually)

HEADS OF DEPARTMENTS

Anatomy 1: Prof. SHIGETAKA YOSHIDA
Anatomy 2: Prof. TSUYOSHI WATANABE
Physiology 1: Prof. AKIRA TAKAI
Physiology 2: Prof. MAKOTO KASHIWAYANAGI
Biochemistry 1: Prof. TAKANOBU TANIGUCHI
Biochemistry 2: Prof. HIROSHI SUZUKI
Pharmacology: Prof. FUMITAKA USHIKUBI
Pathology 1: Prof. KATSUHIRO OGAWA
Pathology 2: Prof. MASATOSHI TATENO
Microbiology and Immunochemistry: Prof. NOBUTAKA WAKAMIYA
Health Science: Prof. TAKAHIKO YOSHIDA
Parasitology: Prof. AKIRA ITOH
Legal Medicine: (vacant)
Internal Medicine 1: Prof. KENJIROH KIKUCHI
Internal Medicine 2: Prof. MASAKAZU HANEDA
Internal Medicine 3: Prof. YUTAKA KOHGO
Psychiatry and Neurology: Prof. SHIGERU CHIBA
Paediatrics: Prof. KENJI FUJIEDA
Surgery 1: Prof. TADAHIRO SASAJIMA
Surgery 2: Prof. SHINICHI KASAI
Orthopaedic Surgery: Prof. TAKEO MATSUNO
Dermatology: Prof. HAJIME IIZUKA
Urology: (vacant)
Ophthalmology: Prof. AKITOSHI YOSHIDA
Otorhinolaryngology and Head and Neck Surgery: Prof. YASUAKI HARABUCHI
Obstetrics and Gynaecology: Prof. KAZUO SENGOKU
Radiology: Prof. TAMIO ABURANO
Anaesthesiology and Critical Care Medicine: Prof. HIROSHI IWASAKI
Neurosurgery: Prof. TATSUYA TANAKA
Laboratory Medicine: Prof. YOSHIHISA ITOH
Oral and Maxillo-Facial Surgery: Prof. MITSUYASHI MATSUDA
Emergency Medicine: Prof. KAZUTOMO GOH
Nursing: Prof. JUN IWAMOTO, Prof. SYOJI KIMURA, Prof. KUMIKO KITAMURA, Prof. NORIKO NOMURA, Prof. YOSHIKATSU MOCHIZUKI, Prof. YOHKO OKADA, Prof. YUKARI HATTORI, Prof. KAZUYO MATSUURA
History and Philosophy: Prof. HITOSHI KONDOH
Psychology: Prof. MASAHARU TAKAHASHI
Sociology: (vacant)
Mathematics: Prof. KAZUNARI YAMAUCHI
Mathematical Information Science: (vacant)
Physics: Prof. MITSUHO TANIMOTO
Chemistry: Prof. MASAO NAKAMURA
Biology: Prof. YUJIROH KAMIGUCHI
Life Science: Prof. YOHKICHI HAYASHI
English: (vacant)
German: (vacant)

ATTACHED INSTITUTES

Animal Laboratory for Medical Research: Dir FUMITAKA USHIKUBI.

Central Laboratory for Research and Education: Dir HIROSHI SUZUKI.

BUNKYO UNIVERSITY

3-2-17 Hatanodai, Shinagawa-ku, Tokyo 142-0064
Telephone: (3) 3783-5511
Fax: (3) 3783-8300
E-mail: interex@hatanodai.bunkyo.ac.jp
Internet: www.bunkyo.ac.jp

Founded 1927

President: TSUNEYOSHI ISHIDA
Number of students: 8,600

Library of 546,000 vols

Faculties of Education, Human Science, Language and Literature, Culture.

CHIBA UNIVERSITY

1-33 Yayoi-cho, Inage-ku, Chiba-shi, Chiba 263-8522
Telephone: (43) 251-1111
Fax: (43) 290-2041
E-mail: kokusai@office.chiba-u.jp
Internet: www.chiba-u.jp

Founded 1949
Independent
Academic year: April to March

President: TOYOKI KOZAI
Director-General: TETSUO YAMANE
Library Director: SYUN TUTIYA

Number of teachers: 1,267 full-time
Number of students: 14,460

Publications: *Annual Report of the Center for Co-operative Research*, *Annual Report of the Center for Environmental Remote Sensing* (annually), *Annual Report of the Center for Frontier Science*, *Annual Report of Chiba University Graduate School of Social Sciences and Humanities*, *Annual Report of the IMIT*, *Annual Report of the Marine Biosystems Research Center* (every 2 years), *Annual Report of the Research Center for Pathogenic Fungi and Microbial Toxicoses* (annually), *Bulletin of the Faculty of Education* (annually), *Chemical Analysis Center Research Achievements*, *Chiba University Social Sciences and Humanities* (annually), *Economics Journal*, *Journal of Humanities* (annually), *Journal of Law and Politics*, *Journal of the School of Nursing* (annually), *Laboratory Waste Treatment Plant Bulletin* (annually), *Newsletter of the Research Center for Pathogenic Fungi and Microbial Toxicoses* (2 a year), *Outline of the Research Center for Pathogenic Fungi and Microbial Toxicoses* (every 2 years), *Record of Research Activities of the Faculty of Pharmaceutical Science*, *Research Activities and Interests of the Faculty of Engineering* (2 a year), *Research Report of the Center for Co-operative Research*, *Technical Bulletin of the Faculty of Horticulture* (annually), *Technical Reports of Mathematical Sciences*

DEANS

Faculty of Letters: Y. NISHIMURA
Faculty of Education: H. FUJISAWA
Faculty of Law and Economics: R. MIYAZAKI
Faculty of Science: K. OGAWA
School of Medicine: Y. FUKUDA
Faculty of Pharmaceutical Sciences: K. YAMAMOTO
School of Nursing: K. ISHIGAKI
Faculty of Engineering: K. MIYAZAKI
Faculty of Horticulture: H. AMANO
Graduate School of Science and Technology: T. OBINATA
Graduate School of Humanities and Social Sciences: S. MIURA
Graduate School of Medical and Pharmaceutical Sciences: T. ISHIKAWA

DIRECTORS

University Hospital: T. FUJISAWA
Health Sciences Center: K. NAGAO
Chemical Analysis Center: T. IMAMOTO
Center for Environmental Remote Sensing: T. TAKAMURA
Center for Frontier Science: N. UENO
International Student Center: M. HIROHASHI
Radioisotope Research Center: Y. ARANO
Research Center for Pathogenic Fungi and Microbial Toxicoses: K. NISHIMURA
Center for Foreign Languages: M. KUBOTA
Center of Co-operative Research: O. SAITO
Marine Biosystems Research Center: T. YAMAGUCHI
Center for Frontier Electronics and Photonics: T. UEMATSU
Gene Research Center: T. TOKUHISA
Institute of Media and Information Technology: S. SHIMAKURA
Toxic Waste Treatment Plant: K. MIYAZAKI
Research Center for Frontier Medical Engineering: Y. MIYAKE
Center for Environment, Health and Field Sciences: T. KOZAI

PROFESSORS

Faculty of Letters:
- AKIYAMA, K., Comparative Literature, French Modern Literature, Japanese Modern Literature
- CHOI, K., History of Korea
- GORYO, K., Psychology
- IIDA, N., Ethics, Bioethics
- INUZUKA, S., Industrial Sociology, Theory of Organization
- JITSUMORI, M., Comparative Cognition, Animal Learning
- KUROSAWA, K., Social Psychology, Law and Psychology, Personality Psychology
- MAEDA, S., German and Austrian Literature, Narratology
- MATSUMOTO, H., Japanese Linguistics (Grammar, Dialectology)
- MINAMIZUKA, S., History of Europe, History of Hungary, Rural Society
- MITSUI, Y., 18th c. French Literature, Philosophy of the Enlightenment
- MIURA, S., Japanese Ancient Literature, Japanese Oral Literature
- MIYAKE, A., Modern Japanese History, Labour History
- MIYANO, H., Psychology
- MIZUKAMI, T., German Literature
- NAGAI, H., Contemporary Western Philosophy
- NAKAGAWA, H., Linguistics, Oral Literature, Ainu Language and Literature
- NISHIMURA, Y., Comparative Studies of Modern Art and Literature
- OGATA, T., Labour Sociology, Foreign Worker Problems, Sociology of Traffic Problems
- OGIHARA, S., Cultural Anthropology of Northern Asia, Ethnology of the Ainu, Oral Traditions of the Ainu and the Northern Peoples
- OGURA, M., Medieval English Philology
- OKAMOTO, T., Japanese Archaeology
- ONO, K., American Literature
- OZAWA, H., Modern and Contemporary History of Europe

SAKURAI, A., Life – History Approach, Sociology of Social Problems, Research of Japanese Minorities (Buraku People etc.)
SATO, H., History
SUGAHARA, K., History of Tokugawa Shogunate
TAKAGI, G., Japanese Early Modern Literature
TAKAHASHI, K., Ancient Philosophy
TAKEI, H., Medical Anthropology, Cultural Anthropology, Amazonian Aboriginal Culture
TAKITO, M., Modern Japanese Literature
TOKIZANE, S., American Literature, Novel, Theory of Literature
TUTIYA, S., Philosophy, Ethics, Cognitive Science, Spoken Dialogue Studies, Document Processing
YANAGISAWA, S., Prehistory of Japan
YASUDA, H., Modern Japanese Literature

Faculty of Education (fax (43) 290-2519; e-mail hd2504@office.chiba-u.jp; internet www.e.chiba-u.jp):
ABE, A., Physical Education and School Health Education
AKASHI, Y., Sociology of Education
AMAGAI, Y., Developmental Clinical Psychology
AMAGASA, S., School Management
FUJII, T., Constitutional Law
FUJIKAWA, D., Development of Teaching
FUJISAWA, H., Art Education
FUSHIMA, Y., Psychology of School Learning
HIRAIDE, S., English and American Literature
HOSAKA, T., Clinical Studies in School Education
INABA, H., Physical Chemistry
INAGAKI, K., Early Childhood Education
ISAKA, J., Japanese Linguistics
ISHII, K., Food and Cookery Science
INOUE, T., Sociology
ISOBE, K., Orthopaedics
ISOZAKI, I., Political Science
IWAGAKI, O., Teaching Methods
IWATA, M., Developmental Psychology
IWATSUKI, K., Educational Psychology
KAMIYA, N., Musical Expression in Early Childhood Education
KAMO, H., Philosophy
KANAMORI, R., Painting
KATAOKA, Y., Sports Physiology
KATAYAMA, T., Sports Management
KATO, S., Chinese Literature
KENMOCHI, N., Analysis and Applied Mathematics
KIKUCHI, T., Teaching Methods of Physical Education and Sports
KOBAYASHI, K., Theory of School Nursing and School Health
KOMIYAMA, T., Motor Control
KOSHIKAWA, H., Differential Topology
KUMABE, T., Mechanics
KURANO, M., Analysis and Applied Mathematics
KUSAKARI, H., Nuclear Physics
MISAWA, M., Climatology
MIWA, S., School Management
MIYAMOTO, M., Sociology of the Family
MIYANO, M., Teaching of Music
MIYASHITA, K., Adolescent Psychology
MIZUUCHI, H., Curriculum Development
MOROTOMI, Y., Educational Counselling
MURAMATSU, S., Sports and Nutrition
NAGANE, M., School Psychology
NAGASAWA, S., Social Education
NAGATA, K., Comparative Theory of Art
NAKAZAWA, J., Developmental Psychology
NUKUI, M., Teaching of Science
OASHI, O., Psychology of Learning
OHGAMA, T., Wood Science and Technology
OHKOCHI, N., Agriculture Education
OHTA, T., Special Education
OI, K., English Pedagogy
OKAMOTO, K., Solid State Physics
OKI, T., Industrial Design
OTSUKA, T., English Linguistics
SADAHIRO, S., Educational Administration
SATO, F., Home Economics Education
SATO, K., Ethics
SATO, M., Movement Theory of Sport
SATO, M., Children's Literature
SHIMADA, K., Teaching of Mathematics
SHIMIZU, T., English and American Literature in School Education
SHUTO, H., Japanese Language Education
SHIBATA, M., Aesthetics of Costume
SUGITA, K., Paediatric Neurology
SUZUKI, A., Physiology and Ecology of Fungi
TAKEUCHI, H., Teaching of Social Studies
TAKIZAWA, F., Philosophy of Physical Education and Sport
TAMURA, T., Greek History
TANAKA, T., Teaching of Social Studies
TERAI, M., Japanese Language Education
TERAKADO, Y., Housing and the Living Environment
TOKUYAMA, I., Sports Pedagogy
TOZAKI, K., Physics
TSURUOKA, Y., Science Education
UENO, H., Sculpture
UESUGI, K., Moral Education
UKAWA, M., Music Education (Piano)
UMETANI, T., Psychology of Handicapped Children
URANO, T., Teaching of Calligraphy
WATANABE, S., Vocal Music
YAMAMURA, J., Human Geography
YAMANO, Y., Electrical Engineering
YAMAUCHI, K., Group Representation Theory
YAMAZAKI, Y., Geology
YODA, A., Technology Education

Faculty of Law and Economics:
ABE, K., International Economics
ABIKO, S., Contemporary Economic Theory
AKIMOTO, E., American Economic History
AMANO, M., Monetary Economics, Business Cycles
AMEMIYA, A., German Socio-Economic History
AOTAKE, S., Corporate Law
ENDOH, Y., Commercial Law, Anti-monopoly Law
FURUUCHI, H., Modern European Economic History
HANDA, Y., Civil Law
HAYASHI, W., International Co-operation Law, Anglo-Japanese Alliance Relations
HAYASHI, Y., Criminal Law
HIROI, Y., Social and Health Policy
INABA, H., Econometrics
IWAMA, A., Constitutional Law, Parliamentary System
IWATA, M., Comparative Economic Systems, Yugoslav Politics and Political Economy
KAKIHARA, K., Macroeconomics
KAMANO, K., Civil Law, Environmental Law
KINPARA, K., Religion and Law, Civil Procedure
KURITA, M., Economic Law, Competition Law
KUDO, H., History of Social Thought
MARUYAMA, E., Condominium Law, Housing Law, Urban Law, Property Law, Civil Law
MARUYAWA, T., German Studies
MATSUDA, C., Public Finance
MIYAZAKI, R., Japanese Government and Politics
MURAYAMA, M., Sociology of Law
MUSASHI, T., Industrial Organization
NAKAHARA, H., International Research and Development, Company Management
NAKAKUBO, H., Labour and Employment Law
NOMURA, Y., Mathematical Economics
NOZAWA, T., History of Political Economy
OGANO, S., Civil Law, Environmental Law, Property Law
OKUMOTO, Y., Economic Statistics, Seasonal Adjustment
OMORI, W., Public Administration, Local Government
SAKAKIBARA, K., Macroeconomics, Money, Constitutional Economics
SAKAMOTO, T., Japanese Legal History
SHIMAZU, I., Philosophy of Law
SHINDO, M., Public Administration
SUZUKI, T., Administrative Law, Local Government Law
TAGAYA, K., Information Law, Administrative Law
TEZUKA, K., Foreigners and Law, Employment Security in Japan, Germany and USA
UEKI, S., Comparative Studies of Civil Law, Contracts and Torts
WATANABE, Y., Constitutional Law
YAMASHINA, T., Middle High German
YUMOTO, K., Political Consciousness in the Chinese Republican Era
YOSHIZUMI, Y., Financial Accounting

Faculty of Science:
FUNABASHI, M., Carbohydrate Chemistry
HINO, Y., Mathematical Analysis
HIROI, Y., Metamorphic Petrology
IMAMOTO, T., Organic Chemistry
INOUE, A., Clay Mineralogy
ISIMURA, R.
ISEZAKI, N., Geophysics
ITO, M., Sedimentology
ITO, T., Structural Geology
KANEKO, K., Surface Solid State Chemistry, Molecular Science, Adsorption Science
KIMURA, T., High Energy Physics
KITAZUME, M., Finite Group Theory, Algebraic Combinatorics
KOBAYASHI, K., Cell Biology
KOHORI, Y., Low-temperature Physics
KOSHITANI, S., Algebra
KOYAMA, N., Biochemistry
KURASAWA, H., Nuclear Physics
MATSUMOTO, R., Astrophysics
NAGISA, M., Operator Algebra
NAKAGAMI, J., Statistics, Mathematical Programming
NAKAMURA, K., Coding Theory, Cryptography and Information Security
NAKANO, M., Biochemistry
NAKAYAMA, T., Nanoscience
NISHIDA, T., Mineralogy
NOZAWA, S., Algebra
OBINATA, T., Developmental Biology
OGAWA, K., Nuclear Physics
OHARA, S., Environmental Geology
OHASHI, K., Cell Physiology
SAKURA, Y., Hydrogeology
TAGURI, M., Statistics
TAKAGI, R., Geometry
TAKEDA, Y., Co-ordination Chemistry, Solution Chemistry
TSUJI, T., Computer Software, Theory of Programmes
TUTIYA, T., Echophysiology
YAMADA, I., Solid State Physics
YAMAMOTO, K., Molecular Physiology
YANAGISAWA, A., Organic Chemistry
YASUDA, M., Statistics
WATANO, Y., Plant Biosystems, Molecular Ecology

Graduate School of Medicine (1-8-1 Inohana, Chuo-Ku, Chiba-shi, Chiba 260-8670; tel. (43) 222-7171; fax (43) 226-2005; e-mail g5004@office.chiba-u.jp; internet www.m.chiba-u.ac.jp):
BUJO, H., Genome Research and Clinical Application

FUJISAWA, T., Thoracic Surgery
FUKUDA, Y., Autonomic Physiology
HARIGAYA, K., Molecular and Tumour Pathology
HATA, A., Public Health
HATTORI, T., Neurology
HIRASAWA, H., Emergency and Critical Care Medicine
ICHINOSE, M., Plastic Surgery
ISHIKURA, H., Molecular Pathology
ITO, H., Radiology
ITO, H., Urology
IWASE, H., Legal Medicine
IYO, M., Psychiatry
KIMURA, S., Biochemistry and Molecular Pharmacology
KOHNO, Y., Paediatrics
KOMURO, I., Cardiovascular Science and Medicine
KOSEKI, H., Molecular Embryology
KURIYAMA, T., Respirology
KUWAKI, T., Molecular and Integrative Physiology
MIYAZAKI, M., General Surgery
MORI, C., Bioenvironmental Medicine
MORIYA, H., Orthopaedic Surgery
NAKAYA, H., Pharmacology
NAKAYAMA, T., Medical Immunology
NISHINO, T., Anaesthesiology
NODA, M., Molecular Infectology
NOGAWA, K., Occupational and Environmental Medicine
NOMURA, F., Molecular Diagnosis
OCHIAI, T., Academic Surgery
OHNUMA, N., Paediatric Surgery
OKAMOTO, Y., Otorhinolaryngology
SAISHO, H., Medicine and Clinical Oncology
SAITO, T., Molecular Genetics
SAITO, Y., Clinical Cell Biology
SEKIYA, S., Reproductive Medicine
SHINKAI, H., Clinical Biology of Extracellular Matrix
SHIRASAWA, H., Molecular Virology
SUZUKI, N., Environmental Biochemistry
TAKIGUCHI, M., Biochemistry and Genetics
TANIGUCHI, M., Molecular Immunology
TANZAWA, H., Clinical Molecular Biology
TOKUHISA, T., Developmental Genetics
TOSHIMORI, K., Anatomy and Developmental Biology
YAMAMOTO, S., Ophthalmology and Visual Science
YAMAURA, A., Neurological Surgery
YANO, A., Infection and Host Disease

Graduate School of Pharmaceutical Sciences (1-33 Yayoi-cho, Inage-ku, Chiba-shi, Chiba 263-8522; tel. (43) 251-1111; fax (43) 290-2974):

AIMI, N., Molecular Structure and Biological Function
ARANO, Y., Radiopharmaceutical Chemistry
CHIBA, K., Pharmacology and Toxicology
HAMADA, Y., Pharmaceutical Chemistry
HORIE, T., Biopharmaceutics
IGARASHI, K., Clinical Biochemistry
ISHIBASHI, M., Natural Products Chemistry
ISHIKAWA, T., Medicinal Organic Chemistry
KOBAYASHI, H., Biochemistry
MURAYAMA, T., Chemical Pharmacology
NEYA, S., Physical Chemistry
NISHIDA, A., Synthetic Organic Chemistry
SAITOH, K., Molecular Biology and Biotechnology
SUZUKI, K. T., Toxicology and Environmental Health
TOIDA, T., Bio-analytical Chemistry
UEDA, S., Drug Information and Communication
UENO, K., Geriatric Pharmacology and Therapeutics
YAMAGUCHI, N., Molecular Cell Biology
YAMAMOTO, K., Pharmaceutical Technology
YAMAMOTO, T., Microbiology and Molecular Genetics
YANO, S., Molecular Pharmacology and Pharmacotherapeutics

School of Nursing (1-8-1 Inohana, Chuo-Ku, Chiba-shi, Chiba 260-8672; tel. (43) 222-7171):

FUNASHIMA, N., Nursing Education
HONDA, A., Continuing Nursing
ISHIGAKI, K., Home Care Nursing
IWASAKI, Y., Psychiatric Nursing
KITAIKE, T., Health Science
MASAKI, H., Gerontological Nursing
MIYAZAKI, M., Community Health Nursing
MORI, M., Maternity Nursing
NAKAMURA, N., Child Nursing
OHTA, S., Gerontological Nursing
OMURO, R., Nursing Administration
SATO, R., Adult Nursing
TESHIMA, M., Hospital Nursing Care
YAMADA, S., Physiology and Biochemistry
YOSHIMOTO, T., Geriatric Community Nursing, Care Systems Management

Faculty of Engineering:

AKUTSU, F., Synthetic Polymer Chemistry
ANDO, M., Construction and Production of Buildings
AOKI, H., Materials Planning for Design
AOYAGI, S., Bio-organic Chemistry
FUJITA, T., Synthetic Organic Chemistry
FUKASAWA, A., Communication and Information Networks
FUKUKAWA, Y., Urban Planning and Design, Historic Conservation
HASEGAWA, A., Photophysics
HATTORI, T., Ceramic Sciences
HIBINO, H., Design Psychology and Colour Science
HIROHASHI, M., Materials Science
HISIDA, M., Heat Engine Engineering
HONDA, T., Optical Engineering, Image Processing
HOTTA, A., Industrial Design
IKEDA, H., Computer Science
KAGEGAWA, K., Inorganic Material
KAMAIKE, M., Product Design
ITO, K., Antenna Engineering
KATO, H., Optimization of Manufacturing
KATSUURA, T., Ergonomics
KITAHARA, T., City Planning
KITAMURA, A., Fundamentals of Materials Science
KITAMURA, T., Electronic Image Processing
KOBAYASHI, H., Organic Memory and Display Materials
KOTERA, H., Printing Image Processing
KUDO, K., Physical Electronics
KURYU, A., Architectural Design
LIU, H., Biomechanical Engineering
MAENO, K., Thermofluid Dynamics
MATSUBA, I., Engineering of Information Processing
MIYAKE, Y., Measurement and Analysis of Image Information
MIYATA, T., Interior Design
MIYAZAKI, K., Philosophy and History of Design
MIYAZAKI, M., Visual Communication Design
MORITA, H., Laser Chemistry on Nanomaterials
MORITA, K., Structural Planning
NAKAHIRA, T., Polymer Chemistry
NAKAI, S., Disaster Prevention
NAKAMOTO, T., Micro Machining
NAKAMURA, M., Plastic Working
NISHIKAWA, N., Fluids Engineering
NOGUCHI, K., Visual Perception
NONAMI, K., Control and Robotics
OCHIAI, Y., Advanced Device Materials
OGUMA, K., Analytical Chemistry
OGURA, K., Synthetic Organic Chemistry
OKAMOTO, H., Optical Properties of Semiconductors
OTANI, S., Earthquake Engineering
OTSUBO, Y., Rheology
SAITO, O., Semiconductor Rhotonics
SHIMIZU, T., Environmental Design
SUGITA, K., Information Recording Materials
TAMAI, T., History of Architecture
TANAKA, K., Physical Electronics
TATEDA, M., Opto-electronics
TATSUMOTO, H., Systems Design in Water and Wastewater Treatment
UEMATSU, T., Industrial Physical Chemistry
UENO, N., Molecular Quantum Assemblies
UNO, M., Architecture and Urban Design
WATANABE, T., Micro-machine Elements
YAGUCHI, H., Visual Science
YAMAGUCHI, M., Electrical Circuits
YAMAMOTO, M., Synthetic Organic Chemistry
YAMAOKA, T., Imaging Materials
YASHIRO, K., Microwave Theory and Technology
YOSHIKAWA, A., Quantum Electronics

Faculty of Horticulture (648 Matsudo, Matsudo-shi, Chiba 271-8510; tel. (47) 308-8706; fax (47) 308-8720; e-mail n8703@office.chiba-u.jp; internet www.h.chiba-u.ac.jp):

AMANO, H., Applied Entomology and Zoology
AMEMIYA, Y., Green Space Environmental Technology
AMEMIYA, Y., Plant Pathology
ANDO, T., Ornamental Plant Science
FUJII, T., Microbial Engineering
HARADA, K., Genetics and Plant Breeding
HONJO, T., Planting Design
IIMOTO, M., Plant Production Engineering
INUBUSHI, K., Soil Science
KEINO, S., Agricultural Marketing
KIKUCHI, M., Agricultural Economics
KON, H., Green Space Meteorology
KOZAI, T., Environmental Control Engineering
MASADA, M., Biochemistry
MATSUI, H., Fruit Science
MII, M., Plant Cell Technology
MINAMIDA, S., Horticultural Management and Information
MOTOYAMA, N., Pesticide Toxicology
NAGATA, Y., Molecular Biology
NAKAGAWA, H., Biotechnology of Agroresources
NAKAMURA, O., Town and Country Planning
OHE, Y., Horticultural Information Science
OKITSU, S., Forest Ecology
ONO, S., Garden Design
SAITO, O., Farm Business Management
SANADA, H., Food and Nutrition
SHINOHARA, Y., Vegetable Science
TASHIRO, Y., Urban Landscape Design
WATANABE, Y., Plant Nutrition
YAMAUCHI, S., Humanistic Study on Environment

Graduate School of Science and Technology:

ANDO, A., Proteins Engineering
ASANO, Y., Environmental Plant Science
FUJIKAWA, T., XAFS Theory
FURUYA, T., Applied Geomorphology
HATTORI, M., Architectural Design Study
HIRATA, H., Systems Engineering
ICHIKAWA, A., Knowledge Engineering
INABA, T., Differential Topology
IWADATE, Y., Physics and Chemistry of Liquids and Amorphous Materials
KOHMOTO, S., Organic Photochemistry
MAJIMA, T., Mechanics and Strength of Materials
MATSUDA, T., Electronic Commerce and Agribusiness
NATSUME, Y., Condensed Matter Theory
NISHIKAWA, K., Physical Chemistry
OHNO, T., Imaging Materials
SATO, T., Plant Molecular Biology
SHIGA, H., Complex Manifolds
SHIMAKURA, S., Fundamentals of Electrical and Electronic Engineering

SUGIYAMA, K., Design Systems Planning
TAGAWA, A., Agricultural Process Engineering
TAMURA, T., Molecular Biology
UESUGI, H., Fireproofing of Buildings
YAHAGI, T., Digital Signal Processing
YOSHIDA, H., Complex Analysis

Graduate School of Medical and Pharmaceutical Sciences:

CHIBA, T., Neurobiology

Health Sciences Center (1-33 Yayoi-cho, Inage-ku, Chiba-shi, Chiba 263-8522; tel. (47) 290-2210; fax (47) 290-2220; e-mail inf@hsc.chiba-u.ac.jp; internet hschome-gw.hsc.chiba-u.ac.jp):

NAGAO, K., Internal Medicine

Center for Environmental Remote Sensing (tel. (43) 290-3832; fax (43) 290-3857; internet www.cr.chiba-u.jp):

MIWA, T., Dept of Geoinformation Analysis
NISHIO, H., Dept of Data Base Research
SUGIMORI, Y., Dept of Geoinformation Analysis
TAKAMURA, T., Dept of Sensor and Atmospheric Radiation
TAKEUCHI, N., Dept of Sensor and Atmospheric Radiation

Research Center for Pathogenic Fungi and Microbial Toxicology (1-8-1 Inohana, Chuo-ku, Chiba 260-8670; tel. (43) 222-7171; fax (43) 226-2486; internet www.pf.chibau.ac.jpf. 1946; Dir: YUZURU MIKAMI):

FUKUSHIMA, K., Division of Fungal Resources and Development
KAMEI, K., Division of Fungal Infection
MIKAMI, Y., Division of Molecular Biology and Therapeutics
NISHIMURA, K., Division of Phylogenetics
TAKEO, K., Division of Ultrastructure and Function

International Student Center (tel. (43) 290-2197; fax (43) 290-2198; e-mail bm2198@office.chiba-u.jp):

HATA, H., Teaching Japanese as a Second Language
NIIKURA, R., Cross-cultural Psychology

Center for Foreign Languages:

BOSWELL, P. D., Psychology of Teaching
KUBOTA, M., Linguistics
MIKOSHIBA, M., Russian Intellectual History
SHIINA, K., Methodology for English Teaching
TABATA, T., Linguistics, Phonology
YAMAOKA, K., French Literature

Marine Biosystems Research Center (1 Uchiura, Amatsu-kominato-cho, Awagun, Chiba 299-5502; tel. (47) 095-2201; fax (47) 095-2271; internet www-es.s.chiba-u.ac.jp/kominato/index_eng.html):

MIYAZAKI, T., Aquatic Ecology
YAMAGUCHI, T., Palaeobiology

Center for Frontier Science (1–33 Yayoi-cho, Inage-ku, Chiba-shi, Chiba 263-8522; tel. (43) 290-3522; fax (43) 290-3523; e-mail info@cfs.chiba-u.jp; internet www.cfs.chiba-u.ac.jp):

HANAWA, T., Astrophysics
OHTAKA, K., Applied Physics

Institute of Media and Information Technology (1–33 Yayoi-cho, Inage-ku, Chiba-shi, Chiba 263-8522; tel. (43) 290-3535; fax (43) 290-3581; internet www.imit.chiba-u.jp):

KOMORI, Y., Mathematical Logic
SOHMIYA, Y., German Linguistics, Semantics, Corpus Linguistics
ZEN, H., Intelligent Information Media

University Hospital (1-8-1 Inohana, Chuo-ku, Chiba-shi, Chiba 260-8670; tel. (43) 222-7171; fax (43) 224-3830; e-mail wad6005@office.chiba-u.jp; internet www.ho.chiba-u.jp):

IKUSAKA, M., Dept of General Medicine
KITADA, M., Pharmacy
KOUZU, T., Dept of Endoscopic Diagnostics and Therapeutics
SATOMURA, Y., Medical Informatics
TONABE, M., Postgraduate Education Center

Research Centre for Frontier Medical Engineering:

HACHIYA, H., Medical Image Processing
IGARASHI, T., Surgical Device Design
ITO, K., Antenna Engineering
SHIMOYAMA, I., Human Neurophysiology
TATKSUOKA, H., Neuroscience

Center for Environment, Health and Field Sciences (6-2-1 Kashiwanoha, Kawashi-shi, Chiba 277-0882; tel. (4) 7134-8401; fax (4) 7134-8437):

ANDO, T., Ornamental Plant Science
KOZAI, T., Environmental Control Engineering
KURIYAMA, T., Respirology
NOMA, Y., Experimental Farms
OHGAMA, T., Wood Science and Technology
TOKUYAMA, I., Sports Pedagogy

ATTACHED INSTITUTES

Center for Education and Research in Nursing Practice.

Center for Research, Training and Guidance in Educational Practice.

Institute for Training Radiological Technicians.

University Hospital.

University Farms.

CHUKYO UNIVERSITY

101-2 Yagoto Honmachi, Showa-ku, Nagoya-shi, Aichi-ken 466-8666
Telephone: (52) 835-7111
E-mail: ic@mng.chukyo-u.ac.jp
Internet: www.chukyo-u.ac.jp
Founded 1923
President: EIJI OGAWA
Chancellor and Chairman of the Board of Directors: KIYOHIRO UMEMURA
Director of the Library: HITOSHI YASUMURA
Director, Administration Bureau: KAZUHIRO HANAMURA

DEANS

Faculty of Letters: TAKASHI SATO
Faculty of English: SANZO SAKAI
Faculty of Psychology: KENZO SORAI
Faculty of Sociology: MASAO ONO
Faculty of Law: HIDEFUMI KOBAYASHI
Faculty of Economics: MASATOSHI SHIRAI
School of Management: KYOHEI IRIE
School of Commerce: HIDEO TAKAHASHI
School of Computer and Cognitive Sciences: JUNICHI TANAHASHI
School of Health and Sport Sciences: KAORU KITAGAWA
College of Liberal Arts: TETSUO KUWAMURA

HEADS OF DEPARTMENTS

SATO, S., Graduate School of Letters
TSUJI, K., Graduate School of Psychology
MATSUDA, N., Graduate School of Sociology
ITO, N., Graduate School of Law
SENDA, J., Graduate School of Economics
MASAKI, S., Graduate School of Business Administration
TSUKAMOTO, T., Graduate School of Commerce
TAMURA, K., Graduate School of Computer and Cognitive Sciences
NAKAGAWA, T., Graduate School of Health and Sport Sciences
NAKAGAKI, N., Graduate School of Business Innovation

CHUO GAKUIN UNIVERSITY

451 Kujike, Abiko, Chiba 270-1196
Telephone: (4) 7183-6501
Fax: (4) 7183-6532
Founded 1900
President: TERUO OKUBO
Faculties of Commerce and Law.

EHIME UNIVERSITY

10-13 Dogo-Himata, Matsuyama City 790-8577
Telephone: (89) 927-9000
Fax: (89) 927-9025
Internet: www.ehime-u.ac.jp
Founded 1949
Independent
Academic year: April to March (two terms)
President: MASAYUKI KOMATSU
Administrative Officer: I. KUBONIWA
Dean of Students' Affairs Office: T. SAITO
Library Director: KOJI SANUKI
Library of 1,144,000 vols
Number of teachers: 976 full-time
Number of students: 9,858

DEANS

Faculty of Law and Arts: MOTOJI IMAIZUMI
Faculty of Education: YASUNOBU KINTO
Faculty of Science: YASUNOBU YANAGISAWA
Faculty of Medicine: KOJI HASHIMOTO
Faculty of Engineering: KOICHI SUZUKI
Faculty of Agriculture: MASAYA SHIRAISHI
United Graduate School of Agricultural Sciences: TADAAKI WAKIMOTO

FUKUI UNIVERSITY

9-1 Bunkyo 3-chome, Fukui City 910-8507
Telephone: (776) 23-0500
Fax: (776) 27-8030
E-mail: kaiho@sec.icpc.fukui-u.ac.jp
Internet: www.fukui-u.ac.jp
Founded 1949
Independent
Academic year: April to March
President: SHINPEI KOJIMA
Director of Administration: YUZO SATO
Librarian: TOSHIYUKI KODAIRA
Library of 453,403 vols
Number of teachers: 367
Number of students: 4,159

DEANS

Faculty of Education and Regional Studies: YOSHIHIKO HAYATA
Faculty of Engineering: SHINGO TAMAKI

FUKUSHIMA UNIVERSITY

1 Kanayagawa, Fukushima 960-1296
Telephone: (24) 548-8084
Fax: (24) 548-3180
Faculties of Education, Administration and Social Sciences, Economics.

FUKUYAMA UNIVERSITY

985-1 Aza-Sanzou, Higashimuracho, Fukuyama-shi, Hiroshima 729-0292
Telephone: (84) 936-2111
Fax: (84) 936-2213
E-mail: soumu@fucc.fukuyama-u.ac.jp
Internet: www.fukuyama-u.ac.jp
Founded 1975
Chancellor: TAKASHI MIYACHI
President: KIYOHISA NISHIZAKI
Vice-President: MINORU ABE

Vice-President: RYUSUKE YOSIHARA
Vice-President: IWAO OTANI
Librarian: TOSHIRO KATAOKA

Library of 222,700 vols
Number of teachers: 240
Number of students: 5,500

DEANS

Faculty of Human Cultures and Science: KAZUE YOSHIDA
Faculty of Economics: RYUSUKE YOSHIHARA
Faculty of Engineering: RYOUICHI ICHINOMIYA
Faculty of Life Science and Biotechnology: FUMITO MATSUURA
Faculty of Pharmacy and Pharmaceutical Sciences: TSUYOSHI GOROMARU

GIFU UNIVERSITY

1-1 Yanagido, Gifu-shi, Gifu-ken 501-1193
Telephone: (58) 230-1111
Fax: (58) 230-2021
E-mail: www-staff@cc.gifu-u.ac.jp
Internet: www.gifu-u.ac.jp

Founded 1949
Independent

President: T. KINJOH
Secretary-General: Y. KIJIMA
Librarian: T. UNO

Library of 822,409 vols, 13,000 periodicals
Number of teachers: 738 full-time
Number of students: 5,995

Publication: Research Bulletins and Reports from each faculty (annually)

DEANS

Faculty of Education: YOSHIMI SASAKI
School of Medicine: Y. NOZAWA
Faculty of Engineering: H. SHIMIZU
Faculty of Agriculture: T. NAKAMURA
Faculty of Regional Studies: Y. MATSUDA

ATTACHED INSTITUTES

Curriculum Research and Development Center: Dir Prof. G. CHUMAN.

Institute of Equilibrium Research: Dir Prof. K. MATSUNAMI.

Institute of Anaerobic Bacteriology: Dir Prof. K. WATANABE.

Institute of Basin Ecosystem Studies: Dir Prof. A. YUASA.

Center for Cooperative Research: Dir Prof. S. YAMASHITA.

Molecular Genetics Research Center: Dir Prof. K. WAWAI.

GUNMA UNIVERSITY

4-2 Aramaki-machi, Maebashi City, Gunma 371-8510
Telephone: (27) 220-7111
E-mail: s-research@jimu.gunma-u.ac.jp
Internet: www.gunma-u.ac.jp

Founded 1949
Academic year: April to March

President: MAMORU SUZUKI
Vice-President (General, Financial Affairs and Facilities): HIROYUKI SHIRAI
Vice-President (Research): SEIJI OZAWA
Vice-President (Student Affairs): KIMIO NAKAMURA
Director, University Hospital: YASUO MORISHITA
Director of Management: MOTOHARU IUE
Administrator: TADEDNORI IKENOUE
Librarian: YOUICHI NAKAZATO

Library of 651,576 vols
Number of teachers: 849 full-time
Number of students: 7,021

Publication: *Journal of Social and Information Studies* (annually)

DEANS

Faculty of Education: TADASHI MATSUDA
Faculty of Engineering: TAKAYUKI TAKARADA
Faculty of Medicine: FUMIO GOTO
Faculty of Social and Information Studies: NOBUTAKA OCHIAI
Institute of Molecular and Cellular Regulation: ITARU KOJIMA

HIROSAKI UNIVERSITY

1 Bunkyo-cho, Hirosaki 036-8560
Telephone: (172) 36-2111
Fax: (172) 37-6594
E-mail: webmaster@cc.hirosaki-u.ac.jp
Internet: www.hirosaki-u.ac.jp

Founded 1949
Independent
Academic year: April to March

President: MASAHIKO ENDO
Vice-President: Y. MIZUNE
Registrar: R. SHIBATA
Librarian: E. OKAZAKI
Director of the Hospital: S. HARATA

Number of teachers: 692
Number of students: 5,512

Publication: *School Outline* (annually)

DEANS

Faculty of Agriculture and Life Science: K. TOYOKAWA
Faculty of Education: H. OZAWA
Faculty of Humanities: T. TANNO
Faculty of Science and Technology: H. OHNUKI
School of Medicine: M. ENDO

PROFESSORS

Faculty of Agriculture and Life Science (3 Bunkyo-cho, Hirosaki 036-8561; internet nature.cc.hirosaki-u.ac.jp):

ANDO, Y., Entomology
AOYAMA, M., Soil Science
ARAKAWA, O., Pomology
ASADA, Y., Applied Microbiology, Microbial Technology
BOKURA, T., Agricultural Meteorology
FUKUDA, H., Horticulture
HARADA, Y., Plant Pathology
ISHIGURO, S., Biochemistry of the Eye, Developmental Biology
KANDA, K., Co-operative Study
KUDO, A., Irrigation, Drainage and Hydraulic Engineering
MAKITA, H., Vegetation Geography, Environmental Science
MIYAIRI, K., Biochemistry
MOTOMURA, Y., Science of Horticultural Bioproducts
MUTO, A., Molecular Engineering
NAKAMURA, S., Biochemical Engineering
NIIZEKI, M., Plant Breeding and Genetics
OBARA, Y., Cytogenetics
OHMACHI, T., Molecular Biology, Applied Microbiology
OKUNO, T., Organic Chemistry and Biochemistry
SASAKI, C., Agricultural Land Engineering
SAWADA, S., Plant Ecophysiology
SAWARA, Y., Animal Behaviour
SHIOZAKI, Y., Pomology
SUGIYAMA, K., Virology, Molecular Biology
SUGIYAMA, S., Crop Science, Plant Evolutionary Biology
TAKAHASHI, H., Regional Economy
TAKAMURA, K., Morphogenesis
TAKEDA, K., Microbial Ecology
TANIGUCHI, K., Rural Planning
TOYOKAWA, K., Feeds and Feeding
UNO, T., Agricultural Economics
YURUGI, M., Structural Mechanics, Construction Materials, Concrete

Faculty of Education (internet siva.cc.hirosaki-u.ac.jp):

ANDO, F., Education for Children with Disabilities
ANNO, M., Japanese History
ASANO, K., Piano
FUMOTO, N., Psychology of Sport and Physical Activity
GION, Z., Social Studies Education
HAGA, T., Clothing Science
HANDA, S., Mathematics Education
HAYAKAWA, M., Health Education
HIKAGE, Y., Home Economics Education, Laundering and Finishing
HIRAKI, K.
HIRAOKA, K., Adolescent Development, Learning Theory
HORIUCHI, H., Earth Materials Science
HOSHI, K., Art Education
HONMA, M., Movement Theory
HOSHINO, H., Condensed Matter Physics
IMAI, T., Musicology
ITOH, S., Analysis
IWAI, Y., Oil Painting, Tempera and Etching
KAMADA, K., Sedimentology
KAMIYA, K., Rural Sociology
KATO, Y., Food Chemistry
KITADA, T., Harmonic Analysis
KON, M., Differential Geometry
MARUYAMA, M., Japanese Literature
MENZAWA, K., School Health Education and Safety Education, School Health Promotion
MORI, A., School Health Education
MORI, R., Home Economics Education
MURAKAMI, O., Animal Physiology
MURAYAMA, M., Educational Methodology
NANBA, K., Algebra, Foundations of Mathematics, Discrete Mathematics
OHSHIMA, Y., Biomechanics
OHTAKA, A., Animal Taxonomy
OKADA, K., Sculpture, Clay Working (Pottery)
OKUNO, T., English Linguistics
OTA, S., Mathematics Education
OTSUBO, S., Sociology of Education
OYAMA, S., Health and Physical Education
OZAWA, H., Educational System and Administration
SAITO, S., Science Education, Phycology, Limnology
SAITO, T., History of Medieval Japan
SATO, K., Exercise Physiology
SATO, S., Adult Education
SATO, Y., Paediatrics
SATOH, Y., Magnetics
SEKI, H., Photochemistry
TAKANASHI, T., English Teaching Methodology
TANDOH, S., Educational Psychology
TOYOSHIMA, A., Social Clinical Psychology
UEDA, K., Timber Engineering
WATANABE, K., Voice
YAJIMA, T., Philosophy
YAMAGUCHI, T., Sinology
YOSHINO, H., Developmental Psychology, Psychology of Personality

Faculty of Humanities (internet human.cc.hirosaki-u.ac.jp):

AKAGI, K., Public Economics, Law and Economics
ARAI, K., Behavioural Accounting
CARPENTER, V., International Politics
FUJINUMA, K., Japanese Archaeology
FUJITA, M., Business Behaviour, Public Utilities
FUNAKI, Y., Statistics, and Operations Research
HASEGAWA, S., Early Modern Japanese History
HORIUCHI, T., Constitutional Law
HOSHINO, Y., Accounting and Control
IGARASHI, Y., Ethics

ISHIDOU, T., English, American Literature, American Studies, Robert Frost, Mark Twain, McCarthyism
KATORI, K., Science of Information and Systems
KITAJIMA, S., Regional Economy and Regional Policy
MOROOKA, M., Science of Religion
MURAMATSU, K., Political Theory
MURATA, S., English Literature
NAKAZAWA, K., Western Economic History
NITTA, S., Modern German Literature
OKAZAKI, E., Philosophy
OKUNO, K., Linguistics
PHILIPS, J. E., History, African, American and Islamci
SAKUMICHI, S., Social Psychology, Anthropology
SATO, N., English Literature
SATOH, K., Japanese Linguistics
SHIMUZU, A., Philosophy of Information
SHINOMIYA, T., Business History
SUDO, H., History of Art
SUGIYAMA, Y., Cultural Anthropology
SUZUKI, K., Economic Theory
TANAKA, I., German Literary Arts
TERADA, M., French Literature
UEKI, H., Chinese Classical Literature
USUDA, S., Japanese Literature
WARASHINA, K., Japanese Language
YASUDA, M., Marketing

Faculty of Science and Technology (3 Bunkyo-cho, Hirosaki 036-8561; internet www.st.hirosaki-u.ac.jp):
AMENOMORI, M., Cognitive Science, Super-high Energy Physics
ARAKI, T., Applied Electronics
FUKASE, M., VLSI Computer
FURUYA, Y., Intelligent Materials Design and Systems, Materials Processing, Solid State Sensors and Actuators, Non-destructive Evaluation
GOTO, T., Applied Chemistry
IIKURA, Y., Instrumentation Physics, Remote Sensing
INAMURA, T., Spray Engineering and Combustion, Propulsion Engineering
ITO, A., Combustion, Fire Science, Multiple Phase Flow
ITO, S., Organic Syntheses
KATO, H., Solid State Physics, Synchrotron-Radiation Science
KAWAGUCHI, S., Cosmic-ray Physics
KURAMATA, S., Space Physics
KURATSUBO, S., Harmonic Analysis
MAKINO, E., Micro Electromechanical Systems
MASHITA, M., Thin Film and Surface Physics
MIYATA, H., Solid Mechanics, Fracture Mechanics, Strength Evaluation Systems
MORI, T.
MOTOSE, K., Algebra
NAKAZATO, H., Functional Analysis
NANJO, H., High Energy Astrophysics
NENCHEV, D. N., Robotics
OHZEKI, K., Analytical Chemistry
RIKIISHI, K., Physical Oceanography, Meteorology, Glaciology
SAITO, M., Computational Science Approach to Biomolecular Recognition
SAKISAKA, Y., Solid State Physics, Synchrotron-radiation Science
SASAKI, K., Surface Physics
SATO, H., Phase Transformation, Plastic Deformation
SATO, T., Raman Spectra
SATO, T., Seismology
SHIBA, M., Disaster Prevention Geology
SHIMIZU, T., Bioinformatics, Biophysics
SUDO, S., Physical Chemistry
SUTO, S., Physical Chemistry of Polymers
TAJIRI, A., Organic Physical Chemistry
TAKAGUCHI, M., Matrix Analysis
TAKEGAHARA, K., Theoretical Solid State Physics
TANAKA, K., Physical Vulcanology, Seismology
TSURUMI, M., Environmental Chemistry, Geochemistry
UJIIE, Y., Petroleum Geology, Organic Geology
YOSHIOKA, Y., Computer Networks, Computer Architecture
YOSHIZAWA, A., Organic Materials Science

School of Medicine (53 Hon-cho, Hirosaki 036-8563; internet hippo.med.hirosaki-u.ac.jp):
ABE, Y., Radiation Oncology
ENDO, M., Glycobiology of Glycoconjugates
HADA, R., Medical Informatics
HANADA, K., Sun Protection, Laser Therapy, Atopic Dermatitis, Photodynamic Therapy
ICHIMARU, T., Medical Apparatus and Engineering
ICHINOHE, T., Paediatric Nursing, Guidance in Nursing Practice
ITO, E., Paediatric Haematology and Oncology
IWASAKI, A., Medical (Radiation) Physics
KACHI, T., Anatomy
KAGIAYA, A., Obstetrics and Gynaecology
KAMIYA, H., Immunopathology of Parasitic Infection
KANEKO, S., Epiteptology, Clinical and Basic Neuropsychopharmacology
KAWAHARA, R., Gerontological Nursing
KIKUCHI, H., Endocrinology
KIMURA, H., Oral and Maxillo-facial Surgery
KIMURA, K., Nursing of Adults
KUDO, H., Tumour Pathology
KURATA, K., Neurophysiology
KURODA, N., Forensic Pathology
MATSUKI, A., Anaesthesiology, Intensive Care, Pain Clinic
MATSUMOTO, M., Neurophysiology
MATSUNAGA, M., Clinical Neurology, Neuroepidemiology
MINAGAWA, T., Cancer Nursing
MITA, R., Public Health
MIURA, H., Existence Philosophy, Medical Philosophy and Ethics
MIURA, T., Orthopaedic Surgery, Rehabilitation Medicine
MIZUSHIMA, Y., Respirology, Gerontology
MOTOMURA, S., Cardiovascular Pharmacology
MUNAKATA, A., Gastroenterology
MUNAKATA, H., Paediatric Surgery
NAKAMURA, T., Chronic Pancreatitis, Pancreatic Steatorrhoea, Pancreatic Diabetes, Gastric Emptying, Clinical Laboratory Medicine
NAKANE, A., Bacteriology, Immunology
NAKAZAWA, M., Basic and Clinical Research for Retinal Diseases
NIKARA, T., Physiology
OHGUSHI, Y., Nursing Science
OKUMURA, K., Internal Medicine, Cardiology
SASAKI, J., Tumour Immunology, Pathogenic Bacteriology, Food Science
SASAKI, M., Surgery for Digestive Diseases, Hepato-pancreaticobiliary Surgery, Liver Transplantation
SATO, T., Pathology
SATO, Y., Neuroscience
SATOH, K., Biochemistry, Enzymology, Chemical Larcinogenesis
SATOH, K., Basic Studies on the Pathogenesis of Cerebrovascular Diseases
SAWADA, Y., Study of Wound Healing, Burns, Hypertrophic Scan and Keloids, Microcirculation of the Flap
SEIMIYA, Y., Analysis of Daily Activity
SHINKAWA, H., Inner and Middle Ear Morphology Middle Ear Surgery
SHOMURA, K., Neural Anatomy
SUDA, T., Endocrinology and Metabolism
SUGAMARA, K., Pharmacological and Pharmaceutical Drugs Interaction
SUGAWARA, K., Physical Fitness, Nutrition, Immunology
SUZUKI, S., Neurosurgery, Cerebro-vascular Diseases
SUZUKI, T., Oncology of the Urogenital Region
TAKAHASHI, G., Microscopic Anatomy, Cell Biology
TATEISHI, T., Clinical Pharmacology, Pharmacokinetics and Pharmacodynamics
TSUCHIDA, S., Cancer Biochemistry, Biochemical Pharmacology
TSUSHIMA, H., Physical Therapy
WADA, K., Clinical Research in Adult Epilepsy
WAKABAYASHI, K., Neuropathology
WAKUI, M., Cellular Physiology
YAGIHASHI, S., Pathology
YAMABE, H., Nephrology
YAMADA, C., Community Health, Public Health, International Health, International Co-operation
WAKUI, M., Physiology I
YASUJIMA, M., Laboratory Medicine, Hypertension
YODONO, H., Research of Interventional Radiology
YONESAKA, S., Paediatric Cardiology

ATTACHED RESEARCH INSTITUTES

Gene Research Centre: 3 Bunkyo-cho, Hirosaki 036-8561; Dir M. NIIZEKI.

Centre for Computing and Communications: 3 Bunkyo-Cho, Hirosaki 036-8561; Dir Y. YOSHIOKA.

Centre for Education and Research of Lifelong Learning: 1 Bunkyo-cho, Hirosaki 036-8560; Dir S. SATO.

Centre for Joint Research: 3 Bunkyo-cho, Hirosaki 036-8561; Dir A. TAJIRI.

Centre for Educational Research and Practice: 1 Bunkyo-cho, Hirosaki 036-8560; Dir K. FUKIGAI.

Earthquake and Volcano Observatory: 3 Bunkyo-cho, Hirosaki 036-8561; Dir K. TANAKA.

Institute of Brain Science: 5 Zaifu-cho, Hirosaki 036-8562; Dir M. MATSUNAGA.

Institute for Experimental Animals: 5 Zaifu-cho, Hirosaki 036-8562; Dir H. KAMIYA.

University Farms: 7-1 Shitafukuro, Fujisaki-machi, Aomori-ken 038-3802; Dir T. NOMURA.

HIROSHIMA UNIVERSITY

3-2 Kagamiyama 1-chome, Higashi-Hiroshima 739-8511

Telephone: (82) 422-7111
Fax: (82) 424-6179
E-mail: www-admin@hiroshima-u.ac.jp
Internet: www.hiroshima-u.ac.jp/index-j.html

Founded 1949
Independent
Academic year: April to March (two semesters)

President: TAIZO MUTA
Executive Vice-Presidents: S. TAKAHASHI (Education and Student Affairs), N. OKI (University Relations), Y. TSUBAKI (Information), K. MAEKAWA (Finance), T. KUDO (Personnel and General Affairs), O. YUGE (Medical Affairs)
Vice-President for Attached Schools: S. ISHII
Library of 3,197,044 vols, including 1,286,724 in foreign languages
Number of teachers: 1,836
Number of students: 15,294 (incl. 4,346 postgraduate)

Publications: *Hiroshima Mathematical Journal, Journal of Science of the Hiroshima University, Series C (Earth and Planetary Sciences), The Hiroshima University Studies—Graduate School of Letters, Bulletin of the Graduate School of Education, Hiroshima Journal of Mathematics Education, Hiroshima Journal of School Education, Studies in Educational Science, Studies in English Language Education, Hiroshima Journal of Medical Sciences, The Journal of Hiroshima University Dental Society, Bulletin of the Graduate School of Engineering, Proceedings of the Research Institute for Radiation Biology and Medicine, The Hiroshima Economic Studies, The Hiroshima Economic Review, The Economic Studies, The Hiroshima Law Journal, Journal of the Graduate School of Biosphere Science, Studies in Area Culture, Studies in Social Sciences, Studies in Culture and the Humanities, Science Reports, Studies in Language and Culture, Journal of International Development and Co-operation, Bulletin of the Institute for Cultural Studies of the Seto Inland Sea, Annual Report of Research Centre for Regional Geography, Reports of the Miyajima Natural Botanical Garden, Journal of International Co-operation in Education, Bulletin of the Department of Teaching Japanese as a Second Language, The Annual of Research on Early Childhood, Journal of Learning Science, Bulletin of Music Culture Education, Bulletin of Training and Research Center for Clinical Psychology, Hiroshima Psychological Research, Research in Higher Education in Japan, Higher Education Forum, Hiroshima Law Review*

DEANS AND DIRECTORS

Graduate School of Letters: H. KISHIDA
Graduate School of Education: T. NAKAHARA
Graduate School of Social Sciences: N. KAWASAKI
Graduate School of Science: M. TANIGUCHI
Graduate School of Advanced Sciences of Matter: T. JO
Graduate School of Health Sciences: T. MURAKAMI
Graduate School of Engineering: M. OKADA
Graduate School of Biosphere Sciences: K. SUZUKI
Graduate School of Biomedical Sciences: T. USUI
Graduate School for International Development and Co-operation: K. SAITO
Law School: M. TANABE
Faculty of Integrated Arts and Sciences: M. SATO
Faculty of Economics: S. TOMIOKA
Hiroshima University Hospital: T. ASAHARA (Dir)
Research Institute for Radiation Biology and Medicine: F. SUZUKI (Dir)

PROFESSORS

Graduate School of Letters (2-3 Kagamiyama 1-chome, Higashi- Hiroshima 739-8522; tel. (82) 422-7111; fax (82) 424-0315; e-mail bun-kyo-sien@office.hiroshima-u.ac.jp; internet home.hiroshima-u.ac.jp/bungaku/index .html):

ARIMOTO, N., Modern and Contemporary Japanese Literature
FURUSE, K., Archaeology
HARANO, N., French Language and Literature
ICHIKI, T., Chinese Philosophy
IMADA, Y., Linguistics
ITOH, K., Medieval Japanese Literature
ITOH, S., American Literature and Culture
IWAI, T., Ancient History of Europe
JIMURA, A., English Language Studies
KANO, M., Chinese Linguistics
KATSUBE, M., Japanese Modern History
KAWAHARA, T., German Plays and Opera
KISHIDA, H., Ancient and Medieval Japanese History
KONDO, Y., History of Ethical Thought
KUBOTA, K., Modern and Contemporary Japanese Literature
MATSUI, F., History of Ethical Thought, Bioethics
MATSUMOTO, M., Japanese Language Studies
MATSUMOTO, Y., French Language and Literature
MIURA, M., History of Japanese Architecture
MIZUTA, H., History of Western Philosophy
NAKAMURA, H., Shakespeare, Cinema Studies, Cultural Semiotics
NISHIBEPPU, M., Ancient History of Japan
NOMA, F., History of Ancient and Medieval Chinese Thought
OCHI, M., Ethics
OKAHASHI, H., Human Geography, Regional Geography
OKAMOTO, A., Modern and Contemporary Western History
OKUMURA, K., Physical Geography, Quaternary Geology
SATO, T., Chinese Literature
SODA, S., Modern Chinese History
TANAKA, H., Modern Contemporary American Literature
TOMINAGA, K., Chinese Literature
UEDA, Y., Linguistics
UEKI, K., English Literature
UEMURA, Y., Asian History
YAMASHIRO, H., Medieval Western History
YAMAUCHI, H., Western Philosophy
YOSHINAKA, T., English Literature

Graduate School of Education (1-1 Kagamiyama 1-chome, Higashi- Hiroshima 739-8524; tel. (82) 422-7111; fax (82) 422-7171; e-mail kyoiku-kyo-sien@office.hiroshima-u .ac.jp; internet www.ed.hiroshima-u.ac.jp/ index.html):

Doctoral Program in Learning and Curriculum Development; and Master's Program in Learning Science – Learning Development Major:

DOBASHI, T., Lifespan Developmental Education
HIGUCHI, S., Philosophy and Aesthetics of Learning
ISHII, S., Environmental Psychology
MORI, T., Psychology of Learning
NISHINE, K., Sociology of Education
TAKAHASHI, S., Social Psychology

Doctoral Program in Learning and Curriculum Development; and Master's Program in Learning Science – Curriculum and Instruction Development Major:

KIHARA, S., Physical Education
KIMURA, H., Social Studies Education
KUROSE, M., Keyboard Music
MAEDA, S., Human Geography
MATSUDA, Y., Psychology of Physical Education
MOCHIZUKI, T., Food Science
MORITA, N., Japanese Language Education
SHIBA, K., Science Education
TAINOSHO, J., Home Economics Education
WAKAMOTO, S., Art Education

Doctoral Program in Learning and Curriculum Development; and Master's Program in Special Education:

FUNATSU, M., Psychology of Children with Disabilities
HAYASAKA, K., Speech and Language Pathology
OCHIAI, T., Special Educational Systems, Inclusive Education
SHIMIZU, Y., Audiology and Education of Children with Hearing Impairment
YAMANASHI, M., Methods of Teaching Children with Visual Impairment

Doctoral Program in Arts and Science Education; and Master's Program in Science, Technology and Science Education – Science Education Major:

FURUKAWA, Y., Solid State Chemistry, Magnetic Resonance
HAYASHI, T., Regional Geology, Geoinformatics, Earth Science Education
KADOYA, S., Science Education
MAEHARA, T., Particles and Fields, Physics Education
SUZUKI, M., Petrology
TANAKA, H., Inorganic Chemistry
TOKUNAGA, T., Solid State Physics
TORIGOE, K., Zoology, Biology Education
TSUTAOKA, T., Solid State Physics
YAMASHITA, Y., Nuclear Physics, Physics Education

Doctoral Program in Arts and Science Education; and Master's Program in Science, Technology and Science Education – Mathematics Education Major:

IMAOKA, M., Geometry
IWASAKI, H., Mathematics Education
KAGEYAMA, S., Statistics and Combinatorics
MARUO, O., Algebra
NAKAHARA, T., Mathematics Education

Doctoral Program in Arts and Science Education; and Master's Program in Science, Technology and Science Education – Technology and Information Education Major:

BANSHOYA, K., Woodworking
MONDEN, Y., Computer Science
TASHIMA, S., Mechanical Processing
UEDA, K., Technology Educations
YAMAMOTO, T., Computer Control Technology

Doctoral Program in Arts and Science Education; and Master's Program in Science, Technology and Science Education – Social Studies Education Major:

IKENO, N., Social Studies Education
KATAKAMI, S., Social Studies Education
KOBARA, T., Social Studies Education
MIYAKE, T., Modern Japanese History
NAKAYAMA, T., Medieval Japanese History
OBI, T., Eastern History
SATO, S., Western History
SHIMOMUKAI, T., Ancient and Medieval Japanese History
TANAHASHI, K., Social Studies Education

Doctoral Program in Arts and Science Education; and Master's Program in Language and Culture Education – Japanese Language and Culture Education Major:

EBATA, Y., Japanese Language
IWASAKI, F., Japanese Literature
TAKAHASHI, K., Linguistic Geography
TAKEMURA, S., Japanese Literature
YOSHIDA, H., Japanese Language Education

Doctoral Program in Arts and Science Education; and Master's Program in Language and Culture Education – English Language and Culture Education Major:

FUKAKAWA, S., Pragmatics, Classroom Research
HAMAGUCHI, O., American Literature
MIURA, S., English Language Education
NAKAO, Y., English Philology and Linguistics
TANAKA, M., Language Testing in English Language Teaching

Doctoral Program in Arts and Science Education; and Master's Program in Language and Culture Education – Japanese Pedagogy, Linguistics and Culture Studies Major:

KURACHI, A., Intercultural Education
MACHI, H., Study of Japanese Composition and Style

MIZUMACHI, I., Educational Language Technology
MIZUSHIMA, H., Comparative Cultures and Comparative Literature
NAKAMURA, S., Japanese Intellectual History
NUIBE, Y., Japanese Language Pedagogics
NUMOTO, K., Historical Study of Japanese Language
SAKODA, K., Second Language Acquisition
TAWATA, S., Japanese Linguistics and Japanese Language Education

Doctoral Program in Arts and Science Education; and Master's Program in Lifelong Activities Education – Health and Sports Sciences Education Major:

ESASHI, Y., Physical Education
KUROKAWA, T., Sports Training
KUSUDO, K., History of Sport
MATSUOKA, S., Physical Education
WATANABE, K., Physiology, Sports Biomechanics
YANAGIHARA, E., Kinematical Analysis in Sport (Ball Games)

Doctoral Program in Arts and Science Education; and Master's Program in Lifelong Activities Education – Human Life Sciences Education Major:

HIRATA, M., Management of Life
IKAWA, Y., Science of Food Preparation
IWASHIGE, H., House Environment Science
MIYAMOTO, S., Clothing Science
SHIBA, S., Home Economics Education

Doctoral Program in Arts and Science Education; and Master's Program in Lifelong Activities Education – Music Culture Education Major:

CHIBA, J., Musicology
KUROSE, M., Keyboard Music
OKANO, S., Piano
OKUDA, M., Vocal Music
YOSHITOMI, K., Music Education

Doctoral Program in Arts and Science Education; and Master's Program in Lifelong Activities Education – Art Education Major:

ESAKI, A., Product Design
SUGAMURA, T., Science of Arts (History of Japanese Arts
UCHIDA, M., Drawing and Painting

Doctoral Program in Education and Human Science; and Master's Program in Educational Studies:

KOGA, K., Educational Administration and Policy
KOHNO, K., Studies of Educational Leadership
KOIKE, G., Adult and Continuing Education
NAKANO, K., Curriculum Research
NINOMIYA, A., Comparative Education
OKATO, T., Educational Management
OTSUKA, Y., Comparative Education
SAKAKOSHI, M., Educational Thought and Philosophy in Germany
SATOH, H., History of Japanese and Eastern Education
TORIMITSU, M., Early Childhood Education
YAMASAKI, H., Sociology of Higher Education
YASUHARA, Y., History of Western Education

Doctoral Program in Education and Human Science; and Master's Program in Psychology:

FUKADA, H., Social Psychology
KODAMA, K., Clinical Psychology
MAEDA, K., Developmental Psychology
MIYATANI, M., Cognitive Psychology
OKAMOTO, Y., Developmental Clinical Psychology
TOSHIMA, T., Neuropsychology
YAMAZAKI, A., Child Psychology

Doctoral Program in Education and Human Science; and Master's Program in Higher Education Research and Development:

ARIMOTO, A., Sociology of Higher Education
DAIZEN, T., Sociology of Higher Education
HATA, T., History of Higher Education in Japan
KITAGAKI, I., Education Technology, Fuzzy Science
YAMAMOI, A., Sociology of Higher Education

Graduate School of Social Sciences (Higashi-Hiroshima Campus: 2-1 Kagamiyama 1-chome, Higashi-Hiroshima 739-8525 Higashi-Senda Campus: 1-89 Higashisenda-machi 1-chome, Hiroshima 730-0053; tel. (82) 422-7111 (Higashi-Hiroshima), (82) 542-7014 (Higashi-Senda); fax (82) 424-7212 (Higashi-Hiroshima), (82) 542-6964 (Higashi-Senda); e-mail syakai-bucho-sien@office.hiroshima-u.ac.jp):

AGAOKA, Y., Medieval Western History
AIZAWA, Y., Private International Law
EGASHIRA, D., Sociology
FUKIHARU, T., Microeconomics
FUTAMURA, H., Public Finance
GINAMA, I., Macroeconometrics
HINO, S., Product Development Theory
HOSHINO, I., Financial Accounting
INOUE, Z., Management (Strategy Theory)
ISHIDA, M., International Finance
ITOH, T., Economic Policy
KAN, T., Fiscal Policy
KANNO, R., Finance
KATOH, F., Occidental Economic History
KAWASAKI, N., Public Administration
MAEKAWA, K., Financial Econometrics
MAKINO, M., Political History
MATSUDA, M., Political Economy
MATSUMIZU, Y., World Economic Conditions
MATSUURA, K., Finance and Econometrics
MATSUIKE, H., Criminal Law
MORIBE, S., Japanese Politics
MORIOKA, T., Labour Economics
MORITA, K., Comparative Economic Systems
MURAMATSU, J., Marketing Theory
NISHIMURA, H., Constitutional Law
NISHITANI, H., International Law
NOMOTO, R., Industrial Organization
ODAKI, M., Statistics
OKAMURA, M., International Economics, Applied Microeconomics
OTANI, T., Sociology of Law
SAKAGUCHI, K., Management Accounting
SAKANE, Y., Economic History of Japan
TAKAHASHI, H., Civil Law
TAKI, A., Industrial Relations
TERAMOTO, Y., Diplomacy and Diplomatic History
TODA, T., Regional Development Policy
TOMIOKA, S., Economic History
TSUBAKI, Y., Information Resource Management
TSUJI, H., Labour Law
UEDA, Y., Public Choice and Institutional Economics
WAKIMOTO, S., Economic Policy
WATANABE, M., Social Policy
YAMADA, S., History of Political Thought
YANO, J., Macroeconomics
YOSHIDA, O., Asian Politics
YOSHIHARA, T., Legal History

Graduate School of Science (3-1 Kagamiyama 1-chome, Higashi- Hiroshima 739-8526; tel. (82) 422-7111; fax (82) 424-0709; e-mail ri-bucho-sien@office.hiroshima-u.ac.jp; internet www.sci.hiroshima-u.ac.jp/english):

Mathematics:

ENOMOTO, H., Graph Theory, Discrete Mathematics
KAMADA, S., Knots, Topology
MATSUMOTO, M., Galois Group, Arithmetic Fundamental Group, Random Number Generation
MATUMOTO, T., Topology
MIZUTA, Y., Potential Theory
MORITA, T., Dynamic Systems, Ergodic Theory
NAGAI, T., Differential Equations
TSUZUKI, N., Arithmetic Geometry, Number Theory
YOSHINO, M., Differential Equations

Physical Science:

HASHIMOTO, E., Physics of Perfect Crystals, Synchrotron Radiation Physics
HIRAYA, A., Molecular Photophysics and Photochemistry
HORI, T., Particle Accelerator Physics, Synchrotron Radiation Physics
KOJIMA, Y., Theory of Relativity and Astrophysics
MARUYAMA, H., Solid State Physics, X-Ray Spectroscopy
NAMATAME, H., Solid State Physics, Synchrotron Radiation Physics
OHSUGI, T., High Energy Particle Physics, Gamma-ray Astrophysics
OKAWA, M., Elementary Particle Theory, Lattice QCD
SUGITATE, T., High Energy Nuclear Physics
TANAKA, K., Photochemistry and Photophysics
TANIGUCHI, M., Solid State Physics, Synchrotron Radiation Science

Chemistry:

AIDA, M., Quantum Chemisty
EBATA, T., Laser Chemistry and Molecular Spectroscopy
FUJIWARA, T., Analytical Chemistry
FUKAZAWA, Y., Organic Stereochemistry
INOUE, K., Molecular Magnetism
MIYOSHI, K., Coordination and Organometallic Chemistry
OHKATA, K., Synthesis and Isolation of Natural Products
OHNO, K., Physical Chemistry and Vibrational Spectroscopy
YAMAMOTO, Y., Organic Main Group Element Chemistry
YAMASAKI, K., Chemical Kinetics and Dynamics

Biological Science:

DEGUCHI, H., Plant Taxonomy and Ecology, Bryology
HOSOYA, H., Cell Biology, Signal Transduction
MICHIBATA, H., Molecular Physiology
SUZUKI, K., Molecular Genetics, Yeast and Agrobacterial Genetics
TAKAHASHI, Y., Plant Molecular Biology
YOSHIZATO, K., Developmental Biology, Regeneration Biology

Earth and Planetary Systems Science:

HIDAKA, H., Isotope Geochemistry
SHIMIZU, H., Trace Element Geochemistry
TAJIMA, F., Solid Earth Geophysics
WATANABE, M., Ore Petrology and Ore Genesis

Mathematical and Life Sciences:

GEKKO, K., Physical Chemistry of Biopolymers
HIRATA, T., Biological Chemistry and Biotechnology
IDE, H., DNA Damage and Repair
KOBAYASHI, R., Self-Organization in Material and Life Science
MORIKAWA, H., Molecular Plant Biology
NISHIMORI, H., Complex Systems and Nonlinear Dynamics
SAKAMOTO, K., Dynamical Systems
TANIMOTO, Y., Magneto-Science
YAMAMOTO, T., Molecular Developmental Biology
YOSHIDA, K., Partial Differential Equations

Marine Biological Laboratory:

YASUI, K., Development and Bio-history of Marine Deuterostomes

Miyajima Natural Botanical Garden:

DEGUCHI, H., Plant Taxonomy and Ecology, Bryology

Institute for Amphibian Biology:

KASHIWAGI, A., Endocrine Disruptors, Space Biology, Apoptosis, Transgenesis
SUMIDA, M., Evolutionary Genetics, Molecular Phylogeny
YAOITA, Y., Developmental Biology, Metamorphosis, Programmed Cell Death

Laboratory of Plant Chromosome and Gene Stock:

KONDO, K., Plant Demography, Chromosome Science and Gene Resources

Graduate School of Advanced Sciences of Matter (3-1 Kagamiyama 1-chome, Higashi-Hiroshima 739-8530; tel. (82) 422-7111; fax (82) 424-7000; internet www.hiroshima-u.ac.jp/en/adsm/):

Department of Quantum Matter:

ENDO, I., Photon Physics
JO, T., Theory of Condensed Matters
KADOYA, Y., Solid State Quantum Optics
OGUCHI, T., Computational Physics
OKAMOTO, H., Beam Physics
SERA, M., Experimental Researches of Strongly Correlated Electron Systems
SUZUKI, T., Low Temperature Physics
TAKABATAKE, T., Magnetism and Magnetic Materials
TAKAHAGI, T., Nanotechnology

Department of Molecular Biotechnology:

HIRATA, D., Molecular Biology
KATO, J., MMolecular Environmental Biotechnology
KINASHI, H., Microbiology and Natural Product Chemistry
KURODA, A., Biochemistry
MIYAKAWA, T., Molecular Biotechnology in Yeast
NISHIO, N., Environmental Bioengineering
ONO, K., Molecular Biochemistry
TSUCHIYA, E., Molecular Cell Biology
YAMADA, T., Plant/Microbe Interactions

Department of Semiconductor Electronics and Integration Science:

IWATA, A., Integrated Circuits
MIURA-MATTAUSCH, M., Semiconductor Device Technology
MIYAZAKI, S., Semiconductor Electronics

Graduate School of Engineering (4-1 Kagamiyama 1-chome, Higashi- Hiroshima 739-8527; tel. (82) 422-7111; fax (82) 422-7039; internet www.eden.hiroshima-u.ac.jp):

Mechanical Systems Engineering:

ISHIZUKA, S., Combustion Science and Technology
KIKUCHI, Y., Heat Transfer, Biomass Energy, Carbon Nanotube
KUROKI, H., Powder Metallurgy and Ceramics
MAEKAWA, H., Fluid Engineering
NAGAMURA, K., Machine Elements, Gear Design and Vibration, Tribology
NAKAGAWA, N., Dynamics of Machines
NAKASA, K., Strength and Fracture of Materials, Vibration and Sound, Acoustic Energy
OBA, F., Manufacturing Systems
SAEKI, M., Automatic Control
SAWA, T., Strength of Material, Elasticity, Solid Mechanics
SHINOZAKI, K., Welding and Joining
SHIZUMA, K., Quantum Energy Applications
TAKI, S., Reactive Gas Dynamics
TAKIYAMA, K., Plasma Spectroscopy
YAMANE, Y., Machining, Machine Tools and Mechatronics
YANAGISAWA, O., Control of Material Properties
YOSHIDA, F., Engineering Elasto-Plasticity

Artificial Complex Systems Engineering:

HINAMOTO, T., Electronic Control, Digital Signal Processing
IWASE, K., Mathematical Statistics and Data Analysis
KADO, T., Nano-electronics
KANEKO, M., Robotics, Active Sensing
NAKANO, K., Computer Engineering
NISHIZAKI, I., Decision Analysis and Game Theory
SAKAWA, M., Systems Optimization
SHIBATA, T., Differential Equations and their Application
TAKAHASHI, K., Production Systems Engineering
TSUJI, T., Biological Systems Engineering
YOKOGAWA, K., Computational Materials Science
YORINO, N., Electric Power System Engineering

Information Engineering:

DOHI, T., Systems Reliability Engineering
HARADA, K., Graphics Geometry
HIRASHIMA, T., Computer-based Learning Environment
KUBO, F., Algebraic Deformation Theory
KUWADA, M., Experimental Designs
MORITA, K., Theoretical Computer Science
SHIBA, M., Complex Analysis and its Applications
WATANABE, T., Computer Science and Information Technology

Chemistry and Chemical Engineering:

ASAEDA, M., Separation and Purification Technology
HARIMA, Y., Materials Physical Chemistry
HIROKAWA, T., Applied Instrumental Analysis
KUNAI, A., Organic Materials Chemistry
OKADA, M., Environmental Chemical Engineering
OKUYAMA, K., Thermal Fluids Engineering
OTSUBO, T., Applied Organic Chemistry
SAKOHARA, S., Polymer Technology
SHIONO, T., Advanced Polymer Chemistry
TAKISHIMA, S., Chemical Engineering Thermodynamics
YAMANAKA, S., Applied Inorganic Materials Chemistry
YOSHIDA, H., Fine Particle Technology

Social and Environmental Engineering:

DOI, Y., Marine Hydrodynamics
FUJIKUBO, M., Strength of Structures
FUJIMOTO, Y., Reliability of Structures and Systems
KANEKO, A., Ocean-Atmosphere Environment
KAWAHARA, Y., Hydraulic Engineering
KITAMURA, M., Computational Mechanics for Structural Design
KOSE, K., Management of Human–Technology–Environment Systems
MATSUO, A., Building Structures
MIURA, K., Building Disasters Prevention
MURAKAWA, S., Community Environmental Science
NAKAMURA, H., Structural Engineering
OHKUBO, T., Building Materials and Components
SASAKI, Y., Soil Mechanics and Earthquake Geotechnical Engineering
SATO, R., Concrete and Concrete Structural Engineering
SUGANO, S., Earthquake Engineering
SUGIE, Y., Transportation Planning
SUGIMOTO, T., Architectural History and Design Theory
TAKAKI, M., Ocean Space Engineering
TSUCHIDA, T., Geotechnical and Geo-environmental Engineering
YASUKAWA, H., Naval Architecture
YOKOBORI, H., Architecture, Urban Planning and International Co-operation

Graduate School of Biosphere Science (4-4 Kagamiyama 1-chome, Higashi- Hiroshima 739-8528; tel. (82) 424-7905; fax (82) 424-2459; e-mail sei-bucho-sien@office.hiroshima-u.ac.jp; internet home.hiroshima-u.ac.jp/gsbstop/English/top/index-e.html):

Department of Sciences for Biospheric Co-existence:

NAKAI, T., Fish-pathogenic Bacteria and Viruses
TANAKA, H., Consumer Food Co-operatives
UEMATSU, K., Neural Basis for Fish Swimming
YAMAO, M., Locally Based Coastal Resource Management in Asia, Sustainable Coastal Fisheries Management and 'Code of Conduct for Responsible Production', People's Participation in Community Development and their Responsibility, Development and Export-oriented Food Production and its Impact on the Resource Environment

Department of Bioresource Science and Technology:

ESAKA, M., Function and Biosynthesis of Ascorbic Acid in Plants
FUJITA, M., Environmental Physiology of Farm Animals
FURASAWA, S., Basic and Applied Immunobiology
GOTO, N., Enology and Viticulture
GUSHIMA, K., Foraging Ecology of Coral Reef Fishes
HORI, K., Structures, Functions and Applications of Lectins from Marine Organisms
IEFUJI, H., Environmental and Food Biotechnology
IMABAYASHI, H., Larval Settlement of Benthic Organisms
KATO, N., Nutrition and Cancer
KONO, K., Cellular Immunology
MATSUDA, H., Chicken Monoclonal Antibodies
MITANI, K., Holistic Management of Farm Animals
MIZUTA, K., Molecular and Cellular Biology of Yeast
NAGAMATSU, Y., Applied Biochemistry of Microbial Proteins
NAKANO, H., Behaviour and Control of Foodborne Bacterial Pathogens
NISHIMURA, T., Structure and Function of Proteases in Muscle Foods
OHTA, T., Physiological Phenomena and Molecules, Identification and Mechanism Analysis
SATO, K., Physical Chemistry of Lipids
SUZUKI, K., Emulsifying Characteristics and Properties of Food Emulsions
SUZUKI, N., Bio-organic Chemistry, Active Oxygen, Antioxidative Activity, Bio- and Chemiluminescence
TANIGUCHI, K., Ruminant Nutrition and Feeding
TERADA, T., Nuclear Transfer in the Bovine and Porcine Embryo
TSUDUKI, M., Animal Breeding and Genetics
YOSHIMURA, Y., Endocrine Control of Avian Reproductive Functions

Department of Environmental Dynamics and Management:

FUJITA, K., Source–Sink Relationship
HOSHIKA, Y., Mechanism of Material Circulation and its Control in Coastal Seas
ISEKI, K., Marine Ecology and Biogeochemical Cycle

KONO, K., Biology and Fertility of Soils
MARAYAMA, T., Biology of Symbiotic Relationships between Marine Invertebrates and Micro-organisms, Biology of Hyperthermophiles
MASAOKA, Y., Enhancement of Metal Stress Tolerance in Plants
NAKANE, K., Environmental Chemistry
SAKUGAWA, H., Environmental Ecosystem Ecology
TAKASUGI, Y., Monitoring and Diagnosis of the Physical Environment in Semi-enclosed Sea
UYE, S., Production Ecology of Marine Zooplankton
YAMAMOTO, K., Microbial Ecology and Marine Ecology
YAMAMOTO, T., Aquatic Environmental Management
YAMAUCHI, M., Development of Ecophysiological Soil and Water Management Technology for Environmental Protection

Graduate School of Biomedical Sciences (2-3 Kasumi 1-chome, Minami-ku, Hiroshima 734-8513; tel. (82) 257-5555; fax (82) 257-5278; e-mail bimes-kyou@office.hiroshima-u.ac.jp; internet www.hiroshima-u.ac.jp/bimes/):

Programs for Biomedical Research:

AOYAMA, H., Anatomy and Developmental Biology
ASAHARA, T., Surgery, Gastroenterological Surgery, Organ Transplantation
CHAYAMA, K., Medicine and Molecular Science, Gastroenterology, Hepatology
DOHI, T., Dental Pharmacology
HAZEKI, O., Physiological Chemistry, Cellular Signal Transduction
HIDE, M., Dermatology, Allergology and Immunopharmacology in Skin
IDE, T., Cellular and Molecular Biology
KANNO, M., Immunology, Parasitology, Molecular Immunology
KATAOKA, K., Histology and Cell Biology, Histochemistry and Cell Biology of the Digestive Organs
KATO, Y., Dental and Medical Biochemistry, Biochemistry and Oral Biology
KIKUCHI, A., Biochemistry, Intracellular Signal Transduction
KURIHARA, H., Periodontal Medicine, Periodontal Tissue Regeneration, Endodontology
KURISU, K., Neurosurgery, Neuro-oncology, Neuroradiology, Surgery of Brain Tumours and Cerebro-vascular Disease, Skull Base Surgery
MASUJIMA, T., Analytical Molecular Medicine and Devices, Videonanoscopes, Cell Dynamics, Pharmaco-dynamics, Bioanalysis
MATSUMOTO, M., Clinical Neuroscience and Therapeutics, Neurology, Strokology, Gerontology
MISHIMA, H., Ophthalmology and Visual Science, Glaucoma, Ocular Cell Biology, Ocular Pharmacology, Retinal Disease
OGATA, N., Neurophysiology
OHTA, S., Xenobiotic Metabolism and Molecular Toxicology, Neurochemistry, Drug Metabolism
OKAMOTO, T., Molecular Oral Medicine and Maxillofacial Surgery
OKAZAKI, M., Biomaterials Science, Dental Materials
SAKAI, N., Molecular and Pharmacological Neuroscience, Molecular Neurobiology, Neuropharmacology
SHIBA, Y., Oral Physiology
SUGAI, M., Bacteriology, Oral Microbiology
SUGIYAMA, M., Molecular Microbiology and Biotechnology, Antibiotics, Enzymology, Molecular Genetics, Applied Microbiology
TAKATA, T., Oral Maxillofacial Pathobiology, Oral Oncology, Periodontal Tissue Engineering, Diagnostic Pathology
UCHIDA, T., Oral Biology, Oral Anatomy
USUI, T., Urology, Andrology, Oncology, Endo-urology
YAMAWAKI, S., Psychiatry and Neurosciences, Biological Psychiatry, Psychopharmacology, Affective Disorders, Neuroleptic Malignant Syndrome, Psychosomatic Medicine, Liaison Psychiatry, Psycho-oncology
YASUI, W., Molecular Pathology, Molecular Pathology of Gastrointestinal Cancer
YOSHIDA, T., Virology, Paramyxovirus, Bacteriology
YOSHIZUMI, M., Cardiovascular Physiology and Medicine, Cardiology and Vascular Biology

Programs for Applied Biomedicine:

AKAGAWA, Y., Advanced Prosthodontics, Implantology
EBOSHIDA, A., Public Health and Health Policy, Health Science, Epidemiology, Environmental Health
HAMADA, T., Geriatric Dentistry, Prosthodontics, Stomatognathic Dysfunction
HIRAKAWA, K., Otorhinolaryngology, Head and Neck Surgery and Oncology, Rhinology
INAI, K., Pathology, Tumour Pathology
ITO, K., Radiology, Diagnostic Imaging, Interventional Radiology
KANBE, M., Clinical Laboratory Medicine, Clinical Physiology, ME, Medical Informatics, Gene Engineering
KAWAHARA, M., Dental Anaesthesiology, Pain Clinic
KAMATA, N., Oral and Maxillofacial Surgery
KIMURA, K.
KOBAYASHI, M., Paediatrics, Child Health
KOHNO, N., Molecular and Internal Medicine, Respiratory Diseases, Cancer Therapeutics
KOZAI, K., Paediatric Dentistry
KUDO, Y., Obstetrics and Gynaecology
MAEDA, N., Oral Growth and Developmental Biology, Development of Masticatory System
MORIKAWA, N., Clinical Pharmacotherapy, Pharmacokinetics, Therapeutic Drug Monitoring
OCHI, M., Orthopaedic Surgery, Sports Medicine, Knee Surgery
OZAWA, K., Pharmacotherapy, Clinical Pharmacology
SUEDA, T., Surgery, Thoracic and Cardiovascular Surgery, Bioengineering
TAKAHASHI, I., Preventive Dentistry, Mucosal Immunology
TANIGAWA, K., Emergency and Critical Care Medicine, Cardiopulmonary Resuscitation, Airway Management, Free Radicals and Reperfusion Injury
TANIMOTO, K., Oral and Maxillofacial Radiology, Dysphagia
TANNE, K., Orthodontics and Craniofacial Developmental Biology, Biomechanics
YAJIN, K., Otorhinolaryngology, Head and Neck Surgery, Head and Neck Oncology, Rhinology
YOSHIZAWA, K., Infectious Disease Control and Prevention, Seroepidemiology of Viral Hepatitis
YUGE, O., Anaesthiology and Critical Care

Programs for Pharmaceutical Sciences:

KOIKE, T., Functional Molecular Sciences, Medicinal Chemistry, Bioinorganic Chemistry
NAKATA, Y., Pharmacology, Neuropharmacology, Molecular Pharmacology
OOTSUKA, H., Pharmacognosy and Natural Product Chemistry, Molecular Pharmaceutics
TAKANO, M., Pharmaceutics and Therapeutics, Drug Transporters and Metabolizing Enzymes, Drug Delivery Systems
TAKEDA, K., Synthetic Organic Chemistry, Mechanistic Organic Chemistry, Synthetic Methodology

Graduate School for International Development and Co-operation (5-1 Kagamiyama 1-chome, Higashi- Hiroshima 739-8529; tel. (82) 424-6905; fax (82) 424-6904; e-mail idec@hiroshima-u.ac.jp; internet home .hiroshima-u.ac.jp/idec):

Division of Development Science:

FUJIWARA, A., Transportation Planning, Environmental Engineering
HIGO, Y., Ocean Engineering
KINBARA, T., Management and Organization
KOMATSU, M., Development Economics
MATSUOKA, S., Environmental Economics
NAKAZONO, K., International Relations
NOHARA, H., Comparative Study of Industrial Organizations
SAITO, K., Marine Development Technology
TOMINAGA, K., Disaster Prevention on Geotechnical Engineering

Division of Educational Development and Cultural and Regional Studies:

IKEDA, H., Content-based Science Education (Biology Education), International Co-operation in Science Education
KASAI, T., Motor Neurophysiology and Motor Rehabilitation Medicine
TABATA, Y., Educational Administration (Educational System, Teacher Education)
UEHARA, A., Intercultural Communication

Faculty of Integrated Arts and Sciences (7-1 Kagamiyama 1-chome, Higashi- Hiroshima 739-8521; tel. (82) 422-7111; fax (82) 424-0751; e-mail souka-bucho-sien@office .hiroshima-u.ac.jp; internet home .hiroshima-u.ac.jp/souka/e/ias.html):

Division of Area Studies:

FUJITA-SANO, M., Cultural Anthropology, American Studies
IIDA, M., English Literature and Culture
ITOH, S., American Literature and Culture
KASHIHARA, O., Modern Japanese Literature
KOHATA, F., Biblical Studies
KUSUNOSE, M., Modern Chinese History
MIKI, N., Contemporary Chinese Culture
OKAMOTO, M., American Social History
SATAKE, A., Japanese History and Culture
SATO, M., History of German Literature, Everyday Life and Customs in the Early Modern Age
TAKATANI, M., Cultural Anthropology, Southeast Asian Studies

Division of Socio-Environmental Studies:

AKIBA, S., Rural Sociology
FUKIHARA, S., Regions and Economy
ICHIKAWA, H., History of Technology
YASUNO, M., Contemporary History

Division of Creative Arts and Sciences:

GOLDSBURY, P. A., Philosophy of Language, Comparative Culture
HARA, M., Comparative Philosophy and Music Aesthetics
KOTOH, T., Comparative Philosophy
MURASE, N., French Theatre, French Studies
NAKAMURA, H., Shakespeare, Cinema Studies, Cultural Semiotics
SAITO, T., Modern Science and Mysticism
TAKAHASHI, N., Ancient Greek Philosophy

Division of Language and Culture:

ANIYA, S., Linguistics
HIGUCHI, M., English Philology

IMAZATO, C., History of the English Language, Lexicography
INOUE, K., Linguistics
KOBAYASHI, H., Applied Linguistics, TESOL
NISHIDA, T., Applied Linguistics
OGAWA, Y., Comparative Study of Japanese and Chinese
SKAER, P. M., Linguistics
TANAKA, S., German Literature
YAMADA, J., Psycholinguistics
YOON, K. B., Korean Literature
YOSHIDA, M., Linguistics

Division of Behavioural and Biological Sciences:

ANDO, M., Integrative Physiology
FURUKAWA, Y., Neurobiology
HORI, T., Psychophysiology
IWATA, K., Comparative Politics and Diplomacy
KAWAHARA, A., Developmental Biology
KUSUDO, K., History of Sport
SEIWA, H., Psychology of Personality
TSUTSUI, K., Brain Science
URA, M., Social Psychology
WADA, M., Biochemistry of Exercise
YAMASAKI, M., Exercise Physiology

Division of Mathematical and Information Sciences:

AGAOKA, Y., Differential Geometry
HARADA, K., Geometry Graphics
KUWADA, M., Experimental Design
MIZUTA, Y., Function Theory
YOSHIDA, K., Applied Analysis

Division of Materials Science:

FUKAMIYA, N., Bioactive Natural Products Chemistry
HATAKENAKA, N., Theoretical Condensed Matter Physics
HIKOSAKA, M., Soft Materials Physics
HOSHINO, K., Condensed Matter Physics
ITOH, T., Molecular Spectroscopy and Quantum Chemistry
KOJIMA, K., Condensed Matter Physics
KOMINAMI, S., Biophysical Chemistry
NAGAI, K., Theoretical Solid State Physics
TAKEDA, T., Condensed Matter Physics
UDAGAWA, M., Condensed Matter Physics

Division of Natural Environmental Sciences:

FUKUOKA, M., Research of Earth Resources
HAYASE, K., Environmental Sciences
HONDA, K., Chemical Ecology
HORIKOSHI, T., Microbiology
KAIHOTSU, I., Hydrology
NAKAGOSHI, N., Landscape Ecology
NARISADA, K., Science Studies
OHO, Y., Environmental Geology
SAKURAI, N., Environmental Plant Physiology
TOGASHI, K., Applied Ecology

Graduate School of Biosphere Science:

NAKANE, K., Environmental Ecosystem Ecology
SAKUGAWA, H., Environmental Chemistry

Law School (1-89 Higashisenda 1-chome, Hiroshima 730-0053; tel. (82) 542-7014; fax (82) 542-6964; e-mail senda-bk-sien@office.hiroshima-u.ac.jp; internet www.law.hiroshima-u.ac.jp/lawschool/ls-top.htm):

GOTOH, K., Commercial Law
HIRANO, T., Legal Philosophy
KAMITANI, Y., Civil Law
KATAGI, H., Commercial Law
KINOSHITA, M., Commercial Law
KOHAMA, S., Civil Law
KOHARI, Y., International Law
MITSUI, M., Labour Law
MONDEN, T., Constitutional Law
NAKA, T., Administrative Law
ODA, N., Criminal Law
OHKUBO, T., Criminal Procedure
OKAMOTO, T., Civil Law
SAEKI, Y., Administrative Law
TANABE, M., Civil Procedure
TORIYABE, S., Civil Law

Graduate School of Medicine (2-3 Kasumi 1-chome, Minami-ku, Hiroshima 734-8553; tel. (82) 257-5555; fax (82) 257-5278; e-mail bimes-kyou@office.hiroshima-u.ac.jp; internet www.hiroshima-u.ac.jp/hsc/):

Health Sciences:

INAMIZU, T., Sports Medicine and Sciences
INOUE, M., Gastroenterology, Gastrointestinal Physiology and Treatment of Acid-related Diseases
KAKEHASHI, M., Health Science, Health Statistics, Mathematical Modelling, Public Health
KATAOKA, T., Health Care for Adults
KAWAMATA, S., Anatomy of Musculoskeletal System, Anatomy of Calcified Tissue
KINJYO, T., Geriatric Nursing
KOBAYASHI, T., Health Development
MATSUKAWA, K., Physiology, Neural Control of the Cardiovascular System, Motor Control
MIYAGUCHI, H., Occupational Behavioural Science Laboratory
MIYAKOSHI, Y., Fundamentals of Nursing Theory and Practice, Nursing Management and Education
MORIYAMA, M., Medical-Surgical Nursing, Adult Health Nursing
MURAKAMI, T., Rheumatoid Surgery, Elbow Surgery, Sports Medicine
OKAMURA, H., Psycho-oncology, Psychosocial Rehabilitation
ONO, M., Community Health and Home Care Nursing
SHIMIZU, H., Science of Occupational Therapy
SHINKODA, K., Physical Therapy, Kinesiology
TANAKA, Y., Paediatrics, Health Science, Nursing Education
TOBIMATSU, Y., Rehabilitation Medicine and Science for the Elderly and People with Disabilities
TSUSHIMA, H., Community and School Health Nursing
URABE, Y., Athletic Rehabilitation
YAMAKATSU, H., Occupational Therapy for Physical Dysfunction and ADL Disorder
YOKOO, K., Neonatal Nursing, Maternal and Child Health Nursing, Midwifery
YUGE, R., Nerve and Muscle Regeneration

Research Institute for Radiation Biology and Medicine (2-3 Kasumi 1-chome, Minami-ku, Hiroshima 734-8553; tel. (82) 257-5555; fax (82) 255-8339; e-mail bimes-gen@office.hiroshima-u.ac.jp; internet www.rbm.hiroshima-u.ac.jp/index.html):

HONDA, H., Developmental Biology
HOSHI, M., Radiation Biophysics
INABA, T., Molecular Oncology, Haematology
KAMIYA, K., Radiation Biology, Oncology
KIMURA, A., Haematology and Oncology
MATSUURA, S., Human Genetics
MIYAGAWA, K., Molecular Oncology
NISHIYAMA, M., Molecular Oncology, Preclinical Development
OHTAKI, M., Biometrics, Environmetrics
SUZUKI, F., Radiation Biology
TAKIHARA, Y., Stem Cell Biology, Haematology, Regenerative Medicine
TASHIRO, S., Molecular Cell Biology

ATTACHED INSTITUTES

Research Institute for Higher Education: 2-2 Kagamiyama 1-chome, Higashi-Hiroshima 739-8521; Dir A. ARIMOTO.

Information Media Center: 4-2 Kagamiyama 1-chome, Higashi-Hiroshima 739-8526; Dir T. WATANABE.

Research Center for Nanodevices and Systems: 4-2 Kagamiyama 1-chome, Higashi-Hiroshima 739-8527; Dir A. IWATA.

Natural Science Center for Basic Research and Development: 3-1 Kagamiyama 1-chome, Higashi-Hiroshima 739-8526; Dir I. YAMASHITA.

International Student Center: 1-2 Kagamiyama 1-chome, Higashi-Hiroshima 739-8523; Dir S. TAWADA.

Community Co-operation Center: 3-2 Kagamiyama 1-chome, Higashi-Hiroshima 739-8511; Dir T. ANDO.

Collaborative Research Center: 10-31 Kagamiyama 3-chome, Higashi-Hiroshima 739-0046; Dir Y. YAMANE.

Health Service Center: 7-1 Kagamiyama 1-chome, Higashi-Hiroshima 739-8511; Dir M. YOSHIHARA.

Institute for Peace Science: 1-89, Higashisenda-machi 1-chome, Naka-ku, Hiroshima 730-0053; Dir M. MATSUO.

Saijo Seminar House: Misonou, Saijo-cho, Higashi-Hiroshima 739-0024; Dir S. TAKAHASHI.

Environmental Research and Management Centre: 5-3 Kagamiyama 1-chome, Higashi-Hiroshima 739-8513; Dir S. OTA.

Hiroshima Synchrotron Radiation Center: 313 Kagamiyama 2-chome, Higashi-Hiroshima 739-8526; Dir M. TANIGUCHI.

Center for the Study of International Co-operation in Education: 5-1 Kagamiyama 1-chome, Higashi-Hiroshima 739-8529; Dir A. NINOMIYA.

Research Center for Regional Geography: 2-3 Kagamiyama 1-chome, Higashi-Hiroshima 739-8522; Dir H. OKAHASHI.

Beijing Research Center: College of International Education, Capital Nomal University, 105 Xisanhuan Beilu, Beijing 00037, China; Dir T. SATO.

HITOTSUBASHI UNIVERSITY

2-1 Naka, Kunitachi-city Tokyo 186-8601
Telephone: (42) 580-8000
Fax: (42) 580-8006
Internet: www.hit-u.ac.jp
Independent
Founded 1875
Academic year: April to March
President: HIROMITSU ISHI
Vice-President: JYURO TERANISHI
Director-General: SAKASHI KAMATA
Dean of Students: TAKEHIKO SUGIYAMA
Librarian: MAKOTO IKEMA
Library of 1,739,884 vols
Number of teachers: 465 full-time
Number of students: 6,429
Publications: *The Hitotsubashi Review* (monthly), *Hitotsubashi Journal of Commerce and Management* (annually), *Hitotsubashi Journal of Economics* (2 a year), *Hitotsubashi Journal of Law and Politics* (annually), *Hitotsubashi Journal of Social Studies* (2 a year), *Hitotsubashi Arts and Sciences* (annually), *Gengo Bunka – Cultura Philologica* (annually)

DEANS

Graduate School and Faculty of Commerce and Management: K. ITO
Graduate School and Faculty of Social Sciences: N. TASAKI
Graduate School and Faculty of Economics: E. TAJIKA
Graduate School and Faculty of Law: T. YAMAUCHI
Graduate School of Language and Society: Y. SANO

Graduate School of International Corporate Strategy: H. TAKEUCHI

ATTACHED INSTITUTES

Institute of Economic Research: Tokyo; f. 1940; 41 teachers; Dir M. KUBONIWA; publ. *Economic Review* (4 a year).

Institute of Innovation Research: Tokyo; f. 1997; 11 teachers; Dir S. NAGAOKA; publ. *Hitotsubashi Business Review* (4 a year).

HOKKAIDO UNIVERSITY

Nishi 5, Kita 8, Kita-ku, Sapporo 060-0808
Telephone: (11) 706-2334
Fax: (11) 706-2095
E-mail: kouryu@general.hokudai.ac.jp
Internet: www.hokudai.ac.jp

Founded 1876
Independent
Academic year: April to March
President: MUTSUO NAKAMURA
Vice-Presidents: YOSHIRO INOUE, HIROSHI SAEKI, YOSHIHITO OSADA MASAAKI HEMMI TAKESHI KISHINAMI
Director-General, Administration Bureau: HAJIME ENDO
Director, University Library: MASAAKI HEMMI
Library of 3,422,052 vols
Number of teachers: 2,154
Number of students: 17,559
Publications: various faculty bulletins
Publications: *Hokudai Jiho* (monthly), *Newsletter* (irregular)

DEANS

Graduate School of Letters: TAKAHIKO NITTA
Graduate School of Education: TOSHIMASA SUZUKI
Graduate School of Law: KATSUMI YOSHIDA
Graduate School of Economics and Business Administration: KAZUO UCHIDA
Graduate School of Science: HISATAKE OKADA
Graduate School of Medicine: KENICHI HOMMA
Graduate School of Dental Medicine: YASUNORI TOTSUKA
Graduate School of Pharmaceutical Sciences: HIDEYOSHI YOKOZAWA
Graduate School of Engineering: TSUNEYOSHI NAKAYAMA
Graduate School of Agriculture: MASAAKI SUWA
Graduate School of Veterinary Medicine: HIROSHI KIDA
Graduate School of Fisheries Science: KOHEI YAMAUCHI
Graduate School of Environmental Earth Science: MOTOYOSHI IKEDA
Graduate School of International Media and Communication: MASANORI TSUKUWA
Graduate School of Information Science and Technology: TOSHIHISA HOMMA
Institute of Language and Culture Studies: TOSHITAKA NOZAWA

PROFESSORS

Graduate School of Letters (Kita 10, Nishi 7, Kita-ku, Sapporo; tel. (11) 726-7728; fax (11) 706-4803; e-mail wwwadmin@letters.hokudai.ac.jp; internet www.hokudai.ac.jp/letters/english/index_e.html):

ABE, J., Psychology
AKASHI, M., Occidental History
ANDO, A., Western Literature
ANZAI, M., Western Literature
FUJII, K., Religious Studies and Indian Philosophy
GOTO, Y., Japanology
HANAI, K., Philosophy
HISHITANI, S., Psychology
INOUE, K., Japanese History
IRIMOTO, T., Northern Culture Studies
ISHIZUKA, H., Linguistic Sciences
ITO, T., Sinology
KADOWAKI, S., Linguistic Sciences
KAMEDA, T., Behavioural Sciences
KANEKO, I., Sociology
KIKUCHI, T., Asian History
KITAMURA, K., Theory and History of Art
KOCHI, S., Japanese History
KURYUZAWA, T., OccidentalHistory
KUWAYAMA, H., History and Anthropology
MATSUOKA, M., Sociology
MIKI, S., Asian History
MISAKI, H., Japanology
MIYATAKE, K., History and Anthropology
MIYAZAWA, T., Japanology
NAGAO, T., Western Literature
NAKA, M., Psychology
NAKATOGAWA, K., Philosophy
NAKAYAMA, A., Japanology
NAMBU, N., Japanese History
NISHIKAWA, Y., Psychology
NITTA, T., Ethics and Applied Philosophy
ONO, Y., Linguistics Sciences
OTA, K., History and Anthropology
RADFORD, M., Behavioural Sciences
SAKAI, A., Ethics and Applied Ethics
SAKURAI, Y., Sociology
SATO, R., Sinology
SEKI, T., Regional Sciences
SHIMIZU, M., Linguistics and Western Languages
SHIRAKIZAWA, A., Japanese History
SUTO, Y., Sinology
TAKAHASHI, H., Linguistics and Western Languages
TAKAHEI, H., Philosophy
TAKEDA, M., Sinology
TAKIGAWA, T., Psychology
TAYAMA, T., Philosophy
TOMITA, Y., Japanology
TSUMAGARI, T., Northern Culture Studies
TUDA, Y., Asian History
UEKI, M., Linguistics and Western Languages
URAI, Y., Linguistics and Western Languages
UTSUNOMIYA, T., Religious Studies and Indian Philosophy
YAMADA, T., Philosophy
YAMADA, T., Western Literature
YAMAGISHI, T., Behavioural Sciences

Graduate School of Education (Kita 11, Nishi 7, Kita-ku, Sapporo; tel. (11) 707-6586; fax (11) 706-4951; e-mail jimubu@edu.hokudai.ac.jp; internet www.hokudai.ac.jp/educat/english.html):

ANEZAKI, Y., Higher and Continuing Education
AOKI, O., Education and Social Work
CHEN, S. J., Infant Developmental Psychology, Cross-cultural Comparison of Childrearing
HEMMI, M., History of Education
KAWAGUCHI, A., Prevention and Health Education for Life-Style Related Diseases
MORIYA, K., Adaptation Physiology, Health Science
MUROHASHI, H., Clinical Cognitive Neuroscience
ONAI, T., Sociology of Education
SATO, K., Psychology of Learning
SHIINA, K., Construction Labour Studies and Industrial Education
SUDA, K., Teaching Methods for Mathematics
SUDA, T., Exercise Physiology
SUZUKI, T., Community Adult Education
SUZUKI, T., History of Sport and Physical Education
TANAKA, Y., Developmental Psychopathology
TOKORO, S., Comparative History of Education
TSUBOI, Y., Educational Administration
YANO, T., Exercise Physiology

Graduate School of Law (Kita 9, Nishi 7, Kita-ku, Sapporo; tel. (11) 706-3074; fax (11) 706-4948; e-mail shomu@juris.hokudai.ac.jp; internet www.juris.hokudai.ac.jp/english/home.html):

DOKO, T., Labour Law
FUJIWARA, M., Civil Law
FURUYA, J., Political History
GONZA, T., History of Political Thought
HASEGAWA, K., Philosophy of Law
HAYASHI, N., Criminal Law (Legal Practice)
HAYASHI, T., Commercial Law
HAYASHIDA, S., Economic Analysis of Law
HIENUKI, T., Economic Law
HITOMI, T., Administrative Law
IKEDA, S., Civil Law
IMAI, H., Philosophy of Law
KURATA, S., Social Security Law
MATSUHISA, M., Civil Law
MATSUMURA, Y., Sociology of Law
MATSUURA, M., Japanese Political History
MUNESUE, T., Constitutional Law
MURAKAMI, H., Administrative Law
NAGAI, T., Criminal Law
NAKAYAMA, H., Law of Criminal Procedure
OHTSUKA, R., Commercial Law
OKADA, N., Constitutional Law
ONAGI, A., Criminal Law
SASADA, E., Constitutional Law
SEGAWA, N., Civil Law
SHIRATORI, Y., Law of Criminal Procedure
SONO, H., Civil Law
SUZUKI, K., AsianLaw
TAGUCHI, M., Western Legal History
TAKAMI, S., Law of Civil Procedure
TAMURA, Y., Intellectual Property Law
TSUJI, Y., Political Theory
TSUNEMOTO, T., Constitutional Law
WATARI, T., Administrative Law
YAMANAKA, Y., Civil Law (Legal Practice)
YOSHIDA, KATSUMI, Civil Law
YOSHIDA, KUNIHIKO, Civil Law
WATARI, Y., Administrative Law

Public Policy School (Kita 9, Nishi 7, Kita-ku, Sapporo; tel. (11) 706-3074; fax (11) 706-4947; e-mail shomu@juris.hokudai.ac.jp; internet www.hops.hokudai.ac.jp):

ISHII, Y., Regional Policy
KAGAYA, S., Infrastructure Planning
KOMORI, T., International Law
KURATA, K., Technology Policy
MACHINO, K., Applied Game Theory
MIYAMOTO, T., Comparative Political Economy
MIYAWAKI, A., Public Administration
NAKAMURA, K., International Politics
SASAKI, T., International Political Economy
SATO, K., Transportation Intelligence
SHIBATA, F., Social Security Administration
TSUJI, Y., Political Theory
YAMAGUCHI, J., Public Administration
YAMASHITA, R., Administrative Law
YOSHIDA, F., Environmental Economics

Graduate School of Economics and Business Administration (Kita 9, Nishi 7, Kita-ku, Sapporo; tel. (11) 706-4058; fax (11) 706-4947; e-mail keizai@pop.econ.hokudai.ac.jp; internet www.econ.hokudai.ac.jp/en/):

HAMADA, Y., Money and Banking
HASEGAWA, H., Econometrics
INOUE, H., International Investment and Finance
ITAYA, J., Public Economics
KANDA, K., Disclosure System and Financial Accounting
KANIE, A., Auditing
KARATO, O., Political Economics
KIMURA, T., Operations Research
KOJIMA, H., Management of Non-Profit Organizations
KOYAMA, K., Public Finance
MIYAMOTO, K., Economic History of Asia
MOHRI, S., Management by Networking

OKABE, H., Social Economy
ONO, H., Microeconomics
SASAKI, K., History of Economics
SEKIGUCHI, Y., Managerial Informatics
SONO, S., Foundations of Statistics
TANAKA, S., Socio-EconomicHistory
UCHIDA, K., Macroeconomics
YONEYAMA, K., Human Resource Development
YONEYAMA, Y., Financial Accounting
YOSHIMI, H., Accounting System
YOSHINO, E., Comparative Socio-Economic Systems

Graduate School of Science (Kita 10, Nishi 8, Kita-ku, Sapporo; tel. (11) 716-2111; fax (11) 756-1244; e-mail shomu@sci.hokudai.ac.jp; internet www.hokudai.ac.jp/science/english/index_e.htm):

AMITSUKA, H., Condensed Matter Physics
ARAI, A., Mathematical Physics
ARITA, K., Geotectonics
FUJIMOTO, M., Theoretical Physics
FUJINO, K., Mineralogy
GONG, J. P., Polymer Science
HARIMAYA, T., Meteorology
HAYASHI, M., Function Theory
HAYASHI, Y-Y., Geophysical Fluid Dynamics
HEKI, K., Space Geodesy
HINATSU, Y., Solid State Chemistry
IDO, M., Solid State Physics
IKAWA, S., Structural Chemistry
IKEDA, R., Geophysical Hydrology
INABE, T., Solid State Physics
ISHIGAKI, T., Philosophy of Science
ISHIKAWA, K., Theoretical Physics
ISHIMORI, K., Structural Chemistry
IZUMIYA, S., Geometry
JIMBO, S., Applied Mathematics
KASAHARA, M., Seismology and Geodesy
KATAKURA, H., Speciation of Terrestrial Invertebrates
KATO, A., Plant Molecular Genetics
KATO, K., Nuclear Physics
KAWABATA, K., Biophysics
KAWAMOTO, N., Theoretical Physics
KAWANO, K., Structural Biology
KISHIMOTO, A., Operator Algebra
KITAMURA, N., Analytical Chemistry
KODA, T., Molecular Biology
KOIKE, K., Solid State Physics
KOIKE, T., Molecular and Cellular Neurobiology
KOYAMA, J., Solid Earth Science
KOZASA, T., Astrophysics and Planetary Science
KUMAGAI, K., Solid State Physics
MASUDA, M., Plant Systematics
MAWATARI, S., Taxonomy of Invertebrates
MINOBE, S., Physical Oceanography, Climate and Meteorology
MIYAKE, T., Number Theory
MIYASHITA, M., Organic Chemistry
MURAKOSHI, K., Material Chemistry
NAKAGAWA, M., Volcanology and Petrology
NAGAHARA, J., Condensed Matter Physics
NAGASAKA, Y., Theory of Function
NAKAMURA, G., Partial Differential Equations
NAKAMURA, I., Algebraic Geometry
NAKAZI, T., Functional Analysis
NISHIMURA, S., Bio-organic Chemistry
NOMURA, K., Solid State Physics
OHGIYA, S., Promoter and Expression
OHKAWA, F., Theoretical Physics
OIKAWA, H., Bio-organic Chemistry
OKADA, H., Micropalaeontology and Palaeo-oceanography
OKADA, H., Volcanology
ONO, K., Geometry
ONODERA, A., Solid State
OSADA, Y., Polymer Chemistry
OZAWA, T., Partial Differential Equations
SAKAGUCHI, K., Biological Chemistry
SASAKI, N., Tissue Science and Mechanobiology
SASAKI, Y., Co-ordination Chemistry
SAWAMURA, M., Organometallic Chemistry
SHIMAMURA, H., Seismology and Geophysics
SUGIYAMA, S., History of Science
SUWA, T., Algebraic Geometry
SUZUKI, N., Organic Geochemistry
SUZUKI, N., Molecular Cell Biology
SUZUKI, T., Physicalorganic Chemistry
TAKAHASHI, T., Cellular Biochemistry
TAKAHATA, M., Behavioural Physiology
TAKEDA, S., Physical Chemistry
TAKESHITA, T., Structural Geology and Tectonics
TAKETSUGU, T., Quantum Chemistry
TANAKA, I., Protein Crystallography
TANAKA, K., Quantum Chemistry
TSUDA, I., Applied Mathematics
TSUDA, S., Biophysical Chemistry
UOSAKI, K., Physical Chemistry
URANO, A., Neuroendocrinology
WATANABE, S., Planetary Atmosphere
YAMAGUCHI, J., Plant Biology and Biochemistry
YAMAGUCHI, K., Differential Geometry
YAMAMOTO, K., Plant Physiology
YAMAMOTO, S., Condensed-Matter Theory
YAMASHITA, H., Representation Theory
YAMASHITA, M., Reproductive Biology
YAZAWA, M., Biochemistry
YOMOGIDA, K., Seismology
YOSHIDA, T., Group Theory and Combination
YURI, M., Complex Systems and Ergodic Theory
YOSHIDA, T., Group Theory and Combination

Graduate School of Medicine (Kita 15, Nishi 7, Kita-ku, Sapporo; tel. (11) 716-2111; fax (11) 717-5286; e-mail webmaster@med.hokudai.ac.jp; internet www.med.hokudai.ac.jp):

AKITA, H., Medical Oncology
ARIGA, T., Paediatrics
ARIKAWA, J., Laboratory Animal Science
ASAKA, M., Gastroenterology and Hematology
FUJITA, H., Environmental Biology
FUKUDA, S., Otolaryngology, Head and Neck Surgery
FUKUSHIMA, K., Sensorimotor and Cognitive Research
GANDO, S., Acute and Critical Care Medicine
HATAKEYAMA, S., Molecular Chemistry
HONMA, K., Chronobiology
IMAMURA, M., Haematology and Oncology
IWANAGA, T., Histology and Cytology
IWASAKI, Y., Neurosurgery
KAMIYA, H., Molecular Neuroanatomy
KASAHARA, M., Pathology
KATO, H., Surgical Oncology
KAWAGUCHI, H., Laboratory Medicine
KISHI, R., Public Health
KOIKE, T., Clinical Immunology
KONDO, S., Surgical Oncology
KOYAMA, T., Psychiatry
MINAKAMI, H., Obstetrics
MINAMI, A., Orthopaedic Surgery
MIWA, S., Cellular and Molecular Pharmacology
MORIMOTO, Y., Anaesthesiology
NISHIMURA, M., Respiratory Medicine
NONOMURA, K., Renal and Genito-urinary Surgery
OHNO, S., Ophthalmology
SAKURAGI, N., Gynecology
SAKURAI, T., Medical Informatics
SASAKI, F., Paediatric Surgery
SASAKI, H., Neurology
SAWAGUCHI, T., Neurobiology
SEYA, T., Microbiology
SHIMIZU, H., Dermatology
SUGIHARA, T., Plastic Surgery
TAMAKI, N., Nuclear Medicine
TAMASHIRO, H., Health for Senior Citizens
TERAZAWA, K., Forensic Medicine
TODO, S., General Surgery
TSUTSUI, H., Cardiovascular Medicine
WATANABE, M., Anatomy and Embryology
YAMAMOTO, Y., Plastic Surgery
YASUDA, K., Joint Reconstruction Surgeryand Sports Medicine
YASUDA, K., Cardiovascular Surgery
YOSHIOKA, M., Neuropharmacology

Health Sciences:

BUTOH, M., Adult and Gerontological Nursing
CHIBA, H., Biomedical Informatics
DAIGUJI, M., Clinical Occupational Therapy
DATE, H., Medical Engineering and Science
FUKUSHIMA, J., Physical Therapy
HATTA, T., Clinical Occupational Therapy
INOUE, K., Basic Occupational Therapy
IWATA, G., Maternal Nursing and Child Nursing
KOBAYASHI, S., Biomedical Informatics
MATSUNO, K., Clinical Pathophysiology
MATSUSHITA, M., Adult and Gerontological Nursing
MIKAMI, T., Clinical Pathophysiology
MIYAMOTO, K., Clinical Physical Therapy
MORISHITA, S., Fundamental Nursing
MORIYAMA, T., Biomedical Informatics
MURUMATSU, T., Community Health Nursing
MURATA, W., Basic Occupational Therapy
NAKAMURA, N., Clinical Pathophysiology
NAKASHIO, S., Biomedical Informatics
NISHIOKA, T., Radiological Technology
SAGAWA, T., Maternal Nursing and Child Nursing
SAITO, T., Community Health Nursing
SAKAI, M., Radiological Technology
SATO, Y., Maternal Nursing and Child Nursing
SHIMIZU, T., Radiological Technology
SHIMOZUMA, M., Medical Engineering and Science
TAKANAMI, S., Community Health Nursing
TAKEDA, N., Basic Physical Therapy
UENO, T., Adult and Gerontological Nursing
YAMAMOTO, T., Medical Engineering and Science
YAMANAKA, M., Clinical Physical Therapy
YOSHIMURA, S., Fundamental Nursing

Graduate School of Dental Medicine (Nishi 7, Kita 13, Kita-ku, Sapporo 060-8586; tel. (11) 716-2111; fax (11) 706-4919; e-mail syomu@den.hokudai.ac.jp; internet www.den.hokudai.ac.jp):

AKAIKE, T., Oral Functional Science
FUKUSHIMA, K., Oral Pathobiological Science
IIDA, J., Oral Functional Science
INOUE, N., Oral Health Science
KAWANAMI, M. ., Oral Health Science
KITAGAWA, K., Oral Pathobiological Science
MORITA, M., Oral Health Science
NAKAMURA, M., Oral Pathobiological Science
OHATA, N., Oral Functional Science
SANO, H., Oral Health Science
SHIBATA, K., Oral Pathobiological Science
SUZUKI, K., Oral Pathobiological Science
TAMURA, M., Oral Health Science
TOTSUKA, Y., Oral Pathobiological Science
WAKITA, M., Oral Health Science
WATARI, F., Oral Health Science
YAWAKA, Y., Oral Functional Science
YOSHIDA, S., Oral Functional Science

Graduate School of Pharmaceutical Sciences (Kita 12, Nishi 6, Kita-ku, Sapporo; tel. (11) 716-2111; fax (11) 706-4989; e-mail shomu@

pharm.hokudai.ac.jp; internet www.hokudai.ac.jp/pharma/english.html):

ARIGA, H., Molecular Biology
HARASHIMA, H., Molecular Design and Pharmaceutics
HASHIMOTO, S., Synthetic and Industrial Chemistry
IGARASHI, Y., Biomembrane and Biofunctional Chemistry
INAGAKI, F., Structural Biology
ISEKI, K., Clinical Pharmaceutics and Therapeutics
KAMATAKI, T., Drug Metabolism
KAMO, N., Biophysical Chemistry
KOBAYASHI, J., Natural Products Chemistry
MATSUDA, A., Medicinal Chemistry
MATSUDA, T., Hygienic Chemistry
MINAMI, M., Pharmacology
MIURA, T., Analytical Chemistry
SATO, Y., Fine Synthetic Chemistry
SHUTO, S., Organic Chemistry for Drug Development
SUZUKI, T., Neuroscience
YOKOSAWA, H., Biochemistry

Graduate School of Engineering (Kita 13, Nishi 8, Kita-ku, Sapporo; tel. (11) 716-8832; fax (11) 706-7895; e-mail shomu@eng.hokudai.ac.jp; internet www.eng.hokudai.ac.jp):

AKAGAWA, S., Freezing and Frozen Soil Engineering
AKERA, H., Theoretical Solid State Physics
ARAI, M., Chemical Reaction Engineering
ASAKURA, K., Fundamental and Practical Study on Multi-phase Flows
BABA, N., Astronomical Optics
CHIKAHISA, T., Energy Systems for Reducing Greenhouse Gases
ENAI, M., Measurement and Analysis of Buoyant Air Circulation
ENOTO, T., Plasma Physics
FUJII, Y., Rock Mechanics
FUJIKAWA, S., Molecular Thermofluid Dynamics
FUJITA, O., Combustion
FUNAMIZU, N., Sustainable Sanitation
FURUSAKA, M., Theory of Neutron Diffraction Scattering
FURUICHI, T., Environmental Systems Planning
GOHARA, K., Nonlinear Dynamics
HARA, S., Synthetic Organic Chemistry
HASEGAWA, K., River Engineering and River Hydraulics
HAYASHIKAWA, T., Structural Dynamics and Earthquake Engineering
HINO, T., Plasma Wall Interactions in Nuclear Fusion Devices
IBAMOTO, T., Grand Thermal Energy System
ICHIKAWA, T., Applied Physical Chemistry
IGUCHI, M., Transport Phenomena and Materials Processing
IKEGAWA, M., Computational Fluid Dynamics
ISHIJIMA, Y., Design and Evaluation of CAES and Geological Disposal
ISHIMASA, T., Physics of Metals
ITAGAKI, M., Fusion Plasma Engineering
JOH, O., Earthquake-Resistant Design of Reinforced Concrete
KADO, Y., Modern Architectural History of Japan
KAGAMI, H., Earthquake Engineering
KAGAYA, S., Regional, City and Transport Planning
KAGIWADA, T., Theories of Material Cutting and Grinding
KAKUCHI, T., Polymer Chemistry
KAMIDATE, T., Bioanalytical Chemistry
KANEKO, K., Rock Mechanics
KIKKAYA, S., Ceramic Science
KIYANAGI, Y., Neutron Engineering
KOBAYASHI, H., Urban Planning and Design
KOBAYASHI, Y., Vibration of Continuous Systems
KONNO, H., Analytical Chemistry
KOSHIZAWA, A., Environmental City Planning
KUBOTA, H., Heating, Ventilating and Air Conditioning Systems
KUDO, I., Spacecraft Design
KUDO, K., Analytical Study of Radiation and other Heat Transfer
KUDOH, M., Solidification
MASUDA, T., Chemical Process Engineering
MIDORIKAWA, M., Building Structural Engineering
MIKAMI, T., Structural Mechanics
MITACHI, T., Geotechnical Engineering
MIURA, S., Geotechnical Engineering
MIYAURA, N., Synthetic Organic Chemistry
MOHRI, T., Computational Materials Science
MORITA, R., Non-linear Optics, Quantum Optics, Laser Physics and Quantum
MORIYOSHI, A., Highway Engineering
MUNEKATA, M., Cell Technology
MUTO, S., Physics of Superlattices and Quantum Structures
NAKAYAMA, T., Very-Low-Temperature Physics
NARITA, T., Applied Materials Science of Ceramics
NARITA, Y., Analysis and Design of Composite Structures
NAWA, T., Concrete Engineering
NISHI, N., Bio-related Polymer Chemistry
NOGUCHI, T., Housing Design and Planning
NOGUCHI, T., Structural Materials and Foundry Engineering
OGAWA, H., Internal Combustion Engines
OHKUMA, T., Organic Synthesis and Molecular Catalysis
OHNUKI, S., Radiation Damage
OHNUMA, H., Materials Engineering
OHSHIMA, N., Machine Engineering and Fluid Mechanics
OHTA, S., Air Pollution Modelling
OHTSUKA, T., Corrosion Science
ORIHARA, H., Soft Matter Physics
SASAKI, K., Theory of Elasticity and Plasticity
SATO, K., Safety and Risk Management
SATO, S., Nuclear Reactor Materials
SAWAMURA, S., Quantum Beam Science and Engineering
SENBU, O., Building Materials
SEO, M., Surface Electrochemistry
SHIMADA, S., Solid State Chemistry
SHIMAZU, Y., Nuclear Reactor Engineering
SHINOHARA, K., Chemical Engineering
SUGIYAMA, K., Nuclear Reactor Safety
TADANO, S., Biomechanics
TAGUCHI, S., Environmental Microbiology and Biotechnology
TAKAGI, M., Tissue Engineering
TAKAHASHI, J., Ceramic Science and Engineering
TAKAHASHI, H., Anodizing of Aluminium
TAKAHASHI, M., Aquatic Environmental Protection Engineering
TAKEDA, Y., Flow Transition to Turbulence
TAMURA, S., Condensed Matter Physics
TANAKA, K., Amorphous Materials
TANAKA, N., Sanitary Landfill Engineering
TANNDA, S., Solid-State Physics, Low Temperature Physics and Quantum-Phase Transition
TSUNEKAWA, M., Minerals Processing and Utilization of Solid Waste
UEDA, T., Structural Performance Assessment during product Life-Cycle
UEDA, M., Structural Engineering
WATANABE, Y., Water and Sewage Works
WRIGHT, O., Phonon Physics
YAMASHITA, M., Femtosecond Optical-Pulse Technology
YAMASHITA, T., Coastal Engineering and Ecological Engineering
YAMAYA, K., Solid State Physics
YOKOYAMA, S., Environmental Ergonomics
YONEDA, T., Applied Geology

Graduate School of Agriculture (Kita 9, Nishi 9, Kita-ku, Sapporo; tel. (11) 716-2111; fax (11) 716-0879; e-mail shomu@agr.hokudai.ac.jp):

ARIGA, S., Biological Science
ASAKAWA, S., Ornamental Plants and Landscape Architecture
ASANO, K., Applied Microbiology
BANDO, H., Molecular Entomology
DEMURA, K., Comparative Agricultural Policy
FUJIKAWA, S., Wood Biology
HARA, H.
HASEGAWA, S., Soil Amelioration
HATA, S., Production Engineering
HATANO, R., Soil Science
HATTORI, A., Meat Science
HIRAI, T., Timber Engineering
ISHII, Y., Forest Policy
IWAMA, K., Crop Science
KAWABATA, J., Food Biochemistry
KIMURA, A., Molecular Enzymology
KITAMURA, K., Plant Genetics and Evolution
KOBAYASHI, Y., Animal Nutrition
KODA, Y., Crop Physiology
KONDO, S., Animal Production Systems
KUROKAWA, I., Farm Management
MARUTANI, T., Erosion Control
MASUDA, K., Plant Functions Development
MASUTA, C., Cell Biology and Manipulation
MATSUDA, J., Agricultural Systems Engineering
MATSUI, H., Biochemistry
MIKAMI, T., Genetic Engineering
MISHIMA, T., Agricultural Marketing
NABETA, K., Natural Product Chemistry
NAGASAWA, T., Land Improvement and Management
NAITO, S., Molecular Biology
NAITO, S., Plant Pathology
NAKAMURA, F., Animal By-products Science
NAKAMURA, F., Forest Management
NOGUCHI, N., Agricultural Vehicle Systems Engineering
OOSAWA, K., Horticultural Science
OSAKI, M., Plant Nutrition
OSANAMI, F., Agricultural Development
SAITO, Y., Animal Ecology
SAKASHITA, A., Agricultural Co-operatives
SANO, Y., Plant Breeding
SHIMAZAKI, K., Dairy Science
SUWA, M., Systematic Entomology
TAHARA, S., Ecological Chemistry
TAKAHASHI, K., Silviculture
TERAZAWA, M., Forest Chemistry
UBUKATA, M., Wood Chemistry
URANO, S., Agricultural Physics
UYEDA, I., Pathogen–Plant Interaction
WADA, T., Applied Bioproduction Engineering
WATANABE, T., Animal Breeding and Reproduction
YAJIMA, T., Forest Resources Biology
YAZAWA, M., Environmental Information of Land
YOKOTA, A., Microbial Resources and Ecology

Graduate School of Veterinary Medicine (Kita 18, Nishi 9, Kita-ku, Sapporo; tel. (11) 716-2111; fax (11) 706-5190; e-mail syomu@vetmed.hokudai.ac.jp; internet www.hokudai.ac.jp/veteri):

AGUI, T., Disease Control
FUJINAGA, T., Veterinary Clinical Sciences
FUJITA, S., Environmental Veterinary Sciences
HABARA, Y., Biomedical Sciences
INABA, M., Veterinary Clinical Sciences
HORIUCHI, M., Prion Diseases

ITO, S., Biomedical Sciences
KATAKURA, K., Disease Control
KIDA, H., Disease Control
KON, Y., Biomedical Sciences
KUWABARA, M., Environmental Veterinary Sciences
MAEDE, Y., Veterinary Clinical Sciences
ONUMA, M., Disease Control
SAITO, M., Biomedical Sciences
TAKAHASHI, Y., Veterinary Clinical Sciences
TAKASHIMA, I., Environmental Veterinary Sciences
UMEMURA, T., Veterinary Clinical Sciences
WATANABE, T., Disease Control

Graduate School of Fisheries Science (3-1-1 Minato-cho, Hakodate; tel. (13) 840-5505; fax (13) 843-5015; e-mail shomu@fish.hokudai.ac.jp; internet www.fish.hokudai.ac.jp):

ABE, S., Aquagenomics and Resources Management
ADACHI, K., Molecular Cell Biology and Histology
ARAI, K., Embryology and Genetics
GOSHIMA, S., Zooplankton Taxonomy and Ecology
HARA, A., Comparative Biochemistry of Fish Serum Protein
HIROYOSHI, K., Fisheries Business Economics
IIDA, K., Underwater Acoustics; Fisheries and Plankton Acoustics
IKEDA, T., Zooplankton Ecology
INOUE, N., Freeze Denaturation of Fish Muscular Proteins
ITABASHI, Y., Marine Lipid Chemistry
KAWAI, Y., Preservation of Fishery Products by Physicochemical Techniques
KIMURA, N., Seakeeping Qualities of Small Fishing Vessels by the Application of Neural Network Models
KISHI, J. M., Numerical Modelling of Marine Ecosystems
KONNO, K., Marine Food Science
KUMA, K., Chemical Oceanography and Marine Biogeochemistry
MEGURO, T., Marine Environment
MIURA, T., Scientific Gears for Fish Sampling
MIYAKE, H., Environmental Physical Oceanography
MIYASHITA, K., Liquid Oxidation and Antioxidant
MONTANI, S., Biogeochemical Oceanography
NAKAYA, K., Phylogeny; Taxonomy; Sharks
SAEKI, H., Functional Improvement of Marine Food Proteins and Marine Food Allergy
SAGA, N., Marine Biology; Developmental Biology
SAITOH, S., Satellite Oceanography
SAKURAI, Y., Marine Ecology; Reproductive Ecology of Marine Fish and Cephalopods
SEKI, N., Food Biochemistry
TAJIMA, K., Classification
TAKAGI, Y., Mechanism of Biomineralization
TAKAHASHI, K., Convert Fisheries By-products into Value Added Products
TAKAHASHI, T., Life History of Righteye Flounders
UEDA, H., Fish Reproductive Physiology
YAMAMOTO, K., Strength of Fishing Gear Materials
YAMAUCHI, K., Regulatory Mechanisms of Gametogenesis in Fish
YOSHIMIZU, M., Viral and Bacterial Fish Diseases
YOSHIMURA, Y., Control and Design of Fishing Boat and Fisheries Machinery

Graduate School of Environmental Earth Science (Kita 10, Nishi 5, Kita-ku, Sapporo; tel. (11) 716-2111; fax (13) 706-4867; e-mail somu@ees.hokudai.ac.jp; internet www.ees.hokudai.ac.jp):

ARAKI, H., Agricultural Environment
ARAKI, Y., Glycoscience
EBUCHI, N., Physical Oceanography
FUJIYOSHI, Y., Mesoscale Meteorology
FUKUDA, M., Cryogeomorphology
FUKUI, M., Microbial Ecology
GREVE, R. G., Dynamics of Ice Sheets and Glaciers
HARA, T., Plant Ecology
HASEBE, F., Atmospheric Science
HIGASHI, S., Behavioural Ecology and Sociobiology
HIRAKAWA, K., Glacial and Periglacial Geomorphology
HIURA, T., Forest Ecology
HONDOH, T., Solid State Physics
IKEDA, M., Numerical Modelling and Remote Sensing of Ocean and Sea Ice
IWAKUMA, T., Freshwater Ecology
KANUMA, K., Forest Economics
KAWAMURA, K., Atmospheric Chemistry and Organic Geochemistry
KIMURA, M., Ecological and Physiological Genetics
KISHI, J. M., Numerical Modelling and Remote Sensing of Ocean- and Sea-Ice
KOHYAMA, T., Ecosystem Ecology and Plant Ecology
KOIKE, T., Forest Rehabilitation
KOUCHI, A., Planetary Science
KUBOKAWA, A., Dynamic Oceanology
KUMA, K., Chemical Oceanography and Marine Biogeochemistry
MAEKAWA, K., Animal Ecology
MATSUDA, F., Synthetic Organic Chemistry and Natural Product Chemistry
MATSUSHIMA, T., Dynamics of Surface Reaction Site
MINAGAWA, M., Isotope Biogeochemistry
MITSUDERA, H., Physical Oceanography and Geophysical Fluid Dynamics
MONTANI, S., Biogeochemical Oceanography
MORIKAWA, M., Extremology and Molecular Microbiology
MOTOMURA, T., Cell Biology of Algae
MUKAI, H., Marine Ecology
NAKAMURA, H., Photochemistry and Analytical Chemistry
NAKAMURA, T., Physical Chemistry
NORIKI, S., Environmental Science and Ocean Science
OHARA, M., Plant Ecology
OHTA, N., Dynamics of photoexcited species and Molecular Photonics
OHTANI, J. M., Photocatalytic and Catalytic Reactions
OKUHARA, T., Catalytic Chemistry
ONO, Y., Environmental Geography
OSAWA, M., Electrochemistry and Surface Chemistry
SAKAIRI, N., Synthetic Carbohydrate Chemistry
SASA, K., Environmental Forestry
SATOH, F., Forest Influence
SHIMAZU, K., (Environmental Electrochemistry and Interfacial Nanotechnology)
SUGIMOTO, A., Biogeoscience
SUZUKI, N., Molecular Cell Biology
TANAKA, A., Plant Physiology
TANAKA, S., Environmental Remediation and Analytical Chemistry
TANAKA, T., Mathematical and Theoretical Ecology
TODA, M. J., Ecology and Taxonomy
UEDA, H., Environmental Biology
WAKATSUCHI, M., Ocean and Sea-Ice Observation
YAMADA, E., Fish Embryology
YAMADA, E., Forage Science
YAMAMURA, E., Regional Planning
YAMAZAKI, K., Climate Data Analysis and Climate Modelling
YOSHIKAWA, H., Ocean and Atmospheric Science
YOSHIDA, K., Crop Science

Institute of Language and Culture Studies (Kita 17, Nishi 8, Kita-ku, Sapporo; tel. (11) 716-2111; fax (11) 706-7801; e-mail soumu@ilcs.hokudai.ac.jp; internet www.hokudai.ac.jp/lang):

HASHIMOTO, H., English
INOUE, K., English
ISHIBASHI, M., German
ISHIKAWA, K., German
KOBAYAKAWA, M., International Public Relations
KOGA, H., Italian
MIYASHITA, M., English
NAGAI, Y., Chinese
NISHI, M., French
OHIRA, T., French
OHNO, K., English
SATOH, S., German
SATOH, T., German
SONODA, K., English
SUGIURA, S., Russian
TAKAHASHI, Y., German
TAKAI, K., Chinese
TAKENAKA, M., French
TSUKUWA, M., German
UEDA, M., English
USAMI, S., Russian
YANADA, N., English
YOSHIDA, T., German

Graduate School of International Media and Communication (Kita 17, Nishi 8, Kita-ku, Sapporo; fax (11) 706-7801; internet www.hokudai.ac.jp/lang/imc):

Most of the Professors in this School also belong to the Institute of Language and Culture Studies

HASHIMOTO, H., English
INOUE, K., English
ISHIKAWA, K., German
ISHIBASHI, M., German
KOGA, H., Italian
KUDOH, M., Russian
MIYASHITA, M., English
NAGAI, Y., Chinese
NISHI, M., French
NOZAWA, Y., Chinese
OGAWA, Y., English
OHIRA, T., French
OHNO, K., English
SATOH, S., German
SATOH, T., German
SONODA, K., English
STAPLETON, P., English
SUGIURA, S., Russian
TAKAHASHI, Y., German
TAKEMOTO, K., English
TAKENAKA, N., French
TSUKUWA, M., German
UEDA, M., English
USAMI, S., Russian
YOSHIDA, T., German

Graduate School of Information Science and Technology (Kita 14, Nishi 9, Kita-ku, Sapporo; tel. (11) 706-6514; fax (11) 706-7890; e-mail jimusitu@ist.hokudai.ac.jp; internet www.ist.hokudai.ac.jp):

AMEMIYA, Y., Semiconductor Devices
ARAKI, K., Natural Language Processing
ARIMURA, H., Computer Science
ENDO, T., Bioinformatics (Molecular Evolution)
FUKUI, T., Growth and Characterization of Quantum Structures
HARAGUCHI, M., Knowledge Representation
HASEGAWA, H., Semiconductor Devices and Integrated Electronics
HOMMA, T., Computational Electromagnetics

IGARASHI, H., Computational Electromagnetism
KANEKO, S., Computer Vision
KAWAHARA, K., Biological Cybernetics
KITAJIMA, H., Image Coding
KOSHIBA, M., Optical Fiber Science and Integrated Photonics
KUDO, M., Pattern Recognition
KURIHARA, M., Artificial Intelligence
MISHIMA, T., Optoelectronics and Nonlinear Optics
MITAMURA, Y., Biomedical Engineering
MIYAKOSHI, M., Functional Analysis and Fuzzy Set Theory
MIYANAGA, Y., Intelligent Communication Systems and Signal Processing
NOJIMA, T., Microwave Engineering and EMC
OGAWA, Y., Communication Engineering
OHUCHI, A., Tourism Information
OMORI, T., Formative Engineering
ONOSATO, M., Field Informatics
SAKAI, Y., Plasma Processing
SATO, Y., Computational Statistics
SHIMIZU, K., Biological Measurement
SUEOKA, K., Surface Spin Analysis
TAKAHASHI, Y., Single-Electronics
TANAKA, Y., Media Architecture
WADA, M., Human Informatics and Robotics
WATANABE, H., Comparative Genomics
YAMAMOTO, K., Non-invasive Measurement
YAMAMOTO, M., Quantum Electron Devices
YAMAMOTO, T., Computer Graphics
YAMASHITA, Y., Nonlinear control theory
ZEUGMANN, T., Learning algorithms for data mining applications

ATTACHED RESEARCH INSTITUTES

Institute of Low Temperature Science: f. 1941; Dir T.HONDOH.

Institute for Genetic Medicine: f. 2000; Dir K. TAKADA; publ. *Collected Papers* (annually).

Research Institute for Electronic Science: f. 1943; Dir T. YAGI.

Catalysis Research Center: f. 1989; Dir T. TAKAHASHI; publ. *Annual Report*.

Slavic Research Center: f. 1955; Dir O. IEDA; publ. *Acta Slavica Iaponica* (annually).

Research Center for Integrated Quantum Electronics: f. 2001; Dir H. HASEGAWA.

Research Center for North Eurasia and North Pacific Regions: Dir M. FUKUDA.

Central Institute of Radioisotope Science: f. 1978; Dir K. MIYASAKA.

Center for Instrumental Analysis: f. 1979; Dir S. HASHIMOTO.

Center for Advanced Research ofEnergy Technology: f. 1994; Dir H. TAKAHASHI.

Center for Research and Development in Higher Education: f. 1995; Dir H SAEKI.

College of Medical Technology: f. 1980; Dir K. MATSUNO.

Centre for Advanced Science and Technology: f. 1996; Dir T. YOSHIKI.

Field Science Center for the Northern Biosphere: f. 2001; Dir N. SUZUKI.

Hokkaido University Museum: f. 1999; Dir S. FUJITA.

IBARAKI UNIVERSITY

1-1, Bunkyo 2-chome, Mito-Shi, Ibaraki-ken 310-8512
Telephone: (29) 228-8007
Fax: (29) 228-8019
Internet: www.ibaraki.ac.jp

Founded 1949
Independent
Academic year: April to March

President: TAKEO MIYATA
Administrator: T. MIYATA
Dean of Student Affairs: F. IKEYA
Librarian: Y. ASANO

Library of 939,000 vols
Number of teachers: 584 full-time
Number of students: 8,864

Publications: bulletins (in Japanese), journals of the faculties (in Japanese)

DEANS

Faculty of Education: R. KIKUCHI
Faculty of Humanities: T. MURANAKA
Faculty of Science: T. WATANABE
Faculty of Engineering: K. YAMAGATA
School of Agriculture: T. MATUDA

PROFESSORS

Faculty of Humanities:

AIZAWA, Y., English and American Culture
AMEMIYA, S., Politics
AOKI, K., French
ARIIZUMI, S., Economic Structure
ARITOMI, M., Psychology
ASANO, Y., Human Geography
CHEANG, K., Linguistics
FUJII, F., Linguistics
FUKAYA, N., Law
FUKAZAWA, Y., European History
FUSHIMI, K., German
IIZUKA, K., Law
IIJIMA, H., Management Science
KAMATA, A., Social Structure
KAMIYA, T., Social Structure
KANAMOTO, S., Japanese Education
KANOU, Y., Asian Culture
KATAYAMA, Y., Philosophy
KIMURA, M., Southeast Asia Area Study
KISHIMOTO, N., Linguistics
KOIDO, M., French and European Culture
KOIZUMI, Y., English and American Culture
KOMIYAJI, M., Business Administration
LIENG, J., Sinology
MATUMURA, N., Social Structure
MAYANAGI, M., Oriental History
MOGI, M., Comparative Culture
MORIYA, S., Logic
MORIYA, T., Sociology
MURANAKA, M., Sociology
NAKURA, B., Economic Structure
NOSAKA, M., Law
OHATA, K., English and American Culture
OKUBO, N., French Culture
SAITO, M., Regional Societies
SAITO, Y., Local Administration
SANO, H., Media Studies
SASAKI, H., History
SASAKURA, S., English
SATO, K., Economic Structure
SATO, K., German Culture
SIBUYA, A., Sociology
SIMAOKA, S., English
SUGII, K., Oriental History
SUGISHITA, T., International Cooperation Theory
SUMIKAWA, H., European and American Economy Theory
SUZUKI, T., Communication
SUZUKI, Y., Psychology
SUZUKI, Y., German
TAKAHASHI, T., English
TAMURA, T., Law
TANAKA, S., Regional Societies
TATEWAKI, I., Regional Societies
TATEYAMA, Y., International Economics
TOKUE, K., Economic Policy
UENO, H., Social Anthropology
UMEDA, T., Law
WATANABE, K., European Culture
YAMAMOTO, H., Asian Economics

Faculty of Education:

ADACHI, K., School Education
AKISAKA, M., Clinical Medicine
AKUTA, N., Clinical Psychology
ARAKAWA, C., Housing and Domestic Science
EBATA, H., School Education
FUJIHIRA, S., German Literature
HASEGAWA, S., Vocal Music
HASHIURA, H., Japanese Literature
HATTORI, K., Physical Activity Science
HAYAKAWA, K., Composition
HAYAKAWA, T., Geomorphology
HONNDA, T., Information Education
IKEYA, F., European History
INABA, K.
INAMI, Y., Computer Science
KAIZU, S., Applied Mathematics
KAJIWARA, S., Instrumental Music
KANEKO, K., Art Education
KIKUCHI, R., Adult Education
KIMURA, K., Philosophy
KOIZUMI, S., Art History
KOJIMA, H., Information Education
KOMURO, K., Technical Education
KUSAKA, Y., Physical Education
MAEKAWA, Y., Sinology
MAKINO, Y., Geology
MATSUDA, M., Art Education
MATSUI, M., Information Sciences
MATSUMURA, T., Education for Handicapped Children
MATSUZAKA, A., Health and Physical Education
MIURA, T., Health and Physical Education
NAGASAWA, K., English Language Teaching
NAKAMURA, T., Health Education
NAMIKI, T., English Morphology
OGATA, T., Health and Physical Education
OKAMOTO, K., Physical Education
ONO, Y., Mycology
ONODERA, A., Historical Geography
OSHIMA, K., Earth Science
OTA, S., Physical Education
OTAKE, H., Women's Studies
OTANI, H., School Nursing
OTSUKI, I., Economic History of Modern Japan
OUCHI, Z., Language Ethics Education
OZAKI, H., Physiology for Handicapped Children
SASAKI, Y., Japanese Language Teaching
SATO, A., Musicology
SATO, E., Mathematical Education
SATO, H., Technical Education
SOGA, H., Mathematical Science
SOGO, M., Painting
SUGANUMA, K., Clinical Psychology
SUZUKI, E., Social Studies Teaching
TAKIZAWA, T., Hygienics
TANAKA, K., Music Education
TANIGUCHI, T., School Education
TASHIRO, T., School Education
TATSUMI, N., Physical Education
TERAMOTO, T., Industrial Arts
TOGASHI, T., Physical Education
TOSHIYASU, Y., Science Education
YAMAMOTO, H., Organic Chemistry
YAMAMOTO, K., Household Management Education
YAMANE, S., Insect Ecology
YAMASHITA, T., School Education
YANAGIDA, N., Mathematics
YASUDA, K., Home Economics Education
YOSHIDA, H., Home Economics Education

Faculty of Science:

AMANO, T., Science of Cosmic Matter
FUJII, Y., Co-ordination Chemistry
FUJIWARA, T., Physics
HORI, Y., Botany
HORIUCHI, T., Analysis
ICHIMASA, M., Cell Biology
ICHIMASA, Y., Physiology
IKEDA, Y., Geochemistry
IMURA, H., Analytical Chemistry
ISIZUKA, T., Astrophysics
IZUOKA, A., Physical Chemistry
KANEKO, M., Chemistry

KANNO, S., Atomic Physics
KAWADA, Y., Chemistry
KIMURA, M., Geochemistry
KOJIMA, J., Entomology
MATSUDA, R., Algebra
MISHIMA, S., Biology
MIWA, I., Biology
MORINO, H., Systematics
NAKANO, Y., Structural Chemistry
NISHIHARA, Y., Magnetism and Superconductivity
NODA, F., Theoretical High Energy
OHASHI, K., Analytical Chemistry
ONISHI, K., Applied Mathematics
ONOSE, H., Statistics
ORIYAMA, T., Organic Chemistry
OSHIMA, H., Topology
SAKATA, F., Mathematical Science
SAKUMA, T., Solid-State Physics
TAGIRI, M., Earth and Planetary Physics
TAKANO, K., Mathematics
URABE, T., Geometry
WATANABE, T., Earth Science
YAMADA, M., Physics
YAMAGAMI, S., Quantum Physics
YANAGIDA, R., Cosmic Ray Physics
YOKOSAWA, M., Astrophysics

Faculty of Engineering:

ABE, O., Ceramics Engineering
ARAKI, T., Computer Science
EDA, H., Production Engineering and Machine Tools
ENOMOTO, M., Materials Physics
FUJII, K., Laser and Plasma
FUKUZAWA, K., Concrete Engineering
HAMAMATSU, Y., Modelling and Simulation
HARIU, T., Electronic Material Systems
HOSHI, T., Systems Information and Remote Sensing
ICHIMURA, M., Materials Physics
IGARASHI, S., Analytical Chemistry
IKEHATA, T., Plasma Science
IMAI, Y., Communication Engineering
INUI, M., Systems Engineering
ISHIGURO, M., Computer Applications
ITO, G., Plastic Working Science
KAGOSHIMA, K., Antennae
KAMINAGA, H., Energy Conversion
KANO, M., Discrete Mathematics and its Application
KAZITANI, S., Energy Conservation
KIKUMA, I., Electronic Materials
KISHI, Y., Intelligent Systems
KOBAYASHI, M., Systems Information
KOBIYAMA, M., Electromagnetic Systems
KOUNOSU, S., Design Engineering
KOYAMADA, Y., Photonic Systems
KOYANAGI, T., Landscape Planning and Design
KUROSAWA, K., Plasma Science
MAEKAWA, K., Materials Science and Engineering
MASUI, M., Electronic Materials
MASUZAWA, T., Dynamics of Machines
MIMURA, N., Global Environment Engineering
MOMOSE, Y., Surface Chemistry
MOTOHASHI, Y., Materials Science and Engineering
MURANOI, T., Electronic Materials for Functionality
NAITO, K., Analytical Chemistry
NAKAMOTO, R., Functional Analysis
NARA, K., Electrical Power Systems
NIIMURA, N., Physics
NIREI, H., Environmental Asset Science
NUMAO, T., Architect
OGUCHI, K., Dynamics of Machines
OKADA, Y., Dynamics of Machines
ONO, K., Polymer Science
ONUKI, J., Materials Technology
OZAWA, S., Computational Physics
SASAKI, Y., Foundation and Design of Precision Engineering
SENBA, I., Computer Science
SHIRAISHI, M., Systems and Controls
SIOHATA, K., Design Engineering
SUGITA, R., Electrical and Electronics Engineering
SUZUKI, H., Mechanical Design
SUZUKI, T., Energy Conversion
TAKAHASHI, M., Organic Chemistry
TAKEUCHI, M., Electrical Materials
TAZUKE, Y., Applied Physics
TOMODA, Y., Mechanical Metallurgy
TOZUNE, A., Electric Machines
TURUTA, K., High Voltage and Plasma Science
WU, Z., Structural Engineering
YAMANAKA, K., Systems and Controls
YASUHARA, K., Geotechnical Engineering
YOKOYAMA, K., Structural Engineering
ZYOU, M., CAD/CAM/CAE

School of Agriculture:

AKUTSU, K., Plant Pathology
GOTO, T., Applied Physics
KARUBE, J., Farmland Engineering
KASHIWAGI, M., Regional Planning Science
KINOSE, K., Hydraulic Engineering
KODAMA, O., Bio-regulation Chemistry
KOSUGIYAMA, M., Animal Breeding
KOUNO, Y., Chemical Ecology
KUBOTA, M., Soil Science and Plant Nutrition
KURUSU, Y., Industrial Microbiology
MACHIDA, T., Agricultural Systems
MARUBASHI, W., Plant Breeding
MASAKI, T., Enzymatic Chemistry
MATSUDA, T., Horticulture
MATSUZAWA, Y., Animal Husbandry and Behaviour
MORIIZUMI, S., Agricultural Machinery
NAKAGAWA, M., Agricultural Economics
NAKAJIMA, M., Farm Science
NAKAMURA, Y., Feed Science
NAKANE, K., Algebra
NAKASONE, H., Agricultural and Environmental Engineering
OTA, H., Microbial Ecology
SAGO, R., Cultivation Science
SHIO, K., Information Science
SHIRAI, M., Molecular Microbiology
TAKAHARA, H., Bioresource Engineering
TSUKIHASHI, T., Horticulture
YONEKURA, M., Crop Production

ATTACHED RESEARCH INSTITUTES

Centre for Research and Development in Higher Education: Dir H. SOGA.

Centre for Co-operative Research and Development: Dir K. FUKUZAWA.

Centre for Educational Research and Training: Dir H. OZAKI.

Centre for Water Environment Studies: Dir H. NIREI.

Experimental Farm: Dir U. NAKAMURA.

Centre for Instrumental Analysis: Dir H. IMURA.

Centre for Education and Research of Lifelong Learning: Dir M. MATSUI.

Information Processing Centre: Dir S. OZAWA.

Izura Institute of Arts and Culture: Dir S. KOIZUMI.

International House: Dir Y. AIZAWA.

Institute of Regional Studies: Dir Y. SAITO.

Gene Research Centre: Dir M. SHIRAI.

IWATE UNIVERSITY

3-18-8 Ueda, Morioka, Iwate 020-8550

Telephone: (19) 621-6006
Fax: (19) 621-6014
E-mail: ssomu@iwate-u.ac.jp
Internet: www.iwate-u.ac.jp

Founded 1949
Independent
Academic year: April to March

President: KENICHI HIRAYAMA
Chief Administrative Officer: TOSHIAKI KIKUCHI
Librarian: YOSHIYA NAKASHIMA

Library of 760,434 vols
Number of teachers: 835
Number of students: 6,218

Publications: *Journal of the Faculty of Agriculture, Report on Technology of Iwate University, Annual Report of the Faculty of Education, Artes Liberales*

DEANS

Faculty of Agriculture: YOSHINOBU OTA
Faculty of Technology: KUNIO MORI
Faculty of Education: TAKAO FUJIWARA
College of Humanities and Social Sciences: TATSUYUKI TAKATSUKA

KAGAWA UNIVERSITY

1-1 Saiwai-cho, Takamatsu-shi 760-8521

Telephone: (87) 832-1025
Fax: (87) 832-1053
E-mail: kokusait@jimu.ao.kagawa-u.ac.jp
Internet: www.kagawa-u.ac.jp

Founded 1949
Independent
Academic year: April to March

President: Dr YOSHITSUGU KIMURA
Vice-President: Dr HIROAKI TAKEUCHI
Vice-President: Dr TAKUMI YOSHIZAWA
Secretary-General: KUNIO SEKI
Librarian: MASAYUKI SATO

Library of 650,000 vols
Number of teachers: 473 (incl. teachers at attached schools)
Number of students: 5,261

DEANS

Faculty of Agriculture: MASAHIKO ICHII
Faculty of Economics: MICHIYO IHARA
Faculty of Education: YOSHIMASA KANO
Faculty of Law: SADAMI UEMURA
Faculty of Engineering: HIROSHI ISHIKAWA
Faculty of Medicine: AKINOBU OKABE

KAGOSHIMA UNIVERSITY

21–24, 1-chome, Korimoto, Kagoshima-shi 890-8580

Telephone: (992) 85-7111
Internet: www.kagoshima-u.ac.jp

Founded 1949
Independent

President: YUKIHIRO NAGATA
Director-General: MASATOSHI TANIGUCHI

Library of 1,338,169 vols
Number of teachers: 1,200 full-time
Number of students: 11,000

DEANS

Faculty of Law, Economics and the Humanities: Y. TATSUMURA
Faculty of Education: Y. NAKAYAMA
Faculty of Science: M. INOUE
Faculty of Medicine: H. YOSHIDA
Faculty of Dentistry: T. NISHIKAWA
Faculty of Medicine and Dentistry: T. AIKO
Faculty of Engineering: Y. NAGASAWA
Faculty of Agriculture: E. SHIMOKAWA
Faculty of Fisheries: K. UEDA

KANAGAWA UNIVERSITY

3-27-1 Rokkakubashi, Kanagawaku, Yokohama 221-8686

Telephone: (45) 491-1701
Internet: www.kanagawa-u.ac.jp

Founded 1949

Library of 800,000 vols
Faculties of Law, Economics, Business Administration, Foreign Languages, Science, Engineering.

KANAZAWA UNIVERSITY

Kakuma-machi, Kanazawa-shi 920-1192
Telephone: (76) 264-5111
Fax: (76) 234-4010
E-mail: now@kanazawa-u.ac.jp
Internet: www.kanazawa-u.ac.jp

Founded 1949
Independent
Academic year: April to March

President: YUJIRO HAYASHI
Vice-President (Finance): S. NAKAMURA
Vice-President (General Affairs and Human Resources): N. ASAKURA
Vice-President (Hospital): Y. WATANABE
Vice-President (Information): T. HASHIMOTO
Vice-President (Research and International Affairs): A. OMURA
Director (Office of Community Relations): T. HASHIMOTO
Director (Office of Intellectual Property): N. YOSHIKUNI
Director (University Library): T. HASHIMOTO

Library: Libraries with 1,749,982 vols
Number of teachers: 1,031
Number of students: 10,794

DEANS

Faculty of Economics: T. YOKOYAMA
Faculty of Education: K. KATAGIRI
Faculty of Engineering: J. ODA
Faculty of Law: T. MAEDA
Faculty of Letters: I. KUBOTA
Faculty of Medicine: M. FURUKAWA
Faculty of Pharmaceutical Sciences: H. ISHIBASHI
Faculty of Science: S. NAKAO
Graduate School of Medical Science: H. YAMAMOTO
Graduate School of Natural Science and Technology: (vacant)
Graduate School of Socio-environmental Studies: K. GOGA
Law School: Y. HATA

DIRECTORS

Advanced Science Research Center: K. YAMAGUCHI
Cancer Research Institute: H. SATO
Center for Co-operative Research: S. MURAKAMI
Environmental Preservation Center: S. MORI
Extension Institute: M. SOMEI
Foreign Language Institute: T. YABUCHI
Health Service Center: H. NAKABAYASHI
Information Media Center: M. IWAHARA
Institute for Nature and Environmental Technology: K. KASHIWAYA
International Student Center: M. KITAURA
Research Center for Higher Education: T. AONO
University Hospital: S. KOIZUMI

PROFESSORS

Faculty of Economics (tel. (76) 264-5440; fax (76) 264-5444):

BENNOU, S., Economic History of Modern China
GOKA, K., Labour Economics
HORIBAYASHI, T., Theory of Economic Planning
IKARIYAMA, H., Public Finance
KAMIJO, I., History of Economic Thought
MAEDA, T., Modern Economics
MARUYAMA, K., Comparative Social Philosophy
MIYATA, M., Banking and Financial Systems
MURAKAMI, K., Principles of Economics
NAKASHIMA, K., World-System Theory and the Financial History of Medieval and Modern Europe
NAMU, S., Education
NISHIDA, Y., Japanese Contemporary Agricultural History
NISHIJIMA, Y., Contrastive Sociolinguistics
NOMURA, M., History of Social Thought
SAWADA, M., Industrial Relations and Human Resource Management in Japan and the USA, General Theory of Business Management
SHIRAISHI, H., Business Administration
TSURUZONO, Y., Korean History
UNNO, Y., Economic Policy
YOKOYAMA, T., Social Security
YOSHINO, Y., Sports Science

Faculty of Education (tel. (76) 264-5555; fax (76) 234-4100):

DEMURA, S., Lifelong Sports
EMORI, I., Pedagogy
GOMI, T., Historical Geography
HATANAKA, H., Magnetic Resonance
IHARA, Y., Inorganic Chemistry
IKEGAMI, K., Developmental Psychology
ISHIMURA, U., Physical Education
ITOH, S., Geography and Planning
IZUMI, N., Dielectrics
KATAGIRI, K., Developmental Neuropsychology of Mental Retardation
KATOH, K., Japanese Linguistics
KAWABATA, K., Freshwater Biology
KAYAHARA, M., Clinical Psychology
KIMURA, M., Education for the Handicapped
KONDOH, A., Japanese Linguistics
KUJIRA, Y., Crop Science
KUROBORI, T., Applied Optics
MAEDA, H., Modern Japanese Literature
MATSUBARA, M., Teaching of Science
MATSUDAIRA, M., Textile Science
MATSUNAKA, H., Instrumental Music
MATSUSHITA, R., Philosophy of Education
MATSUURA, N., Graphic Design
MIYASHITA, T., History of European Art
MIYOSHI, Y., Information Science
MORI, E., Japanese Literature
MOROOKA, K., Teaching Methods
MURAI, A., Research on Method of Teaching 'Social Studies'
OHTSUKA, I., English Linguistics
OI, M., Communication Disorders
OKAZAKI, F., Philosophy
OKUBO, H., History of Physical Education and Sports
OKUDA, H., Japanese History
SAKAYORI, A., Igneous Petrology
SASAK, T., Materials Science and Engineering
SHINOHARA, H., Music Education
SUGIMOTO, M., Geology
SUNADA, R., Practice and Research for Clinical Psychology and Education
TANABE, S., Educational Administration and Management
UEDA, J., Chemistry
YAKURA, K., Plant Molecular Biology
YAMAGISHI, M., Housing Science
YAMAMOTO, H., Biomechanics in Sports
YAMAMOTO, H., Classic Japanese Literature
YAMAMOTO, T., Teaching Methods
YASUKAWA, T., History of Foreign Education

Faculty of Law (tel. (76) 264-5403; fax (76) 264-5405):

CHEN, I., Conflict of Laws
IKUTA, S., English Literature
INOUE, H., Social Security Law
KASHIMA, M., International Relations
KUSUNE, S., International Communication
MAEDA, T., Labour Law
NAKAMASA, M., Social Philosophy
NAKAMURA, M., Chinese Legal History
NAKAYAMA, H., Criminal Procedure
NISHIMURA, S., Political Sociology
SAKURAI, T., European Legal History
TAKAHASHI, R., Sociology
TOKUMOTO, S., Civil Law
UMEDA, Y., Japanese Legal History
YAMAGATA, K., Developmental Psychology

Faculty of Letters (tel. (76) 264-5360; fax (76) 264-5362):

FUJII, S., Prehistory of the Near East
FURUHATA, T., Oriental History
HASHIMOTO, K., Sociology
HONMA, T., American Literature
IWATA, R., Chinese Linguistics
KAGAMI, H., Cultural Anthropology
KAJIKAWA, S., Russian History
KAJIKAWA, Y., Geography
KAMIYA, H., Geography
KASAI, J., Japanese History
KASUYA, Y., French Literature
KIGOSHI, O., Japanese Literature
KUBOTA, I., German Literature
KUBUKI, S., Comparative Culture
MATSUKAWA, J., Cognitive Psychology
MIZOBE, A., Sociology
MOCHII, Y., Oriental History
MURAKAMI, K., American Literature
NAKABAYASHI, N., Cultural Anthropology
NAKAMURA, Y., English Language
NISHIMURA, S., Japanese Literature
NITTA, T., Linguistics
OHTAKI, S., Chinese Language
SASAKI, T., Archaeology
SHIMA, I., Comparative Culture
SHIBATA, M., Philosophy
SUNAHARA, Y., Philosophy
TAKADA, S., English Literature
TAKAHAMA, S., Archaeology
TAKEUCHI, Y., German Linguistics
TOHDA, M., British History
TSUGE, Y., Linguistics
UCHIDA, H., French Literature
UEDA, M., Japanese Literature

Faculty of Medicine (5-11-80 Kodatsuno, Kanazawa, Ishikawa; tel. (76) 265-2500; fax (76) 234-4351):

AMANO, R., Radiochemistry and Radiobiology
ASAI, H., Physical Therapy
HASEGAWA, M., Mental Health and Psychiatric Nursing
HOSO, M., Pathology and Anatomy
HOSOMI, H., Ethics and Bioethics
HOSONO, R., Neurobiology
IKUTA, M., Human Activity Analysis
INAGAKI, M., Fundamental Nursing and Division of Health Science
IZUMI, K., Gerontological and Rehabilitation Nursing
KARASAWA, T., Bacterial Pathogenesis
KAWAHARA, E., Pathology
KAWAI, K., Radiopharmaceutical Chemistry
KIDO, T., Occupational and Environmental Health
KIKUCHI, Y., Radiation Oncology
KIMURA, R., Child Development and Paediatric Nursing
KOJIMA, K., Medical Electronics and Information Sciences
KOSHIDA, K., Medical Radiation Protection
KOYAMA, Y., Psychiatry and Neuropsychology
MIZUKAMI, Y., Radiation Pathology
NAKASHIMA, H., Bioinformatics
NAKATANI, T., Anatomy and Biology of Cutaneous Wound
NEMOTO, T., Medical Engineering, Bioengineering, Biomedical Measurement
NOTOYA, M., Neuropsychology and Speech Pathology
OGIWARA, S., Physical Therapy
OHTAKE, S., Haematology and Oncology
SAEKI, K., Community Health Nursing
SAKAI, A., Maternal and Child Nursing and Midwifery

SANADA, S., Radiological Technology and Medical Physics
SEKI, H., Child and Adolescent Health
SHIMADA, K., Women's Health and Midwifery
SHOSAKU, T., Neurophysiology
SOMEYA, F., Rehabilitation Medicine
SUZUKI, M., Neuroradiology
TACHINO, K., Rehabilitation Medicine
TAKATA, S., Clinical Physiology
TAKAYAMA, T., Nuclear Medicine Technology
TANAKA, J., Virology
YACHIE, A., Immunology and Host Defence

Graduate School of Medical Science (13-1 Takara-machi, Kanazawa, Ishikawa; tel. (76) 265-2100; fax (76) 234-4202):

FUJIWARA, K., Human Movement and Health
FUKUDA, R., Molecular Genetics (Dept. of Biochemistry)
FURUKAWA, M., Otorhinolaryngology, Head and Neck Surgery
HASHIMOTO, T., Laboratory Medicine
HIGASHIDA, H., Biophysical Genetics
ICHIMURA, H., Viral Infection and International Health
INABA, H., Emergency Medical Science (Department of Emergency and Critical Care Medicine)
INOUE, M., Molecular Reproductive Biology
ISEKI, S., Histology and Embryology
KANEKO, S., Cancer Gene Regulation, Gastroenterology and Nephrology
KANO, M., Cellular Neurophysiology
KATO, S., Molecular Neurobiology
KOIZUMI, S., Angiogenesis and Vascular Development (Department of Paediatrics)
KOSHINO, Y., Psychiatry and Neurobiology
MATSUI, O., Radiology
NAKANISHI, Y., Molecular and Cellular Biochemistry
NAKANUMA, Y., Morpho-Functional Pathology (Department of Human Pathology)
NAKAO, S., Cellular Transplantation Biology (Haemato-oncology and Respiratory Medicine)
NAMIKI, M., Integrative Cancer Therapy and Urology
OGAWA, S., Biotargeting
OGINO, K., Environmental and Preventive Medicine
OHSHIMA, T., Forensic and Social Environmental Medicine
OOI, A., Molecular and Cellular Pathology
SAIJOH, K., Environmental and Molecular Bio-informatics
SHIMIZU, T., Bacteriology
SUGIYAMA, K., Ophthalmology
TAKEHARA, K., Angiogenesis and Connective Tissue Metabolism (Department of Dermatology)
TAKUWA, Y., Molecular Vascular Physiology
TANAKA, S., Anatomy and Neuroembryology
TOMITA, K., Restorative Medicine of Neuromusculoskeletal System (Department of Orthopaedic Surgery)
TONAMI, N., Biotracer Medicine (Department of Nuclear Medicine)
WATANABE, G., Thoracic, Cardiovascular and General Surgery (Department of Surgery 1)
YAMADA, M., Neurology and Neurobiology of Ageing
YAMAMOTO, E., Oral and Maxillofacial Surgery
YAMAMOTO, H., Biochemistry and Molecular Vascular Biology
YAMAMOTO, K., Organ Function Restoratology (Department of Anaesthesiology and Intensive Care Medicine)
YOKOI, T., Drug Metabolism and Molecular Toxicology
YOKOTA, T., Stem Cell Biology
YOSHIMOTO, T., Molecular and Medical Pharmacology

Graduate School of Natural Science and Technology (tel. (76) 264-6821; fax (76) 234-6844):

ADACHI, M., Optical Metrology
ANDO, T., Biophysics
AOKI, K., Theoretical Physics
ARAI, S., Petrology
CHIKATA, Y., Bridge Maintenance Management
ENDO, K., Theoretical Chemistry
FUJIMAGARI, T., Mathematical Analysis
FUJISHITA, H., Quantum Physics of Condensed Matter
FUJIWARA, N., Systems and Control
FUKUMORI, Y., Physiological Chemistry
FUNADA, T., Vehicle Automation
FURUMOTO, M., Geophysics
HASHIMOTO, H., Visual Communication, Video Coding, Multimedia Processing
HATANE, I., Numerical Analysis, Computational Physics and Mathematics
HAYAKAWA, K., Hygienic Chemistry
HAYASHI, Y., Separation Engineering
HIRAO, M., Production Engineering
HIROSE, Y., Computational Mechanics
HIWATARI, Y., Theory of Material Physics
HOJO, A., Strength of Materials
HONJO, T., Analytical Chemistry
ICHINOSE, T., Functional Analysis
IKEDA, O., Electrochemistry
INOMATA, K., Organic Chemistry
ISHIBASHI, H., Synthetic Organic Chemistry
ISHIDA, H., Coastal Engineering
ISHIWATARI, A., Geology and Petrology
ISOBE, K., Inorganic Chemistry
ITO, H., Differential Equations
ITO, S., Discrete Dynamical System and its Application
ITO, T., Algebraic Combinatorics
IWAHARA, M., Power Electronics, Applied Magnetics
IWATA, Y., Dynamics of Machinery
KAJIKAWA, Y., Structural Engineering
KAMIYA, Y., Robotics
KANJIN, Y., Harmonic Analysis
KANOH, S., Synthetic Polymer Chemistry
KASUE, A., Geometry
KATO, M., Stratigraphy and Palaeontology
KAWAKAMI, M., Urban and Regional Planning
KIHARA, K., Mineralogy and Crystallography
KIMATA, N., Infrastructure Planning, System Simulation
KIMURA, H., Artificial Intelligence
KIMURA, K., Drug Management and Policies
KIMURA, S., Fluid Mechanics and Thermal Sciences
KINOSHITA, H., Organic Chemistry
KITAGAWA, K., Mechanical Properties of Engineering Materials
KITAGAWA, M., Deformation and Strength of Man-made and Naturally Produced Materials
KITAURA, M., Earthquake Engineering
KODAMA, A., Geometry
KOMURA, A., Electrochemistry
KUBO, J., Theoretical Physics
KUMEDA, M., Electronic Materials
KUNIMOTO, K., Bio-organic Chemistry, Environmental Technology
MAEGAWA, K., Structural Engineering
MAGAI, T., Defects in Solids
MATSUDA, Y., Integrated Circuits
MASUYA, H., Structural Engineering
MATSUMOTO, T., Pile Foundations, Pile Dynamics, Numerical Analysis
MATSUNAGA, T., Molecular Human Genetics
MATSUURA, K., Instrumentation by Image Processing
MIKAGE, M., Herbal Medicine and Natural Resources
MIYAGISHI, S., Applied Physical Chemistry
MIYAJIMA, M., Earthquake Engineering
MIYAKAWA, T., Partial Differential Equations
MONZEN, R., Metallic Materials
MORI, S., Heat and Mass Transfer
MORIMOTO, A., Electronic Materials
MOTOI, M., Organic Chemistry of Polymers
MUKAI, C., Pharmaceutical and Organic Chemistry
MURAKAMI, T., Astrophysics
MURAMOTO, K., Image Information Systems
NAGANO, I., Radio Wave Engineering
NAKAGAKI, R., Physical Chemistry
NAKAMOTO, Y., Polymer Chemistry
NAKANISHI, T., Radiochemistry
NAKAO, S., Applied Mathematics
NAKAYAMA, K., Adaptive Systems
NAOE, S., Optical Properties of Materials
NISHIKAWA, K., Digital Signal Processing
NISHIKAWA, K., Theoretical Chemistry
NITTA, K., Polymer Physics
ODA, J., Bionic Design
OHASHI, N., Molecular Physics
OHGISHI, M., Cognitive Engineering
OHKUMA, S., Biochemistry and Molecular Cell Biology
OHTA, T., Pharmacognosy and Chemistry of Natural Products
OKUNO, M., Mineralogy and Non-crystalline Material Science
OMATA, S., Partial Differential Equations and Numerical Analysis
OTANI, Y., Aerosol Technology
SAITOU, M., Computational Materials Science
SAKURAI, S., Developmental Biology
SAKURAI, T., Biochemistry
SATO, H., Non-linear Vibration
SATO, Y., Organic Physical Chemistry
SEKI, H., Environmental Engineering
SEKIZAKI, M., Physical Chemistry of Crystals
SENDA, H., Co-ordination Chemistry
SHIMADA, K., Clinical Analytical Sciences
SHINTAKU, S., Textile Machinery
SOMEI, M., Chemistry
SUGANO, T., Algebra
SUZUKI, H., Solid State Physics
SUZUKI, M., Co-ordination Chemistry
SUZUKI, N., Holistic Pharmacotherapy
TAGO, Y., Computational Science
TAKAHASHI, K., Photo-function Material Chemistry
TAKAMIYA, S., Microwave/Optoelectronic Semiconductor Devices
TAKANOBU, S., Stochastic Analysis
TAKAYAMA, J., Traffic Engineering and Transport Planning
TAKIMOTO, A., Heat and Mass Transfer, Energy Conversion and Environmental Conservation
TAMAI, N., River Engineering, River Planning
TAMURA, K., Chemical Engineering Fundamentals and Thermodynamics
TANAKA, I., History of Science and Technology
TAZAKI, K., Environmental Earth Science
TORII, K., Civil Engineering Materials
TSUCHIYA, M., Mathematics (Theory of Stochastic Processes)
TSUJI, A., Innovative Pharmaceutics
UCHIYAMA, Y., Tribology (Friction and Wear Mechanisms of Rubbers and Plastics)
UEDA, K., Phylogenetics
UEDA, K., Separation and Analytical Chemistry

UEDA, T., Precision Machining, Laser Processing
UENO, H., Fluid Machinery, Fluid Power
UESUGI, Y., Plasma Science, Fusion Plasma Engineering
USUDA, M., Materials Working
YAJIMA, T., Ecology
YAMADA, K., Neuropsychopharmacology
YAMADA, M., Combinatorics
YAMADA, M., Opto-electronics
YAMADA, T., Polymer Processing, Reaction Engineering and Phase Equilibria
YAMADA, Y., Mechanical Properties of Materials
YAMAKOSHI, K., Biomedical Engineering
YAMANE, S., Computer Science
YAMAZAKI, K., Structural Optimization
YASUMURA, N., Classic Greek and Latin Literature
YATOMI, C., Non-linear Continuum Mechanics
YOKOI, T., Drug Metabolism and Molecular Toxicology
YONEDA, Y., Molecular Pharmacology
YONEYAMA, T., Metal Forming, Machine Design

Law School (tel. (76) 264-5968; fax (76) 234-4167):

ATARASHI, M., Constitutional Law
FURITSU, T., Criminal Law
HASEGAWA, T., Civil Law
HATA, Y., Comparative Constitutional Law
HIGASHI, I., Criminal Procedure
HOSOKAWA, T., Administrative Law
KASHIMI, Y., Civil Law
NAKAJIMA, F., Commercial Law
NAKO, M., Labour Law
NISHIMURA, S., Criminal Law
NOSAKA, Y., Civil Law
OJIMA, S., Family Law
SATO, M., Criminal Procedure
TAJIMA, J., Civil Law

Advanced Science Research Center (13-1 Takara-machi, Kanazawa, Ishikawa; tel. (76) 265-2771; fax (76) 234-4537; e-mail yamaguti@kenroku.kanazawa-u.ac.jp; internet web.kanazawa-u.ac.jp/~asrc):

ASANO, M., Experimental Animal Science
MORI, H., Nuclear Medicine
YAMAGUCHI, K., Molecular Genetics

Cancer Research Institute (13-1 Takara-machi, Kanazawa, Ishikawa; tel. (76) 265-2799; fax (76) 234-4527):

HARADA, F., Molecular and Cellular Biology
HIRAO, A., Molecular and Cellular Biology
MINAMOTO, T., Basic and Clinical Oncology
MUKAIDA, N., Molecular Oncology
MURAKAMI, S., Molecular Genetics
SATO, H., Molecular Oncology
SAWABU, N., Basic and Clinical Oncology
SUDA, T., Molecular and Cellular Immunology
TAKAKURA, N., Molecular and Cellular Biology
YAMAMOTO, K., Molecular and Cellular Biology
YOSHIOKA, K., Molecular and Cellular Biology

Center for Co-operative Research (tel. (76) 264-6111; fax (76) 234-4019):

SERYO, K., Mechanical Engineering
YOSHIKUNI, N., Intellectual Property Management

Environment Preservation Center (tel. (76) 234-6893; fax (76) 234-6895):

OHTA, T., Chemical Engineering Thermodynamics

Extension Institute (tel. (76) 264-5271; fax (76) 234-4045):

HATTORI, E., Adult Education (Life-long Education), Extramural Education

Foreign Language Institute (tel. (76) 264-5760; fax (76) 264-5993):

AISAWA, K., German
KANEKO, Y., German
KIKUCHI, E., German
KUWANO, H., English
MIKAMI (KIMURA), J., French
OYABU, K., English
SANBAI, R., English
SAWADA, S., English
WATANABE, A., English
YABUCHI, T., Chinese

Health Service Center (tel. (76) 264-5251; fax (76) 234-4044; e-mail nakabaya@kenroku.kanazawa-u.ac.jp):

NAKABAYASHI, H., Endocrinology and Metabolism

Information Media Center (tel. (76) 264-6911; fax (76) 234-6918):

SHAKO, M., Network Security
SUZUKI, T., Computational Physics, Particle Physics

Institute of Nature and Environmental Technology (tel. (76) 264-6141; fax (76) 234-4016):

IWASAKA, Y.
KASHIWAYA, K., Hydro-geomorphology
KIMURA, S., Heat Transfer and Fluid Mechanics
KOMURA, K., Environmental Radioactivity
NAKAMURA, K., Ecology
SASAYAMA, Y., Biodiversity
SHIMIZU, N., Bioengineering
YAMADA, S., Magnetic Technology
YAMAMOTO, M., Nuclear Geochemistry

International Student Center (tel. (76) 264-5188; fax (76) 234-4043):

MATSUSHITA, M., Psychology
MIURA, K., Japanese Language Education
OKAZAWA, T., Insect Ecology

Research Center for Higher Education (tel. (76) 264-5837; fax (76) 234-4172):

AONO, T., Medical Law
HAYATA, Y., Evaluation

University Hospital (13-1 Takara-machi, Kanazawa, Ishikawa; tel. (76) 265-2000; fax (76) 234-4320):

KOIZUMI, J., Department of General Medicine
MIYAMOTO, K., Department of Hospital Pharmacy

KITAMI INSTITUTE OF TECHNOLOGY

165 Koen-cho, Kitami, Hokkaido 090-8507
Telephone: (157) 26-9106
Fax: (157) 26-9117
Internet: www.kitami-it.ac.jp

Founded 1960
Independent
Academic year: April to March (2 semesters)

President: HIDEYUKI TSUNEMOTO
Vice-Presidents: KOICHI AYUTA, NOBUO TAKAHASHI
Director of Administration: AKIHIRO SHIBAZAKI
Library Director: TOSHIYUKI OSHIMA

Number of teachers: 150 full-time
Number of students: 2,103

Publication: *Memoirs of Kitami Institute of Technology*

HEADS OF DEPARTMENTS

Mechanical Engineering: HANIU, H.
Electrical and Electronic Engineering: TAMURA, J.
Computer Sciences: SUZUKI, M.
Applied and Environmental Chemistry: SUZUKI, T.
Material Science: INOUE, S.
Civil Engineering: MAEDA, H.
Common Course: TERUI, H.

KOBE UNIVERSITY

1-1 Rokkodai-cho, Nada-ku, Kobe 657-8501, Hyogo
Telephone: (78) 881-1212
E-mail: www-admin@kobe-u.ac.jp
Internet: www.kobe-u.ac.jp

Founded 1902
Independent
Academic year: April to March

President: TOMOYUKI NOGAMI
Directors: MASAHIRO TAKASAKI, SHIGEYUKI MAYAMA, SHINZO KITAMURA, SHOJI NISHIJIMA, KUNIO SAKAMOTO, MASAYUKI SUZUKI, OSAMI NISHIDA, SADAO KAMIDONO
Director of Administration: KUNIO SAKAMOTO
Library Director: KENICHI SUDO

Library of 3,365,000 vols
Number of teachers: 1,674 full-time
Number of students: 17,598

Publications: *Law Review* (annually), *Economic Review* (annually), *Business Research* (irregular), *Journal of Mathematics* (2 a year), *Kobe Journal of Medical Sciences* (6 a year), *Bulletin of Allied Medical Sciences* (annually), *Memoirs of the Graduate School of Science and Technology* (annually), *Journal of International Cooperation Studies* (3 a year), *Economic and Business Review* (annually), *Journal of Economics and Business Administration* (monthly), *Kobe Economic and Business Review* (annually)

DEANS

Faculty and Graduate School of Letters: TAKAJI MATSUSHIMA
Faculty of Cross-Cultural Studies: SATOSHI MUNAKATA
Faculty of Human Development: SUSUMU WADA
Faculty and Graduate School of Law: EIJI TAKIZAWA
Faculty and Graduate School of Economics: TAKASHI NAKATANI
Faculty and Graduate School of Business Administration: HISAKATSU SAKURAI
Faculty of Science: HIROSHI TAKEDA
School and Graduate School of Medicine: SAKAN MAEDA
Faculty of Engineering: HIROMOTO USUI
Faculty of Agriculture: CHIHARU NAKAMURA
Faculty of Maritime Sciences: KINZO INOUE
Graduate School of Humanities and Social Sciences: TAKAJI MATSUSHIMA
Graduate School of Cultural Studies and Human Science: SUSUMU WADA
Graduate School of International Co-operation Studies: YUTAKA KATAYAMA
Graduate School of Science and Technology: HIDEKI FUKUDA
Research Institute for Economics and Business Administration: HIDETOSHI YAMAJI

PROFESSORS

Faculty of Letters (tel. (78) 803-5591; fax (78) 803-5589; e-mail lsoumu@lit.kobe-u.ac.jp; internet www.lit.kobe-u.ac.jp):

DONOHASHI, A., Art History
EDAGAWA, M., French Literature
FUJI, M., Sociology
FUJITA, H., Geography
FUKUNAGA, S., Japanese Literature and Language
HASEGAWA, K., Geography
HISHIKAWA, E., British and American Literature
IWASAKI, N., Sociology
KAMATANI, T., Chinese Language and Literature
KAZASHI, N., Philosophy
KUBOZONO, H., Linguistics
MATSUDA, H., French Literature
MATSUDA, T., Philosophy
MATSUMOTO, Y., Linguistics

MATSUSHIMA, T., Psychology
MOHRI, A., European and American History
MORI, N., Asian History
NAGANO, J., Art Theory
NISHIMITSU, Y., Linguistics
OGURA, T., Psychology
OHTSURU, A., European and American History
RINBARA, S., Japanese Literature and Language
SAITO, S., British and American Literature
SASAKI, M., Sociology
SUZUKI, Y., Japanese Literature and Language
TAKAHASHI, M., Japanese History
YAMAGUCHI, K., German Literature
YAMAMOTO, M., Philosophy
YUI, K., Sociology

Faculty of Cross-Cultural Studies (1-2-1 Tsurukabuto, Nada-ku, Kobe 657-8501; tel. (78) 803-7515; fax (78) 803-7509; e-mail shomudai@ofc.kobe-u.ac.jp; internet ccs.cla.kobe-u.ac.jp/kohou/eigo):

AMANO, K., Comtemporary Culture and Society Division
CHO, S., Comtemporary Culture and Society Division
FUJINO, K., Contemporary Culture and Society Division
GODA, T., Intercultural Communication Division
HAYASHI, H., Human Communication and Information Science Division
ICHIDA, Y., Comtemporary Culture and Society Division
ISHIHARA, K., Area Studies Division
ISHIKAWA, T., Area Studies Division
ISHIZUKA, H., Area Studies Division
KABURAGI, M., Human Communication and Information Science Division
KAGEYAMA, S., Area Studies Division
KIBA, H., Intercultural Communication Division
KINOSHITA, M., Area Studies Division
KOMURASAKI, S., Intercultural Communication Division
LU, X., Area Studies Division
MIKAMI, T., Contemporary Culture and Society Division
MIKIHARA, H., Comtemporary Culture and Society Division
MIURA, N., Intercultural Communication Division
MIZUGUCHI, S., Human Communication and Information Science Division
MIZUTA, K., Comtemporary Culture and Society Division
MORIMOTO, M., Intercultural Communication Division
MORISHITA, J., Human Communication and Information Science Division
MUNAKATA, S., Comtemporary Culture and Society Division
NOTANI, K., Intercultural Communication Division
OHTSUKI, K., Human Communication and Information Science Division
SADANOBU, T., Human Communication and Information Science Division
SAKAMOTO, C., Area Studies Division
SAKANO, T., Intercultural Communication Division
SASAE, O., Area Studies Division
SHIBATA, Y., Intercultural Communication Division
SONE, H., Area Studies Division
SUDO, K., Area Studies Division
SUZAKI, S., Area Studies Division
TANIMOTO, S., Area Studies Division
TERAUCHI, N., Area Studies Division
TODA, M., Intercultural Communication Division
UCHIDA, M., Intercultural Communication Division
UOZUMI, K., Contemporary Culture and Society Division
UTSUKI, N., Human Communication and Information Science Division
WANG, K., Area Studies Division
YAMAZAKI, Y., Contemporary Culture and Society Division
YOKOYAMA, R., Area Studies Divison
YOSHIDA, N., Contemporary Culture and Society Division
YOSHIOKA, M., Intercultural Communication Division

Faculty of Human Development (3-11 Tsurukabuto, Nada-ku, Kobe 657-8501; tel. (78) 803-7905; fax (78) 803-7939; e-mail info@h.kobe-u.ac.jp; internet www.h.kobe-u.ac.jp):

AMAKAWA, T., Sciences for the Natural Environment
AOKI, T., Human Life Environment
ASANO, S., Studies of Social Environment
EBINA, K., Sciences for the Natural Environment
ENOMOTO, T., Sciences for the Natural Environment
FUNAKI, T., Educational Science
FUNAKOSHI, S., Childhood Development and Education
GOMI, K., Childhood Development and Education
HAMAGUCHI, H., Human Life Environment
HIRAKAWA, K., Sports Science
HIRAYAMA, Y., Human Life Environment
HIROKI, K., Childhood Development and Education
HOUNOKI, K., Adult Learning
ICHIHASHI, H., Human Life Environment
IMATANI, N., Studies of Social Environment
INAGAKI, N., Educational Science
ISHIKAWA, T., Health Education
ITO, K., Development Psychology
IWAI, M., Music
JOH, H., Human Life Environment
KAWABATA, T., Health Education
KAWABE, S., Sports Science
KISHIMOTO, H., Childhood Development and Education
MARUYA, N., Human Life Environment
MIKAMI, K., Educational Science
NAKABAYASHI, T., Developmental Psychology
NAKAGAWA, K., Sciences for the Natural Environment
NAKAMURA, K., Developmental Psychology
NAKAYAMA, S., Art and Design
NINOMIYA, A., Studies of Social Environment
ODA, T., Behavioural Development Studies
ODAKA, N., Art and Design
OGAWA, M., Educational Science
OKADA, S., Behavioural Development Studies
SAIDA, Y., Music
SAITO, K., Sciences for the Natural Environment
SATO, M., Developmental Psychology
SHIBA, M., Sports Performance
SHIRAKURA, T., Mathematics and Computer Studies
SUEMOTO, M., Adult Learning
SUGINO, K., Developmental Psychology
TAINOSHO, Y., Sciences for the Natural Environment
TAKAHASHI, J., Mathematics and Computer Studies
TAKAHASHI, M., Mathematics and Computer Studies
TAKAHASHI, T., Mathematics and Computer Studies
TANAKA, Y., Health Education
TERAKADO, Y., Sciences for the Natural Environment
TSUCHIYA, M., Educational Science
TSUKAWAKI, J., Art and Design
UEZI, S., Sciences for the Natural Environment
WADA, S., Studies of Social Environment
WAKAO, Y., Music
YAMAGUCHI, Y., Sport Sciences
YAMASAKI, T., Studies of Social Environment
YANAGIDA, Y., Sport Sciences
YANO, S., Human Life Environment

Graduate School of Law (2-1 Rokkodai-cho, Nada-ku, Kobe 657-850; tel. (78) 803-7232; fax (78) 803-7292; e-mail j1shomu@ofc.kobe-u.ac.jp; internet www.law.kobe-u.ac.jp):

AKASAKA, M., Constitutional Law
AMIYA, R., Western Political History
BABA, K., Sociology of Law
FUJIWARA, A., Japanese Legal History
HAMADA, F., Labour Law
HASUNUMA, K., Philosophy of Law
HATA, M., Civil Procedure
IIDA, F., Political Theory
INOUE, N., Constitutional Law
INOUE, Y., Intellectual Property Law
IOKIBE, M., Japanese Political History, Comparative Politics
ISHIKAWA, T., Professional Legal Education
ISOMURA, T., Civil Law
ITO, M., Comparative Politics
JI, W. D., Chinese Law, Comparative Studies in Legal Culture
KASHIMURA, S., Sociology of Law
KIKKAWA, G., International Relations
KOMURO, N., International Economic Law
KONDO, M., Commercial Law, Securities Regulation
KUBOTA, A., Civil Law
MARUYAMA, E., Anglo-American Law, Medical Law
MASUJIMA, K., International Relations
MORISHITA, T., Russian Law, Principles of Social Sciences
NAKAGAWA, T., Administrative Law
NAKANISHI, M., Civil Procedure
NAKANO, S., Private International Law, International Civil Procedure
NEGISHI, A., Economic Law
OSHIMA, S., Professional Legal Education
OTSUKA, H., Criminal Law
OUCHI, S., Labour Law
SAITO, A., International Trade Law, Private International Law
SAKAMOTO, S., International Law
SATO, H., Tax Law
SENSUI, F., Economic Law
SHINADA, Y., Political Data Analysis, Election System
SHITANI, M., Commercial Law
SUDO, M., Professional Legal Education
TAKIZAWA, E., Western Legal History, Roman Law
TEJIMA, Y., Civil and Medical Law
TSUKIMURA, T., International Relations
USHIMA, K., Criminal Law
YAMADA, S., Civil Law
YAMADA, T., Professional Legal Education
YAMAMOTO, H., Civil Procedure
YAMAMOTO, K., Civil Law
YASUNAGA, M., Civil Law
YONEMARU, T., Administrative Law
YUKIZAWA, K., Commercial Law, Commercial Transactions

Graduate School of Economics (2-1 Rokkodai-cho, Nada-ku, Kobe 657-8501; tel. (78) 803-7246; fax (78) 803-7293; e-mail esoumu@ofc.kobe-u.ac.jp; internet www.econ.kobe-u.ac.jp):

ADACHI, M., Social Policy
AMANO, M., Modern Japanese Economic History
FUJITA, S., International Monetary System
FUKUDA, W., Economic System Theory
HAGIWARA, T., Contemporary Technology Theory
HAMORI, S., Statistical Analysis of Economic Time Series Data

HARA, M., International Investment Theory
HARUYAMA, T., Economic Growth Theory
IRITANI, J., Public Finance Policy
ISHIGURO, K., International Politics and Economics
ISHIKAWA, M., Environmental Economics
JINUSHI, T., American Economy
KATO, H., Chinese Economy
KUBO, H., European Economy
MARUYA, R., Theory of Economic Policy
MATSUBAYASHI, Y., Empirical Analysis of International Macroeconomy
MITANI, N., Labour Economics
NAKAMURA, T., Macroeconomics, Investment Theory
NAKATANI, T., Macrodynamic Theory
NAKANISHI, N., International Economics
OHKUBO, H., Monetary Policy
OHTANI, K., Theory of Statistical Inference
OKUNISHI, T., European Economic History
OSHIO, T., Social Security
SHIGETOMI, K., Economic History of Modern Britain
TAKAHASHI, S., World Economic Geography
TAKIGAWA, Y., Monetary Economics
TANAKA, Y., Theory of Economic Structure
TANIZAKI, H., On Estimation and Test in Simulation-Base Econometrics
UEMIYA, S., History of Economic Theory
URANAGASE, T., Japanese Economic History
YAMAGUCHI, M., Agricultural Policy
YANAGAWA, T., Industrial Organization
YOSHII, M., Comparative Economics

Graduate School of Business Administration (2-1 Rokkodai-cho, Nada-ku, Kobe, 657-8501; tel. (78) 803-7256; fax (78) 803-6969; e-mail bwebmstr@kobe-u.ac.jp; internet www.b.kobe-u.ac.jp):

DEI, F., International Economics, International Investments
FUJIWARA, K., Money and Financial Systems
GOTOH, M., Financial Reporting and Accounting Systems
HARADA, T., Industrial Organization
ISHII, J., Marketing Management and Business Strategy
KAGONO, T., Business Strategy and Corporate Behaviour
KANAI, T., Organizational Behaviour
KATO, H., Finance
KATO, Y., Management Accounting
KOGA, T., International Accounting
KOKUBU, K., Social and Environmental Accounting
KOMBAYASHI, N., Human Resource Management
KOU, L., Marketing
KUTSUNA, K., Entrepreneurial Finance
KUWAHARA, T., Business History
MARUYAMA, M., Applied Microeconomics, Distribution Systems
MATSUO, H., Supply Chain Management, Production Planning and Scheduling
MIZUTANI, F., Public Utility Economics and Regulatory Economics
NAITO, F., Financial Accounting and Auditing
NAKANO, T., Accounting Systems and History
OGAWA, S., Marketing
SAKAKIBARA, S., Corporate Finance and Portfolio Management
SAKASHITA, A., Organizational Behaviour and Corporate Culture
SAKURAI, H., Financial Accounting, Financial Statement Analysis
SHOJI, K., Transport Economics and Policy
TAKAO, A., Insurance Industry Analysis
TAKASHIMA, K., Marketing and Distribution Systems
TANI, T., Management Accounting and Control

Faculty of Science (tel. (78) 803-5761; fax (78) 803-5770; e-mail rishomu@ofc.kobe-u.ac.jp; internet www.sci.kobe-u.ac.jp):

FUKE, K., Physical Chemistry
FUKUDA, Y., Optical Physics
FUKUYAMA, K., Analysis
GUNJI, Y., Planetary Science
HARIMA, H., Condensed Matter Theory
HAYASHI, F., Biology of Living Functions
HAYASHI, M., Organic Chemistry
HIGUCHI, Y., Applied Mathematics
HIMENO, S., Inorganic Chemistry
IKEDA, H., Applied Mathematics
KADONO, Y., Biology of Living Structures
LIM, C. S., High Energy Theory
MATSUDA, T., Planetary Science
MIMURA, T., Biology of Living Structures
MIYATA, T., Earth Science
NAKAGAWA, Y., Planetary Science
NAKAMURA, N., Planetary Science
NAKANISHI, Y., Algebra and Geometry
NORO, M., Applied Mathematics
ONISHI, H., Physical Chemistry
OTOFUJI, Y., Earth Science
SAITO, M., Algebra and Geometry
SAKAMOTO, H., Biology of Living Functions
SASAKI, T., Algebra and Geometry
SATO, H., Earth Science
SETSUNE, J., Inorganic Chemistry
TAKANO, K., Analysis
TAKAYAMA, N., Analysis
TAKEDA, H., Particle Physics
TOMEOKA, K., Planetary Science
TSUCHIYA, T., Biology of Living Functions
WADA, S., Condensed Matter Physics
WATANABE, K., Biology of Living Structures
YAMADA, Y., Analysis
YAMAMURA, K., Organic Chemistry
YAMAZAKI, T., Algebra and Geometry

School and Graduate School of Medicine (7-5-1 Kusunoki-cho, Chuo-ku, Kobe 650-0017; tel. (78) 382-5111; fax (78) 382-5050; e-mail webmst@med.kobe-u.ac.jp; internet www.med.kobe-u.ac.jp/WelcomeJ.html):

AIBA, A., Cell Biology
AKITA, H., General Medical Science
ANDO, H., Basic Allied Medicine
AZUMA, T., Polygenic Disease Research
CHIHARA, K., Endocrinology; Metabolism, Neurology and Haematology; Oncology
FUJIMARA, M., Urulogy
FURUKAWA, H., Applied Occupational Therapy
GU, E., Advanced Medical Research and Treatment
HASHIMOTO, T., Basic Occupational Therapy
HAYASHI, Y., Molecular Medicine and Medical Genetics
HOTTA, H., Microbiology and Genomics
ISHII, N., Disaster and Emergency Medicine
ISHIKAWA, Y., Health Sciences and Basic Nursing
KASUGA, M., Diabetes, Digestive and Kidney Diseases
KATAOKA, T., Molecular Biology
KAWABATA, M., International Health
KAWAGUCHI, Y., Psychiatric Nursing and Mental Health
KAWAMATA, T., Applied Occupational Therapy
KITA, A., Maternal Nursing and Midwifery
KOHMURA, E., Neurosurgery
KOMORI, T., Oral and Maxillofacial Functional Science
KUMAGAI, S., Clinical Pathology and Immunology
KUNO, T., Molecular Pharmacology and Pharmacogenomics
KURODA, Y., Gastroenterological Surgery
KUROSAKA, M., Orthopaedic Surgery
MAEDA, K., Psychiatry and Neurology
MAEDA, S., Molecular Pathology
MARUO, T., Women's Medicine
MATSUDA, N., Community Health Nursing
MATSUMURA, S., Biochemistry
MATSUO, H., Maternity Nursing
MATSUO, M., Paediatrics
MIKI, A., Basic Physical Therapy
MINAMI, Y., Biomedical Regulation and Parasitology
MURATA, K., Clinical Nursing
NAKAMURA, S., Biochemistry
NAKAZONO, N., Applied Medical Technology
NEGI, A., Ophthalmology
NIBU, K., Otorhinolaryngology – Head and Neck Surgery
NISHIGORI, C., Dermatology
NISHIO, H., Public Health
NISHIYAMA, K., Basic Medical Technology
OBARA, H., Perioperative Medicine and Pain Management
OKAMURA, H., Molecular Brain Science
OKITA, Y., Cardiovascular, Thoracic and Paediatric Surgery
OKUMURA, K., Clinical Pharmacokinetics
RYO, R., Applied Medical Technology, Haematology and Blood Transfusion Medicine
SAKAMOTO, N., Medical Informatics
SEINO, S., Cell Biology and Neurophysiology
SEKI, K., Applied Occupational Therapy
SHIMADA, T., Applied Physical Therapy
SHIOZAWA, S., Rheumatology
SUGIMURA, K., Radiology
TABUCHI, Y., Clinical Oncology and Surgical Nursing
TAHARA, S., Plastic Surgery
TAKADA, S., Maternal and Child Health Science
TAMURA, Y., Basic Nursing
TERASHIMA, T., Developmental Neurobiology
TSUTOU, A., Basic Allied Medicine
UENO, Y., Legal Medicine
UGA, S., Parasitology
USAMI, M., Basic Medical Technology, Surgical Metabolism and Nutrition
WATANABE, M., Applied Medical Technology
YADA, M., Clinical Nursing
YAMAGUCHI, M., Applied Occupational Therapy
YAMAMURA, H., Proteomics
YAMAZAKI, I., Applied Occupational Therapy
YOKONO, K., Internal and Geriatric Medicine
YOKOYAMA, M., Cardiovascular and Respiratory Internal Medicine
YOKOZAKI, H., Surgical Pathology

Faculty of Engineering (tel. (78) 803-6333; fax (78) 803-6396; e-mail kousyomu@ofc.kobe-u.ac.jp; internet www.eng.kobe-u.ac.jp/index.html):

ADACHI, H., Theory and History of Architecture
DEKI, S., Applied Inorganic Chemistry
FUJII, S., Energy Conversion Engineering
FUJITA, I., Hydraulic Engineering
HAYASHI, S., Mathematical Theory of Programming
HIRASAWA, S., Heat Transfer and Thermal Engineering
KAKUDA, Y., Mathematical Logic and Mathematical Design Theory
KANKI, H., Machine Dynamics and Control
KAWATANI, M., Structural Dynamics
KAYA, N., Space Solar Power Systems
KIKYO, H., Mathematical Logic and Computer Science
KONDO, A., Biochemical Engineering
KURODA, K., Transportation Engineering and Infrastructure Planning
MASUDA, S., Algorithms and Data Structures
MATSUYAMA, H., Membrane Technology
MICHIOKU, K., River Hydraulics

MITANI, I., Ultimate Design of Steel and Composite Structures
MIYOSHI, T., Quantum Electronics
MORII, M., Information Theory, Computer Networks, Internet Security and Cryptography
MORIMOTO, M., Environmental Acoustics
MORIYAMA, M., Architectural and Urban Environmental Engineering
MORIWAKI, T., Intelligent Manufacturing Systems and Ultraprecision Machining
NAGAO, T., Design and Performance of Building Structures
NAKAGIRI, S., Control and Identification of Distributed Systems
NAKAI, Y., Fatigue and Fracture of Engineering Materials
NAMBU, T., Control of PDE
NISHINO, T., Polymer Chemistry
NUMA, M., VLSI Design and CAD
OGAWA, M., Semiconductor Electronics
OHI, K., Quake-proof Structural Engineering
OHMAE, N., Micro- and Nano-Tribology and Surface Engineering
OHMURA, N., Transport Science
OHTA, Y., Control Engineering
OKUBO, M., Polymer Colloid Chemistry
OSUKA, K., Advanced Control Engineering
SHIBUYA, S., Geotechnical Engineering
SHIGEMURA, T., Urban and Architectural Design
SHIOZAKI, Y., Urban and Housing Study
SHIRASE, K., Autonomous Machine Tools and Intelligent Manufacturing Systems
TADA, Y., Optimum Design of Systems
TAKADA, S., Earthquake Engineering
TAKENAKA, N., Multiphase Flow Engineering
TAKI, K., Computer Science and Engineering
TOMITA, Y., Solid Mechanics
TOMIYAMA, A., Energy and Environmental Engineering
TSUKAMOTO, M., Computer Systems and Networking
TSURUYA, S., Catalytic Chemistry
UEDA, Y., Applied Physical Chemistry
USUI, H., Non-Newtonian Fluid Mechanics
WADA, O., Optoelectronic Materials and Devices
YASAKA, Y., Plasma Science and Power Engineering
YASUDA, C., Architectural Planning and Urban Design
YASUDA, H., Nanomaterials Science
YOSHIMOTO, M., VLSI System Engineering
YOSHIMURA, T., Applied Optics and Image Processing

Faculty of Agriculture (1-1 Rokkodai-cho, Nada-ku, Kobe 657-8501; tel. (78) 803-5921; fax (78) 803-5931; e-mail ashomu@ofc.kobe-u.ac.jp; internet www.ans.kobe-u.ac.jp/indexe.html):

AE, N., Soil Science and Plant Nutrition
AOKI, K., Applied Biofunctional Chemistry
ASHIDA, H., Applied Biofunctional Chemistry
HASEGAWA, S., Animal Nutrition, Morphology and Microbiology
HATA, T., Regional and Environmental Engineering
HORIO, H., Biosystems Engineering
HOSAKA, K., Food Resources Education and Research Centre
HOSHI, N., Animal Nutrition, Morphology and Microbiology
INAGAKI, N., Horticultural Science
KAKO, T., Food and Environmental Economics
KAMIJIMA, O., Plant Breeding and Production Science
KANAZAWA, K., Biofunctional Molecules
KAWAMURA, T., Biosystems Engineering
MAYAMA, S., Plant Protection
MIYAKE, H., Biofunctional Chemistry
MIYANO, T., Animal Breeding and Reproduction
MIZUNO, M., Plant Resource Science
MUKAI, F., Animal Breeding and Reproduction
NAITO, T., Plant Protection
NAKAMURA, C., Plant Genetics and Physiology
NAKANISHI, T., Horticultural Science
OHNO, T., Biofunctional Molecules
OKAYAMA, T., Applied Biofunctional Chemistry
OHSAWA, R., Animal Science
SHIMIZU, A., Animal Nutrition, Morphology and Microbiology
SUGIMOTO, T., Genetics and Physiology
SUGIMOTO, Y., Applied Biofunctional Chemistry
TAKADA, O., Food and Environmental Economics
TANAKA, T., Regional and Environmental Science
TERAI, H., Horticultural Science
TOYODA, K., Biosystems Engineering
UCHIDA, K., Regional and Environmental Science
UCHIDA, N., Plant Breeding and Production Science
YAMAGATA, H., Biofunctional Molecules
YASUDA, T., Plant Genetics and Physiology

Faculty of Maritime Sciences (5-1-1 Fukaeminamimachi, Higashinada-ku, Kobe 658-0022; tel. (78) 431-6206; fax (78) 431-6355; e-mail mssoumu@ofc.kobe-u.ac.jp; internet www.maritime.kobe-u.ac.jp):

AZUKIZAWA, T., Marine Mechatronics
FUKUDA, K., Maritime Energy Engineering
FUKUOKA, T., Machine Design Engineering
FUKUSHI, K., Analytical Chemistry
FURUSHO, M., Seamanship and Traffic Psychology at Sea
HASHIMOTO, M., Internal Combustion Engines
HAYASHI, Y., Ship Navigation
IMAI, A., Logistics Planning
INOUE, K., Marine Traffic Engineering and Maritime Safety Management
INOUE, T., Network and Communication Systems Engineering
ISHIDA, H., Marine Meteorology
ISHIDA, K., Disaster Science
ISHIDA, T., Marine Power and System Engineering
ISOGAI, T., Statistical Science and Quality Management
KATO, E., Functional Polymer Materials Science
KIMURA, R., Acoustical Engineering and Maintenance Engineering
KITAMURA, A., Particle Beam Engineering
KOBAYASHI, E., Maritime Science and Naval Architecture
KOGUCHI, N., Navigation
KOZAI, K., Satellite Oceanography
MARUO, K., Partial Differential Equations
NISHIDA, O., Energy and Environmental Engineering
NISHIO, S., Naval Architecture
NISHIOKA, T., Fracture Mechanics, Computational Mechanics, Experimental Mechanics
ODA, K., Radiation Dosimetry and Applications
OTSUJI, T.
SADAKANE, H., Naval Architecture
SAKAMOTO, K., Power Electronics
SATO, M., Material Chemistry for Transportation
SHIOTANI, S., Numerical Ship Hydrodynamics
SIMADA, H., Cognitive Science
SUGITA, H., Management for Marine Power Plants
SUZUKI, S., Marine Traffic Laws
TAKAHASHI, R., Statistics
TANAKA, S., Fluid Mechanics of Engineering
YAMAMURA, S., Information Engineering
YOSHIDA, S., Shipping Economics

Research Institute for Economics and Business Administration (2-1 Rokkodai-cho, Nada-ku, Kobe 657-8501; tel. (78) 803-7270; fax (78) 803-7059; e-mail office@rieb.kobe-u.ac.jp; internet www.rieb.kobe-u.ac.jp):

GOTO, J., International Economy and Business
IGAWA, K., International Economy and Business
ISOBE, T., International Economy and Business
IZAWA, H., International Economy and Business
KAMIHIGASHI, T., Information Economy and Business
KATAYAMA, S., International Economy and Business
KOJIMA, K., Information Economy and Business
KONISHI, Y., Information Economy and Business
LEE, H., Information Economy and Business
MIYAO, R., RIEB Liaison Centre
NISHIJIMA, S., International Economy and Business
NOBEOKA, K., RIEB Liaison Centre
SHIMOMURA, K., Information Economy and Business
TOMITA, M., International Economy and Business
YAMAJI, H., Information Economy and Business

Graduate School of Humanities and Social Sciences (1-1 Rokkodai-cho, Nada-ku, Kobe 657-8501; tel. (78) 803-5591; fax (78) 803-5589; e-mail lsoumo@lit.kobe-u.ac.jp; internet www.lit.kobe-u.ac.jp/index_bunka.html):

IWASAKI, N., Theory of Social Risks

Graduate School of Cultural Studies and Human Science (3-1-1 Tsurukabuto, Nada-ku, Kobe 657-8501; tel. (78) 803-7905; fax (78) 803-7939; e-mail inkouhou@ccs.cla.kobe-u.ac.jp; internet www.cla.kobe-u.ac.jp/sojinka):

HARIMA, T., Clinical Psychology
HOUNOKI, K., Human and Community Empowerment
KAWABATA, T., Human and Community Empowerment
SUEMOTO, M., Human and Community Empowerment

Graduate School of International Co-operation Studies (2-1 Rokkodai-cho, Nada-ku, Kobe 657-8501; tel. (78) 803-7265; fax (78) 803-7295; e-mail kokusomu@ofc.kobe-u.ac.jp; internet www.kobe-u.ac.jp/~gsics/indexj.html):

ALEXANDER, R. B., Endogenous Security
CHEN, K., Economic Development and Regional Inequality
FUKUI, S., Development Microeconomics
IGARASHI, M., International Law
KATAYAMA, Y., Political Development in Southeast Asia
KIMURA, K., Nation-Building and State Formation in Korea
MATSUNAMI, J., Comparative Study on Deregulation, Privatization and Local Government
MATSUNAGA, N., International Trade and Economic Growth
MIZUNO, T., Review and Future Assessment on International Issues
NISHINA, K., Development Finance
OHTA, H., Applied Microeconomics
SHIBATA, A., International Law

SURUGA, T., Economic Development and Employment
TAKADA, H., Local Public Administration and Finance
TAKAHASHI, M., African Economics
TATEBAYASHI, M., Policy Activities of Political Elites in Japan
TOSA, H., Critical Theory and its Application in International Relations
UCHIDA, Y., Social Sector Management in Developing Countries
UENO, H., Transition Economy Policies

Graduate School of Science and Technology (tel. (78) 803-5332; fax (78) 803-5349; e-mail drkikaku@ofc.kobe-u.ac.jp; internet www.scitec.kobe-u.ac.jp/English/index.html):

ABE, S., Function Control
ARAI, T., Information Mathematics
ASAKURA, Y., Space Formation Engineering
BOKU, S., Environmental Science of Bioresource Production
FUKUDA, H., Applied Molecular Assembly
KANAZAWA, Y., Bioresource and Energy Creation
KATO, S., Material Production Process Engineering
KITAGAWA, H., Relational Biosystems
KOJIMA, F., Structural Design
MAEKAWA, S., Bioinformation
MATSUSHITA, T., Fire Safety Engineering, Thermal Environmental Engineering in Building
MIYAKE, M., Biosystem Applications
MUKAI, T., Space and Planetary Materials
NAKAYAMA, A., Regional Environment
NANBA, T., Material Functions
NOUMI, M., Mathematical Structures
NOZAKI, M., Material Structures
ODANI, M., Urban Transportation Planning, Urban and Regional Planning
OHKAWA, T., Intelligent Bioinformatics
ONO, M., Food Marketing
SASAKI, M., Organic Chemistry
TABUCHI, M., Creation of Spatial Systems
TAKEDA, M., Molecular Cellular Science
TAKEUCHI, T., Molecular Structure and Function
TANAKA, S., Theoretical Life Science and Computational Molecular Biology
TAURA, T., Intelligent Artificial Systems
TSUBAKI, M., Functional Molecular Assembly
TSUTAHARA, M., Biological Resource Utilization
UEHARA, K., Media Technology and its Production
YAMANAKA, M., Earth Sciences

Biosignal Research Center (tel. (78) 803-5332; fax (78) 803-5972; e-mail drkikaku@ofc.kobe-u.ac.jp; internet inherit:biosig.kobe-u.ac.jp/biosignal/english/index.html):

KIKKAWA, U., Biochemistry
ONO, Y., Biology of Living Functions
SAITO, N., Pharmacology
YONEZAWA, K., Biochemistry

Research Institute for Higher Education (1-2-1- Tsurukabuto, Nada-ku, Kobe 657-8501; tel. (78) 803-7522; fax (78) 803-7539; e-mail dakaikei@ofc.kobe-u.ac.jp; internet www.kurihe.kobe-u.ac.jp):

KAWASHIMA, T., Sociology of Education
MAIYA, K., Experimental Psychology
YAMANOUCHI, K., Sociology of Education

Research Center for Inland Seas (tel. (78) 803-5761; fax (78) 803-5770; e-mail rishomu@ofc.kobe-u.ac.jp; internet www.kobe-u.ac.jp/kurcis):

HYODO, M., Earth Science
KAWAI, H., Marine Biology
NAGATA, S., Environmental Biochemistry

Research Center for Urban Safety and Security (tel. (78) 803-6437; fax (78) 803-6394; e-mail rcuss@kobe-u.ac.jp; internet www.kobe-u.ac.jp/~tosi):

ARIKI, Y., Media Engineering
IIZUKA, A., Geo-environmental Engineering and Geoinformatics
ISHIBASHI, K., Seismotectonics
KAMAE, I., Health Informatics and Decision Sciences
OKIMURA, T., Slope Stability and Geotechnical Engineering
TANAKA, Y., Soft Ground Engineering and Earthquake Geotechnical Engineering

International Student Center (tel. (78) 803-5265; fax (78) 803-5289; e-mail ryugaku@ofc.kobe-u.ac.jp; internet www.kobe-u.ac.jp/~kisc):

NAKANISHI, Y., Education in Japanese Language
SEGUCHI, I., Intercultural and Transcultural Education

Medical Center for Student Health (tel. (78) 803-5245; fax (78) 803-5254; e-mail healthy@kobe-u.ac.jp; internet www.kobe-u.ac.jp/medicalc):

BABA, H., Internal Medicine, Biosignal Pathophysiology

Research Center for Environmental Genomics (tel. (78) 803-5332; fax (78) 803-5349; e-mail drkikaku@ofc.kobe-u.ac.jp; internet www.rceg.biosig.kobe-u.ac.jp/hpj.html):

FUKAMI, Y., Biology of Living Structures
NANMORI, T., Plant Molecular Biology
OONO, K., Plant Cell Biology

Molecular Photoscience Research Center (tel. (78) 803-5761; fax (78) 803-5770; e-mail rishomu@ofc.kobe-u.ac.jp; internet www.kobe-u.ac.jp/mprc):

OHTA, H., Condensed Matter Physics
TOMINAGA, K., Condensed Phase Dynamics

School of Languages and Communication (1-2-1 Tsurukabuto, Nada-ku, Kobe 657-8501; tel. (78) 803-7522; fax (78) 803-7539; e-mail dakaikei@ofc.kobe-u.ac.jp; internet solac.cla.kobe-u.ac.jp):

GREER, T., Conversation Analysis, Applied Linguistics, Bilingualism
IGUCHI, J., Applied Linguistics
ISHIKAWA, S., Applied Linguistics
KASHIWAGI, H., English Language Education
KATO, M., English Education
MASUDA, Y., German Linguistics
MIKI, Y., European Maritime Culture
MURATA, R., The Later Enlightenment in German
NAKAGAWA, M., Contrastive Linguistics
OKIHARA, K., Applied Linguistics and English Language Education
SHIMAZU, A., American Literature
TSUJIMOTO, Y., British Journalism of the 18th and 19th c.
URITA, S., English Literature
YOKOKAWA, H., Psycholinguistics
ZHU, C., Phonetics and Foreign Language Education

KUMAMOTO UNIVERSITY

39-1 Kurokami 2-chome, Kumamoto-shi 860-8555
Telephone: (96) 344-2111
Fax: (96) 342-3110
E-mail: message@svml.jimu.kumamoto-u.ac.jp
Internet: www.kumamoto-u.ac.jp
Founded 1949
Independent
Academic year: April to March (two terms)
President: Dr TATSURO SAKIMOTO
Director of Administration Bureau: MASAHARU CHOKI
Vice-Presidents: Prof. TOMOMICHI ONO, Prof. CHUICHI HIRAYAMA, Prof. CHIUCHI HIRAYAMA
Librarian: Prof. NAKAMASA IWAOKA
Number of teachers: 1,022
Number of students: 9,836
Publications: *Kumamoto Journal of Culture and Humanities* (annually), *Kumamoto Law Review* (4 a year), *Kumamoto Journal of Mathematics* (annually), *Kumamoto Journal of Science (Earth Sciences)* (annually), *Memoirs of the Faculty of Engineering* (2 a year), *Physics Report of Kumamoto University* (every 2 years), *Cryogenics Report of the Shockwave and Condensed Matter Research Center* (annually), *Kumamoto University Studies in Social and Cultural Sciences* (annually)

DEANS

Faculty of Letters: Prof. MASATO MORI
Faculty of Education: Prof. SHOICHI ISHIHARA
Faculty of Law: Prof. YATARO YOSHINAGA
Faculty of Science: Prof. MITSUHIKO KOHNO
Faculty of Medical and Pharmaceutical Sciences: Prof. NOBUO SAKAGUCHI
Faculty of Engineering: Prof. ISAO TANIGUCHI
School of Law: Prof. ITARU YAMANAKA
Graduate School of Science and Technology: Prof. KATSUHIKO SUGAWARA
Graduate School of Social and Cultural Sciences: Prof. YASUTOSHI YUKAWA

PROFESSORS

Faculty of Letters (40-1 Kurokami 2-chome, Kumamoto 860-8555; tel. (96) 342-2313; fax (96) 342-2310; e-mail bun-somu@jimu.kumamoto-u.ac.jp; internet www.let.kumamoto-u.ac.jp/let/index.html):

FUKAHORI, K., German Literature
FUKUZAWA, K., Linguistics
HOHGETSU, T., Geography
IHARA, S., Japanese Language
IKEDA, M., Cultural Anthropology and Medical Humanities
KAMIMURA, N., German Language
KINOSHITA, N., Archaeology
KOMATSU, H., Cultural History
KOMOTO, M., Archaeology
KUMAMOTO, S., English Language
MARUYAMA, S., Regional Sociology
MORI, M., Japanese Literature
OGINO, K., German Language
OKABE, T., Aesthetics
OOKUMA, K., French Literature
SAKATA, M., German Literature
SHINOZAKI, S., Ethics
SUGITANI, K., German Literature
TAGUCHI, H., Sociology
TAKAHASHI, T., Ethics
TANAKA, Y., German Literature
TANIKAWA, N., English Literature
TERADA, M., French Literature
TOKUNO, S., Regional Sociology
TONE, T., Psychology
WATANABE, I., Psychology
YASUDA, M., Folklore
YOSHIKAWA, E., Chinese Language
YOSIMURA, T., Japanese History

Faculty of Education (40-1 Kurokami 2-chome, Kumamoto 860-8555; tel. (96) 342-2514; fax (96) 342-2510; e-mail kyo-somu@jimu.kumamoto-u.ac.jp; internet www.educ.kumamoto-u.ac.jp):

ASAKAWA, M., Food
BABA, K., Biology
CHIKUMA, Y., Educational Philosophy
FUKUSHIMA, K., Physics
HARADA, I., Electricity
HIGASHI, T., Electricity
HIRAMINE, Y., Algebra
HIRAWA, T., Vocal Music

HORIHATA, M., Japanese Linguistics
ICHIMURA, K., School Health
ISHIHARA, S., Sculpture
ITOH, J., Algebra
KAWAMINAMI, H., Teaching of Social Studies
KIMURA, M., School Health
KIYOZUMI, M., School Health
KOGA, N., Sociology
KUWAHATA, M., Teaching of Domestic Sciences
MAEDA, K., Teaching of Science
MASAMOTO, K., Biology
MIYAMOTO, M., Teaching of Social Studies
NAGATA, N., Teaching of School Health
NAKATA, Y., Educational Administration
NAKAYAMA, T., Theory and History of Music
NISHIKAWA, M., English Linguistics
OGATA, A., Psychology of Handicapped Children
OGAWA, K., Japanese Literature
OGO, K., Exercise and Hygiene
SHIBAYAMA, K., Clinical Psychology
SHIN, K., Education of Handicapped Children
SHINOHARA, H., Educational Psychology
SUGI, S., Teaching of Japanese
SUGOU, H., History of Handicraft Education
SUZUKI, R., English and American Literature
SUZURIKAWA, S., Social Welfare
TAKAGI, N., Teaching of English
TAKAMORI, H., Clothing
TANIGUCHI, K., Physiology of Exercise
TODA, T., English Linguistics
TORIKAI, K., Home Management
TSURUSHIMA, H., History
TSUZINO, T., Mechanics
UMEDA, M., Design and Crafts
WATANABE, K., Earth Science
YAMAMOTO, S., Teaching of Mathematics
YAMANAKA, M., Economics
YANAGI, H., Educational Sociology
YOKOYAMA, S., Geography
YONEMURA, K., Clinical Medicine and Nursing
YOSHIDA, M., Group Dynamics
YOSHIKAWA, N., Theory and History of Art
YOSHINAGA, S., Teaching of Music

Faculty of Law (40-1 Kurokami 2-chome, Kumamoto 860-8555; tel. (96) 342-2315; fax (96) 342-2310; e-mail jsj-somu@jimu.kumamoto-u.ac.jp; internet www.law.kumamoto-u.ac.jp):

FUKAMATI, K., International Law
HAYASHI, I., International Law
INADA, T., Criminal Procedure
ITO, H., Politics
IWAOKA, N., Politics
KAWAMOTO, T., English Literature
KITAGAWA, K., Philosophy
KIZAKI, Y., Civil Law
MORI, M., German Literature
NAKAMURA, N., Philosophy of Law
OHSAWA, H., Politics
SATO, M., Economic Policy
SUZUKI, K., Politics
WAKASONE, K., European Legal History
YAMASHITA, T., Economics
YAMAZAKI, K., Tax Law
YOSHIDA, I., Sociology of Law
YOSHINAGA, Y., Social Law

Faculty of Science (39-1 Kurokami 2-chome, Kumamoto 860-8555; tel. (96) 342-3314; fax (96) 342-3320; e-mail rig-some@jimu.kumamoto-u.ac.jp; internet www.sci.kumamoto-u.ac.jp/index.html):

ABE, S. I., Developmental Biology
ANIYA, M., Fundamental Physics
ARAI, K., Fundamental Physics
FUJII, A., Solid State Spectroscopy
FURUSHIMA, M., Algebra and Geometry
HAMANA, Y., Probability Theory
HASE, Y., Palaeobotany and Environmental Science
HARAOKA, Y., Analysis and Applied Analysis
HASEGAWA, S., Palaeontology and Environmental Science
HASENAKA, T., Volcanology and Igneous Petrology
ICHIKAWA, F., Superconductivity
ICHIMURA, K., Physical Chemistry
IMAFUKU, K., Organic Chemistry
ISHIDA, A., Dynamics of Environments
ITOH, K., Magnetic Thin Films
KIMURA, H., Analysis and Applied Analysis
KOBAYASHI, O., Algebra and Geometry
KOHNO, M., Analysis and Applied Analysis
MATSUMOTO, N., Inorganic Chemistry
MATSUSAKA, T., Dynamics of Environments
MATSUZAKI, S., Physical Chemistry
MITSUNAGA, M., Quantum Optics
MOMOSHIMA, N., Environmental Analysis
MOTOYOSHI, A., Fundamental Physics
NISHINO, H., Organic Chemistry
NISHIYAMA, T., Petrology, Mineralogy and Geodynamics
NOHDA, S., Environmental Analysis
OHWAKI, S., Integrated Mathematics
SAKAMOTO, N., Polymer Chemistry
SANEMASA, I., Environmental Analysis
SHIBUYA, H., Palaeomagnetism and Geodynamics
SHIMADA, J., Groundwater Circulation
SHIODA, M., Molecular Cell Biology
TANI, T., Molecular Biology
UCHINO, A., Dynamics of Environments
WATANABE, A., Algebra and Geometry
YAMAKI, H., Algebra and Geometry
YOSHIASA, A., Geodynamics and Condensed Matter Physics

Faculty of Medical and Pharmaceutical Sciences (1-1 Honjo 1-chome, Kumamoto 860-8556; tel. (96) 373-5904; fax (96) 373-5906; e-mail iys-somu@jimu.kumamoto-u.ac.jp; internet www.medphas.kumamoto-u.ac.jp):

ARAKI, E., Metabolic Medicine
EKINO, S., Histology
ENDO, F., Paediatrics
FUTATUKA, M., Public Health
GOTO, M., Structure-Function Physical Chemistry
HARADA, S., Medical Virology
HARANO, K., Computational Molecular Design
HORIUCHI, S., Medical Biochemistry
IMAI, T., Drug Metabolism and Disposition
INOMATA, Y., Paediatric Surgery
IRIE, T., Clinical Chemistry and Informatics
ITO, T., Pathology and Experimental Medicine
KAI, H., Molecular Medicine
KAMASUJI, M., Cardiovascular Surgery
KIKAWA, K., General Medicine
KINOSHITA, Y., Aggressology and Critical Care Medicine
KITAMURA, T., Clinical Behavioural Sciences
KODAMA, K., Anatomy
KURATSU, J., Neurosurgery
MIIKE, T., Child Development
MITSUYA, H., Haematology
MITSUYAMA, S., Pharmacology and Molecular Therapeutics
MIURA, R., Molecular Enzymology
MIYATA, T., Chemico-Pharmacological Sciences
MIZUSHIMA, T., Pharmaceutical Microbiology
MORI, M., Molecular Genetics
NAKAGAWA, K., Pharmacology and Therapeutics
NAKAJIMA, M., Organic Chemistry
NAKANISHI, H., Molecular Pharmacology
NAKAYAMA, H., Molecular Cell Function
NISHIMURA, Y., Immunogenetics
NOHARA, T., Natural Medicines
OGAWA, H., Sensory and Cognitive Physiology
OGAWA, H., Cardiovascular Medicine
OHTSUKA, M., Bioorganic Medicinal Chemistry
OKABE, H., Diagnostic Medicine
OKAMURA, H., Reproductive Medicine and Surgery
OTAGIRI, M., Biopharmaceutics
SAITO, H., Pharmacy
SAKAGUCHI, N., Immunology
SASAKI, Y., Gastroenterology and Hepatology
SAYA, H., Tumour Genetics and Biology
SHIGA, K., Molecular Physiology
SHINOHARA, M., Oral and Maxillofacial Surgery
SHOJI, S., Pharmaceutical Biochemistry
TAKAHAMA, K., Environmental and Molecular Health Sciences
TAKEYA, M., Cell Pathology
TANAKA, H., Developmental Neurobiology
TANIHARA, H., Ophthalmology and Visual Science
TERASAKI, H., Anaesthesiology
TOMITA, K., Nephrology
TSUNENARI, S., Forensic Medicine
UCHINO, M., Neurology
UEDA, M., Pharmaceutical Microbiology
UEDA, S., Urology
UEKAMA, K., Physical Pharmaceutics
UNO, T., Analytical and Biophysical Chemistry
YAMAGATA, Y., Structural Biology
YAMAMOTO, T., Molecular Pathology
YAMASHITA, Y., Diagnostic Imaging
YOSHIHARA, H., Medical Informatics
YUMOTO, E., Otolaryngology – Head and Neck Surgery

Faculty of Engineering (39-1 Kurokami 2-chome, Kumamoto 860-8555; tel. (96) 342-3513; fax (96) 342-3510; internet www.eng.kumamoto-u.ac.jp/english/index.htm):

AKIYAMA, H., Electrical Energy System
EBIHARA, K., Electrical Energy Systems
FURUKAWA, K. Water Environmental Engineering
GOTO, M., Bio-related Molecular Science
HARADA, H., Intelligent Systems Engineering
HIROE, T., High Pressure Science and Materials Processing
HIROSE, T., Biochemical Engineering
IHARA, H., Bio-related Molecular Science
IKEGAMI, T., Advanced Technology of Electrical and Computer Systems
IKUNO, H., Electronic and Communication Systems
IMURA, H., Thermal and Fluid Energy Systems
INOUE, T., Electronic and Communication Systems
ISHIHARA, O., Regional Planning and Management
IWAI, Z., Intelligent Systems for Measurement and Control
JYO, A., Chemistry of Molecular Engineering
KASHIWAGI, H., Intelligent Systems for Measurement and Control
KAWAJI, S., Computer Science and Engineering
KAWAMURA, Y., Advanced Materials Technology
KITANO, T., Regional Planning and Management
KITAZANO, Y., Water Environmental Engineering
KOBAYASHI, I., Water Environmental Engineering
KURODA, N., Advanced Materials Technology

MACHIDA, M., Chemistry for Molecular Engineering
MAKINO, Y., Architectural Planning and Design
MAZDA, T., Structural Engineering
MITA, N., Advanced Technology of Electrical and Computer Systems
MITSUI, Y., Architectural Planning and Design
MIYAHARA, K., Electronic and Communication Systems
MIZOKAMI, S., Disaster Prevention Engineering
MOROZUMI, M., Regional Planning and Management
MURAYAMA, N., Advanced Technology of Electrical and Computer Systems
NAITOU, K., Mathematical Science
NAKAMURA, R., Intelligent Systems Engineering
NAKAMURA, Y., Advanced Technology of Electrical and Computer Systems
NISHIDA, M., Advanced Materials Technology
NONAKA, T., Chemistry for Material Science
OBARA, Y., Geotechnical Engineering
ODA, I., Intelligent Machine Design and Manufacturing
OGAWA, K., Architectural Planning and Design
OHMOTO, T., Water Environmental Engineering
OHNO, Y., Materials Development Systems
OHTANI, J., Water Environmental Engineering
OSHIMA, Y., Mathematical Science
SADATOMI, M., Thermal and Fluid Energy Systems
SAISHO, M., Disaster Prevention Engineering
SAKURADA, K., Disaster Prevention Engineering
SATONAKA, S., Intelligent Machine Design and Manufacturing
SHOSENJI, H., Chemistry for Molecular Engineering
SUEYOSHI, T., Computer Science and Engineering
SUZUKI, A., Geotechnical Engineering
TAKADA, Y., Mathematical Science
TANIGUCHI, I., Biorelated Molecular Science
TONDA, H., Materials Development Systems
TORII, S., Intelligent Machine Design and Manufacturing
UCHIYAMA, O., Architectural Planning and Design
UMENO, H., Computer Science and Engineering
USAGAWA, T., Intelligent Systems Engineering
WATANABE, J., Thermal and Fluid Energy Systems
YAMAO, T., Structural Engineering
YANO, T., Structural Engineering
YASUI, H., Intelligent Machine Design and Manufacturing
YOKOI, Y., Mathematical Science

Graduate School of Social and Cultural Sciences (40-1 Kurokami 2-chome, Kumamoto 860-8555; tel. (96) 342-2313; fax (96) 342-2130; e-mail bun-somu@jimu.kumamoto-u.ac.jp; internet www.let.kumamoto-u.ac.jp/gsscs/index_e.html):

YAMANAKA, S., Geography
YUKAWA, Y., Linguistics

Graduate School of Science and Technology (39-1 Kurokami 2-chome, Kumamoto 860-8555; tel. (96) 342-3013; fax (96) 342-3010; e-mail dcjimu@gpo.kumamoto-u.ac.jp; internet 133.95.161.1/index-en.html):

HASEGAWA, S., Natural Environmental Sciences
HIYAMA, T., Energy Systems
ICHIMURA, K., Basic Chemistry and Physics for Materials Sciences
IKI, K., Human-Environmental Engineering
ISHITOBI, M., Intelligent Manufacturing Systems
KAWAHARA, M., Materials Science and Technology
KIDA, K., Applied Chemistry for Materials and Life Sciences
MATSUMOTO, Y., Applied Chemistry of Materials
OHBA, H., Mechanical Systems Design
OHTSU, M., Disaster-Preventive Structural Engineering
OKUNO, Y., Electrical and Computer Engineering
SUGAWARA, K., Environmental Conservation Engineering
UCHIMURA, K., Intelligent Systems and Computer Science
YAMAKI, H., Mathematics
YOSHITAMA, K., Bioinformational Science

School of Law (40-1 Kurokami 2-chome, Kumamoto 860-8555; tel. (96) 342-2315; fax (96) 342-2310; e-mail jsj-somu@jimu.kumamoto-u.ac.jp; internet www.kumamoto-ua.ac.jp/lawschool):

FUKUYAMA, M., Law
HARADA, T., Law
HASHIMOTO, M., Civil Law
HAYASHI, M., Local Government Law
HIRATA, H., Criminal Procedure
ISHIBASHI, H., Social Law
KUBOTA, M., Commercial Law
MATSUBARA, H., Civil Procedure Law
NAKAGAWA, Y., Administrative Law
NAKAMURA, S., Criminal Law
ONO, Y., Civil Law
ONODERA, M., Prosecutor
SAWATARI, K., Law
TADA, N., International Private Law
YAMAMOTO, E., Constitutional Law
YAMANAKA, I., Legal Theory and History

Center for Multimedia and Information Technologies (39-1 Kurokami 2-chome, Kumamoto 860-8555; tel. (96) 342-3824; fax (96) 342-3829; internet www.cc.kumamoto-u.ac.jp):

IRIGUCHI, N.
NAKANO, Y.
SUGITANI, K.

Co-operative Research Center (2081-7 Tabaru, Mashiki-machi, Kumamoto 861-2202; tel. (96) 286-1212; fax (96) 286-1067; internet www.kcr.kumamoto-u.ac.jp/index-j.html):

HIROSUE, H., Liaison between University and Industry
MATSUSHITA, H., Technology Transfer between University and Industry

Institute of Resource Development and Analysis (2-2-1 Honjo, Kumamoto 860-0811; tel. (96) 373-6637; fax (96) 373-6638; e-mail iys-senter@jimu.kumamoto-u.ac.jp):

NAKAGATA, N., Reproductive Engineering
URANO, T., Microbiology and Genetics
YAMADA, G., Transgenic Technology

International Student Center (40-1 Kurokami 2-chome, Kumamoto 860-8555; tel. (96) 342-2133; fax (96) 342-2130; e-mail gji-ryugaku@jimu.kumamoto-u.ac.jp; internet center.ryu.kumamoto-u.ac.jp/index_e.html):

KOWAKI, M., Linguistics (Semitic Languages)

Center for AIDS Research (2-1 Honjo 2-chome, Kumamoto 860-0811; tel. (96) 373-6531; fax (96) 373-6532; internet www.caids.kumamoto-u.ac.jp):

MATSUSHITA, S., Clinical Retrovirology and Infectious Diseases
OKADA, S., Haematopoiesis
TAKIGUCHI, M., Viral Immunology

Shock Wave and Condensed Matter Research Center (39-1 Kurokami 2-chome, Kumamoto 860-8555; tel. (96) 342-3299; fax (96) 342-3293; internet www.shocomarec.kumamoto-u.ac.jp):

FUJII, A., Division of Low Temperature Science
ITO, S., Division of Shock Processing and its Applications
KUBOTA, H., Division of Solid State Physics under Multi-Extreme Conditions

Institute of Molecular Embryology and Genetics (24-1 Kuhonji 4-chome, Kumamoto 862-0976; tel. (96) 344-2111; fax (96) 373-6638; e-mail imeg@kaiju.medic.kumamoto-u.ac.jp; internet www.imeg.kumamoto-u.ac.jp):

KUME, S., Stem Cell Biology
NAGAFUCHI, A., Cellular Interactions
NAKAO, M., Organ Development
NISHINAKAMURA, R., Integrative Cell Biology
OGURA, T., Molecular Cell Biology
OGAWA, M., Cell Differentiation
OKUBO, H., Molecular Neurobiology
SHIMAMURA, K., Morphogenesis
TAGA, T., Cell Fate Modulation
YAMAIZUMI, M., Cell Genetics
YAMAMURA, K., Developmental Genetics
YOKOUCHI, Y., Pattern Formation

Research Center for Lifelong Learning (40-1 Kurokami 2-chome, Kumamoto 860-8555; tel. (96) 342-3281; fax (96) 342-3281; e-mail sos-tiiki@kumamoto-u.ac.jp; internet www.lifelong.kumamoto-u.ac.jp):

SAGA, T., Philosophy, Bio-ethics
UENO, S., Political Science
YANAGI, H., Educational Sociology

Center for Marine Environment Studies (39-1 Kurokami, 2-chome, Kumamoto 860-8555; tel. (96) 342-3448; fax (96) 342-3448; internet www.engan.dc.kumamoto-u.ac.jp/index.html):

HENMI, Y., Analysis of Cyclization Systems for Natural Resources
TAKIKAWA, K., Hydro- and Geosphere Environments
TAKIO, S., Conservation and Development of Natural Resources

Research Center for Higher Education (40-1 Kurokami 2-chome, Kumamoto 860-8555; tel. (96) 342-2716; fax (96) 342-2710; e-mail gak-kyomu@jimu.kumamoto-u.ac.jp; internet www.ge.kumamoto-u.ac.jp):

OHMORI, F., Education Policy
SUGAWARA, T., Educational Evaluation
YAMADA, M., Advanced and Applied Education of European History

ATTACHED RESEARCH INSTITUTES

Center for Multimedia and Information Technologies: Dir TSUYOSHI USAGAWA.

Co-operative Research Center: Dir Prof. HIROYOSHI IKUNO.

Institute of Resource Development and Analysis: Dir HIDEYUKI SAYA.

International Study Center: Dir Prof. TAKASHI HIYAMA.

Center for AIDS Research: Dir Prof. MASAFUMI TAKIGUCHI.

Shock Wave and Condensed Matter Research Center: Dir Prof. SHIGERU ITOH.

Institute of Molecular Embryology and Genetics: Dir Prof. TETSUYA TAGA.

Research Center for Lifelong Learning: Dir Prof. HARUO YANAGI.

Center for Marine Environmental Studies: Dir Prof. AKINORI UCHINO.

Research Center for Higher Education: Dir Prof. YOSHITAKA HASE.

KYOTO INSTITUTE OF TECHNOLOGY

Hashigami-cho, Matsugasaki, Sakyo-ku, Kyoto 606-8585
Telephone: (75) 724-7111
Fax: (75) 724-7010
E-mail: webmaster@adm.kit.ac.jp
Internet: www.kit.ac.jp/index.html
Founded 1949
Independent
Academic year: April to March
President: YOSIMITI EJIMA
Vice-Presidents: SATOSHI HIRAYAMA, KATSUHIKO YAMAGUCHI
Director-General: KIMIO MURAMATSU
Librarian: SHIGEYUKI YAMAGUCHI
Library of 363,140 vols
Number of teachers: 317
Number of students: 4,327
Publications: *Memoirs of the Faculty of Engineering and Design – JINBUN* (Series of Science and Technology, annually), *Bulletin of the Faculty of Textile Science* (annually)

DEANS

Faculty of Engineering and Design: RIKUO OTA
Faculty of Textile Science: SHIGERU KUNUGI

KYOTO UNIVERSITY

Yoshida-Honmachi, Sakyo-ku, Kyoto 606-8501
Telephone: (75) 753-7531
E-mail: koryu52@mail.adm.kyoto-u.ac.jp
Internet: www.kyoto-u.ac.jp
Founded 1897
Independent
Academic year: April to March
President: KAZUO OIKE
Vice-Presidents: AKIHIRO KINDA, HIROHISA HIGASHIYAMA, KOJIRO IRIKURA, MASAO HOMMA, SHIGEAKI TANAKA, BUNZO TSUJI
Library: see Libraries and Archives
Number of teachers: 2,911
Number of students: 22,192
Publication: Publications include faculty memoirs and reviews

DEANS

Graduate School of Agriculture and Faculty of Agriculture: S. YAZAWA
Graduate School of Asian and African Area Studies: M. ICHIKAWA
Graduate School of Biostudies: M. YANAGIDA
Graduate School of Economics and Faculty of Economics: S. NISHIMURA
Graduate School of Education and Faculty of Education: Y. KAWASAKI
Graduate School of Energy Science: M. KASAHARA
Graduate School of Engineering and Faculty of Engineering: M. ARAKI
Graduate School of Global Environmental Studies: M. NAITO
Graduate School of Human and Environmental Studies and Faculty of Integrated Human Studies: H. TOMITA
Graduate School of Informatics: M. FUNAKOSHI
Graduate School of Law and Faculty of Law: S. MORIMOTO
Graduate School of Letters and Faculty of Letters: J. FUJII
Graduate School of Medicine and Faculty of Medicine: T. HONJO
Graduate School of Pharmaceutical Sciences and Faculty of Pharmaceutical Sciences: M. HASHIDA
Graduate School of Science and Faculty of Science: N. SASAO
Law School: Y. NAKAMORI

PROFESSORS

Graduate School of Agriculture and Faculty of Agriculture (Kitashirakawa, Oiwake-cho, Sakyo, Kyoto, 606-8502; tel. (75) 753-6490; fax (75) 753-6020; internet www.kais.kyoto-u.ac.jp):

ADACHI, S., Bioengineering
AOYAMA, S., Agricultural Facility Engineering
AZUMA, J., Forest Biochemistry
ENDO, T., Plant Genetics
FUJISAKI, K., Insect Ecology
FUJITA, M., Structure of Plant Cells
FUJIWARA, T., Fisheries Oceanography
FUSHIKI, T., Nutrition Chemistry
FUTAI, K., Environmental Mycoscience
HIRATA, T., Marine Bioproducts Technology
HIROOKA, H., Animal Science
HORIE, T., Crop Science
IMAI, H., Animal Reproduction
INOUYE, K., Enzyme Chemistry
IWAI, Y., Forest Resources and Society
KAGATSUME, M., Regional Environmental Economics
KANO, K., Bioelectroanalytical Chemistry
KAWACHI, T., Water Resources Engineering
KAWADA, T., Food Biochemistry
KITA, K., Bioenergy Conversion
KITABATAKE, N., Food and Environmental Science
KOSAKI, T., Soil Science
KUME, S., Environmental Physiology
MATSUMOTO, T., Fibrous Biomaterials
MATSUMURA, Y., Quality Analysis and Assessment
MITSUNO, T., Irrigation, Drainage and Hydrological Environment Engineering
MIYAGAWA, H., Bioregulation Chemistry
MIZUYAMA, T., Erosion Control
MORIMOTO, Y., Landscape Architecture
MURATA, K., Molecular Biotechnology
NAKAHARA, H., Marine Microbial Ecology
NAKATSUBO, F., Chemistry of Biomaterials
NIIYAMA, Y., Farm Management
NISHIDA, R., Chemical Ecology
NISHIO, Y., Chemistry of Composite Materials
NISHIOKA, T., Biofunction Chemistry
NOBUCHI, T., Forest Utilization
NODA, K., Comparative Agricultural History
ODA, S., Farm Management Information and Accounting
OHIGASHI, H., Organic Chemistry in Life Science
OHNISHI, O., Crop Evolution
OHTA, S., Tropical Forest Resources and Environments
OIDA, A., Agricultural Systems Engineering
OKUMURA, S., Wood Processing
OKUNO, T., Plant Pathology
SAKO, Y., Marine Microbiology
SAKUMA, M., Behavioural Physiology and Chemical Ecology of Insects
SAKURATANI, T., Tropical Agriculture
SASAKI, Y., Animal Breeding and Genetics
SEKIYA, J., Plant Nutrition
SHIMIZU, S., Fermentation Physiology and Applied Microbiology
SUEHARA, T., Principles of Agricultural Science
TAKAFUJI, A., Ecological Information
TAKEBE, T., Agricultural and Environmental Policy
TAKEDA, H., Forest Ecology
TANAKA, M., Fish Biology
TANI, M., Forest Hydrology
TANISAKA, T., Plant Breeding
TOMINAGA, T., Weed Ecology
UEDA, K., Cellular Biochemistry
UEDA, M., Biomacromolecular Chemistry
UMEDA, M., Field Robotics
UTSUMI, S., Food Quality Design and Development
YAMADA, T., Plant Production Management
YAMASUE, Y., Physiological Aspects of Agricultural Systems
YANO, H., Animal Nutrition
YAZAWA, S., Vegetable and Ornamental Horticulture
YONEMORI, K., Pomology
YOSHIDA, M., Forest Policy and Economics
YOSHIKAWA, M., Physiological Function of Food

Graduate School of Asian and African Area Studies (46 Shimoadachi-cho, Yoshida, Sakyo-ku, Kyoto 606-8501; tel. (75) 753-7302; fax (75) 753-7350; e-mail soumu@cseas.kyoto-u.ac.jp; internet www.asafas.kyoto-u.ac.jp):

ADACHI, A., The Hindu World
ARAKI, S., Agricultural Ecology
HIRAMATSU, K., Natural Hisory
ICHIKAWA, M., Socio-Ecological History
KAJI, S., Culture and Ethnicity
KAKEYA, M., Livelihood and Economy
KOBAYASHI, S., Environmental Ecology
KOSUGI, Y., The Islamic World
OHTA, I., Nature–Human Interaction
SHIMADA, S., Socio-Cultural Integration
SUGISHIMA, T., Comparative Social Transformation

Graduate School of Biostudies:

INABA, K., Laboratory of Science Communication and Bioethics
INOUE, T., Laboratory of Gene Biodynamics
ISHIKAWA, F., Laboratory of Cell Cycle Regulation
KAKIZUKA, A., Laboratory of Functional Biology
KOCHI, T., Laboratory of Plant Molecular Biology
KOZUTUMI, Y., Laboratory of Membrane Biochemistry and Biophysics
MINATO, N., Laboratory of Immunology and Cell Biology
NAGAO, M., Laboratory of Biosignals and Response
NEGISHI, M., Laboratory of Molecular Neurobiology
NISHIDA, E., Laboratory of Signal Transduction
SATO, F., Laboratory of Molecular and Cellular Biology of Totipotency
TAKEYASU, K., Laboratory of Plasma Membrane and Nuclear Signalling
UEMURA, T., Laboratory of Cell Recognition and Pattern Formation
YAMAMOTO, K., Laboratory of Molecular Biology of Bioresponse
YONEHARA, S., Laboratory of Molecular and Cellular Biology

Graduate School of Economics and Faculty of Economics (tel. (75) 753-3400; fax (75) 753-3492; e-mail kyoumu@econ.kyoto-u.ac.jp; internet www.econ.kyoto-u.ac.jp):

FUJII, H., International Accounting
FURUKAWA, A., Money and Finance
HIOKI, K., Organization Theory
HISAMOTO, N., Labour Economics
HORI, K., Economic History
IMAKUBO, S., Economic Policy
IWAMOTO, T., International Economics
KAZUSA, Y., Managerial Accounting
KIJIMA, M., Financial Engineering
KOJIMA, H., Principles of Economics
MORIMUNE, K., Econometrics
MOTOYAMA, Y., World Economy
NARIU, T., Applied Economics
NEI, M., Modern Economics
NISHIMURA, S., Applied Economics
NISHIMUTA, Y., Business History
OHNISHI, H., Economic Statistics

OKADA, T., Regional Economy
SHIMOTANI, M., Japanese Economy
SHIOJI, H., Japanese Economy
TACHIBANAKI, T., Economic Policy
TANAKA, H., History of Social Thought
TAO, M., Business Policy
TOKUGA, Y., Accounting for Venture Business
UETA, K., Public Finance
UNI, H., Economic Theory
WAKABAYASHI, Y., Marketing
YAGI, K., Economic Theory
YAMAMOTO, H., Chinese Economy
YOSHIDA, K., Contemporary Economics

Graduate School of Education and Faculty of Education (tel. (75) 753-3010; fax (75) 753-3025; e-mail kyoumu@kyoumu.educ.kyoto-u.ac.jp; internet www.educ.kyoto-u.ac.jp):
FUJIWARA, K., Clinical Psychology
INAGAKI, K., Sociology of Education
ITOH, Y., Clinical Psychology
IWAI, H., Sociology of the Course of Life
KAWAI, T., Clinical Psychology
KAWASAKI, Y., Library and Information Science
KOYASU, M., Cognitive Psychology in Education
MAEHIRA, Y., Lifelong Education
OKADA, Y., Clinical Personality Psychology
SUGIMOTO, H., Comparative Education
SUZUKI, S., Pedagogy
TAKAMI, S., Educational Finance
TANAKA, K., Curriculum Development and Assessment
TSUJIMOTO, M., Japanese History of Education
YAMADA, Y., Developmental Psychology
YANO, S., Clinical Pedagogy
YOSHIKAWA, S., Cognitive Psychology in Education

Graduate School of Energy Science (tel. (75) 753-4871; fax (75) 753-4745; internet www.energy.kyoto-u.ac.jp/index-eng.html):
HOSHIDE, T., Fracture Mechanics for System Integrity
ISHIHARA, K., Social Engineering of Energy
ISHII, R., Space Energy and Resources
ISHIYAMA, T., Combustion Engine Technology
IWASE, M., Physical Chemistry of Iron- and Steelmaking and Related High-Temperature Processes
KASAHARA, M., Atmospheric Environmental Engineering
KONDO, K., Plasma Diagnostics
MABUCHI, M., Materials Science and Engineering
MAEKAWA, T., Plasma Physics
MATSUMOTO, E., Non-linear Continuum Mechanics
NOZAWA, H., Physics and Technology of VLSI
SAKA, S., Ecosystems of Biomass for Energy Use
SHIOJI, M., Combustion Science and Engineering
SHIOTSU, M., Thermal Hydraulics in Energy Systems
TAKUDA, H., Advanced Processing of Resources and Energy
TEZUKA, T., Energy Economics
YAO, T., Solid-State Energy Chemistry
YOSHIKAWA, H., Man–Machine Systems

Graduate School of Engineering and Faculty of Engineering:
AOKI, K., Rarefied Gas Dynamics
AOKI, K., Resources Development Engineering
AOYAMA, Y., Biorecognition
AOYAMA, Y., Urban and Regional Planning
ARAKI, M., Control Engineering
ASAKURA, T., Tunnel Engineering
ASHIDA, Y., Exploration Geophysics
AWAKURA, Y., Materials Electrochemistry
CHUJO, Y., Polymerization Chemistry
EGUCHI, K., Catalyst Science and Catalyst Design Engineering
FUJII, S., Division of Environmental Quality Control
FUKUYAMA, A., Basic Quantum Engineering
HAGIWARA, T., Automatic Control Engineering
HAMACHI, I., Bio-organic Chemistry
HASEBE, S., Process Systems Engineering
HAYASHI, Y., Disaster Risk Management of Built Environment
HIGASHITANI, K., Surface Control Engineering
HIGUCHI, T., Landscape and Environmental Planning
HIKIHARA, T., Power Conversion and Control Laboratory
HIRAO, K., Inorganic Structural Chemistry
HIYAMA, T., Organic Chemistry of Natural Products
HOJO, M., Continuum Mechanics
HOKOI, S., Thermal Analysis and Design
HOSODA, T., River Engineering
ICHIKAWA, A., Systems and Control
IEMURA, H., Earthquake Engineering
IMAHORI, H., Applied Molecular Science
IMANAKA, T., Biotechnology
INAMURO, T., Fluid Dynamics
INOUE, K., Space Development and Structural Systems
INOUE, M., Energy Conversion Chemistry
INUI, H., Intermetallic Alloys for Structural and Functional Uses
ISHIKAWA, J., Charged Particle Devices
ITO, S., Polymer Structure and Function
ITOH, A., Applied Beam Materials Engineering
ITOH, S., Urban Sanitary Engineering
KAKIUCHI, T., Functional Solution Chemistry
KATO, N., Architectural Information Systems
KAWAI, J., Process Chemical Physics
KIDA, S., Fluid Dynamics
KIMURA, K., Mesoscopic Materials Engineering
KIMURA, S., Design of Functional Materials
KITAGAWA, S., Functional Chemistry
KITAMURA, R., Transport Planning and Engineering
KITAMURA, T., Mechanical Behaviour of Materials
KITANO, M., Quantum Optical Engineering
KOBAYASHI, K., Civil Engineering Systems Analysis
KOBAYASHI, T., Biomedical Engineering
KOMORI, S., Fluids Engineering
KOTERA, H., Mechanical Systems
KUBO, A., Machine Design
MAE, K., Environmental Process Engineering
MAEDA, T., Theory for Architecture and Environmental Design
MAKI, T., Mechanical Properties of Steel
MAKINO, T., Thermophysical Properties of Materials
MASUDA, H., Powder Technology
MASUDA, T., Polymer Physics and Rheology
MATSUBARA, A., Precision Measurement and Machining
MATSUBARA, E., Structural Characterization by X-ray Diffraction
MATSUHISA, H., Vibration Engineering
MATSUMOTO, M., Wind Engineering
MATSUOKA, T., Engineering Geology
MATSUSHIGE, K., Molecular Nano-electronics
MITSUDO, T., Catalysis
MIYAHARA, M., Fluids Confined in Nano-space Order Formation by Nano-colloids
MIURA, K., Environmental Process Engineering
MIYAGAWA, T., Durability of Reinforced Concrete
MIYAZAKI, N., Computational Solid Mechanics
MONNAI, T., Architecture and Human Environmental Planning
MORI, Y., Molecular Biology
MORISAWA, S., Environmental Risk Analysis
MORISHIMA, N., Neutron Science
MORIYAMA, H., Nuclear Materials
MUNEMOTO, J., Architectural Planning
MURAKAMI, M., Thin Film Metallurgy
MURAKAMI, M., Organometallic Chemistry
NAGATA, M., Gas Dynamics
NAKATSUJI, H., Quantum Chemistry
NEZU, I., Fluid Mechanics and Hydraulics
NISHIMOTO, S., Excited-state Hydrocarbon Chemistry
NODA, S., Quantum Optoelectronics Engineering
OGUMI, Z., Electrochemistry
OHE, K., Organometallic Chemistry
OHNISHI, Y., Rock Mechanics
OHSAWA, Y., Electric Power System Engineering
OHSHIMA, M., Materials Process Engineering
OKA, F., Soil Mechanics
ONO, K., Propulsion Engineering
OSAMURA, K., Science of Materials
OSHIMA, K., Organic Reaction Chemistry
OTSUKA, K., Analytical Chemistry of Materials
SAITO, T., Mining and Rock Mechanics
SAKAI, T., Coastal Engineering
SAKAKI, S., Quantum Molecular Science and Technology
SAWAMOTO, M., Living Cationic Polymerization
SAWARAGI, T., Design Systems Engineering
SCAWTHORN, C., Natural Hazard Risk Management
SERIZAWA, A., Nuclear Reactor Engineering
SHIMA, S., Engineering Plasticity
SHIMASAKI, M., Computational Electromagnetic Field Analysis
SHIRAKAWA, M., Biophysical Chemistry
SUGIMURA, H., Nanoscopic Surface Architecture
SUGINOME, M., Organic Synthesis and System Design
SUZUKI, M., Integrated Function Engineering
TABATA, O., Micro Electro-Mechanical Systems
TACHIBANA, A., Quantum Theory of Condensed Matter
TACHIBANA, K., Plasma Physics and Technology
TAKADA, M., Housing and Environmental Design
TAKAHASHI, H., Architectural Design and Theory
TAKAHASHI, Y., History of Architecture
TAKAMATSU, S., Architectural Design
TAKAOKA, G., Ion Engineering, Cluster Science
TAKEDA, N., Solid Waste Management
TAKEWAKI, I., Earthquake Resistant Engineering
TAKIGAWA, T., Physics of Polymer Materials
TAMON, H., Separation Engineering
TAMURA, K., Structural Properties of Materials
TAMURA, M., Environmental Remote Sensing
TAMURA, T., Applied Mechanics
TANAKA, F., Polymer Core Physical Chemistry
TANAKA, H., Environmental Evaluation
TANAKA, I., Ceramic Materials Science
TANAKA, K., Inorganic Solid-State Chemistry
TANAKA, K., Molecular Energy Conservation

TANAKA, T., Molecular Science and Technology of Catalysis
TANIGUCHI, E., Urban Infrastructure Systems
TSUCHIYA, K., Dynamics and Control of Space Vehicles
TSUNO, H., Water Quality Conservation
UCHIYAMA, I., Environmental Health
UETANI, K., Mechanics of Building Structures
WADA, O., Circuit Theory and Applications
WATANABE, F., Reinforced and Pressed Concrete Structures
YAMAMOTO, K., Quantum Physics
YAMASHINA, H., Computer-integrated Manufacturing
YOSHIDA, H., Urban Environment and Safety Engineering
YOSHIDA, J., Organic Chemistry
YOSHIKAWA, T., Robotics
YOSHIMURA, M., Knowledge and Information Systems
YOSHIZAKI, T., Polymer Statistical Mechanics
YOSIDA, H., Thermal Systems Engineering

Graduate School of Global Environmental Studies (tel. (75) 753-9167; fax (75) 753-9187; internet www.adm.kyoto-u.ac.jp/ges):

KAMON, M., Environmental Infrastructure Engineering
KAWASAKI, M., Environmental Atmospheric Chemistry
KOBAYASHI, M., Global Environment Architecture
KOBAYASHI, S., Regional Planning
KOSAKI, T., Terrestrial Ecosystems Management
MATSUI, S., Environmentally Friendly Industries for Sustainable Development
MATSUOKA, Y., Global Integrated Assessment Modelling
MATSUSHITA, K., Global Environmental Policy
MIMURO, M., Environmental Biotechnology
MORIMOTO, Y., Landscape Ecology and Planning
NAKAHARA, H., Conservation of Coastal Ecosystems
OGAWA, T., Philosophical Theory of Human and Environmental Symbiosis
SHIBA, M., Circulation of Environmental Resources
TAKEBE, T., Global Resource Economics
TAMURA, R., Environmental Materials Science
UETA, K., Global Ecological Economics
YOKOYAMA, T., Towards a Theory of Global Civilization

Graduate School of Human and Environmental Studies (Yoshida Nihonmatsu-cho, Sakyo, Kyoto; tel. (75) 753-2950; fax (75) 753-2957; internet www.adm.kyoto-u.ac.jp/jinkan):

ADACHI, Y., Socio-Cultural Environments
ATSUJI, T., Chinese Linguistics
BECKER, C., Comparative Religion, Ethics, Death and Dying
EDA, K., History of Modern China
FUKUI, K., Cultural Anthropology of Ethiopia
FUKUOKA, K., American Literature
FUNAHASHI, S., Neurophysiology
HATTORI, F., Linguistics and Slavonic Languages
HORI, T., Natural Environments
INAGAKI, N., Modern French Literature
ISHIDA, A., Modern German Philology and Literature
ISHIHARA, A., Neurochemistry and Physiology
IYORI, T., Common Environmental System
KAMATA, H., Volcanology
KANASAKA, K., Human Societies
KATO, M., Co-existing Systems of Nature and Human Beings
KAWASHIMA, A., Modern British History
KIMURA, T., Russian Literature
KIWAMOTO, Y., Plasma Physics
KOYAMA, S., History of Japanese Education
KUJIRAOKA, T., Human Development
MAEGAWA, S., Low Temperature Magnetism
MAMIYA, Y., Common Environmental System
MARUHASHI, Y., English Drama
MATSUDA, K., History of Western Learning in Japan
MATSUI, M., Systematic Zoology
MATSUMARU, M., Neurophysiology
MATSUURA, S., History of North-Eastern Asia
MICHIHATA, T., German Literature
MIHARA, O., German Literature
MITANI, K., Slavic Linguistics
MIYAMOTO, Y., Polymer Physics
MORIMOTO, Y., Theory of Partial Differential Equations
MORITANI, T., Environmental Conservation and Development
MOTOKI, Y., Medieval History of Japan
MURANAKA, S., Solid State Chemistry
NAGAYA, M., History and Theory of Social Statistics
NAKANISHI, T., International Relations
NISHII, M., Environmental Conservation and Development
NISHIMURA, M., History of Western Law
NISHIWAKI, T., History of Chinese Philosophy
NISHIYAMA, R., Ancient History of Japan
NIWA, T., American Literature
OKADA, A., Art History and Criticism
OKADA, K., Pedagogy
OKI, M., Linguistics and French Language
ONO, S., Middle High German Literature
OTAGI, H., History of Medieval China
SAEKI, K., Social-environmental System
SAITO, H., Comparative Linguistics and German Language
SAKAGAMI, M., Gravity and Relativity
SHIKAYA, T., Philosophy of Aesthetics
SHIMADA, M., Contemporary History of the United States
SHINGU, K., Fundamental Human Ontology
SHINOHARA, M., Aesthetics and Philosophy
SUGAWARA, K., Social Anthropology and Communication
SUGIMAN, T., Group Dynamics
SUZUKI, M., 18th-Century English Culture and Literature
TAKAHASHI, Y., Environmental Conservation and Development
TAKASAKI, K., Algebraic Analysis and Mathematical Physics
TAMADA, O., Environmental Conservation and Development
TANABE, R., German Literature
TOGO, Y., French Linguistics
TOMIDA, Y., Philosophy and History of Philosophy
TOMITA, H., Statistical Physics
TORISSEN, E., Comparative Culture
TSUDA, K., Internal Medicine
UCHIDA, M., Grammar of the Japanese Language
USHIKI, S., Co-existing Systems of Nature and Human Beings
YAMADA, M., Urban Geography
YAMADA, T., Anthropology and Cognition, Shamanism and Ethnicity
YAMAGUCHI, R., Co-existing Systems of Nature and Human Beings
YAMAMOTO, Y., Organic Chemistry
YAMANASHI, M., Cognitive Linguistics
YASUI, K., Human Development
YODA, Y., Shakespeare

Graduate School of Informatics (tel. (75) 753-3599; fax (75) 753-5379; e-mail jimu-soumu@i.kyoto-u.ac.jp; internet www.i.kyoto-u.ac.jp):

EIHO, S., Image Processing Systems
FUJISAKA, H., Non-equilibrium Dynamics
FUKUSHIMA, M., Systems Optimization
FUNAKOSHI, M., Non-linear Dynamics
GOTOH, O., Bioinformatics
INUI, T., Cognitive Science
ISHIDA, T., Global Information Network
ISO, Y., Analysis of Inverse Problems
IWAI, T., Dynamical Systems Theory
IWAMA, K., Logic Circuits, Algorithms and Complexity Theory
KATAI, O., Symbiotic Systems
KATAYAMA, T., Control Systems Theory
KIGAMI, J., Nonlinear Analysis
KOBAYASHI, S., Biological Information
KUMAMOTO, H., Human Systems
MATSUDA, T., Biomedical Engineering
MATSUYAMA, T., Visual Information Processing
MORIHIRO, Y., Integrated-Media Communications
MORIYA, K., Bioresource Informatics
MUNAKATA, T., Physical Statistics
NAKAMURA, Y., Applied Mathematical Analysis
NAKAMURA, Y., Processor Architecture and Systems Synthesis
NISHIDA, T., Artificial Intelligence
NOGI, T., Fundamentals of Complex Systems
OKUNO, H. G., Speech Media Processing
ONODERA, H., Integrated Circuits Design Engineering
SAKAI, H., Mathematical Systems Theory
SAKAI, T., Environmental Informatics
SATO, M., Foundations of Software Science
SATO, T., Advanced Signal Processing
SUGIE, T., Mechanical Systems Control
TAKAHASHI, T., Intelligent Communication Networks
TAKAHASHI, Y., Information Systems
TANAKA, K., Digital Library
TOMITA, S., Computer Architecture
YAMAMOTO, A., Foundations of Artificial Intelligence
YAMAMOTO, Y., Intelligent and Control Systems
YOSHIDA, S., Digital Communications
YUASA, T., Computer Software

Graduate School of Law and Faculty of Law (fax (75) 753-3290; internet www.kyodai.jp/I-English.htm):

AKIZUKI, K., Public Administration
ASADA, M., International Law
DOI, M., Constitutional Law
HATTORI, T., German Law
HAYASHI, N., Roman Law
IDA, R., Law of International Organizations
ITO, T., Japanese Legal History
ITO, Y., Political and Diplomatic History of Japan
KAMEMOTO, H., Legal Philosophy
KARATO, T., Political and Diplomatic History
KASAI, M., Law of Civil Procedure
KAWAHAMA, N., Economic Law
KAWAKAMI, R., European Legal History
KIMURA, M., Comparative Politics
KINAMI, A., Anglo-American Law
KITAMURA, M., Commercial Law
MABUCHI, M., Public Policy
MAEDA, M., Commercial Law
MATOBA, T., Political Science
MATSUOKA, H., Civil Law
MORI, T., Constitutional Law
MORIMOTO, S., Commercial Law
MURANAKA, T., Labour Law
NAKAMORI, Y., Criminal Law
NAKANISHI, H., International Politics
NISHIGORI, S., Civil Law
NISHIMURA, K., Social Security Law
OISHI, M., Constitutional Law
OKAMURA, S., Administrative Law
OKAMURA, T., Tax Law
ONO, N., History of Political Thought

OTAKE, H., Political Process
SAKAI, H., International Law
SAKAMAKI, T., Criminal Law
SAKUMA, T., Civil Law
SAKURADA, Y., Private International Law
SHIBAIKE, Y., Administrative Law
SHINKAWA, T., Political Process
SHIOMI, J., Criminal Law
SHIOMI, Y., Civil Law
SHIYAKE, M., Constitutional Law
SUZAKI, H., Commercial Law
SUZUKI, M., International Politics and Economy
TANAKA, S., Legal Philosophy
TAKAYAMA, K., Criminal Law
TANASE, T., Sociology of Law
TERADA, H., Oriental Legal History
TOKUDA, K., Law of Civil Procedure
YAMAMOTO, K., Law of Civil Procedure
YAMAMOTO, K., Civil Law
YAMAMOTO, Y., Civil Law
YOKOYAMA, M., Civil Law
YOSHIOKA, K., Criminology

Graduate School of Letters and Faculty of Letters:

AKAMATSU, A., History of Indian Philosophy
FUJII, J., Japanese History
FUJITA, K., Psychology
FUJITA, M., Japanese Philosophy
FUMA, S., Oriental History
HAMADA, M., Asian History
HATTORI, Y., European History
HAYASHI, S., Humanistic Informatics
HIRATA, S., Chinese Language and Literature
IKEDA, S., History of Chinese Philosophy
ISHIKAWA, Y., Geography
ITO, K., Philosophy
ITO, K., Sociology
IWAKI, K., Aesthetics and Art History
IZUMI, T., Archaeology
KAMADA, M., Japanese History
KATAYANAGI, E., Christian Studies
KATSUYAMA, S., Japanese History
KAWAI, K., Chinese Language and Literature
KAWAZOE, S., History of Western Medieval Philosophy
KETA, M., Philosophy of Religion
KIDA, A., Japanese Language and Literature
KIHIRA, E., Contemporary History
KINDA, A., Geography
KOBAYASHI, M., History of Western Philosophy
MATSUDA, M., Sociology
MIMAKI, K., Buddhist Studies
MINAMIKAWA, T., European History
MIYAUCHI, H., English Language and Literature
NAGAI, K., Contemporary History
NAKAMURA, K., American Literature
NAKAMURA, T., Art History
NAKATSUKASA, T., Greek and Latin Classics
NEDACHI, K., Aesthetics and Art History
NISHIMURA, M., German Language and Literature
OCHIAI, E., Sociology
OSAKA, N., Psychology
OTANI, M., Japanese Language and Literature
SAITO, Y., Italian Language and Literature
SAKURAI, Y., Psychology
SATO, A., Slavic Languages and Literature
SHOGAITO, M., Linguistics
SUGIMOTO, Y., Twentieth-century Studies
SUGIURA, K., Geography
SUGIYAMA, M., Oriental History
TAGUCHI, N., French Language and Literature
TAKAHASHI, H., Greek and Latin Classics
TAKUBO, Y., Linguistics
TOKUNAGA, M., Sanskrit Language and Literature
UCHII, S., Philosophy and History of Science
UEHARA, M., Archaeology
WAKASHIMA, T., English Language and Literature
YOSHIDA, J., French Language and Literature
YOSHIDA, K., Linguistics
YOSHIMOTO, M., Oriental History

Graduate School of Medicine and Faculty of Medicine (Yoshida konoe-cho, Sakyo-ku, Kyoto 606-8501; tel. (75) 753-4300; fax (75) 753-4348; e-mail shomu06@mail.adm.kyoto-u.ac.jp; internet www.med.kyoto-u.ac.jp):

CHIBA, T., Gastroenterology and Hepatology
FUJII, S., Gynaecology and Obstetrics
FUJITA, J., Clinical Molecular Biology
FUKUDA, K., Anaesthesia
FUKUHARA, S., Epidemiology and Health Care Research
FUKUI, T., Clinical Epidemiology
FUKUSHIMA, M., Pharmacoepidemiology
FUKUYAMA, H., Functional Brain Imaging
HASHIMOTO, N., Neurosurgery
HAYASHI, T., Psychiatry
HIRAIDE, A., Center for Medical Education
HIRAOKA, M., Radiation Oncology and Image-applied Therapy
HONJO, T., Immunology and Genomic Medicine
ICHIYAMA, S., Clinical Laboratory Medicine
IDE, C., Anatomy and Neurobiology
IMANAKA, Y., Healthcare Economics and Quality Management
INAGAKI, M., Metabolism and Clinical Nutrition
INUI, K., Pharmacy
ITO, J., Otolaryngology, Head and Neck Surgery
KANEKO, T., Morphological Brain Science
KAWANO, K., Integrative Brain Science
KIHARA, M., Global Health and Socio-Epidemiology
KITA, T., Cardiovascular Medicine
KOIZUMI, A., Health and Environmental Sciences
KOMEDA, M., Cardiovascular Surgery
KOSUGI, S., Biomedical Ethics
MAEKAWA, T., Transfusion Medicine and Cell Therapy
MANABE, T., Diagnostic Pathology
MATSUDA, F., Genome Epidemiology
MIMORI, T., Rheumatology and Clinical Immunology
MINATO, N., Immunology and Cell Biology
MISHIMA, M., Respiratory Medicine
MITSUYAMA, M., Microbiology
MIYACHI, Y., Dermatology
NABESHIMA, Y., Pathology and Tumour Biology
NAKAHARA, T., Public Health and International Health
NAKAHATA, T., Paediatrics
NAKAMURA, T., Orthopaedic and Musculoskeletal Surgery
NAKANISHI, S., Biological Sciences
NAKAO, K., Medicine and Clinical Science
NARUMIYA, S., Cell Pharmacology
NODA, M., Molecular Oncology
NOMA, A., Physiology and Biophysics
OGAWA, O., Urology
OHMORI, H., Physiology and Neurobiology
SAKAMOTO, J., Epidemiological and Clinical Research Information Management
SATO, T., Biostatistics
SERIKAWA, T., Laboratory Animals
SHIMIZU, A., Human Genome Analysis
SHINOHARA, T., Molecular Genetics
SHIOTA, K., Anatomy and Developmental Biology
SHIRAKAWA, T., Health Promotion and Human Behaviour
SUZUKI, S., Plastic and Reconstructive Surgery
TAKAHASHI, R., Neurology
TAKEDA, S., Radiation Genetics
TAKETO, M., Pharmacology
TAMAKI, K., Legal Medicine
TANAKA, K., Transplantation and Immunology
TOGASHI, L., Diagnostic Imaging and Nuclear Medicine
TSUKITA, S., Cell Biology
UCHIYAMA, T., Haematology and Oncology
WADA, H., Thoracic Surgery
YOKODE, M., Clinical Innovative Medicine
YOSHIHARA, H., Medical Informatics
YOSHIMURA, N., Ophthalmology and Visual Sciences

Graduate School of Pharmaceutical Sciences and Faculty of Pharmaceutical Sciences (46-29 Yoshida Shimoadachi-cho, Sakyo-ku, Kyoto 606-8501; tel. (75) 753-4510; fax (75) 753-4502; internet www.pharm.kyoto-u.ac.jp):

AKAIKE, A., Pharmacology
FUJII, N., Bio-organic Medicinal Chemistry
HANDA, T., Biosurface Chemistry
HASHIDA, M., Drug Delivery Research
HONDA, G., Pharmacognosy
ITOH, N., Genetic Biochemistry
KANEKO, S., Molecular Pharmacology
KATO, H., Structural Biology
KAWAI, A., Molecular Microbiology
SAJI, H., Patho-Functional Bioanalysis
TAKAKURA, Y., Biopharmaceutics and Drug Metabolism
TAKEMOTO, Y., Organic Chemistry
TOMIOKA, K., Synthetic Medicinal Chemistry
TSUJIMOTO, G., Genomic Drugs Discovery

Graduate School of Science and Faculty of Science:

AGATA, K., Developmental Biology
AOYAMA, H., Theory of Elementary Particles
ARUGA, T., Surface Chemistry
AWAJI, T., Physical Oceanography
FUJIYOSHI, Y., Molecular Biophysics
FUKAYA, K., Geometry
HANADA, T., Inorganic Materials Chemistry
HARA-NISHIMURA, I., Plant Cell Biology
HATA, H., Theoretical Particle Physics
HAYASHI, T., Organic Chemistry
HIRAJIMA, T., Petrology
HIRANO, T., Neurobiology
HORI, M., Animal Ecology
HORIUCHI, H., Theoretical Nuclear Physics
IYEMORI, T., Solar Terrestrial Physics
IKAWA, M., Partial Differential Equations
IMAFUKU, M., Ethology
IMAI, K., Experimental Nuclear Physics
IMANISHI, H., Foliation and Symplectic Geometry
INAGAKI, S., Astrophysics
KAJIMOTO, O., Physical Chemistry
KATAYAMA, K., Biological Anthropology
KATO, K., Number Theory
KATO, S., Theoretical Chemistry
KATO, S., Representation Theory
KAWAI, H., Theoretical Particle Physics
KIDA, H., Climate Physics
KITAMURA, M., Mineralogy
KONO, A., Topology
KOYAMA, K., Cosmic Ray Physics
KUROKAWA, H., Solar Physics
MACHIDA, S., Geomagnetism and Space Physics
MAIHARA, T., Astrophysics
MARUOKA, K., Synthetic Organic Chemistry
MARUYAMA, M., Algebraic Geometry
MASUDA, F., Stratigraphy and Sedimentology
MATSUDA, Y., Solid State Physics
MATSUKI, T., Lie Groups

MIKI, K., Structural Biochemistry and Protein Crystallography
MIWA, T., Algebraic Analysis
MIZUSAKI, T., Low-Temperature Physics
MORI, K., Molecular Biology
MORIWAKI, A., Algebraic Geometry
NAGATA, T., Astrophysics
NAGATANI, A., Plant Physiology
NAKAJIMA, H., Representation Theory and Geometry
NAKAMURA, T., Nuclear Astrophysics
NISHIDA, G., Algebraic Topology
NISHIKAWA, K., Experimental High Energy Physics
NISHIWADA, K., Differential Equations, Financial Mathematics
OBATA, M., Petrology
OIKE, K., Seismology and Physics of the Earth's Interior
OKADA, A., Active Tectonics and Geomorphology
OKADA, K., Plant Molecular Genetics
ONUKI, A., Statistical Physics
OSUKA, A., Organic Chemistry
SAITO, G., Organic Solid State Chemistry
SAITO, H., Number Theory
SASAO, N., Experimental High Energy Physics
SATOH, N., Developmental Genomics
SETOGUCHI, T., Vertebrate Palaeontology
SHIBATA, K., Solar and Cosmic Plasma Physics
SHICHIDA, Y., Molecular Physiology
SHIGEKAWA, I., Probability Theory
SHIMAMOTO, T., Structural Geology and Rock Rheology
SHIRAYAMA, Y., Marine Biology
SHISHIKURA, M., Dynamical System
SUGIYAMA, H., Chemical Biology, Bioorganic Chemistry
TAKEMOTO, S., Geodesy
TAKEMURA, K., Quaternary Geology and Geothermal Sciences
TAKADA, S., Developmental Biology
TANAKA, K., Solid State Spectroscopy, Laser Spectroscopy
TANAKA, Y., Volcano Magnetism
TANIMORI, T., Cosmic Ray Physics
TANIMURA, Y., Theoretical Chemical Physics
TERAO, T., Chemical Physics
TERAZIMA, M., Physical Chemistry, Biophysical Chemistry
TOBE, H., Plant Systematics and Evolution
TSUTSUMI, Y., Nonlinear Partial Differential Equations
UE, M., Low-dimensional Topology
UEDA, T., Complex Analysis in Several Variables
UEMATSU, T., Theory of Elementary Particles
UENO, K., Theory of Complex Manifolds
YAMADA, K., Theory of Condensed Matter
YAMAGIWA, J., Primatology and Anthropology
YAMAUCHI, J., Physical Chemistry and Electron Spin Resonance
YAMAUCHI, M., Number Theory
YAO, M., Physics of Disordered Systems
YODEN, S., Meteorology
YONEI, S., Radiation Biology
YOSHIDA, H., Number Theory
YOSHIKAWA, K., Chemical Physics, Biological Physics
YOSHIMURA, K., Inorganic Chemistry, Solid State Chemistry and Physics, Nuclear Magnetic Resonance
YUSA, Y., Hydrology and Geothermal Sciences

School of Health Sciences, Faculty of Medicine (53 Syogoin Kawahara-cho, Sakyo-ku, Kyoto 606-8507):

AMANO, S., Experimental Epileptology and Neuropathology
EGAWA, T., Diabetes, Teaching Renal Failure, Foot Care
FUJITA, M., Cardiology
FUKUDA, K., Nuclear Magnetic Resonance
FUKUDA, Y., Hepatology. Clinical Immunology
FUNATO, T., Laboratory Medicine and Molecular Diagnostics
HAYASHI, Y., Adult Health Nursing
HINOKUMA, F., Maternal Nursing, Midwifery
INAMOTO, T., Surgery and Clinical Oncology
KABEYAMA, K., Midwifery, Mother and Child Nursing, Women's Health
KATSURA, T., Preventive Nursing, Community Health Nursing
KAWASAKI, N., Biochemistry and Glycobiology
KONISHI, N., Occupational Therapy, Developmental Delay
MITANI, A., Rehabilitation and Brain Science
MIYAJIMA, A., Environmental Health Nursing
NARUKI, H., Community Health Nursing
NOMURA, S., Neuroanatomy and Functional Human Anatomy
SAITO, Y., Basic Nursing, Hospital Infection Control
SAKURABA, S., Psychiatric and Mental Health Nursing
SASADA, M., Haematology and Infectious Diseases
SUGA, S., Clinical Psychology
TOICHI, M., Psychiatry, Cognitive Neuroscience
TSUBOYAMA, T., Orthopaedics, Musculoskeletal Oncology, Bone Metabolism
TSUKITA, S., Cell Biology
UMEMURA, S., Biomedical Ultrasonics
YAMANE, H., Occupational Therapy for Mental Disorders

Law School (fax (75) 753-3290; internet www.kyodai.jp/I-LS.htm):

ASADA, M., International Law
DOI, M., Constitutional Law
ENDO, K., Law Practice Unit
HAMAMOTO, S., Law Practice Unit
HATTORI, T., German Law
HAYASHI, N., Roman Law
HONDA, M., Law Practice Unit
IDA, R., International Law
IIMURA, Y., Law Practice Unit
ITO, T., Japanese Legal History
ITO, Y., Political and Diplomatic History of Japan
KAMEMOTO, H., Legal Philosophy
KAMIKO, A., Law Practice Unit
KASAI, M., Law of Civil Procedure
KAWAHAMA, N., Economic Law
KAWAKAMI, R., European Legal History
KINAMI, A., Anglo-American Law
KITAGAWA, K., Law Practice Unit
KITAMURA, M., Commercial Law
MAEDA, M., Commercial Law
MATSUDA, K., Law Practice Unit
MATSUOKA, H., Civil Law
MORI, T., Constitutional Law
MORIKAWA, S., Law Practice Unit
MORIMOTO, S., Commercial Law
MURAKAMI, K., Law Practice Unit
MURANAKA, T., Labour Law
NAKAGAWA, H., Law Practice Unit
NAKAMORI, Y., Criminal Law
NISHIGORI, S., Civil Law
NISHIMURA, K., Social Security Law
OISHI, M., Constitutional Law
OKAMURA, S., Administrative Law
OKAMURA, T., Tax Law
SAKAMAKI, T., Criminal Law
SAKAI, H., International Law
SAKUMA, T., Civil Law
SAKURADA, Y., Private International Law
SHIBAIKE, Y., Administrative Law
SHIMIZU, M., Law Practice Unit
SHIOMI, J., Criminal Law
SHIOMI, Y., Civil Law
SHIYAKE, M., Constitutional Law
SUZAKI, H., Commercial Law
TAKAYAMA, K., Criminal Law
TANASE, T., Sociology of Law
TERADA, H., Oriental Legal History
TOKUDA, K., Law of Civil Procedure
YAMAGAMI, K., Law Practice Unit
YAMAMOTO, K., Law of Civil Procedure
YAMAMOTO, K., Civil Law
YAMAMOTO, Y., Civil Law
YASUKI, K., Law Practice Unit
YOKOYAMA, M., Civil Law
YOSHIOKA, K., Criminology

ATTACHED RESEARCH INSTITUTES

Institute for Chemical Research: Gokasho, Uji City, Kyoto; f. 1926; Dir Prof. N. ESAKI; publ. *ICR Annual Report*.

Institute for Research in Humanities: Ushinomiya-cho, Yoshida, Sakyo-ku, Kyoto; f. 1939; Dir Prof. B. KIN; publ. *Journal of Oriental Studies* (annually), *Journal of Humanities Studies* (annually, in Japanese), *Annual Bibliography of Oriental Studies*, *Annals ZINBUN* (irregular, in European languages), *News Letter ZINBUN* (annually, in Japanese).

Institute for Frontier Medical Sciences: 53 Kawahara-cho, Shogoin, Sakyo-ku, Kyoto 606-8507; f. 1998; Dir Prof. N. NAKATSUJI; publ. *Annual Report*.

Institute of Advanced Energy: Gokasho, Uji City, Kyoto; f. 1941; Dir Prof. K. YOSHIKAWA; publ. *Annual Report*.

Disaster Prevention Research Institute: Gokasho, Uji City, Kyoto; f. 1951; Dir Prof. Y. KAWATA; publ. *DPRI Newsletter* (4 a year, in Japanese), *Annuals*.

Yukawa Institute for Theoretical Physics: Kitashirakawa, Sakyo-ku, Kyoto; f. 1953; Dir Prof. T. KUGO; publ. *Progress of Theoretical Physics* (monthly).

Institute for Virus Research: Kawara-cho, Shogoin, Sakyo-ku, Kyoto; f. 1956; Dir Prof. K. SHIMOTOHNO; publ. *Annual Report*.

Institute of Economic Research: Yoshida Honmachi, Sakyo-ku, Kyoto; f. 1962; library of 75,722 vols; Dir Prof. Dr T. SAWA.

Research Institute for Mathematical Sciences: Kitashirakawa, Sakyo-ku, Kyoto; f. 1963; research and postgraduate training in mathematical sciences; library of 78,931 vols; Dir Prof. Y. TAKAHASHI.

Research Reactor Institute: Kumatori-cho, Sennan-gun, Osaka; f. 1963; library of 45,300 vols; Dir Prof. S. SHIROYA; publ. *KUR Report* (in Japanese), *KUR Technical Report* (in Japanese), *Progress Report* (annually, in English).

Primate Research Institute: Kanrin 41-2, Inuyama City, Aichi Prefecture; f. 1967; Dir Prof. N. SHIGEHARA; publ. *Annual Report*.

Center for Southeast Asian Studies: Shimoadachi-cho 46, Yoshida, Sakyo-ku, Kyoto; f. 1965; Dir Prof. Dr K. TANAKA; publ. *Southeast Asian Studies* (4 a year), *Report* (2 a year, in English), *Bulletin* (2 a year, in Japanese), *Kyoto Review of Southeast Asia* (in English).

Academic Center for Computing and Media Studies: Yoshida-Honmachi, Sakyo-ku, Kyoto; f. 2002; Dir Prof. T. MATSUYAMA.

Radiation Biology Center: Yoshida Konoecho, Sakyo-ku, Kyoto; f. 1976; research and postgraduate training in radiation biology; Dir Prof. K. KOMATSU; publ. *Annual Report*.

Center for Ecological Research: 509-3 2-chome, Hirano, Otsu, Shiga 520-2113; f. 1991; Dir Prof. T. OHGUSHI.

Radioisotope Research Center: Yoshida Konoecho, Sakyo-ku, Kyoto; f. 1971; Dir Prof. Dr Y. ISOZUMI.

Environment Preservation Center: Yoshida Honmachi, Sakyo-ku, Kyoto; f. 1977; Dir Prof. K. OSHIMA.

Center for the Promotion of Excellence in Higher Education: Yoshida-nihon-matsu-cho, Sakyo-ku, Kyoto; f. 2003; Dir Prof. Dr M. MARUYAMA.

Kyoto University Museum: Yoshida Honmachi, Sakyo-ku, Kyoto; f. 1997; Dir Prof. Dr T. NAKABO.

Kyoto University International Innovation Center: Kyoto-Daigaku-katsura, Nishikyo-ku, Kyoto; f. 2001; Dir Prof. K. MAKINO.

Research Center for Low Temperature and Materials Science: Oiwake-cho, Kitashirakawa, Sakyo-ku, Kyoto; f. 2002; Dir Prof. T. MIZUSAKI.

Field Science Education and Research Center: Oiwake-cho, Kitashirakawa, Sakyo-ku, Kyoto; f. 2003; Dir Prof. M. TANAKA.

Kyoto University Archives: Yoshida Honmachi, Sakyo-ku, Kyoto; f. 2000; Dir Prof. Dr J. SASAKI; publ. *Newsletter* (2 a year, in Japanese), *Bulletin* (annually, in Japanese).

Center for Archaeological Operations: Yoshida Honmachi, Sakyo-ku, Kyoto; f. 1977; Dir Prof. Dr M. UEHARA; publ. *Annual Report*.

Center for African Area Studies: Shimoadachi-cho 46, Yoshida, Sakyo-ku, Kyoto; f. 1986; Dir Prof. Dr S. ARAKI.

Fukui Institute for Fundamental Chemistry: Takanonishihiraki-cho, Sakyo-ku, Kyoto; f. 2002; Dir Prof. H. NAKATSUJI.

Research Institute for Sustainable Humanosphere: Gokasho, Uji City, Kyoto; f. 2004; Dir Prof. H. MATSUMOTO; publ. *RISH Annual Report* (1 a year, in English).

ATTACHED COLLEGE

College of Medical Technology: 53 Shogoin Kawahara-cho, Sakyo-ku, Kyoto 606-8507; f. 1975; Dean Prof. M. SASADA.

KYUSHU INSTITUTE OF DESIGN

Shiobaru 4-9-1, Minami-ku, Fukuoka-shi 815-8540
Telephone: (92) 553-4407
Fax: (92) 553-4593
E-mail: syomuka@kyushu-id.ac.jp
Internet: www.kyushu-id.ac.jp

Founded 1968
Independent
Academic year: April to March (two semesters)

President: SHO YOSHIDA
Director-General: MAKOTO OHYA
Dean of Students: MASAMICHI OHKUBO
Library Director: RYUZO TAKIYAMA

Number of teachers: 96
Number of students: 1,208 (929 undergraduate, 279 postgraduate)

Publication: *Annual Bulletin*

PROFESSORS

Department of Environmental Design:
- DOI, Y., History of Architecture and Industrial Design
- HIROKAWA, S., Theory of Environmental Design
- ISHII, A., Environmental Systems, Building and Environment Engineering
- KATANO, H., Environmental Systems and Building Construction
- KATO, H. M., Environmental Planning and Design
- MIYAMOTO, M., Environmental Planning and Design
- OHKUBO, M., Environmental Systems and Structural Engineering
- SHIGEMATSU, T., Theory of Environmental Design

Department of Industrial Design:
- FUKATA, S., Intelligent Mechanics and Control
- ISHIMURA, S., Industrial History
- ITOI, H., Industrial Design
- MORITA, Y., Public Space and Element Design
- SAKATA, T., Mathematical Statistics
- SAKI, K., Tribology
- SATO, H., Ergonomics
- TOCHIHARA, Y., Environmental Ergonomics
- YASUKOUCHI, A., Physiological Anthropology

Department of Visual Communication Design:
- FUKUSHIMA, S., Artificial Intelligence
- GENDA, E., Image Design
- NAGASHIMA, K., Image Engineering
- SATO, M., Research and Design on Sign Communication
- URAHAMA, K., Image Information Processing
- WAKIYAMA, S., Visual Image Design
- YAMASHITA, S., Vision Science and Neurobiology
- YAMASHITA, Y., Vision Science and Psychophysics

Department of Acoustic Design:
- FUJIEDA, M., Science of Sound Culture
- FUJIWARA, K., Science of Acoustical Environment
- IWAMIYA, S., Science of Acoustical Environment
- KAWABE, T., Science of Acoustical Environment
- NAKAJIMA, Y., Science of Acoustic Information
- NAKAMURA, S., Science of Sound Culture
- YOSHIKAWA, S., Science of Acoustic Information

Department of Art and Information Design:
- FUJIMURA, N., Media Design
- KUROSAWA, S., Media Art and Culture
- OHNISHI, S., Media Art and Culture
- OTA, S., Information Environment Sciences
- SASABUCHI, S., Information Environment Sciences

KYUSHU INSTITUTE OF TECHNOLOGY

1-1 Sensui-sho, Tobata-ku, Kitakyushu-shi, Fukuoka 804-8550
Telephone: (93) 884-3000
Fax: (93) 884-3015
E-mail: sou-kikaku@jimu.kyutech.ac.jp
Internet: www.kyutech.ac.jp

Founded 1909
Independent
Language of instruction: Japanese
Academic year: April to March

President: TERUO SHIMOMURA
Registrar: MAKOTO YOSHIDA
Librarian: MORIO MATSUNAGA

Library of 489,867 vols
Number of teachers: 636 full-time
Number of students: 6,307

Deans
Faculty of Computer Science and Systems Engineering: T KODAMA
Faculty of Engineering: T. KOBAYASHI
Graduate School of Computer Science and Systems Engineering: H. TSUKAMOTO

Publications: *Bulletin*, *Memoirs*.

ATTACHED INSTITUTES

Information Science Center: f. 1987; Dir NAOYUKI OKADA.

Center for Co-operative Research: f. 1989; Dir MORIO MATSUNAGA.

Center for Microelectronic Systems: f. 1990; Dir TSUTOMU SASAO.

Center for Instrumental Analysis: f. 1993; Dir NOBUTAKA NARITA.

Satellite Venture Business Laboratory: f. 1995; Dir YOSHINOBU KUBO.

Center for Health: Dir KENTARO HIRATA.

KYUSHU UNIVERSITY

6-10-1 Hakozaki, Higashi-ku, Fukuoka 812-8581
Telephone: (92) 642-2111
Fax: (92) 642-2113
Internet: www.kyushu-u.ac.jp

Founded 1911
Independent
Academic year: April to March

President: T. KAJIYAMA
Vice-Presidents: H. NAKANO, S. ARIKAWA, Y. SHIBATA, W. KOTERAYAMA, Y. IMANISHI, M. YANAGIHARA
Administrator: K. HAYATA
Librarian: Y. IMANISHI

Library of 3,741,114 vols
Number of teachers: 2,338
Number of students: 18,202

DEANS

Faculty of Agriculture: K. IMAIZUMI
Faculty of Dental Science: A. AKAMINE
Faculty of Design: H. SATO
Faculty of Economics: Y. OGINO
School of Education: T. INABA
Faculty of Engineering: K. OGI
Faculty of Engineering Sciences: T. TSUTSUI
Faculty of Human–Environment Studies: T. WATANABE
Faculty of Humanities: Y. KAWAMOTO
Faculty of Information Science and Electrical Engineering: M. TATEIBA
Faculty of Languages and Cultures: K. YAMASHITA
Faculty of Law: N. UEDA
Faculty of Mathematics: M. T. NAKAO
Faculty of Medical Sciences: H. KANAIDE
Faculty of Pharmaceutical Sciences: YUKIHIRO SHOYAMA
Faculty of Sciences: T. ODAGAKI
Faculty of Social and Cultural Studies: K. TAKADA
Law School (Professional Graduate School): Y. ODE
Graduate School of Systems Life Sciences: T. MURAKAMI

DIRECTORS

Medical Institute of Bioregulation: Y. YOSHIKAI
Institute for Materials Chemistry and Engineering: N. IMAISHI
Research Institute for Applied Mechanics: S. IMAWAKI
Institute of Health Science: K. UEZONO
Computing and Communications Centre: K. MURAKAMI
Biotron Institute: J. CHIKUSHI
Institute of Tropical Agriculture: H. YAHATA
Radioisotope Center: M. HIRATA
Center of Advanced Instrumental Analysis: K. MATSUMOTO
International Student Center: M. YANAGIHARA
Kyushu University Museum: T. MURAE
System LSI Research Center: H. YASUURA

Space Environment Research Center: K. YUMOTO
Research Center for Korean Studies: S. ISHIKAWA
Research Center for Education in Health Care Systems: M. TSUNEYOSHI
Research and Development Centre for Higher Education: H. SHIMA
Research Institute of Superconductor Science and System: K. FUNAKI
Kansei Center for Arts and Science: K. OGI
Art, Science and Technology Centre for Co-operative Research: W. KOTERAYAMA
Research Laboratory for High Voltage Electron Microscopy: Y. TOMOKIYO
Laboratory for Waste Water Treatment: H. KOYAMA
Natural Disaster Information Center of Western Japan: K. ZEN
Institute for Ionized Gas and Laser Research: M. TSUJI
Institute for Irradiation and Analysis of Quantum Radiation: K. ISHIBASHI
Venture Business Laboratory: A. SUEOKA
Kyushu University Asia Research Organization: T. OKAZAKI
Hydrogen Technology Research Centre: T. KONOMI
Steel Research Centre: S. TAKAKI
Centre for Future Chemistry: S. SHINKAI
Bio-Architecture Centre: S. KUHARA
Admission Center: Y. SHIBATA

PROFESSORS

Faculty of Agriculture (6-10-1 Hakozaki, Higashi-ku, Fukuoka 812-8581; tel. (92) 642-2802; fax (92) 642-2804; internet www .agr.kyushu-u.ac.jp):

EGASHIRA, K., Soil Mineralogy and Chemistry
FUJII, H., Silkworm Genetic Resources
FURUKAWA, K., Applied Microbiology
FURUSE, M., Advanced Animal and Marine Bioresources
HATTORI, M.-A., Reproductive Physiology and Biotechnology
HIRAMATSU, K., Water Environmental Engineering
HONJO, T., Marine Environmental Science
IIDA, S., Forest Resources Management
IKEDA, M., Plant Nutrition and Soil Fertility
IKEUCHI, Y., Chemistry and Technology of Animal Products
IMAIZUMI, K., Nutrition Chemistry
ISHINO, Y., Protein Chemistry and Engineering
ITO, M., Marine Bioresource Chemistry and Technology
IWAMOTO, H., Functional Anatomy of Domestic Animals
IWAYA-INOUE, M., Crop Science
KAI, S., Agricultural Marketing
KANAZAWA, S., Microbiological Biochemistry of Soils
KAWAGUCHI, Y., Silkworm Science
KIMURA, M., Biochemistry
KOBAYASHI, Y., Plant Metabolic Physiology
KONDO, R., Systematic Forest and Forest Products Sciences
KUBOTA, F., Plant Production Physiology
KUHARA, S., Molecular Gene Technology
KURODA, K., Wood Chemistry
KUWANO, E., Pesticide Chemistry
MAKI, T., Applied Meteorology
MASUDA, Y., Grassland Science
MATSUI, S., Fish Production Technology
MATSUMOTO, K., Food Analysis
MATSUYAMA, M., Marine Biology
MIYAMOTO, T., Food Hygiene Chemistry
MOHRI, T., Zoology and Reproductive Biology
MORI, K., Bioproduction and Environment Information Sciences
MORITA, M., Biomacromolecular Materials Science
MURASE, Y., Wood Material Technology
NADA, Y, Agricultural Ecology
NAKANO, Y., Irrigation and Water Utilization
NAKAO, M., Marine Biochemistry
NAKAZONO, A., Fish Ecology and Fisheries Biology
ODA, K., Wood Science
OHBA, M., Bioresources and Management
OHTSUBO, M., Environmental Soil Engineering
OKAMOTO, M., Applied Biological Regulation Technology
OKUBO, H., Horticultural Science
OMURA, H., Erosion Control
OTSUKI, K., Forest Ecosphere Sciences and Management
RYUKOH, H., Forest Policy and Resource Management
SATOH, H., Plant Genetic Resources
SHIMIZU, S., Insect Pathology and Microbial Control
SHIMODA, M., Food Process Engineering
SHIRAHATA, S., Cellular Regulation Technology
SHIRAISHI, S., Silviculture
SONOMOTO, K., Microbial Technology
SUZUKI, N., Quantitative Analysis of Agricultural Economics
TADAUCHI, O., Entomology
TAKAGI, M., Insect Natural Enemies
TAKANAMI, Y., Plant Pathology
TANAKA, S., Postharvest Sciences
TSUJI, M., Farm Management
WARIISHI, H., Bioresources Chemistry
YAMADA, K., Food Chemistry
YAMASHITA, S., Agricultural Biophysics
YOKOGAWA, H., Agricultural Economics
YOSHIDA, S., Forest Management
YOSHIMURA, A., Plant Breeding

Faculty of Dental Science (3-1-3 Maidashi, Higashi-ku, Fukuoka 812-8582; tel. (92) 641-1151; internet www.dent.kyushu-u.ac.jp):

AKAMINE, A., Endodontology and Operative Dentistry
HIRATA, M., Molecular and Cellular Biochemistry
IIJIMA, T., Oral Anatomy and Cell Biology
IKEMOTO, Y., Dental Anaesthesiology
ISHIKAWA, K., Biomaterials
KOYANO, K., Removable Prosthodontics
MAEDA, K., Periodontology
NAKAMURA, S., Oral and Maxillofacial Oncology
NAKANISHI, H., Oral Ageing Science
NAKASIMA, A., Orthodontics
NINOMIYA, Y., Oral Neuroscience
NONAKA, K., Paediatric Dentistry
SAKAI, H., Oral Pathology and Medicine
SHIRASUNA, K., Oral and Maxillofacial Surgery
TANAKA, T., Mineralized Tissue Biology
TERADA, Y., Fixed Prosthodontics
YAMAMOTO, K., Biochemical and Molecular Pharmacology
YAMASHITA, Y., Preventive Dentistry
YOSHIURA, K., Oral and Maxillofacial Radiology

Faculty of Design (4-9-1 Shiobaru, Minami-ku, Fukuoka 815-8540; tel. (92) 553-4400; fax (92) 553-4593; internet www.design .kyushu-u.ac.jp):

DOI, Y., History of Architecture and Urban Design
FUJIEDA, M., Composition
FUJIMURA, N., Contents Engineering
FUJIWARA, K., Architectural Acoustics
FUKATA, S., Mechatronics
FUKUSHIMA, S., Image Information Engineering
GENDA, E., Image Design
ISHIDA, T., Architecture Design Theory
ISHII, A., Urban and Building Environmental Engineering
ISHII, A., Industrial Design
ISHIMURA, S., Industrial History
ITABASHI, Y., Contact Comparative Linguistics
IWAMIYA, S., Psychological Acoustics and Acoustic Engineering
KADOTA, H., Media-processing Architecture and Algorithm
KANEKIYO, H., Landscape Architecture
KATANO, H., Building Construction
KAWABE, T., Elementary Particle Physics, High Energy Physics
KIYOSUMI, M., Design Strategy and Design for Branding
KUROSAWA, S., Copyright
MIYAMOTO, M., History of Japanese Cities and Architecture
MORITA, Y., Public Space and Element Design, Industrial Design
NAKAJIMA, Y., Perceptual Psychology
NAKAMURA, S., Composition and Media Art
NISHIYAMA, N., Urban Planning and Design, Landscape Architecture
OHNISHI, S., Art History of Korea and Japan
OTA, S., Functional Analysis
SAKAMOTO, H., Image Engineering
SAKATA, T., Mathematical Statistics
SAKI, K., Tribology
SASABUCHI, S., Mathematical Statistics
SATO, H., Ergonomics
SATO, M., Design and Research on the Sign Communication
SHIGEMATSU, T., Landscape Conservation and Restoration
TAKEDA, T., Virtual Reality
TOCHIHARA, Y., Environmental Ergonomics
URAHAMA, K., Image Information Processing
WAKIYAMA, S., Multiple Image
WATANUKI, S., Kansei Science
YAMASHITA, S., Neurobiology
YAMSHITA, Y., Psychophysics of Vision
YASUKOUCHI, A., Physiological Anthropology
YOSHIKAWA, S., Musical Instrument Acoustics

Faculty of Economics (6-19-1 Hakozaki, Higashi-ku, Fukuoka 812-8581; tel. (92) 642-2357; fax (92) 642-2349; e-mail kzssyomu@jimu.kyushu-u.ac.jp; internet www.en.kyushu-u.ac.jp):

FUJII, Y., International Economic Analysis
FUKAGAWA, H., International Economic Analysis
FURUKAWA, T., Mathematics and Computer Sciences
HAMASUNA, K., International Economic Analysis
HISANO, K., Industrial Systems
HORIE, Y., Economic Analysis and Policy
HOSOE, M., Economic Systems Analysis
INATOMI, M., International Business Analysis
IWAMOTO, S., Mathematics and Computer Sciences
IWASAKI, I., Business and Technology Management
IWATA, K., International Economic Analysis
KAKU, S., Management Systems
KAWANAMI, Y., International Economic Analysis
KONISHI, Y., Business and Technology Management
MAESONO, Y., Mathematics and Computer Sciences
MIURA, I., Economic Systems Analysis
MURAFUJI, I., Business and Technology Management
MUROYAMA, Y., Economic Analysis and Policy

NAGAIKE, K., Business and Technology Management
NAKAI, T., Mathematics and Computer Sciences
NAKAMURA, H., Business and Technology Management
OGINO, Y., Industrial Systems
OSHITA, J., Accounting Systems
OSUMI, K., Economic Systems Analysis
SAEKI, C., Economic Systems Analysis
SEKI, G., Economic Analysis and Policy
SHINOZAKI, A., International Business Analysis
SHIOTSUGU, K., Management Systems
SHUTTO, N., Business and Technology Management
TAKITA, H., International Economic Analysis
TOKINAGA, S., Mathematics and Computer Sciences
USHIYAMA, M., Management Systems
YOSHIDA, M., Business and Technology Management

Faculty of Engineering (6-10-1 Hakozaki, Higashi-ku, Fukuoka 812-8581; tel. (92) 642-3244; fax (92) 642-3243; e-mail kossyomu@jimu.kyushu-u.ac.jp; internet www.eng.kyushu-u.ac.jp/research):

AKIMOTO, F., Urban and Regional Planning
ANDO, J., Marine Hydrodynamics
ARAI, Y., Molecular Systems Chemistry
ASO, S., Space Systems Dynamics
EHARA, S., Geothermics
ESAKI, T., Environmental Geotechnology
FUKAI, J., Heat Transfer
FUKUCHI, N., Functional Design of Marine Systems
FUKUDA, K., Energy Environment, Economic Systems and Hydrodynamics in Nuclear Reactors
FUKUSHIMA, H., Electrochemistry of Materials
FURUKAWA, A., Hydraulic Machinery
FURUKAWA, M., Aerodynamics of Machinery
FURUTA, H., Applied Organic Chemistry
GOTO, M., Biochemical Engineering, Separation Technology
GOTO, N., Guidance and Control
HARA, K., Gel Properties and Applications in Environmental Engineering
HASHIMOTO, N., Coastal Engineering
HINO, S., Structural Mechanics
HIRAJIMA, T., Mineral Processing and Recycling
HIROKAWA, S., Graphic Science, Biomechanics
HISAEDA, Y., Artificial Enzyme Chemistry, Electroorganic Chemistry
HOJO, J., Applied Inorganic Chemistry
HORITA, Z., Microstructure Control and Characterization
IDEMITSU, K., Nuclear Fuel and Waste Management
IDOGAKI, T., Applied Quantum Physics
IKEDA, N., Applied Nuclear Physics
IMASAKA, T., Applied Analytical Chemistry
IMATO, T., Electroanalytical Chemistry
IRIE, M., Advanced Materials Chemistry
ISHIBASHI, K., Radiation Measurement and Safety
ISHIHARA, T., Inorganic Advanced Materials Chemistry
ITOI, R., Geothermal Reservoir Engineering
JINNO, K., Water Resources Engineering
KAI, S., Applied Physics
KAJIWARA, H., Systems Engineering
KAJIWARA, T., Polymer Engineering, Biochemical Engineering
KAMIHIRA, M., Biotechnology, Cell and Tissue Engineering
KANAYAMA, H., Computational Mechanics
KANEMITSU, Y., Sound and Vibration Control of Mechanical System
KATAYAMA, Y., Bioengineering, DDS and Biochip
KAWAKAMI, K., Bioreaction Engineering
KIDO, H., Reactive Gas Dynamics
KIJIMA, K., Hydrodynamics and Ship Dynamics
KIMIZUKA, N., Molecular Organization Chemistry
KISHIDA, M., Reaction Engineering and Advanced Materials Processing
KOMATSU, T., Environmental Hydraulics
KONDO, E., Systems Mathematics and Engineering
KONDO, Y., Materials Strength, Fatigue
KONDOU, T., Dynamics of Machinery, Mechanical Vibration
KONOMI, T., Fuel Cell Systems
KUDO, K., Nuclear Reactor Engineering
KUNOO, K., Aerospace Structural Systems
KUSUDA, T., Environmental Engineering
MASUDA, M., Materials Science
MATSUI, K., Rock Engineering and Mining Machinery
MATSUMIYA, H., Fluid Dynamics
MATSUMURA, S., Irreversible Processes in Materials
MATSUSHITA, H., Construction Materials and Concrete Structure
MINEMOTO, M., Fluid Mechanics and Transport Phenomena
MIURA, H., Advanced Powder Metallurgy
MORI, H., Thermal Energy Conversion
MOTOOKA, T., Materials Science
MUKAIDA, M., Materials Science
MURAKAMI, T., Bionic Design, Biomechanics and Biotribology
MURAKAMI, Y., Fatigue and Fracture
MURASE, E., Engine Systems
NAGAMURA, T., Polymer Science and Ultrafast Molecular Photonics
NAGAYAMA, K., Advanced Microphysics
NAKAO, Y., Fusion Plasma Science
NAKASHIMA, K., Physicochemical Property for Materials
NAKASHIMA, N., Nanocarbon and Supramolecular Chemistry
NOGUCHI, H., Solid Mechanics
OCHIAI, H., Geotechnical and Geoenvironmental Engineering
OGI, K., Processing of Composite Materials
OHTA, H., Space Utilization Science and Technology
OHTA, K., Vibration and Acoustics
ONIKURA, H., Machining Systems
OTSUKA, H., Earthquake Engineering
SAKAGUCHI, K., Innovation System Analysis
SAKURAI, A., Flight Dynamics
SAWADA, R., Nano and Micro Systems, Bioengineering
SHIMAOKA, T., Environmental Engineering and Solid Waste Management
SHIMATANI, Y., River Engineering
SHIMIZU, M., Reaction Engineering for Materials
SHINKAI, A., Ship Design and Maritime Intelligence Technology
SHINKAI, S., Molecular Recognition Chemistry
SUEOKA, A., Dynamics of Machinery
SUGIMURA, J., Machine Design and Tribology
SUMI, T., Transport Planning
TAKAKI, S., Phase Transformation and Structure Control
TAKAMATSU, H., Bio Heat and Mass Transfer, Thermal Engineering
TAKATA, Y., Thermal Engineering
TOYOSADA, M., Fracture and Welding Mechanics
TSUGE, Y., Process Systems Engineering
USHIJIMA, K., Engineering Geophysics
WATANABE, K., Economic Geology
YAMADA, S., Applied Photochemistry, Nanoparticle Technology
YAMAMOTO, Y., Tribology
YAMASAKI, N., Aerospace Propulsion
YOSHIKAWA, T., Structural Design of Marine Systems
ZEN, K., Geotechnical and Disaster Prevention Engineering

Faculty of Engineering Sciences (6-1 Kasuga-koen, Kasuga, Fukuoka 816-8560; tel. (92) 583-7555; fax (92) 583-7060; internet www.tj.kyushu-u.ac.jp):

AOKI, T., High Speed Gas Dynamics
AOKI, Y., Theoretical Chemistry
HARATA, A., Analytical Chemistry
HAYASHI, T., Thermal Environment Systems
HONJO, H., Non-linear Physics
KUWABARA, M., Electroceramics
KYOZUKA, Y., Coastal Environmental Research
MASUDA, M., Laser-Aided Fluid Diagnostics
MATSUNAGA, N., Environmental Fluid Dynamics
MIYOSHI, E., Quantum Materials Physics
NAKASHIMA, H., Advanced Energy Conversion Engineering
NISHIKAWA, M., Energy Chemical Engineering
OHTA, S., Complex Dynamic Systems
SASADA, I., Applied Electromagnetics
SHIMANOE, K., Functional Materials
SHIMIZU, A., Thermal Hydraulics in Extreme Conditions
TANABE, T., Energy Materials Science and Engineering
TAKASAKI, K., Engines and Combustion
TANIMOTO, J., Urban Architectural Environmental Engineering
TERAOKA, Y., Functional Inorganic Materials Chemistry
TOCHIHARA, H., Surface Science
TOMOKIYO, Y., Crystal Physics and Engineering
TSUTSUI, T., Organic Materials Chemistry
UCHINO, K., Plasma and Quantum Electronics
YOKOYAMA, S., Electric Energy Systems

Faculty of Human–Environment Studies (6-19-1 Hakozaki, Higashi-ku, Fukuoka 812-8581; tel. (92) 642-2353; fax (92) 642-3104; internet www.human.kyushu-u.ac.jp):

FUJIMOTO, K., Environmental Planning in Architecture
FURUKAWA, H., Social and Organizational Psychology
HAKODA, Y., Cognitive Psychology
HARIZUKA, S., Clinical Psychology for Disabled Children
HORI, Y., History of Ancient Roman Architecture and Urbanization
INABA, T., Comparative and International Education III
KAWANO, A., Steel Structures and Structural Analysis
KAWASE, H., Earthquake Disaster Mitigation
KIKUCHI, S., Housing Design and Planning
KITAYAMA, O., Psychoanalysis
MAEDA, J., Wind Disaster Mitigation
MARUNO, S., Cognitive Developmental Psychology
MATSUDA, T., Sociology of Educational Organization
MATSUZAKI, Y., Clinical Psychology
MINAMI, H., Environmental Psychology
MIURA, K., Psychology of Art and Cognition
MOCHIDA, K., Comparative and International Education I
NAKAMIZO, S., Psychology and Visual Perception
NANRI, Y., Planning of Adult and Community Education
NOJIMA, K., Counselling Psychology
OBA, N., Clinical Psychology
OGAWA, T., Sociology
OHGAMI, H., Developmental Psychology

SAKINO, K., Reinforced Concrete Structures and Structural Mechanics
SEKI, K., Comparative Religion
SINYA, Y., History of Japanese Education
SUZUKI, Y., Sociology
TAJIMA, S., Clinical Psychology
TAKESHITA, T., Architectural Planning
TOMOEDA, T., Sociology
TSUCHIDO, T., Philosophy of Education II
WATANABE, T., Building, Environmental Design and Control
YAOSAKA, O., Educational Administration
YOSHITANI, T., Intercultural Education

Faculty of Humanities (6-19-1 Hakozaki, Higashi-ku, Fukuoka 812-8581; tel. (92) 642-2351; fax (92) 642-2349; internet www.lit.kyushu-u.ac.jp):

ASAI, K., German Literature
ANDO, T., Japanese History
HAMADA, K., Korean History
HOSOKAWA, R., Ethics
IDE, S., Aesthetics and History of Fine Arts
IMANISHI, Y., Japanese Literature
INADA, T., Linguistics
KAWAMOTO, Y., East Asian History
KIKUCHI, E., Occidental Philosophy
MIYAMOTO, K., Archaeology
OKANO, K., Indian Philosophy
SAEKI, K., Japanese History
SAKAMOTO, T., Linguistics
SAKAUE, Y., Japanese History
SAKONO, F., Japanese Language
SHIBATA, A., Chinese Philosophy
SHIMIZU, K., History of Islamic Civilization
SHINPO, H., Occidental History
TAKAGI, A., Geography
TAKEMURA, N., Chinese Literature
TANI, R., Occidental Philosophy
TUBURAYA, Y., Occidental Philosophy
UENO, Y., Japanese Literature
USHIROSHOJI, M., Aesthetics and History of Fine Arts
YAMANOUCHI, A., Occidental History
YOSHII, A., French Literature

Faculty of Information Science and Electrical Engineering (6-10-1 Hakozaki, Higashi-ku, Fukuoka 812-8581; tel. (92) 642-3244; fax (92) 642-3243; e-mail kossyomu@jimu.kyushu-u.ac.jp; internet www.isee.kyushu-u.ac.jp/indexE.html):

AKAIWA, Y., Digital Radio Communications
AMAMIYA, M., Architecture of Intelligent Systems
ARAKI, K., Software Engineering and Internetworking
ARIKAWA, S., Discovery Science
ENPUKU, K., Superconducting Electronics
FUKUDA, A., Systems Software
FUNAKI, K., Applied Superconductivity
HARA, M., Electric Power Engineering
HASEGAWA, R., Machine Intelligence and Systems Architecture
HASEGAWA, T., Robotics
IRAMINA, K., Biomedical Engineering
KAWABE, T., Robust Control
KAWAHARA, Y., Theoretical Computer Science
KOHDA, T., Communication Systems
KUROKI, Y., Microelectronics
MAKINOUCHI, A., Data and Knowledge Science
MATSUYAMA, K., Solid-State Functional Devices
MIYAO, M., Silicon Heterostructural Materials and Devices
MURAKAMI, K., Computer Systems Architecture
NIIJIMA, K., Signal and Image Analysis
NINOMIYA, T., Electronic Circuits and Systems
OKADA, T., Laser Engineering
SAKOE, H., Media Signal Recognition
SAKURAI, K., Cryptography and Information Security
TAKEDA, M., Text Algorithms and Data Mining
TAKEO, M., Superconducting Magnet and Device Technology
TANIGUCHI, R., Computer Vision
TATEIBA, M., Electromagnetic Wave Sensing and Satellite Communications
TOKO, K., Advanced Biomimetic Materials and Sensors
WADA, K., Control Engineering
YAMASHITA, M., Theoretical Computer Science
YASUMOTO, K., Microwave Engineering and Photonics
YASUURA, H., VLSI Systems Design
YOKOO, M., Multi-agent Systems, Artificial Intelligence
YOSHIDA, K., Electrical Machinery and Control
YOSHIDA, K., RF Microelectronics

Faculty of Languages and Cultures (4-2-1 Ropponmatsu, Chuo-ku, Fukuoka 810-8560; tel. (92) 726-4508; fax (92) 726-4511; internet www.rc.kyushu-u.ac.jp/~ilc/index-e.html):

ABE, Y., German
AO, Y., French
FUJISAKI, M., English
HAGA, K., French
INOUE, N., English
KOTANI, K., English
MATSUMURA, Y., English
MICHEL, W., German
MORI, S., French
OHTA, K., English
OKANO, S., German
TAJIMA, M., English
TANAKA, T., German
TANAKA, Y., French
TANIGUCHI, H., English
TOKUMI, M., English
TSUMURA, M., German
TSUNEKAWA, M., German
TSUNEYOSHI, N., German
YAMAMURA, H., Spanish
YAMASHITA, K., English

Faculty of Law (6-19-1 Hakozaki, Higashi-ku, Fukuoka 812-8581; tel. (92) 642-2354; fax (92) 642-2349; e-mail kashomu3@jimu.kyushu-u.ac.jp; internet www.law.kyushu-u.ac.jp):

ABE, M., International Business Law
AGO, S., International Economic Law
DOI, M., Criminology and Criminal Policy
EGUCHI, A., Legal Culture
GONG, R., Legal Culture
ISHIDA, M., International Political History
ISHIKAWA, S., Political History
ISOGAWA, N., Civil Law
KAWASHIMA, S., Civil Procedure
KISA, S., Administrative Law
KOCHI, H., Civil Law
KONO, T., International Private Law
KUMAGAI, K., Intellectual Property Law
KUMANO, N., Political History
MATSUO, M., Criminal Law
NAKAKUBO, H., Labour and Social Law
NAOE, S., Western Legal History
NISHIMURA, S., Roman Law
NISHIYAMA, Y., Commercial Law, Company Law
NODA, S., Labour Law
ODE, Y., Law of Criminal Procedure
OHASHI, Y., Administrative Law
OHKUMA, Y., Constitutional Law
OHKAWARA, N., Comparative Politics
PEJOVIC, C., Maritime Law
SAKAMOTO, M., Constitutional Law
SAKO, I., Philosophy of Law
SEKIGUCHI, M., History of Political Thought
SHICHINOHE, K., Civil and Water Law
SHIMIZU, I., Commercial Law I, Consumer Law
TANAKA, N., Civil Law
UCHIDA, H., Criminal Law
UEDA, K., Criminal Defence
UEDA, N., Japanese Legal History
WATANABE, T., Tax Law
WATANABE, Y., Constitutional Law
YABUNO, Y., Contemporary Japanese Politics
YANAGIHARA, M., International Law

Faculty of Mathematics (6-10-1 Hakozaki, Higashi-ku, Fukuoka 812-8581; tel. (92) 642-2773; fax (92) 642-2522; internet www.math.kyushu-u.ac.jp):

BANNAI, E., Algebra and Combinatorics
EI, S.-I., Nonlinear Analysis
FUKUMOTO, Y., Fluid Mechanics
HAMACHI, T., Dynamic Systems
HARA, T., Mathematical Physics
IWASAKI, K., Geometry and Differential Equations
KANEKO, M., Number Theory
KATO, M., Topology
KAWASHIMA, S., Partial Differential Equations
KAZAMA, H., Complex Analysis
KOIKE, M., Number Theory
KONISHI, S., Mathematical Statistics
KOSAKI, H., Operator Algebra and Operator Theory
MATSUI, T., Mathematical Physics
MIYAOKA, R., Differential Geometry
MORISHITA, M., Topology and Number Theory
NAKAO, M., Partial Differential Equations
NAKAO, M. T., Computational Mathematics
NISHII, R., Statistical Learning Theory
NOMURA, T., Representation Theory and Harmonic Analysis
OSADA, H., Probability Theory
SAEKI, O., Topology
SATO, E., Algebraic Geometry
SUZUKI, M., Complex Analysis
TABATA, M., Numerical Analysis
TANIGUCHI, S., Stochastic Differential Equations and the Malliavin Calculus
TEZUKA, S., Statistical Computation, Randomness and Computational Finance
WAKAYAMA, M., Representation Theory and Zeta Functions
WATATANI, Y., Operator Algebra
YAMADA, K., Differential Geometry
YOSHIDA, M., Complex Analysis
YOSHIKAWA, A., Mathematical Analysis

Faculty of Medical Sciences (3-1-1 Maidashi, Higashi-ku, Fukuoka 812-8582; tel. (92) 641-1151; internet www.med.kyushu-u.ac.jp):

ARAKI, T., Health Care Administration and Management
FURUE, M., Dermatology
HAMASAKI, N., Clinical Chemistry and Laboratory Medicine
HARA, T., Paediatrics
HARADA, M., Medicine and Biosystemic Science
HASHIZUME, M., Disaster and Emergency Medicine
HAYASHI, J., Environmental Medicine and Infectious Diseases
HIMENO, K., Parasitology
HONDA, H., Clinical Radiology
IIDA, M., Medicine and Clinical Science
IKEDA, N., Forensic Pathology and Science
ISHIBASHI, T., Ophthalmology
ITO, Y., Pharmacology and Cell Signalling
IWAKI, T., Neuropathology
IWAMOTO, Y., Orthopaedic Surgery
KANAIDE, H., Molecular Cardiology
KANBA, S., Neuropsychiatry
KATANO, M., Cancer Therapy and Research
KIRA, J., Neurology
KOMUNE, S., Otorhinolaryngology
KONO, S., Preventive Medicine
KOSAKA, T., Anatomy and Neurobiology
KUBO, C., Psychosomatic Medicine
MAEHARA, Y., General Surgery
MATSUDA, T., Biomedical Engineering
MIHARA, K., Molecular Biology
MOHRI, S., Biomedicine

NAITO, S., Urology
NAKANISHI, Y., Respiratory Medicine
NISHIOKA, K., Health Care Administration and Management
NOBUTOMO, K., Health Services Management and Policy
NOSE, Y., Medical Information Science
OGATA, H., Health Care Administration and Management
SASAKI, T., Neurosurgery
SASAGURI, T., Clinical Pharmacology
SHIBATA, Y., Developmental Molecular Anatomy
SUEISHI, K., Pathophysiological and Experimental Pathology
SUNAGAWA, K., Cardiovascular Medicine
TAKAHASHI, S., Anaesthesiology and Critical Care Medicine
TAKAYANAGI, R., Geriatric Medicine
TAKESHIGE, K., Molecular and Cellular Biology
TANAKA, M., Surgery and Oncology
TOBIMATSU, S., Clinical Neurophysiology
TSUNEYOSHI, M., Anatomic Pathology
TSUZUKI, T., Medical Biophysics and Radiation Biology
YANAGI, Y., Virology
YOSHIDA, M., Medical Education
YOSHIDA, S., Bacteriology
YOSHIMURA, M., Integrative Physiology

Faculty of Pharmaceutical Sciences (3-1-1 Maidashi, Higashi-ku, Fukuoka 812-8582; tel. (92) 641-1151; internet www.phar.kyushu-u.ac.jp):

HIGUCHI, R., Natural Products Chemistry
HIGUCHI, S., Clinical Pharmacokinetics
INOUE, K., Pharmacology
KATAYAMA, T., Molecular Biology
KOGA, N., Functional Molecular Science
KUROSE, H., Pharmacology and Toxicology
MAEDA, M., Biomolecular Recognition Chemistry
MINE, K., Clinical Pharmacology
OHDO, S., Medico-Pharmaceutical Sciences
SASAKI, S., Bioorganic and Synthetic Chemistry
SHOYAMA, Y., Medicinal Resources Regulation
SUEMUNE, H., Pharmaceutical Synthetic Chemistry
TANAKA, Y., Pharmaceutical Cell Biology
UEDA, T., Immunology
UTSUMI, H., Bio-functional Science
YAMADA, H., Molecular Life Sciences
ZAITSU, K., Bio-analytical Chemistry

Faculty of Sciences (6-10-1 Hakozaki, Higashi-ku, Fukuoka 812-8581; tel. (92) 642-2521; fax (92) 642-2522; internet www.science.scc.kyushu-u.ac.jp):

ANNAKA, M., Physical Chemistry
ARATONO, M., Physical Chemistry
FUJIKI, Y., Molecular Cell Biology
HASHIMOTO, M., Theoretical Astrophysics
HIROOKA, T., Middle Atmosphere Dynamics
IBA, K., Plant Physiology and Plant Molecular Biology
INOUE, S., Solid State Physics
ISHIGURO, S., Solution Chemistry
ISHIHARA, T., Molecular Genetics
ITOH, H., Large-Scale Atmospheric Dynamics
IWASA, Y., Theoretical Biology
KATO, T., Mineral Physics
KATSUKI, T., Synthetic Organic Chemistry
KAWABATA, S., Protein Chemistry
KAWAGUTI, T., Low-dimensional Systems
KAWATO, T., Constructive Organic Chemistry
KIMURA, M., Quantum Chemistry
KIMURA, Y., Soft Condensed Matter Physics
KITAGAWA, H., Inorganic Chemistry
KOYAMA, H., Constructive Organic Chemistry
KUGE, O., Biological Chemistry
MAEDA, Y., Radiochemistry
MATSUKUMA, A., Palaeobiology
MIYAHARA, S., Geophysical Fluid Dynamics
MURAE, T., Organic Cosmochemistry and Geochemistry
NAKADA, M., Mantle Dynamics
NAKANISHI, H., Statistical Physics
NAKANO, H., Quantum Chemistry
NORO, T., Experimental Nuclear Physics
ODAGAKI, T., Condensed Matter Theory
OOMI, G., Solid State Physics
SAGARA, K., Experimental Nuclear Physics
SAGATA, N., Molecular and Developmental Cell Biology
SAKAI, K., Co-ordination Chemistry
SANO, H., Stratigraphy and Sedimentology
SEKIYA, H., Structural Chemistry
SEKIYA, M., Planetary System Formation
SHIMAZAKI, K., Plant Physiology
SHIMIZU, H., Seismology, Volcanic Seismology
SHIMOHIGASHI, Y., Biological Chemistry
SHINOZAKI, B., Low-dimensional Systems
SUGIYAMA, H., Molecular and Cellular Neurobiology
TACHIDA, H., Molecular Evolution, Population Genetics
TAKAHASHI, K., Marine Geology
TAKEDA, S., Liquids and Disordered Systems
TANAKA, T., Solar–Terrestrial Physics
TOH, Y., Animal Physiology
TOKESHI, M., Aquatic Ecology, Community Ecology
TOKITA, M., Polymer Physics
TORAMARU, A., Volcanology
TSURIMOTO, T., DNA Replication and Chromosomal Functions
WADA, H., Magnetism
WATANABE, Y., Solid State Physics
YAHARA, T., Ecology and Evolution
YAHIRO, M., Theoretical Nuclear Physics
YOKOYAMA, T., Inorganic Reaction Chemistry
YOSHIMURA, K., Analytical Chemistry
YUMOTO, K., Space and Earth Electromagnetism

Faculty of Social and Cultural Studies (4-2-1 Ropponmatsu, Chuo-ku, Fukuoka 810-8560; tel. (92) 726-4508; fax (92) 726-4511; internet www.scs.kyushu-u.ac.jp/index.html):

ARIMA, M., Japanese History
FURUYA, Y., Cultural Anthropology
GOYAMA, K., Chinese Classical Literature
HATTORI, H., Japanese History
KITA, I., Geochemistry
KOIKE, H., Prehistoric Ecology
KUSAKA, M., Chinese Literature
MATSUMOTO, T., Modern Japanese Literature
MIYAKAWA, Y., Regional Studies
MORI, T., Greek Philosophy
MORIKAWA, T., Asian History
NAKAHASHI, T., Physical Anthropology
NEI, Y., Philosophy
OSANAI, Y., Geology and Petrology
OTA, Y., Cultural Anthropology
SAKAI, H., Sedimentological Sciences
SHIMA, H., Environmental Biology and Entomology
SHIMIZU, H., Cultural Anthropology
SHIMIZU, Y., Japanese Political Thought
TAKADA, K., International Relations
TAKAHASHI, K., History of Science
TAKANO, N., Japanese History
TANAKA, Y., Archaeology
YATA, O., Environmental Biology and Entomology
YOSHIDA, M., Modernization of Japan
YOSHIOKA, H., Political Economy of Sciences

Institute for Materials Chemistry and Engineering (6-1 Kasuga-koen, Kasuga, Fukuoka 816-8580; tel. (92) 583-7555; fax (92) 583-7060; internet www.cm.kyushu-u.ac.jp):

FUJII, M., Physical Properties
HAYAMI, H., Nanoscale Evaluation
IMAISHI, N., Photonic Materials
INANAGA, J., Synthetic Methodology and Catalysis
KANEMASA, S., Advanced Organic Synthesis
KIKUCHI, H., Design of Nanosystems
KOYAMA, S., Microprocess Control
MARUYAMA, A., Integrated Biomaterials
MATAKA, S., Systems of Functional Molecules
MISHIMA, M., Physical Organic Chemistry
MORI, A., Chemistry of Functional Molecules
NAGASHIMA, H., Cluster Chemistry
NARUTA, Y., Advanced Molecular Conversion
SATO, O., Nanostructured Integrated Materials
SHINMYOZU, T., Chemistry of Molecular Assemblies
TAKAHARA, A., Hybrid Molecular Assemblies
TSUJI, M., Heterogeneous Integrated Materials
YAMAKI, J., Energy Storage Materials
YOSHIZAWA, K., Theoretical Chemistry

Medical Institute of Bioregulation (3-1-1 Maidashi, Higashi-ku, Fukuoka 812-8582; tel. (92) 641-1151; internet www.bioreg.kyushu-u.ac.jp):

FUKUI, Y., Immunogenetics
FUKUMAKI, Y., Disease Genes
HAYASHI, K., Genome Analysis
KOHDA, D., Structural Biology
MAKINO, N., Molecular and Clinical Gerontology
MORI, M., Molecular and Surgical Oncology
NAKABEPPU, Y., Neurofunctional Genomics
NAKAYAMA, K., Cell Biology
NISHIMURA, J., Clinical Immunology
SUMIMOTO, H., Biochemistry and Molecular Biology
TAKEDA, K., Embryonic and Genetic Engineering
TANI, K., Molecular and Clinical Genetics
TOH, H., Genome Informatics
WAKE, N., Molecular and Cell Therapeutics
YOSHIKAI, Y., Host Defence
YOSHIMURA, A., Molecular and Cellular Immunology

Research Institute for Applied Mechanics (6-1 Kasuga-koen, Kasuga, Fukuoka 816-8580; tel. (92) 583-7502; fax (92) 583-7701; internet www.riam.kyushu-u.ac.jp):

ARAKAWA, K., Fracture Mechanics and Materials
HANADA, K., Advanced Fusion Research Center
IMAWAKI, S., Ocean Eddy Dynamics
ITOH, S.-I., High-Energy Plasma Physics
KAKIMOTO, K., Nano-Mechanics
KASHIWAGI, M., Free Surface/Interface Dynamics
KOTERAYAMA, W., Ocean Engineering
KURAMOTO, E., High-Energy Solid State Physics
MASUDA, A., Dynamics Simulation Research Center
MATSUNO, T., Ocean Circulation Dynamics
NAKAMURA, K., Plasma Surface Interaction
OHYA, Y., Wind Engineering
OIKAWA, M., Nonlinear Dynamics
SATO, K., Advanced Fusion Research Center
TAKAO, Y., Heterogeneous Solid Mechanics
UNO, I., Atmospheric Dynamics
WAKATA, Y., Geophysical Fluid Dynamics
YANAGI, T., Dynamics Simulation Research Center
YOON, J.-H., Dynamics Simulation Research Center
YOSHIDA, N., Extreme-Circumstances Structural Materials

ZUSHI, H., Advanced Fusion Research Center

Institute of Health Science (6-1 Kasuga-koen, Kasuga, Fukuoka 816-8580; tel. (92) 583-7555; fax (92) 583-7060):

HASHIMOTO, K., Sports Psychology
ICHIMIYA, A., Psychiatry, Mental Health
KUMAGAI, S., Health and Exercise Epidemiology
NISHIMURA, H., Sports Psychology
OGAKI, T., Exercise Physiology
UEZONO, K., Applied Chronobiology
YAMAMOTO, K., Applied Physiology

Institute of Tropical Agriculture (6-10-1 Hakozaki, Higashi-ku, Fukuoka 812-8581; tel. (92) 642-3076; e-mail njm3076@agr.kyushu-u.ac.jp; fax (92) 642-3077; internet www.agr.kyushu-u.ac.jp/english/tropic):

OGATA, K., Tropical Crops and Environment
YAHATA, H., Global Environment Conservation (Forest Ecophysiology)

Radioisotope Centre (6-10-1 Hakozaki, Higashi-ku, Fukuoka 812-8581; tel. (92) 642-2703; fax (92) 642-2706; e-mail jimurad@mbox.nc.kyushu-u.ac.jp; internet www.scc.kyushu-u.ac.jp/RI):

OSAKI, S., Radiation Protection

International Student Centre (6-10-1 Hakozaki, Higashi-ku, Fukuoka 812-8581; tel. (92) 642-2141; fax (92) 642-2144; e-mail intlrkoryu@jimu.kyushu-u.ac.jp; internet www.isc.kyushu-u.ac.jp):

KASHIMA, E., Japanese Language Education
OKAZAKI, T., Japanese Language Education
POLLACK, J., Exchange Student Programmes (Anthropology)
SCULLY, E., Multicultural Education
SHIMIZU, Y., Japanese Language Education

Research and Development Centre for Higher Education (4-2-1 Ropponmatsu, Chuo-ku, Fukuoka 810-8560; tel. (92) 726-4508; fax (92) 726-4511; internet www.rche.kyushu-u.ac.jp/index-e.html):

FUCHITA, Y., Organometallic Chemistry
KIRA, Y., Clinical Psychology
SOEJIMA, Y., Crystal Physics
TAKEYA, S., Student Selection, Information Science, Databases

Art, Science and Technology Centre for Co-operative Research (6-1 Kasuga-koen, Kasuga, Fukuoka 816-8580; tel. (92) 583-7883; fax (92) 573-8729; internet www.astec.kyushu-u.ac.jp):

KUWANO, N., Advanced Functional Materials
MASE, A., Ionized Gas and Laser
MIURA, N., Environment and New Energy
NAKASHIMA, H., Advanced Functional Devices
TANIGAWA, T., Liaison Division
YUMOTO, N., Design Division

Computing and Communications Centre (6-10-1 Hakozaki, Higashi-ku, Fukuoka 812-8581; tel. (92) 642-2303; fax (92) 642-2294; e-mail syomu@cc.kyushu-u.ac.jp; internet www.cc.kyushu-u.ac.jp):

AOYAGI, M., Computational Science
FUJINO, S., Computing
HIROKAWA, S., Information Science
TABATA, Y., German

Biotron Institute (6-10-1 Hakozaki, Higashi-ku, Fukuoka 812-8581; tel. (92) 642-3066; fax (92) 642-3069; e-mail seikan@agr.kyushu-u.ac.jp; internet 133.5.207.201/index.html):

CHIKUSHI, J., Soil Environment

Research Center for Korean Studies (6-10-1 Hakozaki, Higashi-ku, Fukuoka 812-8581; tel. (92) 642-4358; fax (92) 642-4359; e-mail rcks.uok@mbox.nc.kyushu-u.ac.jp; internet rcks.isc.kyushu-u.ac.jp):

MATSUBARA, T., Cultural History of Japanese-Korean Relations

Centre for Future Chemistry (6-10-1 Hakozaki, Higashi-ku, Fukuoka 812-8581; tel. and fax (92) 642-3609; e-mail ogawatcm@mbox.nc.kyushu-u.ac.jp):

OGAWA, M., Functional Materials Technology, Life Sciences

Bio-Architecture Centre (6-10-1 Hakozaki, Higashi-ku, Fukuoka 812-8581; tel. (92) 642-7282):

FURUYA, S., Metabolic Regulation Research
KONDO, T., Biomaterial Design
SHIRAISHI, F., Bioprocess Design

Kyushu University Museum (6-10-1 Hakozaki, Higashi-ku, Fukuoka 812-8581; tel. and fax (92) 642-4252; e-mail office@museum.kyushu-u.ac.jp; internet www.museum.kyushu-u.ac.jp):

IWANAGA, S., Japanese Prehistory
MATSUKUMA, A., Paleobiology

Admission Center (6-10-1 Hakozaki, Higashi-ku, Fukuoka 812-8581; tel. (92) 642-4488; fax (92) 642-4485; e-mail info@ac.kyushu-u.ac.jp; internet www.ac.kyushu-u.ac.jp):

TAKEYA, S., Information Science

MIE UNIVERSITY

1515 Kamihama-cho, Tsu-shi, Mie 514
Telephone: (592) 32-1211
Fax: (592) 31-9000
Internet: www.mie-u.ac.jp

Founded 1949
Independent
Academic year: April to March

President: RYUICHI YATANI
Chief Administration Officer: KATSUYUKI KUROSAKI
Librarian: HIROYUKI NODA

Library of 783,000 vols
Number of teachers: 1,740
Number of students: 7,505

Publications: *Outline of Mie University* (every 2 years), *The Journal of Law and Economics* (Hōkei Ronsō), various faculty bulletins

DEANS

Faculty of Humanities and Social Sciences: HIDEKAZU HIROSE
Faculty of Education: TAKESHI KINOSHITA
School of Medicine: RYUICHI YATANI
Faculty of Engineering: GORO SAWA
Faculty of Bioresources: HITOSHI OBATA
College of Medical Sciences: KATSUMI DEGUCHI

UNIVERSITY OF MIYAZAKI

1-1 Gakuen Kibanadai Nishi, Miyazaki-shi, Miyazaki 889-2192
Telephone: (985) 58-7104
Fax: (985) 58-2896
E-mail: kokusai@miyazaki-u.ac.jp
Internet: www.miyazaki-u.ac.jp

Founded 1949; present name and status 2003 following integration of Miyazaki Medical College
Independent
Academic year: April to March (two semesters)

President: A. SUMIYOSHI
Registrar: K. OHTANI
Librarian: C. TAMURA

Number of teachers: 624
Number of students: 5,450

Publications: Bulletins and memoirs of the faculties

DEANS

Faculty of Agriculture: S. KOBAYE
Faculty of Education and Culture: T. IWAMOTO
Faculty of Engineering: K. HIRANO
Miyazaki Medical College: H. KANNAN

ATTACHED INSTITUTES

Center of Educational Research and Planning: Dir H. IMOU.

Co-operative Research Center: Dir K. KUROSAWA.

Education and Research Center for Lifelong Learning: Dir H. KAMIJOU.

Frontier Science Research Center: Dir T. NAKAYAMA.

Information Processing Center: Dir K. TAKAGISHI.

Total Hygiene Safety Health Center: Dir C. TERAI.

MURORAN INSTITUTE OF TECHNOLOGY

Mizumoto-cho 27-1, Muroran 050-8585, Hokkaido
Telephone: (143) 46-5022
Fax: (143) 46-5033
Internet: www.muroran-it.ac.jp

Founded 1949
Independent
Academic year: April to March

President: HIROAKI TAGASHIRA
Administrative Officer: YASHUTO UEMARA
Chief Librarian: KEN-ICHI MATSUOKA

Library of 284,300 vols
Number of teachers: 360
Number of students: 3,500

Publication: *Memoirs* (annually)

HEADS OF DEPARTMENTS

Structural Engineering: KAZUO OHTSUKI
Urban Environmental Planning: KAZUTAKA KUROSAWA
Environmental Engineering: HITOSHI HOZUMI
Information Processing Engineering: HIROSHI KUBO
Materials Process Engineering: SHINJI HIRAI
Electrical and Electronic Engineering: M MIYAO
Common Subject Division: EIKO ANDO

NAGAOKA UNIVERSITY OF TECHNOLOGY

1603-1 Kamitomioka, Nagaoka, Niigata 940-2188
Telephone: (258) 46-6000
Fax: (258) 47-9000
E-mail: syomugroup@jcom.nagaokaut.ac.jp
Internet: www.nagaokaut.ac.jp

Founded 1976
State control
Language of instruction: Japanese, English
Academic year: April to March

President: Prof. YO KOJIMA
Vice-President (Academic Affairs): Professor YASUNORI MIYATA
Vice-President (Evaluation): Profressor IKUZO NISHIGUCHI
Vice-President (Graduate School): Professor YASUNOBU INOUE
Vice-President (Industry–Academia Cooperation and Information): ATSUSHI KAWASAKI
Vice-President (International Affairs): Professor KOZO ISHIZAKI
Vice-President (Research, Admission and Student Affairs): Professor KYUICHI MARUYAMA
Director of Administration: SATO MASARU

Library of 140,000 vols
Number of teachers: 212
Number of students: 2,469

Departments of Mechanical Engineering, Electrical Engineering, Materials Science and Technology, Civil and Environmental Engineering, Bioengineering, Management and Information System Science, System Safety

DEANS

School of Engineering: Prof. YASUNOBU INOUE
Graduate School of Engineering: Prof. YASUNOBU INOUE
Graduate School of Management of Technology: Prof. YASUNORI MIYATA

HEADS OF DEPARTMENTS

Bioengineering: Prof. KUNITSUGU SODA
Civil and Environmental Engineering: Prof. SHOJI MATSUMOTO
Electrical Engineering: Prof. MASASUKE TAKATA
Management and Information System Science: Prof. KAZUO NAKAMURA
Materials Science and Technology: Prof. KEIZO UEMATSU
Mechanical Engineering: Prof. SHIGEO YANABE
System Safety: Prof. YOSHIHARU MUTOH

NAGASAKI UNIVERSITY

1-14 Bunkyo-machi, Nagasaki 852-8521
Telephone: (95) 819-2042
Fax: (95) 819-2044
E-mail: www_admin@ml.nagasaki-u.ac.jp
Internet: www.nagasaki-u.ac.jp

Founded 1949
Academic year: April to March
Independent

President: HIROSHI SAITO
Vice-Presidents: TSUYOSHI SAKIYAMA, HARUHIKO MASAKI, SHIGERU KATAMINE
Director-General: SYUSUKE MORITA
Library Director: TAKATOSHI OKABAYASHI

Library of 1,078,347 vols
Number of teachers: 1,067 full-time
Number of students: 8,935

Publications: *Bulletin of the Faculty of Education*, *Journal of Business and Economics* (4 a year), *Annual Review of South East Asian Studies*, *Annual Review of Economics*, *Nagasaki Medical Journal* (4 a year), *Acta Medica Nagasakiensia* (2 a year), *Annual Report of Nagasaki University School of Dentistry*, *Report of the Faculty of Engineering* (2 a year), *Journal of Environmental Studies* (2 a year), *Bulletin of the Faculty of Fisheries*, *Bulletin of the School of Allied Medical Sciences*, *Seasonal Report of the Education and Research Centre for Life-long Learning*

DEANS

Faculty of Education: Prof. TATEO HASHIMOTO
Faculty of Economics: Prof. TOSHIO SUGIHARA
School of Medicine: Prof. TAKASHI KANEMATSU
School of Dentistry: Prof. MITSURU ATSUTA
School of Pharmaceutical Sciences: Prof. KENICHIRO NAKASHIMA
Faculty of Engineering: Prof. JUN OYAMA
Faculty of Environmental Studies: Prof. YOSHIHIKO INOUE
Faculty of Fisheries: Prof. MUTSUYOSHI TSUCHIMOTO
Institute of Tropical Medicine: Prof. YOSHIKI AOKI
Graduate School of Science and Technology: Prof. TADASHI ISHIHARA
Graduate School of Biomedical Sciences: Prof. KOHTARO TANIYAMA
School of Allied Medical Sciences: Prof. AKEMI TERASAKI

DIRECTORS

Center for Educational Research and Training: Prof. AKIFUMI FUKUI
University Hospital attached to School of Medicine: Prof. KOJI SUMIKAWA
Atomic Bomb Disease Institute: Prof. MASAO TOMONAGA
Center for Frontier Life Sciences: Prof. HIROSHI SATO
Division of Radiation Biology and Protection: Prof. YUTAKA OKUMURA
Division of Comparative Medicine: HIROSHI SATO
Division of Functional Genomics: NORIO NIIKAWA
University Hospital attached to School of Dentistry: Prof. HIROYUKI FUJII
Garden for Medicinal Plants: Prof. ISAO KONO
Research Center for Tropical Infectious Diseases: Prof. MASAAKI SHIMADA
Animal Research Center: Prof. MICHIO NAKAMURA
Marine Research Institute: Prof. HIDEAKI NAKATA
Health Center: Prof. NOBUKO ISHII
Education and Research Center for Life-long Learning: Prof. KAGEHIRO ITOYAMA
Science Information Center: Prof. HIDEO KURODA
Joint Research Center: Prof. MAKOTO EGASHIRA
Environmental Protection Center: Prof. TAKEHIRO TAKEMASA
Center for Instrumental Analysis: Prof. SUSUMI HATAKEYAMA
International Student Center: Prof. YOSHIHIRO MATSUMURA
Research and Development Center for Higher Education: Prof. SHIGERU KATAMINE

PROFESSORS

Faculty of Education (fax (95) 819-2265; internet www.edu.nagasaki-u.ac.jp):

ADACHI, K., Analysis and Applied Mathematics
AIKAWA, K., School for Intellectually-impaired Children
AKASAKI, M., Teaching of Home Economics
ARITA, Y., Teaching of Social Studies
AZUMA, M., Biology
FUKUI, A., Music Education
FUKUYAMA, Y., Physics
FUNAKOE, K., Law
FURUYA, Y., Materials Science and Engineering
GOTO, Y., Early Childhood Education and Care
HAMASAKI, K., German Literature
HARADA, J., Educational Psychology
HASHIMOTO, T., Science Education
HIGUCHI, S., Analytical Chemistry
HORIUCHI, I., Pianoforte Playing
IIZUKA, T., Philosophy
IKAWA, S., Painting
INOUE, I., American Literature
ITOYAMA, K., Teaching of Technology
IYAMA, K., Social Education
JINNO, N., Biology
KABASHIMA, S., Physics
KAMIZONO, K., Moral and Philosophy Education
KATSUMATA, T., Japanese Literature
KITAMURA, Y., Analysis
KOGA, M., Solid State Physics
MATUNAGA, J., Teaching of Health and Physical Education
MIYAZAKI, M., Developmental Psychology
MURATA, Y., Developmental Psychology
NAKAMURA, M., American Literature
NAKAMURA, Y., English and American Literature
NAKANISHI, H., Biology
NISHIZAWA, S., Physical Fitness
OBARA, T., Exercise Physiology
ODA, M., Design
OSAKI, Y., Astronomy
OTSUBO, Y., Teaching of English
SATO, K., Sculpture
SINNO, T., Psychological Study of Preschool Children's Play
SINOHARA, S., Philosophy
SUGAWARA, M., Exercise Physiology
SUGAWARA, T., Geometry
SUGIYAMA, S., Wood Working
TAHARA, Y., School Health and Sports Physiology
TAKAHASHI, S., International Law, Constitutional Law
TAKAHASHI, S., Sociology
TAMARI, M., Food and Nutritional Chemistry
TANIGAWA, M., Politics
TOMONAGA, S., Psychology
WASHIO, T., Algebra
YAMAGUCHI, T., History
YAMAMOTO, T., Teaching of Japanese
YAMANO, S., Theory of Music
YAMAUCHI, M., Physical Education
YANAGIDA, Y., Educational Sociology
YASUKOUCHI, Y., Teaching of Japanese
YOKOYAMA, M., Politics
YOSHIOKA, H., Educational Psychology

Faculty of Economics (4-2-1 Katafuchi, Nagasaki 850-8506; tel. (95) 820-6300; fax (95) 820-6370; internet www.econ.nagasaki-u.ac.jp):

AOYAMA, S., Development Economics
BASU, D., International Economics
FUJINO, T., Japanese Corporations and Management
FUJITA, W., Economics of Natural Resources and Energy
FUKAURA, A., Monetary Economics
FUKUZAWA, K., Labour Economics
FURUYAMA, M., Law and Finance
GUNN, G., International Relations
IDE, K., Modern Asian Economies
IMADA, T., Accounting
KANKE, M., Business Management
KASAHARA, T., Business Enterprise and Human Evolution
KAWAMURA, Y., Corporate Planning of Financial Institutions, Investment Banking
KIHARA, T., Co-operation among Nations, and International Economics
KOREEDA, M., Microeconomics
MARUYAMA, Y., Decision Making
MATSUMOTO, M., Economic History of the British Empire
MATSUNAGA, A., Small Business Administration
MIHARA, Y., Human Resource Management
MURATA, S., Microeconomics
MURATA, Y., Mathematics
OKADA, H., Financial Accounting
SHIBATA, K., Japanese Economic History
SUGIHARA, T., Management Engineering
SUSAI, M., International Finance
TAGUCHI, N., International Investment
TAKAHASHI, Y., Intellectual Property and Licensing
TAKAKURA, Y., Political Economy
TATEYAMA, S., Business Enterprises and Asian Economics
UCHIDA, S., Monetary Economics
UENO, K., Financial Accounting
UNOTORO, Y., Japanese Economy
YAJIMA, K., Derivative Securities

School of Medicine (1-12-4 Sakamoto, Nagasaki 852-8523; tel. (95) 849-7000; fax (95) 849-7166; internet www.med.nagasaki-u.ac.jp):

AIKAWA, T., Physiology of Visceral Function and Body Fluid
AOYAGI, K., Preventive Health Sciences and Community Health
EGUCHI, K., Immunology, Endocrinology and Metabolism
EISHI, K., Cardiovascular Surgery

FUNASE, K., Human Motor Control, Exercise Physiology
HAMANO, K., Foundations of Nursing
HAYASHI, K., Radiological Science
ISHIHARA, K., Adult Nursing, Cancer Nursing
ISHIMARU, T., Obstetrics and Gynaecology
ITO, T., Biochemistry
KAMIHIRA, S., Laboratory Medicine
KANEMATSU, T., Surgery
KANETAKE, H., Nephro-urology
KATAMINE, S., Cellular and Molecular Biology
KATAYAMA, I., Dermatology
KATO, K., Anatomy of Locomotor Systems, Physical Anthropology
KOHNO, S., Molecular and Clinical Microbiology
KOJI, T., Histology and Cell Biology
KONDO, T., Clinical Biochemistry and Molecular Biology in Ageing-related Vascular Diseases and Cancer
MATSUMOTO, T., Paediatrics
MATSUSAKA, N., Rehabilitation Medicine, Orthopaedic Surgery
MATSUYAMA, T., Cytokine Signalling
MIYASHITA, H., Child Nursing, Rehabilitation
MORISHITA, M., Community Health Nursing
MORIUCHI, H., Medical Virology
NAGAO, T., Occupational Therapy, Assistive Technology
NAGASHIMA, S., Macroscopic Morphology
NAGATA, I., Clinical Neuroscience, Neurology and Neurosurgery
NAKAGOMI, O., Molecular Epidemiology
NAKAJIMA, H., Gynaecological Oncology, Obstetrics
NAKAZONO, I., Forensic Pathology and Science
NIIKAWA, N., Human Genetics
NIWA, M., Neurosensory Pharmacology
OHISHI, K., Midwifery
OHTA, Y., Psychiatry, Mental and Physical Health
OKUMURA, Y., Radiation Biophysics
SATO, H., Comparative Medicine
SEKINE, I., Molecular Pathology
SENJYU, H., Physical Therapy, Pulmonary Rehabilitation
SHIBATA, Y., Radiation Epidemiology
SHIMOKAWA, I., Pathology and Gerontology
SHINDO, H., Orthopaedic Pathomechanism
SHINOHARA, K., Physiology
SUMIKAWA, K., Anaesthesiology
TAGAWA, Y., Thoracic Surgery and Cytometry
TAGUCHI, T., Pathology
TAHARA, H., Physical Therapy, Quality of Life
TAKAHASHI, H., Otorhinolaryngology
TANIYAMA, K., Pharmacology and Therapeutics
TASHIRO, T., Respirology, Infectious Diseases
TERASAKI, A., Adult Health Nursing
TOKUNAGA, M., Public Health Nursing
TOMONAGA, M., Molecular Medicine and Haematology
URATA, H., Adult Nursing, Surgical Nursing
YAMASHITA, S., Molecular Medicine
YANO, K., Cardiovascular Medicine
YOSHIMURA, T., Neurology (Morphology in Neuromuscular Diseases)
YUI, K., Immunology

School of Dentistry (1-7-1 Sakamoto, Nagasaki 852-8588; tel. (95) 849-7600; fax (95) 849-7608; internet www.de.nagasaki-u.ac.jp):

ATSUTA, M., Fixed Prosthodontics
FUJII, H., Removable Prosthodontics
FUJIWARA, T., Paediatric Dentistry
HARA, Y., Periodontology
HAYASHI, Y., Endodontics and Operative Dentistry
HISATSUNE, K., Dental Materials Science
INOKUCHI, T., Oral and Maxillofacial Surgery II
KATO, Y., Dental Pharmacology
MIZUNO, A., Oral and Maxillofacial Surgery I
NAKAMURA, T., Radiology and Cancer Biology
NAKAYAMA, K., Oral Bacteriology
NEMOTO, T., Oral Biochemistry
OI, K., Dental Anaesthesiology
ROKUTANDA, A., Oral Anatomy
SHINSHO, F., Preventive Dentistry
TAKANO, K., Oral Histology
TODA, K., Oral Physiology
YAMAGUCHI, A., Oral Pathology
YOSHIDA, N., Orthodontics

School of Pharmaceutical Sciences (fax (95) 819-2412; internet www.ph.nagasaki-u.ac.jp/indexj.html):

FUJITA, K., Pharmaceutical Chemistry
HATAKEYAMA, S., Pharmaceutical Organic Chemistry
KAI, M., Chemistry of Biofunctional Molecules
KOBAYASHI, N., Molecular Biology of Diseases
KOHNO, M., Cell Regulation
KOUNO, I., Pharmacognosy
KURODA, N., Analytical Chemistry for Pharmaceutics
MURATA, I., Pharmacotherapeutics
NAKAMURA, J., Pharmaceutics
NAKASHIMA, K., Analytical Research for Pharmacoinformatics
NAKAYAMA, M., Hygienic Chemistry
NATSUMARA, Y., Synthetic Chemistry for Pharmaceutics
UEDA, H., Molecular Pharmacology and Neuroscience
WATANABE, M., Radiation and Life Science
YOSHIMOTO, T., Biotechnology

Faculty of Engineering (fax (95) 849-4999; internet www.eng.nagasaki-u.ac.jp):

AOYAGI, H., Biochemistry
EGASHIRA, M., Materials Chemistry
FUJIYAMA, H., Plasma Science
FUKUNAGA, H., Magnetics
FURUMOTO, K., Hydraulics
HARADA, T., Reinforced and Prestressed Concrete Structures
HASAKA, M., Materials Physics and Engineering
IMAI, Y., Fracture Mechanics
ISHIMATSU, T., Measurement and Control Engineering
IWANAGA, H., Analysis of Crystal Structure
IWAO, M., Synthetic Organic Chemistry
KAGAWA, A., Metal Science
KANEMARU, K., Heat Transfer
KAWAZOE, T., Tribology
KISU, H., Computational Mechanics
KOBAYASHI, K., Network Systems
KODAMA, Y., Fluid Dynamics
KUDO, A., Algebra
KUDO, T., Solid State Electrochemistry
MATSUDA, H., Structural and Engineering Mechanics
MATSUO, H., High-Voltage Engineering
MIYAHARA, S., Pattern Recognition and Information Retrieval Systems
NOGUCHI, M., Hydraulics
OGURI, K., Computer and Information Science
OKABAYASHI, T., Dynamics and Control of Structures
ONISHI, M., Co-ordination Chemistry
OYAMA, J., Electrical Machinery
SAKIYAMA, T., Structural Analysis
SETOGUCHI, K., Fatigue
SHIGECHI, T., Thermal Engineering
SHUGYO, M., Inelastic Behaviour of Steel Structures
TAKAHASHI, K., Structural Vibration
TAKENAKA, T., Electromagnetic Wave Theory
TAMARU, Y., Organic Chemistry
TANABASHI, Y., Soil Mechanics
TANAKA, K., Engineering Optics
TSUJI, M., Electrical Control Systems
UCHIYAMA, Y., Ceramics Science and Technology

Faculty of Environmental Studies (fax (95) 819-2716; internet www.env.nagasaki-u.ac.jp/mainJ.shtml):

ARAO, K., Meteorology and Climatology
FUKUSHIMA, K., Anthropology of Religion
GOTO, N., Solid State Physics
HAMA, T., Labour Environment
HAYASE, T., Environmental Politics
HIMENO, J., History of Economics
IDE, Y., Environmental Business Management
IKENAGA, T., Plant Functional Science
IKUNO, M., Civil Law
INOUE, Y., Philosophy
ISHIZAKI, K., Environmental Engineering
KOHRA, S., Environmental Chemistry
MASAKI, H., Oriental Philosophy and Bioethics
MIYA, Y., Crustacean Taxonomy
NAKAMURA, T., Biostatistics and Risk Analysis
NAKAMURA, T., Coastal Oceanography
ONO, T., Environment Economics
SAKUMA, T., Japanese Intellectual History
SONODA, N., German Literature
TAIMURA, A., Exercise Physiology
TAKAZANE, Y., French Culture and Culture Exchange
TAKEMASA, T., Soil Physics
TANIMURA, K., Living Environment
TSUCHIYA, K., Environmental Physiology
UEDA, K., Peptide Chemistry
WAKAKI, T., Japanese Literature
YAMAZAKI, S., Environmental Biochemistry
YOSHIDA, M., Greek Philosophy
YOSHIKAWA, I., Radiation Genetics

Faculty of Fisheries (fax (95) 819-2799; internet www.fish.nagasaki-u.ac.jp/index.htm):

ARAKAWA, O., Marine Food Hygiene
GODA, M., Navigation, Nautical Instruments
HARA, K., Biochemistry
HASHIMOTO, J., Deep-Sea Biology
ISHIHARA, T., Aquatic Biochemistry
ISHIMATSU, A., Fish Physiology
ISHIZAKA, J., Biological Oceanography, Ocean Colour Remote Sensing
KATAOKA, C., Marine Social Science
KITAMURA, H., Marine Chemical Ecology, Effects of Pollution on Marine Life
MATSUBAYASHI, N., Colloid and Interface Science
MATSUOKA, K., Micropalaeontology and Coastal Environment Science
MATSUYAMA, M., Limnology and Oceanography
MORII, H., Ecology and Physiology of Marine and Food Bacteria
NAKATA, H., Fisheries Oceanography and Coastal Oceanography
NATSUKARI, Y., Fisheries Biology, Invertebrates, Cephalopoda
NISHINOKUBI, H., Fishing Boat Seamanship, Fishing Gear Engineering
NOZAKI, Y., Chemistry and Technology of Marine Food Materials
ODA, T., Marine Biochemistry
TACHIBANA, K., Nutritional Chemistry of Marine Food
TAKEMURA, A., Acoustical Behaviour of Marine Animals, Life History of Marine Mammals and Sharks
TAMAKI, A., Ecology of Marine Benthos
TSUCHIMOTO, M., Nutritional Physiology of Marine Food

YAMAGUCHI, Y., Fishing Technology Science, Fishing Ground Ecology
YOSHIKOSHI, K., Fish Pathology

Institute of Tropical Medicine (1-12-4 Sakamoto, Nagasaki 852-8523; tel. (95) 849-7800; fax (95) 849-7805; internet www.tm.nagasaki-u.ac.jp):

AOKI, Y., Parasitology
HIRAYAMA, K., Molecular Immunogenetics
HIRAYAMA, T., Bacteriology
IWASAKI, T., Pathology
KANBARA, H., Protozoology
MIZOTA, T., Social Environment
MOJI, K., Human Ecology
MORITA, K., Virology
NAGATAKE, T., Internal Medicine
NAKAMURA, M., Biochemistry
SHIMADA, M., Eco-epidemiology
TAKAGI, M., Medical Entomology
YAMAMOTO, N., Preventive Medicine and AIDS Research

Graduate School of Science and Technology (fax (95) 819-2491; internet www.seisan.nagasaki-u.ac.jp):

FUJITA, Y., Marine Phycology
FURUKAWA, M., Polymer Science
GOTOH, K., Remote Sensing
HAGIWARA, A., Marine Invertebrate Zoology, Live Food Science, Applied Planktology
ISHIDA, M., Diesel Combustion Engineering
KURODA, H., Computer and Information Science
MATSUO, H., Electronic and Digital Control
NAKASHIMA, N., Chemistry and Materials Science of Nanocarbons
YOSHITAKE, Y., Vibration of Structures

NAGOYA INSTITUTE OF TECHNOLOGY

Gokiso-cho, Showa-ku, Nagoya 466-855
Telephone: (52) 735-5000
Fax: (52) 735-5009
Internet: www.nitech.ac.jp

Founded 1949
Independent
Language of instruction: Japanese
Academic year: April to March

President: HIROAKI YANAGIDA
Vice-Presidents: NOBUYUKI MATSUI, IWATA AKIRA, TETSUMI HORIKOSHI
Director-General: HIDESHI SUDA
Director, University Library: KOICHIRO KAWASHIMA

Library of 463,169 vols
Number of teachers: 372
Number of students: 6,516

Publication: *Bulletin* (annually)

HEADS OF DEPARTMENTS

Applied Chemistry: HIROMICHI YAMADA
Materials Science and Engineering: MINORU DOI
Mechanical Engineering: KOICHI TANAKA
Systems Engineering: KEISUKE GOTO
Electrical and Computer Engineering: KOICHI WADA
Intelligence and Computer Science: RYOHEI NAKANO
Architecture and Civil Engineering: AKIO MIZUTANI
Systems Management and Engineering: HITOSHI TATEMITSU
General Studies: YOSHIHIKO YAMAZAKI

ATTACHED INSTITUTES

Ceramics Research Laboratory: 6-29 Asahigaoka 10-chome, Tajimi, Gifu; Dir SUGURU SUZUKI.

Center for Information and Media Studies: Gokiso-cho, Showa-ku, Nagoya 466-8555; e-mail staff@center.nitech.ac.jp; Dir YUKIE KOYAMA.

Instrument and Analysis Center: Gokiso-cho, Showa-ku, Nagoya 466-8555; Dir YOSHIHARU TSUJITA.

Co-operative Research Center: Gokiso-cho, Showa-ku, Nagoya; Dir KOICHI NAKAMURA.

Research Center for Micro-structure Devices: Gokiso-cho, Showa-ku, Nagoya; Dir MASAYOSHI UMENO.

NAGOYA UNIVERSITY

Furo-cho, Chikusa-ku, Nagoya 464-8601
Telephone: (52) 789-2044
Fax: (52) 789-2045
E-mail: intl@post.jimu.nagoya-u.ac.jp
Internet: www.nagoya-u.ac.jp

Founded 1939
Independent
Language of instruction: Japanese
Academic year: April to March (two semesters)

President: SHIN-ICHI HIRANO
Vice-Presidents: KOJUN YAMASHITA, HIDEKI MORI, YUJI WAKAO, YASUO SUGIURA, SHIN-ICHI YAMAMOTO
Director-General for Administration: SABURO TOYODA
Director of the Library: YOSHITO ITOH

Library: see Libraries and Archives
Number of teachers: 1,831 full-time
Number of students: 16,537

Publication: *Nagoya University Bulletin*

DEANS

School of Letters: H. SUGIYAMA
School of Education: T. MURAKAMI
School of Law: H. SABURI
School of Economics: Y. TOMOSUGI
School of Informatics and Sciences: M. SANO
School of Science: I. OHMINE
School of Medicine: M. HAMAGUCHI
School of Engineering: N. SAWAKI
School of Agricultural Sciences: T. MATSUDA
Graduate School of Bioagricultural Sciences: T. MATSUDA
Graduate School of Economics: Y. TOMOSUGI
Graduate School of Education and Human Development: T. MURAKAMI
Graduate School of Engineering: N. SAWAKI
Graduate School of Environmental Studies: T. KURODA
Graduate School of Information Science: K. AGUSA
Graduate School of International Development: H. NAKANISHI
Graduate School of Languages and Culture: K. KONDO
Graduate School of Law: H. SABURI
Graduate School of Letters: H. SUGIYAMA
Graduate School of Mathematics: Y. NAMIKAWA
Graduate School of Medicine: M. HAMAGUCHI
Graduate School of Science: I. OHMINE

DIRECTORS

Research Institute of Environmental Medicine: I. KODAMA
Solar–Terrestrial Environment Laboratory: R. FUJII
Radioisotope Research Center: K. NISHIZAWA
Center for Gene Research: M. ISHIURA
Center for Chronological Research: K. SUZUKI
Bioscience and Biotechnology Center: M. KOBAYASHI
Education Center for International Students: M. EZAKI
Research Center for Materials Science: K. TATSUMI
Center for Studies of Higher Education: K. TODAYAMA
Hydrospheric Atmospheric Research Center: H. UYEDA
Center for Developmental Clinical Psychology and Psychiatry: S. HONJO
Research Center of Health, Physical Fitness and Sports: K. SHIMAOKA
University Hospital: A. IGUCHI
International Co-operation Center for Agricultural Education: H. TAKEYA
Nagoya University Museum: M. ADACHI
Center for Asian Legal Exchange: K. SUGIURA
Information Technology Center: T. WATANABE
EcoTopia Science Institute: T. MATSUI
Center for Co-operative Research in Advanced Science and Technology: G. OBINATA
Center for Information Media Studies: I. YAMAMOTO

PROFESSORS

School of Agricultural Sciences and Graduate School of Bioagricultural Sciences (tel. (52) 789-5266; fax (52) 789-4005; e-mail info@agr.nagoya-u.ac.jp; internet www.agr.nagoya-u.ac.jp):

AOI, K., Polymer Chemistry
DOKE, N., Plant Pathology
EBIHARA, S., Animal Behavioural Physiology
FUKUSHIMA, K., Forest Chemistry
FUKUTA, K., Animal Morphology and Function
HATTORI, K., Plant Genetics and Breeding
HATTORI, S., Forest Resources Utilization
HIRASHIMA, Y., Biomaterials Engineering
ISOBE, M., Organic Chemistry
KIMURA, M., Soil Biology and Chemistry
KITAGAWA, Y., Stem Cell Engineering
KOBAYASHI, M., Biodynamics of Insect–Virus Interactions
KOBAYASHI, T., Gene Regulation
MAEDA, K., Reproductive Science
MAESHIMA, M., Cell Dynamics
MAKI, M., Molecular and Cellular Regulation
MATSUDA, T., Molecular Bioregulation
MIYAKE, H., Plant Resources and Environment
MIZUNO, T., Molecular Biology and Molecular Genetics
MORI, H., Developmental Signalling Biology
NAKAMURA, K., Biological Chemistry
NAKANO, H., Molecular Biotechnology
NAMIKAWA, T., Animal Genetics
NOGUCHI, T., Molecular Physiological Chemistry
OHTA, T., Forest Meteorology and Hydrology
OJIKA, M., Molecular Function Modelling
OMATA, T., Molecular Plant Physiology
OSAWA, T., Food and Biodynamics
SAKAGAMI, Y., Bioactive Natural Products Chemistry
SHIBATA, E., Forest Protection
SHIMADA, K., Animal Physiology
SOMIYA, H., Animal Information Biology
TAKABE, T., Biosphere Symbiosis
TAKENAKA, C., Forest Environment and Resources
TAKEYA, H., Socioeconomic Science of Food Production
TANAKA, T., Applied Entomology
TOMARU, N., Forest Ecology and Physiology
TSUCHIKAWA, S., Mechanical Engineering for Biological Materials
TSUGE, T., Microbes and Plant Production
YAGINUMA, T., Sericulture Entomological resources
YAMAUCHI, A., Biosphere Resources Cycling
YAMAKI, S., Horticultural Science
YOKOTA, H., Animal Feeds and Production
YOSHIMURA, T., Biomacromolecules

School and Graduate School of Economics (tel. (52) 789-4920; fax (52) 789-4921; internet www.soec.nagoya-u.ac.jp):

ANDO, T., History of European Economic Thought
ARAYAMA, Y., Agricultural Policy and Economic Growth
HIRAKAWA, H., Asian Economics
KANAI, Y., British Monetary History during the Inter-war Period
KIMURA, S., Management Accounting
KISIDA, T., Organization
MINAGAWA, T., Microeconomic Foundations of Macroeconomics
NAGAO, S., History of Economic and Social Thought, Political Economy
NAKANISHI, S., Japanese Economic History
NABESHIMA, N., History of Economic Thought, Political Economy
NEMOTO, J., Applied Econometrics and Productivity Analysis
NOGUCHI, A., Financial Accounting
OHTA, S., Labour Economics
OKUMURA, R., Intertemporal Open-economy Macroeconomics
SATO, M., Conceptual Framework of Business Accounting
TAKAKUWA, S., Business Administration
TAKEUCHI, J., Comparative Study on Economic Development
TAKEUCHI, N., Stabilization Policy
TAMARU, M., Globalization and Japanese Economy
TAWADA, M., International Trade Theory
TOMOSUGI, Y., Management Audit
TSUKADA, H., Mathematical Finance
WAGO, H., Econometrics Analysis
YAMAMOTO, T., Financial Statement Analysis
YAMORI, N., Monetary Economics and Banking Theory

School and Graduate School of Education and Human Development (tel. (52) 789-2602; fax (52) 789-2666; internet www.educa.nagoya-u.ac.jp):

HAYAKAWA, M., Philosophy of Human Becoming
HAYAMIZU, T., Psychology of Personality
IMAZU, K., Sociology of Education
KAGEYAMA, H., School Psychology
KANAI, A., Clinical Psychology
KATOH, S., History of Education
MATOBA, M., Methods of Education
MATUSHITA, H., Philosophy of Human Becoming
MORITA, M., Family Psychology
MURAKAMI, T., Psychometrics
NAKAJIMA, T., Educational Administration
NISHINO, S., Comparative Education
NOGUCHI, H., Psychometrics
OKADA, T., Cognitive Psychology
OTANI, T., Technologies in Education
TAKAGI, Y., School Environment
TERADA, M., Vocational and Technical Education
UEDA, T., Educational Management
YOSHIDA, T., Social Psychology

School and Graduate School of Engineering (Furo-cho, Chikusa-ku, Nagoya 464-8603; tel. (52) 789-3405; fax (52) 789-3100; internet www.engg.nagoya-u.ac.jp):

ANDO, H., Mathematical Information Systems
ASAI, S., Electromagnetic Processing of Materials
ASAOKA, A., Soil Mechanics
BABA, Y., Applied Analytical Chemistry
FUJIMAKI, A., Integrated Quantum Devices Engineering
FUKUDA, T., Micro-Nano System Control Engineering
FURUHASHI, T., Complex Systems
HAYAKAWA, Y., Intelligent Mechatronics
HIRASAWA, M., Nano-integration Engineering
HONDA, H., Bio-process Engineering
HOSOE, S., Mechatronics Control
ICHIMIYA, A., Fundamental Quantum Engineering
IGUCHI, T., Quantum Beam Measurement and Instrumentation
IIDA, T., Energy Environmental Safety Engineering
IIJIMA, S., Molecular Biology and Genetic Engineering
IKUTA, K., Biomedical Micro— and Nano-Mechatronics
INOUE, J., Solid State Engineering
IRITANI, E., Mechanical Separation Process Engineering
ISHIDA, Y., Intelligent Manufacturing Machinery
ISHIHARA, K., Chemistry of Biologically Active Materials
ISHIKAWA, T., Deformation Processing of Materials
ITOH, Y., Infrastructure System Design
KAMIGAITO, M., Organic Chemistry of Macromolecules
KANEDA, Y., Computational Fluid Mechanics
KANETAKE, N., Structure and Morphology Control Engineering
KAWAIZUMI, F., Diffusional Process Engineering
KITANO, T., Radiation Chemistry
KODA, S., Chemical Physics of Condensed Matters
KONO, A., Optical Electronics
KOUMOTO, K., Solid State Materials
KUKITA, Y., Energy Transport Engineering
KURODA, K., Nano-Material Characterization
KURODA, S., Quantum Material Physics and Engineering
KUWABARA, M., Materials Reaction Process Engineering
MATSUDA, H., Thermal Energy Engineering
MATSUDA, I., Design of Catalytic Reactions
MATSUI, M., Magnetism of Materials and Magnetics
MATSUI, T., Energy Functional Materials Engineering
MATSUMOTO, T., Knowledge-Based Design
MATSUMURA, T., High Current and Power Engineering
MATSUSHITA, Y., Physical Chemistry of Materials
MITAKU, S., Biophysical Engineering
MITSUYA, Y., Micro- and Nano-Instrumentation Engineering
MIYATA, T., Fatigue and Fracture of Materials
MIZUTANI, N., Coastal and Maritime Engineering
MIZUTANI, T., Quantum Nano-devices Engineering
MORINAGA, M., Materials Design
MURAMATSU, N., Human System Engineering
MUTO, S., Energy Materials Science under Extreme Conditions
NAKAMURA, A., Optical Physics
NAKAMURA, H., Concrete Materials and Structures
NAKAMURA, Y., Fluid Dynamics
NAKAMURA, M., Resources and Environment
NAKAZATO, K., Intelligent Devices
NIIMI, T., Micro Thermofluid Engineering
NISHIYAMA, H., Selective Organic Synthesis
NOMURA, H., Casting and Solidification Process Engineering
OHNO, N., Computational Solid Mechanics
OKIDO, M., Surface-Interface Engineering
OKUMA, S., Information and Control Systems
ONOGI, K., Process Systems Engineering
SAITO, Y., Nano-Structure Analysis
SAKAI, Y., Statistical Fluid Engineering
SAKATA, M., Structural Physics Engineering
SATO, K., Micro- and Nano-Process Engineering
SATO, K., Communication Networks
SATSUMA, A., Catalyst Design
SAWADA, Y., Disaster Prevention, Geotechnical Engineering
SAWAKI, N., Semiconductor Electronics
SEKI, T., Molecular Assembly, Systems Engineering
SHAMOTO, E., Ultra Precision Engineering
SHIMADA, T., Super Microcomputing
SHINODA, T., Fabrication of Materials Engineering
SODA, K., Quantum Beam Materials Engineering
SOGA, T., Physical Gas Dynamics
SUGAI, H., Plasma Electronics
SUZUOKI, Y., Energy System and Engineering
TAGAWA, T., Chemical Reaction Engineering
TAKAGI, K., Functional Crystalline Chemistry
TAKAI, Y., Energy Device Engineering
TAKAMURA, S., Plasma Science and Technology
TAKEDA, K., Physical Chemistry of Materials
TAKEDA, Y., Nano-Materials and Devices
TANAKA, E., Biomechanics
TANAKA, K., Materials and Mechanics
TANIGUCHI, G., Architectural Planning
TANIMOTO, M., Visual Information
TORIMOTO, T., Material Design Chemistry
TSUBAKI, J., Processes for the Functional Development of Materials
TSUJIMOTO, T., River, Coastal and Estuarine Hydro-Morphodynamics
TSUNASHIMA, S., Spin Electronics
UEDA, T., Structural Mechanics
UMEHARA, N., Manufacturing Process Technology
UMEMURA, A., Propulsion Energy Systems Engineering
URITANI, A., Applied Nuclear Physics
USAMI, T., Structural Analysis
YAMADA, K., Control Systems Engineering
YAMAMOTO, I., Energy Materials Recycling Engineering
YAMANE, T., Protein Crystallography and Structural Biology
YAMANE, Y., Reactor Physics and Engineering
YAMASHITA, H., Heat Transfer and Combustion
YAMAZAKI, K., Energy Materials Science Engineering
YASHIMA, E., Polymer Materials Design
YOSHIKAWA, N., Aerospace Microsystems
ZAIMA, S., Nano-Structured Electronic Device Engineering

Graduate School of Environmental Studies (tel. (52) 789-3454; fax (52) 789-3452; internet www.env.nagoya-u.ac.jp):

AGETA, Y., Glaciology
ANDO, M., Seismology and Geodesy
ENAMI, M., Metamorphic Petrology and Rock-Forming Mineralogy
FUJII, N., Volcanology and Planetary Physics
FUKUWA, N., Earthquake Engineering
HATTA, T., Neuropsychology
HAYASHI, N., Economic and Urban Geography
HAYASHI, Y., Sustainable Transport and Spatial Development
HIBINO, T., Electrochemistry
HIRAHARA, K., Seismology
HIROSE, Y., Environmental Social Psychology
HOSHINO, M., Surface Material Systems

IKADATSU, Y., Jurisprudence
IMURA, H., Environmental Systems Analysis and Planning
ISHII, K., Associative Learning
ITAKURA, T., Sociology
ITO, Y., Counselling and Clinical Psychology (Person-Centred Approach and Focusing-Oriented Psychotherapy)
KAI, K., Meteorology, Climatology and Remote Sensing
KAINUMA, J., Sociology
KANZAWA, H., Meteorology
KATAGI, A., Architectural Design and Theory
KAWABE, I., REE Geochemistry, Geochemical Earthquake Prediction
KAWADA, M., History of Political Thought in Japan
KAWAGUCHI, J., Cognitive Psychology, Human Memory
KAWAI, T., Environmental Science
KAWASAKI, S., Economics
KUNO, S., Environmental Engineering, Environmental Psychology
KURODA, T., Urban Economics, Regional Science, Economic Theory
MASUZAWA, T., Inorganic Biogeochemistry
MATSUBARA, T., Environmental Science, Microbiology, Biochemistry
MATSUMOTO, E., Geochemistry
MIZOGUCHI, T., Historical Geography, Regional Study of South Asia
MORIKAWA, T., Transport Planning
MORIMOTO, H., Mathematical Biology
MURATA, S., Organic Chemistry, Physical Organic Chemistry, Environmental Materials Science
NISHIHARA, K., Sociology, Phenomenological Sociology, Social Theory
OKAMOTO, K., Geography, Behavioural Geography, Urban Geography
OHKAWA, M., Constitutional Law, Environmental Law
OHMORI, H., Structural Mechanics and Computational Analysis
OKUMIYA, M., Optimization of Energy Supplies in Building and Urban Scale
OZAWA, T., Geobiology, Evolutionary Biology
SANO, M., Fuel Cell, Secondary Battery, Energy Systems
SHIMIZU, H., Architectural Planning and Design, Theatre Planning and Administration
SUGIMOTO, T., Heterocyclic Chemistry
SUZUKI, Y., Active Tectonics
TANAKA, S., Urban Sociology
TANAKA, T., Isotope Geochemistry
TANOUE, E., Marine Biogeochemistry
TESHIGAWARA, M., Reinforced Concrete Structures
UMITSU, M., Geomorphology, Quaternary Geology, Geo-environmental Studies
YAMADA, I., Seismology and Planetary Physics
YAMADA, K., Structural Engineering, Bridge Engineering
YAMAGUCHI, Y., Remote Sensing for Environmental Monitoring

Graduate School of Information Science (tel. (52) 789-4716; fax (52) 789-4800; e-mail syomuk@info.human.nagoya-u.ac.jp; internet www.is.nagoya-u.ac.jp):

AGUSA, K., Information Engineering
ARITA, T., Complex Systems Science
AZEGAMI, H., Complex Systems Science
HAYAKAWA, Y., Complex Systems Science
HIRATA, T., Computer Science and Mathematical Informatics
HIROKI, S., Complex Systems Science
ISHII, K., Systems and Social Informatics
JINBO, M., Computer Science and Mathematical Informatics
KOGA, N., Complex Systems Science
MATSUBARA, Y., Computer Science and Mathematical Informatics
MATSUMOTO, H., Computer Science and Mathematical Informatics
MATSUO, S., Complex Systems Science
MITSUI, T., Computer Science and Mathematical Informatics
MIWA, K., Media Science
MORI, M., Complex Systems Science
MORI, T., Complex Systems Science
MURASE, H., Media Science
NAGAOKA, M., Complex Systems Science
OHNISHI, N., Media Science
SAITO, H., Media Science
SAKABE, T., Information Engineering
SAKAI, M., Computer Science and Mathematical Informatics
SASAI, M., Complex Systems Science
SUENAGA, Y., Media Science
SUGIYAMA, Y., Complex Systems Science
TAKADA, H., Information Engineering
TAKAGI, N., Information Engineering
TAKAHAMA, M., Information Engineering
TAKEDA, K., Media Science
TODAYAMA, K., Systems and Social Informatics
WATANABE, T., Systems and Social Informatics
YASUDA, T., Systems and Social Informatics
YASUMOTO, M., Computer Science and Mathematical Informatics
YOKOI, S., Systems and Social Informatics
YOKOSAWA, H., Complex Systems Science
YONEYAMA, M., Systems and Social Informatics

Graduate School of International Development (tel. (52) 789-4952; fax (52) 789-4951; e-mail webmaster@gsid.nagoya-u.ac.jp; internet www.gsid.nagoya-u.ac.jp):

EZAKI, M., Development Information Systems
FUTAMURA, H., Drug Trafficking in Latin America
HIROSATO, Y., Educational Development
KIMURA, H., Dynamics of Regional Politics, International Co-operation Policy I, II, Dynamics of Regional Politics
KINOSHITA, T., Second Language Acquisition, Learning, Language Assessment, TESOL and Applied Linguistics
NAKANISHI, H., International and Regional Politics, Organization for International Co-operation
NISHIMURA, Y., Development Management
OHASHI, A., South-east Asian Studies
OMURO, T., Dynamic Theory of Language
OSADA, H., Integrated Development Planning
OTSUBO, S., International Development Economics
SAKURAI, T., Theory of Intercultural Communication
SUGIURA, M., Second Language Acquisition
TAKAHASHI, K., Multi-Culturalism I, Social Change during Modernization
YASUDA, N., Comparative Asian Legal Systems, Introduction to Law and Development Studies

Graduate School of Languages and Cultures (tel. (52) 789-4881; fax (52) 789-4873; e-mail lcoffice@lang.nagoya-u.ac.jp; internet www.lang.nagoya-u.ac.jp):

ANDO, S., 16th and 17th Century English Poetry
ARIKAWA, K., German Literature in the Age of the Enlightenment
FUKUDA, M., Comparative Literature and Culture, Medical History
HIGH, P., Intellectual History of Japanese Film
IIDA, H., Contrastive Study of Japanese, Korean and English
INOUE, I., English Linguistics
KAMIYA, O., Modern Chinese Language
KATO, S., American Literature, Japanese and American Environmental Literature
KONDO, K., Language Typology
KOSAKA, K., Contrastive Linguistics
MAENO, M., Cultural History of Early Modern Europe
MATSUMOTO, I., Women's Studies
MATSUOKA, M., Victorian Literature
MURANUSHI, K., William Shakespeare
NAGAHATA, A., American Literature
NAKAI, M., Trend of Thought in Modern Chinese Literature
NAKAJIMA, T., German Lyric Poems of the Nineteenth Century
OCHI, K., Obliteration of the Feminine in the Western Culture
SHIBATA, S., Modern Literature in Japan and Germany
SUZUKI, S., Emblem and Religious Poetry in the Sixteenth and Seventeenth Centuries
TADOKORO, M., Comparative Literature and Culture
TANO, I., Modern American Literature and Culture
YANAGISAWA, T., Language Typology, North-Western Caucasian Languages
YOSHIMURA, M., English Romanticism

School and Graduate School of Law (tel. (52) 789-4910; fax (52) 789-4900; e-mail info@nomolog.nagoya-u.ac.jp; internet www.nomolog.nagoya-u.ac.jp):

AIKYO, K., Constitutional Law
AKANE, T., Criminal Procedure
CHIBA, E., Civil Law
FUJITA, S., Role of the Attorney in Legal Practice
FUKE, T., Public Finance Law and Tax Law
HACHISUKA, T., Role of the Attorney in Legal Practice
HAMADA, M., Corporate Law
HASEGAWA, Y., Civil Procedure
HASHIDA, H., Criminal Law
HONMA, Y., Civil Procedure
ICHIHASHI, K., Administrative Law
ISHII, M., Western Legal History
ISOBE, T., History of Western Political Thought
JIMBO, F., Japanese Legal History
KAGAYAMA, S., Civil Law
KAMINO, K., Administrative Law
KATO, H., Environmental Law
KATO, M., Civil Law
KAWANO, M., Civil Procedure
KITAZUMI, K., Western Political History
KOBAYASHI, R., Commercial Law
MAKINO, J., Business Law Practice
MASUDA, T., Japanese Political History
MATSUURA, Y., Legal Informatics, History of Legal Thought
MORI, H., Constitutional Law
MORIGIWA, Y., Jurisprudence
MOTO, H., Constitutional Law
NAKAHIGASHI, -M., Corporate Law
NAKAYA, H., Civil Law
OBATA, K., International Law
OHSAWA, Y., Criminal Procedure
ONO, K., Political Science
SABURI, H., International Law
SADAKATA, M., International Politics
SINDO, H., Urban Politics
SUGAWARA, I., Sociology of Law
SUGIURA, K., Russian Law
SUZUKI, M., Intellectual Property Law
URABE, N., Constitutional Law
USHIRO, F., Public Administration
WADA, H., Labour Law
YAMAMOTO, T., Criminal Law

School and Graduate School of Letters (tel. (52) 789-2202; fax (52) 789-2272; internet www.lit.nagoya-u.ac.jp):

ABE, Y., Anthropology, Study of Religions and the History of Japanese Thought
AMANO, M., English Linguistics
EMURA, H., Asian History

HAGA, S., Japanese History
IKEUCHI, S., Japanese History
INABA, N., Japanese History
INOUE, S., Asian History
KAMIO, M., English and American Literature
KAMITSUKA, Y., Chinese Philosophy
KANAYAMA, Y., Philosophy
KASUGA, Y., Japanese Culture
KIMATA, M., Aesthetics and Art History
KUGINUKI, T., Japanese Linguistics
MACHIDA, K., Linguistics
MATSUZAWA, K., French Literature
MIYAJI, A., Aesthetics and Art History
ODA, Y., Japanese Culture
OGAWA, M., Classics
SATO, S., Western History
SHIMADA, Y., Anthropology, Study of Religions and the History of Japanese Thought
SHIMIZU, S., German Literature
SHIOMURA, K., Japanese Literature
SUGIYAMA, H., Chinese Literature
SUTO, Y., Western History
TAKAHASHI, T., Japanese Literature
TAKEUCHI, H., Chinese Philosophy
TAKIKAWA, M., English and American Literature
TAMURA, H., Philosophy
TSUBOI, H., Japanese Culture
WADA, T., Indian Studies
WAZAKI, H., Anthropology, Study of Religions and the History of Japanese Thought
YAMADA, H., Philosophy
YAMAMOTO, N., Archaeology
YOSHIDA, J., Chinese Philosophy

Graduate School of Mathematics (Furo-cho, Chikusa-ku, Nagoya 464-8602; tel. (52) 789-2429; fax (52) 789-2829; internet www.math.nagoya-u.ac.jp/en):

FUJIWARA, K., Algebraic Geometry
GYOJA, A., Representation Theory
KANAI, M., Geometry and Dynamic Systems
KANNO, H., Mathematical Physics
KIMURA, Y., Fluid Dynamics
KOBAYASHI, R., Differential Geometry
KONDO, S., Algebraic Geometry
MATSUMOTO, K., Number Theory
MIYAKE, M., Partial Differential Equations
NAMIKAWA, Y., Algebraic Geometry
NAYATANI, S., Conformal Geometry
OHSAWA, T., Complex Analysis
SATO, H., Geometry
SHIOTA, M., Real Algebraic Geometry
SHOJI, T., Representational Theory
TSUCHIYA, A., Geometry and Mathematical Physics
UMEMURA, H., Algebraic Geometry
UZAWA, T., Representational Theory

School and Graduate School of Medicine (65 Tsurumai-cho, Showa-ku, Nagoya 466-8550; tel. (52) 744-2500; fax (52) 744-2428; internet www.med.nagoya-u.ac.jp):

ANDO, H., Paediatric Surgery
ANDO, S., Clinical Nursing
AOYAMA, A., International Health
AOYAMA, T., Basic Radiological Technology
ASANO, M., Human Development Nursing and Midwifery
BAN, N., Family and Community Medicine
FUJIMOTO, T., Molecular Cell Biology
FURUKAWA, K., Molecular and Cellular Biology
GOTO, H., Therapeutic Medicine
GOTO, S., Fundamentals of Nursing
HAMAGUCHI, M., Molecular Pathogenesis
HAMAJIMA, N., Preventive Medicine
HIRAI, M., Public Health and Home Care Nursing
HIROSE, K., Cell Physiology
HOSHIYAMA, M., Basic Occupational Therapy
IDA, K., Basic Physical Therapy
IGUCHI, A., Geriatrics
IKEMATSU, Y., Clinical Nursing
ISHIGAKI, T., Radiology
ISHIGURE, N., Medical Radiological Technology
ISHIGURO, N., Orthopaedics
ISOBE, K., Immunology
ITO, H., Basic Medical Technology
ITO, K., Medical Administration and Politics
ITO, S., Basic Radiological Technology
KAIBUCHI, K., Cell Pharmacology
KAJITA, E., Public Health and Home Care Nursing
KATSUMATA, Y., Legal Medicine and Bioethics
KAWAMURA, M., Basic Physical Therapy
KAWATSU, Y., Fundamentals of Nursing
KIKKAWA, F., Obstetrics and Gynaecology
KIKUCHI, A., Molecular Mycology and Medicine
KIUCHI, T., Transplant Surgery
KOBAYASHI, K., Basic Physical Therapy
KODERA, Y., Medical Radiological Technology
KOIKE, Y., Medical Laboratory Technology
KOJIMA, S., Paediatrics
KOJIMA, T., Medical Laboratory Technology
KOMORI, K., Vascular Surgery
MAEDA, H., Medical Radiological Technology
MAEKAWA, A., Public Health and Homecare Nursing
MATSUMURA, Y., Clinical Nursing
MATSUO, S., Clinical Immunology
MIYATA, T., Cell Biology
MIZUTANI, M., Clinical Nursing
MORI, N., Biological Response
MORITA, S., Human Development Nursing and Midwifery
MURATE, T., Medical Laboratory Technology
MUROHARA, T., Cardiology
NABESHIMA, T., Clinical Pharmacy
NAGASE, F., Medical Laboratory Technology
NAKAMURA, S., Clinical Pathophysiology
NAKAO, A., Gastroenterological Surgery
NAKASHIMA, T., Otorhinolaryngology
NAOE, T., Haematology
NARAMA, M., Human Development Nursing and Midwifery
NASU, T., Occupational and Environmental Health
NIMURA, Y., Surgical Oncology
NISHIYAMA, Y., Molecular Virology
OBATA, Y., Medical Radiological Technology
OHNO, K., Neurogenetics and Bioinformatics
OHTA, M., Molecular Bacteriology
OISO, Y., Diabetology and Endocrinology
OTA, K., Fundamentals of Nursing
OZAKI, N., Psychiatry
SAKAKIBARA, H., Public Health and Home Care Nursing
SHIMADA, Y., Anaesthesiology
SHIMAMOTO, K., Medical Radiological Technology
SHIMOKATA, K., Clinical Preventive Medicine
SOBUE, G., Neurology
SOKABE, M., Cell Biophysics
SUGIMURA, K., Basic Occupational Therapy
SUZUKI, K., Basic Occupational Therapy
SUZUKI, K., Human Development Nursing and Midwifery
SUZUKI, S., Applied Physical Therapy
TABUSHI, K., Basic Radiological Technology
TACHIKAWA, K., Hospital and Healthcare Business Management
TAGAWA, Y., Applied Occupational Therapy
TAKAGI, K., Basic Medical Technology
TAKAHASHI, M., Tumour Pathology
TAKAMATSU, J., Transfusion Medicine
TAKAHASHI, T., Molecular Carcinogenesis
TAKEZAWA, J., Emergency and Critical Care Medicine
TERASAKI, H., Protective Care for Sensory Disorders
TOMITA, Y., Dermatology
TORII, S., Plastic and Reconstructive Surgery
TOYOSHIMA, H., Public Health
UEDA, M., Maxillofacial Surgery
UEDA, Y., Cardio-thoracic Surgery
WAKUSAWA, S., Basic Medical Technology
WATANABE, N., Clinical Nursing
YAMADA, S., Applied Physical Therapy
YAMAUCHI, K., Medical Information and Management Science
YAMAUCHI, T., Fundamentals of Nursing
YOKOI, T., Medical Laboratory Technology
YOSHIDA, J., Neurosurgery

School and Graduate School of Science (Furo-cho, Chikusa-ku, Nagoya 464-8602; tel. (52) 789-2394; fax (52) 789-2800; internet www.sci.nagoya-u.ac.jp/index.html):

AIBA, H., Molecular Biology
AWAGA, K., Materials Chemistry
ENDO, T., Biochemistry
FUKUI, Y., Astrophysics
HIRASHIMA, D., Condensed Matter Physics
HOMMA, M., Bioenergetics
HORI, H., Evolutionary Genetics
IIO, T., Biophysics
ISHII, K., Theoretical Biology
ITOH, M., Solid State Physics
ITOH, S., Biophysics, Bioenergetics
KATOU, K., Physiology of Plant Growth
KONDO, S., Pattern Formation
KONDO, T., Plant Physiology
KOUYAMA, T., Biophysics
KUNIEDA, H., Astrophysics
KUROIWA, A., Developmental Biology
MACHIDA, Y., Molecular Biology
MATSUMOTO, K., Molecular Biology
MORI, I., Molecular Neurobiology
NAKANISHI, T., Nuclear and Particle Physics
NISHIDA, Y., Animal Development
NIWA, K., Nuclear and Particle Physics
NOZAKI, K., Nonlinear Physics
ODA, Y., Developmental Biology
OHMINE, I., Physical Chemistry
OHSAWA, Y., Plasma Physics
OHSHIMA, T., Nuclear and Particle Physics
OKAMOTO, Y., Theoretical Biophysics
OWARIBE, K., Cell Adhesion and Cytoskeleton
SANDA, I., Particle Physics and Fields
SATO, M., Solid State Physics
SATO, S., Astrophysics
SAWADA, H., Marine Biochemistry
SHIBAI, H., Astrophysics
SHINOHARA, H., Physical Chemistry
SUGAI, S., Solid State Physics
SUZUMURA, Y., Solid State Physics
TOMIMATSU, A., Theory of Gravitation
UEMURA, D., Organic Chemistry
WADA, N., Low Temperature Physics
WATANABE, Y., Bioinorganic Chemistry
YAMAGUCHI, S., Organic Chemistry
YAMAWAKI, K., Elementary Particle Physics and Fields

Center for Gene Research (Furo-cho, Chikusa-ku, Nagoya 464-8602; tel. (52) 789-3080; fax (52) 789-3081; internet www.gene.nagoya-u.ac.jp/index-e.html):

ISHIURA, M., Genome Biology, Molecular Biology
SUGITA, M., Plant Molecular Biology

Research Center of Health, Physical Fitness and Sports (tel. (52) 789-3946; fax (52) 789-3957; internet www.htc.nagoya-u.ac.jp):

HIRUTA, S., Workload in Care Services
IKEGAMI, Y., Biomechanical Analysis of Human Movement
ISHIDA, K., Cardio-Respiratory Responses during Exercise

IZUHARA, Y., Class Work Study of Physical Education
KONDO, T., Exercise and Gastrointestinal Function, Pancreatic Diseases, Breath and Skin Gas in Health and Diseases
NISHIDA, T., Achievement Motivation in Physical Education and Sports
OGAWA, T., Phenomenological Psychopathology, Psychoanalytic Psychotherapy of Adolescents
OSHIDA, Y., Exercise for Insulin Resistance
SHIMAOKA, K., Teaching of Exercise in Health Promotion Programmes
SHIMAOKA, M., Health and Physical Fitness in Workers
YAMAMOTO, Y., Motor Control and Learning from a Dynamical System Approach

Research Institute of Environmental Medicine (tel. (52) 789-3886; fax (52) 789-3887; internet www.riem.nagoya-u.ac.jp/e/index.html):

KAMIYA, K., Molecular and Genomic Regulation of the Heart
KODAMA, I., Molecular and Cellular Cardiology
KOMATSU, Y., Synaptic Plasticity in the Visual Cortex
MIZUMURA, K., Neurophysiology of Pain
MURATA, Y., Molecular Genetics
SAWADA, M., Molecular and Cellular Neuroscience
SEO, H., Molecular Mechanism of Hormone Action
SUZUMURA, A., Neuroimmunology
YASUI, K., Bioinformation Analysis

Solar–Terrestrial Environment Laboratory (Honohara 3-13, Toyokawa, Aichi Pref., 442-8507; tel. (533) 86-3154; fax (533) 86-0811; internet www.stelab.nagoya-u.ac.jp):

FUJII, R., Space Science (Magnetosphere and Ionosphere Physics
ITOW, Y., Cosmic Ray, Dark Matter and Neutrino Physics
KAMIDE, Y., Solar–Terrestrial Physics
KIKUCHI, T., Solar-Terrestrial Physics
KOJIMA, M., Interplanetary Space Physics
MATSUMI, Y., Atmospheric Photochemistry and Chemical Kinetics
MIZUNO, A., Atmospheric Chemistry and Radio Astronomy
MURAKI, Y., Solar Cosmic Ray Physics
OGAWA, T., Upper Atmosphere Physics
OGINO, T., Space Plasma Physics

Research Center for Materials Science (Furo-cho, Chikusa-ku, Nagoya 464-8602; tel. (52) 789-5902; fax (52) 789-5902; internet www.rcms.nagoya-u.ac.jp/intro/):

IMAE, T., Physical Chemistry
KITAMURA, M., Synthetic Organic Chemistry
SEKI, K., Physical Chemistry
TATSUMI, K., Inorganic Chemistry

International Co-operation Center for Agricultural Education (tel. (52) 789-4225; fax (52) 789-4222; e-mail iccae@agr.nagoya-u.ac.jp; internet www.agr.nagoya-u.ac.jp/~iccae/index-j.html):

ASANUMA, S., Network Development
MATSUMOTO, T., Project Development

Center for Studies of Higher Education (tel. (52) 789-5696; fax (52) 789-5695; e-mail Webmaster@cshe.nagoya-u.ac.jp; internet www.cshe.nagoya-u.ac.jp):

NATSUME, T., Comparative Study on Higher Education

Radioisotope Research Center (Furo-cho, Chikusa-ku, Nagoya 464-8602; tel. (52) 789-2563; fax (52) 789-2567; internet www.ric.nagoya-u.ac.jp):

NISHIZAWA, K., Radiation Protection

Nagoya University Museum (Furo-cho, Chikusa-ku, Nagoya 464-8601; tel. (52) 789-5767; fax (52) 789-5896; internet www.num.nagoya-u.ac.jp):

ADACHI, M., Sedimentation and Tectonics
NISHIKAWA, T., Taxonomy and Phylogeny of Marine Invertebrates

Center for Co-operative Research in Advanced Science and Technology (tel. (52) 789-3921; fax (52) 789-3922; internet www.ccrast.nagoya-u.ac.jp):

IWATA, S., Magnetic Materials and Magnetic Devices
KASAHARA, K., Quantum Electronics, Optical Communication
MORI, S., Environment Process Technology
OBINATA, G., Modelling and Control in Robotics, Human-Robot Interfaces, Biocybernetics
OGAWA, M., Semiconductor Devices
TAKAHASHI, H., Copyright

Center for Information Media Studies (tel. (52) 789-3903; fax (52) 789-3900; internet www.media.nagoya-u.ac.jp):

NAGAO, K., Digital Content Technology, Media Informatics, Image and Language Processing, Agent Technology, Artificial Intelligence

Center for Chronological Research (Furo-cho, Chikusa-ku, Nagoya 464-8602; tel. (52) 789-2579; fax (52) 789-3092; internet www.nendai.nagoya-u.ac.jp/en/index.html):

NAKAMURA, T., Geochemistry and Radiochronometry
SUZUKI, K., Petrology and Geochronology

Bioscience and Biotechnology Center (tel. (52) 789-5194; fax (52) 789-5195; internet www.agr.nagoya-u.ac.jp/~nubs/index.html):

HATTORI, T., Plant Cell Function
KITAJIMA, K., Animal Cell Function
KITANO, H., Plant Bioresources
MATSUOKA, M., Plant Molecular Breeding
UOZUMI, T., Molecular Biosystems
WAKAMATSU, Y., Freshwater Fish Stocks

Hydrospheric–Atmospheric Research Center (tel. (52) 789-3466; fax (52) 789-3436; e-mail koho@hyarc.nagoya-u.ac.jp; internet www.hyarc.nagoya-u.ac.jp/hyarc):

NAKAMURA, K., Satellite Meteorology
SAINO, T., Ocean Climate Biology
UYEDA, H., Meteorology
YASUNARI, T., Meteorology, Climate System Study

Center for Asian Legal Exchange (tel. (52) 789-2325; fax (52) 789-4902; e-mail cale@nomolog.nagoya-u.ac.jp; internet www.nomolog.nagoya-u.ac.jp):

AIKYO, M., Asian Law

Information Technology Center (tel. (52) 789-4352; fax (52) 789-4385; internet www.itc.nagoya-u.ac.jp):

ISHII, K., Computational Fluid Dynamics
MASE, K., Computer Mediated Communication
MIYAO, M., Ergonomics
YOSHIKAWA, M., Database Systems

Center for Developmental Clinical Psychology and Psychiatry (tel. (52) 789-2656; fax (52) 789-5059):

HONJO, S., Child Psychiatry
TSURUTA, K., School Counselling
UJIIE, T., Clinical Support of the Mother-Child Relationship

Education Center for International Students (tel. (52) 789-2198; fax (52) 789-5100; internet www.ecis.nagoya-u.ac.jp):

KASHIMA, T., Phonetics, Teaching Pronunciation of Japanese as a Foreign Language
MATSUURA, M., International Student Advisory and Resource Services
MURAKAMI, K., Teaching Japanese as a Foreign Language
NOMIZU, T., Instrumental Analytical Chemistry, Student Exchange Programme Education
OZAKI, A., Teaching Japanese as a Foreign Language

EcoTopia Science Institute (tel. (52) 789-5262; fax (52) 789-5265; e-mail jimu@esi.nagoya-u.ac.jp; internet www.esi.nagoya-u.ac.jp):

ENOKIDA, Y., Nuclear Fuel Engineering
FUJISAWA, T., High Temperature Physical Chemistry
HASEGAWA, T., Environmental Thermo-Fluid Technologies
HASEGAWA, Y., Energy Science
ICHIHASHI, M., Electron Optics
ITHO, H., Solid Waste Treatment
KATAYAMA, A., Bioremediation and Bioreclamation
KATAYAMA, M., Communication and Information Systems
KITAGAWA, K., Advanced Energy Conversion Systems and Technologies
NAGASAKI, T., Materials Science
OKUBO, H., Electric Power Engineering
SUZUKI, K., Environmental Research
TAKAI, O., Materials Science and Engineering
TANAKA, N., High Resolution Electron Microscopy and Electron Diffraction of Clusters, Wires and Think-Film Related to Nanotechnology
TATEISHI, K., Structural Engineering
TONOIKE, T., Linguistics, Lexicology and Optimality Theory
WATANABE, T., Fluid Informatics and Computational Fluid Dynamics
YOGO, T., Materials Chemistry

NARA WOMEN'S UNIVERSITY

Kita-Uoya-Higashi-Machi, Nara City 630-8506

Telephone: (742) 20-3204
Fax: (742) 20-3205
E-mail: admin@jimu.nara-wu.ac.jp
Internet: www.nara-wu.ac.jp

Founded 1908
Independent
Academic year: April to March

President: MASAKO NIWA
Secretary-General: MASAMI KOTANI
Librarian: NANAKO SHIGESADA

Library of 514,000 vols
Number of teachers: 222
Number of students: 2,746

Publications: *Annual Report of Studies in Humanities and Social Sciences*, *Studies in Home Economics*, *Graduate School of Human Culture*

DEANS

Faculty of Letters: Prof. T. HIRAI
Faculty of Science: Prof. Y. TAKAGI
Faculty of Human Life and Environment: Prof. M. MIYOSHI
Graduate School of Human Culture (Doctorate Course): Prof. N. FUJIWARA

NIIGATA UNIVERSITY

8050 Ikarashi 2-no cho, Niigata City 950-2181

Telephone: (25) 223-6161
Fax: (25) 262-6539
E-mail: info@admin.niigata-u.ac.jp
Internet: www.niigata-u.ac.jp

Founded 1949
Independent
Academic year: April to March

President: AKIRA HASEGAWA
Vice Presidents: SUKEO FUKASAWA, TAKEHIKO BANDO

Director General: Yasushi. Sato
Director of University Library: Takashi Ookuma

Library: see Libraries and Archives
Number of teachers: 1,285
Number of students: 13,088

DEANS

Faculty of Humanities: K. Yoshii
Faculty of Education and Human Sciences: T. Ikuta
Faculty of Law: S. Kuniya
Faculty of Economics: Y. Sugahara
Faculty of Science: Y. Masuda
Faculty of Medicine: M. Yamamoto
Faculty of Dentistry: Y. Yamada
Faculty of Engineering: M. Sengoku
Faculty of Agriculture: A. Suzuki
Graduate School of the Study of Modern Society and Culture: T. Fujii
Graduate School of Science and Technology: N. Tamura
Graduate School of Humanities: K. Yoshii
Graduate School of Education: T. Ikuta
Graduate School of Law: S. Kuniya
Graduate School of Economics: Y. Sugahara
Graduate School of Medicine: M. Yamamoto
Graduate School of Dentistry: Y. Yamada
Graduate School of Medical and Dental Sciences: K. Hanada

ATTACHED RESEARCH INSTITUTES

Brain Research Institute: Dir N. Tsuneki.

Research Institute for Hazards in Snowy Areas: Dir N. Takahama.

Research Laboratory for Molecular Genetics: Dir R. Kominami.

Center for Co-operative Research: Dir T. Hara.

Radioisotope Center: Dir M. Naito.

Center for Instrumental Analysis: Dir I. Tokue.

Integrated Information Processing Center: Dir M. Miyazaki.

Research Institute for Faculty Development: Dir S. Hamaguchi.

OBIHIRO UNIVERSITY OF AGRICULTURE AND VETERINARY MEDICINE

Inada-cho, Obihiro, Hokkaido 080-8555
Telephone: (155) 49-5111
Fax: (155) 49-5229
E-mail: soumo@obihiro.ac.jp
Internet: www.obihiro.ac.jp

Founded 1941
Independent
Academic year: April to March

President: Naoyoshi Suzuki
Director of Administration Bureau: M. Kikuchi
Director of University Library: T. Kawabata

Library of 190,426 vols
Number of teachers: 149
Number of students: 1,431

Department of Basic Veterinary Science: Junzo Yamada
Department of Pathobiological Science: Masakazu Nishimura
Department of Applied Veterinary Science: Toshikazu Shirahata
Department of Clinical Veterinary Science: Takao Sarashina
Research Unit of Animal Physiology and Function: Ikichi Arai
Research Unit of Molecular Cell-Regulation Science: Hiroshi Masuda
Research Unit of Animal Production Science: Mikami Masayuki
Research Unit of Plant Bioscience: Souhei Sawada
Research Unit of Engineering in Agricultural and Biological Systems: Kenichi Ishibashi
Research Unit of Farm Management: Ichio Sasaki
Department of Agro-Environmental Science: Junko Maruyama
Research Unit of Environmental and Rural Engineering: Fujio Tsuchiya
Research Unit of Food and Resource Economics: Shigeru Ito
Research Unit of Socio-Environmental Science: Masaru Umetsu

Publication: *Research Bulletin* (on Natural Sciences and on Humanities and Social Sciences, each 2 a year).

ATTACHED RESEARCH INSTITUTE

Research Centre for Protozoan Molecular Immunology

OCHANOMIZU UNIVERSITY

2-1-1, Otsuka, Bunkyo-ku, Tokyo 112-8610
Telephone: (3) 5978-5106
Fax: (3) 5978-5890
E-mail: syomu2@cc.ocha.ac.jp
Internet: www.ocha.ac.jp

Founded 1874; reorganized 1949 as National University
Independent
Academic year: April to March

President: Masuko Honda
Administrator: Hidetoshi Yakabe

Number of teachers: 322
Number of students: 2,738

Publications: *Natural Science Report* (2 a year), *Studies in Art and Culture* (annually)

DEANS

Faculty of Letters and Education: Yamamoto Hideyuki
Faculty of Science: Kasahara Yuji
Faculty of Human Life and Environmental Science: Itakura Toshiro
Graduate School of Humanities and Sciences: Tokumaru Yoshihiko

OITA UNIVERSITY

700 Dannoharu, Oita City
Telephone: (97) 569-3311
Fax: (97) 554-7413
E-mail: webmaster@ad.oita-u.ac.jp
Internet: www.oita-u.ac.jp

Founded 1949
Independent
Language of instruction: Japanese
Academic year: April to March (two semesters)

President: Iwao Nakayama
Director General of Administration Bureau: Takanobu Irie
Director of University Library: Koichi Oba

Library of 541,000 vols
Number of teachers: 569
Number of students: 5,802

DEANS

Faculty of Education and Welfare Science: Makoto Oshima
Faculty of Economics: Minoru Uno
Faculty of Engineering: Tadao Ezaki
Graduate School of Social Service Administration: Takatomi Ninomiya

ATTACHED INSTITUTE

Tsurumi Seaside Research Institute: Aza-Hirama, Oaza-Ariakeura, Tsurumi-machi, Minamiamabe-gun, Oita 876-1204; tel. (972) 33-1133.

OKAYAMA UNIVERSITY

1-1-1, Tsushima-Naka, Okayama 700-8530
Telephone: (86) 252-1111
Fax: (86) 254-6104
E-mail: ACE7038@adm.okayama-u.ac.jp
Internet: www.okayama-u.ac.jp

Founded 1949
Independent
Academic year: April to March (2 semesters)

President: Iichiro Kono
Vice-Presidents: Kyozo Chiba, Kiichi Matsuhata, Hirokazu Osaki, Hajime Inoue
Director-General: T. Abe

Library: see Libraries and Archives
Number of teachers: 1,341 full-time
Number of students: 14,091

Publication: *Okayama University Bulletin*

DEANS

Faculty of Letters: F. Takahashi
Faculty of Law: S. Tani
Faculty of Education: N. Morikawa
Faculty of Economics: T. Matsumoto
Faculty of Science: K. Kase
Medical School: K. Oguma
Dental School: T. Watanabe
Faculty of Pharmaceutical Sciences: T. Kimura
Faculty of Engineering: H. Totsuji
Faculty of Environmental Science and Technology: T. Adachi
Faculty of Agriculture: T. Shiraishi
Graduate School of Environmental Science (Doctorate Course): F. Nakasuji
Graduate School of Humanities and Social Sciences (Doctorate Course): T. Takahashi
Graduate School of Natural Science and Technology (Doctorate Course): J. Takada
Graduate School of Medicine, Dentistry and Pharmaceutical Science (Doctorate Course): H. Kumon
School of Law: M. Okada

PROFESSORS

Faculty of Letters (tel. (86) 251-7345; fax (86) 251-7350):

Eguchi, Y., Japanese Linguistics
Hasegawa, Y., Psychology
Hisano, N., History of Japanese Culture
Inada, T., Archaeology
Inamura, S., Ethics
Jiang, K., Modern History of Japanese Culture
Kanaseki, T., Comparative Study of Cultures
Kitamura, K., Cultural Anthropology
Kitaoka, T., Religious Philosophy
Kobayashi, T., Sociology
Kurachi, K., History of Japanese Culture
Matsumoto, M., English Historical Linguistics
Miyake, S., Operatic Studies
Nagase, H., French Literature
Nagata, R., European History
Niimura, Y., History of Chinese Culture
Niiro, I., Archaeology
Nishimae, T., American Literature
Shimosada, M., Chinese Literature
Takahashi, F., Ethics
Takahashi, T., Old German Language and Literature
Takuma, F., Modern German History
Tanaka, T., Psychology
Taya, R., Psychology
Teraoka, T., History of German Literature
Tsuji, S., Linguistics
Uchida, K., Geography
Wada, M., Linguistics
Watanabe, M., Japanese Literature
Yamaguchi, K., Aesthetics
Yamaguchi, N., History of French Thought
Yoshioka, F., English Literature

Faculty of Law (tel. (86) 251-7345; fax (86) 251-7350):

ARAKI, M., Western Political History
ATAKA, K., Local Tax and Finance Law
HARANO, A., Administrative Law
HATANO, S., European Legal History
KAWAHARA, Y., International Politics
KOYAMA, H., Administrative Law
KUROKAMI, N., Law of International Organizations
NAKAMURA, M., Information Law and Policy
NAKATOMI, K., Constitutional Law
NISHIHARA, J., Civil Law
OBATA, T., Japanese Political History
SANO, H., Private International Law
TANI, S., Political Process
TONAI, K., Labour Law
YAMAGUCHI, K., Constitutional Law
YONEYAMA, K., Commercial
ZHANG, H., Chinese Law

Faculty of Economics (tel. (86) 251-7345; fax (86) 251-7350):

CHINO, T., Health Economics
ENOMOTO, S., Strategic Management
GENKA, T., Comparative Economic Systems
HARUNA, S., Industrial Organization
HIRANO, M., Local Public Finance
KONISHI, N., Accounting
KOYAMA, Y., Financial Management
KUROKAWA, K., Economic History of the United States
MATSUDA, Y., Organizational Behaviour and Organizational Change
MATSUMOTO, T., Economic History of Modern Asia
NAGAHATA, H., Statistics, Information Science
NAKAMURA, R., Urban and Regional Economics
NIIMURA, S., History of Economic Thought
OTA, Y., History of Economic Thought
SHIMONO, K., Economic History of Modern Japan
TAKEMURA, S., Theory of the Firm, Industrial Organisation
WADA, Y., Social Economics
YOSHIDA, T., Social Statistics, Econometrics
ZHANG, X., Economic Statistics

Faculty of Education (tel. (86) 251-7584; fax (86) 251-7755):

ARIYOSHI, H., Teacher Training
DOI, Y., Algebra
FUCHIGAMI, K., School Organizational Psychology
FUJITA, R., Housing and Living Design
FUKUNAGA, S., British Literature
FURUICHI, Y., Educational Psychology
IDO, K., Music Education
IKEDA, A., Geometry
INADA, T., Japanese Literature
INOUE, S., Educational Psychology
KAGA, M., Biomechanics
KANETA, Y., Composition
KANI, K., Material Engineering
KASAI, Y., Science of Food Preparation
KAWATA, T., Food Science
KISHIMOTO, H., Political Science
KITA, H., Chemistry
KITAGAMI, M., School Management
KOSAKO, M., English Philology
KUSACHI, I., Mineralogy
KONDO, I., Information Technology
MATSUOKA, Y., Clinical Psychology
MIZUNO, M., Developmental Psychology
MONDEN, S., Education for School Health Care
MORI, K., Chinese Philosophy
MORIKAWA, N., Pedagogy
MUSHIAKI, M., Vocal Music
NAKAO, Y., Chemistry
NII, I., Arts and Crafts Education
NISHIYAMA, M., Paintings
NOBE, M., Sociology
OGAWA, T., Paintings
OGURA, H., Biology
OHASHI, K., Manufacturing Education
OHASHI, Y., Physical Education
OKU, S., Music Education
ONO, H., Curriculum Development
ONOYAMA, K., Ceramics
SAKATA, N., Physical Education
SANADA, S., Education for Handicapped Children
SANEKATA, N., Mathematical Analysis
SUGAHARA, M., Japanese Education
SUGIHARA, R., Clothing Science
TAKAHASHI, K., Medicine for School Health Care
TAKAHASHI, T., Mathematics Education
TAKATSUKA, S., English Language Teaching
TAKAYAMA, Y., Social Studies Education
TANAKA, K., Science Education
TANAKA, K., Social Psychology
TANAKA, M., European History
TOKUNAGA, T., Sport Education
UEHARA, K., History
YAMAGUCHI, H., Computer Education
YAMAGUCHI, S., Psychology of Pre-school Children
YAMAMOTO, H., Musicology
YAMAMOTO, H., Systems Engineering
YAMAMOTO, T., Clinical Psychology
YAMANAKA, Y., History of Japanese Education
YAMASHITA, N., Solid State Spectroscopy
YANAGIHARA, M., Psychology of Handicapped Children
YOSHIDA, N., Japanese Language

Faculty of Science (tel. (86) 251-7764; fax (86) 251-7777):

ASAMI, M., Petrology
CHIBA, H., Isotope Geochemistry
HARADA, I., Theoretical Physics
HIROKAWA, M., Mathematical Physics
ISHIDA, H., Structural Chemistry
IWAMI, M., Thin Films and Surface Physics
KAGAWA, H., Molecular Biology
KAMADA, T., Molecular Cell Biology
KASE, K., Resources Geology
KAWAGUCHI, K., Molecular Spectroscopy
KIMURA, M., Organic Function Chemistry
KIYOHARA, K., Differential Geometry
KOBAYASHI, T., Physics of Strongly Correlated Systems
KOJIMA, M., Co-ordination Chemistry
KURODA, Y., Inorganic Chemistry
KUTSUKAKE, K., Molecular Genetics
MACHIDA, K., Mathematical Physics
MOTOMIZU, S., Analytical Chemistry
NAGAO, M., Surface Chemistry
NAKAMURA, H., Number Theory
NAKANO, I., High Energy Physics
NARAOKA, H., Organic Cosmogeochemistry
NOGAMI, Y., Low Dimensional Material Physics
ODA, H., Seismology
OSHIMA, K., Physics of Quantum Materials
ONO, F., Physics of Materials under Extreme Conditions
SAKAI, T., Differential Geometry
SAKAMOTO, T., Marine Biology
SAKUDA, M., Neutrino Physics
SATAKE, K., Organic Chemistry
SATO, R., Analysis
SAWADA, A., Quantum Electromagnetic Physics
SHEN, J.-R., Plant Physiology and Structural Biology
SHIBATA, T., Geology
SHIMAKAWA, K., Petrology and Marine Geology
SUZUKI, I., Geophysics
TAKAGI, K., Synthetic Organic Chemistry
TAKAHASHI, S., Endocrinology
TAKAHASHI, T., Plant Molecular Genetics
TAKAHASHI, Y., Plant Physiology and Plant Molecular Biology
TAMURA, H., Analysis
TANAKA, H., Theoretical Chemistry
TOMIOKA, K., Chronobiology
TSUKAMOTO, O., Atmospheric Science
UEDA, H., Molecular and Developmental Biology
YAMADA, H., Representation Theory
YAMAMOTO, H., Organic Chemistry
YAMAMOTO, S., Physical Chemistry
YAMAMOTO, Y., Plant Physiology and Biochemistry
YOKOYA, T., Photo-emission Condensed Matter Physics
YOSHIKAWA, Y., Inorganic Chemistry
YOSHIMURA, H., Particle Physics-based Cosmology
YOSHINO, Y., Algebra
ZHENG, G.-Q., Low Temperature Condensed Matter Physics

Medical School:

AKIMOTO, N., Adult Nursing
ARAO, Y., Clinical Biology
ASARI, S., Adult Nursing
FUJINO, F., Adult Nursing
FUKAI, K., Human Nursing
IKEDA, S., Clinical Pathology
JOJA, I., Medical Radiotechnology
KAGEYAMA, J., Adult Nursing
KANDA, A., Community Health Nursing
KATAOKA, M., Clinical Biology
KATO, H., Medicinal Radioscience
KATO, K., Human Nursing
KAWASAKI, S., Medical Radioscience
KURAZONO, H., Clinical Biology
KUSACHI, S., Clinical Pathology
NAKAGIRI, Y., Medical Radiotechnology
NAKATA, Y., Clinical Pathology
NISHIDA, M., Adult Nursing
ODA, M., Maternal and Child Health Nursing
OHTA, N., Maternal and Child Health Nursing
OKA, H., Clinical Biology
OKAMOTO, M., Clinical Biology
OKANO, H., Community Health Nursing
OKUDA, H., Maternal and Child Health Nursing
ONO, K., Maternal and Child Health Nursing
SENDA, Y., Adult Nursing
SUMIMOTO, T., Medical Radioscience
TAKAHASHI, K., Clinical Pathology
TAGUCHI, T., Medical Radiotechnology
TAKEDA, Y., Medical Radiotechnology
YAMAMOTO, Y., Medical Radioscience
YAMAOKA, K., Medical Radioscience
YOKOYAMA, Y., Community Health Nursing

Faculty of Pharmaceutical Sciences (tel. (86) 251-7913; fax (86) 251-7926):

HARAYAMA, T., Synthetic and Medicinal Chemistry
HIROTA, T., Pharmaceutical Chemistry
KAMEI, C., Pharmacology
KAWASAKI, H., Clinical Pharmaceutical Science
KIMURA, T., Pharmaceutics
KUROSAKI, Y., Pharmaceutics
MORIYAMA, Y., Neurochemistry
NARIMATSU, S., Health Chemistry
OKAMOTO, K., Bio-organic Chemistry
SAITO, Y., Pharmaceutical Analytical Chemistry
SASAKI, K., Pharmaceutical Fundamental Science
SHINODA, S., Environmental Hygiene
TAMAGAKE, K., Pharmaceutical Physical Chemistry
TSUCHIYA, T., Microbiology
WATAYA, Y., Medicinal Information
YAMAMOTO, I., Immunochemistry
YAMAMOTO, S., Molecular Microbiology
YOSHIDA, T., Pharmacognosy

Faculty of Engineering (tel. (86) 251-8004; fax (86) 251-8021):

FUNABIKI, N., Distributed Systems
GOFUKU, A., Systems Applications
GOTO, K., Functional Materials Chemistry
HASHIGUCHI, K., Foundations of Information Science
HATA, M., Distributed Systems
INABA, H., Energy Engineering
INOUE, A., Systems Theory
KAMIURA, Y., Electronics
KANATANI, K., Foundations of Information Science
KISHIMOTO, A., Functional Materials Chemistry
KOGA, R., Network Architecture
KONISHI, M., Electrical Engineering
MASAKI, A., Information-based Engineering Systems
MIYAZAKI, S., Systems Intelligence
MORIKAWA, Y., Foundations of Information and Communication
NAKANISHI, K., Biotechnology
NARA, S., Electronics
NOGI, S., Electronics
NORITSUGU, T., Systems Control
OHMORI, H., Applied Bioscience
OSAKA, A., Bioactive Materials
SAITO, S., Bioactive Materials
SAKAI, H., Biotechnology
SAKAI, T., Molecular Transformation Chemistry
SAKATA, Y., Functional Materials Chemistry
SENUMA, T., Control of Material Properties
SHAKUNAGA, T., Artificial Intelligence
SHIMAMURA, K., Functional Materials Chemistry
SISHIDO, M., Biomolecular Engineering
SUGIYAMA, Y., Foundations of Information and Communication
SUZUKI, K., Systems Theory
SUZUMORI, K., Systems Control
TADA, N., Material Engineering
TAKADA, J., Functional Materials Chemistry
TAKAHASHI, N., Electrical Engineering
TAKAI, K., Molecular Transformation Chemistry
TANAKA, H., Molecular Transformation Chemistry
TANAKA, Y., Systems Applications
TANIGUCHI, H., Information Based Engineering Systems
TOMITA, E., Energy Engineering
TORAYA, T., Applied Bioscience
TORII, T., Materials Engineering
TOTSUJI, H., Electronics
TUKADA, K., Electronics
TUKAMOTO, S., Manufacturing Engineering
UNEYAMA, K., Molecular Transformation Chemistry
UNO, Y., Design and Manufacturing Technology
WASHIO, S., Engineering Measurement
YAMADA, H., Biomolecular Engineering
YAMASAKI, S., Artificial Intelligences
YANASE, S., Engineering Measurement
YOKOHIRA, T., Network Architecture
YOSHIDA, A., Design and Manufacturing Technology

Faculty of Agriculture (tel. (86) 251-8273; fax (86) 251-8388):

BABA, N., Chemistry of Biological Functions
ICHINOSE, Y., Genetic Engineering
INABA, A., Postharvest Agriculture
INAGAKI, K., Applied Biochemistry and Biotechnology
IZUMIMOTO, M., Animal Food Technology
KAMIMURA, K., Microbial Function
KANZAKI, H., Chemistry and Biochemistry of Bioactive Compounds
KIMURA, Y., Bioapplied Enzymology
KOMATSU, Y., Farm Management and Data Processing Methods
KONDO, Y., Animal Physiology and Pharmacology
KUBOTA, N., Horticultural Crop Production
KUNIEDA, T., Animal Genetics
KURODA, T., Crop Production Science
MASUDA, M., Olericulture
MIYAMOTO, T., Animal Food Function
NAKAJIMA, S., Chemistry and Biochemistry of Bioactive Compounds
NAKASUJI, F., Integrated Pest Management
NIWA, K., Animal Reproduction
OIKAWA, T., Animal Genetics and Breeding
OKAMOTO, G., Pomology
OKUDA, K., Animal Reproduction
SAKAGUCHI, E., Animal Nutrition
SAKAMOTO, K., Applied Plant Ecology
SASAKAWA, H., Rhizosphere Biological Chemistry
SATO, K., Animal Genetics and Breeding
SATOH, T., Resources Management
SHIMOISHI, Y., Biological Information of Chemistry
SHIRAISHI, T., Plant Pathology
SUGIO, T., Microbial Function
TADA, M., Biological Chemistry of Foods
TAHARA, M., Cell Engineering
TSUDA, M., Crop Whole-plant Physiology
YOKOMIZO, I., Farm Managment and Date Processing Methods
YOSHIKAWA, K., Physiological Plant Ecology

Graduate School of Medicine, Dentistry and Pharmaceutical Sciences:

ABE, K., Neuroscience
AWAYA, T., Legal Medicine and Bioethics
DATE, I., Neuroscience
FUKUI, K., Oral Pathobiology
GOHDA, E., Immunochemistry
HARAYAMA, T., Synthetic and Medicinal Chemistry
HATANO, T., Natural Product Chemistry
HIRAMATSU, Y., Obstetrics and Gynaecology
HIROTA, T., Pharmaceutical Chemistry
HUH, N., Basic Oncology
ISHIZU, H., Legal Medicine and Bioethics
IWATSUKI, K., Sensory and Locomotory Function Medicine
KAMEI, C., Pharmacology
KANAZAWA, S., Radiology and Laboratory Medicine
KATO, N., Basic Oncology
KATSU, T., Pharmaceutical Physical Chemistry
KAWAKAMI, N., Social Medicine and Environmental Health Sciences
KAWASAKI, H., Clinical Pharmaceutical Science
KIMATA, Y., Sensory and Locomotory Function Medicine
KIMURA, T., Pharmaceutics
KISHI, K., Oral and Maxillofacial Surgery and Diagnostic Medicine
KITAYAMA, S., Oral Pathobiology
KOIDE, N., Radiology and Laboratory Medicine
KUBOKI, T., Oral Functional Reconstruction
KUMON, H., Basic and Clinical Pathophysiology
KURODA, S., Basic and Clinical Neuroscience
KUROSAKI, Y., Pharmaceutics
MAKINO, H., Basic and Clinical Pathophysiology
MATSUI, H., Basic and Clinical Neuroscience
MATSUO, R., Oral Biology
MINAGI, S., Oral Functional Reconstruction
MIYOSHI, S., Environmental Hygiene
MORISHIMA, T., Obstetrics and Gynaecology
MORITA, K., Anaesthesiology and Emergency Medicine
MORIYAMA, Y., Neurochemistry
NAGAI, N., Oral Pathobiology
NAKAYAMA, E., Infection and Immunology
NARIMATSU, S., Health Chemistry
NINOMIYA, Y., Human Biology
NISHIZAKI, K., Sensory and Locomotory Function Medicine
OGAWA, N., Basic and Clinical Neuroscience
OGUMA, K., Infection and Immunology
OHE, T., Cardiovascular Medicine
OHTSUKA, A., Human Biology
OHTSUKA, Y., Basic and Clinical Neuroscience
OKAMOTO, K., Bio-organic Chemistry
SAITO, Y., Pharmaceutical Analytical Chemistry
SANO, S., Cardiovascular Pathophysiology
SASAKI, A., Oral and Maxillofacial Surgery and Diagnostic Medicine
SASAKI, J., Anatomy
SASAKI, K., Pharmaceutical Fundamental Science
SHIMADA, M., Oral and Maxillofacial Surgery and Diagnostic Medicine
SHIMIZU, K., Basic Oncology
SHIMIZU, N., Basic and Clinical Pathophysiology
SHIMONO, T., Oral Health, Growth and Devlopment
SHIRATORI, Y., Basic and Clinical Pathophysiology
SUGAHARA, T., Oral and Maxillofacial and Diagnostic Medicine
SUGIMOTO, T., Oral Biology
SUZUKI, K., Oral Functional Reconstruction
TAKASHIBA, S., Oral Health, Growth and Development
TAKEI, K., Human Biology
TAKIGAWA, M., Oral Biology
TANAKA, N., Basic and Clinical Pathophysiology
TANIMOTO, M., Basic and Clinical Pathophysiology
TSUCHIYA, T., Microbiology
TSUTSUI, K., Human Biology
WATANABE, T., Oral Health, Growth and Developmnet
WATAYA, Y., Medicinal Information
YAMADA, M., Infection and Immunology
YAMAMOTO, S., Molecular Microbiology
YAMAMOTO, T., Oral Biology
YAMAMOTO, T., Oral Health, Growth and Development
YASUDA, T., Basic and Clinical Pathpphysiology
YOSHINO, T., Basic and Clinical Pathophysiology
YOSHIYAMA, M., Oral Functional Reconstruction

School of Law (tel. (86) 251-7345; fax (86) 251-7350):

AKAMATSU, H., Civil Law
FUJITA, H., Civil Law
FUJIWARA, K., criminal Procedure
HAGA, R., Commercial Law
HAGIWARA, S., Criminal Law
IGUCHI, F., Constitutional Law
KITAGAWA, K., Criminal Law
MATSUMURA, K., Civil Procedure
MIURA, O., Commercial Law
OKADA, M., Administrative Law
SATO, S., Investigative Law
UEDA, S., Criminal Procedure

ATTACHED INSTITUTES

Institute for Study of the Earth's Interior: 827, Yamada, Misasa-cho, Tohaku-gun, Tottori 682-0193; tel. (858) 43-1215; fax (858) 43-2184; f. 1985; Dir Prof. E. NAKAMURA.

Research Institute for Bioresources: 2-20-1, Chuo, Kurashiki, Okayama 710-0046; tel. (86) 424-1661; fax (86) 434-1249; f. 1914; affiliated 1951; Dir Prof. K. TAKEDA.

OSAKA UNIVERSITY

1-1 Yamadaoka, Suita, Osaka 565-0871
Telephone: (6) 6877-5111
Fax: (6) 6879-7106
E-mail: kokusai@hpc.cmc.osaka-u.ac.jp
Internet: www.osaka-u.ac.jp

Founded 1931
Independent
Academic year: April to March

President: Dr HIDEO MIYAHARA
Vice-Presidents (Trustees): NAOSHI SUZUKI, KIYOKAZU WASHIDA, YUKICHI UMAKOSHI, AKEMICHI BABA, KAZUHIKO NISHINA
Chief Directors-General of Administration Bureau: KOICHI KITAMI
Director of University Library: HIRONOBU NAKAMURA

Library: see Libraries and Archives
Number of teachers: 2,387
Number of students: 21,104

Publications: *Osaka Journal of Mathematics, Medical Journal, Law Review, Osaka Economic Papers, Journal of Osaka University Dental Society, Memoirs of the Graduate School of Letters, Memoirs of the Institute of Scientific and Industrial Research, Studies in Language and Culture, Journal of the Faculty of Health and Spirit Science, International Public Policy Studies, Osaka University Papers in English Linguistics, Machikaneyama Ronso*

DEANS

Graduate School and School of Letters: TAKAO KASHIWAGI
Graduate School and School of Human Sciences: JUNJI KOIZUMI
Graduate School of Law and Politics and School of Law: KENJI MITSUNARI
Graduate School of Law: KEN-ICHI YOSHIMOTO
Graduate School and School of Economics: HIROAKI NAGATANI
Graduate School and School of Science: SHINICHI KOTANI
Graduate School and Faculty of Medicine: MASAYA TOHYAMA
Graduate School and School of Dentistry: KENJI TAKADA
Graduate School and School of Pharmaceutical Sciences: HIROSHI YAMAMOTO
Graduate School and School of Engineering: MASAO TOYODA
Graduate School and School of Engineering Science: SHOGO NISHIDA
Graduate School of Language and Culture: KENJI KIMURA
Graduate School of Information Science and Technology: SHOJIRO NISHIO
Graduate School of Frontier Biosciences: TOSHIO HIRANO
Osaka School of International Public Policy: AKIRA KOHSAKA

PROFESSORS

Graduate School and School of Letters (1-5 Machikaneyama-cho, Toyonaka, Osaka 560-8532; tel. (6) 6850-6111; fax (6) 6850-5091; e-mail web-admin@www.let.osaka-u.ac.jp; internet www.let.osaka-u.ac.jp):

AKITA, S., Western History
AMANO, F., Theatre Studies
AOKI, N., Japanese Linguistics
ARAKAWA, M., Central Asian History
EGAWA, A., Western History
ENOMOTO, F., Indian Philosophy and Buddhist Studies
FUJIKAWA, T., Western History
FUJITA, H., Environmental Aesthetics
FUKUNAGA, S., Archaeology
GOTO, A., Japanese Language and Literature
HACHIYA, M., Japanese Language and Literature
HAYASHI, M., German Literature
IIKURA, Y., Japanese Language and Literature
IKAI, T., Japanese History
IRIE, Y., Philosophy and History of Philosophy
IZUHARA, T., Japanese Language and Literature
KAMIKURA, T., Aesthetics
KASHIWAGI, T., French Literature
KATAYAMA, T., Asian History
KAWAMURA, K., Historical Studies of Cultural Exchanges
KINSUI, S., Japanese Language and Literature
KOBAYASHI, S., Human Geography
KODERA, T., Art History
KUDO, M., Japanese Linguistics
MOMOKI, S., Asian History
MORIOKA, Y., American Literature
MORIYASU, T., Central Asian History
MURATA, M., Japanese History
NAGATA, Y., Theatre Studies
NAITO, T., Comparative Literature
NAKAOKA, N., Clinical Philosophy and Ethics
NEGISHI, K., Musicology
OBA, Y., English Linguistics
OHASHI, R., Philosophy and Aesthetics
OKUDAIRA, S., Art History
SANADA, S., Japanese Linguistics
SUGIHARA, T., Historical Studies of Cultural Exchanges
SURO, N., Philosophy, Modern Thought and Cultural Studies
TAIRA, M., Japanese History
TAKAHASHI, B., Chinese Literature
TAKENAKA, T., Western History
TAMAI, A., English Literature
TOKI, S., Japanese Linguistics
UENO, O., Philosophy and History of Philosophy
UMEMURA, T., Japanese History
WADA, A., French Literature
WAKAYAMA, E., Art History
WASHIDA, K., Clinical Philosophy and Ethics
YUASA, K., Chinese Philosophy

Graduate School and School of Human Sciences (1-2 Yamadaoka, Suita, Osaka 565-0871; tel. (6) 6877-5111; fax (6) 6879-8010; internet www.hus.osaka-u.ac.jp/english):

ABE, A., Educational Policy and Administration
ADACHI, K., Behavioural Data Science
DAIBO, I., Social Psychology
FUJIOKA, J., Educational Psychology
FUJITA, A., Clinical Thanatology and Geriatric Behavioural Science
HINOBAYASHI, T., Comparative and Developmental Psychology
HIRASAWA, Y., Lifelong Education
IMURA, O., Clinical Psychology
KASUGA, N., People and Culture
KAWABATA, A., Advanced Empirical Sociology
KIMAE, T., Sociology of Modern Society
KOIZUMI, J., Cultural and Social Anthropology
KONDO, H., Sociology of Education
KOTO, Y., Sociological Theory
KUGIHARA, N., Social Psychology
KUMAKURA, H., Biological Anthropology
KURIMOTO, E., Cultural and Social Anthropology
KUWANO, S., Environmental Psychology
MAESAKO, T., Communication and Media
MINAMI, T., Comparative and Developmental Psychology
MIURA, T., Applied Cognitive Psychology
MIYATA, K., Clinical Psychology
MORIKAWA, K., Fundamental Psychology
MUTA, K., Sociology of Communication
NAKAGAWA, S., Cultural and Social Anthropology
NAKAMURA, T., Quantitative Psychology of Expression and Cognition
NAKAMURA, Y., International Collaboration
NAKAYAMA, Y., Logical Studies, Foundation of Science
NAOI, A., Information Technology and Human Sciences
OIMATSU, K., Clinical Psychology
ONODA, M., Educational Policy and Administration
SHIMIZU, K., Cultural Studies of Education
SUGAI, K., Educational Technology
SUGENO, T., Philosophical Anthropology
TSUTSUMI, S., Social Policy and Community Empowerment Studies
USUI, S., Human Risk Studies
UTSUMI, S., International Collaboration
YAMAMOTO, T., Behavioural Physiology

Graduate School of Law and Politics and School of Law (1-6 Machikaneyama-cho, Toyonaka, Osaka 560-0043; tel. (6) 6850-6111; fax (6) 6850-5091):

HAYASHI, T., Comparative Law and Politics
KAWATA, J., Centre for Legal and Political Practice
KUNII, K., Comparative Law and Politics
MITSUNARI, K., Independent Study Centre
NAKAO, T., Comparative Law and Politics
NAKAYAMA, R., Governance and Law
OKUBO, N., Governance and Law
SAKAMOTO, K., Governance and Law
TAGO, K., Governance and Law
TAKADA, A., Governance and Law
TAKAHASHI, A., Independent Study Course
TAKENAKA, Y., Independent Study Course
TAKIGUCHI, T., Comparative Law and Politics
YAMASHITA, M., Comparative Law and Politics
YOON, K. C., International and Comparative Law Course

Graduate School of Law (1-6 Machikaneyama-cho, Toyonaka, Osaka 560-0043; tel. (6) 6850-6111; fax (6) 6850-5091):

AOE, H., Department of Legal Practice
AOTAKE, S., Department of Legal Practice
CHAEN, S., Department of Legal Practice
HIRATA, K., Department of Legal Practice
IKEDA, T., Department of Legal Practice
KOJIMA, N., Department of Legal Practice
KOSUGI, S., Department of Legal Practice
MATSUI, S., Department of Legal Practice
MATSUKAWA, T., Department of Legal Practice
MATSUMOTO, K., Department of Legal Practice
MISAKA, Y., Department of Legal Practice
MIZUTANI, N., Department of Legal Practice
MURAKAMI, T., Department of Legal Practice
SAKUMA, O., Department of Legal Practice
SHIMOMURA, M., Department of Legal Practice
SUENAGA, T., Department of Legal Practice
SUZUKI, H., Department of Legal Practice
TANIGUTCHI, S., Department of Legal Practice
YOSHIDA, M., Department of Legal Practice
YOSHIMOTO, K., Department of Legal Practice

Graduate School and School of Economics (1-7 Machikaneyama-cho, Toyonaka, Osaka 560-0043; tel. (6) 6850-6111; fax (6) 6850-5205):

ABE, K., Economics
ABE, T., Historical Analysis
ASADA, T., Business Information
BAN, K., Economics
DOME, T., Political Analysis
FUKUSHIGE, M., Management of Technology
FUTAGAMI, K., Economics
HONDA, Y., Policy Analysis

HONMA, M., Economics
IMAI, Y., Theoretical Analysis
KANAI, K., Business Information
KOBAYASHI, T., Business Information
MINO, K., Theoretical Analysis
MIYAMOTO, M., Historical Analysis
NAGATANI, H., Theoretical Analysis
NAKAJIMA, N., Business
OHNISHI, M., Business
OHYA, K., Business Analysis
SAITO, S., Policy Analysis
SAMURA, T., Historical Analysis
SAWAI, M., Historical Analysis
SUGIHARA, K., Economics
TABATA, Y., Business Analysis
TAKAO, H., Business
TAKEDA, E., Business Analysis
YAMADA, M., Theoretical Analysis

Graduate School and School of Science (1-1 Machikaneyama-cho, Toyonaka, Osaka 560-0043; tel. (6) 6850-6111; fax (6) 6850-5288; internet www.sci.osaka-u.ac.jp):

AKAI, H., Quantum Physics
AKUTSU, Y., Quantum Physics
AOSHIMA, S., Polymer Synthesis
ASAKAWA, M., Hadronic Physics
DOI, S., Analysis
FUJIKI, A., Global Geometry and Analysis
FUKASE, K., Natural Product Chemistry
FUKUYAMA, K., Structural Biology
HARADA, A., Supermolecular Science
HASE, S., Organic Biochemistry
HAYASHI, N., Applied Mathematics
HIGASHIJIMA, K., Particle Physics
HOSOTANI, Y., Fundamental Physics
IBUKIYAMA, T., Algebra
INABA, A., Structural Thermodynamics
KAIZAKI, S., Inorganic Chemistry
KANAZAWA, H., Molecular Biology
KASAI, T., Reaction Dynamics, Molecular Thermodynamics
KATAKUSE, I., Interdisciplinary Physics
KAWAMURA, H., Solid State and Statistical Physics
KAWARAZAKI, S., Solid State Physics
KISHIMOTO, T., Particle and Nuclear Physics
KOISO, N., Geometry
KOTANI, S., Analysis
KONNO, K., Algebra
KONNO, T., Co-ordination Chemistry
KUNO, Y., Elementary Particle Physics
KURAMITSU, S., Biophysical Chemistry
MABUCHI, T., Global Mathematics
MASUKATA, H., Molecular Genetics
MATSUDA, J., Planetary Science
MUNAKATA, T., Chemistry
MURATA, M., Biomolecular Chemistry
NAKASHIMA, S., Physical Geochemistry
NAKAZAWA, Y., Condensed Matter Physical Chemistry
NAMIKAWA, Y., Algebra
NISHIDA, H., Development Biology
NISHITANI, T., Analysis
NOMACHI, M., Quark Nuclear Physics
NORISUYE, T., Polymer Solutions
NOZUE, Y., Condensed Matter Physics
OGAWA, T., Quantum Physics
OGIHARA, S., Cell Biology
OHSHIKA, K., Geometry
ONUKI, Y., Condensed Matter Physics
SATO, T., Polymer Chemical Physics
SHIMODA, T., Nuclear Physics
SHINOHARA, A., Nuclear Chemistry
SUGITA, H., Analysis
SUZUKI, S., Bioinorganic Chemistry
TAJIMA, S., Condensed Matter Physics
TAKAHARA, F., Theoretical Astrophysics
TAKEDA, S., Condensed Matter Physics
TAKISAWA, H., Molecular Cell Biology
TERASHIMA, I., Plant Ecophysiology
TOKUNAGA, F., Extreme-Environment Biology
TSUCHIYAMA, A., Experimental Planetology
TSUNEKI, K., Comparative Zoology
TSUNEMI, H., Astrophysics
UMEHARA, M., Global Mathematics
USUI, S., Algebra
WATANABE, T., Algebra
WATARAI, H., Analytical Chemistry
YAMAGUCHI, K., Quantum Chemistry, Physical Chemistry of Condensed Matter
YAMANAKA, T., Physics of Matter
YAMANAKA, T., High Energy Physics
YONESAKI, T., Microbial Genetics

Graduate School and Faculty of Medicine (2-2 Yamadaoka, Suita, Osaka 565-0871; fax (6) 6879-3070; internet www.med.osaka-u.ac.jp):

AOZASA, K., Molecular Pathology
ARAKIDA, M., Health Promotion Science
ASO, Y., Health Promotion Science
BEPPU, S., Functional Diagnostic Physics
FUJIKADO, T., AppliedVisual Science
FUJIWARA, C., Child and Reproductive Health
FUJIWARA, H., Medical Physics and Engineering
FUKUZAWA, M., Paediatric Surgery
HARUNA, M., Medical Physics and Engineering
HATAZAWA, J., Nuclear Medicine
HAYAKAWA, K., Health Promotion Science
HAYASHI, N., Molecular Therapeutics
HIRANO, T., Immunology and Molecular Biology
HORI, M., Cardiovascular Medicine
HOSOKAWA, K., Plastic Surgery
INAGAKI, S., Bioinformatics
INOUE, O., Medical Physics and Engineering
INOUE, T., Radiation Oncology
IWATANI, Y., Bioinformatics
JOHKOH, T., Functional Diagnostic Science
KANAKURA, Y., Haematology and Oncology
KANEDA, Y., Gene Therapy Science
KANOH, M., Cellular Neuroscience
KATAYAMA, I., Dermatology
KAWANO, S., Functional Diagnostic Science
KAWASE, I., Respirology
KIDO, Y., Evidence-based Clinical Nursing
KINOSHITA, H., Biomechanic and Motor Control
KUBO, T., Otorhinolaryngology
KURACHI, Y., Pharmacology
KUROKAWA, N., Pharmacy
MAKIMOTO, K., Evidence-based Clinical Nursing
MASHIMO, T., Anaesthesiology and Critical Care Medicine
MATOBA, R., Legal Medicine
MATSUURA, N., Functional Diagnostic Science
MIKAMI, H., Health Promotion Science
MIYASAKA, M., Immunodynamics
MIYAZAKI, J., Stem Cell Regulation Research
MONDEN, M., Surgery
MORIMOTO, K., Hygiene and Preventive Medicine
MURASE, K., Medical Physics and Engineering
MURATA, Y., Obstetrics and Gynaecology
NAGAI, T., Child and Reproductive Health
NAGATA, S., Genetics
NAKAMURA, H., Radiology
NAKAMURA, T., Molecular Regenerative Medicine
NAKANO, T., Stem-Cell Biology
NOGUCHI, S., Surgical Oncology
OGASAWARA, C., Health Promotion Science
OGIHARA, T., Geriatric Medicine
OGINO, S., Evidence-based Clinical Nursing
OHASHI, K., Child and Reproductive Health
OHIRA, Y., Applied Psychology
OHNO, Y., Health Promotion Science
OKAMOTO, M., Molecular Physiological Chemistry
OKUMIYA, A., Evidence-based Clinical Nursing
OKUYAMA, A., Urology
OZONO, K., Paediatrics
SAKODA, S., Neurology
SATO, H., Cognitive Neuroscience
SHIMADA, M., Child and Reproductive Health
SHIMOMURA, I., Internal Medicine
SHIRAKURA, R., Organ Transplantation
SOBUE, K., Neuroscience
SUGIMOTO, H., Traumatology and Acute Critical Medicine
SUGIMOTO, N., Applied Bacteriology
SUGIYAMA, H., Functional Diagnostic Science
SUZUKI, S., Evidence-based Clinical Nursing
TODA, T., Clinical Genetics
TAKAI, Y., Molecular Biology and Biochemistry
TAKEDA, H., Medical Information Science
TAKEDA, J., Environmental Genetics
TAKEDA, M., Psychiatry
TAMURA, S., Interdisciplinary Image Analysis
TANIGUCHI, N., Biochemistry
TANO, Y., Ophthalmology
TESHIMA, T., Medical Physics and Engineering
TOHYAMA, M., Anatomy and Neuroscience
TSUJIMOTO, Y., Molecular Genetics
UCHIYAMA, Y., Cell Biology and Neuroscience
YAMAMOTO, Y., Bioinformatics
YAMAMURA, T., Bioinformatics
YAMATODANI, A., Medical Physics and Engineering
YANAGIDA, T., Physiology and Biosignalling
YONEDA, Y., Anatomy and Cell Biology
YORIFUJI, S., Functional Diagnostic Science
YOSHIDA, T., Applied Psychology
YOSHIKAWA, H., Orthopaedic Surgery
YOSHIMINE, T., Neurosurgery

Graduate School of Frontier Biosciences (1-3 Yamadaoka, Suita, Osaka 565-0871; fax (6) 6879-4420; internet www.fbs.osaka-u.ac.jp):

FUJITA, I., Neuroscience
HAMADA, H., Organismal Biosystems
HANAOKA, F., Integrated Biology
HIRANO, T., Organismal Biosystems
KAWAMURA, S., Nanobiology
KINOSHITA, S., Biophysical Dynamics
KONDOH, H., Biomolecular Networks
KURAHASHI, T., Biophysical Dynamics
MURAKAMI, F., Neuroscience
NAGATA, S., Integrated Biology
NAKANO, T., Integrated Biology
NAMBA, K., Nanobiology
NORIOKA, S., Biophysical Dynamics
OGURA, A., Neuroscience
OHZAWA, I., Neuroscience
OKAMOTO, M., Biomolecular Networks
SHIMOMURA, I., Organismal Biosystems
SUGINO, A., Biomolecular Networks
TANAKA, K., Organismal Biosystems
YAGI, T., Integrated Biology
YAMAMOTO, N., Neuroscience
YANAGIDA, T., Nanobiology
YONEDA, Y., Biomolecular Networks

Graduate School and School of Dentistry (1-8 Yamadaoka, Suita, Osaka 565-0871; fax (6) 6879-2832; internet www.dent.osaka-u.ac.jp/index-e.html):

AMANO, A., Oral Science Methodology
EBISU, S., Endodontology
FURUKAWA, S., Oral and Maxillofacial Radiology
KAMISAKI, Y., Pharmacology
KAN, Y., Oral Physiology
KOGO, M., Management of Oral and Maxillofacial Diseases
MAEDA, Y., Interdisciplinary Dentistry
MORISAKI, I., Nursing Dentistry
MURAKAMI, S., Periodontology
NIWA, H., Dental Anaesthesiology

NOKUBI, T., Oromaxillofacial Prosthodontics
OHSHIMA, T., Paediatric Dentistry
SHIZUKUISHI, S., Preventive Dentistry
TAKADA, K., Orthodontics and Dentofacial Orthopaedics
TOYOSAWA, S., Oral Pathology
WAKISAKA, S., Oral Anatomy and Developmental Biology
YATANI, H., Occlusion, TMD and Advanced Prosthodontics
YONEDA, T., Molecular and Cellular Craniofacial Biology
YOSHIDA, A., Oral Anatomy and Neurobiology
YURA, Y., Oral and Maxillofacial Oncology

Graduate School and School of Pharmaceutical Sciences (1-6 Yamadaoka, Suita, Osaka 565-0871; fax (6) 6879-8154; internet www.phs.osaka-u.ac.jp):

AZUMA, J., Clinical Evaluation of Medicines and Therapeutics
BABA, A., Molecular Neuropharmacology
DOI, T., Protein Molecular Engineering
HIRATA, K., Environmental Bioengineering
IMANISHI, T., Bioorganic Chemistry
KITA, Y., Synthetic Organic Chemistry
KOBAYASHI, M., Natural Product Chemistry
MAEDA, M., Biochemistry and Molecular Biology
MATSUDA, T., Medicinal Pharmacology
MURAKAMI, N., Medicinal Plant Resource Exploration
NAKAGAWA, S., Biopharmaceutics
NASU, M., Environmental Science and Microbiology
NISHIKAWA, J., Environmental Biochemistry
OHKUBO, T., Biophysical Chemistry
TAKAGI, T., Pharmaceutical Information Science
TANAKA, K., Toxicology
TANAKA, T., Medicinal and Organic Chemistry
UNO, T., Analytical Chemistry
YAGI, K., Bio-Functional Molecular Chemistry
YAMAMOTO, H., Immunology

Graduate School and School of Engineering (2-1 Yamadaoka, Suita, Osaka 565-0871; fax (6) 6879-7210; internet www.eng.osaka-u.ac.jp):

Department of Advanced Science and Biotechnology:

AONO, M., Applied Surface Science
FUKUI, K., Dynamic Cell Biology
FUKUZUMI, S., Physical Chemistry for Life Science
HARASHIMA, S., Molecular Genetics
ITO, K., Applied Optics and Optical Information Processing
KANAYA, S., Biological Extremity Engineering
KOBAYASHI, A., Cell Technology
MIYATA, M., Molecular Recognition Chemistry
OHTAKE, H., Biochemical Engineering
SHIOYA, S., Bioprocess Systems Engineering
TAKAI, Y., Theoretical Computation Physics
URABE, I., Enzyme Engineering
YOKOYAMA, M., Molecular System Engineering

Department of Applied Chemistry:

AKASHI, M., Industrial Organic Chemistry
BABA, A., Resources Chemistry
CHATANI, N., Molecular Interaction Chemistry
HIRAO, T., Material Synthetic Chemistry
IMANAKA, N., Material Synthetic Chemistry
INOUE, Y., Molecular Interaction Chemistry
KAI, Y., Structural Physical Chemistry
KAMBE, N., Synthesis and Catalysis
KOMATSU, M., Synthetic Organic Chemistry
KUROSAWA, H., Organometallic Chemistry
KUWABATA, S., Applied Chemistry
OHSHIMA, T., Theoretical Organic Chemistry
UYAMA, H., Theoretical Organic Chemistry

Department of Materials Chemistry:

HIRAO, T., Materials Synthetic Chemistry
IMANAKA, N., Materials Synthetic Chemistry
KAI, Y., Structural Physical Chemistry
KOMATSU, M., Synthetic Organic Chemistry
KUWABATA, S., Applied Electrochemistry
OSHIMA, T., Theoretical Organic Chemistry
UYAMA, H., Structural Organic Chemistry

Department of Biotechnology:

FUKUI, K., Dynamic Cell Biology
HARASHIMA, S., Molecular Genetics
KOBAYASHI, A., Cell Technology
OTAKE, H., Biochemical Engineering
SHIOYA, S., Bioprocess Systems Engineering
URABE, I., Enzyme Engineering

Department of Precision Science, Technology and Applied Physics:

HIROSE, K., Computational Physics
KASAI, H., Materials Physics Theory
KATAOKA, T., Quantum Measurement and Instrumentation
KAWAKAMI, N., Condensed Matter Physics and Statistical Physics
MASUHARA, H., Laser Photochemistry and Microspectroscopy
MORITA, M., Scientific Hardware Systems
SUGAWARA, Y., Engineering Physics
YAGI, A., Non-linear Analysis and its Applications
YAMAUCHI, K., Ultra-precision Machining
YASUTAKE, K., Atomically-controlled Processes
YOSHII, K., Functional Materials

Department of Applied Physics:

KASAI, H., Materials Physics Theory
KAWAKAMI, N., Condensed Matter Physics and Statistical Physics
MASUHARA, H., Laser Photochemistry and Microspectroscopy
SUGAWARA, Y., Engineering Physics
YAGI, A., Nonlinear Analysis and its Applications

Department of Adaptive Machine Systems:

ASADA, M., Emergent Robotics
ISHIGURRO, H., Evolution Dynamics
MINAMINO, Y., Intelligent Materials
NAKATANI, A., Microdynamics
OHJI, T., Advanced Materials Processing
YASUDA, H., Materials Processing and Devices

Department of Mechanophysics Engineering:

FUJITA, K., Design and Manufacturing Engineering
HURUSHO, J., Real-World Active Intelligence
IKEDA, M., Control Engineering
INABA, T., Morphology in Machine Phenomena
KAJISHIMA, T., Fluid Engineering and Thermohydrodynamics
KATAOKA, I., Quantum Measurement
KUBO, S., Materials and Structures Evaluation
MINOSHIMA, K., Intelligent Materials
MIYOSHI, T., Production and Measurement Systems Engineering
MORI, N., Complex Fluid Mechanics
OTA, Y., Control Engineering
SHIBUTANI, Y., Solid Mechanics
TAKEISHI, K., Thermal Science and Engineering
TAKEUCHI, Y., Design and Manufacturing Engineering
TANAK, T., Mechanical Systems Analysis and Solid Mechanics
TSUJI, Y., Complex Fluid Mechanics
UMEDA, Y., Design and Manufacturing Engineering

Department of Mechanical Engineering and Systems:

KUBO, S., Materials and Structures Evaluation
MINOSHIMA, K., Materials and Structures Evaluation
MIYOSHI, T., Production and Measurement Systems Engineering
SHIBUTANI, Y., Solid Mechanics
TANAKA, T., Mechanical Systems Analysis and Solid Mechanics

Department of Computer-controlled Mechanical Systems:

FUJITA, K., Design and Manufacturing Engineering
FURUSHO, J., Real World Active Intelligence
IKEDA, M., Control Engineering
OTA, Y., Control Engineering
SHIRAI, Y., Real World Active Intelligence
TAKEUCHI, Y., Design and Manufacturing Engineering

Department of Materials Science and Processing:

ARAI, E., Advanced Manufacturing Systems
FUJIMOTO, S., Environmental Materials and Surface Processing
FUJIMOTO, K., Micro-nano Systems
FUJIWARA, Y., Crystal Growth
HIRATA, Y., Intelligent Materials Processing Systems
HUJIMOTO, S., Environmental Materials and Surface Processing
HIROSE, K., Computational Physics
KAKESHITA, T., Quantum Physics of Solids
KOBAYASHI, K., Smart Materials Processing
MATSUO, S., Intelligent Materials Processing
MINAMI, F., Materials Evaluation for Structuring
NISHIMOTO, K., Materials Joining
TANAKA, T., Interface Science and Technology
TOYODA, M., Strength/Fracture Evaluation for Manufacturing
USUI, T., Materials Processing and Metallurgy
YAMAMOTO, M., Physics of Surface and Interface
YAMASHITA, H., Thermophysics of Materials

Department of Materials Science and Engineering:

FUJIWARA, Y., Crystal Growth
KAKESHITA, T., Quantum Physics of Solids
YAMAMOTO, M., Physics of Surface and Interface

Department of Manufacturing Science:

ARAI, E., Advanced Manufacturing Systems
FUJIMOTO, K., Micro-nano Systems
HIRATA, Y., Intelligent Materials Processing Systems
KOBAYASHI, K., Smart Materials Processing
MINAMI, F., Materials Evaluation for Structuring
MIYAMOTO, I., Intelligent Materials Processing Systems
NISHIMOTO, K., Materials Joining
TOYODA, M., Strength/Fracture Evaluation for Manufacturing

Department of Communications Engineering:

BABAGUCHI, N., Telecommunications and Systems Engineering

IIDA, T., Fusion Engineering
ISE, T., Systems and Electric Power Engineering
ITO, T., Electro-Materials Engineering
KAWASAKI, Z., Fundamentals for Communications Engineering
KODAMA, R., Laser Engineering
KOMAKI, S., Microwave and Optical Communication Systems
KUMAGAI, S., Control Engineering
MORITA, S., Microscopic Quantum Engineering
NISHIKAWA, M., Supra-High-Temperature Engineering
SANPEI, S., Telecommunication and System Engineering
SASAKI, T., Applied Electro-Physics
SUGINO, T., Science and Technology of Electrical Materials
SUHARA, T., Integrated Electronic Engineering
TAKINE, T., Advanced Communications and Photonic Networks
SUHARA, T., Integrated Electronic Engineering
TANAKA, K., Laser Engineering
TANIGUCHI, K., Quantum Devices
TANINO, T., Systems Analysis and Optimization
TSUJI, K., Systems Engineering
YAGI, T., Control System Engineering

Department of Sustainable Energy and Environmental Engineering:

HORIIKE, H., Neutronics and Nuclear Instrumentation
KAGA, A., Engineering for the Atmospheric Environment
MIZUNO, M., Environment and Energy Systems
MORIOKA, T., Environmental Management
NISHIJIMA, S., Nuclear Chemical Engineering
SAWAKI, M., Environmental Management
TAKEDA, T., Nuclear Reactor Physics
YAMANAKA, S., Nuclear Fuels

Department of Global Architecture:

DEGUCHI, I., Social Systems Engineering
HASEGAWA, K., Naval Architecture
IMAI, K., Regional Environment and Global Transport
KOHZU, I., Structural Engineering
KATO, N., Naval Architecture
MATSUI, S., Structural and Geotechnical Engineering
NAITO, S., Marine Systems Engineering
NAKATSUJI, K., Social Systems Engineering
NITTA, Y., Social System Engineering
OHNO, Y., Structural Engineering
SAGARA, K., Architectural Design
TACHIBANA, E., Structural Engineering
TANIMOTO, C., Sustainable Development and Strategy
TOKIDA, K., Structural and Geotechnical Engineering
YAMAGUCHI, K., Sustainable Development and Strategy
YAO, T., Naval Architecture

Department of Environmental Engineering:

FUJITA, M., Water Science and Environmental Biotechnology
KAGA, A., Engineering for the Atmospheric Environment
MIZUNO, M., Environment and Energy Systems
MORIOKA, T., Environmental Management

Department of Management for Industry and Technology:

NARUMI, S., Management of Technology Knowledge
SATO, T., Technology Design
YAMAMOTO, T., Management of Technology Knowledge
ZAKO, M., Technology Design

Science Center for Atoms, Molecules and Ions Control:

FUKUDA, T., Plasma Particle Control Division
HAMAGUCHI, S., Plasma Particle Control Division
NAKATANI, R., Micro-composite Research Division
OKADA, S., Plasma Particle Control Division
SHIRAI, Y., Micro-structures Division

Research Center for Ultra-Precision Science and Technology:

ENDO, K., Precision Science and Technology

Graduate School and School of Engineering Science (1-3 Machikaneyama-cho, Toyonaka, Osaka 560-8531; tel. (6) 6850-6111; fax (6) 6850-6151; internet www.es.osaka-u.ac.jp/index-e.html):

Department of Materials Engineering Science:

HIRAI, T., Solar Energy Chemistry
HIRATA, Y., Environment and Energy System
HIYAMIZU, S., Quantum Physics of Nanoscale Materials
IMOTO, N., Quantum Physics of Nanoscale Materials
INOUE, Y., Environment and Energy System
ITOH, T., Dynamics of Nanoscale Materials
IWAI, S., Molecular Organization Chemistry
KANEDA, K., Chemical Reaction Engineering
KITAOKA, Y., Frontier Materials
KITAYAMA, T., Synthetic Chemistry
KUBOI, R., Bioprocess Engineering
MASHIMA, K., Synthetic Chemistry
MATSUMURA, M., Solar Energy Chemistry
MIYAKE, K., Electron Correlation Physics
MIYASAKA, H., Dynamics of Nanoscale Materials
NAKANO, M., Chemical Reaction Engineering
NAKATO, Y., Molecular Organization Chemistry
NAOTA, T., Synthetic Chemistry
OHGAKI, K., Environment and Energy System
SHIMIZU, K., Quantum Science in Extreme Conditions
SUGA, S., Electron Correlation Physics
SUZUKI, N., Frontier Materials
SUZUKI, Y., Electron Correlation Physics
TADA, H., Quantum Physics of Nanoscale Materials
TAYA, M., Bioprocess Engineering
TOBE, Y., Frontier Materials
UEYAMA, K., Chemical Reaction Engineering
YOSHIDA, H., Quantum Science in Extreme Conditions

Department of Mechanical Science and Bioengineering:

ARAKI, T., Biomedical and Biophysical Measurements
HIRAO, M., Mechanics of Solid Materials
KOBAYASHI, H., Mechanics of Solid Materials
MIYAZAKI, F., Mechano-informatics
NOMURA, T., Biophysical Engineering
OHSHIRO, O., Biomedical and Biophysical Measurements
OSAKADA, K., Mechano-informatics
SUGIMOTO, N., Mechanics of Fluids and Thermo-fluids
TANAKA, M., Biomedical Engineering
TSUJIMOTO, Y., Propulsion Engineering
WAKABAYASHI, K., Biophysical Engineering

Department of Systems Innovation:

AIDA, S., Mathematical and Statistical Finance
AKASAKA, Y., Solid State Electronics
ARAI, T., Intelligent Systems
FUJII, T., System Theory
IIGUNI, Y., System Theory
INAGAKI, N., Mathematical and Statistical Finance
INUIGUCHI, M., Theoretical Systems Science
ITOSAKI, H., Advanced Quantum Devices and Electronics
KANO, Y., Statistical Science
KITAGAWA, M., Advanced Quantum Devices and Electronics
KOBAYASHI, T., Optical Electronics
NAGAI, H., Mathematical and Statistical Finance
NAWA, H., Mathematical Modelling
NISHIDA, S., Intelligent Systems
OKAMOTO, H., Solid State Electronics
OKAMURA, Y., Optical Electronics
OKUYAMA, M., Solid State Electronics
SATO, K., Intelligent Systems
SHIRAHATA, S., Statistical Science
SUZUKI, T., Mathematical Modelling
URABE, S., Optical Electronics
USHIO, T., Theoretical Systems Science
YACHIDA, M., Intelligent Systems

Graduate School of Information Science and Technology (1-5 Yamadoaka, Suita, Osaka 565-0871; tel. (6) 6877-5111; fax (6) 6879-4570; internet www.ist.osaka-u.ac.jp):

Department of Pure and Applied Mathematics:

DATE, E., Mathematical Science
HIBI, T., Combinatorics
KAWANAKA, N., Discrete Structures
MATSUMURA, A., Applied Analysis
ODANAKA, S., Computer Assisted Mathematics
SAKANE, Y., Applied Geometry

Department of Information and Physical Sciences:

ISHII, H., Operations Research
MORITA, H., Computing with Complexity and Nonlinearity
NUMAO, M., Architecture for Intelligence
TANIDA, J., Physical Sciences
UOSAKI, K., Nonlinear Systems, Modelling and Optimization

Department of Computer Science:

HAGIHARA, K., Supercomputing Engineering
INOUE, K., Software Engineering
KUSOMOTO, S., Software Science
MASUZAWA, T., Algorithm Engineering
YAGI, Y., Intelligent Media Systems

Department of Information Systems Engineering:

CHIBA, T., Advanced System Architecture
IMAI, M., Integrated System Design
KAWATA, T., Advanced Systems Architecture
KIKUNO, T., Dependability Engineering
ONOYE, T., Information Systems Synthesis
TAKEMURA, H., Integrated Media Environment

Department of Information Networking:

HIGASHINO, T., Mobile Computing
IMASE, M., Information Sharing Platform
MURAKAMI, K., Intelligent Networking Systems
NAKANO, H., Advanced Network Architecture
OBASHI, Y., Cyber Communication
SATO, T., Cyber Communication

Department of Multimedia Engineering:

FUJIWARA, T., Information Security Engineering
KATAGIRI, Y., Multimedia Agent Systems

KISHINO, F., Human Interface Engineering
KOGURE, K., Multimedia Agent Systems
KOMODA, N., Business Information Systems
NISHIO, S., Multimedia Data Engineering
SHIMOJO, S., Applied Media Engineering

Department of Bioinformatic Engineering:
AKAZAWA, K., Human Information Engineering
KASHIWABARA, T., Bio-network Engineering
MATSUDA, H., Genome Information Engineering
SHIMIZU, H., Metabolic Engineering

Graduate School of Language and Culture (1-8 Machikaneyama-cho, Toyonaka, Osaka 560-0043; tel. (6) 6850-6111; fax (6) 6850-5865):
DYUBOVSKI, A., Language and Technology
HARUKI, Y., Language and Communication
HAYASHI, Y., Language and Information Science
HUKAZAWA, Y., Language and Communication
IWANE, H., Language and Technology
KANASAKI, H., Area Studies in Language and Culture
KANEKO, M., Area Studies in Language and Culture
KIMURA, K., Area Studies in Language and Culture
KIMURA, S., Interdisciplinary Cultural Studies
KITAMURA, T., Interdisciplinary Cultural Studies
NAKA, N., Language and Culture in International Relations
NAKANO, Y., Language and Culture in International Relations
NARITA, H., Education in Language and Culture
OKADA, N., Education in Language and Culture
OKITA, T., Education in Language and Culture
SENBA, Y., Language and Technology
TAKAOKA, K., Language and Culture in International Relations
TSUDA, A., Language and Communication
TSUKUI, S., Area Studies in Language and Culture
WATANABE, S., Language and Information Science
YOKOTA, G., Interdisciplinary Cultural Studies

Osaka School of International Public Policy (1-31 Machikaneyama-cho, Toyonaka, Osaka 560-0043; tel. (6) 6850-6111; fax (6) 6850-5208):
HASHIMOTO, Y., Comparative Public Policy
HOSHINO, T., System Integration
KOHSAKA, A., Systems Integration
KOJIMA, N., Comparative Corporate Behaviour
KUROSAWA, M., International Public System
MATSUSHIGE, H., Systems Integration
MURAKAMI, M., International Public System
NAKANO, T., Comparative Corporate Behaviour
NOMURA, Y., Systems Integration
SAITO, S., Comparative Economic Development
SAWAI, M., Comparative Economic Development
SUGIHARA, S., Contemporary Japanese Law and Economy
TAKENAKA, H., International Trade Relations
TANIGUCHI, S., International Trade Relations
TOKOTANI, F., Comparative Public Policy
YAMAUCHI, N., Contemporary Japanese Law and Economy
YONEHARA, K., Contemporary Japanese Law and Economy

ATTACHED INSTITUTES

Institute for Protein Research: Suita Campus, Yamadaoka, Suita, Osaka; Dir HIDEO AKUTSU.

Institute of Scientific and Industrial Research: Suita Campus, Mihogaoka, Ibaraki, Osaka; Dir TOMOJI KAWAI.

Institute of Social and Economic Research: Suita Campus, Mihogaoka, Ibaraki, Osaka; Dir SHINSUKE IKEDA.

Joining and Welding Research Institute: Suita Campus, Mihogaoka, Ibaraki, Osaka; Dir KIYOSHI NOGI.

Research Institute for Microbial Diseases: Suita Campus, Yamadaoka, Suita, Osaka; Dir TAROH KINOSHITA.

OSAKA UNIVERSITY OF FOREIGN STUDIES

8-1-1 Aomatani-higashi, Minoo City, Osaka 562-8558
Telephone: (727) 30-5005
Fax: (727) 30-5009
E-mail: sosoumu@post01.osaka-gaidai.ac.jp
Internet: www.osaka-gaidai.ac.jp

Founded 1949
Independent
Academic year: April to March (two semesters)

President: SHUN KORENAGA
Librarian: Prof. MASARU HASHIMOTO

Library of 612,340 vols
Number of teachers: 206
Number of students: 4,528 (Faculty of Foreign Studies), 354 (Graduate School), 127 (Center for Japanese Language)

Publications: *Journal*, *Japanese Language and Culture: Bulletin of the Center for Japanese Language*, *Journal of the Association for Integrated Studies in Language and Society*.

OTARU UNIVERSITY OF COMMERCE

3-5-21, Midori, Otaru, 047-0851, Hokkaido
Telephone: (134) 27-5200
Fax: (134) 27-5213
E-mail: inl@office.otaru.ac.jp
Internet: www.otaru-uc.ac.jp

Founded 1949
Independent

President: IEMASA YAMADA
Chief Administrative Officer: HIROSHI AIBA
Librarian: YOICHIRO YUKI

Library of 420,000 vols
Number of teachers: 134
Number of students: 2,260

Depts of economics, commerce, law, information and management sciences, teacher-training programme in commerce and graduate school

PROFESSORS

Department of Economics: HAJIME IMANISHI
Department of Commerce: HAJIME ITOH
Department of Law: MASAHIRO MICHINO
Department of Information Technology: HARUHIKO OGASAWARA

UNIVERSITY OF THE RYUKYUS

1 Senbaru, Nishihara-cho, Okinawa 903-0213
Telephone: (98) 895-2221
Fax: (98) 895-8037
E-mail: webmaster@www.u-ryukyu.ac.jp
Internet: www.u-ryukyu.ac.jp

Founded 1950
Academic year: April to March
Independent
Language of instruction: Japanese

President: MOSHIN MORITA
Vice-Presidents: HARUO NAKAZATO, KIYOHIRO MIYAGI
Administrator: MAKOTO UDA
Dean of Students: KATSUMA YAGASAKI
Librarian: TOMONORI ISHIKAWA

Library of 930,000 vols
Number of teachers: 879
Number of students: 8,195

DEANS

Faculty of Law and Letters: K. YOGI
Faculty of Education: T. TAIRA
Faculty of Science: Y. OHMURA
Faculty of Medicine: T. IWAMASA
Faculty of Engineering: Y. YAMASHIRO
Faculty of Agriculture: S. MURAYAMA

PROFESSORS

Faculty of Law and Letters:
AKAMINE, K., American Literature
AKAMINE, M., Japanese Folklore
AKAMINE, M., Modern Chinese History, Modern Okinawa History
ANDO, Y., Sociology
ARAKAKI, S., Civil Law
ASHITOMI, T., Civil Law
CHINEN, S., Monetary Economics
CHINEN, Y., Public Finance
EGAMI, T., Science of Public Administration, Comparative Politics
ENDO, M., Cognitive Psychology
GABE, M., International Relations
HAMASAKI, M., Greek Philosophy
HESHIKI, T., International Marketing
HIYANE, T., History of Political Thought, Political Science
HOSAKA, H., Journalism
IHA, M., Marketing
IKEDA, Y., Japanese Archaeology, Museography
IKEMIYA, M., Ryukyuan Literature
IMURA, O., Clinical Psychology
INABA, Y., Criminal Procedure
IREI, T., Human Resources Management, Business Administration
ISHIKAWA, T., Regional Geography, Human Geography
ISHIMINE, K., Constitutional Law
KABIRA, N., Economic History
KARIMATA, S., Japanese Linguistics, Study of Ryukyuan Dialects
KAWASOE, M., Social Services for the Aged
KOMATSU, M., Economic History
KUDEKEN, K., Community Development in Social Welfare
MACHIDA, M., Settlement Geography, Geographical Information Systems
MAEKADO, A., Geomorphology
MIYARA, S., Linguistics
NAKAHODO, M., Modern Japanese Literature
NAKACHI, H., Administrative Law
NAKACHI, K., American Literature
NAKAHARA, T., Business and Corporation Laws
NAKAMURA, T., Social Psychology
NAMIHIRA, T., Political Philosophy and Theory, Political Science
NISHIKAWA, H., Contemporary Philosophy
OSABE, Y., Asian History
OSHIRO, H., International Economics
OSHIRO, I., Theoretical Economics
OSHIRO, M., Managerial Finance
OSHIRO, T., Regional Development Policy
OYAKAWA, T., Linguistics
SAKIMA, N., European History
SHIMABUKURO, S., Human Geography
SHIMABUKURO, T., Commercial Law, Law of Securities Regulation
SHIMIZU, K., Criminal Law
SHIMOJI, Y., English Linguistics

SHIMURA, K., Quality Management
SUZUKI, N., International Sociology
TAIRA, M., American Literature
TAIRA, T., Applied Linguistics
TAKARA, K., Ryukyuan History
TAKARA, T., Constitutional Law, Administrative Law
TAMAKI, I., Civil Procedure Law
TAMAKI, M., Ryukyuan Literature
TANAKA, H., Economic Statistics
TOMA, S., Theoretical Economics
TOMINAGA, H., Econometrics
TOYOOKA, T., Accounting Information Theory, Accounting Systems
TSUHA, T., Social Anthropology
TSUNODA, M., Civil Law, European Private Law
UEZATO, K., Chinese Literature
UEZU, Y., Accounting
YAMAZATO, J., Japanese History
YAMAZATO, K., American Literature
YOGI, K., Linguistics
YONAHARA, T., Strategic Management
YOSHII, K., German
YOSHIMURA, K., English Literature
YOSHIZAWA, T., Sociology of Education

Faculty of Education:
AIZAWA, T., Chinese Literature
ARATA, Y., Biophysics Engineering
FUJIE, T., Homemaking Education, Aesthetics in Costume
FUJIWARA, Y., Didactics
HAMAMOTO, M., Sports Methodology
HANASHIRO, R., Consumer Education
HIGA, Z., Technical Education
HIGASIMORI, K., Food Science
HIRATA, E., Education for the Handicapped
IKEDA, K., Judo
INOUE, K., Lifelong Education
ISHIGURO, E., Optics
ISHIKAWA, K., Social Development in Children
ITOKAZU, T., Educational Music of Wind Instruments
IZUMI, K., Vocal Music
KAKAZU, T., Psychology
KAMIYAMA, T., Woodcut
KAMIZONO, S., Developmental Psychology of Mentally Retarded and Handicapped Children
KATO, M., Complex Analysis
KAWANA, T., Physical Geography
KINJO, M., Mathematics Education
KINJO, S., Culinary Science
KINJO, Y., Inorganic Chemistry
KOBASHIGAWA, H., Sports Psychology
KOBAYASHI, M., Theory and History of Art
KOJIMA, Y., Japanese Literature
KOYANAGI, M., Physical Chemistry
MAEHARA, H., Discrete Geometry
MAEHARA, T., Psychology
MAESHIRO, R., Regional Economics
MATSUMOTO, S., Mathematical Physics
MIZUNO, M., Criminal Law
NAGAYAMA, T., Piano Playing
NAKAMURA, I., Meteorology
NAKAMURA, T., Education for the Handicapped
NAKAMURA, T., Theory of Music
NAKASONE, Y., Ecology
NAKAZATO, H., Algebra
NISHIMURA, S., Sculpture
NISHIZATO, K., History of East Asia
NOHARA, T., Palaeontology
OKUDA, M., Ceramic Art
OZAWA, Y., Japanese Literature
SEKINE, H., Electricity and Electrical Engineering
SHIMABUKURO, Z., English Linguistics
SHIMOJANA, M., Animal Ecology and Taxonomy (especially spiders)
SHINZATO, R., Clinical Psychology
SHINZATO, S., Kinematics and Dynamics of Mechanisms
SIMABUKURO, T., Psychology of Personality
TAIRA, K., Health Promotion
TAIRA, T., Physical Education
TAKASHIMA, N., Social Studies
TAKEDA, H., International Peace Studies
TAMAKI, A., Physical Education
TOMINAGA, D., Psychophysiology
UEZU, E., Nutrition and Physiology
YAMAUTI, S., TESL/TEFL
YONEMORI, T., Educational Information Technology

Faculty of Science:
FUKUHARA, C., Inorganic Chemistry
GINOZA, M., Condensed Matter Physics
GOYA, E., Functional Analysis
HAGIHARA, A., Forest Ecophysiology
HAYASHI, D., Structural Geology
HENNA, J., Mathematical Statistics
HIDAKA, M., Coral Biology
HIGA, M., Organic Chemistry
HIGA, T., Marine Natural Products Chemistry
HOSOYA, M., Computer Physics
IKEHARA, N., Physiology and Biochemistry
ISA, E., Calcification
ISHIJIMA, S., Atmospheric Science
KAKAZU, K., Mathematical Physics
KATO, Y., Petrology
KIMURA, M., Marine Geology
KODAKA, K., Functional Analysis
KUNIYOSHI, M., Marine Natural Products Chemistry
MAEDA, T., Algebraic Geometry
MAEHARA, R., Topology
MATAYOSHI, S., Quantum Physics
MIYAGI, Y., Molecular Spectroscopy
NAKAMURA, S., Cytology
NIKI, H., Solid State Physics
NISHISHIRAHO, T., Approximation Theory
OHMURA, Y., Condensed Matter Physics
OOMORI, T., Marine Geochemistry
SHIGA, H., Topology
SHOKITA, S., Fisheries Biology
SUZUKI, T., Number Theory
TAIRA, H., Analytical Chemistry
TAKUSHI, E., Solid State Optics
TEZUKA, M., Topology
TOKUYAMA, A., Environmental Chemistry
TOMOYOSE, T., Solid State Physics
TSUCHIYA, M., Ecology
UEHARA, T., Embryology
UEHARA, Y., Physical Chemistry
YAGASAKI, K., Solid State Physics
YAMAGUCHI, M., Coral-Reef Biology
YAMAMOTO, S., Sedimentology
YAMAZATO, M., Probability Theory
YOGI, S., Organic Chemistry
YONASHIRO, K., Condensed Matter Physics

Faculty of Medicine:
ANIYA, Y., Biochemical Pharmacology
ARAKI, K., Haematology
ARIIZUMI, M., Preventive Medicine
FUKUNAGA, T., Virology
HOKAMA, T., Health Care
IMAMURA, T., Bacteriology
ISHIZU, H., Mental Health Science
ISIDA, H., Anatomy
ITO, E., Pathology
IWAMASA, T., Pathology
IWANAGA, M., Bacteriology
KANAYA, F., Hand Surgery, Microsurgery
KANAZAWA, K., Gynaecological Oncology, Reproductive Immunology
KARIYA, K., Biochemistry
KOJA, K., Surgery
KONO, S., Obstetrics and Gynaecology, Endocrinology
KOSUGI, T., Physiology, Haematology
MAEHIRA, F., Clinical Biochemistry, Biochemistry
MIYAGI, I., Medical Entomology
MIYAZAKI, T., Forensic Medicine
MURAYAMA, S.
MUTO, Y., Digestive Surgery
NAKA, K., Health Administration
NODA, Y., Otorhinolaryngology, Head and Neck Surgery
NONAKA, S., Dermatology, Photobiology
OGAWA, Y., Urology
OGURA, C., Neuropsychiatry
OHTA, T., Paediatrics
SAITO, A., Internal Medicine
SAKANASHI, M., Pharmacology
SAKIHARA, S., Health Sociology, Community Health
SATO, Y., Parasitology
SAWAGUCHI, S., Ophthalmology
SHIMADA, K., Human Pathology
SHIMAJIRI, S., Maternal Nursing
SUGAHARA, K., Anaesthesiology
SUNAGAWA, Y., Adult Nursing, Geriatric Nursing
SUNAKAWA, H., Oral and Maxillofacial Surgery
TAKASU, N., Internal Medicine
TANAKA, T., Biochemistry
TERASHIMA, S., Physiology
UZA, M., Health Care
YAMANE, N., Laboratory Medicine
YASUZUMI, F., Anatomy
YOSHII, Y., Neurosurgery

Faculty of Engineering:
AMANO, T., Wind Engineering for Building Structures
ASHARIF, M. R., Adaptive Digital Signal Processing, Speech in Images
FUKUSHIMA, S., Architectural Planning
IKEDA, T., Urban and Regional Planning
KANESHIRO, H., Fatigue Fracture
KINA, S., Sanitary Engineering
KODAMA, M., Microwave
MEKARU, S., Plastic Working
MIYAGI, H., Intelligent Systems
MIYAGI, K., High Velocity Impact
MORITA, D., Conservation Science and Environmental Planning for Architecture
NAGAI, M., Mechanics and Fluid Engineering
NAGATA, T., Thermal Engineering
NAKAMURA, I., Electronic Circuits
NAKAO, Z., Mathematical Informatics
OSHIRO, T., Structural Analysis and Materials
OYAKAWA, K., Heat Transfer Augmentation
SHINZATO, T., Thermal Engineering
TAKAHASHI, H., Power Systems Engineering and Surge Analysis
TAKARA, T., Spoken Language Processing
TAMAKI, S., Digital Control
TOGUCHI, M., Electronic Materials
TSUKAYAMA, S., Coastal Engineering
TSUTSUI, S., Coastal Engineering
UEZATO, K., Electric Machinery
YABUKI, T., Bridge and Structural Engineering
YAFUSO, T., Strength of Materials
YAMAKAWA, T., Reinforced Concrete Structures
YAMAMOTO, T., Neuro-control
YAMASHIRO, Y., Electrical Materials
YARA, H., Welding Engineering
YOSHIYA, K., Intelligent Information Processing
ZUKERAN, C., Multiple-valued Logic Circuit

Faculty of Agriculture:
AKINAGA, T., Postharvest Handling
CHINEN, I., Applied Biochemistry
GIBO, S., Land Conservation
HAYASHI, H., Woody Materials and Processing
HIGA, T., Tropical Horticulture
HIGOSHI, H., Animal Hygiene
HIRATA, E., Forestry Measurement
HONGO, F., Chemistry of Animal Products and Applied Bioresource Utilization
ISHIMINE, Y., Economic Plants
IWAHASHI, O., Insect Ecology
KAWASHIMA, Y., Comparative Anatomy
KOBAMOTO, N., Applied Biophysics

Koki, Z., Preventive Forestry Engineering
Kuroda, T., Environmental Information Sciences
Miyagi, N., Soil Engineering
Murayama, S., Crop Science
Nakada, T., Animal Reproduction
Nakasone, Y., Food Chemistry
Oshiro, S., Animal Science, Environmental Physiology
Sato, S., Genetics and Breeding of Rice Plants
Shinjo, A., Animal Breeding
Shinjo, T., Geomechanics
Shinohara, T., Forest Policy and Economics
Tawata, S., Pesticide Chemistry
Tokashiki, Y., Soil Science
Ueno, M., Agricultural Engineering
Uesato, K., Floricultural Plant Science
Yaga, S., Wood Chemistry and Wood Preservation
Yamashiro, S., Agricultural Engineering
Yasuda, M., Food Microbiology
Yonaha, T., Plant Pathology
Yoshida, S., Agricultural Marketing Theory

Tropical Biosphere Research Center:

Aramoto, M., Terrestrial Resources
Fujimori, K., Cell Biology
Kumazawa, N., Environmental Microbiology Epidemiology
Murai, M., Animal Ecology
Nakamura, M., Reproductive Biology
Takaso, T., Plant Morphology

Education and Research Center of Lifelong Learning (Senbaru, Nishihara-cho, Okinawa):

Daizen, T., Sociology of Schooling, Sociology of Higher Education

University Hospital (Uehara, Nishihara-cho, Okinawa):

Hirose, Y., Hospital Information System, Knowledge-Base System
Hobara, N., Pharmacokinetic Drug Interaction, Quality Control of Medicine

Okinawa–Asia Research Center of Medical Science (Uehara, Nishihara-cho, Okinawa):

Jinno, Y., Molecular Genetics
Tanaku, Y.

ATTACHED INSTITUTES

Tropical Biosphere Research Center: Senbaru, Nishihara-cho, Okinawa; Dir K. Fujimori.

Attached stations:

Sesoko Station: Sesoko Motobu-cho, Okinawa; Chief M. Murai.

Iriomote Station: Uehara Taketomi-cho, Yaeyama Okinawa; Chief T. Takaso.

Gene Research Center: Senbaru, Nishihara-cho, Okinawa; Dir N. Kobamoto.

Center for Co-operative Research: Senbaru, Nishihara-cho, Okinawa; Dir H. Yara.

Instrumental Research Center: Senbaru, Nishihara-cho, Okinawa; Dir Y. Uehara.

Education and Research Center for Lifelong Learning: Senbaru, Nishihara-cho, Okinawa; Dir T. Yoshizawa.

Computing and Networking Centre: Senbaru, Nishihara-cho, Okinawa; Dir H. Miyagi.

Health Administration Center: Senbaru, Nishihara-cho, Okinawa; Dir H. Takara.

Radioisotope Laboratory: Senbaru, Nishihara-cho, Okinawa; Dir E. Isa.

Language Center: Senbaru, Nishihara-cho, Okinawa; Dir Y. Shimoji.

Academic Museum (Fujukan): Senbaru, Nishihara-cho, Okinawa; Dir Y. Kawashima.

Environmental Science Center: Senbaru, Nishihara-cho, Okinawa; Dir Y. Miyagi.

Low Temperature Center: Senbaru, Nishihara-cho, Okinawa; Dir H. Niki.

University Education Center: Senbaru, Nishihara-cho, Okinawa; Dir H. Nakachi.

Center for Educational Research and Practice: Senbaru, Nishihara-cho, Okinawa; Dir T. Yonemori.

Center for Educational Research and Training of Handicapped Children: Senbaru, Nishihara-cho, Okinawa; Dir S. Kamizono.

University Hospital: Uehara, Nishihara-cho, Okinawa; Dir K. Kanazawa.

Okinawa–Asia Research Center of Medical Science: Uehara, Nishihara-cho, Okinawa; Dir K. Naritomi.

Research Laboratory Center: Uehara, Nishihara-cho, Okinawa; Dir M. Sakanashi.

Institute for Animal Experiments: Uehara, Nishihara-cho, Okinawa; Dir E. Ito.

University Experimental Farm: Senbaru, Nishihara-cho, Okinawa; Dir Y. Ishimine.

University Experimental Forest: Yona, Kunigami-son, Okinawa; Dir E. Hirata.

SAGA UNIVERSITY

Honjo-cho 1, Saga City 840
Telephone: (952) 28-8168
Fax: (952) 28-8819
Internet: www.saga-u.ac.jp

Founded 1949
Academic year: April to March

President: Haruo Uehara
Vice-Presidents: Gunji Aramaki, Yasuhisa Shintomi
Director of General Administration Bureau: Toshiji Ueda
Director of University Library: Keiichi Miyajima

Library of 600,341 vols
Number of teachers: 471
Number of students: 595 graduate, 5,808 undergraduate

Publication: various faculty reports and bulletins

DEANS

Faculty of Culture and Education: Kenji Tsuji
Faculty of Economics: Kazafumi Koga
Faculty of Science and Engineering: Akira Hasegawa
Faculty of Agriculture: Takayuki Kojima

DIRECTORS

Joint Research and Development Center: Kohei Arai
Analytical Research and Development Center: Keiichi Watanabe
Computer and Network Center: Yoshiaki Watanabe
International Student Center: Tatsuya Komoto
Institute of Lowland Technology: Shigenori Hayashi
Institute of Ocean Energy: Masanori Monde
Coastal Bioenvironment Center: Osamu Kato
Synchrotron Light Application Centre: Hiroshi Ogawa
Venture Business Laboratory: Masayoshi Aikawa

SAITAMA UNIVERSITY

255 Shimo-Okubo, Sakura-ku, Saitama City, Saitama 338-8570

Telephone: (48) 858-9624
Fax: (48) 858-9675
E-mail: kokusai@post.saitama-u.ac.jp
Internet: www.saitama-u.ac.jp

Founded 1949
Independent
Academic year: April to March

Pres.: Mitsuo Tasumi
Exec. Dirs: Masatoshi Hara, Michihiro Kaiama, Juzo Nakayama, Iwao Matsushima

Library of 758,521 vols, 19,265 periodicals
Number of teachers: 561
Number of students: 8,946

Publication: *Saitama Mathematical Journal* (annual)

DEANS

Faculty of Liberal Arts: Jun Sekiguchi
Faculty of Education: Haruyoshi Shibuya
Faculty of Economics: Yoshihiko Kamii
School of Science: Takeo Machida
School of Eng.: Masaaki Kawahashi
Graduate School of Cultural Science: Jun Sekiguchi
Graduate School of Education: Haruyoshi Shibuya
Graduate School of Economic Science: Yoshihiko Kamii
Graduate School of Science and Eng.: Yuzuru Husimi

ATTACHED INSTITUTES

Co-operative Research Center: Dir Susumu Takada.

Geosphere Research Institute: Dir Kunio Watanabe.

Information Technology Center: Dir Hitoshi Maekawa.

Molecular Analysis and Life Science Center: Dir Kinji Inoue.

SHIGA UNIVERSITY

1-1-1 Banba, Hikone, Shiga 522-8522
Telephone: (749) 27-1172
Fax: (749) 27-1174
E-mail: koho@biwako.shiga-u.ac.jp
Internet: www.shiga-u.ac.jp

Founded 1949
Independent
Academic year: April to March

President: Kenichi Miyamoto
Vice-Presidents: Seiji Oguri, Hideki Sumioka
Administrative Director: Osahiro Todoroki
Librarian: Takeo Terayoko

Library of 550,208 vols
Number of teachers: 315
Number of students: 3,981

Publications: *Fuzoku-shiryo-kan Kenkyu-Kiyo* (bulletin of the Archival Museum, annually), *Kenkyu-Nenpo* (Annals of Human and Social Sciences, annually), *The Hikone Ronso* (economics, several a year), *Kyoiku-Gakubu Kiyo* (memoirs of the Faculty of Education, annually), *Shiga-Eibun-Gakkai-Ronbunshu* (English Studies Review, every 2 years)

DEANS

Faculty of Education: Shobu Sato
Faculty of Economics: Hiroaki Kitamura
Graduate School of Education: Shobu Sato
Graduate School of Economics: Hiroaki Kitamura

ATTACHED RESEARCH INSTITUTES

Archives Museum: Dir Hideki Usami.

Center for Educational Research and Practice: 2-5-1 Hiratsu, Otsu, Shiga 520-0862; Dir Tsutomu Kuboshima.

Center for Environmental Education and Lake Science: 2-5-1 Hiratsu, Otsu, Shiga 520-0862; Dir SHUICHI ENDO.

Institute for Economic and Business Research: Dir NAOKI UMEZAWA.

Information Processing Center: Dir SABURO HORIMOTO.

Joint Research Center: Dir ISAO OGAWA.

Research Center for Lifelong Learning: 2-5-1 Hiratsu, Otsu, Shiga 520-0862; Dir OSAMU UMEDA.

SHIMANE UNIVERSITY

1060 Nishikawatsu-cho, Matsue-shi, Shimane-ken 690-8504
Telephone: (852) 32-6100
Fax: (852) 32-6019
E-mail: webinfo@jn.shimane-u.ac.jp
Internet: www.shimane-u.ac.jp

Founded 1949
Independent
Academic year: April to March
President: YUICHI HONDA
Registrar: T. KAMADA
Librarian: S. WATANABE
Library of 692,000 vols
Number of teachers: 500
Number of students: 5,550

DEANS

Faculty of Law and Literature: Y. MATSUI
Faculty of Education: M. YAMASHITA
Faculty of Science and Engineering: A. TAKUNA
Faculty of Life and Environmental Sciences: H. YAMAMOTO

SHINSHU UNIVERSITY

Asahi 3-1-1, Matsumoto, 390-8621 Nagano-ken
Telephone: (263) 35-4600
Fax: (263) 36-6769
E-mail: shinhp@jm.shinshu-u.ac.jp
Internet: www.shinshu-u.ac.jp

Founded 1949
Independent
President: ATSUSHI KOMIYAMA
Number of teachers: 1,107 full-time
Number of students: 11,478 (9,344 undergraduates, 2,134 in Graduate School)

DEANS

Faculty of Arts: S. OSHIMA
Faculty of Science: T. ITO
Faculty of Education: S. AKAHANE
Faculty of Economics: T. MATASAKA
School of Medicine: T. OHHASHI
Faculty of Engineering: A. NOMURA
Faculty of Agriculture: Y. KARASAWA
Faculty of Textile Science and Technology: A. HACHIMORI

SHIZUOKA UNIVERSITY

Ohya 836, Shizuoka-shi 422-8529
Telephone: (54) 238-4407
Fax: (54) 237-0089
E-mail: koho@gene1.adb.shizuoka.ac.jp
Internet: www.shizuoka.ac.jp

Founded 1949
Independent
President: YOSHIMITSU AMAGISHI
Vice-Presidents: NOBUYUKI ARAKI, HIROKAZU NAKAI
Director General: SHIGENOBU MORI
Director of University Library: KIMIO BAMBA
Number of teachers: 744 full-time
Number of students: 11,112

DEANS

Faculty of Humanities and Social Sciences: YOSHIHIKO YAMAMOTO
Faculty of Education: SHOJI KANAI
Faculty of Information Sciences: HIROYUKI TOKUYAMA
Faculty of Science: KATSUTOSHI ISHIKAWA
Faculty of Engineering: HITOSHI ISHII
Faculty of Agriculture: KIYOSHI OKAWA

DIRECTORS

Research Institute of Electronics: KENZO WATANABE
Center for Joint Research: NAOMICHI OKAMOTO
Center for Education and Research Lifelong Learning: KINJI TAKI
Institute for Genetic Research and Biotechnology: KOICHI YOSHINAGA
Information Processing Center: NAOKAZU YAMAKI
International Student Center: TAKASHIGE HONDA
Satellite Venture Business Laboratory: NORIHIRO INAGAKI

TOHOKU UNIVERSITY

2-1-1 Katahira, Aoba-ku, Sendai 980-8577
Telephone: (22) 217-4844
Fax: (22) 217-4846
E-mail: kokusai@bureau.tohoku.ac.jp
Internet: www.tohoku.ac.jp

Founded 1907
Independent
Academic year: April to March
President: TAKASHI YOSHIMOTO
Vice-Presidents: YOSHIO WASEDA, KUNIAKI SUGAI, HITOSHI OHNISHI, TETSUO SHYOJI, MICHITERU TOKUSHIGE, TOSHIFUMI TAKADA, HIROYUKI YOSHIKAWA
Director of Main Library: KEIICHI NOE

Library: see Libraries and Archives
Number of teachers: 2,581
Number of students: 18,035 (10,912 undergraduate, 7,123 postgraduate)

Publications: *Tohoku University Bulletin* (annually), *Tohoku Journal of Experimental Medicine* (monthly), *Annual Research Bulletin of the Graduate School of Pharmaceutical Sciences* (annually), *Graduate School of Engineering and Faculty of Engineering* (annually), *Tohoku Journal of Agricultural Research* (2 a year), *Reports of the Institute of Fluid Science* (annually), *CYRIC Annual Report* (annually), *Research Report of the Laboratory of Nuclear Science* (annually), *Northeast Asian Study* (annually), *Annual Report of the Economic Society* (4 a year), *Interdisciplinary Information Science* (2 a year), *Tohoku Geophysical Journal* (3 a year)

DEANS

School of Agriculture and Graduate School of Agricultural Science: YUKIO AKIBA
School and Graduate School of Arts and Letters: KEIICHI NOE
School and Graduate School of Dentistry: MAKOTO WATANABE
School and Graduate School of Economics and Management: SHUITSU HINO
School and Graduate School of Education: KATSUHIRO ARAI
Graduate School of Educational Informatics, Research Division: TOSHIRO HAGIHARA
School and Graduate School of Engineering: MITSUNOBU MIYAGI
Graduate School of Environmental Studies: AKITSUGU OKUWAKI
Graduate School of Information Sciences: AKIRA MARUOKA
Graduate School of International Cultural Studies: CHIKAYOSHI YONEYAMA
School and Graduate School of Law: TOSHIYA UEKI
Graduate School of Life Sciences: HIROYUKI IDE
School and Graduate School of Medicine: MAKOTO TAMAI
School and Graduate School of Pharmaceutical Sciences: HIDEO TAKEUCHI
School and Graduate School of Science: OSAMU HASHIMOTO

PROFESSORS

School of Agriculture and Graduate School of Agricultural Science (1-1 Tsutsumidori-Amamiyamachi, Aoba-ku, Sendai 981-8555; tel. (22) 717-8603; fax (22) 717-8607; e-mail agr-syom@bureau.tohoku.ac.jp; internet www.agri.tohoku.ac.jp):

AKIBA, Y., Animal Nutrition
GOMI, K., Microbial Biotechnology
HASEBE, T., Environmental Economics
IKEDA, I., Food and Biomolecular Science
IKEGAMI, M., Plant Pathology
KAMIO, Y., Applied Microbiology
KANAHAMA, K., Horticultural Science
KATSUMATA, R., Animal Microbiology
KIJIMA, A., Ecological Genetics (Field Science Center)
KOKUBUN, M., Crop Science
KOMAI, M., Nutrition
KUDO, A., Farm Business Management
KUWAHARA, S., Applied Bio-organic Chemistry
MAE, T., Plant Nutrition and Function
MATSUDA, K., Insect Science and Bioregulation
MINAMI, T., Fisheries Biology and Ecology
MIYAZAWA, T., Biodynamic Chemistry
MOROZUMI, K., Regional Planning
MUROGA, K., Aquacultural Biology
NAKAI, Y., Animal Health and Management
NANZYO, M., Soil Science
NISHIDA, A., Animal Breeding and Genetics
NISHIMORI, K., Molecular Biology
NISHIO, T., Plant Breeding and Genetics
OBARA, Y., Animal Physiology
OHKAMA, K., Agricultural and Resource Economics
OMORI, M., Fisheries Biology and Ecology
SAIGUSA, M., Environmental Crop Science (Field Science Center)
SAITO, G., Remote Sensing (Field Science Center)
SAITO, T., Animal Products Chemistry
SATO, E., Animal Reproduction
SATO, M., Marine Biochemistry
SATO, S., Land Ecology
SEIWA, K., Forest Ecology
SUZUKI, T., Marine Biotechnology
TANIGUCHI, A., Biological Oceanography
TANIGUCHI, K., Applied Aquatic Botany
TANIGUCHI, N., Applied Population Genetics
TORIYAMA, K., Environmental Biotechnology
YAMAGUCHI, T., Functional Morphology
YAMASHITA, M., Biophysical Chemistry
YAMAYA, T., Plant Cell Biochemistry
YONEKURA, H., Resource Management and Development Policy

School and Graduate School of Arts and Letters (Kawanchi, Aoba-ku, Sendai 980-8576; tel. (22) 795-6003; fax (22) 795-6086; e-mail art-syom@bureau.tohoku.ac.jp; internet www.sal.tohoku.ac.jp/index-j.html):

ABE, H., Western Literature and Languages
AKOSHIMA, K., Japanese History and Archaeology
CHIGUSA, S., Linguistics
GOTO, H., Linguistics
GOTO, T., Indology and History of Indian Buddhism
GYOBA, J., Psychology

HANATO, M., Sinology
HARA, E., Western Literature and Languages
HARA, J., Behavioural Science
HARA, K., Western Literature and Languages
HASEGAWA, K., Sociology
IMAIZUMI, T., Japanese History and Archaeology
KANEKO, Y., Western Literature and Languages
KAWAI, Y., Oriental History
KOBAYASHI, T., Japanese Linguistics
KUMAMOTO, T., Oriental History
MASAMURA, T., Sociology
MATSUMOTO, N., European History
MIURA, S., Sinology
MORIMOTO, K., Western Literature and Languages
NAKAOKA, R., History of Fine Arts
NAKAJIMA, R., Sinology
NAKAMURA, M., Western Literature and Languages
NIHEI, M., Japanese Literature and History of Japanese Philosophy
NIHEI, Y., Psychology
NOE, K., Philosophy and Ethics
NUMAZAKI, I., Cultural Anthropology and Science of Religions
OHBUCHI, K., Psychology
OHTO, O., Japanese History and Archaeology
ONO, Y., European History
OZAKI, A., History of Fine Arts
SAITA, I., Applied Japanese Linguistics
SAITO, M., Japanese Linguistics
SAITO, Y., Western Literature and Languages
SAKURAI, M., Indology and History of Indian Buddhism
SATO, H., Japanese Literature and History of Japanese Philosophy
SATO, M., European History
SATO, N., Japanese Literature and History of Japanese Philosophy
SATO, Y., Behavioural Science
SHIMA, M., Cultural Anthropology and Science of Religions
SHIMIZU, T., Philosophy and Ethics
SHINO, K., Philosophy and Ethics
SUTO, T., Japanese History and Archaeology
SUZUKI, A., Applied Japanese Linguistics
SUZUKI, I., Cultural Anthropology and Science of Religions
TAKAGI, K., Sociology
UMINO, M., Behavioural Science
YOSHIHARA, N., Sociology
ZAKOTA, Y., Philosophy and Ethics

School and Graduate School of Dentistry (4-1 Seiryo-machi, Aoba-ku, Sendai 980-8575; tel. (22) 717-8244; fax (22) 717-8279; e-mail den-syom@bureau.tohoku.ac.jp; internet www.ddh.tohoku.ac.jp/index.html):

ECHIGO, S., Oral Surgery
HAYASHI, H., Oral Physiology
IGARASHI, K., Oral Dysfunction Science
KAWAMURA, H., Maxillofacial Surgery
KIKUCHI, M., Oral and Craniofacial Anatomy
KIMURA, K., Fixed Prosthodontics
KOMATSU, M., Operative Dentistry
KOSEKI, T., Preventive Dentistry
MAYANAGI, H., Paediatric Dentistry
OKUNO, O., Dental Biomaterials
ŌOYA, K., Oral Pathology
OSAKA, K., International Oral Health
SASAKI, K., Advanced Prosthetic Dentistry
SASANO, T., Oral Diagnosis and Radiology
SASANO, Y., Craniofacial Development and Regeneration
SHIMAUCHI, H., Periodontology and Endodontology
SHINODA, H., Dental Pharmacology
SUGAWARA, S., Oral Molecular Bioregulation
SUZUKI, O., Craniofacial Function Engineering
TAKADA, H., Oral Microbiology
TAKAHASHI, M., Dento-oral Anaesthesiology
TAKAHASHI, N., Oral Ecology and Biochemistry
WATANABE, M., Ageing and Geriatric Dentistry

School and Graduate School of Economics and Management (27-1 Kawauchi, Aoba-ku, Sendai 980-8576; tel. (22) 795-6263; fax (22) 795-6270; e-mail webmaster@econ.tohoku.ac.jp; internet www.econ.tohoku.ac.jp/indexj.html):

AKITA, J., International Finance
AOKI, K., Comparative Economic Systems
AOKI, M., Cost Accounting
DOLAN, D., Business Communication
FUJII, T., International Accounting
FUKAI, T., Auditing
HASEBE, H., History of Japanese Economy
HAYASHIYAMA, Y., Environmental Economics
HINO, S., Modern Political Economy
HIRAMOTO, A., Japanese Economy
HOSOYA, Y., Econometrics
ITO, T., Information Systems Management
IPPOSHI, N., Accounting
KAMOIKE, O., Money and Banking
KANAZAKI, Y., Financial Management
KOHNO, D., Business Administration
KOHNO, S., Personnel Administration
KWEON, K. C., Research and Development Management
MASUDA, S., Regional Planning
MIYAKE, M., Macroeconomics
MORI, K., Political Economy
NAKAGAWA, T., International Management
NISHIZAWA, A., Policies for New Venture Creation
NOMURA, M., Social Policy
ODONAKA, N., Socio-Intellectual History
OMURA, I., Political Economy
OTAKI, S., Business Policy
OTOMASA, S., Corporate Governance
SARUWATARI, K., Comparative Business Studies
SATO, H., International Economics
SEKITA, Y., Welfare Information System
SHIMOMURA, H., Tax Law
SUZUKI, T., Business History
TANIGUCHI, A., Types of Business Enterprise
TERUI, N., Marketing
TSUGE, N., Agricultural Economics
TSUKUDA, Y., Business Statistics
YASUDA, K., Management Information System

School and Graduate School of Education (Kawauchi, Aoba-ku, Sendai 980-8576; tel. (22) 795-6103; fax (22) 795-6110; internet www.sed.tohoku.ac.jp/index-j.html):

AKINAGA, Y., Sociology of Education
ARAI, K., Educational Policy and Planning
HASEGAWA, K., Clinical Psychology
HONGO, K., Psychology and Disability
HOSOKAWA, T., Developmental Disorders
IKUTA, K., Philosophy of Education
KAJIYAMA, M., History of Japanese Education
KATO, M., History of Foreign Education
KAWASUMI, R., Compensation and Welfare of Disabilities
KIKUCHI, T., Developmental Psychology
KOIZUMI, S., Educational Process Studies
MIYAKOSHI, E., Comparative Educational Systems
MIZUHARA, K., Curriculum Studies
NAKAZIMA, N., Socio-cultural Study of Sport
OMOMO, T., Educational Administration
ONODERA, T., Educational Psychology
TAKAHASHI, M., Adult Education
UENO, T., Clinical Community Psychology
UNO, S., Educational Psychology

Graduate School of Educational Informatics, Research Division (Kawauchi, Aoba-ku, Sendai 980-8576; tel. (22) 795-6103; fax (22) 795-6110; internet www.ei.tohoku.ac.jp):

HAGIHARA, T., Theory of an Open University
IWASAKI, S., Information Technology Educational Architecture
MURAKI, E., Information Technology Education System Theory
WATABE, S., Information Technology Cognitive Science

School and Graduate School of Engineering (6-6-04, Aramaki Aza Aoba, Aoba-ku, Sendai 980-8579; tel. (22) 795-5817; fax (22) 795-5824; e-mail dean@eng.tohoku.ac.jp; internet www.eng.tohoku.ac.jp):

ABE, H., Urban Design
ABE, K., Fusion Reactor Engineering
ADACHI, F., Communication Systems
ANZAI, K., Casting and Advanced Solidification Processing
ASAI, H., Experimental Aerodynamics
ASAI, K., Solid State Physical Chemistry
ASO, H., Network Theory
CHONAN, S., Biomechatronics
EMURA, T., Intelligent Mechatronics
ESASHI, M., Micromachines
FUKINISHI, Y., Fluid Mechanics
FUKUNAGA, H., Space Structures
GALSTER, W., Energy Physics Engineering
HAMAJIMA, T., Applied Power Systems Engineering
HANE, K., Mechanoptics Design
HARA, N., Materials Electrochemistry
HARAYAMA, Y., Technology Policy
HASHIZUME, H., Fusion and Electromagnetic Engineering
HASHIDA, T., Complex Fracture Systems Design
HATAKEYAMA, R., Basic Plasma Engineering
HINO, M., Ferrous Process Metallurgy
HOKKIRIGAWA, K., Intelligent Systems Engineering
HOSHIMIYA, N., Biomedical Electronics
ICHINOKURA, O., Power Electronics
IGUCHI, Y., Socio-Engineering
IIBUCHI, K., History of Architecture
IKEDA, K., Mathematical Systems Design
IMAMURA, F., Tsunami Engineering
INOMATA, H., Supercritical Fluid Technology
INOMATA, K., Spin-electronics Materials
INOUE, K., Machine Design
INOUE, N., Structural Engineering
INOUE, Y., Applied Organic Synthesis
INUTAKE, M., Magneto–Plasma–Dynamics Engineering
ISHIDA, K., Computational Microstructure Design
ISHII, K., Radiation Science and Engineering
ITAYA, K., Electrochemical Science and Technology
ITO, T., Solid State Electronics
IWAKUMA, T., Structural Mechanics
IWASAKI, S., Engineers Education and Educational Informatics
KAJITANI, T., Applied X-ray and Neutron Spectroscopy
KANAI, H., Electronic Control Engineering
KANNO, M., Architectural Planning
KATO, K., Tribology
KAWAMATA, M., Intelligent Electronic Circuits
KAWASAKI, A., Micro-power Processing and Systems
KAZAMA, M., Geotechnical Engineering
KISHINO, Y., Mechanics of Materials
KIYONO, S., Nanosystem Engineering

KOIKE, J., Device Reliability Science and Engineering
KOIKE, Y., Low Temperature Physics and Superconductivity Physics
KOKAWA, H., Interface Science and Engineering of Joining
KONNO, M., Material Processing
KOSUGE, K., System Robotics
KOYANAGI, M., Advanced Bio-nano Devices
KUMAGAI, I., Protein Technology
KURIYAGAWA, T., Nanoprecision Mechanical Fabrication
KUSHIBIKI, J., Instrumentation and Ultrasonic Micro-spectroscopy Network
KUWANO, H., Informative Nanotechnology
MAKINO, S., Intelligent Communication Engineering
MANO, A., Disaster Potential Research
MASUYA, G., Aerospace Systems
MATSUBARA, F., Applied Mathematical Physics
MATSUKI, H., Bio-electromagnetics
MATSUMOTO, S., Process Control
MIHASHI, H., Building and Materials Science
MIMURA, H., Nuclear Energy Flow, Environmental Engineering
MIURA, H., Fracture Control of Microstructures
MIURA, T., Energy Process Engineering
MIYAZAKI, T., Magnetism and Magnetic Materials
MIZOGUCHI, T., Environmental Chemistry
MOTOSAKA, M., Earthquake Engineering
NAGAHIRA, A., Management of Technology
NAKAHASHI, K., Aerodynamic Design
NAKAMURA, K., Acoustic Physics Engineering
NISHIMURA, O., Ecological Engineering
NISHIZAWA, M., Biomicromachine Engineering
NISINO, T., Applied Life Chemistry
NOIKE, T., Environmental Protection Engineering
NITTA, J., Materials Quantum Science
OHMI, T., Urban Planning and Analysis
OHTSU, H., Applied Nuclear Medical Engineering
OKADA, M., Energy Materials
OMURA, T., Water Quality Engineering
OOJI, A., Energy Conversion Technology
OTA, T., Control of Heat Transfer
OUCHI, C., Biomedical Materials
OYAMA, Y., Opto-electronic Materials
SAHASHI, M., Magnetic Microelectronics
SAITOH, H., Engineering for Information Society
SAKA, M., Mechanics of Materials Systems
SAKUMA, A., Solid-state Physics
SASAO, M., Fusion Plasma Diagnostics
SATO, M., Cell Biomechanics
SAWADA, K., Computational Aerodynamics
SAWAMOTO, M., Hydro-Environment Systems
SAWAYA, K., Electromagnetic Wave Engineering
SEKINE, H., Smart System for Materials and Structures
SHINDO, Y., Mechanics and Design of Material Systems
SHODA, S., Functional Macromolecular Chemistry
SHOJI, K., Precision Machining
SMITH, R. L., Supercritical Fluid Technology
SOYAMA, H., Intelligent Sensing of Materials
SUGAWA, S., Advanced Functional Systems Engineering
SUGIMURA, Y., Structural Mechanics
SUZUKI, M., Structural Design Engineering
SUZUKI, M., Physicochemistry of Biomolecular Systems
TAKIZAWA, H., Synthetic Chemistry of Advanced Materials
TANAKA, H., Environmental Hydrodynamics
TOCHIYAMA, O., Nuclear Fuel Engineering
UCHIDA, S., Science and Engineering of Particle Beams
UCHIDA, T., Image Electronics
UCHIYAMA, M., Science and Engineering of Particle Beams
UEMATSU, Y., Wind Engineering
WADA, H., Biomechanical Engineering
WAKABAYASHI, T., Foundation of Risk Assessment and Management
WAKABAYASHI, T., Nuclear Energy Systems Safety Engineering
WATANABE, T., Material Design and Interface Engineering
YAMADA, M., Hydrocarbon Chemistry
YAMADA, M., Architectural Disaster Prevention Engineering
YAMADA, Y., Particle-Beam Substance Reaction Engineering
YAMAGUCHI, M., Electromagnetic Theory
YAMAGUCHI, T., Computational Biomechanics
YAMAMURA, T., Physics and Chemistry of Fluids
YAMANAKA, K., Materials Evaluation and Sensing
YOKOBORI, T., Materials Design and Interface Engineering
YONEMOTO, T., Reaction Process Engineering
YOSHIDA, K., Space Exploration
YOSHINO, H., Building Environmental Engineering
YOSHINOBU, T., Biomedical Electronics
YUGAMI, H., New Energy Engineering

Graduate School of Environmental Studies (Aobayama, Sendai 980-8579; tel. (22) 795-4504; fax (22) 795-4309; e-mail s-ara@bureau.tohoku.ac.jp; internet www.kankyo.tohoku.ac.jp):

ARAI, K., Environmental Chemical Engineering
ASANO, Y., East Asian Philosophy
CHIDA, T., Geoenvironmental Remediation
ENOMOTO, H., Environmental Processing for Energy Resources
HATTORI, T., Environmentally Benign Sythesis
HOSHINO, H., Analytical Environmental Chemistry
ISHIDA, H., Environmentally Harmonized Materials
KAYA, K., Environmental Ecology Design
KIMUTA, Y., Middle Eastern and Central Asian Studies
MARUYAMA, K., Structural Materials for Eco-friendly Systems
MATSUE, T., Environmental Bioengineering
MATSUKI, K., Environmental Geomechanics
NAGASAKA, T., Environmental Impact Assessment
NARISAWA, M., Korean Ethnoculture
NIITSUMA, H., Earth System Monitoring and Instrumentation
SAITO, T., Urban Environment
SAKAIDA, K., Physical Environmental Geography
SATAKE, M., International Economic and Environmental Studies
TAKAHASHI, H., Earth Exploitation Environmental Studies
TANIGUCHI, S., Materials Process for Circulatory Society
TOHJI, K., Design of Eco-nanomaterials
TSUCHIYA, N., Environmental Geochemistry
YAMASAKI, N., Environmental Hydrothermal Processes
YOSHIOKA, T., Recycling Chemistry

Graduate School of Information Sciences (Aoba, Aramaki, Aobu-ku, Sendai 980-8579; tel. (22) 795-5813; fax (22) 795-5815; e-mail is-syom@bureau.tohoku.ac.jp; internet www.is.tohoku.ac.jp):

ADACHI, Y., Media and Semiotics
AKAMATSU, T., Road Transportation and Traffic
ANDO, A., Econometric System Analysis
AOKI, T., Computer Structures
DEGUCHI, K., Image Analysis
EBISAWA, H., Physical Fluctuaomatics
FUKUCHI, H., Verbal Text Analysis
HASHIMOTO, K., Intelligent Control Systems
HIAI, F., Mathematical Systems Analysis III
HIDA, W., Health Informatics
HORIGUCHI, S., Firmware Science
INAMURA, H., International and Intermodal Transportation
ITOI, K., Information Biology
IWASAKI, S., Cognitive Psychology
KAMEYAMA, M., Intelligent Integrated Systems
KANEKO, M., Mathematical Structures II
KATO, N., Information Technology
KINOSHITA, T., Communication Software Science
KOBAYASHI, H., Ultra-high-speed Information Processing Algorithm
KOBAYASHI, K., Theory of Social Structure and Change
KOBAYASHI, N., Foundations of Software Science
KUDOH, J., Environmental Informatics
MARUOKA, A., Computation Theory
MORISUGI, H., Regional and Urban Planning
MUNEMASA, A., Mathematical Structures I
NAKAJIMA, K., Brain Function Integration
NAKAMURA, T., Computer Architecture
NAKAO, M., Biomodelling
NEMOTO, Y., Communication Science
NISHIZEKI, T., Algorithm Theory
NUMASAWA, J., Information Storage Systems
OBATA, N., Mathematical Systems Analysis II
OBAYASHI, S., Fusion Flow Informatics
OHORI, A., Logic for Information Science
OZAWA, M., Mathematical Structures III
SASAKI, K., Socio-economic Analysis of Urban Systems
SASOH, S., Flow System Informatics
SEKIMOTO, E., Media and Culture
SHINOHARA, A., System Information Sciences
SHIOIRI, S., Visual Recognition and Systems
SHIRATORI, N., Communication Theory
SHIZUYA, H., Information Security
SONE, H., Information Network Systems
SUNOUCHI, C., Mathematical Structures IV
SUZUKI, Y., Acoustic Information
TADOKORO, S., Human-Robot Informatics
TAKEUCHI, O., Philosophy of Human Information
TOKUYAMA, T., Design and Analysis of Information Systems
TOYAMA, Y., Logic for Information Science
TSUBOKAWA, H., Life Fluctuaomatics
URAKAWA, H., Mathematical Systems Analysis I
YAMAMOTO, H., Political Analysis of the Information Society
YAMAMOTO, S., Mathematical Modelling

Graduate School of International Cultural Studies (Kawauchi, Aoba-ku, Sendai 980-8576; tel. (22) 795-7541; fax (22) 795-7583; internet www.intcul.tohoku.ac.jp):

ASAKAWA, T., Language System
ASANO, Y., Asian Cultural Studies
FUJITA, M., Comparative Cultural Studies

FUJIWARA, I., Comparative Cultural Studies
HOLDEN, T., Multi-Cultural Societies
ICHIKAWA, M., Cultural Uses of Language
IGAWA, M., American Studies
ISHIHATA, N., Cultural Uses of Language
ISHIKAWA, H., Asian Cultural Studies
KAWAHIRA, Y., Language Generation
KITAGAWA, S., Islamic Areas and Cultural Studies
KOBAYASHI, F., European Cultural Studies
KUSUDA, I., Language Systems
NUNOTA, T., European Cultural Studies
SASAKI, K., Linguistic Communication
SATO, K., Language Systems
SATO, S., Language Generation
SHIGAKI, M., Language Education
SUZUKI, M., Cultural Uses of Language
TAKAHASHI, R., Science, Technology and Environment
TAKENAKA, K., American Studies
TANAKA, T., Multi-Cultural Societies
TATSUYOSHI, T., Monetary Economics
YAMAGUCHI, N., Linguistic Function
YAMASHITA, H., Multi-Cultural Societies
YOKOKAWA, K., International Economic Relations
YONEYAMA, C., Linguistic Function

School and Graduate School of Law (27-1 Kawauchi, Aoba-ku, Sendai 980-8576; tel. (22) 795-6173; fax (22) 795-6249; e-mail law-jm@bureau.tohoku.ac.jp; internet www.law.tohoku.ac.jp):

AOI, H., Jurisprudence
ARIKAWA, T., Constitutional Law
HIRATA, T., European Political History
IKUTA, O., Land Law
INABA, K., Administrative Law
KAISE, Y., International Civil Procedure
KAWAKAMI, S., Civil Law
KAWATO, S., Political Science, Modern Political Analysis
KOGAYU, T., Civil Law
MIZUNO, N., Civil Law, Family Law
MORITA, K., Administrative Law
OHNISHI, H., International Politics
OKAMOTO, M., Criminal Law
OUCHI, T., Western Legal History
OZAKI, K., International Law
SAITO, T., Criminology
SAKATA, H., Civil Procedure
SERIZAWA, H., Anglo-American Law, Transnational Law of Information
SHIBUYA, M., Tax Law
TSUJIMURA, M., Constitutional Law, Comparative Constitutional Law
UEKI, T., International Law
UEMURA, T., Current Japanese Administration
YAGYU, K., History of Political Theory
YAMAMOTO, H., Constitutional Law, Comparative Constitutional Law
YOSHIDA, M., Japanese Legal History
YOSHIHARA, K., Commercial Law, Commercial Law

Graduate School of Life Sciences (tel. (22) 795-5702; fax (22) 795-5704; internet www.lifesci.tohoku.ac.jp/index.html):

ARIMOTO, H., Biostructrual Chemistry
HIGASHITANI, A., Genomic Reproductive Biology
IDE, H., Organogenesis
IIJIMA, T., Systems Neuroscience
KATOW, H., Developmental Biology
KAWATA, M., Evolutionary Biology
KUMAGAI, T., Genetic Ecology in Critical Environments
KUSANO, T., Plant Molecular and Cellular Biology
MAEDA, Y., Control of Growth and Differentiation
MINAMISAWA, K., Environmental Microbiology
MIZUNO, K., Molecular Cell Biology
MURAMOTO, K., Functional Biomolecules
NAKAMURA, H., Molecular Neurobiology
NISHITANI, K., Plant Physiology
OHSHIMA, Y., Bio-organic Chemistry
SASAKI, M., Biostructural Chemistry
SOGAWA, K., Gene Regulation
TAKAGI, T., Molecular Diversity
TAKAHASHI, H., Space and Adaptation Biology
TSUDA, M., Microbial Genetics
URABE, J., Community and Ecosystem Ecology
WATANABE, M., Plant Reproductive Biology
WATANABE, T., Organella Research
YAMAMOTO, D., Neurogenetics
YAMAMOTO, K., Molecular Genetics
YAWO, H., Molecular and Cellular Neurosciences

School and Graduate School of Medicine (2-1 Seiryo-machi, Aoba-ku, Sendai 980-8575; tel. (22) 717-8005; fax (22) 717-8021; e-mail med-som@bureau.tohoku.ac.jp; internet www.med.tohoku.ac.jp/index-j.html):

ABE, T., Clinical Cell Biology
AIBA, S., Dermatology
ARAI, Y., Urology
DODO, Y., Anatomy and Anthropology
DOHURA, K., Prion Biology
FUKUDO, S., Behavioural Medicine
FUNAYAMA, M., Forensic Medicine
HANDA, Y., Restorative Neuromuscular Rehabilitation
HATTORI, T., Allergy and Infectious Diseases
HAYASHI, Y., Paediatric Surgery
HONGO, M., Comprehensive Medicine (University Hospital)
HORII, A., Molecular Pathology
IGARASHI, K., Biochemistry
ITOH, S., Nephrology, Endocrinology and Vascular Medicine
ITOH, T., Immunology and Embryology
ITOYAMA, Y., Neurology
IZUMI, S., Physical Medicine and Rehabilitation
KAKU, M., Molecular Diagnostics
KASAI, N., Institute for Animal Experimentation
KATAGIRI, H., Advanced Therapeutics for Metabolic Diseases
KATOH, M., Anaesthesiology
KITAMOTO, T., Creutzfeldt–Jacob Disease Science and Technology
KOBAYASHI, T., Otolaryngology, Head and Neck Surgery
KOHZUKI, M., Internal Medicine and Rehabilitation Science
KOINUMA, N., Health Administration and Policy
KOKUBUN, S., Orthopaedic Surgery
KONDO, H., Histology
KONDO, Y., Medical Informatics
MARUYAMA, Y., Physiology I
MATSUBARA, Y., Medical Genetics
MATSUOKA, H., Psychiatry
MORI, E., Behavioural Neurology and Cognitive Neuroscience
NAGATOMI, R., Medicine and Science in Sport and Exercise
NAKAYAMA, K., Developmental Genetics
NODA, T., Molecular Genetics
OHUCHI, N., Surgical Oncology
OKA, Y., Molecular Metabolism and Diabetes
OKAMURA, K., Obstetrics
ONO, T., Genome and Radiation Biology
OSUMI, N., Developmental Neuroscience
SAIJO, Y., Molecular Medicine
SASAKI, I., General Surgery, Biological Regulation and Oncology
SASAKI, T., Rheumatology and Haematology
SASANO, H., Anatomical Pathology
SATOH, H., Environmental Health Sciences
SATOMI, S., Advanced Surgical Science and Technology
SHIBAHARA, S., Molecular Biology and Applied Physiology
SHIMOSEGAWA, T., Gastroenterology
SHINOZAWA, Y., Emergency and Critical Care Medicine
SHIRATO, K., Cardiovascular Medicine
SORA, I., Psychobiology
SUGAMURA, K., Immunology
TABAYASHI, K., Cardiovascular Surgery
TAKAHASHI, A., Neuroendovascular Therapy
TAKAHASHI, S., Diagnostic Radiology
TAKESHIMA, H., Biochemistry and Molecular Biology
TOMINAGA, T., Neurosurgery
TSUJI, I., Epidemiology
UEHARA, N., International Health
YAEGASHI, N., Gynaecological Oncology
YAMADA, A., Plastic and Reconstructive Surgery
YAMADA, S., Therapeutic Radiology
YAMAMURO, M., Pain Control
YANAGISAWA, T., Molecular Pharmacology
YANAI, K., Pharmacology
YOSHIMOTO, T., Neurosurgery

School and Graduate School of Pharmaceutical Sciences (Aoba, Aramaki, Aoba-ku, Sendai 980-8578; tel. (22) 795-6801; fax (22) 795-6805; e-mail ph-som@bureau.tohoku.ac.jp; internet www.pharm.tohoku.ac.jp):

ANZAI, J., Pharmaceutical Physicochemistry
ENOMOTO, T., Molecular Cell Biology
FUKUNAGA, K., Pharmacology
IHARA, M., Medicinal Chemistry
IMAI, Y., Clinical Pharmacology and Therapeutics
IWABACHI, Y., Synthetic Chemistry
KONDO, Y., Molecular Transformation
KOSUGI, H., Organoreaction Chemistry
NAGANUMA, A., Molecular and Biochemical Toxicology
NAKAHATA, N., Cellular Signaling
OHIZUMI, Y., Pharmaceutical Molecular Biology
OHUCHI, K., Pathophysiological Biochemistry
OSHIMA, Y., Natural Products Chemistry
SAKAMOTO, T., Heterocyclic Chemistry
TAKEUCHI, H., Bio-structural Chemistry
TERASAKI, T., Membrane Transport and Drug Targeting
YAMAGUCHI, M., Organometallic Chemistry
YAMOZOE, Y., Drug Metabolism and Molecular Toxicology

School and Graduate School of Science (6-3 Aoba, Aramaki, Aoba-ku, Sendai 980-8578; tel. (22) 795-6346; fax (22) 795-6363; e-mail sci-syom@bureau.tohoku.ac.jp; internet www.sci.tohoku.ac.jp):

AOKI, S., Atmospheric Physics
ASANO, S., Atmospheric Radiation, Physical Climatology
BANDO, S., Differential Geometry
CHIBA, M., Astrophysics
EZAWA, Z. F., Theoretical High Energy Physics, Condensed Matter Physics
FUJIMAKI, H., Geochemistry and Petrology
FUJIMOTO, H., Geodynamics of Subduction Zones
FUJIMURA, Y., Theoretical Chemistry
FUKUMURA, H., Physical Chemistry
FUKUNISHI, H., Upper Atmosphere Physics
FUTAMASE, T., Cosmology, General Relativity
HAMA, H., Beam Physics
HANAMURA, M., Algebraic Geometry
HANAWA, K., Physical Oceanography
HASEGAWA, A., Seismology
HASHIMOTO, O., Experimental Nuclear Physics
HATTORI, T., Mathematical Physics
HIKASA, K., Theoretical High Energy Physics
HINO, M., Human Geography

HIRAMA, M., Organic Chemistry
IGARASHI, G., Volcanology and Planetary Science
IMAIZUMI, T., Active Tectonics
INOUE, K., Experimental Particle Physics
ISHIDA, M., Algebraic Geometry
ISHIHARA, T., Solid State Photophysics
IWASAKI, T., Atmospheric Science
KABUTO, K., Organic Chemistry
KAIHO, K., Palaeontology
KASAGI, J., Nuclear Physics
KAWAKATSU, T., Physics of Soft Materials
KAWAMURA, H., Satellite Oceanography
KENMOTSU, K., Differential Geometry
KIRA, M., Organometallic Chemistry
KOBAYASHI, N., Functional Molecular Chemistry
KOBAYASHI, T., Experimental Nuclear Physics
KOZONO, H., Functional Analysis
KUDOH, Y., Mineralogy and Crystallography
KURAMOTO, Y., Theoretical Condensed Matter Physics
MIKAMI, N., Physical Chemistry
MINOURA, K., Palaeontology
MIYASE, H., Experimental Nuclear Physics
MORIOKA, A., Planetary Space Science
MORITA, N., Organic Chemistry
MORITA, Y., Number Theory
MURAKAMI, Y., Solid State Physics
NAKAMURA, T., Number Theory
NAKAZAWA, T., Atmospheric Physics
NIIZEKI, K., Theoretical Condensed Matter Physics
NISHIKAWA, S., Differential Geometry
ODA, M., Micropalaeontology
OGAWA, T., Partial Differential Equations and Applied Analysis
OHKI, K., Biophysics
OHNO, K., Physical Chemistry
OHTANI, E., Geochemistry and Planetology
OKAMOTO, H., Atmospheric Radiation
OKANO, S., Planetary Spectroscopy
ONO, T., Planetary Plasma Physics
ONODERA, H., Microscopic Research on Magnetism
OTSUKI, K., Tectonics and Structural Geology
SAIKAN, S., Non-linear Laser Spectroscopy
SAIO, H., Astrophysics
SAITO, R., Solid State Theory Nanotube
SATO, H., Seismology
SATOH, T., Experimental Ultra Low Temperature Physics
SEKI, M., Astrophysics
SHIMIZU, H., Nuclear Physics
SUTO, S., Surface Physics
SUZUKI, A., Experimental Particle Physics
SUZUKI, M., Plant Anatomy
TAKAGI, I., Partial Differential Equations
TAKAHASHI, T., Photoemission Solid State Physics
TAKAHASHI, T., Number Theory
TAKEDA, M., Probability Theory
TAKIGAWA, N., Theoretical Nuclear Physics
TAMURA, S., Astronomy
TANAKA, K., Mathematical Logic and Foundations of Mathematics
TANIGAKI, K., Solid-State Physics
TERAMAE, N., Analytical Chemistry
TOBITA, H., Inorganic Chemistry
TOSA, M., Astronomy
TOYOTA, N., Molecular Metals
TSUBOTA, H., Experimental Nuclear Physics
UEDA, M., Natural Product Chemistry
UMINO, N., Seismotectonics
YAMAGUCHI, A., Experimental High Energy Physics
YAMAMOTO, H., Experimental High Energy Physics
YAMAMOTO, Y., Organic Chemistry
YAMASHITA, M., Co-ordination Chemistry
YANAGIDA, E., Partial Differential Equations
YASUDA, N., Meteorology
YOSHIDA, T., Volcanology and Petrology
YOSHIFUJI, M., Organic Chemistry
YUKIE, A., Number Theory

Institute for Materials Research (2-1-1 Katahira, Aoba-ku, Sendai 980-8577; tel. (22) 215-2181; fax (22) 215-2184; e-mail imr-som@imr.tohoku.ac.jp; internet www.imr.tohoku.ac.jp):

CHEN, M., International Frontier Center for Advanced Materials
FUKUYAMA, H., International Frontier Center for Advanced Materials
GOTO, T., Multi-Functional Materials Science
HASEGAWA, M., Irradiation Effects in Nuclear and Related Materials
INOUE, A., Non-Equilibrium Materials
IWASA, Y., Low-Temperature Condensed State Physics
KAWASAKI, M., Superstructured Thin Film Chemistry
KAWAZOE, Y., Materials Design by Computer Simulation
KOBAYASHI, N., Low-Temperature Physics
MAEKAWA, S., Theory of Solid State Physics
MATSUI, H., Nuclear Materials Engineering
MATSUOKA, T., Advanced Electronic Materials
NAKAJIMA, K., Crystal Physics
NOJIRI, H., Magnetism
SAKURAI, T., Surface and Interface Research
SATO, Y., Non-Equilibrium Materials
SHIKAMA, T., Nuclear Materials Science
SHIOKAWA, Y., Radiochemistry of Metals
TAKANASHI, K., Magnetic Materials
UDA, S., Crystal Chemistry
WAGATSUMA, K., Analytical Science
WATANABE, K., High Field Laboratory for Superconducting Materials
YAMADA, K., Neuron and Gamma-Ray Spectroscopy on Condensed Matters

Institute of Multidisciplinary Research for Advanced Materials (2-1-1 Katahira, Aoba-ku, Sendai 980-8577; tel. (22) 795-5202; fax (22) 795-5211; internet www.tagen.tohoku.ac.jp):

AJIRI, T., Organic Resources Chemistry
ARIMA, T., Strongly Correlated Electron Systems
HARADA, N., Chemistry of Molecular Chirality
ISSHIKI, M., High Purity Materials
ITAGAKI, K., Nonferrous Chemical Metallurgy
ITO, O., Photochemistry
KAINO, T., Materials Chemistry
KAKIHANA, M., Chemical Engineering
KASAI, E., Iron Steel Engineering
KAWAMURA, J., Solid State Ion Physics
KITAMURA, S., Ferrous Process Metallurgy
KITAKAMI, O., Magnetic Materials and Devices
KOMEDA, T., Molecular Chemistry
KONO, S., Surface Physics
KOYAMA, T., Biochemistry
KURIHARA, K., Surface Forces
KYOTANI, T., Applied Chemistry
MIYASHITA, T., Materials Chemistry
MIZUSAKI, J., Solid State Ion Devices
MURAMATSU, A., Solid State Chemistry
NAKAMURA, T., Physical Process Engineering
NAKANISHI, H., Materials Chemistry
NODA, Y., Electronic Properties of Solids
OTSUKA, Y., Catalytic and Chemical Processes
OKA, Y., Solid State Spectroscopy
SAITO, F., Chemical Engineering, Powder Technology
SAITO, M., Chemistry
SATO, S., Metal Industrial Engineering
SATO, T., Inorganic Materials Chemistry
SHIMIZU, T., Bio-inorganic Chemistry
SINDO, D., Atomic Scale Morphology Analysis
SODEOKA, M., Chemistry
SUITO, H., Physico-Chemical Metallurgy
SUZUKI, S., Physical Metallurgy
TERAUCHI, M., Electronic Diffraction and Spectrology
TERO, S., Physical Chemistry
TOCHIYAMA, O., Atomic Energy Engineering
TSAI, A., Materials Control
UDAGAWA, Y., X-ray Physics
UEDA, K., Molecular Physics
UMETSU, Y., Aqueous Processing, Physical Chemistry of Metals
YAMAMOTO, M., Soft X-ray Microscopy
YAMAUCHI, S., Physical Chemistry
YANAGIHARA, M., Soft X-ray Microscopy
YOKOYAMA, T., Chemical Engineering

Institute of Development, Ageing and Cancer (4-1 Seiryo-machi, Aoba-ku, Sendai 980-8575; tel. (22) 717-8443; fax (22) 717-8452):

FUKUDA, H., Radiation Medicine
FUKUMOTO, M., Pathology
ISHIOKA, C., General Internal Medicine, Gastroentorology, Molecular Biology
KONDO, T., Thoracic Surgery, Lung Cancer, Lung Transplantation
MATSUI, Y., Developmental Biology
NUKIWA, T., Chest Physician, Molecular Biology
OBINATA, M., Cell Biology
OGURA, T., Developmental Neurobiology, Developmental Biology, Molecular Biology
SATAKE, M., Molecular Biology
SATO, Y., Vascular Biology
TAKAI, T., Experimental Immunology
TAMURA, S., Biochemistry and Molecular Biology
TSUCHIYA, S., Paediatrics
YAMAMOTO, T., Molceular Biology, General Medical Chemistry, Pathological Medical Chemistry
YAMBE, T., Artificial Organs, Cardiovascular Medicine
YASUI, A., DNA Repair and Ageing

Institute of Fluid Science (2-1-1 Katahira, Aoba-ku, Sendai 980-8577; tel. (22) 795-5302; fax (22) 795-5311; e-mail shomu@ifs.tohoku.ac.jp; internet www.ifs.tohoku.ac.jp):

FUJISHIRO, I., Complex Dynamics
HAYASE, T., Super-Real Time Medical Engineering
HAYASHI, K., Molten Geomaterials
IKOHAGI, T., Complex Flow Systems
INOUE, O., Advanced Computational Fluid Dynamics
ISHIMOTO, J., Reality-Coupled Computation
KOBAYASHI, H., Complex Dynamics
KOHAMA, Y., Ultimate Flow Environment
MARUYAMA, S., Heat Transfer Control
NANBU, K., Gaseous Electronics
NISHIYAMA, H., Electromagnetic Intelligent Fluids
OBAYASHI, S., Integrated Fluid Informatics
OHARA, T., Molecular Heat Transfer
OHIRA, K., Cryogenic Flow
OTA, M., Biofluids Control
QIU, J., Intelligent Systems
SAMUKAWA, S., Intelligent Nano-process
SASOH, A., Ultra-high Enthalpy Flow
SUN, M., Interdisciplinary Shockwave Research
TAKAGI, T., Advanced Systems and Materials Evaluation
TAKEUCHI, S., Advanced Systems
TOKUYAMA, M., Theoretical Fluid Dynamics
TSUCHIYAMA, T., Advanced Technology for Environment and Energy

Research Institute of Electrical Communication (2-1-1 Katahira, Aobaku, Sendai 980-8577; tel. (22) 795-5420; fax (22) 795-5426;

e-mail shomu@jm.riec.tohoku.ac.jp; internet www.riec.tohoku.ac.jp/index-j.html):

AOI, H., Information Storage Systems
CHO, Y., Dialectric Nano-devices
EDAMATSU, K., Quantum Optics and Optical Spectroscopy
HANYU, T., Next-generation VLSI Computing
ITO, H., Quantum and Optoelectronics
MASUOKA, F., Electron Devices
MATSUOKA, H., Advanced Practical Information Technology Development
MIZUNO, K., Electron Devices
MURAOKA, H., Information Recording Devices
MUROTA, J., Atomically Controlled Processing
NAKAJIMA, K., Intelligent Integrated Systems
NAKAMURA, Y., Information Storage Engineering
NAKAZAWA, M., Ultra High Speed Optical Communication
NIWANO, M., Molecular Electronics, Silicobioelectronics
NUMAZAWA, J., Video Storage Systems
OHNO, H., Compound Semiconductors, Quantum Structures and Spintronics
OHORI, A., Computer Science
OTSUJI, H., Ultrafast and Ultrabroadband Electronics
SHIRAI, M., Advanced Functional Materials
SHIRATORI, N., Information Communication Systems
SIOIRI, S., Visual Cognition and Systems
SUGIURA, A., Electromagnetic Compatibility
SUZUKI, Y., Acoustic Signal Processing
TAKAGI, T., Wireless Mobile Systems
TANEICHI, M., Advanced Practical Information Technology Development
TOYAMA, Y., Computer Science
TSUBOUCHI, K., Wireless Internet System, Circuits and Devices
YANO, M., Informatics in Biological Systems

School of Health Science, Faculty of Medicine (2-1 Seiryo-machi, Aoba-ku, Sendai 980-8575; tel. (22) 717-7903; fax (22) 717-7910; e-mail cms-syom@bureau.tohoku.ac.jp; internet www.cms.tohoku.ac.jp):

HAYASHI, S., Molecular Oncology
ISHIDA, M., Management of Nursing
ITAGAKI, K., Fundamental Nursing
KOBAYASHI, K., Clinical Investigation
KUROKAWA, T., Microbiology
MARUOKA, S., Nuclear Medicine
MASUDA, T., Pathology
MORI, I., Medical Imaging
NEMOTO, R., Adult Nursing
OISHI, M., Image Engineering
OOTAKA, T., Haematology
SAITO, H., Community Health Nursing
SAITO, H., Psychiatry
SAITO, K., Midwifery
SHINDOH, C., Respiratory Physiology
SHIWAKU, H., Child Health Nursing
TAKABAYASHI, T., Maternity Investigation
TAMURA, H., Neuroradiology
ZUGUCHI, M., Diagnostic Radiology

Information Synergy Center (6-3 Aoba, Aramaki, Aoba-ku, Sendai 980-8578; tel. (22) 795-3407; fax (22) 795-6098; internet www.isc.tohoku.ac.jp):

KINOSHITA, T., Knowledge Engineering
KOBAYASHI, H., High-performance Computer Systems
SONE, H., Communication Networks
YOSHIZAWA, M., Communication Networks

Cyclotron Radioisotope Center (6-3 Aoba, Aramaki, Aoba-ku, Sendai 980-8578; tel. (22) 795-7800; fax (22) 795-7997; e-mail admin@cyric.tohoku.ac.jp; internet www.cyric.tohoku.ac.jp):

BABA, M., Radiation Physics
ITOH, M., Nuclear Medicine
IWATA, R., Radioisotope Production and Radiopharmaceutical Chemistry
OKAMURA, H., Nuclear Physics

Center for the Advancement of Higher Education (41 Kawauchi, Aoba-ku, Sendai 980-8576; tel. (22) 795-7551; fax (22) 795-7647; e-mail center@high-edu.tohoku.ac.jp; internet www.he.tohoku.ac.jp/index.html):

HIDA, W., Respiratory Medicine
HORIE, K., Linguistic Typology and Japanese-Korean Contrastive Linguistics
NAWATA, T., Applied Research Section
SAITOH, K., Applied Research Section
SEKIUCHI, T., Basic Research Section
SHIZUYA, H., Theoretical Computer Science
SUZUKI, T., Applied Clinical Psychology
YOSHIMOTO, K., Formal Linguistics, Cognitive Science

International Exchange Center (Kawauchi, Aoba-ku, Sendai 980-8576; tel. (22) 795-7776; fax (22) 795-7826; e-mail ryugaku@bureau.tohoku.ac.jp; internet www.insc.tohoku.ac.jp):

HORIE, K., Linguistic Typology and Japanese–Korean Comparative Linguistics
KASUKABE, Y., Development of the Short-Term Student Exchange Programme
SATO, S., Japanese Language Teaching
SHIGENO, Y., Technologies of Resource and Material Processing
UEHARA, S., Linguistics and Phonetics
YOSHIMOTO, K., Formal Syntax and Japanese Intonation

Center for Interdisciplinary Research (Aoba, Aramaki, Aoba-ku, Sendai 980-8578; tel. (22) 795-5757; fax (22) 795-5756; e-mail office@cir.tohoku.ac.jp; internet www.cir.tohoku.ac.jp):

KASUYA, A., Materials Science
SUEMITSU, M., Materials Science
YAMANE, H., Solid-state Chemistry
YAO, T., Department of Applied Physics

Center for Northeast Asian Studies (41 Kawauchi, Aoba-ku, Sendai 980-8576; tel. (22) 795-6009; fax (22) 795-6010; e-mail asiajimu@cneas.tohoku.ac.jp; internet www.cneas.tohoku.ac.jp/index-j.html):

HIRAKAWA, A., Political Economy
ISOBE, A., Cultural Studies
KIKUCHI, E., Regional Ecosystem Studies
KUDOH, J., North Asian Societies
KURIBAYASHI, H., Linguistic Studies
MIYAMOTO, K., Socio-economic Studies on the Environment
SATO, M., Environmental and Resources Survey
SEGAWA, M., Social Ecology
TANIGUCHI, H., Geochemistry
YAMADA, K., Social Structure

Center for Low-temperature Science (2-1-1 Katahira, Aoba-ku, Sendai 980-8577; tel. (22) 215-2181; fax (22) 215-2184; e-mail ltcenter@imr.tohoku.ac.jp; internet www.clts.tohoku.ac.jp):

AOKI, H., Low-temperature Physics

New Industry Creation Hatchery Center (Aoba 6-6-10, Aramaki, Aoba-ku, Sendai 980-8579; tel. (22) 795-7105; fax (22) 795-7985; e-mail liaison-office@niche.tohoku.ac.jp; internet www.niche.tohoku.ac.jp):

ICHIE, M., Music and Acoustical Medicine
ISHIDA, K., Advanced Materials based on Computer-aided Design and Microstructural Control
KAWASHIMA, R., Functional Brain Imaging
KOHNO, M., Research and Development on Genomics-Protemics Technology and Free Radical Control
MIYAMOTO, A., Quantum Design of Nano-functional Materials
OHMI, T., DIIN (New Intelligence for IC Differentiation) Project
TAKAHASHI, M., Development of Self-assembled Monodisperse Nano-particles, Thin-film Media for Terabit Recording
TERASAKI, T., Drug Discovery and Development
UEMATSU, Y., Development of Technology for Preserving the Environment and Reducing Wind-Induced Disaster
YAMANAKA, K., Advanced Ultrasonic Non-destructive Evaluation and Sensing
YOKOYAMA, H., Ultrabroadband Coherent Light Sources

Tohoku University Museum (Aoba 6-3, Aramaki, Aoba-ku, Sendai 980-8578; tel. (22) 795-6767; fax (22) 795-6767; e-mail staff@museum.tohoku.ac.jp; internet www.museum.tohoku.ac.jp):

EHIRO, M., Geology and Palaeontology
YANAGIDA, T., Archaeology

Botanical Gardens (12-2 Kawauchi, Aoba-ku, , Sendai 980-0862; tel. (22) 795-6760; fax (22) 795-6766; e-mail garden-tu@biology.tohoku.ac.jp; internet www.biology.tohoku.ac.jp/garden):

SUZUKI, M., Plant Anatomy

ATTACHED RESEARCH INSTITUTES

Institute for Materials Research: Dir AKIHISA INOUE.

Institute of Development, Ageing and Cancer: Dir MASUO OBINATA.

Institute of Fluid Science: Dir TOSHIAKI IKOHAGI.

Research Institute of Electrical Communication: Dir HIROMASA ITO.

Cyclotron and Radioisotope Center: Dir KEIZO ISHII.

Admissions Research Center: Dir KUNIHIKO AOKI.

Institute of Multi-disciplinary Research for Advanced Materials: Dir HACHIRO NAKANISHI.

UNIVERSITY OF TOKUSHIMA

2-24 Shinkura-cho, Tokushima 770-8501
Telephone: (88) 656-7000
Fax: (88) 656-7012
E-mail: hibunsyok@jim.tokushima-u.ac.jp
Internet: www.tokushima-u.ac.jp

Founded 1949
National University Corporation
Academic year: April to March

President: TOSHIHIRO AONO
Vice-Presidents: HIROSHI KAWAKAMI, HISASHI KITAJIMA, YASUHIRO KURODA, HIROSHI NAKAMURA, MASAYUKI SHIBUYA
Secretary-General: HIROSHI NAKAMURA
Director of University Library: KAZUO HOSOI

Number of teachers: 895 full-time
Number of students: 7,744

Publications: *Bulletin of the Faculty of Engineering* (annually), *Journal of Human Sciences* (annually), *Journal of Human Sciences and Arts* (annually), *Journal of Language and Literature* (annually), *Journal of Mathematics* (annually), *Journal of Medical Investigation* (2 a year), *Natural Science Research* (annually), *Social Sciences Research* (annually)

DEANS

Faculty of Dentistry: EIICHI BANDO
Faculty of Engineering: YONEO YANO
Faculty of Integrated Arts and Sciences: MAKOTO WADA
Faculty of Medicine: SABURO SONE
Faculty of Pharmaceutical Sciences: TAKSAHI YAMAUCHI
Institute of Health Biosciences, Graduate School: SABURO SONE

PROFESSORS

Faculty of Dentistry, Graduate School of Oral Sciences and Institute of Health Biosciences (3-18-15 Kuramoto-cho, Tokushima 770-8504; tel. (88) 633-9100; fax (88) 631-4215; e-mail isysoumu2k@jim.tokushima-u.ac.jp):

ASAOKA, K., Biomaterials and Bio-engineering
BANDO, E., Fixed Prosthodontics
HANEJI, T., Anatomy and Histology
HAYASHI, Y., Oral Molecular Pathology
HONDA, E., Oral and Maxillofacial Radiology
HOSOI, K., Molecular Oral Physiology
ICHIKAWA, T., Removable Prosthodontics and Oral Implantology
KAWANO, F., Oral Care and Clinical Education
KITAMURA, S., Anatomy
MATSUO, T., Conservative Dentistry
MIYAKE, Y., Microbiology
MORIYAMA, K., Orthodontics and Dentofacial Orthopaedics
NAGATA, T., Periodontology and Endodontology
NAGAYAMA, M., Oral and Maxillofacial Surgery
NAKAJO, N., Dental Anaesthesiology
NISHINO, M., Paediatric Dentistry
NOMA, T., Molecular Biology
SATO, M., Oral and Maxillofacial Surgery and Oncology
YOSHIMOTO, K., Molecular Pharmacology

Faculty of Engineering (2-1 Minamijosanjima-cho, Tokushima 770-8506; tel. (88) 656-7304; fax (88) 656-7328; e-mail kgsoumuk@jim.tokushima-u.ac.jp; internet www.e.tokushima-u.ac.jp/English/main.html):

AKAMATSU, N., Neural Networks and Speech Recognition
AOE, J., Intelligent Systems Engineering
FUKUI, M., Optoelectronics
FUKUTOMI, J., Fluid Engineering and Turbomachinery
HANABUSA, T., Production Systems Engineering
HASHIMOTO, C., Construction Materials
HASHINO, M., Stochastic Hydrology, Water Resources Engineering
HIRAO, K., Structural Engineering and Seismic Design
HORI, H., Biological Science
IMAEDA, M., Process Dynamics and Control
IMAI, H., Mathematics and Applied Mathematics
INOUE, K., Applied Superconductivity and High-Field Generation
INOUE, T., Crystal Growth and Crystal Engineering
IRITANI, T., Spread Spectrum Communications
ISAKA, K., Electric Energy Engineering
INOUE, T., Crystal Growth and Crystal Engineering
IWATA, T., Applied Spectroscopy and Optical Measurement
KAIEDA, Y., Plastic Forming and Powder Metallurgy
KANESHINA, S., Biological Science
KAWAMURA, Y., Organic Chemistry
KAWASHIRO, K., Enzyme Engineering
KINOUCHI, Y., Biomedical Electronics
KITAYAMA, S., Digital Signal Processing
KONAKA, S., Integrated Circuits
KONDO, A., Geotechnical Engineering
KORAI, H., Microbiology and Microbiological Control
KONISHI, K., Robot and Computer Vision
MASUDA, S., Synthetic and Polymer Chemistry
MIWA, K., Combustion Engineering and Energy Conversion
MIZUGUCHI, H., Urban Planning and Landscape Design
MOCHIZUKI, A., Foundations Engineering and Soil Mechanics
MORIOKA, I., Heat Transfer
MOTONAKA, J., Analytical Chemistry
MURAKAMI, H., Risk and Environmental Assessment
MURAKAMI, R., Metal Fatigue, Surface Modification
NAGAMACHI, S., Mathematics and Applied Mathematics
NIKI, N., Medial Imaging, Pattern Recognition
NISHIDA, N., Optical Information Science
NOJI, S., Molecular Biology and Devlopmental Biology
OHNO, T., Nuclear Magnetic Resonance
OHNO, Y., Electron Devices
OKABE, T., River Engineering, Environmental Hydraulics
ONISHI, T., Power Engineering
ONO, N., Multi-agent Systems and Reinforcement Learning
OOSHIMA, T., Enzymology and Genome Engineering
OUSAKA, A., Thermal Engineering, Multiphase Flow
OYA, K., Particle-Surface Collisions and Nuclear Fusion
REN, F., Computer Science Technology, Natural Language Processing
SAKAI, S., Semiconductor Photonic Devices
SAWADA, T., Structural Engineering, Earthquake Engineering
SHIMOMURA, T., Soft Engineering, Algorithnic Debugging
SUEDA, O., Well-being Engineering and Assistive Engineering
TAJIMA, K., All-Optical Devices
TAKEUCHI, T., Numerical Analysis
TAMESADA, T., Design and Test of Electronic Circuits
TAMURA, K., Biophysical Chemistry
TANAKA, H., Polymer Synthesis and Functional Organic Materials
TOMIDA, T., Chemical Processes Engineering
TSUJI, A., Biochemistry and Protein Engineering
TSUKAYAMA, M., Synthetic and Polymer Chemistry
YAMADA, K., Elasticity and Micromechanics
YAMAGAMI, T., Geotechnical and Landslide Engineering
YAMANAKA, H., Urban Transport Planning and Design
YANO, Y., Intelligent Systems Engineering
YOSHIDA, K., Material Evaluation and Acoustic Emission
YOSHIMURA, T., Vehicle Suspensions and Fuzzy Control

School of Health Sciences (3-18-15 Kuramoto-cho, Tokushima 770-8503; tel. (88) 633-9003; fax (88) 633-9015; e-mail isysoumu4k@jim.tokushima-u.ac.jp; internet www2.medsci.tokushima-u.ac.jp):

FUJII, M., Neuroradiology
HARADA, M., Neuroradiology
KAGAWA, N., Human Pathology
KAWANISHI, C., Fundamental Nursing
KONDO, H., Fundamental Nursing
KONDO, T., Nutritional Biochemistry
MAEZAWA, H., Radiation Medicine
MORIMOTO, T., Breast Surgery
NAGAMINE, I., Clinical Neurpsychiatry
NAGASHINO, H., Biomedical Engineering
NINOMIYA, T., Psychosomatic Medicine
ONISHI, C., Adult and Gerontological Nursing
ONO, T., Bacterial Genetics
SAITOH, K., Cardiology
SEKIDO, K., Dermatological Science
TADA, T., Gerontological Nursing
TAKEGAWA, Y., Radiotherapy
TAMURA, A., Adult Nursing
TERAO, T., Maternal Health
UENO, J., Diagnostic Radiology
YAMANO, S., Artificial Reproductive Technology
YOSHINAGA, T., Medical Image Reconstruction

Faculty of Integrated Arts and Sciences (1-1 Minamijosanjima-cho, Tokushima 770-8502; tel. (88) 656-7103; fax (88) 656-7298; e-mail sksoumks@jim.tokushima-u.ac.jp; internet www.ias.tokushima-u.ac.jp):

ABE, E., Kimono Cloth Shrinkage and Repair
ANDO, M., Chinese Literature
ARAKI, H., Motor and Behavioural Physiology
ARIMA, T., Philosophy of the Qin and Han Dynasties
AZUMA, K., Calligraphy
AZUMA, U., Asian Archaeology
BABA, T., German Language and Literature
GOTO, T., Comparative Biochemistry and Physiology
HAMADA, J., Visual Perception
HARAMIZU, T., Japanese Literature
HAYASHI, H., Environmental Biology
HAYASHI, K., Constitutional Law
HIOKI, Z., Theoretical High Energy Physics
HIRAI, S., Historical Geography
HIRAKI, M., Study of Painting Expression
IMAI, S., Applied Spectrocopy, Atomic Spectrometry and Trace Analysis
INOUE, N., English Corpus Linguistics, English Lexicography
ISHIDA, K., Microfossil Geology
ISHIDA, M., Philosophy of the Mind-Body Problem
ISHIHARA, T., Differential Geometry
ISHII, K., Image Conservation Techniques
ISHIKAWA, E., German Language and Literature
ITO, M., Partial Differential Equations
ITO, T., Computational Mathematics and Sciences
ITO, Y., Functional Analysis
KATAOKA, K., Musicology
KATAYAMA, S., Algebraic Number Theory
KATSURA, S., German Language and Literature
KAWAKAMI, S., German Language and Literature
KISHIE, S., Japanese Dialects
KOORI, N., Nuclear Physics
KOYAMA, K., Solid State Physics
KUWABARA, M., Japanese History
KUWABARA, R., Global Analysis
MAEDA, S., Applied Mathematics
MASUDA, T., Bio-organic Chemistry
MATOBA, H., Exercise Physiology
MATSUMOTO, M., Physical Chemistry
MATSUO, Y., Genetics
MATSUSHITA, M., English Literature
MAYUMI, K., Environmental Economics
MIKI, M., Financial Accounting
MITSUI, A., Industrial Technology
MIURA, T., Physical Education
MIYAZAKI, T., English Literature
MIYAZAWA, K., Composition, Music using Computers
MIZUSHIMA, T., Middle Eastern Economics
MORI, Y., Psychotherapy
MORIOKA, Y., English Linguistics
MOTOKI, Y., English Linguistics
MURATA, A., Geology
NAKAGAWA, H., Marine Physiology and Biochemistry
NAKAJIMA, M., Economic History
NAKAMURA, H., Physical Education
NAKAYAMA, S., Nuclear Physics
NISHIDE, K., American History
OBARA, S., Exercise Physiology
OHASHI, M., Mathematical Programming
OHASHI, M., Immunobiology
OHBUCHI, A., Algebraic Geometry

OYAMA, Y., Analytical Cytology
SAKUMA, R., Social and Imperial History of Modern Britain
SANO, K., Physiological Psychology
SEKIZAWA, J., Risk Assessment for Environmental Protection and Safety
SENBA, M., Japanese Linguistics
SEO, I., English Literature
SHIOTA, T., Geology
TACHIBANA, Y., Economic Theory
TAJIMA, T., French Literature
TAKEDA, Y., Natural Products Chemistry
TERAO, H., Inorganic Chemistry
UENO, K., Sociology of Social Problems
WADA, M., Organic Chemistry
YAMADA, K., Labour Law
YAMAMOTO, M., Developmental Disorders
YOKOIGAWA, K., Applied Microbiology
YOSHIDA, H., Theoretical Sociology
YOSHIDA, S., Ancient Greek Philosophy
YOSHIMORI, K., Chinese Medieval History

Faculty of Medicine, Graduate School of Medical Sciences and Institute of Health Biosciences (3-18-15 Kuramoto-cho, Tokushima 770-8503; tel. (88) 633-9116; fax (88) 633-9028; e-mail isysoumu1k@jim.tokushima-u.ac.jp; internet www.hosp.med.tokushima-u.ac.jp/university/servlet/index):

ADACHI, A., Virology
ARASE, S., Dermatological Science
DOI, T., Clinical Biology and Medicine
FUKUI, Y., Anatomy and Developmental Neurobiology
IRAHARA, M., Gynaecology and Obstetrics
ISHIMURA, K., Anatomy and Cell Biology
ITO, S., Digestive and Cardiovascular Medicine
IZUMI, K., Molecular and Environmental Pathology
KAJI, R., Clinical Neuroscience
KITAGAWA, T., Cardiovascular Surgery
KISHI, K., Nutritional Physiology
KUBO, S., Legal Medicine
MATSUMOTO, T., Medicine and Bioregulatory Sciences
MIYAMOTO, K., Nutritional Biochemistry
MORITA, Y., Integrative Physiology
NAGAHIRO, S., Neurosurgery
NAKAHORI, Y., Human Genetics and Public Health
NAKANISHI, H., Plastic and Reconstructive Surgery
NAKAYA, Y., Nutrition and Metabolism
NISHITANI, H., Radiology
OHMORI, T., Psychiatry
OSHITA, S., Anaesthesiology
OTA, F., Food Microbiology
SANO, T., Human Pathology
SASAKI, T., Biochemistry
SHIOTA, H., Ophthalmology and Visual Science
SONE, S., Internal Medicine and Molecular Therapeutics
TAKEDA, E., Clinical Nutrition
TAKEDA, N., Otorhinolaryngology and Communicative Neuroscience
TAMAKI, T., Pharmacology
TASHIRO, S., Digestive and Paediatric Surgery
TERAO, J., Food Science
YAMAMOTO, S., Applied Nutrition
YASUI, N., Orthopaedic Surgery
YASUMOTO, K., Immunology and Parasitology
YOSHIZAKI, K., Physiology

Faculty of Pharmaceutical Sciences and Graduate School of Pharmaceutical Sciences (1-78-1 Shomachi, Tokushima 770-8505; tel. (88) 633-7245; fax (88) 633-9517; e-mail isysoumu3k@jim.tokushima-u.ac.jp; internet www.ph.tokushima-u.ac.jp):

ARAKI, T., Drug Metabolism and Therapeutics
BABA, Y., Molecular and Pharmaceutical Biotechnology
CHUMAN, H., Molecular and Analytical Chemistry
FUKUI, H., Molecular Pharmacology
FUKUZAWA, K., Health Chemistry
HIGUCHI, T., Molecular Cell Biology and Medicine
ITO, K., Medicinal Biotechnology
KIHARA, M., Pharmaceutical Information Science
KIWADA, H., Pharmacokinetics and Biopharmaceutics
KUSUMI, T., Marine Medicinal Resources
NAGAO, Y., Molecular Medicinal Chemistry
OCHIAI, M., Pharmaceutical Organic Chemistry
SHIMABAYASHI, S., Physical Pharmacy
SHISHIDO, K., Organic Synthesis
TAKAISHI, Y., Pharmacognosy
TAKIGUCHI, Y., Clinical Pharmacology
YAMAUCHI, T., Biochemistry

Center for Advanced Information Technology (2-1 Minamijosanjima-cho, Tokushima 770-8506; tel. (88) 656-7555; fax (88) 656-9122; e-mail kokusai1@jim.tokushima-u.ac.jp; internet www.ait.tokushima-u.ac.jp):

KITA, K., Computer Science, Information Retrieval, Natural Language Processing
OE, S., Image Processing and Visual Pattern Processing

Center for University Extension (1-1 Minamijosanjima-cho, Tokushima 770-8502; tel. (88) 656-7276; fax (88) 656-7277; e-mail kygakusk@jim.tokushima-u.ac.jp; internet www.cue.tokushima-u.ac.jp):

HIROWATARI, S., Adult and Continuing Education
MORITA, H., Analytical Chemistry
SODA, K., Function of Narrative
WAKAIZUMI, S., High Energy Physics
YOSHIDA, A., Educational Technology

Institute for Animal Experimentation, Institute of Health Biosciences (3-18-15 Kuramoto-cho, Tokushima 770-8503; tel. (88) 633-9116; fax (88) 633-9028; e-mail isysoum1k@jim.tokushima-u.ac.jp; internet www.anex.med.tokushima-u.ac.jp):

SASAKI, T., Biochemistry

Institute for Enzyme Research (3-18-15 Kuramoto-cho, Tokushima 770-8503; tel. (88) 633-9420; fax (88) 633-9422; e-mail kenkyu@jim.tokushima-u.ac.jp; internet mms1.ier.tokushima-u.ac.jp/index2.html):

EBINA, Y., Molecular Genetics
FUKUI, K., Gene Regulatorics
KIDO, H., Molecular Enzyme Chemistry
MATSUMOTO, M., Informative Cytology
SUGINO, H., Molecular Cytology
TANIGUCHI, H., Molecular Enzyme Physiology

Institute for Genome Research (3-18-15 Kuramoto-cho, Tokushima 770-8503; tel. (88) 633-9420; fax (88) 633-9422; e-mail kenkyu@jim.tokushima-u.ac.jp; internet www.genome.tokushima-u.ac.jp):

HARA, E., Division of Protein Information
ITAKURA, M., Division of Genetic Information
SHINOHARA, Y., Division of Gene Expression
SIOMI, H., Division of Gene Function Analysis
TAKAHAMA, Y., Division of Experimental Immunology

Institute for Medicinal Resources, Institute of Health Biosciences (1-78-1 Shomachi, Tokushima 770-8505; tel. (88) 633-7245; fax (88) 633-9517; e-mail isysoum3k@jim.tokushima-u.ac.jp; internet www.ph.tokushima-u.ac.jp):

ITO, K., Medicinal Biotechnology

International Student Center (1-1 Minamijosanjima-cho, Tokushima 770-8502; tel. (88) 656-7082; fax (88) 656-9873; e-mail ryugakuk@jim.tokushima-u.ac.jp; internet www.isc.tokushima-u.ac.jp):

JIN, C. H., Computing Science
MISUMI, T., Teaching Japanese as a Foreign Language
OISHI, Y., Teaching Japanese as a Foreign Language

Radioisotope Center (3-18-15 Kuramoto-cho, Tokushima 770-8503; tel. (88) 633-9416; fax (88) 633-9417; e-mail kenkyu@jim.tokushima-u.ac.jp; internet ricb.ri.tokushima-u.ac.jp/RIRC.html):

ADACHI, A., HIV/AIDS treatment

UNIVERSITY OF TOKYO

7-3-1 Hongo, Bunkyo-ku, Tokyo 113-8654
Telephone: (3) 3812-2111
Fax: (3) 5689-7344
E-mail: kokusai@ml.adm.u-tokyo.ac.jp
Internet: www.u-tokyo.ac.jp

Founded 1877
Independent
Academic year: April to March

President: HIROSHI KOMIYAMA
University Librarian: KAZUHIKO SAIGO

Library: see Libraries and Archives
Number of teachers: 4,165
Number of students: 28,386

DEANS

Graduate School of Arts and Sciences and College of Arts and Sciences: Y. KIBATA
Graduate School of Economics and Faculty of Economics: N. JINNO
Graduate School of Humanities and Sociology and Faculty of Letters: TAKESHI INAGAMI
Graduate School for Law and Politics: H. TAKAHASHI
Graduate School of Education and Faculty of Education: M. SATOH
Graduate School of Engineering and Faculty of Engineering: K. HIRAO
Graduate School of Science and Faculty of Science: Y. IWASAWA
Graduate School of Agricultural and Life Sciences and Faculty of Agriculture: KATSUMI AIDA
Graduate School of Medicine and Faculty of Medicine: NOBUTAKA HIROKAWA
Graduate School of Pharmaceutical Sciences and Faculty of Pharmaceutical Sciences: Y. EBIZUKA
Graduate School of Mathematical Sciences: J. SATSUMA
Graduate School of Information Science and Technology: M. TAKEICHI
Graduate School of Frontier Sciences: MICHIKATA KONO
Interfaculty Initiative in Information Studies and Graduate School of Interdisciplinary Information Studies: T. HANADA
Graduate School of Public Policy: A. MORITA

PROFESSORS

Graduate School of Arts and Sciences and College of Arts and Sciences (3-8-1 Komaba, Meguro-ku, Tokyo 153-8902; tel. (3) 5454-6827; fax (3) 5454-4319; e-mail info-komaba@adm.c.u-tokyo.ac.jp; internet www.c.u.-tokyo.ac.jp):

ADACHI, H., History of Japanese Technology
ADACHI, N., Area Studies
AIZAWA, T., German, German History
AOKI, M., German
ARAI, Y., Human Geography
ARAMAKI, K., International Finance
ASASHIMA, M., Developmental Biology
ATOMI, Y., Sports Sciences
BOCCELLARI, J., English, Comparative Literature

ELLIS, T., Japanese as a Foreign Language
ENDO, Y., Physical Chemistry
ENDO, Y., American Studies
ERIGUCHI, Y., Astrophysics
FUKAGAWA, Y., Development Studies, Korean Studies
FUNABIKI, T., Cultural Anthropology
GOTO, N., Environmental Economics
HASEGAWA, T., Behavioural Ecology
HAYAKAMA, S., Law
HAYASHI, F., American Literature
HIKAMI, S., Statistical Physics
HIROMATSU, T., Statistics
HYODO, T., Physics
IKEDA, N., German
IKEGAMI, S., European Medieval History
IKEUCHI, M., Biology
IMAI, T., Philosophy
ISHIDA, A., International Relations
ISHIDA, Y., German History, Comparative Genocide Studies
ISHII, A., International Relations
ISHII, N., Sports Sciences
ISHII, Y., French
ISHIMITSU, Y., German Literature
ISHIURA, S., Neuroscience
ISOZAKI, Y., Earth Science
ITO, A., Cultural Anthropology
ITOH, T., English
IWASA, T., French, Contemporary Art
IWASAWA, Y., International Law
KADOWAKI, S., Philosophy
KAGOSHIMA, S., Solid State Physics
KAJI, T., German
KANEKO, K., Nonlinear Physics, Statistical Physics
KARIMA, F., Chinese
KATO, M., Architectural Composition Theory
KAWAI, S., Graphics
KAWANAGO, Y., German, History of Christian Thought
KAWATO, S., Biophysics
KAZAMA, Y., Theory of Elementary Particles
KIBATA, Y., English, British History
KIMURA, H., Anthropology
KITAGAWA, S., Philosophy
KOBAYASHI, K., Sports Sciences
KOBAYASHI, Y., French, Modern Thought
KODA, K., German
KOJIMA, N., Chemistry
KOJO, Y., Political Science
KOMAKI, K., Radiation Physics
KOMIYAMA, S., Theory of Solid State Physics
KOMORI, Y., Japanese Literature
KONDOH, A., Japanese
KONOSHI, T., Japanese Literature
KOTERA, A., International Law
KUBOTA, S., Sports Science
KUGA, T., Quantum Electronics, Quantum Optics
KURODA, R., Biochemistry of DNA
KUROZUMI, M., Ethics, Japanese Intellectual History
LAMARRE, C., Linguistic Analysis
MABUCHI, I., Biochemistry and Biophysics
MARUYAMA, M., Economics
MASUDA, K., French, French Philosophy
MASUDA, S., Chemistry
MATSUBARA, R., Economic Thought, Social Economics
MATSUI, T., Theoretical Nuclear Physics
MATSUO, M., Environmental and Analytical Chemistry
MATSUOKA, S., Japanese Literature
MATSUURA, H., Multimedia Analysis
MISUMI, Y., Japanese Literature
MITANI, H., Japanese History
MIYAMOTO, H., Philosophy
MIYASHITA, S., French
MORI, M., Political and Social Philosophy
MOTOMURA, R., European History
MURATA, J., Philosophy
MURATA, M., Cell Biology and Biophysics
MURATA, Y., China Studies
NAGATA, T., Physical Chemistry
NAKAI, K., International Relations
NAKANISHI, T., Economics
NAKAZAWA, H., Crosscultural Communication
NAMIKI, Y., Chinese History
NISHINAKAMURA, H., Russian
NIWA, K., Research Management
NOMURA, T., Japanese
NOTOJI, M., American Literature
OE, H., International Relations, Human Security
OGOSHI, N., Korean
OHTA, K., Theoretical Nuclear Physics
OKA, H., English
OKABE, Y., German, Comparative Literature
OKOSHI, Y., Criminal Law
ONAKA, M., Catalysis Chemistry
ONUKI, T., Hellenistic and Early Christian Literature
OTSUKI, T., Sports Sciences
ROSSITTER, P., English
SAKAHARA, S., French
SAKAI, T., Political Science
SASAKI, C., History and Philosophy of Science
SATO, N., Plant Biology
SATO, Y., English, American Literature
SATO, Y., Law, Dispute Processing, Peace Building
SATOMI, D., Biology
SHIBA, N., Serbo-Croat, History
SHIBATA, T., History of Political Thought
SHIGEMASU, K., Bayesian Statistics
SHIMADA, M., Population and Evolutionary Ecology
SHIMOI, M., Inorganic Chemistry, Co-ordination Chemistry
SHIROTA, T., Chinese Literature
SUGAWARA, K., English
SUGAWARA, T., Physical Organic Chemistry
SUGIHASHI, Y., German, Literature and Aesthetics
SUGITA, H., Arabic
SUTOH, K., Molecular Cell Biology
SUYAMA, A., Biophysics
SUZUKI, H., English and Music
SUZUKI, K., French
SUZUKI, K., Graphics
TAJIRI, M., German
TAKADA, Y., English Literature
TAKAHASHI, H., History
TAKAHASHI, N., Political Science
TAKAHASHI, S., German Literature
TAKAHASHI, T., Philosophy
TAKATSUKA, K., Theoretical Molecular Science
TAKEUCHI, N., French, Comparative Literature
TAKITA, Y., English
TAMAI, T., Software Engineering
TANIUCHI, T., Human Geography
TANJI, A., English Literature
TOMODA, S., Organic Chemistry
TSUNEKAWA, K., Political Science
UCHIDA, R., Contemporary Society
UEDA, H., Spanish
URA, M., Russian Literature
USUI, R., German
WAKABAYASHI, M., Chinese, Modern History of East Asia
WILSON, B., English
YAMADA, H., French Literature, Psychoanalytic Criticism
YAMAKAGE, S., International Relations
YAMAMOTO, S., English
YAMAMOTO, T., Philosophy
YAMAMOTO, Y., Culture and Social Change
YAMASHITA, S., Cultural Anthropology
YAMAUCHI, M., Asian History
YAMAWAKI, N., History of Social Thought
YAMAZAKI, Y., Atomic Physics
YONEYA, T., Theoretical Physics
YOSHIE, A., Japanese History
YOSHIOKA, D., Theory of Solid State Physics
YUASA, H., French
YUI, D., American and International History

Graduate School for Law and Politics (7-3-1 Hongo, Bunkyo-ku, Tokyo 113-0033; tel. (3) 5841-3104; fax (3) 5841-3291; e-mail jshomu@j.u-tokyo.ac.jp; internet www.j.u-tokyo.ac.jp):

AIHARA, R., Litigation, Finance and Corporate Law
ARAKI, T., Labour and Employment Law
ASAKA, K., Anglo-American Law
BABA, Y., European Political History
CH'EN, P. H.-C., Principles of Comparative Law, Chinese Legal System
DOGAUCHI, H., Civil Law, Trust Law
EBIHARA, A., German Law
EGASHIRA, K., Commercial Law
FOOTE, D. H., Sociology of Law
FUJITA, T., Commercial Law
FUJIWARA, K., International Politics, Southeast Asian Studies
FURUE, Y., Criminal Procedure
HASEBE, Y., Constitutional Law
HIBINO, T., Constitutional Theory
HIGUCHI, N., Anglo-American Law
HIROSE, H., Consumer Law
IGARASHI, T., Comparative Politics
INOUE, T., Philosophy of Law
INOUYE, M., Criminal Procedure
ISHIGURO, K., Private International Law, Conflict of Laws
ISHIKAWA, K., Constitutional Law
ITO, M., Civil Procedure
ITO, Y., European Law
IWAHARA, S., Corporation Law, Regulation of Financial Institutions
IWAMURA, M., Social Security Law
KABASHIMA, I., Japanese Politics
KANDA, H., Commercial Law
KANSAKU, H., Commercial Law
KATO, J., Comparative Politics
KAWAIDE, Y., History of Western Political Thought
KITAMURA, I., French Law
KOBA, A., Roman Law
KOBAYAKAWA, M., Administrative Law
KOKETSU, H., Administrative Law
KUBO, F., American Government and History
MASUI, Y., Tax Law
MATSUSHITA, J., Insolvency Law
MIYASAKO, Y., International Business Law
MORITA, A., Public Administration
MORITA, H., Civil Law
MORITA, O., Civil Law
NAKATANI, K., International Law
NAKAYAMA, N., Intellectual Property Law
NAKAZATO, M., Tax Law
NISHIDA, N., Criminal Law
NISHIKAWA, Y., Occidental Legal History
NITTA, I., Japanese Legal History
NOMI, Y., Civil Law, Trust Law
NOZAKI, K., General Legal Practice
OBUCHI, T., Intellectual Property Law
OCHIAI, S., Commercial Law
OHGUSHI, K., Latin American Politics
OKUWAKI, N., International Law
OMURA, A., Civil Law
ONUMA, Y., International Law
OTA, S., Law and Social Science, Law and Economics, Civil Dispute Resolution, Legal Negotiation
SAEKI, H., Criminal Law
SAITO, M., Administrative Law, Law of Local Government
SHIOKAWA, N., Russian and Post-Soviet Politics
SHIRAISHI, T., Competition Law
TAKAHARA, A., Politics of East Asia
TAKAHASHI, H., Civil Procedure
TAKAHASHI, K., Constitutional Law
TAKAHASHI, S., History of International Politics

TAKATA, H., Civil Procedure
TANABE, K., Policy Studies
TERAO, Y., Anglo-American Law
UCHIDA, T., Civil Law
UGA, K., Administrative Law
USUI, M., Public Finance Law
WATANABE, H., History of Japanese Political Thought
YAMAGUCHI, A., Criminal Law
YAMAMOTO, R., Administrative Law
YAMAMURO, M., Criminal Procedure
YAMASHITA, T., Commercial Law

Graduate School of Economics and Faculty of Economics (7-3-1 Hongo, Bunkyo-ku, Tokyo 113-0033; tel. (3) 5841-5543; fax (3) 5841-5521; e-mail advisefs@e.u-tokyo.ac.jp; internet www.e.u-tokyo.ac.jp):

ABE, M., Marketing
ARAI, T., Corporate Finance, Securities Investment
BABA, S., Economic History of the Western World, History of Industrializationand Urbanization in Germnay
DAIGO, S., Financial Accounting
FUJIMOTO, T., Technology and Operations Management
FUJIWARA, M., Applied Microeconomics
FUKUDA, S., Money and Banking, Macroeconomics
HANNAH, L., Comparative Business History
HAYASHI, F., Applied Econometrics, Macroeconomics
HIROTA, I., Economic History of Modern France
ICHIMURA, H.
IHORI, T., Public Finance and Economics
ITO, T., International Finance, Finance and Macroeconomics
ITOH, MASANAO, Japanese Economy, Financial History in Japan
ITOH, MOTOSHIGE, International Economics
IWAI, K., Economic Theory
IWAMI, T., International Economics
IWAMOTO, Y., Public Economics, Macroeconomics
JINNO, N., Public Finance
KAMIYA, K., Microeconomics, Mathematical Programming
KANDORI, M., Microeconomic Theory, Game Theory
KANEMOTO, Y., Urban Economics
KOBAYASHI, T., Theory of Investments and Capital Markets
KUBOKAWA, T., Mathematical Statistics
KUNITOMO, N., Statistics, Econometrics and Financial Econometrics
MATSUI, A., Game Theory, Information Economics, Monetary Theory
MATSUSHIMA, H., Microeconomics, Game Theory, Theory of Finance, Informational Economics
MIWA, Y., Economics of Regulations, Corporate Governance, Law and Economics
MOCHIDA, N., Public Finance, Intergovernmental Fiscal Relations
MORI, T., Industrial Relations
OBATA, M., Economic Theory
OKAZAKI, T., Japanese Economic History
OKUDA, H., Russian Economic History
ONOZUKA, T., Economic History of the Western World
SAGUCHI, K., Industrial Relations
SHIBATA, T., Modern Capitalism, Institutional Economics
TABUCHI, T., Urban Economics
TAKAHASHI, N., Organization Theory
TAKEDA, H., Japanese Economic History
TAKENOUCHI, M., International Economics
UEDA, K., Macroeconomics, Financial Theory, Theory of International Finance
WADA, K., Comparative Business History
YAJIMA, Y., Statistics and Econometrics
YOSHIKAWA, H., Macroeconomics

Graduate School of Humanities and Sociology and Faculty of Letters (7-3-1 Hongo, Bunkyo-ku, Tokyo 113-0033; tel. (3) 5841-3705; fax (3) 5841-3817; e-mail shomu@l.u-tokyo.ac.jp; internet www.l.u-tokyo.ac.jp):

AKIYAMA, H., Social Psychology of Ageing
AMANO, M., Philosophy
FUJII, S., Modern Chinese Literature
FUJITA, K., Aesthetics
FUJIWARA, K., Japanese Literature of Heian Era
FUJITA, S., Early Modern Japanese History
FUKASAWA, K., History of Early Modern Europe
GOMI, F., Medieval Japanese History
GOTO, T., Japanese Archaeology
HASEMI, K., Russian and Polish Literature
HATTORI, T., Korean Studies (Sociology)
HAYASI, T., Turkic Languages
HIRAISHI, T., American Literature
HIRANO, Y., German Language and Literature
ICHIKAWA, H., History of Religion, the Bible and Judaism
IKEDA, K., Political Behaviour and Communication, Social Reality and Mediated Communication
IMAMURA, K., Japanese and Asian Archaeology
IMANISHI, N., English Linguistics and Syntax Theory
ISHII, N., History of Modern Europe
ITUMI, K., Classical Language and Literature
KANAZAWA, M., Russian Literature
KANNO, K., Japanese Ethical Thoughts
KATAYAMA, H., Classical Languages and Literature
KAWAHARA, H., History of the Science of Chance
KIMURA, H., Chinese Language
KINOSHITA, N., Cultural Resource Studies
KISHIMOTO, M., Chinese History
KOJIMA, T., Medieval Japanese Literature
KOMATSU, H., Central Asian History
KONDO, K., History of Modern Europe
KONO, M., History of Japanese Art
KUMAMOTO, H., Indo-European Linguistics
MARUI, H., Indian Philosophy
MATSUMOTO, M., Sociology of Science and Technology, Environmental Sociology
MATSUMURA, K., Uralic Linguistics
MATSUNAGA, S., Philosophy
MATSUURA, J., German Language
MIZUSHIMA, T., South Asian History
MURAI, S., Medieval Japanese History
NAGAMI, S., Italian Language and Literature
NAGASHIMA, H., Early Modern Japanese Literature
NAKAJI, Y., French Language and Literature
NISHIMURA, K., Aesthetics
NITAGAI, K., Urban Sociology
NUMANO, M., Russian and Polish Literature
OHASI, Y., English Literature
ONUKI, S., East Asian Archaeology
OSANO, S., History of Western Art
SAITO, A., Indian Philosophy
SAKURAI, M., Ancient Greek History
SAKURAI, Y., Southeast Asian History
SATO, M., Ancient Japanese History
SATO, S., Intellectual History of Modern China
SATO, T., Visual Perception
SATO, Y., Ethics and Social Thought
SATO, Y., History of Japanese Art
SEIYAMA, K., Mathematical Sociology
SEKINE, S., Occidental Ethical Thought
SHIBATA, M., American Literature
SHIGETO, M., German Linguistics
SHIMAZONO, S., Japanese Religious Thought
SHIOKAWA, T., French Language and Literature
SHITOMI, Y., West Asian History
SUEKI, F., Japanese Buddhism
SUZUKI, T., Japanese Language
TACHIBANA, M., Visual Neuroscience
TADA, K., Ancient Japanese Literature
TAKAHASHI, K., English Literature
TAKAHASHI, T., Dravidian Language and Literature
TAKANO, Y., Cognitive Psychology
TAKAYAMA, H., Medieval European History
TAKAYAMA, M., Philosophy
TAKEGAWA, S., Sociology of Social Policy
TAKESHITA, M., Islamic Studies
TAKEUCHI, S., Japanese Ethical Thought
TAMURA, T., French Language and Literature
TOKURA, H., Chinese Literature
TSUCHIDA, R., Sanskrit Language and Literature
TSUKIMURA, T., French Language and Literature
TSUNODA, T., Australian Aboriginal Linguistics
TSURUOKA, Y., Christian Mysticism
UENO, C., Family and Gender Studies
UTAGAWA, H., East Asian Archaeology
UWANO, Z., Accentology and Dialectology
WATANABE, H., Aesthetics
YAMAGUCHI, S., Experimental Social Psychology
YOSHIDA, M., Korean History
YOSHIDA, N., Early Modern Japanese History

Graduate School of Education and Faculty of Education (7-3-1 Hongo, Bunkyo-ku, Tokyo 113-0033; tel. (3) 5841-3904; fax (3) 5841-3914; e-mail edushomu@p.u-tokyo.ac.jp; internet www.p.u-tokyo.ac.jp/index-j.html):

AKITA, K., Action Research on Training
ETO, T., Health Education
HAEBARA, T., Educational Measurement
HIROTA, T., Sociology of Education
HIJIKATA, S., History of Japanese Education
ICHIKAWA, S., Cognitive Psychology
KAMEGUCHI, K., Clinical Psychology
KANAMORI, O., Methods of Education
KANEKO, M., Higher Education
KARIYA, T., Sociology of Education
KAWAMOTO, T., History of Western Education
MUTOH, Y., Physical Education
NAKADA, M., Methods of Education
NEMOTO, A., Library and Information Science
OGAWA, M., Educational Administration
SASAKI, M., Methods of Education
SATOH, K., Lifelong Learning
SATOH, M., Action Research on Teaching
SHIMOYAMA, H., Clinical Psychology
SHIOMI, T., Science of Education
SHIRAISHI, S., Anthropology of Education
TANAKA, C., Clinical Psychology
WATANABE, H., Educational Measurement
YAMAMOTO, Y., Physiology of Education
YANO, M., Higher Education

Graduate School of Engineering and Faculty of Engineering (7-3-1 Hongo, Bunkyo-ku, Tokyo 113-8656; tel. (3) 5841-7662; fax (3) 5841-7446; e-mail octo@t-adm.t.u-tokyo.ac.jp; internet www.t.u-tokyo.ac.jp):

AIDA, T., Macromolecular Chemistry, Supramolecular Chemistry, Bioinorganic Chemistry
AOKI, T., Aerospace Structures, Mechanics of Composite Materials, Smart Structures
ARAI, T., Automatic Assembly, Robotics, Artificial Intelligence and Service Engineering
ARAKAWA, Y., Electric Propulsion
DOI, M., Soft Matter Physics, Polymer Physics, Rheology

DOMEN, K., Heterogeneous Catalysis
FUJIMOTO, K., Deformation and Fracture of Solids, Tribology
FUJINO, Y., Structural Engineering, Dynamics, Control and Monitoring of Structures and Bridges, Wind and Earthquake
FUJITA, M., Organic Co-ordination Chemistry
FUJITA, T., Mineral and Material Processing, Recycling Technology, Intelligent Fluid
FUJIWARA, T., Solid State Physics, Electronic Structure in Condensed Matter
FURUMAI, H., Urban Drainage and Water Quality Management
FURUTA, K., Cognitive Systems Engineering, Technology for Safe and Secure Society
GONOKAMI, M., Non-Linear Optics, Quantum Optics, Quantum Electronics, Optical Processes in Solids
HANAKI, K., Urban and Global Environmental Management, Urban Environment Systems
HARATA, N., Urban Transport Planning
HASHIMOTO, K., Intelligent Materials
HASHIMOTO, T., Science and Technology Studies
HIDAKA, K., High Voltage Engineering, Electrical Insulation, Electrical Discharge and Plasma Physics
HIGUCHI, T., Mechatronics, Micro Electromechanical Systems
HIRAO, K., Theoretical Chemistry and Electronic Structure Theory
HORI, K., Artificial Intelligence
HORII, H., Sociotechnology, Rock Mechanics, Applied Mechanics
HOTATE, K., Photonic Sensing, Photonic Signal Processing, Optical Devices
ICHIKAWA, M., Semiconductor Nano-science and Technology
IEDA, H., Transport and City Planning
IIZUKA, Y., Systems Analysis and Design, Structured Knowledge Engineering, Health Care Social System Engineering
IKUHARA, Y., Interface and Grain Boundary Engineering
ISHIHARA, K., Biomaterials
ISHIHARA, S., Nanomechanics, Nanofabrication
ITO, T., Urban and Architectural History
KAGEYAMA, K., Composite Materials Engineering, Smart Material and Structure Systems
KAMATA, M., Equipment and Environmental Engineering
KAMATA, M., Noise and Vibration Control, Vehicle Engineering, Assistive Technology
KANEKO, S., Flow-Induced Vibration, Vibration Control, Micro Gas Turbine Engineering
KANNO, M., Metallic Materials
KANODA, K., Experimental Physics of Low-dimensional Correlated Electronic Systems
KASAGI, N., Thermal and Fluids Engineering, Energy Systems Engineering, Turbulence Engineering
KATAOKA, K., Biomaterials and Drug Delivery Systems
KATO, T., Materials Chemistry, Polymer Chemistry, Supramolecular Chemistry
KATO, T., Surface Engineering, Tribology, Nanotribology
KATSUMURA, Y., Radiation Chemistry, Applied Radiation Chemistry
KAWACHI, K., Flight Dynamics, Biokinetics, Helicopter Engineering
KIMURA, F., Design Engineering, CAD/CAM, Manufacturing Systems, Computer-Aided Technology in Manufacturing Engineering
KISHIO, K., Solid State Chemistry, Ionic and Electronic Transport in Solids, Superconductivity
KITAMORI, T., Integration of Micro Chemical Systems, Micro Space Chemistry
KOBAYASHI, I., Environmental Information Network, Light Communications
KOIDE, O., Evaluation of Regional Risks and Multimedia Database System for Historical Disasters
KOIKE, T., Hydrology and Water Resources, Remote Sensing
KOMIYAMA, H., Global Environmental Engineering, Materials Science and Engineering
KOSAKO, T., Radiation Safety, Radiation shielding, radiation Dosimetry
KOSEKI, T., Metals and Alloys
KOSHI, M., Chemical Reaction Kinetics, Laser-Induced Chemistry
KOSHIZUKA, S., Computational Fluid Dynamics
KUBO, T., Structural and Earthquake Engineering, Reinforced Concrete Structures
KUWAMURA, H., Structural Engineering, Steel Structures, Welding Mechanics, Reliability Analysis and New Materials
MABUCHI, K., Advanced Biomedical Engineering and Life Sciences
MADARAME, H., Nuclear Safety
MAEDA, K., Defects in Solids, Nanoscopic Analysis
MAEKAWA, K., Concrete Engineering, Modelling of Concrete Performance
MARUYAMA, S., Science and technology of Carbon Nanotubes, Nanoscale Thermal Engineering
MATSUMOTO, Y., Fluid Engineering, Molecular Dynamics
MATSUSHIMA, K., Business and Innovation Modelling
MITSUISHI, M., Intelligent Manufacturing Systems, Network-Based Manufacturing Systems, Active Thermal Compensation for High-Speed Machine Tools
MIYATA, H., Computational Fluid Dynamics, Systems Design, Technology Management
MIZUNO, N., Catalytic Chemistry, Inorganic Chemistry
MOHRI, N., Manufacturing Systems Control, Precision Machining
MORISHITA, E., High-speed Gas Dynamics
NAGAMUNE, T., Biotechnology, Biochemical Engineering, Protein Engineering
NAGAOSA, N., Condensed Matter Theory, Superconductivity
NAGASAKI, S., Safety Research on the Nuclear Fuel Cycle
NAGASAWA, Y., Architectural Planning and Design
NAGASHIMA, T., Aerospace Propulsion
NAGASUKA, S., Space Engineering
NAITO, H., Architectural Design, Landscape Design
NAKAO, M., Nano-Micro Manufacturing, Information Instrument Design, Mechanical Engineering for Science
NAKAO, S., Membrane Science and Technology
NAKAZAWA, M., Radiation Measurement, Quantum Beam Engineering
NAMBA, K., Sustainable Design in Architecture and Urban Space
NAWATA, K., Econometrics, Statistics
NISHIMURA, Y., Urban Conservation Planning, Urban Design
NITTA, T., Applied Superconductivity, Electrical Machinery, Power Systems
NOZAKI, K., Organometallic Chemistry, Homogeneous Catalysis
ODA, T., Electrostatics, Plasma Application for Environmental Protection and Magnetic Separation
OHASHI, H., Thermal Hydrodynamics, Advanced Models for Complex Phenomena
OHBA, Z., Education Systems Project
OHGAKI, S., Environmental Engineering
OHTSU, M., Nanophotonics
OKA, Y., Nuclear Reactor Design and Analysis
OKABE, A., Urban and Regional Analysis, Geographical Information Science
OKABE, Y., Information Devices, Superconductive Electronics, Brain Computer
OKAMOTO, K., Visualization, Micro-,Nano- and Biofluids
OKATA, J., Urban Planning
OKUBO, S., Mining Machinery, Rock Mechanics
OKUDA, H., Computational Mechanics, Digital Value Engineering
OSHIMA, M., Semiconductor Surface Chemistry, Synchrotron Radiation Science
OZAWA, K., Construction, Project and Infrastructure Management
RINOIE, K., Aircraft Design, Separated Flow Aerodynamics
ROKUGAWA, S., Exploration Geophysics, Earth Observing Systems
SAKAI, S., Strength of Materials, Life Cycle Assessment, Fracture Mechanics
SAKAMOTO, I., Building Construction, Timber Structures
SAKAMOTO, Y., Environmental Control Engineering, Air Conditioning
SATO, K., Petroleum Engineering
SATO, S., Coastal and Environmental Engineering
SEKIMURA, N., Maintenance Engineering, Nuclear Materials, Effects of Radiation on Materials
SHIBATA, T., Semiconductor Devices and Integrated Circuits, Integrated Human Intelligence Systems
SHIMIZU, E., Geoinformatics, Regional Planning
SHINOHARA, O., Landscape Planning and Civic Design
SHIOYA, T., Aerospace Materials, Mechanical Behaviour of Materials
SUGA, T., Microsystem Integration and Packaging, Eco-Design
SUZUKI, H., Computer-Aided Design and Manufacture, Geometric Modelling
SUZUKI, H., History of Architecture, History of Modern Architecture
SUZUKI, H., Structural Engineering, Ocean Engineering
SUZUKI, S., Flight Mechanics, Control Engineering
SUZUKI, T., Systems Engineering in Materials Science
TAIRA, K., RNA as Origin of Life and RNA Technology
TAKADA, T., Structural Reliability, Earthquake Engineering, Computational Mechanics, Risk Analysis, Decision Theory
TAKAHASHI, H., Digital Signal Processing
TAKAMASU, K., Precision Metrology, Nanometer Measurement, Coordinate Metrology
TAMAKI, K., Marine Geology
TANAKA, M., Materials and Device Physics, Spintronics
TANAKA, S., Fusion Engineering, Nuclear Waste Management
TARUCHA, S., Electronic Properties of Semiconductor Nanostructures
TERAI, T., Materials Science for Nuclear Systems, Fusion Reactor Engineering, Synthesis and Property Control of Advanced Materials by High-energy Particle Processing
TOKURA, Y., Materials Physics
TORIUMI, A., Advanced Devices Engineering
TOWHATA, I., Geotechnical Engineering

UEDA, T., Cost-Benefit Analysis, Infrastructure Economics
UESAKA, M., Quantum Beam Engineering and Applied Electro-Magnetics
WADA, K., Microphotonics
WASHIZU, M., Bio-nanotechnology
WATANABE, S., Computational Engineering of Nanomaterials
YAGI, O., Applied Microbiology
YAMADA, I., Lifestyle and Environmental Information Technology, Network Sensing, Telecommunication Energy Systems
YAMAGUCHI, H., Polar Environment Engineering, Cavitation
YAMAGUCHI, S., Solid State Ionics
YAMAGUCHI, Y., Nanomaterials Technology, Chemical System Engineering
YAMAJI, K., Energy Systems Engineering
YAMASHITA, K., Theoretical Chemistry and Chemical Reaction Dynamics, Computational Molecular Engineering
YAMATOMI, J., Rock Engineering and Mining Engineering
YOKOYAMA, A., Power Systems Engineering, Control Engineering
YOSHIDA, M., Education Systems Project
YOSHIDA, T., Plasma Materials Engineering
YUHARA, T., Energy Engineering and Policy, Engineering for Naval Architecture and Ocean Engineering, Management of Engineering Projects

Graduate School of Science and Faculty of Science (7-3-1 Hongo, Bunkyo-ku, Tokyo 113-0033; tel. (3) 5841-4570; fax (3) 5841-8776; e-mail shomu@adm.s.u-tokyo.ac.jp; internet www.s.u-tokyo.ac.jp):

AIHARA, H., High Energy Physics
AKASAKA, K., Evolutional and Developmental Biology
AOKI, H., Theoretical Condensed-matter Physics
AOKI, K., Population Biology
EGUCHI, T., Theoretical Particle Physics
FUKADA, Y., Biochemistry and Molecular Biology
FUKUDA, H., Plant Cell Biology
GELLER, R., Seismology
HAMAGUCHI, H., Physical Chemistry
HAMANO, Y., Earth Dynamics
HASEGAWA, T., Solid State Chemistry
HATSUDA, T., Theoretical Hadron Physics
HAYANO, R., High Energy Nuclear Physics Experiment
HIBIYA, T., Ocean Dynamics
HIRANO, H., Evolutionary Genetics
HOSHINO, M., Space Physics
IWASAWA, Y., Surface Chemistry and Catalysis
KAMIYA, R., Cell Biology
KAWASHIMA, T., Organic Chemistry
KIMURA, G., Tectonics, Structural Geology
KOBAYASHI, A., Materials Chemistry, Structural Chemistry
KOBAYASHI, T., Quantum Electronics
KOMAMIYA, S., Experimental Elementary Particle Physics
KOMEDA, Y., Plant Molecular Genetics
KUBO, T., Physiological Chemistry, Molecular Biology
KUBONO, S., Nuclear Physics, Nuclear Astrophysics
KUWAJIMA, K., Biophysics
MAKISHIMA, K., Experimental High Energy Astrophysics
MATSUMOTO, R., Sedimentology and Geochemistry
MATSU'URA, M., Earthquake Physics, Tectonics
MINOWA, M., Experimental Particle Physics without Accelerators
MIYAMOTO, M., Evolution of Planetary Material
MIYASHITA, S., Statistical Mechanics, Magnetism, Condensed Matter
MURAKAMI, T., Environmental Mineralogy
MURATA, J., Plant Systematics
NAGAHARA, H., Petrology, Planetary Science
NAGAO, K., Geochemistry
NAGATA, T., Plant Physiology and Plant Molecular Biology
NAKADA, Y., Stellar Astrophysics
NAKAMURA, E., Organic Chemistry
NAKANO, A., Developmental Cell Biology
NARASAKA, K., Synthetic Organic Chemistry
NISHIHARA, H., Inorganic Chemistry
NOMOTO, K., Theoretical Astrophysics
NONAKA, M., Molecular Immunology
NOTSU, K., Geochemistry
OHTA, T., Solid-State Physical Chemistry
OKA, Y., Neurobiology
OKAMURA, S., Extragalactic Astronomy
ONAKA, T., Astrophysics
OTSUKA, T., Nuclear Theory
OZAWA, K., Petrology
SAIGO, K., Molecular Biology
SAKAI, H., Nuclear Physics
SAKANO, H., Molecular Biology
SANO, M., Nonlinear Dynamics, Fluid Dynamics
SATO, K., Astrophysics and Cosmology
SHIBAHASHI, H., Theoretical Astrophysics
SHIMOURA, S., Nuclear Physics
SHIONOYA, M., Bioinorganic Chemistry
SOFUE, Y., Radio Astronomy
SUGIURA, N., Planetary Science
TACHIBANA, K., Chemistry of Natural Products
TADA, R., Sedimentology and Palaeoceanography
TAJIMA, F., Molecular Population Genetics
TAKEDA, H., Developmental Genetics
TANABE, K., Palaeontology
TERASAWA, T., Space and Magnetospheric Physics
TOHE, A., Yeast Genetics
TSUBONO, K., Experimental Relativity
UCHIDA, S., Solid State Physics, High-Tc Superconductivity
UEDA, S., Human Molecular Evolution
UMEZAWA, Y., Analytical Chemistry
URABE, T., Chemical Geology, Economic Geology
WADATI, M., Statistical Physics and Condensed-Matter Physics
YAMAGATA, T., Ocean–Atmosphere Dynamics
YAMAGISHI, A., Clay Mineralogy
YAMAMOTO, M., Molecular Genetics
YAMAMOTO, S., Astrophysics, Astrochemistry, Molecular Spectroscopy
YAMANOUCHI, K., Physical Chemistry
YANAGIDA, T., Elementary Particle Physics
YOKOYAMA, J., Cosmology and Astrophysics
YOKOYAMA, S., Biophysics, Biochemistry and Molecular Biology
YOSHII, Y., Galactic Astronomy

Graduate School of Agricultural and Life Sciences and Faculty of Agriculture (1-1-1 Yayoi, Bunkyo-ku, Tokyo 113-8657; tel. (3) 5841-5486; fax (3) 5841-8122; e-mail oice@ofc.a.u-tokyo.ac.jp; internet www.a.u-tokyo.ac.jp/english/index.html):

ABE, H., Biochemistry of Aquatic Animals
ABE, K., Biological Function Development
AIDA, K., Fish Physiology
AKASHI, H., Veterinary Microbiology
ANDO, N., Wood-based Materials and Timber Engineering
AOKI, I., Fisheries Biology
CHIDA, K., Cell Regulation
DOI, K., Veterinary Pathology
FUKUDA, K., Biological Function Development
FUKUI, Y., Biological Chemistry
FUKUYO, Y., Aquatic Biology
FURUYA, K., Fisheries Oceanography
HAYASHI, Y., Veterinary Anatomy
HIGUCHI, H., Wild Life Biology
HINO, A., Aquaculture Biology
HOGETSU, T., Plant Physiology and Plant Ecology, Silviculture
HONMA, M., Economics
HORI, S., Landscape and Sustainable Tourism
HORINOUCHI, S., Microbiology and Fermentation
IDE, Y., Forestry Gene Science
IGARASHI, Y., Applied Microbiology
INOUE, M., Forest Policy
ISOGAI, A., Pulp and Paper Sciences
ITOH, K., Veterinary Public Health
IWAMOTO, N., Agricultural History and History of Agricultural Sciences
IZUMIDA, Y., International Food System
KISHINO, H., Biometrics and Statistical Genetics
KITAHARA, T., Organic Chemistry
KOBAYASHI, H., Forest Utilization
KOBAYASHI, K., Agricultural Ecosystems
KUGA, S., Structural Biopolymers
KUMAGAI, S., Veterinary Public Health
KUMAGAI, Y., Evaluation of the Natural Environment
KURATA, K., Bio-environmental Engineering
KUROKURA, H., Aquatic Biology
KUROHMARU, M., Veterinary Anatomy
MASAKI, H., Molecular and Cellular Breeding
MATSUNAGA, S., Aquatic Natural Products Chemistry
MESHITSUKA, G., Wood Chemistry and Pulping Chemistry
MIYAZAKI, T., Soil Physics and Soil Hydrology
MORI, Y., Veterinary Ethology
NAGASAWA, H., Bio-organic Chemistry
NAGATA, S., Forest Ecology and Society
NAGATO, Y., Plant Breeding and Genetics
NAKANISHI, T. M., Radio-Plant Psychology
NANBA, S., Bioresource Technology
NISHIHATA, M., Veterinary Physiology
NISHIYAMA, M., Cell Biotechnology
NISHIZAWA, N. K., Plant Nutrition and Biotechnology
OGAWA, H., Veterinary Emergency Medicine
OGAWA, K., Fish Pathology
OHSHITA, S., Bioprocess Engineering
OHSUGI, R., Crop Physiology
OHTA, A., Cellular Genetics
OHTA, M., Wood-based Materials and Timber Engineering, Wood Physics
OMASA, K., Biological and Environmental Information Engineering
ONO, H., Polymeric Materials
ONO, K., Veterinary Clinical Pathobiology
ONODERA, T., Molecular Immunology
OYAIZU, H., Soil Science
OZAKI, H., Veterinary Pharmacology
SAGARA, Y., Food Informatics and Engineering
SAKAI, H., Forest Utilization
SAKAI, S., Animal Breeding
SAMEJIMA, M., Forest Chemistry
SASAKI, N., Veterinary Surgery
SATO, R., Food Chemistry
SENOO, K., Soil Microbiology
SHIMADA, T., Insect Genetics and Bioscience
SHIMIZU, K., Bioinformation Engineering
SHIMIZU, M., Food Chemistry
SHIMOMURA, A., Forest Landscape Planning and Design
SHIOTA, K., Cellular Biochemistry
SHIRAKO, Y., RNA Virology
SHIOZAWA, S., Physical Planning and Environmental Engineering
SHIRAISHI, N., Forest Management
SHOGENJI, S., Food and Resource Economics

SHOUN, H., Enzymology and Applied Microbiology
SUGIYAMA, N., Horticultural Science
SUZUKI, M., Forest Hydrology and Erosion Control
TAKAHASHI, N., Nutritional Biochemistry
TAKEUCHI, K., Landscape Ecology and Planning
TANAKA, T., Water Environmental Engineering
TANGE, T., Forest Ecophysiology
TANIGUCHI, N., Agricultural Structure and Policy
TANOKURA, M., Food Engineering
TATSUKI, S., Applied Entomology
TOJO, H., Applied Genetics
TSUBONE, H., Comparative Pathophysiology
TSUJIMOTO, H., Veterinary Internal Medicine
TSUTSUMI, N., Plant Molecular Genetics
WASHITANI, I., Conservation Ecology
WATANABE, H., Organic Chemistry
WATABE, S., Aquatic Molecular Biology and Technology
YAGI, H., Farm Business Management
YAMAGUCHI, I., Pesticide and Natural Products Chemistry
YAMAGUCHI-SHINOZAKI, L., Plant Molecular Biology
YAMAMOTO, H., Forest Planning
YAMANE, H., Environmental Biochemistry
YATAGAI, M., Plant Material Sciences
YODA, K., Microbiology Biotechnology
YOKOYAMA, S., Biomass Energy Conversion Technology
YONEYAMA, T., Plant Nutrition and Fertilizers
YOSHIKAWA, Y., Laboratory Animal Science
YOSHIMURA, E., Plant Molecular Physiology

Graduate School of Medicine and Faculty of Medicine (7-3-1 Hongo, Bunkyo-ku, Tokyo 113-0033; tel. (3) 5841-3303; fax (3) 5841-3670; e-mail liaison@m.u-tokyo.ac.jp; internet www.m.u-tokyo.ac.jp):

AKABAYASHI, A., Biomedical Ethics
ANDO, J., Systems Physiology
ARAIE, M., Ophthalmology
ETO, F., Rehabilitation Medicine
FUJITA, T., Nephrology and Endocrinology
FUKAYAMA, M., Human Pathology and Diagnostic Pathology
HANAOKA, K., Anaesthesiology and Pain Medicine
HASHIZUME, K., Paediatric Surgery
HIROKAWA, N., Cell Biology and Anatomy
IGARASHI, T., Paediatrics
IHARA, Y., Neuropathology
IINO, M., Cellular and Molecular Pharmacology
KADOWAKI, T., Nutrition and Metabolism
KAGA, K., Otorhinolaryngology, Head and Neck Surgery
KAI, I., Social Gerontology
KAMINISHI, M., Gastrointestinal Surgery, Surgical Sensory Motor Neuroscience Metabolic Care and Endocrine Surgery
KANDA, K., Nursing Administration
KATO, N., Neuropsychiatry
KAZUMA, K., Adult Nursing; Terminal and Long-term Care Nursing
KIRINO, T., Neurosurgery
KITA, K., Biomedical Chemistry
KITAMURA, T., Urology
KIUCHI, T., Medical Information Network Research
KOBAYASHI, Y., Public Health
KOIKE, K., Infection Control and Prevention
KOSHIMA, I., Plastic and Reconstructive
KURIHARA, H., Physiological Chemistry and Metabolism
MAKUUCHI, M., Hepatobiliary Pancreatic Surgery, Artificial Organ and Transplantation
MATSUSHIMA, K., Molecular Preventive Medicine
MISHINA, M., Molecular Neurobiology
MIYASHITA, Y., Physiology
MIYAZONO, K., Molecular Pathology
MORI, K., Cellular and Molecular Physiology
MURASHIMA, S., Community Health Nursing
NAGAI, R., Cardiology
NAGASE, T., Respiratory Medicine
NAGAWA, H., Surgical Oncology
NAKAMURA, K., Orthopaedic Surgery
NOMOTO, A., Microbiology
OHASHI, Y., Biostatistics; Epidemiology and Preventive Health Sciences
OHE, K., Medical Informatics and Economics
OHTOMO, K., Diagnostic Radiology
OKAYAMA, H., Molecular Biology
OMATA, M., Gastroenterology
OUCHI, Y., Ageing Science, Geriatric Medicine
OYAMA, H., Clinical Bioinformatics
SANADA, H., Gerontological Nursing
SHIMIZU, T., Cellular Signalling
SUZUKI, H., Pharmaceutical Services
TAKAHASHI, K., Transfusion Medicine
TAKAHASHI, T., Neurophysiology
TAKAMOTO, S., Cardiothoracic Surgery
TAKATO, T., Oral and Maxillofacial Surgery
TAKETANI, Y., Obstetrics and Gynaecology
TAMAKI, K., Dermatology
TANIGUCHI, T., Immunology
TOHYAMA, C., Disease Biology and Interpretative Medicine
TOKUNAGA, K., Human Genetics
TSUJI, S., Neurology
TSUTSUMI, O., Obstetrics and Gynaecology
UENO, S., Bioimaging and Biomagnetics
USHIDA, T., Biomedical Materials and Systems
USHIJIMA, H., Developmental Medical Sciences
WAKAI, S., International Community Health
WATANABE, C., Human Ecology
YAHAGI, N., Emergency and Critical Care Medicine
YAMAMOTO, K., Allergology and Rheumatology
YAMAZAKI, T., Clinical Bioinformatics
YATOMI, Y., Clinical Laboratory Medicine
YOSHIDA, K., Forensic Medicine

Graduate School of Pharmaceutical Sciences and Faculty of Pharmaceutical Sciences (7-3-1 Hongo, Bunkyo-ku, Tokyo 113-0033; tel. (3) 5841-4878; fax (3) 5841-4711; e-mail adviser@mol.f.u-tokyo.ac.jp; internet www.f.u-tokyo.ac.jp/index-e.html):

ARAI, H., Health Chemistry
EBIZUKA, Y., Natural Products Chemistry
FUKUYAMA, T., Synthetic Natural Products Chemistry
FUNATSU, T., Biophysics
ICHIJO, H., Cell Signalling
IRIMURA, T., Cancer Biology and Molecular Immunology
IWATSUBO, T., Neuropathology and Neuroscience
KATADA, T., Physiological Chemistry
KIRINO, Y., Neurobiophysics
KOBAYASHI, S., Organic and Organometallic Chemistry
MATSUKI, N., Neuropharmacology and Neuroscience
MIURA, M., Molecular Neurobiology
NAGANO, T., Chemical Biology and Medicinal Chemistry
OHWADA, T., Organic and Medicinal Chemistry
SATOW, Y., Protein Structural Biology
SEKIMIZU, K., Biochemistry, Molecular Biology
SHIBASAKI, M., Synthetic Organic Chemistry
SHIMADA, I., Structural Biology, NMR Spectroscopy, Physical Chemistry
SUGIYAMA, Y., Molecular Pharmacokinetics

Graduate School of Mathematical Sciences (3-8-1 Komaba, Meguro-ku, Tokyo 153-8914; tel. (3) 5465-7014; fax (3) 5465-7012; e-mail suriso@ms.u-tokyo.ac.jp; internet www.ms.u-tokyo.ac.jp):

ARAI, H., Real Analysis, Harmonic Analysis, Theory of Function Spaces
FUNAKI, T., Probability Theory
FURUTA, M., Global Analysis, Low-dimensional Topology
GIGA, Y., Nonlinear Analysis
HORIKAWA, E., Algebraic Geometry
JIMBO, M., Integrable Systems, Representation Theory
KATAOKA, K., Partial Differential Equations
KATSURA, T., Algebraic Geometry
KAWAHIGASHI, Y., Operator Algebras
KAWAMATA, Y., Algebraic Geometry and Complex Manifolds
KIKUCHI, F., Numerical Analysis
KOHNO, T., Three-manifolds, Quantum Groups
KUSUOKA, S., Probability Theory and its Application
MATANO, H., Nonlinear Partial Equations, Dynamical Systems
MATSUMOTO, Y., Topology
MIYAOKA, Y., Algebraic Geometry
MORITA, S., Topology of Manifolds
NAKAMURA, S., Differential Equations and Mathematical Physics
NOGUCHI, J., Complex Analysis in Several Variables, Complex Geometry
ODA, T., Number Theory
OKAMOTO, K., Differential Equations Complex Analysis
OSHIMA, T., Algebraic Analysis, Theory of Unitary Representations
SAITO, S., Arithmetic Geometry, Algebraic Geometry
SAITO, T., Arithmetic Geometry
TOKIHIRO, T., Mathematical Physics, Solid State Physics
TSUBOI, T., Foliations, Diffeomorphism Groups
YOSHIDA, N., Mathematical Statistics, Stochastic Analysis

Graduate School of Information Science and Technology (7-3-1 Hongo, Bunkyo-ku, Tokyo 113-8656; tel. (3) 5841-7662; fax (3) 5841-7446; e-mail octo@t-adm.t.u-tokyo.ac.jp; internet www.i.u-tokyo.ac.jp):

ANDO, S., Sensors, Measurement, Image Processing
AOYAMA, T., Communication Networks and Systems
DOHI, T., Computer-aided Surgery
ESAKI, H., Computer Networks. Internet Architecture
FUJII, M., Economics and Finance
HAGIYA, M., Formal Verification, Programming Languages, Biocomputing
HARA, S., Control Theory, Learning and Optimization
HARASHIMA, H., Human Communications Engineering
HIRAKI, K., Parallel Processing, Computer Architecture, High Speed Networks
HIROSE, K., Speech Information Processing
HIROSE, M., Virtual Reality, Human Interface
IMAI, H., Alogorithms, Optimization, Complexity, Quantum Computing
ISHIKAWA, M., Robotics, Vision, VLSI, Optics in Computing
ISHIZUKA, M., Artificial Intelligence, Multimodal Lifelike Agents, WWW Intelligence

KANZAKI, R., Neural Mechanisms of Behaviour
MABUCHI, K., Advanced Biomedical Engineering and Life Science
MUROTA, K., Discrete Mathematics
NAKAMURA, Y., Robotics, Mechatronics, Automatic Control
NANYA, T., Dependable Computing and VLSI Design
OKABE, Y., Time Series Analysis and Financial Technology
OTSU, N., Real-world Intelligence, Pattern Recognition
OYANAGI, Y., Numerical Analysis, Parallel Processing
SAGAYAMA, S., Speech Recognition, Signal Processing, Spoken Dialogue System, Music Information Processing
SAKAI, S., Computer Systems and Applications
SATO, T., Intelligent Mechanics Human Machine Systems, Human Co-operative Robotics
SHIMOYAMA, I., Micro Electro-Mechanical Systems, Robotics
SUGIHARA, K., Computational Geometry, Robust Scientific Computation
SUGIHARA, M., Numerical Analysis
TACHI, S., Advanced Robotics, Virtual Reality, Telexistence and Retro-reflective Projection Technology
TAKEICHI, M., Programming Language Theory and its Implementation
TAKEUCHI, I., Real-time Distributed Co-operative Systems
TAKEMURA, A., Statistical Science
YONEZAWA, A., Foundation for Computer Software, Programming Language, Software Security

Graduate School of Frontier Sciences (5-1-5 Kashiwanoha, Kashiwa-shi, Chiba 277-8562; tel. (4) 7136-5506; fax (4) 7136-4021; e-mail souiki@k.u-tokyo.ac.jp; internet www.k.u-tokyo.ac.jp):

AIDA, H., High-quality Networking, Parallel and Distributed Processing
AIZAWA, K., Image Processing, Multimedia Technologies
AMEMIYA, Y., X-ray Physics and Instrumentation
ASAI, K., Stochastic Models in Bioinformatics
CHIKAYAMA, T., Information Engineering
FUJIMORI, A., Condensed Matter Physics
FUJIWARA, H., Insect Molecular Biology
HAMANO, Y., Content Production
HARATA, N., Urban Transport Planning, Environmental Information Systems in Spatial Planning and Policy
HASEZAWA, S., Plant Cell Biology
HIHARA, E., Refrigeration Engineering, Heat Transfer, Multi-phase Flows
HIROSE, K., Speech Information Processing
HISADA, T., Finite Element Method, Biomechanics
HOSAKA, H., Information Mechatronics and Microdynamics
IBA, H., Evolutionary Computation, Evolutionary Robotics, Genome Informatics
ISOBE, M., Coastal Environment
ITO, K., Polymer Physics
ITO, T., Functional Genomics
IWATA, S., Design Science, Environmental Studies
KAGEMOTO, H., Environmental Hydrodynamics
KAJI, M., Forest Ecology
KANDA, J., Structural Engineering
KATAOKA, H., Biochemistry
KAWAI, M., Surface Science, Nano-Science
KAWANO, S., Molecular Cell Biology
KIMURA, K., Nano-space Function Design, Applied Solid State Physics
KITOH, S., Environmental Ethics
KOBAYASHI, I., Laboratory of Social Genome Sciences
KOJI, O., Environmental Visualization
KONO, M., Energy Conversion, Aerospace Propulsion
KUMAGAI, Y., Landscape Architecture, Forest Landscape Planning and Design
KUNISHIMA, M., International Infrastructure Development and Management
MATSUHASHI, R., Environment Systems and Economics
MATSUI, T., Comparative Planetology
MINO, T., Water Environment Control, Environmental Biotechnology
MITANI, H., Molecular Genetics, Radiation Biology
MIYAMOTO, Y., Molecular Physiology
MORISHITA, S., Computational Biology, Bioinformatics, Data Mining, Database Systems, Computational Logic
NAGATA, M., Insect Pathology
NAKAYAMA, M., Weather Resources Management and Regional Planning
NAMBA, S., Molecular Plant-microbe Interactions
NISHITA, T., Computer Graphics
OHMORI, H., Natural Environmental Structures
OHNO, H., Living Environmental Design
OHSAWA, M., Plant Ecology
OHYA, Y., Signal Transduction
OKADA, M., Brain Science Information Theory and Physics
ONABE, K., Semiconductor Materials Engineering
SAIGO, K., Synthetic Organic Chemistry, Synthetic Macromolecular Chemistry
SAIKI, K., Surface Science
SAKUMA, I., Biomedical Engineering, Computer-aided Surgery, Precision Engineering
SASAKI, K., Mechatronics, Signal Processing
SHIBATA, T., Semiconductor Electronics
SUGANO, S., Functional Genomics
SUGIURA, S., Cardiology, Physiology of Cardiac Muscle
TAKAGI, H., Solid State Physics and Chemistry
TAKAGI, S., Semiconductor Device Engineerinf
TAKAGI, T., Computational Biology
TAKAGI, Y., Development Economics
TAKASE, Y., Plasma Physics
TAKEDA, N., Smart Structures and Composite Materials
TAKEDA, T., Brain Science
TORIUMI, M., Petrology, Structural Geology
TORO, S., Ocean Environmental Engineering
TSUJI, S., Environmental Archaeology and Ethnology
TSUJI, T., Biomedical Engineering, Cardiovascular Surgery, Biomaterials
TSUKIHASHI, F., Physical Chemistry of Materials
UEDA, T., Molecular Biology
WADA, H., Magneto-Science and Technology
WATANABE, S., Natural Environment Formation
WATANABE, T., Molecular Oncology, Human Retrovirology
YAMAJI, E., Agro-environmental Engineering
YAMAJI, K., Energy Systems Analysis
YAMAMOTO, H., Information Theory and Cryptology
YAMAMOTO, K., Glycobiology
YAMATO, H., Industrial Information Systems and Environment
YANAGISAWA, Y., Chemical Analysis of Air and Indoor Air Pollution, Systems Analysis of Global Environment
YANAGITA, T., International Monetary Economics
YOSHIDA, T., Transnational Infrastructure Management
YOSHIDA, Z., Plasma Physics and Nonlinear Sciences
YOSHIMURA, S., Simulation and Virtual Environment

Interfaculty Initiative in Information Studies and Graduate School of Interdisciplinary Information Studies (7-3-1 Hongo, Bunkyo-ku, Tokyo 113-0033; tel. (3) 5841-5900; fax (3) 3811-5970; e-mail info@iii.u-tokyo.ac.jp; internet www.iii.u-tokyo.ac.jp):

ARAKAWA, C., Computational Fluid Dynamics, Simulation
BABA, A., Historical Informatics, Japanese Early Modern Economic History, Digital Archive Science
EINCO, S., Indian Philology, Ritual and Religion in India
HAMADA, J., Information Law and Policy
HANADA, T., Media Studies
HARA, Y., Economic Development Theory, Southeast Asian Economics
HARASHIMA, H., Communication Engineering and Face Studies
HASHIMOTO, Y., Social Psychology
HIROI, O., Social Psychology, Sociology of Disasters
IKEUCHI, K., Computer Vision
ISHIDA, H., Information Semiotics
KAN, S., Investigation of Possibilities for Regional Union in North-east Asia
KAWAGUCHI, Y., Computer Art
KUNIYOSHI, Y., Intelligent Systems and Informatics
NISHIGAKI, T., Information and Media Studies
SAKAMURA, K., Computer Architecture
SASAKI, M., Ecological Psychology
SUDOH, O., Economics of the Knowledge-based Society
TSUJII, J., Computational Linguistics, Natural Language Processing
YAMAGUCHI, Y., Graphics
YOSHIMI, S., Popular Culture and Media Events

Graduate School of Public Policy (7-3-1 Hongo, Bunkyo-ku, Tokyo 113-0033; tel. (3) 5841-3104; fax (3) 5841-3291; e-mail ppin@j.u-tokyo.ac.jp; internet www.pp.u-tokyo.ac.jp):

HAYASHI, R., Economic Policy
ICHIMURA, H., Econometrics
IHORI, T., Public Finance, Public Economics
ITO, T., International Finance, Macroeconomics
KANEMOTO, Y., Urban Economics
KAWAI, M., Basic Macroeconomics
MORITA, A., Public Management
OKUWAKI, N., International Law and Organization, Law of the Sea, Air and Outer Space
TANABE, K., Politics, Policy Analysis, Policy Process

ATTACHED RESEARCH INSTITUTES

Institute of Medical Science: 4-6-1 Shirokanedai, Minato-ku, Tokyo 108-8639; f. 1892; Dir T. YAMAMOTO; publ. *Annual Report*.

Earthquake Research Institute: 1-1-1 Yayoi, Bunkyo-ku, Tokyo 113-0032; f. 1925; Dir S. OKOBU; publ. *Bulletin of the Earthquake Research Institute* (4 a year).

Institute of Oriental Culture: 7-3-1 Hongo, Bunkyo-ku, Tokyo 113-0033; f. 1941; Dir A. TANAKA; publ. *Memoirs* (2 a year), *Oriental Culture* (annually).

Institute of Social Science: 7-3-1 Hongo, Bunkyo-ku, Tokyo 113-0033; f. 1946; Dir A. KOMORIDA; publ. *Shakai Kagaku Kenkyu* (Journal of Social Science, 6 a year), *Social Science Japan Journal* (2 a year), *Social Science Japan* (newsletter, 3 a year).

Institute of Industrial Science: 4-6-1 Komaba, Meguro-ku, Tokyo 153-8505; f. 1949; Dir M. MAEDA; publ. *Seisan-Kenkyu* (monthly), *Annual Report* (annually).

Historiographical Institute: 7-3-1 Hongo, Bunkyo-ku, Tokyo 113-0033; f. 1869; Dir M. HOTATE; publ. *Shiryo Hensan – Sho Ho* (annually), *Shiryo Hensan – Jo Kenkyu Kiyo* (annually).

Institute of Molecular and Cellular Biosciences: 1-1-1 Yayoi, Bunkyo-ku, Tokyo 113-0032; f. 1953; Dir A. MIYAJIMA.

Institute for Cosmic Ray Research: 5-1-5 Kashiwanoha, Kashiwa-shi, Chiba 277-8582; f. 1953; Dir Y. SUZUKI; publ. *ICRR Report* (irregular), *ICRR News* (4 a year), *ICRR Hokoku*, *Annual Report*.

Institute for Solid State Physics: 5-1-5 Kashiwanoha, Kashiwa-shi, Chiba 277-8581; f. 1957; Dir K. UEDA; publ. *Technical Report* (irregular).

Ocean Research Institute: 1-15-1 Minamidai, Nakano-ku, Tokyo 164-8639; f. 1962; Dir M. TERAZAKI; publ. *Bulletin*, *Preliminary Cruise Report* (irregular).

Cryogenic Center: 2-11-16 Yayoi, Bunkyo-ku, Tokyo 113-0032; f. 1967; Dir M. MINOWA.

Radioisotope Center: 2-11-16 Yayoi, Bunkyo-ku, Tokyo 113-0032; f. 1970; Dir Y. MAKIDE.

Environmental Science Center: 7-3-1 Hongo, Bunkyo-ku, Tokyo 113-0033; f. 1975; Dir K. YAMAMOTO.

Molecular Genetics Research Laboratory: 7-3-1 Hongo, Bunkyo-ku, Tokyo 113-0033; f. 1983; Dir M. YAMAMOTO.

Research Center for Advanced Science and Technology: 4-6-1 Komaba, Meguro-ku, Tokyo 153-8904; f. 1987; Dir K. HASHIMOTO.

Research into Artifacts Center for Engineering: 5-1-5 Kashiwanoha, Kashiwa-shi, Chiba 277-8568; f. 1992; Dir K. UEDA.

Biotechnology Research Center: 1-1-1 Yayoi, Bunkyo-ku, Tokyo 113-8657; f. 1993; Dir S. HORINOUCHI.

Asian Natural Environmental Science Center: 1-1-1 Yayoi, Bunkyo-ku, Tokyo 113-8657; f. 1995; Dir K. TAKEUCHI.

Center for Research and Development of Higher Education: 7-3-1 Hongo, Bunkyo-ku, Tokyo 113-0033; f. 1996; Dir K. OKAMOTO.

Center for Collaborative Research: 4-6-1 Komaba, Meguro-ku, Tokyo 153-8505; f. 1996; Dir H. YOKOI.

Center for Spatial Information Science: 5-1-5 Kashiwanoha, Kashiwa-shi, Chiba 277-8568; f. 1998; Dir R. SHIBASAKI.

High Temperature Plasma Center: 5-1-5 Kashiwanoha, Kashiwa-shi, Chiba 277-8568; f. 1999; Dir Y. OGAWA; publ. *Annual Report*.

Intelligent Modelling Laboratory: 2-11-16 Yayoi, Bunkyo-ku, Tokyo 113-8656; f. 1996; Dir K. HIRAO.

Center for Climate System Research: 5-1-5 Kashiwanoha, Kashiwa-shi, Chiba 277-8568; f. 1991; Dir T. NAKAJIMA.

International Center for Elementary Particle Physics: 7-3-1 Hongo, Bunkyo-ku, Tokyo 113-0033; f. 2004; Dir S. KOMAMIYA.

VLSI Design and Education Center: 2-11-16 Yayoi, Bunkyo-ku, Tokyo 113-8656; f. 1996; Dir K. ASADA; publ. *Annual Report*.

International Center: 7-3-1 Hongo, Bunkyo-ku, Tokyo 113-8654; f. 1990; Dir G. MESHITSUKA; publ. *Bulletin* (annually), *News* (4 a year).

International Research Center for Medical Education: 7-3-1 Hongo, Bunkyo-ku, Tokyo 113-0033; f. 2000; Dir K. KAGA; publ. *Annual Report*, *Newsletter* (2 a year).

Komaba Open Laboratory: 4-6-1 Komaba, Meguro-ku, Tokyo 153-8904; f. 1998; Dir T. NANYA.

University Museum: 7-3-1 Hongo, Bunkyo-ku, Tokyo 113-0033; f. 1965; Dir S. TAKAHASHI; publ. *Ouroboros* (newsletter, 3 a year), *Bulletin* (irregular), *Material Reports* (irregular), *UMUT Monograph* (irregular).

Health Service Center: 7-3-1 Hongo, Bunkyo-ku, Tokyo 113-0033; f. 1967; Dir (vacant); publ. *Kenko Kanri Gaiyo* (annually).

Information Technology Center: 2-11-16 Yayoi, Bunkyo-ku, Tokyo 113-8658; f. 1999; Dir Y. OKABE.

TOKYO INSTITUTE OF TECHNOLOGY

2-12-1, Ookayama, Meguro-ku, Tokyo 152-8550
Telephone: (3) 5734-3827
Fax: (3) 5734-3685
E-mail: iad@jim.titech.ac.jp
Internet: www.titech.ac.jp

Founded 1881
Independent
Academic year: April to March

President: MASUO AIZAWA
Vice-Presidents: CHITOSHI MIKI (Academic), MITSUHARU SEKIGUCHI (Finance), YOSHIMORI HONKURA (Planning), AKIRA SHIMOKOHBE (Research)
Director-General of Administration Bureau: DAISUKE IKEDA
Director of Institute Library: EIJI FUJIWARA

Library of 886,484 vols
Number of teachers: 743 full-time
Number of students: 5,007

DEANS

School of Bioscience and Biotechnology: SHIGEHISA HIROSE
School of Engineering: NOBUO FUJII
School of Science: KIYOSHI NAZAKAWA
Graduate School of Bioscience and Biotechnology: SHIGEHISA HIROSE
Graduate School of Decision Science and Technology: HIROMITSU MUTA
Graduate School of Engineering: NOBUO FUJII
Graduate School of Information Science and Engineering: YUKIO TAKAHASHI
Graduate School of Innovation Management: TAKAO ENKAWA
Graduate School of Science and Engineering: KIYOSHI NAKAZAWA
Interdisciplinary Graduate School of Science and Engineering: YOSHINAO MISHIMA

DIRECTORS

Chemical Resources Laboratory: MASASUKE YOSHIDA
Materials and Structures Laboratory: KENICHI KONDOU
Precision and Intelligence Laboratory: SHINICHI YOKOTA
Research Laboratory for Nuclear Reactors: MASAO OGAWA

PROFESSORS

Graduate School of Bioscience and Biotechnology:

AKAIKE, T., Biomaterial Design
AONO, R., Microbial Physiology, Genetic Engineering
FUJIHIRA, M., Biomolecular Processes
HAMAGUCHI, Y., Cell Biology
HANDA, H., Biotechnology
HASHIMOTO, H., Bio-organic Chemistry
HIROSE, S., Biochemistry
ICHINOSE, H., Neurochemistry and Neuropharmacology
IKAI, A., Biodynamics
INOUE, Y., Enzyme Functions
ISHIKAWA, T., Biofunctional Engineering
KISHIMOTO, T., Cell and Developmental Biology
KITAMURA, N., Molecular Biology
KITAZUME, T., Bio-organic Chemistry
KUDO, A., Molecular Immunology
MOTOKAWA, T., Animal Physiology
NAKAMURA, S., Genetic Engineering
OKADA, N., Molecular Evolution
OKAHATA, Y., Fundamentals of Biomolecules
OKURA, I., Biophysical Chemistry, Enzyme Chemistry
SATO, F., Molecular Design of Biological Importance
SEKINE, M., Bio-organic Chemistry
SHISHIDO, K., Molecular Biology
TAKAMIYA, K., Plant Physiology
TANAKA, N., Protein Crystallography
UENO, A., Bio-organic Chemistry, Molecular Recognition
UNNO, H., Biochemistry

Graduate School of Decision Science and Technology:

ENKAWA, T., Production Management
HASHIZUME, D., Sociology
HAYASAKA, M., History of Politics (Slavic Studies)
HIDANO, N., Regional Planning and Infrastructure Project Appraisal
HIGUCHI, Y., Socio-Economic Networks
IGUCHI, T., Japanese Literature
IIJIMA, J., Systems Theory
IMADA, T., International Relations
ISHII, M., Sports Psychology
ITO, K., Ergonomics, Production Control
KIJIMA, K., Management Systems
KIMOTO, T., History of Technology
KUWAKO, T., Philosophy
KYOMOTO, N., Intellectual Property Strategy, Licensing, Software Protection
MAYEKAWA, S., Psychometrics, Educational Statistics, Multivariate Data Analysis
MIYAJIMA, M., Industrial Management
MIYAKAWA, M., Applied Statistics, Quality Control
MIZUNO, S., Operations Research
MURAKI, M., Process Management
MUTA, H., Educational Planning, Economics of Education
MUTO, S., Game Theory
NAKAGAWA, M., Educational Psychology
NAKAHARA, Y., Exercise Physiology
NAKAI, N., Urban Planning
SAIKI, T., Patenting of Pharmaceutical Inventions
SAITO, T., Sociometrics
SAITO, U., Regional Landscape Planning and Design
TANAKA, Z., Political Science
WARAGAI, T., Philosophy, Logic
WATANABE, C., Technology Policy, Technology Management
YAMAMURO, K., Document Analysis
YAMATO, T., Economic Theory
YAMAZAKI, M., History of Science
YANO, M., Social Planning

Graduate School of Information Science and Engineering:

FUJII, S., Environmental Engineering
FUJIWARA, E., Coding Theory, Computer Systems
FURUI, S., Speech Recognition, Human Interfaces
HIGUCHI, Y., Socio-Economic Networks
HIROSE, S., Applied Solid Mechanics, Ultrasonic Nondestructive Evaluation, Numerical Analysis using Boundary Element Method
KIMEI, H., Geophysical Prospecting

KIMURA, K., Vibration, Stochastic Dynamics, Nonlinear Dynamics
KOJIMA, M., Mathematical Programming
KOJIMA, S., Geometry and Topology
MASE, S., Spatial Statistics
MORI, K., Computer Systems, Distributed Computing
NADAOKA, K., Environmental Systems Analysis, Coastal and Ocean Engineering, Mesoscale Meteorology, Applied Remote Sensing, Coastal-Space Design, Applied Fluid Dynamics
NAKAJIMA, M., Computer Graphics, Image Processing
NAKAMURA, H., Strength of Materials
OGAWA, H., Pattern Recognition, Image Processing
SAEKI, M., Software Engineering
SASAJIMA, K., Precision Engineering, Measuring Systems
SASSA, M., Computer Software, Programming Environments
SATO, T., Artificial Intelligence and Logic Programming
SHIBAYAMA, E., Software Science, Parallel and Distributed Computing
SHIMIZU, M., Biomechanics, Fluid Dynamics
TAKAHASHI, W., Functional Analysis and its Applications
TAKAHASHI, Y., Applied Probability, Operations Research
TAKIGUCHI, K., Mechanics of Building Structures, Disaster Prevention Systems, Concrete Engineering
TANAKA, H., Natural Language Processing
TOKUDA, T., Software Engineering
UJIHASHI, S., Biomechanics, Sports Engineering, Safety Engineering
WATANABE, O., Theory of Computation
YONEZAKI, N., Applied Logic, Software Science

Graduate School of Science and Engineering:
ABE, M., Electronic Properties of Matter
AKAGI, H., Power Engineering, Power Electronics, Electrical Machines
ANDO, I., Polymer Structure, NMR Spectroscopy, Electronic Structure of Polymers
ANDO, M., Antennas, Electromagnetic Wave Theory
ANDO, T., Physics, Condensed Matter Theory, Quantum Hall Effect, Semiconductor Quantum Structures
AOKI, Y., Urban Planning
ARAKI, K., Coding Theory, Digital Communication Systems
ASAHI, K., Experimental Nuclear Physics
DAIMON, M., Cement Chemistry, Porous Materials, Hydrochemical Synthesis
ENDO, M., Solid Vibrations
ENOKI, T., Physical Chemistry
FUJII, N., Electronic Circuits and Networks
FUJIMOTO, Y., Bio-organic Chemistry
FUJIOKA, H., History of Architecture, Architectural Design
FUJITA, T., Algebraic Geometry
FURUYA, K., Optical and Quantum Electronics
FUTAKI, A., Differential Geometry
HAGIWARA, I., Collaboration Engineering
HANNA, J., Imaging Materials
HASHIMOTO, T., Polymer Processing, Thermal Properties of Polymers
HIGUCHI, Y., Exercise Physiology
HINODE, H., Inorganic Synthesis of Solids, Inorganic Industrial Chemistry
HIRAO, A., Polymer Syntheses
HIROSE, S., Robotics, Biomechanics
HONKURA, Y., Geophysics
HOSOYA, A., Theoretical Cosmology
ICHIMURA, T., Molecular Spectroscopy
IGUCHI, I., Condensed Matter Physics and Superconducting Electronics
IIO, K., Experimental Condensed Matter Physics
IKARIYA, T., Homogeneous Catalysis, Synthetic Organic Chemistry
IKEDA, S., Hydraulics and Environmental Fluid Mechanics
INOU, N., Biomechanics, Autonomous Decentralized Systems, Robotics
INOUE, A., Singularity, Algebraic Geometry
INOUE, T., Physical Chemistry of Polymer Materials
ISHII, S., Singularity and Bifurcation
ISHII, S., Electric Power Engineering, Plasma
ISHIZU, K., Polymer Syntheses, Polymer Reactions
IWAMOTO, M., Electronic Materials
IWASAWA, N., Synthetic Organic Chemistry
IWATSUKI, N., Robotics
KAIZU, Y., Co-ordination Chemistry
KAJIUCHI, T., Biochemical Engineering, Environmental Chemical Engineering
KAKIMOTO, F., Experimental Cosmic Ray Physics
KAKIMOTO, M., Polymer Syntheses, Thin Polymer Films
KAKINUMA, K., Bio-organic Chemistry
KAWAI, N., Astrophysics
KAWAMURA, K., Physics, Inorganic Chemistry, Mineral Physics
KAWASAKI, J., Mass Transfer Operations
KAWASHIMA, K., Earthquake Engineering
KIKUTANI, T., Fibre and Polymer Processing, Physical Properties of Polymers
KISHIMOTO, K., Strength of Materials, Computational Mechanics
KITAGAWA, A., Fluid Power Control
KOBAYASHI, A., Industrial Measurement
KOBAYASHI, H., Fracture Mechanics and Fatigue
KONAGAI, M., Semiconductors
KOSHIHARA, S., Materials Science
KOUCHI, N., Physical Chemistry of Atomic and Molecular Processes
KUMAZAWA, I., Human Interface
KUNIEDA, H., Integrated Circuits, Signal Processing
KURODA, C., Process Information Systems
KUROKAWA, N., Number Theory
KUSAKABE, O., Geotechnical Engineering
KYOGOKU, K., Tribology, Machine Elements
MARUYAMA, S., Geology, Tectonics
MARUYAMA, T., Physical Chemistry in Advanced Materials
MATSUI, Y., Advanced Thermo-Fluid Dynamics
MASUKO, M., Tribology, Applied Surface Chemistry
MATSUO, T., Physical Metallurgy of Iron and Steels, High Temperature Deformation in Alloys
MATSUO, Y., Mechanical Properties of Ceramics
MATSUZAWA, A.
MIKI, C., Structural Mechanics and Engineering
MIMACHI, K., Special Functions, Material Physics, Representation Theory, Holonomic Systems
MINAMI, F., Solid State Physics and Laser Spectroscopy
MITA, T., Control Theory, Applications of Control Theory, Robotics
MIYAUCHI, T., Fluid Dynamics, Reactive Gas Dynamics
MIYAZAKI, K., Technology Strategy and Diffusion
MIZUTANI, N., Advanced Ceramics, Ceramic Processing, Electro-ceramics, Thin Films
MOCHIMARU, Y., Computational Fluid Dynamics
MORIIZUMI, T., Bioelectronics
MUNEKATA, H., Applied Physics of Property and Crystallography
MURAI, T., Wanderology
MURAKAMI, H., Workshop Processes and Production Engineering
MURATA, M., Differential Equations
NAGAHASHI, H., Image Processing
NAGAI, T., Solar–Terrestrial Physics
NAGATA, K., High Temperature Physical Chemistry and Electronic Materials
NAKAHARA, T., Lubrication Technology, Two-Phase Flow, Oil Hydraulics
NAKAJIMA, K., Chemical Engineering
NAKAMURA, Y., Diffraction Crystallography, Magnetic Thin Film
NAKASHIMA, S., Experimental Physical Geochemistry, Geochemical Spectroscopy and Kinetics, Physicochemical Properties of Water in the Earth, Organic–Inorganic Interactions and the Origin of Life, Geochemistry of Resources and the Environment
NAKAZAWA, K., Planetary Physics
NISHI, T., Polymer Alloys, Soft Materials, Polymer Nanotechnology
NISHIDA, N., Experimental Condensed Matter Physics, Low Temperature Physics
NISHIMORI, H., Statistical Physics
NIWA, J., Structural Concrete
OBIKAWA, T., Machining, Materials Science, Mechanical Processing Systems
OGAWA, K., Mechanical Operations
OGAWA, T., Steel and Shell Structures
OGUNI, M., Physical Inorganic Chemistry
OHASHI, H., Power Semiconductor Devices
OHASHI, Y., Crystal Chemistry
OHTA, H., Geotechnical Engineering
OHTAGUCHI, K., Biochemical Reaction Engineering
OKA, M., Theoretical Nuclear Physics
OKADA, K., Ceramic Raw Materials, Mineralogical Science
OKADA, T., Analytical Chemistry
OKAZAKI, K., Thermal and Environmental Engineering
OKUDA, Y., Low Temperature Physics
OKUI, N., Organic Thin Films, Physical Properties of Polymers
OKUMA, M., Dynamics, Optimum Design
OKUTOMI, M., Computer Vision
ONO, K., Dynamics of Machinery
ONZAWA, T., Welding and Materials Science
OTSUKA, K., Heterogeneous Catalysis, Electrocatalysis
OTSUKI, N., Construction Materials, Environmental Materials Design
SAITO, A., Thermal Engineering
SAITO, S., Theoretical Condensed Matter Physics
SAITO, Y., Manufacturing Engineering, CAD, CAM, Computer Intelligent Manufacturing
SAJI, T., Electrochemistry, Surface Chemistry
SAKAI, N., Theoretical Elementary Particle Physics
SAKAI, Y., Communication Systems
SAKAMOTO, K., Architectural Design
SAKANIWA, K., Communication Theory
SAMPEI, M., Control Theory (Linear and Non-Linear) and its Application, Nonholonomic Systems
SATO, T., Materials Development, Magnetic Materials, Amorphous Metals
SATOH, I., Thermal Engineering, Heat Transfer Measurement
SENDA, M., Environmental Design
SHIBATA, S., Inorganic Materials Engineering
SHIBATA, T., Experimental Nuclear Physics
SHIBUYA, K., Physical Chemistry
SHIGA, H., Complex Analysis
SHIGA, T., Stochastic Processes
SUMITA, M., Solid Structure and Physical Properties of Organic Materials, Polymer Composites

SUSA, M., Physical Chemistry of Materials
SUZUKI, H., Organometallic Chemistry
SUZUKI, H., Radio Communications Engineering
SUZUKI, K., Organic Chemistry
SUZUKI, M., Plasma Engineering, Nuclear Chemical Engineering
SUZUMURA, A., Joining, High Temperature Materials
TAKAGI, S., Analogue Integrated Circuits, Analogue Signal Processing
TAKAHASHI, E., Petrology, Geochemistry, Solid Geophysics
TAKAHASHI, T., Synthetic Organic Chemistry, Synthetic Processes for Natural Products
TAKATA, T., Supramolecular and Polymer Chemistry
TAKAYANAGI, K., Diffraction, Crystal Physics, Surface Physics
TAKEZOE, H., Optical and Electrical Properties of Organic Materials
TANIOKA, A., Physical Chemistry of Organic Materials, Membrane Science
TOKIMATSU, K., Geotechnical Engineering
TOKURA, H., Processing Technologies
TSUDA, K., Chemical Plant Materials
TSUNAKAWA, H., Geophysics
TSURU, T., Chemistry of Metal Surfaces, Electrochemistry, Corrosion and Passivity of Metals
TSURUMI, T., Electrical Properties and Structure of Inorganic Materials
UCHIYAMA, K., Stochastic Processes and Applied Probability
UEDA, M., Polymer Syntheses
UEDA, M., Wave Information Processing
UEDA, M., Condensed Matter Theory, Quantum Optics
UENO, S., Theory of Parallel and VLSI Computation
UYEMATSU, T., Information Theory, Data Compression
WAKIHARA, M., Inorganic Solid State Chemistry
WATANABE, J., Structure and Properties of Polymer Liquid Crystals
WATANABE, Y., Experimental Particle Physics
YABE, T., Laser Nuclear Fusion, Computational Fluid Dynamics
YAGI, K., Experimental Condensed Matter Physics, Crystal and Surface Physics
YAI, T., Transport Planning and Engineering
YAMAJI, A., Materials Science
YOSHIDA, T., Topology
YOSHINO, J., Experimental Condensed Matter Physics

Interdisciplinary Graduate School of Science and Engineering (4259 Nagatsuta-cho, Midori-ku, Yokohama 226-8502; tel. (45) 922-1111):

AOYAGI, Y., Information Devices
ASADA, M., Quantum Electronics
DEGUCHI, H., Polymer Synthesis
DOI, Y., Polymer Synthesis
FUCHIGAMI, T., Catalytic Chemistry
HARA, M., Nanotechnology
HARASHINA, S., Environmental Planning, Conflict Resolution
HATORI, Y., Visual Communication System, Network Interface
HIROTA, K., Information Systems
HORIOKA, K., High Power Beam Technology, Laser Engineering
HOTTA, E., Plasma Engineering, Pulsed Power Technology
HOYANO, A., Urban and Building Environment
ISHIWARA, M., Nanomaterials
ISHIKAWA, T., Hydraulics and Hydrology
ITO, K., Computational Brain Science, Design and Control of Robotics and Prostheses
KABASHIMA, Y., Information and Communication Engineering
KANNO, R., Lithium Battery, Solid State Ionics, Inorganic Materials Chemistry, Solid State Electrochemistry, High Pressure and Thin-film Synthesis
KATO, M., Fracture and Deformation
KINUGASA, Y., Earthquake Geology, Environmental Geology
KOBAYASHI, S., Knowledge Information Processing
KOBAYASHI, T., Digital Signal Processing
KOHNO, T., Nuclear Physics, Heavy Ion-Beam Science
KOSUGI, Y., Neural Networks
KUMAI, S., Nano-Electronics
MAEJIMA, H., Microprocessors, Special Purpose Processors, On-chip Systems
MIDORIKAWA, S., Earthquake Engineering
MISHIMA, Y., Physical Metallurgy and Alloy Design
NAKAMURA, K., Computational Neuroscience
NAKANO, Y., Environmental Engineering, Separation Process Engineering
NITTA, K., Artificial Intelligence, Regal Reasoning
ODAWARA, O., Electrochemistry of Metals
OHMACHI, T., Earthquake Engineering
OHNO, R., Architectural Design and Planning, Environmental Psychology
OHSAKA, T., Molten Salt Chemistry, Electrochemistry, Electroanalytical Chemistry, Bioelectrochemistry
OHTSU, M., Opto-quantum Electronics
OKAMURA, T., Cryogenic and Energy Conversion Engineering
ONAKA, S., Mechanical Properties of Materials
SAKAI, T., Semiconductor Devices
SASANO, S., History of Urban and Architectural Design
SATO, A., Strengthening Mechanism and Lattice Imperfections
SEO, K., Engineering Seismology
TAMURA, T., Environmental Atmospheric Turbulence, Urban Wind Climate, Aerodynamic Control
TEHRANO, T., Intelligent Informatics
UCHIKAWA, K., Visual Information Processing
WATANABE, M., Physical Geography
YAI, T., Transport Planning and Engineering
YAMAMURA, M., DNA Computing
YAMASAKI, H., Energy Conversion Engineering
YAMAZAKI, Y., Solid State Physics and Chemistry
YOKOYAMA, M., Automated Machine Design
YOSHIKAWA, K., High Temperature Energy Conversion, Environmental Fluid Dynamics

Chemical Resources Laboratory:

AKITA, M., Organometallic Chemistry
DOMEN, K., Surface Chemical Reaction
FUJII, M.
IKEDA, T., Polymer Chemistry and Photochemistry
ISHIDA, M., Chemical Engineering and Chemical Environmental Process Design
IWAMOTO, M., Heterogeneous Catalysis
IYODA, T., Functional Molecular Materials, Nano-structured Materials, Materials Electrochemistry
NAKA, Y., Process Systems Engineering
OSAKADA, K., Co-ordination and Organometallic Chemistry
SHODA, M., Biochemical Engineering, Applied Microbiology
TANAKA, M., Industrial Organic Chemistry
YAMAMOTO, T., Inorganic and Organometallic Chemistry
YAMASE, T., Photochemistry and Photoelectrochemistry
YOSHIDA, M., Biochemistry

Materials and Structures Laboratory:

ATAKE, T., Materials Science, Physical Chemistry
HAYASHI, S., Structural Engineering
ITOH, M., Physical Properties of Inorganic Materials
KASAI, K., Structural Engineering, Earthquake Engineering
KONDO, K., Inorganic Materials and Properties, Applied Physics of Property and Crystallography
SASAKI, S., Synchotron Radiation Science, X-Ray Crystallography, Solid-State Physics
TANAKA, K., Inorganic Materials and Properties, Building Materials
WAKAI, F., Inorganic Materials and Properties
YAMAUCHI, H., Materials Science, Applied Physics of Property and Crystallography, Strongly-Correlated Electron Materials, Superconducting Oxides
YASUDA, E., Ceramic Base Composites, Carbon Alloys and Materials
YOSHIMURA, M., Inorganic Materials and Properties, Soft Processing, Advanced Ceramics

Precision and Intelligence Laboratory:

HATSUZAWA, T., Precise Measurement
HIGO, Y., Physical Metallurgy, Nondestructive Evaluation
HORIE, M., Kinematics of Machinery
HOUJOH, H., Acoustic Measurement, Machine Dynamics
KAGAWA, T., Process Control
KOBAYASHI, K., Opto-electronics, Optical Communications, Photonic Integrated Semiconductor Devices
KOYAMA, F., Optical Semiconductor Devices
MASU, K., Advanced Microdevices
OHTSUKI, S., Bio-medical Ultrasonics, Acoustic Engineering
SATO, M., Pattern Recognition Image Processing
SHINNO, H., Ultraprecision Machining, Machine Tool Engineering
SIMOKOBE, A., Dynamics and Control of Precision Mechanisms
UEHA, S., Ultrasonic Engineering, Applied Optics
WATANABE, S., Mathematics and Information Science
WAKASHIMA, K., Materials Science, Micromechanics of Composites
YOKOTA, S., Fluid Power Control

Research Laboratory for Nuclear Reactors:

ARITOMI, M., Nuclear Thermal Engineering
FUJII, Y., Fusion Fuel Chemistry, Tritium Chemistry
HATTORI, T., Accelerator Physics, Heavy Ion Inertial Fusion
KATO, Y., Advanced Nuclear Reactor Systems Design, Complex Flow Computer Simulation
NINOKATA, H., Reactor Safety, Reactor Physics
OGAWA, M., Beam Plasma Sciences, Nuclear Fusion, Nuclear Physics
SEKIMOTO, H., Neutronics, Nuclear Reactor Design
SHIMADA, R., Fusion Reactor Control, Plasma Engineering
TORII, H., Energy Policy
YANO, T., Composite Materials and their Properties
YOSHIZAWA, Y., Thermal Engineering, Energy System, Combustion

ATTACHED RESEARCH INSTITUTES

Imaging Science and Engineering Laboratory (at Nagatsuta): Dir H. NAGAHASHI.

Center for Research and Development of Educational Technology: Dir N. OTSUKI.

Global Scientific Information and Computing Center: Dir Y. SAKAI.

Research Center for Low Temperature Physics: Dir T. ENOKI.

Frontier Collaborative Research Center (at Nagatsuta): Dir I. OKURA.

Research Center for Educational Facilities: Dir K. SAKAMOTO.

Volcanic Fluid Research Center: Dir M. OGUNI.

Research Center for Carbon Recycling and Energy: Dir K. OKAZAKI.

Research Center for Quantum Nanelectronics: Dir K. FURUYA.

Center for Biological Resources and Informatics: Dir N. OKADA.

Foreign Language Research and Teaching Center: Dir K. IKEDA.

Resources Recycling Process Laboratory: Dir M. SHODA.

Center for Materials Design: Dir E. YASUDA.

Microsystems Research Center: Dir Y. HIGO.

Center for Research in Advanced Financial Technology: Dir S. MIZUNO.

Center for Urban Earthquake Engineering: Dir T. OHMACHI.

International Student Centre: Dir O. KUSAKABE.

TOKYO MEDICAL AND DENTAL UNIVERSITY

5-45, Yushima 1-chome, Bunkyo-ku, Tokyo 113

Telephone: (3) 3813-6111
E-mail: webmaster.isc@tmd.ac.jp
Internet: www.tmd.ac.jp

Founded 1946
Independent
Academic year: April to March (two semesters)

President: AKIO SUZUKI
Director-General: O. KIKUKAWA
Director, University Library: KEIICHI OHYA

Library of 334,132 vols
Number of teachers: 696
Number of students: 2,921

Publications: *Bulletin*, *Bulletin of the Department of General Education*, *Reports of the Medical Research Institute*, *Reports of the Institute for Medical and Dental Engineering*

DEANS

Faculty of Medicine: KATSUIKU HIROKAWA
Faculty of Dentistry: KAZUHIRO ETO
Graduate School of Allied Health Sciences: RYUICHI KAMIYAMA
College of Liberal Arts and Sciences: SAKUMI ITABASHI

HEADS OF DEPARTMENTS

Faculty of Medicine:
- Anatomy 1: K. WAKE
- Anatomy 2: T. SATO
- Anatomy 3: Y. NAKAMURA
- Physiology 1: G. SINODA
- Physiology 2: K. KAMINO
- Biochemistry: S. HANDA
- Pharmacology: T. TANABE
- Pathology: K. NAKAMURA
- Microbiology: N. YAMAMOTO
- Hygiene: Y. YUASA
- Public Health: T. TAKANO
- Medical Zoology: K. FUJITA
- Forensic Medicine: H. HASEKURA
- Internal Medicine 1: N. MIYASAKA
- Internal Medicine 2: F. MARUMO
- Internal Medicine 3: F. NUMANO
- Neurology: (vacant)
- Neuropsychiatry: M. TOORU
- Paediatrics: J. YATA
- Surgery 1: M. ENDO
- Surgery 2: Y. MISHIMA
- Neurosurgery: K. HIRAKAWA
- Thoracic Surgery: (vacant)
- Orthopaedic Surgery: K. FURUYA
- Dermatology: K. NISIOKA
- Urology: H. OSHIMA
- Ophthalmology: T. TOKORO
- Oto-Rhino-Laryngology: A. KOMATSUZAKI
- Radiology: (vacant)
- Obstetrics and Gynaecology: T. ASO
- Anaesthesiology and Intensive Care Medicine: K. AMAHA
- Laboratory Medicine: N. NARA

Faculty of Dentistry:
- Oral Anatomy 1: Y. YAMASHITA
- Oral Anatomy 2: (vacant)
- Oral Physiology: Y. NAKAMURA
- Biochemistry: (vacant)
- Oral Pathology: M. TAKAGI
- Oral Microbiology: N. TSUCHIDA
- Dental Pharmacology: K. OHYA
- Dental Technology 1: F. NISHIMURA
- Dental Technology 2: A. SATO
- Preventive Dentistry and Oral Hygiene: S. OKADA
- Conservative Dentistry 1: J. TAGAMI
- Conservative Dentistry 2: I. ISHIKAWA
- Conservative Dentistry 3: H. SUDA
- Oral Surgery 1: M. AMAGASA
- Oral Surgery 2: S. ENOMOTO
- Prosthodontics 1: M. AI
- Prosthodontics 2: S. HASEGAWA
- Orthodontics 1: K. SOMA
- Orthodontics 2: T. KURODA
- Paedodontics: H. ONO
- Dental Radiology: T. SASAKI
- Dental Anaesthesiology: M. UMINO
- Stomatognathic Dysfunction: T. OYAMA

Department of General Education:
- Literature: T. HIOKI
- History of Social Thought: T. SASAKI
- Mathematics 1: K. KERA
- Mathematics 2: K. NOMURA
- Physics 1: G. IMADATE
- Physics 2: T. CHIBA
- Chemistry 1: K. MURAMATSU
- Chemistry 2: H. FUNAKOSHI
- Biology 1: G. IMADATE
- Biology 2: M. WADA
- English: K. MATSUOKA
- German: T. SUZUKI
- Health and Physical Education: Y. FUSE
- Science History: T. SATO
- Sociology: S. ITABASHI

ATTACHED INSTITUTES

Institute for Medical and Dental Engineering: 3-10, Kandasurugadai 2-chome, Chiyoda-ku, Tokyo 101; Dir T. TOGAWA.

Medical Research Institute: 3-10, Kandasurugadai 2-chome, Chiyoda-ku, Tokyo 101; Dir A. SAKUMA.

TOKYO NATIONAL UNIVERSITY OF FINE ARTS AND MUSIC

12-8 Ueno Park, Taito-ku, Tokyo 110-8714

Telephone: (3) 5685-7500
Fax: (3) 5685-7760
Internet: www.geidai.ac.jp

Founded 1949

President: IKUO HIRAYAMA
Director of University Library: HIROMICHI UENO
Secretary-General: YOSHIYUKI OTAWA

Library: see Libraries
Number of teachers: 218 full-time
Number of students: 2,785

DEANS

Faculty of Fine Arts: KIJO ROKKAKU
Faculty of Music: AKIO SONODA

DIRECTORS

University Art Museum: JUNICHI TAKEUCHI
Performing Arts Center: TERUO SANBAYASHI
Training centre for Foreign Languages and Declamation: SHUN'ICHIRO HATA
Media Art Center: TAKAMICHI ITO

TOKYO UNIVERSITY OF AGRICULTURE AND TECHNOLOGY

2-8-1 Harumi-cho, Fuchu-shi, Tokyo 183

Telephone: (423) 64-3311
Fax: (423) 60-7376
Internet: www.tuat.ac.jp

Founded 1949
Independent
Language of instruction: Japanese
Academic year: April to March

President: SEIZO MIYATA
Vice-Presidents: NAOTOSHI KANDA, MASARU MASUDA
Library Director: NOBUHIKO NISHIWAKI

Library of 346,639 vols
Number of teachers: 405
Number of students: 4,482

Publications: *Report* (every 2 years), faculty bulletins (annually)

DEANS

Faculty of Agriculture: AKIRA SASAO
Faculty of Technology: TADASHI MATSUNAGA
United Graduate School of Agricultural Science: YASUHISA KUNIMI
Graduate School of Bio-Applications and Systems Engineering: HIDEFUMI KOBATAKE

TOKYO UNIVERSITY OF FISHERIES

5–7 Konan 4, Minato-ku, Tokyo 108-8477

Telephone: (3) 5463-0400
Fax: (3) 5463-0359
E-mail: www-master@tokyo-u-fish.ac.jp
Internet: www.tokyo-u-fish.ac.jp

Founded 1888
Academic year: April to March

President: Dr FUMIO TAKASHIMA
Vice-Presidents: Dr K. SATO, Dr R. TAKAI
Administrative Director: M. SATO
Librarian: Dr E. WATANABE

Library of 268,000 vols
Number of teachers: 171
Number of students: 1,745

Publications: *Journal of the TUF* (2 a year), *Report of the TUF* (annually)

HEADS OF LABORATORIES

Ocean Sciences:
- Marine Ecosystem Studies: Dr T. ISHIMARU, Dr M. MAEDA, Dr M. NAMIKOSHI, Dr Y. YAMAGUCHI
- Physics and Environmental Modelling: Prof. Y. ANDO, Dr K. KIHARA, Dr M. MATSUYAMA, Dr T. MORINAGA, Dr H. NAGASHIMA, Dr H. OHASHI, Dr N. SHIOTANI

Marine Science and Technology:
- Fishing Science and Technology: Dr T. ARIMOTO, Dr C. ITOSU, Dr H. KANEHIRO, Dr T. TOKAI

Ocean Systems Engineering: Dr T. AKITA, Prof. Y. NAKAMURA, Dr K. SATOHH, Dr M. FURUSAWA, Dr S. YADA, Dr S. MURAMATSU

Aquatic Biosciences:

Aquatic Biology: Dr K. FUJITA, Prof. M. OMORI, Dr S. SEGAWA, Prof. J. TANAKA, Dr S. WATANABE

Aquaculture: Dr T. TAKEUCHI, Dr M. NOTOYA, Dr N. OKAMOTO, Dr T. WATANABE, Dr H. FUKUDA

Genetics and Biochemistry: Dr T. AOKI

Fisheries Resource Management:

Fisheries Resource Management System: Dr T. KITAHARA, Dr S. YAMADA, Dr K. TAYA, Y. SATO, Dr K. UENO, Prof. Y. SATO

Ecology and Economics of Fisheries Resources: Dr Y. NAKAI, Dr A. OHNO, Dr R. ISEDA, Dr N. KOIWA, Prof. Y. NAKAI

International Economics of Fisheries and Food Industries: Dr K. SAKURAI

Food Science and Technology:

Food Chemistry: Dr T. SUZUKI, Dr T. FUJII, Dr S. WADA, Dr M. TANAKA

Food Engineering: Dr H. WATANABE, Prof. T. MIHORI, Dr R. TAKAI

Marine Biochemistry: Dr S. KIMURA, Dr K. SHIOMI, Dr H. YAMANAKA, Dr T. HAYASHI, Dr T. WATANABE

Applied Microbiology: Dr E. WATANABE

International and Interdisciplinary Studies:

Psychology: Dr K. NAKAMURA

History: O. KANAMORI

English: Dr S. MIURA

French: T. SHIMANO

Ethics: T. AMEMIYA

TOKYO UNIVERSITY OF FOREIGN STUDIES

3-11-1 Asahicho, Fuchu-shi, Tokyo 183-8534

Telephone: (42) 330-5126

Fax: (42) 330-5140

E-mail: ml-zhenhp@tufs.ac.jp

Internet: www.tufs.ac.jp/index-j.html

Founded 1899; reorganized 1949

Semi-private institution

President: SETSUHO IKEHATA

Director-General: M. KOTANI

Library Director: N. TOMIMORI

Library: see Libraries and Archives

Number of teachers: 241 full-time

Number of students: 4,282

Publication: *Area and Culture Studies* (2 a year)

DEANS

Faculty of Foreign Studies: AKIRA BABA

ATTACHED INSTITUTE

Research Institute for Languages and Cultures of Asia and Africa: 3-11-1 Asahicho, Fuchu-shi, Tokyo 183-8534; tel. (42) 330-5600; fax (42) 330-5610; f. 1964; Dir Dr K. MIYAZAKI; publ. *Journal of Asian and African Studies* (2 a year), *Newsletter* (3 a year).

TOKYO UNIVERSITY OF MERCANTILE MARINE

2-1-6 Etchujima, Koto-ku, Tokyo 135-8533

Telephone: (3) 5245-7312

Internet: www.tosho-u.ac.jp

Founded 1875

Independent

President: AKIO M. SUGISAKI

Director of Administration Bureau: TAKAO OKA

Library Director: SUUSHIN SATO

Number of teachers: 110 full-time

Number of students: 1,093

Publication: *Journals* (natural sciences, humanities and social sciences)

PROFESSORS

Information Systems Engineering and Navigation Systems: HAYAMA IMAZU

Navigational Electronics: SHOGO HAYASHI

Marine Engineering and Guidance Control: KOHEI OHTSU

Floating Facilities: KUNIAKI SHOJI

Mathematical Science: OSAMU MATSUSHITA

Power Systems Engineering and Steam Power: MASAHIRO OSAKABE

Internal Combustion Engines: HIROSHI OKADA

Nuclear Power: TOMOJI TAKAMASA

Machinery and Equipment: TOSHIHIKO FUJITA

Electric Power: YOSHIHIRO HATANAKA

Marine Science and Technology: HIROSHI YAMAGISHI

International Cultural Studies: TAKAKO NIWA

Logistics Engineering: IWAO TAMINAGA

UNIVERSITY OF ELECTRO-COMMUNICATIONS

1-5-1 Chofugaoka, Chōfu City, Tokyo 182-8585

Telephone: (424) 43-5014

Fax: (424) 43-5108

E-mail: kenkyo-k@office.uec.ac.jp

Internet: www.uec.ac.jp

Founded 1949

Independent

Academic year: April to March

President: M. KAJITANI

Director of Secretariat: I. ISHIOKA

Library Director: T. MIKI

Number of teachers: 360 full-time

Number of students: 5,452 (4,347 undergraduate, 1,105 postgraduate)

Publication: *Bulletin* (2 a year)

PROFESSORS

Information Transfer: Theory and Practice: KIYOSHI ANDO

Information Photonics and Wave Signal Processing: YOSHIO KAMI

Information and Communications Systems: TAKASHI S. FUKUDA

Computer and Media Science: KAZUHIKO OZEKI

Department of Computer Science: RIKIO ONAI

Department of Electronic Engineering: KIMURA TADAMASA

Department of Applied Physics and Chemistry: K. HAKUTA

Department of Mechanical Engineering and Intelligent Systems: S. KURODA

Department of Systems Engineering: MASAYUKI MATSUI

Department of Human Communications: HARUYUKI INOUE

TOTTORI UNIVERSITY

4-101 Minami, Koyama-cho, Tottori City 680-0945

Telephone: (857) 31-5010

Fax: (857) 31-5018

E-mail: net_adm@jim.tottori-u.ac.jp

Internet: www.tottori-u.ac.jp

Founded 1949

Academic year: April to March

President: MASANORI MICHIUE

Director-General of Administration: Y. SUZUKI

Librarian: K. KOSAKA

Number of teachers: 762 full-time

Number of students: 6,090

DEANS

Faculty of Education and Regional Sciences: M. NAGAYAMA

Faculty of Medicine: T. NOSE

Faculty of Engineering: H. KIYAMA

Faculty of Agriculture: M. IWASAKI

TOYAMA UNIVERSITY

3190 Gofuku, Toyama City 930-8555

Telephone: (764) 45-6011

E-mail: info@toyama-u.ac.jp

Internet: www.toyama-u.ac.jp

Founded 1949; Toyama Medical and Pharmaceutical University, Takaoka National College and Toyama University merged May 2003

Academic year: April to March (two terms)

President: HIROSHI TAKIZAWA

Chief Administrative Officer: O. IMADA

Librarian: H. FUJITA

Library of 965,300 vols

Number of teachers: 445 full-time

Number of students: 7,400

DEANS

Faculty of Economics: S. YOSHIHARA

Faculty of Education: M. KASE

Faculty of Engineering: M. TOKIZAWA

Faculty of Humanities: N. KOTANI

Faculty of Science: K. MATSUMOTO

ATTACHED INSTITUTES

Center for Co-operative Research: Dir C. TATUYAMA.

Center for Research and Training in Teacher Education: Dir S. NAGAI.

Health Administration Center: Dir K. INAZAWA.

Hydrogen Isotope Research Center: Dir K. MATUMOTO.

TOYOHASHI UNIVERSITY OF TECHNOLOGY

Tempaku, Toyohashi, Aichi 441-8580

Telephone: (532) 47-0111

Fax: (532) 44-6509

Internet: www.tut.ac.jp

Founded 1976

Independent

Academic year: April to March

President: Dr TATAU NISHINAGA

Vice-Presidents: TOSHIRO KOBAYASHI, HIROYUKI MATSUI

Director-General of Administration Bureau: TAKASHI NORIZUKI

Librarian: HIROO YONEZU

Library of 170,000 vols

Number of teachers: 213

Number of students: 2,144

DEANS

Department of Architecture and Civil Engineering: AKIRA OHGAI

Department of Ecological Engineering: TOSHIHIRO KITADA

Department of Electrical and Electronic Engineering: AKIO OOTA

Department of Humanities and Management Science and Engineering: JUN YAMAMOTO

Department of Information and Computer Sciences: SEIICHI NAKAGAWA

Department of Knowledge-Based Information Engineering: YOSHIMASA TAKAHASHI

Department of Materials Science: KATSUYUKI AOKI

Department of Mechanical Engineering: MASAO UEMURA

Department of Production Systems Engineering: MASAHIRO KAWAKAMI

UNIVERSITY OF TSUKUBA

1-1-1 Tennodai, Tsukuba, Ibaraki-ken 305-8577
Telephone: (29) 853-2056
Fax: (29) 853-2059
E-mail: koryuka@sakura.cc.tsukuba.ac.jp
Internet: www.tsukuba.ac.jp

Founded 1973
Independent
Language of instruction: Japanese
Academic year: April to March

Pres.: YOICHI IWASAKI
Vice-Pres: NORIO KUDO, HIROSHI MIZUBAYASHI, TAKESHI KOSHIZUKA, SHIN-ICHIRO IZUMI, SUMIO HATANO, HIROMICHI YOSHITAKE, AKIHIDE TANIKAWA
Exec. Advisors to the Pres.: AKIRA UKAWA, ISAO INOUE, YUTAKA TSUJINAKA
Dirr of Univ. Hospital: NOBUHIRO YAMADA
Dir of Education Bureau of Attached Laboratory Schools: AKIHIDE TANIKAWA
Dir of Univ. Library: SADAO UEMATSU

Library of 2,457,258 vols, 23,001 periodicals
Number of teachers: 1,659
Number of students: 16,241

PROVOSTS AND DEANS

Undergraduate Programmes

School of Humanities and Culture:
NORIO YAMADA (Provost)
College of Humanities: MAKOTO ITOH (Dean)
College of Comparative Culture: KIICHIROU TAKEMURA (Dean)
College of Japanese Language and Culture: HIDEICHI ETO (Dean)

School of Social and International Studies:
NOBUHIKO KITAWAKI (Provost)
College of Social Sciences: MIYOKO MOTOZAWA (Dean)
College of International Studies: YUKIO FUKUI (Dean)

School of Human Sciences:
SHINYA MIYAMOTO (Provost)
College of Education: KAZUO HORI (Dean)
College of Psychology: TOSHIKI OGAWA (Dean)
College of Disability Sciences: SHIGEKI SONOYAMA (Dean)

School of Life and Environmental Sciences:
JUN-ICHI HAYASHI (Provost)
College of Biological Sciences: SHINOBU SATOH (Dean)
College of Agro-Biological Resource Sciences: YUKIO KANAI (Dean)
College of Geoscience: KATSUO SASHIDA (Dean)

School of Science and Engineering:
KEN-ICHI OKAMOTO (Provost)
College of Mathematics: MITSUHIRO ITO (Dean)
College of Physics: KAZUHIRO YABANA (Dean)
College of Chemistry: TATSUO ARAI (Dean)
College of Engineering Sciences: KEN-ICHI OHSHIMA (Dean)
College of Engineering Systems: SEIJI YASUNOBU (Dean)
College of Policy and Planning Sciences: REIJJI OBASE (Dean)

School of Informatics:
YOSHIHIKO EBIHARA (Provost)
College of Information Science: YOSHINORI YAMAGUCHI (Dean)
College of Media Arts, Science and Technology: JUN'ICHI ISOYA (Dean)
College of Knowledge and Library Sciences: HIROTOYO ISHII (Dean)

School of Medicine and Medical Sciences:
FUJIO OTSUKA (Provost)
School of Medicine: AKIRA HARA (Dean)
School of Nursing: YUKA SAEKI (Dean)
School of Medical Sciences: OSAMU URAYAMA (Dean)

School of Health and Physical Education:
YOSHIKAZU NOMURA (Provost)

School of Art and Design:
KIYOSHI NISHIKAWA (Provost)

Masters Degree Programmes:
NORIO KUDO (Provost)
depts of Area studies, Art and design, Education, Environmental sciences, Health and sport sciences

Doctoral Degree Programmes

Graduate School of Humanities and Social Sciences:
YOSHIKI TSUBOI (Provost)
depts of History and anthropology, International political economy, Literature and linguistics, Modern cultures and public policies, Philosophy, Social sciences

Graduate School of Business Sciences:
TAKAHIRO EGUCHI (Provost)
depts of Advanced studies of business law, Law School programme, MBA programme in international business, Systems management, Systems management and business law

Graduate School of Pure and Applied Sciences:
MASAFUMI AKAHIRA (Provost)
depts of Applied physics, Chemistry, Frontier science, Materials science, Materials science and engineering, Mathematics, Physics

Graduate School of Systems and Information Engineering:
JIRO TANAKA (Provost)
depts of Business administration and public policy, Computer science, Engineering mechanics and energy, Intelligent interaction technologies, Policy and planning sciences – Consecutive doctoral programme, Quantitative finance and management, Risk engineering, Social systems and management, Social systems engineering – Divided doctoral programme,

Graduate School of Life and Environmental Sciences:
OSAMU NUMATA (Provost)
depts of Advanced agricultural technology and sciences, Agro-bioresourses science and technology, Appropriate technology and sciences for sustainable development, Bioindustrial sciences, Biological sciences, Biosphere resource science and technology, Earth evolution sciences – Consecutive doctoral programme, Earth evolution sciences – Doctoral programme, Environmental science – Master's programme, Functional biosciences, Geoenvironmental sciences – Consecutive doctoral programme, Geoenvironmental sciences – Doctoral programme, Geosciences – Master's programme, Integrative environmental sciences, Life sciences and bioengineering, Structural biosciences, Sustainable environmental studies – Doctoral programme

Graduate School of Comprehensive Human Sciences:
KAZUHIKO SHIMIZU (Provost)
depts of Advanced biomedical applications, Art and design – Consecutive doctoral programme, Art and design – Doctoral programme, Art and design – Master's programme, Biomolecular and integrated medical sciences, Coaching science, Disability sciences, Education, Human care sciences, Functional and regulatory medical sciences, Kansei, behavioural and brain sciences, Medical sciences, Medical sciences for control pathological processes, Nursing sciences, Physical education, health and sport sciences, Psychology, School education, Social and environmental medicine, Sports medicine, World cultural heritage studies, World heritage studies

Graduate School of Library, Information and Media Studies:
SHIN-ICHI NAKAYAMA (Provost)
dept of Library, Information and Media Studies

DIRECTORS OF CENTRES

Centre for Computational Physics: MITSUHISA SATO
Plasma Research Centre: TERUJI CHO
Centre for Tsukuba Advanced Research Alliance: AKIYOSHI FUKAMIZU
Foreign Language Centre: IZUMI YASUI
Sport and Physical Education Centre: KEN MIYASHITA
Agricultural and Forestry Research Centre: NAOKI SAKAI
Terrestrial Environment Research Centre: TADASHI TANAKA
Laboratory Animal Resource Centre: KEN-ICHI YAGAMI
Shimoda Marine Research Centre: KAZUO INABA
Sugadaira Montane Research Centre: SEIJI TOKUMASU
International Student Centre: STEFAN KAISER
Gene Research Centre: HIROSHI KAMADA
Research Centre for University Studies: HISATOSHI SUZUKI
Proton Medical Research Centre: AKIRA MATSUMURA
Admission Centre: TOMONORI SHIRAKAWA
Tsukuba Industrial Liaison and Co-operative Research Centre: SHIN'ICHI YUTA
Centre for Research on International Co-operation in Educational Development: HIDEO NAKATA
Research Centre for Knowledge Communities: SHIGEO SUGIMOTO
Tsukuba Research Centre for Interdisciplinary Materials Science: YOUICHI OOTSUKA
Special Support Education Research Centre: HISAO MAEKAWA
Alliance for Research on North Africa: KAZUKO SHIOJIRI
Academic Computing and Communications Centre: KOUZOU ITANO
Research Facility for Science and Technology: KAZUO MATSUUCHI
Radioisotope Centre: HIROKI OSHIO
Tsukuba Critical Path Research and Education Integrated Leading Centre: NAOYUKI OCHIAI
University Health Centre: MORIO OHTSUKA

UTSUNOMIYA UNIVERSITY

350 Mine-machi, Utsunomiya-shi, Tochigi 321-8505
Telephone: (286) (36) 1515
Internet: www.utsunomiya-u.ac.jp

Founded 1949

Independent
Language of instruction: Japanese
Academic year: April to March

President: HIROTO TABARA
Vice-Presidents: HIDEKI KASUYA, SHIGERU KITAJIMA
Director of University Library: HIROTAKA KOIKE

Library of 551,376 vols
Number of teachers: 476
Number of students: 5,411

DEANS

Faculty of Education: KIYOSHI NAKAMURA
Faculty of Engineering: YASUSHI NISHIDA
Faculty of Agriculture: TADATAKE MIZUMOTO
Faculty of International Studies: KAZUKO FUJITA

WAKAYAMA UNIVERSITY

Sakaedani 930, Wakayama-shi 640-8510
Telephone: (73) 454-0361
Fax: (73) 457-7000
Internet: www.wakayama-u.ac.jp

Founded 1949
Academic year: April to March

President: S. MORIYA
Chief Administrative Officer: M. TANIGUCHI
Librarian: H. TACHIBANA

Library of 741,765 vols
Number of teachers: 371
Number of students: 4,460

Publications: *Bulletin of the Faculty of Education*, *The Wakayama Economic Review*

DEANS

Faculty of Education: K. MORISUGI
Faculty of Economics: T. KINOUCHI
Faculty of Systems Engineering: O. OTSUKI

YAMAGATA UNIVERSITY

1-4-12, Koshirakawa-machi, Yamagata 990-8560
Telephone: (23) 628-4006
Fax: (23) 628-4013
Internet: www.yamagata-u.ac.jp

Founded 1949
Independent
Academic year: April to March (two semesters)

President: FUJIRO SENDO
Secretary-General: DAISUKE IKEDA
Librarian: MASANOBU HAYAKAWA

Library of 991,330 vols
Number of teachers: 1,800
Number of students: 9,436

Publications: *Bulletin of Humanities* (annually), *Bulletin of Social Sciences* (2 a year), *Bulletin of Educational Science* (annually), *Bulletin of Natural Sciences* (annually), *Medical Journal* (2 a year), *Bulletin of Engineering* (annually), *Bulletin of Agricultural Science* (annually)

DEANS

Faculty of Literature and Social Sciences: KOICHI TAKAGI
Faculty of Education: TSUNEO ISHIJIMA
Faculty of Science: SEIGO KATO
School of Medicine: MASAO ENDOH
Faculty of Engineering: TAKESHI ENDO
Faculty of Agriculture: TAKESHI SASSA

YAMAGUCHI UNIVERSITY

1677-1 Yoshida, Yamaguchi 753-8511
Telephone: (83) 933-5026
Fax: (83) 933-5029
E-mail: sh033@office.cc.yamaguchi-u.ac.jp
Internet: www.yamaguchi-u.ac.jp

Founded 1949
National University Corporation
Academic year: April to March

President: HIROSHI KATO
Vice-Presidents: SHINYA KAWAI, KYOSUKE SAKATE TAKUYA MARUMOTO YOSHIKAZU SUGIHARA, OSAMU FUKUMASA
Secretary-General: YUTAKA MATSUYAMA
Director of University Library: OSAMU FUKUMASA

Library: see Libraries and Archives
Number of teachers: 889
Number of students: 10,785 (9,099 undergraduates, 1,686 postgraduates)

DEANS

Faculty of Humanities: SUSUMU TANAKA
Faculty of Education: ISSEI YOSHIDA
Faculty of Economics: OSAMU TAKIGUCHI
Faculty of Science: HIROYUKI MASHIYAMA
School of Medicine: TOKUHIRO HIROSHI ISHIHARA
Faculty of Engineering: TOSHIKATSU MIKI
Faculty of Agriculture: DAIZO KOGA
United Graduate School of Veterinary Science: TOSHIHARU HAYASHI
Graduate School of East Asian Studies: NORIKO OTANI
Graduate School of Innovation and Technology Management: KEN KAMINISH

ATTACHED INSTITUTES

Collaborative Research Center: Dir NORIKAZU SHIMIZU.

Science Research Center: Dir YASUO KISO.

University Hospital: Dir MASUNORI MATSUZAKI.

Media and Information Technology Center: Dir YOSHIHIKO HAMAMOTO.

Education Promoting Center: Dir TADASHI WATANABE.

Venture Business Laboratory: Dir SETSUZO YAMAMOTO.

Business Incubation Square: Dir SETSUZO YAMAMOTO.

UNIVERSITY OF YAMANASHI, NATIONAL UNIVERSITY CORPORATION

4-4-37 Takeda Kofu, Yamanashi 400-8510
Telephone: (55) 220-8004
Fax: (55) 220-8024
Internet: www.yamanashi.ac.jp

Founded 1949
Independent
Academic year: April to March

President: YOJI YOSHIDA
Registrar: KENJI TAMARU
Dean of Students: KUNIO OOHARA
Librarian: TOSHIAKI OTOMO

Library of 556,439 vols
Number of teachers: 600
Number of students: 5,150

Publications: *Bulletin of the Faculty of Education and Human Sciences* (2 a year), *Report of the Faculty of Engineering* (annually), *Journal of Applied Educational Research* (annually), *Report of the Faculty of Medicine*

DEANS

Faculty of Education: TETSUO HORI
Faculty of Medicine: HIDEAKI NUKUI
Faculty of Engineering: KOKI YOKOTSUKA

ATTACHED INSTITUTES

Co-operative Research and Development Center: 4-3-11 Takeda, Kofu 400-8511.

Center for Instrumental Analysis: 4-3-11 Takeda, Kofu 400-8511.

Integrated Information Processing Center: 4-3-11 Takeda, Kofu 400-8511; Dir KOJI IWANUMA.

Clean Energy Research Center: 7 Miyamae-cho, Kofu 400-0021.

Institute of Enology and Viticulture: attached to the Faculty of Engineering.

Center for Crystal Science and Technology: attached to the Faculty of Engineering.

Center for Life Science Research: 1110 Shimokato, Tamaho-cho, Nakakoma-gun 409-3898.

International Student Center: 4-4-37 Takeda, Kofu 400-8510.

YOKOHAMA NATIONAL UNIVERSITY

79-1 Tokiwadai, Hodogaya-ku, Yokohama 240-8501
Telephone: (45) 339-3036
Fax: (45) 339-3039
E-mail: international@nuc.ynu.ac.jp
Internet: www.ynu.ac.jp

Founded 1949
National University Corporation
Language of instruction: Japanese
Academic year: April to March (2 semesters)

President: YOSHIHIRO IIDA
Executive Directors: S. KISUGI, A. NAGASHIMA, S. WATANABE, K. YANAI
Secretary-General: N. MURATA

Library: see Libraries and Archives
Number of teachers: 619 full-time
Number of students: 10,711

DEANS

Faculty of Business Administration: K. YAMAKURA
Faculty of Economics: Y. HASEBE
Faculty of Education and Human Sciences: S. FUKUDA
Faculty of Engineering: M. SHIRATORI
Faculty of Environment and Information Sciences: S. INOUE
Graduate School of Education: S. FUKUDA
Graduate School of Engineering: M. SHIRATORI
International Graduate School of Social Sciences: F. KANAZAWA

PROFESSORS

Faculty of Business Administration (79-4 Tokiwadai, Hodogaya-ku, Yokohama 240-8501; tel. (45) 339-3654; fax (45) 339-3656; e-mail int.somu@nuc.ynu.ac.jp; internet www.business.ynu.ac.jp):

ABE, S., Marketing
CHO, D., Business Administration
HIGASHIDA, A., Econometrics
INOUE, T., Industrial Economics
IZUMI, H., Financial Accounting
KIJIMA, Y., Mathematics
MITO, H., Corporate Ownership and Control, Business Ethics, Business and Society
MIZOGUCHI, S., Management Accounting
MOGAKI, H., International Personnel Management
NAKAMURA, H., Strategic Accounting, Capital Budgeting
OKADA, E., International Accounting
OHTSUKA, E., Game Theory
SHIBATA, H., International and Comparative Human Resource Management
SHIRAI, H., Management Information Systems, Business Modelling
USUI, I., Business Mathematics
YAGI, H., Environmental Accounting
YAMAKURA, K., Strategic Management
YONEZAWA, Y., Corporate Finance

Faculty of Economics (79-3 Tokiwadai, Hodogaya-ku, Yokohama 240-8501; tel. (45) 339-

3510; fax (45) 339-3504; e-mail int.somu@nuc.ynu.ac.jp; internet www.econ.ynu.ac.jp):

AKIYAMA, T., Macroeconomics
FUKAGAI, Y., History of Economic Thought, Economic Ethics
HAGINARA, S., US Macroeconomic Policy
HASEBE, Y., Comparative Economic Systems
ISHIYAMA, Y., History of European Economic Integration
KIZAKI, M., Chinese Economy
NAKAMURA, Y., Comparative Economics
OHMORI, Y., Labour Economics
OKADO, M., Economic History of Modern Japan
TOMIURA, E., International Economics
UI, T., Microeconomics
YAMAZAKI, K., Developing Economics, Brazilian Economy

Faculty of Education and Human Sciences (79-2 Tokiwadai, Hodogaya-ku, Yokohama 240-8501; tel. (45) 339-3253; fax (45) 339-3264; e-mail edu.somu@nuc.ynu.ac.jp; internet www.edhs.ynu.ac.jp):

ARAI, H., Educational Administration
ARAI, M., Mechanical Engineering
ARIMITSU, Y., History of Japan
BABA, Y., Operations Research
CHOMABAYASHI, T., Total Conditioning
EBIHARA, O., Sports Sociology
ETO, T., Geology
FENG, L., Ancient Chinese Language, Ancient Japanese, Chinese Language and Culture
FUJIMORI, T., Sculpture
FUKAWA, G., Teaching of Japanese as a Native Language
FUKUDA, S., Experimental Psychology
FUKUOKA, T., Teaching of Science
HARADA, H., Ecology
HARADA, M., Architecture
HASHIMOTO, Y., Teaching of Mathematics
HAYASHIBE, H., Psycholinguistics
HORI, M., Environmental Safety Engineering
HORI, N., Teaching of Art
IMOTO, S., European Culture
ISHIDA, J., Mathematics Education
KAGEYAMA, S., Social Studies
KANAI, Y., Gender Studies
KANAZAWA, H., Teaching Japanese as a Foreign Language
KANEKO, K., Food and Nutrition
KASAHARA, M., Cultural Anthropology
KIKUCHI, T., Biological Oceanography
KIMURA, M., Sports Methodology
KITAGAWA, Y., Human Rights
KOBAYASHI, K., Modern European Theology
KOBAYASHI, N., Formative Design
KOBAYASHI, Y., Special Education
KOIZUMI, H., Teaching Methods
MAEDA, M., Differential Geometry
MAJIMA, R., Palaeontology
MATSUISHI, T., Psychiatry and Neurology
MIYAKE, A., Japanese Literature in the 14th and 15th Centuries
MIYASAKA, M., Teaching of Art
MOCHIDA, Y., Plant Ecology
MORIMOTO, S., Teaching of Science
MORIMOTO, S., Physiology and Exercise Physiology
MOTEKI, K., Music Appreciation
MURATA, T., Modern Chinese History
MUTO, Y., Child Studies
MUROI, H., Aesthetics
NAGANAWA, M., History of Russian Thought
NAKAGAWA, T., Aural Rehabilitation
NAKAMURA, E., Analytical Chemistry
NEGAMI, S., Topology and Graph Theory
NEMOTO, M., German Literature and Culture
NISHIMURA, T., Consumer Affairs
NISHIWAKI, Y., Teaching of Geography
NUKATA, J., Computer-embedded Education
NUSHI, A., Educational Psychology
OCHIAI, M., Sports Psychology
OKADA, M., Classical Chinese Literature
OKADA, M., School Psychology
ONO, Y., Aesthetics
OOISHI, A., Commutative Ring Theory
OSHIMA, A., Educational Technology
OTAKI, F., Piano Music
SAKAI, Y., Computational Mechanics
SAKATA, S., Teaching English as a Foreign Language
SANO, H., Outdoor Recreation
SASAKI, H., Educational Systems
SATOH, Y., Plant Morphology
SHIROUZU, N., Modern Chinese Literature
SUGIYAMA, T., Piano Music
SUKAWA, H., Korean Economic History
SUZUKI, K., Geophysics
SUZUKI, T., Teaching of Home Economics
TAJIMA, F., Information Technology
TAKAGI, H., Adolescent Psychology
TAKAGI, M., Japanese as a Native Language Education
TAKAGI, N., Teaching Methodology
TAKAHASHI, K., Teaching of Dance
TAKAHASHI, K., English Linguistics
TAKAHASHI, M., Philosophy of Education
TAKAYAMA, Y., Special Education
TAKEZAWA, T., Electronics
TAKUSARI, D., Music Compostion
TAMAKI, Y., Animal Genetics and Physiology
TANAKA, H., Exercise and Environmental Physiology
TANEDA, Y., Developmental Biology
TANISHO, S., Biochemical Engineering
UMEMOTO, Y., French New Wave Cinema
WATABE, M., Sociology of Education
YAMAMOTO, I., Physics
YAMAMOTO, M., Special Education
YATA, S., Wood Science and Technology
YOKOYAMA, N., Physical Education

Faculty of Engineering (79-5 Tokiwadai, Hodogaya-ku, Yokohama 240-8501; tel. (45) 339-3804; fax (45) 339-3827; e-mail eng.somu@nuc.ynu.ac.jp; internet www.eng.ynu.ac.jp):

AMEMIYA, N., Electromagnetics of Superconductors
ANDO, K., Fracture Mechanics of Ceramics
AOKI, H., Design and Analysis of Steel Structures
ARAI, H., Electromagnetics
ARAI, M., Ship Design
ASAMI, M., Synthetic Organic Chemistry
AZUSHIMA, A., Tribology in Metal Forming
BABA, T., Semiconductor Layers
FUKUTOMI, H., Granular Boundary Phenomena, Texture and Microstructure Control
HABUKA, H., Chemical Engineering
HANEJI, N., Semiconductor Materials and Processing
HIRAYAMA, T., Dynamics of Ships and Offshore Structures in Waves
HIROSE, Y., Laser Applications, Opto-electronic Devices and Electronic Circuits
IGUCHI, E., Strongly Correlated Electron Systems
IMAI, G., Soil Mechanics and Geotechnical Engineering
ISHIHARA, O., Plasma Physics
ISHII, R., Digital Signal Processing and Digital Image Processing
KAMEMOTO, K., Unsteady and Separated Flow and Fluid Engineering
KAMINOYAMA, M., Rheology and Flow Fluids
KAMIYA, N., Industrial Electrochemistry
KAWAI, K., Metal Forming and Numerical Simulation
KAWAMURA, A., Power Electronics, Digital Control and Robotics
KIMISHIMA, Y., Low-Temperature Physics
KITADA, Y., Topology of Manifolds
KITAYAMA, K., Architecture Design
KOBAYASHI, K., Bioanalytical Chemistry
KOBAYASHI, S., City Planning and Housing
KOHNO, R., Information Theory
KOIZUMI, J., Bioengineering
KOKUBUN, Y., Photonic Integrated Circuits
KONNO, N., Interacting Particle Systems
KUROKAWA, J., Internal Flow and Performances of Fluid Machinery
MAEKAWA, T., Computer Aided Design and Manufacturing
MATSUMOTO, K., Biochemical Engineering
MIURA, K., Physical Metallurgy
MIZUGUCHI, J., Optical Properties of Organic Molecular Crystals
NAITOH, A., Biophysics, Structural Biology, Nuclear Magnetic Resonance Spectroscopy
NISHIMURA, S., High Voltage Engineering and Electric Power Engineering
NISHINO, K., Turbulence
OGAWA, T., Mechanism of Explosion Phenomena
OGINO, T., Surface Science and Nanotechnology of Semiconductors
OHARA, K., Theory of Architecture
OHNO, K., Computer Physics, Condensed Matter Theory, Nanoscale Science
OHTANI, H., Chemical Safety Engineering
OKUYAMA, K., Boiling Heat Transfer
ONO, T., Quantum Field Theory
OTA, K., Applied Electrochemistry
OYAMA, T., Electric Power Systems Engineering
SAKAKIBARA, K., Physical Organic Chemistry
SANADA, K., Power-Assisted Equipment for the Elderly
SASAKI, K., Elementary Particle Physics
SEKINE, K., Fracture of Materials
SHIBATA, M., Cosmic Ray Physics
SHIBAYAMA, T., Coastal Hydrodynamics
SHIRATORI, M., Strength of Materials
SUMI, Y., Structural Mechanics of Ships and Fracture Mechanics
SUZUKI, K., Numerical Ship Hydrodynamics
SUZUKI, K., Solid State Chemistry
TAGAWA, Y., Steel Structures
TAKADA, H., Mechanical Vibration
TAKAGI, J., Analysis of Grinding
TAKAHASHI, F., Space Geodesy (ULBI/GPS and Network Computing)
TAKANO, S., Information Theory and Applied Probability Analysis
TAKEDA, J., Solid State Physics
TAMANO, K., Topology
TAMURA, A., Environmental Psychology
TANAKA, H., Machine Design
TANAKA, M., Surface Physics
TANI, K., Geotechnical Engineering
TASAI, A., Reinforced Concrete Structures
TOMOI, M., Polymer Chemistry
TSUBAKI, T., Structural Mechanics, Concrete Engineering and Computational Mechanics
TSUBOI, T., Shock Tubes, Waves and Combustion
TSUKAMOTO, O., Application of Superconductivity and Electric Machine Control
UEDA, K., Polymer Solution Chemistry
UTAKA, Y., Thermal Engineering
WATANABE, M., Medical Engineering, Carcinogenesis and Pathology
WATANABE, M., Electrochemistry and Polymer Chemistry
YABUTA, T., Machine Intelligence
YAGI, M., Excited States of Molecules
YAKOU, T., Bauschinger Effect
YAMAGUCHI, M., Electromagnetism of Materials
YAMAZAKI, Y., Earthquake Engineering
YOKOYAMA, Y., Chemistry of Organic Photoresponsive Materials

YOSHIDA, K., History of European Architecture and Modern Architecture
YOSHIKAWA, N., Digital Integrated Circuit

Graduate School of Education (79-2 Tokiwadai, Hodogaya-ku, Yokohama 240-8501; tel. (45) 339-3253; fax (45) 339-3264; e-mail edu.somu@nuc.ynu.ac.jp; internet www.edhs.ynu.ac.jp):

INUZUKA, F., Extracurricular Activities

Faculty of Environmental and Information Sciences (79-7 Tokiwadai, Hodogaya-ku, Yokohama 240-8501; tel. (45) 339-4422; fax (45) 339-4430; e-mail env-inf.somu@nuc.ynu.ac.jp; internet www.eis.ynu.ac.jp/e/index.html):

ARIMA, M., Petrology
ARISAWA, H., Theory of Database and Knowledge Base Systems
FUJIWARA, K., Vegetation Science
GOTOH, T., Computer Graphics
HARA, T., Catalysis by Metal Complexes
HIRANO, N., Functional Analysis
HIRATSUKA, K., Molecular and Cellular Biology, Plant Pathology, Plant Physiology, Plant Biotechnology
INOUE, S., Synthetic Organic Chemistry
INOUE, Y., Design of Ships and Ocean Structures
ITOH, K., Environmental Physical Chemistry
KAGEI, S., Fuzzy Control
KANEKO, N., Soil Ecosystem
KONDO, M., Innovation Policy, Research and Development Management, Technology Strategy in Developing Countries
KUNIEDA, H., Surface and Solution Chemistry
MASUNAGA, S., Monitoring and Assessment of Environmental Pollution
MATSUDA, H., Risk Management
MATSUMOTO, T., Computation Theory
MEGURO, T., Inorganic Materials Ceramics
MITSUI, I., Local Economies and Small and Medium Enterprises (especially Comparative Studies of Policies in Japan and the EU)
MORISHITA, S., Vibration Control
NAGAO, T., Artificial Intelligence, Computer Vision
NAKAI, S., Environmental Epidemiology
NAKAMURA, F., Urban Transportation Planning
OHNO, K., Psytosociology
SADOHARA, S., Urban Environmental Planning
SASAMOTO, H., Plant Biotechnology, Plant Cell Engineering, Plant Cell and Tissue Culture, Plant Physiology
SHIDA, K., Mathematical Sociology
SHIGEOKA, T., Environmental Risk Management for Bio- and Ecosystems
SHUSA, Y., Globalization of Firms
SUZUKI, A., Chemical Physics
SUZUKI, K., Atmospheric Spectroscopy
TAMURA, N., Natural Language Processing
TERADA, T., Topology
UENO, S., Optimal Control of Flight Path
UESUGI, S., Bio-organic Chemistry
URANO, K., Evaluation Methods of Environmental Pollution
YAMADA, H., Structural Engineering

International Graduate School of Social Sciences (79-4 Tokiwadai, Hodogaya-ku, Yokohama 240-8501; tel. (45) 339-3602; fax (45) 339-3661; internet www.igss.ynu.ac.jp/index-e.htm):

ARAKI, I., International Economic Law
ARIE, D., History and Methodology of Social Science
DOI, H., Marxist Theory of Value
FUJIMORI, T., Industrial Psychology
GONJO, Y., Economic History of Modern France
HAMAMOTO, M., Accounting
HARADA, K., Constitutional Law
IKEDA, T., Development Assistance Programmes, Infrastructure Development
IMAMURA, Y., Civil Law
IWASAKI, M., Tax Law
KAMIKAWA, T., International Finance
KATO, M., Environmental Law
KAWABATA, Y., Tax Law
KAWASHIMA, K., General Civil and Commercial Practice
KIMIZUKA, M., Constitutional Law
KOBAYASHI, M., Econometric Theory
KOBAYASHI, M., Sociolinguistics
KOHDA, K., Macroeconomics
KOIKE, O., Comparative Public Policy
KURASAWA, M., Theory of Finance, Law and Economics
KURUSHIMA, T., Commercial Law
MATSUI, Y., Production and Operation Management
MORIKAWA, T., International Law
NAGAI, M., Criminal Law and Procedure
NAKAMURA, K., Regional and Local International Development
NAKANO, H., English Literature
NAKAMURA, Y., Linguistics
NEMOTO, Y., Private International Law
NOMURA, H., Civil Procedure Law
OKABE, J., Economic Statistics
OKUYAMA, K., Civil Law, Comparative Family Law, Latin-American Law
OSAWA, Y., Commercial Law
SAINO, H., Criminal Law
SAITO, S., Accounting
SANBE, N., Administrative Law
SATO, M., Criminal and Procedure Law
SUGIHARA, M., Financial, Commercial and Civil Law
SUMITA, K., Governmental and Nonprofit Accounting
TAKAHASHI, J., Civil Law, Land Law, Sociology Law
TAKAHASHI, M., Cost Accounting
TANAKA, M., Business Enterprise
TANAKA, T., Criminal Law
TASHIRO, Y., Agricultural Policy
TSUBURAYA, T., Contract Law
TOKUE, Y., Criminal and Procedure Law
UEMURA, H., Institutional Economics, Macroeconomics
USUI, I, Business Mathematics
YAMASHITA, S., National Accounting
YOO, H., International Law
YOSHIKAWA, T., Management Accounting

International Student Center (79-1 Tokiwadai, Hodogaya-ku, Yokohama 240-8501; tel. (45) 339-3186; fax (45) 339-3189; e-mail ryugakusei.center@nuc.ynu.ac.jp; internet www.isc.ynu.ac.jp):

ISHIKAWA, Y., Applied Surface Science, Industrial Ecology
KADOKURA, M., Japanese Studies
OGAWA, Y., Japanese Linguistics
YOMOTA, C., Japanese as a Second Language
YOSHIDA, S., Phonology, Linguistics

ATTACHED RESEARCH INSTITUTES

Center for Risk Management and Safety Sciences: 79-5 Tokiwadai, Hodogayaku, Yokohama; tel. (45) 339-3776; fax (45) 339-4294; e-mail anshin@ynu.ac.jp; internet www.anshin.ynu.ac.jp; Dir KAZUYOSHI SEKINE.

Cooperative Research and Development Center: 79-5 Tokiwadai, Hodogayaku, Yokohama; tel. (45) 339-4381; fax (45) 339-4387; e-mail cordec@nuc.ynu.ac.jp; internet www.crd.ynu.ac.jp; Dir SHIN MORISHITA.

Education Center: tel. (45) 339-3135; fax (45) 339-3141; e-mail kyomu.gakumu@nuc.ynu.ac.jp; internet www.yec.ynu.ac.jp; Dir KUNIO SUZUKI.

Health Service Center: tel. (45) 339-3153; fax (45) 339-3156; e-mail healths@nuc.ynu.ac.jp; internet www.hoken.ynu.ac.jp; Dir ETSUKO TANAKA.

Information Processing Center: Dir Y. MATSUI.

Instrumental Analysis Center: 79-5 Tokiwadai, Hodogayaku, Yokohama; tel. (45) 339-4406; fax (45) 339-4406; e-mail iac@nuc.ynu.ac.jp; internet www.iac.ynu.ac.jp; Dir YASUSHI YOKOHAMA.

Radio-Isotope (RI) Center: 79-5 Tokiwadai, Hodogayaku, Yokohama; tel. (45) 339-4410; fax (45) 339-4410; internet www.tech.ynu.ac.jp/%7Ecolombai/ricenter/index-j.html; Dir TOMOHIKO KIKUCHI.

Venture Business Laboratory: 79-5 Tokiwadai, Hodogayaku, Yokohama; tel. (45) 339-4280; fax (45) 339-4280; e-mail ec-kanri@ynu.ac.jp; internet www.vbl.ynu.ac.jp; Dir AKIHIRO TAMURA.>

Municipal Institutions

AOMORI UNIVERSITY OF HEALTH AND WELFARE

Mase 58-1 Hamadate, Aomori 030-8505
Telephone: (17) 765-2000
Fax: (17) 765-2188
E-mail: webmaster@auhw.ac.jp
Founded 1999
President: SACHIE SHINDO
Faculty of Health Sciences, including Nursing, Therapy and Social Welfare.

DAIDO INSTITUTE OF TECHNOLOGY

10-3 Takiharu-cho, Minami-ku, Nagoya
Internet: www.daido-it.ac.jp
Founded 1961
President: AKIRA SAWAOKA
Library of 170,000 vols
Number of teachers: 100
Number of students: 3,620
Schools of Informatics, Engineering, Liberal Arts and Sciences.

EDOGAWA UNIVERSITY

Komaki 474, Nagareyama-shi, Chiba-ken 270-0198
Telephone: (4) 7152-0661
Fax: (4) 7154-2490
E-mail: webmaster@edogawa-u.ac.jp
Internet: www.edogawa-u.ac.jp
Founded 1990
College of Sociology.

FUJI WOMEN'S UNIVERSITY

Kita 16-jo Nishi 2, Kita-ku, Sapporo-shi, Hokkaido 001-0016
Telephone: (11) 736-0311
Fax: (11) 709-8541
E-mail: somu@fujijoshi.ac.jp
Internet: www.fujijoshi.ac.jp
Founded 1961
President: YOSHIKO NAGATA
Library of 300,000 vols
Number of teachers: 89
Number of students: 2,250
Faculties of Humanities, Life Sciences.

FUJITA HEALTH UNIVERSITY

1-98 Dengakugakubo, Kutsukake-cho, Toyoake, Aichi-ken 470-1192
Telephone: (562) 93-2504
Fax: (562) 93-4595

Founded 1964
President: TAKAHIKO FUNABIKI
Library of 172,000 vols
Faculties of Medical Technology, Nursing, Radiological Technology, Rehabilitation.

FUKUI UNIVERSITY OF TECHNOLOGY

3-6-1 Gakuen, Fukui City, Fukui 910-8505
Telephone: (776) 22-8111
Fax: (776) 29-7891
E-mail: kouhou@ccmails.fukui-ut.ac.jp
President: Dr MASANOBU MIYAKE
Number of teachers: 160
Departments of Electrical and Electronic Engineering, Mechanical Engineering, Architecture and Civil Engineering, Environmental and Biotechnological Frontier Engineering, Management Science, Space Communication Engineering.

FUKUOKA INSTITUTE OF TECHNOLOGY

3-30-1 Wajiro-Higashi, Higashi-ku, Fukuoka 811-0295
Telephone: (92) 606-3131
Fax: (92) 606-8923
E-mail: www-staff@fit.ac.jp
Internet: www.fit.ac.jp
President: KAZUO AOKI
Faculties of Engineering, Information Engineering, Social and Environmental Studies.

FUKUSHIMA MEDICAL UNIVERSITY

1 Hikariga-oka, Fukushima City 960-1295
Telephone: (24) 547-1111
Fax: (24) 547-1995
E-mail: sshigeta@fmu.ac.jp
Internet: www.fmu.ac.jp
Founded 1950
Academic year: April to March
President: SHIRO SHIGETA
Director of Library: T. SUZUKI
Secretary: Y. YOSHIDA
Hospital Director: S. NIWA
Library of 138,738 vols
Number of teachers: 330
Number of students: 820
Publications: *Fukushima Igaku Zasshi* (Fukushima Medical Journal, 4 a year), *Fukushima Journal of Medical Science* (2 a year)
Faculty of medicine, faculty of nursing, postgraduate research institute, hospital

DEANS

School of Medicine: HIDEO KOCHI
School of Nursing: YOKO NAKAYAMA

GIFU PHARMACEUTICAL UNIVERSITY

5-6-1, Mitahora-higashi, 5-chome, Gifu 502-8585
Telephone: (58) 237-3931
Fax: (58) 237-5979
E-mail: goto@gifu-pu.ac.jp
Internet: www.gifu-pu.ac.jp
Founded 1932
Municipal Control
Academic year: April to March
President: Prof. MASAYUKI KUZUYA
Chief Administrative Officer: TAKASHI SHINODA
Library Director: Prof. HIROICHI NAGAI
Library of 59,000 vols
Number of teachers: 70
Number of students: 649
Publications: *Proceedings* (annually), *Bulletin of Liberal Arts*

DEANS

Faculty of Pharmaceutical Science: Prof. KAZUYUKI HIRANO
Faculty of Manufacturing Pharmacy: Prof. TADASHI KATAOKA

PROFESSORS

FURUKAWA, S., Molecular Biology
GOTO, M., Pharmaceutical Analytical Chemistry
HARA, A., Biochemistry
HIRANO, K., Pharmaceutics
HIROTA, K., Medicinal Chemistry
INOUE, K., Pharmacognosy
KATAOKA, T., Pharmaceutical Chemistry
KAWASHIMA, Y., Pharmaceutical Engineering
KUZUYA, M., Pharmaceutical Physical Chemistry
MASAKI, Y., Pharmaceutical Synthetic Chemistry
MORI, H., Microbiology
NAGAI, H., Pharmacology
NAGASE, H., Hygienics

HACHINOHE INSTITUTE OF TECHNOLOGY

88-1 Ohbiraki Myo, Hachinohe, Aomori 031-8501
Telephone: (178) 25-3111
E-mail: www-admin@hi-tech.ac.jp
Founded 1972
President: SANKICHI TAKAHASHI
Library of 100,000 vols
Number of students: 5,000
Faculties of Mechanical Systems on Information Technology, Electronic Intelligence and Systems, Environmental and Civil Engineering, Architectural Engineering, Chemical Engineering on Biological Environments, System and Information Engineering, Liberal Arts and Technology.

HAKUOH UNIVERSITY

1117 Daigyoji, Oyama City, Tochigi Prefecture 323-8585
Telephone: (285) 22–1111
Fax: (285) 22-8989
E-mail: nyuushi@hakuoh.ac.jp
Internet: www.hakuoh.ac.jp
Founded 1915
Number of students: 3,000
Library of 136,000 vols
Faculties of Business Management and Law.

HAKUSEI GAKUEN UNIVERSITY

2-3-1 Ohyachi-nishi, Atsubetsu-ku, Sapporo-shi, Hokkaido 004-8631
Telephone: (11) 891-2731
Fax: (11) 894-3690
E-mail: soumu@hokusei.ac.jp
Founded 1962
President: HIROSHI OHTOMO
Dean (Curriculum and Academic Affairs): HIDEHITO YONEMOTO
Dean (Student Affairs): HIRONORI YAMAGUCHI
Dean (Media and Information Affairs): TOSHIYUKI KATAYAMA
Chief Administrative Officer: AKIRA SAKAI
Number of teachers: 137
Number of students: 4,177

DEANS

School of Humanities: TADAO NOGUCHI
School of Economics: SHIN'ICHI TAMURA
School of Social Welfare: NAOTO SUGIOKA

HAMAMATSU UNIVERSITY SCHOOL OF MEDICINE

3600 Handa-cho, Hamamatsu City 431-3192
Telephone: (53) 435-2111
Fax: (53) 433-7290
E-mail: staff@hama-med.ac.jp
Internet: www.hama-med.ac.jp
Founded 1974
Number of teachers: 273
Medical school.

HANNAN UNIVERSITY

5-4-3 Amami, Higashi, Matsubara, Osaka 580-8502
Telephone: (72) 332-1224
E-mail: webmaster@hannan-u.ac.jp
Internet: www.hannan-u.ac.jp
Founded 1965
President: SHINICHI OTSUKI
Faculties of Business, Economics, Management Information, International Communication.

HEALTH SCIENCES UNIVERSITY OF HOKKAIDO

Ishikari-Tobetsu, Hokkaido 061-0293
Telephone: (1332) 3-1211
Fax: (1332) 3-1669
E-mail: soumuka@hoku-iryo-u.ac.jp
Founded 1974
Library of 145,000 vols
Number of students: 2,400
Faculty of Pharmaceutical Sciences.

HIMEJI INSTITUTE OF TECHNOLOGY

2167 Shosha, Himeji City, Hyogo 671-2201
Telephone: (792) 66-1661
Fax: (792) 66-8868
E-mail: www-adm@cnth.himeji-tech.ac.jp
Internet: www.himeji-tech.ac.jp
Founded 1944 as Hyogo Prefectural Special College of Technology, 1949 under present name
Academic year: April to March
President: TADAO HAKUSHI
Dean of Students: HIROSHI NAKAYAMA
Director of Administration: TOSHIAKI SUZUKI
Library Director: HIDEHIKO NAKANO
Library of 173,000 vols
Number of teachers: 354
Number of students: 3,222
Publication: *Reports of Himeji Institute of Technology* (annually)

DEANS

Faculty of Engineering: MOTOYOSHI HASEGAWA
Faculty of Science: SHIGERU TERABE
School of Humanities for Environmental Policy and Technology: JUNJI KIHARA
Department of General Education: YASUKAGE ODA

ATTACHED INSTITUTES

Institute of Natural and Environmental Sciences: Dir AKINORI NAKANISHI.

Laboratory of Advanced Science and Technology for Industry: Dir HARUSIGE TSUBAKINO.

HOSHI UNIVERSITY

2-4-41 Ebara, Shinagawa, Tokyo 142-8501
Telephone: (3) 5498-5821
Fax: (3) 3787-0036
E-mail: www@hoshi.ac.jp
Internet: www.hoshi.ac.jp
Library of 85,000 vols

Number of students: 1,200
Faculty of Pharmaceutical Sciences.

IWATE PREFECTURAL UNIVERSITY

152-52 Takizawa-aza-sugo, Takizawa, Iwate 020-0193
Telephone: (19) 694-2012
Fax: (19) 694-2011
E-mail: Kyoumu@m1.iwate-pu.ac.jp
Founded 1988
President: JUNICHI NISHIZAWA
Vice-President: TETSUO TSUKAMOTO

DEANS

Faculty of Nursing: YURIKO KENMATSU
Faculty of Social Welfare: TAKESHI TAKAZAWA
Faculty of Software and Information Science: MASATOSHI MIYAZAKI
Faculty of General Policy: NOBORU HOSOYA

KITAKYUSHU UNIVERSITY

4-2-1 Kitagata, Kokuraminami-ku, Kitakyushu-shi, Fukuoka 802-8577
Telephone: (93) 962-1837
E-mail: shomu@kitakyu-u.ac.jp
Internet: www.kitakyu-u.ac.jp
Founded 1946, university status 1950
Library of 379,000 vols
Number of students: 5,456.

KOBE CITY UNIVERSITY OF FOREIGN STUDIES

9-1 Gakuen-higashi-machi, Nishi-ku, Kobe 673
Telephone: (78) 794-8111
E-mail: www-admin@kobe-cufs.ac.jp
Internet: www.kobe-cufs.ac.jp
Founded 1946
President: YOSHIO YUKIDA
Registrar: YOSHIO WATANABE
Librarian: SUSUMU KURANAKA
Library of 353,800 vols
Number of teachers: 98
Number of students: 2,000.

KOBE UNIVERSITY OF COMMERCE

Gakuen-nishimachi, Nishi-ku, Kobe 651-2197
Telephone: (78) 794-6161
Fax: (78) 794-6166
E-mail: shomuka@kobuec.ac.jp
Internet: www.kobeuc.ac.jp/index_e.htm
Founded 1929
State control
Language of instruction: Japanese
Academic year: April to March
President: YASUO SAKAMOTO
Registrar: NOBUHIDE FUJIWARA
Librarian: KENTARO NOMURA
Library of 406,000 vols
Number of teachers: 103
Number of students: 2,050

HEADS OF DEPARTMENTS

Economics: Prof. H. OKAMOTO
Business Administration: Prof. S. TORIBE
Management Science: Prof. M. FUJISAKI
Marketing and International Business: Prof. N. KAWANABE
Graduate schools of economics, business administration and management science

KUMAMOTO PREFECTURAL UNIVERSITY

3-1-100 Tsukide, Kumamoto City 862-8502
Telephone: (96) 383-2929
Fax: (96) 384-6765
E-mail: www-admin@pu-kumamoto.ac.jp
Internet: www.pu-kumamoto.ac.jp
Founded 1947
Library of 250,000 vols
Faculties of Letters, Environmental and Symbiotic Sciences, Administration, Cultural Studies.

KYOTO PREFECTURAL UNIVERSITY OF MEDICINE

465 Kajii-cho, Kawaramachi, Hirokoji, Kamikyo-ku, Kyoto 602-8566
Telephone: (75) 251-5111
E-mail: kikaku01@koto.kpu-m.ac.jp
Internet: www.kpu-m.ac.jp
Founded 1873
President: IBATA YASUHIKO
Dean of Students: MARUNAKA YOSHINORI
Director of University Hospital: YAMAGISHI HISAKAZU
Director of Library: NISHIMURA TSUNEHIKO
Library of 218,000 vols
Number of teachers: 304
Number of students: 649 undergraduate, 193 postgraduate
Publication: *Kyoto Furitsu Ikadaigaku Zasshi* (Journal)

DEANS

Faculty of Culture and Education: M. SANO
College of Medical Technology: T. REIKO
Graduate School: F. SHINJI

KYOTO SANGYO UNIVERSITY

Motoyama, Kamigamo, Kita-ku, Kyoto City 603-8555
Telephone: (75) 705-1408
Fax: (75) 705-1409
E-mail: info-adm@star.kyoto-su.ac.jp
Internet: www.kyoto-su.ac.jp
Founded 1965
President: TOYOH SAKAI
Number of teachers: 561
Number of students: 13,254
Faculties of Business Administration, Cultural Studies, Economics, Engineering, Foreign Languages, Law, Science.

KYUSHU SANGYO UNIVERSITY

3-1 Matsukadai 2-chome, Higashi-ku, Fukuoka 813-8503
Telephone: (92) 673-5050
Fax: (92) 673-5599
Internet: www.ip.kyusan-u.ac.jp
Founded 1960
Chairman: NARASAKI KENJIRO
President: UDAGAWA NORITO
Library of 712,310 vols
Number of teachers: 330
Number of students: 15,200
Faculties of Economics, Commerce, Management, Engineering, Fine Arts, International Culture, Information Science.

NAGANO UNIVERSITY

Shimonogo 658-1, Ueda-shi, Nagano-ken 386-1298
Telephone: (268) 39-0001
Fax: (268) 39-0002
E-mail: kouhou@nagano.ac.jp
Founded 1966
President: YOSHINORI IDE
Library of 127,000 vols
Number of teachers: 120
Number of students: 1,656
Faculties of Social Science and Social Welfare.

NAGASAKI PREFECTURAL UNIVERSITY

123 Kawashimo-cho, Sasebo-shi, Nagasaki-ken 858-8580
Telephone: (956) 47-2191
Fax: (956) 47-6941
Founded 1967
Departments of Economics and Distribution.

NAGOYA CITY UNIVERSITY

1 Kawasumi, Mizuho-cho, Mizuho-ku, Nagoya
Telephone: (52) 841-6201
Fax: (52) 841-6201
E-mail: admin@cc.nagoya-cu.ac.jp
Internet: www.nagoya-cu.ac.jp
Founded 1950
President: YOSHIRO WADA
Secretary-General: S. ISOBE
Library Director: S. SAITO
Library of 502,973 vols
Number of teachers: 536
Number of students: 3,500
Publications: *Nagoya Medical Journal* (quarterly, English), *Annual Report of the Faculty of Pharmaceutical Sciences, NCU* (Japanese), *Oikonomika* (quarterly, Japanese)

DEANS

Medical School: M. SASAKI
Faculty of Pharmaceutical Sciences: H. IKEZAWA
Faculty of Economics: Y. NAITO
School of Humanities and Social Sciences: T. KIDO
School of Design and Architecture: T. YANAGISAWA

OSAKA CITY UNIVERSITY

3-3-138, Sugimoto, Sumiyoshi-ku, Osaka 558-8585
Telephone: (6) 6605-3453
Fax: (6) 6605-2058
E-mail: okamoto@ado.osaka-cu.ac.jp
Internet: www.osaka-cu.ac.jp
Founded 1949
Academic year: April to March
President: T. KODAMA
Vice-Presidents: T. KAJIURA N. SOURI
Secretary-General: T. KOHNO
Dean of Bureau for Students' Affairs: K. NAKAGAWA
Dean of Bureau for Admissions and Education: Y. MIYAMOTO
Dir of Media Centre: TAKEO MATSUDA
Library of 2,000,000 books, 9,000 periodicals
Number of teachers: 895
Number of students: 8,676
Publications: *Business Review* (annually), *Journal of Economics* (4 a year), *Economic Review* (6 a year), *Journal of Law and Politics* (4 a year), *Studies in the Humanities* (annually), *Osaka Journal of Mathematics* (4 a year), *Journal of Geosciences*, *Memoirs of the Faculty of Engineering* (annually), *Osaka City Medical Journal* (2 a year), *Quarterly Journal of Economic Studies* (4 a year)

DEANS

Graduate School and Faculty of Business: OSAMI TOMIZAWA
Graduate School and Faculty of Economics: H. SATO
Graduate School and Faculty of Law: T. MATSUDA

Graduate School and Faculty of Literature and Humanities: H. SAKAGUCHI
Graduate School and Faculty of Science: T. KAMAE
Graduate School and Faculty of Engineering: T. FUKUDA
Graduate School and Faculty of Human Life Science: S. TOGASHI
Graduate School of Medicine and Medical School: S. OTANI
College of Nursing: M. NAGAYAMA

ATTACHED INSTITUTES

Research Center for Finance and Securities: Dir K. FURUSAWA.
University Hospital: Dir S. OGITA.
Institute for Health and Sport Sciences: Dir T. HAZAMA.
Research Center for Human Rights: Dir M. NOGUCHI.
Media Center: Dir T. MATSUDA.

OSAKA GAKUIN UNIVERSITY

2-36-1 Kishibe-Minami, Suita-shi, Osaka 564-8511
Telephone: (6) 6381-8434
Fax: (6) 6382-4363
E-mail: www-admin@uta.osaka-gu.ac.jp
Internet: www.osaka-gu.ac.jp
President: YOSHIYASU SHIRAI
Library of 720,000 vols
Faculties of Distribution and Communication Sciences, Administrative Sciences, Economics, Law, Foreign Languages, International Studies, Informatics, Corporate Intelligence.

OSAKA PREFECTURE UNIVERSITY

1-1 Gakuen-cho, Sakai, Osaka 599-8531
Telephone: (72) 252-1161
Fax: (72) 254-9900
Internet: www.osakafu-u.ac.jp
Founded 1949 as Naniwa University; present name 1955
Prefectural control
Academic year: April to March
President: TSUTOMU MINAMI
Administrator: TOSHIHIKO HONDA
Director of Library and Science Information Centre: YOJI HIMENO
Library of 1,072,033 vols
Number of teachers: 871
Number of students: 6,332
Publications: *Journal of Economics, Business and Law*, *British and American Language and Culture*, *DMSIS Research Report*

DEANS

College of Agriculture: MITSUNORI KIRIHATA
College of Economics: KATSUHIRO MIYAMOTO
College of Engineering: YOJI TAKEDA
College of Integrated Arts and Sciences: SIGEMITSU NAKANISI
College of Social Welfare: YOICHI DOI

ATTACHED INSTITUTE

Research Institute for Advanced Science and Technology: Dir TAKAAKI DOMARU.

SAPPORO MEDICAL UNIVERSITY

Nishi 17-chome, Minami 1-jo, Chuo-ku, Sapporo, Hokkaido 060
Telephone: (11) 611-2111
Fax: (11) 612-5861
E-mail: info@sapmed.ac.jp
Internet: www.sapmed.ac.jp
Founded 1945 as Hokkaido Prefectural School of Medicine; became Sapporo Medical College 1950; present name 1993
Academic year: April to March
President: A. YACHI
Chief Administrative Officer: M. WATANABE
Librarian: S. URASAWA
Library of 214,000 vols
Number of teachers: 373
Number of students: 1,026
Publication: *Sapporo Igaku Zassi* (Sapporo Medical Journal, with English summaries, 6 a year)

DEANS

School of Health Sciences: T. SATO
School of Medicine: M. MORI

ATTACHED INSTITUTES

Cancer Research Institute: Dir K. FUJINAGA.
Marine Biomedical Institute: Dir M. MORI.

SHIMONOSEKI UNIVERSITY

2-1-1 Daigakucho, Shimonoseki City, Yamaguchi Prefecture 751-8510
Telephone: (832) 52-0288
Fax: (832) 52-8099
E-mail: www-admin@shimonoseki-cu.ac.jp
Internet: www.shimonoseki-cu.ac.jp
Founded 1962
Library of 171,200 vols
Number of students: 2,270
Schools of Economics and International Commerce.

TOKYO METROPOLITAN UNIVERSITY

Minami-Ohsawa 1-1, Hachioji-shi, Tokyo 192-0397
Telephone: (426) 77-1111
Fax: (426) 77-1221
Internet: www.metro-u.ac.jp
Founded 1949
Municipal control
Language of instruction: Japanese
Academic year: April to March (two terms)
President: K. OGIUE
Director of Administrative Bureau: T. MORUOKA
Librarian: M. MAEDA
Library: see Libraries and Archives
Number of teachers: 646
Number of students: 6,540
Publications: *Bulletin* (annually), *Gakuhou* (2 a year), *Daigakuhiroba* (6 a year)

DEANS

Faculty of Social Sciences and Humanities: SATORU NAGUMO
Faculty of Law: MASAHIDE MAEDA
Faculty of Economics: TOSHINAO NAKATSUKA
Faculty of Science: HIDEYUKI SATO
Faculty of Engineering: KOHEI SUZUKI
Center for Urban Studies: TOSHIHIKO MOGI

PROFESSORS

Faculty of Social Sciences and Humanities:
EBARA, Y., Theoretical Sociology
FUKUI, A., French Philosophy
FUKUMA, K., Modern English Poetry
FUKUMOTO, Y., German Linguistics
FUKUSHIMA, F., African Literature
HARA, K., European Culture
HIRAI, H., Modern Chinese Literature
ICHIHARA, S., Psychology of Perception
IDE, H., English Novels
INADA, A, Classical Literature
INUI, A., Secondary Education and Educational Practice
ISHIHARA, K., Family Studies, Social Research
ISHIKAWA, T., French Philosophy of the 17th Century
ISHINO, K., French Semantics
ITO, C., English Novels
JIN, K., Comparative Linguistics
JITSUKAWA, T., French Philosophy
KAI, H., Ethics
KANZAKI, S., Ancient Greek Philosophy
KATO, M., Modern English Poetry
KIMURA, M., Ancient Korean History
KISHI, Y., German Literature
KOBAYASHI, K., History of Japanese Language
KOBAYASHI, R., Social Studies and Administration
KOTANI, H., Indian History
KUROSAKI, I., Educational Administration
MANZAWA, M., Modern German Literature
MOGI, T., Educational Psychology
MORIOKA, K., Urban Sociology, Comparative Sociology
MURAYAMA, K., American Novels
NAGAI, T., Clinical Psychology
NAGUMO, S., Modern Chinese Literature
NAKAJIMA, H., Theoretical Linguistics
NAKANO, T., Modern French History
NARASAKI, H., Contemporary American Novel
NISHIKAWA, N., French Poetry of the 19th Century
OCHIAI, M., Chinese Dialectology
OGINO, T., Sociolinguistics
OHGUSHI, R., Adult Education
OKABE, H., Modern German Literature
OKABE, T., Social Welfare System
OKADA, E., History of Social Welfare
OKADA, M., Middle French Literature
OKADA, N., German Philosophy
OKAZAWA, S., Contemporary German Literature
OKUBO, Y., French Literature of the 16th Century
OKUMURA, S., Capitalism in Pre-communist China
ONO, A., Archaeology
ORISHIMA, M., American Novels
OTSUKA, K., Social Anthropology
PEARSON, H. E., Applied Linguistics, TESOL
SATAKE, Y., Federal Chinese History
SATO, S., Chinese Philology
SEO, I., German Literature of the 20th Century
SOEDA, A., Social Methodology
SUDA, O., Developmental Study of Communication
SUZUKI, T., Contemporary Austrian Literature
TAKAHASHI, K., Political Sociology
TAKAYAMA, H., English Poetry of the 18th Century
TANJI, N., Philosophy of Science
UENO, Y., Shakespearian Studies
WATANABE, Y., Social Anthropology
YASUDA, T., Reading Process Research
YOSHIKAWA, K., French Literature of the 20th century

Faculty of Law:
ASAKURA, M., Labour Law, Social Security Law
FUCHI, M., European Legal History
HITOMI, T., Decentralization and Local Autonomy
IKEDA, T., Civil Law, Law of Land Property
ISHIDA, A., Domestic Politics and International Politics
ISHII, M., Civil Law, Medical Law
ISHIKAWA, K., Constitutional Law
ISOBE, T., Administrative Law
KIMURA, M., Criminal Law
MAEDA, M., Criminal Law
MIYAMURA, H., History of Japanese Political Thought

MIZUBAYASHI, T., Japanese Legal History
MORIYAMA, S., East Asian Politics
MORITA, A., Outside Application of National Control
NAKAJIMA, H., Civil Procedure
NAWATA, Y., Philosophy of Law
NOGAMI, K., Political History of Western Countries
NOMURA, Y., Civil Law, Environmental Law
SHIBUYA, T., Commercial Law, Intellectual Property Law, Competition Law

Faculty of Economics:
ASANO, H., Marketing Science
ASANO, S., Econometrics
CHIBA, J., Financial Accounting
FUKAGAI, Y., History of Economic Thought
FUKUSHIMA, T., Public Economics, International Economics
HIGANO, M., Money and Banking
KANAYA, S., Fiscal and Monetary Policy
KUWATA, K., Management Strategy
MIYAKAWA, A., Marxian Economic Theory, History of Economic Thought
MURAKAMI, N., Chinese Enterprise Location
NAKAMURA, J., Labour Economics
NAKATSUKA, T., Business Administration, Operations Research
OMORI, Y., Econometrics
TODA, H., Econometrics
WAKITA, S., Japanese Labour Market
YAGO, K., French Economic History
YAMATO, T., Distribution Mechanism
YAMAZAKI, S., Distribution Policy

Faculty of Science:
ABE, T., Physical Training
ACHIBA, Y., Laser Chemistry
AIHARA, Y., Ageing and Temperature Regulation
EBIHARA, M., Space Chemistry
FUKUSAWA, H., Classical Oceanography
GUEST, M., Geometry
HIROSE, T., Experimental High-Energy Physics
HISANAGA, S., Cell Biology
HORI, N., Environmental Geography
HUYAMA, Y., Genetics
IKEMOTO, I., Solid State Chemistry
IMANAKA, K., Human Motor Behaviour, Perception and Motor Control
ISOBE, T., Biological Chemistry
ISOZAKI, H., Partial Differential Equations
IWATA, S., Glacial Geomorphology
IYODA, M., Organic Chemistry
IZAWA, T., Biochemistry and Physiology of Exercise
KACHI, N., Botanical Ecology
KAINOSHO, M., Biochemistry
KAMIGATA, N., Organic Chemistry
KAMISHIMA, Y., Topology
KATADA, M., Physical Inorganic Chemistry and Radiochemistry
KATO, T., Physical Chemistry
KIKUCHI, T., Topography
KOBAYASHI, N., Atomic and Molecular Physics (Experimental)
KOMANO, T., Molecular Genetics
KORANAGA, T., Micro-nano System
KOUGI, M., Neutron Scattering and Solid State Physics
KUWASAWA, K., Neurobiology
MIKAMI, T., Climatology, Climate Change, Urban Climate
MINAKATA, H., High-energy Physics
MIYAHARA, T., Solid State Spectroscopy
MIYAKE, K., Number Theory
MIZOGUCHI, K., Solid State Physics and Magnetic Resonance
MOCHIZUKI, K., Partial Differential Equations
NAKAMURA, K., Algebraic Number Theory and Algorithms
OHASHI, T., X-ray Astronomy
OHNITA, Y., Differential Geometry and Lie Groups
OKA, M., Singularity Theory and Algebraic Geometry
OKABE, Y., Theoretical Condensed-Matter Physics
OKADA, M., Harmonious Analysis
OKUNO, K., Atomic Physics
PRICE, W. S., Biochemistry
SAITO, S., Elementary Particle Basic Theory
SAKAI, M., Analytic Functions
SATO, H., Electron Theory of Metals
SHIMADA, K., Bacteriology
SUGIURA, Y., Human Geography
SUZUKI, T., Atomic Nuclear Physics
TAKII, S., Microbial Ecology
TERAO, H., Singularities and Combinatorics
WADA, M., Photobiology
WAKABAYASHI, M., Systematic Botany
WATANABE, Y., Aquatic Ecology
YAMASAKI, H., Seismo-tectonics, Quaternary Geology
YAMASAKI, T., Systematic Zoology
YASUGI, S., Developmental Biology
YOMASHITA, M., Inorganic Chemistry

Faculty of Engineering:
ANDO, Y., River Engineering, Applied Hydrology
ASAKO, Y., Heat and Mass Transfer
CHIKAZAWA, M., Physical Chemistry of Solid Surfaces
FUKAO, S., Building Construction
FURUKAWA, Y., Precision Machining and Computer-Aided Manufacturing Systems
HOBO, T., Analytical Chemistry and Instrumental Analysis
IGOSHI, M., Computer-Aided Design and Manufacturing
IKUTA, S., Parallel Algorithms
INOUE, H., Physical Organic Photochemistry
ISHIKAWA, H., E-business Model and Database
ISHINO, H., Building Service Engineering
ITO, D., Superconductors and their Applications
IWASAKI, K., Computer Architecture
IWATATE, T., Geomechanics
IYODA, T., Molecular Functional Materials
KATAKURA, M., Traffic Engineering and Infrastructure Planning
KAWAI, T., Organic Chemistry
KAWATA, S., Control Engineering
KIMURA, G., Electrical Machinery and Power Electronics
KIYA, T., Digital Signal Management
KITSUTAKA, Y., Building Material Engineering
KOBAYASHI, K., Architectural Theory and Design
KOIZUMI, A., Sanitary Engineering
KOKUBU, K., Concrete Technology
MAEDA, K., Bridge and Structural Engineering
MASUDA, H., Electrical Chemistry
MISAWA, H., Strength of Materials
MORIYA, T., Applications of Ultrasonics
NAGAHAMA, K., Chemical Engineering, Phase Equilibrium and Related Properties
NAGAOKA, S., Functional Materials
NAGASAWA, S., Applications of Lasers and Remote Sensing
NAKAMURA, I., Robotics and Mechatronics
NISHIKAWA, T., Structural Engineering
NISHIMURA, K., Geomechanics
NISHIMURA, H., Plasticity and New Materials Processing
OKUMURA, T., Semiconductor Physics, Optoelectric Devices
OTA, M., Power Engineering
SAKAKI, T., Strength of Metals and Alloys
SEKIMOTO, H., Piezo-electrical Vibrations and their applications
SUZUKI, K., Structural Dynamics
TAKAMIZAWA, K., City Planning
TAKI, M., Bioelectromagnetics, Noise Control Engineering
UENO, J., Architectural Planning
UMEGAKI, T., Ceramics, Inorganic Phosphate Chemistry
UMEYAMA, M., Water Environmental Engineering
WATANABE, K., Hydrodynamics, Hydraulic Machinery
WATANABE, T., Environment and Energy Saving
YAMADA, M., Chemical Sensing and Instrumentation
YAMAGISHI, T., Synthetic Organic Chemistry
YAMAZAKI, S., Structural Engineering
YOKOYAMA, R., Control and Optimization of Large-Scale Systems
YOSHIBA, M., High Temperature Material

Center for Urban Studies:
AKIYAMA, T., City Transportation Planning
HAGAI, M., Comparative Urban Public Administration
HAGIHARA, K., Urban and Regional Economics
HOSHI, T., Health Science
MATSUMOTO, Y., Social Network Theory
NAKABAYASHI, I., Urban Geography and City Planning
TAMAGAWA, H., Urban Space Analysis

WAKAYAMA MEDICAL UNIVERSITY

811-1 Kimiidera Wakayama City 641-8509
Telephone: (73) 447-2300
E-mail: admin@wakayama-med.ac.jp
Internet: www.wakayama-med.ac.jp

Founded 1945

President: HIROYUKI YAMAMOTO

Library of 63,250 vols
Number of teachers: 260
Number of students: 399

Publications: *Wakayama Igaku* (in Japanese, 4 a year), *Wakayama Medical Reports* (in English, 4 a year).

YOKOHAMA CITY UNIVERSITY

22-2 Seto, Kanazawa-ku, Yokohama 236-0027
Telephone: (45) 787-2311
Fax: (45) 787-2316
E-mail: netadmin@yokohama-cu.ac.jp
Internet: www.yokohama-cu.ac.jp

Founded 1928
Municipal control
Academic year: April to March

Chancellor and President: KEICHI OGAWA
Chief Administrative Officer: ROKUROU TAKAI
Library Director: MASATAKA OZAKI

Library of 677,610 vols
Number of teachers: 640
Number of students: 5,480

Publications: *Yokohama Shiritu Daigaku Ronso* (Bulletin, 8 a year), *Yokohama Shiritu Daigaku Kiyo* (Journal, annually), *Keizai-to-Boeki* (Industry and Trade, 2 a year), *Yokohama Medical Bulletin* (English, annually), *Yokohama Igaku* (Medical Journal, 6 a year), *Yokohama Mathematical Journal* (English, 2 a year)

DEANS

Faculty of Economics and Business Administration: KAWAUCHI YOSHITADA
Faculty of Humanities and International Studies: FUNIO KANEKO
Faculty of Science: MAKI KUNISUKE
School of Medicine: OKUDA KENJI

ATTACHED INSTITUTES

Economics Research Institute: Dir MASATO OKA.

Kihara Biological Research: Dir HIDEKI KOYAMA.

University Hospital (at Fukuura): Dir HARA MASAMICHI.

University Hospital (at Urafune): Dir SUGIYAMA MITUGI.

Private Universities and Colleges

AICHI UNIVERSITY

1-1 Machihata-cho, Toyohashi-shi, Aichi-ken 441-8522

Telephone: (532) 47-4131
Fax: (532) 47-4144
E-mail: inted@aichi-u.ac.jp
Internet: www.aichi-u.ac.jp

Founded 1946
Academic year: April to March

President: NOBUTERU TAKEDA
Registrar: MASASHI WATANABE
Librarian: MITSUSHI TAMAKI

Library of 1,458,362 vols
Number of teachers: 714 (254 full-time, 460 part-time)
Number of students: 10,084

DEANS

Faculty of Business Administration: TATSUHISA MINAMI
Faculty of Economics: MOTOHIKO SATO
Faculty of International Communication: KENICHI TAMOTO
Faculty of Law: KOUJI SHINDO
Faculty of Letters: MASAYOSHI KATANO
Faculty of Modern Chinese Studies: SATOSHI IMAI
Graduate School of Business Administration: MITSUO FUJIMOTO
Graduate School of Chinese Studies: TSUYOSHI BABA
Graduate School of Economics: KOICHI MIYAIRI
Graduate School of Humanities: KAZUYOSHI SHIMIZU
Graduate School of International Communication: SHIN KOUNO
Graduate School of Law: KATSUYOSHI KATO
Junior College: TAKAO KUROYANAGI

ATTACHED INSTITUTES

Community Research Institute: Dir Dr SHOICHIRO ARIZONO.

Comprehensive Chinese–Japanese Dictionary Editing Centre: Dir SATORU ABE.

Institute of International Affairs: Dir MASAHIRO MIYOSHI.

Institute of Managerial Research: Dir HIROYOSHI KOUZO.

International Centre for Chinese Studies: Dir MITSUYUKI KAGAMI.

Research Institute of Industry in Chubu District: Dir YOSHIHARU HIGUCHI.

AICHI GAKUIN UNIVERSITY

Araike, Iwasaki-cho, Nisshin-shi, Aichi-gun, Aichi-ken 470-0195

Telephone: (5617) 3-1111
Fax: (5617) 3-4449
E-mail: kohoka@dpc.aichi-gakuin.ac.jp
Internet: www.aichi-gakuin.ac.jp

Founded 1876
Private control
Language of instruction: Japanese
Academic year: April to March

President: TADATAKA KOIDE
Registrar: TAICHI HAYAKAWA
Librarian: YUKEI HASEBE

Library of 770,332 vols
Number of teachers: 459
Number of students: 13,044

Publications: *Transactions of the Institute for Cultural Studies* (annually), *Business Review of Aichi Gakuin University* (quarterly), *Aichi Gakuin Law Review* (quarterly), *Journal of the Research Institute of Zen* (annually), *The Journal of Aichi Gakuin University* (quarterly), *Foreign Languages and Literature* (annually), *Journal of Aichi Gakuin University Dental Society* (quarterly), *Regional Analysis* (2 a year)

DEANS

Faculty of Letters: TATSUYAKI HASHIMOTO
Faculty of Commerce: KUNIHIRO TAKARADA
Faculty of Management: YOSHINOBU SATO
Faculty of Law: YOSHISHIGE KURODA
Faculty of Dentistry: JIRO HASEGAWA
Faculty of General Education: MICHIYOSHI KUROBE
Japanese Language Course for Foreign Students: TOSHIO TAKEUCHI
Faculty of Policy Science For The Information Society: (vacant)

UNIVERSITY OF AIZU

Aizu-Wakamatsu, Fukushima-ken 965-8580

Telephone: (242) 37-2500
Fax: (242) 37-2528
E-mail: daigakuin@u-aizu.ac.jp
Internet: www.u-aizu.ac.jp

Founded 1993

President: TETSUHIKO IKEGAMI

Number of teachers: 89
Number of students: 1,039

HEADS OF DEPARTMENTS

Dean of Graduate School of Computer Science and Engineering: SATOSHI OKAWA
Chairman of Department of Information Systems: RYUICHI OKA
Chairman of Department of Computer Systems: VICTOR I. RYZHII
Head of Department of Computer Software: HIDESADA KANDA
Head of Department of Computer Hardware: KAZUYUKI SAITO

AOYAMA GAKUIN UNIVERSITY

4-4-25 Shibuya, Shibuya-ku, Tokyo 150-8366

Telephone: (3) 3409-8111
Fax: (3) 3409-0927
E-mail: iec-office@iec.aoyama.ac.jp
Internet: www.aoyama.ac.jp

Founded 1874
Academic year: April to March

Chancellor: M. FUKAMACHI
President: Dr M. HANDA
Vice-Presidents: Dr M. NISHIZAWA, Dr M. TSUJI
Administrative Officer: T. MUNEKATA
Library Director: Dr H. TAKAMORI

Library of 1,442,666 vols, 16,262 periodicals
Number of teachers: 1,422 (including 976 part-time)
Number of students: 19,372

Publications: *Aoyama Journal of Business*, *Aoyama Journal of Economics*, *Aoyama Law Review* (all 4 a year), *Aoyama Journal of General Education*, *Thought Currents in English Literature*, *Educational Inquiry*, *KIYO* (Journal of Literature), *Aoyama Gobun* (Journal of Japanese Literature), *Aoyama Shigaku* (Journal of History), *Aoyama Business Review*, *Aoyama Journal of International Politics, Economics and Business*, *Etudes Françaises*, *Aoyama International Communication Studies*, *Aoyama Management Review*

DEANS

College of Literature: H. ISHIZAKI
College of Economics: Dr Y. YOSHIZOE
College of Law: Dr T. YAMAZAKI
School of Business Administration: S. HASEGAWA
School of International Politics, Economics and Business Administration: S. HAKAMADA
College of Science and Engineering: Dr K. UOZUMI
Graduate School of International Management: Dr F. ITOH

CHAIRS OF DEPARTMENTS

College of Literature (internet www.cl.aoyama.ac.jp):
- Department of Education: Y. SAKAI
- Department of Education (Evening Division): Dr M. KITAMOTO
- Department of English: M. AKIMOTO
- Department of English (Evening Division): Y. SAKUMA
- Department of French: Dr T. TSUYUZAKI
- Department of Japanese: Y. HIJIKATA
- Department of History: Dr S. WATANABE
- Department of Psychology: K. ENDO

College of Economics (internet www.econ.aoyama.ac.jp):
- Department of Economics: N. HIRASAWA
- Department of Economics (Evening Division): S. SUGIURA

College of Law (internet www.als.aoyama.ac.jp):
- Department of Law: T. DOBASHI

School of Business Administration (internet www.agub.aoyama.ac.jp):
- Department of Business Administration: Dr O. SATO
- Department of Business Administration (Evening Division): Dr N. IWATA

School of International Politics, Economics and Business (internet www.sipeb.aoyama.ac.jp):
- Department of International Politics: Dr J. TSUCHIYAMA
- Department of International Economics: K. SENBA

College of Science and Engineering (internet www.agnes.aoyama.ac.jp):
- Department of Physics: Dr I. NISHIO
- Department of Chemistry: Dr H. ITOH
- Department of Mechanical Engineering: Dr S. OHISHI
- Department of Electrical Engineering and Electronics: Dr A. SAWABE
- Department of Industrial and Systems Engineering: Dr M. KURODA
- Deparment of Integrated Information Technology: Dr S. NINOMIYA

ASIA UNIVERSITY

5-24-10 Sakai, Musashino-shi, Tokyo 180-8629

Telephone: (422) 36-3255
Fax: (422) 36-4869
E-mail: koryu@asia-u.ac.jp
Internet: www.asia-u.ac.jp/english

Founded 1941
Academic year: April to March

President: SHINICHI KOIBUCHI
Librarian: SEIJI NAKAMURA

Library of 548,000 vols
Number of teachers: 466 (174 full-time, 292 part-time)
Number of students: 8,029

DEANS

Graduate School of Business Administration: K. Kasai
Graduate School of Economics: Y. Tozawa
Graduate School of Law: T. Morimoto
Faculty of Business Administration: H. Oshima
Faculty of Economics: T. Kato
Faculty of Law: H. Nakano
Faculty of International Relations: H. Ogawa
Faculty of Liberal Arts: T. Watanabe
Asia University Junior College: S. Usui

ATTACHED INSTITUTES

Institute for Asian Studies: f. 1973; Dir T. Kimura; publ. *Journal* (annually), *Bulletin* (quarterly).

Center for English Language Education: f. 1989; Dir F. Takemae; publ. *Journal* (2 a year).

Intensive Japanese Course: f. 1953; Dir H. Kawaguchi.

AZABU UNIVERSITY

1-17-71 Fuchinobe, Sagamihara City, Kanagawa 229-8501
Telephone: (42) 754-7111
Fax: (42) 754-7661
Internet: www.azabu-u.ac.jp

Founded 1890

President: Tsunenori Nakamura
Librarian: Hideo Fujitani

Library of 135,000 vols
Number of teachers: 182
Number of students: 2,300

Publication: *Bulletin*

DEANS

School of Veterinary Medicine: Toshio Masaoka
College of Environmental Health: Tsuyoshi Hirata

BUKKYO UNIVERSITY

96 Kitahananobo-cho, Murasakino, Kita-ku, Kyoto 603-8301
Telephone: (75) 491-2141
Fax: (75) 495-5723
E-mail: mmc-info@bukkyo-u.ac.jp
Internet: www.bukkyo-u.ac.jp

Founded 1868
Private control
Academic year: April to March

President: S. Nakai
Vice-President: E. Nakamura
Registrar: H. Ohkita
Librarian: Y. Yamada

Library of 684,000 vols
Number of teachers: 164
Number of students: 6,457

Publications: *Journal of the Faculty of Letters* (annually), *Journal of the Faculty of Education* (annually), *Journal of the Faculty of Sociology* (annually), *Bukkyo University Graduate School Review* (annually)

DEANS

Faculty of Letters: M. Shimizu
Faculty of Education: J. Kakumoto
Faculty of Sociology: M. Hamaoka
Postgraduate Programs in Literature: M. Shimizu
Postgraduate Programs in Education: J. Kakumoto
Postgraduate Programs in Sociology: M. Hamaoka
Independent Postgraduate Programs in Buddhism: S. Onoda
Training Program for the Jodo Priesthood: T. Todo

CHIKUSHI JOGAKUEN UNIVERSITY

2-12-1 Ishizaka, Dazaifu City, Fukuoka Prefecture 818-0192
Telephone: (92) 924-4369
Fax: (92) 924-4369

Founded 1988

Departments of Japanese Language and Literature, English, Asian Studies, Human Welfare, Clinical Psychology.

CHUBU UNIVERSITY

1200 Matsumoto-cho, Kasugai-shi, Aichi-ken 487-8501
Telephone: (568) 51-1111
Fax: (568) 51-1141
E-mail: cucip@office.chubu.ac.jp
Internet: www.chubu.ac.jp

Founded 1964
Language of instruction: Japanese
Academic year: April to March

Chancellor: Kazuo Yamada
President: Atsuo Iiyoshi

Library of 427,000 vols
Number of teachers: 491 (including 244 part-time)
Number of students: 8,000 (including 200 postgraduate)

Publications: *Memoirs of the College of Engineering* (annually), *Sogo Kogaku* (Journal of the Research Institute for Science and Technology, annually), *Journal of the College of Business Administration and Information Science* (2 a year), *Journal of the College of International Studies* (2 a year), *Journal of the Research Institute for International Studies* (annually), *Journal of the Research Institute for Industry and Economics* (annually), *Journal of Information Science* (annually), *Journal of the College of Humanities* (annually)

DEANS

College of Engineering: Dr Makoto Watanabe
College of Business Administration and Information Science: Dr Nobuo Kamata
College of International Studies: Dr Nobuhiro Nagashima
College of Humanities: Yukio Akatsuka
Graduate School of Engineering: Dr Makoto Watanabe
Graduate School of International Studies: Dr Nobuhiro Nagashima
Graduate School of Business Administration and Information Science: Dr Nobuo Kamata

HEADS OF DEPARTMENTS

College of Engineering:
- Mechanical Engineering: Dr Toshiyuki Sakata
- Electrical Engineering: Dr Keiju Matsui
- Electronic Engineering: Dr Kenji Ota
- Civil Engineering: Dr Naoki Matsuo
- Architecture: Dr Keiji Sato
- Industrial Chemistry: Dr Hidehiko Mori
- Engineering Physics: Dr Takashi Aoki
- Science Laboratory: Hiroyuki Ueda
- Information Science: Dr Koji Miyake

College of Business Administration and Information Science:
- Business Administration and Information Science: Dr Yoshinori Adachi

College of International Studies:
- International Relations: Katsuhiko Tsunoda
- Department of Comparative Cultures: Akira Ishii

College of Humanities:
- Japanese Language and Culture: Ryuichi Adachi
- English Language and Culture: Kiyoshi Shimokawa
- Communication Studies: Yotaro Konaka
- Psychology: Toshio Uchida

Graduate School of Engineering:
- Mechanical Engineering: Dr Toshiyuki Sakata
- Electrical and Electronic Engineering: Dr Toshiyuki Ido
- Architecture and Civil Engineering: Dr Eiji Mizuno
- Industrial Chemistry: Dr Jugo Koketsu
- AppliedPhysics: Dr Takatoshi Izumi
- Computer Science: Masayasu Hata

Graduate School of International Studies:
- International Studies: Sadao Ogura (Chair.)

Graduate School of Business Administration and Information Science:
- Business Administration and Information Science: Toshio Yoshida (Chair.)

Other Academic Programmes:
- Humanities: Dr Masamichi Tsuruta
- Faculty of Social Sciences: Sumitaka Maekawa
- Natural Science and Mathematics: Dr Satoko Titani
- Information Science: Dr Akitsugu Mizushima
- Modern Languages: Tetsu Kido
- Health Science: Masatoshi Yamasaki
- Course for Teacher Certification: Dr Sadao Ohkido

ATTACHED RESEARCH INSTITUTES

Research Institute for Industry and Economics: Dir Dr Masao Ishida.

Institute of International Regional Studies: Dir Dr Masao Yoshida.

Research Institute of Information Science: Dir Dr Shoji Mizushima.

High Technology Research Center: Dir Dr Koji Iwata.

Chubu Institute for Advanced Studies: Dir Dr Hidetoshi Kato.

Innovation Center for Production Engineering: Dir Dr Yoshiharu Namba.

Research Institute for Biological Function: Dir Dr Koji Iwata.

Center for Education.

Center for Information Data Processing.

Media Education Center.

Language Center.

Center for International Programs.

Lifelong Learning Center.

Center for Regional Exchange and Linkage.

Center for Physical Education and Cultural Activities.

CHUO UNIVERSITY

742-1 Higashinakano, Hachioji-shi, Tokyo 192-0393
Telephone: (426) 74-2111
Fax: (426) 74-2214
E-mail: intlcent@tamajs.chuo-u.ac.jp
Internet: www.chuo-u.ac.jp

Founded 1885
Academic year: April to March (two semesters)

President and Chancellor: Koji Suzuki
Secretary-General: Shunsuke Hodoshima
Dean of Students: Hisao Fukuchi
Library Director: Ken Nagasaki

Library: see Libraries
Number of teachers: 2,009
Number of students: 29,573 (3,171 evening course), 1,833 graduates
Publications: various faculty bulletins, journals

DEANS

Faculty of Law: K. NAGAI
Faculty of Economics: A. ICHII
Faculty of Commerce: K. KITAMURA
Faculty of Science and Engineering: N. OKUBO
Faculty of Literature: S. HAYASHI
Faculty of Policy Studies: M. KONO
Correspondence Division, Faculty of Law: M. SUGAWARA
Graduate School of Law: T. SHIIBASHI
Graduate School of Economics: H. TANAKA
Graduate School of Commerce: M. TATEBE
Graduate School of Science and Engineering: K. SUGIYAMA
Graduate School of Literature: S. MUTO
Graduate School of Policy Studies: T. MASUJIMA

DIRECTORS

Institute of Comparative Law in Japan: T. KINOSHITA
Institute of Accounting Research: Y. WATABE
Institute of Economic Research: Y. KOGUCHI
Institute of Business Research: T. ISHIZAKI
Institute of Social Science: Y. KAWASAKI
Institute of Cultural Science: M. IRINODA
Institute of Health and Physical Science: A. NISHITANI
Institute of Science and Engineering: M. IRI
Computer Center: T. SEKIGUCHI
International Center: H. HAYASHIDA
Health Center: T. TSUKADA

DAITO BUNKA UNIVERSITY

1-9-1 Takashimadaira, Itabashi-ku, Tokyo 175-8571
Telephone: (3) 5399-7323
Fax: (3) 5399-7823
E-mail: info@ic.daito.ac.jp
Internet: www.daito.ac.jp

Founded 1923
Private Control
Academic year: April to March

Chairman of Board: T. TAKEUCHI
President: M. WADA
Managing Directors: K. SOEDA, S. TSUJINO
Director of Administrative Office: S. TSUJINO
Director of Academic Affairs: S. WATABE
Librarian: I. MIYOSHI

Library of 1,204,490 vols
Number of teachers: 1,070
Number of students: 13,315

Publications: *Daito Bunka Daigaku* (Bulletin), *Daito Bunka News* (10 a year)

DEANS

Faculty of Business Administration: M. IMASHIRO
Faculty of Economics: K. UENO
Faculty of Foreign Languages: S. YAMAZAKI
Faculty of International Relations: N. OSHIKAWA
Faculty of Law: Y. FURUKAWA
Faculty of Literature: M. OTA
Faculty of Social–Human Environmentology: Y. TAKAYAMA
Faculty of Sports and Health Science: Y. AOBA

HEADS OF DEPARTMENTS

Faculty of Business Administration (tel. (3) 5399-7462; fax (3) 5399-7342):
- Business Management: T. INOUE
- Business Studies and Informatics: R. HASEGAWA

Faculty of Economics (tel. (3) 5399-7326; fax (3) 5399-7342):
- Socio-economics: M. NAKAJIMA
- Modern Economics: T. KIMURA

Faculty of Foreign Languages (tel. (3) 5399-7329; fax (3) 5399-7381):
- Chinese Languages: K. NAKAMURA
- English Language: H. KITABAYASHI
- Japanese Language: H. TANAKA

Faculty of International Relations (560 Iwadono, Higashimatsuyama-shi, Saitama 355-8501; tel. (493) 31-1513; fax (493) 31-1528):
- International Relations: E. USUKI
- International Culture: K. TANABE

Faculty of Law (tel. (3) 5399-7338; fax (3) 5399-7342):
- Law: F. ISHIYAMA
- Political Science: K. UCHIDA

Faculty of Literature (tel. (3) 5399-7324; fax (3) 5399-7381):
- Japanese Literature: J. SHIMOYAMA
- Sinology: H. KADOWAKI
- English and American Literature: A. AMISHIRO
- Education: H. SHISHIKURA
- Calligraphy: Y. TANAKA

Social-Human Environmentology (tel. (3) 5399-7356; fax (3) 5399-7357):
- Social–Human Environmentology: A. SHINOHARA

Sports and Health Science (tel. (493) 31-1552; fax (493) 31-1512):
- Health Science: M. KANO
- Sports Science: J. OHASHI

HEADS OF GRADUATE SCHOOLS

Asian Area Studies: M. TAKAKUWA
Business Administration: K. SUZUKI
Economics: H. SUESHIGE
Foreign Languages: E. NISHIKAWA
Law: H. TOKI
Law School: K. ONO
Literature: J. KOYANO

JAPANESE LANGUAGE PROGRAMME FOR FOREIGN STUDENTS

Japanese Language Course: T. MIKAMI

ATTACHED INSTITUTES

Institute of Business Research: Dir T. TANAKA.

Institute of Calligraphy: Dir H. TANAKA.

Institute of Contemporary Asian Studies: Dir N. OSHIKAWA.

Institute of Economic Research: Dir T. NAKAMURA.

Institute of the Humanities: Dir M. HIYOSHI.

Institute of International Comparative Politics: Dir T. NAGAI.

Institute of Language Education Research: Dir M. TERAMURA.

Institute of Legal Studies: Dir M. KIHARA.

Institute of Oriental Studies: Dir T. FUKUDA.

DOHTO UNIVERSITY

149 Nakanoswawa, Kitahiroshima-shi, Hokkaido 061-1196
Telephone: (11) 372-3111

Founded 1964

Chancellor: Dr JUN SAKURAI

Faculties of Social Welfare, Fine Arts, Management.

DOKKYO UNIVERSITY

1-1 Gakuen-cho, Soka-shi, Saitama-ken 340-0042
Telephone: (489) 42-1111
Fax: (489) 41-6621
E-mail: info@dokkyo.ac.jp
Internet: www.dokkyo.ac.jp

Founded 1964
Private control

President: YASUO KUWAHARA
Head Administrator: IKUO TOI
Librarian: KO KAJIYAMA

Library of 675,000 vols
Number of teachers: 410
Number of students: 8,925

Publication: *Dokkyo International Review* (annually)

DEANS

Faculty of Foreign Languages: YUJI NAKAJIMA
Faculty of Economics: MASAMICHI CHIYOURA
Faculty of Law: SHOICHI KOSEKI
Graduate School of Foreign Languages: YUJI NAKAJIMA
Graduate School of Law: SHOICHI KOSEKI
Graduate School of Economics: MASAMICHI CHIYOURA

HEADS OF DEPARTMENTS

German: TAMIKO KURODA
English: HAJIME ABE
French: JUNICHI IMURA
Language and Culture: HISAO MATSUMARU
Economics: MASANOBU MATSUMOTO
Law: NOBUO SAKAMOTO
International Legal Studies: AKIYOSHI HOSHINO
Management Science: YASUMASA NAKAMURA

ATTACHED INSTITUTES

Center for Data Processing and Computer Science: Dir MASARU HONDA.

International Center: Dir YASUO KUWAHARA.

Research Institute of Foreign Language Teaching: Dir YOSHISABURO HONDA.

DOSHISHA UNIVERSITY

Karasuma Imadegawa, Kamigyo-ku, Kyoto 602-580
Telephone: (75) 251-3110
Fax: (75) 251-3075
E-mail: ji-shomu@mail.doshisha.ac.jp
Internet: www.doshisha.ac.jp

Founded 1875
Academic year: April to March

Chancellor: M. OYA
President: E. HATTA
Dean of Academic Affairs: N. TABATA
Dean of Student Affairs: A. MORITA
Administrative Officer: I. HARA

Library: Libraries with 715,027 vols
Number of teachers: 489 full-time
Number of students: 24,166

Publications: *Studies in Christianity, Studies in Humanities, Doshisha Studies in English, Social Science Review, Doshisha Law Review, Economic Review, Doshisha Business Review, Science and Engineering Review of Doshisha University, Doshisha American Studies, The Social Sciences, The Humanities, The Study of Christianity and Social Problems, Shuryu, Doshisha Literature, L.L.L., Annual Report of Cultural Studies, Studies in Cultural History, Annual of Philosophy, Philosophical Review, Journal of Education and Culture, Doshisha Psychological Review, Bigaku Geijutsugaku, Doshisha Kokubungaku, Doshisha Review of Sociology, Doshisha*

Kogaku Kaiho, *Doshisha Studies in Language and Culture*, *Doshisha Policy and Management Review*, *Doshisha Hokentaiiku*, *Doshisha Danso*, *Neesima Studies*

DEANS

Faculty of Theology: K. MORI
Faculty of Letters: Y. KUROKI
Faculty of Law: A. SEGAWA
Faculty of Economics: T. NISHIMURA
Faculty of Commerce: T. UKAI
Faculty of Engineering: M. SENDA
Graduate School of American Studies: T. KAMATA
Graduate School of Policy and Management: S. OTA

DIRECTORS

Institute for the Study of Humanities and Social Sciences: T. TAKITA
Center for American Studies: N. YAMAUCHI
Science and Engineering Research Institute: O. YAMAGUCHI
Institute for Language and Culture: I. KOIKE

DOSHISHA WOMAN'S COLLEGE OF LIBERAL ARTS

Kodo, Kyotanabe-shi, Kyoto-fu 610-0395
Telephone: (774) 65-8411
Fax: (774) 65-8461
E-mail: somu-t@dwc.doshisha.ac.jp
Internet: www.dwc.doshisha.ac.jp

Founded 1876
Academic year: April to March

Chancellor: M. OYA
President: J. MORITA
Registrar: Y. HONMA
Librarian: Y. YODEN

Library of 445,983 vols
Number of teachers: 750
Number of students: 5,948

Publication: *Annual Reports of Studies*

DEANS

Liberal Arts: M. TERAKAWA
Academic Affairs: Y. HONMA
Student Affairs: Y. KOMOTO
General Affairs: K. KOSAKA
Admissions Centre: N. YOSHIKAI
Career Support Centre: N. MORISHITA
Accounting and Finance: S. TAKAMOTO
Religious Affairs: J. KONDO
Human Life and Science: N. NISHIMURA
Contemporary Social Studies: T. KONO
Pharmaceutical Sciences: K. MORITA
Library and information Services Centre: Y. YODEN
Academic Research Promotion Centre: K. MOROI
International Exchange Centre: T. TAGUCHI

FUKUOKA UNIVERSITY

8-19-1, Nanakuma, Jonan-ku, Fukuoka 814-0180
Telephone: (92) 871-6631
Fax: (92) 862-4431
E-mail: fupr@adm.fukuoka-u.ac.jp
Internet: www.fukuoka-u.ac.jp

Founded 1934
Private control
Academic year: April to March

President: HIROYUKI YAMASHITA
Vice-Presidents: KENROU KAWAIDA, KUNIHIDE MIHASHI, MASAHIRO KIKUCHI
Secretary-General: K. SUETSUGU
Librarian: H. NAGATA

Library of 1,400,000 vols
Number of teachers: 928 full-time
Number of students: 22,319

Publications: *Reviews*, *Bulletin*, *Reports*

DEANS

Faculty of Humanities: S. MAMOTO
Faculty of Law: N. ASANO
Faculty of Economics: T. TANAKA
Faculty of Commerce: T. ETO
Faculty of Science: M. SAIGO
Faculty of Engineering: H. YAMASHITA
School of Medicine: Y. IKEHARA
Faculty of Pharmaceutical Sciences: H. SHIMENO
Faculty of Sports and Health Science: K. KANAMORI

DIRECTORS

Takamiya Evening School: M. MORI
Central Research Institute: Y. TOMINAGA
Computer Centre: K. SHUDO
Radioisotope Centre: S. TASAKI
Animal Care Unit: S. KASHIMURA
Language Training Centre: K. TACHIBANA
Fukuoka University Hospital: A. ARIYOSHI
Fukuoka University Chikushi Hospital: T. YAO

GAKUSHUIN UNIVERSITY

1-5-1 Mejiro, Toshima-ku, Tokyo 171-8588
Telephone: (3) 3986-0221
Fax: (3) 5992-1005
E-mail: webmaster@gakushuin.ac.jp
Internet: www.gakushuin.ac.jp/univ

Founded 1949
Private control
Language of instruction: Japanese
Academic year: April to March

Chancellor: Y. TAJIMA
President: Y. NAGATA
Chief Administrative Officer: M. MUNAKATA
Dean of Students: H. ENDO
Librarian: I. ARAKAWA

Library of 1,300,000 vols
Number of teachers: 202 full-time, 645 part-time
Number of students: 8,616 (8,082 undergraduate, 534 postgraduate)

Publications: *Gakushuin Daigaku Bungaku-Bu Kenkyu Nenpo* (Annual Collection of Essays and Studies, Faculty of Letters), *Gakushuin Daigaku Hogakkai Zasshi* (Gakushuin Review of Law and Politics, 2 a year), *Gakushuin Daigaku Keizai Ronshu* (Gakushuin Economic Papers, 4 a year), *Gakushuin Daigaku Kenkyusosho* (Gakushuin University Studies, annually)

DEANS

Faculty of Economics: Y. SUGITA
Faculty of Law: T. INOUE
Faculty of Letters: N. FUKUI
Faculty of Sciences: D. FUJIWARA

CHAIRMEN

Graduate School of Economics: T. KAWASHIMA
Graduate School of Humanities: N. FUKUI
Graduate School of Law: T. OKA
Graduate School of Management: Y. AOKI
Graduate School of Politics: T. KATSURAGI
Graduate School of Sciences: D. FUJIWARA

HEADS OF DEPARTMENTS

Faculty of Economics:
- Economics: A. WAKISAKA
- Management: A. KOYAMA

Faculty of Law (tel. (3) 3986-0221; fax (3) 5992-1006; e-mail law-dean@gakushuin.ac.jp; internet www.gakushuin.ac.jp/univ/law):
- Law: M. OKINO
- Political Studies: N. SUDO

Faculty of Letters:
- English: M. HASHIMOTO
- French: K. YOSHIDA
- German: A. ONUKI
- History: T. TAKANO
- Japanese: Y. NAGASHIMA
- Philosophy: S. SAKONJI
- Psychology: S. SHINOHARA
- Teachers' Training Course: K. TSURUMA

Faculty of Sciences (tel. (3) 3986-0221 ext. 6450; fax (3) 5992-1029; e-mail sci-off@gakushuin.ac.jp):
- Chemistry: M. AKAOGI
- Mathematics: K. YAJIMA
- Physics: A. KAWABATA

PROFESSORS

Faculty of Economics:
- AOKI, Y., Consumer Behaviour
- ARAI, K., Stochastic Processes and Statistics
- ASABA, S., Business Economics and Strategic Management
- ENDO, H., Health Economics and Business Policy
- FUKUCHI, J., Statistics, Statistical Finance
- HOSONO, K., Macroeconomics
- IMANO, K., Human Resource Management
- ISHII, S., Economic History of Japan
- ITSUMI, Y., Public Finance
- IWATA, K., Japanese Economic Studies, Land and Housing Economics
- KAMBE, S., Microeconomic Theory and Game Theory
- KANEDA, N., Accounting
- KATSUO, Y., Financial Accounting
- KAWASHIMA, T., Special Economics and Econometrics
- KOYAMA, A., Business Finance and International Management
- MITSUI, K., Public Economics
- MIYAGAWA, T., Macroeconomics, Japanese Economy
- MORITA, M., Management Science and Strategic Management
- MUKUNOKI, H., International Economics
- NAMBU, T., Industrial Economics
- OKUMURA, H., Japanese Economic Studies, International Finance
- SHIROTA, Y., Computer Science
- SUGITA, Y., Marketing Science
- SUZUKI, T., Business History
- TANAKA, N., Systems and Simulation
- TATSUMI, K., Financial Markets and Investment
- UCHINO, T., Management and Organization Theory
- UEDA, T., Marketing
- WADA, T., Business Economics and Strategic Management
- WAKISAKA, A., Economics of Work and Pay
- WAKOH, J., Game Theory, Mathematical Economics
- YUZAWA, T., Business History

Faculty of Law:
- ENDO, K., Sociology
- FUKUMOTO, K., Politics
- HASEBE, Y., Law of Civil Procedure
- HASHIMOTO, Y., Labour and Employment Law
- HIRANO, H., Social Psychology
- IIDA, Y., Political History of Europe
- INOUE, T., History of Politics and Diplomacy in Japan
- ISOZAKI, N., Political Change in East Asia
- KAMIYA, M., Anglo-American Law
- KANZAKI, T., Conflict of Laws
- KATSUNAGI, T., Public Policy and Jurisprudence
- MAEDA, A., Commercial Law
- MIZUNO, K., Civil Law
- MORINAGA, T., History of Western Political Thought
- MURAMATSU, M., Public Administration
- MURANUSHI, M., International Politics
- NAKAI, Y., Comparative Politics
- NOMURA, T., Civil Law
- NONAKA, N., Principles of Political Science
- NOSAKA, Y., Constitutional Law

OKA, T., Civil Law
OKINO, M., Civil Law
SAKAMOTO, K., Political Process of Japan
SAKURAI, K., Administrative Law
SASAKI, T., Political Theory
SHIBAHARA, K., Criminal Law
SHIZUMI, M., Criminal Law
SUDO, N., Sociology
SUNADA, I., American Government and Politics
TAKAGI, H., Administrative Law
TOMATSU, H., Constitutional Law
TSUMURA, M., Law of Criminal Procedure
TSUNEOKA, T., Administrative Law

Faculty of Letters:

ABE, S., History of Japanese Language and Dialectology
ARIKAWA, H., History of European Art
CHUJOH, S., 19th-century French Novel
FITZSIMMONS, A., Irish Literature, Modern British Poetry
FUKUI, N., Contemporary European History
HARADA, Y., French 17th-century Philosophy and Literature
HASHIMOTO, M., Modern English Literature, Irish Literature
HOSAKA, Y., Semantics, Syntax (German)
HYODO, H., Japanese Medieval Literature, Culture of Japanese Performing Arts
IENAGA, J., Medieval Japanese History
INOUE, I., Modern Japanese History
ITOH, K., Clinical Psychology, Supportive Psychotherapy
IWASAKI, H., 20th-century French Novel
KAMENAGA, Y., Medieval European History
KAMIOKA, N., Contemporary American Novels
KANDA, T., Medieval Japanese Literature
KANEGAE, H., Ancient Japanese History
KAWAGUCHI, Y., Educational Methodology
KAWASAKI, Y., Psychotherapy, Transference
KOBAYASHI, T., History of Japanese Art
KOMATSU, E., Linguistics
MAEDA, N., Modern Japanese Linguistics
MANO, Y., British Novels
MARÉ, T., French Literature
MATSUSHIMA, S., English Romantic Poetry
MIYASHITA, S., German Poetry
MURANO, R., Cross-cultural Communication, Teaching Japanese as a Foreign Language
NAGANUMA, Y., Volunteer Learning
NAGASHIMA, Y., Linguistics (Semantics)
NAGATA, Y., Social Psychology
NAKAJIMA, H., English Linguistics
NAKAMURA, I., History of Japanese Thought
NAKANO, H., Elizabethan Drama
NINOMIYA, R., 17th- and 18th-century French Literature
NOMURA, R., 17th- and 18th-century French Literature
OHNUKI, A., Cultural Studies
OKAMOTO, J., German Linguistics, Cognitive Semantics, Linguistic Theory
PEKAR, T., German Literature, Cultural Studies
SAEKI, T., French Drama
SAITOH, T., Educational History
SAKAI, K., Comparative Philosophy, Modern (18th- and 19th-century) Philosophy, Phenomenology
SAKONJI, S., Greek Philosophy, Neoplatonism, Renaissance Philosophy
SANO, M., History of Japanese Art
SASAKI, T., Ancient Japanese Linguistics
SHIMADA, M., Ancient Roman History
SHIMOKAWA, K., British Philosophy (Locke and Hume), Ethics and Political Philosophy
SHINKAWA, T., Medieval Thought and Buddhism in Japan
SHINODA, A., Comparative Psychology
SHINOHARA, S., Learning Theories
SHIOTANI, K., 18th- and 19th-century English Literature
SUGIYAMA, N., French Philosophy
SUWA, T., Cultural Geography
TAKADA, H., German Linguistics, History of the German Language, Historical Pragmatics
TAKAHASHI, H., History of European Art
TAKAMI, K., Linguistics (Syntax and Semantics)
TAKANO, T., Early Modern Japanese History
TAKETSUNA, S., Educational Psychology
TAKEUCHI, F., Modern Asian History
TANABE, C., American Literature
TOGAWA, S., Modern Japanese Literature
TOYAMA, M., Social Cognition, Causal Attribution
TSURUMA, K., Ancient Chinese History
UCHIDA, T., American Literature
WATANABE, M., History of German Linguistics, Sociolinguistics, Comparative Linguistics
YAHAGI, S., 19th-century American Literature
YAMAMOTO, M., Child Development, Developmental Disorder
YAMAMOTO, Y., Modern Japanese Literature
YOSHIDA, K., French Poetry and Poets
YOSHIKAWA, M., Clinical Psychology, Clinical Assessment

Faculty of Science (tel. (3) 3986-0221 ext.6450; fax (3) 5992-1029; e-mail sci-off@gakushuin.ac.jp):

AKAO, K., Complex Manifolds
AKAOGI, M., Science of the Earth's Materials under High Pressure
AKIYAMA, T., Synthetic Organic Chemistry
ARAKAWA, I., Surface and Vacuum Science
FUJIWARA, D., Functional Analysis, Theory of Partial Differential Equations
HIRANO, T., Quantum Optics
IDA, D., Gravity and Relativistic Cosmology
IITAKA, S., Algebraic Geometry, Birational Geometry
ISHII, K., Vibrational Spectroscopy of Molecular Systems
KATASE, K., Differential Topology, Complex Dynamic Systems
KAWABATA, A., Theory of Solid State Physics, Mesoscopic Physics
KAWASAKI, T., Topology and Geometry of Surfaces
KOTANI, M., Photochemistry and Photophysics of Organic Solids
MIZOGUCHI, T., Materials Science, Spin-polarized Electron Spectroscopy, Magnetism, Amorphous Materials
MIZUTANI, A., Numerical Analysis
MOCHIDA, K., Organometallic Chemistry of Group 14 Elements
MURAMATSU, Y., Geo- and Environmental Chemistry of Trace Elements and Isotopes
NAKAJIMA, S., Number Theory
NAKAMURA, H., Organic Synthesis
NAKANO, S., Number Theory
NISHIZAKA, T., Biophysics of Macromolecular Motion
TAKAHASHI, T., Electronic Properties of Small-dimensional Conductors, Organic Conductors and Superconductors
TASAKI, H., Theoretical Physics and Mathematical Physics
WATANABE, M., Physics of Crystal Growth
YAJIMA, K., Mathematical Physics, Partial Differential Equations

Centre for Sports and Health Science (tel. (3) 3971-8989; fax (3) 5992-9306):

HANEDA, Y., Sports Biomechanics
HIRO, N., Sports Methodology
ONO, T., Exercise Physiology
SATO, Y., Applied Physiology, General Principle of Ball Game Strategy and Tactics
TAKAMARU, Y., Coaching Sciences
YAGI, Y., Sports Psychology

ATTACHED INSTITUTES

Gakushuin Daigaku Gaikokugo Kyoiku Kenkyu Sentah (Gakushin University Foreign Language Teaching and Research Centre): f. 1997; Dir K. MOCHIDA.

Gakushuin Daigaku Jinbun Kagaku Kenkyujo (Research Institute for Humanities): f. 1976; Dir Y. NAGASHIMA.

Gakushuin Daigaku Keisanki Sentah (Gakushuin University Computer Centre): f. 1974; Dir K. ARAI.

Gakushuin Daigaku Keizai Keiei Kenkyujo (Gakushuin University Research Institute for Economics and Management): f. 1984; Dir K. IMANO.

Gakushuin Daigaku Kokusai Kouryu Sentah (Gakushuin University Centre for International Exchange): f. 1990; Dir K. SHIOTANI.

Gakushuin Daigaku Seimei Bunshi Kagaku Kenkyujo (Gakushuin University Institute for Biomolecular Science): f. 1991; Dir T. HAGA.

Gakushuin Daigaku Shiryokan (Gakushuin University Museum of History): f. 1975; Dir T. SHINKAWA.

Gakushuin Daigaku Sports Kenkoh Kagaku Sentah (Gakushuin University Centre for Sports and Health Sciences): f. 1994; Dir Y. YAGI.

Gakushuin Daigaku Toyo Bunka Kenkyu-Jo (Gakushuin University Research Institute for Oriental Cultures): f. 1952; Dir T. OKA.

HAKODATE UNIVERSITY

5-1 Takaoka-cho, Hakodate 042-0955
Telephone: (138) 57-1181
Fax: (138) 57-0298
E-mail: post@hakodate-u.ac.jp
Internet: www.hakodate-u.ac.jp

Founded 1938

President: HAKUSHI KAWAMURA
Number of students: 1,200

Faculty of Commerce.

HIROSHIMA JOGAKUIN UNIVERSITY

4-13-1, Ushita-higashi, Higashi-ku, Hiroshima 732-0063

Telephone: (82) 228-0386
Fax: (82) 227-4502
E-mail: kokusai@gaines.hju.ac.jp
Internet: www.hju.ac.jp

Founded 1886, as college 1949
Academic year: April to March

President: HIROSHI IMADA
Vice-President: SHIGEKI SATOH
Registrar: YUJI MAEWAKA
Chief Administrative Officer: SHIGENOBU HATAKEYAMA

Library of 200,000 vols
Number of teachers: 75
Number of students: 2,062

Publication: *Bulletin* (annually)

Departments of Japanese Language and Literature, English Studies, Human and Cultural Studies, Environmental Science, Environmental Culture, Graduate School of Language and Culture, Human Life Science.

HIROSHIMA UNIVERSITY OF ECONOMICS

5-37-1 Gion, Asaminami-ku, Hiroshima City 731-0192
Telephone: (82) 871-1002
Fax: (82) 871-1666
E-mail: int-sc@hue.ac.jp
Internet: www.hue.ac.jp

Founded 1967
Academic year: April to March

Chancellor: MASAO ISHIDA
President: TSUNEO ISHIDA
Chief Administrative Officer: SHIGEMITSU ARICHI
Librarian: HIROSHI SEIKE

Library of 281,050 vols
Number of teachers: 150 full-time
Number of teachers: 106 part-time
Number of students: 5,000

DEANS

Faculty of Economics: TOSHIYUKI MIZOGUCHI
Graduate School of Economics: TOSHIYUKI MIZOGUCHI

HIROSHIMA SHUDO UNIVERSITY

1-1-1 Ozuka-higashi, Asaminami-ku, Hiroshima 731-3195
Telephone: (82) 830-1103
Fax: (82) 830-1303
Internet: www.shudo-u.ac.jp

President: MASANORI KODAMA

Library of 640,594 vols in Japanese and other languages; 4,999 periodicals, 655,112 other items
Number of teachers: 179
Number of students: 6,204

Publications: *Monographs of the Institute for Advanced Studies*, *Papers of the Research Society of Commerce and Economics*, *Studies in the Humanities and Sciences*, *Shudo Hogaku: Shudo Law Review*, *Journal of Human Environmental Studies*, *Journal of Economic Sciences*

Faculties of Commercial Sciences, Economic Sciences, Human Environmental Sciences, Humanities and Human Sciences and Law.

HOKKAI-GAKUEN UNIVERSITY

4-1-40, Asahi-machi, Toyohira-ku, Sapporo 062-8605
Telephone: (11) 841-1161
Fax: (11) 824-3141
Internet: www.hokkai-t-u.ac.jp

Founded 1952
Academic year: April to March

Chairman: MASAO MORIMOTO
President: T. ASAKURA
Librarian: M. KOBAYASHI

Library of 810,912 vols
Number of teachers: 233 full-time
Number of students: 8,856

Publications: *Keizai Ronshu* (Journal of Economics, 4 a year), *Hogaku Kenkyu* (Journal of the Faculty of Law, 4 a year), *Gakuen Ronshu* (Journal of Hokkai-Gakuen University, 4 a year), *Kogakubu Kenkyu Hokoku* (Bulletin of the Faculty of Engineering, annually), *Jinbun Ronshu* (Studies in Culture, 3 a year), *Keiei Ronshu* (Journal of Business Administration, 4 a year)

DEANS

Faculty of Business Administration: M. UCHIDA
Faculty of Economics: K. KODA
Faculty of Engineering: N. YOGO
Faculty of Humanities: T. KUWAHARA
Faculty of Law: K. NIIYAMA

CHAIRMEN

Graduate School of Business Administration: T. TOCHINAI
Graduate School of Economics: K. KIMURA
Graduate School of Engineering: Y. MOMOUCHI
Graduate School of Law: Y. YOSHIDA
Graduate School of Literature: T. OHAMA
Law School: A. SUDA

ATTACHED INSTITUTE

Development Research Institute: f. 1957; Dir H. OKUDA; publ. *Kaihatsu Ronshu* (Journal of Policy Studies, 2 a year).

General Education and Research Center: Dir M. TAKEDA.

HOKURIKU UNIVERSITY

1-1 Taiyogaoka, Kanazawa City, Ishikawa Prefecture 920-1180
Telephone: (76) 229-1161
Fax: (76) 229-1393
E-mail: koho@hokuriku-u.ac.jp
Internet: www.hokuriku-u.ac.jp

Founded 1975
Academic year: April to March

President: S. KAWASHIMA
Librarian: Y. KITANO

Library of 209,000 vols
Number of teachers: 144
Number of students: 3,000

Publications: *Hokuriku Daigaku Kiyo* (bulletin, annually), *Hokuriku Hogaku* (journal of law and political science, 4 a year)

DEANS

Faculty of Future Learning: S. SONOYAMA
Faculty of Pharmaceutical Sciences: T. SAWANISHI
Graduate School of Pharmaceutical Research: T. SAWANISHI (Chair)

HOSEI UNIVERSITY

2-17-1, Fujimi, Chiyoda-ku, Tokyo 102-8160
Telephone: (3) 3264-9662
Fax: (3) 3238-9873
E-mail: ic@i.hosei.ac.jp
Internet: www.hosei.ac.jp

Founded 1880
Private control
Language of instruction: Japanese
Academic year: April to March

President: TADAO KIYONARI
Vice-Presidents: CHIMAKI HIRABAYASHI, MASAFUMI KANEKO, GORO SHIRAI, TAKUMITSU HORIE
Registrar: JITSUKAZU WADA
Library Director: YASUTAKA SHIRAI

Library of 1,750,000 vols
Number of teachers: 2,226 (558 full-time, 1,668 part-time)
Number of students: 29,399, graduate 1,512, correspondence education 13,448

Publications: *Hogaku-Shirin* (Law and Political Sciences Review, 4 a year), *Hosei Daigaku Bungakubu Kiyo* (Bulletin of Faculty of Letters, annually), *Keizai-Shirin* (Economic Review, 4 a year), *Shakai Shirin* (Sociology and Social Sciences, 4 a year), *Keiei Shirin* (Business Journal, 4 a year), *Hosei Daigaku Kogakubu Kenkyu Shuho* (College of Engineering Bulletin, annually), *Daigakuin Kiyo* (Graduate School Bulletin, 2 a year), *Ningen Kankyo Ronshu* (Journal of Humanity and the Environment, 2 a year), *Ibunka* (Journal of Intercultural Communication, annually)

DEANS

Faculty of Law: HIROMI MUTO
Faculty of Letters: TSUTOMU HOSHINO
Faculty of Economics: MASAYOSHI TSURUMI
Faculty of Engineering: HISAMATSU NAKANO
Faculty of Social Sciences: HIROSHI KUMON
Faculty of Business Administration: KOSUKE OGAWA
Lifelong Learning and Career Studies: KOICHI SASAGAWA
Graduate Division: MASATOSHI YOSHIDA
Faculty of Intercultural Communication: SATORU OSAWA
Faculty of Humanity and the Environment: KUNIO KIKUCHI
Faculty of Social Policy and Administration: TADASHI MATSUZAKI
Faculty of Computer and Information Sciences: KENJI OMORI

ATTACHED INSTITUTES

Institute of Nogaku Studies: 2-17-1 Fujimi, Chiyoda-ku, Tokyo 102-8160; f. 1952; Dir H. NISHINO; publ. *Catalogue Noh Drama Collections*.

Ohara Institute for Social Research: 4342 Aihara-machi, Machida-shi, Tokyo 194-0298; f. 1919; Dir S. HAYAKAWA; publ. *Labour Yearbook of Japan* (annually), *Report* (monthly).

Institute of Okinawan Studies: 2-17-1 Fujimi, Chiyoda-ku, Tokyo 102-8160; f. 1972; Dir T. YASUE; publ. *Bulletin*, *Report* (annually).

Boissonade Institute of Modern Laws and Politics: 2-17-1 Fujimi, Chiyoda-ku, Tokyo 102-8160; f. 1977; Dir D. KISHII.

Japan Statistics Research Institute: 4342 Aihara-machi, Machida-shi, Tokyo 194-0298; f. 1946; Dir H. MORI; publ. *Bulletin* (annually).

Research Center of Ion Beam Technology: 3-7-2 Kajino-cho, Koganei-shi, Tokyo 184-8584; f. 1979; Dir T. NAKAMURA; publ. *Report* (annually).

Computational Science Research Center: 3-7-2 Kajino-cho, Koganei-shi, Tokyo 184-8584; f. 1969; Dir M. KUSAKABE.

Sports and Physical Education Research Center: 2-17-1 Fujimi, Chiyoda-ku, Tokyo 102-8160; f. 1976; Dir K. GOMYO.

Institute of Comparative Economic Studies: 4342 Aihara-machi, Machida-shi, Tokyo 194-0298; f. 1984; Dir K. ODAKA; publ. *Journal* (annually).

Research and Service Center for Tama Community: 2-17-1 Fujimi, Chiyoda-ku, Tokyo 102-8160; Dir C. HIRABAYASHI; publ. *Newsletter* (quarterly).

Information Research Technology Center: 2-17-1 Fujimi, Chiyoda-ku, Tokyo 102-8160; f. 2000; Dir G. SHIRAI.

Information Research Institute, California: 800 Airport Blvd, Suite 504, Burlingame, CA 94010, USA; f. 2000; Dir K. YANA.

INTERNATIONAL CHRISTIAN UNIVERSITY

10-2, Osawa 3-chome, Mitaka-shi, Tokyo 181-8585
Telephone: (422) 33-3038
Fax: (422) 33-9887
E-mail: webmaster@icu.ac.jp
Internet: www.icu.ac.jp

Founded 1949

An ecumenical university, accepting students of high academic ability from all countries
Languages of instruction: Japanese, English
Academic year: April to March or September to June

President: NORIHIKO SUZUKI
Vice-President (Academic Affairs): KAZUAKI SAITO

Vice-President (Financial Affairs): ICHIRO NISHIDA
Library Director: YUKI NAGANO
Library: see Libraries
Number of teachers: 147 (full-time)
Number of students: 2,887
Publications: *Humanities-Christianity and Culture*, *Educational Studies*, *Language Research Bulletin*, *Asian Cultural Studies*, *Social Science*

DEANS

College of Liberal Arts: M. OKANO
Graduate School: S. KAWASHIMA
Student Affairs: A. AOI

ATTACHED INSTITUTES

Institute of Asian Cultural Studies: f. 1971, replacing Committee f. 1958; Dir W. STEELE; publ. *Asian Cultural Studies* (annually).

Institute of Educational Research and Service: f. 1953; Dir J. MAHER; publ. *Educational Studies* (annually).

Institute for the Study of Christianity and Culture: f. 1963; Dir A. TANAKA; publ. *Humanities-Christianity and Culture* (annually).

Social Science Research Institute: f. 1953; Dir S. ISHIWATA; publ. *The Journal of Social Science* (2 a year).

Hachiro Yuasa Memorial Museum: f. 1982; collections of Japanese archaeology and folk art; Dir K. SAITO; publ. *Annual Report*.

Peace Research Institute: f. 1991; Dir J. WASILEWSKI.

Research Center for Japanese Language Education: f. 1991; Dir M. HIROSE.

ISHINOMAKI SENSHU UNIVERSITY

1 Shinmito, Minamisakai, Ishinomaki-shi, Miyagi 986-8580
Telephone: (225) 22-7711
Fax: (225) 22-7809
Chairman: Dr MASAYOSHI DEUSHI
President: RYOUJI KOBAYASHI
Library of 100,000 vols
Faculty of Science and Engineering and Faculty of Business Administration.

IWATE MEDICAL UNIVERSITY

19-1 Uchimaru, Morioka, Iwate 020-8505
Telephone: (19) 651-5111
Fax: (19) 624-1231
E-mail: webmaster@iwate-med.ac.jp
Internet: www.iwate-med.ac.jp
Founded 1928, University 1952
Private control
President: SHIGERU ONO
Librarian: TOKIO NAWA
Library of 249,221 vols
Number of teachers: 500
Number of students: 1,037
Publications: *Journal of the Iwate Medical Association* (6 a year), *Annual Report of the School of Liberal Arts and Sciences*, *Dental Journal* (4 a year)

DEANS

School of Medicine: CHUICHI ITO
School of Dentistry: KIMIO SAKAMAKI
School of Liberal Arts and Sciences: KOKI KANNO

HEADS OF DEPARTMENTS

School of Medicine:

Anatomy I: Prof. MASAHARU HORIGUCHI
Anatomy II: Prof. YOICHI SATO
Physiology I: Prof. KAZUHIKO SASAKI
Physiology II: Prof. MANABU KUBOKAWA
Biochemistry: Prof. SABURO HORIUCHI
Pharmacology: Prof. TAKESHI KASHIMOTO
Pathology I: Prof. TAKASHI SAWAI
Pathology II: Prof. TOMOYUKI MASUDA
Bacteriology: Prof. SHIGEHIRO SATO
Hygiene and Public Health: Prof. NOBUO NISHI
Legal Medicine: Prof. YASUHIRO AOKI
Medicine I: Prof. KAZUYUKI SUZUKI
Medicine II: Prof. KATSUHIKO HIRAMORI
Medicine III: Prof. HIROSHI INOUE
Neurology: Prof. HIDEO TOHGI
Psychiatry: Prof. AKIO SAKAI
Paediatrics: Prof. SHOICHI CHIDA
Surgery I: Prof. KAZUYOSHI SAITO
Neurosurgery: Prof. AKIRA OGAWA
Surgery III: Prof. KOHEI KAWAZOE
Orthopaedic Surgery: Prof. TADASHI SHIMAMURA
Dermatology: Prof. TOSHIHIDE AKASAKA
Urology: Prof. TOMOAKI FUJIOKA
Ophthalmology: Prof. YUTAKA TAZAWA
Otolaryngology: Prof. KAZUO MURAI
Radiology: Prof. SHIGERU EHARA
Obstetrics and Gynaecology: Prof. TERUO KAKABU
Anaesthesiology: Prof. NAOHISA MORI
Plastic Reconstructive Surgery: Prof. SEIICHIRO KOBAYASHI
Laboratory Medicine: Prof. AKIRA SUWABE
Clinical Pathology: Prof. SHINICHI NAKAMURA
Critical Care and Emergency Center: Prof. SHIGERU TANIGUCHI

School of Dentistry:

Oral Anatomy I: Prof. YOHICHIRO NOZAKA
Oral Anatomy II: Prof. Y. SATOH
Oral Physiology: Prof. YASUYUKI KITADA
Biochemistry: Prof. HIROYA KAWASAKI
Oral Biochemistry: Prof. NOBUKO SATO
Oral Pathology: Prof. MASANOBU SATO
Oral Microbiology: Prof. SHIGENOBU KIMURA
Dental Pharmacology: Prof. HIRHISA KATO
Dental Technology: Prof. YOSHIMA ARAKI
Conservative Dentistry I: Prof. MINORU KUBOTA
Conservative Dentistry II: Prof. KAZUYUKI UENO
Oral Surgery I: Prof. KEIGO KUDO
Oral Surgery II: Prof. SABURO SEKIYAMA
Prosthetic Dentistry I: Prof. HISATOSHI TANAKA
Prosthetic Dentistry II: Prof. KANJI ISHIBASHI
Orthodontics: Prof. HIROYUKI MIURA
Paedodontics: Asst Prof. KUMIKO NOSAKA
Dental Radiology: Prof. KIMIO SAKAMAKI
Oral Diagnosis: Prof. MORIO TOTSUKA
Medicine: Prof. EIJI TAKAHASI
Dental Anaesthesiology: Prof. SHIGEHARU JOH
Preventive Dentistry: Prof. MASAMI YONEMITSU

School of Liberal Arts and Sciences:

Philosophy: Asst Prof. HISAKAZU ENDO
Jurisprudence: Prof. KOKI KANNO
Mathematics: Asst Prof. HIROSHI YANAMOTO
Physics: Asst Prof. EIICHI SATO
Chemistry: Prof. HIROKO HIRANO
Biology: Prof. SUSUMU KIKUCHI
German: Prof. SADAAKI WATANABE
English: Asst Prof. MICHIKO ONO
Literature: Prof. TSUTOMU KUROSAWA
Physical Education: Asst Prof. MASAMI SAKUYAMA
Psychology: Prof. SENJIRO TANAKA

JAPAN ADVANCED INSTITUTE OF SCIENCE AND TECHNOLOGY

1-1 Asahidai, Tatsunokuchi, Nomi, Ishikawa 923-1292
Telephone: (761) 51-1111
Fax: (761) 51-1116
E-mail: kouhou@jaist.ac.jp
Internet: www.jaist.ac.jp
Founded 1990
President: SUKEKATSU USHIODA
Vice-Presidents: AKIO MAKISHIMA, AKIO KAMEOKA
Director of the Library: HIDENOBU HORI
Number of teachers: 202
Number of students: 1,940

DEANS

School of Knowledge Science: YOSHITERU NAKAMORI
School of Information Science: AKIRA SHIMAZU
School of Materials Science: NOBUO OTSUKA

JAPAN WOMEN'S UNIVERSITY

2-8-1 Mejirodai, Bunkyou-ku, Tokyo 112-8681
E-mail: n-abroad@atlas.jwu.ac.jp
Internet: www.jwu.ac.jp
Founded 1901
President: SHOKO GOTO
Number of teachers: 200
Number of students: 5,900
Faculties of Home Economics, Humanities, Integrated Arts and Social Sciences, Science.

JIKEI UNIVERSITY

3-25-8 Nishi-Shinbashi, Minato-ku, Tokyo 105-8461
Telephone: (3) 3433-1111
Fax: (3) 3435-1922
Internet: www.jikei.ac.jp
Founded 1881
Private control
Academic year: April to March
President: SATOSHI KURIHARA
Library of 227,036 vols
Number of teachers: 2,151
Number of students: 1,545
Publications: *Tokyo Jikeikai Medical Journal* (6 a year, in Japanese), *Jikeikai Medical Journal* (4 a year, in English), *Kyoiku Kenkyu Nenpo* (annually, in Japanese), *Research Activities* (annually, in English)

DEANS

School of Medicine and School of Nursing: S. KURIHARA

ATTACHED INSTITUTE

Research Center for Medical Sciences: Dir S. KURIHARA.

KANSAI UNIVERSITY

3-3-35 Yamate-cho, Suita-shi, Osaka 564-8680
Telephone: (6) 6368-1121
Fax: (6) 6330-3027
E-mail: www-adm@www.kansai-u.ac.jp
Internet: www.kansai-u.ac.jp
Founded 1886
Academic year: April to March
President: TEIICHI KAWATA
Chairman of Board of Trustees: SEIICHIRO MORIMOTO
Director of Educational Affairs Bureau: YASUHIRO KONISHI
Librarian: NOBORU TANAKA

Library: see Libraries and Archives
Number of teachers: 1,827
Number of students: 26,674

Publications: *Bungaku Ronshu* (Literary Essays, 3 a year), *Hogaku Ronshu* (Law Review, quarterly), *Shakaigaku Kiyo* (Journal of Sociological Research, 2 a year), *Keizai Ronshu* (Economic Review, 6 a year), *Shogaku Ronshu* (Business Review, 5 a year), *Kogaku Kenkyu Hokoku* (Technology Reports, annually), *Keizai-Seiji Kenkyusho Kenkyu Shoho* (Economic and Political Studies), *Tozaigakujutsu Kenkyusho Kiyo* (Bulletin of Institute of Oriental and Occidental Studies), *Kogaku to Gijutsu* (Engineering and Technology), *Hogaku Kenkyusho Kenkyu Shoho*, *Gien* (Industrial Technology), *Review of Law and Politics*, *Review of Economics*, *Review of Business and Commerce*, *Joho Kenkyu* (Informatics Research), *Senri eno Muchii* (Journal of Graduate School of Foreign Language Education and Research, annually), *Hakubatsukan Kiyo* (annually), *Kokogakutsu Shiryoshitsu Kiyo* (annually), *Jinken Mondai Kenkyu Kiyo* (annually)

DEANS

Faculty of Commerce: Prof. HIROMI TSURUTA
Faculty of Economics: Prof. KANJI MORIOKA
Faculty of Engineering: Prof. TETSUAKO TSUCHIDO
Faculty of Informatics: Prof. TAKASHI KATO
Faculty of Law: Prof. KUMIHIRO OHNUMA
Faculty of Letters: Prof. KEIJI SHIBAI
Faculty of Sociology: Prof. ICHIRO MATSUHARA
School of Law: Prof. KEIICHI YAMANAKA
Institute of Foreign Language Education and Research: Prof. TAICHI USAMI

PROFESSORS

Faculty of Law

Department of Jurisprudence:

OHNUMA, K., Labour Law II
FUKUTAKI, H., Commercial Law
GOTO, M., Civil Law
ICHIHARA, Y., History of Legal Thought
ICHIKAWA, K., Japanese Legal History
IKEDA, T., Administrative Law
IWASAKI, K., Insurance Law and Shipping Law
KAMEDA, K., Administrative Law II
KOCHU, N., Constitutional Law
KOIZUMI, Y., Constitutional Law
KOKUBU, T., Family Law and Succession Law
KURITA, K., Maritime Law
KURITA, T., Debtors' and Creditors' Rights
KUZUHARA, R., Criminal Law
NAGATA, S., Civil Law
OHNUMA, K., Labour Law
OKA, T., European Legal History
SASAMOTO, Y., Insurance Law
SATO, Y., Private International Law
SENTO, Y., Family Law and Succession Law
TSUKIOKA, T., Law of Real Property
YOSHIDA, E., Comparative Constitutional Law
YOSHIDA, N., Emancipation of Buraku

Department of Politics:

MANABE, S., Diplomatic History
MORIMOTO, T., Political and Governmental Organization
OTSURU, C., International Politics
TERAJIMA, T., Political Philosophy
TOKURA, K., European Politics
WAKATA, K., Political Psychology
YAMAMOTO, K., Information Processing
YAMANO, H., Political History of Modern Japan

Faculty of Letters

Course of English Language and Literature:

AKIMOTO, H., American Literature
AOYAMA, T., Linguistics
HASEGAWA, A., English Linguistics
HOSHII, Y., Introductory Seminar
IRIKO, F., Study of American Literature
ISHIZAKA, K., Middle English
KAMIMURA, T., Modern British Novels
KIRWAN, J.
MAKIN, P. J., Modern British and American Poetry
SAKAMOTO, T., History of English Literature
SHIMAZAKI, M., British and American Prose
TANIGUCHI, Y., Modern American Literature
TSUTSUI, O., British and American Drama

Course of Japanese Language and Literature:

ENDO, K., Japanese Linguistics
FUJITA, S., Japanese Literature (Edo Period)
KAMITANI, E., Japanese Linguistics
OHHAMA, M., Early Ancient Japanese Literature
SEKIYA, T., Textual Criticism of Noh Plays
TANAKA, N., Literature in the Heian Period
URANISHI, K., Modern and Contemporary Japanese Literature
YAMAMOTO, T., Early Modern Japanese Fiction
YAMAMOTO, T., Literature in the Heian Period
YOSHIDA, N., History of Modern Japanese Literature

Course of Philosophy:

INOUE, K., Comparative Study of Eastern and Western Thought
KIOKA, N., Philosophy
NAKATANI, N., History of Art in the Far East
ODA, Y., History of Religions
SHINAGAWA, T., Ethics
YAMAMOTO, I., Philosophy

Course of French Language and Literature:

HIRATA, S., Modern French Literature
HONDA, T., French Linguistics
ITOH, M., French Philology
KASHIWAGI, O., French Literature
KAWAKAMI, M., Modern French Literature
NONAMI, T., French Literature
OKU, J., History of French Literature

Course of German Language and Literature:

HAMAMOTO, T., German Cultural Studies
KUDO, Y.
SHIBATA, T., German Literature
TAKEICHI, O., German Linguistics
USAMI, Y., Modern German Literature
WATANABE, Y., German Linguistics
YAKAME, T., German Literature

Course of History and Geography:

ASAJI, K., European Medieval History
FUJITA, T., History of Early China
HASHIMOTO, S., Human Geography
ITOH, O., Human Geography
KOBA, M., Physical Geography
MATSUURA, A., History of Early Modern China
MORI, T.
NAKAMURA, H., History of Modern Russia
NISHIMOTO, M., History of Ancient Japan
NOMA, H., Human History
OHYA, W., History of Modern Japan
SHIBAI, K., History of Modern and Contemporary Europe
SHINTANI, H., History of West Asia
SUITA, H., History of Ancient Orient
TAKAHASHI, S., Human Geography
TAKAHASHI, T., History of Medieval Japan
YABUTA, Y., History of Early Modern Japan
YONEDA, F., Archaeology

Course of Chinese Language and Literature:

AZUMA, J., History of Chinese Philosophy
HAGINO, S., Modern and Contemporary Chinese Literature
INOUE, T., Early Modern Chinese Literature
KAWATA, T., History of Chinese Philosophy
KITAOKA, M., Modern Chinese Literature
KUSAKA, T., Chinese Linguistics
MORISE, T., Classical Chinese Poetry
NIKAIDO, Y., Chinese Popular Religion
TAKEUCHI, Y., Sociology of Education
TAO, D., History of Chinese Philosophy
UCHIDA, K., Chinese Linguistics

Course of Education:

AKAO, K., Adult Education Theory
FUJII, M., Psychology
HATASE, N., Clinical Psychology
MATSUMURA, N., Developmental Psychology
NAKATA, Y., Psychology
NOMURA, Y., Experimental Psychology
OKAMURA, T., Public Administration of Education
TAMADA, K., Pedagogy
TANAKA, T., Psychology
TANAKA, Y., Sociology of Education
YAMAMOTO, F., Pedagogy
YAMAZUMI, K., Educational Research

Inter-Departmental Course:

HAZAMA, K., Social Welfare
KURAHASHI, E., Library and Information Science
SAWAI, S.
SHIBATA, H., Information Processing
UEDA, Y., Liberation of Buraku

Course of Physical Arts:

AOKI, S., Health and Physical Education
BAN, Y., Health and Physical Education
KAWAMOTO, T., Health and Physical Education
KIMURA, S., Health and Physical Education
MIURA, T., Health and Physical Education
MIZOHATA, K., Health and Physical Education
OITA, K., Health and Physical Education
SHIRAFUJI, I., Health and Physical Education
TAKECHI, H., Health and Physical Education
TAMURA, N., Health and Physical Education
ZAKO, T., Health and Physical Education

Faculty of Economics:

AKIOKA, H., Microeconomics
HAMANO, K., Economic History of Japan
HASHIMOTO, K., Public Finance
HASHIMOTO, N., Econometrics
HASHIMOTO, S., History of Economic Theories
HAYASHI, H., Public Finance
HIROE, M., Monetary Policy
ICHIEN, M., Social Security
ICHIKAWA, K., Commercial Economics
ISHIDA, H., Economics of Modern China
IWAI, H., Economic Statistics
KASEDA, H., Economic History
KASHIHARA, M., Agricultural Economics
KASUGA, J., Principles of Economics
KITAGAWA, K., European Economic History
KOIKE, H., Introduction to Political Economy
KUSUNOKI, S., International Economics
LEE, Y., Social Economics
MATSUO, A., Mathematical Statistics
MATSUSHITA, K., Demography
MORIOKA, K., Introduction to Political Economy
MOTOKI, H., Macrodynamics
NAGAHISA, R., Principles of Economics
OTSUKA, T., Social Policy
SATO, M., Macroeconomics
TAKESHITA, K., Theory of Economic System
TANIDA, N., Information Processing
UEMURA, K., History of Social Thought
WAKAMORI, F., Political Economy
YASUKI, H., Industrial Organization
YOSHINAGA, K., Economic Statistics

Faculty of Commerce:

ABE, S., Public Sector Economics
ARAKI, T., Information Processing Practice
HABARA, K., Non-Life Insurance
HATORI, Y., International Relations
HIROSE, M., General Management
HIROTA, T., Corporate Strategy
IKEJIMA, M., Securities Markets
INOUE, S., Business History
ITO, K., Human Resources Management
IWASA, Y., Financial Intermediation and Institutions
KATO, Y., Distribution Theory
MATSUMOTO, Y., Monitoring Theory for Fair Disclosure
MATSUO, N., Financial Accounting
MIKAMI, H., Economics of Transport and Communication
MIZUNO, I., Management Accounting
MYOJIN, N., Book-keeping
NAGANUMA, H., History of Commerce
NAKAJIMA, M., Cost Accounting and Accounting History
NAKAMURA, M., Business Communication
OKU, K., Theory of International Trade
OKURA, Y., Tax Accounting
SASAKURA, A., International Accounting
SHIBA, K., Accounting Information Theory
SUYAMA, K., Marketing Management
TAKAHASHI, N., International Transport
TAKAYA, S.
TSURUTA, H., Public Finance
UE, K., Monetary Theory
YOKOTA, S., European and American Economy
YOSHIDA, T., Management of International Trade

Faculty of Sociology

Major in Sociology:

ISHIMOTO, K., Theory of Buraku Liberation
IWAMI, K., Understanding Modern Societies
KAKEBA, H., Sociology of Knowledge
KATAGIRI, S., Theoretical Sociology
KUMANO, T., Cultural Anthropology
MATSUHARA, I., Social Policy and Planning
NAGAI, Y., Urban Studies
SUGINO, A., Social Welfare Policy and Planning
YAMAMOTO, Y., Sociology of Knowledge
YAMATO, R., Sociology of Family

Major in Industrial Psychology:

AMEMIYA, T., Ergonomics
ENDO, Y., Social Cognition
HIGASHIMURA, T., Information Processing
IIDA, N., Psychiatry
KAWASAKI, T., Vocational Guidance
KURATO, Y., Clinical Psychology
SEKIGUCHI, R., Experimental Psychology
SHIMIZU, K., Psychometrics
TAKAGI, O., Interpersonal Psychology
TERASHIMA, S., Clinical Psychology
TSUCHIDA, S., Social Psychology

Major in Mass Communication:

FUJIOKA, S., Journalism
KIMURA, Y., Social Communication
KURODA, I., Sociology of Broadcasting Culture
MIZUNO, Y.
OGAWA, H., Media and Culture
SENO, G., Human Communication
TSUNEKI, T., Communication Behaviour
YOSHIOKA, I., Communication Theory

Major in Industrial Sociology:

ASADA, M., Policy for Economic Stabilization
FUNABA, T., Human Resource Studies
HASHIMOTO, K., Philosophy of Science
MORITA, M., Personnel Management
OH, Y., Industrial Information Theory
ONISHI, M., Labour–Management Relations
SAITOU, Y., Industrial Technology
TAKASE, T., Industrial Sociology
WAKABAYASHI, M., Business Administration
YANO, H., Economic Theory
YOSANO, A., Mathematical Sociology

Faculty of Informatics:

AOYAMA, C., Global Environmentology
ATSUJI, S., Organizational Decision Making
COOK, N. D., General Systems Theory
EZAWA, Y., Computer Science
FUKADA, Y., Image Processing and Pattern Recognition
FUKE, H., International Networks
FURUTA, H., Fuzzy Logic, Theory and Application
HAYASHI, I., Information Systems Management
HAYASHI, T., Computer Graphics
HIJIKATA, H., Mathematics
HIROKAME, M., Mathematics
HORI, M., File Structure
ITO, T., Computer Simulation
KAMEI, K., Management
KATO, M., Philosophy
KATO, T., Cognitive Science
KATO, T., Computer Crime
KITAJIMA, O., Business Behaviour
KITANI, S., Public Administration
KOMATSU, Y., Business Administration
KUBOTA, K., Audiovisual Media Production
KUBOTA, M., Communication
KUROKAMI, H., Multimedia Education
KUROKUZU, H., Accounting Information Systems
KUWABARA, T., Psychology
MIYASHITA, F., Computer Science
NAKAGAWA, Y., Data Structure and Algorithm
NOGUCHI, H., Business Information
OKAMOTO, T., Public Policy
SANO, M., Community Networks
SHIOMURA, T., Microeconomic Models
SHYI, S. C., Management Information Systems
SUGA, T., Computer-based Communication
TANAKA, S., Knowledge Information Processing
TSUJI, M., Software Architecture
UESHIMA, S., Principles of Database Management
UKAI, Y., Economic Policy
YAMAGUCHI, S., Cultural Studies of Information Society
YAMANA, T., Macroeconomic Models
YOSHIDA, N., Principles of Computer Electronics

Faculty of Engineering

Department of Mechanical Engineering:

ARAI, Y., Measurement Systems
ISHIHARA, I., Thermal Engineering
KITAJIMA, K., Manufacturing Processes
SHINGUABARA, S., Nanophysics and Nanofabrication Technology
SHINKE, N., Strength of Materials
TAGAWA, N., Micromechatronics
TAKUMA, M., Experiments on Mechanical Engineering

Department of Mechanical Systems Engineering:

BANDO, K., Computational Fluid Dynamics
FUJITA, T., Analytical Dynamics
HIGUCHI, M., Production Engineering
IWATSUBO, T., Measurement Systems
MORI, A., Machine Design and Engineering Tribology
OHBA, K., Fluids Engineering and Biomechanics
OZAWA, M., Engineering Thermodynamics
UCHIYAMA, H., Control Engineering

Department of Electrical Engineering and Computer Science:

HARA, T., Theory of Electricity and Magnetism
HORIBA, Y., System LSI
KUMAMOTO, A., Flexible and Intelligent Image Processing
MAEDA, Y., Control Theory and Neural Computation
OHNISHI, M., Study of Ion Beam Colliding Fusion Neutron Source
TAMURA, H., Applied Systems Science
YAMAMOTO, M., Computer Networking

Department of Electronics:

IIDA, Y., Microwave and Millimetre-Wave Engineering
KOJIMA, T., Optical and Electromagnetic Engineering
MUNEYASU, M., Image Processing
MURAMAKA, N., Computer Systems Engineering
NOMURA, Y., Information and Intelligent Systems
OKADA, H., Information Networks
OMURA, Y., Device Physics and Modelling
YOKOTA, K., Semiconductor Engineering

Department of Chemical Engineering:

MIYAKE, T., Catalyst Engineering
MIYAKE, Y., Separation Engineering
MUROYAMA, K., Chemical Reaction Engineering
ODA, H., Physical Chemistry
OKADA, Y., Nanoparticle Engineering
SHIBATA, J., Physical Chemistry
SUZUKI, T., Catalyst Engineering
YAMAMOTO, H., Experimental Chemical Engineering

Department of Applied Chemistry:

ARAKAWA, R., Analytical Chemistry
ISHII, Y., Organometallic Chemistry
ISHIKAWA, T., Electrochemistry and Electrochemical Devices
MATSUMOTO, A., Polymer Chemistry
OCHI, M., Polymer Engineering
OUCHI, T., Functional Polymers
TANEKA, K., Organic Supramolecular Chemistry

Department of Materials Science and Engineering:

AKAMATSU, K., Functional Materials
IKEDA, M., Environmental Conscious Materials Laboratory
KOBAYASHI, T., Processing of Molten Metals
KOMATSU, S., Strength of Materials
KOZUKA, H., Ceramic Engineering
MIYAKE, H., Foundry Engineering
OISHI, T., Physical Chemistry of Materials Processing
SUGIMOTO, T., Nonferrous Metallic Materials

Department of Systems Management Engineering:

AOYAGI, S., Automatic Control Theory
FUYUKI, M., Production Systems Engineering
HORII, K., Human Factors Engineering
MORI, K., Production Management
NAKAI, T., Operations Research
UEMURA, T., Visual Information Engineering

Department of Civil and Environmental Engineering:

DOGAKI, M., Structural Mechanics
ISHIGAKI, T., Hydraulic Engineering for Environment and Disaster Prevention
KAWAKAMI, S., Traffic Engineering
KUSUMI, H., Rock Mechanics and Geological Engineering
MIKAMI, I., Design of Civil Engineering Structures
SAKANO, M., Structural Engineering
TOYOFUKU, T., Construction Materials

WADA, Y., Sanitary Engineering

Department of Architecture:

ASANO, K., Structural Engineering
EGAWA, N., Architectural Environmental Design Laboratory
KAWAI, Y., Environmental Engineering
KAWAMICHI, R., Architectural Theory and Design
MARUMO, H., Urban Design
NAGAI, N., History of Architecture
NOGUCHI, T., Environmental Engineering
YAO, S., Structural Engineering

Department of Biotechnology:

HASEGAWA, Y., Genetic Engineering
OBATA, H., Microbial Technology
TSUCHIDO, T., Biocontrol Technology
UESATO, S., Pharmaceutical Technology
YAGI, H., Biochemical Engineering
YOSHIDA, M., Food Biotechnology

General Education in Natural Sciences:

AKI, S.
FUKUSHIMA, M., Probability Theory
ICHIHARA, K., Probability Theory
IKEUCHI, I., Intracellular Signals Transduction Mechanism of Neuronal Cells
KURISU, T., Game Theory
KURIYAMA, A., Mathematical Physics
KUSUDA, M., Functional Analysis
SAITO, T.
SEKI, M., Fluid Dynamics
SHIRAIWA, T., Chiral Molecular Chemistry
TAJITSU, Y.
TAMURA, H., Naturally Occurring Polymer Chemistry
TATSUMI, M., Applied Analytical Chemistry
URAGAMI, T., Functional Polymer Science
YAMAMURA, M., Quantum Many-body Physics
YAMAUCHI, O., Bio-inorganic Chemistry
YANAGAWA, T., Knot Group Theory

Institute of Foreign Language Education and Research:

FUKUI, N., Study of Japanese Culture and Ruth Benedict
GEN, YUKIKOI, Diachronic Study of Colloquial Chinese
GIBBS, A. S., Approach to Foreign-language Communication through Pragmatics, Stylistics and Discourse Analysis, Reading and Writing for Academic Purposes
HIRATA, W., Spanish and Latin American Literature
ISHIHARA, T., American Literature
JOHNSON, G. S., Presentation, Oral Interpretation
KAWAI, T., English Education, English Linguistics
KIKUCHI, A., Linguistics
KIKUCHI, U., Experimental Phonetics
KITAMURA, Y., Cognitive Science, Education Technology
KITE, Y., Sociolinguistics, Second Language Acquisition
KONDO, M., Russian Literature
KUMATANI, A., Korean Linguistics, Sociolinguistics
MOCHIZUKI, M., Applied Linguistics, Japanese Linguistics
NISHIKAWA, K., Chinese Linguistics
SAITO, E., English Education
SCHAUWECKER, D. F., Japanese–German Relationships
SHEN, G., Chinese Language Education
SUGITANI, M., German Language, Education and Intercultural Communication
TAKAHASHI, H., Sociolinguistics
TAKAHASHI, T., English Language Education
TAKEUCHI, O., Applied Linguistics, Educational Technology
USAMI, T., English Literature, English Education
WADA, Y., Medieval Manuscript Studies
YAMANE, S., English Phonetics
YAMAMOTO, E., English Linguistics
YASHIMA, T., Applied Linguistics, Intercultural Communication
YOSHIZAWA, K., Applied Linguistics

School of Law:

FUJITA, H., International Law
HAYAKAWA, T., Commercial Law
IMANISHI, Y., Civil Law
ISHII, K., Criminal Procedure
KAMEDA, K., Administrative Law
KAWAGUCHI, M., Labour Law
KIMURA, T., Civil Law
KINOSHITA, S., Constitutional Law
KITAGAWA, T., Law of International Transactions
KUBO, H., Civil Law
MURATA, H., Constitutional Law
MUROTA, G.
NOVO, M., Administrative Law
ODO, Y., Civil Law
SHIMADA, R., Civil Procedure
TAKESHITA, K., Philosophy of Law
TAKIGAWA, T., Economic Law, International Economic Law
TATSUMI, N., Intellectual Property Law
YAMANAKA, K., Criminal Law
YAMATO, M., Commercial Law
WAKAMATSU, Y., Civil Law

KEIO UNIVERSITY

2-15-45 Mita, Minato-ku, Tokyo 108-8345
Telephone: (3) 3453-4511
Fax: (3) 3769-1564
E-mail: www@info.keio.ac.jp
Internet: www.keio.ac.jp/index-en.html

Founded 1858
Private control
Academic year: April to March

President: YUICHIRO ANZAI
Vice-Presidents: M. KURODA, T. SEKIBA, M. SHIMIZU, T. SARUTA, N. SAITO, H. YAMAZAKI, T. TANAKA, N. KUDO, K. YOSHIDA
Secretary-General: T. ISHIKAWA
Registrar: T. TOIZUMI
Directors of Libraries: K. HOSONO (Mita Media Centre), Y. ITO (Hiyoshi Media Centre), S. KOYASU (Medical Information and Media Center), K. HARADA (Information and Media Center for Science and Technology), M. OOE (SFC Media Center)

Library of 3,700,000 vols
Number of teachers: 1,859 full-time
Number of students: 32,137 (regular course), 11,661 (correspondence course)

Publications: *Keio Business Review* (annually), *Keio Communication Review* (annually), *Keio Economic Studies* (2 a year), *Keio Journal of Medicine* (4 a year)

DEANS

Faculty of Business and Commerce: H. SAKURAMOTO
Faculty of Economics: E. HOSODA
Faculty of Environmental Information: K. KUMASAKA
Faculty of Law: S. MORI
Faculty of Letters: T. NISHIMURA
School of Medicine: M. KITAJIMA
Faculty of Policy Management: T. KOJIMA
Faculty of Science and Technology: I. INASAKI
Faculty of Nursing and Medical Care: K. YOSHINO

CHAIRPERSONS

Graduate School of Business Administration: M. AOI
Graduate School of Business and Commerce: H. SAKURAMOTO
Graduate School of Economics: K. IKEO
Graduate School of Health Management: K. YOSHINO
Graduate School of Human Relations: H. MITSUI
Graduate School of Law: S. MORI
Graduate School of Letters: T. NISHIMURA
Graduate School of Media and Governance: H. TOKUDA
Graduate School of Medicine: M. KITAJIMA
Graduate School of Science and Technology: I. INASAKI
Law School: T. HIRARAGI

DIRECTORS

International Center: T. SAKAMOTO
Institute of Cultural and Linguistic Studies: S. NAKAGAWA
Institute for Media and Communications Research: M. SEKINE
Institute for Economic and Industry Studies (Keio Economic Observatory): K. TSUJIMURA
Institute of Physical Education: R. TAKAMINE
Institute of Oriental Classics: T. SEKIBA
Fukuzawa Memorial Center for Modern Japanese Studies: M. KOMURO
Teacher Training Center: K. SAKAKIBARA
Keio Institute of East Asian Studies: C. YOKOYAMA
Keio Research Center for Foreign Language: S. SAKOMURA
Centre for Japanese Studies: T. SAKAMOTO
Sports Medicine Research Center: H. YAMAZAKI
Research Centre for the Arts and Arts Administration: F. MAEDA
Institute of Computer Education: Y. OHNO
Keio Research Institute at SFC: J. MURAI
Intellectual Property Centre: K. SHIMIZU
Institute for Advanced Biosciences: M. TOMITA
Keio Research Centre for the Liberal Arts: I. HADA
Information Technology Center: S. SUGIYAMA
Institute for Advanced Medical Research: M. KITAJIMA
Center for Integrated Medical Research: Y. IKEDA
Global Security Research Institute: A. SETH
Research Institute for Digital Media and Content: Y. ANZAI
Organization for Global Initiatives: Y. ANZAI
Leading-Edge Laboratory of Science and Technology: Y. KOIKE

KINKI UNIVERSITY

Kowakae 3-4-1, Higashiosaka-shi, Osaka 577-8502
Telephone: (6) 6721-2332
Fax: (6) 6721-2353
E-mail: koho@msa.kindai.ac.jp
Internet: www.kindai.ac.jp

Founded 1925
Private control
Language of instruction: Japanese
Academic year: April to March

President: HIROYUKI HATA
Head Administrator: HIROAKI SEKOH

Library of 1,200,000 vols
Number of teachers: 1,563
Number of students: 29,794

Publications: *Acta Medica Kinki University* (2 a year), *Annals of the Molecular Engineering Institute* (annually), *Annual Report of Kinki University Atomic Energy Research Institute* (annually), *Bulletin of the Fisheries Laboratory of Kinki University* (irregular), *Bulletin of the Pharmaceutical Research and Technology Institute* (annually), *Bulletin of the School of Literature, Arts and Cultural Studies* (annually), *Ikoma Journal of Economics* (2 a year), *Journal of Business Administration and Marketing Strategy* (3 a year), *Journal of the Faculty of Science and Engineering at Kinki University* (annually), *Law Review of Kinki University*

(4 a year), *Medical Journal of Kinki University* (2 a year), *Memoirs of the Faculty of Agriculture of Kinki University* (annually), *Memoirs of the Institute of Advanced Technology* (2 a year), *Memoirs of the School of Biology-Oriented Science and Technology* (annually), *Multimedia Education* (annually), *Research Journal of the Department of Teacher Education* (2 a year), *Research Reports of the Faculty of Engineering of Kinki University* (annually), *Science and Technology* (annually)

DEANS

School of Agriculture: KOICHIRO KOMAI
School of Biology-Oriented Science and Technology: KAZUO YAMAMOTO
School of Business Administration: HIROYASU OKITSU
School of Economics: KYOUZOU TAKECHI
School of Engineering: HIROSHI TSUBAKIHARA
School of Humanity-Oriented Science and Engineering: MASAYUKI ONO
School of Law: HIDEJIRO ISHIDA
School of Literature, Arts and Cultural Studies: YUTAKA ARAMAKI
School of Medicine: HARUMASA OYANAGI
School of Pharmaceutical Sciences: KAZUAKI KAKEHI
School of Science and Engineering: MEGUMU MUNAKATA

ATTACHED RESEARCH INSTITUTES

Atomic Energy Research Institute: Dir HIROSHIGE MORISHIMA.

Centre for Human Rights: Dir SUEHIRO KITAGUCHI.

Ethnology Research Centre: Dir KANICHI NOMOTO.

Experimental Farms: Dir NAOKI UTSUNOMIYA.

Fisheries Laboratory: Dir HIDEMI KUMAI.

Industrial and Law Information Institute: Dir HIDEO UENO.

Institute of Advanced Technology: Dir AKIRA IRITANI.

Institute of Immunotherapy for Cancer: Dir KOJIN KARATANI.

Institute of Resource Recycling: Dir KOICHIRO KOMAI.

Kinki University Hospital: Dir HITOSHI SHIOZAKI.

Life Science Research Institute: Dir KINJI ISHIKAWA.

Molecular Engineering Institute: Dir MASAKUNI YOSHIHARA.

Nara Hospital, Kinki University School of Medicine: Dir YOSHIKI INOUE.

Pharmaceutical Research and Technology Institute: Dir KAZUAKI KAKEHI.

Research Institute of Industrial Technology: Dir YASUHIRO FUKAYA.

Research Institute of Oriental Medicine: Dir MASAYUKI YASUTOMI.

Research Institute for Science and Technology: Dir OSAMU FUJINO.

Sakai Hospital, Kinki University School of Medicine: Dir TAKAHIRO AKIYAMA.

KOBE GAKUIN UNIVERSITY

518 Arise, Ikawadani-cho, Nishiku, Kobe 651-2180
Telephone: (78) 974-1551
Fax: (78) 974-5689
E-mail: kgu@j.kobegakuin.ac.jp
Internet: www.kobegakuin.ac.jp

Founded 1966
Academic year: April to March

President: TADANORI MAYUMI
Administrative Officer: YOSHIHIRO MIYAMOTO
Librarian: HIROMI YOSHIDA

Library of 793,950 vols
Number of teachers: 220
Number of students: 8,838

Publications: *Kobe Gakuin Hogaku* (Law and Politics Review), *Kobe Gakuin Economic Papers, Annual Report of the Faculty of Nutrition, Memoirs of the Faculty of Pharmaceutical Sciences, Faculty Bulletin of Humanities and Sciences, Report of the High Technology Research Centre* (annually), *Asia-Pacific Research Centre Annual Report, Journal of Business Management*

DEANS

Faculty of Business Administration: NOBUO TSUNO
Faculty of Economics: YOSHIO TANAKA
Faculty of Humanities and Sciences: HIRONORI MIZUMOTO
Faculty of Law: TOYOKI OKADA
Faculty of Nutrition: KIYOSHI GODA
Faculty of Pharmaceutical Sciences: HIROSHI OKAMOTO
Faculty of Rehabilitation: ISAO NARA
Graduate School of Economics: YOSHIO TANAKA
Graduate School of Food and Medicinal Sciences: KIYOSHI GODA
Graduate School of Humanities and Sciences: HIRONORI MIZUMOTO
Graduate School of Law: TOYOKI OKADA
Graduate School of Law Practices: KENJI SANEKATA
Graduate School of Nutrition: KIYOSHI GODA
Graduate School of Pharmaceutical Sciences: HIROSHI OKAMOTO

ATTACHED RESEARCH INSTITUTES

Asia Pacific Research Centre: Dean HIROYUKI TANIGUCHI.

Center for Area Research and Development: Dean HIROYUKI SHIMIZU.

Center for High-Technology Research: Dean YOSHIO OKADA.

Co-operative Research Centre of Life Sciences: Dir TADANORI MAYUMI.

East Asian Industry and Economy Research Center: Dean MEGUMI NAKAMURA.

KOGAKUIN UNIVERSITY

1-24-2, Nishi-shinjuku, Shinjuku-ku, Tokyo 163-8677
Telephone: (3) 3342-1211
Fax: (3) 3342-5304
Internet: www.kogakuin.ac.jp

Founded 1887, university status 1949
Academic year: April to March

President: HIROFUMI MIURA
Registrar: YUJI KIMURA
Librarian: EIJI YODOGAWA

Library of 256,000 vols
Number of teachers: 200
Number of students: 7,050 (6,500 undergraduates, 520 graduate students, 30 doctoral students)

Publications: *Kogakuin Daigaku Kenkyu Hokoku* (research reports, 2 a year), *Kogakuin Daigaku Kyotukatei Kenkyu Ronso* (research reports, 2 a year)

HEADS OF DEPARTMENTS

Mechanical Engineering: Prof. AKISATO MIZUNO
Mechanical Systems Engineering: Prof. HIROFUMI MIURA
Basic Engineering in Global Environment: Prof. OKITSUGU FRUYA
Applied Chemistry: Prof. MORIO HIRANO
Environmental Chemical Engineering: Prof. NAOTAKE KATO
Materials Science and Technology: Prof. SHINYA TERAMACHI
Electrical Engineering: Prof. SHUICHI YOKOYAMA
Electronic Engineering: Prof. HIDEO KAWANISHI
Computer Science and Communication Engineering: Prof. HISAO SHIIZUKA
Architecture: Prof. TAKURO YOSHIDA
Design in Architecture and Urbanism: Prof. SADAO WATANABE

KOKUGAKUIN UNIVERSITY

4-10-28, Higashi, Shibuya-ku, Tokyo 150-8440
Telephone: (3) 5466-0111
Fax: (3) 5778-7061
E-mail: kokusai@kokugakuin.ac.jp
Internet: www.kokugakuin.ac.jp

Founded 1882
Academic year: April to March

President: Prof. MASAHIKO ASOYA
Secretary-General: SHOZO SANAGI
Librarian: T. SAWANOBORI

Library: see Libraries
Number of teachers: 790
Number of students: 10,319

Publications: *Kokugakuin Zasshi* (Journal of Kokugakuin University), *Kokugakuin Keizaigaku* (Kokugakuin University Economic Review), *Kokugakuin Hogaku* (Journal of the Faculty of Law and Politics), *Kokugakuin Daigaku Kiyo* (Transactions of Kokugakuin University), *Kokugakuin Daigaku Daigakuin Bungaku Kenkyuka ronshu* (Journal of the Graduate School, Kokugakuin University), *Kokugakuin Daigaku Kenzaigaku Kenkyuka Kiyo* (Kokugakuin University Economic Studies), *Kokugakuin Hokenronso* (Journal of Law and Politics, Graduate School of Law), *Nihonbunka-Kenkyusho-Kiyo* (Transactions of the Institute for Japanese Culture and Classics)

DEANS

Faculty of Letters: SHUHEI AOKI
Faculty of Economics: HIRONORI KON'I
Faculty of Law: SEIICHI NAGAMORI
Faculty of Shinto Studies: SOJI OKADA
Graduate School: TSUYOSHI FUJIMOTO
Law School: KATSUMASA HIRABAYASHI

ATTACHED RESEARCH INSTITUTES

Institute for Japanese Culture and Classics: 4-10-28, Higashi, Shibuya-ku, Tokyo 150-8440.

KOKUSHIKAN UNIVERSITY

4-28-1 Setagaya, Setagaya-ku, Tokyo 154-8515
Telephone: (3) 5481-3112
Fax: (3) 3413-7420
E-mail: wwwadmin@kiss.kokushikan.ac.jp
Internet: www.kokushikan.ac.jp

Founded 1917
Private control
Academic year: April to March

Chairman: HARUO NISHIHARA
President: HIDEO OSAWA
General Director: ATSUSHI MATSUMOTO
Librarian: SHOICHI YAMAMOTO

Library of 630,638 vols
Number of teachers: 310
Number of students: 12,677

Publications: *Politics and Economics Review, Kokushikan Law Review*, various faculty journals and reviews

DEANS

Faculty of Political Science and Economics: HIROYUKI YAMAZAKI
Faculty of Political Science and Economics (Evening Session): RYOZO SHIROGANE
Faculty of Physical Education: KAZUYUKI NISHYAMA
Faculty of Engineering: KATSUHIKO WAKABAYASHI
Faculty of Law: NORIYOSHI WATANABE
Faculty of Letters: AKIRA ABE
School of Asia 21: KAGEAKI KAJIWARA
Junior College: HIROSHI TASHIRO

HEADS OF DEPARTMENTS

Faculty of Political Science and Economics (tel. (3) 5481-3151; fax (3) 5481-3153):

Political Philosophy: KICHIZO FUJIMOTO
Economics: SHUNSUKI AOKI
Business Administration: YOSHINORI NAGAI

Faculty of Political Science and Economics (Evening Session) (tel. (3) 5481-3146; fax (3) 5481-3141):

Economics: KEIICHI SATO
Politics: HIROMI INO

Faculty of Physical Education (7-3-1 Nagayama, Tama-shi, Tokyo 206-8515; tel. (42) 339-7200; fax (42) 339-7238):

Martial Arts: YASUFUMI KOYAMA
Physical Education: TOYOJI HASHIMOTO
Sports and Medical Science: KEISUKE AMAHA

Faculty of Engineering (tel. (3) 5481-3251; fax (3) 5481-3253):

Mechanical Engineering: YOSHINORI NAKAZAWA
Electrical Engineering: NOZOMI MORIOKA
Civil Engineering: HIDEO KANARI
Architectural Engineering: NAOHITO HORI

Faculty of Law (tel. (3) 5481-3311; fax (3) 5481-3328):

Law: YOSHITADA KOMATSU
Modern Business Law: TADASHI WATANABE

Faculty of Letters (tel. (3) 5481-3231; fax (3) 5481-3328):

Education: YOTARO MOURI
Ethics: HIROMUNE MASHIBA
Elementary Education: TAMOTSU UMEBARA
Japanese History: SATORU HOSAKA
Oriental History: TAKAO ISHIBASHI
Geography: HITOSHI HASEGAWA
Chinese Literature: YOSHIHIDO UCHIMURA
Japanese Language and Literature: SHOICHI YAMAMOTO

School of Asia 21 (1-1-1 Hirohakama, Machida-shi, Tokyo 195-8550; tel. (42) 736-1050; fax (42) 735-3680; e-mail asia21jim@kiss.kokushikan.ac.jp):

Head of Department: NOBUO HARADA

Junior College (1-1-1 Hirohakama, Machida-shi, Tokyo 195-8550; tel. (42) 736-2345; fax (42) 736-2348):

Japanese Literature: KIYOSHI OMOTE

ATTACHED INSTITUTES

Institute for the Study of Politics: Dir JINSEI SATOU.

Institute for Cultural Studies of Ancient Iraq: Dir KATSUHIKO ONUMA.

Institute for Research on Martial Arts and Ethics: Dir MASANORI NOGI.

Center for Information Science: Dir HARUO KAWASAKI.

Asia-Japan Research Center: Dir NOBUYUKI MIURA.

Lifetime Learning Center: Dir KUNITOSHI MATSUBA.

KOMAZAWA UNIVERSITY

1-23-1 Komazawa, Setagaya-ku, Tokyo 154-8525
Telephone: (3) 3418-9010
Fax: (3) 3418-9017
E-mail: info-soumu@komazawa-u.ac.jp
Internet: www.komazawa-u.ac.jp
Academic year: April to March

President: TETSUO OTANI
Vice-President: MITSUNORI TAKEHANA
Registrar: RYOKO HIROSE
Librarian: TATSUYA HAYASHI

Library of 1,076,500 vols
Number of teachers: 328
Number of students: 15,422

Publications: *Journal of the Faculty of Buddhism*, *Journal of Buddhist Studies*, *Komazawa Educational Review*, *Regional Views*, *Journal of the Faculty of Letters*, *Komazawa Japanese Literature*, *Studies in British and American Literature*, *Komazawa Geography*, *Journal of the Historical Association of Komazawa.*, *Komazawa Journal of Sociology*, *Journal of the Faculty of Economics*, *The Economic Review of Komazawa Univ.*, *Journal of the Faculty of Law of Komazawa University*, *Komazawa Law and Political Science Review*, *Komazawa Business Studies*, *Komazawa Business Review*, *Journal of the Faculty of Foreign Languages*, *The Review of Foreign Languages*, *Bunka* (Komazawa University Journal of Culture), *Journal of Health Sciences of Komazawa University*, *Journal of Radiological Sciences of Komazawa University*, *Komazawa Annual of Sociology*, *Komazawa University Journal of Health and Physical Education*

DEANS

Faculty of Buddhism: RENTARO IKEDA
Faculty of Business Administration: SHIGERU HATORI
Faculty of Economics: SHUJI KOSUGI
Faculty of Health Sciences: MASAKI KOYAMA
Faculty of Law: SANAE URATA
Faculty of Letters: MASAHIRO TAKAGI

CHAIRMEN

Graduate Division of Arts and Sciences: TAKETSUGI IIJIMA
Graduate Division of Business Administration: TOMOMORI NAGATA
Graduate Division of Buddhism: MASASHI NAGAI
Graduate Division of Commerce: YOSHIHARU HIYAKUTA
Graduate Division of Economics: MASASHI NAGAI
Graduate Division of Law: MASATAKA ARAKI
Graduate Division of Legal Research and Training: HIROYUKI AONO

ATTACHED INSTITUTES

Institute for Applied Geography.

Institute for Comparative Buddhist Literature.

Institute of Legal Research.

Institute of Mass Communication.

Institute of Zen Buddhism and Economics.

Research Institute for Accounting.

Zen Institute.

KONAN UNIVERSITY

8-9-1 Okamoto, Higashinada-ku, Kobe 658-8501
Telephone: (78) 431-4341
Fax: (78) 435-2306
E-mail: d-jimu@adm.konan-u.ac.jp
Internet: www.konan-u.ac.jp

Founded 1918

President: Y. SUGIMURA

Library of 775,000 vols
Number of teachers: 240 full-time
Number of students: 9,578

Publications: *Journal of Konan University Faculty of Letters* (irregular), *Memoirs of Konan University* (science and engineering series, 2 a year), *Konan Economic Papers* (irregular), *Konan Hogaku* (Konan Law Review, irregular), *Konan Business Review* (irregular), *Journal of the Institute for Language and Culture* (irregular)

DEANS

Faculty of Business Administration: Y. NAKATA
Faculty of Economics: H. KOBAYASHI
Faculty of Law: T. MAEDA
Faculty of Letters: T. HISATAKE
Faculty of Science and Engineering: T. SHIGEMATSU

KOSHIEN UNIVERSITY

Momijigaoka, Takarazuka, Hyogo 665-0006
Telephone: (797) 87-5111
Fax: (797) 87-5666
E-mail: info@koshien.ac.jp
Internet: www.koshien.ac.jp

Founded 1967

President: TOMIO KINOSHITA

Library of 106,942 vols
Number of teachers: 170
Number of students: 1,428

Colleges of Nutrition, Business Administration, Information Sciences, Humanities.

KURUME UNIVERSITY

67 Asahi-Machi, Kurume 830-0011
Telephone: (942) 35-3311
Fax: (942) 32-5191
E-mail: soumu@med.kurume-u.ac.jp
Internet: www.kurume-u.ac.jp

Founded 1928

President: KYOZO KOKETSU
Director of Administrative Office: KATSUMI YOSHIHISA

Library of 415,000 vols
Number of teachers: 534
Number of students: 5,808

Publications: *The Kurume Medical Journal* (quarterly), *The Journal of the Kurume Medical Association* (monthly), *The Journal for Studies on Industrial Economics* (quarterly)

Faculties of Literature, Economics, Commerce, Medicine and Law.

KWANSEI GAKUIN UNIVERSITY

1-1-155 Uegahara, Nishinomiya, Hyogo 662-8501
Telephone: (798) 51-0952
Fax: (798) 51-0954
E-mail: ciec@kwansei.ac.jp
Internet: www.kwansei.ac.jp

Founded 1889
Academic year: April to March

Chancellor: MICHIYA HATA
President: KAZUO HIRAMATSU
Vice-Presidents: KOHEI ASANO, TOKUTOSHI INOUE, HIDEKI MINE
Library Director: TAKUTOSHI INOUE

Library: see Libraries and Archives
Number of teachers: 435 full-time
Number of students: 18,702

Publications: *Theological Studies*, *Humanities Review*, *Journal of the School of Sociology*, *Journal of Law and Politics*,

Journal of Economics, Journal of Business Administration, Law Review, Economic Review, Journal of Policy Studies, Review of Economics and Business Management, Studies in Computer Science, Language and Culture, Studies in Teacher Development, Social Sciences Review, Natural Sciences Review

DEANS

School of Business Administration: AKIRA MIYAMA
School of Economics: SHIN NEGISHI
School of Humanities: ATSUHIDE SAKAKURA
School of Law and Politics: YOZO SAWADA
School of Policy Studies: TOYOO FUKUDA
School of Science: YAICHI SHINOHARA
School of Sociology: MICHIHITO TSUSHIMA
School of Theology: ETSURO KINOWAKI
Law School: TOORU KATO
Graduate School of Language, Communication and Culture: TAKAAKI KANZAKI
Institute of Business and Accounting: MARTIN COLLICK

KYOTO PHARMACEUTICAL UNIVERSITY

5, Misasagi-Nakauchi-cho, Yamashina-ku, Kyoto 607-8414
Telephone: (75) 595-4600
Fax: (75) 595-4750
E-mail: kpu-koho@mb.kyoto-phu.ac.jp
Internet: www.kyoto-phu.ac.jp

Founded 1884

President: MASAZUMI IKEDA
Registrar: Dr NORIAKI FUNASAKI
Librarian: Dr TAKESI NISINO

Library of 91,260 vols
Number of teachers: 104
Number of students: 1,821

PROFESSORS

FUJIMOTO, S., Environmental Biochemistry
FUNASAKI, N., Physical Chemistry
HAMAZAKI, H., Health and Sports Sciences
HATAYAMA, T., Biochemistry
HIRAYAMA, T., Public Health
UENISHI, J., Pharmaceutical Chemistry
KAMBE, T., Mathematics
KIM, J., Cell Biology
KISO, Y., Medicinal Chemistry
KITAMURA, K., Analytical Chemistry
KOHNO, S., Pharmacology
KOIKE, C., Physics Laboratory
KONOSHIMA, T., Pharmaceutical Sciences and Natural Resources
MURANISHI, S., Pharmaceutics
NAKATA, T., Clinical Pharmacology
NISHINO, T., Microbiology
NODE, M., Pharmaceutical Manufacturing Chemistry
OHTA, S., Chemistry of Functional Molecules
OKABE, S., Applied Pharmacology
SAKURAI, H., Analytical and Bioinorganic Chemistry
SATO, T., Pathological Biochemistry
TAKADA, K., Pharmacokinetics
TAKEUCHI, K., Pharmacology and Experimental Therapeutics
TANIGUCHI, T., Neurobiology
YAMAMOTO, A., Biopharmaceutics
YOKOYAMA, T., Hospital Pharmacy
YOSHIKAWA, M., Pharmacognosy

ATTACHED INSTITUTE

Institute of Molecular and Cellular Biology for Pharmaceutical Sciences.

Center for Frontier Research in Medicinal Sciences.

MATSUYAMA UNIVERSITY

4–2 Bunkyo-cho, Matsuyama Ehime 790-8578
Telephone: (89) 925-7111
Fax: (89) 922-6064
E-mail: mu-koho@matsuyama-u.ac.jp
Internet: www.matsuyama-u.ac.jp

Founded 1923
Academic year: April to March

President: Prof. SATORU KANIMORI
Registrar: SANIMOTU OCHI

Library: see Libraries and Archives
Number of teachers: 308
Number of students: 5,730

Publications: *Matsuyama Daigaku Ronshu* (every 2 months), *Studies in Language and Literature* (2 a year)

DEANS

Faculty of Business Administration: Prof. N. IDIIDA
Faculty of Economics: Prof. J. IRIE, Prof. Y. SEINO
Faculty of Humanities: Prof. T. KANAMURA
Faculty of Law: Prof. T. TAKEMIYA
Junior College: Prof. K. YAGI

MEIJI UNIVERSITY

1-1 Kanda-Surugadai, Chiyoda-ku, Tokyo 101-8301
Telephone: (3) 3296-4545
Fax: (3) 3296-4339
E-mail: koho@isc.meiji.ac.jp
Internet: www.meiji.ac.jp

Founded 1881
Private control
Academic year: April to March (two semesters)

Chancellor: HIROMI NAYA
President: HIROMI NAYA
Director of Library: SHUICHI NOGAMI

Library of 1,930,000 vols
Number of teachers: 2,025 (716 full-time, 1,309 part-time)
Number of students: 35,504 (33,155 undergraduate, 1,358 postgraduate, 991 women's junior college)

DEANS

School of Agriculture: INATOMI HIDEO
School of Arts and Letters: TAKEHIKO YOSHIMURA
School of Business Administration: KATSUHIKO HIRAI
School of Commerce: YOSHIO SUZUKI
School of Information and Communication: YOSHIYUKI NAKAMURA
School of Law: KEIICHIRO TSUCHIYA
School of Political Science and Economics: KAZUTO IIDA
School of Science and Technology: MASAO MUKAIDONO
Graduate School: AKIRA NAKAMURA

GRADUATE SCHOOL CHAIRMEN

Department of Agriculture: YUKIO HIROMASA
Department of Arts and Letters: KAZUMASA HINATA
Department of Business Administration: ETSUO ABE
Department of Commerce: KUNIO FUKUDA
Department of Governance Science: HIROO ICHIKAWA
Department of Global Business: TAKEAKI KARIYA
Department of Law: MAKOTO OKANO
Department of Political Science and Economics: AKIRA SAITO
Department of Professional Accountancy: HIROMI NAYA
Department of Science and Technology: MASAO MUKAIDONO

ATTACHED INSTITUTES

Institute of Humanities: Dir MASAHIKO HAYASHI.

Institute of Social Sciences: Dir KOHEI YAMADA.

Institute of Sciences and Technology: Dir KATSUMI YONEYAMA.

Museum: Dir TAKASHI KOAZE.

Computer Centre: Dir HARUO SHIMOSAKA.

Centre for International Programmes: Dir SHIGEHIKO ARAI.

MEIJI GAKUIN UNIVERSITY

1-2-37 Shirokanedai, Minato-ku, Tokyo 108-8636
Telephone: (3) 5421-5152
Fax: (3) 5421-5458
E-mail: cicet@mguad.meijigakuin.ac.jp
Internet: www.meijigakuin.ac.jp

Founded 1877
Private control
Language of instruction: Japanese
Academic year: April to July, September to March

Chancellor: Prof. SATORU KUZE
President: Prof. YOSHIKAZU WAKITA
Vice-Presidents: Prof. MIKIKO YAMAZAKI, Prof. TOSHIO HASHIMOTO, Prof. TOMOYOSHI KOIZUMI
Administrative Officer: SHUJI SHIBASAKI
Librarian: Prof. KUNIO IWAYA

Library of 825,000 vols
Number of teachers: 256
Number of students: 13,639

Publications: *Meiji Gakuin Review, English Language and Literature, Papers and Proceedings of Economics, Proceedings of Integrated Arts and Sciences, Law Review* (3 a year), *International and Regional Studies* (2 a year), *French Literature, Art Studies, Psychology, Sociology and Social Welfare Review* (annually)

DEANS

Faculty of Literature: Prof. RYUUICHI HIGUCHI
Faculty of Economics: Prof. TAKESHI OSHIO
Faculty of Sociology and Social Work: Prof. KATSUYOSHI KAWAI
Faculty of Law: Prof. MITSURU ABE
Faculty of International Studies: Prof. NOZOMO AKIZUKI
Faculty of General Education: Prof. YASUO IKEGAMI
Graduate School of Literature: Prof. MASAAKI TSUTSUI
Graduate School of Economics: Prof. MASAAKI TAKAMATSU
Graduate School of Sociology and Social Work: Prof. KIYOSHI MATSUI
Graduate School of Law: Prof. AKIRA OKI
Graduate School of International Studies: Prof. SHIGEMOCHI HIROSHIMA

MEIJO UNIVERSITY

1-501 Shiogamaguchi, Tempaku-ku, Nagoya, Aichi 468-8502
Telephone: (52) 832-1151
Fax: (52) 833-9494
E-mail: kikaku@meijo-u.ac.jp
Internet: www.meijo-u.ac.jp

Founded 1949
Private control
Academic year: April to March

President: MASAKI AMINAKA
Administrative Officer: RYOICHI ARAI
Library Director: YUICHIROU OZAKI

Library of 735,994 vols, 7,047 periodicals
Number of teachers: 431 (full-time)
Number of students: 15,495

Publications: *Meijo Hogaku, Meijo Ronsou*, faculty bulletins and reports

DEANS

Faculty of Law: Yuzou Kimura
Faculty of Business: Hitoshi Imai
Faculty of Economics: Umegaki
Faculty of Science and Technology: Tetso Hujimoto
Faculty of Agriculture: Naosuke Nii
Faculty of Pharmacy: Yoshio Suzuki
Faculty of Urban Science: Todashi Ushijima
Faculty of Education: Kouji Itou
Junior College: Shinji Morita

MEISEI UNIVERSITY

2-1-1 Hodokubo, Hino-shi, Tokyo 191-8506
Campuses at Hino and Ome
Telephone: Hino: (42) 591-5111; Ome: (428) 25-5111
Fax: Hino: (42) 591-8181; Ome: (428) 25-5182
E-mail: office@flc.meisei-u.ac.jp
Internet: www.meisei-u.ac.jp

Founded 1964
Private control
Academic year: April to March

President: Jun'ichi Ujihara
Vice-Presidents: Tetsuo Ogawa, Takehiko Maruyama
Directors of Student Affairs: Kazuyoshi Yamanaka, Toshiaki Ueda
Secretary-General: Katsunori Kanatani
Library Director: Yoshiaki Fiunatsu

Library of 880,305 vols, 4,300 periodicals
Number of teachers: 243
Number of students: 8,651 (correspondence courses 8,152)

Publications: *Research Bulletin of Meisei University. Humanities and Social Sciences* (annually), *Research Bulletin of Meisei University. Physical Sciences and Engineering* (annually), *Bulletin of Meisei University. Department of Arts, Faculty of Japanese Culture* (annually), *Research Bulletin of Meisei University. Faculty of Informatics* (annually), *Annual Bulletin of the Graduate School of Humanities and Social Sciences, Meisei University*

DEANS

Faculty of Physical Sciences and Engineering (Hino): Prof. Munekazu Takano
Faculty of Humanities (Hino): Prof. Koichi Tsukada
Faculty of Informatics (Ome): Prof. Kanji Otsuka
Faculty of Japanese Culture (Ome): Prof. Kenji Ikawa
Faculty of Economics (Hino): Prof. Yoshihiko Nishino

CHAIRMEN OF DEPARTMENTS

Faculty of Physical Sciences and Engineering:
- Physics: Prof. Kyoji Nariai
- Chemistry: Prof. Tomoya Machinami
- Mechanical Engineering: Prof. Nobuyuki Yamaguchi
- Electrical Engineering: Prof. Hiroyuki Sato
- Civil Engineering: Prof. Masafumi Yasui

Faculty of Humanities and Social Sciences:
- English Language and Literature: Prof. John Ingulsrud
- Sociology: Prof. Shigeatsu Nakata
- Psychology: Prof. Makoto Kuroiwa
- Pedagogy: Prof. Takeo Miyakama
- Correspondence Course in Education: Prof. Yosho Sato

Faculty of Informatics:
- Electronics and Computer Science: Prof. Shinya Hasebe
- Management Information: Prof. Toyoaki Mitsunari

Faculty of Japanese Culture:
- Japanese and Comparative Literature: Assoc. Prof. Masao Shibata
- Arts: Prof. Noriyoshi Takaragi

Faculty of Economics:
- Economics: Prof. Haruo Kataoka

ATTACHED INSTITUTES

Tokyo Lincoln Center.

Shakespeare Center.

Postwar Educational History Research Center.

Material Science Research Center.

Information Science Research Center.

International Studies Center.

Frontier Research Center for Global Environment Science.

Asian Center for Environmental Research.

MEJIRO UNIVERSITY

4-31-1 Nakaochiai, Shinjuku-ku, Tokyo 161-8539
Telephone: (3) 5996-3121
Fax: (3) 5996-3238
E-mail: webmaster@mejiro.ac.jp
Internet: www.mejiro.ac.jp

Founded 1923

President: Koki Sato

DEANS

Faculty of Humanities: Kisaku Kudo
Faculty of Human and Social Sciences: Osami Hukushima
Faculty of Business Administration: (vacant)

MOMOYAMA GAKUIN UNIVERSITY (ST ANDREW'S UNIVERSITY)

1-1 Manabino, Izumi, Osaka 594-1198
Telephone: (725) 54-3131
Fax: (725) 54-3215
E-mail: kokusai@andrew.ac.jp
Internet: www.andrew.ac.jp

Founded 1959
Languages of instruction: Japanese, English
Academic year: April to March

President: Michio Matsuura
Vice-Presidents: Akira Hasegawa, Yoji Iwatsu, Jiro Kimura
Library Director: Norio Kitagawa

Library of 646,000 vols
Number of teachers: 156
Number of students: 7,387

Publications: *Economic & Business Review, English Review, Human Sciences Review, Intercultural Studies, Journal of Christian Studies, Pan-Pacific Business Review, Research Institute Bulletin, St. Andrew's University Law Review, Sociological Review*

DEANS

Faculty of Business Administration: Kichizo Akashi
Faculty of Economics: Norio Takehara
Faculty of Law: Noriyuki Honma
Faculty of Letters: Natsuki Kunimatsu
Faculty of Sociology: Yoshifumi Shimizu

CHAIRS OF GRADUATE SCHOOLS

Graduate School of Business Administration: Shinshi Kataoka
Graduate School of Economics: Mitsuhiko Iyoda
Graduate School of Letters: Nobuaki Teraki
Graduate School of Sociology: Osamu Ueda

MIYAGI GAKUIN WOMEN'S COLLEGE

1-1 Sakuragaoka 9-chome, Aoba-ku, Sendai Miyagi 981-8557
Telephone: (22) 279-1311
Fax: (22) 279-7566
E-mail: shomu@mgu.ac.jp
Internet: www.mgu.ac.jp

Founded 1886; first degree courses
Private control
Language of instruction: Japanese
Academic year: April to March

Chancellor: K. Matsuzaki
President: M. Anbe
Librarian: T. Onodera

Library of 320,000 vols
Number of teachers: 100
Number of students: 3,094

Publications: *Bulletin of English Department* (annually), *Christianity and Culture* (annually), *Japanese Literature Note* (annually), *Journal of Miyagi College for Women* (annually), *Annals of the Institute for Research in Humanities and Social Sciences* (annually), *Annual Report of the Institute of Living Sciences, Annual Report of the Institute of Early Childhood Education*

DEANS

Department of Music: T. Sumikawa
Department of English Literature: K. Isozaki
Department of Japanese Literature: M. Hakazawa
Department of Cultural Studies: W. Takahashi
Department of Food and Nutritional Science: H. Hiramoto
Department of Domestic and Cultural Sciences: N. Okabo
Department of Developmental and Clinical Studies: T. Adaohi
Department of Intercultural Studies: M. Kurotaki

NAGOYA UNIVERSITY OF COMMERCE AND BUSINESS

4-4 Sagamine, Komenoki-cho, Nisshin-shi, Aichi 470-0193
Telephone: (561) 73-2111
Fax: (561) 75-2430
E-mail: aanghel@nucba.ac.jp
Internet: www.nucba.ac.jp

Founded 1953
Private control
Language of instruction: Japanese
Academic year: April to February (2 terms)

President: Hiroshi Kurimoto
Director: Masahide Kurimoto
Director of Library (vacant)

Library of 70,000 vols
Number of teachers: 160 (102 full-time, 58 part-time)
Number of students: 3,389

Publications: *Journal of Economics and Management* (2 a year), *Journal of Language, Culture and Communication* (2 a year), *Bulletin of the Yuichi Kurimoto Memorial Graduate School of Business Administration* (annually)

HEADS OF DEPARTMENTS

Faculty of Accounting and Finance: Prof. Akira Kobashi
Faculty of Business Administration: Prof. Hiroko Kakitani
Faculty of Foreign Languages and Asian Studies: Prof. George Watt
Faculty of Management Information Science: Prof. Namio Honda

NANZAN UNIVERSITY

18 Yamazato-cho, Showa-ku, Nagoya 466-8673
Telephone: (52) 832-3111
Fax: (52) 833-6985
E-mail: webmaster@nanzan-u.ac.jp
Internet: www.nanzan-u.ac.jp

Founded 1949

Academic year: April to March

President: H-J. MARX
Vice-Presidents: M. MARUYAMA, M. HAMANA, R. SZIPPL
Chief of General Affairs Section: T. AIZAWA
Librarian: M. OMORI

Library of 605,942 vols, 14,262 periodicals, 2,689 audiovisual titles
Number of teachers: 727 (301 full-time, 426 part-time)
Number of students: 9,622

Publications: *Academia (Literature and Language)* (2 a year), *Academia (Humanities and Social Sciences)* (2 a year), *Academia (Natural Science and Health and Physical Education)* (in Japanese and English, annually), *The Nanzan Journal of Economic Studies* (in Japanese and English, 3 a year), *Nanzan Management Review* (in Japanese and English, 3 a year), *Nanzan Law Review* (in Japanese, 4 a year), *Nanzan Journal of Theological Studies* (in Japanese and English, annually), *Academia (Mathematical Sciences and Information Engineering)* (in Japanese and English, annually), *Nanzan Studies on Japanese Language and Culture* (in Japanese, annually)

DEANS

Faculty of Arts and Letters: Y. ABE
Faculty of Business Administration: K. SAITO
Faculty of Economics: S. HANAI
Faculty of Foreign Studies: N. KINOSHITA
Faculty of Law: K. AOKI
Faculty of Mathematical Sciences and Information Engineering: M. NORO
Faculty of Policy Studies: M. FUJIWARA
General Education: S. ENOMOTO

ATTACHED INSTITUTES

Center for American Studies: study of American politics, economics, diplomacy, culture and society and US relationship with Japan; publ. *Nanzan Review of American Studies* (in English, annually).

Center for Asia-Pacific Studies: interdisciplinary study of the politics, economics and society of the Asia-Pacific region; publ. *Bulletin* (annually).

Centre for European Studies: interdisciplinary study of European politics, economics and society; publ. *Bulletin* (in Japanese, annually).

Center for the Study of Human Relations: ; publ. *Journal of Human Relations* (in Japanese, annually).

Center for Latin American Studies: study of Latin America, particularly the humanities and social sciences (history, anthropology, education, economics, literature, philosophy, politics, archaeology and linguistics); publ. *Perspectivas Lantinoamericanas* (in Spanish, Portuguese and English, annually).

Center for Japanese Studies: a one-semester or one-year programme for international students from all countries who wish to study all aspects of Japanese language, culture and area studies.

Center for Linguistics: conducts research in theoretical linguistics including language acquisition.

Center for Management Studies: specializing in the study of management issues of firms.

Center for Mathematical Sciences and Information Engineering: research into information engineering and quantitative sciences; co-ordination of collaboration between industry and academia.

Institute for Social Ethics: research on the ethical problems in the modern and post-industrial society; publ. *Society and Ethics* (in Japanese, 2 a year).

Nanzan Anthropological Institute: research in cultural anthropology, mainly in SE, East and South Asia; publ. *Nanzan Studies in Cultural Anthropology* (in Japanese, irregular), *Asian Folklore Studies* (in English, 2 a year), *Newsletter* (in Japanese, annually).

Nanzan Institute for Religion and Culture: research in the area of world religions with special reference to the religions of Asia and to the dialogue between religions; publ. *Nanzan Symposia* (in Japanese, irregular), *Religious Studies Today* (in Japanese, irregular), *Bulletin* (in Japanese and English, annually), *Japanese Journal of Religious Studies* (in English, 2 a year), *Nanzan Library of Asian Religion and Culture* (in English, irregular), *Nanzan Studies in Asian Religions* (in English, irregular), *Nanzan Studies in Religion and Culture* (in English, irregular).

NIHON UNIVERSITY

8–24, Kudan-Minami 4-chome, Chiyoda-ku, Tokyo 102-8275
Telephone: (3) 5275-8116
Fax: (3) 5275-8315
E-mail: intldiv@adm.nihon-u.ac.jp
Internet: www.nihon-u.ac.jp

Founded as Nihon Law School 1889, University status 1903

Private control

Academic year: April to March

Chairman of Board: K. MORITA
President: Y. SEZAI
Vice-Presidents: T. MAKINO, M. ONOZAWA, S. SASAKI

Library of 5,680,481 vols
Number of teachers: 2,830 full-time
Number of students: 82,677

Publications: *Genshiryoku Kenkyujo Hokoku* (annual report of the Atomic Energy Research Institute), *Johokagaku Kenkyu* (information science studies), *Journal of Oral Science*, *Kaikeigaku Kenkyu* (accounting), *Kenkyu Kiyo* (humanities and social sciences), *Kenkyu Kiyo* (proceedings of the Institute of Natural Sciences), *Kenkyu Kiyo Nihon Daigaku Shigakubu (Ippan Kyouiku)* (transactions of the School of Dentistry (General Studies)), *Kokusai Kankei Gakubu Nenpo* (international relations), *Kokusai Kankei Kenkyu* (international relations), *Kokusai Chiiki Kenkyujo Shoho* (RRIAP proceedings of symposium), *Nenji Kenkyu Houkokusho* (annual report of the Institute of Information Sciences), *Nichidai Igaku Zasshi* (journal of Nihon University Medical Association), *Nihon Daigaku Geijutsu Gakubu Kiyo Ronbunhen* (research in fine art at the College of Art), *Nihon Daigaku Geijutsu Gakubu Kiyo Sousakuhen* (artistic works of the College of Art), *Nihon Daigaku Kokusai Kankei Gakubu Seikatsu Kagaku Kenkyujo Hokoku*, *Nihon Daigaku Kou Gakubu Kiyo* (journal of the College of Engineering), *Nihon Daigaku Kyouiku Seido Kenkyujo Kiyo* (bulletin of the Educational Systems Research Institute), *Nihon Daigaku Igakubu Kiyo* (bulletin of the liberal arts and sciences), *Nihon Daigaku Seibutsushigenkagakubu Sogokenkyujo Kenkyugyosekishu* (proceedings of the General Research Institute, College of Bioresource Sciences), *Nihon Daigaku Seibutsushigenkagakubu ei Kenkyu* (proceedings of the Life Science Research Center, College of Bioresource Sciences), *Nihon Daigaku Seisanko Gakubu Kenkyu Houkoku* (journal of the College of Industrial Technology, in editions A and B), *Nihon Daigaku Seisankogaku Kenkyujo Shohou* (journal of the College of Industrial Technology), *Nihon Daigaku Seishin Bunka Kenkyujo Kiyo* (bulletin of the Culture Research Institute), *Nihon Daigaku Tsushinkyoikubu Kenkyu Kiyo* (bulletin of the Correspondence Division of Nihon University), *Nihon Daigaku Yakugakubu Kenkyu Kiyo* (bulletin of the College of Pharmacy), *Nihon Hogaku* (law), *Nihon University Comparative Law*, *Rikogaku Kenkyu Shoho* (journal of the Institute of Science and Technology), *PRIAP Circular*, *Sou-Ka-Ken Nyusu* (URC news), *Seikei Kenkyu* (political science and economics), *Shogaku Kenkyu* (business and industry), *Nihon University Journal of Medicine*

DEANS

College of Law: T. NUMANO (acting)
College of Humanities and Sciences: K. SHIMAKATA
College of Economics: T. MAKINO
College of Commerce: S. KATSUYAMA
College of Art: K. ICHINOSE
College of International Relations: S. SATO
College of Science and Technology: K. KOJIMA
College of Industrial Technology: T. OTANI
College of Engineering: M. ONOZAWA
School of Medicine: T. HORIE
School of Dentistry: Y. TODA
School of Dentistry at Matsudo: S. OTAKE
College of Bioresource Sciences: S. SASAKI
College of Pharmacy: K. ANZAI
Correspondence Division: Y. SEZAI
Junior College: Y. SEZAI

NIPPON DENTAL UNIVERSITY

1-9-20 Fujimi, Chiyoda-ku, Tokyo 102
Telephone: (3) 3261 8311
Fax: (3) 3264-8399
E-mail: web-master@tokyo.ndu.ac.jp
Internet: www.ndu.ac.jp

Founded 1907

Academic year: April to March

President: SOH NAKAHARA
Deans: SHIGEO YOKODUKA (Tokyo Faculty), SEN NAKAHARA (Niigata Faculty)
Registrars: SHINICHI TAKIZAWA (Tokyo), KENEI OHBA (Niigata)
Librarians: TAKEJI AYUKAWA (Tokyo Faculty), KAN KOBAYASHI (Niigata Faculty)

Library of 96,822 vols (Tokyo Faculty), 89,217 vols (Niigata Faculty)
Number of teachers: 474 full-time
Number of teachers: 264 part-time
Number of students: 1,580

Publications: *Odontology* (every 2 months), *Annual Publications*, *Bulletin* (annually)

PROFESSORS

Tokyo:

AIYAMA, S., Anatomy
AOBA, T., Pathology
FURUTA, Y., Anatomy
FURUYA, H., Anaesthesiology
ISHIKAWA, H., Orthodontics
KAMOI, K., Periodontology
KATSUUMI, I., Conservative Dentistry
KOBAYASHI, Y., Prosthodontics
MATSUMOTO, S., Physiology

NAKAHARA, S., Dentistry in Society
NIWA, M., Hygiene
OGIWARA, K., Paedodontics
SANADA, K., Biochemistry
SATO, T., Anatomy
SIRAKAWA, M., Oral Surgery
SUZUKI, T., Surgery
TANAKA, H., Conservative Dentistry
TSUTSUI, T., Pharmacology
UCHIDA, M., Oral and Maxillofacial Surgery
YOKOZUKA, S., Prosthodontics
YOSHIDA, T., Dental Materials Science
YOSIKAWA, M., Microbiology
YOSUE, T., Radiology

Niigata

1-8 Hamauracho, Niigata-shi, Niigata 951; tel. (25) 267-1500; fax (25) 267-1134

HASEGAWA, A., Periodontology
HATA, Y., Prosthodontics
HATATE, S., Prosthodontics
IGARASHI, F., Otorhinolaryngology
KAMEDA, A., Orthodontics
KANRI, T., Anaesthesiology
KATAGIRI, M., Oral Pathology
KATOH, Y., Conservative Dentistry
KAWASAKI, K., Conservative Dentistry
KIMURA, T., Dental Pharmacology
KOBAYASHI, K., Oral Anatomy
MATAGA, I., Oral Surgery
MATSUKI, H., Surgery
MORITA, O., Prosthodontics
MURAKAMI, T., Oral Physiology
NAKAHARA, S., Dentistry in Society
OGURA, H., Dental Materials Science
NISHIMURA, K., Oral Surgery
SAITO, K., Oral Microbiology
SHIBAZAKI, K., Internal Medicine
SHIMAMURA, H., Oral Biochemistry
SHIMOOKA, S., Paedodontics
SUETAKA, T., Oral Hygiene
TSUCHIKAWA, K., Oral Surgery
TSUCHIMOTO, M., Radiology

NOTRE DAME WOMEN'S COLLEGE

1–2 Minami Nonogami-cho, Shimogamo, Sakyo-ku, Kyoto 606-0847
Telephone: (75) 781-1173
Fax: (75) 702-4060
E-mail: international@notredame.ac.jp
Internet: www.notredame.ac.jp

Founded 1961
Private control
Language of instruction: Japanese
Academic year: April to March

President: M. HONDA
Secretary-General: K. TOI
Librarian: Y. OKAZAKI

Library of 133,000 vols
Number of teachers: 36 full-time
Number of teachers: 69 part-time
Number of students: 1,443

Publications: *Kiyo*, *Insight* (annually)

Departments of English Language and Literature and Cultural Living.

OBIRIN UNIVERSITY

3758 Tokiwa-machi, Machida-shi, Tokyo 194-0294
Telephone: (42) 797-5419
E-mail: cis@obirin.ac.jp

Founded 1966

President: TOYOSHI SATOW
Number of students: 7,000

Colleges of Humanities, Economics, International Studies, Business and Public Administration.

OSAKA MEDICAL COLLEGE

2–7 Daigakumachi, Takatsuki City, Osaka 569-8686
Telephone: (72) 683-1221
Fax: (72) 683-3723
E-mail: hp-info@poh.osaka-med.ac.jp
Internet: www.osaka-med.ac.jp

Founded 1927
Private control
Language of instruction: Japanese
Academic year: April to March

Chairman: TADAHIRO TANAKA
President: MASAHISA SHIMADA
Secretary-General (vacant)
Librarian: AKIRA SHIMIZU

Library of 221,160 vols
Number of teachers: 362
Number of students: 601

Publications: *Journal* (annually, in Japanese), *Bulletin* (annually, in English)

HEADS OF DEPARTMENTS

Anatomy I: Prof. Dr YOSHINORI OTSUKI
Anatomy II: (vacant)
Physiology I: (vacant)
Physiology II: Prof. Dr TAKAHIRO KUBOTA
Medical Chemistry: Prof. Dr HIROYUKI KAGAMIYAMA
Pathology I: Prof. Dr YURO SHIBAYAMA
Pathology II: Prof. Dr HIROSHI MORI
Microbiology: Prof. Dr KOICHI SANO
Pharmacology: Prof. Dr MIZUO MIYAZAKI
Forensic Medicine: Prof. Dr KOICHI SUZUKI
Hygiene and Public Health: Prof. Dr KOICHI KOUNO
Internal Medicine I: Prof. Dr TOSHIAKI HANAFUSA
Internal Medicine II: Prof. Dr KEN-ICHI KATSU
Internal Medicine III: Prof. Dr YASUSHI KITAURA
General Gastrointestinal Surgery: Prof. Dr NOBUHIKO TANIGAWA
Thoracic and Cardiovascular Surgery: (vacant)
Neurosurgery: Prof. Dr TOSHIHIKO KUROIWA
Orthopaedic Surgery: Prof. Dr MUNEAKI ABE
Paediatrics: Prof. Dr HIROSHI TAMAI
Obstetrics and Gynaecology: Prof. Dr MINORU UEKI
Dermatology: Prof. Dr KIMIHIRO KIYOKANE
Urology: Prof. Dr YOHJI KATSUOKA
Otorhinolaryngology: Prof. Dr HIROSHI TAKENAKA
Ophthalmology: Prof. Dr TSUNEHIKO IKEDA
Neuropsychiatry: Prof. Dr HIROSHI YONEDA
Radiology: Prof. Dr ISAMU NARABAYASHI
Anaesthesiology: Prof. Dr TOSHIAKI MINAMI
Clinical Pathology: Prof. Dr AKIRA SHIMIZU
Oral Surgery: Prof. Dr MASASHI SHIMAHARA
Plastic Surgery: (vacant)

OSAKA SANGYO UNIVERSITY

3-1-1 Nakagaito, Daito-shi, Osaka 574-8530
Telephone: (72) 875-3001
Fax: (72) 875-6551
Internet: www.osaka-sandai.ac.jp

Founded 1965

Chairman of the Board of Trustees: SHIMEJI FURUTANI
President: JUN-ICHIRO SEJIMA

Number of teachers: 250
Number of students: 15,634

Faculties of Human Environment, Business Management, Economics, Engineering; College of General Education; Graduate School.

OTEMON GAKUIN UNIVERSITY

1-15 Nishiai 2-chome, Ibaraki, Osaka 567-8502
Telephone: (72) 641-9631
Fax: (72) 643-5651
E-mail: webmaster@www.otemon.ac.jp
Internet: www.otemon.ac.jp

Founded 1966

Library of 400,000 vols

Faculties of Economics, Management, Humanities, Letters.

RIKKYO UNIVERSITY (St Paul's University)

3-34-1 Nishi-Ikebukuro, Toshima-ku, Tokyo 171-8501
Telephone: 3985-2204
Fax: 3986-8784
E-mail: cis@grp.rikkyo.ne.jp
Internet: www.rikkyo.ne.jp

Founded 1874
Private control
Academic year: April to March

Chancellor: Rev. TOSHIHIKO HAYAMI
President: TERUO OSHIMI
Registrar: Prof. Y. HIKITA
Librarian: Prof. H. SENGOKU

Library of 1,540,558 vols
Number of teachers: 1,110
Number of students: 15,000

Publications: *Rikkyo* (quarterly), *Rikkyo Daigaku Toshokan Dayori* (library news), *Rikkyo Daigaku Shokuin Kiyo* (administrative staff research proceedings, annually), *Kiristokyo Kyoiku Kenkyu* (Studies in Christian Education), *Rikkyo University Bulletin* (every 2 years), *Rikkyo Koho* (Rikkyo news bulletin every 2 months), and numerous faculty journals

DEANS

Faculty of Arts: H. MAEDA
Faculty of Economics: N. OIKAWA
Faculty of Science: T. MOTOBAYASHI
Faculty of Social Relations: N. SHIRAISHI
Faculty of Law and Politics: T. AWAJI
Faculty of Tourism: N. OKAMOTO
Faculty of Community and Human Services: M. SEKI
Faculty of General Curriculum Development: Y. SHOJI

RISSHO UNIVERSITY

4-2-16 Osaki, Shinagawa-ku, Tokyo 141
Telephone: (3) 3492-5262
Fax: (3) 5487-3343
E-mail: kint@ris.ac.jp
Internet: www.ris.ac.jp

Founded 1872
Private control
Language of instruction: Japanese
Academic year: April to March

Chancellor: N. TANAKA
President: H. SAKAZUME
Vice-President: Z. KITAGAWA
Registrar (vacant)
Chief Librarians: H. FUJITA (Osaki), Y. IKOMA (Kumagaya)

Number of teachers: 217 full-time
Number of teachers: 483 part-time
Number of students: 11,900

Publications: *Journal of Nichiren Buddhism* (annually), *Journal of Buddhist Studies*, *Bulletin* (annually), *Quarterly Report of Economics*, etc

DEANS

Faculty of Buddhist Studies: K. MITOMO
Faculty of Letters: S. TEGAWA
Faculty of Economics: K. FUKUOKA

Faculty of Business and Management: Y. KATO
Faculty of Law: S. IWAI
Faculty of Social Welfare: T. HOSHINO
Faculty of Geo-Environmental Science: Y. YOSHIDA
Graduate School (Economics): K. FUKUOKA
Graduate School (Literature): Y. TAKAGI
Graduate School (Business Administration): T. OKUMURA
Graduate School (Law): T. SUZUKI

ATTACHED INSTITUTES

Institute for the Comprehensive Study of the Lotus Sutra: Dir K. SASAKI.

Institute for Nichiren Buddhist Studies: Dir H. WATANABE.

Institute of Humanistic Sciences: Dir T. NAKAO.

Institute of Economic Studies: Dir M. TAKUMI.

Institute of Business and Management: Dir S. ABE.

Institute of Legal Studies: Dir K. OCHIAI.

Institute of Environmental Sciences: Dir T. ARAI.

RITSUMEIKAN UNIVERSITY

56-1 Tojiin Kitamachi, Kita-ku, Kyoto 525-8577
Telephone: (75) 465-1111
E-mail: kokusai@st.ritsumei.ac.jp
Internet: www.ritsumei.ac.jp
Founded 1900
Private control
Academic year: April to March
President: TOYO OMI NAGATA
Vice-Presidents: SADAO KAWAMURA, KIMIO YAKUSHIJI
Dean (Academic Affairs): MITSURU SATO
Dean (Graduate Affairs): YOSHINOBU KUSAKABE
Dean (Research Affairs): MAKOTO SATO
Dean (Student Affairs): KATSUO NAKAGAWA
Dean (Library): YOSHIHIRO TANIGUCHI
Library of 2,532,945 vols
Number of teachers: 1,312 full-time
Number of students: 35,604 full-time
Publications: *Ritsumeikan Business Review, Ritsumeikan Economic Review, Ristumeikan Journal of International Studies, Ritsumeikan Journal of International Relations and Area Studies, Ritsumeikan International Affairs, Ritsumeikan Shigaku, Memoirs of Research Institute of Humanities and Social Science, Journal of Ritsumeikan Geographical Society, Proceedings of the Philosophical Society of Ritsumeikan University, Ritsumeikan Law Review, Memoirs of the SR Center, Ritsumeikan University, Ritsumeikan Annual Review of International Studies* (in English), *Ritsumeikan Eibei Bungaku, Ritsumeikan Torena Haiho, Ritsumeikan Toyoshigaku, Core Ethics, Ritsumeikan Sangyo Shyakaironsyu, Memoirs of the Institute of Humanities, Human and Social Science, Ritsumeikan Seisaku Kagaku, Studies in Language and Culture, Ritsumeikan Bungaku, Journal of Human Science, Art Research, Ritsumeikan Ronkyu Nihon Bungaku, Ritsumeikan Gakurin, Social Systems Studies*

DEANS

College and Graduate School of Business Administration: TERUYOSHI TANAKA
Graduate School for Core Ethics and Frontier Sciences: KOZO WATANABE
College of Economics: JUNICHI HIRATA
Graduate School of Economics: SHUJI MATSUKAWA
College of Information Science and Engineering: TAKEO IIDA
College and Graduate School of International Relations: HIROFUMI OGI
Graduate School of Language Education and Information Science: JUNSAKU NAKAMURA
College of Law: RYOICHI YOSHIMURA
School of Law: MASATO ICHIKAWA
Graduate School of Law: SHIRO AKAZAWA
College of Letters: KAZUAKI KIMURA
Graduate School of Letters: HIROHIDE TAKEYAMA
College and Graduate School of Policy Science: KIYOFUMI KAWAGUCHI
College and Graduate School of Science and Engineering: HIDEYUKI TAKAKURA
Graduate School of Science for Human Services: CHUICHIRO TAKAGAKI
College and Graduate School of Social Sciences: KUNIHIRO TOSHIFUMI

PROFESSORS

College and Graduate School of Law:
AKAZAWA, S., Politics, History
ARAKAWA, S., Civil Law, Sociology of Law
DEGUCHI, M., Civil Procedure Law
HANATATE, F., Civil Law
HIRANO, H., Basic Science of Law
HISAOKA, Y., Criminal Law, Criminal Procedure Law
HONDA, M., German Criminal Law
HORI, M., Politics
IKUTA, K., Criminal Law, Criminal Procedure Law
ISHIHARA, H., English Literature
KATSUI, H., Civil Law
KOBORI, M., Modern British Politics
KOYAMA, Y., Civil Law
KURATA, M., Human Rights Theory, Constitutional Law
KUZUNO, H., Criminal Justice and Juvenile Justice
MIKI, Y., Taxation Law
MIYAI, M., International Economic Law
MIZUGUCHI, N., Public Administration, Regional Autonomy
MOTOYAMA, A., Family Law
MURAKAMI, H., Political Science
NAKAJIMA, S., Public Law
NAKAMURA, Y., French Modern Legal History, French Criminal Procedure
NAKATANI, Y., Politics
NISHIMURA, M., International Politics
NOGUCHI, M., English
OHGAKI, H., Financial Law
OHIRA, Y., Japanese Legal History
OKAWA, S., Civil Law
SATO, K., Social Law
SO, S., East Asian Law and Human Rights
SUTO, Y., Proportional Doctrines
TAKEHAMA, O., Insurance
TAKEHARU, S., German, German Literature
TANIMOTO, K., German Language and Literature
TOKUGAWA, S., Civil Law
UNOKI, Y., Chinese Language and Literature
YAKUSHIJI, K., International Law
YAMAMOTO, T., Social Security Law
YASUMOTO, N., Public Administrative Law
YOSHIDA, M., Labour Law
YOSHIMURA, R., Law of Damage
YOSHIOKA, K., Literary Theory

College and Graduate School of Economics:
AGATSUMA, N., Economic Policy
ASADA, K., Public Finance, Money and Banking
FUJIOKA, A., Economic Analysis of Nuclear-based Military Expansion
FURUKAWA, A., Economic Policy
HAMADA, S., Corporate Law
HATANAKA, T., Early Modern Japanese History
HIRATA, J., Economic Statistics
INABA, K., Economic Statistics
IWATA, K., International Economics
IZAWA, H., Economic Theory
KAJIYAMA, N., Currency Exchange System and Economic Development
KAKIHARA, H., Economic Policy, Medicine
KAKUTA, S., Economic Theory
KANEMARU, Y., East Asian Economic History and Modern Chinese History
KASAI, T., International Economic Cooperation
MATSUBARA, T., Agricultural Economics
MATSUI, S., Political Economy, Economic Philosophy
MATSUKAWA, S., General Theory of Economics
MATSUMOTO, A., Political, Financial and Monetary Economics
MATSUNO, S., East Asian Economic Relations
NISHIGUCHI, K., Economic Theory of Developing Nations
NOZAWA, T., Phonology, Psycholinguistics
OHKAWA, M., Economic Theory, International Economics
OHKAWA, T., Industrial Organization
OKAO, K., History of Modern Sports
SAITO, T., Modern Chinese Literature
SAKAMOTO, K., Economic Policy
SATO, T., Social Policy
SATOU, Y., Sport Psychology
SHIMADA, Y., Area Environmental Systems
SHIMIZU, Y., Educational Technology, Intercultural Communication
TAKAGI, A., Contemporary Capitalism
TANAKA, H., Russian and Eastern European Economic Studies
TANAKA, Y., International Economics
TANIGAKI, K., International Trade Theory
TOMATSURI, T., Tourism
TSUJII, E., English
UCHIYAMA, A., Public Finance
WAKABAYASHI, H., Comparative Research of Policy Theories, Regional Policy
YAMADA, H., Econometrics
YAMAI, T., German Economics
YAMAMOTO, S., Actuarial Economics, Insurance, US-Japanese Comparative Economics and Portfolio Theory
YOKOYAMA, M., International Economics
YOSHIDA, C., International Economics
ZHENG, X., Urban and Regional Economics

College and Graduate School of Business Administration:
ANDO, T., Technology Transfer
BAILEY, A. A., English
CHIYODA, K., Accounting
DOI, Y., Transportation
ENNO, B., Corporate Culture and Governance
FUJITA, T., Business Accounting
HARA, Y., International Corporations
HASHIMOTO, T., Business Administration History
HATTORI, Y., Modern Financial Markets
HIRAI, T., Environmental Accounting Theory
HYOUDO, T., Contemporary Science and Technology
IDA, T., English
IKEDA, S., Cultural Studies, Total Quality Management
IMADA, O., Production Management
ITO, T., Politics and Literature in the Weimar Republic
IWATA, N., Japanese Language Education and Linguistics
KINOSHITA, A., Distribution Procedures
KOEZUKA, H., Product Planning, Marketing Channels
KOKUBO, M., Industrial and Social Psychology
KOSAKA, K., Communicative and Cognitive Mechanisms
MATSUI, T., Medium Enterprises

MATSUMURA, K., Business Financial Management
MIURA, I., Japanese Retail Business
MIURA, M., Health Science
MIYOSAWA, T., Managerial Accounting
MUKAI, J., International Finance
MURAYAMA, T., International Investment
NAGASHIMA, O., Japanese Economy
NAKAMURA, M., Multinationals
NAKANISHI, I., Industrial Economics, Comparative Economic Studies
NAKATA, M., General Business Administration
NAMIE, I., Labour Problems
OKAMOTO, N., Physical Fitness
OKUMURA, Y., Business Strategies
SAITO, M., Business Administration
SASABE, A., History of Science and Engineering
SATO, N., Design Management
SHIOMI, K., Cross-cultural Communication
SCHLUNZE, R. D., International Management, Economic Geography
SUZUKI, Y., French
TAKEDA, M., Management Organization and Information Systems
TAKI, H., Corporations and Accounting
TAMAMURA, H., Privatization
TANAKA, A., Asian Enterprises
TANAKA, T., History of Business Thought
TANAKA, T., Statistics
TANEDA, Y., Managerial Accounting
WATANABE, T., Business Management
YAMAZAKI, S., Spanish
YAMAZAKI, T., Business Administration
YANAGASE, K., Public Finance, Public Economics, Development Policy
YOSHIDA, K., Mathematical Programming

College and Graduate School of Social Sciences:

AKAI, S., Sociology
ARAKI, H., Human Development
ARUGA, I., Turn-Verein
FUKASAWA, A., French Labour and Social History
HIGASHI, J., Critical Applied Linguistics, Sociology of Education
HOGETSU, M., Sociology of Deviance and Sociological Theories
IIDA, T., Sociology
IKEUCHI, Y., American Playwrights
IKUTA, M., Welfare and Information Technology
INUI, K., Social Planning
ISHIKURA, Y., Welfare Sociology, Child and Clinical Psychiatry
JINBO, T., Alternative Media, Media Ethics and Journalism
KANAI, J., Sports Sociology
KIDA, A., Japanese Sociology
KOIZUMI, H., Advertising
KUNIHIRO, T., Political Sociology
KUSAFUKA, N., Physical Education
KUTSUNAI, K., French Literature
LIM, B., Urban Planning
MAEDA, N., Welfare Sociology and Comparative Research in Welfare
MATSUBA, M., German Capitalism
MATSUDA, H., History of Modern Social Thought
MINESHIMA, A., Welfare for the Disabled
MIYASHITA, S., History of Science and Technology
MONDEN, K., History of Science and Technology
MORINISHI, M., History of the Performing Arts
NAGASAWA, K., General Theory of Economics, Economical Statistics
NAKAFUMI, S., Chinese Language and Study of the Tales of Heike
NAKAGAWA, K., Sociology
NAKAMA, Y., Art History
NAKAMURA, T., Cultural Anthropology
NODA, M., Judicial Welfare
OGAWA, E., Elderly Home Care
OKADA, M., Health Education and Social Work
OKUGAWA, O., Cross-cultural Communication
OZAWA, W., Cross-cultural Communication
SAKAMOTO, T., Sociology
SAKATA, K., Local Media Theory, Broadcast Media Theory
SAKURADANI, M., Sociology
SASAKI, K., Cultural Anthropology
SATO, Y., Sociology, Philosophy
SATOU, H., Sociology, Social Security
SHIBATA, H., Social Security
SHINODA, T., Theory of Political Economy
SUDO, Y., Modern Capitalism
SUZUKI, M., Social Consciousness
TAKAGAKI, C., Mass Communication
TAKAGI, M., Clinical Psychology
TAKAHASHI, M., Sociology
TAKEHAMA, A., Consumer Behaviour
TSUDA, M., Public Access
TSUDOME, M., Social Welfare
TSUJI, K., Disaster Behaviour
WADA, T., Labour Sociology
WEN, C., Tale of the Heike, Chinese Language
YAMAMOTO, T., Welfare Budget and Administration
YAMASHITA, T., Leisure and Sports Sociology
YANAGISAWA, S., Sociology
YOSHIDA, M., Psycholinguistics

College and Graduate School of Letters:

AKAMA, R., Modern Drama, Literature and Ukiyoe
ASAO, K., Applied Linguistics
EGUCHI, N., Caribbean Studies
FOX, C. E., Modern Japanese Verse
FUJI, K., Experimental Analysis of Behaviour
FUJIMAKI, M., Human Geography, Urban Social Geography
HATTORI, K., Philosophy of Nature and Social Philosophy
HAYASHI, N., Study of True Human Education
HIEDA, Y., Comparative Literature
HIGASHIYAMA, A., Psychology of Sensation and Perception, Geometry of Visual Space
HIKOSAKA, Y., History of Japanese Dialects
HONDA, O., History of Agricultural Development
HONGO, M., National Law of Ancient Japan, Royal Authority and Religion
HOSHINO, Y., Human Memory and Learning, Cognitive Processes
HOSOI, K., Personality
IKEDA, Y., Modern Philosophy
IKUTA, M., Comparative Study of Large Asian Cities
ISE, T., Philosophy
ISHII, F., German Literature in the Pre-March Revolution Period
KASUGAI, T., Clinical Education
KATAHIRA, H., Land Use in the Semi-arid Regions of Australia, Landscape Reproduction
KATSURAJIMA, N., Japanese Early Modern History, Tokugawa Intellectual History
KAWAGUCHI, Y., The English Novel: Forster, Austen, Golding
KAWASHIMA, K., Study of Artisan Guilds and the Rural Traditional Handicraft Industry
KAWASHIMA, M., Life and Culture in Late Medieval Japan
KIDACHI, M., Archaeology
KIMURA, K., Modern Japanese Literature
KITAMURA, M., Political and Cultural Development in the Republic of China
KITAO, H., Ethics and Philosophy
KITANO, K., Film Studies
KO, J. Y., Korean Archaeology
KOBAYASHI, K., Poetry and Painting of William Blake
KUSAKABE, Y., Greek Philosophy, History of Ontology
MACLEAN, R., English and American Literature since the 18th Century
MARUYAMA, M., 20th-century American Literature
MASHIMO, A., Ancient Japanese Literature, Manyoshu and Oral Literature
MATSUDA, K., English Romantic Poets of the 18th and 19th Centuries
MATSUDA, T., Perception and Cognition
MATSUMOTO, H., Late 19th- to Early 20th-century Politics
MATSUMOTO, Y., Medieval Chinese History, Political System of the Tang Dynasty
MOCHIZUKI, A., Applied Behaviour Analysis, Behavioural Human Serviceology
MUKAI, T., Hegelian Philosophy, Culture and Ideology
MURASHIMA, Y., Educational Philosophy, Moral Education
NAGATA, T., Modern and Contemporary American History
NAKAGAWA, S., Modern Japanese Literature
NAKAGAWA, Y., American Literature, Women's Studies
NAKAGAWA, Y., Holistic Education, Women's Studies
NAKANISHI, K., Heian Literature
ODA, M., Cognitive Science, Concept and Imagery
ODAUCHI, T., Religious Movements and Heresy in Medieval Europe
OHTO, C., Greek and Hellenistic History
OKADA, H., Contemporary Chinese Literature
OUJI, T., Area Studies
OZEKI, M., Political Thought and History in Modern Japan, Cultural Theory
PEATY, D., English Language Education
SAITO, T., Research on Altered States of Consciousness
SANO, M., Generative-grammatical Analyses of Japanese and English
SATO, T., Educational and Social Psychology, Experimental Psychology
SHIMA, H., Studies in Tang Dynasty Thought
SHIMIZU, Y., Medieval Chinese Literature and Criticism
SHIMOKAWA, S., Life and Works of Stendhal
SUGIHASHI, T., History of the Warrior Government Formation
TADAI, T., Evidence-based Clinical Psychology and Psychiatry
TAKAGI, K., Developmental Psychology
TAKAHASHI, H., Contemporary German History
TAKAHASHI, M., Natural Environmental Changes and Relationship to Human Lifestyles
TAKASHIMA, K., 19th-century American Literature
TAKEYAMA, H., Italian Literature, Ethnography and Comparative Culture
TAKIMOTO, K., Modern Japanese Literature, Mori Ogai
TANI, T., Phenomenology and Contemporary Philosophy
TOBINO, K., Philosophical Study in Education and Human Relations
TSUCHIDA, N., Developmental Psychology
TSUKAMA, Y., Linguistics, Phonetics, Foreign Language Education
UEDA, H., Meiji Japanese Literature
UEDA, T., History of Contemporary Western Art, Art Criticism
UENO, R., Classical Chinese Literature
WADA, S., Archaeological Research of the Yayoi and Kofun Peirods
WELLS, K., American Poetry, Folklore and Folksong, Comparative Culture

YAGI, Y., Psychology of Self; Personality and Social Psychology
YAMAMOTO, M., Psychotherapy and Psychoanalysis
YANO, K., Archaeology
YANO, K., Human Geography
YONEYAMA, H., American History, Japanese American History
YOSHIDA, H., Learning Psychology
YOSHIKOSHI, A., Human Impact on the Hydrological Environment
YOSHIMURA, H., Chinese Tang Dynasty Literature
YUKAWA, E., Applied Linguistics and Bilingualism

College and Graduate School of International Relations:

ANDO, T., Western Political History
ANZAI, I., International Peace Theory
ASAHI, M., Contemporary Global Economics
HARA, T., South American Anthropology
HOSHINO, K., European Economics, Monetary Integration
INOUE, J., Cultural Sociology
ITAKI, M., Social Science Methodology
KA, G., Japanese and Chinese Comparative Studies
KATO, T., Black African-American Literature
KATSURA, R., Asian and International Social Welfare, Family Welfare and Policy
KIMIJIMA, A., Peace Studies, Constitutional Law
KIYOMOTO, O., Contemporary South East Asian History
KOBAYASHI, M., Political Science
KOYAMA, M., International Relations
MATSUSHITA, K., Politics of Developing Countries
MINAMINO, Y., Comparative Politics, Political History, Irish Political History
MIYAKE, M., Linguistic Analysis
MUN, G. S., North East Asian History
NAGASU, M., Japanese Development Assistance, International Co-operation
NAKAGAWA, R., Asian Economics
NAKATSUJI, K., Modern Political History
ODAIRA, K., International Co-operation Law, Francophone and EU Studies
OGI, H., Asian Studies, Chinese Education and Literature
OIKAWA, M., Contemporary American Theatre
OKUDA, H., International Finance
OZORA, H., Mass Media
SATO, M., Comparative Sociology, African Politics
TAKAHASHI, N., Japanese Economy
TAKEUCHI, T., Comparative Analysis of Family Structure
TATSUZAWA, K., International Law Relations, Islamic Law, Space Law
WAKANA, M., American Literature
WASSERMAN, M., Theatrical Arts of the West and Japan
YAMADA, H., Japanese Language

College and Graduate School of Policy Science:

HIRAO, H., Use of Computers in English Education
HONDA, Y., Econometrics
HOSOI, K., Modern Management Theory
JIDOU, Y., History of Industrial Technology
KAWAGUCHI, K., Citizen Participation, Co-operatives and NPOs
KISHIMOTO, T., International Politics and Economics
MIKAMI, T., Artificial Intelligence, Memory and Decision-Making
MIKAMI, T., Administrative Law, Planning Law
MURAYAMA, H., Political Attitude and Political Behaviour
OBATA, N., Environmental Policy
RATZLAFF, G. L., Second Language Acquisition, Multilingualism
SATOH, M., Policy Formation
SHIGEMORI, T., Political Theory
SHIRAKAWA, I., Economic Policy, International Economics
TAKADA, S., Urban and Regional Planning
TAKAO, K., Environmental Policies, Development Economics
TONEGAWA, K., System Simulation and Management Problems
UMESAKI, A., English Education
YAMAMOTO, R., Obligation, Medical Malpractice and Consumer Law
YAMANE, H., Post-war German Literature
YASUE, N., EU and Other International Organizations
ZHOU, W., Environmental Policy, Energy Systems Engineering

College and Graduate School of Science and Engineering:

ABE, A., Technology Management
AKISHITA, S., Active Noise Control in Machinery, Robotics
AMANO, K., Environmental Systems Analysis
AMASAKI, S., Concrete Engineering
AMEYAMA, K., Physical Metallurgy, Microstructure Control, Electron Microscopy
AOYAMA, A., Life-Cycle Engineering
ARAI, M., Spectral Theory of Differential Operators
ARAKI, Y., Educational Technology
ARASE, M., Linguistics, English, Japanese, Substance-Dependence Research
ARIMOTO, S., Robotics, Mechatronics, Machine Intelligence
CHEN, E., Image-Processing, Radioactive Rays Image Measurement, Soft Computing
EGASHIRA, S., Solid Particle and Water Tow Phase Flows, Watercourse and Riverbed Variations
ENDO, A., Community Structure of Terrestrial Invertebrate Animals
FUJIEDA, I., Graphic Information Machinery
FUJIMURA, S., Riemannian Geometry
FUJINO, T., Electrical Engineering
FUKAGAWA, R., Geomechanics, Geomechatronics
FUKUI, M., System LSIs
FUKUMOTO, T., Soil Mechanics and Geotechnical Engineering
FUKUYAMA, T., Elementary Particles, High Energy Astrophysics
HARUNA, M., Urban and Regional Planning Systems
HAYAKAWA, K., Traffic-induced Ground Vibration Propagation and Reduction Measures
HIRAI, S., Robotic Manipulation
IIDA, T., Ergonomics
IKEDA, K., Nonlinear Physical Phenomena
IMAI, S., Atomic Layer CVD and Fabrication of Single Electron Devices
IMAMURA, N., Chemistry of Bio-active Compounds produced by Micro-organisms
ISAKA, T., Sports Biomechanics, Analysis of Human Movement
ISHII, A., Robot Vision, Sensors and Image Analysis
ISHII, H., Number Theory of Automorphic Forms
ISONO, Y., Computational Material Science
ITO, M., Strength and Design of Steel Structures
IWASHIMIZU, Y., Solid Mechanics, Ultrasonic Materials Evaluation
IZUNO, K., Earthquake Resistant Design of Structures
KAITO, C., Quantum Dots Formation
KANEKO, H., Contemporary German Poetry
KASAHARA, K., Optical Communication Devices
KATO, M., Physical Chemistry
KAWABATA, T., Power Electronics
KAWAGUCHI, A., Preparation of Functional Polymer Materials Using Epitaxies, and Study of their Properties
KAWAMURA, K., English as a Foreign or Second Language
KAWAMURA, S., Robotics
KIDO, Y., Investigation of Surface and Interface Structures
KIMATA, M., Engineering
KITAZAWA, T., Numerical Analysis of Electromagnetic Wave Problems
KOBAYASHI, H., Wind-tunnel Experiments and Analyses of Long Bridges Subject to Wind Load
KOJIMA, K., Material and Inorganic Chemistry, Optical Materials
KOJIMA, T., FEM Analysis of Hybrid Concrete Structures Using Discrete Elements
KOMATSU, Y., Online Parameter Estimations of the Induction Machine Utilizing Extension Slip Method
KONDO, K., Synthesis of Functional Polymers
KONISHI, S., Micronanomechatronics and Micromachines, Systems Engineering, Electronic Devices
KOYANAGI, S., Parallel Computation, Database Computer Engineering, Data Mining
KUBO, M., Applied Microbiology
KURATSUJI, H., Quantum Phenomenology
KUSAKA, T., Fracture Mechanics
MAEDA, H., Robot Intelligence for Action and Tasks
MAKIKAWA, M., Biomedical Engineering, Application of Human Motion for Engineering
MATSUDA, T., Separation Analysis, Electroanalysis, Environmental Analysis Chemistry
MATSUOKA, M., Nickel-hydride Batteries, Solar Cells Electrocatalysis, Titanium Dioxide Photocatalysis
MIKI, H., Semiconductor Materials, Solid-state Devices
MIYANO, T., Complex Systems Science, Artificial Intelligence
MIZOSHIRI, I., Medical Electronics and Biological Engineering
MORIMOTO, A., Ultrafast Photonics, Ultrafast Laser Technology, and Terahertz Optoelectronics
MORISAKI, H., Analysis of the Surface Characteristics of Microbial Cells, and the Interaction between Micro-organisms and Interfaces
MURAHASHI, M., Regional and Urban Structure Analyses and Development Techniques
NAKADA, T., Surface Properties
NAKAJIMA, H., Theoretical Analysis of the Interaction Structures of Multi-component Systems
NAKAJIMA, J., Waste Water Treatment Systems, Nitrogen and Phosphorus Removal
NAKAJIMA, K., Homogeneous Kähler Manifolds
NAKAMURA, N., Structure and Physical Properties of Normal Long Chain Compounds, Ionomers and Liquid Crystals
NAKAMURA, Y., French Thought and Literature, Contemporary Japanese Literature
NAKANISHI, T., Measurement and Estimation of Automobile Traffic Flow
NAKAYA, Y., Human Interface, Artificial Intelligence, Recognition Engineering
NAMBA, H., Surfaces as New Materials, Surface Chemical Dynamics

NANISHI, Y., Semiconductor Optoelectronic Devices, Physical Properties of Quantum Structures, Plasma-excited Semiconductor Processes
NARUKI, I., Analysis and Geometry of Complex Manifolds
NISHIO, S., Surface Science
NISHIWAKI, K., Gas Flow, Turbulence, Heat Transfer and Combustion in Combustion Chambers
NUMAI, T., Optical Electronics
OGAMI, Y., Fluid Dynamics
OGASAWARA, H., Geophysics
OGAWA, H., Intelligence Information Science
OGAWA, S., Analysis of Moduli Spaces
OGURA, T., Si System Architecture
OIKAWA, K., Architectural and Urban Space Planning, Environmental Design
OKADA, M., Magnetic and Dielectric Materials, Semiconductor Lasers
ONO, B., Cellular and Molecular Study of the Biological Functions of the Budding Yeast
ONO, Y., Optical Periodic Microstructure
OSAKA, H., Operator Algebras
OZUTSUMI, K., Structural and Thermodynamic Studies of Metal Complexes in Solution
SAITO, S., Optical Communications
SAKAI, J., Optical Fibre Communications and Optical Information Processing
SAKAI, T., Statistical Research on Reliability Engineering
SAKANE, M., Strength Evaluation of Heat-resistant Materials at High Temperatures
SATOMI, J., Basic Physiological and Biochemical Study of Sports Training
SAWAMURA, S., High-pressure Physical Chemistry of Solutions
SHAWBACK, M., Foreign Languages, General Studies
SHIMAKAWA, H., Social Systems, Computer Software, Information Systems
SHINODA, H., Environmental Studies
SHINYA, H., Functional Analysis
SHIRAISHI, H., Electro-analytical Chemistry
SUGIMOTO, S., Systems and Control Engineering
SUGINO, N., Teaching English as a Foreign Language
SUGIYAMA, S., Microsystem Technology
SUZUKI, K., MEMS for Information and Telecommunication
SUZUKI, K., Pharmaceutical Development, Molecular Biology
TACHIKI, T., Physiology, Biochemistry and the Breeding of Useful Micro-organism-sTAKAKURA, H., High-efficiency Solar Cell Research
TAKANO, N., Computational Mathematics
TAKAYAMA, S., Advanced Sensing Systems and Measurement Science
TAKAYAMA, Y., Computative Algebra
TAKENAKA, A., Properties of Elementary Particles and their Interactions
TAMAKI, J., Design of Functional Interface between Inorganic Materials for Gas-sensing Devices
TAMIAKI, H., Bio-organic Chemistry
TAMURA, H., Information Engineering, Virtual Reality
TANAKA, H., Computer Vision, Visual Communication, Intelligent Information Systems
TANAKA, K., Micro-electric Machine Systems
TANAKA, S., Computer Graphics Systems
TANAKA, T., Precision Processing
TANIGUCHI, Y., High-pressure Physical Chemistry of Liquids, Solutions and Biological Materials
TANIKAGA, R., Organic Synthesis Using Biocatalysts and Organic Sulphurous Reagents
TATEYAMA, K., Construction Engineering
TERAI, H., Research into Computer and LSI Design Automation Systems
THAWONMAS, R., Artificial Intelligence, Entertainment Computing
TOKI, K., Earthquake Engineering, Natural Disaster Science
TORIYAMA, T., Optical Applied Measurements
TSUDAGAWA, M., Analysis and Application of Space Filters
TSUKAGUCHI, H., Transport System Planning and Management
UKITA, H., Optomechatronics
WAKAYAMA, M., Food and Nutrition
WAKAYAMA, M., Food and Nutrition, Micro-organisms
WATANABE, T., Control Engineering
XU, G., Pattern Recognition, Computer Science, Robotics
YAMADA, H., Development of Free-electron Laser
YAMADA, K., Water Demand Analyses and Predictions
YAMADA, O., Mathematical Analysis
YAMADA, T., Probability and Statistics
YAMADA, T., Telecommunication
YAMAMOTO, N., Biomechanics and Function of Living Systems
YAMAMOTO, S., American Drama
YAMASAKI, M., Urban Landscape Planning
YAMAUCHI, H., System VLSI Architecture and Implementation
YAMAZAKI, K., Parallel Computing, Computer Graphics, Case-based Reasoning
YOSHIDA, M., Ecology, Ethology
YOSHIHARA, Y., Formation Mechanisms of Harmful Combustion Products and Methods for their Reduction
YOSHIMURA, Y., Structural Phase Transition in Alkali Metal Cyanide

College of Information Science and Engineering:

ASANO, S., Bioscience and Bio-informatics
CHEN, Y. W., Media Technology
ENDO, H., Computer Science
FUJITA, N., Bioscience and Bio-informatics
FUKUMOTO, J., Natural Language Processing
FUSAOKA, A., Human and Computer Intelligence
HACHIMURA, K., Media Technology
HAGIWARA, H., Human and Computer Intelligence
HATTORI, F., Information and Communication Science
HAYANO, T., Proteomics, Molecular Biology, Biochemistry
HAYASHI, T., Media Technology
HIGUCHI, N., Media Technology
IIDA, T., Human and Computer Intelligence
IKEDA, H., Computer Science
INOUE, Y., Information Systems Engineering
KAMEI, K., Human and Computer Intelligence
KAWAI, M., Wireless and Network Systems
KAWAGOE, K., Information and Communication Science
KIKUCHI, M., Bioscience and Bio-informatics
KIKUCHI, T., Bioscience and Bio-informatics
KISHIMOTO, R., Information and Communication Science
KITAMOTO, S., Computer-Generated Animation
KOTSUKI, S., Genetic Informatics
KUNIEDA, Y., Computer Science
KUWABARA, K., Knowledge Processing, Communication Science
MAEDA, T., Electromagnetic Waves and Data Transmission
NAGANO, S., Systems Biology
NAKATANI, Y., Information and Communication Science
NISHIKAWA, I., Human and Computer Intelligence
NISHIO, N., Computer Science
NOZAWA, K., Educational Technology, Inter-cultural Communication
OGAWA, E., Knowledge Engineering
OHNISHI, A., Operating Systems
OKUBO, E., Computer Science
OSHIMA, T., Artificial Reality
OYANAGI, S., Computer Science
RINALDO, F. J., Artificial Intelligence, Expert Systems and Knowledge Information Processing
SHIMAKAWA, H., Computer Science
SHINODA, H., Human and Computer Intelligence
SHIRAI, Y., Robot Intelligence
SUGINO, N., Teaching English as a Foreign Language
SUZUKI, K., Bioscience and Bio-informatics
TAMURA, H., Media Technology
TANAKA, H., Human and Computer Intelligence
TANAKA, S., Media Technology
THAWONMAS, R., Intelligent Entertainment Computing
XU, G., Media Technology
YAMASHITA, Y., Media Technology
YOSHIKAWA, T., Mechatronics, Control Engineering and Robotics

College and Graduate School of Policy Science:

HATTORI, T., Management of Knowledge, Management Accounting
HIRAO, H., English Linguistics
HIRAOKA, K., Regional Economics, Public Finance, Local Public Finance
HONDA, Y., Economic Policy, Econometrics
HOSOI, K., Business Administration
ISHIHARA, K., Urban Planning
JIDOU, Y., History of Industrial Technology
KANAGAE, H., Planning Science and Technology, Sustainable Development
KAWAGUCHI, K., Socio-Economic Systems, Policy and Economic Studies
KISHI, M., Public Management Theory, Administrative and Financial Reform
KISHIMOTO, T., International Finance
MIKAMI, T., Property and Land Law
MIKAMI, T., Computer Networks, Cognitive Science
MURAYAMA, H., Politics
OBATA, N., Social System Engineering, Environmental Preservation
RATZLAFF, G., Second Language Pedagogy
SATOH, M., Political Process
SHIGEMORI, T., Politics, History of Philosophy, Ethics
TABAYASHI, Y., American Literature, Feminism, Cultural Studies
TAKADA, S., City and Building Planning
TAKAO, K., Development Economics and Environmental Policy
TONEGAWA, K., Systems Simulation, Management Information Systems
UMESAKI, A., Teaching English as a Foreign Language
YAMAMOTO, R., Civil Law
YAMANE, H., Contemporary German Literature, Modern Japanese Culture
YASUE, N., Politics, Public and International Law, International Organizations
ZHOU, W., Environmental Policy, Energy Systems Engineering

Graduate School of Sciences for Human Services:

AKIRA, H., Genetic Psychology
DAN, S., Family Medical Treatment Methods
FUJI, N., Clinical Psychology
HAYASHI, N., Education, Theory of Character Building

MOCHIZUKI, A., Experimental Action Analysis
MURAMOTO, K., Clinical Psychology, Trauma
NAKAGAWA, Y., Clinical Pedagogics
NAKAMURA, J., Intelligence Development, Life-Span development, Counselling
NAKAMURA, T., Sociology, Social Welfare
NODA, M., Administration of Welfare Justice, Child Welfare
TADAI, T., Clinical Psychology, Psychiatry
TAKAGAKI, C., Clinical Psychology
TAKINO, I., Clinical Psychology
TOKUDA, K., Clinical Psychology

Graduate School for Core Ethics and Frontier Sciences:

AKAMA, R., Japanese Literature
DUMOUCHEL, P., Economic Philosophy
ENDO, A., Symbiosis Theory
GOTO, R., Economic Philosophy
KAMBAYASHI, T., Aesthetics, Art
KOIZUMI, Y., Philosophy
MATSUBARA, Y., History of Science, Scientific Theory
NISHI, M., Comparative Literature
NISHIKAWA, N., French Language, Japanese History, European History
TATEIWA, S., Ethics
UEMURA, M., Television Gaming
WATANABE, K., Cultural Anthropology, African Studies, History of Anthropology

Graduate School of Language Education and Information Science:

AZUMA, S., Code-switching, Socio-linguistic Significance
LEE, N., Linguistics
MATSUDA, K., English Literature
NAKAMURA, J., English Corpus Linguistics
NOZAWA, K., Teaching English as a Foreign Language
OHNO, Y., Japanese Pedagogics, Formal Language Studies
OKURA, M., Japanese Language Teaching Methodology
RATZLAFF, G., Second Language Pedagogy and Acquisition
SHIMIZU, Y., Teaching English as a Foreign Language
SUGIMORI, M., Applied Linguistics
TSUKUMA, Y., Linguistics, Phonetics
UMESAKI, A., English Corpus Linguistics
YAMADA, H., Linguistics, Phonetics
YOSHIDA, S., Psychology Linguistics

Law School:

DANBAYASHI, K., Women and Law, Trial Procedure
FUJITA, M., Criminal Practice Law
HANATATE, F., Civil Law
HIRAI, T., Civil, Merchant and Medical Law
IBUSUKI, M., Legal Informatics, Criminal Procedure
ICHIKAWA, M., Constitutional Case Law
KATSUI, H., Civil Law
KITAMURA, K., Public Law
KOMATSU, Y., Bankruptcy Law, Consumer Law and Intellectual Property Law
KURONO, Y., Civil Law
MATSUI, Y., International Law
MATSUMIYA, T., Criminal Law
MATSUMOTO, K., Civil Liability, Limitation Act
MORISHITA, H., Criminal Law and Criminal Defence
NINOMIYA, S., Civil Law
OKAHARA, F., Civil Law
OKAMOTO, M., Real Estate Law
OKAWA, S., Civil Case Law, Criminal Case Law
OKUBO, S., Public Law
SAGAMI, Y., Civil Law
SAKAI, H., International Civil Procedure
SHINATANI, T., Corporate Law, Securities Regulation
TANAKA, T., Enterprise Law
UEDA, K., Criminology
WADA, S., Civil Law
WATANABE, S., International Private Law and Civil Procedure
YAMAGUCHI, K., Consumer Protection and International Trade
YAMAMOTO, T., International Conflict Management
YAMANA, T., Tax and Inheritance Tax Law
YASUMOTO, N., Administrative Law, Tax Law

ATTACHED INSTITUTES

Center for American Studies: Dir H. YONEYAMA.

Institute of International Relations and Area Studies: Dir M. TAKAHASHI.

Institute of International Language and Culture Studies: Dir S. NAKAGAWA.

Art Research Center: Dir T. KANBAYASHI.

Institute of Humanities and Human and Social Sciences: Dir S. NAKAJIMA.

Institute of Human Sciences: Dir A. MOCHIZUKI.

Regional Information Research Center: Dir H. KANEGAE.

Institute of Social Systems: Dir M. NAKATA.

Research Center for Finance: Dir S. OGAWA.

Research Center for Management Strategy: Dir Y. TANEDA.

Institute of Science and Engineering: Dir H. NAKAJIMA.

Research Organization of Science and Engineering: Dir H. KOBAYASHI.

Research Center for Advanced Materials and Production Technology: Dir T. SAKAI.

Biwaka Environmental Research Centre: Dir K. YAMADA.

Center for Eco-technology: Dir M. HIRAOKA.

Research Institute for Micro System Technology: Dir S. SUGIYAMA.

Research Institute for Sports and Healthcare Technology: Dir M. MAKIKAWA.

Synchroton Radiation (SR) Center: Dir H. OKAMOTO.

Very Large Scale Integration (VLSI) Center: Dir H. YAMAUCHI.

Research Organization of Science and Engineering: Dir TORU WATANABE.

Institute of Science and Engineering: Dir HISAO NAKAJIMA.

Advanced Robotics Research Centre: Dir TORU WATANABE.

Glycotechnology Research Centre: Dir TOSHISUKE KAWASAKI.

Frontier Semiconductor Nano Electronics: Dir YASUSHI NANISHI.

Research Centre for Functional Materials Chemistry: Dir TAMAKI JUN.

Center for Super-Human Intelligent System: Dir MASAHIRO FUKUI.

Research Institute for Innovation Technological Management: Dir SHOTARU KAZUKI.

Research Center for Disaster Mitigation Systems: Dir KOJIMA TAKAYUKI.

21st Century Center of Excellence Organization: Dir HIRONARI YAMADA.

The Synchrotron Light Life Science Center: Dir HIRONARI YAMADA.

Research Centre for Disaster Mitigation of Urban Cultural Heritage: Dir KENZO TOKI.

New Frontiers Research Centre: Dir KENZO TOKI.

RITSUMEIKAN ASIA PACIFIC UNIVERSITY

1-1 Jumonjibaru, Beppu-shi, Oita 874-8577
Telephone: (977) 78-1111
Fax: (977) 78-1123
E-mail: ritsapu2003@apu.ac.jp
Internet: www.apu.ac.jp

Founded 2000
Private control
Languages of instruction: English, Japanese
Academic year: September to July andApril to February
President: Prof. MONTE CASSIM
Vice-Presidents: Dr HAYASHI KENTARO, Prof. NAKAGAMI KEN'ICHI, Prof. YAKUSHIJI KIMIO, NISHIDA MUNEAKI
Dean of Academic Affairs: Prof. NAKANO MASAHIRO
Dean of Student Affairs: Prof. YAMAGAMI SUSUMU
Dean of International Affairs: Dr A. MANI
Library of 65,000 vols
Number of teachers: 120
Number of students: 4,240 (4,000 undergraduate, 240 postgraduate)
Publications: *Journal of Asia Pacific Studies* (3 a year), *Polyglossia* (2 a year)

DEANS

College of Asia Pacific Studies: Dr HAYAO FUKUI
College of Asia Pacific Management: KUNIO IGUSA
Graduate School of Asia Pacific Studies: Dr HAYAO FUKUI
Graduate School of Management: Dr RONALD PATTEN

RYUKOKU UNIVERSITY

67 Tsukamoto-cho, Fukakusa, Fushimi-ku, Kyoto 612-8577
Telephone: (75) 642-1111
Fax: (75) 642-8867
E-mail: ric@rnoc.fks.ryukoku.ac.jp
Internet: www.ryukoku.ac.jp

Founded 1639
Private control
Academic year: April to March
President: EGUN MIKOGAMI
Vice-Presidents: YOSHIO KAWAMURA, TAKESHI HORIKAWA
Secretary-General: CHIKO IWAGAMI
Librarian: JITSUZO SHIGETA
Library: see libraries
Number of teachers: 472
Number of students: 18,310
Publications: *Bulletin of Buddhist Cultural Institute* (annually), *Annual Bulletin of Research Institute for Social Science*, *Ryukoku Law Review* (quarterly), *Journal of Economic Studies* (quarterly), *Journal of Ryukoku University* (2 a year), *Ryukoku Journal of Humanities and Sciences* (2 a year), *Journal of Intercultural Communication* (annually)

DEANS

Faculty of Letters: EGUN MIKOGAMI
Faculty of Economics: HIROKUNI TERADA
Faculty of Business Administration: RINPACHI MISHIMA
Faculty of Law: KEIJI NAGARA
Faculty of Science of Technology: YOUICHI KOBUCHI
Faculty of Sociology: KAZUNORI KOGA
Faculty of Intercultural Communication: MASANORI HIGA
Junior College: DOSHO WAKAHARA

Japanese Culture and Language Programme: ITSUYO HIGASHINAKA

PROFESSORS

Faculty of Letters:

AKAMATSU, T., History of Japanese Buddhism
AKIMOTO, M., Japanese Language and Literature
ASADA, M., Japanese Tendai Sect
ASAI, N., Shin Buddhism
CHIN, K., Chinese Language and Literature
DOI, J., Modern Japanese Literature
ECHIZENYA, H., Modern Japanese Culture
FUKUSHIMA, H., Modern Japanese History
FUROMOTO, T., Anglo-Irish Literature
HAYASHIDA, Y., Eastern History
HIGASHINAKA, I., English Romantic Literature
HIRATA, A., Modern Japanese Thought
ICHIMURA, T., Psychology
ITOI, M., Japanese Language
IZUMOJI, O., Japanese Literature
KAGOTANI, M., Japanese History
KATSUBE, M., Japanese Archaeology
KIDA, T., Modern Chinese History
KITANO, A., Modern Japanese Literature
KODAMA, D., History of Indian Buddhism
KODAMA, S., History of Japanese Religion
KODANI, S., English Literature
KOJIMA, M., Intercultural Pedagogy
LAZARIN, M., Philosophy
MARUYAMA, T., Philosophy
MASUDA, R., English Literature
MIKOGAMI, E., Modern Western Philosophy
MIKOGAMI, E., Indian Philosophy
MITSUKAWA, T., Indian Buddhism
MIYAMA, Y., Japanese Literature of the Edo Period
MIYAMOTO, S., Modern English Novels
MIZOGUCHI, K., Philosophy
NAGAKAWA, H., American Literature
NAKAYAMA, S., Chinese Buddhism
NISHIYAMA, R., Mathematics
ODA, Y., Eastern History
OHMINE, A., Philosophy
OHTA, T., Shin Buddhism
OHTORI, K., Tanka Poetry in the Middle Ages
OKA, R., Thought of Shiran
OKAZAKI, K., Japanese Archaeology
SHIYOUBO, T., English Linguistics
TAKEDA, H., History of Indian Buddhism
TAKEDA, R., Buddhism
TANAKA, M., Educational Psychology
TANAKA, S., Psychology
TATSUGUCHI, M., Buddhist Theology
TOKUNAGA, D., Shin Buddhism
TOMITA, M., Educational Technology
TSUNEYOSHI, K., Methods and Curriculum of Education
TSUZUKI, A., East Asian History
UESUGI, T., Philosophy of Education
UMITANI, N., Philosophy of Education
UWAYOKOTE, M., Japanese History
WATANABE, K., History of Sports Philosophy
WATANABE, T., Chinese Buddhist Theory
YAMADA, Y., English Literature
YATA, R., History of Shin Buddhism

Faculty of Economics:

AZUMA, T., Applied Physiology
FUJIMOTO, M., American Culture
HATA, N., Health Industry Economics
HIGUCHI, M., Middle Spanish Literature
IGUCHI, T., Industrial Organization
ISHIKAWA, R., Labour Economics
ITOH, T., Mathematics
KANEKO, H., Economic Theory
KAWAMURA, T., German Literature
KAWAMURA, Y., Development Sociology
LAKSHMAN, W. D., Economic Theory
MATSUOKA, K., Economic Policy
MATSUOKA, T., Theory of Modern Capitalism
MISAKI, S., Economic Theory
MIZUHARA, S., Economic Thought
NAKAMURA, H., Regional Economics
NISHIBORI, F., Theoretical Economics
OBAYASHI, M., African American Development
OISHI, M., English Language
OKACHI, K., International Economic Theory
OMAE, S., Social Policy
OTSUKI, M., German Economic History
SHIMUZU, K., American Literature
TAJIRI, E., Teaching Japanese
TAKADA, M., Public Finance
TAKENAKA, E., Labour Economics
TANAKA, Y., Economic Systems Theory
TERADA, H., Financial Theory
TSUBOUCHI, R., Sociology
YAMAMOTO, S., International Economics
YOSHIMURA, H., Indian Mahayanist Buddhist Thought
YUNO, T., International Finance

Faculty of Business Administration:

ABE, D., Theoretical Economics
FUJITA, N., Japanese Business History
HARA, M., International Accounting Theory
HAYASHI, A., Corporate Accounting
HAYASHI, K., Cost Accounting
HITOMI, K., Manufacturing Systems Engineering
HONDA, H., Corporate Finance Theory
INOUE, H., Business Management
INOUE, K., Finance Theory
INOUE, Y., English Language
KAMEI, M., International Business Management
KANEKO, A., Insurance Theory
KATAGIRI, M., Marketing Theory
KAWASHIMA, M., Marketing Theory
KITAZAWA, Y., Small Business Management
KOIKE, T., Information Processing Management
KONNO, T., Information Processing Management
KUDARA, K., Buddhism
MASAOKA, M., Managerial Accounting
MISHIMA, R., Business Administration Psychology
MORIYA, H., Merchandise Studies
NAKAYAMA, J., German Literature
NATSUME, K., International Business Strategy
NISHIHARA, J., Japanese Language Education
NISHIKAWA, K., Labour Management
NOMA, K., Marketing Research
OHGAI, T., International Business
OHNISHI, K., Information Industry
OHSUGI, M., International Finance Theory
ONO, K., Accounting
SATO, K., Marketing
SHIGEMOTO, N., Business Organization Theory
SHIMADA, H., Business Management
SHIMADA, M., English Linguistics
SUGIMURA, M., French Literature
TAKADA, S., Religion
TAKAYANAGI, K., Astronomy
TERASHIMA, K., Information Management
TOGAMI, M., Sociology
TOYOSHIMA, M., Engineering Management
YAMASHITA, A., Macroeconomics
YOKOYAMA, K., Regional Sociology
YOSHIHIRO, S., Primate Ecology
YUI, H., Industrial Engineering

Faculty of Law:

FUJIWARA, H., Civil Law
FUKUSHIMA, I., Criminal Law
HAYASHI, T., Buddhism
HIGASHI, F., Physical Education
HIRANO, T., Political Processes
HIRANO, T., The Constitution; Religious Law
HONMA, Y., Civil Proceedings Act
ISHIDA, T., Political Theory
ISHII, K., Philosophy of Law
ISHIZUKA, S., Criminology
IWATA, N., Chinese Language
KATSURA, F., English Language and Literature
KAWABATA, M., African Politics
KAWASUMI, Y., Civil Law
KIM, D., International Human Rights Laws
KISAKA, J., Japanese Political History
KONDO, H., 18th-century English Novel
KUBOTA, M., Sports Sociology
MIKAMI, T., Administrative Law
MIZUNO, T., Tax Law
NAGARA, K., Administrative Law
NISHIO, Y., Commercial Law
SAKAI, S., Current Middle East Politics
SAKAMOTO, M., Administration
SHIRAISHI, K., Public Administration
TAKAHASHI, S., Italian Fascism
TAKEHISA, S., Commercial Law
TAKITA, R., Commercial Politics
TANAKA, N., International Law
TODORIKI, K., Sports Sociology
TOMINO, K., Regional Autonomy
TSUJITA, J., Astrophysics
UEDA, K., Constitutional Law
WAKITA, S., Labour Law
YOROI, T., Labour Law

Faculty of Science and Technology:

ABE, H., Plasma Physics
ARIKI, Y., Pattern Recognition
DOHSHITA, S., Speech and Audio Media Processing
ENAMI, K., Materials Science and Engineering
FUJIMOTO, Y., Information Engineering
GOTOH, Y., Materials Science
HARADA, T., Catalytic Chemistry
HAYASHI, H., Polymer Science
HORIKAWA, T., Mechanical Engineering and Materials Science
IIDA, S., Solid State Physics
IKEDA, T., Applied Analysis and Computational Science
IWAMOTO, T., Robot Engineering
JIKU, F., Environmental Engineering
KAIYOH, H., Communications Engineering
KAMIJOH, E., Inorganic Functional Materials
KATOH, K., Multivariable Functions
KAWASHIMA, H., Mechanical Engineering
KOBAYASHI, K., Metallic Materials Chemistry
KOBUCHI, Y., Information Science
KOKUBU, H., Mathematics and Dynamic Systems
KONDOH, H., Germanic Literature and Languages
KUNIHIRO, T., Nuclear and Elementary Particle Physics
KUTSUNA, H., Mechanical Engineering
MATSUMOTO, W., Mathematics (Analysis)
MATSUSHITA, T., Co-ordination Chemistry
MIYASHITA, T., Mechanical Physics
MORITA, Y., Nonlinear Differential Equations
NAKAMURA, T., Computer Science
NAKANISHI, S., Mechanical Engineering
NISHIHARA, H., Superconductivity; Physics
OHJI, K., Mechanical Engineering
OHTSUKA, N., Materials Strength and Fracture Mechanics
OKADA, Y., Information Processing
OKAMOTO, Y., Anglo-Irish Literature
OZAWA, T., Information Technology
SAITOH, M., Optics
SOHMA, K., Buddhism
TAGUCHI, T., Health and Physical Education
TAKAHASHI, T., Science Education and Educational Technology

TSUBOI, Y., Mechatronics and Electronic Control
TSUTSUMI, K., Intelligent Robotic Systems
UDO, A., Systems Engineering
URABE, K., Ceramics
WADA, T., Inorganic Materials Chemistry
YOTSUTANI, S., Mathematics (Analysis)
YUKIMOTO, Y., Semiconductor Electronics

Faculty of Sociology:
FUKUZAKI, S., Health Science
FUNAHASHI, K., Community and Regional Studies
FUSHIMI, Y., Social Welfare Finance
HAYASE, K., Senior Citizens' Welfare
KAMEYAMA, Y., Sociology
KANBAYASHI, S., Social Technology for the Disabled
KASAHARA, S., Industrial Sociology
KISHIDA, H., Clinical Psychology
KODAMA, N., Sociology
KOGA, K., Religion
KOSHII, I., Social Psychology
KUCHIBA, M., Comparative Sociology
MATSUSHITA, K., Population Economics
MATSUTANI, N., Social Security Theory
MORI, Y., Social Welfare Institutions
MUKAI, T., Rural Sociology
MURAI, R., Welfare for the Disabled
NORIKUMO, S., Information Engineering
ODA, K., Social Welfare
OGASAWARA, M., Theoretical Sociology
OSHIDA, E., Mass Media Civilization
SASAKI, M., Social Work
SEKIGUCHI, S., Psychology
SHIMIZU, H., Everyday Life and Religion
SHIMIZU, K., Social Welfare
TAKEHARA, H., Principles of Education
TANAKA, S., Industrial Sociology
TANO, T., Health and Physical Education
TERAKAWA, Y., Religious Psychology
WATARI, H., English Philology

Faculty of Intercultural Communication:
AKAGI, H., Japanese Industrial Arts
FUKUDA, K., The United Nations and Japan
FURMANOVSKY, M., American History, TESOL
HABITO, R., Indian and Buddhist Philosophy
HAMANO, S., Human Rights Law, Western Political Thought
HIGA, M., Applied Linguistics
KIGLICS, I., Economics
KIMURA, B., Psychiatry
KOIZUMI, T., Comparative Study of Civilizations
KWON, O., Education
MACADAM, J., Comparative Culture
MATSUBARA, H., Western History
MATSUI, K., Energy Economics
MIYAKAWA, C., French Literature and Language
MURATA, S., Comparative Study of Educational Systems
NAGASAKI, N., Modern South Asian History
PANG, C., Japanese Language, Chinese Language
SAKAMOTO, S., Food Culture, Ethnobotany
SIMPSON, J., World Agriculture
SUDO, M., Comparative Study of Folklore
SUEHARA, T., Cultural Anthropology, Economic Anthropology
SUGIMURA, T., History of Middle Eastern Art
TOH, N., International Communications and Relations
TSURUTA, K., Comparative Literature
UEYAMA, D., Buddhist Studies

Junior College:
ASAEDA, Z., History of Japanese Buddhism
HAMAGAMI, Y., Child Welfare
IHARA, K., Nursing Technology
IIDA, K., International Social Welfare
IKUTA, M., Social Welfare for the Elderly
KATOH, H., History of Social Welfare Policy
KAWAZOE, T., Shin Buddhism
NAGAI, T., Developmental Psychology
OHNISHI, M., Community Health
TANIMOTO, M., Philosophy
TATSUDANI, A., History of Shin Buddhism
WAKAHARA, D., Pedagogy
YAMADA, M., Indian Buddhism
YAMADA, Y., Shin Buddhism
YOSHIDA, K., Discrimination Problems

ATTACHED RESEARCH INSTITUTES

Institute of Buddhist Cultural Studies: Shichijo Ohmiya, Shimogyo-ku, Kyoto 600; Dir KYOSHIN ASANO.

Research Institute for the Social Sciences: 67 Tsukamoto-cho, Fukakusa, Fushimi-ku, Kyoto; Dir TAKESHI HIRANO.

Socio-cultural Research Institute: 1-5 Yokoya, Seta Ohe-cho, Otsu, Shiga 520-21; Dir KENICHI MATSUI.

Joint Research Centre for Science and Technology: 1-5 Yokoya, Seta Ohe-cho, Otsu, Shiga 520-21; Dir KEISUKE KOBAYASHI.

UNIVERSITY OF THE SACRED HEART, TOKYO

Hiroo 4 chome 3-1, Shibuya-ku, Tokyo 150-8938
Telephone: (3) 3407-5811
Fax: (3) 5485-3884
E-mail: wwwadmin@u-sacred-heart.ac.jp
Internet: www.u-sacred-heart.ac.jp
Founded 1948
Private control
Academic year: April to March
President: Prof. KIYO YAMAGATA
Business Chief: H. SHIMAOKA
Registrar: Y. YOSHIDA
Librarian: Prof. K. TORIGOE
Library of 310,000 vols
Number of teachers: 65
Number of students: 2,243
Publications: *Seishin Ronso* (Seishin Studies, 2 a year), *Kiyo* (Publications of the Research Institute for the Study of Christian Culture, annually)

DEANS

Dean of Students: T. KUBOTA
Dean of Studies: K. KITAMURA

SANNO INSTITUTE OF MANAGEMENT

6-39-15 Todoroki, Setagaya, Tokyo 158-8630
Telephone: (3) 3704-1111
Fax: (3) 3704-1608
Internet: www.sanno.ac.jp
Founded 1925
Consists of SANNO Graduate School (MBA Programme), SANNO University Isehara (4-year degree course in Management and Informatics, and distance education course), SANNO College Jiyugaoka (2-year degree course, and distance education course)
Academic year: April to March
Chairman: SHUNICHI UENO
President, Sanno University: MASAAKI HARADA
Executive Director: TOSHIKAZU TAMURA
Library of 345,000 vols
Number of teachers: 126
Number of students: 7,410 (excluding distance education course students)
Publications: *SANNO College Bulletin* (2 a year), *SANNO College Jiyugaoka Bulletin* (annually), *Journal of the Management Research Centre* (irregular)

DEANS

Graduate School: TOSHIKAZU TAMURA
School of Management and Information Science: MINAMI MIYAUCHI
Business Administration: MICHIKO MORIWAKI

SAPPORO GAKUIN UNIVERSITY

11-Banchi, Bunkyodai, Ebetsu, Hokkaido 069-8555
Telephone: (11) 386-8111
Fax: (11) 386-8113
E-mail: kyoumu@ims.sgu.ac.jp
Internet: www.sgu.ac.jp
Founded 1946
President: FUSE AKIKO
Faculties of Economics, Humanities, Law, Social Information.

SAPPORO UNIVERSITY

3-7-3-1 Nishioka, Toyohira-ku, Sapporo 062-8520
Telephone: (11) 852-1181
E-mail: koho@sapporo-u.ac.jp
Internet: www.sapporo-u.ac.jp
Founded 1967
Private Control
Academic year: April to March
President: MASAYUKI KIMURA
Head Administrator: K. KUROSAWA
Librarian: N. TAKAMATSU
Library of 426,000 vols
Number of teachers: 162
Number of students: 6,700
Publications: *Sapporo Law Review* (2 a year), *Journal of Comparative Cultures* (2 a year), *Sapporo University Journal* (2 a year), *Industrial and Business Journal* (2 a year)

DEANS

Faculty of Foreign Languages: M. KATO
Faculty of Economics: K. MOTODA
Faculty of Business Administration: J. ARAKAWA
Faculty of Law: H. TANAKA
Faculty of Cultural Studies: M. YAMAGUCHI
Women's Junior College: A. TODA
Graduate School of Law: K. SAKAI

SEIJO UNIVERSITY

6-1-20 Seijo, Setagaya-ku, Tokyo 157-8511
Telephone: (3) 3482-1181
Fax: (3) 3484-2698
E-mail: info@seijo.ac.jp
Internet: www.seijo.ac.jp
Founded 1950
Private control
Academic year: April to March
President: KENJI AGATSUMA
Administrative Secretary: N. SAKAMOTO
Librarian: K. SHINYAMA
Library of 660,000 vols
Number of teachers: 530 (141 full-time, 389 part-time)
Number of students: 5,612

DEANS

Faculty of Arts and Literature: JUNICHI TOBE
Faculty of Economics: SHUICHIRO KIMURA YUI
Faculty of Law: KUNIHIRO ONUMA
Junior College: MASUMI ISHINABE

ATTACHED INSTITUTES

Institute of Economic Studies.

Institute of Folklore Studies.

SEIKEI UNIVERSITY

3-3-1 Kichijoji-Kitamachi, Musashino City, Tokyo 180-8633
Telephone: (422) 37-3531
Fax: (422) 37-3883
Internet: www.seikei.ac.jp

Founded 1949
Academic year: April to March

President: KEISUKE KURITA
Librarian: HARUO TANAKA

Library of 742,000 vols
Number of teachers: 183 full-time
Number of students: 8,840 (8,584 undergraduate, 256 postgraduate)

Publications: *Seikei Daigaku Ippankenkyu Hokoku* (Bulletin), *Seikei Daigaku Kogaku Hokoku* (Technology Report), *Journal of Asian and Pacific Studies*

DEANS

Faculty of Economics: C. KOMURA
Faculty of Engineering: Y. KAWADA
Faculty of Humanities: K. AONO
Faculty of Law: E. UEMURA

DIRECTORS

Information Processing Center: A. NAKAZATO
Center for Asian and Pacific Studies: T. TOMITA

SENSHU UNIVERSITY

8 Kandajimbo-cho 3-chome, Chiyoda-ku, Tokyo 101-8425
Telephone: (44) 911-1250
Fax: (44) 911-1243
E-mail: iaffairs@acc.senshu-u.ac.jp
Internet: www.senshu-u.ac.jp

Founded 1880
Academic year: April to March

President: YOSHIHIRO HIDAKA
Librarian: T. OBA

Library of 1,110,000 vols
Number of teachers: 400 full-time
Number of students: 20,472

DEANS

School of Business Administration: K. UOTA
School of Commerce: K. ONISHI
School of Economics: S. SAKAI
School of Law: B. KOHATA
School of Literature: T. ARAKI
School of Network and Information: M. SAKAMOTO
Graduate School of Business Administration: N. TAKEMURA
Graduate School of Commerce: N. OGUCHI
Graduate School of Economics: M. YABUKI
Graduate School of Humanities: T. SUZUKI
Graduate School of Law: T. TAKAGAI
Professional School of Legal Affairs: Y. HIRAI

ATTACHED INSTITUTES

Imamura Institute of Legal Studies.
Institute of Accounting Studies.
Institute of Business Administration.
Institute of Commercial Sciences.
Institute for Development of Social Intelligence.
Institute for Humanities.
Institute of Information Science.
Institute of Natural Sciences.
Institute of Social Sciences.
Institute of Sports, Physical Education and Research.
Law Institute.
Psychological Counselling Centre.

SETSUNAN UNIVERSITY

17-8 Ikedanakamachi, Neyagawa-shi, Osaka 572-8508
Telephone: (72) 839-9102
Fax: (72) 826-5100
Internet: www.setsunan.ac.jp

Founded 1975

Chancellor and Chairman: Dr TAKAOMI TOMATSU
President: Dr SENNOSUKE KURIYAMA

DEANS

Faculty of Law: MASUYUKI MORIMOTO
Faculty of International Languages and Cultures: MITSUNORI IMAI
Faculty of Business Administration and Information: TATSUMI SHIMADA
Faculty of Engineering: YOSHIO NAMITA
Faculty of Pharmaceutical Sciences: NOBORU YATA

SHIKOKU UNIVERSITY

Ojin-cho, Tokushima-shi, Tokushima, 771-1192
Telephone: (88) 665-9911
Fax: (88) 665-8037
E-mail: oip@shikoku-u.ac.jp

Founded 1966

Chairman: HISAKO SATO

Library of 317,470 vols
Number of teachers: 163
Number of students: 3,114

Faculty of Literature; Graduate School of Management and Information Science.

SOKA UNIVERSITY

1-236, Tangi-cho, Hachioji, Tokyo 192-8577
Telephone: (426) 91-8200
Fax: (426) 91-2039
E-mail: adm@j.soka.ac.jp
Internet: www.soka.ac.jp

Founded 1971
Private control
Academic year: April to March

President: Prof. Dr MASAMI WAKAE
Vice-Presidents: Prof. KATSUHIKO FUKUSHIMA, Prof. MASASUKE NIHEI
Librarian: Prof. EIICHI IMAGAWA

Library of 1,005,000 vols
Number of teachers: 295
Number of students: 7,842

Publication: *SUN* (Soka University News, 4 a year)

DEANS

Faculty of Economics: Prof. Dr HIDETAKA HASEBE
Faculty of Law: Prof. AKIRA KIRIGAYA
Faculty of Letters: Prof. YUTAKA ISHIGAMI
Faculty of Business Administration: Prof. KAORU YAMANAKA
Faculty of Education: Prof. RIKIO KIMATA
Faculty of Engineering: Prof. YOSHIMI TESHIGAWARA
Division of Correspondence Education: Prof. TADASHIGE TAKAMURA
Graduate School of Economics: Prof. KINJI UEDA
Graduate School of Law: Prof. KAZUO KAWASAKI
Graduate School of Letters: Prof. KAZUNORI KUMAGAI
Graduate School of Engineering: Prof. KOJIRO KOBAYASHI
Institute of Japanese Language: Prof. KEIKO ISHIKAWA

DIRECTORS

Peace Research Institute: T. TAKAMURA
Institute of Asian Studies: E. IMAGAWA
Institute for the Comparative Study of Cultures: M. KITA
Institute of Life Science: M. WAKAE
Institute of Systems Science: M. WAKAE
International Research Institute for the Advanced Study of Buddhism: H. KANNO

SOPHIA UNIVERSITY (Jôchi University)

Chiyoda-ku, Kioicho 7-1, Tokyo 102-8554
Telephone: (3) 3238-3111
Fax: (3) 3238-3885
Internet: www.sophia.ac.jp

Founded 1913
Private control (Society of Jesus)
Languages of instruction: Japanese, English
Academic year: April to March

Chancellor: TOSHIAKI KOSO
President: YOSHIAKI ISHIZAWA
Vice-Presidents: S. IKEO, S. YAMAOKA, L. GROVE
Registrar: H. YAMAMOTO

Library: see Libraries and Archives
Number of teachers: 526
Number of students: 11,714

Publications: *Monumenta Nipponica* (4 a year in English), *Sophia* (4 a year in Japanese)

DEANS

Faculty of Humanities: A. OSHIMA
Faculty of Law: M. KOJO
Faculty of Economics: T. SUGIMOTO
Faculty of Foreign Studies: K. YOSHIDA
Faculty of Science and Technology: K. SOGABE
Faculty of Theology: T. SAKUMA
Faculty of Comparative Culture: R. GARDNER
Faculty of Human Sciences: H. OKAMOTO

DIRECTORS

Institute of Medieval Thought: H. OGINO
Iberoamerican Institute: K. IMAI
Institute of Christian Culture and Oriental Religions: K. MATSUOKA
Counselling Institute: Y. YAMANAKA
Life Science Institute: K. KUMAKURA
Institute of Asian Cultures: Y. MURAI
Institute for the Culture of German-speaking Areas: S. KOIZUMI
Linguistic Institute for International Communication: K. YOSHIDA
Institute of American and Canadian Studies: T. OTSUKA
Institute of Comparative Culture: J. OKADA
Institute for the Study of Social Justice: H. MACHINO
Institute for Studies of the Global Environment: K. SEGAWA

HEADS OF DEPARTMENTS

Faculty of Theology:
- Theology: S. YAMAOKA

Faculty of Humanities:
- Philosophy: Y. OHASHI
- Education: Y. YUKAWA
- Psychology: Y. AKETA
- History: K. YAMAUCHI
- Japanese Literature: M. SEMA
- English Literature: T. IINO
- German Literature: A. TAKAHASHI
- French Literature: K. YOSHIMURA
- Journalism: Y. TAJIMA
- Sociology: S. WATANABE
- Social Welfare: T. AMINO

Faculty of Law:
- Law: S. TAGASHIRA
- International Legal Studies: K. DEGUCHI
- Legal Studies of the Global Environment: Y. KITAMURA

Faculty of Economics:
- Economics: T. UEYAMA

Management: J. Kobayashi
Faculty of Foreign Studies:
English Language and Studies: M. Tanno
German Language and Studies: Y. Takahashi
French Language and Studies: M. Takai
Spanish Language and Hispanic Studies: A. Edelmira
Russian Language and Studies: T. Ueno
Portuguese Language and Luso-Brazilian Studies: M. João
Faculty of Comparative Culture (4 Yonban-cho, Chiyoda-ku, Tokyo 102-0081; tel. (3) 3238-4000; fax (3) 3238-4076):
Comparative Culture: V. Ozaki
Japanese Language and Studies: M. Yonekura
Faculty of Science and Technology:
Mechanical Engineering: M. Yoshida
Electrical and Electronics Engineering: A. Kawanaka
Mathematics: S. Ouchi
Physics: T. Sekine
Chemistry: T. Sakaizumi

TAKUSHOKU UNIVERSITY

3-4-14 Kohinata, Bunkyo-ku, Tokyo 112
Telephone: (3) 3947-2261
E-mail: web_int@ofc.takushoku-u.ac.jp
Internet: www.takushoku-u.ac.jp
Founded 1900
Campuses at Hachioji and Bunkyo
Chancellor: S. Odamura
President: T. Osakai
Chairman of Board of Directors: T. Fujito
Librarian: S. Kori
Library of 440,000 vols
Number of teachers: 528
Number of students: 10,377
Publications: *Takushoku Daigaku Ronshu* (every 2 months), *Kaigai Jijo* (Journal of World Affairs, monthly), *Hokoku* (annually)

DEANS
Faculty of Commerce: T. Takahashi
Faculty of Political Science and Economics: K. Kobayashi
Faculty of Foreign Languages: T. Wada
Faculty of Engineering: M. Sakata
Special Japanese Language Course for Foreign Students: M. Araki
Takushoku Junior College: T. Goto
Hokkaido Takushoku Junior College: T. Ishikawa
Graduate School: T. Osakai

TAMAGAWA UNIVERSITY

6-1-1 Tamagawa Gakuen 6-chome, Machida, Tokyo 194-8610
Telephone: (427) 39-8111
Fax: (427) 39-1181
E-mail: webmaster@tamagawa.ac.jp
Internet: www.tamagawa.ac.jp
Founded 1929
Private control
Language of instruction: Japanese
Academic year: April to March
President: Yoshiaki Obara
Registrar: Takashi Urata
Librarian: Harua Toda
Library of 775,000 vols
Number of teachers: 351 full-time
Number of teachers: 436 part-time
Number of students: 7,774
Publications: *Zenjin Education* (monthly), *Shoho* (annually), *Mitsubachi Kagaku* (4 a year)

DEANS
Faculty of Agriculture: Tadayuki Ishiyama
Faculty of Engineering: Hidetake Tanibayashi
Faculty of Arts and Education: Hiroshi Yoneyama
Department of Education by Correspondence: Hiroshi Yoneyama
Junior College for Women: Michiaki Nagai
Graduate School for Education and Letters: Yasutada Takahashi
Graduate School for Agriculture: Mitsuo Matsuka
Graduate School for Engineering: Takuro Koike
Associate Degree Junior College for Women: Tomio Ozawa

TEZUKAYAMA UNIVERSITY

7-1-1 Tezukayama, Nara City 631-8501
Telephone: (742) 48-9122
Fax: (742) 48-9135
E-mail: webmaster@tezukayama-u.ac.jp
Internet: www.tezukayama-u.ac.jp
Founded 1941
Library of 280,000 vols
Number of teachers: 109
Number of students: 4,166
Faculties of Humanities, Economics, Business Administration, Law and Policy.

TOHOKU GAKUIN UNIVERSITY

1-3-1 Tsuchitoi, Aoba-ku, Sendai 980-8511
Telephone: (22) 264-6425
Fax: (22) 264-6515
E-mail: ico@tscc.tohoku-gakuin.ac.jp
Internet: www.tohoku-gakuin.ac.jp
Founded 1886
Private control
Language of instruction: Japanese
Academic year: April to March
Library of 1,000,000 vols
President: Nozomu Hoshimiya
Vice-Presidents: Koji Otsuka, Noboru Sekiya
Number of teachers: 674
Number of students: 12,518
Publications: *Church and Theology* (2 a year), *Economics* (3 a year), *History and Geography* (2 a year), *Human, Jurisprudence* (2 a year), *Linguistic and Information Sciences* (3 a year), *Science and Engineering Report* (2 a year), *Tohoku Gakuin University Review English Language and Literature* (2 a year)

DEANS
Faculty of Economics: Kazuo Endo
Faculty of Engineering: Ginro Endo
Faculty of Law: Makoto Saito
Faculty of Letters: Kenichi Endo
Faculty of Liberal Arts: Shunzo Sasaki

CHAIRS OF DEPARTMENTS
Faculty of Economics:
Business Administration: Y. Saito
Business Administration (Eveninig Course): S. Saito
Economics: Y. Saito
Economics (Evening Course): A. Nozaki
Faculty of Engineering:
Mechanical Engineering and Intelligent Systems: H. Endo
Electrical Engineering and Information Technology: H. Echigo
Electronic Engineering: Y. Hoshi
Civil and Environmental Engineering: M. Nakazawa
Faculty of Law:
Law: K. Ito
Faculty of Letters:
Christian Studies: K. Sasaki
English: O. Yagawa
English (Evening Course): H. Muranoi
History: H. Tsuji
Faculty of Liberal Arts:
Human Science: Y. Horike
Information Science: A. Sato
Language and Culture: H. Ito
Regional Planning: M. Sakuma

TOKAI UNIVERSITY EDUCATIONAL SYSTEM

2-28-4 Tomigaya, Shibuya-ku, Tokyo 151-8677
Telephone: (3) 3467-2211
Fax: (3) 3467-0197
E-mail: pr@yyg.u-tokai.ac.jp
Internet: www.pr.tokai.ac.jp
Founded 1942
Chairman and President: Tatsuro Matsumae

DIRECTORS
Strategic Peace and International Affairs Research Institute: Norio Matsumae
Research Institute for Educational Development: Sounosuke Katori
Research Institute of Science and Technology: Sounosuke Katori
Tokai University Research and Information Center: Yoshiaki Matsumae
Tokai University Space Information Center: Haruhisa Shimoda
Okinawa Regional Research Center: Sounosuke Katori
Tokai University European Center (Denmark): Morito Takahashi
Tokai University Pacific Center (Hawaii): Kiyoshi Yamada
Research Institute of Modern Civilization: Tatsuro Matsumae

CONSTITUENT UNIVERSITIES

Tokai University

Telephone: (463) 58-1211
Fax: (463) 50-2052
E-mail: kikaku@tsc.u-tokai.ac.jp
Internet: www.u-tokai.ac.jp
Shonan Campus: 1117 Kitakaname, Hiratsuka-shi, Kanagawa 259-1292; tel. (463) 58-1211; fax (463) 35-2458
Yoyogi Campus: 2-28-4 Tomigaya, Shibuya-ku, Tokyo 151-8677; tel. (3) 3467-2211
Shimizu Campus: 3-20-1 Orido, Shimizu-shi, Shizuoka 424-8610; tel. (543) 34-0411
Isehara Campus: Bouseidai, Isehara-shi, Kanagawa 259-1193; tel. (463) 93-1121
Numazu Campus: 317 Nishino, Numazu-shi, Shizuoka 410-0395; tel. (559) 68-1111
Founded 1946
Academic year: April to March
President: Jiro Takano
Librarian: Tasuku Hayami
Library of 1,801,220 vols
Number of teachers: 1,461 full-time
Number of students: 31,481
Publications: *Tokai Journal of Experimental and Clinical Medicine*, bulletins of the various schools, etc

CHAIRMEN
Graduate School of Letters: Nobuyuki Watase
Graduate School of Political Science: Yoshiteru Makita
Graduate School of Economics: Osamu Takenaka
Graduate School of Law: Shigeru Otsuka
Graduate School of Arts: Harumi Koshiba

Graduate School of Physical Education: NAOHISA MATSUNAGA
Graduate School of Science: JIRO TAKANO
Graduate School of Engineering: HIROMASA TAKEUCHI
Graduate School of High Technology for Human Welfare: MASAAKI SHINJI
Graduate School of Marine Science and Technology: YOSHIMASA TOYOTA
Graduate School of Medicine: KIYOSHI KUROKAWA
Graduate School of Health Sciences: KEIKO SHICHITA

DEANS

School of Letters: YASUO TANAKA
School of Political Science and Economics: YASUSHI INOUE
School of Law: SHIGERU OTSUKA
School of Humanities and Culture: HIROSHI NINOMIYA
School of Physical Education: NOBUYUKI SATO
School of Science: KENZOU NANRI
School of Engineering: HIROHISA UCHIDA
School of Engineering II (Evening Session): HIROHISA UCHIDA
School of High Technology for Human Welfare: CHIKAO UEMURA
School of Marine Science and Technology: YOSHIMASA TOYOTA
School of Medicine: TOMOMITSU HOTTA
School of Health Sciences: RIYUUKO FUJIMURA
Japanese Language Course for Foreign Students: FUSATO TANIGUCHI (Head)
Foreign Language Centre: KIYOICHI ONO (Head)
Licensed Professional Training Center: YUUKO MIYASAKA (Head)
International Student Education Center: FUSATO TANIGUCHI (Head)
School of Information Technology and Electronics: NOBUAKI TAKAHASHI

HEADS OF DEPARTMENTS

School of Letters:

- Civilization: TOSHIHARU HARADA
- Asian Civilization: TAKASHI UHARA
- European Civilization: TADATOSHI KUBOTA
- American Civilization: RYOZOU MATSUMOTO
- Nordic Studies: NOBUYOSHI MORI
- Japanese History: FUSAO SONE
- Oriental History: MOTOI ASAI
- Occidental History: YASUO KINBARA
- Archaeology: HITOSHI KAMURO
- Japanese Literature: KOICHIRO KOIZUMI
- Creative Writing: NOBURU TSUJIHARA
- English: SHUNJI KAGAYA
- Media Studies: FUMIHIKO YOSHIDA
- Psychological and Sociological Studies: KOUICHI OGAWA

School of Political Science and Economics:

- Political Science: KAZUO YAMAUCHI
- Economics: AKIRA KONAKAYAMA
- Business Administration: KATSUTOSHI AYANO

School of Law:

- Law: SHIGERU OOTSUKA

School of Humanities and Culture:

- Human Development: YASUHIRO FUJINO
- Arts: YATSUHIRO NIIZEKI
- International Studies: YUSUKE DAN

School of Physical Education:

- Physical Education: MASARU UNO
- Judo and Kendo: TOSHIAKI HASHIMOTO
- Physical Recreation: TAEKO KAWAMUKAI

School of Science:

- Mathematics: MAKOTO DOI
- Mathematical Sciences: HIDEYUKI DOUKE
- Physics: TSUNENORI SUZUKI
- Chemistry: YASUYUKI MIURA

School of Information Technology and Electronics:

- Human and Information Science: KENJU OTSUKA
- Information Media Technology: SHIGEYUKI OHARA
- Management Systems Engineering: MASANOBU MATSUMARU
- Applied Computer Engineering: RYOUSUKE MASUDA
- Electronics: TOMIO IZUMI
- Communications Engineering: SHIGENORI TOMIYAMA
- Electrical and Electronic Engineering: YOSHIBUMI MIZUTANI

School of Engineering:

- Applied Biochemistry: TAKAO HONMA
- Applied Chemistry: YASUO AZUMA
- Applied Science: Optics and Photonics: MORIAKI WAKAKI
- Applied Science: Energy Engineering: AKIRA YOKOCHI
- Architecture and Building Engineering: KAZUHIKO MASHITA
- Civil Engineering: YOJI SHIMAZAKI
- Materials Science: ITARU JIMBO
- Mechanical Engineering: TAKANE ITO
- Precision Engineering: YOSHIDA KAZUNARI
- Prime Mover Engineering: TOSHIO IIJIMA
- Aeronautics and Astronautics: FUMIO TOYAMA

School of Engineering II (Evening Session):

- Electrical Engineering: YOSHIBUMI MIZUTANI
- Information Systems: KOUHEI CHIYOU
- Construction Engineering: SHUUJI HANYUU
- Mechanical Engineering: KAZUHISA ISHIBASHI

School of High Technology for Human Welfare:

- Information and Communication Technology: MIYAO SHIINA
- Material Science and Technology: KOUZABURO NISHIYAMA
- Biological Science and Technology: MASAO HYODO
- Bio-Medical Engineering: KENTARO YODA

School of Marine Science and Technology:

- Geo-Environmental Technology: OSAMU WATARAI
- Marine Civil Engineering: HIROMICHI TANAKA
- Marine Mineral Resources: TADASHI MASUYAMA
- Fisheries: SHO TANAKA
- Marine Design and Engineering: KOICHIRO YOSHIDA
- Marine Science: YOSHIO SATO
- Nautical Engineering: MUNEO IKEDA

School of Medicine:

- Medicine: KIYOSHI KUROKAWA

School of Health Sciences:

- Nursing: KAZUKO SUZUKI
- Social Work: IKUKO NAKANO

Foreign Language Center:

- Group I (English): SHIGETOSHI SATO
- Group II (German, French, Chinese, Korean, Spanish, Russian): NAOKI OTA

Licensed Professional Training Center

- YUUKO MIYASAKA
- Teacher Training Program: TAMOTSU SUGAI
- Librarian Training Program: YUUKO MIYASAKU
- Curator Training Program: YUUKO MIYASAKU

International Student Education Center:

- Intensive Japanese Language Program: SACHIE MIYAGI
- Foreign Student Program: SACHIE MIYAGI

DIRECTORS

Research Institute of Civilization: RYOUZOU MATSUMOTO
Institute of Oceanic Research and Development: JIRO SEGAWA
Medical Research Institute: KIYOSHI KUROKAWA
Research Institute of Higher Education: TAKASHI YASUOKA
Research Institute of Sports Medical Science: MASARU SAITO
Advanced Science and Technology Co-operative Research Center: HIROHISA UCHIDA

Kyushu Tokai University

Telephone: (96) 382-1141
Fax: (96) 381-7956
E-mail: kikaku@jsmail.js.ktokai-u.ac.jp
Internet: www.ktokai-u.ac.jp

Kumamoto Campus: 9-1-1 Toroku, Kumamoto-shi, Kumamoto 862-8652; tel. (96) 382-1141; fax (96) 381-7956

Aso Campus: Kawayou, Choyo-son, Aso-gun, Kumamoto 869-1404; tel. (9676) 7-0611; fax (9676) 7-2053

Founded 1973
Academic year: April to March

President: YOSHIAKI MATSUMAE
Librarian: TAKAAKI TSUKIJI

Library of 240,965 vols
Number of teachers: 138 full-time
Number of students: 3,437

CHAIRMEN

Graduate School of Engineering: CHIKAE WATANABE
Graduate School of Agriculture: KIHACHIROU NOBUKUNI

DEANS

School of Information Science: SHOJI KAIDA
School of Engineering: CHIKAE WATANABE
School of Agriculture: KIHACHIROU NOBUKUNI

HEADS OF DEPARTMENTS

School of Information Science:

- Management Science: YOICHI IWASAKI
- Information Science: HIDEO KUGISAWA

School of Engineering:

- Mechanical Systems Engineering: EIICHIROU KAWAHARA
- Architecture: MASANORI MIYAZAKI
- Civil Engineering: YASUHIRO MIGITA
- Management Engineering: NAOTOSHI SUMIKURA
- Space and Earth Information Technology: KIYOSHI SHIMAMURA
- Electrical and Electronic Systems: DAISUKE OKANO

School of Agriculture:

- Plant Science: TASTUROU MURATA
- Animal Science: FUKASHI KOYANAGI
- Bioscience: KEIJI IGOSHI

DIRECTORS

Institute of Industrial Science and Technology: ICHIRO TAKAGI
Agricultural Research Institute: TAKAO TORIKATA

Hokkaido Tokai University

Telephone: (11) 571-5111
Fax: (11) 571-7879
E-mail: kikaku@ss.htokai.ac.jp
Internet: www.htokai.ac.jp

Sapporo Campus: 5-1-1-1 Minamisawa, Minami-ku, Sapporo, Hokkaido 005-8601; tel. (11) 571-5111; fax (11) 571-7879

Asahikawa Campus: 224 Chuwa, Kamui-cho, Asahikawa, Hokkaido 070-8601; tel. (166) 61-5111; fax (166) 62-8180

Founded 1977

Academic year: April to March
President: Shunmei Mitsuzawa
Librarian: Eiichi Sato

Library of 179,000 vols
Number of teachers: 112 full-time
Number of students: 2,515

CHAIRMEN

Graduate School of Arts: Jun Mikami
Graduate School of Science and Engineering: Tetsuo Shimono

DEANS

School of Art and Technology: Jun Mikami
School of International Cultural Relations: Kouji Kobayashi
School of Engineering: Minoru Koutaki

HEADS OF DEPARTMENTS

School of Art and Technology:
Design: Yoshinori Arai
Architecture: Hiroshi Kitajima
School of International Cultural Relations:
Comparative Culture: Satora Mabuchi
Intercultural Communications: Takuya Yoshimura
Northern Regions Cultural Studies: Kazuhito Kawasaki
School of Engineering:
Electronic and Information Science Technology: Tatsuo Iwata
Marine Science and Technology: Kenji Yano
Bioscience and Technology: Takeshi Sakkaki

DIRECTORS

Research Institute for Higher Education Programs: Yasunari Kurihara
Cultural Institute of Northern Region: Tsutomu Kokawa
Environmental Research Institute: Hiroyuki Nishimura

TOKIWA UNIVERSITY

1-430-1 Miwa, Mito-shi, Ibaraki Prefecture 310-8585
Telephone: (29) 232-2511
Fax: (29) 231-6078
E-mail: kouhou@tokiwa.ac.jp
Internet: www.tokiwa.ac.jp

Founded 1983

Chairman: Hidemichi Morosawa
President: Satoshi Ohori

Colleges of Human Science, Applied International Studies, Community Development; Graduate School of Human Science.

TOKYO UNIVERSITY OF PHARMACY AND LIFE SCIENCES

1432-1 Horinouchi, Hachioji, Tokyo 192-03
Telephone: (426) 76-5111
Internet: www.toyaku.ac.jp

Founded 1880

President: Dr T. Yamakawa
Librarian: Prof. A. Ohta

Library of 85,000 vols
Number of teachers: 200
Number of students: 2,200

Publication: *Annual Report*

Departments of pharmaceutical sciences, biopharmacy and pharmaceutical technology.

TOKYO DENTAL COLLEGE

1-2-2 Masago, Mihama-ku, Chiba 261-8502
Telephone: (43) 270-3764
Fax: (43) 270-3765
E-mail: int@tdc.ac.jp
Internet: www.tdc.ac.jp

Founded 1890
Academic year: April to March

Dean: Prof. Yuzuru Kaneko
Vice-Deans: Prof. Masashi Yakushiji

Library of 198,000 vols
Number of teachers: 306
Number of students: 983 (802 undergraduate, 181 postgraduate)

Publications: *Bulletin* (in English, 4 a year), *Shikwa Gakuho* (research journal, in Japanese, every 2 months).

TOKYO KEIZAI UNIVERSITY

1-7-34 Minami-cho, Kokubunji-shi, Tokyo 185-8502
Telephone: (42) 328-7711
Internet: www.tku.ac.jp

Founded 1900 as Okura Commerce School
Private control
Academic year: April to March

President: Katsuhiko Murakami
Chief Administrative Officer: Touru Sasaki
Librarian: Shigekazu Kukita

Library of 640,000 vols
Number of teachers: 445
Number of students: 7,673

Publications: *Journal of Tokyo Keizai University* (6 a year), *Journal of Humanities and Natural Sciences* (2 a year), *Journal of Communication Studies* (2 a year), *Tokyo Kezai Law Review* (2 a year)

DEANS

Faculty of Economics: Masahiro Fukushi
Faculty of Business Administration: Yoshiaki Jinnai
Faculty of Contemporary Law: Kazuo Shimada
Faculty of Communication Studies: Kaoru Yamazaki
Graduate School of Economics: Hisashi Watanabe (Chair.)
Graduate School of Business Administration: Kenji Omori (Chair.)
Graduate School of Communication Studies: Teruo Ariyama (Chair.)
Graduate School of Contemporary Law: Yoshio Miyazaki (Chair.)

TOKYO UNIVERSITY OF AGRICULTURE

1-1-1 Sakuragaoka, Setagaya-ku, Tokyo 156-8502
Telephone: (3) 5477-2560
Fax: (3) 5477-2635
E-mail: tuacip@nodai.ac.jp
Internet: www.nodai.ac.jp

Founded 1891
Academic year: April to March

President: Dr Isoya Shinji
Chief Administrative Officer: Dr Akio Shibakazi
Librarian: Dr Shigeyuki Miyabayashi

Library of 665,000 vols
Number of teachers: 357
Number of students: 13,000

Publication: *Journal of Agricultural Science* (annually)

DEANS

Faculty of Agriculture: Dr Takashi Amano
Faculty of Applied Bioscience: Dr Kanju Osawa
Faculty of Bio-Industry: Dr Masao Ito
Faculty of International Agriculture and Food Studies: Dr Katsutoshi Niinuma
Faculty of Regional Environmental Science: Dr Masaharu Komamura
Graduate School of Agriculture: Dr Tai Uchimura
Graduate School of Bio-Industry: Dr Yoshie Momonoki
Junior College: Dr Tadashi Yasuhara

TOKYO DENKI DAIGAKU (Tokyo Denki University)

2-2 Kanda-Nishiki-cho, Chiyoda-ku, Tokyo 101-8457
Telephone: (3) 5280-3555
Fax: (3) 5280-3623
E-mail: gakuchoshitsu@jim.ac.jp
Internet: www.dendai.ac.jp

Founded 1907
Academic year: April to March

President: Dr Yoshihiro Toma
General Director of Multimedia Resource Centre and Library: Dr T. Saito

Library of 321,481 vols, 2,975 periodicals
Number of teachers: 748 (355 full-time, 393 part-time)
Number of students: 11,563

DEANS

Graduate School of Engineering: J. Iwamoto
School of Engineering: T. Ibamoto
School of Engineering (Evening Programme): S. Murakami
Graduate School of Science and Engineering: M. Takizawa
School of Science and Engineering: Y. Kashimura
School of the Information Environment: S. Nakamura

DIRECTORS

Research Institute for Technology: H. Inaba
Applied Superconductivity Research Laboratory: I. Nemoto
Research Institute for Construction Technology: M. Tachibana
Centre for Research Collaboration: H. Tomita
Frontier Research and Development Centre: Y. Uchikawa

TOKYO UNIVERSITY OF SCIENCE

1-3 Kagurazaka, Shinjuku-ku, Tokyo 162-8601
Telephone: (3) 3260-4271
Internet: www.tus.ac.jp

Founded 1881
Private control

President: Hiroyuki Okamura
Deputy Presidents: Yoshimoto Abe, Tsunehiro Manabe
Librarian: Masaaki Ueki

Library of 948,592 vols
Number of teachers: 782
Number of students: 19,825

Publication: *Science Forum* (monthly)

DEANS

Faculty of Engineering Division I: Shinji Honami
Faculty of Engineering Division II: Takayuki Teramoto
Faculty of Industrial Science and Technology: Tsuneo Watanabe
Faculty of Pharmaceutical Sciences: Ken Takeda
Faculty of Science Division I: Tetsuo Kanamoto
Faculty of Science Division II: Hiroshi Niitsuma
Faculty of Science and Technology: Hiroyuki Seto
School of Management: Masayoshi Hirota

HEADS OF DEPARTMENTS

Faculty of Engineering Division I:
- Architecture: YUZO SHINOZAKI
- Electrical Engineering: MASATOSHI SANO
- Industrial Chemistry: TATSUHIKO TANAKA
- Management Science: TOSHIKAZU YAMAGUCHI
- Mechanical Engineering: SHIGEKA YOSHIMOTO
- General Education: HIDEKAZU TACHIZAKI

Faculty of Engineering Division II:
- Architecture: HIDEO NAOI
- Electrical Engineering: NORIAKI MASUI
- Management Science: YUKIO NOGUCHI
- General Education: TAMIO HARA

Faculty of Industrial Science and Technology (2641 Yamazaki, Noda-shi, Chiba 278-8510; tel. (4) 7124-1501; fax (4) 7124-2150):
- Applied Electronics: MANABA YAMAMOTO
- Biological Science and Technology: YASUHIRO TOMOOKA
- Materials Science and Technology: YASUO KOGO
- General Education: SHIRO FUJII

Faculty of Pharmaceutical Sciences (2641 Yamazaki, Noda-shi, Chiba 278-8510; tel. (4) 7124-1501; fax (4) 7124-2150):
- Pharmaceutical Sciences: JUNZO SUZUKI
- Pharmaceutical Technochemistry: HIROSHI HARA

Faculty of Science Division I:
- Applied Chemistry: IZUMI NAKAI
- Applied Physics: TAKESHI HATTORI
- Chemistry: KOICHI TSUKIYAMA
- General Education: YOSHIHIRO MARUYAMA
- Mathematical Information Science: HIROSHI YABE
- Mathematics: NOBORO OKAZAWA
- Physics: AKIRA SUZUKI

Faculty of Science Division II:
- Chemistry: TSUYOSHI SATO
- Mathematics: MITSUO YOSHIZAWA
- Physics: TADASHI MIYAZAKI
- General Education: SHIZUTAKA SAITO

Faculty of Science and Technology (2641 Yamazaki, Noda-shi, Chiba 278-8510; tel. (4) 7124-1501; fax (4) 7124-2150):
- Applied Biological Science: KENGO SAKAGUCHI
- Architecture: MASATO KAWAMUKAI
- Civil Engineering: TSUKASA NISHIMURA
- Electrical Engineering: SUMIO KOGOSHI
- Industrial Administration: TAKESHI ARAI
- Information Science: YOSHIO TOGAWA
- Mathematics: TAKAO KOBAYASHI
- Mechanical Engineering: HIROSHI KAWAMURA
- Physics: ATSUO MORINAGA
- Pure and Applied Chemistry: MASAHIKO ABE
- General Education: AKIRA SASAKI

School of Management (500 Shimokiyoku, Kuki-shi, Saitama 346-8512; tel. (480) 21-7600; fax (480) 21-7603):
- Management: TAKESHI KOSAKA

ATTACHED INSTITUTES

Research Education Organization for Information Science and Technology: 1–3 Kagurazaka, Shinjuku-ku, Tokyo 162-8601; tel. (3) 3260-4271; Principal MASANORI OHYA.

Research Institute for Biological Sciences: 2641 Yamazaki, Noda-shi, Chiba 278-8510; tel. (4) 7124-1501; Principal TAKACHIKA AZUMA.

Research Institute for Science and Technology: 2641 Yamazaki, Noda-shi, Chiba 278-8510; tel. (4) 7124-1501; Principal YOSHIMASA NIHEI.

TOKYO WOMEN'S CHRISTIAN UNIVERSITY

2-6-1, Zempukuji, Suginami-ku, Tokyo 167-8585

Telephone: (3) 3395-1211
Fax: (3) 3399-3123
E-mail: iec@office.twcu.ac.jp
Internet: www.twcu.ac.jp

Founded 1918
Private control
Language of instruction: Japanese
Academic year: April to March

President: AKIKO MINATO
Librarian: SHINSUKE MUROFUCHI

Library of 557,000 vols
Number of teachers: 142
Number of students: 4,208, including 78 graduates

Publications: *Japanese Literature* (2 a year), *Essays and Studies in British and American Literature* (2 a year), *Historica* (annually), *Sociology and Economics* (annually), *Annals of Institute for Comparative Studies of Culture* (annually), *Science Reports* (annually), *Essays and Studies* (2 a year), *University Bulletin* (monthly)

DEANS

Graduate School: HIROSHI IMAI
College of Arts and Sciences: SANAE INOUE
College of Culture and Communication: YUKO KOBAYASHI

CHAIRMEN

Graduate School of Humanities: HIROSHI IMAI
Graduate School of Science: MASAHIKO SHINOHARA
Graduate School of Culture and Communication: RYOICHI SATO

DIRECTORS

Institute for Comparative Studies of Culture: AIKO KOZAKI
Institute for Women's Studies: HIROKO SATO

HEADS OF DEPARTMENTS

College of Arts and Sciences:
- Philosophy: MITSUSHI KUBO
- Japanese Literature: AKIRA KANEKO
- English: YUTAKA KURONO
- History: TESSEI MATSUZAWA
- Sociology and Economics: NOZOMU KAWAMURA
- Psychology: HIROTADA HIROSE
- Mathematics: MASAHIKO SHINOHARA

College of Culture and Communication:
- Communication: MEIKO SUGIYAMA
- Cross-Cultural Studies: AKIRA TAKEDA
- Languages: TAZUKO UENO

TOKYO WOMEN'S MEDICAL UNIVERSITY

8-1 Kawada-cho, Shinjuku-ku, Tokyo 162-8666

Telephone: (3) 3353-8111
Fax: (3) 3353-6793
Internet: www.twmu.ac.jp

Founded 1900
Private control
Language of instruction: Japanese
Academic year: April to March

President: K. TAKAKURA
Registrar: H. YOSHIOKA
Librarian: M. KOBAYASHI

Library of 227,850 vols
Number of teachers: 2,178
Number of students: 961

Publication: *Journal of Tokyo Women's Medical University* (monthly, in English or Japanese).

ATTACHED INSTITUTES

Heart Institute of Japan: Dir H. KASANUKI.

Institute of Biomedical Engineering: Dir T. OKANO.

Institute of Gastroenterology: Dir Dr K. TAKASAKI.

Neurological Institute: Dir M. IWATA.

Kidney Center: Dir K. NITTA.

Diabetes Center: Dir Y. IWAMOTO.

Maternal and Perinatal Center: Deputy Dir H. NISHIDA.

Institute of Clinical Endocrinology: Dir K. TAKANO.

Critical Care Medical Center: Dir T. SUZUKI.

Institute of Rheumatology: Dir N. KAMATANI.

Chest Institute: Dir A. NAGAI.

Institute of Oriental Medicine: Dir H. TAKAHASHI.

TOYO UNIVERSITY

28-20 Hakusan 5-chome, Bunkyo-ku, Tokyo 112-8606

Telephone: (3) 3945-7557
Fax: (3) 3942-2489
E-mail: ipo@hakusrv.toyo.ac.jp
Internet: www.toyo.ac.jp

Founded 1887
Private control
Academic year: April to March

President: TOMONORI MATSUO
Director of Academic Affairs: MIKIO AKIYAMA
Librarian: TAKITARO MORIKAWA

Library of 1,101,256 vols
Number of teachers: 1,269 (523 full-time, 746 part-time)
Number of students: 29,819

Publications: faculty bulletins, journals, etc

DEANS

Undergraduate School of Literature: TASHIAKI YAMADA
Undergraduate School of Economics: SHUNICHI KIGAWA
Undergraduate School of Business Administration: YOUICHI KAKIZAKI
Undergraduate School of Law: HIDETOSHI KOBAYASHI
Undergraduate School of Sociology: MAMORA FUNATSU
Undergraduate School of Engineering: MASAHIDE YONEYAMA
Undergraduate School of Regional Development Studies: HAJIME NAGAHAMA
Undergraduate School of Life Sciences: AKIRA SAKURAI
Graduate School of Literature: KAZUO ARITA
Graduate School of Sociology: KOJUN FURUKAWA
Graduate School of Law: MASUO IMAGAMI
Graduate School of Business Administration: YASUHIRO OGURA
Graduate School of Engineering: TOHRU IUCHI
Graduate School of Economics: KIYOSHI ASUNO
Graduate School of Regional Development Studies: TOMONORI MARSUO
Graduate School of Life Sciences: AKIRA INOUE

ATTACHED INSTITUTES

Institute of Human Sciences: Dir TSUNEYUKI MATSUMOTO.

Institute of Social Sciences: Dir SHUSAKU YAMAYA.

Institute of Oriental Studies: Dir KIYOMI TAKEUCHI.

Institute of Asian Cultures: Dir YUTEN HIGA.

Institute of Regional Vitalization Studies: Dir HIROHIDE KONAMI.

Research Institute of Industrial Technology: Dir MASAO YANO.

TSUDA COLLEGE

2-1-1 Tsuda-machi, Kodaira-shi, Tokyo 187-8577

Telephone: (42) 342-5111
Fax: (42) 341-2444
E-mail: info-admin@tsuda.ac.jp
Internet: www.tsuda.ac.jp

Founded 1900

Academic year: April to March

Chairman: KAZUYOSHI ISHIZAKA

Library of 270,000 vols, 3,000 periodicals
Number of teachers: 87 full-time
Number of students: 2,837 (incl. 109 postgraduate)

Publications: *The Tsuda Review* (annually), *Journal of Tsuda College* (annually), *The Study of International Relations* (annually)

Faculty of liberal arts, departments of English language and literature, mathematics and computer science, international and cultural studies; postgraduate schools of literary studies, international and cultural studies, mathematics.

TSURU UNIVERSITY

3-8-1 Tahara, Tsuru, Yamanashi 402-8555

Telephone: (554) 43-4341
Fax: (554) 43-4347
E-mail: mail@tsuru.ac.jp
Internet: www.tsuru.ac.jp

Founded 1955

Number of teachers: 74 (full-time)
Number of students: 3,000

Teacher training college.

WASEDA UNIVERSITY

1-104 Totsuka-machi, Shinjuku-ku, Tokyo 169-8050

Telephone: (3) 3203-4141
Fax: (3) 3203-7051
E-mail: intl-ac@list.waseda.jp
Internet: www.waseda.jp

Founded 1882
Private control
Academic year: April to February

Pres.: KATSUHIKO SHIRAI

Vice-Pres: KENICHI ENATSU, SEIGO HIRAYAMA, SEIJI HONDA, KENJI HORIGUCHI, YOSHIJI HORIKOSHI, EI'ICHIRO KOBAYASHI, EIKO KONO, ISAO MURAOKA, AKIRA NISHITANI, EI'ICHIRO NOJIMA, AKIRA SESHIMO, SATOSHI SHIMIZU, NAOJI TAKAGI, HIDEAKI TAUCHI, TERUAKI TAYAMA, KENJIRO TSUCHIDA, NOBUHIRO TSUMOTO, KATSUICHI UCHIDA, YASUMASA UMESATO, SHOTARO WATANABE

Dir of Library: NOBUYUKI KAMIYA

Library of 5,100,000 vols
Number of teachers: 5,885
Number of students: 54,228 (45,757 undergraduate, 8,471 postgraduate)

The Schools of Letters, Arts and Sciences I and II will be terminated when all existing students graduate; they are replaced from 2007 by the School of Culture, Media and Society and the School of Humanities and Social Sciences. The Schools of Science and Engineering will also be terminated when all existing students graduate; they are replaced from 2007 by the School of Fundamental Science and Engineering, the School of Creative Science and Engineering and the School of Advanced Science and Engineering.

DEANS

School of Political Science and Econ.: SHOZO IIJIMA
School of Law: TATSUO UEMURA
School of Letters, Arts and Sciences I: TERUHISA TAJIMA
School of Letters, Arts and Sciences II: TERUHISA TAJIMA
School of Culture, Media and Society: TERUHISA TAJIMA
School of Humanities and Social Sciences: TERUHISA TAJIMA
School of Education: TOMOKI WARAGAI
School of Commerce: NOBUTAKE YOKOTA
School of Science and Eng.: SHUJI HASHIMOTO
School of Fundamental Science and Eng.: SUNAO KAWAI
School of Creative Science and Eng.: HIROSHI YAMAKAWA
School of Advanced Science and Eng.: ATSUSHI ISHIYAMA
School of Social Science: YASUHIRO ONISHI
School of Human Sciences: MIHO SAITO
School of Sport Science: TSUNEO SOGAWA
School of Int. Liberal Studies: PAUL SNOWDEN
Graduate School of Political Science: SEISHI SATO
Graduate School of Econ.: RYO NAGATA
Graduate School of Law: TAKEHIKO SONE
Graduate School of Letters, Arts and Sciences: TERUHISA TAJIMA
Graduate School of Commerce: MASATAKA OTA
Graduate School of Science and Eng.: SHUJI HASHIMOTO
Graduate School of Fundamental Science and Eng.: SUNAO KAWAI
Graduate School of Creative Science and Eng.: HIROSH YAMAKAWA
Graduate School of Advanced Science and Eng.: ATSUSHI ISHIYAMA
Graduate School of Education: TOSHIMICHI MIYAGUCHI
Graduate School of Social Sciences: YASUHIRO ONISHI
Graduate School of Sport Sciences: TETSUO FUKUNAGA
Graduate School of Asia Pacific Studies: SATOSHI AMAKO
Graduate School of Global Information and Telecommunication Studies: YOSHIYORI URANO
Graduate School of Japanese Applied Linguistics: YOSHIKAZU KAWAGUCHI
Graduate School of Information Production, and Systems: KOTARO HIRASAWA
Graduate School of Environment and Energy Eng.: KATSUYA NAGATA
The Okuma School of Public Management: MITSUYOSHI ISHIDA
Waseda Law School: KAORU KAMATA
Graduate School of Finance, Accounting and Law: JUN UNO
Graduate School of Accountancy: YOSHITAKA KOBAYASHI

ATTACHED INSTITUTES

Advanced Research Centre for Human Sciences: Dir Y. MORIKAWA.

Advanced Research Institute for Science and Engineering: Dir Y. HAMA.

Aizu Museum: Dir K. OHASHI.

Athletic Center: Dir H. SATO.

Center for Finance Research: Dir JUN UNO.

Center for International Education: Dean T. OHNO.

Center for Japanese Language: Dir H. YOSHIOKA.

Center for Professional Legal Education and Research: Dir KAORU KAMATA.

Comprehensive Research Organization: Chief J. YOSHIDA.

Consolidated Research Institute for Advanced Science and Medical Care: Dir K. SHIRAI.

Distance Learning Center: Dir M. NAKANO.

Environmental Research Institute: Dir K. NAGATA.

Environmental Safety Center: Dir T. NAGOYA.

Extension Center: Dir K. NAKAJIMA.

Global Information and Telecommunications Institute: Dir Y. URANO.

Hirayama Ikuo Volunteer Center: Dir K. SHIRAI.

Human Service Center: Dir M. ODA.

Information, Production and Systems Research Center: Dir KOTARO HIRASAWA.

Information Technology Research Organization: Dir T. OHTSUKI.

Institute for Advanced Studies in Education: Dir T. ISHIDO.

Institute of Asia–Pacific Studies: Dir Y. NISHIMURA.

Institute of Comparative Law: Dir S. KIDANA.

Institute for Nanoscience and Nanotechnology: Dir I. OHDOMARI.

Institute for Research in Business Administration: Dir S. UGAI.

Institute for Research in Contemporary Political and Economic Affairs: Dir T. SUZUKI.

Kagami Memorial Laboratory for Materials Science and Technology: Dir H. NAKAE.

Media Network Center: Dir S. HIRASAWA.

Open Education Center: Dir K. KOYAMA.

Organization for Asian Studies: Dir TAKAYASU OKUSHIMA.

Tsubouchi Memorial Theatre Museum: Dir M. TAKEMOTO.

Waseda Institute for Advanced Study: Dir KUNIAKI TATSUTA.

Waseda Institute for Sport Sciences: Dir TETSUO FUKUNAGA.

Waseda University Archives: Dir H. KOGUCHI.

Schools of Art and Music

Elizabeth University of Music: 4–15 Noboricho, Naka-ku, Hiroshima; tel. (82) (221) 0918; fax (82) 221-0947; f. 1952; library: 88,750 vols, 15,000 sound recordings; 47 full-time, 70 part-time teachers; 656 undergraduates, 53 postgraduates; Pres. J. M. BENÍTEZ; Dean of Academic Affairs K. NAGAI; publ. *Kenkyuu Kiyoo* (annually).

Kanazawa College of Art: 5-11-1, Kodatsuno, Kanazawa, Ishikawa 920-8656; tel. (76) 262-3531; fax (76) 262-6594; e-mail admin@kanazawa-bidai.ac.jp; f. 1946; depts of Fine Art, Design, Crafts; Graduate School; Research Institute of Art and Craft, f. 1972; 67 full-time staff, 200 part-time staff; 665 students; library: 72,000 vols; Pres. YOSHIAKI INUI; publ. *Bulletin* (annually).

Kunitachi College of Music: 5-5-1 Kashiwa-cho, Tachikawa-shi, Tokyo 190-8520; tel. (42) 536-0321; fax (42) 535-2313; internet www.kunitachi.ac.jp; f. 1950; library: 155,000 books, 120,000 vols of sheet music, 170,000 audio-visual items; 417 teachers; 2,439 students; Pres. NORIKO TAKANO; publs *Kenkyu Kiyo* (Memoirs, annually), *Daigakuin Nempo* (annual publication of the postgraduate school), *Ongaku Kenkyujo Nempo* (annual publication of the research institute).

Kyoto City University of Arts: 13-6 Kutsukake-cho, Ohe, Nishikyo-ku, Kyoto 610-11; 500 students.

Musashino Academia Musicae: 1-13-1 Hazawa, Nerima-ku, Tokyo 176-8521; tel. (3) 3992-1121; fax (3) 3991-7599; internet www.musashino-music.ac.jp; f. 1929; 382 teachers; 2,269 students; library: 200,000 vols; Pres. NAOKATA FUKUI; Librarian HACHIRO CHIKURA; publ. *Review of Studies* (in Japanese, annually).

Osaka College of Music: 1-1-8, Shonai-saiwaimaohi, Toyonaka City, Osaka 561-8555; tel. (6) 6334-2131; fax (6) 6333-0286; e-mail info@daion.ac.jp; internet www.daion.ac.jp; f. 1915; courses in composition, vocal music and instrumental music; library: 123,500 vols; 376 teachers; 1,171 students; Pres. NOBUO NISHIOKA; publ. *Bulletin*.

Tama Art University: 3-15-34 Kaminoge, Setagaya-ku, Tokyo 158; tel. (3) 3702-1141; fax 03-702-2235; e-mail pro@tamabi.ac.jp; internet www.tamabi.ac.jp; f. 1935; undergraduate division established 1953; departments within the Faculty of Art and Design: painting; sculpture; ceramic, glass and metal works; graphic design; product and textile design; environmental design; information design; art science; 415 teachers; 4,718 students, incl. 3,491 undergraduates and 235 graduates; Pres. SHIRO TAKAHASHI.

Toho Gakuen School of Music: 41-1 1-chome, Wakaba-cho, Chofu-shi, Tokyo 182-8510; tel. (3) 3307-4101; fax (3) 3307-4354; internet www.tohomusic.ac.jp; f. 1961; 83 teachers; 1,400 students; library: 133,000 vols; Pres. T. TSUTSUMI.

Tokyo College of Music: 3-4-5, Minami-Ikebukuro, Toshima-ku, Tokyo 171-8540; tel. (3) 3982-3186; fax (3) 3982-2883; f. 1907; 1,702 students; library: 130,000 vols, 11,300 CDs; Pres. KIYOTATSU MIYOSHI.

Ueno Gakuen University: Department of Music, Faculty of Music and Cultural Studies, 24-12 Higashi-Ueno 4-chome, Taito-ku, Tokyo 110-8642; tel. (3) 3842-1021; fax (3) 3843-7548; e-mail info@uenogakuen.ac.jp; internet www.uenogakuen.ac.jp; f. 1904; library: 175,000 vols; 184 teachers; 580 students; Pres. Prof. HIRO ISHIBASHI

DEAN

Faculty of Music and Cultural Studies: Prof. Y. ARIMURA

JORDAN

The Higher Education System

In 1920 Jordan (formerly Transjordan) became a League of Nations mandate under British administration. The mandate was terminated in 1946 and Jordan became a independent sovereign state. Wars with Israel in 1948 and 1967 led to an influx of Palestinian refugees; moreover, after the Six Day War (1967) Jerusalem and the West Bank fell wholly under Israeli control. Until 1967 the oldest institution of higher education in Jordan was Birzeit University in the West Bank, which was founded as a school in 1924, added post-secondary courses in 1953 and became a two-year junior college in 1961. However, after 1967 Birzeit University came under Israeli jurisdiction and since 1994 has been part of the Palestinian (National) Authority (PA). The oldest university is now the University of Jordan (founded 1962). The Ministry of Higher Education and Scientific Research and the Council of Higher Education are the bodies responsible for higher education, which consists of public and private universities. In addition, there are approximately 40 community colleges offering diploma-level post-secondary programmes of study.

Universities admissions operate on the basis of the General Secondary Examination. Jordanian universities operate a US-style 'credit semester' system, under which students are required to accumulate a given number of credits each semester in order to graduate. The standard undergraduate Bachelors degree is a four-year programme of study and requires at least 132 credits. Degrees in professional fields of study, such as medicine, engineering and dentistry, may last from five to six years. In 2005 the Council of Higher Education introduced the University Achievement Examination, to be taken by all undergraduates in the final year of the Bachelors degree. The purpose of this examination is to develop a standard measure for evaluating students and courses at both public and private institutions on a subject by subject basis. Success in this examination leads to the award of the University Achievement Examination Qualification Certificate. There are three postgraduate degrees: the Higher Diploma, Masters and Doctor of Philosophy. The Higher Diploma is a one- to three-year course in a professional field of study. The Masters is often a two-year course requiring at least 33 credits. Finally, the Doctor of Philosophy lasts for three to five years, and is a combination of both coursework and original research. The full scope of postgraduate degrees is only available at public universities.

Post-secondary vocational and technical education is serviced in the main by community colleges. There are also accredited workplace-based training schemes. Courses at community colleges last two to three years, require at least 66 credits for completion and lead to the award of a Diploma. All public community colleges are affiliated to Al-Balqa' Applied University. In 1999 a law was passed establishing a five-tier framework for post-secondary non-university education, graded Semi-Skilled, Skilled, Craftsman, Technician and Professional.

Learned Societies

GENERAL

Aal Albayt Foundation for Islamic Thought: POB 950361, Amman 11195; tel. (6) 5539471; fax (6) 5526471; e-mail alalbait@index.com.jo; f. 1980; research is divided into 2 main categories: long-term projects such as the issuing of the *Encyclopedia of Arab Islamic Civilization*, the *Comprehensive Catalogue of Arab Islamic MSS*, the *Annotated Bibliographies of Islamic Economy and Islamic Education* and the Great Tafsirs project; and medium-term projects dealing with contemporary Muslim life and thought; 130 mems from 42 countries; library of 26,146 vols, 562 periodicals; special collections: Hashemite and Jordanian Collections; Pres. Prof. IBRAHIM CHABBOUH; Librarian NOUZAT ABU LABAN.

UNESCO Office Amman: POB 2270, Amman 11181; located at: Wadi Saqra St, Amman 11181; tel. (6) 5516559; fax (6) 5532183; e-mail amman@unesco.org; f. 1973; Dir NDEYE FALL.

BIBLIOGRAPHY, LIBRARY SCIENCE AND MUSEOLOGY

Jordan Library Association: POB 6289, Amman; tel. and fax (6) 4629412; f. 1963; 600 mems; Pres. FADIL KLAYB; Sec. YOUSRA ABU AJAMIEH; publs *Directory of the Libraries in Jordan*, *Directory of Periodicals in Jordan*, *Jordanian National Bibliography 1979–*, *Palestinian Bibliography*, *Palestinian-Jordanian Bibliography*, *Rissalat al-Maktaba* (The Message of the Library) (quarterly), etc.

LANGUAGE AND LITERATURE

British Council: First Circle, Jebel Amman, POB 634, Amman 11118; tel. (6) 4636147; fax (6) 4656413; e-mail bcamman@britishcouncil.org.jo; internet www.britishcouncil.org.jo; teaching centre; offers courses and exams in English language and British culture and promotes cultural exchange with the UK; Dir TIM GORE.

Goethe Institut: POB 1676, Amman 11118; tel. (6) 4641993; fax (6) 4612383; e-mail giammvw@go.com.jo; internet www.goethe.de/na/amm/enindex.htm; offers courses and exams in German language and culture and promotes cultural exchange with Germany; library of 3,000 vols; Dir Dr WOLFGANG ULE.

Instituto Cervantes: Mohammad Hafiz Ma'ath St 10, POB 815467, Amman 11180; tel. (6) 4610858; fax (6) 4624049; e-mail cenamm@cervantes.es; internet amman.cervantes.es; offers courses and exams in Spanish language and culture and promotes cultural exchange with Spain and Spanish-speaking Latin and Central America; library: library of 14,000 vols; Dir MARÍA CARMEN ORDÓÑEZ CARVAJAL.

Research Institutes

AGRICULTURE, FISHERIES AND VETERINARY SCIENCE

Department of Agricultural and Scientific Research and Extension: POB 226, Amman; f. 1958; covers all branches of agricultural research, information and extension; library of 18,500 vols; Dir SAID GHEZAWI.

HISTORY, GEOGRAPHY AND ARCHAEOLOGY

Council for British Research in the Levant: POB 519, Jubaiha, Amman 11941; tel. (6) 5341317; fax (6) 5337197; e-mail n.qaisi@cbrl.org.uk; internet www.cbrl.org.uk; f. 1996 as the merger of the British Institute in Amman for Archaeology and History with the British School of Archaeology in Jerusalem; supports British post-doctoral research in social sciences and the contemporary Levant; provides some limited grant funding and a hostel, library and lab facilities to members; 296 individual mems, 27 institutional mems; library of 24,000 vols, divided between Amman and Jerusalem; Dir Prof. BILL FINLAYSON; publs *Levant* (annual), *Bulletin* (annual), *Levant Supplementary Series* (monograph series).

TECHNOLOGY

Royal Scientific Society: POB 1438, Al-Jubaiha 11941; tel. (6) 5344701; fax (6) 5340520; e-mail rssinfo@rss.gov.jo; internet www.rss.gov.jo; f. 1970; independent, non-profit industrial research and development centre; electronic services and training centre, computer systems, mechanical engineering, chemical industry, building research centre, economics, wind and solar energy research centre; library: see Libraries and Archives; Pres. Prof. SA'AD HIJAZI; publs *Current List of Periodicals Holdings*, *Monthly Accession List*.

Libraries and Archives

Amman

Abdul Hameed Shoman Public Library: POB 940255, Amman 11194; tel. (6) 4649514; fax (6) 4610470; e-mail library@shoman.org; internet www.shoman.org; f. 1986; 120,000 vols, 1,200 periodicals; Librarian EMAD ABU-EID.

Greater Amman Public Library: POB 182181, Amman; tel. (6) 4627718; fax (6) 4649420; f. 1960; 257,179 vols in Arabic and

English; 500,000 vols, 256 current periodicals; 31 brs for adults and children, Deposit Library for UNESCO (5,000 vols); Jordanian publications; Chief Officer MOHAMED AL-KFAWIN.

National Library: POB 6070, Amman 11118; tel. (6) 4610311; fax (6) 4616832; e-mail nl@nic.net.jo; internet www.nl.gov.jo; f. 1994; prepares and issues the nat. bibliography and union catalogue; responsible for copyrights and legal deposits; responsible for enforcing Jordanian copyright law; depository for nat., UNESCO and WIPO publs; 100,000 vols; Dir-Gen. MAMOUN THARWAT TALHOUNI.

Scientific and Technical Information Centre: POB 925819, Amman; tel. (6) 4844701; fax (6) 4844806; f. 1986; core collection includes energy, civil engineering, construction, industrial chemistry, mechanical engineering, computer science, economics, electronics; 47,000 vols, 1,670 periodicals, 200 theses, 2,000 non-print media, 450 maps, 15,000 specifications; on-line service from Dialog, BRS, Infoline; Dir Dr YOUSEF NUSSEIR.

University of Jordan Library: University of Jordan, Amman; tel. (6) 5355000; fax (6) 5355570; e-mail library@ju.edu.jo; internet library.ju.edu.jo; f. 1962; 789,000 vols, 350 current Arabic periodicals, 19,977 online periodicals, mainly in English; 15 reading rooms; legal deposit for UN, WHO, FAO, World Bank, UNESCO, IMF, SIPRI, UNU, ILO, Institute for Peace Research documents; legal deposit for dissertations from all Arab universities; Dir Dr MOHAMMAD RAQAB; publs *Bibliographical list and indexes* (irregular), Directory for Theses Deposited at University Library (2 a year), *Library Guide* (annually).

Irbid

Irbid Public Library: POB 348, Irbid; f. 1957; 30,000 vols; Librarian ANWAR ISHAQ AL-NSHIWAT.

Museums and Art Galleries

Amman

Folklore Museum: POB 88, Amman; housed by the Department of Antiquities; f. 1972; collection of national traditional costumes; Curator Mrs SA'DIYA AL-TEL.

Jordan Archaeological Museum: POB 88, Amman; tel. and fax (6) 46319768; e-mail doa@nic.net.jo; f. 1951; 13,000 objects, 36,000 coins; 20 staff; library of 3,560 vols; Curator AIDA NAGHAURY.

Popular Life Museum: POB 88, Amman; f. 1973; local domestic history; brs in Petra, Madaba, Salt and Kerak; Curator IMAN QUDA.

Universities

AL-BALQA' APPLIED UNIVERSITY

POB 19117, Salt, Al-Balqa' Governorate
Telephone: (5) 3552519
Fax: (5) 3557518
Internet: www.bau.edu.jo

Founded 1997
State control

President: Prof. OMAR EL-REEMAWI

Library of 24,500 vols (17,500 in Arabic, 7,000 in English), 200 periodicals
Number of teachers: 200
Number of students: 21,246

There are 15 affiliated University Colleges and around 35 affiliated private, military and UN-operated colleges.

DEANS

Faculty of Engineering: Prof. AMEN AL-RBEDI
Faculty of Planning and Management: Dr SEDQE AL-MOMANI
Faculty of Graduate Studies and Scientific Research: Dr NAJI ABDELHALEEM
Faculty of Agriculture: Dr ATIF AL-KHARABSHIH
Faculty of Engineering Technology: Dr MOHAMED AL-KHARABSHIH
Faculty of Science and Information Technology: Dr SALEH OQEILI
Faculty of Planning and Management: Dr AHMAD FAR'RAS ORAN
Institute of Traditional Islamic Arts: Dr KHALED AL-AZAM

AL AL-BAYT UNIVERSITY

POB 130040, 25113 Mafraq
Telephone: (2) 6297000
E-mail: programmer@alalbayt.aabu.edu.jo
Internet: www.aabu.edu.jo

Founded 1993
State control

President: Prof. ABDUL-SALAM AL-ABADI
Registrar: QFTAN AL-MONANI

Library of 164,890 vols, 121 periodicals
Number of teachers: 200
Number of students: 11,733

Publications: *Al-Manara* (Journal of Academic Research, English and Arabic, quarterly), *Al-Zahra* (newsletter, English and Arabic, monthly)

DEANS

Faculty of Arts and Sciences: Dr HIND ABU ALSHA'R
Faculty of Economics and Administrative Sciences: Dr OGLAH MBAYDEEN
Faculty of Islamic Information Technology: Dr ISMAIL ABABNEH
Faculty of Islamic Jurisprudence and Law: Dr ZIAD AL-DAGAM
Faculty of Nursing: Dr MUNTAHA GHARAYBEH
Faculty of Scientific Research: Prof. AZME TAHA
Faculty of Graduate Studies: Prof. RAJAB ABU HALAWA

ATTACHED RESEARCH INSTITUTES

Institute of Architecture and Islamic Arts: Dir Dr ABDELMAJEED AL-REJOUB.

Institute of Bayt al-Hikmah (Islamic Studies and Political Science): Dir MOHAMED AL-ARNA'OUT.

Institute of Earth and Environmental Sciences: Dir Prof. NADHIR AL-ANSARI.

THE HASHEMITE UNIVERSITY

POB 150459, 13115 Zarqa
Telephone: (5) 3903333
Fax: (5) 3826613
E-mail: huniv@hu.edu.jo
Internet: www.hu.edu.jo

Founded 1992
State control

President: Dr OMAR SHDEIFAT
Vice-President: Prof. MOHAMAD ABU-QUDAIS

Library of 120,000 vols, 5,000 periodicals
Number of teachers: 329
Number of students: 9,254

DEANS

Faculty of Allied Health Sciences: Dr SULEIMAN A. SALEH
Faculty of Economics and Administrative Science: Dr SULTAN N. ABU-TAYEH
Faculty of Educational Sciences: Prof. MAJED ABU-JABER
Faculty of Engineering: Dr AYMAN H. AL-MOMANI
Faculty of Information Technology: Dr ALI SHATNAWI
Faculty of Natural Resources and Environment: Dr DR. MUNIR JAMIL MOHAMMAD
Faculty of Nursing: Dr SALWA AL-OBEISAT
Faculty of Research and Graduate Studies: Dr AHMAD S. ABUSHAMLEH
Faculty of Science and Arts: Dr ABDEL-FATTAH T. SHIHADA
Faculty of Sports Science: Dr IBRAHIM MOUSA ADEL

ATTACHED RESEARCH INSTITUTES

Queen Rania Institute of Tourism and Heritage.

UNIVERSITY OF JORDAN

Amman 11942
Telephone: (6) 5355000
Fax: (6) 5355522
E-mail: edu@ju.edu.jo
Internet: www.ju.edu.jo

Founded 1962
State and autonomous control
Languages of instruction: Arabic, English
Academic year: September to August (two semesters and a summer session)

President: ABDELRAHIM A. HUNAITI
Vice-President for Administrative Affairs: Dr SALMAN ALBDOUR
Academic Vice-President for Humanities and Social Sciences: Dr SAMI KHASAWNIH
Academic Vice-President for Scientific and Medical Faculties: Dr ABDULLAH AL-MUSA
Director of Registration and Admission: GHALEB AL-HOURANI
Director of the Library: Dr HANI AL-AMAD

Number of teachers: 931
Number of students: 23,623

Publications: *Al-Majallah al-Thaqafiyyah* (quarterly), *Annual Report*, *Campus News* (in English, monthly), *Dirasat* (scientific research), *University News/Anba' al-Jami'ah* (in Arabic, monthly), *Yearbook*

DEANS

Faculty of Agriculture: Dr MOHAMMAD SHATANAWI
Faculty of Arts: Dr SALEH SULEIMAN
Faculty of Business Administration: Dr AMAL H. EL-FARHAN
Faculty of Dentistry: Dr GHAZI BAKA'EEN
Faculty of Educational Sciences: Dr AYESH ZAITOUN
Faculty of Engineering and Technology: Dr MOHAMMAD HAMDAN
Faculty of Humanities and Social Sciences: Dr SHAFIQ AL-OTOUM
King Abdullah II Faculty for Information Technology: Dr AHMAD AL-JABER
Faculty of Law: Dr BASHAR ABDUL-HADI
Faculty of Medicine: Dr AKRAM SHANNAK
Faculty of Nursing: Dr RAGHDA SHUKRI
Faculty of Pharmacy: Dr FATMA AFIFI
Faculty of Physical Education: SAMI HAMDAN
Faculty of Rehabilitation Sciences: Dr AKRAM SHANNAK
Faculty of Science: Dr AHMAD ALAWNEH
Faculty of Shari'a (Islamic Studies): Dr MOHAMMAD HASSAN ABU-YAHYA
Faculty of Graduate Studies: Dr LEWIS MUKATTASH

JORDAN UNIVERSITY OF SCIENCE AND TECHNOLOGY (JUST)

POB 3030, Irbid 22110
Telephone: (2) 7201000
Fax: (2) 7095123
E-mail: just@just.edu.jo
Internet: www.just.edu.jo

Founded 1986
State control
Languages of instruction: Arabic, English
Academic year: September to September

President: Prof. WAJIH M. OWAIS
Vice-Presidents: Prof. AHMAD ABU EL-HAIJA, Prof. ANWAR BATIKHI
Registrar: FAISAL AL-RIFAIE
Librarian: ISSA LELLO

Library of 90,000 vols
Number of teachers: 452
Number of students: 7,934

DEANS

Faculty of Agriculture: Assoc. Prof. MARWAN MUWALLA (acting)
Faculty of Dentistry: Asst Prof. MOHAMMAD AL-OMARI (acting)
Faculty of Engineering: Prof. TAISIR KHEDAYWI
Faculty of Medicine: Assoc. Prof. IBRAHIM BANI-HANI (acting)
Faculty of Nursing: Assoc. Prof. ROWAIDA AL-MAAITAH (acting)
Faculty of Pharmacy: Prof. MUTAZ SHEIKH SALEM
Faculty of Science: Prof. NABIL AL-BASHIR (acting)
Faculty of Veterinary Medicine: Prof. ORHAN ALPAN (acting)
Graduate Studies: Prof. NAJI NAJIB
Scientific Research: Prof. ABDULRAHMAN TAMIMI
Student Affairs: Assoc. Prof. ZIAD QUDAH (acting)

ATTACHED CENTRES

Centre for Agricultural Research and Production: Dir Asst Prof. RIDA SHIBLI.

Centre for Environmental Sciences and Technology: Dir Asst Prof. WAIL ABU-EL-SHA'R.

Computer Centre: Dir Asst Prof. ALI SHATNAWI.

Consultative Centre for Science and Technology: Dir Prof. ABDULRAHMAN TAMIMI.

KING HUSSEIN UNIVERSITY

POB 20, Ma'an
Telephone: (3) 2133020
Fax: (3) 2133025
E-mail: ahu@nic.net.jo
Internet: www.ahu.edu.jo

Founded 1999
State control

President: ADEL TWEISSI

Number of teachers: 58
Number of students: 1,948

Publication: *Al-Haq Ya'lu* (2 a year)

DEANS

College of Arts: ISSA QWAIDER
College of Educational Sciences: YOUSEF ABU HELALA
College of Science: ISMAEL GARIABEH

MU'TAH UNIVERSITY

POB 7, Mu'tah, Al Karak
Amman Liaison Office: POB 5076, Amman
Telephone: (6) 4617860
Fax: (6) 4654061
Internet: www.mutah.edu.jo

Founded 1981
State control
Languages of instruction: Arabic, English
Academic year: October to June

President: Prof. EID DAHIYAT
Vice-Presidents: Prof. MOHAMED SHAHIN (Humanities Faculties), Prof. ABDELRAHIM HUNAITI (Science Faculties), Prof. NOMAN KHATEEB
Registrar: TAHA AL-ADAILA
Librarian: AMIN AL-NAJDAWI

Library of 240,000 vols
Number of teachers: 370
Number of students: 7,193

Publications: *Humanities and Social Sciences* (4 a year), *Mu'tah Journal for Research and Studies, Natural and Applied Sciences* (4 a year)

DEANS

Arts: Dr MOHAMED SHAWBKIH
Economics and Administrative Sciences: Prof. FAIZ ZOOBI
Education: Dr MOUSA NABHAN
Engineering: Dr YOUSEF JARAFRIH
Law: Dr NIZAM AL-MAJALI
Science and Arts (Ma'an branch): Dr RATIB OWRAN
Sciences: Dr MOHAMED SAWI
Scientific Research and Graduate Studies: Prof. ANEES KHASAWNEH
Student Affairs: Prof. ADEL TAWISSI

YARMOUK UNIVERSITY

POB 566, Irbid
Telephone: (2) 7271100
Fax: (2) 7274725
E-mail: yarmouk@yu.edu.jo
Internet: www.yu.edu.jo

Founded 1975
National and autonomous control
Languages of instruction: Arabic, English
Academic year: October to June

President: Prof. Dr FAYEZ I. KHASAWNEH
Vice-President (Administrative Affairs): Prof. Dr MOHAMMED S. SUBBARINI
Vice-President (Academic Affairs): Prof. Dr HISHAM S. GHARAIBEH
Registrar: ZACHARIAH ABU-ALDAHAB
Librarian: Dr MOHAMMAD SARAYRAH

Library: Central Library of 402,951 vols, 1,150 current periodicals
Number of teachers: 687
Number of students: 21,205

Publications: *Abhath al-Yarmouk* (Yarmouk Research Journal), *Al'anba* (Institute of Archaeology and Anthropology Newsletter), *Al-Sanabel* (Yearbook), *Forced Migration Network* (newsletter), *Majallat al-Yarmouk* (Yarmouk Magazine), *Qadaya Allajjeen Wannaziheen* (newsletter), *Sahafat al-Yarmouk* (Yarmouk Newspaper), *Yarmouk Numismatics* (journal)

DEANS

Hijjawi Faculty of Applied Engineering: Prof. Dr OMAR ASFAR
Faculty of Arts: Prof. Dr HANNA J. HADDAD
Faculty of Economics and Administrative Sciences: Prof. Dr REFAT ABDEL HALIM ALFAOURI
Faculty of Education: Prof. Dr AHMAD AUDEH
Faculty of Fine Arts: Prof. Dr ABDEL-HAMID ABDEL-WAHHAB HAMAM
Faculty of Law: Dr ABDEL-MOHDI MASSADEH
Faculty of Physical Education: Prof. Dr ZIAD AL-KURDI
Faculty of Science: Prof. Dr SAMI MAHMOUD
Faculty of Shari'a (Islamic Law): Dr ABDULNASER ABUL BASAL
Graduate Studies and Research: Prof. Dr SAMI K. ABDEL-HAFEZ
Student Affairs: Prof. Dr SULTAN T. ABU-ORABI

PROFESSORS

ABDUL-ALMAJED, M., Usul al-Din
ABDUL-HAFEZ, S., Biology
ABDULHAY, W., Political Science
ABDUL-RAHMAN, A., Arabic
ABO-ZEID, M., Electronic Engineering
ABU AL-JARAYESH, I., Physics
ABU HELOU, Y., Education
ABU-HILAL, A., Geology
ABU-RAHMAH, K., Arabic
ABU-SALEH, M., Statistics
ABUL-UDOUSS, Y., Arabic
ADWAN, Y., Public Administration
AL-ADWAN, S., Chemistry
AL-AHMADI, A., Usul al-Din
ALARAIBI, M., Fine Arts
ALAWNEH, S., Education Psychology
AL-FAYOUMI, I., Arabic
AL-HAQ, F., Linguistics
AL-HASSAN, K., Chemistry
AL-HASSAN, S., English
AL-HIARY, H., Education
AL-JUBOORY, K., Epigraphy
AL-KATIB, R., Education
AL-KAYSI, M., Islamic Studies
AL-MUHEISEN, Z., Archaeology
AL-NOURI, Q., Anthropology
AL-QUDAH, M., Chemistry
AL-QURAISH, T., Semitic and Oriental Languages
AL-SAADI, W., Public Law
AL-SALEM, H., Physical Education
AL-SALIM, M., Business Administration
AL-SHEIKH, K., Arabic
AL-SHMAI, F., Private Law
AL-TELL, SH., Education
ARAJI, A., Public Administration
AREDAH, F., Sports Science
ASFAR, O., Engineering Science and Mechanics
ATHAMNEH, N., English
ATIYYAT, A., Chemistry
ATOUM, A., Education
AWAD, A., History
AYYOUB, N., Physics
BADER, Y., Linguistics
BAKKAR, Y., Arabic
BANI HANI, A., Economics
BARQAWI, K., Chemistry
BATAYNEH, M., History
DAIRY, A., Physical Education
DARABSEH, M., Arabic
DWAIRI, I., Geology
ESMADI, F., Chemistry
FAOURI, R., Public Administration
FARGHAL, M., English
FATAFTAH, Z., Chemistry
FORA, A., Mathematics
GHARAIBEH, H., Banking and Finance
GHARAIBEH, S., Geology
GHAWANMEH, Y., History
GHAZWI, F., Sociology
GHAZZAWI, M., Education
HADDAD, H., Arabic
HADDAD, M., Anthropology
HADDAD, N., Arabic
HAJ-HUSSEIN, A. T., Chemistry
HAMAD, A., Arabic
HAMAM, A., Music
HAMDAN, A., Linguistics
HAMMAD, KH., Economics
HIJAZI, M., Usul al-Din
HIJJEH, M., Mathematics
HMEDAT, W., Economics
HUNAITI, A., Biology
IDRES, A., Fiqh
JIBRIL, I., Chemistry
KAFAFI, Z., Archaeology
KHARBUTLI, M., English
KHASAWNEH, F., Biology
KHASAWNEH, I., Chemistry
KHATEEB, A., Education
KHAWALDEH, M., Education

KHRAIWISH, H., Arabic
KOFAHI, M., Physics
KURDI, Z., Physical Education
LAHAM, N., Physics
LAHHAM, J., Biology
MADAN, K., Statistics
MAHADIN, R., Linguistics
MAHMOUD, S., Physics
MAKKI, A., Electrical Power Engineering
MARI, T.A., Education
MASHAGBAH, F., English
MOMANI, Q., Arabic
MOMANI, R., Economics
MOMANI, R., Islamic Economy
MRYYAN, N., Economics
NAFI, A., Arabic
NAJJAR, M., Anthropology
NUSAIR, N., Public Administration
ODEH, A., Education
OGLAH, A., Biology
OLAIMAT, M., Education
OLWAN, M., Law
OMARI, M, Usul al-Din
OWEIS, W., Biology
QASSEM, W., Biomechanics
QUDAH, S., Arabic
QUTTOUS, B., Arabic
RABABAH, M., Arabic
RABBA'I, A., Arabic
RASHID, M., Chemistry
RAWI, Z., Statistics
RAYYAN, M., History
REFAI, M., Mathematics
REFAIE, S., Electronic Engineering
RHAYYEL, A., Mathematics
SABBAGH, Z., Business Administration
SADEDDIN, W., Geology
SADIQ, M., Fine Arts
SAFA, F., Arabic
SALEM, A., Physics
SALHIEH, M., History
SARI, S., Archaeology
SERYANI, M., Geography
SHARE'E, M., Economics
SHARI, A., Arabic
SHAYEB, F., Arabic
SHORFAT, M., Linguistics
SMADI, A., Education Psychology
STATIYYEH, S., Arabic
SUBBARINI, M., Education
SULEIMAN, I., Journalism
TALAFHA, H., Economics
TALIB, M., Chemistry
TASHTOUSH, H., Chemistry
THALJI, A., English
UGAILI, S., Computer Science
UGLAH, M., Fiqh and Islamic Studies
WARDAT, R., Linguistics
WAZARMAS, I., Physical Education
YOUNIS, M., Mathematics
YUSUF, N., Physics
ZAGHAL, A., Sociology
ZAGHAL, M., Chemistry
ZIADAT, A., Journalism
ZUBI, A., Arabic
ZUGHOUL, M., English

ATTACHED INSTITUTES

Center for Consultation and Community Service: Dir Prof. Dr WALEED M. HMEDAT.

Center for Theoretical and Applied Physics: Dir Prof. Dr NABIL MOHAMMAD LAHAM.

Computer and Information Center: Dir Dr SAMEH HUSSEIN GHWANMEH.

Educational Research and Development Center: Dir Prof. Dr AHMAD AUDEH.

Institute of Archaeology and Anthropology: Dir Dr ZIYAD AL-SAAD.

Jordanian Studies Center: Dir Dr RASLAN BANI YASIN.

Language Center: Dir Prof. Dr RADWAN MAHADIN.

Marine Sciences Station: jointly with Univ. of Jordan

Aqaba; Dir Dr MOHAMAD BADRAN.

Refugees, Displaced Persons and Forced Migration Studies Center: Dir Prof. Dr ALI ZAGHAL.

Speech and Hearing Center: Dir Prof. Dr SAMEER STATIYYEH.

Colleges

Al-Husn Polytechnic: POB 50, Al-Husn; tel. (2) 7210397; f. 1981; library: 10,000 vols; 60 teachers; 800 students; 2-year diploma courses; Dean Dr HUSEIN SARHAN.

Amman University College for Applied Engineering: POB 15008, Marka, Amman; tel. (6) 4892345; f. 1975; two-year diploma course; four-year Bachelor of Applied Engineering; library: 17,000 vols; 91 teachers; 2,000 students; Dean MOHAMMAD A. K. ALIA

HEADS OF DEPARTMENTS

Chemical Engineering: Dr ADNAN MUSTAFA
Civil Engineering: Dr MOHAMAD KHARABSHI
Electrical Engineering: Dr RATIB ISA
Mechanical Engineering: Dr SALAMA AHMAD

Jordan Institute of Public Administration: POB 960383, Amman; tel. (6) 4664155; fax (6) 4680731; f. 1968; administrative training, research and consultation; library: 5,386 vols; Dir-Gen. ABDULLAH ELAYYAN.

Jordan Statistical Training Centre: POB 2015, Amman; tel. (6) 4842171; fax (6) 4833518; f. 1964 for the training of government employees and other applicants in statistical methods; library: *c.* 700 vols; Dir ABDULHADI ALAWIN; publs *Annual Report*, *Students' Reports*.

Princess Sumaya University College for Technology: POB 925819, Amman; tel. (6) 4844701; fax (6) 4844806; f. 1991; BSc courses in computer studies; 10 teachers; 120 students; Dean Dr MOHAMMAD QASEM AL-QUARYOTY; Registrar MOHAMMAD HARB ATIYEH.

University of Petra: POB 961343, Amman 11196; tel. (6) 5715579; e-mail president@uop.edu.jo; internet www.uop.edu.jo; f. 1991 as Jordan University for Women; library: 45,000 vols, 300 periodicals; 160 teachers; 4,000 students; Pres. Prof. AMIN MAHMOUD; publs *Al-Basair* (scientific journal, 2 a year), *Awraq Jamie'ya* (2 a year).

KAZAKHSTAN

The Higher Education System

The Kazakh (formerly Kyrgyz) Autonomous Soviet Socialist Republic was founded in 1920 and became a full Union Republic of the USSR in 1936. In 1991 Kazakhstan declared independence from the USSR, and was renamed the Republic of Kazakhstan. The oldest institutions of higher education date from the Soviet period, and include Almaty Abai State University (founded 1928), Western Kazakhstan State University (founded 1932; current name and status 2000) and Al-Farabi Kazakh National University (founded 1934; current name and status 1994). The Ministry of Education and Science oversees higher education, which is governed according to the Law on Higher Education (1993). The languages of instruction are Kazakh and Russian, although Kazakhs constitute the majority of students in higher education and ethnic Russians mostly choose to attend institutions outside Kazakhstan. Among institutions offering higher education are universities, academies, institutes, conservatories, higher schools and higher vocational schools. In 2005/06 there was a total of 181 State-run higher schools (including universities), with a total enrolment of 775,800 students. Additionally, in 2003/04 there were 134 non-governmental higher education institutes with 297,900 students.

Since 2004 admission to higher education has been on the basis of both the old Diploma of Completed Secondary Education and the new Unified National Testing Examination. The university awards system is moving away from the Soviet-era Specialist Diploma (undergraduate), Candidate of Sciences and Doctor of Sciences (both postgraduate) and towards the European-style Bachelors, Masters and Doctor of Philosophy (PhD) degrees. In effect, Kazakhstan is implementing the Bologna Process to establish a European Higher Education Area (although it is not a signatory to that agreement), the first phase of which is to adopt a credit-based system of comparable degrees with two main cycles (undergraduate and graduate). The undergraduate-level Specialist Diploma is still offered in most disciplines, notably professional fields of study, and lasts up to six years. Graduates with this degree may advance straight to doctoral-level studies. The Bachelors is a four-year degree; students pursue a general programme of studies in the first two years before majoring in one subject in the final two years. Graduates with the Bachelors may then study for a Masters degree, a two-year course of study (or one year following the Specialist Diploma). The Candidate of Sciences (Aspirantura) is a research-based degree lasting two to three years, following which the student must defend a thesis. Finally, the highest university-level degree is the Doctor of Sciences, a period of study with no fixed duration which allows the student to pursue a career in academia or research.

Technical and vocational education at post-secondary level is offered by vocational schools, technical schools and colleges. The standard entry requirement is 11–12 years of completed education or the Diploma of Completed Secondary Education. Courses leading to the award of the Diploma of Completed Vocational Secondary Education last between six months to one year. There are also vocational colleges which administer courses of two to three years leading to the award of the Specialized Secondary Education in a professional field of study.

The Ministry of Education and Science is responsible for quality assurance and accreditation, which consists of a three-stage process: licensing, attestation and accreditation. First, an institution's legal status is affirmed by the award of an operational licence. Secondly, a process of attestation assesses the institution's compliance with minimum educational standards defined by the Ministry of Education and Science. Thirdly, and finally, institutions which have met the appropriate standards of quality assurance receive accreditation, which is then dependent on future five-yearly attestation processes.

Learned Societies

GENERAL

National Academy of Sciences of Kazakhstan: 050021 Almaty, Shevchenko 28; tel. (3272) 69-55-93; fax (3272) 69-57-09; e-mail aukeev@academset.kz; f. 1947; sections of Biological and Medical Sciences, Chemical Engineering, Earth Sciences, Humanities and Social Sciences, Physical and Mathematical Sciences; attached research institutes: see Research Institutes; Pres. Serikbek Daukeyev; Sec.-Gen. Murat Mukhamedzhanov.

UNESCO Office Almaty: 480091 Almaty, Ul. Tole Bi 67, 4th Fl., UN Bldg; tel. (3272) 58-26-46; fax (3272) 69-58-63; e-mail almaty@unesco.org; internet www.unesco.kz; designated Cluster Office for Kazakhstan, Kyrgyzstan and Tajikistan; Dir (vacant).

LANGUAGE AND LITERATURE

British Council: 050013 Almaty, Republic Sq. 13; tel. (3272) 72-01-11; fax (3272) 72-01-13; e-mail general@kz.britishcouncil.org; internet www.britishcouncil.kz; offers courses and exams in English language and British culture and promotes cultural exchange with the UK; attached office in Astana; also responsible for British Council work in Kyrgyzstan; library of 10,000 vols; Dir James Kennedy.

Goethe-Institut: 050040 Almaty, Dschandosowa 2; tel. (3272) 47-27-04; fax (3272) 47-29-72; e-mail il-goethe@nursat.kz; internet www.goethe.de/oe/alm/deindex.htm; offers courses and exams in German language and culture and promotes cultural exchange with Germany; library of 5,000 vols; Dir Richard Künzel.

Research Institutes

AGRICULTURE, FISHERIES AND VETERINARY SCIENCE

Akmola Agricultural Research Institute: 021231 Akmola obl., Zerendinsky raion, Selo Charlinka; tel. (31172) 2-41-86; fax (31172) 2-17-33; f. 1984; Dir Bakytzhan Zhanaidarovich Khamzin.

Aral Scientific and Research Institute of Agroecology and Agriculture: 467918 Kyzylorda obl., Aralsk, Lenina 2A; fax (32422) 7-45-63; f. 1995; Dir Torekhan Karlkikhanovich Karlikhanov.

Atyrau Scientific and Research Institute of Agriculture: 060002 Atyrau, Azattyk 1; tel. (31022) 2-90-46; fax (31022) 2-91-41; f. 1995; Dir Gulsym Sisengaliyeva.

Barayev, A. I., Research Centre for Grain Farming: 021600 Akmola obl., Shortandy, Nauchnyi; tel. and fax (31631) 2-10-59; e-mail kanal@kepter.kz; f. 1956; library of 56,000 vols; Dir Zh. A. Kaskarbayev.

Central Kazakhstan Scientific and Research Institute of Agriculture: 100435 Karaganda obl., Buchar Zhyrau raion, Selo Tsentralnoye; tel. (32138) 3-12-51; fax (32138) 3-18-48; f. 1937; Dir Elaman Shakhanovich Shakhanov.

East Kazakhstan Scientific and Research Institute of Agriculture: 070512 Eastern Kazakhstanv obl., Glubokovsky raion, Pos. Opytnoye Pole, Ul. Nagornaya 3A; tel. (3272) 29-56-54; fax (3272) 29-56-65; Dir Sainelhan Zheksekenovich Zheksekenov.

Kazakh Research Technological Institute for Operation and Maintenance of Agricultural Machinery: 020100 Akmola obl., Akkol, Lenina 176; tel. (31638) 2-12-75; fax (31638) 2-06-43; e-mail kazniti@mail.kz; f. 1962; Dir A. P. Solomkin.

Kazakh Scientific and Research Institute of Astrakhan Sheep Breeding: 160019 Shymkent, Pr. Lenina 3; tel. (3252) 12-04-09; f. 1962; Dir Abdrahman Moldanasarovich Ombaev.

Kazakh Scientific and Research Institute of Feedstuffs Production and Pasture: 050035 Almaty, Ul. Dzhandosova 51; tel. (3272) 21-45-86; f. 1969; Dir Kasym Abuovich Asanov.

Kazakh Scientific and Research Institute of Fruit Growing and Viticulture: 050035 Almaty, Pr. Gagarina 238A; tel. (3272) 48-47-92; fax (3272) 48-10-50; e-mail kazniipv@fastline.kz; f. 1978; Dir EDUARD DAULETOVICH MADENOV.

Kazakh Scientific and Research Institute of Grain and Processed Grain Products: 478000 Astana, Ul. Ugolnaya 26; tel. (3172) 31-01-93; fax (3172) 31-01-96; f. 1953; Dir A. A. OSPANOV.

Kazakh Scientific and Research Institute of Mechanization and Electrification in Agriculture: 050005 Almaty, Pr. Raimbeka 312; tel. (3272) 40-48-00; fax (3272) 77-52-61; f. 1978; Dir ASAN BEKENOVICH OSPANOV.

Kazakh Scientific and Research Institute of Poultry: 040933 Almaty obl., Karasaisky raion, Pos. 50 Let Kazakhskoi SSR, Ul. Maslieva 8; tel. (32771) 9-56-31; fax (32771) 9-56-45; f. 1966; Dir AIDAR KALDYBEKOVICH SABDENOV.

Kazakh Scientific and Research Institute of the Economics and Organization of the Agroindustrial Complex: 050057 Almaty, Ul. Tsatpaeva 30B; tel. (3272) 43-64-11; f. 1934; Dir GANI ALIMOVICH KALIEV.

Kazakh Scientific and Research Institute of the Fishing Industry: 050016 Almaty, Ul. Suyunbay 89A; fax (3272) 30-47-93; e-mail npcrh@itte.kz; Dir SHOKAN ASHENOVICH ALPEYISOV.

Kazakh Scientific and Research Institute of the Food Industry: 050060 Almaty, Pr. Gagarina 238A; tel. (3272) 48-28-90; fax (3272) 48-10-50; e-mail kazniipv@fastline.kz; f. 1993; Dir DUISENBAY SAILAUBAYEVICH IZBASAROV.

Kazakh Scientific and Research Institute of Water Management: 487822 Taraz, Ul. Koigeldy 12; fax (32622) 2-47-78; f. 1950; Dir VALIAHMET NURIAHMETOVICH MUHAMEDZHANOV.

Kazakh Scientific, Research and Design Institute of the Meat and Milk Industry: 490035 Semipalatinsk, Ul. Baitursunova 29; tel. (3222) 44-26-15; fax (3222) 44-09-90; e-mail nikimmp@ok.kz; f. 1958; Dir MEIRAM ARYNOVICH MYRZABAYEV.

Kazakh Veterinary Scientific and Research Institute: 480029 Almaty, Pr. Raimbeka 223; tel. (3272) 32-17-55; fax (3272) 32-16-11; e-mail kaznivi@itte.kz; f. 1925; Dir ABYLAI RYSBAIULY SANSYZBAI.

Kostanai Scientific and Research Institute of Agriculture: 485000 Kostanai, 50 Let Oktobra 94; tel. (3142) 27-80-34; fax (3142) 54-24-72; f. 1984; Dir BERIKZHAN BALAPANULY KAIYPAI.

National Academic Centre of Agrarian Research: 480091 Almaty, 79 Abylai Khan; tel. (3272) 62-52-17; fax (3272) 62-38-31; e-mail nacar@itte.kz; departments: economics and information in agriculture; crop science and plant breeding; farming, agrochemistry, water and forest production and agroecology; livestock production and veterinary science; mechanization of agricultural production; processing and storing agricultural produce.

Northern Kazakhstan Research Institute of Animal Breeding and Veterinary Science: 150700 Northen Kazakhstan obl., Bishkul raion, Bishkul, Ul. Institutskaya 1; tel. (31538) 2-13-44; fax (31538) 2-12-53; f. 1962; library of 41,000 vols; Dir KANAT. R. MYNZHASOV.

Pavlodar Scientific and Research Institute of Agriculture: 140909 Pavlodar obl., Pavlodar raion, Pos. Krasnoarmeika; fax (3182) 32-50-61; f. 1993; Dir KENZHE KOZHAHMETOVICH ABDULLAYEV.

Research and Technological Institute of Livestock Raising: 040918 Almaty obl., Kaskelensky raion, Tausamaly; tel. (3272) 34-16-45; f. 1974; library of 18,000 vols, 3,300 journals; Dir A. M. MELDEBEKOV.

Research Institute for Plant Protection: 040924 Almaty obl., Karasai raion, Selo Rakhat; fax (3272) 29-56-22; e-mail kazniizr@nursat.kz; f. 1958; library of 29,134 vols; Dir ABAI ORAZULY SAGITOV.

Research Institute of Forestry and Agroforestry Reclamation: 020000 Akmola obl., Shchuchinsk, Ul. Kirova 58; tel. (31622) 2-14-62; f. 1957; library of 140,000 vols; Dir V. M. KOSTROMIN.

Research Institute of Potato and Vegetable Growing: 040917 Almaty obl., Karasai raion, Pos. Kainar; tel. and fax (3272) 98-37-06; f. 1945; Dir TIMUR AITPAYEV.

Research Institute of Sheep Breeding: 040622 Almaty obl., Zhambulsky raion, Mynbayeva; tel. (32770) 6-41-20; f. 1933; sheep, goat, horse and camel breeding; library of 100,000 vols; Dir B. S. SEYIDALIYEV; publ. *Proceedings* (annually).

South Kazakhstan Scientific and Research Institute of Agriculture: 160813 Shymkent, Soviyetskaya 111; tel. (3252) 22-20-98; fax (3252) 55-16-30; f. 1988; Dir MUHTAR ZHANBYRBAYEVICH ZHANBYRBAYEV.

Taldykorgan Agricultural Research Institute: 040000 Almaty obl., Taldykorgan raion, Pos. Zarya; tel. (32822) 9-94-45; fax (32822) 7-12-34; f. 1992; Dir M. K. KOZHAHMETOV.

Tselinny Scientific and Research Institute of Mechanization and Electrification in Agriculture: 110011 Kostanai, Pr. Abaya 34; fax (3142) 55-81-47; e-mail celin@mail.kz; Dir VLADIMIR LEONIDOVICH ASTAFEV.

Uspanov Institute of Soil Science: 050060 Almaty, Akademgorodok; fax (3272) 48-14-69; e-mail soil@nursat.kz; f. 1945; attached to Nat. Acad. of Sciences of Kazakhstan; Dir A. S. SAPAROV.

ECONOMICS, LAW AND POLITICS

Institute of Economics: 050010 Almaty, Kurmangazy 29; tel. (3272) 93-01-75; fax (3272) 62-78-19; e-mail ieconom@academset.kz; f. 1952; attached to Nat. Acad. of Sciences of Kazakhstan; Dir M. B. KENGHEGUZIN.

Institute of State and Law: 050000 Almaty, Kurmangazy 29; tel. (3272) 69-59-11; f. 1961; attached to Nat. Acad. of Sciences of Kazakhstan; Dir E. K. NURPEISOV.

HISTORY, GEOGRAPHY AND ARCHAEOLOGY

Institute of Geography: 050010 Almaty, Ul. Kalinina 69A; tel. (3272) 61-81-29; f. 1983; attached to Nat. Acad. of Sciences of Kazakhstan; Dir N. K. MUKITANOV.

Margulan Institute of Archaeology: 050010 Almaty, Pr. Dostvyk 44; tel. and fax (3272) 61-86-63; e-mail margulan@freenet.kz; f. 1991; attached to Nat. Acad. of Sciences of Kazakhstan; Dir A. K. MARGULANA.

Valikhanov, Ch. Ch., Institute of History and Ethnology: 050021 Almaty, Ul. Shevchenko 28; tel. (3272) 62-92-37; f. 1945; attached to Nat. Acad. of Sciences of Kazakhstan; Dir M. K. KOZYBAYEV.

LANGUAGE AND LITERATURE

Auezov, M. O., Institute of Literature and Arts: 050010 Almaty, Ul. Kurmangazy 29; tel. (3272) 72-74-11; fax (3272) 72-79-43; e-mail lit_art@academset.kz; internet http://litart.mindlab.kz; f. 1934; attached to Min. of Education and Nat. Acad. of Sciences of Kazakhstan; Dir SEIT ASKAROVICH KASKABASOV; publ. *Keruen* (quarterly).

Baitursynov Institute of Linguistics: 050021 Almaty, Ul. Kurmangazy 29; tel. (3272) 69-10-34; e-mail adm@kaztil.alma-ata.su; f. 1961; attached to Nat. Acad. of Sciences of Kazakhstan; Dir A. T. KAIDAROV.

MEDICINE

Central Asian Plague Prevention Research Institute: 050034 Almaty, Kopalskaya ul. 14; tel. (3272) 35-75-48; Dir V. M. STEPANOV.

Dermatovenereological Research Institute of the Committee for Health: Ministry of Education, Culture and Health, 050002 Almaty, Ul. Raimbeka 60; tel. (3272) 30-40-85; fax (3272) 50-23-77; f. 1931; library of 250,000 vols; Dir ZURA B. KESHILEVA.

Institute of Microbiology, Epidemiology and Infectious Diseases: 050002 Almaty, Ul. Pastera 34; tel. (3272) 33-04-26; Dir I. K. SHURATOV.

Institute of Nutrition: 050008 Almaty, Ul. Klochkova 66; tel. (3272) 42-92-03; fax (3272) 42-97-20; f. 1974; attached to Nat. Acad. of Sciences of Kazakhstan; Dir T. SH. SHARMANOV; publs *Voprosy pitaniya*, *Zdravookhranenie Kazakhstana* (8–10 a year).

Kazakhstan Paediatrics Research Institute: 050000 Almaty, Al-Farabi 146; tel. (3272) 48-81-21; fax (3272) 63-12-07; f. 1932; library of 36,000 vols; Dir A. K. MASKAKEYEV.

National Centre of Labour Hygiene and Occupational Diseases: 100027 Karaganda, Pr. Lenina 71; tel. and fax (3272) 52-10-21; e-mail ncgtpz@mail.kz; f. 1958 as Institute of Physiology and Occupational Diseases; present name 2002; attached to Min. of Education and Science; Dir G. A. KULKYBAYEV; publ. *Occupational Hygiene and Medical Ecology* (quarterly).

National Center for Tuberculosis Problems: 050000 Almaty, Bekhozhin ul. 5; tel. (3272) 91-86-57; fax (3272) 91-86-58; e-mail ncpt@itte.kz; f. 1932; library of 11,000 vols; Dir Prof. G. B. RAKISHEV.

Research Institute of Clinical and Experimental Surgery: 050003 Almaty, Ul. Mira 62; Dir M. A. ALIEV.

NATURAL SCIENCES

Biological Sciences

Aitkhozhin, M. A., Institute of Molecular Biology and Biochemistry: 050012 Almaty, Ul. Dosmuhamedova 86; tel. (3272) 67-63-06; fax (3272) 67-19-47; e-mail genome@imbb.almaty.kz; f. 1983; attached to Nat. Acad. of Sciences of Kazakhstan; Dir Prof. N. A. AITKHOZHIN (acting).

Institute of Botany: 050029 Almaty, Timiryazeva 36D; tel. (3272) 47-66-92; fax (3272) 47-90-42; f. 1995; attached to Nat. Acad. of Sciences of Kazakhstan; Dir S. A. ABIYEV.

Institute of Experimental Biology: 050022 Almaty, Pr. Abaya 38; tel. (3272) 67-23-03; attached to Min. of Education and Science; Dir A. M. MURZAMADIEV.

Institute of General Genetics and Cytology: 050040 Almaty; f. 1995; attached to Nat. Acad. of Sciences of Kazakhstan.

Institute of Human and Animal Physiology: 480032 Almaty, Akademgorodok; tel.

(3272) 48-04-88; f. 1945; attached to Nat. Acad. of Sciences of Kazakhstan; Dir KH. D. DUISEMBIN.

Institute of Microbiology and Virology: 050010 Almaty, Ul. Kirova 103; tel. (3272) 61-84-97; e-mail adm@imv.academ.alma-ata.su; f. 1956; attached to Nat. Acad. of Sciences of Kazakhstan; Dir A. N. ILYALETDINOV.

Institute of Zoology: 050034 Almaty, Akademgorodok; tel. (3272) 48-19-32; e-mail common@zoo/2.academ.alma-ata.su; f. 1943; attached to Nat. Acad. of Sciences of Kazakhstan; Dir T. N. DOSZHANOV.

Mathematical Sciences

Institute of Mathematics: 050010 Almaty, Pushkina 125; tel. and fax (3272) 91-37-40; e-mail azh@math.kz; internet www.math.kz; f. 1965; attached to Nat. Acad. of Sciences of Kazakhstan; Dir A. A. ZHENSYKBAYEV.

Institute of Theoretical and Applied Mathematics: 050021 Almaty, Ul. Pushkina 125; tel. (3272) 61-37-40; e-mail bliev@itpm.alma-ata.su; f. 1965; attached to Nat. Acad. of Sciences of Kazakhstan; Dir N. K. BLIEV.

Physical Sciences

Akhmedsafin, U. M., Institute of Hydrogeology and Hydrophysics: 050010 Almaty, Ul. Krasina 94; tel. (3272) 61-50-51; f. 1965; attached to Nat. Acad. of Sciences of Kazakhstan; Dir V. V. VESELOV.

Bekturov Institute of Chemical Sciences: 050010 Almaty, Ualikhanov 106; tel. (3272) 91-23-89; fax (3272) 91-24-80; e-mail labsp@ics.scinet.kz; internet www.chemistry.kz/labsp.php?page=ics&lang=en; f. 1945; attached to Min. of Education and Science and Nat. Acad. of Sciences of Kazakhstan; library of 83,000 vols; Dir Prof. Dr E. E. ERGOZHIN; publ. *Chemical Journal of Kazakhstan* (quarterly).

Chemical-Metallurgical Institute: 100009 Karaganda, Ermekov 63; tel. and fax (3212) 43-31-61; e-mail hmi@mail.krg.kz; f. 1958; attached to Nat. Acad. of Sciences of Kazakhstan; Dir Dr BOLAT KHASSEN.

Fesenkov Astrophysical Institute: 480068 Almaty, Kamenskoe plato; tel. (3272) 65-00-40; e-mail adm@afi.academ.alma-ata.su; f. 1950; attached to Nat. Acad. of Sciences of Kazakhstan; Dir B. T. TASHENOV.

Geological Surveying Oil Research Institute: 060002 Atyrau, Ul. Ordzhonikidze 43; tel. (31222) 3-33-86; Dir S. U. UTGALIYEV.

Institute of Nuclear Physics: 050032 Almaty, Ibragimova 1; tel. (3272) 54-64-67; fax (3272) 54-65-17; e-mail kadyrzhanov@inp1.sci.kz; internet inp1.sci.kz; f. 1957; attached to Nat. Acad. of Sciences of Kazakhstan; Dir K. K. KADYRZHANOV.

Institute of Organic Catalysis and Electro-chemistry: 050010 Almaty, D. Kunayev 142; tel. (3272) 61-58-08; fax (3272) 91-57-22; e-mail orgcat@nursat.kz; internet www.catalysis.nsk.su; f. 1969; attached to Nat. Acad. of Sciences of Kazakhstan; Dir M. Z. ZHURINOV.

Institute of Organic Synthesis and Carbon Chemistry: 100000 Karaganda, Ul. 40-let Kazakhstana; tel. (3272) 52-60-85; f. 1983; attached to Nat. Acad. of Sciences of Kazakhstan; Dir S. M. MOLDAKHMETOV.

Institute of Petroleum Chemistry and Natural Salts: 060002 Atyrau, Ul. Lenina 2; tel. (3122) 22-26-74; f. 1960; attached to Nat. Acad. of Sciences of Kazakhstan; Dir N. R. BUKEIKHANOV.

Institute of Physics and Technology: 050032 Alatau, Ibragimova 11; tel. (3272) 26-24-95; fax (3272) 26-25-11; e-mail mukashev@sci.kz; internet www.sci.kz; f. 1991; attached to Nat. Acad. of Sciences of Kazakhstan; depts of: condensed matter physics, material science and nanotechnology; spectroscopic methods of research; high-energy physics and cosmic rays; information technology; Dir Dr B. N. MUKASHEV.

Institute of Phytochemistry: 100009 Karaganda, Ministry of Education and Science, ul. Gazalieva, 4; e-mail kms@phyto.karaganda.su; f. 1995; attached to Nat. Acad. of Sciences of Kazakhstan.

Institute of Seismology: 050060 Almaty, Pr. Al-Farabi 75; tel. (3272) 48-21-34; fax (3272) 49-44-17; e-mail adm@seism.academ.alma-ata.su; f. 1976; attached to Nat. Acad. of Sciences of Kazakhstane; Dir A. K. KURSKEYEV.

Institute of Space Research: 050034 Almaty, Akademgorodok; tel. (3272) 62-38-96; e-mail silakaziki@akma-ata.su; f. 1991; attached to Nat. Acad. of Sciences of Kazakhstan; Dir U. M. SULTANGAZIN.

Institute of the Ionosphere: 050020 Almaty, Kamenskoe plato; tel. (3272) 54-80-74; fax (3272) 65-09-93; e-mail adm@ionos.alma-ata.su; f. 1983; attached to Nat. Acad. of Sciences of Kazakhstan; Dir V. I. DROBZHEV.

National Nuclear Centre: 071100 Kurchatov, Lenina 6; tel. (32251) 2-33-33; fax (32251) 2-38-58; e-mail nnc@nnc.kz; internet www.nnc.kz; f. 1992; Dir S. T. TUKHVATULIN.

Physical Technical Institute: 050032 Almaty, Alatau; tel. (3272) 69-05-66; fax (3272) 54-52-24; e-mail mukashev@sci.kz; internet www.sci.kz; f. 1991; attached to Nat. Acad. of Sciences of Kazakhstan; Dir Prof. B. N. MUKASHEV; publ. *Annual Report*.

Satpaev, K. I., Institute of Geological Sciences: 050010 Almaty, Ul. Kalinina 69A; tel. (3272) 61-56-08; e-mail adm@geol.academ.alma-ata.su; f. 1940; attached to Nat. Acad. of Sciences of Kazakhstan; Dir A. A. ABDULLIN.

PHILOSOPHY AND PSYCHOLOGY

Institute of Philosophy: 050021 Almaty, Ul. Kurmangazy 29; tel. and fax (3272) 69-59-11; e-mail adm@phil.academ.south-capital.kz; f. 1991; attached to Nat. Acad. of Sciences of Kazakhstan; Dir Prof. A. N. NYSANBAYEV.

RELIGION, SOCIOLOGY AND ANTHROPOLOGY

Institute of Orient Studies: 050010 Almaty, Ul. Pushkina 111/113; tel. (3272) 61-53-71; f. 1996; attached to Nat. Acad. of Sciences of Kazakhstan; Dir K. T. TALIPOV.

TECHNOLOGY

Eastern Mining and Metallurgical Research Institute of Non-ferrous Metals: 070002 Ust-Kamenogorsk, Promyshlennaya 1; tel. (3232) 47-37-73; fax (3232) 47-37-71; e-mail vniitsvetmet@ukg.kz; internet vcm.ukg.kz; f. 1950; attached to Min. of Industry and Trade; carries out research and semi-commercial scale tests; provides scientific and technical assistance in the introduction of technologies and equipment in the fields of polymetal ores mining and dressing, heavy non-ferrous metals metallurgy, applied and analytical chemistry, and environment protection; library of 167,000 vols; Dir N. N. USHAKOV.

Institute of Informatics and Control Problems: 050010 Almaty, Pushkina 125; tel. and fax (3272) 62-77-15; e-mail office@ipic.kz; f. 1991; attached to Nat. Acad. of Sciences of Kazakhstan; Dir M. B. AIDARKHANOV.

Institute of Metallurgy and Ore Enrichment: 050010 Almaty, Ul. Shevchenko 29/33; tel. (3272) 91-57-81; fax (3272) 91-46-60; e-mail imo-almaty@nursat.kz; internet www.imo.nursat.kz; f. 1945; attached to Nat. Acad. of Sciences of Kazakhstan; Dir Prof. Dr BAGDAULET KENZHALIEV; publ. *Kompleksnoe Ispolzovanie Mineralnogo Siria* (6 a year).

Kunayev Institute of Mining: 050046 Almaty, Pr. Abaya 191; tel. (3272) 46-98-76; fax (3272) 46-89-80; e-mail igdrk@mail.ru; internet www.igdnckpms.kz; f. 1944; attached to Nat. Acad. of Sciences of Kazakhstan; development of efficient and environmentally-safe technologies; consulting in the field of mining law, economics of mining production, health and safety; training of mining professionals; library of 36,019 vols, 21,397 periodicals; Dir Prof. Dr GALIEV SEITGALI ZHOLDASOVICH.

National Centre for Complex Processing of Mineral Raw Materials: 050036 Almaty, Dzhandosov 67; tel. (3272) 59-00-70; fax (3272) 59-00-75; e-mail cmrp@itte.kz; internet www.innovation.kz; attached to Nat. Academy of Sciences of Kazakhstan; Dir A. ZHARMENOV.

Scientific and Technological Centre of Machinery Construction: 480064 Almaty, Pr. Abaya 191; tel. (3272) 46-97-50; e-mail mntc@mail.ru; f. 1998; Dir S. U. JOLDASBEKOV.

Libraries and Archives

Almaty

Al-Farabi Kazakh State University Central Library: 050010 Almaty, Timiryazeva ul. 42; tel. (3272) 47-27-61; fax (3272) 49-26-09; e-mail guljan_m@kazsu.kz; internet lib.kazsu.kz; f. 1934; 1,500,000 vols; Dir E. D. ABULKAYIROVA.

Central Library of the former Kazakh Academy of Sciences: 050021 Almaty, Ul. Shevchenko 28; tel. (3272) 62-83-41; f. 1932; 6,186,000 vols, 2,041 MSS; Dir K. K. ABUGALIEYEVA.

National Library of the Republic of Kazakhstan: 050013 Almaty 13, Pr. Abaya 14; tel. (3272) 62-79-56; fax (3272) 69-65-86; e-mail info@nlpub.freenet.kz; internet www.nlrk.kz; f. 1910; legal deposit library; 5,448,000 vols; Dir R. A. BERDIGALIYEVA.

Scientific and Technical Library of Kazakhstan: 050026 Almaty, S. Mukanov 223B; tel. and fax (3272) 68-26-79; e-mail rootbb@nursat.kz; internet www.rntb.kz; f. 1960; 22,600,000 vols (including patents); Dir-Gen. K. G. URMURZINA.

Karaganda

Karaganda State University Library: 100026 Karaganda, Ul. Universitetskaya 28; tel. (3212) 74-53-00; fax (3212) 74-47-67; e-mail root@lib.kargu.ksu.kz; internet library.ksu.kz; 400,000 vols; Dir S. M. ZHERZHISOVA.

Museums and Art Galleries

Almaty

Central State Museum of Kazakhstan: 050059 Almaty, Samal-1 44; tel. (3272) 64-22-00; e-mail csmrk@hotmail.kz; internet www.unesco.kz/heritagenet/kz/participant/museum/csmrk/rus/default.htm; history and natural history of Kazakhstan; Dir NURSAN ALIMBAY.

Kasteyev Kazakh State Art Museum: 050040 Almaty, Ul. Satpayeva 30A; tel. (3272) 47-82-49; fax (3272) 47-86-69; e-mail kazart@nursat.kz; internet www.art.nursat.kz; f. 1976; Kazakh art, folk art, Soviet and European art; library of 23,000 vols; Dir BAYTURSUN E. UMORBEKOV.

Universities

AKTAU SH. YESENOV UNIVERSITY

466200 Aktau, Mikro raion 14
Telephone: (3292) 43-85-68
Fax: (3292) 33-42-21
E-mail: aktau_university@hotmail.com
State control
Rector: ASHIMZHAN S. AKHMETOV.

AKTOBE K. ZHUBANOV STATE UNIVERSITY

030014 Aktobe, Molgagulova 34
Telephone: (3132) 55-37-56
Fax: (3132) 57-78-43
E-mail: zhubanov@samgau.kz
State control.

AL-FARABI KAZAKH NATIONAL UNIVERSITY

050038 Almaty, Al-Farabi 71
Telephone: (3272) 47-16-71
Fax: (3272) 47-26-09
E-mail: anurmag@kazsu.kz
Internet: www.kazsu.kz
Founded 1934 (fmrly Kazakh S.M. Kirov State University), present name and status 1994
State control
Languages of instruction: Kazakh, Russian
Academic year: September to July (two semesters)
Rector: Prof. T. A. KOZHAMKULOV
Pro-Rectors: Dr G. K. AKHMETOVA, Prof. ZH. D. DADEBAYEV, Prof. A. I. KUPCHISHIN, Prof. Z. A. MANSUROV, Prof. N. O. OMASHEV, Dr S. T. SHALGYMBAYEV
Librarian: E. DZ. ABULKAIROVA
Library: see Libraries and Archives
Number of teachers: 1,618
Number of students: 14,500
Publication: *Vestnik KazGNU* (annually)

DEANS

Department of Biology: Prof. R. I. BERSIMBAYEV
Department of Chemistry: Prof. Z. A. ABILOB
Department of Economics and Business: Prof. R. Y. YELEMESSOV
Department of Geography: Dr K. M. BAIMYRZAYEV
Department of History: Prof. ZH. K. TAIMAGAMBETOV
Department of International Relations: Prof. Y. B. ZHATKANBAYEV
Department of Journalism: Prof. B. O. ZHAKYP
Department of Law: Prof. D. L. BAIDELDINOV
Department of Literary and Language Studies: Prof. K. A. ABDEZULY
Department of Mechanics and Mathematics: Prof. M. K. ORUNKHANOV
Department of Oriental Studies: Prof. S. M. SYZDYKOV
Department of Philosophy and Political Science: Prof. G. Y. YESSIM
Department of Physics: Prof. A. S. ASKAROVA
Preparatory Department for Foreign Citizens: Dr G. Y. UTEBALIYEVA

ATTACHED INSTITUTES

Al-Farabi Research Center: Dir A. A. KASSYMZHANOVA.

Centre of Physico-Chemical Methods of Research and Analysis: Dir K. S. BAISHEV.

Chinese Language Centre: Dir A. S. SHAKABAYEV.

Combustion Problems Institute: Dir T. A. KETEGENOV.

Ecological-Educational Innovation Complex: Dir S. T. SHALGYMBAYEV.

Educational Research Centre of Ancient Turkik Written Memorials: Dir S. M. SYZDYKOV.

Educational Research Centre for Ethnopedagogics and Ethnopsychology: Dir K. B. ZHARIKBAYEV.

European Documentation Centre: Dir K. I. BAIZAKOVA.

French Centre for Education, Science, Language and Culture: Dir S. I. NURGOZHINA.

Kazakhstan-Indian Centre of Information Technologies: Dir G. T. BALAKAYEVA.

Research Institute of Biology and Biotechnology Problems: Dir A. K. BISSENBAYEV.

Research Institute of Ecological Problems: Dir T. M. SHALAKHMETOVA.

Research Institute of Experimental and Theoretical Physics: Dir T. S. RAMAZANOV.

Research Institute of Mathematics and Mechanics: Dir Prof. N. T. DANAYEV.

Research Institute of New Chemical Technologies and Materials: Dir Prof. K. A. ZHUBANOV.

Scientific-Technological Park: Dir A. K. TULESHOV.

ALMATY ABAI STATE UNIVERSITY

050010 Almaty, Dostyk 12
Telephone: (3272) 91-63-39
Fax: (3272) 91-30-50
E-mail: rector@bai.uni.sci.kz
Internet: www.abai.uni.sic.kz
Founded 1928
State control
Languages of instruction: Kazakh, Russian
Academic year: September to June
Rector: TOKMUKHAMED S. SADYKOV
Library of 1,000,000 vols
Number of teachers: 730
Number of students: 8,877

DEANS

Arts and Graphics: BAIMURAT OSPANOV
Finance and Economics: MIRSEDA ALIMBAYEVA
Geography and Ecology: AZIMKHAN SEITZHANOV
History: SAIYN BORBASOV
International Relations: EUGENI KUZNETSOV
Kazakh Philology: SAUL DAUTOVA
Law: KAMAL BURKHANOV
Physics and Mathematics: MAKTAGALI BEKTEMISOV
Psychology and Pedagogy: ROMSEIT KOJANBAYEV
Russian Philology: MANAT MUSATAYEVA

ALMATY TECHNOLOGICAL UNIVERSITY

050012 Almaty, Tole-bi 100
Telephone: (3272) 68-83-35
Fax: (3272) 68-63-30
E-mail: atukz@mail.kz
Internet: www.atu.kz
Founded 1952
State control
Rector: K. S. KULAZHANOV
Faculties of Economics and Cybernetics, Extra-mural Studies, Food Science and Technology.

ATYRAU H. DOSMUHAMEDOV STATE UNIVERSITY

465017 Atyrau, Ul. Pushkina 12
Telephone: (3122) 23-30-44
Fax: (3122) 23-30-17
State control
Rector: ASHAT IMANGALIYEV.

DZHAMBUL UNIVERSITY

080003 Taraz, Dzhambul 16A
Telephone: (3262) 23-19-78
State control.

EASTERN KAZAKHSTAN STATE UNIVERSITY

070002 Ust-Kamenogorsk, 30 Gvardeiskoy Divisii 34B
Telephone: (3232) 27-29-11
Fax: (3232) 28-64-07
E-mail: vkgu@ukg.kz
Founded 1952
State control
Languages of instruction: Kazakh, Russian
Academic year: September to June
Rector: ABDUMUTALIP A. ABZHAPPAROV
First Vice-Rector: GENADIJ I. MOSTOVENKO
Library of 805,000 vols
Number of teachers: 841
Number of students: 9,615

DIRECTORS

Adult Education: FARXAD KURMANOV
Continuing Education: MAJAK ZHAKSILIKOV
Economics and Law: TOXTAR BOLGAJOV
History, Psychology and Culture: ALBINA ZHANBOSINOVA
Natural Sciences, Ecology and Medicine: GULBANY SADIKOVA
Philology and Journalism: LUISA ABDULLINA
Physics, Mathematics and Technology: MAZIN SKAKOV

GUMILEV, L. N., EURASIAN UNIVERSITY

010008 Astana, Tsiolkovsky 6
Telephone: (3172) 24-32-93
Fax: (3172) 24-30-90
E-mail: root@lceu.ricc.kz
Founded 1962 as teacher-training institute; became Akmola University 1992; present name 1996
State control
Languages of instruction: Kazakh, Russian
Academic year: September to June
Rector: Prof. Dr AMANGHELDY HUSSAYNOVICH HUSSAINOV
Pro-Rector for Co-ordination and Academic Programmes: MUKHTAR USSINOVICH ISMAGAMBETOV
Pro-Rector for Financial Administration: MUKHTAR MUKHAMEDIEVICH URAZALIN
Pro-Rector for Research and International Relations: Prof. Dr RAHMETULLA SHARAPIDENOVICH YERKASSOV
Pro-Rector for Social Activities: MINA EMANUILOVNA ROMANENKO
Senior Adminstrative Officer: Prof. AMANGHELDY ZHAKSYLIKOVICH ISMAILOV
Library of 1,000,000 vols

Publication: *Bulletin of the Eurasian University* (3 a year)

DEANS

Faculty of Culture and Art: IRINA UMANGIREEVNA AUSHEVA

Faculty of Economics: Prof. SAYRAN KABDRAKHMANOVNA SURAGANOVA

Faculty of Engineering: Prof. Dr SERIK NURAKOV

Faculty of Engineering and Economics (extramural): Prof. VYACHESLAV VIKTOROVICH TARASSOV

Faculty of Foreign Languages: SAULE BAZYLOVNA ZAGATOVA

Faculty of History and International Relations: KADYR ABILZHANOVICH AKHMETOV

Faculty of Humanities (extramural): MARAT TOKENOVICH ZHOLBARISSOV

Faculty of Law: ZHUMAHAN ZHARKINBEKOVICH UTENOV

Faculty of Natural Sciences and Physical Education: Prof. AMANZHOL KUSSEPOVICH KUSSEPOV

Faculty of Oriental Studies: Prof. Dr SEYIT ASKAROVICH KASKABASOV

Faculty of Philology: GALINA ALEXANDROVNA CHERNETSKAYA

Faculty of Physics and Mathematics: YERLAN SERIKOVICH BAIGOZHIN

KARAGANDA E. A. BUKETOV STATE UNIVERSITY

100026 Karaganda, Universitetskaya ul. 28

Telephone: (3212) 74-49-50

Fax: (3212) 74-47-67

E-mail: root@ksu.kz

Internet: www.ksu.kz

Founded 1972

State control

Academic year: September to June

Rector: ZH. AKYLBAYEV

Number of teachers: 1,022

Number of students: 15,294

Publication: *Vestnik* (4 a year)

Faculties of philology, economics, law, history, mathematics, physics, chemistry, biology, philosophy and psychology, education, foreign languages, physical culture and sport, social sciences, vocational and continuing improvement.

KAZAKH HUMANITARIAN LAW UNIVERSITY

050008 Almaty, Pr. Abaya 50A

Telephone: (3272) 42-52-25

Fax: (3272) 77-97-53

Founded 1994

State control

Languages of instruction: Kazakh, Russian

Academic year: September to June

Rector: MAKSUT NARIKBAYEV

Vice-Rector: BOLAT BEYEKENOV

Library of 100,237 vols

Number of teachers: 545

Number of students: 1,883

Publication: *State and Law* (3 a year)

DEANS

Commercial Law: SERGEY MARKIN

Criminal Law and Trial Investigation Law: RAMASAN NURTAYEV

International Law: IRINA KHAN

Judicial and State Prosecution Law: OMIRBAY KYSTAUBAY

KAZAKH K. I. SATBAYEV NATIONAL TECHNICAL UNIVERSITY

050013 Almaty, Satbayev 22

Telephone: (3272) 92-60-25

Fax: (3272) 92-60-26

E-mail: allnt@kazntu.sci.kz

Internet: www.ntu.kz

Founded 1934 as Kazakh Polytechnic Institute; present name and status *c.* 1996

State control

Academic year: September to July

Rector: Prof. DOSYM K. SULEYEV

Library of 1,207,803 vols

Number of teachers: 1,354

Number of students: 10,142

Publication: *KazNTU Herald*

Attached Institutes of Geological Prospecting, Mining, Oil and Gas, Metallurgy and Polygraphy, Information Technology, Machinery Construction, Ecology Economics, Natural Humanities.

KAZAKH STATE WOMEN'S PEDAGOGICAL INSTITUTE

480083 Almaty, Aiteke-bi 99

Telephone: (3272) 39-42-83

Founded 1944

State control

Languages of instruction: Kazakh, Russian

Academic year: September to July

Rector: SELIKBEK ISAYEV

Library of 860,000 vols

Number of teachers: 650

Number of students: 2,600

Faculties of Economics, Education, History, Library Science, Modern Languages, Music Education, Natural Sciences, Philology, Philosophy, Primary Education, Sports, Teacher Training.

KAZAKH-TURKISH HODJA AHMET YESEVI INTERNATIONAL UNIVERSITY

487010 Turkistan, Maydan Yesim-Khan 2

Telephone: (3253) 34-11-44

Fax: (3253) 34-14-47

E-mail: webmaster@mktu.turkistan.kz

Internet: www.turkistan.kz

Founded 1991 jtly by govts of Kazakhstan and Turkey

State control

Languages of instruction: Kazakh, Turkish

Languages of instruction: Russian, English

Academic year: September to July

Rector: MURAT ZHURINOV

Library of 480,000 vols

Number of teachers: 700

Number of students: 10,200

Publications: *Bulletin*, *Scientific Methodological Articles* (26 a year)

Faculties of Art, Art Studies, Ecology, Economics, History, History and Philology, Languages and Literature, Law, Mathematics and Economics, Medicine, Natural sciences, Oriental studies.

KOKSHETAU SH. VALIHANOV UNIVERSITY

100001 Kokshetau, Ul. Karla Marksa 76

Telephone: (3162) 25-55-84

Fax: (3162) 25-55-83

E-mail: universi@kokc.kz

Founded 1962

State control

Languages of instruction: Kazakh, Russian

Academic year: September to July

Rector: ABAI A. AITMUHAMBETOV

Library of 600,000 vols

Number of teachers: 450

Number of students: 4,900

DEANS

Faculty of Agriculture and Technology: ALEKSANDR PODDUBNY

Faculty of Chemistry and Biology: TOLEGEN SEILHANOV

Faculty of Economics: KOSYBAI AITKOZHIN

Faculty of Foreign Languages: NATALYA ZHUMANGULOVA

Faculty of History and Art: ZHARAS ERMEKBAYEV

Faculty of Philology: OLGA ANITSHENKO

Faculty of Physics and Mathematics: KADYRHAN MUSABAYEV

KOSTANAI A. BAITURSYNOV STATE UNIVERSITY

110000 Kostanai, ul. Baitursynova 47

Telephone: (3142) 54-25-94

Fax: (3142) 54-25-94

E-mail: ksu47@mail.kz

Internet: www.ksu.kst.kz

Founded 1939, present status 1992

State control

Rector: KHUSAIN KH. VALIYEV

Publications: *Bilim zharysy* (monthly), *Zharsken-Kostanai* (6 a year), *Mezhvuzovskii nauchnyi zhurnal* (Intercollegiate Scientific Journal), *Vestnik Nauki* (Herald of Science, 4 a year)

Faculty of Journalism; Institutes of Agriculture, Economy and Management, Engineering and Physics, Humanities, Law, Mathematics and Information Technology, Veterinary Studies; college of Kazakh State University.

KYZYLORDA KORKYT ATA HUMANITARIAN UNIVERSITY

120000 Kyzylorda, Zheltoksan 40

State control.

KYZYLORDA KORKYT ATA STATE UNIVERSITY

467021 Kyzylorda, Aiteke-bi 29A

Telephone: (32422) 6-17-95

Fax: (32422) 6-17-25

E-mail: ksu@kyzstun.asdc.kz

Founded 1937

State control

Languages of instruction: Kazakh, Russian

Academic year: September to June

Rector: KYLYSHBAI A. BISSENOV

Library of 1,780,000 items

Number of teachers: 460

Number of students: 8,000

Publications: *Vestnik* (sciences, 4 a year), *Syr Tulegu* (news)

Faculties of Correspondence and Evening Courses, Economics and Engineering, Economics and Management, Engineering and Ecology, History and Law, Natural Sciences, Philology and Arts, Physics and Mathematics.

NORTHERN KAZAKHSTAN N. KOZEYBAYEV UNIVERSITY

150000 Petropavlovsk, Ul. Universitetskaya 18

Telephone: (3152) 49-33-52

Fax: (3152) 49-33-52

E-mail: mail@nkzu.edu

Internet: www.nkzu.edu

Founded 1937

State control

Languages of instruction: Kazakh, Russian

Academic year: September to June

Rector: UNDASSYIN ASHIMOV

Pro-Rector: FELIKS A. SYM

Library of 647,136 vols
Number of teachers: 440
Number of students: 4,920

DEANS

Faculty of Economics: IVAN G. KENDUH
Faculty of History and Philology: SABYR I. IBRAYEV
Faculty of Information Technology: VICTOR P. GUSSAKOV
Faculty of Law: NATALYA K. BARANOVA
Faculty of Mechanical Engineering: KAIRAT T. KOSHEKOV
Faculty of Music: ANATOLIY E. SLEZKO
Faculty of Natural Sciences: NIKOLAI N. SEMENOV
Faculty of Physical Education and Sports: VICTOR K. KULAYEV
Faculty of Transport and Construction Engineering: TULEGEN H. HAIRULLIN
Faculty of Welfare and Protective Services: TAKHIR M. MUHAMADIYEV

SEMEY STATE SHAKARIM UNIVERSITY

490035 Semipalatinsk, Ul. Gleynky 20A
Telephone: (3222) 42-29-37
Fax: (3222) 35-95-49
E-mail: info@semgu.kz
Internet: www.semgu.kz

Founded 1995
State control
Languages of instruction: Kazakh, Russian
Academic year: September to June

Rector: YERLAN SYDYKOV
Vice-Rector: MIKHAIL PANIN

Library of 1,000,000 vols
Number of teachers: 648
Number of students: 8,682

DEANS

Faculty of Economics: SERIKTAY BAIMUKHANOV
Faculty of Engineering and Technology: SERIK TUMENOV
Faculty of Finance: BEGMAN KOZHEGELDIYEV
Faculty of Humanities: ALMAGUL MUKHAMEDKHANOVA
Faculty of Natural Sciences: BENUR MUSABALINA
Faculty of Philology: FARIDA ZHAKSYBAYEVA
Faculty of Veterinary Medicine and Agriculture: ZEINOLLA TOKAYEV

SOUTHERN KAZAKHSTAN AUZEV HUMANITIES UNIVERSITY

160018 Shymkent, Beibitshilik 3
Telephone: (32522) 44-99-88
E-mail: ukrgi-smh@nursat.kz
State control.

SOUTHERN KAZAKHSTAN MEDICAL ACADEMY

160000 Shymkent, Lenina 1

Founded 1944
State control.

STATE FINANCIAL INSTITUTE

071403 Semipalatinsk, Ul. Shugajeva 159
Telephone: (3222) 63-59-20
Fax: (3222) 66-28-83

Founded 1995
State control

Rector: GENNADI N. GARMANIC.

TARAZ M. KH. DULATI STATE UNIVERSITY

080012 Taraz, Suleimanov 7
Telephone: (32622) 44-42-20
Fax: (32622) 45-97-25
E-mail: targu@nursat.kz
Internet: www.tarsu.kz

Founded 1998
State control

Rector: A. E. BEKTURGANOV

Number of teachers: 1,414
Number of students: 10,500

HEADS OF DEPARTMENTS

Economics and Management: B. ALDASHOV
Engineering and Techniques: D. SAHIYEV
Food and Processing Industry: M. SAHI
Information Technology: M. SHAIZHANOV
Languages: R. SEYIDUALIYEVA
Law: S. USHAROVA
Light Textile Industry: ZH. MYRKALYKOV
Mechanization and Energetics: S. MYRZASHEV
Natural Sciences: O. SALIMABAYEV
Natural Management and Construction: A. AIMEN
Pedagogy: B. MUSILMOV

ZHETYSU I. ZHANSUGUROV UNIVERSITY

040009 Taldykorgan, Ul. I. Zhansugurova 187A
Telephone: (32722) 2-00-20
Fax: (32722) 1-22-61
E-mail: tk_jgu@mail.ru

Founded 1972
State control
Languages of instruction: Kazakh, Russian
Academic year: September to June

Rector: ESENGELDY MEDEUYOV
Pro-Rector: ASKHAT SARSENBAYEV

Number of teachers: 307
Number of students: 6,985

Faculties of Business and Commerce, Computer Education, Finance, Foreign Languages, Humanities, Law, Mathematics and Pedagogy.

ZHEZKAZGAN O. A. BAIKONUROV UNIVERSITY

100600 Zhezkazgan, Pr. Alashahana 1
Telephone: (83102) 73-63-24
Fax: (83102) 73-01-15
E-mail: univer@iftc.zhez.kz

Founded 1956
State control
Languages of instruction: Kazakh, Russian, English

Rector: ZHUMAGALI NAURYZBAI
Vice-Rector: KALI KISHAUOV

Library of 1,100,000 vols
Number of teachers: 1,035
Number of students: 3,061

DIRECTORS

Institute of Economics and Law: GULNAR TEMIRBAYEVA
Institute of Mining Engineering: MUHAMEDZHAN AUEZOV
Institute Natural Sciences: OMITRAI ZHALELOV
Institute of Philology and Arts: MURAT ABEUOV

Other Higher Educational Institutes

Aktobe State Medical Institute: 463022 Aktobe, Ul. Lenina 52; tel. (3132) 54-39-04; library: 62,000 vols.

Almaty Institute of Power Engineering and Telecommunication: 050013 Almaty, Ul. Baytursynova 126; tel. (3272) 92-57-40; fax (3272) 92-50-57; e-mail aipet@aipet.kz; internet www.aipet.kz; f. 1975; faculties: thermal engineering, radio engineering, power engineering; part-time courses and retraining; pre-institutional training; ENTEL College; br. in Ust Kamenogorsk; library: 465,000 vols; 284 teachers; 4,856 students; Rector GUMARBEK ZH. DAUKEYEV; publs *Collections of Scientific Works* (2 a year), *Collections of Postgraduate Works* (annually).

Almaty Kurmangazy State Conservatoire: 480091 Almaty, Ablaikhan pr. 90; tel. (3272) 62-76-40; courses: piano, orchestral and folk instruments, academic and folk singing, choral and symphonic conducting, musicology, composition, cultural management; library: 266,060 vols.

Almaty State Theatrical and Cinema Institute: 480091 Almaty, Ul. Bogenbai Batyr 136; tel. (3272) 63-66-52; fax (3272) 50-62-84; f. 1992; acting and directing apprenticeship; 10 teachers; library: 400 vols.

Astana State Medical Academy: 473013 Astana, Pr. Mira 51A; tel. (3172) 26-07-829; fax (3172) 26-39-18; e-mail akma@asdc.kz; f. 1964, present name and status 1997; faculties: medicine and biological sciences, medicine, paediatrics; library: 381,500 vols; 370 teachers; 2,100 students; Rector R. K. TULEBAYEV.

'D. Serikbaev' East Kazakhstan State Technical University: 69 H. K. O., 070004 Ust-Kamenogorsk; tel. (3232) 26-28-89; fax (3232) 26-74-09; e-mail ekstu@ektu.kz; internet www.ektu.kz; f. 1958; academic divisions: Institute of Economics and Management, Institute of Mining and Metallurgical Engineering, Institute of Building Technologies and Architecture, Institute of Mechanics and Technology, Postgraduate and New Technologies Institute, Institute of Information Technologies, Faculty with the the Kazakh Language of Instruction, Virtual Institute, Centre of Humanities Education; bachelors degrees, specialist diplomas, masters degrees and doctoral programmes; library: 859,800 vols; 660 teachers; 10,400 students; Rector GALYMKAIR MUTANOV; First Vice-Rector ZHENIS KULSEITOV; Vice-Rector (Science and International Co-operation Matters) TULEGEN IPALAKOV; publs *Collections of Scientific Works* (annually), *Vestnik* (scientific journal, quarterly), *Za znanie!* (To Knowledge!, monthly).

Karaganda Kazpotrebsoyuz University of Economics: 100009 Karaganda, Ul. Akademicheskaya 9; tel. (3212) 44-16-22; fax (3212) 44-16-32; e-mail keu@city.krg.kz; internet www.keu.pmicro.kz; f. 1966; finance and credit, accountancy and audit, computer systems, economics and management, law, customs business, marketing and commerce, merchandizing, state and local government, commodity management and analysis, standardization and certification; brs in Aktobe, Astana, Kostanai, Pavlodar, Shymkent; library: 580,000 vols; 170 teachers; 5,000 students; Rector Prof. Dr ERKARA AIMAGAMBETOV.

Karaganda Metallurgical Institute: 101400 Temirtau, Pr. Lenina 34; tel. (3213) 91-56-26; fax (3213) 91-62-80; e-mail karmeti@temirtau.kz; f. 1963; library: 288,000 vols; faculties: mechanical engineering, metallurgy, chemical engineering; 175 teachers; 2,500 students; Rector Prof. ABDRAKHMAN NAIZABEKOV.

Karaganda State Medical Academy: 100008 Karaganda, Ul. Gogolya 40; tel. (3212) 51-34-79; fax (3212) 51-89-31; e-mail kgma@nursat.kz; internet www.ksma.kz; f. 1950, present name and status 1997; faculties: biology, dentistry, eastern medicine,

medicine, paediatrics, pharmacy, postgraduate studies, public health; 520 teachers; 2,954 students; library: 400,000 vols, 186 periodicals; Rector I. KOOLMAGEMBETOV; publ. *Medicine and Ecology* (6 a year).

Karaganda State Technical University: 100027 Karaganda, Bulvar Mira 56; tel. (3212) 56-88-95; fax (3212) 56-88-95; e-mail ivc@kstu.kz; internet www.kstu.kz; f. 1953 as Karaganda Mining Institute; present name and status 1996; faculties of business management, economics and management, civil engineering, information technology, electromechanical engineering, geoecology, machine building, mining, transport and road engineering; library: 1,500,000 books; 762 teachers; 8,166 students; Rector GENNADY G. PIVEN.

Kazakh Ablai Khan University of International Relations and World Languages: Muratbaev 200, 050022 Almaty; tel. (3272) 92-19-97; fax (3272) 92-19-91; e-mail kazumo@ablaikhan.kz; internet www.ablaikhan.kz; f. 1941; faculties: English, German, French; 668 teachers; 5,000 students; library: 630,000 vols; Rector SALIMA S. KUNANBAEVA; Vice-Rectors NAGIMA A. SARSEMBAEVA (Study Department), KUSAYIN T. RYSSALDY (Scientific and Research Work), SATIMA S. ZHUMAGULOVA (Study and Methodical Work), ZHUMAGUL A. ISMAGAMBETOVA (Social Work); publs scientific papers.

Kazakh Leading Academy of Architecture and Civil Engineering:e-mail inter.rel@mail.ru Ul. Ryskulbekov 28, 050043 Almaty; tel. (3272) 29-46-11; fax (3272) 20-59-79; e-mail kazgasa@itte.kz; internet www.kazgasa.kz; f. 1980; State control; academic year September to July; undergraduate and postgraduate courses and scientific research, PhD programmes; faculties: architecture, civil engineering, environmental engineering, economics and management in construction, social sciences; 309 teachers; 4,262 students; Pres. AMIRLAN KUSSAINOV; Rector GULZADA MUKTAPOVA; publ. *Messenger of KazGASA* (quarterly).

Kazakh S. D. Asfendijarov National Medical University: 050012 Almaty, Ul. Tole-bi 88; tel. (3272) 92-78-85; fax (3272) 92-69-97; e-mail kaznmu@arna.kz; internet www.kaznmu.kz; f. 1931; present name and status 2001; faculties: dentistry, general medicine, health sciences, paediatrics, pharmacy, public health; library: 221,000 vols; 883 teachers; 5,349 students; Rector T. MUMINOV.

Kazakh S. Seifullin Agrarian University: 473032 Astana, Pr. Pobedy 116; tel. (3172) 31-75-47; fax (3172) 32-22-94; e-mail agun@kepter.kz; internet www.agun.kz; f. 1957; library: 400,000 vols; 402 teachers; 2,043 students; Rector B. ALIMZHANOV.

Kazakh State University of Agriculture: 050010 Almaty, Pr. Abaya 8; tel. (3272) 65-19-48; fax (3272) 62-44-09; e-mail info@kgau.almaty.kz; internet www.agriun.almaty.kz; f. 1996 by merger of Kazakh State Institute of Agriculture (f. 1929) and Alma-Ata Veterinary Institute (f. 1910); depts: agricultural biology, engineering, forestry and horticulture, microbiology, veterinary medicine; library: 800,000 vols; 670 teachers; 7,600 students; Rector K. A. SAGADIYEV.

Kazakh 'T. Ryskulov' Economic University: 050035 Almaty, Ul. Dzhandosova 55; tel. (3272) 20-28-45; fax (3272) 21-96-31; e-mail kazeu@pisem.net; internet www.kazeu.com; f. 1963; faculties: management and marketing, finance and credit, accounting and information technology, world economy and international relations; banking and finance management research institute, faculty development institute; market economy research institute; Kazakh economic, finance and international trade university; 520 teachers; 5,177 students; Rector N. K. MAMYROV.

Kazakhstan Institute of Management, Economics and Strategic Research: 050100 Almaty, Ul. Abaya 4; tel. (3272) 70-42-00; fax (3272) 70-43-38; internet www.kimep.kz; f. 1992; colleges of business, social sciences and continuing education; 184 teachers; 3,529 students; Pres. Dr CHAN YOUNG BANG.

Kustanai Agricultural Institute: 110000 Kustanai, Pr. Sverdlova 28; tel. (3142) 25-12-23; fax (3142) 25-34-76; f. 1966; library: 341,000 vols; Dirs L. M. OVCHINIKOVA, V. S. PROKURATOVA.

Rudnyi Industrial Institute: 111500 Rudnyi, Ul. 50 let Oktyabrya 38; tel. and fax (31431) 5-07-03; e-mail rii@krcc.kz; f. 1958; faculties: mining, automation of production processes, construction, economics; attached institute in Lisakovsk; 200 teachers; 4,250 students; Rector Prof. U. T. ABDRAKHIMOV.

Semipalatinsk State Medical Academy: 490019 Semipalatinsk, Abaya ul. 103; tel. (3222) 62-39-65; fax (3222) 66-34-01; f. 1953; library: 315,000 vols; 900 teachers; 2,500 students; Rector T. K. RAISSOV.

South Kazakhstan Technical University: 160018 Shymkent, Tauke-han 5; tel. (3252) 53-50-48; f. 1943; faculties: mechanical, chemical technology, economics; library: 524,000 vols; Rector T. SH. KALMENOV; publ. *Science and Education in South Kazakhstan*.

Taraz State Pedagogical University: 080000 Taraz, Zhambyl obl., Ul. Tole-bi 62; tel. (3262) 45-13-94; fax (3262) 34-35-30; e-mail gylym_targpi@mail.ru; f. 1967; teacher training and research; Rector Prof. Dr MACHMETGALY N. SARYBEKOV.

Western Kazakhstan State University: 090000 Uralsk, Ul. Krasnoarmejskaja 19; tel. and fax (3112) 51-26-32; e-mail zapkazgu@wkau.kz; internet www.wkau.kz; f. 1932, current name and status following merger of Western Kazakhstan Agrarian University, Western Kazakhstan Humanities University and Western Kazakhstan Dauletkerey Institute of Arts 2000; faculties: agri-business and ecology, culture and library science, economics, finance and accountancy, fine arts, geography and natural sciences, history and human rights, musical arts, oil and gas, pedagogy, philology, physics and mathematics, polytechnic, sports and physical training, veterinary medicine and sanitation; library: 1,160,000 vols; 899 teachers; 17,052 students; Rector B. K. DAMITOV.

KENYA

The Higher Education System

Until independence was achieved in 1963 Kenya was part of British East Africa. The oldest institutions of higher education were established during British colonial rule, such as Egerton University (founded 1939; current name and status 1987), the University of Nairobi (founded 1956; current name and status 1970) and Strathmore University (founded 1961; current name and status 1993). In 2003/04 there were 106,407 students enrolled in higher education. There are public and private universities, which are both accredited by the Commission for Higher Education. In both public and private universities the senior officer is the Chancellor, who in public universities is appointed by the President and in private universities is an appropriate or distinguished personage. University governance is handled by the Governing Council or Board of Trustees, and the chief executive is the Vice-Chancellor, who is also head of the University Senate, which is responsible for academic affairs, and financial and administrative management. Faculty boards and Departments are the main units of academic administration. The Ministry of Education is the government ministry in charge of higher education, acting through the aegis of the Commission for Higher Education. Universities are funded by the state budget and by students' tuition fees.

Admission to university undergraduate degree programmes is on the basis of at least an average C+ score in the Kenya Certificate of Secondary Education. Admission to Diploma or Certificate programmes requires at least C− or D+ respectively. Students who have been awarded the Diploma or Certificate may be admitted to degree-level programmes. Diplomas and Certificates are awarded after up to a year of intensive study at universities and polytechnics or through 'open' and distance learning schemes. The standard undergraduate Bachelors degree lasts for four years, except in disciplines such as veterinary medicine (five years), architecture and medicine (both six years). Upon completion of the Bachelors degree, students may take either a one-year Postgraduate Diploma course or a one- to three-year Masters degree. The most advanced university-level degree programme is the Doctorate, which requires two years of study following award of the Masters.

Post-secondary vocational and technical education is available through a number of different institutions: craft training institutes, youth polytechnics, institutes of technology and polytechnics. Although there is not yet a uniform national framework for vocational qualifications, they are roughly separated into four levels: artisan, craftsman, technician and technologist. The Kenya Institute of Education and Kenya National Examinations Council are responsible for developing curriculum and testing at these four levels. Qualifications offered include Higher Diploma, Higher Technician Diploma, Ordinary Diploma and Ordinary Technician Diploma.

Learned Societies

GENERAL

African Network of Scientific and Technological Institutions (ANSTI): UNESCO Nairobi Office, POB 30592, Nairobi; tel. (20) 622620; fax (20) 622750; e-mail info@ansti.org; internet www.ansti.org; f. 1980 under the auspices of UNESCO and UNDP, aided by the Fed. Repub. of Germany and based at the Unesco Regional Office for Science and Technology (*q.v.*); aims to bring about collaboration between African engineering, scientific and technological institutions involved in postgraduate training, and to undertake research and development in areas of developmental significance in the region; mems: 85 institutions in 32 countries; Co-ordinator Prof. J. G. MASSAQUOI; publs *African Journal of Science and Technology*, *Directory of ANSTI Institutions*.

Kenya National Academy of Sciences: POB 39450, Nairobi; tel. (20) 311714; fax (20) 311715; e-mail secretariat@knascience.org; internet www.knascience.org; f. 1977; advancement of learning and research; 200 mems; Hon. Chair. Prof. JOSEPH O. MALO; Hon. Sec. Prof. FELIX M. LUTI; publs *Kenya Journal of Science and Technology* (2 a year), *Newsletter*, *Post Magazine*, *Proceedings of Symposia*.

National Council for Science and Technology: POB 30623, Nairobi; tel. (20) 336173; f. 1977; attached to Ministry of Regional Development, Science and Technology; semi-autonomous government agency; provides advisory services to the Government; 35 council mems; library of 3,000 vols, collection of research reports; Sec. Prof. P. GACII; publs *Annual Report*, *NCST Newsletter*.

UNESCO Nairobi Regional Bureau for Science and Technology for Sub-Saharan Africa and Cluster Office: POB 30592, Nairobi 00100 GPO; located at: United Nations Offices, Gigiri, Block C, United Nations Ave, Gigiri, Nairobi; tel. (20) 622353; fax (20) 622750; e-mail nairobi@unesco.org; internet www.unesco-nairobi.org; f. 1965; regional office for 47 African countries; designated Cluster Office for Burundi, Kenya, Rwanda and Uganda; library of 10,000 vols, 400 periodicals; Dir PAUL VITTA; publ. *African Journal of Science and Technology* (2 a year).

AGRICULTURE, FISHERIES AND VETERINARY SCIENCE

Agricultural Society of Kenya: POB 30176, Nairobi; tel. (20) 566655; fax (20) 573838; e-mail chiefexecutive@ask.kenya.com; f. 1901; encourages and assists agriculture in Kenya; holds 12 shows a year and farming competitions; sponsors Young Farmers' Clubs of Kenya; 12,000 mems; Chair. TIMOTHY O. OMATO; Chief Exec. BATRAM M. MUTHOKA; publ. *The Kenya Farmer* (monthly).

BIBLIOGRAPHY, LIBRARY SCIENCE AND MUSEOLOGY

Kenya Library Association: POB 46031, Nairobi; tel. (20) 811622; fax (20) 811455; e-mail arbulogosi@avu.org; f. 1956 to organize, unite and represent the professions concerned with information work in Kenya, to promote professional integrity and to govern the members of the association in all matters of professional practice, etc.; 200 mems; Chair. JACINTA WERE; Sec. ALICE BULOGOSI; publs *Kelias News* (every 2 months), *Maktaba—Official Journal* (2 a year).

ECONOMICS, LAW AND POLITICS

Law Society of Kenya: POB 72219-00200, Nairobi; Professional Centre, First Floor, Parliament Rd, Nairobi; tel. (20) 311337; fax (20) 223997; e-mail lsk@lsk.or.ke; internet www.lsk.or.ke; f. 1949; 4,000 mems; Sec. GEORGE KEGORO; publ. *The Advocate* (4 a year).

HISTORY, GEOGRAPHY AND ARCHAEOLOGY

Historical Association of Kenya: c/o Prof. B. A. Ogot, Moi University, POB 3900, Eldoret; f. 1966; Chair. Prof. BETHWELL A. OGOT; Sec. Dr KARIM K. JANMOHAMED; publs *Hadith Series* (annually), *Kenya Historical Review* (2 a year).

LANGUAGE AND LITERATURE

Alliance Française: Maison Française Monrovia, Loila St, POB 45475, 0100 Nairobi; tel. (20) 340054; fax (20) 315207; e-mail afnairob@africaonline.co.ke; offers courses and exams in French language and culture and promotes cultural exchange with France; attached teaching centre in Mombasa.

British Council: Upperhill Rd, POB 40751, 00100 Nairobi; tel. (20) 2836000; fax (20) 2836500; e-mail information@britishcouncil.or.ke; internet www.britishcouncil.org/kenya; teaching centre; offers courses and exams in English language and British culture and promotes cultural exchange with the UK; Dir, Kenya and Regional Dir, East Africa PHILIP GOODWIN.

Teaching Centre:

Teaching Centre: opp. Norfolk Hotel, Harry Thuku Rd, POB 40751, 00100 Nairobi; tel. (20) 334855; fax (20) 244968; e-mail teaching.centre@britishcouncil.or.ke; Man. PHILIP RYLAH.

Goethe-Institut: Maendeleo House, POB 49468, 00100 Nairobi; tel. (20) 224640; fax (20) 340770; e-mail info@nairobi.goethe.org; internet www.goethe.de/nairobi; offers courses and exams in German language and culture and promotes cultural exchange with Germany; library of 5,000 vols; Dir BARBARA MEYER-MARROTH.

MEDICINE

Kenya Medical Association: Chyulu Road, Upper Hill, POB 48502, Nairobi; tel. (20) 724617; f. 1962; 1,500 mems; Chair. Dr JAMES W. NYIKAL; Sec. Dr KAVOO KILONZO; publs *East African Medical Journal* (monthly), *Medicus* (monthly).

NATURAL SCIENCES

Biological Sciences

East African Wildlife Society: POB 20110, 00200 City Sq., Riara Rd, off Ngong Rd, Nairobi; tel. (20) 574145; fax (20) 570335; e-mail info@eawildlife.org; internet www.eawildlife.org; f. 1961; non-profit org.; safeguards and promotes the conservation and sustainable management of wildlife resources and their natural habitats in East Africa; 6,000 mems; Exec. Dir ALI AKBER KAKA; publs *African Journal of Ecology* (4 a year), *Swara* (4 a year), *Wildlife Info* (4 a year).

Nature Kenya, the East Africa Natural History Society: POB 44486, GPO, 00100 Nairobi; tel. (20) 3749957; fax (20) 3741049; e-mail office@naturekenya.org; internet www.naturekenya.org; f. 1909; 1,000 mems; library of 10,000 vols; Chair. Dr IAN GORDON; publs *Journal of East African Natural History* (2 a year), *Kenya Birds* (2 a year), *Nature East Africa (the EANHS Bulletin)* (2 a year).

Physical Sciences

Kenya Astronomical Society: POB 59224, Nairobi.

RELIGION, SOCIOLOGY AND ANTHROPOLOGY

Theosophical Society: 55A Third Parklands Ave, POB 45928, Nairobi; e-mail cprdunn@nbnet.co.ke; Gen. Sec. C. P. ROBERTSON-DUNN; publ. *The Theosophical Light* (2 a year).

TECHNOLOGY

Institution of Engineers of Kenya: 1st Fl., KRBC Annex, POB 41346, 00100 Nairobi; tel. (20) 729326; fax (20) 716922; e-mail iek@iekenya.org; internet www.iekenya.org; f. 1945, present name 1973; 2,100 mems; Hon. Sec. Eng. J M. WANYOIKE; publ. *Kenya Engineer* (every 2 months).

Research Institutes

AGRICULTURE, FISHERIES AND VETERINARY SCIENCE

Coffee Research Foundation: CRF Coffee Research Station, POB 4, Ruiru; tel. (151) 54027; fax (151) 54133; f. 1949; research on coffee cultivation, agronomy and management, marketing and economics of production; Dir W. R. OPILE; publs *Annual Report*, *Kenya Coffee Bulletin*.

Interafrican Bureau for Animal Resources: Maendeleo House, Monrovia St, POB 30786, Nairobi; tel. (20) 338544; fax (20) 220546; e-mail oau-ibar@africaonline.co.ke; internet www.au-ibar.org; f. 1951; veterinary and livestock health and production covering all mem. states of the OAU; library: library of over 5,000 vols; Dir Dr J. T. MUSIIME; publ. *Bulletin of Animal Health and Production in Africa* (quarterly).

Kenya Agricultural Research Institute: City Square, POB 57811, Nairobi; tel. (20) 4183720; fax (20) 4183344; e-mail resource.center@kari.org; internet www.kari.org; f. 1979; agricultural and veterinary sciences research; Dir Dr R. M. KIOME.

Attached centre:

National Veterinary Research Centre (MUGUGA): POB 32, Kikuyu; preparation and issue of biological products and research into animal health and animal diseases; Dir D. P. KARIUKI; publs *Annual Report*, *Record of Research*.

Ministry of Agriculture and Livestock Development, Department of Veterinary Services: Private Bag Kangemi (00625) Nairobi; tel. (20) 632231; fax (20) 631273; f. 1903; control and diagnosis of animal diseases, advisory service to farmers, animal health policy formulation, veterinary research and investigation services, veterinary regulation services; library of 27,500 vols; Dir Dr WILLIAM TOROITICH K. GHONG'; publ. *Annual Report*.

National Agricultural Research Laboratories: POB 14733, Nairobi; tel. and fax (20) 444144; f. 1908; soil science research, crop protection research; library of 4,000 vols; Dir Dr F. N. MUCHENA; publs *Annual Report*, *Soil Survey Report*.

National Horticultural Research Centre: POB 220, Thika; tel. (67) 21283; fax (67) 21285; e-mail karithika@africaonline.co.ke; internet www.kari.org; f. 1955; research into crop protection, seed production, citriculture, viticulture, floriculture, temperate and tropical fruits, post-harvest physiology, vegetables; breeds for multiple disease resistance to common bean diseases; Dir Dr C. N. WATURU.

Plant Breeding Station: Ministry of Agriculture, PO Njoro; tel. (51) 48150; fax (51) 47986; f. 1927; 20 professional staff; Officer-in-Charge Dr R. C. MCGINNIS; improvement of wheat, barley and oats.

Pyrethrum Board of Kenya: POB 420, Nakuru; tel. (51) 211567; fax (51) 210466; e-mail pbk@kenya-pyrethrum.com; internet www.kenya-pyrethrum.com; f. 1948; research and information on pyrethrum as a natural insecticide; Dir SAMUEL KIHIU; publ. *Pyrethrum Post* (2 a year).

Tea Research Foundation of Kenya: POB 820, 20200 Kericho; tel. (52) 20598; fax (52) 20575; e-mail lib-trfk@kenyaweb.com; f. 1951; research and technology devt on the production and manufacture of tea, with special emphasis on agronomic, botanical, environmental and physical parameters; pests and diseases management; tea biochemistry and processing of tea, technology, knowledge and information transfer, training and advisory services; value addition, product diversification and market research; library of 10,000 vols; Dir Dr WILSON K. RONNO; publs *Tea Growers Handbook*, *Tea Journal* (2 a year), *TRFK Quarterly Bulletin*.

HISTORY, GEOGRAPHY AND ARCHAEOLOGY

British Institute in Eastern Africa: POB 30710, GPO 0100 Nairobi; tel. (20) 4343190; fax (20) 4343365; e-mail bieanairobi@africaonline.com; internet www.britac.ac.uk/institutes/eafrica; f. 1960; library of 5,000 vols, 100 periodicals; research into the history and archaeology of Eastern Africa, for which occasional grants and studentships are offered; 350 mems; Dir Dr PAUL J. LANE; publ. *Azania* (annually).

MEDICINE

Alupe Leprosy and Other Skin Diseases Research Centre (The John Lowe Memorial): POB 3, Busia; tel. and fax (55) 22410; f. 1952; part of KEMRI; Dir Dr P. A. OREGE; publ. *Annual Report*.

Institute for Medical Research and Training: National Public Health Laboratory Services, POB 20750, Nairobi; f. 1964 for research and medical training; see also College of Health Professions, Medical School, under Colleges.

Kenya Medical Research Institute (KEMRI): POB 54840-00200, Nairobi; tel. (20) 722541; fax (20) 720030; e-mail kemri-hq@nairobi.mimcom.net; internet www.kemri.org; f. 1979; under the Min. of Health; research in biomedical sciences, co-operates with other instns in training programmes and research, co-operates with the relevant ministries, the Nat. Ccl for Science and Technology and the Medical Science Advisory Research Cttee; 11 centres: Centre for Biotechnology Development Research, Centre for Clinical Research, Centre for Virus Research, Centre for Infections and Parasitic Diseases Research, Centre for Traditional Medicines and Drugs Research, Centre for Microbiology Research, Centre for Respiratory Diseases Research, Centre for Vector Biology and Control Research, Centre for Geographic Medicine Research, Centre for Public Health Research, Eastern and Southern Africa Centre of International Parasite Control (ESACIPAC); co-ordinates the annual African Health Sciences Congress and is secretariat for African Forum for Health Sciences (AFHES); library of 3,000 vols, collection of scientific reprints, theses and dissertations; Dir Dr DAVY KOECH; publs *African Journal of Health Sciences* (quarterly), *AIDS Update* (6 a year), *Annual Report*, *KEMRI Abstracts*, *KEMRI Newsletter* (annually).

National Public Health Laboratory Services (Medical Department): POB 20750, Nairobi; tel. (20) 725601; fax (20) 729504; all branches of medicine; library; Dir Dr JACK NYAMONGO.

Respiratory Diseases Research Centre: POB 47855, Nairobi; tel. (20) 724262; fax (20) 720030; f. 1960; part of KEMRI; research on all aspects of respiratory diseases, with special reference to diagnostic and treatment procedures relevant to developing country situations and to the epidemiology of respiratory diseases; Dir Dr J. A. ODHIAMBO; publ. *Annual Report*.

NATURAL SCIENCES

Biological Sciences

Institute of Primate Research: National Museums of Kenya, POB 24481, Nairobi; tel. (20) 882571; fax (20) 882546; e-mail iprdirector@ipr.or.ke; internet www.ipr.or.ke; research in primate medicine, virology, reproductive biology, infectious diseases, and ecology and conservation; Dir Dr EMMANUEL O. WANGO; publ. *IPR Report* (annually).

TECHNOLOGY

Kenya Industrial Research and Development Institute: Lusaka Rd, Dunga, POB 30650, Nairobi; tel. (20) 535966; fax (20) 555738; e-mail kirdi@arcc.or.ke; internet www.kirdi.go.ke; f. 1948; provides advice for established local industrial concerns and gives assistance in the establishment of new industries on the utilization of local materials; Dir Dr P. M. MUTURI; publs *Annual Report*, *Newsletter*, brochures.

Mines and Geological Department: Madini House, Machakos Rd, POB 30009,

00100 Nairobi; tel. (20) 541040; e-mail cmg@bidii.com; f. 1932; geological survey and research; mineral resources development; administers mineral and explosives laws; library of 32,000 vols, 10,000 periodicals; Commr L. K. BIWOTT; publs *Annual Report*, *Mineral Statistics Data*, bulletins, maps, reports, statistics.

National Fibre Research Centre, Kibos: POB 1490, Kisumu; Dir J. H. BRETTELL.

Libraries and Archives

Kisumu

British Council Library: opp. Alpha House, Odinga Odinga Rd, POB 454, Kisumu; tel. (57) 21613; fax (57) 21717; e-mail kisumu@britishcouncil.or.ke; internet www.britishcouncil.org/kenya; Information Centre Man. TEDMAN ALOO.

Mombasa

British Council Library: Jubilee Insurance Bldg, Moi Ave, POB 90590, Mombasa; tel. (41) 2223076; fax (41) 2315349; e-mail mombasa@britishcouncil.or.ke; 3,000 vols, 32 periodicals; Information Centre Man. MARY STEVENS.

Nairobi

Desai Memorial Library: POB 1253, Nairobi; f. 1942; public library and reading room; 31,800 vols; books in Swahili, English, Gujarati, Gurumukhi, Hindi and Urdu; reference, newspaper and periodic sections; 1,151 mems; Pres. A. M. SADARUDDIN; Sec. HARSHAD JOSHI.

High Court of Kenya Library: Law Courts, POB 30041, Nairobi; tel. (20) 221221; e-mail hck.lib@nbnet.co.ke; f. 1935; comprises High Court Library and Court of Appeal Library in Nairobi and 10 major br. libraries at Mombasa, Kisumu, Eldoret, Kakamega, Nakuru, Nyeri, Kisumu, Bungoma, Machakos and Kisii; 100,000 vols, 65 periodicals on practitioner's law, with special emphasis on Kenyan and English law; Head Librarian E. N. JUMA.

Ismail Rahimtulla Trust Library: POB 40333, Nairobi; tel. (20) 212660; f. 1953; 7,200 vols; Librarian P. GITAU.

Kenya Agricultural Research Institute Library: POB 57811, Nairobi; tel. (20) 583720; fax (20) 583344; e-mail resource.centre@kari.org; internet www.kari.org; f. 1928; extends current scientific awareness service to all agricultural research and academic centres and official depts within Kenya; 150,000 vols; Research Librarian VIVIENNE OGUYA; publs *East African Agricultural and Forestry Journal* (quarterly), *Record of Research* (annual report).

Kenya National Archives and Documentation Service: POB 49210, Moi Ave, 00100 Nairobi; tel. (20) 228959; fax (20) 228020; e-mail knarchives@kenyaweb.com; internet www.kenyarchives.go.ke; f. 1965; preservation and custody of public records; assists government offices in the maintenance of public records; over 1 million items, incl. reports, maps, films, microfilms, photographs, slides; archival materials accessible to national and international researchers; five records centres in Mombasa, Nairobi, Nakuru, Kisumu and Kakamega; 50,000 vols and periodicals, incl. 9,000 government monographs; 600 annual reports from government ministries and depts; Kenya Gazette, Laws of Kenya and parliamentary debates; 20,000 general and Africana vols; 700 theses and dissertations; 5,000 legal deposit collections; 1,600 periodicals and journals, incl. 30 current titles; the library prepares accession lists for all collections, and alphabetical lists for annual reports and periodicals, and publs indexes and guides to public records; databases accessible via website; Dir MUSILA MUSEMBI.

Kenya National Library Services: POB 30573, Ngong Rd, Nairobi; tel. (20) 725550; fax (20) 721749; e-mail knls@nbnet.co.ke; internet www.knls.or.ke; f. 1967; 621,000 vols, 120 periodicals; public library services through Nat. Lending Library in Nairobi, 19 brs and 8 mobile units; Nat. Reference and Bibliographic Dept f. 1980; special collections: East Africana and Kenyana; Chair. Archbishop STEPHEN ONDIEKI; Dir S. K. NG'ANG'A; publs *Kenya National Bibliography* (annually), *Kenya Periodical Directory* (every 2 years), annual report.

McMillan Memorial Library: POB 40791, Banda St, Nairobi; tel. (20) 221844; f. 1931; two branch libraries at Kaloleni and Eastlands; comprises Nairobi City Library Services; colls of old photographs, microfilms of East Africa, serial publs; Africana colln of 20,000 vols; 400,000 vols; Chief Librarian A. O. ESILABA.

University of Nairobi Libraries: POB 30197, 00100 Nairobi; tel. (20) 318262; internet www.library.uonbi.ac.ke; f. 1959; 850,000 vols, 600 periodicals, 7,000 electronic journals; 11 brs; acts as legal nat. depository and UN deposit library; Librarian SALOME MUNAVU (acting).

Museums and Art Galleries

Nairobi

National Museums of Kenya: Museum Hill, POB 40658, 00100 Nairobi; tel. (20) 742131; fax (20) 741424; e-mail dgnmk@museums.or.ke; internet www.museums.or.ke; f. 1910 by the East African Natural History Society; all branches of natural sciences, pre-history, geology, education, ethnography; library: joint library with East Africa Natural History Society, 30,000 vols; Dir Dr IDLE OMAR FARAH; Librarian A. H. K. OWANO; publs *Horizons*, *Journal of East Africa Natural History*, *Kenya Past and Present*.

Attached museums:

Fort Jesus Museum: POB 82412, Mombasa; tel. (41) 312839; fax (41) 227797; e-mail nmkfortj@swiftmombasa.com; f. 1960; inside 16th c. Portuguese fortress overlooking Mombasa harbour; finds from various coastal Islamic sites, from Fort Jesus, and from a 17th c. Portuguese wreck show the history of the Kenya coast; library of 1,000 vols and numerous offprints; Curator ALI BAAKABE.

Kisumu Museum: POB 1779, Kisumu; tel. (57) 40804; e-mail kisumuse@africaonline.co.ke; Curator PETER NYAMENYA.

Kitale Museum: POB 1219, Kitale; tel. (54) 20670; f. 1926; history and science, emphasis on education; library of 5,000 vols; Curator ABEL ATITI.

Lamu Museum: POB 48, Lamu; tel. (42) 633073; e-mail lamuse@hotmail.com; internet www.museums.or.ke; Curator ATHMAN HUSSEIN.

Universities

AFRICA NAZARENE UNIVERSITY

POB 53067-00200, Nairobi
Telephone: (45) 24350
Fax: (45) 24352
E-mail: admit@anu.ac.ke
Internet: www.anu.ac.ke

Founded 1994
Private control; administered by Church of the Nazarene International
Academic year: September to August (3 trimesters)

Vice-Chancellor: Prof. LEAH MARENGU
Deputy Vice-Chancellor (Academic): Prof. MARY JONES

Number of teachers: 50
Number of students: 850

Departments of Commerce, Computer Science and Theology.

AFRICAN VIRTUAL UNIVERSITY

POB 25405, Nairobi
Located at: 71 Maalim Juma Rd, Kilimani, POB 25405-006o3, Nairobi
Telephone: (20) 2712056
Fax: (20) 2712071
E-mail: contact@avu.org
Internet: www.avu.org

Founded 1997
Independent distance-learning institution sponsored by the World Bank, providing education in 18 African countries through a network of 33 Learning Centres
Languages of instruction: English, French

Rector: KUZVINETSA PETER DZVIMBO
Chief Financial Officer: DEREK PIERSON
Director, Academic Programmes Management and Development: Dr FRED BARASA

Bachelor degree and diploma courses in business studies and computer science; short courses in journalism, information technology and business communication.

CATHOLIC UNIVERSITY OF EASTERN AFRICA

POB 24205, Nairobi
Telephone: (20) 891601
Fax: (20) 891261
E-mail: admin@cuea.edu
Internet: www.cuea.edu

Founded 1984 as Catholic Higher Institute of Eastern Africa; present name and status 1992
Private control

Rector: Rev. Prof. JOHN C. MAVIIRI
Vice-Rector and Deputy Vice-Chancellor (Academic): Prof. PAUL OGULA
Vice-Rector and Deputy Vice-Chancellor (Administration): FRANCIS MUCHOKI
Vice-Rector and Deputy Vice-Chancellor (Finance) (vacant)

Library of 58,303 vols, 11,445 periodicals
Number of teachers: 240 (120 full-time, 120 visiting)
Number of students: 3,000

Publications: *African Christian Studies* (4 a year), *Eastern Africa Journal of Humanities and Science* (annually)

DEANS

Faculty of Arts and Social Sciences: SELLINE OKETCH
Faculty of Commerce: ATHERU KALENYWA
Faculty of Science: THUO GATHOGO
Faculty of Theology: Rev. Dr DEODONE NGONA

ATTACHED RESEARCH INSTITUTES

Centre for Social Justice and Ethics: Dir Rev. Prof. J. BAITU.

DAYSTAR UNIVERSITY

Athi River Campus, POB 17, 90145 Nairobi
Telephone: (45) 22601
Fax: (45) 22420
E-mail: vc@daystar.ac.ke
Internet: www.daystar.ac.ke
Founded 1994
Private control; non-profit, non-denominational Christian
Vice-Chancellor: Rev. Prof. GODFREY MBITI NGURU
Deputy Vice-Chancellor for Finance, Administration and Planning: AUSTIN EVANS
Library of 10,000 vols
Number of teachers: 180
Number of students: 1,900
campus in Nairobi

DEANS

Arts: Dr PHILIP KITUI
Science and Technology: Dr JON MASSO
Social Science: Dr STEPHEN NYAMBEGERA

UNIVERSITY OF EASTERN AFRICA, BARATON

POB 2500, Eldoret
Telephone: (53) 52625
Fax: (53) 52263
E-mail: dvc@ueab.ac.ke
Internet: www.ueab.ac.ke
Private control; Seventh-Day Adventist
Founded 1980
Chancellor: GEOFFREY MBWANA
Vice-Chancellor: Prof. R. TIMOTHY MCDONALD
Deputy Vice-Chancellor: Dr NATHANIEL WALEMBA
Dean of Students: BENSON NYAGWENCHA
Library of 50,000 vols
Number of teachers: 89
Number of students: 1,502 (1,286 full-time, 216 part-time)

DEANS

School of Business: SAMUEL OYIEKE
School of Education: Prof. DENFORD MUSVOSVI
School of Humanities and Social Sciences: Prof. WA-GITHUMO MWANGI
School of Science and Technology: Prof. ASAPH MARADUFU

EGERTON UNIVERSITY

POB 536, Njoro
Telephone: (51) 62277
Fax: (51) 62442
E-mail: eu-vc@net2000ke.com
Founded 1939; university status 1987
State control
Language of instruction: English
Academic year: August to May
Vice-Chancellor: Prof. E. K. MARITIM
Deputy Vice-Chancellors: Prof. J. K. TUITOEK (Administration and Finance), Prof. E. M. WATHUTA (Academic Affairs), Prof. S. A. ABDULRAZAK (Research and Extension)
Registrars: Prof. N. J. K. KATHURI (Academic), Dr T. K. SEREM (Administration and Finance)
Principal of Kisii College Campus: Prof. J. S. CHACHA
Principal of Laikipia Campus: Prof. A. M. SINDABI
Dean of Students: C. C. CHERUIYOT (acting)
Librarian: S. C. OTENYA
Library of 160,000 vols
Number of teachers: 800
Number of students: 10,000
Publications: *Agricultural Bulletin* (2 a year), *Annual Report*, *Educational Journal* (2 a year), *Egerton Journal* (2 a year), *'Kumekucha'* (2 a year)

DEANS

Agriculture: E. M. NJOKA
Arts and Social Sciences: Dr M. M. THEURI
Commerce (Kisii Campus): P. A. C. KAPSOOT
Education (Laikipia Campus): Dr L. W. CHIURI
Education and Human Resources: Dr B. N. GITHUA
Engineering: P. K. KIMANI
Environmental Science and Natural Resources: Prof. F. K. LELO
Health Sciences: Dr D. K. NGOTHO
Science: Dr S. M. NGARI
Graduate School: Prof. D. K. NASSIUMA (Dir)
School of Continuing Education: Prof. F. N. WEGULO (Dir)
School of Education: Dr F. S. BARASA (Dir)

HEADS OF DEPARTMENTS

Agricultural Economic and Business Management: Dr G. A. OBARE (acting)
Agricultural Education and Extension: Dr J. K. KIBET (acting)
Agricultural Engineering: Dr M. C. CHEMELIL
Agriculture and Home Economics: Dr D. R. ODERO (acting)
Agronomy: Dr E. M. NJOKA
Animal Health: Dr A. CHINGI
Animal Science: Prof. H. K. MUIRURI
Biochemistry and Molecular Biology: Prof. M. LIMO
Botany: Dr ANASTASIA MUIA
Chemistry: Prof. KAGWANJA
Computer Science: GEORGE NDIRANGU
Curriculum and Instruction: Dr J. CHANGEYWO
Dairy and Food Science and Technology: Dr JACKIN NANUA
Economics: Dr D. E. OUMA
Educational Administration and Planning: Dr M. W. NGWARE
Educational Materials Centre: JOHN NKANATHA
Educational Psychology and Counselling: Fr Dr S. N. MBUGUA
Environmental Science: Dr W. A. SHIVOGA
Geography: Dr C. M. GICHABA (acting)
History: Dr R. M. MATHEKA
Horticulture: Dr D. K. ISUTSA
Languages: Dr C. KITETU
Literature: Prof. EMILIA ILLIEVA
Mathematics: Dr I. S. ISLAM
Natural Resources: Dr D. K. TOO
Philosophy and Religious Studies: Dr M. M. THEURI
Physics: Dr H. S. A. GOLICHA
Sociology: B. ONSARINGO
Zoology: Dr J. MATHOOKO

JOMO KENYATTA UNIVERSITY OF AGRICULTURE AND TECHNOLOGY

POB 62000, City Sq., 0200 Nairobi
Telephone: (67) 52711
Fax: (67) 52030
E-mail: vc@jkuat.ac.ke
Internet: www.jkuat.ac.kec
Founded 1981; university status 1994
State control
Language of instruction: English
Academic year: August to June
Chancellor: Prof. ALI A. MAZRUI
Vice-Chancellor: Prof. NICK G. WANJOHI
Deputy Vice-Chancellors: Prof. H. M. THAIRU (Academic Affairs), Prof. S. G. AGONG (Administration, Planning and Development), Prof. S. K. SINEI (Research, Production and Extension)
Registrar (Academic Affairs): ANTHONY MUTUA KISWII
Registrar (Administration, Planning and Development): P. D. M. MUCHAI
Librarian: L. M. WANYAMA
Library of 45,000 vols
Number of teachers: 350
Number of students: 2,349
Publications: *Horizon DAT* (architecture, annually), *Journal of Agriculture Science and Technology* (2 a year), *Journal of Civil Engineering* (annually)

DEANS

Faculty of Agriculture: Prof. F. K. LENGA
Faculty of Engineering: Prof. R. N. MUTUKU
Faculty of Science: Prof. R. O. ODHIAMBO
School of Architecture and Building Sciences: Dr B. O. MOIRONGO

CHAIRMEN OF DEPARTMENT

Agricultural Engineering: Dr J. W. KALULI
Architecture: Dr C. C. OCHIENG
Biochemistry: Dr P. LOMO
Botany: Dr V. W. NGUMI
Chemistry: Dr G. T. THIONG'O
Civil Engineering: Dr K. S. MAKHANU
Construction Management: B. M. OTOKI
Electrical Engineering: Dr E. N. NDUNG'U
Food Science: Dr F. M. MATHOOKO
Horticulture: Dr C. K. NDUNG'U
Landscape Architecture: S. KIGONDU
Mathematics and Statistics: Dr R. O. ODHIAMBO
Mechanical Engineering: Dr S. P. NG'ANG'A
Physics: Dr D. M. MULATI
Zoology: Dr J. K. MAGAMBO

DIRECTORS OF INSTITUTES AND BOARDS

Institute for Biotechnology Research: Prof. E. M. KAHANGI
Institute of Computer Science and Information Technology: J. M. WAFULA
Institute of Continuing Education: Dr J. K. KWANZA
Institute of Energy and Environmental Technology: Prof. I. K. INOTI
Institute of Human Resource Development: W. N. KARUGU
Institute of Tropical Medicine and Infectious Diseases: Prof. J. K. MAGAMBO
Alternative Degree Programme: Dr V. W. NGUMI
Board of Postgraduate Studies: Prof. S. M. UPPAL
JKUAT Information Technology Centre: Dr L. M. GITONGA
JKUAT Nairobi Centre: Dr H. A. OUMA

KENYA METHODIST UNIVERSITY

POB 267, Meru
Telephone: (164) 30301
Fax: (164) 30162
E-mail: info@kemu.ac.ke
Internet: www.kemu.ac.ke
Founded 1997
Private control
Chancellor: Dr. Rev. STEPHEN KANYARU M'IMPWI
Vice-Chancellor: Prof. MUTUMA MUGAMBI
Registrar: Dr. Rev. STEPHEN KANYARU M'IMPWI
Librarian: JOE C. NYAMULUI

CHAIRS OF FACULTY

Agriculture and Natural Resources: Prof. KABURU M'RIBU
Applied Biology: Prof. ALICE N. MURITHI
Business Administration: Prof. BENJAMIN MAKUYU
Education and Counselling: JOHN GIKUNDA MARIENE

Maths and Computer Science: Prof. LUHAHI LAHI
Theology: Rev. PETER MUKUCCIA

KENYATTA UNIVERSITY

POB 43844, GPO 00100, Nairobi
Telephone: (20) 810901
Fax: (20) 811575
Internet: www.ku.ac.ke
Founded 1972 as constituent college of University of Nairobi, present status 1985
State control
Language of instruction: English
Academic year: September to July
Chancellor: Prof. HARRIS MULE
Vice-Chancellor: Prof. E. M. STANDA
Deputy Vice-Chancellors: Prof. J. J. ONGONG'A (Academic), Prof. M. S. RAJAB (Administration), Prof. O. M. MUGENDA (Finance, Planning and Development)
Registrars: Dr G. KATANA (Academic), Dr M. N. ETYANG (Administration), Dr N. M. KARAGU (Finance, Planning and Development)
Librarian: R. N. NDEGWA (acting)
Library of 267,581 vols, 6,550 vols of periodicals
Number of teachers: 651
Number of students: 17,000
Publication: *East African Journal of Science*

DEANS

School of Business: Dr E. KHAKAME
School of Education: Prof. J. OTIENDE
School of Environmental and Human Sciences: Dr D. N. MUGENDI
School of Humanities and Social Sciences: Prof. MARY GETUI
School of Pure and Applied Sciences: Dr G. MULUVI
School of Graduate Studies: Prof. WANJIRU E. MWATHA

MASENO UNIVERSITY

Private Bag, Maseno
Telephone: (57) 351008
Fax: (57) 351153
E-mail: vc-maseno@maseno.ac.ke
Internet: www.maseno.ac.ke
Founded 2000 upon independence of Moi University's Maseno University College
State control
Chancellor: THE PRESIDENT OF THE REPUBLIC OF KENYA
Vice-Chancellor: Prof. FREDRICK N. ONYANGO
Deputy Vice-Chancellor: Prof. RICHARD MIBEY
Librarian: G. D. OJUANDO
Library of 350,000 vols
Number of teachers: 285
Number of students: 3,681
Publications: *Equator News* (quarterly), *Maseno Journal of Education, Arts and Science* (2 a year)

DEANS

Faculty of Arts and Social Sciences: FRANCIS ANG'AWA
Faculty of Education: LUCAS OTHUON
Faculty of Science: MARY ABAKUTSA ONYANGO
Institute of Research and Postgraduate Studies: WILLIAM OCHIENG
Institute of Undergraduate Studies: MONICA AYIEKO
School of Family, Consumer Science and Technology: MARY K. WALINGO (Dir)
School of Public Health and Community Development: ROSEBELLA ONYANGO (Dir)

MOI UNIVERSITY

POB 3900, Eldoret 30100
Telephone: (53) 43620
Fax: (53) 43047
E-mail: vcmu@mu.ac.ke
Internet: www.mu.ac.ke
Founded 1984
State control
Language of instruction: English
Academic year: September to June
Chancellor: Prof. BETHWEL ALLAN OGOT
Vice-Chancellor: Prof. DAVID K. SOME
Deputy Vice-Chancellor (Planning and Development) : Prof. S. GUDU
Deputy Vice-Chancellor (Research and Extension): Dr M. J. KAMAR
Chief Academic Officer: Prof. K. OLE KAREI
Chief Administrative Officer: Dr J. K. SANG
Principal of Chepkoilel Campus: Dr J. K. LONYANGAPUO
Finance Officer: BENSON MUIRURI
Librarian: TIRONG ARAP TANUI
Library of 200,000 vols, 50,000 periodicals
Number of teachers: 709
Number of students: 5,266

DEANS

School of Agriculture and Biotechnology: Dr REUBEN M. MUASYA
School of Arts and Social Sciences: Dr PETER O. NDEGE
School of Economics and Business Management: Prof HENRY K. MARITIM
School of Education: Prof. RUTH N. OTUNGA
School of Engineering: Prof ABEL N. MAYAKA
School of Environmental Sciences: Prof. WILSON K. YABANN
School of Human Resources Development: Dr MARY C. LUTTA-MUKKHEBI
School of Information Sciences: Prof. JOSEPH B. OJIAMBO
School of Law: Prof. JOHN K. CHEBII
School of Medicine: Dr FABIAN ESAMAI
School of Natural Resources Management: Prof. ERICK KOECH
School of Public Health: Prof. JOSEPH ROTICH
School of Science: Dr PETER K. TORONGEY

HEADS OF DEPARTMENTS

School of Agriculture and Biotechnology:
- Agricultural Marketing and Co-operatives: Prof. M. O. ODHIAMBO
- Crop Production and Seed Technology: Dr P. W. MATHENGE
- Rural Engineering: J. K. KORIR
- Soil Science: Prof. C. O. OTHIENO

School of Arts and Social Sciences:
- Anthropology: Prof. J. AKONG'A
- Government and Public Administration: Dr A. LOKUJI
- History: Dr ODHIAMBO-NDEGE
- Kiswahili and Other African Languages: Dr N. SHITEMI
- Linguistics and Foreign Languages: J. AGALO
- Literature: BUSOLO WEGESA
- Philosophy: Fr Dr C. MUNGA
- Religion: Dr A. CHEPKWONY
- Sociology: Dr S. CHESSA

School of Economics and Business Management:
- Business Management: Dr A. MADUT
- Economics: J. OBILO

School of Education:
- Educational Administration, Planning and Curriculum Development: Prof. S. A. OMULANDO
- Educational Foundations: Dr I. N. KIMENGI
- Educational Psychology: S. O. KEBAYA
- Education, Communications and Technology: Dr PATRICK KAFU
- Science Education: Dr LOIS KONANA
- Teaching Practice Unit: Dr A. M. SIMIYU
- Technology Education: C. W. WOSYANJU

School of Engineering:
- Chemical and Process Engineering: A. KUMAR
- Civil and Structural Engineering: Dr S. M. SHITOTE
- Computer Services and Instrumentation Centre: R. ONYANCHA
- Electrical and Communications Engineering: Dr A. J. M. CHOL
- Production Engineering: Dr T. M. OGADA
- Textile Engineering: P. M. WAMBUA

School of Environmental Studies:
- Biological Sciences: Prof. S. MANOHAR
- Environmental Economics and Human Ecology: Prof. M. P. TOLE
- Environmental Health: Prof. T. D. DAVIES
- Environmental Law: Dr W. K. YABAN
- Environmental Monitoring and Cartography: Dr E. UCAKUWUN
- Environmental Planning and Management: Dr E. UCAKUWUN
- Physical Sciences: Prof. T. C. SHARMA

School of Information Sciences:
- Archives and Records Management: Dr J. WAMUKOYA
- Desktop Publishing Unit: T. OUKO
- Information and Media Technology: G. WANYEMBI
- Library and Information Studies: M. K. MAJANJA
- Publishing and Book Trade: F. MUREITHI

School of Law:
- Archives and Records Management: Assoc. Prof. F. X. NJENGA

School of Natural Resources Management:
- Fisheries: Dr M. MUCHIRI
- Forestry: Dr E. KOECH
- Tourism: B. M. MUSYOKI
- Wildlife Management: Dr B. E. L. WISHITEMI
- Wood Science and Technology: Prof. J. G. MWANGI

School of Public Health:
- Aesthesiology and Critical Health: Dr J. O. WAMBANI
- Behavioural Sciences: Dr D. NGARE
- Child Health, Paediatrics and Adolescence: Dr F. ESAMAI
- Dental Health: Dr C. KIBOSIA
- Environmental Health: G. RUKUNGA
- Epidemiology and Preventive Medicine: Prof. P. R. KENYA
- Forensic Medicine and Toxicology: W. OCHIENG
- Haematology and Blood Transfusion: Dr N. BUZIBA
- Health Management and Health Economics: Dr W. ODERO
- Histopathology and Cytology: Prof. VLADIMIR KOZLOV
- Human Anatomy: Dr M. NDIEMA
- Immunology: Prof. A. K. CHEMTAI
- Medical Biochemistry: Dr J. WAKHISI
- Medical Education: VINCENT NAWEYA
- Medical Physiology: Prof. J. NSHAHO
- Nursing Sciences and Emergency Medicine: P. MANG'ERA
- Nutrition and Dietetics: Dr ETTYANG
- Medicine: Dr P. AYUO
- Mental Health: Dr O. F. OMOLO
- Microbiology and Parasitology: Dr K. K. KAMAR
- Pharmacology and Therapeutics: Dr A. MARITIM
- Radiology and Imageing: G. D. E. ONDITI
- Reproductive Health: Dr E. O. WERE
- Surgical Sciences and Traumatology: Prof. B. O. KHWA-OTSYULU

School of Science:
- Botany: S. GUDU

Chemistry: Dr P. KIPKEMBOI
Mathematics: Dr M. M. MUTISO
Physics: Prof. K. M. KHANNA
Zoology: Dr F. M. F. WANJALA

Institute for Human Resources Development:
Communication Studies: L. CHEMAI
Development Studies: E. G. CHAHENZA
Quantitative Skills: E. L. W. SIMIYU

UNIVERSITY OF NAIROBI

POB 30197, Nairobi
Telephone: (20) 318262
Fax: (20) 246655
E-mail: postmaster@unics.gn.apc.org
Internet: www.uonbi.ac.ke

Founded 1956 as Royal Technical College of East Africa; present name 1970
State control
Language of instruction: English
Academic year: October to July

Chancellor: JOE B. WANJUI
Vice-Chancellor: Prof. G. A. O. MAGOHA
Deputy Vice-Chancellor (Academic): Prof. J. T. KAIMENYI
Deputy Vice-Chancellor (Administration and Finance) (vacant)
Registrars: S. MBALU (Academic), C. O. OMBATI (Administration), W. J. ASILLA (Planning, acting)
Librarian: S. MATHANGANI
Number of teachers: 2,169
Number of students: 35,000
Publications: *Annual Report*, *University of Nairobi Varsity Focus* (research activity newsletter)

PRINCIPALS

College of Agriculture and Veterinary Medicine: Prof. P. M. MBITHI
College of Architecture and Engineering: Prof. F. W. O. ADUOL
College of Biological and Physical Sciences: Prof. L. IRUNGU
College of Education and External Studies: Prof. H. MUTORO
College of Health Sciences: Prof. J. K. KITONYI
College of Humanities and Social Sciences: Prof. I. M. MBECHE

DEANS

Agriculture: Prof. A. W. MWANGOMBE
Architecture, Design and Development: W. OLIMA
Arts: Prof. P. WANYANDE
Commerce: Prof. J. KENDWIWO
Dental Sciences: Prof. S. GUTHUA
Education: Prof. L. KIBERA
Engineering: Prof. B. NJOROGE (acting)
External Studies: Dr R. AYOT
Law: Prof. M. OKECH-OWITI
Medicine: Prof. D. MAKAWITI
Pharmacy: Prof. I. KIBWAGE
Science: Prof. N. OKETCH
Social Sciences: Dr J. H. WERE
Veterinary Medicine: Prof. P. KANYARI

PROFESSORS

Faculty of Agriculture (POB 29053, Nairobi; tel. (20) 631340; fax (20) 632121):
IMUNGI, J. K., Food Technology and Nutrition
KARUE, C. N., Range Management
MICHIEKA, R. W., Crop Protection
MITARU, B., Animal Production
MUKUNYA, D. M., Crop Protection
MWANGOMBE, A., Crop Protection
OGUTU, A., Agricultural Economics
WAITHAKA, K., Crop Science

Faculty of Architecture (tel. (20) 724521):
SYAGGA, P. M., Land Development

Faculty of Arts (tel. (20) 318362; e-mail arts@uonbi.ac.ke):
ABDULAZIZ, M. H., Linguistics and African Languages
CHESAINA, C., Literature
INDANGASI, H., Literature
MUGAMBI, J. N. K., Religious Studies
MUREITHI, L. P., Economics
MURIUKI, G., History
MWABU, G. M., Economics
NYASANI, J., Philosophy
OCHOLA AYAYO, A. B. C., Population Studies
ODINGO, R. S., Geography
OJANY, F. F., Geography
OMONDI, L. N., Linguistics and African Languages
OYUGI, W. O., Political Science and Public Administration

Faculty of Commerce (tel. (20) 742261):
KIBERA, F. N., Business Administration

Faculty of Dental Sciences (tel. (20) 720322; fax (20) 723252):
GUTHUA, S. W., Oral Surgery
KAIMENYI, J. T., Periodontology and Community Dentistry
OPINYA, G. N., Paediatric Dentistry, Orthodontics

Faculty of Education (POB 97, Kikuyu; tel. (66) 32021; e-mail deanedu@uonbi.ac.ke):
KARANI, F. A., Educational Communication and Technology
MACHARIA, D., Education
OKOMBO, O., Linguistics and Literature
WANJALA, Linguistics and Literature

Faculty of Engineering (tel. (20) 339061):
ADUOL, F. W. O., Surveying
GICHAGA, F. J., Civil Engineering
LUTI, F. M., Mechanical Engineering
OBUDHO, R. A., Urban and Regional Planning
OTIENO, A. V., Electrical and Electronics Engineering
SHARMA, T. C., Agricultural Engineering

Faculty of Law (tel. (20) 742261):
MUTUNGI, O. K., Commercial Law
OJWANG, J. B., Private Law
OKOTH-OGENDO, H. W. O., Public Law

Faculty of Medicine (tel. (20) 725102; fax (20) 714048):
ATINGIA, J. E. U., Orthopaedic Surgery
BHATT, S. M., Medicine
BWIBO, N. O., Paediatrics
KIGONDU, C., Clinical Chemistry
KIMANI, J. K., Human Anatomy
KUNGU, A., Human Pathology
KYAMBI, J. M., Surgery
MAGOHA, G. A., Surgery
MAKAWITI, D. W., Biochemistry
MALEK, A. K., Human Anatomy
MATTA, W. M., Human Anatomy
MEME, J. S., Paediatrics
NDELE, J., Pharmacology
NDETEI, D. M., Psychiatry
ODHIAMBO, P. A., Surgery
OJWANG, S. B. O., Obstetrics and Gynaecology
OLIECH, J. S., Surgery
OTIENO, L. S., Medicine
PAMBA, H. O., Medical Microbiology
SINEI, S. K., Obstetrics and Gynaecology
THAIRU, K., Physiology
WAMOLA, I. A., Medical Microbiology
WASUNA, A. E. U., Surgery

Faculty of Pharmacy (tel. (20) 711132; fax (20) 714048):
GUANTAI, A.
KIBWAGE, I. O., Pharmaceutical Chemistry
KOKWARO, G. O., Pharmaceutics and Pharmacy Practice
MAITAI, C. K., Pharmacology and Pharmacognosy
MWANGI, J. W., Pharmacology and Pharmacognosy

Faculty of Science (tel. (20) 4443181; e-mail deanscience@uonbi.ac.ke):
GENGA, R., Physics
GITU, P. M., Chemistry
KAMAU, G. N., Chemistry
KHAMALA, C. P. M., Zoology
KOKWARO, J. O., Botany
MIBEY, R. K., Botany
MIDIWO, J. O., Chemistry
MUKIAMA, T. K., Botany
MUNAVU, R. M., Chemistry
MWANGI, R. W., Zoology
NYAMBOK, I. O., Geology
ODADA, E., Geology
ODHIAMBO, J. W., Mathematics
OGALLO, L. T., Meteorology
OGANA, B. W., Mathematics
ONYANGO, F. N., Physics
OTIENO-MALO, J. B., Physics
PATEL, P. J., Physics
POKHRIYAL, G. P., Mathematics
WANDIGA, S. O., Chemistry

Faculty of Social Sciences (POB 97, Kikuyu; tel. (66) 321178):
ONIANGO, C. M. P., Philosophy and Religious Studies

Faculty of Veterinary Sciences (POB 29053, Nairobi; tel. (20) 631007; fax (20) 631007; e-mail deanfvm@uonbi.ac.ke):
AGUMBAH, G. J. O., Clinical Studies
GATHUMA, J. M., Public Health, Pharmacology and Toxicology
KIPTOON, J. C., Clinical Studies
MAINA, J. N., Veterinary Anatomy
MAITHO, T. E., Public Health, Pharmacology and Toxicology
MALOIY, G. M. O., Physiology
MITEMA, S. E. O., Public Health, Pharmacology and Toxicology
MUGERA, G. M., Veterinary Pathology
MUNYUA, W. K., Veterinary Pathology
MUTIGA, E. R., Clinical Studies
NYAGA, P. N., Veterinary Pathology
ODUOR-OKELLO, D., Veterinary Anatomy

Institutes:
ALILA, P., Institute for Development Studies
OCHOLLA-AYAYO, A. B. C., Population Studies and Research Institute
OKIDI, C. O., Institute for Development Studies
RODRIGUES, A. J., School of Informatics and Computing
SUDA, C., Institute for African Studies
WANDIBBA, S. B. A., Institute of African Studies

ATTACHED INSTITUTES

Institute of African Anthropology and Gender Studies: tel. (20) 742078; Dir Dr I. NYAMONGO.

Institute for Development Studies: tel. (20) 334244; e-mail idsdirector@swiftkenya.com; Dir Prof. D. MCCORMICK.

Institute of Diplomacy and International Studies: tel. (20) 339014; fax (20) 339014; Dir Dr M. MWAGIRU.

Institute of Nuclear Science: Dir D. M. MAINA.

Population Studies and Research Institute: tel. (20) 318262; Dir Dr L. IKAMARI.

School of Computing and Informatics: e-mail consult@uonbi.ac.ke; Dir K. GITAO.

School of Journalism and Mass Communication: tel. (20) 229168; e-mail SOJ@uonbi.ac.ke; Dir W. KIAI.

STRATHMORE UNIVERSITY

POB 59857, 00200 City Square, NairobiTelephone: (20) 606155
Fax: (20) 607498
E-mail: admissions@strathmore.edu
Internet: www.strathmore.edu

Founded 1961 as Strathmore College; present name *c.* 1993
Private control (non-profit)
Academic year: January to December

Principal: C. SOTZ

Library of 15,000 vols
Number of teachers: 96
Number of students: 2,700 (1,200 full-time, 1,500 evening)

School of Accountancy, School of Administration and Management, Information Technology Centre, Distance Learning Centre.

Colleges

Bukura Agricultural College: POB 23, Sigalagala-Butere Rd, Bukura; tel. (56) 20023; f. 1958; language of instruction: English; academic year October to October; departments: agricultural engineering, agronomy, basic sciences, horticulture, home economics, agricultural economics, agricultural education and extension; 240 students; Principal F. O. ANDITI.

Eldoret Polytechnic: POB 4461, Eldoret; tel. (53) 32661; fax (53) 33188; e-mail eldopoly@africaonline.co.ke; offers certificate and diploma courses in library and information studies; Principal CLEOPHAS LAGAT.

Kenya Conservatoire of Music: POB 41343, Nairobi; tel. (20) 222933; f. 1944; library of instrumental and vocal scores; Dir CAROL NGANGA; publ. *Newsletter* (irregular).

Kenya Institute of Administration: POB 23030, Lower Kabete, Nairobi; tel. (20) 582311; fax (20) 582306; e-mail kia@africaonline.co.ke; f. 1961; residential training for the Kenya Public Service in public administration, project development and management, senior management seminars, research and consultancy, computer courses, effective management communication, management information systems, policy analysis, management of public enterprises, French courses, finance management, environmental management, performance improvement programmes, human resource management, customer care and ethics, disaster management, training for trainers; library: 47,067 vols, 30 current periodicals and a fully equipped audio-visual aids centre; 30 teachers; 280 students; Dir TITUS J. K. GATEERE; publs *K. I. A. Occasional Papers* (monthly), *Newsline* (3 a year).

Kenya Medical Training College: POB 30195, Nairobi; tel. (20) 725711; fax (20) 722907; e-mail kmtc@nbnet.ke; f. 1924; library: 18,000 vols, 150 periodicals; 195 teachers; 2,000 students; Principal W. K. A. BOIT.

Kenya Polytechnic: POB 52428 Nairobi; f. 1961 with UNDP aid; depts of mechanical, electrical and electronic engineering, science, building, business studies, printing, institutional management, library and archive studies, general studies, mathematics, statistics, computing, media services; library: 40,000 vols, 150 periodicals; 300 teachers; 6,504 students; Principal P. O. OKAKA; Librarian S. K. NG'ANG'A.

Kenya School of Law: POB 30369, Nairobi; tel. (20) 890044; fax (20) 891722; e-mail lawschool@kenyaschooloflaw.com; f. 1963; library: 4,730 vols; 13 teachers; 400 students; Principal Prof. W. KULUNDU-BITONYE; Senior Principal Lecturer ANTHONY MUNENE; Librarian BENTA NARKISO.

Kiambu Institute of Science and Technology: POB 414, Kiambu; tel. (66) 22236; fax (66) 22319; f. 1973; library: 10,000 vols; depts of building, business education, electrical engineering, electronics, computer studies, bakery technology; 61 teachers; 600 students; Principal SIMON IRUNGU.

Kisumu Polytechnic: POB 143 Kisumu; tel. (35) 40161; fax (35) 44417; f. 1997; courses offered in electrical engineering, electronics, mechanical engineering, automotive engineering, analytical chemistry, food and beverage management, building, computer studies, personnel management, accounting and business administration; 112 teachers; 2,000 students; Principal FRANCIS IMBO.

Mombasa Polytechnic: POB 90420, Mombasa; tel. (41) 492222; fax (41) 495632; e-mail msapoly@kenyaweb.com; internet www.mombasapoly.ac.ke; f. 1948; full-time, sandwich, block-release and day-release courses; library: 20,000 vols; 200 teachers; 4,037 students; Principal C. T. AKUMU OWUOR; Registrar A. M. GEKONGE; Librarian R. KASINA

HEADS OF DEPARTMENT

Applied Sciences: P. OCHOLA
Building and Civil Engineering: J. K. KARIO
Business Studies: H. M. SALIM
Computing and Information Technology: K. G. ARIF
Electrical and Electronic Engineering: F. O. OTIENO
Enterprise and Development Centre: K. A. NYANGUN
Mechanical Engineering: M. W. MBUGUA
Media and Graphic Design: K. D. MWARINGA
Medical Engineering: S. M. MWANGI

Rift Valley Institute of Science and Technology: POB 7182, Nakuru; tel. (37) 211974; fax (37) 45656; f. 1972; library: 9,000 vols; 125 teachers; 1,200 students; Principal FRANCIS Z. K. MENJO.

Western University College of Science and Technology: POB 190, Kakamega; tel. (56) 20724; e-mail weco@africaonline.co.ke; f. 1977; library: 4,000 vols; 56 teachers; 500 students; Principal ALFRED F. O. MACHUKI; Librarian ROBERT KIMAKWA.

KIRIBATI

The Higher Education Systme

In 1979 the Gilbert Islands became an independent republic within the Commonwealth, under the name of Kiribati. Higher education consists mostly of a branch of the University of the South Pacific. In addition, there are the Kiribati Teachers College and the Tarawa Technical Institute, both operated by the Government. All these institutions are located on the Tarawa Atoll. Students from Kiribati also attend establishments of higher education in Australia, New Zealand and Canada. The Ministry of Youth, Education and Sport Development is responsible for tertiary education. The Ministry of Health and Medical Services runs a School of Nursing, also based on Tarawa.

Library

Bairiki

National Library and Archives: POB 6, Bairiki, Tarawa; tel. 21337; fax 28222; f. 1979 (fmrly Gilbert Islands National Archives); lending section of 30,000 vols; reference library of 2,000 vols; 18,000 vols in small library units throughout Kiribati; National Collection (housed in Archives) of 3,500 published items; archives records of 70,000 items; special collections include 600 rolls of microfilm and 4,000 microfiches; small philatelic, photograph, and sound recording collections; Librarian and Archivist KUNEI ETEKIERA.

Museum

Bairiki

National Museum: POB 75, Bairiki, Tarawa; in process of formation; items stored in National Archives; Cultural Affairs Officer BWERE ERITAIA.

College

University of the South Pacific, Kiribati Extension Centre: POB 59, Bairiki, Tarawa; tel. 21085; fax 21419; internet www.usp.ac.fj; f. 1973; an external campus of the University of the South Pacific; part-time undergraduate and diploma courses; 5 staff; library: 5,000 vols; 300 students; Dir URIAM TIMITI (acting).

Attached institute:

Atoll Research Activities: POB 206, Bikenibeu, Tarawa; marine science and biology; Programme Man. TEMAKEI TEBANO; publ. *Atoll Bulletin*.

DEMOCRATIC PEOPLE'S REPUBLIC OF KOREA

The Higher Education System

The Democratic People's Republic of Korea (North Korea) occupies the northern part of the Korean peninsula. In 1945 Korea was divided into military occupation zones, with Soviet forces in the North and US forces in the South. A provisional People's Committee, led by Kim Il Sung of the Korean Communist Party, was established in the North in 1946 and accorded government status. In 1948 the Democratic People's Republic of Korea was proclaimed. The oldest university is Kim Il Sung University, founded in 1946. A report submitted to UNESCO by the North Korean Government in 2000 stated that there were more than 300 universities and colleges with 1.89m. students and academics. In March 2001 the Ministry of Education announced plans for the establishment of a university of information science and technology in Pyongyang, in co-operation with a South Korean education foundation. The new university, named the Pyongyang University of Science and Technology (PUST), was due to open in September 2007 and 50 teachers, mostly from South Korea, were expected to teach around 200 North Korean postgraduate students.

Learned Societies

GENERAL

Academy of Sciences: Ryonmot-dong, Jangsan St, Sosong District, Pyongyang; tel. 51956; f. 1952; brs of Biology (Pres. SON KYONG NAM), Construction and Building Materials (Pres. KIM MAN HYONG), Electronics and Automation Design (Pres. LI SON BONG), Light Industry (Pres. PYON SOK CHON), and brs in Pyongsong (Chair. HAN BYONG HUI) and Hamhung (Pres. . RI HYO SON); attached research institutes: see Research Institutes; libraries: see Libraries and Archives; Pres. PYON YONG-RIP; publs *Bulletin* (6 a year), journals for Physics, Mathematics, Biology, Mechanical Engineering, Metals, Analysis (all 4 a year) and for Chemistry and Chemical Engineering, Mining, Electronic and Automatic Engineering, Geology and Geography (all 6 a year).

Academy of Social Sciences: Central District, Pyongyang; f. 1952; attached research institutes: see Research Institutes; library: see Libraries and Archives; Pres. KIM SOK HYONG.

AGRICULTURE, FISHERIES AND VETERINARY SCIENCE

Academy of Agricultural Science: Ryongsong District, Pyongyang; f. 1948; attached to Acad. of Sciences; attached research institutes: see Research Institutes; Pres. KYE YONG SAM.

Academy of Fisheries: Namgang-dong, Sung Ho District, Pyongyang; attached to Acad. of Sciences; f. 1969; 6 attached research institutes; Chair SO GYONG HO.

Academy of Forestry: Samsin-dong, Taesong District, Pyongyang; f. 1948; attached to Acad. of Sciences; 5 attached research institutes; Pres. IM ROK JAE.

LANGUAGE AND LITERATURE

Goethe-Informationszentrum: Chollima Cultural House, 8-33 Jonggwang St, Central Area, Pyongyang; internet www.goethe.de/seoul; library of 4,000 vols; promotes cultural exchange with Germany; Dir Dr UWE SCHMELTER (based in Seoul).

MEDICINE

Academy of Medical Sciences: Saemaul-dong, Pyongchon District, POB 305, Pyongyang; tel. 46924; attached to Acad. of Sciences; attached research institutes: see Research Institutes; Pres. RI CHOL.

TECHNOLOGY

Academy of Light Industry Science: Kangan 1-dong, Songyo District, Pyongyang; f. 1954; 7 attached research institutes; Chair. LI JU UNG.

Academy of Railway Sciences: Namgyo-dong, Hyongjaesan District, Pyongyang; attached to Acad. of Sciences; 5 attached research institutes; Chair. MAENG YUN CHOL.

Research Institutes

AGRICULTURE, FISHERIES AND VETERINARY SCIENCE

Agricultural Chemical Research Institute: Ryongsong District, Pyongyang; attached to DPRK Acad. of Agricultural Science; Dir PAK JAE KUN.

Agricultural Irrigation Research Institute: Onchon County, South Pyongan Province; attached to DPRK Acad. of Agricultural Science; Dir HWANG CHANG HONG.

Agricultural Mechanization Research Institute: Sadong District, Pyongyang; attached to DPRK Acad. of Agricultural Science; Dir KANG SONG RYONG.

Crop Cultivation Research Institute: Ryongsong District, Pyongyang; attached to DPRK Acad. of Agricultural Science; Dir RYEM DOK SU.

Crop Science Research Institute: Sunchon City, South Pyongan Province; attached to DPRK Acad. of Agricultural Science; Dir PAK BYONG MUK.

Fruit Cultivation Research Institute: Sukchon County; South Pyongan Province; attached to DPRK Acad. of Agricultural Science; Dir JANG HY KUNG.

Poultry Science Research Institute: Hyongjaesan District, Pyongyang; attached to DPRK Acad. of Agricultural Science; Dir CHOI MAN SANG.

Reed Research Institute: Haeju City, South Hwanghae Province; attached to DPRK Acad. of Agricultural Science; Dir KIM IN SU.

Rice Research Institute: Ryongsong District, Pyongyang; attached to DPRK Acad. of Agricultural Science; Dir KIM SANG RYEN.

Sericulture Research Institute: Dongrim County, North Pyongan Province; attached to DPRK Acad. of Agricultural Science; Dir KIM SUN JONG.

Soil Science Research Institute: Ryongsong District, Pyongyang; attached to DPRK Acad. of Agricultural Science; Dir LI KUN HAENG.

Vegetable Science Research Institute: Sadong District, Pyongyang; attached to DPRK Acad. of Agricultural Science; Dir KIM HAK SON.

Veterinary Science Research Institute: Ryongsong District, Pyongyang; attached to DPRK Acad. of Agricultural Science; Dir PAK WON KUN.

Zoology Research Institute: Sariwon City, North Hwanghae Province; attached to DPRK Acad. of Agricultural Science; Dir KIM KYANG JUNG.

ARCHITECTURE AND TOWN PLANNING

Institute of Architecture and Building Engineering: C/o Academy of Sciences, Namgang-dong, Sung Ho District, Pyongyang; attached to DPRK Acad. of Science; Dir SIN DONG CHOL.

ECONOMICS, LAW AND POLITICS

Institute of International Affairs: C/o Academy of Social Sciences, Central District, Pyongyang; attached to DPRK Acad. of Social Sciences; Dir KIM HYONG U.

Institute of Law: C/o Academy of Social Sciences, Central District, Pyongyang; attached to DPRK Acad. of Social Sciences; Dir SIM HYONG IL.

Institute of Trade and Economics: C/o Academy of Social Sciences, Central District, Pyongyang; attached to DPRK Acad. of Social Sciences; Dir (vacant).

HISTORY, GEOGRAPHY AND ARCHAEOLOGY

Institute of Archaeology: C/o Academy of Social Sciences, Central District, Pyongyang; attached to DPRK Acad. of Social Sciences; Dir KIM MYONG NAM.

Institute of Geography: Ryonmot-dong, Jangsan St, Sosong District, Pyongyang; attached to DPRK Acad. of Sciences; Dir KIM JONG RAK.

Institute of History: C/o Academy of Social Sciences, Central District, Pyongyang;

attached to DPRK Acad. of Social Sciences; Dir CHON YONG RYUL.

LANGUAGE AND LITERATURE

Institute of Ethnic Classics: C/o Academy of Social Sciences, Central District, Pyongyang; attached to DPRK Acad. of Social Sciences; Dir KIM SUNG PHIL.

Institute of Juche Literature: C/o Academy of Social Sciences, Central District, Pyongyang; attached to DPRK Acad. of Social Sciences; Dir KIM HA MYONG.

Institute of Linguistics: C/o Academy of Social Sciences, Central District, Pyongyang; attached to DPRK Acad. of Social Sciences; Dir JONG SUN GI.

MEDICINE

Industrial Medicine Institute: Sapo-dong, Sapo District, Hamhung City; tel. 2810; attached to DPRK Acad. of Medical Sciences; Dir JO UN HO.

Research Institute for the Cultivation of Medicinal Herbs: Wonju-dong, Sariwon City, North Hwanghae Province; attached to DPRK Acad. of Medical Sciences; Dir KIM KWANG SOP.

Research Institute of Antibiotics: Ryonpo-dong, Sunchon City, South Pyongan Province; attached to DPRK Acad. of Medical Sciences; Dir CHOE SUN JONG.

Research Institute of Biomedicine: Dongsan-dong, Rangnang District, Pyongyang; tel. 23545; attached to DPRK Acad. of Medical Sciences; Dir PAK YUI SUN.

Research Institute of Child Nutrition: Dangsan-dong, Mangyongdae District, Pyongyang; tel. 73430; attached to DPRK Acad. of Medical Sciences; Dir KIM YONG KWANG.

Research Institute of Endocrinology: Mirim-dong, Sadong District, Pyongyang; tel. 623828; attached to DPRK Acad. of Medical Sciences; Dir JANG HON CHOL.

Research Institute of Experimental Therapy: C/o Academy of Medical Sciences, Chonsong-dong, Haesang District, Hamhung City, South Hamgyong Province; attached to DPRK Acad. of Medical Sciences; Dir NAM ON GIL.

Research Institute of Hygiene: Dangsan-dong, Mangyongdse District, Pyongyang; tel. 44925; attached to DPRK Acad. of Medical Sciences; Dir JE HYONG DO.

Research Institute of Microbiology: Pyongsong City, South Pyongan Province; attached to DPRK Acad. of Medical Sciences; Dir KIM CHANG JIN.

Research Institute of Natural Drugs: Somun-dong, Donghumsan District, Hamhung City, South Hamgyong Province; tel. 53905; attached to DPRK Acad. of Medical Sciences; Dir LI HWAI SU.

Research Institute of Oncology: Saemaul-dong, Pyongchon District, Pyongyang; tel. 42208; attached to DPRK Acad. of Medical Sciences; Dir KIM CHUN WON.

Research Institute of Pharmacology: Daehung-dong, Songyo District, Pyongyang; tel. 623868; attached to DPRK Acad. of Medical Sciences; Dir RYU GYONG HUI.

Research Institute of Psychoneurology: Uiju County, North Pyongan Province; attached to DPRK Acad. of Medical Sciences; Dir LI GYUN.

Research Institute of Radiological Medicine: Saemaul-dong, Pyongchon District, Pyongyang; tel. 45347; attached to DPRK Acad. of Medical Sciences; Dir O SOK ROK.

Research Institute of Respiratory Ducts and Tuberculosis: C/o Academy of Medical Sciences, Chongsong-dong, Haesang District, Hamhung City, South Hamgyong Province; attached to DPRK Acad. of Medical Sciences; Dir LI CHU WAN.

Research Institute of Surgery: C/o Academy of Medical Sciences, Chongsong-dong, Haesang District, Hamhung City, South Hamgyong Province; attached to DPRK Acad. of Medical Sciences; Dir HAN BYONG GAP.

Research Institute of Synthetic Pharmacy: Sapo-dong, Sapo District, Hamhung City, South Hamgyong Province; attached to DPRK Acad. of Medical Sciences; Dir LI GI SOP.

NATURAL SCIENCES

General

Central Institute of Experimental Analysis: C/o Academy of Sciences, Kwahak-Idong, Unjong District, Pyongsong City, South Pyongan Province; tel. (02) 422-5044; f. 1983; attached to DPRK Acad. of Sciences; Dir RIM CHUN RYOB; publs *Punsok* (analysis, 4 a year), *Bulletin*.

Institute of Environmental Protection: Ryusong-dong, Central District, Pyongyang; attached to DPRK Acad. of Sciences; Dir KIM YONG CHAN.

Biological Sciences

Institute of Botany: Kosan-dong, Daesong District, Pyongyang; attached to DPRK Acad. of Sciences; Dir GUAK JONG SONG.

Institute of Genetics: C/o Academy of Sciences, Ryonmot-dong, Jangsan St, Sosong District, Pyongyang; attached to DPRK Acad. of Sciences; Dir BAEK MUN CHAN.

Institute of Molecular Biology: C/o Academy of Sciences, Ryonmot-dong, Jangsan St, Sosong District, Pyongyang; attached to DPRK Acad. of Sciences; Dir KO GWANG UNG.

Institute of Plant Physiology: C/o Academy of Sciences, Ryonmot-dong, Jangsan St, Sosong District, Pyongyang; attached to DPRK Acad. of Sciences; Dir KIM SONG OK.

Institute of Zoology: Daesong-dong, Daesong District, Pyongyang; attached to DPRK Acad. of Sciences; Dir BAEK JONG HWAN.

Mathematical Sciences

Institute of Mathematics: C/o Academy of Sciences, Doksan-dong, Pyongsong City, South Pyongan Province; attached to DPRK Acad. of Sciences; Dir HO GON.

Physical Sciences

Institute of Analytical Chemistry: C/o Academy of Sciences, Chongsong-dong, Hoesang District, Hamhung City, South Hamgyong Province; attached to DPRK Acad. of Sciences; Dir RIM CHUN RYOP.

Institute of Ferrous Metals: Sae Gori-dong, Chollima District, Nampo City; attached to DPRK Acad. of Sciences; Dir LI BANG GUN.

Institute of Geology: C/o Academy of Sciences, Doksan-dong, Pyongsong City, South Pyongan Province; attached to DPRK Acad. of Sciences; Dir KIM ZONG HUI.

Institute of Inorganic Chemistry: C/o Academy of Sciences, Chongsong-dong, Hoesang District, Hamhung City, South Hamgyong Province; attached to DPRK Acad. of Sciences; Dir CHU SUNG.

Institute of Macromolecular Chemistry: C/o Academy of Sciences, Chongsong-dong, Hoesang District, Hamhung City, South Hamgyong Province; attached to DPRK Acad. of Sciences; Dir LI JANG HYOK.

Institute of Non-Ferrous Metals: Jungdaedu-dong, Hangku District, Nampo City; attached to DPRK Acad. of Sciences; Dir KIM MYONG RIN.

Institute of Physical Chemistry: C/o Academy of Sciences, Chongsong-dong, Hoesang District, Hamhung City, South Hamgyong Province; attached to DPRK Acad. of Sciences; Dir KIM JUNG BAE.

Institute of Physics: C/o Academy of Sciences, Doksan-dong, Pyongsong City, South Pyongan Province; attached to DPRK Acad. of Sciences; Dir RYO IN KWANG.

Institute of Pure Metals: Kumbit-dong, Ryongsong District, Hamhung City, South Hamgyong Province; attached to DPRK Acad. of Sciences; Dir LI SANG BOM.

Pyongyang Astronomical Observatory: Daesong-dong, Daesong District, Pyongyang; attached to DPRK Acad. of Sciences; Dir KIM YONG HYOK.

Research Centre for Atomic Energy: Mangyongdae District, Pyongyang; fax (2) 3814416; attached to General Dept of Atomic Energy; Pres. RIM PONG SIK.

PHILOSOPHY AND PSYCHOLOGY

Institute of Philosophy: C/o Academy of Social Sciences, Central District, Pyongyang; attached to DPRK Acad. of Social Sciences; Dir KIM CHANG WON.

TECHNOLOGY

Institute of Chemical Engineering: C/o Academy of Sciences, Chongsong-dong, Hoesang District, Hamhung City, South Hamgyong Province; attached to DPRK Acad. of Sciences; Dir LI JAE OP.

Institute of Constructional Mechanization: C/o Academy of Sciences, Namgang-dong, Sung Ho District, Pyongyang; attached to DPRK Acad. of Sciences; Dir PAK RYANG SOP.

Institute of Electricity: C/o Academy of Sciences, Doksan-dong, Pyongsong City, South Pyongan Province; attached to DPRK Acad. of Sciences; Dir CHOE WON GYONG.

Institute of Fuel: Dongsan-dong, Songrim City, North Hwanghe Province; attached to DPRK Acad. of Sciences; Dir KO YONG JIN.

Institute of Hydraulic Engineering: C/o Academy of Sciences, Namgang-dong, Sung Ho District, Pyongyang; attached to DPRK Acad. of Sciences; Dir KIM RYONG GYUN.

Institute of Industrial Biology: C/o Academy of Sciences, Doksan-dong, Pyongsong City, South Pyongan Province; attached to DPRK Acad. of Sciences; Dir LI CHUN HO.

Institute of Mechanical Engineering: C/o Academy of Sciences, Doksan-dong, Pyongsong City, South Pyongan Province; attached to DPRK Acad. of Sciences; Dir KIM UNG SAM.

Institute of Ore Dressing Engineering: C/o Academy of Sciences, Doksan-dong, Pyongsong City, South Pyongan Province; attached to DPRK Acad. of Sciences; Dir LI WON SOK.

Institute of Organic Building Materials: C/o Academy of Sciences, Namgang-dong, Sung Ho District, Pyongsong; attached to DPRK Acad. of Sciences; Dir PAK CHANG SUN.

Institute of Paper Engineering: Songdori, Anju City, South Pyongan Province; attached to DPRK Acad. of Sciences; Dir RYU SAM JIP.

Institute of Silicate Engineering: Sijong-gu, Taedong County, South Pyongan Province; attached to DPRK Acad. of Sciences; Dir KIM UNG SANG.

Institute of Thermal Engineering: C/o Academy of Sciences, Doksan-dong, Pyongsong City, South Pyongan Province; attached to DPRK Acad. of Sciences; Dir HAN DONG SIK.

Institute of Tideland Construction: C/o Academy of Sciences, Namgang-dong, Sung Ho District, Pyongyang; attached to DPRK Acad. of Sciences; Dir CHO SOK.

Institute of Welding: Ponghwa-dong, Chollima District, Nampo City; attached to DPRK Acad. of Sciences; Dir CHAE HON MUK.

Research Centre of Electronics and Automation: C/o Academy of Sciences, Doksan-dong, Pyongsong City, South Pyongan Province; attached to DPRK Acad. of Sciences; incorporates institutes of Electronics, of Computer Science, of Automation, of Technical Cybernetics, of Electronic Materials; Gen. Dir LI SON BONG.

Research Institute of Medical Instruments: Daesin-dong, Dongdaewon District, Pyongyang; tel. 623839; attached to DPRK Acad. of Medical Sciences; Dir JO MYONG SAM.

Libraries and Archives

Chongjin

Chongjin City Library: Chongjin; Librarian KANG CHAE GUM.

Chongjin Historical Library: Chongjin; Curator EU JAI GYONG.

North Hamgyong Provincial Library: Chongjin; Librarian CHOI MYONG OK.

Haeju

South Hwanghae Provincial Library: Haeju; Librarian CHOI CHI DO.

Hamhung

South Hamgyong Provincial Library: Hamhung; Librarian KIM SOOK JONG.

Hesan

Ryanggang Provincial Library: Hesan; Librarian KIM CHOL WOO.

Kaesong

Kaesong City Library: Kaesong; Librarian HAN IL.

Kaesong Historical Library: Kaesong; Curator CHOI SAE YONG.

Kangge

Chagang Provincial Library: Kangge; Librarian SONG AAI GUN.

Pyongsong

South Pyongan Provincial Library: Pyongsong; Librarian KIM DUK KWAN.

Pyongyang

Academy of Sciences Library: POB 330, Kwahakdong 1, Unjong District, Pyongyang; tel. 32353968; fax 814580; f. 1952; 3,200,000 vols; Dir Prof. KIM HYON OK; Chief Librarian Assoc. Prof. HONG SANG SU; publ. *Bulletin*.

Academy of Social Sciences Library: Central District, Pyongyang; Chief Librarian KIM SAE SONG.

Grand People's Study House/State Central Library: POB 200, Pyongyang Central District; tel. (2) 321-5614; fax (2) 381-4427; f. 1982; in charge of nat. bibliography; also functions as correspondence univ.; 20,000,000 vols; Dir CHOE HUI JONG.

Pyongyang Scientific Library: Central District, POB 109, Pyongyang; tel. (2) 321-2314; f. 1978.

Sariwon

North Hwanghae Provincial Library: Sariwon; Librarian KIM HYO DAL.

Shinuiju

North Pyongan Provincial Library: Shinuiju; Librarian LI YONG SIK.

Wonsan

Kangwon Provincial Library: Wonsan; Librarian JI GYU HYOK.

Museums and Art Galleries

Haeju

Haeju Historical Museum: Haeju, South Hwanghae Province.

Hamhung

Hamhung Historical Museum: Hamhung, South Hamgyong Province; Curator KIM IK MYON.

Hyangsan county

Mt Myohyang-san Museum: Hyangsan County, North Pyongan Province; Curator CHOI HYONG MIN.

Pyongyang

Korean Art Gallery: Pyongyang; Curator KIM SANG CHOL.

Korean Central Historical Museum: Central District, Pyongyang; prehistory to early 20th century; Curator JANG JONG SIN.

Korean Ethnographic Museum: Central District, Pyongyang; Curator JON MOON JIN.

Korean Revolutionary Museum: Central District, Pyongyang; history from second half of 19th century to the present; Dir HWANG SUN HUI.

Memorial Museum of the War of Liberation: Moranbong District, Pyongyang; history from second half of the 19th century to the present; Dir THAE PYONG RYOL.

Shinchon county

Shinchon Museum: Shinchon County, South Hwanghae Province; Curator PAK IN CHAIK.

Shinuiju

Shinuiju Historical Museum: Shinuiju, North Pyongan Province; Curator PAK YONG GWAN.

Wonsan

Wonsan Historical Museum: Wonsan, Kangwon Province; Curator JO GANG BAIK.

Universities and Colleges

KIM IL SUNG UNIVERSITY

Daesong District, Pyongyang
Telephone: 54946

Founded 1946
State control
Academic year: September to August

President: SONG JA RIP
Vice-Presidents: CHOE JAND RYONG, JO CHOL, KIM IL GWANG, O KIL BANG, PAEK CHOL, PAEK JAE UK, RI JAE MYON, RI SONG CHOL, RO SONG CHAN

Number of teachers: 2,000
Number of students: 12,000

Publication: Publications: natural science magazine, social science magazine

Faculties of history, philosophy, economics, law, religion, foreign literature, geography, geology, physics and mathematics, chemistry, biology, atomic energy, computer science.

ATTACHED RESEARCH INSTITUTES

Computer Science College: Dir KIM YONG JUN.

Doctoral Institute: Dir HAN YONG GU.

Literature College: Dir UN JONG SOP.

Kim Chaek University of Technology: Waesong District, Pyongyang; faculties of geology, mining, metallurgy, mechanical and electrical engineering, shipbuilding, electronics, nuclear technology; Pres. HONG SO HON.

Kim Hyong-Jik University of Education: Pyongyang; f. 1946; Faculties of revolutionary history, pedagogy, history and geography, language and literature, foreign languages, mathematics, physics, biology, music, fine arts, physical education; 2,500 students; 5-year degree course, short-term courses for teachers, correspondence and post-graduate courses; Pres. HONG IL CHON.

Pyongyang University of Agriculture: Pyongyang; f. 1981; depts of fruit and vegetable cultivation, stockbreeding, poultry; Pres. CHON SI GON.

Pyongyang University of Medicine: Woesong District, Pyongyang; Pres. RI WON GIL;

There are colleges of higher and professional education (engineering, agriculture, fisheries, teacher training) situated in all the main towns; there are also Factory (Engineering) Colleges.

REPUBLIC OF KOREA

The Higher Education System

The country's oldest institutions of higher education were founded during the final years of the Joseon dynasty (1392–1910), among them Yonsei and Paichai Universities (both founded 1885), Ewha Women's University (founded 1886), Korea University (founded 1905; formerly Posung College) and Dongguk University (founded 1906). Several were established during the early years of the Japanese occupation of the Korean peninsula (1910–45), including Jinju National University (founded 1910), Seoul Theological College (founded 1911), Chung-Ang University (founded 1918) and Miryang National University (founded 1923). Consequently, the Korean education system at all levels displayed strong Japanese influences. Following the Allied defeat of Japan in 1945 Korea was divided at latitude 38°N into military occupation zones, with Soviet forces in the north and US forces in the south. In 1948 the US-administered south became the independent Republic of Korea, while the Democratic People's Republic of Korea was proclaimed in the Soviet-administered north. A three-year war between north and south ended in 1953, and the two countries remain divided at the cease-fire line, separated by a UN-supervised demilitarized zone. Post-1945 education became influenced by the US system and from 1945 has been structured with six years of primary education, six years of secondary education and four years of higher education. A consequence of military control from the 1960s, and particularly during the 1980s, was that specialized and technical education became more respected than the general cultural knowledge traditionally held in high esteem. In recent years a high value has been placed upon scientific education, which resulted in South Korea becoming one of the world's most technologically advanced countries by the 1980s.

Higher education consists of seven types of institution: Junior Colleges, Colleges and Universities, Broadcast and Correspondence Universities, Industrial Universities, Universities of Education, Technical Colleges and miscellaneous colleges. Junior Colleges are distinguished from the other types of institutions by the fact that they do not offer four-year undergraduate Bachelors degree programmes. Instead, they offer two- to three-year mainly technical and professionally-oriented programmes. Junior Colleges are regulated by the Korean Council for College Education. The remaining six types of institution are grouped under the term Colleges and Universities, and are coordinated by the Korean Council for University Education (KCUE). The acronym 'SKY' is used to denote the three most prestigious universities: Seoul National University, Korea University and Yonsei University. In 2005 there were 853,089 students enrolled at 158 junior colleges; 1,859,639 at 173 universities and colleges; and 282,225 at 1,051 graduate schools.

Since 1993 the US-style College Scholastic Aptitude Test has been the main basis for admission to higher education. Applicants are also assessed on their scholastic record and institutions may set their own entrance examination. The College Scholastic Aptitude Test is administered by the Institute of Curriculum and Evaluation. The main undergraduate degree is the four-year Bachelors (Haksa), although programmes in professional disciplines such as dentistry and medicine last up to six years. Degrees are awarded on the basis of the US-style 'credit semester' system, and students usually need to accrue 140 credits for award of the Bachelors, of which 35 must be in a designated 'major' subject. The postgraduate (or graduate) Masters (Suksa) and Doctorate (Paksa) degrees are offered primarily by university graduate schools. The Masters lasts two years and requires 24–36 credits, the Doctorate two years and 36 credits. Junior colleges, specialist vocational and technical schools are the leading institutions of vocational and technical education. Students usually work towards a vocational qualification and then sit the examination for the National Technical Certificate.

Learned Societies

GENERAL

Korea Foundation: Seocho POB 227, Diplomatic Center Building 1376-1 Seocho 2-dong Seocho-gu, Seoul 137-072; tel. (2) 3463-5600; fax (2) 3463-6086; e-mail webmaster@kf.or.kr; internet www.kf.or.kr; f. 1992 (fmrly Int. Cultural Soc. of Korea); promotes mutual understanding and friendship between Korea and the rest of the world; 60 mems; library of 8,000 vols; Pres. LEE IN-HO; publs *Koreana* (4 a year in English and Chinese), *Korea Focus* (6 a year, in English).

National Academy of Sciences: San-94, Panpo-dong, Seocho-gu, Seoul 137-044; tel. (2) 534-0737; fax (2) 537-3183; e-mail academ@nas.go.kr; internet www.nas.go.kr; f. 1954; 150 mems; library of 15,000 vols; Pres. Dr HO WANG LEE; Sec.-Gen. YOUNG SEON CHUNG; publs *NAS Annual Bulletin* (in Korean), *Journal of NAS* (in Korean, annually), *Proceedings of the International Symposium* (in Korean, annually), *NAS Bulletin* (in English, every 2 years), *Development of Science Study in Korea* (in Korean, annually).

Royal Asiatic Society, Korea Branch: CPO Box 255, Seoul; tel. (2) 763-9483; fax (2) 766-3796; f. 1900 to encourage interest in, and promote study and dissemination of knowledge about the arts, history, literature and customs of Korea and the neighbouring countries; 1,600 mems; library: reference library of 1,000 vols; Gen. Man. SUE J. BAE; publ. *Transactions* (annually).

AGRICULTURE, FISHERIES AND VETERINARY SCIENCE

Korean Forestry Society: C/o Department of Forest Resources, Seoul National University, Suwon, Kyonggido 441-744; tel. (331) 290-2330; f. 1960 to foster the study of all aspects of forestry, to promote co-operation among members; 800 mems; Pres. Prof. JONG HWA YOUN; Sec. Assoc. Prof. JOO SANG CHUNG; publ. *Journal* (quarterly).

BIBLIOGRAPHY, LIBRARY SCIENCE AND MUSEOLOGY

Korean Library Association: San 60-1, Banpo-dong, Seocho-gu, Seoul 137-702; tel. (2) 535-4868; fax (2) 535-5616; e-mail klanet@hitel.net; internet www.korla.or.kr; f. 1945; a social and academic institution comprising all the libraries and librarians in Korea; 1,115 institutional, 1,865 individual mems; Pres. KI-NAM SHIN; Exec.-Dir KYUNG-KU LEE; publs *KLA Bulletin* (6 a year), *Statistics on Libraries in Korea* (annually).

Korean Research and Development Library Association: Room 0411, KIST Library, POB 131, Cheongryang, Seoul; tel. 967-3692; fax (82) 2963-4013; f. 1979; Pres. KE HONG PARK; Sec. KEON TAK OH.

ECONOMICS, LAW AND POLITICS

Korean Association of Sinology: c/o Asiatic Research Center, Korea University, Anam-dong, Seoul; f. 1955; 100 mems; Chair. JUN-YOP KIM; publ. *Journal of Chinese Studies*.

Korean Economic Association: 45, 4–ga, Namdae-mun-ro, Chung-gu, Seoul; tel. (2) 757-9738; fax (2) 775-5505; e-mail kea1952@kea.ne.kr; internet www.kea.ne.kr; f. 1952; theory, policy and history of economics and business administration; 2,800 mems; library of 3,000 vols; Pres. PYUNG-JOO KIM; Sec.-Gen. JOON-WOO NAHM; publ. *Korean Economic Review* (2 a year).

FINE AND PERFORMING ARTS

Music Association of Korea: Building 1-117, Dongsung-dong, Chongro-gu, Seoul; f. 1961; to develop Korean national music and to promote and protect Korean musicians; organizes concerts, encourages musical composition and nation-wide singing, is active in the international musical exchange and in music education; awards the Prize of Musical Culture; 700 mems; small library; Pres. Dr TAI JOON PARK; Sec. DAE YUP SOHN.

HISTORY, GEOGRAPHY AND ARCHAEOLOGY

Korean Geographical Society: Dept of Geography, College of Social Sciences, Seoul National University, Seoul 151-746; tel. (2) 875-1463; fax (2) 876-2853; e-mail kgeos@hanmail.net; internet society.kordic.re.kr/~kgs/korindex.html; f. 1945 to promote mutual co-operation in academic work and international understanding; 772 individual mems, 69 institutional mems; Pres. WOO-KUNG HUH; Sec.-Gen. YONG-CHUL SHIN; publ. *Journal* (5 a year).

LANGUAGE AND LITERATURE

Alliance Française: 63-2, Hoehyun-dong 1-ga, Jung-gu, POB 9412, Seoul 100-051; tel. (2) 755-5702; fax (2) 774-4252; e-mail alliance@nuri.net; internet www.afcoree.co.kr; offers courses and exams in French language and culture and promotes cultural exchange with France; attached teaching centres in Busan, Chonju, Daegu, Daejon, Gwangju, Jeonju; Dir RÉGIS CRISTIN.

British Council: 4th Fl., Hungkuk Life Insurance Bldg, 226 Shinmunro 1-ga, Jongro-gu, Seoul 110-786; tel. (2) 3702-0600; fax (2) 3702-0660; e-mail info@britishcouncil.or.kr; internet www.bckorea.or.kr; teaching centre; offers courses and exams in English language and British culture and promotes cultural exchange with the UK; Dir SHOBA PONNAPPA.

Goethe-Institut: 339-1, Huam-dong, Yongsan-ku, Seoul 140-901; tel. (2) 754-9831; fax (2) 754-9834; e-mail giseoul@seoul.goethe.org; internet www.goethe.de/os/seo/deindex.htm; offers courses and exams in German language and culture and promotes cultural exchange with Germany; library of 12,000 vols; Dir DR UWE SCHMELTER.

MEDICINE

Korean Medical Association: CPO Box 2062, Seoul; tel. (02) 794-2474; fax (02) 792-1296; e-mail intl@kma.org; internet www.kma.org; f. 1908; to develop the medical sciences and medical education by encouraging research and investigation; 59,292 mems; library of 10,000 vols; Pres. KWANG-SU HAN; publs *Journal* (monthly), *The KMA News* (2 a week).

PHILOSOPHY AND PSYCHOLOGY

Korean Psychological Association: Dept of Psychology, Seoul National University, Shinrim 2-dong, Kwanak-gu, Seoul; tel. 877-0101, ext. 2528; f. 1946; 420 mems; Pres. BONGYUN SUH; Sec. Gen. JUNGOH KIM; publs *Korean Journal of Psychology* (2 a year), *Korean Journal of Clinical Psychology* (2 a year), *Korean Journal of Social Psychology*, *Korean Journal of Industrial Psychology*, *Korean Journal of Developmental Psychology* (all annually).

Research Institutes

GENERAL

Academy of Korean Studies: 50 Unjung-dong, Songnam-si, Pundang-gu, Kyonggi-do 463-791; tel. (342) 709-8111; fax (342) 709-1531; f. 1978 to research and re-evaluate traditional Korean culture; library of 361,000 vols incl. 35,000 in Western languages; Pres. LEE YOUNG-DUG; publ. *Chongsin Munhwa/Academy News* (3–4 a year).

AGRICULTURE, FISHERIES AND VETERINARY SCIENCE

Rural Development Administration: 250 Seodun-dong, Kwonsun-ku, Suwon 441-707; tel. (31) 299-2200; fax (31) 299-2469; internet www.rda.go.kr; f. 1906 to carry out agricultural research and rural community development; 11 subordinate research organizations, 9 provincial offices, 34 regional specialized crop stations; library of 190,000 vols; Administrator MOO-NAM CHUNG; publs *Annual Research Report* (Korean and English editions), *Research and Extension* (in Korean, monthly), *Agricultural Technology* (in Korean, monthly).

ECONOMICS, LAW AND POLITICS

Korea Development Institute: POB 113, Cheongryang, Seoul 131-012; tel. 958-4114; fax 961-5092; internet www.kdiux.kdi.re.kr; f. 1971 to help determine the basic direction of the nation's development by formulating long-term goals and strategies based on accurate economic analysis; to conduct policy-oriented research relating to individual sectors of the economy that will help the country to maintain high economic growth with price stability; to provide consultation on policy issues relating to short-term economic management and planning; library of 100,000 vols, 39,000 research reports, govt documents, also data bank; Pres. JIN SOON LEE; publs *KDI Journal of Economic Policy* (quarterly, in Korean), *KDI Economic Outlook* (quarterly, in Korean).

Korea Institute for Industrial Economics and Trade (KIET): POB 205, Chongryang-ri, Seoul; tel. 962-6211-8; fax 963-8540; f. 1976; advises govt on industrial, trade and commercial policies; analyses Korean industry, int. economies, new technology and promotion of trade; library of 45,000 vols, 1,500 periodicals; Pres. KYU UCK LEE; publs *KIET Real Economy* (every 2 weeks), *Journal of Industrial Competitiveness* (annually), *KIET Economic Outlook* (2 a year).

Korean Research Center: 228 Pyong-dong, Chongno-gu, Seoul; f. 1956; research in social sciences; library; Pres. MUNAM CHON; publs *Journal of Social Sciences and Humanities*, *Korean Studies Series*.

EDUCATION

Korean Educational Development Institute: 92–6 Umyeon-dong, Seocho-gu, Seoul 137-791; tel. (2) 3460-0216; fax (2) 3460-0156; e-mail oirc@kedi.re.kr; internet eng.kedi.re.kr; f. 1972; independent, government-funded research and development institute; undertakes research and development activities on education; assists government in formulation of educational policies and in long-term development of education; library of 121,197 vols, 88 periodicals, 499,018 microfiches; Pres. Dr HYUNG-YEEL KOH; publs *KEDI Journal of Education Policy* (in English, 2 a year), *KEDI Newsletter* (in English, 2 a year), *Research Abstracts* (in English, annually), *Statistical Yearbook of Education* (in Korean and English, annually).

National Institute for Training of Educational Administrators: C/o Ministry of Education 77, Sejong-ro, Chongro-ku, Seoul 110-760; tel. (2) 733-2741; fax (2) 733-0149; f. 1970; government institute; attached to Ministry of Education; library of 21,000 vols; Dir CHONG-TAEK CHANG.

NATURAL SCIENCES

Physical Sciences

Korea Meteorological Administration: 460-18 Sindaebang-dong, Dongjak-gu, Seoul 156-720; tel. (2) 836-2385; fax (2) 836-2386; internet www.kma.go.kr; under the control of the Ministry of Science and Technology; Dir H. J. SON; publ. monthly and annual meteorological reports.

PHILOSOPHY AND PSYCHOLOGY

Korean Institute for Research in the Behavioural Sciences: 1606-3 Socho-Dong, Kangnam-gu, Seoul 137-071; tel. 581-8611; f. 1968; basic and applied research in five areas: social, child, learning, organization, and psychological testing; 70 researchers; library of 5,000 vols; Dir SUNG JIN LEE; publs *Research Bulletin*, *Research Notes*, *Research Monograph*.

TECHNOLOGY

Electronics and Telecommunications Research Institute (ETRI): 161 Gaejong-dong, Yuseong-gu, Daejeon City 305-350; tel. (860) 6114; fax (861) 1033; f. 1976; undertakes research and development in field of advanced information technology; library of 40,000 vols, 30,000 technical reports, and ETLARS databases; Pres. CHU-HWAN YIM; publs include, *Weekly Technology Trends* (weekly), *ETRI Journal* (quarterly), *Electronics and Telecommunications Trends* (quarterly), *Patent Announcement* (every 2 weeks), *Patent Information* (monthly).

Korea Atomic Energy Research Institute (KAERI): POB 105, Yu-Seong, Taejon 305-600; tel. 868-2000; fax 868-2702; f. 1959; reactor-related research and development, security and R&D of nuclear fuel, nuclear policy research, radiation application technology development and research and treatment of nuclear radiation, nuclear personnel training and other aspects of nuclear energy; library of 61,000 vols, 700,000 technical reports and 950 periodicals; Pres. SEONG-YUN KIM; publs *Won Woo* (6 a year), *Annual Report*, *KAERI Research Papers* (annually), *Journal*, etc.

Korea Institute of Energy and Research: POB 5, Taedok Science Town, Taejon 305-343; tel. (42) 861-9700; fax (42) 861-6224; f. 1977 to conduct research on energy and technology; supported by Ministry of Science and Technology; 500 mems; library of 30,000 vols; Pres. P. CHUNG MOO AUH; publs *Energy R&D*, *Technical Trends on NRSE*, *Annual Report*.

Korea Institute of Science and Technology (KIST): 39-1 Hawolkok-dong, Songbuk-ku, Seoul; tel. (2) 958-6114; fax (2) 958-5478; f. 1966; research in applied science, chemical engineering, polymer engineering, materials science and engineering, mechanical and control systems, electronics and information technology, environment and CFC alternatives technology, systems engineering, genetic engineering, science and technology policy; library of 50,000 vols, 15,000 technical reports; Pres. Dr WON HOON PARK; publs *Newsletter* (Korean, every 2 weeks), *KIST2000 Newsletter* (Korean, every 2 weeks), *Collection of Abstracts* (Korean and English, annually).

Libraries and Archives

Pusan

Pusan National University Library: 30 Jangjeon-dong, Keumjeong-gu, Pusan 609-735; tel. (51) 510-1800; fax (51) 513-9787; f. 1946; 650,000 vols, 5,000 periodicals; Dir DONG-HYUN JUNG.

Seoul

Chung-Ang University Library: 221 Huk-suk-dong, Dongjak-ku, Seoul; f. 1949; 442,667 vols; Dir Too Young Lee.

Dongguk University Library: 263-ga, Pil-dong, Seoul; f. 1906; Buddhist and Oriental studies; 350,000 vols, 1,100 periodicals; Dir Dr Bo Hwan Kim.

Ewha Woman's University Library: 11–1, Daehyun-dong, Sudaemun-gu, Seoul 120-750; tel. 3277-3124; fax 3277-2857; e-mail jnam@mm.ewha.ac.kr; internet lib.ewha.ac.kr; f. 1923; 1,720,471 vols; Dir Bong Hee Kim.

Government Archives and Records Service: 117 Chansong-dong, Chongno-gu, Seoul 110-034; tel. 720-4415; fax 739-8944; f. 1969; 336,275 vols, 1,188,226 diagrams, 1,539,666 cards, 181,311 rolls of microfilm; 740,463 audiovisual items; collection of records of the Yi dynasty; Archivist Sun-Young Kim.

Korea University Library: 1 Anam-dong, Sungbuk-gu, Seoul 136-701; tel. (2) 3290-1472; fax (2) 924-0751; f. 1937; 400,132 vols; Dir Hwa-Young Kim.

National Assembly Library: 1 Yoido-dong, Seoul; tel. 784-3565; fax 788-4193; f. 1952; library service for members of the National Assembly, the Executive, the Judiciary, and for scholars and legislative research activities and int. book exchange with 360 institutions worldwide; 900,000 vols, 12,101 current periodicals, 700 newspapers; Librarian Chong-Il Park; publs *National Assembly Library Review* (monthly), *Index to Korean-Language Periodicals* (every 2 months and annually), *Acquisitions List* (annually), *Index to National Assembly Debates* (irregular), *Index to Korean Laws and Statutes* (2 a year), *Issue Briefs* (irregular), *Legislative Information Analysis* (quarterly), *List of Theses for the Doctor's and Master's Degree in Korea* (annually).

National Library of Korea: 60–1, Panpo-Dong, Seocho-gu, Seoul 137-702; tel. (2) 590-0544; fax (2) 590-0546; e-mail nlkpc@www.nl.go.kr; internet www.nl.go.kr; f. 1945; 3,889,298 vols; legal deposit library for Korean publications, ISBN, ISSN nat. centre, KOLIS-NET (Korean Library Information System Network) centre, international exchange, research in library and information science, publishes nat. bibliographies, operates National Digital Library (www.dlibrary.go.kr) and training centre for librarians; Dir Gi-Young Jeong; publ. *Doseogwan* (4 a year).

Seoul National University Library: San 56-1, Shillim-dong, Kwanak-gu, Seoul 151-742; tel. (2) 880-5284; fax (2) 871-2972; f. 1946; 2,077,000 vols, 13,000 periodicals, incl. Agricultural Library (121,000 vols), Medical Library (123,000 vols), Law Library (65,000 vols), Business Library (11,000 vols), Social Sciences Library (20,000 vols), Dental Library (9,000 vols) and Kyujang-gak Archives (special collection on Choseon Dynasty, 152,000 vols); collections on the arts, sciences, law, education, music, medicine, engineering, economics and commerce; Dir Kyo-Hun Chin; publs *Library Newsletter* (2 a year), *Kyujang-gak* (annually), *Ko-munseo* (annually).

Transport Library: 168, 2-ka, Bongnae-dong, Seoul; f. 1920; 32,000 vols; Dir Cho Woo Hyun; Chief Librarian Kim Doo Ho; publ. *Korean National Railroad Bulletin* (monthly).

United Nations Depository Library: Korea University, 1 An-Am-dong, Sungbuk-gu, Seoul; tel. (2) 3290-1492; fax (2) 922-4633; e-mail mgc@kulib.korea.ac.kr; f. 1957; 38,000 vols; Dir Hwa-Young Kim; Librarian Mi-Gyoung Cho.

Yonsei University Library: Yonsei University, 134 Sinchon-dong, Sudaemoon-gu, Seoul; tel. 361-3308; f. 1915; 1,538,000 vols including Korean archives, 10,700 periodicals; Dir Jong Chul Han; publs *Dong Bang Hak Chi* (Journal of Korean Studies), *Inmun Kwahak* (Journal of Humanities), *International Journal of Korean Studies*, *Journal of East and West Studies*, *Kyo Yuk Non Jib* (Journal of Education), *Yonsei Non-Chong* (Journal of Graduate School), *Yonsei Social Science Review*, *Abstracts of Faculty Research Report*, *Yonsei Magazine*.

Taegu

Kyungpook National University Library: 1370, Sankyuk-dong, Puk-ku, Taegu 702-701; tel. (53) 950-6510; fax (53) 950-6533; e-mail cmseo@knu.ac.kr; internet kudos.knu.ac.kr; f. 1952; 2,115,000 vols; Dir Seo, Jong-moon.

Museums and Art Galleries

Pusan

Pusan National University Museum: Pusan; Korean archaeology with special collection of historical remains of Kyongsang-Namdo province, arts, ethnology, etc.; Dir Prof. Suk-Hee Kim; publ. *Research Reports* (irregular).

Seoul

National Museum of Contemporary Art: Deoksugung, 5-1 Jeong-Dung, Jung-gu, Seoul 100-120.

National Museum of Korea: 1 Sejong-ro, Chongno-gu, Seoul; tel. (2) 720-2714; fax (2) 734-7255; f. 1908; Korean archaeology, culture and folklore; *c.* 100,000 artefacts representing over 5,000 years of human endeavour on the Korean peninsula; education centre; library: *c.* 20,000 vols; brs in 8 other towns; Dir-Gen. Yang-Mo Chung; publs *Report of Researches of Antiquities*, *Misul Charyo* (Materials in Art, 2 a year), *Bakmulkwan Sinmun* (Museum News, monthly).

National Science Museum: 2 Waryong-dong, Chongno-gu, Seoul 110; tel. 762-5209; f. 1926; holds National Science Fair, exhibitions, science classrooms, film service, etc.; library of 2,000 vols on science and technology; Dir Chi-Eun Kim; publ. *Bulletin*.

Seoul National University Museum: San 56–1, Sinlim-dong, Kwanak-gu, Seoul 151-742; tel. (2) 874-5693; fax (2) 874-3999; f. 1941; exhibition of Korean culture totalling 8,058 artefacts; library specializing in Korean archaeology, art history, anthropology and folklore; Dir Dr Nak-kyu Park; publ. *Bulletin* (annually).

Yonsei University Museum: Shinchon-dong, Sudaemun-gu, Seoul; f. 1965; research; prehistory, history, fine arts, ethnic customs, medicine, geology, etc.; Dir Prof. Whang Won-Koo; publs occasional papers, excavation reports.

Universities

AJOU UNIVERSITY

5 Wonchun-Dong, Yeongtong-Gu, Suwon 443-749

Telephone: (2) 231-7121

Internet: www.ajou.ac.kr

Founded 1973

President: Jae Yoon Park
Registrar: Joon Yop Kim
Librarian: Jae Suk Lee

Library of 230,000 vols
Number of teachers: 750
Number of students: 10,954

Colleges of engineering, business administration, natural sciences, medicine, social sciences, humanities; graduate school.

ANDONG NATIONAL UNIVERSITY

388 Songcheon-dong, Angong, Kyung-buk 460-380

Telephone: (55) 1661

Internet: www.andong.ac.kr

Founded 1979

President: Kim Yub
Registrar: Kim Jong-sik
Librarian: Ku Sang-man

Library of 55,000 vols
Number of teachers: 113
Number of students: 2,900

HEADS OF DEPARTMENTS

Korean: Sir Bo-woul
Sino-Korean Literature: Kim Sar-han
History: Kim Ho-jong
Folklore: Chang Chul-soo
Oriental Philosophy: Oh Suk-won
Law: Kwon Yeong-jun
Public Administration: Lee Byung-kap
Business Administration: Choi Sung-ki
International Trade: Rhee Sang-chool
Accounting: Sir Yong-su
Physics: Sohn Yeon-kyu
Chemistry: Yeh Jin-hae
Biology: Lee Hee-moo
Computer Science and Statistics: Cha Young-joon
Home Economics: Choi Yong-ok
Food Economics: Yoon Suk-kyung
National Ethics Education: Yi Chong-kyun
English: Kim Yang-su
Mathematics: Kim Si-joo
Music: Cho In-chan
Fine Arts: Song Ki-suk
Physical Education: Kim Cheong-han
General Education: Pak Chae-uk

CATHOLIC UNIVERSITY OF KOREA

Songeui Campus, 505 Banpo-dong, Socho-gu, Seoul 137-701
Songsin Campus, 90-1 Hyehwa-dong, Chongro-gu, Seoul 110-758
Songsim Campus, 43-1 Yokkok 2-dong, Wonmi-gu, Puchon City, Kyonggi-do 420-743

Telephone: (2) 740-9714
Fax: (2) 741-2801
E-mail: webmaster@catholic.ac.kr
Internet: www.cuk.ac.kr

Founded 1995 by merger of Catholic University (f. *c.* 1984 from existing colleges) and Songsim Women's University (f. 1957)

President: Most Rev. Peter Kang

Number of teachers: 914

Library of 160,000
Number of students: 8,075 (6,772 undergraduate, 1,303 postgraduate)

Publication: Catholic Theology and Thoughts (annually)

Songeui Campus: incl. Colleges of Medicine, and Nursing; Graduate Schools of Occupational Health, and Health Management. Songsin Campus: incl. College of Theology. Songsim Campus: incl. Colleges of Humanities, Social Sciences, Science and Technology, and Human Ecology.

CATHOLIC UNIVERSITY OF TAEGU-HYOSUNG

330 Kumnak 1-ri, Hayang-up, Kyongsan-shi, Kyongbuk 712-702
Telephone: (53) 850-3001
Fax: (53) 850-3600
E-mail: presid@cuth.cataegu.ac.kr
Internet: www.cataegu.ac.kr

Founded 1995 as a result of merger of Hyosung Women's University and Taegu Catholic University
Private control
President: SOO-EUP KIM
Library of 410,000 vols
Number of teachers: 780
Number of students: 11,132
Publications: *Research Bulletin* (annually), *University Bulletin* (annually)
Colleges of Humanities, Theology, Foreign Studies, Natural Sciences, Engineering, Medicine, Social Sciences, Law and Politics, Economics and Commerce, Home Economics, Pharmacy, Education, Music, and Fine Arts.

CHANGWON NATIONAL UNIVERSITY

9 Sarim-dong, Changwon, Kyongnam 641-773
Telephone: (551) 279-7000
Fax: (551) 283-2970
E-mail: webmaster@sarim.changwon.ac.kr
Internet: www.changwon.ac.kr

Founded 1969 as Masan Junior College of Education; became Changwon National College 1984; present name 1991
President: Dr SOO-O LEE.

CHEJU NATIONAL UNIVERSITY

Chejudaehakno 66, Cheju, Cheju-do 690-756
Telephone: (64) 754-2114
Fax: (64) 755-6130
E-mail: cnu@cheju.ac.krr
Internet: www.cheju.ac.kr

Founded 1952 as Cheju Provincial Junior College; became Cheju National College 1962; present name 1982
Academic year: March to February
President: Dr CHUNG-SUK KOH
Number of teachers: 500
Number of students: 10,000.

CHEONGJU UNIVERSITY

36 Naedok-dong, Sangdang-ku, Chongju 360-764
Telephone: (43) 229-8114
Fax: (43) 229-8110
Internet: www.cheongju.ac.kr

Founded 1946 as Chongju Commercial College; became Chongju College 1951; present name 1981
President: KIM YOON BAE.

CHEONGJU NATIONAL UNIVERSITY OF EDUCATION

135 Sugok-Dong, Heung Duk-Gu, Cheongju, Chungbuk 361-712
Telephone: (43) 279-0800
Fax: (43) 279-0797
Internet: www.chongju-e.ac.kr

Founded 1941
President: YONG-WOO LIM
Library of 100,000 vols
Departments of Ethics Education, Korean Education, Social Studies, Mathematics, Science, Physical Education, Music, Fine Arts, Practical Arts; Graduate School of Education.

CHONBUK NATIONAL UNIVERSITY

664-14 Deogjin-dong 1-ka, Chonju 561-756, Chonbuk
Telephone: 70-2114
Fax: 0652-70-2188
Internet: www.chonbuk.ac.kr

Founded 1947
State control
Academic year: March to February (two semesters)
President: Dr MYUNG SOO CHANG
Library Director: JIN KON OH
Library of 385,000 vols
Number of teachers: 800
Number of students: 24,000
Publications: *The Chonbuk University Newspaper*, *The Chonbuk University Herald* (weekly), *Chonbuk National University Bulletin* (annually), annual bulletins of research institutes

VICE-PRESIDENTS

Academic Affairs: YEONG CHUL KIM
Student Affairs: EUNG KYO RYU
Research and Development: JEONG KEUN PARK
Graduate School: SUN YUNG CHO
Graduate School of Agricultural Development: SUNG YUN KANG
Graduate School of Business Administration: SUNG WOO HYUNG
Graduate School of Education: GWANG HYUN CHOI
Graduate School of Public Administration: YOUNG MIN HEO
Graduate School of Environmental Studies: JE BIN IM
Graduate School of Industrial Technology: SUK PYO HONG
College of Engineering: CHUL RO YU
College of Agriculture: JAI SIK HONG
College of Humanities: YOUNG CHUEL KIM
College of Law: KYU SUK SUH
College of Social Science: JAE YOUNG KIM
College of Education: SEUNG TAI PARK
College of Commerce: YEONG HEE CHEONG
College of Natural Science: CHOON HO LEE
Medical School: NO SUK KI
College of Dentistry: CHAN UN PARK
College of Arts: KYE IL SONG
College of Veterinary Medicine: JOO MOOK LEE
College of Home Economics: KEUM SODU CHI

DIRECTORS

Language Research Institute: KYU TAE CHO
Research Institute of Agricultural Development: SUN YOUNG CHOI
Institute of Local Government and Autonomy: CHEOL JONG RYU
Social Science Research Institute: SOON GOO CHO
Institute of Basic Science: KWANG HO SO
Institute of Science Education: SEUK BEUM KO
Institute of Social Education: DAE WOON CHANG
Research Institute of Engineering Technology: HAK SHIN KIM
Institute for Medical Science: HONG BAI EUN
Research Institute of Urban and Environmental Studies: EUNG KYO RYU
Laboratory of Electronics Industry and Development: SUNG JOONG KIM
Research Institute of Semiconductors: HYUNG JAE LEE
Research Institute of Sports Science: SANG JONG LEE
Institute of Rural Development: DONG HO LEE
Cholla Cultural Research Centre: HEE KWON LEE
Institute of Advanced Materials Development: CHONG KYO KIM
Biosafety Research Institute: BYUNG MOO LIM
Institute for Molecular Biology and Genetics: KWANG YEOP JANG
American Studies Research Institute: JANG RYUNG KIM
Research Institute of Law: KYU SUK SUH
Research Institute of Industry and Economy: SEUNG KI PARK
Electric and Electronic Circuit and Systems Research Institute: DONG YONG KIM
Research Institute of Communist Countries: WON HO YOON
Information Industry Research Institute: OK BAE CHANG
Humanities Research Institute: KANG JE KWAK
Institute of Animal Research and Development: WON JIB SHIN
Institute of Dental Science: EUN CHUNG JHEE

HEADS OF DEPARTMENTS

College of Agriculture:

- Agricultural Biology: HYUNG MOO KIM
- Agricultural Chemistry: YOUNG HEE MOON
- Agricultural Economics: DONG HO LEE
- Agricultural Engineering: JAE YOUNG LEE
- Engineering of Agricultural Machinery: CHUL SOO KIM
- Agronomy: SUNG YOUNG CHOI
- Animal Science: WON JIB SHIN
- Food Science and Technology: DONG HWA SHIN
- Forest Products and Technology: CHEOL SOO HAN
- Forest Resources: KAE HWAN KIM
- Horticulture: JAE CHEOL KIM
- Landscape Architecture: SEI CHEON KIM

College of Arts:

- Korean Music: HEOI CHUN CHUNG
- Dance: WON KIM
- Fine Arts: SEUNG TAEG LIM
- Industrial Design: CHONG KI KIM
- Music: HYUN JIN KIM

College of Commerce:

- Accounting: JAE DUCK CHA
- Business Administration: SANG MAN LEE
- Economics: SEUNG KI PARK
- International Trade: NAK PIL CHOI

College of Dentistry:

- Dentistry: KWANG JOON KOH

College of Education:

- Biology Education: MU YEOL KIM
- Chemistry Education: SEUK BEUM KO
- Earth Science Education: CHUL HEE KIM
- Education: DONG HO SO
- English Language Education: BYEONG HWA JEONG
- Arts Education: IN HYUN PARK
- German Language Education: MUN HI YI
- Home Economics Education: HEE SOOK SOHN
- Korean Language Education: BONG GEUN KANG
- Mathematics Education: SANG CHEOL LEE
- Music Education: JE HYUN PARK
- National Ethics Education: CHANG SOON CHOI
- Physical Education: KIL HWAN JUNG
- Social Science Education: HEE HWAN LEE

College of Engineering:

- Aerospace Engineering: SHIN JAE KANG
- Architectural Engineering: YANG SEOB SOH
- Chemical Engineering: KI JU KIM
- Chemical Technology: DAI SOO LEE
- Civil Engineering: JU SEONG BAE
- Computer Engineering: YOUNG CHON KIM
- Control Instrumentation Engineering: SUNG JOONG KIM
- Electrical Engineering: DONG YONG KIM
- Electronic Engineering: HEUNG KI BAIK
- Environmental Engineering: CHAN HEE WON

Industrial Engineering: DONG WON KIM
Information and Telecommunications Engineering: MOON HO LEE
Mechanical Design: JAE KYOO LIM
Mechanical Engineering: YOUNG TAIG OH
Metallurgical Engineering: DONG KEON KIM
Materials Engineering: BOK HEE KIM
Mining and Mineral Resources Engineering: SEUNG GON KIM
Polymer Science and Technology: JOHNG MOON LEE
Precision Engineering: TAE YOUNG KIM
Textile Engineering: PYONG KI PARK

College of Humanities:
Korean Language and Literature: JEONG KU CHON
English Language and Literature: SOO GIL KIM
French Language and Literature: YOUNG KYUNG CHOU
Chinese Language and Literature: YOUNG JUN CHOI
German Language and Literature: CHO WANG JEONG
Japanese Language and Literature: CHANG KEE PARK
Spanish Language and Literature: NAK WON CHOI
Archaelogy and Anthropology: POOK KIM
History: GIL WON KANG
Philosophy: JEON KYU PARK

College of Law:
Civil Law: YOUNG MIN HEO
Private Law: JAI KIL CHUNG
Public Law: YANG KYUN SHIN

College of Natural Science:
Biology: GOOK HYUN CHUNG
Chemistry: IN HO CHO
Computer Science: YUNG SUNG KIM
Statistics: KYUNG SOO HAN
Geology: JUNG HOO LEE
Mathematics: YANG KOHN KIM
Molecular Biology: CHUNG UNG PARK
Physics: CHAI HO RIM
Preliminary course in Medicine: WON KU LEE
Preliminary course in Dentistry: HWA SIN PARK

College of Social Science:
Journalism and Communication: JOON MANN KANG
Political Science and Diplomacy: CHEOL JONG RYU
Psychology: HYUCK CHEL KWON
Public Administration: IN JAE KANG
Social Welfare: WON KYU CHOI
Sociology: HARK SERB CHUNG

College of Veterinary Medicine:
Veterinary Medicine: IN HYUK CHOI

Medical School:
Medicine: MOO SAM LEE
Nursing: MYUNG JA KIM

College of Home Economics:
Home Management: (vacant)
Clothing and Textiles: (vacant)

CHONNAM NATIONAL UNIVERSITY

300 Yongbong-dong, Puk-Gu, Kwangju 500-757
Telephone: (62) 530-0114
Fax: (62) 530-1015
E-mail: admiss@altair.chonnam.ac.kr
Internet: www.chonnam.ac.kr

Founded 1952
State control
Language of instruction: Korean
Academic year: March to February (two semesters)

President: Dr CHUNG SEOK-JONG
Dean of Academic Affairs: Dr JONG MOK LEE
Dean of Student Affairs: Dr JUNG MOOK YOON
Dean of Planning and Research: Dr SUNG SOO PARK
Librarian: Dr YOON JUNG HAN

Library of 600,000 vols, 6,000 periodicals
Number of teachers: 2,435
Number of students: 24,000

Publications: *Rural Development Review, The Journal of Research Institute for Catalysis, The Journal of Natural Science, Journal of Unification Studies, Research on Honam Culture, Journal of Humanities Studies, Language Teaching, Chonnam Review of American Studies, Social Science Review, The Journal of Regional Development, Industrial Relations Research, The Journal of Sports Science, Chonnam Medical Journal, Technological Review, Journal of Agricultural Science and Technology, Journal of Sciences for Better Living, Journal of Drug Development, Journal of Arts, Yongbong Review*

DEANS

Graduate School: HA IL PARK
Graduate School of Education: KEUN HO CHUNG
Graduate School of Business Administration: SOUG SHIN CHOI
Graduate School of Public Administration: SEONG KIE KIM
Graduate School of Industry: KWAN SOO LEE
College of Education: KEUN HO CHUNG
College of Business Administration: SOUG SHIN CHOI
College of Engineering: KWAN SOO LEE
College of Agriculture: JAE HONG KIM
College of Law: SEONG KIE KIM
College of Medicine: YOUNG HONG PAIK
College of Dentistry: MONG SOOK VANG
College of Natural Sciences: JAE KEUN KIM
College of Pharmacy: BYUNG HO CHUNG
College of Arts: JONG IL KIM
College of Veterinary Medicine: NAM YONG PARK
College of Social Sciences: YOUNG KWAN CHOI
College of Home Economics: DUCK SOON HWANG

ATTACHED RESEARCH INSTITUTES

Management Research Centre: Dir JAE JEON KIM.

Educational Research Institute: Dir YONG NAM LEE.

American Studies Institute: Dir KIL HO SUNG.

Law and Administration Institute: Dir KYONG UN LEE.

Social Sciences Institute: Dir KEUN SIK CHUNG.

Arts Institute: Dir JONG IL KIM.

5.18 Institute: Dir SU SUNG OH.

Humanities Studies Institute: Dir DONG SOO KIM.

Culture and Religious Studies Institute: Dir JUNG HEE KIM.

Centre for Regional Development: Dir SUNG WOO HONG.

Research Institute for Asia and the Pacific Rim: Dir MOON JI BYUNG.

Honam Culture Research Centre: Dir KYU PARK MAN.

Science for Better Living Institute: Dir HYUN SOOK LIM.

Research Institute of Nursing Science: Dir HYE YOUNG KANG.

Engineering Research Institute: Dir NAM SOO SHIN.

Science Education Institute: Dir HEE KYUN OH.

Basic Sciences Institute: Dir WON KI CHOI.

Agricultural Science and Technology Institute: Dir YOUNG MAN LEE.

Veterinary Medicine Research Centre: Dir NAM YONG PARK.

Occupational Medicine Institute: Dir JAE DONG MUN.

Biotechnology Institute: Dir BAIK HO CHO.

Sports Science Centre: Dir DONG WON YANG.

Research Institute for Drug Development: Dir BYUNG HO CHUNG.

Research Institute for Medical Science: Dir SUNG SIK PARK.

Automobile Research Centre: Dir YOUNG KIL KIM.

Information and Research Communications Institute: Dir HYUN JAE KIM.

Research Institute for Catalysis: Dir CHANG SHIN SUNWOO.

Dental Science Institute: Dir BYUNG JOO PARK.

Environmental Research Institute: Dir CHONG BIN LEE.

Hormone Research Centre: Dir HYUK BANG KWON.

Advanced Materials Research Centre: Dir YONG HYUCK BAIK.

Polymer Science and Technology Research Centre: Dir KYU HO CHAE.

Research Centre for High Quality Electric Components and Systems: Dir YOUNG CHUL LIM.

Electronic Telecommunication Technology Research Centre: Dir YOUNG MIN KIM.

Construction, Environment and Cleaner Production Technology Research Centre: Dir CHONG JUN LEE.

CHOSUN UNIVERSITY

375, Seosuk-dong, Dong-gu, Kwangju, 501-759
Telephone: (62) 230-7114
E-mail: haksa@mail.chosun.ac.kr
Internet: www.chosun.ac.kr

Founded 1946
Private control
Language of instruction: Korean
Academic year: March to February

President: KIM JOO-HOON
Dean of Academic Affairs: CHAI-KYUN PARK
Dean of Student Affairs: YANG-SOO SON
Dean of General Affairs: PYUNG-JOON PARK
Dean of Finance: JEI-WON KOH
Librarian: KI-SANG KIM

Library of 597,032 vols
Number of teachers: 556
Number of students: 26,164

Publications: various research journals.

DEANS

College of Humanities: JEONG-SEOK KANG
College of Natural Science: HAK-JIN JUNG
College of Law and Political Science: CHANG-HYEON KOH
College of Business Administration: BYUNG-KYU KIM
College of Engineering: WHAN-KYU PARK
College of Education: HONG-WON PARK
College of Foreign Languages: YONG-HERN LEE
College of Physical Education: DONG-YOON CHOE
College of Medicine: YO-HAN JUNG
College of Dentistry: CHANG-KEUN YOON

College of Pharmacy: YEONG-JONG YOO
College of Industry: HEUNG-KYU JOO
College of Arts: YONG-HYUN KUK
Evening College: JEONG-JOO CHOE
Graduate School: JOON-CHAE PARK
Graduate School of Education: SEOK-CHEOL PARK
Graduate School of Industry: SEONG-HYU JO

CHAIRMEN OF DEPARTMENTS

College of Humanities:
- Korean Language and Literature: TAE-JIN JANG
- English Language and Literature: HAK-HAENG JO
- French Language and Literature: WOO-HYUN JO
- History: OH-RYONG JUNG
- Philosophy: MOON-JEONG PARK

College of Natural Science:
- Mathematics: JONG-HO CHOE
- Computer Science and Statistics: KYU-JUNG CHOE
- Physics: SANG-YEOL LEE
- Chemistry: IL-DOO KIM
- Biology: HONG-SEOB KIM
- Genetic Science: SEONG-JUN KIM

College of Law and Political Science:
- Law: YEONG-KYU KIM
- Public Administration: YEONG-KYU KIM
- Political Science and Diplomacy: YANG-SOO SON

College of Business Administration:
- Economics: IK-HYUN KIM
- Management: BYUNG-KYU KIM
- Accounting: OK-YOON PARK
- Trade: MOON-SOO YOO

College of Engineering:
- Civil Engineering: BYEONG-DAE LIM
- Architectural Engineering: JEONG-SOO JANG
- Mechanical Engineering: JONG-IL KIM
- Precision Mechanical Engineering: SEON-JONG PARK
- Mechanical Design Engineering: TAE-KWON JUNG
- Electrical Engineering: BYEONG-SOO YOO
- Electronics Engineering: JOON-HYUN KIM
- Computer Systems Engineering: CHEOL SONG
- Metallurgical Engineering: HWAN-JONG JO
- Resource Engineering: DONG-WOO SUH
- Chemical Engineering: BYUNG-OOK JO
- Industrial Management: HAK-YEONG BYUN
- Environmental Engineering: SEONG-EUI SHIN
- Aerospace Engineering: CHEOL-HYUNG JO
- Nuclear Engineering: SEUNG-PYUNG CHOE
- Naval Architecture Engineering: CHANG-EUN PARK

College of Education:
- Korean Language: OK-KEUN HAN
- Foreign Languages: KYU-EUL YUM
- English Major: KYU-EUL YUM
- German Major: JAE-MAN PARK
- Mathematics Education: SEOK-JOO PARK
- Sciences: HEE-NAM KIM
- Physics Major: KWAN-KYO LEE
- Chemistry Major: JAE-HEUNG JO
- Biology Major: SEONG-YONG KANG
- Earth Science Major: HEE-NAM KIM
- Home Economics: YEONG-SOOK KIM
- Music: KYU-YEOL CHAI

College of Foreign Languages:
- Spanish Language: KI-TAEK KIM
- German Language: YEONG-SOO JUNG
- Chinese Language: KIL-JANG PARK
- Japanese Language: SANG-IK PARK
- Arabic Language: HEE-MAN SAH
- Russian Language: SOO-HEE KIM

College of Physical Education:
- Physical Education: HYUNG-CHULL NO
- Dance: JOON-YEONG SONG

College of Medicine:
- Medicine: KWANG-SAM KOH
- Nursing: SONG-JA KIM

College of Pharmacy:
- Pharmacy: MYEONG-HYEON JUNG

College of Industry:
- Electronic Data Processing: HACK-JOO AHN
- Food and Nutrition: WHA-JOONG SUH
- Industrial Design: KIL-YONG SUH

College of Arts:
- Fine Arts: JONG-SOO KIM
- Applied Arts: JONG-HOON PARK
- Sculpture: JEONG-SOO KOH

Evening College:
- Law: YEONG-KON KIM
- Economics: KWANG-SOO JEE
- Management: KANG-OK LEE
- Accounting: KI-PYONG KIM
- Trade: SUNG-MIN LEE
- Civil Engineering: CHEOL-SOON KIM
- Architectural Engineering: MAN-TAEK LIM
- Mechanical Engineering: JIN-HEUNG KIM
- Mechanical Design Engineering: IN-YEONG YANG
- Precision Mechanical Engineering: JAE-KI SHIM
- Electrical Engineering: SANG-IL LEE
- Electronics Engineering: CHANG-KYOON PARK

ATTACHED INSTITUTES

Ja-yang Ultramodern Science and Technology Research Institute: Dir CHYULL WOONG PARK.

Humanities Research Institute: Dir CHANG-WHAN KOO.

Social Science Research Institute: Dir CHANG-HYUN KOH.

Natural Science Research Institute: Dir HAK-JIN JUNG.

Production Technology Research Institute: Dir CHEOL-HYEONG JO.

National Development Research Institute: Dir BYEONG-DAE LIM.

Atomic Energy Research Institute: Dir BOK-NAM PARK.

Energy and Resources Research Institute: Dir JONG-IL KIM.

Korean History Research Institute: Dir HYUNG-KWAN PARK.

National Unification Research Institute: Dir JEONG-JOO CHOE.

Foreign Cultural Research Institute: Dir JEONG-SEOK KANG.

Educational Research Institute: Dir YONG-SUB CHOE.

Medical Research Institute: Dir YO-HAN JUNG.

Dental-Biology Research Institute: Dir CHANG-KEUN YOON.

Pharmaceutical Research Institute: Dir DON-IL LEE.

Management Research Institute: Dir OH-YOON PARK.

Environment and Pollution Research Institute: Dir JIN-WHAN LEE.

Agricultural Research Institute: Dir NAM-KI JO.

Saemaul Research Institute: Dir MOON-SOO YOO.

Student Guidance Research Institute: Dir IL-HOUN KIM.

Arts Research Institute: Dir YONG-HYUN KUK.

CHUNG-ANG UNIVERSITY

221 Heukseok Dong, Dongjak-gu, Seoul 156-756
Telephone: (2) 820-6124
Fax: (2) 813-8069
E-mail: interedu@cau.ac.kr
Internet: www.cau.ac.kr
Founded 1918
Private control
Academic year: March to February (two semesters)
Chairman and Chancellor: HEE SU KIM
President: BUM HONN PARK
Vice-Presidents: DAE SIK KIM (Seoul Campus): SANG YOON LEE (Ansung Campus): YUN-WON HWANG
Provost of Medical Centre: CHANG KWUN HONG
Directors of Libraries: TAE WOO NAM (Seoul Campus): YANG HYUN LEE (Ansung Campus)
Library of 1,150,000 vols
Number of teachers: 2,127
Number of students: 22,071 (undergraduate), 4,563 (graduate)
Publications: *Theses Collection*, *College Journals* (annually), *Korean Studies Journal* (quarterly), *Journal of Chung-Ang Pharmacy*, *Korean Journal of Comparative Law*, *Korean Education Index*, *Journal of Economic Development* (all annually), *Chung-Ang Press* (weekly), *Chung-Ang Herald* (monthly)

ACADEMIC DEANS

College of Construction Engineering: KI BONG KIM
College of Arts: SANG JUE SHIN
College of Education: YOUNG DUCK CHOI
College of Engineering: SUNG SUN KIM
College of Foreign Languages: SUNG MOO YANG
College of Home Economics: YANG HEE KIM
College of Industrial Studies: KWANG RO YOON
College of Law: YOUNG SOL KWON
College of Liberal Arts: NAM JOON CHANG
College of Medicine: IM WON CHANG
College of Music: LEE SUK CHEH
College of Pharmacy: IN HOI HUH
College of Political Science and Economics: IN KIE KIM
College of Sciences: SUK YONG LEE
College of Social Sciences: CHI SOON JANG
Graduate School: JO SUP CHUNG
Graduate School of Construction Engineering: SUNG SUN KIM
Graduate School of Education: JAE WOO LEE
Graduate School of the Information Industry: YOUNG CHAN KIM
Graduate School of International Management: HUN CHU
Graduate School of Mass Communication: SANG CHUL LEE
Graduate School of Public Administration: SANG YOON REE
Graduate School of Social Development: KYONG SUH PARK

DIRECTORS

Institute of Advertising and Public Relations: JUN IL RYEE
Institute of Arts: SEUNG KIL KOH
Institute of Basic Sciences: KYUNG HEE CHOI
Institute of Economic Research: YEN KYUN WANG
Institute of Environmental Science: SEI KWAN SOHN
Institute of Family Life: HYUN OK LEE
Institute of Food Resource: SOO SUNG LEE
Institute of Genetic Engineering: YUNG CHAI CHUNG
Institute of Humanities: JOONG SHIK HYUN

Institute of Industrial Construction Technology: YONG JU HWANG
Institute of Industrial Design: WON MO KWAK
Institute of Industrial Management: SEONG MU SUH
Institute of International Trade: JU SUP HAHN
Institute of International Women's Studies: JAE WOO LEE
Institute of Japanese Studies: KYUN IL KIM
Institute of Korean Education: SUNG YOON HONG
Institute of Korean Folklore: SEON POONG KIM
Institute of Legal Research: HYUK JU LEE
Institute of Management Research: DONG SUNG KWAK
Institute of Medical Science: DAE YONG UHM
Institute of North-East Asian Studies: JAE SUN CHOI
Institute of Overseas Korean Residents: SANG MAN LEE
Institute of Pharmaceutical Science: KI HO KIM
Institute of Production Engineering: SOO SAM KIM
Institute of Public Policy and Administration: SANG YOON RHEE
Institute of Social Sciences: HYUNG KOOK KIM
Institute of Sports Sciences Research: JIN YOO
Institute of Technology and Science: YOUNG CHAN KIM
Institute of Third World Studies: UJIN YI
Chung-Ang Music Institute: HAK WON YOON
Australian Studies Institute: HYUNG SHIK KIM

CHUNGBUK NATIONAL UNIVERSITY

48 Gaesin-dong, Cheongju, Chungbuk 361-763
Telephone: (43) 261-3299
E-mail: jdoh@libl.chungbuk.ac.kr
Internet: www.chungbuk.ac.kr

Founded 1951 as Agricultural College, university status 1970
Academic year: March to July, September to December

President: BANG-WOONG SHIN
Director of Administration: KEE UN CHUNG
Dean of Academic Affairs: YOUNG SOO JEONG
Dean of Student Affairs: SUNG HOO HONG
Dean of Planning and Research Affairs: SOON SEOP KWAK
Director of Library: SOON KEY JUNG

Library of 520,000 vols
Number of teachers: 700
Number of students: 18,000

Publications: *Journal of the Industrial Science and Technology Institute, Review of Industry and Management, Journal of the Institute of Construction Technology, Journal of Agricultural Science Research, Journal of Genetic Engineering Research, Law Journal, Journal of Humanities, Journal of Pharmaceutical Science, Journal of Social Science, Juris Forum, Jungwon Munhwa Nonchong, Journal of the Research Institute for Computer and Information Communication, Journal of Language and Literature*

DEANS

College of Humanities: JANG SUNG JOONG
College of Social Science: HEE KYUNG KANG
College of Natural Science: BYUNG CHOON LEE
College of Engineering: LEE JAE KI
College of Commerce and Business Administration: DO WON SUH
College of Education: SHEON JOO CHIN
College of Pharmacy: HAN KUN
College of Medicine: YOUNG JIN SONG
College of Law: JUN HUR
College of Home Economics: KI NAM KIM
College of Veterinary Medicine: YOUNG WON YUN

ATTACHED INSTITUTES

Computer Center: Dir Y. S. KOO.
Student Guidance Institute: Dir D. J. PARK.
Health Center: Dir Y. J. OH.
Saemaul Research Institute: Dir S. W. KANG.
Natural Science Institute: Dir S. Y. HONG.
Institute of Unification Research of the Korean Peninsula: Dir H. K. AHN.
Institute of Construction Technology: Dir B. K. KOO.
Language Research Institute: Dir H. K. KIM.

CHUNGJU NATIONAL UNIVERSITY

123 Geomdan-ri, Iryu-Myeon, Chungju, Chungbuk 380-702
Telephone: (43) 841-5011
Fax: (43) 841-5017
Internet: www.chungju.ac.kr

Founded 1962 as Chungju Technical Junior College

President: KI-TAE SUNG

Number of teachers: 188
Number of students: 8,140

Colleges of Techno-System Engineering, Electrical-Electronic and Information Engineering, Construction and Applied Chemistry, Engineering, Humanities and Social Sciences, Division of Liberal Arts.

CHUNGNAM NATIONAL UNIVERSITY

220 Gung-dong, Yuseong-gu, Daejon, Chungnam 305–764
Telephone: (42) 821-5114
Fax: (42) 823-1469
Internet: www.chungnam.ac.kr

Founded 1952
Academic year: March to June, September to December

President: KWANG-JIN RHEE
Dean of Academic Affairs: CHUL KYU CHOI
Dean of Student Affairs: KUN MOOK CHOI
Registrar: MYUNG KYUN KIM
Librarian: JONG UP CHO

Number of teachers: 880
Number of students: 20,000

Publications: journals of 24 research institutes (annually).

DEANS

Graduate School: CHONG HOE PARK
Graduate School of Business Administration: KEAN SHIK LEE
Graduate School of Education: SANG CHUL KANG
Graduate School of Public Administration: JAE CHANG KA
Graduate School of Industry: GUNG SUCK NAM
Graduate School of Public Health: SAE JIN CHOI
College of Humanities: HAE KIL SUH
College of Social Sciences: TONG HOON KIM
College of Natural Sciences: JONG SUK CHOI
College of Economics and Management: CHUL HWAN CHUN
College of Engineering: SOO YOUNG CHUNG
College of Agriculture: JONG WOO KIM
College of Law: KANG YONG LEE
College of Pharmacy: BYUNG ZUN AHN
College of Home Economics: YOUNG JIN CHUNG
College of Medicine: JIN SUN BAI
College of Fine Arts and Music: CHEOL NAM
College of Veterinary Medicine: MOO HYUNG JUN

HEADS OF DEPARTMENTS

College of Humanities:
- Korean Language and Literature: BYEONG WOOK KIM
- English Language and Literature: JAE IK YU
- German Language and Literature: SANG KUN CHUNG
- French Language and Literature: MI YUN KIM
- Chinese Language and Literature: JOON HO WOO
- Japanese Language and Literature: MOON KI HUR
- Sino-Korean Literature: JONG-UP CHO
- History: SANG CHUL CHA
- Korean History: SOO TAE KIM
- Archaeology: KANG SEUNG LEE
- Philosophy: MYEONG JIN NAM
- Education: SAM HWAN JOO

College of Social Sciences:
- Sociology: NO YOUNG PARK
- Literary and Information Science: BOCK HEE HAHN
- Psychology: KYO HEON KIM
- Mass Communication: SEUNG MOCK YANG
- Public Administration: KEUN BOK KANG
- Local Government: DONG IL YOOK
- Political Science and Diplomacy: KE HEE LEE

College of Natural Sciences:
- Mathematics: KANG JOO MIN
- Statistics: NAK YOUNG LEE
- Computer Science: JI HOON KANG
- Physics: JAE SHIK JUN
- Chemistry: JUN GILL KANG
- Biology: KWAN HEE YOU
- Biochemistry: TAE IK KWON
- Microbiology: PIL JAE MAENG
- Geology: WON SA KIM
- Oceanology: TAE WON LEE
- Physical Education: DAE WOO CHOI
- Pre-medicine: NAK YOUNG LEE
- Socio-physical Education: CHOON-KI MIN
- Astronomy and Space Science: KWANG TEA KIM

College of Economics and Management:
- Economics: TECK SUNG KWON
- Business Administration: TAE GYU YI
- Accounting: SEH DO OH
- International Management: JONG SOON KOO

College of Engineering:
- Architectural Engineering Education: DEOG SEONG OH
- Metallurgical Engineering Education: HONG RO LEE
- Mechanical Engineering Education: JONG HO WON
- Electrical Engineering Education: HEUNG HO LEE
- Electronic Engineering Education: DAE YOUNG KIM
- Civil Engineering Education: JAE CHUL SHIN
- Industrial Technology Education: PAN WOOK KIM
- Chemical Engineering Education: SEUNG KON RYU
- Textile Engineering: KI SEA BAE
- Naval Architecture and Ocean Engineering: CHANG SUP LEE
- Material Engineering: GIL MOO KIM
- Mechanical Design Engineering: SEONG YEON YOO
- Computer Engineering: OH-SEOK KWON
- Polymer Engineering: SUNG KWON
- Environmental Engineering: CHOUNG KEUN WONG

College of Agriculture:

Agronomy: CHOONG SOO KIM
Horticulture: JONG-SUK LEE
Forestry: HO KYUNG SONG
Agricultural Biology: KWAN SAM CHOC
Animal Science: CHANG SIK PARK
Dairy Science: IN DUK LEE
Agricultural Engineering: TAI CHEOL KIM
Agricultural Machinery Engineering: MAN-SOO KIM
Agricultural Chemistry: KYU SEUNG LEE
Forest Products Technology: YANG JUN
Food Technology: NAM JIN OH

College of Veterinary Medicine:

Veterinary Medicine: DUCK KWAM KIM

College of Law:

Public Law: SANG OH BAC
Private Law: YOUNG WOO PARK

College of Pharmacy:

Pharmacy: KWANG IL KWON
Pharmaceutics: KYUNG LAE PARK

College of Home Economics:

Home Economics Education: JOON HO LEE
Clothing and Textiles: KYUNG HEE HONG
Food and Nutrition: MEE REE KIM

College of Medicine:

Medicine: JIN SUN BAI
Nursing: HEE YOUNG SO

College of Fine Arts and Music:

Music: SANG LOCK PARK
Wind & Strings: BYUNG HOON
Painting: NYUNG BAC KIM
Sculpture: CHEOL NAM
Industrial Arts: BYUNG JIN CHOI

ATTACHED RESEARCH INSTITUTES

Basic Science Research Institute: Dir SOCK YUN YUN.

Language Research Institute: Dir BONG JOO HWANG.

Educational Research and Development Institute: Dir CHOONG HOE KIM.

Canadian-American Studies Institute: Dir JAE SUK CHOI.

Unification Research Institute: Dir KI-DON CHUNG.

Institute of Environmental Science and Technology: Dir MOO YOUNG SONG.

Research Institute of Biological Engineering: Dir SANG GI PAIK.

Paekche Research Institute: Dir JOO TACK SEONG.

Industrial Education Research Centre: Dir TAE KYUN KIM.

Humanities Research Institute: Dir JAI YOUNG SONG.

Natural Sciences Research Institute: Dir YOUN DOO KIM.

Institute of Medicine Development: Dir GYE JU LEE.

Institute of Management and Economics: Dir SEUNG EUI PARK.

Industrial Technology Research Institute: Dir TAIK KEE KIM.

Institute of Law: Dir KEUN RYUK CHOI.

Institute of Agricultural Science and Technology: Dir JAE CHANG LEE.

Institute of Community Medicine: Dir KIL CHUN KANG.

Research Institute of Physical Education and Sports Science: Dir Prof. SEONG-PYO HONG.

Research Institute of Home Economics: Dir JAE SOOK KIM.

Community Development Research Institute: Dir BYANG GI AHN.

Co-operative Cancer Research Institute: Dir KI SUB SON.

Institute of Social Science: Dir YEONG SEONG KIM.

Art-Culture Research Institute: Dir OUN MO SHIN.

SEOUL NATIONAL UNIVERSITY OF EDUCATION

Seocho-dong 1650, Seocho-gu, Seoul 137-742
E-mail: center@ns.snue.ac.kr
Internet: www.seoul-e.ac.kr

Founded 1945

President: HO-SEONG KIM.

DAEBUL UNIVERSITY

72 Samho-ri, Samho-myeun, Yangam-gun, Chonnam
Telephone: (693) 469-1114
Fax: (693) 462-2510
E-mail: webmaster@mail.daebul.ac.kr
Internet: www.daebul.ac.kr

Founded 1994 as Daebul Institute of Technology and Science; present name 1996
Private control

President: Dr KYUNG-SOO LEE.

DAEGU NATIONAL UNIVERSITY OF EDUCATION

1797-6 Daemyong-dong 2-8, Namgu, Daegu
Telephone: (53) 620-1114
Fax: (53) 651-5369
E-mail: webmaster@dnue.ac.kr
Internet: www.dnue.ac.kr

Founded 1950

President: LEE-KEON CHANG

Number of teachers: 112
Number of students: 3,512 (2,775 undergraduates, 737 graduates)

Teacher-training university.

DAEGU UNIVERSITY

Jinryang, Gyeongsan, Gyeongbuk 712-714
Telephone: (53) 850-5000
Fax: (53) 850-5009
E-mail: nsadmin@taegu.ac.kr
Internet: www.taegu.ac.kr

President: JAE-KYOO LEE
Number of students: 16,000

Colleges of Humanities, Law, Public Administration, Economics and Business Administration, Social Sciences, Natural Sciences Engineering, Natural Resources, Arts and Design, Education, Rehabilitation Sciences, Health Science.

DANKOOK UNIVERSITY

147 Hannam-ro, Yongsan-gu, Seoul
Telephone: (2) 709-2122
Internet: www.dankook.ac.kr

Founded 1947, university status 1967
Private control
Language of instruction: Korean
Academic year: March to February

Chancellor: CHOONG-SIK CHANG
President: SEUNG-KOOK KIM
Registrar: YONG-WOO LEE

Library of 140,000 vols
Number of teachers: 321
Number of students: 13,557

Publications: Reviews, *Dan Won.*

DEANS

College of Liberal Arts and Sciences: MOON-SUP CHA
College of Law: YOO-HYUK KIM
College of Commerce and Economics: HAENG-XUH KIM
College of Engineering: MYUNG-WON KO
College of Education: SEUNG-KOOK KIM

HEADS OF DEPARTMENTS

Seoul Campus:

College of Liberal Arts and Sciences:

Korean and Korean Literature: SUN-MOOK YIM
English and English Literature: TAE-JU LEE
Chinese and Chinese Literature: YOUNG-ZAI CHI
German and German Literature: SUNG-DAE KIM
Japanese and Japanese Literature: MUN-KI HUR
History: NAE-HYUN YOON
Counting and Statistics: GANG-SUP LEE
Chemistry: CHANG-BAE KIM
Food and Nutrition: SOON-JA CHUNG
Pottery Arts: BOO-WOONG LEE

College of Law and Political Science:

Law: DONG-SUB AHN
Administration: DONG-SHIM KEUM
Political Science: TAE-HOON KANG
Regional Development: KI-YONG HONG

College of Commerce and Economics:

Economics: DONG-UN PARK
Foreign Trade: SI-KYUNG KIM
Management: KWANG-JU LEE
Accounting: SEUNG-HIE KOH

College of Engineering:

Architectural Engineering: JUNG-SHIN KIM
Civil Engineering: KIL-CHOUM LEE
Mechanical Engineering: HIE-SONG KIM
Electrical Engineering: SEUK-YONG HWANG
Electronic Engineering: YEON-KANG JIN
Chemical Engineering: IL-HYUN JUNG
Textile Engineering: KANG JOO

College of Education:

Sino-Korean Education: CHUN-GUY PARK
Special Education: DO-SU KIM
Mathematics Education: YOUNG-SIK CHANG
Science Education: MOON-NAM LEE
Music Education: JOUNG-MON KOH
Physical Education: TAE-KYUN YOO

Cheonan Campus:

College of Humanities and Science:

Korean and Korean Literature: MIN-YOUNG YOO
English and English Literature: YONG-HOON LEE
German and German Literature: CHA-SIK SHIN
French and French Literature: SUNG-GYU BOK
Chinese and Chinese Literature: TAE-HOON LEE
Spanish and Spanish Literature: HAE-SUN KOH
History: IL-BEOM SHIN
Industrial Arts: MYUNG-HYUNG CHO

College of Social Science:

Law: YONG-WOO KWOM
Administration: SOO-YOUNG KIM
Economics: BYUNG-SUP KWAK
Foreign Trade: BYUNG-JIN AHN
Management: DOO-HYU SHIN
Accounting: YONG-GI CHUN

College of Science and Engineering:

Applied Physics: SUNG-WON CHOI
Chemistry: IL KIM
Biology: KYEONG-SOOK LEE
Mathematics: SONG-KI CHUN
Agriculture: JAE-CHUN CHE
Agricultural Economics: DONG-HI KIM
Architectural Engineering: MOO-UNG CHUNG
Civil Engineering: YONG-KI CHA

Mineral and Petroleum Engineering: MYUNG-SUN GONG
Electronic Engineering: KUANG-JUN WOO
Industrial Chemistry: SEUNG-JAE CHOI
Physical Education: JONG-HAN OH

College of Dentistry:
Dentistry: KYEONG-UK KIM

ATTACHED INSTITUTES

Institute of Saemaul Studies: Dir Dr YOO-HYUK KIM.

Institute of Oriental Studies: Dir Dr PAE-KANG HWANG.

Industrial Research Institute: Dir Dr HE-CHEOL LIM.

Chinese Studies Institute: Dir Dr YOUNG-CHOON HAN.

Folk Arts Institute: Dir Dr JOO-SUN SUK.

Institute of Technological Research: Dir JEONG-RYEON HAN.

Statistics Studies Institute: Dir Dr HYUNG-BO KIM.

Institute of Anglo-American Studies: Dir Dr DAUK-RYONG KONG.

DONG-A UNIVERSITY

840, Hadan 2-dong, Saha-gu, Pusan 604-714
Telephone: (51) 200-6212
Fax: (51) 200-6214
E-mail: president@donga.ac.kr
Internet: www.donga.ac.kr

Founded 1946
Private control
Language of instruction: Korean
Academic year: March to February

President: JAE-RONG CHOI
Vice-President: BYUNG-TAE CHO
Head of Secretariat: YEONG-GI LEE
Dean of Academic Affairs: CHANG-OCK CHOI
Dean of Student Affairs: DAE-KYU LEE
Dean of Financial Affairs: YOON-SIK HWANG
Dean of Research: SOON-KYU CHOI
Dean of Administration: LI-KYOO KIM
Director of Library: KUN-BAE HAHN

Library of 582,134 vols

Number of professors: 513
Number of students: 17,217

Publications: faculty journals and bulletins, *General Culture Series* (2 a year).

DEANS

Graduate School: WOONG-DAL RYOO
Graduate School of Business Administration: YONG-DAE KIM
Graduate School of Education: CHONG-IL TCHOI
Graduate School of Industry: KUN-MO HAN
Graduate School of Mass Communication: MIN-NAM KIM
College of Humanities: SANG-BAK CHUNG
College of Natural Sciences: TAE-SEOP UHM
College of Law: MAN-HEE JEONG
College of Social Sciences: KWANG-SUK SUL
College of Business Administration: TAE-YOON JUN
College of Agriculture: DAE-SOO CHUNG
College of Engineering: CHUN-KEUN PARK
College of Physical Education: CHEOL-HO PARK
College of Arts: SOO-CHUL PARK
College of Human Ecology: SEOK-HWAN KIM
College of Medicine: DUCK-HWAN CHUNG

DIRECTORS

Agricultural Resources Research Institute: YOUNG-KIL KIM
Institute of Korean Resources Development: SUNG-GYO CHUNG
Environmental Problems Research Institute: JANG-HO KIM
Business Management Research Institute: SEONG-HWAN KIM
Sokdang Academic Research Institute of Korean Culture: HYENG-JU KIM
Social Science Research Institute: JAE-GYONG KIM
Population Research Centre: SOON CHOI
Language Research Institute: CHI-GUN HA
Research Institute of Sports Science: YOUNG-PIL AN
German Studies Institute: SANG-UG RHIE
Institute for the Study of Law: SANG-HO KIM
Basic Science Research Institute: WAN-SE KIM
Ocean Resources Research Institute: JIN-HOO KIM
Research Institute for Genetic Engineering: CHUNG-HAN CHUNG
MIS Research Institute: KAY-SEOB HAN
Research Institute for Humanities: YOUNG-DO CHUNG
Research Institute for Human Ecology: EUN-JOO PARK
Tourism and Leisure Research Institute: YUNG-MYUN AHN
Industrial Technology Research Centre: TAE-OK JUN
Institute of Data Communication: CHANG-HI HONG
Plastic Arts Research Institute: SUNG-DO BACK
Life Science Research Institute: YONG-CHUN CHOI
Industrial Medicine Research Institute: JUNG-MAN KIM
Research Institute for Clinical Medicine: JEONG-MAN KIM

DONGDUK WOMEN'S UNIVERSITY

23-1 Wolgok-dong, Sungbuk-ku, Seoul 136-714
Telephone: (2) 940-4000
Fax: (2) 940-4182
E-mail: master@dongduk.ac.kr
Internet: www.dongduk.ac.kr

Founded 1950
Private control
Language of instruction: Korean
Academic year: March to February (2 semesters)

Chancellor: WON-YOUNG CHO
Vice-Chancellor: YOUNG-YON YOON
Registrar: DO-SEOK CHANG
Librarian: YOON-SIK KIM

Library of 232,000 vols
Number of teachers: 154
Number of students: 6,155

Publications: *Journal of Dongduk Women's University*, *Dongduk News Letter* (2 a year), *Treatise* (annually), *Dongduk Women's Newspaper* (weekly)

DEANS

College of Humanities: SANG-GI CHO
College of Social Sciences: SAE-YOUNG OH
College of Natural Sciences: SANG-SOON LEE
College of Computer and Information Sciences: YANG-HEE LEE
College of Pharmacy: IN-KOO CHUN
College of Arts: SUN-BAEK JANG
College of Design: DONG-JO KOO
College of Performing Arts: (vacant)
General Studies and Teaching Profession Division: HONG-TAE PARK

ATTACHED RESEARCH INSTITUTES

Research Institute for Humanities: Dir DOK-BONG LEE.

Industrial Research Institute: Dir YOON-SUNG LIM.

Research Institute for Life Sciences: Dir NAM-HEE WOO.

Central Pharmaceutical Research Institute: Dir HYO-JIN KIM.

Design Research Institute: Dir CHEOL-WOONG SIM.

DONG-EUI UNIVERSITY

24 Kaya-dong, Pusanjin-ku, Pusan 614-714
Telephone: (51) 890-1114
Fax: (51) 890-1234
E-mail: wwwadmin@www.dongeui.ac.kr
Internet: www.dongeui.ac.kr

Founded 1976 as Kyungdong Engineering Technical College; became Dong-Eui College 1979; present name 1983
Private control

President: Dr KEUN-WU PAK

Library of 336,000 vols
Number of students: 3,704 (3,420 undergraduate, 284 postgraduate).

DONGSHIN UNIVERSITY

252 Daehohong, Naju, Chonnam 520-714
Telephone: (61) 330-3014
Internet: www.dongshinu.ac.kr

President: KYUM-BUM LEE

Library of 500,000
Number of students: 1,604

Colleges of Engineering, Humanities and Social Science, Information and Science, Arts, Oriental Medicine.

DONGGUK UNIVERSITY

26 3-ga, Pil-dong, Chung-gu, Seoul 100-715
Telephone: 260-3114
Fax: 277-1274
Internet: www.dongguk.ac.kr

Founded 1906, university status 1953
Private control

Chairman: IN-GAB OH
President: Dr SUK-KU SONG
Librarian: Dr BO HWAN KIM

Library: see Libraries
Number of teachers: 500
Number of students: 16,050

Publications: *Dongguk Shinmun* (weekly), *Dongguk Post* (monthly), *Pulgyo Hakpo* (Journal of Buddhist Studies), *Dongguk Journal*, *Dongguk Sasang* (Dongguk Thought), and 20 others

Colleges of Buddhism, liberal arts and sciences, law and political science, economics and commerce, agriculture and forestry, engineering, education, medical science; graduate school, graduate school of public administration, graduate school of business administration, graduate school of education, graduate school of information industry; colleges on Kyongju Campus.

Research Institutes: Buddhist culture, comparative literature, statistical science, law and political science, business management, agriculture and forestry, overseas development, national security, computer, Middle Eastern and East European affairs, Korean studies, Saemaul research, landscape art, industrial technology, translation of Buddhist scriptures.

DONGSEO UNIVERSITY

San 69-1, Churye-Dong, Sasang-gu, Pusan 617-716
Telephone: (51) 320-2092
Fax: (51) 320-2094
E-mail: anna1974@dongseo.ac.kr
Internet: www.dongseo.ac.kr

Founded 1991 as Dongseo College of Technology; present name 1996

President: DONG-SOON PARK
Executive Director, International Cooperation Committee: JEKUK CHANG

Number of students: 7,000.

DONGYANG UNIVERSITY

1 Kyochon-dong, Punggi, Youngju, Kyungbuk 750-711
Telephone: (572) 630-1114
Fax: (572) 636-8523
E-mail: wwwadmin@phenix.dyu.ac.kr
Internet: www.dyu.ac.kr

Founded 1994
Private control
Academic year: March to December

President: Dr SUNG-HAE CHOI
Vice-President: Dr YOUNG-HWAN PARK
Librarian: BOK-SOO BYUN

Library of 150,000 vols
Number of teachers: 80
Number of students: 3,100 (3,000 undergraduate, 100 postgraduate)

Colleges of Science and Engineering, Human and Social Science, Arts and Graduate Schools of Information and Education.

DUKSUNG WOMEN'S UNIVERSITY

419 Ssangmoon-dong, Dobong-gu, Seoul 132-714
Telephone: 901-8114
Fax: 902-8125
Internet: www.duksung.ac.kr

Founded 1950
Private control
Language of instruction: Korean
Academic year: March to February

President: YONG-NAE KIM
Registrar: SOOK-JA LIM
Librarian: YOUNG-HWAN CHUNG

Library of 328,000 vols
Number of teachers: 148 full-time
Number of teachers: 162 part-time
Number of students: 5,250

Publications: *Duksung Women's University Journal*, *Geunmack* (annually), *Duksung Women's University Newsletter* (24 a year), *Duksung Women's University Newsletter*

DEANS

College of Humanities: JUNG-BOON YOON
College of Social Sciences: SUNG-CHUL KIM
College of Natural Science: SUK-IM YOON
College of Pharmacy: KI-HWA JUNG
College of Fine Arts: AIE-YUNG KIM

EWHA WOMEN'S UNIVERSITY

11–1 Daehyun-dong, Sodaemun-gu, Seoul 120-750
Telephone: (2) 3277-3160
Fax: (2) 364-8019
E-mail: iei@ewha.ac.kr
Internet: www.iei.ewha.ac.kr

Founded 1886
Languages of instruction: Korean, English
Academic year: March to December (two semesters)

Chancellor: HOO-JUNG YOON
President: Dr IN-RYUNG SHIN
Librarian: BONG-HEE KIM

Library: see Libraries
Number of teachers: 800
Number of students: 21,000 (graduates 6,000; undergraduates 15,000)

Publications: *Ewha Voice* (monthly, in English), *Edae Hakbo* (weekly, in Korean), *Ewha News* (monthly, in Korean)

DEANS

Graduate School: Dr PIL-WHA CHANG
Institute of Science and Technology: Dr WON KIM
Graduate School of International Studies: Dr JANG-HEE YOO
Graduate School of Translation and Interpretation: Dr YOUNG CHOI
Graduate School of Education: Dr WOUN-SIK CHOI
Graduate School of Design: Dr YOUNG-KI KIM
Graduate School of Social Welfare: Dr WOUN-SIK CHOI
Graduate School of Information Science: Dr HONG-SIK AHN
Graduate School of Theology: Dr MYUNG-SU YANG
Graduate School of Policy Sciences: Dr HONG-SIK AHN
Graduate School of Practical Music: Dr YOO-RI CHOI
Graduate School of Business Administration: Dr YOON-SUK SUH
Graduate School of Clinical Health Sciences: Dr CHOON-MI KIM
College of Liberal Arts: Dr HYUN-JA KIM
College of Social Sciences: Dr HONG-SIK AHN
College of Natural Sciences: Dr NAM-SOO LEE
College of Engineering: Dr YEONG-SOO SHIN
College of Music: Prof. KYU-DO LEE
College of Arts and Design: Prof. YOUNG-KI KIM
College of Human Movement and Performance: Dr KEE-WOONG KIM
College of Education: Dr YOUNG-JU JU
College of Law: Dr MYEONG-CHO YANG
College of Business Administration: Dr YOON-SUK SUH
College of Medicine: Dr HWA-SOON CHUNG
College of Nursing: Dr YOUNG-SOON BYUN
College of Pharmacy: Dr CHOON-MI KIM
College of Home Science and Management: Dr SEONG-YEON PARK

DIRECTORS OF ATTACHED RESEARCH INSTITUTES

Korean Cultural Research Institute: Dr HYUN-JA KIM.

Korean Women's Institute: Dr JUNG-WHA OH.

Asian Center for Women's Studies: Dr EUN-SHIL KIM.

Asian Food and Nutrition Research Institute: Dr JONG-MI LEE.

Environmental Research Institute: Dr SEOK-SOON PARK.

Research Institute for Basic Sciences: Dr GIL-JA JEON.

Ewha Colour and Design Research Institute: Dr GYOUN-SIL CHOI.

Institute of Information and TeleCommunication: Dr KI-JOON CHAE.

Institute of International Trade and Co-operation: Dr KI-SOOK CHO.

Korean Language and Literature Research Institute: Dr KI-OK SUNG.

Ewha Historical Research Center: Dr SO-JA CHOI.

Institute for Semiotic Studies: Dr MIN-SUK CHOI.

Ewha Institute for Women's Theological Studies: Dr KYUNG-SUK LEE.

Research Institute of Natural History: Dr IN-SOOK LEE.

Ewha Center for Engineering Research: Dr YOUNG-SOO SHIN.

Music Institute: Prof. BOK-JOO JHONG.

Ceramic Research Institute: Dr SUK-YOUNG KANG.

Research Institute of Movement Science: Dr KEE-WOONG KIM.

Research Institute for the Science of Education: Dr HEE-JIN KIM.

Research Institute of Curriculum Instruction: Dr WOON-SIK CHOI.

Management Research Center: Dr SEONG-KOOK KIM.

Research Institute of Nursing Science: Dr YOUNG-SOON BYUN.

Research Institute of Pharmaceutical Science: Dr HEA-YOUNG PARK.

Medical Research Center: Dr KYUNG-KYU CHOI.

Human Ecology and Environmental Institute: Dr SUNG-YEON PARK.

Ewha Legal Science Institute: Dr YOUNG-MIN CHANG.

GYEONGSANG NATIONAL UNIVERSITY

900 Gazwa-dong, Chinju 660-701
Telephone: (55) 751-5047
Fax: (55) 751-6087
E-mail: webadmin@nongae.gsnu.ac.kr
Internet: www.gsnu.ac.kr

Founded 1948 as Gyeongnam Provincial Junior Agricultural College; became Gyeongnam National College 1968 and Gyeongsang National College 1972; present name 1979

President: CHOONG-SAENG PARK
Number of teachers: 670
Number of students: 23,300 (21,100 undergraduate, 2,200 postgraduate)

Colleges of Humanities, Social Sciences, Natural Sciences, Business Administration, Engineering, Agriculture and Life Science, Law, Education, Veterinary Medicine, Medicine and Marine Science.

HALLYM UNIVERSITY

39 Hallymdaehak-gil, Chunchon, Kangwon-do 200-702
Telephone: (33) 248-1000
Fax: (33) 256-3333
E-mail: parkphil@hallym.ac.kr
Internet: www.hallym.ac.kr

Founded 1982
Private control
Academic year: March to December

President: Dr SANG-WOO RHEE
Vice-President: Dr SIL HAN
Dean for Academic Affairs: Dr SOO-YOUNG CHOI
Dean for Student Affairs: Dr CHOONG-IL LEE
Dean for General Affairs: NAK-SUNG SUNG
Dean for Planning and Co-ordination: Dr KI-WON LEE
Library Director: Dr GEUN-GAB BAK

Library of 373,000 books
Number of teachers: 591
Number of students: 10,119 (9,353 undergraduate, 766 postgraduate)

Publication: *Hallym News* (every 2 weeks)

DEANS

College of Humanities: Prof. CHUN-TAEK OH
College of Social Sciences: Prof. YUNG-MYUNG KIM
College of Natural Sciences: Prof. RAK-JOONG KIM
College of Information and Electronics Engineering: Prof. CHANG-GEUN SONG
College of Medicine: Prof. HYOUNG-JIN PARK

HANKUK AVIATION UNIVERSITY

200-1, Hwajon-dong, Koyang City, Kyonggi-do 412-791
Telephone: (2) 300-0114
Fax: (2) 3158-5769
Internet: www.hangkong.ac.kr

Founded 1952 as National Aviation College; became Hankuk Aviation College 1968

President: SOON-KIL HONG
Dean of Academic Affairs: YEONG-HOOK LEE
Dean of Student Affairs: CHIL-YOUNG KIM
Dean of Planning and International Affairs: JOON-HONG BOO
Dean of Research Affairs and Faculty Evaluation: SOO-CHAN HWANG

Library of 247,000

DEANS

Graduate School: YUN-HYUN LEE
Graduate School of Aviation and Information Industry: SOON-KIL HONG
Graduate School of Business Administration: GUN-HO CHA

HANKUK UNIVERSITY OF FOREIGN STUDIES

270 Imun-dong, Dongdaemun-gu, Seoul
Telephone: 965-7001
E-mail: iso@hufs.ac.kr
Internet: www.hufs.ac.kr

Founded 1954
Private control

President: Prof. BYONG MAN AHN
Dean of Academic Affairs: Prof. SUNG RAE PAK
Dean of Student Affairs: Prof. CHANG BOK LEE
Chief Administration Officer: SEOK JOO YOON
Librarian: Prof. KYU CHUL CHO

Library of 303,900 vols
Number of teachers: 292
Number of students: 12,838

Publications: *Argus* (monthly, English and other foreign languages), *Journal* (annually), *Oe-Dae Hakbo* (weekly, Korean)

DEANS

Graduate School: Prof. JOUNG YOLE REW
Graduate School of International Trade: Prof. HEE JOON LEE
Graduate School of Interpretation and Translation: Prof. I BAE KIM
Graduate School of Education: Prof. JIN KWON RHIM
Graduate School of Management Information Systems: Prof. JAE SEOK JUNG
College of Occidental Languages: Prof. YOUNG GUL LEE
College of Oriental Languages: Prof. KI IOB CHUNG
College of Law and Political Science: Prof. DEOK KIM
College of Trade and Economics: Prof. HEE JOON LEE
College of Education: Prof. HAN-JIN OH
College of Liberal Arts and Sciences: Prof. JIK HYUN KIM
Academic and Student Affairs (Evening Courses): Prof. DUCK YONG WOO
College of Foreign Languages: Prof. JONG SOO CHOI
College of Social Sciences: Prof. BYUNG HO PARK

DIRECTORS

Audio-Visual Education Institute: Prof. SOON-HAM PARK
Foreign Language Training and Research Centre: Prof. JAI MIN KIM
Institute for Research in Languages and Linguistics: Prof. SEONG JOON REW
Research Institute for Economics and Business Administration: Prof. BYUNG KWOON MIN
Chinese Studies Institute: Prof. KWAN-JANG CHOI
Russian and East European Institute: Prof. KYU WHA CHO
Institute of Latin-American Studies: Prof. MAN SHIK MIN
Institute of the Middle East: Prof. SOON NAM HONG
Institute of African Studies: Prof. WON TAK PARK
Institute of Korean Regional Studies: Prof. BYONG MAN AHN
Institute of International Communication: Prof. JONG KI KIM
Institute of History: Prof. SUNG RAE PAK
Institute of Foreign Language Studies: Prof. YOUNG JO KIM
Institute of Humanities: Prof. SUNG WI KANG
Student Guidance Center: Prof. JONG GEON YOON
Interpretation and Translation Center: Prof. I-BAE KIM

HANKYONG NATIONAL UNIVERSITY

67 Sukjong-dong, Ansung-City, Kyonggi-do 456-749
Telephone: (334) 670-5114
Fax: (334) 673-2704
E-mail: kosoon@hnu.hankyong.ac.kr
Internet: www.hankyong.ac.kr

Founded 1939
State control
Academic year: March to February

President: WON-WOO LEE
Director of the Office for Academic Affairs: II-SHIN CHOE
Director of the Office of Student Affairs: JAE-HO AN
Director of the Office of General Affairs: JONG-NAM LEE
Director of the Office of Strategy Department: HO-SANG RYU
Library Director: SHI-GYUN YOU

Library of 82,000 books, 175 periodicals
Number of teachers: 458
Number of students: 7,718 (7,558 undergraduate, 160 postgraduate)

DEANS

College of Agriculture and Life Science: YOUNG-HO KIM
College of Science and Engineering: HAK-YOUNG LEE
College of Humanities and Social Sciences: WAN-PYO HONG
Graduate School of Industry: SONG-KAP RHEE

HAN NAM UNIVERSITY

133 Ojung-dong, Taeduk-gu, Taejon 306-791
Telephone: (42) 629-7114
Fax: (42) 625-5874
E-mail: webmaster@hannam.ac.kr
Internet: www.hannam.ac.kr

Founded 1956
Academic year: March to December

Colleges of Liberal Arts, Education, Natural Sciences, Engineering, Economics and Business Administration, Law, Social Sciences

President: Dr SANG-YOON LEE
Vice-President: Dr HYUNG TAE KIM
Director of International Relations Center: Dr KYU TAE JUNG

Library: University possesses Central Library, Central Museum, Natural History Museum, Academic Information Center
Number of teachers: 965
Number of students: 11,441.

HANSEO UNIVERSITY

360 Daegok-ri, Haemi-Myun, Seosan City, Chungnam 356-820
Telephone: (455) 660-1139
E-mail: webmaster@hanseo.ac.kr
Internet: www.hanseo.ac.kr

Founded 1989
Number of students: 1,927
President: KEE-SUN HAM

Colleges of Liberal Arts, Social Science, Aeronautical Engineering, Engineering, Science, Health Science, Arts, Graduate School.

HANSHIN UNIVERSITY

Hanshin
Telephone: (31) 370-6546
Fax: (31) 372-3343
E-mail: am0124@hs.ac.kr
Internet: www.hanshin.ac.kr

Founded 1980
Number of students: 6,000
President: YOUNG-SUCK OH

Colleges of Theology, Humanities, Social Sciences, Management and Trade, Information Sciences.

HANSUNG UNIVERSITY

389 Samseon-Dong, Sungbuk-gu, Seoul
Telephone: (2) 760-4114
Fax: (2) 745-8943
E-mail: getsmile@hansung.ac.kr
Internet: www.hansung.ac.kr

Founded 1945
President: HAN WAN-SANG

Colleges of Humanities, Social Sciences, Arts, Engineering, Liberal Arts and Science.

HANYANG UNIVERSITY

17 Haengdang-dong, Sungdong-gu, Seoul 133-791
Telephone: (2) 2290-0046
Fax: (2) 2281-1784
E-mail: webmaster@ihanyang.ac.kr
Internet: www.hanyang.ac.kr

Founded 1939 as Hanyang Institute of Technology; present status 1959
Private control
Academic year: March to July, September to December

President: Dr CHONG YANG KIM
Academic Dean: Dr CHANG SEOP SONG

Library of 350,000 vols
Number of teachers: c. 958
Number of students: c. 24,508

Publications: *Hanyang Nonmun Dzip*, *Journal of Economic Studies*, *Sino-Soviet Affairs*, *Journal of Korean Studies*, *Journal of Student Guidance Research*, and numerous others

Colleges of engineering (including architectural engineering), liberal arts and sciences (including journalism and cinema), commerce and economics, law and political science, music, physical education, education, medicine; evening engineering college; graduate school, graduate school of industrial management.

HONAM UNIVERSITY

48 Ssangchon-dong, Seo-Ku, Kwangju City
E-mail: jgms@honam.honam.ac.kr
Internet: www.honam.ac.kr

Founded 1978
President: SOO-IL LEE
Library of 400,000

Colleges of Humanities, Social Sciences, Business Administration, Natural Science, Engineering, Internet and Media, Arts and Physical Education.

HONG-IK UNIVERSITY

72–1 Sangsu-dong, Mapo-gu, Seoul 121-791
Telephone: (2) 320-1114
Fax: (2) 320-1122
E-mail: webm@wow.hongik.ac.kr
Internet: hongik.ac.kr

Founded 1946
Private control
Language of instruction: Korean
Academic year: March to June, September to December

Chairman: Dr MYEON YOUNG LEE
President: BYUNG KEE JANG
Vice-President for Academic Affairs: SANG PIL SHIM
Vice-President for General Affairs: SEUNG EUI NAM
Director of University Library: SHIN YUE LEE

Library of 1,010,000 vols
Number of teachers: 463 full-time
Number of teachers: 390 part-time
Number of students: 16,679

Publications: *Hong-Ik University Journal* (annually), *Hong-Ik Economic Review* (annually), *Journal of Student Life* (annually), *Management Review* (annually), *Papers on the Study of Education* (annually)

DEANS

College of Engineering: YEON GON PARK
College of Business Administration: BUM YONG SUNG
College of Fine Arts: SANG HO SHIN
College of Education: SIN JAE JANG
College of Liberal Arts: WON PYO JUNG
College of Law and Economics: DOO HYUN HWANG
College of Business Management: JONG DAE JIN
College of Science and Technology: DOO BOK LEE
College of Design and Arts: KEUN JAE OH
Graduate School: YOUNG TAE JANG
Graduate School of Industrial Arts: HYUN CHIL CHOI
Graduate School of Architecture and Urban Design: JAE WOO SONG
Graduate School of Education: JAE CHANG LEE
Graduate School of Advanced Technology and Administration: SEUNG EUI NAM
Graduate School of Information: DO SUUN PARK
Graduate School of International Business Administration: CHANG HEE LIM
Graduate School of Tax Studies: CHANG HEE LIM
Graduate School of Industry: HEE GU KIM
Graduate School of Educational Management: JAE CHANG LEE
Graduate School of Advertising and Public Relations: MYUNG KWANG KWON

ATTACHED INSTITUTES

Environmental Development Institute.

Research Institute of Business Administration.

Institute of Economic Research.

Educational Research Institute.

Research Institute of Eastern and Western Cultures.

Research Center of Ceramic Art.

Research Institute for Science and Technology.

Research Institute of Modern Plastic Arts.

Research Institute of Industrial Design.

Research Institute of Law.

Research Institute of Industrial Technology.

Research Institute of Humanities.

Tribology Research Institute.

North-East Asia Research Institute.

HOSEO UNIVERSITY

29-1 Sechul-ri, Baebang-myun, Asan Chungnam 336-795
Telephone: (41) 540-5017
Fax: (41) 540-5019
E-mail: webmaster@office.hoseo.ac.kr
Internet: www.hoseo.ac.kr

Founded 1978
Private control

President: IL-KU KANG

Library of 300,000 vols
Number of teachers: 520
Number of students: 12,000.

HOWON UNIVERSITY

727 Wolha-ri, Impi, Kunsan, Chonbuk 450-7114
Telephone: (6) 450-7114
Fax: (6) 450-7777
E-mail: webmaster@howon.ac.kr
Internet: www.howon.ac.kr

Founded 1977 as Kunsan Technical Advanced School; renamed Sohae Technical Junior College 1979; became Chonbuk Sanup University 1988; present name 1998
Private control
Academic year: March to February

President: Dr HEE-SUNG KANG.

UNIVERSITY OF INCHEON

177 Dowha-dong, Nam-gu, Incheon
Telephone: (32) 770-8114
Fax: (32) 761-1549
Internet: www.inchon.ac.kr

President: HONG CHUL

Colleges of Humanities, Natural Sciences, Social Sciences, Law, Engineering, Economics and Business Administration, North-east Asian Studies, Arts and Physical Education.

INHA UNIVERSITY

253 Yonghyn-dong, Nam-gu, Inchon 402-751
Telephone: (32) 860-7030
Fax: (32) 867-7222
E-mail: orir@inha.ac.kr
Internet: www.inha.ac.kr

Founded 1954
Private control
Academic year: March to February

President: Dr SEOUNG-YONG HONG
Vice-President: Dr BYUNG-HA CHOI
Registrar: Dr CHONG-BO KIM
Librarian: Dr MYUNG-KOO YUN

Library of 350,000 vols
Number of teachers: 644
Number of students: 18,116

Publications: bulletins of the research institutes.

DEANS

Graduate School: Dr JI-HOON CHOI
Graduate School of Business Administration: Dr YONG-HWI SHINN
Graduate School of Education: Dr KI-HO CHUNG
Graduate School of Engineering: Dr DONG-IL KIM
Graduate School of Public Administration: Dr YOUNG-SANG SHIN
Engineering: Dr BYUNG-HEE KANG
Natural Sciences: Dr DAE-YOON PARK
Business and Economics: Dr KI-MYUNG KIM
Education: Dr CHANG-GEOL KIM
Law and Political Science: Dr YOUNG-HEE LEE
Humanities: Dr WOO-JIN KIM
Home Economics: (vacant)
Medicine: Dr SEH-HWAN KIM

ATTACHED RESEARCH INSTITUTES

Aviation Management Research Institute: Dir Dr YOUNG-SIK HONG.

Basic Science Research Institute: Dir Dr SUH-YUNG YANG.

Center for International Studies: Dir Dr BYUNG-WON PARK.

Center for Korean Studies: Dir Dr PYONG-SUK YUN.

Environmental Research Institute: Dir Dr KWANG-MYEUNG CHO.

Humanities Research Institute: Dir Dr MOON-CHANG KIM.

Institute for Business and Economic Research: Dir Dr DAE-HWAN KIM.

Institute for Information and Electronics Research: Dir Dr SEUNG-HONG HONG.

Institute of Advanced Materials: Dir Dr WON-KOO PARK.

Institute of Computer Science and Applications: Dir Dr CHANG-JONG WANG.

Institute of Polymer Science and Engineering: Dir Dr DONG-CHOO LEE.

Management Research Institute: Dir Dr MYUNG-SUP CHUN.

Medicinal Toxicology Research Institute: Dir Dr YONG-NAM CHA.

Ocean Science and Technology Institute: Dir Dr YONG-CHUL LEE.

Science and Technology Research Institute: Dir Dr BONG-GOO WOO.

Social Science Research Institute: Dir Dr YONG-WOO KIM.

Sports Science Research Institute: Dir Dr YOUNG-JUN HA.

Student Life Research Institute: Dir Dr YOUNG-SOO JUNG.

Education Research Institute: Dir Dr HEUNG-KYU KIM.

Domestic Science Research Institute: Dir Dr CHAN-BOO PARK.

INJE UNIVERSITY

607 Obang-Dong, Gimhae, Gyeongnam 621-749
Telephone: (55) 334-7111
Fax: (55) 334-0712
E-mail: webmaster@ijnc.inje.ac.kr
Internet: www.inje.ac.kr

Founded 1983

Chairman: NAK WHAN PAIK
President: CHANGMO SUNG

Library of 500,000

Colleges of Medicine, Biomedical Science and Engineering, Humanities and Social Sciences, Natural Sciences, Engineering, Design, Music.

JEONJU UNIVERSITY

1200 Hyoja-dong, Wansangu, Chonju Jeollabukdo 520-759
Telephone: (652) 220-2122
Fax: (652) 220-2074
Internet: www.jeonju.ac.kr

Colleges of Christian Studies, Language and Culture, Law and Public Administration, Social Science, Economics and Information, Business Administration, Natural Science, Information Technology and Computer Science, Engineering, Architecture,

Arts, Athletics and Visual Communication, Culture and Tourism, Teachers' College.

JINJU NATIONAL UNIVERSITY

150 Chilamdong, Jinju, Kyongnam Kyongnam 660-758
Telephone: (55) 751-3114
Fax: (55) 752-9554
Internet: www.chinju.ac.kr
Founded 1910
President: JUNG HAE-JU
Colleges of Agriculture, Science and Engineering, Humanities and Social Services.

KANGNAM UNIVERSITY

San 6-2 Kukal-ri, Kihueng-eup, Yonasin-shi, Kyunggi-do 449-702
Telephone: (331) 280-3421
Fax: (331) 280-3428
E-mail: master@venus.kangnam.ac.kr
Internet: www.kangnam.ac.kr
Founded 1946
Private control
Academic year: March to December
Chairman: DO-HAN YOON
President: BYOUNG-JOON CHOE
Chief Librarian: SEUNG-HWAN KIM
Library of 240,000 books
Number of teachers: 170
Number of students: 6,534 (6,433 undergraduate, 101 postgraduate)

DEANS

College of Theology: Prof. SOOK-JONG LEE
College of Humanities: Prof. SUNG-MO JO
College of Social Sciences: Prof. CHANG-SUK LEE
College of Social Welfare: Prof. YOUNG-HO KIM
College of Management and Economics: Prof. JAE-HA HWANG
College of Science and Engineering: Prof. KI-SUNG PARK
College of Art and Physical Education: Prof. JAE-YONG YANG
Graduate School: SANG-HAK NO (Pres.)

KANGNUNG NATIONAL UNIVERSITY

123 Chibyon-dong, Kangnung, Kangwon-do 210-702
Telephone: (33) 640-2766
Fax: (33) 640-2768
E-mail: ciec@kangnung.ac.kr
Internet: www.kangnung.ac.kr
Founded 1968 as Kangnung Educational College; became Kangnung Junior College 1977 and Kangnung National College 1979; present name 1991
State control
Academic year: March to December (two semesters)
Colleges of Humanities, Social Sciences, Natural Sciences, Engineering, Life Sciences, Arts and Physical Education, Dentistry; 17 research institutes, museum, gallery
President: Dr SONG HAN
Director of Center for International Exchange and Cooperation: Dr SANG-HOON LEE
Library of 340,000 vols, 970 periodicals
Number of teachers: 258 full-time, 370 part-time
Number of students: 7,321.

KANGWEON NATIONAL UNIVERSITY

192-1 Hyoja-dong, Chuncheon 200-701, Kangweon-do
Telephone: (33) 250-7192
Fax: (33) 253-1964
E-mail: intn@cc.kangwon.ac.kr
Internet: www.kangwon.ac.kr
Founded 1947
President: YONG SOO PARK
Registrar: HYUNG-SIK LIM
Librarian: KYUNG-HO PARK
Library of 206,000 vols
Number of teachers: 378
Number of students: 16,000

DEANS

College of Business Administration: JONG-SEOP SHIM
College of Engineering: JE-SEON PARK
College of Agriculture: SANG-YOUNG LEE
College of Law: JEUNG-HU KIM
College of Education: KEUN-SEONG CHOI
College of Humanities and Social Science: HAN-SEOL PARK
College of Forestry: SU-CHANG KIM
College of Natural Sciences: CHONG-HYEOK LEE

KAYA UNIVERSITY

120 Jisan-ri, Koryong-kun, Kyungbuk 717-800
Telephone: (543) 954-1438
Fax: (543) 954-6094
E-mail: webmaster@kaya.ac.kr
Internet: www.kaya.ac.kr
Founded 1993
Private control
Languages of instruction: Korean, English
Academic year: March to December
President: Dr KYUNG-HEE LEE
Librarian: Prof. DONG-HAE LEE
Library of 2,800,000 vols
Number of teachers: 103
Number of students: 4,120 (4,000 undergraduate, 120 postgraduate)

DEANS

Faculty of Social Sciences: Prof. CHANG-HUN OK
Department of Engineering: Prof. SANG-HEE PARK

KEIMYUNG UNIVERSITY

1000 Shindang-dong, Dalseo-Gu, Taegu 704-701
Telephone: (53) 580-6022
Fax: (53) 580-6025
E-mail: intl_aff@kmu.ac.kr
Internet: www.kmu.ac.kr
Founded 1954
Private control
Academic year: March to February
President: SYNN ILHI
Vice-President for Academic Affairs: PAEK SEUNG KYUN
Vice-President for Medical Affairs: KANG JIN-SUNG
Dean of Dongsan Library: PARK JOON-SHIK
Library of 1,174,000 vols
Number of teachers: 1,284 (604 full-time, 680 part-time)
Number of students: 21,126
Publications: *Journal of the Institute for Cross-Cultural Studies, Business Management Review, Asian Journal of Business and Entrepreneurship, Bulletin of the Institute for International Science, Proceedings of Mathematical Science, Journal of the Institute of Natural Sciences, Journal of Social Sciences, Journal of Art and Culture, Journal of Nakdonggang Environmental Research Institute, Journal of Life Science Research, Keimyung Journal of Nursing Science, Keimyung University Medical Journal, Journal of the Institute for Japanese Studies, Journal of International Studies, Keimyung Law Review, Accounting Information Review*

DEANS

Graduate School: PARK YOUNG CHOON
Graduate School of Education: KIM KI-HAN
Graduate School of Business Administration: KIM JIN TAK
Graduate School of Policy Development: CHOI BONG KI
Graduate School of Women's Studies: JOO KWANG JEE
Graduate School of Industrial Technology: KIM HONG YOUNG
Graduate School of International Studies: OH SEI-CHANG
Graduate School of Pastoral Theology: CHONG JOONG-HO
Graduate School of Arts: KIM JEONG GIL
Graduate School of Industrial Design: HUR YONG
Graudate School of the Sports Industry: KIM SANG-HONG
Graduate School of Medical Management: PARK YOUNG NAM
Faculty of Language and Literature: KIM JONG SUN
Faculty of Humanities: JIN WON-SUK
College of Education: SIM HO TACK
Faculty of International Studies: LI JONG-KWANG
Faculty of Commerce: OH SEI-CHANG
Faculty of Business Administration: PARK MYUNG-HO
Faculty of Social Sciences: KIM SE SHUL
Faculty of Politics and Economics: CHO YONG SANG
Faculty of Police Sciences: CHOI EUNG RYUL
Faculty of Law: CHOI SANG-HO
Faculty of Basic Sciences: UHM JAE-KUK
Faculty of Applied Sciences: MIN HYUNG-JIN
Faculty of Environmental Studies: KIM IN-HWAN
Faculty of Construction Systems Engineering: KIM JONG YOUNG
Faculty of Automotive Engineering: SHIN SUNG-HEON
Faculty of Computer and Electronic Engineering: SON YOO-EK
Faculty of Chemical and Materials Engineering: SYNN DONG-SU
School of Medicine: PARK YOUNG NAM
Faculty of Nursing: KIM JEONG NAM
Faculty of Human Life Sciences: JOO KWANG JEE
Faculty of Music: KIM JEONG GIL
Faculty of Fine Arts: HUR YONG
Faculty of Fashion: JON KYONG-TAE
Faculty of Physical Education: KIM SANG HONG

ATTACHED INSTITUTES

Research Institute for the Humanities: Dir LEE JIN-WOO.

Institute for International Studies: Dir LIM MOUN-YOUNG.

Research Institute for Social Science: Dir KIM SE SHUL.

Institute of Industrial Management Research: Dir CHO BONG JIN.

Research Institute for Natural Sciences: Dir UHM JAE KUK.

Research Institute for Industrial Technology: Dir KIM JEONG HWAN.

Research Institute for the Arts: Dir WOO CHUNG-IL.

Research Institute of Life Sciences: Dir YOON JIN-SOOK.

Research Institute for Medical Science: Dir KWAK CHUN SIK.

Research Institute for Medical Heredity: Dir PARK YOUNG NAM.

Research Institute for Nursing Science: Dir KIM JEONG NAM.

Institute for Brain Research: Dir YIM MAN BIN.

KONGJU NATIONAL UNIVERSITY

182 Shinkwan-dong, Kongju, Chungnam
Telephone: (416) 850-8114
Fax: (416) 853-3517
Internet: www.kongju.ac.kr
Founded 1948 as Kongju Provincial Teachers' College; became Kongju National Teachers' College 1950; present name 1991
President: Dr SUCK-WON CHOI
Dean, Office of Academic Affairs: HYUNG-TAE MOON
Director General: CHANG-YONG PARK
Library of 360,000
Number of teachers: 602
Number of students: 13,560

DEANS

College of Education: BYUNG-MOO KIM
College of Humanities and Social Sciences: PIL-YOUNG LEE
College of Sciences: YOUNG-KYUN WOO
College of Engineering: KUM-BAE LEE
College of Industrial Sciences: SEONG-MIN KIM

KON-KUK UNIVERSITY

1 Hwayang-dong, Gwangjin-gu, Seoul 143-701
Telephone: (2) 450-3259
Fax: (2) 450-3257
Internet: www.konkuk.ac.kr
Founded 1946, university status 1959
Private control
Academic year: March to February
Chairman: KYUNG-HEE KIM
President: KIL-SAENG CHUNG
Vice-Presidents: YUNG-KYE KANG (Seoul Campus): MOON-JA UM (Chungju Campus)
Registrar: HYEON-LYONG KIM
Librarian: YUNG-KWON KIM
Library of 1,130,000 vols
Number of teachers: 589 (full time)
Number of students: 17,177
Publications: *Newspaper* (weekly), *English Newspaper* (monthly)

ACADEMIC DEANS

College of Agriculture: CHONG-CHON KIM
College of Animal Husbandry: CHANG-WON KANG
College of Architecture: YONG-SIK KIM
College of Art: HO-CHANG RYU
College of Arts and Design: HYUNG-JAE MAENG
College of Arts and Home Economics: WON-JA LEE
College of Business Administration: THOMAS T. H. JOH
College of Commerce and Economics: JEONG-PYO CHOL
College of Education: II HWANG
College of Engineering: KWANG-SOO KIM
College of Humanities: SOON-BONG PACK
College of Information & Telecommunication: SUN-YOUNG HAN
College of Law: SEUNG-HO LEE
College of Life Environment: SUK-HUN KYUNG
College of Medicine: TAE-KYU PACK
College of Natural Sciences: LEE-CHOI CHANG
College of Social Sciences: YOUNG-BOON LEE
College of Veterinary Medicine: BYUNG-JOO KIM
Graduate School: JOO-YOUNG LEE
Graduate School of Agriculture and Animal Science: SUN-JOO KIM
Graduate School of Architecture: BYOUNG-KEUN KANG
Graduate School of Business Administration: DAE-HO KIM
Graduate School of Design: LEE-SANG EUN
Graduate School of Education: DONG-OK LEE
Graduate School of Engineering: JOONG-RIN SHIN
Graduate School of Information and Telecommunication: CHUN-HYON CHANG
College of Liberal Arts: OH-HYUN CHO
Graduate School of Mass Communication: DAE-IN KANG
Graduate School of Medicine: KYUNG-YUNG LEE
College of Political Science: SUNG-BOK LEE
Graduate School of Public Administration: EUN-JAE LEE
Graduate School of Real Estate Studies: CHO-JOO HYUN
College of Sciences: JUNE-TAK RHEE
Graduate School of Social Sciences: NAM-KYU PARK

ATTACHED INSTITUTES

Humanities Research Institute.

Basic Science Research Institute.

Institute of Industrial Science and Technology.

Social Science Research Institute.

Public Administration Research Institute.

Institute of Economics and Management.

Animal Resources Research Center.

Research Institute of Agricultural Resources Development.

Institute of Life Culture.

Education Research Institute.

Joong Won Research Institute of Humanities.

Institute for Social Development and Policy.

Research Institute of Natural Science.

Arts and Design Research Institute.

Research Institute of Medical Sciences.

Research Institute of Chinese Affairs.

Research Institute of Korean Affairs.

Institute of Korean Reunification Studies.

Environmental Science Research Institute.

Law Research Institute.

Center for Real Estate Policy.

Research Center for the Korean History of Technology.

Research Institute of Korean Politics and Society.

Research Institute of Livestock Management and Environmental Economics

KONYANG UNIVERSITY

26 Nae-Dong, Nonsan, Chungnam 320-711
Telephone: (41) 730-5114
Fax: (41) 733-2070
E-mail: webmaster@konyang.ac.kr
Internet: www.konyang.ac.kr
Founded 1991
President: HEE-SOO KIM
Library of 250,000 .

KOOKMIN UNIVERSITY

861-1, Chongnung-dong, Songbuk-ku, Seoul 136-702
Telephone: (2) 910-4114
Internet: www.kookmin.ac.kr
Founded 1946
President: MOON-HWAN KIM
Dean of Academic Affairs: Prof. KIM YOUNG-JEON
Dean of Student Affairs: Prof. LEE JONG-EUN
Dean of General Affairs: KIL YEONG-BAE
Dean of Planning and Development Affairs: Prof. KANG SIN-DON
Library: *c.* 200,000 vols
Number of teachers: 159 full-time
Number of teachers: 211 part-time
Number of students: 15,000
Publications: *Kookmin University Press* (weekly), *Kookmin Tribune* (English, monthly), *Kookmin University Bulletin* (annually), *Theses* (annually), *Journal of Language and Literature, Papers in Chinese Studies, Theses of Korean Studies, Law and Political Review, Economic and Business Administration Review, Theses of Engineering, Design Review, Education Review, Journal of the Scientific Institute, Journal of Sports Science Research*

DEANS

Graduate School: CHOI HWAN-YOL
Graduate School of Education: CHOI HWAN-YOL
Graduate School of Business Administration: CHOI HWAN-YOL
Graduate School of Public Administration: LEE YOUNG-SUN
College of Liberal Arts: Prof. LEE JUNG-KEE
College of Law and Political Science: LEE YONG-SUN
College of Economics and Business Administration: NAH OH-YOUN
College of Engineering: Prof. YOON TAI-YOON
College of Architecture and Design: Prof. KIM CHUL-SOO
College of Education: SHIN JOONG-SHIK
College of Forestry: KO YUNG-ZU

ATTACHED RESEARCH INSTITUTES

Economic Research Institute.

Institute for Saemaul Undong.

Institute for Korean Studies.

Institute of Language and Literature.

Legal Research Institute.

Institute of Industrial Technology.

Educational Research Institute.

Environmental Design Research Institute.

Myongwon Tea Ceremony Research Institute.

Sports Science Institute.

Basic Science Institute.

Institute for Chinese Studies.

Social Sciences Institute

KOREA ADVANCED INSTITUTE OF SCIENCE AND TECHNOLOGY (KAIST)

373-1 Kusong-dong, Yusong-ku, Taejon 305-701
Telephone: (42) 869-2114
Fax: (42) 869-2260
E-mail: oir@sorak.kaist.ac.kr
Internet: www.kaist.ac.kr
Founded 1981 by merger of Korea Advanced Institute of Science (KAIS) and Korea Institute of Science and Technology (KIST); KIST separated from KAIST 1989; Korea Institute of Technology (KIT) merged with KAIST 1989
State control
Academic year: March to February
President: CHANG-SUN HONG
Colleges of Natural Science, Engineering, Humanities and Social Science, Graduate School of Management.

KOREA MARITIME UNIVERSITY

1 Dongsam-Dong, Yeongdo-gu, Busan 606-791
E-mail: webmaster@hhu.ac.kr
Internet: www.kmaritime.ac.kr
Colleges of Maritime Sciences, Ocean Science and Technology, Engineering, International Studies.

KOREA NATIONAL OPEN UNIVERSITY

169 Dongsung-dong, Chongro-ku, Seoul 110-791
Telephone: (2) 7404-114
Fax: (2) 744-5882
E-mail: webmaster@knou.ac.kr
Internet: www.knou.ac.kr
Founded 1972
State control
Academic year: March to February
President: Dr KYOO-HYANG CHO
Registrar: EUI-DONG KIM
Library Director: SUNG-KIH KIM
Library of 412,000 vols
Number of teachers: 112
Number of students: 199,000
Publications: *KNOU Journal*, *Distance Education*, *KNOU Newsletter*, *KNOU Weekly*

DEANS

College of Liberal Arts: YONG-HAK LEE
College of Social Science: SOO-SIN KIM
College of Natural Science: HYE-SEON KIM
College of Education: CHONG-SOOK CHOI
School of General Education: YUNG-HO LEE

HEADS OF DEPARTMENTS

Korean: YONG-SHIK YOON
English: DONG-KOOK LEE
Chinese: SEONG-KON KIM
French: YONG-CHOL LEE
Law: NOHYUN KWAK
Public Administration: JI-WON KIM
Economics: KYWON KIM
Business Administration: DONG-HEE CHUNG
Trade: JONG-SUNG KIM
Media Arts and Science: CHUL-JU LEE
Agricultural Science: HYON-WON LEE
Home Economics: YOUNG-JA BAIK
Computer Science: EON-BAI LEE
Education: HWA-TAE CHO
Early Childhood Education: SUN-HEE PARK
Applied Statistics: TAE-RIM LEE
Health Hygienics: SOO-YOUL KWON

ATTACHED INSTITUTES

Institute of Distance Education: Dir SOON-JEONG HONG.

Educational Media Development Centre: Dir DUK-HUN KWAK.

KOREA NATIONAL UNIVERSITY OF THE ARTS

San 1-5 Seokgwan-dong, Seongbuk-gu, Seoul 136-716
Telephone: (2) 958-2553
Fax: (2) 958-2549
E-mail: global@knua.ac.kr
Founded 1993
President: GEON-YONG LEE
Number of teachers: 730
Number of students: 2,600
Colleges of Music, Drama, Film, Television and Multimedia, Dance, Visual Arts, Korean Traditional Arts.

KOREA NATIONAL UNIVERSITY OF EDUCATION

7 Darak-ri, Kangnae-myon, Chongwon-gun, Chungbuk 363-791
Telephone: (43) 230-3114
Fax: (43) 233-2207
E-mail: internat@knuecc-sun.knue.ac.kr
Internet: www.knue.ac.kr
Founded 1984
President: BAE-HUN PARK
Library of 300,000 vols
Number of teachers: 331
Number of students: 6,060.

KOREA UNIVERSITY

1, 5-ga, Anam-dong, Sungbuk-gu, Seoul 136-701
Telephone: (2) 3290-1152
Fax: (2) 922-5820
Internet: www.korea.ac.kr
Founded 1905, as Posung College
Private control: financed by the Korea-Choongang Educational Foundation
Language of instruction: Korean
Academic year: March to February (two semesters)
President: YOON-DAE EUH (acting)
Dean of Planning and Public Relations: MANN-JANG PARK
Dean of Academic Affairs: CHANG-YIL AHN
Dean of Students: SONG-BOK KIM
Dean of General Affairs: SA-SOON YOUN
Dean of Construction and Facility Management: YOUNG-HYUN PAIK
Librarian: IL-CHUL SHIN
Library: see Libraries
Number of teachers: 627 full-time
Number of teachers: 781 part-time
Number of students: 21,685
Publications: *Kodai Shinmoon* (Korean, weekly), *The Granite Tower* (English, every 2 weeks), *Gyongyong Shinmoon* (Korean, weekly), *Kodai Moonwha* (Korean, annually), *Phoenix* (bilingual, annually), *Korea University Bulletin* (English, annually), and many other periodicals

DEANS

College of Agriculture: BEYOUNG-HWA KWACK
College of Business Administration: JANG RHO LEE
College of Education: IN-JONG YOU
College of Engineering: JONG-HWI HONG
College of Law: JONG-DAE BAE
College of Liberal Arts: PONG-HEUM HAN
College of Medicine: SUNG-YONG PARK
College of Political Science and Economics: YONG-BUM CHO
College of Science: SI-JOONG KIM
Graduate School: BONG-WHAN LAU
Graduate School of Business Administration: DONG-KI KIM
Graduate School of Education: SUNG-TAI KIM
Graduate School of Food and Agriculture: HAN-CHUL YANG
College of Liberal Arts and Science (Jochiwon campus): JUNG-BAI KIM
College of Economics and Commerce (Jochiwon campus): JUNG-BAI KIM

CHAIRMEN OF DEPARTMENTS

College of Agriculture:
- Agricultural Chemistry: SE-YONG LEE
- Agricultural Economics: YOUNG-SIK KIM
- Agronomy: HYOK-JI KWON
- Animal Science: YONG-SUK SON
- Food Technology: CHUL-RHEE
- Forestry: KI-HYON PAIK
- Genetic Engineering: YONG-JIN CHOI
- Horticulture: KUEN-WOO PARK
- Plant Protection: BYUNG-KOOK HWANG

College of Business Administration:
- Business Administration: PHIL-SANG LEE
- International Trade: BYUNG-GUK HWANG

College of Education:
- Education: KI-HANG WANG
- English Language Education: CHONG-KEON KIM
- Geography Education: YOUNG-JOON CHOE
- History Education: HYUN-KOO KIM
- Home Economics: OCK-BOON CHUNG
- Korean Language Education: KWANG-SOO SUNG
- Mathematics Education: JUNG-SOOK SAKONG
- Physical Education: SANG-KYEM KIM

College of Engineering:
- Architectural Engineering: DONG-YANG YANG
- Chemical Engineering: SUK-IN HONG
- Civil Engineering: EUI-SO CHOI
- Electrical Engineering: GWI-TAE PARK
- Electronic and Computer Engineering: KYUN-HYON TCHAH
- Industrial Systems and Information Engineering: SUNG-SHICK KIM
- Materials Science: DOK-YOL LEE
- Mechanical Engineering: HYO-WHAN CHANG

College of Law:
- Law: CHONG-BOK LEE

College of Liberal Arts:
- Chinese Language and Literature: DONG-HYANG LEE
- English Language and Literature: KYOUNG-JA PARK
- French Language and Literature: SUNG-GI JON
- German Language and Literature: SUNG-OCK KIM
- History: IN-SUN YU
- Japanese Literature: CHOON-MIE KIM
- Korean Language and Literature: IN-HWAN KIM
- Philosophy: HONG-BIN LIM
- Psychology: MAHN-YOUNG LEE
- Russian Language and Literature: SUN CHOI
- Spanish Language and Literature: HYOUNG-NAM NOH
- Sociology: CHOON YANG

College of Medicine:
- Premedical Course: YONG-HYUCK CHUN
- Medicine: BOE-GWUN CHUN
- Nursing: PYOUNG-SOOK LEE

College of Political Science and Economics:
- Economics: CHANG-HO YOON
- Political Science and International Relations: SUNG-JOO HAN
- Statistics: MYUNG-HOE HUH
- Public Administration: YOUNG-PYOUNG KIM

College of Science:
- Chemistry: YOUNG-SANG CHOI
- Earth and Environmental Science: CHIL-SUP SO
- Mathematics: IN-SUK WEE
- Physics: JOO-SANG KANG

College of Economics and Commerce (Jochiwon campus):
- Management Information Systems: MOON-CHAN RIEW
- Business Administration: GYUN-HWA JUNG
- International Trade: GWANG-HYUN LEE
- Economics: YEONG-DAE HAHN
- Public Administration: SI-YUL PYO

AFFILIATED RESEARCH INSTITUTES

Anglo-American Studies Institute: Dir Prof. CHONG-WHA CHUNG.

Asiatic Research Center: Dir Prof. SUNG-JOO HAN.

Behavioural Science Research Center: Dir Prof. SUNG-CHICK HONG.

Business Management Research Center: Dir Prof. CHUNG JEE.

German Studies Institute: Dir Prof. PONG-HEUM HAN.

Institute of Economic Development: Dir Prof. SANG-KYUNG KWAK.

Institute of Environmental Health: Dir Prof. CHUL-WHAN CHA.

Institute of Industrial Science and Technology: Dir Prof. BYUNG-HOON CHUN.

Institute of Law: Dir Prof. ZAI-WOO SHIM.

Institute of Medico-Legal Affairs: Dir Prof. KOOK-JIN MOON.

Institute of Plastic Reconstruction and Special Surgery: Dir Prof. SE-MIN BAEK.

Institute of Statistics: Dir Prof. JAE-CHANG LEE.

Institute of Tropical Endemic Diseases: Dir Prof. HAN-JONG RIM.

Institute of Viral Diseases: Dir Prof. HO-WANG LEE.

Korea Nutrition Research Institute: Dir Prof. WOO-IK HWANG.

Korean Cultural Research Center: Dir Prof. IL-SIK HONG.

Korean Entomological Institute: Dir Prof. HAK-RYUL KIM.

Labor Education and Research Institute: Dir Prof. TSCHONG-NAE SONG.

Mass Communications Research Institute: Dir Prof. YONG-YOON.

Research Institute of Basic Sciences: Dir Prof. TAE-HWAN CHANG.

Research Institute of Education: Dir Prof. SUK-KEE CHA.

Research Institute for Food Resources: Dir Prof. YONG-KYO KIM.

Research Institute for Sports Science: Dir Prof. BYUNG-KI SUN.

Russian Studies Institute: Dir Prof. HAK-SOON KIM.

Student Guidance Center: Dir Prof. CHANG-YIL AHN.

KOSIN UNIVERSITY

149-1 Dongsam-dong, Yeongdo-gu, Busan 606-701

Telephone: (51) 990-2114
Fax: (51) 911-2525
E-mail: jhpark@kosin.ac.kr
Internet: www.kosin.ac.kr

Founded 1946

President: CHUNG HYUN-KEE

Library of 120,000 vols

Colleges of Theology, Humanities and Social Sciences, Natural Sciences, Health Sciences, Human Ecology, Computer Sciences, Arts, Medicine.

KUMOH NATIONAL UNIVERSITY OF TECHNOLOGY

188 Shinpyung, Kumi, Kyungbuk 730-701

Telephone: (546) 467-4114
Fax: (546) 461-0136
E-mail: webmaster@kumoh.kumoh.ac.kr
Internet: www.kumoh.ac.kr

Founded 1979 as Kumoh Institute of Technology; became Kumoh National Institute of Technology 1990; present name 1993

President: Dr JAE-HUN KIM.

KUNSAN NATIONAL UNIVERSITY

San 68 Miryong-dong, Kunsan, Chonbuk-do 573-701

Telephone: (63) 469-4134
Fax: (63) 469-4197
E-mail: inter@kunsan.ac.kr
Internet: www.kunsan.ac.kr

Founded 1979

Language of instruction: Korean, English
Academic year: March to February

President: Dr HEE-YEON LEE

Library of 280,000 vols
Number of teachers: 327
Number of students: 11,065

PROFESSORS

College of Arts, School of Fine Arts and Design:
- CHO, Y. B., Department of Industrial Design
- KIM, S. T., Department of Industrial Ceramic Arts
- KIM, Y. O., Department of Music

College of Engineering, Faculty of Electronic and Information Engineering:
- LEE, J. I., Electronic and Information Engineering
- HEO, B. M., Department of Mechanical Design Engineering
- LIM, B. Y., Department of Civil Engineering
- KIM, S. G., Materials Science and Engineering
- LEE, H. Y., Department of Chemical Engineering
- MOON, C. H., Department of Architectural Engineering

College of Humanities, Faculty of Oriental Language and Literature:
- MOON, C.-S., Department of Japanese Language and Literature
- PARK, B.-S., Department of Chinese Language and Literature
- LIM, K.-J., Department of Philosophy
- PAE, B. H., Department of German Literature and Language
- CHO, S. H., Department of Korean Language and Literature
- SEO, H. S., Department of English Language and Literature
- LEE, H. H., Department of History

College of Natural Sciences:
- YOON, C. S., Department of Physics
- LEE, K. S., Department of Biological Science
- CHOI, H. S., Department of Chemistry
- HANG, T. S., Department of Mathematics
- PARK, Y. S., Department of Informatics and Statistics
- RYOU, O. S., Department of Human Ecology
- KIM, S. Y., Department of Food Science and Nutrition
- KIM, A. S., Department of Clothing and Textiles

College of Ocean Science and Technology:
- CHUNG, E. Y., Department of Aquaculture and Biotechnology
- KIM, Y. G., Department of Marine Life Science
- LEE, K. R., Department of Marine Science and Production
- JEONG, K. J., Department of Marine Engineering
- CHANG, S. H., Department of Food Science and Technology
- SEO, S. W., Department of Ocean System Engineering
- YIH, W. H., Department of Ocean Information Science

College of Social Sciences:
- KIM, Y.-J., Public Administration
- LIM, H. J., Economics and Trade
- HWANG, H. M., International Trade
- KWON, E. M., Business Administration and Accounting

KWANDONG UNIVERSITY

522 Naegok-dong, Kangnung-si, Gangwon-do 210-701

Telephone: (33) 641-1011
Fax: (33) 641-1010
Internet: www.kwandong.ac.kr

Founded 1959

President: BYONG-JIN YOU
Number of students: 8,000

Colleges of Humanities, Law and Politics, Arts, Education, Science and Engineering, Medicine.

KWANGJU UNIVERSITY

Kwangju 503-703
Internet: kwangju.ac.kr

Founded 1981 as Kwangju Kyung Sang Junior College; became Kwangju Open College 1984; present name 1989

President: Dr JAE-WOON LEE

Library of 230,000 vols

Colleges of Management, Commerce and Social Welfare, Humanities and Social Sciences, Engineering, Arts; Graduate School.

KWANGWOON UNIVERSITY

447-1 Wolgye-dong, Nowon-gu, Seoul 139-701

Telephone: (2) 940-5114
E-mail: hsk@kw.ac.kr
Internet: www.kwangwoon.ac.kr

President: YOUNG-SHIK PARK

Colleges of Electronics and Information, Engineering, Natural Sciences, Humanities and Social Sciences, Law, Business.

KYONGGI UNIVERSITY

94-6 Yiu-dong, Yeongtong-gu, Suwon, Kyonggi-do 443-760
E-mail: webmaster@kyonggi.ac.kr
Internet: www.kyonggi.ac.kr

Founded 1957

Chairman: CHEONG-SOO CHU
Chancellor: CHONG-KUK SON
Number of students: 13,000

Colleges of Humanities and Arts, Social Sciences, Natural Sciences and Engineering, Graduate Schools of Architecture, Politics and Policy, Tourism Management, Service Business Administration, Education International Studies, Industrial Technology and Information, Traditional Arts, Public Administration, Information and Communication, Arts and Design, Sports Sciences, Alternative Medicine, Social Welfare.

KYONGJU UNIVERSITY

San. 42-1 Hyohyun-dong, Kyongju, Kyungbuk 780-712

Telephone: (54) 770-5114
Fax: (54) 748-5553
E-mail: webmaster@gyeongju.ac.kr
Internet: www.kyongju.ac.kr

Founded 1988 as Korea Tourism University; present name 1993

Private control

President: Dr CHEONG-KON HAN

Colleges of Tourism Studies, Foreign Languages and Tourism, Law and Public Administration, Construction and Environment, Business Administration and Advertising, Computer and Information Science.

KYUNG HEE UNIVERSITY

1 Hoegi-dong, Dongdaemun-ku, Seoul 130-701
Telephone: (2) 961-0031
Fax: (2) 962-4343
E-mail: cie@nms.kyunghee.ac.kr
Internet: www.kyunghee.ac.kr
Founded 1949; renamed 1952
Private control
Academic year: March to December (two terms)
Founder-Chancellor: Dr YOUNG SEEK CHOUE
President: BYUNG-MOOK KIM
Vice-Presidents: BYUNG MOOK KIM (Seoul Campus): KYU HONG PARK (Suwon Campus): MYUNG KWAN PARK (Development)
Registrars: DONG JOON CHOO (Seoul Campus): WON-KYUNG CHO (Suwon Campus)
Librarians: JAE HONG KIM (Seoul Campus): HAN WON KIM (Suwon Campus)
Library of 1,200,000 vols, separate medical library of 15,000 vols
Number of teachers: 2,300
Number of students: 29,080
Publications: *University Life* (in English, monthly), *University Weekly* (in Korean), *Kohwang* (in Korean, annually), *Peace Forum* (in English, every 2 years), research bulletins for each college

DEANS

Seoul Campus:

College of Liberal Arts and Sciences: BOK-KEUN CHUNG
College of Law: SHIYOON LEE
College of Political Science and Economics: SUNG-HAN SUH
College of Tourism and Hotel Management: KON-JO YOO
College of Human Ecology: HYUN-SUH PARK
College of Medicine: YOUG HO CHO
College of Oriental Medicine: HYUNG KOO LEE
College of Dentistry: SANG RAE LEE
College of Pharmacy: YOUNG SOO RHO
College of Music: SUN HWANG
Graduate School: KWANG SHIK SOHN
Graduate School of East–West Medicine: KI-WON RYU
Graduate School of Business Administration: KEUN SOO LEE
Graduate School of Public Administration: SEI DEUK OH
Graduate School of Education: KEE-SAW PARK
Graduate School of Journalism and Mass Communication: SUK-WOO LEE
Graduate School of Physical Education: KI CHAE KOH
Graduate School of International Legal Affairs: MYUNG-SUNG YUN
Graduate School of Tourism: KONG-JO YOO
Graduate School of NGO: KUN WOO PARK
Graduate School of Peace Studies: JAE-SHIK SOHN

Suwon Campus:

College of Foreign Languages: JONG HUH
College of Social Sciences and Department of Management and International Relations: WON-KYU PARK
College of Natural Sciences and Department of the Environment and Applied Chemistry: SUK JIN CHOUNG
College of Engineering and Department of Electronics and Information Technology: KYE SUK JUN
College of Industry and Department of Life Science: JAE SUN JO
College of Sports Science and Department of Physical Education: JIN HO KIM
Department of Mechanical and Industrial Systems Engineering: KYOUNG SUK PARK
Department of Civil and Architectural Engineering: YOUNG TAE ON
Department of Art and Design: HEON LOOK LEE
Graduate School of Industry and Information Science: KYE TAK LEE
Graduate School of Pan-Pacific International Studies: CHONGSOO KIM
Graduate School of Information and Communication: YONG-OHK CHIN

DEPARTMENTS

College of Humanities (1 Hoegi-dong, Dongdaemun-ku, Seoul 130-701; tel. (2) 961-0221; e-mail khsc0100@khu.ac.kr; fax (2) 963-3152):

- Korean Language and Literature
- English Language and Literature
- Philosophy
- History

College of Law (1 Hoegi-dong, Dongdaemun-ku, Seoul 130-701; tel. (2) 961-0611; fax (2) 961-0615; e-mail khsc0200@khu.ac.kr):

- Legal Science
- International Legal Affairs

College of Political Science and Economics (1 Hoegi-dong, Dongdaemun-ku, Seoul 130-701; tel. (2) 961-0621; fax (2) 961-0622):

- Social Sciences
- Economics and International Trade
- Sociology
- Journalism and Communication

College of Business Administration (1 Hoegi-dong, Dongdaemun-ku, Seoul 130-701; tel. (2) 961-0511; fax (2) 961-0151; e-mail khsc0320@khu.ac.kr):

- Business Administration
- Accounting
- Health Service Management
- e-Business

College of Tourism and Hotel Management (1 Hoegi-dong, Dongdaemun-ku, Seoul 130-701; tel. (2) 961-0803; fax (2) 964-2537; e-mail khsc1600@khu.ac.kr):

- School of Tourism
- Hotel and Tourism Management
- Tourism Interpretation
- Food Service Management
- Culinary Science and Arts

College of Sciences (1 Hoegi-dong, Dongdaemun-ku Seoul 130-701; tel. (2) 961-0230; fax (2) 961-9154; e-mail sobas@khu.ac.kr):

- Mathematics
- Physics
- Chemistry
- Biology
- Geography

College of Human Ecology (1 Hoegi-dong, Dongdaemun-ku, Seoul 130-701; tel. (2) 961-0551; fax (2) 561-0550; e-mail khsc0500@khu.ac.kr):

- Housing, Child and Family Studies
- Food and Nutrition
- Clothing and Textiles
- Housing and Interior Design

College of Medicine (1 Hoegi-dong, Dongdaemun-ku, Seoul 130-701; tel. (2) 961-0274; fax (2) 969-6958; e-mail haih@khu.ac.kr):

- Pre-Medical Science
- Medical Science

College of Oriental Medicine (1 Hoegi-dong, Dongdaemun-ku, Seoul 130-701; tel. (2) 961-0321; fax (2) 965-5969; e-mail khsc0700@khu.ac.kr):

- Pre-Oriental Medical Science
- Oriental Medical Science

College of Dentistry (1 Hoegi-dong, Dongdaemun-ku, Seoul 130-701; tel. (2) 961-0341; fax (2) 960-1457; e-mail khsc0800@khu.ac.kr):

- Dentistry

College of Pharmacy (1 Hoegi-dong, Dongdaemun-ku, Seoul 130-701; tel. (2) 961-0356; fax (2) 966-3885; e-mail haih@khu.ac.kr):

- Pharmaceutical Science
- Oriental Pharmaceutical Science

College of Nursing Science (1 Hoegi-dong, Dongdaemun-ku Seoul 130-701; tel. (2) 961-0305; fax (2) 961-9398):

- Nursing Science

College of Music (1 Hoegi-dong, Dongdaemun-ku, Seoul 130-701; tel. (2) 961-0571; fax (2) 967-6192; e-mail ingyum@khu.ac.kr):

- Composition
- Vocal Music
- Instrumental Music

College of Fine Art:

- Korean Painting
- Drawing and Painting
- Sculpture

College of Art and Design:

- Korean Dancing
- Modern Dancing
- Ballet

Graduate School (1 Hoegi-dong, Dongdaemun-ku, Seoul 130-701; tel. (2) 961-0122; fax (2) 966-0902):

- Korean, English, French, Chinese, Japanese and Spanish Languages and Literatures
- History
- Philosophy
- Law
- Public Administration
- Political Science
- Mass Communication
- Economics
- Management
- International Trade and Business
- Accounting
- Sociology
- Mathematics
- Physics
- Chemistry
- Biology
- Geography
- Genetic Engineering
- Food Science and Technology
- Environmental Science
- Astronomy and Space Science
- Food and Nutrition
- Clothing and Textiles
- Home Economics
- Agronomy
- Forestry
- Landscape Architecture
- Horticulture
- Mechanical Engineering
- Chemical Engineering
- Textile Engineering
- Electronic Engineering
- Computer Engineering
- Nuclear Engineering
- Civil Engineering
- Architectural Engineering
- Industrial Engineering
- Radio Engineering
- Medicine
- Oriental Medicine
- Dentistry
- Nursing
- Pharmacy
- Dance
- Music
- Fine Arts
- Ceramic Arts

Graduate School of East–West Medicine (1 Hoegi-dong, Dongdaemun-ku, Seoul 130-701; tel. (2) 961-9214; fax (2) 961-9215):

- East–West Medicine
- Oriental Medical Science
- Oriental Medical Industry

Graduate School of Business Administration (1 Hoegi-dong, Dongdaemun-ku, Seoul 130-701; tel. (2) 961-0127; fax (2) 961-0738):

Business Administration
Tax Management
Foreign Trade Management
Management Consulting
Branding Strategy

Graduate School of Public Administration (1 Hoegi-dong, Dongdaemun-ku, Seoul 130-701; tel. (2) 961-0131; fax (2) 962-1213):

Public Administration

Graduate School of Education (1 Hoegi-dong, Dongdaemun-ku, Seoul 130-701; tel. (2) 961-0135; fax (2) 964-6674):

Taekwando Education
Earth Science Education
Design Education
Educational Administration
Civil Ethics Education
Social Studies Education
Korean Language Education
Mathematics Education
Geography Education
History Education
Fine Arts Education
Music Education
Elementary Education
Japanese Education
Chinese Education
Business Education
Environmental Education
Agricultural Education
Ceramic Arts Education
Chemistry Education
Biology Education
Engineering Education
Computer Science Education
Educational Technology
Nursing Education
Early Child Education
Educational Psychology
Home Economics Education

Graduate School of Journalism and Mass Communication (1 Hoegi-dong, Dongdaemun-ku, Seoul 130-701; tel. (2) 961-0561; fax (2) 967-7083):

Journalism
Strategic Communication
Media Arts

Graduate School of Physical Education (1 Hoegi-dong, Dongdaemun-ku, Seoul 130-701; tel. (2) 961-0771; fax (2) 961-9219):

Physical Education
Sports Science

Graduate School of International Legal Affairs (1 Hoegi-dong, Dongdaemun-ku, Seoul 130-701; tel. (2) 961-0905; fax (2) 961-9134):

International Trade Law
Insurance and Maritime Law
Intellectual Property Law
International Tax Law
International Environment

Graduate School of Tourism (1 Hoegi-dong, Dongdaemun-ku, Seoul 130-701; tel. (2) 961-0813; fax (2) 961-0811):

Hotel and Tourism Management
Convention Industry
Culinary Science
Food Service Management

Graduate School of Non-Governmental Organization (1 Hoegi-dong, Dongdaemun-ku, Seoul 130-701; tel. (2) 961-9240; fax (2) 961-9242; e-mail ngo@khu.ac.kr; internet web .kyunghee.ac.kr/~ngo):

Non-Governmental Organization Management
Non-Governmental Organization Policy
Volunteer Management

Graduate Institute of Peace Studies (Jingop-eup, Namyangju-gun, Kyonggi-do 423-860; tel. (31) 528-7622; fax (31) 528-7630):

Peace and Security
Northeast Asian Studies
Public and International Policy
Human Welfare

College of Foreign Languages (1 Sochen-ni, Kihung-eup, Yongin, Kyongki-do 449-701; tel. (31) 201-2201; fax (31) 204-8112):

English Language and Literature
French Language and Literature
Spanish Language and Literature
Russian Language and Literature
Japanese Language and Literature
Chinese Language and Literature
Korean Language and Literature

College of Social Sciences and Department of Management and International Relations (1 Sochen-ni, Kihung-eup, Yongin, Kyongki-do 449-701; tel. (31) 201-2301; fax (31) 204-8113):

Global Management
Taxation and Accounting
Business Management and Venture Business
International Relations
Area Studies

College of Natural Sciences and Department of the Environment and Applied Chemistry (1 Sochen-ni, Kihung-eup, Yongin, Kyongki-do 449-701; tel. (31) 201-2401; fax (31) 204-8114):

Chemical Engineering and New Materials Science
Chemistry
Environmental Science
Polymer and Textile Engineering

College of Engineering and Department of Electronics and Information Technology (1 Sochen-ni, Kihung-eup, Yongin, Kyongki-do 449-701; tel. (31) 201-2501; fax (31) 204-8115):

Electronic Engineering
Computer Engineering
Radio Engineering
Mathematics
Physics
Optoelectronics
Information and Communications Engineering
Astronomy and Space Science
Oriental Medicine Systems Engineering

College of Industry and Department of Life Science (1 Sochen-ni, Kihung-eup, Yongin, Kyongki-do 449-701; tel. (31) 201-2601; fax (31) 204-8116):

Genetic Engineering
Agronomy
Forest Science
Horticultural Science
Food Science and Technology

College of Sports Science and Department of Physical Education (1 Sochen-ni, Kihung-eup, Yongin, Kyongki-do 449-701; tel. (31) 201-2701; fax (31) 204-8117):

Coaching
Golf Management
Physical Education
Sports Medicine
Taekwando

Department of Mechanical and Industrial Systems Engineering (1 Sochen-ni, Kihung-eup, Yongin, Kyongki-do 449-701; tel. (31) 201-2601; fax (31) 204-8116):

Mechanical Engineering
Industrial Engineering
Advanced Materials and Process Engineering
Nuclear Engineering

Department of Civil and Architectural Engineering (1 Sochen-ni, Kihung-eup, Yongin, Kyongki-do 449-701; tel. (31) 201-2939; fax (31) 201-1354):

Architectural Engineering
Civil Engineering

Department of Art and Design (1 Sochen-ni, Kihung-eup, Yongin, Kyongki-do 449-701; tel. (31) 201-2672; fax (31) 207-8127):

Industrial Design
Visual Design
Landscape Architecture
Textile and Fashion Design
Digital Art and Design
Ceramic Art
Drama and Film

Graduate School of Industry and Information Science (1 Sochen-ni, Kihung-eup, Yongin, Kyongki-do 449-701; tel. (31) 201-2131; fax (31) 201-2777):

Regional Development Administration
Management and Information
International Trade Information
Accounting
Small and Medium Sized Firms
Taxation
Mechanical Engineering
Electronic Engineering
Computer Science
Information Communication
Control and Instrumentation
Advanced Materials and Process Engineering
Industrial Engineering
Automotive Engineering
Electromagnetic Wave and Broadcasting Engineering
Civil Engineering
Food Science and Technology
Industrial Design
Sports Diplomacy

Graduate School of Pan-Pacific International Studies (1 Sochen-ni, Kihung-eup, Yongin, Kyongki-do 449-701; tel. (31) 201-2146; fax (31) 204-8119):

International Trade and Economic Cooperation
International Business
Area Studies on Latin America

ATTACHED INSTITUTES

Centre for the Reconstruction of Human Society: Dir JONG-IL RA.

Institute of International Peace Studies: Dir JAE-SIK SOHN.

Institute for a Brighter Society: Dir BYUNG-KON HWANG.

Research Centre for Land Development: Dir YONG-HYUN KIL.

Research Institute of Educational Affairs: Dir MI-SOP SONG.

Kyung Hee Language Institute: Dir BYUNG-SOO PARK.

Research Institute of Social Science: Dir MYUNG-SIK LEE.

East-West Pharmaceutical Research Institute: Dir YOUNG SOO RHO.

Institute of Genetic Engineering: Dir TAE-RYONG HAHN.

Korean Institute of Ornithological Studies: Dir JEONCHIL YOO.

Research Institute of Physical Education: Dir YOUNG-KEUN CHOI.

Institute of Industrial Relations: Dir KI-AN PARK.

Kyung Hee Institute of Legal Studies: Dir BYUNG-MOOK KIM.

Research Centre for Student Life: Dir CHONG-KYU KIM.

Research Institute for Basic Science: Dir Bok-Keun Chung.
Institute of Architecture and Urban Studies: Dir Chang-Han Cho.
Institute of Korean Classical Medicine: Dir Won-Seek Hong.
Institute of Archaeology and Art History: Dir Byung-Ik Soh.
Institute of Korean Political Studies: Dir Byung-Key Song.
Institute of Oral Biology: Dir Han-Guk Cho.
Institute of Campus Development: Dir Byung-Ik So.
Institute of Landscape Architecture: Dir Bong-Won Ahn.
Institute of Materials Science and Technology: Dir Young-Nam Paik.
Communication Research Institute: Dir Kwang-Jae Lee.
Institute of Korean Culture: Dir Tae-Yeong Kim.
Institute of Food Development: Dir Jae-Sun Jo.
Solar Energy Research Institute: Dir Hyun-Chae Jung.
Institute for Laser Engineering: Choo-Hie Lee.
Institute of Folklore: Dir Mi-Won Lee.
Research Institute for East-West Medicine: Dir Hwan-Jo Suh.
Kyung Hee Institute of Economic Research: Dir Myung-Kwang Park.
Center for Asian Pacific Studies: Dir Dal-Hyun Kim.
Kyung Hee Research Institute of Public Affairs: Yun-Ho Park.
Institute of Hazardous Substances: Dir Hyung-Suk Kim.
Research Institute for Endocrinology: Dir Young-Kil Choi.
Business Management Research Institute: Dir Sung-Soo Kim.
Telematic Systems Engineering Research Institute: Dir Yong-Wook Jin.
Research Institute for Taekwondo: Dir Kyung-Ji Kim.
Institute for Information Society Studies: Dir Kyu-Hong Park.

KYUNGIL UNIVERSITY

33 Puho-ri, Hayang-up, Kyungsan-si, Kyungsangpuk-do 712-701
Telephone: (53) 853-8001
Fax: (53) 853-8800
E-mail: webmaster@kiu.ac.kr
Internet: www.kyungil.ac.kr
Founded 1963 as Technical High School attached to Chunggu College; renamed Junior Technical College attached to Yeungnam University 1967; seperated from Yeungnam University as Yeungnam Junior Technical College 1975; renamed Kyungpook Junior Technical College 1976; renamed Kyungpook Junior College of Technology 1978; became Kyungpook Open University 1985; renamed Kyungpook Sanup University 1988; became Kyungil University 1997
Private control
Academic year: March to December
President: Mu-Keun Lee
Director for General Affairs: Jong-Seok Kim
Director of the Office for Planning and Development: Weon-Sik Lee
Chief Librarian: Ha-Yong Park
Number of teachers: 250
Number of students: 10,000

DEANS
College of Engineering: Myung-Jin Yoon
College of Information Technology: Lee-Kok Kim
College of Humanities and Social Sciences: Yool-Chong Anh
College of Formative Arts: Jung-Won Kim
School of General Education: Bo-Gun Suh
Graduate School: Jin-Ho Kim
Graduate School of Industry: Jin-Ho Kim
Graduate School of Design: Jin-Ho Kim

KYUNGNAM UNIVERSITY

449 Wolyoung-dong, Masan, Kyungnam 631-701
Telephone: (55) 245-5000
Fax: (55) 246-6184
E-mail: webmaster@kyungnam.ac.kr
Internet: www.kyungnam.ac.kr
Founded 1946
Private control
President: Dr Jae Kyu Park
Registrar: Dr Jae In Yang
Librarian: Dr Dock Joung Youn
Library of 537,887 vols
Number of teachers: 674
Number of students: 15,000

DEANS
College of Arts: Dr Jin Ki Cho
College of Science: Dr Sue Dae Lee
College of Education: Dr Seok Zoo Lee
College of Engineering: Dr Soo Heum Lee
College of Law and Political Science: Dr Kyung Sik Ra
College of Business Administration: Dr Hyun Wook Koh
Graduate School: Dr Choong Kyun Chong

KYUNGPOOK NATIONAL UNIVERSITY

1370 Sankyuk-dong, Puk-ku, Taegu 702-701
Telephone: (53) 950-6823
Fax: (53) 950-6093
E-mail: interknu@kyungpook.ac.kr
Internet: www.knu.ac.kr
Founded 1946
State control
Academic year: March to February (two semesters)
President: Dr Dal Ung Kim
Dean of Academic Affairs: Dr Kee Chan Kim
Dean of Student Affairs: Dr Min Hyung Lee
Dean of Planning and Research Support: Dr Jae Keun Sohn
Dean of General Affairs: Dr Seung Tae Park
Library: see Libraries
Number of teachers: 825
Number of students: 24,504
Publication: *Research Review* (annually)

DEANS
Graduate School: Dr Yon-Ung Kwon
College of Agriculture and Life Sciences: Dr Jong-Uck Choi
College of Dentistry: Dr Hee-Moon Kyung
College of Economics and Commerce: Dr Byeong-Hae Sohn
College of Engineering: Dr Dong-Ho Lee
College of Human Ecology: Dr Young-Sun Yoo
College of Humanities: Dr Kee-Chan Kim
College of Law: Dr Tae-Seong Kang
College of Medicine: Dr Joung-Sik Kwak
College of Music and Visual Arts: Dr Ki-Duck Kwon
College of Natural Sciences: Dr Byung-Jo Moon
College of Social Sciences: Dr Jae-Hong Kim
College of Veterinary Medicine: Dr Cha-Soo Lee
School of Electrical Engineering and Computer Science: Dr Yong-Hyun Lee

PROFESSORS
College of Agriculture and Life Sciences (#223 College of Agriculture and Life Sciences Building I, Kyungpook National University, Taegu 702-701; tel. (53) 950-5700; fax (53) 950-6701):
Cho, R.-K., Food Chemistry
Cheong, S.-T., Fruit Science, Plant Propagation
Choi, J., Soil Science
Choi, J.-U., Food Preservation Engineering
Choi, K., Forest Management and Economics
Choi, K.-S., Animal Breeding
Choi, K.-S., Economic Statistics
Choi, S.-T., Floriculture, Protected Cultivation
Choi, Y.-H., Food Engineering
Chung, J.-D., Plant Tissue Culture
Chung, M.-S., Tree Cultivation
Chung, S.-K., Food Analysis and Sanitation
Chung, S.-O., Irrigation and Drainage Engineering
Eom, T.-J, Woody Plant Biochemistry
Hong, S.-C., Forest Ecology
Hwang, Y.-H., Plant Genetics
Jang, I.-J., Agricultural Robot for Control Measurements
Jo, J.-K., Grass Physiology
Jung, S.-K., Landscape Construction
Kim, B.-S., Vegetable Cultivation, Pepper Cultivation
Kim, C.-S., Agricultural Policy
Kim, D.-S., Dairy Microbiology
Kim, D.-U., Plant Molecular Biology
Kim, J.-E., Environmental Chemistry
Kim, K.-U., Weed Science
Kim, S.-G., Agricultural Marketing
Kim, S.-K., Maize Breeding
Kim, T.-H., Agricultural Power Energy Conservation
Kim, Y.-S., Landscape Planning
Kwon, M.-N., Geotechnical and Foundation Engineering
Kwon, Y.-J., Systematic Entomology
Lee, H.-C., Agricultural Economic History
Lee, H.-T., Landscape Design
Lee, J.-T., Fungal Plant Pathology
Lee, J.-Y., Wood Chemistry
Lee, K.-C., Landscape Management
Lee, K.-M., Terramechanics, Greenhouse Controls
Lee, K.-W., Viral Plant Pathology
Lee, S.-C., Crop Production and Management
Lee, S.-G., Agricultural Buildings
Noh, S.-K., Insect Genetic Resources
Park, I.-H., Landscape Plants
Park, K.-K., Post-Harvest Process, Systems Mechanics
Park, S.-J., Wood Anatomy
Park, W.-C., Plant Nutrition
Park, Y.-G., Forest Genetics
Rhee, I.-J., Fibre Materials Science
Rhee, I.-K., Biochemistry
Ryu, J.-C., Agricultural Crops
Sohn, J.-K., Rice Cultivation
Sohn, H.-R., Sericulture
Son, D.-S., Forest Cultivation
Suh, S.-D., Hydrology, Land Engineering
Syn, Y.-B., Fruit Science, Plant Physiology
Uhm, J.-Y., Bacterial Plant Pathology
Yeo, Y.-K., Lipid Chemistry

College of Dentistry (#211 College of Dentistry, Kyungpook National University, Taegu 702-701; tel. (53) 420-6801; fax (53) 425-6025):
Bae, Y.-C., Oral Anatomy
Cho, S.-A., Prosthodontics
Choi, J.-K., Oral Medicine

Jo, K.-H., Prosthodontics
Kim, C.-S., Oral and Maxillofacial Surgery
Kim, K.-H., Dental Materials
Kim, Y.-J., Paediatric Dentistry
Kwon, O.-W., Orthodontics
Kyoung, H.-M., Orthodontics
Lee, S.-H., Oral and Maxillofacial Surgery
Nam, S.-H., Paediatric Dentistry
Song, S.-B., Preventive Dentistry and Public Health Dentistry
Sung, J.-H., Orthodontics

College of Economics and Commerce (#213 College of Economics and Commerce, Kyungpook National University, Taegu 702-701; tel. (53) 950-5403; fax (53) 950-5405):

Bae, B.-H., Managerial Accounting
Chang, H.-S., Marketing
Chang, J.-S., Industrial Organization
Cho, S.-P., Financial Accounting
Choe, J.-M., Managerial Accounting
Choi, Y.-H., Korean Economy
Ha, I.-B., Macroeconomics
Han, D.-H., International Economics
Jung, C.-Y., Operations Management
Kang, H.-Y., Managerial Accounting
Kim, H.-K., Labour Economics
Kim, J.-J., Marketing
Kim, S.-H., Monetary Economics, International Economics
Kim, Y.-H., Economic Development, Korean Economic History
Kwon, C.-T., Financial Accounting
Kwon, S.-C., Financial Accounting
Kwon, S.-K., Financial Accounting
Lee, D.-M., Management Information Systems
Lee, H.-W., Operations Management
Lee, J.-D., Financial Management
Lee, J.-K., International Commercial Law
Lee, J.-W., Income Distribution, Comparative Economics
Lee, J.-W., Personnel and Organization Management
Lee, S.-D., Personnel and Organization Management
Lee, S.-H., Marketing
Lee, Y.-S., International Transportation and Logistics
Moon, S.-H., Operations Management
Nah, K.-S., Economic History
Park, C.-S., Financial Management
Park, J.-H., Macroeconomics
Shin, M.-S., Financial Management
Sohn, B.-H., International Economics

College of Engineering (#211 College of Engineering Building VI, Kyungpook National University, Taegu 702-701; tel. (53) 950-5500; fax (53) 958-5054):

Ahn, K.-S., Digital Engineering
Bae, K.-S., Digital Signal Processing, Speech Signal Processing, Digital Communication
Bae, S.-K., Geochemical Engineering
Baek, Y.-S., Power Systems Analysis
Chien, S.-I., Vision
Cho, J.-H., Bioelectronics, Electronic Measurements
Cho, S.-H., Ceramics for Electronics
Cho, Y.-J., Computer Networks
Cho, Y.-K., Antenna and Propagation, Ultrasonics
Choi, H.-C., Wave Propagation
Choi, H.-M., Parallel Distributed Processing, Processors, Logic Design
Choi, M.-H., Architectural Planning and Design
Choi, S.-J., Water Supply and Waste Water Treatment Engineering
Choi, S.-Y., Semiconductor Engineering
Choi, T.-H., Robotics
Chung, I.-S., Mechanical Metallurgy
Ha, J.-M., Urban Design and City Planning
Ha, Y.-H., Image Processing and Computer Vision Digital Signal Processing
Han, K.-J., Computer Networks
Han, K.-Y., Water Resources Engineering
Heo, N.-H., Zeolite Chemistry, Physical Chemistry
Hong, J.-K., Speech Signal Processing
Hong, S.-M., Control Theory
Hwang, C.-S., Visual Communication
Jeon, G.-J., Intelligent Control, Systems Engineering
Ji, B.-C., Polymer and Fibre Physics
Joo, E.-K., Digital Communication
Kang, I.-K., Biopolymers
Kang, M.-M., Architectural Structure
Kim, C.-H., Applied Mechanics
Kim, C.-J., Architectural Design
Kim, C.-Y., Microwave Engineering
Kim, D.-G., Power Electronics
Kim, D.-H., Reaction Engineering
Kim, D.-R., Surface Science and Engineering
Kim, H.-G., Power Electronics
Kim, H.-J., Pattern Recognition
Kim, H.-S., Synthetic Organic Chemistry
Kim, J.-J., Structural Ceramics
Kim, N.-C., Digital Communications, Image Communications
Kim, N.-K., Dielectric Materials
Kim, S.-H., Computational Geometry
Kim, S.-H., Synthetic Functional Dyes
Kim, S.-J., Geometry, Numerical Analysis
Kim, S.-J., Optical Signal Processing, Circuits and Systems
Kim, S.-M., Automata Theory
Kim, S.-S., Tribology
Kim, T.-J., Inorganic and Organometallic Chemistry, Homogeneous Catalysis
Kim, W.-J., Architectural Construction
Kim, W.-S., Architectural Construction
Kim, W.-S., Polymer Synthesis
Kim, Y.-M., Computer Graphics, Image Processing
Kim, Y.-S., Geotechnical Engineering
Kwon, O.-J., Powder Metallurgy
Kwon, S.-B., Fluid Mechanics
Kwon, W.-H., Powder Electronics
Kwon, Y.-D., Structural Analysis
Kwon, Y.-H., Architectural Structure
Lee, B.-K., Powder Synthesis
Lee, C.-W., Combustion
Lee, D.-D., Semiconductor Engineering
Lee, D.-H., Polymerization Catalysis
Lee, J.-H., Semiconductor Technology
Lee, J.-T., Process Control
Lee, K.-I., Audio and Video Engineering, Electronic Measurements
Lee, K.-K., Non-linear Control Theory
Lee, M.-H., Instrumental Analysis, NMR Spectroscopy
Lee, S.-J., Natural Language
Lee, S.-R., Control and Automation
Lee, T.-J., Process and Property Thermodynamics
Lee, Y.-H., Semiconductor Engineering
Lee, Y.-M., Precision Machining
Lim, Y.-J., Dyeing Chemistry
Min, K.-E., Physical Properties of Solid Polymers
Min, K.-S., Water Quality Engineering
Moon, J.-D., Applied Electrostatics and High Voltage Applications
Oh, C.-S., Computation, Analysis and Design of Electrical Machinery
Oh, T.-J., Polymer and Fibre Chemistry
Park, B.-O., Composite Materials
Park, H.-B., Robust Control Theory
Park, J.-K., Biochemical Engineering and Transport Phenomena
Park, J.-S., Instrumentation, CAD, VLSI Design
Park, K.-C., Joining and Metal Forming
Park, K.-H., Robotics and Control
Park, L.-S., Physical Properties of Polymer Solutions
Park, M.-H., Structural Engineering
Park, S.-K., Microelectronics
Park, S.-T., Computer Networks, Databases
Riu, K.-J., Heat Transfer
Ryu, K.-W., Parallel Algorithms
Seo, B.-H., Automatic and Digital Control, Computer Applications
Seo, K.-H., Polymer Processing
Shim, S.-C., Petroleum Chemistry, Organic and Organometallic Chemistry
Shin, S.-K., Semiconductor Engineering
Sohn, B.-K., Semiconductor Engineering
Sohn, J.-R., Catalytic Chemistry, Inorganic Material
Sohng, K.-I., Video Engineering, Multiple Valued Logic Systems
Song, D.-I., Polymer Rheology
Song, J.-W., Optical Communication
Suh, C.-M., Materials and Mechanics
Ye, B.-J., Casting, Solidification
Yoo, K.-Y., Parallel Processing
Yu, S.-D., Integrated Circuits

College of Human Ecology (#212 College of Human Ecology, Kyungpook National University, Taegu 702-701; tel. (53) 950-6200; fax (53) 950-6205):

Choi, B.-G., Child Development
Choi, M.-S., Nutritional Biochemistry
Kang, M.-Y., Nutrition
Lee, H.-S., Nutrition

College of Humanities (#209 College of Humanities, Kyungpook National University, Taegu 702-701; tel. (53) 950-5100; fax (53) 950-6101):

Bang, I., Oriental Philosophy
Cheon, K.-S., Korean Syntax
Cho, M.-H., British and American Drama
Choi, S.-S., German Literature, Classic Literature
Choy, C.-H., Korean History
Chung, I.-S., Chinese Linguistics
Chung, J.-S., English Linguistics, Syntax
Eun, J.-N., Modern Anglo-American Literature
Han, S.-Z., German Literature
Hong, S.-M., Korean Linguistics
Hwang, W.-Z., Korean Literature
Jang, T.-W., Chinese Linguistics
Ju, B.-D., Korean History
Kim, C.-D., Political and Economic Anthropology
Kim, C.-G., Western History
Kim, C.-S., British Poetry
Kim, C.-W., German Drama
Kim, D.-M., Oriental Philosophy
Kim, I.-L., Korean Classical Literature
Kim, K.-C., English Linguistics
Kim, K.-S., Korean Classical Literature
Kim, S.-W., Korean Chinese Literature
Kim, Y.-D., Western Philosophy
Kim, Y.-K., Western Philosophy
Kwon, K.-H., Modern Korean Literature
Kwon, T.-R., Chinese Linguistics
Kwon, Y.-U., Korean History
Lee, C.-S., Chinese Literature
Lee, D.-H., German Literature
Lee, E.-Y., French Phonology
Lee, H.-J., Archaeology
Lee, H.-J., Chinese Literature
Lee, J.-H., Japanese Literature
Lee, K.-E., Russian Literature
Lee, K.-J., German Idealism
Lee, P.-S., French Syntax
Lee, S.-G., Korean Dialectology
Lee, W.-K., English Literature
Paek, D.-H., Korean Philology
Park, C.-B., English Literature
Park, J.-G., French Literature
Park, S.-W., German Linguistics
Park, Y.-H., Korean Chinese Literature
Shin, O.-H., Western Philosophy
Sohn, H.-S., English Linguistics
Yi, B.-K., Bronze Age Archaeology, Museology
Yi, K.-S., Chinese History
Yoo, K.-S., Western History

College of Law (#305 College of Law, Kyungpook National University, Taegu 702-701; tel. (53) 950-5456; fax (53) 950-5455):

CHANG, J.-H., Civil Law
KANG, T.-S., Civil Law
KIM, S.-T., Local Public Administration and Finance
KIM, Y.-S., Land Policy
LEE, Y.-J., Financial Administration
MOON, K.-S., Policy Sciences, Financial Management
PARK, J.-H., Urban Planning
PARK, J.-T., Commercial Law
RHEE, W.-W., Urban Administration

College of Medicine (#208 College of Medicine, Kyungpook National University, Taegu 702-701; tel. (53) 420-6901; fax (53) 421-6585; internet med.knu.ac.kr):

BAEK, W.-Y., Intensive Care Therapy
BAIK, B.-S., Craniofacial Surgery
CHAE, J.-M., Forensic Pathology
CHAE, S.-C., Cardiology
CHANG, S.-I., Surgery, Paediatric Surgery
CHANG, S.-K., Transplantation, Tumours
CHO, D.-K., Nephrology
CHO, D.-Y., Molecular Genetics
CHO, H.-J., Neuroanatomy
CHO, T.-H., Oncology
CHO, Y.-L., Gynaecological Oncology
CHOI, Y.-H., Gastroenterology
CHUN, B.-Y., Health Care Administration and Health Policy
CHUN, S.-S., Reproductive Endocrinology and Infertility
CHUNG, B.-Y., Adult Nursing, Cancer Nursing
CHUNG, J.-M., Gastroenterology
CHUNG, S.-L., Dermatology, Leprosy
CHUNG, T.-H., Immunology
DOH, B.-N, Psychiatric and Mental Health Nursing
HAMM, I.-S., Cerebrovascular Disease, Neuro-Oncology
HONG, H.-S., Anatomy, Medical Genetics
HONG, J.-G., Pain Clinic
HWANG, S.-K., Paediatric Neurosurgery
IHN, J.-C., Joint Reconstructive Surgery
JUN, J.-B., Dermatology, Mycology, Dermatopathology
JUN, J.-E., Cardiology
JUN, S.-H., Surgery, Colorectal Surgery
JUNG, M.-S., Women's Health Nursing
JUNG, S.-K., Paediatric Urology, Traumatology
KANG, D.-J., Psychiatry, Psychopharmacology
KANG, D.-S., Thoracic Radiology
KIM, B.-W., Endocrinology, Metabolism
KIM, B.-W., Tumours
KIM, C.-Y., Cardiovascular Pharmacology
KIM, D.-W., Dermatology
KIM, H.-M., Paediatrics, Neonatology
KIM, I.-T., Vitreous Humour and Retina
KIM, J.-C., Cellular and Molecular Immunology
KIM, K.-T., Paediatric Cardiovascular Surgery
KIM, M.-Y., Paediatric Nursing
KIM, N.-S., Allergology, Rheumatology
KIM, P.-T., Hand Surgery
KIM, S.-L., Cerebrovascular Disease
KIM, S.-Y., Vitreous Humour and Retina
KIM, T.-H., Diagnostic Radiology
KIM, Y.-I., Surgery
KIM, Y.-J., Interventional Radiology
KIM, Y.-W., Vascular Surgery
KOO, J.-H., Paediatrics, Nephrology
KWAK, J.-S., Forensic Pathology
KWAK, Y.-S., Pharmacy
KWON, J.-Y., Paediatric Ophthalmology
LEE, J.-B., Family Medicine
LEE, J.-T., Cardiovascular Surgery
LEE, J.-Y., Occupational Neurology
LEE, K.-B., Nuclear Medicine
LEE, K.-S., Paediatrics, Haemato-Oncology and Genetics
LEE, M.-G., Neuropsychological Pharmacology
LEE, S.-B., Paediatrics, Cardiology
LEE, S.-H., Otology, Neuro-Otology
LEE, S.-K., Biostatistics and Nutritional Epidemiology
LEE, S.-N., Psychiatry, Psychotherapy
LEE, W.-J., Renal Physiology
LEE, W.-K., Clinical Microbiology
LEE, Y.-C., Virology
LEE, Y.-H., Surgery, Head and Neck Endoscrine Surgery
PARK, B.-C., Paediatric and Spinal Surgery
PARK, I.-H., Oncology and Infection
PARK, I.-K., Radiation Oncology, Radiation Biology
PARK, I.-S., Gynaecological Oncology
PARK, J.-H., Fundamentals of Nursing
PARK, J.-S., Cardiovascular Physiology
PARK, J.-S., Head and Neck Oncology
PARK, J.-W., Vascular Pharmacology and Anaesthesia
PARK, J.-Y., Health Care Administration and Health Policy
PARK, S.-Y., Adult Nursing
PARK, W.-H., Cardiology
PARK, Y.-K., Andrology
PARK, Y.-M., Spinal Neuro-Oncology, Neurotrauma
RIM, H.-D., Psychiatry, Psychosomatics
SEOL, S.-Y., Molecular Epidemiology
SOHN, Y.-K., Neuropathology
SUH, C.-K., Neurology
SUH, I.-S., Pathology of the Gastrointestinal Tract
SUH, J.-S., Diagnostic Haematology
SUH, S.-R., Adult Nursing
YEO, M.-H., Epidemiology and Population Dynamics
YU, W.-S., Surgery, Surgical Oncology
YUN, Y.-K., Surgery, Hepatobiliary Surgery

College of Music and Visual Arts (#217 College of Music and Visual Arts, Kyungpook National University, Taegu 702-701; tel. (53) 950-5650; fax (53) 950-5655):

BYUN, Y.-B., Sculpture
CHONG, H.-I., Kayagum (12-Stringed Zither)
CHUNG, H.-C., Composition
JUNG, W.-H., Piano
KANG, C.-S., Piano
KIM, G.-J., Voice (Soprano)
KIM, J.-W., Voice (Baritone)
KIM, K.-I., Piano
KIM, W.-S., Korean Painting
KU, Y.-K., Komungo (6-Stringed Zither)
KWON, K.-D., Visual Design
LEE, D.-C., Oil Painting
LEE, E.-S., Piano
LEE, K.-J., Kayagum (12-Stringed Zither)
LEE, W.-S., Visual Design
LIM, H.-S., Clarinet
OH, H.-C., Oil Painting
PARK, N.-H., Art History
SHIM, S.-H., Voice (Tenor)
YOO, H., Korean Painting
YI, T.-B., Theory of Korean Music and Taegum (Korean Transverse Flute)
YOON, J.-R., Cello
YUN, M.-G., Piri (Korean Oboe)

College of Natural Sciences (#201 College of Natural Sciences, Kyungpook National University, Taegu 702-701; tel. (53) 950-5300; fax (53) 957-0431):

BAE, Z.-U., Analytical Chemistry
CHANG, T.-W., Structural Geology
CHO, K.-H., Statistical Inference
CHOI, J.-K., Probability, Stochastic Processes
CHOI, S.-D., Condensed Matter Theory
HA, J.-H., Microbial Genetics
HUH, T.-L., Molecular Genetics
JEE, J.-G., Physical Chemistry
JEONG, J.-H., Inorganic Chemistry
JIN, I.-N., Enzymology
JO, S.-G., High Energy Physics Theory
JUNG, I.-B., Analysis
KANG, H.-D., Experimental Nuclear Physics
KANG, S.-S., Biochemistry and Animal Physiology
KIM, E.-S., Algebra
KIM, H.-S., Analysis
KIM, I.-S., Biochemistry
KIM, J.-G., Microbial Genetics
KIM, K.-E., Precipitation Mechanism
KIM, S.-W., Computer Languages
KIM, S.-W., Petrology
KIM, Y.-H., Cellular Immunobiology
KOH, I.-S., Sedimentology, Sedimentary Petrology
KWAK, Y.-W., Organic Chemistry
LEE, E.-W., Surface and Thin Films Experiments
LEE, H.-H., Analysis
LEE, H.-L., Analytical Chemistry
LEE, H.-R., Condensed Matter Theory
LEE, I.-S., Statistical Inference, Theoretical Statistics
LEE, J.-K., Organic Chemistry
LEE, J.-Y., Virology
LEE, K.-M., Radiative Transfer, Upper Atmosphere
LEE, S.-H., Analysis
LEE, S.-K., Information Visualization
LEE, S.-Y., Thin Film and Electroluminescence Experiments
LEE, Y.-H., Biochemical Engineering
LEE, Y.-S., Cellular Biochemistry
MIN, K.-D., Atmospheric Energetics
MOON, B.-J., Biochemistry
PARK, B.-G., Reliability Analysis
PARK, C.-Y., Topology
PARK, H.-C., Animal Taxonomy
PARK, J.-H., Plant Systematics
PARK, J.-W., Biochemical Carcinogenesis
PARK, W., Molecular Biology
PARK, Y.-B., Biochemistry
PARK, Y.-C., Database Systems
PARK, Y.-C., Inorganic Chemistry
PARK, Y.-S., Algebra
PARK, Y.-T., Organic Chemistry
SEO, B.-B., Genetics
SOHN, J.-K., Bayesian Decision Theory, Statistical Computing
SOHN, K.-S., Condensed Matter Theory
SOHN, U.-I., Molecular Biology
SON, D.-C., Experimental High Energy Physics
SONG, J.-K., Mulitivariate Data Analysis
SONG, S.-D., Plant Physiology
SUH, Y.-J., Geometry

College of Social Sciences (#315 College of Social Sciences, Kyungpook National University, Taegu 702-701; tel. (53) 950-5200; fax (53) 950-5205):

CHIN, S.-M., Industrial Sociology
CHO, H.-C., Counselling Psychology
CHOI, C.-M., Social Welfare Administration
CHOI, K.-S., Social Psychology
HAN, N.-J., Sociology of Family
JIN, Y.-S., Cognitive Psychology
KIM, J.-H., Ethics and Legal Studies in Mass Communication
KIM, W.-H., International Relations
KIM, Y.-H., Clinical Psychology
KIM, Y.-H., Social Policy
LEE, J.-H., Regional Geography
LEE, Y.-J., Information Science
NAM, K.-H., Bibliography
NOH, D.-I., Korean Politics
PARK, B.-S., Clinical Social Work
PARK, J.-S., Political Communication Theory
PARK, J.-W., Population Studies
PARK, K.-S., Broadcasting
PARK, S.-D., Social Security

PARK, Y.-C., Regional Development, Economic Geography
SHON, J.-P., Library Management
YOON, Y.-H., Comparative Politics

College of Veterinary Medicine (#205 College of Veterinary Medicine, Kyungpook National University, Taegu 702-701; tel. (53) 950-5950; fax (53) 950-5955):

BYUN, M.-D., Veterinary Obstetrics
CHOI, W.-P., Veterinary Microbiology
JANG, I.-H., Veterinary Surgery, Veterinary Obstetrics
KIM, B.-H., Veterinary Microbiology
KIM, Y.-H., Veterinary Obstetrics
LEE, C.-S., Veterinary Pathology
LEE, J.-H., Veterinary Medicine
MOON, M.-H., Veterinary Parasitology
PARK, C.-K., Veterinary Microbiology
TAK, R.-B., Veterinary Public Health
YU, C.-J., Veterinary Physiology

Teachers' College:

AHN, B.-H., Space Physics
BAE, H.-D., Politics, Political Thought
BAE, J.-E., English Literature
CHAE, H.-W., Training
CHANG, D.-I., Medieval Korean History
CHUNG, D.-H., German Linguistics
CHUNG, H.-P., Philosophy of Education
CHUNG, H.-S., Cell Biology, Photosynthesis
CHUNG, S.-T., Sport Psychology
CHUNG, W.-W., Mineralogy
HONG, Y.-P., Politics, Political Thought
HWANG, S.-G., Algebra
HWANG, B.-S., French Linguistics
IM, J.-R., Korean Linguistics
JANG, H.-S., Nutrition
JANG, Y.-O., Home Management
JO, P.-G., Clothing
JO, W.-R., Geomorphology
JUN, B.-Q., English Linguistics
KANG, Y.-H., Astronomy
KI, U.-H., Geometry
KIM, B.-K., Counselling
KIM, H.-K., Economic Development
KIM, H.-S., Early Modern East Asian History
KIM, J.-J., Dance
KIM, J.-T., Korean Linguistics
KIM, J.-W., Contemporary Western History
KIM, K.-H., Measurement and Evaluation for Physical Education
KIM, M.-H., Educational Administration
KIM, M.-K., Korean Literature
KIM, M.-N., Philosophy of Education
KIM, S.-H., Educational Psychology
KIM, Y.-H., Geometry
KOH, J.-K., Particle Physics, Physics Education
LEE, A.-H., Educational Psychology
LEE, B.-H., Early Modern Korean History
LEE, J.-H., Korean Literature
LEE, J.-H., Politics, International Politics
LEE, J.-W., Population Geography, Geographical Education
LEE, M.-H., Biomechanics
LEE, M.-J., Educational Psychology
LEE, M.-K., Ancient Korean History
LEE, M.-S., Physical Chemistry
LEE, N.-G., Rural Sociology
LEE, O.-B., Social Education
LEE, S.-B., Statistics and Critical Phenomena
LEE, S.-C., Sports Nutrition
LEE, S.-T., Korean Linguistics
LEE, W.-B., Organic Chemistry
LEE, Y.-J., Petrology
LIM, C.-K., German Literature
MOON, S.-H., Western Philosophy
OH, C.-H., Optics, Quantum Electronics
OH, D.-S., History of Physical Education
OH, Y.-S., Public Economics
PAK, J.-S., Geometry
PARK, C.-Y., Educational Administration
PARK, D.-K., Plasma Physics
PARK, J.-Y., English Literature
PARK, K.-S., Teaching English as a Second Language
PARK, T.-H., Urban Geography
RIM, S.-H., Algebra
RYU, S.-E., German Drama
SEO, J.-M., Korean Literature
SHIN, K.-J., French Literature
SHIN, Y.-G., Teaching of Physical Education
SOHN, J.-K., Animal Physiology
SONG, B.-H., Microbiology, Molecular Biology
SONG, W.-C., Politics, Political Thought
YANG, H.-J., Animal Morphology, Ecology
YANG, J.-S., Climatology
YANG, S.-Y., Palaeobiology
YI, M.-S., French Linguistics
YOH, S.-D., Organic Chemistry
YOO, Y.-J., Analysis
YOON, I.-H., Micrometeorology
YOON, J.-L., Educational Psychology

ATTACHED INSTITUTES

Toigye Research Institute.
Institute of Regional Development.
Peace Research Institute.
Research Institute for Economics and Business Administration.
Institute of Humanities.
Law Research Institute.
Institute for Social Science.
Institute of Pacific Rim Studies.
Institute for Local Autonomy.
Institute for City and Province Management.
Institute of Secondary Education.
Public Opinion and Public Relations Research Institute.
Institute of Korean Residents in Foreign Countries.
Institute of Geographic Information Systems.
Institute of Basic Sciences.
Research Institute for Genetic Engineering.
Environmental Science Institute.
Topology and Geometry Research Centre.
Science Education Research Institute.
Institute for Material Chemistry.
Radiation Science Research Institute.
Research Institute of Industrial Technology.
Sensor Technology Research Centre.
Institute of Electronic Technology.
Research Institute of Engineering Design Technology.
Engineering Tribology Research Institute.
Advanced Materials Research Institute.
Research Institute of Dyeing and Finishing.
Information Institute of Dyeing and Finishing.
Machinery Technology Institute.
Institute of Agricultural Science and Technology.
Institute of Veterinary Medical Sciences.
Post-Harvest Technology Research Institute.
International Agricultural Research Institute.
Research Institute of the Environment and Open Spaces.
Research Institute of Physical Education and Sports Science.
Liver Research Institute.
Cancer Research Institute.
Cardiovascular Research Institute.
Medical Imaging Research Institute.
Institute of Biomaterials Research and Development.
Medical Research Institute.
Research Institute of Nursing Science.
Language Institute.

KYUNGSUNG UNIVERSITY

110-1 Daeyeon-dong, Nam-gu, Pusan 608-736
Telephone: (51) 620-4114
E-mail: www@www.ks.ac.kr
Internet: kyungsung.ac.kr
Founded 1955
Chairman: KIM DAE-SEONG
President: KYUNG MOON-PARK
Library of 500,000 vols
Number of students: 12,000
Colleges of Liberal Arts, Law and Political Science, Commerce and Economics, Science, Engineering, Pharmacy, Arts, Theology, Multimedia; Graduate Schools of International Business, Multimedia, Social Welfare, Education, Clinical Pharmacology, Digital Design.

KYUNGWON UNIVERSITY

San 65 Bokjeong-dong, Sujeong-gu, Seongnam, Gyeonggi-do
Telephone: (31) 750-5901
E-mail: webmaster@kyungwon.ac.kr
Founded 1978
Chairman: MEN JEONG GWANG-MO
President: LEE GIL-YA
Number of teachers: 254
Number of students: 8,600
Colleges of Humanities, Business and Economics, Law and Science, Engineering, Natural Science, Software, Arts, Music, Oriental Medicine, Human Ecology.

MIRYANG NATIONAL UNIVERSITY

1025-1 Naei-dong, Miryang, Kyungnam 627-702
Telephone: (527) 354-3181
Fax: (527) 355-3186
E-mail: sdlee@arang.miryang.ac.kr
Internet: www.miryang.ac.kr
Founded 1923 as a public school of agricultural sericulture
President: TAE-KIL CHOI

DEANS AND CHAIRMEN

Graduate School: YON-GYU PARK
School of Computer, Information and Communication Engineering: SUN-JONG KIM
School of Food Science and Environmental Engineering: DONG-SEOP KIM
School of Materials Engineering: SU-CHAK RYU
School of Architecture: KANG-GEUN PARK

MOKPO NATIONAL MARITIME UNIVERSITY

571-2 Jugkyo-dong, Mokpo, Chonnam 530-729
Telephone: (631) 240-7045
E-mail: ryujb@mmu.ac.kr
Internet: www.mmu.ac.kr
Founded 1950
President: Dr BYUNGJU OH
Number of teachers: 72
Number of students: 1,800

Divisions of Maritime Transportation Systems, Nautical Science, Navigation System Engineering, Maritime Safety Systems Engineering, Maritime Information Systems, International Logistics Systems, Maritime Policing.

MOKPO NATIONAL UNIVERSITY

61 Torim-ri, Chonggye-myon, Muan-gun, Chonnam 534-729
Telephone: (61) 450-2114
Fax: (61) 452-4793
Internet: www.mokpo.ac.kr

Founded 1946 as Mokpo Teacher-Training School; became Mokpo Teachers' College 1963, Mokpo Junior College 1978 and Mokpo National College 1979; present name and status 1990

President: WOONG-BAE KIM

Number of teachers: 334
Number of students: 9,986

Colleges of Humanities, Social Sciences, Natural Sciences, Engineering, Home Ecology, Business Administration.

MOKWON UNIVERSITY

Doan-dong 800, Seo-ku, Taejon 302-729
Telephone: (42) 829-7114
Fax: (42) 825-5020
E-mail: webmaster@mokwon.ac.kr
Internet: www.mokwon.ac.kr

Founded 1954

President: KEUN JOHN LYU

Library of 340,000

Colleges of Theology, Humanities, Natural Sciences, Engineering, Social Sciences, Music, Fine Arts.

PAICHAI UNIVERSITY

14 Yeon-Ja, 1-gil, Seo-gu, Daejeon 302-735
Telephone: (42) 520-5114
E-mail: jd1234@mail.pcu.ac.kr
Internet: www.paichai.ac.kr

Founded 1885

President: CHUNG SOON-HOON

Colleges of Humanities, Foreign Studies, Business Administration, Social Sciences, Tourism, Natural Sciences, Engineering, Arts.

POHANG UNIVERSITY OF SCIENCE AND TECHNOLOGY

San 31 Hyoja-dong, Nam-gu, Pohang, Kyungbuk 790-784
Telephone: (54) 279-2910
Fax: (54) 279-3590
E-mail: iao@postech.ac.kr
Internet: www.postech.ac.kr

Founded 1986

Academic year: March to January

President: Prof. CHAN-MO PARK
Vice-President: Prof. IN-SIK NAM
Dean of Policy and Planning (International Affairs): Prof. YUSHIN HONG

Number of teachers: 263
Number of students: 2,736 (1,329 undergraduate, 1,407 postgraduate)

HEADS OF DEPARTMENTS

Division of Molecular Life Sciences: CHI-BOM CHAE
Department of Chemistry: HYOM-YUNG LEE
Department of Mathematics: DONG-WOO KWAK
Department of Physics: TONG-NYONG LEE
Department of Chemical Engineering: CHANG-KUN SOO
Department of Computer Science and Engineering: KYOUNG-CHAN KIM
Division of Electronic and Electrical Engineering: JEONG-YOON HA
Division of Material Sciences and Engineering: SOON-JU KWON
Department of Industrial Engineering: KWANG-SOO KIM
Department of Mechanical Engineering: JE-HYUN BAEK
Division of Humanities and Social Sciences: JUNG KIM

PUKYONG NATIONAL UNIVERSITY

559-1 Daeyon-dong, Nam-gu, Busan
Telephone: (51) 620-6114
Fax: (51) 620-1114
E-mail: web@pknu.ac.kr
Internet: www.pknu.ac.kr

Founded 1996 by the amalgamation of National Fisheries University of Pusan and Pusan National University of Technology

President: CHU-KANG NAM
Dean of Academic Affairs: SONG-WOO NAM
Dean of Student Affairs: IL-PARK HEUNG
Dean of Planning Office: HYUN-CHAN JUNG
Dean of General Affairs: IN-CHUL HWANG
Director of Library: YONG-SOO PYO

Number of teachers: 664
Number of students: 23,671 (23,336 undergraduates, 335 graduates)

DEANS

Faculty of Business Administration: JONG-WOOK HA
Faculty of Engineering: HYUNG-GI LEE
Faculty of Environmental and Marine Science and Technology: DAE-CHOUL KIM
Faculty of Fisheries Science: DAE-SEOK BYUN
Faculty of Humanities and Social Sciences: RAE-LEE SEUNG
Faculty of Natural Sciences: SE-KWON KIM

PUSAN NATIONAL UNIVERSITY

30 Jangjeon-dong, Kumjeong-ku, Pusan 609-735
Telephone: 510-1293
Fax: 512-9049
Internet: www.pusan.ac.kr

Founded 1946

Academic year: March to February

President: INN-SE KIM
Dean of Academic Affairs: SANG-WOOK PARK
Dean of Student Affairs: IN-BO SIM
Dean of Planning and Research: JUNG-DUK LIM
Director of General Affairs: SANG-WOO HAN
Director of Library: DONG-HYUN JUNG

Library: see Libraries

Museum: see Museums

Number of teachers: 967
Number of students: 24,670

Publications: *University Academic Journal* (annual collection of theses), *PNU Weekly Newsletter*, *College Academic Journal*

DEANS

Graduate School: JUNG-KEUN KIM
Graduate School of Management: BEUNG-GEUN MUN
Graduate School of Public Administration: KI-HYUNG RYU
Graduate School of Environment: MAN-HYUNG LEE
Graduate School of Education: HONG-WOOK HUH
Graduate School of Industry: MAN-HYUNG LEE
College of Humanities: JIN-NONG CHUNG
College of Natural Sciences: SANG-JOON LEE
College of Engineering: MAN-HYUNG LEE
College of Law: BAE-WON KIM
College of Education: HONG-WOOK HUH
College of Social Sciences: HYUN-JUNG SHIN
College of Business: BEUNG-GEUN MUN
College of Arts: EUL-MEE PARK
College of Pharmacy: JEE-HYUNG JUNG
College of Medicine: YONG-KI KIM
College of Dentistry: LI-HEE YUN
College of Human Ecology: YEONG-OK SONG

ATTACHED INSTITUTES

Research Institute of Basic Sciences.

Research Institute for Science Education.

Research Institute of Mechanical Technology.

Research Institute of Genetic Engineering.

Research Institute of Information and Communication.

Language Research and Education Institute.

Research Institute of Korean National Unity.

Industrial Technology Research Institute.

Institute of Environmental Studies.

Urban Affairs Research Institute.

Institute of Law Studies.

Social Welfare Research Institute.

Institute for European and American Studies.

Institute of Korean Cultural Studies.

Research Institute of Physical Education and Sports Science.

Local Government Research Institute.

Educational Research Institute.

Institute of Labour Problems.

Research Institute for Oral Biotechnology.

Research Institute of Medical Science.

Research Institute for Drug Development.

Social Survey Research Center.

Research Center for Dielectric Advanced Matter Physics.

Center for Women's Studies.

Industrial Development Research Center.

Asian Research Institute.

Research Institute of Computer Engineering.

Engineering Research Center for Net-Shape and Die Manufacturing.

Center for Information and Communication Studies.

PUSAN NATIONAL UNIVERSITY OF EDUCATION

Pusan
Internet: www.pusan-e.ac.kr

Founded 1946 as Pusan Normal School; became Pusan Teachers' College 1955 and Pusan College of Education 1961; name reverted to Pusan Teachers' College 1963; present name 1993

President: Dr CHI-YUL OK.

PUSAN UNIVERSITY OF FOREIGN STUDIES

55-1 Uan-Dong, Nam-gu, Pusan 608-738
Telephone: (51) 640-3000
Fax: (51) 645-4525
E-mail: webmaster@www.pufs.ac.kr
Internet: www.pufs.ac.kr

Library of 320,000 vols

Colleges of Occidental Studies, Oriental Studies, Humanities and Social Sciences, Commerce and Business, Information and Sciences, Leisure Sports Studies.

PUSAN WOMEN'S COLLEGE

74 Yangjung-dong, Pusan Jin-ku, Pusan 614-734

Telephone: (51) 852-0081
Fax: (51) 867-4705
Internet: www.pwc.ac.kr

Founded 1954

Divisions of Child Education, Tourism, Welfare and Health, Art, Business and Management, Applied Art.

SAMCHOK NATIONAL UNIVERSITY

253 Gyodong, Samchok, Kangwon-do 245-080

Telephone: (397) 572-8611
Fax: (397) 572-8620
E-mail: webadmin@samchok.ac.kr
Internet: www.samchok.ac.kr

Founded 1939 as Samchok Public Vocational School; became Samchok Public Industrial School 1944, Samchok Public Industrial Middle School 1946 and Samchok Industrial High School 1950; present name 1991

President: Dr TAE-YUN CHANG.

SANGJI UNIVERSITY

660 Woosan-dong, Wonju, Kangwon-do

Telephone: (371) 730-0182
Fax: (371) 730-0128
E-mail: webmaster@mail.sangji.ac.kr
Internet: www.sangji.ac.kr

Founded 1962

President: Dr SUNG-HOON KIM

Number of teachers: 473

Colleges of Humanities and Social Sciences, Life Science and Natural Resources, Oriental Medicine, Science and Engineering, Economics and Business Administration, Art and Sports.

SANGMYUNG UNIVERSITY

7 Hongji-dong, Chongno-gu, Seoul 110-743

Telephone: (2) 396-7465
Fax: (2) 395-1896
E-mail: secint@smu.ac.kr
Internet: www.sangmyung.ac.kr

Founded 1965
Private control
Academic year: March to December

President: Prof. MYUNG-DUCK SEO
Vice-President: Prof. DONG-WOOK KIM
Vice-President (Planning and Co-ordination): Prof. JAE-KUN KIM

Library of 600,000 books, 8,000 vols of periodicals
Number of teachers: 750
Number of students: 10,296 (9,499 undergraduate, 797 postgraduate)

DEANS

College of Arts: Prof. KUN-SUNG CHOI
College of Arts and Physical Education: Prof. SOON-IM JEE
College of Design: Prof. HAN-DAL SEO
College of Education: Prof. JUNG-JA PARK
College of Humanities and Social Sciences: Prof. MYUNG-JAE LEE
College of Industry: Prof. YONG-JUN YANG
College of Language and Literature: Prof. KI-HUN KU
College of Natural Sciences: Prof. JI-HWAN LEE

SEJONG UNIVERSITY

98 Kunja-dong, Kwangjin-gu, Seoul

Telephone: (2) 3408-3499
Fax: (2) 3408-3561
E-mail: semyaje@sejong.ac.kr
Internet: sejong.ac.kr

Founded 1947

President: Dr CHUL-SU KIM
Vice-Presidents: Dr SUK-MO KOO (Academic Affairs, and Provost), Dr HYUN-JU SHIN (International Programs and Christian Ministry), YOUNG-HWAN CHOI (Research and Development)
Dean of Academic Affairs: Dr YONG-U SOK
Dean of Student Support: Dr EUI-JANG KO
Dean of Finance: KWANG-HO PARK
Dean of Admissions and Planning: Dr JA-MO KANG
Number of students: 7,337

DEANS

Graduate School: Dr YANG-JA YOO
Graduate School of Business: Dr B J. YANG
Graduate School of Public Administration: Dr KYUNG-SHIK JOO
Graduate School of Education: Dr HYUN-WOOK NAM
Graduate School of Information and Communication: Dr JOUNG-WON KIM
Graduate School of Tourism: Dr CHOL-YONG KIM
Graduate School of Mass Communication: DON-SHIK CHOO
College of Liberal Arts: Dr CHON-SUN IHM
College of Social Sciences: Dr KI-SANG LEE
College of Business Administration: Dr SOO-SUP SONG
College of Tourism: Dr SO-YOON CHO
College of Natural Sciences: Dr SUNG-CHUNG AN
College of Engineering: Dr HOON-IL OH
College of Music, Fine Arts and Physical Education: Dr DUCK-BOON LEE

SEOKYEONG UNIVERSITY

16-1 Jungneung-dong, Sungbuk-ku, Seoul 136-704

Telephone: (2) 940-7114
Fax: (2) 919-0345
E-mail: webadmin@bukak.seokyeong.ac.kr
Internet: www.seokyeong.ac.kr

Founded 1947

President: CHUL-SOO HAN

Colleges of Humanities, Social Sciences, Natural Science and Engineering, Arts.

SEOUL NATIONAL UNIVERSITY

San 56-1, Shilim-dong, Kwanak-gu, Seoul 151-742

Telephone: (2) 880-5114
Fax: (2) 885-5272
Internet: www.snu.ac.kr

Founded 1946
State control
Academic year: March to February

President: UN-CHAN CHUNG
Vice-President: HO-IN LEE
Dean of Academic Affairs: CHANG-KU BYUN
Dean of Student Affairs: MI-NA LEE
Dean of Research Affairs: JIN-HO CHUNG
Dean of Planning and Co-ordination: SEONGHWAN OH
Director-General of General Administration: SUNGMOO LEE
Director-General of Library: NAM JIN HUH

Library: see Libraries and Archives
Number of teachers: 1,675
Number of students: 31,974
Publication: *University Gazette* (weekly)

DEANS

College of Agriculture and Life Sciences: MOO HA LEE
College of Business Administration: SANG HUNG AHN
College of Dentistry: PILL HOUN CHOUNG
College of Education: CHUNG-IL YUN
College of Engineering: MIN KOO HAN
College of Fine Arts: YOUNG GULL KWON
College of Human Ecology: IN KYEONG HWANG
College of Humanities: DU HWAN KWON
College of Law: NAK-IN SUNG
College of Medicine: KYU-CHANG WANG
College of Music: MIN KIM
College of Natural Sciences: SE-JUNG OH
College of Nursing: SUNG-AE PARK
College of Pharmacy: SANG-SUP JEW
College of Social Sciences: SAM-OCK PARK
College of Veterinary Medicine: IL-SUK YANG
Graduate School: TAE SOO LEE
Graduate School of Environmental Studies: KEE WON HWANG
Graduate School of Public Administration: DAI GON LEE
Graduate School of Public Health: BONG MIN YANG

ATTACHED RESEARCH INSTITUTES

Asian Music Research Institute: Dir SA JOON KANG.

Automation and Systems Research Institute: Dir JIN WOO PARK.

Cancer Research Institute: Dir YUNG-JUE BANG.

Center for Advanced Material Research: Dir HUN-JOON SOHN.

Centre for Educational Research: Dir NAM-KEE CHANG.

Centre for International Studies: Dir IN-SUNG JANG.

Centre for Social Sciences: Dir KWANG OK KIM.

Center for Theoretical Physics: Dir CHOON KYU LEE.

Dental Research Institute: Dir PILL-HOON CHOUNG.

Environmental Planning Institute: Dir KEE WON HWANG.

Graduate Institute for International and Area Studies: Dir-Gen. WON-TACK HONG.

Institute of Advanced Aerospace Technology: Dir YONG HYUP KIM.

Institute of Advanced Machinery and Design: Dir JUNG YUL YOO .

Institute of American Studies: Dir YOUNG-SUN HA.

Institute of Chemical Processes: Dir EN SUP YOON.

Institute of Cognitive Sciences: Dir JUNG-OH KIM.

Institute of Communication Research: SUG MIN YOUN.

Institute of Economic Research: Dir KWANG-HA KANG.

Institute of Environmental Science and Engineering: Dir WHA-YOUNG LEE.

Institute of Finance and Banking: Dir JEONG SIK PARK.

Institute for Gender Research: Dir CHIN-SUNG CHUNG.

Institute of Health and Environment: Dir BONG MIN YANG.

Institute of Humanities: Dir JEONG-HYUN SHIN.

Institute of Industrial Relations: Dir WEN WOO PARK.

Institute of Information and Operation Management: Dir SUCK-CHUL YOON.

Institute of International Affairs: Dir TAE-HO BARK.

Institute for Japanese Studies: Dir YONG DEOK KIM.

Institute for Korean Regional Studies: Dir WOO-IK YU.

Institute of Korean Studies: Dir TAE JIN YI.

Institute of Management Research: Dir SANG HYUNG AHN.

Institute of Microbiology: Dir YEONG-JAE SEOK.

Institute for Molecular Biology and Genetics: Dir BYEONG GAE LEE.

Institute of New Media and Communications: Dir SANG WOOK NAM.

Institute of Oceanography: Dir KYUNG RYUL KIM.

Institute of Philosophical Research: Dir IN-RAE JO.

Institute of Psychological Science: Dir IN CHOL CHOI.

Institute for Social Development and Policy Research: Dir JUNG-OH KIM.

Inter-University Semiconductor Research Centre: Dir KUK JIN CHUN.

Korea Bio-MAX Center: Dir JEONG BIN YIM.

Korea Institute of Public Affairs: Dir SEUNG-JONG LEE.

Korean Language Education Research Institute: Dir HANYONG WOO.

Language Research Institute: Dir MYONG-YOL KIM.

Law Research Institute: Dir BYOUNG JO CHOE.

Liver Research Institute: Dir HYO-SUK LEE.

Medical Research Centre: Dir KYU-CHANG WANG.

NANO Systems Institute: Dir YOUNG JUNE PARK.

Natural Products Research Institute: Dir YOUNG SIK KIM.

Opera Research Institute: Dir MIN KIM.

Research Institute of Advanced Computer Technology: Dir MYUNG SOO KIM.

Research Institute of Advanced Materials: Dir HU-CHUL LEE.

Research Center for Agricultural Biomaterials: Dir YIN WON LEE.

Research Institute for Agriculture and Life Sciences: Dir MOO HA LEE.

Research Institute for Basic Sciences: Dir SE-JUNG OH.

Research Institute of Energy and Resources: Dir JOO MYUNG KANG.

Research Institute of Engineering Science: Dir CHOONG KI CHUNG.

Research Institute of Human Ecology: Dir YEON SOOK LEE.

Research Institute of Marine Systems Engineering: Dir KYU YEUL LEE.

Research Institute of Mathematics: Dir HYEONG-IN CHOI.

Research Institute of Nursing Science: Dir MYOUNG-AE CHOE.

Research Institute of Pharmaceutical Sciences: Dir SANG-SUP JEW.

Research Institute of Public Information Management: Dir JONG-WON CHOI.

Visual Arts Institute: Dir YOUNG GULL KWON.

Western Music Research Centre: Dir HEE SOOK OH.

SEOUL THEOLOGICAL UNIVERSITY

Kyungki-do, Buchon City
E-mail: admin@stui.net
Internet: www.stu.ac.kr

Founded 1911

President: JOSEPH JONG JIN CHOE

Departments of Theology, Christian Education, Social Welfare, Church Music, Mission English, Childcare, Education.

SEOUL WOMEN'S UNIVERSITY

126 Kongnung 2-dong, Nowon-gu, Seoul 139-144

Telephone: (2) 970-5114
Fax: (2) 978-7931
E-mail: webmaster@mail.swu.ac.kr
Internet: www.swu.ac.kr

Founded 1961
Private control
Academic year: March to February

President: Dr KWANG-JA LEE
Dean of Academic Affairs: Dr KI SUK PARK
Dean of Student Affairs: Dr JU HAN PARK
Dean of General Affairs: Dr HEI JUNG CHUN
Dean of Planning and Budget: Dr EON HO CHOI
Chief Librarian: Dr ON ZA PARK

Number of teachers: 136
Number of students: 5,911

Publications: *Seoul Women's University News* (every 2 weeks), *Journal of the Social Science Research Institute* (annually), *Journal of Art and Design* (annually), *Journal of Women's Studies* (annually), *Journal of the Institute of Humanities* (annually), *Journal of the Natural Science Institute* (annually), *Journal of Student Guidance and Counselling* (annually), *Journal of Child Studies* (annually), *Journal of the Graduate School Seoul Women's University* (annually)

DEANS

Collegeof Humanities: Prof YOUNG CHUL LEE
College of Information and Communication: Dr MOON HEE KANG
College of Natural Sciences: Dr JONG SUK LEE
College of Social Sciences: Dr MOON HEE KANG
Division of Fine Arts: Prof. BOK HEE CHEON

HEADS OF DEPARTMENTS

Division of Humanities:

- Korean Language and Literature: Dr SOONG WON LEE
- English Language and Literature: Dr EUN JOO HAN
- French Language and Literature: Dr DON TCHANE BAK
- German Language and Literature: Dr WON UNG BONG
- History: Dr TAEK JOONG KIM
- Chinese Language and Literature: Dr KWANG HOON HONG
- Japanese Language and Literature: (vacant)
- Christian Studies: Dr KYOUNG CHUL JANG
- International Relations: Dr EUN SANG YU
- Creative Writing: Dr HEE CHUL KIM

Division of Economics, Business Administration and Information Science:

- Business Administration: Dr DONG CHUL HAN
- Economics: Dr CHONG OOK RHEE
- Library and Information Science: Dr SARAH YOO
- Mass Communication: Dr JUNG IM AHN

Divsion of Natural Sciences:

- Horticultural Science: Dr EUN HEUI LEE
- Clothing Science: Dr MI JA KIM
- Food and Microbial Technology: Dr DONG SUN JUNG
- Nutrition: Dr KYUNG WON KIM
- Chemistry: Dr IN SOOK RHEE
- Biology: Dr YEON JAE BAE
- Mathematics: Dr SOOK HEU JUN
- Computer Science and Engineering: Dr HYON WOO SEUNG
- Multimedia and Computer Communications: Dr HYON WOO SEUNG
- Environmental Studies: Dr CHANG SEOK LEE
- Human Movement Sciences: Dr JIN PARK

Division of Human Development:

- Social Work: Dr SOON HAE HONG
- Child Studies: Dr MI OK MOON
- Public Administration: Dr SEE WOO LEE
- Adolescence Studies: Dr SEE WOO LEE
- Gerontology: Dr YOON LOO LEE
- Educational Psychology: Dr HO SOON BAE

Division of Art and Design:

- Ceramics and Fibre Arts: Prof. HYANG SOOK PARK
- Visual Design: Prof. HAK JUNG YOON
- Product Design: Prof. HAK JUNG YOON
- Interior Design: Prof. HAK JUNG YOON
- Painting: Prof. SOO FAN OH

SEOWON UNIVERSITY

231 Mochung-dong, Hongduk-ku, Cheongju 361-742

Telephone: (43) 299-8114
Fax: (43) 283-8822
Internet: www.seowon.ac.kr

Founded 1968

Number of teachers: 506
Number of students: 8,760

Colleges of Art, Education, Liberal Arts, Social Sciences, Natural Sciences.

SILLA UNIVERSITY

617-736 San 1-1 Gwaebop-dong, Sasang-gu, Busan

Telephone: (51) 999-5000
E-mail: webadm@silla.ac.kr
Internet: silla.ac.kr

Chairman: HAE-GON PARK
President: BYUNG-HWA LEE

Colleges of Humanities and Social Sciences, Economics and Business Administration, Natural Sciences, Engineering, Information Technology Design, Education, Arts.

SOGANG UNIVERSITY

CPO 1142, Seoul 100-611

Telephone: (2) 705-8114
Fax: (2) 705-8119
E-mail: interrel@sogang.ac.kr
Internet: www.sogang.ac.kr

Founded 1960
Private control
Languages of instruction: Korean, English
Academic year: March to December (two semesters)

President: CHANG-SUP CHOI (acting)
Manager (Academic Affairs): MOON-SEOB YOUM
Manager (Student Affairs): MYEONG-HOON CHEON
Director of Library: SEOG PARK

Number of teachers: 302
Number of students: 10,900

Publications: *Sogang Herald* (monthly), *Sogang Hakbo* (weekly)

DEANS

Graduate School: CHUL AN
Graduate School of Business: WOON YOUL CHOI
Graduate School of Economics: YOUNG GOO LEE
Graduate School of Education: JUNG TAEK KIM
College of Humanities: IN CHAI CHUNG
Graduate School of Information and Technology: JUNG YUN SEO
Graduate School of International Studies: SE YOUNG AHN
Graduate School of Mass Communication: HAK SOO KIM
Graduate School of Media Communications: KAK YOON
Graduate School of Public Policy: KAP YUN LEE
Graduate School of Theology: TAE SU HA
College of Engineering: YOUNG GOO LEE
College of Natural Sciences: KWAE HI LEE
College of Social Science: KAP YUN LEE
School of Business Administration: JANG HO LEE
School of Economics: BOK UNG KIM
General Education Division: HEE NAM CHOI

PROFESSORS

College of Engineering:

AN, C., Electronic Engineering
CHANG, I. S., Electronic Engineering
CHANG, J. H., Computer Science
CHOI, C. S., Chemical Engineering
CHOI, J.-W., Chemical Engineering
CHOI, M., Computer Science
HONG, D.-H., Electronic Engineering
HUR, N., Mechanical Engineering
HWANG, S. Y., Electronic Engineering
IHM, I., Computer Science
JANG, J. W., Electronic Engineering
JEE, Y., Electronic Engineering
JEON, D., Mechanical Engineering
JEONG, S., Mechanical Engineering
KIM, N., Mechanical Engineering
KIM, S. C., Computer Science
KOO, K. K., Chemical and Biomolecular Engineering
LEE, H. Y., Mechanical Engineering
LEE, J. W., Chemical Engineering
LEE, K. H., Electronic Engineering
LEE, K. S., Chemical Engineering
LEE, S. H., Electronic Engineering
LEE, T. S., Mechanical Engineering
NANG, J., Computer Science
OH, K. W., Computer Science
OH, S. Y., Chemical and Biomolecular Engineering
PARK, H. M., Chemical and Biomolecular Engineering
PARK, H. S., Chemical and Biomolecular Engineering
PARK, R. H., Electronic Engineering
PARK, S., Computer Science
RHEE, H. W., Chemical and Biomolecular Engineering
RIM, C. S., Computer Science
SEO, J., Computer Science
YOO, K.-P., Chemical and Biomolecular Engineering
YUN, S. W., Electronic Engineering

College of Humanities:

AN, S. J., English Language and Literature
BAIK, I. H., History
BAK, J. S., French Language and Literature
CHANG, S. N., German Language and Literature
CHANG, Y. H., English Language and Literature
CHO, B. H., History
CHO, S. W., English Language and Literature
CHOI, H.-M., French Language and Literature
CHUNG, D. H., History
CHUNG, I. C., Philosophy
JEONG, Y. I., Korean Language and Literature
KANG, Y. A., Philosophy
KEEL, H. S., Religious Studies
KIM, G., Chinese Culture
KIM, H. G., History
KIM, S. H., Religious Studies
KIM, S. N., Religious Studies
KIM, W. S., Philosophy
KIM, Y. H., History
KIM, Y. S., English Language and Literature
KWAK, C. G., Korean Language and Literature
LEE, J. D., German Language and Literature
LEE, J. W., History
LEE, S. B., English Language and Literature
LIM, S. W., History
PAK, C. T., Philosophy
SEONG, Y., Philosophy
SHIN, K., English Language and Literature
SHIN, S. W., English Language and Literature
SONG, H. S., Korean Language and Literature
SONG, W. Y., German Language and Literature
SPALATIN, C. A., Philosophy
SUH, C. M., Korean Language and Literature
SUNG, H. K., Korean Language and Literature
UM, J., Philosophy

College of Natural Sciences:

CHIN, C. S., Chemistry
CHO, K., Physics
CHO, S. H., Mathematics
CHUNG, D. M., Mathematics
CHUNG, S. Y., Mathematics
HONG, S. S., Mathematics
KANG, J., Chemistry
KIM, D. S., Mathematics
KIM, J., Mathematics
KIM, S. R., Life Science
KIM, W. S., Life Science
KIM, W. T., Physics
LEE, B. H., Physics
LEE, D., Chemistry
KIM, D. H., Chemistry
LEE, H., Chemistry
LEE, J. B., Mathematics
LEE, J. G., Mathematics
LEE, J. K., Life Science
LEE, W. K., Chemistry
PARK, G. S., Physics
PARK, S. A., Mathematics
PARK, S. H., Mathematics
PARK, Y. J., Physics
RHEE, B. K., Physics
SHIN, C. E., Mathematics
SHIN, W., Chemistry
SO, H., Chemistry
YANG, J. M., Life Science
YOON, K. B., Chemistry

College of Social Science:

CHANG, Y. H., Mass Communication
CHO, H., Sociology
CHO, O., Sociology
CHOI, C. S., Mass Communication
CHOI, O. C., Law
CHUNG, H.-J., Law
EOM, D. S., Law
HONG, S. B., Law
KANG, J. I., Political Science
KIM, H. S., Mass Communication
KIM, K. M., Sociology
KIM, Y. S., Political Science
LEE, K. Y., Political Science
OH, B. S., Law
PARK, H. S., Political Science
PARK, S. T., Sociology
SHIN, Y. H., Political Science
SONN, H. C., Political Science
SUH, K. M., Law
YOON, Y. D., Sociology

School of Business Administration:

CHEE, Y. H., Business Administration
CHOI, J. H., Business Administration
CHOI, S. J., Business Administration
CHOI, W. Y., Business Administration
CHUN, S. B., Business Administration
HA, Y. W., Business Administration
JON, J. S., Business Administration
KANG, H. S., Business Administration
KIM, S. K., Business Administration
KOOK, C. P., Business Administration
LEE, C., Business Administration
LEE, D. S., Business Administration
LEE, J. B., Business Administration
LEE, J. H., Business Administration
LEE, J. J., Business Administration
LEE, K. L., Business Administration
LEE, N. J., Business Administration
LEE, W. Y., Business Administration
LIM, C. U., Business Administration
MIN, J. H., Business Administration
PARK, K. K., Business Administration
PARK, N. H., Business Administration
PARK, Y. S., Business Administration
RHO, B. H., Business Administration
SUH, C. J., Business Administration

School of Economics:

CHO, C. O., Economics
GILL, I. S., Economics
JEON, S. H., Economics
KIM, B. U., Economics
KIM, K. D., Economics
KIM, K. H., Economics
KIM, S. Y., Economics
KWACK, T., Economics
LEE, D. S., Economics
LEE, H. K., Economics
LEE, H. S., Economics
LEE, Y. G., Economics
NAHM, J. W., Economics
NAM, S. I., Economics
SONG, E. Y., Economics
SUH, J. H., Economics
WANG, G. H., Economics

Graduate School of International Studies:

AHN, S. Y.
CHO, Y. J.

Graduate School of Media Communications:

BYUN, D. H.
JUNG, M.-R.
KIM, C. H.
KIM, Y. Y.
LEE, S. W.
SHIN, H. C.
YOON, K.

Graduate School of Theology:

CHUNG, W. S.
MOON, J. Y.
SIM, J. H.

General Education Division:

CHO, G. H., General Education
CHOI, H. N., General Education
KIM, J.-W., General Education
KIM, O. S., General Education

ATTACHED RESEARCH INSTITUTES

Institute for Applied Sciences and Technology: Dir S. Y. JEONG.

Institute for Business Research: Dir S. CHUN.

Institute for Economic Research: Dir K. KIM.

Institute for Entrepreneurial Studies: Dir Y. H. CHEE.

Institute for Information and Technology: Dir D. H. HONG.

Institute of International and Area Studies: Dir K. Y. LEE.
Institute of Language and Information: Dir W. Y. SONG.
Institute for Philosophical Studies: Dir Y. A. KANG.
Institute for Religion: Dir C. Y. KIM.
Institute for Social Sciences: Dir H. C. SONN.
Institute for the Study of Media and Culture: Dir D. W. HYUN.
Legal Science Institute: Dir B. S. OH.
Research Institute for Basic Science: Dir J. B. LEE.
Research Institute for East Asian Studies: Dir Y. H. SHIN.
Research Institute for Humanities: Dir J. D. LEE.
Research Institute for Life and Culture: Dir J. M. WOO.
Research Institute for Theology: Dir J. PARK.
Technology Management Institute: Dir B. KIM.

SOOKMYUNG WOMEN'S UNIVERSITY

53-12 Chungpa-dong 2-ka, Yongsan-gu, Seoul 140
Telephone: (2) 710-9114
Fax: (2) 718-2337
E-mail: kslee@sookmyung.ac.kr
Internet: www.sookmyung.ac.kr

Founded 1906
Private control
Language of instruction: Korean
Academic year: March to February

President: KYUNG-SOOK LEE
Dean of Academic Affairs: EUN-GYUN MOK
Dean of Student Affairs: YOUNG-SOOK SUH
Dean of Administrative Affairs: CHUN-HAK OH
Dean of Planning: MOO-SEUCK CHO
Library Director: HEE-JAE LEE
Library of 628,688
Number of teachers: 370
Number of students: 13,315

Publications: *Sookdae Shinbo* (in Korean, weekly), *Newsletter* (in Korean, 3 a year), *Bulletin* (in English and Korean, annually), *Sookmyung Times* (in English, monthly), *Asian Women* (in English)

DEANS

Graduate School: JUNG-WOO LEE
Graduate Schools of Special Subjects: SOOK-HEE PARK
College of Liberal Arts: JUNG-SHIN HAN
College of Natural Sciences: YOUNG-HEE HONG
College of Home Economics: SUN-JAE LEE
College of Political Science and Law: SANG-KWANG LEE
College of Economics and Commerce: WON-BAE YOON
College of Music: MAN-BANG YI
College of Pharmacy: AN-KEUN KIM
College of Fine Arts: HAK-SEONG KIM

HEADS OF DEPARTMENTS

Division of the Humanities: JONG-JIN PARK
Division of English Language and Literature: IN-CHAN PARK
Division of Foreign Language and Literature: HYE-YANG SHIN
Division of Education: BYUNG-HEE YOON
Department of Culture and Tourism: MAENG-SUN KIM
Division of Natural Sciences: YOUNG-JA PARK
Division of Mathematics and Statistics: KI-SUK LEE
Division of Information Science: KYUNG-MOOK OH
Department of Physical Education: JUNG-H CHO
Department of Dance: IN-JA PARK
Division of Home Management and Child Welfare: YOUNG-HYE SUNG
Division of Life Sciences: YOUNG-SIL HAN
Division of Political Science and Public Administration: EUGENE LEE
Division of Law: SHIN-YUNG CHOE
Division of Communication: BO-SEOB AN
Division of Economics: YONG-JA KIM
Division of Business Administration: KWANG-JAE LEE
Department of Instrumental Music: HEE-CHUE CHAI
Department of Vocal Music: YUN-JA KIM
Department of Composition: SOON-HO KWON
Division of Pharmacy: JUNG-HWAN CHO
Division of Design: JUN-JA PARK
Department of Painting: HYUN-HAW KIM
Department of Arts and Crafts: SEOL KIM

ATTACHED INSTITUTES

Research Institute for Asian Women: Dir MEE-SOK PARK.
Research Institute for Korean Unification: Dir KI-BYEOM LEE.
Research Institute of Science for Health and Better Living: Dir HYUN-SOOK KIM.
Research Institute of Pharmaceutical Sciences: Dir HEE-DOO KIM.
Socio-Educational Research Unit: Dir IN-SUB SONG.
Institute for Child Study: Dir SO-HEE LEE.
Research Institute of Natural Sciences: Dir KWANG-HYUN NO.
Research Institute of the Global Environment: Dir JUNG-JIN OH.
Research Institute of Regional Studies: Eugene Lee.
Research Institute of Economics and Business Administration: Dir CHONG-EUI KIM.
Research Institute of Industrial Design: Dir HAN-TAI YOO.
Moonshin Institute of Fine Arts: Dir SUNG-SOOK CHOI.
Drug Information Research Institute: Dir HYUN-TAEK SHIN.
Research Institute of Traditional Korean Food: Dir YOUNG-SIL HAN.

SOONGSIL UNIVERSITY

1-1 Sangdo 5-dong, Dongjak-ku, Seoul 156-743
Telephone: (2) 820-0111
Fax: (2) 814-7362
Internet: www.ssu.ac.kr

Founded 1897
Private control
Academic year: March to December

Chancellor: SUN-HEE KWAK
President: YOON-BAE OUH
Vice-President for International Affairs: HAE-SEOK OH
Vice-President for Academic Affairs: BONG-CHUL SEO
Librarian: PYUNG-SYK RO
Library of 367,000 vols
Number of teachers: 586 (252 full-time, 334 part-time)
Number of students: 10,167

DEANS

College of Humanities: HONG-ZIN KIM
College of Natural Sciences: YOUNG-JA YUN
College of Law: SUNG-SOOK KIM
College of Social Sciences: KWANG-SEOB SHIN
College of Economics and Commerce: WON-WOO LEE
College of Engineering: MUN-HEON KIM
College of Information Science: CHUL-HEE LEE

HEADS OF SCHOOLS

School of Basic Sciences (in the College of Natural Sciences): CHANG-BAE KIM
School of Economics and World Commerce (in the College of Economics and Commerce): SUNG-SUP RHEE
School of Business Administration (in the College of Economics and Commerce): (vacant)
School of Electronics, Electrics and Information Telecommunication (in the College of Engineering): SOON-CHUL JO
School of Computing (in the College of Information Science): CHAE-WOO YOO
Evening Courses: YOUNG-JONG KIM
Graduate School (General): YOUNG-HOON KIM
Graduate School of Industry: HYEON-TAE CHO
Graduate School of Small Business: DONG-KIL YOO
Graduate School of Information Science: SUNG-YUL RHEW
Graduate School of Labour and Industrial Relations: WOO-HYEON CHO
Graduate School of Unification Policy: TUK-CHU CHUN
Graduate School of International and Regional Studies: LEE-SOO KANG
Graduate School of Education: JAE-HYEON HAN
Graduate School of Christian Studies: YOUNG-HAN KIM

DIRECTORS

Institute of Humanities: HONG-ZIN KIM
Institute of Social Science: SOO-EON MOON
Institute of Korean Christian Culture Research: YOUNG-HAN KIM
Institute of Law: DOO-HWAN KIM
Christian Institute of Social Studies: SAM-YEUL LEE
Institute of Industrial Technology: YOUNG-PIL KWON
Institute for Adult and Continuing Education: KWANG-MYUNG KIM
Institute of Business and Economic Strategies: DAE-YONG JEONG
Institute of Natural Sciences: CHONG-IN YU
Resource Recycling Research Centre: KAP-SOO DOH

HEADS OF DEPARTMENTS

College of Humanities:

Korean Language and Literature: CHONG-CHUL PARK
English Language and Literature: JUN-EON PARK
German Language and Literature: YONG-SAM PARK
French Language and Literature: SAI-LYONG LEE
Chinese Language and Literature: JONG-SEONG KIM
Philosophy: SAM-YEUL LEE
History: EUN-KOO PARK

College of Natural Sciences:

Mathematics: EUN-SOON PARK
Statistics: GUN-SEOG KANG

School of Basic Sciences:

Physics: CHANG-BAE KIM
Chemistry: KUAN-SOO SHIN

College of Law:

Law: CHEOL-HONG YOON

College of Social Sciences:

Social Work: HE-LEN NOH
Public Administration: YOON-SHIK LEE

Political Science and Diplomacy: JANG-KWON KIM
Japanese Studies: JANG-CHUL SHIN

College of Economics and Commerce

School of Economics and World Commerce:

Economics: YOU-YOUNG PARK
World Commerce: HEON-DEOK YOON

School of Business Administration:

Business Administration: JAE-KWAN LEE
Small Business: DAE-YONG CHUNG
Accounting: DAE-KEUN KIM

College of Engineering:

Chemical Engineering: YOUNG-WOO NAM
Textile Engineering: YONG-HO KIM
Mechanical Engineering: YOUNG-PIL KWON
Architectural Engineering: MOON-SANG CHO
Industrial Engineering: IN-SOO CHOI

School of Electronics, Electrics and Information Telecommunication:

Electronics Engineering: SUN-TAE JEONG
Electrical Engineering: JAE-CHUL KIM
Information Telecommunication Engineering: CHUL-HUN SEO

SUNCHON NATIONAL UNIVERSITY

315 Maegok-dong, Sunchon, Chonnam 540-742
Telephone: (661) 750-3114
Fax: (661) 750-3117
E-mail: webmaster@sunchon.ac.kr
Internet: www.sunchon.ac.kr

Founded 1935
State control
Academic year: March to December

President: Dr JAE-KI KIM
Deans: Dr WON-OG YANG (Academic Affairs), Dr JONG-CHUN CHOI (Student Affairs), Dr NAM-HOON CHO (University Planning and Research), DOO-HEE LEE (General Affairs)
Librarian: Dr JIN-IL DOO

Library of 211,000 books
Number of teachers: 340
Number of students: 12,560 (11,117 undergraduate, 1,443 postgraduate)

DEANS

College of Agriculture and Life Science: Dr DONG-HWAN OH
College of Humanities and Social Sciences: Dr JUNG-SUN SHIM
College of Natural Sciences: Dr MAN-CHAI JANG
College of Engineering: Dr BONG-CHAN BAN
College of Education: Dr SANG-WOOK HAN

SUNGKYUL CHRISTIAN UNIVERSITY

147-2 Anyang 8-dong, Manan-gu, Anyang, Kyungki-do 430-742
Telephone: (343) 467-8114
Internet: www.sungkyul.ac.kr

Founded 1962 as a seminary; present name 1992

President: Dr KEE-HO SUNG

Library of 170,000 vols.

SUNGKYUNKWAN UNIVERSITY

Humanities and Social Sciences Campus, 53 Myongnyun-dong 3-ga, Chongo-gu, Seoul 110-745
Natural Sciences Campus, 300 Chunchun-dong, Changan-gu, Suwon, Kyonggi-do 440-746
Telephone: (2) 760-0114
Fax: (2) 744-2453
E-mail: webmaster@www.skku.ac.kr
Internet: www.skku.ac.kr

Founded 1398; university status 1953
Private control
Academic year: March to February

Chairman of the Board of Trustees: E-HOUCK KWON
President: JUNG DON SEO
Vice-Presidents: CHAE-WOONG LEE (Humanities and Social Sciences Campus), YUN-HEUM PARK (Natural Sciences Campus)
Academic Affairs Officer: HYUK KIM
Librarian: PYUNG-U PARK

Library of 1,448,259 vols
Number of teachers: 980
Number of students: 24,098

Publications: *Journal of Humanities Sciences* (in Korean, annually), *Journal of Eastern Culture* (in Korean, annually), *Journal of Social Sciences* (in Korean, annually), *Journal of Korean Economics* (annually), *Journal of Human Life Sciences* (in Korean, annually), *Sung Kyun Law Review* (in Korean, 2 a year), *Learned Papers in Science and Technology* (in Korean, 2 a year), *Learned Papers in the Natural Sciences* (in Korean, 2 a year), *Journal of Modern China* (in Korean, annually), *Suson Learned Papers* (in Korean, annually)

DEANS

School of Confucian and Oriental Studies: YOUNG-JIN CHOI
School of Language and Literature: BONG-WON CHOI
School of Humanities: HAN-GU LEE
College of Law: KYU-SANG JUNG
School of Social Sciences: CHANG-SOO CHUNG
School of Economics: SUNG-SOON LEE
School of Business Administration: YOUNG-KYU KIM
School of Human Life Sciences: YANG-HEE LEE
College of Education: YOUNG-EUN CHIN
School of Art: HAK-SUN LIM
School of Natural Sciences: SANG-TAE LEE
School of Electrical and Computer Engineering: CHIL-GEE LEE
School of Chemical, Polymer and Textile Engineering: BOONG-SOO JEON
School of Metallurgical and Materials Engineering: JOEN-GEON HAN
School of Mechanical Engineering: HYUN-SOO KIM
School of Architecture, Landscape Architecture and Civil Engineering: SANG-HAE CHOI
School of Systems Management Engineering: HOO-GON CHOI
School of Pharmacy: WON-HUN HAM
School of Life Sciences and Technology: KYU-SEUNG LEE
School of Sports Science: EUNG-NAM AHM
School of Medicine: DAY-YONG UHM

HEADS OF DEPARTMENTS

School of Confucian and Oriental Studies (tel. (2) 760-1030; fax (2) 760-0909; e-mail confuorsch@skku.edu; internet www.skkuscos.ac.kr):

Confucian Philosophy: IL-BEOM CHOI
Korean Philosophy: IL-BEOM CHOI
Chinese Philosophy: IL-BEOM CHOI

School of Language and Literature (tel. (2) 760-1031; fax (2) 760-0910; e-mail lanlitsch@skku.edu; internet web.skku.edu/human):

Korean Language and Literature: WOO-SHIK KANG
English Language and Literature: DONG-WOOK KIM
French Language and Literature: JEE-SOON LEE
Chinese Language and Literature: HYUNG-WOO BYUN
German Language and Literature: JEONG-JUN LEE
Russian Language and Literature: JONG-WOO OH
Korean Literature in Classical Chinese: MYOUNG-HO KIM

School of Humanities (tel. (2) 760-1039; fax (2) 760-0910; e-mail humansch@skku.edu; internet web.skku.edu/human):

History: HAE-SOON SHIN
Philosophy: JWA-YONG LEE
Library and Information Science: YOUNG-MAN KOH

College of Law (tel. (2) 760-1032; fax (2) 760-0920; e-mail lawdept@skku.edu; internet law.skku.ac.kr):

Law: SEUNG-WOO LEE

School of Social Sciences (tel. (2) 760-1033; fax (2) 760-0930; e-mail socischsch@skku.edu; internet www.skku.ac.kr/~sscience):

Public Administration: KEUN-SEI KIM
Political Science and Diplomacy: IN-SUB MAH
Journalism and Mass Communications: EUN-KYUNG HAN
Sociology: SANG-WOOK KIM
Social Welfare: KYUNG-ZOON HONG
Psychology: DUK-WOONG HAN

School of Economics (tel. (2) 760-1034; fax (2) 744-5717; e-mail econsch@skku.edu; internet web.skku.edu/~ecostat):

Economics: KWANG-SU KIM
Statistics: CHONG-SUN PARK

School of Business Administration (tel. (2) 760-1040; fax (2) 760-0950; e-mail bizsch@skku.edu; internet biz.skku.ac.kr):

Business Administration: YOUNG-GYU KIM

School of Human Life Sciences (tel. (2) 760-1035; fax (2) 760-0960; e-mail humlisci@skku.edu; internet lifetech.skku.ac.kr):

Family Life Management and Consumer Studies: KEE-OK KIM
Fashion Design: HEA-YOUNG KIM
Child Psychology and Education: IN-SOO CHOE

College of Education (tel. (2) 760-1036; fax (2) 760-0960; e-mail edudept@skku.edu; internet www.skku.ac.kr/~coe):

Education: DUK-HEE CHUN
Education in Classical Chinese: MYONG-HAK LEE
Mathematics Education: OK-KEE KANG
Computer Education: JAE-HYUN KIM

School of Art (tel. (2) 760-1038; fax (2) 760-0900; e-mail artsch@skku.edu; internet www.skkuart.ac.kr):

Fine Art: JIN-SOO JUNG
Design: MYOUN KIM
Dance: KYUNG-HEE KIM
Film, Television and Multimedia: JIN-OH CHUNG

School of Natural Sciences (tel. (31) 291-5523; fax (31) 291-5809; e-mail natscisch@skku.edu; internet jayun.skku.ac.kr):

Life Sciences: KIL-LYONG KIM
Mathematics: MEE-KYOUNG KIM
Physics: SEONG-WOO HONG
Chemistry: YONG-KEUN SON

School of Electrical and Computer Engineering (tel. (31) 291-5524; fax (31) 291-5819; e-mail eceng@skku.edu; internet ece.skku.ac.kr):

Electrical and Computer Engineering: YUN-HO LEE

School of Chemical, Polymer and Textile Engineering (tel. (31) 291-5525; fax (31) 291-5829; e-mail chemeng@skku.edu; internet nature.skku.ac.kr/~hwagosum):

Chemical Engineering: TAE-HO KIM
Textile Engineering: JUN-YOUNG LEE

School of Metallurgical and Materials Engineering (tel. (31) 291-5526; fax (31) 291-5829; e-mail mateng@skku.edu; internet mse.skku.ac.kr):

Metallurgical Engineering: JIN-HO JOO
Materials Engineering: JAI-CHAN LEE

School of Mechanical Engineering (tel. (31) 291-5827; fax (31) 291-5849; internet mecha.skku.ac.kr):

Mechanical Engineering: MU-JIN KANG

School of Architecture, Landscape Architecture and Civil Engineering (tel. (31) 291-5529; fax (31) 291-5859; internet www.skku.ac.kr/~oas):

Architecture: SANG-HAE LEE
Civil and Environmental Engineering: DONG-YUP KIM
Landscape Architecture: HYUN-MOK SHIN

School of Systems Management Engineering (tel. (31) 291-5531; fax (31) 291-5859; internet www.skku.ac.kr/~sme):

Systems Management Engineering: SUNG-IL LEE

School of Pharmacy (tel. (31) 291-5528; fax (31) 291-6000; internet pharm.skku.ac.kr):

Pharmacy: KYU-HYUCK JUNG

School of Life Sciences and Technology (tel. (31) 291-5532; fax (31) 291-6000; internet lifeeng.skku.ac.kr):

Food and Life Sciences: KI-MOON PARK
Bio-mechatronic Engineering: DAE-WON LEE
Genetic Engineering: SUK-CHAN LEE

School of Sports Science (tel. (31) 291-5533; fax (31) 291-6000; e-mail hobbytool@hananet.net; internet www.skkusport.com):

Sports Science: BUM-SIK KIM
Coaching Science: BUM-SIK KIM

School of Medicine (tel. (31) 291-6020; fax (31) 291-6029; e-mail jdseo@smc.samsung.co.kr; internet medicine.skku.ac.kr):

Medicine: JUNG-DON SEO

ATTACHED RESEARCH INSTITUTES

Academy for East Asian Studies: Dir JAMES PALAIS.

SUNGSHIN WOMEN'S UNIVERSITY

249-1 Dongseon-dong 3-ga, Seongbuk-do, Seoul 136-742
Telephone: (2) 920-7114
E-mail: www@cc.sungshin.ac.kr
Internet: www.sungshin.ac.kr

Founded 1936

Library of 500,000 vols
Number of students: 13,000

Colleges of Humanities, Social Sciences, Natural Sciences, Human Ecology, Education, Arts, Music.

SUWON UNIVERSITY

445-743 San 2-2 Wawoo-ri, Bongnam-myun, Hwasung-si, Gyeonggi-do
E-mail: info@suwon.mail.co.kr
Internet: www.suwon.ac.kr

Founded 1982

Chairman: IN-SOO LEE
President: D. Y. YOON.

TAEJON UNIVERSITY

96-3 Yongun-dong, Tong-gu, Taejon 300-716
Telephone: (42) 282-0231
Fax: (42) 283-8808
E-mail: taejon@dragon.taejon.ac.kr
Internet: www.taejon.ac.kr.

UNIVERSITY OF SEOUL

90 Jeonnong-dong, Dongdaemun-gu, Seoul 130-743
Telephone: (2) 2210-2114
Fax: (2) 2243-2732
E-mail: w3adm@uos.ac.kr
Internet: www.uos.ac.kr

Founded 1918; Seoul City University until 1996
Maintained by Seoul Metropolitan Government
Language of instruction: Korean
Academic year: March to February

President: Dr SANG-BUM LEE
Provost of Academic Affairs: Dr HYUN-SOO MIN
Provost of General Administration: IN-SONG CHANG
Provost of Planning and Development: Dr EUI-YOUNG SON
Provost of Student Affairs: Dr KEUN-HEE CHOI
Director of Central Library: Dr YONG-GUN KIM

Library of 554,895 vols
Number of teachers: 302
Number of students: 14,867

Publication: *University Press* (every 2 weeks)

DEANS

College of Economics and Business Administration: Dr JONG-DAE LEE
College of Engineering: Dr SUNG-IL CHO
College of Law and Public Administration: Dr YONG-CHAN PARK
College of Liberal Arts and Natural Sciences: Dr JUN-HO SONG
College of Urban Sciences: Dr HYUNG-SU HAN
Liberal Arts Division: Dr DONG-HA LEE
Graduate School: Dr JAE-BOK PARK
Graduate School of Business Administration: Dr JONG-DAE LEE
Graduate School of Engineering: Dr SUNG-IL CHO
Graduate School of Urban Administration: Dr HYUNG-SU HAN

ATTACHED INSTITUTES

E-Government Research Institute: Dir Dr HYUN-SUNG KIM.

Institute of Humanities: Dir Dr SUNG-BAEK LEE.

Institute of Industrial Management: conducts various economic and business management research; promotes a close relationship between business corporations and the university; Dir Dr JONG-DAE LEE.

Institute of Industrial Technology: Dir Dr MYUNG-DO O.

Institute of Information and Technology: Dir Dr SUNG-HWAN KIM.

Institute of Law and Administration: Dir Dr YOUN-CHAN PARK.

Institute of Quantum Information Processing and System: Dir Dr DO-YUL AN.

Institute of Seoul Studes: aims to rediscover important values imbedded in the cultural and historical city of Seoul and to develop them academically and systematically; Dir Dr WU-TAE LEE.

Institute of Tax Research: Dir Dr SANG JONG SONG.

Institute of Urban Sciences: f. 1976; multidisciplinary research and other academic activities to solve problems arising in a rapidly expanding metropolis; Dir Dr CHAN-HWAN CHOI.

Seoul Institute for Transparency: Dir Dr IL-TAE KIM.

Student Guidance Center: contributes to development of students through counselling and studying every phase of student activities; Dir Dr SUNG-HO LEE.

Urban Anti-Disaster Research Center: Dir Dr MYUNG-O YUN.

UNIVERSITY OF ULSAN

POB 18, Ulsan 680-049
Telephone: (52) 277-3101
Fax: (52) 277-3419
E-mail: webmaster@mail.ulsan.ac.kr
Internet: uou.ulsan.ac.kr

Founded 1970
Private control
Academic year: March to December

Chairman: MONG-JOON CHUNG
President: CHUNG-KIL CHUNG
Head of Academic Information Centre: Prof. JEONG-SEOK HEO

Library of 700,000 books, 909 periodicals
Number of teachers: 723
Number of students: 11,659 (6,121 undergraduate, 5,538 postgraduate)

DEANS

College of Natural Sciences: TAE-SOO KIM
College of Engineering: DONG-KEE LEE
College of Social Sciences: YEON-JAE SHIN
College of Human Ecology: HYE-KYUNG KIM
College of Humanities: CHUNG-HOO SUH
College of Business Administration: HI-KYOON LEE
College of Fine Arts: PYUNG-HUI PARK
College of Design: SANG-HYE HAN
College of Industry and Management: KYU-CHO LEE
College of Music: HYUN-KYUNG CHAE
College of Medicine: WON-DONG KIM
Graduate School: KANG-MOON KOH
Graduate School of Education: MYEUNG-HAK YANG
Graduate School of Industrial Technology: SEONG-DEUK KIM I
Graduate School of Business Administration: JOONG-HEON NAM
Graduate School of Regional Development: WOO-SUNG KIM
Graduate School of Information and Communications Technology: KYUNG-SUP PARK

WON KWANG UNIVERSITY

344-2 Shinyong-Dong, Iksan, Chonbuk 570-749
Telephone: 50-5114
Internet: www.wonkwang.ac.kr

Founded 1946
Private control
Academic year: March to August, September to February

President: GAB-WOEN JEONG
Vice-President (Academy): SONG CHON-EUN
Vice-President (Medicine): CHON PAL-KHN
Dean of Academic Affairs: GO GUN-IL
Dean of Planning Office: CHOI SEONG-SIK
Dean of Student Affairs: KIM JONG-SU
Dean of Financial and General Affairs: OH HAE-GEUM
Director of Library: LEE MAN-SANG

Number of teachers: 462
Number of students: 23,200

DEANS

Graduate School: YU GI-SU
Graduate School of Education: YU JAE-YEONG
Graduate School of Industry: YUN YANG-WOONG
College of Won Buddhism: KIM HONG-CHULO
College of Liberal Arts and Sciences: OHM JEONG-OAK
College of Education: SHIN YO-YOUNG
College of Law: KIM DAE-KYOO
College of Agriculture: LEE KAP-SANG
College of Pharmacy: OCK CHI-WAN

College of Oriental Medicine: MAENG UNG-JAEO
College of Engineering: CHUNG SA-HEE
College of Social Sciences: KIM GUY-KON
College of Management: PARK JAE-ROK
College of Home Economics: MOON BUM-SOO
College of Dentistry: KIM SU-NAM
School of Medicine: CHUNG YEUN-TAI

HEADS OF DEPARTMENTS

College of Won Buddhism:
- Won Buddhism: KIM SEONG-JANG
- Won Buddhist Oriental Religion: RO KWON-YONG

College of Liberal Arts and Sciences:
- Korean Language and Literature: CHAE KYU-PAN
- English Language and Literature: YONG BYUNG-SEOK
- German Language and Literature: KIM CHANG-RYOL
- French Language and Literature: WON YOO-SANG
- Chinese Language and Literature: KANG TAE-KWON
- History: LEE JU-CHEON
- Dance: RHEE GIL-JU
- Philosophy: KIM SEONG-KWAM

College of Natural Science:
- Archaeology and Art History: SHIN SOON-CHUL
- Mathematics: LEE SEUNG-WOO
- Physics: LIM SUNG-WOO
- Statistics: KIM TAE-SUNG
- Chemistry: BAEK SEUNG-HWA
- Molecular Biology: KIM BYUNG-JIN
- Physical Education: KIM YONG-KYU

College of Law:
- Law: PEE JUNG-HYUN

College of Management:
- Management: CHUNG SOO-JIN
- International Trade: KIM JOONG-SHIK
- Accounting: SUL SUNG-JIN

College of Social Sciences:
- Public Administration: LIM KWANG-HYUN
- Mass Communication and Journalism: SONG HAE-RYONG
- Economics: JEONG GAB-WON
- Information Management: PARK RYUN
- Politics and Diplomacy: LEE WOO-JUNG
- Social Welfare: KIM SUNG-CHUN
- Health Policy and Management: KIM JONG-IN

College of Pharmacy:
- Pharmacy: OK CHIN-WAN

College of Education:
- Korean Language Education: JEONG MYUNG-GI
- English Language Education: JUNG TAE-JIN
- Japanese Language Education: PARK JUNG-EUI
- Chinese Language Education: KIM DAE-HYUN
- History Education: YOON YONG-EE
- Education: KIM JUN-GI
- Commercial Education: KO YONG-BU
- Child Education: PARK HWA-YOUN
- Mathematical Education: CHOI KYU-HYUCK
- Physics Education: LEE HYUN-SOON
- Biology Education: PARK EUN-KYU
- Home Economics Education: PARK IL-ROCK
- Music Education: KIM YOUNG-SUN
- Physical Education: SHIN JONG-SOUN

College of Agriculture:
- Agriculture: LEE JOONG-HO
- Agricultural Chemistry: HAN SEONG-SOO
- Horticulture: YU SUNG-OH
- Forestry: RYU TAEK-KYU

College of Oriental Medicine:
- Pre-Oriental Medicine: YU HEUI-YOUNG
- Oriental Medicine: MAENG WOONG-JAE

College of Engineering:
- Construction Engineering: YANG KEEK-YOUNG
- Electric Engineering: JANG SUNG-HWAN
- Civil Engineering: LEE BYUNG-KOO
- Electronic Engineering: KANG YUNG-JIN
- Urban Planning Engineering: JUNG JUNG-KWEON
- Computer Engineering: HAN SUNG-KOOK
- Mechanical Engineering: KIM DONG-HYUN
- Control and Instrumentation Engineering: AHN TAE-CHON
- Materials Engineering: PARK HEE-SOON

College of Home Economics:
- Clothing: LEE SUN-HEUI
- Home Management: CHAE OCK-HI
- Food Nutrition: KIM IN-SOOK

College of Dentistry:
- Pre-Dentistry: KIM SANG-CHUL
- Dentistry: JIN TAI-HO

School of Medicine:
- Pre-Medicine: CHOI BONG-KYU
- Medicine: PARK SUK-DON

College of Fine Arts:
- Applied Fine Arts: NAM SANG-JAE
- Ceramic Crafts: KIM GI-CHUN
- Western Painting: LEE CHUNG-HEE
- Metal Crafts: OH YOUNG-KYUNG
- Korean Painting: KIM GUM-CHAUL
- Sculpture: YUN SEK-KU
- Calligraphy: KIM YANG-DONG

ATTACHED INSTITUTE

Won Kwang Medical Center: Dir JEON PAL-KEUN.

YEUNGNAM UNIVERSITY

Gyongsan 632
Telephone: Taegu 82-5111
Internet: www.yu.ac.kr

Founded 1967 by amalgamation of Taegu College and Chunggu College
Private control
Academic year: March to February (two semesters)

President: Dr LEW JOON
Dean of Academic Affairs: Dr PARK BONG MOK
Dean of Student Affairs: Dr KIM JUNG YUEP
Dean of Business Affairs: Dr PARK SUNG KYU
Dean of Planning and Development: Dr YOON BYUNG TAE
Director of Library: Dr OH MYUNG-KUN

Library of 398,690 vols
Number of teachers: 549
Number of students: 22,506

Publications: *Yeungnam University Theses Collection*, *Library Guide*, *Yeungdae Munha* (Yeungnam University Culture), *Student Guide* (annually), and various faculty and institutional publs

DEANS

College of Liberal Arts: KIM TAIK-KYOO
College of Science: KIM JONG DAE
College of Engineering: LEE DONG IN
College of Law and Political Science: RHEE CHANGWOO
College of Commerce and Economics: RYU CHANG OU
College of Medicine: KIM WON JOON
College of Pharmacy: SEO BYEONG CHEON
College of Agriculture and Animal Sciences: SYE YOUNG-SYEK
College of Home Economics: LEE KAP RANG
College of Education: SONG BYUNG SOON
College of Fine Arts: HONG SUNG MOON
College of Music: KIM SHIN WHAN
Evening College: BYUN JAE-OCK
Graduate School: KIM HOGWON
Graduate School of Business Administration: KIM KIE-TAEK
Graduate School of Environmental Studies: JIN KAP DUCK
Graduate School of Education: CHUNG SOON MOK

PROFESSORS

College of Liberal Arts:
- CHAE, S. H., Buddhist Philosophy
- CHANG, H. K., Psychology
- CHO, K.-S., Korean Language and Literature
- CHUNG, Y. W., Archaeology
- HU, J. W., Western Philosophy
- HUH, C. Y., European History
- HWANG, S.-M., English and Linguistics
- KEWN, S.-H., English Drama
- KIM, B. K., Western Philosophy
- KIM, C. S., Korean Language and Literature
- KIM, S. H., English Novel
- KIM, S. J., Korean History
- KIM, S. K., English Literature
- KIM, S. M., English Poetry
- KIM, T. K., Anthropology
- KIM, W.-W., English Poetry
- KWON, Y. G., English Language and Literature
- LEE, B. J., Asian History
- LEE, B. L., Korean Language and Literature
- LEE, C. H., Western Philosophy
- LEE, J. W., Chinese Prose, Phonology
- LEE, S.-T., English Literature
- LEE, S.-D., English Poetry
- LEE, S. K., Korean History
- LEE, Y. K., Philosophy of History, Social Philosophy
- LEE, W. J., Philosophy
- LIM, B.-J., French Language
- MUN, C.-B., English Philosophy
- O, S. C., Korean History
- OH, M.-K., Sociology
- SUH, I., American Literature
- SUH, K. B., Chinese Poetry
- YOH, K. K., English Language
- YOUN, Y.-O., Korean Literature

College of Science:
- CHANG, G. S., Physics
- CHANG, K., Mathematics
- CHO, H. S., Physics
- CHO, Y., Mathematics
- CHOE, O.-S., Physics
- DOH, M. K., Inorganic Chemistry
- KANG, S. G., Physics
- KIM, D. S., Analytical Chemistry
- KIM, J. D., Organic Chemistry
- KIM, J.-C., Mathematics
- KIM, M. M., Physics
- KIM, Y. H., Physics
- PAHK, G.-H., Mathematics
- PARK, B. K., Physical Chemistry
- PARK, H.-S., Mathematics
- PARK, W. H., Biology
- RO, H. K., Physics
- WOO, J., Statistics

College of Engineering:
- BAE, J. H., Electrical Engineering
- BYUN, D. K., Civil Engineering
- CHANG, D. H., Textile Engineering
- CHO, B., Chemical Engineering
- CHO, H., Textile Engineering
- CHOI, S.-G., Electronic Engineering
- CHOI, S.-H., Mechanical Design
- CHUNG, K.-H., Eletronic Engineering
- CHUNG, W.-G., Textile Engineering
- HA, Z.-H., Mechanical Engineering
- JOO, H., System Engineering
- KANG, S. H., Chemical Engineering
- KIM, D. O., Traffic Engineering
- KIM, G.-C., Civil Engineering
- KIM, H. S., Architectural Engineering
- KIM, I.-J., Architectural Engineering

KIM, J. Y., Mechanical Engineering
KIM, K. S., Industrial Chemistry
KIM, S.-K., Textile Engineering
LEE, D. H., Control Engineering
LEE, D.-I., Electrical Engineering
LEE, J. H., Industrial Chemistry
LEE, K. S., Mechanical Engineering
LEE, M. H., Industrial Chemistry
LEE, M. Y., Electronic Communication
LEE, S. T., Civil Engineering
LEE, T.-S., Marine Engineering
PARK, J. Y., Civil Engineering
PARK, W.-K., Chemical Engineering
PARK, Y.-K., Industrial Chemistry
RO, C. K., Electrical Engineering
RO, H. J., Architectural Engineering
SOHN, Y. K., Computer Engineering
SONG, J. S., Textile Engineering
UM, W.-T., Urban Engineering
WU, M. J., Civil Engineering

College of Law and Political Science:

BYUN, J.-O., Constitutional and Administrative Law
CHANG, T.-O., Public Administration
CHO, C.-H., Civil Law
CHOI, J.-C., Public Administration
CHEUNG, W. J., International Law
KIM, J.-S., Public Administration
KIM, K.-D., Civil Law
KWON, H. K., Political Science and Diplomacy
LEE, W. S., Political Science and Diplomacy
PAIK, S. K., Public Administration
PARK, S.-W., Criminal Law
RHEE, C.-W., Political Science and Diplomacy
YOON, B. T., Public Administration

College of Commerce and Economics:

BAE, Y. S., Economics
HAR, C. D., Business Policy
KIM, J. H., Foreign Trade
KIM, K.-T., Economics
KIM, T. W., Business Administration
KWON, B. T., Economics
LEE, W.-D., Economics
PARK, S.-K., Business Administration
RYU, C. O., Foreign Trade
SANG, M. D., Business Administration
SHIN, H. J., International Theory and Policy
YI, Y. W., Economics
YOON, I. H., Economics
YU, H. K., Economics

College of Medicine:

CHUNG, J. H., Preventive Medicine
CHUNG, J. K., Microbiology
CHUNG, W. Y., Obstetrics and Gynaecology
HAH, Y. M., Dermatology
HAHN, D. K., Ophthalmology
HAM, D. S., Anatomy
IHIN, J. C., Orthopaedic Surgery
KIM, C. S., Internal Medicine
KIM, C. S., Pathology
KIM, S. H., General Surgery
KIM, W. J., Pharmacology
KWUN, K. B., General Surgery
LEE, S. K., Physiology
LEE, T. S., Pathology
LEE, Y. C., Anatomy
PARK, C. S., Neurology
SONG, K. W., Oto-rhino-laryngology

College of Pharmacy:

CHANG, U. K., Pharmacy
CHUNG, K. C., Pharmacy
CHUNG, S. R., Pharmacy
DO, J. C., Industrial Pharmacy
HAN, B. S., Industrial Pharmacy
HUH, K., Pharmacy
JIN, K. D., Pharmacy
KIM, J. Y., Industrial Pharmacy
LEE, M. K., Industrial Pharmacy
LEE, S. W., Pharmacology
SEOH, B. C., Industrial Pharmacy

College of Agriculture and Animal Sciences:

BYUN, J. K., Horticulture
CHOI, C., Food Technology and Science
CHUNG, H. D., Horticulture
CHUNG, Y. G., Food Science and Technology
JUNG, K. J., Animal Science
KIM, B. D., Community Development
KIM, J. K., Applied Microbiology
LEE, H. C., Animal Science
PARK, C. H., Agronomy
SON, J. Y., Animal Science
SYE, Y. S., Animal Science
YOON, W., Community Development

College of Home Economics:

CHO, S. Y., Food and Nutrition
HAN, J. S., Food Preparation
KIM, K. S., Food Science
LEE, J. O., Clothing Science
LEE, J. S., Home Management
LEE, K. R., Food and Nutrition
PARK, J. R., Food Science

College of Education:

AHN, Y. T., Business Education
BAEK, U. H., Developmental Psychology
CHO, D. B., Personality and Education
CHUN, B. K., Audio-Visual Method
CHUNG, S. M., History of Korean Education
CHUNG, Y. K., Linguistics
KIM, H., Evaluation
KIM, J. R., Physical Education
KWON, J. W., Educational Psychology
LEE, J. H., Physical Education
LEE, K. T., English Language Education
LEE, S. B., Mathematics Education
LIM, M. S., Physical Education
PARK, B. M., Philosophy of Education
PARK, Y. B., Curriculum and Instruction
SONG, B. S., Educational Psychology

College of Fine Arts:

HONG, S. M., Sculpture
KIM, Y. Z., Painting

College of Music:

KIM, S. W., Vocal Music

ATTACHED RESEARCH CENTRES

National Unification Research Center: Dir LEE WEON SUL.

Institute of Industrial Technology: Dir Prof. CHOI SUN-HO.

Institute of Social Science: Dir Prof. KIM KI-DONG.

Institute of Resources Development: Dir CHO SEO YEUL.

Saemaul and Regional Development Research Institute: Dir YOON WOOK.

Institute of Korean Culture: Dir Prof. O SEI CHANG.

Institute of Environmental Studies: Dir CHANG TAI-OK.

Institute of Natural Science: Dir KIM DONG SOO.

Institute of Humanities: Dir SHIN GUI HYUN.

Institute of Management and Economics Research: Dir HONG YOON-IL.

Marine Science Institute: Dir KIM KI TAE.

Institute of Basic Medicine: Dir HAM DOCK SANG.

Institute of Clinical Medicine: Dir HAHN DUK KEE.

YONSEI UNIVERSITY

134 Shinchon-dong, Sudaemoon-gu, Seoul 120-749
Telephone: (2) 2123-2114
Fax: (2) 392-0618
E-mail: ewebmaster@yonsei.ac.kr
Internet: www.yonsei.ac.kr

Founded 1885
Private control
Languages of instruction: Korean, English
Academic year: March to February (two semesters)

President: CHANG-YOUNG JUNG
Vice-President for Academic Affairs: KYUNG-DUCK MIN
Vice-President for Medical Affairs: JIN-KYUNG KANG
Vice President for Wonju Campus: DAI-WOON LEE
Vice President for External Affairs and Alumni: HAN-JOONG KIM
Director of University Planning and Public Relations: IN-KI JOO
Dean of Academic Affairs: HI-SOO MOON
Dean of Admissions: YONG-HAK KIM
Dean of Student Affairs and Services: TAE-SEUNG PAIK
Director of General Affairs: HYUK-GEUN CHOI
Director of the Central Library: YOUNG-SOO SHIN

Library: see Libraries and Archives
Number of teachers: 3,331
Number of students: 52,410

Publications: *Yonsei Chunchu*, *Yonsei Annals*, *Yonsei Non-Chong*, *Abstracts of Faculty Research Reports*, *Journal of Humanities*, *Journal of Far Eastern Studies*, *Journal of East and West Studies*, *Social Science Review*, *Journal of Education Science*, *Engineering Review*, *Business Review*, *Journal of Korean Studies*, *Journal of Korean Informatics*, *Theology and Modern Times*, *Yonsei Philosophy Review*, *Korean Journal of Nursing Questions*, *Global Economic Review*, *Yonsei Law Journal*, *Yonsei Law Review*, *Yonsei Journal of Social Science*, *Journal of Engineering Research*, *New Energy and Environmental Systems*, *Theological Forum*, *Yonsei Review of Theology and Culture*, *Yonsei Economics Review*, *Yonsei Review of Educational Research*, *Yonsei Journal of Medical History*, *Yonsei Engineering Magazine*, *Yonsei Social Welfare Review*, *Yonsei Journal of Language and Literature*, *Yonsei Journal of Women's Studies*, *Yonsei Communication*, *Yonsei Journal of Public Administration*, *Journal of the Radio Communication Research Centre*, *Yonsei Journal of Sport and Leisure Studies*, *Yonsei Unification Studies*, *Focus on Genetic Science*, *Journal of the Research Institute of ASIC Design*, *Yonsei Medical Journal*, *Journal of the Research Institute of Information and Telecommunications*, *Annual Report of the Natural Science Research Institute*, *Journal of Nursing Science*, *Yonsei Nursing Journal*, *Infection Control Newsletter*, *Korean Journal of Health Science*, *Yonsei Journal of Human Ecology*, *Journal of the Institute of Basic Science*, *Journal of the Natural Science Research Institute*, *Yonsei Health Science*, *Yonsei University Counseling Center Research Review*, *Yonsei Biochemistry*, *Journal of the Yonsei Institute for Cancer Research*, *Yonsei Journal of Medical Education*, *Yonsei Journal of Clinical Orthodontics*, *Yonsei Journal of Dental Science*, *Tropical Medicine News*, *Journal of Medical Technology*

DEANS

Graduate School: SOO-IL KIM
United Graduate School of Theology: YANG-HO LEE
Graduate School of Business Administration: JOON-SEUK KIM
Graduate School of Education: SANG-WAN HAN
Graduate School of Public Administration: MYUNG-SOON SHIN

Graduate School of Engineering: JINHO LEE
Graduate School of Health Science and Management: SEUNG-HUM YU
Graduate School of International Studies: YOUNG-SUN LEE
Graduate School of Administrative Science: KYUNG-SIHK AHN
Graduate School of Communcation and Arts: YOUNG-SEOK KIM
Graduate School of Law: SANG-KI PARK
Graduate School of Human Environmental Science: CHUNG-SOOK YOON
Graduate School of Economics: SUNG-KUN HA
Graduate School of Information: KAP-YOUNG JEONG
Graduate School of Mass Communication: YANG-SOO CHOI
Graduate School of Social Welfare: HYE-KYUNG LEE
Graduate School of Nursing: SO YA JA KIM
Graduate School of Health and Environment: SOO-HONG NOH
College of Liberal Arts: IN-CHO JUN
College of Business and Economics: SUNG-KUN HA
College of Science: YOUNG-MIN KIM
College of Engineering: DAE-HEE YOON
College of Theology: YANG-HO LEE
College of Social Science: WOO-SUH PARK
College of Law: SANG-KI PARK
College of Music: MYUNG-JA CHO
College of Home Ecology: YOUNG LEE
College of Education: INTACK OH
University College: KYUNG-CHAN MIN
College of Medicine: SE-JONG KIM
College of Dentistry: HEUNG-KYU SOHN
College of Nursing: SO YA JA KIM
College of Liberal Arts and Science: BAE-SUN JI
College of Commerce and Law: PYEONG-JUN YU
College of Health Science: SOO-HONG NOH
Wonju College of Medicine: SEONG-JOON KANG

AFFILIATED INSTITUTES

Institute of Korean Studies: e-mail yskh@yonsei.ac.kr; Dir Prof. IN-CHO JUN.

Institute of East and West Studies: e-mail iphiy@yonsei.ac.kr; Dir Prof. TAE-KYU PARK.

Center for Language and Information Development: e-mail holee@yonsei.ac.kr; Dir Prof. IK-HWAN LEE.

Institute for Korean Unification Studies: Dir Prof. DONG-CHEON SHIN.

Center for Information Storage Devices: e-mail disd@yonsei.ac.kr; Dir Prof. YOUNG-PIL PARK.

Center for Space Astrophysics: e-mail josephin@csa.yonsei.ac.kr; Dir Prof. YOUNG-WOOK LEE.

Center for Noncrystalline Materials: e-mail ysle@yonsei.ac.kr; Dir Prof. DO-HYANG KIM.

Technology Innovation Center for Medical Instruments: e-mail mhlee@rimire.yonsei.ac.kr; Dir Prof. HYUNG-RO YOON.

Institute of Life Science & Biotechnology: e-mail ilb@yonsei.ac.kr; Dir Prof. YOUNG-MIN KIM.

Protein Network Research Center: e-mail pnrc@yonsei.ac.kr; Dir Prof. YU-SAM KIM.

Cancer Metastasis Research Center: e-mail tskangcc@yumc.yonsei.ac.kr; Dir Prof. JAE-KYUNG ROH.

Center for Ultra fast Optical Characteristics Control: e-mail eunjung@alchemy.yonsei.ac.kr; Dir Prof. DONG-HO KIM.

Yonsei Proteome Research Center: e-mail yprc@yonsei.ac.kr; Dir Prof. YOUNG-KI PAIK.

Center for Genome Regulation: e-mail jjy77@yonsei.ac.kr; Dir Prof. YOUNG-JOON KIM.

Center for Women's Studies & Development: e-mail jisook@yonsei.ac.kr; Dir Prof. KYUNG-JA OH.

Center for Supramolecular Nano-Assembly: e-mail csna@yonsei.ac.kr; Dir Prof. MYONG-SOO LEE.

Biometrics Engineering Research Center: e-mail berc@yonsei.ac.kr; Dir Prof. JAE-HIE KIM.

Molecular Ageing Research Center: e-mail marc@yonsei.ac.kr; Dir Prof. IN-KWON CHUNG.

Center for Chronic Metabolic Disease Research: e-mail mrc@yumc.yonsei.ac.kr; Dir Prof. YONG-HO AHN.

Institute of State Governance, Yonsei University: e-mail terese7@yonsei.ac.kr; Dir Prof. CHANG-YOUNG JUNG.

Institute of Medical Engineering: e-mail mhlee@rimire.yonsei.ac.kr; Dir Prof. HYUNG-RO YOON.

Center for Bioactive Molecular Hybrids: e-mail cbmh@yonsei.ac.kr; Dir Prof. KWAN-SOO KIM.

Research Center for Orofacial Hard Tissue Regeneration: e-mail dmrc@yonsei.ac.kr; Dir Prof. KYOUNG-NAM KIM.

Center for Atomic Wires & Layers: e-mail cellmeeting@hanmail.net; Dir Prof. HAN-WOONG YEOM.

Educational Research Institute: e-mail eduresearch@yonsei.ac.kr; Dir Prof. MOON-HEE YON.

Institute of Urban and Regional Planning: e-mail wonny0924@hanmail.net; Dir Prof. EUN-KOOK LEE.

Research Institute for ASIC Design: e-mail asic@yonsei.ac.kr; Dir Prof. JAE-SEOK KIM.

Center for Signal Processing Research: e-mail cspr@yonsei.ac.kr; Dir Prof. DAESIK HONG.

Institute for the Study of Korean Modernity: e-mail zeong@dragon.yonsei.ac.kr; Dir Prof. HYON-KEE ZEONG.

Center for Cognitive Science: e-mail c_cogsci@yonsei.ac.kr; Dir Prof. CHAN-SUP CHUNG.

Institute of Media Art: e-mail matd@yonsei.ac.kr; Dir Prof. IN-CHEOL PARK.

Yonsei ERP Research Center: e-mail ebrc@yonsei.ac.kr; Dir Prof. CHOON-SEONG LEEM.

Yonsei Research Institute of Ageing Science: e-mail yrias@yonsei.ac.kr; Dir Prof. YANG-SOO JANG.

Institute of Millennium Environmental Design and Research: e-mail medr@yonsei.ac.kr; Dir Prof. YEUNSOOK LEE.

Institute of Human Identification: e-mail kdkim@yumc.yonsei.ac.kr; Dir Prof. CHONG-YOUL KIM.

Institute of Functional Biomaterial Science: e-mail song5002@yonsei.ac.kr; Dir Prof. SUNG-SIK YOON.

The Asian Institute for Bioethics and Medical Law: e-mail byuly74@yonsei.ac.kr; Dir Prof. MYONG-SEI SOHN.

Research Institute of Hospital management: e-mail yiha@yonsei.ac.kr; Dir Prof. HYE-JONG LEE.

Nano Science & Technical Research Institute: e-mail shiwoni@yonsei.ac.kr; Dir Prof. JUNG-HYUN KIM.

Institute of the Humanities: e-mail inmun509@yonsei.ac.kr; Dir Prof. YOUNGSEO BAIK.

Institute of Literary Translation: e-mail kolitra@yonsei.ac.kr; Dir Prof. KYUNG-HWAN MOON.

Institute for Social Development Studies: e-mail scbillee@hanmail.net; Dir Prof. YONG-HAK KIM.

Research Institute for Human Behavior: e-mail kims@yonsei.ac.kr; Dir Prof. YOUNG-WOO SOHN.

Research Institute for Philosophy: e-mail wittshi@hanmail.net; Dir Prof. IN-HEUI LYU.

European Culture & Information Center: e-mail europe@yonsei.ac.kr; Dir Prof. SU-YOUNG KIM.

Management Research Center: e-mail ysmrc@yonsei.ac.kr; Dir Prof. SEJO OH.

Economic Institute: e-mail yeri@base.yonsei.ac.kr; Dir Prof. SEOUNG-HWAN SUH.

Yonsei Institute of Statistical Science: e-mail ahnyk503@yonsei.ac.kr; Dir Prof. YUNKEE AHN.

Natural Science Research Institute: e-mail nsri@yonsei.ac.kr; Dir Prof. MUN-SUK CHUN.

Institute for Mathematical Science: Dir Prof. KUN SOO CHANG.

Global Environment Laboratory: e-mail cej@atmos.yonsei.ac.kr; Dir Prof. TAE-YOUNG LEE.

Research Institute of Ground water and Soil Environment: e-mail yin5004@ieg.or.kr; Dir Prof. HI-SOO MOON.

Molecular Science Research Institute: e-mail office@alchemy.yonsei.ac.kr; Dir Prof. DONG-SOO LEE.

Atomic Scale Surface Science Research Center: e-mail cnwhang@yonsei.ac.kr; Dir Prof. KWANGHO JEONG.

Engineering Research Institute: e-mail bsjin@yonsei.ac.kr; Dir Prof. MIGNON PARK.

New Energy and Environmental System Research Institute: e-mail ktlee@yonsei.ac.kr; Dir Prof. YUNG-IL JOE.

Automation Technology Research Institute: e-mail codling@control.yonsei.ac.kr; Dir Prof. JIN-BAE PARK.

Institute of Medical Instruments Technology: e-mail mhlee@yonsei.ac.kr; Dir Prof. MYOUNG-HO LEE.

Institute of Automotive Technology: e-mail car3557@yonsei.ac.kr; Dir Prof. KWANG-MIN CHUN.

Information and Telecommunications Research Institute: e-mail savant21@itl.yonsei.ac.kr; Dir Prof. DAESIK HONG.

Disaster Research Center: e-mail civil@yonsei.ac.kr; Dir WON-CHOEL CHO.

Research Institute of Radiological Science: Dir HYUNG-SIK YOO.

Institute for Human Tissue Restoration: Dir BYUNG-YOON PARK.

Radion Communications Research Center: e-mail kangjy@yonsei.ac.kr; Dir Prof. JONG-SOO SEO.

Advanced Building Science and Technology Research Center: e-mail archi@yonsei.ac.kr; Dir Prof. SUNG-JIN SONG.

Urban-Transportation Science Research Center: e-mail urban@yonsei.ac.kr; Dir Prof. WANN YU.

Research Institute of Iron and Steel Technology: e-mail ymetal@yonsei.ac.kr; Dir Prof. TO HOON KIM.

Institute of Microbial Cultures: e-mail ezet@yonsei.ac.kr; Dir Prof. CHUL SOO SHIN.

Research Institute for Software Application: e-mail ikheart@cs.yonsei.ac.kr; Dir Prof. HYE-RAN BYUN.

Bio Products Research Center: e-mail brc@yonsei.ac.kr; Dir Prof. BAIK-LIN SEONG.

Institute of Christianity and Korean Culture: e-mail isic1@hanmail.net; Dir Prof. KYUN JIN KIM.

Social Science Research Institute: e-mail solki@dreamwiz.com; Dir Prof. YANG-SOO CHOI.

Institute for Communication Research: e-mail dongkim@yonsei.ac.kr; Dir Prof. YOUNG-SEOK KIM.

Center for Social Welfare Research: e-mail welfareri@yonsei.ac.kr; Dir Prof. ICK-SEOP LEE.

Institute of Legal Research: e-mail yslaw@yonsei.ac.kr; Dir Prof. DAE-SOON KIM.

Music Research Institute: e-mail oyeonk@chol.com; Dir Prof. SEI WON HONG.

Human Ecology Research Institute: e-mail humaneco@yonsei.ac.kr; Dir Prof. EUN AE KIM.

Research Institute of Food and Nutritional Sciences: e-mail sujeongg@yonsei.ac.kr; Dir Prof. JONG HO LEE.

Research Institute of Clothing and Textile Sciences: e-mail clothing@yonsei.ac.kr; Dir Prof. GILSOO CHOI.

Institute of Sport, Physical Education and Leisure Studies: e-mail yoonyj@yonsei.ac.kr; Dir Prof. YONG-JIN YOON.

Institute of Sport Science: e-mail kni8993@yumc.yonsei.ac.kr; Dir Prof. JUN-HEE SUL.

Institute of Health Services Research: e-mail prev@yumc.yonsei.ac.kr; Dir Prof. SEUNG-HUM YU.

Institute of Tropical Medicine: e-mail para@yumc.yonsei.ac.kr; Dir Prof. TAI-SOON YONG.

Institute for Environmental Research: e-mail iery@yumc.yonsei.ac.kr; Dir Prof. DONG-CHUN SHIN.

Institute of Handicapped Children: e-mail joonsl96@yumc.yonsei.ac.kr; Dir Prof. JOON-SOO LEE.

Institute for Occupational Health: e-mail ojko@yumc.yonsei.ac.kr; Dir Prof. JAEHOON ROH.

Institute for Cancer Research: e-mail gekim@yumc.yonsei.ac.kr; Dir Prof. GWI EON KIM.

Institute of Logopedics and Phoniatrics: e-mail hschoi@yumc.yonsei.ac.kr; Dir Prof. HONG SHIK CHOI.

Cardiovascular Research Institute: e-mail cgc@yumc.yonsei.ac.kr; Dir Prof. SUNG SOON KIM.

Institute of Genetic Science: e-mail kyungsup59@yumc.yonsei.ac.kr; Dir Prof. KYUNG SUP KIM.

Institute of Gastroenterology: e-mail ingas@yumc.yonsei.ac.kr; Dir Prof. SANG IN LEE.

Institute of Chest Diseases: e-mail ysamkim@yumc.yonsei.ac.kr; Dir Prof. SUNG KYU KIM.

Institute of Endocrinology: e-mail yumie@yumc.yonsei.ac.kr; Dir Prof. DUK HEE KIM.

Institute for Transplantation Research: e-mail yukim@yumc.yonsei.ac.kr; Dir Prof. KI-IL PARK.

Brain Research Institute: e-mail bilee@yumc.yonsei.ac.kr; Dir Prof. BYUNG-IN LEE.

Institute of Vision Research: e-mail opth@yumc.yonsei.ac.kr; Dir Prof. JONG BOK LEE.

Rehabilitation Institute of Muscular Diseases: e-mail kje@yumc.yonsei.ac.kr; Dir Prof. JAE HO MOON.

Institute of Kidney Diseases: e-mail dshan@yumc.yonsei.ac.kr; Dir Prof. DAE SUK HAHN.

Institute of Andrology: e-mail urology@yumc.yonsei.ac.kr; Dir Prof. SEOUNG CHOUL YANG.

Research Institute of Traditional Medicine: e-mail kapark@yumc.yonsei.ac.kr; Dir Prof. KYUNG AH PARK.

Institute for Immunology and Immunological Diseases: e-mail jsshin6203@yumc.yonsei.ac.kr; Dir Prof. DONGSOO KIM.

Research Institute of Rehabilitation Medicine: e-mail jcsevrm@yumc.yonsei.ac.kr; Dir Prof. CHANG-IL PARK.

Institute of Allergy: e-mail cshong@yumc.yonsei.ac.kr; Dir Prof. CHEIN-SOO HONG.

Research Institute of Radiological Science: e-mail jscho@yumc.yonsei.ac.kr; Dir Prof. KI-WHANG KIM.

Institute for Tissue Restoration: e-mail plastic@yumc.yonsei.ac.kr; Dir Prof. BEYOUNG-YUN PARK.

Research Institute of Bacterial Resistance: e-mail leekcp@yumc.yonsei.ac.kr; Dir Prof. KYUNGWON LEE.

Cutaneous Biology Research Institute: e-mail yderm@yumc.yonsei.ac.kr; Dir Prof. DONG-SIK BANG.

Medical Behaviour Science Research Institute: e-mail skmin518@yumc.yonsei.ac.kr; Dir Prof. SUNG-KIL MIN.

Institute of Women's Life Science: e-mail kh8730@yumc.yonsei.ac.kr; Dir Prof. KI-HYUN PARK.

AIDS Research Institute: e-mail aidsri@yumc.yonsei.ac.kr; Dir Prof. JUNE-MYUNG KIM.

Research Institute of Anesthesia and Pain Medicine: e-mail ywhong@yumc.yonsei.ac.kr; Dir Prof. YONG-WOO HONG.

Spine and Spinal Cord Institute: e-mail ydnscho@yumc.yonsei.ac.kr; Dir Prof. YONG-EUN CHO.

Oral Science Research Center: e-mail obiol@yumc.yonsei.ac.kr; Dir Prof. SEOUNG-ILL LEE.

Dental Materials Institute: e-mail yridm@yumc.yonsei.ac.kr; Dir Prof. KWANG MAHN KIM.

Institute of Craniofacial Deformity: e-mail deform@yumc.yonsei.ac.kr; Dir Prof. HYOUNG-SEON BAIK.

Research Institute for Periodontal Regeneration: e-mail perioinst@yumc.yonsei.ac.kr; Dir Prof. CHONG-KWAN KIM.

Institute of Oral Cancer Research: e-mail op3@yumc.yonsei.ac.kr; Dir Prof. JIN KIM.

Nursing Policy Research Institute: e-mail nupolicy@yumc.yonsei.ac.kr; Dir Prof. SO JA YA KIM.

Research Institute for Home Health Care: e-mail hhres@yumc.yonsei.ac.kr; Dir Prof. WON HEE LEE.

Institute of Basic Science: e-mail skyun@dragon.yonsei.ac.kr; Dir Prof. JIN CHUL CHOI.

Institute for Regional Studies and Development: e-mail kslew@dragon.yonsei.ac.kr; Dir Prof. KWANG-SOO LEW.

Institute of Health Science: e-mail ych0406@dragon.yonsei.ac.kr; Dir Prof. OK DOO AWH.

Institute of Environmental Science and Technology: e-mail yiest@dragon.yonsei.ac.kr; Dir Prof. YONG-CHIL SEO.

YOSU NATIONAL UNIVERSITY

96-1 Dundeok-dong, Yosu-shi, Chollanam-do 550-749

Telephone: (662) 659-2114

Fax: (662) 659-3003

Internet: www.yosu.ac.kr

Founded 1917 as Yosu Public Fisheries School; became Yosu Public Fisheries Middle School 1946, Yosu National Fisheries High School 1963, Yosu National Fisheries Junior College 1979, Yosu National Fisheries College 1987, Yosu National Fisheries University 1993; present name 1998

President: HA-JOON KIM

Number of teachers: 212

Number of students: 5,064

Colleges of Humanities and Social Science, Natural Science, Engineering, Fisheries and Ocean Science, Graduate School of Industry and Technology; Graduate School of Education.

KUWAIT

The Higher Education System

University-level education in Kuwait comprises of Kuwait University (founded 1962) and a branch of the Arab Open University (founded 2002). The Ministry of Education is responsible for overseeing higher education. It is Government policy to provide free education for all Kuwaiti citizens from primary to tertiary level. Students for courses not offered by Kuwait University are offered scholarships to study abroad. In May 1996 the National Assembly approved a draft law to regulate students' behaviour, dress and activities, with regard to observance of the teachings of Shari'a (Islamic) law, and to eradicate coeducational classes at Kuwait University over a five-year period. A KD-1,000m. project to build a new university campus and to gather the institution's dispersed facilities onto one site was in the planning stages in early 2005.

Admission to university-level undergraduate courses is on the basis of the General Secondary Education Certificate (Shahadat-al-thanawia-al-a'ama). The Bachelors degree is arranged on a US-style 'credit semester' system and usually last four years, except for professional programmes such as engineering and medicine, which last five and seven years respectively. Masters degrees at Kuwait University last up to two years and are available in most subjects.

The Public Authority for Applied Education and Training oversees technical and vocational education. The institutions which offer vocational education are the Vocational Training Centre, Industrial Training Centre at Shuwaikh, College of Technological Studies, Nursing Institute and Telecommunications and Navigation Institute. There are also Colleges of Basic Education, Business Studies and Health Studies offering two- to four-year courses leading to the award of a professional Diploma.

Learned Societies

GENERAL

National Council for Culture, Arts and Letters: POB 23996, 13100 Safat; tel. 2469090; fax 2432331; e-mail info@nccal.org.kw; f. 1973; guidance and support in all fields of culture; sponsors art exhibitions, drama, publishes books and periodicals; Sec.-Gen. BADER S. A. AL-REIFA; publs *Al-Thaqafa al-'Alamiyah*, *Alam al-Fikr*, *Alam Al-Ma'arifa*, *Ibda'at 'Alamiyah*, *Al-Fonon*.

LANGUAGE AND LITERATURE

British Council: 2 Al Arabi St, Block 2, POB 345, 13004 Safat, Mansouria, Kuwait City; tel. 2520067; fax 2520069; e-mail Bc.Enquiries@kw.britishcouncil.org; internet www.britishcouncil.org/kuwait; teaching centre; offers courses and exams in English language and British culture and promotes cultural exchange with the UK; library of 9,000 vols; Dir (acting), Teaching Centre Man. JOHN PARE.

Research Institutes

ECONOMICS, LAW AND POLITICS

Arab Planning Institute, Kuwait: POB 5834, 13059 Safat; tel. 4843130; fax 4842935; e-mail api@api.org.kw; internet www.arab-api.org; f. 1966 with assistance from the UN Devt Programme, and since 1972 financed by 15 Arab mem. states; trains personnel in economic and social devt planning; undertakes research and advisory work and organizes conferences and seminars on problems affecting economic and social devt in the Arab world; library: information centre consisting of 56,000 vols, (22,000 Arabic, 34,000 English) 400 periodicals (in English and Arabic); Dir Dr ESSA M. AL-GHAZALI; publs *Development Bridge* (in Arabic, 10 a year), *Journal of Development and Economic Policies* (in Arabic and English, 2 a year).

EDUCATION

Gulf Arab States Educational Research Center: POB 12580, 71656 Shamia; tel. 4835203; fax 4830571; e-mail gaserc@kuwait.net; internet www.gaserc.edu.kw; f. 1978 as part of Arab Bureau of Education for the Gulf States (see under Saudi Arabia); research on all educational topics; also provides training courses in developed curricula, educational statistics, educational evaluation, and educational research; Dir Prof. MARZOUG Y. ALGHOUNIAM; Librarian MOHEI A. HAK; publ. *Al-Hasaad Al-Terbawi (Arabic Text)* (6 a year).

MEDICINE

Arabization Center for Medical Science: POB 5225, 13053 Safat; tel. 5338610; fax 5338618; f. 1983; part of Council of Arab Ministers of Health—Arab League; aims: the Arabization of medical literature and translation into Arabic of medical sciences, development of a current bibliographic database, issuing of Arabic medical directories, training of manpower in the field of medical information and library science; library of 1,000 vols; Sec.-Gen. Dr ABDEL RAHMAN AL-AWADI; publs *Arab Medical Doctors Directory*, *Directory of Health Education and Research Organizations in Arab Countries*, *Directory of Hospitals and Clinics in Arab World*, and other titles.

NATURAL SCIENCES

General

Kuwait Institute for Scientific Research: POB 24885, 13109 Safat; tel. 4836100; fax 4830643; e-mail public_relations@safat.kisr.edu.kw; internet www.kisr.edu.kw; f. 1967 to promote and conduct scientific research in the fields of food resources, water resources, oil sector support, environmental studies, infrastructure services and urban development, and economics and applied systems; scientific and technical information centre (see below); Dir-Gen. Dr ABDULHADI AL-OTAIBI; publs *Annual Report*, *Annual Research Report*.

Libraries and Archives

Kuwait City

Kuwait University Libraries: POB 23558, Kuwait City; e-mail jacl@kuniv.edu; internet library.kuniv.edu.kw; f. 1966; 323,514 vols, 2,898 periodicals, 1,298 electronic journals, 20,000 audiovisual items; Dir DHIYA' ALJASIM.

Safat

National Library of Kuwait: POB 26182, 13122 Safat; tel. 2415191; fax 2415195; e-mail library@nlk.gov.kw; f. 1936; nat. and UN depository library; national ISBN agency; national bibliographic centre; special colln *Kuwaitiana*; over 300,000 vols in Arabic and English, 750 periodicals; Dir-Gen. WAFA'A H. AL-SANE.

National Scientific and Technical Information Centre: Kuwait Institute for Scientific Research, POB 24885, 13109 Safat; tel. 4818713; fax 4836097.

Museums and Art Galleries

Safat

Department of Antiquities and Museums: POB 23996, 13100 Safat; tel. 2426521; fax 2404862; Dir Dr FAHED AL-WOHAIBI.

Museums controlled by the Department:

Failaka Island Archaeological Museum: exhibits from excavations.

Failaka Island Ethnographic Museum: collection of material from Failaka Island, housed in the old residence of the island's Sheikh.

Kuwait National Museum: Arabian Gulf St, Kuwait City; f. 1957; antiquities from late Bronze Age to Hellenistic period, found at Failaka Island; ethnographic material.

Educational Science Museum: Ministry of Education, POB 7, 13001 Safat; tel. 2421268; fax 2446078; f. 1972; lectures, exhibitions, film shows, etc.; sections on natural history, science, space, oil, health; planetarium, meteorology; library of 2,000 vols; Dir ADNAN AL-ALI.

University

KUWAIT UNIVERSITY

POB 5969, 13060 Safat, Kuwait

Telephone: 4811188

Fax: 4848648

E-mail: info@kuniv.edu
Internet: www.kuniv.edu.kw

Founded 1962, inaugurated 1966
State control

Language of instruction: Arabic, except in faculties of science, engineering and petroleum, allied health science and nursing, medicine and department of English

Academic year: September to June (2 semesters)

Chancellor: HE The Minister of Higher Education
President: Prof. NADER AL-JALLAL
Vice-President for Academic Affairs: Prof. HASSAN AL-ALAWI
Vice-President for Planning and Evaluation: Dr MOUDI AL-HUMOUD
Vice-President for Research and Graduate Studies: Dr ASSAD ISMAEL
Dean of Admissions and Registration: Dr ABDULLA AL-FUHAID
Secretary-General: Dr AHMED AL-DEKHIL (acting)
Library Director: Dr HUSEIN AL-ANSARI

Library: see Libraries and Archives
Number of teachers: 4,530
Number of students: 19,320

Publications: *Annals of the Faculty of Arts* (monthly), *Arab Journal for the Humanities* (4 a year), *Arab Journal of Linguistics*, *Arab Journal of Management Sciences* (3 a year), *Educational Journal* (4 a year), *Islamic Studies Magazine* (3 a year), *Journal of Gulf and Arabian Peninsula* (4 a year), *Journal of Law* (4 a year), *Journal of Palestine Studies*, *Journal of Science* (2 a year), *Journal of the Social Sciences* (4 a year), *Medical Principles and Practice* (4 a year)

DEANS

College of Allied Health Sciences and Nursing: Dr HABIB ABUL
College of Arts: Dr SHAFIQA BASTAKI
College of Business Administration: Dr ADEL AL-HUSSAINAN
College of Dentistry: Dr JAWAD BEHBEHANI
College of Education: Dr RASHID ALI AL-SAHEL
College of Engineering and Petroleum: Prof. ABDUL-LATEEF AL-KHALEEFI
College of Graduate Studies: Dr ABDULLA AL-SHEIKH
College of Law: Dr FADEL NASRALLAH
College of Medicine: Dr JAWAD BEHBEHANI
College of Pharmacy: Dr LADISLAV NOVOTNY
College of Science: Prof. REDHA AL-HASAN
College of Sharia and Islamic Studies: Dr MOHAMMED AL-TABTABAIE
College of Social Sciences: Dr ALI A. AL-TARRAH
Women's College: Dr AHMET YIGIT

HEADS OF DEPARTMENTS

College of Allied Health Sciences and Nursing:

Health Information: Dr MAKHDOOM A. SHAH
Medical Technology: Prof. SARFAN KUMARSITI
Nursing: Dr WINNIFRED OGUNDEYIN
Physical Therapy: Dr MAKHDOOM ALI SHAH (acting)
Radiology: Prof. GEOFFREY DOUGHERTY

College of Arts:

Arabic Language and Literature: Dr SUAD ABDEL WAHAB
English Language and Literature: Dr LEILA AL-MALEH
History: Prof. Dr FATOUH AL-KHATRASH
Media: Dr JAMEL AL-MENAYES
Philosophy: Prof. MICHAEL MITIAS

College of Business Administration:

Accounting: Dr YOUSEF AL-ADLY
Economics: Dr IQBAL AL-REHMANI
Finance and Financial Institutions: Dr TALLA MOHAMMED AL-DEEHANI
Management and Marketing: Dr MONA RASHID AL-GAIS
Public Administration: Dr ADAM GHAZI AL-OTAIBI
Quantitative Methods and Management Information Systems: Dr JAFAR MOHAMMED

College of Dentistry:

Bioclinical Science: Prof. Dr NATHANIEL SALAKO
Developmental and Preventative Science: Prof. Dr JON ARTUN
Diagnostic Science: Assoc. Prof. BOBBY K. JOSEPH (acting)
Restorative Sciences: Prof. Dr ENOSAKHRE SAMUEL AKPATA
Surgical Sciences: Prof. Dr TRYGGVE LIE

College of Education:

Curriculum and Methodology: Dr ALI AL-HABIB
Educational Administration and Planning: Dr AHMED AL-BUSTAN
Educational Foundation: Dr MOHAMMAD MAHMOUD ALABDULGHAFOOR
Educational Psychology: Dr FAWZIYA ABBAS HADI

College of Engineering and Petroleum:

Architecture: Dr EL-SAYED AMER
Chemical Engineering: Prof. HABIB SHABAN
Civil Engineering: Dr HASHEM MUSAED AL-TABTABAI
Computer Engineering: Dr SABAH AL-FADAGHI
Electrical Engineering: Prof. MOHAMED MUSTAFA SAIED
Mechanical and Industrial Engineering: Dr FAISAL AL-JEWAIHEL
Petroleum Engineering: Prof. RIDHA BEN CHERIF GHARBI

College of Law:

Criminal Law: Dr NUR-EDDIN HINDAWI
International Law: Dr MEDWIS AL-RESHAIDI
Private Law: Dr JAMAL AL-NAKAS
Public Law: Dr AZIZA SHARIF

College of Medicine:

Anatomy: Dr MAHMOUD SHERIF
Biochemistry: Dr B. CHENG
Community Medicine: Prof. PHILIP MOODY
Medicine: Prof. K. V. JOHNY
Microbiology: Prof. TULSI TSHOG
Nuclear Medicine: Prof. A. ELGAZZAR
Obstetrics and Gynaecology: Prof. A. OMU
Paediatrics: (vacant)
Pathology: Prof. T. A. JUNAID
Pharmacology-Toxicology: Prof. CHARLES PILCHER
Physiology: Prof. J. S. JUGGI
Psychiatry: Dr A. FIDO
Radiology: Prof. ABDULLAH BEHBEHANI
Surgery: Dr HILAL AL-SAYER

College of Pharmacy:

Applied Therapeutics: Prof. JAGDISH SHARMA
Pharmaceutical Chemistry: Assoc. Prof. DOTUN PHILLIPS
Pharmaceutics: Dr ALY NADA
Pharmacy Practice: Dr IVAN EDAFIOGHO

College of Science:

Biological Sciences: Dr REDA AL-HASSAN
Chemistry: Dr AHMED KAREEMI
Geology: Dr FAWZIA AL-RUWAIH
Mathematics and Computer Science: Dr ISMAEL ALI
Physics: Dr AMINA AL-FARHAN
Statistical and Operational Research: Dr ABU BAKR HUSSEIN

College of Sharia and Islamic Studies:

Comparative Jurisprudence: Prof. LASHEYN AL-GAYATI
Faith and Propagation: Dr MOHAMMED METWALLI
Islamic Jurisprudence: Dr MOHAMMED BAYANOUNI
Quranic Interpretation and Hadith: Prof. AL-SAYED M. NOAH

College of Social Sciences:

Geography: Dr FATMA AL-ABDUL REZZAQ
Library and Information Science: Prof. Dr TAGHREED ALQUDSI-GHABRA
Political Sciences: Dr MASOOMA AL-MUBAREK
Psychology: Dr OWAID MESHAAN
Sociology and Social Work: Prof. Dr MOHAMMED AL-RUMAIHI

Colleges

College of Basic Education: POB 3405, 73251 Adailiya; tel. 2514200; fax 2518852; f. 1973; BA degree courses in Education; depts of Islamic Sciences, Sciences, Psychology, Social Studies, Education, Library Sciences, Teaching of Arts, Interior Design, Educational Technology, Music Education, Home Economics, Mathematics, Physical Education, Arabic Language; Dean Dr ABDULLAH A. AL-KANDRI.

College of Business Studies: POB 43197, 32046 Hawalli; tel. 2614962; fax 2660362; f. 1975; depts of Administration and Secretarial Studies, English Language, Insurance and Banking, Economics, Typewriting, Office Training, Accountancy; Dean Dr JABER AL-MERRI.

College of Health Sciences: POB 14281, 72853 Shuwaikh; tel. 2541044; fax 4811920; f. 1974; Assoc. Degree courses; depts of Oral and Dental Health, Natural Sciences, Environmental Health, Nursing, Food Sciences and Nutrition, Pharmaceutical and Medical Sciences, Medical Records; Dean Dr FATMA AL-KANDRI.

College of Technological Studies: POB 42325, 70654 Shuwaikh; tel. 4816122; fax 4843143; f. 1976; Assoc. Degree courses; depts of Electrical Engineering, Air Conditioning and Refrigeration, and Power Engineering, Electronic Engineering, Chemical Engineering, Civil Engineering, Motor Vehicle and Marine Engineering, Production Engineering and Welding, and Applied Sciences; library: 6,510 vols, 180 periodicals; 322 teachers; 1,950 students; Dean Dr FAISAL MANDANI.

KYRGYZSTAN

The Higher Education System

Following the Russian revolution in 1917, Kyrgyzstan was established as an autonomous region within the Russian Soviet Federated Socialist Republic (RSFSR). In 1936 it was recognized as a full Union member of the Soviet Union and became the Kyrgyz Soviet Socialist Republic. The oldest institutions of higher education were founded during the early years of Soviet rule, among them Jalal-Abad State University (founded 1926), Kyrgyz National University 'Zhusup Balasagyn' (founded 1932; current name 1993) and Kyrgyz Agrarian Academy (founded 1933). In August 1991 Kyrgyzstan declared its independence from the Soviet Union. The Ministry of Education and Science is responsible for the administration of higher education, which in 2004/05 consisted of 49 public and private establishments, with total enrolment of 218,273 students. Higher education is governed according to the Law on Education (1992). Some institutions of a specialist or professional nature are administered by the appropriate Government ministry, and several universities are run on a co-operative basis between the Kyrgyz Government and governments of other countries, such as Kyrgyz–Russian Slavic University (founded 1992) and Kyrgyz–Turkish University 'Manas' (founded 1995).

Admission to higher education is on the basis of the Certificate of Completed Secondary Education and success in university entrance examinations (which have been administered since 2003 by the United States Agency for International Development—USAID). Kyrgyzstan operates a dual system of the old Soviet-style degrees alongside Bachelors and Masters degrees. The old-style Specialist Diploma is a five-year programme of study, followed the by the Candidate of Science (two years) and Doctor of Science (research only) programmes. Alternatively, an undergraduate may study for four years for the Bachelors degree, followed by a two-year Masters degree, before progressing onto the Candidate of Science and Doctor of Science programmes.

In 2002 the Ministry of Education and Science established a quality assurance department and universities are now required to introduce measures for quality assurance.

Learned Societies

GENERAL

National Academy of Sciences of the Kyrgyz Republic: 720071 Bishkek, Chuy pr. 265A; tel. (312) 61-00-93; fax (312) 24-36-07; e-mail interdep@aknet.kg; internet academ.aknet.kg; f. 1954; depts of Physical-Engineering, Mathematical and Mining-Geological Sciences, Chemical-Technological, Medical-Biological and Agricultural Sciences, Humanities; 133 mems (42 permanent, 58 corresp., 33 foreign); attached research institutes: see Research Institutes; library: see Libraries and Archives; Pres. J. JEYENBAYEV; Chief Sec. Academician A. ALDASHEV; publ. *Izvestiya* (bulletin).

BIBLIOGRAPHY, LIBRARY SCIENCE AND MUSEOLOGY

Library Association of Kyrgyzstan: 720044 Bishkek, pr. Tynchtyk 27; tel. (312) 48-41-34; fax (312) 48-40-35; Pres. T. SHAYMERGENOVA.

HISTORY, GEOGRAPHY AND ARCHAEOLOGY

Kyrgyz Geographical Society: 720081 Bishkek, Bul. Erkindik 30; tel. (312) 26-47-21; Chair. S. U. UMURZAKOV.

LANGUAGE AND LITERATURE

Alliance Française: 720026 Bishkek, c/o French Consulate, ul. Razakov 49; tel. (312) 66-03-64; fax (312) 66-04-41; e-mail alliancefrancokirghiz@yahoo.fr; offers courses and exams in French language and culture and promotes cultural exchange with France.

British Council:see entry in Kazakhstan chapter.

Research Institutes

AGRICULTURE, FISHERIES AND VETERINARY SCIENCE

Institute of Forest and Walnut Studies: 720015 Bishkek, Karagachovaya rosha 15; tel. (312) 67-90-82; e-mail institute@lesic.elcat.kg; f. 1992; attached to Nat. Acad of Sciences of the Kyrgyz Republic; Dir E. TURDUKULOV.

ECONOMICS, LAW AND POLITICS

Center for Economic Research: 720071 Bishkek, Chuy pr. 265A; tel. (312) 65-56-80; fax (312) 24-36-07; e-mail cer@hotmail.kg; f. 1998; attached to Nat. Acad. of Sciences of the Kyrgyz Republic; Dir T. S. DYIKANBAYEVA.

Institute of Philosophy and Law: 720071 Bishkek, Chuy pr. 265A; tel. (312) 24-38-27; e-mail togusakov@mail.ru; f. 1958; attached to Nat. Acad. of Sciences of the Kyrgyz Republic; Dir O. A. TOGUSAKOV.

FINE AND PERFORMING ARTS

National Centre for 'Manas' Studies and Fine Arts: 720071 Bishkek, Chuy pr. 265A; tel. (312) 24-34-68; f. 1995; attached to Nat. Acad. of Sciences of the Kyrgyz Republic; Dir A. AKMATALIYEV.

HISTORY, GEOGRAPHY AND ARCHAEOLOGY

Institute of History: 720071 Bishkek, Chuy pr. 265A; tel. (312) 65-54-95; e-mail inst_history@hotmail.kg; f. 1954; attached to Nat. Acad. of Sciences of the Kyrgyz Republic; Dir J. JUNASHALIYEV.

LANGUAGE AND LITERATURE

Institute of Linguistics: 720071 Bishkek, Chuy pr. 265A; tel. (312) 24-34-95; f. 1924; attached to Nat. Acad. of Sciences of the Kyrgyz Republic; Dir T. AHMATOV.

MEDICINE

Institute of Medical Problems: 714000 Osh, Ozgon 52; tel. (3222) 2-84-44; f. 1994; attached to Kyrgyz Acad. of Sciences; Dir R. TOYCHUYEV.

Kyrgyz Research Institute of Obstetrics and Paediatrics: 720040 Bishkek, Togolok Moldo 1; tel. (312) 22-67-19; fax (312) 26-42-75; e-mail oroz@uzakov.bishkek.su; f. 1961; library of 14,000 vols; Dir DUYSHA KUDAYAROV.

Research and Development Institute of Molecular Biology and Medicine: 720040 Bishkek, Togolok Moldo 3; e-mail cardio@elcat.kg; f. 2002; library of 5,000 vols; Dir A. ALDASHEV.

Scientific and Production Centre for Preventive Medicine: 720005 Bishkek, Baitik Baatyr 34; tel. (312) 54-45-78; e-mail shainak@intranet.kg; f. 1938; research into public health, and environment and health; library of 13,500 vols; Dir Prof. O. T. KASYMOV.

NATURAL SCIENCES

Biological Sciences

Institute of Biology and Soil Studies: 720071 Bishkek, Chuy pr. 265; tel. (312) 65-56-87; f. 1994; attached to Nat. Acad. of Sciences of the Kyrgyz Republic; Dir S. KASIYEV.

Institute of Biotechnology: 720071 Bishkek, Chuy pr. 265; tel. (312) 64-03-02; e-mail junushov@yandex.ru; f. 1964; attached to Nat. Acad. of Sciences of the Kyrgyz Republic; Dir A. JUNUSHOV.

Mathematical Sciences

Institute of Mathematics: Chui pr. 265, 720071 Bishkek; tel. (312) 24-35-61; fax (312) 24-36-07; e-mail mathnas@aknet.kg; internet www.math.aknet.kg; f. 1984; attached to Nat. Acad. of Sciences of the Kyrgyz Republic; fields of research: integro-differential equations, singular preturbations, reverse and ill-posed problems, computer proof of theorems, economical-mathematical methods; 55 mems; Dir MURZABEK I. IMANALIEV; Scientific Sec. MARYAM A. ASANKULOVA.

Physical Sciences

Institute of the Biosphere: 715600 Dzhalal-Abad, Uzbekistan 130; tel. (3722) 5-26-00; attached to Nat. Acad. of Sciences of the Kyrgyz Republic; Dir T. RAHMANOV.

Institute of Geology: 720481 Bishkek, Bul. Erkindik 30; tel. (312) 66-47-37; fax (312) 66-42-56; e-mail geol@aknet.kg; f. 1943; attached to Nat. Acad. of Sciences of the Kyrgyz Republic; Dir A. B. BAKIROV.

Institute of High-Altitude Physiology and Experimental Pathology of High Rocks: 720048 Bishkek, Ul. Gorkogo 1/5; tel. (312) 23-93-52; f. 1954; attached to Nat. Acad. of Sciences of the Kyrgyz Republic; Dir A. SHANAZAROV.

Institute of Physics: 720071 Bishkek, Pr. Chuy 265; tel. (312) 25-52-59; fax (312) 24-36-07; e-mail interdep@aknet.kg; internet academ.aknet.kg; f. 1984; attached to Nat. Acad. of Sciences of the Kyrgyz Republic; Dir Prof. Dr TOKTOSUN OROZOBAKOV.

Institute of Rocks, Physics and Mechanics: 720815 Bishkek, Ul. Mederova 98; tel. (312) 54-11-15; fax (312) 54-11-17; e-mail ifmgp@totel.kg; internet www.ifmgp.to.kg; f. 1960; attached to Nat. Acad. of Sciences of the Kyrgyz Republic; library of 500,000 vols; Dir I. T. AITMATOV; publ. *Proceedings* (every 2 years).

Institute of Seismology: 720060 Bishkek, Asanbay 52/1; tel. (312) 46-29-42; fax (312) 46-29-04; e-mail kis@mail.elcat.kg; f. 1975; attached to Nat. Acad. of Sciences of the Kyrgyz Republic; Dir A. TURDULKULOV.

RELIGION, SOCIOLOGY AND ANTHROPOLOGY

Centre for Dungan Studies: 720071 Bishkek, Chuy pr. 265A; tel. (312) 24-34-89; f. 1954; attached to Nat. Acad. of Sciences of the Kyrgyz Republic; Dir M. IMAZOV.

Centre for Social Research: 720071 Bishkek, Chuy pr. 265A; tel. (312) 24-37-35; e-mail nurbekcsr@freenet.kg; attached to Nat. Acad. of Sciences of the Kyrgyz Republic; Dir N. OMURALIYEV.

Institute of Social Sciences: 714000 Osh, Mominova 11; tel. (3222) 2-92-44; f. 1994; attached to Kyrgyz Acad. of Sciences; Dir E. SULAYMANOV.

TECHNOLOGY

Institute for the Complex Utilization of Natural Resources (ICUNR): 714000 Osh, Mominova 11; tel. (3222) 2-60-10; fax (3222) 2-03-42; e-mail ikipr@aknet.kg; f. 1988; attached to Nat. Acad. of Sciences of the Kyrgyz Republic; f. 1988; Dir Prof. JAPAR TEKENOVICH TEKENOV.

Institute of Automatics: 720071 Bishkek, Chuy pr. 265; tel. (312) 65-55-22; e-mail automatics@aknet.kg; f. 1960; attached to Nat. Acad. of Sciences of the Kyrgyz Republic; Dir T. OMOROV.

Institute of Chemistry and Chemical Technology: 720071 Bishkek, Chuy pr. 267; tel. (312) 65-79-45; e-mail chem_institute@mail.ru; f. 1994; attached to Nat. Acad. of Sciences of the Kyrgyz Republic; Dir K. SULAIMANKULOV.

Institute of Machinery Research: 720055 Bishkek, Ul. Skryabina 23; tel. (312) 54-11-13; fax (312) 42-27-85; e-mail impulse@elcat.kg; attached to Nat. Acad. of Sciences of the Kyrgyz Republic; Dir Prof. M. DZHUMATAEV; publ. *Collected Scientific Articles of the Institute for Machinery Research* (every 2 years).

Institute of New Technologies: 714000 Osh, Ermaka 301; tel. (3222) 2-45-32; f. 1993; attached to Nat. Acad. of Sciences of the Kyrgyz Republic; 3 laboratories; Dir JOROMAMAT ARZIEV.

Institute of Power Engineering and Microelectronics: 715600 Dzhalal-Abad, Toktogul 43; tel. (3722) 5-24-85; f. 1993; attached to Nat. Acad. of Sciences of the Kyrgyz Republic; Dir S. KYDYRALIYEV.

Institute of Water Problems and Hydropower: Ul. Frunze 533, 720033 Bishkek; tel. (312) 21-45-72; fax (312) 21-06-74; e-mail iwp@istc.kg; internet www.caresd.net/iwp; f. 1992; attached to Nat. Acad. of Sciences of the Kyrgyz Republic; 60 mems; Dir Acad. DUSHEN MAMATKANOV.

Libraries and Archives

Bishkek

Central Library of the National Academy of Sciences of the Kyrgyz Republic: 720071 Bishkek, Chuy pr. 265A; tel. (312) 24-27-59; e-mail tokonovatt@hotmail.kg; f. 1943; 985,000 vols; Dir L. A. BONDAREVA.

Kyrgyz State National University Library: 720024 Bishkek, Ul. Frunze 547; tel. (312) 9-98-26; 931,500 vols; Dir M. A. ASANBAYEV.

National Library of the Kyrgyz Republic: 720000 Bishkek, Ul. Sovetskaya 208; tel. (312) 66-20-90; fax (312) 66-21-55; e-mail library@nlpub.bishkek.gov.kg; internet www.nlkr.org.kg; 3,514,700 vols; Dir ANARA CHYNYBAEVA.

Scientific and Technical Library of Kyrgyzstan: 720302 Bishkek, Chuy pr. 106; tel. (312) 6-23-66; f. 1967; 5,817,000 vols (not incl. patents); Dir S. I. MAKAROV.

Museums and Art Galleries

Bishkek

Botanical Garden: 720064 Bishkek, Akhunbayev 1A; tel. (312) 43-53-55; e-mail bigarden@mail.ru; internet bigarden.by.ru; f. 1938; attached to Nat. Acad. of Sciences of the Kyrgyz Republic; library of 15,000 vols; Dir I. SODOMBEKOV; publ. *Introduktsiya i Akklimatizatsiya Rastenii v Kyrgyzstane* (annually).

Kyrgyz State Museum of Fine Art: 720000 Bishkek, Baytyk Batyr 196; tel. (312) 66-16-23; fax (312) 66-16-24; e-mail kmmii@mail.ru; modern art; Dir K. N. UZUBALIYEVA.

State Historical Museum of Kyrgyzstan: Bishkek, Krasnooktyabrskaya ul. 236; f. 1925; Dir N. M. SEITKAZIYEVA.

Universities

ACADEMY OF MANAGEMENT UNDER THE PRESIDENT OF THE KYRGYZ REPUBLIC

720040 Bishkek, Ul. Panfilova 237
Telephone: (312) 22-13-85
Fax: (312) 66-36-14
E-mail: reception@amp.aknet.kg
Internet: www.amp.aknet.kg

Founded 1992
State control
Languages of instruction: Russian, English
Academic year: September to June

Rector: ASKAR KUTANOV
Provost: GROGORI FREIUK
Dean: ANARBEK ADYJAPAROV

Library of 17,394 vols
Number of teachers: 90
Number of students: 678.

BISHKEK HUMANITIES UNIVERSITY

720044 Bishkek, Pr. Tynchtyk
Telephone: (312) 48-40-35
Fax: (312) 54-14-05
E-mail: rectorat@bgupub.freent.bishkek.su
Internet: www.bhu.kg

Founded 1979
State control

Rector: ISHENGUL BOLJUROVA
Librarian: ROSA TURDUKEEVA

Library of 300,000 vols
Number of teachers: 280
Number of students: 6,000

Faculties of Administration and Sociology, Ecology and Management, German Philology, Information, Social work and Psychology, Kyrgyz and Russian Philology, Oriental Studies and International Relations, Turkish Relations.

INTERNATIONAL UNIVERSITY OF KYRGYZSTAN

720001 Bishkek, Pr. Chui 255
Telephone: (312) 21-76-15
Fax: (312) 21-96-15
E-mail: iuk@lmflko.bishkek.su
Internet: www.iuk.kg

Founded 1993
State control
Language of instruction: Russian
Academic year: September to June

President: ASYLBEK AIDARALIYEV

Library of 100,000 vols
Number of teachers: 209
Number of students: 1,627

DEANS

College of Ecology and Biotechnology: ALMAZBEK SHANAZAROV
College of Economics and Business: SHAYLOOBEK MUSAKODJOYEV
College of Foreign Languages: ZINAIDA KARAYEVA (Dir)
Polytechnic College: AMAN TOHLUKOV (Dir)

ISSYK-KUL STATE UNIVERSITY 'K. TYNYSTANOV'

722360 Karakol, Abdrahmanova 103
Telephone: (3922) 5-01-23
Fax: (3922) 5-04-98
E-mail: igu@issy-kul.kg

Founded 1940
State control
Language of instruction: Russian

President: MUSTAFA M. KIDIBAYEV

Number of teachers: 434
Number of students: 6,626

DEANS

Faculty of Art and Modelling: DOCTURBEK IBRAYEV
Faculty of Chemistry and Biology: SHARIPA KACHEKOVA
Faculty of Foreign Languages: TEMIRBEK SULAIMANOVICH
Faculty of Mathematics and Computer Science: JEKSHENBEK MAMYROV
Faculty of Medicine and Technology: HAIRINISIO AISAKULOVA
Faculty of Natural Resources and Geography: MONOLDAR JUMAKULOV
Faculty of Pedagogy and Physical Education: ASKAR IMANBAYEV
Faculty of Philology: AYIDA ABDYLDAYEVA
Faculty of Physics and Technology: DOOLOTBETK AKANOV

JALAL-ABAD STATE UNIVERSITY

715600 Jalal-Abad, Ul. Lenina 57
Telephone: (3722) 5-59-68
Fax: (3722) 5-03-33
E-mail: jasu@infotel.kg
Founded 1926
State control
Languages of instruction: Russian, Kyrgyz
Academic year: September to June
Rector: JAMGYRBEK BOKOSHOV
Vice-Rector: NURMAT JAILOOBAYEV
Library of 58,000 vols
Number of teachers: 600
Number of students: 16,000

DEANS
Faculty of Agriculture and Biology: TALCHA AMANKULOVA
Faculty of Economics: BEKMAMAT JOOSHBAYEV
Faculty of Engineering and Technology: EGEMBERDI UMETOV
Faculty of Foreign Languages: ASKAR MURZAKULOV
Faculty of Medicine: SHAIRBEK SULAIMANOV
Faculty of Philology: ANARA KADYROVA
Faculty of Technology: MANAS SOORONBAYEV

KYRGYZ NATIONAL UNIVERSITY 'ZHUSUP BALASAGYN'

720024 Bishkek, Ul. Frunze 537
Telephone: (312) 26-26-34
Internet: www.knu.kg
Founded 1932 as Kyrgyz State Pedagogical University; became Kyrgyz State University 1951; present name 1993
State control
Rector: ISHENGUL BOLJUROVA
Pro-Rectors: SHARSHENBEK B. SALPIEV (Academic), ANVAR M. MAKEEV (International Ties and Investment), VYACHESLAV I. SHAPOVALOV (Scientific)
Number of teachers: 600
Number of students: 22,000
Faculties of Mathematics, Informatics and Cybernetics, Economics and Finance, Physics and Electronics, Geography and Ecology, Accountancy and Commerce, Chemical Technology, Journalism, History and Regional Government, Kyrgyz Philology, Russian Philology, Biology, Military Studies.

KYRGYZ–RUSSIAN SLAVIC UNIVERSITY

720000 Bishkek, Ul. Kievskaya 44
Telephone: (312) 28-28-59
Fax: (312) 28-28-59
E-mail: krsu@krsu.edu.kg
Internet: www.krsu.edu.kg
Founded 1992
State control
Rector: Prof. VLADIMIR I. NIFADEV
Pro-Rectors: Prof. IMIL A. AKKOZIEV (Academic), Prof. EDNAN O. KARABAEV (Foreign Relations), Prof. VALERI M. LELEVKIN (Scientific)
Number of teachers: 234
Number of students: 2,200

DEANS
Faculty of Economics: Prof. VICKTOR K. GAIDAMAKO
Faculty of Humanities: Prof. ABDYKADYR O. ORUSBAEV
Faculty of International Relations: (vacant)
Faculty of Law: Asst. Prof. LEILA CH. SYDYKOVA
Faculty of Medicine: Prof. ANES G. ZARUFYAN
Faculty of Science and Technology: Asst. Prof. VLADIMIR A. YURIKOV
Faculty of Distance Education: Asst. Prof. YURI D. SURODIN

KYRGYZ STATE PEDAGOGICAL UNIVERSITY 'I. ARABAYEV'

720024 Bishkek, Razakova 51
Telephone: (312) 66-03-47
Fax: (312) 66-05-88
E-mail: el_dar@netmail.kg
Founded 1952
State control
Languages of instruction: Kyrgyz, Russian
Rector: ABLABEK ASANKANOV
Vice-Rector for Academic Affairs: SVETLANA MUSAYEVA
Number of teachers: 1,190
Number of students: 4,000
Faculties of Chemistry and Biology, Physics and Mathematics and Teacher Training.

KYRGYZ STATE UNIVERSITY OF CONSTRUCTION, TRANSPORT AND ARCHITECTURE

720020 Bishkek, Ul. Maldybayeva 34
Telephone: (312) 44-35-61
Fax: (312) 44-51-36
E-mail: ksucta@elcat.kg
Founded 1954
State control
Rector: JUMABEK TENTIYEV
Faculties of Humanities, Kyrgyz and Arabic, Military Studies.

KYRGYZ TECHNICAL UNIVERSITY 'I. RAZZAKOV'

720044 Bishkek, Pr. Mira 66
Telephone: (312) 54-51-25
Fax: (312) 54-51-62
E-mail: ktu@transfer.kg
Internet: ktu.edu.kg
Founded 1954 as Frunze Polytechnic Institute; present name 1992
State control
Academic year: September to July
Rector: Prof. MURAT JAMANBAEV
Vice-Rector for Academic Affairs: Prof. SAGYNBEK DJUMAGULOV
Vice-Rector for Economics and Finance: Prof. TURAT DUISHENALIEV
Vice-Rector for Marketing and External Affairs: Prof. ADYLBEK SULTANBEKOV
Vice-Rector for Science: Prof. SARBAGYSH ABRAHAMANOV
Library of 520,000 vols
Number of teachers: 534
Number of students: 9,540
Publications: *Herald* (2 a year), *Science and New Technologies* (4 a year)
Faculties of Power Engineering, Food and Textile Technologies, Information Technology, Machine Building and Transport; Institute of Business and Management; Center of Distance Education.

KYRGYZ–TURKISH UNIVERSITY 'MANAS'

720000 Bishkek, Ul. Manasa 56
Telephone: (312) 54-19-42
Fax: (312) 54-19-35
E-mail: webmaster@manas.kg
Internet: www.manas.kg
Founded 1995 by govts of Kyrgyzstan and Turkey
State control
Languages of instruction: Kyrgyz, Turkish
Academic year: September to June
Rectors: Prof. Dr SEYFULLAH ÇEVIK (acting), Prof. Dr KARYBEK MOLDOBAEV
Pro-Rector: Prof. Dr ANVAR MOKEEV
Library of 44,000 books
Number of teachers: 179
Number of students: 1,369
Publications: *Sosyal Bilimler Dergisi* (Journal of Social Sciences, 2 a year), *Fen Bilimleri Dergisi* (Journal of Science and Engineering, 2 a year)

DEANS
Faculty of Arts and Sciences: Assoc. Prof. SUAYIP KARAKAŞ
Faculty of Management: Asoc. Prof. SEYFULLAH ÇEVİK
Faculty of Technology: Prof. Dr EROL ÖZTEKİN
Faculty of Communication: Prof. Dr YÜKSEL KAVAK
Higher Vocational School: Dr HALIL SEVAL
Higher Modern Language School: Assoc. Prof. ZAMIRA DERBİŞEVA

KYRGYZ–UZBEK UNIVERSITY

714000 Osh, Ul. Aitiyeva 27
Telephone: (3222) 5-70-55
Fax: (3222) 2-54-73
E-mail: kuu@oshmail.kg
Founded 1994
State control
Languages of instruction: Russian, Kyrgyz, Uzbek
Rector: MUHAMMAD MAMASAIDOV
Vice-Rector: IDRIS ERGESHOV
Library of 108,272 vols
Number of teachers: 520
Number of students: 11,793

HEADS OF DEPARTMENTS
Energy Engineering: ANVARJON ISMANJANOV
Engineering and Technology: ISMANALY BAKIROV
Fashion Design: AIGUL NAVATOVA
Finance and Economics: GULOMJON MAMATUREDIYEV
History and Philology: RANO ALIYEVA
Law and Customs: ANIPA SARYKOVA
Pedagogy: SHUHRAT TASHHODJAYEV
Preventive Medicine: JANYBEK MURATOV
World Languages and International Relations: ARAP ANARBAYEV

NARYN STATE UNIVERSITY

722600 Naryn, Ul. Sagynbay Orozbak Uulu 25
Telephone: (3522) 5-08-14
Fax: (3522) 5-08-14
E-mail: nsu@ktnet.kg
Founded 1996
State control
Languages of instruction: Kyrgyz, Russian
Rector: ALMAZ AKMATALIYEV
Vice-Rector: TASHTANBEK SIYAYEV
Number of teachers: 240
Number of students: 4,500

DEANS
Faculty of Agro-Technology: KUBANYEBBEK DUISHEKEYEV
Faculty of Economics: DAMIRA OMURALIYEVA
Faculty of Humanities: YRYS JAKEYEVA
Faculty of Information Technologies: ALMANBET AMANALIEYEV
Faculty of Law: SALIDIN KALDYBAYEV
Faculty of Philology: ALI TURDUGULOV

OSH STATE UNIVERSITY

714000 Osh, Ul. Lenina 331
Telephone: (33222) 2-29-12
Fax: (33222) 5-75-58
E-mail: oshsu@rambler.ru

Internet: www.oshsu.kg

Founded 1951 as Osh Pedagogical Institute; present name and status 1992

State control

Academic year: September to July

Rector: Acad. Prof. Dr BEKTEMIR M. MURZUBRAIMOV

First Pro-Rector (Academic): Prof. Dr TASHMANBET K. KENENSARIEV

Pro-Rectors: Asst Prof. AVAZBEK R. ASANOV (Scientific Work and International Relations), Prof. Dr SHAMSHI B. BAZARBAEV (Correspondence Education), Prof. Dr MUKHTAR O. OROZBEKOV (Contract Education), Prof. Dr AVAZBEK K. ATAHANOV (International Affairs and Educational Projects), Col BURKHAN B. MAMATISAKOV (Planning and Provision)

Number of teachers: 1,200

Number of students: 26,000

Publication: *Vestnik* (research, monthly)

DEANS

Faculty of History: Asst. Prof. TURDUMAMAT KADYROV

Faculty of Philology: Asst Prof. NAZIRA K. SALAKHITDINOVA

Faculty of Natural Sciences and Geography: Asst Prof. ABDUVALI T. TOKTOMAMATOV

Faculty of Law: Asst Prof. EGEMBERDI S. TOKTOROV

Faculty of Law (Correspondence Courses): Asst Prof. ERKIN E. DUISENOV

Faculty of Kyrgyz Philology: Asst Prof. SATKANBAI M. MOMUNALIEV

Faculty of World Languages: Asst Prof. SHUKRI V. MARASH-OGLY

Faculty of Arts: Asst Prof. ABDYKARIM KALYKOV

Faculty of Education and Physical Training: Asst Prof. ABDYKERIM A. ISAEV

Faculty of Medicine: Prof. Dr DAMIR ZH. RISALIEV

Faculty of Physics, Mathematics and Information Technology: Asst Prof. ABDYGANY O. ABDUVALIEV

Faculty of Theology: Asst Prof. TEMIR A. ZHOROBEKOV

Faculty of Business and Management: Asst Prof. ZHYLDYZ K. AKNAZAROVA

Faculty of Uzbek Humanities and Education: Asst Prof. EDGOR YU. ZHALALOV

Faculty of Philosophy and Management: Asst Prof. ERKAIM ZHOROBEKOVA

Faculty of International Education Intergration: Asst Prof. ABDUGANY ZH. SHERIEV

OSH TECHNOLOGICAL UNIVERSITY

714018 Osh, Ul. Isanova 81

Telephone: (3222) 5-40-87

Fax: (3222) 5-38-68

E-mail: site@oshtu.osh.kg

Internet: www.oshtu.osh.kg

Founded 1993; previously Osh Higher College of Technology

State control

Rector: Prof. ZHANIBEK SH. SHARSHENALIEV

Number of teachers: 482

Number of students: 16,607

Faculties: Construction Engineering; Cybernetics and Information Technology; Transport and Service Technology; Finance and Economics; State Administration and Business; Law; Ecology and Geology; Technological Engineering; Energetics and New Energy Technology; Language Technology and Social Sciences; Basic and Professional Education; Evening and Correspondence Education.

TALAS STATE UNIVERSITY

722720 Talas, Ul. Karla Marksa 25

Telephone: (3422) 5-20-15

Fax: (3422) 5-25-80

E-mail: tsu1exrel@hotmail.kg

Founded 1996

State control

Languages of instruction: Kyrgyz, Russian, English

Academic year: September to June

Rector: TOROKBEK OMURBEKOV

Library of 101,000 vols

Number of teachers: 248

Number of students: 2,983

DEANS

Faculty of Ecology and Agronomy: AIBEK UPENOV

Faculty of Economics and Law: ESENGUL OMUSHEV

Faculty of Education: ERKIN ABDRAIMOV

Faculty of Modern Languages: MANAS KALMANBETOV

Faculty of Technology: NURLAN ASYLBEKOV

TŠUJ UNIVERSITY

720023 Bishkek, Kievskaya 187

Telephone: (312) 24-77-95

Fax: (312) 24-78-84.

Other Higher Educational Institutes

Bishkek Academy of Finance and Economics: 720010 Bishkek, Bul. Molodoi Gvardii 55; tel. (312) 65-04-86; fax (312) 65-02-17; e-mail kubat@freenet.kg; internet bafe .freenet.kg; f. 1994; 53 teachers; 567 students; Rector Prof. ABDRAKHMAN S. MAVLYANOV.

Kyrgyz Agrarian Academy: 720005 Bishkek, Ul. Mederova 68; tel. (312) 54-52-10; fax (312) 54-05-45; e-mail kaa@imfiko.bishkek .su; f. 1933; depts: agronomy, agricultural engineering, veterinary science, agricultural economics, zootechnics, irrigation and land reclamation, agricultural business; library: 1,043,000 vols; 280 teachers; 4,547 students; Pres. J. AKIMALIYEV.

Kyrgyz State Academy of Medicine: 720020 Bishkek, Akhunbaeva 92; tel. (312) 54-58-81; fax (312) 54-58-59; e-mail is@ksma .elcat.kg; internet www.ksma.edu.kg; f. 1939; faculties of general medicine, sanitation and hygiene, paediatric medicine, stomatology, pharmaceutics, and foreign and contract students; 408 teachers; 2,646 students; Rector (vacant).

Kyrgyz State Institute of Fine Art: 720460 Bishkek, Ul. Dzhantosheva 115; tel. (312) 47-02-25; f. 1967; music, cultural studies, language and literature, theatre, ballet; library: 4,500 vols; 186 teachers; 765 students; Rector A. ASAKEYEV.

LAOS

The Higher Education System

In 1946 the French Indo-China provinces of Luang Prabang, Vientiane and Champasak were united as the Kingdom of Laos, which became independent within the French Union in 1949 and achieved sovereignty in 1953. Sisavangvong University, the country's first university and named for the King, was founded in 1958. However, in 1975 the insurgent Neo Lao Haksat (Lao Patriotic Front) gained control of the country, abolished the monarchy and established the Lao People's Democratic Republic; Sisavangvong University was dissolved into separate colleges. In 1995 National University of Laos was created from a merger of various institutions of higher education. In 2004/05 there were 10,500 students enrolled at three university-level institutions and 18,500 students enrolled at 19 other institutions of higher education. The Ministry of Education has overall responsibility for higher education.

Admission to higher education requires the main secondary school certificate (Baccalauréat) and the applicant is requires to sit an entrance examination. The undergraduate degree is the Bachelors and lasts four years; however, some disciplines, notably pharmacy, dentistry, engineering (all five years) and medicine (six years) require longer. There are no postgraduate degrees.

Vocational and technical education is offered by three kinds of institution: Vocational Schools, specializing in accountancy, teaching and nursery nursing; Middle Technical Schools, for training middle-level technicians; and Higher Technical Schools of Institutes, providing training for higher-level technicians. Both the Middle and Higher Technical Schools offer Diploma courses.

Learned Society

RELIGION, SOCIOLOGY AND ANTHROPOLOGY

Lao Buddhist Fellowship: Maha Kudy, That Luang, Vientiane; f. 1964; Pres. Rev. THONG KHOUNE ANANTASUNTHONE; Vice-Pres. Rev. PHONG SAMALEUX, Rev. PRECHA SOUTHAMAKOSANE; Sec.-Gen. Rev. SIHO SIHAVONG.

Libraries and Archives

Vientiane

Bibliothèque Nationale: BP 122, Ministry of Information and Culture, Vientiane; tel. 21-21-24-52; fax 21-21-30-29; e-mail pfd-mill@pan.laos.net.la; f. 1956; compiles nat. bibliography; 300,000 vols, 120 periodicals, 250 maps, 6,000 MSS; spec. collns include palm leaf MSS; Dir KONGDEUANE NETTAVONGS; publs magazine on preservation of Lao palm-leaf MSS (3 a year), *Vannasinh* (3 a year), *Siengkhene* (3 a year).

National University of Laos Central Library: Dongdok, Vientiane; f. 1995; 50,000 vols.

Museums and Art Galleries

Vientiane

Ho Phakeo: Setthathiraj Rd, Vientiane; built 1563 by King Setthathiraj, became national museum 1965.

That Luang: Saysettha District, Vientiane; built 1566 by King Saysetthathiraj, restored 1930.

Wat Sisaket: Lane Xang Ave, Vientiane; f. 1828 by King Anuvong.

University

NATIONAL UNIVERSITY OF LAOS

POB 7322, Vientiane
Telephone: 21-41-60-70
Fax: 21-41-23-81
E-mail: nuolpu@laotel.com
Internet: www.nuol.edu.la

Founded 1995 by merger of 10 existing institutions of higher education and a centre of agriculture
State control
Language of instruction: Lao
Academic year: September to June

Rector: Dr SOMKOT MANGNOMEK
Vice-Rectors: TUYEN DONGVAN (Planning and International Co-operation), LAMMAY PHIPHAKKHAVONG (Student Affairs), SAYAMANG VONGSAK (Academic Affairs)
Chief Administrative Officer and Director of Rectorate Cabinet: Dr KONGSY SENGMANY
Director of Central Library: CHANSY PHUANGSOUKET

Library of 120,000 vols
Number of teachers: 852
Number of students: 15,791

Publication: *Mahavithagnalay Heang Xath Lao* (Activities in the National Univeristy of Laos, quarterly)

DEANS

Faculty of Agriculture: THONGPHANH KOUSONSAVATH
Faculty of Economics and Management: KHAMLUSA NOUANSAVANH
Faculty of Education: KHAM-ANE SAYASONE
Faculty of Engineering and Architecture: Dr SOMKOT MANGNOMEK
Faculty of Forestry: SOUCKONGSENG SAYALEUT
Faculty of Humanities and Social Sciences: SOUPHAP KHOUANGVICHITH
Faculty of Law and Political Science: BOUN OUM PAPHATSALANG
Faculty of Medical Science: Dr BOUNSAY THOVISOUK
Faculty of Philology: PHETSAMONE KHOUNSAVAT
Faculty of Sciences: BOUAKHAYKHONE SVENGSUKSA
School of Foundation Studies: INPENG KHIEUVONGPHACHANH (Dir)

ATTACHED INSTITUTIONS

Centre of Teacher Development: Dir BOUNTHEUNG CHANMANY.

School of Foundation Studies: Dir INPENG KHIEOVONGPHACHANH.

LATVIA

The Higher Education System

Until Latvia first achieved independence in 1921 it was under Russian Tsarist and then Russian Bolshevik rule. The earliest surviving institutions of higher education were established during the period (1918–20) of *de facto* civil war involving the Latvian provisional Government, the Russian Bolsheviks, German volunteers and White Russians (Mensheviks). Institutions dating from this period include the University of Latvia, the Latvian Academy of Music and the Transport and Telecommunications Institute (all founded 1919). Institutions founded during the early independent period include Daugavpils University and the Latvian Academy of Arts (both founded 1921). In June 1940 the USSR invaded and occupied Latvia, which then became a Soviet Socialist Republic until regaining independence in 1991. The higher education system is administered according to the Education Act (1991) and Law on Higher Education Institutions (1995). A legal distinction is made between 'academic' and 'professional' higher education: university-level institutions offer both academic and professional qualifications, however non-university level institutions of higher education offer only professional qualifications. The Ministry of Education and Science is the Government body responsible for higher education. Latvia participates in Bologna Process to establish a European Higher Education Area, the first phase of which is to adopt a credit-based system of comparable degrees with two main cycles (undergraduate and graduate). In 2004/05 higher education was offered at 56 institutions, with a total enrolment of 130,706 students.

Admission to higher education is on the basis of relevant passes in the General Secondary Education Certificate, often based on criteria established by individual institutions. In 2000 Latvia ratified the Bologna process and a two-tier Bachelors (Bakalaurs) and Masters (Magistrs) degree system has been established for both the academic and professional streams of higher education (although old-style professional diplomas are still offered by non-university level institutions). Degrees are awarded on a credits accrued basis. The standard undergraduate Bachelors lasts three to fours years and students must acquire 120–60 credits. Only a four-year Bachelors programme is regarded as a complete degree; a three-year Bachelors is regarded as an intermediate qualification. Bachelors degrees in professional fields may last longer, such as dentistry (five years) and medicine (six years), and are regarded as equivalent to the Masters. The Masters is either a one to two-year degree requiring 40–80 credits, taken after the Bachelors, or a five-year undergraduate and postgraduate combined professional degree requiring 200 credits for completion. The Doctorate (Doktors) is the highest university-level degree and involves three to four years of full-time study, culminating with public defence of a thesis.

Technical and vocational education is principally available at post-secondary vocational colleges. The main award is the First Level (Higher) Vocational Diploma, which requires two to three years of study.

Learned Societies

GENERAL

Latvian Academy of Sciences: Akadēmijas laukums 1, Rīga 1524; tel. 6722-5361; fax 6782-1153; e-mail lza@ac.lza.lv; internet www.lza.lv; f. 1946; divs of Chemical, Biological and Medical Sciences (Chair. R. Valters, Scientific Sec. B. Ādamsone), Physical and Technical Sciences (Chair. J. Jansons, Scientific Sec. S. Negrejeva), Social Sciences and Humanities (Chair. T. Jundzis, Scientific Sec. I. Tālberga); 318 mems (91 full, 55 hon., 84 corresp., 88 foreign); attached research institutes: see Research Institutes; library: see Libraries and Archives; Pres. Juris Ekmanis; Sec.-Gen. A. Siliņš; publs *Automātika un Skaitlošanas Tehnika* (Automation and Computer Engineering), *Heterociklisko Savienojumu Ķīmija* (Chemistry of Heterocyclic Compounds), *Kompozītmateriālu Mehānika* (Mechanics of Composite Materials), *Latvijas Fizikas un Tehnisko Zinātnu Žurnāls* (Latvian Journal of Physical and Technical Sciences), *Latvijas Kīmijas Žurnāls* (Latvian Chemical Journal), *Magnitnaya Gidrodinamika* (Magnetic Hydrodynamics), *Proceedings of the Academy* (in 2 sections: humanitarian sciences, and natural, exact and applied sciences).

LANGUAGE AND LITERATURE

Alliance Française: Merkela iela 13, Rīga 1050; tel. 6714-0175; offers courses and examinations in French language and culture and promotes cultural exchange with France.

British Council: Blaumana iela 5a-2, Rīga 1011; tel. 6728-1730; fax 6750-4100; e-mail mail@britishcouncil.lv; internet www.britishcouncil.lv; offers courses and examinations in English language and British culture and promotes cultural exchange with the UK; library; Dir Agita Kalvina.

Goethe-Institut: Torna iela 1, via Klostera iela, Rīga 1050; tel. 6750-8194; fax 6732-3999; e-mail info@riga.goethe.org; internet www.goethe.de/ms/pra/deindex.htm; offers courses and examinations in German language and culture and promotes cultural exchange with Germany; library of 7,000 vols; Dir Rudolf de Baey.

Research Institutes

ECONOMICS, LAW AND POLITICS

Institute of Economics: Akadēmijas laukums 1, Rīga 1050; tel. and fax 6782-1289; e-mail raimara@ac.lza.lv; internet www.economics.lv; f. 1997; attached to Latvian Acad. of Sciences; Dir Raita Karnīte.

EDUCATION

Educator Training Support Centre: Brivibas iela 72, Rīga 1011; tel. 6731-2081; fax 6731-2082; e-mail jvvpvd@acad.latnet.lv; f. 1995; responsible for implementing and supporting govt policy on teacher-training and the devt of teaching skills; attached to Min. of Education and Science; Dir Dr Sarmis Mikuda; publ. *Skolotājs*.

HISTORY, GEOGRAPHY AND ARCHAEOLOGY

Institute of History of Latvia: Akadēmijas laukums 1, Rīga 1050; tel. 6522-3715; fax 6722-5044; internet www.lza.lv/en/inst/in18.htm; f. 1936; attached to Latvian Acad. of Sciences; Univ. of Latvia; library of 4,000 vols; Dir A. Caune; publ. *Latvijas Vēstures Institūta Žurnāls* (Journal, quarterly).

LANGUAGE AND LITERATURE

Institute of Literature, Folklore and Art: Akadēmijas laukums 1, Rīga 1050; tel. 6721-2872; fax 6722-9017; e-mail litfom@lza.lv; f. 1992; attached to Univ. of Latvia; Dir Benedikts Kalnačs; publ. *Letonica* (2 a year).

Latvian Language Institute: Akadēmijas laukums 1, Rīga 1050; tel. and fax 6722-7696; e-mail latv@ac.lza.lv; attached to Latvian Acad. of Sciences; Dir J. Valdmanis; publ. *Linguistica Lettica* (2 a year).

MEDICINE

Institute of Experimental and Clinical Medicine, University of Latvia: O. Vaciesa iela 4, Rīga 1004; tel. 6761-2038; e-mail ekmi@lu.lv; internet www.lu.lv; f. 1946; physiology, oncology; Dir Dr Peteris Tretjakovs.

NATURAL SCIENCES

Biological Sciences

Institute of Biology: Miera iela 3, Salaspils 2169; tel. 6794-4988; fax 6794-4986; e-mail office@email.lubi.edu.lv; internet www.lubi.edu.lv; f. 1951; attached to Univ. of Latvia; 100 mems; library of 22,000 vols; Dir Dr Viesturs Melecis.

Institute of Wood Chemistry: Dzērbenes iela 27, Rīga 1006; tel. 6755-3063; e-mail koks@edi.lv; internet www.lza.lv/en/inst/in10.htm; f. 1946; library of 5,000 vols; Sci. Dir Dr Janis Dolacis.

Kirchenstein, A., Institute of Microbiology and Virology: Ratsupites iela 1, Rīga 1067; tel. 6742-6197; fax 6742-8036; e-mail vaira@latnet.lv; internet www.micro.lv; f. 1946, re-f. 1993; attached to Min. of Education and Science and Univ. of Latvia; Dir VAIRA SAULĪTE.

Latvian Institute of Organic Synthesis: Aizkraukles iela 21, Rīga 1006; tel. 6755-1822; fax 6755-0338; e-mail sinta@osi.lv; f. 1957; attached to Latvian Acad. of Sciences; Dir Prof. I. KALVINSH; publ. *Chemistry of Heterocyclic Compounds* (in Russian and English, monthly).

Physical Sciences

Institute of Astronomy of the University of Latvia: Raiņa bulv. 19, Rīga 1586; tel. 6703-4580; fax 6703-4582; e-mail astra@acad.latnet.lv; internet www.astr.lu.lv; f. 1946; Dir Dr MĀRIS ĀBELE; publs *Astronomiskais kalendārs* (Astronomical Calendar, annual), *Zvaigžņotā Debess* (The Starry Sky, quarterly).

Institute of Inorganic Chemistry: Miera iela 34, Rīgas rajons, Salaspils 2169; tel. 6794-4711; fax 6780-0779; e-mail nki@nki.lv; internet www.nki.lv; f. 1946; attached to Rīga Technical Univ. and Latvian Acad. of Sciences; Dir Dr Ing. JANIS GRABIS; publ. *Latvijas kīmijas žurnāls* (Latvian Journal of Chemistry, quarterly).

Institute of Physical Energetics: Aizkraukles iela 21, Rīga 1006; tel. 6755-2011; fax 6755-0839; e-mail fei@edi.lv; internet www.innovation.lv/fei; f. 1946; attached to Latvian Acad. of Sciences; Dir Prof. J. A. EKMANIS; publ. *Latvian Journal of Physics and Technical Sciences* (6 a year).

Institute of Physics: Miera iela 32, Rīgas rajons, Salaspils 2121; tel. 6794-4700; fax 6790-1214; e-mail fizinst@sal.lv; internet www.iph.sal.lv; Dir Dr JĀNIS FREIBERGS.

Nuclear Research Centre: Miera iela 31, Salaspils 2169; tel. 6790-1210; fax 6790-1212; e-mail brzs@lanet.lv; attached to Latvian Acad. of Sciences; Dir A. LAPENAS.

PHILOSOPHY AND PSYCHOLOGY

Institute of Philosophy and Sociology: Akadēmijas laukums 1, Rīga 1940; tel. 6722-9208; fax 6721-0806; e-mail fsi@lza.lv; internet www.fsi.lv; f. 1981; attached to Univ. of Latvia; Dir MAIJA KŪLE; publs *Filozofia* (annual), *Religiski-filozofiski raksti* (religious-philosophical writings).

TECHNOLOGY

Institute of Electronics and Computer Science: Dzērbenes iela 14, Rīga 1006; tel. 6755-4500; fax 6755-5337; e-mail info@edi.lv; internet www.edi.lv; f. 1960; attached to Univ. of Latvia; library of 10,000 vols; Dir Prof. IVARS BILINSKIS; publ. *Avtomatika i vychislitelnaya technika* (6 a year).

Institute of Polymer Mechanics: Aizkraukles iela 23, Rīga 1006; tel. 6755-1145; fax 6782-0467; e-mail polmech@edzi.lza.lv; f. 1963; attached to Latvian Acad. of Sciences; Dir J. JANSONS; publ. *Mechanics of Composite Materials* (6 a year).

Research Institute of Water and Land Management: Dobeles iela 43, Jelgava 3000; tel. 6302-5517; fax 6302-7180; e-mail janis.valters@apollo.lv; f. 1940; Dir Dr JANIS VALTERS.

Scientific Research Institute of Microdevices: Maskavas iela 240, Rīga 1063; tel. 6725-1619; fax 6725-1000; f. 1962; semiconductor devices and integrated circuits; Dir ARNIS KUNDZINS.

Libraries and Archives

Rīga

Latvian Academic Library: Rūpniecības iela 10, Rīga 1235; tel. 6710-6206; fax 6710-6202; e-mail acadlib@lib.acadlib.lv; internet www.acadlib.lv; f. 1524; 3,100,000 vols, incunabula, MSS; spec. collns incl. Latvian literature; Dir VENTA KOCERE.

National Library of Latvia: Kr. Barona iela 14, Rīga 1423; tel. 6736-5250; fax 6728-0851; e-mail lnb@lnb.lv; internet www.lnb.lv; f. 1919; 4,478,424 vols; Dir ANDRIS VILKS; publs *Bibliotēku zinātnes aspekti* (irreg.), *Latviešu Zinātne un Literatūra* (irreg.).

Patent and Technology Library: Šķūņu 17, Rīga 1974; tel. 6722-7310; fax 6721-0767; e-mail patbib@patbib.lv; internet www.patbib.lv; f. 1949; located at Patent Office of the Republic of Latvia; 31m. patents, 303,000 standards; Dir AGNESE BUHOLTE.

University of Latvia Library: Kalpaka bulvāris 4, Rīga 1820; tel. 6722-0087; fax 6722-3984; e-mail biblioteka@lu.lv; internet www.lu.lv/biblioteka; f. 1862; 1,997,081 vols; Dir IVETA GUDAKOVSKA.

Museums and Art Galleries

Bauska

Bauska Castle Museum: Pilskalns, Bauska 3901; tel. and fax 6392-3793; e-mail bauska.pils@e-apollo.lv; f. 1990; Bauska Castle history; Dir M. SKANIS.

Cēsis

Cēsis Museum of History and Art: Pils laukums 9, Cēsis 4100; tel. 6412-2615; f. 1925; history, ethnography; library of 8,000 vols; Dir A. VANADZIŅŠ.

Rīga

History Museum of Latvia: Pils laukumā 3, Rīga 1050; tel. 6722-3004; fax 6722-0586; e-mail museum@history-museum.lv; f. 1869; Dir A. RADIŅŠ.

Latvian Museum of Natural History: K. Barona iela 4, Rīga 1050; tel. 6735-6023; fax 6735-6027; e-mail ldm@dabasmuzejs.gov.lv; internet www.dabasmuzejs.gov.lv; f. 1846; geology, natural history; library of 18,000 vols; Dir MĀRA EIPURE; publ. *Daba un Muzejs* (annual).

Latvian Open-Air Ethnographical Museum: Brīvības iela 440, Rīga 1056; tel. 6799-4510; fax 6799-4178; e-mail info@brivdabas-muzejs.lv; internet www.muzejs.lv; f. 1924; wooden architecture since 17th century; archive of 70,000 units; Dir JURIS INDĀNS.

Museum of Foreign Art: Pils laukumā 3, Rīga 1050; tel. 6722-6467; fax 6722-8776; e-mail arzemju.mm@apollo.lv; internet www.amm.lv; f. 1773; library of 15,300 vols; Dir DAIGA UPENIECE.

Museum of the History of Rīga and Navigation: Palasta iela 4, Rīga 1050; tel. 6721-1358; fax 6721-0226; e-mail direkt@rigamuz.lv; internet www.vip.latnet.lv/museums/riga; f. 1773; library of 24,000 vols; Dir K. RADZIŅA.

Rainis Museum of the History of Literature and Arts: Pils laukums 2, Rīga 1050; tel. and fax 6721-6425; e-mail pumpurs@acad.latnet.lv; f. 1925; Dir I. ZUKULIS.

State Museum of Art: K. Valdemāra iela 10A, Rīga 1010; tel. 6732-5051; fax 6735-7408; e-mail vmm@latnet.lv; internet www.vmm.lv; f. 1905; Dir MĀRA LĀCE.

Stradiņ Museum of the History of Medicine: Antonijas iela 1, Rīga 1360; tel. 722-29-14; fax 721-13-23; e-mail museum2@apollo.lv; internet www.mwm.lv; f. 1957; library of 39,851 vols, 16,368 rare books; Dir E. BERZINA; publ. *Acta medico-historica Rigensia*.

Salaspils

National Botanical Gardens: Miera iela 1, Salaspils 2169; tel. and fax 6794-5460; e-mail sekretare@nbd.apollo.lv; internet www.nbd.gov.lv; f. 1956; attached to Min. of Education and Science; library of 24,000 vols; Dir Prof. Dr GEDERTS ĪEVINSH; publs *Index Seminum* (annual), *The Baltic Botanical Gardens* (2 a year).

Universities

DAUGAVPILS UNIVERSITY

Vienības ielā 13, Daugavpils 5400
Telephone: 6542-1606
Fax: 6542-2922
E-mail: dau@dau.lv
Internet: www.dau.lv
Founded 1921
State control
Rector: Prof. ZAIGA IKERE
Pro-Rector for Research: Prof. ARVĪDS BARŠEVSKIS
Pro-Rector for Studies: IRĒNA KAMINSKA
Library of 400,000 vols
Number of teachers: 260
Number of students: 4,700

DEANS

Faculty of Humanities: VALENTĪNA LIEPA
Faculty of Music and Art: VOLDEMĀRS SKUTĀNS
Faculty of Natural Sciences and Mathematics: ANTONIJS SALĪTIS
Faculty of Pedagogy and Psychology: ILGA SALĪTE
Faculty of Social Sciences: VLADIMIRS MENĐIKOVS
Dept of Sports Pedagogy: JĀNIS JAUJA (Head)

UNIVERSITY OF LATVIA

Raiņa bulvāris 19, Rīga 1586
Telephone: 6703-4300
Fax: 6703-4302
E-mail: lu@lanet.lv
Internet: www.lu.lv
Founded 1919
Language of instruction: Latvian
Academic year: September to June
Rector: Prof. Dr IVARS LĀCIS
Vice-Rectors: JURIS KRŪMIŅŠ, INDRIĶIS MUIŽNIEKS
Librarian: IVETA GUDAKOVSKA
Number of teachers: 1,148
Number of students: 28,115
Publications: *Acta Universitatis Latviensis* (10 a year), *Agora* (2 a year), *Automatic Control and Computer Sciences* (6 a year), *Ceļš* (theology, annual), *Humanities and Social Sciences Latvia* (quarterly), *Journal of Baltic Psychology* (annual), *Journal of the Latvian Institute of History*, *Latvijas Vēsture* (History of Latvia, quarterly), *Law and Rights* (monthly), *Latvian Human Rights Quarterly* (2 a year), *Lettonics* (every 2 years), *Linguistica Lettica* (every 2 years), *Magnetohydrodynamics* (quarterly), *Mechanics of Composite Materials* (6 a year), *Terra* (9 a year), *The Starry Sky* (quarterly)

DEANS

Faculty of Biology: Assoc. Prof. ULDIS KONDRATOVICS
Faculty of Chemistry: Assoc. Prof. J. ŠVIRKSTS
Faculty of Economics and Management: Prof. E. VASERMANIS
Faculty of Education and Psychology: Assoc. Prof. A. KANGRO
Faculty of Geography and Earth Sciences: Prof. M. KLAVIŅŠ
Faculty of History and Philosophy: Doc. G. STRAUBE
Faculty of Law: Doc. K. BALODIS
Faculty of Medicine: Prof. U. VIKMANIS
Faculty of Modern Languages: Assoc. Prof. E. OŠIŅŠ
Faculty of Philology: Prof. J. KURSITE-PAKULE
Faculty of Physics and Mathematics: Prof. M. AUZIŅŠ
Faculty of Social Sciences: Assoc. Prof. INTA BRIKŠE
Faculty of Theology: Assoc. Prof. J. CĀLĪTIS

ATTACHED RESEARCH INSTITUTES

August Kirhenshtein Institute of Microbiology and Virology: Dir Dr VAIRA SAULĪTE.

Biomedical Research and Study Centre: Dir Dr ZINAIDA ŠOMSTEINE.

Institute of Accountancy: Dir Dr INTA BRUNA.

Institute of Aquatic Ecology: Dir Dr chem. JURIS AIGANS.

Institute of Astronomy: Dir Dr ARTURS BALKAVS-GRĪNHOFS.

Institute of Atomic Physics and Spectroscopy: Dir Dr hab. ph. JANIS SPIGULIS.

Institute of Biology: Dir Dr VIESTURS MELECIS.

Institute of Chemical Physics: Dir Dr chem. DONATS ERTS.

Institute of Educational Research: Dir Dr ANDRIS KANGRO.

Institute of Electronics and Computer Science: Dir Dr IVARS BILINSKIS.

Institute of Environmental Science and Management: Dir Dr RAIMONDS ERNŠTEINS.

Institute of Experimental and Clinical Medicine: Dir Dr RENATE LIGENE.

Institute of Finance: Dir Prof. Dr ELMĀRS ZELGALVIS.

Institute of Geodesy and Geoinformatics: Dir Dr JĀNIS BALODIS.

Institute of Geology: Dir Assoc. Prof. EDVINS LUKSHEVICHS.

Institute of History of Latvia: Dir Dr hist. JANIS BERZINŠ.

Institute of Human Rights: Alternate Dir GITA FELDHŪNE.

Institute of International Affairs: Dir Prof. Dr JURIS BOJĀRS.

Institute of Literature, Folklore and Art: Dir Dr BENEDIKTS KALNAČS.

Institute of Marketing and Quality Management: Dir Prof. Dr VALĒRIJS PRAUDE.

Institute of Mathematics: Dir Dr ANDREJS REINFELDS.

Institute of Mathematics and Computer Science: Dir Prof. Dr JĀNIS BĀRZDIŅŠ.

Institute of Microbiology and Biotechnology: Dir Prof. Dr ULDIS VIESTURS.

Institute of National Economy: Dir Dr ROBERTS ŠKAPARS.

Institute of Philosophy and Sociology: Dir Prof. Dr MAIJA KŪLE.

Institute of Physics: Dir Dr JĀNIS FREIBERGS.

Institute of Polymer Mechanics: Dir Dr JURIS JANSONS.

Institute of Postgraduate Education in Medicine: Dir Dr JUNIS ZEMMERIS.

Institute of Solid State Physics: Dir Dr ANDRIS ŠTERNBERGS.

Latvian Language Institute: Dir Prof. Dr JĀNIS VALDMANIS.

LATVIA UNIVERSITY OF AGRICULTURE

Lielā iela 2, Jelgava 3001
Telephone: 6302-2584
Fax: 6302-7238
E-mail: rector@llu.lv
Internet: www.llu.lv

Founded 1939 as Jelgava Agricultural Acad.; present name and status 1991
State control
Languages of instruction: Latvian, English, German and Russian

Rector: JURIS SKUJĀNS
Vice-Rector for Research: PĒTERIS RIVŽA
Vice-Rector for Studies: ARNIS MUGURĒVIČS

Library of 509,173 vols
Number of teachers: 482
Number of students: 4,691

Publication: *Works* (annual).

RĪGA STRADIŅS UNIVERSITY

Dzirciema iela 16, Rīga 1007
Telephone: 6740-9232
Fax: 6747-1815
E-mail: rsu@rsu.lv
Internet: www.rsu.lv

Founded 1951 as Rīga Medical Institute; present name and status 2002
State control
Languages of instruction: Latvian, English
Academic year: September to June
Rector: JĀNIS VĒTRA
Vice-Rector for Clinics: JĀNIS GARDOVSKIS
Vice-Rector for Economics and Management: MARINA GULMANE
Vice-Rector for Science: IVETA OZOLANTA
Vice-Rector for Teaching: ILZE AKOTA
Library of 320,000 vols
Number of teachers: 795
Number of students: 5,226

Publications: *Dentistry* (annual), *Kirurģija* (Surgery, 2 a year), *Zinātniskie raksti* (medicine and pharmacy)

Faculties of European studies, Medicine, Nursing, Pharmacy, Public health, Rehabilitation medicine, Stomatology.

RĪGA TECHNICAL UNIVERSITY

Kaļķu iela 1, Rīga 1658
Telephone: 6708-9333
Fax: 6782-0094
Internet: www.rtu.lv
Founded 1990
Rector: Dr IVARS KNĒTS

Library of 2,000,000 vols
Number of teachers: 589
Number of students: 15,330

Publications: *Jaunais Inzenieris* (newspaper), *Scientific Proceedings of RTU* (quarterly)

Brs in Daugavpils, Liepaja and Ventspils.

DEANS

Faculty of Architecture and Urban Planning: Prof. Dr IVARS STRAUTMANIS
Faculty of Building and Civil Eng.: Dr Ing. JURIS SMIRNOVS
Faculty of Computer Science and Information Technology: Dr Ing. JANIS GRUNDSPENKIS
Faculty of Electronics and Telecommunications: Assoc. Prof. ILMARS SLAIDINS
Faculty of Eng. Economics: Prof. Dr KONSTANTĪNS DIDENKO
Faculty of Materials Science and Applied Chemistry: Prof. VALDIS KAMPAR
Faculty of Power and Electrical Eng.: Prof. JĀNIS GERHARDS
Faculty of Transport and Mechanical Eng.: Prof. GUNDARS LIBERTS

ATTACHED CENTRES

Institute of Humanities: Āzenes iela 16/20, Rīga 1048; e-mail huminst@bf.rtu.lv; internet www.bf.rtu.lv; Dir Dr ANITA LANKA.

Institute of Languages: Meža iela 1/1 – 409, Rīga 1048; e-mail valodu.instituts@rtu.lv; internet omega.rtu.lv/vi; Dir Dr LARISA ILJINSKA.

Rīga Business School: Skolas iela 1, Rīga 1010; e-mail admin@rbs.lv; internet www.rbs.lv; Dir Dr JĀNIS GRĒVIŅŠ.

Other Higher Educational Institutions

Latvian Academy of Arts: Kalpaka bulvāris 13, Rīga 1867; tel. 6733-2202; fax 6722-8963; e-mail lma@latnet.lv; internet www.lma.lv; f. 1921; depts of Painting, Sculpture, Graphic arts, Industrial design, Textiles, Fashion design, Art history and theory, Interior design, Environmental art, Graphic design, Metal design, Ceramics, Glass, Art education; library: 32,000 vols; 100 teachers; 638 students; Rector Prof. JĀNIS ANDRIS OSIS; Dean of Students Assoc. Prof. UGIS AUZIŅŠ.

Latvian Academy of Music: Krishyana Barona iela 1, Rīga 1050; tel. 6722-8684; fax 6782-0271; e-mail academy@music.lv; internet www.lmuza.lv; f. 1919; piano, orchestral instruments, singing, choral conducting, music education, composition, musicology; library: 150,000 vols, 47,000 tape recordings, 36,000 records, 1,300 audio cassettes, 2,800 CDs, 1,000 video cassettes; 246 teachers; 426 students; Rector Prof. JURIS KARLSONS.

Transport and Telecommunication Institute: Lomonosova str. 1, Rīga 1019; tel. 6710-0650; fax 6710-0660; e-mail tsi@tsi.lv; internet www.tsi.lv; f. 1919 (formerly Riga Aviation Univ., present status 1999); faculties of Management, Economics and transport, Computer science and electronics; library: 15,000 vols; 140 teachers; 3,500 students; Rector EUGENE KOPYTOV.

LEBANON

The Higher Education System

The two oldest universities in Lebanon are private institutions founded by Christian denominations in the 19th century while Lebanon was still under Ottoman Turkish rule; they are University of Beirut (founded 1866; formerly Syrian Protestant College) and Université Saint Joseph (founded 1875; Jesuit control). Following the dissolution of the Ottoman Empire after the First World War (1914–18), a Greater Lebanese state was created by the Allied powers, administered by France under a League of Nations mandate from 1920 until independence was declared in 1941. Institutions of higher education established in this period include Lebanese American University (founded 1924 by the United Presbyterian Church, USA), Near East School of Theology (founded 1932) and Académie Libanaise des Beaux Arts (founded 1937). The higher education system displays strong French and US influences, which vary from institution to institution reflecting whether they were set up by American missionaries or the French authorities. Furthermore, higher education is dominated by private institutions; only Université Libanaise (founded 1951) and Académie Libanaise des Beaux Arts are under State control. In 1998 Lebanon secured a loan of US $60m. from the World Bank, in order to restructure the country's system of technical and vocational education. Some 142,951 Lebanese students were enrolled in higher education in the 2001/02 academic year.

Admission to university undergraduate courses is on the basis of the secondary school qualification (Baccalauréat), and student may also be required to sit an entrance examination. Depending on the institution, the main undergraduate degree is known as the Licence, Bachelors, Maîtrise or Diploma, and is usually three to five years in duration. Medical students are awarded a professional degree called the Doctorat after seven years. A range of degrees is also available at the first stage of postgraduate study, including Masters, Maîtrise or Diplôme d'Etudes Supérieures. The final state of university-level degrees is the Doctorat d'Etat.

Learned Societies

GENERAL

UNESCO Office Beirut and Regional Bureau for Education in the Arab States: POB 5244, Beirut; located at: Cité Sportive Blvd, Beirut; tel. (1) 850013; fax (1) 824854; e-mail beirut@unesco.org; internet www.unesco.org.lb; designated Cluster Office for Iraq, Jordan, Lebanon, Syria and Palestinian Autonomous Territories; Regional Bureau for Education in the Arab States; Dir Ramzi Salamé.

BIBLIOGRAPHY, LIBRARY SCIENCE AND MUSEOLOGY

Lebanese Library Association: POB 113/5367 Beirut; or c/o American University of Beirut, University Library/Serials Dept, Beirut; tel. (1) 350000; fax (1) 744703; f. 1960; 218 mems; Pres. Fawz Abdallah; Sec. Rudaynah Shoujah; publ. *Newsletter* (3 a year).

ECONOMICS, LAW AND POLITICS

Association Libanaise des Sciences Juridiques: Faculté de Droit et des Sciences politiques, Université Saint Joseph, BP 17-5208, Beirut; tel. (1) 421000; fax (1) 421045; f. 1963; represents the Lebanon in the Int. Asscn of Legal Science; study of legal problems in Lebanon, conferences etc; 40 mems; Pres. Pierre Gannagé; Sec.-Gen. Nabil Maamazi; publ. *Proche-Orient* (judicial studies).

LANGUAGE AND LITERATURE

British Council: Sadat/Sidani St, Azar Bldg, Ras Beirut; tel. (1) 740123; fax (1) 739461; e-mail general.enquiries@lb.britishcouncil.org; internet www.britishcouncil.org/lebanon; teaching centre; offers courses and exams in English language and British culture and promotes cultural exchange with the UK; Dir Dr Ken Churchill; Teaching Centre Man. Andrew Mackenzie.

Goethe-Institut: 11 Rue Bliss, Beirut; tel. (1) 740524; fax (1) 743524; e-mail goethe_v@cyberia.net.lb; internet www.goethe.de/na/bei/enindex.htm; offers courses and exams in German language and culture and promotes cultural exchange with Germany; library of 7,000 vols; Dir Rolf Stehle.

Instituto Cervantes: Centre Ville, 287 A/B Maarad St, BP 11-1202, Beirut; tel. (1) 970253; fax (1) 970291; e-mail cenbei@cervantes.es; internet beirut.cervantes.es; offers courses and exams in Spanish language and culture and promotes cultural exchange with Spain and Spanish-speaking Latin and Central America; library of 5,000 vols; Dir Andrés Pérez Sánchez-Morate.

Research Institutes

GENERAL

Centre d'Etudes et de Recherches sur le Moyen-Orient Contemporain, Beirut: c/o Ambassade de France au Liban, (valise diplomatique), 128 bis rue de l'Université, 75531 Paris 07 SP, France; tel. (1) 420291; fax (1) 420295; e-mail cermoc.adm@lb.refer.org; internet www.lb.refer.org/cermoc; f. 1977; study of the Middle East in all its aspects: history, sociology, economy, human geography, physical geography, towns; library of 20,000 vols; Dir Henry Laurens.

Orient-Institut der Deutschen Morgenländischen Gesellschaft Beirut (Orient Institute of the German Institute of Oriental Studies, Beirut): POB 11-2988, Riad el-Solh 1107 2120, Beirut; tel. (1) 376598; fax (1) 376599; e-mail oib-dir@oidmg.org; internet www.oidmg.org; f. 1961; activities in the field of Oriental research (Islamic, Arabic, Persian, Turcological, Semitic), philology, and contemporary history, incl. field research, history of the eastern Churches; co-operation with universities in the Middle East and Germany; library of 150,000 vols; Dir Prof. Dr Manfred Kropp; publs *Bibliotheca Islamica — Beiruter Texte und Studien, Beiruter Blätter*.

ECONOMICS, LAW AND POLITICS

Centre for Arab Unity Studies: Sadat Tower Bldg, 9th floor, Lyon St, Hamra POB 113-6001, Beirut 1103 2090; tel. (1) 801582; fax (1) 865548; e-mail info@caus.org.lb; internet www.caus.org.lb; f. 1975; an independent, non-political centre for scientific research on all aspects of Arab society and Arab unity, particularly in the fields of economics, politics, sociology and education; activities are governed and implemented by three bodies: Board of Trustees, Executive Committee and General Secretariat; library of 11,000 vols, 650 periodicals; Dir-Gen. Dr Khair El-Din Haseeb; publ. *Al-Mustaqbal Al-Arabi* (The Arab Future, monthly).

Institut de Recherches d'Economie Appliquée: Faculté de Sciences Economiques, Université Saint Joseph, BP 293, Beirut; f. 1980; economic studies of the Lebanon and other Middle Eastern countries; Pres. Prof. Louis Hobeika; publs *Proche-Orient, études économiques* (quarterly).

Institute for Palestine Studies, Publishing and Research Organization: POB 11-7164, Anis Nsouli St (off Verdun St), Beirut 1107-2230; tel. (1) 868387; fax (1) 814193; e-mail ipsbrt@palestine-studies.org; internet www.palestine-studies.org *or* 3501 M St, NW, Washington, DC 20007, USA; tel. (202) 342-3990; fax (202) 342-3927 *or* POB 25658, Nicosia, Cyprus; tel. 319124; fax 756324; f. 1963; ind. non-profit Arab research org.; promotes a better understanding of the Palestine problem and the Arab-Israeli conflict; 25 mems; library of 58,000 vols (Arabic, Hebrew, English, French, German, Spanish and Russian); microfilm colln, private papers and archives; Chair. Dr Hisham Nashabe; Exec. Sec. Prof. Walid Khalidi; publs *Journal of Palestine Studies* (English, quarterly), *Majallat al-Dirasat al-Filistiniyah* (Arabic, quarterly), *Revue d'études palestiniennes* (French, quarterly).

Lebanese Center for Policy Studies: POB 55-215, Tayar Center (3rd Fl., Block C), Sin al-Fil, Beirut; tel. (1) 486429; fax (1) 490375; e-mail info@lcps-lebanon.org; internet www.lcps-lebanon.org; f. 1989; research into political, social and economic development; library facilities; Pres. Dr Elie A. Salem; Dir Dr Paul Salem (acting).

HISTORY, GEOGRAPHY AND ARCHAEOLOGY

Institut Français d'Archéologie du Proche Orient: Rue de Damas, POB 11-1424, Beirut; tel. (1) 615844; fax (1) 615866; e-mail ifapo@lb.refer.org; f. 1946; Dir JEAN-LOUIS HUOT; library of 45,000 vols; brs in Syria and Jordan; publs *Syria, Revue d'Art et d'Archéologie, Bibliothèque Archéologique et Historique*.

Libraries and Archives

Beirut

American University of Beirut Libraries: POB 11/0236, Riad El-Solh 1107 2020, Beirut; tel. (1) 340460 ext. 2600; fax (1) 744703; e-mail library@aub.edu.lb; internet www.aub.edu.lb/libraries; f. 1866; 586,363 vols, 1,386 MSS, 2,604 current periodicals, 1,063,240 audiovisual items, 1,596 maps; Librarian HELEN BIKHAZI.

Beirut Arab University Library: POB 11-5020, Beirut; tel. (1) 300110; fax (1) 818402; e-mail bau@inco.com.lb; f. 1960; important collections on Lebanese, Arabic and Islamic studies; 110,000 vols and 1,500 periodicals; Chief Librarian SAID TAYARA.

Bibliothèque Nationale du Liban: Immeuble Hatab, 6th Fl., rue Madame Curie, Beirut; tel. (1) 756321; fax (1) 756319; e-mail info@bnlb.org; internet www.bnlb.org; f. 1921; library closed and collections put in storage 1979, due to civil war; restoration and reconstruction of the library began 2003; 150,000 vols, 2,500 MSS.

Bibliothèque Orientale: Rue de l'Université St Joseph, POB 166 775, Achrafieh, Beirut 1100-2150; tel. (1) 202421; fax (1) 339287; e-mail bo@usj.edu.lb; internet www.usj.edu.lb; f. 1875; 200,000 vols, 1,800 periodicals, 3,500 MSS, 40,000 photographs, 1,000 maps; attached Centre Pouzet d'Etude des Civilisations Anciennes et Médiévales; Dir MAY SEMAAN SEIGNEURIE; publ. *Mélanges de L'Universités Saint-Joseph* (annually).

Bibliothèques de l'Université St Joseph: BP 175 208, Beirut; faculties of law, economics, politics, administration: 100,000 vols, 550 periodicals; medical sciences (POB 115076): 12,000 vols, 125 periodicals; engineering (POB 1514): 10,000 vols, 115 periodicals; arts: 65,000 vols, 300 periodicals.

Attached library:

Bibliothèque de la Faculté des Lettres et des Sciences Humanies: Rue de Damas, BP 17-5208, Beirut 1104 2020; tel. (1) 611456 ext. 5105; fax (1) 611359; e-mail flsh.biblio@usj.edu.lb; f. 1977; 85,000 vols; Librarian LEILA BOU NADER ELIAN.

Near East School of Theology Library: POB 13-5780, Chouran, Beirut 1102 2070; tel. (1) 354194; fax (1) 347129; e-mail library@theonest.edu.lb; internet www.pcusa.org/pcusa/wmd/globaled/institutes/nest.htm; f. 1932; 40,000 vols; collection of MSS, collection of The American Press; 135 religious periodicals (of which 80 are current); Librarian RITA KHARRAT; publ. *Theological Review* (2 a year).

Daroon-Harissa

Library of the Syrian Patriarchal Seminary: Seminary of Charfet, Daroon-Harissa; tel. (9) 903040; f. 1786; 36,000 vols and 3,100 Syriac and Arabic MSS; Librarian Fr JOSEPH MELKI; publ. *Trait d'Union*.

Khonchara

Library of the St John Monastery: Khonchara; f. 1696; Basilian Shweiriet Order; 12,000 vols, 372 MSS; the Order preserves the first printing press in the Middle East with Arabic and Greek letters (first book 1734); Abbot-General Rt Rev. Mgr ATHANASE HAGE.

Saïda

Library of the Monastery of Saint-Saviour: Saïda; f. 1711; Basilian Missionary Order of Saint-Saviour; 28,500 vols and 2,550 MSS; Librarians SLEIMAN ABOU-ZEID, MAKARIOS HAIDAMOUS; publs *Ar-Riçalat* (monthly), *Al-Wahdat* (quarterly), *L'Ordo Grec-Catholique*, *An-Nahlat* (quarterly), *Nafhat Al-Moukhalles* (quarterly).

Museums and Art Galleries

Beirut

American University Museum: Ras Beirut; tel. (1) 340549; fax (1) 363235; e-mail museum@aub.edu.lb; internet ddc.aub.edu.lb/projects/museum; f. 1868; Stone Age flint implements; bronze tools and implements from Early Bronze Age to Byzantine period; pottery and other artefacts from the Bronze and Iron Ages, and Classical, Hellenistic, Roman and Byzantine periods; Arabic pottery from the 8th–16th c.; Phoenician glassware; Egyptian artefacts from Neolithic to the Dynastic period; pottery from the Neolithic period of Mesopotamia and cylinder seals and cuneiform tablets from Sumer and Akkad; numismatics of the countries in the eastern basin of the Mediterranean; Dir Dr LEILA BADRE; publs *Newsletter* (2 a year), *Berytus* (annually).

Daheshite Museum and Library: POB 202, Beirut; contains aquarelles, gouaches, original paintings, engravings, sculptures in marble, bronze, ivory and wood carvings; library of 30,000 vols (20,000 Arabic, 10,000 English and French), on arts, philosophy, history, literature, religions, etc.; Dir Dr A. S. M. DAHESH.

Musée des Beaux-Arts: POB 3939, Beirut; Dir Dr DAHESH.

Musée National (National Museum of Lebanon): Rue de Damas, Beirut; f. 1920; exhibits: royal jewellery, arms and statues of the Phoenician epoch; sarcophagus of King Ahiram (13th century BC), with first known alphabetical inscriptions; the collection of Dr G. Ford of 25 sarcophagi of the Greek and Hellenistic epoch; large collection of terracotta statuettes of the Hellenistic period; Roman and Byzantine mosaics; Arabic woods and ceramics; Dir-Gen. Dr CAMILE ASMAR; publ. *Bulletin and monographs*.

Sursock Museum: Sursock St, Ashrafieh, Beirut.

Besharre

Musée Khalil Gibran: Besharre; dedicated to the life and works of the author.

Universities

AL-IMAM AL-OUZAI UNIVERSITY

POB 14-5355, Beirut 2802-1105

Telephone: (1) 704452
Fax: (1) 704449
E-mail: islamic-studies@ouzai.org
Internet: www.ouzai.org

Founded 1979
Private control
Academic year: October to June

Chairman: TOUFIC AL-HOURI
Library Administrator: SAMIR OMARI

Number of teachers: 110
Number of students: 2,500

DEANS

Imam Ouzai College of Islamic Studies: Prof. Dr KAMEL MOUSA
Islamic College of Business Administration: Prof. Dr MOHAMED ISKANDARANI

DIRECTORS

Documentation Centre for Bibliographic Information on Islam and the Muslim World: Dr BASSAM ABDEL HAMID
Documentation Centre on World Countries and Major Cities: Dr IBRAHIM ASSAL
Documentation Centre on World Leading Banks: ANWAR SOUBRA
Islamic Institute for the Supervision of Food Products: Dr IBRAHIM ADHAM

AMERICAN UNIVERSITY OF BEIRUT

Bliss St, Beirut

Telephone: (1) 350000
Fax: (1) 351706
Internet: www.aub.edu.lb

Founded 1866
Private control
Language of instruction: English
Academic year: October to June

President: JOHN WATERBURY
Vice-Presidents: MAKHLUF HADDADIN (Academic), GEORGES TOMEY (Administration), GEORGE NAJJAR (Regional External Programmes)
Provost: PETER HEATH
Registrar: SALIM KANAAN (acting)
Librarian: HELEN BIKHAZI

Number of teachers: 420
Number of students: 5,000

Publications: *Al-Abhath* (Arab Studies, in English and Arabic, annually), *Berytus Archaeological Studies* (English, annually), *Research Report* (2 a year)

DEANS

Faculty of Agricultural and Food Sciences: NUHAD DAGHIR
Faculty of Arts and Sciences: KHALIL BITAR
Faculty of Engineering and Architecture: IBRAHIM HAJJ
Faculty of Health Sciences: HUDA ZURAYK
Faculty of Medicine and Medical Center: NADIM CORTAS
Student Affairs: DEAN KEULIN

BEIRUT ARAB UNIVERSITY

POB 11-5020, Riad El-Solh 1107 2809, Beirut

Telephone: (1) 300110
Fax: (1) 818402
E-mail: bau@bau.edu.lb
Internet: www.bau.edu.lb

Founded 1960
Private control; established by the El-Ber Wa El-Ehsan Association; academically associated with the University of Alexandria
Languages of instruction: Arabic, English, French
Academic year: September to May

President: Prof. Dr MOSTAFA HASSAN MOSTAFA
Secretary-General: ISSAM HOURY
Director of Student Affairs: MOHAMED HAMOUD
Chief Librarian: SAEED TAYARA

Library of 125,000 vols
Number of teachers: 784
Number of students: 12,194

Publications: *Architecture and Planning Journal* (annually), *Human Sciences Journal* (2 a year), *Journal of Commercial*

Research and Studies (2 a year), *Revue des Etudes Juridiques* (2 a year)

DEANS

Faculty of Architecture: Prof. Dr RAMADAN ABDEL MAKSOUD
Faculty of Arts: Prof. Dr OLGA MATTAR MOHAMED GHAZI
Faculty of Commerce: Prof. Dr SAID ABDEL AZIZ OSMAN
Faculty of Dentistry: Prof. Dr MOSTAFA FAKHRI KHALIL
Faculty of Engineering: Prof. Dr IBRAHIM ABDEL-SALAM AWAD
Faculty of Law: Prof. Dr HAFIZA EL-HADDAD
Faculty of Medicine: Prof. Dr MOUNIR MOHAMED ZEERBAN
Faculty of Pharmacy: Prof. Dr FAWZI ALI YAZIBI
Faculty of Science: Prof. Dr SAMY HAMED CHAABAN

PROFESSORS

Faculty of Architecture:
ABDEL MAKSOUD, R., Building Science and Technology
HAMDI, E. F., Environmental Design

Faculty of Arts:
ABDUL RAHMAN, A. M., Sociology
EBRAHEEM, E. A., Geography
FAHMI, N. A., English Language and Literature
GHAZI, O. M. M., General and Applied Linguistics

Faculty of Commerce and Business Administration:
OSMAN, S. A., Public Economics

Faculty of Dentistry:
AMER, W. A-A., Oral Medicine, Periodontics and Diagnosis
EL-MULHALLAWI, A. S., Oral and Maxillofacial Surgery
KHALIL, M. F., Dental Biomaterials
MOSTAFA, A. M. M., Conservative Dentistry, Operative Dentistry
SEGAAN, G. I., Prosthodontics

Faculty of Engineering:
AWAD, I. A., Computer Engineering and Systems
BAGHDADI, K. H., River Engineering
ELGHAMMAL, M. A., Electrical Systems
EL-GHAZOULY, H. G., Surveying and Geodesy
EL-SHERBINY, M. M., Electrical and Computer Engineering
FARROUKH, O. O., Electro-magnetics and Optics
FATAH EL-BAB, F. A. I., Stability and Analysis of Space Structures
GHABASHI, M. A-L., Theoretical Physics and Materials Science
HASAB, M. A. H., Design of Thermal Systems
KHALIL, M. F., Fluid Mechanics
MOSTAFA, M. A. F., Mechanical Vibrations
RAJAB, M. M. E., Microelectronics
RASHED, A. M. H., Power Systems Analysis
SOROUR, M. K., Thermal Engineering

Faculty of Law:
ABD AL-WAHHAB, M. A., Public Law
AL-HADDAD, H. S. A., Private International Law
DWIDAR, M. H. I., Economy Planning
EL-MAGZOUB, M. M., Public International Law
KHALIL, A. A. S., Procedure Law

Faculty of Medicine:
ABOU AL-OLA, M. M., Histology: Histochemistry and Electron Microscope
AHMED, S. I., Internal Medicine – Gastrointestinal
EL-BAHEI, N. M., Clinical Pharmacology
EL-GEBALY, F. F., Embryology and Genetics
EL-SAWWA, E. A-K., Anatomy: Embryology and Genetics
KHEDR, M. M. S., Clinical Pharmacology
MADWAR, A., Histology: Histochemistry and Electron Microscopy
MASHALI, N. A-R., Gynaecological Pathology and Haematopathology
SALEH, M. N-D. A., Anatomy: Genetics of Development
ZEERBAN, M. M., Cardiothoracic Surgery

Faculty of Pharmacy:
BORAI, N. A., Pharmaceutics
EL-KHODAIRY, K. A-H., Microencapsulation and Drug Delivery Systems
EL-LAKANY, A. M., Chemistry of Natural Products
EL-YAZBI, F. A., Pharmaceutical Analysis and Drug Quality Control
MOHYEEDIN, M. M., Neurohumoral Transmission in Pharmacology
OSHBA, N. H. M., Synthetic Medicinal Chemistry

Faculty of Science:
ABD EL-JAWAD, N. M. A., Enzymology
ALI, A. M. A. M., Nuclear Physics
BADAWI, N. S. A., Cell Biology
DUKAINESH, S. I. A., Invertebrate Ecology
FALTAS, M. S., Fluid Dynamics
HAMAD, H. H. A., Fluid Dynamics
IBRAHIM, H. I., Solid State Physics
KOREK, M., Molecular Physics
MANSOUR, S. M. S., Organic Chemistry
SHAALAN, S. H., Phycology

LEBANESE AMERICAN UNIVERSITY

POB 13-5053, Chouran, Beirut 1102 2801
Telephone: (1) 786456
Fax: (1) 867098
Internet: www.lau.edu.lb

Founded 1924 by the United Presbyterian Church, USA
Private control
Language of instruction: English
Academic year: October to September

President: Dr JOSEPH JABBRA
Vice-President (Academic Affairs): Dr ABDALLAH SFIER
Vice-President (Development): ROBERT STODDARD
Vice-President (Finance and Administration): ELIAS BAZ
Vice-President (Student Affairs): Dr LAYLA NIMAH
Registrars: VATCHE PAPAZIAN (Beirut Campus): FOUAD SALIBI (Byblos Campus)
Librarians: AIDA NAAMAN (Beirut campus): FAWZ ABDALLAH (Byblos campus)

Libraries with 282,000 vols, 1,600 periodicals
Number of teachers: 170 full-time
Number of teachers: 347 part-time
Number of students: 6,300

Publications: *Al-Raida magazine* (4 a year), *LAU magazine* (4 a year)

DEANS

School of Arts and Sciences (Beirut campus): Dr SAMIRA AGHACY
School of Arts and Sciences (Byblos campus): Dr FOUAD HASHWA
School of Business (Beirut campus): Dr TAREK MIKDASHI
School of Business (Byblos campus): Dr WASSIM SHAHINE
School of Engineering and Architecture: Dr ELIE BADR (acting)
School of Pharmacy: Dr GABRIEL MALIHA

ATTACHED INSTITUTES

Beirut Institute for Media Arts.

Center for Lebanese Heritage.

Centre for Sponsored Research and Development.

Human Resources Institute.

Institute for Banking and Finance.

Institute of Family and Entrepreneurial Business.

Institute of Hospitality and Tourism Management Studies.

Institute for Peace and Justice Education.

Institute for Professional Journalists.

Institute for Water Resources and Environmental Technologies.

Institute for Women's Studies in the Arab World.

Software Institute.

Summer Institute for Intensive Arabic Language and Culture.

Teacher Training Institute.

Urban Planning Institute.

NOTRE DAME UNIVERSITY LOUAIZE

POB 72, Zouk Mikael, Zouk Mosbeh, Kesrwan
Telephone: (9) 218950
Fax: (9) 218771
E-mail: webm@ndu.edu.lb
Internet: www.ndu.edu.lb

Founded 1987 by the Maronite Order of the Holy Virgin Mary
Private control
Academic year: October to September

President: Rev. BOUTROS TARABAY
Vice-President (Academic Affairs): Dr GEORGE M. EID
Vice-President (Sponsored Research and Development): Dr AMEEN A. RIHANI
Director of Administration: Fr ROGER CHUKRI
Director of Admissions: ELHAM HASHEM
Director of Finance: Fr SAMIR GHSOUB
Director of Public Relations and Presidential Counsellor: SUHEIL MATAR
Director of Student Affairs: Fr BOULOS WEHBEH
Registrar: LEA EID
Director of Libraries: LESLIE A. HAGE

Number of teachers: 233
Number of students: 4,263

Publications: *PALMA Journal* (2 a year), *Spirit* (4 a year)

DEANS

Faculty of Architecture, Art and Design: Dr SHAHWAN KHOURY (acting)
Faculty of Business Administration and Economics: Dr ELIE YACHOUI
Faculty of Engineering: Dr SHAHWAN KHOURY
Faculty of Humanities: Dr BOULOS SARRU'
Faculty of Natural and Applied Sciences: Dr JEAN FARES
Faculty of Political Science, Public Affairs and Diplomacy: Dr MICHEL NEHME

DIRECTORS

North Lebanon campus: SALIM KARAM
Shouf campus: Dr ASSAAD EID
Division of Continuing Education: FAWZI BAROUD

ATTACHED RESEARCH INSTITUTES

Center for Digitization and Preservation.

Lebanese Emigration Research Center.

Water Energy and Environment Research Center.

UNIVERSITÉ ANTONINE

BP 40016, Hadath Baabda
Telephone: (5) 924076

Fax: (5) 924075
E-mail: contact@upa.edu.lb
Internet: www.upa.edu.lb

Founded 1996
Private control
Academic year: October to July
Number of teachers: 120
Number of students: 850

Publications: *Al-Antouniyah* (annually), *Our Liturgic Life* (2 series: research, 2 a year; celebrations, 4 a year)

Faculties of Biblical Studies, Computer Studies, Ecumenical and Religious Studies, Multimedia and Telecommunications Engineering, Nursing and Theology and Pastoral Studies; Higher Institute of Music; Institute of Physical Education and Sport; University Technical Institute of Laboratory Science and Dental Prosthetics.

UNIVERSITÉ DE BALAMAND

Box 100, Tripoli; Located at: Balamand-Koura
Telephone: (6) 930250
Fax: (6) 930278
E-mail: pr@balamand.edu.lb
Internet: www.balamand.edu.lb

Founded 1988

Organized in three campuses: Balamand Campus (fine arts, theology, arts and social sciences, business administration, sciences, engineering, medicine); Sin El Fil Campus, POB 55251, Beirut, Tel. (1) 502370, Fax (1) 502371 (fine arts); Achrafieh Campus, St Georges Health Complex, Youssef Sursok St, Achrafieh, POB 166378, Beirut, Tel. (1) 562108, Fax (1) 562110 (health sciences, postgraduate medical education)
Private control
Languages of instruction: Arabic, English, French
Academic year: October to June

Chancellor: GHASSAN TUENI
President: ELIE A. SALEM
Vice-Presidents: GEORGES N. NAHAS
Dean of Admissions and Registration: WALID MOUBAYYED
Dean of Student Affairs: ANTOINE GERJESS
Librarian: SAMEERA BASHIR

Library of 70,000 vols
Number of teachers: 350
Number of students: 2,550

Publications: *Al-Inaa* (irregular), *Al-Markab* (annually), *Chronos* (2 a year), *Hawliyat* (annually), *Revue Médicale Libanaise* (4 a year)

DEANS

Faculty of Arts and Social Sciences: NADIM NAIMY
Faculty of Business Administration: KARIM NASR (acting)
Faculty of Engineering: MICHEL NAJJAR
Faculty of Health Sciences: NADIM KARAM
Faculty of Medicine: CAMILLE NASSAR
Faculty of Sciences: MUCHEL NAJJAR
St George Faculty of Postgraduate Medical Education: CAMILLE NASSAR
St John of Damascus Institute of Theology: Bishop PAUL YAZIGI
Lebanese Academy of Fine Arts: GEORGES HADDAD

UNIVERSITÉ LIBANAISE

Place du Musée, Beirut
Telephone: (1) 612624
Fax: (1) 612572
E-mail: sgul@ul.edu.lb
Internet: www.ul.edu.lb

Founded 1951
State control
Languages of instruction: Arabic, French, English
Academic year: October to June

Rector: Dr IBRAHIM KOBEISSI
Secretary-General: MOHAMAD EL BABA
Librarian: DINA SUKKAR

Number of teachers: 3,118
Number of students: 69,627

Publications: *Dirassat* (annually), *Hannoun* (annually), *Pedagogic Research* (annually), *Social Sciences* (annually)

DEANS

Faculty of Agronomy: Dr MOUSTAFA MROUEH
Faculty of Dentistry: Dr FADIA ABOU DAGHER
Faculty of Economics and Business Administration: Dr NASRALLAH NASRALLAH
Faculty of Engineering: Dr MOHAMAD ZEAÏTER
Faculty of Law, Political and Administrative Sciences: Dr FARÈS KERBAGE
Faculty of Literature and Humanities: Dr RIAD KASSEM
Faculty of Medical Sciences: Dr PHILIPPE CHEDID
Faculty of Pedagogy: Dr ABDEL RAOUF SENNO
Faculty of Pharmacy: Dr AZIZ GAHCHANE
Faculty of Public Health: Dr ELIAS CHAMOUM
Faculty of Sciences: Dr ALI MNEIMNEH
Faculty of Tourism: Dr MOHAMAD CHAÏA
Institute of Fine Arts: Dr HACHEM EL-AYOUBI
Institute of Social Sciences: Dr NASSIF NASSAR
University Institute of Technology: Dr ALI ISMAIL

ATTACHED INSTITUTES

Institute of Legal Information: Dir Dr PHILIPPE NABHANE.

UNIVERSITÉ SAINT-ESPRIT DE KASLIK

POB 446, Jounieh
Telephone: (9) 934444
Fax: (9) 642333
E-mail: rectorat@usek.edu.lb
Internet: www.usek.edu.lb

Founded 1950
Private control (Lebanese Maronite Order of Monks)
Languages of instruction: French, English, Arabic
Academic year: October to July

Chancellor: Abbé ÉLIAS KHALIFE
Rector: Père ANTOINE AL AHMAR
Vice-Rectors: Abbé PAUL NAAMAN (First Vice-Rector), Père ANTOINE AL-AHMAR (Administration), Père GEORGES HOBEIKA (External Relations and Research)
Secretary-General: Père PIERRE BOU ZEIDAN
Librarian: Père JOSEPH MOUKARZEL

Library of 250,000 vols
Number of teachers: 620
Number of students: 5,180

Publications: *Actes de Colloques tenus à l'Université Saint-Esprit de Kaslik*, *Annales de Philosophie et des Sciences Humaines* (annually), *Annales de Recherches Scientifiques* (annually), *Bibliothèque de l'Université Saint-Esprit de Kaslik*, *Bulletin de l'Université Saint-Esprit de Kaslik* (2 a year), *Cahiers Annuels* (annually), *Parole de l'Orient* (annually), *Revue de la Faculté des Beaux Arts* (annually), *Revue Juridique* (annually)

DEANS

Faculty of Agricultural Sciences: Fr JOSEPH WAKIM
Faculty of Business Administration and Commercial Sciences: Fr KARAM RIZK
Faculty of Fine Arts: ALEXIS MOUZARKEL
Faculty of Law: Dr President JOSEPH CHAOUL
Faculty of Literature: Dr ANTOINE NOUJAIM
Faculty of Medicine: Fr GÉDÉON MOHASSEB
Faculty of Music: Fr LOUIS HAJJE
Faculty of Philosophy and Human Sciences: Fr JEAN AKIKI
Faculty of Sciences and Computer Engineering: Fr ANTOINE AL-AHMAR
Pontifical Faculty of Theology: Fr THOMAS MOUHANNA

DIRECTORS

Institute of History: Dr ANTOINE NOUJAIM
Institute of Liturgy: Fr AYOUB CHAHWAN
Institute of Nursing: Dr JEAN-CLAUDE LAHOUD
Institute of Sacred Art: Fr ABDO BADWI
Department of Architecture: ALEXIS MOUZARKEL
Department of Graphic Design: ELIE KHOURY
Department of Interior Design: PIERRE HAGE BOUTROS
Department of Visual and Scenic Arts: PAUL ZGHEIB

UNIVERSITÉ SAINT JOSEPH

Rue de Damas, BP 17-5208, Mar Mikhaël, Beirut 1104 2020
Telephone: (1) 421000
Fax: (1) 421001
E-mail: rectorat@usj.edu.lb
Internet: www.usj.edu.lb

Founded 1875
Private control (Jesuit)
Languages of instruction: French, Arabic, English
Academic year: September to June (2 semesters)

Rector: Rev. Fr RENÉ CHAMUSSY
Vice-Rector for Admin.: Rev. Fr BRUNO SION
Vice-Rector for Arabic and Islamic Studies: AHYAF SINNO
Vice-Rector for Research: MOUNIR CHAMOUN
Vice-Rector for Int. Relations: Dr ANTOINE HOKAYEM
Secr.-Gen.: HENRI AWIT

Library: see Libraries and Archives
Number of teachers: 1,602
Number of students: 10,832

Publications: *ACES–Actualités Cliniques et Scientifiques* (dental medicine, 2 a year), *Annales de la Faculté de Droit* (irreg.), *Annales de Géographie–Géosphères* (annual), *Annales d'Histoire—Tempora* (annual), *Annales de l'Institut de Langues et de Traduction—Al-Kimiya* (annual), *Annales de l'Institut de Lettres Orientales* (annual), *Annales de Lettres Françaises—Acanthe* (annual), *Annales de Philosophie—Iris* (annual), *Annales de Psychologie et des Sciences de l'Education—Psyécho* (annual), *Annales de Sociologie et d'Anthropologie* (annual), *Bulletin Annuel de la Faculté de Médecine* (annual), *Bulletin intérieur de l'Institut libanais d'éducateurs* (annual), *Chroniques du CEMAM* (modern Arab world, annual), *Chroniques Politiques* (annual), *Chroniques Sociales* (irregul), *Conférences de l'ALDEC* (annually), *Enseignement Continu Post-universitaire* (medicine, annually), *Etudes de droit libanais* (irreg.), *Hommes et Sociétés du Proche-Orient* (annual), *Journées d'Etudes Post-universitaires* (midwifery, annual), *L'Orient des Dieux* (annual), *Mélanges de l'Université Saint-Joseph* (annual), *Proche Orient Chrétien* (2 a year), *Proche Orient, Etudes Economiques* (irreg.), *Proche Orient, Etudes Juridiques* (irreg.), *Proche Orient, Etudes en Management* (irreg.), *Publications techniques et scientifiques de l'Ecole supérieure d'ingé-*

nieurs de Beyrouth (irreg.), *Regards* (theatre, audiovisual studies and cinema, annual), *Revue de l'Institut Libanais d'Educateurs* (annual), *Travaux et Jours* (2 a year)

DEANS AND DIRECTORS

Faculty of Arts and Human Sciences: JARJOURA HARDANE
Faculty of Business Admin.: TONI GIBEILY
Faculty of Dentistry: Dr NADA NAAMAN
Faculty of Economics: HENRI AWIT
Faculty of Education Sciences: NADA NASR
Faculty of Eng.: WAJDI NAJEM
Faculty of Law and Political Science: FAYEZ HAGE-CHAHINE
Faculty of Medicine: Dr FERNAND DAGHER
Faculty of Nursing: CLAIRE ZABLIT
Faculty of Pharmacy: DOLLA SARKIS
Faculty of Religious Studies: Rev. Fr LOUIS BOISSET
Faculty of Sciences: TOUFIC RIZK
School of Agro-Industrial Engineers: YOLLA GHORRA
School of Mediterranean Agricultural Engineers: YOLLA GHORRA
School of Eng.: WAJDI NAJEM
School of Laboratory Technicians in Medical Analysis: MARIE-GABRIELLE HINDI
School of Midwifery: NAYLA DOUGHANE
Lebanese School of Social Work: MAY HAZZAZ
School of Translators and Interpreters of Beirut: HENRI AWAISS
Higher Institute of Insurance Sciences: NADI JAZZAR
Higher Institute of Religious Studies: Rev. Fr. FADI DAOU
Higher Institute of Speech Therapy: Dr KAMAL KALLAB
Institute of Business Admin.: PHILIPPE FATTAL
Nat. Institute of Communication and Information: HADY SAWAYA
Lebanese Institute for Educators: GARINE ZOHRABIAN
Institute of Health and Social Protection Management: TOBIE ZAKHIA
Institute of Islamic-Christian Studies: Rev. Fr SALAH ABOU JAOUDÉ
Institute of Languages and Translation: HENRI AWAISS
Institute of Oriental Arts: AHYAF SINNO
Institute of Physiotherapy: PIERRE FILFILI
Institute of Political Science: FADIA KIWAN
Institute of Psychomotricity: CARLA ABI ZEID DAOU
Institute of Theatrical, Audiovisual and Cinema Studies: PAUL MATTAR
Centre of Banking Studies: FADWA MANSOUR
Open Univ.: MOUNIR CHAMOUN

ATTACHED RESEARCH INSTITUTES

Centre for Arab-Christian Research and Documentation: Dir Rev. Fr SAMIR KHALIL SAMIR.

Centre for Computer Modelling and Information Technology: Dir MAROUN CHAMOUN.

Centre for Economic Documentation and Research: Dir IRMA MAJDALANI.

Centre for European Union Studies: Dir CHIBLI MALLAT.

Centre for Modern Arab World Research: Dir CHRISTOPHE-HENRI VARIN.

Centre for Strategic Studies and Research: Dir PIERRE VALLAUD.

Centre for Studies and Research in Arabic Terminology: Dir MAY HADDAD.

Centre for the Study and Interpretation of Religious Fact: Dir GRACE HOMSY.

Centre for the Study of Law in the Arab World: Dir ANTOINE KHAIR.

Centre for the Study of Markets and Distribution in the Middle East: Dir CAMILLE ASSAF.

Centre for Telecommunications and the Electrical Industry: Dir RAGI GHOSN.

Centre for Water and the Environment: Dir WAJDI NAJEM.

Chemistry Centre: Dir TOUFIC RIZK.

Euro-Lebanese Intercultural Centre: Dir Rev. Fr LOUIS BOISSET.

Francis Hours Centre for Prehistory and Archaeology: Dir LEVON NORDIGUIAN.

Laboratory of Calcified Tissues: Dir NADA NAAMAN.

Laboratory for Documentation and Research in Tourism: Dir LILIANE BARAKAT.

Laboratory of Experimental Psychology: Project Dir ANTOINE ROUMANOS.

Laboratory of Molecular and Cytogenetic Biology: Dir Rev. Fr JOHAN DE WIT.

Laboratory for University Technology: Dir NADA NASR.

Lebanese Centre of Building Studies and Research: Dir MUHSEN ELIE RAHAL.

Louis Pouzet Centre for the Study of Ancient and Medieval Civilizations: Dir EMMA GANNAGÉ.

Mapping Laboratory: Dir PIERRE-CHARLES GERARD.

Medical Computer Science Unit: Dir Dr RAMZI ASHOUSH.

Medical Genetic Unit: Dir ANDRÉ MEGARBANE.

Michel Henri Studies Centre: Dir JAD HATEM.

Molecular Biology Laboratory: Dir DOLLA SARKIS.

New Technologies Teaching Unit: Dir STEFAN BAZAN.

Professional Centre for Mediation: Dir JOHANNA BOURJEILI.

Research Centre for Surgical Sciences: Dir VICTOR GEBANA.

Teledetection Laboratory: Dir JANNINE SOMMA.

Toxicology Laboratory: Dir HAYAT TANNOUS.

University Ethics Centre: Dir Rev. Fr JEAN DUCRUET.

University Observatory of Socio-economic Reality: Dir CHOGHIH KASPARIAN.

Colleges

Académie Libanaise des Beaux-Arts: POB 55251, Sin-El-Fil, Beirut; tel. (1) 480056; f. 1937; schools of architecture, decorative arts, publicity, plastic arts; library: 4,300 vols; 180 teachers; 600 students; Chair. Mgr GEORGES KHODR; Dir-Gen. GEORGES HADDAD.

Haigazian University: POB 11-1748, Beirut; tel. (1) 349230; fax (1) 350926; e-mail rartinian@haigazian.edu.lb; internet www.haigazian.edu.lb; f. 1955; private control; academic year: October to June; BA and BSc in Arabic Studies, Armenian Studies, Biology, Business Administration, Chemistry, Christian Education, Computer Science, Education, English Literature, History, Hospitality Management, Mathematics, Medical Laboratory Technology, Physics, Political Science, Psychology; M.A. programmes in Educational Administration and Supervision, General Psychology and Clinical Psychology; MBA; library: libraries (Armenian, Arabic and English) of 66,000 vols; 63 teachers (23 full-time, 40 part-time); 743 students; Pres. Rev. PAUL HAIDOSTIAN; Deans ARDA EKMEKJI (Arts and Sciences), FADI ASRAWI (Business and Economics); Librarian ZEVART TANIELIAN; publs *Haigazian Herald* (4 a year), *Armenological Review* (annually), *In Spirit* (2 a year), *Business News* (4 a year), *Haigazian Focus* (annually).

Middle East University: POB 90481, Jdeidet El Matn 1202-2040; tel. (1) 685800; fax (1) 684800; e-mail meu@meu.edu.lb; internet www.meu.edu.lb; f. 1939; private control; language of instruction: English; academic year October to June; offers degrees in business administration, computer science, education (elementary and secondary), religion; MBA; also diploma courses; library: 20,000 vols; 29 teachers (13 full-time, 16 part-time); 200 students; Pres. S. MYKLEBUST; Registrar S. ISSA.

Near East School of Theology: POB 13–5780, Beirut 1102 2070; tel. (1) 354194; fax (1) 347129; e-mail nest.adm@inco.com.lb; internet www.pcusa.org/pcusa/wmd/globaled/institutes/nest.htm; f. 1932; a Protestant ecumenical institution of higher learning; offers theological education and pastoral training to qualified candidates for church ministries, as well as to lay candidates regardless of church affiliation, sex, race or nationality; library: 40,000 vols; 7 teachers; 36 students; Pres. Dr MARY MIKHAEL; publ. *Theological Review*.

LESOTHO

The Higher Education System

The Roman Catholic Hierarchy of South Africa founded Pius XII College in 1945, while Lesotho was part of the British protectorate of Basutoland. Pius XII College became known as University of Basutoland, Bechuanaland and Swaziland in 1963, and after the Kingdom of Lesotho was declared an independent state in 1966 it was renamed University of Botswana, Lesotho and Swaziland. In 1975 the University of Botswana, Lesotho and Swaziland was divided into separate national universities and the branch at Roma, Lesotho was reconstituted as National University of Lesotho. Higher education is funded by the central Government, which accounts for about 90% of the National University of Lesotho's income. Some 3,266 students were enrolled at the National University of Lesotho, at Roma, in 2002. A total of 4,582 students were enrolled at tertiary-level institutions in 1998/99.

Governance of the National University of Lesotho consists of the Council (appointed by the Head of State), Senate, Congregation, Student Union, non-academic staff and external members. The Head of State is the Chancellor of the University, and the Vice-Chancellor, Pro-Vice Chancellor, Registrar, Bursar and Librarian are the primary management staff, responsible for the day-to-day affairs of the university. Overall responsibility for Policy lies with the Council, and the Senate oversees all academic affairs. Deans of Faculty and Directors of Institutes are the heads of academic units.

Admission to the National University of Lesotho is on the basis of the Cambridge Overseas School Certificate in the first or the second division. A Diploma is awarded in theology and agriculture after two years, otherwise the undergraduate Bachelors degree last four years, divided into two two-year cycles. Award of the Bachelors of Law requires a further two years of study. The postgraduate Masters degree lasts two years and is awarded in arts, science and education. Doctoral degree programmes are available in agriculture, education and the humanities, and last for two years after the award of Masters.

Technical and vocational education consists of a College Certificate or Diploma. Courses are offered by a number of different institutions, including home economics and craft schools, trade schools, Lesotho Agricultural College and Lerotholi Polytechnic.

Learned Societies

BIBLIOGRAPHY, LIBRARY SCIENCE AND MUSEOLOGY

Lesotho Library Association: Private Bag A26, Maseru; tel. 213420; fax 340000; f. 1978; 60 individual mems, 22 institutions; Chair. S. M. MOHAI; Sec. N. TAOLE; publ. *Journal* (annually).

LANGUAGE AND LITERATURE

Alliance Française: cnr Pioner Rd and Kingsway, Private Bag A106, Maseru 100; tel. 325722; fax 310475; e-mail maseru@alliance.org.za; internet www.alliancefrancaise.co.za/lesotho/; offers courses and exams in French language and culture and promotes cultural exchange with France.

Research Institutes

AGRICULTURE, FISHERIES AND VETERINARY SCIENCE

Department of Agricultural Research: POB 829, Maseru 100; tel. 22312395; research station at Maseru and field experimental stations.

NATURAL SCIENCES

Physical Sciences

Geological Survey Department: Dept of Mines and Geology, POB 750, Maseru 100; tel. 323750; fax 310498; Dir MATSEPO C. RAMAISA.

Libraries and Archives

Maseru

Lesotho National Archives: POB 52, Maseru 100; tel. 312047; fax 310194; f. 1958; undertakes research and preservation of national documents since 1869; Senior Archivist M. QHOBOSHEANE.

Lesotho National Library Service: POB 985, Maseru 100; tel. 323100; fax 310194; f. 1976; 30,000 vols; Senior Librarian M. MABATHOANA (acting).

University

NATIONAL UNIVERSITY OF LESOTHO

PO Roma 180
Telephone: 340601
Fax: 340000
E-mail: registrar@nul.ls
Internet: www.nul.ls

Founded 1945 as Pius XII College, became campus of University of Botswana, Lesotho and Swaziland 1966; present name 1975
Language of instruction: English
Academic year: August to May

Chancellor: HM King LETSIE III
Vice-Chancellor: Dr T. H. MOTHIBE
Pro-Vice-Chancellor: Dr N. L. MAHAO
Registrar: J. M. HLALELE
Librarian: A. M. LEBOTSA

Library of 205,150 vols, 500 periodicals
Number of teachers: 171
Number of students: 3,266

Publications: *Announcer*, *Lesotho Law Journal*, *Light in the Night*, *Mohlomi Journal* (History), *Mophatlatsi*, *NUL News*, *NUL Research Journal*

DEANS

Faculty of Agriculture: Prof. P. M. SUTTON
Faculty of Education: Dr E. M. MARUPING
Faculty of Health Science: Prof. P. O. ODONKOR
Faculty of Humanities: Rev. J. KHUTLANG
Faculty of Law: O. M. OWORI
Faculty of Postgraduate Studies: (vacant)
Faculty of Science and Technology: Prof. K. K. GOPINATHAN
Faculty of Social Sciences: Prof. S. G. HOOHLO

DIRECTORS

Institute of Education: S. T. MOTLOMELO
Institute of Extra-Mural Studies: Prof. D. BRAIMOH, Prof. Y. D. BWATWA, Dr A. M. SETSABI
Institute of Labour Studies: S. SANTHO (acting)
Institute of South African Studies: Dr M. MOCHEBELELE

PROFESSORS

Faculty of Agriculture:
BRAIDE, F. G.
EBENENE, A. C.
OKELW-UMA, I.
SUTTON, P. M.

Faculty of Education:
MATS'ELA, Z. A., Language and Social Education

Faculty of Law:
KUMAR, U., Private Law

Faculty of Postgraduate Studies:
BALOGUN, T. A.

Faculty of Science and Technology:
GOPINATHAN, K. K., Physics
MALU, O.

Faculty of Social Sciences:
EJIGOU, A., Statistics

Institute of Southern African Studies:
PRASAD, G.

College

Lesotho Agricultural College: Box 139, Maseru; tel. 322484; fax 400022; f.1955; state control; language of instruction: English; academic year: August to May (two semesters); library: 60,000 vols; Principal Dr S. L. RALITS'OELE.

LIBERIA

The Higher Education System

From 1821 onwards emancipated slaves from the southern states of the USA were resettled along the West Guinean coast, and in 1847 the independent sovereign state of Liberia was declared, with a Constitution based on that of the USA. Liberia College, the first institution of higher education, was founded in 1862 and became a university in 1951. In 1889 Cuttington University College was founded by the Episcopal Church in the USA, by whom it is still maintained in conjunction with the Episcopal Church in Liberia. Other institutions of higher education include the William V. S. Tubman College of Technology (founded 1970; formerly Harper Technical College) and the Booker Washington Institute (founded 1929). There are also junior colleges offering two-year degree programmes. In the academic year 1999/2000 there were 44,107 students enrolled in university-level institutions and 15,631 students enrolled in post-secondary and vocational education.

Universities must be chartered by the Ministry of Education but higher education in Liberia is decentralized in that each institution is autonomous and governed by a Board of Trustees. The Minister of Education is the Government representative on each Board of Trustees, which is advised by an Administrative Council, comprising all academic and administrative staff, two elected faculty members and two elected student representatives. The Council also advises the President of the University and co-ordinates the day-to-day running of the institution. The State provides funding to both public and private institutions and also offers financial aid to students, which covers half the cost of tuition and study materials.

Applicants must hold the Senior High School certificates to gain admission to higher education and are also required to sit entrance examinations in English and Mathematics. Students at junior colleges study for the two-year Associate degree and university undergraduates take a four-year Bachelors degree. The Bachelors of Law degree is awarded after five years and medical degrees last seven years. Postgraduate degrees, such as the Masters, are available on a limited basis.

In addition to junior colleges, post-secondary technical and vocational education is offered by technical colleges.

Learned Societies

LANGUAGE AND LITERATURE

Alliance Française: 28 Payne Ave, POB 10, 3016 Sinkor 14th/15th Sts, 1000 Monrovia 10; tel. and fax 226888; e-mail alliancefr_monrovia@yahoo.com; offers courses and exams in French language and culture and promotes cultural exchange with France.

Society of Liberian Authors: POB 2468, Monrovia; f. 1959; aims to encourage general interest in writing and encourage literature in local vernacular; publ. *Kaafa* (2 a year).

TECHNOLOGY

Geological, Mining and Metallurgical Society of Liberia: POB 902, Monrovia; f. 1964; 78 mems; Pres. CLETUS S. WOTORSON; Sec. Dr MEDIE-HEMIE NEUFVILLE; publ. *Bulletin* (2 a year).

Liberia Arts and Crafts Association: POB 885, Monrovia; f. 1964; 14 mems; aims to encourage artists and craftsmen through exhibitions, sales, workshops; Pres. R. VANJAH RICHARDS.

Research Institutes

AGRICULTURE, FISHERIES AND VETERINARY SCIENCE

Central Agriculture Research Institute: Mailbag 3929, Suakoko; tel. 223443; f. 1946; under Ministry of Agriculture; research on crops, animal husbandry, horticulture, soil, and inland fisheries; bilateral and international agencies; service centre for supply of improved seeds, plant material and animals; library of 8,700 vols; Dir WALTER T. WILES; publ. *CARI News*.

MEDICINE

Liberian Institute for Biomedical Research: POB 10-1012, 1000 Monrovia 10; f. 1952, renamed 1975; administrative centre for biomedical research; conducts research and attracts research projects; Dir Dr ALOYSIUS P. HANSON.

NATURAL SCIENCES

Biological Sciences

Nimba Research Laboratory: c/o Lamco J. V. Operating Co., Grassland, Nimba, Robertsfield; (POB 69, Monrovia); f. 1962; under supervision of Nimba Research Committee of International Union for Conservation of Nature and Natural Resources, in conjunction with UNESCO; biological and ecological exploration and conservation in the Mount Nimba region and conservation; library of 100 vols and access to LAMCO library, Yekepa; Chair. KAI CURRY-LINDAHL.

Libraries and Archives

Monrovia

Government Public Library: Ashmun St, Monrovia; f. 1959; 15,000 vols.

Liberian Information Service Library: POB 9021, Monrovia; reference.

University of Liberia Libraries: University of Liberia, POB 9020, Monrovia; tel. 222448; f. 1862; general library and separate law library; 107,384 vols, 2,118 periodicals; Dir ANNABEL U. TINGBA (acting).

Museums and Art Galleries

Cape Mount

Tubman Centre of African Cultures: Cape Mount; local art, history and ethnology.

Monrovia

Africana Museum: Cuttington University College, c/o Episcopal Church Office, POB 277, Monrovia; f. 1960; items from Liberia and neighbouring countries; traditional arts and crafts, ethnographical material; 2 traditional houses representing Kpelle and Grebo architecture; depository for archaeological collections; serves as a teaching collection for the College and as a research facility for visiting scholars; specialized research library in the college; Dir EDWARD O. N'GELE.

National Museum: Broad and Buchanan Sts, POB 3223, Monrovia; f. 1962; Liberian history, art and ethnography; Dir BURDIE UREY-WEEKS.

University

UNIVERSITY OF LIBERIA

POB 9020, Monrovia

Telephone: 224670

Fax: 226418

Founded as Liberia College 1862; university status 1951

State control

Language of instruction: English

Academic year: March to December (two semesters)

President: Dr BEN ROBERTS

Vice-President for Academic Affairs: Dr FREDERICK S. GREGBE

Vice-President for Administration: Dr WINGROVE C. DWAMINA (acting)

Dean of Admissions: MOORE T. WORRELL

Libraries: see Libraries and Archives

Number of teachers: 260

Number of students: 3,400

Publications: *Liberian Law Journal*, *This Week on Campus*, *University of Liberia Catalogue and Announcements*, *University of Liberia Journal*, *Varsity Pilot*

DEANS

College of Agriculture and Forestry: Dr BISMARCK REEVES

College of Business and Public Administration: Prof. WILLIE BELLEH Jr

A. M. Douglas College of Medicine: Dr TAIWO DARAMOLA

College of Social Sciences and Humanities (Liberia College): Dr BEN A. ROBERTS

College of Science and Technology: Prof. FREDERICK D. HUNDER (acting)
Louis Arthur Grimes School of Law: Cllr LUVENIA ASH-THOMPSON
William V. S. Tubman Teachers College: Dr JOSHUA D. CLEON
Student Affairs: HARRISON MLE-SIE WOART

CO-ORDINATORS OF SCHOOLS
School of Pharmacy: Dr ARTHUR S. LEWIS
Graduate School of Education Administration: Dr HENRY KWEKWE
Graduate School of Regional Planning: Dr JAMES N. KOLLIE Sr

Colleges

Booker Washington Institute: POB 273, Kakata; tel. 331048; f. 1929; state control; 52 teachers; 750 students; agricultural and industrial courses; secondary high school courses; basic computer literacy; Principal MULBAH JACKOLLIE.

Cuttington University College: c/o Episcopal Church Building, POB 10-277, 1000 Monrovia 10; tel. 227413; fax 226059; e-mail cuttingtonuniversity@yahoo.com; internet cuttington.org; f. 1889; maintained by intl donors, incl. Episcopal Church in the USA, Episcopal Church of Liberia; applied for subsidies from the Liberian Government; language of instruction: English; academic year September to June; library stock subjected to looting during civil war (1990–1996), 250 periodicals; 110 teachers; 1,545 undergraduate students, 225 graduate students; Pres. Dr HENRIQUE F. TOKPA; Vice-Pres. (Academic) Dr JAMES E. MOCK; Vice-Pres. for Administration Dr CHARLES K. MULBAH; Dean of Students HILARY W. COLLINS; Registrar and Dean of Admissions BENGALY M. KAMARA; Librarian FORKPA H. KEMAH.

William V. S. Tubman College of Technology: POB 3570, Monrovia; f. 1970; state control; language of instruction: English; academic year: March to December; 21 teachers; 200 students; three-year associate degree course in engineering technology; Pres. Dr THEOPHILUS N. SONPON; Dean/Admin. Dr SOLOMON S. B. RUSSELL.

LIBYA

The Higher Education System

All current institutions of higher education have been founded since Libya became an independent kingdom in 1951. (Following a military coup in 1969 it became known as the Libyan Arab Republic and since 1986 it has been known as the Great Socialist People's Libyan Arab Jamhariya.) The oldest university is University of Garyounis, which was founded in 1957 as the Faculty of Arts and Education, Benghazi, became the University of Benghazi in 1973 and adopted its current name in 1976. Both University of Garyounis and Al-Fateh University (also founded 1957; formerly Faculty of Science, Tripoli) were part of the former federal University of Libya until 1973. In 2002/03 there were an estimated 375,028 students in recognized institutions of higher education. The Secretariat for Higher Education is the responsible body for higher education, which is financed from the State budget. However, due to the expansion in student numbers and growing pressure on Government funding, greater autonomy has been granted to local public administrations in allowing the establishment of new, mostly private universities.

A People's Committee, headed by a Dean (who acts as the Secretary), is the management body of each University. The main academic units are the Faculty and the Department. Faculties are also governed by a People's Committee, the Secretary of which represents the Faculty on the University People's Committee. Heads of Department are members of the Faculty People's Committee. Students sit on University and Faculty People's Committees.

Admission to higher education is on the basis of the Secondary Education Certificate, with different pass marks depending on the type of institution or degree applied for. Most undergraduate Bachelors degrees from universities require four years of study, but architecture, engineering (both five years) and medicine (six years) require longer. There are also technical and vocational institutions which offer four to five-year Bachelors degrees in the sciences, technology and engineering. The main postgraduate degrees are the Masters and Doctorate. The Masters is a two-year programme of study following award of the Bachelors, and study for the Doctorate also lasts two years, culminating in public defence of a thesis.

Technical and vocational training at post-secondary level is offered by technical institutes.

Learned Societies

LANGUAGE AND LITERATURE

British Council: c/o British Embassy, 24th Fl., Burj al Fatah, POB 4206 Tripoli; tel. (21) 3351473; fax (21) 3351471; e-mail info.libya@britishcouncil-ly.org; internet www.britishcouncil.org/libya; offers courses and exams in English language and British culture and promotes cultural exchange with the UK; Dir CARL REUTER.

Union of Libyan Authors, Writers and Artists: POB 1017, Tripoli; f. 1980; all fields of culture, education and art; 800 mems; library of 4,000 vols; Pres. AMIN MAZEN.

Research Institutes

GENERAL

National Academy for Scientific Research: POB 12312, Tripoli; tel. (21) 3339101; fax (21) 3338412; f. 1981 to conduct, finance and support scientific studies and research in all branches of knowledge; 330 mems; library of 19,000 vols; Dir-Gen. Dr TAHER H. JEHEMI; publs *Al-Fikr Al-Arabi*, *Al-Fikr Al-Istratiji Al-Arabi*, *Al-Ilm Wa Atteknolojia*.

HISTORY, GEOGRAPHY AND ARCHAEOLOGY

Libyan Studies Centre: POB 5070, Sidi Munaider, Tripoli; tel. (21) 3333996; fax (21) 3331616; f. 1978; historical studies and documentation; 140 mems; library of 100,000 vols, 700 periodicals, 3,000 MSS, 60,000 photographs; Dir Dr MOHAMED T. JERARY; publs *Al Insaf* (annually), *Al-Kunnasha* (The Scrap Book, 2 a year), *As-Shahid* (The Martyr, annually), *Al-Wathaiq wa al-Makhtutat* (annually), *Index of Libyan Periodicals* (annually), *Majallat al-Buhuth at-Tarikhia* (2 a year).

Libraries and Archives

Benghazi

National Library of Libya: POB 9127, Benghazi; tel. (61) 9097073; e-mail nat-lib-libya@hotmail.com; f. 1973; Gen. Sec. MOHAMMAD A. ESHOWEIHDI.

Public Library: Shar'a 'Umar al-Mukhtar, Benghazi; f. 1955; 11,000 vols; Librarian AHMAD GALLAL.

University of Garyounis Library: POB 1308, Benghazi; tel. (61) 87633; f. 1955; 294,844 vols; 2,170 periodicals; 7 depts, including 2,360 MSS, 70,000 documents, 10,000 microfilms and rare books; Chief Librarian AHMED GALLAL; publs available for exchange.

Tripoli

Agricultural Research Centre Library: POB 2480, Tripoli; f. 1973; 6,000 vols, 220 periodicals; Librarian LAMIS AL-GABSI.

Government Library: 14 Shar'a al-Jazair, Tripoli; f. 1917; 35,500 vols; Librarian BASHIR AL-BADRI.

National Archives: Castello, Tripoli; tel. (21) 40166; internet www.nll.8m.com; f. 1928; controlled by Department of Antiquities, General People's Committee for Education, Tripoli; extensive collection of documents relating to the history of Libya mostly in Turkish from the Ottoman period; 5 libraries, 55,000 vols; Curator ABDULAALI OWN; publ. *Libya Antiqua*.

Museums and Art Galleries

Shahat

Department of Antiquities, Shahat (Cyrene): responsible for archaeological sites from Shahat west to the frontiers of Tocra, east to Msa'd; Controller BRAYEK ATTIYA.

Tripoli

Department of Antiquities: Assarai al-Hamra, Tripoli; responsible for all museums and archaeological sites in Libya; Pres. Dr ABDULLAH SHAIBOUB.

Museums controlled by the Department:

- **Apollonia Museum:** Marsa Soussa.
- **Archaeological, Natural History, Epigraphy, Prehistory and Ethnography Museums:** Assarai al-Hamra, Tripoli.
- **Benghazi Museum:** Benghazi; mausoleum of Omar el Mukhtar.
- **Cyrene Museum:** Cyrene (Shahat).
- **Gaigab Museum:** Gaigab (near Cyrene).
- **Germa Museum:** Germa (Fezean).
- **Islamic Museum:** Tripoli.
- **Leptis Magna Museum:** Leptis Magna.
- **Ptolemais Museum:** Tolmeitha.
- **Sabratha Museum of Antiquities:** Sabratha.
- **Tauchira Museum:** Tokra.
- **Zanzur Museum:** Zanzur (Tripoli).

Universities

AL-ARAB MEDICAL UNIVERSITY

POB 18251, Benghazi
Telephone: (61) 225007
Fax: (61) 222195

Founded 1984
State control
Languages of instruction: Arabic, English
Academic year: September to May

President: Dr AMER RAHIL
Registrar: ABU-BAKER AMMARI
Librarian: MOHAMMED EL-SAID

Library of 30,000 vols, 600 periodicals
Number of teachers: 256
Number of students: 1,615

Publication: *Garyounis Medical Journal*

DEANS

Faculty of Dentistry: Dr ABDULLA OMAR DOURDA
Faculty of Medicine: Dr ABDUL HADI MOUSSA
Faculty of Pharmacy: Dr ABDUSALAM A. AL-MAYHOUB

AL-FATEH UNIVERSITY

POB 13482, Tripoli
Telephone: (22) 605441
Fax: (22) 605460
E-mail: m.alfituri@hotmail.com
Founded 1957
State control
Language of instruction: Arabic
Academic year: September to June
President: Dr MOHAMED L. FARHAT
Vice-President: Dr NAJAH S. ELGABSI
Secretary-General: Dr YOUNIS ALAGILI
General Registrar: Dr AWEDAT GANDOUR
Librarian: Dr MOHAMED ABDUL JALEEL
Number of teachers: 3,200
Number of students: 75,000
Publications: *Bulletin of the Faculty of Education*, *Bulletin of the Faculty of Engineering*, *Bulletin of the Faculty of Law*, *Libyan Journal of Agriculture*, *Libyan Journal of Sciences*

DEANS

Faculty of Agriculture: Dr AMER ELMIGRI
Faculty of Economics and Political Science: Dr HAFAD SHAILI
Faculty of Education: Dr TOHAMI TARHOUNI
Faculty of Engineering: Dr ABDULHAMID ASHOUR
Faculty of Fine Arts: Dr HAMID
Faculty of Law: Dr OMAR HUSSIN
Faculty of Physical Education: Dr SADDIK EL KABOLI
Faculty of Science: Dr OMAR ELHAJI
Faculty of Veterinary Medicine: Dr SALAH ZWAI (acting)

AL-FATEH UNIVERSITY FOR MEDICAL SCIENCES

POB 13040, Tripoli
Telephone: (21) 3336010
Fax: (21) 3602971
Founded 1986
State control
Languages of instruction: Arabic, English
Faculties of Dentistry, Medical Technology, Medicine and Pharmacy.

AL-TAHADI UNIVERSITY

POB 674, Sirt
Telephone: (54) 60636
Fax: (54) 62152
E-mail: tahdi51@hotmail.com
Founded 1989
State control
President: ABOULGASIM AL-SHAIKH
Faculties of Agriculture, Arts, Economics and Political Science, Engineering, Mechanical and Electrical Engineering, Medicine and Science.

BRIGHT STAR UNIVERSITY OF TECHNOLOGY

POB 58158, Ajdabia
Telephone: (64) 23012
Fax: (21) 600185
Founded 1981
State control
Language of instruction: Arabic
Academic year: October to June
Chancellor: Engr ALI SALEH ELFAZZANI
Registrar: Engr MANSOOR MASOOD FARAJ
Chief of Administration: Engr ABD ELSALAM ELZAROUG
Librarian: IBRAHIM MOHAMED AMIR
Number of teachers: 67
Number of students: 1,160

HEADS OF DEPARTMENTS

Basic Engineering Science: Dr SHAHADA ELASADI
Chemical Engineering: Dr MOHAMED ABD ELAZIZ
Electrical and Electronic Engineering: Dr SAMI ESSA MOUSA
Mechanical and Production Engineering: Dr ABD ELATIF ELGIZAWI
Petroleum Engineering: Dr MUSTAFA AWAD

DERNA UNIVERSITY

Derna
Founded 1995
State control
Languages of instruction: Arabic, English
Faculties of Accountancy and Economics, Fine Arts and Architecture, Law, Medical Technology and Social Sciences.

UNIVERSITY OF GARYOUNIS

POB 1308, Benghazi
Telephone: (61) 20148
Internet: www.garyounis.edu
Founded 1955 as University of Libya, renamed 1973, present name 1976
State control
Language of instruction: Arabic
Chancellor: Dr MUHAMID A. ALMAHDAWI
Registrar: MAHMUD M. FAKHRI
Library: see Libraries and Archives
Number of teachers: 610
Number of students: 15,000
Publications: various faculty bulletins.

DEANS

Faculty of Arts and Education: Dr FATHI AL-HARIM
Faculty of Economics: Dr ABDELGADIR AMIR
Faculty of Engineering: Dr BELAID EIKWARI
Faculty of Law: Dr SULMAN AL-GURISH
Faculty of Science: Dr MUHAMID EL-AWIME

UNIVERSITY OF MORAGAB

POB 40414-40937 Ain Zara
Telephone: (31) 629365
Fax: (31) 629366
Founded 1987
State control
Faculties of Economics, Education and Science, Engineering, Law and Literature.

NASIR UNIVERSITY

POB 48222, Al-Khums Tripoli
Telephone: (325) 660080
Fax: (325) 660048
Founded 1986
State control
Faculties of Arts, Economics and Political Science, Education and Science, Engineering, Law and Science.

OMAR AL-MUKHTAR UNIVERSITY

POB 991, Al-Bayda
Telephone: (84) 6310719
Fax: (84) 632233
Founded 1985
State control
President: ABDALLA A. M. ZAIED
Faculties of Agriculture, Engineering, Literature and Education, Science and Veterinary Medicine.

OPEN UNIVERSITY

POB 13375, Tripoli
Telephone: (21) 4625507
Fax: (21) 4625527
E-mail: info@libopenuniv.edu.org
Internet: www.libopenuniv.edu.org
Founded 1987
State control
Language of instruction: Arabic
Academic year: September to July
President: IBRAHIM ABU-FARWA
Number of teachers: 47
Number of students: 8,000
Faculties of Accountancy, Administration, Arabic, Economics, Education and Psychology, Geography, History, Islamic Studies, Law, Political Science, Sociology and Social Work; Dept of Continuing Education.

SEBHA UNIVERSITY

POB 18758, Sebha
Telephone: (71) 21575
Fax: (71) 29201
Founded 1983 from the Faculty of Education of Al-Fateh University
State control
Languages of instruction: Arabic, English
Academic year: October to August
Chancellor: Dr ABU BAKR ABDULLAH OTMAN
Vice-Chancellor: SALEM ABDULLAH SAID
Registrar: MISBAH AL-GHAWIL
Librarian: ZIDAN AL-BREIKY
Number of teachers: 280
Number of students: 3,000
Publications: *Al-Shifa* (medicine, annually), *Physical Education Magazine* (every 6 months)

DEANS

Faculty of Agriculture: Dr MOHAMMAD ABDUL KARIM
Faculty of Arts and Education: HAMED MASHMOOR
Faculty of Dentistry: Dr HASAN AL-BUSAIFY
Faculty of Economics and Accountancy: Dr BASHIR ABU-QILA
Faculty of Engineering and Technology: MOHAMMAD ARAHOOMA
Faculty of Medicine: Dr OMAR IBRAHIM AL-SHAIBANI
Faculty of Physical Education: ABDUL RAHMAN AL-ANSARI
Faculty of Science: Dr MOHAMMAD BASHIR HASAN

SEVENTH OF APRIL UNIVERSITY

POB 16418, Al-Zawia
Telephone: (23) 26882
Founded 1988
State control
Languages of instruction: Arabic, English
Faculties of Education, Engineering, Physical Education (women only) and Science.

Colleges

African Centre for Applied Research and Training in Social Development (ACARTSOD): POB 80606, Tripoli; tel. (21) 4835103; fax (21) 4835066; e-mail fituri_acartsod@hotmail.com; f. 1977 as an intergovernmental institution under the auspices of the UN Economic Comm. for Africa and the OAU; aims to promote and co-ordinate applied research and training in the field of social development at regional and sub-regional levels, organizes seminars, etc.; Deputy Exec. Dir Dr AHMED SAID FITURI; publs *ACARTSOD Newsletter* (2 a year), *African Social Challenges* (annually).

Higher Institute of Mechanical and Electrical Engineering: POB 61160, Hoon; tel. (57) 602841; fax (57) 602842; e-mail aisa_jadi@yahoo.com; f. 1976; BSc level studies; library: 22,000 vols, 100 periodicals; 48 teachers; 336 students; Dean AISA S. JADI.

Higher Institute of Technology: POB 68, Brack; tel. (71) 45300; fax (71) 27600; f. 1976; first degree courses in general sciences, medical technology, food technology and environmental sciences; library: 10,000 vols; 60 teachers; 500 students; Dean Dr ABDUSSALAM M. ALMETHNANI.

Islamic Arts and Crafts School: Shar'a 1 September, Tripoli; tel. (21) 3334315.

National Institute of Administration: POB 3651, Tripoli; tel. (21) 4623420; fax (21) 4623423; f. 1953; offers higher diploma in administration and accounting; library: 10,000 vols; 30 teachers; publ. *National Magazine of Administration*.

Posts and Telecommunications Institute: POB 2428, Tripoli; f. 1963; library: 510 vols; Dir K. MARABUTACI.

LIECHTENSTEIN

The Higher Education System

The Principality's first university was not founded until 1992 when the former Liechtensteinische Ingenieurschule (founded 1961; formerly Abendtechnikum Vaduz) achieved university status; it is now know as Hoschschule Liechtenstein (Liechtenstein University of Applied Sciences) and is a state-run institution. A private university, Universität für Humanwissenschaften (University of Human Sciences), was founded in Triesen in 1991 and there is also a publicly-funded music school in Vaduz. Many Liechtensteiners continue their studies at universities in Austria and Switzerland.

Admission to higher education depends upon completion of secondary education and award of the Matura. The undergraduate degree is the Bachelors, a three-year programme of study. Following the Bachelors, postgraduate students may be awarded the Nachdiplom (a short-course degree), Magister Philosophiae (requiring five years of study) and finally Doctor of Philosophy.

Vocational and technical training consists of either workplace-oriented apprenticeship schemes or four-year professional courses in civil engineering, mechanical engineering, economics and architecture at Hoschschule Liechtenstein.

Learned Societies

HISTORY, GEOGRAPHY AND ARCHAEOLOGY

Historischer Verein für das Fürstentum Liechtenstein (Historical Society for the Principality of Liechtenstein): Plankner Str. 39, Schaan; tel. 392-17-47; fax 392-17-05; e-mail info@hvfl.li; internet www.hvfl.li; f. 1901; 814 mems; library of 3,000 vols; Sec. Lic. phil. KLAUS BIEDERMANN; publ. *Jahrbuch*.

NATURAL SCIENCES

General

Liechtensteinische Gesellschaft für Umweltschutz (Liechtenstein Society for Environmental Protection): Im Bretscha 22, 9494 Schaan; tel. 232-52-62; fax 237-40-31; e-mail info@lgu.li; internet www.lgu.li; f. 1973; 750 mems; Pres. REGULA MOSBERGER; publs *LGU-Mitteilungen* (quarterly), *LGU-Schriftenreihe*, *Liechtensteiner Umweltbericht* (1 or 2 a year).

Research Institute

ECONOMICS, LAW AND POLITICS

Liechtenstein-Institut: Auf dem Kirchhügel, St Luziweg 2, 9487 Bendern; tel. 373-30-22; fax 373-54-22; e-mail admin@liechtenstein-institut.li; internet www.liechtenstein-institut.li; f. 1986; research on topics related to Liechtenstein in the fields of law, political science, economics and social science, history; Pres. Dr iur. GUIDO MEIER; Dir Dr ANDREA WILLI; publ. *Annual Report* (in German).

Libraries and Archives

Vaduz

Liechtensteinische Landesbibliothek: 9490 Vaduz; tel. 236-63-62; fax 233-14-19; e-mail info@landesbibliothek.li; internet www.landesbibliothek.li; f. 1961; public, academic and nat. library; 230,000 vols; Dir BARBARA VOGT.

Liechtensteinisches Landesarchiv: Städtle 51, 9490 Vaduz; tel. 236-63-40; fax 236-63-59; e-mail info@la.llv.li; internet www.la.llv.li; f. 1961; nat. archives; reference library of 6,000 shelf m of documents; Archivist Lic. phil. PAUL VOGT; publ. *Veröffentlichungen des Liechtensteinischen Landesarchivs*.

Museums and Art Galleries

Vaduz

Kunstmuseum Liechtenstein: Städtle 32, Postfach 370, 9490 Vaduz; tel. 235-03-00; fax 235-03-29; e-mail mail@kunstmuseum.li; internet www.kunstmuseum.li; f. 2000; museum of fine arts, incl. private collns of the Prince of Liechtenstein and state collns of international modern art; Dir Dr FRIEDEMANN MALSCH.

Liechtensteinisches Landesmuseum (Liechtenstein National Museum): Städtle 43, Postfach 1216, 9490 Vaduz; tel. 236-75-50; fax 236-75-52; e-mail landesmuseum@llm.llv.li; internet www.landesmuseum.li; f. 1954; includes items from the collections of the Prince, the State, and the Liechtenstein Historical Soc.; Pres. EVA PEPIC.

Postmuseum des Fürstentums Liechtenstein: Städtle 37, 9490 Vaduz; tel. 236-64-44; fax 236-66-55; e-mail briefmarken-fl@llv.li; internet www.pwz.li; f. 1930; Liechtenstein stamps, historical postal documents, postal machinery; Dir NORBERT HASLER.

Universities

HOCHSCHULE LIECHTENSTEIN
(Liechtenstein University of Applied Sciences)

Fürst-Franz-Josef-Str., 9490 Vaduz
Telephone: 265-11-11
Fax: 265-11-12
E-mail: info@hochschule.li
Internet: www.hochschule.li
Founded 1961 as Abendtechnikum Vaduz; renamed Liechtensteinische Ingenieurschule 1985; university status 1992; renamed Fachhochschule Liechtenstein 1997; present name 2005
State control
Languages of instruction: German, English
Rector: KLAUS NÄSCHER
Librarian: ULRIKE BRUNHART
Number of students: 500
Publication: *Denkfabrik* (magazine, 2 a year)

DEANS

Faculty of Architecture: Prof. Dipl. Ing. HANSJÖRG HILTI
Faculty of Business Studies: Dipl. Ing. HARTWIG BISCHOF
Faculty of Humanities: Dr ROBERT BLUNDER

PROFESSORS

BALDEGGER, U., Entrepreneurship
EISINGER, A., Urban Construction and Development
HILTI, H., Design and Woodwork
KÄFERSTEIN, J., Design and Construction
MEISTER, U., Design and Construction
MENICHETTI, M. J., Business Economics
WEINMANN, S, Information Technology for Business
WENZ, M., Business Management and International and Liechtenstein Tax Law
WINNING, H.-H., Urban Construction, Planning and Transport

UNIVERSITÄT FÜR HUMANWISSENSCHAFTEN
(University of Human Sciences)

Dorfstr. 24, 9495 Triesen
Telephone: 399-40-10
Fax: 399-40-11
E-mail: info@ufl.li
Internet: www.unilie.li
Founded 2000
Private control
Rector: Prof. Dr WILLI A. RIBI
Courses in medical science and mediation and conflict resolution

PROFESSORS

AMMER, R., Medicine
DEANGELIS, C. D., Medicine
DREXEL, H., Internal Medicine
FURRER, M., Surgery
GALEAZZI, R. L., Medicine
GLOSSMANN, H., Biochemical Pharmacology
GOTTWALD, W., Mediation
HERRLING, P. L., Medicine
HÖLAND, W., Medicine
KESSELRING, J., Neurology
MOONS, K. G. M., Medicine
PFEIFFER, K. P., Biostatistics
REINHART, W., Internal Medicine
RENNIE, D., Medicine
RIESEN, W. F., Medicine
SCHREIBER, H.-P., Medical Ethics
STEURER, J., Medicine

College

Liechtensteinische Musikschule: St Florinsgasse 1, 9490 Vaduz; tel. 232-46-20; fax 232-46-42; e-mail info@musikschule.li; internet www.musikschule.li; f. 1963; 93 teachers; 2,450 students; library: 12,000 vols, special collection of works of composer Josef Gabriel Rheinberger; intl master classes June to September; Dir JOSEF FROMMELT.

LITHUANIA

The Higher Education System

The oldest existing institution of higher education in Lithuania is Vilnaius Universitetas (Vilnius University), founded in 1579 when Lithuania was united in a Commonwealth with Poland. The next oldest institution is Vilnaius Dailes Akademija (Vilnius Academy of Fine Arts), founded in 1793. In 1795 Lithuania was annexed by the Russian Empire and remained under Russian (and later, Bolshevik) rule until 1920, when the USSR recognized Lithuanian independence. In 1922 Lithuania was declared a parliamentary democracy under the terms of its first constitution. Several university-level institutions date from this year, among them Kauno Medicinos Universitetas (Kaunas Medical University), Kauno Technologijos Universitetas (Kaunas University of Technology) and Vytauto Didžiojo Universitetas (Vytautas Magnus University). According to the 'Secret Protocols' to the 1939 Treaty of Non-Aggression signed by the USSR and Nazi Germany, Lithuania was to come under German influence. However, the subsequent Nazi-Soviet Treaty on Friendship and Existing Borders granted the USSR control of Lithuania. In 1940 the Lithuanian Government was forced to resign and a Soviet Socialist Republic was established. In 1990 Lithuania was the first Soviet republic to declare independence, although this was not recognized by the USSR State Council until 1991. In February of that year the Supreme Council of the Republic of Lithuania adopted the Law on Science and Studies which established the guidelines of higher education reform, with the intention of bringing Lithuania's research and higher education system closer to that of Western Europe. Following the introduction of the Law on Education in 2000, Lithuania participates in Bologna Process to establish a European Higher Education Area, the first phase of which is to adopt a credit-based system of comparable degrees with two main cycles (undergraduate and graduate). From 2003 a uniform tuition fee was introduced for students in higher education, although there were exemptions for the highest achievers. In 2004/05 there were 38 schools of higher education and 21 universities. In that year total enrolment in institutions of higher education was an estimated 195,600.

The main requirement for admission to university is the Certificate of Maturity (Brandos Atestatas), the main secondary school qualification. Institutions receiving more applications than places available set competitive entrance examinations. Lithuania has established a two-tier Bachelors (Bakalauras) and Masters (Magistras) degree system in accordance with the principles of the Bologna Process. The Bachelors is a four-year programme of study and students are required to accrue 160 credits for award of the degree. Following the Bachelors is the Masters, the first postgraduate-level degree. This is a programme of study lasting one-and-a-half to two years, and may be awarded in conjunction with a professional title. The Doctorate (Daktaras) follows the Masters and requires up to four years of study, covering classroom-based instruction and original thesis research.

Technical and vocational education at post-secondary level is available at junior colleges and vocational schools (Aukstesnioji mokykla). Qualifications offered include the Higher Education Diploma (Aukštojo Mokslo Diplomas) and College Diploma (Aukštesniojo Mokslo Diplomas).

Learned Societies

GENERAL

Lithuanian Academy of Sciences: 3 Gedimino pr., 01103 Vilnius; tel. (5) 261-36-51; fax (5) 261-84-64; e-mail prezidiumas@ktl.mii.lt; internet neris.mii.lt/lma; f. 1941; divisions of Agriculture and Forestry (Head Prof. ALBINAS KUSTA), Biological, Medical and Geosciences (Head Prof. VYTAS ANTANAS TAMOSIUNAS), Humanities and Social Sciences (Head Prof. LEONARDAS SAUKA), Mathematics, Physics and Chemistry (Head Prof. VALDEMARAS RAZUMAS), Technical Sciences (Head Prof. VYTAUTAS OSTASEVICIUS); 194 mems (40 full, 60 corresp., 50 expert, 44 foreign); library: see Libraries and Archives; Pres. Prof. ZENONAS ROKUS RUDZIKAS; Sec.-Gen. Prof. VALDEMARAS RAZUMAS; publs *Acta medica Lituanica* (3 or 4 a year), *Arts Studies* (5 a year), *Journal of Agricultural Sciences* (4 a year), *Journal of Biology* (4 a year), *Journal of Chemistry* (4 a year), *Journal of Ecology* (3 or 4 a year), *Journal of Geography* (4 a year), *Journal of Geology* (4 a year), *Journal of Philosophy and Sociology* (3 or 4 a year), *Journal of Power Engineering* (4 a year), *Lithuanian Science* (5 or 6 a year), *Lituanistica* (3 or 4 a year), *Science and Technology* (monthly).

LANGUAGE AND LITERATURE

Alliance Française: Mykolo Romerio Universitetas, Ateities g. 20-118 Vilnius, 08303; tel. (5) 271-46-72; fax (5) 271-45-22; offers courses and exams in French language and culture and promotes cultural exchange with France.

British Council: Jogailos 4, 01116 Vilnius; tel. (5) 264-48-90; fax (5) 264-48-93; e-mail mail@britishcouncil.lt; internet www.britishcouncil.org/lithuania; f. 1992; offers courses and exams in English language and British culture and promotes cultural exchange with the UK; library of 5,201 vols; Dir LINA BALENAITE; Information Centre Man. RIMA KLUSOVSKIENE.

Goethe-Institut: Tilto g. 3-6, 01101 Vilnius; tel. (5) 231-44-33; fax (5) 231-44-32; e-mail info@vilnius.goethe.org; internet www.goethe.de/ne/vil/deindex.htm; offers courses and exams in German language and culture and promotes cultural exchange with Germany; Dir IRMTRAUT HUBATSCH.

PEN Centre of Lithuania: K. Sirvydo 6, 01101 Vilnius; tel. (5) 269-19-77; fax (5) 212-65-56; e-mail platelis@takas.lt; f. 1989; promotes friendship and co-operation among writers internationally; campaigns for freedom of expression, human rights and democratic causes; 34 mems; Pres. KORNELIJUS PLATELIS; Sec. LAIMANTAS JONUSYS.

Research Institutes

AGRICULTURE, FISHERIES AND VETERINARY SCIENCE

Lithuanian Forest Research Institute: Liepų 1, 53101 Girionys, Kauno raj.; tel. (37) 54-73-10; fax (37) 54-74-46; e-mail miskinst@mi.lt; internet www.mi.lt; f. 1950; main areas of research: biodiversity and sustainability of forest ecosystems; reforestation; forest productivity increment, protection and usage; forest genetic resources and breeding of forest trees; forest policy, social and economic problems; library of 60,000 vols; Dir Prof Dr habil. REMIGIJUS OZOLINČIUS; Scientific Sec. Dr DIANA MIZARAITĖ; publs *Baltic Forestry* (2 a year), *Miškininkystė* (Silviculture, 2 a year).

ECONOMICS, LAW AND POLITICS

Institute of Economics: Goštauto g. 12, 01108 Vilnius; tel. (5) 262-35-02; fax (5) 212-75-06; e-mail ei@ktl.mii.lt; f. 1941; attached to Lithuanian Acad. of Sciences; library of 5,000 vols; Dir Prof. EDUARDAS VILKAS.

Lithuanian Institute of Philosophy and Sociology: Saltoniškių 58, 08105 Vilnius; tel. and fax (5) 275-18-98; e-mail lfsi@ktl.mii.lt; internet neris.mii.lt/LFSI/; f. 1977; 92 mems; Dir Dr VACYS BAGDONAVIČIUS; publs *Humanistika*, *Logos*, *Philosophy and Sociology* (4 a year).

FINE AND PERFORMING ARTS

Institute of Culture and Arts: Tilto 4, 01101 Vilnius; tel. (5) 262-60-91; fax (5) 261-09-89; Dir Prof. Dr A. MATULIONIS; Scientific Sec. Dr A. ŠIMĖNIENĖ; publ. *The Art Studies* (2 a year).

HISTORY, GEOGRAPHY AND ARCHAEOLOGY

Institute of Geology and Geography: T. Ševčenkos 13, 03223 Vilnius; tel. (5) 210-46-90; fax (5) 210-46-95; e-mail giedre.kulviciene@geo.lt; internet www.geo.lt; f. 1990; Dir A. ZUZEVIČIUS; publs *Geografija* (Geography), *Geografijos metraštis* (Geographical Yearbook, annually), *Baltica* (annually), *Geologija* (Geology, 4 a year).

Institute of Lithuanian History: Kražių g. 5, 01108 Vilnius; tel. (5) 261-44-36; fax (5) 261-44-33; e-mail istorija@istorija.lt; internet www.istorija.lt; library of 142,000 vols; Dir Habil. dr. doc. ALVYDAS NIKŽENTAITIS; publs *Archeologija Baltica* (Lithuanian Archaeology), *Lietuvos archeologija* (Lithuanian Archaeology), *Lithuanian Ethnology*, *Lithuanian Historical Studies*, *Lithuanian Metrica*, *Lituanistica*, *Urban Past*, *Yearbook of Lithuanian History*.

LANGUAGE AND LITERATURE

Institute of Lithuanian Language: P. Vileisio 5, 10308 Vilnius 55; tel. (5) 234-64-72; fax (5) 234-70-00; e-mail lki@lki.lt; internet www.lki.lt; f. 1939; 40 mems; library: Archives of Lithuanian Dialects; Dir Asst Prof. JOLANTA ZABARSKAITE; publs *Acta Linguistica Lithuanica* (2 a year), *Culture of Language* (annually), *Terminology* (annually), *Archivum Lithuanicum* (annually).

Institute of Lithuanian Literature and Folklore: Antakalnio 6, 10308 Vilnius; tel. (5) 262-19-43; fax (5) 261-62-54; e-mail llti@ktl.mii.lt; internet www.llti.lt; f. 1939; library of 240,000 vols and other printed matter; Dir LEONARDAS SAUKA; publs *Lituanistica* (4 a year), *Senoji Lietuvos literatura* (Old Lithuanian Literature, annually), *Tautosakos darbai* (Folklore Studies, annually).

MEDICINE

Institute of Hygiene: Didžioji 22, 01128 Vilnius; tel. (5) 262-45-83; fax (5) 262-46-63; e-mail institutas@hi.lt; internet www.hi.lt; f. 1808; library of 8,000 vols; Dir Prof. habil Dr JULIUS KALIBATAS; publ. *Public Health* (4 a year).

Institute of Immunology: Moletu pl. 29, 08409 Vilnius; tel. (5) 246-92-22; fax (5) 246-92-10; e-mail imi@imi.lt; internet www.imi.lt; f. 1990; attached to Vilnius University; immunology, immunochemistry, molecular biology and virusology; Dir Prof. habil.dr. VYTAS TAMOŠIŪNAS.

Institute of Oncology, Vilnius University: Santariškių 1, 08660 Vilnius; tel. (5) 278-67-00; fax (5) 272-01-64; e-mail administracija@loc.lt; internet www.loc.lt; f. 1990; Dir Prof. Dr K. VALUCKAS.

NATURAL SCIENCES

Biological Sciences

Institute of Biochemistry: Mokslininkų 12, 08412 Vilnius; tel. (5) 272-91-44; fax (5) 272-91-96; e-mail biochemija@bchi.lt; internet www.bchi.lt; f. 1967; Dir Prof. Dr. habil. VALDAS LAURINAVICIUS.

Institute of Botany: Žaliųjų ežerų 49, 08406 Vilnius; tel. (5) 271-16-18; fax (5) 272-99-50; e-mail botanika@botanika.lt; internet www.botanika.lt/bi; f. 1959; Dir Dr VALERIJUS RAŠOMAVIČIUS; publ. *Botanica Lithuanica* (4 a year).

Institute of Ecology of Vilnius University: Akademijos g. 2, 08412 Vilnius 21; tel. and fax (5) 272-93-52; e-mail ekoi@ekoi.lt; internet www.ekoi.lt; f. 1945; attached to Vilnius Univ.; library of 77,000 vols; Dir Dr habil. MEČISLOVAS ŽALAKEVIČIUS; publ. *Acta Zoologica Lituanica* (in English, 4 a year).

Mathematical Sciences

Institute of Mathematics and Informatics: Akademijos g. 4 08663 Vilnius; tel. (5) 210-93-00; fax (5) 272-92-09; e-mail mathematica@ktl.mii.lt; internet www.mii.lt; f. 1956; Dir Prof. Dr. habil. GINTAUTAS DZEMYDA; publs *Informatica*, *Informatics in Education*, *Lithuanian Mathematical Journal* (quarterly), *Mathematical Modelling and Analysis*, *Nonlinear Analysis: Modelling and Control*.

Physical Sciences

Institute of Chemistry: A. Goštauto 9, 01108 Vilnius; tel. (5) 261-26-63; fax (5) 261-70-18; e-mail chemins@ktl.mii.lt; internet www.chi.lt; f. 1945; Dir Prof. Dr. habil. EIMUTIS JUZELIŪNAS.

Institute of Physics: Savanorių pr. 231, 02300 Vilnius; tel. (5) 266-16-40; fax (5) 260-23-17; e-mail fi@fi.lt; internet www.fi.lt; f. 1977; Dir Assoc. Prof. dr VIDMANTAS REMEIKIS; publ. *Environmental and Chemical Physics* (4 a year).

Institute of Theoretical Physics and Astronomy: A. Goštauto g. 12, 01108 Vilnius; tel. (5) 262-09-47; fax (5) 212-53-61; e-mail atom@itpa.lt; internet www.itpa.lt; f. 1990; attached to Lithuanian Acad. of Sciences and Vilnius University; library of 112,000 vols; Dir and Head of Astronomical Observatory Dr Hab. GRAŽINA TAUTVAIŠIENĖ; publs *Baltic Astronomy* (quarterly), *Lithuanian Journal of Physics* (quarterly), *Lietuvos dangus* (Sky of Lithuania; in Lithuanian, annual).

TECHNOLOGY

Institute of Biotechnology: V. Graičiūno g. 8, 02241 Vilnius; tel. (5) 260-21-03; fax (5) 260-21-16; e-mail office@ibt.lt; internet www.ibt.lt; f. 1975; genetic and molecular studies of DNA and research and development of recombinant biomedical proteins; Dir Dr habil. A. PAULIUKONIS.

Institute of Semiconductor Physics: A. Goštauto g. 11, 01108 Vilnius; tel. (5) 261-97-59; fax (5) 262-71-23; e-mail spiadm@pfi.lt; internet www.pfi.lt; f. 1967; Dir Prof. Dr Hab. STEPONAS ASMONTAS.

Lithuanian Energy Institute: Breslaujos 3, 44403 Kaunas; tel. (37) 35-14-03; fax (37) 35-12-71; e-mail rastine@mail.lei.lt; internet www.lei.lt; f. 1956; library of 40,000 vols; Dir Prof. Dr Hab. EUGENIJUS UŠPURAS; publs *Energetika* (Power Engineering, quarterly), *Environmental Research, Engineering and Management* (quarterly).

Libraries and Archives

Vilnius

Library of the Lithuanian Academy of Sciences: Žygimantu 1/8, 01102 Vilnius; tel. (5) 262-95-37; fax (5) 262-13-24; e-mail biblioteka@mab.lt; internet www.mab.lt; f. 1941; 3,733,000 vols incl. 250,610 manuscripts; Dir Dr JUOZAS MARCINKEVIČIUS.

Lithuanian Technical Library: Šv. Ignoto 6, 01120 Vilnius; tel. (5) 261-87-18; fax (5) 261-03-79; e-mail info@tb.lt; internet www.tb.lt; f. 1957; patent information centre; publishes official bulletins and patent documents of the State Patent Bureau; 36,768,138 vols; Dir KAZYS MACKEVIČIUS.

Martynas Mažvydas National Library of Lithuania: Gedimino pr. 51, 01109 Vilnius; tel. (5) 262-90-23; fax (5) 262-71-29; e-mail biblio@lnb.lrs.lt; internet www.lnb.lt; f. 1919; incorporated National Printing Archive 1992; 7,000,000 vols in total, including 4m. books, periodicals, and reference publications, 70,000 MSS, 103,000 microforms, 63,000 audiovisual items, 30,000 old and rare books; National Printing Archive consists of 2,174,574 items, including books, maps and periodicals since 16th c., as well as books printed in Lithuania since 16th c. in Latin, Polish and Russian; Rare Book and Manuscript department contains 70,000 items, including 30,000 books from 15–18th c. (including works by early Church reformers, Martin Luther and Philip Melanchton, and the humanist, Erasmus), private archives of prominent Lithuanians since 19th c., 149 parchments (including privileges of the Grand Dukes of Lithuania and the Kings of Poland), as well as autographs, legal documents and photographs since 15th c.; 200,000 items in Music Department, including 100,000 items of printed music since 16th c., 500 rare music scores and 55,000 audiovisual items; Dir VYTAUTAS GUDAITIS; publ. *Tarp Knygų* (monthly).

Vilnius University Library: Universiteto g. 3, 01122 Vilnius; tel. (5) 268-71-01; fax (5) 268-71-04; e-mail mb@mb.vu.lt; internet www.mb.vu.lt; f. 1570; 5,349,881 vols, 251,320 MSS, 87,928 graphic art items, 437,367 UN publs; Dir BIRUTĖ BUTKEVIČIENĖ.

Museums and Art Galleries

Kaunas

Čiurlionis, M. K., National Museum of Art: Vlado Putvinskio 55, 44248 Kaunas; tel. (37) 22-94-75; fax (37) 22-26-06; e-mail mkc@takas.lt; internet www.ciurlionis.lt; f. 1921; Lithuanian and European art, folk art, oriental and ancient Egyptian art, numismatics; named after Lithuanian artist M. K. Čiurlionis (1875–1911); library of 30,000 vols; Dir OSVALDAS DAUGELIS.

Kaunas Botanical Garden: Ž. E. Žilibero 6, 46324 Kaunas; tel. (37) 39-00-33; fax (37) 39-01-33; e-mail bs@bs.vdu.lt; internet www.vdu.lt/Botanika/Bot_garden.htm; f. 1923; attached to Vytautas Magnus University; 62 hectares; research into botany, ecology and the natural environment; library of 10,000 vols; Dir Dr REMIGIJUS DAUBAZAS.

Vytautas the Great War Museum: K. Donelaičio 64, 44248 Kaunas; tel. (37) 42-21-46; fax (37) 42-07-65; e-mail v.d.karomuziejus@takas.lt; f. 1921; archaeological finds, weapons, firearms, ammunition, army uniforms, objects and documents relating to the transatlantic flight of the 'Lituanica'; colln of ethnographic photographs by Balys Buracas (1897–1972); Dir JUOZAPAS JUREVIČIUS.

Trakai

Trakai Historical Museum: Kęstučio 4, Trakai 21104; tel. (528) 5-82-41; e-mail trakai.museum@is.lt; f. 1948; 16th–17th c. tiles, coins, pottery, bone chessmen and other artefacts discovered during excavations at Trakai Castle; also ethnographic and applied art collections; Dir VIRGILIJUS POVILIŪNAS.

Vilnius

Lithuanian Art Museum: Didžioji 4, 01128 Vilnius; tel. (5) 262-80-30; fax (5) 212-60-06; e-mail muziejus@ldm.lt; internet www.ldm.lt; f. 1933; library of 25,166 vols; Lithuanian and foreign works of fine and applied art; br. museums incl. Vilnius Picture Gallery, Museum of Applied Art, Foreign Art Gallery, Pranas Gudynas Restoration Centre of Museum Treasures, Klaipėda Picture Gallery, Clock Museum, Palanga Amber Museum, Juodkrantė Exhibition Hall; Dir ROMUALDAS BUDRYS; publ. *Issues of the Museum* (annually).

National Museum of Lithuania: Arsenalo 1, 01100 Vilnius; tel. (5) 262-77-74; fax (5) 261-10-23; e-mail muziejus@lnm.lt; internet www.lnm.lt; f. 1855; history, ethnography, numismatics, archaeology, iconography; library of 55,000 vols; Dir BIRUTĖ KULNYTĖ; publs *Archaeology*, *Ethnography* (annually),

Museum (annually), *Numismatics* (annually).

Universities

KAUNO MEDICINOS UNIVERSITETAS (Kaunas Medical University)

A. Mickevičiaus 9, 44307 Kaunas
Telephone: (37) 32-72-01
Fax: (37) 22-07-33
E-mail: info@kmu.lt
Internet: www.kmu.lt
Founded 1922 as Faculty of Medicine of Kaunas University; Kaunas Medical Institute 1950; Kaunas Medical Academy in 1989; university status 1998
State control
Rector: REMIGIJUS ŽALIŪNAS
Vice-Rector for Research: Prof. IRENA MISEVICIČIENĖ
Vice-Rector for Studies: Prof. JULIJA BRAŽDŽIONYTĖ
Vice-Rector for University Clinics: JUOZAS PUNDZIUS
Library of 782,000 vols (53% in Russian, 28% in Lithuanian, 19% in English, German, French and Polish)
Number of teachers: 600 (including researchers)
Number of students: 2,100

DEANS
Faculty of Medicine: Prof. Dr ROMUALDAS GAILYS
Faculty of Nursing: Prof. ARVYDAS ŠEŠKEVIČIUS
Faculty of Odontology: Dr sci. habil. RIČARDAS KUBILIUS
Faculty of Pharmacy: Dr sci. habil. PAULIUS VAINAUSKAS
Faculty of Public Health: Dr sc. habil. RAMUNĖ KALĖDIENĖ

ATTACHED RESEARCH INSTITUTES
Institute for Biomedical Research: Dir IRENA MISEVICIČIENĖ.
Institute of Cardiology: Dir Dr RIMANTAS BENETIS.
Institute of Endocrinology: Dir Dr sci. habil. ANTANAS NORKUS.
Institute of Psychophysiology and Rehabilitation: Dir Dr habil. DAIVA RASTENYTĖ.

KAUNO TECHNOLOGIJOS UNIVERSITETAS (Kaunas University of Technology)

K. Donelaičio 73, 44029 Kaunas
Telephone: (37) 30-00-11
Fax: (37) 32-41-44
E-mail: rastine@cr.ktu.lt
Internet: www.ktu.lt
Founded 1922
State control
Academic year: September to June
Rector: Prof. RAMUTIS BANSEVIČIUS
Vice-Rectors: Prof. RAIMUNDAS ŠIAUČIŪNAS (Academic Affairs), Prof. VYTAUTAS OSTAŠEVIČIUS (Research)
Head of Administration: Prof. ALGIMANTAS NAVICKAS
Librarian: GENOVAITE DUOBINIENĖ
Library of 1,700,000 vols
Number of teachers: 1,030
Number of students: 18,224
Publications: *Chemical Technology* (4 a year), *Economics of Engineering* (5 a year), *Electronics and Electrical Engineering* (6 a year), *Environmental Research* (4 a year), *Humanistica* (2 a year), *Information Technology and Control* (4 a year), *Language Teaching and Learning in the Context of Social Changes* (2 a year), *Measurements* (4 a year), *Mechanics* (6 a year), *Materials Science* (4 a year), *Social Sciences* (5 a year), *Ultrasound* (4 a year)

DEANS
Faculty of Chemical Technology: Prof. ZIGMUNTAS JONAS BERESNEVIČIUS
Faculty of Civil Engineering and Architecture: Dr HENRIKAS ELZBUTAS
Faculty of Design and Technology: Dr SIGITAS STANYS
Faculty of Economics and Management: Dr BRONIUS NEVERAUSKAS
Faculty of Electrical Engineering and Control Systems: Prof. JONAS DAUNORAS
Faculty of Fundamental Sciences: Dr VYTAUTAS JANILIONIS
Faculty of Humanities: Prof. GIEDRIUS KUPREVIČIUS
Faculty of Informatics: Prof. ALEKSANDRAS TARGAMADZĖ
Faculty of Mechanical Engineering: Prof. ALGIMANTAS FEDARAVIČIUS
Faculty of Social Sciences: Dr VIKTORIJA BARŠAUSKIENĖ
Faculty of Telecommunications and Electronics: Dr BRUNONAS DEKERIS
International Studies Centre: Dr KĘSTUTIS PILKAUSKAS
Panevėžys Institute: Prof. ALGIRDAS JURKAUSKAS

ATTACHED RESEARCH INSTITUTES
Computational Technologies Centre: Dir Prof. RIMANTAS BARAUSKAS.
Institute of Biomedical Engineering: Dir Prof. ARŪNAS LUKOŠEVIČIUS.
Institute of Defence Technologies: Dir Prof. ALGIMANTAS FEDARAVIČIUS.
Institute of Environmental Engineering: Dir Prof. JURGIS STANIŠKIS.
Institute of Europe: Dir Prof. KĘSTUTIS KRIŠČIŪNAS.
Institute of Materials Science: Dir Prof. SIGITAS TAMULEVIČIUS.
Institute of Metrology: Dir Prof. RIMVYDAS ŽILINSKAS.
Institute of Piezomechanics: Dir Prof RAMUTIS PETRAS BANSEVIČIUS.
Institute of Technological Systems Diagnostics: Dir Prof VITALIJUS VOLKOVAS.
Prof. K. Baršauskas Ultrasound Research Institute: Dir Prof. RYMANTAS JONAS KAŽYS.
Research Centre for Microsystems and Nanotechnology: Dir Prof. VALENTINAS SNITKA.

KLAIPĖDOS UNIVERSITETAS (Klapėida University)

H. Manto 84, 92294 Klaipėda
Telephone: (46) 39-89-00
Fax: (46) 39-89-02
E-mail: vladas.zulkus@ku.lt
Internet: www.ku.lt
Founded 1991
State control
Academic year: September to June
Rector: Prof. Dr habil. VLADAS ŽULKUS
Vice-Rector for Academic Affairs: Prof. Dr VAIDUTIS LAURĖNAS
Vice-Rector for Administration: Doc. Dr ADOLFAS BRĖSKIS
Vice-Rector for International Relations: Prof. Dr VILIJA TARGAMADZĖ
Vice-Rector for Research and Art: Prof. Dr habil. BENEDIKTAS TILICKIS
Library Director: JANINA PUPELIENĖ
Library of 458,275 books, 30,453 periodicals
Number of teachers: 431 full-time
Number of students: 7,666 (7,578 undergraduate, 88 postgraduate)
Publications: *Acta Historica Universitatis Klavpeolencis* (annually), *Archiviem Lituanuciem* (annually), *Jura ir aplinka* (Sea and Environment, 4 a year), *Sociologija: miutis ir veolumas* (Sociology: Thought and Action, 2 a year), *Tiltai* (Bridges, 4 a year)

DEANS
Faculty of Arts: Prof. VYTAUTAS TETENSKAS
Faculty of Education: Doc. ANTANAS LUKOŠEVIČIUS
Faculty of Health Sciences: Prof. Dr habil. ALGIMANTAS KIRKUTIS
Faculty of Humanities: Doc. ALEKSANDRAS ŽALYS
Faculty of Marine Engineering: Prof. Dr VYTENIS ALBERTAS ZABUKAS
Faculty of Science and Mathematics: Doc. PETRAS GRECEVIČIUS
Faculty of Social Sciences: Doc. ANTANAS BUČINSKAS

ATTACHED INSTITUTES
Coastal Research and Planning Institute: Dir Doc. ARTŪRAS RAZINKOV.
Institute of Continuing Studies: Dir Doc. RUTA-MARIJA ANDRIEKIENE.
Institute of Regional Policy and Planning: Dir Prof. STASYS VAITEKŪNAS.
Maritime Institute: Dir Doc. Dr VIKTORAS SENČILA.

LIETUVOS ŽEMĖS ŪKIO UNIVERSITETAS (Lithuanian University of Agriculture)

Akademija, Studentu 11, 53361 Kaunas
Telephone: (37) 39-75-00
Fax: (37) 39-75-00
E-mail: laa@nora.lzuu.lt
Internet: www.lzuu.lt
Founded 1924
Rector: Prof. dr habil. ALBINAS KUSTA
Vice-Rector for Research: Prof. dr habil. ROMUALDAS DELTUVAS
Vice-Rector for Studies: Prof. dr habil. ANTANAS JUODVALKIS
Library of 520,338 vols, 200 periodicals
Number of teachers: 525
Number of students: 6,032
Publications: *Agricultural Engineering*, *Agriculture*, *Baltic Forestry*, *Silviculture*, *Water Management*

DEANS
Faculty of Agricultural Engineering: Prof. dr. habil. ALGIRDAS JONAS RAILA
Faculty of Agronomy: Assoc. Prof. dr EGIDIJA EGIDIJA VENSKUTONIENĖ
Faculty of Economics and Management: Assoc. Prof. dr JONAS ČAPLIKAS
Faculty of Forestry: Assoc. Prof. dr EDMUNDAS BARTKEVIČIUS
Faculty of Water and Land Management: Assoc. Prof. dr VIDMANTAS GURKLYS

ATTACHED RESEARCH INSTITUTES
Institute of the Environment: Dir Assoc. Prof. dr VIDA RUTKOVIENĖ.
Institute of Information Technologies: Dir Assoc. Prof. dr ALEKSANDRAS SAVILIONIS.
Institute of Rural Culture: Dir Assoc. Prof. dr SVETLANA STATKEVIĖIENĖ.

MYKOLO ROMERIO UNIVERSITETAS
(Mykolas Romeris University)

Ateities 20, 08303 Vilnius
Telephone: (5) 271-46-47
Fax: (5) 267-00-00
E-mail: roffice@mruni.lt
Internet: www.mruni.lt
Founded 1990 as Law University of Lithuania; present name 2000
State control
Rector: Prof. Dr ALVYDAS PUMPUTIS
University Secretary: ANTANAS KERAS
Librarian: ALMONE JAKUBCIONIENE
Library of 156,042 vols, 188 periodicals
Number of students: 16,000

DEANS

Faculty of Economics and Management: Assoc. Prof. Dr VITALIJA RUDZKIENĖ
Faculty of Law: Prof. Dr JUOZAS ZILYS
Faculty of Public Administration: Dr TADAS SUDNICKAS
Faculty of Social Policy: Assoc. Prof. Dr LETA DROMANTIENE
Faculty of Strategic Management and Policy: Prof. habil. dr VYGANDAS K. PAULIKAS
Kaunas Faculty of Police: ANTANAS BUTAVIČIUS

ATTACHED RESEARCH INSTITUTES

Center for Research: Deputy Dir SAULĖ MAČIUKAITĖ-ŽVINIENĖ.

ŠIAULIŲ UNIVERSITETAS
(Siauliai University)

Vilniaus g. 88, 76285 Šiauliai
Telephone: (41) 59-58-00
Fax: (41) 59-58-09
E-mail: all@cr.su.lt
Internet: www.su.lt
Founded 1997 by merger of Šiauliai Pedagogical Institute and Siauliai Polytechnical Faculty of Kaunas University of Technology
State control
Rector: Prof. habil. dr VINCAS LAURUTIS
Librarian: LORETA BURBAITĖ
Library of 400,000 vols, 550 periodicals
Number of teachers: 840
Number of students: 10,000
Publications: *Jaunųjų mokslininkų darbai* (Young Researchers' Works; 3 a year), *Kūrybos erdvės* (Spaces of Creation; 2 a year), *Special Education*

DEANS

Faculty of Arts: Assoc. Prof. Dr. LEONAS PAULAUSKAS
Faculty of Education: Assoc. Prof. Dr AUŠRINĖ GUMULIAUSKIENĖ
Faculty of Humanities: Prof. GENOVAITĖ KAČIUŠKIENĖ
Faculty of Physics and Mathematics: Assoc. Prof. Dr ALFREDAS LANKAUSKAS
Faculty of Social Sciences: Assoc. Prof. Dr TEODORAS TAMOŠIŪNAS
Faculty of Special Education: Assoc. Prof. Dr JUOZAS PUMPUTIS
Faculty of Technology: Prof. Dr VIDAS LAURUŠKA

ATTACHED RESEARCH INSTITUTES

Continuing Education Institute: Dean Assoc. Prof. Dr LIDIJA UŠECKIENĖ.

VILNIAUS GEDIMINO TECHNIKOS UNIVERSITETAS
(Vilnius Gediminas Technical University)

Saulėtekio alėja 11, 10223 Vilnius
Telephone: (5) 274-50-30
Fax: (5) 270-01-12
E-mail: rastine@adm.vtu.lt
Internet: www.vtu.lt
Founded 1956
State control
Languages of instruction: Lithuanian, English
Academic year: September to June
Chancellor: ARŪNAS KOMKA
Rector: ROMUALDAS GINEVIČIUS
Vice-Rectors: Assoc. Prof. ALFONSAS DANIŪNAS, RAIMUNDAS KIRVAITIS, Prof. Dr habil. ALGIRDAS VACLOVAS VALIULIS, Prof. Dr habil. EDMUNDAS KAZIMIERAS ZAVADSKAS
Librarian: R. PŪGŽLIENĖ
Library of 679,960 vols
Number of teachers: 827
Number of students: 13,000
Publications: *Aviation* (annually), *Business: Theory and Practice* (2 a year), *Geodesy and Cartography* (4 a year), *International Journal of Strategic Property Management* (2 a year), *Journal of Civil Engineering and Management* (4 a year), *Journal of Environmental Engineering and Landscape Management* (4 a year), *Technological and Economic Development of Economy* (4 a year), *Town Planning and Architecture* (4 a year), *Transport* (4 a year)

DEANS

Faculty of Architecture: RIMANTAS BUIVYDAS
Faculty of Business Management: Prof. Dr habil ALEXANDRAS VYTAUTAS RUTKAUSKAS
Faculty of Civil Engineering: Assoc. Prof. Dr P. VAINIŪNAS
Faculty of Electronics: ROMA RINKEVIČIENĖ
Faculty of Environmental Protection: Assoc. Prof. Dr D. ČYGAS
Faculty of Fundamental Sciences: ALGIRDAS CIUČELIS
Faculty of Mechanics: Prof. Dr habil M. MARIŪNAS
Faculty of Transport Engineering: Prof. Dr habil L. P. LINGAITIS
Institute of Aviation: Prof. Dr habil J. STANKŪNAS

PROFESSORS

Faculty of Architecture (Pylimo g. 26/1, Vilnius 01118; tel. (5) 274-50-12; fax (5) 274-52-13; e-mail archdek@ar.vtu.lt):

ANUŠKEVIČIUS, J.
BUIVYDAS, R.
DIČIUS, V.
DINEIKA, A.
ŠEIBOKAS, J.
STAUSKIS, V. J.
VANAGAS, J.
ZIBERKAS, L. P.

Faculty of Business Management (tel. (5) 274-48-88; fax (5) 274-48-92; e-mail management@vv.vtu.lt):

BIVAINIS, J.
GINEVIČIUS, R.
MELNIKAS, B.
PALIULIS, N.
RUTKAUSKAS, V.
STAŠKEVIČIUS, J.

Faculty of Civil Engineering (tel. (5) 274-52-39; fax (5) 274-50-16; e-mail povva@st.vtu.lt):

ATKOČIŪNAS, J.
ČYRAS, P.
KAKLAUSKAS, A.
KAKLAUSKAS, G.
KALANTA, S.
KVEDARAS, A. K.
MAČIULAITIS, R.
MARČIUKAITIS, J. G.
PARASONIS, J.
USTINOVIČIUS, L.
VAINIŪNAS, P.
ZAVADSKAS, E. K.

Faculty of Electronics (Naugarduko g. 41, 03225 Vilnius; tel. (5) 274-47-53; fax (5) 274-47-70; e-mail dekanatas@el.vtu.lt):

DAMBRAUSKAS, A.
JANKAUSKAS, Z.
KAJACKAS, A.
KVEDARAS, V.
MARCINKEVIČIUS, A.
MARTAVIČIUS, R.
POŠKA, A.
RINKEVIČIENĖ, R.
SKUDUTIS, J.
ŠMILGEVIČIUS, A.
ŠTARAS, S.

Faculty of Environmental Engineering (tel. (5) 274-47-27; fax (5) 274-47-31; e-mail info@ap.vtu.lt):

BALTRĖNAS, P.
BURINSKIENĖ, M.
BUTKUS, P.
ČYGAS, D.
GINIOTIS, V.
JAKOVLEVAS-MATECKIS, K.
JUŠKEVIČIUS, P.
JUODIS, E. S.
LAURINAVIČIUS, A.
LUKIANAS, A.
MARTINAITIS, V.
MATUZEVIČIUS, A.
SAKALAUSKAS, K.
ZAKAREVIČIUS, A.

Faculty of Fundamental Sciences (tel. (5) 274-48-43; fax (5) 274-48-44; e-mail fmf@fm.vtu.lt):

ADOMĖNAS, P.
BAUŠYS, R.
BELEVIČIUS, R.
ČESNYS, A.
ČIEGIS, R.
ČIŽAS, A.
KAČIANAUSKAS, R.
KAZRAGIS, A.
KERIENĖ, J.
KIRJACKIS, E.
KULVIETIS, G.
KULYS, J.
LEONAVIČIUS, M. K.
SAKALAUSKAS, L.
SAULIS, L.
STYRO, D.

Faculty of Mechanics (J. Basanavičiaus 28, 2009 Vilnius; tel. (5) 274-47-45; fax (5) 274-50-43; e-mail mechanik@me.vtu.lt):

AUGUSTAITIS, V.
MARCINKEVIČIUS, A. H.
MARIŪNAS, M.
VALIULIS, A.
VEKTERIS, V.

Faculty of Transport Engineering (J. Basanavičiaus 28B, 03224 Vilnius; tel. (5) 274-47-97; fax (5) 274-48-00; e-mail tif@ti.vtu.lt):

BIDEVIČIUS, M.
BUTKUS, A.
LINGAITIS, L.
LUKOŠEVIČIENĖ, O.
PALŠAITIS, R.
PIKŪNAS, A.
SILEVIČIUS, H.
SPRUOGIS, B.
ŽVIRBLIS, A.

Institute of Aviation (Rodūnios Kelias g. 30, 02187 Vilnius; tel. (5) 274-48-09; fax (5) 274-50-58; e-mail avinst@ai.vtu.lt):

STANKŪNAS, J.

Institute of Humanities (Saulėtekio alėja 28, 10225 Vilnius; tel. (5) 269-87-60; fax (5) 269-86-95; e-mail hinst@hi.vtu.lt):

TAMOŠAUSKAS, P.

ATTACHED INSTITUTES

International Studies Centre: tel. (5) 274-48-95; fax (5) 274-48-97; e-mail tsc@ts.vtu.lt; Dir Prof. Dr habil ZENONAS KAMAITIS.

VILNIAUS PEDAGOGINIS UNIVERSITETAS
(Vilnius Pedagogical University)

Studentų g. 39, 08106 VilniusTelephone: (5) 279-02-81
Fax: (5) 279-02-81
E-mail: studsk@vpu.lt
Internet: www.vpu.lt

Founded 1935 as National Pedagogical Institute in Klaipeda; moved to Vilnius 1939; present name and status 1992
State control
Rector: Acad. Prof. Dr. habil. ALGIRDAS GAIŽUTIS
Librarian: EMILIJA BANIONYTE
Number of teachers: 420
Number of students: 12,400

DEANS

Faculty of Foreign Languages: Dr ALGIMANTAS MARTINKĖNAS
Faculty of History: Prof. Dr LIBERTAS KLIMKA
Faculty of Lithuanian Philology: DALIA PŪRIENĖ
Faculty of Mathematics and Informatics: Assoc. Prof. Dr DALIA KUMPONIENĖ
Faculty of Natural Sciences: Assoc. Prof. Dr BRONISLOVAS ŠALKUS
Faculty of Pedagogy and Psychology: Dr RITA MAKARSKAITĖ-PETKEVIČIENĖ
Faculty of Physics and Technology: Dr KAZIMIERAS SADAUSKAS
Faculty of Slavonic Philology: Dr GINTAUTAS KUNDROTAS

ATTACHED RESEARCH INSTITUTES

Cultural and Arts Education Institute: Dir Prof. habil. Dr VAIDAS MATONIS.

Social Communication Institute: Dir Assoc. Prof. Dr GIEDRĖ KVIESKIENĖ.

VILNIAUS UNIVERSITETAS
(Vilnius University)

Universiteto g. 3, 01513 Vilnius
Telephone: (5) 268-70-10
Fax: (5) 268-70-09
E-mail: infor@cr.vu.lt
Internet: www.vu.lt

Founded 1579
State control
Language of instruction: Lithuanian
Academic year: September to July
Rector: Prof. BENEDIKTAS JUODKA
Pro-Rectors: Prof. JUOZAS RIMANTAS LAZUTKA, Prof. JUOZAS VIDMANTIS VAITKUS, Dr BIRUTĖ POCIŪTĖ, Prof. ALGIMANTAS RAUGALĖ, Dr ALEKSAS PIKTURNA
Director of the Library: Prof. AUDRONĖ GLOSIENĖ

Library: see Libraries and Archives
Number of teachers: 1,266
Number of students: 24,793

Publications: *Information Sciences* (4 a year), *Journal of Baltic Linguistics (Baltistica)* (3 a year), *Studies of Lithuanian History* (2 a year), *Problems* (2 a year), *Psychology* (2 a year), *Economics* (4 a year), *Law* (4 a year), *Linguistics* (2 a year), *Literature* (4 a year), *Book Science* (2 a year), *Acta Paedagogica Vilnensia* (2 a year), *Journal of Political Sciences* (4 a year), *Archaeologica Lituana* (annually), *Acta Orientalia Vilnensia* (annually), *STEP: Social Theory, Empirics, Policy and Practice* (2 a year), *Transformation in Business and Economics* (annually), *Lithuanian Political Science Yearbook* (annually), *Sociology, Thought and Action* (2 a year), *Respectus Philologicus* (1–2 a year)

DEANS

Faculty of Chemistry: Prof. AIVARAS KAREIVA
Faculty of Communication: Prof. DOMAS KAUNAS
Faculty of Economics: Dr BIRUTĖ GALINIENĖ
Faculty of History: Prof. ZENONAS BUTKUS
Faculty of Humanities in Kaunas: Dr STASYS ALBINAS GIRDZIJAUSKAS
Faculty of Law: Prof. VYTAUTAS NEKROŠIUS
Faculty of Mathematics and Informatics: Prof. FELIKSAS IVANAUSKAS
Faculty of Medicine: Prof. ZITA KUČINSKIENĖ
Faculty of Natural Sciences: Prof. KĘSTUTIS KILKUS
Faculty of Philology: Dr ANTANAS SMETONA
Faculty of Philosophy: Dr KĘSTUTIS DUBNIKAS
Faculty of Physics: Prof. JŪRAS BANYS

PROFESSORS

Faculty of Chemistry (Naugarduko g. 24, 03225 Vilnius; tel. (5) 233-09-87; fax (5) 233-09-87; e-mail chf@chf.vu.lt; internet www.chf.vu.lt):

- ABRUTIS, A., Inorganic Chemistry
- ARMALIS, S., Analytical Chemistry
- BALTRŪNAS, G., Electrochemistry
- BARKAUSKAS, J., Inorganic Chemistry
- DAUJOTIS, V., Surface and Boundary-layer Chemistry
- KAREIVA, A., Inorganic Chemistry
- KAZLAUSKAS, R., Analytical Chemistry
- MAKUŠKA, R., Polymer Chemistry
- PADARAUSKAS, A., Analytical Chemistry
- RAMANAVIČIUS, A., Biochemistry, Immunology
- TAUTKUS, S., Analytical Chemistry
- TUMKEVIČIUS, S., Organic Chemistry
- VAINILAVIČIUS, P., Organic Chemistry

Faculty of Communication (Saulėtekio alėja 9, 10222 Vilnius; tel. (5) 236-61-00; fax (5) 236-61-04; e-mail kf@kf.vu.lt; internet www.kf.vu.lt):

- KAUNAS, D., Book History, Book Science

Faculty of Economics (Saulėtekio alėja 9, 10222 Vilnius; tel. (5) 236-61-20; fax (5) 236-61-27; e-mail ef@ef.vu.lt; internet www.ef.vu.lt):

- BERŽINSKAS, G., Quality Management
- GYLYS, P., Economics Theory
- LAKIS, V., Audit
- MACKEVIČIUS, J., Accounting and Audit
- MARČINSKAS, A., Management
- MARTIŠIUS, S., Econometrics
- PRANULIS, V., Marketing
- RUŽEVIČIUS, J., Quality Management
- SIMANAUSKAS, L., Economic Informatics
- VENGRAUSKAS, P. V., Research in field of Co-operative Trade
- ŽEBRAUSKAS, A., Chemical Technology

Faculty of History (Universiteto g. 7, 01122 Vilnius; tel. (5) 268-72-80; fax (5) 268-72-82; e-mail if@if.vu.lt; internet www.if.vu.lt):

- BUMBLAUSKAS, A., Theory of History and History of Culture
- BUTKUS, Z., Contemporary History since 1914
- GUDAVIČIUS, E., Medieval History
- LUCHTANAS, A., Archaeology
- MICHELBERTAS, M., Archaeology, Numismatics
- VALIKONYTĖ, J., Medieval History

Faculty of Humanities in Kaunas (Muitinės g. 8, 44280 Kaunas; tel. (37) 42-25-23; fax (37) 42-32-22; e-mail dekanas@vukhf.lt; internet www.vukhf.lt):

- ČIEGIS, R., Economics
- GRONSKAS, V., Economics
- POLIAKOVAS, O., Diachronic Balto-Slavic Linguistics

Faculty of Law (Saulėtekio alėja 9, 10222 Vilnius; tel. (5) 236-61-60; fax (5) 2236-61-63; e-mail tf@tf.vu.lt; internet www.tf.vu.lt):

- MARCIJONAS, A., Environmental Law
- NEKROŠIUS, V., Civil Proceedings, Roman Law
- ŠILEKIS, E., Constitutional Law
- VANSEVIČIUS, S., History of Lithuanian State and Law

Faculty of Mathematics and Informatics (Naugarduko g. 24, 03225 Vilnius; tel. (5) 233-60-28; fax (5) 215-15-85; e-mail maf@maf.vu.lt; internet www.mif.vu.lt):

- BAGDONAVIČIUS, V., Probability Theory and Mathematical Statistics
- BIKELIS, A., Probability Theory and Mathematical Statistics
- BLOZNELIS, M., Probability Theory
- ČEKANAVIČIUS, V., Probability Theory and Mathematical Statistics
- IVANAUSKAS, F., Numerical Analysis
- KUBILIUS, J., Probabilistic Number Theory, History of Mathematics
- LAURINČIKAS, A., Probabilistic Number Theory
- LEIPUS, R., Probability Theory and Mathematical Statistics
- MACKEVIČIUS, V., Theory of Probability
- MANSTAVIČIUS, E., Probabilistic Number Theory
- PAULAUSKAS, V., Theory of Probability
- RAČKAUSKAS, A., Theory of Probability

Faculty of Medicine (M.K. Čiurlionio g. 21, 03101 Vilnius; tel. (5) 239-87-00; fax (5) 239-87-05; e-mail mf@mf.vu.lt; internet www.mf.vu.lt):

- AMBROZAITIS, A., Infectious Diseases
- BALČIŪNIENĖ, I., Cariology
- BARKAUSKAS, E. V., Vascular Surgery
- BAUBINAS, A., Environmental Hygiene, Paediatric Hygiene
- BUBNYS, A., Surgery
- ČESNYS, G., Anatomy, Anthropology
- DAINYS, B., Transplantation, Urology, Nephrology
- DEMBINSKAS, A., Psychiatry
- DUBAKIENĖ, R., Allergology
- IRNIUS, A., Gastroenterology
- IVAŠKEVIČIUS, J., Anaesthesiology, Intensive Care
- JANILIONIS, R., Pulmonology
- KALIBATIENĖ, D., Gastroenterology, Therapy, Nursing
- KALTENIS, P., Paediatrics, Paediatric Nephrology
- KUČINSKAS, V., Human Genetics
- KUČINSKIENĖ, Z. A., Medical Biochemistry
- LAUCEVIČIUS, A., Cardiology
- NOREIKA, L. A., Surgery
- PARNARAUSKIENĖ, R., Neurology, Neurophysiology
- PLIUŠKYS, J. A., Internal Medicine
- PORVANECKAS, N., Traumatology-Orthopaedics
- PRONCKUS, A., Surgery
- RAMANAUSKAS, J., Pharmacology
- RAUGALĖ, A., Paediatrics
- SIAURUSAITIS, B. J., Paediatric Surgery
- SIRVYDIS, V., Cardiac Surgery
- STRUPAS, K., Surgery
- TRIPONIS, V. J., Vascular Surgery
- USONIS, V., Paediatric Infectology
- UŽDAVINYS, G., Cardiac Surgery
- VAIČEKONIS, V., Pulmonology
- VALANTINAS, J., Hepatology
- VALIULIS, A., Paediatric Pulmonology
- VENALIS, A., Rheumatology
- VITKUS, K., Reconstructive Surgery
- ŽVIRONAITĖ, V., Cardiology

Faculty of Natural Sciences (M.K. Čiurlionio g. 21/27, 03101 Vilnius; tel. (5) 239-82-00; fax (53) 239-82-04; e-mail gf@gf.vu.lt; internet www.gf.vu.lt):

- BUKANTIS, A., Climatology

ČESNULEVIČIUS, A., Geomorphology
ČITAVIČIUS, D. J., Molecular Genetics of Microorganisms
DUNDULIS, K. J., Engineering Geology
GAIGALAS, A. J., Lithology
JANKAUSKAS, T. R., Palaeontology and Stratigraphy
JUODKA, B., Molecular Biology
JURGAITIS, A., Lithology and Mineral Deposits
KABAILIENĖ, M., Palaeontology and Stratigraphy
KAVALIAUSKAS, P., Land Management
KILKUS, K., Hydrology
KIRVELIENĖ, V., Cell Biochemistry
LAZUTKA, J. R., Human Cytogenetics
MOKRIK, R., Palaeohydrogeology, Hydrochemistry, Groundwater Formation
NAUJALIS, J. R., Botany
PODĖNAS, S., Entomology
RAKAUSKAS, R., Entomology
RANČELIS, V. P., Genetics
SLAPŠYTĖ, G., Animal Genetics
TRIMONIS, A. E., Oceanology
VALENTA, V. J., Biology
ŽAROMSKIS, R. P., Oceanology

Faculty of Philology (Universiteto g. 5, 01122 Vilnius; tel. (5) 268-72-02; fax (5) 268-72-08; e-mail flf@flf.vu.lt; internet www.flf.vu.lt):

GIRDENIS, A. S., General Linguistics, Baltic Linguistics
JAKAITIENĖ, E. M., Lexicology, Semantics
KOSTIN, E., Russian Literature
KOŽENAUSKIENĖ, R., Stylistics
LASSAN, E., Syntax, Cognitive Linguistics
NASTOPKA, K. V., Literary Theory, Lithuanian Literature
NORKAITIENĖ, I. N., History of German Language, German Philology, Semantics, Semiotics
PAKERIENĖ-DAUJOTYTĖ, V., History and Philosophy of Literature
PAULAUSKIENĖ, A., Grammar
ROSINAS, A., Comparative Linguistics, History of Baltic Languages
STUNDŽIA, B., Phonetics, Phonology
TEMČINAS, S., Old Church Texts, Balto-Slavic Linguistics
ULČINAITĖ, E., Neolatin Literature
USONIENĖ, A., English Linguistics, Semantics, Syntax

Faculty of Philosophy (Universiteto g. 9/1, 01513 Vilnius; tel. (5) 266-76-06; fax (5) 266-76-00; e-mail fsf@fsf.vu.lt; internet www.fsf.vu.lt):

BAGDONAS, A., Developmental Psychology
DOBRYNINAS, A., Philosophy of Social Sciences, Criminology
GAILIENĖ, D., Differential and Individual Psychology
KALENDA, C., Ethics
KOČIŪNAS, R. A., Clinical Psychology
NORKUS, Z., History of Philosophy
PLEČKAITIS, R., History of Philosophy
PŠIBILSKIS, V., Political Science
SAULAUSKAS, M. P., Contemporary Philosophy, Theories of Social Change, Postmodern Theories
ŠLIOGERIS, M. A., Metaphysics
VAITKEVIČIUS, P. H., Applied and Experimental Psychology
VALICKAS, G., Social Psychology

Faculty of Physics (Saulėtekio alėja 9, 10222 Vilnius; tel. (5) 236-60-00; fax (5) 236-60-03; e-mail ff@ff.vu.lt; internet www.ff.vu.lt):

ARLAUSKAS, K., Solid State Physics, Noncrystalline Materials
BALEVIČIUS, V., Theoretical Physics, Optics, Spectroscopy
BANDZAITIS, A., Atomic Physics
BANYS, J., Solid State Physics, Ferroelectrics
DIKČIUS, G., Optics, Spectroscopy
GADONAS, R. E., Optics
GARŠKA, E., Acoustics
GAVRIUŠINAS, V., Semiconductor Physics
GRIGAS, J., Ferroelectrics and Phase Transitions
IVAŠKA, V., Electromagnetism
JARAŠIUNAS, K., Semiconductor Physics
JURŠĖNAS, S. A., Semiconductor Physics
JUŠKA, G., Solid State Physics, Noncrystalline Materials
KAŽUKAUSKAS, V., Semiconductor Physics
KIMTYS, L., Magnetic Resonance, Relaxation, Spectroscopy
MONTRIMAS, E., Semiconductor Physics, Electronics Structure
ORLIUKAS, A. F., Solid State Ionics
PALENSKIS, V., Superconductor Physics
PISKARSKAS, A., Optics
ROTOMSKIS, R., Biophysics
SAKALAUSKAS, S., Electronics and Physical Instrumentation
SIRUTKAITIS, V., Optics
SMILGEVIČIUS, V., Optics
STABINIS, A. P., Optics
STORASTA, J., Semiconductor Physics
TAMULAITIS, G., Semiconductor Physics
VAITKUS, J. V., Semiconductor Physics
VALKŪNAS, L., Clinical Physics, Biophysics
ŽILINSKAS, P. J., Metrology, Physical Instrumentation
ŽUKAUSKAS, A., Semiconductor Physics

Sports Centre (Saulėtekio alėja 2, 10222 Vilnius; tel. (5) 269-87-20; fax (5) 269-88-56; e-mail sveikata.sportas@kkc.vu.lt):

JANKAUSKAS, J. P., Sports Education
SAPLINSKAS, J., Physiology

ATTACHED INSTITUTES

Algirdas Greimas Centre for Semiotics: Universiteto g. 5, Vilnius; tel. (5) 268-71-61; e-mail greimocentras@cr.vu.lt; internet www.gc.vu.lt; Head Dr DALIA SATKAUSKYTĖ.

Centre for Environmental Studies: Head Dr STASYS SINKEVIČIUS

PROFESSORS

LEKEVIČIUS, E., General Ecology

Centre for Gender Studies: Head Dr DALIA MARCINKEVIČIENĖ.

Centre for Oriental Studies: Head AUDRIUS BEINORIUS.

Centre for Religious Studies and Research: Head Habil. Dr RITA ŠERPYTYTĖ.

International Centre of Knowledge Economy and Knowledge Management: Dir Prof. RENALDAS GUDAUSKAS.

Institute of Foreign Languages: Dir Dr NIJOLĖ BRAŽĖNIENĖ

PROFESSORS

IDZELIS, R. V., Linguistics, Semantics

Institute of International Relations and Political Science: Dirs Prof. RAIMUNDAS LOPATA, Prof. J. ČIČINSKAS

PROFESSORS

JOKUBAITIS, A. (Political Philosophy)
NEKRAŠAS, E. (Theory of International Relations)

Institute of Materials Science and Applied Research: Dir Prof. ARTŪRAS ŽUKAUSKAS.

Stateless Cultures Centre: Head Dr GRIGORIJUS POTAŠENKO.

Vilnius Distance Education Study Centre: Dir Dr POVILAS ABARIUS.

VYTAUTO DIDŽIOJO UNIVERSITETAS (Vytautas Magnus University)

K. Donelaicio 58, 44248 Kaunas
Telephone: (37) 22-27-39
Fax: (37) 20-38-58
E-mail: info@adm.vdu.lt
Internet: www.vdu.lt

Founded 1922, closed 1950, re-opened 1989
State-funded
Languages of instruction: Lithuanian, English
Academic year: September to June

Rector: V. KAMINSKAS
Vice-Rector for Academic Affairs: P. ZAKAREVIČIUS
Vice-Rector for International Affairs: K. PUKELIS
Vice-Rector for Science: L. PRANEVIČIUS
University Secretary: N. KLEBANSKAJA
Chair. of the Senate: E. ALEKSANDRAVIČIUS
Chair. of the University Council: S. TAMKEVIČIUS
Librarian: J. MASALSKIENĖ

Library of 179,588 vols
Number of teachers: 430
Number of students: 9,000

Publications: *Management of Organizations: Systematic Research, SOTER, Vocational Training: Research and Realities, Works and Days*

DEANS

Faculty of Catholic Theology: V. VAIČIŪNAS
Faculty of Economics and Management: P. ŽUKAUSKAS
Faculty of Humanities: R. APANAVIČIUS
Faculty of Informatics: I. SKUČAS
Faculty of Natural Sciences: D. MICKEVIČIUS
Faculty of Social Sciences: R. LAUŽACKAS
School of Fine Arts: V. LEVANDAUSKAS
School of Law: T. KLIMAS
School of Political Sciences and Diplomacy: L. DONSKIS
School of Social Work: A. JAGELAVIČIUS
Kaunas Botanical Gardens: R. DAUBARAS

PROFESSORS

Faculty of Catholic Theology:

MOTUZAS, A.
NARBEKOVAS, A.
PUZARAS, P.
ŽEMAITIS, K.

Faculty of Economics and Management:

CEPINSKIS, J.
KVEDARAVIČIUS, P.
ZAKAREVIČIUS, P.
ZUKAUSKAS, P.

Faculty of Humanities:

ALEKSANDRAVIČIUS, E.
APANAVIČIUS, R.
DONSKIS, L.
GAMZIUKAITE-MAŽIULIENĖ, R.
GENZELIS, B.
GUDAITIS, L. F.
KARALIŪNAS, S.
KERBELYTE, B.
KIAUPA, Z.
MARCINKEVICIENE, R.
SKRUPSKELYTE, V.

Faculty of Informatics:

AUGUTIS, J.
KAMINSKAS, V.
SAPAGOVAS, M.
SKUČAS, I.

Faculty of Natural Sciences:

GRAŽULEVIČIENE, R.
JUKNYS, R.
KAMUNTAVIČIUS, G.
MARUSKA, A.
MILDAŽIENE, V.
PRANEVIČIUS, L.
STRAVINSKIENE, V.

Faculty of Social Sciences:

GOŠTAUTAS, A.
LAUŽACKAS, R.
PUKELIS, K.
TERRESEVIČIENE, M.

VAŠTOKAS, R.

School of Fine Arts:

LEVANDAUSKAS, V.

STAUSKAS, V.

VAŠKELIS, B.

School of Political Science and Diplomacy:

PRAZAUSKAS, A.

ATTACHED CENTRES

Business Consulting and Continuous Education Centre: Dir P. ZAKAREVIČIUS.

Centre for Social Research: Dir N. KASATKINA.

Centre for Asian Studies: Dir A. PRAZAUSKAS.

Centre for Civil Tolerance: Dir E. BENDIKAITE.

Centre of Computational Linguistics: Dir R. MARCINKEVIČIENÉ.

Centre for Educational Studies: Dir G. M. LINKAITYTE.

Centre for European Studies: Dir K. FUCHS.

Centre of Lithuanian Catholic Church History: Dir A. MOTUZAS.

Centre for Quality of Studies and Research: Dir K. PUKELIS.

Centre for Slavic Studies: Dir CZESLAW MILOSZ.

Çentre for Social Anthropology: Dir V. ČIUBRIUSKAS.

Centre for Social Integration: Dir J. PIVORIENE.

Centre for Social Welfare Education: Dir V. IVANAUSKIENÉ.

Centre for Vocational Training Studies: Dir R. LAUŽACKAS.

Culture Research Centre: Dir E. KIŠKINA.

Diaspora Study Centre: Dir E. ALEKSANDRAVIČIUS.

Environmental Research Centre: Dir V. MILDAŽIENÉ.

Foreign Languages Centre: Dir N. MAČIANSKIENÉ.

Japanese Study Centre: Dir A. ALIŠAUSKAS.

Latvian Studies Centre: Dir A. BUTKUS.

Prof. B. Vaskelis Çomparative Literature Centre: Dir I. ŽEKEVIČIUTE.

Sports Centre: Dir L. KALVAITIENE.

Statistics Centre: Dir V. KOPSTINSKAS.

War History Studies Centre: Dir V. RAKUTIS.

Other Higher Educational Institutes

Generolo Jono Žemaičio Lietuvos Karo Akademija (General Jono Žemaičio Military Academy of Lithuania): Šilo g. 5a, 10322 Vilnius; tel. (5) 210-36-88; fax (5) 212-73-18; e-mail info@lka.lt; internet www.lka.lt; f. 1994; state control; depts of foreign languages, management, department of political science, engineering management, humanities, applied sciences; military depts of tactics, combat support and physical training; Center of Science; Military History Center; Strategic Research Centre; library: 132,000 vols and periodicals; 424 cadets; Dir Col. ALGIMANTAS VYŠNIAUSKAS; publ. *The Military Archives*.

International School of Management: E. Ozeskienes 18, 44254 Kaunas; tel. (37) 30-24-02; fax (37) 20-56-76; e-mail ism@ism.lt; internet www.ism.lt; f. 1999; private control; library: 7,518 vols; 60 teachers; 900 students (600 undergraduate, 300 postgraduate); President VIRGINIJUS KUNDROTAS; publ. *Business Training Centre News* (monthly).

Lietuvos Kūno Kultūros Akademija (Lithuanian Academy of Physical Education): Sporto 6, 44221 Kaunas; tel. (37) 30-26-21; internet www.lkka.lt; f. 1945 as Lithuanian National Institute of Physical Education; state control; faculties of sports education, sports biomedicine and sports technologies and tourism; Rector ALBERTAS SKURVYDAS; publ. *Education. Physical Training. Sport.*

Lietuvos Muzikos ir Teatro Akademija (Lithuanian Academy of Music and Theatre): Gedimino pr. 42, 01110 Vilnius; tel. (5) 261-26-91; fax (5) 212-69-82; e-mail rektoratas@lma.lt; internet www.lma.lt; f. 1933; study programmes: musicology, ethnomusicology, music performance (piano, singing, orchestral instruments, folk instruments, accordion, choir conducting, symphony orchestra and opera-conducting), composition, musical education, drama (theory, history, acting and directing), television, film and sound directing, camera, arts management; library: libraries with 213,000 vols, record libraries with 29,000 records; 274 teachers; 1,167 students; Rector Prof. Dr EDUARDAS GABNYS; publ. *Menotyra* (Science of Art, annually).

Lietuvos Veterinarijos Akademija (Lithuanian Veterinary Academy): Tilžės g. 18, 47181 Kaunas; tel. (37) 36-23-83; fax (37) 36-24-17; e-mail reklva@lva.lt; internet www.lva.lt; f. 1936; faculties: veterinary medicine and animal husbandry technology; library: 231,486 vols; 120 teachers; 1,369 students; Rector HENRIKAS ŞILINSKAS; publ. *Veterinary Science and Zootechnics* (annually).

Vilniaus Dailes Akademija (Vilnius Academy of Fine Arts): Maironio 6, 01124 Vilnius; tel. (5) 210-54-30; fax (5) 210-54-63; e-mail vda@vda.lt; internet www.vda.lt; f. 1793; depts: painting, sculpture, printmaking, ceramics, architecture, textiles, art theory and history, design, interior and furnishing, industrial art, fashion design, monumental and decorative arts; library; museum; 280 teachers; 1,700 students; Rector Prof. ADOMAS BUTRIMAS.

LUXEMBOURG

The Higher Education System

In 1867 the London Congress declared Luxembourg to be an independent, sovereign state, although it remained under Dutch hegemony until 1890. The oldest existing institution of higher education is the Conservatoire de Musique de la Ville de Luxembourg (founded 1906), but the first university-level institution, the Université de Luxembourg, was not established until 2003. Prior to the foundation of the Université de Luxembourg an Act of 1969 permitted the recognition of qualifications awarded by overseas universities in Luxembourg; one such institution is Sacred Heart University in Luxembourg (founded 1991; attached to Sacred Heart University, CT, USA). Under the Law of 11 January 1995, a new higher education qualification, the Diplôme d'ingénieur industriel, was introduced.

The Université de Luxembourg participates in the Bologna Process to establish a European Higher Education Area, the first phase of which is to adopt a credit-based system of comparable degrees with two main cycles (undergraduate and postgraduate). The Bachelors is the primary undergraduate degree and requires three years of study; the first postgraduate degree is the Masters, and lasts two years; and the Doctorate is the highest university degree, lasting three years. Students at all levels are required to spend a period studying abroad. There are several non-university institutions offering a variety of two- to four-year diploma courses.

Technical and vocational education takes the form of adult and continuing programmes, and is offered by a range of institutions and agencies, including Centres of Continuing Vocational Training, Ministry of Education, Chambers of Commerce and Trades, the Communes and Private Associations.

Learned Societies

GENERAL

Institut Grand-Ducal: 2a rue Kalchesbruck, 1852 Luxembourg; tel. 478-2790; fax 478-2792; internet www.igd.lu; includes six sections: (*a*) History (Pres. PAUL SPANG), (*b*) Medicine (Pres. HENRI METZ), (*c*) Natural Sciences (Pres. PIERRE SECK), (*d*) Linguistic, Thnology and Place Names (Pres. HENRI KLEES), (*e*) Arts and Literature (Pres. PIERRE SCHUMACHER), (*f*) Moral and Political Sciences (Sec. GASTON REINESCH).

LANGUAGE AND LITERATURE

Institut Pierre Werner: 28, rue Münster, 2162 Luxembourg; tel. 490-4431; fax 490-643; e-mail info@ipw.lu; internet www.ipw.lu; f. 2003 jtly by the Centre Culturel Français, Goethe-Institut (Germany) and Ministère de la Culture Luxembourgeois; promotes cultural diversity and exchange in Europe; named after fmr Luxembourgeois Prime Minister; Dir CLAUDIA VOLKMAR-CLARK.

MEDICINE

Collège Médical: Ministère de la Santé, 57 blvd de la Pétrusse, Luxembourg; f. 1818; governmental consultative body; 11 mems; Pres. Dr GEORGES ARNOLD; Sec. PIERRE SCHROEDER.

NATURAL SCIENCES

Biological Sciences

Société des Naturalistes Luxembourgeois: BP 327, 2013 Luxembourg; e-mail info@snl.lu; internet www.snl.lu; f. 1890 to study the natural environment of Luxembourg and modifications of the animal and plant communities caused by environmental changes and to promote nature conservation; working groups: botany, mycology, and entomology; organizes conferences and guided excursions; 580 mems; Pres. CHRISTIAN RIES; Sec. YVES KRIPPEL; publ. *Bulletin* (annual).

Research Institutes

ECONOMICS, LAW AND POLITICS

Service Central de la Statistique et des Etudes Economiques: located at: 13, rue Erasme, 1468 Luxembourg; BP 304, 2013 Luxembourg; tel. 478-4272; e-mail secretariat@statec.etat.lu; internet www.statec.public.lu; f. 1962; attached to Min. of Economics; library of 9,000 vols, 500 periodicals; Dir SERGE ALLEGREZZA; publs *Annuaire Statistique du Luxembourg* (annually), *Cahiers Economiques* (irregular), *Indicateurs Rapides* (13 series), *Le Bulletin du STATEC* (8 a year), *Le Luxembourg en Chiffres*, *Le Recueil de Statistiques par Commune*, *Note de Conjoncture* (quarterly), *Recensements de la Population*, *Répertoire des Entreprises*, *Statistiques Historiques*.

EDUCATION

Commission Grand-Ducale d'Instruction: 29 rue Aldringen, 2926 Luxembourg; tel. 478-5254; fax 478-5188; internet www.men.lu; f. 1843; Pres. FRANCIS JEITZ; Sec. PAUL KLEIN.

MEDICINE

Centre de Recherche Public de la Santé: 18 rue Dicks, 1417 Luxembourg; tel. 453-2131; fax 453-219; e-mail secretariat@crp-sante.lu; internet www.crp-sante.lu; f. 1988; applied, clinical and public health research; Pres. FERNAND WAGNER.

TECHNOLOGY

Centre de Recherche Public Henri Tudor: 29 ave John F. Kennedy, 1855 Luxembourg-Kirchberg; tel. and fax 425-991; e-mail info@tudor.lu; internet www.crpht.lu; f. 1988; applied science; Pres. JEAN DE LA HAMETTE; Dir CLAUDE WEHENKEL; publ. *Cahiers de l'Innovation*.

Libraries and Archives

Esch-sur-Alzette

Bibliothèque de la Ville: 26 rue Emile Mayrisch, Esch-sur-Alzette; tel. 547-383; fax 552-037; e-mail bibliotheque@villeesch.lu; internet www.bibliotheque.esch.lu; f. 1919; German, French, English and Italian literature; popular science books; 60,000 vols; special collection of Luxembourgensia; Record Library; Chief Librarian HENRI LUTGEN.

Luxembourg

Archives Nationales: Plateau du Saint-Esprit, BP 6, 2010 Luxembourg; tel. 478-6660; fax 474-692; e-mail archives.nationales@an.etat.lu; internet www.etat.lu/an; f. 19th c.; Dir JOSEE KIRPS.

Bibliothèque Nationale: 37 blvd F. D. Roosevelt, 2450 Luxembourg; tel. 229755-1; fax 475672; e-mail info@bnl.etat.lu; internet www.bnl.lu; f. 1798, reorganized 1897, 1945, 1958, 1973, 1988 and 2004; nat. and research library open to the general public; 1,000,000 items; Dir Dr MONIQUE KIEFFER; publs *Bibliographie d'histoire luxembourgeoise* (online), *Bibliographie luxembourgeoise* (online).

Mersch

Centre National de Littérature: 2 rue Emmanuel Servais, 7565 Mersch; tel. 326-955; fax 327-090; e-mail cnl@cnl.etat.lu; internet www.literaturarchiv.lu; f. 1986; 40,000 vols, 300 periodicals; special collection of works published in Luxembourg; Dir GERMAINE GOETZINGER; Chief Librarian MARIE-FRANCE KREMER; publ. *Bibliographie courante de la littérature luxembourgeoise* (annually).

Museum

Luxembourg

Musée National d'Histoire et d'Art (National Museum of History and Art): Marché-aux-Poissons, 2345 Luxembourg; tel. and fax 479-330; e-mail musee@mnha.etat.lu; internet www.mnha.public.lu; f. 1845; archaeology, fine arts, industrial and popular arts, history of Luxembourg; library of 25,000 vols; Dir PAUL REILES; publ. *Newsletter*.

University

UNIVERSITÉ DU LUXEMBOURG

Limpertsberg Campus: 162A ave de la Faïencerie, 1511 Luxembourg
Kirchberg Campus: 6 rue Richard Coudenhove-Kalergi, 1359 Luxembourg
Walferdange Campus: BP 2, route de Diekirch, 7201 Walferdange

Telephone: 466-644-1
Fax: 466-644-508
Internet: www.uni.lu

Founded 1969; present name and status 2003
State control
Languages of instruction: French, German, English
Academic year: October to June
Rector: ROLF TARRACH
Vice-Rector: Dr ADELHEID EHMKE
Director (Administration): JEAN-PAUL MOSSONG
Library of 120,000 vols
Number of teachers: 350 (mostly part-time)
Number of students: 1,600

Publications: *Avis de la CNE*, *Cahiers d'Economie*, *Cahiers d'Histoire*, *Cahiers ISIS*, *Cahiers de Pédagogie*, *Cahiers de Philosophie – série A*, *Cahiers de Philosophie – série B*, *Cahiers de Physique*, *Editions Spéciales*, *English Studies*, *Etudes de Biologie*, *Etudes Classiques*, *Etudes de Géographie*, *Etudes de Philosophie*, *Etudes Romanes*, *Germanistik*, *Les Droits de l'Homme*, *Travaux de Linguistique*, *Travaux de Mathématiques*

DEANS

Faculty of Law, Economics and Finance: Prof. Dr FRANCK LEPREVOST (acting)
Faculty of Letters, Human Sciences, Arts and Educational Science: Prof. LUCIEN KERGER
Faculty of Science, Technology and Communication: Prof. Dr MASSIMO MALVETTI

Colleges

Conservatoire de Musique d'Esch-sur-Alzette: 50 rue d'Audun, BP 145, 4002 Esch-sur-Alzette; tel. 549-725; fax 549-731; internet www.conservatoire-esch.lu; f. 1926 as Ecole Municipale de Musique; present status 1969; 60 teachers; 1,000 students; Principal Prof. FRED HARLES; publ. *Annuaire* (Year Book).

Conservatoire de Musique de la Ville de Luxembourg: 33 rue Charles Martel, 2134 Luxembourg; tel. 456-555; fax 449-686; f. 1906; 150 teachers; Dir FERNAND JUNG; Sec. PIERRE BERG; publ. *Compte rendu* (annually).

Institut Supérieur de Technologie: Rue Richard Coudenhove-Kalergi, 1359 Luxembourg-Kirchberg; tel. 420-101; fax 432-124; e-mail admin@ist.lu; f. 1979; mechanical engineering, electrical engineering, civil engineering, industrial computing; library: 10,000 vols; 70 teachers; 400 students; Pres. PROSPER SCHROEDER; Dir ALBERT RETTER.

Institut Universitaire International de Luxembourg: Château de Munsbach, 31 rue du Parc, 5374 Luxembourg; located at: BP 73, 6905 Niederanven; tel. 2615-9212; fax 2615-9228; internet www.iuil.lu; f. 1974; Dir POL WAGNER

DEPARTMENTS

Centre International d'Economie Politique
Centre International d'Etudes Juridiques et de Droit Comparé
Centre International d'Etudes et de Recherches Européennes

Sacred Heart University in Luxembourg: 25B Blvd Royal, 2449 Luxembourg; tel. 227-613; fax 227-623; e-mail admissions@shu.lu; internet www.shu.lu; f. 1991; US-accredited MBA program; attached to Sacred Heart University, Connecticut, USA; Dirs Dr THOMAS D. QUEISSER (Academic Programs), VICTORIA GEHRING (Graduate Admissions).

FORMER YUGOSLAV REPUBLIC OF MACEDONIA

The Higher Education System

After the First World War (1914–18) Vardar Macedonia, the area now known as the former Yugoslav republic of Macedonia (FYRM), became part of the new Kingdom of Serbs, Croats and Slovenes (formally named Yugoslavia in 1929). Following the Second World War (1939–45) Macedonia became part of the new communist-led Federative People's Republic of Yugoslavia. In 1991 the Macedonian Sobranie (Assembly) declared the republic of Macedonia to be a sovereign territory. Macedonian secession was effectively acknowledged by the Federal Republic of Yugoslavia in 1992. Univerzitet 'SV. Kiril I Metodij' (University of Skopje—founded 1949) is the oldest of the three universities in Macedonia; the others are Univerzitet 'Sv. Kiliment Ohridski' Bitola (St Klement Ohridski University of Bitola—founded 1979) and Universiteti I Ejl (South-East European University—founded 2001). The last of these was established following new legislation in 2000 which permitted the use of Albanian and other languages in private tertiary institutions, and in 2004, under further amendments to legislation on higher education, it became the third state-funded university. In 2003/04 some 46,637 students were enrolled at the universities at Skopje and at Bitola.

Admission to higher education is on the basis of the Secondary Leaving Diploma and entrance examinations. Higher education is divided between colleges and universities/university faculties. Colleges specialize in two- to three-year diploma courses leading to a professional title. Universities and university faculties offer four- to six-year diploma and degree programmes. The first postgraduate degree is the Masters (Magister) and is a two-year research degree culminating in public defence of a thesis. The final university-level degree is the Doctor of Science (Doktor na nauiki).

Learned Societies

GENERAL

Društvo za nauka i umetnost (Association of Sciences and Arts): 97000 Bitola, POB 145; tel. (97) 22-683; f. 1960; main activities: scientific meetings, symposia, research; 154 mems; 25 assocs; sections of social sciences and law, natural and mathematical sciences, medical, technical and applied sciences, arts, linguistics and literature, history and geography; Pres. SOTIR PANOVSKI; Sec.-Gen. TRAJKO OGNENOVSKI; publs *Prilozi* (Contributions, 2 a year), *Scientific Thought*.

Makedonska Akademija na Naukite i Umetnostite (Macedonian Academy of Sciences and Arts): 1000 Skopje, Bulevar Krste Misirkov 2, POB 428; tel. (2) 323-5400; fax (2) 323-5500; e-mail makakad@manu.edu.mk; internet www.manu.edu.mk; f. 1967; sections of Arts (Sec. PETRE M. ANDREEVSKI), Biological and Medical Sciences (Sec. VLADIMIR SERAFIMOSKI), Linguistics and Literary Sciences (Sec. ZUZANNA TOPOLIŃSKA), Mathematical and Technical Sciences (Sec. BOJAN ŠOPTRAJANOV), Social Sciences (Sec. TAKI FITI); 72 mems (43 ordinary, 29 foreign); library of 100,000 vols; Pres. CVETAN GROZDANOV; Chief Scientific Sec. KRUM TOMOVSKI; publs *Letopis* (annually), *Prilozi na Oddelenieto za biološki i medicinski nauki* (Contributions of the Dept of Biological and Medical Sciences, 2 a year), *Prilozi na Oddelenieto za lingvistika i literaturna nauka* (Contributions of the Dept of Linguistics and Literary Sciences, 2 a year), *Prilozi na Oddelenieto za matematičko-tehnički nauki* (Contributions of the Dept of Mathematical and Technical Sciences, 2 a year), *Prilozi na Oddelenieto za opštestveni nauki* (Contributions of the Dept of Social Sciences, 2 a year).

AGRICULTURE, FISHERIES AND VETERINARY SCIENCE

Sojuz na Društvata na Veterinarnite Lekari i Tehničari na Makedonija (Union of Associations of Veterinary Surgeons and Technicians of Macedonia): Veterinaren institut, 1000 Skopje, Lazar Pop-Trajkov 5, POB 95; f. 1950; 450 mems; Pres. SILJAN ZAHARIEVSKI; Sec. ADŽIEVSKI BLAŽE; publ. *Makedonski veterinaren pregled* (Macedonian Veterinary Review).

Sojuz na Inženeri i Tehničari po Sumarstvo i Industrija za Prerabotka na Drvo na Makedonija (Union of Forestry Engineers and Technicians of Macedonia): Šumarski institut, 1000 Skopje, Engelsova 2; f. 1952; 500 mems; Pres. Dipl. Ing. ŽIVKO MINČEV; Sec. Dipl. Ing. MILE STAMENKOV; publ. *Sumarski pregled* (Forester's review).

Zdruzenie na Zemjodelski Inženeri na Makedonija (Association of Agricultural Engineers of Macedonia): Zemjodelski fakultet, P. Fah. 297, 1000 Skopje; tel. (2) 311-5277; fax (2) 323-8218; f. 1994; 3,000 mems; publ. *Macedonian Agriculture Review* (annually).

BIBLIOGRAPHY, LIBRARY SCIENCE AND MUSEOLOGY

Bibliotekarsko Drushtvo na Makedonija (Macedonian Library Association): Narodna i univerzitetska biblioteka 'Kliment Ohridski', 1000 Skopje Bul. Goce Delčev, br 6; tel. (2) 321-2736; fax (2) 322-6846; e-mail lanam@freemail.org.mk; f. 1949; 250 mems; Pres. SVETLANA MARKOVIK; Sec. (vacant); publ. *Bibliotekarska iskra* (2 a year).

Društvo na Muzejskite Rabotnici na Makedonija (Museum Society of Macedonia): Muzej na grad Skopje, 1000 Skopje, Mito Hadži-Vasilev-Jasmin b.b.; f. 1951; 100 mems; Pres. KUZMAN GEORGIEVSKI; Sec. GALENA KUCULOVSKA.

Sojuz na društvata na arhivskite rabotnici na Makedonija (Union of Societies of Archivists of Macedonia): 1001 Skopje, Gligor Prličev 3, POB 496; tel. (2) 323-7211; fax (2) 323-4461; f. 1954; 340 mems; publ. *Makedonski arhivist* (annually).

ECONOMICS, LAW AND POLITICS

Društvo za Filozofija, Sociologija i Politikologija na Makedonija (Society for Philosophy, Sociology and Politics of Macedonia): Institut za sociološki i političko-pravni istražuvanja, 1000 Skopje, Bul. Partizanski odredi b.b.; f. 1960; 170 mems; Pres. Dr DRAGAN TAŠKOVSKI; Sec. SVETA ŠKARIĆ; publ. *Zbornik* (Collected Papers).

Sojuz na Ekonomistite na Makedonija (Union of Economists of Macedonia): 1000 Skopje, Ekonomiski Fakultet, K. Misirkov b.b.; tel. (2) 322-4311; fax (2) 322-4973; f. 1950; 3,000 mems; Pres. Prof. Dr TAKI FITI; Sec. ACO SPASOVSKI; publ. *Stopanski pregled* (Economic review).

Sojuz na Združenijata na Pravnicite na Makedonija (Union of Associations of Jurists of Macedonia): Ustaven sud na Makedonija, 1000 Skopje, XII udarna brigada 2; f. 1946; 4,000 mems; Pres. BORO DOGANDŽISKI; Sec. PETAR GOLUBOVSKI; publ. *Pravna misla* (Legal opinion).

FINE AND PERFORMING ARTS

Društvo na Istoričarite na Umetnosta od Makedonija (Society of Art Historians of Macedonia): Arheološki muzej na Makedonija, 1000 Skopje, Curčiska b.b.; f. 1970; 130 mems; Pres. MILANKA BOŠKOVSKA; Sec. MATE BOŠKOVSKI; publ. *Likovna umetnost* (Plastic Arts).

Društvo na Likovnite Umetnici na Makedonija (Society of Plastic Arts of Macedonia): 1000 Skopje, 13 Noemvri b.b., PF 438; tel. (2) 321-1533; f. 1944; 333 mems; Pres. GLIGOR ČEMERSKI; Sec. BRANISLAV MIRČEVSKI.

Sojuz na Kompozitorite na Makedonija (Society of Macedonian Composers): 1000 Skopje, Maksim Gorki 18; tel. (2) 322-0567; fax (2) 323-5854; f. 1950; 49 mems; Pres. VLASTIMIR NIKOLOVSKI; Sec. MARKO KOLOVSKI; publ. *Informer*.

HISTORY, GEOGRAPHY AND ARCHAEOLOGY

Geografsko Društvo na R. Makedonija (Geographical Society of Macedonia): Geografski institut pri Prirodnomatematički fakultet, 1000 Skopje, PF 146; f. 1949; 600 mems; Pres. Prof. VASIL GRAMATNIKOVSKI; Sec. Ass. NIKOLA PANOV; publs *Geografski razgledi* (Geographical surveys), *Geografski vidik* (Geographical outlook).

Sojuz na Društvata na Istoričarite na Republika Makedonija (Union of Societies of Historians of the Republic of Macedonia): Institut za nacionalna istorija, 1000 Skopje, ul. Grigor Prličev br.3, POB 591; tel. (2) 311-4078; fax (2) 311-5831; f. 1952; Pres. Dr TODOR CHEPREGANOV; Sec. GHORGHI CHAKARJANEVSKI; publ. *Istorija* (History).

Združenie na Arheolozite na Makedonija (Archaeological Society of Macedonia): Muzej na Makedonija, Ćurčiska b. b., 1000 Skopje (Kuršumlian); tel. (2) 311-6044; fax (2) 311-6439; f. 1970; 150 mems; Pres. VOISLAV SANEV; Sec. DRAGIŠA ZDRAVKOVSKI; publ. *Macedoniae acta archaeologica*.

LANGUAGE AND LITERATURE

Alliance Française: Bitola 7000, M. U. B. 'Sv. Kliment Ohridski', Leninova 39; tel. and fax (47) 232-363; e-mail afbitola@yahoo.fr; offers courses and exams in French language and culture and promotes cultural exchange with France; attached office in Tetovo; Dir JEAN-FRANÇOIS SAINT-DIZIER.

British Council: Bulevar Goce Delcev 6, POB 562, 1000 Skopje; tel. (2) 313-5035; fax (2) 313-5036; e-mail info@britishcouncil.org.mk; internet www.britishcouncil.org/macedonia; f. 1996; offers courses and exams in English language and British culture and promotes cultural exchange with the UK; library of 6,000 vols; Dir ANDREW HADLEY.

Društvo na Literaturnite Preveduvači na Makedonija (Society of Literary Translators of Macedonia): 1000 Skopje, PF 3; f. 1955; 102 mems; Pres. Prof. Dr BOŽIDAR NASTEV; Sec. TAŠKO ŠIRILOV.

Društvo na Pisatelite na Makedonija (Society of Writers of Macedonia): 1000 Skopje, Maksim Gorki 18; tel. (2) 311-7668; fax (2) 322-8345; f. 1947; 269 mems; Pres. JOVAN PAVLOVSKI; Secs PASKAL GILOVSKI, SVETLANA HRISTOVA-JOCIĆ.

Sojuz na Društvata za Makedonski Jazik i Literatura (Union of Asscns for Macedonian Language and Literature): Filološki fakultet, 1000 Skopje, Bul. Krste Misirkov b.b.; f. 1954; 700 mems; Pres. ELENA BENDEVSKA; Sec. LJUPČO MITREVSKI; publ. *Literaturen zbor* (Literary word).

Združenie na Folkloristite na Makedonija (Association of Folklorists of Macedonia): Institut za folklor, 1000 Skopje, Ruzveltova 3; tel. (2) 323-3876; f. 1952; 60 mems; Pres. GORGI SMOKVARSKI; Sec. ERMIS LAFAZANOVSKY; publ. *Narodno Stvaralaštvo* (1 or 2 a year).

MEDICINE

Farmaceutsko Društvo na Makedonija (Pharmacological Society of Macedonia): 1000 Skopje, Ivo Ribar Lola MI/6; Pres. LAZAR TOLOV; Sec. GALABA SRBINOVSKA; publ. *Bilten* (Bulletin).

Makedonsko Lekarsko Društvo (Medical Society of Macedonia): 1000 Skopje, Gradski zid blok 11/6; f. 1946; 2,000 mems; publ. *Makedonski medicindki pregled* (Macedonian Medical Review).

NATURAL SCIENCES

Mathematical Sciences

Sojuz na Društvata na Matematičarite na Makedonija (Society of Mathematicians of Macedonia): 1000 Skopje, PF 162; tel. (2) 311-7055 ext. 105; fax (2) 322-8141; e-mail pandeski@iunona.phf.ukim.edu.mk; f. 1950; Chief Officers Prof. Dr BORKO ILIEVSKI, Prof. Dr NIKOLA PANDESKI; publ. *Matematički Bilten* (Mathematical Bulletin).

Physical Sciences

Društvo na Fizičarite na Makedonija (Society of Physicists of Macedonia): 1000 Skopje, POB 162; tel. (2) 311-7055; fax (2) 322-8141; e-mail blagoj@iunona.pmf.ukim.edu.mk; f. 1949; 60 mems; Pres. Prof. Dr BLAGOJA VELJANOSKI; Sec. Asst Prof. NACE STOJANOV; publs *Bilten* (Bulletin), *Impuls*.

Makedonsko Geološko Društvo (Macedonian Geological Society): Geološki zavod, 1001 Skopje, POB 28; tel. (2) 323-0873; f. 1954; 300 mems; library of 20,000 vols; Pres. NIKOLA TUDŽAROV; Sec. ROZA PETROVSKA.

TECHNOLOGY

Sojuz na Inženeri i Tehničari na Makedonija (Society of Engineers and Technicians of Macedonia): 1000 Skopje, Nikola Vapcarov b.b.; f. 1945; 27,000 mems; Pres. Prof. Dr Ing. DIME LAZAROV; Sec. BORO RAVNJANSKI.

Research Institutes

AGRICULTURE, FISHERIES AND VETERINARY SCIENCE

Institut za Južni Zemjodelski Kulturi (Institute of Southern Crops): 2400 Strumica, Goce Delčev b.b.; tel. (34) 345-096; fax (34) 345-096; e-mail admin@isc.ukim.edu.mk; internet www.isc.ukim.edu.mk; f. 1956; Dir Dr SAŠA MITREV; publ. *Zbornik* (Collected Papers).

Institut za Ovoštarstvo (Institute of Pomology): 1000 Skopje, Prvomajska 5; tel. (2) 323-0557; f. 1953; attached to Skopje University; fruit research; library of 3,670 vols; Dir Dr IVAN KUZMANOVSKI.

Institut za Stočarstvo (Institute of Animal Sciences): 1000 Skopje, Ile Ilievski 92A; tel. (2) 306-3523; fax (2) 306-2358; f. 1952; Dir Dr BONE PALASEVSKI.

Institut za Tutun (Tobacco Institute): 97500 Prilep, Kičevsko Džade; tel. (48) 416-760; fax (48) 416-763; f. 1924; library of 5,000 vols; Dir Dr KIRIL FILIPOSKI; publ. *Tutun* (Tobacco, every 2 months).

Veterinaren Institut na Makedonija (Veterinary Institute of Macedonia): 1000 Skopje, Univerzitet Kiril i Metodij, Ul. Lazar Pop Trajkov 5-7; f. 1927; Dir CANE PEJKOVSKI; Sec. DIMITAR ANASTASOV.

Zavod za Unapreduvanje na Lozarstvoto i Vinarstvoto na Makedonija (Institute for the Advancement of Viticulture of Macedonia): 1000 Skopje, Naselba Butel 1; f. 1952; Dir Dr DIME PEMOVSKI; publs *Lozarstvo i vinarstvo* (Viticulture), *Godišen izveštaj* (Annual Report).

Zavod za Unapreduvanje na Stočarstvoto na Makedonija (Institute for the Advancement of Animal Husbandry of Macedonia): 1000 Skopje, Avtokomanda; f. 1952; Dir Prof. Dr BLAGOJ VASKOV.

ECONOMICS, LAW AND POLITICS

Ekonomski Institut na Univerzitetet 'Sveti Kiril i Metodij' (Institute of Economics of Sts Cyril and Methodius University): 1000 Skopje, Prolet 1, POB 250; tel. (2) 311-5076; fax (2) 322-6350; e-mail eis@ek-inst.ukim.edu.mk; internet www.ek-inst.ukim.edu.mk; f. 1952; library of 19,000 vols; Dir Prof. Dr ANTONIJA JOSIFOVSKA; publ. *Economic Development Journal* (4 a year).

HISTORY, GEOGRAPHY AND ARCHAEOLOGY

Institut za Nacionalna Istorija (Institute of National History): 1000 Skopje, Ul. Gligor Prlicev br.3; tel. (2) 311-4078; fax (2) 311-5831; e-mail inimak@on.net.mk; f. 1948; history of Macedonian peoples, history of Balkan peoples, history of ethnic communities; 56 mems; library of 27,350 vols; library: 37,500 periodicals, 1,300 vols newspapers; Dir Prof. Dr TODOR CEPREGANOV; publ. *Glasnik* (Journal).

LANGUAGE AND LITERATURE

Institut za Folklor (Institute of Folklore): 1000 Skopje, Ruzveltova 3, POB 319; tel. (2) 338-0176; fax (2) 338-0177; f. 1950; Dir Dr TRPKO BICEVSKI; publ. *Makedonski folklor* (2 a year).

Institut za Makedonski Jazik 'Krste Misirkov' (Krste Misirkov Institute of Macedonian Language): 1000 Skopje, Grigor Prličev 5; tel. (2) 311-4733; fax (2) 322-2225; e-mail kvesna@ukim.edu.mk; f. 1953; Dir MARIJA KOROBAR-BELČEVA; publs *Makedonski jazik* (The Macedonian Language), *Stari tekstovi* (Ancient Texts), *Makedonistika* (Macedonian Studies).

TECHNOLOGY

Geološki Zavod (Geology Institute): 1001 Skopje, POB 28; f. 1944; geological mapping, exploration of mineral deposits, drilling, mining, grouting; *c.* 700 mems; library: *c.* 10,000 vols; Gen Dir DRAGAN ANGELESKY; publ. *Trudovi* (Transactions).

Zavod za vodostopanstvo na R. Makedonija (Water Development Institute of Macedonia): 1000 Skopje, Železnička 62, PF 310; tel. (2) 322-8028; fax (2) 323-9401; f. 1951; library of 1,800 vols; Dir Ing. METODI BOEV; publ. *Vodostopanski problemi* (Water Development Problems, every 5 years).

Libraries and Archives

Bitola

Istoriski arhiv na Bitola (Historical Archives of Bitola): 97000 Bitola, 1 May 171; f. 1954; conservation, collection and printing of archive materials; 3,946 vols; Dir JOVAN KOCHANKOVSKY.

Matična i Univerzitetska Biblioteka 'Kliment Ohridski' ('St Climent Ohridski' University Library): 97000 Bitola, Leninova 39; tel. and fax (47) 220-515; e-mail nuubbt@uklo.edu.mk; internet www.nuubbt.uklo.edu.mk; f. 1945; 450,000 vols; Dir JELENA PETROVSKA; publ. *Library Trend* (quarterly).

Ohrid

Arhiv na Makedonija: 97300 Ohrid; tel. (96) 32-104; f. 1957; 3,000 vols; special collections: Old Church Slavonic MSS, early Greek and Arabic books; Dir DIMITAR SMILESKI.

Skopje

Arhiv na Makedonija (State Archives of the Former Yugoslav Republic of Macedonia): Gligor Prličev 3, 1000 Skopje; tel. (2) 311-5783; fax (2) 316-5944; e-mail arhiv@unet.com.mk; internet www.arhiv.gov.mk; f. 1951; 70,274,587 documents; 9 regional depts: Skopje, Bitola, Prilep, Tetovo, Shtip, Strumica, Kumanovo, Ohrid and Veles; Dir Dr ATANAS VANGELOV; publ. *Makedonski archivist*.

Arhiv na Skopje (Archives of Skopje): 1000 Skopje, Moskovska 1, reon 45; tel. (2) 325-9420; f. 1952; 3,000 vols; *c.* 1.5 km of archive records, 333,152 units of published information; Dir Dr MILOŠ KONSTANTINOV; publ. *Dokumenti i materiali za istorijata na Skopje* (irregular).

Biblioteka 'Braka Miladinovci' (District of Skopje Public Library): 1000 Skopje, Partizanski odredi b.b.; tel. (2) 323-2544; f. 1935; 800,000 vols; 27 brs; Dir GOJKO IKONOMOV.

Narodna i univerzitetska biblioteka 'Sv. Kliment Ohridski' (National and University Library 'St Kliment Ohridski'): 1000 Skopje, Bul. Goce Delčev 6; tel. (2) 311-5177; fax (2) 322-6846; e-mail kliment@nubsk.edu.mk; internet www.nubsk.edu.mk; f. 1944; State copyright, central and deposit library; 3,000,000 vols; special collections: Slav MSS, incunabula and rare books, oriental, music, cartography, doctoral theses, fine art; Dir POSKOL GILEVSKI; publ. *Makedonska bibliografija* (in 3 series, each 4 a year).

Museums and Art Galleries

Bitola

Zavod, muzej i galerija (Institute, Museum and Gallery): 7000 Bitola, Ul. Kliment Ohridski b.b.; tel. (47) 233-187; fax (47) 229-525; e-mail grafik@freemail.com.mk; internet www.muzejbt.org.mk; f. 1948; archaeology, history, ethnology, art; library of 10,000 vols; Dir IVAN JOLEVSKI.

Skopje

Muzej na Grad Skopje (Museum of Skopje): 1000 Skopje, Mito Hadzivasilev b.b.; tel. (2) 311-5367; f. 1949; Dir KLIME KOROBAR.

Muzej na Makedonija (Museum of Macedonia): 1000 Skopje, Curčiska b.b.; tel. (2) 311-6044; fax (2) 311-6439; e-mail musmk@mpt.com.mk; internet www.artisoft.net/museum; f. 1924; archaeology, history, ethnology; library of 19,000 vols; Dir Dr DRAGI MITREVSKI; publs *Numizmatičar* (annually), *Zbornik* (Collected Papers, annually).

Muzej na Sovremena Umetnost (Museum of Contemporary Art): 1000 Skopje, Samoilova b.b., PF 482; tel. (2) 311-7735; f. 1964; Dir ZORAN PETROVSKI.

Prirodonaučen muzej na Makedonija (Natural History Museum of Macedonia): 1000 Skopje, 55 Bulevar Ilinden 86; f. 1926; library of 44,000 vols; Dir BRANISLAVA MIHAJLOVA; publs *Acta*, *Fragmenta Balcanica*, *Fauna na Makedonija*.

Umetnička Galerija (Art Gallery): 1000 Skopje, Kruševska 1A, POB 278; tel. (2) 323-3904; f. 1948; modern art; Dir VIKTORIJA VASEVA-DIMESKA.

Universities

UNIVERSITETI I EJL (South-East European University—SEE)

1200 Tetovo, 'Ilindenska' p.n.

Telephone: (44) 356-000

Internet: www.seeu.edu.mk

Founded 2001

State control

Languages of instruction: Albanian, English

Rector: Dr ALAJDIN ABAZI

Pro-Rector for Academic Issues: Dr ABDYLMENAF BEXHETI

Pro-Rector for Research Issues: Dr ZAMIR DIKA

Secretary-General: Dr BLERIM REKA

Library of 16,139 vols

Number of teachers: 300

Number of students: 6,000

DEANS

Faculty of Business Administration: Dr NASIR SELIMI

Faculty of Communication Sciences and Technologies: Dr VLLADIMIR RADEVSKI

Faculty of Law: Dr ASLLAN BILALLI

Faculty of Public Administration: Dr ETEM AZIRI

Faculty of Teacher Training: Dr TEUTA ARIFI

Director of Graduate Programmes and Research: PAUL FOSTER

UNIVERZITET 'SV. KIRIL I METODIJ' (University of Skopje)

1000 Skopje, POB 576, Bulevar Krste Misirkov b.b.

Telephone: (2) 311-6323

Fax: (2) 311-6370

E-mail: postmaster@ukim.edu.mk

Internet: www.ukim.edu.mk

Founded 1949

State control

Language of instruction: Macedonian

Academic year: October to June

Rector: Prof. Dr GJORGJI MARTINOVSKI

Vice-Rector for Finance, Investments and Development: Prof. BORIS KRSTEV

Vice-Rector for International Co-operation: Prof. LJUBICA SUTURKOVA

Vice-Rector for Science: Prof. VELIMIR STOJKOVSKI

Vice-Rector for Teaching: Prof. ZORAN VELKOVSKI

Secretary-General: DUŠKO SEKOVSKI

Number of teachers: 2,600

Number of students: 36,700

Publications: *Univerzitetski bilten*, *Univerzitetski vesnik i Studentski zbor*

DEANS

Faculty of Agriculture and Food: Prof. Dr ORDAN CUKALIEV

Faculty of Architecture: Prof. Dr VLATKO P. KOROBAR

Faculty of Civil Engineering: Prof. Dr SANDE ATANASOVSKI

Faculty of Dentistry: Prof. Dr MARIJA NAKOVA

Faculty of Drama: Prof. GOCE KOLAROVSKI

Faculty of Economics: Prof. Dr BOBEK SUKLEV

Faculty of Education (Skopje): Prof. Dr NIKOLA PETROV

Faculty of Education (Stip): Prof. SPASKO SIMONOVSKI

Faculty of Electrical Engineering: Prof. Dr VANGEL FUSTIĆ

Faculty of Fine Arts: Prof. VELJO TASOVSKI

Faculty of Forestry: Prof. Dr KOLE VASILEVSKI

Faculty of Law: Prof. Dr GALE GALEV

Faculty of Mechanical Engineering: Prof. Dr MILAN COSEVSKI

Faculty of Medicine: Prof. Dr MAGDALENA ZANTEVA-NAUMOVSKA

Faculty of Mining and Geology: Prof. Dr TODOR DELIPETROV

Faculty of Music: Prof. Dr DIMITRIJE BUZAROVSKI

Faculty of Natural and Mathematical Sciences: Prof. Dr ICKO GJORGJOSKI

Faculty of Pedagogy: Prof. Dr MURAT MURATI

Faculty of Pedagogy: Prof. Dr METODI SIMONOVSKI

Faculty of Pharmacy: Prof. Dr SVETLANA KULEVANOVA

Faculty of Philology: Prof. Dr MAKSIM KARANFILOVSKI

Faculty of Philosophy: Prof. Dr TRAJAN GOCEVSKI

Faculty of Physical Education: Prof. Dr DUSKO IVANOV

Faculty of Technology and Metallurgy: Prof. Dr BLAGOJ PAVLOVSKI

Faculty of Veterinary Medicine: Prof. Dr JOSIF TOSEVSKI

ATTACHED RESEARCH INSTITUTES

Institute of Agriculture: Dir Dr SLOBODAN BANXO.

Institute of Cattle-Breeding: Dir Dr MIRJANA MENKOVSKA.

Institute of Earthquake Engineering and Seismology: Dir Dr MIHAIL GAREVSKI.

Institute of Economics: Dir Dr ANTONIJA JOSIFOVSKA.

Institute of Folklore: Dir Dr SEVIM PILICKOVA.

Institute of the Macedonian Language 'Krste Misirkov': Dir Dr SNEZANA VENOVSKA-ANTEVSKA.

Institute of Macedonian Literature: Dir Dr JOVANKA STOJANOVSKA.

Institute of National History: Dir Dr TODOR CEPERGANOV.

Institute of Sociological, Political and Juridical Research: Dir Dr PANDE LAZAREVSKI.

Institute of Southern Crops: Dir Dr SASO MITREV.

UNIVERZITET 'SV. KLIMENT OHRIDSKI' BITOLA (St Kliment Ohridski University of Bitola)

97000 Bitola, Bulevar 1 Maj b.b.

Telephone: (97) 223-788

Fax: (97) 223-594

E-mail: rektorat@uklo.edu.mk

Internet: www.uklo.edu.mk

Founded 1979

Languages of instruction: Macedonian, Serbian

Rector: Prof. Dr BOŽIDAR MASLINKOV

Secretary-General: Dipl. pravnik JORDAN MITREVSKI

Library of 160,000 vols, 500 periodicals, 1,000 microforms

Number of teachers: 248

Number of students: 9,150

Faculties of Biotechnology, Economics, Law, Teacher Training, Technology and Tourism and Hotel Management; Higher School of Medicine; Institutes of Agriculture, Ancient Slavic Culture, Education, Hydrobiology and Tobacco Research.

MADAGASCAR

The Higher Education System

In 1896 Madagascar came under French colonial rule and in 1958 became an autonomous state (as the Malagasy Republic) within the French Community; full independence was achieved in 1960. The Université d'Antananarivo (founded 1961) is the oldest current institution of higher education; it was formed from a merger of pre-existing colleges. The Ministry of National education and Scientific Research has overall responsibility for higher education, which consists of universities, technical institutes and teacher training colleges. In 2003/04 there were an estimated 42,100 students in higher education, and In 2005/06 there were six universities and 14 private institutions of higher education. The degree system (see below) is based upon the French cyclical model.

The Rector or President is the head of the University, governing in conjunction with Councils for administrative and academic affairs. The Administrative Council oversees the institutional budget, stipulates rules and regulations and ensures good governance. The Academic Council is responsible for matters of teaching and research.

The secondary school Baccalauréat is required for admission to university. The university degree system consists of three cycles. The first cycle lasts for two years after which a student receives one of two diplomas, either Diplôme Universitaire d'Etudes Littéraires or Diplôme Universitaire d'Etudes Scientifiques. Engineering students are awarded either the Diplôme Universitaire de Technicien Supérieur en Informatique or the Diplôme Universitaire d'Etudes Technologiques before studying for another two to three years for the Diplôme d'Ingénieur. Law students are awarded the Capacité en Droit after two years, and can then stake the four-year Licence. The Doctorat de Médecine is a seven-year programme. The second cycle is a period of specialization of either one year, resulting in award of the Licence (undergraduate degree), or two years, resulting in award of the Maîtrise (postgraduate degree). Following the Maîtrise, the third cycle is a two-year period of study leading to the award of the Diplôme d'Etudes Supérieures, followed by research and thesis for the degree of Doctorat de Troisième Cycle.

The main post-secondary qualification for technical and vocational education is the Brevet de Technicien, awarded after three years' study at technical institutes.

Learned Societies

GENERAL

Académie Nationale Malgache: BP 6217, Tsimbazaza, Antananarivo; f. 1902; studies in human and natural sciences; four sections: language, literature and arts, moral and political sciences, basic sciences, applied sciences; 140 mems, 60 foreign mems in each section; library of 100,000 vols; Pres. Dr C. RABENORO; publs *Bulletin de l'Academie* (annually), *Bulletin d'Information et de Liaison*, *Mémoires*.

BIBLIOGRAPHY, LIBRARY SCIENCE AND MUSEOLOGY

Association des Bibliothécaires, Documentalistes, Archivistes et Muséographes de Madagascar: Bibliothèque Nationale, BP 257, Antananarivo; tel. (20) 22-258-72; f. 1976; promotion, development, preservation and conservation of national collections; Pres CHRISTIANE ANDRIAMIRADO; Secs SAMOELA ANDRIANKOTONIRINA, FRANÇOISE RAMANANDRAISOA; publ. *Haren-tsaina* (2 a year).

LANGUAGE AND LITERATURE

Alliance Française: Ambavamamba 101, BP 916 Antananarivo; tel. (20) 22-232-63; fax (20) 22-225-04; e-mail dgfranc@dts.mg; internet www.alliancefrancaise.mg; offers courses and exams in French language and culture and promotes cultural exchange with France; attached teaching centres in Ambanja, Ambatondrazaka Ambilobe, Ambositra, Ambovombe, Andapa, Antalaha, Antananarivo, Antsahabe, Antsalova, Antsirabé, Antsiranana, Antsohihy, Fandriana, Farafangana, Fianarantsoa, Fort Dauphin, Mahajanga, Maintirano, Manakara, Mananjary, Moramanga, Morombe, Morondava, Nosy Be, Sainte Marie, Sambava, Toamasina, Tolagnaro, Toliara, Tsiroanomandidy, and Vohemar; Dir of Operations, Madagascar HERVÉ LE PORZ.

British Council: see chapter on Mauritius.

Research Institutes

GENERAL

Institut de Recherche pour le Développement (IRD): BP 434, Antananarivo 101; tel. (20) 22-330-98; fax (20) 22-369-82; e-mail irdmada@ird.mg; internet www.ird.mg; research into economics, statistics, fisheries, environment, health, deforestation, biodiversity and water; library of 200 vols; Dir CHRISTIAN FELLER; (see main entry under France).

AGRICULTURE, FISHERIES AND VETERINARY SCIENCE

Centre National de Recherche Appliquée au Développement Rural (CENRADERU): BP 1690, Antananarivo; e-mail fofifa@bow.ats.mg; f. 1994; research into agriculture, forestry and fisheries, zoology, veterinary studies and rural economy; publ. *Rapport d'activité* (annually).

Attached institute:

CENRADERU—IRCT: BP 227, Mahajanga; research on cotton and other fibres; main research station at Toliary; regional station at Tanandava; sisal research at Mandrare.

Centre Technique Forestier Tropical: BP 745, Antananarivo; f. 1961; silviculture, genetics, soil conservation; Dir J. P. BOUILLET; (see main entry under France).

Département de Recherches Agronomiques de la République Malgache: BP 1690, Antananarivo 101; tel. (20) 320-7190; fax (20) 224-0130; e-mail fofifa@dts.mg; stations at Alaotra, Antalaha, Ambanja, Ambovombe, Ivoloina, Mahajanga, Fianarantsoa, Ilaka Est, Kianjavato, Kianjasoa, Tanandava; Dir CLAUDE RATSIMBAZAFY.

Institut de Recherches Agronomiques Tropicales (IRAT): 4 rue Rapiera, Anjohy, BP 853, Antananarivo; tel. (20) 22-271-82; attached to Centre de Co-operation Internationale en Recherche Agronomique pour le Développement (CIRAD).

Institut d'Elevage et de Médecine Vétérinaire des Pays Tropicaux: Antananarivo; central laboratory, research stations at Kianjasoa and Miadana; (see main entry under France).

FINE AND PERFORMING ARTS

Institut Malgache des Arts Dramatiques et Folkloriques (IMADEFOLK): Centre Culturel Albert Camus, Ave de l'Indépendance, Antananarivo; f. 1964; traditional songs and dances; Dir O. RAKOTO.

HISTORY, GEOGRAPHY AND ARCHAEOLOGY

Institut Géographique et Hydrographique National: Rue Dama-Ntsoha, Ambanidia, BP 323, Antananarivo 101; tel. (20) 22-229-35; fax (20) 22-252-64; e-mail ftm@dts.mg; internet www.ftm.mg; f. 1945; Dir ANDRIANJAFIMBELO RAZAFINAKANGA.

NATURAL SCIENCES

Biological Sciences

Institut Pasteur: BP 1274, Antananarivo 101; tel. (20) 22-412-72; fax (20) 22-415-34; e-mail ipm@pasteur.mg; internet www.pasteur.mg; f. 1898; biological research; library of 6,200 vols; Dir Dr MAUCLÈRE; publ. *Archives* (2 a year).

Physical Sciences

Institute and Observatory of Geophysics at Antananarivo: University of Antananarivo (Rectorate), Antananarivo 101; tel. and fax (20) 22-253-53; e-mail ioga@syfed.refer.mg; f. 1889, affiliated to the University 1967; study of seismology, geomagnetism, applied geophysics, exploration geophysics, time service, meteorological and astronomical observation; library of 3,000 vols, 800 periodicals; Dir J. B. RATSIMBAZAFY; publs

Bulletin Magnetique (monthly and annually), *Bulletin Méteorologique* (monthly), *Bulletin Sismique* (annually), *Mada–Geo* (4 a year).

Service Géologique: BP 322, Antananarivo 101; tel. (20) 22-400-48; fax (20) 22-418-73; internet www.cite.mg/mine; f. 1926; library of 3,000 vols; Dir A. RANANDARIVELO; publs *Annales géologiques*, *Atlas des fossiles caractéristiques de Madagascar*, *Documentation du Service Géologique*, *Rapport annuel*, *Travaux du Bureau Géologique*.

TECHNOLOGY

Bureau de Recherches Géologiques et Minières (BRGM): BP 458, Antananarivo; Dir G. BOURNAT; (see main entry under France).

Libraries and Archives

Antananarivo

Archives Nationales: BP 3384, Antananarivo; tel. and fax (20) 22-235-34; e-mail rijandriamihamina@malagasy.com; f. 1958; historical library of 30,000 vols; Dir SAHONDRA ANDRIAMIHAMINA.

Bibliothèque Municipale: Ave du 18 juin, Antananarivo; f. 1961; 22,600 vols.

Bibliothèque Nationale: Anosy, BP 257, Antananarivo; tel. (20) 22-258-72; fax (20) 22-294-48; f. 1961; 236,800 books, 2,660 periodicals, 2,912 MSS, 2,600 maps; special collections: history, literature, the arts, applied sciences, information on Madagascar; Dir L. RALAISAHOLIMANANA; publ. *Bibliographie Nationale de Madagascar* (annually).

Bibliothèque Universitaire d'Antananarivo: Campus Universitaire d'Ambohitsaina, BP 908, Antananarivo 101; tel. (20) 22-612-28; fax (20) 22-612-29; e-mail bu@univ-antananarivo.mg; internet www.bu.univ-antananarivo.mg; f. 1960; 301,500 vols; special MSS collection: Madagascar and Indian Ocean; Dir JEAN-MARIE ANDRIANIAINA; publ. *Bibliographie Annuelle de Madagascar*.

Médiathèque du Centre Culturel 'Albert Camus': 14 ave de l'Indépendance, BP 488, Antananarivo 101; tel. (20) 22-236-47; fax (20) 22-213-38; e-mail mediatheque@ccac.mg; internet www.ccac.mg; f. 1962; 40,000 vols, 111 periodicals, 111 CD-ROMs, 1,339 CDs, 3000 videos; Dir GUY MAURETTE; Librarian CATHERINE CAUDAN.

Antsirabé

Bibliothèque Municipale: Antsirabé; tel. 44-484-57; f. 1952; 2,700 vols; Librarian ALBERT DENIS RAKOTO.

Museums and Art Galleries

Antananarivo

Musée d'Art et d'Archéologie de l'Université de Madagascar: Isoraka, 17 rue Dr Villette, BP 564, Antananarivo 101; f. 1970; art, archaeology and social sciences; library of 1,800 vols; Dir J.-A. RAKOTOARISOA; publs *Taloha* (annually), *Travaux et Documents* (irregular).

Musée Historique: Rue Pasteur Ravelojaona, Antananarivo; tel. (20) 22-200-91; f. 1897; history and arts; Curator ALDINE RAVAONATOANDRO.

Universities

UNIVERSITÉ D'ANTANANARIVO

Campus Universitaire Ambohitsaina, BP 566, 101 Antananarivo
Telephone: (20) 22-326-39
Fax: (20) 22-279-26
Internet: www.univ-antananarivo.mg
Founded 1961
Rector: Dr PASCAL RAKOTOBE
Library: see Libraries and Archives
Number of teachers: 635
Number of students: 14,069

HEADS OF FACULTIES AND HIGHER SCHOOLS

Agriculture: DANIEL RAZAKANINDRIANA
Law, Economics, Business Studies, Sociology: RADO RAKOTOARISON
Literature and Humanities: JEAN-MARIUS SOLO RAHARINJANAHARY
Medicine: Prof. PAUL RAJAONARIVELO
Sciences: BRUNO ANDRIANANTENAINA
Ecole Normale Supérieure: YVES RENÉ RASOANAIVO
Ecole Supérieure Polytechnic: BENJAMIN RANDRIANOELINA
Ecole Supérieure des Sciences Agronomiques: Prof. ARMAND R PANJA RAMANOELINA

UNIVERSITÉ DE FIANARANTSOA

BP 1264, 301 Fianarantsoa
Telephone: (20) 75-508-02
Fax: (20) 75-506-19
E-mail: ufianara@syfed.refer.mg
Internet: www.misa.mg/univ
Founded 1988
State control
Language of instruction: French
Academic year: November to July
Rector: MARIE DIEUDONNÉ MICHEL RAZAFINDRANDRIATSIMANIRY
Administrative and Financial Director: DOMINIQUE RAZAFIMANAMPY
Director of Studies and Research: RIVO RAKOTOZAFY
Librarian: BRUNO JEAN ROMUALD RANDRIAMORA
Number of teachers: 63
Number of students: 1,836

DEANS

Faculty of Law: PATRICE GOUSSOT
Faculty of Sciences: TSILAVO MANDRESY RAZAFINDRAZAKA
École Nationale d'Informatique: JOSVAH PAUL RAZFIMANDIMBY
École Normale Supérieure: ROGER RATOVONJANAHARY
Institut des Sciences et Techniques de l'Environnement: PASCAL RATALATA

UNIVERSITÉ DE MAHAJANGA

BP 652, 401 Mahajanga
Telephone: (20) 62-227-24
Fax: (20) 62-233-12
E-mail: nocline@dts.mg
Founded 1977
State control
Academic year: October to July
Rector: Prof. ANDRIANAIVO RALISON
Registrar: JEANNETTE RAZAFINDRALINE
Librarian: JUSTINE RAZANAMANITRA
Number of teachers: 80 full-time
Number of students: 1,532
Publications: *IOSTM Bulletin* (public health, 4 a year), *JSPM* (2 a year)

DEANS

Faculty of Medicine: Prof. RANDRIANJAFISAMINDRAKOTROKA
Faculty of Natural Sciences: MARTIAL ZOZIME RASOLONJATOVO
Institute of Dentistry and Stomatology: Dr NOËLINE RAZANAMIHAJA

UNIVERSITÉ NORD MADAGASCAR

BP 0, 201 Antsiranana
Telephone: (20) 82-29-409
Fax: (20) 82-29-409
E-mail: umnm@dts.mg
Founded 1976
State control
Academic year: January to September
President: CÉCILE MARIE ANGE MANOROHANTA-DOMINIQUE
Administrative Director: ALY AHMAD
Librarian: VIRGINIE MILISON
Number of teachers: 64 permanent
Number of teachers: 33 temporary
Number of students: 826

DEANS

Faculty of Arts and Humanities: (vacant)
Faculty of Science: JEAN VICTOR RANDRIANOHAVY

DIRECTORS

Ecole Normale Supérieure pour l'Enseignement Technique: ANDRÉ TOTOHASIN
Ecole Supérieur Polytechnique: MAX ANDRIANANTENAINA

UNIVERSITÉ DE TOAMASINA

BP 591, 501 Toamasina
Telephone: (20) 53-322-44
Fax: (20) 53-335-66
E-mail: univtoam@dts.mg
Internet: www.univ-toamasina.mg
Founded 1977 as Centre Universitaire Régional de Toamasina, present status 1988
State control
Language of instruction: French
Rector: ROGER RAJAONARIVELO
Secretary-General: ANDRÉ BIAS RAMILAMANANA
Librarian: ELIANE JOSÉPHINE RENÉ
Number of teachers: 54
Number of students: 3,391

DEANS

School of Arts and Research: ABRAHAM LATSAKA
School of Economics and Management: SETH ARSÈNE RATOVOSON

HEADS OF DEPARTMENTS

Economics: JEANNOT RAMIARAMANANA
French Literature: MONIQUE ANDRÉA DJISTERA
Geography: JACQUES RANDRIANATOANDRO
History: SOLOFO RANDRIANJA
Management: ARISTIDE RAMANANTSALAMA
Philosophy: ETIENNE RAZAFINDEHIBE

UNIVERSITÉ DE TOLIARA

BP 185, Maninday, Toliara 601
Telephone: (20) 94-417-73
E-mail: rectul@syfed.refer.mg
Internet: www.refer.mg/madag_ct/madag_ct/edu/minesup/toliara/toliara
Founded 1977 as Regional Centre of Université de Madagascar; independent university status 1988
State Control
Languages of instruction: French, Malagasy
Academic year: November to July
Rector: M. THEODORET
Library of 8,000 vols

DEANS

Faculty of Arts and Humanities: MARC JOSEPH RAZAFINDRAKOTO

Faculty of Science: HERY ANTENAINA RAZAFIMANDIBY

Ecole Normale Supérieure: JEAN RAKOTOARIVELO

ATTACHED RESEARCH INSTITUTES

Institut Halieutique et des Sciences Marines: Dir MAN WAI RABENIEVANANA.

Colleges

Collège Rural d'Ambatobe: BP 1629, Antananarivo; Dir M. ROGER RAJOELISOLO.

Institut National des Sciences Comptables et de l'Administration d'Entreprises: Maison des Produits, 67 Ha, BP 946, Antananarivo 101; tel. (20) 22-660-65; fax (20) 22-308-95; e-mail drinscae@simicro.mg; f. 1986; 4-year courses and in-service training in accountancy, management and banking; library: 17,230 vols, 24 periodicals; 24 teachers; 1,051 students (325 full-time, 726 in-service); Dir-Gen. VICTOR HARISON.

Institut National des Sciences et Techniques Nucléaires: BP 4279, Antananarivo 01; tel. (20) 22-611-81; fax (20) 22-355-83; e-mail instn@dts.mg; internet www.geocities.com/mada_instn; f. 1976 as laboratory; institute status 1992; depts of Dosimetry and Radiation Protection, X-Ray Fluorescence Techniques and Environment, Nuclear Techniques and Analysis, Theoretical Physics, Instrumentation and Maintenance, Computer Science and Renewable Energies; Dir RAOELINA ANDRIAMBOLOLONA; publ. *Journal des Sciences et Techniques Nucléaires*.

Institut National des Télécommunications et des Postes: Antanetibe, 101 Antananarivo; f. 1968; 200 students.

MALAWI

The Higher Education System

The former British protectorate of Nyasaland gained independence, as Malawi, in 1964 and became a republic in 1966. Higher education consists of two state universities, the University of Malawi (founded 1964) and the University of Mzuzu (founded 1999).

The University of Malawi has a federal structure, consisting of five colleges, each headed by a Principal, assisted by a Vice-Principal, Registrar and Deans of Faculty. The Head of State is the Chancellor of the University, and the Vice-Chancellor is the senior governing officer, overseeing the day-to-day running of the institution. The Chancellor is guided by the University Council, the University policy-making body. There were 4,757 university students in 2003. Some students attend institutions in the United Kingdom and the USA. The Ministry of Education and Human Resources is responsible for providing higher education.

Admission to university is mainly on the basis of the Malawi School Certificate of Education, but O-levels and the Cambridge Overseas Higher School Certificate are also accepted. The colleges of the University of Malawi offer three-year Diploma courses, and the main undergraduate degree is the Bachelors, which lasts either four years for the Bachelors (General) or five to six years for the Bachelors (Honours). On completion of the Bachelors postgraduates can study for one to two years for the Masters. The final university-level degree is the PhD, lasting three to five years.

The National Apprenticeships Scheme is the principal form of post-secondary technical and vocational education. Programmes last for four years and are offered in a number of professional fields. The main qualifications are the Craft Certificate and Trade Test Certificate.

Learned Societies

GENERAL

Society of Malawi: POB 125, Blantyre; f. 1948; study and records of history and natural sciences; 400 mems; library of 1,650 vols, 3,000 journals; Chair. A. SCHWARZ; Sec. Mrs P. ROYLE; publ. *Journal* (2 a year).

BIBLIOGRAPHY, LIBRARY SCIENCE AND MUSEOLOGY

Malawi Library Association: POB 429, Zomba; tel. (1) 524265; fax (1) 525225; e-mail fkachala@sobomw.com; f. 1976; 340 mems; trains library assistants, provides professional advice, holds seminars and workshops; Pres. GEOFFREY F. SALANJE; Sec.-Gen. FRANCIS F. C. KACHALA; publs *MALA Bulletin* (annually), *MALA Trends* (every 2 years), *MALA Update*.

LANGUAGE AND LITERATURE

British Council: Plot no. 13/20 City Centre, POB 30222, Lilongwe 3; tel. (1) 773244; fax (1) 772945; e-mail info@britishcouncil.org.mw; internet www.britishcouncil.org/malawi; offers courses and exams in English language and British culture and promotes cultural exchange with the UK; library of 5,991 vols; Dir BRENDAN BARKER.

MEDICINE

Medical Association of Malawi: Private Bag 360, Chichiri, Blantyre 3; tel. (1) 630333; fax (1) 631353; f. 1967; 265 mems; 100 assoc. mems; Chair. Dr B. MWALE; Sec. Dr E. MTITIMILA; publ. *Malawi Medical Journal*.

Research Institutes

AGRICULTURE, FISHERIES AND VETERINARY SCIENCE

Agricultural Research and Extension Trust: P/Bag 9, Lilongwe; tel. (1) 761148; fax (1) 761615; e-mail aret@malawi.net; f. 1995; attached to Tobacco Asscn of Malawi; applied research on improvement of burley, flue-cured and fire-cured tobacco in Malawi; Dir Dr E. H. C. CHILEMBWE; publs *Coresta Bulletin* (4 a year), *Tobacco Science*.

Baka Agricultural Research Station: POB 97, Karonga; f. 1974; attached to Min. of Agriculture; applied research on the general agronomy of the Karonga and Chitipa regions.

Bvumbwe Agricultural Research Station: POB 5748, Limbe; tel. (1) 662206; f. 1940; attached to Min. of Agriculture; conducts applied research into tree and horticultural crops, especially tung, macadamia, cashew, vegetables, spices, coffee, mushrooms, roots and tubers, and the general agronomy of the Southern uplands; Head N. NSANJAMA.

Central Veterinary Laboratory: POB 527, Lilongwe; tel. (1) 766341; fax (1) 766010; e-mail dahi.cvl@malawi.net; f. 1974; attached to Min. of Agriculture; research into endemic diseases.

Chitala Agricultural Research Station: Private Bag 13, Salima; e-mail agric-research@sdnp.org.mw; f. 1978; attached to Min. of Agriculture; part of Lakeshore Rural Development Programme; conducts research on cereals, cotton, groundnuts, mango, roots and tubers, livestock; Station Man. L. R. NTUANA.

Chitedze Agricultural Research Station: POB 158, Lilongwe; tel. (1) 773252; fax (1) 773184; e-mail icrisat-malawi@cgiar.com; f. 1948; attached to Min. of Agriculture; conducts applied research into cereals, grain legumes, oil seeds, pasture and the general agronomy of the Central Region and into livestock improvement, especially of local Zebu cattle; library of 10,000 vols, 300 periodicals; Head Dr P. SIBALE.

Fisheries Research Unit: POB 27, Monkey Bay; tel. and fax (1) 587249; f. 1954; attached to Min. of Forestry and Natural Resources; research into fisheries of Lake Malawi; social economic surveys; Chief Fisheries Research Officer B. J. MKOKO; publs *Fisheries Bulletin* (monthly), *Survey Reports* (quarterly), *Technical Reports* (monthly).

Forest Research Institute of Malawi: POB 270, Zomba; attached to Min. of Forestry and Natural Resources; research into silviculture, tree breeding, pathology, entomology, soils, mycorrhizae and wood products.

Kasinthula Agricultural Research Station: POB 28, Chikwawa; tel. (1) 423207; e-mail agric-research@sdnp.org.mw; f. 1976; attached to Min. of Agriculture; irrigation research; Officer in Charge JULIAN W. MCHOWA.

Lifuwu Agricultural Research Station: POB 102, Salima; tel. (1) 829661; fax (1) 788801; e-mail agric-research@sdnp.org.mw; f. 1973; attached to Dept of Agricultural Research and Technical Services; rice research; Officer in Charge T. R. MZENGEZA.

Lunyangwa Agricultural Research Station: POB 59, Mzuzu; tel. (1) 332633; f. 1968; attached to Min. of Agriculture; conducts applied research into the general agronomy of the Northern Region, specializing in rice, coffee, tea, cassava, pasture work, and tropical fruits at its Mkondezi sub station; Head Dr A. LOWOLE.

Makoka Agricultural Research Station: Private Bag 3, Thondwe; tel. (1) 534254; e-mail cgmproject@malawi.net; f. 1967; cultivation of cotton, cassava, sweet potato, maize, groundnuts, soya beans, pigeon peas, cowpeas, sunflowers, sorghum and rice; agroforestry species and domestication of wild fruits; library of 1,300 vols; Head Dr CHARLES T. KISYOMBE; publs *Makoka Agricultural Research Station, Report*.

Mbawa Agricultural Research Station: POB 8, Embangweni; tel. (1) 342362; fax (1) 332687; e-mail agric-research@sdnp.org.mw; internet www.agricresearch.gov.mw; f. 1936; attached to Dept of Agricultural Research Services, Min. of Agriculture; applied research into livestock, cereals, grain legumes and technology transfer initiatives; publs *Quarterly Report*, *Station Guide* (annually).

Mikolongwe Livestock Improvement Centre: POB 5193, Limbe; f. 1955; attached to Min. of Agriculture; seeks to improve productive capacity of local Zebu cattle and fat-tailed sheep; the station also contains the Poultry Improvement Unit and the Veterinary Staff training school.

Mwimba Tobacco Research Station: POB 224, Kasungu; f. 1979; attached to Min. of

Agriculture; applied research on improvement and production of flue cured and oriental tobacco in Malawi.

Tea Research Foundation (Central Africa): POB 51, Mulanje; tel. (1) 467277; fax (1) 467209; e-mail trfca@africa-online.net; f. 1966; conducts research on the genetic improvement of tea and associated agronomic research and training for the tea industry in southern Africa; Dir Dr A. S. KUMWENDA; publ. *Newsletter* (2 a year).

NATURAL SCIENCES

Physical Sciences

Geological Survey of Malawi: POB 27, Zomba; tel. (1) 524166; fax (1) 524716; e-mail geomalawi@chirunga.sdnp.org.mw; f. 1921; attached to Ministry of Mines, Natural Resources and Environmental Affairs; geological mapping and surveys; mineral investigation, engineering, geology, geophysics, drilling, seismology; library of 5,000 vols; Dir C. E. KAPHWIYO; publs *Annual Report*, *Bulletin*.

Libraries and Archives

Lilongwe

Malawi National Library Service: POB 30314, Lilongwe 3; tel. (1) 773700; fax (1) 771616; e-mail gnyali@nlsmw.org; f. 1968; provides public library services; publishes children's books; 1,000,000 vols; Nat. Librarian G. L. NYALI; publ. *Accessions Bulletin*.

Zomba

National Archives of Malawi: Mkulichi Rd, POB 62, Zomba; tel. and fax (1) 525240; e-mail archives@sdnp.org.mw; internet chambo.sdnp.org.mw/ruleoflaw/archives; f. 1947, as branch of Central African Archives, became National Archives of Malawi 1964; public archives, records management, historical manuscripts, legal deposit library, films, tapes, microfilms, gramophone records, philatelic collection, maps, and plans; national ISBN agency; 30,000 vols, 240 periodicals; Dir PAUL LIHOMA; Librarian STANLEY S. GONDWE; publ. *Malawi National Bibliography* (annually).

University of Malawi Libraries: POB 280, Zomba; tel. (1) 524222; fax (1) 525225; e-mail smwiyeriwa@chirunga.sdnp.org.mw; f. 1965; 391,000 vols; Librarian S. MWIYERIWA; publs *Library Bulletin*, *Nthambi Zisanu*, *Report to Senate* (annually).

Museums

Blantyre

Museums of Malawi: POB 30360, Chichiri, Blantyre 3; tel. (1) 672438; fax (1) 676615; e-mail museums@malawi.net; f. 1959; Dir of Museums Dr M. E. D. NHLANE; publ. *Ndiwula* (newsletter, annually).

Universities

UNIVERSITY OF MALAWI

POB 278, Zomba
Telephone: (1) 524282
Fax: (1) 524031
E-mail: uniregistrar@usdnp.org.mw
Internet: www.unima.mw

Founded 1964
Language of instruction: English
State control
Academic year: January to September

Number of teachers: 710
Number of students: 5,400

Chancellor: THE PRESIDENT OF MALAWI
Vice-Chancellor: Prof. J. D. RUBADIRI
Registrar: BEN WOKOMAATANI MALUNGA
Librarian: F. G. HOUSE (acting)

Publications: *Journal of Humanities*, *Journal of Social Science*, *Malawi Journal of Science and Technology*, *Research Report to Senate*.

CONSTITUENT INSTITUTES

Bunda College of Agriculture: POB 219, Lilongwe; tel. (1) 277226; fax (1) 277364; library of 50,000 vols; 131 teachers; 681 students; Principal Dr G. Y. KANYAMA-PHIRI; Registrar F. T. ZALIRA MSONTHI

DEANS

Faculty of Agriculture: Dr D. M. CHILIMA
Faculty of Development Studies: Dr C. M. MASANGANO
Faculty of Environmental Science: Prof. M. B. KWAPATA
Postgraduate Studies: Dr R. K. D. PHOYA

PROFESSORS

EL-SHAZLY ABU-AGWA, F., Crop Science
KAMWANJA, L. A., Animal Science
KWAPATA, M. B., Forestry and Horticulture
MTIMUNI, J. P., Animal Science
PHOYA, R. K. D., Animal Science
SAKA, V. W., Crop Science

Chancellor College: POB 280, Zomba; tel. (1) 524222; fax (1) 524046; library of 300,000 vols; 250 teachers; 1,812 students; Principal Dr F. B. MOTO; Registrar J. A. KADZANJA

DEANS

Faculty of Education: Dr D. MALUWA-BANDA
Faculty of Humanities: Dr E. KAYAMBAZINTHU
Faculty of Law: N. MHURA
Faculty of Science: Dr E. SAMBO
Faculty of Social Science: Dr L. MALEKANO
Postgraduate Studies: Prof. K. PHIRI

PROFESSORS

CHIRWA, W. C., History
DUDLEY, C. O., Biology
JOSHUA, S. J., Physics
KADZAMIRA, Z. D., Political and Administrative Studies
KALUWA, B. M., Economics
KISHINDO, P. A. K., Sociology
PHIRI, K. M., History
SAKA, J. D. K., Chemistry
ULEDI-KAMANGA, B. J., English

College of Medicine: PB 360, Chichiri, Blantyre 3; tel. (1) 671911; fax (1) 674700; e-mail registrar@admin.medicol.mw; library of 18,000 vols; 87 teachers; 169 students; Principal Prof. ROBIN BROADHEAD; Registrar C. TRIGU-LEMANI

DEANS

Faculty of Medicine: Prof. J. E. CHISI
Postgraduate Studies: Prof. E. BERGSTEIN

PROFESSORS

ADELOYE, A., Surgery
BROADHEAD, R. L., Paediatrics
KOMOLAFE, O. O., Microbiology
LIOMBA, G. N., Pathology
MADUAGWU, E. N., Biochemistry
MOLYNEUX, M. E., Paediatrics
MSAMATI, B. C., Anatomy
MUKIIBI, J. M., Haematology
ZIJLSTRA, E. E., Medicine

Kamuzu College of Nursing: PB 1, Lilongwe; tel. (1) 751622; fax (1) 756424; library of 24,000 ; 66 teachers; 300 students; Principal D. NKOMBA-JERE; Registrar N. D. MABVUMBE

DEANS

Faculty of Nursing: E. B. CHILEMBA
Postgraduate Studies: C. KAPONDA

Malawi Polytechnic: PB 303, Chichiri, Blantyre 3; tel. (1) 670411; fax (1) 670578; library of 38,745 vols; 176 teachers; 2,549 students; Principal Y. A. ALIDE (acting); Registrar A. KUMWENDA

DEANS

Faculty of Applied Sciences: A. MADHLOPA
Faculty of Commerce: B. T. NJOBVU
Faculty of Engineering: N. T. BEN
Faculty of Education and Media Studies: G. MANGANDA
Postgraduate Studies: F. GOMILE CLUDYAONGA

MZUZU UNIVERSITY

Private Bag 201, Luwinga, Mzuzu 2
Telephone: (1) 333575
Fax: (1) 333497
E-mail: mzuni@sdnp.org.mw

Founded 1999
State control

Chancellor: THE PRESIDENT OF MALAWI
Vice-Chancellor: Prof. PETER N. MWANZA
Deputy Vice-Chancellor: Prof. DAN CHIMWENJE
Registrar: REGINALD MISHANI
Librarian: Prof. JOSEPH UTA

DEANS

Faculty of Education: DAVID K. MPHANDE
Faculty of Environmental Sciences: LUSAYO M. MWABUMBA

HEADS OF DEPARTMENTS

Faculty of Education:
- Biology: Assoc. Prof. GODWIN Y. MKAMANGA (acting)
- Chemistry: ELLEN MULAGA (acting)
- Education: RUBEN D. HANGO (acting)
- English: Assoc. Prof. MARY MUKHEBI-LUTTA (acting)
- French: BOSTON J. SOKO (acting)
- Geography: (vacant)
- History: DONALD P. CHIPETA (acting)
- Mathematics: JOHN RYAN
- Physics: (vacant)
- Theology and Religious Studies: Dr DAVID K. MPHANDE (acting)

Faculty of Environmental Sciences:
- Environmental Sciences: LUSAYO M. MWABUMBA

ATTACHED RESEARCH INSTITUTES

Centre for Continuing Education: Coordinator DOMINIC M. NDENGU.

MALAYSIA

The Higher Education System

The country's oldest existing institution of higher education is Universiteti Teknologi Malaysia (Malayasia University of Technology), Johor, which was founded in 1904 (current name and status 1972) when Johor was still an independent Malay state (it came under British control in 1914). The next oldest institution is Universiteti Pendidikan Sultan Idris (Sultan Idris University of Education—founded 1922). Malaya was granted independence, within the Commonwealth, in 1957 and Malaysia was established in 1963, through the union of the independent Federation of Malaya (renamed the States of Malaya), Singapore, and the former British colonies of Sarawak and Sabah. Subsequently, Singapore left the federation and the States of Malaya were styled Peninsular Malaysia. In October 1994 the Government introduced a bill that would allow foreign universities to establish branch campuses in Malaysia. From the end of that year the Government permitted the use of English as a medium of instruction in science and engineering subjects at tertiary level. In 1998 the government incorporation of higher education gave greater powers of autonomy to the universities, which are governed by an executive body (Board of Governors) and academic council (Senate). At the seventh ASEAN summit meeting in November 2001 it was decided that the town of Bandar Nusajaya in Johor would be the location for the first ASEAN university. It would be Malaysia's second international university. There are 15 public and private universities.

The main criteria for admission to higher education are the Malaysia Higher Certificate of Education and Matriculation Certificate. Applications are made through the central Unit Pusat Universiti (Central University Unit). The undergraduate Bachelors degree lasts three to four years, though some disciplines require longer periods of study, such as medicine and dentistry (which require five years). Following the Bachelors, the Masters is the first postgraduate degree, requiring one to years further study; finally, after award of the Masters, study for a PhD lasts a minimum of two years.

Post-secondary vocational and technical education is available at specialist schools.

Learned Societies

ARCHITECTURE AND TOWN PLANNING

Malaysian Institute of Architects: 4–6 Jl. Tangsi, POB 19855, 50726 Kuala Lumpur; tel. (3) 2928733; fax (3) 2982878; e-mail info@pammy.org; f. 1967; 2,267 mems; library of 1,000 vols; Pres. P. KASI; publs *Berita Akitek* (monthly), *Majalah Akitek* (6 a year), *Panduan Akitek* (annually).

BIBLIOGRAPHY, LIBRARY SCIENCE AND MUSEOLOGY

Librarians' Association of Malaysia: POB 12545, 50782 Kuala Lumpur; tel. (3) 26947390; fax (3) 26947390; e-mail ppm55@po.jaring.my; internet www.pnm.my/ppm; f. 1955; 600 mems; Pres. ZAWIYAH BABA; Sec. NAFISAH AHMAD; publ. *Jurnal PPM* (annually).

HISTORY, GEOGRAPHY AND ARCHAEOLOGY

Malaysian Historical Society: 958 Jl. Hose, 50460 Kuala Lumpur; tel. (3) 2481469; fax (3) 2487281; f. 1953; activities include restoration and preservation of historical sites; 200 indiv. and institutional mems; Pres. Dato MUSA HITAM; publs *Malaysia in History*, *Malaysia Dari Segi Sejarah* (annually).

LANGUAGE AND LITERATURE

Alliance Française: 15 Lorong Gurney, 54100 Kuala Lumpur; tel. (3) 26925929; fax (3) 26930502; e-mail afkuala@tm.net.my; internet www.alliancefrancaise.org.my; offers courses and exams in French language and culture and promotes cultural exchange with France; attached teaching centre in Penang; Dir ERIC SZCZUREK.

British Council: Ground Fl., West Block, Wisma Selangor Dredging, 142C Jalan Ampang, 50450 Kuala Lumpur; POB 10539, 50916 Kuala Lumpur; tel. (3) 27237900; fax (3) 27136599; e-mail kualalumpur@britishcouncil.my; internet www.britishcouncil.org.my; teaching centre; offers courses and exams in English language and British culture and promotes cultural exchange with the UK; attached offices in Kota Kinabalu, Kuching, Penang (teaching centre) and Subang Jaya (teaching centre); library of 14,000 vols, 100 periodicals; Dir GERRY LISTON; Dir, English Language STEVE BATES.

Dewan Bahasa dan Pustaka (National Language and Literary Agency): POB 10803, 50926 Kuala Lumpur; tel. (3) 21481011; fax (3) 21489245; internet www.dbp.gov.my; f. 1956 to develop and enrich the Malay language; aims: to develop literary talent, to standardize spelling and pronunciation and devise technical terms, etc. in Malay, to print or assist in the production of publs in Malay and the translation of books into Malay; 1,171 mems; library: see Libraries and Archives; Dir-Gen. Dato' Hj. A. AZIZ DERAMAN; publs *Dewan Sastera* (monthly), *Dewan Budaya* (monthly), *Dewan Bahasa* (monthly), *Pelita Bahasa* (monthly).

Goethe-Institut: 1, Jalan Langgak Golf, 55000 Kuala Lumpur; tel. (3) 21422011; fax (3) 21422282; e-mail goethekl@tm.net.my; internet www.goethe.de/so/kua/deindex.htm; offers courses and exams in German language and culture and promotes cultural exchange with Germany; Dir Dr VOLKER WOLF.

Tamil Language Society: c/o Department of Indian Studies, University of Malaya, Kuala Lumpur; f. 1957; 350 mems; aims at the promotion and propagation of the Tamil language and Indian culture; Pres. M. JAYAKUMAR; Hon. Sec. L. KRISHNAN; publ. *Tamil Oli* (Tamil, English and Bahasa Malaysia, annually).

MEDICINE

Academy of Family Physicians of Malaysia: Room 6, 5th Floor, MMA House, 124 Jalan Pahang, 53000 Kuala Lumpur; tel. (3) 40417735; fax (3) 40425206; e-mail afpm@po.jaring.my; f. 1973; 800 mems; Pres. Dr M. K. RAJAKUMAR; Chair. (vacant); publ. *The Family Physician* (3 a year).

Malaysian Medical Association: 4th Floor, MMA House, 124 Jl. Pahang, 53000 Kuala Lumpur; tel. (3) 40420617; fax (3) 40418187; e-mail mma@tm.net.my; internet www.mma.org.my; f. 1959; 7,000 mems; Pres. Dato' Datuk Dr P. KRISHNAN; Admin Officer Ms SUMATHI; publs *Medical Journal of Malaysia* (quarterly), *MMA Newsletter* (monthly).

NATURAL SCIENCES

General

Malaysian Scientific Association: Room 1, 2nd Floor, Bangunan Sultan Salahuddin Adbul Aziz Shah, 16 Jalan Utara, POB 48, 46700 Petaling Jaya; tel. (3) 79578930; fax (3) 79541644; e-mail malsci@tm.net.my; f. 1955; 388 mems, engaged in scientific and technological works; Pres. Dr SOON TING KUEH; Hon. Sec. Dr ZURAINEE MOHD NOR.

Biological Sciences

Malaysian Nature Society: POB 10750, 60724 Kuala Lumpur; tel. (3) 22879422; fax (3) 22878773; e-mail natsoc@po.jaring.my; internet www.mns.org.my; f. 1940; an independent society to promote the study, appreciation and conservation of nature; 5,000 mems; library: small library; Pres. Dato' Dr SALLEH MOHD NOR; Exec. Dir Dr LOH CHI LEONG; publs *The Malayan Nature Journal* (4 a year), *Malaysian Naturalist* (4 a year).

Malaysian Society for Biochemistry and Molecular Biology: c/o Biochemistry Dept, Faculty of Medicine, University of Malaya, 50603 Kuala Lumpur; f. 1973; lectures, workshops and seminars, annual conference; 120 mems; Pres. Prof. PERUMAL RAMASAMY; Sec. Dr SHEILA NATHAN; publs *Proceedings of Annual Conference*, *Malaysian Journal of Biochemistry and Molecular Biology*.

Malaysian Zoological Society: 68000 Ampang Selangor, Darul Ehsan; tel. (603) 4083422; fax (603) 4075375; e-mail zoonegara@tm.net.my; f. 1961; Pres. Y. B. Tan Sri Dato V. M. HUTSON; Sec.-Treas. YUEN TANG & CO.

RELIGION, SOCIOLOGY AND ANTHROPOLOGY

Royal Asiatic Society, Malaysian Branch: 130M Jl. Thamby Abdullah, off Jl. Tun Sambanthan, Brickfields, 50470 Kuala Lumpur; tel. (3) 22748345; fax (3) 22743458; e-mail mbras@tm.net.my; internet www.mbras.org.my; f. 1877; 935 mems; history, literature, sociology, anthropology; Pres. Datuk ABDULLAH BIN ALI; Sec. Datuk BURHANUDDIN BIN AHMAD TAJUDIN; publ. *Journal* (2 a year).

Research Institutes

AGRICULTURE, FISHERIES AND VETERINARY SCIENCE

Department of Agriculture: Ministry of Agriculture, Wisma Tani, Jl. Mahameru, 50624 Kuala Lumpur; f. 1905; undertakes all aspects of research and extension for improvement of crops; pest forecasting and surveillance; establishing Agricultural Information System; library of 15,000 vols; Dir ABU BAKAR BIN MAHMUD; publs *Malaysian Agricultural Journal*, *Statistical Digest*.

Forest Research Institute Malaysia (FRIM): Kepong, 52109, Selangor Darul Ehsan, Kuala Lumpur; tel. (3) 62797000; fax (3) 62731314; internet www.frim.gov.my; f. 1929; consists of 1,319 ha of experimental plantations, 5 arboreta, a nursery, a museum, a herbarium of 125,000 sheets of tree species, a wood collection of nearly 10,000 specimens, and a library (see Libraries); 3 substations; Rattan Information Centre est. 1982; Dir-Gen. Dato' Dr ABDUL RAZAK MOHD ALI; publs *Annual Report*, *Bamboo Bulletin*, *FRIM Technical Information*, *Journal of Tropical Forest Products*, *Journal of Tropical Forest Science*, *Malayan Forest Records*, *Research Pamphlets*, *Research Programme*, *RIC Bulletin*, *Urban Forestry Bulletin*.

Freshwater Fisheries Research Centre: Batu Berendam, 75350 Malacca; tel. (6) 8172485; fax (6) 3175705; e-mail pppat@po.jaring.my; f. 1957; attached to Dept of Fisheries Malaysia; research on freshwater fisheries and aquaculture; special emphasis on indigenous carp, study of fishes in lakes and reservoirs, breeding of indigenous freshwater fish; air-breathing fish, cichlid (Tilapia), aquarium fish, and aquatic plants; library of 3,800 vols; Chief Officer HAMBAL HANAFI; publ. *Annual Report*.

Malaysian Agricultural Research and Development Institute (MARDI): POB 12301, GPO, 50774 Kuala Lumpur; tel. (3) 943711; fax (3) 9483664; e-mail dg@mardi.my; internet www.mardi.my; f. 1969; an autonomous organization which conducts scientific, technical, economic and sociological research in Malaysia with respect to the production, utilization and processing of all crops (except rubber and oil palm), and livestock; library of 50,000 vols; Dir-Gen. Dr SAHARAN BIN ANANG; Librarian KHADIJAH IBRAHIM; publs *Journal of Tropical Agriculture and Food Sciences* (2 a year), *Agromedia* (4 a year).

Malaysian Rubber Research and Development Board: 148 Jl. Ampang, POB 10508, 50716 Kuala Lumpur; tel. (3) 2614422; fax (3) 2613139; f. 1959 to plan and determine policies and programmes for natural rubber research, technical development and promotion nationally and worldwide; to collate and interpret information pertaining to the rubber industry; to co-ordinate all research, development and publicity financed by the Board; dependent units are the Rubber Research Institute of Malaysia (see below), the Tun Abdul Razak Research Centre, UK, and Malaysian Rubber Bureaux located in major rubber consuming areas; Controller of Rubber Research and Chair. ENCIK HARON BIN SIRAJ; publs *Annual Report*, *Malaysian Rubber Review* (quarterly), *Rubber Developments* (2 a year).

Rubber Research Institute of Malaysia: POB 10150, 50908 Kuala Lumpur; tel. (3) 4567033; fax (3) 4573512; f. 1925, operates under the Rubber Research Institute of Malaysia (RRIM) Extension and Amendment Bill, 1972; consists of a Directorate, 4 depts (11 divisions), 3 sections, research laboratories, 3 experimental stations of over 10,000 acres; engaged in research, extension services, technical advisory service and information on all aspects of rubber production; library: see Libraries; Dir Datuk Dr ABDUL AZIZ BIN S. A. KADIR; Deputy Dir (Research) Dr WAN RAHMAN BIN WAN YACOB (acting); publs *Annual Report*, *Chung Tze Jen Chee Kan* (Mandarin, quarterly), *Journal* (3 a year), *Jurnal Sains* (Malay, 2 a year), *Natural Rubber Research* (quarterly), *Planters' Bulletin* (quarterly), *Siaran Pekebun* (Malay, quarterly), divisional reports.

ECONOMICS, LAW AND POLITICS

Asian and Pacific Development Centre: Pesiaran Duta, POB 12224, 50770 Kuala Lumpur; tel. (3) 6511088; fax (3) 6510316; e-mail info@apdc.po.my; internet www.apdc.com.my/apdc; f. 1980; promotes and undertakes research and training, acts as a clearing house for information on development, offers consultancy services; current programme: to overcome poverty, to assist development instns to manage national development and change, to increase the policy-making capacity of Asian-Pacific countries, to increase the capacity of the region to adjust to the changing world environment; 19 full mem. govts, 1 assoc. mem., 1 contributing non-mem.; library of 43,200 vols; Dir Dr MOHD NOOR H. HARUN; publs *APDC Annual Report*, *APDC Newsletter* (2 a year), *Asia-Pacific Development Monitor* (2 a year), *Issues in Gender and Development*.

MEDICINE

Institute for Medical Research (IMR): Jl. Pahang, 50588 Kuala Lumpur; tel. (3) 2986033; f. 1901; now research branch of Ministry of Health; researches into biomedical and social aspects of tropical diseases, provides specialised diagnostic, consultative and information services, trains medical and paramedical staff, also WHO Centre for Research and Training in Tropical Diseases for the Western Pacific Region, and SEAMEO-TROPMED National Centre, WHO Collaborating Centre for Taxonomy and Immunology of Filariasis and Screening and Clinical Trials of Drugs against Brugian Filariasis, and WHO Collaborating Centre for Ecology, Taxonomy and Control of Vectors of Malaria, Filariasis and Dengue; 598 staff; library of 20,000 vols; Dir Dr M. S. LYE (acting); publs *IMR Quarterly Bulletin*, *Bulletin of the Institute for Medical Research* (irregular), *Study of the Institute for Medical Research* (irregular), *Annual Report*, *International Medical Journal*, *IMR Handbook*.

NATURAL SCIENCES

Physical Sciences

Geological Survey of Malaysia, Ipoh: Scrivenor Rd, Ipoh, Perak; f. 1903; 792 mems; basic geological information on East and West Malaysia with special emphasis on mineral resources; library of 18,720 vols (East Malaysia), 34,000 vols (West Malaysia); Dir-Gen. E. H. YIN; publs *Annual Report*, regional memoirs, reports and bulletins (East), map reports and proceedings (W. Malaysia), economic bulletins, annual reports and professional papers (West), *Geochemical Report*.

Geological Survey of Malaysia, Sarawak: POB 560, 93712 Kuching, Sarawak; tel. (82) 240152; fax (82) 415390; f. 1949; 183 staff; geological mapping, mineral investigations, engineering geology, hydrogeology; library of 18,000 vols; Dir CHEN SHICK-PEI; publs *Annual Report*, *Bulletins*, *Geological Papers*, *Technical Papers*, *Maps*, *Memoirs*, *Reports*.

Mineral and Geoscience Department, Malaysia: Locked Bag 2042, 88999 Kota Kinabalu, Sabah; tel. (88) 260311; fax (88) 240150; e-mail jmgsbh@p.sabah.gov.my; f. 1949; geological mapping, minerals research, engineering geology, hydrogeology, geophysics, mineralology and petrology, laboratory analysis; library of 3,500 vols; Dir N. K. ANG; publs *Annual Report* (industrial mineral production statistics and directory of producers in Malaysia), *Malaysian Mineral Yearbook*.

TECHNOLOGY

Malaysian Institute of Microelectronic Systems (MIMOS): MIMOS Berhad, Technology Park Malaysia, 57000 Kuala Lumpur; tel. (3) 89965000; fax (3) 89960527; e-mail tbcc@mimos.my; internet www.mimos.my; f. 1985; research and development in microelectronics, information technology and related areas; provides advisory and technical services to the govt and the private sector; encourages and supports the creation of new industries based on high technology and modern microelectronics; collaborates with other bodies in the fields; library of 6,200 vols, 202 periodicals; Dir-Gen. Dr TENGKU MOHD AZZMAN SHARIFFADEEN; publs *MIMOS IT Paper* (2 a year), *MIMOS Teknologi Buletin* (quarterly), *MOSMEDIA* (quarterly).

Standards and Industrial Research Institute of Malaysia (SIRIM): POB 35, 40700 Shah Alam, Selangor; tel. (3) 5591630; fax (3) 5508095; f. 1975 by merger of National Institute of Scientific and Industrial Research and the Standards Institution of Malaysia; facilitates industrial development through research into existing and future problems relating to engineering and production of processed and fabricated industrial products; provides a range of technical services that include quality assurance, metrology, industry testing, technology modification and improvement, technology transfer, consultancy, industrial information and extension services; undertakes applied research and prototype production to adapt or modify known processes and technologies; finds new uses for locally available raw materials and by-products, and develops new products and processes based on indigenous raw materials; the drafting and publications of Malaysian standards and standards testing; library of 13,000 vols; 165,000 standards and specifications, 400 periodicals; Controller Dr AHMAD TAJUDDIN ALI; publs *Annual Report*, *Berita SIRIM* (SIRIM News, quarterly), *Malaysian Standards*.

Libraries and Archives

Alor Setar

Kedah State Public Library Corporation: Jalan Kolam Air, 05100 Alor Setar, Kedah Darul Aman; tel. (4) 7333592; fax (4) 7336232; f. 1974; includes Alor Setar Public

Library, five branch libraries, six mobile libraries and seven village libraries; 684,776 vols; Dir Mrs MAZIZAH BT. HJ. MD DARUS; publs *Annual Report*, *Bibliographies*, *Guide to the Library*, *Indexes*.

Ipoh

Tun Razak Library: Jl. Panglima Bukit Gantang Wahab, 30000 Ipoh, Perak Darul Ridzuan; tel. (5) 508073; f. 1931; special collections on Malaysia and Singapore; UNESCO depository; special language section; 245,816 vols in English, Chinese, Malay and Tamil; Asst Librarian NOOR AFITZA H. PAWAN CHIK; publs *Annual Reports*, *Malaysiana Collection*.

Jitra

Perpustakaan, Universiti Utara Malaysia: Sintok, 06010 Jitra, Kedah; tel. (4) 9241740; fax (4) 9241959; f. 1984; 183,000 vols, 6,000 periodicals; Chief Librarian PUAN JAMILAH MOHAMED.

Johor Baharu

Perpustakaan Sultan Ismail: Jl. Dato Onn, Johor Baharu; f. 1964; administered by the Town Council; 40,600 vols in Chinese, English, Malay and Tamil; Librarian (vacant); publ. *Lapuran Tahunan* (Annual Report).

Perpustakaan Sultanah Zanariah, Universiti Teknologi Malaysia: 81310 Utm Skudai, Johor; tel. (7) 5576160; fax (7) 5572555; internet www.psz.utm.my; f. 1972; 344,000 vols, 9,300 periodicals; audio-visual collection; Chief Librarian ROSNA TAIB; publs *Berita Perpustakaan Sultanah Zanariah* (2 a month), *Buletin MAKIN*.

Kota Baharu

Kelantan Public Library Corporation: Jl. Mahmood, 15200 Kota Baharu, Kelantan; tel. (9) 7444522; fax (9) 7487736; e-mail ppak@kel.lib.edu.my; f. 1938, present name 1974; 261,000 vols; special collection: Kelantan Collection; State Librarian NIK ARIFF BIN NIK MANSOR.

Kota Kinabalu

Sabah State Library/Perpustakaan Negeri Sabah: 88572 Kota Kinabalu, Sabah; tel. (88) 54333; fax (88) 233167; f. 1951; now a state department within the Ministry of Social Services (Sabah); public reference and lending library of 841,914 vols, mainly in Bahasa Malaysia, English and Chinese; special local history collection on Borneo; comprises 20 brs (in addition to main library), 10 mobile libraries for rural areas and 26 village libraries; Dir ADELINE LEONG.

Kuala Lumpur

Kuala Lumpur Public Library: Sam Mansion, Jl. Tuba, Kuala Lumpur; f. 1966; 45,000 vols; Librarian SOONG WAN YOONG.

Library, Forest Research Institute Malaysia: Kepong, 52109 Selangor; tel. (3) 62797497; fax (3) 62804624; e-mail zaki@frim.gov.my; internet www.frim.gov.my; f. 1929; 55,000 vols on forestry and related subjects; colln consists of books, scientific and technical reports, reprints, standards, conference papers, theses, newspaper clippings, gazettes, maps; services incl. SDI, Rattan Information Centre, current awareness services, literature searches, etc.; Head Librarian MOHAMAD ZAKI HAJI MOHD ISA; publs *FRIM in Focus* (quarterly), *FRIM Technical Information* (irreg.), *Journal of Tropical Forest Science* (3 a year), *Timber Technology Bulletin* (irreg.), *FRIM Reports* (irregular), *FRIM Research Pamphlet* (irreg.).

Malaysian Rubber Board Library: Jl. Ampang, POB 10150, 50908 Kuala Lumpur; tel. 4567033; fax (3) 4573512; e-mail rabiah@lgm.gov.my; f. 1925; 150,000 vols, mainly science and technology, particular emphasis on subjects relating to rubber research; Librarian RABIAH BT MOHD. YUSOF; publs *Bibliographies*, *Recent Additions to the Library*, *List of RRIM Translations*, *List of Journal Holdings*, *List of Forthcoming Conferences*, etc.

Ministry of Agriculture Library: Wisma Tani, Jl. Sultan Salahuddin, 50624 Kuala Lumpur; tel. (3) 2982011; fax (3) 2913758; f. 1906; 80,000 vols; publs *Bulletin* (irregular), *Malaysian Agricultural Journal* (2 a year).

National Archives of Malaysia: Jl. Duta, 50568 Kuala Lumpur; tel. (3) 6510688; fax (3) 6515679; e-mail query@arkib.gov.my; internet www.arkib.gov.my; f. 1957; public records, archives, audio-visual records, private and business records; Prime Minister's archives; 10,471 vols; Dir-Gen. Dato' HABIBAH ZON; publs *Annual Report*, *Hari ini Dlm. Sejarah* (Today in History, 4 a year), *National Archives of Malaysia*.

National Library of Malaysia: 232 Jalan Tun Razak, 50572 Kuala Lumpur; tel. (3) 2943488; fax (3) 2927899; e-mail pnmweb@www.pnm.my; f. 1966; national bibliographic centre, national depository, national centre for Malay MSS, national centre for ISBN and ISSN; depository for UN publs; 1,413,348 vols; Dir-Gen. CIK SHAHAR BANUN JAAFAR; publs *Jurnal Filologi Melayu* (annually), *Selitan Perpustakaen* (2 a year).

Pusat Dokumentasi Melayu (Dewan Bahasa dan Pustaka) (Malay Documentation Centre, Institute of Language and Literature): POB 10803, 50926 Kuala Lumpur; tel. (3) 21481030; fax (3) 21484208; e-mail aizan@dbp.gov.my; internet www.dbp.gov.my; f. 1956; 122,830 vols, 138 periodicals, 3,290 audiovisual items; directory of Malaysian writers; bibliography of modern Malaysian literature; Chief Librarian AIZAN MOHD ALI; publs *Mutiara Pustaka* (annually), *Subject Bibliography* (irregular).

University of Malaya Library: Pantai Valley, 50603 Kuala Lumpur; tel. (3) 7575887; fax (3) 7573661; f. 1957; 1,239,749 vols, 8,040 periodicals; special collections include medical (124,339 vols), legal (99,382 vols), Malay language and culture (75,525 vols), Chinese (61,406 vols), Tamil (16,658 vols); Librarian ZAITON OSMAN; publs *Maklumat Semasa* (bulletin, monthly), *Kekal Abadi* (quarterly newsletter).

Kuching

Sarawak State Library: Jl. P. Ramlee, 93572 Kuching; tel. (82) 242911; fax (82) 246552; f. 1950; administered by the Ministry of Environment; 1,232,780 vols in Bahasa Malaysia, English, Iban and Chinese; State Librarian JOHNNY K. S. KUEH.

Melaka

Malacca Public Library Corporation: 242-1 Jalan Bukit Baru, 75150 Melaka; tel. (6) 2824859; fax (6) 2824798; e-mail admin@perpustam.edu.my; internet www.perpustam.edu.my; f. 1977; 526,375 vols; Librarian RIZA FEISAL BIN SHEIK SAID.

Penang

Penang Public Library Corporation: 2nd Floor, Dewan Sri Pinang, 10200 Penang; tel. (4) 2622255; fax (4) 2628820; e-mail ppapp@png.lib.edu.my; f. 1817; reorganized 1973; 415,000 vols; Chair. Y. B. Dr TOH KIN WOON; Dir ENCIK ONG CHAI LIN; publ. *Buletin Mutiara* (4 a year).

Perpustakaan Universiti Sains Malaysia: Minden, 11800 Penang; tel. (4) 6577888; fax (4) 6571526; e-mail chieflib@usm.my; internet www.lib.usm.my; f. 1969; 809,000 vols (main library 644,000 vols, 5,500 periodicals; medical library 87,000 vols, 1,370 periodicals; engineering library 78,000 vols, 487 periodicals), media 122,916 items, 9,969 reels microfilm, 105,809 sheets microfiche; Chief Librarian Hon. Datin MASRAH HAJI ABIDIN; publ. *MIDAS Bulletin* (every 2 months).

Serdang

Perpustakaan Universiti Putra Malaysia: 43400 UPM Serdang, Selangor Darul Ehsan; tel. (3) 89468601; fax (3) 89483745; e-mail lib@lib.upm.edu.my; internet www.lib.upm.edu.my; f. 1971; 460,000 vols and bound periodicals; Chief Librarian AMIR HUSSAIN MOHAMMAD ISHAK (acting).

Shah Alam

Selangor Public Library Corporation: c/o Perpustakaan Raja Tun Uda, Persiaran Bandaraya, 40572 Shah Alam, Selangor; tel. (3) 55197667; fax (3) 55196045; e-mail jothi@ppas.org.my; internet www.ppas.org.my; f. 1971; 1,435,803 vols; main library; 8 brs; 4 township libraries, 55 village libraries and 13 mobile units; Dir SHAHANEEM HANOUM; publs *Accession List* (monthly), *PPAS Newsletter* (quarterly).

Tun Abdul Razak Library: MARA Institute of Technology, 40450 Shah Alam, Selangor; tel. (3) 5564041; fax (3) 5503648; f. 1957; two main libraries and 10 brs; 898,000 vols; Chief Librarian RAHMAH MUHAMAD.

Museums and Art Galleries

Kota Kinabalu

Sabah Museum: Jl. Muzium, 88300 Kota Kinabalu, Sabah; tel. (88) 253199; fax (88) 240230; e-mail muzium.sabah@sabah.gov.my; internet www.mzm.sabah.gov.my; f. 1886 in Sandakan; anthropological, archaeological, natural history and historical, ethno-botanical and ethnological collections; Islamic Civilization Museum, Agop Batu Tulug museum, Kinabatangan, Sandakan Heritage Museum, Sandakan Agnes Keith House, Sandakan Memorial Tun Abdul Razak, Tambunan Datu Paduka Mat Salleh Memorial, Kinarut Panoramic Mansion House, Tenom Murut Culture Museum, Semporna Bukit Tengkorak and Kunak Tingkayu open archaeological site; library of 7,000 vols; Dir Datuk JOSEPH POUNIS GUNTAVID; publs *Journal* (annually), *Buletin Muzium* (annually), *Annual Report*.

Kuala Lumpur

Islamic Arts Museum Malaysia: Jalan Lembah Perdana, 50480 Kuala Lumpur; tel. (3) 22742020; fax (3) 22740529; e-mail info@iamm.org.my; internet www.iamm.org.my; f. 1999; art and culture of Islam from 7th century to the present; Dir SYED MOHAMAD ALBUKHARY.

National Museum of Malaysia/Muzium Negara: Jl. Damansara, 50566 Kuala Lumpur; tel. (3) 22826255; fax (3) 22827294; e-mail info@jma.gov.my; internet www.jma.gov.my; f. 1963; houses collections of ethnographical, archaeological and zoological materials; comprehensive reference library on Malaysia and many Asian subjects, reference collections of archaeology, zoology and ethnography are also preserved in the Perak Museum, Taiping; Dir-Gen. Dr ADI HAJI TAHA; publ. *Federation Museums Journal* (annually).

Kuching

Sarawak Museum: Jl. Tun Abang Haji Openg, 93566 Kuching, Sarawak; tel. (82) 258388; fax (82) 246680; f. 1886; ethnographic, archaeological, natural history and historical collections; reference library; State archives; Dir SANIB SAID; publ. *Sarawak Museum Journal*.

Penang

Penang Museum and Art Gallery: Farquhar St, Penang; tel. (4) 2613144; f. 1963; Chair., Penang State Museum Board NAZIR ARIFF; Curator Encik KHOO BOO CHIA; publ. *Annual Report*.

Taiping

Perak Museum: Taiping, Perak; f. 1883; antiquities, Perak archives, ethnography, zoology and a library; Dir-Gen. SHAHRUM BIN YUB.

Universities

INTERNATIONAL ISLAMIC UNIVERSITY MALAYSIA

Jalan Gombak, 53100 Kuala Lumpur
Telephone: (3) 20564000
Fax: (3) 20564053
E-mail: pro@iiu.edu.my
Internet: www.iiu.edu.my

Founded 1983
Ministry of Education control
Languages of instruction: Arabic, English
Open to Muslims and non-Muslims from Malaysia and abroad
Constitutional Head: HRH THE SULTAN OF PAHANG
President: Y.B. Tan Sri Dato' SERI SANUSI BIN JUNID
Rector: Prof. Dr MOHD. KAMAL HASSAN
Deputy Rector (Academic Affairs): Assoc. Prof. Dato' Haji JAMIL HAJI OSMAN
Deputy Rector (Planning and Development): Prof. Dr ISMAWI HAJI ZEN
Deputy Rector (Student Affairs and Discipline): Assoc. Prof. Dr SIDEK BABA
Chief Librarian: Assoc. Prof. SYED SALIM AGHA BIN SYED AZAMTHULLA

Library of 356,700 vols
Number of teachers: 1,166
Number of students: 16,649

Publications: *At-Tajdid* (in Arabic, 2 a year), *Gombak Review* (in English, 2 a year), *IIUM* (in English, 2 a year), *IIUM Journal of Economics and Management* (in English, 2 a year), *IIUM Law Journal* (in English, 2 a year), *Intellectual Discourse* (in English, 2 a year)

DEANS OF KULLIYYAH

Kulliyah of Architecture and Environmental Design: Assoc. Prof. Dr CHE MUSA CHE OMAR
Kulliyyah of Economics and Management Sciences: Assoc. Prof. Dr MOHD. AZMI OMAR
Kulliyah of Education: Assoc. Prof. Dr MOHD. SAHARI NORDIN
Kulliyah of Engineering: Assoc. Prof. Dr AHMAD FARIS ISMAIL
Kulliyah of Information and Communications Technology: Dr MOHD. ADAM SUHAIMI
Kulliyyah of Islamic Revealed Knowledge and Human Sciences: Prof. Dr MOHAMED ARIS HAJI OSMAN
Ahmad Ibrahim Kulliyyah of Laws: Assoc Prof. Dr NIK AHMAD KAMAL NIK MAHMOD
Kulliyah of Medicine: Prof. Dato' Dr MD. TAHIR AZHAR
Kulliyyah of Pharmacy: Prof. Dr TARIQ ADBUL RAZAK
Kulliyah of Science: Assoc. Prof. Dr TORLA HAJI HASSAN

ATTACHED INSTITUTE

International Institute of Islamic Thought and Civilization (ISTAC): 205A Jl. Damansara, Bukit Damansara, 50480 Kuala Lumpur; tel. (3) 2544444; fax (3) 2548343; f. 1991; financed by Ministry of Education; postgraduate research and teaching in fields of Islamic thought and civilization; library of 149,686 vols; Dir Prof. Dr SYED MUHAMMAD NAQUIB AL-ATTAS.

UNIVERSITI KEBANGSAAN MALAYSIA
(National University of Malaysia)

43600 UKM Bangi, Selangor
Telephone: (3) 89214187
Fax: (3) 89254890
E-mail: kbha@pkrisc.cc.ukm.my
Internet: www.ukm.my

Founded 1970
State control
Languages of instruction: Malay, English, Arabic
Academic year: May to April
Chancellor: Tuanku JAAFAR IBNI AL-MARHUM TUANKU ABDUL RAHMAN
Vice-Chancellor: Prof. Dato' Dr MOHD SALLEH MOHD. YASIN
Deputy Vice-Chancellors: Prof. Dr SUKIMAN SARMANI (Academic and International Affairs), Prof. Dato' Dr MOHD WAHID SAMSUDIN (Students and Alumni Affairs)
Registrar: Hj. MOHAMED MUSTAFA MOHTAR
Bursar: Hj. MOHD ABDUL RASHID MOHD FADZIL
Chief Librarian: PUTRI SANIAH MEGAT ABDUL RAHMAN

Library of 945,000 vols, 4,000 journals
Number of teachers: 1,781
Number of students: 24,487

Publications: *Jurnal Sari*, *Jurnal Islamiyyat*, *Jurnal Jebat*, *Jurnal Pendidikan*, *Jurnal Pengurusan*, *Jurnal Psikologi Malaysia*, *Jurnal Kejuruteraan* (2 a year), *Jurnal Ekonomi Malaysia*, *Jurnal Perubatan UKM*, *Jurnal Akademika*, *Sains Malaysiana* (4 a year), *Jurnal Undang-Undang and Masyarakat*, *Buletin Pusat Pengajian Umum*, *Journal of Language Teaching, Linguistics and Literature*

DEANS

Faculty of Allied Health Sciences: Prof. Dr MOHD AZMAN ABU BAKAR
Faculty of Dentistry: Prof. Dato' Dr Hj. MOHD ARIFFIN HJ. MOHAMED
Faculty of Economics and Business: Prof. Dr NOOR AZLAN GHAZALI
Faculty of Education: Assoc. Prof. Dr LILIA HALIM
Faculty of Engineering: Prof. Ir. Dr HASSAN BASRI
Faculty of Islamic Studies: Prof. Dr ZAKARIA SETAPA
Faculty of Law: Assoc. Prof. KAMAL HALILI HASSAN
Faculty of Medicine: Prof. Dr LOKMAN SAIM
Faculty of Social Sciences and Humanities: Prof. Dr YUSUF ISMAIL
Faculty of Science and Technology: Prof. Dr ABDUL JALIL ABDUL KADER
Faculty of Science and Information Technology: Prof. AZIZ DERAMAN
Centre for General Studies: Prof. Dr ABDUL LATIF SAMIAN
Institute for Environment and Development (LESTARI): Prof. Dr IBRAHIM KOOMOO
Institute of Malay World and Civilization (ATMA): Prof. Dato' Dr SHAMSUL AMRI BAHARUDDIN
Institute of Malaysian and International Studies (IKMAS): Prof. Dr ROGAYAH HJ. MAT ZIN
Institute of Microengineering and Nanoelectronics (IMEN): Prof. Dr BURHANUDDIN YEOP MAJLIS
Institute of Medical Molecular Biology (UMBI): Prof. Dr A. RAHMAN A. JAMAL
Institute of Occidental Studies (IKON): Prof. Dato' Dr SHAMSUL AMRI BAHARUDDIN
Institute of Space (ANGKASA): Prof. Dr BAHARUDDIN YATIM
National Institute for Genomics and Molecular Biology–Malaysia: Prof. Dr NOR MUHAMMAD MAHADI

PROFESSORS

ABDUL HAMID, Z., Genetics and Plant Biotechnology
ABDUL KADER, A. J., Microbial Physiology
ABDUL KADIR, K., Endocrinology and Metabolism
ABDUL RAHMAN, R., Environmental Engineering
ABDUL RASHID, A. H., Anatomy
ABDULLAH, A., Food Science and Nutrition
ABDULLAH, I., Structural Geology and Tectonics
ABDULLAH, M., Statistics
ABDULLAH, P., Analytical and Environmental Chemistry
ABU BAKAR, M. A., Lipid Biochemistry
ABU TALIB, I., Material Physics
AHMAD, I., Virology
AHMAD, Z., Political Science
ALI, A., Industrial Planning and Strategies
ALI, O., Community Health
ALI JAMAL, A. R., Paediatric Haematology
ALI RAHIM, S., Development Communications
AZMAN ALI, RAYMOND, Neurology, Epilepsy and Stroke Medicine
BABA, I., Inorganic Chemistry
BABJI, A. S., Food Science
BAHARUDDIN, S. A., Anthropology and Sociology
BASRI, H., Civil and Environmental Engineering
BIDIN, A. A., Toxonomy of Lower Plants
BOO NEM YUN, Neonatology
CHOO, O. L., Child Neurology and Development Paediatrics
DAUD, W. R. W., Drying, Separation and Fuel Cell Technology
DIN, L., Organic Chemistry
EMBI, M. N., Protein Biochemistry
GEORGE, E., Haematology
HADI, A. S., Urbanization, Industrialization and Migration
HAMDAN, A. R., Artificial Intelligence
HASAN, M. N. H., Zoology
HASAN, Z. A. A., Parasitology
HASSAN, H. R., Psychiatry
HASSAN, S. Z. S., Anthropology of Religion, Gender Studies
ISKANDAR, T. M., Internal Control and Auditing
ISMAIL, M. Y., Minority and Sub-culture Studies
IZHAM CHEONG, Medicine
ISMAIL, N. M. N., Obstetrics and Gynaecology
JAHI, J. M., Physical Geography
JAMAL, F., Clinical Bacteriology
JASIN, B., Micropalaeontology
KADRI, A., Zoology
KAMIS, A., Animal Physiology, Comparative Endocrinology
KENG, C. S., Haematology
KOMOO, I., Engineering Geology and Conservation Geology
KONG, C. T. N., Nephrology
KRISHNASWAMY, S., Psychiatry
LAZAN, H., Plant Physiology and Biochemistry
LIEW, C. G., Family Medicine
LIM, A., Clinical Microbiology and Antimicrobial Chemotherapy

LONG, J., Education
MAHADI, N. M., Environmental Microbiology
MAJLIS, B. Y., Integrated Circuit Technology
MAJZUB, R. M., Pre-school and Adolescent Education and Development
MANSOR, M., Cytogenetics, Cytology
MAT SALLEH, M., Solid State Physics
MEERAH, T. S. M., Science Education
MD. HASHIM MERICAN, Z. M., Neuromuscular Pharmacology
MEAH, F. A., Surgery
MISIRAN, K., Anaesthesiology
MOHAMAD, A. L., Plant Systematics
MOHAMED, M. A., Oral Health
MOHAMED YASIN, M. S., Medical Mycology
MOHAMED, R., Bacterial Serology
MOHD NOOR, N., Plant Tissue Culture
MOHD SALLEH, K., Science and Society
MOHAMAD, H., Petrology and Geochemistry
MOHAMMED ZAIN, S. BIN, Mathematics
NGAH, W. Z. W., Medical Biochemistry
NIK ABD. RAHMAN, N. H. S., Archaeology
NOOR, M. I., Nutrition
NOR, G. M., Oral Surgery
OTHMAN, A. H., Co-ordination Chemistry
OTHMAN, B. H. R., Marine Biology
OTHMAN, M., Signals Processing
OTHMAN, M. Y. H., Energy Physics
PIHIE, A. H. L., Clinical Biochemistry
SAHID, I., Weed and Enviromental Science
SAID, I. M., Organic Chemistry
SAIM, L., Otology and Neuro-otology
SALLEH, A. R., Algebraic Topology, Ethnomathematics
SALLEH, RAMLI MD, Malay Syntax and Translation
SALLEH, S. H. H., Traditional Malay Literature
SAMSUDIN, A. R., Geophysics
SAMSUDIN, M. W., Organic Chemistry
SARMANI, S., Radiochemistry
SHAH, F. H., Molecular Biology
SHAMSUDIN, A. H., Mechanical Engineering
SIWAR, C., Rural Economics
SULAIMAN, N. A., Bioscience and Clinical Pharmacology
SULAIMAN, S., Vector Control, Vectorecology
SYED HUSSAIN, S. N. A., Histopathology, Cytopathology
TAHIR, U. M. M., Modern Malay Literature, Literary Criticism
TAMIN, N. M., Eco-engineering Restoration
TAP, A. O. M., Pure Mathematics
TEH, W. H. W., Rural Culture and Society
TENGKU SEMBOK, T. M., Information Retrieval
YAHAYA, MUHAMMAD, Physics
YAMIN, B. M., Chemistry
YATIM, B., Applied Physics
YONG, O., Investment
YUSOFF, K., Cardiology
YUSUF, M. H., Social Psychology
ZAMAN, H. B., Information Technology Policy and Strategic Studies

UNIVERSITI MALAYA
(University of Malaya)

Lembah Pantai, 50603 Kuala Lumpur
Telephone: (3) 7560022
Fax: (3) 7564004
Internet: www.cc.um.edu.my

Founded 1962
State control
Languages of instruction: Bahasa Malaysia, English
Academic year: May to April (2 semesters)
Chancellor: Duli Yang Maha Mulia Paduka Seri Sultan Perak Darul Ridzuan Sultan AZLAN MUHIBBUDDIN SHAH
Pro-Chancellors: Duli Yang Teramat Mulia Raja Muda Perak Darul Ridzuan Raja NAZRIN SHAH, Yang Amat Berbahagia Orang Kaya Bendahara Seri Maharaja Tun Haji SYED ZAHIRUDDIN BIN SYED HASSAN
Vice-Chancellor: Tan Sri Dato' Dr ABDULLAH SANUSI AHMAD
Deputy Vice-Chancellors: Prof. Dato' Dr FIRDAUS H. ABDULLAH, Prof. Dato' Dr OSMAN BAKAR, Assoc. Prof. Dr HAMZAH ABDUL RAHMAN
Registrar: YAACOB HUSSEIN
Librarian: Dr ZAITON OSMAN

Number of teachers: 1,571
Number of students: 24,345

Publications: *Annual Report*, *Berita UM* (newsletter, 2 a month), *Budiman* (4 a year), *University of Malaya Gazette* (annually)

DEANS

Faculty of Arts and Social Sciences: Prof. Datuk Dr ZAINAL KLING
Faculty of Business and Accounting: Prof. Dr MANSOR MD ISA
Faculty of Computer Science and Information Technology: Prof. Dr MASHKURI H. YAACOB
Faculty of Dentistry: Prof. Dato' Dr HASHIM YAACOB
Faculty of Economics and Administration: Prof. Dr JAHARA YAHAYA
Faculty of Education: Prof. Dr RAHIMAH BT. H. AHMAD
Faculty of Engineering: Prof. Dr WAN ABU BAKAR WAN ABAS
Faculty of Languages and Linguistics: Prof. Dato' Dr ASMAH H. OMAR
Faculty of Law: Prof. Dato' Dr N. S. SOTHI RACHAGAN
Faculty of Medicine: Prof. Dato' Dr ANUAR ZAINI MOHD. ZAIN
Faculty of Science: Prof. Dr MUHAMAD RASAT MUHAMAD
Institute of Postgraduate Studies and Research: Prof. Dr ANSARY AHMED
Academy of Islamic Studies: Prof. Dato' Dr MAHMOOD ZUHDI HJ. ABDUL MAJID (Dir)
Academy of Malay Studies: Prof. Dr WAN ABDUL KADIR WAN YUSOFF (Dir)
Centre for Foundation Studies in Science: Assoc. Prof. MOHD SAID MOHD KADIR (Dir)

PROFESSORS

Faculty of Arts and Social Sciences:
ABDULLAH ZAKAVIA, G., History
ALI, S. H., Sociology
AZIZAH, K., Anthropology and Sociology
CHENG, G. N., Chinese Studies
FATIMAH HASNAH, D., Anthropology and Sociology
LEE, B. T., Geography
LIM, C. S., English Studies
MOHD FAUZI, Y., Anthropology and Sociology
MOHD YUSOFF, H., History
NATHAN, K. S.
RAMLAH, A., History
RANJIT SINGH, D. S., History
SHAHARIL, T. R., Southeast Asia Studies
VOON, P. K., Land Use Studies
ZAINAL, K., Anthropology and Sociology

Faculty of Business and Accounting:
MANSOR, M. I., Financial Management
SIEH, M. L., Business Administration

Faculty of Computer Science and Information Technology:
MASHKURI, Y., Computer Science

Faculty of Dentistry:
HASHIM, Y., Oral Pathology and Oral Medicine
ISHAK, A. R., Preventive Dentistry
LIAN, C. B., Oral Surgery
LING, B. C., Prosthetics
LUI, J. L., Conservative Dentistry
RAHIMAH, A. K., Community Dentistry
SIAR, C. H., Periodontology
TOH, C. G., Conservative Dentistry
ZUBAIDAH ABD, R., Oral Biology

Faculty of Economics and Administration:
FIRDAUS, A., Administration and Political Science
JAHARA, Y., Development Studies
JAMILAH, M. A., Development Studies
JOMO, K. S., Applied Economics
KOK, K. L., Applied Economics
LEE, K. H., Analytical Economics
NAGARAJ, S., Applied Statistics
NAIDU, G., Applied Economics
TAN, P. C., Applied Statistics

Faculty of Education:
CHEW, S. B., Sociology of Education
CHIAM, H. K., Social Psychology of Education
GAUDART, H. M., Language Education
ISHAK, H., Pedagogy and Educational Psychology
NIK AZIS, N. P., Mathematics and Science Education
RAHIMAH HJ., A., Educational Development
RAMIAH, A. L., Educational Development
SAFIAH, O., Language Education
SURADI, S., Pedagogy and Educational Psychology
YONG, M. S. LEONARD, Pedagogy and Educational Psychology

Faculty of Engineering:
ABDUL GHANI, K., Computer-aided Design and Manufacturing
EZRIN, A., Built Environment
FAISAL, A., Civil and Environmental Engineering
GOH, S. Y., Mechanical and Material Engineering
KHALID, M. N., Electrical and Telecommunications Engineering
LU, S. K. S., Electrical Engineering
MASITAH, H., Chemical Engineering
MOHD ALI, H., Chemical Engineering
MOHD ZAKI, A. M., Mechanical and Material Engineering
RAMACHANDRAN, K. B., Biochemical Engineering
WAN ABU BAKAR, W. A., Mechanical Engineering
WOODS, P. C., Built Environment

Faculty of Law:
BALAN, P., Company Law and Civil Procedure
HARI, C., Jurisprudence and Legal Philosophy
KHAW, L. T., Law of Intellectual Property and Land Law
MIMI KAMARIAH, A. M., Family Law and Criminal Procedures
SOTHI RACHAGAN, N. S., Environmental and Consumer Law
SURYA, P. S., International Law

Faculty of Medicine:
ALJAFRI, A. M., Surgery
ANUAR ZAINI, M. Z., Medicine
ASMA, O., Paediatrics
CHANDRA, S. N., Parasitology
CHUA, C. T., Medicine
DELLIKAN, A. E., Anaesthesiology
DEVA, M. P., Psychological Medicine
EL-SABBAN, FAROUK M. F., Physiology
GOH, K. L., Medicine
KHAIRULL, A. A., Parasitology
KULENTHRAN, A., Obstetrics and Gynaecology
LAM, S. K., Medical Microbiology
LANG, C. C., Medicine
LIM, C. T., Paediatrics
LIM, Y. C., Surgery
LIN, H. P., Paediatrics
LOOI, L. M., Pathology
MENAKA, N., Pathology
NGEOW, Y. F., Medical Microbiology

Ong, S. Y. G., Anaesthesiology
Paramsothy, M., Medicine
Perumal, R., Biochemistry
Prasad, U., Oto-rhino-laryngology
Puthucheary, S. D., Medical Microbiology
Raman, A., Physiology
Ramanujam, T. M., Surgery
Rokiah, I., Medicine
Ruby, H., Physiology
Sengupta, S., Orthopaedic Surgery
Sivanesaratnam, V., Obstetrics and Gynaecology
Subramaniam, K., Anatomy
Tan, C. T., Medicine
Tan, N. H., Biochemistry
Tan, S. K. P.
Teoh, S. T., Social and Preventive Medicine
Yap, S. F., Pathology
Yeoh, P. N., Pharmacy

Faculty of Science:

Ansary, A., Microbiology and Bacteriology
Hamid, A. H. A., Natural Product Chemistry
Harith, A., Physics
Koh, C. L., Genetics
Lim, M. H., Multilinear Algebra
Low, K. S., Lasers and Optoelectronics
Mak, C., Plant Breeding
Mohamed, A. M., Taxonomy and Ecology
Muhamad Rasat, M., Molecular Electronics
Muhamad, Z., Botany
Mukherjee, T. K., Genetics
Nair, H., Plant Physiology
Osman, B., Philosophy of Science
Rahim, S., Semiconductor Physics
Raj, J. K., Engineering Geology
Ramli, A., Zoology
Wong, C. S., Plasma Physics
Yeap, E. B., Geology

Academy of Islamic Studies:

Abdullah Alwi, H., Syariah and Economics
Mahmood Zuhdi, A. M., Figh and Usul
Mahfodz, M., Syariah and Law

Academy of Malay Studies:

Abu Hassan, M. S., Malay Literature
Asmah, O., Malay Linguistics
Hashim, M., Linguistics
Norazit, S., Economic Anthropology
Rahmah, B., Malay Culture and Arts
Wan Abdul Kadir, W. Y., Popular Culture Studies
Yaacob, H., Development Studies and Change

UNIVERSITI MALAYSIA SABAH

Tingkat 9, Gaya Centre, Jalan Tun Fuad Stephens, Locked Bag 2073, 88999 Kota Kinabalu, Sabah
Telephone: (88) 320789
Fax: (88) 320223
E-mail: pejcslor@ums.edu.my
Internet: www.ums.edu.my

Founded 1994
Academic year: June to March

Vice-Chancellor: Prof. Datuk Seri Panglima Dr Abu Hassan Othman
Deputy Vice-Chancellors: Prof. Dr Mohd Zahedi Daud (Academic), Prof. Datuk Dr Kamaruzzaman Ampon (Research and Development), Prof. Datuk Dr Mohd Noh Dalimin (Student Affairs)
Registrar: Hela Ladin bin Mohd Dahalan
Librarian: Che Salmah Mehamood

Number of teachers: 476
Number of students: 8,300

Publications: *Borneo Science* (2 a year), *Kinabalu* (annually), *Manu* (annually)

DEANS

School of Business and Economics: Assoc. Prof. Syed Azizi Syed Wafa
School of Business and Finance, Labuan: Assoc. Prof. Dr Zainal Abidin Said
School of Arts Studies: Assoc. Prof. Haji Inon Shaharuddin Abd. Rahman
School of Social Sciences: Assoc. Prof. Hassan bin Mat Nor
School of Education and Social Development: Prof. Dr Shukery Mohamed
School of Engineering and Information Technology: Assoc. Prof. Dr Sazali Yaacob
School of Food Science and Nutrition: Assoc. Prof. Dr Mohd Ismail Abdullah
School of International Forestry: Assoc. Prof. Dr Aminuddin Mohamed
School of Psychology and Social Work: Prof. Dato' Dr Abdul Halim Othman
School of Science and Technology: Assoc Prof. Dr Amran Ahmed
School of Informatic Sciences, Labuan: Awang Asri Awang Ibrahim (acting)
Centre for Postgraduate Studies: Prof. Dr Zainodin Hj Jubok
Centre for the Promotion of Knowledge and Language Learning: Prof. Dr Ahmat Adam

ATTACHED RESEARCH INSTITUTES

Biotechnology Research Institute: Dir Prof. Datin Dr Ann Anton.

Borneo Marine Research Institute: Dir Prof. Dr Hj Ridzwan Abd Rahman.

Tropical Biology and Conservation Research Institute: Dir Prof. Datin Dr Maryati Mohamed.

UNIVERSITI MALAYSIA SARAWAK (UNIMAS)

Jalan Dato' Mohd Musa, 94300 Kota Samarahan, Sarawak
Telephone: (82) 671000
Fax: (82) 672411
Internet: www.unimas.my

Chairman: Tan Sri Datuk Amar Haji Bujang Mohd Nor
Chancellor: Tun Yang Terutama Tun Datuk Patinggi Abang Haji Muhammad Salahuddin
Pro-Chancellor: Yang Amat Berhormat Pehin Sri Dr Haji Abdul Taib Mahmud
Vice-Chancellor: Prof. Dr Abdul Rashid Abdullah
Deputy Vice-Chancellors: Prof. Haji Sulaiman Hanapi (Student Affairs and Alumni), Prof. Dr Mohd Azib Salleh (Academic and Internationalization)
Registrar: Prof. Dr Hamsawi Sani

Library of 108,000 vols, 10,000 journals
Number of teachers: 464
Number of students: 5,675 (5,112 undergraduate, 563 postgraduate)

DEANS

Faculty of Applied and Creative Arts: Assoc. Prof. Mohd Fadzil Abdul Rahman
Faculty of Cognitive Science and Human Development: Prof. Dr Datin Napsiah Mahfoz
Faculty of Computer Science and Information Technology: Assoc. Prof. Narayanan Kulathuramaiyer
Faculty of Economy and Business: Assoc. Prof. Dr Shazali Abu Mansor
Faculty of Engineering: Prof. Dr Khairuddin Ab Hamid
Faculty of Medicine and Health Sciences: Prof. Dr Syaed Hassan AL Mashoor
Faculty of Resource Science and Technology: Assoc. Prof. Dr Sabdin Mohd Long
Faculty of Social Sciences: Assoc. Prof. Dr Mutalip Abdullah

PROFESSORS

Abdullah, M. S., Medicine and Health Sciences
Ab Hamid, K., Engineering
Abu Mansor, S., Engineering
Al Mashoor, S. H., Medicine and Health Sciences
Bohari, H., Medicine and Health Sciences
Gudum, H., Medicine and Health Sciences
Hadi, Y., Resource Science and Technology
Harun, W. S. W., Resource Science and Technology
Long, P. K., Medicine and Health Sciences
Mahfoz, N., Cognitive Science and Human Development
Malik, A. S., Medicine and Health Sciences
Ngidang, D., Social Sciences
Said, S., Engineering
Singh, B., Medicine and Health Sciences
Thambyrajah, V., Medicine and Health Sciences

MALAYSIA UNIVERSITY OF SCIENCE AND TECHNOLOGY (MUST)

GL 33 (Ground Fl.), Block C, Kelana Square, 17 Jl. SS 7/26, 47301, Kelana Jaya, Petaling Jaya, Selangor Darul Ehsan
Telephone: (3) 78801777
Fax: (3) 78801762
E-mail: admin@must.edu.my
Internet: www.must.edu.my

Private control
Academic year: September to June

Postgraduate research university; collaborative programme with Massachusetts Institute of Technology (MIT)

Provost: Dr Nor Adnan Yahaya (acting)
Vice-President for Finance and Business Affairs: Badly Shah bin Ariff Shah
Registrar and Head of Administration: Stephen John Lee
Chief Librarian: Johari Affandi Omar

DEANS

Biotechnology: Assoc. Prof. Dr Lim Saw Hoon
Construction Engineering and Management: Assoc. Prof. Dr Chan Toong Khuan
Energy and Environment: Asst Prof. Dr Scott Kennedy
Information Technology: Assoc. Prof. Dr Nor Adnan Yahya
Materials Science and Engineering: Prof. Dr Zanuldin Ahmad
Systems Engineering and Management: Asst Prof. Dr Indra Gunawan
Transportation and Logistics: Assoc. Prof. Dr Leong Choon Heng

MULTIMEDIA UNIVERSITY

Jalan Multimedia, 63100 Cyberjaya, Selangor
Telephone: (3) 83125018
Fax: (3) 83125022
E-mail: mkt@mmu.edu.my
Internet: www.mmu.edu.my

Chancellor: Yang Amat Berbahagia Dato' Seri Dr Siti Hasmah binti Haji Mohd Ali
President: Prof. Dr Ghauth Jasmon

DEANS

Faculty of Creative Multimedia (Cyberjaya Campus): Assoc. Prof. Dr Abu Hassan Ismail
Faculty of Engineering (Cyberjaya Campus): Prof. Chuah Hean Teik
Faculty of Information Technology (Cyberjaya Campus): Prof. Lee Poh Aun
Faculty of Management (Cyberjaya Campus): Assoc. Prof. Dr Mohd Ismail Sayyed Ahmad

Faculty of Business and Law (Melaka Campus): Dr GOH PEK CHEN (acting)
Faculty of Engineering and Technology (Melaka Campus): (vacant)
Faculty of Information Science and Technology (Melaka Campus): (vacant)

UNIVERSITI PENDIDIKAN SULTAN IDRIS
(Sultan Idris University of Education)

35900 Tanjong Malim, Perak Darul Ridzuan
Telephone: (5) 4506000
Fax: (5) 4595488
E-mail: admin@upsi.edu.my
Internet: www.upsi.edu.my

Founded 1922

Chancellor: MAHA MULIA RAJA PERMAISURI
Vice-Chancellor: Prof. Dato' MOHAMMAD NOOR B. HAJI SALEH
Vice-Chancellor: Datuk Dr MUHAMMAD RAIS BIN ABDUL KARIM
Pro-Vice-Chancellor (Academic Affairs): Prof. Dr KHADIJAH ROHANI BINTI MOHAMMAD YUNUS
Pro-Vice-Chancellor (Planning and Development): Prof. Dr MOHAMMAD NOOR BIN SALEH
Pro-Vice-Chancellor (Student Welfare): Prof. Dr MOHAMMAD YUSOF BIN ABU BAKAR
Registrar: RUSLEY BIN TAIB
Chief Librarian: CIK ZAHARIAH BINTI MOHAMED SHAHAROON

DEANS

Faculty of Business and Economics: Madya HARIRI BIN KAMIS
Faculty of Cognitive Science and Human Development: Prof. Datin NORAN FAUZIAH BINTI YAAKUB
Faculty of Drama and Music: Prof. MADYA HAJI IBERAHIM BIN HASSAN
Faculty of Foreign Languages: Encik NOR AZMI BIN MOHAMMAD
Faculty of Information Technology and Communication: Encik ABD SAMAD BIN HANIF
Faculty of Science and Technology: Prof. Madya Dr OMAR BIN MOHAMMAD YUSOH

ATTACHED RESEARCH INSTITUTES

Centre for Modern Languages: Dir PUAN AINON BINTI OMAR.

Centre for Research and Consultancy: Dir Prof. Dato' Dr ABU BAKAR BIN NORDIN.

Institute of Education, Technology and Multimedia: Dir Prof. Madya Dr ABD LATIF B. HAJI GAPOR.

Institute of International Relations: Dir (vacant).

Institute of Koranic Studies: Dir Prof. Dr BACHOK M. TAIB.

Institute of Malay Civilisation: Dir Prof. Emeritus Dato' Dr ASMAH HAJI OMAR.

Institute of Quality Assurance: Dir Prof. Madya Dr NAGENDRALINGAN RATNAVADIVEL.

Institute of Technology and Communication: Dir Prof. Madya Dr MOHAMAD BIN IBRAHIM.

UNIVERSITI PUTRA MALAYSIA
(Putra University, Malaysia)

43400 Serdang, Selangor Darul Ehsan
Telephone: (3) 89486101
Fax: (3) 89483244
E-mail: cans@admin.upm.edu.my
Internet: www.upm.edu.my

Founded 1971
State control
Languages of instruction: Malay, English
Academic year: May to November (two semesters)

Chancellor: The Governor of Penang
Vice-Chancellor: Prof. Dato' Dr MOHD ZOHADIE BARDAIE
Deputy Vice-Chancellors: Prof. Dr MUHAMAD AWANG (Academic), Assoc. Prof. Dr MAKHDZIR MARDAN (Development), Assoc. Prof. Dr Haji IDRIS ABDOL (Student Affairs)
Registrar: KAMALUL ARIFFIN MUSA
Librarian: KAMARIAH BT ABDUL HAMID

Number of teachers: 1,074
Number of students: 33,566

Publication: *Tribun Putra* (monthly)

DEANS

Faculty of Agriculture: Prof. Dr MOHD. YUSOF HUSSEIN
Faculty of Computer Science and Information Technology: Dr ABD. AZIM BIN ABD. GHANI
Faculty of Design and Architecture: Assoc. Prof. Dr MUSTAFA KAMAL
Faculty of Economics and Management: Prof. Dr NIK MUSTAFA RAJA ABDULLAH
Faculty of Educational Studies: Assoc. Prof. KAMARIAH BT ABU BAKAR
Faculty of Engineering: Prof. Dr Ir. RADIN UMAR RADIN SOHADI
Faculty of Food Science and Biotechnology: Prof. Dr GULAM RUSUL BIN RAHMAT ALI
Faculty of Forestry: Prof. Dato' Dr NIK MUHAMAD NIK MAJID
Faculty of Human Ecology: Prof. Dr ABDULLAH AL-HADI HJ. MUHAMED
Faculty of Medicine and Health Sciences: Assoc. Prof. Dr JAMMAL AHMAD ESSA
Faculty of Modern Languages and Communication: Prof. Dr SHAIK MOHD NOOR ALAM SHAIK MOHD HUSSEIN
Faculty of Science and Environmental Studies: Prof. Dr WAN ZIN WAN YUNUS
Faculty of Veterinary Medicine: Prof. Dato' Dr Sheik OMAR ABDUL RAHMAN
School of Graduate Studies: Prof. Dr AINI IDERIS
Graduate School of Management: Assoc. Prof. ZAINAL ABIDIN KIDAM
External Programme Centre: Assoc. Prof. Dr ABDUL AZIZ SAHAREE (Dir)
Institute for Distance Education and Learning: Assoc. Prof. AZAHARI ISMAIL (Dir)
Islamic Centre: Assoc. Prof. Dr Haji MUHD. FAUZI BIN MOHAMAD (Dir)

HEADS OF DEPARTMENTS

Faculty of Agriculture (tel. (3) 89486930; fax (3) 89433097; e-mail yusof@agri.upm.edu.my):
- Agribusiness and Information Systems: Prof. Dr MAD NASIR SHAMSUDIN
- Agricultural Technology: Dr RAJA AHMAD TAJUDIN SHAH RAJA ABDUL RASHID
- Animal Sciences: Assoc. Prof. Dr ZAINAL AZNAM BIN MOHD. JELAN
- Crop Science: Assoc. Prof. Dr MOHD RIDZWAN ABDUL HALIM
- Land Management: Assoc. Prof. Dr SITI ZANYAH DARUS
- Plant Protection: Assoc. Prof. Dr DZOLKHIFLI OMAR

Faculty of Computer Science and Information Technology (tel. (3) 89486101 ext. 3549; fax (3) 89482102; e-mail azim@fsktm.upm.edu.my; internet www.fsktm.upm.edu.my):
- Communication Technology and Networking: AZIZOL BIN HJ. ABDULLAH
- Computer Science: Dr ALI BIN MAMAT
- Information Systems: Assoc. Prof. Dr Haji HASAN BIN SELAMAT
- Multimedia: Dr FATIMAH BT. DATO' AHMAD

Faculty of Design and Architecture (tel. (3) 89480014; fax (3) 89480017; e-mail mustafa@frsb.upm.edu.my; internet www.frsb.upm.edu.my):
- Architecture: Prof. RUSLAN BIN KHALID
- Landscape Architecture: OSMAN MOHD TAHIR

Faculty of Economics and Management (tel. (3) 89432714; fax (3) 89486188; e-mail nmra@econ.upm.edu.my; internet www.econ.upm.edu.my):
- Accounting and Finance: Assoc. Prof. Dr ANUAR MD. NASIR
- Economics: Assoc. Prof. Dr ZAKARIAH ABD. RASHID
- Hospitality and Recreation: Assoc. Prof. Dr AHMAD SHUIB
- Management and Marketing: Assoc. Prof. Dr SAMSINAR MD. SIDIN

Faculty of Educational Studies (tel. (3) 89480588; fax (3) 89480119; e-mail kamarab@educ.upm.edu.my; internet www.educ.upm.edu.my):
- Education: Assoc. Prof. Dr OTHMAN DATO' HJ. MOHAMED
- Professional Development and Continuing Education: Prof. Dr AMINAH AHMAD

Faculty of Engineering (tel. (3) 89486655; fax (3) 89434641; e-mail radinumx@eng.upm.edu.my; internet www.eng.upm.edu.my):
- Aerospace Engineering: Assoc. Prof. Dr WAQAR ASRAR
- Biological and Agricultural Engineering: Dr ABDUL RASHID MUHAMAD SHARIF
- Chemical and Environmental Engineering: Dr FAKHRU'L-RAZI AHAMADUN
- Civil Engineering: Dr SALLEH JAAFAR
- Computer and Communication Systems Engineering: Assoc. Prof. Dr BORHANUDDIN BIN MOHD. ALI
- Electrical and Electronic Engineering: Dr BAMBANG SUNARYO BIN SUPARJO
- Mechanical and Manufacturing Engineering: Dr MEGAT MOHAMAD HAMDAN BIN MEGAT AHMAD
- Process and Food Engineering: Dr WAN MUHAMAD WAN ABDULLAH

Faculty of Food Science and Biotechnology (tel. (3) 89486314; fax (3) 89423552; e-mail gulam@fsb.upm.edu.my; internet www.fsb.upm.edu.my):
- Biotechnology: Assoc. Prof. Dr MOHD ALI HASSAN
- Food Sciences: Assoc. Prof. Dr AZIZAH BT. OSMAN
- Food Technology: Assoc. Prof. Dr RUSSLY BIN ABDUL RAHMAN

Faculty of Forestry (tel. (3) 89487835; fax (3) 89432514; e-mail nik@forr.upm.edu.my; internet www.forr.upm.edu.my):
- Forest Management: Dr AHMAD AINUDDIN BIN NURUDDIN
- Forest Production: Dr ZAIDON ASHAARI

Faculty of Human Ecology (tel. (3) 89424371; fax (3) 89435385; e-mail abdhadi@ecol.upm.edu.my; internet www.ecol.upm.edu.my):
- Family Development Studies: Dr ROHANI ABDULLAH
- Music: NOR AZHAR MOHD YUSOF
- Resource Management and Consumer Studies: Assoc. Prof. Dr NURIZAN YAHAYA
- Social Development Studies: Dr ZAHID BIN EMBY

Faculty of Medicine and Health Sciences (tel. (3) 89488822; fax (3) 89426957; e-mail jammal@medic.upm.edu.my):
- Biomedical Science: Dr MOHD ROSLAN SULAIMAN
- Clinical Laboratory Sciences: Dr HAIRUZAH ITHNIN
- Community Health: Dr LONG SEH CHIN
- Human Growth and Development: Assoc. Prof. Dr NOVAIHAN
- Medicine: Assoc. Prof. Dr NG TIAN SENG
- Nutrition and Health Sciences: Dr MAZNAH ISMAIL

Surgery: Assoc. Prof. Dr YUNUS GUL ALIF GUL

Faculty of Modern Languages and Communication (tel. (3) 89485886; fax (3) 89439951; e-mail shaik@fbm.upm.edu.my):

Communication Studies: Dr EZHAR TAMAM
English Language: Assoc. Prof. Dr ROSLI TALIF
Foreign Languages: ANG LAY HOON
Malay Language: Tuan Hj. MOHD AMIN ARSHAD

Faculty of Science and Environmental Studies (tel. (3) 89486646; fax (3) 89432508; e-mail wanzin@fsas.upm.edu.my; internet www.fsas.upm.edu.my):

Biochemistry and Microbiology: Assoc. Prof. Datin Dr KALIJAH MD. YUSOFF
Biology: Dr JAPAR SIDIK BUJANG
Chemistry: Assoc. Prof. Dr MAWARDI BIN RAHMANI
Environmental Sciences: Dr RAMDZANI ABDULLAH
Mathematics: Prof. Dr KAMEL ARIFFIN
Physics: Assoc. Prof. Dr Hj. W. MAHMOOD MAT YUNUS

Faculty of Veterinary Medicine (tel. (3) 8943587; fax (3) 89486317; e-mail sheikh@vef.upm.edu.my; internet www.vet.upm.edu.my):

University Veterinary Hospital: Dr NADZARIAH CHENG ABDULLAH

ATTACHED RESEARCH INSTITUTES

Institute of Bioscience: Dir Prof. Dr ABDUL RANI BAHAMAN.

Institute of Multimedia: Dir Assoc. Prof. Dr BACHOK TAIB (acting).

Sultan Salahuddin Abdul Aziz Shah Cultural and Arts Centre: Dir Assoc. Prof. Dr NAIM HAJI MOHAMAD.

Technology Research Park: Dir Prof. Dr JINAP BT. SELAMAT.

University Business Centre: Dir Dr JOHARI ENDAN.

UNIVERSITI SAINS MALAYSIA
(University of Science, Malaysia)

Minden, 11800 Penang
Telephone: (4) 6533888
Fax: (4) 6565401
E-mail: kpp_pnc@notes.usm.my
Internet: www.usm.my
Founded 1969
Federal control
Languages of instruction: Bahasa Malaysia, English
Academic year: June to June
Chancellor: HM Queen Tuanku FAUZIAH BINTI ALMARHUM TENGKU ABDUL RASHID
Pro-Chancellors: Hon. Tan Sri RAZALI ISMAIL, Hon. Tan Sri Datuk Dr LIN SEE YAN
Vice-Chancellor: Hon. Prof. Dato' DZULKIFLI ABDUL RAZAK
Deputy Vice-Chancellors: Hon. Dato' Prof. MUHAMMAD IDIRIS SALEH, Hon Dato' Prof. SYED AHMAD HUSSEIN, Hon. Dato' Assoc. Prof. JAMALUDIN MOHAIADIN
Registrar: AZMAN ABDULLAH
Library: see Libraries and Archives
Number of teachers: 1,528
Number of students: 27,325 (21,744 undergraduate, 5,581 postgraduate)
Publications: *Frontiers* (3 a year), *Perantara* (3 a year), *Mediskop* (3 a year), *Graduate Infolink* (3 a year), *Kejuruteran* (3 a year)

DEANS

School of Aerospace Engineering: ILLYIA MOHAMAD YUSOF
School of Arts: Dr MOHAMAD NAJIB AHMAD DAWA
School of Biological Sciences: Prof. MASHHOR MANSOR
School of Chemical Engineering: Assoc. Prof. ABDUL LATIF AHMAD
School of Chemical Sciences: Assoc. Prof. WAN AHMAD KAMIL MAHMOOD
School of Civil Engineering: Assoc. Prof. WAN JASHIM WAN IBRAHIM
School of Communications: Dr MOHAMED ZIN NORDIN
School of Computer Sciences: Assoc. Prof. ROSNI ABDULLAH MUSTAFA
School of Dentistry: Assoc. Prof. AB. RANI SAMSUDIN
School of Distance Education: OMAR MAJID
School of Education Studies: Assoc. Prof. AMINAH AYOB
School of Electrical and Electronics Engineering: Assoc. Prof. OTHMAN SIDEK
School of Health Sciences: Assoc. Prof. ZAINUL F. ZAINUDDIN
School of Housing, Building and Planning: Prof. MAHYUDDIN RAMLI
School of Humanities: Assoc. Prof. NORIZAN MOHD NOOR
School of Industrial Technology: Prof. WAN ROSLI WAN DAUD
School of Management: Hon. Dato' Prof. DAING MOHAMAD NASIR DAING IBRAHIM
School of Materials and Mineral Resources Engineering: Assoc. Prof. KHAIRUN AZIZI MOHD AZIZLI
School of Mathematical Sciences: Assoc. Prof. AHMAD IZANI MD ISMAIL
School of Mechanical Engineering: Prof. ABDUL AZIZ BABA
School of Medical Sciences: Assoc. Prof. ZABIDI AZHAR MOHD HUSSIN
School of Pharmaceutical Sciences: Assoc. Prof. ABAS HUSSIN
School of Physics: Assoc. Prof. HASLAN ABU HASSAN
School of Social Sciences: Assoc. Prof. ABDUL RAHIM IBRAHIM
Biomedical and Health Sciences Platform: Prof. NORAZMI MOHAMAD NOOR
Clinical Platform: Prof. WAN MOHAMAD WAN BEBAKAR
Engineering and Technology Platform: Assoc. Prof. AHMAD FARHAN MOHAMAD SADULLAH
Fundamental Science Platform: Prof. ABDUL AZIZ TAJUDIN
Information and Communication Technology Platform: Prof. ZAHARIN YUSOFF
Life Sciences Platform: Prof. MOHAMED ISA ABDUL MAJID
Institute of Postgraduate Studies: Prof. AHMAD SHUKRI MUSTAPA KAMAL

DIRECTORS

Advanced Medical and Dental Institute: Dr RAMLI SAAD
Centre for Archaeological Research Malaysia: Hon. Dato' Prof. STIL ZURAINA ABDUL MAJID
Centre for Instructional Technology and Multimedia: Assoc. Prof. WAN MOHAMAD FAUZY WAN ISMAIL
Centre for Knowledge, Communication and Technology: Prof. AHMAD YUSOFF HASSAN
Centre for Languages and Translation: Dr NORISHAM MOHAMAD
Centre for Marine and Coastal Studies: Prof. ZUBIR DIN
Centre for Policy Research: Prof. MUHAMAD JANTAN
Corporate Development Division: Assoc. Prof. OMAR OSMAN
Doping Control Centre: Prof. AISHAH ABDUL LATIFF
Drug Research Centre: Prof. SHARIF MAHSUFI MANSOR
Health Campus: Hon. Prof. Dato' MAFAUZY MOHAMAD
Health Centre: Dr NURULAIN ABDULLAH BAYANUDDIN
Human Genome Centre (Virtual): (vacant)
Institute for Research in Molecular Medicine: Prof. ASMA ISMAIL
IPv6 Centre of Excellence: Assoc. Prof. SURESEWAN RAMADASS
Islamic Centre: NASIRUN MOHAMAD SALLEH
Museum and Art Gallery: HASNUL JAMAL SAIDON
National Poison Centre: Assoc. Prof. RAHMAT AWANG
River Engineering and Urban Drainage Research Centre: Assoc. Prof. NOR AZAZI ZAKARIA
University Hospital: Dr ZAIDUN KAMARI
University Hospital: Dr RAMLI SAAD
USAINS Holding: Hon. Dato' Dr GAN EE KIANG
Women's Development Research Centre: Hon. Datin Assoc. Prof. RASHIDAH SHUIB

PROFESSORS

ABDUL AZIZ, B., Medical Oncology, Haematology and Palliative Medicine
ABDUL AZIZ, T., Radiation Biophysics, Medical Physics
ABDUL GHANI, S., Urban and Regional Planning
ABDUL RASHID, A. R., Clinical Pharmacology and Therapeutics
ABDUL WAHAB, A. R., Vector Ecology
AB RANI, S., Maxillofacial Surgery, Tissue Banking, Bone Banking
ABU HASSAN, A., Mosquito and Urban Pest Control, Aquatic Insect, Insect Ecology
ABU TALIB, A., South-east Asian History
AHMAD PAUZI, M. Y., Physiology
AHMAD SHUKRI, M. K., Radiation Biophysics, Medical Physics
AHMAD YUSOFF, H., Mechanical Computer-Aided Engineering, CAD-CAM
AISHAH, A. L., Pharmacology
AMBIGAPATHY, P., English as a Second Language and Sociolinguistics
AMINAH, A., Science Education
AMIR HUSSIN, B., Economics
ASMA, I., Medical Microbiology, Molecular Biology of Infectious Diseases, Rapid Diagnosis of Infectious Diseases esp. Typhoid and Paratyphoid Fevers
BAHARUDDIN, S., Plant Pathology
BAHRUDDIN, S., Chemical Resistance Measurements
BOEY, P. L., Palm Oil Chemistry and Technology
CHAN, K. L., Pharmaceutical Chemistry
CHAN, N. W., Water Resources, Hydrology and Flood Hazard Management, Climatology
CHONG, C. S., Biophysics
DAING MOHD NASIR, D. I., Accounting, Business Administration
DZULKIFLI, A. R., Pharmacology
FARID, G., Digital and Data Communication
FUN, H. K., Solid State Physics
GOON, W. K., Environmental Studies, Mangrove Ecosystem, Tropical Rain Forest
HANAFI, I., Plastic Composite and Rubber
HARBINDAR JEET SINGH, G. S., Calcium Metabolism
HASSAN, S., Applied Mathematics
IBRAHIM, C. O., Biotechnology
IBRAHIM, W., Transport Planning
ILYAS, M., Geophysics
ITAM, S., Medical Parasitology and Entomology
JAFRI MALIN, A., Neurosurgery
JAMIL, I., Polymers
JEYARATNAM, K., Policy Studies
JUNAIDAH, O., Scattering of Electromagnetic Waves
KAMARULAZIZI, I., Semiconductor Energy Studies, Clean Room Fabrication Technology
KOH, H. L., Environmental and Ecosystem Modelling EIA Simulation

LEE, C. Y., Geophysics Exploration, Applied Geophysics
LIM, K. O., Biophysics
LIM, P. E., Waste Water Treatment
LOH, K. W., Economics
MAFAUZY, M., Endocrinology, Effect of Natural Products on Diabetes
MAHYUDDIN, R., Building Technology
MASHHOR, M., Botany
MASHUDI, K., Linguistics
MD SALLEH, Y., Literature
MOHAMAD AZEMI, M. N., Food Technology
MOHAMAD, S., Literature
MOHAMED, S., Marketing
MOHAMED ISA, A. M., Biodegradable Plastics, Biotechnology
MOHAMMAD MAHFOOZ, A. A., Management
MOHAMED GHOUSE, N., Theatre and Dance
MOHAMED OMAR, K., Environmental Technology
MOHAMED RAZALI, S., Social Psychiatry and Rehabilitation
MOHAMED SHUKRI, S., Planning and Development Management
MORSHIDI, S., Urban Planning and Development
MUHAMAD, J., Management Science, Statistics, Operations Management
MUHAMMAD IDIRIS, S., Analytical Chemistry
MUSTAFFA, E., Medicine
NAVARATNAM, V., Clinical Pharmacology
NORZAMI, M. N., Immunology
NOR HAYATI, O., Surgical Pathology with special interest in Gynaepathology, Dermatopathology and Oncopathology
OMAR, S., Inorganic Chemistry
ONG, B. H., Computer-aided Geometric Design
OSMAN, M., Marketing
PLOTNIKOV IOURI, P., Flight Dynamics and Control Systems, Applied Optimal Control
POH, B. L., Organic Chemistry
QUAH, S. H., Applied Mathematics
RADZALI, O., Materials and Bioceramics Engineering
RAHMAT, A., Clinical Pharmacy and Toxicology
RAMLI, M., Persuasive Communication
ROGAYAH, J., Curriculat Development and Problem-based Learning
ROSHADA, H., Biomedical Analysis
ROSHIHAN, M. A., Quality Control
ROZHAN, M. I., Solid State Physics
ROZMAN, D., Chemistry of Wood
RUSLAN, R., Geographic Information Systems
RUSLI, N., Public Health, Islamic Occupational and Health Medicine, AIDS Prevention and Counselling, Islamic Perspectives in Medicine and Health, Occupational Health and Safety
SARINGAT, B., Quality Control Tablets, Capsules, Herbal Formulations
SEETHARAMU, K. N., Heat Transfer, Computational Fluid Dynamics, Stress Analysis
SHARIF MAHSUFI, M., Pharmacokinetics, Drug Metabolism
SITI ZURAINA, A. M., Anthropology and Sociology
SUBASH, B., Chemical Reaction Engineering, Zeolyte Catalysis, Environmental Catalysis, Process Design and Development
SUKOR, K., Poverty-focussed Micro-credit Programme
SURESH, N., Economics
SYED IDRIS, S. H., Communications, Radar Systems, Microwave, Antenna and Propagation
SYED MOHSIN, S. S. J., Pharmacology
TENG, C. S., Chemical Engineering
TEOH, S. G., Inorganic and Organo-metallic Chemistry
WAN ABDUL MANAN, W. M., Nutrition, Public Health and Quality of Life
WAN MOHAMAD, W. B., Endocrinology, Impaired Glucose Tolerance Test
WAN ROSLI, W. D., Paper Technology
YUEN, K. H., Pharmaceutical Technology
ZABIDI AZHAR, H., Paediatric Neurology
ZAHARIN, Y., Computational Linguistics and Algebraic Geometry
ZAINAL ABIDIN, A., Electroplating, Waste Water Treatment
ZAINAL ARIFIN, A., Materials, Ceramics
ZAINAL ARIFIN, M. I., Polymer Technology
ZAINUL FADZIRUDDIN, Z., Molecular Biology
ZAKARIA, M. A., Colloid Surface and Cement Sciences
ZHARI, I., Pharmaceuticals
ZUBIR, D., Pollution
ZULFIGAR, Y., Coral and Marine Biology
ZULMI, W., Hand and Reconstructive Surgery

UNIVERSITI TEKNOLOGI MALAYSIA
(Malaysia University of Technology)

Skudai, 81310 Johor
Telephone: (7) 5576160
Fax: (7) 5561722
E-mail: pendaftar@utm.my
Internet: www.utm.my

Founded 1904; university status 1972
State control
Languages of instruction: Bahasa Malaysia, English
Academic year: June to March
Vice-Chancellor (President): Datuk Prof. Ir.Dr MOHD ZULKIFKI TAN SRI MOHD GHAZALI
Deputy Vice-Chancellors: Prof. Dr AZMAN HJ. AWANG (Academic), Prof. Ir. Dr MOHD AZRAAI KASSIM (Development), Dato' Prof. Dr Hj. MOHAMED MANSOR ABDULLAH (Student Affairs)
Registrar: RAHANI ABU BAKAR
Librarian: ROSNA TAIB

Library: see Libraries and Archives
Number of teachers: 1,633
Number of students: 31,529
Publication: *Journal of Technology* (in 6 series, each 2 a year)

DEANS

Faculty of Built Environment: Prof. Dr SUPIAN AHMAD
Faculty of Chemical and Natural Resources Engineering: Prof. Dr AHMAD KAMAL B. IDRIS
Faculty of Civil Engineering: Assoc. Prof. Dr Ir. HASANAN MD NOR
Faculty of Computer Science and Information Systems: Prof. Dr AHMAD ZAKI ABU BAKAR
Faculty of Education: Prof. Dr ABU BAKAR HJ. HASHIM
Faculty of Electrical Engineering: Prof. Dr AHMAD DARUS
Faculty of Geoinformation Engineering and Science: Prof. Dr MOHD IBRAHIM SEENI MOHAMAD
Faculty of Management and Human Resources Development: Assoc. Prof. Dr MOHD TAIB HJ. DORA
Faculty of Mechanical Engineering: Prof. Dr ALIAS MOHD NOOR
Faculty of Science: Prof. Dr Hj. RASHIDI MD RAZALI
School of Graduate Studies: Prof. Dr RAHMALAN AHMAD
School of Professional and Continuing Education: Prof. Dr BAHROM SANUGI

HEADS OF DEPARTMENTS

Faculty of Built Environment (tel. (7) 550201; fax (7) 5566155; e-mail fab@mel.utm.my; internet www.fab.utm.my):
- Architecture: MAHMUD MOHD JUSAN
- Quantity Surveying: ISMAIL HARON
- Urban and Regional Planning: Assoc. Prof. Dr AHMAD NAZRI MUHAMMAD LUDIN

Faculty of Chemical and Natural Resources Engineering (tel. (7) 5505304; fax (7) 558143; e-mail mis@fkkksa.utm.my; internet www.fkkksa.utm.my):
- Bioprocess Engineering: Dr ROSLI B. MD. ILLIAS
- Chemical Engineering: Assoc. Prof. ZAINUDDIN ABD. MANAN
- Gas Engineering: Assoc. Prof. Dr RAHMAT MOHSIN
- Petroleum Engineering: ZULKAFLI HASSAN
- Polymer Engineering: Dr WAN AIZAN WAN ABD. RAHMAN

Faculty of Civil Engineering (tel. (7) 5503081; fax (7) 5566157; e-mail FKA@fka.utm.my; internet www.fka.utm.my):
- Environmental Engineering: Assoc. Prof. Dr MOHD ISMID MOHD SAID
- Geotechnics and Transport: Assoc. Prof. Dr RAMLI NAZIR
- Hydraulics and Hydrology: Assoc. Prof. Dr AHMAD KHAIRI ABD. WAHAB
- Structures and Materials: Assoc. Prof. Ir. Dr WAHID OMAR

Faculty of Computer Science and Information Systems (tel. (7) 5503570; fax (7) 5565044; e-mail tp@fsksm.utm.my; internet web.fsksm.utm.my):
- Computer Graphics and Multimedia: Dr SITI MARIYAM HJ. SHAMSUDIN
- Computer Systems and Communicaton: Assoc Prof. Dr SYAMSUL B. SHAHIBUDIN
- Information Systems: MD HAFIZ SELAMAT
- Modelling and Industrial Computing: Assoc. Prof. Dr ABD. RAHMAN AHMAD
- Software Engineering: Assoc. Prof. Dr SAFAAI DERIS

Faculty of Education (tel. (7) 5504372; fax (7) 5560542; e-mail fp@utm.my; internet www.fp.utm.my):
- Basic Education: Assoc. Prof. Dr MOHD NAJIB ABD. GHAFAR
- Educational Multimedia: Assoc. Prof. Dr BAHARUDDIN ARIS
- Science and Mathematics: Assoc. Prof. Dr MUHAMMAD YUSOF HJ. ARSHAD
- Social Education: Assoc. Prof. Dr ABD. HAFIDZ HJ. OMAR
- Technical and Vocational Education: Assoc. Prof. Dr MUHAMMAD RASHID HJ. RAJUDDIN

Faculty of Electrical Engineering (tel. (7) 5505021; fax (7) 5566272; e-mail fke@suria.fke.utm.my; internet www.fke.utm.my):
- Control Engineering and Instrumentation: Assoc. Prof. Dr RUZAIRI H. ABD. RAHIM
- Electronic Engineering: Assoc. Prof. Dr ABU KHARI A'AIN
- Energy Conversion: Prof. Dr Ir. ABD. HALIM MOHD YATIM
- Energy and Power Systems: Prof. Dr HUSSEIN AHMAD
- Mechatronics and Robotics: Dr ROSBI MAMAT
- Microelectronics and Computer Engineering: Assoc. Prof. Dr SHEIKH HUSSAIN SHEIKH SALLEH
- Radio Communications Engineering: Assoc. Prof. Dr MAZLINA HJ. ESA
- Telematics and Optics: Assoc. Prof. Dr ABU BAKAR MOHAMAD

Faculty of Geoinformation Engineering and Science (tel. (7) 5502801; fax (7) 5566163; e-mail admin@fksg.utm.my; internet www.fksg.utm.my):
- Geoinformatics: Assoc. Prof. GHAZALI DESA
- Geoinformatics Engineering: Assoc. Prof. Dr ABD. MAJID ABD. KADIR
- Land Administration and Development: Dr ISMAIL OMAR
- Property Management: Assoc. Prof. DZURLLKANIAN ZULKARNAIN DAUD

Remote Sensing: Assoc. Prof. Dr Hj. MAZLAN HASHIM

Faculty of Management and Human Resources Development (tel. (7) 5503373; fax (7) 5566911; e-mail fppsm@utmjb.utm .my; internet www.fppsm.utm.my):

Human Resources Management: SHAHRI HJ. ABD. MAJID
Linguistics: Dr ZUBAIDAH AWANG
Management: Dr HISHAMUDDIN SOM

Faculty of Mechanical Engineering (tel. (7) 5504554; fax (7) 5566159; e-mail maklumat@ fkam.utm.my; internet fkam.utm.my):

Aeronautics and Automation: Dr THOLUDDIN MAT LAZIM
Applied Mechanics: Assoc. Prof. Dr MOHD NASIR TAMIM
Design: Assoc. Prof. Dr DZULKIFLI AWANG
Manufacturing and Industry: Assoc Prof. Dr Sha'ri Hj. MOHD YUSUF
Marine Engineering: Assoc. Prof. Dr ADI MAIMUN ABDUL MALIK
Materials Engineering: Assoc. Prof. Dr ESAH HAMZAH
Thermofluids: Assoc. Prof. Dr AZHAR ABDUL AZIZ

Faculty of Science (tel. (7) 5504042; fax (7) 5566162; e-mail fsains@fs.utm.my; internet www.fs.utm.my):

Biology: Assoc. Prof. Dr NOOR AINI ABDUL RASHID
Chemistry: Assoc Prof. Dr RAZAK ALI
Mathematics: Assoc. Prof. Dr JAMALUDIN TALIB
Physics: Assoc. Prof. Dr ZULKEFLI OTHMAN

ATTACHED RESEARCH INSTITUTES

Autodesk Training Centre: Dir Prof. AZMI ABDULLAH.

Business Advanced Technology Centre: Dir Prof. Dr NAOH ABU BAKAR.

Centre for Advanced Software Engineering: Dir Prof. Dr NORBIK BASHAH IDRIS.

Centre for Artificial Intelligence and Robotics: Dir Prof. Dr MARZUKI KHALID.

Centre for Automotive Development: Dir Assoc. Prof. Dr Ir. AZHAR ABD. AZIZ.

Centre for Gas Technology: Dir Dr ZULKIFLI B. YAAKOB.

Centre for Geodetic and Geodynamic Studies: Dir Assoc. Prof. KAMALUDIN HJ. MOHD OMAR.

Centre for Geographic Information and Analysis: Dir Dr ALIAS ABD. RAHMAN.

Centre for Hydrographic Studies: Dir Assoc. Prof. Dr RAZALI MAHMUD.

Centre for Industrial Measurement and Engineering Surveying: Dir Dr HALIM SETAN.

Centre for Lipids Engineering and Applied Research (CLEAR): Dir Assoc. Prof. MUSTAFFA KAMAL TUN ABD. AZIZ.

Centre for Rural Planning Studies: Dir Prof. Dr NOOR SHARIPAH SUTAN SIDI.

Centre for the Study of the Built Environment in the Malay World: Dir Assoc. Prof. Dr MOHD. TAJUDDIN MOHD RASDI.

Centre for Technology Design: Dir KAMAL AZAM BANI HASHIM.

Chemical Engineering Pilot Plant: Dir Prof. RAMLAN AZIZ.

Coastal and Off-Shore Engineering Institute: Dir Prof. ADIBAH ISMAIL.

Composite Technology Research Centre: Dir Assoc. Prof. Dr AB. SAMAN ABD. KADER.

Construction Technology and Management Centre: Dir Assoc. Prof. Dr MUDH ZAIMI ABD. MAJID.

High Voltage and High Current Institute: Dir Dr ZULKURNAIN ABDUL MALIK.

Ibnu Sina Fundamental Science Studies Institute: Dir Prof. Dr HALIMATON HAMDAN.

Information Technology Centre: Dir Assoc. Prof. SARUDIN KARI.

Information Technology Training Centre: Dir Assoc. Prof. WARDAH ZAINAL ABIDIN.

Institute of Environment and Water Resources Management: Dir Assoc. Prof. Dr ZAINI UJANG.

Institute of Noise and Vibration: Dir Prof. Dr MOHD SALMAN LEONG ABDULLAH.

Institute of Software Technology: Dir YM. RAJA BAHARUDDIN ANOM.

Membrane Research Centre: Dir Prof. Dr HAMDANI SAIDI.

Remote Sensing Centre: Dir ABDUL RAZAK MOHD YUSOFF.

Steel Technology Centre: Dir Assoc. Prof. Dr. MAHMOOD MD TAHIR.

Sultan Iskandar Institute for Highrise and Urban Habitats: Dir Prof. Dr AZMAN AWANG.

Technology Policy Research Centre: Dir Prof. Dr ROGAYAH MOHAMED.

UNIVERSITI TEKNOLOGI MARA

40450 Shah Alam, Selangor, Darul Ehsan
Telephone: (3) 55442000
Fax: (3) 55442223
E-mail: webadmin@www.uitm.edu.my
Internet: www.uitm.edu.my

Founded 1956 as Dewan Latihan RIDA; became Maktab MARA 1965 and Institut Teknologi MARA 1967; present name 1999
Academic year: May to April

Vice-Chancellor: Dato' Seri Prof. Dr IBRAHIM ABU SHAH

Number of teachers: 4,200
Number of students: 100,000

Publications: *Accountancy Newsletter*, *Info UiTM*, *International Research Journal*

DEANS

Faculty of Accountancy: Prof. Dr Hj IBRAHIM KAMAL ABDUL RAHMAN
Faculty of Administration and Law: Prof. Madya RAMLA BINTI MOHD NOH
Faculty of Applied Science: Prof. Madya Dr AHMAD SAZALI HAMZAH
Faculty of Architecture, Planning and Surveying: Prof. Madya Dr MOHAMED YUSOFF ABBAS
Faculty of Art and Design: Prof. Madya Dr BAHARUDIN UJANG
Faculty of Business and Management: Prof. Madya Dr JAMIL HAMALI
Faculty of Chemical Engineering: Prof. Madya Dr SHARIFAH AISHAH AYED A. KADIR
Faculty of Civil Engineering: Prof. Madya Ir Dr Hj MOHD YUSOF ABD RAHMAN
Faculty of Communication and Media Studies: Prof. Madya ALIAS MD SALLEH
Faculty of Education: Prof. Dr HAZADIAH MOHD DAHAN
Faculty of Electrical Engineering: Prof. Madya Dr YUSOF MD SALLEH
Faculty of Health Science: Prof. Dr ABD RAHIM MD NOOR
Faculty of Hotel and Tourism Management: EN ABDUL AZIZ ABDUL MAJID
Faculty of Information Science: Prof. Madya Dr LAILI HJ HASHIM
Faculty of Information Technology and Quantitative Science: Prof. Madya AZIZI NGAH TASIR
Faculty of Mechanical Engineering: Prof. Madya Dr SHANRANI ANUAR
Faculty of Medicine: Y. Bhg Dato'Prof. Dr KHALID YUSOF
Faculty of Office Management and Technology: Prof. Madya Dr HALIMATON HJ KHALID
Faculty of Performing Arts: Prof. Madya Md RUSHDIE KUBON MD SHARIFF
Faculty of Pharmacy: Prof. Dr ABU BAKAR ABD MAJEED (acting)
Faculty of Sports Science and Recreation: Prof. Madya Dr Muhd KAMIL IBRAHIM
Centre for Graduate Studies: Datin ZUBAIDAH ALSREE

UNIVERSITI TEKNOLOGI PETRONAS

31750 Tronoh, Perak Darul Ridzuan
Telephone: (5) 3678018
Fax: (5) 3678
E-mail: utp@petronas.com.my
Internet: www.utp.edu.my

Founded 1995 as Institute of Technology Petronas; present name 1997.

UNIVERSITI TENAGA NASIONAL

Km.7 Jalan Kajang-Puchong, 43009 Kajang, Selangor
Telephone: (3) 89212020
Fax: (3) 89263504
E-mail: infor@uniten.edu.my
Internet: www.uniten.edu.my

Founded 1976 as Institut Latihan Sultan Ahmad Shah; re-named Tenaga Nasional Berhad 1990 and Institut Kerjuruteraan Teknologi Tenaga Nasional 1994; present name 1997
Private control
Languages of instruction: English, Bahasa Malaysia
Academic year: June to May

Vice-Chancellor: Prof. Ir Dr ZAINUL ABIDIN MOHD SHARRIF
Deputy Vice-Chancellor (Academic): Prof. Ir Dr ZAINUL ABIDIN MOHD SHARRIF
Deputy Vice-Chancellor (Management): Dr MOHD ZAMZAM JAAFAR
Special Advisor to the Vice-Chancellor: Prof. Ir Dr SYED ABDUL KADER AL JUNID
Registrar: Dr TENGKU AZIZ TENGKU ZAINAL
Librarian: SUHAIMI HAJI ABU HASSAN

Library of 73,846 vols
Number of teachers: 350
Number of students: 6,500 (6,240 undergraduate, 260 postgraduate)

DEANS

College of Business Management: Dr Hj. SHAARI MOHD NOR
College of Engineering: Dr IBRAHIM HUSSEIN
College of Information Technology: Dr ZAINUDDIN HASSAN (Deputy Dean)
Institute of Liberal Studies: Prof. Datin Dr Hjh. KOBKUA SUWANNATHAT-PIAN
Bandar Muadzam Shah Branch Campus: Prof. Dr ZULKIFLI ABDUL HAMID (Provost)

UNIVERSITI UTARA MALAYSIA
(Northern University of Malaysia)

06010 UUM Sintok, Kedah Darul Aman
Telephone: (4) 9284000
Fax: (4) 9283046
Internet: www.uum.edu.my

Founded 1984
State control
Languages of instruction: Malay, English
Academic year: July to June (two semesters)

Chancellor: HRH THE SULTAN OF KEDAH
Vice-Chancellor: Prof. Dato' Dr AHMAD FAWZI B. HJ MOHD BASRI
Deputy Vice-Chancellor (Academic Affairs): Assoc. Prof. Dr ABDUL RAZAK CHIK
Deputy Vice-Chancellor (Development): Prof. Dr MAHMOOD NAZAR MOHAMED

Deputy Vice-Chancellor (Student Affairs): Assoc. Prof. Dr MOHAMAD MUSTAFA ISHAK
Bursar: Dato' MAIDIN B. SYED ALI
Registrar: LATIFAH BT HJ. HASSAN
Librarian: JAMILAH BT MOHAMMED

Number of teachers: 1,076
Number of students: 20,000

Publications: *Annual Report*, *Mutakhir* (weekly), *Uniutama* (quarterly)

DEANS AND DIRECTORS

Faculty of Accountancy: Assoc. Prof. Dr MAHAMAD TAYIB
Faculty of Business Management: Assoc. Prof. Dr ABDUL JUMAAT B. MAHAJAR
Faculty of Cognitive Sciences and Education: Prof. Dr ROSNA BT AWANG HASHIM
Faculty of Communication and Modern Languages: Assoc. Prof. Dr CHE SU BT. MUSTAFFA
Faculty of Economics: Assoc. Prof. Dr ROSLAN B. ABDUL HAKIM
Faculty of Finance and Banking: Assoc. Prof. Dr YUSNIDAH BT. IBRAHIM
Faculty of Information Technology: Prof. Dr KU RUHANA BT KU MAHAMUD
Faculty of International Studies: Assoc. Prof. Dr AHMAD FAIZ B. HJ. ABD. HAMID
Faculty of Management of Technology: ABDUL NASIR BIN ZULKIFLI
Faculty of Public Management and Law: Assoc. Prof. Dr ABDUL RAHMAN B. ABDUL AZIZ
Faculty of Quantitative Science: Assoc. Prof. Dr ABD. RAZAK B. YAAKUB
Faculty of Social and Human Development: Assoc. Prof. Dr HAJI AZMI SHAARI
Faculty of Tourism, Hospitality and Environmental Management: Assoc Prof. Dr HAJI IBRAHIM B. ABD. HAMID
Centre for Research and Consultancy: Assoc. Prof. Dr ZULKHAIRI MD DAHALIN
Institute for Entrepreneurship Development: Assoc. Prof. Dr CHE ANI B. MAD.
Institute for Quality Management: KAMARULZAMAN B. MD ALI
Computer Centre: Dir: AZMAN B. TA'A
Executive Development Programme: Prof. Dr JUHARY OMAR B. ALI MAT ALI

Colleges

Co-operative College of Malaysia: 103 Jl. Templer, 46700 Petaling Jaya, Selangor; tel. (3) 7574911; fax (3) 7570434; e-mail mkm@mkm.edu.my; f. 1956; provides in-service and pre-service training; Diploma and Certificate courses in co-operative management; specialized courses in business management, accounting, computer studies, co-operative management; library: 30,000 vols; 2,905 students; Dir ARMI HJ. ZAINUDIN.

Institut Bahasa Melayu Malaysia (Malaysian Institute of the Malay Language): Lembah Pantai, 59990 Kuala Lumpur; tel. (3) 22822389; fax (3) 22826076; internet www2.moe.gov.my/ibmm; f. 1958; 81 teachers; 778 students; offers a 3-year pre-service diploma course, a 14-week in-service course in the teaching of the Malay language, to trained teachers; students are selected by the Ministry of Education; also offers short courses of Malay language as a foreign and second language; Principal ENCIK SALLEH BIN MOHD. HUSEIN.

KDU College: Jl. SS 22/41, 47400 Petaling Jaya, Selangor; tel. (3) 77288123; fax (3) 77277096; e-mail best@kdu.edu.my; internet www.kdu.edu.my; f. 1983 as Kolej Damansara Utama; library: 25,300 vols; 250 teachers; 6,000 students; pre-university and foundation courses, diploma courses in business administration, computer science, engineering, hotels and tourism; degrees in business, accounting and finance, economics; CEO Dr YAP CHEE SING; Registrar TAN JING KUAN.

Politeknik Kuching, Sarawak: Km. 22, Jl. Matang, Locked Bag 3094, 93050 Kuching, Sarawak; tel. (82) 428796; fax (82) 428023; f. 1989; library: 10,000 vols; 130 teachers; 1,200 students; diploma and certificate courses in civil, electrical and mechanical engineering and commerce/business, apprentice training in oil, gas and petroleum technology in co-operation with PETRONAS; Principal AYOB BIN Haji JOHARI (acting).

Tunku Abdul Rahman College: POB 10979, 50932 Kuala Lumpur; tel. (3) 4214977; fax (3) 4226336; f. 1969; library: 122,715 vols; 290 teachers; 8,123 students; Principal Dr LIM KHAIK LEANG; Registrar CHEE AH KIOW

HEADS OF SCHOOLS

Arts and Science: Dr CHENG SU CHIAU (acting)
Business Studies: YOONG LAI THYE (acting)
Pre-University Studies: TSEN WEI KONG (acting)
Technology: HEW HIOEN ON

Ungku Omar Polytechnic: Dairy Rd, 31400 Ipoh, Perak; tel. (5) 5457656; fax (5) 5471162; f. 1969 with Unesco aid; library: 33,300 vols, 60 periodicals; 549 teachers; 6,451 students; Principal Mej. Ir HAJI MOHAMED ZAKARIA B. MOHD NOOR; Admin. Officer ROFBIAH BT KAMARUDDIN; Librarian NOR AINON B. ZAKARIA

HEADS OF DEPARTMENTS

Civil Engineering: NAIMAH MOHD KHALIL
Commerce: HJ. NOORANI NURUDDIN
Electrical Engineering: CHAN CHEONG LOONG
General Studies: YAAKUB MAT DIN
Marine Engineering: MOHD FISAL B. HAROON
Mechanical Engineering: MOHD NOR B. YUSOFF

Yayasan Pengurusun Malaysia (Malaysian Institute of Management): 227 Jl. Ampang, 50450 Kuala Lumpur; tel. (3) 2425255; fax (3) 2643168; f. 1966; MBA, BA, diploma and certificate courses; Pres. Raja Tun MOHAR BIN RAJA BADIOZAMAN; CEO Dr TARCISIUS CHIN; publs *Malaysian Management Review* (2 a year), *Management Newsletter* (4 a year).

MALDIVES

The Higher Education System

The Maldives became fully independent, outside the Commonwealth, on 26 July 1965. The first institution of higher education, the Maldives College of Higher Education, was founded in 1998. All higher, technical and vocational qualifications in the Maldives are awarded by this institution. The first Bachelors degree programme was launched in 2000 and in 2001 the Ministry of Education established the Maldives National Qualifications Framework. The Maldives Accreditation Board is responsible for quality assurance and accreditation of higher education programmes of study. In 2003 6,898 students were enrolled at Maldives College of Higher Education.

Bachelors degrees are three-year programmes of study. The only postgraduate award is the Graduate Certificate. Technical and vocational education consists of Certificate and Diploma courses run by the Maldives College of Higher Education.

Research Institutes

GENERAL

Institute of Islamic Studies: Male'; tel. 3322718; fax 3313953; e-mail rasheed .moosa@thauleem.net; f. 1980; attached to Min. of Education; aims to provide educational opportunities for the country's young people, to encourage the spread of the Arabic language, to provide training and refresher courses for imams, lawyers, judges, and teachers of the Quran and Islamic studies, to promote study of the Quran, to upgrade the Islamic curriculum in accordance with the needs of the country, to publish and translate books on all aspects of Islam; library of 19,000 vols; Dir-Gen. IBRAHIM RASHEED MOOSA; publ. *Al-Manhaj* (annually).

National Centre for Linguistic and Historical Research: Sosun Magu, Male' 20-05, Henveiru; tel. 3323206; fax 3326796; e-mail nclhr@dhivehinet.net.mv; internet www.qaumiyyath.gov.mv; f. 1982; research on history, culture and language of the Republic of Maldives; restoration and preservation of the nation's heritage; preservation and promotion of the Dhivehi language; Dir IBRAHIM ZUHOOR; publs *Faiythoora* (monthly), *Dhivehinge Tharika* (2 a year).

Libraries and Archives

Male'

Islamic Library: Islamic Centre, Medhuziyaaraiy Magu, Male' 20-02; tel. 3323623; f. 1985; Islamic Studies and literature; 4,500 vols; Dir Imaam AHMED SHATHIR.

National Library: 59 Majeedi Magu, Galolhu, Male' 20-04; tel. 3323945; fax 3313712; f. 1945; public library facilities; 40,272 vols; special collections: Dhivehi, English, Arabic, Urdu, Maldives; Dir-Gen. HABEEBA HUSSAIN HABEEB; publs *Bibliography of Dhivehi Publications*, *Bibliography of English Publications*.

Museum

Male'

National Museum: National Centre for Linguistic and Historical Research, Male' 20-05; tel. 3322254; fax 3326796; e-mail nclhr@dhivehinet.net.mv; internet www .geocities.com/bnaseem/welcome.htm; f. 1952; conservation and display of historical items; Senior Curator ALI WAHEED.

College

Maldives College of Higher Education: Nikagas Magu, Machchangolhi, Male'; tel. 3345155; fax 3315411; internet www.mche .edu.mv; f. 1998; academic year January to November (2 terms); campuses at Hithadhoo (2), Kulthudhuffushi and Thinadhoo; faculties of Education, Eng. technology, Shari'a and law, Health sciences, Hospitality and tourism studies, Management and computing; centres of Maritime studies, Open learning; Vice-Rector for Admin. HUSSAIN HALEEM.

MALI

The Highed Education System

Mali, the former French colony of Soudan, became an independent state in 1960, following the secession of Senegal from the Federation of Mali, founded in 1959. Tertiary education facilities include the national Université de Bamako (founded 1993) and several colleges of higher education. Many students also receive higher education abroad, mainly in France and Senegal. In 2004/05 there were 32,609 students enrolled at the Université de Bamako.

The Ministry of National Education controls higher education, but the State-run Université de Bamako is financially autonomous. The University Council is the policy-making body of the Université and the Rector acts as chief executive. The main academic divisions are the Colleges, Schools and Institutes.

The secondary school Baccalauréat is the main requirement for admission to higher education. The first (undergraduate) stage of higher education last four years in most fields and leads to the award of a Diplôme; some disciplines such as medicine and pharmacy last five to six years. Students at the Ecoles are awarded specialist Diplômes, depending on the field of study. The second (postgraduate) level of higher education is the two-year Diplôme d'Etudes Approfondies, which is only offered by the Institut Supérieur pour la Formation et la Recherche Appliquée, and the three-year Doctorat Malien research degree, awarded after submission of a thesis.

Post-secondary technical and vocational education consists of programmes of study and professional training leading to the award of Brevet de Technicien, Diplôme de Technicien Supérieur and Diplôme des Sciences Appliquées.

Learned Society

GENERAL

UNESCO Office Bamako: Badalabougou Est, BP E 1763 Bamako; tel. 223-34-92; fax 223-34-94; e-mail bamako@unesco.org; designated Cluster Office for Burkina Faso, Mali and Niger; Dir AHMED OULD DEIDA.

Research Institutes

GENERAL

Centre National de la Recherche Scientifique et Technologique: BP 3052, Bamako; tel. 222-90-85; f. 1986; co-ordinates all research activity in Mali; 57 research instns, 443 staff; Dir-Gen. Dr MAMADOU DIALLO IAM; publs *Revue Malienne de Science et de Technologie* (annually), *Vie de la Recherche* (quarterly).

Institut de Recherche pour le Développement (IRD): BP 2528, Bamako; tel. 221-05-01; fax 221-64-44; e-mail granjon@sahel.ird.ml; environmental and social sciences for development; library of 4,000 books and journals; Dir JOSEPH BRUNET-JAILLY; (see main entry under France); publ. *Actualités de la Recherche au Mali* (6 a year).

AGRICULTURE, FISHERIES AND VETERINARY SCIENCE

Centre National de Recherches Fruitières: BP 30, Bamako; f. 1962; controls experimental plantations, phytopathological laboratory, technological laboratory and pilot schemes; Dir P. JEANTEUR.

Centre National de Recherches Zootechniques: BP 262, Bamako; f. 1927; experimental farm with sections on genetics (bovine, swine, poultry), nutrition and biochemistry, pasture, veterinary medicine; library of 1,000 vols; Dir Dr FERNAND TRAORE.

Centres de Recherche Rizicole: 2 rice research centres, at Kankan and at Ibetemi.

Institut de Recherches Agronomiques Tropicales et des Cultures Vivrières (IRAT): BP 438, Bamako; f. 1962; controls stations at Bamako, Koulikoro, Kogoni par Nioro, Ibetemi (Mopti), and sub-stations at Kita and Koporokenie-Pe; general agronomy, land amelioration, cultivation techniques, fertilization needs, plant breeding (sorghum, pennisetum, short and floating rices, maize, wheat, groundnuts and formerly sugar cane); Dir M. THIBOUT; (see main entry under France).

Institut du Sahel: BP 1530, Bamako; tel. 222-21-48; fax 222-59-80; e-mail administration@insah.org; internet www.insah.org; f. 1976; a specialized institution of the Comité Interétats de Lutte contre la Sécheresse dans le Sahel (CILSS); aims to combat effects of drought and achieve food security in the Sahel (consisting of Burkina Faso, Cape Verde, Gambia, Guinea-Bissau, Mali, Mauritania, Niger, Senegal, Chad), through the promotion and coordination of research, circulating scientific and technical information; library of 12,000 vols, 240 periodicals; Dir Gen. MOUSTAPHA AMADOU; publs *Actes, Etudes & Travaux, Etudes et Recherches, Recherche et Développement*.

Office du Niger: BP 106, Ségou; tel. 232-02-92; fax 232-01-41; f. 1932, taken over by Mali govt 1958; research stations at Bougomi and Sahel (cotton), Kayo (rice), Soninkoura (fruit); Dir-Gen. NANCOMA KEITA.

MEDICINE

Institut Marchoux: BP 251, Bamako; tel. 222-51-31; fax 222-95-44; f. 1935; part of *Organisation de Co-ordination et de Coopération pour la Lutte contre les Grandes Endémies* (*q.v.*); medical research, teaching, treatment and epidemiology, specializing in leprosy; Dir SOMITA KEITA.

Institut d'Ophtalmologie Tropicale de l'Afrique de l'Ouest Francophone: BP 248, Bamako; tel. 222-27-22; fax 222-51-86; e-mail iota@malinet.ml; f. 1953; research in tropical eye diseases and prevention of blindness, training courses for technicians and doctors specializing in ophthalmology; Dir Dr ALAIN AUZEMERY.

NATURAL SCIENCES

Physical Sciences

Direction Nationale de la Météorologie: BP 237, Bamako; tel. and fax 229-21-01; e-mail dnm@afribone.net.ml; library of 1,265 vols; Dir K. KONARE; publs *Bulletin Agrométéorologique, Bulletin Climatologique* (monthly).

TECHNOLOGY

Société Nationale de Recherches et d'Exploitation des Ressources Minières de Mali (SONAREM), Service de Documentation: BP 2, Kati; tel. 222-41-84; fax 222-21-60; f. 1961; geology, mining (gold mining in Kalana, phosphates in Bourem), hydrogeology; 5 staff; library of 5,000 vols; Dir DAOUDA DIAKITE.

Libraries and Archives

Bamako

Bibliothèque Nationale du Mali: BP 159, Ave Kassé Keïta, Bamako; tel. 222-49-63; f. 1913; *c.* 60,000 vols, 2,000 current periodicals; Dir MAMADOU KONOBA KEÏTA.

Attached institution:

Archives Nationales du Mali: Koulouba, Bamako; tel. 222-58-44; f. 1913; Archivist LAMINE CAMARA.

Centre Culturel Français: Blvd de l'Indépendance, BP 1547, Bamako; tel. 222-40-19; fax 222-58-28; e-mail ccfmedia@afribone.net.ml; internet www.ccfbamako.org; f. 1962; public library of 27,000 vols; Dir NICOLE SEURAT.

Timbuktu

Centre d'Etudes, de Documentation et de Recherches Historiques 'Ahmed Baba' (CEDRAB): BP 14, Timbuktu; tel. and fax 292-10-81; e-mail centre@tombouctou.org.ml; f. 1970; to preserve the historical heritage of the region; collects and conserves Arabic MSS; 15,000 archives; Dir MOHAMED GALLAH DICKO.

Museum

Bamako

Musée National du Mali: BP 159, Bamako; tel. 222-34-86; fax 223-19-09; e-mail musee@malinet.ml; library of 1,900 vols; Dir Dr SAMUEL SIDIBE.

University

UNIVERSITÉ DE BAMAKO

BP 2528, Rue Baba Diarra Porte 113, Bamako
Telephone: 222-19-33
Fax: 222-19-32
E-mail: universiteaml@refer.org
Internet: www.ml.refer.org/univ-mali/
Founded 1993 as Université de Mali; present name 2005
State Control
Language of instruction: French
Rector: SIBY GINETTE BELLEGARDE
Number of teachers: 510
Number of students: 11,250

DEANS

Faculty of Law and Economics: ANTOINE FERNAND CAMARA
Faculty of Letters, Languages, Arts and Humanities: DRISSA DIAKITE
Faculty of Medicine, Pharmacy and Dentistry: MOUSSA TRAORÉ
Faculty of Science and Technology: ABDOUL KARIM SANOGO
School of Administration: (vacant)
School of Engineering: MOUSSA KANTE (Dir)
School of Teacher Training: BOUBA DIARRA (Dir)

ATTACHED RESEARCH INSTITUTES

Institut Malien de Technologie: Dir DAOUDA KONÉ.

Institut Polytechnique Rural: Dir FAFRÉ SAMAKÉ.

Institut des Sciences Fondamentales de la Recherche Appliquée: Dir N'GOLO DIARRA.

Institut Universitaire de Gestion: Dir SIBY GINETTE BELLEGARDE.

Colleges

Ecole des Hautes Etudes Pratiques: BP 242, Bamako; tel. 222-21-47; f. 1974, present name 1979; diploma courses in accountancy, business studies; 35 teachers; 471 students; Dir-Gen. SIDI MOHAMED TOURE.

Ecole Nationale d'Ingénieurs: BP 242, Bamako; tel. 222-21-47; Dir MAMADOU DIAKITE.

Ecole Normale Supérieure: BP 241, Bamako; tel. 222-21-89; f. 1962; 150 teachers; 1,754 students; Dir SÉKOU B. TRAORÉ; publ. *Cahiers de l'ENSup*.

Faculté de Médecine, de Pharmacie et d'Odonto-Stomatologie: BP 1805, Bamako; tel. 222-52-77; fax 222-96-58; f. 1969 (formerly Ecole Nationale de Médecine et de Pharmacie); library: 6,800 vols, 289 periodicals; 100 teachers; 1,800 students; Dir Prof. ISSA TRAORE; publ. *Mali Médical*.

Faculté des Sciences Juridiques et Economiques: 1185 Ave de la Liberté (Route de Koulouba), BP 276, Bamako; tel. 222-27-19; fax 223-18-95; e-mail sacko@ena.ena.ml; f. 1958 (formerly École Nationale d'Administration); Dean DUSMANE O. SIDIBE; publ. *Cahier du CERES*.

Institut de Productivité et de Gestion Prévisionnelle: BP 1300, Bamako; tel. 222-55-11; f. 1971; library: 3,000 vols; in-service training, business advice; 15 staff; Dir-Gen. SIDIKI TRAORE.

Institut Polytechnique Rural de Katibougou: BP 6, Koulikoro; tel. 226-20-12; f. 1965; teaching and research in agronomy, agricultural economics, stockbreeding, forestry, veterinary science, rural technology; 300 teachers; 12,000 students; Dir-Gen. OUSMANE BELCO TOURE.

MALTA

The Higher Education System

In 1592 the Jesuit Order founded the Collegium Melitense and in 1769 it was elevated to university status by Grandmaster Manoel Pinto de Fonseca; it is now known as the University of Malta (L-Università ta' Malta). From 1814 to 1964 Malta was a Crown Colony of the United Kingdom, before becoming an independent sovereign state, within the Commonwealth, in 1964. Malta became a republic in 1974. Education is governed by the Education Act (1988), which is the responsibility of the Education Division of the Ministry of Education, Youth and Employment. Education is free at all levels. The Council and the Senate are the supreme governing bodies of the University, which is an autonomous institution funded by the Government. In 2006/07 there were 9,416 students enrolled at the University. Malta participates in the Bologna Process to establish a European Higher Education Area, the first phase of which is to adopt a credit-based system of comparable degrees with two main cycles (undergraduate and graduate).

Admission to the University is on the basis of the Matriculation Certificate Examination. The University operates a US-style 'credit semester' system, under which students have to accrue a minimum number of credits each semester in order to earn a degree. A full-time year of study is usually equivalent to 60 credits. Non-degree university studies last one to two years and result in award of either a Certificate or Diploma. The undergraduate Bachelors degree is classified as either 'Ordinary' or 'Honours': the former requires three years of study, and the latter at least three, usually four. Dual subject Honours degrees require a minimum of four years, and degrees in professional field of study may last longer, such as medicine (five years) and law (six years). The first postgraduate-level degree at the University is the Masters, which is open to anyone with a Bachelors (Honours) degree of at least second-class classification. A Masters lasts one to two years and may be either a 'research' or a 'taught' degree. Finally the second postgraduate and highest university-level degree is the Doctor of Philosophy, awarded after three to six years of original research and submission of a thesis.

Learned Societies

AGRICULTURE, FISHERIES AND VETERINARY SCIENCE

Agrarian Society: Palazzo de la Salle, 219 Triq ir-Repubblika Valletta VLT 1116; tel. 21244339; fax 21246074; agraria@searchmalta.com; f. 1844; 200 mems; Pres. JOSEPH BORG; Hon. Sec. PAUL DEBATTISTA.

ARCHITECTURE AND TOWN PLANNING

Kamra tal-Periti Malta (Chamber of Architects and Civil Engineers): The Professional Centre, Triq Tas-Sliema, Gzira GZR 1633; tel. and fax 21314265; e-mail kamratalperiti@nextgen.net.mt; internet www.ktpmalta.com; f. 1920; mem. of Malta Fed. of Professional Asscns; 570 mems; Pres. DAVID FELICE; publ. *The Architect* (quarterly).

BIBLIOGRAPHY, LIBRARY SCIENCE AND MUSEOLOGY

Malta Library and Information Association: c/o Univ. Library, Msida MSD 2080; tel. 21239225; fax 21249841; e-mail robert.mizzi@gov.mt; internet www.malia-malta.org; f. 1969; professional assctn to safeguard the interests of librarians and promote legislation concerning libraries; holds courses in librarianship; 125 mems; Chair. ROBERT MIZZI; Sec. VERONICA CALLEJA; publ. *Informalia* (Newsletter, quarterly).

ECONOMICS, LAW AND POLITICS

Malta Society of Arts, Manufactures and Commerce: Palazzo De La Salle, 219 Triq ir-Republika, Valletta VLT 1116; tel. 21244339; fax 21246074; e-mail info@artsmalta.org; internet www.artsmalta.org; f. 1852; Pres. PAUL ASCIAK; Hon. Sec. CHARLES MERCIECA.

FINE AND PERFORMING ARTS

Malta Cultural Institute: 'La Paloma', 16 Triq Sant'Enriku, Sliema SLM 1321; tel. (21) 338923; fax (21) 333831; e-mail maltacultinst@yahoo.com; internet geocities.com/maltacultinst; f. 1948; concerts, ballet, book presentations, painting and sculpture and ceramic exhibitions; 800 mems; Dir MARIE THERESE VASSALLO DIPLICH; publ. *MCI Bulletin* (monthly).

LANGUAGE AND LITERATURE

British Council: Whitehall Mansions, Ix-Xatt Ta' Xbiex, Ta' Xbiex XBX 1026; tel. 23232403; fax 23232402; e-mail information@britishcouncil.org.mt; internet www.britishcouncil.org/malta; offers courses and examinations in English language and British culture and promotes cultural exchange with the UK; Dir RONNIE MICALLEF.

NATURAL SCIENCES

Biological Sciences

Malta Ecological Foundation (ECO): Dar ECO, 10B Triq Sant' Andrija, Valletta VLT 1341; tel. 21641486; fax 21338780; e-mail eco@ecomalta.org; internet www.ecomalta.org; f. 1992; 4,018 mems; library of 5,100 vols; Dir DUNSTAN HAMILTON; publ. *Stakeholder*.

Libraries and Archives

Gozo

Gozo Public Library: Triq Vajringa, Victoria, Gozo VCT 1310; tel. 21556200; fax 21560599; e-mail gozo.libraries@gov.mt; internet www.libraries-archives.gov.mt/gpl; f. 1853, merged with the Royal Malta (now Nat.) Library 1948; nat. and reference library; copyright deposit library; 35,000 vols; Librarian GEORGE V. BORG.

Msida

University of Malta Library: Msida MSD 2080; tel. 21310239; fax 21314306; e-mail dls@lib.um.edu.mt; internet www.lib.um.edu.mt; f. 1954 at the Old Univ. Bldgs in Valletta; transferred to the new Univ. campus in Msida 1967; 750,000 vols, 1,331 current print journals 6,150 electronic journals; Dir ANTHONY MANGION.

Valletta

National Library of Malta: POB 2025, Triq it-Tezorerija, Valletta VLT 2000; tel. 21243297; fax 21235992; internet www.libraries-archives.gov.mt/nlm; f. 1555; incorporates the archives of the Order of St John of Jerusalem; Dir PHILIP BORG; publ. *Bibljografija Nazzjonali Malta/Malta National Bibliography* (annual).

Museum

Valletta

Sovrintendenza Tal-Patrimonju Kulturali (Superintendence of Cultural Heritage): POB 2008, 138 Triq Melita, Valletta VLT 2000; tel. 21230711; fax 21251140; e-mail heritage.superintendence@gov.mt; internet www.culturalheritage.gov.mt; f. 2002, replaces Museums Dept (f. 1903); govt agency; fulfils duties of the State in ensuring the protection and accessibility of Malta's cultural heritage; responsible for all scientific investigation regarding cultural assets such as the conduction of field work and archaeological excavation, and for the full record keeping and management of documentation resulting from such interventions; evaluates art objects, objects of cultural value and collns of such items; advises and co-ordinates with the Malta Environment and Planning Authority on issues regarding land use and devt to safeguard cultural heritage when considering applications for planning permission; monitors and controls import and export of goods which are of cultural significance, whether the movement is temporary (for example, for exhibition or restoration purposes) or permanent; issues permits needed for such movements; has a number of direct commitments with regional and int. instns relating to the conservation and promotion of Malta's cultural heritage on int. basis; liases with UNESCO, the Council of Europe and the European Union; participates in European and Euro-Med programmes; responsible for policy, standards, and guidelines related to cultural heritage and regulates heritage management plans;

advises govt on heritage matters; Superintendent ANTHONY PACE.

University

UNIVERSITY OF MALTA

Msida, MSD 2080
Telephone: 21333903
Fax: 21336450
E-mail: comms@um.edu.mt
Internet: www.um.edu.mt
Founded as Collegium Melitense 1592, elevated to univ. status by Grandmaster Pinto 1769
Language of instruction: English
Academic year: October to July
Chancellor: Prof. J. RIZZO NAUDI
Pro-Chancellor: Prof. D. J. ATTARD
Rector: Prof. JUANITO CAMILLERI
Pro-Rectors: Prof. R. MUSCAT, Prof. A. J. VELLA, Dr M. A. LAURI
Registrar: A. GELLEL
Dir of Finance: R. ATTARD
Dir of Library Services: A. MANGION
Library of 700,000 vols, 5,500 periodicals (print and electronic full text
Number of teachers: 865
Number of students: 9,416 (7,709 full-time, 2,207 part-time)
Publications: *Journal of Anglo-Italian Studies*, *Journal of Education*, *Journal of Maltese Studies*, *Journal of Mediterranean Studies*, *Mediterranean Journal of Educational Studies*, *Mediterranean Human Rights Journal*, *Malta Medical Journal*, *Journal of Baroque Studies*

DEANS OF FACULTIES

Faculty of Architecture and Civil Eng.: J. FALZON
Faculty of Arts: Prof. D. FENECH
Faculty of Dental Surgery: Dr S. CAMILLERI
Faculty of Economics, Management and Accountancy: Prof. D. DARMANIN
Faculty of Education: Dr C. BORG
Faculty of Eng.: Prof. R. GHIRLANDO
Faculty of Laws: Prof. I. REFALO
Faculty of Medicine and Surgery: Prof. G. LAFERLA
Faculty of Science: Prof. A. VELLA
Faculty of Theology: Rev. Prof. E. AGIUS

HEADS OF DEPARTMENTS

Faculty of Architecture and Civil Engineering (tel. 21346225; fax 21346225; e-mail arch-ce@um.edu.mt):
- Architecture and Urban Design: Prof. D. DE LUCCA
- Building and Civil Engineering: J. FALZON

Faculty of Arts (tel. 23403085; fax 21317938; e-mail arts@um.edu.mt; internet www.arts.um.edu.mt):
- Arabic and Near Eastern Studies: Prof. A. J. FRENDO
- Classics and Archaeology: Prof A. BONANNO
- English: Dr I. CALLUS
- French: Dr C. DEPASQUALE
- History: Prof. D. FENECH
- History of Art: Prof. M. BUHAGIAR
- International Relations: Prof. J. PIROTTA
- Italian: Prof. J. BRINCAT
- Maltese: Prof. M. MIFSUD
- Philosophy: Prof. J. FRIGGIERI
- Sociology: Prof. J. TROISI
- Translation and Interpreting Studies: Prof. J. EYNAUD

Faculty of Dental Surgery (Medical School, G'Mangia; tel. 21221019; fax 21235638; e-mail med-school@um.edu.mt):
- Dental Surgery: Dr S. CAMILLERI

Faculty of Economics, Management and Accountancy (tel. 21333997; fax 21317782; e-mail fema@um.edu.mt):
- Accountancy: Prof. D. DARMANIN
- Banking and Finance: Prof. J. FALZON (acting)
- Economics: Prof. P. L. BRIGUGLIO
- Management: C. FSADNI
- Marketing: (vacant)
- Public Policy: Prof. G. PIROTTA
- Social Policy and Social Work: Rev. Dr C. TABONE

Faculty of Education (tel. 21324639; fax 21317938; e-mail educ@um.edu.mt; internet www.educ.um.edu.mt):
- Arts and Languages in Education: Prof. C. L. MIFSUD
- Education Studies: Dr J. GIORDMAINA
- Mathematics, Science and Technical Education: Dr L. BEZZINA
- Primary Education: Dr V. SOLLARS
- Psychology: Dr E. TANTI BURLÒ
- Youth and Community Studies: Dr M. CLARK

Faculty of Engineering (tel. 21343567; fax 21343577; e-mail eng@um.edu.mt; internet www.eng.um.edu.mt):
- Communications and Computer Engineering: Dr V. BUTTIGIEG
- Electrical Power and Control Engineering: Dr S. FABRI
- Electronic Systems Engineering: Dr K. CAMILLERI
- Manufacturing Engineering: Dr J. BORG
- Mechanical Engineering: Prof. R. GHIRLANDO
- Metallurgy and Materials Engineering: Prof. M. GRECH

Faculty of Laws (tel. 21333998; fax 21324478; e-mail laws@um.edu.mt; internet home.um.edu.mt/laws):
- Civil Law: Dr P GALEA
- Commercial Law: Dr R. CAMILLERI
- Criminal Law: Dr S. CAMILLERI
- European and Comparative Law: Prof. P. G. XUEREB
- International Law: Prof. D. ATTARD
- Public Law: Prof. I. REFALO

Faculty of Medicine and Surgery (Medical School, G'Mangia; tel. 21221019; fax 21235638; e-mail med-school@um.edu.mt; internet home.um.edu.mt/med-surg):
- Anatomy: Prof. A. CUSCHIERI
- Clinical Pharmacology and Therapeutics: Prof. R. ELLUL-MICALLEF
- Family Medicine: Dr D. SOLER
- Medicine: Prof. J. M. CACCIOTTOLO
- Obstetrics and Gynaecology: Prof. M. BRINCAT
- Paediatrics: Dr S. ATTARD MONTALTO
- Pathology: Dr B. ELLUL
- Pharmacy: Prof. A. SERRACINO INGLOTT
- Physiology and Biochemistry: Prof. J. V. BANNISTER
- Psychiatry: Dr D. CASSAR
- Public Health: Dr J. MAMO
- Surgery: Prof. G. LAFERLA

Faculty of Science (tel. 21330430; fax 21312110; e-mail science@um.edu.mt; internet home.um.edu.mt/science):
- Biology: Prof. V. AXIAK
- Chemistry: Prof. A. J. VELLA
- Computer Information Systems: Prof. A. LEONE GANADO
- Computer Science and Artificial Intelligence: M. ROSNER
- Mathematics: Prof. A. BUHAGIAR
- Physics: Dr A. MICALLEF
- Statistics and Operations Research: Prof. L. SANT

Faculty of Theology (tel. 21314982; fax 21314982; e-mail theology@um.edu.mt; internet home.um.edu.mt/theology):
- Church History: Mgr. Dr J. BEZZINA
- Fundamental and Dogmatic Theology: Rev. Dr H. SCERRI
- Moral Theology: Rev. Prof. E. AGIUS
- Pastoral Theology: Rev. Dr P. GALEA
- Philosophy: Prof. J. FRIGGIERI
- Sacred Scripture, Hebrew and Greek: Rev. Dr A. ABELA

ATTACHED CENTRES AND INSTITUTES

Centre for Communication Technology: University of Malta, Msida MSD 2080; tel. 23402417; fax 21345655; e-mail cct@um.edu.mt; Dir Prof. S. CHIRCOP.

Edward de Bono Institute for the Design and Development of Thinking: University of Malta, Msida MSD 2080; tel. 23402434; fax 21323981; e-mail instituteofthinking@um.edu.mt; internet home.um.edu.mt/create; Dir Dr S. DINGLI.

Euro-Mediterranean Centre for Educational Research: University of Malta, Msida MSD 2080; tel. 21338126; fax 21317938; e-mail emcer@um.edu.mt; internet www.educ.um.edu.mt/mep; Dir Prof. R. SULTANA.

European Centre for Gerontology: University of Malta, Msida MSD 2080; tel. 23402237; fax 21319526; e-mail eurgeront@um.edu.mt; internet home.um.edu.mt/eurgeront; Dir Prof. J. TROISI.

European Documentation and Research Centre: University of Malta, Msida MSD 2080; tel. 23402001; fax 21337624; e-mail edrc@um.edu.mt; internet home.um.edu.mt/edrc; Chair. Prof. P. G. XUEREB.

Foundation for International Studies: Old University Building, St Paul's St, Valletta; tel. 21234121; fax 21230551; internet www.um.edu.mt/intoff/fiss.html; Chief Exec. Prof. P. L. BRIGUGLIO.

Attached research institutes:

Euro-Mediterranean Centre on Insular Coastal Dynamics: Foundation for International Studies, Old University Building, St Paul's St, Valletta; tel. 21240746; fax 21230551; e-mail icod@icod.org.mt; internet www.icod.org.mt; Dir Dr A. MICALLEF.

International Environment Institute: Foundation for International Studies, Old University Building, St Paul's St, Valletta; tel. 21240741; fax 21230551; e-mail iei@um.edu.mt; Exec. Co-ordinator Dr L. F. CASSAR.

Islands and Small States Institute: Foundation for International Studies, Old University Building, St Paul's St, Valletta; tel. 21248218; fax 21230551; e-mail islands@um.edu.mt; internet home.um.edu.mt/islands; Dir Prof. P. L. BRIGUGLIO.

Gozo Centre: Mgarr Rd, Xewkija, Gozo; tel. 21564559; fax 21564550; e-mail ugc@um.edu.mt; internet home.um.edu.mt/ugc; Dir Prof. P. L. BRIGUGLIO.

Institute of Agriculture: University of Malta, Msida MSD 2080; tel. 23402322; fax 21346519; e-mail ioa@um.edu.mt; internet home.um.edu.mt/ioa; Dir Dr G. ATTARD.

Institute of Anglo-Italian Studies: University of Malta, Msida MSD 2080; tel. 23402266; fax 21317938; e-mail angloitalian@um.edu.mt; internet home.um.edu.mt/angloitalian; Dir Prof. P. VASSALLO.

Institute for Energy Technology: Triq il-Port Ruman, M'Xlokk BBG 05; tel. 21650675; fax 21650615; e-mail ietmalta@um.edu.mt; internet home.um.edu.mt/ietmalta; Exec. Dir. M. FSADNI.

Institute of Forensic Studies: University of Malta, Msida MSD 2080; tel. 21346016; fax 23402771; e-mail forensic.criminology@um.edu.mt; Chair. Dr B. Ellul.

Institute of Health Care: IHC, G'Mangia; tel. 21250530; fax 21244973; e-mail ihc@um.edu.mt; internet home.um.edu.mt/ihc; Dir Dr S. Buttigieg.

Institute of Linguistics: University of Malta, Msida MSD 2080; tel. 23402947; fax 21345655; e-mail ling@um.edu.mt; internet home.um.edu.mt/ling; Chair. Prof. A. Borg.

Institute for Maltese Studies: University of Malta, Msida MSD 2080; tel. 23402297; fax 21322885; Dir Prof. H. Frendo.

Institute for Masonry and Construction Research: University of Malta, Msida MSD 2080; tel. 23402867; fax 21346225; e-mail masonry-construction@um.edu.mt; internet home.um.edu.mt/masonry-construction/index.html; Dir Prof. A. Torpiano.

Institute for Physical Education and Sport: University of Malta, Msida MSD 2080; tel. 23402032; fax 21317082; e-mail pesp@um.edu.mt; Dir M. Aquilina.

Institute of Public Administration and Management: University of Malta, Msida MSD 2080; tel. 23402555; fax 21331916; e-mail ipam@um.edu.mt; Dir Dr E. Warrington.

International Institute for Baroque Studies: University of Malta, Msida MSD 2080; tel. 21316619; fax 21333919; e-mail iibs@um.edu.mt; internet home.um.edu.mt/iibs; Dir Prof. D. DeLucca.

Mediterranean Academy of Diplomatic Studies: University of Malta, Msida MSD 2080; tel. 23402821; fax 21483091; e-mail medac@um.edu.mt; internet home.um.edu.mt/medac; Dir Prof. S. Calleya.

Mediterranean Institute: University of Malta, Msida MSD 2080; tel. 21346580; fax 21320717; e-mail medinst@um.edu.mt; internet home.um.edu.mt/medinst/index.html; Dir Dr S. Mercieca.

Centre for Labour Studies: University of Malta, Msida MSD 2080; tel. 21340251; fax 21340251; e-mail cls@um.edu.mt; internet home.um.edu.mt/cls; Dir Prof. G. Baldacchino.

Centre for Literacy: University of Malta, Msida MSD 2080; tel. 23402038; fax 21317938; e-mail literacy@um.edu.mt; Dir Prof. C. L. Mifsud.

Centre for Environmental Education and Research: University of Malta, Msida MSD 2080; tel. 23402331; fax 21317938; e-mail ceer@um.edu.mt; internet home.um.edu.mt/ceer; Dir Dr P. Pace.

MARSHALL ISLANDS

The Higher Education System

The Republic of the Marshall Islands lies within the area of the Pacific Ocean known as Micronesia. In 1947 the UN authorized the USA to administer the Islands within a Trust Territory of the Pacific Islands. The 1986 Compact of Free Association between the Marshall Islands and the USA was renewed in May 2003. The College of the Marshall Islands (which became independent from the College of Micronesia in 1993) is based on Majuro and had 903 students enrolled in 2000/01. In 1995 the University of the South Pacific opened an extension centre on Majuro. The Fisheries and Nautical Center offers vocational courses for Marshall islanders seeking employment in the fishing industry or on passenger liners, cargo ships and tankers. The Minsitry of Education is responsible for providing higher education.

Learned Societies

NATURAL SCIENCES

Biological Sciences

Marshall Islands Conservation Society (MICS): POB 649, Majuro 96960; e-mail info@coralatolls.org; internet www.coralatolls.org; f. to help Marshallese to manage and protect their atoll environments and to use their resources sustainably; promotes community-based fisheries management, protection for endangered species (humphead wrasse, giant groupers, turtles and sharks); organizes community awareness workshops, conservation practitioner and fisheries observer training; monitors live reef food fish trade and aquarium trade exports.

Research Institutes

AGRICULTURE, FISHERIES AND VETERINARY SCIENCE

Marshall Islands Marine Resources Authority (MIMRA): POB 860, Majuro 96960; tel. 625-8262; fax 625-5447; e-mail mimra@ntamar.com; internet www.mimra.com; research and devt to generate awareness and promote involvement of the local population in sustainable management of coastal resources, incl. outer island fish market, community based fisheries management projects; grant aid projects in partnership with Japanese govt.

HISTORY, GEOGRAPHY AND ARCHAEOLOGY

Historic Preservation Office: POB 1454, Majuro 96960; tel. and fax 625-4476; e-mail rmihpo@ntamar.com; internet members.tripod.com/~alelemuseum/hpo.html; f. 1991 by the Historic Preservation Act of 1991 (amended in 1992) to preserve Marshallese culture; operates with advice and assistance from Advisory Council on Historic Preservation; conducts archaeological survey and inventory, outer island surveys, underwater surveys, oral history and ethnography; maintains RMI Register of Historic Places; attached to Cultural Affairs Div., Min. of Internal Affairs; Historic Preservation Officer FREDERICK DEBRUM; Chief Archaeologist RICHARD WILLIAMSON.

Nuclear Institute: Oscar deBrum Memorial Hall, Majuro; f. 1997; promotes research on and public understanding of history of nuclear weapons and their effects on culture and diplomacy, incl. US nuclear testing program in the Marshall Islands; partnership with Nuclear Studies Institute of the American Univ. (Washington, DC—*q.v.*) incl. exchange program for students and faculty; attached to College of the Marshall Islands; Dir MARY SILK.

Museum

Majuro

Alele Museum, Library and National Archives: POB 629, Majuro 96960; tel. 625-3372; fax 625-3226; e-mail alele@ntamar.com; internet members.tripod.com/~alelemuseum/; f. 1981; Joachim deBrum Colln of over 2,500 glassplate negatives showing Marshallese life and landscapes during 1880–1930; Bogan Colln of Marshallese crafts from 1940s; recordings of traditional oral literature, video documentaries on cultural and community themes; organizes annual cultural festival (*Lutok Kobban Alele*); incorporates Nat. Archives, c. 2,500 microfilms covering Trust Territory of the Pacific Islands, Marshall Islands High Court Proceedings, Congress and *Nitijela* legislation, journal colln, Joachim deBrum Memorial Trust Corpn colln, birth and death certificates; library: incl. Pacific Colln of published and unpublished material specific to the Marshall Islands and Oceania; Curator TERRY MOTE.

University

UNIVERSITY OF THE SOUTH PACIFIC, MARSHALL ISLANDS CAMPUS

POB 3537, Majuro 96960
Telephone: 625-7279
Fax: 625-7282
E-mail: uspmaj@ntamar.com
Internet: www.usp.ac.fj/index.php?id=marshall_centre
Founded 1993
Dir: Dr IRENE TAAFAKI
Sec.: LYDIA TIBON
Number of teachers: 10.

Colleges

College of the Marshall Islands: POB 1258, Majuro 96960; e-mail webmaster@cmi.edu; internet www.cmi.edu; f. 1989 as College of Micronesia-Majuro, a constituent body of the Community College of Micronesia; accredited and adopted present name 1991; became independent institution 1993; campuses at Arrak (Marshall Islands Science Station) and at Gugeegue on Kwajalein Atoll; Pres. WILSON G. HESS; library: 15,000 vols, 140 periodicals, CD-ROMS, videos, DVDs, maps, microfilm; spec. collns incl. Micronesian Colln (articles, books, proceedings and reports on the area), Marshall Islands Colln (local flora and fauna, historical and cultural materials); 42 teachers; 903 students.

Fisheries and Nautical Training Centre: POB 860 Majuro 96960; tel. 625-7449; fax 625-6221; e-mail mimra@ntamar.com; offers vocational courses for Marshall islanders seeking employment in the fishing industry or on passenger liners, cargo ships and tankers; attached to Marshall Islands Marine Resources Authority; Instructor WILLIAM SOKOMI.

MAURITANIA

The Higher Education System

Mauritania, formerly part of French West Africa, achieved full independence on 28 November 1960 (having become a self-governing member of the French Community two years earlier). The earliest institution of higher education was the Institut National des Hautes Etudes Islamiques (founded 1961). Université de Nouakchott, the only university-level institution, was founded in 1981. In 2003/04 there were 9,292 students enrolled in tertiary education. The Ministry of Higher Education and Scientific Research is the responsible government body for higher education, which is free (barring a nominal registration fee).

Université de Nouakchott is governed by the University Assembly, the membership of which is made up from the staff, students and government officials. The University Assembly is headed by the university President or Rector. the Vice-Chancellor is in charge of administration, and the senior academic officers are the Deans, Vice-Deans and General Secretary.

The secondary school Baccalauréat is the main requirement for admission to tertiary education. The university degree systems is based on the old-style French model and consists of two cycles. The first cycle lasts for two years and results in award of the Diplôme d'Etudes Universitaires Générales. An exception to this is the Ecole Nationale d'Administration, which awards a Diplôme after five years of study. The second cycle is two years in duration and culminated with the award of the Maîtrise. There are no postgraduate-level degrees; students usually complete their higher education abroad.

The Centre Supérieur d'Enseignement Technique is the leading institution of technical and vocational education, and specializes in mechanical and electrical engineering.

Learned Societies

BIBLIOGRAPHY, LIBRARY SCIENCE AND MUSEOLOGY

Association Mauritanienne des Bibliothécaires, Archivistes et Documentalistes: c/o Bibliothèque Nationale, BP 20, Nouakchott; f. 1979; Pres. O. DIOUWARA; Sec. SID'AHMED FALL.

LANGUAGE AND LITERATURE

Alliance Française: BP 5022, Nouakchott; tel. and fax 525-31-48; e-mail afm@mauritel .mr; offers courses and exams in French language and culture and promotes cultural exchange with France; attached teaching centres in Atar, Kaedi and Nouadhibou.

Research Institutes

GENERAL

Institut Mauritanien de Recherche Scientifique: BP 196, Nouakchott; Dir Prof. MOHAMED LEMINE OULD HAMMADI.

AGRICULTURE, FISHERIES AND VETERINARY SCIENCE

Institut Supérieur des Sciences et Techniques Halieutiques: Nouadhibou-Cansado; tel. 554-90-47; fax 554-90-28; f. 1983; part of Economic Community of West Africa; research and training in the fisheries industry; Dir-Gen. D. SOGUI.

TECHNOLOGY

Direction des Mines et de la Géologie: Ministère des Mines et de l'Industrie, BP 199, Nouakchott; tel. 225-30-83; fax 225-69-37; e-mail mmi@mauritania.mr; f. 1968; 17 mems; library of 3,000 vols; Dir WANE IBRAHIMA LAMINE.

Libraries and Archives

Boutilimit

Arab Library: Boutilimit; library of the late Grand Marabout, Abd Allah Ould Chelkh Sidya.

Chinguetti

Arab Library: Chinguetti; several private religious libraries, with a total of 3,229 vols, including pre-Islamic MSS; Librarian MOHAMED ABDALLAHI OULD FALL.

Kaédi

Arab Library: Kaédi; ancient religious texts.

Nouakchott

Archives Nationales: BP 77, Nouakchott; tel. 22-523-17; fax 22-526-36; f. 1955; 3,000 vols, 1,000 periodicals; documentation centre; Dir NAGI OULD MOHAMED MAHMOUD; publ. *Chaab* (daily).

Bibliothèque Nationale: BP 20, Nouakchott; tel. 24–35; dependent on Ministry of Culture; f. 1965; depository for all the country's publications; documentation centre for western Africa; 10,000 vols, collection of over 4,000 old MSS; 8 mems; Head Librarian OUMAR DIOUAWARA; Historian Prof. MOKTAR OULD HAMIDOU.

Centre de Documentation Pédagogique: BP 171, Nouakchott; f. 1962; 1,000 vols; 58 periodicals; educational and general works; Librarian MOHAMMED SAID.

Oualata

Arab Library: Oualata.

Tidjikja

Arab Library: Tidjikja; Librarian AHMEDOU OULD MOHAMED MAHMOUD.

University

UNIVERSITÉ DE NOUAKCHOTT

BP 798, Nouakchott
Telephone: 525-13-82
Fax: 525-39-97
E-mail: webmaster@univ-nkc.mr
Internet: www.univ-nkc.mr

Founded 1981
State control
Languages of instruction: Arabic, French, English
Academic year: October to June

Rector: MOHAMED EL HACEN OULD LEBATT
Librarian: ISSA OULD MOHAMED AHMED

Library of 20,059 vols
Number of teachers: 254
Number of students: 10,000

Publications: *Annales de la Faculté des Lettres et Sciences Humaines* (annually), *Revue d'Études Juridiques et Économiques* (annually)

DEANS

Faculty of Law and Economics: SIDI MOHAMED ABDELLAHI
Faculty of Letters and Human Sciences: DIALLO IBRAHIMA MOUSSA
Faculty of Science and Technology: AHMEDOH OULD HAOUBA

Colleges

Ecole Nationale d'Administration: BP 252, Nouakchott; tel. 525-32-22; fax 525-75-17; f. 1966; library: 8,000 vols; a documentation and research centre for the study of administration and politics in Mauritania; first degree courses; 33 teachers; 266 students; Librarian YARBA FALL; Dir CHEIK MOHAMED SALEM OULD MOHAMED LEMINE; publs *Annales*, *Futurs Cadres* (3 a year).

Institut National des Hautes Etudes Islamiques: Boutilimit; f. 1961; 300 students.

Institut Supérieur Scientifique: BP 5026, Nouakchott; tel. 525-11-68; fax 525-39-97; f. 1986; mathematics, physics, chemistry, biology, geology, computer studies, natural resources, ecology; library: 30,000 vols; Dir AHMEDOU OULD HAMED.

MAURITIUS

The Higher Education System

Mauritius became independent, within the Commonwealth, in 1968. In 1992 the Republic of Mauritius was proclaimed. The University of Mauritius (founded 1965) is the oldest existing institution of higher education in Mauritius. In 2005/06 6,602 students were enrolled at the University (35% of whom were part-time students), out of a total of 16,852 students in higher education; in addition, many students receive further education abroad. Government funding accounts for an estimated 85% of the University's running costs; the rest is made up from students' tuition fees, consultancy work and commercial rent.

The Council is the University policy-making body with control of administration and finance, and the Senate is the highest academic body. The Court is a body which meets annually to discuss general plans. The five Faculty Boards co-ordinate all teaching and research, administer examinations and evaluate programmes of study, and act on the instructions of the Vice-Chancellor and Senate.

Two GCE A-levels are the minimum requirement for admission to higher education, although for one- to three-year Certificate and Diploma courses the minimum requirement is the Cambridge Overseas School Certificate. Undergraduate Bachelors degrees at the University last three to four years, depending on the subject, but students wishing to study for professional degrees in dentistry or medicine must attend institutions outside the country. Following the Bachelors, the first postgraduate degree is the Masters, which last two to three years. The Masters of Philosophy is a research-based degree available in a number of subject areas. Finally, the Doctor of Philosophy is the highest university-level degree and is a research-based period of study lasting at least three year.

Post-secondary vocational and technical qualifications include several Brevets and Diplomas.

Learned Societies

GENERAL

Royal Society of Arts and Sciences of Mauritius: c/o Mauritius Sugar Industry Research Institute, Réduit; tel. 454-1061; fax 454-1971; e-mail rsas@msiri.intnet.mu; internet www.msiri.intnet.mu; f. 1829; Royal title 1847; 186 mems; Pres. JEAN-ALAIN LALOUETTE; Hon. Sec. ROSEMAY NG KEE KWONG; publ. *Proceedings* (irreg.).

AGRICULTURE, FISHERIES AND VETERINARY SCIENCE

Société de Technologie Agricole et Sucrière de Maurice: Mauritius Sugar Industry Research Institute, Réduit; tel. 454-1061; fax 454-1971; e-mail rngcheong@msiri.intnet.mu; f. 1910; 400 mems; Pres. G. DE FONTENAY; Hon. Sec. R. NG CHEONG; publ. *Revue Agricole et Sucrière de l'Ile Maurice*.

HISTORY, GEOGRAPHY AND ARCHAEOLOGY

Société de l'Histoire de l'Ile Maurice: rue de Froberville, Curepipe Rd, BP 150, Port Louis; e-mail societehistoire@intnet.mu; f. 1938; 810 ordinary mems; Hon. Sec. G. RAMET; publs *Bulletin*, *Dictionary of Mauritian Biography*.

LANGUAGE AND LITERATURE

Alliance Française: 1, rue Victor Hugo, Bell Village, Port Louis; tel. 212-2949; fax 212-2812; e-mail info@afmccf.com; internet www.afmccf.com; offers courses and exams in French language and culture and promotes cultural exchange with France; six attached teaching centres in Port-Louis.

British Council: Royal Rd, POB 111, Rose Hill, Mauritius; tel. 454-9550; fax 454-9553; e-mail general.enquiries@mu.britishcouncil.org; internet www.britishcouncil.org/mauritius; offers courses and exams in English language and British culture and promotes cultural exchange with the UK; also responsible for British Council work in Madagascar and the Seychelles; Dir ROSALIND BURFORD.

Research Institutes

AGRICULTURE, FISHERIES AND VETERINARY SCIENCE

Mauritius Sugar Industry Research Institute: 1 Moka Rd, Réduit; tel. 454-1061; fax 454-1971; e-mail m.s.i.r.i.@msiri.intnet.mu; internet www.msiri.mu; f. 1953; research on cane breeding, agronomy, soils, diseases, pests, weeds, botany, mechanization, biotechnology, sugar manufacture, by-products, also on food crops cultivated in association with sugar-cane and between cane cycles; library: see Libraries and Archives; Dir Dr JEAN CLAUDE AUTRY; publs *Occasional Papers* (irreg.), *Occasional Reports & Monographs* (irreg.), *Flore de Mascareignes* (irreg.).

NATURAL SCIENCES

Biological Sciences

Research Centre for Mauritius Flora and Fauna: c/o Mauritius Institute, POB 54, Port Louis; tel. 212-0639; fax 212-5717; attached to Mauritius Institute.

Libraries and Archives

Coromandel

National Archives: Devt Bank of Mauritius Complex, Coromandel; tel. 233-4469; fax 233-4299; e-mail arc@mail.gov.mu; f. 1815; contains records of the French Administration (1721–1810) and the British Administration (1810–1968); comprises Divisions of MS Records, Printed Records, Notarial Registers, Land Court Registers, Maps and Plans, Photographic Service, Microfilm Section, Oral History Unit and Restoration Unit; 300,000 items; Chief Officer PIERRE ROLAND CHUNG SAM WAN.

Curepipe

Carnegie Library: Queen Elizabeth II Ave, Curepipe; tel. 674-2287; fax 676-5054; f. 1920; spec. colln on Indian Ocean islands; 90,000 vols; Senior Librarian T. K. HURRYNAG-RAMNAUTH.

Port Louis

City Library: City Hall, POB 422, Port Louis; tel. 212-0831 ext. 163; fax 212-4258; internet mpl.intnet.mu/library.htm; f. 1851; 110,000 vols; important collections on Mauritius and archives of Port Louis Municipal Council; music scores; depository for WHO publications; Head Librarian BENJAMIN SILARSAH; publs *Annual Report*, *Subject Bibliography on Mauritius* (annually), *Subject Index to Local Newspapers* (2 a year).

Mauritius Institute Public Library: POB 54, Port Louis; tel. 212-0639; fax 212-5717; f. 1902; legal deposit library and depository library for UNESCO; 60,000 vols, including an extensive collection of books, articles and reports on Mauritius; Head Librarian S. ANKIAH.

Réduit

Mauritius Sugar Industry Research Institute (MSIRI) Library: Réduit; tel. 454-1061; fax 454-1971; e-mail library@msiri.intnet.mu; internet www.msiri.mu; f. 1953; 31,150 vols; representative colln on all aspects of sugar cane cultivation and sugar manufacture, and expanding colln on food crops; wide coverage of technical periodical literature; colln of prints and drawings and early pbls on sugar cane; in-house databases and int. colln of CD-ROM databases and full texts; Head of Library, Scientific Information Service and Pbls Dept ROSEMAY NG KEE KWONG.

University of Mauritius Library: Réduit; tel. 454-1041; fax 464-0905; e-mail uomlibrary@uom.ac.mu; internet www.uom.ac.mu; f. 1965; important collns in fields of administration, social sciences, agriculture, science and technology, law, textile engineering, medical research and Mauritiana; partial depository for UN and World Bank publs; 175,000 vols (140,000 books, 35,000 bound vols of periodicals); Chief Librarian ISHWARDUTH DASSYNE.

Museums and Art Galleries

Mahebourg

Historical Museum: Mahebourg; tel. 631-9329; f. 1950; a branch of the Mauritius Institute; comprises collection of old maps, engravings, water-colours and naval relics of local interest, exhibited in an 18th-c. French house; Dir R. GAJEELEE.

Port Louis

Port Louis Museum: Mauritius Institute, Port Louis; tel. 212-2815; fax 212-5717; e-mail mimuse@intnet.mu; f. 1880; comprises a Natural History Museum, collections of fauna, flora and geology of Mauritius and of the other islands of the Mascarene region; Dir S. ABDOOLRAHAMAN.

Réduit

Mauritius Herbarium: c/o Mauritius Sugar Industry Research Institute, Réduit; tel. 454-1061; fax 454-1971; e-mail msiri@msiri.intnet.mu; internet webmsiri.intnet.mu; f. 1960; public herbarium for education and research; specializes in flora of Mascarene Islands; Curator CLAUDIA BAIDER; publ. *Flore des Mascareignes* (irregular).

Universities

UNIVERSITY OF MAURITIUS

Réduit

Telephone: 454-1041
Fax: 454-9642
E-mail: webmaster@uom.ac.mu
Internet: www.uom.ac.mu

Founded 1965
Languages of instruction: English, French
Academic year: August to July

Chancellor (vacant)
Pro-Chancellor: S. BISSOONDOYAL
Vice-Chancellor: Prof. I. FAGOONEE
Pro-Vice-Chancellors: Prof. V. HOOKOOMSING (Research and Consultancy)
Registrar: CHAN CHIM YUK
Chief Librarian: I. DASSYNE (acting)

Library: see Libraries and Archives
Number of teachers: 400 (231 full-time, 169 part-time)
Number of students: 5,760
Publications: *Annual Report*, *Calendar* (annually), *Research Journal* (annually), *University Newsletter* (4 a year), *Vice-Chancellor's Report*

DEANS

Faculty of Agriculture: Assoc. Prof. Dr D. R. VENCATASAMY (acting)
Faculty of Engineering: Prof. Dr H. C. S. RUGHOOPUTH
Faculty of Law and Management: Assoc. Prof. C. FY-THIN AH HEN
Faculty of Science: Prof. B. A. F. GURIB-FAKIM
Faculty of Social Studies and Humanities: Assoc. Prof. Dr P. P. VEERAPEN

PROFESSORS

GURIB FAKIM, A., Chemistry
MATHUR, H., Social Studies
MEHTA, H., Management
NATH, S., Economics and Statistics
RUGHOOPUTH, H. C. S., Electrical and Electronic Engineering
RUGHOOPUTH, S. D. D. V., Physics
SENTENI, A., Virtual Centre for Innovative Learning Technologies
JOYNATHSING, M., Centre for Applied Social Research

UNIVERSITY OF TECHNOLOGY, MAURITIUS

La Tour Koenig, Pointe-aux-Sables

Telephone: 234-7624
Fax: 234-1660
E-mail: registrar@utm.intnet.mu
Internet: www.utm.ac.mu

Founded 2000 by Act of Parliament
Language of instruction: English
Academic year: August to June
State Control

Director-General: PETER STEVEN COUPE
Registrar: SASSITA DEVI GOORDYAL
Librarian: GEETA DWARKAN

Library of 12,000
Number of teachers: 100 (full-time and part-time)
Number of students: 1,407 (440 full-time, 967 part-time)

HEADS OF SCHOOLS

School of Business Informatics and Software Engineering: Dr N. MOHAMUDALLY
School of Public Sector Policy and Management: Dr RAMESH DURBARRY

Colleges

Mahatma Gandhi Institute: Moka; tel. 403-2000; fax 433-2235; e-mail vkoonjal@intnet.mu; internet mgi.intnet.mu; f. 1970; serves as a centre for the study of Indian culture and traditions, and the promotion of education and culture; courses in Indian Music and Dance, Fine Arts, Indian Languages, Mandarin and Indian Philosophy; research in Indian and Immigration Studies, Culture and Civilization, Bhojpuri, Folklore and Oral Traditions and Mauritian History, Geography and Literature; library: 100,000 vols; 218 secondary teachers, 76 in tertiary sector; 2,336 students; special collections: Gandhi, Mauritius, archives relating to Indian immigration to Mauritius 1842–1912; Chair. L. NUCKCHADY; Dir-Gen. S. NIRSIMLOO GAYAN (acting); Registrar Dr V. D. KOONJAL; publs *Journal of Mauritian Studies* (English, 2 a year), *Vasant* (Hindi, 4 a year), *Rimjhim* (Hindi, 4 a year).

Mauritius College of the Air: Réduit; tel. 403-8200; fax 464-8854; e-mail mca@mca.ac.mu; internet www.mca.ac.mu; f. 1972; runs distance education programmes; provides the national broadcasting organization with programmes for schools; produces audio-visual material for use by children and adults in formal and non-formal education; acquires pre-recorded media-based educational material from overseas and makes it available to schools in Mauritius; library: 9,500 vols; 62 part-time tutors; 1,780 students; Dir MEENA SEETULSINGH.

Robert Antoine Sugar Industry Training Centre: Royal Rd, Réduit; tel. 454-7024; fax 454-7026; e-mail rasitc@intnet.mu; internet pages.intnet.mu/rasitc; f. 1980; courses in sugarcane agronomy, cane sugar manufacture and chemical control in sugar factories, mechanization of field operations, power generation for sugar factories, management skills, supervisory skills, leadership development, communications; courses in English and French at various levels; 100 part-time specialists; 800 part-time students; Dir Dr LINDA MAMET.

MEXICO

The Higher Education System

From the 1520s until independence in 1821 Mexico was under Spanish rule. The oldest current institutions of higher education date from this period, among them Universidad Nacional Autónoma de Mexico (founded 1551), Universidad de Guanajuato (founded 1732; current name 1945), Universidad Autónoma de Campeche (founded 1756) and Universidad de Guadalajara (founded 1792). The Secretaria de Educación Pública (SEP) is the government ministry responsible for the administration of education at all levels, but following legislation enacted in 1992 granting greater autonomy to the Federal States, there has been an increase in the number of privately-run institutions of higher education. In early 2006 the Congreso de la Unión (Parliament) passed legislation requiring all public and private institutions of higher education who offered degree programmes to be accredited; prior to this there were no national standards for accreditation or quality assurance. In 2004/05 there were an estimated 4,876 institutes of higher education, attended by 2,322,900 students in 2003/04. Institutions of higher education are classified as Universities, Technological Universities or Institutes, Polytechnics or Teachers' Colleges.

To gain admission to a first degree programme, an applicant must possess the certificate for completion of secondary school, the Bachillerato, and sit an entrance examination. The Technological Universities have introduced a specialist two-year course (Técnico Superior Universitario) which can either used to transfer to the four-year Licenciado (see below) or as a complete qualification in its own right. The Licenciado is offered at undergraduate level by all institutions of higher education and usually last fours years, although degrees awarded in conjunction with a professional title may last longer. The first postgraduate degree is the Maestría, which is a one- or three-year research-based course of study. Finally, the Doctorado is a two- to three-year period of research and represents the highest level of university qualifications.

Post-secondary awards for vocational and technical education include the Salida Lateral or Carrera Corta (two to three years) leading to a Diploma or Titulo Técnico.

Regulatory and Representative Bodies

GOVERNMENT

Secretariat of State for Public Education: Dinamarca 84, 5o, Col. Juárez, 06600 México, DF; tel. (55) 5510-255; fax (55) 5329-6873; e-mail educa@sep.gob.mx; internet www.sep.gob.mx; Sec. of Public Education JOSEFINA VÁZQUEZ MOTA.

NATIONAL BODIES

Asociación Nacional de Universidades e Instituciones de Educación Superior (ANUIES) (National Association of Universities and Institutions of Higher Education): Tenayuca 200, Col. Santa Cruz Atoyac, 03310 México, DF; tel. (55) 5420-4900; e-mail ric@anuies.mx; internet www.anuies.mx; f. 1950; co-ordinates and represents instns of higher education, studies academic and admin. problems of the nat. higher education system; promotes exchange of personnel, information and services between the affiliated instns; 144 affiliated univs, centres and colleges; library of 11,500 vols; Exec. Sec.-Gen. Dr RAFAEL LÓPEZ CASTAÑARES; publs *Confluencia* (monthly), *Revista de la Educación Superior* (every 3 months).

Centro de Co-operación Regional para la Educación de Adultos en América Latina y el Caribe (CREFAL)/Centre for Regional Co-operation for Adult Education in Latin America and the Caribbean: Avda Lázaro Cárdenas s/n, Col. Revolución, 61609 Pátzcuaro, Mich.; tel. (434) 342-8200; fax (434) 342-8151; e-mail crefal@crefal.edu.mx; internet tariacuri.crefal.edu.mx/crefal; f. 1951 by UNESCO and OAS, now administered by a Board of Dirs from mem. countries; regional technical assistance, specialist training in literary and adult education, research; library of 80,416 vols; library: CEDEAL/CREFAL Adult Education documentation centre for Latin America: database of 17,347 entries; Dir HUMBERTO SALAZAR HERRERA; publs *Decisio – saberes para la Acción en Educación de Adultos* (3 a year), *Revista Interamericana de Educación de Adultos* (3 a year).

Dirección General de Relaciones Educativas, Científicas y Culturales (Board of Educational, Scientific and Cultural Relations): Secretaría de Educación Pública, Brasil 31, 2o piso, México 1, DF; f. 1960; comprises Sections of Technical Assistance, Int. Relations in the fields of Education, Science and Culture and Exchange; serves as co-ordinating agency between the UN, UNESCO, the OAS and the Mexican Govt; Dir Dr ENRIQUE G. LEÓN LÓPEZ.

Federación de Instituciones Mexicanas Particulares de Educación Superior (Federation of Mexican Higher-Education Institutions): Río Guadalquivir 50, 4o piso, Col. Cuauhtémoc, 06500 México, DF; tel. (55) 5514-5514; fax (55) 5207-0581; e-mail vcampuza@fimpes.org.mx; internet www.fimpes.org.mx; f. 1981; comprises 114 higher-education instns incl. the principal private univs; works to improve communication and collaboration between its mems and the other educational instns in the country; promotes high academic standards; Exec. Sec. Lic. VICTOR CAMPUZANO TARDITI.

Learned Societies

GENERAL

Colegio Nacional (National College): Luis González Obregón 23, Centro Histórico, 06020 México, DF; tel. (55) 5789-4330; fax (55) 5702-1779; e-mail colnal@mx.inter.net; internet www.colegionacional.org.mx; f. 1943 by the Government for the dissemination of national culture; 37 mems; library of 30,000 vols, 10,000 periodicals; Sec./Administrator Lic. FAUSTO VEGA Y GÓMEZ; publ. *Memoria* (annually).

UNESCO Office Mexico: Pte Masaryk no. 526, 3er piso, Colonia Polanco, 11560 México, DF; tel. (55) 5230-7600; fax (55) 5230-7602; e-mail mexico@unesco.org; internet www.unescomexico.org; f. 1967; Dir LUIS MANUEL TIBURCIO.

AGRICULTURE, FISHERIES AND VETERINARY SCIENCE

Sociedad Agronómica Mexicana (Mexican Agricultural Society): Mariano Azuela 121, 2° piso, Del. Cuauhtémoc, 06400 México, DF; f. 1921.

Sociedad Forestal Mexicana (Mexican Forestry Society): Calle de Jesús Terán 11, México 1, DF; f. 1921; 225 mems; Exec. Pres. Ing. RIGOBERTO VÁSQUEZ DE LA PARRA; Sec.-Gen. Lic. ADOLFO AGUILAR Y QUEVEDO; publ. *México Forestal* (every 2 months).

ARCHITECTURE AND TOWN PLANNING

Asociación de Ingenieros y Arquitectos de México (Association of Mexican Engineers and Architects): 3A Calle del Puente de Alvarado 58, México, DF; f. 1868; 560 mems; library of 7,565 vols; Pres. Ing. FEDERICO DOVALI RAMOS; Sec. Ing. JOSÉ ACOSTA SÁNCHEZ; publ. *Revista Mexicana de Ingeniería y Arquitectura* (quarterly).

BIBLIOGRAPHY, LIBRARY SCIENCE AND MUSEOLOGY

Asociación Mexicana de Bibliotecarios, AC (Mexican Library Association): Apdo 12-792, Administración de Correos 12, 03001 México, DF; Angel Urraza 817-A, Col. Del Valle, 03100 México, DF; tel. (55) 5575-3396; fax (55) 5575-1135; e-mail correo@ambac.org.mx; internet www.ambac.org.mx; f. 1924; 1,061 mems; Pres. FELIPE BECERRIL TORRES; Sec. ELÍAS CID RAMÍREZ; publs *Memorias de las Jornadas Mexicanas de Biblioteconomía* (annually), *Noticiero de la AMBAC* (4 a year), *Revista Liber*.

Dirección General de Bibliotecas (Main Directorate of Libraries): Universidad Nacional Autónoma de México, Ciudad Universitaria, Apdo 70–392, 04510 México, DF; tel. (55) 5622-3960; fax (55) 5622-4938; e-mail sinfo@dgb.unam.mx; internet http://dgb.unam.mx; f. 1966; documentation service, current awareness and SDI services, computerized bibliographical searches; Digital Library of 6,000 periodical titles with full text; 140 specialized databases; library of 3,485 vols; special collection of 230 titles of abstracting and indexing periodicals; 2,500 Latin American periodicals; Dir Dra SILVIA GONZÁLEZ MARÍN; publs *Biblioteca Universitaria* (electronic, irregular), *CLASE* (quarterly index of Latin American citation in social sciences and humanities), *PERIODICA* (quarterly index of Latin American science and technology journals).

ECONOMICS, LAW AND POLITICS

Barra Mexicana—Colegio de Abogados (Mexican Bar Association—College of Advocates): Varsovia No. 1, Colonia Juárez, 06600 México, DF; tel. (55) 5208-3115; fax (55) 5208-3117; e-mail labarra@bma.org.mx; internet www.bma.org.mx; f. 1922; 1,732 mems; library of 5,260 vols; Pres. Lic. FABIÁN AGUINACO BRAVO; Sec. Lic. CARLOS PASTRANA Y ÁNGELES; publs *El Foro* (2 a year), *La Barra* (6 a year).

Instituto Nacional de Estadística, Geografía e Informática (National Institute of Statistics, Geography and Informatics): Avda Héroe de Nacozari sur 2301, Fracc. Jardines del Parque, 20270 Aguascalientes, Ags; tel. (449) 916-78-15; fax (449) 918-22-32; e-mail atencion.usuarios@inegi.gob.mx; internet www.inegi.gob.mx; f. 1983; integrates and develops the National System of Statistics and the Geographic Information System; undertakes the National Census; library of 15,000 vols; Pres. Dr GILBERTO CALVILLO VIVES; publs *Agenda Estadística de los Estados Unidos Mexicanos* (annually), *Anuario de Estadísticas por Entidad Federativa* (annually), *Anuario Estadístico del Comercio Exterior* (electronic, annually), *Anuario Estadístico del Estado* (separate volume for each state of Mexico), *Anuario Estadístico de los Estados Unidos Mexicanos* (electronic, annually), *Boletín de los Sistemas Nacionales Estadístico y de Información Geográfica* (electronic, annually), *Cuaderno Estadístico de la Zona Metropolitana de la Ciudad de México* (electronic, annually), *Encuesta Nacional de Ocupación y Empleo* (electronic, annually), *La Industria Automotriz en México* (annually), *La Industria Maquiladora de Exportación*, *La Industria Química en México* (annually), *La Industria Siderúrgica en México* (annually), *La Industria Textil y del Vestido en México* (annually), *México en el Mundo* (every 2 years), *La Minería en México* (annually), *El Sector Alimentario en México* (annually).

EDUCATION

Centro Nacional de Documentación e Información Pedagógica y Museo Pedagógico Nacional (National Centre for Educational Documentation and Information and National Educational Museum): Calle Presidente Masaryk 526, México 5, DF; f. 1971; library of 10,000 vols; Dir Prof. MARIANO CRUZ PÉREZ; publs *Documentación e Información* (monthly), *Lista de Canje* (2 a year), *Sep-Forjadores* (monthly).

FINE AND PERFORMING ARTS

Asociación Musical Manuel M. Ponce, AC (Manuel M. Ponce Musical Association): Bucareli No. 12, Desp. 411, México 1, DF; tel. (55) 521-7260; f. 1949 to promote annual concert seasons of traditional, modern and contemporary Mexican and foreign music; library of musical scores, tapes, records and books; Pres. LUIS HERRERA DE LA FUENTE; Vice-Pres. JESÚS ALVARADO ORTÍZ; Musical Dir MARÍA DE LOS ANGELES CALCÁNEO; Secs VÍCTOR URBAN, EDELMIRA ZUÑIGA.

Ateneo Veracruzano (Veracruz Athenaeum): Edif. Lonja Mercantil, Independencia 924, Vera Cruz; f. 1933; 68 mems (18 corresp.); Pres. C.P.T. FRANCISCO BROISSIN A.; Sec. Prof. ANTONIO SALAZAR PÁEZ; publ. *Boletín* (monthly).

Instituto Nacional de Bellas Artes y Literature (National Institute of Fine Arts and Literature): Paseo de la Reforma y Campo Marte s/n, Col. Chapultepec Polanco, 11560 México, DF; tel. (55) 5521-9251; internet www.cnca.gob.mx/cnca/buena/inba/intro.html; f. 1947; consists of depts of music, visual arts, opera, literature, dance, theatrical production, architecture, artistic education and administration; responsible for cultural insts throughout Mexico; Dir GERARDO ESTRADA; publs *Boletín de Literatura* (6 a year), *Revista de Educación Artística* (4 a year), *Revista Hetereofonía* (3 a year), *Revista Pauta* (6 a year).

Affiliated institution:

Centro Nacional de Conservación y Registro del Patrimonio Artístico Mueble (National Centre for Conservation and Registry of Movable Art Heritage): San Ildefonso 60, Col. Centro, Del. Cuauhtémoc, México DF; tel. (55) 5702-2197; fax (55) 5702-2143; f. 1958; restoration of works of art; Dir WALTHER BOELSTERLY.

HISTORY, GEOGRAPHY AND ARCHAEOLOGY

Academia Mexicana de la Historia (Mexican Academy of History): Plaza Carlos Pacheco 21, Col. Centro, Cuauhtémoc, 06070 México, DF; tel. (55) 5518-2708; fax (55) 5521-9653; e-mail informes@acadmexhistoria.org.mx; internet www.acadmexhistoria.org.mx; f. 1919; 30 mems; correspondent of Real Academia, Madrid; library of 10,000 vols; Dir Dr MIGUEL LEÓN-PORTILLA; Sec. Dr GISELA VON WOBESER; publ. *Memorias* (2 a year).

Academia Nacional de Historia y Geografía (National Academy of History and Geography): Londres 60, México 6, DF; f. 1925; 179 mems; Dir Dr JESÚS FERRER GAMBOA; publ. *Revista*.

Departamento de Antropología e Historia de Nayarit (Department of Anthropology and History in Nayarit): Avda México 91, Tepic, Nayarit; f. 1946; Dir EVERARDO PEÑA NAVARRO; Sec. MARÍA A. GONZÁLEZ A..

Sociedad Mexicana de Geografía y Estadística (Mexican Society of Geography and Statistics): Calle de Justo Sierra 19, Apdo 10739, Del. Cuauhtémoc, 06020 México, DF; tel. (55) 5542-7340; e-mail smexgeoyesta@aol.com; f. 1833; 1,204 active mems, 640 corresponding mems; library of 450,000 vols; Pres. Lic. CUAUHTÉMOC CISNEROS MADRID; Sec.-Gen. LEOPOLDO CHAGOYA MORGAN; publs *Boletín* (3 a year), *and special works*.

Sociedad Mexicana de Historia de la Ciencia y la Tecnología (Mexican Society for History of Science and Technology): Edif. de las Sociedades Científicas, Avda Cipreses s/n, Col. San Andrés Totoltepec, Tlalpan, 14400 México, DF; tel. (55) 5849-6830; fax (55) 5849-6831; e-mail info@smhct.org; internet www.smhct.org; f. 1964; Pres. Dr JUAN JOSÉ SALDAÑA; publs *Anales*, *Memorias*, *Quipu*.

LANGUAGE AND LITERATURE

Academia Mexicana de la Lengua (Mexican Academy of Letters): Liverpool 76, Col. Juárez, 06600 México, DF; tel. (55) 5208-2526; fax (55) 5208-2416; e-mail academia@academia.org.mx; internet www.academia.org.mx; f. 1875; corresp. of the Real Academia Española (Madrid); 178 mems; Dir JOSÉ G. MORENO DE ALBA; Sec. MANUEL ALCALÁ ANAYA.

Alliance Française–Alianza Francesa México: Apdo 105-136, Socrates 156, Esq. Homero, Col. Los Morales Polanco, 11510 México, DF; tel. (55) 1084-4200; fax (55) 5395-5182; e-mail fafdg@alianzafrancesa.org.mx; internet www.alianzafrancesa.org.mx; f. 1884; Pres. AGUSTÍN LEGORRETA CHAUVET; Gen. Dir BERNARD FRONTERO; offers courses and exams in French language and culture and promotes cultural exchange with France; attached teaching centres in Acapulco, Ciudad del Carmen, Cozumel, Cuautla, Guadalajara, Guanajuato, Irapuato, Léon, Martínez de la Torre, Querétaro and Tijuana.

British Council: Lope de Vega 316, Col. Chapultepec Morales, 11570 México, DF; tel. (55) 5263-1900; fax (55) 5263-1940; e-mail bcmexico@britishcouncil.org.mx; internet www.britishcouncil.org.mx; f. 1943; teaching centre; offers courses and exams in English language and British culture and promotes cultural exchange with the UK; Dir CLIVE BRUTON.

Goethe-Institut (Goethe Institute): Tonalá 43, Col. Roma, 06700, México, DF; tel. (55) 5207-0487; fax (55) 5533-1057; e-mail info@mexiko.goethe.org; internet www.goethe.de/hn/mex/deindex.htm; offers courses and exams in German language and culture and promotes cultural exchange with Germany; attached centre in Guadalajara; library of 13,000 vols, 35 periodicals; Dir FOLCO NÄTHER.

PEN Club de México (PEN Club of Mexico): Heriberto Frías 1452-407, Col. del Valle, 03100 México, DF; tel. (55) 5564-5078; e-mail presidencia@penmexico.org.mx; internet www.penmexico.org.mx; f. 1924; 62 mems; Pres. MARÍA ELENA RUIZ CRUZ; Sec. JAIME RAMÍREZ GARRIDO; publ. *Directory of Writers* (annually).

MEDICINE

Academia Mexicana de Cirugía (Mexican Academy of Surgery): Avda Cuauhtémoc 330, Bloque B 3o piso, Col. Doctores, 06725 México DF; tel. (55) 5761-2581; e-mail amc06@prodigy.net.mx; internet www.amc.org.mx; f. 1933; Pres. FERNANDO BERNAL SAHAGÚN; Sec. FRANCISCO JAVIER OCHOA CARRILLO; publ. *Revista* (monthly).

Academia Mexicana de Dermatología (Mexican Academy of Dermatology): Georgia 114, Despacho 503, Col. Nápoles. Del. Benito Juárez, 03810 México, DF; tel. (55) 5682-2545; fax (55) 5682-8963; e-mail academiadermatologia@prodigy.net.mx; internet www.amd.org.mx; f. 1952; Dir Dr GILBERTO ADAME MIRANDA; Sec. Dra GABRIELA FRIAS ANCONA.

Academia Nacional de Medicina de México (Mexican National Academy of Medicine): Apdo 7–813, Avda Cuauhtémoc 330, Bloque B planta baja, Col. Doctores, 06725 México, DF; tel. (55) 5519-8679; e-mail contacto@anmm.org.mx; internet www.anmm.org.mx; f. 1865; 14 sections; 340 mems; library of 20,000 vols; Pres. Dr MISAEL URIBE ESQUIVEL; Gen. Sec. Dra TERESA CORONA VÁZQUEZ; publ. *Gaceta Médica de México*.

Asociación de Médicas Mexicanas, AC (Mexican Association of Women Doctors): Bruselas 10 Int. 403, Col. Juárez, 06600 México, DF; tel. (55) 5591-0159; fax (55) 5546-8202; f. 1925; 3,000 mems; represents members' interests as doctors, citizens and women; Pres. Dra IRENE TALAMAS V.; publ. *Revista*.

Asociación Mexicana de Facultades y Escuelas de Medicina (Mexican Association of Faculties and Schools of Medicine): López Cotilla 754, Col. del Valle, 03100 México, DF; tel. (55) 5682-9482; fax (55) 5687-9323; e-mail amfem@prodigy.net.mx; internet www.amfem.edu.mx; f. 1957; mems 30 medical schools; Pres. Dr HUMBERTO A. VERAS GODOY; Admin. Sec. Lic. YVONNE E. FISCHER HESS.

Consejo Mexicano de Dermatología, AC (Mexican Dermatological Council): Instituto Dermatológico de Jalisco, Guadalajara; tel. (33) 3660-1515 ext. 200; f. 1974; 349 mems; qualifies specialists as part of Nat. Academy of Medicine Comm. of Postgraduate Studies; Gen. Sec. Prof. ERNESTO MACOTELA RUÍZ; publ. *Roster*.

Federación Mexicana de Ginecología y Obstetricia (Mexican Federation of Gynaecology and Obstetrics): Nueva York 38, Col. Nápoles, 03810 México, DF; tel. (55) 5669-0211; fax (55) 5682-0160; e-mail secretario@femego.org.mx; internet www.femego.org.mx; f. 1961; 4,600 mems; Pres. Dr JESÚS LEAL DEL ROSAL; Sec. Dr FERNANDO GAVIÑO GAVIÑO; publ. *Ginecología y Obstetricia de México*.

Sociedad Mexicana de Cardiología (Mexican Cardiological Society): Juan Badiano 1, Sección XVI Tlalpan, 14080 México, DF; tel. (55) 5655-7694; fax (55) 5573-2111; e-mail info@smcardiologia.org.mx; internet www.smcardiologia.org.mx; f. 1935; 1,250 mems; Pres. Dr ALFONSO BUENDÍA HERNÁNDEZ; Sec. Dr JUAN VERDEJO PARÍS; publs *Arch.Cardio.-Méx.*, *Revista Mexicana de Enfermería Cardiológica* (3 a year).

Sociedad Mexicana de Nutrición y Endocrinología, AC (Mexican Society for Nutrition and Endocrinology): Ohio 27, Col. El Rosedal, Del. Coyoacán , 04330 México, DF; tel. (55) 5636-2216; e-mail endocrinologia_smne@prodigy.net.mx; internet www.endocrinologia.com.mx; f. 1960; 660 mems; Pres. Dr ALFONSO VILLASEÑOR RUÍZ; Sec. Dr RAÚL GUTIÉRREZ GUTIÉRREZ; publ. *Revista de Endocrinología y Nutrición*.

Sociedad Mexicana de Parasitología, AC (Mexican Parasitological Society): Casa Tlalpan, Avenida Cipreses S/N, Km. 23.5 de la Antigua Carretera México-Cuernavaca, Col. San Andrés Totoltepec, 14400 México, DF; tel. (55) 5849-4054; fax (55) 5335-3422; e-mail flisser@servidor.unam.mx; internet www.facmed.unam.mx/smp; f. 1960; 20 active mems and 31 hon. mems from 14 countries; Pres. Dra ANA FLISSER; Sec. Dr FIDEL DE LA CRUZ HERNÁNDEZ HERNÁNDEZ.

Sociedad Mexicana de Pediatría (Mexican Paediatrics Society): Tehuantepec 86-503, Col. Roma Sur, Del. Cuauhtémoc, 06760 México, DF; tel. (55) 5564-8371; e-mail smp1930@socmexped.org.mx; internet www.socmexped.org.mx; f. 1930; 1,200 mems; Pres. Dr XAVIER DE JESÚS NOVALES CASTRO; Gen. Sec. Dr MARIO GONZÁLEZ VITE; publ. *Revista Mexicana de Pediatría* (6 a year).

Sociedad Mexicana de Salud Pública (Mexican Public Health Society): Herschel 109, Col. Anzures, Del. Miguel Hidalgo, 11590 México, DF; tel. (55) 5203-4291; fax (55) 5203-4229; e-mail smsp@prodigy.net.mx; internet www.smsp.org.mx; f. 1944; 6,000 mems; small library; Exec. Dir HUMBERTO MUÑOZ GRANDÉ; publ. *Higiene* (3 a year).

NATURAL SCIENCES

General

Academia Mexicana de Ciencias (Mexican Academy of Science): Calle Cipreses s/n, Km. 23.5 de la Carretera federal México-Cuernavaca, San Andrés Totoltepec, Tlalpan, 14400 México, DF; tel. (55) 5849-4905; fax (55) 5849-5112; e-mail academia@amc.unam.mx; internet www.amc.unam.mx; f. 1959; library of 420,000 vols; 1,847 mems; Pres. Dr JUAN PEDRO LACLETTE SAN ROMÁN; Sec. Dr OSVALDO MÁXIMO MUTCHINICK BARINGOLTZ; publ. *Revista* (4 a year).

Ateneo Nacional de Ciencias y Artes de México (National Athenaeum of Sciences and Arts): Bucareli 12, México, DF; f. 1920 as Ateneo Estudiantil de Ciencias y Artes, then Ateneo de Ciencias y Artes de México 1926, present name 1934; comprises sections of architecture, astronomy and mathematics, biology, broadcasting, cinematography, criminology and penal law, engineering, eugenics, geography, history, hygiene, law (civil, industrial, and international), literature, medicine, military studies, music, pedagogics, political economy, natural science, statistics; 7 corresp. centres: Monterrey, Mérida, Veracruz, Chiapas, Tijuana, Oaxaca, Tlaxcala; over 1,000 mems, including hon. and corresponding; library of 10,000 vols; Hon. Pres. Dr ALFONSO PRUNEDA; Pres. EMILIO PORTES GIL; Vice-Pres LUIS GARRIDO, Arq. EDMUNDO ZAMUDIO; Sec.-Gen. JOSÉ L. COSSIO; publs *Boletín*, *pamphlets*.

Biological Sciences

Asociación Mexicana de Microbiología, AC (Mexican Microbiological Association): Centro de Ciencias Genómicas, Avda Universidad s/n, Col. Chamilpa, Cuernavaca, Mor.; e-mail informes@microbiologia.org.mx; internet www.microbiologia.org.mx; f. 1949; Pres. Dra ESPERANZA MARTÍNEZ-ROMERO; Sec. BRENDA VALDERRAMA; publ. *Revista Latinoamericana de Microbiología*.

Sociedad Botánica de México, AC (Mexican Botanical Society): Centro de Investigaciones en Ecosistemas, Universidad Nacional Autónoma de México, Campus Morelia, Antigua Carretera a Pátzcuaro 8701, Col. San José de La Huerta, 58190 Morelia, Mich.; e-mail sbm@socbot.org.mx; internet www.socbot.org.mx; f. 1941; promotes the study, teaching and technology of botany; organizes the National Botanic Congress every 3 years; 1,000 mems; library of 850 vols, 350 periodicals; Pres. Dr MIGUEL MARTÍNEZ RAMOS; Exec. Sec. Dr JORGE ARTURO MEAVE DEL CASTILLO; publs *Boletín* (2 a year), *Macpalxochitl* (monthly newsletter).

Sociedad Mexicana de Biología (Mexican Biological Society): Avda de Brasil, México 1, DF; f. 1921; Pres. FERNANDO OCARANZ; publ. *Revista Mexicana de Biología*.

Sociedad Mexicana de Entomología (Mexican Entomological Society): Apdo 63, 91000 Jalapa, Veracruz; e-mail sme@campus.iztacala.unam.mx; internet www.iztacala.unam.mx/sme; f. 1952; 650 mems; Pres. CÁNDIDO LUNA LEÓN; publs *Boletín* (irregular), *Folia Entomológica Mexicana* (3 a year).

Sociedad Mexicana de Fitogenética (Mexican Society of Plant Genetics): Apdo 21, 56230 Chapingo, Edo de México; tel. (55) 5954-2200; fax (55) 5954-6652; e-mail somefi@taurus1.chapingo.mx; internet www.uaaan.mx/eventos/somefi/somefi.htm; f. 1965; 1,000 mems; Pres. Dr RAFAEL ORTEGA PACZKA; Sec. JUAN MOLINA MORENO; publs *Revista Fitotecnia Mexicana*, *Revista Germen*.

Sociedad Mexicana de Fitopatología, AC (Mexican Society of Phytopathology): Apdo postal 85, 56230 Chapingo, Edo de México; e-mail sandoval@colpos.mx; internet www.colpos.mx/ifit/smf/somefit.htm; f. 1958; 400 mems; holds one national meeting per year; Pres. Dr GUSTAVO MORA AGUILERA; Sec. Dr SERGIO SANDOVAL; publs *El Vector*, *Revista Mexicana de Fitopatología* (2 a year).

Sociedad Mexicana de Historia Natural (Mexican Natural History Society): Avda Dr Vertiz 724, Col. Vertiz Narvarte, 03020 México, DF; tel. (55) 5519-4505; fax (55) 5538-4505; e-mail info@smhn.com.mx; internet smhn.org.tripod.com; f. 1868, refounded 1936; 400 mems; library of 5,000 vols; Pres. Dr RAUL GIO ARGAEZ; publ. *Revista*.

Sociedad Mexicana de Micología (Mexican Society of Mycology): Apdo 41, 67700 Linares, Nuevo León; tel. (55) 5541-1333; e-mail smdm@tap-ecosur.edu.mx; internet www.smdm.org.mx; f. 1965; 400 mems; library of 12,000 vols; Pres. Dr FORTUNATO GARZA OCAÑAS; Sec. Dr RICARDO VALENZUELA GARZA (acting); publ. *Revista Mexicana de Micología* (annually).

Mathematical Sciences

Centro de Investigación en Computación (Computing Research Centre): Avda Juan de Dios Batiz s/n, Casi esq. Miguel Othón de Mendizabal, Unidad Profesional Adolfo López Mateos, Col. Nueva Industrial Vallejo, Del. Gustavo A. Madero, 07738 México, DF; tel. (55) 5729-6000 ext. 56604; fax (55) 5586-2936; e-mail webmaster@cic.ipn.mx; internet www.cic.ipn.mx; f. 1996; 250 mems; library of 4,000 vols; Dir Dr OSCAR CAMACHO NIETO; publs *Computación y Sistemas* (4 a year), *Research on Computing Science* (6 a year).

Sociedad Matemática Mexicana (Mexican Mathematical Society): Apdo 70-450, Coyoacán, 04510 México, DF; tel. (55) 5622-4481; fax (55) 5622-4479; e-mail smm@smm.org.mx; internet www.smm.org.mx; f. 1943; 1,100 mems, 20 institutional mems; promotes mathematics, sponsors National Congresses and Regional Assemblies of mathematicians, and The National Mathematical Olympics; Pres. Dr EMILIO LLUIS-PUEBLA; Sec. Dr PABLO PADILLA-LONGORIA; publs *Aportaciones Matemáticas*, *Boletín de la SMM* (2 a year), *Carta informativa* (4 a year), *Miscelánea Matemática* (2 a year).

Physical Sciences

Asociación Mexicana de Geólogos Petroleros (Mexican Association of Petroleum Geologists): Torres Bodet 176, 06400 México, DF; e-mail presidencia@amgp.org; internet www.amgp.org; f. 1949; 600 mems; Pres. J. ANTONIO ESCALERA ALCOCER; Sec. JOSÉ GPE. GALICIA BARRIOS; publ. *Boletín* (quarterly).

Sociedad Astronómica de México, AC (Mexican Astronomical Society): Apdo M 9647, Jardín Felipe Xicoténcatl, Colonia Alamos, 03400 México, DF; tel. (55) 5519-4730; e-mail socastmx@mx.inter.net; internet sam.astro.org.mx; f. 1902; library of 5,000 vols; 500 mems; Pres. MARTE TREJO SANDOVAL; Sec.-Gen. JORGE RUBÍ GARZA; publ. *El Universo* (quarterly).

Sociedad Geológica Mexicana, AC (Mexican Geological Society): Torres Bodet 176, Del. Cuauhtémoc, 06400 México, DF; tel. (55) 5541-0879; e-mail publigl@geologia.igeolcu.unam.mx; internet www.geociencias.unam.mx/SGM.html; f. 1904; 1,000 mems; library of 4,500 vols; Pres. Ing. BERNARDO MARTELL ANDRADE; Vice-Pres. Ing. HERIBERTO PALACIOS; Sec. Ing. LUIS VELÁZQUEZ AGUIRRE; publs *Boletín* (3 a year), *Revista Mexicana de Ciencias Geológicas* (jtly, 3 a year).

Sociedad Química de México (Mexican Chemical Society): Barranca del Muerto 26, Esquina Hércules, Col. Crédito Constructor, Del. Benito Juárez, 03940 México, DF; tel. (55) 5662-6837; fax (55) 5662-6823; e-mail soquimex@prodigy.net.mx; internet www.sqm.org.mx; f. 1956; 2,300 mems; Pres. ANDRÉS CERDA ONOFRE; Sec. (vacant); publ. *Revista de la SQM* (4 a year).

PHILOSOPHY AND PSYCHOLOGY

Sociedad Mexicana de Estudios Psico-Pedagógicos (Mexican Society for Psycho-Pedagogical Studies): Nayarit 86, México, DF.

RELIGION, SOCIOLOGY AND ANTHROPOLOGY

Sociedad Mexicana de Antropología (Mexican Anthropological Society): Apdo 100, C. A. P. Polanco, 11550 México, DF; tel. (55) 5622-9570; fax (55) 5622-9651; e-mail somedean@yahoo.com.mx; internet morgan.iia.unam.mx/usr/sma/index.html; f. 1937; 480 mems; Sec. Dr LEONARDO LÓPEZ LUJÁN; publ. *Revista Mexicana de Estudios Antropológicos* (annually).

TECHNOLOGY

Sociedad Mexicana de Ingeniería Sísmica, AC (Mexican Society of Seismic Engineering): Camino de Santa Teresa 187, Col. Parques del Pedregal, Tlalpan, 14020 México, DF; tel. (55) 5606-1314; e-mail smis@prodigy.net.mx; internet www.smis.org.mx; f. 1962; 350 mems; Pres. Dr EDUARDO REINOSO ANGULO; Sec. M.I. FRANCISCO GARCÍA ÁLVAREZ; publ. *Revista de Ingeniería Sísmica* (3 a year).

Research Institutes

GENERAL

Institut de Recherche pour le Développement (IRD) (Development Research Institute): Cicerón 609, Col. Los Morales, 11530 México, DF; tel. (55) 5280-7688; fax (55) 5282-0800; e-mail ird@irdmex.org; internet www.mx.ird.fr; Rep. GHANI CHEHBOUNI; (see main entry under France).

AGRICULTURE, FISHERIES AND VETERINARY SCIENCE

Campo Agrícola Experimental Río Bravo (Río Bravo Agricultural Research Station): Apdo 172, Río Bravo, Tamps; f. 1965; research into regional problems and diversification; Dir Ing. Agr. MANUEL CARNERO HERNÁNDEZ.

Instituto Nacional de Investigaciones Forestales, Agrícolas y Pecuarias (National Institute of Forestry, Agriculture and Livestock Research): Serapio Rendón 83, Col. San Rafael, Del. Cuauhtémoc, 06470 México, DF; tel. (55) 5484-1900; e-mail contactenos@inifap.gob.mx; internet www.inifap.gob.mx; f. 1985 through the integration of Instituto Nacional de Investigaciones Agrícolas, Instituto Nacional de Investigaciones Pecuarias and Instituto Nacional de Investigaciones Forestales; conducts research in all aspects of agricultural development and production; agronomy library, livestock library and forestry library; Gen. Dir Dr PEDRO BRAJCICH GALLEGOS; publs *Agricultura Técnica en México* (2 a year), *Ciencia Forestal* (2 a year).

BIBLIOGRAPHY, LIBRARY SCIENCE AND MUSEOLOGY

Instituto de Investigaciones Bibliográficas (Institute of Bibliographical Research): c/o Biblioteca Nacional de México and Hemeroteca Nacional de México, Centro Cultural Universitario, Ciudad Universitaria, Del. Coyoacán,, 04510 México, DF; tel. (55) 5622-6827; fax (55) 5665-0951; e-mail webmast@biblional.bibliog.unam.mx; internet http://biblional.bibliog.unam.mx; f. 1899, present name 1967; compiles the national bibliographies and books on bibliographical subjects; Dir VICENTE QUIRARTE CASTAÑEDA; publs *Boletín* (2 a year), *Nueva Gaceta Bibliográfica* (4 a year).

ECONOMICS, LAW AND POLITICS

Centro de Estudios Demográficos, Urbanos y Ambientales (Centre for Demographic, Urban and Environmental Studies): Camino al Ajusco 20, 14200 México, DF; tel. (55) 5449-3000; fax (55) 5645-0464; e-mail direccion.ceddu@colmex.mx; internet www.colmex.mx/centros/ceddu; f. 1964; library of 500,000 vols; Dir Dr JOSÉ LUIS LEZAMA DE LA TORRE; publ. *Revista de Estudios Demográficos y Urbanos* (3 a year).

Centro de Estudios Económicos (Centre for Economic Studies): Camino al Ajusco 20, Pedregal de Santa Teresa, Apdo 20671, 10740 México, DF; tel. (55) 5449-3000; fax (55) 5645-0464; e-mail webmaster@colmex.mx; internet www.colmex.mx; f. 1981; research areas include microeconomics, macroeconomics, economic development, statistics, game theory, environmental economics, industrial organization, international economics, public finance; master's and doctorate programmes; library of 8,000 vols; Dir JAIME SEMPERE CAMPELLO; publ. *Estudios Económicos* (2 a year).

Centro de Estudios Internacionales (Centre for International Studies): Camino al Ajusco 20, Col. Pedregal de Sta. Teresa, 10740 México, DF; tel. (55) 5449-3000 ext. 3110; fax (55) 5645-0464; e-mail direccion.cei@colmex.mx; internet www.colmex.mx/centros/cei/index.htm; f. 1960; research areas include international relations, politics, federal and local public administration, Mexico's political system and foreign policy, and regional studies of North America, Europe and Latin America; undergraduate programmes in Politics and Public Administration, and International Relations; Dir GUSTAVO VEGA; publ. *Foro Internacional* (4 a year).

Centro de Relaciones Internacionales: Ciudad Universitaria, FCPS, UNAM, 04510 México, DF; tel. (55) 5622-9412; fax (55) 5622-9413; attached to the Faculty of Political and Social Sciences of the Universidad Nacional Autónoma de México; f. 1970; coordinates and promotes research in all aspects of international relations and Mexico's foreign policy, as well as the training of researchers in different fields: Disciplinary construction problems, Co-operation and International Law, Developing nations, Actual problems in world society, Africa, Asia, Peace Research; 30 full mems; library of 6,000 vols, 35 special collections, 16,000 journals, etc; Dir Lic. ROBERTO PEÑA GUERRERO; publs *Boletín Informativo del CRI*, *Cuadernos*, *Relaciones Internacionales* (quarterly).

Instituto Mexicano del Desarrollo, AC: M. Escobedo 510, 8° piso, México 5, DF; tel. (55) 5531-0823; research on socio-economic development and planning; 470 staff; Dir-Gen. Lic. ERNESTO SANCHEZ AGUILAR.

EDUCATION

Centro de Estudios Educativos, AC (Centre for Educational Studies): Avda Revolución 1291, Col. Tlacopac–San Angel, Del. Alvaro Obregón, 01040 México, DF; tel. (55) 5593-5719; fax (55) 5651-6374; e-mail cee@cee.edu.mx; internet www.cee.edu.mx; f. 1963; scientific research into the problems of education in Mexico and Latin America; library of 31,500 vols, 642 periodicals; Dir-Gen. Dr LUIS MORFIN LÓPEZ; publ. *Revista Latinoamericana de Estudios Educativos* (4 a year).

HISTORY, GEOGRAPHY AND ARCHAEOLOGY

Centro de Estudios de Asia y África (Centre for Asian and African Studies): Camino al Ajusco 20, Pedregal de Santa Teresa, 10740 México, DF; tel. (55) 5449-3000; fax (55) 5645-0464; e-mail coord.acad.ceaa@colmex.mx; internet ceaa.colmex.mx/sitioceaa; f. 1964; studies of and research on Africa, China, Korea, Japan, South Asia, Southeast Asia, Middle East and North Africa; master's and doctorate programmes; library of 30,000 vols, 130 periodicals; Dir JUAN JOSÉ RAMÍREZ BONILLA; publs *Anuario Asia Pacífico* (annually), *Cuadernos de Trabajo*, *Estudios de Asia y África* (3 a year).

Centro de Estudios Históricos (Centre for Historical Studies): Coordinación Académica, Centro de Estudios Históricos, Camino al Ajusco 20, 10740 México, DF; tel. (55) 5449-3000 ext. 3132; fax (55) 5645-0464; e-mail coord.acad.ceh@colmex.mx; internet www.colmex.mx/centros/ceh; f. 1941; history of Mexico and Latin America; Dir Dr GUILLERMO PALACIOS; publ. *Historia Mexicana* (4 a year).

Instituto Nacional de Estudios Históricos de las Revoluciones de México (INEHRM) (National Institute for Historical Studies of the Mexican Revolutions): Francisco I. Madero 1, Colonia San Ángel, 01000 México, DF; tel. (55) 5616-3808; e-mail contactoinehrm@segob.gob.mx; internet www.inehrm.gob.mx; f. 1953; library of 43,000 vols; Man. Dr PABLO SERRANO ÁLVAREZ.

LANGUAGE AND LITERATURE

Centro de Estudios Lingüísticos y Literarios (Centre for Linguistic and Literary Studies): Coordinación Académica, Centro de Estudios Lingüísticos y Literarios, Camino al Ajusco 20, 10740 México, DF; tel. (55) 5255-5449; fax (55) 5255-5645; e-mail coord.acad.cell@colmex.mx; internet www.colmex.mx/centros; f. 1947; Spanish linguistics and literature, Indian languages, translation; Dir AURELIO GONZÁLEZ PÉREZ; publ. *Nueva Revista de Filología Hispánica* (2 a year).

MEDICINE

Instituto Nacional de Cardiología 'Ignacio Chávez' (National Cardiological Institute): Juan Badiano 1, Col. Sección XVI, Del. Tlalpan, 14080 México, DF; tel. (55) 5573-2911; fax (55) 5573-0994; e-mail webmaster@cardiologia.org.mx; internet www.cardiologia.org.mx; f. 1944; 390 medical mems; library of 8,465 vols, 569 periodicals; Dir Dr FAUSE ATTIÉ CURY; Sub-Dirs L. C. CUAUHTÉMOC SOTO CASTILLO (Administrative Division), Dr MARCO ANTONIO MARTÍNEZ RÍOS (Medical Attendance), Dr JOSÉ FERNANDO GUADALAJARA BOO (Medical Education Division), Dr PEDRO ANTONIO REYES LÓPEZ (Research Division); Library Dir MARIO FLAVIO FUENTES INIESTRA; publ. *Archivos de Cardiología de México* (6 nos, 1 vol per year).

Instituto Nacional de Diagnóstico y Referencia Epidemiológicos (National Institute of Epidemiological Diagnosis and Reference): Calle de Carpio 470, Santo Tomás, Miguel Hidalgo, 11340 México, D.F.; tel. (55) 5341-4389; fax (55) 5341-3264; e-mail indre@cenids.ssa.gob.mx; f. 1938; performs epidemiological laboratory reference services nationwide; carries out technological development and research in laboratory for support of epidemiological surveillance; trains and supervises laboratory personnel and performs quality control procedures for the National Laboratory Network; library of 3,930 vols, 603 journals. MEDLINE terminal; Dir Dr ANA FLISSER.

Instituto Nacional de Higiene de la S.S.A. (National Institute of Hygiene): Gerencia General de Biológicas y Reactivos, Czda Mariano Escobedo 20, Col. Popotla, Del. Miguel Hidalgo, 11400 México, DF; tel. (55) 5527-7368; fax (55) 5527-6693; f. 1895; 300 mems; library of 10,000 vols; Dir (vacant).

Instituto Nacional de Neurología y Neurocirugía (National Institute of Neurology and Neurosurgery): Insurgentes Sur 3877, Col. La Fama, Deleg. Tlalpan, 14269 México, DF; tel. (55) 5606-3822; fax (55) 5606-3245; e-mail webmaster@innn.edu.mx; internet www.innn.edu.mx; f. 1964; library of 2,700 vols, 270 periodicals; Dir-Gen. Dr JULIO SOTELO MORALES; publ. *Archivos de Neurociencias* (review, 4 a year).

Instituto Nacional de Salud Pública (National Institute of Public Health): Avda Universidad 655, Col. Santa María Ahuacatitlán, 62508 Cuernavaca, Morelos; e-mail webmaster@insp.mx; internet www.insp.mx; f. 1987; incorporates School of Public Health in Mexico (f. 1922), and research centres on Public Health, Health Systems; Infectious Diseases, Malaria, and Nutrition and Health; master's and doctorate programmes; library of 35,000 vols; Dir Dr MAURICIO HERNÁNDEZ AVILA; publ. *Salud Pública de México* (6 a year).

NATURAL SCIENCES

General

Centro de Investigación y de Estudios Avanzados del Instituto Politécnico Nacional (Centre for Research and Advanced Studies, National Polytechnic Institute): Apdo 14-740, 07000 México, DF; Avda Instituto Politécnico Nacional 2508, Col. San Pedro Zacatanco, 07360 México, DF; tel. (55) 5061-3800; fax (55) 5061-3901; e-mail buzon@mail.cinvestav.mx; internet www.cinvestav.mx; f. 1961; postgraduate research and training centre in sciences; integrates the work of the depts of biochemistry, physics, applied physics, physiology, biophysics and neurosciences, electrical engineering, mathematics, genetics and molecular biology, cellular biology, marine resources, experimental pathology, chemistry, biotechnology and bioengineering, biotechnology and biochemistry, pharmacology, bioelectronics, educational mathematics, toxicology, metallurgical engineering, computer science, mechatronics, solid-state electronics, automatic control, molecular biomedicine, communications, ceramic engineering, genetic engineering, materials, engineering drawing, human ecology and educational research; library of 256,000 vols, 3,200 special collections; Dir Dra ROSALINDA CONTRERAS THEUREL; publs *Avance y Perspectiva* (4 a year), *Morfismos* (2 a year).

Consejo Nacional de Ciencia y Tecnología (CONACYT) (National Council for Science and Technology): Avda Insurgentes Sur 1582, Col. Crédito Constructor, Del. Benito Juárez, 03940 México, DF; tel. (55) 5322-7700; e-mail magarciag@conacyt.mx; internet www.conacyt.mx; f. 1970; co-ordinates scientific research and development and formulates policy; Dir GUSTAVO ADOLFO CHAPELA CASTAÑARES; publ. *Ciencia y Desarrollo* (monthly).

Instituto Mexicano de Recursos Naturales Renovables, AC (Institute for the Conservation of Natural Resources): Dr Vertiz 724, Narvarte, 03020 México, D.F.; tel. (55) 5519-4505; fax (55) 5519-1633; e-mail imernar@hotmail.com; internet www.imernar.org; f. 1952; library of 7,000 vols and 200 regular periodicals; Dir (vacant).

Biological Sciences

Instituto de Ecología, AC (Institute of Ecology): Apdo Postal 63, Km 2½ Carretera Antigua a Coatepec No. 351, Congregación el Haya, 91070 Jalapa, Veracruz; tel. (228) 842-1800; fax (228) 818-7809; e-mail correo.electronico@inecol.edu.mx; internet www.ecologia.edu.mx; f. 1975; plant and animal ecology and taxonomy, biogeography, dynamics and structure of ecosystems, conservation and management of natural resources, environmental biotechnology, wood technology, coastal management, entomology, flora and fauna inventory; postgraduate programmes in Ecology and Natural Resources Management, in Wildlife Management and in Systematics; library of 24,000 vols, 535 current periodicals, 500 maps, 60 electronic reference titles; Dir-Gen. Dr DANIEL PIÑERO DALMAU; publs *Acta Zoológica Mexicana* (3 a year), *Acta Botánica Mexicana* (4 a year), *Flora del Bajío y de Regiones Adyacentes*, *Flora de Veracruz*, *Madera y Bosques* (2 a year).

Instituto Nacional de la Pesca (National Fishery Institute): Pitágoras 1320, Col. Santa Cruz Atoyac, Del. Benito Juárez, 03310 México, DF; tel. (55) 5605-2424; e-mail correoweb@inp.sagarpa.gob.mx; internet www.inp.sagarpa.gob.mx; f. 1962; research in marine biology; library of 3,000 vols; Dir Dr GUILLERMO ALBERTO COMPEÁN JIMÉNEZ.

Instituto Tecnológico del Mar (Institute of Marine Technology): Km. 12 Carretera Veracruz-Córdoba, Apdo Postal 68, 94290 Boca del Río, Ver.; tel. (229) 986-0189; fax (229) 986-1894; internet www.itmar1.edu.mx; f. 1975, renamed 1981; 150 mems; library of 4,500 vols; Dir ALMILCAR SUÁREZ ALLEN.

Mathematical Sciences

Instituto de Matemáticas (Institute of Mathematics): Area de la Investigación Científica, Circuito Exterior, Ciudad Universitaria, Coyoacán, 04510 México, DF; tel. (55) 5622-4523; fax (55) 5550-1342; e-mail rosi@matem.unam.mx; internet www.matem.unam.mx; f. 1942; research in mathematics; 59 mems; library of 20,000 vols; Dir Dr JAVIER BRACHO CARPIZO; publs *Anales* (annually), *Aportaciones Matemáticas* (irregular), *Monografías* (irregular), *Publicaciones Preliminares*.

Physical Sciences

Instituto de Astronomía (Institute of Astronomy): Apdo postal 70–264, 04510 México, DF; tel. (55) 5622-3906; fax (55) 5616-0653; e-mail direc@astroscu.unam.mx; internet www.astroscu.unam.mx; f. 1878; an Institute of the National Autonomous University of Mexico; research in astronomy and astrophysics; library of 7,000 vols, 1,550 journals; Dir Dr JOSÉ FRANCO; publs *Anuario del Observatorio Astronómico Nacional* (annually), *Revista Mexicana de Astronomía y Astrofísica* (2 a year).

Instituto Nacional de Astrofísica, Optica y Electrónica (National Institute of Astrophysics, Optics and Electronics): Luis Enrique Erro 1, Apdos 216 y 51, 72000 Tonantzintla, Pue.; tel. (222) 266-3100; fax (222) 247-2231; e-mail astrofi@inaoep.mx; internet www.inaoep.mx; f. 1971 formerly Observatorio Nacional de Astrofísica, f. 1942; 22 research mems; library of 7,000 vols, 144 periodicals; Gen. Dir Dr ALFONSO SERRANO PÉREZ-GROVAS; Gen. Academic Sec. Dr MANUEL G. CORONA GALINDO; publ. *Boletín del Instituto de Tonantzintla*.

Instituto Nacional de Investigaciones Nucleares (National Institute of Nuclear Research): Km 36.5, Carretera México-Toluca, 52045, Ocoyoacac, Edo. de México; tel. (55) 5329-7200; fax (55) 5329-7299; e-mail webmastr@nuclear.inin.mx; internet www.inin.mx; f. 1979 (previously part of *Instituto Nacional de Energía Nuclear*, f. 1955); planning, research and development of atomic technology, including non-military use of atomic energy; library of 41,500 vols (incl. theses), 75,000 periodicals, 7,300 consulting works, 6,000 pamphlets, 1,000 official pubs, 125 video tapes, 835,000 reports on microfiche and 25,000 in printed form; Gen. Dir JOSÉ RAÚL ORTÍZ MAGAÑA; Technical Sec. Dr JULIÁN SÁNCHEZ GUTIERREZ; publ. *Contacto Nuclear* (4 a year).

Servicio Meteorológico Nacional (National Meteorological Dept): Avda Observatorio 192, Col. Observatorio, Del. M. Hidalgo, 11860 México, DF; tel. (55) 2636-4600; fax (55) 5271-0878; e-mail webmaster@mailsmn.cna.gob.mx; internet smn.cna.gob.mx; f. 1915; library of 80,000 vols, 90,180 pamphlets; Dir Dr MICHEL ROSENGAUS MOSHINSKY.

RELIGION, SOCIOLOGY AND ANTHROPOLOGY

Centro Co-ordinador y Difusor de Estudios Latinoamericanos (Co-ordinating and Information Centre for Latin American Studies): Piso 8, Torre II de Humanidades, Ciudad Universitaria, 04510 México, DF; tel. (55) 5623-0211; e-mail moce@servidor.unam.mx; internet www.ccydel.unam.mx; f. 1978; attached to Universidad Nacional de México; study of Latin America and the Caribbean in all disciplines (history, literature, philosophy, etc.); library of 11,898 monographs, 8,700 magazines, 3,000 pamphlets, 160 theses and 150 records; Dir Dra ESTELA MORALES CAMPOS; publs *Archipiélago, Revista Cultural de Nuestra América* (4 a year), *Latinoamérica. Revista de Estudios Latinoamericanos*.

Centro de Estudios Sociológicos (Centre for Sociological Studies): Camino al Ajusco 20, 10740 México, DF; tel. (55) 5449-3000; fax (55) 5645-0464; e-mail direccion.ces@colmex.mx; internet www.colmex.mx; f. 1973; research areas include sociological theory, economic sociology and the sociology of work, social movements and civil organizations, class and family, political parties, elections and politics, education, labour markets, migration and emigration, reproductive health, religion, culture; doctorate programme in Social Science; Dir ROBERTO BLANCARTE PIMENTEL; publ. *Estudios Sociológicos*.

Comisión Nacional para el Desarrollo de los Pueblos Indígenas (National Commission for the Development of Indian Peoples): Avda México-Coyoacán 343, Col. Xoco, Del. Benito Juárez 03330 México, DF; tel. (55) 9183-2100; e-mail dirgral@cdi.gob.mx; internet www.cdi.gob.mx; f. 1948; forms links with indigenous communities of Mexico; organs incl. 23 co-ordinating centres in the interior, radio stations transmitting in 31 indigenous languages, 29 regional documentation and information centres; library: specialized library of 25,000 vols; Dir-Gen. XÓCHITL GÁLVEZ RUIZ; publs *Colección Historia de los Pueblos Indígenas de México*, *México Indígena*.

Instituto Indigenista Interamericano (Inter-American Indian Institute): Avda de las Fuentes 106, Col. Jardines de Pedregal, Del. Álvaro Obregón, 01900 México, DF; tel. (55) 5595-8410; e-mail ininin@prodigy.net.mx; internet www.indigenista.org; f. 1940; supplies technical assistance to member governments for the Indian population of the continent; library of 40,000 vols; Dir GUILLERMO ESPINOSA VELASCO; publ. *América Indígena* (4 a year).

Instituto Nacional de Antropología e Historia (National Institute of Anthropology and History): Córdoba 45, Col. Roma, 06700 México, DF; tel. (55) 5533-2015; fax (55) 5525-2213; e-mail difusion@inah.gob.mx; internet www.inah.gob.mx; f. 1939; govt organization for research, conservation and promotion of Mexican cultural heritage, especially archaeological and historical sites; controls 105 museums, incl. Museo Nacional de Antropología, Museo Nacional de Historia, Museo Nacional del Virreinato, Museo Nacional de las Intervenciones, Museo Nacional de las Culturas, Museo del Templo Mayor and Galería de Historia; manages Escuela Nacional de Antropología e Historia, Escuela Nacional de Conservación, Restauración y Museografía, National Anthropology and History Library, National Photographic Archives and Phonographic Archive; Dir-Gen. SERGIO RAÚL ARROYO GARCÍA; publs *Boletín* (anthropology, ethnology, history and archaeology, 4 a year), *Arqueología* (archaeology, 2 a year), *Historias* (history and related subjects, 3 a year), *Alquimia* (conservation and photographic archives, 3 a year), *Dimensión Antropológica* (anthropology, linguistics and ethnology, 3 a year), *Museos de México y del Mundo* (museology, in English and Spanish, 2 a year).

TECHNOLOGY

Instituto de Investigaciones Eléctricas (Institute of Electrical Research): Calle Reforma No. 113, Col. Palmira, 62490 Cuernavaca, Mor.; tel. (777) 362-3811; fax (777) 318-9854; e-mail difusion@iie.org.mx; internet www.iie.org.mx; f. 1975 to promote and undertake research and experimental development in the electrical industry; consulting service; library of 61,284 vols; Exec. Dir Ing. OSWALDO GANGOITI RUÍZ; publs *Boletín IIE*, *Referencias IIE*.

Instituto Mexicano de Investigaciones Tecnológicas (IMIT, AC): Calz. Legaria 694, Col. Irrigación, Del. Miguel Hidalgo, 11500 Mexico DF; tel. (55) 5557-1022; fax (55) 5395-4147; f. 1950; applied research on natural resources and development of industrial processes; pre-investment studies, reports process and conceptual engineering; library: specialized library in chemical technology of 12,000 vols, 250 periodicals; Dir Dr MARTÍNEZ FRÍAS.

Instituto Mexicano del Petróleo (Mexican Petroleum Institute): Eje Central Norte L. Cárdenas 152, Col. San Bartolo Atepehuecan, Apdo 14–805, 07730 México, DF; tel. (55) 9175-6000; fax (55) 9175-8000; e-mail sabugalp@imp.mx; internet www.imp.mx; f. 1967; research on petroleum products and equipment, petroleum and petrochemical industries, economic studies, exploration, refining; training and specialist courses; 5,000 mems; library of 46,000 vols; Gen. Dir JOSÉ LUIS GARCÍA LUNA H.; publ. *Revista* (quarterly).

Libraries and Archives

Chapingo

Biblioteca Central–Universidad Autónoma Chapingo (Central Library–Chapingo Autonomous University): Km. 38.5 Carretera México-Texcoco, 56230 Texcoco, Edo de México; tel. (595) 952-1500 ext. 5741; fax (595) 952-1501; e-mail biblioteca_central@correo.chapingo.mx; internet www.ceres.chapingo.mx; f. 1870; 175,000 vols, 3,100 periodicals, 8500 maps; spec. colln on the Mexican Agricultural Congress; Dir Lic. VÍCTOR HERNÁNDEZ GÓMEZ; publs *Revista de Chapingo* (in 3 series, irregular), *Revista de Geografía Agrícola* (in 3 series, irregular).

Guadalajara

Coordinación de Bibliotecas, Universidad de Guadalajara (University of Guadalajara Library Services): Avda Juárez 976, Edif. Cultural y Administrativo, piso 7, 44100 Guadalajara, Jal.; tel. (33) 3134-2277; fax (33) 3134-2205; e-mail sergiolr@redudg.udg.mx; internet www.rebiudg.udg.mx; f. 1861, new name 1994; depository for UNESCO publs; 1,660,353 vols, 13,588 periodicals (2,068 print, 11,520 electronic); Dir Mtro. SERGIO LÓPEZ RUELAS.

Mexico City

Archivo General de la Nación (National Archives): Avda Eduardo Molina y Albañiles s/n, Col. Penitenciaría Ampliación, Deleg. Venustiano Carranza, 15350 México, DF; tel. (55) 5133-9900; fax (55) 5789-5296; e-mail argena@segob.gob.mx; internet www.agn.gob.mx; f. 1795; documents relating to the vice-regal administration of New Spain, the Inquisition, independence 1821–40, the 19th c., the Mexican Revolution 1910, and the years up to 1976 (50 km of documents); 49,000 books; 1,050 prehispanic paintings; newspaper collection of 1,272,000 copies; microfilm service and library; Dir-Gen. Mtro JORGE RUIZ DUEÑAS; publ. *Boletín* (4 a year).

Biblioteca Central de la Universidad Nacional Autónoma de México (Central Library of the National Autonomous University of Mexico): Ciudad Universitaria, 04510 México, DF; tel. (55) 5622-1603; fax (55) 5616-0664; e-mail web-bc@dgb.unam.mx; internet bc.unam.mx; f. 1924; 350,000 vols, 2,883 periodicals, 265,000 theses; Dir-Gen. of Libraries Dra SILVIA GONZÁLEZ MARÍN; Sub-Dir of the Central Library Lic. ADRIANA HERNÁNDEZ SÁNCHEZ.

Biblioteca de Derecho y Legislación de la Secretaría de Hacienda (Law Library, Finance Ministry): Correo Mayor 31, México, DF; f. 1925, present form 1928; 13,000 vols; specialized library relating to ancient and existing federal laws, tax laws from 1831, foreign and international laws; Librarian SOFÍA SILVA.

Biblioteca de Historia de la Secretaría de Hacienda (Historical Library, Finance Ministry): Palacio Nacional, 06066 México, DF; f. 1939 with the collections of the old library of the Finance Ministry and those of Genaro Estrada acquired by the Government; 8,750 vols, 14,000 pamphlets relating to Mexico.

Biblioteca de la Secretaría de Comercio y Industria: Avda Cuauhtémoc y Dr Liceaga, México 7, DF; f. 1918; economic material, statistical annuals, census returns for population, livestock, etc; trade statistics; 42,250 vols; Librarian Lic. MARÍA TERESA HERNÁNDEZ G.

Biblioteca de la Secretaría de Comunicaciones y Transportes (Library of the Ministry of Communications and Transport): Tacuba y Xicotecatl, México, DF; f. 1891; 10,000 vols; Dir RENATO MOLINE ENRÍQUEZ.

Biblioteca de la Secretaría de Gobernación (Library of the Ministry of the Interior): Bucareli 99, 06699 México, DF; f. 1917; 45,000 vols.

Biblioteca 'José Ma. Lafragua' ('José Ma. Lafragua' Library): Ex Colegio de la Santa Cruz de Tlatelolco, Plaza de las Tres Culturas, Avda R. Flores Magón 1, Col. Guerrero, 06995 México, DF; tel. (55) 5063-3000, ext. 4102; e-mail sgaytan@sre.gob.mx; internet www.gob.mx/wb/egobierno/egob_Biblioteca_Jose_Ma_Lafragua; f. 19th c.; 35,000 vols; specializes in international relations and social sciences; Dir Dra MERCEDES DE VEGA ARMIJO.

Biblioteca Vasconcelos (Vasconcelos Library): Eje 1 Norte esq Aldama, Buenavista, México, DF; tel. (55) 1253-9100 ext. 8102; e-mail bvasconcelos@correo.conaculta.gob.mx; internet www.bibliotecavasconcelos.gob.mx; f. 1946; 500,000 vols, special collections, hall for the blind and visually-impaired; Dir JORGE VON ZIEGLER; publ. *Biblioteca de México* (6 a year).

Biblioteca del Honorable Congreso de la Unión (Congress Library): Biblioteca Unidad Centro Histórico, Edif. de la ex-Iglesia de Santa Clara, Tacuba 29, 06000 México, DF; tel. (55) 5510-3866; fax (55) 5512-1085; e-mail emolina@servidor.unam.mx; internet www.cddhcu.gob.mx/bibcong; f. 1936; 110,000 vols, 95 periodicals; Dir ENRIQUE MOLINA LEÓN.

Attached institution:

Sistema Integral de Información y Documentación (SIID) (Integral System of Information and Documentation): Palacio Legislativo de San Lázaro, Avda Congreso de la Unión s/n, 15969 México, DF; tel. (55) 5628-1318; fax (55) 5522-1463; e-mail siid@info.cddhcu.gob.mx; internet www.cddhcu.gob.mx/bibcongr/integra/siid.htm; f. 1991; collns of the old libraries of the Chamber of Deputies and the Chamber of Senators; 60,000 vols, 489 periodicals; Dir Lic. D. M. LIAHUT BALDOMAR.

Biblioteca del Instituto Nacional de Salud Pública (National Institute of Public Health Library): Insp-Biblioteca, Avda Universidad 655, Col. Santa Maria Ahuacatitlán, 62508 Cuernavaca, Mor.; tel. (777) 311-29-30-00 ext. 6252; fax (777) 101-29-10; e-mail atalani@insp.mx; internet www.insp.mx; f. 1922; specialized collections in public health medical administration, hygiene, preventive medicine, epidemiology, statistics, mental hygiene, nutrition, rehabilitation, occupational safety, industrial hygiene and water, air, noise and waste pollution engineering; 35,000 vols, 800 periodicals; Librarian Lic. NATALIA LÓPEZ LÓPEZ; publ. *Salud Pública de México* (6 a year).

Biblioteca 'Miguel Lerdo de Tejada' de la Secretaría de Hacienda y Crédito Público (General Library, Finance Ministry): Avda República de El Salvador 49, Centro Histórico, México, DF; tel. (55) 9158-9837; fax (55) 5709-5144; e-mail unidpc06@hacienda.gob.mx; internet www.shcp.gob.mx/servs/dgpcap/bmlt; f. 1928; 250,000 vols; Dir ROMÁN BELTRÁN MARTÍNEZ.

Biblioteca Nacional de Antropología e Historia 'Dr Eusebio Dávalos Hurtado' (National Library of Anthropology and History): Avda Paseo de la Reforma y Calzada Gandhi, 1er. Piso, Col. Polanco, 11560 México, DF; tel. (55) 5553-6865; fax (55) 5286-1743; e-mail subtec.bnah@inah.gob.mx; internet www.bnah.inah.gob.mx; f. 1888 as Library of the Instituto Nacional de Antropología e Historia de México (see Research Institutes); 550,000 vols, 8,000 periodicals; Dir CÉSAR MOHENO; publs *Arqueología* (4 a year), *Arqueología Mexicana* (6 a year), *Alquimía* (4 a year), *Dimensión Antropológica* (3 a year), *Historias* (2 a year).

Biblioteca Nacional de México (National Library): Centro Cultural Universitario, C.U., Delegación Coyoacán, 04510 México, DF; tel. (55) 5622-6800; fax (55) 5665-0951; e-mail gasca@biblional.bibliog.unam.mx; internet www.bibliog.unam.mx/bib/biblioteca.html; f. 1867; run by Bibliographic Research Institute of the National University of Mexico; 1,250,000 vols, and other items relating to the political, social, artistic, literary and historical development of Mexico; Library Co-ordinator Mtra. ROSA MARÍA GASCA NUÑEZ.

Hemeroteca Nacional de México (National Library of Periodicals): Centro Cultural Universitario, C.U., Delegación Coyoacán, 04510 México, D.F.; tel. (55) 5622-6818; fax (55) 5665-0951; e-mail curielg@biblional.bibliog.unam.mx; internet www.bibliog.unam.mx/hem/hemeroteca.html; f. 1912; run by Bibliographic Research Institute of the National University of Mexico; 250,000 vols; newspapers and periodicals; Mexican Gazette of 18th c.; Co-ordinator Mtra GUADALUPE CURIEL DEFOSSÉ.

Instituto Nacional de Bellas Artes y Literatura (Educación e Investigación Artísticas) (National Institute of Fine Arts and Literature (Art Education and Research)): Paseo de la Reforma y Campo Marte s/n, Col. Chapultepec Polanco, 11560 México, DF; tel. (55) 5521-9251; fax (55) 5280-5364; internet www.cnca.gob.mx/cnca/buena/inba; f. 1947; incorporates several centres, each of which inherited specialist material from the former Biblioteca Ibero-Americana y de Bellas Artes.

Incorporated centres:

Centro de Documentación y Biblioteca (Documentation Centre and Library): Eje Lázaro Cárdenas 2, 3er Piso (Torre Latinoamericana), Col. Centro, 06007 México, DF; f. 1984; specializes in Mexican literature; 3,500 vols; database LIME-INBA of the Mexican literature contained in the principal libraries of Mexico City; Dir Lic. JORGE PEREZ-GROVAS.

Centro Nacional de Investigación y Documentación de las Artes Plásticas (National Centre for Research and Documentation on the Plastic Arts): Calle Nueva York 224, Col. Nápoles, 03810 México, DF.

Centro Nacional de Investigación de Información y Documentación de la Danza José Limón (José Limón National Centre for Research, Information and Dance Documentation): Campos Eliseos 480, Col. Polanco, 11560 México, DF.

Centro Nacional de Investigación y Documentación Musical Carlos Chávez (Carlos Chávez National Centre for Research and Music Documentation): Liverpool 16, Col. Juárez, 06600 México, DF.

Centro Nacional de Investigación e Información Teatral Rodolfo Usigli (Rodolfo Usigli National Centre for Research and Theatre Information): Chihuahua 216, Esquina Monterrey, Col. Roma, 06760 México, DF.

Monterrey

Biblioteca del Instituto Tecnológico y de Estudios Superiores de Monterrey (Library of the Monterrey Institute of Technology and Higher Studies): Avda Eugenio Garza Sada 2501 Sur, Sucursal de Correos 'J', Col. Tecnológico, 64849 Monterrey (Nuevo León); tel. (81) 8328-4096; fax (81) 8328-4067; e-mail miguel_arreola@itesm.mx; internet biblioteca.mty.itesm.mx; f. 1943; more than 200 library instructional workshops annually; nat. and int. interlibrary loan (to USA and Europe); organizes int. book fair, conferences, academic congresses.; 400,000 vols, 19,000 periodicals of which more than 18,000 are electronic; digital library with more than 64 databases; Dir Ing. MIGUEL ARREOLA; publs *Calidad Ambiental* (quarterly), *Integratec* (6 a year), *Revista de Humanidades* (2 a year), *Transferencia* (quarterly).

Puebla

Biblioteca de la Universidad de las Américas (Library of the Universidad de las Américas): POB 100, Santa Catarina Mártir, San Andrés, 72820 Cholula, Pue.; tel. (222) 229-2257; fax (222) 229-2078; e-mail bibinfo@mail.udlap.mx; internet ciria.udlap.mx/bibliotecas; f. 1940; humanities, science and technology; 400,000 vols, 2,200 periodicals; special collection; M. Covarrubias archives, R. Barlow archives, Herrera Carrillo archives, Porfirio Díaz archives; Dir Mtro ARTURO ARRIETA.

Toluca

Biblioteca Pública Central del Estado de México (Main Public Library of México State): Centro Cultural Mexiquense, 50000 Toluca (Estado de México); f. 1827; 40,012 vols, 128 periodicals; Dir MARÍA CRISTINA PÉREZ GÓMEZ.

Tuxtla Gutiérrez

Biblioteca Pública del Estado de Chiapas (Public Library of Chiapas State): Blvd Angel Albino Corzo Km 1087, Tuxtla Gutiérrez, Chiapas; tel. (961) 3-06-64; f. 1910; 45,000 vols; Dir JOSÉ LUIS CASTRO.

Zacatecas

Bibliotecas Públicas de Zacatecas (Zacatecas Public Libraries): Plaza Independencia 1, 98000 Zacatecas; internet www.angelfire.com/nh/luishugo; f. 1832; consists of the following libraries: Biblioteca Central Estatal 'Mauricio Magdaleno', Biblioteca de Colecciones Especiales 'Elias Amador'; Dir (vacant).

Museums and Art Galleries

Campeche

Museo Regional de Campeche (Campeche Regional Museum): Calle 59 entre 16 y 14, Campeche, Camp.; f. 1985; archaeology and history; Dir Arq. JOSÉ E. ORTÍZ LAN.

Guadalajara

Casa Taller José Clemente Orozco (House and Studio of José Clemente Orozco): Calle Aurelio Aceves 27, Col. Arcos Vallarta, 44120 Guadalajara, Jalisco; tel. (33) 3818-2800 ext. 31063; fax (33) 3818-2800 ext. 31014; e-mail museocabanas_lpb@yahoo.com.mx; internet http://vive.guadalajara.gob.mx/puntos/puntose.asp?which=221; f. 1951; paintings and sketches by the artist; Dir MARGARITA V. DE OROZCO.

Museo del Estado de Jalisco (Jalisco State Museum): Liceo 60, Centro Histórico, 44100 Guadalajara, Jalisco; tel. (33) 3613-2703; fax (33) 3614-5257; f. 1918; collections of early Mexican objects; folk art and costumes; archaeological discoveries; anthropological, archaeological and historical research; library of 6,000 vols; Dir CARLOS R. BELTRÁN BRISEÑO.

Museo Regional de Guadalajara (Guadalajara Regional Museum): Liceo 60, Zona Centro, 44100 Guadalajara, Jalisco; tel. (33) 3613-2705; fax (33) 3614-5257; e-mail mrg-inahjalisco@prodigy.net.mx; internet vive.guadalajara.gob.mx/puntos/puntose.asp?which=221; f. 1918; special collections of pre-Spanish and Colonial period art and paintings; archaeological and palaeontological collections; Dir Lic. CRISTINA SÁNCHEZ DEL REAL.

Guanajuato

Museos de la Universidad de Guanajuato (University Museums): Lascuraín de Retana 5, 36000 Guanajuato, Guan.; f. 1870; comprise: Natural History, Geology, Mineralogy, and include the natural history collection of Alfredo Duges with many rare specimens.

Madero

Museo de la Cultura Huasteca (Museum of Huastec Culture): POB 12, 89050 Madero, Tamaulipas; located at: Blvd A. López Mateos s/n, Tampico, Tamaulipas; tel. and fax (833) 210-2217; f. 1960; attached to the Instituto Nacional de Antropología e Historia; library of 1,750 vols, 95 discs; Dir C. P. MA. ALEJANDRINA ELÍAS ORTIZ.

Mérida

Museo Regional de Antropología (Regional Museum of Anthropology): Palacio Canton, Calle 43 por Paseo de Montejo, Mérida, Yucatán; tel. and fax (999) 923-0557; f. 1920; attached to the Instituto Nacional de Antropología e Historia; collections of Pre-Hispanic Mayan and Olmec culture, precious stones, ceramics, jade, objects in copper and gold; Dir AGUSTÍN PEÑA CASTILLO.

Mexico City

Laboratorio Arte Alameda (Alameda Laboratory of Arts): Dr Mora 7, Col. Centro Histórico, 06050 México, DF; tel. (55) 5510-2793; fax (55) 5512-2079; e-mail info.artealameda@gmail.com; internet www.artealameda.inba.gob.mx; f. 1962 as Pinacoteca Virreinal de San Diego, a museum of Mexican colonial arts; present name and collections 2000; attached to Instituto Nacional de Bellas Artes; collections of new media and electronic art; library of 5,000 vols; Dir MARIANA MUNGUIA; Curator PRÍAMO LOZADA.

Museo de Arte Alvar y Carmen T. de Carrillo Gil (Alvar and Carmen T. de Carrillo Gil Museum of Art): Avda Revolución 1608, Col. San Angel, Del. Alvaro Obregón, 01000 México, DF; tel. (55) 5550-3983; fax (55) 5550-4232; e-mail macg.cashida@correo.inba.gob.mx; internet www.macg.inba.gob.mx; f. 1974; contemporary Mexican art; library of 3,500 vols; Dir CARLOS ASHIDA; publ. *Gazeta del Museo* (monthly).

Museo de Arte Contemporáneo Rufino Tamayo (Rufino Tamayo Museum of Contemporary Art): Paseo de la Reforma y Gandhi s/n, Bosque de Chapultepec, Del. Miguel Hidalgo, 11580 México, DF; tel. (55) 5286-5839; fax (55) 5286-6539; f. 1981; permanent collection of contemporary art, permanent exhibition of Rufino Tamayo's work; temporary exhibits of international artists; library specializing in Rufino Tamayo, contemporary art and artists; Dir CRISTINA GÁLVEZ GUZZY.

Museo de Arte Moderno (Museum of Modern Art): Bosque de Chapultepec, Paseo de la Reforma y Gandhi, 11560 México, DF; tel. (55) 5553-6233; fax (55) 5553-6211; e-mail mam.direccion@conaculta.inba.gob.mx; internet www.conaculta.gob.mx/mam; f. 1964; mainly Mexican collection of modern and contemporary art and temporary exhibitions of modern Mexican and foreign art; Dir Prof. LUIS- MARTIN LOZANO.

Museo de Historia Natural de la Ciudad de México (Natural History Museum of the City of Mexico): 2° Sección del Bosque de Chapultepec, Apdo Postal 18–845, Del. Miguel Hidalgo, 11800 México, DF; tel. (55) 5515-6304; fax (55) 5515-2222; e-mail mhn@df.gob.mx; internet www.sma.df.gob.mx/mhn; f. 1964; exhibitions on the universe, the earth, the origin of life, plant and animal taxonomy, evolution and adaptation of species, biology, man and bio-geographical areas; contains replicas of prehistoric creatures; library of 6,000 vols; Dir Biol. NEMESIO CHÁVEZ ARREDONDO.

Museo del Palacio de Bellas Artes (Museum of the Palace of Fine Arts): Avda Juárez y Eje Central 'Lázaro Cardenas', Centro Histórico, Del. Cuauhtémoc, 06050 México, DF; tel. (55) 5512-2593; fax (55) 5510-1388; e-mail difusion@museobellasartes.artte.com; internet www.cnca.gob.mx/palacio/museo.htm; f. 1934; attached to the Instituto Nacional de Bellas Artes; permanent exhibition 'Los Grandes Muralistas'; Dir Arq. AGUSTÍN ARTEAGA.

Museo Estudio Diego Rivera (Museum of Diego Rivera's Studio): Calle Diego Rivera s/n esq. Avda Altavista, Col. San Angel Inn, 01060 México, DF; tel. (55) 5550-1518; fax (55) 5550-1004; internet www.cnca.gob.mx/cnca/buena/inba/subbellas/museos/rivera.html; f. 1986; permanent exhibition 'Estudio Taller de Diego Rivera'.

Museo Nacional de Antropología (National Museum of Anthropology): Avda Paseo de la Reforma y Calzada Gandhi s/n, Col. Chapultepec Polanco, Delegación Miguel Hidalgo, 11560 México, DF; tel. (55) 5553-6266; fax (55) 5286-1791; e-mail atencion.mna@inah.gob.mx; internet www.mna.inah.gob.mx; f. 1940; attached to the Instituto Nacional de Antropología e Historia; anthropological, ethnological, and archaeological subjects relating to Mexico; 6,000 exhibits; library of 300,000 vols; Dir Arqlgo. FELIPE SOLÍS OLGUÍN; publs *Cuadernos*, *Guides*.

Museo Nacional de Arquitectura (National Museum of Architecture): Palacio de Bellas Artes, Avda Juárez 4, Centro Histórico, Del. Cuauhtémoc, 06050 México, DF; tel. (55) 5510-2475; fax (55) 5510-2853; e-mail mnalarq@correo.inba.gob.mx; internet www.inba.gob.mx; f. 1984; important examples of Mexican architecture through the ages; photographic archive; original plans by Adamo Boari, Federico Mariscal, Juan O'Gorman, Carlos Obregón Santacilia, Mario Pani, Enrique del Moral, José Villagrán, Juan Segura, Francisco Centeno and Francisco J. Serrano; original drawings of the Palacio de Bellas Artes; Dir XAVIER GUZMÁN.

Museo Nacional de Arte (National Museum of Art): Tacuba 8, Centro Histórico, Del. Cuauhtémoc, 06010 México, DF; tel. (55) 5130-3400; fax (55) 5130-3401; e-mail munal@munal.com.mx; internet www.munal.com.mx; f. 1982; permanent exhibitions of Mexican art from 16th c. to 1950; library of 39,000 vols; Dir ROXANA VELÁSQUEZ; publ. *Revista Memoria*.

Museo Nacional de Artes e Industrias Populares del Instituto Nacional Indigenista (National Museum of Traditional Arts and Crafts, National Institute of Indigenous People): Avda Juárez 44, 06050 México, DF; internet www.cuauhtemoc.df.gob.mx/turismo/museos/corpus.html; f. 1951; examples of traditional Mexican art of all periods, conservation and encouragement of traditional handicrafts; Dir MARÍA TERESA POMAR.

Museo Nacional de las Culturas (National Museum of Cultures): Calle de Moneda 13, Col. Centro Histórico, 06060 México, DF; tel. (55) 5542-0165; fax (55) 5542-0422; e-mail direccion.cmuseo@inah.gob.mx; internet www.inah.gob.mx/muse1/html/muse13.html; attached to the Instituto Nacional de Antropología e Historia; f. 1965; collections of archaeology and ethnology from all over the world; public lectures, special courses for teachers, training in plastic arts; library of 11,862 vols; Dir Antrop. MOISÉS LEONEL DURÁN SOLÍS.

Museo Nacional de la Estampa: Avda Hidalgo 39, Col. Centro, Delg. Cuauhtémoc, 06050 México, DF; tel. (55) 5521-2244; fax (55) 5521-2244; permanent exhibition 'Proceso Histórico de la Estampa en México'.

Museo Nacional de Historia (National Historical Museum): Reforma y Gandhi, 1a Sección del Bosque de Chapultepec, Delegación Miguel Hidalgo, 11580 México, DF; tel. (55) 5241-3100; fax (55) 5241-3132; e-mail difusion.mnh@inah.gob.mx; internet www.mnh.inah.gob.mx; f. 1944; attached to the Instituto Nacional de Antropología e Historia; history of Mexico since the 16th c.; historical paintings, flags, weapons, documents, jewellery, textiles, ceramics, furniture, clothing and other objects of social and cultural history; Dir Lic. LUCIANO CEDILLO ÁLVAREZ.

Museo Nacional de las Intervenciones (National Museum of the Interventions in Mexico): General Anaya y 20 de agosto, Del. Coyoacán, 04100 México, DF; tel. (55) 5604-0699; fax (55) 5604-0981; internet www.cnca.gob.mx/cnca/inah/museos/munaint.html; f. 1981; government-owned museum attached to the Instituto Nacional de Antropología e Historia; exhibitions show history of foreign interventions and Mexican independence; library of 800 vols; Dir Lic. MONICA CUEVAS Y LARA.

Museo Nacional de San Carlos (San Carlos Museum): Puente de Alvarado 50, Col. Tabacalera, 06030 México, DF; tel. (55) 5566-8085; fax (55) 5535-1256; e-mail mnsancarlos@mail.com; internet www.bellasartes.gob.mx/INBA/TemplateINBA; f. 1968; attached to Instituto Nacional de Bellas Artes; colln of 14th–19th c. European panels, paintings, sculpture, drawings and prints; housed within the Palace of the Counts of Buenavista designed by Manuel Tolsá; library of 2,633 vols; Dir MARÍA FERNANDA MATOS MOCTEZUMA; publ. *Bulletin* (3 a year).

Monterrey

Museo Regional de Nuevo León (Regional Museum of Nuevo León): Rafael José Verger s/n, Col. Obispado, Apdo 291, 64010 Monterrey, Nuevo León; tel. (81) 833-9588; fax (81) 8346-0404; f. 1956; regional and Mexican history, archaeology and painting; Dir Arq. JAVIER SÁNCHEZ GARCÍA.

Morelia

Museo Regional Michoacano (Michoacan Museum): Calle de Allende 305 esq. con Abasolo, Centro Histórico de Morelia, 58000 Morelia, Michoacán; tel. and fax (443) 12-0407; f. 1886; archaeological, ecological, ethnographical and prehistoric collections of the district; library of 10,000 vols; Dir Arq. PAUL DELGADO LAMAS; publ. *Anales*.

Oaxaca

Museo de las Culturas de Oaxaca (Museum of the Cultures of Oaxaca): Apdo 68000, 'Ex-Convento de Santo Domingo', Macedonio Alcalá y Adolfo Gurrión s/n, Oaxaca, Oax.; tel. (951) 6-2991; internet www.inah.gob.mx/muse2/htme/mure2001.html; f. 1933; anthropology, archaeology, ethnography and religious art; contains the famous archaeological treasures found in Tomb No. 7, Monte Albán, jewellery; Dir JESÚS MARTÍNEZ ARVIZU.

Patzcuaro

Museo Regional de Artes Populares (Regional Museum of Arts and Crafts): Enseñanza y Alcantarilla s/n, Pátzcuaro, Michoacán; f. 1935; ancient and modern ethnographical exhibits relating to the Tarascan Indians of Michoacán; colonial and contemporary native art; Dir RAFAELA LUFT DÁVALOS.

Puebla

Museo de Arte 'José Luis Bello y González' ('José Luis Bello y González' Museum of Art): Avda 3 Poniente 302, Puebla, Pue.; f. 1938, opened to the public 1944; contains: ivories, porcelain, wrought iron, furniture, clocks, watches, musical instruments, etc., Mexican, Chinese and European paintings, sculptures, pottery, vestments, tapestries, ceramics, miniatures, etc.

Museo Regional de Santa Mónica (Santa Monica Regional Museum): Avda Poniente 103, Puebla, Pue.; f. 1940; religious art; comprises the collections of various disbanded convents and now housed in that of Santa Mónica.

Museo Regional del Estado de Puebla (Puebla State Regional Museum): Casa del Alfeñique, 4 Oriente No. 416, Puebla, Pue.; f. 1931; notable historical collections; Dir JUAN ARMENTA CAMACHO.

Querétaro

Museo Regional de Querétaro (Querétaro Historical Museum): Calle Corregidora Sur 3, 76000 Querétaro, Qro; tel. (442) 20-2031; internet www.queretaro-mexico.com.mx/coneculta/regional.html; f. 1936; local history and art; Dir MANUEL OROPEZA SEGURA.

Tepotzotlán

Museo Nacional del Virreinato (National Museum of the Vice-Royalty): Plaza Hidalgo 99, 54600 Tepotzotlán, Estado de México; tel. (55) 5876-0245; fax (55) 5876-0332; e-mail virreinato.museo@inah.gob.mx; internet www.munavi.inah.gob.mx; f. 1964; attached to the Instituto Nacional de Antropología e Historia; collections on the art and culture of the Colonial period; housed in 17th–18th c. building, formerly belonging to the Jesuits; library of 4,000 vols from 16th–19th c.; Dir MIGUEL EMIGDIO FERNÁNDEZ FÉLIX.

Toluca

Museo de las Bellas Artes (Museum of Fine Arts): Calle de Santos Degollado 102, Toluca Edo. de México; internet www.turista.com.mx/edomexico; paintings, sculptures, Mexican colonial art; Dir Prof. JOSÉ M. CABALLERO-BARNARD.

Tuxtla Gutiérrez

Museo Regional de Chiapas (Chiapas Regional Museum): Calzada de los Hombres Ilustres s/n, Parque Madero, 29000 Tuxtla Gutiérrez, Chiapas; tel. (961) 622-0459; fax (961) 623-4554; f. 1939; archaeological and historical collections; Dir ROBERTO RAMOS MAZO.

Tzintzuntzan

Museo Etnográfico y Arqueológico (Ethnographical and Archaeological Museum): Tzintzuntzan, Michoacán; f. 1944; ethnographical and archaeological collections relating to the Tzinztuntzan and Tarascan zones of Lake Pátzcuaro.

Xalapa

Museo de Antropología de Xalapa, Universidad Veracruzana (Xalapa Museum of Anthropology, Veracruzana University): Avda Xalapa s/n, 91010 Xalapa, Veracruz; tel. (228) 815-0910; fax (228) 815-4952; e-mail museo@uv.mx; internet www.uv.mx/max; f. 1959; special regional archaeological collections of the Olmec, Totonac and Huastec cultures of ancient Mexico; Dir Dra SARA LADRÓN DE GUEVARA.

Universities

UNIVERSIDAD NACIONAL AUTÓNOMA DE MÉXICO

Ciudad Universitaria, Del. Coyoacán, 04510 México, DF
Telephone: (55) 5622-0958
Fax: (55) 5616-0245
E-mail: lal@hp.fciencias.unam.mx
Internet: www.unam.mx
Founded 1551
Language of instruction: Spanish
Academic year: August to May
Rector: Dr JUAN RAMÓN DE LA FUENTE RAMÍREZ
Secretary-General: Lic. ENRIQUE DEL VAL BLANCO
Administrative Secretary: Dr DANIEL BARRERA PÉREZ
Director of the Postgraduate Studies Office: Dra ROSAURA RUIZ GUTIÉRREZ
Director of the Office for Interinstitutional Collaboration: Mtra MÓNICA VEREA CAMPOS
Librarian: Dra SILVIA GONZÁLEZ MARÍN
Library: in addition to the National Library and Central Library (see under Libraries and Archives), there are 142 specialized libraries
Number of teachers: 29,979
Number of students: 269,000
Publications: *Acta Poética* (annually), *Acta Sociológica* (3 a year), *Anales de Antropología* (annually), *Anales del Instituto de Biología: Serie Botánica* (2 a year), *Anales del Instituto de Biología: Serie Zoología* (2 a year), *Anales del Instituto de Investigaciones Estéticas* (2 a year), *Anuario Jurídico* (annually), *Anuario de Letras* (annually), *Anuario de Letras Modernas* (annually), *Anuario de la Historia del Derecho Mexicano* (annually), *Antropológicas* (3 a year), *Antropología Física Latinoamericana* (annually), *Archivos Hispanoamericanas de Sexología* (2 a year), *Atmósfera* (4 a year), *Bibliografía Filosófica Mexicana* (annually), *Bibliografía Latinoamericana* (2 a year), *Biblioteca Universitaria* (2 a year), *Bien. Boletín de Investigación, Educación y sus Nexos* (3 a year), *Bien. Revista Especializada en Ciencias Sociales y la Educación* (2 a year), *Boletín Mexicano de Derecho Comparado* (3 a year), *Boletín de la Escuela Nacional de Música* (monthly), *Boletín del Instituto de Investigaciones Bibliográficas* (2 a year), *Carrizos* (4 a year), *Ciencias* (4 a year), *Clase: Citas Latinoamericanas en Ciencias Sociales y Humanidades* (4 a year), *¿Cómo ves?* (monthly), *Contaduría y Administración* (4 a year), *Crítica Jurídica* (2 a year), *Crítica: Revista Hispanoamericana de Filosofía* (3 a year), *Cuadernos Americanos* (6 a year), *Chicomóztoc: Boletín del Seminario de Estudios para la Descolonización de México* (annually), *Demos: Carta Demográfica sobre México* (annually), *Desde el Sur: Humanismo y Ciencia* (4 a year), *Dianoia: Anuario de Filosofía* (annually), *Diógenes* (4 a year), *Discurso: Cuadernos de Teoría y Análisis* (2 a year), *Economía Informa* (monthly), *Educación Química* (6 a year), *Emprendedores* (6 a year), *Estudios de Antropología Biológica* (every 2 years), *Estudios de Cultura Maya* (every 2 years), *Estudios de Cultura Náhuatl* (every 2 years), *Estudios de Cultura Otopame* (every 2 years), *Estudios de Historia Moderna y Contemporánea de México* (annually), *Estudios de Historia Novohispana* (annually), *Estudios de Lingüística Aplicada* (2 a year), *Estudios Latinoamericanos* (2 a year), *Estudios Políticos* (3 a year), *Experiencia Literaria* (irregular), *Ingeniería, Investigación y Tecnología* (4 a year), *Investigación Bibliotecológica* (2 a year), *Investigación Económica* (4 a year), *Investigaciones Geográficas* (2 a year), *La Experiencia Literaria* (irregular), *Latinoamérica: Anuario de Estudios Latinoamericanos* (irregular), *Los Universitarios* (6 a year), *Mathesis* (4 a year), *Medievalia* (2 a year), *Momento Económico–Información y Análisis de la Conjuntura Económica* (6 a year), *Nova Tellus: Anuario del Centro de Estudios Clásicos* (2 a year), *Nuevo Consultorio Fiscal–Laboral y Contable-Financiero* (26 a year), *Omnia* (4 a year), *Perfiles Educativos* (4 a year), *Pluralitas* (electronic, monthly), *Poligrafías–Revista de Literatura Comparada* (annually), *Periódica: Indice de Revistas Latinoamericanas en Ciencias* (4 a year), *Problemas del Desarrollo: Revista Latinoamericana de Economía* (4 a year), *Punto de Partida* (6 a year), *Relaciones Internacionales* (3 a year), *Revista CIHMECH* (annually), *Revista de Derecho Privado* (3 a year), *Revista de la Facultad de Medicina* (6 a year), *Revista de Zoología* (2 a year), *Revista Mexicana de Astronomía y Astrofísica* (2 a year), *Revista Mexicana de Ciencias Geológicas* (2 a year), *Revista Mexicana de Ciencias Políticas y Sociales* (4 a year), *Revista Mexicana de Sociología* (4 a year), *Revista Veterinaria – México* (4 a year), *Sinopsis* (annually), *Tempus* (irregular), *Theoría: Revista del Colegio de Filosofía* (3 a year), *Tip. Revista Especializada en Ciencias Químicas Biológicas* (2 a year), *Tip. Tópicos de Investigación y Posgrado* (3 a year), *Trabajo Social* (4 a year), *UNAM Hoy* (6 a year), *Universidad de México* (monthly), *Vertientes–Revista Especializada en Ciencias de la Salud* (2 a year), *Voices of México* (4 a year)

DIRECTORS OF FACULTIES AND SCHOOLS

Faculty of Accounting and Administration: Mtro ARTURO DÍAZ ALONSO
Faculty of Architecture: Arq. FELIPE GERARDO LEAL FERNÁNDEZ
Faculty of Basic Sciences: Dr RAMÓN PERALTA Y FABI
Faculty of Chemistry: Dr ENRIQUE RODOLFO BAZÚA RUEDA
Faculty of Economics: Dr ROBERTO IVÁN ESCALANTE SEMERENA
Faculty of Engineering: Mtro GERARDO FERRANDO BRAVO
Faculty of Law: Lic. FERNANDO SERRANO MIGALLÓN
Faculty of Medicine: Dr JOSÉ NARRO ROBLES
Faculty of Odontology: Dr JOSÉ ANTONIO VELA CAPDEVILLA
Faculty of Philosophy and Literature: Dr AMBROSIO FRANCISCO JAVIER VELASCO GÓMEZ
Faculty of Political and Social Sciences: Dr FERNANDO PÉREZ CORREA
Faculty of Psychology: Dra LUCY MARÍA REIDL MARTÍNEZ
Faculty of Veterinary Medicine and Animal Husbandry: Dr LUIS ALBERTO ZARCO QUINTERO
National Schools:
- National School of Music: Mtro LUIS ALFONSO ESTRADA RODRÍGUEZ
- National School of Nursing and Obstetrics: Lic. SEVERINO RUBIO DOMÍNGUEZ
- National School of Plastic Arts: Dra LUZ DEL CARMEN VILCHIS ESQUIVEL
- National School of Social Work: Mtro CARLOS ARTEAGA BASURTO

Multidisciplinary Units of Professional Studies:
- Faculty of Advanced Studies Cuautitlán: Dr JUAN ANTONIO MONTARAZ Y CRESPO
- Faculty of Advanced Studies Iztacala: Dr RAMIRO JESÚS SANDOVAL
- Faculty of Advanced Studies Zaragoza: Mtro JUAN FRANCISCO SÁNCHEZ RUIZ
- National School of Professional Studies Acatlán: Lic. HERMELINDA OSORIO CARRANZA
- National School of Professional Studies Aragón: Arq. LILIA TURCOTT GONZÁLEZ

ATTACHED RESEARCH INSTITUTES, CENTRES AND PROGRAMMES

Sciences:

Instituto de Astronomía (Institute of Astronomy): Dir Dra SILVIA TORRES DE PEIMBERT.

Instituto de Investigaciónes en Matemáticas Aplicadas y en Sistemas (Institute of Applied Mathematics and Systems Research): Dir Dr FRANCISCO JORGE O'REILLY TOGNO.

Instituto de Biología (Institute of Biology): Dir Dr HÉCTOR MANUEL HERNÁNDEZ MACÍAS.

Instituto de Investigaciones Biomédicas (Institute of Biomedical Research): Dir Dr JUAN PEDRO LACLETTE SAN ROMÁN.

Instituto de Química (Institute of Chemistry): Dir Dr RAYMUNDO CEA OLIVARES.

Instituto de Ingeniería (Institute of Engineering): Dir Dr SERGIO ALCOCER MARTÍNEZ DE CASTRO.

Instituto de Geografía (Institute of Geography): Dir Dr JOSÉ LUIS PALACIO PRIETO.

Instituto de Geología (Institute of Geology): Dir Dr GUSTAVO TOLSON JONES.

Instituto de Geofísica (Institute of Geophysics): Dir Dr JAIME URRUTIA FUCUGAUCHI.

Instituto de Matemáticas (Institute of Mathematics): Dir Dr JOSÉ ANTONIO DE LA PEÑA MENA.

Instituto de Física (Institute of Physics): Dir Dr FERNANDO MATÍAS MORENO YNTRIAGO.

Instituto de Ciencias del Mar y Limnología (Institute of Marine Sciences and Limnology): Dir Dr ADOLFO GRACIA GASCA.

Instituto de Investigaciones en Materiales (Institute of Materials Research): Dir Dr LUIS ENRIQUE SANSORES CUEVAS.

Instituto de Ciencias Nucleares (Institute of Nuclear Sciences): Dir Dr OCTAVIO CASTAÑOS GARZA.

Instituto de Fisiología Celular (Institute of Cellular Physiology): Dir Dr ADOLFO GARCÍA SÁINZ.

Instituto de Biotecnología (Institute of Biotechnology): Dir Dr FRANCISCO XAVIER SOBERÓN MAINERO.

Instituto de Ecología (Institute of Ecology): Dir Dr HÉCTOR ARITA WATANABÉ.

Centro de Ciencias de la Atmósfera (Centre for Atmospheric Sciences): Dir Dr CARLOS GAY GARCÍA.

Centro de Investigación sobre Fijación del Nitrógeno (Centre for Research on Nitrogen Fixation): Dir Dra GEORGINA HERNÁNDEZ DELGADO.

Instituto de Neurobiología (Institute of Neurobiology): Dir Dr CARLOS ARÁMBURO DE LA HOZ.

Centro de Investigación en Energía (Energy Research Centre): Dir Dr MANUEL MARTÍNEZ FERNÁNDEZ.

Centro de Ciencias de la Materia Condensada (Centre for Condensed Matter Science): Dir Dr LEONEL SUSANO COTA ARAIZA.

Centro de Ciencias Físicas (Centre for Physical Sciences): Dir Dr JORGE FLORES VALDÉS.

Centro de Ciencias Aplicadas y Desarrollo Tecnológico (Centre for Applied

Sciences and Technological Development): Dir Dr FELIPE LARA ROSANO.

Centro de Física Aplicada y Tecnología Avanzada (Centre for Advanced Technology and Applied Physics): Dir Dr VÍCTOR MANUEL CASTAÑO MENESES.

Centro de Geociencias Aplicadas (Centre for Applied Geosciences): Dir Dr LUCA FERRARI PEDRAGLIO.

Programa Universitario de Energía (University Programme on Energy): Dir Dr ARTURO REINKING CEJUDO.

Programa Universitario del Medio Ambiente y Diversidad (University Programme on the Environment and Diversity): Dir Dra IRMA ROSAS PÉREZ.

Programa Universitario de Alimentos (University Programme on Food): Dir Dr ALEJANDRO POLANCO JAIME.

Programa Universitario de Investigación en Salud (University Programme for Health Research): Dir Dr RAÚL AGUILAR ROBLERO.

Programa Universitario de Materiales (University Programme on Materials): Dir Dr RAMIRO PÉREZ CAMPOS.

Dirección de Programas Universitarios (Administration for University Programmes): Dir Dr PABLO MULÁS DEL POZO.

Humanities:

Instituto de Investigaciones Antropológicas (Institute of Anthropological Research): Dir Dra MARI CARMEN SERRA PUCHE.

Instituto de Investigaciones Estéticas (Institute of Aesthetics Research): Dir Dra MARÍA TERESA URIARTE CASTAÑEDA.

Instituto de Investigaciones Bibliográficas (Institute of Bibliographical Research): Dir Dr VICENTE QUIRARTE CASTAÑEDA.

Instituto de Investigaciones Económicas (Institute of Economic Research): Dir Dr JORGE BASAVE KUNHARDT.

Instituto de Investigaciones Históricas (Institute of Historical Research): Dir Dra VIRGINIA GUEDEA RINCÓN GALLARDO.

Instituto de Investigaciones Jurídicas (Institute of Legal Research): Dir Dr DIEGO VALADÉZ RÍOS.

Instituto de Investigaciones Filológicas (Institute of Philological Research): Dir Dr FERNANDO CURIEL DEFOSSÉ.

Instituto de Investigaciones Filosóficas (Institute of Philosophical Research): Dir Dra PAULETTE DIETERLEN STRUCK.

Instituto de Investigaciones Sociales (Institute of Social Research): Dir Dr RENÉ MILLÁN VALENZUELA.

Centro de Estudios sobre la Universidad (Centre for Studies on the University): Dir Dr AXEL DIDRIKSSON TAKAYANAGUI.

Centro de Investigaciones Interdisciplinarias en Ciencias y Humanidades (Centre for Interdisciplinary Research in Science and Humanities): Dir Dr DANIEL CAZÉZ MENCHE.

Centro Regional de Investigaciones Multidisciplinarias (Regional Centre for Multidisciplinary Research): Dir Mtro HÉCTOR HIRÁM HERNÁNDEZ BRINGAS.

Centro Universitario de Investigaciones Bibliotecológicas (University Centre for Library Science Research): Dir Dr FILBERTO FELIPE MARTÍNEZ ARELLANO.

Centro de Investigaciones sobre América del Norte (Centre for Research on North America): Dir Dr JOSÉ LUIS VALDÉS UGALDE.

Centro Coordinador y Difusor de Estudios Latinoamericanos (Centre for the Co-ordination and Promotion of Latin American Studies): Dir Dra ESTELA MORALES CAMPOS.

Programa Universitario de Estudios de Género (University Programme on Gender Studies): Dir Dra GRACIELA HIERRO PÉREZCASTRO.

Programa Universitario de Estudios sobre la Ciudad (University Programme on Studies of the City): Dir Dr MANUEL PERLÓ COHEN.

Attached Extension and Cultural Centres:

Centro de Enseñanza de Lenguas Extranjeras (Centre for Foreign Language Teaching): Dir Mtra MA. AURORA MARRÓN OROZCO.

Centro de Enseñanza para Extranjeros (Educational Centre for Foreign Students): Dir Dr GUILLERMO PULIDO GONZÁLEZ.

Centro de Enseñanza para Extranjeros en Taxco (Educational Centre for Foreign Students in Taxco): Dir Lic. GUSTAVO PEÑA HERNÁNDEZ.

Centro Universitario de Estudios Cinematográficos (University Centre for Cinematographic Studies): Dir Mtro MITL VALDEZ SALAZAR.

Centro Universitario de Teatro (University Centre for Theatre Studies): Dir Mtro JOSÉ RAMÓN ENRÍQUEZ.

Dirección General de Música (General Administration for Music): Dir Mtro SERGIO VELA.

Dirección de Literatura (Administration for Literature): Dir Mtro FELIPE GARRIDO.

Dirección de Teatro y Danza (Administration for Dramatic Arts and Dance): Dir Lic. MARIO ANTONIO VERA CRESTANI.

Dirección General de Actividades Cinematográficas (General Administration for Cinematographic Activities): Dir Biol. SERGIO IVÁN TRUJILLO.

Dirección General de Artes Plásticas (General Administration for Plastic Arts): Dir Dra LILY KASSNER.

Escuela Permanente de Extensión en San Antonio, Texas (Permanent Extension School, San Antonio, Texas, USA): Dir Lic. MARIO MELGAR.

Escuela de Extensión en Hull, Quebec, Canadá (Extension School, Hull, Quebec, Canada): Dir Mtra ESPERANZA GARRIDO REYES.

Dirección General de Radio UNAM (General Administration for Radio UNAM): Dir Lic. FERNANDO ESCALANTE SOBRINO.

Dirección General de Televisión Universitaria (General Administration for University Television): Dir Lic GUADALUPE FERRER.

UNIVERSIDAD AUTÓNOMA DEL ESTADO DE MÉXICO

Avda Instituto Literario No. 100 OTE. Col. Centro, 50000 Toluca

Telephone: (722) 26-23-00
Fax: (722) 14-55-46
Internet: www.uaemex.mx

Founded 1956
State control
Language of instruction: Spanish
Academic year: September to August

Rector: M. en A. URIEL GALICIA HERNANDEZ
Academic Secretary: M. en S.P. EZEQUIEL JAIMES FIGUEROA
Administrative Secretary: M.A.E. PEDRO LIZOLA MARGOLIS
Librarian: M. en E.L. RUPERTO RETANA RAMIREZ

Library of 292,000 vols
Number of teachers: 3,045
Number of students: 36,642

DIRECTORS

School of Anthropology: M. en E.L. RODRIGO MARCIAL JIMENEZ
School of Sciences: Biol. PEDRO DEL AGUILA JUAREZ
School of Nursing: L. en Enf. LUZ MARIA FRANCO BERNAL
School of Art and Architecture: M. en Pl. JESUS AGUILUZ LEON
School of Agricultural Sciences: Ing. ARTURO MAYA GOMEZ
School of Behavioural Sciences: Lic. en Psic. TERESA PONCE DAVALOS
School of Political Sciences and Public Administration: M. en C.P. JOSE MARTINEZ VILCHIS
School of Accountancy and Administration: M.A.E. IGNACIO MERCADO
School of Law: M. en D. JOAQUIN BERNAL SANCHEZ
School of Economics: M. en E. RICARDO RODRIGUEZ MARCIAL
School of Geography: L. en G. VICENTE PEÑA MANJARREZ
School of Humanities: L. en E.L. GERARDO MEZA GARCIA
School of Engineering: M. en I. ANGEL ALBITER RODRIGUEZ
School of Medicine: M.C. GABRIEL GERARDO HUITRON BRAVO
School of Veterinary Medicine: M. en C.E. EDUARDO GASCA PLIEGO
School of Dentistry: C.D. FRANCISCO MONTIEL CONZUELO
School of Urban and Regional Planning: M. en Pl. ALBERTO VILLAR CALVO
School of Chemistry: M. en C. JUAN CARLOS SANCHEZ MEZA
School of Tourism: L. en T. MARICRUZ MORENO ZAGAL

UNIVERSIDAD FEMENINA DE MÉXICO

Avda Constituyentes 151, 11850 México, DF

Telephone: (55) 5515-1311

Founded 1943
Private control
Language of instruction: Spanish
Academic year: September to June

Rector: Dra ELIZABETH BAQUEDANO
Secretary-General: Lic. LUIS SILVA GUERRERO
Registrar: Lic. PABLO TORRES MORÁN
Librarian: Srta AGUEDA CANEDO GUTIÉRREZ

Library of 12,000 vols
Number of teachers: 243
Number of students: 1,300

Publications: *Catálogo General Anual*, *Periódico Bimestral*

DEANS

School of Law: Lic. ANTONIO ADOLFO LÓPEZ GARCÍA
School of Education: Lic. LUZ BEATRIZ UNNA DE TORRES
School of Pharmacobiological Chemistry: Q.F.B. ENRIQUE CALDERÓN GARCÍA
School of Interior Decoration: Arq. CARLOS CANTÚ BOLLAND
School of Pedagogy: Lic. MARÍA ELENA NAVARRETE TOLEDO
School of Social Work: Profa T.S. MARÍA DEL SOCORRO SUSANA CAMPOS GARCÍA
School of Psychology: Lic. LUZ ANTONIETA POLANCO DE GARZÓN
School of Tourist Business Administration: Lic. ARMANDO GONZÁLEZ FLORES
School of International Relations: Lic. EMILIA WITTE MONTES DE OCA

School of Clinical Laboratories: Q.B.P. VÍCTOR MANUEL SÁNCHEZ HIDALGO, Dr JOSÉ AGUILAR CASTILLO (daytime courses)
School of Museology: Lic. ROBERTO ALARCÓN
School of History of Art: ELIZABETH BAQUEDANO
School of Interpreting and Translating: Lic. MAUREEN ANNE IVENS MCCULLAGH

UNIVERSIDAD AUTÓNOMA DE AGUASCALIENTES

Avda Universidad 940, 20100 Aguascalientes, Ags
Telephone: (449) 910-7410
Fax: (449) 910-7409
Internet: www.uaa.mx

Founded 1973
State control
Language of instruction: Spanish
Academic year: August to June (two semesters)

Rector: Dr. ANTONIO AVILA STORER
Secretary-General: Mtro. JASÉ RAMIRO ALEMÁN LÓPEZ
Librarian: C.P. IRMA DE LEON DE MUÑOZ

Library of 152,150 vols
Number of teachers: 1,461
Number of students: 11,501

Publications: *Gaceta Universitaria* (monthly), *Correo Universitario*, *Evaluación* (annually), *Caleidoscopio* (2 a year), *Scientiae Naturae* (2 a year), *Investigacion y Ciencia* (2 a year)

DEANS

Centre for Biomedical Sciences: Dra RUBY S. LIBREROS AGUDELO
Centre for Agricultural Sciences: I.B.Q. NARA AURORA GUERRERO GARCÍA
Centre for Arts and Humanities: Mtro JOSÉ ALFREDO ORTIZ GARZA
Centre for Secondary Education: Lic. ERNESTINA LEÓN RODRÍGUEZ
Centre for Economics and Administration: C.P. RICARDO GONZÁLEZ ALVAREZ
Centre for Design and Construction Sciences: Ing. JORGE PIO MONSIVAIS SANTOYO
Centre for Basic Sciences: Ing ANGEL DÍAZ PALOS

UNIVERSIDAD DE LAS AMÉRICAS – PUEBLA

Sta Catarina Mártir, Apdo Postal 100, 72820 Cholula, Puebla
Telephone: (222) 229-2000
Fax: (222) 229-2009
Internet: www.udlap.mx

Founded 1940 as Mexico City College; became Universidad de las Américas in 1963
Private control
Languages of instruction: Spanish, English
Academic year: August to May

President: Dra NORA LUSTIG TENENBAUM
Academic Vice-President: Dr EDUARDO LASTRA Y PÉREZ SALAZAR
Vice-President (Administration and Finance): Mtro JOSÉ MANUEL BLANCO ASPURU
Registrar: Mtra MARTHA FERNÁNDEZ DE LARA
Librarian: Dr ALFREDO SÁNCHEZ HULTRÓN SANTOS

Library: see Libraries
Number of teachers: 325 full-time
Number of students: 8,300

Publications: *UDLA Informa*, *La Catarina*

DEANS

Faculty of Administration: Dr FRANCISCO GUERRA VÁZQUEZ
Faculty of Business: Dr ROBERTO SOLANO
Faculty of Engineering: Dr JUAN MANUEL RAMÍREZ
Faculty of Arts and Humanities: Dra LUISA VILAR PAYÁ
Faculty of Social Sciences: Dr ISIDRO MORALES MORENO
Research and Graduate Studies: Dr GERARDO AYALA SAN MARTÍN

HEADS OF DEPARTMENTS

Accounting and Finance: Dr LUIS FELIPE JUÁREZ VALDÉS
Actuarial Sciences and Statistics: Dr LEOVIGILDO LEANDRO LÓPEZ GARCÍA
Anthropology: Dra PATRICIA SCARBOROUGH PLUNKET NAGODA
Applied Arts: Mtra SUNNY CECILE SAVOY RAWLS
Architecture: Dr MARIO VERGARA BALDERAS
Graphic Design: Mtro JUAN MANUEL BADA DOSAL
Business Administration: Dr FELIPE RODOLFO BURGOS OCHOÁTEGUI
Chemical and Food Engineering: Mtro LUIS GABRIEL RÍOS CASAS
Chemistry and Biology: Dr PEDRO ALFREDO WESCHE EBELING
Civil Engineering: Dr JOSÉ ANGEL RAYNAL VILLASEÑOR
Communications: Mtro JORGE ALBERTO CALLES SANTILLANA
Computer Systems Engineering: Dr DAVID SOL MARTÍNEZ
Economics: Dr CARLOS ALBERTO IBARRA NINO
Education: Dr ALEJANDRO RAMÍREZ JOSÉ
Electronics Engineering: Dr RUBÉN ALEJOS PALOMARES
Hotel Management: Mtra MARÍA DEL CARMEN MILAGROS MORFÍN HERRERA
International Relations: Mtro JOSÉ LUIS GARCÍA AGUILAR
Languages: Mtra PATRICIA ANN MCCOY BABALLE
Law: Dr MOISÉS ROMERO BERISTÁIN
Literature: Mtro JESÚS VILLEGAS GUZMÁN
Mechanical Engineering: Mtro CARLOS ENRIQUE JORGE ACOSTA MEJÍA
Physics and Mathematics: Dr ANDRÉS RAMOS RAMÍREZ
Psychology: Dra NÉLIDA NORMA ASILI PERUCCI

UNIVERSIDAD ANÁHUAC

Apdo 10-844, 11000 México, DF
Located at: Avda Universidad Anáhuac s/n, Lomas Anáhuac, 52760 Huixquilucan, Estado de México
Telephone: (55) 5627-0210
Fax: (55) 5589-9796
E-mail: anahuac@anahuac.mx
Internet: www.anahuac.mx

Founded 1963
Private control
Academic year: August to June (two terms)

Rector: Lic. RAYMUND COSGRAVE
Secretary-General: Arq. JOSÉ MATEOS
General Academic Director: Dr CRISTIAN NAZER
Librarian: Mtro DANIEL MATTES

Library of 163,500 vols
Number of teachers: 1,100
Number of students: 7,000

Publications: *Medicina y Etica* (4 a year), *Iuris Tantum* (annually), *Generación Anáhuac* (6 a year), *Carta Económica–Boletín Instituto Desarrollo Empresarial Anáhuac (IDEA)* (6 a year)

DEANS

School of Actuarial Sciences: Act. OLIVA SÁNCHEZ
School of Architecture: Arq. FERNANDO PAZ Y PUENTE
School of Communication Sciences: Dr CARLOS GÓMEZ PALACIO
School of Economics and Business: Dr RAMÓN LECUONA
School of Industrial and Graphic Design: Lic. LEONOR AMOZURRUTIA
School of Law: Dr JOSÉ ANTONIO NÚÑEZ
School of Medicine: Dr TOMÁS BARRIENTOS
School of Psychology: Mtro JOSÉ MARÍA LÓPEZ
School of Tourism Administration: Prof. LOUIS PASCAL
Faculty of Bioethics: Dr JOSÉ KUTHY PORTER
Faculty of Education: Mtra LUZ DEL CARMEN DÁVALOS
Faculty of Engineering: Dr ALEJANDRO MONTANO

UNIVERSIDAD AUTÓNOMA AGRARIA 'ANTONIO NARRO'

Buenavista, Saltillo, 25315 Coahuila
Telephone: (844) 411-0275
Fax: (844) 411-0207
E-mail: docencia@uaaan.mx
Internet: www.uaaan.mx

Founded 1923, University status 1975
Academic year: January to December

Rector: Ing. EDUARDO FUENTES RODRÍGUEZ
Vice-Rector: M. V. Z. JOSÉ L. BERLANGA FLORES
Registrar: Ing. GUSTAVO OLIVARES SALAZAR
Librarian: LUZ ELENA PEREZ MATA (acting)

Number of teachers: 430
Number of students: 2,583

CO-ORDINATORS OF FACULTIES

Animal Science: Dr EDUARDO AIZPURU GARCIA
Agronomy: Dr MARCO ANTONIO BUSTAMANTE G.
Engineering: M. C. LUIS M. LASSO MENDOZA
Social and Economics Science: Ing. FRANCISCO MARTINEZ GOMEZ

UNIVERSIDAD AUTÓNOMA DE BAJA CALIFORNIA

Apdo Postal 459, Avda Alvaro Obregón y Julian Carrillo s/n, 21100 Mexicali, Baja California
Telephone: (686) 554-2200
Fax: (686) 554-2200
Internet: www.uabc.mx

Founded 1957
Language of instruction: Spanish
Academic year: August to June

Rector: C.P. VÍCTOR EVERARDO BELTRÁN CORONA
Vice-Rector: M.C. RENÉ ANDRADE PETERSON
Secretary-General: M.C. JUAN JOSÉ SEVILLA GARCÍA
Librarian: Lic. ALMA LORENA CAMARENA FLORES

Number of teachers: 3,099
Number of students: 21,548

Publications: *Caláfia*, *Cuadernos de Ciencias Sociales*, *Cuaderno de Taller Literario*, *Estudios Fronterizos*, *Revistas Universitarias*, *Divulgare*, *Semillero*, *Yubai*, *Paradigmas*, *Ciencias Marinas*, *Revista de Investigación Educativa*

PRINCIPALS

Mexicali Campus:

School of Accountancy and Administration: C.P. PLACIDO VALENCIANA MORENO
Faculty of Architecture: Arq. AARÓN G. BERNAL RODRÍGUEZ
Faculty of Odontology: C.D. MANUEL OSCAR LARA BETANCOURT
Faculty of Humanities: M.C. ANGEL MANUEL ORTIZ MARÍN
School of Engineering: Ing. CÉSAR RAÚL REYES MAZÓN

Faculty of Law: Lic. MA. AURORA LACAVEX BERUMEN
School of Medicine: Med. SERGIO ROMO BARRAZA
School of Nursing: Lic. ANDREA VERDUGO BATIZ
School of Social Sciences: Lic. MIGUEL ANGEL RENDÓN MARTÍNEZ
School of Pedagogy: Prof. JESÚS ACEVES GUTIÉRREZ
School of Languages: Lic. KORA EVANGELINA BASICH PERALTA

Tijuana Campus:

Faculty of Accountancy and Administration: C.P. LUIS MEZA ARISTIGUE
Faculty of Chemistry: M.C. MA. EUGENIA PÉREZ MORALES
Faculty of Law: Lic. JOSÉ DE JESÚS DÍAZ DE LA TORRE
Faculty of Economics: Dra SONIA YOLANDA LUGO MORONES
Faculty of Medicine: Dra ADRIANA CAROLINA VARGAS OJEDA
Faculty of Odontology: Dr MIGUEL ANGEL CADENA ALCÁNTAR
School of Tourism: Lic. ONÉSIMO CUAMEA VELÁZQUEZ
School of Humanities: Lic. JORGE GUSTAVO MENDOZA GONZÁLEZ

Ensenada Campus:

School of Accountancy and Administration: Lic. SAÚL MÉNDEZ HERNÁNDEZ
Faculty of Marine Sciences: Dr ROBERTO MILLÁN NÚÑEZ
Faculty of Sciences: M.C. ERNESTO CAMPOS GONZÁLEZ
School of Engineering: M.C. JOSÉ DE JESÚS ZAMARRIPA TOPETE

Tecate Campus:

School of Engineering: Quim. SERGIO VALE SÁNCHEZ (Dir)

DIRECTORS OF RESEARCH INSTITUTES

Geography Institute (Mexicali Campus): (vacant)
Engineering Institute (Mexicali Campus): M.C. MOÍSES RIVAS LÓPEZ
Social Research Institute (Mexicali Campus): M.C. AGUSTÍN SÁNDEZ PÉREZ
Agriculture and Stockbreeding Research Institute: Ing. VÍCTOR MANUEL VEGA KURI
Veterinary Science and Research Institute: Dr EDUARDO SÁNCHEZ LÓPEZ
Educative Development and Research Institute: Mtro EDUARDO BACKHOFF ESCUDERO
Oceanology Research Institute (Ensenada Campus): Dr JOSÉ A. ZERTUCHE GONZÁLEZ
History Research Centre (Tijuana Campus): Dra CATALINA VELÁZQUEZ MORALES

UNIVERSIDAD AUTÓNOMA DE BAJA CALIFORNIA SUR
(Autonomous University of Baja California Sur)

Carretera al Sur $5^1/_2$km, 23080 La Paz, BCS
Telephone: (612) 128-0440
Fax: (612) 128-0880
Internet: www.uabcs.mx

Founded 1975
State control
Language of instruction: Spanish

Rector: JORGE ALBERTO VALE SÁNCHEZ
Secretary-General: PUBLIO OCTAVIO ROMERO MARTÍNEZ
Director of Plannning and Programming: Dr ARTURO HERNÁNDEZ PRADO
Head Librarian: Lic. JOSÉ ALFREDO VERDUGO SÁNCHEZ

ACADEMIC AREA CO-ORDINATORS

Agricultural Sciences: JOSÉ GUADALUPE LOYA RAMÍREZ
Marine Sciences: JORGE GARCÍA PÁMANES
Social Sciences and Humanities: Ma. LUISA CABRAL BOWLING

HEADS OF DEPARTMENTS

Agricultural Sciences (tel. (612) 128-0802; e-mail jloya@uabcs.mx):
- Agronomy: ARTURO ESCOBAR ESTRADA
- Zootechnology: JUAN MANUEL AVILA SANDOVAL

Marine Sciences (tel. (612) 128-0801; e-mail jgarciap@uabcs.mx):
- Computer Systems: MIGUEL ANGEL NORZAGARAY COSIO
- Fisheries Engineering: Dr MARCO ANTONIO CADENA ROA
- Marine Biology: EMILIO BARJAU GONZÁLEZ
- Marine Geology: Ing. JOSÉ ANTONIO PÉREZ VENZOR

Social Sciences and Humanities (tel. (612) 128-0800; e-mail mlcabral@uabcs.mx):
- Economics: JOAQUÍN SERMEÑO LIMA
- Humanities: Dr HUMBERTO GÓNZALEZ GALVÁN
- Political Sciences and Public Administration: Lic. ALFONSO GUILLÉN VICENTE

UNIVERSIDAD DEL BAJIO

Apdo Postal 1-444, 37000 Léon, Gto
Telephone: (47) 17-17-40
Fax: (47) 18-55-11

Founded 1968
Private control
Academic year: August to December, February to June

Rector: Mtro RONALDO HENDERSON CALDERON
Vice-Rector: Mtro CESAR RANGEL BARRERA
Registrar: Lic. JOSE L. REGULES FAJARDO
Librarian: Lic. ALMA ROSA HERNÁNDEZ GARCÍA

Number of teachers: 730
Number of students: 6,450

Publications: *Espíritu Lasallista* (monthly), *Cuadernos* (2 a year)

DIRECTORS OF FACULTIES

Accountancy Administration and International Marketing: SARA BERTHA ROCHA VILLASEÑOR
Agronomy: Ing. PATRICIA MENA HERNANDEZ
Architecture: Arq. MIGUEL ANGEL GARCÍA GÓMEZ
Communication Sciences: Lic. GERARDO GONZALEZ DEL CASTILLO SILVA
Computing Engineering: Ing. EDEL ESPINO LEDESMA
Dentistry: Dr JOSÉ ALEJANDRO SEGOVIA GALLARDO
Engineering: Ing. RAFAEL BONILLA LIRA
Industrial, Environmental and Graphic Design: Lic. LUIS E. CERVANTES FERNANDEZ
Law: Lic. CARLOS V. MUÑOZ JIMÉNEZ
Telecommunications Engineering: Ing. JAIME PALACIOS CASTAÑÓN
Tourism and Hotel Studies: RODOLFO MUJICA SANTOYO
Veterinary Studies: M. V. Z. JESÚS ALVAREZ PEREZ
Preparatory School: Dr SALVADOR MUÑOZ SOLIS
Graduate School of Administration: Lic. GUSTAVO A. HERNÁNDEZ MORENO
Graduate School of Architecture: M. A. GREGORIO G. DE LA ROSA FALCON
Graduate School of Dentistry: Dr ENRIQUE NIEMBRO CAMPUZANO
Graduate School of Education: Lic. MANUEL CASTRO VILLICAÑA
Graduate School of Electronics and Computational Engineering: Ing. JAIME PALACIOS CASTAÑÓN

CAMPUSES

San Francisco del Rincón Campus: ; 550 students; Dir Ing. FELIPE AGUILERA MOTA.

Salamanca Campus: ; 750 students; Dir Lic. LUIS ERNESTO RIOS PEREZ.

UNIVERSIDAD AUTÓNOMA DE CAMPECHE

Avda Universidad y Agustín Melgar, 24030 Campeche, Camp.
Telephone: (981) 19800
Internet: www.uacam.mx

Founded 1756, refounded 1965
State control
Academic year: September to June

Rector: Ing. JAVIER CÚ ESPEJO
Secretary-General: Lic. JOAQUÍN UC VALENCIA
Librarian: Lic. ARACELI MAY CANUL

Number of teachers: 443
Number of students: 4,760

Publications: *Panorama* (6 a year), *Pinceladas* (6 a year)

DIRECTORS OF FACULTIES AND SCHOOLS

Faculty of Humanities: Lic. JOSÉ MANUEL ALCOCER BERNÉS
Faculty of Social Sciences: Dr GERARDO MIXCOATL TINOCO
Faculty of Law: Lic. JORGE RODRÍGUEZ VARGAS
School of Accounting and Administration: M. en C. ENNA SANDOVAL CASTELLANOS
Faculty of Chemical and Biological Sciences: Mtra ANGELICA SOTO MARTÍNEZ
Faculty of Engineering: Ing. DOMINGO BERMAN ORDAZ
School of Dentistry: CD LUIS HERRERA LÓPEZ
School of Medicine: Dr CARLOS EDUARDO GARCÍA SOLIS
Higher School of Nursing: Lic. MARÍA CANDELARIA AGUILAR BRICEÑO
'Lic. Ermilo Sandoval Campos' Preparatory School: Lic. VÍCTOR ORTIZ PASOS
'Dr Nazario Víctor Montejo Godoy' Preparatory School: Lic. ALMA LORENA GUZMAN GARCÍA

UNIVERSIDAD DEL CARIBE

Lote 1, Manzana 1, Region 78, Esq. Fracc Tabachines, 77528 Cancún, Quintana Roo 77528
Telephone: (998) 881-4400
Fax: (998) 881-4400
E-mail: rectoria@unicaribe.edu.mx
Internet: www.unicaribe.edu.mx

Founded 2000
State control
Academic year: August to May

President: JOSÉ LUIS PECH VÁRGUEZ
Rector: FERNANDO ESPINOSA DE LOS REYES AGUIRRE
Academic Secretary: ANA CRISTINA ÁVILA LÓPEZ
Administrative Secretary: LUIS MANUEL ROSAS TORRES

Number of teachers: 120
Number of students: 1,214

HEADS OF DEPARTMENTS

Economics and International Business: ENRIQUE CORONA SANDOVAL
Human Professional Development: ARACELI NAVA NAVARRO
Natural Sciences and Engineering: HILARIO LÓPEZ GARACHANA
Tourism, Hotel Management and Gastronomy: ANA PRICILA SOSA FERREIRA

UNIVERSIDAD AUTÓNOMA DEL CARMEN

Calle 31 x 56 s/n, 24176 Ciudad del Carmen, Camp.
Telephone: (938) 381-1018 ext. 1006
Fax: (938) 381-1018 ext. 1328
Internet: www.unacar.mx

Founded 1967

Rector: Ing. PEDRO OCAMPO CALDERÓN
Secretary-General: Lic. RAFAEL HUGO GARCÍA MORENO
Chief Administrative Officer: Lic. HILDA LÓPEZ LÓPEZ
Librarian: C. OLGA SÁNCHEZ PÉREZ

Number of teachers: 340
Number of students: 4,484

Publications: *Voz Universitaria*, *Senda Universitaria*

Faculties of commerce and administration, law, chemistry, education.

UNIVERSIDAD AUTÓNOMA CHAPINGO

Km 38.5 Carretera México-Veracruz, Texcoco, Edo de México
Telephone: (595) 952-1500
Fax: (595) 952-1565
Internet: www.chapingo.mx

Founded 1854 as Escuela Nacional de Agricultura; named changed 1978
Government control
Academic year: August to June

Rector: Dr JOSÉ SERGIO BARRALES DOMINGUEZ
Director-General (Academic): Dr JAVIER RUIZ LEDESMA
Director-General (Administration): JOSÉ SOLIS RAMÍREZ
Director-General (Research): Dr ENRIQUE SERRANO GÁLVEZ
Librarian: ROSA MARÍA OJEDA TREJO

Library: see Libraries and Archives
Number of teachers: 1,200
Number of students: 6,800 (6,500 undergraduates, 300 graduates)

Publications: *Revista Chapingo* (every 2 months), *Revista de Geografía Agrícola* (every 2 months), *Textual* (social sciences, 2 a year)

DEANS

Agroecology: Dr LAKSMI REDDIAR KRISHNMURTHY
Forestry: ANGEL LEYVA OVALLE
Agricultural Mechanical Engineering: MARTÍN SOTO ESCOBAR
Agricultural Parasitology: FRANCISCO PONCE GONZALEZ
Agroindustrial Engineering: Dr LUIS RAMIRO GARCÍA CHAVEZ
Dry Area Science: SANTIAGO RAMON MENDOZA MORENO
Earth Science: Dr DAVID CRISTÓBAL ACEVEDO
Economic and Administrative Science: JAIME RUVALCABA LIMON
Forestry: ANGEL LEYVA OVALLE
Irrigation: RENE MARTINEZ ELIZONDO
Phytotechnics: Dr MARIO PEREZ GRAJALES
Rural Sociology: JESUS CARLOS MORETT SANCHEZ
Zootechnology: MELITON CORDOBA ALVAREZ

ATTACHED RESEARCH INSTITUTES

Centre for Global Economic, Social, Technological Research in Agriculture and Agroindustry: Dir Dr RITA SCHWENTESIUS RINDERMAN.

UNIVERSIDAD AUTÓNOMA DE CHIAPAS

Colina Universitaria, Carretera Panamericana Km. 1080, Blvd Belisario Domínguez, 29000 Tuxtla Gutiérrez, Chiapas
Telephone: (961) 5-08-27
Fax: (961) 5-06-64
Internet: www.unach.mx

Founded 1975
Private control
Academic year: September to July (two semesters)

Rector: Ing. PEDRO RENÉ BODEGAS VALERA
Secretary-General: LUIS MANUEL MARTÍNEZ ESTRADA
Academic Secretary: Ing. ROBERTO CRUZ DE LEÓN
Librarian: Lic. DOLORES SERRANO CANCINO

Number of teachers: 906
Number of students: 12,052

Publication: *Gaceta Universitaria*

DIRECTORS

Campus I (Tuxtla Gutiérrez):
Faculty of Accounting and Administration: C.P. CESAR MAZA GONZÁLEZ
School of Civil Engineering: Ing. ROBERTON Y CRUZ DIAZ
Faculty of Architecture: Arq. RICARDO GUILLÉN CASTAÑEDA

Campus II (Tuxtla Gutiérrez):
Faculty of Human Medicine: Dr JOSÉ LUIS AQUINO HERNÁNDEZ
School of Veterinary Medicine and Zootechnics: MVZ. ALBERTO YAMAZAKI MAZA

Campus III (San Cristóbal de las Casas):
Faculty of Law: Lic. ALFONSO RAMÍREZ MARTÍNEZ
Faculty of Social Sciences: JORGE ALBERTO LÓPEZ AREVALO

Campus IV (Tapachula):
Faculty of Accounting: C.P. JORGE FERNANDO ORDAZ RUÍZ
Faculty of Administration Sciences: KENY ORDAZ ESCOBAR
School of Chemical Sciences: JOSÉ RAMÓN PUIG COTA
Faculty of Agriculture: Ing. ALFONSO PÉREZ ROMERO

Campus V (Villaflores):
School of Agronomy: Dr ALFREDO MEDINA MELÉNDEZ

Campus VI (Tuxtla Gutiérrez):
Faculty of Humanities: CARLOS RINCÓN RAMÍREZ

UNIVERSIDAD POPULAR DE LA CHONTALPA

Galeana s/n Esq. Morelos, Centro, 86500 Cárdenas, Tabasco
Telephone: (937) 372-5743
Fax: (937) 372-5743
E-mail: informacion@upchontalpa.edu.mx
Internet: www.upchontalpa.edu.mx

Founded 1998
State control

Rector: Ing. RAMÓN ALEJANDRO FIGUEROA CANTORAL
Secretary (Academic): Dr ARQUÍMEDES ORAMAS VARGAS
Secretary (University Extension and Social Services): MANUEL AYSA JIMÉNEZ
Secretary (Administration and Finance): ELVIS SEGURA CÓRDOVA

Publications: *Gaceta Enlace Universitario*, *Expresión Universitaria*, *Revista Tecnociencia Universitaria*

Main subject areas: agricultural engineering, civil engineering, petrochemical engineering, electrical and mechanical engineering, zootechnical engineering, business and international finance, political science and public administration, psychology, pharmaceutical chemistry.

UNIVERSIDAD DE CIENCIAS Y ARTES DEL ESTADO DE CHIAPAS (UNICACH)
(Chiapas State University of Arts and Sciences)

1a Sur Poniente 1460, Tuxtla Gutiérrez, Chiapas
Located at: Calz. Samuel León Brindis 151, Tuxtla Gutiérrez, Chiapas
Telephone: (961) 602-8176
E-mail: desacad@unicach.edu.mx
Internet: www.unicach.edu.mx

Founded 1893, as Industrial School of Chiapas; current name and status 1995
State control
Language of instruction: Spanish

Rector: Mtra MARÍA ELENA TOVAR GONZÁLEZ
Secretary-General: Dra ALMA ROSA GONZÁLEZ ESQUINCA
Director of Information: Ing. MARINO PEREZ MARTINEZ

DIRECTORS

School of Biology: Mtra ADELINA SCHLIE GUZMAN
School of Music: Lic. LUIS FELIPE MARTÍNEZ GORDILLO
School of Nutrition: Lic. VIDALMA DEL ROSARIO BEZARES SARMIENTO
School of Odontology: C.D. JUAN JOSÉ ORTEGA ALEJANDRE
School of Psychology: Lic. GERMAN ALEJANDRO GARCIA LARA
School of Topography: Ing. LISANDRO MARTÍNEZ POZO
Centre for Human Development: Lic. MARINA IDALIA GUIZAR CORDOVA
University Centre for Information and Documentation: Ing. ARQUIMEDES R. LÓPEZ ROBLERO

UNIVERSIDAD AUTÓNOMA DE CHIHUAHUA

Escorza y Venustiano Carranza s/n, Apdo Postal 324, 31000 Chihuahua, Chih.
Telephone: (614) 439-1530
Fax: (614) 439-1529
E-mail: xvenegas@uachnet.mx
Internet: www.uach.mx

Founded 1954
Language of instruction: Spanish
Academic year: August to June

Rector: Dr JESÚS ENRIQUE GRAJEDA HERRERA
Secretary-General: Dr JESÚS XAVIER VENEGAS HOLGUÍN
Administrative Director: C.P. y L.A.E. GABRIELA RICO CABRERA
Librarian: C.P. FERNANDO SALOMÓN BEYER

Number of teachers: 1,428
Number of students: 12,429

Publications: various faculty journals.

DIRECTORS

Faculty of Accountancy and Administration: C.P. y M.A. FRANCISCO JAVIER LUJÁN DE LA GARZA
Faculty of Engineering: Ing. ARTURO LEAL BEJARANO
Faculty of Medicine: Dr CARLOS ENRIQUE MORALES ORTEGA
Faculty of Law: Lic. MARIO TREVISO SALAZAR
Faculty of Chemical Sciences: Ing. MANUEL RUÍZ ESPARZA MEDINA
School of Nursing and Nutrition Science: M.E.M.I. ROSA MARÍA DOZAL MOLINA

Faculty of Stockbreeding: Dr GUILLERMO VILLALOBOS VILLALOBOS
Faculty of Agriculture and Forestry: M.S. ARTURO JAVIER OBANDO RODRÍGUEZ
Faculty of Agricultural Engineering: M.C. ALMA PATRICIA HERNÁNDEZ RODRÍGUEZ
Faculty of Physical Education and Sport Science: L.E.F. PRIMO ALBERTO GONZÁLEZ ARZATE
Faculty of Philosophy and Literature: Lic. ISELA YOLANDA DE PABLO PORRAS
Faculty of Political and Social Sciences: Lic. SAMUEL GARCÍA SOTO
School of International Economics: Lic. MANUEL PARGA MUÑOZ
School of Dentistry: Dr JESÚS DUARTE MAYAGOITIA
Institute of Fine Arts: Lic. RUBEN TINAJERO MEDINA

ATTACHED INSTITUTES

Higher School of Graphic Communication: Dir Ing. JUAN RUÍZ TRUJILLO.

School of Architecture of Chihuahua: Dir Arq. EDUARDO GONZÁLEZ TEJEDA.

School of Psychology: Dir Lic. ROSARIO VALDÉZ CARAVEO.

Sigmund Freud School of Psychology and Pedagogy: Dir Lic. ELVA HERNÁNDEZ ALVÍDREZ.

Higher Institute of Architecture and Design: Dir Arq. CARLOS HÉCTOR CARRERA ROBLES.

School of Nursing of the Centro Médico de Especialidades, S.A., Ciudad Juárez: Dir Dr SERGIO ANTONIO ESPEJO POSADAS.

School of Nursing and Obstetrics of the General Hospital, Ciudad Juárez: Dir Dra ADRIANA SAUCEDO GARCÍA.

School of Nursing, Hidalgo del Parral: Dir Enf. LETICIA S. DE CHÁVEZ.

School of Nursing of the Hospital de Jesús: Dir Lic. NATALIA MORALES MONFIL.

School of Nursing of the Regional Hospital, Ciudad Cuauhtémoc: Dir Enf. CARMEN GUTIÉRREZ.

Nursing Educational Centre, El Parque: Dir Lic. Enf. TERESA DE JESÚS MENDOZA VIDAÑA.

School of Nursing and Obstetrics of the Sanatorio Palmore: Dir Enf. MARISELA PÉREZ DE LEÓN.

School of Nursing and Health Science Skills: Dir Enf. ARMIDA AVITIA DE RODRÍGUEZ.

School of Nursing, Ciudad Delicias: Dir Enf. FRANCISCO JAVIER LÓPEZ DÁVALOS.

UNIVERSIDAD POPULAR DE LA CHONTALPA
(People's University of Chontalpa)

Galeana s/n Esq. Morelos, Centro, 86500 Cárdenas, Tabasco
Telephone: (937) 372-5743
Fax: (937) 372-5743
E-mail: informacion@upchontalpa.edu.mx
Internet: www.upchontalpa.edu.mx

Founded 1998
State control

Rector: Ing. RAMÓN ALEJANDRO FIGUEROA CANTORAL
Secretary (Academic): Dr ARQUÍMEDES ORAMAS VARGAS
Secretary (University Extension and Social Services): MANUEL AYSA JIMÉNEZ
Secretary (Administration and Finance): ELVIS SEGURA CÓRDOVA

Publications: *Gaceta Enlace Universitario, Expresión Universitaria, Revista Tecnociencia Universitaria*

Main subject areas: agricultural engineering, civil engineering, petrochemical engineering, electrical and mechanical engineering, zootechnical engineering, business and international finance, political science and public administration, psychology and pharmaceutical chemistry.

UNIVERSIDAD AUTÓNOMA DE COAHUILA

Blvd V. Carranza esq. González Lobo, Col. República Oriente, 25280 Saltillo, Coahuila
Telephone: (844) 438-1729
Fax: (844) 438-1622
Internet: www.uadec.mx

Founded 1867, refounded 1957
State control
Language of instruction: Spanish
Academic year: August to June (two terms)

Rector: L.Ab. OSCAR VILLEGAS RICO
Secretary-General: L.Ab.L. ALBERTO L. SALAZAR RODRÍGUEZ
Librarian: ANTONIO MALACARA

Number of teachers: c. 900
Number of students: 13,923.

UNIVERSIDAD DE COLIMA

Avda Universidad 333, 28040 Colima, Col.
Telephone: (312) 316-1000
E-mail: rectoria@volcan.ucol.mx
Internet: www.ucol.mx

Founded 1940 as Universidad Popular de Colima, reorganized 1962
State control
Language of instruction: Spanish
Academic year: August to July

Rector: Dr CARLOS SALAZAR SILVA
Secretary-General: Dr JUSTINO PINEDA LARIOS
Librarian: Dra EVANGELINA SERRANO

Number of teachers: 1,204
Number of students: 19,000

Publication: *Estudios Sobre las Culturas Contemporáneas*

DEANS

Faculty of Social and Political Sciences: Lic. FERNANDO H. ALCARAZ INIGUEZ
Faculty of Economics: Dr ERNESTO RANGEL DELGADO
Faculty of Arts and Communications: Lic. LUIS MIGUEL BUENO SÁNCHEZ
Faculty of Social Studies: Licda MARISA MESINA POLANCO
Faculty of Educational Science: Prof. JOSÉ FRANCISCO BALLESTEROS SILVA
Faculty of Nursing: Licda ANA MARÍA CHAVEZ ACEVEDO
School of Languages: Licda GRISELDA P. CEBALLOS LLERENAS
Faculty of Chemical Science: M.C. SANTIAGO E. VELASCO VILLALPANDO
Faculty of Accountancy and Administration 1: C.P. TOBIAS ALVAREZ LUNA
Faculty of Accountancy and Administration 2: JOSÉ MARTÍN TORRES RÍOS
Faculty of Veterinary Studies and Zoology: Dr ENRIQUE SILVA PENA
Faculty of Electro-mechanical Engineering: M.C. ANDRÉS G. FUENTES COVARRUBIAS
Faculty of Marine Science: O.Q. ADRÍAN TINTOS GÓMEZ
Faculty of Accountancy and Administration: M.A. JOSÉ ALFREDO CANO ANGUIANO
Faculty of Law: Lic. MARIO DE LA MADRID ANDRADE
Faculty of Medicine: Dr RAMÓN A. CEDILLO NAKAY
Faculty of Education: Mtra CARMEN ALICIA SANTOS ANDRADE
Faculty of Architecture: Arq. JULIO DE JESÚS MENDOZA JIMÉNEZ
Faculty of Civil Engineering: M.C. GERARDO CERRATO OSEGUERA
Faculty of Biological Sciences and Agronomy: Mtro. ARNOLDO MUCHEL ROSALES
Faculty of Telematics: M.C. RAUL AQUINO SANTOS

UNIVERSIDAD DEL EJÉRCITO Y FUERZA AÉREA
(University of the Army and Air Force)

Calzada México Tacuba s/n, Popotla, Delegación Miguel Hidalgo, México, DF
Telephone: (55) 5396-9106
Internet: www.sedena.gob.mx/educacion/index.html

Founded 1975

Rector: JUAN HERNÁNDEZ ÁVALOS.

CONSTITUENT MILITARY SCHOOLS

Escuela Militar de Graduados de Sanidad (Graduate Military School of Public Health)

Cerrada de Palomas s/n, Lomas de San Isidro, CP 11620, México, DF
Telephone: (55) 5520-2079
Internet: www.sedena.gob.mx/educacion/planteles/emgs/index.htm

Founded 1970

Dir: Gen. de Brigada Dr LUIS GONZÁLEZ Y GUTIÉRREZ.

Escuela Médico Militar (Military Medical School)

Cerrada de Palomas esq. con Periférico s/n, Lomas de San Isidro, Delegación Miguel Hidalgo, CP 11200, México, DF
Telephone: (55) 5540-7726
Internet: www.sedena.gob.mx/educacion/planteles/emm/index.html

Founded 1881

Dir: Gen. de Brigada Dr RODOLFO LERMA SHIUMOTO.

Escuela Militar de Odontología (Military School of Dentistry)

Calle Batalla de Celaya e Idelfonso Vázquez s/n, Lomas de Sotelo, México, DF
Telephone: (55) 5520-2591
Internet: www.sedena.gob.mx/educacion/planteles/emo/index.html

Founded 1976

Dir: Gen. Brig. C. D. MIGUEL ANGEL GUTIÉRREZ PÉREZ.

Escuela Militar de Ingenieros (Military School of Engineers)

Calzada México Tacuba s/n, Popotla, Delegación Miguel Hidalgo, México, DF
Telephone: (55) 5396-3596
Internet: www.sedena.gob.mx/educacion/planteles/emi/index.htm

Founded 1822

Dir: Gen. Brig. I. C. GILBERTO GARCIA CAMPANTE.

Heroico Colegio Militar (Heroic Military College)

Carretera México-Cuernavaca Km 22, San Pedro Mártir, Tlalpan, México, DF
Telephone: (55) 5676-5044
Internet: www.sedena.gob.mx/educacion/planteles/hcm/index.html

Founded 1818

Dir: Gen. de Brigada D. E. M. CARLOS GARCÍA PRIANI.

Escuela Militar de Enfermeras (Military School of Nurses)

Calle Idelfonso Vázquez e Industria Militar, Jardines Poniente del Hospital Central Militar, Lomas de Sotelo, México, DF

Telephone: (55) 5580-6913

Internet: www.sedena.gob.mx/educacion/planteles/eme/index.html

Founded 1938

Dir: Lt-Col IRMA RÍOS SANDOVAL.

Escuela Militar de Oficiales de Sanidad (Military School of Public Health Officers)

Calle General Francisco Murguía s/n, Unidad Habitacional Militar, Lomas de Sotelo, México, DF

Telephone: (55) 5557-6807

Internet: www.sedena.gob.mx/educacion/planteles/emos/index.htm

Founded 1927

Dir: Col Dr ROBERTO CASTILLO MARÍN.

Escuela Militar de Aviación (Military School of Aviation)

Colegio del Aire, Base Aérea Militar No. 5, Zapopan, Jalisco

Telephone: (33) 3624-1470

Internet: www.sedena.gob.mx/educacion/planteles/ema/index.htm

Founded 1915

Dir: Col PEDRO VALENCIA SAUCEDO.

Escuela Militar de Transmisiones (Military School of Signals)

Campo Militar No. 1-H, Los Leones Tacuba, México, DF

Telephone: (55) 5387-8943

Internet: www.sedena.gob.mx/educacion/planteles/emt/index.htm

Founded 1925

Dir: Gen. de Brigada LEOVIGILDO MUÑOZ HERNÁNDEZ.

Escuela Militar de Especialistas de Fuerza Aérea (Military School of Air Force Specialists)

Colegio del Aire, Base Aérea Militar No. 5, Zapopan, Jalisco

Telephone: (33) 3624-1470

Internet: www.sedena.gob.mx/educacion/planteles/emefa/index.htm

Founded 1934

Dir: Col RAMIRO MARMOLEJO GUZMÁN.

Escuela Militar de Mantenimiento y Abastecimiento (Military School of Supply and Maintenance)

Colegio del Aire, Base Aérea Militar No. 5, Zapopan, Jalisco

Telephone: (33) 3624-1470

Internet: www.sedena.gob.mx/educacion/planteles/emma/index.htm

Founded 1942

Dir: Col JESÚS ULLOA GONZÁLEZ.

Escuela Militar de Materiales de Guerra (Military School of War Materials)

Campo Militar 1-F, Santa Fe, DF

Telephone: (55) 5570-2549

Internet: www.sedena.gob.mx/educacion/planteles/emmg/index.htm

Founded 1946

Dir: Col FELIPE VARGAS TAPIA.

Escuela Militar de Clases de Transmisiones (Military School of Signals Classes)

Campo Militar No. 15-A, General Ramón Corona en la Mojonera, Zapopan, Jalisco

Telephone: (33) 3832-0462

Internet: www.sedena.gob.mx/educacion/planteles/emct/index.htm

Founded 1953

Dir: Col SAÚL CONTRERAS OJEDA.

Escuela Militar de Tropas Especialistas de Fuerza Aérea (Military School of Specialist Air Force Troops)

Campo Militar No. 37-D, Santa Lucia, México, DF

Telephone: (55) 5557-6070

Internet: www.sedena.gob.mx/educacion/planteles/emtefa/index.htm

Founded 1981

Dir: Gen. JAVIER POSADAS MEJÍA.

UNIVERSIDAD JUÁREZ DEL ESTADO DE DURANGO

Constitución 404, Sur, 34000 Durango, Durango

Telephone: (618) 2-00-44

Internet: www.ujed.mx

Founded as a Civil College 1856, became University 1957

Private control

Language of instruction: Spanish

Academic year: January to December (2 terms)

Rector: Dr JORGE RAMÍREZ DÍAZ

Secretary-General: C.P. JUAN FRANCISCO SALAZAR BENITEZ

Chief Administrative Officer: T.S. ADRIANA AVELAR VILLEGAS

Librarian: A.B. JOSÉ LINO HERNÁNDEZ CAMPOS

Number of teachers: 1,116

Number of students: 20,160

DEANS

Faculty of Accountancy and Administration: C.P. MARÍA MAGDALENA MEDINA CÓRDOBA M.A.

Faculty of Law: Lic. VICENTE GUERRERO ITURBE

Faculty of Medicine: Dr JORGE RUIZ LEÓN

Faculty of Veterinary Medicine and Zootechnics: M.V.Z. RAÚL RANGEL ROMERO

School of Dentistry: C.D. MIGUEL ROJAS REGALADO

School of Social Work: T.S. MARÍA ANTONIA HERNÁNDEZ ESCAREÑO

School of Chemical Sciences: Ing. ENRIQUE TORRES CABRAL

School of Applied Mathematics: Ing. UBALDO ARENAS JUÁREZ

School of Forestry: Ing. ALFONSO HERRERA AYÓN

School of Nursing and Obstetrics: Lic. MARÍA ELENA VALDEZ DE REYES

School of Music: Prof. ABRAHAM E. VIGGERS ARREOLA

School of Painting, Sculpture and Crafts: Prof. FRANCISCO MONTOYA DE LA CRUZ

Gómez Palacio Campus:

School of Agriculture and Stockbreeding: Ing. JESÚS JOSÉ QUIÑONES VERA

School of Biology: BIOL. M.C. RAÚL DÍAZ MORENO

School of Medicine: Dr LUIS DE VILLA VÁZQUEZ

School of Civil Engineering: Ing. EVERARDO F. DELGADO SOLIS

School of Food Science and Technology: Ing. GERARDO FRANCISCO ALDANA RUIZ

ATTACHED INSTITUTES

Instituto de Investigación Científica (Institute of Scientific Research): Dir MARÍA DEL ROSARIO RUIZ A..

Instituto de Ciencias Sociales (Institute of Social Sciences): Dir Lic. MIGUEL PALACIOS MONCAYO.

Instituto de Investigaciones Históricas (Institute of Historical Research): Dir Lic. MARÍA GUADALUPE RODRIGUEZ LÓPEZ.

Instituto de Investigaciones Jurídicas (Institute of Legal Research): Dir Lic. ANGEL ISMAEL MEJORADO OLAGUEZ.

Museo de Antropología e Historia (Anthropology and History Museum): Dir Lic. ANGEL RODRÍGUEZ SOLÓRZANO.

UNIVERSIDAD PEDAGÓGICA DE DURANGO

Avda 16 de Septiembre 132, Col Silvestre Dorador, 3407 Durango, Durango

Telephone: (618) 812-9509

Fax: (618) 812-9509

E-mail: upndgo@gauss.logicnet.com.mx

Founded 1997

State control

Dir: Prof. BERNARDO DEL REAL SARMIENTO.

UNIVERSIDAD ESTATAL DEL VALLE DE ECATEPEC

Avda Central s/n, Esq. Leona Vicario, Valle de Anáhuac, 66120 Ecatepec, México, DF

Telephone: (55) 710-4560

Fax: (55) 710-2688

E-mail: israelrios413@hotmail.com

Founded 2001

State control

Rector: ISMAEL SÁENZ VILLA.

UNIVERSIDAD DEL GOLFO

Obregón 203 Pte, Zona Centro, 89000 Tampico, Tamaulipas

Telephone: (833) 212-9222

Fax: (833) 212-9222

E-mail: publicidad@univgolfo.edu.mx

Internet: www.unigolfo.edu.mx

Founded 1972

Private control

Languages of instruction: English, German, Spanish

Academic year: September to July

Rector: Dr HERIBERTO FLORENCIA MENÉNDEZ

Vice-Rector: Lic. HILARIO ZUÑIGA MENCHACA

Chief Administrative Officer: Lic. MARCO ANTONIO MALDONADO LUGO

Librarian: JUANA PIZAÑA MÁRQUEZ

Library of 25,000 vols

Number of teachers: 148 (25 full-time, 123 part-time)

Number of students: 4,800

DIRECTORS

Faculty of Accounting and Administration: Lic. SERGIO ARTURO ROMO BECERRA

Faculty of Law: Lic. ELSA EMILIA PAREDES RAMÍREZ

Faculty of Economics and Computing: Ing. FRANCISCO DÍAZ FERNÁNDEZ

European Faculty for Foreign Students: Dr HERIBERTO FLORENCIA MENÉNDEZ

Postgraduate Studies: Lic. PABLO JOSÉ JIMÉNEZ ALCORTA

UNIVERSIDAD DE GUADALAJARA

Avda Juárez 975, Sector Juárez, 44100 Guadalajara, Jal.

Telephone: (33) 3825-8888

Fax: (33) 3626-0668

E-mail: webudg@cencar.udg.mx
Internet: www.udg.mx
Founded 1792, restructured 1925
State control
Academic year: March to February
Rector: Lic. José Trinidad Padilla López
Secretary-General: Mtro Carlos Briseño Torres
Chief Administrative Officer: Mtro Gustavo Alfonso Cárdenas Cutiño
Librarian: Mtro Sergio Lópes Ruelas
Library: see Libraries and Archives
Number of teachers: 11,784
Number of students: 180,776
Publications: *Revista Universidad de Guadalajara* (4 a year), *Gaceta*, *Jures*.

UNIVERSITY CENTRES

Art, Architecture and Design: Rector Arq. Carlos Correa Ceseña.
Health Sciences: Rector Dr Raúl Vargas López.
Exact and Engineering Sciences: Rector Mtro Hector Enrique Salgado Rodríguez.
Biological Sciences and Farming: Rector M. en C. Salvador Mena Munguia.
Economic and Administrative Sciences: Rector Mtro Ixcoatl Tonatiuh Bravo Padilla.
Social Sciences and Humanities: Rector Dr Juan Manuel Durán Juárez.
El Sur: Rector Lic. Jesús Alberto Espinoza Arias.
La Cienega: Rector Mtro Pedro Javier Guerrero Medina.
La Costa: Rector M. en C. Jeffry Steven Fernández Rodríguez.
La Costa Sur: Rector Dr Juan José Palacios Lara.
Los Altos: Rector Dr Héctor Armando Macías Martínez.
Los Valles: Executive Co-ordinator Dr Miguel Angel Navarro Navarro.
Del Norte: Executive Co-ordinator Dr Cándido González Pérez.

UNIVERSIDAD AUTÓNOMA DE GUADALAJARA

Apdo Postal 1-440, 44100 Guadalajara, Jalisco
Located at: Avda Patria No. 1201, Lomas del Valle, 3a Sección, Guadalajara, Jalisco
Telephone: (33) 3638-8463
E-mail: uag@uag.mx
Internet: www.uag.mx
Founded 1935
Private control
Language of instruction: Spanish
Academic year: August to May
Rector: Lic. Antonio Leaño Alvarez del Castillo
Vice-Rector: Ing. Juan José Leaño Alvarez del Castillo
Chief Administrative Officer: Lic. Rubén Quiroz V.
Chief Academic Officer: Dr Néstor Velasco P.
Librarian: Lic. Alberto Olivares Duarte
Library of 178,000 vols, 3,760 maps, 3,400 periodicals
Number of teachers: 1,622
Number of students: 14,102
Publications: *Docencia* (3 a year), *Actas de la Facultad de Medicina* (2 a year), *Academia* (6 a year), *Item Histórico* (monthly)

DEANS

College of Humanities and Social Sciences: Lic. Ismael Zamora Tovar
College of Architecture and Design: Arq. Raúl Mendoza R.
College of Law: Lic. Humberto López Delgadillo
College of Business: C.P. Javier González C.
College of Engineering: Ing. Rafael Jaime A.
College of Sciences: Ing. Jaime Hernández O.
College of Health Sciences: Dr Néstor Velasco P.
Postgraduate Studies: Dr Mauricio Alcocer Ruthling (Dir)
Research Administration: Dr Rodolfo Casillas V. (Dir)
Universidad en la Comunidad (UNICO, Junior College): Lic. Pedro Rodríguez L. (Dir)
Continuing Education: Dr José Morales G. (Dir)

DIRECTORS

College of Humanities and Social Sciences (Avda Patria 1202, Lomas del Valle, 44100 Guadalajara, Jalisco; tel. (33) 6610-1010 ext. 32237; fax (33) 6610-1610; e-mail izamora@uagunix.gdl.uag.mx; internet www.uag.edu):
- School of Anthropology, Philosophy and Letters: Lic. Cristina Ruíz de Hernández
- School of Linguistics: Lic. María Esther de la Cuesta Díaz
- School of Communication Sciences: Lic. Víctor Escalante Vera
- School of Psychology: Lic. Gabriel Morales Hernández
- School of Pedagogy: Lic. Ismael Zamora T.
- School of International Relations: Prof. Fernando Torres de la T.
- International Language Centre: Lic. Ma. Esther de la Cuesta D.

College of Architecture and Design (Avda Patria 1201, Lomas del Valle, 45110 Guadalajara, Jalisco; tel. (33) 6610-1010 ext. 32669; fax (33) 6610-1610; e-mail rmendoz@cu.gdl.uag.mx; internet www.uag.edu):
- School of Architecture: Arq. Raúl Mendoza R.
- School of Graphic Design: Lic. Carlos Herrera P.
- School of Landscape and Interior Design: Lic. Susana Maytorena
- School of Industrial Design: Arq. Alfredo Ambriz T.

College of Law (Avda Patria 1201, Lomas del Valle, 45110 Guadalajara, Jalisco; tel. (33) 6610-1010 ext. 32739; fax (33) 6610-1610 ext. 32276; e-mail hdelgadi@uagunix.gdl.uag.mx):
- School of Law: Lic. Humberto López D.
- School of of Social Work: Lic. Elsa Espinoza T.

College of Business (Avda Patria 1201, Lomas del Valle, 45110 Guadalajara, Jalisco; tel. (33) 6610-0412; fax (33) 6610-0412; e-mail jgcastil@uagunix.gdl.uag.mx):
- School of Business Administration: Lic. Ma. Elena Monroy L.
- School of Public Accountancy: C.P. José Arzate V.
- School of Economics: Lic. José Luis Sánchez de la F.
- School of Tourism: Lic. Celina Gallegos S.
- School of International Business: Lic. Atala Sosa H.

College of Engineering (Avda Patria 1202, Lomas del Valle, 45110 Guadalajara, Jalisco; tel. (33) 6610-1010 ext. 32216; fax (33) 6610-1010 ext. 32211; e-mail rjaime@uagunix.gdl.uag.mx):
- School of Mechanical and Electrical Engineering: Ing. Manuel Uriarte Razo
- School of Civil Engineering: Ing. Miguel Angel Parra Mena
- School of Information Management and Computer Systems: Ing. Gonzalo Osuna
- School of Computer Engineering: Ing. Rafael Jaime Alejo
- School of Electronic Engineering: Ing. Ramón Vázquez E.

College of Sciences (Avda Patria 1202, Lomas del Valle, 45110 Guadalajara, Jalisco; tel. (33) 6610-1010 ext. 32813; fax (33) 6610-1010 ext. 32219; e-mail jhernan@uagunix.gdl.uag.mx):
- School of Chemical Sciences: Ing. Antonio Peimbert V.
- School of Natural Sciences and Agriculture: Biol. Jorge Flores M.
- School of Mathematics: Ing. Eduardo Ojeda P.

College of Health Sciences (Avda Patria 1201, Lomas del Valle, 45110 Guadalajara, Jalisco; tel. (33) 6610-1010 ext. 32737; fax (33) 6610-0244; e-mail nperez@med.gdl.uag.mx):
- School of Medicine: Dr. Ricardo León B.
- School of Nursing: Enf. Gloria de la Cerda
- School of Dentistry: Dr Rafael Chacón V.

ATTACHED INSTITUTES

Institute of Biological Sciences: Dir Dr Francisco Rodríguez González.
Institute of Exact and Natural Sciences: Dir Ing. Ignacio Sánchez R..
Institute of Humanities and Social Sciences: Dir Lic. Ismael Zamora Tovar.
Institute of Co-operative International Higher Education: Dir Lic. Ricardo Beltrán Rojas.
Hospital 'Dr Angel Leaño': Dir Dr Leonel Solís Mena.
Hospital 'Ramón Garibay': Dir Dr Jesús Castillo Pacheco.
Dental Clinic: Dir Dr Rogelio Hinojosa Torre.
Centre for Asian and Latin American Studies: Dir Prof. Fernando Torres de la T.
Centre for Canadian Studies: Dir Lic. Francisco Lancaster-Jones.

UNIVERSIDAD DE GUANAJUATO

Lascuráin de Retana 5, 36000 Guanajuato, Gto.
Telephone: (473) 732-0006
Fax: (473) 735-1902
E-mail: info@quijote.ugto.mx
Internet: www.ugto.mx
Founded 1732 as Colegio de la Purísima Concepción; changed in 1928 to Colegio del Estado; present name 1945
State control
Academic year: August to June
Rector: Dr Arturo Lara López
Secretary: Dra María Guadalupe Martínez Cadena
Librarian: Mtra Rosalía del Carmen Macías Rodríguez
Library of 372,963 vols
Number of teachers: 2,900 (808 full-time, 2,092 part-time)
Number of students: 24,406
Publications: *Colmena Universitaria* (2 a year), *Acta Universitaria* (every 2 months), *Comunidad Universitaria* (2 a year), *Investigaciones Jurídicas* (2 a year), *Regiones* (2 a year), *Azogue* (2 a year), *Gaceta Naturaleza* (2 a year), *Voces, Laboratorio de Historia Oral* (2 a year), *Centro, Textos de la Historia Guanajuatense* (every 8 months), *Tarea Universitaria* (every 2 months)

DIRECTORS

Faculty of Accountancy and Administration: Mtro PORFIRIO TAMAYO CONTRERAS
Faculty of Administrative Sciences: C.P. EMIGDIO ARCHUNDIA FERNÁNDEZ
Faculty of Architecture: Arq. J. JESÚS OCTAVIO HERNÁNDEZ DÍAZ
Faculty of Chemical Sciences: Dr ALBERTO FLORENTINO AGUILERA ALVARADO
Faculty of Civil Engineering: Ing. CARLOS ARNOLD OJEDA
Faculty of Electronics, Mechanical and Electronic Engineering: OSCAR G. IBARRA MANZANO
Faculty of Geophysics and Hydraulic Engineering: Ing. JUAN MANUEL TOVAR ALCANTAR
Faculty of Industrial Relations: L.R.I. DOMINGO HERRERA BRIBIESCA
Faculty of Law: Lic. JUAN RENÉ SEGURA RICAÑO
Faculty of Mathematics: Dr IGNACIO BARRADAS BRIBIESCA
Faculty of Medicine: Dr FRANCISCO JAVIER GUERRERO MARTÍNEZ
Faculty of Mining, Metallurgy and Geology: Ing. RENÉ ECHEGOYEN GUZMÁN
Faculty of Nursing and Midwifery (Celaya): M.A.E. ROSALINA DÍAZ GUERRERO
Faculty of Nursing and Midwifery (Guanajuato): L.E. LETICIA SOTO FRANCO
Faculty of Nursing and Midwifery (Irapuato): Mtra LETICIA CAMPOS ZERMEÑO
Faculty of Nursing and Midwifery (León): ROSA MA. RICO VENEGAS
Faculty of Philosophy, History and Letters: GENARO ANGEL MARTELL AVILA
Faculty of Psychology: M.C. LETICIA CHACÓN GUTIÉRREZ

ATTACHED INSTITUTES

Institute of Experimental Biological Research: Dir CARLOS ALBERTO LEAL MORALES.

Institute of Agricultural Sciences: Dir M.I. MANUEL COLLADO MANÉ.

Center of Humanities Research: Dir Dr ARMANDO SANDOVAL PIERRES.

Inorganic Chemistry Research Centre: Dir Mtro JUAN JOSÉ GUZMÁN ANDRADE.

Medical Research Institute: Dir Dra ELVA LETICIA PÉREZ LUQUE.

Institute of Scientific Research: Dir Dr MARTÍN PICÓN NÚÑEZ.

Institute of Educational Sciences: Dir M. en I. HÉCTOR ERNESTO RUÍZ ESPARZA MURILLO.

Institute of Physics: Dir Dr JOSÉ LUIS LUCIO MARTÍNEZ.

Centre for Social Sciences Research: Dir Dr LUIS MIGUEL RIONDA RAMÍREZ.

Institute of Labour Research: Dir Dr CARLOS MENDIOLA ANDA.

UNIVERSIDAD AUTÓNOMA DE GUERRERO

Abasolo 33, 03900 Chilpancingo, Guerrero
Internet: www.uagro.mx

Founded 1869
Private control
Language of instruction: Spanish
Academic year: August to June

Rector: Ing. Agron. RAMÓN REYES CARRETO
General Secretary: M. C. CATALINO MACEDO VENCES
Librarian: Lic. ROBERT ALEXANDER ENDEAN GAMBOA

Number of teachers: 1,600
Number of students: 49,000

Publications: *Revista de la UAG*, *Gaceta Popular*, *Otatal*

DIRECTORS

Higher School of Agriculture: Q.B. GILBERTO BIBIANO MORENO
School of Engineering: Ing. RODOLFO VÁZQUEZ ZEFERINO
School of Chemical-Biological Sciences: Q. B. P. MARCO ANTONIO LEYVA VÁZQUEZ
School of Marine Ecology: Biol. ARMANDO YOKOYAMA KANO
School of Medicine: Dr ASCENCIO VILLEGAS ARRIZON
School of Commerce and Administration: C.P. SALVADOR OLIVAR CAMPOS
Higher School of Tourism: Lic. ARMANDO BELLO RODRÍGUEZ
School of Economics: M. C. S. ANGEL CRESPO ACEVEDO
School of Law: Lic. ALEJANDRO BERNABE GONZÁLEZ
School of Philosophy: Lic. FAUSTO AVILA JUÁREZ
School of Veterinary Medicine and Animal Husbandry: M. V. Z. SALVADOR SÁNCHEZ PADILLA
School of Social Sciences: Lic. ANGEL ASCENCIO ROMERO
School of Architecture and Town Planning: Arq. CLAUDIO RIOS TORRES
Regional School of Earth Sciences: Geol. GERMÁN URBAN LAMADRID

UNIVERSIDAD AUTÓNOMA DE HIDALGO

Abasolo No. 600, Centro, 42000 Pachuca, Hidalgo
Telephone: (771) 7-2000

Founded 1869 as the Instituto Científico y Literario, present status 1961
Academic year: September to June

Rector: Lic. JUAN ALBERTO FLORES ÁLVAREZ
Secretary: Lic. JORGE HIRAM ROSSETTE PENAGOS
Registrar: L.A.E. JORGE DEL CASTILLO TOVAR
Librarian: Lic. EVARISTO LUVIAN TORRES

Number of teachers: c. 700
Number of students: c. 9,000

Publications: *Revista Técnica de Información*, *Boletín Informativo*, *Informe Anual de Rectoría*

COURSE CO-ORDINATORS

Science and Technology: Ing. CARLOS HERRERA ORDOÑEZ
Professional Studies: Lic. YOLANDA MEJÍA VELASCO
Education: Quim. F.B. SILVIA PARGA MATEOS
Special Studies: Lic. FRANCISCO MURILLO BUTRON

DIRECTORS OF SCHOOLS AND INSTITUTES

Institute of Accountancy and Administration: C.P. HORACIO SOLIS LEYVA
Institute of Exact Sciences: Ing. JOSÉ CALDERÓN HERNÁNDEZ
Institute of Social Sciences: Lic. ALEJANDRO STRAFFON ARTEAGA
School of Medicine: Dr LUIS CORZO MONTAÑO
School of Odontology: Dr MIGUEL ANGEL ANTON DE LA C.
School of Nursing: Enf. LUZ MARÍA FLORES RAMÍREZ
School of Social Work: T.S. IMELDA MONROY DEL ANGEL
Preparatory School I: Ing. ERNESTO HERNÁNDEZ OCAÑA
Preparatory School II: Lic. LAURO PEREA MONTIEL
Preparatory School III: Lic. JUAN MANUEL CAMACHO BERTRAN

UNIVERSIDAD IBEROAMERICANA

Prolongación Paseo de la Reforma 880, Col. Lomas de Santa Fé, 01210 México, DF
Telephone: (55) 5950-4000
Fax: (55) 5267-4005
Internet: www.uia.mx

Founded 1943, University status 1954
Private control
Language of instruction: Spanish
Academic year: August to July

Rector: Mtro ENRIQUE GONZÁLEZ TORRES
Director-General (Academic): Mtro ENRIQUE BEASCOECHEA ARANDA
Director of Research and Graduate Programmes: Mtro JESÚS L. GARCÍA
Librarian: Ing. PILAR VERDEJO

Library of 204,000 vols, 1,395 periodicals
Number of teachers: 1,668 (279 full-time, 1,389 part-time)
Number of students: 10,508 (9,770 undergraduate, 738 postgraduate)

Publications: *Boletín Bibliográfico* (monthly), *Boletín Bolsa de Trabajo* (monthly), *Didac* (2 a year), *Gallo* (5 a year), *Jurídica* (annually), *El Ladrillo* (weekly), *Poesía y Poética* (3 a year), *Revista de Filosofía* (quarterly), *Revista del Departamento de Psicología* (3 a year), *Umbral XXI* (quarterly), *Prometeo* (3 a year), *Historia y Grafía* (3 a year)

DIRECTORS OF DEPARTMENTS

Architecture, Urban Planning and Design: Arq. JORGE BALLINA
Art: Lic. AÍDA SIERRA
Business Administration and Accounting: Mtro JAVIER CERVANTES
Basic Sciences: Mtro ARTURO FREGOSO
Engineering: Ing. SANTIAGO MARTÍNEZ
Communication: Mtro JOSÉ CARREÑO
International Studies: Lic. AGUSTÍN GUTIÉRREZ
Economics: Dr GERARDO JACOBS
History: Dra VALENTINA TORRES-SEPTIÉN
Human Development: Lic. JORGE MARTÍNEZ
Health: Dr FELIPE VADILLO
Law: Lic. LORETTA ORTIZ
Literature: Mtra SILVIA RUÍZ
Philosophy: Lic. FRANCISCO GALÁN
Political and Social Sciences: Dra CARMEN BUENO
Psychology: Dr PEDRO ALVAREZ
Religious Sciences: Dr CARLOS SOLTERO

REGIONAL CAMPUSES

Universidad Iberoamericana – León

Libramiento Norte Km 3, Apdo Postal 26, 37000 León, Guanajuato
Telephone: (477) 11-38-60
Fax: (477) 11-54-77

Founded 1978
Private control
Language of instruction: Spanish
Academic year: August to July

Rector: Ing. CARLOS ALBERTO SEBASTIÁN SERRA MARTÍNEZ
Director-General (Academic): Biol. ARTURO MORA ALVA
Director-General (University Educational Services): Lic. DAVID MARTÍNEZ MENDIZÁBAL
Registrar: Quím. MARIO ALBERTO ARREDONDO MORALES
Librarian: Ing. AMADOR CENDEJAS MELGOZA

Library of 41,000 vols, 691 periodicals
Number of teachers: 86 (48 full-time, 38 part-time)
Number of students: 2,319 (1,864 undergraduate, 455 postgraduate)

Publication: *Presencia Universitaria* (monthly)

HEADS OF DEPARTMENTS

Art and Design: Arq. JOSÉ LUIS MARTÍNEZ COSSIO
Economic and Administrative Sciences: C.P. PATRICIA MAGDALENA GARCÍA VILLASEÑOR
Human Sciences: Mtro HÉCTOR GÓMEZ
Law and Political Science: Lic. ALFONSO FRAGOSO GUTIÉRREZ
Engineering and Applied Sciences: Ing. GONZALO BAYOD BARRON
Basic Sciences and Mathematics: Fís. WENCESLAO OÑATE MORENO

Universidad Iberoamericana – Torreón

Calz. Iberoamericana No. 2255, C.P. 27010, Sucursal Torreón, Coahuila
Telephone: (871) 729-1010
Fax: (871) 729-1080
Internet: www.lag.uia.mx

Founded 1982
Private control
Academic year: August to July

Rector: Ing. HECTOR ACUÑA NOGUEIRA
Director-General (Academic): Ing. GABRIEL MONTERRUBIO ALVAREZ
Director-General (University Educational Services): Mtro FELIPE ESPINOZA TORRES
Registrar: C.P. CLAUDIA RODRÍGUEZ TORRES
Librarian: Lic. MARTHA I. MCANALLY SALAS

Library of 23,000 vols, 307 periodicals
Number of teachers: 387
Number of students: 2,299 (2,125 undergraduate, 174 graduate)

Publications: *Acequias* (4 a year), *Notilaguna* (monthly)

HEADS OF DEPARTMENTS

Human Sciences: Lic. SERGIO GARZA SALDIVAR
Economic and Administrative Sciences: Lic. ENRIQUE MACÍAS GONZÁLEZ
Physics and Mathematics: Ing. HARRY DE LA PEÑA
Art and Design: D. G. AMPARO ARJONA GRANADOS

Universidad Iberoamericana – Tijuana

Apdo 185, 22200 Tijuana, Baja California
Located at: Avda Centro Universitario 2501, Playas de Tijuana, 22200 Tijuana, Baja California
Telephone: (664) 630-1577
Fax: (664) 630-1591
Internet: www.tij.uia.mx

Founded 1982
Language of instruction: Spanish
Academic year: August to July

Rector: Mtro HUMBERTO BARQUERA GÓMEZ
Director-General (Academic): Dr ALBERTO ODRIOZOLA
Director-General: Lic. ARIEL GARCÍA
Registrar: Lic. ISABEL HUERTA

Library of 29,000 vols, 465 periodicals
Number of teachers: 328
Number of students: 1,221 (823 undergraduate, 398 postgraduate)

HEADS OF DEPARTMENTS

Art and Communication: Mtro BERNARDO TORRES
Economic and Administrative Sciences: Lic. RAFAEL LUNA
Human Sciences: Dr MARCELO CHAVARRÍA
Law: Lic. JESÚS VARGAS
Engineering and Sciences: Ing. FRANCISCO SALOMÓN GONZÁLEZ
Health Sciences: Dr MARCELO CHAVARRÍA
Language: Lic. MARIO HERNÁNDEZ

Universidad Iberoamericana – Puebla

Blvd del Niño Poblano 2901, U. Territorial Atlixcayotl, 72430 Puebla, Puebla
Telephone: (222) 229-0700
E-mail: webmaster@uiagc.pue.uia.mx
Internet: www.pue.uia.mx

Founded 1983
Private control
Academic year: August to July

Rector: Arq. CARLOS VELASCO ARZAC
Director-General (Academic): Mtro JAVIER SÁNCHEZ DÍAZ DE RIVERA
Director-General (University Educational Services): Mtro RAMIRO BERNAL CUEVAS
Registrar: Lic. FRANCISCO JAVIER GARCÍA GARCÍA
Librarian: Lic. LUISA GONZÁLEZ GARDEA

Library of 66,000 vols, 480 periodicals
Number of teachers: 132 (126 full-time, 6 part-time)
Number of students: 5,139 (4,181 undergraduate, 958 postgraduate)

Publications: *Magistralis* (every 2 years), *Comunidad* (3 a year)

HEADS OF DEPARTMENTS

Economic and Administrative Sciences: Mtro MANUEL RODRÍGUEZ AGUIRRE
Art, Design and Architecture: Arq. FRANCISCO VALVERDE DÍAZ DE LEÓN
Human and Social Sciences: Dr EDUARDO ALMEIDA ACOSTA
Engineering and Sciences: Ing. LUIS ENRIQUE FERNÁNDEZ LOMELIN

UNIVERSIDAD AUTÓNOMA INDÍGENA DE MÉXICO

Juárez 39, Mochicahui, 81890 El Fuerte, Sinaloa
Telephone: (698) 892-0008
Fax: (698) 892-0042
E-mail: uaim@uaim.edu.mx
Internet: www.uaim.edu.mx

Founded 2001

President: Lic. JOAQUÍN VEGA ACUÑA
Rector: JESÚS ÁNGEL OCHOA ZAZUETA
Secretary-General: MANUEL DE JESÚS VALDEZ ACOSTA
Director-General (Academic): ERNESTO GUERRA GARCÍA
Director-General (Administration): CARLOS ERNESTO VILLA PANQUIÁN
Director-General (Institutional Development): JOSÉ HUMBERTO GALAVIZ ARMENTA
Librarian: ERNESTO GAXIOLA ENCINAS

DIRECTORS

Los Mochis Campus: Lic. ROSARIO ROCHÍN NAPUS
Mochicahui Campus: Lic. JUAN ANTONIO DELGADO MORALES
Sinaloa de Leyva Campus: (vacant)

UNIVERSIDAD INTERCONTINENTAL

Insurgentes Sur 4303, Col. Santa Ursula Xitle, Del. Tlalpan, 14420 México, DF
Telephone: (55) 5487-1300
Internet: www.uic.edu.mx

Founded 1976
Private control
Academic year: August to July

Rector: JUAN JOSÉ CORONA LÓPEZ
General Secretary: JOSÉ-LUIS VEGA ARCE
Administrative Officer: C.P. JOSÉ LUIS LEON ZAMUDIO
Librarian: MIGUEL ANGEL SÁNCHEZ BEDOLLA

Number of teachers: 773
Number of students: 4,500

Publications: *Extensiones*, *Voces*, *Psicología y Educación Turismo*, *Traduic*, *Intersticios*, *Boletín Jurídico*

HEADS OF DEPARTMENTS

Architecture: Arq. FRANCISCO TERRAZAS URBINA
Communication Sciences: CARLOS CHÁVEZ LÓPEZ
Accountancy: ALBERTO GONZÁLEZ CARRERA
Administration: Dr SERGIO CHAVARRÍA Y ALDANA
Graphic Design: D. I. MARCELA CASTRO CANTU
Informatics: Dra VICTORIA RAQUEL BAJAR
International Commercial Relations: VALENTINA PEREA HERRERA
Law: Dr CARLOS CASILLAS VELEZ
Philosophy: ALEJANDRO GUTIÉRREZ ROBLES
Languages: Lic. LUZ MARIA VARGAS ESCOBEDO
Odontology: Dr ALFREDO LOCHT MIRO
Pedagogy: MARIA ELENA NAVARRETE TOLEDO
Psychology: Dr SALVADOR CASTRO AGUILERA
Theology: SERGIO ESPINOSA GONZÁLEZ
Tourism: OMAR AVENDAÑO REYES

UNIVERSIDAD AUTÓNOMA DE CIUDAD JUÁREZ

Henry Dunant 4016, Zona Pronaf, Ciudad Juárez, Chihuahua
Telephone: (656) 688-2100
E-mail: intdac@uacj.mx
Internet: www.uacj.mx

Founded 1973
State control
Language of instruction: Spanish
Academic year: August to June

President: RUBÉN LAU ROJO
General Secretary: CARLOS GONZÁLEZ HERRERA
Chief Administrative Officer: FERNANDO ROVELO CAMILO
Dean of Academic Affairs: Dr JESÚS LAU NORIEGA
Director of Graduate Studies and Research: M.C. MANUEL LOERA DE LA ROSA

Number of teachers: 710
Number of students: 12,200

Publications: *Entorno*, *Nóesis*

DEANS

College of Social Sciences and Administration: Lic. LUIS A. MAYORGA
College of Engineering and Technology: Dr RAMÓN PARRA
College of Biomedical Sciences: Dr FELIPE FORNELLI
College of Architecture, Design and Art: Arq. ARTURO MARTÍNEZ LASSO

UNIVERSIDAD ESTATAL DE ESTUDIOS PEDAGÓGICOS

Fresnillo y Cañitas 310, Ex-ejido, Zacatecas, 21090 Mexicali, Baja California
Telephone: (686) 555-4959
Fax: (686) 555-4959
State control

Dir: Prof. ALFONSO SEPÚLVEDA ORNELAS

Teacher training.

UNIVERSIDAD DE LA CIUDAD DE MÉXICO

Fray Servando Teresa de Mier 99, Centro, 06080 Cuauhtémoc, México, DF
Telephone: (55) 5134-9804
E-mail: rectoria_ucm@df.gob.mx
Internet: www.ucm.df.gob.mx

Founded 2001
State control

Rector: Ing. MANUEL PÉREZ ROCHA
Director (Academic): FLORINDA RIQUER FERNÁNDEZ
Director (Administrative): PATRICIA FUENTES RANGEL
Director (University Development): Lic. OSCAR GONZÁLEZ

Librarian: Lic. BLANCA ESTELA VELÁZQUEZ MORALES
Publications: *Mano Vuelta*, *Noticiario*
Campuses in Iztapalapa, Del Valle and San Lorenzo Tezonco.

ATTACHED RESEARCH INSTITUTES

Centro de Estudios sobre La Ciudad: Fray Servando Teresa de Mier 92, Cubículos 9 y 10, Tercer piso Col. Centro, 06080 Cuauhtémoc, México, DF; tel. (55) 5134-9804; e-mail centroestudiosucm@yahoo.com.mx; Dirs SILVIA BOLOS JACOB, ANA HELENA TREVIÑO CARRILLO.

UNIVERSIDAD DEL VALLE DE MÉXICO

Tehuantepec 250, Col. Roma Sur, Del. Cuauhtémoc, 06760 México, DF
Telephone: (55) 5264-7933
Fax: (55) 5574-0422
E-mail: jnajera@uvmnet.edu
Internet: www.uvmnet.edu
Founded 1960
Private control
Languages of instruction: Spanish, English, French
Academic year: August to June
President: C.P. JESÚS M. NAJERA MARTÍNEZ
Rectors: Lic. LUIS SILVA GUERRERO (Region A), Ing. JAIME PACHECO CHÁVEZ (Region B), Lic. PATRICIA PUENTE H. (Region C), Lic. SILVIA RIVERA DAMIÁN (Region D)
Vice-Rector (Academic Affairs): Lic. SERGIO LINARES
Head of Administration: Lic. JESÚS CARRANZA
Registrar: Lic. EDITH TERÁN
Librarian: Lic. SALVADOR CIPRES
Number of teachers: 2,300
Number of students: 25,500
Publications: *Adelante* (monthly), *Lince* (monthly), *Academias* (monthly)

DEANS OF CAMPUSES

San Rafael: Lic. MARÍA DE LA LUZ DÍAZ MIRANDA
Roma: Lic. GUADALUPE ZUÑIGA
San Angel: Lic. GRISELDA VEGA TATO
Tlalpan: Lic. LUIS SILVA GUERRERO
Xochimilco: Lic. SALVADOR SILVA
Guadalupe Insurgentes: Lic. MARTHA ANIDES
Chapultepec: Lic. ELIZABETH MANNING
Lomas Verdes: Lic. PATRICIA PUENTE
Querétaro: Lic. SILVIA RIVERA
San Miguel de Allende: Dr FRANCISCO MARTÍNEZ
Lago Guadalupe: Lic. GABRIELA MOTA

UNIVERSIDAD LA SALLE DE MÉXICO

Benjamin Franklin 47, Col. Condesa, Del. Cuauhtémoc, 06140 México, DF
Telephone: (55) 5728-9500
Fax: (55) 5271-8585
Internet: www.ulsa.edu.mx
Founded 1962
Private control
Campuses at Cancún, Cuernavaca, Guadalajara, Morelia, Obregón and Pachuca
Language of instruction: Spanish
Academic year: August to June
Rector: Mtro LUCIO TAZZER DE SCHRIJVER
Vice-Rector: Ing. AMBROSIO LUNA SALAS
Registrar: HORTENSIA NEGRETTI
Librarian: ALICIA GRAVE DE VARGAS DE ALBA
Number of teachers: 1,100
Number of students: 10,311
Publications: *Gaceta*, *Diez Días*, *Boletín de Preparatoria*, *Boletín de Biblioteca*, *Revista Dirección*, *Revista Médica La Salle*, *Revista Logos*, *Humanitas*, *Reflexiones Universitarias*, *Siempre Unidos*

DIRECTORS

School of Preparatory Studies: Mtro MARIO RAMÍREZ PÉREZ
School of Administrative Sciences: Lic. JOSÉ FRANCISCO PULIDO MACÍAS
School of Architecture and Graphic Design: Arq. OSCAR GONSENHEIM PAILLÉS
School of Chemistry: Quím. MARÍA TERESA ESTRADA DE GÓMEZ
Faculty of Law: Lic. JAIME A. VELA DEL RÍO
Faculty of Medicine: Dr MIGUEL AHUMADA AYALA
School of Philosophy: Mtro JOSÉ ANTONIO DACAL ALONSO
School of Engineering: Ing. EDMUNDO BARRERA MONSIVAIS
School of Religious Sciences: Dr JORGE BONILLA SORT DE SANTZ
Postgraduate Studies: Mtra MARÍA ELENA ESCALERA JIMÉNEZ
School of Education: Mtro CARLOS DAVID DOMÍNGUEZ TROLLE
Research Centre: Mtra ESTHER VARGAS MEDINA
Humanities: Lic. RAFAEL RUIZ RAMÍREZ

UNIVERSIDAD AUTÓNOMA METROPOLITANA

Rectoría General, Prolongación Canal de Miramontes 3855, Col. Ex-Hacienda San Juan de Dios, Delegación Tlalpan, 14387 México, DF
Telephone: (55) 5723-5644
Fax: (55) 5576-6888
E-mail: riebeling@tonatiuh.uam.mx
Internet: www.uam.mx
Founded 1973
State control
Language of instruction: Spanish
Academic year: September to July
Rector-General: JULIO RUBIO OCA
Secretary-General: MAGDALENA FRESAN OROZCO
Librarian: KAMILA KNAP ROUBAL
Number of teachers: 3,700
Number of students: 45,000
Publications: *Semanario de la UAM* (weekly), *Casa del Tiempo* (monthly), *Revista Iztapalapa* (2 a year), *Revista A* (2 a year), *Diseño UAM* (3 a year), *Economía, Teoría y Práctica Sociológica*, *Pauta*, *Contactos* (6 a year), *Alegatos* (3 a year), *El Cotidiano* (6 a year), *Reencuentro* (irregular), *Topodrilo* (6 a year), *Universidad Futura* (irregular), *Argumentos* (3 a year).

CONSTITUENT CAMPUSES

Azcapotzalco Campus

Avda San Pablo 180, Col. Reynosa-Tamaulipas, Del. Azcapotzalco, 02000 México, DF
Telephone: (55) 5485-9510
Internet: www.azc.uam.mx
Rector: EDMUNDO JACOBO MOLINA
Secretary: JORDY MICHELI THIRIÓN
Librarian: FERNANDO VELÁZQUEZ MERLO

DIRECTORS

Basic Sciences and Engineering: ANA MARISELA MAUBERT FRANCO
Social Sciences and Humanities: MONICA DE LA GARZA MALO
Design, Arts and Sciences: JORGE SÁNCHEZ DE ANTUÑANO BARRANCO

HEADS OF DEPARTMENTS

Basic Sciences: JOSÉ RUBÉN LUEVANO ENRÍQUEZ
Electronics: RAFAEL QUINTERO TORRES
Energy: SILVYE TURPIN MORION
Materials: ANTONIO MARTÍN LUNAS ZARANDIETA
Systems: ANGEL HERNÁNDEZ RODRÍGUEZ
Business: ANAHÍ GALLARDO VELÁZQUEZ
Law: GERARDO GONZÁLEZ ASCENCIO
Economics: ERNESTO TURNER BARRAGÁN
Humanities: BEGOÑA ARTETA GAMERDINGER
Sociology: PAZ TRIGUEROS LEGARRETA
Evaluation and Design: FRANCISCO JOSÉ SANTOS ZERTUCHE
Design Research and Information: JULIA VARGAS RUBIO
Environment: SAÚL ALCANTARA ONOFRE
Realization and Technique: HECTOR SCHWABE MAYAGOITIA

Iztapalapa Campus

San Rafael Atlixco 186, Col. Vicentina, Del. Iztapalapa, 09340 México, DF
Telephone: (55) 5612-4665
Internet: www.iztapalapa.uam.mx
Rector: JOSÉ LUIS GÁZQUEZ MATEOS
Secretary: ANTONIO AGUILAR AGUILAR
Librarian: ALFONSO ROMERO SÁNCHEZ

DIRECTORS

Basic Sciences and Engineering: LUIS MIER Y TERÁN CASANUEVA
Biological and Health Sciences: JOSÉ LUIS ARREDONDO FIGUEROA
Social Sciences and Humanities: JOSÉ GREGORIO VIDAL BONIFÁZ

HEADS OF DEPARTMENTS

Physics: SALVADOR CRUZ JIMÉNEZ
Electrical Engineering: MIGUEL CADENA MÉNDEZ
Hydraulics and Process Engineering: ALBERTO SORIA LÓPEZ
Mathematics: RODOLFO SUÁREZ CORTÉS
Chemistry: FERNANDO ROJAS GONZÁLEZ
Biology: CAROLINA MÜDESPACHER ZIEHL
Biology of Reproduction: JORGE HERNANDO HARO CASTELLANOS
Biotechnology: JORGE SORIANO SANTOS
Health Sciences: ERNESTO RODRÍGUEZ AGUILERA
Hydrobiology: MARGARITA GALLEGOS MARTÍNEZ
Anthropology: RODRIGO DÍAZ CRUZ
Economics: RAÚL CONDE HERNÁNDEZ
Philosophy: JOSÉ LEMA LABADIE
Sociology: OCTAVIO NATERAS DOMÍNGUEZ

Xochimilco Campus

Calzada del Hueso 1100, Col. Villa Quietud, Del. Coyoacán, 04960 México, DF
Telephone: (55) 5594-6656
Internet: cueyatl.uam.mx
Rector: JAIME KRAVZOV JINICH
Secretary: MARINA ALTAGRACIA MARTÍNEZ
Librarian: MARGARITA LUGO HUBP

DIRECTORS

Biological and Health Sciences: NORBERTO MANJARRÉZ ALVAREZ
Social Sciences and Humanities: GUILLERMO VILLASEÑOR GARCÍA
Art and Design: EMILIO PRADILLA COBOS

HEADS OF DEPARTMENTS

Health Education: JOSÉ BLANCO GIL
Man and His Environment: JOSÉ A. VICCON PALE
Agricultural and Animal Production: SALVADOR VEGA Y LEÓN
Biological Systems: CARLOS TOMÁS QUIRINO BARREDA
Education and Communication: JORGE ALSINA VALDÉS Y CAPOTE
Politics and Culture: ERNESTO SOTO REYES GARMENDIA
Economic Production: CUAUHTÉMOC VLADIMIR PÉREZ LLANAS

Social Relations: ALBERTO PADILLA ARIAS
Methods and Systems: SALVADOR DUARTE YURIAR
Creative Synthesis: MARÍA TERESA DEL PANDO ALONSO
Technology and Production: JAVIER SANTACRUZ ACEVES
Theory and Analysis: FRANCISCO PÉREZ CORTÉS

UNIVERSIDAD MICHOACANA DE SAN NICOLÁS DE HIDALGO

Edif. 'TR', Ciudad Universitaria, 58030 Morelia, Michoacán
Telephone: (443) 316-7020
Fax: (443) 316-8835
Internet: www.umich.mx

Founded 1539, University in 1917
State control
Language of instruction: Spanish
Academic year: September to June

Rector: Lic. DANIEL TRUJILLO MESINA
Secretary-General: Dr ARMANDO ROMAN LUNA ESCALANTE
Administrative Secretary: L.A.E. DOMINGO BAUTISTA FARIAS
Director of Library: Lic. ADALBERTO ABREGO GUTIERREZ

Library of 150,000 vols
Number of teachers: 2,158
Number of students: 31,769

Publications: *Boletín de Rectoría*, *Cuadernos de Derecho*, *Polemos*, *Cuadernos de Centro de Investigación de la Cultura Puehépecha*.

UNIVERSIDAD TECNOLÓGICA DE LA MIXTECA
(Mixteca Technological University)

69000 Huajuápan de León, Oaxaca
Telephone: (919) 532-0214
E-mail: escolar@nuyoo.utm.mx
Internet: www.utm.mx

Founded 1990
State control
Language of instruction: Spanish

Rector: Dr MODESTO SEARA VÁZQUEZ
Vice-Rector (Academic): Ing. GERARDO GARCÍA HERNÁNDEZ
Vice-Rector (Administration): C.P. JAVIER JOSÉ RUIZ SANTIAGO
Vice-Rector (University Relations and Research): Lic. SERGIO GUERRERO VERDEJO
Librarian: Lic. MANUEL BARRAGÁN ROJAS

HEADS OF STUDIES

Applied Mathematics: Mtro JUAN CARLOS MENDOZA SANTOS
Computer Engineering: Ing. FRANCISCO ESPINOSA MACEDA
Design: D.I. ROBERTO ESQUIVEL JAIME
Electrical Engineering: ENRIQUE GUZMÁN RAMÍREZ
Food Science: Q.F.B. JUANA RAMÍREZ ANDRADE
Industrial Engineering: Dr DANIEL ERASTE SANTOS REGES
Management Sciences: Lic. MARÍA GUADALUPE NORIEGA GÓMEZ

ATTACHED INSTITUTES

Institute of Agroindustry: Dir Mtro ENRIQUE LEMUS FUENTES.

Institute of Design: Dir Lic. ALFONSO ACOSTA ROMERO.

Institute of Electronics and Computers: Dir Mtro LUIS ANSELMO ZARZA LÓPEZ.

Centre for Humanities and Social Sciences: Head Lic. JOSÉ AARON SALAZAR DEL CARMEN.

Institute of Hydrology: Dir Ing. SAÚL MARTÍNEZ RAMÍREZ.

Mineral Institute: Dir Ing. ENRIQUE CONTRERAS GONZÁLEZ.

UNIVERSIDAD DE MONTEMORELOS

Apdo 16-5, Montemorelos, 67530 Nuevo León
Telephone: (826) 263-0900
Fax: (826) 263-6185
E-mail: umontemorelos@edu.mx
Internet: um.edu.mx

Founded 1973
Private control
Language of instruction: Spanish
Academic year: August to May

President: Dr ISMAEL CASTILLO OSUNA
Vice-Presidents: RAQUEL KORNIEJCZUK (Academic), RUBEN MEZA (Administrative), BENJAMIN LAZARO (Finance), ABRAHAM MURILLO (Student Affairs)
Director of Admissions and Records: EKEL COLLINS
Librarian: ADÁN SURIANO

Number of teachers: 175
Number of students: 2,350

Publications: *Logos* (annually), *Memorias del Centro de Investigaciones Educativas* (annually), *Perspectivas Teológicas* (annually), *Revista Internacional de Estudios en Educación* (2 a year)

DEANS

School of Administrative Sciences: ARIEL QUINTEROS
School of Arts and Communications: EUNICE AGUILAR
School of Biomedical Sciences: ALEJANDRO GIL
School of Education: JULIAEMY DE FLORES
School of Engineering and Technology: JORGE MANRIQUE
School of Health Sciences: ZENO CHARLES MICHEL
School of Music: NORKA DE CASTILLO
School of Theology: OMAR VELÁZQUEZ

ATTACHED INSTITUTES

Institute of Modern Languages: Dir ELIA HENAO.

Music Conservatory: Dir NORKA CASTILLO.

Preparatory School: Dir ISRAEL ESCOBEDO.

UNIVERSIDAD DE MONTERREY

Avda Ignacio Morones Prieto 4500 Pte, 66238 San Pedro Garza García, Nuevo León
Telephone: (81) 8124-1000
Fax: (81) 8124-1010
Internet: www.udem.edu.mx

Founded 1969
Private control
Language of instruction: Spanish
Academic year: August to May

President: Dr FRANCISCO J. AZCÚNAGA GUERRA
Vice-President (Administrative): Ing. CARLOS MAURICIO RODRÍGUEZ CHAPA
Vice-President (High School and Integral Education): GUADALUPE ELENA RAMOS VILLAREAL
Vice-President (Institutional Development) (vacant)
Vice-President (Undergraduate and Graduate Programmes): Lic. RAFAEL GARZA MENDOZA
Registrar: JUAN MARTÍNEZ VILLAREAL
Librarian: SAUL HIRAM SOUTO FUENTES

Library of 409,796 units
Number of teachers: 250
Number of students: 9,139

HEADS OF ACADEMIC DIVISIONS

School of Architecture, Design and Engineering: Ing. JOSÉ ALFREDO GALVÁN GALVÁN
School of Business: Dr MARIO ALANIS GARZA
School of Health Sciences: Dr EDUARDO GARCÍALUNA MARTÍNEZ
School of Humanistic Studies and Education: Dr VÍCTOR AURELIO ZÚÑIGA GONZÁLEZ
School of Law and Social Sciences: Lic. JORGE MANUEL AGUIRRE HERNÁNDEZ
Graduate Studies: Dr ARNAUD CHEVALLIER DELABASLE

HEADS OF UNDERGRADUATE PROGRAMMES

Accountancy and Finance: GABRIELA GARZA
Architecture: (vacant)
Arts: ROBERTO SALINAS
Biomedical Engineering: JESÚS VÁZQUEZ
Business Administration: CLAUDIA ENRÍQUEZ
Computer Science: ELIZABETH GUTIÉRREZ
Digital Graphic Design: ELIZABETH GUTIÉRREZ
Economics: LAURA ZÚÑIGA
Education: LUIS FERNANDO MÁRQUEZ
Graphic Design: JESÚS GAYTÁN
Human Resources: CLAUDIA ENRÍQUEZ
Humanities and Social Studies: MARÍA GLORIA CARBAJAL
Industrial Design: CARLOS CHAVEZNAVA
Industrial Engineering: IRASEMA VARGAS
Information Systems: ELIZABETH GUTIÉRREZ
Information Technology: ELIZABETH GUTIÉRREZ
Interior Design: CARLOS CHAVEZNAVA
International Business: MIREYA MALDONADO
International Finance: GABRIELA GARZA
International Marketing: MARTHA ALICIA CHAPA
International Studies: CELINA FERNÁNDEZ
International Tourism: LAURA ZÚNIGA
Law: SARA SILLER
Mechanical Engineering: DEMÓFILO MALDONADO
Mechatronic Engineering: DEMÓFILO MALDONADO
Medicine: CARLOS CANTÚ
Political Science and Public Administration: CELINA FERNÁNDEZ
Psychology: EVANGELINA REYES
Psychopedagogy: LUIS FERNANDO MÁRQUEZ
Textiles and Fashion Design: JESÚS GAYTÁN POLANCO

UNIVERSIDAD AUTÓNOMA DEL ESTADO DE MORELOS

Avda Universidad 1001, Col. Chamilpa, 62210 Cuernavaca, Morelos
Telephone: (777) 329-7083
Fax: (777) 329-7083
E-mail: dicodi@uaem.mx
Internet: www.uaem.mx

Founded 1953
State control
Language of instruction: Spanish
Academic year: September to July

Rector: RENÉ SANTOVEÑA ARREDONDO
Secretary-General: Lic. MANUEL PRIETO GÓMEZ
Academic Secretary: ELISEO GUAJARDO RAMOS
Librarian: Arq. JORGE SALAZAR DÍAZ

Number of teachers: 1,473
Number of students: 17,500

DEANS AND DIRECTORS

Faculty of Accountancy, Administration and Informatics: REY MARTÍNEZ MENDOZA
Faculty of Agriculture: Lic. ARTURO TAPIA DELGADO
Faculty of Architecture: Arq. EFRÉN ROMERO BENÍTEZ
Faculty of Arts: Dr JESÚS NIETO SOTELO
Faculty of Biological Sciences: ALFONSO VIVEROS MIRAMONTES
Faculty of Chemical and Industrial Sciences: MODESTO MÉNDEZ RDRÍGUEZ

School of Educational Sciences: Antonio Arana Pineda
Faculty of Human Communication: Lic. Liliana Arce Flores
Faculty of Human Sciences: Dra Angélica Tornero Salinas
School of Laboratory Technicians: María Isabel Neri Figueroa
Faculty of Law and Social Sciences: Lic. Jorge Arturo García Rubí
Faculty of Medicine: Dr Miguel Ángel Castañeda Cruz
School of Nursing: Alejandra Rivera Gutiérrez
Faculty of Pharmacy: Dr Alejandro Nieto Rodríguez
Faculty of Psychology: Dr Fernando Bilbao Marcos
Faculty of Sciences: Dr Verónica Narváez Padilla
Institute of the Eastern Region: Lic. José Patricio Durán Campoamor
Institute of the Southern Region: Lic. Aurora Cedillo Martínez
Language Centre: Prof. J. Reyes Aguirre Palacios
Spanish School for Foreign Learners: Wilfrido Ávila García

There are also 9 Preparatory Schools

UNIVERSIDAD MOTOLINIA AC

Cerrado de Ameyalco 227, Col. del Valle, 03100 México, DF
Telephone: (55) 5568-0559
Fax: (55) 5568-8324
E-mail: motolinia_promocion@yahoo.com
Internet: www.motolinia.com.mx

Founded 1918
Private control
Language of instruction: Spanish
Academic year: August to July

Principal: Luz María Portillo Arroyo
Chief Administrative Officer: María del Refugio Herrera Flores
Librarian: Juana María Camargo Muñoz

Schools of law and chemistry. There is also a campus at Pedregal.

UNIVERSIDAD AUTÓNOMA DE NAYARIT

Ciudad de la Cultura Amado Nervo, 63190 Tepic, Nayarit
Telephone: (311) 211-8800
Internet: www.uan.mx

Founded 1930 as Instituto de Ciencias y Letras de Nayarit, refounded as university 1969

Rector: Lic. Rubén Hernández de la Torre
Secretary-General: Lic. Fermín Fletes A.

Number of teachers: 230
Number of students: 2,400

Schools of agriculture, dentistry, nursing, commerce and administration, law, economics, chemical engineering, medicine, zoology, veterinary medicine.

UNIVERSIDAD AUTÓNOMA DEL NORESTE

Monclova 1561, Col. República, 25280 Saltillo, Coahuila
Telephone: (844) 416-3033
Fax: (844) 416-3153
Internet: www.uane.edu.mx

Founded 1974
Private control
Academic year: January to December (2 terms)

Rector: Lic. Francisco Aguirre Fuentes
Vice-Rectors: Lic. María del Carmen Ruíz Esparza (Academic), C.P. Gabriel Durán Maltos (Administrative)
Librarian: Lic. Nelly Bermúdez Arrazate

Number of teachers: 708
Number of students: 4,225

Courses in business administration, accountancy, education and psychology, law, tourism, architecture, computer studies, industrial and systems engineering, political science, graphic design.

UNIVERSIDAD AUTÓNOMA DE NUEVO LEÓN

Ciudad Universitaria, 66451 San Nicolás de los Garza, Nuevo León
Telephone: (81) 8329-4000
Internet: www.uanl.mx

Founded 1933
Academic year: August to July

Rector: Dr Reyes S. Tamez Guerra
Vice-Rector: Dr Jesús Galán Wong
Secretary for Administration and Finance: C.P. J. Ovidio Buentello Garza

Number of teachers: 7,211
Number of students: 104,300 (incl. attached schools)

DEANS

Faculty of Agronomy: Dr Juan F. Villarreal Arredondo
Faculty of Architecture: Arq. Guillermo Roberto Wah Robles
Faculty of Biological Sciences: M.C. Juan M. Adame Rodríguez
Faculty of Chemical Sciences: Ing. José Manuel Martínez Delgado
Faculty of Civil Engineering: Ing. Francisco Gámez Treviño
Faculty of Communication Sciences: Lic. Juan Mario Gámez Cruz
Faculty of Earth Sciences: Dr Cosme Pola Simuta
Faculty of Economics: Lic. Jorge Meléndez Barrón
Faculty of Forestry Sciences: Dr Alfonso Martínez Muñoz
Faculty of Law and Social Sciences: Lic. Alejandro Izaguirre González
Faculty of Mechanical and Electrical Engineering: Ing. Cástulo E. Vela Villarreal
Faculty of Medicine: Dr Jesús Z. Villarreal Pérez
Faculty of Music: Lic. Juan Luis Rodríguez Trujillo
Faculty of Nursing: Lic. María Gpe. Martínez de Dávila
Faculty of Odontology: Dr Roberto Carrillo González
Faculty of Philosophy and the Arts: Lic. Ricardo C. Villarreal Arrambide
Faculty of Physical and Mathematical Sciences: Ing. José Oscar Recio Cantú
Faculty of Political Science and Public Administration: Lic. Ricardo A. Fuentes Cavazos
Faculty of Psychology: Lic. Guillermo Hernández Martínez
Faculty of Public Accounting and Administration: C.P. Ramiro Soberón Pérez
Faculty of Public Health: Lic. Elizabeth Solís de Sánchez
Faculty of Social Work: Lic. Ma. Irene Cantú Reyna
Faculty of Sports Administration: Lic. René Salgado Méndez
Faculty of Veterinary Medicine and Zootechnics: Dr José Antonio Salinas Meléndez
Faculty of the Visual Arts: Arq. Mario Armendariz Velázquez

UNIVERSIDAD AUTÓNOMA 'BENITO JUÁREZ' DE OAXACA

Apdo 76, Ciudad Universitaria, 68120 Oaxaca, Oax.
Telephone: (951) 511-0688
Internet: www.uabjo.mx

Founded 1827, university status 1955
Private control
Academic year: September to July

Rector: Dr Cesar Mayoral Figueroa
General Secretary: Dr Eduardo L. Perez Campos
Librarian: Lic. Donaji Mendoza Luna

Library of 77,237 vols
Number of teachers: 980
Number of students: 15,000

Publication: *Planeación*

DEANS

School of Architecture: Arq. Jorge Vargas Guzmán
School of Law and Social Sciences: Lic. Abel García Ramírez
School of Medicine: Dr Alfonso Santos Ortíz
Faculty of Commerce and Administration: L.A.E. Severino Rojas Lázaro
School of Chemistry: Dr Arturo Santaella V.
School of Nursing and Obstetrics: Enf. Noemi Córdova Vargas
School of Fine Arts: Lic. Evelio Bautista Torres
School of Odontology: C.D. Austreberto Martínez Molina
School of Veterinary Studies: M.V.Z. Carlos A. de J. León Ledezma
Language Centre: Prof. Eric O'Connel

UNIVERSIDAD DE OCCIDENTE

Apdo 81200, B. Juárez 435 pte, Los Mochis, Sinaloa
Telephone: (668) 816-1000
Internet: culiacan.udo.mx

Founded 1978
Academic year: September to August

Chancellor: Dr Francisco Cuauhtemoc Frias Castro
Rector: Ruben Elias Gil Leyva
Secretary-General: M. S. P. Jose Guillermo Alvarez Guerrero
Chief Administrative Officer: Lic. Fernando Orpinela Lizarraga
Librarian: Delpha Della Rocca King

Number of teachers: 414
Number of students: 4,344

Publications: *Ciencia Jurídica*, *Un Sueño del Paraíso*, *Los Mochis*.

CONSTITUENT INSTITUTIONS

Campus Los Mochis: Carretera Internacional y Blvd Macario Gaxiola, Los Mochis; tel. (668) 816-1000; Dir Cila Maria Hernandez Rojo

HEADS OF DEPARTMENTS

Accountancy: Arq. R. Rodríguez Beltran
Administration: Lic. J. R. Cabreras García
Psychology: Lic. P. Ceballos Rendon
Communication: Lic. I. Torres Santini
Biology: Ocean. F. G. Cupul Magaña
Mathematics: Ing. F. Barreras Manzanarez
Law: Lic. F. Frías Loaiza
Engineering: Ing. M. Soler Rivera

Campus Culiacan: Blvd Madero 34 pte, Culiacan; tel. (667) 540-495; Dir Lic. Gilberto Higuera Bernal

HEADS OF DEPARTMENTS

Administration: Lic. A. González Luna
Economics: Lic. E. Damken Alatorre

Communication: Lic. M. L. Zambada Gallardo
Mathematics: Ing. M. Morín del Rincón
Law: Lic. R. Rodríguez Leal
Sociology: Lic. C. Habermann Gastélum
Engineering: Ing. L. Carlos Medina Aguilar

Campus Guasave: Corregidora y Zaragoza, Guasave; tel. (667) 872-0065; Dir Lic. Jesus Teodoro Ramirez Jacobo

HEADS OF DEPARTMENTS

Administration: Lic. R. Rivera Montoya
Accountancy: Lic. M. A. Camacho Crespo
Communication: Lic. C. J. Pérez Delaumeau
Mathematics: Ing. M. Narvaez Fernandez
Law: Lic. P. Hernández Benítez
Sociology: Lic. Y. A. Gutiérrez Alvarez

Campus Mazatlan: Avda del Mar 1200, Mazatlan; Dir Lic. Luis O. Montoya Higuera

HEADS OF DEPARTMENTS

Psychology: Lic. L.E. Sánchez Leyva
Administration: Lic. F. Arellano Ontiveros
Mathematics: Ing. A. Gutiérrez Márquez
Language: Lic. A. G. Ramirez Zertuche

Campus Guamuchil: Jose Maria Vigil y Blvd Lazaro Cardenas, Guamuchil, Sinaloa; tel. (673) 2-03-83; Dir Lic. Benito Gomez Urbalejo.

UNIVERSIDAD PANAMERICANA

Augusto Rodin 498, Col. Mixcoac, 03920 México, DF

Telephone: (55) 5563-2655
Fax: (55) 5611-2265
Internet: www.mixcoac.upmx.mx

Founded 1966
Private control
Academic year: August to June

Rector: Dr Ramón Ibarra
Vice-Rectors: Jesús Magaña Bravo, Lic. Sergio Raimond-Kedilhac Navarro
Administrative Director: Dr Víctor Manuel Pizá
Librarian: Elisa Riva Palacio

Library of 45,000 vols
Number of teachers: 450
Number of students: 5,000

Publications: *Boletín* (monthly), *Revista Istmo* (every 2 months), *Tópicos Journal of Philosophy* (2 a year), *Ars Juris* (2 a year)

Preparatory and first degree courses.

DIRECTORS

School of Administration: Ing. Amadeo Vázquez
School of Law: Dr Roberto Ibáñez Mariel
School of Economics: Lic. Flavia Rodríguez
School of Philosophy: Dr Rocio Mier y Terán
School of Education: Dra Carmen Ramso
School of Engineering: Ing. Pedro Creuheras
School of Accounting: Claudio M. Rivas

AFFILIATED INSTITUTIONS

Instituto de Capacitación de Mandos Intermedios (Mid Management Institute): Mar Mediterráneo 183, Col. Popotla, 11400 México, DF; tel. (55) 5399-7272; f. 1966; 170 teachers; 2,400 students; library of 1,200 vols; business administration to supervisor and head of dept level; Dir Conrado Antonio Larios.

Instituto de Desarrollo para Operarios: Norte 182, No. 477, Col. Peñón de los Baños, 15520 México, DF; tel. (55) 5760-3464; f. 1968; 45 teachers; 550 students; library of 500 vols; courses for worker-management; Dir Enrique Sierra.

Instituto Panamericano de Alta Dirección de Empresa (Pan-American Institute of Higher Business Studies): Floresta 20, Col. Clavería, 02080 México, DF; tel. (55) 5527-0260f. 1967; library of 8,000 vols; 40 teachers; 1,900 students; Dir Sergio Raimond-Kedilhac Navarro.

Instituto Panamericano de Ciencias de la Educación (Pan-American Institute of Education): Augusto Rodin 498, Col. Mixcoac, 03920 México, DF; Dir Dra Marcela Chavarría.

UNIVERSIDAD PANAMERICANA DE NUEVO LAREDO

Ave Morelos 2311, Col. Juárez, Nuevo Laredo, Tam.

Telephone: (867) 715-2731
Fax: (867) 715-2562
E-mail: universipanameri@netscape.net
Internet: www.unipanam.edu.mx

Founded 1980
Private control
Academic year: September to July

Rector: Lic. Francisco Balderas García
Secretary-General: C.P. Victor M. Castillo Avendaño
Director of Academic Affairs: Profa Guadalupe Jasso Juárez
Director of Services: Profa Ma. Monica Balderas Alcocer
Director of Preparatory Division: Prof. Carlos Camacho Mancillas
Director of Undergraduate Division: Profa Norma Gallegos Calderón
Director of Postgraduate Division: Dr José de Jesús Leal Mahmuud
Librarian: Lic. Abelardo Gloria Hinojosa

Number of teachers: 105
Number of students: 1,800 (1,200 undergraduate, 600 postgraduate)

DEANS

Faculty of Education: Prof. Carlos Camacho Mancillas
Faculty of Law, Public Finance and Administration: Lic. Fernando Ríos Rodríguez
Faculty of Medicine: Dr Wenceslao Lozano Rendón
Faculty of Primary School Education: Profa Juana María Cerda Torres
Faculty of Psychology: Lic. Virginia Zapata Rodríguez
Faculty of Secondary School Education: Profa Norma Gallegos Calderón
Faculty of Veterinary and Zoological Sciences: MVZ Alejandro Gurrola Granados
Faculty of Master's Degree Courses: Profa Ma. Balderas Alcocer

UNIVERSIDAD PEDAGÓGICA NACIONAL
(National Pedagogic University)

Carretera al Ajusco No. 24 Col. Héroes de Padierna Delegación, Tlalpan, 14200 México, DF

Telephone: (55) 5645-6213
Fax: (55) 5645-5340
E-mail: rectoria@upn.mx
Internet: www.upn.mx

State control
Language of instruction: Spanish

Rector: Marcela Santillán Nieto
Director of Planning: Abraham Sánchez Contreras
Director of Studies: Elsa Mendiola Sanz
Director of Library and Academic Support Services: Fernando Velázquez Merlo

Number of teachers: 3,989
Number of students: 69,300

Major subject areas: methods of teaching: education administration, pedagogy, educational psychology, educational sociology, indigenous education; part-time teaching: pre-school, primary and adult education; distance-learning: teaching French.

BENEMÉRITA UNIVERSIDAD AUTÓNOMA DE PUEBLA

4 Sur No 104, 72000 Puebla, Pue.

Telephone: (222) 229-5500
Fax: (222) 211-0821
E-mail: ciari@siu.buap.mx
Internet: www.buap.mx

Founded 1937
State control
Academic year: August to May

Rector: Dr Enrique Doger Guerrero
Secretary-General: Lic. Guillermo Nares Rodríguez
Librarian: Mtro Enrique Huitzil Muñoz

Number of teachers: 3,608
Number of students: 42,055

DIRECTORS

School of Public Administration: Mtra Sara Amalia Vélez Mejía
School of Architecture: Arq. José Antonio Ruíz Tenorio
School of Public Accountancy: M.A. María de Lourdes Medina Hernández
School of Chemical Sciences: M.C. José Javier Sosa Rivadeneira
School of Law and Social Sciences: Lic. Emiliano Perea Pelaez
School of Economics: Mtro Dante Méndez Jiménez
School of Philosophy and Letters: Dr Roberto Hernández Oramas
School of Arts: Mtro David Cornish Becerra
School of Communication: Lic. Eduardo Garzón Valdés
School of Languages: Mtro Antonio Vera García de León
School of Physics and Mathematics: Dra Soraya Gómez y Estrada
School of Chemical Engineering: Mtro Ignacio Rojas
School of Civil and Technological Engineering: Mtro Nicolás Fueyo MacDonald
School of Computing: Dr Guillermo de Ita Luna
School of Electronics: M.C. Jaime Cid Monjaraz
School of Medicine: Dr Manuel Morales Camacho
School of Physical Culture: Mtra María Vélez Mora
School of Stomatology: M.C. Luis Antonio González Salazar
School of Psychology: Psic. J. Fernando Turrent Rodríguez
School of Veterinary Medicine and Animal Husbandry: Dr Francisco Javier Franco Guerra
School of Biology: Biol. Gonzalo Yanes Gómez
School of Nursing and Obstetrics: Lic. en Enf. María Margarita Campos Vázquez
Hospital: Dr Adalberto Baights
School of Agricultural Engineering: Ing. Rosalba Solís Gómez
Institutes of Sciences: Dra María Lilia Cedillo Ramírez
Institute of Social Sciences and Humanities: Mtro Roberto M. Vélez Pliego
Institute of Physics: Dr Rutilo Nicolás Silva González
Institute of Physiology: Dr José Ramón Eguibar Cuenca

UNIVERSIDAD POPULAR AUTÓNOMA DEL ESTADO DE PUEBLA

21 Sur 1103, Col. Santiago, 72160 Puebla, Pue.

Telephone: (222) 229-9400

Fax: (222) 232-5251
Internet: web.upaep.mx
Founded 1973
Private control
Academic year: August to July
Chancellor: MANUEL RODRÍGUEZ CONCHA
President: MARIO IGLESIAS GARCÍA TERUEL
Vice-President: Ing. VICENTE PACHECO CEBALLOS
Registrar: Lic. MARÍA DE LOS ANGELES RONDERO CHEW
Public Relations Officer: Arq. JOSÉ M. ARGÜELLES REYES NIEVA
Librarian: Lic. LEOBARDO REYES JIMÉNEZ
Number of teachers: 652
Number of students: 5,084
Publication: *Vertebracíon* (6 a year)

HEADS OF DEPARTMENTS

Medicine: Dr JORGE BAUTISTA O'FARRILL
Dentistry: C.D. CARLOS PINEDA Y RÍOS
Nursing: Dra DULCE MA. PÉREZ SUÁREZ
Accountancy: C.P. GERMÁN GONZÁLEZ MARTIÑÓN
Agriculture and Animal Sciences: Ing. GERARDO VALLE FLORES
Architecture: Arq. FERNANDO RODRÍGUEZ CONCHA
Business Administration: Ing. TITO LIVIO DE LA TORRE
Civil Engineering: Ing. MARIO JIMÉNEZ SUÁREZ
Chemical Engineering: Ing. MA. JOSEFINA RIVERO VILLAR
Communication Sciences: Lic. VICTOR MANUEL SÁNCHEZ STEINPREIS
Industrial Engineering: Ing. JUAN ANTONIO ANAYA SANDOVAL
Political Sciences: Lic. JUAN DE DIOS ANDRADE MARTÍNEZ
Law: Lic. MATÍAS RIVERO AGUILAR
Psychology: Lic. MARTHA PATRICIA GUTIÉRREZ C.
Philosophy: Lic. JORGE LUIS NAVARRO CAMPOS
Education: Lic. PATRICIA CABALLERO CERVANTES
Computer Systems: Ing. JOSÉ MARÍA BEDOLLA CORDERO
International Business: Lic. JAVIER AGUAYO ORDÓÑEZ
Ecology: Mtro RUBEN P. RODRÍGUEZ TORRES
Institutional Administration: Lic. MARIA ELBA AMEZCUA DE N.
Economics: Lic. ALONSO IBÁÑEZ Y DURÁN
Advertising Design and Production: Arq. MIGUEL ANGEL BALANDRA JARA
Graduate Programmes and Continuous Education: Lic. GUADALUPE ESPINOSA ROMERO
English: Lic. HERLINDA CANTO VALENCIA
Social Studies: Arq. EDUARDO RAZO CISNEROS
Mathematics: Mtro ALEJANDRO NARVÁEZ H.
Physics: Ing. ROSARIO ACOSTA DE GALVÁN
Division of Art and Architecture: Arq. MIGUEL ANGEL BALANDRA JARA
Division of Basic Sciences: Ing. JOSÉ MARÍA BEDOLLA CORDERO
Division of Engineering: Ing. RAFAEL RANGÉL GONZÁLEZ
Division of Economics and Administration Sciences: Ing. TITO LIVIO DE LA TORRE
Division of Humanities: Lic. JOSÉ ANTONIO ARRUBARRENA ARAGÓN
Division of Health Sciences: Dr OCTAVIO CASTILLO Y LÓPEZ

UNIVERSIDAD DEL MAR, PUERTO ÁNGEL
(University of the Sea, Puerto Ángel)

Ciudad Universitaria, 70902 Puerto Ángel, Oaxaca
Telephone: (958) 584-3078
E-mail: web@angel.umar.mx
Internet: www.umar.mx
Founded 1992
State control
Language of instruction: Spanish
Rector: Dr MODESTO SEARA VAZQUEZ
Vice-Rector (Academic): Biol. MARIO FUENTE CARRASCO
Vice-Rector (Administration): C.P. ANDRÉS HERNÁNDEZ SANTIAGO
Vice-Rector (Relations and Research): Lic. MARTHA ISABEL PÉREZ HERNÁNDEZ
Head of Postgraduate Studies: Dra BEATRIZ AVALOS SARTORIO
Head Librarian: Lic. URSULA NAVARRO ALVARADO
Publication: *Ciencia y Mar*

HEADS OF STUDIES

Puerto Ángel campus:
Aquiculture: M.C. JOSÉ ARTURO MARTÍNEZ VEGA
Environment: M.C. HÉCTOR LÓPEZ ARJONA
Fisheries: (vacant)
Marine Biology: Hidrobiol. GABRIELA MEDINA GONZALEZ
Maritime Studies: M.C. CARLOS GABRIEL ARGUELLES REDONDO
Oceanology: (vacant)
Puerto Escondido campus:
Biology: (vacant)
Forestry: (vacant)
Zootechnology: (vacant)
Huatulco campus:
International Relations: (vacant)
Tourism Administration: Lic. GUILLERMO CHÁVEZ MUÑOZ

ATTACHED RESEARCH INSTITUTES

Ecology Institute: Dir Dra JUDITH AMADOR HERNÁNDEZ.

Industrial Institute: Dir M.C. SAÚL SERRANO GUZMÁN.

Research Institute: Dir Oceanól. MIGUEL A. AHUMADA SEMPOAL.

UNIVERSIDAD AUTÓNOMA DE QUERÉTARO

Centro Universitario, Cerro de las Campanas, 76010 Querétaro, Qro
Telephone: (442) 216-3242
Fax: (442) 216-4917
Internet: www.uaq.mx
Founded 1951
State control
Language of instruction: Spanish
Academic year: July to June
Rector: JOSÉ ALFREDO ZEPEDA GARRIDO
Academic Secretary: HUGO SANCHEZ VELEZ
Administrative Secretary: MIGUEL ANGEL ESCAMILLA SANTANA
Librarian: ARTURO HERNÁNDEZ SIERRA
Number of teachers: 1,428
Number of students: 18,000
Publications: *Revista de Egresados de Contabilidad*, *Revista Extensión Universitaria*, *Revista de Informática*, *Revista de Sociología*, *Revista de Medicina*, *Revista de Investigación*, *Revista Auriga*, *Revista Bellas Artes*, *Autonomía*

DEANS

Faculty of Engineering: JESÚS HERNÁNDEZ ESPINO
Faculty of Chemistry: J. MERCED ESPARZA AGUILAR
Faculty of Psychology: ANDRES VELÁZQUEZ ORTEGA
Faculty of Humanities: GABRIEL CORRAL BASURTO
Faculty of Law: ARSENIO DURAN BECERRA
Preparatory Faculty: DOLORES CABRERA MUÑOZ
School of Medicine: Dr SALVADOR GUERRERO SERVIN
School of Sociology: CARLOS DORANTES GONZALEZ
School of Veterinary Science and Zoology: M.V.Z. GUILLERMO DE LA ISLA HERRERA
School of Nursing: ALEJANDRINA FRANCO ESGUERRA
School of Journalism: LUIS ROBERTO AMIEBA PEREZ
School of Social Enterprise Management: FELIPE SAMAYOA
School of Computer Science: LUIS F. SAAVEDRA URIBE
School of Languages: AURORA IVETTE SILVA RODRIGUEZ
School of Fine Arts: JOSÉ ROBERTO GONZÁLEZ GARCÍA

UNIVERSIDAD DE QUINTANA ROO
(University of Quintana Roo)

Blvd Bahía s/n, esquina Ignacio Comonfort Col. del Bosque, 77019 Chetuma, Quintana Roo
Telephone: (983) 835-0300
Internet: www.uqroo.mx
State control
Language of instruction: Spanish
Rector: EFRAÍN VILLANUEVA ARCOS
Director of Administration and Finance: FELIPE CRIOLLO RIVERO
Director of Planning: CARLOS BRACAMONTES Y SOSA
Secretary-General: FRANCISCO MORIENTES DE ORCA GARRO
Head Librarian: ELÍAS LEÓN ISLAS
Library of 30,479 vols
Publication: *Revista* (scientific journal, 2 a year)

ACADEMIC DIRECTORS

Economic, Management and Social Sciences: FERNANDO CABRERA CASTELLANOS
Engineering and Sciences: MEDINA LEYVA LUIS FELIPE
Humanities and International Studies: ANTONIO HIGUERA BONFIL

HEADS OF DEPARTMENTS

Economic, Management and Social Sciences:
- Economic and Management Sciences: CRUCITA KEN
- Social Sciences: MANUEL BUENROSTO ALBA

Engineering and Sciences:
- Engineering: MAGDALENA MALDONADO
- Sciences: DAVID VELÁZQUEZ TORRES

Humanities and International Studies:
- Humanities: RAÚL ARISTIDES PÉREZ AGUILAR
- International Studies: RAFAÉL VELÁZQUEZ FLORES
- Languages: CARIDAD MARCOLA ROJO

UNIVERSIDAD REGIOMONTANA

Villagrán 238 Sur, Apdo Postal 243, CP 64000 Monterrey, NL
Telephone: (81) 8220-4600
Fax: (81) 8344-3470
Internet: www.ur.mx
Founded 1969
Private control
Language of instruction: Spanish
Academic year: September to August
Rector: Dr PABLO A. LONGORIA TREVIÑO
Administrative Director: Ing. GUILLERMO CHARLES LOBO
Registrar: Ing. GERARDO GONZÁLEZ
Librarian: Ing. JORGE MERCADO SALAS
Library of 42,952 vols
Number of teachers: 450
Number of students: 4,500

Publications: *Espresión* (weekly), *Veritas* (annually)

DEANS

Faculty of Engineering and Architecture: Dr RODOLFO SALINAS HERNÁNDEZ
Faculty of Economic and Administrative Sciences: Dr CARLOS OLIVARES LEAL
Faculty of Humanities and Social Sciences: Lic. DORA ANTINORI CARLETTI
Preparatory Division: Lic. NICOLÁS PALACIOS LOZANO

UNIVERSIDAD AUTÓNOMA DE SAN LUIS POTOSÍ

Alvaro Obregón 64 Antiguo, Centro Histórico, 78000 San Luis Potosí
Telephone: (444) 826-1381
Fax: (444) 812-3343
Internet: www.uaslp.mx
Founded 1826 as Instituto Científico y Literario
Federal control
Language of instruction: Spanish
Academic year: August to June
Rector: Lic. MARIO GARCÍA VALDEZ
General Secretary: Arq. MANUEL F. VILLAR RUBIO
Particular Secretary: Lic. MARÍA DEL PILAR DELGADILLO SILVA
Administrative Secretary: RICARDO SEGOVIA MEDINA
Finance Director: JOSÉ E. HERNÁNDEZ GARZA
Libraries System Director: Dr LUIS DEL CASTILLO MORA
Library of 3,000,000 vols in 28 libraries
Number of teachers: 2,290
Number of students: 19,400
Publications: *Alfa y Omega* (every 6 months), *Convergencia* (2 a year), *Escenario* (2 a year), *Hábitat* (annually), *Horizonte Administrativo* (3 a year), *La Rueda* (2 a year), *Lex Universitatis* (3 a year), *Revista del Instituto de Investigaciones Jurídicas* (every 6 months), *Universitarios Potosinos* (2 a year)

DEANS

Accountancy and Administration: JUAN MANUEL BUENROSTRO MORÁN
Agronomy: M. C. MIGUEL ANGEL TISCAREÑO IRACHETA
Chemistry: Dr JORGE F. TORO VÁZQUEZ
Communications: Lic. JORGE ARTURO MIRABAL MARTÍNEZ
Economics: Lic. DAVID VEGA NIÑO
Engineering: Ing. ARNOLDO GONZÁLEZ ORTÍZ
Habitat: Arq. ALEJANDRO GALVÁN ARELLANO
Law: Lic. RICARDO SANCHEZ MARQUEZ
Library Science: Lic. ROSA MARÍA MARTÍNEZ RIDER
Medicine: Dr JESUS EDUARDO NOYOLA BERNAL
Nursing: Mtra. MAGDALENA MIRANDA
Psychology: Lic. VICTOR MANUEL ARREGUÍN ROCHA
Science: M. C. BENITO PINEDA REYES
Stomatology: Dr MARIO AREVALO MENDOZA

AFFILIATED INSTITUTES

Educative Sciences: Dir M. C. FERNANDO MENDOZA SAUCEDO.
Geology: Dir Dr J. RAFAEL BARBOZA GUDIÑO.
Humanistic Studies: Dir C. P. ABRAHAM SÁNCHEZ FLORES.
Metallurgy: Dir Dr JOSÉ DE JESÚS NEGRETE SÁNCHEZ.
Optical Communications: Dir Dr ALFONSO LASTRAS MARTINEZ.
Physics: Dir Dr PEDRO VILLASEÑOR GONZÁLEZ.

UNIVERSIDAD COMUNITARIA DE SAN LUIS POTOSÍ

Arista 1000, Barrio del Tequis, San Luis Potosí, SLP
Telephone: (444) 815-3190
E-mail: salsilca@terra.com.mx
Founded 2002
State control
Rector: Prof. SALVADOR SILVA CARRILLO
Main subject areas: anthropology, community health, indigenous law, administrative information technology and economic development

DIRECTORS

Tamanzunchale Campus: Lic. RAFAEL MURGÍA FRANCISCO
Tamuín Campus: MARTHA INÉS FLORES PACHECO
Tonkanhuitz Campus: Ing. ALFREDO GURROLA GRAVE

UNIVERSIDAD POLITÉCNICA DE SAN LUIS POTOSÍ

Iturbide 140, Centro, 78000 San Luis Potosí, SLP
Telephone: (444) 814-4714
Fax: (444) 812-6519
Founded 2001
Rector: JUAN ANTONIO MARTÍNEZ MARTÍNEZ.

UNIVERSIDAD DE LA SIERRA

Carretera Moctezuma-Cumpas Km 2, 84561 Moctezuma, Sonora
Telephone: (634) 342-9600
Fax: (634) 342-9600
E-mail: rectoria@universidaddelasierra.edu.mx
Internet: www.universidaddelasierra.edu.mx
Founded 2002
State control
Academic year: August to May
Rector: Prof. JESÚS TORRES GALLEGOS
Secretary-General (Academic): Lic. JESUS ENRIQUE CHÁVEZ RAMIREZ
Librarians: Lic. IMELDA MONTAÑO AGUILAR, Lic. MARIA ELENA CORDOVA SALIDO

HEADS OF DEPARTMENTS

Economics and Business Administration: Lic. RUBÉN ÁNGEL VASQUEZ NAVARRO
Biological Sciences: HUGO SILVA KURUMIYA
Engineering and Technology: Ing. CRISTIAN VINICIO LÓPEZ DEL CASTILLO

UNIVERSIDAD AUTÓNOMA DE SINALOA

Apdo Postal 1919, Calle Angel Flores s/n, 80000 Culiacán, Sinaloa
Internet: www.uasnet.mx
Founded 1873
State control
Rector: Lic. DAVID MORENO LIZÁRRAGA
Secretary-General: Lic. ARTURO ZAMA ESCALANTE
Registrar: Lic. J.B. GAXIOLA COTA
Number of teachers: c. 400
Number of students: c. 6,000
Schools of law and social science, chemistry, physics and mathematics, accountancy, administration, economics, nursing, agriculture, social work. Campuses in Mazatlán, Los Mochis, Guamúchil, Juan José Ríos.

UNIVERSIDAD DE SONORA

Apdo Postal 336 y 106, 83000 Hermosillo, Sonora
Telephone: (662) 259-2136
Fax: (662) 259-2135
Internet: www.uson.mx
Founded Charter granted 1938; opened and officially inaugurated 1942
Private control
Language of instruction: Spanish
Academic year: September to June
Rector: Ing. MANUEL RIVERA ZAMUDIO
Secretary-General: Ing. MANUEL BALCÁZAR MEZA
Librarian: Lic. ANA LILYA MOYA
Library of 45,000 vols
Number of teachers: 1,025
Number of students: 18,000
Publications: *Gaceta Universitaria* (monthly), *Revista de la Universidad* (quarterly), *Poemarios* (every 2 months), *Revista de Física* (2 a year), *Revista de Economía* (2 a year), *Sonora Agropecuario* (every 2 months)

CO-ORDINATORS

School of Social Work: T.S. AMELIA I. DE BLANCO
School of Nursing: Prof. ELVIRA COTA
School of Advanced Studies: Ing. IGNACIO AYALA ZAZUETA
School of Law and Social Sciences: Lic. MIGUEL CÁRDENAS
School of Chemical Sciences: Ing. OSVALDO LANDAVAZO
School of Engineering: Ing. MIGUEL A. MORENO N.
School of Accountancy and Administration: C.P. RAMÓN CÁRDENAS VALDÉS
School of Economics: Lic. RODOLFO DÍAZ CASTAÑEDA
School of Agriculture and Animal Husbandry: Ing. MARIO GUZMÁN
School of Psychology and Communication Sciences: Lic. DANIEL C. GUTIÉRREZ C.
Department of Biochemistry: HECTOR ESCÁRCEGA
Department of Mathematics: EDUARDO TELLECHEA ARMENTA
Department of Physics: ANTONIO JAUREGUI D.
Department of Humanities: JOSÉ SAPIEN DURÁN
Department of Geology: Ing. EFRÉN PÉREZ SEGURA

CAMPUS DIRECTORS

Unidad Sur: Lic. JOSÉ A. VALENZUELA
Unidad Norte: Ing. RODOLFO GUZMÁN
Unidad Santana: Ing. MARIO TARAZÓN H.

UNIVERSIDAD JUÁREZ AUTÓNOMA DE TABASCO

Avda Universidad s/n, Zona de la Cultura, 86000 Villahermosa, Tabasco
Telephone: (993) 314-0698
Internet: www.ujat.mx
Founded 1958
State control
Academic year: September to August
Rector: Dr FERNANDO RABELO RUIZ DE LA PEÑA
Academic Secretary: Dr WALTER RAMÍREZ IZQUIERDO
Administrative Secretary: Ing. ARMANDO MORALES MURILLO
Secretary of the Rectorate: L.A. RICARDO SAIZ CALDERON
Librarian: Lic. TOMASA BARRUETA GARCÍA
Library of 174,608 vols
Number of teachers: 1,050
Number of students: 20,470
Publications: *Revista de la Universidad*, *Perspectivas Docentes*, *Universidad y Cien-*

cias, Revista de la División de Ciencias Sociales y Humanidades, Revista Temas Biomédicos, Gaceta Juchiman, Revista Hitos de la División de Ciencias Economico-Administrativas/Centro, Revista Zenzontle de la División de Educación y Artes, Revista de la Unidad Chontalpa

DIRECTORS

Division of Health Sciences: Dr ESMELIN TRINIDAD VÁZQUEZ
Division of Agricultural Sciences: M. V. Z. VICTOR DE JESUS PEREZPRIEGO COBIAN
Division of Humanities and Social Sciences: Lic. FREDDY PRIEGO PRIEGO
Division of Economic and Administrative Sciences: C.P. OLGA YERI GONZÁLEZ LÓPEZ (Centre Unit)
Division of Engineering and Technology: Ing. ARTURO ARIAS RODAS
Division of Biological Sciences: M. C. ANDRÉS ARTURO GRANADOS BERBER
Division of Arts and Education: Lic. EFRAIN PÉREZ CRUZ
Division of Basic Sciences: Fis. CARLOS GONZÁLEZ ARIAS
Chontalpa Unit: Ing. JUAN LUIS RAMIREZ MARROQUIN (Dir-Gen.)

UNIVERSIDAD AUTÓNOMA DE TAMAULIPAS

Apdo Postal 186, 87000 Ciudad Victoria, Tamaulipas
Internet: www.uat.mx

Founded 1955
Private control
Language of instruction: Spanish
Academic year: August to June

Rector: Ing. HUMBERTO FILIZOLA HACES
Secretary-General: M.V.Z. FERNANDO ARIZPE GARCÍA
Academic Secretary: C.P. URIEL DAVILA HERRERA
Administrative Secretary: Ing. MIGUEL CANTU CABALLERO
Director of Planning and Institutional Development: Dr. MARCO AURELIO NAVARRO

Number of teachers: 2,848 (912 full-time, 1,936 part-time)
Number of students: 36,000

Publications: *Sociotam* (2 a year), *Biotam* (2 a year)

DIRECTORS

Tampico Campus:
Faculty of Medicine: Dr ATENOGENES SALDIVAR
Faculty of Dentistry: Dr DELFINO ALVISO
Faculty of Law and Social Sciences: Lic. SALVADOR ESTEVE
Faculty of Engineering: Ing. MOISES BARCENAS
Faculty of Architecture: Arq. JUAN JOSÉ CUEVAS
Faculty of Commerce and Administration: C.P. JOSÉ LUIS LIZARDI
Faculty of Nursing and Obstetrics: Mtra PAULINA AGUILERA
Higher School of Music: Mtro EDGAR ZARAGOZA

Victoria Campus:
Faculty of Veterinary Medicine: M.V.Z. SERGIO GARZA
Faculty of Agriculture: Ing. MARIO LARA
Faculty of Commerce and Administration: Mtro HUGO VALLADARES
Faculty of Education: Lic. VALENTÍN AVILA
Faculty of Law and Social Sciences: Lic. J. LAVIN
Faculty of Social Work: Lic. GONZALO HERNÁNDEZ
School of Nursing: Lic CINTHYA IBARRA

Mante Campus:
Faculty of Agriculture: Ing. ALEJANDRO HERNÁNDEZ

Matamoros Campus:
Faculty of Human Medicine: Dr JUAN CARLOS CANTÓ
Faculty of Nursing: Mtra ANTONIA HERNÁNDEZ

Reynosa Campus:
Faculty of Chemical Sciences: L.Q.I. RENE FUENTES
Faculty of Agro-industrial Sciences: Ing. JOSE SUÁREZ FERNÁNDEZ

Nuevo Laredo Campus:
Faculty of Commerce and Administration: Lic RAMIRO GARZA
Faculty of Nursing: Lic ROSALINDA MEDINA

UNIVERSIDAD AUTÓNOMA DE TLAXCALA

Avda Universidad 1, 90000 Tlaxcala, Tlax.
Telephone: (246) 462-1167
Fax: (246) 462-1167
E-mail: rectoria@cci.uatx.mx
Internet: www.uatx.mx

Founded 1976
Academic year: July to June

Rector: J.A. RENÉ GRADA YAUTENTZI
Administrative Director: DOROTEO NAVA
Librarian: OSVALDO RAMÍREZ ORTIZ

Number of teachers: 700
Number of students: 10,000

Depts: social sciences, biomedical sciences, education, humanities. Research centres: animal physiology and behaviour, animal reproduction, biological sciences and biotechnology, genetics and environment, regional development.

UNIVERSIDAD VERACRUZANA

Zona Universitaria, Lomas del Estadio s/n, 91090 Jalapa, Ver.
Telephone: (228) 842-17-63
Fax: (228) 817-63-70
E-mail: rarias@uv.mx
Internet: www.uv.mx

Founded 1944
Academic year: September to August

Rector: Dr RAÚL ARIAS LOVILLO
Vice-Rector (Veracruz Campus): EMILIO ZILLI DEBERNARDI
Vice-Rector (Orizaba-Córdoba Campus): Arq. ROBERTO OLAVARRIETA MARENCO
Vice-Rector (Poza Rica-Tuxpan Campus): Dra CLARA CELINA MEDINA SAGAHÓN
Vice-Rector (Coatzacoalcos-Minatitlán Campus): ENRIQUE RAMÍREZ NAZARIEGA
Academic Secretary: Mtra MARIA DEL PILAR VELASCO MUÑOZ LEDO
Dean of Planning and Institutional Research: Mtra LAURA ELENA MARTÍNEZ MÁRQUEZ
Librarian: Lic. DIANA GONZÁLEZ ORTEGA

Number of teachers: 5,064
Number of students: 44,903

Publications: *La Palabra y el Hombre, La Ciencia y el Hombre*

HEADS OF DIVISIONS

Health Sciences: Dr RAMÓN FLORES LOZANO
Humanities: Dr Ma MAGDALENA HERNÁNDEZ ALARCÓN
Agricultural and Biological Sciences: Mtro ERNESTO RODRÍGUEZ LUNA
Technology: Mtro WALTER LUIS SAIZ GONZÁLEZ
Economics: Dr MARIO MIGUEL OJEDA RAMÍREZ
Arts: Mtro ENRIQUE SALMERÓN CÓRDOBA

DIRECTORS

Xalapa Campus:
Faculty of Architecture: Arq. MIGUEL ÁNGEL CORTÉS ZAHAR
Faculty of Law: Lic. MANLIO FABIO CASARÍN NAVARRETE
Faculty of Economics: Dr REY ACOSTA BARRADAS
Faculty of Psychology: Mtro AGUSTÍN AGUIRRE PITALÚA
Faculty of Fine Arts: Mtro HÉCTOR VINICIO REYES CONTRERAS
Faculty of Dance: Mtra NATALIA JUAN GIL
Faculty of Music: Mtra PATRICIA CASTILLO DÍAZ
Faculty of Theatre: Mtra ELKA FEDIUK WALCZEWSKA
Faculty of Medicine: Dr RAFAEL CANO ORTEGA
Faculty of Dentistry: MARINA FERNÁNDEZ CONTI
Faculty of Nutrition: CONCEPCIÓN SÁNCHEZ ROVELO
Faculty of Clinical Chemistry: SANDRA LUZ GONZÁLEZ HERRERA
Faculty of Nursing: CRISTINA SAAVEDRA VÉLEZ
Faculty of Accounting and Business Management: LUIS RICARDO OLIVARES MENDOZA
Faculty of Anthropology: Mtro FRANCISCO JAVIER KURI CAMACHO
Faculty of Philosophy: Mtro ALBERTO C. RUIZ QUIROZ
Faculty of History: Mtro HÉCTOR MÁRTINEZ DOMÍNGUEZ
Faculty of Languages: Mtra ROSALBA HESS MORENO
Faculty of Spanish Language and Literature: Lic. NIDIA VINCENT ORTEGA
Faculty of Education: Mtra ROCÍO L. GONZÁLEZ GUERRERO
Faculty of Agriculture: Ing. GABRIEL MAY MORA
Faculty of Biology: Biol. SOLEDAD ROCHA FLORES
Faculty of Civil Engineering: Ing. ARURO ORTIZ CEDANO
Faculty of Mechanical and Electrical Engineering: Mtro RAFAEL LOZANO GONZÁLEZ
Faculty of Chemical Engineering: Mtro MIGUEL ÁNGEL FRAGOSO LÓPEZ
Faculty of Chemical Biological Pharmacy: Dr RAFAEL DÍAZ SOBAC
Faculty of Statistics and Computing: ALMA ROSA GARCÍA GAONA
Faculty of Administrative and Social Sciences: ADELAIDA RODRÍGUEZ ARCOS
Faculty of Sociology: Mtro LUIS MAGAÑA CUELLAR
Faculty of Physics: Dr CÉSAR RENÉ DE LA CRUZ LASO
Faculty of Electronic Instrumentation: Mtro ÁNGEL BARRIENTOS SANTIAGO
Faculty of Mathematics: Dr JOSÉ RIGOBERTO GABRIEL ARGÜELLES

Veracruz Campus:
Faculty of Communications Science: Lic. JOSÉ LUIS CERDÁN DÍAZ
Faculty of Medicine: Dr FRANCISCO MANUEL SANTIAGO SILVA
Faculty of Dentistry: Dra EMMA HERNÁNDEZ FIGUEROA
Faculty of Nutrition: Lic. MA. DE LOURDES MALPICA CARLÍN
Faculty of Veterinary Medicine and Zootechnics: CARLOS LAMONTHE ZAVALETA
Faculty of Nursing: SOFÍA DELFÍN BADUY
Faculty of Physical Education, Sports and Recreation: Mtro SERGIO HERNÁNDEZ LÓPEZ
Faculty of Education: Mtra LETICIA SÁNCHEZ TETUMA
Faculty of Clinical Chemistry: MA. DEL REFUGIO SALAS ORTEGA
Faculty of Psychology: Psic. MA. EUGENIA PADILLA FARÍAS
Faculty of Accounting: CELIA DEL PILAR GARRIDO VARGAS

Faculty of Business Management: LILIANA IVONNE BETANCOURT TRAVENDHAN
Faculty of Engineering: Ing. JOSÉ A. TELLO ALLENDE

Orizaba-Córdoba Campus:

Faculty of Chemical Sciences: SOFÍA CANALES CHÁVEZ
Faculty of Nursing: Enf. INÉS HUERTA VÁSQUEZ
Faculty of Medicine: Dr JORGE E. LÓPEZ GONZÁLEZ
Faculty of Mechanical and Electrical Engineering: Ing. GUILLERMO CABALLERO LEÓN
Faculty of Architecture: Arq. ABEL COLORADO SAINZ
Faculty of Dentistry: GUILLERMO MERAZ ZÚÑIGA
Faculty of Biological and Agricultural Sciences: ANTONIO PÉREZ PACHECO
Faculty of Accountancy and Business Management: IDELFONSO VÍCTOR MUÑOZ ROSAS

Poza Rica-Tuxpan Campus:

Faculty of Social Work: Lic. VIRGINIA CALLEJAS MATEOS
Faculty of Education: Lic. ADORACIÓN BARRALES VILLEGAS
Faculty of Accountancy: Mtro MARIO SOTO DEL ÁNGEL
Faculty of Medicine: Dr JORGE C. VILLEGAS PATIÑO
Faculty of Dentistry: JAVIER AGUIRRE BACEROT
Faculty of Psychology: Mtro FRANCISCO BERMÚDEZ JIMÉNEZ
Faculty of Nursing: JUANA PERALTA SANTIAGO
Faculty of Civil Engineering: Ing. ALEJANDRO CÓRDOVA CEBALLOS
Faculty of Chemical Sciences: Ing. SERGIO NATAN GONZÁLEZ ROCHA
Faculty of Architecture: Arq. LUIS MANUEL VILLEGAS SALGADO
Faculty of Biology, Agriculture and Animal Husbandry: Biol. JOSÉ LUIS ALANIS MÉNDEZ
Faculty of Electronic Engineering and Communications: SILVERIO PÉREZ CÁCERES
Faculty of Mechanical and Electrical Engineering: Ing. JOSÉ LUIS JUÁREZ SUÁREZ

Coatzacoalcos-Minatitlán Campus:

Faculty of Accounting and Business Management: JAVIER ARENAS WAGNER
Faculty of Medicine: Dr FRANCISCO ORTIZ GUERRERO
Faculty of Engineering: Ing. CIRO CASTILLO PÉREZ
Faculty of Dentistry: Dr JAVIER GASTÓN PÉREZ ORTIZ
Faculty of Social Work: Lic. LUCINDA MIRANDA CHIÑAS
Faculty of Nursing: MORAIMA KATZ
Faculty of Agricultural Production Systems Engineering: Ing. ALBERTO HERNÁNDEZ QUIROZ
Faculty of Chemistry (Coatzacoalcos): ERUVIEL FLANDÉS ALEMÁN

UNIVERSIDAD PEDAGÓGICA VERACRUZANA

Calle Museo 133, Unidad Magisterial, 91010 Xalapa, Veracruz

Telephone: (228) 814-1594
Fax: (228) 814-0036
E-mail: sec.academica@secupv.org
Internet: www.secupv.org

Founded 1980
State control

Rector: Dr MARCO WILFREDO SALAS MARTÍNEZ
Academic Secretary: REYNALDO CASTILLO AGUILAR

HEADS OF DEPARTMENTS

Primary Education: GUSTAVO SALVADOR TRUJILLO
Education and Educational Research: MARÍA MARCELA GONZÁLEZ ARENAS
Postgraduate Studies: Dr MARCO ANTONIO RODRÍGUEZ REVOREDO

UNIVERSIDAD AUTÓNOMA DE YUCATÁN

Calle 60 491–A x 57 Centro, 97000 Mérida, Yucatán

Telephone: (999) 930-0900
Internet: www.uady.mx

Founded 1922
Independent
Academic year: September to July

Rector: Dr RAÚL HUMBERTO GODOY MONTAÑEZ
Director General for Academic Development: ALFREDO F. J. DÁJER ABIMERHI

Library: 20 libraries with 227,022 vols, 7,401 periodical titles
Number of teachers: 1,158 (640 full-time)
Number of students: 15,823

Publication: *Revista*

DIRECTORS

Faculty of Accountancy and Administration: MANUEL ESCOFFIÉ AGUILAR
Faculty of Anthropology: Dr FRANCISCO FERNÁNDEZ REPETTO
Faculty of Architecture: Arq. EDGARDO BOLIO ARCEO
Faculty of Chemical Engineering: CARLOS ESTRADA PINTO
Faculty of Chemistry: WENDY F. BRITO LOEZA
Faculty of Dentistry: VÍCTOR M. ALONZO SOSA
Faculty of Economics: Dr RODOLFO CANTO SÁENZ
Faculty of Education: Ing. MARÍA ELENA BARRERA BUSTILLOS
Faculty of Engineering: Ing. JOSÉ ANTONIO GONZÁLEZ FAJARDO
Faculty of Law: Abog. RENÁN SOLÍS SÁNCHEZ
Faculty of Mathematics: Dr LUIS RODRÍGUEZ CARVAJAL
Faculty of Medicine: Dra GLORIA HERRERA CORREA
Faculty of Nursing: Lic. LIZBETH PADRÓN AKÉ
Faculty of Psychology: Mtro EFRAÍN DUARTE BRICEÑO
Faculty of Veterinary Studies: FERNANDO HERRERA Y GÓMEZ
Preparatory School 1: Ing. MIGUEL SUMÁRRAGA CERVERA
Preparatory School 2: TERESITA DE J. GÓMEZ LIZARRAGA

ATTACHED INSTITUTE

Centro de Investigaciones Regionales 'Dr Hideyo Noguchi': Dir Dra JUDITH ORTEGA CANTO.

UNIVERSIDAD AUTÓNOMA DE ZACATECAS

Jardin Juárez 147, 98000 Zacatecas, Zac.
Internet: www.ciu.reduaz.mx

Founded 1832
State control

Rector: FRANCISCO FLORES SANDOVAL
Secretary-General: DELFINO GARCÍA HERNÁNDEZ
Administrative Secretary: SALVADOR SANTILLÁN HERNÁNDEZ
Academic Secretary: FRANCISCO VALERIO QUINTERO
Librarian: JUAN IGNACIO PIÑA MARQUINA

Library of 35,265 vols
Number of teachers: 1,100
Number of students: 14,800

Publications: *Cuadernos de investigación, Diálogo, Gaceta universitaria, Azogue*

DIRECTORS

School of Law: Lic. VIRGILIO RIVERA DELGADILLO
School of Engineering: Ing. JUAN FRANCISCO ROCHÍN SALINAS
School of Chemistry: JUANA MARÍA VALADEZ CASTREJÓN
School of Nursing: MA ISABEL MEDINA HERNÁNDEZ
School of Accounting and Administration: JESÚS LIMONES HERNÁNDEZ
School of Economics: Lic. RODOLFO GARCÍA ZAMORA
School of Animal Breeding and Veterinary Medicine: ANTONIO MEJÍA HARO
School of Dentistry: Dr RAÚL BERMEO PADILLA
School of Medicine: Dr GERARDO DE JESÚS FÉLIX DOMÍNGUEZ
School of Agronomy: Ing. PEDRO ZESATI DEL VILLAR
School of Social Sciences: PEDRO GÓMEZ SÁNCHEZ
School of Mines and Metallurgy: Ing. RUBEN DE JESÚS DEL POZO MENDOZA
School of Mathematics: Lic. JUAN ANTONIO PÉREZ
School of Psychology: Lic. RICARDO BERMEO PADILLA
School of Music: Lic. ESAUL ARTEAGA DOMÍNGUEZ
School of Humanities: Lic. VEREMUNDO CARRILLO TRUJILLO
School of Physics: Lic. HUMBERTO VIDALES ROQUE
School of Education: SERGIO ESPINOSA PROA

ATTACHED INSTITUTES

Centro de Investigaciones Agronómicas: Dir Ing. JULIO LOZANO GUTIÉRREZ.

Centro de Investigaciones en Ciencias Químicas: Dir Dr MIGUEL ANGEL JUÁREZ PÉREZ.

Centro de Investigaciones en Medicina Veterinaria y Zootecnia: Dir Lic. ARMANDO TALAMANTES ROQUE.

Centro de Investigaciones en Ingeniería Mecánica y Eléctrica: Dir Ing. MANUEL RETA HERNÁNDEZ.

Centro de Investigaciones Jurídicas: Dir Lic. JOSÉ ANTONIO VALENZUELA RIOS.

Centro de Investigaciones Históricas: Dir CUAUHTEMOC ESPARZA SÁNCHEZ.

Centro Regional de Estudios Nucleares: Dir LEOPOLDO QUIRINO TORRES.

Centro de Estudios Literarios: Dir Lic. DAVID OJEDA ALVAREZ.

Centro de Estudios en Ciencias Minerales y de la Tierra: Dir Ing. VICTOR MANUEL NAVARRO HERNÁNDEZ.

Centro Universitario de Investigación y Docencia: Dir Dr RAFAEL HERRERA ESPARZA.

Centro de Investigación y Análisis de la Economía Regional: Dir Lic. RIGOBERTO VILLA VÁSQUEZ.

Centro de Investigaciones Astronómicas: Dir Ing. MANUEL RIOS HERRERA.

Centro de Instrumentos: Dir Ing. ALFONSO MACÍAS LÓPEZ.

Instituto de Investigaciones Odontológicas: Dir Dr OSCAR SAUCEDO QUINTERO.

Instituto de Investigaciones Economico-Sociales: Dir Ing. PEDRO CARRERA HERNÁNDEZ.

UNIVERSIDAD POLITÉCNICA DE ZACATECAS

Carretera Zacatecas-Guadalupe Km 4, Dependencias Federales, 98600 Guadalupe, Zacatecas

Telephone: (492) 923-6966
Fax: (492) 923-9666

E-mail: demsys@zac.sep.gob.mx
Founded 2002
State control
Rector: JOSÉ GUADALUPE ESTRADA.

Technical Universities

INSTITUTO POLITÉCNICO NACIONAL

Unidad Profesional Zacatenco, Col. Lindavista, 07738 México, DF
Telephone: (905) 754-4102
Fax: (905) 754-4102
Internet: www.ipn.mx

Founded 1936
State control
Language of instruction: Spanish
Academic year: September to July

Director-General: C.P. OSCAR JOFFRE VELÁZQUEZ
Secretary-General: Ing. ALFREDO LÓPEZ HERNÁNDEZ
Administrative Director: Ing. HÉCTOR URIEL MAYAGOITIA PRADO
Librarian: Lic. CESAR SANTÓME FIGUEROA

Number of teachers: 12,356
Number of students: 107,200

Publications: *Gaceta Politécnicá; Acta Politécnica*, *Acta Médica*, *Anales de la Escuela Nacional de Ciencias Biológicas*, *Economía Política*

DIRECTORS

Higher School of Mechanical and Electrical Engineering: Ing. ARTURO ZEPEDA SALINAS
Higher School of Engineering and Architecture: Ing. SALVADOR PADILLA ALONSO
Higher School of Chemical Engineering and Mining Industries: Ing. TIMOTEO PASTRANA APONTE
Higher School of Textile Engineering: Ing. CASSIN FRANCISCO ALE GUERRERO
Higher School of Physics and Mathematics: M. en C. OLGA LETICIA HERNÁNDEZ CHÁVEZ
Higher School of Medicine: Dr JUAN ORDORICA VARGAS
National School of Medicine and Homeopathy: Dr JAIME ERNESTO SÁNCHEZ GONZÁLEZ
National School of Biological Sciences: Dra THELMA LILIA VILLEGAS GARRIDO
Higher School of Commerce and Administration: C.P. JOSÉ DE JESÚS VÁZQUEZ BONILLA
Higher School of Tourism: Lic. VÍCTOR CHALE GÓNGORA
Higher School of Economics: Lic. MIGUEL ANGEL CORREA JASSO
Interdisciplinary Professional Unit of Engineering and Social and Administrative Sciences: Ing. ERNESTO ANGELES MEJÍA
Interdisciplinary Centre for Health Sciences: Lic. Nut. ADRIÁN GUILLERMO QUINTERO GUTIÉRREZ
Interdisciplinary Centre for Marine Sciences: M. en C. JULIAN RENÉ TORRES VILLEGAS
Interdisciplinary Research Centre for Regional Development (Michoacán): M. en C. VÍCTOR MANUEL LÓPEZ LÓPEZ
Interdisciplinary Research Centre for Regional Development (Durango Centre): Dr JÓSE ANGEL L. ORTEGA HERRERA
Interdisciplinary Research Centre for Regional Development (Oaxaca Centre): Ing. FERNANDO ELI ORTÍZ HERNÁNDEZ
Centre for Research and Development in Digital Technology (in Tijuana): Dr JOSÉ MÁRIA MONTOYA FLORES
Project for Technological and Scientific Social Studies: M. en C. LUIS FERNANDO CASTILLO GARCÍA
Interdisciplinary Project for the Environment and Integrated Development: Dr JUAN MANUEL NAVARRO PINEDA

ATTACHED INSTITUTION

Centro de Investigación y de Estudios Avanzados: see under Research Institutes.

INSTITUTO TECNOLÓGICO Y DE ESTUDIOS SUPERIORES DE MONTERREY

Eugenio Garza Sada 2501, Col. Tecnológico 64849 Monterrey, Nuevo León
Telephone: (81) 8358-2000
Fax: (81) 8358-8931
Internet: www.itesm.mx

Founded 1943
Private control
Language of instruction: Spanish
Academic year: August to May

President: Dr RAFAEL RANGEL SOSTMANN
Academic Vice-President: Dr HÉCTOR MOREIRA
Financial Vice-President: Ing. ELISEO VÁZQUEZ OROZCO
President of Monterrey Campus: Ing. RAMÓN DE LA PEÑA MANRIQUE
President of Eugenio Garza Sada Campus: Dr JOSÉ TREVIÑO ABREGO
Presidents for Out-of-State Campuses: Dr CÉSAR MORALES HERNÁNDEZ (Southern Zone), Ing. LUIS CARAZA (Central Zone), C. P. DAVID NOEL RAMÍREZ (Northern Zone), Ing. JUAN MANUEL DURÁN GUTIÉRREZ (Pacific Zone), Ing. CARLOS CRUZ LIMÓN (Virtual University)
Registrars: Lic. SERGIO SIERRA CABADA (Monterrey Campus): Ing. JOSÉ PANTOJAO (State of Mexico Campus): Lic. SERGIO BRAVO (Pacific Zone): Lic. MARCO VINICIO LÓPEZ (Querétaro Campus): Ing. JUAN MANUEL RUIZ (Northern Zone)
Librarian: Ing. MIGUEL ARREOLA

Library of 110,000 vols, 2,500 periodicals, 698,000 vols (Out-of-State Campuses)
Number of teachers: 5,148
Number of students: 68,947

DIRECTORS OF ACADEMIC DIVISIONS (MONTERREY CAMPUS)

Division of Administration and Social Sciences: C. P. GERARDO LUJÁN
Division of Agricultural and Marine Sciences: Dr JUAN D. VEGA
Division of Sciences and Humanities: Ing. PATRICIO LOPEZ DEL PUERTO
Division of Graduate Studies and Research: Dr FERNANDO JAIMES
Division of Engineering and Architecture: Dr TEÓFILO RAMOS
Division of Health Sciences: Dr CARLOS DÍAZ MONTEMAYOR

The Institute comprises 24 campuses in addition to the main Monterrey and Eugenio Garza Sada campuses.

Colleges

CETYS UNIVERSIDAD – CENTRO DE ENSEÑANZA TÉCNICA Y SUPERIOR

Calzada CETYS s/n, Col. Rivera, 21259 Mexicali, Baja California
Telephone: (686) 567-3701
Fax: (686) 565-0241
E-mail: info@cetys.mx
Internet: www.cetys.mx

Founded 1961
Academic year: September to June

Rector: Ing. ENRIQUE CARLOS BLANCAS DE LA CRUZ
Vice-Rector (Academic): Dr FERNANDO LEÓN GARCÍA
Director-General of Mexicali Campus: Ing. SERGIO REBOLLAR MCDONOUGH
Director-General of Tijuana Campus: Lic. MIGUEL ANGEL SALAS MARRÓN
Director-General of Ensenada Campus: Ing. FRANCISCO VILLALBA ROSARIO

Library: Libraries with 57,000 vols
Number of teachers: 487
Number of students: 3,700

Courses in fields of engineering (industrial, mechanical, manufacturing, electronics, computers, digital graphic design), computer sciences, corporate information systems, international business, management, finance, accountancy, behavioural sciences, international and corporate law, continuous education, executive development programmes.

COLEGIO DE LA FRONTERA SUR

Carretera Panamericana y Periférico Sur s/n, Apdo Postal 63, 29290 San Cristóbal de las Casas, Chiapas
Telephone: (967) 678-1883
Fax: (962) 628-1015
Internet: www.ecosur.mx

Founded 1994

Director-General: Dr PABLO FARÍAS CAMPERO

Divisions of Alternative Means of Production, of Agroecological Technology, of Health and Population, of the Conservation and Exploitation of Biodiversity.

COLEGIO DE MÉXICO

Apdo 20671, 01000 México
Located at: Camino al Ajusco 20, Pedregal de Santa Teresa, 10740 México, DF
Telephone: (55) 5449-3000
Fax: (55) 5645-0464
E-mail: webmaster@colmex.mx
Internet: www.colmex.mx

Founded 1940
Academic year: September to July

President: Dr JAVIER GARCIADIEGO DANTÁN
Secretary-General: MANUEL ORDORICA MELLADO
Academic Co-ordinator: JEAN FRANÇOIS PRUD'HOMME
Library Director: MICAELA CHÁVEZ VILLA

Library of 780,000 vols
Number of teachers: 305 (incl. researchers)
Number of students: 313

Publications: *Estudios de Asia y África* (3 a year), *Estudios Demográficos y Urbanos* (3 a year), *Estudios Económicos* (2 a year), *Estudios Sociológicos* (3 a year), *Foro Internacional* (4 a year), *Historia Mexicana* (4 a year), *Nueva Revista de Filología Hispánica* (2 a year)

DIRECTORS

Centre for Asian and African Studies: JUAN JOSÉ RAMÍREZ BONILLA
Centre for Demographic, Urban and Environmental Studies: JOSÉ LUIS LEZAMA
Centre for Economic Studies: JAIME SEMPERE CAMPELLO
Centre for Historical Studies: GUILLERMO PALACIOS Y OLIVARES
Centre for International Studies: GUSTAVO VEGA
Centre for Linguistics and Literary Studies: AURELIO GONZÁLEZ PÉREZ
Centre for Sociological Studies: ROBERTO BLANCARTE PIMENTEL

ESCUELA NACIONAL DE ANTROPOLOGÍA E HISTORIA (National School of Anthropology and History)

Periférico Sur y Zapote s/n, Col. Isidro Fabela, C.P. 14030, México, DF

Telephone: (55) 5606-8946
Fax: (55) 5606-0197
E-mail: enahdir@yahoo.com
Internet: www.enah.inah.gob.mx

Founded 1938

Academic year: January to December

Director: FRANCISCO ORTIZ PEDRAZA
Librarian: MARÍA DE LOURDES MÉNDEZ CAMPOS

Library of 37,575 vols
Number of teachers: 395
Number of students: 2,296

Publications: *Folleto de Información Básica y Cuadernos de Trabajo* (irregular), *Revista Cuicuilco* (quarterly)

Faculties of Physical Anthropology, Social Anthropology, Archaeology, Ethno-history, Linguistics and History.

ESCUELA NACIONAL DE BIBLIOTECONOMÍA Y ARCHIVONOMÍA (National School of Librarianship and Archives)

Calz. Ticoman 645, Col. Santa Ma. Ticoman, CP 07330 México, DF

Telephone: (55) 3752-7475
Fax: (55) 2752-7575

Founded 1945

Director: Mtro NAHUM PEREZ PAZ

Library of 5,000 vols
Number of teachers: 72
Number of students: 420

Publication: *Bibliotecas y Archivos*.

ESCUELA NACIONAL DE CONSERVACIÓN, RESTAURACIÓN Y MUSEOGRAFÍA 'MANUEL DEL CASTILLO NEGRETE' (Manuel del Castillo Negrete National School of Conservation, Restoration and Museography)

Ex-Convento de Churubusco, Xicoténcatl y Gral Anaya, 04120 México, DF

Telephone: (55) 5604-5188
Fax: (55) 5604-5163
E-mail: inahmex@telecomm.net.mx
Internet: www.telecomm.net.mx/encrym

Founded 1968

Academic year: September to July

Director: M. A. MERCEDES GOMEZ-URQUIZA
Deputy Director: DANIEL CAMACHO URIBE
Head of Academic Extension: GINA SALDAÑA LOZANO

Library of 15,000 vols
Number of teachers: 116
Number of students: 126.

INSTITUTO TECNOLÓGICO AUTÓNOMO DE MÉXICO

Campus Rio Hondo: Río Hondo 1, Col. Tizapán San Ángel, Del. Alvaro Obregón, 01000 México, DF
Campus Santa Teresa: Cetro de Investigación y Estudios de Posgrado (CIEP), Avda Camino Santa Teresa 930, Col. Héroes de Padierna, Del. Magdalena Contreras, 10700 México, DF

Telephone: (55) 5628-4000
Fax: (55) 5628-4102
E-mail: arturof@rectoria.rhon.itam.mx
Internet: www.itam.mx

Founded 1946

Academic year: January to December

President: ALBERTO BAILLERES
Rector: ARTURO FERNÁNDEZ PÉREZ

Library of 106,000 vols, 1,202 periodicals
Number of students: 3,500

Publication: *Revista Estudios* (4 a year)

Courses in business administration, economics, accounting, mathematics, law, computer sciences, public policy, literature, history, statistics and social sciences.

INSTITUTO TECNOLÓGICO Y DE ESTUDIOS SUPERIORES DE OCCIDENTE, AC

Apdo 31-175, 45051 Zapopan, Jal.
Located at: Periférico Sur Manuel Gómez Morín 8585, 45090 Tlaquepaque, Jal.

Telephone: (33) 3669-3434
Fax: (33) 3669-3435
E-mail: rectoria@iteso.mx
Internet: www.iteso.mx

Founded 1957

Academic year: January to December

Rector: DAVID FERNÁNDEZ DÁVALOS
Secretary-General: CARLOS LUNA CORTÉS

Library of 113,000 vols
Number of teachers: 945
Number of students: 6,796

Publications: *Sinectica* (2 a year), *Renglones* (Review 3 a year), *Huella* (3 a year)

Undergraduate courses in architecture, business administration, communications, environmental engineering, finance, international business, international relations, management of information systems, mechanical engineering, philosophy, public accountancy, civil, industrial and electronic engineering, chemical processing and administration, computer systems, design, psychology, industrial relations, educational sciences, law, marketing. Postgraduate courses in business management, education, engineering, communications, human development, industrial electronics, applied information systems, global marketing, politics, public management.

INSTITUTO TECNOLÓGICO DE CELAYA

Avda Tecnológico y Antonio García Cubas, Apdo Postal 57, 38010 Celaya, Gto

Telephone: (461) 611-7575
Fax: (461) 611-7979
Internet: www.itc.mx

Founded 1958

Director: Dr JUAN SILLERO PÉREZ
Academic Vice-Director: M.C. SAMUEL DOMÍNGUEZ TAMAYO
Administrative Vice-Director: M.C. RUBEN MARTÍNEZ BALDERAS
Librarian: Lic. TEODORO VILLALOBOS SALINAS

Library of 16,600 vols
Number of students: 2,623

Publications: *Apertura*, *Pistas Educativas*

Courses in industrial engineering, mechanics, chemistry and biochemistry, production and business administration, computer systems, electronics.

INSTITUTO TECNOLÓGICO DE CHIHUAHUA

Apdo Postal 2-1549, Ave. Tecnológico No 2909, 31310 Chihuahua, Chih.

Telephone: (614) 413-7474
Fax: (614) 413-5187
Internet: www.itch.edu.mx

Founded 1948

Director: Ing. MANUEL GALLARDO RODRÍGUEZ
Administrative Vice-Director: Ing. JUAN DE DIOS RUIZ
Academic Vice-Director: Ing. ANTONIO TREVIÑO RUIZ

Library of 29,000 vols
Number of teachers: 350
Number of students: 4,400

Publication: *Electro* (annually)

Degree courses in industrial, electrical, mechanical, chemical, electronic and materials engineering; postgraduate courses in electronics; degree and postgraduate courses in administration.

INSTITUTO TECNOLÓGICO DE DURANGO

Blvd F. Pescador 1830 Ote., Apdo Postal 465, 34080 Durango

Fax: (618) 818-4813
Internet: www.itdgo.mx

Founded 1948

Dependent on the Dirección General de Institutos Tecnológicos Regionales, SEP

Director: Ing. HÉCTOR ARREOLA SORIA
Librarian: JESÚS LAU

Library of 19,000 vols
Number of teachers: 267
Number of students: 2,677

First degree courses in industrial engineering in electronics, electricity, biochemistry, mechanics, information science, chemistry and civil engineering; Masters in industrial planning, biochemistry, civil engineering.

INSTITUTO TECNOLÓGICO DE CIUDAD JUÁREZ

Blvd Tecnológico 1340, 32000 Ciudad Juárez, Chihuahua

Telephone: (656) 688-2500
Fax: (656) 688-2515
Internet: www.itcj.mx

Founded 1964

Director: ROBERTO ARANA MORAN
Vice-Directors: HUMBERTO C. MORALES MORENO (Administrative), ALFREDO ESTRADA GARCÍA (Academic), SALVADOR SÁNCHEZ CRUZ (Academic Support)

Library of 13,300 vols
Number of teachers: 268
Number of students: 4,468.

INSTITUTO TECNOLÓGICO DE CIUDAD MADERO

1° de Mayo s/n, 89440 Ciudad Madero, Tamaulipas

Telephone: (833) 210-0415
Fax: (833) 210-5381
E-mail: itcm@itcm.edu.mx
Internet: www.itcm.edu.mx

Founded 1954

Director: Ing. JUAN MANUEL TURRUBIATE MARTÍNEZ

Library of 17,781 vols
Number of students: 5,000.

INSTITUTO TECNOLÓGICO DE MÉRIDA

Avda Tecnológico km. 5, Apdo Postal 9–11, 97118 Mérida, Yucatán

Telephone: (999) 944-8171
Fax: (999) 944-8171
E-mail: itm@uxmal.itmerida.mx
Internet: www.itmerida.mx

Founded 1961

Academic year: August to June

Director: Ing. GELASIO LUNA CONZUELO

Vice-Director (Administration): Ing. WILLIAM RAMÍREZ ROMERO
Vice-Director (Academic): Ing. ISIDRO CALDERÓN ACOSTA
Vice-Director (Planning): Ing. HERBERT LORÍA SUNZA
Librarian: Ing. NORINA LIZARRAGA CETINA

Library of 20,000 vols
Number of teachers: 369
Number of students: 4,146

Publications: *Revista del Centro de Graduados e Investigación* (quarterly), *La Quincena* (every 2 weeks)

HEADS OF DEPARTMENTS

Chemistry and Biochemistry: Dr CARLOS REYES SOSA
Earth Sciences: Ing. RAÚL ESTRADA SOSA
Electricity and Electronics: Ing. RAÚL CHIU NAZARALA
Economics and Management: Lic. SOLEDAD SOSA GÓMEZ
Industrial Engineering: Ing. EMANUEL CONDE ONTIVEROS
Metal-Mechanics: Ing. JOSÉ D. BORGES PASOS
Systems and Computing: Ing. JORGE CETINA SAURI
Graduate Studies and Research: Ing. GILBERTO CANTO BURGOS

INSTITUTO TECNOLÓGICO DE MORELIA

Avda Tecnológico 1500, Col. Lomas de Santiaguito, 58120 Morelia, Michoacán
Telephone: (443) 312-1570
Fax: (443) 312-1570 ext. 211
E-mail: direccion@itmorelia.edu.mx
Internet: www.itmorelia.edu.mx

Founded 1965

Director: Ing. JAIME ZORAGOZA BUENO

Library of 15,000 vols
Number of students: 3,500

Courses in industrial engineering and iron and steel industry.

INSTITUTO TECNOLÓGICO DE OAXACA

Calz. Tecnológico y Wilfrido-Massieu s/n, 68030 Oaxaca, Oax.
Internet: www.itox.mx

Founded 1968

Director: Ing. ARMANDO D. PALACIOS GARCÍA

Number of teachers: 280
Number of students: 3,000

Publication: *Itrosíntesis*

Courses in mechanical, electrical, chemical and civil engineering, business management and industrial planning.

INSTITUTO TECNOLÓGICO DE ORIZABA

Col Emiliano Zapata, 94320 Orizaba, Ver.
Telephone: (272) 724-4096
Fax: (272) 725-1728
Internet: www.itorizaba.edu.mx

Founded 1957

Director: Ing. ENRIQUE LEAL CRUZ
Administrative Assistant Director: Ing. BLAS REYES T.
Assistant Director (Planning): Ing. ROSENDO MARTÍNEZ
Academic Assistant Director: Ing. KIKEY GONZÁLEZ F.

Number of teachers: 308
Number of students: 2,994

Courses in chemical, industrial mechanical, electrical and electronic engineering, and computer science.

INSTITUTO TECNOLÓGICO DE QUERÉTARO

Avda Tecnológico s/n esq. Escbedo, Col. Centro, 76000 Querétaro, Qro
Telephone: (442) 216-3597
Fax: (442) 216-9931
Internet: www.itq.edu.mx

Founded 1967

Director: Ing. JUAN VALDESPINO MARTÍNEZ
Academic Vice-Director: Ing. JORGE MARIO ELIAS MARTÍNEZ
Vice-Director (Planning and Extension): Ing. FERNANDO QUIROZ GATICA

Library of 28,000 vols
Number of teachers: 314
Number of students: 3,596

Courses in industrial and mechanical engineering, architecture, systems engineering, electrical and electronic engineering and industrial administration.

INSTITUTO TECNOLÓGICO DE SALTILLO

Venustiano Carranza 2400, Col. Tecnológico, 25280 Saltillo, Coahuila
Telephone: (844) 438-9500
Internet: www.its.mx

Founded 1951

Director: Ing. JOSÉ C. TAMEZ SAENZ

Library: *c.* 15,100 vols
Number of students: 3,000

Publications: *Boletín de Seguridad Industrial*, *Boletín de Fundación*, *Boletín de Microenseñanza*, faculty bulletins

Courses in industrial, metallurgical and computer science engineering and technology.

INSTITUTO TECNOLÓGICO DE SONORA

5 de Febrero 818 Sur, 85000 Ciudad Obregón, Son.
Telephone: (644) 417-0783
Fax: (644) 417-0244
E-mail: orusso@itson.mx
Internet: www.itson.mx

Founded 1955 as Preparatory school, became University in 1973

Rector: Dr OSCAR RUSSO VOGEL
Vice-Rector for Academic Affairs: Lic. JAVIER VALES GARCÍA
Vice-Rector for Administrative Affairs: Lic. JORGE OROZCO PARRA

Library of 87,000 vols
Number of teachers: 914
Number of students: 16,355

Publications: *Revista de la Sociedad Académica* (2 a year), *ITSON-DIEP* (research reports, 2 a year)

Courses in biotechnological, electrical, electronic, systems and industrial, civil, chemical and agricultural engineering, chemistry, business administration, accounting, management information systems, education, psychology, veterinary medicine, natural resources and water resources management.

INSTITUTO DE ESTUDIOS SUPERIORES EN CIENCIA Y TECNOLOGÍA DEL MAR

Circunvalación Norte e Icazo, Veracruz, Ver.

Founded 1957

Dependent on the Dirección General de Enseñanzas Tecnológicas (Ministry of Education)

Director: Ing. JOSÉ LÓPEZ MEDINA.

School of Music

Conservatorio Nacional de Música (National Conservatoire): Avda Presidente Masaryk 582, México 5, DF; tel. (55) 5280-6347; fax (55) 5280-3726; f. 1866; 170 teachers; Dir Maestro LEOPOLDO TELLEZ; library: 48,900 vols; publs *Heterofonía*, *Gaceta de la Biblioteca*.

FEDERATED STATES OF MICRONESIA

The Higher Education System

The Federated States of Micronesia is comprised of the four named and autonomous states, namely Chuuk, Pohnpei, Yap and Kosrae. It is a small, developing nation made up of 87 islands and islets spread over four major island groups in 2.5m. sq. km of the Western Pacific. Its citizens speak 17 different languages and dialects. Higher Education is limited to one institution: the College of Mirconesia. The Department of Education is the government ministry responsible for overseeing the education sector. Education is governed by Act PL 7-97, which was approved by Congress in 1992.

Learned Societies

NATURAL SCIENCES

Chuuk Conservation Society: Chuuk; f. 2005 to protect and preserve local natural resources in order to sustain community livelihoods; Chair JOE KONNO; Sec. MARY ROSE NAKAYAMA.

Conservation Society of Pohnpei: POB 2461, Kolonia, Pohnpei 96941; tel. 320-5409; fax 320-5063; e-mail csp@mail.fm; internet www.serehd.org; f. 1998; aims to increase community involvement in the conservation and management of Pohnpei's natural resources, to build local capacity through public and private partnerships, to develop alternatives to unsustainable practices and to promote laws and policies that support these objectives; current programmes: marine, terrestrial and educational awareness; Exec. Dir PATTERSON SHED.

Kosrae Conservation and Safety Organization: POB 539, Tofol, Kosrae 96944; tel. 370-3391; fax 370-3000; e-mail kcso@mail.fm; promotes conservation of the natural environment and awareness creation; Chair. MADISON NENA; Exec. Dir ANDY GEORGE.

Micronesia Conservation Trust: POB 2177, Kolonia, Pohnpei 96941; tel. 320-5670; fax 320-8903; e-mail mct@mail.fm; internet mctconservation.org; f. 2002 to support biodiversity conservation and related sustainable development for the people of Micronesia; provides long-term, sustained funding to community-based orgs and other NGOs through a grants programme; Exec. Dir WILLY KOSTKA.

Yap Institute of Natural Science: POB 215, Colonia, Yap 96943; tel. 350-4630; e-mail mfalanruw@mail.fm; promotes sustainable use of local resources; Dir Dr MARJORIE C. FALANRUW.

Libraries and Archives

Kolonia

College of Micronesia Learning Resources Center: POB 159, Kolonia, Pohnpei 96941; tel. 320-2480; e-mail comfsmlib@comfsm.fm; internet www.comfsm.fm/library; comprises general library, serials section, US Govt documents library; Micronesia-Pacific Research Center; depository for the Secretariat of the Pacific Community materials and a partial depository for UN documents; Nat. Archives contains materials from the Navy and Trust Territory eras; 34,000 vols; Dir SUE CALDWELL.

Pohnpei Public Library: POB 284, Kolonia, Pohnpei 96941; tel. 320-2423; f. 1988; 8,000 vols; 1 mobile library; Head Librarian CARMINA LIHPAI.

Palikir

Congress Library: POB PS3, Palikir, Pohnpei 96941; tel. 320-2324; fax 320-5122; e-mail liwi@mail.fm; f. 1978; library of the legislative br. of nat. Govt; 15,000 vols, 30 periodicals; Librarian MARIETA J. PAIDEN.

Museums and Galleries

Kolonia

Lidorkini Museum: Kolonia, Pohnpei 96941; tel. 320-5299; artefacts from the Nan Madol site, pounding stones, handicrafts, items from the Japanese occupation of the islands (1914–44); Curator HENTER LAWRENCE.

Tofol

Kosrae State Museum: Tofol, Kosrae; artefacts, photographs of Kosrae history and culture.

College

College of Micronesia: National Campus, POB 159, Kolonia, Pohnpei 96941; tel. 320-2480; fax 320-2479; e-mail national@comfsm.fm; internet www.comfsm.fm; f. 1963; offers assoc. of arts and assoc. of science degrees; other campuses located in Chuuk State, Kosrae State, Pohnpei State and Yap State; its Fisheries and Maritime Institute is located on Yap; library: Library: see Libraries and Archives; 798 students; Pres. SPENSIN JAMES.

MOLDOVA

The Higher Education System

The oldest institution of higher education is the Academia de Mizică, Teatru şi Arte Plastice (Academy of Music, Theatre and Fine Arts of Republic of Moldova—founded 1919), which was established when the former Russian territory of Bessarabia was part of Romania. Other institutions dating from the period of Romanian control include Universitatea Agrară de State din Moldova (Moldovan State Agrarian University—founded 1933) and Universitatea Pedagogică de Stat 'Ion Creangă' (Ion Creangă Pedagogical State University—founded 1940). However, the USSR refused to recognize Romania's claims to the territory, and in October 1924 formed a Moldovan Autonomous Soviet Socialist Republic (ASSR) on the eastern side of the Dniester, in the Ukrainian Soviet Socialist Republic (SSR). The current institution of Universitatea de Stat din Tirasapol (Tirasapol State University), was founded in the Moldovan ASSR in 1930 (it was re-located to the capital Chişinău in 1999). In June 1940 Romania was forced to cede Bessarabia and northern Bucovina to the USSR, under the terms of the Treaty of Non-Aggression (the 'Molotov-Ribbentrop Pact'), concluded with Nazi Germany in August 1939. Northern Bucovina, southern Bessarabia and the Kotovsk-Balţa region of the Moldovan ASSR were incorporated into the Ukrainian SSR. The remaining parts of the Moldovan ASSR and of Bessarabia were merged to form the Moldovan SSR, which formally joined the USSR on 2 August 1940 and remained under Soviet rule until independence was declared in 1991. Following independence the self-styled 'Transnistrian Moldovan Republic' (formerly 'Transnistrian Moldovan SSR') was declared on the eastern side of the Dniester. The Law on Education of 1995 classified higher education as either long-term study programmes offered by universities, academies, and institutes or short-term study programmes offered by vocational colleges. In 2000 Moldova adopted the European Credit Transfer System in public universities.

Admission to higher education is determined by fixed quotas (numerus clauses/numerus fixus) drawn up by the Government. Consequently, students are usually required to sit a competitive entrance examination as well as holding the Diplomă de Bacalaureat, the main secondary school-leavers' certificate. Undergraduate degrees are divided into short- and long-terms programmes of study. The Diploma of Short-Term Higher Education (Diplomă de Studii Superioare de Scurtă Durată) is the primary programme of short-term study and lasts two to three years. These are the only kinds of degrees offered by vocation colleges. The Diplomă de Licentă is a long-term programme of study lasting four to six years and culminates with the defence of a thesis. Students who do not defend their thesis are awarded the Diploma of University Higher Studies (Diplomă de Studii Superioare Universitare). The first postgraduate-level degree is the Diplomă de Magistru, awarded upon completion of one to two years of research following the Diplomă de Licentă. There are two doctoral degrees, Doctor of Sciences (Doctor în Stiinte) and Doctor Abilitat. The Doctor în Stiinte is awarded after three years of research and successful defence of a thesis. Doctor Abilitat is a post-doctoral degree, awarded after two years following the Doctor în Stiinte.

Post-secondary technical and vocational education is available mainly through colleges and is regarded as short-term higher education.

Learned Societies

GENERAL

Academy of Sciences of Moldova: 2001 Chişinău, bd. Ştefan cel Mare şi Sfînt 1; tel. (22) 27-14-78; fax (22) 54-28-23; e-mail consiliu@asm.md; internet www.asm.md; f. 1946; sections of Agricultural Sciences (Academician-Co-ordinator SIMION TOMA), Biological, Chemical and Ecological Sciences (Academician-Co-ordinator ION TODERAS), Economical and Mathematical Sciences (Academician-Co-ordinator GHEORGE MISCOI), Humanities and Arts (Academician-Co-ordinator ALEXANDRU ROSCA), Medical Sciences (Academician-Co-ordinator GHEORGHE GHIDIRIM), Physical and Engineering Sciences (Academician-Co-ordinator VALERIUS CANTER); 112 mems (48 full, 64 corresp.); attached research institutes: see Research Institutes; library: see Libraries and Archives; Pres. GHEORGHE DUCA; General Scientific Sec. BORIS GAINA; publs *Buletinul* (Biological and Chemical and Agricultural Sciences, every 3 months; Mathematics, , every 4 months), *Computer Science Journal of Moldova* (quarterly), *Economy and Sociology* (quarterly), *Elektronnaya Obrabotka Materialov* (Electronic Processing of Materials, every 2 months), *Moldavian Journal of Physical Sciences* (quarterly), *Revista de Filozofie şi Drept* (Journal of Philosophy and Law, every 2 months), *Revista de Istorie a Moldovei* (Moldovan Historical Journal, quarterly), *Revista de Lingvistică şi Ştiinţă Literară* (Journal of Linguistics and Study of Literature, every 2 months).

HISTORY, GEOGRAPHY AND ARCHAEOLOGY

Geographical Society of Moldova: 2028 Chişinău, str. Academiei 1; tel. (22) 73-96-18; e-mail geography_md@yahoo.com; Head of Laboratory Dr NICOLAE BOBOC.

LANGUAGE AND LITERATURE

Alliance Française: 2012 Chişinău, str. Sfatul Tarii 18; tel. (22) 23-45-10; fax (22) 23-72-34; e-mail alfr@alfr.md; internet www.alfr.md; offers courses and exams in French language and culture and promotes cultural exchange with France; Dir OLIVIER JACQUOT.

Goethe-Institut: see entry in Romania chapter.

PEN Centre of Moldova: 2012 Chişinău, bd. Ştefan cel Mare şi Sfînt 134, PO 12, POB 231; tel. (22) 23-24-79; e-mail contrafort@moldnet.md; f. 1991; 25 mems; Pres. VITALIE CIOBANU.

NATURAL SCIENCES

Biological Sciences

Entomological Society of Moldova: 2028 Chişinău, str. Academiei 1; tel. (22) 73-98-96; Chair B. V. VEREŞCIAGHIN.

Microbiological Society of Moldova: 2028 Chişinău, str. Academiei 1; tel. (22) 73-98-78; e-mail acadrudic@yahoo.com; Chair. Prof. VALERY RUDIC.

Ornithological Society of Moldova: 2028 Chişinău, str. Academiei 1; tel. (22) 73-75-09; Chair. (vacant).

Society of Botanists of Moldova: 2002 Chişinău, str. Pădurii 18; tel. (22) 52-38-96; Chair. A. G. NEGRU.

Society of Geneticists of Moldova: 2049 Chişinău, str. Mirceşti 44; tel. (22) 43-23-08; Chair. V. D. SIMINEL.

Society of Plant Physiology and Biochemistry of Moldova: 2002 Chişinău, str. Pădurii 26/1; tel. (22) 56-79-59; fax (22) 55-00-26; e-mail sbiochim@bio.asm.md; f. 1988; 40 mems; Pres. Prof. SIMION I. TOMA.

Society of Hydrobiologists and Ichthyologists: 2028 Chişinău, str. Academiei 1; tel. (22) 57-75-30; fax (22) 73-12-55; e-mail izoolasm@mail.md; f. 1968; 36 mems; Chair. Prof. ION TODERAŞ.

Teriological Society of Moldova: 2028 Chişinău, str. Academiei 1 (Room 220); tel. (22) 72-55-66; fax (22) 73-12-55; e-mail amunteanu@asm.md; 19 mems; Chair. Dr ANDREI MUNTEANU.

Physical Sciences

Physical Society of Moldova: 2928 Chişinău, str. Academiei 5; tel. and fax (22) 73-90-60; e-mail kantser@lises.asm.md; Chair. Acad. Prof. VALERIU KANTSER.

RELIGION, SOCIOLOGY AND ANTHROPOLOGY

Moldovan Sociological Association: 3121 Balti, str. Puşkin 38; tel. (231) 2-44-79; Chair. N. V. ŢURCANU.

Research Institutes

AGRICULTURE, FISHERIES AND VETERINARY SCIENCE

National Institute of Animal Husbandry and Veterinary Medicine: 6525 Anenii Noii, s. Maximovca; tel. and fax (22) 42-93-50; e-mail inzmv2004@yahoo.com; f. 1958; library of 19,000 vols; Dir Dr. hab. MIHAIL BAHCIVANJI; publ. *Scientific Transactions* (annually).

National Institute for Viticulture and Vinification: 2070 Chişinău, s. Codru, str. Vierul 59; tel. (22) 28-50-25; fax (22) 28-50-35; e-mail invv@agriculture.md; internet www.agriculture.md/invv; f. 1909; prepares national strategies and for the development of viticulture; creates of new types of grapes, resistant to diseases and frost; elaboration of modern technologies for producing cuttings without viruses; of storage methods and use of grapes with nutritive and therapeutic purposes; creation of new wines, champagnes and liqueurs; design and sale of machines and equipment for viticulture.

Research Institute for Maize and Sorghum: 4834 Criuleni, s. Paşcani; tel. and fax (22) 24-10-07; e-mail porumbeni@agriculture.md; internet www.agriculture.md/porumbeni; f. 1973; research into the improvement of seed strains, seed production and cultivation of maize, sorghum, vegetables, medicinal and aromatic plants; Dir Dr MICU VASILE.

Tobacco Research Institute: Chişinău, s. Gratieşti, str. Prieteniei 1; tel. (22) 46-06-86; fax (22) 46-04-87; e-mail tutunix@agriculture.md; internet www.agriculture.md/tutun; f. 1968; Dir Dr TUDOR ZAGORNEANU.

ECONOMICS, LAW AND POLITICS

Centre for the Study of Marketing Problems: 2001 Chişinău, bd. Ştefan cel Mare şi Sfînt; tel. and fax (22) 26-23-91; attached to Acad. of Sciences of Moldova; Dir P. V. COJUCARI.

Institute of Economic Research: 2001 Chişinău, bd. Ştefan cel Mare şi Sfînt 1; tel. (22) 26-24-01; attached to Acad. of Sciences of Moldova; Dir V. CIOBANU.

FINE AND PERFORMING ARTS

Institute of the History and Theory of Art: 2001 Chişinău, bd. Ştefan cel Mare şi Sfînt 1; tel. (22) 26-06-02; fax (22) 22-33-48; f. 1991; attached to Acad. of Sciences of Moldova; fine art, architecture, music, performing arts; Dir LEONID M. CEMORTAN; publ. *Arta* (2 series: fine arts and architecture, and music and the performing arts, each annually).

HISTORY, GEOGRAPHY AND ARCHAEOLOGY

Institute of Archaeology and Ancient History: 2712 Chişinău, str. Mitropolitul Banulescu-Bodoni 35; tel. and fax (22) 22-22-42; attached to Acad. of Sciences of Moldova; Dir VALENTIN DERGACEV.

Institute of Geography: 2028 Chişinău, str. Academiei 1; tel. and fax (22) 73-98-38; e-mail geography@cc.acad.md; f. 1992; attached to Acad. of Sciences of Moldova; Dir TATIANA S. CONSTANTINOVA.

Institute of History: 2012 Chişinău, str. 31 August 1989 82; tel. (22) 23-33-10; e-mail iist_asm@mtc.md; f. 1958; attached to Acad. of Sciences of Moldova; Dir DEMIR DRAGNEV.

LANGUAGE AND LITERATURE

Institute of Linguistics: 2012 Chişinău, str. 31 August 1989 82; tel. (22) 23-33-05; fax (22) 23-77-52; e-mail lingva@moldova.md; f. 1991; attached to Acad. of Sciences of Moldova; library of 10,000 vols; Dir Acad. SILVIU BEREJAN; publ. *Revistă de Lingvistică şi Ştiinţă Literară* (6 a year).

Institute of Literature and Folklore: 2001 Chişinău, bd. Ştefan cel Mare şi Sfînt; tel. (22) 27-27-19; e-mail ilfasm@yahoo.it; f. 1991; attached to Acad. of Sciences of Moldova; Dir Acad. HARALAMBIE CORBU; publ. *Revistă de Lingvistică şi Ştiinţă Literară* (6 a year).

MEDICINE

National Centre of Preventive Medicine: 2025 Chişinău, str. Gh. Asachi 67A; tel. (22) 72-96-47; fax (22) 72-97-25; e-mail ncpm@obenesh.mldnet.com; Dir-Gen. MIHAI MAGDEI.

NATURAL SCIENCES

Biological Sciences

Botanical Gardens and Institute of Botany: 2002 Chişinău, str. Pădurii 18; tel. (22) 55-04-43; fax (22) 52-38-98; e-mail grbot@moldova.md; f. 1950; attached to Acad. of Sciences of Moldova; library of 43,000 items; Dir Acad. ALEXANDRU CIUBOTARU; publ. *Botanical Research* (annually).

Centre for Pathology and Pathobiology: 2004 Chişinău, str. 31 August 1989 151; tel. (22) 22-75-19; attached to Acad. of Sciences of Moldova; Dir. Acad. VASILE ANESTIADE.

Institute of Genetics: 2002 Chişinău, str. Pădurii 20; tel. (22) 77-04-47; fax (22) 55-61-80; e-mail dobynda@mail.md; f. 1985; attached to Acad. of Sciences of Moldova; Dir ANATOL JACOTĂ.

Institute of Microbiology and Biotechnology: 2028 Chişinău, str. Academiei 1; tel. (22) 72-55-24; fax (22) 72-57-54; e-mail microbiologie@mail.md; internet www.asm.md; f. 1992; attached to Acad. of Sciences of Moldova; Dir Acad. VALERIU RUDIC; publ. *Bulletin* (2 a year).

Institute of Physiology and Sanocreatology: 2028 Chişinău, str. Academiei 1; tel. (22) 72-51-55; attached to Acad. of Sciences of Moldova; specialized in study into the pancreas; Dir Acad. TEODOR FURDUI.

Institute of Plant Physiology: 2002 Chişinău, str. Pădurii 26/1; tel. (22) 56-79-59; fax (22) 55-00-26; e-mail ifpdirect@asm.md; f. 1961; attached to Acad. of Sciences of Moldova; library of 9,000 vols; Dir Dr GHEROGHE TUDORACHE.

Institute of Zoology: 2028 Chişinău, str. Academiei 1; tel. (22) 73-98-09; fax (22) 73-12-55; e-mail izoolasm@mail.md; attached to Acad. of Sciences of Moldova; Dir ION TODERAŞ.

Research Institute for Biological Plant Protection: 2060 Chişinău, bd. Dacia 58; tel. (22) 56-83-58; fax (22) 77-96-41; e-mail icpp@agriculture.md; attached to Acad. of Sciences of Moldova; Dir ION S. POPUŞOI.

Mathematical Sciences

Institute of Mathematics and Computer Science: 2028 Chişinău, str. Academiei 5; tel. (22) 72-59-82; fax (22) 73-80-27; e-mail imam@math.md; internet www.math.md; f. 1964; attached to Acad. of Sciences of Moldova; Dir Dr hab. CONSTANTIN V. GAINDRIC; Scientific Sec. Dr SVETLANA COJOCARU; publs *Buletinul Academiei de Ştiinţe a Republicii Moldova: Matematica* (3 a year), *Computer Science Journal of Moldova* (3 a year), *Quasigroups and Related Systems* (annually).

Physical Sciences

Center of Experimental Seismology, Central Station: 2028 Chişinău, str. Academiei 3; tel. (22) 73-71-79; attached to Acad. of Sciences of Moldova; forms the central unit of the Institute of Geophysics and Geology's seismic network; operates in conjunction with four local stations and four strong-motion recorders; Dir I. ILIEŞ.

Institute of Applied Physics: 2028 Chişinău, str. Academiei 5,; tel. (22) 73-81-50; fax (22) 73-81-49; e-mail director@phys.asm.md; internet www.phys.asm.md; f. 1964; attached to Acad. of Sciences of Moldova; 66 scientific personnel; Dir Prof. L. KULYUK; publs *Moldavian Journal of Physical Sciences* (4 a year), *Surface Engineering and Applied Electrochemistry* (6 a year).

Institute of Chemistry: 2028 Chişinău, str. Academiei 3; tel. (22) 72-54-90; fax (22) 73-99-54; e-mail ichem@asm.md; f. 1959; attached to Acad. of Sciences of Moldova; Dir Dr hab. TUDOR LUPASCU.

Institute of Geophysics and Geology: 2028 Chişinău, str. Academiei 3; tel. (22) 73-90-27; fax (22) 73-96-63; e-mail neagavi@mail.ru; attached to Acad. of Sciences of Moldova; Dir Dr VASILE ALCAZ; Scientific Sec. Dr VASILE NEAGA.

RELIGION, SOCIOLOGY AND ANTHROPOLOGY

Institute of Ethnography and Folklore: 2001 Chişinău, bd. Ştefan cel Mare şi Sfînt 1; tel. (22) 26-45-14; f. 1991; attached to Acad. of Sciences of Moldova; Dir N. A. DEMCENCO; publ. *Revista de Etnologie* (annually).

Institute of National Minorities Studies: 2001 Chişinău, bd. Ştefan cel Mare şi Sfînt 1; tel. (22) 26-44-91; attached to Acad. of Sciences of Moldova; Dir C. F. POPOVICI.

Institute of Philosophy, Sociology and Political Sciences: 2001 Chişinău, bd. Ştefan cel Mare şi Sfînt 1; tel. (22) 27-05-37; fax (22) 27-14-69; e-mail ifilos@cc.acad.md; internet www.asm.md; attached to Acad. of Sciences of Moldova; f. 2006; philosophy; sociology; political sciences; mythology; history of religion; social-demographic researches on families; 54 mems; Dir Dr ION RUSANDU; publs *Iconomie şi Sociologie* (Economy and Sociology), *Revistă de Filosofie şi Drept* (Philosophy and Law).

TECHNOLOGY

Institute of Power Engineering: 2028 Chişinău, str. Academiei 5; tel. (22) 72-70-40; fax (22) 73-53-86; e-mail mkiorsak@cc.asm.md; f. 1964; attached to Acad. of Sciences of Moldova; Dir Dr MIHAI V. CHIORSAC.

Libraries and Archives

Bălţi

Bălţi Municipal Library: 3121 Bălţi, str.A. Puskin 34; tel. (231) 2-34-59; f. 1880; Dir INGA COJOCARU.

Chişinău

Central Scientific Library of the Moldovan Academy of Sciences: 2001 Chişinău, bd. Ştefan cel Mare şi Sfînt 1; tel. (22) 27-42-79; fax (22) 54-28-23; e-mail corotenco@cc.acad.md; internet www.amlib.asm.md; f. 1947; 1,406,887 vols; Dir ELENA COROTENCO.

Centre for Scientific Information in the Social Sciences: 2001 Chişinău, bd. Ştefan cel Mare şi Sfînt 1; tel. (22) 23-23-39; attached to Acad. of Sciences of Moldova; Dir V. I. MOCREAC.

Moldovan State University Library: 2009 Chişinău, str. A. Mateevici 60; tel. (22) 57-75-05; e-mail library@usm.md; internet www.usm.md/bcu; f. 1946; 1,810,000 vols; Dir ECATERINA ZASMENCO.

National Library of the Republic of Moldova: 2012 Chişinău, str. 31 August 1989 78A; tel. and fax (22) 22-14-75; e-mail bnrm@bnrm.md; internet www.bnrm.md; f. 1832; national library and principal depository of Moldova; national centre of inter-library Loans; national centre for library automation and information; national centre for library science; 2,507,055 vols, 834 periodicals; Dir A. A. RĂU.

Scientific and Technical Library of Moldova: Chişinău, str. Creanga 45; tel. (22) 62-87-42; fax (22) 62-34-47; f. 1968; 560,000 vols, 11,000,000 patents, 750,000 standards; Dir P. T. RACU.

Tighina

Tighina Country Public Library: Tighina; e-mail bpjt@fromru.com; internet ournet.md/~bpjt; f. 1943; 3 brs; 106,787 vols; Dir LARISA CAMENSCIC.

Museum

Chişinău

National Museum of Fine Arts of Moldova: Chişinău, str. 31 August 1989 115; tel. (22) 24-17-30; f. 1944; Dir VASILE NEGRUŢĂ.

Universities

UNIVERSITATEA AGRARĂ DE STAT DIN MOLDOVA
(Moldovan State Agrarian University)

2049 Chişinău, str. Mirceşti 44
Telephone: (22) 31-22-58
Fax: (22) 31-22-76
E-mail: cimpoies@uasm.md
Internet: www.uasm.md
Founded 1933
State control
Languages of instruction: Romanian, English, Russian
Rector: Prof. Dr GHEORGHE P. CIMPOES
Library of 785,000 vols
Number of teachers: 400
Number of students: 7,670 (5,435 on campus, 2,235 distance)

DEANS

Faculty of Accountancy: Assoc. Prof. Dr RUSLAN BABALAU
Faculty of Agricultural Engineering and Transport: Assoc. Prof. Dr GRIGORE MARIAN
Faculty of Agronomy: Prof. Dr ANDREI PALII
Faculty of Animal Breeding: Prof. Dr ANDREI SUMANSCHII
Faculty of Economics: Assoc. Prof. Dr PETRU TOMITA
Faculty of Horticulture: Prof. Dr VALERIAN BALAN
Faculty of Land Surveying and Law: Assoc. Prof. Dr OLEG HORJAN
Faculty of Veterinary Medicine: Assoc. Prof. Dr GHEORGHE DONICA

UNIVERSITATEA CO-OPERATIST COMERCIALĂ DIN MOLDOVEI
(Co-operative Trade University of Moldova)

2027 Chişinău, bd. Gagarin 8
Telephone: (22) 27-07-84
Fax: (22) 54-12-10
E-mail: webmaster@uccm.md
Internet: www.uccm.md
Founded 1993
State control
Languages of instruction: Romanian, English
Languages of instruction: French, Russian
Rector: Dr TUDOR MALECA
Pro-Rector: LARISA ŞAVGA
Library of 92,000 vols
Number of teachers: 200
Number of students: 1,200

DEANS

Faculty of Accountancy and Business Informatics: Dr SERGIU OPREA
Faculty of Management and Economics: Dr ELENA GRAUR
Faculty of Marketing and the Science of Commodities: Dr FEODOSIE PITUŞCAN
Faculty of Part-Time Studies: Dr SVETLANA MUŞTUC

UNIVERSITATEA DE STAT DIN BĂLŢI 'ALECU RUSSO'
('Alecu Russo' Bălţi State University)

3121 Bălţi, str. Puşkin 38
Telephone: (231) 2-30-66
Fax: (231) 2-30-39
E-mail: rumleanschi@usb.moldnet.md
Internet: www.usb.md
Founded 1945
State control
Languages of instruction: Romanian, English
Languages of instruction: French, German
Languages of instruction: Russian, Ukrainian
Rector: Dr NICOLAE FILIP
First Vice-Rector: Dr VAERIU CABAC
Library of 1,200,000 vols
Number of teachers: 425
Number of students: 4,200
Publications: *Bulletin of Administration* (monthly), *Scientific Papers* (every 2 years), *University Yearbook* (every 5 years)

DEANS

Faculty of Economics: Dr GHEORGHE PLĂMĂDEALĂ
Faculty of Foreign Languages and Literatures: Dr ION MANOLI
Faculty of Law: Dr GHEORGHE NEAGU
Faculty of Music and Music Teaching: Dr ION GAGIM
Faculty of Pedagogy and Psychology: Dr LIDIA STUPACENCO
Faculty of Philology: Dr MARIA ŞLEAHTIŢCHI
Faculty of Technology, Physics and Mathematics: Dr ALEXANDRU URSU

UNIVERSITATEA DE STAT 'BOGDAN PETRICEICU HASDEU' DIN CAHUL
('Bogdan Petriceicu Hasdeu' State University of Cahul)

3901 Cahul, str. Piaţa Independenţei 1
Telephone: (299) 2-24-81
Founded 1999
Rector: Dr ION ŞIŞCANU.

UNIVERSITATEA DE STAT DIN COMRAT
(Comrat State University)

3900 Comrat, str. A. Galaţan 17
Telephone: (298) 2-43-45
Fax: (298) 2-40-91
E-mail: kdu@moldnet.md
Founded 1991
State control
Languages of instruction: Romanian, Bulgarian, Russian
Rector: Dr STEFANN VARBAN
Library of 50,200 vols
Number of teachers: 190
Number of students: 1,780
Faculties of Agricultural Technology, Economics and National Culture.

UNIVERSITAŢEA DE STAT DE MEDICINĂ ŞI FARMACIE 'N. TESTEMIŢANU'
('Nicolae Testemiţeanu' State Medical and Pharmaceutical University)

2004 Chişinău, bd. Ştefan cel Mare şi Sfînt 165
Telephone: (22) 24-34-08
Fax: (22) 24-23-44
E-mail: rector@usmf.md
Internet: www.usmf.md
Founded 1945
State control
Languages of instruction: Romanian, Russian
Rector: Prof. Dr ION ABABII
First Vice-Rector and Vice-Rector for Academic Affairs: Prof. Dr NICOLAE V. ESANU
Vice-Rector for Administrative Affairs: CONSTANTIN NICHIFOR AVASILOAIE
Vice-Rector for International Relations: Dr VALERIU TEODOR CHICU
Vice-Rector for Medical Affairs and Postgraduate Education: Prof. Dr VLADIMIR T. HOTINEANU
Vice-Rector for Research: Prof. Dr VIOREL I. PRISACARU
Library of 786,000 vols
Publication: *Curieurul medical* (every 2 months)

DEANS

Faculty of Continuing Medical Training: Dr STEFAN GROPPA
Faculty of General Medicine: Prof. Dr GHEORGHE PLĂCINTĂ
Faculty of Pharmacy: Prof. Dr Hab. VASILE PROCOPIŞIN
Faculty of Stomatology: Prof. Dr PAVEL GODOROJA

UNIVERSITATEA DE STAT DIN MOLDOVA
(Moldova State University)

2009 Chişinău, str. A. Mateevici 60
Telephone: (22) 57-74-01
Fax: (22) 24-42-48
E-mail: stahi@usm.md
Internet: www.usm.md
Founded 1946
State control
Languages of instruction: Romanian, Russian
Academic year: September to June
Rector: GH. RUSNAC
Pro-Rectors: P. CHETRUŞ, A. CRIVOI, P. GAUGAŞ E. MURARU
Registrar: T. LUCHIAN
Librarian: ECATERINA ZASMENCO
Library: see Libraries and Archives
Number of teachers: 1,300
Number of students: 23,000
Publications: *Scientific Annals* (annually), *Universitatea* (monthly)

DEANS

Faculty of Biology and Soil Science: V. CIOBANU
Faculty of Chemistry and Chemical Technology: G. DRAGALINA
Faculty of Economic Sciences: V. CUJBĂ
Faculty of Foreign Languages and Literature: E. AXENTI
Faculty of History and Psychology: C. SOLOMON

Faculty of International Relations, Political and Administrative Sciences: V. CUJBĂ
Faculty of Journalism and Communication: C. MARIN
Faculty of Law: G. AVORNIC
Faculty of Letters: I. CINDREA
Faculty of Mathematics and Informatics: G. CIOCANU
Faculty of Physics: P. GAŞIN
Faculty of Social Protection, Sociology and Philosophy: M. BULGARU

UNIVERSITATEA DE STAT DIN TIRASPOL (Tiraspol State University)

2069 Chişinău, str. Ghenadie Iablocichin 5
Telephone: (22) 75-49-24
Fax: (22) 75-49-24
E-mail: scs_ust@moldova.cc

Founded 1930; moved from Tirasopol to present location in 1992, due to civil unrest
State control
Languages of instruction: Romanian, Russian

Rector: Prof. LAURENTIU CALMUTCHI
Vice-Rector: Prof. IGOR POSTOLACHI
Number of students: 3,140
Publication: *Light* (monthly)

DEANS

Faculty of Biology and Chemistry: BORIS NEDBALIUC
Faculty of Geography: ION MIRONOV
Faculty of Pedagogy: VASILE PANICO
Faculty of Philology: LUDMILA SOLOVIOV
Faculty of Physics and Mathematics: BORIS KOROLEVSKI

UNIVERSITATEA PEDAGOGICĂ DE STAT 'ION CREANGĂ' (Ion Creangă Pedagogical State University)

2069 Chişinău, str. I. Creangă 1
Telephone: (22) 74-54-14
Fax: (22) 74-99-14
E-mail: ups@upm.moldnet.md

Founded 1940
State control
Languages of instruction: Romanian, English
Languages of instruction: French, German, Russian

Rector: Dr ION GUŢU
Number of teachers: 423
Number of students: 5,545, (3,945 full-time, 1,600 part-time)
Publication: *Annual Scientific Edition*

DEANS

Faculty of Fine Arts: ALEXANDRU VATAVU
Faculty of Foreign Languages and Literatures: VALENTIN CUŞCA
Faculty of History and Ethno-Pedagogy: NICOLE CHICUŞ
Faculty of Pedagogy: PETRU JELESCU
Faculty of Philology: ALEXANDRA BARBĂNEAGRĂ
Faculty of Psychology and Special Psycho-Pedagogy: IGOR RACU

UNIVERSITATEA TEHNICĂ A MOLDOVEI (Technical University of Moldova)

2004 Chişinău, bd. Ştefan cel Mare şi Sfînt 168
Telephone: (22) 23-78-61
Fax: (22) 23-22-52
E-mail: extrel@adm.utm.md
Internet: www.utm.md

Founded 1964
State control
Languages of instruction: Romanian, Russian
Academic year: September to June

Rector: Acad. Prof. ION BOSTAN
First Vice-Rector for Education: Prof. Dr PETRU TODOS
Vice-Rector for Administration and Capital Construction: PAVEL SPÂNU
Vice-Rector for Continuing Education and International Relations: Assoc. Prof. Dr VALENTIN AMARIEI
Vice-Rector for Part-Time Studies and Distance Education: Assoc. Prof. Dr TIMOFEI ANDROS
Vice-Rector for Research: Prof. Dr hab. VALERIAN DOROGAN
Vice-Rector for Studies and Relations with Colleges: Prof. Dr DUMITRU UNGUREANU
Dean of Students: Dr CONSTANTIN STRATAN
Library of 1,080,000 vols
Number of teachers: 750
Number of students: 17,000
Publications: *Meridian Ingineresc* (4 a year), *Mesager* (newspaper, monthly)

DEANS

Faculty of Computers, Informatics and Microelectronics: Assoc. Prof. Dr ION BALMUS
Faculty of Economic Engineering and Business: Prof. Dr NICOLAE TURCANU
Faculty of Engineering and Management in Machine-Building: Assoc. Prof. Dr ALEXEI TOCA
Faculty of Engineering and Management in Mechanics: Assoc. Prof. Dr VASILE CARTOFEANU
Faculty of Power Engineering: Prof. Dr ION STRATAN
Faculty of Radioelectronics and Telecommunications: Assoc. Prof. Dr SERGIU ANDRONIC
Faculty of Surveying, Geodesy and Civil Engineering: Assoc. Prof. Dr VICTOR TOPOREŢ
Faculty of Technology and Management in the Food Industry: Assoc. Prof. Dr GRIGORE MUSTEATA
Faculty of the Textile Industry: Assoc. Prof. Dr CONSTANTIN SPINU
Faculty of Urban Planning and Architecture: Assoc. Prof. Dr NISTOR GROZAVU

Other Higher Educational Institutions

Academia de Mizică, Teatru şi Arte Plastice (Academy of Music, Theatre and Fine Arts of Republic of Moldova): 2014 Chişinău, str. A. Mateevici 87; tel. and fax (22) 22-19-49; e-mail usam@moldovacc.md; internet www.amtap.mdl.net; f. 1919; 1,500 students; Rector Dr AURELIAN DANILĂ.

Academia de Studii Economice (Academy of Economic Studies): 2005 Chişinău, str. Mitropolit Bănulescu-Bodoni 61; tel. (22) 22-41-28; fax (22) 22-19-68; e-mail r_gb@ase.md; internet www.ase.md; f. 1991; library: 317,000 vols; faculties of accountancy, business and administration, economics and law, finance, information technology and statistics and international economic relations; Rector Prof. Dr Hab. GRIGORII BELOSTECINIC.

Institutul Naţional de Educaţie Fizică şi Sport (National Institute of Physical Education and Sport): 2024 Chişinău, str. A. Doga 28/2; tel. (22) 49-40-81; fax (22) 49-76-71; e-mail inefs@mdl.net; faculties of part-time studies, pedagogy, sports and teacher development; Rector VEACESLAV MANOLACHE.

Institutul de Relaţii Internaţionale din Moldova (International Relations Institute of Moldova): 2009 Chişinău, str. Gh. Caşu 28/2; tel. (22) 73-59-43; fax (22) 73-59-42; e-mail infoirim@mail.ru; f. 2003; Rector CONSTANTIN MARIN.

MONACO

The Higher Education System

In 1861 Monaco became an independent state under the protection of France. There is only one public institution of higher education, the Académie de Musique Prince Rainier III de Monaco (founded 1993), and one private university of business studies, International University of Monaco (founded 1986). Most Monagesque students undertake higher education in France. Post-secondary technical and vocational education is provided by the Sections de Technicien Supérieur. Programmes of study last for two years and lead to the award of the Higher Technician Certificate (Brevet de Technicien Supérieur).

Learned Societies

HISTORY, GEOGRAPHY AND ARCHAEOLOGY

Association Monégasque de Préhistoire: Musée d'Anthropologie, 56 *bis* blvd du Jardin exotique, 98000 Monte Carlo; tel. 93-15-80-06; fax 93-30-02-46; e-mail ssimone@gouv.mc; f. 1984; 100 mems; Pres. SUZANNE SIMONE.

LANGUAGE AND LITERATURE

Alliance Française: Maison de France, 42 rue Grimaldi, BP 300, 98006 Monte Carlo; tel. 93-50-08-24; offers courses and exams in French language and culture and promotes cultural exchange with France.

Research Institute

NATURAL SCIENCES

General

Centre Scientifique de Monaco: Villa Girasole, 16 blvd de Suisse, Monte Carlo 98000; tel. 93-25-89-54; fax 93-25-70-90; e-mail centre@centrescientifique.mc; internet www.centrescientifique.mc; f. 1960; pure and applied research in the fields of oceanography, marine biology and the protection and regeneration of the marine environment; laboratories in Musée Océanographique de Monaco (*q.v.*); Pres. of Admin. Council ROGER PASSERON; Sec.-Gen. MICHEL BOISSON; publ. *Bulletin* (in French and in English, annually).

Libraries and Archives

Monte Carlo

Archives du Palais Princier de Monaco: BP 518, Monaco 98015 Cedex; tel. 93-25-18-31; private archives of the princes of Monaco; Curator RÉGIS LÉCUYER.

Bibliothèque Louis Notari: 8 rue Louis Notari, 98000 Monaco; tel. 93-15-29-40; fax 93-15-29-41; f. 1909; 310,000 vols, 18,000 phonograms, 4,000 videos; Librarian HERVÉ BARRAL; publ. *Bibliographie de Monaco* (data base).

Princess Grace Irish Library: 9 rue Princesse Marie de Lorraine, 98000 Monaco-Ville; tel. 93-50-12-25; fax 93-50-66-65; e-mail pglib@monaco.mc; internet www.monaco.mc/pglib; f. 1984; functions under the aegis of the Fondation Princesse Grace; Irish and Celtic studies library; 10,000 vols, 2,000 sheet items of Irish music and folk songs, 250 theses, 250 video cassettes and DVDs; reproduction of the Book of Kells; paintings, prints, sculptures; young readers' colln; English language activities for local school students; theatre, writing and poetry workshops; Administrator JUDITH GANTLEY.

Museums and Art Galleries

Monte Carlo

Musée d'Anthropologie Préhistorique: 56 *bis* blvd du Jardin exotique, 98000 Monte Carlo; tel. 93-15-80-06; fax 93-30-02-46; e-mail musant@gouv.mc; f. 1902; prehistory, quaternary geology; library of 3,000 vols, 200 periodicals; Curator PATRICK SIMON; publ. *Bulletin* (annually).

Musée National: 17 ave Princess Grace, 98000 Monaco; tel. 93-30-91-26; fax 92-16-73-21; e-mail musee-national@monte-carlo.mc; f. 1972; Galéa collection: automatons, miniature furniture, antique dolls, nativity scenes; Dir BÉATRICE BLANCHY.

Musée Océanographique de Monaco: Ave Saint-Martin, 98000 Monaco-Ville; tel. 93-15-36-00; fax 93-50-52-97; e-mail biblio@oceano.mc; internet www.oceano.mc; inaugurated 1910 by Prince Albert I of Monaco; part of Institut Océanographique, Paris; aquarium containing 6,000 fishes of 450 species, and coral reefs; mother-of-pearl holy art shells; library of 50,000 vols; Dir JEAN JAUBERT; publs *Bulletin de l'Institut OOéanographique* (irreg.), *Mémoires de l'Institut océanographique* (irreg.).

College

Académie de Musique Prince Rainier III de Monaco: 1 Blvd Albert 1er, 98000 Monaco; tel. 93-15-28-91; f. 1933; 53 professors; 650 students; Dir JOËL RIGAL.

MONGOLIA

The Higher Education System

Mongolia was formerly the Manchu province of Outer Mongolia. In 1911, following the republican revolution in China, Mongolian princes declared the province's independence. Russia (and later, the USSR) competed with China for control of Mongolia and in November 1924 the Mongolian People's Republic was proclaimed. The oldest institutions of higher education date from this year, among them the Academy of Management, Higher School of Finance and Economics and Higher School of Trade and Industry. The oldest multi-faculty university-level institution is the National University of Mongolia (founded 1942). Higher education consists of universities, higher schools and colleges. In 2004/05 there were 46 state-owned universities and colleges with 84,041 students, and 137 private universities and colleges with 39,405 students. Many Mongolian students continue their academic careers at universities and technical schools in Russia, Germany, the United Kingdom and the USA. Higher education is the responsibility of the Ministry of Education, Culture and Science, while the Consortium of Mongolian Universities and Colleges (founded 1995) is a non-governmental body representing 18 public and private universities.

Admission to higher education is on the basis of the Certificate of Secondary Education, students' academic records and relevant entrance examinations according to the programme of study applied for. The first stage of undergraduate study is the Diploma of Higher Education, which is awarded after two to three years. The second stage of undergraduate higher education is the Bachelors degree, which lasts four years (including time spent on the Diploma) for which students are required to accumulate 120 'credit hours' for successful completion of the degree. After the Bachelors has been awarded students are eligible to study for the Masters, which usually lasts a year and requires 30 credit hours. Finally, the Doctorate is the highest university-level degree, and requires a minimum of 60 credit hours.

The Certificate of Vocational Education is the main qualification for technical and vocational education, which is widely available at junior, senior and post-secondary levels.

Learned Societies

GENERAL

Mongolian Academy of Sciences: Sükhbaataryn talbai 3, Ulan Bator; tel. and fax (11) 321638; e-mail mas@magicnet.nm; f. 1921; depts of Agriculture (Dir N. ALTANSÜKH), Geology and Geography (Dir, vacant), Medicine and Biology (Dir P. NYAMDAVAA), Physics, Mathematics, Chemistry and Technology (Dir D. KHAISAMBUU), Social Sciences (Dir KH. NAMSRAI); attached research institutes: see Research Institutes; Pres. BAATARYN CHADRAA; Scientific Sec. DÜGERIN REGDEL; publs *Proceedings of the Mongolian Academy of Sciences* (4 a year), *Studia Archaeologica*, *Studia Ethnographica*, *Studia Folclorica*, *Studia Historica*, *Studia Mongolica*, *Studia Museologica*.

AGRICULTURE, FISHERIES AND VETERINARY SCIENCE

Academy of Agricultural Sciences: Ulan Bator; f. 1998; Pres. N. ALTANSÜKH.

Association of Private Veterinary Surgeons: Ulan Bator; Pres. GOTOVYN BATTULGA.

BIBLIOGRAPHY, LIBRARY SCIENCE AND MUSEOLOGY

Academy of Information Sciences: Ulan Bator; f. 2004; Vice-Pres. CH. DALAI.

ECONOMICS, LAW AND POLITICS

Academy of State and Law: Ulan Bator; f. 2003; Pres. T. SENGEDORJ.

EDUCATION

Association of Mongolian Universities and Higher Schools: Ulan Bator; Pres. B. ERDENESÜREN.

Consortium of Mongolian Universities and Higher Schools: c/o University of Health Sciences, Ulan Bator; Pres. TS. LKHAGVASÜREN.

FINE AND PERFORMING ARTS

Academy of Cinematic Art: Ulan Bator; f. 2003; Pres. T. GANDI.

LANGUAGE AND LITERATURE

Association of Mongolian Writers: Ulan Bator; Exec. Dir KHAIDAVYN CHILAAJAV.

MEDICINE

Academy of Health Management: Ulan Bator; Pres. N. UDVAL.

Academy of Medical Sciences: Ulan Bator; f. 2005; Pres. PAGVAJAVYN NYAMDAVAA.

Society of Mongolian Surgeons: Ulan Bator; Pres. B. GOOSH.

NATURAL SCIENCES

General

Academy of Natural Sciences: Ulan Bator; f. 1998; Pres. JAMTSYN GARIDKHÜÜ; Learned Sec. T. ERDENEJAV.

RELIGION, SOCIOLOGY AND ANTHROPOLOGY

Academy of Anthropology: Ulan Bator; f. 1998; Pres. L. DASHNYAM.

Academy of Astrology: Mongolian Youth Association Bldg, Baga Toiruu, Sükhbaatar district, Ulan Bator; tel. and fax (11) 322982.

Academy of Nomadic Culture and Civilization: 'Ikh Zasag' University Building, 4th khoroo, Bayanzurkh district, Ulan Bator; tel. (11) 457826; fax (11) 455736; e-mail ihkzasag@ikhzasag.edu.mn; internet www.ikhzasag.edu.mn; f. 2002; 80 mems; Pres. NAMSRAIN NYAM-OSOR; publ. *Ikh Zasag* (2 a year).

Genghis Khan World Academy: Bldg 6, 2nd sub-district, Bayanzürkh district, Ulan Bator (POB 21/174); fax (11) 315846; e-mail wack@magicnet.mn; internet www.chinggesacademy.mn.

Mongolian Muslims' Society: Ulan Bator; f. 1990; Pres. KADYRYN SAIRAAN.

TECHNOLOGY

Association of Academies of Science and Technology: Ulan Bator; f. 1998; Pres. L. DASHNYAM.

Mongolian Civil Engineers' Association: Baruun Dörvön Zam, Ikh Toiruu 1, Ulan Bator (POB 44/7); tel. (11) 328097; fax (11) 325580; e-mail midiid@magicnet.mn.

Mongolian National Mining Association: Ulan Bator; f. 2003; Dir N. ALGAA.

Mongolian National Water Association: Ulan Bator; f. 2000; Pres. S. CHULUUNKHUYAG.

National Academy of Engineering: Ulan Bator; f. 1998; Pres. P. OCHIRBAT.

Science and Technology Foundation: Ulan Bator; Dir KH. TSOOKHÜÜ.

Research Institutes

AGRICULTURE, FISHERIES AND VETERINARY SCIENCE

Agricultural Economics Research Institute: c/o Academy of Sciences, Sükhbaataryn talbai 3, Ulan Bator; attached to Mongolian Acad. of Sciences; Dir YU. ADYAA.

Agricultural Research Institute: Khovd; tel. (43) 3720; f. 1994; library of 10,000 vols; Dir P. BAATARBILEG.

Institute of Forestry and Hunting: Ulan Bator; Dir D. ENKHSAIKHAN.

Institute of Pasture and Fodder: Darkhan; Dir D. TSEDEV.

Institute of Veterinary Research: Zaisan, Ulan Bator; tel. (11) 341553; f. 1960; attached to Mongolian Agricultural Univ.; library of 4,000 vols; Dir B. BYAMBAA; publ. *Proceedings of the Institute of Veterinary Research and Training*.

Research Institute of Animal Husbandry 'J. Sambuu': Zaisan, Ulan Bator; tel. (11) 341572; e-mail riah@magicnet.mn; f. 1961; attached to Mongolian Acad. of Sciences; library of 800 vols; Dir DONDOVYN

ALTANGEREL; publ. *Proceedings* (in Mongolian, with English summary).

Research Institute of Pastoral Animal Husbandry in the Gobi Region: Bulgan district, Ömnögobi province; f. 1959; attached to Mongolian Acad. of Sciences; camel and goat husbandry; Dir N. BIICHEE.

Research Institute of Plant Protection: c/o Academy of Sciences, Sükhbaataryn talbai 3, Ulan Bator; attached to Mongolian Acad. of Sciences; Dir D. TSEDEV.

Research Institute of Vegetable Growing and Land Cultivation Training: Darkhan-Uul province; tel. and fax (37) 24132; attached to Mongolian Agricultural Univ.; 138 teachers; 1,050 students.

ARCHITECTURE AND TOWN PLANNING

Building Institute: c/o Academy of Sciences, Sükhbaataryn talbai 3, Ulan Bator; attached to Mongolian Acad. of Sciences; Dir D. LKHANAG.

Construction and Architecture Research, Experimental, Production and Business Corporation: c/o Academy of Sciences, Sükhbaataryn talbai 3, Ulan Bator; tel. (11) 341437; Exec. Dir D. KHAISAMBUU.

Institute of Agricultural Architecture: Ulan Bator; Dir O. JADAMBA.

Institute of Architecture and Town Planning: c/o Academy of Sciences, Sükhbaataryn talbai 3, Ulan Bator; attached to Mongolian Acad. of Sciences; Dir (vacant).

Research Institute of Soils and Foundations Engineering: c/o Academy of Sciences, Sükhbaataryn talbai 3, Ulan Bator; attached to Mongolian Acad. of Sciences; Dir Dr A. ANAND.

ECONOMICS, LAW AND POLITICS

Centre for North-East Asian Studies: Mongolian Technical University Bldg (2nd Fl.), Ulan Bator (POB 51/4); tel. (11) 458317; fax (11) 458317; f. 1990; attached to Mongolian Acad. of Sciences; library of 2,000 vols; Dir Prof. CH. DALAI; publ. *North-East Asian Studies* (2 a year).

Institute of Economics: Ulan Bator; tel. (11) 320802; fax (11) 322216; f. 1962; attached to National University of Mongolia; fmrly attached to Mongolian Acad. of Sciences; library of 2,000 vols; Dir P. LUVSANDORJ.

Institute of International Studies: Room 806, Soyolyn töv örgöö, Sükhbaataryn talbai, Ulan Bator; tel. and fax (11) 322613; attached to Mongolian Acad. of Sciences; Dir LUVSANGIIN KHAISANDAI; Scientific Sec. D. SHÜRKHÜÜ.

Institute of Management Development: Ulan Bator; Dir D. TSERENDORJ.

Institute of Market Studies: Chamber of Commerce and Industry, Ulan Bator; Dir S. DEMBEREL.

Institute of Mongol Studies: c/o Academy of Sciences, Sükhbaataryn talbai 3, Ulan Bator 11; attached to Mongolian Acad. of Sciences; Dir SH. BIRA.

Institute of National Development: Ulan Bator; attached to Mongolian Acad. of Sciences and the Presidential Secretariat; Dir RADNAASÜMBERELIIN RENCHINBAZAR; Scientific Sec. L. TSEDENDAMBA.

Institute of Oriental and International Studies: c/o Academy of Sciences, Sükhbaataryn talbai 3, Ulan Bator; attached to Mongolian Acad. of Sciences; Dir A. OCHIR.

Institute of Strategic Studies: Partizany gudamj, Ulan Bator (POB 870); tel. (11) 328188; fax (11) 324055; e-mail abat@magicnet.mn; attached to Ministry of Defence; Dir Maj.-Gen. CHOYJAMTSYN ULAANKHÜÜ.

Mongolian Development Research Centre: Room 50, Baga Toiruu 13, Chingeltei district, Ulan Bator (POB 20A/63); tel. and fax (11) 315686; internet www.mdrc.mn.

'Prognoz' Institute of Socio-Political Studies: Ulan Bator; attached to Mongolian People's Revolutionary Party; Dir O. ERDENECHIMEG.

Research Institute for Land Policy: Chingünjavyn gudamj 2, Ulan Bator; tel. (11) 60506; f. 1975; library of 1,100 vols; Dir Dr G. PÜREVSÜREN.

Research Institute of Economic Studies: Ulan Bator; f. 1991; microeconomics; Dir Prof. T. DORJ.

FINE AND PERFORMING ARTS

Research Institute of Culture and Arts: c/o Academy of Sciences, Sükhbaataryn talbai 3, Ulan Bator 11; attached to Mongolian Acad. of Sciences; Dir S. TSERENDORJ.

HISTORY, GEOGRAPHY AND ARCHAEOLOGY

Institute of Archaeology: c/o Academy of Sciences, Sükhbaataryn talbai 3, Ulan Bator; attached to Mongolian Acad. of Sciences; Dir D. TSEVEENDORJ; Scientific Sec. B. TSOGTBAATAR.

Institute of Geography: c/o Academy of Sciences, Sükhbaataryn talbai 3, Ulan Bator; tel. (11) 350472; attached to Mongolian Acad. of Sciences; Dir Dr S. DORJGOTOV.

Institute of History: Jukovyn gudamj 77, Bayanzürkh district, Ulan Bator; tel. and fax (11) 458305; e-mail history@mongol.net; attached to Mongolian Acad. of Sciences; archaeology, Mongolian history, ethnography; Dir D. DASHDAVAA.

LANGUAGE AND LITERATURE

Folk Literature Research Institute: Ulan Bator; Dir B. KATUU.

Institute of Mongolian Language and Literature: c/o Academy of Sciences, Sükhbaataryn talbai 3, Ulan Bator; tel. (11) 451762; attached to Mongolian Acad. of Sciences; Dir KH. SAMPILDENDEV.

MEDICINE

Institute of Hygiene, Epidemiology and Microbiology: c/o Academy of Sciences, Sükhbaataryn talbai 3, Ulan Bator; attached to Mongolian Acad. of Sciences; Dir J. KUPUL.

Institute of Public Health: Enkh taivny gudamj 17, Ulan Bator; tel. (11) 458645; fax (11) 458645; e-mail pubhealth@magicnet.mn; Dir L. NARANTUYAA.

Institute of Traditional Medicine: c/o Academy of Sciences, Sükhbaataryn talbai 3, Ulan Bator; attached to Mongolian Acad. of Sciences; Dir D. DAGVATSEREN.

Medical Research Institute: c/o Academy of Sciences, Sükhbaataryn talbai 3, Ulan Bator; attached to Mongolian Acad. of Sciences; Dir YO. BODIKHÜÜ.

National Centre for Communicable Diseases: Bayanzürkh district, Ulan Bator; tel. and fax (11) 458699; e-mail nccd@magicnet.mn; f. 2001; Dir TOGOOGIIN ALTANTSETSEG.

National Forensic Research Centre: Ulan Bator; Dir CH. ALTANKHISHIG.

National Institute of Medicine: c/o Academy of Sciences, Sükhbaataryn talbai 3, Ulan Bator; attached to Mongolian Acad. of Sciences; Learned Sec. B. TSERENDASH.

Research and Production Centre of Biotechnology: Ulan Bator; attached to Min. of Health and Inst. of Public Health; Dir J. OYUUNBILEG.

Research and Production Institute of Biological Preparations and Blood: Ulan Bator; Dir A. DANDII.

State Research Centre for Maternal and Child Health: Amarsanaagiin gudamj, Bayangol district, Ulan Bator; tel. (11) 362633; fax (11) 302316; e-mail mcrcch@magicnet.mn; f. 1930; attached to Mongolian Acad. of Sciences; Dir G. CHOIJAMTS; publ. *Mother and Child* (2 a year).

NATURAL SCIENCES

General

Institute of Scientific and Technical Development: Ulan Bator; Dir D. NYAMAA.

Biological Sciences

Institute of Biology: Ulan Bator; tel. (11) 458851; f. 1965; attached to Mongolian Acad. of Sciences; Dir TS. JANCHIV.

Institute of Botany: Ulan Bator; tel. (11) 451837; fax (11) 323158; e-mail ibot@mongol.net; attached to Mongolian Acad. of Sciences; Learned Sec. D. MAGSAR.

Institute of Geoecology: c/o Academy of Sciences, Sükhbaataryn talbai 3, Ulan Bator; tel. (11) 321862; attached to Mongolian Acad. of Sciences; Dir J. TSOGTBAATAR.

Palaeontology Centre: Enkh Taivny gudamj 63, Ulan Bator; fax (11) 458935; e-mail barsgeodin@magicnet.mn; attached to Mongolian Acad. of Sciences; Dir R. BARSBOLD.

Mathematical Sciences

Institute of Mathematics: Ulan Bator; attached to National University of Mongolia; fmrly attached to Mongolian Acad. of Sciences; Dir A. MEKEI.

Physical Sciences

Astronomical Observatory: Khürel-Togoot, Ulan Bator (CPOB 788); tel. (11) 52929; f. 1961; attached to Mongolian Acad. of Sciences; library of 1,500 vols; Dir G. NOONOI.

Centre of Seismology and Geomagnetism: c/o Academy of Sciences, Sükhbaataryn talbai 3, Ulan Bator; attached to Mongolian Acad. of Sciences; Dir U. SÜKHBAATAR.

Institute of Chemistry and Chemical Technology: Züün Dörvön Zam, Bayanzürkh district, Ulan Bator; tel. (11) 453133; e-mail monchemi@magicnet.mn; attached to Mongolian Acad. of Sciences; Dir B. PÜREVSÜREN.

Institute of Geology and Mineral Enrichment: CPO Box 118, Ulan Bator; Enkh taivny örgön chölöö 63, Ulan Bator; tel. (11) 457858; fax (11) 457858; f. 1973; attached to Mongolian Acad. of Sciences; library of 1,000 vols; Dir O. TÖMÖRTOGOO; publ. *Khaiguulchin* (4 a year).

Institute of Meteorology and Hydrology: Khudaldaany gudamj 5, Ulan Bator; tel. and fax (11) 326614; e-mail meteoins@magicnet.mn; f. 1966; library of 13,000 vols; Dir D. AZZAYAA; publ. *Environment*.

Institute of Physics and Technology: Enkh Taivny gudamj 54B, Ulan Bator; tel. (11) 458397; fax (11) 458397; e-mail instphys@magicnet.mn; f. 1961; attached to Mongolian Acad. of Sciences; library of 50,000 vols; Dir TS. BAATAR.

Research Centre for Astronomy and Geophysics: c/o Academy of Sciences, Sükhbaataryn talbai 3, Ulan Bator; tel. (11) 458849; attached to Mongolian Acad. of Sciences; Dir B. BEKHTÖR.

RELIGION, SOCIOLOGY AND ANTHROPOLOGY

Institute of Astrology: Ulan Bator; Dir SH. JARGALSAIKHAN.

Institute of Buddhist Studies: Ulan Bator; Dir G. LUVSANTSEREN.

Institute of Philosophy, Sociology and Law: Jukovyn gudamj 77, Ulan Bator; tel. (11) 453752; f. 1972; attached to Mongolian Acad. of Sciences; Dir G. CHULUUNBAATAR.

Social Sciences Institute: Ulan Bator; attached to National University of Mongolia (fmrly attached to Mongolian Acad. of Sciences); Dir O. MÖNKHBAT.

TECHNOLOGY

Agricultural Technology Science, Technology and Production Corporation: Ulan Bator; tel. (11) 341155; attached to Mongolian Academy of Sciences.

Communications Research and Production Corporation: c/o Academy of Sciences, Sükhbaataryn talbai 3, Ulan Bator; attached to Mongolian Acad. of Sciences; Dir D. LKHAGVAA.

Electronic Equipment and Machine Studies Science, Technology and Production Corporation: Ulan Bator; tel. (11) 328025; attached to Mongolian Acad. of Sciences.

Experimental and Research Centre for Leather: c/o Academy of Sciences, Sükhbaataryn talbai 3, Ulan Bator; attached to Mongolian Acad. of Sciences; Dir D. GANBOLD.

Experimental and Research Centre for Wool: c/o Academy of Sciences, Sükhbaataryn talbai 3, Ulan Bator; attached to Mongolian Acad. of Sciences; Dir G. YONDONSAMBUU.

Forestry and Wood Processing Industry Institute: c/o Academy of Sciences, Sükhbaataryn talbai 3, Ulan Bator; attached to Mongolian Acad. of Sciences; Dir SAINBAYAR.

Geodesic and Geological Engineering Institute: Ulan Bator; Dir TS. TSERENBAT.

Heat Technology and Industrial Ecology and Institute: Ikh Surguuliin gudamj 2A, Sükhbaatar district, Ulan Bator; tel. 324959; attached to Mongolian Acad. of Sciences; Dir S. BATMÖNKH.

Informatics Institute: c/o Academy of Sciences, Sükhbaataryn talbai 3, Ulan Bator; tel. (11) 458090; attached to Mongolian Acad. of Sciences; Dir MAIDARJAVYN GANZORIG.

Information Technology Science, Technology and Production Corporation: Ulan Bator; tel. (11) 327133; attached to attached to Mongolian Acad. of Sciences.

Light Industry Scientific, Technological and Production Corporation (ARMONO): Chingisiin örgön chölöö, Ulan Bator; tel. and fax (11) 342536; e-mail armono@mongol.net; f. 1997; research into leather and timber industrial products; attached to Mongolian Acad. of Sciences.

Military Science Research Institute: Ministry of Defence, Ulan Bator; Dir SH. PALAMDORJ.

Mining Institute: c/o Academy of Sciences, Sükhbaataryn talbai 3, Ulan Bator; attached to Mongolian Acad. of Sciences; Dir S. MANGAL.

Natural Freezing and Food Technology Institute: c/o Academy of Sciences, Sükhbaataryn talbai 3, Ulan Bator; attached to Mongolian Acad. of Sciences; Dir N. LONJID.

Petrochemical Technology Research Centre: Ulan Bator; tel. (11) 24779.

Power Institute: c/o Academy of Sciences, Sükhbaataryn talbai 3, Ulan Bator; attached to Mongolian Acad. of Sciences; Dir D. BUMAYUUSH.

Renewable Energy Science, Technology and Production Corporation: Chingisiin örgön chölöö, Khan-Uul district, Ulan Bator (POB 35/479); tel. and fax (11) 342377; attached to Mongolian Acad. of Sciences; Dir B. CHADRAA.

Roads Research and Production Corporation: c/o Academy of Sciences, Sükhbaataryn talbai 3, Ulan Bator; attached to Mongolian Acad. of Sciences; Dir B. KHUNDGAA.

Standardization and Metrology National Centre: Enkh Taivny gudamj 46A, Ulan Bator (POB 51/48); tel. (11) 458349; fax (11) 458032; e-mail mncsm@magicnet.mn; f. 1953; attached to Min. of Industry and Trade; library of 130,000 vols; Dir NYAMJAVYN JANCHIVDORJ; publ. *Standards and Metrology* (monthly).

Traditional Medicine Science, Technology and Production Corporation: Ulan Bator; tel. (11) 343103; attached to Mongolian Acad. of Sciences.

Transport Research and Production Corporation: c/o Academy of Sciences, Sükhbaataryn talbai 3, Ulan Bator; attached to Mongolian Acad. of Sciences; Dir L. TÜDEV.

Water Policy Research Institute: Baruunselbe 13, Ulan Bator 211238; tel. (11) 325487; fax (11) 321862; f. 1965; library of 3,500 vols; Dir N. CHULUUNKHUYAG.

Libraries and Archives

Ulan Bator

Gandan Library: Gandantegchinlen Buddhist Monastery, Ulan Bator; tel. (11) 360023; f. 1838; Buddhist theology and philosophy, xylographs, secular works of science and literature.

National Archives of Mongolia: Ulan Bator 210646; tel. (11) 324533; fax (11) 324533; e-mail jganbold@magicnet.mn; f. 1996; history, art, literature, science, technology, film, sound recordings; Dir-Gen. DEMBERELIIN ÖLZIIBAATAR; publ. *Archives News* (2 a year).

Natsagdorj Central Public Library: 2nd sub-district, Sükhbaatar district, Ulan Bator; tel. (11) 327873; fax (11) 329950; internet www.mclibrary.edu.mn; Dir T. MIJIDDORJ.

State Central Library: Söüliin gudamj, Sükhbaatar district, Ulan Bator; tel. and fax (11) 323100; e-mail nat.lib@magicnet.mn; f. 1921; 4,000,000 vols, incl. rare and ancient editions; Dir GOTOVYN AKIM.

Museums and Art Galleries

Arkhangai

Ethnographical Museum: Arkhangai; located in the Zayain Gegeenii Süm (temple founded in 1536).

Bayan-Ölgii

Town Museum: Bayan-Ölgii; Kazakh culture, especially costume and artefacts.

Dornogobi

Danzan Ravjaa Museum: Dornogobi; commemorates the life and works of the 19th c. writer and lama, Danzan Ravjaa.

Khentii

Ethnographical Museum: Khentii; located in the home of the former Tsetseg Khan.

Ulan Bator

Botanical Garden: Ulan Bator; attached to Mongolian Acad. of Sciences; Dir G. OCHIRBAT.

Memorial Museum of Victims of Political Persecution: Olimpiin örgön chölöö, Ulan Bator; tel. (11) 320592; located in home of executed Prime Minister Genden; commemorates in documents and photographs the victims of the 1930s Stalinist purges; Dir S. BEKHBAT.

Mongolian National Gallery of Modern Art: Ulan Bator; tel. (11) 327177; fax (11) 313191; e-mail mnartgallery@mongolnet.mn; internet www.ulaanbaatar.net/artgallery; f. 1991; Dir D. ENKHTSETSEG.

Museum of Asian Art: Juulchny gudamj, Ulan Bator; private collection of religious art and artefacts in precious metals; Dir A. ALTANGEREL.

Museum of Military History: Enkh Taivny örgön chölöö, Ulan Bator; tel. (11) 454292; Dir Col P. BYAMBASÜREN.

Museum of Mongolian Costume: Enkhtaivny örgön chölöö, Ulan Bator; f. 2005; folk costume, felt tents and artefacts since the Genghis Khan period.

Museum of Mongolian Traditional Medicine: Next to Bogd Khan's Winter Palace (Museum of Religious History), Ulan Bator; f. 2005; Dir D. TSERENSODNOM.

Museum of Religious History: Chingis Khaany örgön chölöö, Ulan Bator; tel. (11) 324788; housed in Choyjin Lamyn Khüree, a former lamasery, and Bogd Khan's Winter Palace; Dir G. TÖVSAIKHAN.

National Museum of Mongolian History: Khudaldaany gudamj, Ulan Bator (POB 46/332); tel. (11) 326802; fax (11) 326802; e-mail nmmh@mongol.net; f. 1924 as Mongolian National Museum; present name 1990 by merger of State Central Museum and Museum of the Revolution; 46,000 historical and ethnographical objects from prehistory to present day; Dir Dr S. IDSHINNOROV; publ. *Museologia* (annually).

Natsagdorj Museum: Chingis Khaany örgön chölöö, Ulan Bator; tel. (11) 327879; life and works of the author and poet Dashdorjiin Natsagdorj.

Natural History Museum: Khuvisgalchdyn örgön chölöö, Ulan Bator; tel. (11) 321716; natural history, Gobi desert dinosaur eggs and skeletons; Dir P. ERDENEBAT.

Theatre Museum: Cultural Palace, Sükhbaatar Square, Ulan Bator; tel. (11) 326820.

Ulan Bator Museum: Enkh Taivny örgön chölöö, Ulan Bator; located in old Russian house; history of Ulan Bator.

Wildlife Museum: Öndör Gegeen Zanabazaryn gudamj, Ulan Bator; tel. (11) 360248; fax (11) 360067.

Zanabazar Fine Arts Museum: Barilgachdyn talbai, Ulan Bator; sculptures by Mongolia's first Buddhist leader and *tankas* (religious paintings); Dir D. GUNGAA.

Zhukov, G. K., House Museum: Enkh Taivny örgön chölöö, 15th sub-district, Ulan Bator; tel. (11) 453781; career of Soviet Marshal Zhukov.

Universities

'CHOI LUVSANJAV' UNIVERSITY OF LANGUAGE AND CIVILIZATION

11th microraion, 7th sub-district, Sükhbaatar district, Ulan Bator (POB 13/550)
Telephone: (11) 353524
Fax: (11) 353524
Founded 1993
Vice-President: SOYOMBO LUVSANJAV
Number of teachers: 40 (22 full-time, 18 part-time)
Number of students: 380
Library of 10,000 vols
Mongolian and Chinese studies; training of English- and Japanese-speaking teachers and interpreters.

MONGOLIAN AGRICULTURAL UNIVERSITY

Zaisan, Ulan Bator
Telephone: (11) 341592
Fax: (11) 341770
E-mail: haaint@magicnet.mn
Internet: www.msua.edu.mn
Founded 1942 as veterinary dept of Mongolian State University; became Institute of Agriculture 1958; university status 1991; present name 1996
State control
Director: Dr J. GANBOLD
Rector: B. BYAMBAA
Pro-Rector: L. NYAMBAT
Library of 200,000 vols
Number of teachers: 300
Number of students: 6,700

DEANS

Faculty of Agricultural Economics: A. BAKEI
Faculty of Agricultural Engineering and Product Technology: L. LUVSANSHARAV
Faculty of Agronomy: BEGZIIN DORJ
Faculty of Animal Husbandry: (vacant)
Faculty of Basic Education: H. KHÜRELTOGOO
Faculty of Veterinary Medicine: B. LUVSANSHARAV

ATTACHED RESEARCH INSTITUTES

Altai Region Agricultural Research Institute.

Beekeeping Research Institute.

Dalanzadgad Camel Research Centre.

Darkhan Research Institute of Plant Science and Agriculture.

Eastern Region Agricultural Research Institute.

Gobi Region Pastoral Livestock Research Institute.

Research Institute of High-Mountain Agriculture.

Research Institute of Agricultural Engineering.

Research Institute of Animal Husbandry.

Tsetserleg Yak Research Centre.

Ulaangom Crop Research Institute.

MONGOLIAN UNIVERSITY OF ARTS AND CULTURE

Baga Toiruu 22, Chingeltei district, Ulan Bator
Telephone: (11) 327335
Fax: (11) 325205
Founded 1990
State control
Academic year: September to June
Rector: D. TSEDEV
Vice-Rector: JAMBALYN ENEBISH
Registrar: ALTANGERELIIN GANBAATAR
Librarian: DAMBAJAVYN NYAMDULAM
Number of teachers: 230
Number of students: 1,900

DEANS

College of Culture: L. BATCHULUUN
College of Music: CH. CHINBAT
College of Radio and Television: (vacant)
College of Theatre Art: (vacant)

MONGOLIAN STATE EDUCATION UNIVERSITY

Baga toiruu 14, Sükhbaatar district, Ulan Bator
Telephone: (11) 326010
Fax: (11) 322705
E-mail: togmid@mspu.edu.mn
Internet: www.mspu.edu.mn
Founded 1951
State control
Academic year: September to June
Rector: Prof. B. JADAMBA
Vice-Rectors: Prof. B. JADAMBAA (International Relations and Information), Prof. D. TÖMÖRTOGOO (Research), Prof. TS. BATSUURI (Teaching)
Head of Academic Affairs: Prof. D. PÜREVDORJ
Head of Graduate Studies: Prof. N. JADAMBAA
Library of 300,000 vols
Number of teachers: 330
Number of students: 5,261
Publication: *Teacher Education* (2 a year)

DIRECTORS

School of Art and Technology: Prof. G. BATDORJ
School of Computer Science and Information Technology: Prof. L. CHOIJOOVAANCHIG
School of Education Studies: Prof. TS. SUMYAA
School of Foreign Languages: Prof. Z. GULIRAANZ
School of History and Social Sciences: Prof. D. NARANTSETSEG
School of Mongolian Studies: Prof. TS. ÖNÖRBAYAN
School of Mathematics and Statistics: Prof. TS. BATKHÜÜ
School of Natural Sciences: Prof. M. ÜINDEN
School of Physical Education: Prof. S. JAMTS
School of Physics and Technology: Prof. R. BAZARSÜREN
School of Pre-School Education: Prof. J. BATDELGER
School of Teacher Training: Prof. S. BATKHUYAG

UNIVERSITY OF HEALTH SCIENCES

Choidogiin gudamj 3, Sükhbaatar district, Ulan Bator (POB 48/111)
Telephone: (11) 328670
Fax: (11) 321249
E-mail: nmumtlhs@magicnet.mn
Internet: www.nmum.cjb.net
Founded 1942
State control
Academic year: September to August
Director: Prof. TS. LKHAGVASÜREN
Deputy Director: D. DUNGERDORJ
Scientific Secretary: G. BATMÖNKH
Chief Administrative Officer: N. BATKHÜREL
Librarian: N. TSAGAACH
Number of teachers: 310
Number of students: 2,300

DEANS

Faculty of Biomedicine: (vacant)
Faculty of Health Economics: B. ERDENESAIKHAN
Faculty of Medicine: (vacant)
Faculty of Pharmacy: S. TSETSEGMAA
School of Dentistry: B. OYUUNBAT
School of Public Health: CH. TSOLMON
School of Traditional Medicine: Prof. N. TÖMÖRBAATAR

ATTACHED COLLEGES

Medical College in Darkhan.

Medical College in Dornogobi Province.

Medical College in Gobi-Altai Province.

Medical College in Ulan Bator.

UNIVERSITY OF THE HUMANITIES

Baga Toiruu, Sükhbaatar district, Ulan Bator
Telephone: (11) 322702
Fax: (11) 322702
E-mail: UH@mongol.net
Founded 1979 as Higher School of Russian Language Teachers; present name and status 2000
State control
Dir: Prof. BEGZIIN CHULUUNDORJ
Schools of foreign languages, social sciences; departments of journalism, human resource management, foreign languages, literature, culture and American and British studies.

NATIONAL UNIVERSITY OF MONGOLIA

Ikh Surguuliin gudamj 1, Sükhbaatar district, Ulan Bator (POB 46A/523)
Telephone: (11) 320892
Fax: (11) 320668
E-mail: numelect@magicnet.mn
Internet: www.num.edu.mn
Founded 1942
State control
Academic year: September to June
President: TSERENSODNOMYN GANTSOG
Vice-Presidents: SÜRENGIIN DAVAA (Academic), R. SAMYAA (Research)
Library of 350,000 vols
Number of teachers: 500
Number of students: 6,500
Publication: *Proceedings*.

FACULTIES AND TRAINING AND RESEARCH INSTITUTES

Faculty of Biology: incl. depts of zoology, botany, ecology, forestry, biochemistry and microbiology, biophysics, and genetics; Dir R. SAMYAA.

Faculty of Chemistry: incl. depts of general chemistry (analytical and physical chemistry), organic chemistry (coal and petrochemistry), ferrous-metal and rare-element chemistry, chemistry and technology of new materials; Dean D. DORJ.

Faculty of Earth Sciences: Dean CH. GONCHIGSUMLAA.

School of Economic Studies: incl. depts of the theory of economics, management, accountancy, credit and finance, statistics, economic data processing, marketing, demography, mathematics, and foreign languages; Dir CH. HASHCHULUUN.

School of Foreign Languages and Cultures: English, Russian, French, German, Korean, Japanese, Chinese, Czech, Polish.

School of Foreign Service: training of diplomats.

School of Information Technology.

School of International Relations: postgraduate studies in foreign relations; Dir J. BOR.

School of Law: incl. depts of constitutional law, civil law, state administration, international law, and criminal process law; Dir S. NARANGEREL.

School of Mathematics and Computer Science: incl. depts of algebra, geometry, mathematical analysis, probability theory and mathematical statistics, applied mathematics, and methods of teaching mathematics, computer programming; Dean JAMTSYN BAATAR.

School of Mongolian Language and Culture: incl. depts of linguistics, Mongolian language, literature, and journalism; Dir D. BADAMDORJ.

School of Physics and Electronics: incl. depts of theoretical physics, nuclear physics, geophysics, optics, radiophysics, solid-state physics, hydrology, electronics, and meteorology; Dean CHÜLTEMIIN BAYARKHÜÜ.

School of Social Sciences: incl. depts of philosophy, sociology, history, politics, and culture and art; Dean SH. SODNOM.

Graduate School: Dean A. MEKEI.

Office of International Affairs: Dean S. ALTANTSETSEG.

Office of Undergraduate Studies: Dean N. BATCHIMEG.

'ORKHON' UNIVERSITY

Chinggis Khaany örgön chölöö, Khan-Uul district, Ulan Bator (POB 36/176)
Telephone: (11) 342696
Fax: (11) 341276
E-mail: info@orkhon.edu.mn
Internet: www.orkhon.edu.mn

Founded 1992
Private control

Director: Prof. Dr NYAMAAGIIN KHAJIDSÜREN

Library of 25,000 vols
Number of teachers: 70
Number of students: 1,000

BA degree courses in languages (English, German, French, Russian, Japanese, Korean) and law; MA degree courses in linguistics.

MONGOLIAN UNIVERSITY OF SCIENCE AND TECHNOLOGY

Baga Toiruu 34, Sükhbaatar district, Ulan Bator (POB 46/520)
Telephone: (11) 325109
Fax: (11) 324121
E-mail: info@must.edu.mn
Internet: www.must.edu.mn

Founded 1969
State control
Academic year: September to July

Rector: D. DASHJAMTS (acting)
Vice-Rectors: Z. TSERENDORJ (Academic Affairs), L. BOLDBAATAR (Finance and Development), D. DASHJAMTS (Research and Technology)
Chief Administrative Officer: O. NASANBAT
Librarian: G. PÜREV

Library of 170,000 vols
Number of teachers: 781
Number of students: 17,000

Publications: *MUST News* (in Mongolian, monthly), *Science and Technology* (in Mongolian, 4 a year), *Scientific Transactions* (in Mongolian, 4 a year)

DIRECTORS

School of Civil Engineering: Z. BINDERYAA
School of Computer Technology and Management: (vacant)
School of Food and Biotechnology: D. NANSALMAA
School of Foreign Languages: T. BATBAYAR
School of Geology: D. CHULUUN
School of Humanities: A. ENKHBAATAR
School of Industrial Technology and Design: B. DAVAASÜREN
School of Mathematics: J. BAASANDORJ
School of Materials Technology: P. MÖNKHBAATAR
School of Mechanical Engineering: G. BATKHÜREL
School of Mining Engineering: B. PÜREVTOGTOKH
School of Power Engineering: H. ENKHJARGAL
School of Technology in Darkhan: S. TSEVEL
School of Technology in Erdenet: S. DAVAANYAM
School of Technology in Övörhangai Province: J. JANTSANDORJ
School of Technology in Sükhbaatar Province: MAJIGIIN KHÜRLEE
School of Telecommunications and Information Technology: B. DAMDINSÜREN
Graduate Study Centre: H. BUYANNEMEKH

ULAANBAATAR UNIVERSITY

Bayanzürkh district, Ulan Bator (POB 44/658)
Telephone: (11) 450179
Fax: (11) 311080
E-mail: ubuniv@mongol.net
Internet: www.ulaanbaatar.edu.mn

Founded 1993 as Higher Technical School; received charter 1996
State control
Academic year: September to July

Rector: YONG SUNG JE
Vice-Rector: D. BOLD
Scientific Sec.: T. NAMJIL

Number of teachers: 78
Number of students: 800

Publication: *Proceedings of the Ulaanbaatar University* (annually)

Faculties of Language and Literature, Social Sciences and Technology.

Higher Schools

Academy of Management: Chingisiin örgön chölöö 7, Khan-Uul district, Ulan Bator; tel. and fax (11) 343037; e-mail td@aom.edu.mn; f. 1924; govt agency; depts of public administration, management, economics, computer science, English language; 52 teachers; 739 students; Rector TOGOOCHIN LKHAGVAA; publs *Public Administration* (in Mongolian, 4 a year), *Management* (in Mongolian, 4 a year).

Darkhan Higher School: 4th sub-district, Darkhan district, Darkhan-Uul Province (Darkhan CPOB 520); tel. and fax (372) 35652; internet www.darkhandeed.mn; f. 1997; tourism, hotel and restaurant management, accounting, English, Korean, Chinese, Japanese; library: 25,000 vols; 90 teachers; 1,000 students.

Defence Academy: 16th sub-district, Bayanzükh district, Ulan Bator; tel. (11) 458673; law, accounting, state administration, operation of motor vehicles, tracked vehicles and bridge-building machinery, electronics, communications, military science, military history; Dir Col N. JALBAJAV.

Genghis Khan 'Ikh Zasag' University: Baatar B. Dorjiin gudamj, 4th sub-district, Bayanzürkh district, Ulan Bator (POB49/349); tel. (11) 457826; fax (11) 455736; e-mail ikhzasag@edu.mn; internet www.ikhzasag.edu.mn; schools of international relations, international trade and economics, international law, tourism management, American, Japanese and Chinese studies, English, Japanese and Chinese interpreting; 146 teachers; 3,660 students; Pres. NAMSRAIN NYAM-OSOR; Vice-Pres J. KHAIDAV (Finance), N. TUUL (International Relations), J. TSETSEGMAA (Management), B. NASAN (Marketing); publs *Ikh Zasag* (newspaper, every 3 months), *Ikh Zasag* (journal, jtly with Academy of Nomadic Civilization and Culture, 2 a year).

Higher School of Arts and Crafts: Ulan Bator.

Higher School of Culture: Erkh Chölöönii talbai, Chingeltei district, Ulan Bator (POB 46/982); tel. (11) 326759; fax (11) 329328; e-mail cclib@mongol.net; internet www.moncollege.150m.com; training of librarians, cultural managers, museum workers and archivists, printers, and music, song and dance teachers; Dir G. BAATAR.

Higher School of European Languages: located at: Ikh Surguuliin gudamj 9, Sükhbaatar district, Ulan Bator (POB 46/982); tel. (11) 320993; f. 1993; English, French, Russian and German interpreting; 52 teachers (11 full-time, 41 part-time); 632 students; Rector T. PELJID.

Higher School of Finance and Economics: Enkh Taivny gudamj 12A, Bayanzürkh district, Ulan Bator 49; tel. and fax (11) 458378; internet www.ife.edu.mn; f. 1924; 65 teachers; 1,200 students; depts of banking and finance, business and management, international studies, information technology, accounting and audit, economics and econometrics; Dir JAMYANDORJIIN BATKHUYAG.

Higher School of Information Technology: Ulan Bator; Dir G. TSOGBADRAKH.

Higher School of International Economics and Business: 20th sub-district, Bayangol district, Ulan Bator; tel. (11) 681525; fax (11) 452067; e-mail iieb_elselt@yahoo.com; internet www.iieb.edu.mn; international economics, banking and accounting, business management, taxation and audit.

Higher School of International Studies: Ikh Surguuliin gudamj 2A, Sükhbataar district, Ulan Bator, (POB 46/205); tel. (11) 329860; fax (11) 329450; Dir NARANDULAM.

Higher School of Labour: Erkh Chölöönii talbai (bldg behing the Tengis cinema), Chingeltei district, Ulan Bator; tel. (11) 318176; fax (11) 312629; e-mail mli_999@yahoo.com; attached to attached to the Mongolian Confederation of Trade Unions; labour economics and management, finance, business management, accountancy and social work.

Higher School of Legal Studies: Ulan Bator; tel. (11) 529798; Dir L. DASHNYAM.

Higher School of Literature: Ulan Bator; Dir SHIRSEDIIN TSEND-AYUUSH.

Higher School of Mongolian Language and Literature: Chingisiin örgön chölöö 29, 3rd sub-district, Khan-Uul district, Ulan Bator; tel. (11) 342210; fax (11) 342210; trains teachers and interpreters in French, German and Japanese; English-language journalism.

Higher School of Oriental Literature: Ulan Bator; Dir S. BATMÖNKH.

Higher School of Oriental Philosophy and Anthropology: 17th sub-district, Bayangol district, Ulan Bator; tel. and fax (11) 361461; e-mail ophsi@mongolnet.mn; Dir NANSALYN SARANTUYAA.

Higher School of Religion: Ulan Bator; tel. (11) 457454; Dir SH. SONINBAYAR.

Higher School of Social Studies: 2nd sub-district, Bayanzürkh district, Ulan Bator (POB 23/277); tel. and fax (11) 460356; e-mail uuds@magicnet.mn; f. 1993; library: 12,000 vols; Dir TS. ENKHEE.

Higher School of Technology: Darkhan, Darkhan-Uul province; tel. (372) 23368; fax (372) 23760; e-mail Technol@mongol.net; fmr polytechnic and technical college; electrical and heating engineering, mining and ore concentration, geology, power supply management.

Higher School of Trade and Industry: Oyuutny gudamj 14, Enkhtaivny Örgön Chölöö, Ulan Bator, (POB 48/404); tel. (11) 325724; fax (11) 326748; e-mail icbm@magicnet.mn; f. 1924; business management, marketing, international trade, accountancy; library: two libraries, with 22,000 vols; 60 teachers; 1,200 students; Rector S. BUDNYAM; publ. *Mercury* (3 a year).

'Khalkha Juram' Higher School of Law: Tulga Co. Bldg, Ikh Toiruu 20, Sükhbaatar district, Ulan Bator, (POB 51/128); tel. and fax (11) 350480; Dir T. DOOKHÜÜ.

Khan-Uul Higher School: located at: Tulga Co. Bldg, Ikh Toiruu 20, Sükhbaatar district, Ulan Bator (POB 46/419); tel. (11) 351032; e-mail khan-uul@mongol.net; internet www.khan-uul.mn; f. 1994; business economics, applied mathematics, computer programming, computer technology; 25 teachers; 280 students; Dir TSERENGIIN DEMBEREL.

'Mongol' Higher School: Ulan Bator; Dir NAMJAAGIIN DASHZEVEG.

Mongolian Business Institute: Enkhtaivny örgön chölöö, Bayangol district, Ulan Bator, (POB 24/715); tel. (11) 361589; e-mail mbi_191@mol.mn; internet www.mbi.edu.mn; f. 1991; degree courses in management, economics, finance, marketing; 40 teachers; 500 students; Dir Dr B. ERDENESÜREN.

Mongolian National Higher School: Enigma Centre, 11th sub-district, Bayangol district, Ulan Bator; tel. (11) 300900; fax (11) 300799; e-mail MNI@Mongolnet.mn; f. 1998; law, economics, financial and business management, economics of tourism, hotel and restaurant management, marketing, international trade; Dir TÖMÖRBAATARYN KHERÜÜGA.

'Monos' Higher School of Medicine: Songolongiin toiruu 5, 20th sub-district, Songinokhairkhan district, Ulan Bator; tel. (11) 633235; medicine and pharmacy.

'Otgontenger' University: Jukovyn örgön chölöö, Bayanzürkh district, Ulan Bator, (POB 51/35); tel. (11) 454560; e-mail Oy_oyun@magicnet.mn; internet www.otgontenger.edu.mn; f. 1991; training of Russian- and English-language teachers and interpreters, Japanese-, German-, French-, Chinese- and Korean-language business and tourism managers, and Japanese-language international tour guides, and training in English-language journalism; 48 teachers; 650 students; Founder and Chair. DULAMSÜRENGIIN OYUUNKHOROL; Rector D. NARANCHIMEG.

'Otoch Maramba' Higher School of Medicine: 2nd sub-district, Bayanzürkh district, Ulan Bator (POB 49/235); tel. (11) 457489; fax (11) 358489; f. 1991; study of traditional medicine; 6 teachers; 68 students; Dir TSERENSODNOM.

Private Higher School of Oriental Philosophy and History: Enkh Taivny gudamj 35 Ulan Bator (POB 44/283); tel. (11) 322628; fax (11) 320210; f. 1992; library: 5,000 vols; 150 students; Dir R. NANSAL.

Radio and Television Higher School: Mongolian Radio and Television Bldg, Khuvisgalyn zam 3, Ulan Bator 11; tel. (11) 369223; training of radio and television journalists and producers, television cameramen and engineers.

Railway College: Enkhtaivny örgön chölöö 44, Bayangol district, Ulan Bator (POB 35/76); tel. (11) 322723; fax (11) 322797; e-mail mtzcoll@mongolnet.mn; railway transport organization, management, construction, maintenance, automation and telecommunications, passenger services, rolling-stock maintenance; trains staff for Mongolian Railways, the country's largest employer; Dir B. SERÜÜD.

'Shikhikhutug' Higher School of Law: Ikh Surguuliin gudamj 1, 6th sub-district, Ulan Bator (POB 46/1033); tel. and fax (11) 323392; e-mail shihihutug@mongol.net; Dir D. OYUUNTSETSEG.

'Shonkhor' Higher School of Physical Culture: Baga Toiruu 55, 8th sub-district, Sükhbaatar district, Ulan Bator (CPOB 960); tel. and fax (11) 319858; Dir KH. BAYANMÖNKH.

'Tenger' Socio-Economic Higher School: Chinggissin örgön chölöö, 2nd sub-district, Khan-Uul district, Ulan Bator; tel. (11) 342651; social sciences, anthropology, accounting, business economics, trade economics, state administration, tourism, social work; Chinese language jtly with Shandong University, China.

'Zanabazar' Buddhist University: Ulan Bator; attached to Gandantegchinlen monastery; Dir SH. SONINBAYAR.

Colleges

College of Agriculture: Darkhan; hydrology, land improvement, meteorology.

'O. Tleikhan' Building College: Baruun Dörvön Zam, Enkhtaivny örgön chölöö 35, Ulan Bator (POB 24/643); tel. (11) 322723; fax (11) 322797; e-mail cwc@magicnet.mn; civil engineering, utilities, electrical engineering, machine and vehicle repair, computer operations; Dir B. CHIMIDDORJ.

Ulan Bator College: Construction College Bldg, West side of road to Gandan monastery, Baruun Dörvön Zam, Bayangol district, Ulan Bator; depts of business management and computer programming, Korean-language teacher-training and interpreting; 10 teachers; 140 students; Rector YUM SUN JE.

MONTENEGRO

The Higher Education System

Following the dissolution of the Socialist Federal Republic of Yugoslavia in 1992, Montenegro became part of the Federal Republic of Yugoslavia, which was renamed the State Union of Serbia and Montenegro in 2003. In 2006 Montenegro declared independence from the State Union of Serbia and Montenegro. The Univerzitet Crne Gore Podgorica (University of Montenegro, Podgorica—founded 1974) is the main institution of higher education and was established while Montenegro was part of the Socialist Federal Republic of Yugoslavia. The newly-established Ministry of Education has assumed responsibility for higher education, which is still strongly based on the former Yugoslav system. In 2002 the New University Law introduced a range of reforms, including adoption of the European Credit Transfer System and increased autonomy for institutions of higher education. Consequently, Montenegro also participates in the Bologna Process to establish a European Higher Education Area, the first phase of which is to adopt a credit-based system of comparable degrees with two main cycles (undergraduate and graduate).

Under the old system, admission to higher education was based on completion of general secondary education or four-year vocational certificate programmes and award of the Secondary School Leaving Diploma. Universities also set their own entrance examinations. Quotas for admissions were set by the Government. The new undergraduate Bachelors degree (four years) replaces the old-style awards of Diplom Višeg Obrazovanje (two to three years) and Diplom Visokog Obrazovanja (four to six years). The Masters degree (Magistarska Dimploma) is a one-year programme of study following the Bachelors. Finally, the Doctorate (Doktorat Nauka) is the highest university-level degree and is awarded after a period of research culminating with defence of a thesis.

Learned Societies

GENERAL

Crnogorska akademija nauka i umjetnosti (CANU) (Montenegrin Academy of Sciences and Arts): Rista Stijovića 5, 81000 Podgorica; tel. (81) 655-456; fax (81) 655-451; e-mail canu@cg.yu; internet www.canu.cg.yu; depts of Arts, Natural Sciences, of Social Sciences; 37 mems; Pres. MOMIR ĐUROVIĆ; Sec.-Gen. RANISLAV BULATOVIĆ; publs *Bibliografije* (Bibliographies), *Glasnik* (Review), *Godišnjak CANU* (annually), *Istorijski izvori* (Historical Issues), *Naučni skupovi* (Symposia), *Posebna izdanja* (Special Editions), *Posebni radovi* (Special Works), *Zbornici radova* (Works).

LANGUAGE AND LITERATURE

Montenegrin PEN Centre: Bul. Lenjina 93, 21325 Podgorica; e-mail sreten@cg.yu; internet www.montenegro.org/pen.html; f. 1990; promotes friendship and co-operation among writers, and defends freedom of expression; Pres. SRETEN PEROVIC; publ. *Doclea*.

Research Institutes

BIBLIOGRAPHY, LIBRARY SCIENCE AND MUSEOLOGY

Republički zavod za zaštitu spomenika kulture (Institute for the Protection of Cultural Monuments of Montenegro): Bajova 150, 81250 Cetinje; tel. (86) 231-039; fax (86) 231-753; e-mail rzzsk@cg.yu; internet www.heritage.cg.yu/rzzsk_e.htm; f. 1948; research, registration and protection of cultural property in Montenegro; library of 2,500 vols; Dir SLOBODAN MITROVIĆ; publ. *Starine Crne Gore* (annually).

HISTORY, GEOGRAPHY AND ARCHAEOLOGY

Istorijski institut Crne Gore (Historical Institute of Montenegro): Bulevar Revolucije 3, 81000 Podgorica; tel. (81) 241-624; fax (81) 241-336; e-mail biicg@cg.yu; f. 1948; Dir Prof. Dr DJORDJE BOROZAN; publ. *Istorijski zapisi* (4 a year).

NATURAL SCIENCES

Institut za biologiju mora (Institute of Marine Biology): Dobrota 66, POB 69, 85330 Kotor; tel. (82) 334-569; fax (82) 334-570; e-mail biokotor@cg.yu; internet www.ibmk.org; f. 1961; scientific investigation, exploitation, control and protection of the sea; Dir Dr SRETEN MANDIĆ; publ. *Studia Marina* (2 or 3 a year).

Libraries and Archives

Cetinje

Biblioteka državnog muzeja Crne Gore (Library of the National Museum of Montenegro): Novice Cerovica bb, 81250 Cetinje; tel. (86) 231-313; e-mail mncgb@cg.yu; internet www.heritage.cg.yu/nm_e.htm; f. 1926; over 20,000 vols.

Centralna narodna biblioteka Crne Gore (Central National Library of Montenegro): Pf. 57, Bulevar crnogorskih junaka 163, 81250 Cetinje; tel. (86) 231-143; fax (86) 231-726; e-mail cnb@cg.yu; internet cnbct.cnb.cg.ac.yu; f. 1946; 1,600,000 vols; special collection of MSS, maps, picture postcards, photographs, records, exhibition catalogues; Federal copyright and deposit library; Dir JELENA ĐUROVIC; publ. *Bibliografski vjesnik* (3 a year).

Državni arhiv Crne Gore (Public Records Office of Montenegro): Novice Cerovica 2, 81250 Cetinje; tel. (86) 231-045; fax (86) 232-670; internet www.heritage.cg.yu/da_e.htm; f. 1951; inherited documents of the State Archive of Montenegro (f. 1895); official state documents of Montenegro since 1878; 3,760 m of documents; oldest document dates from 1539; Dir STEVAN RADUNOVIC; publ. *Arhivski zapisi* (Archive Records).

Podgorica

Biblioteka istorijskog instituta Crne Gore (Library of the Historical Institute of Montenegro): Bul. revolucije 3, 81000 Podgorica; tel. (81) 241-336; fax (81) 241-624; f. 1948; 38,000 vols.

Museums and Art Galleries

Cetinje

Narodni muzej Crne Gore (National Museum of Montenegro): Novice Cerovića bb, 81250 Cetinje; tel. (86) 231-303; fax (86) 231-682; e-mail mncgb@cg.yu; internet www.heritage.cg.yu/nm_e.htm; f. 1896; consists of five separate museums: Art Museum of Montenegro; Ethnographic Museum of Montenegro; Historical Museum of Montenegro; King Nikola's Palace; and Njegos' Museum; library of 30,000 vols; Dir PETAR ĆUKOVIĆ; publ. *Glasnik Cetinjskih Muzeja*.

Kotor

Pomorski muzej (Maritime Museum): 81330 Kotor; tel. (82) 325-146; internet www.visit-montenegro.org/kultura/muz_kotor.htm; f. 1900; models, paintings, weapons, Turkish guns, navigation instruments and compasses; library of 10,000 vols; Dir JOVAN MARTINOVIĆ; publ. *Godišnjak Pomorskog Muzeja u Kotoru* (Yearbook).

Podgorica

Arheoloska zbirka Crne Gore (Archaeological Collection of Montenegro): Vuka Karadzica 8, 81000 Podgorica; tel. (81) 631-349; f. 1961; collection, arrangement, maintenance, study and presentation of archaeological excavation sites in Montenegrol.

Muzej grada Podgorice (Museum of the City of Podgorica): Miljana Vukova 59, Podgorica; tel. (81) 632-006; e-mail pgmuzej@cg.yu; f. 1950; four areas of study: archeological, ethnographic, historical and cultural-historical; colln of displays from the classical period to the present; Roman fibula, Illyrian jewellery, old coins, everyday objects made of metal and bones related to the settlements and influences of different civilizations and cultures in the area.

Prirodnjacki muzej (Natural History Museum): Trg Nikole Kovacevica br. 7, 81000 Podgorica; tel. (81) 633-184; fax (81) 620-968; e-mail prmuzej@cg.yu; internet www.pmcg.cg.yu; f. 1961; exhibits on the fauna and palaeontology of Montenegro; publ. *Natura Montenegrina*.

University

UNIVERZITET CRNE GORE, PODGORICA
(University of Montenegro, Podgorica)

Cetinjski put b.b., 81000 Podgorica
Telephone: (81) 241-888
Fax: (81) 242-301
E-mail: rektor@cg.ac.yu
Internet: www.ucg.cg.ac.yu

Founded 1974 from existing faculties and high schools in Podgorica, Nikšić and Kotor
State control
Academic year: October to July

Rector: Prof. Dr LJUBIŠA STANKOVIĆ
Vice-Rectors: Prof. Dr PREDRAG IVANOVIĆ (Finance and Development), Prof. ŽARKO MIRKOVIĆ (International Relations), Prof. Dr MITAR MIŠOVIĆ (Teaching and Science)
Secretary-General: DRAGIŠA IVANOVIĆ
Librarian: Dr VASO JOVOVIĆ

Library of 25,000 vols, 1,097 periodicals
Number of teachers: 700
Number of students: 11,000
Publication: *Bilten* (quarterly)

DEANS

Civil Engineering: RADENKO PEJOVIĆ
Drama (Cetinje): NENAD VUKOVIĆ
Economics:
Electrical Engineering: MILUTIN OSTOJIĆ
Fine Arts (Cetinje): PAVLE PEJOVIĆ
Law: DRAGAN VUKČEVIĆ
Maritime Studies (Kotor): BORISLAV IVOŠEVIĆ
Mechanical Engineering: MILAN VUKČEVIĆ
Medicine: MILORAD BAKIĆ
Metallurgy and Technology: VLADIMIR KOMNENIĆ
Natural Sciences: SLOBODAN BACKOVIĆ
Philosophy: MILADIN VUKOVIĆ
Academy of Music: RADOVAN POPOVIĆ
College of Physiotherapy: VUKAŠIN MIHAJLOVIĆ

ATTACHED RESEARCH INSTITUTES

Biotechnical Agriculture Institute: Cetinjski put bb, 81000 Podgorica; tel. (81) 268-437; fax (81) 268-432; e-mail bti@cg.ac.yu; internet www.ucg.cg.ac.yu/biotehnicki_ins.htm; Dir Dr LJUBOMIR PEJOVIĆ.

Historical Institute of Montenegro: Bul. revolucije 3, 81000 Podgorica; tel. (81) 241-336; fax (81) 241-624; internet www.ucg.cg.ac.yu/istorijski_ins.htm; Dir DJORDJE BOROZAN.

Institute of Foreign Languages: Jovana Tomasevica 37, 81000 Podgorica; tel. and fax (81) 245-334; e-mail isj@cg.ac.yu; internet www.institut.cg.yuf. 1979; Dir Dr IGOR LAKIC.

Institute of Marine Sciences, Kotor: see Research Institutes: Natural Sciences.

MOROCCO

The Higher Education System

Université Quaraouyine Fès (founded 859), an institution for Koranic, Islamic and Arabic studies, is among the oldest universities in continuous existence in the world. From 1912 until 1958 Morocco was a French protectorate and, consequently, the higher education system displays strong French influences. The Université Mohammed V Agdal (founded 1957) is the oldest multi-disciplinary institution of secular studies. In 1998/99 there were 68 state university-level institutions and in 2003/04 there were 277,442 students enrolled at state universities and equivalent-level institutions.

The Ministry of National Education, Higher Education, Training and Scientific Research is the supreme authority of higher education, which is free to Moroccan students. The senior officers of universities, such as Presidents and Deans of Faculty, are state appointees, and are responsible for running universities in conjunction with University Councils, Faculty Councils and Faculty Scientific Councils. The main types of institutions of higher education are universities, higher schools (grandes écoles), teacher-training institutes and other specialist institutes.

Admission to higher education is often on the basis of the secondary school awards Diplôme du Baccalauréat and Diplôme du Baccalaureat Technique, but additional two-year courses (classes prépartoires aux grandes écoles) are required for entry to the grandes écoles. Most university degrees fall into one of three cycles, with some exceptions; these include degrees for disciplines that require longer periods of undergraduate study than the standard four years, such as engineering (five years), veterinary medicine and agronomy (six years) and medicine (seven years). The first cycle of higher education consist of certificates and diplomas awarded after two years of a broad-based programme of study in one of four subject groups (arts and humanities, science and economics, applied sciences, engineering and agriculture) appropriate to the intended area of specialization. Students in the arts and humanities are awarded the Certificat Universitaire d'Etudes Littéraires; students in science and economics receive the Certificat Universitaire d'Etudes Scientifiques; students in applied sciences are awarded Diplôme d'Etudes Universitaires de Générales or Diplôme d'Etudes Universitaires de Technologie; while students in engineering and agriculture undertake a two-year preparatory programme of study. The second cycle of higher education is a period of specialist training and culminates in the award of either the Licence or the Maîtrise. Students who have the Certificat Universitaire d'Etudes Littéraires or Certificat Universitaire d'Etudes Scientifiques undertake a further two years of study for the Licence, while holders of the Diplôme d'Etudes Universitaires de Générales or Diplôme d'Etudes Universitaires de Technologie are awarded the Maîtrise after the same period. Professional titles are awarded in some disciplines, like engineering (Diplôme d'Ingénieur d'Etat), veterinary medicine (Docteur Vétérinaire) and medicine (Doctorat en Médecine). The third cycle of higher education awards consists mainly of three degrees, Diplôme d'Etudes Supérieures Approndies, Diplôme d'Etudes Supérieures Spécialisées and Doctorat D'état. Holders of the Licence are eligible for admission to the Diplôme d'Etudes Supérieures Approndies, a two-year programme of study and research, culminating in submission of a dissertation, that allows admission to doctoral-level studies. The Diplôme d'Etudes Supérieures Spécialisées is also a two-year course, open to holders of either the Licence or Maîtrise, but does not qualify the student for doctoral-level studies. The Doctorat D'état is the highest university-level degree and comprises three to five years of research. Outside the university system, the grandes écoles offer specialist degrees such as Diplôme de Technicien Supérieur and Diplôme d'Ingénieur d'Etat.

Students with Diplôme du Baccalauréat and the Diplôme du Baccalaureat Technique may attend post-secondary vocational and technical education and study for the Brevet de Technicien Supérieur, which requires successful completion of a two-year programme of study.

The national accreditation body for tertiary education is the National Accreditation and Evaluation Committee (Commission Nationale d'Accreditation et d'Evaluation).

Learned Societies

GENERAL

Académie du Royaume du Maroc: Charia Imam Malik, Km 11, BP 5062, Rabat; tel. 37-75-51-13; fax 37-75-51-01; e-mail alacademia@iam.net.ma; f. 1977; 65 mems; promotes the devt of research and reflection in the principal fields of intellectual activity; library of 16,000 vols; Permanent Sec. Dr Abdellatif Berbich; publs *Academia* (annual), *Proceedings of Sessions* (2 a year).

UNESCO Office Rabat: BP 1777 RP, Rabat; located at: 35 ave du 16 Novembre, Agdal, Rabat; tel. 37-67-03-72; fax 37-67-03-75; e-mail rabat@unesco.org; f. 1991; designated Cluster Office for Algeria, Libya, Mauritania, Morocco and Tunisia; Dir Rosamaria Durand.

AGRICULTURE, FISHERIES AND VETERINARY SCIENCE

Société d'Horticulture et d'Acclimatation du Maroc: BP 13.854, Casablanca 01; f. 1914; 260 mems; Pres. Josette Duplat; Sec. René Tripotin.

ECONOMICS, LAW AND POLITICS

Société d'Etudes Economiques, Sociales et Statistiques du Maroc: BP 535, Rabat–Chellah; f. 1933; 20 mems; Dir Nacer el Fassi; publ. *Signes du Présent* (quarterly).

FINE AND PERFORMING ARTS

Association des Amateurs de la Musique Andalouse: c/o 133 ave Ziraoui, Casablanca; f. 1956 to preserve and catalogue traditional Moroccan (Andalusian) music; maintains a School of Andalusian music at Casablanca, directed and subsidized by the Ministry of Culture; Dir Hadj Driss Benjelloun.

HISTORY, GEOGRAPHY AND ARCHAEOLOGY

Association Nationale de Géographie Marocaine: Faculté des Lettres et des Sciences Humaines, Université Mohammed V, Rabat; tel. 37-77-18-93; fax 37-77-20-68; f. 1916; Sec.-Gen. Taoufik Agoumi; publ. *Revue de Géographie du Maroc* (2 a year).

LANGUAGE AND LITERATURE

Alliance Française: 22 Ave de la Marche Verte, 24000 El Jadida; tel. 23-34-21-06; fax 23-35-31-82; e-mail afm.eljadida@iam.net.ma; internet www.ambafrance-ma.org/institut/afm-eljadida; offers courses and examinations in French language and culture and promotes cultural exchange with France; attached teaching centre in Essaouira.

British Council: 36 Rue de Tanger, BP 427 Rabat; tel. 37-76-08-36; fax 37-76-08-50; e-mail bc@britishcouncil.org.ma; internet www.britishcouncil.org/morocco; teaching centre; offers courses and examinations in English language and British culture and promotes cultural exchange with the United Kingdom; attached teaching centre in Casablanca; library of 8,000 vols, 20 periodicals; Dir Steve Mcnulty; Teaching Centre Man. Ian Winter.

Goethe-Institut: 7 rue Sana'a, 10000 Rabat; tel. 37-70-65-44; fax 37-70-82-66; e-mail rabatkul@goethe.org.ma; internet www.goethe.de/wm/rab/deindex.htm; offers courses and examinations in German language and culture and promotes cultural exchange with Germany; attached centre in Casablanca; library of 15,000 vols; Dir Dr Dieter Strauss.

Instituto Cervantes: 5 Zankat Madnine, 10000 Rabat; tel. 37-70-87-38; fax 37-70-02-79; e-mail cenrabat@cervantes.org.ma;

internet rabat.cervantes.es; offers courses and examinations in Spanish language and culture and promotes cultural exchange with Spain and Spanish-speaking Latin and Central America; attached centres in Casablanca, Fez, Tangier and Tétouan; library; Dir XABIER MARKIEGI CANDINA.

Research Institutes

GENERAL

Centre National pour la Recherche Scientifique et Technique: 52 Charii Omar Ibn Khattab, BP 8027, 10102 Agdal-Rabat; tel. 37-77-28-03; fax 37-77-12-88; e-mail cnr@cnr.ac.ma; internet www.cnr.ac.ma; f. 1976; under Min. of Higher Education; research fields include food and agriculture, communication, environment, natural resources, astronomy, geophysics, biotechnology, geology, computer science, mathematics, social sciences, int. business, environmental science, energy and maintenance; library of 3,500 vols, 70 periodicals; Dir SAID BELCADI (acting); Sec.-Gen. (vacant); publ. *Lettre d'Information* (annual).

Attached Institute:

Institut Marocain de l'Information Scientifique et Technique (IMIST): Rabat; e-mail imist@cnr.ac.ma; internet www.cnr.ac.ma/imist/site; scheduled to open 2005 to provide technical documentation to scientific and industrial researchers.

AGRICULTURE, FISHERIES AND VETERINARY SCIENCE

Institut National de la Recherche Agronomique: BP 6512 RI, Rabat; tel. 37-77-55-30; fax 37-77-40-03; internet www.inra.org.ma; f. 1930; research in agronomy; library of 40,000 vols, 300 periodicals; Dir A. ARIFI; publs *Al Awamia* (quarterly), *Les Cahiers de la Recherche Agronomique* (irreg.).

Institut National de Recherche Halieutique: 2 rue de Tiznit, Casablanca; tel. 22-22-88-70; fax 22-26-88-57; f. 1947; applied fisheries oceanography, marine biology, evaluation of resources, aquaculture, environmental studies, fishing gear technology, fish processing technology, fisheries management; library of 1,050 vols, 70 periodicals; Dir MOHAMED SEDRATI; publs *Bulletin*, *Travaux et Documents*, *Notes d'Information*.

Mission Pédologique: Ministère de la Réforme Agraire, BP 432, Rabat; pedology; Dir J. L. GEOFFROY.

ECONOMICS, LAW AND POLITICS

Centre d'Etudes, de Documentation et d'Informations Economiques et Sociales (CEDIES–Informations): Angle ave des Forces Armées Royales et angle rue Mohamed Errachid, Casablanca 20100; tel. 22-25-26-96; fax 22-25-38-39; Pres. ABDERRAHIM LAHJOUJI; publ. *CEDIES Informations*.

La Fondation du Roi Abdul Aziz pour les Etudes Islamiques et les Sciences Humaines: BP 12585, Casablanca 20052; located at: Blvd de la Corniche, Ain Diab, Anfa, Casablanca 20050; tel. 22-39-10-27; fax 22-39-10-31; e-mail secretariat@fondation.org.ma; internet www.fondation.org.ma; f. 1985; to promote the study of social sciences and humanities in the Maghreb, by means of documentation and cultural activities; library of 310,000 , 1,289 periodicals; Dir PRINCE ABDULLAH IBN ABDUL AZIZ AL-SAOUD; publ. *Lettre d'Information* (2 a year).

HISTORY, GEOGRAPHY AND ARCHAEOLOGY

Comité National de Géographie du Maroc: Institut Universitaire de la Recherche Scientifique, BP 2122 Riad, Rabat; f. 1959; Pres. THE MINISTER OF EDUCATION; Sec.-Gen. A. LAOUINA; publ. *Atlas du Maroc*.

LANGUAGE AND LITERATURE

Instituto Muley El Hassan: PB 84, Tétouan; research on Hispano-Muslim works; library of 5,500 vols; Dirs MOHAMMED BEN TAUÍT, MARIANO ARRIBAS PALAU.

MEDICINE

Direction de l'Epidémiologie et de Lutte Contre les Maladies: 71 ave Ibn Sina, Agdal, Rabat; tel. 37-67-12-71; fax 37-67-12-98; e-mail delm@sante.gov.ma; internet www.sante.gov.ma/departements/delm/index--delm.htm; f. 1990; applied research in epidemiology and environmental health; Dir Dr NOUREDDINE CHAOUKI; publ. *Bulletin Epidémiologique* (3 a year).

Institut National d'Hygiène: POB 769, Rabat Agdal; tel. 37-77-19-02; fax 37-77-20-67; e-mail relaouad@sante.gov.ma; f. 1930; depts of microbiology, parasitology, physics and chemistry, toxicology, serology, immunology, molecular biology, genetics, entomology; Nat. Poison Control Centre; 266 mems; library: Toxicological Documentation Centre of 400 vols; library of 3,000 vols; Dir Prof. RAJAE EL AOUAD.

Institut Pasteur du Maroc: 1 pl. Louis Pasteur, Casablanca 20100; tel. 22-43-44-50; fax 22-26-09-57; e-mail pasteur@pasteur.ma; internet www.pasteur.ma; f. 1911; research into infectious diseases, bacteriology, parasitology and virology, biochemistry and genetics, food and environmental safety; promotion of public health; Dir Prof. MOHAMMED HASSAR.

NATURAL SCIENCES

Physical Sciences

Direction de la Géologie: c/o Ministry of Energy and Mines, BP 6208, Rabat-Instituts; tel. 37-68-87-01; fax 37-68-87-13; e-mail kafif@mem.gov.ma; f. 1921; Nat. Geological Survey; library of 25,000 vols; Dir Dr MOHAMMED SADIFUI; publs *Mines, Géologie et Energie*, *Notes et Mémoires du Service Géologique du Maroc*.

TECHNOLOGY

Bureau de Recherches et de Participations Minières (BRPM): 5 Charia Moulay Hassan, BP 99, Rabat; tel. 37-76-30-35; fax 37-76-24-10; f. 1928; state agency to develop mining research and industry; Gen. Man. ASSOU LHA TOUTE; publ. *Rapport d'Activité* (annual).

Laboratoire Public d'Essais et d'Etudes: 25 rue d'Azilal, Casablanca; tel. 22-30-04-50; fax 22-30-15-50; f. 1947; hydraulics, environment, roads, study of soil, materials and methods of construction; library of 7,000 vols; Dir-Gen. MOHAMED JELLALI; publs *LPEE-Magazine* (quarterly), *Revue Marocaine de Génie Civil* (quarterly).

Libraries and Archives

Casablanca

Bibliothèque de la Communauté Urbaine de Casablanca: 142 ave des Forces Armées Royales, Casablanca; tel. 22-31-41-70; f. 1917; law, political economy, sciences, philosophy, history, literature, the arts, geography, medicine, sport, travel, fiction; 91,307 vols in Arab section, 267,149 vols in foreign section; 137 periodicals, several foreign daily newspapers; Dir HAJ MOHAMED BOUZID.

Fez

Bibliothèque de l'Université Quaraouyine Fès: Place des Seffarines, Fez; 22,071 vols, 5,157 MSS, 38 archives.

Marrakesh

Bibliothèque Ben Youssef: Ave 11 Janvier, Hay Mohamadi Daoudiat, Marrakesh; 21,223 vols, 586 periodicals, 1,840 MSS; Dir SEDDIK BELLARBI.

Rabat

Bibliothèque de l'Institut Scientifique: Ave Ibn Battota, BP 703, Agdal, 10106 Rabat; tel. 37-77-45-48; fax 37-77-45-40; f. 1920; zoology, botany, geomorphology, cartography, ecology, earth sciences, geophysics, remote detection; 15,700 vols, 1,728 periodicals; Librarian ABDELLATIF BAYED; publs *Bulletin de l'Institute Scientifique*, *Travaux de l'Institut Scientifique*.

Bibliothèque Générale et Archives: BP 1003, Ave Ibn Battouta, Rabat; tel. 37-77-18-90; fax 37-77-60-62; f. 1920; 600,000 vols, 31,000 MSS and 2,000 linear metres of archives; Dir AHMED TOUFIQ; publ. *Bibliographie Nationale* (2 a year).

Centre National de Documentation:; tel. 37-77-49-44; fax 37-77-31-34; e-mail cnd@mpep.gov.ma; internet www.abhatoo.net.ma; f. 1966; documentation on the economic, social, scientific and technical development of Morocco; library depository of World Bank publications; regional reps in Fès, Tangier, Casablanca, Agadir, Marrakesh, Meknès, Oujda; mem. of FID and IFLA; 9,000 vols, 120,000 microfiches, 350 periodicals; Dir ADNANE BENCHAKROUN; publ. *KATAB* (bibliography).

Tangier

Biblioteca Española: Instituto Cervantes, 99 ave Sidi Mohamed Ben Abdellah, 90000 Tangier; tel. 39-93-23-99; fax 39-94-76-03; e-mail bibtan@cervantes.es; internet http://tanger.cervantes.es/menubiblioteca_35_1.htm; f. 1941; main collection in the Spanish language; antique Spanish publications from 18th and 19th centuries; periodical library includes Spanish, Arab and African titles; Spanish sheet music from early 20th century; photographic archive from former Spanish Tourist office in Tangier; 70,000 vols; Dir and Librarian JAUME BOVER PUJOL; publ. *Miscelanea de la Biblioteca Española*.

Tétouan

Bibliothèque Générale et Archives: 32 ave Mohammed V, BP 692, Tétouan; tel. 39-96-32-58; fax 39-96-10-04; e-mail bgatetou@iam.net.ma; f. 1939; research and public library; 50,000 books, 3,500 periodicals, 2,400 MSS, 23,000 historical archive items, 1,200,000 admin. archive items, 45,000 photographs, 1,429 numismatic items; Dir Dr M. ZOUAK.

Museums and Art Galleries

Chefchaouen

Musée Ethnographique de Chefchaouen: Kasbah Outa Hammam, Chefchaouen; tel. 39-98-67-61; f. 1985; musical instruments, arms, embroidery, carved boxes, local pottery.

Essaouira

Musée Sidi Mohamed ben Abdellah: Derb Laalouj, Essaouira; tel. 24-47-23-00; f. 1981; musical instruments, jewellery, arms, carved wooden objects.

Fez

Musée d'Armes du Borj-Nord: Borj-Nord, Fez; tel. 35-64-52-41; built as a military fort in the 16th century, converted into a museum in 1963; collection of 1,100 military artefacts; Curator MOHAMED ZAIM.

Musée Batha: Ksar el Batha, Fez; tel. 35-63-41-16; built as a royal residence in 19th century; converted into a museum in 1915; colln incl. sculpted wood and plaster objects, cast iron, local blue ceramics, embroidery, coins, carpets, jewellery, astrological instruments; Curator HNIA CHIKHAOUI.

Larache

Musée Archéologique: Larache; tel. 39-51-20-92; f. 1973; remains found primarily at the Lixus archaeological site, from the Phoenician, Carthaginian, Mauritanian, Roman and Islamic ages.

Marrakesh

Musée Dar Si Saïd: Derb el Bahia, Riad El Zaitoun El Jadid, Marrakesh; tel. 24-44-24-64; internet www.minculture.gov.ma/fr/Musee%20Dar%20Si%20Said.htm; f. as a royal residence in 19th century, converted into a museum in 1932; artefacts from the Marrakesh region and southern Morocco, incl. wooden objects, jewellery, pottery and ceramics, arms, carpets and woven materials; archaeological remains; Dir HASSAN BEL ARBI.

Meknès

Musée Dar El Jamaï: Pl. El Hedime, Meknès; tel. 35-53-08-63; f. 1920; handicraft items from the region, incl. embroidery, wood carvings, leatherwork, carved chests, carpets, ceramics, ancient jewellery, wrought ironwork, copper and brass objects, painted woodwork, traditional costumes and ancient Korans; Chief Curator HASSAN CHERRADI.

Moulay Driss Zerhoun

Site Archéologique de Volubilis: Conservation du Site de Volubilis, Moulay Driss Zerhoun, Meknès; tel. and fax 35-54-41-03; e-mail volubilisarcheosite@yahoo.fr; f. 1950; archaeological site; library of 250 vols; Archaeologist YOUSSEF BOKBOT.

Rabat

Musée Archéologique: 23 rue Al-Brihi, Rabat; tel. 37-70-19-19; fax 37-75-08-84; e-mail abdelbuencer@canomail.com; f. 1931; history of Morocco from prehistory until the Islamic era; collns incl. stone tools, primitive furniture, Roman divinities, bronze and marble statues, early Islamic ceramics; Curator ABDELWAHED BEN-NCER.

Musée Ethnographique des Oudaïa: Kasba des Oudaïa, Rabat; tel. 37-72-64-61; f. 1915; clothing from various regions of Morocco, jewellery, astronomical tools, carpets, pottery, musical instruments; Curator HOUCEINE EL KASRI.

Musée de la Kasbah: 23 rue el Brihi, Rabat; archaeology and folklore; Curator MOHAMMED HABIBI.

Safi

Musée National de la Céramique: Kachla, Safi; tel. 24-46-38-95; f. 1990; originally a military fort; Curator NOUREDDINE ESSAFSAFI.

Tangier

Musée d'Art Contemporain: 52 Ave d'Angleterre, Tangier; tel. 39-94-99-72; f. 1990; constructed as British consulate; modern Moroccan art.

Tangier American Legation Museum: 8 Zankat America, Tangier; tel. 39-93-59-60; e-mail legation@maroc.net; internet www.maroc.net/legation; f. 1976; operated by the Tangier American Legation Museum Soc., Inc.; permanent colln paintings since 16th century, etchings, aquatints, prints and maps of Morocco; also documentation and artefacts concerning Moroccan-American relations; sponsors short-term exhibitions of contemporary artists; library: research library of 4,500 vols on North Africa and Morocco in English, French, Spanish, Arabic and Portuguese; Dir THOR H. KUNIHOLM.

Tétouan

Musée Archéologique: 2 rue Ben Hssain, Tétouan; tel. 39-96-73-03; f. 1939; prehistoric and pre-Islamic archaeological remains from northern Morocco; mosaics and coins.

Musée des Arts Traditionnels: Tétouan; Curator AMRANI AHMED.

Musée Ethnographique: BP 41 Tétouan; located at: Zankat Skala, 65 Bab El Okla, 93000 Tétouan; tel. 39-97-05-05; f. 1928; originally a fortress; carved wooden objects, copperware, pottery, embroidery.

Universities

UNIVERSITÉ ABDELMALEK ESSAÂDI TÉTOUAN

BP 211, Route de l'Aéroport, Tétouan

Telephone: 39-99-51-34
Fax: 39-97-91-51
Internet: www.uae.ac.ma

Founded 1989
State control
Languages of instruction: Arabic, French

Rector: MUSTAPHA BENNOUNA

Number of teachers: 632
Number of students: 17,150

Publication: *Tourjouman* (Journal of the School of Translation)

Campus in Tangier; Faculties of Arts and Humanities, Law, Economics and Social Sciences and Science and Technology; Schools of Commerce and Management and Translation.

UNIVERSITÉ AL AKHAWAYN IFRANE

BP 104, ave Hassan II, 53000 Ifrane

Telephone: 35-86-20-00
Fax: 35-56-71-50
E-mail: devcom@alakhawayn.ma
Internet: www.alakhawayn.ma

Founded 1995
Private control
Language of instruction: English
Academic year: September to July

President: Prof. RACHID BENMOKHTAR BENABDELLAH
Vice-President for Academic Affairs: Prof. ABDELLATIF BENCHERIFA
Vice-President for Finance and Administration: ABDELILAH KAMAL
Executive Director for Development and Communication: RACHID SLIMI
Dean of Student Affairs: Dr CHARIF BELFEKIH

Library of 65,000 books, 400 periodicals
Number of teachers: 90
Number of students: 1,012 (899 undergraduate, 113 postgraduate)

DEANS

School of Business Administration: Dr AHMED DRIOUCHI
School of Humanities and Social Sciences: Dr MOHAMED DAHBI (acting)
School of Science and Engineering: Dr AMINE BENSAID

DIRECTORS

Center for Academic Development and Study Skills: CATHERINE OWENS
Center of Environmental Issues and Regional Development: Dr BACHIR RAISSOUNI
Executive Education Center: NADIA SANDI
Hillary Rodham Clinton Women's Empowerment Center: LEÏLA BOUASRIA
Institute of Economic Analysis and Prospective Studies: RACHID SLIMI
Language Center: MONCEF LAHLOU

UNIVERSITÉ CADI AYYAD MARRAKECH

Blvd Prince Moulay Abdellah, BP 511, Marrakesh

Telephone: 24-43-48-13
Fax: 24-43-44-94
Internet: www.ucam.ac.ma

Founded 1978
State control
Languages of instruction: Arabic, French
Academic year: September to July

Rector: Prof. MOHAMED KNIDIRI
Secretary-General: SALAH EDDINE BERRAHOU

Number of teachers: 897
Number of students: 36,522

Publications: *Revue de la Faculté de Droit*, *Revue de la Faculté des Lettres*, *Revue de la Faculté des Sciences*

DEANS

Faculty of Law, Economics and Social Sciences: Prof. AHMED TRACHEN
Faculty of Letters and Humanities (Beni Mellal): MOHAMED ESSAOURI
Faculty of Letters and Humanities (Marrakech): Prof. MOHAMED BOUGHALI
Faculty of Sciences: Prof. ABDELKADER MOUKHLISSE
Faculty of Science and Technology: MOHAMED ARSALANE
Institute of Technology: AHMED SOUISSI

UNIVERSITÉ CHOUAÏB DOUKKALI EL JADIDA

BP 299, 2 bis, ave Mohamed ben Larbi Alaoui, Koudiate ben Driss, 24000 El Jadida

Telephone: 23-34-44-47
Fax: 23-34-44-49
Internet: www.ucd.ac.ma

Founded 1989
State control
Languages of instruction: Arabic, French, English

Rector: ABDELHAMID AHMADY

Library of 14,460 vols
Number of teachers: 440
Number of students: 8,100

Publications: *Magazine de la Faculté des Lettres Parallèles*, *Revue de la Faculté des Lettres*

Faculties of Arts and Humanities and Science.

UNIVERSITÉ HASSAN I SETTAT

BP 539, 50 rue Ibn Al Haithem, 26000 Settat

Telephone: 23-72-12-75
Fax: 23-72-12-74
Internet: www.uh1.ac.ma
State control

Rector: MOHAMED RAHJ

Number of teachers: 204

Number of students: 6,679
Faculties of Law, Economics and Social Sciences and Science and Technology; School of Commerce and Management.

UNIVERSITÉ HASSAN II AÏN CHOCK CASABLANCA

BP 9167, 19 rue Tarik Bnou Ziad, Casablanca
Telephone: 22-27-37-37
Fax: 22-27-51-60
Founded 1975
Languages of instruction: Arabic, French
Academic year: September to July
Rector: Aziz Hasbi
Chief Administrative Officer: Noreddine Siraj
Librarian: K. El Hamzaoui
Number of teachers: 1,190
Number of students: 33,213
Publication: faculty reviews

DEANS

Faculty of Arts and Human Sciences: Ahmed Boucharb
Faculty of Dentistry: Latifa Tricha
Faculty of Law: Bachir El Kouhlani
Faculty of Medicine and Pharmacy: Najib Zerouali Ouariti
Faculty of Sciences: Driss El Khyari
National Higher School of Electronics and Mechanics: Abdelilah Smili (Director)
Technology High School: Mohammed Barkaoui (Director)

HEADS OF DEPARTMENTS

Faculty of Arts and Human Sciences:
Arabic Language and Literature: Mohammed Balaji
English Language and Literature: M'barek Rouane
French Language and Literature: Kacem Bassfou
Geography: El Mostafa Chouiki
German Language and Literature: Fathallah El Badri
History: (vacant)
Islamic Studies: Zinelabidine Belafrej
Spanish Language and Literature: (vacant)

Faculty of Dentistry:
Biology and Basic Sciences: Nezza El Alami
Children's Dentistry: Souâd Lamseffer
Conservative Dentistry: Houssine Hirche
Dental Surgery: Ishak Benyahia
Paradontology: Jamila El Kassa
Prosthesis: Samira Belmkhneth

Faculty of Law, Economics and Social Sciences:
Economics: Bachir el Kouhlani
Judicial Science: Mohammed El Kachbour
Political Science: Omar Bouziane

Faculty of Medicine and Pharmacy:
Cardio-Vascular Diseases: Nacer Chraibi
Clinical Biology: Naima M'daghri
Medicine: Ahmed Farouqi
Medico-Surgical Emergency: Rajae Aghzadi
Oto-Neuro-Ophthalmology: Mostapha Touhami
Paediatrics: Abderrahman Abid
Preclinic Biology: Khadija Zarrouck
Respiratory Diseases: Mohammed Bartal
Social and Community Medicine: Said Louahlia
Surgery: Abdelmajid Bouzidi

Faculty of Sciences:
Biology: Mohammed Lotfi
Chemistry: El Mahjoub Lakhdar
Geology: Omar Seddiki
Mathematics: Mohamed Khalid Bouhaia
Physics: Mohammed Saghir El Aadi

National Higher School of Electronics and Mechanics:
Electrical Engineering: Hassan Bazi
Mechanical Engineering: Abdelkhalek Latrach
Principles of Engineering: Ali Zaki

Technology High School:
Electrical Engineering: Boumhdi El Hanouni
Management: Moussa Yassafi
Mechanical Engineering: Abdelhak Bouaziz
Process Engineering: Abelkrim Omoumou

UNIVERSITÉ HASSAN II MOHAMMEDIA

BP 150, 279 Cité Yassmina, Mohammedia
Telephone: 23-31-46-35
Fax: 23-31-46-34
Internet: www.uh2m.ac.ma
Founded 1992
State control
Rector: Rahma Bourqia

DEANS

Faculty of Arts and Humanities, Ben Msik Campus: Abdelhak Hamam
Faculty of Arts and Humanities, Mohammedia Campus: Abdeljawad Sekkat
Faculty of Economics, Law and Social Science, Mohammedia Campus: Mohamed Dasser
Faculty of Science, Ben Msik Campus: Mohammed Berrada
Faculty of Science and Technology, Mohammedia Campus: Mohamed Rafiq

UNIVERSITÉ IBNOU ZOHR AGADIR

BP 3215, Agadir
Founded 1989
Rector: Mustapha Dkhissi
Number of students: 9,724
Faculties of Letters and Humanities and of Sciences.

UNIVERSITÉ IBN TOFAIL KÉNITRA

BP 242, 104 rue Ahmed Boughaba, Bir rami Est, 14000 Kénitra
Telephone: 37-37-28-09
Fax: 37-37-40-52
E-mail: ruitk@iam.net.ma
Founded 1989
State control
Rector: Mohamed Essouari
Library of 42,007 vols
Number of teachers: 405
Number of students: 11,778

DEANS

Faculty of Arts and Humanities: Fouzia El Ghissassi
Faculty of Science: Allal El Bakkali

UNIVERSITÉ MOHAMMED I OUJDA

BP 524, 60000 Oujda
Telephone: 36-74-47-83
Fax: 36-74-47-79
Internet: www.univ-oujda.ac.ma
Founded 1978
State control
Languages of instruction: Arabic, French
Academic year: October to June
Rector: El-Madani Belkhadir
Secretary-General: Abderrahman Houtech
Librarian: Zoubida Chahi
Number of teachers: 593
Number of students: 19,872
Publications: *Al Mayadine*, *Cahiers du CEMM*, *Revue de la Faculté des Lettres*

DEANS

Faculty of Law and Economics: El-Larbi M'rabet
Faculty of Letters and Human Sciences: Mohammed Laamiri
Faculty of Science: Benaïssa N'ciri
Institute of Technology: Mohammed Barboucha (Dir)

HEADS OF DEPARTMENTS

Arabic Language and Literature: Hassan Lamrani
Biology: Mohamed Seghrouchni
Chemistry: Assou Zahidi
Economics: Hachemi Bentahar
Electrical Engineering: Mohammed Mokhtari
English Language and Literature: Mostafa Shoul
French Language and Literature: Mohammed Hammouti
Geography: Mohammed Ben Brahim
Geology: Mimoun Boughriba
History: Mohammed Menfaa
Islamic Studies: Rachid Belahbib
Management Techniques: Yahya Houat
Mathematics: Omar Anane
Physics: Larbi Roubi
Private Law: Abderrahman Oussama
Public Law: (vacant)

ATTACHED CENTRE

Centre d'Etudes sur les Mouvements Migratoires Maghrébins: f. 1990.

UNIVERSITÉ MOHAMMED V AGDAL

BP 554, 3 rue Michlifen, Agdal, Rabat
Telephone: 37-67-13-18
Fax: 37-67-14-01
E-mail: presidence@um5a.ac.ma
Internet: www.um5a.ac.ma
Founded 1957
State control
Languages of instruction: Arabic, French
Academic year: September to July
President: Hafid Boutaleb Joutei
Secretary-General: Mohamad Maniar
Librarian: Hafida Belouafi
Number of teachers: 1,209
Number of students: 24,996
Publications: *Annales du Centre des Études Stratégiques*, *Bulletin de l'Institut Scientifique*, *Bulletin Magnétique*, *Bulletin Séismologique*, *Documents de l'Institut Scientifique*, *Hespéris Tamuda* (annually, in French, Spanish and English), *Langues et Littératures* (annually, in European languages), *Revue de la Faculté des Lettres et des Sciences Humaines* (annually, in Arabic), *Revue Marocaine de l'Automatique, de l'Informatique et du Traitement du Signal*, *Revue Marocaine Juridique, Politique et Economique*, *Revue des Sciences de la Terre*, *Travaux de l'Institut Scientific*

DEANS

Faculty of Law and Economics: Abdelghani Kadmiri
Faculty of Letters and Human Sciences: Saïd Bensaïd Alaoui
Faculty of Sciences: Hassan Chlyah
Higher School of Technology (Salé): Mohammed Rhachi
Mohammadia School of Engineering: Ramdane Khalid
Science Institute: Mohamed Saghi

HEADS OF DEPARTMENTS

Faculty of Law and Economics (BP 721, ave des Nations Unies, Rabat; tel. 37-77-27-32; fax 37-77-26-16; internet www.dfc.gov.ma/fdroit):

Economics: LAHCEN OULHAJ
Private Law: AÏCHA CHERKOUI MALKI
Public Law: TAHAR BAHBOUHI

Faculty of Letters and Human Sciences (BP 1040, ave Ibn Battouta, Rabat; tel. 37-77-19-89; fax 37-77-20-68):

Arabic Language and Literature: SAÄD YAQTINE
Communication: MOHAMED SADID
English Language and Literature: SABER LASRI
French Language and Literature: JAMAL EDDINE EL-HANI
Geography: MOHAMED REFFAS
German Language and Literature: RAJAA TAZI
History: ALI MUHAMMEDI
Islamic Studies: MOHAMED ROUGUI
Italian Language and Literature: MOHAMMED MOKHTARY
Philosophy, Psychology and Social Sciences: SALEM YAFOUT
Spanish Language and Literature: MOHAMMED SALHI

Faculty of Sciences (BP 1014, ave Ibn Battouta, Rabat; tel. 37-77-18-34; fax 37-77-42-61; e-mail chlyah@fsr.ac.ma; internet www.fsr.ac.ma):

Biology: MOHAMED TIJANE
Chemistry: FATIMA CHERKAOUI
Geology: MOHAMED BENZAKOUR
Mathematics and Computer Studies: BENSALEM JENNANE
Physics: MOHAMED ELFERDE

Higher School of Technology (BP 227, ave Prince Héritier Sidi Mohammed, Salé Médina; tel. 37-88-15-61; fax 37-88-15-64; e-mail administration@estsale.ac.ma; internet www.estsale.ac.ma):

Industrial Maintenance: AZIZ ET-TAHIR
Management Techniques: SIDI EL HASSAN DRISSI
Marketing and Communication Techniques: ABDELAZIZ BAHOUSSA
Urban and Environmental Engineering: MOHAMMED GAROUM

Mohammadia School of Engineering (BP 765 Ave Ibn Sina, Rabat; tel. 37-68-71-50; fax 37-77-88-53; e-mail diremi@emi.ac.ma; internet www.emi.ac.ma):

Civil Engineering: AHMED NEJJAR
Computer Engineering: NAJIB TOUNSI
Electrical Engineering: MOHAMED CHERKAOUI
General and Technical Education: RAJAE ABOULAICH
Mechanical Engineering: LAHCEN BELFALS
Mining Engineering: MY LAHCEN SBAI
Process Engineering: ABDELLATIF TOUZANI

Science Institute (BP 703, Ave Ibn Battouta, Rabat; tel. 37-77-45-48; fax 37-77-45-40; e-mail direction@israbat.ac.ma; internet www.israbat.ac.ma):

Botany and Plant Ecology: MOHAMED FENNANE
Geology: HASSAN ASSEBRY
Geomorphology and Cartography: BOUCHTA EL-FALLAH
Geophysics: MIMOUN HARNAFI
Teledetection: ANAS EMRAN
Zoology and Animal Ecology: MOHAMED FEKHAOUI

UNIVERSITÉ MOHAMMED V SOUISSI RABAT

BP 8007, N.U. Agdal, Rabat
located at: ave Med Benabdellah Regragui, Madinat al-Irfane, Rabat
Telephone: 37-68-11-60
Fax: 37-68-11-63
E-mail: presidence@um5s.ac.ma
Internet: www.um5s.ac.ma
Founded 1993
Academic year: September to July
President: TAIEB CHKILI
Secretary-General: ABDURRAHMANE RIDA
Number of teachers: 2,000
Number of students: 22,000
Publications: *Al Irfane* (information bulletin, monthly), *Reflexions* (science, quarterly)

DEANS

Faculty of Dentistry: BOUCHAÏB JIDAL
Faculty of Education: MOHAMMED ZGOR
Faculty of Law: ABDERRAZAK TLY RACHID
Faculty of Law, Salé: MOHAMED BENALLAL
Faculty of Medicine and Pharmacy: ABDELMJID BELMAHI
National Higher School of Informatics and Systems Analysis: ABDELFADIL BENNANI (Dir)

ATTACHED RESEARCH INSTITUTES

Institute of African Studies: Dir HALIMA FERHAT.

Institute for Research and Study in Arabization: Dir ABDELKADER FASSI FIHRI.

University Scientific Research Institute: Dir ABDELKÉBIR EL-KHATIBI.

UNIVERSITÉ MOULAY ISMAIL MEKNÈS

BP 298, Marjane I, Meknès
Telephone: 35-46-73-06
Fax: 35-46-73-05
Founded 1982; univ. status 1989
State control
President: MOHAMED BENNANI
Number of teachers: 691
Number of students: 24,094
Publications: *Maksanat* (Journal of the Faculty of Arts), *Minbar Al Mamiaa* (annual)

DEANS

Faculty of Arts and Human Sciences: MUSTAPHA BENCHEIKH
Faculty of Law, Economics and Social Studies: ABDELKADER HASSANI
Faculty of Science: AMAR KAFANI
Faculty of Science and Technology: MOHAMED HNACH
Higher School of Industrial Engineering: MOHAMED BOUIDIDA (Dir)

ATTACHED RESEARCH INSTITUTES

Higher Institute of Technology: Dir ABDELKADER HASSANI.

UNIVERSITÉ QUARAOUYINE FÈS

Dhar Mahraz, BP 2509, Fez
Telephone: 35-64-10-06
Fax: 35-64-10-13
Founded AD 859, enlarged in 11th century, reorganized 1963
State control
Language of instruction: Arabic
Academic year: September to July
Rector: Prof. ABDELOUAHHAB TAZI SAOUD
Secretary-General: MOHAMMED BENNANI ZOUBIR
Number of teachers: 115
Number of students: 6,000.

CONSTITUENT INSTITUTES

Faculty of Arabic Studies: ave Allal Al-Fassi, BP 1483, Marrakesh; Dean Prof. HASSAN JELLAB.

Faculty of Sharia: BP 52, Agadir; Dean Prof. MOHAMMED ATTAHIRI.

Faculty of Sharia (Law): BP 60, Saïs, Fez; Dean Prof. MOHAMMED YESSEF.

Faculty of Theology: blvd Abdelkhalek Torres, BP 95, Tétouan; Dean Prof. DRISS KHALIFA.

UNIVERSITÉ SIDI MOHAMED BEN ABDELLAH FÈS

BP 2626, ave des Almohades, Fez
Telephone: 35-62-55-85
Fax: 35-62-24-01
Founded 1975
State control
Languages of instruction: Arabic, French
Academic year: September to July
President: TAOUFIK OUAZZANI CHAHDI
Vice-Presidents: ABDERRAHMAN TENKOUL (Academic and Pedagogy), RACHID BENSLIMANE (Research and Co-operation)
Sec.-Gen.: MOHAMED FERHANE
Libraries with 225,000 vols
Number of teachers: 1,010
Number of students: 35,088

DEANS

Faculty of Law, Economics and Social Sciences: SKALI HOUSSAINI ALI
Faculty of Letters and Human Sciences (Dhar Mehrez): CHAD MOHAMED
Faculty of Letters and Human Sciences (Saiss): MOHAMED MEZZINE
Faculty of Science (Dhar Mehrez): SAGHI MOHAMED
Faculty of Science and Technology (Saiss): ABDELILAH HALLAOUI
High School of Technology: OUAZZANI CHAHDI TAOUFIK (Dir)

HEADS OF DEPARTMENTS

Faculty of Law, Economics and Social Sciences:

Economics: IDRISSI HASSAN
Private Law: ABDELGHANI DHIMEN
Public Law: AHMED ELGOURARI

Faculty of Letters and Human Sciences (Dhar Mehrez):

Arabic: ABDELMALEK CHAMI
English: KHALID EL-BERKAOUI (Co-ordinator)
French: ABDERRAHMANE TENKOUL
Geography: MOHAMED REHHOU (Co-ordinator)
German: MASLEK ABDERRAZAK
History: MOULAY HACHEM ALAOUI KACIMI
Islamic Studies: HAMID FETAH
Philosophy, Psychology and Sociology: ALI AFERFAR
Spanish: IMAMI ABDELLATIF

Faculty of Letters and Human Sciences (Saiss):

Arabic: MOHAMED BOUTAHER
English: ABDELJALIL NAOUI ELKHIR
French: FATOUMA MELOUK
Geography: IBRAHIM ACDIM
History: MOHAMED LABBAR
Islamic Studies: LAHSEN ZIN FILALI

Faculty of Science (Dhar Mehrez):

Biology: BOUYA DRISS
Chemistry: KARBAL ABDELALI
Geology: ABDELLAH BOUSHABA
Mathematics: AMEZIANE HASSANI RACHID
Physics: FOUAD LAHLOU

Faculty of Science and Technology (Saiss):
- Biology: YAMANI JAMAL
- Chemistry: LHOUSINE EL-GHADRAOUI
- Mathematics: OUAKILI HASSAN
- Physics: CHARKANI EL-HASSANI MOHAMED

High School of Technology:
- Electrical Engineering: BENSLIMANE RACHID
- Industrial Maintenance: ABDELLATIF SAFOUAN
- Management: ALI BEN GHAZI AKHLAKI
- Mechanical and Production Engineering: KIHEL BACHIR
- Process Engineering: BENTAMA JILALI

Colleges

Conservatoire de Casablanca: Complexe Culturel Benmsik, Casablanca; tel. 22-37-21-89; 120 students; Dir MOHAMED LACHHAB.

Conservatoire de Fès: rue Mustapha Lamaani, Dar Adaîl, Fez; tel. 35-62-39-93; f. 1960; 366 students; Dir MOHAMED BRIOUEL.

Conservatoire de Marrakech: Arçat al Hamed Bab Doukkala, 40000 Marrakech; tel. 24-38-70-66; f. 1948; teaches Western classical and modern music and classical Moroccan and Arab music; 320 students; Dir MOHAMED MAHASSIN.

Conservatoire National de Musique et de Danse, Rabat: 33 rue Tensift-Agdal, Rabat; tel. 37-77-37-94; trains students in Western and Arabic music and classical dance; the Conservatoire has an orchestra for modern Arab music, an orchestra for Andalusian and Moroccan music, two youth orchestras and a big-band orchestra; 1,685 students; Dir MOHAMMED EL BAHJA.

Ecole des Métiers d'Art (School of Native Arts and Crafts): Bab Okla, BP 89, Tétouan; f. 1921; textiles, carpets, rugs, ceramics, engraving, plaster inlays, woodwork, precious metal work, leather and Arabic woodcarving; 350 mems; Dir ABDELLAH FEKHAR.

Ecole des Métiers d'Art (School of Native Arts and Crafts): Bab Okla, BP 89, Tétouan; f. 1921; textiles, carpets, rugs, ceramics, engraving, plaster inlays, woodwork, precious metal work, leather and Arabic woodcarving; 350 mems; Dir ABDELLAH FEKHAR.

Ecole Hassania des Travaux Publics: Km 7, route d'El Jadida, BP 8108, Oasis, Casablanca; tel. 22-23-07-06; fax 22-23-07-17; e-mail ehtpdg@menara.ma; internet www.ehtp.ac.ma; f. 1971; civil engineering, industrial engineering and telecommunication systems, meteorology, sciences of geographical information, computer engineering; MBA, Master's programmes, specialized courses, seminaries; 7 research and study centres; library: 15,000 vols; 73 full-time teachers, 180 visiting teachers; 480 students; Dir ABDESLAM MESSOUDI.

Ecole Nationale d'Administration: BP 165, 2 ave de la Victoire, Rabat; tel. 37-73-14-50; fax 37-73-09-29; f. 1948; library: 18,000 vols; 36 teachers; 646 students; Dir AMINE MZOURI; publ. *Administration et Société* (3 a year).

Ecole Nationale d'Architecture: BP 6372, Chariaa Allal El Fassi, Rabat; tel. 37-77-52-29; fax 37-77-52-76; e-mail e.n.a@smartnet.net.ma; f. 1980 under the Ministry of Territorial Administration, Water Resources and the Environment; courses in architecture, regional town planning and housing; 60 teachers; 400 students; Dir ABDERRAHMANE CHORFI.

Ecole Nationale des Beaux-Arts: Ave Mohamed V, Cité Scolaire BP 89, Tétouan; f. 1946; drawing, painting, sculpture, decorative arts; Dir MOHAMMED M. SERGHINI.

Ecole Nationale Forestière d'Ingénieurs: BP 511, Salé; tel. 37-78-97-04; fax 37-78-71-49; f. 1968; library: 5,000 vols; 20 teachers; 160 students; Dir MY Y. ALAOUI.

Ecole Nationale de l'Industrie Minérale: rue Hadj Ahmed Cherkaoui, BP 753, Agdal, Rabat; tel. 37-68-02-28; fax 37-77-10-55; e-mail info@enim.ac.ma; internet www.enim.ac.ma; f. 1972; specializes in geology, material sciences, mining sciences, chemical process engineering, electro-mechanical engineering, energy sciences, computer science, industrial maintenance, production systems, energy systems; library: 11,000 vols; 86 teachers; 420 students; Dir OMAR DEBBAJ; publs *Liaison Bulletin* (monthly), *Report* (annually).

Ecole des Sciences de l'Information: BP 6204, Rabat-Instituts; tel. 37-77-49-04; fax 37-77-02-32; e-mail esi@esi.ac.ma; internet www.esi.ac.ma; f. 1974; 4-year undergraduate courses and 2-year postgraduate courses for archivists, librarians, documentalists; language of instruction: English; library: 18,000 vols, 50 current periodicals, 415 audio-visual documents; also UNESCO publications, research papers, courses, syllabuses etc.; 64 teachers; 512 students; Dir MOHAMED BENJELLOUN.

Ecole Supérieure de l'Agro-Alimentaire (Higher School of Food Science): 22 rue Catelet, Belvedère, Casablanca; tel. 22-24-54-05; fax 22-24-53-99; e-mail supagro@casanet.net.ma; f. 1997; 90 teachers; 70 students; Dir ABDELRHAFOUR TANTAOUI ELARAKI.

Institut Agronomique et Vétérinaire Hassan II: BP 6202, Madinat El-Irfane-Instituts, Rabat; tel. 37-77-17-58; fax 37-77-81-35; e-mail dg@iav.ac.ma; internet www.iav.ac.ma; f. 1966; library: 45,000 documents, 1,200 periodicals; 327 teachers; 1,606 students; Dir Prof. FOUAD GUESSOUS; Sec.-Gen. Prof. MOSTAFA AGBANI; publs *Actes de l'Institut Agronomique et Vétérinaire Hassan II* (in French and English, 4 a year), *AgroVet Magazine* (in French, 4 a year), *IAVinfo* (6 a year), *Rapport d'activités* (annually).

Instituto Español de Enseñanza Secundaria 'Severo Ochoa' (Spanish Institute in Tangier): Plaza El Koweit 1, Tangier; tel. 39-93-63-38; fax 39-93-60-22; e-mail luisbadosa@hotmail.com; internet arce.cnice.mecd.es/instituto.severo.ochoa; f. 1949; Dir LUIS BADOSA ORTUÑO; library: 8,000 vols; 38 teachers; 360 students; publs *Revista Babel* (several languages, annual), *Revista Kasbah* (Spanish, annual).

Institut National des Sciences de l'Archéologie et du Patrimoine: ave Kennedy, route des Zaers, 10000 Rabat-Souissi; tel. 37-75-09-61; fax 37-75-08-84; e-mail archeo@iam.net.ma; f. 1986; departments of anthropology, archaeology and cultural heritage, heritage studies, Islamic studies and archaeology and prehistory; 60 teachers; 50 students; Dir JOUDIA HASSAR-BENSLIMANE; publ. *Bulletin d'Archéologie Marocaine* (annually).

Institut National de Statistique et d'Economie Appliquée: BP 6217, Rabat; tel. 37-77-09-15; fax 37-77-94-57; f. 1961; library: 15,000 vols; 398 students; Dir ABDELAZIZ EL GHAZALI; publ. *Revue* (annual).

Institut Supérieur d'Art Dramatique et d'Animation Culturelle: Charia Al Mansour Eddahbi, BP 1355, Rabat; tel. 37-72-17-02; fax 37-70-34-23; internet www.miniculture.gov.ma/fr/isadac.htm; f. 1985; provides practical and academic training in all areas of the dramatic arts; Dir AHMED MASSAIA.

MOZAMBIQUE

The Higher Education System

From the 19th century until independence in 1975 Mozambique was a Portuguese colony. The oldest current institutions of higher education were founded during the period of Portuguese rule, most prominently the state-run Universidade Eduardo Mondlane (founded 1962; current name 1976). The other leading state institution is the Universidade Pedagógica (founded 1986); a third public university, the Universidade Lúrio, was founded in 2007. The main private institutions include the Catholic University and Higher Polytechnic Institute. The Ministry of Education is the agency responsible for state provision of higher education, which is publicly funded.

Students must be awarded the Certificado de Habilitações Literarias upon completion of secondary education and sit an entrance examination in order to be admitted to higher education. Currently, only undergraduate degrees are available. The Bacharelato is awarded after the first cycle of higher education, which lasts three years and is available in most subject areas. Depending on 'good' or 'very good' grades, students may be admitted to a Licenciatura programme of study, which lasts two years following the Bacharelato. Students of architecture, medicine and veterinary medicine study for the Licenciatura. Since 1976, students have been required to spend as many years in state employment (usually teaching) as the length of the course, their degree being awarded once their public service has been completed.

Technical and vocational education is offered by technical schools and institutes controlled by the Secretary of State for Technical and Professional Education. Completion of medium-level technical and vocational education results in award of either the Engenheiro Técnico (technician engineer) or Tecnico Medio (middle level technician).

Learned Societies

GENERAL

UNESCO Office Maputo: CP 1397, Maputo; located at: 515 Av. Frederick Engels, Maputo; tel. (1) 494450; fax (1) 493431; e-mail maputo@unesco.org; Dir BENOÎT SOUSSOU.

LANGUAGE AND LITERATURE

British Council: Rua John Issa, 226, POB 4178 Maputo; tel. (1) 226776; fax (1) 421577; e-mail general.enquiries@britishcouncil.org.mz; internet www.britishcouncil.org/mozambique; offers courses and exams in English language and British culture and promotes cultural exchange with the UK; Dir SIMON INGRAM-HILL.

Research Institutes

AGRICULTURE, FISHERIES AND VETERINARY SCIENCE

Instituto de Algodão de Moçambique (Mozambique Institute for Cotton): Av. Eduardo Mondlane No. 2221 (1° andar), CP 806, Maputo; tel. (1) 431015; fax (1) 430679; e-mail iampab@zebra.uem.mz; f. 1991; departments of fibre technology and quality, administration and finance, development studies and projects; library of 2,500 vols, 210 journals and reviews; Dir Eng. Agr. ERASMO MUHATE; publs *Relatório Anual de Actividades* (annually), *Relatório Trimestral* (4 a year).

Instituto Nacional de Investigação Agronómica: CP 3658, Maputo 4; tel. (1) 460190; fax (1) 460074; e-mail inia@iniadta.uem.mz; f. 1965; Dir Dr CALISTO BIAS; publ. *Comunicacões / INIA.*

MEDICINE

Instituto Nacional de Saúde (National Health Institute): Av. Eduardo Mondlane 296, CP 264, Maputo; fax (1) 423726; f. 1980; study, research and training in ecology, epidemiology, immunology, malaria, microbiology, parasitology, trypanosomiasis; traditional medicine; documentation and information depts; 32 staff; library of 6,500 vols; Dir Dr RUI GAMA VAZ; publ. *Revista Médica de Moçambique.*

NATURAL SCIENCES

Physical Sciences

Direcção Nacional de Geologia: CP 217, Maputo; tel. (1) 427121; fax (1) 420796; e-mail geologia@zebra.uem.mz; f. 1928; regional geology, geological mapping and mineral exploration; library of 30,000 vols, maps, technical material, etc; Dir ELIAS XAVIER DAUDI; publs *Bibliografia Geológico-Mineira de Moçambique* (annually), *Boletim Geológico de Moçambique* (annually), *Boletim Informativo da DNG* (4 a year), *Notíćias Explicativas da Geológico de Moçambique* (irregular), *Relatório Anual* (annually).

Instituto Nacional de Meteorologia: CP 256, Maputo; tel. and fax (1) 491150; e-mail mozmet@inam.gov.mz; internet www.inam.gov.mz; f. 1907; library of 750 vols; Dir FILIPE DOMINGOS FREIRES LÚCIO; publs *Anuário de Observações* (in 2 vols: I *Observações Meteorológicas de Superficie*, II *Observações Meteorológicas de Altitude*), *Boletim Meteorológico para a Agricultura* (every 10 days), *Informações de Carácter Astronómico* (annually).

Libraries and Archives

Maputo

Arquivo Histórico de Moçambique: Av. Filipe Samuel Magaia 717, CP 2033, Maputo; tel. (1) 431296; fax (1) 423428; e-mail jneves@zebra.uem.mz; internet www.ahm.uem.mz; f. 1934; attached to the University; 25,000 vols, 11,600 periodicals; special collections: written reports of administrative or governmental offices and business; cartography; iconography; oral history; Dir Prof. Dr JOEL DAS NEVES TEMBE; publs *Arquivo*, *Documentos* (series), *Estudos* (series), *Instrumentos de Pesquisa* (series).

Biblioteca Nacional de Moçambique (National Library of Mozambique): Av. 25 de Setembro 1384, CP 141, Maputo; tel. (1) 425676; f. 1961; 110,000 vols; Dir ANTÓNIO M. B. COSTA E SILVA.

Centro Nacional de Documentação e Informação de Moçambique: CP 4116, Maputo; tel. (1) 426666; f. 1977; part of Council of Ministers Secretariat; 12,000 vols; Dir RICARDO SANTOS; publ. *Documento Informativo.*

Direcção Nacional de Geologia, Centro de Documentação: CP 217, Maputo; tel. (1) 420797; fax (1) 429216; e-mail geologia@zebra.uem.mz; f. 1928; documentation centre for geology and mineral exploration; 10 special collections; Dir ELIAS XAVIER DAUDI; publs *Bibliografia Geológico-Mineira* (annually), *Boletim Geológico* (annually), *Bolentim Informativo* (4 a year), *Notícias Explicativas da Geologia de Moçambique* (irregular), *Relatório Anual da DNG* (annually).

Museum

Maputo

Museu de História Natural: Praça da Travessia do Zambeze, CP 1780, Maputo; tel. (1) 491145; fax (1) 490879; e-mail mnhi@zebra.uem.mz; internet www.museu.org.mz; f. 1911; natural history museum and ethnographic gallery; attached to the University; Dir AUGUSTO J. PEREIRA CABRAL.

Universities

UNIVERSIDADE EDUARDO MONDLANE

CP 257, Maputo

Telephone: (1) 427851
Fax: (1) 326426
Internet: www.uem.mz

Founded 1962
State control
Language of instruction: Portuguese
Academic year: February to December

Rector: Prof. Dr BRAZÃO MAZULA
Vice-Rector for Academic Affairs (vacant)
Vice-Rector for Administration and Resources (vacant)
Director of Documentation Services: POLICARPO MATIQUITE

Number of teachers: 1,069
Number of students: 9,712

DEANS

Faculty of Agriculture: Prof. Dr ANDRADE F. EGAS
Faculty of Architecture: Prof. JOSÉ FORJAZ
Faculty of Arts and Social Science: Prof. Dr ARMINDO NGUNGA
Faculty of Economics: Dr FERNANDO LICHUCHA (acting)
Faculty of Education: Prof. Dr MOUZINHO MÁRIO (acting)
Faculty of Engineering: Prof. Dr GABRIEL AMOS
Faculty of Law: Dr TAÍBO MUCOBORA (acting)
Faculty of Medicine: Prof. Dr EMILIA NOORMAHOMED
Faculty of Veterinary Science: Dr LUÍS NEVES
Faculty of Science: Dr FRANCISCO VIEIRA

ATTACHED INSTITUTES

Centre for African Studies: Dir Prof. Dr MARCELINO LIPHOLA.

Centre for Informatics: Dir Eng. AMÉRICO MUCHANGA.

UNIVERSIDADE LÚRIO

Av. Eduardo Mondlane 39, CP 364, Nampula
Internet: www.unilurio.ac.mz

Founded 2007
State control

Courses in Dentistry, Pharmacology and Medicine

Rector: Prof. Dr JORGE FERRÃO.

UNIVERSIDADE PEDAGÓGICA

Com. Augusto Cardoso 135, Maputo
Telephone: (1) 420860
Fax: (1) 422113
E-mail: grupsede@zebra.uem.mz

Founded 1986
State Control
Language of instruction: Portuguese
Academic year: August to June

Rector: CARLOS MACHILI

Number of teachers: 215
Number of students: 1,400

Faculties of Languages, Natural Sciences and Mathematics, Pedagogy, Physical Education and Sports and Social Sciences.

MYANMAR

The Higher Education System

In the 19th century Burma (now Myanmar) was annexed to British India and remained under British rule until independence was achieved in 1948 (with a period under Japanese occupation in 1942–45). The oldest current institutions of higher education date from the 1920s, among them University of Yangon (founded 1920), Institute of Forestry (founded 1923), Yangon Technical University and Yezin Agricultural University (both founded 1924). The Ministry of Education has overall responsibility for higher education, with the exception of specialized institutions attached to other ministries. In 2001/02 there were an estimated 587,300 students at 958 institutions of tertiary education.

Admission to higher education is on the basis of results in the secondary school Matriculation and, in some instances, an entrance examination. Bachelors degrees are classified as either 'Pass' or 'Honours' depending on the length of study: fours years for Bachelors (Pass) and five years for Bachelors (Honours). Bachelors degrees in professional fields of study (engineering, forestry, medicine) take upwards of six years. Postgraduate degrees include the ordinary Masters and Masters of Research.

Admission to post-secondary technical and vocational education is also on the basis of secondary school Matriculation and entrance examination. State-run technical institutes specialise in three-year training programmes leading to the award of the Diploma.

Learned Societies

LANGUAGE AND LITERATURE

British Council: 78 Kanna Rd, POB 638, Yangon; tel. (1) 254658; fax (1) 245345; e-mail enquiries@britishcouncil.org.mm; internet www.britishcouncil.org/burma; offers courses and exams in English language and British culture and promotes cultural exchange with the UK; teaching centre; Dir Dr MARCUS MILTON; Teaching Centre Man. MICHAEL GORDON.

Research Institutes

AGRICULTURE, FISHERIES AND VETERINARY SCIENCE

Forest Research Institute: Yezin, Pyinmana; tel. (67) 22600; fax (1) 665592; e-mail friyezin@myanmar.com.mm; f. 1978; library of 9,207 vols; Dir HTUN PAW OO.

ECONOMICS, LAW AND POLITICS

Department of Research and Management Studies: Institute of Economics, Hlaing Campus, Yangon; conducts research into various aspects of the Burmese economy; current activities include investigation of problems of modernization and development of agriculture, industrial development, planning and economic management, trade and development, etc.; also conducts courses for senior management personnel; Head (vacant); publs. occasional papers and research monographs.

MEDICINE

Department of Medical Research (Lower Myanmar): 5 Ziwaka Rd, Dagon PO, Yangon 11191; tel. (1) 251508; fax (1) 251514; e-mail dmrlowerm@mptmail.net .mm; formerly Burma Medical Research Institute; f. 1963; 24 divisions and 7 clinical research units: animal services, bacteriology, biochemistry, computer diagnostics and vaccine research, epidemiology, experimental medicine, finance and budget, health systems research, clinical research, immunology, instrumentation, library, medical entomology, medical research statistics, nuclear medicine, nutrition, parasitology, pathology, pharmacology, physiology, publications, radioisotope and virology; clinical research units: malaria (DSGH), malaria (2MH), cerebral and complicated malaria (DMR), snakebites, traditional medicine, HIV/AIDS, research unit (IM II), oncology; Dir-Gen. Prof. Dr PAING SOE; publs *DMR Bulletin*, *Myanmar Health Sciences Research Journal*, *DMR CBL Newsletter*.

National Health Laboratories: Yangon; f. 1968 by amalgamating the Harcourt-Butler Institute of Public Health, the Pasteur Institute, Office of the Chemical Examiner and Office of the Public Analyst; composed of five divisions: Administration, Public Health, Chemical, Food and Drugs and Clinical; Dir Dr MEHM SOE MYINT.

RELIGION, SOCIOLOGY AND ANTHROPOLOGY

Department of Religious Affairs: Kaba-aye Pagoda compound, Yangon; a government-supported centre for research and studies in Buddhist and allied subjects; library of 17,000 vols, 7,000 periodicals, 7,650 palm-leaf MSS, etc; Dir-Gen. U ANT MAUNG.

TECHNOLOGY

Myanmar Scientific and Technological Research Department: Kanbe, Yankin Post Office, Yangon; tel. (1) 665695; fax (1) 665292; a dept of the Ministry of Science and Technology; composed of the Analysis Dept, Metallurgy Research Dept, Physics and Engineering Research Dept, Technical Information Centre, Fine Instruments Dept and Workshop, Applied Chemistry Research Dept, Ceramics Research Dept, Standards and Specifications Dept, Polymer Research Dept, Pharmaceutical Research Dept, Food Technology Research Dept; research in applied sciences; library of 17,000 vols, 1,200 periodicals; Dir-Gen. Col TIN HTUT.

Union of Myanmar Atomic Energy Centre: Central Research Organization, 6 Kaba Aye Pagoda Rd, Yangon; f. 1955; environmental radiation monitoring, nuclear instrumentation; Chair U ANG KOE.

Libraries and Archives

Bassein

Bassein Degree College Library: Bassein; f. 1958; 27,560 vols; Librarian NYAN HTUN.

State Library: Bassein; f. 1963; 1,453 vols.

Kyaukpyu

State Library: Kyaukpyu; f. 1955; 8,651 vols.

Magwe

Magway University Library: Magway; tel. (62) 21522 ext.108; f. 1958; 50,000 vols; Dir KHIN MYINT MYINT.

Mandalay

Institute of Medicine Library: Seiktaramahi Quarters, Mandalay; f. 1964; 28,362 vols, 47 periodicals; Librarian KAUNG NYUNT.

State Library: Mandalay; f. 1955; 7,004 vols.

University of Mandalay Library: University Estate, Mandalay; 146,000 vols; Librarian U NYAN TUN.

Mawlamyine

Mawlamyine University Library: Mawlamyine, Mon State; f. 1964; 60,916 vols, 35 periodicals; Librarian U THEIN LWIN; publ. *Newsletter* (every 2 months).

State Library: Mawlamyine; f. 1955; 13,265 vols; 1,262 MSS.

Myitkyina

Myitkyina Degree College Library: Myitkyina, Kachin State; Librarian (vacant).

Pyinmana

Institute of Animal Husbandry and Veterinary Science Library: Yezin, Pyinmana; tel. (67) 22449; fax (67) 642927; e-mail drhsuvs@myanmar.com.mm; f. 1964; 4,500 vols; Librarian HTAY HTAY KHIN.

Yezin Agricultural University Library: Yezin, Pyinmana; tel. (67) 21098; fax (67) 21437; f. 1924, autonomous 1964; 26,000 vols, 130 periodicals; Chief Librarian Dr MYINT THAUNG.

Tyaunggyi

Taunggyi Degree College Library: Taunggyi, Shan State; Librarian (vacant).

Yangon

Central Biomedical Library: Department of Medical Research (Lower Myanmar), 5 Ziwaka Rd, Dagon PO, Yangon 11191; tel. (1) 251508; fax (1) 251504; e-mail dmrlower@baganmail.net.mm; formerly Burma Medical Research Institute Library; f. 1963; 27,000 vols, 250 periodicals on health and biomedical sciences; Chief Librarian DAW NYUNT NYUNT SWE.

Institute of Computer Science and Technology Library: Yangon; Library Asst Daw YU YU TIN.

Institute of Economics Library: University Estate, POB 473, Yangon 11041; tel. (1) 532433; e-mail rector@eco.edu.mm; f. 1964; 87,000 vols; Librarian Daw KHIN KYU.

Institute of Education Library: University Estate, Yangon; f. 1964; 36,166 vols; Librarian Daw GILDA TWE.

Institute of Medicine I Library: 245 Myoma Kyaung Rd, Lanmadaw P.O. 11131, Yangon; f. 1929; 40,000 vols; Librarian KHIN MAW MAW TUN.

Institute of Medicine II Library: North Okkalapa, Yangon 11031; tel. (1) 699467; fax (1) 690265; f. 1964; 25,000 vols; Librarian U THI TAR.

Myanmar Education Research Bureau: 426 Pyay Rd, University PO 11041, Yangon; tel. (1) 531468; fax (1) 525049; f. 1965; a dept of the Ministry of Education; 56,000 vols; educational materials resource centre; Chair. U MYINT HAN; publ. *The World of Education* (quarterly).

National Library: Strand Rd, Yangon; tel. (1) 272058; f. 1952; incorporating the Bernard Free Library; 158,800 vols, 12,321 MSS, 411,426 periodicals; Chief Librarian U KHIN MAUNG TIN.

Sarpay Beikman Public Library: 529 Merchant St, Yangon; f. 1956; 74,404 vols (56,729 Burmese, 17,675 English); Librarian NU NU.

Universities' Central Library: University PO, Yangon; f. 1929; 350,000 vols; central library for all higher education institutes; specializes in Burmese books, palm-leaf MSS (over 11,000), and books on Burma and Asia; Chief Librarian THAW KAUNG.

University of Yangon Library: Yangon; tel. (1) 537250; fax (1) 510721; f. 1927; 200,000 vols; Head Librarian KHIN HNIN OO.

Workers' College Library: Yangon; f. 1964; 19,500 vols; Librarian KHIN THIN KYU.

Yangon Institute of Technology Library: Insein PO, Gyogon, Yangon; f. 1964; 48,000 vols, 560 periodicals; Librarian U TIN MAUNG LWIN.

Museums and Art Galleries

Bagan

Bagan Archaeological Museum: opposite Gawdawpalin Temple, Bagan, Mandalay Division; f. 1904, new bldg opened 1975; site museum for ancient capital of 11th- to 14th-century; lithic inscriptions, Buddha images, statuary and artefacts; administered by Dept of Archaeology; Curator U KYAW NYEIN.

Mandalay

State Museum: Corner of 24th and 80th Sts, Mandalay; f. 1955; over 1,500 exhibits; also br. museum in fmr Mandalay Palace grounds; Curator U SOE THEIN.

Mawlamyine

Mon State Museum: Dawei Tada Rd, Mawlamyine; f. 1955; over 750 exhibits; Curator U MIN KHIN MAUNG.

Sitture

Rakhine State Museum: Chin Pyan Rd, Kyaung-gyi Quarter, Sitture, Rakhine State; f. 1955; over 500 exhibits (silver coins, costumes etc.); also site museum at Mrauk-U, ancient capital; Curator Daw NU MYA ZAN.

Taunggyi

Shan State Museum: Min Lan, Thittaw Quarter, Taunggyi, Shan State; f. 1957; over 600 exhibits; Curator U SAN MYA.

Yangon

Bogyoke Aung San Museum: 25 Bogyoke Museum Rd, Bahan PO, Yangon; tel. (1) 250600; f. 1959; 571 exhibits relating to the life and work of General Aung San.

National Museum of Art and Archaeology: 26/42 Pansodan, Yangon; f. 1952; 1,652 antiquities; 354 paintings; replica of King Mindon's Mandalay Palace; Dir-Gen. Dr YE TUT; Chief Curator U KYAW WIN.

Universities

UNIVERSITY OF CULTURE

No. 26 Quarter, Aung Zeta Rd, South Dagon Myothit Township, Yangon
Telephone: (1) 590250
Fax: (1) 590250
Founded 1993
Language of instruction: English
Academic year: November to September
Rector: TIN SOE
Number of teachers: 135
Number of students: 733
Departments of Fine Arts, Dance, Music, Drama, Painting and Sculpture.

DAGON UNIVERSITY

North Dagon Township, Yangon
Telephone: (1) 584550Myanmar
Academic year: July to March
Faculties of Arts and Humanities, Mathematics and Computer Science and Natural Sciences.

UNIVERSITY OF FOREIGN LANGUAGES, YANGON

119–131 University Ave, 11041 Yangon
Telephone: (1) 513193
Fax: (1) 513194
E-mail: rectorufly@mptmail.net.mm
Founded 1964
Rector: Dr SOE WIN
Librarian: Daw HLA HLA MYINT
Rector: Dr SOE WIN
Librarian: Daw HLA HLA MYINT
Library of 26,000 vols
Number of teachers: 100
Number of students: 3,000
Language courses in Chinese, English, French, German, Japanese, Korean, Russian and Thai; Myanmar language courses for foreign students.

MAGWE UNIVERSITY

University Campus, Magwe
Telephone: (63) 21030
Founded 1958
Number of teachers: 130
Number of students: 3,550.

UNIVERSITY OF MANDALAY

University Estate, Mandalay
Telephone: (2) 21211
Founded 1925 as a college of the University of Rangoon; independent university status 1958
Language of instruction: Myanmar
Academic year: July to March
Rector: U TIN MAUNG
Pro-Rector: U LU NI
Registrars: U WIN MYINT (Student Affairs and Hostels), Daw SEIN SEIN (Examination and Convocation)
Librarian: U NYAN TUN
Library of 175,000 vols
Number of teachers: 860
Number of students: 22,700

HEADS OF DEPARTMENTS

Botany: U NYUNT LWIN
Chemistry: U KHIN MG KYI
Economics: Daw KHIN SAN MAY
English: Daw WINNIE MURRAY
Geography: Daw FAITH WILLIAM LAY
Geology: Dr MYINT THEIN
History: Daw SAN SAN AYE
International Relations: Daw KHIN HTWE YI
Law: U KHIN MG THEIN
Mathematics: Dr KYAW NYUNT
Myanmar: Daw HLA MYAT
Oriental Studies: U BA SUN
Philosophy: Daw MYA KYAING
Physics: U KYEE MYINT
Psychology: U KHIN MAUNG THAN
Zoology: Dr KHIN MG AYE

9 affiliated colleges.

MANDALAY TECHNOLOGICAL UNIVERSITY

Patheingyi, M. T. U., PO, Mandalay
Telephone: (2) 88712
Fax: (2) 88702
Founded 1991
Number of teachers: 144
Number of students: 2,418
Pro-Rector: Prof. Dr AUNG KYAW MYAT
Bachelor's, Master's and doctoral courses.

MAWLAMYINE UNIVERSITY

Taung Waing Rd, Mawlamyine, Mon State
Telephone: (32) 21180
Founded 1953, university status 1986
Languages of instruction: Myanmar, English
State control
Academic year: November to September
Rector: HLA TUN AUNG
Pro-Rector: HLA PE
Librarian: THEIN LWIN
Number of teachers: 300
Number of students: 8,100
Library of 78,000 vols (36,000 in Myanmar, 42,000 in English)

HEADS OF DEPARTMENTS AND PROFESSORS

Botany: Assoc. Prof. SANN TINT
Chemistry: Prof. MAUNG MAUNG HTAY
English: Assoc. Prof. SEINE SEINE MYINT
Geography: Prof. THAN MYA
Geology: Prof. NYAN THIN
History: Assoc. Prof. MYINT MYINT THAN
Marine Science: Assoc. Prof. KYI WINN
Mathematics: Assoc. Prof. KHIN MAUNG LATT
Myanmar: Assoc. Prof. YIN YIN MYINT
Oriental Studies: TIN OO
Philosophy: Assoc. Prof. TIN HLA
Physics: Prof. SEIN HTOON
Zoology: Assoc. Prof. MYA MYA NU

AFFILIATED COLLEGES

Bago College: Principal HLA MYINT.

Dawei College: Principal THIN HLAING.

Hpa-an College: Principal LAWRENCE THAW.

MONYWA UNIVERSITY

Sagging Division, Monywa

Founded 1996

Rector: MAUNG HTOO

Faculties of Arts and Humanities, Mathematics and Computer Science and Natural Sciences.

PATHEIN UNIVERSITY

Ayeyarwaddy Division, Pathein

Founded 1996

Faculties of Arts and Humanities, Mathematics and Computer Science and Natural Sciences.

SITTWE UNIVERSITY

Sittwe, Rakhine State

Telephone: (1) 246704
E-mail: hivdig@indp.org

Founded 1996

Rector: SEIN MOE MOE

Faculties of Arts and Humanities, Mathematics and Computer Science and Natural Sciences.

TAUNGGYI UNIVERSITY

Taunggyi, Shan State

Telephone: (81) 21160

Founded 1961

Number of teachers: 125
Number of students: 3,500

Faculties of Arts and Humanities, Mathematics and Computer Science and Natural Sciences.

UNIVERSITY OF VETERINARY SCIENCE, YEZIN

Yezin, Pyinmana

Telephone: (1) 22447
Fax: (1) 642927
E-mail: tintinmyaing@mail4u.com.mm

Founded 1964, formerly part of University of Yangon

Languages of instruction: Myanmar, English

Rector: Dr MAUNG MAUNG SAN
Librarian: HTAY HTAY SAN

Library of 13,204 vols, 53 periodicals
Number of teachers: 65
Number of students: 620

Faculties of Animal Husbandry and Veterinary Science.

UNIVERSITY OF YANGON

University Avenue Rd, Kamayut Yangon

Telephone: (1) 514908

Founded 1920
Academic year: July to March

Campuses in Hling Region, Kyimyindine Region, Botataung Region

Rector: TIN OO HLAING
Registrar: NYUNT NYUNT WIN

Number of teachers: 2,060
Number of students: 47,131

HEADS OF DEPARTMENTS

Anthropology: SEIN TAN
Botany: Dr KYAW SOE
Chemistry: Dr NYUNT WIN
English: HAN TIN
Geography: TIN AYE
Geology: Dr MAUNG THEIN
History: TUN AUNG CHEIN
Industrial Chemistry: Dr MIN MYINT
International Relations: KHIN KHIN MA
Law: Dr TIN AUNG AYE
Library Studies: THAW KAUNG
Mathematics: SEIN MIN
Myanmar: SHWE THWIN
Oriental Studies: LAY MYING
Philosophy: (vacant)
Physics: Dr ZIN AUNG
Psychology: AYE THAN
Zoology: KYI KYI

3 affiliated degree-granting colleges in Pathein, Sittwe and Yangon, and 2 colleges in Hinthada and Pyay.

YANGON TECHNOLOGICAL UNIVERSITY

Gyogon, Insein Yangon 11014

Telephone: (1) 642410
Fax: (1) 642564

Founded 1924, independent status 1961
Ministry of Science and Technology
Academic year: October to July

Rector: Prof. U. NYI HLA NGE

6-year first degree courses, 1-year postgraduate diploma and 2- and 3-year postgraduate degree courses

Number of teachers: 204
Number of students: 1,120

HEADS OF DEPARTMENTS

Aerospace Engineering: Prof. Dr KHIN THAN YU
Architecture: Prof. Dr SWE SWE AYE
Chemical Engineering: Prof. Dr MYA MYA OO
Civil Engineering: Prof. Dr HTIN AUNG
Electrical Engineering: Prof. Dr KHIN AYE WIN
Information Technology, Electronic and Mechatronic Engineering: Prof. Dr KYAWT KHIN
Material Science and Metal Engineering: Prof. Dr VICTORIA SIMONS
Mechanical Engineering: Prof. Dr YIN YIN HTUN
Mining Engineering: Prof. Dr AUNG SHEIN
Petroleum Engineering: Prof. Dr MYINT SOE
Textile Engineering: Prof. Dr NAW MU MU AYE

YEZIN AGRICULTURAL UNIVERSITY

Yezin, Pyinmana

Telephone: (67) 21434

Founded 1924, independent status 1964

Rectors: Dr KYAW THAN
Pro-Rectors: Dr CHO CHO MYINT (Academic), HLA TUN (Administration)
Registrars: TIN WAN, AUNG SAN

Number of teachers: 121
Number of students: 1,200.

University-Level Institutions

Institute of Computer Science and Technology: Thaimaing Campus, Hlaing PO 11052, Yangon; tel. (1) 665686; fax (1) 665292; f. 1988 as Universities Computer Centre); library: 11,000 vols; 20 teachers; 100 students; language of instruction: English; academic year July to March; Rector Dr TIN MAUNG; Pro-Rector Dr KYAW THEIN; Registrar U KYIN HTWE; Librarian Daw KHIN MAR AYE.

Institute of Dental Medicine: Thanthumar Rd, Thingankyun POB, Yangon; tel. (1) 571270; fax (1) 571269; f. 1964, Institute status 1974; language of instruction: English; academic year November to September; 120 teachers; 500 students; library: 7,500 vols; publ. *Myanmar Dental Journal* (annually); Rector PAING SOE; Courses in Dentistry, Dental Technology, Nursing and Surgery.

Institute of Economics: University Estate, Kamaryut Township Yangon 11041; tel. (1) 532433; f. 1964; library: 87,000 vols; 237 teachers; 5,096 students; academic year November to September; publ. *Annual Magazine*; Rector U MAW THAN.

Institute of Education: Pyay Rd, University PO, Kamayut Township, Yangon; tel. (1) 504772; fax (1) 504773; e-mail rectoryjoe@mptmail.net.mm; f. 1931, present status since 1964; languages of instruction: Myanmar, English; academic year June to March; 126 teachers; 2,535 students; publ. *Magazine* (annually); Pro-Rector KHIN ZAW.

Institute of Forestry: Yezin, Pyinmana; tel. (67) 21436; e-mail teaknet@mtpt400.stems.com; f. 1923, present status since 1992; language of instruction: English; academic year November to September; library: 10,000 vols; 45 teachers; 300 students; Rector AUNG THAN.

Institute of Medicine (I): 245 Myoma Kyaung Rd, Lanmadaw, POB 11131, Yangon; tel. (1) 26065; fax (1) 243910; e-mail rct.imy@mptmail.net.mm; f. 1964; languages of instruction: Myanmar, English; library: 52,000 vols; 440 teachers; 2,200 students; publs *Annual Magazine*, *Scientific Paper Reports*; Rector Prof. MYO MYINT.

Institute of Medicine (II): 13 Mile Pyay Rd, Mingaladon, Yangon; tel. (1) 45507; f. 1964; languages of instruction: Myanmar, English; academic year November to July; library: 24,000 vols; 320 teachers; 1,500 students; publs *Medical Education Report* (quarterly), *Annual Magazine*; Rector Dr THA HLA SHWE.

Institute of Medicine (III): 30th St, between 73rd and 74th Sts, Mandalay; tel. (2) 30311; f. 1954, present status and title since 1964; languages of instruction: Myanmar, English; academic year September to August; library: 18,000 vols; 190 teachers; 900 students; Rector Dr TUN THIN.

Institute of Technology: Insein PO, Gyogon, Yangon 11011; tel. (1) 665678; fax (1) 663357; e-mail yiy.yangon@pemail.net; internet http://welcome.to/yit; f. 1924, independent status 1964; languages of instruction: Myanmar, English; academic year October to July; library: 48,000 vols, 560 journals; 250 teachers; 4,500 students; Departments of Civil Engineering, Mechanical Engineering, Electrical Engineering, Electronic Engineering, Chemical Engineering, Textile Engineering, Mining Engineering, Petroleum Engineering, Metallurgical Engineering, Aeronautical Engineering and Architecture.

Colleges

Defence Services Academy: Maymyo; f. 1955; an independent degree college under the Ministry of Defence; degree courses for cadets training for service as regular commissioned officers in the Burma Army, Navy and Air Force; 120 staff; 400 students; Commanding Officer Col. AUNG WIN.

Magway Degree College: University Campus, Magway, Magway Division; tel. (63) 21030; 129 teachers; 3,555 students; Principal U SEIN WIN.

Myitkyina Degree College: University Campus, Myitkyina, Kachin State; tel. (101) 21053; 90 teachers; 1,752 students; Principal U SUM HLOT NAW.

Pathein Degree College: University Campus, Pathein, Ayeyarwady Division; tel. (42)

21135; 178 teachers; 5,158 students; Principal Dr MAUNG KYAW.

Sittwe Degree College: University Campus, Sittwe, Rakhine State; tel. (43) 21236; 97 teachers; 1,730 students; Principal U KWAW MYA THEIN.

State School of Fine Arts: Mandalay; f. 1953; Principal KAN NYUNT.

State School of Fine Arts: Kanbawza Yeiktha, Kaba Aye Pagoda Rd, Bahan PO, Yangon; tel. (1) 52176; f. 1952; courses in drawing, fine art, commercial art, sculpture and wood-carving; Principal U SOE TINT.

State School of Music and Drama: East Moat Rd, Mandalay; tel. (2) 21176; f. 1953; courses in dancing, singing, Burmese harp and orchestra, xylophone, piano, oboe, stringed instruments and stave notation; Principal KAN NYUNT.

State School of Music and Drama: Kanbawza Yeiktha, Kaba Aye Pagoda Rd, Bahan PO, Yangon; tel. (1) 52176; f. 1952; courses in dancing, singing, Burmese harp and orchestra, piano, oboe, xylophone, stringed instruments, stave notation and Burmese verse; Principal U AUNG THWIN.

Taunggyi State College: Taunggyi Shan State; tel. (81) 21160; 125 teachers; 3,456 students; Principal U SAW HLINE.

Workers' College: 273/279 Konthe Lan, Botahtaung PO, Yangon; tel. (1) 92825; 47 teachers; 5,650 students; Principal U SAN MAUNG.

The Europa Regional Surveys of the World 2008

'Europa's Regional Surveys of the World are justly renowned for their exceptionally high levels of production, content and accuracy.' - *Reference Reviews*

A nine-volume library of historical, political, geographical and economic data, providing an accurate and impartial overview of the major regions of the world.

These exhaustive surveys bring together a unique collection of information, from description and analysis of the principal issues affecting each region, to statistical data and directory information.

Meticulously researched and updated every year, these Surveys are an indispensable information source on which you can rely.

Available as a set or individually, the nine titles that make up the series are as follows: *Africa South of the Sahara; Central and South-Eastern Europe; Eastern Europe, Russia and Central Asia; The Far East and Australasia; The Middle East and North Africa; South America, Central America and the Caribbean; South Asia; The USA and Canada; Western Europe.*

Bibliographic Details
November 2007: 285x220mm: 9 volumes
Set: 978-1-85743-442-2

To order your set or for further information about individual volumes please contact:
Tel: + 44 (0) 20 7017 6629
Fax: + 44 (0) 20 7017 6720
E-mail: sales.europa@tandf.co.uk

Also available online!

Europa World *Plus*

Europa World and the Europa Regional Surveys of the World online

www.europaworld.com

Europa World Plus enables you to subscribe to Europa World together with as many of the nine Europa Regional Surveys of the World online as you choose, in one simple annual subscription.

The Europa Regional Surveys of the World complement and expand upon the information in Europa World with in-depth, expert analysis at regional, sub-regional and country level.

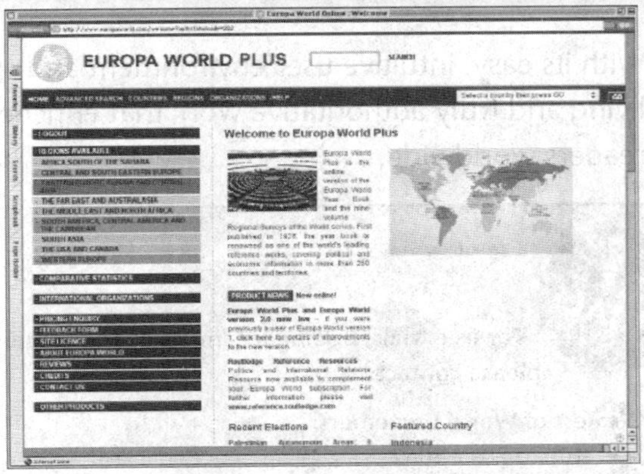

For further information and to register for a free trial please contact us at:
Tel: + 44 (0) 20 7017 6062; Fax: + 44 (0) 20 7017 6720
E-mail: reference@routledge.co.uk

Routledge
Taylor & Francis Group